Statistics Sources

ISSN 0585-198X

Statistics Sources

26th Edition
2003

A Subject Guide to Data on Industrial,
Business, Social, Educational, Financial, and
Other Topics for the United States
and Internationally

Volume 2
J-Z
Appendixes

Steven R. Wasserman
Editor

GALE GROUP

THOMSON LEARNING

Detroit • New York • San Diego • San Francisco
Boston • New Haven, Conn. • Waterville, Maine
London • Munich

Steven R. Wasserman, *Editor*
Peggy Barrett, *Editor and Word Processor*

Gale Group Staff

Amanda C. Quick, *Managing Editor, Business Product*
Jeffrey Matlock, *Technical Specialist*

Dorothy Maki, *Manufacturing Manager*
Nekita McKee, *Buyer*

The paper used in this publication meets the minimum requirements of American National Standard for Information Sciences—Permanence Paper for Printed Library Materials, ANSI Z39.48-1984.

This book is printed on recycled paper that meets Environmental Protection Agency standards.

Copyright © 2002 by Steven R. Wasserman
Library of Congress Catalog Card Number: 84-82356
ISBN 0-7876-6327-1 (set)
ISBN 0-7876-6328-X (Volume 1)
ISBN 0-7876-6329-8 (Volume 2)
ISSN 0585-198X

Printed in the United States of America

CONTENTS

Volume 1

Volume 2

PREFACE

As *Statistics Sources* approaches its twenty-seventh edition (the present volume is the twenty-sixth edition), the constant and painstaking effort to continue to bolster and add value to its content in the interest of its users continues unabated. The work continues to be an easy-to-use alphabetically arranged dictionary and guide to current sources of factual quantitative information on well over 20,000 specific subjects, incorporating almost 100,000 citations and more than 2,000 sources readily leading users to the widest possible range of print and non-print, published and unpublished, and electronic and other forms of U.S. and international statistical sources for economic, business, financial, industrial, cultural, social, educational, and other topics.

Preparation of This Edition

This twenty-sixth edition of *Statistics Sources* fully and thoroughly updates, revises, and extends the scope and content of the twentieth-fifth edition. Complete revisions incorporate a wider range of current data sources from the "Selected Bibliography of Key Statistical Sources" and "Federal Statistical Telephone Contacts" sections, through the main body of the work, and throughout the appendixes.

During the preparation of this edition, as in each earlier edition, the editors thoroughly analyzed and indexed hundreds of American information sources, several years of *Statistical Abstract of the United States*, numerous basic statistical publications from many organizations, and special statistical issues of professional, technical, and trade journals. Additional sources of international statistics are cited in this edition, increasing the range of access points within a user's reference shelves.

Arrangement and Content

The familiar and convenient arrangement of the basic work continues as a straight alphabetic list of subjects. Sources of statistical information are arranged alphabetically by issuing organization within each subject category. In addition to both print and machine-readable sources, a considerable number of organizations, government agencies, trade and professional groups, and international bodies are cited because they are important sources of statistical data, even if they do not ordinarily publish all of the statistics they compile. In such instances, specific inquiries may be addressed to the organization mentioned. As in earlier editions, the street address of the publisher of any work cited has been provided wherever possible, followed by the telephone number of the source.

Interfiled within the subject categories are geographic headings for states and individual countries. Listings for state data center agencies that make census information and data available to the public are included with the citations of sources for each state. These listings appear under the heading "State Data Center Agencies," which immediately follows the citation for "Primary Statistics Source" under each state subheading.

Individual citations for each country are subarranged by an alphabetic list of specific subjects, enabling the user to pinpoint sources of statistics on subjects such as agriculture, education, energy, imports, population, and consumer prices. Two types of key statistical sources are cited in listings for countries (as applicable and available) and precede the alphabetical listing of specific subjects for the country. The first citation is to the National Statistical Office, if the country has such an office. This is followed by a reference to the major printed sources for the country, termed the Primary Statistics Source or Sources. These sources should be consulted by users seeking more in-depth data, particularly for technical and commercial activities in countries other than the U. S. and Canada.

Introductory Materials Pinpoint
Key Sources and Individuals

The "Selected Bibliography of Key Statistical Sources" and "Federal Statistical Telephone Contacts" sections precede the main section of *Statistics Sources*. The "Selected Bibliography" provides an annotated guide to a selected group of major, general statistical compendia and related works, and includes dictionaries of terms, almanacs, census publications, periodical sources, and guides to machine-readable and online data sources. Both governmental and non-governmental sources are cited. A source's availability in machine-readable form or as an online database is noted wherever possible. The "Telephone Contacts" section provides the names and telephone numbers of individuals and agencies within the U. S. federal government with expertise in identifying the most current sources of statistical data.

Appendixes Identify Published and Nonpublished Sources

The two appendixes identify the sources of information used to compile this directory. The "Source Publications" appendix provides an alphabetic listing of the specific publication titles of every printed source mentioned in *Statistics Sources*, along with the issuing or publishing bodies, their addresses and phone numbers. The "Sources of Nonpublished Statistical Data" appendix identifies the agencies, institutions, and other organizations which are cited as sources of nonpublished statistical information in this edition.

Editor's Note

Statistics Sources may best be described as a finding guide to statistics. It does not purport to cite sources of in depth statistics on technical and commercial activities in specific foreign countries. For such purposes, the reader is referred to the Primary Statistics Source, or the National Statistical Office mentioned at the head of the geographic listings, as well as to the particular works cited in the selected bibliography which forms the first component of the work.

The painstaking task of accurately inputting and printing the manuscript for this edition has been the contribution of Peggy Barrett.

Steven R. Wasserman
Editor

J

JAILS

U.S. Department of Justice, Bureau of Justice Statistics, 810 Seventh Street, NW, Washington, D.C. 20531 (800) 732-3277, www.ojp.usdoj.gov/bjs; *Profile of Jail Inmates; Correctional Populations in the United States*; and *Prison and Jail Inmates at Midyear.*

Jamaica - National Statistical Office

Statistical Institute of Jamaica, Nine Swallowfield Road, Kingston 5, Jamaica.

Jamaica - Primary Statistics Sources

Statistical Institute of Jamaica, Nine Swallowfield Road, Kingston 5, Jamaica; *Quarterly Abstract of Statistics; Statistical Abstract;* and *Statistical Yearbook of Jamaica.*

JAMAICA - AGRICULTURE

The Economist Intelligence Unit, 111 West 57th Street, New York, New York 10019 (800) 938-4685; *Jamaica Country Report;* and *The New Latin America Market Atlas.*

Euromonitor International, Inc., 122 South Michigan Avenue, Suite 1200, Chicago, Illinois 60603 (800) 577-EURO; *World Marketing Data and Statistics.*

Europa Publications Limited, 18 Bedford Square, London, WC1B 3JN, England; *The Europa World Year Book.*

Food and Agricultural Organization of the United Nations (FAO), Via delle Terme di Caracalla, 00100 Rome, Italy (Telephone Number in U.S. (202) 653-2400); *The State of Food and Agriculture;* and *Trade Yearbook.*

Inter-American Development Bank, 1300 New York Avenue, NW, Washington,

D.C. 20577 (202) 623-1753; *Economic and Social Progress in Latin America.*

M.E. Sharpe, 80 Business Park Drive, Armonk, New York 10504 (800) 541-6563; *The Illustrated Book of World Rankings.*

St. Martin's Press, Inc., 175 Fifth Avenue, New York, New York 10010 (800) 221-7945; *The Statesman's Year-Book.*

Statistical Office of the United Nations, Publishing Service, New York, New York 10017 (800) 253-9646; *Statistical Yearbook for Latin America and the Caribbean.*

United Nations Conference on Trade and Development, Central Statistical Service, Palais des Nations, Geneva, Switzerland (Telephone in U.S. (800) 253-9646); *UNCTAD Commodity Yearbook.*

JAMAICA - AIRLINE SERVICE

The Economist Intelligence Unit, 111 West 57th Street, New York, New York 10019 (800) 938-4685; *The New Latin America Market Atlas.*

Europa Publications Limited, 18 Bedford Square, London, WC1B 3JN, England; *The Europa World Year Book.*

International Civil Aviation Organization, 999 University Street, Montreal, Quebec, Canada H3C 5H7 (514) 954-8219; *Civil Aviation Statistics of the World.*

M.E. Sharpe, 80 Business Park Drive, Armonk, New York 10504 (800) 541-6563; *The Illustrated Book of World Rankings.*

St. Martin's Press, Inc., 175 Fifth Avenue, New York, New York 10010 (800) 221-7945; *The Statesman's Year-Book.*

Statistical Office of the United Nations, Publishing Service, New York, New York 10017 (800) 253-9646; *Statistical Yearbook.*

JAMAICA - ALUMINUM PRODUCTION AND CONSUMPTION - See JAMAICA - MINING

AND MINERAL PRODUCTS

JAMAICA - ANIMAL HEALTH

Food and Agricultural Organization of the United Nations (FAO), Via delle Terme di Caracalla, 00100, Rome, Italy (Telephone Number in U.S. (202) 653-2400); *Animal Health Yearbook.*

JAMAICA - AREA AND DENSITY OF POPULATION

Central Intelligence Agency, Washington, D.C. 20505 (703) 482-1100, www.cia.gov; *The World Factbook.*

Euromonitor International, Inc., 122 South Michigan Avenue, Suite 1200, Chicago, Illinois 60603 (800) 577-EURO; *International Marketing Data and Statistics;* and *The World Economic Factbook.*

Europa Publications Limited, 18 Bedford Square, London, WC1B 3JN, England; *The Europa World Year Book.*

Food and Agricultural Organization of the United Nations (FAO), Via delle Terme di Caracalla, 00100 Rome, Italy (Telephone Number in U.S. (202) 653-2400); *The State of Food and Agriculture.*

Inter-American Development Bank, 1300 New York Avenue, NW, Washington, D.C. 20577 (202) 623-1753; *Economic and Social Progress in Latin America.*

M.E. Sharpe, 80 Business Park Drive, Armonk, New York 10504 (800) 541-6563; *The Illustrated Book of World Rankings.*

St. Martin's Press, Inc., 175 Fifth Avenue, New York, New York 10010 (800) 221-7945; *The Statesman's Year-Book.*

Statistical Office of the United Nations, Publishing Service, New York, New York 10017 (800) 253-9646; *Statistical Yearbook.*

United Nations Educational, Scientific and Cultural Organization (UNESCO), 7 Place de Fontenoy, F-75700 Paris, France

(Telephone Number in U.S. (212) 963-5981; *Statistical Yearbook.*

The (800) 645-7247, 1818 H Street, NW, Washington, D.C. 20433 (800) 645-7247; *World Development Report.*

JAMAICA - ARMS EXPORTS AND IMPORTS - See JAMAICA - MILITARY

JAMAICA - BALANCE OF PAYMENTS

The Economist Intelligence Unit, 111 West 57th Street, New York, New York 10019 (800) 938-4685; *The New Latin America Market Atlas;* and *The World Market Atlas.*

Europa Publications Limited, 18 Bedford Square, London, WC1B 3JN, England; *The Europa World Year Book.*

Inter-American Development Bank, 1300 New York Avenue, NW, Washington, D.C. 20577 (202) 623-1753; *Economic and Social Progress in Latin America.*

International Monetary Fund, 700 Nineteenth Street, NW, Washington, D.C. 20431 (202) 623-7000; *Balance of Payments Yearbook.*

United Nations Conference on Trade and Development (UNCTAD), New York, New York 10017 (800) 253-9646; *Handbook of International Trade and Development Statistics.*

The World Bank, 1818 H Street, NW, Washington, D.C. 20433 (202) 477-1234; *World Development Report.*

JAMAICA - BANKING

Euromonitor International, Inc., 122 South Michigan Avenue, Suite 1200, Chicago, Illinois 60603 (800) 577-EURO; *World Marketing Data and Statistics.*

Europa Publications Limited, 18 Bedford Square, London, WC1B 3JN, England; *The Europa World Year Book.*

Inter-American Development Bank, 1300 New York Avenue, NW, Washington, D.C. 20577 (202) 623-1753; *Economic and Social Progress in Latin America.*

International Monetary Fund, 700 Nineteenth Street, NW, Washington, D.C. 20431 (202) 623-7000; *International Financial Statistics.*

Organization of American States (OAS), General Secretariat, Washington, D.C. 20006 (202) 458-3533; *Statistical Bulletin of the OAS.*

M.E. Sharpe, 80 Business Park Drive, Armonk, New York 10504 (800) 541-6563; *The Illustrated Book of World Rankings.*

St. Martin's Press, Inc., 175 Fifth Avenue, New York, New York 10010 (800) 221-7945; *The Statesman's Year-Book.*

Statistical Office of the United Nations, Publishing Service, New York, New York 10017 (800) 253-9646; *Statistical Yearbook;* and *Statistical Yearbook for Latin America and the Caribbean.*

JAMAICA - BARLEY PRODUCTION - See JAMAICA - CROPS

JAMAICA - BAUXITE EXPORTS

International Monetary Fund, 700 Nineteenth Street, NW, Washington, D.C. 20431 (202) 623-7000; *International Financial Statistics.*

Organization of American States (OAS), General Secretariat, Washington, D.C. 20006 (202) 458-3533; *Statistical Bulletin of the OAS.*

JAMAICA - BAUXITE PRODUCTION AND CONSUMPTION - See JAMAICA - MINING AND MINERAL PRODUCTS

JAMAICA - BEER PRODUCTION - See JAMAICA - BEVERAGES

JAMAICA - BEVERAGES

M.E. Sharpe, 80 Business Park Drive, Armonk, New York 10504 (800) 541-6563; *The Illustrated Book of World Rankings.*

Statistical Office of the United Nations, Publishing Service, New York, New York 10017 (800) 253-9646; *Statistical Yearbook.*

JAMAICA - BIRTH RATES

Central Intelligence Agency, Washington, D.C. 20505 (703) 482-1100, www.cia.gov; *The World Factbook.*

Euromonitor International, Inc., 122 South Michigan Avenue, Suite 1200, Chicago, Illinois 60603 (800) 577-EURO; *International Marketing Data and Statistics;* and *The World Economic Factbook.*

Europa Publications Limited, 18 Bedford Square, London, WC1B 3JN, England; *The Europa World Year Book.*

M.E. Sharpe, 80 Business Park Drive, Armonk, New York 10504 (800) 541-6563; *The Illustrated Book of World Rankings.*

St. Martin's Press, Inc., 175 Fifth Avenue, New York, New York 10010 (800) 221-7945; *The Statesman's Year-Book.*

Statistical Office of the United Nations, Publishing Service, New York, New York 10017 (800) 253-9646; *Demographic Yearbook; Statistical Yearbook;* and *Statistical Yearbook for Latin America and the Caribbean.*

World Health Organization, Office of Publications, 20 Avenue Appia, CH-1211 Geneva 27, Switzerland (Telephone Number in U.S. (518) 436-9686); *World Health Statistics Annual.*

JAMAICA - BONDS

Inter-American Development Bank, 1300 New York Avenue, NW, Washington, D.C. 20577 (202) 623-1753; *Economic and Social Progress in Latin America.*

Organization of American States (OAS), General Secretariat, Washington, D.C. 20006 (202) 458-3533; *Statistical Bulletin of the OAS.*

Statistical Office of the United Nations, Publishing Service, New York, New York 10017 (800) 253-9646; *Statistical Yearbook.*

JAMAICA - BOOK PRODUCTION

United Nations Educational, Scientific and Cultural Organization (UNESCO), 7 Place de Fontenoy, F-75700 Paris, France (Telephone Number in U.S. (212) 963-5981); *Statistical Yearbook.*

JAMAICA - BROADCASTING

Billboard Limited, Post Office Box 9027, 1006 AA Amsterdam, The Netherlands (Telephone Number in U.S. (212) 764-7300); *World Radio TV Handbook.*

Central Intelligence Agency, Washington, D.C. 20505 (703) 482-1100, www.cia.gov; *The World Factbook.*

Euromonitor International, Inc., 122 South Michigan Avenue, Suite 1200, Chicago, Illinois 60603 (800) 577-EURO; *World Marketing Data and Statistics.*

M.E. Sharpe, 80 Business Park Drive, Armonk, New York 10504 (800) 541-6563; *The Illustrated Book of World Rankings.*

St. Martin's Press, Inc., 175 Fifth Avenue, New York, New York 10010 (800) 221-7945; *The Statesman's Year-Book.*

JAMAICA - BUDGET

Central Intelligence Agency, Washington, D.C. 20505 (703) 482-1100, www.cia.gov; *The World Factbook.*

JAMAICA - BUSINESS

Inter-American Development Bank, 1300 New York Avenue, NW, Washington, D.C. 20577 (202) 623-1517; *Economic and Social Progress in Latin America.*

JAMAICA - BUSINESS AND PROFESSIONAL LICENSES

International Monetary Fund, 700 Nineteenth Street, NW, Washington, D.C. 20431 (202) 623-7000; *Government Finance Statistics Yearbook.*

JAMAICA - CABBAGE PRODUCTION - See JAMAICA - CROPS

JAMAICA - CALORIE SUPPLY

Food and Agricultural Organization of the United Nations (FAO), Via delle Terme di Caracalla, 00100 Rome, Italy (Telephone Number in U.S. (202) 653-2400); *The State of Food and Agriculture.*

Statistical Office of the United Nations, Publishing Service, New York, New York 10017 (800) 253-9646; *Statistical Yearbook for Latin America and the Caribbean.*

JAMAICA - CAPITAL INVESTMENT

Inter-American Development Bank, 1300 New York Avenue, NW, Washington, D.C. 20577 (202) 623-1753; *Economic and Social Progress in Latin America.*

JAMAICA - CAPITAL REVENUE

Inter-American Development Bank, 1300 New York Avenue, NW, Washington, D.C. 20577 (202) 623-1753; *Economic and Social Progress in Latin America.*

International Monetary Fund, 700 Nineteenth Street, NW, Washington, D.C. 20431 (202) 623-7000; *Government Finance Statistics Yearbook.*

JAMAICA - CATTLE - See JAMAICA - LIVESTOCK AND POULTRY

JAMAICA - CEMENT PRODUCTION - See JAMAICA - MINING AND MINERAL PRODUCTS

JAMAICA - CHEMICAL (ORGANIC) PRODUCTION - See JAMAICA - MINING AND MINERAL PRODUCTS

JAMAICA - CHICKENS - See JAMAICA - LIVESTOCK AND POULTRY

JAMAICA - CIGAR AND CIGARETTE PRODUCTION - See JAMAICA - TOBACCO PRODUCTION

JAMAICA - CLIMATE

M.E. Sharpe, 80 Business Park Drive, Armonk, New York 10504 (800) 541-6563; *The Illustrated Book of World Rankings.*

St. Martin's Press, Inc., 175 Fifth Avenue, New York, New York 10010 (800) 221-7945; *The Statesman's Year-Book.*

JAMAICA - COAL PRODUCTION - See JAMAICA - MINING AND MINERAL PRODUCTS

JAMAICA - COCOA (BEANS) PRODUCTION - See JAMAICA - CROPS

JAMAICA - COFFEE PRODUCTION AND CONSUMPTION - See JAMAICA - CROPS

JAMAICA - COMMERCE

St. Martin's Press, Inc., 175 Fifth Avenue, New York, New York 10010 (800) 221-7945; *The Statesman's Year-Book.*

JAMAICA - COMMUNICATIONS - See JAMAICA - TRANSPORTATION AND COMMUNICATIONS

JAMAICA - CONSTRUCTION INDUSTRY

The Economist Intelligence Unit, 111 West 57th Street, New York, New York 10019 (800) 938-4685; *The New Latin America Market Atlas.*

Inter-American Development Bank, 1300 New York Avenue, NW, Washington, D.C. 20577 (202) 623-1753; *Economic and Social Progress in Latin America.*

M.E. Sharpe, 80 Business Park Drive, Armonk, New York 10504 (800) 541-6563; *The Illustrated Book of World Rankings.*

St. Martin's Press, Inc., 175 Fifth Avenue, New York, New York 10010 (800) 221-7945; *The Statesman's Year-Book.*

Statistical Office of the United Nations, Publishing Service, New York, New York 10017 (800) 253-9646; *Statistical Yearbook.*

JAMAICA - CONSUMER PRICE INDEX

Europa Publications Limited, 18 Bedford Square, London, WC1B 3JN, England; *The Europa World Year Book.*

International Labour Office, I.L.O. Publications, CH-1211, Geneva 22, Switzerland; *Yearbook of Labour Statistics.*

Statistical Office of the United Nations, Publishing Service, New York, New York 10017 (800) 253-9646; *Statistical Yearbook.*

JAMAICA - CONSUMER PRICES

The Economist Intelligence Unit, 111 West 57th Street, New York, New York 10019 (800) 938-4685; *The New Latin America Market Atlas.*

Euromonitor International, Inc., 122 South Michigan Avenue, Suite 1200, Chicago, Illinois 60603 (800) 577-EURO; *World Marketing Data and Statistics.*

International Labour Office, I.L.O. Publications, CH-1211, Geneva 22, Switzerland; *Yearbook of Labour Statistics.*

International Monetary Fund, 700

Nineteenth Street, NW, Washington, D.C. 20431 (202) 623-7000; *International Financial Statistics.*

Organization of American States (OAS), General Secretariat, Washington, D.C. 20006 (202) 458-3533; *Statistical Bulletin of the OAS.*

JAMAICA - CONSUMPTION

The Economist Intelligence Unit, 111 West 57th Street, New York, New York 10019 (800) 938-4685; *The New Latin America Market Atlas.*

Inter-American Development Bank, 1300 New York Avenue, NW, Washington, D.C. 20577 (202) 623-1753; *Economic and Social Progress in Latin America.*

Statistical Office of the United Nations, Publishing Service, New York, New York 10017 (800) 253-9646; *Statistical Yearbook for Latin America and the Caribbean.*

The World Bank, 1818 H Street, NW, Washington, D.C. 20433 (202) 477-1234; *World Development Report.*

JAMAICA - CORN PRODUCTION - See JAMAICA - CROPS

JAMAICA - CORPORATE TAXES - See JAMAICA - TAXATION

JAMAICA - COTTON - See JAMAICA - CROPS

JAMAICA - CRIME

Yale University Press, Yale Station, New Haven, Connecticut 06520 (800) 987-7323; *Violence and Crime in Cross-National Perspective.*

JAMAICA - CROPS

The Economist Intelligence Unit, 111 West 57th Street, New York, New York 10019 (800) 938-4685; *The New Latin America Market Atlas.*

Europa Publications Limited, 18 Bedford Square, London, WC1B 3JN, England; *The Europa World Year Book.*

Food and Agricultural Organization of the United Nations (FAO) Via delle Terme di Caracalla, 00100 Rome, Italy (Telephone Number in U.S. (202) 653-2400); *The State of Food and Agriculture;* and *Production Yearbook.*

International Monetary Fund, 700 Nineteenth Street, NW, Washington, D.C. 20431 (202) 623-7000; *International Financial Statistics.*

M.E. Sharpe, 80 Business Park Drive, Armonk, New York 10504 (800) 541-6563;

The Illustrated Book of World Rankings.

Organization of American States (OAS), General Secretariat, Washington, D.C. 20006 (202) 458-3533; *Statistical Bulletin of the OAS.*

St. Martin's Press, Inc., 175 Fifth Avenue, New York, New York 10010 (800) 221-7945; *The Statesman's Year-Book.*

Statistical Office of the United Nations, Publishing Service, New York, New York 10017 (800) 253-9646; *Statistical Yearbook.*

United Nations Conference on Trade and Development, Central Statistical Service, Palais des Nations, Geneva, Switzerland (Telephone in U.S. (800) 253-9646); *UNCTAD Commodity Yearbook.*

JAMAICA - CUSTOMS DUTIES

Inter-American Development Bank, 1300 New York Avenue, NW, Washington, D.C. 20577 (202) 623-1753; *Economic and Social Progress in Latin America.*

International Monetary Fund, 700 Nineteenth Street, NW, Washington, D.C. 20431 (202) 623-7000; *Government Finance Statistics Yearbook.*

St. Martin's Press, Inc., 175 Fifth Avenue, New York, New York 10010 (800) 221-7945; *The Statesman's Year-Book.*

JAMAICA - DAIRY PRODUCTS

Europa Publications Limited, 18 Bedford Square, London, WC1B 3JN, England; *The Europa World Year Book.*

Food and Agricultural Organization of the United Nations (FAO), Via delle Terme di Caracalla, 00100 Rome, Italy (Telephone Number in U.S. (202) 653-2400); *Production Yearbook;* and *The State of Food and Agriculture.*

M.E. Sharpe, 80 Business Park Drive, Armonk, New York 10504 (800) 541-6563; *The Illustrated Book of World Rankings.*

St. Martin's Press, Inc., 175 Fifth Avenue, New York, New York 10010 (800) 221-7945; *The Statesman's Year-Book.*

Statistical Office of the United Nations, Publishing Service, New York, New York 10017 (800) 253-9646; *Statistical Yearbook.*

JAMAICA - DEATH RATES - See JAMAICA - MORTALITY

JAMAICA - DEBT

The Economist Intelligence Unit, 111 West 57th Street, New York, New York 10019 (800) 938-4685; *The New Latin America Market Atlas.*

JAMAICA - DEFENSE

The Economist Intelligence Unit, 111 West 57th Street, New York, New York 10019 (800) 938-4685; *The New Latin America Market Atlas.*

JAMAICA - DEFENSE EXPENDITURES - See JAMAICA - MILITARY

JAMAICA - DEMOGRAPHY

The Economist Intelligence Unit, 111 West 57th Street, New York, New York 10019 (800) 938-4685; *The World Market Atlas.*

Euromonitor International, Inc., 122 South Michigan Avenue, Suite 1200, Chicago, Illinois 60603 (800) 577-EURO; *International Marketing Data and Statistics; The World Economic Factbook;* and *World Marketing Data and Statistics..*

M.E. Sharpe, 80 Business Park Drive, Armonk, New York 10504 (800) 541-6563; *The Illustrated Book of World Rankings.*

Statistical Office of the United Nations, Publishing Service, New York, New York 10017 (800) 253-9646; *Human Development Report.*

JAMAICA - DEVELOPMENT ASSISTANCE

Inter-American Development Bank, 1300 New York Avenue, NW, Washington, D.C. 20577 (202) 623-1753; *Economic and Social Progress in Latin America.*

Statistical Office of the United Nations, Publishing Service, New York, New York 10017 (800) 253-9646; *Statistical Yearbook.*

JAMAICA - DIAMOND PRODUCTION - See JAMAICA - MINING AND MINERAL PRODUCTS

JAMAICA - DISCOUNT RATES - See JAMAICA - BANKING

JAMAICA - DISEASES - See JAMAICA - HEALTH

JAMAICA - DIVORCE RATES

M.E. Sharpe, 80 Business Park Drive, Armonk, New York 10504 (800) 541-6563; *The Illustrated Book of World Rankings.*

Statistical Office of the United Nations, Publishing Service, New York, New York 10017 (800) 253-9646; *Demographic Yearbook;* and *Statistical Yearbook.*

JAMAICA - ECONOMY

Central Intelligence Agency, Washington, D.C. 20505 (703) 482-1100, www.cia.gov; *The World Factbook.*

The Economist Intelligence Unit, 111 West 57th Street, New York, New York 10019 (800) 938-4685; *Jamaica Country Report.*

Euromonitor International, Inc., 122 South Michigan Avenue, Suite 1200, Chicago, Illinois 60603 (800) 577-EURO; *International Marketing Data and Statistics; The World Economic Factbook;* and *World Marketing Data and Statistics..*

Europa Publications Limited, 18 Bedford Square, London, WC1B 3JN, England; *The Europa World Year Book.*

Inter-American Development Bank, 1300 New York Avenue, NW, Washington, D.C. 20577 (202) 623-1753; *Economic and Social Progress in Latin America.*

M.E. Sharpe, 80 Business Park Drive, Armonk, New York 10504 (800) 541-6563; *The Illustrated Book of World Rankings.*

Organization of American States (OAS), General Secretariat, Washington, D.C. 20006 (202) 458-3533; *Statistical Bulletin of the OAS.*

St. Martin's Press, Inc., 175 Fifth Avenue, New York, New York 10010 (800) 221-7945; *The Statesman's Year-Book.*

Statistical Office of the United Nations, Publishing Service, New York, New York 10017 (800) 253-9646; *Economic Survey of Latin America and the Caribbean;* and *World Statistics Pocketbook.*

The World Bank, 1818 H Street, NW, Washington, D.C. 20433 (202) 477-1234; *The World Bank Atlas;* and *World Development Report.*

JAMAICA - EDUCATION

The Economist Intelligence Unit, 111 West 57th Street, New York, New York 10019 (800) 938-4685; *The New Latin America Market Atlas;* and *The World Market Atlas.*

Euromonitor International, Inc., 122 South Michigan Avenue, Suite 1200, Chicago, Illinois 60603 (800) 577-EURO; *International Marketing Data and Statistics; and World Marketing Data and Statistics..*

Europa Publications Limited, 18 Bedford Square, London, WC1B 3JN, England; *The Europa World Year Book.*

International Monetary Fund, 700 Nineteenth Street, NW, Washington, D.C. 20431 (202) 623-7000; *Government Finance Statistics Yearbook.*

M.E. Sharpe, 80 Business Park Drive, Armonk, New York 10504 (800) 541-6563; *The Illustrated Book of World Rankings.*

St. Martin's Press, Inc., 175 Fifth Avenue, New York, New York 10010 (800) 221-7945; *The Statesman's Year-Book.*

Statistical Office of the United Nations, Publishing Service, New York, New York 10017 (800) 253-9646; *Human Development Report;* and *Statistical Yearbook for Latin America and the Caribbean.*

United Nations Educational, Scientific and Cultural Organization (UNESCO), 7 Place de Fontenoy, F-75700 Paris, France (Telephone Number in U.S. (212) 963-5981); *Statistical Yearbook.*

The World Bank, 1818 H Street, NW, Washington, D.C. 20433 (202) 477-1234; *World Development Report.*

JAMAICA - EGG PRODUCTION AND CONSUMPTION - See JAMAICA - DAIRY PRODUCTS

JAMAICA - ELECTRICITY

Central Intelligence Agency, Washington, D.C. 20505 (703) 482-1100, www.cia.gov; *The World Factbook.*

The Economist Intelligence Unit, 111 West 57th Street, New York, New York 10019 (800) 938-4685; *The New Latin America Market Atlas.*

Inter-American Development Bank, 1300 New York Avenue, NW, Washington, D.C. 20577 (202) 623-1753; *Economic and Social Progress in Latin America.*

M.E. Sharpe, 80 Business Park Drive, Armonk, New York 10504 (800) 541-6563; *The Illustrated Book of World Rankings.*

Organization of American States (OAS), General Secretariat, Washington, D.C. 20006 (202) 458-3533; *Statistical Bulletin of the OAS.*

St. Martin's Press, Inc., 175 Fifth Avenue, New York, New York 10010 (800) 221-7945; *The Statesman's Year-Book.*

Statistical Office of the United Nations, Publishing Service, New York, New York 10017 (800) 253-9646; *Human Development Report;* and *Statistical Yearbook.*

JAMAICA - EMPLOYMENT

Euromonitor International, Inc., 122 South Michigan Avenue, Suite 1200, Chicago, Illinois 60603 (800) 577-EURO; *International Marketing Data and Statistics.*

International Labour Office, I.L.O. Publications, CH-1211, Geneva 22, Switzerland; *Yearbook of Labour Statistics.*

M.E. Sharpe, 80 Business Park Drive, Armonk, New York 10504 (800) 541-6563; *The Illustrated Book of World Rankings.*

Statistical Office of the United Nations, Publishing Service, New York, New York 10017 (800) 253-9646; *Statistical Yearbook for Latin America and the Caribbean.*

JAMAICA - ENERGY

The Economist Intelligence Unit, 111 West 57th Street, New York, New York 10019 (800) 938-4685; *The New Latin America Market Atlas.*

Euromonitor International, Inc., 122 South Michigan Avenue, Suite 1200, Chicago, Illinois 60603 (800) 577-EURO; *International Marketing Data and Statistics; The World Economic Factbook; and World Marketing Data and Statistics.*

Food and Agricultural Organization of the United Nations (FAO), Via delle Terme di Caracalla, 00100 Rome, Italy (Telephone Number in U.S. (202) 653-2400); *The State of Food and Agriculture.*

M.E. Sharpe, 80 Business Park Drive, Armonk, New York 10504 (800) 541-6563; *The Illustrated Book of World Rankings.*

St. Martin's Press, Inc., 175 Fifth Avenue, New York, New York 10010 (800) 221-7945; *The Statesman's Year-Book.*

Statistical Office of the United Nations, Publishing Service, New York, New York 10017 (800) 253-9646; *Energy Statistics Yearbook; Human Development Report; Statistical Yearbook; World Statistics Pocketbook;* and *Statistical Yearbook for Latin America and the Caribbean.*

The World Bank, 1818 H Street, NW, Washington, D.C. 20433 (202) 477-1234; *The World Bank Atlas;* and *World Development Report.*

JAMAICA - ENVIRONMENT

The Economist Intelligence Unit, 111 West 57th Street, New York, New York 10019 (800) 938-4685; *Jamaica Country Report.*

Statistical Office of the United Nations, Publishing Service, New York, New York 10017 (800) 253-9646; *Bulletin of Industrial Statistics for the Arab Countries.*

JAMAICA - EXCHANGE RATES

Central Intelligence Agency, Washington, D.C. 20505 (703) 482-1100, www.cia.gov; *The World Factbook.*

Euromonitor International, Inc., 122 South Michigan Avenue, Suite 1200, Chicago, Illinois 60603 (800) 577-EURO;

International Marketing Data and Statistics; and *The World Economic Factbook.*

Europa Publications Limited, 18 Bedford Square, London, WC1B 3JN, England; *The Europa World Year Book.*

Inter-American Development Bank, 1300 New York Avenue, NW, Washington, D.C. 20577 (202) 623-1753; *Economic and Social Progress in Latin America.*

International Civil Aviation Organization, 999 University Street, Montreal, Quebec, Canada H3C 5H7 (514) 954-8219; *Civil Aviation Statistics of the World.*

International Monetary Fund, 700 Nineteenth Street, NW, Washington, D.C. 20431 (202) 623-7000; *International Financial Statistics.*

Organization of American States (OAS), General Secretariat, Washington, D.C. 20006 (202) 458-3533; *Statistical Bulletin of the OAS.*

Statistical Office of the United Nations, Publishing Service, New York, New York 10017 (800) 253-9646; *Statistical Yearbook;* and *World Statistics Pocketbook.*

JAMAICA - EXCISE TAXES - See JAMAICA - TAXATION

JAMAICA - EXPORTS

Central Intelligence Agency, Washington, D.C. 20505 (703) 482-1100, www.cia.gov; *The World Factbook.*

The Economist Intelligence Unit, 111 West 57th Street, New York, New York 10019 (800) 938-4685; *Jamaica Country Report; The New Latin America Market Atlas;* and *The World Market Atlas.*

Euromonitor International, Inc., 122 South Michigan Avenue, Suite 1200, Chicago, Illinois 60603 (800) 577-EURO; *International Marketing Data and Statistics;* and *The World Economic Factbook.*

Europa Publications Limited, 18 Bedford Square, London, WC1B 3JN, England; *The Europa World Year Book.*

Food and Agricultural Organization of the United Nations (FAO) Via delle Terme di Caracalla, 00100 Rome, Italy (Telephone Number in U.S. (202) 653-2400); *The State of Food and Agriculture.*

Inter-American Development Bank, 1300 New York Avenue, NW, Washington, D.C. 20577 (202) 623-1753; *Economic and Social Progress in Latin America.*

International Monetary Fund, 700 Nineteenth Street, NW, Washington,

D.C. 20431 (202) 623-7000; *Direction of Trade Statistics; Government Finance Statistics Yearbook;* and *International Financial Statistics.*

Organization of American States (OAS), General Secretariat, Washington, D.C. 20006 (202) 458-3533; *Statistical Bulletin of the OAS.*

St. Martin's Press, Inc., 175 Fifth Avenue, New York, New York 10010 (800) 221-7945; *The Statesman's Year-Book.*

Statistical Office of the United Nations, Publishing Service, New York, New York 10017 (800) 253-9646; *Statistical Yearbook for Latin America and the Caribbean.*

United Nations Conference on Trade and Development (UNCTAD), New York, New York 10017 (800) 253-9646; *Handbook of International Trade and Development Statistics.*

The World Bank, 1818 H Street, NW, Washington, D.C. 20433 (202) 477-1234; *World Development Report.*

JAMAICA - EXTERNAL FINANCING

Inter-American Development Bank, 1300 New York Avenue, NW, Washington, D.C. 20577 (202) 623-1753; *Economic and Social Progress in Latin America.*

Statistical Office of the United Nations, Publishing Service, New York, New York 10017 (800) 253-9646; *Statistical Yearbook for Latin America and the Caribbean.*

JAMAICA - EXTERNAL INDEBTEDNESS

Inter-American Development Bank, 1300 New York Avenue, NW, Washington, D.C. 20577 (202) 623-1753; *Economic and Social Progress in Latin America.*

Statistical Office of the United Nations, Publishing Service, New York, New York 10017 (800) 253-9646; *Statistical Yearbook for Latin America and the Caribbean.*

The World Bank, 1818 H Street, NW, Washington, D.C. 20433 (202) 477-1234; *World Development Report.*

JAMAICA - EXTERNAL TRADE

Euromonitor International, Inc., 122 South Michigan Avenue, Suite 1200, Chicago, Illinois 60603 (800) 577-EURO; *World Marketing Data and Statistics.*

Food and Agricultural Organization of the United Nations (FAO), Via delle Terme di Caracalla, 00100 Rome, Italy (Telephone Number in U.S. (202) 653-2400); *The State of Food and Agriculture;* and *Trade Yearbook.*

Inter-American Development Bank, 1300 New York Avenue, NW, Washington, D.C. 20577 (202) 623-1753; *Economic and Social Progress in Latin America.*

Statistical Office of the United Nations, Publishing Service, New York, New York 10017 (800) 253-9646; *Statistical Yearbook;* and *Statistical Yearbook for Latin America and the Caribbean.*

JAMAICA - FABRIC PRODUCTION - See JAMAICA - TEXTILE INDUSTRY

JAMAICA - FARM CROPS - See JAMAICA - CROPS

JAMAICA - FEMALE WORKING POPULATION - See JAMAICA - EMPLOYMENT

JAMAICA - FERTILITY RATES

Central Intelligence Agency, Washington, D.C. 20505 (703) 482-1100, www.cia.gov; *The World Factbook.*

M.E. Sharpe, 80 Business Park Drive, Armonk, New York 10504 (800) 541-6563; *The Illustrated Book of World Rankings.*

Statistical Office of the United Nations, Publishing Service, New York, New York 10017 (800) 253-9646; *Human Development Report.*

The World Bank, 1818 H Street, NW, Washington, D.C. 20433 (202) 477-1234; *The World Bank Atlas;* and *World Development Report.*

JAMAICA - FERTILIZER

The Economist Intelligence Unit, 111 West 57th Street, New York, New York 10019 (800) 938-4685; *The New Latin America Market Atlas.*

Food and Agricultural Organization of the United Nations (FAO), Via delle Terme di Caracalla, 00100, Rome, Italy (Telephone Number in U.S. (202) 653-2400); *Fertilizer Yearbook;* and *The State of Food and Agriculture.*

Statistical Office of the United Nations, Publishing Service, New York, New York 10017 (800) 253-9646; *Statistical Yearbook.*

JAMAICA - FETAL MORTALITY - See JAMAICA - MORTALITY

JAMAICA - FINANCE

The Economist Intelligence Unit, 111 West 57th Street, New York, New York 10019 (800) 938-4685; *Jamaica Country Report.*

Europa Publications Limited, 18 Bedford Square, London, WC1B 3JN,

England; *The Europa World Year Book.*

Inter-American Development Bank, 1300 New York Avenue, NW, Washington, D.C. 20577 (202) 623-1753; *Economic and Social Progress in Latin America.*

International Monetary Fund, 700 Nineteenth Street, NW, Washington, D.C. 20431 (202) 623-7000; *International Financial Statistics.*

M.E. Sharpe, 80 Business Park Drive, Armonk, New York 10504 (800) 541-6563; *The Illustrated Book of World Rankings.*

Organization of American States (OAS), General Secretariat, Washington, D.C. 20006 (202) 458-3533; *Statistical Bulletin of the OAS.*

St. Martin's Press, Inc., 175 Fifth Avenue, New York, New York 10010 (800) 221-7945; *The Statesman's Year-Book.*

JAMAICA - FISHERIES

Europa Publications Limited, 18 Bedford Square, London, WC1B 3JN, England; *The Europa World Year Book.*

Food and Agricultural Organization of the United Nations (FAO), Via delle Terme di Caracalla, 00100 Rome, Italy (Telephone Number in U.S. (202) 653-2400); *The State of Food and Agriculture;* and *Yearbook of Fishery Statistics.*

Inter-American Development Bank, 1300 New York Avenue, NW, Washington, D.C. 20577 (202) 623-1753; *Economic and Social Progress in Latin America.*

M.E. Sharpe, 80 Business Park Drive, Armonk, New York 10504 (800) 541-6563; *The Illustrated Book of World Rankings.*

Statistical Office of the United Nations, Publishing Service, New York, New York 10017 (800) 253-9646; *Statistical Yearbook.*

United Nations Conference on Trade and Development, Central Statistical Service, Palais des Nations, Geneva, Switzerland (Telephone in U.S. (800) 253-9646); *UNCTAD Commodity Yearbook.*

JAMAICA - FLOUR PRODUCTION

Statistical Office of the United Nations, Publishing Service, New York, New York 10017 (800) 253-9646; *Statistical Yearbook.*

JAMAICA - FOOD

Food and Agricultural Organization of the United Nations (FAO), Via delle Terme di Caracalla, 00100 Rome, Italy (Telephone Number in U.S. (202) 653-2400); *Production Yearbook;* and *The State of Food and Agriculture.*

Statistical Office of the United Nations, Publishing Service, New York, New York 10017 (800) 253-9646; *Human Development Report.*

United Nations Conference on Trade and Development, Central Statistical Service, Palais des Nations, Geneva, Switzerland (Telephone in U.S. (800) 253-9646); *UNCTAD Commodity Yearbook.*

JAMAICA - FOREIGN AID

Inter-American Development Bank, 1300 New York Avenue, NW, Washington, D.C. 20577 (202) 623-1753; *Economic and Social Progress in Latin America.*

JAMAICA - FOREIGN DEBT

The Economist Intelligence Unit, 111 West 57th Street, New York, New York 10019 (800) 938-4685; *The New Latin America Market Atlas.*

Inter-American Development Bank, 1300 New York Avenue, NW, Washington, D.C. 20577 (202) 623-1753; *Economic and Social Progress in Latin America.*

St. Martin's Press, Inc., 175 Fifth Avenue, New York, New York 10010 (800) 221-7945; *The Statesman's Year-Book.*

JAMAICA - FOREIGN INDEBTEDNESS

Inter-American Development Bank, 1300 New York Avenue, NW, Washington, D.C. 20577 (202) 623-1753; *Economic and Social Progress in Latin America.*

Statistical Office of the United Nations, Publishing Service, New York, New York 10017 (800) 253-9646; *Economic Survey of Latin America and the Caribbean.*

JAMAICA - FOREIGN INVESTMENT

The Economist Intelligence Unit, 111 West 57th Street, New York, New York 10019 (800) 938-4685; *The New Latin America Market Atlas.*

JAMAICA - FOREIGN TRADE

The Economist Intelligence Unit, 111 West 57th Street, New York, New York 10019 (800) 938-4685; *Jamaica Country Report;* and *The New Latin America Market Atlas.*

Euromonitor International, Inc., 122 South Michigan Avenue, Suite 1200, Chicago, Illinois 60603 (800) 577-EURO; *International Marketing Data and Statistics;* and *The World Economic Factbook.*

Europa Publications Limited, 18 Bedford Square, London, WC1B 3JN, England; *The Europa World Year Book.*

Food and Agricultural Organization of the United Nations (FAO), Via delle Terme di Caracalla, 00100 Rome, Italy (Telephone Number in U.S. (202) 653-2400); *The State of Food and Agriculture.*

Inter-American Development Bank, 1300 New York Avenue, NW, Washington, D.C. 20577 (202) 623-1753; *Economic and Social Progress in Latin America.*

International Monetary Fund, 700 Nineteenth Street, NW, Washington, D.C. 20431 (202) 623-7000; *International Financial Statistics.*

M.E. Sharpe, 80 Business Park Drive, Armonk, New York 10504 (800) 541-6563; *The Illustrated Book of World Rankings.*

St. Martin's Press, Inc., 175 Fifth Avenue, New York, New York 10010 (800) 221-7945; *The Statesman's Year-Book.*

Statistical Office of the United Nations, Publishing Service, New York, New York 10017 (800) 253-9646; *Economic Survey of Latin America and the Caribbean; International Trade Statistics Yearbook;* and *Statistical Yearbook.*

United Nations Conference on Trade and Development, Central Statistical Service, Palais des Nations, Geneva, Switzerland (Telephone in U.S. (800) 253-9646); *UNCTAD Commodity Yearbook.*

The World Bank, 1818 H Street, NW, Washington, D.C. 20433 (202) 477-1234; *World Development Report.*

JAMAICA - FORESTRY AND FOREST PRODUCTS

The Economist Intelligence Unit, 111 West 57th Street, New York, New York 10019 (800) 938-4685; *The New Latin America Market Atlas.*

Europa Publications Limited, 18 Bedford Square, London, WC1B 3JN, England; *The Europa World Year Book.*

Food and Agricultural Organization of the United Nations (FAO), Via delle Terme di Caracalla, 00100 Rome, Italy (Telephone Number in U.S. (202) 653-2400); *The State of Food and Agriculture;* and *Yearbook of Forest Products.*

Inter-American Development Bank, 1300 New York Avenue, NW, Washington, D.C. 20577 (202) 623-1753; *Economic and Social Progress in Latin America.*

M.E. Sharpe, 80 Business Park Drive, Armonk, New York 10504 (800) 541-6563; *The Illustrated Book of World Rankings.*

Statistical Office of the United Nations, Publishing Service, New York, New York

10017 (800) 253-9646; *Statistical Yearbook.*

United Nations Conference on Trade and Development, Central Statistical Service, Palais des Nations, Geneva, Switzerland (Telephone in U.S. (800) 253-9646); *UNCTAD Commodity Yearbook.*

United Nations Educational, Scientific and Cultural Organization (UNESCO), 7 Place de Fontenoy, F-75700 Paris, France (Telephone Number in U.S. (212) 963-5981); *Statistical Yearbook.*

The World Bank, 1818 H Street, NW, Washington, D.C. 20433 (202) 477-1234; *World Development Report.*

JAMAICA - GAS PRODUCTION - See JAMAICA - MINING AND MINERAL PRODUCTS

JAMAICA - GENERAL INDUSTRIAL STATISTICS - See JAMAICA - INDUSTRY

JAMAICA - GENERAL MORTALITY - See JAMAICA - MORTALITY

JAMAICA - GEOGRAPHIC DATA

M.E. Sharpe, 80 Business Park Drive, Armonk, New York 10504 (800) 541-6563; *The Illustrated Book of World Rankings.*

JAMAICA - GOATS - See JAMAICA - LIVESTOCK AND POULTRY

JAMAICA - GOLD HOLDINGS

International Monetary Fund, 700 Nineteenth Street, NW, Washington, D.C. 20431 (202) 623-7000; *International Financial Statistics.*

Statistical Office of the United Nations, Publishing Service, New York, New York 10017 (800) 253-9646; *Statistical Yearbook.*

JAMAICA - GOLD PRODUCTION AND CONSUMPTION - See JAMAICA - MINING AND MINERAL PRODUCTS

JAMAICA - GOLD RESERVES

The Economist Intelligence Unit, 111 West 57th Street, New York, New York 10019 (800) 938-4685; *The New Latin America Market Atlas.*

JAMAICA - GOVERNMENT

Central Intelligence Agency, Washington, D.C. 20505 (703) 482-1100, www.cia.gov; *The World Factbook.*

Europa Publications Limited, 18 Bedford Square, London, WC1B 3JN, England; *The Europa World Year Book.*

Inter-American Development Bank, 1300 New York Avenue, NW, Washington,

D.C. 20577 (202) 623-1753; *Economic and Social Progress in Latin America.*

International Monetary Fund, 700 Nineteenth Street, NW, Washington, D.C. 20431 (202) 623-7000; *Government Finance Statistics Yearbook;* and *International Financial Statistics.*

St. Martin's Press, Inc., 175 Fifth Avenue, New York, New York 10010 (800) 221-7945; *The Statesman's Year-Book.*

Statistical Office of the United Nations, Publishing Service, New York, New York 10017 (800) 253-9646; *National Accounts Statistics;* and *Statistical Yearbook.*

The World Bank, 1818 H Street, NW, Washington, D.C. 20433 (202) 477-1234; *World Development Report.*

JAMAICA - GRAIN PRODUCTION - See JAMAICA - CROPS

JAMAICA - GRANTS

International Monetary Fund, 700 Nineteenth Street, NW, Washington, D.C. 20431 (202) 623-7000; *Government Finance Statistics Yearbook.*

JAMAICA - GROSS DOMESTIC PRODUCT

The Economist Intelligence Unit, 111 West 57th Street, New York, New York 10019 (800) 938-4685; *Jamaica Country Report; The New Latin America Market Atlas;* and *The World Market Atlas.*

Euromonitor International, Inc., 122 South Michigan Avenue, Suite 1200, Chicago, Illinois 60603 (800) 577-EURO; *International Marketing Data and Statistics;* and *The World Economic Factbook.*

Europa Publications Limited, 18 Bedford Square, London, WC1B 3JN, England; *The Europa World Year Book.*

Inter-American Development Bank, 1300 New York Avenue, NW, Washington, D.C. 20577 (202) 623-1753; *Economic and Social Progress in Latin America.*

M.E. Sharpe, 80 Business Park Drive, Armonk, New York 10504 (800) 541-6563; *The Illustrated Book of World Rankings.*

Organization of American States (OAS), General Secretariat, Washington, D.C. 20006 (202) 458-3533; *Statistical Bulletin of the OAS.*

Statistical Office of the United Nations, Publishing Service, New York, New York 10017 (800) 253-9646; *Human Development Report; National Accounts Statistics; Statistical Yearbook;* and *Statistical Yearbook for Latin America and the Caribbean.*

The World Bank, 1818 H Street, NW, Washington, D.C. 20433 (202) 477-1234; *World Development Report.*

JAMAICA - GROSS NATIONAL PRODUCT

Euromonitor International, Inc., 122 South Michigan Avenue, Suite 1200, Chicago, Illinois 60603 (800) 577-EURO; *International Marketing Data and Statistics.*

Inter-American Development Bank, 1300 New York Avenue, NW, Washington, D.C. 20577 (202) 623-1753; *Economic and Social Progress in Latin America.*

St. Martin's Press, Inc., 175 Fifth Avenue, New York, New York 10010 (800) 221-7945; *The Statesman's Year-Book.*

U.S. Arms Control and Disarmament Agency, 320 Twenty-first Street, NW, Washington, D.C. 20451 (202) 647-8677; *World Military Expenditures and Arms Transfers.*

The World Bank, 1818 H Street, NW, Washington, D.C. 20433 (202) 477-1234; *The World Bank Atlas;* and *World Development Report.*

JAMAICA - GROUNDNUTS PRODUCTION - See JAMAICA - CROPS

JAMAICA - HEALTH

The Economist Intelligence Unit, 111 West 57th Street, New York, New York 10019 (800) 938-4685; *The New Latin America Market Atlas.*

Euromonitor International, Inc., 122 South Michigan Avenue, Suite 1200, Chicago, Illinois 60603 (800) 577-EURO; *World Marketing Data and Statistics.*

M.E. Sharpe, 80 Business Park Drive, Armonk, New York 10504 (800) 541-6563; *The Illustrated Book of World Rankings.*

St. Martin's Press, Inc., 175 Fifth Avenue, New York, New York 10010 (800) 221-7945; *The Statesman's Year-Book.*

Statistical Office of the United Nations, Publishing Service, New York, New York 10017 (800) 253-9646; *Human Development Report; Statistical Yearbook;* and *Statistical Yearbook for Latin America and the Caribbean.*

United Nations Children's Fund (UNICEF), 3 United Nations Plaza, New York, New York 10017 (800) 253-9646; *State of the World's Children.*

The World Bank, 1818 H Street, NW, Washington, D.C. 20433 (202) 477-1234; *World Development Report.*

World Health Organization, Office of Publications, 20 Avenue Appia, CH-1211 Geneva 27, Switzerland (Telephone Number in U.S. (518) 436-9686); *World Health Statistics Annual.*

JAMAICA - HEALTH EXPENDITURES

International Monetary Fund, 700 Nineteenth Street, NW, Washington, D.C. 20431 (202) 623-7000; *Government Finance Statistics Yearbook.*

Statistical Office of the United Nations, Publishing Service, New York, New York 10017 (800) 253-9646; *Statistical Yearbook for Latin America and the Caribbean.*

JAMAICA - HIDE PRODUCTION

Food and Agricultural Organization of the United Nations (FAO), Via delle Terme di Caracalla, 00100 Rome, Italy (Telephone Number in U.S. (202) 653-2400); *Production Yearbook.*

JAMAICA - HIGHWAYS

Central Intelligence Agency, Washington, D.C. 20505 (703) 482-1100, www.cia.gov; *The World Factbook.*

The Economist Intelligence Unit, 111 West 57th Street, New York, New York 10019 (800) 938-4685; *The New Latin America Market Atlas.*

St. Martin's Press, Inc., 175 Fifth Avenue, New York, New York 10010 (800) 221-7945; *The Statesman's Year-Book.*

JAMAICA - HORSES - See JAMAICA - LIVESTOCK AND POULTRY

JAMAICA - HOURS OF WORK - See JAMAICA - EMPLOYMENT

JAMAICA - HOUSING AND HOUSING UNITS

Euromonitor International, Inc., 122 South Michigan Avenue, Suite 1200, Chicago, Illinois 60603 (800) 577-EURO; *World Marketing Data and Statistics.*

M.E. Sharpe, 80 Business Park Drive, Armonk, New York 10504 (800) 541-6563; *The Illustrated Book of World Rankings.*

Statistical Office of the United Nations, Publishing Service, New York, New York 10017 (800) 253-9646; *Statistical Yearbook for Latin America and the Caribbean.*

JAMAICA - HOUSING EXPENDITURES

International Monetary Fund, 700 Nineteenth Street, NW, Washington, D.C. 20431 (202) 623-7000; *Government Finance Statistics Yearbook.*

JAMAICA - ILLITERACY RATES

The Economist Intelligence Unit, 111 West 57th Street, New York, New York 10019 (800) 938-4685; *The New Latin America Market Atlas.*

JAMAICA - ILLITERATE POPULATION

Central Intelligence Agency, Washington, D.C. 20505 (703) 482-1100, www.cia.gov; *The World Factbook.*

The Economist Intelligence Unit, 111 West 57th Street, New York, New York 10019 (800) 938-4685; *The World Market Atlas.*

Euromonitor International, Inc., 122 South Michigan Avenue, Suite 1200, Chicago, Illinois 60603 (800) 577-EURO; *The World Economic Factbook.*

Statistical Office of the United Nations, Publishing Service, New York, New York 10017 (800) 253-9646; *Human Development Report;* and *Statistical Yearbook for Latin America and the Caribbean.*

United Nations Educational, Scientific and Cultural Organization (UNESCO), 7 Place de Fontenoy, F-75700 Paris, France (Telephone Number in U.S. (212) 963-5981); *Statistical Yearbook.*

JAMAICA - IMPORTS

Central Intelligence Agency, Washington, D.C. 20505 (703) 482-1100, www.cia.gov; *The World Factbook.*

The Economist Intelligence Unit, 111 West 57th Street, New York, New York 10019 (800) 938-4685; *Jamaica Country Report; The New Latin America Market Atlas;* and *The World Market Atlas.*

Euromonitor International, Inc., 122 South Michigan Avenue, Suite 1200, Chicago, Illinois 60603 (800) 577-EURO; *International Marketing Data and Statistics;* and *The World Economic Factbook.*

Europa Publications Limited, 18 Bedford Square, London, WC1B 3JN, England; *The Europa World Year Book.*

Food and Agricultural Organization of the United Nations (FAO), Via delle Terme di Caracalla, 00100 Rome, Italy (Telephone Number in U.S. (202) 653-2400); *The State of Food and Agriculture.*

Inter-American Development Bank, 1300 New York Avenue, NW, Washington, D.C. 20577 (202) 623-1753; *Economic and Social Progress in Latin America.*

International Monetary Fund, 700 Nineteenth Street, NW, Washington,

D.C. 20431 (202) 623-7000; *Direction of Trade Statistics; Government Finance Statistics Yearbook;* and *International Financial Statistics.*

Organization of American States (OAS), General Secretariat, Washington, D.C. 20006 (202) 458-3533; *Statistical Bulletin of the OAS.*

St. Martin's Press, Inc., 175 Fifth Avenue, New York, New York 10010 (800) 221-7945; *The Statesman's Year-Book.*

Statistical Office of the United Nations, Publishing Service, New York, New York 10017 (800) 253-9646; *Statistical Yearbook for Latin America and the Caribbean.*

United Nations Conference on Trade and Development (UNCTAD), New York, New York 10017 (800) 253-9646; *Handbook of International Trade and Development Statistics.*

The World Bank, 1818 H Street, NW, Washington, D.C. 20433 (202) 477-1234; *World Development Report.*

JAMAICA - INCOME DISTRIBUTION

Statistical Office of the United Nations, Publishing Service, New York, New York 10017 (800) 253-9646; *Statistical Yearbook for Latin America and the Caribbean.*

JAMAICA - INCOME TAXES - See JAMAICA - TAXATION

JAMAICA - INDUSTRY

Central Intelligence Agency, Washington, D.C. 20505 (703) 482-1100, www.cia.gov; *The World Factbook.*

The Economist Intelligence Unit, 111 West 57th Street, New York, New York 10019 (800) 938-4685; *Jamaica Country Report.*

Euromonitor International, Inc., 122 South Michigan Avenue, Suite 1200, Chicago, Illinois 60603 (800) 577-EURO; *International Marketing Data and Statistics; World Marketing Data and Statistics;* and *The World Economic Factbook.*

Europa Publications Limited, 18 Bedford Square, London, WC1B 3JN, England; *The Europa World Year Book.*

International Labour Office, I.L.O. Publications, CH-1211, Geneva 22, Switzerland; *Yearbook of Labour Statistics.*

M.E. Sharpe, 80 Business Park Drive, Armonk, New York 10504 (800) 541-6563; *The Illustrated Book of World Rankings.*

St. Martin's Press, Inc., 175 Fifth Avenue, New York, New York 10010 (800)

221-7945; *The Statesman's Year-Book.*

Statistical Office of the United Nations, Publishing Service, New York, New York 10017 (800) 253-9646; *Statistical Yearbook; Industrial Commodity Statistics Yearbook;* and *Economic Survey of Latin America and the Caribbean.*

World Intellectual Property Organization, 34 Chemin des Colombettes, CH-1211 Geneva 20, Switzerland; *Industrial Property Statistics.*

JAMAICA - INFANT AND MATERNAL MORTALITY - See JAMAICA - MORTALITY

JAMAICA - INFLATIONARY FACTORS

Statistical Office of the United Nations, Publishing Service, New York, New York 10017 (800) 253-9646; *Economic Survey of Latin America and the Caribbean.*

JAMAICA - INTEREST RATES

Inter-American Development Bank, 1300 New York Avenue, NW, Washington, D.C. 20577 (202) 623-1753; *Economic and Social Progress in Latin America.*

Organization of American States (OAS), General Secretariat, Washington, D.C. 20006 (202) 458-3533; *Statistical Bulletin of the OAS.*

JAMAICA - INTERNATIONAL FINANCE

Inter-American Development Bank, 1300 New York Avenue, NW, Washington, D.C. 20577 (202) 623-1753; *Economic and Social Progress in Latin America.*

JAMAICA - INTERNATIONAL LIQUIDITY

Inter-American Development Bank, 1300 New York Avenue, NW, Washington, D.C. 20577 (202) 623-1753; *Economic and Social Progress in Latin America.*

International Monetary Fund, 700 Nineteenth Street, NW, Washington, D.C. 20431 (202) 623-7000; *International Financial Statistics.*

JAMAICA - INTERNATIONAL RESERVES

Organization of American States (OAS), General Secretariat, Washington, D.C. 20006 (202) 458-3533; *Statistical Bulletin of the OAS.*

JAMAICA - INTERNATIONAL RESERVES EXCLUDING GOLD

Inter-American Development Bank, 1300 New York Avenue, NW, Washington, D.C. 20577 (202) 623-1753; *Economic and Social Progress in Latin America.*

Statistical Office of the United Nations, Publishing Service, New York, New York 10017 (800) 253-9646; *Statistical Yearbook.*

JAMAICA - INTERNATIONAL STATISTICS

Inter-American Development Bank, 1300 New York Avenue, NW, Washington, D.C. 20577 (202) 623-1753; *Economic and Social Progress in Latin America.*

JAMAICA - INVESTMENT

Inter-American Development Bank, 1300 New York Avenue, NW, Washington, D.C. 20577 (202) 623-1753; *Economic and Social Progress in Latin America.*

Statistical Office of the United Nations, Publishing Service, New York, New York 10017 (800) 253-9646; *Statistical Yearbook for Latin America and the Caribbean.*

JAMAICA - IRON ORE PRODUCTION AND CONSUMPTION - See JAMAICA - MINING AND MINERAL PRODUCTS

JAMAICA - IRRIGATION

Euromonitor International, Inc., 122 South Michigan Avenue, Suite 1200, Chicago, Illinois 60603 (800) 577-EURO; *International Marketing Data and Statistics.*

Inter-American Development Bank, 1300 New York Avenue, NW, Washington, D.C. 20577 (202) 623-1753; *Economic and Social Progress in Latin America.*

JAMAICA - LABOR

Central Intelligence Agency, Washington, D.C. 20505 (703) 482-1100, www.cia.gov; *The World Factbook.*

The Economist Intelligence Unit, 111 West 57th Street, New York, New York 10019 (800) 938-4685; *The New Latin America Market Atlas.*

Euromonitor International, Inc., 122 South Michigan Avenue, Suite 1200, Chicago, Illinois 60603 (800) 577-EURO; *International Marketing Data and Statistics; and World Marketing Data and Statistics..*

Europa Publications Limited, 18 Bedford Square, London, WC1B 3JN, England; *The Europa World Year Book.*

Food and Agricultural Organization of the United Nations (FAO), Via delle Terme di Caracalla, 00100 Rome, Italy (Telephone Number in U.S. (202) 653-2400); *The State of Food and Agriculture.*

International Labour Office, I.L.O. Publications, CH-1211, Geneva 22, Switzerland; *Yearbook of Labour Statistics.*

M.E. Sharpe, 80 Business Park Drive, Armonk, New York 10504 (800) 541-6563; *The Illustrated Book of World Rankings.*

St. Martin's Press, Inc., 175 Fifth Avenue, New York, New York 10010 (800) 221-7945; *The Statesman's Year-Book.*

Statistical Office of the United Nations, Publishing Service, New York, New York 10017 (800) 253-9646; *Human Development Report.*

The World Bank, 1818 H Street, NW, Washington, D.C. 20433 (202) 477-1234; *The World Bank Atlas;* and *World Development Report.*

JAMAICA - LAND AREA

The Economist Intelligence Unit, 111 West 57th Street, New York, New York 10019 (800) 938-4685; *The New Latin America Market Atlas.*

JAMAICA - LAND USE

Central Intelligence Agency, Washington, D.C. 20505 (703) 482-1100, www.cia.gov; *The World Factbook.*

Euromonitor International, Inc., 122 South Michigan Avenue, Suite 1200, Chicago, Illinois 60603 (800) 577-EURO; *International Marketing Data and Statistics.*

Food and Agricultural Organization of the United Nations (FAO), Via delle Terme di Caracalla, 00100 Rome, Italy (Telephone Number in U.S. (202) 653-2400); *Production Yearbook.*

Inter-American Development Bank, 1300 New York Avenue, NW, Washington, D.C. 20577 (202) 623-1753; *Economic and Social Progress in Latin America.*

The World Bank, 1818 H Street, NW, Washington, D.C. 20433 (202) 477-1234; *World Development Report.*

JAMAICA - LIBRARIES

M.E. Sharpe, 80 Business Park Drive, Armonk, New York 10504 (800) 541-6563; *The Illustrated Book of World Rankings.*

United Nations Educational, Scientific and Cultural Organization (UNESCO), 7 Place de Fontenoy, F-75700 Paris, France (Telephone Number in U.S. (212) 963-5981); *Statistical Yearbook.*

JAMAICA - LIFE EXPECTANCY

Central Intelligence Agency, Washington, D.C. 20505 (703) 482-1100, www.cia.gov; *The World Factbook.*

The Economist Intelligence Unit, 111 West 57th Street, New York, New York

10019 (800) 938-4685; *The New Latin America Market Atlas.*

Euromonitor International, Inc., 122 South Michigan Avenue, Suite 1200, Chicago, Illinois 60603 (800) 577-EURO; *The World Economic Factbook.*

Statistical Office of the United Nations, Publishing Service, New York, New York 10017 (800) 253-9646; *Human Development Report; World Statistics Pocketbook;* and *Statistical Yearbook for Latin America and the Caribbean.*

The World Bank, 1818 H Street, NW, Washington, D.C. 20433 (202) 477-1234; *The World Bank Atlas;* and *World Development Report.*

JAMAICA - LITERACY RATE

Euromonitor International, Inc., 122 South Michigan Avenue, Suite 1200, Chicago, Illinois 60603 (800) 577-EURO; *World Marketing Data and Statistics.*

JAMAICA - LIVESTOCK AND POULTRY

Euromonitor International, Inc., 122 South Michigan Avenue, Suite 1200, Chicago, Illinois 60603 (800) 577-EURO; *International Marketing Data and Statistics.*

Europa Publications Limited, 18 Bedford Square, London, WC1B 3JN, England; *The Europa World Year Book.*

Food and Agricultural Organization of the United Nations (FAO), Via delle Terme di Caracalla, 00100 Rome, Italy (Telephone Number in U.S. (202) 653-2400); *Production Yearbook;* and *The State of Food and Agriculture.*

M.E. Sharpe, 80 Business Park Drive, Armonk, New York 10504 (800) 541-6563; *The Illustrated Book of World Rankings.*

St. Martin's Press, Inc., 175 Fifth Avenue, New York, New York 10010 (800) 221-7945; *The Statesman's Year-Book.*

Statistical Office of the United Nations, Publishing Service, New York, New York 10017 (800) 253-9646; *Statistical Yearbook.*

United Nations Conference on Trade and Development, Central Statistical Service, Palais des Nations, Geneva, Switzerland (Telephone in U.S. (800) 253-9646); *UNCTAD Commodity Yearbook.*

JAMAICA - LIVING LEVELS - See JAMAICA - LIFE EXPECTANCY

JAMAICA - MAIL - NUMBER OF PIECES SENT OR RECEIVED

Statistical Office of the United Nations, Publishing Service, New York, New York

10017 (800) 253-9646; *Statistical Yearbook.*

JAMAICA - MAIN ECONOMIC INDICATORS - See JAMAICA - ECONOMY

JAMAICA - MANUFACTURING

The Economist Intelligence Unit, 111 West 57th Street, New York, New York 10019 (800) 938-4685; *The New Latin America Market Atlas.*

Inter-American Development Bank, 1300 New York Avenue, NW, Washington, D.C. 20577 (202) 623-1753; *Economic and Social Progress in Latin America.*

M.E. Sharpe, 80 Business Park Drive, Armonk, New York 10504 (800) 541-6563; *The Illustrated Book of World Rankings.*

Statistical Office of the United Nations, Publishing Service, New York, New York 10017 (800) 253-9646; *Statistical Yearbook for Latin America and the Caribbean;* and *Statistical Yearbook.*

JAMAICA - MARRIAGE RATES

Europa Publications Limited, 18 Bedford Square, London, WC1B 3JN, England; *The Europa World Year Book.*

M.E. Sharpe, 80 Business Park Drive, Armonk, New York 10504 (800) 541-6563; *The Illustrated Book of World Rankings.*

Statistical Office of the United Nations, Publishing Service, New York, New York 10017 (800) 253-9646; *Demographic Yearbook;* and *Statistical Yearbook.*

JAMAICA - MEAT PRODUCTION - See JAMAICA - LIVESTOCK AND POULTRY

JAMAICA - MERCHANT SHIPPING

Europa Publications Limited, 18 Bedford Square, London, WC1B 3JN, England; *The Europa World Year Book.*

St. Martin's Press, Inc., 175 Fifth Avenue, New York, New York 10010 (800) 221-7945; *The Statesman's Year-Book.*

Statistical Office of the United Nations, Publishing Service, New York, New York 10017 (800) 253-9646; *Statistical Yearbook.*

U.S. Department of Transportation, Maritime Administration, 400 Seventh Street, SW, Washington, D.C. 20590 (202) 366-5807, www.marad.dot.gov; *A Statistical Analysis of the World's Merchant Fleets.*

JAMAICA - MILITARY

Central Intelligence Agency, Washington, D.C. 20505 (703) 482-1100, www.cia.gov; *The World Factbook.*

The Economist Intelligence Unit, 111 West 57th Street, New York, New York 10019 (800) 938-4685; *The New Latin America Market Atlas.*

Euromonitor International, Inc., 122 South Michigan Avenue, Suite 1200, Chicago, Illinois 60603 (800) 577-EURO; *World Marketing Data and Statistics.*

The International Institute for Strategic Studies, 23 Tavistock Street, London WC2E 7NQ, England 44 171 3797676; *The Military Balance.*

International Monetary Fund, 700 Nineteenth Street, NW, Washington, D.C. 20431 (202) 623-7000; *Government Finance Statistics Yearbook.*

St. Martin's Press, Inc., 175 Fifth Avenue, New York, New York 10010 (800) 221-7945; *The Statesman's Year-Book.*

Statistical Office of the United Nations, Publishing Service, New York, New York 10017 (800) 253-9646; *Human Development Report.*

U.S. Arms Control and Disarmament Agency, 320 Twenty-first Street, NW, Washington, D.C. 20451 (202) 647-8677; *World Military Expenditures and Arms Transfers.*

JAMAICA - MILK PRODUCTION - See JAMAICA - DAIRY PRODUCTS

JAMAICA - MINING AND MINERAL PRODUCTS

Commodity Research Bureau, Inc., 30 South Wacker Drive, Chicago, Illinois 60606 (312) 454-1801; *Commodity Year Book.*

The Economist Intelligence Unit, 111 West 57th Street, New York, New York 10019 (800) 938-4685; *The New Latin America Market Atlas.*

Europa Publications Limited, 18 Bedford Square, London, WC1B 3JN, England; *The Europa World Year Book.*

Inter-American Development Bank, 1300 New York Avenue, NW, Washington, D.C. 20577 (202) 623-1753; *Economic and Social Progress in Latin America.*

M.E. Sharpe, 80 Business Park Drive, Armonk, New York 10504 (800) 541-6563; *The Illustrated Book of World Rankings.*

St. Martin's Press, Inc., 175 Fifth Avenue, New York, New York 10010 (800) 221-7945; *The Statesman's Year-Book.*

Statistical Office of the United Nations, Publishing Service, New York, New York 10017 (800) 253-9646; *Statistical Yearbook;*

and *Statistical Yearbook for Latin America and the Caribbean.*

United Nations Conference on Trade and Development, Central Statistical Service, Palais des Nations, Geneva, Switzerland (Telephone in U.S. (800) 253-9646); *UNCTAD Commodity Yearbook.*

JAMAICA - MONEY EXCHANGE RATE - See JAMAICA - EXCHANGE RATES

JAMAICA - MONEY RATES - MARKET

Inter-American Development Bank, 1300 New York Avenue, NW, Washington, D.C. 20577 (202) 623-1753; *Economic and Social Progress in Latin America.*

Statistical Office of the United Nations, Publishing Service, New York, New York 10017 (800) 253-9646; *Statistical Yearbook.*

JAMAICA - MONEY RESERVES

Euromonitor International, Inc., 122 South Michigan Avenue, Suite 1200, Chicago, Illinois 60603 (800) 577-EURO; *International Marketing Data and Statistics.*

Inter-American Development Bank, 1300 New York Avenue, NW, Washington, D.C. 20577 (202) 623-1753; *Economic and Social Progress in Latin America.*

JAMAICA - MONEY SUPPLY

The Economist Intelligence Unit, 111 West 57th Street, New York, New York 10019 (800) 938-4685; *Jamaica Country Report.*

Euromonitor International, Inc., 122 South Michigan Avenue, Suite 1200, Chicago, Illinois 60603 (800) 577-EURO; *International Marketing Data and Statistics.*

Europa Publications Limited, 18 Bedford Square, London, WC1B 3JN, England; *The Europa World Year Book.*

Inter-American Development Bank, 1300 New York Avenue, NW, Washington, D.C. 20577 (202) 623-1753; *Economic and Social Progress in Latin America.*

International Monetary Fund, 700 Nineteenth Street, NW, Washington, D.C. 20431 (202) 623-7000; *International Financial Statistics.*

Statistical Office of the United Nations, Publishing Service, New York, New York 10017 (800) 253-9646; *Statistical Yearbook.*

JAMAICA - MORTALITY

Central Intelligence Agency, Washington, D.C. 20505 (703) 482-1100, www.cia.gov; *The World Factbook.*

The Economist Intelligence Unit, 111 West 57th Street, New York, New York 10019 (800) 938-4685; *The New Latin America Market Atlas*.

Euromonitor International, Inc., 122 South Michigan Avenue, Suite 1200, Chicago, Illinois 60603 (800) 577-EURO; *International Marketing Data and Statistics*; and *The World Economic Factbook*.

Europa Publications Limited, 18 Bedford Square, London, WC1B 3JN, England; *The Europa World Year Book*.

St. Martin's Press, Inc., 175 Fifth Avenue, New York, New York 10010 (800) 221-7945; *The Statesman's Year-Book*.

Statistical Office of the United Nations, Publishing Service, New York, New York 10017 (800) 253-9646; *Demographic Yearbook; Human Development Report; World Statistics Pocketbook;* and *Statistical Yearbook*.

United Nations Children's Fund (UNICEF), 3 United Nations Plaza, New York, New York 10017 (800) 253-9646; *State of the World's Children*.

The World Bank, 1818 H Street, NW, Washington, D.C. 20433 (202) 477-1234; *The World Bank Atlas;* and *World Development Report*.

World Health Organization, Office of Publications, 20 Avenue Appia, CH-1211 Geneva 27, Switzerland (Telephone Number in U.S. (518) 436-9686); *World Health Statistics Annual*.

JAMAICA - MOTION PICTURES

St. Martin's Press, Inc., 175 Fifth Avenue, New York, New York 10010 (800) 221-7945; *The Statesman's Year-Book*.

Statistical Office of the United Nations, Publishing Service, New York, New York 10017 (800) 253-9646; *Statistical Yearbook*.

JAMAICA - MOTOR VEHICLE TAXES - See JAMAICA - TAXATION

JAMAICA - MOTOR VEHICLES IN USE

The Economist Intelligence Unit, 111 West 57th Street, New York, New York 10019 (800) 938-4685; *The New Latin America Market Atlas*.

Europa Publications Limited, 18 Bedford Square, London, WC1B 3JN, England; *The Europa World Year Book*.

Statistical Office of the United Nations, Publishing Service, New York, New York 10017 (800) 253-9646; *Statistical Yearbook*.

JAMAICA - MULES - See JAMAICA -

LIVESTOCK AND POULTRY

JAMAICA - MUSEUMS

M.E. Sharpe, 80 Business Park Drive, Armonk, New York 10504 (800) 541-6563; *The Illustrated Book of World Rankings*.

United Nations Educational, Scientific and Cultural Organization (UNESCO), 7 Place de Fontenoy, F-75700 Paris, France (Telephone Number in U.S. (212) 963-5981); *Statistical Yearbook*.

JAMAICA - NATALITY - See JAMAICA - BIRTH RATES

JAMAICA - NATIONAL ACCOUNTS

Europa Publications Limited, 18 Bedford Square, London, WC1B 3JN, England; *The Europa World Year Book*.

Inter-American Development Bank, 1300 New York Avenue, NW, Washington, D.C. 20577 (202) 623-1753; *Economic and Social Progress in Latin America*.

International Monetary Fund, 700 Nineteenth Street, NW, Washington, D.C. 20431 (202) 623-7000; *International Financial Statistics*.

Organization of American States (OAS), General Secretariat, Washington, D.C. 20006 (202) 458-3533; *Statistical Bulletin of the OAS*.

Statistical Office of the United Nations, Publishing Service, New York, New York 10017 (800) 253-9646; *Statistical Yearbook;* and *National Accounts Statistics*.

JAMAICA - NATIONAL INCOME

Inter-American Development Bank, 1300 New York Avenue, NW, Washington, D.C. 20577 (202) 623-1753; *Economic and Social Progress in Latin America*.

M.E. Sharpe, 80 Business Park Drive, Armonk, New York 10504 (800) 541-6563; *The Illustrated Book of World Rankings*.

Statistical Office of the United Nations, Publishing Service, New York, New York 10017 (800) 253-9646; *National Accounts Statistics; Statistical Yearbook;* and *Statistical Yearbook for Latin America and the Caribbean*.

JAMAICA - NATIONAL PRODUCT

M.E. Sharpe, 80 Business Park Drive, Armonk, New York 10504 (800) 541-6563; *The Illustrated Book of World Rankings*.

Statistical Office of the United Nations, Publishing Service, New York, New York 10017 (800) 253-9646; *Statistical Yearbook*.

JAMAICA - NATURAL GAS PRODUCTION - See JAMAICA - MINING AND MINERALS PRODUCTS

JAMAICA - NEWSPAPER PRODUCTION - See JAMAICA - FORESTRY AND FOREST PRODUCTS

JAMAICA - NEWSPRINT - See JAMAICA - FORESTRY AND FOREST PRODUCTS

JAMAICA - NUTRITION

Statistical Office of the United Nations, Publishing Service, New York, New York 10017 (800) 253-9646; *Statistical Yearbook for Latin America and the Caribbean*.

JAMAICA - OCCUPATIONS - See JAMAICA - LABOR FORCE

JAMAICA - PAPER - See JAMAICA - FORESTRY AND FOREST PRODUCTS

JAMAICA - PATENTS, TRADEMARKS AND SERVICE MARKS

Statistical Office of the United Nations, Publishing Service, New York, New York 10017 (800) 253-9646; *Statistical Yearbook*.

JAMAICA - PEANUT PRODUCTION - See JAMAICA - CROPS

JAMAICA - PESTICIDE USE

Food and Agricultural Organization of the United Nations (FAO), Via delle Terme di Caracalla, 00100 Rome, Italy (Telephone Number in U.S. (202) 653-2400); *The State of Food and Agriculture*.

JAMAICA - PETROLEUM INDUSTRY

The Economist Intelligence Unit, 111 West 57th Street, New York, New York 10019 (800) 938-4685; *The New Latin America Market Atlas*.

Food and Agricultural Organization of the United Nations (FAO), Via delle Terme di Caracalla, 00100 Rome, Italy (Telephone Number in U.S. (202) 653-2400); *The State of Food and Agriculture*.

Inter-American Development Bank, 1300 New York Avenue, NW, Washington, D.C. 20577 (202) 623-1753; *Economic and Social Progress in Latin America*.

M.E. Sharpe, 80 Business Park Drive, Armonk, New York 10504 (800) 541-6563; *The Illustrated Book of World Rankings*.

Statistical Office of the United Nations, Publishing Service, New York, New York 10017 (800) 253-9646; *Statistical Yearbook*.

United Nations Conference on Trade and Development, Central Statistical

Service, Palais des Nations, Geneva, Switzerland (Telephone in U.S. (800) 253-9646); *UNCTAD Commodity Yearbook.*

JAMAICA - PIGS - See JAMAICA - LIVESTOCK AND POULTRY

JAMAICA - POPULATION

Central Intelligence Agency, Washington, D.C. 20505 (703) 482-1100, www.cia.gov; *The World Factbook.*

The Economist Intelligence Unit, 111 West 57th Street, New York, New York 10019 (800) 938-4685; *Jamaica Country Report; The New Latin America Market Atlas;* and *The World Market Atlas.*

Euromonitor International, Inc., 122 South Michigan Avenue, Suite 1200, Chicago, Illinois 60603 (800) 577-EURO; *International Marketing Data and Statistics;* and *The World Economic Factbook.*

Europa Publications Limited, 18 Bedford Square, London, WC1B 3JN, England; *The Europa World Year Book.*

Food and Agricultural Organization of the United Nations (FAO), Via delle Terme di Caracalla, 00100 Rome, Italy (Telephone Number in U.S. (202) 653-2400); *Production Yearbook.*

Inter-American Development Bank, 1300 New York Avenue, NW, Washington, D.C. 20577 (202) 623-1753; *Economic and Social Progress in Latin America.*

International Labour Office, I.L.O. Publications, CH-1211, Geneva 22, Switzerland; *Yearbook of Labour Statistics.*

M.E. Sharpe, 80 Business Park Drive, Armonk, New York 10504 (800) 541-6563; *The Illustrated Book of World Rankings.*

Organization of American States (OAS), General Secretariat, Washington, D.C. 20006 (202) 458-3533; *Statistical Bulletin of the OAS.*

St. Martin's Press, Inc., 175 Fifth Avenue, New York, New York 10010 (800) 221-7945; *The Statesman's Year-Book.*

Statistical Office of the United Nations, Publishing Service, New York, New York 10017 (800) 253-9646; *Demographic Yearbook; Human Development Report; Statistical Yearbook; World Statistics Pocketbook;* and *Statistical Yearbook for Latin America and the Caribbean.*

United Nations Educational, Scientific and Cultural Organization (UNESCO), 7 Place de Fontenoy, F-75700 Paris, France (Telephone Number in U.S. (212) 963-5981); *Statistical Yearbook.*

U.S. Arms Control and Disarmament Agency, 320 Twenty-first Street, NW, Washington, D.C. 20451 (202) 647-8677; *World Military Expenditures and Arms Transfers.*

The World Bank, 1818 H Street, NW, Washington, D.C. 20433 (202) 477-1234; *The World Bank Atlas;* and *World Development Report.*

World Health Organization, Office of Publications, 20 Avenue Appia, CH-1211 Geneva 27, Switzerland (Telephone Number in U.S. (518) 436-9686); *World Health Statistics Annual.*

JAMAICA - POST OFFICES

M.E. Sharpe, 80 Business Park Drive, Armonk, New York 10504 (800) 541-6563; *The Illustrated Book of World Rankings.*

St. Martin's Press, Inc., 175 Fifth Avenue, New York, New York 10010 (800) 221-7945; *The Statesman's Year-Book.*

JAMAICA - POTATO PRODUCTION - See JAMAICA - CROPS

JAMAICA - POWER PRODUCTION INDUSTRY

Statistical Office of the United Nations, Publishing Service, New York, New York 10017 (800) 253-9646; *Statistical Yearbook.*

JAMAICA - PRICES

Food and Agricultural Organization of the United Nations (FAO), Via delle Terme di Caracalla, 00100 Rome, Italy (Telephone Number in U.S. (202) 653-2400); *Production Yearbook;* and *The State of Food and Agriculture.*

International Labour Office, I.L.O. Publications, CH-1211, Geneva 22, Switzerland; *Yearbook of Labour Statistics.*

International Monetary Fund, 700 Nineteenth Street, NW, Washington, D.C. 20431 (202) 623-7000; *International Financial Statistics.*

M.E. Sharpe, 80 Business Park Drive, Armonk, New York 10504 (800) 541-6563; *The Illustrated Book of World Rankings.*

Statistical Office of the United Nations, Publishing Service, New York, New York 10017 (800) 253-9646; *Economic Survey of Latin America and the Caribbean;* and *Statistical Yearbook for Latin America and the Caribbean.*

JAMAICA - PRINTING AND WRITING PAPER - See JAMAICA - FORESTRY AND FOREST PRODUCTS

JAMAICA - PRODUCTION

M.E. Sharpe, 80 Business Park Drive, Armonk, New York 10504 (800) 541-6563; *The Illustrated Book of World Rankings.*

JAMAICA - PRODUCTIVITY

Euromonitor International, Inc., 122 South Michigan Avenue, Suite 1200, Chicago, Illinois 60603 (800) 577-EURO; *International Marketing Data and Statistics.*

JAMAICA - PROPERTY TAXES - See JAMAICA - TAXATION

JAMAICA - PUBLIC CONSUMPTION FUND

Inter-American Development Bank, 1300 New York Avenue, NW, Washington, D.C. 20577 (202) 623-1753; *Economic and Social Progress in Latin America.*

JAMAICA - PUBLIC EXPENDITURE

Inter-American Development Bank, 1300 New York Avenue, NW, Washington, D.C. 20577 (202) 623-1753; *Economic and Social Progress in Latin America.*

Organization of American States (OAS), General Secretariat, Washington, D.C. 20006 (202) 458-3533; *Statistical Bulletin of the OAS.*

Statistical Office of the United Nations, Publishing Service, New York, New York 10017 (800) 253-9646; *Statistical Yearbook for Latin America and the Caribbean.*

JAMAICA - PUBLIC FINANCE - See JAMAICA - FINANCE

JAMAICA - PUBLIC REVENUES

Inter-American Development Bank, 1300 New York Avenue, NW, Washington, D.C. 20577 (202) 623-1753; *Economic and Social Progress in Latin America.*

Organization of American States (OAS), General Secretariat, Washington, D.C. 20006 (202) 458-3533; *Statistical Bulletin of the OAS.*

JAMAICA - RADIO BROADCASTING - See JAMAICA - BROADCASTING

JAMAICA - RADIO RECEIVERS

St. Martin's Press, Inc., 175 Fifth Avenue, New York, New York 10010 (800) 221-7945; *The Statesman's Year-Book.*

Statistical Office of the United Nations, Publishing Service, New York, New York 10017 (800) 253-9646; *Statistical Yearbook.*

JAMAICA - RAILWAYS

The Economist Intelligence Unit, 111 West 57th Street, New York, New York 10019 (800) 938-4685; *The New Latin*

America Market Atlas.

Europa Publications Limited, 18 Bedford Square, London, WC1B 3JN, England; *The Europa World Year Book.*

Jane's Information Group, Sentinel House, 163 Brighton Road, Coulsdon, Surrey CR5 2NH, England (Telephone Number in U.S. (703) 683-3700); *Jane's World Railways.*

Statistical Office of the United Nations, Publishing Service, New York, New York 10017 (800) 253-9646; *Statistical Yearbook.*

JAMAICA - RELIGION

Central Intelligence Agency, Washington, D.C. 20505 (703) 482-1100, www.cia.gov; *The World Factbook.*

M.E. Sharpe, 80 Business Park Drive, Armonk, New York 10504 (800) 541-6563; *The Illustrated Book of World Rankings.*

St. Martin's Press, Inc., 175 Fifth Avenue, New York, New York 10010 (800) 221-7945; *The Statesman's Year-Book.*

JAMAICA - RENT PRICES

International Labour Office, I.L.O. Publications, CH-1211, Geneva 22, Switzerland; *Yearbook of Labour Statistics.*

JAMAICA - RESERVES EXCLUDING GOLD

The Economist Intelligence Unit, 111 West 57th Street, New York, New York 10019 (800) 938-4685; *The New Latin America Market Atlas.*

JAMAICA - RETAIL TRADE

Euromonitor International, Inc., 122 South Michigan Avenue, Suite 1200, Chicago, Illinois 60603 (800) 577-EURO; *World Marketing Data and Statistics.*

Inter-American Development Bank, 1300 New York Avenue, NW, Washington, D.C. 20577 (202) 623-1753; *Economic and Social Progress in Latin America.*

JAMAICA - RICE PRODUCTION - See JAMAICA - CROPS

JAMAICA - ROOT AND TUBER PRODUCTION - See JAMAICA - CROPS

JAMAICA - ROUNDWOOD PRODUCTION - See JAMAICA - FORESTRY AND FOREST PRODUCTS

JAMAICA - RUBBER PRODUCTION

M.E. Sharpe, 80 Business Park Drive, Armonk, New York 10504 (800) 541-6563; *The Illustrated Book of World Rankings.*

JAMAICA - SAWNWOOD PRODUCTION - See JAMAICA - FORESTRY AND FOREST PRODUCTS

JAMAICA - SCIENCE AND TECHNOLOGY - EXPENDITURE FOR RESEARCH - See JAMAICA - SCIENTISTS, TECHNICIANS AND ENGINEERS

JAMAICA - SCIENTISTS, TECHNICIANS AND ENGINEERS

Statistical Office of the United Nations, Publishing Service, New York, New York 10017 (800) 253-9646; *Statistical Yearbook.*

JAMAICA - SENIOR CITIZENS

M.E. Sharpe, 80 Business Park Drive, Armonk, New York 10504 (800) 541-6563; *The Illustrated Book of World Rankings.*

JAMAICA - SHEEP - See JAMAICA - LIVESTOCK AND POULTRY

JAMAICA - SILVER PRODUCTION - See JAMAICA - MINING AND MINERAL PRODUCTS

JAMAICA - SOCIAL DATA

M.E. Sharpe, 80 Business Park Drive, Armonk, New York 10504 (800) 541-6563; *The Illustrated Book of World Rankings.*

Statistical Office of the United Nations, Publishing Service, New York, New York 10017 (800) 253-9646; *Bulletin of Industrial Statistics for the Arab Countries.*

JAMAICA - SOCIAL SECURITY

Inter-American Development Bank, 1300 New York Avenue, NW, Washington, D.C. 20577 (202) 623-1753; *Economic and Social Progress in Latin America.*

International Monetary Fund, 700 Nineteenth Street, NW, Washington, D.C. 20431 (202) 623-7000; *Government Finance Statistics Yearbook.*

Statistical Office of the United Nations, Publishing Service, New York, New York 10017 (800) 253-9646; *National Accounts Statistics.*

JAMAICA - SOCIOECONOMIC DATA

Inter-American Development Bank, 1300 New York Avenue, NW, Washington, D.C. 20577 (202) 623-1753; *Economic and Social Progress in Latin America.*

JAMAICA - SOYBEAN PRODUCTION - See JAMAICA - CROPS

JAMAICA - STAMP TAXES AND DUTIES -See JAMAICA - SEE TAXATION

JAMAICA - STATE BUDGET REVENUE AND EXPENDITURES

Euromonitor International, Inc., 122 South Michigan Avenue, Suite 1200, Chicago, Illinois 60603 (800) 577-EURO; *International Marketing Data and Statistics.*

Inter-American Development Bank, 1300 New York Avenue, NW, Washington, D.C. 20577 (202) 623-1753; *Economic and Social Progress in Latin America.*

JAMAICA - STEEL - See JAMAICA - MINING AND MINERAL PRODUCTS

JAMAICA - STOCKS - COMMODITY - MARKET PRICE - INDEX

Food and Agricultural Organization of the United Nations (FAO), Via delle Terme di Caracalla, 00100 Rome, Italy (Telephone Number in U.S. (202) 653-2400); *The State of Food and Agriculture.*

JAMAICA - SUGAR - See JAMAICA - CROPS

JAMAICA - SULPHURIC ACID PRODUCTION - See JAMAICA - MINING AND MINERAL PRODUCTS

JAMAICA - TAXATION

Europa Publications Limited, 18 Bedford Square, London, WC1B 3JN, England; *The Europa World Year Book.*

Inter-American Development Bank, 1300 New York Avenue, NW, Washington, D.C. 20577 (202) 623-1753; *Economic and Social Progress in Latin America.*

International Monetary Fund, 700 Nineteenth Street, NW, Washington, D.C. 20431 (202) 623-7000; *Government Finance Statistics Yearbook.*

Statistical Office of the United Nations, Publishing Service, New York, New York 10017 (800) 253-9646; *Statistical Yearbook for Latin America and the Caribbean.*

JAMAICA - TELEPHONES IN USE

American Telephone and Telegraph Company, 26 Parsippany Road, Whippany, New Jersey 07981 (800) 222-0300; *The World's Telephones.*

Central Intelligence Agency, Washington, D.C. 20505 (703) 482-1100, www.cia.gov; *The World Factbook.*

The Economist Intelligence Unit, 111 West 57th Street, New York, New York 10019 (800) 938-4685; *The New Latin America Market Atlas.*

Europa Publications Limited, 18 Bedford Square, London, WC1B 3JN, England; *The Europa World Year Book.*

St. Martin's Press, Inc., 175 Fifth Avenue, New York, New York 10010 (800) 221-7945; *The Statesman's Year-Book.*

Statistical Office of the United Nations, Publishing Service, New York, New York 10017 (800) 253-9646; *Statistical Yearbook; and World Statistics Pocketbook.*

JAMAICA - TELEVISION BROADCASTING - See JAMAICA - BROADCASTING

JAMAICA - TELEVISION RECEIVER PRODUCTION

Statistical Office of the United Nations, Publishing Service, New York, New York 10017 (800) 253-9646; *Statistical Yearbook.*

JAMAICA - TEXTILE INDUSTRY

Statistical Office of the United Nations, Publishing Service, New York, New York 10017 (800) 253-9646; *Statistical Yearbook.*

United Nations Conference on Trade and Development, Central Statistical Service, Palais des Nations, Geneva, Switzerland (Telephone in U.S. (800) 253-9646); *UNCTAD Commodity Yearbook.*

JAMAICA - THEATRE

United Nations Educational, Scientific and Cultural Organization (UNESCO), 7 Place de Fontenoy, F-75700 Paris, France (Telephone Number in U.S. (212) 963-5981); *Statistical Yearbook.*

JAMAICA - TIRE (MOTOR VEHICLE) PRODUCTION

Statistical Office of the United Nations, Publishing Service, New York, New York 10017 (800) 253-9646; *Statistical Yearbook.*

JAMAICA - TOBACCO PRODUCTION

M.E. Sharpe, 80 Business Park Drive, Armonk, New York 10504 (800) 541-6563; *The Illustrated Book of World Rankings.*

Statistical Office of the United Nations, Publishing Service, New York, New York 10017 (800) 253-9646; *Statistical Yearbook.*

JAMAICA - TOURISM

The Economist Intelligence Unit, 111 West 57th Street, New York, New York 10019 (800) 938-4685; *The New Latin America Market Atlas.*

Euromonitor International, Inc., 122 South Michigan Avenue, Suite 1200, Chicago, Illinois 60603 (800) 577-EURO; *The World Economic Factbook; and World Marketing Data and Statistics.*

Europa Publications Limited, 18

Bedford Square, London, WC1B 3JN, England; *The Europa World Year Book.*

M.E. Sharpe, 80 Business Park Drive, Armonk, New York 10504 (800) 541-6563; *The Illustrated Book of World Rankings.*

Organization of American States (OAS), General Secretariat, Washington, D.C. 20006 (202) 458-3533; *Statistical Bulletin of the OAS.*

St. Martin's Press, Inc., 175 Fifth Avenue, New York, New York 10010 (800) 221-7945; *The Statesman's Year-Book.*

Statistical Office of the United Nations, Publishing Service, New York, New York 10017 (800) 253-9646; *Statistical Yearbook; and Statistical Yearbook for Latin America and the Caribbean.*

World Tourism Organization, Calle Capitan Haya 42, E-28020 Madrid, Spain; *Yearbook of Tourism Statistics.*

JAMAICA - TRACTORS IN USE

The Economist Intelligence Unit, 111 West 57th Street, New York, New York 10019 (800) 938-4685; *The New Latin America Market Atlas.*

Statistical Office of the United Nations, Publishing Service, New York, New York 10017 (800) 253-9646; *Statistical Yearbook.*

JAMAICA - TRADE - See JAMAICA - FOREIGN TRADE

JAMAICA - TRADEMARKS AND SERVICE MARKS

Statistical Office of the United Nations, Publishing Service, New York, New York 10017 (800) 253-9646; *Statistical Yearbook.*

JAMAICA - TRANSPORTATION AND COMMUNICATIONS

Central Intelligence Agency, Washington, D.C. 20505 (703) 351-2053; *The World Factbook.*

The Economist Intelligence Unit, 111 West 57th Street, New York, New York 10019 (800) 938-4685; *The New Latin America Market Atlas.*

Euromonitor International, Inc., 122 South Michigan Avenue, Suite 1200, Chicago, Illinois 60603 (800) 577-EURO; *World Marketing Data and Statistics.*

Europa Publications Limited, 18 Bedford Square, London, WC1B 3JN, England; *The Europa World Year Book.*

Inter-American Development Bank, 1300 New York Avenue, NW, Washington, D.C. 20577 (202) 623-1753; *Economic and*

Social Progress in Latin America.

M.E. Sharpe, 80 Business Park Drive, Armonk, New York 10504 (800) 541-6563; *The Illustrated Book of World Rankings.*

St. Martin's Press, Inc., 175 Fifth Avenue, New York, New York 10010 (800) 221-7945; *The Statesman's Year-Book.*

Statistical Office of the United Nations, Publishing Service, New York, New York 10017 (800) 253-9646; *Human Development Report; and Statistical Yearbook for Latin America and the Caribbean.*

JAMAICA - TREASURY BILL RATES

Organization of American States (OAS), General Secretariat, Washington, D.C. 20006 (202) 458-3533; *Statistical Bulletin of the OAS.*

JAMAICA - UNEMPLOYMENT

Central Intelligence Agency, Washington, D.C. 20505 (703) 351-2053; *The World Factbook.*

The Economist Intelligence Unit, 111 West 57th Street, New York, New York 10019 (800) 938-4685; *The New Latin America Market Atlas.*

Euromonitor International, Inc., 122 South Michigan Avenue, Suite 1200, Chicago, Illinois 60603 (800) 577-EURO; *International Marketing Data and Statistics.*

International Labour Office, I.L.O. Publications, 1828 L Street NW, Suite 801, Washington, D.C. 20036 (301) 638-3152; *Yearbook of Labour Statistics.*

Organization of American States (OAS), General Secretariat, Washington, D.C. 20006 (202) 458-3533; *Statistical Bulletin of the OAS.*

St. Martin's Press, Inc., 175 Fifth Avenue, New York, New York 10010 (800) 221-7945; *The Statesman's Year-Book.*

Statistical Office of the United Nations, Publishing Service, New York, New York 10017 (800) 253-9646; *Statistical Yearbook.*

JAMAICA - VITAL STATISTICS

Euromonitor International, Inc., 122 South Michigan Avenue, Suite 1200, Chicago, Illinois 60603 (800) 577-EURO ; *International Marketing Data and Statistics.*

St. Martin's Press, Inc., 175 Fifth Avenue, New York, New York 10010 (800) 221-7945; *The Statesman's Year-Book.*

Statistical Office of the United Nations, Publishing Service, New York, New York

10017 (800) 253-9646; *Statistical Yearbook.*

World Health Organization, Office of Publications, 20 Avenue Appia, CH-1211 Geneva 27, Switzerland (Telephone Number in U.S. (518) 436-9686); *World Health Statistics Annual.*

JAMAICA - WAGES

International Labour Office, I.L.O. Publications, 1828 L Street NW, Suite 801, Washington, D.C. 20036 (301) 638-3152; *Yearbook of Labour Statistics.*

Organization of American States (OAS), General Secretariat, Washington, D.C. 20006 (202) 458-3533; *Statistical Bulletin of the OAS.*

JAMAICA - WEATHER - See JAMAICA - CLIMATE

JAMAICA - WELFARE

Inter-American Development Bank, 1300 New York Avenue, NW, Washington, D.C. 20577 (202) 623-1753; *Economic and Social Progress in Latin America.*

International Monetary Fund, 700 Nineteenth Street, NW, Washington, D.C. 20431 (202) 623-7000; *Government Finance Statistics Yearbook.*

JAMAICA - WHEAT PRODUCTION AND PRICES - See JAMAICA - CROPS

JAMAICA - WHOLESALE PRICES

Inter-American Development Bank, 1300 New York Avenue, NW, Washington, D.C. 20577 (202) 623-1753; *Economic and Social Progress in Latin America.*

JAMAICA - WHOLESALE TRADE

Inter-American Development Bank, 1300 New York Avenue, NW, Washington, D.C. 20577 (202) 623-1753; *Economic and Social Progress in Latin America.*

JAMAICA - WINE PRODUCTION - See JAMAICA - BEVERAGES

JAMAICA - WOOL PRODUCTION - See JAMAICA - TEXTILE INDUSTRY

Japan - National Statistical Office

Statistics Bureau, Management and Coordination Agency, 19-1 Wakamatsucho, Shinjuku, Tokyo 162, Japan.

Japan - Primary Statistics Sources

Management and Coordination Agency, Statistics Bureau, Tokyo, Japan; *Japan Statistical Yearbook; Monthly Statistics of Japan;* and *Statistical Indicators on Social Life.*

Japan - Databases

I.N. Industry Statistics Database, I.N. Information Corporation, Database Center Building, 6F, 1-7-18, Konan, Minato-ku, Tokyo 108, Japan. Subject coverage: Japanese industry statistics.

Japanese Economic Situation, Nikko Research Center, 1-1-3 Marunouchi, Chiyoda-ku, Tokyo 100, Japan. Subject coverage: Time series of macroeconomic Japanese data.

NIKKEI Financial File, Nihon Keizai Shimbun, Inc., Databook Bureau, 1-9-5 Ohtemachi, Chiyoda-ku, Tokyo 100, Japan. Subject coverage: Full range of financial statistics.

NRI/E Japan Economic and Business Database, Nomura Research Institute, Financial Engineering Department, Data Bank Section, Dai-Ni Yamaman Building, 6-7 Koami-Cho, Nihonbashi, Chuo-ku, Tokyo 103, Japan. Subject coverage: Japan economy and business.

Research/Report Reference Database, Mainichi Newspapers, Media Planning Division, 1-1-1 Hitotsubashi, Chiyoda-ku, Tokyo 100-51, Japan. Subject coverage: Statistical research and policy information.

JAPAN - ABORTIONS

Statistical Office of the United Nations, Publishing Service, New York, New York 10017 (800) 253-9646; *Demographic Yearbook.*

JAPAN - AGRICULTURE

The Economist Intelligence Unit, 111 West 57th Street, New York, New York 10019 (800) 938-4685; *Japan Country Report.*

Euromonitor International, Inc., 122 South Michigan Avenue, Suite 1200, Chicago, Illinois 60603 (800) 577-EURO; *International Marketing Data and Statistics;* and *World Marketing Data and Statistics..*

Europa Publications Limited, 18 Bedford Square, London, WC1B 3JN, England; *The Europa World Year Book.*

European Commission Office of Press and Public Affairs, 2100 M Street, NW, Washington, D.C. 20037 (202) 862-9500; *Basic Statistics of the Community.*

Food and Agricultural Organization of the United Nations (FAO), Via delle Terme di Caracalla, 00100 Rome, Italy (Telephone Number in U.S. (202) 653-2400); *Production Yearbook;* and *The State of Food and Agriculture.*

M.E. Sharpe, 80 Business Park Drive, Armonk, New York 10504 (800) 541-6563; *The Illustrated Book of World Rankings.*

National Technical Information Service, 5285 Port Royal Road, Springfield, Virginia 22161 (800) 553-6847; *Handbook of Economic Statistics.*

Organisation for Economic Co-operation and Development (OECD), 2 rue Andre-Pascal, 75 Paris 16, France (Telephone Number in U.S. (202) 785-6323); *Economic Accounts for Agriculture; Indicators of Industrial Activity;* and *OECD Economic Surveys: Japan.*

St. Martin's Press, Inc., 175 Fifth Avenue, New York, New York 10010 (800) 221-7945; *The Statesman's Year-Book.*

Statistical Office of the United Nations, Publishing Service, New York, New York 10017 (800) 253-9646; *Asia-Pacific in Figures; Statistical Yearbook;* and *Statistical Yearbook for Asia and the Pacific.*

Statistics Bureau, Management and Coordination Agency, Japan; *Statistical Indicators on Social Life.*

United Nations Conference on Trade and Development, Central Statistical Service, Palais des Nations, Geneva, Switzerland (Telephone in U.S. (800) 253-9646); *UNCTAD Commodity Yearbook.*

JAPAN - AIRLINE SERVICE

The Economist Intelligence Unit (Asia) Limited, 10th Floor, Luk Kwok Centre, 72 Gloucester Road, Wanchai, Hong Kong (Phone Number in U.S. (800) 938-4685); *Asian Market Atlas.*

Europa Publications Limited, 18 Bedford Square, London, WC1B 3JN, England; *The Europa World Year Book.*

European Commission Office of Press and Public Affairs, 2100 M Street, NW, Washington, D.C. 20037 (202) 862-9500; *Basic Statistics of the Community.*

International Civil Aviation Organization, 999 University Street, Montreal, Quebec, Canada H3C 5H7 (514) 954-8219; *Civil Aviation Statistics of the World.*

M.E. Sharpe, 80 Business Park Drive, Armonk, New York 10504 (800) 541-6563; *The Illustrated Book of World Rankings.*

National Technical Information Service, 5285 Port Royal Road, Springfield, Virginia

22161 (800) 553-6847; *Handbook of Economic Statistics.*

Organisation for Economic Co-operation and Development (OECD), 2 rue Andre-Pascal, 75 Paris 16, France (Telephone Number in U.S. (202) 785-6323); *Tourism Policy and International Tourism in OECD Member Countries.*

St. Martin's Press, Inc., 175 Fifth Avenue, New York, New York 10010 (800) 221-7945; *The Statesman's Year-Book.*

Statistical Office of the United Nations, Publishing Service, New York, New York 10017 (800) 253-9646; *Statistical Yearbook.*

JAPAN - ALMOND PRODUCTION - See JAPAN - CROPS

JAPAN - ALUMINUM PRODUCTION AND CONSUMPTION - See JAPAN - MINING AND MINERAL PRODUCTS

JAPAN - ANIMAL FEEDINGSTUFFS

Organisation for Economic Co-operation and Development (OECD), 2 rue Andre-Pascal, 75 Paris 16, France (Telephone Number in U.S. (202) 785-6323); *Foreign Trade by Commodities.*

Statistical Office of the United Nations, Publishing Service, New York, New York 10017 (800) 253-9646; *Statistical Yearbook.*

JAPAN - ANIMAL HEALTH

Food and Agricultural Organization of the United Nations (FAO), Via delle Terme di Caracalla, 00100, Rome, Italy (Telephone Number in U.S. (202) 653-2400); *Animal Health Yearbook.*

JAPAN - ANTIMONY AND ANTIMONY ORE - See JAPAN - MINING AND MINERAL PRODUCTS

JAPAN - APPLE PRODUCTION - See JAPAN - CROPS

JAPAN - AREA AND DENSITY OF POPULATION

Central Intelligence Agency, Washington, D.C. 20505 (703) 482-1100, www.cia.gov; *The World Factbook.*

Euromonitor International, Inc., 122 South Michigan Avenue, Suite 1200, Chicago, Illinois 60603 (800) 577-EURO; *International Marketing Data and Statistics;* and *The World Economic Factbook.*

Europa Publications Limited, 18 Bedford Square, London, WC1B 3JN, England; *The Europa World Year Book.*

European Commission Office of Press and Public Affairs, 2100 M Street, NW,

Washington, D.C. 20037 (202) 862-9500; *Basic Statistics of the Community.*

Food and Agricultural Organization of the United Nations (FAO), Via delle Terme di Caracalla, 00100 Rome, Italy (Telephone Number in U.S. (202) 653-2400); *The State of Food and Agriculture.*

M.E. Sharpe, 80 Business Park Drive, Armonk, New York 10504 (800) 541-6563; *The Illustrated Book of World Rankings.*

National Technical Information Service, 5285 Port Royal Road, Springfield, Virginia 22161 (800) 553-6847; *Handbook of Economic Statistics.*

St. Martin's Press, Inc., 175 Fifth Avenue, New York, New York 10010 (800) 221-7945; *The Statesman's Year-Book.*

Statistical Office of the United Nations, Publishing Service, New York, New York 10017 (800) 253-9646; *Statistical Yearbook.*

Statistics Bureau, Management and Coordination Agency, Japan; *Statistical Indicators on Social Life.*

United Nations Educational, Scientific and Cultural Organization (UNESCO), 7 Place de Fontenoy, F-75700 Paris, France (Telephone Number in U.S. (212) 963-5981); *Statistical Yearbook.*

The World Bank, 1818 H Street, NW, Washington, D.C. 20433 (202) 477-1234; *World Development Report.*

JAPAN - ARMS EXPORTS AND IMPORTS - See JAPAN - MILITARY

JAPAN - ARSENIC PRODUCTION AND CONSUMPTION - See JAPAN - MINING AND MINERAL PRODUCTS

JAPAN - BALANCE OF PAYMENTS

The Economist Intelligence Unit, 111 West 57th Street, New York, New York 10019 (800) 938-4685; *The World Market Atlas.*

Europa Publications Limited, 18 Bedford Square, London, WC1B 3JN, England; *The Europa World Year Book.*

European Commission Office of Press and Public Affairs, 2100 M Street, NW, Washington, D.C. 20037 (202) 862-9500; *Basic Statistics of the Community.*

International Monetary Fund, 700 Nineteenth Street, NW, Washington, D.C. 20431 (202) 623-7000; *Balance of Payments Yearbook;* and *International Financial Statistics.*

National Technical Information Service, 5285 Port Royal Road, Springfield, Virginia

22161 (800) 553-6847; *Handbook of Economic Statistics.*

Organisation for Economic Co-operation and Development (OECD), 2 rue Andre-Pascal, 75 Paris 16, France (Telephone Number in U.S. (202) 785-6323); *Economic Outlook; Geographical Distribution of Financial Flows to Developing Countries; Main Economic Indicators - Historical Statistics;* and *OECD Economic Surveys: Japan.*

United Nations Conference on Trade and Development (UNCTAD), New York, New York 10017 (800) 253-9646; *Handbook of International Trade and Development Statistics.*

The World Bank, 1818 H Street, NW, Washington, D.C. 20433 (202) 477-1234; *World Development Report.*

JAPAN - BANKING

Euromonitor International, Inc., 122 South Michigan Avenue, Suite 1200, Chicago, Illinois 60603 (800) 577-EURO; *World Marketing Data and Statistics.*

Europa Publications Limited, 18 Bedford Square, London, WC1B 3JN, England; *The Europa World Year Book.*

International Monetary Fund, 700 Nineteenth Street, NW, Washington, D.C. 20431 (202) 623-7000; *Government Finance Statistics Yearbook;* and *International Financial Statistics.*

M.E. Sharpe, 80 Business Park Drive, Armonk, New York 10504 (800) 541-6563; *The Illustrated Book of World Rankings.*

National Technical Information Service, 5285 Port Royal Road, Springfield, Virginia 22161 (800) 553-6847; *Handbook of Economic Statistics.*

Organisation for Economic Co-operation and Development (OECD), 2 rue Andre-Pascal, 75 Paris 16, France (Telephone Number in U.S. (202) 785-6323); *Economic Outlook; Financial Market Trends;* and *OECD Economic Surveys: Japan.*

St. Martin's Press, Inc., 175 Fifth Avenue, New York, New York 10010 (800) 221-7945; *The Statesman's Year-Book.*

Statistical Office of the United Nations, Publishing Service, New York, New York 10017 (800) 253-9646; *Statistical Yearbook.*

JAPAN - BARLEY PRODUCTION - See JAPAN - CROPS

JAPAN - BAUXITE PRODUCTION AND CONSUMPTION - See JAPAN -MINING AND MINERAL PRODUCTS

JAPAN - BEVERAGES

European Commission Office of Press and Public Affairs, 2100 M Street, NW, Washington, D.C. 20037 (202) 862-9500; *Basic Statistics of the Community.*

M.E. Sharpe, 80 Business Park Drive, Armonk, New York 10504 (800) 541-6563; *The Illustrated Book of World Rankings.*

National Technical Information Service, 5285 Port Royal Road, Springfield, Virginia 22161 (800) 553-6847; *Handbook of Economic Statistics.*

Organisation for Economic Co-operation and Development (OECD), 2 rue Andre-Pascal, 75 Paris 16, France (Telephone Number in U.S. (202) 785-6323); *Indicators of Industrial Activity.*

Statistical Office of the United Nations, Publishing Service, New York, New York 10017 (800) 253-9646; *Statistical Yearbook.*

JAPAN - BIRTH RATES

Central Intelligence Agency, Washington, D.C. 20505 (703) 482-1100, www.cia.gov; *The World Factbook.*

The Economist Intelligence Unit (Asia) Limited, 10th Floor, Luk Kwok Centre, 72 Gloucester Road, Wanchai, Hong Kong (Phone Number in U.S. (800) 938-4685); *Asian Market Atlas.*

Euromonitor International, Inc., 122 South Michigan Avenue, Suite 1200, Chicago, Illinois 60603 (800) 577-EURO; *The World Economic Factbook.*

Europa Publications Limited, 18 Bedford Square, London, WC1B 3JN, England; *The Europa World Year Book.*

European Commission Office of Press and Public Affairs, 2100 M Street, NW, Washington, D.C. 20037 (202) 862-9500; *Basic Statistics of the Community.*

M.E. Sharpe, 80 Business Park Drive, Armonk, New York 10504 (800) 541-6563; *The Illustrated Book of World Rankings.*

Organisation for Economic Co-operation and Development (OECD), 2 rue Andre-Pascal, 75 Paris 16, France (Telephone Number in U.S. (202) 785-6323); *Labour Force Statistics.*

St. Martin's Press, Inc., 175 Fifth Avenue, New York, New York 10010 (800) 221-7945; *The Statesman's Year-Book.*

Statistical Office of the United Nations, Publishing Service, New York, New York 10017 (800) 253-9646; *Asia-Pacific in Figures; Demographic Yearbook;* and *Statistical Yearbook.*

Statistics Bureau, Management and Coordination Agency, Japan; *Statistical Indicators on Social Life.*

World Health Organization, Office of Publications, 20 Avenue Appia, CH-1211 Geneva 27, Switzerland (Telephone Number in U.S. (518) 436-9686); *World Health Statistics Annual.*

JAPAN - BISMUTH PRODUCTION AND CONSUMPTION - See JAPAN - MINING AND MINERAL PRODUCTS

JAPAN - BONDS

European Commission Office of Press and Public Affairs, 2100 M Street, NW, Washington, D.C. 20037 (202) 862-9500; *Basic Statistics of the Community.*

Organisation for Economic Co-operation and Development (OECD), 2 rue Andre-Pascal, 75 Paris 16, France (Telephone Number in U.S. (202) 785-6323); *Financial Market Trends.*

Statistical Office of the United Nations, Publishing Service, New York, New York 10017 (800) 253-9646; *Statistical Yearbook.*

JAPAN - BOOK PRODUCTION

Organisation for Economic Co-operation and Development (OECD), 2 rue Andre-Pascal, 75 Paris 16, France (Telephone Number in U.S. (202) 785-6323); *Indicators of Industrial Activity.*

United Nations Educational, Scientific and Cultural Organization (UNESCO), 7 Place de Fontenoy, F-75700 Paris, France (Telephone Number in U.S. (212) 963-5981); *Statistical Yearbook.*

JAPAN - BROADCASTING

Billboard Limited, Post Office Box 9027, 1006 AA Amsterdam, The Netherlands (Telephone Number in U.S. (212) 764-7300); *World Radio TV Handbook.*

Central Intelligence Agency, Washington, D.C. 20505 (703) 482-1100, www.cia.gov; *The World Factbook.*

The Economist Intelligence Unit (Asia) Limited, 10th Floor, Luk Kwok Centre, 72 Gloucester Road, Wanchai, Hong Kong (Phone Number in U.S. (800) 938-4685); *Asian Market Atlas.*

Euromonitor International, Inc., 122 South Michigan Avenue, Suite 1200, Chicago, Illinois 60603 (800) 577-EURO; *World Marketing Data and Statistics.*

European Commission Office of Press and Public Affairs, 2100 M Street, NW, Washington, D.C. 20037 (202) 862-9500; *Basic Statistics of the Community.*

M.E. Sharpe, 80 Business Park Drive, Armonk, New York 10504 (800) 541-6563; *The Illustrated Book of World Rankings.*

St. Martin's Press, Inc., 175 Fifth Avenue, New York, New York 10010 (800) 221-7945; *The Statesman's Year-Book.*

United Nations Educational, Scientific and Cultural Organization (UNESCO), 7 Place de Fontenoy, F-75700 Paris, France (Telephone Number in U.S. (212) 963-5981); *Statistical Yearbook.*

JAPAN - BUSINESS

Central Intelligence Agency, Washington, D.C. 20505 (703) 482-1100, www.cia.gov; *The World Factbook.*

European Commission Office of Press and Public Affairs, 2100 M Street, NW, Washington, D.C. 20037 (202) 862-9500; *Basic Statistics of the Community.*

JAPAN - BUTTER - See JAPAN - DAIRY PRODUCTS

JAPAN - CABBAGE PRODUCTION - See JAPAN - CROPS

JAPAN - CADMIUM PRODUCTION AND CONSUMPTION - See JAPAN - MINING AND MINERAL PRODUCTS

JAPAN - CALORIE SUPPLY

Food and Agricultural Organization of the United Nations (FAO), Via delle Terme di Caracalla, 00100 Rome, Italy (Telephone Number in U.S. (202) 653-2400); *The State of Food and Agriculture.*

JAPAN - CAPITAL INVESTMENT

National Technical Information Service, 5285 Port Royal Road, Springfield, Virginia 22161 (800) 553-6847; *Handbook of Economic Statistics.*

Organisation for Economic Co-operation and Development (OECD), 2 rue Andre-Pascal, 75 Paris 16, France (Telephone Number in U.S. (202) 785-6323); *Economic Outlook;* and *Financial Market Trends.*

JAPAN - CAPITAL REVENUE

International Monetary Fund, 700 Nineteenth Street, NW, Washington, D.C. 20431 (202) 623-7000; *Government Finance Statistics Yearbook.*

Organisation for Economic Co-operation and Development (OECD), 2 rue Andre-Pascal, 75 Paris 16, France (Telephone Number in U.S. (202) 785-6323); *Economic Outlook;* and *Financial Market Trends.*

JAPAN - CASHEW NUT PRODUCTION - See JAPAN - CROPS

JAPAN - CASTOR BEAN PRODUCTION - See JAPAN - CROPS

JAPAN - CATTLE - See JAPAN - LIVESTOCK AND POULTRY

JAPAN - CAULIFLOWER PRODUCTION - See JAPAN - CROPS

JAPAN - CAUSTIC SODA PRODUCTION - See JAPAN - BEVERAGES

JAPAN - CEMENT PRODUCTION - See JAPAN - MINING AND MINERAL PRODUCTS

JAPAN - CEREAL PRODUCTION - See JAPAN - CROPS

JAPAN - CHEESE - See JAPAN - DAIRY PRODUCTS

JAPAN - CHEMICAL (ORGANIC) PRODUCTION - See JAPAN - MINING AND MINERAL PRODUCTS

JAPAN - CHESTNUT PRODUCTION - See JAPAN - CROPS

JAPAN - CHICKENS - See JAPAN - LIVESTOCK AND POULTRY

JAPAN - CHROMITE PRODUCTION AND CONSUMPTION - See JAPAN - MINING AND MINERAL PRODUCTS

JAPAN - CHROMIUM ORE PRODUCTION AND CONSUMPTION - See JAPAN - MINING AND MINERAL PRODUCTS

JAPAN - CIGAR AND CIGARETTE PRODUCTION - See JAPAN - TOBACCO PRODUCTION

JAPAN - CLASS STRUCTURE

European Commission Office of Press and Public Affairs, 2100 M Street, NW, Washington, D.C. 20037 (202) 862-9500; *Basic Statistics of the Community.*

JAPAN - CLIMATE

M.E. Sharpe, 80 Business Park Drive, Armonk, New York 10504 (800) 541-6563; *The Illustrated Book of World Rankings.*

St. Martin's Press, Inc., 175 Fifth Avenue, New York, New York 10010 (800) 221-7945; *The Statesman's Year-Book.*

Statistics Bureau, Management and Coordination Agency, Japan; *Statistical Indicators on Social Life.*

JAPAN - CLOTHING - PRODUCTION INDEX - See JAPAN - TEXTILE INDUSTRY

JAPAN - CLOTHING EXPORTS AND

IMPORTS - See JAPAN - TEXTILE INDUSTRY

JAPAN - COAL PRODUCTION - See JAPAN - MINING AND MINERAL PRODUCTS

JAPAN - COBALT PRODUCTION AND CONSUMPTION - See JAPAN - MINING AND MINERAL PRODUCTS

JAPAN - COCOA (BEANS) PRODUCTION - See JAPAN - CROPS

JAPAN - COFFEE - See JAPAN - CROPS

JAPAN - COKE OVEN COKE PRODUCTION - See JAPAN - MINING AND MINERAL PRODUCTS

JAPAN - COKE OVEN ORE PRODUCTION AND CONSUMPTION - See JAPAN - MINING AND MINERAL PRODUCTS

JAPAN - COKE PRODUCTION AND CONSUMPTION - See JAPAN - MINING AND MINERAL PRODUCTS

JAPAN - COMMERCE

St. Martin's Press, Inc., 175 Fifth Avenue, New York, New York 10010 (800) 221-7945; *The Statesman's Year-Book.*

JAPAN - COMMUNICATIONS - See JAPAN - TRANSPORTATION AND COMMUNICATIONS

JAPAN - CONSTRUCTION INDUSTRY

European Commission Office of Press and Public Affairs, 2100 M Street, NW, Washington, D.C. 20037 (202) 862-9500; *Basic Statistics of the Community.*

M.E. Sharpe, 80 Business Park Drive, Armonk, New York 10504 (800) 541-6563; *The Illustrated Book of World Rankings.*

Organisation for Economic Co-operation and Development (OECD), 2 rue Andre-Pascal, 75 Paris 16, France (Telephone Number in U.S. (202) 785-6323); *Industrial Structure Statistics; The Iron and Steel Industry; Main Economic Indicators - Historical Statistics;* and *OECD Economic Surveys: Japan.*

St. Martin's Press, Inc., 175 Fifth Avenue, New York, New York 10010 (800) 221-7945; *The Statesman's Year-Book.*

Statistical Office of the United Nations, Publishing Service, New York, New York 10017 (800) 253-9646; *Statistical Yearbook.*

JAPAN - CONSUMER PRICE INDEX

European Commission Office of Press and Public Affairs, 2100 M Street, NW, Washington, D.C. 20037 (202) 862-9500; *Basic Statistics of the Community.*

National Technical Information Service, 5285 Port Royal Road, Springfield, Virginia 22161 (800) 553-6847; *Handbook of Economic Statistics.*

Organisation for Economic Co-operation and Development (OECD), 2 rue Andre-Pascal, 75 Paris 16, France (Telephone Number in U.S. (202) 785-6323); *Economic Outlook.*

JAPAN - CONSUMER PRICE INDEX NUMBERS

Europa Publications Limited, 18 Bedford Square, London, WC1B 3JN, England; *The Europa World Year Book.*

Statistical Office of the United Nations, Publishing Service, New York, New York 10017 (800) 253-9646; Statistical Yearbook.

JAPAN - CONSUMER PRICES

Euromonitor International, Inc., 122 South Michigan Avenue, Suite 1200, Chicago, Illinois 60603 (800) 577-EURO; *World Marketing Data and Statistics.*

European Commission Office of Press and Public Affairs, 2100 M Street, NW, Washington, D.C. 20037 (202) 862-9500; Basic Statistics of the Community.

International Labour Office, I.L.O. Publications, 1828 L Street NW, Suite 801, Washington, D.C. 20036 (301) 638-3152; Yearbook of Labour Statistics.

International Monetary Fund, 700 Nineteenth Street, NW, Washington, D.C. 20431 (202) 623-7000; International Financial Statistics.

Organisation for Economic Co-operation and Development (OECD), 2 rue Andre-Pascal, 75 Paris 16, France (Telephone Number in U.S. (202) 785-6323); Economic Outlook.

JAPAN - CONSUMPTION

European Commission Office of Press and Public Affairs, 2100 M Street, NW, Washington, D.C. 20037 (202) 862-9500; Basic Statistics of the Community.

International Lead and Zinc Study Group, Metro House, 58 St. James's Street, London SW1A 1LD, England; Lead and Zinc Statistics.

International Monetary Fund, 700 Nineteenth Street, NW, Washington, D.C. 20431 (202) 623-7000; International Financial Statistics.

International Rubber Study Group, York House, 8th Floor, Empire Way, Wembley, London HA9 0PA, England; Rubber Statistical Bulletin.

National Technical Information Service, 5285 Port Royal Road, Springfield, Virginia 22161 (800) 553-6847; Handbook. of Economic Statistics.

Organisation for Economic Co-operation and Development (OECD), 2 rue Andre-Pascal, 75 Paris 16, France (Telephone Number in U.S. (202) 785-6323); *The Footwear, Raw Hides and Skins, and Leather Industry in OECD Countries; The Iron and Steel Industry; Meat Balances in OECD Member Countries; The Non-Ferrous Metals Industry; The Pulp and Paper Industry;* and *Textile Industry in OECD Countries.*

Statistics Bureau, Management and Coordination Agency, Japan; *Statistical Indicators on Social Life.*

The World Bank, 1818 H Street, NW, Washington, D.C. 20433 (202) 477-1234; *World Development Report.*

JAPAN - COPPER AND COPPER ORE - See JAPAN - MINING AND MINERAL PRODUCTS

JAPAN - CORN PRODUCTION - See JAPAN - CROPS

JAPAN - CORPORATE INCOME TAXES - See JAPAN - TAXATION

JAPAN - CORPORATE TAXES - See JAPAN - TAXATION

JAPAN - COTTON - See JAPAN - CROPS

JAPAN - CRIME

International Criminal Police Organization (INTERPOL), 50 quai Achille Lignon, F-69006 Lyon, France; *International Crime Statistics.*

Statistics Bureau, Management and Coordination Agency, Japan; *Statistical Indicators on Social Life.*

Yale University Press, Yale Station, New Haven, Connecticut 06520 (800) 987-7323; *Violence and Crime in Cross-National Perspective.*

JAPAN - CROPS

Commodity Research Bureau, Inc., 30 South Wacker Drive, Chicago, Illinois 60606 (312) 454-1801; *Commodity Year Book.*

Europa Publications Limited, 18 Bedford Square, London, WC1B 3JN, England; *The Europa World Year Book.*

European Commission Office of Press and Public Affairs, 2100 M Street, NW, Washington, D.C. 20037 (202) 862-9500; *Basic Statistics of the Community.*

Food and Agricultural Organization of the United Nations (FAO), Via delle Terme di Caracalla, 00100 Rome, Italy (Telephone Number in U.S. (202) 653-2400); *Production Yearbook;* and *The State of Food and Agriculture.*

M.E. Sharpe, 80 Business Park Drive, Armonk, New York 10504 (800) 541-6563; *The Illustrated Book of World Rankings.*

National Technical Information Service, 5285 Port Royal Road, Springfield, Virginia 22161 (800) 553-6847; *Handbook of Economic Statistics.*

Organisation for Economic Co-operation and Development (OECD), 2 rue Andre-Pascal, 75 Paris 16, France (Telephone Number in U.S. (202) 785-6323); *Economic Accounts for Agriculture; Foreign Trade by Commodities; Indicators of Industrial Activity;* and *Textile Industry in OECD Countries.*

St. Martin's Press, Inc., 175 Fifth Avenue, New York, New York 10010 (800) 221-7945; *The Statesman's Year-Book.*

Statistical Office of the United Nations, Publishing Service, New York, New York 10017 (800) 253-9646; *Statistical Yearbook.*

Statistics Bureau, Management and Coordination Agency, Japan; *Statistical Indicators on Social Life.*

United Nations Conference on Trade and Development, Central Statistical Service, Palais des Nations, Geneva, Switzerland (Telephone in U.S. (800) 253-9646); *UNCTAD Commodity Yearbook.*

JAPAN - CUSTOMS DUTIES

European Commission Office of Press and Public Affairs, 2100 M Street, NW, Washington, D.C. 20037 (202) 862-9500; *Basic Statistics of the Community.*

International Monetary Fund, 700 Nineteenth Street, NW, Washington, D.C. 20431 (202) 623-7000; *Government Finance Statistics Yearbook.*

Organisation for Economic Co-operation and Development (OECD), 2 rue Andre-Pascal, 75 Paris 16, France (Telephone Number in U.S. (202) 785-6323); *Economic Accounts for Agriculture;* and *The Non-Ferrous Metals Industry.*

St. Martin's Press, Inc., 175 Fifth Avenue, New York, New York 10010 (800) 221-7945; *The Statesman's Year-Book.*

JAPAN - DAIRY PRODUCTS

Commodity Research Bureau, Inc., 30 South Wacker Drive, Chicago, Illinois 60606 (312) 454-1801; *Commodity Year*

Book.

Europa Publications Limited, 18 Bedford Square, London, WC1B 3JN, England; *The Europa World Year Book.*

European Commission Office of Press and Public Affairs, 2100 M Street, NW, Washington, D.C. 20037 (202) 862-9500; *Basic Statistics of the Community.*

Food and Agricultural Organization of the United Nations (FAO), Via delle Terme di Caracalla, 00100 Rome, Italy (Telephone Number in U.S. (202) 653-2400); *Production Yearbook;* and *The State of Food and Agriculture.*

M.E. Sharpe, 80 Business Park Drive, Armonk, New York 10504 (800) 541-6563; *The Illustrated Book of World Rankings.*

National Technical Information Service, 5285 Port Royal Road, Springfield, Virginia 22161 (800) 553-6847; *Handbook of Economic Statistics.*

Organisation for Economic Co-operation and Development (OECD), 2 rue Andre-Pascal, 75 Paris 16, France (Telephone Number in U.S. (202) 785-6323); *Economic Accounts for Agriculture;* and *Milk, Milk Products, and Egg Balances in OECD Member Countries.*

St. Martin's Press, Inc., 175 Fifth Avenue, New York, New York 10010 (800) 221-7945; *The Statesman's Year-Book.*

Statistical Office of the United Nations, Publishing Service, New York, New York 10017 (800) 253-9646; *Statistical Yearbook.*

JAPAN - DEATH RATES

The Economist Intelligence Unit (Asia) Limited, 10th Floor, Luk Kwok Centre, 72 Gloucester Road, Wanchai, Hong Kong (Phone Number in U.S. (800) 938-4685); *Asian Market Atlas.*

European Commission Office of Press and Public Affairs, 2100 M Street, NW, Washington, D.C. 20037 (202) 862-9500; *Basic Statistics of the Community.*

Statistical Office of the United Nations, Publishing Service, New York, New York 10017 (800) 253-9646; *Statistical Yearbook.*

Statistics Bureau, Management and Coordination Agency, Japan; *Statistical Indicators on Social Life.*

World Health Organization, Office of Publications, 20 Avenue Appia, CH-1211 Geneva 27, Switzerland (Telephone Number in U.S. (518) 436-9686); *World Health Statistics Annual.*

JAPAN - DEFENSE EXPENDITURES - See

JAPAN - MILITARY

JAPAN - DEMOGRAPHY

The Economist Intelligence Unit, 111 West 57th Street, New York, New York 10019 (800) 938-4685; *The World Market Atlas.*

The Economist Intelligence Unit (Asia) Limited, 10th Floor, Luk Kwok Centre, 72 Gloucester Road, Wanchai, Hong Kong (Phone Number in U.S. (800) 938-4685); *Asian Market Atlas.*

Euromonitor International, Inc., 122 South Michigan Avenue, Suite 1200, Chicago, Illinois 60603 (800) 577-EURO; *The World Economic Factbook;* and *World Marketing Data and Statistics.*

European Commission Office of Press and Public Affairs, 2100 M Street, NW, Washington, D.C. 20037 (202) 862-9500; *Basic Statistics of the Community.*

M.E. Sharpe, 80 Business Park Drive, Armonk, New York 10504 (800) 541-6563; *The Illustrated Book of World Rankings.*

Statistical Office of the United Nations, Publishing Service, New York, New York 10017 (800) 253-9646; *Asia-Pacific in Figures;* and *Human Development Report.*

JAPAN - DEVELOPMENT ASSISTANCE

European Commission Office of Press and Public Affairs, 2100 M Street, NW, Washington, D.C. 20037 (202) 862-9500; *Basic Statistics of the Community.*

Organisation for Economic Co-operation and Development (OECD), 2 rue Andre-Pascal, 75 Paris 16, France (Telephone Number in U.S. (202) 785-6323); *Geographical Distribution of Financial Flows to Developing Countries.*

Statistical Office of the United Nations, Publishing Service, New York, New York 10017 (800) 253-9646; *Statistical Yearbook.*

JAPAN - DIAMONDS - See JAPAN - MINING AND MINERAL PRODUCTS

JAPAN - DISCOUNT RATES - See JAPAN - BANKING

JAPAN - DISEASES - See JAPAN - HEALTH

JAPAN - DIVORCE RATES

M.E. Sharpe, 80 Business Park Drive, Armonk, New York 10504 (800) 541-6563; *The Illustrated Book of World Rankings.*

Statistical Office of the United Nations, Publishing Service, New York, New York 10017 (800) 253-9646; *Demographic Yearbook;* and *Statistical Yearbook.*

Statistics Bureau, Management and Coordination Agency, Japan; *Statistical Indicators on Social Life.*

JAPAN - DOMESTIC PRODUCT

European Commission Office of Press and Public Affairs, 2100 M Street, NW, Washington, D.C. 20037 (202) 862-9500; *Basic Statistics of the Community.*

JAPAN - DUCKS - See JAPAN - LIVESTOCK AND POULTRY

JAPAN - ECONOMY

Central Intelligence Agency, Washington, D.C. 20505 (703) 482-1100, www.cia.gov; *The World Factbook.*

The Economist Intelligence Unit, 111 West 57th Street, New York, New York 10019 (800) 938-4685; *Japan Country Report.*

Euromonitor International, Inc., 122 South Michigan Avenue, Suite 1200, Chicago, Illinois 60603 (800) 577-EURO; *International Marketing Data and Statistics; The World Economic Factbook;* and *World Marketing Data and Statistics..*

Europa Publications Limited, 18 Bedford Square, London, WC1B 3JN, England; *The Europa World Year Book.*

European Commission Office of Press and Public Affairs, 2100 M Street, NW, Washington, D.C. 20037 (202) 862-9500; *Basic Statistics of the Community.*

M.E. Sharpe, 80 Business Park Drive, Armonk, New York 10504 (800) 541-6563; *The Illustrated Book of World Rankings.*

National Technical Information Service, 5285 Port Royal Road, Springfield, Virginia 22161 (800) 553-6847; *Handbook of Economic Statistics.*

Organisation for Economic Co-operation and Development (OECD), 2 rue Andre-Pascal, 75 Paris 16, France (Telephone Number in U.S. (202) 785-6323); *Economic Outlook; Geographical Distribution of Financial Flows to Developing Countries; Main Economic Indicators - Historical Statistics; OECD Economic Surveys: Japan;* and *OECD Employment Outlook.*

St. Martin's Press, Inc., 175 Fifth Avenue, New York, New York 10010 (800) 221-7945; *The Statesman's Year-Book.*

Statistical Office of the United Nations, Publishing Service, New York, New York 10017 (800) 253-9646; *World Statistics Pocketbook.*

Statistics Bureau, Management and

Coordination Agency, Japan; *Statistical Indicators on Social Life.*

The World Bank, 1818 H Street, NW, Washington, D.C. 20433 (202) 477-1234; *The World Bank Atlas;* and *World Development Report.*

JAPAN - EDUCATION

The Economist Intelligence Unit, 111 West 57th Street, New York, New York 10019 (800) 938-4685; *The World Market Atlas.*

The Economist Intelligence Unit (Asia) Limited, 10th Floor, Luk Kwok Centre, 72 Gloucester Road, Wanchai, Hong Kong (Phone Number in U.S. (800) 938-4685); *Asian Market Atlas.*

Euromonitor International, Inc., 122 South Michigan Avenue, Suite 1200, Chicago, Illinois 60603 (800) 577-EURO; *World Marketing Data and Statistics.*

Europa Publications Limited, 18 Bedford Square, London, WC1B 3JN, England; *The Europa World Year Book.*

European Commission Office of Press and Public Affairs, 2100 M Street, NW, Washington, D.C. 20037 (202) 862-9500; *Basic Statistics of the Community.*

M.E. Sharpe, 80 Business Park Drive, Armonk, New York 10504 (800) 541-6563; *The Illustrated Book of World Rankings.*

Organisation for Economic Co-operation and Development (OECD), 2 rue Andre-Pascal, 75 Paris 16, France (Telephone Number in U.S. (202) 785-6323); *Education in OECD Countries.*

St. Martin's Press, Inc., 175 Fifth Avenue, New York, New York 10010 (800) 221-7945; *The Statesman's Year-Book.*

Statistical Office of the United Nations, Publishing Service, New York, New York 10017 (800) 253-9646; *Asia-Pacific in Figures; Human Development Report;* and *Statistical Yearbook for Asia and Pacific.*

Statistics Bureau, Management and Coordination Agency, Japan; *Statistical Indicators on Social Life.*

United Nations Educational, Scientific and Cultural Organization (UNESCO), 7 Place de Fontenoy, F-75700 Paris, France (Telephone Number in U.S. (212) 963-5981); *Statistical Yearbook.*

The World Bank, 1818 H Street, NW, Washington, D.C. 20433 (202) 477-1234; *World Development Report.*

JAPAN - EGG PRODUCTION AND CONSUMPTION - See JAPAN - DAIRY

PRODUCTS

JAPAN - EGGPLANT PRODUCTION - See
JAPAN - CROPS

JAPAN - ELECTRICITY

Central Intelligence Agency,
Washington, D.C. 20505 (703) 482-1100,
www.cia.gov; *The World Factbook.*

Commodity Research Bureau, Inc., 30
South Wacker Drive, Chicago, Illinois
60606 (312) 454-1801; *Commodity Year
Book.*

European Commission Office of Press
and Public Affairs, 2100 M Street, NW,
Washington, D.C. 20037 (202) 862-9500;
Basic Statistics of the Community.

M.E. Sharpe, 80 Business Park Drive,
Armonk, New York 10504 (800) 541-6563;
The Illustrated Book of World Rankings.

National Technical Information Service,
5285 Port Royal Road, Springfield, Virginia
22161 (800) 553-6847; *Handbook of
Economic Statistics.*

Organisation for Economic Co-
operation and Development (OECD), 2 rue
Andre-Pascal, 75 Paris 16, France
(Telephone Number in U.S. (202) 785-
6323); *Energy Statistics of OECD Countries;
Indicators of Industrial Activity;* and
Industrial Structure Statistics.

Penn Well Publishing Company, 1421
South Sheridan Road, Post Office Box 1260,
Tulsa, Oklahoma 74101 (800) 752-9764;
International Energy Statistics Sourcebook.

St. Martin's Press, Inc., 175 Fifth
Avenue, New York, New York 10010 (800)
221-7945; *The Statesman's Year-Book.*

Statistical Office of the United Nations,
Publishing Service, New York, New York
10017 (800) 253-9646; *Electric Power in
Asia and the Pacific; Human Development
Report;* and *Statistical Yearbook.*

JAPAN - EMPLOYMENT

Euromonitor International, Inc., 122
South Michigan Avenue, Suite 1200,
Chicago, Illinois 60603 (800) 577-EURO;
International Marketing Data and Statistics.

European Commission Office of Press
and Public Affairs, 2100 M Street, NW,
Washington, D.C. 20037 (202) 862-9500;
Basic Statistics of the Community.

International Labour Office,
I.L.O. Publications, 1828 L Street NW, Suite
801, Washington, D.C. 20036 (301) 638-
3152; *Yearbook of Labour Statistics.*

M.E. Sharpe, 80 Business Park Drive,

Armonk, New York 10504 (800) 541-6563;
The Illustrated Book of World Rankings.

Organisation for Economic Co-
operation and Development (OECD), 2 rue
Andre-Pascal, 75 Paris 16, France
(Telephone Number in U.S. (202) 785-
6323); *The Iron and Steel Industry,; OECD
Employment Outlook; OECD Economic
Surveys: Japan;* and *Textile Industry in
OECD Countries.*

Statistical Office of the United Nations,
Publishing Service, New York, New York
10017 (800) 253-9646; *Asia-Pacific in
Figures;* and *Statistical Yearbook.*

Statistics Bureau, Management and
Coordination Agency, Japan; *Statistical
Indicators on Social Life.*

JAPAN - ENERGY

Euromonitor International, Inc., 122
South Michigan Avenue, Suite 1200,
Chicago, Illinois 60603 (800) 577-EURO;
The World Economic Factbook; and *World
Marketing Data and Statistics.*

European Commission Office of Press
and Public Affairs, 2100 M Street, NW,
Washington, D.C. 20037 (202) 862-9500;
Basic Statistics of the Community.

Food and Agricultural Organization of
the United Nations (FAO), Via delle Terme
di Caracalla, 00100 Rome, Italy (Telephone
Number in U.S. (202) 653-2400); *The State
of Food and Agriculture.*

M.E. Sharpe, 80 Business Park Drive,
Armonk, New York 10504 (800) 541-6563;
The Illustrated Book of World Rankings.

National Technical Information Service,
5285 Port Royal Road, Springfield, Virginia
22161 (800) 553-6847; *Handbook of
Economic Statistics.*

Organisation for Economic Co-
operation and Development (OECD), 2 rue
Andre-Pascal, 75 Paris 16, France
(Telephone Number in U.S. (202) 785-
6323); *Coal Information; Energy Statistics
of OECD Countries; OECD Environmental
Data;* and *Oil and Gas Information.*

Penn Well Publishing Company, 1421
South Sheridan Road, Post Office Box 1260,
Tulsa, Oklahoma 74101 (800) 752-9764;
International Energy Statistics Sourcebook.

St. Martin's Press, Inc., 175 Fifth
Avenue, New York, New York 10010 (800)
221-7945; *The Statesman's Year-Book.*

Statistical Office of the United Nations,
Publishing Service, New York, New York
10017 (800) 253-9646; *Asia-Pacific in
Figures; Energy Statistics Yearbook; Human
Development Report; World Statistics*

Pocketbook; and *Statistical Yearbook.*

The World Bank, 1818 H Street, NW,
Washington, D.C. 20433 (202) 477-1234;
The World Bank Atlas; and *World
Development Report.*

JAPAN - ENGINEERING AND METAL
PRODUCTS - EXPORTS AND IMPORTS

European Commission Office of Press
and Public Affairs, 2100 M Street, NW,
Washington, D.C. 20037 (202) 862-9500;
Basic Statistics of the Community.

JAPAN - ENVIRONMENT

The Economist Intelligence Unit, 111
West 57th Street, New York, New York
10019 (800) 938-4685; *Japan Country
Report.*

Organization for Economic Co-
operation and Development (OECD), 2 rue
Andre-Pascal, 75 Paris 16, France
(Telephone Number in U.S. (202) 785-
6323): *OECD Environmental Data.*

Statistical Office of the United Nations,
Publishing Service, New York, New York
10017 (800) 253-9646; *World Statistics
Pocketbook.*

JAPAN - EXCHANGE RATES

Central Intelligence Agency,
Washington, D.C. 20505 (703) 482-1100,
www.cia.gov; *The World Factbook.*

The Economist Intelligence Unit (Asia)
Limited, 10th Floor, Luk Kwok Centre, 72
Gloucester Road, Wanchai, Hong Kong
(Phone Number in U.S. (800) 938-4685);
Asian Market Atlas.

Euromonitor International, Inc., 122
South Michigan Avenue, Suite 1200,
Chicago, Illinois 60603 (800) 577-EURO;
International Marketing Data and Statistics;
and *The World Economic Factbook.*

Europa Publications Limited, 18
Bedford Square, London, WC1B 3JN,
England; *The Europa World Year Book.*

European Commission Office of Press
and Public Affairs, 2100 M Street, NW,
Washington, D.C. 20037 (202) 862-9500;
Basic Statistics of the Community.

International Civil Aviation
Organization, 999 University Street,
Montreal, Quebec, Canada H3C 5H7 (514)
954-8219; *Civil Aviation Statistics of the
World.*

International Monetary Fund, 700
Nineteenth Street, NW, Washington,
D.C. 20431 (202) 623-7000; *International
Financial Statistics.*

National Technical Information Service, 5285 Port Royal Road, Springfield, Virginia 22161 (800) 553-6847; *Handbook of Economic Statistics.*

Organisation for Economic Co-operation and Development (OECD), 2 rue Andre-Pascal, 75 Paris 16, France (Telephone Number in U.S. (202) 785-6323); *Economic Outlook; Financial Market Trends; Revenue Statistics of OECD Member Countries;* and *Tourism Policy and International Tourism in OECD Member Countries.*

Statistical Office of the United Nations, Publishing Service, New York, New York 10017 (800) 253-9646; *Statistical Yearbook;* and *World Statistics Pocketbook.*

Walden Publishing, Ltd., Two Market Street, Saffron Walden Essex, CB10 1HZ, England; *The World of Information Asia and Pacific Review.*

JAPAN - EXCISE TAXES - See JAPAN - TAXATION

JAPAN - EXPORTS

American Automobile Manufacturers Association, 1401 H Street, NW, Suite 900, Washington, D.C. 20005 (202) 326-5500; *World Motor Vehicle Data.*

Central Intelligence Agency, Washington, D.C. 20505 (703) 482-1100, www.cia.gov; *The World Factbook.*

The Economist Intelligence Unit, 111 West 57th Street, New York, New York 10019 (800) 938-4685; *Japan Country Report;* and *The World Market Atlas.*

The Economist Intelligence Unit (Asia) Limited, 10th Floor, Luk Kwok Centre, 72 Gloucester Road, Wanchai, Hong Kong (Phone Number in U.S. (800) 938-4685); *Asian Market Atlas.*

Euromonitor International, Inc., 122 South Michigan Avenue, Suite 1200, Chicago, Illinois 60603 (800) 577-EURO; *International Marketing Data and Statistics;* and *The World Economic Factbook.*

Europa Publications Limited, 18 Bedford Square, London, WC1B 3JN, England; *The Europa World Year Book.*

European Commission Office of Press and Public Affairs, 2100 M Street, NW, Washington, D.C. 20037 (202) 862-9500; *Basic Statistics of the Community.*

Food and Agricultural Organization of the United Nations (FAO), Via delle Terme di Caracalla, 00100 Rome, Italy (Telephone Number in U.S. (202) 653-2400); *The State of Food and Agriculture.*

International Lead and Zinc Study Group, Metro House, 58 St. James's Street, London SW1A 1LD, England; *Lead and Zinc Statistics.*

International Monetary Fund, 700 Nineteenth Street, NW, Washington, D.C. 20431 (202) 623-7000; *Direction of Trade Statistics;* and *International Financial Statistics.*

International Rubber Study Group, York House, 8th Floor, Empire Way, Wembley, London HA9 0PA, England; *Rubber Statistical Bulletin.*

National Technical Information Service, 5285 Port Royal Road, Springfield, Virginia 22161 (800) 553-6847; *Handbook of Economic Statistics.*

Organisation for Economic Co-operation and Development (OECD), 2 rue Andre-Pascal, 75 Paris 16, France (Telephone Number in U.S. (202) 785-6323); *Economic Outlook; The Footwear, Raw Hides and Skins, and Leather Industry in OECD Countries; Foreign Trade by Commodities; Geographical Distribution of Financial Flows to Developing Countries; Industrial Structure Statistics; The Iron and Steel Industry; Milk, Milk Products, and Egg Balances in OECD Member Countries; OECD Economic Surveys: Japan; The Pulp and Paper Industry;* and *Review of Fisheries in OECD Member Countries.*

St. Martin's Press, Inc., 175 Fifth Avenue, New York, New York 10010 (800) 221-7945; *The Statesman's Year-Book.*

Statistical Office of the United Nations, Publishing Service, New York, New York 10017 (800) 253-9646; *Foreign Trade Statistics of Asia and the Pacific.*

Statistics Bureau, Management and Coordination Agency, Japan; *Statistical Indicators on Social Life.*

United Nations Conference on Trade and Development (UNCTAD), New York, New York 10017 (800) 253-9646; *Handbook of International Trade and Development Statistics.*

Walden Publishing, Ltd., Two Market Street, Saffron Walden Essex, CB10 1HZ, England; *The World of Information Asia and Pacific Review.*

The World Bank, 1818 H Street, NW, Washington, D.C. 20433 (202) 477-1234; *World Development Report.*

JAPAN - EXTERNAL FINANCING

Organisation for Economic Co-operation and Development (OECD), 2 rue Andre-Pascal, 75 Paris 16, France (Telephone Number in U.S. (202) 785-

6323); *Economic Outlook;* and *Financial Market Trends.*

JAPAN - EXTERNAL INDEBTEDNESS

National Technical Information Service, 5285 Port Royal Road, Springfield, Virginia 22161 (800) 553-6847; *Handbook of Economic Statistics.*

Organisation for Economic Co-operation and Development (OECD), 2 rue Andre-Pascal, 75 Paris 16, France (Telephone Number in U.S. (202) 785-6323); *Financial Market Trends;* and *Geographical Distribution of Financial Flows to Developing Countries.*

The World Bank, 1818 H Street, NW, Washington, D.C. 20433 (202) 477-1234; *World Development Report.*

JAPAN - EXTERNAL TRADE

Euromonitor International, Inc., 122 South Michigan Avenue, Suite 1200, Chicago, Illinois 60603 (800) 577-EURO; *World Marketing Data and Statistics.*

European Commission Office of Press and Public Affairs, 2100 M Street, NW, Washington, D.C. 20037 (202) 862-9500; *Basic Statistics of the Community.*

Food and Agricultural Organization of the United Nations (FAO), Via delle Terme di Caracalla, 00100 Rome, Italy (Telephone Number in U.S. (202) 653-2400); *The State of Food and Agriculture;* and *Trade Yearbook.*

National Technical Information Service, 5285 Port Royal Road, Springfield, Virginia 22161 (800) 553-6847; *Handbook of Economic Statistics.*

Statistical Office of the United Nations, Publishing Service, New York, New York 10017 (800) 253-9646; *Asia-Pacific in Figures; Statistical Yearbook;* and *Statistical Yearbook for Asia and the Pacific.*

JAPAN - FABRIC PRODUCTION - See JAPAN - TEXTILE INDUSTRY

JAPAN - FARM CROPS - See JAPAN - CROPS

JAPAN - FEMALE WORKING POPULATION - See JAPAN - EMPLOYMENT

JAPAN - FERTILITY RATES

Central Intelligence Agency, Washington, D.C. 20505 (703) 482-1100, www.cia.gov; *The World Factbook.*

The Economist Intelligence Unit (Asia) Limited, 10th Floor, Luk Kwok Centre, 72 Gloucester Road, Wanchai, Hong Kong

(Phone Number in U.S. (800) 938-4685); *Asian Market Atlas.*

M.E. Sharpe, 80 Business Park Drive, Armonk, New York 10504 (800) 541-6563; *The Illustrated Book of World Rankings.*

Statistical Office of the United Nations, Publishing Service, New York, New York 10017 (800) 253-9646; *Human Development Report.*

The World Bank, 1818 H Street, NW, Washington, D.C. 20433 (202) 477-1234; *The World Bank Atlas;* and *World Development Report.*

JAPAN - FERTILIZER

European Commission Office of Press and Public Affairs, 2100 M Street, NW, Washington, D.C. 20037 (202) 862-9500; *Basic Statistics of the Community.*

Food and Agricultural Organization of the United Nations (FAO), Via delle Terme di Caracalla, 00100, Rome, Italy (Telephone Number in U.S. (202) 653-2400); *Fertilizer Yearbook;* and *The State of Food and Agriculture.*

National Technical Information Service, 5285 Port Royal Road, Springfield, Virginia 22161 (800) 553-6847; *Handbook of Economic Statistics.*

Organisation for Economic Co-operation and Development (OECD), 2 rue Andre-Pascal, 75 Paris 16, France (Telephone Number in U.S. (202) 785-6323); *Economic Accounts for Agriculture;* and *Foreign Trade by Commodities.*

Statistical Office of the United Nations, Publishing Service, New York, New York 10017 (800) 253-9646; *Statistical Yearbook.*

JAPAN - FETAL MORTALITY - See JAPAN - MORTALITY

JAPAN - FIBRE PRODUCTION - See JAPAN - TEXTILE INDUSTRY

JAPAN - FILAMENT PRODUCTION - See JAPAN - TEXTILE INDUSTRY

JAPAN - FILMS - See JAPAN - MOTION PICTURES

JAPAN - FINANCE

The Economist Intelligence Unit, 111 West 57th Street, New York, New York 10019 (800) 938-4685; *Japan Country Report.*

Europa Publications Limited, 18 Bedford Square, London, WC1B 3JN, England; *The Europa World Year Book.*

European Commission Office of Press

and Public Affairs, 2100 M Street, NW, Washington, D.C. 20037 (202) 862-9500; *Basic Statistics of the Community.*

International Monetary Fund, 700 Nineteenth Street, NW, Washington, D.C. 20431 (202) 623-7000; *International Financial Statistics.*

M.E. Sharpe, 80 Business Park Drive, Armonk, New York 10504 (800) 541-6563; *The Illustrated Book of World Rankings.*

National Technical Information Service, 5285 Port Royal Road, Springfield, Virginia 22161 (800) 553-6847; *Handbook of Economic Statistics.*

Organisation for Economic Co-operation and Development (OECD), 2 rue Andre-Pascal, 75 Paris 16, France (Telephone Number in U.S. (202) 785-6323); *Economic Outlook; Financial Market Trends; Geographical Distribution of Financial Flows to Developing Countries; Main Economic Indicators - Historical Statistics; OECD Financial Statistics;* and *Revenue Statistics of OECD Member Countries.*

St. Martin's Press, Inc., 175 Fifth Avenue, New York, New York 10010 (800) 221-7945; *The Statesman's Year-Book.*

Statistical Office of the United Nations, Publishing Service, New York, New York 10017 (800) 253-9646; *Statistical Yearbook for Asia and the Pacific.*

Statistics Bureau, Management and Coordination Agency, Japan; *Statistical Indicators on Social Life.*

JAPAN - FISHERIES

Europa Publications Limited, 18 Bedford Square, London, WC1B 3JN, England; *The Europa World Year Book.*

Food and Agricultural Organization of the United Nations (FAO), Via delle Terme di Caracalla, 00100 Rome, Italy (Telephone Number in U.S. (202) 653-2400); *The State of Food and Agriculture.*

M.E. Sharpe, 80 Business Park Drive, Armonk, New York 10504 (800) 541-6563; *The Illustrated Book of World Rankings.*

National Technical Information Service, 5285 Port Royal Road, Springfield, Virginia 22161 (800) 553-6847; *Handbook of Economic Statistics.*

Organisation for Economic Co-operation and Development (OECD), 2 rue Andre-Pascal, 75 Paris 16, France (Telephone Number in U.S. (202) 785-6323); *Foreign Trade by Commodities;* and *Review of Fisheries in OECD Member Countries.*

St. Martin's Press, Inc., 175 Fifth Avenue, New York, New York 10010 (800) 221-7945; *The Statesman's Year-Book.*

Statistical Office of the United Nations, Publishing Service, New York, New York 10017 (800) 253-9646; *Statistical Yearbook.*

United Nations Conference on Trade and Development, Central Statistical Service, Palais des Nations, Geneva, Switzerland (Telephone in U.S. (800) 253-9646); *UNCTAD Commodity Yearbook.*

JAPAN - FLAX AND FLAX FIBRE PRODUCTION - See JAPAN - TEXTILE INDUSTRY

JAPAN - FLOUR PRODUCTION

Commodity Research Bureau, Inc., 30 South Wacker Drive, Chicago, Illinois 60606 (312) 454-1801; *Commodity Year Book.*

European Commission Office of Press and Public Affairs, 2100 M Street, NW, Washington, D.C. 20037 (202) 862-9500; *Basic Statistics of the Community.*

Statistical Office of the United Nations, Publishing Service, New York, New York 10017 (800) 253-9646; *Statistical Yearbook.*

JAPAN - FOOD

Euromonitor International, Inc., 122 South Michigan Avenue, Suite 1200, Chicago, Illinois 60603 (800) 577-EURO; *Retail Trade International.*

European Commission Office of Press and Public Affairs, 2100 M Street, NW, Washington, D.C. 20037 (202) 862-9500; *Basic Statistics of the Community.*

Food and Agricultural Organization of the United Nations (FAO), Via delle Terme di Caracalla, 00100 Rome, Italy (Telephone Number in U.S. (202) 653-2400); *Production Yearbook;* and *The State of Food and Agriculture.*

Organisation for Economic Co-operation and Development (OECD), 2 rue Andre-Pascal, 75 Paris 16, France (Telephone Number in U.S. (202) 785-6323); *Food Consumption Statistics;* and *Foreign Trade by Commodities.*

Statistical Office of the United Nations, Publishing Service, New York, New York 10017 (800) 253-9646; *Human Development Report;* and *Statistical Yearbook for Asia and the Pacific.*

United Nations Conference on Trade and Development, Central Statistical Service, Palais des Nations, Geneva, Switzerland (Telephone in U.S. (800) 253-9646); *UNCTAD Commodity Yearbook.*

JAPAN - FOOTWEAR - PRODUCTION INDEX

Organisation for Economic Co-operation and Development (OECD), 2 rue Andre-Pascal, 75 Paris 16, France (Telephone Number in U.S. (202) 785-6323); *Indicators of Industrial Activity.*

JAPAN - FOREIGN AID

National Technical Information Service, 5285 Port Royal Road, Springfield, Virginia 22161 (800) 553-6847; *Handbook of Economic Statistics.*

JAPAN - FOREIGN DEBT

International Monetary Fund, 700 Nineteenth Street, NW, Washington, D.C. 20431 (202) 623-7000; *Government Finance Statistics Yearbook.*

Organisation for Economic Co-operation and Development (OECD), 2 rue Andre-Pascal, 75 Paris 16, France (Telephone Number in U.S. (202) 785-6323); *Economic Outlook.*

St. Martin's Press, Inc., 175 Fifth Avenue, New York, New York 10010 (800) 221-7945; *The Statesman's Year-Book.*

Walden Publishing, Ltd., Two Market Street, Saffron Walden Essex, CB10 1HZ, England; *The World of Information Asia and Pacific Review.*

JAPAN - FOREIGN INDEBTEDNESS

Organisation for Economic Co-operation and Development (OECD), 2 rue Andre-Pascal, 75 Paris 16, France (Telephone Number in U.S. (202) 785-6323); *Economic Outlook;* and *Financial Market Trends.*

JAPAN - FOREIGN TRADE

The Economist Intelligence Unit, 111 West 57th Street, New York, New York 10019 (800) 938-4685; *Japan Country Report.*

The Economist Intelligence Unit (Asia) Limited, 10th Floor, Luk Kwok Centre, 72 Gloucester Road, Wanchai, Hong Kong (Phone Number in U.S. (800) 938-4685); *Asian Market Atlas.*

Euromonitor International, Inc., 122 South Michigan Avenue, Suite 1200, Chicago, Illinois 60603 (800) 577-EURO; *International Marketing Data and Statistics;* and *The World Economic Factbook.*

Europa Publications Limited, 18 Bedford Square, London, WC1B 3JN, England; *The Europa World Year Book.*

European Commission Office of Press

and Public Affairs, 2100 M Street, NW, Washington, D.C. 20037 (202) 862-9500; *Basic Statistics of the Community.*

Food and Agricultural Organization of the United Nations (FAO), Via delle Terme di Caracalla, 00100 Rome, Italy (Telephone Number in U.S. (202) 653-2400); *The State of Food and Agriculture.*

International Monetary Fund, 700 Nineteenth Street, NW, Washington, D.C. 20431 (202) 623-7000; *International Financial Statistics.*

M.E. Sharpe, 80 Business Park Drive, Armonk, New York 10504 (800) 541-6563; *The Illustrated Book of World Rankings.*

National Technical Information Service, 5285 Port Royal Road, Springfield, Virginia 22161 (800) 553-6847; *Handbook of Economic Statistics.*

Organisation for Economic Co-operation and Development (OECD), 2 rue Andre-Pascal, 75 Paris 16, France (Telephone Number in U.S. (202) 785-6323); *Economic Outlook; The Footwear, Raw Hides and Skins, and Leather Industry in OECD Countries; Foreign Trade by Commodities; Main Economic Indicators - Historical Statistics; Maritime Transport; Meat Balances in OECD Member Countries;* and *OECD Economic Surveys: Japan.*

St. Martin's Press, Inc., 175 Fifth Avenue, New York, New York 10010 (800) 221-7945; *The Statesman's Year-Book.*

Statistical Office of the United Nations, Publishing Service, New York, New York 10017 (800) 253-9646; *Statistical Yearbook;* and *International Trade Statistics Yearbook.*

United Nations Conference on Trade and Development, Central Statistical Service, Palais des Nations, Geneva, Switzerland (Telephone in U.S. (800) 253-9646); *UNCTAD Commodity Yearbook.*

World Bureau of Metal Statistics, 27-A High Street, Ware, Herts. SG12 9BA, England; *World Metal Statistics.*

The World Bank, 1818 H Street, NW, Washington, D.C. 20433 (202) 477-1234; *World Development Report.*

JAPAN - FORESTRY AND FOREST PRODUCTS

American Forest and Paper Association, 1111 Nineteenth Street, NW, Washington, D.C. 20036 (202) 463-2700; *Wood Pulp and Fiber Statistics.*

The Economist Intelligence Unit (Asia) Limited, 10th Floor, Luk Kwok Centre, 72 Gloucester Road, Wanchai, Hong Kong

(Phone Number in U.S. (800) 938-4685); *Asian Market Atlas.*

Europa Publications Limited, 18 Bedford Square, London, WC1B 3JN, England; *The Europa World Year Book.*

European Commission Office of Press and Public Affairs, 2100 M Street, NW, Washington, D.C. 20037 (202) 862-9500; *Basic Statistics of the Community.*

Food and Agricultural Organization of the United Nations (FAO), Via delle Terme di Caracalla, 00100 Rome, Italy (Telephone Number in U.S. (202) 653-2400); *The State of Food and Agriculture;* and *Yearbook of Forest Products.*

M.E. Sharpe, 80 Business Park Drive, Armonk, New York 10504 (800) 541-6563; *The Illustrated Book of World Rankings.*

National Technical Information Service, 5285 Port Royal Road, Springfield, Virginia 22161 (800) 553-6847; *Handbook of Economic Statistics.*

Organisation for Economic Co-operation and Development (OECD), 2 rue Andre-Pascal, 75 Paris 16, France (Telephone Number in U.S. (202) 785-6323); *Foreign Trade by Commodities; Indicators of Industrial Activity; Industrial Structure Statistics;* and *The Pulp and Paper Industry.*

St. Martin's Press, Inc., 175 Fifth Avenue, New York, New York 10010 (800) 221-7945; *The Statesman's Year-Book.*

Statistical Office of the United Nations, Publishing Service, New York, New York 10017 (800) 253-9646; *Statistical Yearbook.*

United Nations Conference on Trade and Development, Central Statistical Service, Palais des Nations, Geneva, Switzerland (Telephone in U.S. (800) 253-9646); *UNCTAD Commodity Yearbook.*

United Nations Educational, Scientific and Cultural Organization (UNESCO), 7 Place de Fontenoy, F-75700 Paris, France (Telephone Number in U.S. (212) 963-5981); *Statistical Yearbook.*

The World Bank, 1818 H Street, NW, Washington, D.C. 20433 (202) 477-1234; *World Development Report.*

JAPAN - FRUIT PRODUCTION

European Commission Office of Press and Public Affairs, 2100 M Street, NW, Washington, D.C. 20037 (202) 862-9500; *Basic Statistics of the Community.*

Organisation for Economic Co-operation and Development (OECD), 2 rue Andre-Pascal, 75 Paris 16, France

(Telephone Number in U.S. (202) 785-6323); *Economic Accounts for Agriculture;* and *Foreign Trade by Commodities.*

JAPAN - FURNITURE AND WOOD PRODUCTS EXPORTS AND IMPORTS

European Commission Office of Press and Public Affairs, 2100 M Street, NW, Washington, D.C. 20037 (202) 862-9500; *Basic Statistics of the Community.*

Organisation for Economic Co-operation and Development (OECD), 2 rue Andre-Pascal, 75 Paris 16, France (Telephone Number in U.S. (202) 785-6323); *Foreign Trade by Commodities;* and *Industrial Structure Statistics.*

JAPAN - GARLIC PRODUCTION - See JAPAN - CROPS

JAPAN - GAS - See JAPAN - MINING AND MINERAL PRODUCTS

JAPAN - GENERAL INDUSTRIAL STATISTICS - See JAPAN - INDUSTRY

JAPAN - GENERAL MORTALITY - See JAPAN - MORTALITY

JAPAN - GEOGRAPHIC DATA

European Commission Office of Press and Public Affairs, 2100 M Street, NW, Washington, D.C. 20037 (202) 862-9500; *Basic Statistics of the Community.*

M.E. Sharpe, 80 Business Park Drive, Armonk, New York 10504 (800) 541-6563; *The Illustrated Book of World Rankings.*

JAPAN - GLASS AND GLASS PRODUCTS - PRODUCTION INDEX

Organisation for Economic Co-operation and Development (OECD), 2 rue Andre-Pascal, 75 Paris 16, France (Telephone Number in U.S. (202) 785-6323); *Indicators of Industrial Activity.*

JAPAN - GOATS - See JAPAN - LIVESTOCK AND POULTRY

JAPAN - GOLD HOLDINGS

International Monetary Fund, 700 Nineteenth Street, NW, Washington, D.C. 20431 (202) 623-7000; *International Financial Statistics.*

Statistical Office of the United Nations, Publishing Service, New York, New York 10017 (800) 253-9646; *Statistical Yearbook.*

JAPAN - GOLD PRODUCTION AND CONSUMPTION - See JAPAN - MINING AND MINERAL PRODUCTS

JAPAN - GOVERNMENT

Central Intelligence Agency, Washington, D.C. 20505 (703) 482-1100, www.cia.gov; *The World Factbook.*

Europa Publications Limited, 18 Bedford Square, London, WC1B 3JN, England; *The Europa World Year Book.*

European Commission Office of Press and Public Affairs, 2100 M Street, NW, Washington, D.C. 20037 (202) 862-9500; *Basic Statistics of the Community.*

International Monetary Fund, 700 Nineteenth Street, NW, Washington, D.C. 20431 (202) 623-7000; *Government Finance Statistics Yearbook;* and *International Financial Statistics.*

Organisation for Economic Co-operation and Development (OECD), 2 rue Andre-Pascal, 75 Paris 16, France (Telephone Number in U.S. (202) 785-6323); *Economic Outlook;* and *Revenue Statistics of OECD Member Countries.*

St. Martin's Press, Inc., 175 Fifth Avenue, New York, New York 10010 (800) 221-7945; *The Statesman's Year-Book.*

Statistical Office of the United Nations, Publishing Service, New York, New York 10017 (800) 253-9646; *Asia-Pacific in Figures; National Accounts Statistics;* and *Statistical Yearbook.*

The World Bank, 1818 H Street, NW, Washington, D.C. 20433 (202) 477-1234; *World Development Report.*

JAPAN - GRAIN PRODUCTION - See JAPAN - CROPS

JAPAN - GRANTS

International Monetary Fund, 700 Nineteenth Street, NW, Washington, D.C. 20431 (202) 623-7000; *Government Finance Statistics Yearbook.*

National Technical Information Service, 5285 Port Royal Road, Springfield, Virginia 22161 (800) 553-6847; *Handbook of Economic Statistics.*

Organisation for Economic Co-operation and Development (OECD), 2 rue Andre-Pascal, 75 Paris 16, France (Telephone Number in U.S. (202) 785-6323); *Geographical Distribution of Financial Flows to Developing Countries.*

JAPAN - GREEN PEPPER AND CHILIE PRODUCTION - See JAPAN - CROPS

JAPAN - GROSS DOMESTIC PRODUCT

The Economist Intelligence Unit, 111 West 57th Street, New York, New York 10019 (800) 938-4685; *Japan Country Report;* and *The World Market Atlas.*

The Economist Intelligence Unit (Asia) Limited, 10th Floor, Luk Kwok Centre, 72 Gloucester Road, Wanchai, Hong Kong (Phone Number in U.S. (800) 938-4685); *Asian Market Atlas.*

Euromonitor International, Inc., 122 South Michigan Avenue, Suite 1200, Chicago, Illinois 60603 (800) 577-EURO; *International Marketing Data and Statistics;* and *The World Economic Factbook.*

Europa Publications Limited, 18 Bedford Square, London, WC1B 3JN, England; *The Europa World Year Book.*

European Commission Office of Press and Public Affairs, 2100 M Street, NW, Washington, D.C. 20037 (202) 862-9500; *Basic Statistics of the Community.*

International Monetary Fund, 700 Nineteenth Street, NW, Washington, D.C. 20431 (202) 623-7000; *International Financial Statistics.*

M.E. Sharpe, 80 Business Park Drive, Armonk, New York 10504 (800) 541-6563; *The Illustrated Book of World Rankings.*

National Technical Information Service, 5285 Port Royal Road, Springfield, Virginia 22161 (800) 553-6847; *Handbook of Economic Statistics.*

Organisation for Economic Co-operation and Development (OECD), 2 rue Andre-Pascal, 75 Paris 16, France (Telephone Number in U.S. (202) 785-6323); *Economic Outlook; Geographical Distribution of Financial Flows to Developing Countries;* and *Revenue Statistics of OECD Member Countries.*

St. Martin's Press, Inc., 175 Fifth Avenue, New York, New York 10010 (800) 221-7945; *The Statesman's Year-Book.*

Statistical Office of the United Nations, Publishing Service, New York, New York 10017 (800) 253-9646; *Human Development Report; National Accounts Statistics;* and *Statistical Yearbook.*

The World Bank, 1818 H Street, NW, Washington, D.C. 20433 (202) 477-1234; *World Development Report.*

JAPAN - GROSS NATIONAL PRODUCT

Euromonitor International, Inc., 122 South Michigan Avenue, Suite 1200, Chicago, Illinois 60603 (800) 577-EURO; *International Marketing Data and Statistics.*

Europa Publications Limited, 18 Bedford Square, London, WC1B 3JN, England; *The Europa World Year Book.*

European Commission Office of Press and Public Affairs, 2100 M Street, NW,

Washington, D.C. 20037 (202) 862-9500; *Basic Statistics of the Community.*

National Technical Information Service, 5285 Port Royal Road, Springfield, Virginia 22161 (800) 553-6847; *Handbook of Economic Statistics.*

Organisation for Economic Co-operation and Development (OECD), 2 rue Andre-Pascal, 75 Paris 16, France (Telephone Number in U.S. (202) 785-6323); *Economic Outlook;* and *Geographical Distribution of Financial Flows to Developing Countries.*

U.S. Arms Control and Disarmament Agency, 320 Twenty-first Street, NW, Washington, D.C. 20451 (202) 647-8677; *World Military Expenditures and Arms Transfers.*

Walden Publishing, Ltd., Two Market Street, Saffron Walden Essex, CB10 1HZ, England; *The World of Information Asia and Pacific Review.*

The World Bank, 1818 H Street, NW, Washington, D.C. 20433 (202) 477-1234; *The World Bank Atlas;* and *World Development Report.*

JAPAN - GROUNDNUTS PRODUCTION - See JAPAN - CROPS

JAPAN - HAY PRODUCTION - See JAPAN - CROPS

JAPAN - HAZELNUT PRODUCTION - See JAPAN - CROPS

JAPAN - HEALTH

The Economist Intelligence Unit (Asia) Limited, 10th Floor, Luk Kwok Centre, 72 Gloucester Road, Wanchai, Hong Kong (Phone Number in U.S. (800) 938-4685); *Asian Market Atlas.*

Euromonitor International, Inc., 122 South Michigan Avenue, Suite 1200, Chicago, Illinois 60603 (800) 577-EURO; *World Marketing Data and Statistics.*

European Commission Office of Press and Public Affairs, 2100 M Street, NW, Washington, D.C. 20037 (202) 862-9500; *Basic Statistics of the Community.*

M.E. Sharpe, 80 Business Park Drive, Armonk, New York 10504 (800) 541-6563; *The Illustrated Book of World Rankings.*

Organisation for Economic Corporation and Development (OECD), 2 rue Andre-Pascal, 75 Paris 16, France (Telephone Number in U.S. (202) 785-6323); *OECD Health Systems: Facts and Trends.*

St. Martin's Press, Inc., 175 Fifth Avenue, New York, New York 10010 (800)

221-7945; *The Statesman's Year-Book.*

Statistical Office of the United Nations, Publishing Service, New York, New York 10017 (800) 253-9646; *Asia-Pacific in Figures; Human Development Report;* and *Statistical Yearbook.*

Statistics Bureau, Management and Coordination Agency, Japan; *Statistical Indicators on Social Life.*

United Nations Children's Fund (UNICEF), 3 United Nations Plaza, New York, New York 10017 (800) 253-9646; *State of the World's Children.*

The World Bank, 1818 H Street, NW, Washington, D.C. 20433 (202) 477-1234; *World Development Report.*

World Health Organization, Office of Publications, 20 Avenue Appia, CH-1211 Geneva 27, Switzerland (Telephone Number in U.S. (518) 436-9686); *World Health Statistics Annual.*

JAPAN - HEMP FIBRE PRODUCTION - See JAPAN - TEXTILE INDUSTRY

JAPAN - HIDE PRODUCTION

Food and Agricultural Organization of the United Nations (FAO), Via delle Terme di Caracalla, 00100 Rome, Italy (Telephone Number in U.S. (202) 653-2400); *Production Yearbook.*

Organisation for Economic Co-operation and Development (OECD), 2 rue Andre-Pascal, 75 Paris 16, France (Telephone Number in U.S. (202) 785-6323); *The Footwear, Raw Hides and Skins, and Leather Industry in OECD Countries; Foreign Trade by Commodities;* and *Indicators of Industrial Activity.*

JAPAN - HIGHWAYS

Central Intelligence Agency, Washington, D.C. 20505 (703) 482-1100, www.cia.gov; *The World Factbook.*

The Economist Intelligence Unit (Asia) Limited, 10th Floor, Luk Kwok Centre, 72 Gloucester Road, Wanchai, Hong Kong (Phone Number in U.S. (800) 938-4685); *Asian Market Atlas.*

European Commission Office of Press and Public Affairs, 2100 M Street, NW, Washington, D.C. 20037 (202) 862-9500; *Basic Statistics of the Community.*

International Road Federation, 2600 Virginia Avenue, NW, Washington, D.C. 20037 (202) 338-4641; *World Road Statistics.*

St. Martin's Press, Inc., 175 Fifth Avenue, New York, New York 10010 (800)

221-7945; *The Statesman's Year-Book.*

JAPAN - HOME FINANCE

Organisation for Economic Co-operation and Development (OECD), 2 rue Andre-Pascal, 75 Paris 16, France (Telephone Number in U.S. (202) 785-6323); *Main Economic Indicators - Historical Statistics.*

JAPAN - HONEY PRODUCTION

Commodity Research Bureau, Inc., 30 South Wacker Drive, Chicago, Illinois 60606 (312) 454-1801; *Commodity Year Book.*

JAPAN - HOPS PRODUCTION - See JAPAN - CROPS

JAPAN - HORSES - See JAPAN - LIVESTOCK AND POULTRY

JAPAN - HOURS OF WORK - See JAPAN - EMPLOYMENT

JAPAN - HOUSING AND HOUSING UNITS

Euromonitor International, Inc., 122 South Michigan Avenue, Suite 1200, Chicago, Illinois 60603 (800) 577-EURO; *World Marketing Data and Statistics.*

European Commission Office of Press and Public Affairs, 2100 M Street, NW, Washington, D.C. 20037 (202) 862-9500; *Basic Statistics of the Community.*

M.E. Sharpe, 80 Business Park Drive, Armonk, New York 10504 (800) 541-6563; *The Illustrated Book of World Rankings.*

National Technical Information Service, 5285 Port Royal Road, Springfield, Virginia 22161 (800) 553-6847; *Handbook of Economic Statistics.*

Statistical Office of the United Nations, Publishing Service, New York, New York 10017 (800) 253-9646; *Statistical Yearbook.*

Statistics Bureau, Management and Coordination Agency, Japan; *Statistical Indicators on Social Life.*

JAPAN - HOUSING CONSTRUCTION - See JAPAN - CONSTRUCTION INDUSTRY

JAPAN - HOUSING EXPENDITURES

European Commission Office of Press and Public Affairs, 2100 M Street, NW, Washington, D.C. 20037 (202) 862-9500; *Basic Statistics of the Community.*

JAPAN - HYDROCHLORIC ACID PRODUCTION

European Commission Office of Press and Public Affairs, 2100 M Street, NW,

Washington, D.C. 20037 (202) 862-9500; *Basic Statistics of the Community.*

Statistical Office of the United Nations, Publishing Service, New York, New York 10017 (800) 253-9646; *Statistical Yearbook.*

JAPAN - ILLITERATE POPULATION

Central Intelligence Agency, Washington, D.C. 20505 (703) 482-1100, www.cia.gov; *The World Factbook.*

The Economist Intelligence Unit, 111 West 57th Street, New York, New York 10019 (800) 938-4685; *The World Market Atlas.*

Euromonitor International, Inc., 122 South Michigan Avenue, Suite 1200, Chicago, Illinois 60603 (800) 577-EURO; *The World Economic Factbook.*

Statistical Office of the United Nations, Publishing Service, New York, New York 10017 (800) 253-9646; *Asia-Pacific in Figures;* and *Human Development Report.*

United Nations Educational, Scientific and Cultural Organization (UNESCO), 7 Place de Fontenoy, F-75700 Paris, France (Telephone Number in U.S. (212) 963-5981); *Statistical Yearbook.*

JAPAN - IMPORTS

American Automobile Manufacturers Association, 1401 H Street, NW, Suite 900, Washington, D.C. 20005 (202) 326-5500; *World Motor Vehicle Data.*

Central Intelligence Agency, Washington, D.C. 20505 (703) 482-1100, www.cia.gov; *The World Factbook.*

The Economist Intelligence Unit, 111 West 57th Street, New York, New York 10019 (800) 938-4685; *Japan Country Report;* and *The World Market Atlas.*

The Economist Intelligence Unit (Asia) Limited, 10th Floor, Luk Kwok Centre, 72 Gloucester Road, Wanchai, Hong Kong (Phone Number in U.S. (800) 938-4685); *Asian Market Atlas.*

Euromonitor International, Inc., 122 South Michigan Avenue, Suite 1200, Chicago, Illinois 60603 (800) 577-EURO; *International Marketing Data and Statistics;* and *The World Economic Factbook.*

Europa Publications Limited, 18 Bedford Square, London, WC1B 3JN, England; *The Europa World Year Book.*

European Commission Office of Press and Public Affairs, 2100 M Street, NW, Washington, D.C. 20037 (202) 862-9500; *Basic Statistics of the Community.*

Food and Agricultural Organization of the United Nations (FAO), Via delle Terme di Caracalla, 00100 Rome, Italy (Telephone Number in U.S. (202) 653-2400); *The State of Food and Agriculture.*

International Lead and Zinc Study Group, Metro House, 58 St. James's Street, London SW1A 1LD England; *Lead and Zinc Statistics.*

International Monetary Fund, 700 Nineteenth Street, NW, Washington, D.C. 20431 (202) 623-7000; *Direction of Trade Statistics;* and *International Financial Statistics.*

International Rubber Study Group, York House, 8th Floor, Empire Way, Wembley, London HA9 0PA, England; *Rubber Statistical Bulletin.*

National Technical Information Service, 5285 Port Royal Road, Springfield, Virginia 22161 (800) 553-6847; *Handbook of Economic Statistics.*

Organisation for Economic Co-operation and Development (OECD), 2 rue Andre-Pascal, 75 Paris 16, France (Telephone Number in U.S. (202) 785-6323); *Economic Outlook; The Footwear, Raw Hides and Skins, and Leather Industry in OECD Countries; Industrial Structure Statistics; The Iron and Steel Industry; Milk, Milk Products, and Egg Balances in OECD Member Countries; OECD Economic Surveys: Japan; The Pulp and Paper Industry;* and *Review of Fisheries in OECD Member Countries.*

St. Martin's Press, Inc., 175 Fifth Avenue, New York, New York 10010 (800) 221-7945; *The Statesman's Year-Book.*

Statistical Office of the United Nations, Publishing Service, New York, New York 10017 (800) 253-9646; *Foreign Trade Statistics of Asia and the Pacific.*

United Nations Conference on Trade and Development (UNCTAD), New York, New York 10017 (800) 253-9646; *Handbook of International Trade and Development Statistics.*

Walden Publishing, Ltd., Two Market Street, Saffron Walden Essex, CB10 1HZ, England; *The World of Information Asia and Pacific Review.*

The World Bank, 1818 H Street, NW, Washington, D.C. 20433 (202) 477-1234; *World Development Report.*

JAPAN - INCOME TAXES - See JAPAN - TAXATION

JAPAN - INDUSTRIAL METALS PRODUCTION - See JAPAN - MINING AND

MINERAL PRODUCTS

JAPAN - INDUSTRY

Central Intelligence Agency, Washington, D.C. 20505 (703) 482-1100, www.cia.gov; *The World Factbook.*

The Economist Intelligence Unit, 111 West 57th Street, New York, New York 10019 (800) 938-4685; *Japan Country Report.*

Euromonitor International, Inc., 122 South Michigan Avenue, Suite 1200, Chicago, Illinois 60603 (800) 577-EURO; *International Marketing Data and Statistics; The World Economic Factbook;* and *World Marketing Data and Statistics.*

Europa Publications Limited, 18 Bedford Square, London, WC1B 3JN, England; *The Europa World Year Book.*

European Commission Office of Press and Public Affairs, 2100 M Street, NW, Washington, D.C. 20037 (202) 862-9500; *Basic Statistics of the Community.*

International Labour Office, I.L.O. Publications, 1828 L Street NW, Suite 801, Washington, D.C. 20036 (301) 638-3152; *Yearbook of Labour Statistics.*

M.E. Sharpe, 80 Business Park Drive, Armonk, New York 10504 (800) 541-6563; *The Illustrated Book of World Rankings.*

National Technical Information Service, 5285 Port Royal Road, Springfield, Virginia 22161 (800) 553-6847; *Handbook of Economic Statistics.*

Organisation for Economic Co-operation and Development (OECD), 2 rue Andre-Pascal, 75 Paris 16, France (Telephone Number in U.S. (202) 785-6323); *Economic Outlook; Industrial Structure Statistics; Main Economic Indicators - Historical Statistics;* and *OECD Environmental Data.*

St. Martin's Press, Inc., 175 Fifth Avenue, New York, New York 10010 (800) 221-7945; *The Statesman's Year-Book.*

Statistical Office of the United Nations, Publishing Service, New York, New York 10017 (800) 253-9646; *Asia-Pacific in Figures; Industrial Commodity Statistics; Statistical Yearbook;* and *Statistical Yearbook for Asia and the Pacific.*

Statistics Bureau, Management and Coordination Agency, Japan; *Statistical Indicators on Social Life.*

World Intellectual Property Organization, 34 Chemin des Colombettes, CH-1211 Geneva 20, Switzerland; *Industrial Property Statistics.*

JAPAN - INFANT MORTALITY RATE - See JAPAN - MORTALITY

JAPAN - INFLATIONARY FACTORS

National Technical Information Service, 5285 Port Royal Road, Springfield, Virginia 22161 (800) 553-6847; *Handbook of Economic Statistics.*

JAPAN - INTEREST RATES

National Technical Information Service, 5285 Port Royal Road, Springfield, Virginia 22161 (800) 553-6847; *Handbook of Economic Statistics.*

Organisation for Economic Co-operation and Development (OECD), 2 rue Andre-Pascal, 75 Paris 16, France (Telephone Number in U.S. (202) 785-6323); *Economic Outlook; Financial Market Trends; Main Economic Indicators - Historical Statistics;* and *OECD Financial Statistics.*

JAPAN - INTERNAL TRADE

European Commission Office of Press and Public Affairs, 2100 M Street, NW, Washington, D.C. 20037 (202) 862-9500; *Basic Statistics of the Community.*

Organisation for Economic Co-operation and Development (OECD), 2 rue Andre-Pascal, 75 Paris 16, France (Telephone Number in U.S. (202) 785-6323); *Main Economic Indicators - Historical Statistics.*

Statistical Office of the United Nations, Publishing Service, New York, New York 10017 (800) 253-9646; *Statistical Yearbook;* and *Statistical Yearbook for Asia and the Pacific.*

JAPAN - INTERNATIONAL FINANCE

European Commission Office of Press and Public Affairs, 2100 M Street, NW, Washington, D.C. 20037 (202) 862-9500; *Basic Statistics of the Community.*

Organisation for Economic Co-operation and Development (OECD), 2 rue Andre-Pascal, 75 Paris 16, France (Telephone Number in U.S. (202) 785-6323); *Economic Outlook;* and *Financial Market Trends.*

JAPAN - INTERNATIONAL LIQUIDITY

International Monetary Fund, 700 Nineteenth Street, NW, Washington, D.C. 20431 (202) 623-7000; *International Financial Statistics.*

Organisation for Economic Co-operation and Development (OECD), 2 rue Andre-Pascal, 75 Paris 16, France (Telephone Number in U.S. (202) 785-

6323); *Economic Outlook;* and *Financial Market Trends.*

JAPAN - INTERNATIONAL RESERVES EXCLUDING GOLD

National Technical Information Service, 5285 Port Royal Road, Springfield, Virginia 22161 (800) 553-6847; *Handbook of Economic Statistics.*

Statistical Office of the United Nations, Publishing Service, New York, New York 10017 (800) 253-9646; *Statistical Yearbook.*

JAPAN - INTERNATIONAL STATISTICS

Organisation for Economic Co-operation and Development (OECD), 2 rue Andre-Pascal, 75 Paris 16, France (Telephone Number in U.S. (202) 785-6323); *Financial Market Trends;* and *Tourism Policy and International Tourism in OECD Member Countries.*

JAPAN - INVESTMENTS

International Monetary Fund, 700 Nineteenth Street, NW, Washington, D.C. 20431 (202) 623-7000; *International Financial Statistics.*

Organisation for Economic Co-operation and Development (OECD), 2 rue Andre-Pascal, 75 Paris 16, France (Telephone Number in U.S. (202) 785-6323); *Economic Outlook; Financial Market Trends; Industrial Structure Statistics; The Iron and Steel Industry;* and *Textile Industry in OECD Countries.*

JAPAN - IRON ORE - See JAPAN - MINING AND MINERAL PRODUCTS

JAPAN - IRRIGATION

Euromonitor International, Inc., 122 South Michigan Avenue, Suite 1200, Chicago, Illinois 60603 (800) 577-EURO; *International Marketing Data and Statistics.*

JAPAN - JUTE PRODUCTION - See JAPAN - CROPS

JAPAN - LABOR

Central Intelligence Agency, Washington, D.C. 20505 (703) 482-1100, www.cia.gov; *The World Factbook.*

The Economist Intelligence Unit (Asia) Limited, 10th Floor, Luk Kwok Centre, 72 Gloucester Road, Wanchai, Hong Kong (Phone Number in U.S. (800) 938-4685); *Asian Market Atlas.*

Euromonitor International, Inc., 122 South Michigan Avenue, Suite 1200, Chicago, Illinois 60603 (800) 577-EURO; *International Marketing Data and Statistics;* and *World Marketing Data and Statistics..*

Europa Publications Limited, 18 Bedford Square, London, WC1B 3JN, England; *The Europa World Year Book.*

European Commission Office of Press and Public Affairs, 2100 M Street, NW, Washington, D.C. 20037 (202) 862-9500; *Basic Statistics of the Community.*

Food and Agricultural Organization of the United Nations (FAO), Via delle Terme di Caracalla, 00100 Rome, Italy (Telephone Number in U.S. (202) 653-2400); *The State of Food and Agriculture.*

International Labour Office, I.L.O. Publications, 1828 L Street NW, Suite 801, Washington, D.C. 20036 (301) 638-3152; *Yearbook of Labour Statistics.*

M.E. Sharpe, 80 Business Park Drive, Armonk, New York 10504 (800) 541-6563; *The Illustrated Book of World Rankings.*

National Technical Information Service, 5285 Port Royal Road, Springfield, Virginia 22161 (800) 553-6847; *Handbook of Economic Statistics.*

Organisation for Economic Co-operation and Development (OECD), 2 rue Andre-Pascal, 75 Paris 16, France (Telephone Number in U.S. (202) 785-6323); *Economic Outlook; The Iron and Steel Industry; Labour Force Statistics; Main Economic Indicators - Historical Statistics; Maritime Transport; OECD Economic Surveys: Japan; OECD Employment Outlook;* and *Textile Industry in OECD Countries.*

St. Martin's Press, Inc., 175 Fifth Avenue, New York, New York 10010 (800) 221-7945; *The Statesman's Year-Book.*

Statistical Office of the United Nations, Publishing Service, New York, New York 10017 (800) 253-9646; *Human Development Report.*

Statistics Bureau, Management and Coordination Agency, Japan; *Statistical Indicators on Social Life.*

The World Bank, 1818 H Street, NW, Washington, D.C. 20433 (202) 477-1234; *The World Bank Atlas;* and *World Development Report.*

JAPAN - LAND USE

Central Intelligence Agency, Washington, D.C. 20505 (703) 482-1100, www.cia.gov; *The World Factbook.*

Euromonitor International, Inc., 122 South Michigan Avenue, Suite 1200, Chicago, Illinois 60603 (800) 577-EURO; *International Marketing Data and Statistics.*

European Commission Office of Press

and Public Affairs, 2100 M Street, NW, Washington, D.C. 20037 (202) 862-9500; *Basic Statistics of the Community.*

Food and Agricultural Organization of the United Nations (FAO), Via delle Terme di Caracalla, 00100 Rome, Italy (Telephone Number in U.S. (202) 653-2400); *Production Yearbook.*

The World Bank, 1818 H Street, NW, Washington, D.C. 20433 (202) 477-1234; *World Development Report.*

JAPAN - LEAD AND LEAD ORE - See JAPAN - MINING AND MINERAL PRODUCTS

JAPAN - LEATHER - PRODUCTION INDEX

Organisation for Economic Co-operation and Development (OECD), 2 rue Andre-Pascal, 75 Paris 16, France (Telephone Number in U.S. (202) 785-6323); *Indicators of Industrial Activity.*

JAPAN - LEATHER AND FOOTWEAR EXPORTS AND IMPORTS

European Commission Office of Press and Public Affairs, 2100 M Street, NW, Washington, D.C. 20037 (202) 862-9500; *Basic Statistics of the Community.*

Organisation for Economic Co-operation and Development (OECD), 2 rue Andre-Pascal, 75 Paris 16, France (Telephone Number in U.S. (202) 785-6323); *The Footwear, Raw Hides and Skins, and Leather Industry in OECD Countries.*

JAPAN - LIBRARIES

M.E. Sharpe, 80 Business Park Drive, Armonk, New York 10504 (800) 541-6563; *The Illustrated Book of World Rankings.*

United Nations Educational, Scientific and Cultural Organization (UNESCO), 7 Place de Fontenoy, F-75700 Paris, France (Telephone Number in U.S. (212) 963-5981); *Statistical Yearbook.*

JAPAN - LIFE EXPECTANCY

Central Intelligence Agency, Washington, D.C. 20505 (703) 482-1100, www.cia.gov; *The World Factbook.*

The Economist Intelligence Unit (Asia) Limited, 10th Floor, Luk Kwok Centre, 72 Gloucester Road, Wanchai, Hong Kong (Phone Number in U.S. (800) 938-4685); *Asian Market Atlas.*

Euromonitor International, Inc., 122 South Michigan Avenue, Suite 1200, Chicago, Illinois 60603 (800) 577-EURO; *The World Economic Factbook.*

Organisation for Economic Co-operation and Development (OECD), 2 rue Andre-Pascal, 75 Paris 16, France (Telephone Number in U.S. (202) 785-6323); *Economic Outlook.*

St. Martin's Press, Inc., 175 Fifth Avenue, New York, New York 10010 (800) 221-7945; *The Statesman's Year-Book.*

Statistical Office of the United Nations, Publishing Service, New York, New York 10017 (800) 253-9646; *Asia-Pacific in Figures; World Statistics Pocketbook;* and *Human Development Report.*

Statistics Bureau, Management and Coordination Agency, Japan; *Statistical Indicators on Social Life.*

The World Bank, 1818 H Street, NW, Washington, D.C. 20433 (202) 477-1234; *The World Bank Atlas;* and *World Development Report.*

JAPAN - LIGNITE PRODUCTION - See JAPAN - MINING AND MINERAL PRODUCTS

JAPAN - LITERACY RATE

Euromonitor International, Inc., 122 South Michigan Avenue, Suite 1200, Chicago, Illinois 60603 (800) 577-EURO; *World Marketing Data and Statistics.*

JAPAN - LIVESTOCK AND POULTRY

Commodity Research Bureau, Inc., 30 South Wacker Drive, Chicago, Illinois 60606 (312) 454-1801; *Commodity Year Book.*

Euromonitor International, Inc., 122 South Michigan Avenue, Suite 1200, Chicago, Illinois 60603 (800) 577-EURO; *International Marketing Data and Statistics.*

Europa Publications Limited, 18 Bedford Square, London, WC1B 3JN, England; *The Europa World Year Book.*

European Commission Office of Press and Public Affairs, 2100 M Street, NW, Washington, D.C. 20037 (202) 862-9500; *Basic Statistics of the Community.*

Food and Agricultural Organization of the United Nations (FAO), Via delle Terme di Caracalla, 00100 Rome, Italy (Telephone Number in U.S. (202) 653-2400); *Production Yearbook;* and *The State of Food and Agriculture.*

M.E. Sharpe, 80 Business Park Drive, Armonk, New York 10504 (800) 541-6563; *The Illustrated Book of World Rankings.*

National Technical Information Service, 5285 Port Royal Road, Springfield, Virginia 22161 (800) 553-6847; *Handbook of Economic Statistics.*

Organisation for Economic Co-operation and Development (OECD), 2 rue Andre-Pascal, 75 Paris 16, France (Telephone Number in U.S. (202) 785-6323); *Economic Accounts for Agriculture; Indicators of Industrial Activity;* and *Meat Balances in OECD Member Countries.*

St. Martin's Press, Inc., 175 Fifth Avenue, New York, New York 10010 (800) 221-7945; *The Statesman's Year-Book.*

Statistical Office of the United Nations, Publishing Service, New York, New York 10017 (800) 253-9646; *Statistical Yearbook.*

United Nations Conference on Trade and Development, Central Statistical Service, Palais des Nations, Geneva, Switzerland (Telephone in U.S. (800) 253-9646); *UNCTAD Commodity Yearbook.*

JAPAN - LIVING LEVELS - See JAPAN - LIFE EXPECTANCY

JAPAN - MACHINERY - PRODUCTION INDEX

Organisation for Economic Co-operation and Development (OECD), 2 rue Andre-Pascal, 75 Paris 16, France (Telephone Number in U.S. (202) 785-6323); *Indicators of Industrial Activity.*

JAPAN - MAGNESIUM PRODUCTION AND CONSUMPTION - See JAPAN - MINING AND MINERAL PRODUCTS

JAPAN - MAIL - NUMBER OF ITEMS SENT AND RECEIVED

Statistical Office of the United Nations, Publishing Service, New York, New York 10017 (800) 253-9646; *Statistical Yearbook.*

JAPAN - MAIN ECONOMIC INDICATORS - See JAPAN - ECONOMY

JAPAN - MANGANESE AND MANGANESE ORE - See JAPAN - MINING AND MINERAL PRODUCTS

JAPAN - MANPOWER

Statistical Office of the United Nations, Publishing Service, New York, New York 10017 (800) 253-9646; *Statistical Yearbook for Asia and the Pacific.*

JAPAN - MANUFACTURING

American Automobile Manufacturers Association, 1401 H Street, NW, Suite 900, Washington, D.C. 20005 (202) 326-5500; *World Motor Vehicle Data.*

European Commission Office of Press and Public Affairs, 2100 M Street, NW, Washington, D.C. 20037 (202) 862-9500; *Basic Statistics of the Community.*

M.E. Sharpe, 80 Business Park Drive, Armonk, New York 10504 (800) 541-6563; *The Illustrated Book of World Rankings.*

National Technical Information Service, 5285 Port Royal Road, Springfield, Virginia 22161 (800) 553-6847; *Handbook of Economic Statistics.*

Organisation for Economic Co-operation and Development (OECD), 2 rue Andre-Pascal, 75 Paris 16, France (Telephone Number in U.S. (202) 785-6323); *Foreign Trade by Commodities; Indicators of Industrial Activity; Industrial Structure Statistics;* and *OECD Economic Surveys: Japan.*

Statistical Office of the United Nations, Publishing Service, New York, New York 10017 (800) 253-9646; *Statistical Yearbook.*

Statistics Bureau, Management and Coordination Agency, Japan; *Statistical Indicators on Social Life;* and *Statistical Yearbook.*

JAPAN - MARRIAGE RATES

Europa Publications Limited, 18 Bedford Square, London, WC1B 3JN, England; *The Europa World Year Book.*

European Commission Office of Press and Public Affairs, 2100 M Street, NW, Washington, D.C. 20037 (202) 862-9500; *Basic Statistics of the Community.*

M.E. Sharpe, 80 Business Park Drive, Armonk, New York 10504 (800) 541-6563; *The Illustrated Book of World Rankings.*

Statistical Office of the United Nations, Publishing Service, New York, New York 10017 (800) 253-9646; *Demographic Yearbook;* and *Statistical Yearbook.*

Statistics Bureau, Management and Coordination Agency, Japan; *Statistical Indicators on Social Life.*

JAPAN - MEAT PRODUCTION - See JAPAN - LIVESTOCK AND POULTRY

JAPAN - MERCHANT SHIPPING

Europa Publications Limited, 18 Bedford Square, London, WC1B 3JN, England; *The Europa World Year Book.*

European Commission Office of Press and Public Affairs, 2100 M Street, NW, Washington, D.C. 20037 (202) 862-9500; *Basic Statistics of the Community.*

Lloyd's Register of Shipping, 17 Battery Place, New York, New York 10004; *Register of Ships.*

National Technical Information Service, 5285 Port Royal Road, Springfield, Virginia

22161 (800) 553-6847; *Handbook of Economic Statistics.*

Organisation for Economic Co-operation and Development (OECD), 2 rue Andre-Pascal, 75 Paris 16, France (Telephone Number in U.S. (202) 785-6323); *Maritime Transport.*

St. Martin's Press, Inc., 175 Fifth Avenue, New York, New York 10010 (800) 221-7945; *The Statesman's Year-Book.*

Statistical Office of the United Nations, Publishing Service, New York, New York 10017 (800) 253-9646; *Statistical Yearbook.*

U.S. Department of Transportation, Maritime Administration, 400 Seventh Street, SW, Washington, D.C. 20590 (202) 366-5807, www.marad,dot.gov; *A Statistical Analysis of the World's Merchant Fleets.*

JAPAN - MERCURY PRODUCTION AND CONSUMPTION - See JAPAN - MINING AND MINERAL PRODUCTS

JAPAN - METAL PRODUCTS - See JAPAN - MINING AND MINERAL PRODUCTS

JAPAN - MILITARY

Central Intelligence Agency, Washington, D.C. 20505 (703) 482-1100, www.cia.gov; *The World Factbook.*

The Economist Intelligence Unit (Asia) Limited, 10th Floor, Luk Kwok Centre, 72 Gloucester Road, Wanchai, Hong Kong (Phone Number in U.S. (800) 938-4685); *Asian Market Atlas.*

Euromonitor International, Inc., 122 South Michigan Avenue, Suite 1200, Chicago, Illinois 60603 (800) 577-EURO; *World Marketing Data and Statistics.*

The International Institute for Strategic Studies, 23 Tavistock Street, London WC2E 7NQ, England 44 171 3797676; *The Military Balance.*

National Technical Information Service, 5285 Port Royal Road, Springfield, Virginia 22161 (800) 553-6847; *Handbook of Economic Statistics.*

St. Martin's Press, Inc., 175 Fifth Avenue, New York, New York 10010 (800) 221-7945; *The Statesman's Year-Book.*

Statistical Office of the United Nations, Publishing Service, New York, New York 10017 (800) 253-9646; *Human Development Report.*

U.S. Arms Control and Disarmament Agency, 320 Twenty-first Street, NW, Washington, D.C. 20451 (202) 647-8677; *World Military Expenditures and Arms Transfers.*

JAPAN - MILK PRODUCTION - See JAPAN - DAIRY PRODUCTS

JAPAN - MILLET PRODUCTION - See JAPAN - CROPS

JAPAN - MINING AND MINERAL PRODUCTS

Commodity Research Bureau, Inc., 30 South Wacker Drive, Chicago, Illinois 60606 (312) 454-1801; *Commodity Year Book.*

Europa Publications Limited, 18 Bedford Square, London, WC1B 3JN, England; *The Europa World Year Book.*

European Commission Office of Press and Public Affairs, 2100 M Street, NW, Washington, D.C. 20037 (202) 862-9500; *Basic Statistics of the Community.*

International Lead and Zinc Study Group, Metro House, 58 St. James's Street, London SW1A 1LD England; *Lead and Zinc Statistics.*

M.E. Sharpe, 80 Business Park Drive, Armonk, New York 10504 (800) 541-6563; *The Illustrated Book of World Rankings.*

National Technical Information Service, 5285 Port Royal Road, Springfield, Virginia 22161 (800) 553-6847; *Handbook of Economic Statistics.*

Organisation for Economic Co-operation and Development (OECD), 2 rue Andre-Pascal, 75 Paris 16, France (Telephone Number in U.S. (202) 785-6323); *Coal Information; Energy Statistics of OECD Countries; Foreign Trade by Commodities; Indicators of Industrial Activity; Industrial Structure Statistics; The Iron and Steel Industry; The Non-Ferrous Metals Industry;* and *OECD Economic Surveys: Japan.*

Penn Well Publishing Company, 1421 South Sheridan Road, Post Office Box 1260, Tulsa, Oklahoma 74101 (800) 752-9764; *International Energy Statistics Sourcebook.*

St. Martin's Press, Inc., 175 Fifth Avenue, New York, New York 10010 (800) 221-7945; *The Statesman's Year-Book.*

Statistical Office of the United Nations, Publishing Service, New York, New York 10017 (800) 253-9646; *Statistical Yearbook.*

United Nations Conference on Trade and Development, Central Statistical Service, Palais des Nations, Geneva, Switzerland (Telephone in U.S. (800) 253-9646); *UNCTAD Commodity Yearbook.*

World Bureau of Metal Statistics, 27-A High Street, Ware, Herts. SG12 9BA, England; *World Metal Statistics.*

JAPAN - MOLYBDENUM AND MOLYBDENUM ORE - See JAPAN - MINING AND MINERAL PRODUCTS

JAPAN - MONEY AND CREDIT

Organisation for Economic Co-operation and Development (OECD), 2 rue Andre-Pascal, 75 Paris 16, France (Telephone Number in U.S. (202) 785-6323); *OECD Economic Surveys: Japan.*

JAPAN - MONEY EXCHANGE RATE - See JAPAN - EXCHANGE RATES

JAPAN - MONEY RATES - MARKET

European Commission Office of Press and Public Affairs, 2100 M Street, NW, Washington, D.C. 20037 (202) 862-9500; *Basic Statistics of the Community.*

Organisation for Economic Co-operation and Development (OECD), 2 rue Andre-Pascal, 75 Paris 16, France (Telephone Number in U.S. (202) 785-6323); *Economic Outlook;* and *Financial Market Trends.*

Statistical Office of the United Nations, Publishing Service, New York, New York 10017 (800) 253-9646; *Statistical Yearbook.*

JAPAN - MONEY RESERVES

Euromonitor International, Inc., 122 South Michigan Avenue, Suite 1200, Chicago, Illinois 60603 (800) 577-EURO; *International Marketing Data and Statistics.*

European Commission Office of Press and Public Affairs, 2100 M Street, NW, Washington, D.C. 20037 (202) 862-9500; *Basic Statistics of the Community.*

Organisation for Economic Co-operation and Development (OECD), 2 rue Andre-Pascal, 75 Paris 16, France (Telephone Number in U.S. (202) 785-6323); *Economic Outlook;* and *Financial Market Trends.*

JAPAN - MONEY SUPPLY

The Economist Intelligence Unit, 111 West 57th Street, New York, New York 10019 (800) 938-4685; *Japan Country Report.*

Euromonitor International, Inc., 122 South Michigan Avenue, Suite 1200, Chicago, Illinois 60603 (800) 577-EURO; *International Marketing Data and Statistics.*

Europa Publications Limited, 18 Bedford Square, London, WC1B 3JN, England; *The Europa World Year Book.*

European Commission Office of Press and Public Affairs, 2100 M Street, NW, Washington, D.C. 20037 (202) 862-9500;

Basic Statistics of the Community.

International Monetary Fund, 700 Nineteenth Street, NW, Washington, D.C. 20431 (202) 623-7000; *International Financial Statistics.*

Organisation for Economic Co-operation and Development (OECD), 2 rue Andre-Pascal, 75 Paris 16, France (Telephone Number in U.S. (202) 785-6323); *Economic Outlook.*

Statistical Office of the United Nations, Publishing Service, New York, New York 10017 (800) 253-9646; *Statistical Yearbook.*

JAPAN - MORTALITY

Central Intelligence Agency, Washington, D.C. 20505 (703) 482-1100, www.cia.gov; *The World Factbook.*

The Economist Intelligence Unit (Asia) Limited, 10th Floor, Luk Kwok Centre, 72 Gloucester Road, Wanchai, Hong Kong (Phone Number in U.S. (800) 938-4685); *Asian Market Atlas.*

Euromonitor International, Inc., 122 South Michigan Avenue, Suite 1200, Chicago, Illinois 60603 (800) 577-EURO; *The World Economic Factbook.*

Europa Publications Limited, 18 Bedford Square, London, WC1B 3JN, England; *The Europa World Year Book.*

European Commission Office of Press and Public Affairs, 2100 M Street, NW, Washington, D.C. 20037 (202) 862-9500; *Basic Statistics of the Community.*

St. Martin's Press, Inc., 175 Fifth Avenue, New York, New York 10010 (800) 221-7945; *The Statesman's Year-Book.*

Statistical Office of the United Nations, Publishing Service, New York, New York 10017 (800) 253-9646; *Asia-Pacific in Figures; Human Development Report; Demographic Yearbook; World Statistics Pocketbook;* and *Statistical Yearbook.*

Statistics Bureau, Management and Coordination Agency, Japan; *Statistical Indicators on Social Life.*

United Nations Children's Fund (UNICEF), 3 United Nations Plaza, New York, New York 10017 (800) 253-9646; *State of the World's Children.*

The World Bank, 1818 H Street, NW, Washington, D.C. 20433 (202) 477-1234; *The World Bank Atlas;* and *World Development Report.*

World Health Organization, Office of Publications, 20 Avenue Appia, CH-1211 Geneva 27, Switzerland (Telephone

Number in U.S. (518) 436-9686); *World Health Statistics Annual.*

JAPAN - MOTION PICTURES

St. Martin's Press, Inc., 175 Fifth Avenue, New York, New York 10010 (800) 221-7945; *The Statesman's Year-Book.*

Statistical Office of the United Nations, Publishing Service, New York, New York 10017 (800) 253-9646; *Statistical Yearbook.*

United Nations Educational, Scientific and Cultural Organization (UNESCO), 7 Place de Fontenoy, F-75700 Paris, France (Telephone Number in U.S. (212) 963-5981); *Statistical Yearbook.*

JAPAN - MOTOR VEHICLE PRODUCTION

American Automobile Manufacturers Association, 1401 H Street, NW, Suite 900, Washington, D.C. 20005 (202) 326-5500; *World Motor Vehicle Data.*

European Commission Office of Press and Public Affairs, 2100 M Street, NW, Washington, D.C. 20037 (202) 862-9500; *Basic Statistics of the Community.*

National Technical Information Service, 5285 Port Royal Road, Springfield, Virginia 22161 (800) 553-6847; *Handbook of Economic Statistics.*

Organisation for Economic Co-operation and Development (OECD), 2 rue Andre-Pascal, 75 Paris 16, France (Telephone Number in U.S. (202) 785-6323); *Foreign Trade by Commodities;* and *Indicators of Industrial Activity.*

Statistical Office of the United Nations, Publishing Service, New York, New York 10017 (800) 253-9646; *Statistical Yearbook.*

JAPAN - MOTOR VEHICLE TAXES - See JAPAN - TAXATION

JAPAN - MOTOR VEHICLES IN USE

American Automobile Manufacturers Association, 1401 H Street, NW, Suite 900, Washington, D.C. 20005 (202) 326-5500; *World Motor Vehicle Data.*

Europa Publications Limited, 18 Bedford Square, London, WC1B 3JN, England; *The Europa World Year Book.*

European Commission Office of Press and Public Affairs, 2100 M Street, NW, Washington, D.C. 20037 (202) 862-9500; *Basic Statistics of the Community.*

International Road Federation, 2600 Virginia Avenue, NW, Washington, D.C. 20037 (202) 338-4641; *World Road Statistics.*

Statistical Office of the United Nations, Publishing Service, New York, New York 10017 (800) 253-9646; *Statistical Yearbook.*

JAPAN - MULES - See JAPAN - LIVESTOCK AND POULTRY

JAPAN - MUSEUMS

M.E. Sharpe, 80 Business Park Drive, Armonk, New York 10504 (800) 541-6563; *The Illustrated Book of World Rankings.*

Statistics Bureau, Management and Coordination Agency, Japan; *Statistical Indicators on Social Life.*

United Nations Educational, Scientific and Cultural Organization (UNESCO), 7 Place de Fontenoy, F-75700 Paris, France (Telephone Number in U.S. (212) 963-5981); *Statistical Yearbook.*

JAPAN - NATALITY - See JAPAN - BIRTH RATE

JAPAN - NATIONAL ACCOUNTS

Europa Publications Limited, 18 Bedford Square, London, WC1B 3JN, England; *The Europa World Year Book.*

European Commission Office of Press and Public Affairs, 2100 M Street, NW, Washington, D.C. 20037 (202) 862-9500; *Basic Statistics of the Community.*

International Monetary Fund, 700 Nineteenth Street, NW, Washington, D.C. 20431 (202) 623-7000; *International Financial Statistics.*

Organisation for Economic Co-operation and Development (OECD), 2 rue Andre-Pascal, 75 Paris 16, France (Telephone Number in U.S. (202) 785-6323); *Economic Outlook.*

Statistical Office of the United Nations, Publishing Service, New York, New York 10017 (800) 253-9646; *Asia-Pacific in Figures; National Accounts Statistics; Statistical Yearbook;* and *Statistical Yearbook for Asia and the Pacific.*

JAPAN - NATIONAL INCOME

M.E. Sharpe, 80 Business Park Drive, Armonk, New York 10504 (800) 541-6563; *The Illustrated Book of World Rankings.*

Organisation for Economic Co-operation and Development (OECD), 2 rue Andre-Pascal, 75 Paris 16, France (Telephone Number in U.S. (202) 785-6323); *Economic Outlook.*

Statistical Office of the United Nations, Publishing Service, New York, New York 10017 (800) 253-9646; *National Accounts Statistics;* and *Statistical Yearbook.*

JAPAN - NATIONAL PRODUCT

European Commission Office of Press and Public Affairs, 2100 M Street, NW, Washington, D.C. 20037 (202) 862-9500; *Basic Statistics of the Community.*

M.E. Sharpe, 80 Business Park Drive, Armonk, New York 10504 (800) 541-6563; *The Illustrated Book of World Rankings.*

Organisation for Economic Co-operation and Development (OECD), 2 rue Andre-Pascal, 75 Paris 16, France (Telephone Number in U.S. (202) 785-6323); *Economic Outlook;* and *Main Economic Indicators - Historical Statistics.*

Statistical Office of the United Nations, Publishing Service, New York, New York 10017 (800) 253-9646; *Statistical Yearbook.*

JAPAN - NATURAL GAS PRODUCTION - See JAPAN - MINING AND MINERAL PRODUCTS

JAPAN - NATURAL RUBBER PRODUCTION

European Commission Office of Press and Public Affairs, 2100 M Street, NW, Washington, D.C. 20037 (202) 862-9500; *Basic Statistics of the Community.*

International Rubber Study Group, York House, 8th Floor, Empire Way, Wembley, London HA9 0PA, England; *Rubber Statistical Bulletin.*

National Technical Information Service, 5285 Port Royal Road, Springfield, Virginia 22161 (800) 553-6847; *Handbook of Economic Statistics.*

JAPAN - NEWSPAPER PRODUCTION AND CONSUMPTION - See JAPAN - FORESTRY AND FOREST PRODUCTS

JAPAN - NEWSPRINT - See JAPAN - FORESTRY AND FOREST PRODUCTS

JAPAN - NICKEL AND NICKEL ORE - See JAPAN - MINING AND MINERAL PRODUCTS

JAPAN - NITRIC ACID PRODUCTION - See JAPAN - MINING AND MINERAL PRODUCTS

JAPAN - OATS PRODUCTION - See JAPAN - CROPS

JAPAN - OCCUPATIONS - See JAPAN - LABOR FORCE

JAPAN - OIL PRODUCING CROPS

European Commission Office of Press and Public Affairs, 2100 M Street, NW, Washington, D.C. 20037 (202) 862-9500; *Basic Statistics of the Community.*

Organisation for Economic Co-operation and Development (OECD), 2 rue

Andre-Pascal, 75 Paris 16, France (Telephone Number in U.S. (202) 785-6323); *Foreign Trade by Commodities.*

JAPAN - ONION PRODUCTION - See JAPAN - CROPS

JAPAN - ORANGE PRODUCTION - See JAPAN - CROPS

JAPAN - PALM KERNEL PRODUCTION - See JAPAN - CROPS

JAPAN - PAPER - See JAPAN - FORESTRY AND FOREST PRODUCTS

JAPAN - PATENTS, TRADEMARKS AND SERVICE MARKS

Statistical Office of the United Nations, Publishing Service, New York, New York 10017 (800) 253-9646; *Statistical Yearbook.*

World Intellectual Property Organization, 34 Chemin des Colombettes, CH-1211 Geneva 20, Switzerland; *Industrial Property Statistics.*

JAPAN - PEANUT PRODUCTION - See JAPAN - CROPS

JAPAN - PEPPER PRODUCTION - See JAPAN - CROPS

JAPAN - PERIODICALS

United Nations Educational, Scientific and Cultural Organization (UNESCO), 7 Place de Fontenoy, F-75700 Paris, France (Telephone Number in U.S. (212) 963-5981); *Statistical Yearbook.*

JAPAN - PESTICIDE USE

Food and Agricultural Organization of the United Nations (FAO), Via delle Terme di Caracalla, 00100 Rome, Italy (Telephone Number in U.S. (202) 653-2400); *The State of Food and Agriculture.*

JAPAN - PETROLEUM INDUSTRY

European Commission Office of Press and Public Affairs, 2100 M Street, NW, Washington, D.C. 20037 (202) 862-9500; *Basic Statistics of the Community.*

Food and Agricultural Organization of the United Nations (FAO), Via delle Terme di Caracalla, 00100 Rome, Italy (Telephone Number in U.S. (202) 653-2400); *The State of Food and Agriculture.*

M.E. Sharpe, 80 Business Park Drive, Armonk, New York 10504 (800) 541-6563; *The Illustrated Book of World Rankings.*

National Technical Information Service, 5285 Port Royal Road, Springfield, Virginia 22161 (800) 553-6847; *Handbook of Economic Statistics.*

Organisation for Economic Co-operation and Development (OECD), 2 rue Andre-Pascal, 75 Paris 16, France (Telephone Number in U.S. (202) 785-6323); *Energy Statistics of OECD Countries; Foreign Trade by Commodities; Indicators of Industrial Activity;* and *Oil and Gas Information.*

Penn Well Publishing Company, 1421 South Sheridan Road, Post Office Box 1260, Tulsa, Oklahoma 74101 (800) 752-9764; *International Energy Statistics Sourcebook.*

St. Martin's Press, Inc., 175 Fifth Avenue, New York, New York 10010 (800) 221-7945; *The Statesman's Year-Book.*

Statistical Office of the United Nations, Publishing Service, New York, New York 10017 (800) 253-9646; *Statistical Yearbook.*

United Nations Conference on Trade and Development, Central Statistical Service, Palais des Nations, Geneva, Switzerland (Telephone in U.S. (800) 253-9646); *UNCTAD Commodity Yearbook.*

JAPAN - PHOSPHATES AND PHOSPHATE ROCK PRODUCTION - See JAPAN - MINING AND MINERAL PRODUCTS

JAPAN - PIG-IRON AND FERRO-ALLOY PRODUCTION - See JAPAN - MINING AND MINERAL PRODUCTS

JAPAN - PIGS - See JAPAN - LIVESTOCK AND POULTRY

JAPAN - PIPELINES FOR OIL AND PETROLEUM PRODUCTS

National Technical Information Service, 5285 Port Royal Road, Springfield, Virginia 22161 (800) 553-6847; *Handbook of Economic Statistics.*

JAPAN - PLASTIC AND RESIN PRODUCTION

Commodity Research Bureau, Inc., 30 South Wacker Drive, Chicago, Illinois 60606 (312) 454-1801; *Commodity Year Book.*

European Commission Office of Press and Public Affairs, 2100 M Street, NW, Washington, D.C. 20037 (202) 862-9500; *Basic Statistics of the Community.*

Organisation for Economic Co-operation and Development (OECD), 2 rue Andre-Pascal, 75 Paris 16, France (Telephone Number in U.S. (202) 785-6323); *Foreign Trade by Commodities.*

Statistical Office of the United Nations, Publishing Service, New York, New York 10017 (800) 253-9646; *Statistical Yearbook.*

JAPAN - PLATINUM PRODUCTION - See JAPAN - MINING AND MINERAL PRODUCTS

JAPAN - POPULATION

Central Intelligence Agency, Washington, D.C. 20505 (703) 482-1100, www.cia.gov; *The World Factbook.*

The Economist Intelligence Unit, 111 West 57th Street, New York, New York 10019 (800) 938-4685; *Japan Country Report;* and *The World Market Atlas.*

The Economist Intelligence Unit (Asia) Limited, 10th Floor, Luk Kwok Centre, 72 Gloucester Road, Wanchai, Hong Kong (Phone Number in U.S. (800) 938-4685); *Asian Market Atlas.*

Euromonitor International, Inc., 122 South Michigan Avenue, Suite 1200, Chicago, Illinois 60603 (800) 577-EURO; *International Marketing Data and Statistics;* and *The World Economic Factbook.*

Europa Publications Limited, 18 Bedford Square, London, WC1B 3JN, England; *The Europa World Year Book.*

European Commission Office of Press and Public Affairs, 2100 M Street, NW, Washington, D.C. 20037 (202) 862-9500; *Basic Statistics of the Community.*

Food and Agricultural Organization of the United Nations (FAO), Via delle Terme di Caracalla, 00100 Rome, Italy (Telephone Number in U.S. (202) 653-2400); *Production Yearbook.*

International Labour Office, I.L.O. Publications, 1828 L Street NW, Suite 801, Washington, D.C. 20036 (301) 638-3152; *Yearbook of Labour Statistics.*

M.E. Sharpe, 80 Business Park Drive, Armonk, New York 10504 (800) 541-6563; *The Illustrated Book of World Rankings.*

National Technical Information Service, 5285 Port Royal Road, Springfield, Virginia 22161 (800) 553-6847; *Handbook of Economic Statistics.*

St. Martin's Press, Inc., 175 Fifth Avenue, New York, New York 10010 (800) 221-7945; *The Statesman's Year-Book.*

Statistical Office of the United Nations, Publishing Service, New York, New York 10017 (800) 253-9646; *Asia-Pacific in Figures; Demographic Yearbook; Human Development Report; Statistical Yearbook; World Statistics Pocketbook;* and *Statistical Yearbook for Asia and the Pacific.*

Statistics Bureau, Management and Coordination Agency, Japan; *Statistical Indicators on Social Life.*

United Nations Educational, Scientific and Cultural Organization (UNESCO), 7 Place de Fontenoy, F-75700 Paris, France (Telephone Number in U.S. (212) 963-5981); *Statistical Yearbook.*

U.S. Arms Control and Disarmament Agency, 320 Twenty-first Street, NW, Washington, D.C. 20451 (202) 647-8677; *World Military Expenditures and Arms Transfers.*

Walden Publishing, Ltd., Two Market Street, Saffron Walden Essex, CB10 1HZ, England; *The World of Information Asia and Pacific Review.*

The World Bank, 1818 H Street, NW, Washington, D.C. 20433 (202) 477-1234; *The World Bank Atlas;* and *World Development Report.*

World Health Organization, Office of Publications, 20 Avenue Appia, CH-1211 Geneva 27, Switzerland (Telephone Number in U.S. (518) 436-9686); *World Health Statistics Annual.*

JAPAN - POST OFFICES

M.E. Sharpe, 80 Business Park Drive, Armonk, New York 10504 (800) 541-6563; *The Illustrated Book of World Rankings.*

JAPAN - POTATO PRODUCTION - See JAPAN - CROPS

JAPAN - POWER PRODUCTION INDUSTRY

European Commission Office of Press and Public Affairs, 2100 M Street, NW, Washington, D.C. 20037 (202) 862-9500; *Basic Statistics of the Community.*

Statistical Office of the United Nations, Publishing Service, New York, New York 10017 (800) 253-9646; *Electric Power in Asia and the Pacific;* and *Statistical Yearbook.*

JAPAN - PRICES

European Commission Office of Press and Public Affairs, 2100 M Street, NW, Washington, D.C. 20037 (202) 862-9500; *Basic Statistics of the Community.*

Food and Agricultural Organization of the United Nations (FAO), Via delle Terme di Caracalla, 00100 Rome, Italy (Telephone Number in U.S. (202) 653-2400); *Production Yearbook;* and *The State of Food and Agriculture.*

International Labour Office, I.L.O. Publications, 1828 L Street NW, Suite 801, Washington, D.C. 20036 (301) 638-3152; *Yearbook of Labour Statistics.*

International Lead and Zinc Study Group, Metro House, 58 St. James's Street, London SW1A 1LD England; *Lead and Zinc Statistics.*

JAPAN - MINING AND MINERAL PRODUCTS

International Monetary Fund, 700 Nineteenth Street, NW, Washington, D.C. 20431 (202) 623-7000; *International Financial Statistics.*

International Rubber Study Group, York House, 8th Floor, Empire Way, Wembley, London HA9 0PA, England; *Rubber Statistical Bulletin.*

M.E. Sharpe, 80 Business Park Drive, Armonk, New York 10504 (800) 541-6563; *The Illustrated Book of World Rankings.*

National Technical Information Service, 5285 Port Royal Road, Springfield, Virginia 22161 (800) 553-6847; *Handbook of Economic Statistics.*

Organisation for Economic Co-operation and Development (OECD), 2 rue Andre-Pascal, 75 Paris 16, France (Telephone Number in U.S. (202) 785-6323); *Economic Outlook; The Footwear, Raw Hides and Skins, and Leather Industry in OECD Countries; Indicators of Industrial Activity; The Iron and Steel Industry; Main Economic Indicators - Historical Statistics;* and *The Pulp and Paper Industry.*

World Bureau of Metal Statistics, 27-A High Street, Ware, Herts. SG12 9BA, England; *World Metal Statistics.*

JAPAN - PRINTING AND WRITING PAPER - See JAPAN - FORESTRY AND FOREST PRODUCTS

JAPAN - PRODUCTION

American Automobile Manufacturers Association, 1401 H Street, NW, Suite 900, Washington, D.C. 20005 (202) 326-5500; *World Motor Vehicle Data.*

European Commission Office of Press and Public Affairs, 2100 M Street, NW, Washington, D.C. 20037 (202) 862-9500; *Basic Statistics of the Community.*

International Lead and Zinc Study Group, Metro House, 58 St. James's Street, London SW1A 1LD England; *Lead and Zinc Statistics.*

International Rubber Study Group, York House, 8th Floor, Empire Way, Wembley, London HA9 0PA, England; *Rubber Statistical Bulletin.*

M.E. Sharpe, 80 Business Park Drive, Armonk, New York 10504 (800) 541-6563; *The Illustrated Book of World Rankings.*

National Technical Information Service, 5285 Port Royal Road, Springfield, Virginia 22161 (800) 553-6847; *Handbook of Economic Statistics.*

Organisation for Economic Co-operation and Development (OECD), 2 rue

Andre-Pascal, 75 Paris 16, France (Telephone Number in U.S. (202) 785-6323); *Economic Outlook; The Footwear, Raw Hides and Skins, and Leather Industry in OECD Countries; Indicators of Industrial Activity; Industrial Structure Statistics; The Iron and Steel Industry; Meat Balances in OECD Member Countries; Milk, Milk Products, and Egg Balances in OECD Member Countries; The Non-Ferrous Metals Industry; The Pulp and Paper Industry;* and *Textile Industry in OECD Countries.*

Statistics Bureau, Management and Coordination Agency, Japan; *Statistical Indicators on Social Life.*

JAPAN - PRODUCTIVITY

Euromonitor International, Inc., 122 South Michigan Avenue, Suite 1200, Chicago, Illinois 60603 (800) 577-EURO; *International Marketing Data and Statistics.*

European Commission Office of Press and Public Affairs, 2100 M Street, NW, Washington, D.C. 20037 (202) 862-9500; *Basic Statistics of the Community.*

Organisation for Economic Co-operation and Development (OECD), 2 rue Andre-Pascal, 75 Paris 16, France (Telephone Number in U.S. (202) 785-6323); *Economic Outlook.*

JAPAN - PROPERTY TAXES - See JAPAN - TAXATION

JAPAN - PUBLIC CONSUMPTION FUND

European Commission Office of Press and Public Affairs, 2100 M Street, NW, Washington, D.C. 20037 (202) 862-9500; *Basic Statistics of the Community.*

Organisation for Economic Co-operation and Development (OECD), 2 rue Andre-Pascal, 75 Paris 16, France (Telephone Number in U.S. (202) 785-6323); *Revenue Statistics of OECD Member Countries.*

JAPAN - PUBLIC EXPENDITURES

European Commission Office of Press and Public Affairs, 2100 M Street, NW, Washington, D.C. 20037 (202) 862-9500; *Basic Statistics of the Community.*

National Technical Information Service, 5285 Port Royal Road, Springfield, Virginia 22161 (800) 553-6847; *Handbook of Economic Statistics.*

Organisation for Economic Co-operation and Development (OECD), 2 rue Andre-Pascal, 75 Paris 16, France (Telephone Number in U.S. (202) 785-6323); *Revenue Statistics of OECD Member Countries.*

Statistics Bureau, Management and Coordination Agency, Japan; *Statistical Indicators on Social Life.*

JAPAN - PUBLIC FINANCE - See JAPAN - FINANCE

JAPAN - PUBLIC HEALTH - See JAPAN - HEALTH

JAPAN - PUBLIC REVENUES

National Technical Information Service, 5285 Port Royal Road, Springfield, Virginia 22161 (800) 553-6847; *Handbook of Economic Statistics.*

Organisation for Economic Co-operation and Development (OECD), 2 rue Andre-Pascal, 75 Paris 16, France (Telephone Number in U.S. (202) 785-6323); *Revenue Statistics of OECD Member Countries.*

JAPAN - RADIO BROADCASTING - See JAPAN - BROADCASTING

JAPAN - RADIO RECEIVERS

St. Martin's Press, Inc., 175 Fifth Avenue, New York, New York 10010 (800) 221-7945; *The Statesman's Year-Book.*

Statistical Office of the United Nations, Publishing Service, New York, New York 10017 (800) 253-9646; *Statistical Yearbook.*

JAPAN - RAILWAYS

Europa Publications Limited, 18 Bedford Square, London, WC1B 3JN, England; *The Europa World Year Book.*

European Commission Office of Press and Public Affairs, 2100 M Street, NW, Washington, D.C. 20037 (202) 862-9500; *Basic Statistics of the Community.*

Jane's Information Group, Sentinel House, 163 Brighton Road, Coulsdon, Surrey CR5 2NH, England (Telephone Number in U.S. (703) 683-3700); *Jane's World Railways.*

National Technical Information Service, 5285 Port Royal Road, Springfield, Virginia 22161 (800) 553-6847; *Handbook of Economic Statistics.*

St. Martin's Press, Inc., 175 Fifth Avenue, New York, New York 10010 (800) 221-7945; *The Statesman's Year-Book.*

Statistical Office of the United Nations, Publishing Service, New York, New York 10017 (800) 253-9646; *Statistical Yearbook.*

JAPAN - RANCHING

European Commission Office of Press and Public Affairs, 2100 M Street, NW,

Washington, D.C. 20037 (202) 862-9500; *Basic Statistics of the Community*.

JAPAN - RAPESEED PRODUCTION - See JAPAN - CROPS

JAPAN - RELIGION

Central Intelligence Agency, Washington, D.C. 20505 (703) 482-1100, www.cia.gov; *The World Factbook*.

M.E. Sharpe, 80 Business Park Drive, Armonk, New York 10504 (800) 541-6563; *The Illustrated Book of World Rankings*.

St. Martin's Press, Inc., 175 Fifth Avenue, New York, New York 10010 (800) 221-7945; *The Statesman's Year-Book*.

JAPAN - RENT PRICES

International Labour Office, I.L.O. Publications, 1828 L Street NW, Suite 801, Washington, D.C. 20036 (301) 638-3152; *Yearbook of Labour Statistics*.

JAPAN - RETAIL TRADE

Euromonitor International, Inc., 122 South Michigan Avenue, Suite 1200, Chicago, Illinois 60603 (800) 577-EURO; *Retail Trade International*; and *World Marketing Data and Statistics*.

European Commission Office of Press and Public Affairs, 2100 M Street, NW, Washington, D.C. 20037 (202) 862-9500; *Basic Statistics of the Community*.

Statistical Office of the United Nations, Publishing Service, New York, New York 10017 (800) 253-9646; *Statistical Yearbook*.

JAPAN - RICE PRODUCTION - See JAPAN - CROPS

JAPAN - ROOT AND TUBER PRODUCTION - See JAPAN - CROPS

JAPAN - ROUNDWOOD PRODUCTION - See JAPAN - FORESTRY AND FOREST PRODUCTS

JAPAN - RUBBER PRODUCTION AND CONSUMPTION

Commodity Research Bureau, Inc., 30 South Wacker Drive, Chicago, Illinois 60606 (312) 454-1801; *Commodity Year Book*.

European Commission Office of Press and Public Affairs, 2100 M Street, NW, Washington, D.C. 20037 (202) 862-9500; *Basic Statistics of the Community*.

International Rubber Study Group, York House, 8th Floor, Empire Way, Wembley, London HA9 0PA, England; *Rubber Statistical Bulletin*.

M.E. Sharpe, 80 Business Park Drive, Armonk, New York 10504 (800) 541-6563; *The Illustrated Book of World Rankings*.

National Technical Information Service, 5285 Port Royal Road, Springfield, Virginia 22161 (800) 553-6847; *Handbook of Economic Statistics*.

Organisation for Economic Co-operation and Development (OECD), 2 rue Andre-Pascal, 75 Paris 16, France (Telephone Number in U.S. (202) 785-6323); *Foreign Trade by Commodities*.

Statistical Office of the United Nations, Publishing Service, New York, New York 10017 (800) 253-9646; *Statistical Yearbook*.

JAPAN - RYE PRODUCTION - See JAPAN - CROPS

JAPAN - SAFFLOWER SEED PRODUCTION - See JAPAN - CROPS

JAPAN - SALT PRODUCTION - See JAPAN - MINING AND MINERAL PRODUCTS

JAPAN - SAWNWOOD PRODUCTION - See JAPAN - FORESTRY AND FOREST PRODUCTS

JAPAN - SCIENCE AND TECHNOLOGY - EXPENDITURE FOR RESEARCH - See JAPAN - SCIENTISTS, TECHNICIANS AND ENGINEERS

JAPAN - SCIENTISTS, TECHNICIANS AND ENGINEERS

European Commission Office of Press and Public Affairs, 2100 M Street, NW, Washington, D.C. 20037 (202) 862-9500; *Basic Statistics of the Community*.

Statistical Office of the United Nations, Publishing Service, New York, New York 10017 (800) 253-9646; *Statistical Yearbook*.

United Nations Educational, Scientific and Cultural Organization (UNESCO), 7 Place de Fontenoy, F-75700 Paris, France (Telephone Number in U.S. (212) 963-5981); *Statistical Yearbook*.

JAPAN - SENIOR CITIZENS

M.E. Sharpe, 80 Business Park Drive, Armonk, New York 10504 (800) 541-6563; *The Illustrated Book of World Rankings*.

JAPAN - SESAME SEED PRODUCTION - See JAPAN - CROPS

JAPAN - SHEEP - See JAPAN - LIVESTOCK AND POULTRY

JAPAN - SHIPBUILDING - PRODUCTION INDEX

Organisation for Economic Co-

operation and Development (OECD), 2 rue Andre-Pascal, 75 Paris 16, France (Telephone Number in U.S. (202) 785-6323); *Indicators of Industrial Activity*.

JAPAN - SILVER PRODUCTION AND CONSUMPTION - See JAPAN - MINING AND MINERAL PRODUCTS

JAPAN - SISAL PRODUCTION - See JAPAN - CROPS

JAPAN - SOCIAL DATA

European Commission Office of Press and Public Affairs, 2100 M Street, NW, Washington, D.C. 20037 (202) 862-9500; *Basic Statistics of the Community*.

M.E. Sharpe, 80 Business Park Drive, Armonk, New York 10504 (800) 541-6563; *The Illustrated Book of World Rankings*.

Statistical Office of the United Nations, Publishing Service, New York, New York 10017 (800) 253-9646; *World Statistics Pocketbook*.

JAPAN - SOCIAL SECURITY

European Commission Office of Press and Public Affairs, 2100 M Street, NW, Washington, D.C. 20037 (202) 862-9500; *Basic Statistics of the Community*.

Organisation for Economic Co-operation and Development (OECD), 2 rue Andre-Pascal, 75 Paris 16, France (Telephone Number in U.S. (202) 785-6323); *Revenue Statistics of OECD Member Countries*.

St. Martin's Press, Inc., 175 Fifth Avenue, New York, New York 10010 (800) 221-7945; *The Statesman's Year-Book*.

Statistical Office of the United Nations, Publishing Service, New York, New York 10017 (800) 253-9646; *National Accounts Statistics*.

JAPAN - SOCIOECONOMIC DATA

European Commission Office of Press and Public Affairs, 2100 M Street, NW, Washington, D.C. 20037 (202) 862-9500; *Basic Statistics of the Community*.

Organisation for Economic Co-operation and Development (OECD), 2 rue Andre-Pascal, 75 Paris 16, France (Telephone Number in U.S. (202) 785-6323); *Economic Outlook*.

JAPAN - SOYBEAN PRODUCTION - See JAPAN - CROPS

JAPAN - STAMP TAXES AND DUTIES - See JAPAN - TAXATION

JAPAN - STATE BUDGET REVENUE

EXPENDITURES

Euromonitor International, Inc., 122 South Michigan Avenue, Suite 1200, Chicago, Illinois 60603 (800) 577-EURO; *International Marketing Data and Statistics.*

JAPAN - STEEL - See JAPAN - MINING AND MINERAL PRODUCTS

JAPAN - STOCKS - COMMODITY - MARKET PRICE - INDEXES

Food and Agricultural Organization of the United Nations (FAO), Via delle Terme di Caracalla, 00100 Rome, Italy (Telephone Number in U.S. (202) 653-2400); *The State of Food and Agriculture.*

International Lead and Zinc Study Group, Metro House, 58 St. James's Street, London SW1A 1LD England; *Lead and Zinc Statistics.*

Statistical Office of the United Nations, Publishing Service, New York, New York 10017 (800) 253-9646; *Statistical Yearbook.*

World Bureau of Metal Statistics, 27-A High Street, Ware, Herts. SG12 9BA, England; *World Metal Statistics.*

JAPAN - STRAW PRODUCTION - See JAPAN - CROPS

JAPAN - SUGAR AND SUGARBEET PRODUCTION - See JAPAN - CROPS

JAPAN - SULPHUR AND SULPHURIC ACID PRODUCTION - See JAPAN - MINING AND MINERAL PRODUCTS

JAPAN - SUNFLOWER PRODUCTION - See JAPAN - CROPS

JAPAN - TAXATION

Europa Publications Limited, 18 Bedford Square, London, WC1B 3JN, England; *The Europa World Year Book.*

European Commission Office of Press and Public Affairs, 2100 M Street, NW, Washington, D.C. 20037 (202) 862-9500; *Basic Statistics of the Community.*

International Monetary Fund, 700 Nineteenth Street, NW, Washington, D.C. 20431 (202) 623-7000; *Government Finance Statistics Yearbook.*

International Road Federation, 2600 Virginia Avenue, NW, Washington, D.C. 20037 (202) 338-4641; *World Road Statistics.*

Organisation for Economic Co-operation and Development (OECD), 2 rue Andre-Pascal, 75 Paris 16, France (Telephone Number in U.S. (202) 785-6323); *Revenue Statistics of OECD Member Countries.*

JAPAN - TEA PRODUCTION AND CONSUMPTION - See JAPAN - CROPS

JAPAN - TELEGRAPH SERVICE

Statistical Office of the United Nations, Publishing Service, New York, New York 10017 (800) 253-9646; *Statistical Yearbook.*

JAPAN - TELEPHONES IN USE

American Telephone and Telegraph Company, 26 Parsippany Road, Whippany, New Jersey 07981 (800) 222-0300; *The World's Telephones.*

Central Intelligence Agency, Washington, D.C. 20505 (703) 482-1100, www.cia.gov; *The World Factbook.*

The Economist Intelligence Unit (Asia) Limited, 10th Floor, Luk Kwok Centre, 72 Gloucester Road, Wanchai, Hong Kong (Phone Number in U.S. (800) 938-4685); *Asian Market Atlas.*

European Commission Office of Press and Public Affairs, 2100 M Street, NW, Washington, D.C. 20037 (202) 862-9500; *Basic Statistics of the Community.*

St. Martin's Press, Inc., 175 Fifth Avenue, New York, New York 10010 (800) 221-7945; *The Statesman's Year-Book.*

Statistical Office of the United Nations, Publishing Service, New York, New York 10017 (800) 253-9646; *Statistical Yearbook;* and *World Statistics Pocketbook.*

JAPAN - TELEVISION BROADCASTING - See JAPAN - BROADCASTING

JAPAN - TELEVISION RECEIVER PRODUCTION

European Commission Office of Press and Public Affairs, 2100 M Street, NW, Washington, D.C. 20037 (202) 862-9500; *Basic Statistics of the Community.*

National Technical Information Service, 5285 Port Royal Road, Springfield, Virginia 22161 (800) 553-6847; *Handbook of Economic Statistics.*

Statistical Office of the United Nations, Publishing Service, New York, New York 10017 (800) 253-9646; *Statistical Yearbook.*

JAPAN - TELEVISION RECEIVERS - IN USE

Statistical Office of the United Nations, Publishing Service, New York, New York 10017 (800) 253-9646; *Statistical Yearbook.*

JAPAN - TEXTILE INDUSTRY

American Forest and Paper Association, 1111 Nineteenth Street, NW, Washington, D.C. 20036 (202) 463-2700; *Wood Pulp and Fiber Statistics.*

Euromonitor International, Inc., 122 South Michigan Avenue, Suite 1200, Chicago, Illinois 60603 (800) 577-EURO; *Retail Trade International.*

European Commission Office of Press and Public Affairs, 2100 M Street, NW, Washington, D.C. 20037 (202) 862-9500; *Basic Statistics of the Community.*

Food and Agricultural Organization of the United Nations (FAO), Via delle Terme di Caracalla, 00100 Rome, Italy (Telephone Number in U.S. (202) 653-2400); *Production Yearbook.*

M.E. Sharpe, 80 Business Park Drive, Armonk, New York 10504 (800) 541-6563; *The Illustrated Book of World Rankings.*

National Technical Information Service, 5285 Port Royal Road, Springfield, Virginia 22161 (800) 553-6847; *Handbook of Economic Statistics.*

Organisation for Economic Co-operation and Development (OECD), 2 rue Andre-Pascal, 75 Paris 16, France (Telephone Number in U.S. (202) 785-6323); *Economic Accounts for Agriculture; Foreign Trade by Commodities; Indicators of Industrial Activity; Industrial Structure Statistics;* and *Textile Industry in OECD Countries.*

St. Martin's Press, Inc., 175 Fifth Avenue, New York, New York 10010 (800) 221-7945; *The Statesman's Year-Book.*

Statistical Office of the United Nations, Publishing Service, New York, New York 10017 (800) 253-9646; *Statistical Yearbook.*

United Nations Conference on Trade and Development, Central Statistical Service, Palais des Nations, Geneva, Switzerland (Telephone in U.S. (800) 253-9646); *UNCTAD Commodity Yearbook.*

JAPAN - THEATRE

United Nations Educational, Scientific and Cultural Organization (UNESCO), 7 Place de Fontenoy, F-75700 Paris, France (Telephone Number in U.S. (212) 963-5981); *Statistical Yearbook.*

JAPAN - TIMBER - See JAPAN - FORESTRY AND FOREST PRODUCTS

JAPAN - TIN - See JAPAN - MINING AND MINERAL PRODUCTS

JAPAN - TIRE (MOTOR VEHICLE) PRODUCTION

International Rubber Study Group, York House, 8th Floor, Empire Way, Wembley, London HA9 0PA, England; *Rubber Statistical Bulletin.*

National Technical Information Service, 5285 Port Royal Road, Springfield, Virginia 22161 (800) 553-6847; *Handbook of Economic Statistics.*

Statistical Office of the United Nations, Publishing Service, New York, New York 10017 (800) 253-9646; *Statistical Yearbook.*

JAPAN - TOBACCO PRODUCTION

Commodity Research Bureau, Inc., 30 South Wacker Drive, Chicago, Illinois 60606 (312) 454-1801; *Commodity Year Book.*

European Commission Office of Press and Public Affairs, 2100 M Street, NW, Washington, D.C. 20037 (202) 862-9500; *Basic Statistics of the Community.*

M.E. Sharpe, 80 Business Park Drive, Armonk, New York 10504 (800) 541-6563; *The Illustrated Book of World Rankings.*

Organisation for Economic Co-operation and Development (OECD), 2 rue Andre-Pascal, 75 Paris 16, France (Telephone Number in U.S. (202) 785-6323); *Foreign Trade by Commodities; Indicators of Industrial Activity;* and *Industrial Structure Statistics.*

Statistical Office of the United Nations, Publishing Service, New York, New York 10017 (800) 253-9646; *Statistical Yearbook.*

JAPAN - TOURISM

Euromonitor International, Inc., 122 South Michigan Avenue, Suite 1200, Chicago, Illinois 60603 (800) 577-EURO; *The World Economic Factbook,* and *World Marketing Data and Statistics.*

Europa Publications Limited, 18 Bedford Square, London, WC1B 3JN, England; *The Europa World Year Book.*

M.E. Sharpe, 80 Business Park Drive, Armonk, New York 10504 (800) 541-6563; *The Illustrated Book of World Rankings.*

Organisation for Economic Co-operation and Development (OECD), 2 rue Andre-Pascal, 75 Paris 16, France (Telephone Number in U.S. (202) 785-6323); *Tourism Policy and International Tourism in OECD Member Countries.*

St. Martin's Press, Inc., 175 Fifth Avenue, New York, New York 10010 (800) 221-7945; *The Statesman's Year-Book.*

Statistical Office of the United Nations, Publishing Service, New York, New York

10017 (800) 253-9646; *Statistical Yearbook.*

World Tourism Organization, Calle Capitan Haya 42, E-28020 Madrid, Spain; *Yearbook of Tourism Statistics.*

JAPAN - TRACTORS IN USE

Statistical Office of the United Nations, Publishing Service, New York, New York 10017 (800) 253-9646; *Statistical Yearbook.*

JAPAN - TRADE - See JAPAN - FOREIGN TRADE

JAPAN - TRADEMARKS AND SERVICE MARKS - See JAPAN - PATENTS, TRADEMARKS AND SERVICE MARKS

JAPAN - TRANSPORTATION AND COMMUNICATIONS

Central Intelligence Agency, Washington, D.C. 20505 (703) 482-1100, www.cia.gov; *The World Factbook.*

The Economist Intelligence Unit (Asia) Limited, 10th Floor, Luk Kwok Centre, 72 Gloucester Road, Wanchai, Hong Kong (Phone Number in U.S. (800) 938-4685); *Asian Market Atlas.*

Euromonitor International, Inc., 122 South Michigan Avenue, Suite 1200, Chicago, Illinois 60603 (800) 577-EURO; *World Marketing Data and Statistics.*

Europa Publications Limited, 18 Bedford Square, London, WC1B 3JN, England; *The Europa World Year Book.*

European Commission Office of Press and Public Affairs, 2100 M Street, NW, Washington, D.C. 20037 (202) 862-9500; *Basic Statistics of the Community.*

M.E. Sharpe, 80 Business Park Drive, Armonk, New York 10504 (800) 541-6563; *The Illustrated Book of World Rankings.*

St. Martin's Press, Inc., 175 Fifth Avenue, New York, New York 10010 (800) 221-7945; *The Statesman's Year-Book.*

Statistical Office of the United Nations, Publishing Service, New York, New York 10017 (800) 253-9646; *Human Development Report;* and *Statistical Yearbook for Asia and the Pacific.*

JAPAN - TUNGSTEN PRODUCTION AND CONSUMPTION - See JAPAN - MINING AND MINERAL PRODUCTS

JAPAN - TURKEYS - See JAPAN - LIVESTOCK AND POULTRY

JAPAN - UNEMPLOYMENT

Central Intelligence Agency, Washington, D.C. 20505 (703) 482-1100,

www.cia.gov; *The World Factbook.*

Euromonitor International, Inc., 122 South Michigan Avenue, Suite 1200, Chicago, Illinois 60603 (800) 577-EURO; *International Marketing Data and Statistics.*

European Commission Office of Press and Public Affairs, 2100 M Street, NW, Washington, D.C. 20037 (202) 862-9500; *Basic Statistics of the Community;* and *Eurostat Review.*

International Labour Office, I.L.O. Publications, 1828 K Street, NW, Suite 801, Washington, D.C. 20036 (301) 638-3152; *Yearbook of Labour Statistics.*

National Technical Information Service, 5285 Port Royal Road, Springfield, Virginia 22161 (800) 553-6847; *Handbook of Economic Statistics.*

Organisation for Economic Co-operation and Development (OECD), 2 rue Andre-Pascal, 75 Paris 16, France (Telephone Number in U.S. (202) 785-6323); *Economic Outlook; OECD Economic Surveys: Japan;* and *OECD Employment Outlook.*

St. Martin's Press, Inc., 175 Fifth Avenue, New York, New York 10010 (800) 221-7945; *The Statesman's Year-Book.*

Statistical Office of the United Nations, Publishing Service, New York, New York 10017 (800) 253-9646; *Statistical Yearbook.*

Statistics Bureau, Management and Coordination Agency, Japan; *Statistical Indicators on Social Life.*

JAPAN - URANIUM PRODUCTION AND CONSUMPTION - See JAPAN - MINING AND MINERAL PRODUCTS

JAPAN - UTILITIES

European Commission Office of Press and Public Affairs, 2100 M Street, NW, Washington, D.C. 20037 (202) 862-9500; *Basic Statistics of the Community.*

Statistical Office of the United Nations, Publishing Service, New York, New York 10017 (800) 253-9646; *Electric Power in Asia and the Pacific.*

JAPAN - VANADIUM AND VANADIUM ORE - See JAPAN - MINING AND MINERAL PRODUCTS

JAPAN - VITAL STATISTICS

Euromonitor International, Inc., 122 South Michigan Avenue, Suite 1200, Chicago, Illinois 60603 (800) 577-EURO; *International Marketing Data and Statistics.*

European Commission Office of Press

and Public Affairs, 2100 M Street, NW, Washington, D.C. 20037 (202) 862-9500; *Basic Statistics of the Community;* and *Eurostat Review.*

St. Martin's Press, Inc., 175 Fifth Avenue, New York, New York 10010 (800) 221-7945; *The Statesman's Year-Book.*

JAPAN - WELFARE

St. Martin's Press, Inc., 175 Fifth Avenue, New York, New York 10010 (800) 221-7945; *The Statesman's Year-Book.*

JAPAN - WHOLESALE TRADE

European Commission Office of Press and Public Affairs, 2100 M Street, NW, Washington, D.C. 20037 (202) 862-9500; *Basic Statistics of the Community;* and *Eurostat Review.*

Statistical Office of the United Nations, Publishing Service, New York, New York 10017 (800) 253-9646; *Statistical Yearbook.*

JAPAN - WINE PRODUCTION - See JAPAN - BEVERAGES

JAPAN - WOOD AND WOOD PULP - See JAPAN - FORESTRY AND FOREST PRODUCTS

JAPAN - WOOL - PRODUCTION AND CONSUMPTION - See JAPAN - TEXTILE INDUSTRY

JAPAN - YARN PRODUCTION - See JAPAN - TEXTILE INDUSTRY

JAPAN - ZINC AND ZINC ORE - See JAPAN - MINING AND MINERAL PRODUCTS

JAPAN - ZOOS AND BOTANICAL GARDENS

United Nations Educational, Scientific and Cultural Organization (UNESCO), 7 Place de Fontenoy, F-75700 Paris, France (Telephone Number in U.S. (212) 963-5981); *Statistical Yearbook.*

JAPANESE POPULATION

U.S. Department of Commerce, Bureau of the Census, Washington, D.C. 20233 (301) 457-4100, www.census.gov; *Census of Population, General Population Characteristics, United States.*

JAZZ

National Endowment for the Arts, 1100 Pennsylvania Avenue, NW, Washington, D.C. 20506 (202) 682-5400, www.arts.gov; *Arts Survey of Public Participation in the Arts.*

Recording Industry Association of America, 1330 Connecticut Avenue, NW, Suite 300, Washington, D.C. 20036 (202)

775-0101; *Consumer Profile.*

JEWELRY, SILVERWARE, AND PLATED WARE - MANUFACTURING

U.S. Department of Commerce, Bureau of the Census, Washington, D.C. 20233 (301) 457-4100, www.census.gov; *Census of Manufactures;* and *Annual Survey of Manufactures.*

U.S. Department of Labor, Bureau of Labor Statistics, Two Massachusetts Avenue, NE, Washington, D.C. 20212 (202) 691-5200, www.stats.bls.gov; *Employment and Earnings;* and Internet site: http://stats.bls.gov/ceshome .

JEWELRY STORES

U.S. Department of Commerce, Bureau of the Census, Washington, D.C. 20233 (301) 457-4100, www.census.gov; *County Business Patterns; Current Business Reports, Annual Benchmark Report for Retail Trade; Economic Census;* and unpublished data.

JEWISH POPULATION - See RELIGION

JOB CORPS

The Congress of the U.S., Congressional Research Service, 10 First Street, SE, Washington, D.C. 20540 (202) 707-5700; *Cash and Non-Cash Benefits for Persons With Limited Income: Eligibility Rules, Recipient and Expenditure Data.*

JOGGING

National Sporting Goods Association, 1601 Feehanville Drive, Suite 300, Mount Prospect, Illinois 60056 (847) 296-6742; *Sports Participation in 1998;* and *The Sporting Goods Market in 1999.*

JOHNSTON ISLAND - AGRICULTURE

Food and Agricultural Organization of the United Nations (FAO), Via delle Terme di Caracalla, 00100 Rome, Italy (Telephone Number in U.S. (202) 653-2400); *Production Yearbook; The State of Food and Agriculture;* and *Trade Yearbook.*

JOHNSTON ISLAND - ANIMAL HEALTH

Food and Agricultural Organization of the United Nations (FAO), Via delle Terme di Caracalla, 00100, Rome, Italy (Telephone Number in U.S. (202) 653-2400); *Animal Health Yearbook.*

JOHNSTON ISLAND - AREA AND DENSITY OF POPULATION

Central Intelligence Agency, Washington, D.C. 20505 (703) 482-1100, www.cia.gov; *The World Factbook.*

Food and Agricultural Organization of the United Nations (FAO), Via delle Terme di Caracalla, 00100 Rome, Italy (Telephone Number in U.S. (202) 653-2400); *The State of Food and Agriculture.*

St. Martin's Press, Inc., 175 Fifth Avenue, New York, New York 10010 (800) 221-7945; *The Statesman's Year-Book.*

Statistical Office of the United Nations, Publishing Service, New York, New York 10017 (800) 253-9646; *Statistical Yearbook.*

JOHNSTON ISLAND - BIRTH RATES

Central Intelligence Agency, Washington, D.C. 20505 (703) 482-1100, www.cia.gov; *The World Factbook.*

Statistical Office of the United Nations, Publishing Service, New York, New York 10017 (800) 253-9646; *Demographic Yearbook.*

JOHNSTON ISLAND - BROADCASTING

Central Intelligence Agency, Washington, D.C. 20505 (703) 482-1100, www.cia.gov; *The World Factbook.*

JOHNSTON ISLAND - BUDGET

Central Intelligence Agency, Washington, D.C. 20505 (703) 482-1100, www.cia.gov; *The World Factbook.*

JOHNSTON ISLAND - CALORIE SUPPLY

Food and Agricultural Organization of the United Nations (FAO), Via delle Terme di Caracalla, 00100 Rome, Italy (Telephone Number in U.S. (202) 653-2400); *The State of Food and Agriculture.*

JOHNSTON ISLAND - CROPS

Food and Agricultural Organization of the United Nations (FAO), Via delle Terme di Caracalla, 00100 Rome, Italy (Telephone Number in U.S. (202) 653-2400); *The State of Food and Agriculture.*

JOHNSTON ISLAND - DAIRY PRODUCTS

Food and Agricultural Organization of the United Nations (FAO), Via delle Terme di Caracalla, 00100 Rome, Italy (Telephone Number in U.S. (202) 653-2400); *The State of Food and Agriculture.*

JOHNSTON ISLAND - DIVORCE RATES

Statistical Office of the United Nations, Publishing Service, New York, New York 10017 (800) 253-9646; *Demographic Yearbook.*

JOHNSTON ISLAND - ECONOMY

Central Intelligence Agency,

Washington, D.C. 20505 (703) 482-1100, www.cia.gov; *The World Factbook*.

JOHNSTON ISLAND - ELECTRICITY

Central Intelligence Agency, Washington, D.C. 20505 (703) 482-1100, www.cia.gov; *The World Factbook*.

JOHNSTON ISLAND - ENERGY

Food and Agricultural Organization of the United Nations (FAO), Via delle Terme di Caracalla, 00100 Rome, Italy (Telephone Number in U.S. (202) 653-2400); *The State of Food and Agriculture*.

JOHNSTON ISLAND - EXCHANGE RATES

Central Intelligence Agency, Washington, D.C. 20505 (703) 482-1100, www.cia.gov; *The World Factbook*.

JOHNSTON ISLAND - EXPORTS

Central Intelligence Agency, Washington, D.C. 20505 (703) 482-1100, www.cia.gov; *The World Factbook*.

Food and Agricultural Organization of the United Nations (FAO), Via delle Terme di Caracalla, 00100 Rome, Italy (Telephone Number in U.S. (202) 653-2400); *The State of Food and Agriculture*.

JOHNSTON ISLAND - EXTERNAL TRADE

Food and Agricultural Organization of the United Nations (FAO) Via delle Terme di Caracalla, 00100 Rome, Italy (Telephone Number in U.S. (202) 653-2400); *The State of Food and Agriculture;* and *Trade Yearbook*.

JOHNSTON ISLAND - FARM CROPS - See JOHNSTON ISLAND - CROPS

JOHNSTON ISLAND - FERTILITY RATES

Central Intelligence Agency, Washington, D.C. 20505 (703) 482-1100, www.cia.gov; *The World Factbook*.

JOHNSTON ISLAND - FERTILIZER

Food and Agricultural Organization of the United Nations (FAO), Via delle Terme di Caracalla, 00100, Rome, Italy (Telephone Number in U.S. (202) 653-2400); *Fertilizer Yearbook;* and *The State of Food and Agriculture*.

JOHNSTON ISLAND - FISHERIES

Food and Agricultural Organization of the United Nations (FAO), Via delle Terme di Caracalla, 00100 Rome, Italy (Telephone Number in U.S. (202) 653-2400); *The State of Food and Agriculture;* and *Yearbook of Fishery Statistics*.

JOHNSTON ISLAND - FOREIGN TRADE

Food and Agricultural Organization of the United Nations (FAO), Via delle Terme di Caracalla, 00100 Rome, Italy (Telephone Number in U.S. (202) 653-2400); *The State of Food and Agriculture*.

JOHNSTON ISLAND - FORESTRY AND FOREST PRODUCTS

Food and Agricultural Organization of the United Nations (FAO), Via delle Terme di Caracalla, 00100 Rome, Italy (Telephone Number in U.S. (202) 653-2400); *The State of Food and Agriculture;* and *Yearbook of Forest Products*.

JOHNSTON ISLAND - GOVERNMENT

Central Intelligence Agency, Washington, D.C. 20505 (703) 482-1100, www.cia.gov; *The World Factbook*.

JOHNSTON ISLAND - HIGHWAYS

Central Intelligence Agency, Washington, D.C. 20505 (703) 482-1100, www.cia.gov; *The World Factbook*.

JOHNSTON ISLAND - ILLITERATE POPULATION

Central Intelligence Agency, Washington, D.C. 20505 (703) 482-1100, www.cia.gov; *The World Factbook*.

JOHNSTON ISLAND - IMPORTS

Central Intelligence Agency, Washington, D.C. 20505 (703) 482-1100, www.cia.gov; *The World Factbook*.

Food and Agricultural Organization of the United Nations (FAO), Via delle Terme di Caracalla, 00100 Rome, Italy (Telephone Number in U.S. (202) 653-2400); *The State of Food and Agriculture*.

JOHNSTON ISLAND - INDUSTRY

Central Intelligence Agency, Washington, D.C. 20505 (703) 482-1100, www.cia.gov; *The World Factbook*.

JOHNSTON ISLAND - LABOR

Central Intelligence Agency, Washington, D.C. 20505 (703) 482-1100, www.cia.gov; *The World Factbook*.

Food and Agricultural Organization of the United Nations (FAO), Via delle Terme di Caracalla, 00100 Rome, Italy (Telephone Number in U.S. (202) 653-2400); *The State of Food and Agriculture*.

JOHNSTON ISLAND - LAND USE

Central Intelligence Agency, Washington, D.C. 20505 (703) 482-1100,

www.cia.gov; *World Factbook*.

Food and Agricultural Organization of the United Nations (FAO), Via delle Terme di Caracalla, 00100 Rome, Italy (Telephone Number in U.S. (202) 653-2400); *Production Yearbook*.

JOHNSTON ISLAND - LIFE EXPECTANCY

Central Intelligence Agency, Washington, D.C. 20505 (703) 482-1100, www.cia.gov; *The World Factbook*.

JOHNSTON ISLAND - LIVESTOCK AND POULTRY

Food and Agricultural Organization of the United Nations (FAO), Via delle Terme di Caracalla, 00100 Rome, Italy (Telephone Number in U.S. (202) 653-2400); *Production Yearbook;* and *The State of Food and Agriculture*.

JOHNSTON ISLAND - MARRIAGE RATES

Statistical Office of the United Nations, Publishing Service, New York, New York 10017 (800) 253-9646; *Demographic Yearbook*.

JOHNSTON ISLAND - MILITARY

Central Intelligence Agency, Washington, D.C. 20505 (703) 482-1100, www.cia.gov; *The World Factbook*.

JOHNSTON ISLAND - MORTALITY

Central Intelligence Agency, Washington, D.C. 20505 (703) 482-1100, www.cia.gov; *The World Factbook*.

Statistical Office of the United Nations, Publishing Service, New York, New York 10017 (800) 253-9646; *Demographic Yearbook*.

JOHNSTON ISLAND - PESTICIDE USE

Food and Agricultural Organization of the United Nations (FAO), Via delle Terme di Caracalla, 00100 Rome, Italy (Telephone Number in U.S. (202) 653-2400); *The State of Food and Agriculture*.

JOHNSTON ISLAND - PETROLEUM INDUSTRY

Food and Agricultural Organization of the United Nations (FAO), Via delle Terme di Caracalla, 00100 Rome, Italy (Telephone Number in U.S. (202) 653-2400); *The State of Food and Agriculture*.

JOHNSTON ISLAND - POPULATION

Central Intelligence Agency, Washington, D.C. 20505 (703) 482-1100, www.cia.gov; *The World Factbook*.

Food and Agricultural Organization of the United Nations (FAO), Via delle Terme di Caracalla, 00100 Rome, Italy (Telephone Number in U.S. (202) 653-2400); *Production Yearbook.*

St. Martin's Press, Inc., 175 Fifth Avenue, New York, New York 10010 (800) 221-7945; *The Statesman's Year-Book.*

Statistical Office of the United Nations, Publishing Service, New York, New York 10017 (800) 253-9646; *Demographic Yearbook;* and *Statistical Yearbook.*

World Health Organization, Office of Publications, 20 Avenue Appia, CH-1211 Geneva 27, Switzerland (Telephone Number in U.S. (518) 436-9686); *World Health Statistics Annual.*

JOHNSTON ISLAND - PRICES

Food and Agricultural Organization of the United Nations (FAO), Via delle Terme di Caracalla, 00100 Rome, Italy (Telephone Number in U.S. (202) 653-2400); *Production Yearbook;* and *The State of Food and Agriculture.*

JOHNSTON ISLAND - POPULATION

Central Intelligence Agency, Washington, D.C. 20505 (703) 482-1100, www.cia.gov; *The World Factbook.*

JOHNSTON ISLAND - RELIGION

Central Intelligence Agency, Washington, D.C. 20505 (703) 482-1100, www.cia.gov; *The World Factbook.*

JOHNSTON ISLAND - STOCKS - COMMODITY - MARKET PRICE - INDEX

Food and Agricultural Organization of the United Nations (FAO), Via delle Terme di Caracalla, 00100 Rome, Italy (Telephone Number in U.S. (202) 653-2400); *The State of Food and Agriculture.*

JOHNSTON ISLAND - TELEPHONES IN USE

Central Intelligence Agency, Washington, D.C. 20505 (703) 482-1100, www.cia.gov; *The World Factbook.*

JOHNSTON ISLAND - TRANSPORTATION AND COMMUNICATIONS

Central Intelligence Agency, Washington, D.C. 20505 (703) 482-1100, www.cia.gov; *The World Factbook.*

JOHNSTON ISLAND - UNEMPLOYMENT RATE

Central Intelligence Agency, Washington, D.C. 20505 (703) 482-1100, www.cia.gov; *The World Factbook.*

JOHNSTON ISLAND - VITAL STATISTICS

World Health Organization, Office of Publications, 20 Avenue Appia, CH-1211 Geneva 27, Switzerland (Telephone Number in U.S. (518) 436-9686); *World Health Statistics Annual.*

Jordan - National Statistical Office

Department of Statistics, Post Office Box 2015, Amman, Jordan.

Jordan - Primary Statistics Source

Department of Statistics, Post Office Box 2015, Amman, Jordan; *Statistical Yearbook.*

JORDAN - AGRICULTURE

Economic Commission for Western Asia, Post Office Box 27, Baghdad, Iraq; *Statistical Abstract of Western Asia.*

The Economist Intelligence Unit, 111 West 57th Street, New York, New York 10019 (800) 938-4685; *Jordan Country Report.*

Euromonitor International, Inc., 122 South Michigan Avenue, Suite 1200, Chicago, Illinois 60603 (800) 577-EURO; *World Marketing Data and Statistics.*

Europa Publications Limited, 18 Bedford Square, London, WC1B 3JN, England; *The Europa World Year Book.*

Federal Statistical Office, Gustav - Stresemann - Ring 11, D-6200 Wiesbaden, Germany; *Jordanien.*

Food and Agricultural Organization of the United Nations (FAO), Via delle Terme di Caracalla, 00100 Rome, Italy (Telephone Number in U.S. (202) 653-2400); *Production Yearbook; The State of Food and Agriculture;* and *Trade Yearbook.*

M.E. Sharpe, 80 Business Park Drive, Armonk, New York 10504 (800) 541-6563; *The Illustrated Book of World Rankings.*

St. Martin's Press, Inc., 175 Fifth Avenue, New York, New York 10010 (800) 221-7945; *The Statesman's Year-Book.*

Statistical Office of the United Nations, Publishing Service, New York, New York 10017 (800) 253-9646; *Statistical Yearbook.*

United Nations Conference on Trade and Development, Central Statistical Service, Palais des Nations, Geneva, Switzerland (Telephone in U.S. (800) 253-9646); *UNCTAD Commodity Yearbook.*

JORDAN - AIRLINE SERVICE

Economic Commission for Western Asia, Post Office Box 27, Baghdad, Iraq; *Statistical Abstract of Western Asia.*

Europa Publications Limited, 18 Bedford Square, London, WC1B 3JN, England; *The Europa World Year Book.*

International Civil Aviation Organization, 999 University Street, Montreal, Quebec, Canada H3C 5H7 (514) 954-8219; *Civil Aviation Statistics of the World.*

M.E. Sharpe, 80 Business Park Drive, Armonk, New York 10504 (800) 541-6563; *The Illustrated Book of World Rankings.*

St. Martin's Press, Inc., 175 Fifth Avenue, New York, New York 10010 (800) 221-7945; *The Statesman's Year-Book.*

Statistical Office of the United Nations, Publishing Service, New York, New York 10017 (800) 253-9646; *Statistical Yearbook.*

JORDAN - ALUMINUM PRODUCTION - See JORDAN - MINING AND MINERAL PRODUCTS

JORDAN - ANIMAL HEALTH

Food and Agricultural Organization of the United Nations (FAO), Via delle Terme di Caracalla, 00100, Rome, Italy (Telephone Number in U.S. (202) 653-2400); *Animal Health Yearbook.*

JORDAN - AREA AND DENSITY OF POPULATION

Central Intelligence Agency, Washington, D.C. 20505 (703) 482-1100, www.cia.gov; *The World Factbook.*

Economic Commission for Western Asia, Post Office Box 27, Baghdad, Iraq; *Statistical Abstract of Western Asia.*

Euromonitor International, Inc., 122 South Michigan Avenue, Suite 1200, Chicago, Illinois 60603 (800) 577-EURO; *International Marketing Data and Statistics;* and *The World Economic Factbook.*

Europa Publications Limited, 18 Bedford Square, London, WC1B 3JN, England; *The Europa World Year Book.*

Federal Statistical Office, Gustav - Stresemann - Ring 11, D-6200 Wiesbaden, Germany; *Jordanien.*

Food and Agricultural Organization of the United Nations (FAO), Via delle Terme di Caracalla, 00100 Rome, Italy (Telephone Number in U.S. (202) 653-2400); *The State of Food and Agriculture.*

M.E. Sharpe, 80 Business Park Drive, Armonk, New York 10504 (800) 541-6563; *The Illustrated Book of World Rankings*.

St. Martin's Press, Inc., 175 Fifth Avenue, New York, New York 10010 (800) 221-7945; *The Statesman's Year-Book*.

Statistical Office of the United Nations, Publishing Service, New York, New York 10017 (800) 253-9646; *Statistical Yearbook*.

United Nations Educational, Scientific and Cultural Organization (UNESCO), 7 Place de Fontenoy, F-75700 Paris, France (Telephone Number in U.S. (212) 963-5981); *Statistical Yearbook*.

The World Bank, 1818 H Street, NW, Washington, D.C. 20433 (202) 477-1234; *World Development Report*.

JORDAN - ARMS EXPORTS AND IMPORTS - See JORDAN - MILITARY

JORDAN - BALANCE OF PAYMENTS

Economic Commission for Western Asia, Post Office Box 27, Baghdad, Iraq; *Statistical Abstract of Western Asia*.

The Economist Intelligence Unit, 111 West 57th Street, New York, New York 10019 (800) 938-4685; *The World Market Atlas*.

Europa Publications Limited, 18 Bedford Square, London, WC1B 3JN, England; *The Europa World Year Book*.

Federal Statistical Office, Gustav - Stresemann - Ring 11, D-6200 Wiesbaden, Germany; *Jordanien*.

International Monetary Fund, 700 Nineteenth Street, NW, Washington, D.C. 20431 (202) 623-7000; *Balance of Payments Yearbook;* and *International Financial Statistics*.

United Nations Conference on Trade and Development (UNCTAD), New York, New York 10017 (800) 253-9646; *Handbook of International Trade and Development Statistics*.

The World Bank, 1818 H Street, NW, Washington, D.C. 20433 (202) 477-1234; *World Development Report*.

JORDAN - BALANCE OF TRADE

Economic Commission for Western Asia, Post Office Box 27, Baghdad, Iraq; *Statistical Abstract of Western Asia*.

JORDAN - BANKING

Economic Commission for Western Asia, Post Office Box 27, Baghdad, Iraq; *Statistical Abstract of Western Asia*.

Euromonitor International, Inc., 122 South Michigan Avenue, Suite 1200, Chicago, Illinois 60603 (800) 577-EURO; *World Marketing Data and Statistics*.

Europa Publications Limited, 18 Bedford Square, London, WC1B 3JN, England; *The Europa World Year Book*.

International Monetary Fund, 700 Nineteenth Street, NW, Washington, D.C. 20431 (202) 623-7000; *Government Finance Statistics Yearbook;* and *International Financial Statistics*.

M.E. Sharpe, 80 Business Park Drive, Armonk, New York 10504 (800) 541-6563; *The Illustrated Book of World Rankings*.

St. Martin's Press, Inc., 175 Fifth Avenue, New York, New York 10010 (800) 221-7945; *The Statesman's Year-Book*.

Statistical Office of the United Nations, Publishing Service, New York, New York 10017 (800) 253-9646; *Statistical Yearbook*.

JORDAN - BARLEY PRODUCTION - See JORDAN - CROPS

JORDAN - BEER PRODUCTION - See JORDAN - BEVERAGES

JORDAN - BEVERAGES

M.E. Sharpe, 80 Business Park Drive, Armonk, New York 10504 (800) 541-6563; *The Illustrated Book of World Rankings*.

Statistical Office of the United Nations, Publishing Service, New York, New York 10017 (800) 253-9646; *Statistical Yearbook*.

JORDAN - BIRTH RATES

Central Intelligence Agency, Washington, D.C. 20505 (703) 482-1100, www.cia.gov; *The World Factbook*.

Euromonitor International, Inc., 122 South Michigan Avenue, Suite 1200, Chicago, Illinois 60603 (800) 577-EURO; *International Marketing Data and Statistics;* and *The World Economic Factbook*.

Europa Publications Limited, 18 Bedford Square, London, WC1B 3JN, England; *The Europa World Year Book*.

M.E. Sharpe, 80 Business Park Drive, Armonk, New York 10504 (800) 541-6563; *The Illustrated Book of World Rankings*.

St. Martin's Press, Inc., 175 Fifth Avenue, New York, New York 10010 (800) 221-7945; *The Statesman's Year-Book*.

Statistical Office of the United Nations, Publishing Service, New York, New York 10017 (800) 253-9646; *Demographic Yearbook;* and *Statistical Yearbook*.

World Health Organization, Office of Publications, 20 Avenue Appia, CH-1211 Geneva 27, Switzerland (Telephone Number in U.S. (518) 436-9686); *World Health Statistics Annual*.

JORDAN - BONDS

International Monetary Fund, 700 Nineteenth Street, NW, Washington, D.C. 20431 (202) 623-7000; *Government Finance Statistics Yearbook*.

JORDAN - BOOK PRODUCTION

United Nations Educational, Scientific and Cultural Organization (UNESCO), 7 Place de Fontenoy, F-75700 Paris, France (Telephone Number in U.S. (212) 963-5981); *Statistical Yearbook*.

JORDAN - BROADCASTING

Billboard Limited, Post Office Box 9027, 1006 AA Amsterdam, The Netherlands (Telephone Number in U.S. (212) 764-7300); *World Radio TV Handbook*.

Central Intelligence Agency, Washington, D.C. 20505 (703) 482-1100, www.cia.gov; *The World Factbook*.

Euromonitor International, Inc., 122 South Michigan Avenue, Suite 1200, Chicago, Illinois 60603 (800) 577-EURO; *World Marketing Data and Statistics*.

M.E. Sharpe, 80 Business Park Drive, Armonk, New York 10504 (800) 541-6563; *The Illustrated Book of World Rankings*.

St. Martin's Press, Inc., 175 Fifth Avenue, New York, New York 10010 (800) 221-7945; *The Statesman's Year-Book*.

JORDAN - BUDGET

Central Intelligence Agency, Washington, D.C. 20505 (703) 482-1100, www.cia.gov; *The World Factbook*.

JORDAN - BUSINESS AND PROFESSIONAL LICENSES

International Monetary Fund, 700 Nineteenth Street, NW, Washington, D.C. 20431 (202) 623-7000; *Government Finance Statistics Yearbook*.

JORDAN - CABBAGE PRODUCTION - See JORDAN - CROPS

JORDAN - CALORIE SUPPLY

Food and Agricultural Organization of the United Nations (FAO), Via delle Terme di Caracalla, 00100 Rome, Italy (Telephone Number in U.S. (202) 653-2400); *The State of Food and Agriculture*.

JORDAN - CAPITAL REVENUES

International Monetary Fund, 700 Nineteenth Street, NW, Washington, D.C. 20431 (202) 623-7000; *Government Finance Statistics Yearbook.*

JORDAN - CATTLE - See JORDAN - LIVESTOCK AND POULTRY

JORDAN - CAULIFLOWER PRODUCTION - See JORDAN - CROPS

JORDAN - CEMENT PRODUCTION - See JORDAN - MINING AND MINERAL PRODUCTS

JORDAN - CHEESE PRODUCTION - See JORDAN - DAIRY PRODUCTS

JORDAN - CHEMICAL (ORGANIC) PRODUCTION - See JORDAN - MINING AND MINERAL PRODUCTS

JORDAN - CHICK PEA PRODUCTION - See JORDAN - CROPS

JORDAN - CHICKENS - See JORDAN - LIVESTOCK AND POULTRY

JORDAN - CIGARETTE PRODUCTION - See JORDAN - TOBACCO PRODUCTION

JORDAN - CLIMATE

M.E. Sharpe, 80 Business Park Drive, Armonk, New York 10504 (800) 541-6563; *The Illustrated Book of World Rankings.*

St. Martin's Press, Inc., 175 Fifth Avenue, New York, New York 10010 (800) 221-7945; *The Statesman's Year-Book.*

JORDAN - COAL PRODUCTION - See JORDAN - MINING AND MINERAL PRODUCTS

JORDAN - COFFEE PRODUCTION - See JORDAN - CROPS

JORDAN - COMMERCE

St. Martin's Press, Inc., 175 Fifth Avenue, New York, New York 10010 (800) 221-7945; *The Statesman's Year-Book.*

JORDAN - COMMUNICATIONS - See JORDAN - TRANSPORTATION AND COMMUNICATIONS

JORDAN - CONSTRUCTION INDUSTRY

M.E. Sharpe, 80 Business Park Drive, Armonk, New York 10504 (800) 541-6563; *The Illustrated Book of World Rankings.*

St. Martin's Press, Inc., 175 Fifth Avenue, New York, New York 10010 (800) 221-7945; *The Statesman's Year-Book.*

Statistical Office of the United Nations, Publishing Service, New York, New York 10017 (800) 253-9646; *Statistical Yearbook.*

JORDAN - CONSUMER PRICE INDEX

Euromonitor International, Inc., 122 South Michigan Avenue, Suite 1200, Chicago, Illinois 60603 (800) 577-EURO; *World Marketing Data and Statistics.*

Europa Publications Limited, 18 Bedford Square, London, WC1B 3JN, England; *The Europa World Year Book.*

Statistical Office of the United Nations, Publishing Service, New York, New York 10017 (800) 253-9646; *Statistical Yearbook.*

JORDAN - CONSUMER PRICES

International Labour Office, I.L.O. Publications, 1828 K Street, NW, Suite 801, Washington, D.C. 20036 (301) 638-3152; *Yearbook of Labour Statistics.*

International Monetary Fund, 700 Nineteenth Street, NW, Washington, D.C. 20431 (202) 623-7000; *International Financial Statistics.*

JORDAN - CONSUMPTION

The World Bank, 1818 H Street, NW, Washington, D.C. 20433 (202) 477-1234; *World Development Report.*

JORDAN - COPPER PRODUCTION - See JORDAN - MINING AND MINERAL PRODUCTS

JORDAN - CORN PRODUCTION - See JORDAN - CROPS

JORDAN - CORPORATE TAXES - See JORDAN - TAXATION

JORDAN - COTTON PRODUCTION - See JORDAN - CROPS

JORDAN - CRIME

International Criminal Police Organization (INTERPOL), 26 rue Armengaud, 92210 Saint Cloud, France; *International Crime Statistics.*

Yale University Press, Yale Station, New Haven, Connecticut 06520 (800) 987-7323; *Violence and Crime in Cross-National Perspective.*

JORDAN - CROPS

Europa Publications Limited, 18 Bedford Square, London, WC1B 3JN, England; *The Europa World Year Book.*

Food and Agricultural Organization of the United Nations (FAO), Via delle Terme di Caracalla, 00100 Rome, Italy (Telephone Number in U.S. (202) 653-2400); *Production Yearbook;* and *The State of Food and Agriculture.*

M.E. Sharpe, 80 Business Park Drive, Armonk, New York 10504 (800) 541-6563; *The Illustrated Book of World Rankings.*

St. Martin's Press, Inc., 175 Fifth Avenue, New York, New York 10010 (800) 221-7945; *The Statesman's Year-Book.*

Statistical Office of the United Nations, Publishing Service, New York, New York 10017 (800) 253-9646; *Statistical Yearbook.*

United Nations Conference on Trade and Development, Central Statistical Service, Palais des Nations, Geneva, Switzerland (Telephone in U.S. (800) 253-9646); *UNCTAD Commodity Yearbook.*

JORDAN - CUSTOMS DUTIES

International Monetary Fund, 700 Nineteenth Street, NW, Washington, D.C. 20431 (202) 623-7000; *Government Finance Statistics Yearbook.*

St. Martin's Press, Inc., 175 Fifth Avenue, New York, New York 10010 (800) 221-7945; *The Statesman's Year-Book.*

JORDAN - DAIRY PRODUCTS

Economic Commission for Western Asia, Post Office Box 27, Baghdad, Iraq; *Statistical Abstract of Western Asia.*

Food and Agricultural Organization of the United Nations (FAO), Via delle Terme di Caracalla, 00100 Rome, Italy (Telephone Number in U.S. (202) 653-2400); *Production Yearbook;* and *The State of Food and Agriculture.*

M.E. Sharpe, 80 Business Park Drive, Armonk, New York 10504 (800) 541-6563; *The Illustrated Book of World Rankings.*

St. Martin's Press, Inc., 175 Fifth Avenue, New York, New York 10010 (800) 221-7945; *The Statesman's Year-Book.*

Statistical Office of the United Nations, Publishing Service, New York, New York 10017 (800) 253-9646; *Statistical Yearbook.*

JORDAN - DEATH RATES - See JORDAN - MORTALITY

JORDAN - DEFENSE EXPENDITURES - See JORDAN - MILITARY

JORDAN - DEMOGRAPHY

The Economist Intelligence Unit, 111 West 57th Street, New York, New York 10019 (800) 938-4685; *The World Market Atlas.*

Euromonitor International, Inc., 122 South Michigan Avenue, Suite 1200, Chicago, Illinois 60603 (800) 577-EURO; *International Marketing Data and Statistics;*

World Marketing Data and Statistics; and *The World Economic Factbook.*

Federal Statistical Office, Gustav-Stresemann - Ring 11, D-6200, Wiesbaden, Germany; *Jordanien.*

M.E. Sharpe, 80 Business Park Drive, Armonk, New York 10504 (800) 541-6563; *The Illustrated Book of World Rankings.*

Statistical Office of the United Nations, Publishing Service, New York, New York 10017 (800) 253-9646; *Human Development Report.*

JORDAN - DEVELOPMENT ASSISTANCE

Statistical Office of the United Nations, Publishing Service, New York, New York 10017 (800) 253-9646; *Statistical Yearbook.*

JORDAN - DIAMOND PRODUCTION - See JORDAN - MINING AND MINERAL PRODUCTS

JORDAN - DISCOUNT RATES - See JORDAN - BANKING

JORDAN - DISEASES - See JORDAN - HEALTH

JORDAN - DIVORCE RATES

M.E. Sharpe, 80 Business Park Drive, Armonk, New York 10504 (800) 541-6563; *The Illustrated Book of World Rankings.*

Statistical Office of the United Nations, Publishing Service, New York, New York 10017 (800) 253-9646; *Demographic Yearbook;* and *Statistical Yearbook.*

JORDAN - ECONOMY

Central Intelligence Agency, Washington, D.C. 20505 (703) 482-1100, www.cia.gov; *The World Factbook.*

The Economist Intelligence Unit, 111 West 57th Street, New York, New York 10019 (800) 938-4685; *Jordan Country Report.*

Euromonitor International, Inc., 122 South Michigan Avenue, Suite 1200, Chicago, Illinois 60603 (800) 577-EURO; *International Marketing Data and Statistics; World Marketing Data and Statistics;* and *The World Economic Factbook.*

Europa Publications Limited, 18 Bedford Square, London, WC1B 3JN, England; *The Europa World Year Book.*

Federal Statistical Office, Gustav-Stresemann - Ring 11, D-6200, Wiesbaden, Germany; *Jordanien.*

M.E. Sharpe, 80 Business Park Drive, Armonk, New York 10504 (800) 541-6563;

The Illustrated Book of World Rankings.

St. Martin's Press, Inc., 175 Fifth Avenue, New York, New York 10010 (800) 221-7945; *The Statesman's Year-Book.*

Statistical Office of the United Nations, Publishing Service, New York, New York 10017 (800) 253-9646; *World Statistics Pocketbook.*

The World Bank, 1818 H Street, NW, Washington, D.C. 20433 (202) 477-1234; *The World Bank Atlas;* and *World Development Report.*

JORDAN - EDUCATION

Economic Commission for Western Asia, Post Office Box 27, Baghdad, Iraq; *Statistical Abstract of Western Asia.*

The Economist Intelligence Unit, 111 West 57th Street, New York, New York 10019 (800) 938-4685; *The World Market Atlas.*

Euromonitor International, Inc., 122 South Michigan Avenue, Suite 1200, Chicago, Illinois 60603 (800) 577-EURO; *International Marketing Data and Statistics;* and *World Marketing Data and Statistics.*

Europa Publications Limited, 18 Bedford Square, London, WC1B 3JN, England; *The Europa World Year Book.*

Federal Statistical Office, Gustav - Stresemann - Ring 11, D-6200 Wiesbaden, Germany; *Jordanien.*

M.E. Sharpe, 80 Business Park Drive, Armonk, New York 10504 (800) 541-6563; *The Illustrated Book of World Rankings.*

St. Martin's Press, Inc., 175 Fifth Avenue, New York, New York 10010 (800) 221-7945; *The Statesman's Year-Book.*

Statistical Office of the United Nations, Publishing Service, New York, New York 10017 (800) 253-9646; *Human Development Report.*

United Nations Educational, Scientific and Cultural Organization (UNESCO), 7 Place de Fontenoy, F-75700 Paris, France (Telephone Number in U.S. (212) 963-5981); *Statistical Yearbook.*

The World Bank, 1818 H Street, NW, Washington, D.C. 20433 (202) 477-1234; *World Development Report.*

JORDAN - EGG PRODUCTION AND CONSUMPTION - See JORDAN -DAIRY PRODUCTS

JORDAN - EGGPLANT PRODUCTION - See JORDAN - CROPS

JORDAN - ELECTRICITY

Central Intelligence Agency, Washington, D.C. 20505 (703) 482-1100, www.cia.gov; *The World Factbook.*

M.E. Sharpe, 80 Business Park Drive, Armonk, New York 10504 (800) 541-6563; *The Illustrated Book of World Rankings.*

Penn Well Publishing Company, 1421 South Sheridan Road, Post Office Box 1260, Tulsa, Oklahoma 74101 (800) 752-9764; *International Energy Statistics Sourcebook.*

St. Martin's Press, Inc., 175 Fifth Avenue, New York, New York 10010 (800) 221-7945; *The Statesman's Year-Book.*

Statistical Office of the United Nations, Publishing Service, New York, New York 10017 (800) 253-9646; *Human Development Report;* and *Statistical Yearbook.*

JORDAN - EMPLOYMENT

Economic Commission for Western Asia, Post Office Box 27, Baghdad, Iraq; *Statistical Abstract of Western Asia.*

Euromonitor International, Inc., 122 South Michigan Avenue, Suite 1200, Chicago, Illinois 60603 (800) 577-EURO; *International Marketing Data and Statistics.*

Federal Statistical Office, Gustav - Stresemann - Ring 11, D-6200 Wiesbaden, Germany; *Jordanien.*

International Labour Office, I.L.O. Publications, 1828 K Street, NW, Suite 801, Washington, D.C. 20036 (301) 638-3152; *Yearbook of Labour Statistics.*

M.E. Sharpe, 80 Business Park Drive, Armonk, New York 10504 (800) 541-6563; *The Illustrated Book of World Rankings.*

Statistical Office of the United Nations, Publishing Service, New York, New York 10017 (800) 253-9646; *Bulletin of Industrial Statistics for the Arab Countries;* and *Statistical Yearbook.*

JORDAN - ENERGY

Economic Commission for Western Asia, Post Office Box 27, Baghdad, Iraq; *Statistical Abstract of Western Asia.*

Euromonitor International, Inc., 122 South Michigan Avenue, Suite 1200, Chicago, Illinois 60603 (800) 577-EURO; *International Marketing Data and Statistics; World Marketing Data and Statistics;* and *The World Economic Factbook.*

Food and Agricultural Organization of the United Nations (FAO), Via delle Terme di Caracalla, 00100 Rome, Italy (Telephone

Number in U.S. (202) 653-2400); *The State of Food and Agriculture.*

M.E. Sharpe, 80 Business Park Drive, Armonk, New York 10504 (800) 541-6563; *The Illustrated Book of World Rankings.*

Penn Well Publishing Company, 1421 South Sheridan Road, Post Office Box 1260, Tulsa, Oklahoma 74101 (800) 752-9764; *International Energy Statistics Sourcebook.*

St. Martin's Press, Inc., 175 Fifth Avenue, New York, New York 10010 (800) 221-7945; *The Statesman's Year-Book.*

Statistical Office of the United Nations, Publishing Service, New York, New York 10017 (800) 253-9646; *Energy Statistics Yearbook; Human Development Report; World Statistics Pocketbook;* and *Statistical Yearbook.*

The World Bank, 1818 H Street, NW, Washington, D.C. 20433 (202) 477-1234; *The World Bank Atlas;* and *World Development Report.*

JORDAN - ENVIRONMENT

The Economist Intelligence Unit, 111 West 57th Street, New York, New York 10019 (800) 938-4685; *Jordan Country Report.*

Statistical Office of the United Nations, Publishing Service, New York, New York 10017 (800) 253-9646; *World Statistics Pocketbook.*

JORDAN - EXCHANGE RATES

Central Intelligence Agency, Washington, D.C. 20505 (703) 482-1100, www.cia.gov; *The World Factbook.*

Euromonitor International, Inc., 122 South Michigan Avenue, Suite 1200, Chicago, Illinois 60603 (800) 577-EURO; *International Marketing Data and Statistics;* and *The World Economic Factbook.*

Europa Publications Limited, 18 Bedford Square, London, WC1B 3JN, England; *The Europa World Year Book.*

International Civil Aviation Organization, 999 University Street, Montreal, Quebec, Canada H3C 5H7 (514) 954-8219; *Civil Aviation Statistics of the World.*

International Monetary Fund, 700 Nineteenth Street, NW, Washington, D.C. 20431 (202) 623-7000; *International Financial Statistics.*

Statistical Office of the United Nations, Publishing Service, New York, New York 10017 (800) 253-9646; *Bulletin of Industrial Statistics for the Arab Countries; World*

Statistics Pocketbook; and *Statistical Yearbook.*

JORDAN - EXCISE TAXES - See JORDAN - TAXATION

JORDAN - EXPORTS

Central Intelligence Agency, Washington, D.C. 20505 (703) 482-1100, www.cia.gov; *The World Factbook.*

Economic Commission for Western Asia, Post Office Box 27, Baghdad, Iraq; *Statistical Abstract of Western Asia.*

The Economist Intelligence Unit, 111 West 57th Street, New York, New York 10019 (800) 938-4685; *Jordan Country Report;* and *The World Market Atlas.*

Euromonitor International, Inc., 122 South Michigan Avenue, Suite 1200, Chicago, Illinois 60603 (800) 577-EURO; *International Marketing Data and Statistics;* and *The World Economic Factbook.*

Europa Publications Limited, 18 Bedford Square, London, WC1B 3JN, England; *The Europa World Year Book.*

Food and Agricultural Organization of the United Nations (FAO), Via delle Terme di Caracalla, 00100 Rome, Italy (Telephone Number in U.S. (202) 653-2400); *The State of Food and Agriculture.*

International Monetary Fund, 700 Nineteenth Street, NW, Washington, D.C. 20431 (202) 623-7000; *Direction of Trade Statistics; Government Finance Statistics Yearbook;* and *International Financial Statistics.*

St. Martin's Press, Inc., 175 Fifth Avenue, New York, New York 10010 (800) 221-7945; *The Statesman's Year-Book.*

Statistical Office of the United Nations, Publishing Service, New York, New York 10017 (800) 253-9646; *Bulletin of Industrial Statistics for the Arab Countries.*

United Nations Conference on Trade and Development (UNCTAD), New York, New York 10017 (800) 253-9646; *Handbook of International Trade and Development Statistics.*

The World Bank, 1818 H Street, NW, Washington, D.C. 20433 (202) 477-1234; *World Development Report.*

JORDAN - EXTERNAL INDEBTEDNESS

The World Bank, 1818 H Street, NW, Washington, D.C. 20433 (202) 477-1234; *World Development Report.*

JORDAN - EXTERNAL TRADE

Euromonitor International, Inc., 122 South Michigan Avenue, Suite 1200, Chicago, Illinois 60603 (800) 577-EURO; *World Marketing Data and Statistics.*

Food and Agricultural Organization of the United Nations (FAO), Via delle Terme di Caracalla, 00100 Rome, Italy (Telephone Number in U.S. (202) 653-2400); *The State of Food and Agriculture;* and *Trade Yearbook.*

Statistical Office of the United Nations, Publishing Service, New York, New York 10017 (800) 253-9646; *Statistical Yearbook.*

JORDAN - FARM CROPS - See JORDAN - CROPS

JORDAN - FEMALE WORKING POPULATION - See JORDAN - EMPLOYMENT

JORDAN - FERTILITY RATES

Central Intelligence Agency, Washington, D.C. 20505 (703) 482-1100, www.cia.gov; *The World Factbook.*

M.E. Sharpe, 80 Business Park Drive, Armonk, New York 10504 (800) 541-6563; *The Illustrated Book of World Rankings.*

Statistical Office of the United Nations, Publishing Service, New York, New York 10017 (800) 253-9646; *Human Development Report.*

The World Bank, 1818 H Street, NW, Washington, D.C. 20433 (202) 477-1234; *The World Bank Atlas;* and *World Development Report.*

JORDAN - FERTILIZER

Food and Agricultural Organization of the United Nations (FAO), Via delle Terme di Caracalla, 00100, Rome, Italy (Telephone Number in U.S. (202) 653-2400); *Fertilizer Yearbook;* and *The State of Food and Agriculture.*

Statistical Office of the United Nations, Publishing Service, New York, New York 10017 (800) 253-9646; *Statistical Yearbook.*

JORDAN - FETAL MORTALITY - See JORDAN - MORTALITY

JORDAN - FINANCE

Economic Commission for Western Asia, Post Office Box 27, Baghdad, Iraq; *Statistical Abstract of Western Asia.*

The Economist Intelligence Unit, 111 West 57th Street, New York, New York 10019 (800) 938-4685; *Jordan Country Report.*

Europa Publications Limited, 18

Bedford Square, London, WC1B 3JN, England; *The Europa World Year Book.*

Federal Statistical Office, Gustav - Stresemann - Ring 11, D-6200 Wiesbaden, Germany; *Jordanien.*

International Monetary Fund, 700 Nineteenth Street, NW, Washington, D.C. 20431 (202) 623-7000; *Government Finance Statistics Yearbook;* and *International Financial Statistics.*

M.E. Sharpe, 80 Business Park Drive, Armonk, New York 10504 (800) 541-6563; *The Illustrated Book of World Rankings.*

St. Martin's Press, Inc., 175 Fifth Avenue, New York, New York 10010 (800) 221-7945; *The Statesman's Year-Book.*

JORDAN - FISHERIES

Economic Commission for Western Asia, Post Office Box 27, Baghdad, Iraq; *Statistical Abstract of Western Asia.*

Federal Statistical Office, Gustav - Stresemann - Ring 11, D-6200 Wiesbaden, Germany; *Jordanien.*

Food and Agricultural Organization of the United Nations (FAO), Via delle Terme di Caracalla, 00100 Rome, Italy (Telephone Number in U.S. (202) 653-2400); *The State of Food and Agriculture;* and *Yearbook of Fishery Statistics.*

M.E. Sharpe, 80 Business Park Drive, Armonk, New York 10504 (800) 541-6563; *The Illustrated Book of World Rankings.*

United Nations Conference on Trade and Development, Central Statistical Service, Palais des Nations, Geneva, Switzerland (Telephone in U.S. (800) 253-9646); *UNCTAD Commodity Yearbook.*

JORDAN - FLOUR PRODUCTION

Statistical Office of the United Nations, Publishing Service, New York, New York 10017 (800) 253-9646; *Statistical Yearbook.*

JORDAN - FOOD

Food and Agricultural Organization of the United Nations (FAO), Via delle Terme di Caracalla, 00100 Rome, Italy (Telephone Number in U.S. (202) 653-2400); *Production Yearbook;* and *The State of Food and Agriculture.*

Statistical Office of the United Nations, Publishing Service, New York, New York 10017 (800) 253-9646; *Human Development Report.*

United Nations Conference on Trade and Development, Central Statistical Service, Palais des Nations, Geneva,

Switzerland (Telephone in U.S. (800) 253-9646); *UNCTAD Commodity Yearbook.*

JORDAN - FOREIGN DEBT

International Monetary Fund, 700 Nineteenth Street, NW, Washington, D.C. 20431 (202) 623-7000; *Government Finance Statistics Yearbook.*

St. Martin's Press, Inc., 175 Fifth Avenue, New York, New York 10010 (800) 221-7945; *The Statesman's Year-Book.*

JORDAN - FOREIGN TRADE

Economic Commission for Western Asia, Post Office Box 27, Baghdad, Iraq; *Statistical Abstract of Western Asia.*

The Economist Intelligence Unit, 111 West 57th Street, New York, New York 10019 (800) 938-4685; *Jordan Country Report.*

Euromonitor International, Inc., 122 South Michigan Avenue, Suite 1200, Chicago, Illinois 60603 (800) 577-EURO; *International Marketing Data and Statistics;* and *The World Economic Factbook.*

Europa Publications Limited, 18 Bedford Square, London, WC1B 3JN, England; *The Europa World Year Book.*

Federal Statistical Office, Gustav - Stresemann - Ring 11, D-6200 Wiesbaden, Germany; *Jordanien.*

Food and Agricultural Organization of the United Nations (FAO), Via delle Terme di Caracalla, 00100 Rome, Italy (Telephone Number in U.S. (202) 653-2400); *The State of Food and Agriculture.*

International Monetary Fund, 700 Nineteenth Street, NW, Washington, D.C. 20431 (202) 623-7000; *International Financial Statistics.*

M.E. Sharpe, 80 Business Park Drive, Armonk, New York 10504 (800) 541-6563; *The Illustrated Book of World Rankings.*

St. Martin's Press, Inc., 175 Fifth Avenue, New York, New York 10010 (800) 221-7945; *The Statesman's Year-Book.*

Statistical Office of the United Nations, Publishing Service, New York, New York 10017 (800) 253-9646; *Bulletin of Industrial Statistics for the Arab Countries; International Trade Statistics Yearbook;* and *Statistical Yearbook.*

United Nations Conference on Trade and Development, Central Statistical Service, Palais des Nations, Geneva, Switzerland (Telephone in U.S. (800) 253-9646); *UNCTAD Commodity Yearbook.*

The World Bank, 1818 H Street, NW, Washington, D.C. 20433 (202) 477-1234; *World Development Report.*

JORDAN - FORESTRY AND FOREST PRODUCTS

Europa Publications Limited, 18 Bedford Square, London, WC1B 3JN, England; *The Europa World Year Book.*

Federal Statistical Office, Gustav - Stresemann - Ring 11, D-6200 Wiesbaden, Germany; *Jordan.*

Food and Agricultural Organization of the United Nations (FAO), Via delle Terme di Caracalla, 00100 Rome, Italy (Telephone Number in U.S. (202) 653-2400); *The State of Food and Agriculture;* and *Yearbook of Forest Products.*

M.E. Sharpe, 80 Business Park Drive, Armonk, New York 10504 (800) 541-6563; *The Illustrated Book of World Rankings.*

St. Martin's Press, Inc., 175 Fifth Avenue, New York, New York 10010 (800) 221-7945; *The Statesman's Year-Book.*

Statistical Office of the United Nations, Publishing Service, New York, New York 10017 (800) 253-9646; *Statistical Yearbook.*

United Nations Conference on Trade and Development, Central Statistical Service, Palais des Nations, Geneva, Switzerland (Telephone in U.S. (800) 253-9646); *UNCTAD Commodity Yearbook.*

United Nations Educational, Scientific and Cultural Organization (UNESCO), 7 Place de Fontenoy, F-75700 Paris, France (Telephone Number in U.S. (212) 963-5981); *Statistical Yearbook.*

The World Bank, 1818 H Street, NW, Washington, D.C. 20433 (202) 477-1234; *World Development Report.*

JORDAN - GAS PRODUCTION - See JORDAN - MINING AND MINERAL PRODUCTS

JORDAN - GENERAL INDUSTRIAL STATISTICS - See JORDAN - INDUSTRY

JORDAN - GENERAL MORTALITY - See JORDAN - MORTALITY

JORDAN - GEOGRAPHIC DATA

M.E. Sharpe, 80 Business Park Drive, Armonk, New York 10504 (800) 541-6563; *The Illustrated Book of World Rankings.*

JORDAN - GOATS - See JORDAN - LIVESTOCK AND POULTRY

JORDAN - GOLD HOLDINGS

International Monetary Fund, 700 Nineteenth Street, NW, Washington, D.C. 20431 (202) 623-7000; *International Financial Statistics.*

Statistical Office of the United Nations, Publishing Service, New York, New York 10017 (800) 253-9646; *Statistical Yearbook.*

JORDAN - GOLD PRODUCTION AND CONSUMPTION - See JORDAN -MINING AND MINERAL PRODUCTS

JORDAN - GOVERNMENT

Central Intelligence Agency, Washington, D.C. 20505 (703) 482-1100, www.cia.gov; *The World Factbook.*

Economic Commission for Western Asia, Post Office Box 27, Baghdad, Iraq; *Statistical Abstract of Western Asia.*

Europa Publications Limited, 18 Bedford Square, London, WC1B 3JN, England; *The Europa World Year Book.*

International Monetary Fund, 700 Nineteenth Street, NW, Washington, D.C. 20431 (202) 623-7000; *Government Finance Statistics Yearbook;* and *International Financial Statistics.*

St. Martin's Press, Inc., 175 Fifth Avenue, New York, New York 10010 (800) 221-7945; *The Statesman's Year-Book.*

Statistical Office of the United Nations, Publishing Service, New York, New York 10017 (800) 253-9646; *National Accounts Statistics;* and *Statistical Yearbook.*

The World Bank, 1818 H Street, NW, Washington, D.C. 20433 (202) 477-1234; *World Development Report.*

JORDAN - GRAIN PRODUCTION - See JORDAN - CROPS

JORDAN - GRANTS

International Monetary Fund, 700 Nineteenth Street, NW, Washington, D.C. 20431 (202) 623-7000; *Government Finance Statistics Yearbook.*

JORDAN - GREEN PEPPER AND CHILIE PRODUCTION - See JORDAN - CROPS

JORDAN - GROSS DOMESTIC PRODUCT

Economic Commission for Western Asia, Post Office Box 27, Baghdad, Iraq; *Statistical Abstract of Western Asia.*

The Economist Intelligence Unit, 111 West 57th Street, New York, New York 10019 (800) 938-4685; *Jordan Country Report;* and *The World Market Atlas.*

Euromonitor International, Inc., 122 South Michigan Avenue, Suite 1200, Chicago, Illinois 60603 (800) 577-EURO; *International Marketing Data and Statistics;* and *The World Economic Factbook.*

Europa Publications Limited, 18 Bedford Square, London, WC1B 3JN, England; *The Europa World Year Book.*

M.E. Sharpe, 80 Business Park Drive, Armonk, New York 10504 (800) 541-6563; *The Illustrated Book of World Rankings.*

Statistical Office of the United Nations, Publishing Service, New York, New York 10017 (800) 253-9646; *Bulletin of Industrial Statistics for the Arab Countries; Human Development Report; National Accounts Statistics;* and *Statistical Yearbook.*

The World Bank, 1818 H Street, NW, Washington, D.C. 20433 (202) 477-1234; *World Development Report.*

JORDAN - GROSS NATIONAL PRODUCT

Euromonitor International, Inc., 122 South Michigan Avenue, Suite 1200, Chicago, Illinois 60603 (800) 577-EURO; *International Marketing Data and Statistics.*

St. Martin's Press, Inc., 175 Fifth Avenue, New York, New York 10010 (800) 221-7945; *The Statesman's Year-Book.*

U.S. Arms Control and Disarmament Agency, 320 Twenty-first Street, NW, Washington, D.C. 20451 (202) 647-8677; *World Military Expenditures and Arms Transfers.*

The World Bank, 1818 H Street, NW, Washington, D.C. 20433 (202) 477-1234; *The World Bank Atlas;* and *World Development Report.*

JORDAN - GROUNDNUT PRODUCTION - See JORDAN - CROPS

JORDAN - HEALTH

Economic Commission for Western Asia, Post Office Box 27, Baghdad, Iraq; *Statistical Abstract of Western Asia.*

Euromonitor International, Inc., 122 South Michigan Avenue, Suite 1200, Chicago, Illinois 60603 (800) 577-EURO; *World Marketing Data and Statistics.*

Federal Statistical Office, Gustav - Stresemann - Ring 11, D-6200 Wiesbaden, Germany; *Jordanien.*

M.E. Sharpe, 80 Business Park Drive, Armonk, New York 10504 (800) 541-6563; *The Illustrated Book of World Rankings.*

St. Martin's Press, Inc., 175 Fifth Avenue, New York, New York 10010 (800) 221-7945; *The Statesman's Year-Book.*

Statistical Office of the United Nations, Publishing Service, New York, New York 10017 (800) 253-9646; *Human Development Report;* and *Statistical Yearbook.*

United Nations Children's Fund (UNICEF), 3 United Nations Plaza, New York, New York 10017 (800) 253-9646; *State of the World's Children.*

The World Bank, 1818 H Street, NW, Washington, D.C. 20433 (202) 477-1234; *World Development Report.*

World Health Organization, Office of Publications, 20 Avenue Appia, CH-1211 Geneva 27, Switzerland (Telephone Number in U.S. (518) 436-9686); *World Health Statistics Annual.*

JORDAN - HEALTH EXPENDITURES

International Monetary Fund, 700 Nineteenth Street, NW, Washington, D.C. 20431 (202) 623-7000; *Government Finance Statistics Yearbook.*

JORDAN - HIDE PRODUCTION

Food and Agricultural Organization of the United Nations (FAO), Via delle Terme di Caracalla, 00100 Rome, Italy (Telephone Number in U.S. (202) 653-2400); *Production Yearbook.*

JORDAN - HIGHWAYS

Central Intelligence Agency, Washington, D.C. 20505 (703) 482-1100, www.cia.gov; *The World Factbook.*

Economic Commission for Western Asia, Post Office Box 27, Baghdad, Iraq; *Statistical Abstract of Western Asia.*

International Road Federation, 2600 Virginia Avenue, NW, Washington, D.C. 20037 (202) 338-4641; *World Road Statistics.*

St. Martin's Press, Inc., 175 Fifth Avenue, New York, New York 10010 (800) 221-7945; *The Statesman's Year-Book.*

JORDAN - HORSES - See JORDAN - LIVESTOCK AND POULTRY

JORDAN - HOURS OF WORK - See JORDAN - EMPLOYMENT

JORDAN - HOUSING AND HOUSING UNITS

Euromonitor International, Inc., 122 South Michigan Avenue, Suite 1200, Chicago, Illinois 60603 (800) 577-EURO; *World Marketing Data and Statistics.*

M.E. Sharpe, 80 Business Park Drive, Armonk, New York 10504 (800) 541-6563; *The Illustrated Book of World Rankings.*

JORDAN - HOUSING EXPENDITURES

International Monetary Fund, 700 Nineteenth Street, NW, Washington, D.C. 20431 (202) 623-7000; *Government Finance Statistics Yearbook.*

JORDAN - ILLITERATE POPULATION

Central Intelligence Agency, Washington, D.C. 20505 (703) 482-1100, www.cia.gov; *The World Factbook.*

The Economist Intelligence Unit, 111 West 57th Street, New York, New York 10019 (800) 938-4685; *The World Market Atlas.*

Euromonitor International, Inc., 122 South Michigan Avenue, Suite 1200, Chicago, Illinois 60603 (800) 577-EURO; *The World Economic Factbook.*

Statistical Office of the United Nations, Publishing Service, New York, New York 10017 (800) 253-9646; *Human Development Report.*

United Nations Educational, Scientific and Cultural Organization (UNESCO), 7 Place de Fontenoy, F-75700 Paris, France (Telephone Number in U.S. (212) 963-5981); *Statistical Yearbook.*

JORDAN - IMPORTS

Central Intelligence Agency, Washington, D.C. 20505 (703) 482-1100, www.cia.gov; *The World Factbook.*

Economic Commission for Western Asia, Post Office Box 27, Baghdad, Iraq; *Statistical Abstract of Western Asia.*

The Economist Intelligence Unit, 111 West 57th Street, New York, New York 10019 (800) 938-4685; *Jordan Country Report;* and *The World Market Atlas.*

Euromonitor International, Inc., 122 South Michigan Avenue, Suite 1200, Chicago, Illinois 60603 (800) 577-EURO; *International Marketing Data and Statistics;* and *The World Economic Factbook.*

Europa Publications Limited, 18 Bedford Square, London, WC1B 3JN, England; *The Europa World Year Book.*

Food and Agricultural Organization of the United Nations (FAO), Via delle Terme di Caracalla, 00100 Rome, Italy (Telephone Number in U.S. (202) 653-2400); *The State of Food and Agriculture.*

International Monetary Fund, 700 Nineteenth Street, NW, Washington,

D.C. 20431 (202) 623-7000; *Direction of Trade Statistics; Government Finance Statistics Yearbook;* and *International Financial Statistics.*

St. Martin's Press, Inc., 175 Fifth Avenue, New York, New York 10010 (800) 221-7945; *The Statesman's Year-Book.*

Statistical Office of the United Nations, Publishing Service, New York, New York 10017 (800) 253-9646; *Bulletin of Industrial Statistics for the Arab Countries.*

United Nations Conference on Trade and Development (UNCTAD), New York, New York 10017 (800) 253-9646; *Handbook of International Trade and Development Statistics.*

The World Bank, 1818 H Street, NW, Washington, D.C. 20433 (202) 477-1234; *World Development Report.*

JORDAN - INCOME TAXES - See JORDAN - TAXATION

JORDAN - INDUSTRY

Central Intelligence Agency, Washington, D.C. 20505 (703) 482-1100, www.cia.gov; *The World Factbook.*

The Economist Intelligence Unit, 111 West 57th Street, New York, New York 10019 (800) 938-4685; *Jordan Country Report.*

Euromonitor International, Inc., 122 South Michigan Avenue, Suite 1200, Chicago, Illinois 60603 (800) 577-EURO; *International Marketing Data and Statistics; World Marketing Data and Statistics;* and *The World Economic Factbook.*

Europa Publications Limited, 18 Bedford Square, London, WC1B 3JN, England; *The Europa World Year Book.*

Federal Statistical Office, Gustav - Stresemann - Ring 11, D-6200 Wiesbaden, Germany; *Jordanien.*

International Labour Office, I.L.O. Publications, 1828 L Street, NW, Washington, D.C. 20036 (301) 638-3152; *Yearbook of Labour Statistics.*

M.E. Sharpe, 80 Business Park Drive, Armonk, New York 10504 (800) 541-6563; *The Illustrated Book of World Rankings.*

St. Martin's Press, Inc., 175 Fifth Avenue, New York, New York 10010 (800) 221-7945; *The Statesman's Year-Book.*

Statistical Office of the United Nations, Publishing Service, New York, New York 10017 (800) 253-9646; *Bulletin of Industrial Statistics for the Arab Countries;* and *Industrial Commodity Statistics Yearbook.*

JORDAN - INFANT AND MATERNAL MORTALITY - See JORDAN - MORTALITY

JORDAN - INTERNATIONAL LIQUIDITY

International Monetary Fund, 700 Nineteenth Street, NW, Washington, D.C. 20431 (202) 623-7000; *International Financial Statistics.*

JORDAN - INTERNATIONAL RESERVES EXCLUDING GOLD

Statistical Office of the United Nations, Publishing Service, New York, New York 10017 (800) 253-9646; *Statistical Yearbook.*

JORDAN - INVESTMENTS

International Monetary Fund, 700 Nineteenth Street, NW, Washington, D.C. 20431 (202) 623-7000; *International Financial Statistics.*

JORDAN - IRON ORE PRODUCTION AND CONSUMPTION - See JORDAN - MINING AND MINERAL PRODUCTS

JORDAN - IRRIGATION

Euromonitor International, Inc., 122 South Michigan Avenue, Suite 1200, Chicago, Illinois 60603 (800) 577-EURO; *International Marketing Data and Statistics.*

JORDAN - LABOR

Central Intelligence Agency, Washington, D.C. 20505 (703) 482-1100, www.cia.gov; *The World Factbook.*

Economic Commission for Western Asia, Post Office Box 27, Baghdad, Iraq; *Statistical Abstract of Western Asia.*

Euromonitor International, Inc., 122 South Michigan Avenue, Suite 1200, Chicago, Illinois 60603 (800) 577-EURO; *International Marketing Data and Statistics;* and *World Marketing Data and Statistics..*

Europa Publications Limited, 18 Bedford Square, London, WC1B 3JN, England; *The Europa World Year Book.*

Food and Agricultural Organization of the United Nations (FAO), Via delle Terme di Caracalla, 00100 Rome, Italy (Telephone Number in U.S. (202) 653-2400); *The State of Food and Agriculture.*

International Labour Office, I.L.O. Publications, 1828 L Street, NW, Washington, D.C. 20036 (301) 638-3152; *Yearbook of Labour Statistics.*

M.E. Sharpe, 80 Business Park Drive, Armonk, New York 10504 (800) 541-6563; *The Illustrated Book of World Rankings.*

St. Martin's Press, Inc., 175 Fifth Avenue, New York, New York 10010 (800) 221-7945; *The Statesman's Year-Book.*

Statistical Office of the United Nations, Publishing Service, New York, New York 10017 (800) 253-9646; *Human Development Report.*

The World Bank, 1818 H Street, NW, Washington, D.C. 20433 (202) 477-1234; *The World Bank Atlas;* and *World Development Report.*

JORDAN - LAND USE

Central Intelligence Agency, Washington, D.C. 20505 (703) 482-1100, www.cia.gov; *The World Factbook.*

Economic Commission for Western Asia, Post Office Box 27, Baghdad, Iraq; *Statistical Abstract of Western Asia.*

Euromonitor International, Inc., 122 South Michigan Avenue, Suite 1200, Chicago, Illinois 60603 (800) 577-EURO; *International Marketing Data and Statistics.*

Food and Agricultural Organization of the United Nations (FAO), Via delle Terme di Caracalla, 00100 Rome, Italy (Telephone Number in U.S. (202) 653-2400); *Production Yearbook.*

The World Bank, 1818 H Street, NW, Washington, D.C. 20433 (202) 477-1234; *World Development Report.*

JORDAN - LIBRARIES

M.E. Sharpe, 80 Business Park Drive, Armonk, New York 10504 (800) 541-6563; *The Illustrated Book of World Rankings.*

United Nations Educational, Scientific and Cultural Organization (UNESCO), 7 Place de Fontenoy, F-75700 Paris, France (Telephone Number in U.S. (212) 963-5981); *Statistical Yearbook.*

JORDAN - LIFE EXPECTANCY

Central Intelligence Agency, Washington, D.C. 20505 (703) 482-1100, www.cia.gov; *The World Factbook.*

Euromonitor International, Inc., 122 South Michigan Avenue, Suite 1200, Chicago, Illinois 60603 (800) 577-EURO; *The World Economic Factbook.*

St. Martin's Press, Inc., 175 Fifth Avenue, New York, New York 10010 (800) 221-7945; *The Statesman's Year-Book.*

Statistical Office of the United Nations, Publishing Service, New York, New York 10017 (800) 253-9646; *Human Development Report;* and *World Statistics Pocketbook.*

The World Bank, 1818 H Street, NW, Washington, D.C. 20433 (202) 477-1234; *The World Bank Atlas;* and *World Development Report.*

JORDAN - LITERACY RATE

Euromonitor International, Inc., 122 South Michigan Avenue, Suite 1200, Chicago, Illinois 60603 (800) 577-EURO; *World Marketing Data and Statistics.*

JORDAN - LIVESTOCK AND POULTRY

Economic Commission for Western Asia, Post Office Box 27, Baghdad, Iraq; *Statistical Abstract of Western Asia.*

Euromonitor International, Inc., 122 South Michigan Avenue, Suite 1200, Chicago, Illinois 60603 (800) 577-EURO; *International Marketing Data and Statistics.*

Europa Publications Limited, 18 Bedford Square, London, WC1B 3JN, England; *The Europa World Year Book.*

Food and Agricultural Organization of the United Nations (FAO), Via delle Terme di Caracalla, 00100 Rome, Italy (Telephone Number in U.S. (202) 653-2400); *Production Yearbook;* and *The State of Food and Agriculture.*

M.E. Sharpe, 80 Business Park Drive, Armonk, New York 10504 (800) 541-6563; *The Illustrated Book of World Rankings.*

St. Martin's Press, Inc., 175 Fifth Avenue, New York, New York 10010 (800) 221-7945; *The Statesman's Year-Book.*

Statistical Office of the United Nations, Publishing Service, New York, New York 10017 (800) 253-9646; *Statistical Yearbook.*

United Nations Conference on Trade and Development, Central Statistical Service, Palais des Nations, Geneva, Switzerland (Telephone in U.S. (800) 253-9646); *UNCTAD Commodity Yearbook.*

JORDAN - LIVING LEVELS - See JORDAN - LIFE EXPECTANCY

JORDAN - MAIL - NUMBER OF PIECES SENT OR RECEIVED

Statistical Office of the United Nations, Publishing Service, New York, New York 10017 (800) 253-9646; *Statistical Yearbook.*

JORDAN - MANUFACTURING

M.E. Sharpe, 80 Business Park Drive, Armonk, New York 10504 (800) 541-6563; *The Illustrated Book of World Rankings.*

Statistical Office of the United Nations, Publishing Service, New York, New York 10017 (800) 253-9646; *Bulletin of Industrial*

Statistics for the Arab Countries; and *Statistical Yearbook.*

JORDAN - MARRIAGE RATES

Europa Publications Limited, 18 Bedford Square, London, WC1B 3JN, England; *The Europa World Year Book.*

M.E. Sharpe, 80 Business Park Drive, Armonk, New York 10504 (800) 541-6563; *The Illustrated Book of World Rankings.*

Statistical Office of the United Nations, Publishing Service, New York, New York 10017 (800) 253-9646; *Demographic Yearbook;* and *Statistical Yearbook.*

JORDAN - MEAT PRODUCTION - See JORDAN - LIVESTOCK AND POULTRY

JORDAN - MERCHANT SHIPPING

Economic Commission for Western Asia, Post Office Box 27, Baghdad, Iraq; *Statistical Abstract of Western Asia.*

Europa Publications Limited, 18 Bedford Square, London, WC1B 3JN, England; *The Europa World Year Book.*

St. Martin's Press, Inc., 175 Fifth Avenue, New York, New York 10010 (800) 221-7945; *The Statesman's Year-Book.*

Statistical Office of the United Nations, Publishing Service, New York, New York 10017 (800) 253-9646; *Statistical Yearbook.*

JORDAN - MILITARY

Central Intelligence Agency, Washington, D.C. 20505 (703) 482-1100, www.cia.gov; *The World Factbook.*

Euromonitor International, Inc., 122 South Michigan Avenue, Suite 1200, Chicago, Illinois 60603 (800) 577-EURO; *World Marketing Data and Statistics.*

The International Institute for Strategic Studies, 23 Tavistock Street, London WC2E 7NQ, England 44 171 3797676; *The Military Balance.*

International Monetary Fund, 700 Nineteenth Street, NW, Washington, D.C. 20431 (202) 623-7000; *Government Finance Statistics Yearbook.*

St. Martin's Press, Inc., 175 Fifth Avenue, New York, New York 10010 (800) 221-7945; *The Statesman's Year-Book.*

Statistical Office of the United Nations, Publishing Service, New York, New York 10017 (800) 253-9646; *Human Development Report.*

U.S. Arms Control and Disarmament Agency, 320 Twenty-first Street, NW,

Washington, D.C. 20451 (202) 647-8677; *World Military Expenditures and Arms Transfers.*

JORDAN - MILK PRODUCTION - See JORDAN - DAIRY PRODUCTS

JORDAN - MINING AND MINERAL PRODUCTS

Economic Commission for Western Asia, Post Office Box 27, Baghdad, Iraq; *Statistical Abstract of Western Asia.*

Europa Publications Limited, 18 Bedford Square, London, WC1B 3JN, England; *The Europa World Year Book.*

M.E. Sharpe, 80 Business Park Drive, Armonk, New York 10504 (800) 541-6563; *The Illustrated Book of World Rankings.*

Penn Well Publishing Company, 1421 South Sheridan Road, Post Office Box 1260, Tulsa, Oklahoma 74101 (800) 752-9764; *International Energy Statistics Sourcebook.*

St. Martin's Press, Inc., 175 Fifth Avenue, New York, New York 10010 (800) 221-7945; *The Statesman's Year-Book.*

Statistical Office of the United Nations, Publishing Service, New York, New York 10017 (800) 253-9646; *Bulletin of Industrial Statistics for the Arab Countries;* and *Statistical Yearbook.*

United Nations Conference on Trade and Development, Central Statistical Service, Palais des Nations, Geneva, Switzerland (Telephone in U.S. (800) 253-9646); *UNCTAD Commodity Yearbook.*

JORDAN - MONEY EXCHANGE RATES - See JORDAN - EXCHANGE RATES
JORDAN - MONEY RESERVES

Euromonitor International, Inc., 122 South Michigan Avenue, Suite 1200, Chicago, Illinois 60603 (800) 577-EURO; *International Marketing Data and Statistics.*

JORDAN - MONEY SUPPLY

Economic Commission for Western Asia, Post Office Box 27, Baghdad, Iraq; *Statistical Abstract of Western Asia.*

The Economist Intelligence Unit, 111 West 57th Street, New York, New York 10019 (800) 938-4685; *Jordan Country Report.*

Euromonitor International, Inc., 122 South Michigan Avenue, Suite 1200, Chicago, Illinois 60603 (800) 577-EURO; *International Marketing Data and Statistics.*

Europa Publications Limited, 18 Bedford Square, London, WC1B 3JN, England; *The Europa World Year Book.*

Federal Statistical Office, Gustav-Stresemann - Ring 11, D-6200, Wiesbaden, Germany; *Jordanien.*

International Monetary Fund, 700 Nineteenth Street, NW, Washington, D.C. 20431 (202) 623-7000; *International Financial Statistics.*

Statistical Office of the United Nations, Publishing Service, New York, New York 10017 (800) 253-9646; *Statistical Yearbook.*

JORDAN - MONUMENTS AND HISTORICAL SITES

United Nations Educational, Scientific and Cultural Organization (UNESCO), 7 Place de Fontenoy, F-75700 Paris, France (Telephone Number in U.S. (212) 963-5981); *Statistical Yearbook.*

JORDAN - MORTALITY

Central Intelligence Agency, Washington, D.C. 20505 (703) 482-1100, www.cia.gov; *The World Factbook.*

Euromonitor International, Inc., 122 South Michigan Avenue, Suite 1200, Chicago, Illinois 60603 (800) 577-EURO; *International Marketing Data and Statistics;* and *The World Economic Factbook.*

Europa Publications Limited, 18 Bedford Square, London, WC1B 3JN, England; *The Europa World Year Book.*

St. Martin's Press, Inc., 175 Fifth Avenue, New York, New York 10010 (800) 221-7945; *The Statesman's Year-Book.*

Statistical Office of the United Nations, Publishing Service, New York, New York 10017 (800) 253-9646; *Demographic Yearbook; Human Development Report; World Statistics Pocketbook;* and *Statistical Yearbook.*

United Nations Children's Fund (UNICEF), 3 United Nations Plaza, New York, New York 10017 (800) 253-9646; *State of the World's Children.*

The World Bank, 1818 H Street, NW, Washington, D.C. 20433 (202) 477-1234; *The World Bank Atlas;* and *World Development Report.*

World Health Organization, Office of Publications, 20 Avenue Appia, CH-1211 Geneva 27, Switzerland (Telephone Number in U.S. (518) 436-9686); *World Health Statistics Annual.*

JORDAN - MOTION PICTURES

Statistical Office of the United Nations, Publishing Service, New York, New York 10017 (800) 253-9646; *Statistical Yearbook.*

JORDAN - MOTOR VEHICLE TAXES - See JORDAN - TAXATION

JORDAN - MOTOR VEHICLES

Economic Commission for Western Asia, Post Office Box 27, Baghdad, Iraq; *Statistical Abstract of Western Asia.*

Europa Publications Limited, 18 Bedford Square, London, WC1B 3JN, England; *The Europa World Year Book.*

JORDAN - MOTOR VEHICLES IN USE

Europa Publications Limited, 18 Bedford Square, London, WC1B 3JN, England; *The Europa World Year Book.*

International Road Federation, 2600 Virginia Avenue, NW, Washington, D.C. 20037 (202) 338-4641; *World Road Statistics.*

Statistical Office of the United Nations, Publishing Service, New York, New York 10017 (800) 253-9646; *Statistical Yearbook.*

JORDAN - MULES - See JORDAN - LIVESTOCK AND POULTRY

JORDAN - MUSEUMS

M.E. Sharpe, 80 Business Park Drive, Armonk, New York 10504 (800) 541-6563; *The Illustrated Book of World Rankings.*

United Nations Educational, Scientific and Cultural Organization (UNESCO), 7 Place de Fontenoy, F-75700 Paris, France (Telephone Number in U.S. (212) 963-5981); *Statistical Yearbook.*

JORDAN - NATALITY - See JORDAN - BIRTH RATE

JORDAN - NATIONAL ACCOUNTS

Economic Commission for Western Asia, Post Office Box 27, Baghdad, Iraq; *Statistical Abstract of Western Asia.*

Europa Publications Limited, 18 Bedford Square, London, WC1B 3JN, England; *The Europa World Year Book.*

Federal Statistical Office, Gustav - Stresemann - Ring 11, D-6200 Wiesbaden, Germany; *Jordanien.*

International Monetary Fund, 700 Nineteenth Street, NW, Washington, D.C. 20431 (202) 623-7000; *International Financial Statistics.*

Statistical Office of the United Nations, Publishing Service, New York, New York 10017 (800) 253-9646; *National Accounts Statistics;* and *Statistical Yearbook.*

JORDAN - NATIONAL INCOME

M.E. Sharpe, 80 Business Park Drive, Armonk, New York 10504 (800) 541-6563; *The Illustrated Book of World Rankings.*

Statistical Office of the United Nations, Publishing Service, New York, New York 10017 (800) 253-9646; *National Accounts Statistics;* and *Statistical Yearbook.*

JORDAN - NATIONAL PRODUCT

M.E. Sharpe, 80 Business Park Drive, Armonk, New York 10504 (800) 541-6563; *The Illustrated Book of World Rankings.*

JORDAN - NATURAL GAS PRODUCTION - See JORDAN - MINING AND MINERAL PRODUCTS

JORDAN - NEWSPAPER PRODUCTION - See JORDAN - FORESTRY AND FOREST PRODUCTS

JORDAN - NEWSPRINT - See JORDAN - FORESTRY AND FOREST PRODUCTS

JORDAN - OCCUPATIONS - See JORDAN - LABOR

JORDAN - PAPER - See JORDAN - FORESTRY AND FOREST PRODUCTS

JORDAN - PATENTS, TRADEMARKS AND SERVICE MARKS

Statistical Office of the United Nations, Publishing Service, New York, New York 10017 (800) 253-9646; *Statistical Yearbook.*

JORDAN - PEANUT PRODUCTION - See JORDAN - CROPS

JORDAN - PERIODICALS

United Nations Educational, Scientific and Cultural Organization (UNESCO), 7 Place de Fontenoy, F-75700 Paris, France (Telephone Number in U.S. (212) 963-5981); *Statistical Yearbook.*

JORDAN - PESTICIDE USE

Food and Agricultural Organization of the United Nations (FAO), Via delle Terme di Caracalla, 00100 Rome, Italy (Telephone Number in U.S. (202) 653-2400); *The State of Food and Agriculture.*

JORDAN - PETROLEUM INDUSTRY

Food and Agricultural Organization of the United Nations (FAO), Via delle Terme di Caracalla, 00100 Rome, Italy (Telephone Number in U.S. (202) 653-2400); *The State of Food and Agriculture.*

M.E. Sharpe, 80 Business Park Drive, Armonk, New York 10504 (800) 541-6563; *The Illustrated Book of World Rankings.*

Penn Well Publishing Company, 1421 South Sheridan Road, Post Office Box 1260, Tulsa, Oklahoma 74101 (800) 752-9764; *International Energy Statistics Sourcebook.*

Statistical Office of the United Nations, Publishing Service, New York, New York 10017 (800) 253-9646; *Statistical Yearbook.*

United Nations Conference on Trade and Development, Central Statistical Service, Palais des Nations, Geneva, Switzerland (Telephone in U.S. (800) 253-9646); *UNCTAD Commodity Yearbook.*

JORDAN - PHOSPHATE EXPORTS

International Monetary Fund, 700 Nineteenth Street, NW, Washington, D.C. 20431 (202) 623-7000; *International Financial Statistics.*

JORDAN - PHOSPHATE ROCK PRODUCTION - See JORDAN - MINING AND MINERAL PRODUCTS

JORDAN - PIGS - See JORDAN - LIVESTOCK AND POULTRY

JORDAN - POPULATION

Central Intelligence Agency, Washington, D.C. 20505 (703) 482-1100, www.cia.gov; *The World Factbook.*

The Economist Intelligence Unit, 111 West 57th Street, New York, New York 10019 (800) 938-4685; *Jordan Country Report;* and *The World Market Atlas.*

Euromonitor International, Inc., 122 South Michigan Avenue, Suite 1200, Chicago, Illinois 60603 (800) 577-EURO; *International Marketing Data and Statistics;* and *The World Economic Factbook.*

Europa Publications Limited, 18 Bedford Square, London, WC1B 3JN, England; *The Europa World Year Book.*

Federal Statistical Office, Gustav - Stresemann - Ring 11, D-6200 Wiesbaden, Germany; *Jordanien.*

Food and Agricultural Organization of the United Nations (FAO), Via delle Terme di Caracalla, 00100 Rome, Italy (Telephone Number in U.S. (202) 653-2400); *Production Yearbook.*

International Labour Office, I.L.O. Publications, 1828 L Street, NW, Washington, D.C. 20036 (301) 638-3152; *Yearbook of Labour Statistics.*

M.E. Sharpe, 80 Business Park Drive, Armonk, New York 10504 (800) 541-6563; *The Illustrated Book of World Rankings.*

St. Martin's Press, Inc., 175 Fifth Avenue, New York, New York 10010 (800)

221-7945; *The Statesman's Year-Book.*

Statistical Office of the United Nations, Publishing Service, New York, New York 10017 (800) 253-9646; *Demographic Yearbook; Human Development Report; World Statistics Pocketbook;* and *Statistical Yearbook.*

United Nations Educational, Scientific and Cultural Organization (UNESCO), 7 Place de Fontenoy, F-75700 Paris, France (Telephone Number in U.S. (212) 963-5981); *Statistical Yearbook.*

U.S. Arms Control and Disarmament Agency, 320 Twenty-first Street, NW, Washington, D.C. 20451 (202) 647-8677; *World Military Expenditures and Arms Transfers.*

The World Bank, 1818 H Street, NW, Washington, D.C. 20433 (202) 477-1234; *The World Bank Atlas;* and *World Development Report.*

World Health Organization, Office of Publications, 20 Avenue Appia, CH-1211 Geneva 27, Switzerland (Telephone Number in U.S. (518) 436-9686); *World Health Statistics Annual.*

JORDAN - POST OFFICES

M.E. Sharpe, 80 Business Park Drive, Armonk, New York 10504 (800) 541-6563; *The Illustrated Book of World Rankings.*

St. Martin's Press, Inc., 175 Fifth Avenue, New York, New York 10010 (800) 221-7945; *The Statesman's Year-Book.*

JORDAN - POTATO PRODUCTION - See JORDAN - CROPS

JORDAN - POWER PRODUCTION INDUSTRY

Statistical Office of the United Nations, Publishing Service, New York, New York 10017 (800) 253-9646; *Statistical Yearbook.*

JORDAN - PRICES

Economic Commission for Western Asia, Post Office Box 27, Baghdad, Iraq; *Statistical Abstract of Western Asia.*

Federal Statistical Office, Gustav - Stresemann - Ring 11, D-6200 Wiesbaden, Germany; *Jordanien.*

Food and Agricultural Organization of the United Nations (FAO), Via delle Terme di Caracalla, 00100 Rome, Italy (Telephone Number in U.S. (202) 653-2400); *Production Yearbook;* and *The State of Food and Agriculture.*

International Labour Office, I.L.O. Publications, 1828 L Street, NW, Suite

801, Washington, D.C. 20036 (301) 638-3152; *Yearbook of Labour Statistics.*

International Monetary Fund, 700 Nineteenth Street, NW, Washington, D.C. 20431 (202) 623-7000; *International Financial Statistics.*

M.E. Sharpe, 80 Business Park Drive, Armonk, New York 10504 (800) 541-6563; *The Illustrated Book of World Rankings.*

JORDAN - PRINTING AND WRITING PAPER - See JORDAN - FORESTRY AND FOREST PRODUCTS

JORDAN - PRODUCTION

M.E. Sharpe, 80 Business Park Drive, Armonk, New York 10504 (800) 541-6563; *The Illustrated Book of World Rankings.*

JORDAN - PRODUCTIVITY

Euromonitor International, Inc., 122 South Michigan Avenue, Suite 1200, Chicago, Illinois 60603 (800) 577-EURO; *International Marketing Data and Statistics.*

JORDAN - PROPERTY TAXES - See JORDAN - TAXATION

JORDAN - PUBLIC FINANCE - See JORDAN - FINANCE

JORDAN - RADIO BROADCASTING - See JORDAN - BROADCASTING

JORDAN - RADIO RECEIVERS

St. Martin's Press, Inc., 175 Fifth Avenue, New York, New York 10010 (800) 221-7945; *The Statesman's Year-Book.*

JORDAN - RAILWAYS

Europa Publications Limited, 18 Bedford Square, London, WC1B 3JN, England; *The Europa World Year Book.*

Jane's Information Group, Sentinel House, 163 Brighton Road, Coulsdon, Surrey CR5 2NH, England (Telephone Number in U.S. (703) 683-3700); *Jane's World Railways.*

St. Martin's Press, Inc., 175 Fifth Avenue, New York, New York 10010 (800) 221-7945; *The Statesman's Year-Book.*

JORDAN - RELIGION

Central Intelligence Agency, Washington, D.C. 20505 (703) 482-1100, www.cia.gov; *The World Factbook.*

M.E. Sharpe, 80 Business Park Drive, Armonk, New York 10504 (800) 541-6563; *The Illustrated Book of World Rankings.*

St. Martin's Press, Inc., 175 Fifth Avenue, New York, New York 10010 (800) 221-7945; *The Statesman's Year-Book.*

JORDAN - RENT PRICES

International Labour Office, I.L.O. Publications, 1828 L Street, NW, Suite 801, Washington, D.C. 20036 (301) 638-3152; *Yearbook of Labour Statistics.*

JORDAN - RETAIL TRADE

Euromonitor International, Inc., 122 South Michigan Avenue, Suite 1200, Chicago, Illinois 60603 (800) 577-EURO; *World Marketing Data and Statistics.*

JORDAN - RICE PRODUCTION - See JORDAN - CROPS

JORDAN - ROOT AND TUBER PRODUCTION - See JORDAN - CROPS

JORDAN - ROUNDWOOD PRODUCTION - See JORDAN - FORESTRY AND FOREST PRODUCTS

JORDAN - RUBBER PRODUCTION AND CONSUMPTION

M.E. Sharpe, 80 Business Park Drive, Armonk, New York 10504 (800) 541-6563; *The Illustrated Book of World Rankings.*

JORDAN - SALT PRODUCTION - See JORDAN - MINING AND MINERAL PRODUCTS

JORDAN - SAWNWOOD PRODUCTION - See JORDAN - FORESTRY AND FOREST PRODUCTS

JORDAN - SCIENCE AND TECHNOLOGY - EXPENDITURE FOR RESEARCH - See JORDAN - SCIENTISTS, TECHNICIANS AND ENGINEERS

JORDAN - SCIENTISTS, TECHNICIANS AND ENGINEERS

Statistical Office of the United Nations, Publishing Service, New York, New York 10017 (800) 253-9646; *Statistical Yearbook.*

JORDAN - SENIOR CITIZENS

M.E. Sharpe, 80 Business Park Drive, Armonk, New York 10504 (800) 541-6563; *The Illustrated Book of World Rankings.*

JORDAN - SESAME SEED PRODUCTION - See JORDAN - CROPS

JORDAN - SHEEP - See JORDAN - LIVESTOCK AND POULTRY

JORDAN - SILVER PRODUCTION AND CONSUMPTION - See JORDAN - MINING AND MINERAL PRODUCTS

JORDAN - SOCIAL DATA

M.E. Sharpe, 80 Business Park Drive, Armonk, New York 10504 (800) 541-6563; *The Illustrated Book of World Rankings.*

Statistical Office of the United Nations, Publishing Service, New York, New York 10017 (800) 253-9646; *World Statistics Pocketbook.*

JORDAN - SOCIAL SECURITY

International Monetary Fund, 700 Nineteenth Street, NW, Washington, D.C. 20431 (202) 623-7000; *Government Finance Statistics Yearbook.*

Statistical Office of the United Nations, Publishing Service, New York, New York 10017 (800) 253-9646; *National Accounts Statistics.*

JORDAN - STAMP TAXES AND REVENUES - See JORDAN - TAXATION

JORDAN - STATE BUDGET REVENUE AND EXPENDITURES

Euromonitor International, Inc., 122 South Michigan Avenue, Suite 1200, Chicago, Illinois 60603 (800) 577-EURO; *International Marketing Data and Statistics.*

JORDAN - STEEL - See JORDAN - MINING AND MINERAL PRODUCTS

JORDAN - STOCKS - COMMODITY - MARKET PRICE - INDEX

Food and Agricultural Organization of the United Nations (FAO), Via delle Terme di Caracalla, 00100 Rome, Italy (Telephone Number in U.S. (202) 653-2400); *The State of Food and Agriculture.*

JORDAN - SUGAR PRODUCTION AND CONSUMPTION - See JORDAN - CROPS

JORDAN - TAXATION

Europa Publications Limited, 18 Bedford Square, London, WC1B 3JN, England; *The Europa World Year Book.*

International Monetary Fund, 700 Nineteenth Street, NW, Washington, D.C. 20431 (202) 623-7000; *Government Finance Statistics Yearbook.*

International Road Federation, 2600 Virginia Avenue, NW, Washington, D.C. 20037 (202) 338-4641; *World Road Statistics.*

JORDAN - TEA CONSUMPTION - See JORDAN - CROPS

JORDAN - TELEPHONES IN USE

American Telephone and Telegraph

Company, 26 Parsippany Road, Whippany, New Jersey 07981 (800) 222-0300; *The World's Telephones.*

Central Intelligence Agency, Washington, D.C. 20505 (703) 482-1100, www.cia.gov; *The World Factbook.*

Europa Publications Limited, 18 Bedford Square, London, WC1B 3JN, England; *The Europa World Year Book.*

St. Martin's Press, Inc., 175 Fifth Avenue, New York, New York 10010 (800) 221-7945; *The Statesman's Year-Book.*

Statistical Office of the United Nations, Publishing Service, New York, New York 10017 (800) 253-9646; *Statistical Yearbook;* and *World Statistics Pocketbook.*

JORDAN - TELEVISION BROADCASTING - See JORDAN - BROADCASTING

JORDAN - TEXTILE INDUSTRY

M.E. Sharpe, 80 Business Park Drive, Armonk, New York 10504 (800) 541-6563; *The Illustrated Book of World Rankings.*

JORDAN - THEATRE

United Nations Educational, Scientific and Cultural Organization (UNESCO), 7 Place de Fontenoy, F-75700 Paris, France (Telephone Number in U.S. (212) 963-5981); *Statistical Yearbook.*

JORDAN - TOBACCO PRODUCTION

M.E. Sharpe, 80 Business Park Drive, Armonk, New York 10504 (800) 541-6563; *The Illustrated Book of World Rankings.*

Statistical Office of the United Nations, Publishing Service, New York, New York 10017 (800) 253-9646; *Statistical Yearbook.*

JORDAN - TOURISM

Economic Commission for Western Asia, Post Office Box 27, Baghdad, Iraq; *Statistical Abstract of Western Asia.*

Euromonitor International, Inc., 122 South Michigan Avenue, Suite 1200, Chicago, Illinois 60603 (800) 577-EURO; *World Marketing Data and Statistics;* and *World Economic Factbook.*

Europa Publications Limited, 18 Bedford Square, London, WC1B 3JN, England; *The Europa World Year Book.*

Federal Statistical Office, Gustav - Stresemann - Ring 11, D-6200 Wiesbaden, Germany; *Jordanien.*

M.E. Sharpe, 80 Business Park Drive, Armonk, New York 10504 (800) 541-6563; *The Illustrated Book of World Rankings.*

St. Martin's Press, Inc., 175 Fifth Avenue, New York, New York 10010 (800) 221-7945; *The Statesman's Year-Book.*

Statistical Office of the United Nations, Publishing Service, New York, New York 10017 (800) 253-9646; *Statistical Yearbook.*

World Tourism Organization, Calle Capital Haya 42, E-28020 Madrid, Spain; *Yearbook of Tourism Statistics.*

JORDAN - TRACTORS IN USE

Statistical Office of the United Nations, Publishing Service, New York, New York 10017 (800) 253-9646; *Statistical Yearbook.*

JORDAN - TRADE - See JORDAN - FOREIGN TRADE

JORDAN - TRADEMARKS AND SERVICE MARKS - See JORDAN - PATENTS, TRADEMARKS AND SERVICE MARKS

JORDAN - TRANSPORTATION AND COMMUNICATIONS

Central Intelligence Agency, Washington, D.C. 20505 (703) 482-1100, www.cia.gov; *The World Factbook.*

Economic Commission for Western Asia, Post Office Box 27, Baghdad, Iraq; *Statistical Abstract of Western Asia.*

Euromonitor International, Inc., 122 South Michigan Avenue, Suite 1200, Chicago, Illinois 60603 (800) 577-EURO; *International Marketing Data and Statistics;* and *World Marketing Data and Statistics..*

Europa Publications Limited, 18 Bedford Square, London, WC1B 3JN, England; *The Europa World Year Book.*

Federal Statistical Office, Gustav - Stresemann - Ring 11, D-6200 Wiesbaden, Germany; *Jordanien.*

M.E. Sharpe, 80 Business Park Drive, Armonk, New York 10504 (800) 541-6563; *The Illustrated Book of World Rankings.*

St. Martin's Press, Inc., 175 Fifth Avenue, New York, New York 10010 (800) 221-7945; *The Statesman's Year-Book.*

Statistical Office of the United Nations, Publishing Service, New York, New York 10017 (800) 253-9646; *Human Development Report.*

JORDAN - TURKEYS - See JORDAN - LIVESTOCK AND POULTRY

JORDAN - UNEMPLOYMENT

Central Intelligence Agency, Washington, D.C. 20505 (703) 482-1100, www.cia.gov; *The World Factbook.*

Euromonitor International, Inc., 122 South Michigan Avenue, Suite 1200, Chicago, Illinois 60603 (800) 577-EURO; *International Marketing Data and Statistics.*

International Labour Office, I.L.O. Publications, 1828 L Street, NW, Suite 801, Washington, D.C. 20036 (301) 638-3152; *Yearbook of Labour Statistics.*

St. Martin's Press, Inc., 175 Fifth Avenue, New York, New York 10010 (800) 221-7945; *The Statesman's Year-Book.*

JORDAN - VITAL STATISTICS

Euromonitor International, Inc., 122 South Michigan Avenue, Suite 1200, Chicago, Illinois 60603 (800) 577-EURO; *International Marketing Data and Statistics.*

St. Martin's Press, Inc., 175 Fifth Avenue, New York, New York 10010 (800) 221-7945; *The Statesman's Year-Book.*

Statistical Office of the United Nations, Publishing Service, New York, New York 10017 (800) 253-9646; *Statistical Yearbook.*

World Health Organization, Office of Publications, 20 Avenue Appia, CH-1211 Geneva 27, Switzerland (Telephone Number in U.S. (518) 436-9686); *World Health Statistics Annual.*

JORDAN - WAGES

Federal Statistical Office, Gustav - Stresemann - Ring 11, D-6200 Wiesbaden, Germany; *Jordanien.*

International Labour Office, I.L.O. Publications, 1828 L Street, NW, Suite 801, Washington, D.C. 20036 (301) 638-3152; *Yearbook of Labour Statistics.*

Statistical Office of the United Nations, Publishing Service, New York, New York 10017 (800) 253-9646; *Statistical Yearbook.*

JORDAN - WALNUT PRODUCTION - See JORDAN - CROPS

JORDAN - WATERMELON PRODUCTION - See JORDAN - CROPS

JORDAN - WEATHER - See JORDAN - CLIMATE

JORDAN - WELFARE EXPENDITURES

International Monetary Fund, 700 Nineteenth Street, NW, Washington, D.C. 20431 (202) 623-7000; *Government Finance Statistics Yearbook.*

JORDAN - WHEAT PRODUCTION AND PRICES - See JORDAN - CROPS

JORDAN - WHOLESALE PRICES - INDEX NUMBERS

Statistical Office of the United Nations, Publishing Service, New York, New York 10017 (800) 253-9646; *Statistical Yearbook.*

JORDAN - WINE PRODUCTION - See JORDAN - BEVERAGES

JORDAN - WOOL PRODUCTION - See JORDAN - TEXTILE INDUSTRY

JUDICIAL SERVICE, FEDERAL - EMPLOYEES AND PAYROLLS

Office of Personnel Management, 1900 E Street, NW, Washington, D.C. 20415 (202) 606-1800, www.opm.gov; *Federal Civilian*

Workforce Statistics; Employment and Trends; and unpublished data.

JUDICIAL SERVICE, FEDERAL - FEDERAL OUTLAYS

Executive Office of the President, Office of Management and Budget, Executive Office Building, Washington, D.C. 20503 (202) 395-3080, www.whitehouse.gov/omb; *Historical Tables.*

JUICES

U.S. Department of Agriculture, Economic Research Service, 1800 M Street,

NW, Washington, D.C. 20036 (202) 694-5050, www.ers.usda.gov; *Food Consumption, Prices, and Expenditures;* and *Agricultural Outlook.*

JUVENILES - ARREST

U.S. Department of Justice, Federal Bureau of Investigation, 935 Pennsylvania Avenue, NW, Washington, D.C. 20535 (202) 324-3691, www.fbi.gov; *Crime in the United States.*

JUVENILES - COURT CASES

National Center for Juvenile Justice, 710 Fifth Avenue, Pittsburgh, Pennsylvania 15219 (412) 227-6950; *Juvenile Court Statistics.*

K

KANSAS - See also STATE DATA (FOR INDIVIDUAL STATES)

Kansas - Primary Statistics Source

University of Kansas, Institute for Public Policy and Business Research, 607 Blake Hall, Lawrence, Kansas 66045 (785) 864-3701; *Kansas Statistical Abstract; and* Internet site: http://www.ukans.edu/cwis/units/IPPBR/

Kansas - State Data Centers

State Library, State Capitol Building, Room 343-N, Topeka, Kansas 66612, Mr. Marc Galbraith (913) 296-3296.

Center for Economic Development and Business Research, Box 121, Wichita State University, Wichita, Kansas 67260-0121, Ms. Janet Nickel (316) 978-3225.

Division of the Budget, Room 152-E, State Capitol Building, Topeka, Kansas 66612, Mr. David Dallam (913) 296-2436.

Institute for Public Policy and Business Research, 607 Blake Hall, The University of Kansas, Lawrence, Kansas 66045-2960, Ms. Thelma Helyar (913) 864-3701.

Population and Resources Laboratory, Department of Sociology, 204 Waters Hall, Kansas State University, Manhattan, Kansas 66506-4003, Dr. Leonard Bloomquist (913) 532-6865.

KAZAKHSTAN - ABORTIONS

Statistical Office of the United Nations, Publishing Service, New York, New York 10017 (800) 253-9646; *Trends in Europe and North America: The Statistical Yearbook of the Economic Commission for Europe.*

KAZAKHSTAN - AGRICULTURE

Academic International Press, Box

1111, Gulf Breeze, Florida 32562; *Russia and Eurasia Facts and Figures Annual.*

Business International Moscow, 23 Profsoyuznaya Ulitsa 117859, Moscow (Telephone Number in U.S. (800) 938-4685); *The CIS Market Atlas.*

Economist Intelligence Unit, 111 West 57th Street, New York, New York 10019 (800) 938-4685; *Kazakhstan Country Report.*

Euromonitor International, Inc., 122 South Michigan Avenue, Suite 1200, Chicago, Illinois 60603 (800) 577-EURO; *World Marketing Data and Statistics.*

Europa Publications Limited, 18 Bedford Square, London, WC1B 3JN, England; *The Europa World Year Book.*

Food and Agriculture Organization of the United Nations (FAO), Via delle Terme di Caracalla, 00100, Rome, Italy (Telephone Number in U.S. (202) 653-2400); *Production Yearbook; The State of Food and Agriculture;* and *Trade Yearbook.*

St. Martin's Press, Inc., 175 Fifth Avenue, New York, New York 10010 (800) 221-7945; *The Statesman's Year-Book.*

Statistical Office of the United Nations, Publishing Service, New York, New York 10017 (800) 253-9646; *Industrial Commodity Statistics Yearbook;* and *Statistical Yearbook.*

The World Bank, 1818 H Street, NW, Washington, D.C. 20433 (202) 477-1234; *Statistical Handbook: States of the Former USSR;* and *World Development Indicators.*

KAZAKHSTAN - AIRLINE SERVICE

Business International Moscow, 23 Profsoyuznaya Ulitsa 117859, Moscow (Telephone Number in U.S. (800) 938-4685); *The CIS Market Atlas.*

International Civil Aviation Organization, 999 University Street,

Montreal, Quebec, Canada H3C 5H7 (514) 285-8219; *Civil Aviation Statistics of the World.*

St. Martin's Press, Inc., 175 Fifth Avenue, New York, New York 10010 (800) 221-7945; *The Statesman's Year-Book.*

Statistical Office of the United Nations, Publishing Service, New York, New York 10017 (800) 253-9646; *Statistical Yearbook.*

KAZAKHSTAN - ANIMAL HEALTH

Food and Agriculture Organization of the United Nations (FAO), Via delle Terme di Caracalla, 00100, Rome, Italy (Telephone Number in U.S. (202) 653-2400); *Animal Health Yearbook.*

KAZAKHSTAN - AREA AND DENSITY OF POPULATION

Academic International Press, Box 1111, Gulf Breeze, Florida 32562; *Russia and Eurasia Facts and Figures Annual.*

Business International Moscow, 23 Profsoyuznaya Ulitsa 117859, Moscow (Telephone Number in U.S. (800) 938-4685); *The CIS Market Atlas.*

Central Intelligence Agency, Washington, D.C. 20505 (703) 482-1100, www.cia.gov; *The World Factbook.*

Euromonitor International, Inc., 122 South Michigan Avenue, Suite 1200, Chicago, Illinois 60603 (800) 577-EURO; *The World Economic Factbook.*

Europa Publications Limited, 18 Bedford Square, London, WC1B 3JN, England; *The Europa World Year Book.*

St. Martin's Press, Inc., 175 Fifth Avenue, New York, New York 10010 (800) 221-7945; *The Statesman's Year-Book.*

Statistical Office of the United Nations, Publishing Service, New York, New York 10017 (800) 253-9646; *Statistical Yearbook;* and *Trends in Europe and North America: The Statistical Yearbook of the Economic*

Commission for Europe.

United Nations Educational, Scientific and Cultural Organization (UNESCO), 7 Place de Fontenoy, F-75700 Paris, France (Telephone Number in U.S. (212) 963-5981); *Statistical Yearbook*.

The World Bank, 1818 H Street, NW, Washington, D.C. 20433 (202) 477-1234; *World Development Report*.

KAZAKHSTAN - BALANCE OF PAYMENTS

Europa Publications Limited, 18 Bedford Square, London, WC1B 3JN, England; *The Europa World Year Book*.

United Nations Conference on Trade and Development (UNCTAD), New York, New York 10017 (800) 253-9646; *Handbook of International Trade and Development Statistics*.

The World Bank, 1818 H Street, NW, Washington, D.C. 20433 (202) 477-1234; *World Development Report;* and *World Development Indicators*.

KAZAKHSTAN - BANKING

Business International Moscow, 23 Profsoyuznaya Ulitsa 117859, Moscow (Telephone Number in U.S. (800) 938-4685); *The CIS Market Atlas*.

Euromonitor International, Inc., 122 South Michigan Avenue, Suite 1200, Chicago, Illinois 60603 (800) 577-EURO; *World Marketing Data and Statistics*.

KAZAKHSTAN - BEVERAGES

Statistical Office of the United Nations, Publishing Service, New York, New York 10017 (800) 253-9646; *Statistical Yearbook*.

KAZAKHSTAN - BIRTH RATES

Academic International Press, Box 1111, Gulf Breeze, Florida 32562; *Russia and Eurasia Facts and Figures Annual*.

Business International Moscow, 23 Profsoyuznaya Ulitsa 117859, Moscow (Telephone Number in U.S. (800) 938-4685); *The CIS Market Atlas*.

Central Intelligence Agency, Washington, D.C. 20505 (703) 482-1100, www.cia.gov; *The World Factbook*.

Euromonitor International, Inc., 122 South Michigan Avenue, Suite 1200, Chicago, Illinois 60603 (800) 577-EURO; *International Marketing Data and Statistics;* and *The World Economic Factbook*.

Europa Publications Limited, 18 Bedford Square, London, WC1B 3JN, England; *The Europa World Year Book*.

St. Martin's Press, Inc., 175 Fifth Avenue, New York, New York 10010 (800) 221-7945; *The Statesman's Year-Book*.

Statistical Office of the United Nations, Publishing Service, New York, New York 10017 (800) 253-9646; *Statistical Yearbook*.

World Health Organization, Office of Publications, 20 Avenue Appia, CH-1211 Geneva 27, Switzerland (Telephone Number in U.S. (518) 436-9686); *World Health Statistics Annual*.

KAZAKHSTAN - BOOK PRODUCTION

Statistical Office of the United Nations, Publishing Service, New York, New York 10017 (800) 253-9646; *Trends in Europe and North America: The Statistical Yearbook of the Economic Commission for Europe*.

United Nations Educational, Scientific and Cultural Organization (UNESCO), 7 Place de Fontenoy, F-75700 Paris, France (Telephone Number in U.S. (212) 963-5981); *Statistical Yearbook*.

KAZAKHSTAN - BROADCASTING

Central Intelligence Agency, Washington, D.C. 20505 (703) 482-1100, www.cia.gov; *The World Factbook*.

Euromonitor International, Inc., 122 South Michigan Avenue, Suite 1200, Chicago, Illinois 60603 (800) 577-EURO; *World Marketing Data and Statistics*.

St. Martin's Press, Inc., 175 Fifth Avenue, New York, New York 10010 (800) 221-7945; *The Statesman's Year-Book*.

Statistical Office of the United Nations, Publishing Service, New York, New York 10017 (800) 253-9646; *Trends in Europe and North America: The Statistical Yearbook of the Economic Commission for Europe*.

United Nations Educational, Scientific and Cultural Organization (UNESCO), 7 Place de Fontenoy, F-75700 Paris, France (Telephone Number in U.S. (212) 963-5981); *Statistical Yearbook*.

KAZAKHSTAN - BUDGET

Business International Moscow, 23 Profsoyuznaya Ulitsa 117859, Moscow (Telephone Number in U.S. (800) 938-4685); *The CIS Market Atlas*.

Central Intelligence Agency, Washington, D.C. 20505 (703) 482-1100, www.cia.gov; *The World Factbook*.

KAZAKHSTAN - CAPITAL INVESTMENT

The World Bank, 1818 H Street, NW, Washington, D.C. 20433 (202) 477-1234; *Statistical Handbook: States of the Former USSR*.

KAZAKHSTAN - CATTLE - See KAZAKHSTAN - LIVESTOCK AND POULTRY

KAZAKHSTAN - CHEMICALS

Business International Moscow, 23 Profsoyuznaya Ulitsa, 117859, Moscow (Telephone Number in U.S. (800) 938-4685); *The CIS Market Atlas*.

KAZAKHSTAN - COAL PRODUCTION AND CONSUMPTION - See KAZAKHSTAN - MINING AND MINERAL PRODUCTS

KAZAKHSTAN - COMMERCE

St. Martin's Press, Inc., 175 Fifth Avenue, New York, New York 10010 (800) 221-7945; *The Statesman's Year-Book*.

KAZAKHSTAN - COMMUNICATIONS - See KAZAKHSTAN - TRANSPORTATION AND COMMUNICATIONS

KAZAKHSTAN - CONSTRUCTION INDUSTRY

Academic International Press, Box 1111, Gulf Breeze, Florida 32562; *Russia and Eurasia Facts and Figures Annual*.

Business International Moscow, 23 Profsoyuznaya Ulitsa, 117859, Moscow (Telephone Number in U.S. (800) 938-4685); *The CIS Market Atlas*.

St. Martin's Press, Inc., 175 Fifth Avenue, New York, New York 10010 (800) 221-7945; *The Statesman's Year-Book*.

Statistical Office of the United Nations, Publishing Service, New York, New York 10017 (800) 253-9646; *Statistical Yearbook*.

KAZAKHSTAN - CONSUMER PRICE INDEX

Statistical Office of the United Nations, Publishing Service, New York, New York 10017 (800) 253-9646; *Statistical Yearbook;* and *Trends in Europe and North America: The Statistical Yearbook of the Economic Commission for Europe.*

KAZAKHSTAN - CONSUMER PRICES

Euromonitor International, Inc., 122 South Michigan Avenue, Suite 1200, Chicago, Illinois 60603 (800) 577-EURO; *World Marketing Data and Statistics*.

KAZAKHSTAN - CONSUMER PRODUCTS

Business International Moscow, 23 Profsoyuznaya Ulitsa, 117859, Moscow (Telephone Number in U.S. (800) 938-4685); *The CIS Market Atlas*.

KAZAKHSTAN - CONSUMPTION

Business International Moscow, 23 Profsoyuznaya Ulitsa, 117859, Moscow (Telephone Number in U.S. (800) 938-4685); *The CIS Market Atlas.*

The World Bank, 1818 H Street, NW, Washington, D.C. 20433 (202) 477-1234; *World Development Report;* and *Statistical Handbook: States of the Former USSR.*

KAZAKHSTAN - COTTON PRODUCTION AND CONSUMPTION - See KAZAKHSTAN - CROPS

KAZAKHSTAN - CRIME

Academic International Press, Box 1111, Gulf Breeze, Florida 32562; *Russia and Eurasia Facts and Figures Annual.*

Statistical Office of the United Nations, Publishing Service, New York, New York 10017 (800) 253-9646; *Trends in Europe and North America: The Statistical Yearbook of the Economic Commission for Europe.*

KAZAKHSTAN - CROPS

Academic International Press, Box 1111, Gulf Breeze, Florida 32562; *Russia and Eurasia Facts and Figures Annual.*

Europa Publications Limited, 18 Bedford Square, London, WC1B 3JN, England; *The Europa World Year Book.*

Food and Agriculture Organization of the United Nations (FAO), Via delle Terme di Caracalla, 00100, Rome, Italy (Telephone Number in U.S. (202) 653-2400); *Production Yearbook; The State of Food and Agriculture;* and *Trade Yearbook.*

St. Martin's Press, Inc., 175 Fifth Avenue, New York, New York 10010 (800) 221-7945; *The Statesman's Year-Book.*

Statistical Office of the United Nations, Publishing Service, New York, New York 10017 (800) 253-9646; *Industrial Commodity Statistics Yearbook;* and *Statistical Yearbook.*

The World Bank, 1818 H Street, NW, Washington, D.C. 20433 (202) 477-1234; *Statistical Handbook: States of the Former USSR.*

KAZAKHSTAN - DAIRY PRODUCTS

Europa Publications Limited, 18 Bedford Square, London, WC1B 3JN, England; *The Europa World Year Book.*

Food and Agriculture Organization of the United Nations (FAO), Via delle Terme di Caracalla, 00100, Rome, Italy (Telephone Number in U.S. (202) 653-2400); *Production Yearbook; The State of Food and Agriculture;* and *Trade Yearbook.*

St. Martin's Press, Inc., 175 Fifth Avenue, New York, New York 10010 (800) 221-7945; *The Statesman's Year-Book.*

Statistical Office of the United Nations, Publishing Service, New York, New York 10017 (800) 253-9646; *Industrial Commodity Statistics Yearbook;* and *Statistical Yearbook.*

KAZAKHSTAN - DEATH RATES - See KAZAKHSTAN - MORTALITY

KAZAKHSTAN - DEMOGRAPHY

Business International Moscow, 23 Profsoyuznaya Ulitsa, 117859, Moscow (Telephone Number in U.S. (800) 938-4685); *The CIS Market Atlas.*

Euromonitor International, Inc., 122 South Michigan Avenue, Suite 1200, Chicago, Illinois 60603 (800) 577-EURO; *International Marketing Data and Statistics; The World Economic Factbook;* and *World Marketing Data Statistics.*

Statistical Office of the United Nations, Publishing Service, New York, New York 10017 (800) 253-9646; *Demographic Yearbook;* and *Human Development Report.*

The World Bank, 1818 H Street, NW, Washington, D.C. 20433 (202) 477-1234; *Statistical Handbook: States of the Former USSR.*

KAZAKHSTAN - DISEASES - See KAZAKHSTAN - HEALTH

KAZAKHSTAN - DIVORCE RATES

Academic International Press, Box 1111, Gulf Breeze, Florida 32562; *Russia and Eurasia Facts and Figures Annual.*

Statistical Office of the United Nations, Publishing Service, New York, New York 10017 (800) 253-9646; *Demographic Yearbook; Trends in Europe and North America: The Statistical Yearbook of the Economic Commission for Europe;* and *Statistical Yearbook.*

KAZAKHSTAN - DOMESTIC INVESTMENT

Business International Moscow, 23 Profsoyuznaya Ulitsa, 117859, Moscow (Telephone Number in U.S. (800) 938-4685); *The CIS Market Atlas.*

KAZAKHSTAN - ECONOMY

Academic International Press, Box 1111, Gulf Breeze, Florida 32562; *Russia and Eurasia Facts and Figures Annual.*

Business International Moscow, 23 Profsoyuznaya Ulitsa, 117859, Moscow

(Telephone Number in U.S. (800) 938-4685); *The CIS Market Atlas.*

Central Intelligence Agency, Washington, D.C. 20505 (703) 482-1100, www.cia.gov; *The World Factbook.*

Economist Intelligence Unit, 111 West 57th Street, New York, New York 10019 (800) 938-4685; *Kazakhstan Country Report.*

Euromonitor International, Inc., 122 South Michigan Avenue, Suite 1200, Chicago, Illinois 60603 (800) 577-EURO; *World Marketing Data and Statistics;* and *The World Economic Factbook.*

St. Martin's Press, Inc., 175 Fifth Avenue, New York, New York 10010 (800) 221-7945; *The Statesman's Year-Book.*

Statistical Office of the United Nations, Publishing Service, New York, New York 10017 (800) 253-9646; *World Statistics Pocketbook.*

The World Bank, 1818 H Street, NW, Washington, D.C. 20433 (202) 477-1234; *The World Bank Atlas;* and *World Development Report.*

KAZAKHSTAN - EDUCATION

Academic International Press, Box 1111, Gulf Breeze, Florida 32562; *Russia and Eurasia Facts and Figures Annual.*

Business International Moscow, 23 Profsoyuznaya Ulitsa, 117859, Moscow (Telephone Number in U.S. (800) 938-4685); *The CIS Market Atlas.*

Euromonitor International, Inc., 122 South Michigan Avenue, Suite 1200, Chicago, Illinois 60603 (800) 577-EURO; *International Marketing Data and Statistics;* and *World Marketing Data and Statistics.*

Europa Publications Limited, 18 Bedford Square, London, WC1B 3JN, England; *The Europa World Year Book.*

St. Martin's Press, Inc., 175 Fifth Avenue, New York, New York 10010 (800) 221-7945; *The Statesman's Year-Book.*

Statistical Office of the United Nations, Publishing Service, New York, New York 10017 (800) 253-9646; *Human Development Report;* and *Trends in Europe and North America: The Statistical Yearbook of the Economic Commission for Europe.*

United Nations Educational, Scientific and Cultural Organization (UNESCO), 7 Place de Fontenoy, F-75700 Paris, France (Telephone Number in U.S. (212) 963-5981); *Statistical Yearbook.*

The World Bank, 1818 H Street, NW, Washington, D.C. 20433 (202) 477-1234; *World Development Report.*

KAZAKHSTAN - ELECTRICITY

Academic International Press, Box 1111, Gulf Breeze, Florida 32562; *Russia and Eurasia Facts and Figures Annual.*

Business International Moscow, 23 Profsoyuznaya Ulitsa, 117859, Moscow (Telephone Number in U.S. (800) 938-4685); *The CIS Market Atlas.*

Central Intelligence Agency, Washington, D.C. 20505 (703) 482-1100, www.cia.gov; *The World Factbook.*

St. Martin's Press, Inc., 175 Fifth Avenue, New York, New York 10010 (800) 221-7945; *The Statesman's Year-Book.*

Statistical Office of the United Nations, Publishing Service, New York, New York 10017 (800) 253-9646; *Energy Statistics Yearbook; Human Development Report; Trends in Europe and North America: The Statistical Yearbook of the Economic Commission for Europe;* and *Statistical Yearbook.*

The World Bank, 1818 H Street, NW, Washington, D.C. 20433 (202) 477-1234; *Statistical Handbook: States of the Former USSR.*

KAZAKHSTAN - EMPLOYMENT

Euromonitor International, Inc., 122 South Michigan Avenue, Suite 1200, Chicago, Illinois 60603 (800) 577-EURO; *International Marketing Data and Statistics.*

Statistical Office of the United Nations, Publishing Service, New York, New York 10017 (800) 253-9646; *Statistical Yearbook;* and *Trends in Europe and North America: The Statistical Yearbook of the Economic Commission for Europe.*

The World Bank, 1818 H Street, NW, Washington, D.C. 20433 (202) 477-1234; *Statistical Handbook: States of the Former USSR.*

KAZAKHSTAN - ENERGY

Academic International Press, Box 1111, Gulf Breeze, Florida 32562; *Russia and Eurasia Facts and Figures Annual.*

Business International Moscow, 23 Profsoyuznaya Ulitsa, 117859, Moscow (Telephone Number in U.S. (800) 938-4685); *The CIS Market Atlas.*

Euromonitor International, Inc., 122 South Michigan Avenue, Suite 1200, Chicago, Illinois 60603 (800) 577-EURO; *International Marketing Data and Statistics;*

World Marketing Data and Statistics; and *The World Economic Factbook.*

St. Martin's Press, Inc., 175 Fifth Avenue, New York, New York 10010 (800) 221-7945; *The Statesman's Year-Book.*

Statistical Office of the United Nations, Publishing Service, New York, New York 10017 (800) 253-9646; *Energy Statistics Yearbook; Human Development Report; Trends in Europe and North America: The Statistical Yearbook of the Economic Commission for Europe; World Statistics Pocketbook;* and *Statistical Yearbook.*

The World Bank, 1818 H Street, NW, Washington, D.C. 20433 (202) 477-1234; *Statistical Handbook: States of the Former USSR; The World Bank Atlas;* and *World Development Report.*

KAZAKHSTAN - ENVIRONMENT

Business International Moscow, 23 Profsoyuznaya Ulitsa, 117859, Moscow (Telephone Number in U.S. (800) 938-4685); *The CIS Market Atlas.*

Economist Intelligence Unit, 111 West 57th Street, New York, New York 10019 (800) 938-4685; *Kazakhstan Country Report.*

Statistical Office of the United Nations, Publishing Service, New York, New York 10017 (800) 253-9646; *Statistical Yearbook; World Statistics Pocketbook;* and *Trends in Europe and North America: The Statistical Yearbook of the Economic Commission for Europe.*

KAZAKHSTAN - EXCHANGE RATES

Central Intelligence Agency, Washington, D.C. 20505 (703) 482-1100, www.cia.gov; *The World Factbook.*

Euromonitor International, Inc., 122 South Michigan Avenue, Suite 1200, Chicago, Illinois 60603 (800) 577-EURO; *International Marketing Data and Statistics;* and *The World Economic Factbook.*

Europa Publications Limited, 18 Bedford Square, London, WC1B 3JN, England; *The Europa World Year Book.*

Statistical Office of the United Nations, Publishing Service, New York, New York 10017 (800) 253-9646; *Statistical Yearbook; World Statistics Pocketbook;* and *Trends in Europe and North America: The Statistical Yearbook of the Economic Commission for Europe.*

Walden Publishing, Ltd., Two Market Street, Saffron Walden Essex, CB10 1HZ, England; *The World of Information Asia and Pacific Review.*

KAZAKHSTAN - EXPORTS

Academic International Press, Box 1111, Gulf Breeze, Florida 32562; *Russia and Eurasia Facts and Figures Annual.*

Business International Moscow, 23 Profsoyuznaya Ulitsa, 117859, Moscow (Telephone Number in U.S. (800) 938-4685); *The CIS Market Atlas.*

Central Intelligence Agency, Washington, D.C. 20505 (703) 482-1100, www.cia.gov; *The World Factbook.*

Economist Intelligence Unit, 111 West 57th Street, New York, New York 10019 (800) 938-4685; *Kazakhstan Country Report.*

Euromonitor International, Inc., 122 South Michigan Avenue, Suite 1200, Chicago, Illinois 60603 (800) 577-EURO; *International Marketing Data and Statistics;* and *The World Economic Factbook.*

Europa Publications Limited, 18 Bedford Square, London, WC1B 3JN, England; *The Europa World Year Book.*

International Monetary Fund, 700 Nineteenth Street, NW, Washington, D.C. 20431 (202) 623-7000; *Direction of Trade Statistics.*

St. Martin's Press, Inc., 175 Fifth Avenue, New York, New York 10010 (800) 221-7945; *The Statesman's Year-Book.*

Statistical Office of the United Nations, Publishing Service, New York, New York 10017 (800) 253-9646; *International Trade Statistics Yearbook;* and *Trends in Europe and North America: The Statistical Yearbook of the Economic Commission for Europe.*

United Nations Conference on Trade and Development (UNCTAD), New York, New York 10017 (800) 253-9646; *Handbook of International Trade and Development Statistics.*

Walden Publishing, Ltd., Two Market Street, Saffron Walden Essex, CB10 1HZ, England; *The World of Information Asia and Pacific Review.*

The World Bank, 1818 H Street, NW, Washington, D.C. 20433 (202) 477-1234; *Statistical Handbook: States of the Former USSR; World Development Report;* and *World Development Indicators.*

KAZAKHSTAN - EXTERNAL DEBT

The World Bank, 1818 H Street, NW, Washington, D.C. 20433 (202) 477-1234; *World Development Indicators.*

KAZAKHSTAN - EXTERNAL INDEBTEDNESS

The World Bank, 1818 H Street, NW, Washington, D.C. 20433 (202) 477-1234; *World Development Report.*

KAZAKHSTAN - EXTERNAL TRADE

Academic International Press, Box 1111, Gulf Breeze, Florida 32562; *Russia and Eurasia Facts and Figures Annual.*

Euromonitor International, Inc., 122 South Michigan Avenue, Suite 1200, Chicago, Illinois 60603 (800) 577-EURO; *World Marketing Data and Statistics.*

Food and Agriculture Organization of the United Nations (FAO), Via delle Terme di Caracalla, 00100, Rome, Italy (Telephone Number in U.S. (202) 653-2400); *Trade Yearbook.*

Statistical Office of the United Nations, Publishing Service, New York, New York 10017 (800) 253-9646; *Statistical Yearbook.*

The World Bank, 1818 H Street, NW, Washington, D.C. 20433 (202) 477-1234; *Statistical Handbook: States of the Former USSR.*

KAZAKHSTAN - FABRIC PRODUCTION AND CONSUMPTION - See KAZAKHSTAN - TEXTILE INDUSTRY

KAZAKHSTAN - FERTILITY RATES

Central Intelligence Agency, Washington, D.C. 20505 (703) 482-1100, www.cia.gov; *The World Factbook.*

Statistical Office of the United Nations, Publishing Service, New York, New York 10017 (800) 253-9646; *Human Development Report; and Trends in Europe and North America: The Statistical Yearbook of the Economic Commission for Europe.*

The World Bank, 1818 H Street, NW, Washington, D.C. 20433 (202) 477-1234; *Statistical Handbook: States of the Former USSR; The World Bank Atlas; World Development Report; and World Development Indicators.*

World Health Organization, Office of Publications, 20 Avenue Appia, CH-1211 Geneva 27, Switzerland (Telephone Number in U.S. (518) 436-9686); *World Health Statistics Annual.*

KAZAKHSTAN - FERTILIZER

Food and Agriculture Organization of the United Nations (FAO), Via delle Terme di Caracalla, 00100, Rome, Italy (Telephone Number in U.S. (202) 653-2400); *Fertilizer Yearbook.*

Statistical Office of the United Nations, Publishing Service, New York, New York

10017 (800) 253-9646; *Industrial Commodity Statistics Yearbook;* and *Statistical Yearbook.*

KAZAKHSTAN - FINANCE

Economist Intelligence Unit, 111 West 57th Street, New York, New York 10019 (800) 938-4685; *Kazakhstan Country Report.*

Europa Publications Limited, 18 Bedford Square, London, WC1B 3JN, England; *The Europa World Year Book.*

The World Bank, 1818 H Street, NW, Washington, D.C. 20433 (202) 477-1234; *Statistical Handbook: States of the Former USSR.*

KAZAKHSTAN - FISHERIES

Food and Agriculture Organization of the United Nations (FAO), Via delle Terme di Caracalla, 00100, Rome, Italy (Telephone Number in U.S. (202) 653-2400); *The State of Food and Agriculture; and Yearbook of Fishery Statistics.*

Statistical Office of the United Nations, Publishing Service, New York, New York 10017 (800) 253-9646; *Industrial Commodity Statistics Yearbook;* and *Statistical Yearbook.*

KAZAKHSTAN - FOOD

Food and Agriculture Organization of the United Nations (FAO), Via delle Terme di Caracalla, 00100, Rome, Italy (Telephone Number in U.S. (202) 653-2400); *Production Yearbook; The State of Food and Agriculture; and Trade Yearbook.*

Statistical Office of the United Nations, Publishing Service, New York, New York 10017 (800) 253-9646; *Human Development Report; and Industrial Commodity Statistics Yearbook.*

KAZAKHSTAN - FOOTWEAR PRODUCTION AND CONSUMPTION - See KAZAKHSTAN - TEXTILE INDUSTRY

KAZAKHSTAN - FOREIGN DEBT

Walden Publishing, Ltd., Two Market Street, Saffron Walden Essex, CB10 1HZ, England; *The World of Information Asia and Pacific Review.*

KAZAKHSTAN - FOREIGN INVESTMENT

Business International Moscow, 23 Profsoyuznaya Ulitsa, 117859, Moscow (Telephone Number in U.S. (800) 938-4685); *The CIS Market Atlas.*

KAZAKHSTAN - FOREIGN TRADE

Business International Moscow, 23 Profsoyuznaya Ulitsa, 117859, Moscow (Telephone Number in U.S. (800) 938-4685); *The CIS Market Atlas.*

Economist Intelligence Unit, 111 West 57th Street, New York, New York 10019 (800) 938-4685; *Kazakhstan Country Report.*

Euromonitor International, Inc., 122 South Michigan Avenue, Suite 1200, Chicago, Illinois 60603 (800) 577-EURO; *The World Economic Factbook.*

Food and Agriculture Organization of the United Nations (FAO), Via delle Terme di Caracalla, 00100, Rome, Italy (Telephone Number in U.S. (202) 653-2400); *Trade Yearbook.*

International Monetary Fund, 700 Nineteenth Street, NW, Washington, D.C. 20431 (202) 623-7000; *Direction of Trade Statistics.*

St. Martin's Press, Inc., 175 Fifth Avenue, New York, New York 10010 (800) 221-7945; *The Statesman's Year-Book.*

Statistical Office of the United Nations, Publishing Service, New York, New York 10017 (800) 253-9646; *International Trade Statistics Yearbook;* and *Statistical Yearbook.*

The World Bank, 1818 H Street, NW, Washington, D.C. 20433 (202) 477-1234; *Statistical Handbook: States of the Former USSR; World Development Report; and World Development Indicators.*

KAZAKHSTAN - FORESTRY AND FOREST PRODUCTS

Academic International Press, Box 1111, Gulf Breeze, Florida 32562; *Russia and Eurasia Facts and Figures Annual.*

Business International Moscow, 23 Profsoyuznaya Ulitsa, 117859, Moscow (Telephone Number in U.S. (800) 938-4685); *The CIS Market Atlas.*

Food and Agriculture Organization of the United Nations (FAO), Via delle Terme di Caracalla, 00100, Rome, Italy (Telephone Number in U.S. (202) 653-2400); *The State of Food and Agriculture; and Yearbook of Forest Products.*

St. Martin's Press, Inc., 175 Fifth Avenue, New York, New York 10010 (800) 221-7945; *The Statesman's Year-Book.*

Statistical Office of the United Nations, Publishing Service, New York, New York 10017 (800) 253-9646; *Industrial Commodity Statistics Yearbook; Trends in Europe and North America: The Statistical Yearbook of the Economic Commission for*

Europe; and *Statistical Yearbook*.

United Nations Educational, Scientific and Cultural Organization (UNESCO), 7 Place de Fontenoy, F-75700 Paris, France (Telephone Number in U.S. (212) 963-5981); *Statistical Yearbook*.

The World Bank, 1818 H Street, NW, Washington, D.C. 20433 (202) 477-1234; *World Development Report*.

KAZAKHSTAN - GOATS - See KAZAKHSTAN - LIVESTOCK AND POULTRY

KAZAKHSTAN - GOVERNMENT

Academic International Press, Box 1111, Gulf Breeze, Florida 32562; *Russia and Eurasia Facts and Figures Annual*.

Central Intelligence Agency, Washington, D.C. 20505 (703) 482-1100, www.cia.gov; *The World Factbook*.

Europa Publications Limited, 18 Bedford Square, London, WC1B 3JN, England; *The Europa World Year Book*.

St. Martin's Press, Inc., 175 Fifth Avenue, New York, New York 10010 (800) 221-7945; *The Statesman's Year-Book*.

Statistical Office of the United Nations, Publishing Service, New York, New York 10017 (800) 253-9646; *National Accounts Statistics;* and *Statistical Yearbook*.

The World Bank, 1818 H Street, NW, Washington, D.C. 20433 (202) 477-1234; *Statistical Handbook: States of the Former USSR;* and *World Development Report*.

KAZAKHSTAN - GROSS DOMESTIC PRODUCT

Academic International Press, Box 1111, Gulf Breeze, Florida 32562; *Russia and Eurasia Facts and Figures Annual*.

Economist Intelligence Unit, 111 West 57th Street, New York, New York 10019 (800) 938-4685; *Kazakhstan Country Report*.

Euromonitor International, Inc., 122 South Michigan Avenue, Suite 1200, Chicago, Illinois 60603 (800) 577-EURO; *International Marketing Data and Statistics;* and *The World Economic Factbook*.

Statistical Office of the United Nations, Publishing Service, New York, New York 10017 (800) 253-9646; *Human Development Report; National Accounts Statistics; Trends in Europe and North America: The Statistical Yearbook of the Economic Commission for Europe;* and *Statistical Yearbook*.

The World Bank, 1818 H Street, NW,

Washington, D.C. 20433 (202) 477-1234; *Statistical Handbook: States of the Former USSR; World Development Report;* and *World Development Indicators*.

KAZAKHSTAN - GROSS NATIONAL PRODUCT

St. Martin's Press, Inc., 175 Fifth Avenue, New York, New York 10010 (800) 221-7945; *The Statesman's Year-Book*.

Walden Publishing, Ltd., Two Market Street, Saffron Walden Essex, CB10 1HZ, England; *The World of Information Asia and Pacific Review*.

The World Bank, 1818 H Street, NW, Washington, D.C. 20433 (202) 477-1234; *The World Bank Atlas; World Development Report;* and *World Development Indicators*.

KAZAKHSTAN - HEALTH

Academic International Press, Box 1111, Gulf Breeze, Florida 32562; *Russia and Eurasia Facts and Figures Annual*.

Business International Moscow, 23 Profsoyuznaya Ulitsa, 117859, Moscow (Telephone Number in U.S. (800) 938-4685); *The CIS Market Atlas*.

Euromonitor International, Inc., 122 South Michigan Avenue, Suite 1200, Chicago, Illinois 60603 (800) 577-EURO; *World Marketing Data and Statistics*.

Statistical Office of the United Nations, Publishing Service, New York, New York 10017 (800) 253-9646; *Human Development Report; Trends in Europe and North America: The Statistical Yearbook of the Economic Commission for Europe;* and *Statistical Yearbook*.

United Nations Children's Fund (UNICEF), 3 United Nations Plaza, New York, New York 10017 (800) 253-9646; *State of the World's Children*.

The World Bank, 1818 H Street, NW, Washington, D.C. 20433 (202) 477-1234; *World Development Report*.

World Health Organization, Office of Publications, 20 Avenue Appia, CH-1211 Geneva 27, Switzerland (Telephone Number in U.S. (518) 436-9686); *World Health Statistics Annual*.

KAZAKHSTAN - HIGHWAYS

Academic International Press, Box 1111, Gulf Breeze, Florida 32562; *Russia and Eurasia Facts and Figures Annual*.

Business International Moscow, 23 Profsoyuznaya Ulitsa, 117859, Moscow (Telephone Number in U.S. (800) 938-4685); *The CIS Market Atlas*.

Central Intelligence Agency, Washington, D.C. 20505 (703) 482-1100, www.cia.gov; *The World Factbook*.

St. Martin's Press, Inc., 175 Fifth Avenue, New York, New York 10010 (800) 221-7945; *The Statesman's Year-Book*.

Statistical Office of the United Nations, Publishing Service, New York, New York 10017 (800) 253-9646; *Trends in Europe and North America: The Statistical Yearbook of the Economic Commission for Europe*.

KAZAKHSTAN - HOUSING AND HOUSING UNITS

Business International Moscow, 23 Profsoyuznaya Ulitsa, 117859, Moscow (Telephone Number in U.S. (800) 938-4685); *The CIS Market Atlas*.

Euromonitor International, Inc., 122 South Michigan Avenue, Suite 1200, Chicago, Illinois 60603 (800) 577-EURO; *World Marketing Data and Statistics*.

Statistical Office of the United Nations, Publishing Service, New York, New York 10017 (800) 253-9646; *Trends in Europe and North America: The Statistical Yearbook of the Economic Commission for Europe*.

KAZAKHSTAN - ILLITERATE POPULATION

Central Intelligence Agency, Washington, D.C. 20505 (703) 482-1100, www.cia.gov; *The World Factbook*.

Euromonitor International, Inc., 122 South Michigan Avenue, Suite 1200, Chicago, Illinois 60603 (800) 577-EURO; *The World Economic Factbook*.

Statistical Office of the United Nations, Publishing Service, New York, New York 10017 (800) 253-9646; *Human Development Report*.

United Nations Educational, Scientific and Cultural Organization (UNESCO), 7 Place de Fontenoy, F-75700 Paris, France (Telephone Number in U.S. (212) 963-5981); *Statistical Yearbook*.

KAZAKHSTAN - IMPORTS

Academic International Press, Box 1111, Gulf Breeze, Florida 32562; *Russia and Eurasia Facts and Figures Annual*.

Business International Moscow, 23 Profsoyuznaya Ulitsa, 117859, Moscow (Telephone Number in U.S. (800) 938-4685); *The CIS Market Atlas*.

Central Intelligence Agency, Washington, D.C. 20505 (703) 482-1100, www.cia.gov; *The World Factbook*.

Economist Intelligence Unit, 111 West 57th Street, New York, New York 10019 (800) 938-4685; *Kazakhstan Country Report.*

Euromonitor International, Inc., 122 South Michigan Avenue, Suite 1200, Chicago, Illinois 60603 (800) 577-EURO; *International Marketing Data and Statistics;* and *The World Economic Factbook.*

Europa Publications Limited, 18 Bedford Square, London, WC1B 3JN, England; *The Europa World Year Book.*

International Monetary Fund, 700 Nineteenth Street, NW, Washington, D.C. 20431 (202) 623-7000; *Direction of Trade Statistics.*

St. Martin's Press, Inc., 175 Fifth Avenue, New York, New York 10010 (800) 221-7945; *The Statesman's Year-Book.*

Statistical Office of the United Nations, Publishing Service, New York, New York 10017 (800) 253-9646; *International Trade Statistics Yearbook;* and *Trends in Europe and North America: The Statistical Yearbook of the Economic Commission for Europe.*

United Nations Conference on Trade and Development (UNCTAD), New York, New York 10017 (800) 253-9646; *Handbook of International Trade and Development Statistics.*

Walden Publishing, Ltd., Two Market Street, Saffron Walden Essex, CB10 1HZ, England; *The World of Information Asia and Pacific Review.*

The World Bank, 1818 H Street, NW, Washington, D.C. 20433 (202) 477-1234; *Statistical Handbook: States of the Former USSR; World Development Report;* and *World Development Indicators.*

KAZAKHSTAN - INDUSTRY

Academic International Press, Box 1111, Gulf Breeze, Florida 32562; *Russia and Eurasia Facts and Figures Annual.*

Business International Moscow, 23 Profsoyuznaya Ulitsa, 117859, Moscow (Telephone Number in U.S. (800) 938-4685); *The CIS Market Atlas.*

Central Intelligence Agency, Washington, D.C. 20505 (703) 482-1100, www.cia.gov; *The World Factbook.*

Economist Intelligence Unit, 111 West 57th Street, New York, New York 10019 (800) 938-4685; *Kazakhstan Country Report.*

Euromonitor International, Inc., 122 South Michigan Avenue, Suite 1200,

Chicago, Illinois 60603 (800) 577-EURO; *The World Economic Factbook;* and *World Marketing Data and Statistics..*

Europa Publications Limited, 18 Bedford Square, London, WC1B 3JN, England; *The Europa World Year Book.*

St. Martin's Press, Inc., 175 Fifth Avenue, New York, New York 10010 (800) 221-7945; *The Statesman's Year-Book.*

Statistical Office of the United Nations, Publishing Service, New York, New York 10017 (800) 253-9646; *Industrial Commodity Statistics Yearbook; Trends in Europe and North America: The Statistical Yearbook of the Economic Commission for Europe;* and *Statistical Yearbook.*

The World Bank, 1818 H Street, NW, Washington, D.C. 20433 (202) 477-1234; *Statistical Handbook: States of the Former USSR;* and *World Development Indicators.*

KAZAKHSTAN - INFANT MORTALITY RATES - See KAZAKHSTAN - MORTALITY

KAZAKHSTAN - INTERNAL TRADE

Statistical Office of the United Nations, Publishing Service, New York, New York 10017 (800) 253-9646; *Statistical Yearbook.*

KAZAKHSTAN - LABOR

Academic International Press, Box 1111, Gulf Breeze, Florida 32562; *Russia and Eurasia Facts and Figures* Annual.

Business International Moscow, 23 Profsoyuznaya Ulitsa, 117859, Moscow (Telephone Number in U.S. (800) 938-4685); *The CIS Market Atlas.*

Central Intelligence Agency, Washington, D.C. 20505 (703) 482-1100, www.cia.gov; *The World Factbook.*

Euromonitor International, Inc., 122 South Michigan Avenue, Suite 1200, Chicago, Illinois 60603 (800) 577-EURO; *International Marketing Data and Statistics;* and *World Marketing Data and Statistics.*

St. Martin's Press, Inc., 175 Fifth Avenue, New York, New York 10010 (800) 221-7945; *The Statesman's Year-Book.*

Statistical Office of the United Nations, Publishing Service, New York, New York 10017 (800) 253-9646; *Human Development Report;* and *Statistical Yearbook.*

The World Bank, 1818 H Street, NW, Washington, D.C. 20433 (202) 477-1234; *Statistical Handbook: States of the Former USSR; The World Bank Atlas; World Development Report;* and *World Development Indicators.*

KAZAKHSTAN - LAND USE

Central Intelligence Agency, Washington, D.C. 20505 (703) 482-1100, www.cia.gov; *The World Factbook.*

Euromonitor International, Inc., 122 South Michigan Avenue, Suite 1200, Chicago, Illinois 60603 (800) 577-EURO; *International Marketing Data and Statistics.*

Food and Agriculture Organization of the United Nations (FAO), Via delle Terme di Caracalla, 00100, Rome, Italy (Telephone Number in U.S. (202) 653-2400); *Production Yearbook.*

The World Bank, 1818 H Street, NW, Washington, D.C. 20433 (202) 477-1234; *World Development Report.*

KAZAKHSTAN - LIBRARIES

Statistical Office of the United Nations, Publishing Service, New York, New York 10017 (800) 253-9646; *Trends in Europe and North America: The Statistical Yearbook of the Economic Commission for Europe.*

United Nations Educational, Scientific and Cultural Organization (UNESCO), 7 Place de Fontenoy, F-75700 Paris, France (Telephone Number in U.S. (212) 963-5981); *Statistical Yearbook.*

KAZAKHSTAN - LIFE EXPECTANCY

Academic International Press, Box 1111, Gulf Breeze, Florida 32562; *Russia and Eurasia Facts and Figures Annual.*

Business International Moscow, 23 Profsoyuznaya Ulitsa, 117859, Moscow (Telephone Number in U.S. (800) 938-4685); *The CIS Market Atlas.*

Central Intelligence Agency, Washington, D.C. 20505 (703) 482-1100, www.cia.gov; *The World Factbook.*

Euromonitor International, Inc., 122 South Michigan Avenue, Suite 1200, Chicago, Illinois 60603 (800) 577-EURO; *The World Economic Factbook.*

Statistical Office of the United Nations, Publishing Service, New York, New York 10017 (800) 253-9646; *Demographic Yearbook; Trends in Europe and North America: The Statistical Yearbook of the Economic Commission for Europe; World Statistics Pocketbook;* and *Human Development Report.*

The World Bank, 1818 H Street, NW, Washington, D.C. 20433 (202) 477-1234; *The World Bank Atlas; World Development Report;* and *World Development Indicators.*

World Health Organization, Office of Publications, 20 Avenue Appia, CH-1211

Geneva 27, Switzerland (Telephone Number in U.S. (518) 436-9686); *World Health Statistics Annual.*

KAZAKHSTAN - LIVESTOCK AND POULTRY

Academic International Press, Box 1111, Gulf Breeze, Florida 32562; *Russia and Eurasia Facts and Figures Annual.*

Business International Moscow, 23 Profsoyuznaya Ulitsa, 117859, Moscow (Telephone Number in U.S. (800) 938-4685); *The CIS Market Atlas.*

Europa Publications Limited, 18 Bedford Square, London, WC1B 3JN, England; *The Europa World Year Book.*

Food and Agriculture Organization of the United Nations (FAO), Via delle Terme di Caracalla, 00100, Rome, Italy (Telephone Number in U.S. (202) 653-2400); *Production Yearbook; The State of Food and Agriculture;* and *Trade Yearbook.*

St. Martin's Press, Inc., 175 Fifth Avenue, New York, New York 10010 (800) 221-7945; *The Statesman's Year-Book.*

Statistical Office of the United Nations, Publishing Service, New York, New York 10017 (800) 253-9646; *Industrial Commodity Statistics Yearbook;* and *Statistical Yearbook.*

KAZAKHSTAN - MACHINERY

Statistical Office of the United Nations, Publishing Service, New York, New York 10017 (800) 253-9646; *Industrial Commodity Statistics Yearbook.*

KAZAKHSTAN - MAIL - NUMBER OF PIECES SENT OR RECEIVED

Statistical Office of the United Nations, Publishing Service, New York, New York 10017 (800) 253-9646; *Statistical Yearbook.*

KAZAKHSTAN - MANUFACTURING

Statistical Office of the United Nations, Publishing Service, New York, New York 10017 (800) 253-9646; *Industrial Commodity Statistics Yearbook;* and *Statistical Yearbook.*

The World Bank, 1818 H Street, NW, Washington, D.C. 20433 (202) 477-1234; *World Development Indicators.*

KAZAKHSTAN - MARRIAGE RATES

Academic International Press, Box 1111, Gulf Breeze, Florida 32562; *Russia and Eurasia Facts and Figures Annual.*

Statistical Office of the United Nations, Publishing Service, New York, New York 10017 (800) 253-9646; *Demographic*

Yearbook; Trends in Europe and North America: The Statistical Yearbook of the Economic Commission for Europe; and *Statistical Yearbook.*

KAZAKHSTAN - MEAT PRODUCTION - See KAZAKHSTAN - LIVESTOCK AND POULTRY

KAZAKHSTAN - MERCHANT SHIPPING

Statistical Office of the United Nations, Publishing Service, New York, New York 10017 (800) 253-9646; *Statistical Yearbook.*

KAZAKHSTAN - MILITARY

Academic International Press, Box 1111, Gulf Breeze, Florida 32562; *Russia and Eurasia Facts and Figures Annual.*

Central Intelligence Agency, Washington, D.C. 20505 (703) 482-1100, www.cia.gov; *The World Factbook.*

Euromonitor International, Inc., 122 South Michigan Avenue, Suite 1200, Chicago, Illinois 60603 (800) 577-EURO; *World Marketing Data and Statistics.*

The International Institute for Strategic Studies, 23 Tavistock Street, London WC2E 7NQ, England 44 171 3797676; *The Military Balance.*

St. Martin's Press, Inc., 175 Fifth Avenue, New York, New York 10010 (800) 221-7945; *The Statesman's Year-Book.*

Statistical Office of the United Nations, Publishing Service, New York, New York 10017 (800) 253-9646; *Human Development Report.*

KAZAKHSTAN - MINING AND MINERAL PRODUCTS

Academic International Press, Box 1111, Gulf Breeze, Florida 32562; *Russia and Eurasia Facts and Figures Annual.*

Business International Moscow, 23 Profsoyuznaya Ulitsa, 117859, Moscow (Telephone Number in U.S. (800) 938-4685); *The CIS Market Atlas.*

Europa Publications Limited, 18 Bedford Square, London, WC1B 3JN, England; *The Europa World Year Book.*

St. Martin's Press, Inc., 175 Fifth Avenue, New York, New York 10010 (800) 221-7945; *The Statesman's Year-Book.*

Statistical Office of the United Nations, Publishing Service, New York, New York 10017 (800) 253-9646; *Energy Statistics Yearbook;* and *Statistical Yearbook.*

KAZAKHSTAN - MONEY SUPPLY

Economist Intelligence Unit, 111 West

57th Street, New York, New York 10019 (800) 938-4685; *Kazakhstan Country Report.*

KAZAKHSTAN - MONUMENTS AND HISTORICAL SITES

United Nations Educational, Scientific and Cultural Organization (UNESCO), 7 Place de Fontenoy, F-75700 Paris, France (Telephone Number in U.S. (212) 963-5981); *Statistical Yearbook.*

KAZAKHSTAN - MORTALITY

Academic International Press, Box 1111, Gulf Breeze, Florida 32562; *Russia and Eurasia Facts and Figures Annual.*

Business International Moscow, 23 Profsoyuznaya Ulitsa, 117859, Moscow (Telephone Number in U.S. (800) 938-4685); *The CIS Market Atlas.*

Central Intelligence Agency, Washington, D.C. 20505 (703) 482-1100, www.cia.gov; *The World Factbook.*

Euromonitor International, Inc., 122 South Michigan Avenue, Suite 1200, Chicago, Illinois 60603 (800) 577-EURO; *International Marketing Data and Statistics;* and *The World Economic Factbook.*

Europa Publications Limited, 18 Bedford Square, London, WC1B 3JN, England; *The Europa World Year Book.*

St. Martin's Press, Inc., 175 Fifth Avenue, New York, New York 10010 (800) 221-7945; *The Statesman's Year-Book.*

Statistical Office of the United Nations, Publishing Service, New York, New York 10017 (800) 253-9646; *Demographic Yearbook; Human Development Report; Trends in Europe and North America: The Statistical Yearbook of the Economic Commission for Europe; World Statistics Pocketbook;* and *Statistical Yearbook.*

United Nations Children's Fund (UNICEF), 3 United Nations Plaza, New York, New York 10017 (800) 253-9646; *State of the World's Children.*

The World Bank, 1818 H Street, NW, Washington, D.C. 20433 (202) 477-1234; *The World Bank Atlas; World Development Report;* and *World Development Indicators.*

World Health Organization, Office of Publications, 20 Avenue Appia, CH-1211 Geneva 27, Switzerland (Telephone Number in U.S. (518) 436-9686); *World Health Statistics Annual.*

KAZAKHSTAN - MOTION PICTURES

Statistical Office of the United Nations, Publishing Service, New York, New York

10017 (800) 253-9646; *Statistical Yearbook.*

United Nations Educational, Scientific and Cultural Organization (UNESCO), 7 Place de Fontenoy, F-75700 Paris, France (Telephone Number in U.S. (212) 963-5981); *Statistical Yearbook.*

KAZAKHSTAN - MOTOR VEHICLE PRODUCTION

Business International Moscow, 23 Profsoyuznaya Ulitsa, 117859, Moscow (Telephone Number in U.S. (800) 938-4685); *The CIS Market Atlas.*

Statistical Office of the United Nations, Publishing Service, New York, New York 10017 (800) 253-9646; *Statistical Yearbook.*

KAZAKHSTAN - MUSEUMS

United Nations Educational, Scientific and Cultural Organization (UNESCO), 7 Place de Fontenoy, F-75700 Paris, France (Telephone Number in U.S. (212) 963-5981); *Statistical Yearbook.*

KAZAKHSTAN - NATIONAL ACCOUNTS

Statistical Office of the United Nations, Publishing Service, New York, New York 10017 (800) 253-9646; *National Accounts Statistics;* and *Statistical Yearbook.*

The World Bank, 1818 H Street, NW, Washington, D.C. 20433 (202) 477-1234; *Statistical Handbook: States of the Former USSR.*

KAZAKHSTAN - NATIONAL INCOME

Business International Moscow, 23 Profsoyuznaya Ulitsa, 117859, Moscow (Telephone Number in U.S. (800) 938-4685); *The CIS Market Atlas.*

Statistical Office of the United Nations, Publishing Service, New York, New York 10017 (800) 253-9646; *National Accounts Statistics;* and *Statistical Yearbook.*

KAZAKHSTAN - NATIONAL PRODUCT

Statistical Office of the United Nations, Publishing Service, New York, New York 10017 (800) 253-9646; *Statistical Yearbook.*

KAZAKHSTAN - PATENTS, TRADEMARKS AND SERVICE MARKS

Statistical Office of the United Nations, Publishing Service, New York, New York 10017 (800) 253-9646; *Statistical Yearbook.*

KAZAKHSTAN - PERIODICALS

United Nations Educational, Scientific and Cultural Organization (UNESCO), 7 Place de Fontenoy, F-75700 Paris, France (Telephone Number in U.S. (212) 963-

5981); *Statistical Yearbook.*

KAZAKHSTAN - PETROLEUM INDUSTRY

Food and Agriculture Organization of the United Nations (FAO), Via delle Terme di Caracalla, 00100, Rome, Italy (Telephone Number in U.S. (202) 653-2400); *The State of Food and Agriculture.*

St. Martin's Press, Inc., 175 Fifth Avenue, New York, New York 10010 (800) 221-7945; *The Statesman's Year-Book.*

Statistical Office of the United Nations, Publishing Service, New York, New York 10017 (800) 253-9646; *Energy Statistics Yearbook; Industrial Commodity Statistics Yearbook; Trends in Europe and North America: The Statistical Yearbook of the Economic Commission for Europe;* and *Statistical Yearbook.*

KAZAKHSTAN - PIGS - See KAZAKHSTAN - LIVESTOCK AND POULTRY

KAZAKHSTAN - POPULATION

Academic International Press, Box 1111, Gulf Breeze, Florida 32562; *Russia and Eurasia Facts and Figures Annual.*

Business International Moscow, 23 Profsoyuznaya Ulitsa, 117859, Moscow (Telephone Number in U.S. (800) 938-4685); *The CIS Market Atlas.*

Central Intelligence Agency, Washington, D.C. 20505 (703) 482-1100, www.cia.gov; *The World Factbook.*

Economist Intelligence Unit, 111 West 57th Street, New York, New York 10019 (800) 938-4685; *Kazakhstan Country Report.*

Euromonitor International, Inc., 122 South Michigan Avenue, Suite 1200, Chicago, Illinois 60603 (800) 577-EURO; *International Marketing Data and Statistics;* and *The World Economic Factbook.*

Food and Agriculture Organization of the United Nations (FAO), Via delle Terme di Caracalla, 00100, Rome, Italy (Telephone Number in U.S. (202) 653-2400); *Production Yearbook.*

St. Martin's Press, Inc., 175 Fifth Avenue, New York, New York 10010 (800) 221-7945; *The Statesman's Year-Book.*

Statistical Office of the United Nations, Publishing Service, New York, New York 10017 (800) 253-9646; *Demographic Yearbook; Human Development Report; Trends in Europe and North America: The Statistical Yearbook of the Economic Commission for Europe; World Statistics Pocketbook;* and *Statistical Yearbook.*

United Nations Educational, Scientific and Cultural Organization (UNESCO), 7 Place de Fontenoy, F-75700 Paris, France (Telephone Number in U.S. (212) 963-5981); *Statistical Yearbook.*

Walden Publishing, Ltd., Two Market Street, Saffron Walden Essex, CB10 1HZ, England; *The World of Information Asia and Pacific Review.*

The World Bank, 1818 H Street, NW, Washington, D.C. 20433 (202) 477-1234; *Statistical Handbook: States of the Former USSR; The World Bank Atlas; World Development Report;* and *World Development Indicators.*

World Health Organization, Office of Publications, 20 Avenue Appia, CH-1211 Geneva 27, Switzerland (Telephone Number in U.S. (518) 436-9686); *World Health Statistics Annual.*

KAZAKHSTAN - POST OFFICES

Statistical Office of the United Nations, Publishing Service, New York, New York 10017 (800) 253-9646; *Trends in Europe and North America: The Statistical Yearbook of the Economic Commission for Europe.*

KAZAKHSTAN - POULTRY - See KAZAKHSTAN - LIVESTOCK AND POULTRY

KAZAKHSTAN - PRICES

Food and Agriculture Organization of the United Nations (FAO), Via delle Terme di Caracalla, 00100, Rome, Italy (Telephone Number in U.S. (202) 653-2400); *Production Yearbook.*

The World Bank, 1818 H Street, NW, Washington, D.C. 20433 (202) 477-1234; *Statistical Handbook: States of the Former USSR.*

KAZAKHSTAN - PRODUCTION

The World Bank, 1818 H Street, NW, Washington, D.C. 20433 (202) 477-1234; *Statistical Handbook: States of the Former USSR.*

KAZAKHSTAN - PUBLIC FINANCE - See KAZAKHSTAN - FINANCE

KAZAKHSTAN - RADIO RECEIVERS

St. Martin's Press, Inc., 175 Fifth Avenue, New York, New York 10010 (800) 221-7945; *The Statesman's Year-Book.*

Statistical Office of the United Nations, Publishing Service, New York, New York 10017 (800) 253-9646; *Statistical Yearbook.*

KAZAKHSTAN - RAILWAYS

Academic International Press, Box

1111, Gulf Breeze, Florida 32562; *Russia and Eurasia Facts and Figures Annual.*

Business International Moscow, 23 Profsoyuznaya Ulitsa, 117859, Moscow (Telephone Number in U.S. (800) 938-4685); *The CIS Market Atlas.*

St. Martin's Press, Inc., 175 Fifth Avenue, New York, New York 10010 (800) 221-7945; *The Statesman's Year-Book.*

Statistical Office of the United Nations, Publishing Service, New York, New York 10017 (800) 253-9646; *Statistical Yearbook; and Trends in Europe and North America: The Statistical Yearbook of the Economic Commission for Europe.*

KAZAKHSTAN - RELIGION

Academic International Press, Box 1111, Gulf Breeze, Florida 32562; *Russia and Eurasia Facts and Figures Annual.*

Central Intelligence Agency, Washington, D.C. 20505 (703) 482-1100, www.cia.gov; *The World Factbook.*

St. Martin's Press, Inc., 175 Fifth Avenue, New York, New York 10010 (800) 221-7945; *The Statesman's Year-Book.*

KAZAKHSTAN - RETAIL TRADE

Business International Moscow, 23 Profsoyuznaya Ulitsa, 117859, Moscow (Telephone Number in U.S. (800) 938-4685); *The CIS Market Atlas.*

Euromonitor International, Inc., 122 South Michigan Avenue, Suite 1200, Chicago, Illinois 60603 (800) 577-EURO; *World Marketing Data and Statistics.*

Statistical Office of the United Nations, Publishing Service, New York, New York 10017 (800) 253-9646; *Statistical Yearbook.*

KAZAKHSTAN - ROADS - See
KAZAKHSTAN - HIGHWAYS

KAZAKHSTAN - ROUNDWOOD PRODUCTION AND CONSUMPTION -See KAZAKHSTAN - FORESTRY AND FOREST PRODUCTS

KAZAKHSTAN - RUBBER PRODUCTION AND CONSUMPTION

Statistical Office of the United Nations, Publishing Service, New York, New York 10017 (800) 253-9646; *Statistical Yearbook.*

KAZAKHSTAN - SCIENTISTS, TECHNICIANS AND ENGINEERS

Statistical Office of the United Nations, Publishing Service, New York, New York 10017 (800) 253-9646; *Statistical Yearbook.*

KAZAKHSTAN - SHEEP - See
KAZAKHSTAN - LIVESTOCK AND POULTRY

KAZAKHSTAN - SOCIAL DATA

Statistical Office of the United Nations, Publishing Service, New York, New York 10017 (800) 253-9646; *World Statistics Pocketbook.*

KAZAKHSTAN - SOCIAL SECURITY

Statistical Office of the United Nations, Publishing Service, New York, New York 10017 (800) 253-9646; *National Accounts Statistics.*

KAZAKHSTAN - STEEL PRODUCTION AND CONSUMPTION - See KAZAKHSTAN - MINING AND MINERAL PRODUCTS

KAZAKHSTAN - TAXATION

Europa Publications Limited, 18 Bedford Square, London, WC1B 3JN, England; *The Europa World Year Book.*

KAZAKHSTAN - TELEPHONES IN USE

Academic International Press, Box 1111, Gulf Breeze, Florida 32562; *Russia and Eurasia Facts and Figures Annual.*

Central Intelligence Agency, Washington, D.C. 20505 (703) 482-1100, www.cia.gov; *The World Factbook.*

Statistical Office of the United Nations, Publishing Service, New York, New York 10017 (800) 253-9646; *Statistical Yearbook; World Statistics Pocketbook; and Trends in Europe and North America: The Statistical Yearbook of the Economic Commission for Europe.*

KAZAKHSTAN - TEXTILE INDUSTRY

Business International Moscow, 23 Profsoyuznaya Ulitsa, 117859, Moscow (Telephone Number in U.S. (800) 938-4685); *The CIS Market Atlas.*

Statistical Office of the United Nations, Publishing Service, New York, New York 10017 (800) 253-9646; *Industrial Commodity Statistics Yearbook; and Statistical Yearbook.*

KAZAKHSTAN - THEATRE

United Nations Educational, Scientific and Cultural Organization (UNESCO), 7 Place de Fontenoy, F-75700 Paris, France (Telephone Number in U.S. (212) 963-5981); *Statistical Yearbook.*

KAZAKHSTAN - TIRE (MOTOR VEHICLE) PRODUCTION

Statistical Office of the United Nations, Publishing Service, New York, New York

10017 (800) 253-9646; *Statistical Yearbook.*

KAZAKHSTAN - TOBACCO PRODUCTION

Statistical Office of the United Nations, Publishing Service, New York, New York 10017 (800) 253-9646; *Statistical Yearbook.*

KAZAKHSTAN - TOURISM

Business International Moscow, 23 Profsoyuznaya Ulitsa, 117859, Moscow (Telephone Number in U.S. (800) 938-4685); *The CIS Market Atlas.*

Euromonitor International, Inc., 122 South Michigan Avenue, Suite 1200, Chicago, Illinois 60603 (800) 577-EURO; *The World Economic Factbook.*

Statistical Office of the United Nations, Publishing Service, New York, New York 10017 (800) 253-9646; *Statistical Yearbook; and Trends in Europe and North America: The Statistical Yearbook of the Economic Commission for Europe.*

KAZAKHSTAN - TRADEMARKS AND SERVICE MARKS - See KAZAKHSTAN - PATENTS, TRADEMARKS AND SERVICE MARKS

KAZAKHSTAN - TRANSPORTATION AND COMMUNICATION

Academic International Press, Box 1111, Gulf Breeze, Florida 32562; *Russia and Eurasia Facts and Figures Annual.*

Business International Moscow, 23 Profsoyuznaya Ulitsa, 117859, Moscow (Telephone Number in U.S. (800) 938-4685); *The CIS Market Atlas.*

Central Intelligence Agency, Washington, D.C. 20505 (703) 482-1100, www.cia.gov; *The World Factbook.*

Euromonitor International, Inc., 122 South Michigan Avenue, Suite 1200, Chicago, Illinois 60603 (800) 577-EURO; *International Marketing Data and Statistics; and World Marketing Data and Statistics.*

St. Martin's Press, Inc., 175 Fifth Avenue, New York, New York 10010 (800) 221-7945; *The Statesman's Year-Book.*

Statistical Office of the United Nations, Publishing Service, New York, New York 10017 (800) 253-9646; *Human Development Report; and Trends in Europe and North America: The Statistical Yearbook of the Economic Commission for Europe.*

KAZAKHSTAN - UNEMPLOYMENT

Central Intelligence Agency, Washington, D.C. 20505 (703) 482-1100, www.cia.gov; *The World Factbook.*

St. Martin's Press, Inc., 175 Fifth Avenue, New York, New York 10010 (800) 221-7945; *The Statesman's Year-Book.*

Statistical Office of the United Nations, Publishing Service, New York, New York 10017 (800) 253-9646; *Statistical Yearbook;* and *Trends in Europe and North America: The Statistical Yearbook of the Economic Commission for Europe.*

KAZAKHSTAN - VITAL STATISTICS

St. Martin's Press, Inc., 175 Fifth Avenue, New York, New York 10010 (800) 221-7945; *The Statesman's Year-Book.*

Statistical Office of the United Nations, Publishing Service, New York, New York 10017 (800) 253-9646; *Statistical Yearbook.*

World Health Organization, Office of Publications, 20 Avenue Appia, CH-1211 Geneva 27, Switzerland (Telephone Number in U.S. (518) 436-9686); *World Health Statistics Annual.*

KAZAKHSTAN - WAGES

Business International Moscow, 23 Profsoyuznaya Ulitsa, 117859, Moscow (Telephone Number in U.S. (800) 938-4685); *The CIS Market Atlas.*

Statistical Office of the United Nations, Publishing Service, New York, New York 10017 (800) 253-9646; *Statistical Yearbook.*

The World Bank, 1818 H Street, NW, Washington, D.C. 20433 (202) 477-1234; *Statistical Handbook: States of the Former USSR.*

KAZAKHSTAN - WELFARE

Academic International Press, Box 1111, Gulf Breeze, Florida 32562; *Russia and Eurasia Facts and Figures Annual.*

St. Martin's Press, Inc., 175 Fifth Avenue, New York, New York 10010 (800) 221-7945; *The Statesman's Year-Book.*

KAZAKHSTAN - WHOLESALE PRICES

Academic International Press, Box 1111, Gulf Breeze, Florida 32562; *Russia and Eurasia Facts and Figures Annual.*

Statistical Office of the United Nations, Publishing Service, New York, New York 10017 (800) 253-9646; *Statistical Yearbook.*

KAZAKHSTAN - WHOLESALE TRADE

Statistical Office of the United Nations, Publishing Service, New York, New York 10017 (800) 253-9646; *Statistical Yearbook.*

KAZAKHSTAN - WOOL PRODUCTION AND CONSUMPTION - See KAZAKHSTAN -

TEXTILE INDUSTRY

KENTUCKY - See also STATE DATA (FOR INDIVIDUAL STATES)

Kentucky - Primary Statistics Source

Kentucky Cabinet for Economic Development, State Government of Kentucky, Capital Plaza Office Tower, Frankfort, Kentucky. 40601 (502) 564-4886; *Kentucky Deskbook of Economic Statistics;* and Internet site: http://www.edc.state. ky.us.

Kentucky - State Data Centers

Kentucky State Data Center, University of Louisville, 426 W. Bloom Street, Louisville, Kentucky 40208 (502) 852-7990.

Governor's Office of Policy and Management, Capitol Annex, Room 284, Frankfort, Kentucky 40601, Ms. Diane Hancock (502) 564-7300.

State Library Division, Department of Libraries and Archives, 300 Coffeetree Road, Post Office Box 537, Frankfort, Kentucky 40601, Ms. Brenda Fuller (502) 564-8300, ext. 334.

Kenya - National Statistical Offices

Kenya Customs and Excise Department, Ministry of Finance, Post Office Box 40160, Nairobi, Kenya.

Ministry of Planning and National Development, Post Office Box 30266, Nairobi, Kenya.

Kenya - Primary Statistics Sources

Central Bureau of Statistics, Ministry of Planning and National Development, Post Office Box 30266, Nairobi, Kenya; *Statistical Abstract* and *Kenya Statistical Digest.*

KENYA - AGRICULTURE

Central Bureau of Statistics, Ministry of Economic Planning and Development, Post Office Box 30266, Nairobi, Kenya; *Republic of Kenya Statistical Abstract.*

Economist Intelligence Unit, 111 West 57th Street, New York, New York 10019 (800) 938-4685; *Kenya Country Report.*

Euromonitor International, Inc., 122 South Michigan Avenue, Suite 1200,

Chicago, Illinois 60603 (800) 577-EURO; *International Marketing Data and Statistics;* and *World Marketing Data and Statistics.*

Europa Publications Limited, 18 Bedford Square, London, WC1B 3JN, England; *The Europa World Year Book.*

Food and Agricultural Organization of the United Nations (FAO), Via delle Terme di Caracalla, 00100 Rome, Italy (Telephone Number in U.S. (202) 653-2400); *Production Yearbook; The State of Food and Agriculture; Trade Yearbook;* and *Production Yearbook.*

M.E. Sharpe, 80 Business Park Drive, Armonk, New York 10504 (800) 541-6563; *The Illustrated Book of World Rankings.*

St. Martin's Press, Inc., 175 Fifth Avenue, New York, New York 10010 (800) 221-7945; *The Statesman's Year-Book.*

Statistical Office of the United Nations, Publishing Service, New York, New York 10017 (800) 253-9646; *Statistical Yearbook;* and *Survey of Economic and Social Conditions in Africa.*

The World Bank, 1818 H Street, NW, Washington, D.C. 20433 (202) 477-1234; *World Development Indicators.*

United Nations Conference on Trade and Development, Central Statistical Service, Palais des Nations, Geneva, Switzerland (Telephone in U.S. (800) 253-9646); *UNCTAD Commodity Yearbook.*

United Nations Economic Commission for Africa, Africa Hall, Post Office Box 3001, Addis Ababa, Ethiopia (Telephone Number in U.S. (800) 253-9646); *African Statistical Yearbook.*

KENYA - AIRLINE SERVICE

Europa Publications Limited, 18 Bedford Square, London, WC1B 3JN, England; *The Europa World Year Book.*

M.E. Sharpe, 80 Business Park Drive, Armonk, New York 10504 (800) 541-6563; *The Illustrated Book of World Rankings.*

St. Martin's Press, Inc., 175 Fifth Avenue, New York, New York 10010 (800) 221-7945; *The Statesman's Year-Book.*

Statistical Office of the United Nations, Publishing Service, New York, New York 10017 (800) 253-9646; *Statistical Yearbook.*

United Nations Economic Commission for Africa, Africa Hall, Post Office Box 3001, Addis Ababa, Ethiopia (Telephone Number in U.S. (800) 253-9646); *African Statistical Yearbook.*

KENYA - ALUMINUM PRODUCTION - See

KENYA - MINING AND MINERAL PRODUCTS

KENYA - ANIMAL HEALTH

Food and Agricultural Organization of the United Nations (FAO), Via delle Terme di Caracalla, 00100 Rome, Italy (Telephone Number in U.S. (202) 653-2400); *Animal Health Yearbook*.

KENYA - AREA AND DENSITY OF POPULATION

African Development Bank, 01 BP 1387, Abidjan 01, Cote d'Ivoire; *Selected Statistics on Regional Member Countries*.

Central Intelligence Agency, Washington, D.C. 20505 (703) 482-1100, www.cia.gov; *The World Factbook*.

Euromonitor International, Inc., 122 South Michigan Avenue, Suite 1200, Chicago, Illinois 60603 (800) 577-EURO; *International Marketing Data and Statistics;* and *The World Economic Factbook*.

Europa Publications Limited, 18 Bedford Square, London, WC1B 3JN, England; *The Europa World Year Book*.

Food and Agricultural Organization of the United Nations (FAO), Via delle Terme di Caracalla, 00100 Rome, Italy (Telephone Number in U.S. (202) 653-2400); *The State of Food and Agriculture*.

M.E. Sharpe, 80 Business Park Drive, Armonk, New York 10504 (800) 541-6563; *The Illustrated Book of World Rankings*.

St. Martin's Press, Inc., 175 Fifth Avenue, New York, New York 10010 (800) 221-7945; *The Statesman's Year-Book*.

Statistical Office of the United Nations, Publishing Service, New York, New York 10017 (800) 253-9646; *Statistical Yearbook;* and *Survey of Economic and Social Conditions in Africa*.

United Nations Educational, Scientific and Cultural Organization (UNESCO), 7 Place de Fontenoy, F-75700 Paris, France (Telephone Number in U.S. (212) 963-5981); *Statistical Yearbook*.

The World Bank, 1818 H Street, NW, Washington, D.C. 20433 (202) 477-1234; *World Development Report*.

KENYA - BALANCE OF PAYMENTS

African Development Bank, 01 BP 1387, Abidjan 01, Cote d'Ivoire; *Selected Statistics on Regional Member Countries*.

The Economist Intelligence Unit, 111 West 57th Street, New York, New York 10019 (800) 938-4685; *The World Market Atlas*.

Europa Publications Limited, 18 Bedford Square, London, WC1B 3JN, England; *The Europa World Year Book*.

International Monetary Fund, 700 Nineteenth Street, NW, Washington, D.C. 20431 (202) 623-7000; *Balance of Payments Yearbook*.

United Nations Conference on Trade and Development (UNCTAD), New York, New York 10017 (800) 253-9646; *Handbook of International Trade and Development Statistics*.

United Nations Economic Commission for Africa, Africa Hall, Post Office Box 3001, Addis Ababa, Ethiopia (Telephone Number in U.S. (800) 253-9646); *African Statistical Yearbook*.

The World Bank, 1818 H Street, NW, Washington, D.C. 20433 (202) 477-1234; *World Development Report;* and *World Development Indicators*.

KENYA - BANKING

Euromonitor International, Inc., 122 South Michigan Avenue, Suite 1200, Chicago, Illinois 60603 (800) 577-EURO; *World Marketing Data and Statistics*.

International Monetary Fund, 700 Nineteenth Street, NW, Washington, D.C. 20431 (202) 623-7000; *Government Finance Statistics Yearbook;* and *International Financial Statistics*.

M.E. Sharpe, 80 Business Park Drive, Armonk, New York 10504 (800) 541-6563; *The Illustrated Book of World Rankings*.

St. Martin's Press, Inc., 175 Fifth Avenue, New York, New York 10010 (800) 221-7945; *The Statesman's Year-Book*.

United Nations Economic Commission for Africa, Africa Hall, Post Office Box 3001, Addis Ababa, Ethiopia (Telephone Number in U.S. (800) 253-9646); *African Statistical Yearbook*.

KENYA - BARLEY PRODUCTION - See KENYA - CROPS

KENYA - BEER PRODUCTION - See KENYA - BEVERAGES

KENYA - BEVERAGES

M.E. Sharpe, 80 Business Park Drive, Armonk, New York 10504 (800) 541-6563; *The Illustrated Book of World Rankings*.

Statistical Office of the United Nations, Publishing Service, New York, New York 10017 (800) 253-9646; *Statistical Yearbook*.

KENYA - BIRTH RATES

Central Intelligence Agency, Washington, D.C. 20505 (703) 482-1100, www.cia.gov; *The World Factbook*.

Euromonitor International, Inc., 122 South Michigan Avenue, Suite 1200, Chicago, Illinois 60603 (800) 577-EURO; *International Marketing Data and Statistics;* and *The World Economic Factbook*.

Europa Publications Limited, 18 Bedford Square, London, WC1B 3JN, England; *The Europa World Year Book*.

M.E. Sharpe, 80 Business Park Drive, Armonk, New York 10504 (800) 541-6563; *The Illustrated Book of World Rankings*.

Statistical Office of the United Nations, Publishing Service, New York, New York 10017 (800) 253-9646; *Demographic Yearbook; Statistical Yearbook;* and *Survey of Economic and Social Conditions in Africa*.

The World Bank, 1818 H Street, NW, Washington, D.C. 20433 (202) 477-1234; *World Development Indicators*.

KENYA - BONDS

International Monetary Fund, 700 Nineteenth Street, NW, Washington, D.C. 20431 (202) 623-7000; *Government Finance Statistics Yearbook*.

KENYA - BOOK PRODUCTION

Europa Publications Limited, 18 Bedford Square, London, WC1B 3JN, England; *The Europa World Year Book*.

KENYA - BROADCASTING

Billboard Limited, Post Office Box 9027, 1006 AA Amsterdam, The Netherlands (Telephone Number in U.S. (212) 764-7300); *World Radio TV Handbook*.

Central Intelligence Agency, Washington, D.C. 20505 (703) 482-1100, www.cia.gov; *The World Factbook*.

Euromonitor International, Inc., 122 South Michigan Avenue, Suite 1200, Chicago, Illinois 60603 (800) 577-EURO; *World Marketing Data and Statistics*.

M.E. Sharpe, 80 Business Park Drive, Armonk, New York 10504 (800) 541-6563; *The Illustrated Book of World Rankings*.

St. Martin's Press, Inc., 175 Fifth Avenue, New York, New York 10010 (800) 221-7945; *The Statesman's Year-Book*.

KENYA - BUDGET

Central Intelligence Agency,

Washington, D.C. 20505 (703) 482-1100, www.cia.gov; *The World Factbook.*

KENYA - BUSINESS AND PROFESSIONAL LICENSES

International Monetary Fund, 700 Nineteenth Street, NW, Washington, D.C. 20431 (202) 623-7000; *Government Finance Statistics Yearbook.*

KENYA - BUTTER PRODUCTION - See KENYA - DAIRY PRODUCTS

KENYA - CALORIE SUPPLY

African Development Bank, 01 BP 1387, Abidjan 01, Cote d'Ivoire; *Selected Statistics on Regional Member Countries.*

Food and Agricultural Organization of the United Nations (FAO), Via delle Terme di Caracalla, 00100 Rome, Italy (Telephone Number in U.S. (202) 653-2400); *The State of Food and Agriculture.*

KENYA - CAPITAL REVENUE

International Monetary Fund, 700 Nineteenth Street, NW, Washington, D.C. 20431 (202) 623-7000; *Government Finance Statistics Yearbook.*

KENYA - CASHEW NUT PRODUCTION - See KENYA - CROPS

KENYA - CASTOR BEAN PRODUCTION - See KENYA - CROPS

KENYA - CATTLE - See KENYA - LIVESTOCK AND POULTRY

KENYA - CEMENT PRODUCTION - See KENYA - MINING AND MINERAL PRODUCTS

KENYA - CHEESE PRODUCTION AND CONSUMPTION - See KENYA - DAIRY PRODUCTS

KENYA - CHEMICAL (ORGANIC) PRODUCTION - See KENYA - MINING AND MINERAL PRODUCTS

KENYA - CHICKENS - See KENYA - LIVESTOCK AND POULTRY

KENYA - CIGARETTE PRODUCTION - See KENYA - TOBACCO PRODUCTION

KENYA - CLIMATE

Central Bureau of Statistics, Ministry of Economic Planning and Development, Post Office Box 30266, Nairobi, Kenya; *Republic of Kenya Statistical Abstract.*

M.E. Sharpe, 80 Business Park Drive, Armonk, New York 10504 (800) 541-6563; *The Illustrated Book of World Rankings.*

St. Martin's Press, Inc., 175 Fifth Avenue, New York, New York 10010 (800) 221-7945; *The Statesman's Year-Book.*

KENYA - COAL PRODUCTION - See KENYA - MINING AND MINERAL PRODUCTS

KENYA - COFFEE - See KENYA - CROPS

KENYA - COMMERCE

St. Martin's Press, Inc., 175 Fifth Avenue, New York, New York 10010 (800) 221-7945; *The Statesman's Year-Book.*

KENYA - COMMUNICATIONS - See KENYA - TRANSPORTATION AND COMMUNICATIONS

KENYA - CONSTRUCTION INDUSTRY

M.E. Sharpe, 80 Business Park Drive, Armonk, New York 10504 (800) 541-6563; *The Illustrated Book of World Rankings.*

Statistical Office of the United Nations, Publishing Service, New York, New York 10017 (800) 253-9646; *Statistical Yearbook.*

United Nations Economic Commission for Africa, Africa Hall, Post Office Box 3001, Addis Ababa, Ethiopia (Telephone Number in U.S. (800) 253-9646); *African Statistical Yearbook.*

KENYA - CONSUMER PRICE INDEX

African Development Bank, 01 BP 1387, Abidjan 01, Cote d'Ivoire; *Selected Statistics on Regional Member Countries.*

Europa Publications Limited, 18 Bedford Square, London, WC1B 3JN, England; *The Europa World Year Book.*

Statistical Office of the United Nations, Publishing Service, New York, New York 10017 (800) 253-9646; *Statistical Yearbook; and Survey of Economic and Social Conditions in Africa.*

United Nations Economic Commission for Africa, Africa Hall, Post Office Box 3001, Addis Ababa, Ethiopia (Telephone Number in U.S. (800) 253-9646); *African Statistical Yearbook.*

KENYA - CONSUMER PRICES

Euromonitor International, Inc., 122 South Michigan Avenue, Suite 1200, Chicago, Illinois 60603 (800) 577-EURO; *World Marketing Data and Statistics.*

International Labour Office, I.L.O. Publications, 1828 L Street, NW, Suite 801, Washington, D.C. 20036 (301) 638-3152; *Yearbook of Labour Statistics.*

International Monetary Fund, 700

Nineteenth Street, NW, Washington, D.C. 20431 (202) 623-7000; *International Financial Statistics.*

KENYA - CONSUMPTION

African Development Bank, 01 BP 1387, Abidjan 01, Cote d'Ivoire; *Selected Statistics on Regional Member Countries.*

Statistical Office of the United Nations, Publishing Service, New York, New York 10017 (800) 253-9646; *Survey of Economic and Social Conditions in Africa.*

The World Bank, 1818 H Street, NW, Washington, D.C. 20433 (202) 477-1234; *World Development Report.*

KENYA - COPPER AND COPPER ORE PRODUCTION AND CONSUMPTION - See KENYA - MINING AND MINERAL PRODUCTS

KENYA - CORN PRODUCTION - See KENYA - CROPS

KENYA - CORPORATE TAXES - See KENYA - TAXATION

KENYA - COTTON - See KENYA - CROPS

KENYA - CRIME

Yale University Press, Yale Station, New Haven, Connecticut 06520 (800) 987-7323; *Violence and Crime in Cross-National Perspective.*

KENYA - CROPS

Europa Publications Limited, 18 Bedford Square, London, WC1B 3JN, England; *The Europa World Year Book.*

Food and Agricultural Organization of the United Nations (FAO), Via delle Terme di Caracalla, 00100 Rome, Italy (Telephone Number in U.S. (202) 653-2400); *Production Yearbook; and The State of Food and Agriculture.*

International Monetary Fund, 700 Nineteenth Street, NW, Washington, D.C. 20431 (202) 623-7000; *International Financial Statistics.*

M.E. Sharpe, 80 Business Park Drive, Armonk, New York 10504 (800) 541-6563; *The Illustrated Book of World Rankings.*

St. Martin's Press, Inc., 175 Fifth Avenue, New York, New York 10010 (800) 221-7945; *The Statesman's Year-Book.*

Statistical Office of the United Nations, Publishing Service, New York, New York 10017 (800) 253-9646; *Statistical Yearbook.*

United Nations Conference on Trade and Development, Central Statistical

Service, Palais des Nations, Geneva, Switzerland (Telephone in U.S. (800) 253-9646); *UNCTAD Commodity Yearbook.*

United Nations Economic Commission for Africa, Africa Hall, Post Office Box 3001, Addis Ababa, Ethiopia (Telephone Number in U.S. (800) 253-9646); *African Statistical Yearbook.*

KENYA - CUSTOMS DUTIES

International Monetary Fund, 700 Nineteenth Street, NW, Washington, D.C. 20431 (202) 623-7000; *Government Finance Statistics Yearbook.*

St. Martin's Press, Inc., 175 Fifth Avenue, New York, New York 10010 (800) 221-7945; *The Statesman's Year-Book.*

KENYA - DAIRY PRODUCTS

Europa Publications Limited, 18 Bedford Square, London, WC1B 3JN, England; *The Europa World Year Book.*

Food and Agricultural Organization of the United Nations (FAO), Via delle Terme di Caracalla, 00100 Rome, Italy (Telephone Number in U.S. (202) 653-2400); *Production Yearbook;* and *The State of Food and Agriculture.*

M.E. Sharpe, 80 Business Park Drive, Armonk, New York 10504 (800) 541-6563; *The Illustrated Book of World Rankings.*

St. Martin's Press, Inc., 175 Fifth Avenue, New York, New York 10010 (800) 221-7945; *The Statesman's Year-Book.*

Statistical Office of the United Nations, Publishing Service, New York, New York 10017 (800) 253-9646; *Statistical Yearbook.*

KENYA - DEATH RATES - See KENYA - MORTALITY

KENYA - DEFENSE EXPENDITURES - See KENYA - MILITARY

KENYA - DEMOGRAPHY

The Economist Intelligence Unit, 111 West 57th Street, New York, New York 10019 (800) 938-4685; *The World Market Atlas.*

Euromonitor International, Inc., 122 South Michigan Avenue, Suite 1200, Chicago, Illinois 60603 (800) 577-EURO; *International Marketing Data and Statistics; The World Economic Factbook;* and *World Marketing Data and Statistics.*

M.E. Sharpe, 80 Business Park Drive, Armonk, New York 10504 (800) 541-6563; *The Illustrated Book of World Rankings.*

Statistical Office of the United Nations,

Publishing Service, New York, New York 10017 (800) 253-9646; *Human Development Report;* and *Survey of Economic and Social Conditions in Africa.*

KENYA - DEVELOPMENT ASSISTANCE

Statistical Office of the United Nations, Publishing Service, New York, New York 10017 (800) 253-9646; *Statistical Yearbook.*

KENYA - DIAMOND PRODUCTION - See KENYA - MINING AND MINERAL PRODUCTS

KENYA - DIVORCE RATES

M.E. Sharpe, 80 Business Park Drive, Armonk, New York 10504 (800) 541-6563; *The Illustrated Book of World Rankings.*

Statistical Office of the United Nations, Publishing Service, New York, New York 10017 (800) 253-9646; *Demographic Yearbook.*

KENYA - ECONOMY

African Development Bank, 01 BP 1387, Abidjan 01, Cote d'Ivoire; *Selected Statistics on Regional Member Countries.*

Economist Intelligence Unit, 111 West 57th Street, New York, New York 10019 (800) 938-4685; *Kenya Country Report.*

Euromonitor International, Inc., 122 South Michigan Avenue, Suite 1200, Chicago, Illinois 60603 (800) 577-EURO; *International Marketing Data and Statistics; The World Economic Factbook;* and *World Marketing Data and Statistics.*

Europa Publications Limited, 18 Bedford Square, London, WC1B 3JN, England; *The Europa World Year Book.*

M.E. Sharpe, 80 Business Park Drive, Armonk, New York 10504 (800) 541-6563; *The Illustrated Book of World Rankings.*

St. Martin's Press, Inc., 175 Fifth Avenue, New York, New York 10010 (800) 221-7945; *The Statesman's Year-Book.*

Statistical Office of the United Nations, Publishing Service, New York, New York 10017 (800) 253-9646; *Foreign Trade Statistics for Africa;* and *World Statistics Pocketbook.*

The World Bank, 1818 H Street, NW, Washington, D.C. 20433 (202) 477-1234; *The World Bank Atlas;* and *World Development Report.*

KENYA - EDUCATION

African Development Bank, 01 BP 1387, Abidjan 01, Cote d'Ivoire; *Selected Statistics on Regional Member Countries.*

Central Bureau of Statistics, Ministry of Economic Planning and Development, Post Office Box 30266, Nairobi, Kenya; *Republic of Kenya Statistical Abstract.*

The Economist Intelligence Unit, 111 West 57th Street, New York, New York 10019 (800) 938-4685; *The World Market Atlas.*

Euromonitor International, Inc., 122 South Michigan Avenue, Suite 1200, Chicago, Illinois 60603 (800) 577-EURO; *International Marketing Data and Statistics;* and *World Marketing Data and Statistics.*

Europa Publications Limited, 18 Bedford Square, London, WC1B 3JN, England; *The Europa World Year Book.*

International Monetary Fund, 700 Nineteenth Street, NW, Washington, D.C. 20431 (202) 623-7000; *Government Finance Statistics Yearbook.*

M.E. Sharpe, 80 Business Park Drive, Armonk, New York 10504 (800) 541-6563; *The Illustrated Book of World Rankings.*

St. Martin's Press, Inc., 175 Fifth Avenue, New York, New York 10010 (800) 221-7945; *The Statesman's Year-Book.*

Statistical Office of the United Nations, Publishing Service, New York, New York 10017 (800) 253-9646; *Human Development Report;* and *Survey of Economic and Social Conditions in Africa.*

United Nations Economic Commission for Africa, Africa Hall, Post Office Box 3001, Addis Ababa, Ethiopia (Telephone Number in U.S. (800) 253-9646); *African Statistical Yearbook.*

United Nations Educational, Scientific and Cultural Organization (UNESCO), 7 Place de Fontenoy, F-75700 Paris, France (Telephone Number in U.S. (212) 963-5981); *Statistical Yearbook.*

The World Bank, 1818 H Street, NW, Washington, D.C. 20433 (202) 477-1234; *World Development Report;* and *World Development Indicators.*

KENYA - EGG PRODUCTION AND CONSUMPTION - See KENYA - DAIRY PRODUCTS

KENYA - ELECTRICITY

Central Intelligence Agency, Washington, D.C. 20505 (703) 482-1100, www.cia.gov; *The World Factbook.*

M.E. Sharpe, 80 Business Park Drive, Armonk, New York 10504 (800) 541-6563; *The Illustrated Book of World Rankings.*

St. Martin's Press, Inc., 175 Fifth

Avenue, New York, New York 10010 (800) 221-7945; *The Statesman's Year-Book.*

Statistical Office of the United Nations, Publishing Service, New York, New York 10017 (800) 253-9646; *Human Development Report; Statistical Yearbook;* and *Survey of Economic and Social Conditions in Africa.*

United Nations Economic Commission for Africa, Africa Hall, Post Office Box 3001, Addis Ababa, Ethiopia (Telephone Number in U.S. (800) 253-9646); *African Statistical Yearbook.*

KENYA - EMPLOYMENT

Euromonitor International, Inc., 122 South Michigan Avenue, Suite 1200, Chicago, Illinois 60603 (800) 577-EURO; *International Marketing Data and Statistics.*

International Labour Office, I.L.O. Publications, 1828 L Street, NW, Suite 801, Washington, D.C. 20036 (301) 638-3152; *Yearbook of Labour Statistics.*

M.E. Sharpe, 80 Business Park Drive, Armonk, New York 10504 (800) 541-6563; *The Illustrated Book of World Rankings.*

Statistical Office of the United Nations, Publishing Service, New York, New York 10017 (800) 253-9646; *Statistical Yearbook;* and *Survey of Economic and Social Conditions in Africa.*

United Nations Economic Commission for Africa, Africa Hall, Post Office Box 3001, Addis Ababa, Ethiopia (Telephone Number in U.S. (800) 253-9646); *African Statistical Yearbook.*

KENYA - ENERGY

Euromonitor International, Inc., 122 South Michigan Avenue, Suite 1200, Chicago, Illinois 60603 (800) 577-EURO; *International Marketing Data and Statistics; The World Economic Factbook;* and *World Marketing Data and Statistics.*

Food and Agricultural Organization of the United Nations (FAO), Via delle Terme di Caracalla, 00100 Rome, Italy (Telephone Number in U.S. (202) 653-2400); *The State of Food and Agriculture.*

M.E. Sharpe, 80 Business Park Drive, Armonk, New York 10504 (800) 541-6563; *The Illustrated Book of World Rankings.*

St. Martin's Press, Inc., 175 Fifth Avenue, New York, New York 10010 (800) 221-7945; *The Statesman's Year-Book.*

Statistical Office of the United Nations, Publishing Service, New York, New York 10017 (800) 253-9646; *Energy Statistics Yearbook; Human Development Report;*

World Statistics Pocketbook; and *Statistical Yearbook.*

United Nations Economic Commission for Africa, Africa Hall, Post Office Box 3001, Addis Ababa, Ethiopia (Telephone Number in U.S. (800) 253-9646); *African Statistical Yearbook.*

The World Bank, 1818 H Street, NW, Washington, D.C. 20433 (202) 477-1234; *The World Bank Atlas;* and *World Development Report.*

KENYA - ENVIRONMENT

Economist Intelligence Unit, 111 West 57th Street, New York, New York 10019 (800) 938-4685; *Kenya Country Report.*

Statistical Office of the United Nations, Publishing Service, New York, New York 10017 (800) 253-9646; *World Statistics Pocketbook.*

KENYA - EXCHANGE RATES

African Development Bank, 01 BP 1387, Abidjan 01, Cote d'Ivoire; *Selected Statistics on Regional Member Countries.*

Central Intelligence Agency, Washington, D.C. 20505 (703) 482-1100, www.cia.gov; *The World Factbook.*

Euromonitor International, Inc., 122 South Michigan Avenue, Suite 1200, Chicago, Illinois 60603 (800) 577-EURO; *International Marketing Data and Statistics;* and *The World Economic Factbook.*

Europa Publications Limited, 18 Bedford Square, London, WC1B 3JN, England; *The Europa World Year Book.*

International Monetary Fund, 700 Nineteenth Street, NW, Washington, D.C. 20431 (202) 623-7000; *International Financial Statistics.*

Statistical Office of the United Nations, Publishing Service, New York, New York 10017 (800) 253-9646; *Foreign Trade Statistics for Africa; World Statistics Pocketbook;* and *Statistical Yearbook.*

KENYA - EXCISE TAXES - See KENYA - TAXATION

KENYA - EXPORTS

African Development Bank, 01 BP 1387, Abidjan 01, Cote d'Ivoire; *Selected Statistics on Regional Member Countries.*

Central Intelligence Agency, Washington, D.C. 20505 (703) 482-1100, www.cia.gov; *The World Factbook.*

The Economist Intelligence Unit, 111 West 57th Street, New York, New York

10019 (800) 938-4685; *Kenya Country Report;* and *The World Market Atlas.*

Euromonitor International, Inc., 122 South Michigan Avenue, Suite 1200, Chicago, Illinois 60603 (800) 577-EURO; *International Marketing Data and Statistics;* and *The World Economic Factbook.*

Europa Publications Limited, 18 Bedford Square, London, WC1B 3JN, England; *The Europa World Year Book.*

Food and Agricultural Organization of the United Nations (FAO), Via delle Terme di Caracalla, 00100 Rome, Italy (Telephone Number in U.S. (202) 653-2400); *The State of Food and Agriculture.*

International Monetary Fund, 700 Nineteenth Street, NW, Washington, D.C. 20431 (202) 623-7000; *Direction of Trade Statistics; Government Finance Statistics Yearbook;* and *International Financial Statistics.*

St. Martin's Press, Inc., 175 Fifth Avenue, New York, New York 10010 (800) 221-7945; *The Statesman's Year-Book.*

Statistical Office of the United Nations, Publishing Service, New York, New York 10017 (800) 253-9646; *Foreign Trade Statistics for Africa;* and *Survey of Economic and Social Conditions in Africa.*

United Nations Conference on Trade and Development (UNCTAD), New York, New York 10017 (800) 253-9646; *Handbook of International Trade and Development Statistics.*

United Nations Economic Commission for Africa, Africa Hall, Post Office Box 3001, Addis Ababa, Ethiopia (Telephone Number in U.S. (800) 253-9646); *African Statistical Yearbook.*

The World Bank, 1818 H Street, NW, Washington, D.C. 20433 (202) 477-1234; *World Development Report;* and *World Development Indicators.*

KENYA - EXTERNAL INDEBTEDNESS

African Development Bank, 01 BP 1387, Abidjan 01, Cote d'Ivoire; *Selected Statistics on Regional Member Countries.*

Statistical Office of the United Nations, Publishing Service, New York, New York 10017 (800) 253-9646; *Survey of Economic and Social Conditions in Africa.*

The World Bank, 1818 H Street, NW, Washington, D.C. 20433 (202) 477-1234; *World Development Report.*

KENYA - EXTERNAL TRADE

African Development Bank, 01 BP 1387,

Abidjan 01, Cote d'Ivoire; *Selected Statistics on Regional Member Countries.*

Euromonitor International, Inc., 122 South Michigan Avenue, Suite 1200, Chicago, Illinois 60603 (800) 577-EURO; *World Marketing Data and Statistics.*

Food and Agricultural Organization of the United Nations (FAO), Via delle Terme di Caracalla, 00100 Rome, Italy (Telephone Number in U.S. (202) 653-2400); *The State of Food and Agriculture;* and *Trade Yearbook.*

Statistical Office of the United Nations, Publishing Service, New York, New York 10017 (800) 253-9646; *Statistical Yearbook.*

The World Bank, 1818 H Street, NW, Washington, D.C. 20433 (202) 477-1234; *World Development Indicators.*

KENYA - FARM CROPS - See KENYA - CROPS

KENYA - FEMALE WORKING POPULATION - See KENYA - EMPLOYMENT

KENYA - FERTILITY RATES

Central Intelligence Agency, Washington, D.C. 20505 (703) 482-1100, www.cia.gov; *The World Factbook.*

M.E. Sharpe, 80 Business Park Drive, Armonk, New York 10504 (800) 541-6563; *The Illustrated Book of World Rankings.*

Statistical Office of the United Nations, Publishing Service, New York, New York 10017 (800) 253-9646; *Human Development Report;* and *Survey of Economic and Social Conditions in Africa.*

The World Bank, 1818 H Street, NW, Washington, D.C. 20433 (202) 477-1234; *The World Bank Atlas; World Development Report;* and *World Development Indicators.*

KENYA - FERTILIZER

Food and Agricultural Organization of the United Nations (FAO), Via delle Terme di Caracalla, 00100 Rome, Italy (Telephone Number in U.S. (202) 653-2400); *Fertilizer Yearbook;* and *The State of Food and Agriculture.*

Statistical Office of the United Nations, Publishing Service, New York, New York 10017 (800) 253-9646; *Statistical Yearbook.*

KENYA - FETAL MORTALITY - See KENYA - MORTALITY

KENYA - FINANCE

African Development Bank, 01 BP 1387, Abidjan 01, Cote d'Ivoire; *Selected Statistics*

on Regional Member Countries.

Central Bureau of Statistics, Ministry of Economic Planning and Development, Post Office Box 30266, Nairobi, Kenya; *Republic of Kenya Statistical Abstract.*

Economist Intelligence Unit, 111 West 57th Street, New York, New York 10019 (800) 938-4685; *Kenya Country Report.*

Europa Publications Limited, 18 Bedford Square, London, WC1B 3JN, England; *The Europa World Year Book.*

International Monetary Fund, 700 Nineteenth Street, NW, Washington, D.C. 20431 (202) 623-7000; *International Financial Statistics.*

M.E. Sharpe, 80 Business Park Drive, Armonk, New York 10504 (800) 541-6563; *The Illustrated Book of World Rankings.*

St. Martin's Press, Inc., 175 Fifth Avenue, New York, New York 10010 (800) 221-7945; *The Statesman's Year-Book.*

United Nations Economic Commission for Africa, Africa Hall, Post Office Box 3001, Addis Ababa, Ethiopia (Telephone Number in U.S. (800) 253-9646); *African Statistical Yearbook.*

KENYA - FISHERIES

Central Bureau of Statistics, Ministry of Economic Planning and Development, Post Office Box 30266, Nairobi, Kenya; *Republic of Kenya Statistical Abstract.*

Europa Publications Limited, 18 Bedford Square, London, WC1B 3JN, England; *The Europa World Year Book.*

Food and Agricultural Organization of the United Nations (FAO), Via delle Terme di Caracalla, 00100 Rome, Italy (Telephone Number in U.S. (202) 653-2400); *The State of Food and Agriculture.*

M.E. Sharpe, 80 Business Park Drive, Armonk, New York 10504 (800) 541-6563; *The Illustrated Book of World Rankings.*

St. Martin's Press, Inc., 175 Fifth Avenue, New York, New York 10010 (800) 221-7945; *The Statesman's Year-Book.*

Statistical Office of the United Nations, Publishing Service, New York, New York 10017 (800) 253-9646; *Statistical Yearbook;* and *Survey of Economic and Social Conditions in Africa.*

United Nations Conference on Trade and Development, Central Statistical Service, Palais des Nations, Geneva, Switzerland (Telephone in U.S. (800) 253-9646); *UNCTAD Commodity Yearbook.*

United Nations Economic Commission for Africa, Africa Hall, Post Office Box 3001, Addis Ababa, Ethiopia (Telephone Number in U.S. (800) 253-9646); *African Statistical Yearbook.*

KENYA - FLOUR PRODUCTION

Statistical Office of the United Nations, Publishing Service, New York, New York 10017 (800) 253-9646; *Statistical Yearbook.*

KENYA - FOOD

African Development Bank, 01 BP 1387, Abidjan 01, Cote d'Ivoire; *Selected Statistics on Regional Member Countries.*

Food and Agricultural Organization of the United Nations (FAO), Via delle Terme di Caracalla, 00100 Rome, Italy (Telephone Number in U.S. (202) 653-2400); *Production Yearbook;* and *The State of Food and Agriculture.*

Statistical Office of the United Nations, Publishing Service, New York, New York 10017 (800) 253-9646; *Human Development Report.*

United Nations Conference on Trade and Development, Central Statistical Service, Palais des Nations, Geneva, Switzerland (Telephone in U.S. (800) 253-9646); *UNCTAD Commodity Yearbook.*

KENYA - FOREIGN DEBT

International Monetary Fund, 700 Nineteenth Street, NW, Washington, D.C. 20431 (202) 623-7000; *Government Finance Statistics Yearbook.*

St. Martin's Press, Inc., 175 Fifth Avenue, New York, New York 10010 (800) 221-7945; *The Statesman's Year-Book.*

KENYA - FOREIGN TRADE

Economist Intelligence Unit, 111 West 57th Street, New York, New York 10019 (800) 938-4685; *Kenya Country Report.*

Euromonitor International, Inc., 122 South Michigan Avenue, Suite 1200, Chicago, Illinois 60603 (800) 577-EURO; *International Marketing Data and Statistics;* and *The World Economic Factbook.*

Europa Publications Limited, 18 Bedford Square, London, WC1B 3JN, England; *The Europa World Year Book.*

Food and Agricultural Organization of the United Nations (FAO), Via delle Terme di Caracalla, 00100 Rome, Italy (Telephone Number in U.S. (202) 653-2400); *The State of Food and Agriculture.*

International Monetary Fund, 700 Nineteenth Street, NW, Washington,

D.C. 20431 (202) 623-7000; *International Financial Statistics.*

M.E. Sharpe, 80 Business Park Drive, Armonk, New York 10504 (800) 541-6563; *The Illustrated Book of World Rankings.*

St. Martin's Press, Inc., 175 Fifth Avenue, New York, New York 10010 (800) 221-7945; *The Statesman's Year-Book.*

Statistical Office of the United Nations, Publishing Service, New York, New York 10017 (800) 253-9646; *Foreign Trade Statistics for Africa; International Trade Statistics Yearbook;* and *Statistical Yearbook.*

United Nations Conference on Trade and Development, Central Statistical Service, Palais des Nations, Geneva, Switzerland (Telephone in U.S. (800) 253-9646); *UNCTAD Commodity Yearbook.*

United Nations Economic Commission for Africa, Africa Hall, Post Office Box 3001, Addis Ababa, Ethiopia (Telephone Number in U.S. (800) 253-9646); *African Statistical Yearbook.*

The World Bank, 1818 H Street, NW, Washington, D.C. 20433 (202) 477-1234; *World Development Report;* and *World Development Indicators.*

KENYA - FORESTRY AND FOREST PRODUCTS

Central Bureau of Statistics, Ministry of Economic Planning and Development, Post Office Box 30266, Nairobi, Kenya; *Republic of Kenya Statistical Abstract.*

Europa Publications Limited, 18 Bedford Square, London, WC1B 3JN, England; *The Europa World Year Book.*

Food and Agricultural Organization of the United Nations (FAO), Via delle Terme di Caracalla, 00100 Rome, Italy (Telephone Number in U.S. (202) 653-2400); *The State of Food and Agriculture;* and *Yearbook of Forest Products.*

M.E. Sharpe, 80 Business Park Drive, Armonk, New York 10504 (800) 541-6563; *The Illustrated Book of World Rankings.*

St. Martin's Press, Inc., 175 Fifth Avenue, New York, New York 10010 (800) 221-7945; *The Statesman's Year-Book.*

Statistical Office of the United Nations, Publishing Service, New York, New York 10017 (800) 253-9646; *Statistical Yearbook.*

United Nations Conference on Trade and Development, Central Statistical Service, Palais des Nations, Geneva, Switzerland (Telephone in U.S. (800) 253-9646); *UNCTAD Commodity Yearbook.*

United Nations Economic Commission for Africa, Africa Hall, Post Office Box 3001, Addis Ababa, Ethiopia (Telephone Number in U.S. (800) 253-9646); *African Statistical Yearbook.*

United Nations Educational, Scientific and Cultural Organization (UNESCO), 7 Place de Fontenoy, F-75700 Paris, France (Telephone Number in U.S. (212) 963-5981); *Statistical Yearbook.*

The World Bank, 1818 H Street, NW, Washington, D.C. 20433 (202) 477-1234; *World Development Report.*

KENYA - GAS PRODUCTION - See KENYA - MINING AND MINERAL PRODUCTS

KENYA - GENERAL INDUSTRIAL STATISTICS - See KENYA - INDUSTRY

KENYA - GENERAL MORTALITY - See KENYA - MORTALITY

KENYA - GEOGRAPHIC DATA

M.E. Sharpe, 80 Business Park Drive, Armonk, New York 10504 (800) 541-6563; *The Illustrated Book of World Rankings.*

KENYA - GOATS - See KENYA - LIVESTOCK AND POULTRY

KENYA - GOLD HOLDINGS

International Monetary Fund, 700 Nineteenth Street, NW, Washington, D.C. 20431 (202) 623-7000; *International Financial Statistics.*

Statistical Office of the United Nations, Publishing Service, New York, New York 10017 (800) 253-9646; *Statistical Yearbook.*

The World Bank, 1818 H Street, NW, Washington, D.C. 20433 (202) 477-1234; *World Development Indicators.*

KENYA - GOLD PRODUCTION AND CONSUMPTION - See KENYA - MINING AND MINERAL PRODUCTS

KENYA - GOVERNMENT

Central Intelligence Agency, Washington, D.C. 20505 (703) 482-1100, www.cia.gov; *The World Factbook.*

Europa Publications Limited, 18 Bedford Square, London, WC1B 3JN, England; *The Europa World Year Book.*

International Monetary Fund, 700 Nineteenth Street, NW, Washington, D.C. 20431 (202) 623-7000; *Government Finance Statistics Yearbook;* and *International Financial Statistics.*

St. Martin's Press, Inc., 175 Fifth

Avenue, New York, New York 10010 (800) 221-7945; *The Statesman's Year-Book.*

Statistical Office of the United Nations, Publishing Service, New York, New York 10017 (800) 253-9646; *National Accounts Statistics; Statistical Yearbook;* and *Survey of Economic and Social Conditions in Africa.*

The World Bank, 1818 H Street, NW, Washington, D.C. 20433 (202) 477-1234; *World Development Report;* and *World Development Indicators.*

KENYA - GRAIN PRODUCTION - See KENYA - CROPS

KENYA - GRANTS

International Monetary Fund, 700 Nineteenth Street, NW, Washington, D.C. 20431 (202) 623-7000; *Government Finance Statistics Yearbook.*

KENYA - GROSS DOMESTIC PRODUCT

African Development Bank, 01 BP 1387, Abidjan 01, Cote d'Ivoire; *Selected Statistics on Regional Member Countries.*

The Economist Intelligence Unit, 111 West 57th Street, New York, New York 10019 (800) 938-4685; *Kenya Country Report;* and *The World Market Atlas.*

Euromonitor International, Inc., 122 South Michigan Avenue, Suite 1200, Chicago, Illinois 60603 (800) 577-EURO; *International Marketing Data and Statistics;* and *The World Economic Factbook.*

Europa Publications Limited, 18 Bedford Square, London, WC1B 3JN, England; *The Europa World Year Book.*

M.E. Sharpe, 80 Business Park Drive, Armonk, New York 10504 (800) 541-6563; *The Illustrated Book of World Rankings.*

Statistical Office of the United Nations, Publishing Service, New York, New York 10017 (800) 253-9646; *Human Development Report; National Accounts Statistics; Statistical Yearbook;* and *Survey of Economic and Social Conditions in Africa.*

United Nations Economic Commission for Africa, Africa Hall, Post Office Box 3001, Addis Ababa, Ethiopia (Telephone Number in U.S. (800) 253-9646); *African Statistical Yearbook.*

The World Bank, 1818 H Street, NW, Washington, D.C. 20433 (202) 477-1234; *World Development Report;* and *World Development Indicators.*

KENYA - GROSS NATIONAL PRODUCT

Euromonitor International, Inc., 122

South Michigan Avenue, Suite 1200, Chicago, Illinois 60603 (800) 577-EURO; *International Marketing Data and Statistics.*

Europa Publications Limited, 18 Bedford Square, London, WC1B 3JN, England; *The Europa World Year Book.*

St. Martin's Press, Inc., 175 Fifth Avenue, New York, New York 10010 (800) 221-7945; *The Statesman's Year-Book.*

The World Bank, 1818 H Street, NW, Washington, D.C. 20433 (202) 477-1234; *The World Bank Atlas; World Development Report;* and *World Development Indicators.*

KENYA - GROUNDNUT PRODUCTION - See KENYA - CROPS

KENYA - HEALTH

African Development Bank, 01 BP 1387, Abidjan 01, Cote d'Ivoire; *Selected Statistics on Regional Member Countries.*

Euromonitor International, Inc., 122 South Michigan Avenue, Suite 1200, Chicago, Illinois 60603 (800) 577-EURO; *World Marketing Data and Statistics.*

M.E. Sharpe, 80 Business Park Drive, Armonk, New York 10504 (800) 541-6563; *The Illustrated Book of World Rankings.*

St. Martin's Press, Inc., 175 Fifth Avenue, New York, New York 10010 (800) 221-7945; *The Statesman's Year-Book.*

Statistical Office of the United Nations, Publishing Service, New York, New York 10017 (800) 253-9646; *Human Development Report;* and *Statistical Yearbook.*

United Nations Children's Fund (UNICEF), 3 United Nations Plaza, New York, New York 10017 (800) 253-9646; *State of the World's Children.*

United Nations Economic Commission for Africa, Africa Hall, Post Office Box 3001, Addis Ababa, Ethiopia (Telephone Number in U.S. (800) 253-9646); *African Statistical Yearbook.*

The World Bank, 1818 H Street, NW, Washington, D.C. 20433 (202) 477-1234; *World Development Report.*

KENYA - HEALTH EXPENDITURES

International Monetary Fund, 700 Nineteenth Street, NW, Washington, D.C. 20431 (202) 623-7000; *Government Finance Statistics Yearbook.*

KENYA - HIDE PRODUCTION

Food and Agricultural Organization of the United Nations (FAO), Via delle Terme di Caracalla, 00100 Rome, Italy (Telephone Number in U.S. (202) 653-2400); *Production Yearbook.*

KENYA - HIGHWAYS

Central Intelligence Agency, Washington, D.C. 20505 (703) 482-1100, www.cia.gov; *The World Factbook.*

International Road Federation, 2600 Virginia Avenue, NW, Washington, D.C. 20037 (202) 338-4641; *World Road Statistics.*

St. Martin's Press, Inc., 175 Fifth Avenue, New York, New York 10010 (800) 221-7945; *The Statesman's Year-Book.*

Statistical Office of the United Nations, Publishing Service, New York, New York 10017 (800) 253-9646; *Survey of Economic and Social Conditions in Africa.*

United Nations Economic Commission for Africa, Africa Hall, Post Office Box 3001, Addis Ababa, Ethiopia (Telephone Number in U.S. (800) 253-9646); *African Statistical Yearbook.*

KENYA - HORSES - See KENYA - LIVESTOCK AND POULTRY

KENYA - HOURS OF WORK - See KENYA - EMPLOYMENT

KENYA - HOUSING AND HOUSING UNITS

Euromonitor International, Inc., 122 South Michigan Avenue, Suite 1200, Chicago, Illinois 60603 (800) 577-EURO; *World Marketing Data and Statistics.*

M.E. Sharpe, 80 Business Park Drive, Armonk, New York 10504 (800) 541-6563; *The Illustrated Book of World Rankings.*

KENYA - HOUSING EXPENDITURES

International Monetary Fund, 700 Nineteenth Street, NW, Washington, D.C. 20431 (202) 623-7000; *Government Finance Statistics Yearbook.*

KENYA - ILLITERATE POPULATION

Central Intelligence Agency, Washington, D.C. 20505 (703) 482-1100, www.cia.gov; *The World Factbook.*

The Economist Intelligence Unit, 111 West 57th Street, New York, New York 10019 (800) 938-4685; *The World Market Atlas.*

Euromonitor International, Inc., 122 South Michigan Avenue, Suite 1200, Chicago, Illinois 60603 (800) 577-EURO; *The World Economic Factbook.*

Statistical Office of the United Nations,

Publishing Service, New York, New York 10017 (800) 253-9646; *Human Development Report.*

United Nations Educational, Scientific and Cultural Organization (UNESCO), 7 Place de Fontenoy, F-75700 Paris, France (Telephone Number in U.S. (212) 963-5981); *Statistical Yearbook.*

KENYA - IMPORTS

African Development Bank, 01 BP 1387, Abidjan 01, Cote d'Ivoire; *Selected Statistics on Regional Member Countries.*

Central Intelligence Agency, Washington, D.C. 20505 (703) 482-1100, www.cia.gov; *The World Factbook.*

The Economist Intelligence Unit, 111 West 57th Street, New York, New York 10019 (800) 938-4685; *Kenya Country Report;* and *The World Market Atlas.*

Euromonitor International, Inc., 122 South Michigan Avenue, Suite 1200, Chicago, Illinois 60603 (800) 577-EURO; *International Marketing Data and Statistics;* and *The World Economic Factbook.*

Europa Publications Limited, 18 Bedford Square, London, WC1B 3JN, England; *The Europa World Year Book.*

Food and Agricultural Organization of the United Nations (FAO), Via delle Terme di Caracalla, 00100 Rome, Italy (Telephone Number in U.S. (202) 653-2400); *The State of Food and Agriculture.*

International Monetary Fund, 700 Nineteenth Street, NW, Washington, D.C. 20431 (202) 623-7000; *Direction of Trade Statistics; Government Finance Statistics Yearbook;* and *International Financial Statistics.*

St. Martin's Press, Inc., 175 Fifth Avenue, New York, New York 10010 (800) 221-7945; *The Statesman's Year-Book.*

Statistical Office of the United Nations, Publishing Service, New York, New York 10017 (800) 253-9646; *Foreign Trade Statistics for Africa.*

United Nations Conference on Trade and Development (UNCTAD), New York, New York 10017 (800) 253-9646; *Handbook of International Trade and Development Statistics.*

United Nations Economic Commission for Africa, Africa Hall, Post Office Box 3001, Addis Ababa, Ethiopia (Telephone Number in U.S. (800) 253-9646); *African Statistical Yearbook.*

The World Bank, 1818 H Street, NW, Washington, D.C. 20433 (202) 477-1234;

World Development Report; and *World Development Indicators.*

KENYA - INCOME TAXES - See KENYA - TAXATION

KENYA - INDUSTRY

Central Bureau of Statistics, Ministry of Economic Planning and Development, Post Office Box 30266, Nairobi, Kenya; *Republic of Kenya Statistical Abstract.*

Central Intelligence Agency, Washington, D.C. 20505 (703) 482-1100, www.cia.gov; *The World Factbook.*

Economist Intelligence Unit, 111 West 57th Street, New York, New York 10019 (800) 938-4685; *Kenya Country Report.*

Euromonitor International, Inc., 122 South Michigan Avenue, Suite 1200, Chicago, Illinois 60603 (800) 577-EURO; *International Marketing Data and Statistics; The World Economic Factbook;* and *World Marketing Data and Statistics.*

Europa Publications Limited, 18 Bedford Square, London, WC1B 3JN, England; *The Europa World Year Book.*

International Labour Office, I.L.O. Publications, 1828 L Street, NW, Suite 801, Washington, D.C. 20036 (301) 638-3152; *Yearbook of Labour Statistics.*

M.E. Sharpe, 80 Business Park Drive, Armonk, New York 10504 (800) 541-6563; *The Illustrated Book of World Rankings.*

St. Martin's Press, Inc., 175 Fifth Avenue, New York, New York 10010 (800) 221-7945; *The Statesman's Year-Book.*

Statistical Office of the United Nations, Publishing Service, New York, New York 10017 (800) 253-9646; *Statistical Yearbook; Industrial Commodity Statistics Yearbook;* and *Survey of Economic and Social Conditions in Africa.*

United Nations Economic Commission for Africa, Africa Hall, Post Office Box 3001, Addis Ababa, Ethiopia (Telephone Number in U.S. (800) 253-9646); *African Statistical Yearbook.*

The World Bank, 1818 H Street, NW, Washington, D.C. 20433 (202) 477-1234; *Statistical Handbook: States of the Former USSR;* and *World Development Indicators.*

World Intellectual Property Organization, 34 Chemin des Colombettes, CH-1211 Geneva 20, Switzerland; *Industrial Property Statistics.*

KENYA - INFANT AND MATERNAL MORTALITY - See KENYA - MORTALITY

KENYA - INTERNAL TRADE

Statistical Office of the United Nations, Publishing Service, New York, New York 10017 (800) 253-9646; *Statistical Yearbook.*

KENYA - INTERNATIONAL LIQUIDITY

International Monetary Fund, 700 Nineteenth Street, NW, Washington, D.C. 20431 (202) 623-7000; *International Financial Statistics.*

KENYA - INTERNATIONAL RESERVES EXCLUDING GOLD

African Development Bank, 01 BP 1387, Abidjan 01, Cote d'Ivoire; *Selected Statistics on Regional Member Countries.*

Statistical Office of the United Nations, Publishing Service, New York, New York 10017 (800) 253-9646; *Statistical Yearbook.*

The World Bank, 1818 H Street, NW, Washington, D.C. 20433 (202) 477-1234; *World Development Indicators.*

KENYA - IRON ORE PRODUCTION AND CONSUMPTION - See KENYA - MINING AND MINERAL PRODUCTS

KENYA - IRRIGATION

Euromonitor International, Inc., 122 South Michigan Avenue, Suite 1200, Chicago, Illinois 60603 (800) 577-EURO; *International Marketing Data and Statistics.*

KENYA - LABOR

African Development Bank, 01 BP 1387, Abidjan 01, Cote d'Ivoire; *Selected Statistics on Regional Member Countries.*

Central Bureau of Statistics, Ministry of Economic Planning and Development, Post Office Box 30266, Nairobi, Kenya; *Republic of Kenya Statistical Abstract.*

Central Intelligence Agency, Washington, D.C. 20505 (703) 482-1100, www.cia.gov; *The World Factbook.*

Euromonitor International, Inc., 122 South Michigan Avenue, Suite 1200, Chicago, Illinois 60603 (800) 577-EURO; *International Marketing Data and Statistics* and *World Marketing Data and Statistics.*

Europa Publications Limited, 18 Bedford Square, London, WC1B 3JN, England; *The Europa World Year Book.*

Food and Agricultural Organization of the United Nations (FAO), Via delle Terme di Caracalla, 00100 Rome, Italy (Telephone Number in U.S. (202) 653-2400); *The State of Food and Agriculture.*

International Labour Office,

I.L.O. Publications, 1828 L Street, NW, Suite 801, Washington, D.C. 20036 (301) 638-3152; *Yearbook of Labour Statistics.*

M.E. Sharpe, 80 Business Park Drive, Armonk, New York 10504 (800) 541-6563; *The Illustrated Book of World Rankings.*

St. Martin's Press, Inc., 175 Fifth Avenue, New York, New York 10010 (800) 221-7945; *The Statesman's Year-Book.*

Statistical Office of the United Nations, Publishing Service, New York, New York 10017 (800) 253-9646; *Human Development Report.*

The World Bank, 1818 H Street, NW, Washington, D.C. 20433 (202) 477-1234; *The World Bank Atlas; World Development Report;* and *World Development Indicators.*

KENYA - LAND USE

Central Intelligence Agency, Washington, D.C. 20505 (703) 482-1100, www.cia.gov; *The World Factbook.*

Euromonitor International, Inc., 122 South Michigan Avenue, Suite 1200, Chicago, Illinois 60603 (800) 577-EURO; *International Marketing Data and Statistics.*

Food and Agricultural Organization of the United Nations (FAO), Via delle Terme di Caracalla, 00100 Rome, Italy (Telephone Number in U.S. (202) 653-2400); *Production Yearbook.*

The World Bank, 1818 H Street, NW, Washington, D.C. 20433 (202) 477-1234; *World Development Report.*

KENYA - LIBRARIES

M.E. Sharpe, 80 Business Park Drive, Armonk, New York 10504 (800) 541-6563; *The Illustrated Book of World Rankings.*

United Nations Educational, Scientific and Cultural Organization (UNESCO), 7 Place de Fontenoy, F-75700 Paris, France (Telephone Number in U.S. (212) 963-5981); *Statistical Yearbook.*

KENYA - LIFE EXPECTANCY

African Development Bank, 01 BP 1387, Abidjan 01, Cote d'Ivoire; *Selected Statistics on Regional Member Countries.*

Central Intelligence Agency, Washington, D.C. 20505 (703) 482-1100, www.cia.gov; *The World Factbook.*

Euromonitor International, Inc., 122 South Michigan Avenue, Suite 1200, Chicago, Illinois 60603 (800) 577-EURO; *The World Economic Factbook.*

St. Martin's Press, Inc., 175 Fifth

Avenue, New York, New York 10010 (800) 221-7945; *The Statesman's Year-Book*.

Statistical Office of the United Nations, Publishing Service, New York, New York 10017 (800) 253-9646; *Human Development Report;* and *World Statistics Pocketbook*.

The World Bank, 1818 H Street, NW, Washington, D.C. 20433 (202) 477-1234; *The World Bank Atlas;* and *World Development Report*.

KENYA - LITERACY RATE

Euromonitor International, Inc., 122 South Michigan Avenue, Suite 1200, Chicago, Illinois 60603 (800) 577-EURO; *World Marketing Data and Statistics*.

Statistical Office of the United Nations, Publishing Service, New York, New York 10017 (800) 253-9646; *Survey of Economic and Social Conditions in Africa*.

KENYA - LIVESTOCK AND POULTRY

Euromonitor International, Inc., 122 South Michigan Avenue, Suite 1200, Chicago, Illinois 60603 (800) 577-EURO; *International Marketing Data and Statistics*.

Europa Publications Limited, 18 Bedford Square, London, WC1B 3JN, England; *The Europa World Year Book*.

Food and Agricultural Organization of the United Nations (FAO), Via delle Terme di Caracalla, 00100 Rome, Italy (Telephone Number in U.S. (202) 653-2400); *Production Yearbook;* and *The State of Food and Agriculture*.

M.E. Sharpe, 80 Business Park Drive, Armonk, New York 10504 (800) 541-6563; *The Illustrated Book of World Rankings*.

St. Martin's Press, Inc., 175 Fifth Avenue, New York, New York 10010 (800) 221-7945; *The Statesman's Year-Book*.

Statistical Office of the United Nations, Publishing Service, New York, New York 10017 (800) 253-9646; *Statistical Yearbook;* and *Survey of Economic and Social Conditions in Africa*.

United Nations Conference on Trade and Development, Central Statistical Service, Palais des Nations, Geneva, Switzerland (Telephone in U.S. (800) 253-9646); *UNCTAD Commodity Yearbook*.

United Nations Economic Commission for Africa, Africa Hall, Post Office Box 3001, Addis Ababa, Ethiopia (Telephone Number in U.S. (800) 253

KENYA - LIVING LEVELS - See KENYA - LIFE EXPECTANCY

KENYA - MAIL - NUMBER OF ITEMS SENT AND RECEIVED

Statistical Office of the United Nations, Publishing Service, New York, New York 10017 (800) 253-9646; *Statistical Yearbook*.

KENYA - MANUFACTURING

M.E. Sharpe, 80 Business Park Drive, Armonk, New York 10504 (800) 541-6563; *The Illustrated Book of World Rankings*.

Statistical Office of the United Nations, Publishing Service, New York, New York 10017 (800) 253-9646; *Statistical Yearbook;* and *Survey of Economic and Social Conditions in Africa*.

United Nations Economic Commission for Africa, Africa Hall, Post Office Box 3001, Addis Ababa, Ethiopia (Telephone Number in U.S. (800) 253-9646); *African Statistical Yearbook*.

The World Bank, 1818 H Street, NW, Washington, D.C. 20433 (202) 477-1234; *World Development Indicators*.

KENYA - MARRIAGE RATES

M.E. Sharpe, 80 Business Park Drive, Armonk, New York 10504 (800) 541-6563; *The Illustrated Book of World Rankings*.

Statistical Office of the United Nations, Publishing Service, New York, New York 10017 (800) 253-9646; *Demographic Yearbook*.

KENYA - MEAT PRODUCTION - See KENYA - LIVESTOCK AND POULTRY

KENYA - MERCHANT SHIPPING

Europa Publications Limited, 18 Bedford Square, London, WC1B 3JN, England; *The Europa World Year Book*.

St. Martin's Press, Inc., 175 Fifth Avenue, New York, New York 10010 (800) 221-7945; *The Statesman's Year-Book*.

Statistical Office of the United Nations, Publishing Service, New York, New York 10017 (800) 253-9646; *Statistical Yearbook*.

United Nations Economic Commission for Africa, Africa Hall, Post Office Box 3001, Addis Ababa, Ethiopia (Telephone Number in U.S. (800) 253-9646); *African Statistical Yearbook*.

U.S. Department of Transportation, Maritime Administration, 400 Seventh Street, SW, Washington, D.C. 20590 (202) 366-5807, www.marad.dot.gov; *A Statistical Analysis of the World's Merchant Fleets*.

KENYA - MILITARY

Central Intelligence Agency, Washington, D.C. 20505 (703) 482-1100, www.cia.gov; *The World Factbook*.

Euromonitor International, Inc., 122 South Michigan Avenue, Suite 1200, Chicago, Illinois 60603 (800) 577-EURO; *World Marketing Data and Statistics*.

The International Institute for Strategic Studies, 23 Tavistock Street, London WC2E 7NQ, England 44 171 3797676; *The Military Balance*.

International Monetary Fund, 700 Nineteenth Street, NW, Washington, D.C. 20431 (202) 623-7000; *Government Finance Statistics Yearbook*.

St. Martin's Press, Inc., 175 Fifth Avenue, New York, New York 10010 (800) 221-7945; *The Statesman's Year-Book*.

Statistical Office of the United Nations, Publishing Service, New York, New York 10017 (800) 253-9646; *Human Development Report*.

KENYA - MILK PRODUCTION - See KENYA - DAIRY PRODUCTS

KENYA - MILLET PRODUCTION - See KENYA - CROPS

KENYA - MINING AND MINERAL PRODUCTS

Europa Publications Limited, 18 Bedford Square, London, WC1B 3JN, England; *The Europa World Year Book*.

M.E. Sharpe, 80 Business Park Drive, Armonk, New York 10504 (800) 541-6563; *The Illustrated Book of World Rankings*.

St. Martin's Press, Inc., 175 Fifth Avenue, New York, New York 10010 (800) 221-7945; *The Statesman's Year-Book*.

Statistical Office of the United Nations, Publishing Service, New York, New York 10017 (800) 253-9646; *Statistical Yearbook*.

United Nations Conference on Trade and Development, Central Statistical Service, Palais des Nations, Geneva, Switzerland (Telephone in U.S. (800) 253-9646); *UNCTAD Commodity Yearbook*.

United Nations Economic Commission for Africa, Africa Hall, Post Office Box 3001, Addis Ababa, Ethiopia (Telephone Number in U.S. (800) 253-9646); *African Statistical Yearbook*.

KENYA - MONEY EXCHANGE RATE - See KENYA - EXCHANGE RATES

KENYA - MONEY RESERVES

Euromonitor International, Inc., 122

South Michigan Avenue, Suite 1200, Chicago, Illinois 60603 (800) 577-EURO); *International Marketing Data and Statistics.*

KENYA - MONEY SUPPLY

African Development Bank, 01 BP 1387, Abidjan 01, Cote d'Ivoire; *Selected Statistics on Regional Member Countries.*

Economist Intelligence Unit, 111 West 57th Street, New York, New York 10019 (800) 938-4685; *Kenya Country Report.*

Euromonitor International, Inc., 122 South Michigan Avenue, Suite 1200, Chicago, Illinois 60603 (800) 577-EURO; *International Marketing Data and Statistics.*

Europa Publications Limited, 18 Bedford Square, London, WC1B 3JN, England; *The Europa World Year Book.*

International Monetary Fund, 700 Nineteenth Street, NW, Washington, D.C. 20431 (202) 623-7000; *International Financial Statistics.*

Statistical Office of the United Nations, Publishing Service, New York, New York 10017 (800) 253-9646; *Statistical Yearbook.*

The World Bank, 1818 H Street, NW, Washington, D.C. 20433 (202) 477-1234; *World Development Indicators.*

KENYA - MONUMENTS AND HISTORICAL SITES

United Nations Educational, Scientific and Cultural Organization (UNESCO), 7 Place de Fontenoy, F-75700 Paris, France (Telephone Number in U.S. (212) 963-5981); *Statistical Yearbook.*

KENYA - MORTALITY

Central Intelligence Agency, Washington, D.C. 20505 (703) 482-1100, www.cia.gov; *The World Factbook.*

Euromonitor International, Inc., 122 South Michigan Avenue, Suite 1200, Chicago, Illinois 60603 (800) 577-EURO; *International Marketing Data and Statistics;* and *The World Economic Factbook.*

Europa Publications Limited, 18 Bedford Square, London, WC1B 3JN, England; *The Europa World Year Book.*

Statistical Office of the United Nations, Publishing Service, New York, New York 10017 (800) 253-9646; *Demographic Yearbook; Human Development Report; Statistical Yearbook; World Statistics Pocketbook;* and *Survey of Economic and Social Conditions in Africa.*

United Nations Children's Fund (UNICEF), 3 United Nations Plaza, New York, New York 10017 (800) 253-9646; *State of the World's Children.*

The World Bank, 1818 H Street, NW, Washington, D.C. 20433 (202) 477-1234; *The World Bank Atlas; World Development Report;* and *World Development Indicators.*

KENYA - MOTION PICTURES

Statistical Office of the United Nations, Publishing Service, New York, New York 10017 (800) 253-9646; *Statistical Yearbook.*

KENYA - MOTOR VEHICLE TAXES - See KENYA - TAXATION

KENYA - MOTOR VEHICLES IN USE

Europa Publications Limited, 18 Bedford Square, London, WC1B 3JN, England; *The Europa World Year Book.*

International Road Federation, 2600 Virginia Avenue, NW, Washington, D.C. 20037 (202) 338-4641; *World Road Statistics.*

Statistical Office of the United Nations, Publishing Service, New York, New York 10017 (800) 253-9646; *Statistical Yearbook;* and *Survey of Economic and Social Conditions in Africa.*

KENYA - MUSEUMS

M.E. Sharpe, 80 Business Park Drive, Armonk, New York 10504 (800) 541-6563; *The Illustrated Book of World Rankings.*

United Nations Educational, Scientific and Cultural Organization (UNESCO), 7 Place de Fontenoy, F-75700 Paris, France (Telephone Number in U.S. (212) 963-5981); *Statistical Yearbook.*

KENYA - NATALITY - See KENYA - BIRTH RATE

KENYA - NATIONAL ACCOUNTS

African Development Bank, 01 BP 1387, Abidjan 01, Cote d'Ivoire; *Selected Statistics on Regional Member Countries.*

Central Bureau of Statistics, Ministry of Economic Planning and Development, Post Office Box 30266, Nairobi, Kenya; *Republic of Kenya Statistical Abstract.*

Europa Publications Limited, 18 Bedford Square, London, WC1B 3JN, England; *The Europa World Year Book.*

International Monetary Fund, 700 Nineteenth Street, NW, Washington, D.C. 20431 (202) 623-7000; *International Financial Statistics.*

Statistical Office of the United Nations, Publishing Service, New York, New York

10017 (800) 253-9646; *National Accounts Statistics;* and *Statistical Yearbook.*

United Nations Economic Commission for Africa, Africa Hall, Post Office Box 3001, Addis Ababa, Ethiopia (Telephone Number in U.S. (800) 253-9646); *African Statistical Yearbook.*

KENYA - NATIONAL INCOME

M.E. Sharpe, 80 Business Park Drive, Armonk, New York 10504 (800) 541-6563; *The Illustrated Book of World Rankings.*

Statistical Office of the United Nations, Publishing Service, New York, New York 10017 (800) 253-9646; *National Accounts Statistics;* and *Statistical Yearbook.*

KENYA - NATIONAL PRODUCT

M.E. Sharpe, 80 Business Park Drive, Armonk, New York 10504 (800) 541-6563; *The Illustrated Book of World Rankings.*

Statistical Office of the United Nations, Publishing Service, New York, New York 10017 (800) 253-9646; *Statistical Yearbook.*

KENYA - NATURAL GAS PRODUCTION - See KENYA - MINING AND MINERAL PRODUCTS

KENYA - NEWSPAPER PRODUCTION - See KENYA - FORESTRY AND FOREST PRODUCTS

KENYA - NEWSPRINT - See KENYA - FORESTRY AND FOREST PRODUCTS

KENYA - OATS PRODUCTION - See KENYA - CROPS

KENYA - OCCUPATIONS - See KENYA - LABOR

KENYA - PAPER - See KENYA - FORESTRY AND FOREST PRODUCTS

KENYA - PATENTS, TRADEMARKS AND SERVICE MARKS

Statistical Office of the United Nations, Publishing Service, New York, New York 10017 (800) 253-9646; *Statistical Yearbook.*

World Intellectual Property Organization, 34 Chemin des Colombettes, CH-1211 Geneva 20, Switzerland; *Industrial Property Statistics.*

KENYA - PEANUT PRODUCTION - See KENYA - CROPS

KENYA - PESTICIDE USE

Food and Agricultural Organization of the United Nations (FAO), Via delle Terme di Caracalla, 00100 Rome, Italy (Telephone Number in U.S. (202) 653-2400); *The State*

of Food and Agriculture.

KENYA - PETROLEUM INDUSTRY

Food and Agricultural Organization of the United Nations (FAO), Via delle Terme di Caracalla, 00100 Rome, Italy (Telephone Number in U.S. (202) 653-2400); *The State of Food and Agriculture.*

International Monetary Fund, 700 Nineteenth Street, NW, Washington, D.C. 20431 (202) 623-7000; *International Financial Statistics.*

M.E. Sharpe, 80 Business Park Drive, Armonk, New York 10504 (800) 541-6563; *The Illustrated Book of World Rankings.*

St. Martin's Press, Inc., 175 Fifth Avenue, New York, New York 10010 (800) 221-7945; *The Statesman's Year-Book.*

Statistical Office of the United Nations, Publishing Service, New York, New York 10017 (800) 253-9646; *Statistical Yearbook.*

United Nations Conference on Trade and Development, Central Statistical Service, Palais des Nations, Geneva, Switzerland (Telephone in U.S. (800) 253-9646); *UNCTAD Commodity Yearbook.*

KENYA - PIGS - See KENYA - LIVESTOCK AND POULTRY

KENYA - POPULATION

African Development Bank, 01 BP 1387, Abidjan 01, Cote d'Ivoire; *Selected Statistics on Regional Member Countries.*

Central Bureau of Statistics, Ministry of Economic Planning and Development, Post Office Box 30266, Nairobi, Kenya; *Republic of Kenya Statistical Abstract.*

Central Intelligence Agency, Washington, D.C. 20505 (703) 482-1100, www.cia.gov; *The World Factbook.*

The Economist Intelligence Unit, 111 West 57th Street, New York, New York 10019 (800) 938-4685; *Kenya Country Report;* and *The World Market Atlas.*

Euromonitor International, Inc., 122 South Michigan Avenue, Suite 1200, Chicago, Illinois 60603 (800) 577-EURO; *International Marketing Data and Statistics;* and *The World Economic Factbook.*

Europa Publications Limited, 18 Bedford Square, London, WC1B 3JN, England; *The Europa World Year Book.*

Food and Agricultural Organization of the United Nations (FAO), Via delle Terme di Caracalla, 00100 Rome, Italy (Telephone Number in U.S. (202) 653-2400); *Production Yearbook.*

International Labour Office, I.L.O. Publications, 1828 L Street, NW, Suite 801, Washington, D.C. 20036 (301) 638-3152); *Yearbook of Labour Statistics.*

M.E. Sharpe, 80 Business Park Drive, Armonk, New York 10504 (800) 541-6563; *The Illustrated Book of World Rankings.*

St. Martin's Press, Inc., 175 Fifth Avenue, New York, New York 10010 (800) 221-7945; *The Statesman's Year-Book.*

Statistical Office of the United Nations, Publishing Service, New York, New York 10017 (800) 253-9646; *Demographic Yearbook; Human Development Report; Statistical Yearbook; World Statistics Pocketbook;* and *Survey of Economic and Social Conditions in Africa.*

United Nations Educational, Scientific and Cultural Organization (UNESCO), 7 Place de Fontenoy, F-75700 Paris, France (Telephone Number in U.S. (212) 963-5981); *Statistical Yearbook.*

The World Bank, 1818 H Street, NW, Washington, D.C. 20433 (202) 477-1234; *The World Bank Atlas;* and *World Development Report.*

KENYA - POST OFFICES

M.E. Sharpe, 80 Business Park Drive, Armonk, New York 10504 (800) 541-6563; *The Illustrated Book of World Rankings.*

KENYA - POTATO PRODUCTION - See KENYA - CROPS

KENYA - PRICES

Food and Agricultural Organization of the United Nations (FAO), Via delle Terme di Caracalla, 00100 Rome, Italy (Telephone Number in U.S. (202) 653-2400); *Production Yearbook;* and *The State of Food and Agriculture.*

International Labour Office, I.L.O. Publications, 1828 L Street, NW, Suite 801, Washington, D.C. 20036 (301) 638-3152); *Yearbook of Labour Statistics.*

International Monetary Fund, 700 Nineteenth Street, NW, Washington, D.C. 20431 (202) 623-7000; *International Financial Statistics.*

M.E. Sharpe, 80 Business Park Drive, Armonk, New York 10504 (800) 541-6563; *The Illustrated Book of World Rankings.*

United Nations Economic Commission for Africa, Africa Hall, Post Office Box 3001, Addis Ababa, Ethiopia (Telephone Number in U.S. (800) 253-9646); *African Statistical Yearbook.*

KENYA - PRINTING AND WRITING PAPER - See KENYA - FORESTRY AND FOREST PRODUCTS

KENYA - PRODUCTION

M.E. Sharpe, 80 Business Park Drive, Armonk, New York 10504 (800) 541-6563; *The Illustrated Book of World Rankings.*

KENYA - PRODUCTIVITY

Euromonitor International, Inc., 122 South Michigan Avenue, Suite 1200, Chicago, Illinois 60603 (800) 577-EURO; *International Marketing Data and Statistics.*

KENYA - PROPERTY TAXES - See KENYA - TAXATION

KENYA - PUBLIC FINANCE - See KENYA - FINANCE

KENYA - RADIO BROADCASTING - See KENYA - BROADCASTING

KENYA - RADIO RECEIVERS

St. Martin's Press, Inc., 175 Fifth Avenue, New York, New York 10010 (800) 221-7945; *The Statesman's Year-Book.*

KENYA - RAILWAYS

Europa Publications Limited, 18 Bedford Square, London, WC1B 3JN, England; *The Europa World Year Book.*

Jane's Information Group, Sentinel House, 163 Brighton Road, Coulsdon, Surrey CR5 2NH, England (Telephone Number in U.S. (703) 683-3700); *Jane's World Railways.*

St. Martin's Press, Inc., 175 Fifth Avenue, New York, New York 10010 (800) 221-7945; *The Statesman's Year-Book.*

Statistical Office of the United Nations, Publishing Service, New York, New York 10017 (800) 253-9646; *Survey of Economic and Social Conditions in Africa.*

United Nations Economic Commission for Africa, Africa Hall, Post Office Box 3001, Addis Ababa, Ethiopia (Telephone Number in U.S. (800) 253-9646); *African Statistical Yearbook.*

KENYA - RELIGION

Central Intelligence Agency, Washington, D.C. 20505 (703) 482-1100, www.cia.gov; *The World Factbook.*

M.E. Sharpe, 80 Business Park Drive, Armonk, New York 10504 (800) 541-6563; *The Illustrated Book of World Rankings.*

St. Martin's Press, Inc., 175 Fifth Avenue, New York, New York 10010 (800)

221-7945; *The Statesman's Year-Book.*

KENYA - RENT PRICES

International Labour Office, I.L.O. Publications, 1828 L Street, NW, Suite 801, Washington, D.C. 20036 (301) 638-3152; *Yearbook of Labour Statistics.*

KENYA - RETAIL TRADE

Euromonitor International, Inc., 122 South Michigan Avenue, Suite 1200, Chicago, Illinois 60603 (800) 577-EURO; *World Marketing Data and Statistics.*

Statistical Office of the United Nations, Publishing Service, New York, New York 10017 (800) 253-9646; *Statistical Yearbook.*

KENYA - RICE PRODUCTION - See KENYA - CROPS

KENYA - ROOT AND TUBER PRODUCTION - See KENYA - CROPS

KENYA - ROUNDWOOD PRODUCTION - See KENYA - FORESTRY AND FOREST PRODUCTS

KENYA - RUBBER PRODUCTION

M.E. Sharpe, 80 Business Park Drive, Armonk, New York 10504 (800) 541-6563; *The Illustrated Book of World Rankings.*

KENYA - SALT PRODUCTION

Statistical Office of the United Nations, Publishing Service, New York, New York 10017 (800) 253-9646; *Statistical Yearbook.*

KENYA - SAWNWOOD PRODUCTION - See KENYA - FORESTRY AND FOREST PRODUCTS

KENYA - SCIENCE AND TECHNOLOGY - EXPENDITURE FOR RESEARCH - See KENYA - SCIENCE, TECHNICIANS AND ENGINEERS

KENYA - SCIENTISTS, TECHNICIANS AND ENGINEERS

Statistical Office of the United Nations, Publishing Service, New York, New York 10017 (800) 253-9646; *Statistical Yearbook.*

United Nations Educational, Scientific and Cultural Organization (UNESCO), 7 Place de Fontenoy, F-75700 Paris, France (Telephone Number in U.S. (212) 963-5981); *Statistical Yearbook.*

KENYA - SENIOR CITIZENS

M.E. Sharpe, 80 Business Park Drive, Armonk, New York 10504 (800) 541-6563; *The Illustrated Book of World Rankings.*

KENYA - SESAME SEED PRODUCTION - See

KENYA - CROPS

KENYA - SHEEP - See KENYA - LIVESTOCK AND POULTRY

KENYA - SILVER PRODUCTION AND CONSUMPTION - See KENYA - MINING AND MINERAL PRODUCTS

KENYA - SISAL PRODUCTION - See KENYA - CROPS

KENYA - SOCIAL DATA

African Development Bank, 01 BP 1387, Abidjan 01, Cote d'Ivoire; *Selected Statistics on Regional Member Countries.*

M.E. Sharpe, 80 Business Park Drive, Armonk, New York 10504 (800) 541-6563; *The Illustrated Book of World Rankings.*

Statistical Office of the United Nations, Publishing Service, New York, New York 10017 (800) 253-9646; *World Statistics Pocketbook.*

KENYA - SOCIAL SECURITY

Statistical Office of the United Nations, Publishing Service, New York, New York 10017 (800) 253-9646; *National Accounts Statistics.*

KENYA - STAMP TAXES AND DUTIES - See KENYA - TAXATION

KENYA - STATE BUDGET REVENUE AND EXPENDITURES

Euromonitor International, Inc., 122 South Michigan Avenue, Suite 1200, Chicago, Illinois 60603 (800) 577-EURO; *International Marketing Data and Statistics.*

KENYA - STEEL PRODUCTION AND CONSUMPTION - See KENYA - MINING AND MINERAL PRODUCTS

KENYA - STOCKS - COMMODITY - MARKET PRICE - INDEX

Food and Agricultural Organization of the United Nations (FAO), Via delle Terme di Caracalla, 00100 Rome, Italy (Telephone Number in U.S. (202) 653-2400); *The State of Food and Agriculture.*

KENYA - SUGAR PRODUCTION AND CONSUMPTION - See KENYA - CROPS

KENYA - TAXATION

Europa Publications Limited, 18 Bedford Square, London, WC1B 3JN, England; *The Europa World Year Book.*

International Monetary Fund, 700 Nineteenth Street, NW, Washington, D.C. 20431 (202) 623-7000; *Government*

Finance Statistics Yearbook.

International Road Federation, 2600 Virginia Avenue, NW, Washington, D.C. 20037 (202) 338-4641; *World Road Statistics.*

The World Bank, 1818 H Street, NW, Washington, D.C. 20433 (202) 477-1234; *World Development Indicators.*

KENYA - TEA - See KENYA - CROPS

KENYA - TELEGRAPH SERVICE

Statistical Office of the United Nations, Publishing Service, New York, New York 10017 (800) 253-9646; *Statistical Yearbook.*

KENYA - TELEPHONES IN USE

American Telephone and Telegraph Company, 26 Parsippany Road, Whippany, New Jersey 07981 (800) 222-0300; *The World's Telephones.*

Central Intelligence Agency, Washington, D.C. 20505 (703) 482-1100, www.cia.gov; *The World Factbook.*

Europa Publications Limited, 18 Bedford Square, London, WC1B 3JN, England; *The Europa World Year Book.*

Statistical Office of the United Nations, Publishing Service, New York, New York 10017 (800) 253-9646; *Statistical Yearbook;* and *World Statistics Pocketbook.*

KENYA - TELEVISION BROADCASTING - See KENYA - BROADCASTING

KENYA - TEXTILE INDUSTRY

M.E. Sharpe, 80 Business Park Drive, Armonk, New York 10504 (800) 541-6563; *The Illustrated Book of World Rankings.*

St. Martin's Press, Inc., 175 Fifth Avenue, New York, New York 10010 (800) 221-7945; *The Statesman's Year-Book.*

Statistical Office of the United Nations, Publishing Service, New York, New York 10017 (800) 253-9646; *Statistical Yearbook.*

United Nations Conference on Trade and Development, Central Statistical Service, Palais des Nations, Geneva, Switzerland (Telephone in U.S. (800) 253-9646); *UNCTAD Commodity Yearbook.*

KENYA - TOBACCO PRODUCTION

M.E. Sharpe, 80 Business Park Drive, Armonk, New York 10504 (800) 541-6563; *The Illustrated Book of World Rankings.*

Statistical Office of the United Nations, Publishing Service, New York, New York 10017 (800) 253-9646; *Statistical Yearbook.*

KENYA - TOURISM

Central Bureau of Statistics, Ministry of Economic Planning and Development, Post Office Box 30266, Nairobi, Kenya; *Republic of Kenya Statistical Abstract.*

Euromonitor International, Inc., 122 South Michigan Avenue, Suite 1200, Chicago, Illinois 60603 (800) 577-EURO; *The World Economic Factbook;* and *World Marketing Data and Statistics.*

Europa Publications Limited, 18 Bedford Square, London, WC1B 3JN, England; *The Europa World Year Book.*

M.E. Sharpe, 80 Business Park Drive, Armonk, New York 10504 (800) 541-6563; *The Illustrated Book of World Rankings.*

St. Martin's Press, Inc., 175 Fifth Avenue, New York, New York 10010 (800) 221-7945; *The Statesman's Year-Book.*

Statistical Office of the United Nations, Publishing Service, New York, New York 10017 (800) 253-9646; *Statistical Yearbook.*

United Nations Economic Commission for Africa, Africa Hall, Post Office Box 3001, Addis Ababa, Ethiopia (Telephone Number in U.S. (800) 253-9646); *African Statistical Yearbook.*

World Tourism Organization, Calle Capitan Haya 42, E-28020 Madrid, Spain; *Yearbook of Tourism Statistics.*

KENYA - TRACTORS IN USE

Statistical Office of the United Nations, Publishing Service, New York, New York 10017 (800) 253-9646; *Statistical Yearbook.*

KENYA - TRADE - See KENYA - FOREIGN TRADE

KENYA - TRADEMARKS AND SERVICE MARKS - See KENYA - PATENTS, TRADEMARKS AND SERVICE MARKS

KENYA - TRANSPORTATION AND COMMUNICATIONS

Central Bureau of Statistics, Ministry of Economic Planning and Development, Post Office Box 30266, Nairobi, Kenya; *Republic of Kenya Statistical Abstract.*

Central Intelligence Agency, Washington, D.C. 20505 (703) 482-1100, www.cia.gov; *The World Factbook.*

Euromonitor International, Inc., 122 South Michigan Avenue, Suite 1200, Chicago, Illinois 60603 (800) 577-EURO; *International Marketing Data and Statistics;* and *World Marketing Data and Statistics.*

Europa Publications Limited, 18

Bedford Square, London, WC1B 3JN, England; *The Europa World Year Book.*

M.E. Sharpe, 80 Business Park Drive, Armonk, New York 10504 (800) 541-6563; *The Illustrated Book of World Rankings.*

St. Martin's Press, Inc., 175 Fifth Avenue, New York, New York 10010 (800) 221-7945; *The Statesman's Year-Book.*

Statistical Office of the United Nations, Publishing Service, New York, New York 10017 (800) 253-9646; *Human Development Report.*

United Nations Economic Commission for Africa, Africa Hall, Post Office Box 3001, Addis Ababa, Ethiopia (Telephone Number in U.S. (800) 253-9646); *African Statistical Yearbook.*

KENYA - UNEMPLOYMENT

Central Intelligence Agency, Washington, D.C. 20505 (703) 482-1100, www.cia.gov; *The World Factbook.*

Euromonitor International, Inc., 122 South Michigan Avenue, Suite 1200, Chicago. Illinois 60603 (800) 577-EURO; *International Marketing Data and Statistics.*

International Labour Office, I.L.O. Publications, 1828 L Street, NW, Suite 801, Washington, D.C. 20036 (301) 638-3152; *Yearbook of Labour Statistics.*

KENYA - VITAL STATISTICS

Central Bureau of Statistics, Ministry of Economic Planning and Development, Post Office Box 30266, Nairobi, Kenya; *Republic of Kenya Statistical Abstract.*

Euromonitor International, Inc., 122 South Michigan Avenue, Suite 1200, Chicago. Illinois 60603 (800) 577-EURO; *International Marketing Data and Statistics.*

Statistical Office of the United Nations, Publishing Service, New York, New York 10017 (800) 253-9646; *Statistical Yearbook.*

KENYA - WAGES

International Labour Office, I.L.O. Publications, 1828 L Street, NW, Suite 801, Washington, D.C. 20036 (301) 638-3152; *Yearbook of Labour Statistics.*

Statistical Office of the United Nations, Publishing Service, New York, New York 10017 (800) 253-9646; *Statistical Yearbook.*

KENYA - WEATHER - See KENYA - CLIMATE

KENYA - WHEAT PRODUCTION AND PRICES - See KENYA - CROPS

KENYA - WHOLESALE TRADE

Statistical Office of the United Nations, Publishing Service, New York, New York 10017 (800) 253-9646; *Statistical Yearbook.*

KENYA - WINE PRODUCTION - See KENYA - BEVERAGES

KENYA - WOOL PRODUCTION - See KENYA - TEXTILE INDUSTRY

KENYA - YARN PRODUCTION - See KENYA - TEXTILE INDUSTRY

KEOGH PLANS

Board of Governors of the Federal Reserve System, 20th Street and Constitution Avenue, NW, Suite 700, Washington, D.C. 20009 (202) 884-7799, www.bog.frb.fed.us; *Federal Reserve Bulletin.*

U.S. Department of the Treasury, Internal Revenue Service, 1111 Constitution Avenue, NW, Washington, D.C. 20224 (202) 874-0410, www.irs.treas.gov; *Statistics of Income, Individual Income Tax Returns.*

KIDNEY DISEASE AND INFECTIONS - DEATHS

U.S. Department of Health and Human Services, National Center for Health Statistics, 3700 East-West Highway, Hyattsville, Maryland 20782 (301) 436-8500, www.cdc.gov/nchs; *Vital Statistics of the United States; National Vital Statistics Report;* and unpublished data.

Kiribati - National Statistical Office

Statistics Office, Ministry of Finance and Economic Planning, Post Office Box 67, Bariki, Tarawa, Kiribati.

Kiribati - Primary Statistics Source

Statistics Office, Ministry of Finance, P.O. Box 67, Bariki, Tarawa, Kiribati; *National Development Plan, 1983 - 1986.*

KIRIBATI - AGRICULTURE

Asian Development Bank, Post Office Box 789, Manila, 1099 Manila, Philippines; *Key Indicators of Developing Asian and Pacific Countries.*

Euromonitor International, Inc., 122 South Michigan Avenue, Suite 1200, Chicago, Illinois 60603 (800) 577-EURO; *World Marketing Data and Statistics.*

Europa Publications Limited, 18 Bedford Square, London, WC1B 3JN,

England; *The Europa World Year Book.*

Food and Agricultural Organization of the United Nations (FAO), Via delle Terme di Caracalla, 00100 Rome, Italy (Telephone Number in U.S. (202) 653-2400); *Production Yearbook; The State of Food and Agriculture;* and *Trade Yearbook.*

St. Martin's Press, Inc., 175 Fifth Avenue, New York, New York 10010 (800) 221-7945; *The Statesman's Year-Book.*

Statistical Office of the United Nations, Publishing Service, New York, New York 10017 (800) 253-9646; *Asia-Pacific in Figures.*

United Nations Conference on Trade and Development, Central Statistical Service, Palais des Nations, Geneva, Switzerland (Telephone in U.S. (800) 253-9646); *UNCTAD Commodity Yearbook.*

KIRIBATI - AIRLINE SERVICE

Europa Publications Limited, 18 Bedford Square, London, WC1B 3JN, England; *The Europa World Year Book.*

St. Martin's Press, Inc., 175 Fifth Avenue, New York, New York 10010 (800) 221-7945; *The Statesman's Year-Book.*

KIRIBATI - AREA AND DENSITY OF POPULATION

Central Intelligence Agency, Washington, D.C. 20505 (703) 482-1100, www.cia.gov; *The World Factbook.*

Euromonitor International, Inc., 122 South Michigan Avenue, Suite 1200, Chicago. Illinois 60603 (800) 577-EURO; *The World Economic Factbook.*

Europa Publications Limited, 18 Bedford Square, London, WC1B 3JN, England; *The Europa World Year Book.*

Food and Agricultural Organization of the United Nations (FAO), Via delle Terme di Caracalla, 00100 Rome, Italy (Telephone Number in U.S. (202) 653-2400); *The State of Food and Agriculture.*

St. Martin's Press, Inc., 175 Fifth Avenue, New York, New York 10010 (800) 221-7945; *The Statesman's Year-Book.*

KIRIBATI - BALANCE OF PAYMENTS

Europa Publications Limited, 18 Bedford Square, London, WC1B 3JN, England; *The Europa World Year Book.*

KIRIBATI - BANKING

Asian Development Bank, Post Office Box 789, 1099 Manila, Philippines; *Key Indicators of Developing Asian and Pacific*

Countries.

Euromonitor International, Inc., 122 South Michigan Avenue, Suite 1200, Chicago, Illinois 60603 (800) 577-EURO; *World Marketing Data and Statistics.*

KIRIBATI - BIRTH RATES

Central Intelligence Agency, Washington, D.C. 20505 (703) 482-1100, www.cia.gov; *The World Factbook.*

Euromonitor International, Inc., 122 South Michigan Avenue, Suite 1200, Chicago. Illinois 60603 (800) 577-EURO; *International Marketing Data and Statistics;* and *The World Economic Factbook.*

Europa Publications Limited, 18 Bedford Square, London, WC1B 3JN, England; *The Europa World Year Book.*

Statistical Office of the United Nations, Publishing Service, New York, New York 10017 (800) 253-9646; *Asia-Pacific in Figures.*

KIRIBATI - BONDS

Asian Development Bank, Post Office Box 789, 1099 Manila, Philippines; *Key Indicators of Developing Asian and Pacific Countries.*

KIRIBATI - BROADCASTING

Billboard Limited, Post Office Box 9027, 1006 AA Amsterdam, The Netherlands (Telephone Number in U.S. (212) 764-7300); *World Radio TV Handbook.*

Central Intelligence Agency, Washington, D.C. 20505 (703) 482-1100, www.cia.gov; *The World Factbook.*

Euromonitor International, Inc., 122 South Michigan Avenue, Suite 1200, Chicago, Illinois 60603 (800) 577-EURO; *World Marketing Data and Statistics.*

St. Martin's Press, Inc., 175 Fifth Avenue, New York, New York 10010 (800) 221-7945; *The Statesman's Year-Book.*

KIRIBATI - BUDGET

Central Intelligence Agency, Washington, D.C. 20505 (703) 482-1100, www.cia.gov; *The World Factbook.*

KIRIBATI - CALORIE SUPPLY

Asian Development Bank, Post Office Box 789, Manila, 1099 Manila, Philippines; *Key Indicators of Developing Asian and Pacific Countries.*

Food and Agricultural Organization of the United Nations (FAO), Via delle Terme di Caracalla, 00100 Rome, Italy (Telephone

Number in U.S. (202) 653-2400); *The State of Food and Agriculture.*

KIRIBATI - CAPITAL INVESTMENT

Asian Development Bank, Post Office Box 789, 1099 Manila, Philippines; *Key Indicators of Developing Asian and Pacific Countries.*

KIRIBATI - CAPITAL REVENUE

Asian Development Bank, Post Office Box 789, 1099 Manila, Philippines; *Key Indicators of Developing Asian and Pacific Countries.*

KIRIBATI - CHEMICAL (ORGANIC) PRODUCTION - See KIRIBATI - MINING AND MINERAL PRODUCTS

KIRIBATI - CLIMATE

St. Martin's Press, Inc., 175 Fifth Avenue, New York, New York 10010 (800) 221-7945; *The Statesman's Year-Book.*

KIRIBATI - CLOTHING EXPORTS AND IMPORTS - See KIRIBATI - TEXTILE INDUSTRY

KIRIBATI - COAL PRODUCTION - See KIRIBATI - MINING AND MINERAL PRODUCTS

KIRIBATI - COMMERCE

St. Martin's Press, Inc., 175 Fifth Avenue, New York, New York 10010 (800) 221-7945; *The Statesman's Year-Book.*

KIRIBATI - CONSUMER PRICE INDEX

Asian Development Bank, Post Office Box 789, 1099 Manila, Philippines; *Key Indicators of Developing Asian and Pacific Countries.*

Europa Publications Limited, 18 Bedford Square, London, WC1B 3JN, England; *The Europa World Year Book.*

KIRIBATI - CONSUMER PRICES

Euromonitor International, Inc., 122 South Michigan Avenue, Suite 1200, Chicago, Illinois 60603 (800) 577-EURO; *World Marketing Data and Statistics.*

International Labour Office, I.L.O. Publications, 1828 L Street, NW, Suite 801, Washington, D.C. 20036 (301) 638-3152; *Yearbook of Labour Statistics.*

KIRIBATI - CONSUMPTION

South Pacific Commission, Post Box D5, Noumea Cedex, New Caledonia; *Statistical Bulletin of the South Pacific: Retail Price Indexes.*

KIRIBATI - CORN PRODUCTION - See KIRIBATI - CROPS

KIRIBATI - CROPS

Asian Development Bank, Post Office Box 789, 1099 Manila, Philippines; *Key Indicators of Developing Asian and Pacific Countries.*

Europa Publications Limited, 18 Bedford Square, London, WC1B 3JN, England; *The Europa World Year Book.*

Food and Agricultural Organization of the United Nations (FAO), Via delle Terme di Caracalla, 00100 Rome, Italy (Telephone Number in U.S. (202) 653-2400); *The State of Food and Agriculture.*

St. Martin's Press, Inc., 175 Fifth Avenue, New York, New York 10010 (800) 221-7945; *The Statesman's Year-Book.*

United Nations Conference on Trade and Development, Central Statistical Service, Palais des Nations, Geneva, Switzerland (Telephone in U.S. (800) 253-9646); *UNCTAD Commodity Yearbook.*

KIRIBATI - CUSTOMS DUTIES

St. Martin's Press, Inc., 175 Fifth Avenue, New York, New York 10010 (800) 221-7945; *The Statesman's Year-Book.*

KIRIBATI - DAIRY PRODUCTS

Food and Agricultural Organization of the United Nations (FAO), Via delle Terme di Caracalla, 00100 Rome, Italy (Telephone Number in U.S. (202) 653-2400); *The State of Food and Agriculture.*

St. Martin's Press, Inc., 175 Fifth Avenue, New York, New York 10010 (800) 221-7945; *The Statesman's Year-Book.*

KIRIBATI - DEATH RATES - See KIRIBATI - MORTALITY

KIRIBATI - DEMOGRAPHY

Euromonitor International, Inc., 122 South Michigan Avenue, Suite 1200, Chicago. Illinois 60603 (800) 577-EURO; *International Marketing Data and Statistics; The World Economic Factbook;* and *World Marketing Data and Statistics.*

Statistical Office of the United Nations, Publishing Service, New York, New York 10017 (800) 253-9646; *Asia-Pacific in Figures.*

KIRIBATI - DEVELOPMENT ASSISTANCE

Asian Development Bank, Post Office Box 789, 1099 Manila, Philippines; *Key Indicators of Developing Asian and Pacific*

Countries.

KIRIBATI - DISEASES - See KIRIBATI - HEALTH

KIRIBATI - ECONOMY

Asian Development Bank, Post Office Box 789, 1099 Manila, Philippines; *Key Indicators of Developing Asian and Pacific Countries.*

Central Intelligence Agency, Washington, D.C. 20505 (703) 482-1100, www.cia.gov; *The World Factbook.*

Euromonitor International, Inc., 122 South Michigan Avenue, Suite 1200, Chicago. Illinois 60603 (800) 577-EURO ; *The World Economic Factbook;* and *World Marketing Data and Statistics.*

Europa Publications Limited, 18 Bedford Square, London, WC1B 3JN, England; *The Europa World Year Book.*

St. Martin's Press, Inc., 175 Fifth Avenue, New York, New York 10010 (800) 221-7945; *The Statesman's Year-Book.*

Statistical Office of the United Nations, Publishing Service, New York, New York 10017 (800) 253-9646; *World Statistics Pocketbook.*

The World Bank, 1818 H Street, NW, Washington, D.C. 20433 (202) 477-1234; *The World Bank Atlas.*

KIRIBATI - EDUCATION

Euromonitor International, Inc., 122 South Michigan Avenue, Suite 1200, Chicago. Illinois 60603 (800) 577-EURO; *International Marketing Data and Statistics;* and *World Marketing Data and Statistics.*

Europa Publications Limited, 18 Bedford Square, London, WC1B 3JN, England; *The Europa World Year Book.*

St. Martin's Press, Inc., 175 Fifth Avenue, New York, New York 10010 (800) 221-7945; *The Statesman's Year-Book.*

Statistical Office of the United Nations, Publishing Service, New York, New York 10017 (800) 253-9646; *Asia-Pacific in Figures.*

United Nations Educational, Scientific and Cultural Organization (UNESCO), 7 Place de Fontenoy, F-75700 Paris, France (Telephone Number in U.S. (212) 963-5981); *Statistical Yearbook.*

KIRIBATI - EGG PRODUCTION AND CONSUMPTION - See KIRIBATI - DAIRY PRODUCTS

KIRIBATI - ELECTRICITY

Asian Development Bank, Post Office Box 789, 1099 Manila, Philippines; *Key Indicators of Developing Asian and Pacific Countries.*

Central Intelligence Agency, Washington, D.C. 20505 (703) 482-1100, www.cia.gov; *The World Factbook.*

St. Martin's Press, Inc., 175 Fifth Avenue, New York, New York 10010 (800) 221-7945; *The Statesman's Year-Book.*

Statistical Office of the United Nations, Publishing Service, New York, New York 10017 (800) 253-9646; *Electric Power in Asia and the Pacific.*

KIRIBATI - EMPLOYMENT

Euromonitor International, Inc., 122 South Michigan Avenue, Suite 1200, Chicago. Illinois 60603 (800) 577-EURO; *International Marketing Data and Statistics.*

International Labour Office, I.L.O. Publications, 1828 L Street, NW, Suite 801, Washington, D.C. 20036 (301) 638-3152; *Yearbook of Labour Statistics.*

Statistical Office of the United Nations, Publishing Service, New York, New York 10017 (800) 253-9646; *Asia-Pacific in Figures.*

KIRIBATI - ENERGY

Euromonitor International, Inc., 122 South Michigan Avenue, Suite 1200, Chicago. Illinois 60603 (800) 577-EURO; *International Marketing Data and Statistics; The World Economic Factbook;* and *World Marketing Data and Statistics.*

Food and Agricultural Organization of the United Nations (FAO), Via delle Terme di Caracalla, 00100 Rome, Italy (Telephone Number in U.S. (202) 653-2400); *The State of Food and Agriculture.*

St. Martin's Press, Inc., 175 Fifth Avenue, New York, New York 10010 (800) 221-7945; *The Statesman's Year-Book.*

Statistical Office of the United Nations, Publishing Service, New York, New York 10017 (800) 253-9646; *Asia-Pacific in Figures; World Statistics Pocketbook;* and *Statistical Yearbook.*

The World Bank, 1818 H Street, NW, Washington, D.C. 20433 (202) 477-1234; *The World Bank Atlas.*

KIRIBATI - ENVIRONMENT

Statistical Office of the United Nations, Publishing Service, New York, New York 10017 (800) 253-9646; *World Statistics Pocketbook.*

KIRIBATI - EXCHANGE RATES

Asian Development Bank, Post Office Box 789, 1099 Manila, Philippines; *Key Indicators of Developing Asian and Pacific Countries.*

Central Intelligence Agency, Washington, D.C. 20505 (703) 482-1100, www.cia.gov; *The World Factbook.*

Euromonitor International, Inc., 122 South Michigan Avenue, Suite 1200, Chicago. Illinois 60603 (800) 577-EURO; *International Marketing Data and Statistics;* and *The World Economic Factbook.*

Europa Publications Limited, 18 Bedford Square, London, WC1B 3JN, England; *The Europa World Year Book.*

Statistical Office of the United Nations, Publishing Service, New York, New York 10017 (800) 253-9646; *World Statistics Pocketbook.*

Walden Publishing, Ltd., Two Market Street, Saffron Walden Essex, CB10 1HZ, England; *The World of Information Asia and Pacific Review.*

KIRIBATI - EXPORTS

Asian Development Bank, Post Office Box 789, 1099 Manila, Philippines; *Key Indicators of Developing Asian and Pacific Countries.*

Central Intelligence Agency, Washington, D.C. 20505 (703) 482-1100, www.cia.gov; *The World Factbook.*

Euromonitor International, Inc., 122 South Michigan Avenue, Suite 1200, Chicago. Illinois 60603 (800) 577-EURO; *International Marketing Data and Statistics;* and *The World Economic Factbook.*

Europa Publications Limited, 18 Bedford Square, London, WC1B 3JN, England; *The Europa World Year Book.*

Food and Agricultural Organization of the United Nations (FAO), Via delle Terme di Caracalla, 00100 Rome, Italy (Telephone Number in U.S. (202) 653-2400); *The State of Food and Agriculture.*

St. Martin's Press, Inc., 175 Fifth Avenue, New York, New York 10010 (800) 221-7945; *The Statesman's Year-Book.*

South Pacific Commission, Post Box D5, Noumea Cedex, New Caledonia; *Statistical Bulletin of the South Pacific: Overseas Trade.*

Walden Publishing, Ltd., Two Market Street, Saffron Walden Essex, CB10 1HZ, England; *The World of Information Asia and Pacific Review.*

KIRIBATI - EXTERNAL FINANCING

Asian Development Bank, Post Office Box 789, 1099 Manila, Philippines; *Key Indicators of Developing Asian and Pacific Countries.*

KIRIBATI - EXTERNAL INDEBTEDNESS

Asian Development Bank, Post Office Box 789, 1099 Manila, Philippines; *Key Indicators of Developing Asian and Pacific Countries.*

KIRIBATI - EXTERNAL TRADE

Asian Development Bank, Post Office Box 789, 1099 Manila, Philippines; *Key Indicators of Developing Asian and Pacific Countries.*

Euromonitor International, Inc., 122 South Michigan Avenue, Suite 1200, Chicago, Illinois 60603 (800) 577-EURO; *World Marketing Data and Statistics.*

Food and Agricultural Organization of the United Nations (FAO), Via delle Terme di Caracalla, 00100 Rome, Italy (Telephone Number in U.S. (202) 653-2400); *The State of Food and Agriculture;* and *Trade Yearbook.*

Statistical Office of the United Nations, Publishing Service, New York, New York 10017 (800) 253-9646; *Asia-Pacific in Figures.*

KIRIBATI - FARM CROPS - See KIRIBATI - CROPS

KIRIBATI - FERTILITY RATES

Central Intelligence Agency, Washington, D.C. 20505 (703) 482-1100, www.cia.gov; *The World Factbook.*

The World Bank, 1818 H Street, NW, Washington, D.C. 20433 (202) 477-1234; *The World Bank Atlas.*

KIRIBATI - FERTILIZER

Food and Agricultural Organization of the United Nations (FAO), Via delle Terme di Caracalla, 00100 Rome, Italy (Telephone Number in U.S. (202) 653-2400); *The State of Food and Agriculture.*

KIRIBATI - FINANCE

Asian Development Bank, Post Office Box 789, 1099 Manila, Philippines; *Key Indicators of Developing Asian and Pacific Countries.*

Europa Publications Limited, 18 Bedford Square, London, WC1B 3JN, England; *The Europa World Year Book.*

KIRIBATI - FISHERIES

Europa Publications Limited, 18 Bedford Square, London, WC1B 3JN, England; *The Europa World Year Book.*

Food and Agricultural Organization of the United Nations (FAO), Via delle Terme di Caracalla, 00100 Rome, Italy (Telephone Number in U.S. (202) 653-2400); *The State of Food and Agriculture;* and *Yearbook of Fishery Statistics.*

St. Martin's Press, Inc., 175 Fifth Avenue, New York, New York 10010 (800) 221-7945; *The Statesman's Year-Book.*

United Nations Conference on Trade and Development, Central Statistical Service, Palais des Nations, Geneva, Switzerland (Telephone in U.S. (800) 253-9646); *UNCTAD Commodity Yearbook.*

KIRIBATI - FOOD

Food and Agricultural Organization of the United Nations (FAO), Via delle Terme di Caracalla, 00100 Rome, Italy (Telephone Number in U.S. (202) 653-2400); *Production Yearbook,;* and *The State of Food and Agriculture.*

South Pacific Commission, Post Box D5, Noumea Cedex, New Caledonia; *Statistical Bulletin of the South Pacific: Retail Price Indexes.*

United Nations Conference on Trade and Development, Central Statistical Service, Palais des Nations, Geneva, Switzerland (Telephone in U.S. (800) 253-9646); *UNCTAD Commodity Yearbook.*

KIRIBATI - FOREIGN DEBT

Walden Publishing, Ltd., Two Market Street, Saffron Walden Essex, CB10 1HZ, England; *The World of Information Asia and Pacific Review.*

KIRIBATI - FOREIGN TRADE

Asian Development Bank, Post Office Box 789, 1099 Manila, Philippines; *Key Indicators of Developing Asian and Pacific Countries.*

Euromonitor International, Inc., 122 South Michigan Avenue, Suite 1200, Chicago. Illinois 60603 (800) 577-EURO ; *The World Economic Factbook.*

Europa Publications Limited, 18 Bedford Square, London, WC1B 3JN, England; *The Europa World Year Book.*

Food and Agricultural Organization of the United Nations (FAO), Via delle Terme di Caracalla, 00100 Rome, Italy (Telephone Number in U.S. (202) 653-2400); *The State of Food and Agriculture.*

St. Martin's Press, Inc., 175 Fifth

Avenue, New York, New York 10010 (800) 221-7945; *The Statesman's Year-Book.*

South Pacific Commission, Post Box D5, Noumea Cedex, New Caledonia; *Statistical Bulletin of the South Pacific: Overseas Trade.*

United Nations Conference on Trade and Development, Central Statistical Service, Palais des Nations, Geneva, Switzerland (Telephone in U.S. (800) 253-9646); *UNCTAD Commodity Yearbook.*

KIRIBATI - FORESTRY AND FOREST PRODUCTS

Food and Agricultural Organization of the United Nations (FAO), Via delle Terme di Caracalla, 00100 Rome, Italy (Telephone Number in U.S. (202) 653-2400); *The State of Food and Agriculture.*

Statistical Office of the United Nations, Publishing Service, New York, New York 10017 (800) 253-9646; *Statistical Yearbook.*

United Nations Conference on Trade and Development, Central Statistical Service, Palais des Nations, Geneva, Switzerland (Telephone in U.S. (800) 253-9646); *UNCTAD Commodity Yearbook.*

KIRIBATI - GOVERNMENT

Asian Development Bank, Post Office Box 789, 1099 Manila, Philippines; *Key Indicators of Developing Asian and Pacific Countries.*

Central Intelligence Agency, Washington, D.C. 20505 (703) 482-1100, www.cia.gov; *The World Factbook.*

Europa Publications Limited, 18 Bedford Square, London, WC1B 3JN, England; *The Europa World Year Book.*

St. Martin's Press, Inc., 175 Fifth Avenue, New York, New York 10010 (800) 221-7945; *The Statesman's Year-Book.*

Statistical Office of the United Nations, Publishing Service, New York, New York 10017 (800) 253-9646; *Asia-Pacific in Figures.*

KIRIBATI - GRAIN PRODUCTION - See KIRIBATI - CROPS

KIRIBATI - GROSS DOMESTIC PRODUCT

Asian Development Bank, Post Office Box 789, 1099 Manila, Philippines; *Key Indicators of Developing Asian and Pacific Countries.*

Euromonitor International, Inc., 122 South Michigan Avenue, Suite 1200, Chicago. Illinois 60603 (800) 577-EURO; *International Marketing Data and Statistics;*

and *The World Economic Factbook.*

Europa Publications Limited, 18 Bedford Square, London, WC1B 3JN, England; *The Europa World Year Book.*

KIRIBATI - GROSS NATIONAL PRODUCT

Asian Development Bank, Post Office Box 789, 1099 Manila, Philippines; *Key Indicators of Developing Asian and Pacific Countries.*

St. Martin's Press, Inc., 175 Fifth Avenue, New York, New York 10010 (800) 221-7945; *The Statesman's Year-Book.*

Walden Publishing, Ltd., Two Market Street, Saffron Walden Essex, CB10 1HZ, England; *The World of Information Asia and Pacific Review.*

The World Bank, 1818 H Street, NW, Washington, D.C. 20433 (202) 477-1234; *The World Bank Atlas.*

KIRIBATI - HEALTH

Asian Development Bank, Post Office Box 789, 1099 Manila, Philippines; *Key Indicators of Developing Asian and Pacific Countries.*

Euromonitor International, Inc., 122 South Michigan Avenue, Suite 1200, Chicago, Illinois 60603 (800) 577-EURO; *World Marketing Data and Statistics.*

St. Martin's Press, Inc., 175 Fifth Avenue, New York, New York 10010 (800) 221-7945; *The Statesman's Year-Book.*

South Pacific Commission, Post Box D5, Noumea Cedex, New Caledonia; *Statistical Bulletin of the South Pacific: Retail Price Indexes.*

Statistical Office of the United Nations, Publishing Service, New York, New York 10017 (800) 253-9646; *Asia-Pacific in Figures;* and *Statistical Yearbook.*

World Health Organization, Office of Publications, 20 Avenue Appia, CH-1211 Geneva 27, Switzerland (Telephone Number in U.S. (518) 436-9686); *World Health Statistics Annual.*

KIRIBATI - HIGHWAYS

Central Intelligence Agency, Washington, D.C. 20505 (703) 482-1100, www.cia.gov; *The World Factbook.*

St. Martin's Press, Inc., 175 Fifth Avenue, New York, New York 10010 (800) 221-7945; *The Statesman's Year-Book.*

KIRIBATI - HOURS OF WORK - See KIRIBATI - EMPLOYMENT

KIRIBATI - HOUSING AND HOUSING UNITS

Euromonitor International, Inc., 122 South Michigan Avenue, Suite 1200, Chicago, Illinois 60603 (800) 577-EURO; *World Marketing Data and Statistics.*

South Pacific Commission, Post Box D5, Noumea Cedex, New Caledonia; *Statistical Bulletin of the South Pacific: Retail Price Indexes.*

KIRIBATI - ILLITERATE POPULATION

Central Intelligence Agency, Washington, D.C. 20505 (703) 482-1100, www.cia.gov; *The World Factbook.*

Euromonitor International, Inc., 122 South Michigan Avenue, Suite 1200, Chicago. Illinois 60603 (800) 577-EURO; *The World Economic Factbook.*

Statistical Office of the United Nations, Publishing Service, New York, New York 10017 (800) 253-9646; *Asia-Pacific in Figures.*

United Nations Educational, Scientific and Cultural Organization (UNESCO), 7 Place de Fontenoy, F-75700 Paris, France (Telephone Number in U.S. (212) 963-5981); *Statistical Yearbook.*

KIRIBATI - IMPORTS

Asian Development Bank, Post Office Box 789, 1099 Manila, Philippines; *Key Indicators of Developing Asian and Pacific Countries.*

Central Intelligence Agency, Washington, D.C. 20505 (703) 482-1100, www.cia.gov; *The World Factbook.*

Euromonitor International, Inc., 122 South Michigan Avenue, Suite 1200, Chicago. Illinois 60603 (800) 577-EURO; *International Marketing Data and Statistics;* and *The World Economic Factbook.*

Europa Publications Limited, 18 Bedford Square, London, WC1B 3JN, England; *The Europa World Year Book.*

Food and Agricultural Organization of the United Nations (FAO), Via delle Terme di Caracalla, 00100 Rome, Italy (Telephone Number in U.S. (202) 653-2400); *The State of Food and Agriculture.*

St. Martin's Press, Inc., 175 Fifth Avenue, New York, New York 10010 (800) 221-7945; *The Statesman's Year-Book.*

South Pacific Commission, Post Box D5, Noumea Cedex, New Caledonia; *Statistical Bulletin of the South Pacific: Overseas Trade.*

Walden Publishing, Ltd., Two Market

Street, Saffron Walden Essex, CB10 1HZ, England; *The World of Information Asia and Pacific Review.*

KIRIBATI - INDUSTRY

Central Intelligence Agency, Washington, D.C. 20505 (703) 482-1100, www.cia.gov; *The World Factbook.*

Euromonitor International, Inc., 122 South Michigan Avenue, Suite 1200, Chicago. Illinois 60603 (800) 577-EURO ; *The World Economic Factbook;* and *World Marketing Data and Statistics.*

Europa Publications Limited, 18 Bedford Square, London, WC1B 3JN, England; *The Europa World Year Book.*

International Labour Office, I.L.O. Publications, 1828 L Street, NW, Suite 801, Washington, D.C. 20036 (301) 638-3152; *Yearbook of Labour Statistics.*

St. Martin's Press, Inc., 175 Fifth Avenue, New York, New York 10010 (800) 221-7945; *The Statesman's Year-Book.*

Statistical Office of the United Nations, Publishing Service, New York, New York 10017 (800) 253-9646; *Asia-Pacific in Figures.*

KIRIBATI - INTERNATIONAL RESERVES EXCLUDING GOLD

Asian Development Bank, Post Office Box 789, 1099 Manila, Philippines; *Key Indicators of Developing Asian and Pacific Countries.*

KIRIBATI - INTERNATIONAL STATISTICS

Asian Development Bank, Post Office Box 789, 1099 Manila, Philippines; *Key Indicators of Developing Asian and Pacific Countries.*

KIRIBATI - LABOR

Central Intelligence Agency, Washington, D.C. 20505 (703) 482-1100, www.cia.gov; *The World Factbook.*

Euromonitor International, Inc., 122 South Michigan Avenue, Suite 1200, Chicago, Illinois 60603 (800) 577-EURO; *International Marketing Data and Statistics;* and *World Marketing Data and Statistics.*

Europa Publications Limited, 18 Bedford Square, London, WC1B 3JN, England; *The Europa World Year Book.*

Food and Agricultural Organization of the United Nations (FAO), Via delle Terme di Caracalla, 00100 Rome, Italy (Telephone Number in U.S. (202) 653-2400); *The State of Food and Agriculture.*

International Labour Office, I.L.O. Publications, 1828 L Street, NW, Suite 801, Washington, D.C. 20036 (301) 638-3152; *Yearbook of Labour Statistics.*

St. Martin's Press, Inc., 175 Fifth Avenue, New York, New York 10010 (800) 221-7945; *The Statesman's Year-Book.*

The World Bank, 1818 H Street, NW, Washington, D.C. 20433 (202) 477-1234; *The World Bank Atlas.*

KIRIBATI - LAND USE

Central Intelligence Agency, Washington, D.C. 20505 (703) 482-1100, www.cia.gov; *The World Factbook.*

Euromonitor International, Inc., 122 South Michigan Avenue, Suite 1200, Chicago. Illinois 60603 (800) 577-EURO; *International Marketing Data and Statistics.*

Food and Agricultural Organization of the United Nations (FAO), Via delle Terme di Caracalla, 00100 Rome, Italy (Telephone Number in U.S. (202) 653-2400); *Production Yearbook.*

KIRIBATI - LIBRARIES

United Nations Educational, Scientific and Cultural Organization (UNESCO), 7 Place de Fontenoy, F-75700 Paris, France (Telephone Number in U.S. (212) 963-5981); *Statistical Yearbook.*

KIRIBATI - LIFE EXPECTANCY

Central Intelligence Agency, Washington, D.C. 20505 (703) 482-1100, www.cia.gov; *The World Factbook.*

Euromonitor International, Inc., 122 South Michigan Avenue, Suite 1200, Chicago. Illinois 60603 (800) 577-EURO; *The World Economic Factbook.*

Statistical Office of the United Nations, Publishing Service, New York, New York 10017 (800) 253-9646; *Asia-Pacific in Figures;* and *World Statistics Pocketbook.*

The World Bank, 1818 H Street, NW, Washington, D.C. 20433 (202) 477-1234; *The World Bank Atlas.*

KIRIBATI - LITERACY RATE

Euromonitor International, Inc., 122 South Michigan Avenue, Suite 1200, Chicago, Illinois 60603 (800) 577-EURO; *World Marketing Data and Statistics.*

KIRIBATI - LIVESTOCK AND POULTRY

Europa Publications Limited, 18 Bedford Square, London, WC1B 3JN, England; *The Europa World Year Book.*

Food and Agricultural Organization of the United Nations (FAO), Via delle Terme di Caracalla, 00100 Rome, Italy (Telephone Number in U.S. (202) 653-2400); *Production Yearbook;* and *The State of Food and Agriculture.*

St. Martin's Press, Inc., 175 Fifth Avenue, New York, New York 10010 (800) 221-7945; *The Statesman's Year-Book.*

United Nations Conference on Trade and Development, Central Statistical Service, Palais des Nations, Geneva, Switzerland (Telephone in U.S. (800) 253-9646); *UNCTAD Commodity Yearbook.*

KIRIBATI - MANUFACTURING

Asian Development Bank, Post Office Box 789, 1099 Manila, Philippines; *Key Indicators of Developing Asian and Pacific Countries.*

KIRIBATI - MARRIAGES

Europa Publications Limited, 18 Bedford Square, London, WC1B 3JN, England; *The Europa World Year Book.*

KIRIBATI - MEAT PRODUCTION - See KIRIBATI - LIVESTOCK AND POULTRY

KIRIBATI - MERCHANT SHIPPING

Europa Publications Limited, 18 Bedford Square, London, WC1B 3JN, England; *The Europa World Year Book.*

St. Martin's Press, Inc., 175 Fifth Avenue, New York, New York 10010 (800) 221-7945; *The Statesman's Year-Book.*

KIRIBATI - MILITARY

Central Intelligence Agency, Washington, D.C. 20505 (703) 482-1100, www.cia.gov; *The World Factbook.*

Euromonitor International, Inc., 122 South Michigan Avenue, Suite 1200, Chicago, Illinois 60603 (800) 577-EURO; *World Marketing Data and Statistics.*

KIRIBATI - MINING AND MINERAL PRODUCTS

Asian Development Bank, Post Office Box 789, 1099 Manila, Philippines; *Key Indicators of Developing Asian and Pacific Countries.*

United Nations Conference on Trade and Development, Central Statistical Service, Palais des Nations, Geneva, Switzerland (Telephone in U.S. (800) 253-9646); *UNCTAD Commodity Yearbook.*

KIRIBATI - MONEY SUPPLY

Asian Development Bank, Post Office

Box 789, 1099 Manila, Philippines; *Key Indicators of Developing Asian and Pacific Countries.*

KIRIBATI - MORTALITY

Central Intelligence Agency, Washington, D.C. 20505 (703) 482-1100, www.cia.gov; *The World Factbook.*

Euromonitor International, Inc., 122 South Michigan Avenue, Suite 1200, Chicago. Illinois 60603 (800) 577-EURO; *International Marketing Data and Statistics;* and *The World Economic Factbook.*

Europa Publications Limited, 18 Bedford Square, London, WC1B 3JN, England; *The Europa World Year Book.*

Statistical Office of the United Nations, Publishing Service, New York, New York 10017 (800) 253-9646; *Asia-Pacific in Figures;* and *World Statistics Pocketbook.*

The World Bank, 1818 H Street, NW, Washington, D.C. 20433 (202) 477-1234; *The World Bank Atlas.*

World Health Organization, Office of Publications, 20 Avenue Appia, CH-1211 Geneva 27, Switzerland (Telephone Number in U.S. (518) 436-9686); *World Health Statistics Annual.*

KIRIBATI - MOTION PICTURES

St. Martin's Press, Inc., 175 Fifth Avenue, New York, New York 10010 (800) 221-7945; *The Statesman's Year-Book.*

KIRIBATI - MOTOR VEHICLES IN USE

Europa Publications Limited, 18 Bedford Square, London, WC1B 3JN, England; *The Europa World Year Book.*

KIRIBATI - NATIONAL ACCOUNTS

Statistical Office of the United Nations, Publishing Service, New York, New York 10017 (800) 253-9646; *Asia-Pacific in Figures;* and *National Accounts Statistics.*

KIRIBATI - NEWSPAPER PRODUCTION - See KIRIBATI - FORESTRY AND FOREST PRODUCTS

KIRIBATI - OCCUPATIONS - See KIRIBATI - LABOR

KIRIBATI - PESTICIDE USE

Food and Agricultural Organization of the United Nations (FAO), Via delle Terme di Caracalla, 00100 Rome, Italy (Telephone Number in U.S. (202) 653-2400); *The State of Food and Agriculture.*

KIRIBATI - PETROLEUM INDUSTRY

Asian Development Bank, Post Office Box 789, 1099 Manila, Philippines; *Key Indicators of Developing Asian and Pacific Countries.*

Food and Agricultural Organization of the United Nations (FAO), Via delle Terme di Caracalla, 00100 Rome, Italy (Telephone Number in U.S. (202) 653-2400); *The State of Food and Agriculture.*

United Nations Conference on Trade and Development, Central Statistical Service, Palais des Nations, Geneva, Switzerland (Telephone in U.S. (800) 253-9646); *UNCTAD Commodity Yearbook.*

KIRIBATI - POPULATION

Asian Development Bank, Post Office Box 789, 1099 Manila, Philippines; *Key Indicators of Developing Asian and Pacific Countries.*

Central Intelligence Agency, Washington, D.C. 20505 (703) 482-1100, www.cia.gov; *The World Factbook.*

Euromonitor International, Inc., 122 South Michigan Avenue, Suite 1200, Chicago. Illinois 60603 (800) 577-EURO; *International Marketing Data and Statistics;* and *The World Economic Factbook.*

Europa Publications Limited, 18 Bedford Square, London, WC1B 3JN, England; *The Europa World Year Book.*

Food and Agricultural Organization of the United Nations (FAO), Via delle Terme di Caracalla, 00100 Rome, Italy (Telephone Number in U.S. (202) 653-2400); *Production Yearbook.*

International Labour Office, I.L.O. Publications,1828 L Street, NW, Suite 801, Washington, D.C. 20036 (301) 638-3152 ; *Yearbook of Labour Statistics.*

St. Martin's Press, Inc., 175 Fifth Avenue, New York, New York 10010 (800) 221-7945; *The Statesman's Year-Book.*

Statistical Office of the United Nations, Publishing Service, New York, New York 10017 (800) 253-9646; *Asia-Pacific in Figures;* and *World Statistics Pocketbook.*

Walden Publishing, Ltd., Two Market Street, Saffron Walden Essex, CB10 1HZ, England; *The World of Information Asia and Pacific Review.*

The World Bank, 1818 H Street, NW, Washington, D.C. 20433 (202) 477-1234; *The World Bank Atlas.*

World Health Organization, Office of Publications, 20 Avenue Appia, CH-1211 Geneva 27, Switzerland (Telephone Number in U.S. (518) 436-9686); *World*

Health Statistics Annual.

KIRIBATI - POWER PRODUCTION INDUSTRY

Statistical Office of the United Nations, Publishing Service, New York, New York 10017 (800) 253-9646; *Electric Power in Asia and the Pacific.*

KIRIBATI - PRICES

Asian Development Bank, Post Office Box 789, 1099 Manila, Philippines; *Key Indicators of Developing Asian and Pacific Countries.*

Food and Agricultural Organization of the United Nations (FAO), Via delle Terme di Caracalla, 00100 Rome, Italy (Telephone Number in U.S. (202) 653-2400); *Production Yearbook,;* and *The State of Food and Agriculture.*

International Labour Office, I.L.O. Publications, 1828 L Street, NW, Suite 801, Washington, D.C. 20036 (301) 638-3152; *Yearbook of Labour Statistics.*

South Pacific Commission, Post Box D5, Noumea Cedex, New Caledonia; *Statistical Bulletin of the South Pacific: Overseas Trade;* and *Statistical Bulletin of the South Pacific: Retail Price Indexes.*

KIRIBATI - RADIO RECEIVERS

St. Martin's Press, Inc., 175 Fifth Avenue, New York, New York 10010 (800) 221-7945; *The Statesman's Year-Book.*

KIRIBATI - RELIGION

Central Intelligence Agency, Washington, D.C. 20505 (703) 482-1100, www.cia.gov; *The World Factbook.*

St. Martin's Press, Inc., 175 Fifth Avenue, New York, New York 10010 (800) 221-7945; *The Statesman's Year-Book.*

KIRIBATI - RETAIL TRADE

Euromonitor International, Inc., 122 South Michigan Avenue, Suite 1200, Chicago, Illinois 60603 (800) 577-EURO; *World Marketing Data and Statistics.*

KIRIBATI - RICE PRODUCTION - See KIRIBATI - CROPS

KIRIBATI - SOCIAL DATA

Asian Development Bank, Post Office Box 789, 1099 Manila, Philippines; *Key Indicators of Developing Asian and Pacific Countries.*

Statistical Office of the United Nations, Publishing Service, New York, New York

10017 (800) 253-9646; *World Statistics Pocketbook.*

KIRIBATI - STOCKS - COMMODITY - MARKET PRICE - INDEX

Food and Agricultural Organization of the United Nations (FAO), Via delle Terme di Caracalla, 00100 Rome, Italy (Telephone Number in U.S. (202) 653-2400); *The State of Food and Agriculture.*

KIRIBATI - TAXATION

St. Martin's Press, Inc., 175 Fifth Avenue, New York, New York 10010 (800) 221-7945; *The Statesman's Year-Book.*

KIRIBATI - TELEPHONES IN USE

American Telephone and Telegraph Company, 26 Parsippany Road, Whippany, New Jersey 07981 (800) 222-0300; *The World's Telephones.*

Central Intelligence Agency, Washington, D.C. 20505 (703) 482-1100, www.cia.gov; *The World Factbook.*

Europa Publications Limited, 18 Bedford Square, London, WC1B 3JN, England; *The Europa World Year Book.*

St. Martin's Press, Inc., 175 Fifth Avenue, New York, New York 10010 (800) 221-7945; *The Statesman's Year-Book.*

Statistical Office of the United Nations, Publishing Service, New York, New York 10017 (800) 253-9646; *World Statistics Pocketbook.*

KIRIBATI - TEXTILE INDUSTRY

South Pacific Commission, Post Box D5, Noumea Cedex, New Caledonia; *Statistical Bulletin of the South Pacific: Retail Price Indexes.*

United Nations Conference on Trade and Development, Central Statistical Service, Palais des Nations, Geneva, Switzerland (Telephone in U.S. (800) 253-9646); *UNCTAD Commodity Yearbook.*

KIRIBATI - THEATRE

United Nations Educational, Scientific and Cultural Organization (UNESCO), 7 Place de Fontenoy, F-75700 Paris, France (Telephone Number in U.S. (212) 963-5981); *Statistical Yearbook.*

KIRIBATI - TOBACCO PRODUCTION

South Pacific Commission, Post Box D5, Noumea Cedex, New Caledonia; *Statistical Bulletin of the South Pacific: Retail Price Indexes.*

KIRIBATI - TOURISM

Euromonitor International, Inc., 122 South Michigan Avenue, Suite 1200, Chicago. Illinois 60603 (800) 577-EURO; *The World Economic Factbook;* and *World Marketing Data and Statistics.*

Europa Publications Limited, 18 Bedford Square, London, WC1B 3JN, England; *The Europa World Year Book.*

World Tourism Organization, Calle Capitan Haya 42, E-28020 Madrid, Spain; *Yearbook of Tourism Statistics.*

KIRIBATI - TRADE - See KIRIBATI - FOREIGN TRADE

KIRIBATI - TRANSPORTATION AND COMMUNICATIONS

Central Intelligence Agency, Washington, D.C. 20505 (703) 482-1100, www.cia.gov; *The World Factbook.*

Euromonitor International, Inc., 122 South Michigan Avenue, Suite 1200, Chicago. Illinois 60603 (800) 577-EURO; *International Marketing Data and Statistics;* and *World Marketing Data and Statistics.*

Europa Publications Limited, 18 Bedford Square, London, WC1B 3JN, England; *The Europa World Year Book.*

St. Martin's Press, Inc., 175 Fifth Avenue, New York, New York 10010 (800) 221-7945; *The Statesman's Year-Book.*

South Pacific Commission, Post Box D5, Noumea Cedex, New Caledonia; *Statistical Bulletin of the South Pacific: Retail Price Indexes.*

KIRIBATI - UNEMPLOYMENT

Central Intelligence Agency, Washington, D.C. 20505 (703) 482-1100, www.cia.gov; *The World Factbook.*

International Labour Office, I.L.O. Publications, 1828 L Street, NW, Suite 801, Washington, D.C. 20036 (301) 638-3152; *Yearbook of Labour Statistics.*

KIRIBATI - UTILITIES

Statistical Office of the United Nations, Publishing Service, New York, New York 10017 (800) 253-9646; *Electric Power in Asia and the Pacific.*

KIRIBATI - WAGES

International Labour Office, I.L.O. Publications, 1828 L Street, NW, Suite 801, Washington, D.C. 20036 (301) 638-3152; *Yearbook of Labour Statistics.*

KIRIBATI - WHOLESALE PRICES - INDEX

NUMBERS

Asian Development Bank, Post Office Box 789, 1099 Manila, Philippines; *Key Indicators of Developing Asian and Pacific Countries.*

Korea (Democratic People's Republic Of) - National Statistical Office

Central Bureau of Statistics, Pyongyang, Democratic People's Republic of Korea.

Korea (Democratic People's Republic Of) - Primary Statistics Source

Superintendent of Documents, U.S. Government Printing Office, Washington, D.C. 20402; *Area Handbook for North Korea.*

KOREA (DEMOCRATIC PEOPLE'S REPUBLIC OF) - AGRICULTURE

Asian Development Bank, Post Office Box 789, 1099 Manila, Philippines; *Key Indicators of Developing Asian and Pacific Countries.*

Economist Intelligence Unit, 111 West 57th Street, New York, New York 10019 (800) 938-4685; *Korea (North) Country Report.*

Euromonitor International, Inc., 122 South Michigan Avenue, Suite 1200, Chicago, Illinois 60603 (800) 577-EURO; *World Marketing Data and Statistics.*

Europa Publications Limited, 18 Bedford Square, London, WC1B 3JN, England; *The Europa World Year Book.*

Food and Agricultural Organization of the United Nations (FAO), Via delle Terme di Caracalla, 00100 Rome, Italy (Telephone Number in U.S. (202) 653-2400); *The State of Food and Agriculture,;* and *Trade Yearbook.*

M.E. Sharpe, 80 Business Park Drive, Armonk, New York 10504 (800) 541-6563; *The Illustrated Book of World Rankings.*

St. Martin's Press, Inc., 175 Fifth Avenue, New York, New York 10010 (800) 221-7945; *The Statesman's Year-Book.*

Statistical Office of the United Nations, Publishing Service, New York, New York 10017 (800) 253-9646; *Statistical Yearbook.*

United Nations Conference on Trade and Development, Central Statistical Service, Palais des Nations, Geneva, Switzerland (Telephone in U.S. (800) 253-

9646); *UNCTAD Commodity Yearbook.*

KOREA (DEMOCRATIC PEOPLE'S REPUBLIC OF) - AIRLINE SERVICE

The Economist Intelligence Unit (Asia) Limited, 10th Floor, Luk Kwok Centre, 72 Gloucester Road, Wanchai, Hong Kong (Phone Number in U.S. (800) 938-4685); *Asian Market Atlas.*

M.E. Sharpe, 80 Business Park Drive, Armonk, New York 10504 (800) 541-6563; *The Illustrated Book of World Rankings.*

St. Martin's Press, Inc., 175 Fifth Avenue, New York, New York 10010 (800) 221-7945; *The Statesman's Year-Book.*

KOREA (DEMOCRATIC PEOPLE'S REPUBLIC OF) - ALUMINUM PRODUCTION AND CONSUMPTION - See KOREA (DEMOCRATIC PEOPLE'S REPUBLIC OF) - MINING AND MINERAL PRODUCTS

KOREA (DEMOCRATIC PEOPLE'S REPUBLIC OF) - ANIMAL HEALTH

Food and Agricultural Organization of the United Nations (FAO), Via delle Terme di Caracalla, 00100 Rome, Italy (Telephone Number in U.S. (202) 653-2400); *Animal Health Yearbook.*

KOREA (DEMOCRATIC PEOPLE'S REPUBLIC OF) - AREA AND DENSITY OF POPULATION

Central Intelligence Agency, Washington, D.C. 20505 (703) 482-1100, www.cia.gov; *The World Factbook.*

Euromonitor International, Inc., 122 South Michigan Avenue, Suite 1200, Chicago. Illinois 60603 (800) 577-EURO; *International Marketing Data and Statistics;* and *The World Economic Factbook.*

Europa Publications Limited, 18 Bedford Square, London, WC1B 3JN, England; *The Europa World Year Book.*

Food and Agricultural Organization of the United Nations (FAO), Via delle Terme di Caracalla, 00100 Rome, Italy (Telephone Number in U.S. (202) 653-2400); *The State of Food and Agriculture.*

M.E. Sharpe, 80 Business Park Drive, Armonk, New York 10504 (800) 541-6563; *The Illustrated Book of World Rankings.*

St. Martin's Press, Inc., 175 Fifth Avenue, New York, New York 10010 (800) 221-7945; *The Statesman's Year-Book.*

Statistical Office of the United Nations, Publishing Service, New York, New York 10017 (800) 253-9646; *Statistical Yearbook.*

Times Books, 201 East 50th Street, New York, New York 10022 (800) 726-0600; *The Economist Book of Vital World Statistics.*

KOREA (DEMOCRATIC PEOPLE'S REPUBLIC OF) - ARMS EXPORTS AND IMPORTS - See KOREA (DEMOCRATIC PEOPLE'S REPUBLIC OF) - MILITARY

KOREA (DEMOCRATIC PEOPLE'S REPUBLIC OF) - BALANCE OF PAYMENTS

The Economist Intelligence Unit, 111 West 57th Street, New York, New York 10019 (800) 938-4685; *The World Market Atlas.*

KOREA (DEMOCRATIC PEOPLE'S REPUBLIC OF) - BANKING

Asian Development Bank, Post Office Box 789, 1099 Manila, Philippines; *Key Indicators of Developing Asian and Pacific Countries.*

Euromonitor International, Inc., 122 South Michigan Avenue, Suite 1200, Chicago, Illinois 60603 (800) 577-EURO; *World Marketing Data and Statistics.*

M.E. Sharpe, 80 Business Park Drive, Armonk, New York 10504 (800) 541-6563; *The Illustrated Book of World Rankings.*

St. Martin's Press, Inc., 175 Fifth Avenue, New York, New York 10010 (800) 221-7945; *The Statesman's Year-Book.*

KOREA (DEMOCRATIC PEOPLE'S REPUBLIC OF) - BARLEY PRODUCTION - See KOREA (DEMOCRATIC PEOPLE'S REPUBLIC OF) - CROPS

KOREA (DEMOCRATIC PEOPLE'S REPUBLIC OF) - BEER PRODUCTION - See KOREA (DEMOCRATIC PEOPLE'S REPUBLIC OF) - BEVERAGES

KOREA (DEMOCRATIC PEOPLE'S REPUBLIC OF) - BEVERAGES

M.E. Sharpe, 80 Business Park Drive, Armonk, New York 10504 (800) 541-6563; *The Illustrated Book of World Rankings.*

KOREA (DEMOCRATIC PEOPLE'S REPUBLIC OF) - BIRTH RATES

Central Intelligence Agency, Washington, D.C. 20505 (703) 482-1100, www.cia.gov; *The World Factbook.*

The Economist Intelligence Unit (Asia) Limited, 10th Floor, Luk Kwok Centre, 72 Gloucester Road, Wanchai, Hong Kong (Phone Number in U.S. (800) 938-4685); *Asian Market Atlas.*

Euromonitor International, Inc., 122 South Michigan Avenue, Suite 1200, Chicago. Illinois 60603 (800) 577-EURO; *International Marketing Data and Statistics;*

and *The World Economic Factbook.*

Europa Publications Limited, 18 Bedford Square, London, WC1B 3JN, England; *The Europa World Year Book.*

M.E. Sharpe, 80 Business Park Drive, Armonk, New York 10504 (800) 541-6563; *The Illustrated Book of World Rankings.*

St. Martin's Press, Inc., 175 Fifth Avenue, New York, New York 10010 (800) 221-7945; *The Statesman's Year-Book.*

Statistical Office of the United Nations, Publishing Service, New York, New York 10017 (800) 253-9646; *Demographic Yearbook;* and *Statistical Yearbook.*

KOREA (DEMOCRATIC PEOPLE'S REPUBLIC OF) - BONDS

Asian Development Bank, Post Office Box 789, 1099 Manila, Philippines; *Key Indicators of Developing Asian and Pacific Countries.*

KOREA (DEMOCRATIC PEOPLE'S REPUBLIC OF) - BROADCASTING

Billboard Limited, Post Office Box 9027, 1006 AA Amsterdam, The Netherlands (Telephone Number in U.S. (212) 764-7300); *World Radio TV Handbook.*

Central Intelligence Agency, Washington, D.C. 20505 (703) 482-1100, www.cia.gov; *The World Factbook.*

The Economist Intelligence Unit (Asia) Limited, 10th Floor, Luk Kwok Centre, 72 Gloucester Road, Wanchai, Hong Kong (Phone Number in U.S. (800) 938-4685); *Asian Market Atlas.*

Euromonitor International, Inc., 122 South Michigan Avenue, Suite 1200, Chicago, Illinois 60603 (800) 577-EURO; *World Marketing Data and Statistics.*

M.E. Sharpe, 80 Business Park Drive, Armonk, New York 10504 (800) 541-6563; *The Illustrated Book of World Rankings.*

St. Martin's Press, Inc., 175 Fifth Avenue, New York, New York 10010 (800) 221-7945; *The Statesman's Year-Book.*

KOREA (DEMOCRATIC PEOPLE'S REPUBLIC OF) - BUDGET

Central Intelligence Agency, Washington, D.C. 20505 (703) 482-1100, www.cia.gov; *The World Factbook.*

KOREA (DEMOCRATIC PEOPLE'S REPUBLIC OF) - CABBAGE PRODUCTION - See KOREA (DEMOCRATIC PEOPLE'S REPUBLIC OF) - CROPS

KOREA (DEMOCRATIC PEOPLE'S

REPUBLIC OF) - CALORIE SUPPLY

Asian Development Bank, Post Office Box 789, 1099 Manila, Philippines; *Key Indicators of Developing Asian and Pacific Countries.*

Food and Agricultural Organization of the United Nations (FAO), Via delle Terme di Caracalla, 00100 Rome, Italy (Telephone Number in U.S. (202) 653-2400); *The State of Food and Agriculture.*

KOREA (DEMOCRATIC PEOPLE'S REPUBLIC OF) - CAPITAL INVESTMENT

Asian Development Bank, Post Office Box 789, 1099 Manila, Philippines; *Key Indicators of Developing Asian and Pacific Countries.*

KOREA (DEMOCRATIC PEOPLE'S REPUBLIC OF) - CATTLE - See KOREA (DEMOCRATIC PEOPLE'S REPUBLIC OF) - LIVESTOCK AND POULTRY

KOREA (DEMOCRATIC PEOPLE'S REPUBLIC OF) - CEMENT PRODUCTION - See KOREA (DEMOCRATIC PEOPLE'S REPUBLIC OF) - MINING AND MINERAL PRODUCTS

KOREA (DEMOCRATIC PEOPLE'S REPUBLIC OF) - CHEMICAL (ORGANIC) PRODUCTION - See KOREA (DEMOCRATIC PEOPLE'S REPUBLIC OF) - MINING AND MINERAL PRODUCTS

KOREA (DEMOCRATIC PEOPLE'S REPUBLIC OF) - CHESTNUT PRODUCTION - See KOREA (DEMOCRATIC PEOPLE'S REPUBLIC OF) - CROPS

KOREA (DEMOCRATIC PEOPLE'S REPUBLIC OF) - CHICKENS - See KOREA (DEMOCRATIC PEOPLE'S REPUBLIC OF) - LIVESTOCK AND POULTRY

KOREA (DEMOCRATIC PEOPLE'S REPUBLIC OF) - CIGARETTE PRODUCTION - See KOREA (DEMOCRATIC PEOPLE'S REPUBLIC OF) - TOBACCO PRODUCTION

KOREA (DEMOCRATIC PEOPLE'S REPUBLIC OF) - CLIMATE

M.E. Sharpe, 80 Business Park Drive, Armonk, New York 10504 (800) 541-6563; *The Illustrated Book of World Rankings.*

St. Martin's Press, Inc., 175 Fifth Avenue, New York, New York 10010 (800) 221-7945; *The Statesman's Year-Book.*

KOREA (DEMOCRATIC PEOPLE'S REPUBLIC OF) - COAL PRODUCTION - See KOREA (DEMOCRATIC PEOPLE'S REPUBLIC OF) - MINING AND MINERAL PRODUCTS

KOREA (DEMOCRATIC PEOPLE'S REPUBLIC OF) - COFFEE PRODUCTION AND CONSUMPTION - See KOREA (DEMOCRATIC PEOPLE'S REPUBLIC OF) - CROPS

KOREA (DEMOCRATIC PEOPLE'S REPUBLIC OF) - COKE OVEN COKE PRODUCTION AND CONSUMPTION - See KOREA (DEMOCRATIC PEOPLE'S REPUBLIC OF) - MINING AND MINERAL PRODUCTS

KOREA (DEMOCRATIC PEOPLE'S REPUBLIC OF - COMMERCE

St. Martin's Press, Inc., 175 Fifth Avenue, New York, New York 10010 (800) 221-7945; *The Statesman's Year-Book.*

KOREA (DEMOCRATIC PEOPLE'S REPUBLIC OF) - CONSTRUCTION INDUSTRY

M.E. Sharpe, 80 Business Park Drive, Armonk, New York 10504 (800) 541-6563; *The Illustrated Book of World Rankings.*

KOREA (DEMOCRATIC PEOPLE'S REPUBLIC OF) - CONSUMER PRICE INDEX

Asian Development Bank, Post Office Box 789, 1099 Manila, Philippines; *Key Indicators of Developing Asian and Pacific Countries.*

KOREA (DEMOCRATIC PEOPLE'S REPUBLIC OF) - CONSUMER PRICES

Euromonitor International, Inc., 122 South Michigan Avenue, Suite 1200, Chicago, Illinois 60603 (800) 577-EURO; *World Marketing Data and Statistics.*

KOREA (DEMOCRATIC PEOPLE'S REPUBLIC OF) - COPPER AND COPPER ORE - See KOREA (DEMOCRATIC PEOPLE'S REPUBLIC OF) - MINING AND MINERAL PRODUCTS

KOREA (DEMOCRATIC PEOPLE'S REPUBLIC OF) - CORN PRODUCTION - See KOREA (DEMOCRATIC PEOPLE'S REPUBLIC OF) - CROPS

KOREA (DEMOCRATIC PEOPLE'S REPUBLIC OF) - CORPORATE TAXES - See (KOREAN - DEMOCRATIC PEOPLE'S REPUBLIC OF) - TAXATION

KOREA (DEMOCRATIC PEOPLE'S REPUBLIC OF) - COTTON - See KOREA (DEMOCRATIC PEOPLE'S REPUBLIC OF) - CROPS

KOREA (DEMOCRATIC PEOPLE'S REPUBLIC OF) - CRIME

International Criminal Police Organization (INTERPOL), 50 quai Achille Lignon, F-69006 Lyon, France; *International Crime Statistics.*

Yale University Press, Yale Station, New Haven, Connecticut 06520 (800) 987-7323; *Violence and Crime in Cross-National Perspective.*

KOREA (DEMOCRATIC PEOPLE'S REPUBLIC OF) - CROPS

Asian Development Bank, Post Office Box 789, 1099 Manila, Philippines; *Key Indicators of Developing Asian and Pacific Countries.*

Europa Publications Limited, 18 Bedford Square, London, WC1B 3JN, England; *The Europa World Year Book.*

Food and Agricultural Organization of the United Nations (FAO), Via delle Terme di Caracalla, 00100 Rome, Italy (Telephone Number in U.S. (202) 653-2400); *Production Yearbook;* and *The State of Food and Agriculture.*

M.E. Sharpe, 80 Business Park Drive, Armonk, New York 10504 (800) 541-6563; *The Illustrated Book of World Rankings.*

St. Martin's Press, Inc., 175 Fifth Avenue, New York, New York 10010 (800) 221-7945; *The Statesman's Year-Book.*

Statistical Office of the United Nations, Publishing Service, New York, New York 10017 (800) 253-9646; *Statistical Yearbook.*

United Nations Conference on Trade and Development, Central Statistical Service, Palais des Nations, Geneva, Switzerland (Telephone in U.S. (800) 253-9646); *UNCTAD Commodity Yearbook.*

KOREA (DEMOCRATIC PEOPLE'S REPUBLIC OF) - DAIRY PRODUCTS

Europa Publications Limited, 18 Bedford Square, London, WC1B 3JN, England; *The Europa World Year Book.*

Food and Agricultural Organization of the United Nations (FAO), Via delle Terme di Caracalla, 00100 Rome, Italy (Telephone Number in U.S. (202) 653-2400); *The State of Food and Agriculture.*

M.E. Sharpe, 80 Business Park Drive, Armonk, New York 10504 (800) 541-6563; *The Illustrated Book of World Rankings.*

St. Martin's Press, Inc., 175 Fifth Avenue, New York, New York 10010 (800) 221-7945; *The Statesman's Year-Book.*

Statistical Office of the United Nations, Publishing Service, New York, New York 10017 (800) 253-9646; *Statistical Yearbook.*

KOREA (DEMOCRATIC PEOPLE'S REPUBLIC OF) - DEATH RATES - See

KOREA (DEMOCRATIC PEOPLE'S REPUBLIC OF) - MORTALITY

KOREA (DEMOCRATIC PEOPLE'S REPUBLIC OF) - DEFENSE EXPENDITURES

U.S. Arms Control and Disarmament Agency, 320 Twenty-first Street, NW, Washington, D.C. 20451 (202) 647-8677; *World Military Expenditures and Arms Transfers.*

KOREA (DEMOCRATIC PEOPLE'S REPUBLIC OF) - DEMOGRAPHY

The Economist Intelligence Unit, 111 West 57th Street, New York, New York 10019 (800) 938-4685; *The World Market Atlas.*

The Economist Intelligence Unit (Asia) Limited, 10th Floor, Luk Kwok Centre, 72 Gloucester Road, Wanchai, Hong Kong (Phone Number in U.S. (800) 938-4685); *Asian Market Atlas.*

Euromonitor International, Inc., 122 South Michigan Avenue, Suite 1200, Chicago. Illinois 60603 (800) 577-EURO; *International Marketing Data and Statistics; The World Economic Factbook;* and *World Marketing Data and Statistics.*

M.E. Sharpe, 80 Business Park Drive, Armonk, New York 10504 (800) 541-6563; *The Illustrated Book of World Rankings.*

Statistical Office of the United Nations, Publishing Service, New York, New York 10017 (800) 253-9646; *Human Development Report.*

KOREA (DEMOCRATIC PEOPLE'S REPUBLIC OF) - DEVELOPMENT ASSISTANCE

Asian Development Bank, Post Office Box 789, 1099 Manila, Philippines; *Key Indicators of Developing Asian and Pacific Countries.*

KOREA (DEMOCRATIC PEOPLE'S REPUBLIC OF) - DIAMOND PRODUCTION - See KOREA (DEMOCRATIC PEOPLE'S REPUBLIC OF) - MINING AND MINERAL PRODUCTS

KOREA (DEMOCRATIC PEOPLE'S REPUBLIC OF) - DIVORCE RATES

Statistical Office of the United Nations, Publishing Service, New York, New York 10017 (800) 253-9646; *Demographic Yearbook.*

M.E. Sharpe, 80 Business Park Drive, Armonk, New York 10504 (800) 541-6563; *The Illustrated Book of World Rankings.*

KOREA (DEMOCRATIC PEOPLE'S REPUBLIC OF) - ECONOMY

Asian Development Bank, Post Office Box 789, 1099 Manila, Philippines; *Key Indicators of Developing Asian and Pacific Countries.*

Central Intelligence Agency, Washington, D.C. 20505 (703) 482-1100, www.cia.gov; *The World Factbook.*

Economist Intelligence Unit, 111 West 57th Street, New York, New York 10019 (800) 938-4685; *Korea (North) Country Report.*

Euromonitor International, Inc., 122 South Michigan Avenue, Suite 1200, Chicago. Illinois 60603 (800) 577-EURO; *International Marketing Data and Statistics; World Marketing Data and Statistics;* and *The World Economic Factbook.*

Europa Publications Limited, 18 Bedford Square, London, WC1B 3JN, England; *The Europa World Year Book.*

M.E. Sharpe, 80 Business Park Drive, Armonk, New York 10504 (800) 541-6563; *The Illustrated Book of World Rankings.*

St. Martin's Press, Inc., 175 Fifth Avenue, New York, New York 10010 (800) 221-7945; *The Statesman's Year-Book.*

Statistical Office of the United Nations, Publishing Service, New York, New York 10017 (800) 253-9646; *World Statistics Pocketbook.*

The World Bank, 1818 H Street, NW, Washington, D.C. 20433 (202) 477-1234; *The World Bank Atlas.*

KOREA (DEMOCRATIC PEOPLE'S REPUBLIC OF) - EDUCATION

The Economist Intelligence Unit, 111 West 57th Street, New York, New York 10019 (800) 938-4685; *The World Market Atlas.*

The Economist Intelligence Unit (Asia) Limited, 10th Floor, Luk Kwok Centre, 72 Gloucester Road, Wanchai, Hong Kong (Phone Number in U.S. (800) 938-4685); *Asian Market Atlas.*

Euromonitor International, Inc., 122 South Michigan Avenue, Suite 1200, Chicago. Illinois 60603 (800) 577-EURO; *International Marketing Data and Statistics;* and *World Marketing Data and Statistics.*

Europa Publications Limited, 18 Bedford Square, London, WC1B 3JN, England; *The Europa World Year Book.*

M.E. Sharpe, 80 Business Park Drive, Armonk, New York 10504 (800) 541-6563; *The Illustrated Book of World Rankings.*

St. Martin's Press, Inc., 175 Fifth Avenue, New York, New York 10010 (800) 221-7945; *The Statesman's Year-Book.*

Statistical Office of the United Nations, Publishing Service, New York, New York 10017 (800) 253-9646; *Human Development Report.*

KOREA (DEMOCRATIC PEOPLE'S REPUBLIC OF) - EGG PRODUCTION AND CONSUMPTION - See JAPAN - DAIRY PRODUCTS

KOREA (DEMOCRATIC PEOPLE'S REPUBLIC OF) - EGGPLANT PRODUCTION - See KOREA (DEMOCRATIC PEOPLE'S REPUBLIC OF) - CROPS

KOREA (DEMOCRATIC PEOPLE'S REPUBLIC OF) - ELECTRICITY

Asian Development Bank, Post Office Box 789, 1099 Manila, Philippines; *Key Indicators of Developing Asian and Pacific Countries.*

Central Intelligence Agency, Washington, D.C. 20505 (703) 482-1100, www.cia.gov; *The World Factbook.*

M.E. Sharpe, 80 Business Park Drive, Armonk, New York 10504 (800) 541-6563; *The Illustrated Book of World Rankings.*

St. Martin's Press, Inc., 175 Fifth Avenue, New York, New York 10010 (800) 221-7945; *The Statesman's Year-Book.*

Statistical Office of the United Nations, Publishing Service, New York, New York 10017 (800) 253-9646; *Electric Power in Asia and the Pacific; Human Development Report;* and *Statistical Yearbook.*

KOREA (DEMOCRATIC PEOPLE'S REPUBLIC OF) - EMPLOYMENT

Euromonitor International, Inc., 122 South Michigan Avenue, Suite 1200, Chicago. Illinois 60603 (800) 577-EURO; *International Marketing Data and Statistics.*

M.E. Sharpe, 80 Business Park Drive, Armonk, New York 10504 (800) 541-6563; *The Illustrated Book of World Rankings.*

KOREA (DEMOCRATIC PEOPLE'S REPUBLIC OF) - ENERGY

Euromonitor International, Inc., 122 South Michigan Avenue, Suite 1200, Chicago. Illinois 60603 (800) 577-EURO; *International Marketing Data and Statistics; World Marketing Data and Statistics;* and *The World Economic Factbook.*

Food and Agricultural Organization of the United Nations (FAO), Via delle Terme di Caracalla, 00100 Rome, Italy (Telephone Number in U.S. (202) 653-2400); *The State of Food and Agriculture.*

M.E. Sharpe, 80 Business Park Drive, Armonk, New York 10504 (800) 541-6563; *The Illustrated Book of World Rankings.*

St. Martin's Press, Inc., 175 Fifth Avenue, New York, New York 10010 (800) 221-7945; *The Statesman's Year-Book.*

Statistical Office of the United Nations, Publishing Service, New York, New York 10017 (800) 253-9646; *Human Development Report; World Statistics Pocketbook;* and *Statistical Yearbook.*

The World Bank, 1818 H Street, NW, Washington, D.C. 20433 (202) 477-1234; *The World Bank Atlas.*

KOREA (DEMOCRATIC PEOPLE'S REPUBLIC OF) - ENVIRONMENT

Economist Intelligence Unit, 111 West 57th Street, New York, New York 10019 (800) 938-4685; *Korea (North) Country Report.*

Statistical Office of the United Nations, Publishing Service, New York, New York 10017 (800) 253-9646; *World Statistics Pocketbook.*

KOREA (DEMOCRATIC PEOPLE'S REPUBLIC OF) - EXCHANGE RATES

Asian Development Bank, Post Office Box 789, 1099 Manila, Philippines; *Key Indicators of Developing Asian and Pacific Countries.*

Central Intelligence Agency, Washington, D.C. 20505 (703) 482-1100, www.cia.gov; *The World Factbook.*

The Economist Intelligence Unit (Asia) Limited, 10th Floor, Luk Kwok Centre, 72 Gloucester Road, Wanchai, Hong Kong (Phone Number in U.S. (800) 938-4685); *Asian Market Atlas.*

Euromonitor International, Inc., 122 South Michigan Avenue, Suite 1200, Chicago. Illinois 60603 (800) 577-EURO; *International Marketing Data and Statistics;* and *The World Economic Factbook.*

Europa Publications Limited, 18 Bedford Square, London, WC1B 3JN, England; *The Europa World Year Book.*

Statistical Office of the United Nations, Publishing Service, New York, New York 10017 (800) 253-9646; *World Statistics Pocketbook.*

Walden Publishing, Ltd., Two Market Street, Saffron Walden Essex, CB10 1HZ, England; *The World of Information Asia and Pacific Review.*

KOREA (DEMOCRATIC PEOPLE'S REPUBLIC OF) - EXPORTS

American Automobile Manufacturers Association, 1401 H Street, NW, Suite 900, Washington, D.C. 20005 (202) 326-5500; *World Motor Vehicle Data.*

Asian Development Bank, Post Office Box 789, 1099 Manila, Philippines; *Key Indicators of Developing Asian and Pacific Countries.*

Central Intelligence Agency, Washington, D.C. 20505 (703) 482-1100, www.cia.gov; *The World Factbook.*

The Economist Intelligence Unit, 111 West 57th Street, New York, New York 10019 (800) 938-4685; *Korea (North) Country Report;* and *The World Market Atlas.*

The Economist Intelligence Unit (Asia) Limited, 10th Floor, Luk Kwok Centre, 72 Gloucester Road, Wanchai, Hong Kong (Phone Number in U.S. (800) 938-4685); *Asian Market Atlas.*

Euromonitor International, Inc., 122 South Michigan Avenue, Suite 1200, Chicago. Illinois 60603 (800) 577-EURO; *International Marketing Data and Statistics;* and *The World Economic Factbook.*

Europa Publications Limited, 18 Bedford Square, London, WC1B 3JN, England; *The Europa World Year Book.*

Food and Agricultural Organization of the United Nations (FAO), Via delle Terme di Caracalla, 00100 Rome, Italy (Telephone Number in U.S. (202) 653-2400); *The State of Food and Agriculture.*

International Monetary Fund, 700 Nineteenth Street, NW, Washington, D.C. 20431 (202) 623-7000; *Direction of Trade Statistics.*

St. Martin's Press, Inc., 175 Fifth Avenue, New York, New York 10010 (800) 221-7945; *The Statesman's Year-Book.*

Walden Publishing, Ltd., Two Market Street, Saffron Walden Essex, CB10 1HZ, England; *The World of Information Asia and Pacific Review.*

KOREA (DEMOCRATIC PEOPLE'S REPUBLIC OF) - EXTERNAL FINANCING

Asian Development Bank, Post Office Box 789, 1099 Manila, Philippines; *Key Indicators of Developing Asian and Pacific Countries.*

KOREA (DEMOCRATIC PEOPLE'S REPUBLIC OF) - EXTERNAL INDEBTEDNESS

Asian Development Bank, Post Office Box 789, 1099 Manila, Philippines; *Key Indicators of Developing Asian and Pacific Countries.*

KOREA (DEMOCRATIC PEOPLE'S REPUBLIC OF) - EXTERNAL TRADE

Asian Development Bank, Post Office Box 789, 1099 Manila, Philippines; *Key Indicators of Developing Asian and Pacific Countries.*

Euromonitor International, Inc., 122 South Michigan Avenue, Suite 1200, Chicago, Illinois 60603 (800) 577-EURO; *World Marketing Data and Statistics.*

Food and Agricultural Organization of the United Nations (FAO), Via delle Terme di Caracalla, 00100 Rome, Italy (Telephone Number in U.S. (202) 653-2400); *The State of Food and Agriculture;* and *Trade Yearbook.*

KOREA (DEMOCRATIC PEOPLE'S REPUBLIC OF) - FARM CROPS - See KOREA (DEMOCRATIC PEOPLE'S REPUBLIC OF) - CROPS

KOREA (DEMOCRATIC PEOPLE'S REPUBLIC OF) - FEMALE WORKING POPULATION - See KOREA (DEMOCRATIC PEOPLE'S REPUBLIC OF) - EMPLOYMENT

KOREA (DEMOCRATIC PEOPLE'S REPUBLIC OF) - FERTILITY RATES

Central Intelligence Agency, Washington, D.C. 20505 (703) 482-1100, www.cia.gov; *The World Factbook.*

The Economist Intelligence Unit (Asia) Limited, 10th Floor, Luk Kwok Centre, 72 Gloucester Road, Wanchai, Hong Kong (Phone Number in U.S. (800) 938-4685); *Asian Market Atlas.*

M.E. Sharpe, 80 Business Park Drive, Armonk, New York 10504 (800) 541-6563; *The Illustrated Book of World Rankings.*

Statistical Office of the United Nations, Publishing Service, New York, New York 10017 (800) 253-9646; *Human Development Report.*

The World Bank, 1818 H Street, NW, Washington, D.C. 20433 (202) 477-1234; *The World Bank Atlas.*

KOREA (DEMOCRATIC PEOPLE'S REPUBLIC OF) - FERTILIZER

Food and Agricultural Organization of the United Nations (FAO), Via delle Terme di Caracalla, 00100 Rome, Italy (Telephone Number in U.S. (202) 653-2400); *The State of Food and Agriculture.*

Statistical Office of the United Nations, Publishing Service, New York, New York 10017 (800) 253-9646; *Statistical Yearbook.*

KOREA (DEMOCRATIC PEOPLE'S REPUBLIC OF) - FETAL MORTALITY - See KOREA DEMOCRATIC PEOPLE'S REPUBLIC OF) - MORTALITY

KOREA (DEMOCRATIC PEOPLE'S REPUBLIC OF) - FIBRE PRODUCTION - See KOREA (DEMOCRATIC PEOPLE'S REPUBLIC OF) - TEXTILE INDUSTRY

KOREA (DEMOCRATIC PEOPLE'S REPUBLIC OF) - FINANCE

Asian Development Bank, Post Office Box 789, 1099 Manila, Philippines; *Key Indicators of Developing Asian and Pacific Countries.*

Economist Intelligence Unit, 111 West 57th Street, New York, New York 10019 (800) 938-4685; *Korea (North) Country Report.*

Europa Publications Limited, 18 Bedford Square, London, WC1B 3JN, England; *The Europa World Year Book.*

Food and Agricultural Organization of the United Nations (FAO), Via delle Terme di Caracalla, 00100 Rome, Italy (Telephone Number in U.S. (202) 653-2400); *The State of Food and Agriculture.*

M.E. Sharpe, 80 Business Park Drive, Armonk, New York 10504 (800) 541-6563; *The Illustrated Book of World Rankings.*

St. Martin's Press, Inc., 175 Fifth Avenue, New York, New York 10010 (800) 221-7945; *The Statesman's Year-Book.*

Statistical Office of the United Nations, Publishing Service, New York, New York 10017 (800) 253-9646; *Statistical Yearbook.*

KOREA (DEMOCRATIC PEOPLE'S REPUBLIC OF) - FISHERIES

Europa Publications Limited, 18 Bedford Square, London, WC1B 3JN, England; *The Europa World Year Book.*

Food and Agricultural Organization of the United Nations (FAO), Via delle Terme di Caracalla, 00100 Rome, Italy (Telephone Number in U.S. (202) 653-2400); *The State of Food and Agriculture,; and Yearbook of Fishery Statistics.*

M.E. Sharpe, 80 Business Park Drive, Armonk, New York 10504 (800) 541-6563; *The Illustrated Book of World Rankings.*

St. Martin's Press, Inc., 175 Fifth Avenue, New York, New York 10010 (800) 221-7945; *The Statesman's Year-Book.*

United Nations Conference on Trade and Development, Central Statistical Service, Palais des Nations, Geneva, Switzerland (Telephone in U.S. (800) 253-9646); *UNCTAD Commodity Yearbook.*

KOREA (DEMOCRATIC PEOPLE'S REPUBLIC OF) - FOOD

Food and Agricultural Organization of the United Nations (FAO), Via delle Terme di Caracalla, 00100 Rome, Italy (Telephone Number in U.S. (202) 653-2400); *Production Yearbook;* and *The State of Food and Agriculture.*

Statistical Office of the United Nations, Publishing Service, New York, New York 10017 (800) 253-9646; *Human Development Report.*

United Nations Conference on Trade and Development, Central Statistical Service, Palais des Nations, Geneva, Switzerland (Telephone in U.S. (800) 253-9646); *UNCTAD Commodity Yearbook.*

KOREA (DEMOCRATIC PEOPLE'S REPUBLIC OF) - FOREIGN DEBT

Walden Publishing, Ltd., Two Market Street, Saffron Walden Essex, CB10 1HZ, England; *The World of Information Asia and Pacific Review.*

KOREA (DEMOCRATIC PEOPLE'S REPUBLIC OF) - FOREIGN TRADE

Asian Development Bank, Post Office Box 789, 1099 Manila, Philippines; *Key Indicators of Developing Asian and Pacific Countries.*

The Economist Intelligence Unit (Asia) Limited, 10th Floor, Luk Kwok Centre, 72 Gloucester Road, Wanchai, Hong Kong (Phone Number in U.S. (800) 938-4685); *Asian Market Atlas.*

Economist Intelligence Unit, 111 West 57th Street, New York, New York 10019 (800) 938-4685; *Korea (North) Country Report.*

Euromonitor International, Inc., 122 South Michigan Avenue, Suite 1200, Chicago. Illinois 60603 (800) 577-EURO; *International Marketing Data and Statistics;* and *The World Economic Factbook.*

Europa Publications Limited, 18 Bedford Square, London, WC1B 3JN, England; *The Europa World Year Book.*

Food and Agricultural Organization of the United Nations (FAO), Via delle Terme di Caracalla, 00100 Rome, Italy (Telephone Number in U.S. (202) 653-2400); *The State of Food and Agriculture.*

M.E. Sharpe, 80 Business Park Drive, Armonk, New York 10504 (800) 541-6563; *The Illustrated Book of World Rankings.*

St. Martin's Press, Inc., 175 Fifth Avenue, New York, New York 10010 (800) 221-7945; *The Statesman's Year-Book.*

United Nations Conference on Trade and Development, Central Statistical Service, Palais des Nations, Geneva, Switzerland (Telephone in U.S. (800) 253-9646); *UNCTAD Commodity Yearbook.*

KOREA (DEMOCRATIC PEOPLE'S REPUBLIC OF) - FORESTRY AND FOREST PRODUCTS

American Forest and Paper Association, 1111 Nineteenth Street, N.W. Washington, D.C. 20036 (202) 463-2700; *Wood Pulp and Fiber Statistics.*

The Economist Intelligence Unit (Asia) Limited, 10th Floor, Luk Kwok Centre, 72 Gloucester Road, Wanchai, Hong Kong (Phone Number in U.S. (800) 938-4685); *Asian Market Atlas.*

Europa Publications Limited, 18 Bedford Square, London, WC1B 3JN, England; *The Europa World Year Book.*

Food and Agricultural Organization of the United Nations (FAO), Via delle Terme di Caracalla, 00100 Rome, Italy (Telephone Number in U.S. (202) 653-2400); *The State of Food and Agriculture;* and *Yearbook of Forest Products.*

M.E. Sharpe, 80 Business Park Drive, Armonk, New York 10504 (800) 541-6563; *The Illustrated Book of World Rankings.*

St. Martin's Press, Inc., 175 Fifth Avenue, New York, New York 10010 (800) 221-7945; *The Statesman's Year-Book.*

Statistical Office of the United Nations, Publishing Service, New York, New York 10017 (800) 253-9646; *Statistical Yearbook.*

United Nations Conference on Trade and Development, Central Statistical Service, Palais des Nations, Geneva, Switzerland (Telephone in U.S. (800) 253-9646); *UNCTAD Commodity Yearbook.*

United Nations Educational, Scientific and Cultural Organization (UNESCO), 7 Place de Fontenoy, F-75700 Paris, France (Telephone Number in U.S. (212) 963-5981); *Statistical Yearbook.*

KOREA (DEMOCRATIC PEOPLE'S REPUBLIC OF) - GARLIC PRODUCTION - See KOREA (DEMOCRATIC PEOPLE'S REPUBLIC OF) - CROPS

KOREA (DEMOCRATIC PEOPLE'S REPUBLIC OF) - GAS PRODUCTION - See KOREA (DEMOCRATIC PEOPLE'S REPUBLIC OF) - MINING AND MINERAL PRODUCTS

KOREA (DEMOCRATIC PEOPLE'S REPUBLIC OF) - GENERAL MORTALITY - See KOREA (DEMOCRATIC PEOPLE'S REPUBLIC OF) - MORTALITY

KOREA (DEMOCRATIC PEOPLE'S REPUBLIC OF) - GEOGRAPHIC DATA

M.E. Sharpe, 80 Business Park Drive, Armonk, New York 10504 (800) 541-6563; *The Illustrated Book of World Rankings.*

KOREA (DEMOCRATIC PEOPLE'S REPUBLIC OF) - GOATS - See KOREA (DEMOCRATIC PEOPLE'S REPUBLIC OF) - LIVESTOCK AND POULTRY

KOREA (DEMOCRATIC PEOPLE'S REPUBLIC OF) - GOLD PRODUCTION AND CONSUMPTION - See KOREA (DEMOCRATIC PEOPLE'S REPUBLIC OF) - MINING AND MINERAL PRODUCTS

KOREA (DEMOCRATIC PEOPLE'S REPUBLIC OF) - GOVERNMENT

Asian Development Bank, Post Office Box 789, 1099 Manila, Philippines; *Key Indicators of Developing Asian and Pacific Countries.*

Central Intelligence Agency, Washington, D.C. 20505 (703) 482-1100, www.cia.gov; *The World Factbook.*

Europa Publications Limited, 18 Bedford Square, London, WC1B 3JN, England; *The Europa World Year Book.*

St. Martin's Press, Inc., 175 Fifth Avenue, New York, New York 10010 (800) 221-7945; *The Statesman's Year-Book.*

Statistical Office of the United Nations, Publishing Service, New York, New York 10017 (800) 253-9646; *National Accounts Statistics.*

KOREA (DEMOCRATIC PEOPLE'S REPUBLIC OF) - GRAIN PRODUCTION - See KOREA (DEMOCRATIC PEOPLE'S REPUBLIC OF) - CROPS

KOREA (DEMOCRATIC PEOPLE'S REPUBLIC OF) - GREEN PEPPER AND CHILIE PRODUCTION - See KOREA (DEMOCRATIC PEOPLE'S REPUBLIC OF) - CROPS

KOREA (DEMOCRATIC PEOPLE'S REPUBLIC OF) - GROSS DOMESTIC PRODUCT

Asian Development Bank, Post Office Box 789, 1099 Manila, Philippines; *Key Indicators of Developing Asian and Pacific Countries.*

The Economist Intelligence Unit, 111 West 57th Street, New York, New York 10019 (800) 938-4685; *Korea (North) Country Report;* and *The World Market Atlas.*

The Economist Intelligence Unit (Asia) Limited, 10th Floor, Luk Kwok Centre, 72 Gloucester Road, Wanchai, Hong Kong (Phone Number in U.S. (800) 938-4685); *Asian Market Atlas.*

Euromonitor International, Inc., 122 South Michigan Avenue, Suite 1200, Chicago. Illinois 60603 (800) 577-EURO; *International Marketing Data and Statistics;* and *The World Economic Factbook.*

M.E. Sharpe, 80 Business Park Drive, Armonk, New York 10504 (800) 541-6563; *The Illustrated Book of World Rankings.*

Statistical Office of the United Nations, Publishing Service, New York, New York 10017 (800) 253-9646; *Human Development Report;* and *National Accounts Statistics.*

Walden Publishing, Ltd., Two Market Street, Saffron Walden Essex, CB10 1HZ, England; *The World of Information Asia and Pacific Review.*

KOREA (DEMOCRATIC PEOPLE'S REPUBLIC OF) - GROSS NATIONAL PRODUCT

Asian Development Bank, Post Office Box 789, 1099 Manila, Philippines; *Key Indicators of Developing Asian and Pacific Countries.*

Euromonitor International, Inc., 122 South Michigan Avenue, Suite 1200, Chicago. Illinois 60603 (800) 577-EURO; *International Marketing Data and Statistics.*

St. Martin's Press, Inc., 175 Fifth Avenue, New York, New York 10010 (800) 221-7945; *The Statesman's Year-Book.*

U.S. Arms Control and Disarmament Agency, 320 Twenty-first Street, NW, Washington, D.C. 20451 (202) 647-8677; *World Military Expenditures and Arms Transfers.*

The World Bank, 1818 H Street, NW, Washington, D.C. 20433 (202) 477-1234; *The World Bank Atlas.*

KOREA (DEMOCRATIC PEOPLE'S REPUBLIC OF) - HEALTH

The Economist Intelligence Unit (Asia) Limited, 10th Floor, Luk Kwok Centre, 72 Gloucester Road, Wanchai, Hong Kong (Phone Number in U.S. (800) 938-4685); *Asian Market Atlas.*

Euromonitor International, Inc., 122 South Michigan Avenue, Suite 1200, Chicago, Illinois 60603 (800) 577-EURO; *World Marketing Data and Statistics.*

M.E. Sharpe, 80 Business Park Drive, Armonk, New York 10504 (800) 541-6563; *The Illustrated Book of World Rankings.*

St. Martin's Press, Inc., 175 Fifth Avenue, New York, New York 10010 (800) 221-7945; *The Statesman's Year-Book.*

Statistical Office of the United Nations, Publishing Service, New York, New York 10017 (800) 253-9646; *Human Development Report.*

United Nations Children's Fund (UNICEF), 3 United Nations Plaza, New York, New York 10017 (800) 253-9646; *State of the World's Children.*

KOREA (DEMOCRATIC PEOPLE'S REPUBLIC OF) - HEMP FIBRE PRODUCTION - See KOREA (DEMOCRATIC PEOPLE'S REPUBLIC OF) - TEXTILE INDUSTRY

KOREA (DEMOCRATIC PEOPLE'S REPUBLIC OF) - HIDE PRODUCTION

Food and Agricultural Organization of the United Nations (FAO), Via delle Terme di Caracalla, 00100 Rome, Italy (Telephone Number in U.S. (202) 653-2400); *Production Yearbook.*

KOREA (DEMOCRATIC PEOPLE'S REPUBLIC OF) - HIGHWAYS

Central Intelligence Agency, Washington, D.C. 20505 (703) 482-1100, www.cia.gov; *The World Factbook.*

The Economist Intelligence Unit (Asia) Limited, 10th Floor, Luk Kwok Centre, 72 Gloucester Road, Wanchai, Hong Kong (Phone Number in U.S. (800) 938-4685); *Asian Market Atlas.*

International Road Federation, 2600 Virginia Avenue, NW, Washington, D.C. 20037 (202) 338-4641; *World Road Statistics.*

St. Martin's Press, Inc., 175 Fifth Avenue, New York, New York 10010 (800) 221-7945; *The Statesman's Year-Book.*

KOREA (DEMOCRATIC PEOPLE'S REPUBLIC OF) - HORSES - See KOREA (DEMOCRATIC PEOPLE'S REPUBLIC OF) - LIVESTOCK AND POULTRY

KOREA (DEMOCRATIC PEOPLE'S REPUBLIC OF) - HOURS OF WORK - See KOREA (DEMOCRATIC PEOPLE'S REPUBLIC OF) - EMPLOYMENT

KOREA (DEMOCRATIC PEOPLE'S REPUBLIC OF) - HOUSING AND HOUSING UNITS

Euromonitor International, Inc., 122 South Michigan Avenue, Suite 1200,

Chicago, Illinois 60603 (800) 577-EURO; *World Marketing Data and Statistics.*

M.E. Sharpe, 80 Business Park Drive, Armonk, New York 10504 (800) 541-6563; *The Illustrated Book of World Rankings.*

KOREA (DEMOCRATIC PEOPLE'S REPUBLIC OF) - ILLITERATE POPULATION

Central Intelligence Agency, Washington, D.C. 20505 (703) 482-1100, www.cia.gov; *The World Factbook.*

The Economist Intelligence Unit, 111 West 57th Street, New York, New York 10019 (800) 938-4685; *The World Market Atlas.*

Euromonitor International, Inc., 122 South Michigan Avenue, Suite 1200, Chicago. Illinois 60603 (800) 577-EURO; *The World Economic Factbook.*

Statistical Office of the United Nations, Publishing Service, New York, New York 10017 (800) 253-9646; *Human Development Report.*

KOREA (DEMOCRATIC PEOPLE'S REPUBLIC OF) - IMPORTS

American Automobile Manufacturers Association, 1401 H Street, NW, Suite 900, Washington, D.C. 20005 (202) 326-5500; *World Motor Vehicle Data.*

Asian Development Bank, Post Office Box 789, 1099 Manila, Philippines; *Key Indicators of Developing Asian and Pacific Countries.*

Central Intelligence Agency, Washington, D.C. 20505 (703) 482-1100, www.cia.gov; *The World Factbook.*

The Economist Intelligence Unit, 111 West 57th Street, New York, New York 10019 (800) 938-4685; *Korea (North) Country Report;* and *The World Market Atlas.*

The Economist Intelligence Unit (Asia) Limited, 10th Floor, Luk Kwok Centre, 72 Gloucester Road, Wanchai, Hong Kong (Phone Number in U.S. (800) 938-4685); *Asian Market Atlas.*

Euromonitor International, Inc., 122 South Michigan Avenue, Suite 1200, Chicago. Illinois 60603 (800) 577-EURO; *International Marketing Data and Statistics;* and *The World Economic Factbook.*

Europa Publications Limited, 18 Bedford Square, London, WC1B 3JN, England; *The Europa World Year Book.*

Food and Agricultural Organization of the United Nations (FAO), Via delle Terme di Caracalla, 00100 Rome, Italy (Telephone

Number in U.S. (202) 653-2400); *The State of Food and Agriculture.*

International Monetary Fund, 700 Nineteenth Street, NW, Washington, D.C. 20431 (202) 623-7000; *Direction of Trade Statistics.*

St. Martin's Press, Inc., 175 Fifth Avenue, New York, New York 10010 (800) 221-7945; *The Statesman's Year-Book.*

Walden Publishing, Ltd., Two Market Street, Saffron Walden Essex, CB10 1HZ, England; *The World of Information Asia and Pacific Review.*

KOREA (DEMOCRATIC PEOPLE'S REPUBLIC OF) - INDUSTRIAL METALS PRODUCTION - See KOREA (DEMOCRATIC PEOPLE'S REPUBLIC OF) - MINING AND MINERAL PRODUCTS

KOREA (DEMOCRATIC PEOPLE'S REPUBLIC OF) - INDUSTRY

Central Intelligence Agency, Washington, D.C. 20505 (703) 482-1100, www.cia.gov; *The World Factbook.*

Economist Intelligence Unit, 111 West 57th Street, New York, New York 10019 (800) 938-4685; *Korea (North) Country Report.*

Euromonitor International, Inc., 122 South Michigan Avenue, Suite 1200, Chicago. Illinois 60603 (800) 577-EURO; *International Marketing Data and Statistics; World Marketing Data and Statistics;* and *The World Economic Factbook.*

Europa Publications Limited, 18 Bedford Square, London, WC1B 3JN, England; *The Europa World Year Book.*

M.E. Sharpe, 80 Business Park Drive, Armonk, New York 10504 (800) 541-6563; *The Illustrated Book of World Rankings.*

St. Martin's Press, Inc., 175 Fifth Avenue, New York, New York 10010 (800) 221-7945; *The Statesman's Year-Book.*

World Intellectual Property Organization, 34 Chemin des Colombettes, CH-1211 Geneva 20, Switzerland; *Industrial Property Statistics.*

KOREA (DEMOCRATIC PEOPLE'S REPUBLIC OF) - INFANT AND MATERNAL MORTALITY RATE - See KOREA (DEMOCRATIC PEOPLE'S REPUBLIC OF) - MORTALITY

KOREA (DEMOCRATIC PEOPLE'S REPUBLIC OF) - INTERNATIONAL RESERVES EXCLUDING GOLD

Asian Development Bank, Post Office Box 789, 1099 Manila, Philippines; *Key

Indicators of Developing Asian and Pacific Countries.*

KOREA (DEMOCRATIC PEOPLE'S REPUBLIC OF) - INTERNATIONAL STATISTICS

Asian Development Bank, Post Office Box 789, 1099 Manila, Philippines; *Key Indicators of Developing Asian and Pacific Countries.*

KOREA (DEMOCRATIC PEOPLE'S REPUBLIC OF) - IRON ORE - See KOREA (DEMOCRATIC PEOPLE'S REPUBLIC OF) - MINING AND MINERAL PRODUCTS

KOREA (DEMOCRATIC PEOPLE'S REPUBLIC OF) - IRRIGATION

Euromonitor International, Inc., 122 South Michigan Avenue, Suite 1200, Chicago. Illinois 60603 (800) 577-EURO; *International Marketing Data and Statistics.*

KOREA (DEMOCRATIC PEOPLE'S REPUBLIC OF) - LABOR

Central Intelligence Agency, Washington, D.C. 20505 (703) 482-1100, www.cia.gov; *The World Factbook.*

The Economist Intelligence Unit (Asia) Limited, 10th Floor, Luk Kwok Centre, 72 Gloucester Road, Wanchai, Hong Kong (Phone Number in U.S. (800) 938-4685); *Asian Market Atlas.*

Euromonitor International, Inc., 122 South Michigan Avenue, Suite 1200, Chicago. Illinois 60603 (800) 577-EURO; *International Marketing Data and Statistics;* and *World Marketing Data and Statistics.*

Europa Publications Limited, 18 Bedford Square, London, WC1B 3JN, England; *The Europa World Year Book.*

Food and Agricultural Organization of the United Nations (FAO), Via delle Terme di Caracalla, 00100 Rome, Italy (Telephone Number in U.S. (202) 653-2400); *The State of Food and Agriculture.*

M.E. Sharpe, 80 Business Park Drive, Armonk, New York 10504 (800) 541-6563; *The Illustrated Book of World Rankings.*

St. Martin's Press, Inc., 175 Fifth Avenue, New York, New York 10010 (800) 221-7945; *The Statesman's Year-Book.*

Statistical Office of the United Nations, Publishing Service, New York, New York 10017 (800) 253-9646; *Human Development Report.*

The World Bank, 1818 H Street, NW, Washington, D.C. 20433 (202) 477-1234; *The World Bank Atlas.*

KOREA (DEMOCRATIC PEOPLE'S REPUBLIC OF) - LAND USE

Central Intelligence Agency, Washington, D.C. 20505 (703) 482-1100, www.cia.gov; *The World Factbook.*

Euromonitor International, Inc., 122 South Michigan Avenue, Suite 1200, Chicago. Illinois 60603 (800) 577-EURO; *International Marketing Data and Statistics.*

Food and Agricultural Organization of the United Nations (FAO), Via delle Terme di Caracalla, 00100 Rome, Italy (Telephone Number in U.S. (202) 653-2400); *Production Yearbook.*

KOREA (DEMOCRATIC PEOPLE'S REPUBLIC OF) - LEAD AND LEAD ORE PRODUCTION AND CONSUMPTION - See KOREA (DEMOCRATIC PEOPLE'S REPUBLIC OF) - MINING AND MINERAL PRODUCTS

KOREA (DEMOCRATIC PEOPLE'S REPUBLIC OF) - LIBRARIES

M.E. Sharpe, 80 Business Park Drive, Armonk, New York 10504 (800) 541-6563; *The Illustrated Book of World Rankings.*

KOREA (DEMOCRATIC PEOPLE'S REPUBLIC OF) - LIFE EXPECTANCY

Central Intelligence Agency, Washington, D.C. 20505 (703) 482-1100, www.cia.gov; *The World Factbook.*

The Economist Intelligence Unit (Asia) Limited, 10th Floor, Luk Kwok Centre, 72 Gloucester Road, Wanchai, Hong Kong (Phone Number in U.S. (800) 938-4685); *Asian Market Atlas.*

Euromonitor International, Inc., 122 South Michigan Avenue, Suite 1200, Chicago. Illinois 60603 (800) 577-EURO; *The World Economic Factbook.*

St. Martin's Press, Inc., 175 Fifth Avenue, New York, New York 10010 (800) 221-7945; *The Statesman's Year-Book.*

Statistical Office of the United Nations, Publishing Service, New York, New York 10017 (800) 253-9646; *Human Development Report;* and *World Statistics Pocketbook.*

The World Bank, 1818 H Street, NW, Washington, D.C. 20433 (202) 477-1234; *The World Bank Atlas.*

KOREA (DEMOCRATIC PEOPLE'S REPUBLIC OF) - LIGNITE PRODUCTION - See KOREA (DEMOCRATIC PEOPLE'S REPUBLIC OF) - MINING AND MINERAL PRODUCTS

KOREA (DEMOCRATIC PEOPLE'S

REPUBLIC OF) - LITERACY RATE

Euromonitor International, Inc., 122 South Michigan Avenue, Suite 1200, Chicago, Illinois 60603 (800) 577-EURO; *World Marketing Data and Statistics.*

KOREA (DEMOCRATIC PEOPLE'S REPUBLIC OF) - LIVESTOCK AND POULTRY

Euromonitor International, Inc., 122 South Michigan Avenue, Suite 1200, Chicago. Illinois 60603 (800) 577-EURO; *International Marketing Data and Statistics.*

Europa Publications Limited, 18 Bedford Square, London, WC1B 3JN, England; *The Europa World Year Book.*

Food and Agricultural Organization of the United Nations (FAO), Via delle Terme di Caracalla, 00100 Rome, Italy (Telephone Number in U.S. (202) 653-2400); *Production Yearbook;* and *The State of Food and Agriculture.*

M.E. Sharpe, 80 Business Park Drive, Armonk, New York 10504 (800) 541-6563; *The Illustrated Book of World Rankings.*

St. Martin's Press, Inc., 175 Fifth Avenue, New York, New York 10010 (800) 221-7945; *The Statesman's Year-Book.*

Statistical Office of the United Nations, Publishing Service, New York, New York 10017 (800) 253-9646; *Statistical Yearbook.*

United Nations Conference on Trade and Development, Central Statistical Service, Palais des Nations, Geneva, Switzerland (Telephone in U.S. (800) 253-9646); *UNCTAD Commodity Yearbook.*

KOREA (DEMOCRATIC PEOPLE'S REPUBLIC OF) - LIVING LEVELS - See KOREA (DEMOCRATIC PEOPLE'S REPUBLIC OF) - LIFE EXPECTANCY

KOREA (DEMOCRATIC PEOPLE'S REPUBLIC OF) - MANUFACTURING

American Automobile Manufacturers Association, 1401 H Street, NW, Suite 900, Washington, D.C. 20005 (202) 326-5500; *World Motor Vehicle Data.*

Asian Development Bank, Post Office Box 789, 1099 Manila, Philippines; *Key Indicators of Developing Asian and Pacific Countries.*

M.E. Sharpe, 80 Business Park Drive, Armonk, New York 10504 (800) 541-6563; *The Illustrated Book of World Rankings.*

KOREA (DEMOCRATIC PEOPLE'S REPUBLIC OF) - MARRIAGE RATES

M.E. Sharpe, 80 Business Park Drive, Armonk, New York 10504 (800) 541-6563; *The Illustrated Book of World Rankings.*

Statistical Office of the United Nations, Publishing Service, New York, New York 10017 (800) 253-9646; *Demographic Yearbook.*

KOREA (DEMOCRATIC PEOPLE'S REPUBLIC OF) - MEAT PRODUCTION - See KOREA (DEMOCRATIC PEOPLE'S REPUBLIC OF) - LIVESTOCK AND POULTRY

KOREA (DEMOCRATIC PEOPLE'S REPUBLIC OF) - MERCHANT SHIPPING

Europa Publications Limited, 18 Bedford Square, London, WC1B 3JN, England; *The Europa World Year Book.*

Lloyd's Register of Shipping, 17 Battery Place, New York, New York 10004; *Register of Ships.*

St. Martin's Press, Inc., 175 Fifth Avenue, New York, New York 10010 (800) 221-7945; *The Statesman's Year-Book.*

Statistical Office of the United Nations, Publishing Service, New York, New York 10017 (800) 253-9646; *Statistical Yearbook.*

U.S. Department of Transportation, Maritime Administration, 400 Seventh Street, SW, Washington, D.C. 20590 (202) 366-5807, www.marad.dot.gov; *A Statistical Analysis of the World's Merchant Fleets.*

KOREA (DEMOCRATIC PEOPLE'S REPUBLIC OF) - MERCHANT VESSELS - TONNAGE LAUNCHED - See KOREA (DEMOCRATIC PEOPLE'S REPUBLIC OF) - MERCHANT SHIPPING

KOREA (DEMOCRATIC PEOPLE'S REPUBLIC OF) - MILITARY

Central Intelligence Agency, Washington, D.C. 20505 (703) 482-1100, www.cia.gov; *The World Factbook.*

The Economist Intelligence Unit (Asia) Limited, 10th Floor, Luk Kwok Centre, 72 Gloucester Road, Wanchai, Hong Kong (Phone Number in U.S. (800) 938-4685); *Asian Market Atlas.*

Euromonitor International, Inc., 122 South Michigan Avenue, Suite 1200, Chicago, Illinois 60603 (800) 577-EURO; *World Marketing Data and Statistics.*

The International Institute for Strategic Studies, 23 Tavistock Street, London WC2E 7NQ, England 44 171 3797676; *The Military Balance.*

St. Martin's Press, Inc., 175 Fifth Avenue, New York, New York 10010 (800) 221-7945; *The Statesman's Year-Book.*

Statistical Office of the United Nations, Publishing Service, New York, New York 10017 (800) 253-9646; *Human Development Report.*

U.S. Arms Control and Disarmament Agency, 320 Twenty-first Street, NW, Washington, D.C. 20451 (202) 647-8677; *World Military Expenditures and Arms Transfers.*

KOREA (DEMOCRATIC PEOPLE'S REPUBLIC OF) - MILK PRODUCTION - See KOREA (DEMOCRATIC PEOPLE'S REPUBLIC OF) - DAIRY PRODUCTS

KOREA (DEMOCRATIC PEOPLE'S REPUBLIC OF) - MILLET PRODUCTION - See KOREA (DEMOCRATIC PEOPLE'S REPUBLIC OF) - CROPS

KOREA (DEMOCRATIC PEOPLE'S REPUBLIC OF) - MINING AND MINERAL PRODUCTS

Asian Development Bank, Post Office Box 789, 1099 Manila, Philippines; *Key Indicators of Developing Asian and Pacific Countries.*

Europa Publications Limited, 18 Bedford Square, London, WC1B 3JN, England; *The Europa World Year Book.*

M.E. Sharpe, 80 Business Park Drive, Armonk, New York 10504 (800) 541-6563; *The Illustrated Book of World Rankings.*

St. Martin's Press, Inc., 175 Fifth Avenue, New York, New York 10010 (800) 221-7945; *The Statesman's Year-Book.*

Statistical Office of the United Nations, Publishing Service, New York, New York 10017 (800) 253-9646; *Statistical Yearbook.*

United Nations Conference on Trade and Development, Central Statistical Service, Palais des Nations, Geneva, Switzerland (Telephone in U.S. (800) 253-9646); *UNCTAD Commodity Yearbook.*

KOREA (DEMOCRATIC PEOPLE'S REPUBLIC OF) - MONEY EXCHANGE RATES

Euromonitor International, Inc., 122 South Michigan Avenue, Suite 1200, Chicago. Illinois 60603 (800) 577-EURO; *International Marketing Data and Statistics.*

KOREA (DEMOCRATIC PEOPLE'S REPUBLIC OF) - MONEY RESERVES

Euromonitor International, Inc., 122 South Michigan Avenue, Suite 1200, Chicago. Illinois 60603 (800) 577-EURO;

International Marketing Data and Statistics.

KOREA (DEMOCRATIC PEOPLE'S REPUBLIC OF) - MONEY SUPPLY

Asian Development Bank, Post Office Box 789, 1099 Manila, Philippines; *Key Indicators of Developing Asian and Pacific Countries.*

Economist Intelligence Unit, 111 West 57th Street, New York, New York 10019 (800) 938-4685; *Korea (North) Country Report.*

Euromonitor International, Inc., 122 South Michigan Avenue, Suite 1200, Chicago. Illinois 60603 (800) 577-EURO; *International Marketing Data and Statistics.*

KOREA (DEMOCRATIC PEOPLE'S REPUBLIC OF) - MORTALITY

Central Intelligence Agency, Washington, D.C. 20505 (703) 482-1100, www.cia.gov; *The World Factbook.*

The Economist Intelligence Unit (Asia) Limited, 10th Floor, Luk Kwok Centre, 72 Gloucester Road, Wanchai, Hong Kong (Phone Number in U.S. (800) 938-4685); *Asian Market Atlas.*

Euromonitor International, Inc., 122 South Michigan Avenue, Suite 1200, Chicago. Illinois 60603 (800) 577-EURO; *International Marketing Data and Statistics;* and *The World Economic Factbook.*

Europa Publications Limited, 18 Bedford Square, London, WC1B 3JN, England; *The Europa World Year Book.*

St. Martin's Press, Inc., 175 Fifth Avenue, New York, New York 10010 (800) 221-7945; *The Statesman's Year-Book.*

Statistical Office of the United Nations, Publishing Service, New York, New York 10017 (800) 253-9646; *Demographic Yearbook; Human Development Report; World Statistics Pocketbook;* and *Statistical Yearbook.*

United Nations Children's Fund (UNICEF), 3 United Nations Plaza, New York, New York 10017 (800) 253-9646; *State of the World's Children.*

The World Bank, 1818 H Street, NW, Washington, D.C. 20433 (202) 477-1234; *The World Bank Atlas.*

KOREA (DEMOCRATIC PEOPLE'S REPUBLIC OF) - MOTION PICTURES

St. Martin's Press, Inc., 175 Fifth Avenue, New York, New York 10010 (800) 221-7945; *The Statesman's Year-Book.*

KOREA (DEMOCRATIC PEOPLE'S REPUBLIC OF) - MOTOR VEHICLE PRODUCTION

American Automobile Manufacturers Association, 1401 H Street, NW, Suite 900, Washington, D.C. 20005 (202) 326-5500; *World Motor Vehicle Data.*

KOREA (DEMOCRATIC PEOPLE'S REPUBLIC OF) - MOTOR VEHICLES IN USE

American Automobile Manufacturers Association, 1401 H Street, NW, Suite 900, Washington, D.C. 20005 (202) 326-5500; *World Motor Vehicle Data.*

International Road Federation, 2600 Virginia Avenue, NW, Washington, D.C. 20037 (202) 338-4641; *World Road Statistics.*

KOREA (DEMOCRATIC PEOPLE'S REPUBLIC OF) - MULES - See KOREA (DEMOCRATIC PEOPLE'S REPUBLIC OF) - LIVESTOCK AND POULTRY

KOREA (DEMOCRATIC PEOPLE'S REPUBLIC OF) - MUSEUMS

M.E. Sharpe, 80 Business Park Drive, Armonk, New York 10504 (800) 541-6563; *The Illustrated Book of World Rankings.*

KOREA (DEMOCRATIC PEOPLE'S REPUBLIC OF) - NATALITY - See KOREA (DEMOCRATIC PEOPLE'S REPUBLIC OF) - BIRTH RATES

KOREA (DEMOCRATIC PEOPLE'S REPUBLIC OF) - NATIONAL INCOME

M.E. Sharpe, 80 Business Park Drive, Armonk, New York 10504 (800) 541-6563; *The Illustrated Book of World Rankings.*

Statistical Office of the United Nations, Publishing Service, New York, New York 10017 (800) 253-9646; *National Accounts Statistics.*

KOREA (DEMOCRATIC PEOPLE'S REPUBLIC OF) - NATIONAL PRODUCT

M.E. Sharpe, 80 Business Park Drive, Armonk, New York 10504 (800) 541-6563; *The Illustrated Book of World Rankings.*

KOREA (DEMOCRATIC PEOPLE'S REPUBLIC OF) - NATURAL GAS PRODUCTION - See KOREA (DEMOCRATIC PEOPLE'S REPUBLIC OF) - MINING AND MINERAL PRODUCTS

KOREA (DEMOCRATIC PEOPLE'S REPUBLIC OF) - NEWSPAPER PRODUCTION AND CONSUMPTION - See KOREA (DEMOCRATIC PEOPLE'S REPUBLIC OF) - FORESTRY AND FOREST PRODUCTS

KOREA (DEMOCRATIC PEOPLE'S REPUBLIC OF) - NEWSPRINT - See KOREA (DEMOCRATIC PEOPLE'S REPUBLIC OF) - FORESTRY AND FOREST PRODUCTS

KOREA (DEMOCRATIC PEOPLE'S REPUBLIC OF) - OATS PRODUCTION - See KOREA (DEMOCRATIC PEOPLE'S REPUBLIC OF) - CROPS

KOREA (DEMOCRATIC PEOPLE'S REPUBLIC OF) - OCCUPATIONS - See KOREA (DEMOCRATIC PEOPLE'S REPUBLIC OF) - LABOR

KOREA (DEMOCRATIC PEOPLE'S REPUBLIC OF) - PAPER - See KOREA (DEMOCRATIC PEOPLE'S REPUBLIC OF) - FORESTRY AND FOREST PRODUCTS

KOREA (DEMOCRATIC PEOPLE'S REPUBLIC OF) - PATENTS, TRADEMARKS AND SERVICE MARKS

Statistical Office of the United Nations, Publishing Service, New York, New York 10017 (800) 253-9646; *Statistical Yearbook.*

World Intellectual Property Organization, 34 Chemin des Colombettes, CH-1211 Geneva 20, Switzerland; *Industrial Property Statistics.*

KOREA (DEMOCRATIC PEOPLE'S REPUBLIC OF) - PEANUT PRODUCTION - See KOREA (DEMOCRATIC PEOPLE'S REPUBLIC OF) - CROPS

KOREA (DEMOCRATIC PEOPLE'S REPUBLIC OF) - PESTICIDE USE

Food and Agricultural Organization of the United Nations (FAO), Via delle Terme di Caracalla, 00100 Rome, Italy (Telephone Number in U.S. (202) 653-2400); *The State of Food and Agriculture.*

KOREA (DEMOCRATIC PEOPLE'S REPUBLIC OF) - PETROLEUM INDUSTRY

Asian Development Bank, Post Office Box 789, 1099 Manila, Philippines; *Key Indicators of Developing Asian and Pacific Countries.*

Food and Agricultural Organization of the United Nations (FAO), Via delle Terme di Caracalla, 00100 Rome, Italy (Telephone Number in U.S. (202) 653-2400); *The State of Food and Agriculture.*

M.E. Sharpe, 80 Business Park Drive, Armonk, New York 10504 (800) 541-6563; *The Illustrated Book of World Rankings.*

St. Martin's Press, Inc., 175 Fifth Avenue, New York, New York 10010 (800) 221-7945; *The Statesman's Year-Book.*

United Nations Conference on Trade and Development, Central Statistical

Service, Palais des Nations, Geneva, Switzerland (Telephone in U.S. (800) 253-9646); *UNCTAD Commodity Yearbook.*

KOREA (DEMOCRATIC PEOPLE'S REPUBLIC OF) - PHOSPHATE ROCK PRODUCTION - See KOREA (DEMOCRATIC PEOPLE'S REPUBLIC OF) - MINING AND MINERAL PRODUCTS

KOREA (DEMOCRATIC PEOPLE'S REPUBLIC OF) - PIG-IRON AND FERRO-ALLOY PRODUCTION - See KOREA (DEMOCRATIC PEOPLE'S REPUBLIC OF) - MINING AND MINERAL PRODUCTS

KOREA (DEMOCRATIC PEOPLE'S REPUBLIC OF) - PIGS - See KOREA (DEMOCRATIC PEOPLE'S REPUBLIC OF) - LIVESTOCK AND POULTRY

KOREA (DEMOCRATIC PEOPLE'S REPUBLIC OF) - POPULATION

Asian Development Bank, Post Office Box 789, 1099 Manila, Philippines; *Key Indicators of Developing Asian and Pacific Countries.*

Central Intelligence Agency, Washington, D.C. 20505 (703) 482-1100, www.cia.gov; *The World Factbook.*

The Economist Intelligence Unit, 111 West 57th Street, New York, New York 10019 (800) 938-4685; *Korea (North) Country Report;* and *The World Market Atlas.*

The Economist Intelligence Unit (Asia) Limited, 10th Floor, Luk Kwok Centre, 72 Gloucester Road, Wanchai, Hong Kong (Phone Number in U.S. (800) 938-4685); *Asian Market Atlas.*

Euromonitor International, Inc., 122 South Michigan Avenue, Suite 1200, Chicago. Illinois 60603 (800) 577-EURO; *International Marketing Data and Statistics;* and *The World Economic Factbook.*

Europa Publications Limited, 18 Bedford Square, London, WC1B 3JN, England; *The Europa World Year Book.*

Food and Agricultural Organization of the United Nations (FAO), Via delle Terme di Caracalla, 00100 Rome, Italy (Telephone Number in U.S. (202) 653-2400); *Production Yearbook.*

M.E. Sharpe, 80 Business Park Drive, Armonk, New York 10504 (800) 541-6563; *The Illustrated Book of World Rankings.*

St. Martin's Press, Inc., 175 Fifth Avenue, New York, New York 10010 (800) 221-7945; *The Statesman's Year-Book.*

Statistical Office of the United Nations, Publishing Service, New York, New York

10017 (800) 253-9646; *Demographic Yearbook; Human Development Report; World Statistics Pocketbook;* and *Statistical Yearbook.*

U.S. Arms Control and Disarmament Agency, 320 Twenty-first Street, NW, Washington, D.C. 20451 (202) 647-8677; *World Military Expenditures and Arms Transfers.*

Walden Publishing, Ltd., Two Market Street, Saffron Walden Essex, CB10 1HZ, England; *The World of Information Asia and Pacific Review.*

The World Bank, 1818 H Street, NW, Washington, D.C. 20433 (202) 477-1234; *The World Bank Atlas.*

KOREA (DEMOCRATIC PEOPLE'S REPUBLIC OF) - POST OFFICES

M.E. Sharpe, 80 Business Park Drive, Armonk, New York 10504 (800) 541-6563; *The Illustrated Book of World Rankings.*

KOREA (DEMOCRATIC PEOPLE'S REPUBLIC OF) - POTATO PRODUCTION - See KOREA (DEMOCRATIC PEOPLE'S REPUBLIC OF) - CROPS

KOREA (DEMOCRATIC PEOPLE'S REPUBLIC OF) - POWER PRODUCTION INDUSTRY - ESTABLISHMENTS, PAYROLLS, VALUE ADDED, ETC.

Statistical Office of the United Nations, Publishing Service, New York, New York 10017 (800) 253-9646; *Electric Power in Asia and the Pacific.*

KOREA (DEMOCRATIC PEOPLE'S REPUBLIC OF) - PRICES

Asian Development Bank, Post Office Box 789, 1099 Manila, Philippines; *Key Indicators of Developing Asian and Pacific Countries.*

Food and Agricultural Organization of the United Nations (FAO), Via delle Terme di Caracalla, 00100 Rome, Italy (Telephone Number in U.S. (202) 653-2400); *Production Yearbook;* and *The State of Food and Agriculture.*

M.E. Sharpe, 80 Business Park Drive, Armonk, New York 10504 (800) 541-6563; *The Illustrated Book of World Rankings.*

KOREA (DEMOCRATIC PEOPLE'S REPUBLIC OF) - PRINTING AND WRITING PAPER - See KOREA (DEMOCRATIC PEOPLE'S REPUBLIC OF) - FORESTRY AND FOREST PRODUCTS

KOREA (DEMOCRATIC PEOPLE'S REPUBLIC OF) - PRODUCTION

American Automobile Manufacturers

Association, 1401 H Street, NW, Suite 900, Washington, D.C. 20005 (202) 326-5500; *World Motor Vehicle Data.*

M.E. Sharpe, 80 Business Park Drive, Armonk, New York 10504 (800) 541-6563; *The Illustrated Book of World Rankings.*

KOREA (DEMOCRATIC PEOPLE'S REPUBLIC OF) - PRODUCTIVITY

Euromonitor International, Inc., 122 South Michigan Avenue, Suite 1200, Chicago, Illinois 60603 (800) 577-EURO; *International Marketing Data and Statistics.*

KOREA (DEMOCRATIC PEOPLE'S REPUBLIC OF) - PUBLIC FINANCE - See KOREA (DEMOCRATIC PEOPLE'S REPUBLIC OF) - FINANCE

KOREA (DEMOCRATIC PEOPLE'S REPUBLIC OF) - RADIO BROADCASTING - See KOREA (DEMOCRATIC PEOPLE'S REPUBLIC OF) - BROADCASTING

KOREA (DEMOCRATIC PEOPLE'S REPUBLIC OF) - RADIO RECEIVERS

St. Martin's Press, Inc., 175 Fifth Avenue, New York, New York 10010 (800) 221-7945; *The Statesman's Year-Book.*

KOREA (DEMOCRATIC PEOPLE'S REPUBLIC OF) - RAILWAYS

Jane's Information Group, Sentinel House, 163 Brighton Road, Coulsdon, Surrey CR5 2NH, England (Telephone Number in U.S. (703) 683-3700); *Jane's World Railways.*

St. Martin's Press, Inc., 175 Fifth Avenue, New York, New York 10010 (800) 221-7945; *The Statesman's Year-Book.*

KOREA (DEMOCRATIC PEOPLE'S REPUBLIC OF) - RELIGION

Central Intelligence Agency, Washington, D.C. 20505 (703) 482-1100, www.cia.gov; *The World Factbook.*

M.E. Sharpe, 80 Business Park Drive, Armonk, New York 10504 (800) 541-6563; *The Illustrated Book of World Rankings.*

St. Martin's Press, Inc., 175 Fifth Avenue, New York, New York 10010 (800) 221-7945; *The Statesman's Year-Book.*

KOREA (DEMOCRATIC PEOPLE'S REPUBLIC OF) - RETAIL TRADE

Euromonitor International, Inc., 122 South Michigan Avenue, Suite 1200, Chicago, Illinois 60603 (800) 577-EURO; *World Marketing Data and Statistics.*

KOREA (DEMOCRATIC PEOPLE'S REPUBLIC OF) - RICE PRODUCTION - See

KOREA (DEMOCRATIC PEOPLE'S REPUBLIC OF) - CROPS

KOREA (DEMOCRATIC PEOPLE'S REPUBLIC OF) - ROOT AND TUBER PRODUCTION - See KOREA (DEMOCRATIC PEOPLE'S REPUBLIC OF) - CROPS

KOREA (DEMOCRATIC PEOPLE'S REPUBLIC OF) - ROUNDWOOD PRODUCTION - See KOREA (DEMOCRATIC PEOPLE'S REPUBLIC OF) - FORESTRY AND FOREST PRODUCTS

KOREA (DEMOCRATIC PEOPLE'S REPUBLIC OF) - RUBBER PRODUCTION AND CONSUMPTION

M.E. Sharpe, 80 Business Park Drive, Armonk, New York 10504 (800) 541-6563; *The Illustrated Book of World Rankings.*

KOREA (DEMOCRATIC PEOPLE'S REPUBLIC OF) - SALT PRODUCTION

Statistical Office of the United Nations, Publishing Service, New York, New York 10017 (800) 253-9646; *Statistical Yearbook.*

KOREA (DEMOCRATIC PEOPLE'S REPUBLIC OF) - SAWNWOOD PRODUCTION - See KOREA (DEMOCRATIC PEOPLE'S REPUBLIC OF) - FORESTRY AND FOREST PRODUCTS

KOREA (DEMOCRATIC PEOPLE'S REPUBLIC OF) - SENIOR CITIZENS

M.E. Sharpe, 80 Business Park Drive, Armonk, New York 10504 (800) 541-6563; *The Illustrated Book of World Rankings.*

KOREA (DEMOCRATIC PEOPLE'S REPUBLIC OF) - SHEEP - See KOREA (DEMOCRATIC PEOPLE'S REPUBLIC OF) - LIVESTOCK AND POULTRY

KOREA (DEMOCRATIC PEOPLE'S REPUBLIC OF) - SILVER PRODUCTION AND CONSUMPTION - See KOREA (DEMOCRATIC PEOPLE'S REPUBLIC OF) - MINING AND MINERAL PRODUCTS

KOREA (DEMOCRATIC PEOPLE'S REPUBLIC OF) - SOCIAL DATA

Asian Development Bank, Post Office Box 789, 1099 Manila, Philippines; *Key Indicators of Developing Asian and Pacific Countries.*

M.E. Sharpe, 80 Business Park Drive, Armonk, New York 10504 (800) 541-6563; *The Illustrated Book of World Rankings.*

Statistical Office of the United Nations, Publishing Service, New York, New York 10017 (800) 253-9646; *World Statistics Pocketbook.*

KOREA (DEMOCRATIC PEOPLE'S

REPUBLIC OF) - SOCIAL SECURITY

Statistical Office of the United Nations, Publishing Service, New York, New York 10017 (800) 253-9646; *National Accounts Statistics.*

KOREA (DEMOCRATIC PEOPLE'S REPUBLIC OF) - SOYBEANS PRODUCTION - See KOREA (DEMOCRATIC PEOPLE'S REPUBLIC OF) - CROPS

KOREA (DEMOCRATIC PEOPLE'S REPUBLIC OF) - STATE BUDGET REVENUE AND EXPENDITURES

Euromonitor International, Inc., 122 South Michigan Avenue, Suite 1200, Chicago, Illinois 60603 (800) 577-EURO; *International Marketing Data and Statistics.*

KOREA (DEMOCRATIC PEOPLE'S REPUBLIC OF) - STEEL PRODUCTION AND CONSUMPTION - See KOREA (DEMOCRATIC PEOPLE'S REPUBLIC OF) - MINING AND MINERAL PRODUCTS

KOREA (DEMOCRATIC PEOPLE'S REPUBLIC OF) - STOCKS - COMMODITY - MARKET PRICE - INDEX

Food and Agricultural Organization of the United Nations (FAO), Via delle Terme di Caracalla, 00100 Rome, Italy (Telephone Number in U.S. (202) 653-2400); *The State of Food and Agriculture.*

KOREA (DEMOCRATIC PEOPLE'S REPUBLIC OF) - SUGAR PRODUCTION AND CONSUMPTION - See KOREA (DEMOCRATIC PEOPLE'S REPUBLIC OF) - CROPS

KOREA (DEMOCRATIC PEOPLE'S REPUBLIC OF) - TAXATION

International Road Federation, 2600 Virginia Avenue, N.W., Washington, D.C. 20037 (202) 338-4641; *World Road Statistics.*

St. Martin's Press, Inc., 175 Fifth Avenue, New York, New York 10010 (800) 221-7945; *The Statesman's Year-Book.*

KOREA (DEMOCRATIC PEOPLE'S REPUBLIC OF) - TELEPHONES IN USE

American Telephone and Telegraph Company, 26 Parsippany Road, Whippany, New Jersey 07981 (800) 222-0300; *The World's Telephones.*

Central Intelligence Agency, Washington, D.C. 20505 (703) 482-1100, www.cia.gov; *The World Factbook.*

The Economist Intelligence Unit (Asia) Limited, 10th Floor, Luk Kwok Centre, 72 Gloucester Road, Wanchai, Hong Kong (Phone Number in U.S. (800) 938-4685);

Asian Market Atlas.

St. Martin's Press, Inc., 175 Fifth Avenue, New York, New York 10010 (800) 221-7945; *The Statesman's Year-Book.*

Statistical Office of the United Nations, Publishing Service, New York, New York 10017 (800) 253-9646; *World Statistics Pocketbook.*

KOREA (DEMOCRATIC PEOPLE'S REPUBLIC OF) - TELEVISION BROADCASTING - See KOREA (DEMOCRATIC PEOPLE'S REPUBLIC OF) - BROADCASTING

KOREA (DEMOCRATIC PEOPLE'S REPUBLIC OF) - TEXTILE INDUSTRY

American Forest and Paper Association, 1111 Nineteenth Street, NW, Washington, D.C. 20036 (202) 463-2700; *Wood Pulp and Fiber Statistics.*

Food and Agricultural Organization of the United Nations (FAO), Via delle Terme di Caracalla, 00100 Rome, Italy (Telephone Number in U.S. (202) 653-2400); *Production Yearbook.*

M.E. Sharpe, 80 Business Park Drive, Armonk, New York 10504 (800) 541-6563; *The Illustrated Book of World Rankings.*

St. Martin's Press, Inc., 175 Fifth Avenue, New York, New York 10010 (800) 221-7945; *The Statesman's Year-Book.*

United Nations Conference on Trade and Development, Central Statistical Service, Palais des Nations, Geneva, Switzerland (Telephone in U.S. (800) 253-9646); *UNCTAD Commodity Yearbook.*

KOREA (DEMOCRATIC PEOPLE'S REPUBLIC OF) - TOBACCO PRODUCTION

M.E. Sharpe, 80 Business Park Drive, Armonk, New York 10504 (800) 541-6563; *The Illustrated Book of World Rankings.*

Statistical Office of the United Nations, Publishing Service, New York, New York 10017 (800) 253-9646; *Statistical Yearbook.*

KOREA (DEMOCRATIC PEOPLE'S REPUBLIC OF) - TOURISM

Euromonitor International, Inc., 122 South Michigan Avenue, Suite 1200, Chicago, Illinois 60603 (800) 577-EURO; *The World Economic Factbook; and World Marketing Data and Statistics.*

M.E. Sharpe, 80 Business Park Drive, Armonk, New York 10504 (800) 541-6563; *The Illustrated Book of World Rankings.*

St. Martin's Press, Inc., 175 Fifth Avenue, New York, New York 10010 (800)

221-7945; *The Statesman's Year-Book.*

KOREA (DEMOCRATIC PEOPLE'S REPUBLIC OF) - TRACTORS IN USE

Statistical Office of the United Nations, Publishing Service, New York, New York 10017 (800) 253-9646; *Statistical Yearbook.*

KOREA (DEMOCRATIC PEOPLE'S REPUBLIC OF) - TRADE - See KOREA (DEMOCRATIC PEOPLE'S REPUBLIC OF) - FOREIGN TRADE

KOREA (DEMOCRATIC PEOPLE'S REPUBLIC OF) - TRADEMARKS AND SERVICE MARKS - See KOREA (DEMOCRATIC PEOPLE'S REPUBLIC OF) - PATENTS, TRADEMARKS AND SERVICE MARKS

KOREA (DEMOCRATIC PEOPLE'S REPUBLIC OF) - TRANSPORTATION AND COMMUNICATIONS

Central Intelligence Agency, Washington, D.C. 20505 (703) 482-1100, www.cia.gov; *The World Factbook.*

The Economist Intelligence Unit (Asia) Limited, 10th Floor, Luk Kwok Centre, 72 Gloucester Road, Wanchai, Hong Kong (Phone Number in U.S. (800) 938-4685); *Asian Market Atlas.*

Euromonitor International, Inc., 122 South Michigan Avenue, Suite 1200, Chicago, Illinois 60603 (800) 577-EURO; *International Marketing Data and Statistics; and World Marketing Data and Statistics.*

Europa Publications Limited, 18 Bedford Square, London, WC1B 3JN, England; *The Europa World Year Book.*

M.E. Sharpe, 80 Business Park Drive, Armonk, New York 10504 (800) 541-6563; *The Illustrated Book of World Rankings.*

St. Martin's Press, Inc., 175 Fifth Avenue, New York, New York 10010 (800) 221-7945; *The Statesman's Year-Book.*

Statistical Office of the United Nations, Publishing Service, New York, New York 10017 (800) 253-9646; *Human Development Report.*

KOREA (DEMOCRATIC PEOPLE'S REPUBLIC OF) - TUNGSTEN PRODUCTION AND CONSUMPTION - See KOREA (DEMOCRATIC PEOPLE'S REPUBLIC OF) - MINING AND MINERAL PRODUCTS

KOREA (DEMOCRATIC PEOPLE'S REPUBLIC OF) - UNEMPLOYMENT

Central Intelligence Agency, Washington, D.C. 20505 (703) 482-1100, www.cia.gov; *The World Factbook.*

Euromonitor International, Inc., 122 South Michigan Avenue, Suite 1200, Chicago, Illinois 60603 (800) 577-EURO; *International Marketing Data and Statistics.*

KOREA (DEMOCRATIC PEOPLE'S REPUBLIC OF) - UTILITIES

Statistical Office of the United Nations, Publishing Service, New York, New York 10017 (800) 253-9646; *Electric Power in Asia and the Pacific.*

KOREA (DEMOCRATIC PEOPLE'S REPUBLIC OF) - VITAL STATISTICS

Euromonitor International, Inc., 122 South Michigan Avenue, Suite 1200, Chicago, Illinois 60603 (800) 577-EURO; *International Marketing Data and Statistics.*

St. Martin's Press, Inc., 175 Fifth Avenue, New York, New York 10010 (800) 221-7945; *The Statesman's Year-Book.*

Statistical Office of the United Nations, Publishing Service, New York, New York 10017 (800) 253-9646; *Statistical Yearbook.*

KOREA (DEMOCRATIC PEOPLE'S REPUBLIC OF) - WALNUT PRODUCTION - See KOREA (DEMOCRATIC PEOPLE'S REPUBLIC OF) - CROPS

KOREA (DEMOCRATIC PEOPLE'S REPUBLIC OF) - WATERMELON PRODUCTION - See KOREA (DEMOCRATIC PEOPLE'S REPUBLIC OF) - CROPS

KOREA (DEMOCRATIC PEOPLE'S REPUBLIC OF) - WEATHER - See KOREA (DEMOCRATIC PEOPLE'S REPUBLIC OF) - CLIMATE

KOREA (DEMOCRATIC PEOPLE'S REPUBLIC OF) - WHEAT PRODUCTION AND PRICES - See KOREA (DEMOCRATIC PEOPLE'S REPUBLIC OF) - CROPS

KOREA (DEMOCRATIC PEOPLE'S REPUBLIC OF) - WHOLESALE PRICES - INDEX NUMBERS

Asian Development Bank, Post Office Box 789, 1099 Manila, Philippines; *Key Indicators of Developing Asian and Pacific Countries.*

KOREA (DEMOCRATIC PEOPLE'S REPUBLIC OF) - WINE PRODUCTION - See KOREA (DEMOCRATIC PEOPLE'S REPUBLIC OF) - BEVERAGES

KOREA (DEMOCRATIC PEOPLE'S REPUBLIC OF) - WOOD - See KOREA (DEMOCRATIC PEOPLE'S REPUBLIC OF) - FORESTRY AND FOREST PRODUCTS

KOREA (DEMOCRATIC PEOPLE'S REPUBLIC OF) - WOOL PRODUCTION - See KOREA (DEMOCRATIC PEOPLE'S

REPUBLIC OF) - TEXTILE INDUSTRY

KOREA (DEMOCRATIC PEOPLE'S REPUBLIC OF) - ZINC ORE PRODUCTION - See KOREA (DEMOCRATIC PEOPLE'S REPUBLIC OF) - MINING AND MINERAL PRODUCTS

Korea (Republic Of) - National Statistical Office

National Statistical Office, 90 Kyongun-dong, Chongno-gu, Seoul, Korea.

Korea (Republic Of) - Primary Statistics Sources

National Statistical Office, Seoul, Korea; *Korea Statistical Yearbook;* and *Monthly Statistics of Korea.*

KOREA (REPUBLIC OF) - ADMINISTRATIVE DISTRICTS

Korean Overseas Information Service, Ministry of Culture and Information, Seoul 110, Republic of Korea; *Statistical Data on Korea.*

KOREA (REPUBLIC OF) - AGRICULTURE

Economist Intelligence Unit, 111 West 57th Street, New York, New York 10019 (800) 938-4685; *Korea (South) Country Report.*

Euromonitor International, Inc., 122 South Michigan Avenue, Suite 1200, Chicago, Illinois 60603 (800) 577-EURO; *International Marketing Data and Statistics;* and *World Marketing Data and Statistics.*

Europa Publications Limited, 18 Bedford Square, London, WC1B 3JN, England; *The Europa World Year Book.*

Food and Agricultural Organization of the United Nations (FAO), Via delle Terme di Caracalla, 00100 Rome, Italy (Telephone Number in U.S. (202) 653-2400); *Production Yearbook; The State of Food and Agriculture;* and *Trade Yearbook.*

St. Martin's Press, Inc., 175 Fifth Avenue, New York, New York 10010 (800) 221-7945; *The Statesman's Year-Book.*

Statistical Office of the United Nations, Publishing Service, New York, New York 10017 (800) 253-9646; *Asia-Pacific in Figures; Statistical Yearbook;* and *Statistical Yearbook for Asia and the Pacific.*

United Nations Conference on Trade and Development, Central Statistical Service, Palais des Nations, Geneva, Switzerland (Telephone in U.S. (800) 253-9646); *UNCTAD Commodity Yearbook.*

The World Bank, 1818 H Street, NW, Washington, D.C. 20433 (202) 477-1234; *World Development Indicators.*

KOREA (REPUBLIC OF) - AIRLINE SERVICE

The Economist Intelligence Unit (Asia) Limited, 10th Floor, Luk Kwok Centre, 72 Gloucester Road, Wanchai, Hong Kong (Phone Number in U.S. (800) 938-4685); *Asian Market Atlas.*

Europa Publications Limited, 18 Bedford Square, London, WC1B 3JN, England; *The Europa World Year Book.*

International Civil Aviation Organization, 999 University Street, Montreal, Quebec, Canada H3C 5H7 (514) 954-8219; *Civil Aviation Statistics of the World.*

M.E. Sharpe, 80 Business Park Drive, Armonk, New York 10504 (800) 541-6563; *The Illustrated Book of World Rankings.*

St. Martin's Press, Inc., 175 Fifth Avenue, New York, New York 10010 (800) 221-7945; *The Statesman's Year-Book.*

Statistical Office of the United Nations, Publishing Service, New York, New York 10017 (800) 253-9646; *Statistical Yearbook.*

KOREA (REPUBLIC OF) - AIRPORTS

Central Intelligence Agency, Washington, D.C. 20505 (703) 482-1100, www.cia.gov; *The World Factbook.*

KOREA (REPUBLIC OF) - ALUMINUM PRODUCTION AND CONSUMPTION - See KOREA (REPUBLIC OF) - MINING AND MINERAL PRODUCTS

KOREA (REPUBLIC OF) - ANIMAL HEALTH

Food and Agricultural Organization of the United Nations (FAO), Via delle Terme di Caracalla, 00100 Rome, Italy (Telephone Number in U.S. (202) 653-2400); *Animal Health Yearbook.*

KOREA (REPUBLIC OF) - ANTHRACITE PRODUCTION - See KOREA (REPUBLIC OF) - MINING AND MINERAL PRODUCTS

KOREA (REPUBLIC OF) - ANTIMONY ORE PRODUCTION AND CONSUMPTION - See KOREA (REPUBLIC OF) - MINING AND MINERAL PRODUCTS

KOREA (REPUBLIC OF) - AREA AND DENSITY OF POPULATION

Central Intelligence Agency, Washington, D.C. 20505 (703) 482-1100, www.cia.gov; *The World Factbook.*

Euromonitor International, Inc., 122 South Michigan Avenue, Suite 1200,

Chicago, Illinois 60603 (800) 577-EURO; *International Marketing Data and Statistics;* and *The World Economic Factbook.*

Europa Publications Limited, 18 Bedford Square, London, WC1B 3JN, England; *The Europa World Year Book.*

Food and Agricultural Organization of the United Nations (FAO), Via delle Terme di Caracalla, 00100 Rome, Italy (Telephone Number in U.S. (202) 653-2400); *The State of Food and Agriculture.*

M.E. Sharpe, 80 Business Park Drive, Armonk, New York 10504 (800) 541-6563; *The Illustrated Book of World Rankings.*

St. Martin's Press, Inc., 175 Fifth Avenue, New York, New York 10010 (800) 221-7945; *The Statesman's Year-Book.*

Statistical Office of the United Nations, Publishing Service, New York, New York 10017 (800) 253-9646; *Statistical Yearbook.*

United Nations Educational, Scientific and Cultural Organization (UNESCO), 7 Place de Fontenoy, F-75700 Paris, France (Telephone in U.S. (212) 963-5981); *Statistical Yearbook.*

KOREA (REPUBLIC OF) - ARMS EXPORTS AND IMPORTS - See KOREA (REPUBLIC OF) - MILITARY

KOREA (REPUBLIC OF) - BALANCE OF PAYMENTS

The Economist Intelligence Unit, 111 West 57th Street, New York, New York 10019 (800) 938-4685; *The World Market Atlas.*

Europa Publications Limited, 18 Bedford Square, London, WC1B 3JN, England; *The Europa World Year Book.*

International Monetary Fund, 700 Nineteenth Street, NW, Washington, D.C. 20431 (202) 623-7000; *Balance of Payments Yearbook.*

Korean Overseas Information Service, Ministry of Culture and Information, Seoul 110, Republic of Korea; *Statistical Data on Korea.*

United Nations Conference on Trade and Development (UNCTAD), New York, New York 10017 (800) 253-9646; *Handbook of International Trade and Development Statistics.*

The World Bank, 1818 H Street, NW, Washington, D.C. 20433 (202) 477-1234; *World Development Indicators.*

KOREA (REPUBLIC OF) - BANKING

Euromonitor International, Inc., 122

South Michigan Avenue, Suite 1200, Chicago, Illinois 60603 (800) 577-EURO; *World Marketing Data and Statistics.*

Europa Publications Limited, 18 Bedford Square, London, WC1B 3JN, England; *The Europa World Year Book.*

International Monetary Fund, 700 Nineteenth Street, NW, Washington, D.C. 20431 (202) 623-7000; *International Financial Statistics.*

Korean Overseas Information Service, Ministry of Culture and Information, Seoul 110, Republic of Korea; *Statistical Data on Korea.*

M.E. Sharpe, 80 Business Park Drive, Armonk, New York 10504 (800) 541-6563; *The Illustrated Book of World Rankings.*

St. Martin's Press, Inc., 175 Fifth Avenue, New York, New York 10010 (800) 221-7945; *The Statesman's Year-Book.*

Statistical Office of the United Nations, Publishing Service, New York, New York 10017 (800) 253-9646; *Statistical Yearbook.*

KOREA (REPUBLIC OF) - BARLEY PRODUCTION - See KOREA (REPUBLIC OF) - CROPS

KOREA (REPUBLIC OF) - BEER PRODUCTION - See KOREA (REPUBLIC OF) - BEVERAGES

KOREA (REPUBLIC OF) - BEES

Korean Overseas Information Service, Ministry of Culture and Information, Seoul 110, Republic of Korea; *Statistical Data on Korea.*

KOREA (REPUBLIC OF) - BEVERAGES

M.E. Sharpe, 80 Business Park Drive, Armonk, New York 10504 (800) 541-6563; *The Illustrated Book of World Rankings.*

Statistical Office of the United Nations, Publishing Service, New York, New York 10017 (800) 253-9646; *Statistical Yearbook.*

KOREA (REPUBLIC OF) - BIRTH RATES

Central Intelligence Agency, Washington, D.C. 20505 (703) 482-1100, www.cia.gov; *The World Factbook.*

The Economist Intelligence Unit (Asia) Limited, 10th Floor, Luk Kwok Centre, 72 Gloucester Road, Wanchai, Hong Kong (Phone Number in U.S. (800) 938-4685); *Asian Market Atlas.*

Euromonitor International, Inc., 122 South Michigan Avenue, Suite 1200, Chicago, Illinois 60603 (800) 577-EURO; *International Marketing Data and Statistics;*

and *The World Economic Factbook.*

Europa Publications Limited, 18 Bedford Square, London, WC1B 3JN, England; *The Europa World Year Book.*

M.E. Sharpe, 80 Business Park Drive, Armonk, New York 10504 (800) 541-6563; *The Illustrated Book of World Rankings.*

St. Martin's Press, Inc., 175 Fifth Avenue, New York, New York 10010 (800) 221-7945; *The Statesman's Year-Book.*

Statistical Office of the United Nations, Publishing Service, New York, New York 10017 (800) 253-9646; *Asia-Pacific in Figures; Demographic Yearbook;* and *Statistical Yearbook.*

The World Bank, 1818 H Street, NW, Washington, D.C. 20433 (202) 477-1234; *World Development Indicators.*

KOREA (REPUBLIC OF) - BOOK PRODUCTION

Europa Publications Limited, 18 Bedford Square, London, WC1B 3JN, England; *The Europa World Year Book.*

St. Martin's Press, Inc., 175 Fifth Avenue, New York, New York 10010 (800) 221-7945; *The Statesman's Year-Book.*

United Nations Educational, Scientific and Cultural Organization (UNESCO), 7 Place de Fontenoy, F-75700 Paris, France (Telephone in U.S. (212) 963-5981); *Statistical Yearbook.*

KOREA (REPUBLIC OF) - BROADCASTING

Billboard Limited, Post Office Box 9027, 1006 AA Amsterdam, The Netherlands (Telephone Number in U.S. (212) 764-7300); *World Radio TV Handbook.*

Central Intelligence Agency, Washington, D.C. 20505 (703) 482-1100, www.cia.gov; *The World Factbook.*

The Economist Intelligence Unit (Asia) Limited, 10th Floor, Luk Kwok Centre, 72 Gloucester Road, Wanchai, Hong Kong (Phone Number in U.S. (800) 938-4685); *Asian Market Atlas.*

Euromonitor International, Inc., 122 South Michigan Avenue, Suite 1200, Chicago, Illinois 60603 (800) 577-EURO; *World Marketing Data and Statistics.*

M.E. Sharpe, 80 Business Park Drive, Armonk, New York 10504 (800) 541-6563; *The Illustrated Book of World Rankings.*

St. Martin's Press, Inc., 175 Fifth Avenue, New York, New York 10010 (800) 221-7945; *The Statesman's Year-Book.*

United Nations Educational, Scientific and Cultural Organization (UNESCO), 7 Place de Fontenoy, F-75700 Paris, France (Telephone in U.S. (212) 963-5981); *Statistical Yearbook.*

KOREA (REPUBLIC OF) - BUDGET

Central Intelligence Agency, Washington, D.C. 20505 (703) 482-1100, www.cia.gov; *The World Factbook.*

KOREA (REPUBLIC OF) - CABBAGE PRODUCTION - See KOREA (REPUBLIC OF) - CROPS

KOREA (REPUBLIC OF) - CALORIE INTAKE

Korean Overseas Information Service, Ministry of Culture and Information, Seoul 110, Republic of Korea; *Statistical Data on Korea.*

KOREA (REPUBLIC OF) - CALORIE SUPPLY

Food and Agricultural Organization of the United Nations (FAO), Via delle Terme di Caracalla, 00100 Rome, Italy (Telephone Number in U.S. (202) 653-2400); *The State of Food and Agriculture.*

KOREA (REPUBLIC OF) - CASTOR BEAN PRODUCTION - See KOREA (REPUBLIC OF) - CROPS

KOREA (REPUBLIC OF) - CATTLE - See KOREA (REPUBLIC OF) - LIVESTOCK AND POULTRY

KOREA (REPUBLIC OF) - CAUSTIC SODA PRODUCTION - See KOREA (REPUBLIC OF) - BEVERAGES

KOREA (REPUBLIC OF) - CEMENT PRODUCTION - See KOREA (REPUBLIC OF) - MINING AND MINERAL PRODUCTS

KOREA (REPUBLIC OF) - CHEMICAL (ORGANIC) PRODUCTION - See KOREA (REPUBLIC OF) - MINING AND MINERAL PRODUCTS

KOREA (REPUBLIC OF) - CHESTNUT PRODUCTION - See KOREA (REPUBLIC OF) - CROPS

KOREA (REPUBLIC OF) - CHICKENS - See KOREA (REPUBLIC OF) - LIVESTOCK AND POULTRY

KOREA (REPUBLIC OF) - CIGARETTE PRODUCTION - See KOREA (REPUBLIC OF) - TOBACCO PRODUCTION

KOREA (REPUBLIC OF) - CLIMATE

Korean Overseas Information Service, Ministry of Culture and Information, Seoul 110, Republic of Korea; *Statistical Data on Korea.*

M.E. Sharpe, 80 Business Park Drive, Armonk, New York 10504 (800) 541-6563; *The Illustrated Book of World Rankings.*

St. Martin's Press, Inc., 175 Fifth Avenue, New York, New York 10010 (800) 221-7945; *The Statesman's Year-Book.*

KOREA (REPUBLIC OF) - CLOTHING EXPENDITURES

Korean Overseas Information Service, Ministry of Culture and Information, Seoul 110, Republic of Korea; *Statistical Data on Korea.*

KOREA (REPUBLIC OF) - COAL PRODUCTION - See KOREA (REPUBLIC OF) - MINING AND MINERAL PRODUCTS

KOREA (REPUBLIC OF) - COFFEE PRODUCTION AND CONSUMPTION - See KOREA (REPUBLIC OF) - CROPS

KOREA (REPUBLIC OF) - COKE OVEN COKE PRODUCTION AND CONSUMPTION - See KOREA (REPUBLIC OF) - MINING AND MINERAL PRODUCTS

KOREA (REPUBLIC OF) - COMMERCE

St. Martin's Press, Inc., 175 Fifth Avenue, New York, New York 10010 (800) 221-7945; *The Statesman's Year-Book.*

KOREA (REPUBLIC OF) - COMMUNICATION EXPENDITURES

Korean Overseas Information Service, Ministry of Culture and Information, Seoul 110, Republic of Korea; *Statistical Data on Korea.*

KOREA (REPUBLIC OF) - COMMUNICATIONS - See KOREA (REPUBLIC OF) - TRANSPORTATION AND COMMUNICATIONS

KOREA (REPUBLIC OF) - CONSTRUCTION INDUSTRY

M.E. Sharpe, 80 Business Park Drive, Armonk, New York 10504 (800) 541-6563; *The Illustrated Book of World Rankings.*

St. Martin's Press, Inc., 175 Fifth Avenue, New York, New York 10010 (800) 221-7945; *The Statesman's Year-Book.*

Statistical Office of the United Nations, Publishing Service, New York, New York 10017 (800) 253-9646; *Statistical Yearbook.*

KOREA (REPUBLIC OF) - CONSUMER PRICE INDEX

Europa Publications Limited, 18 Bedford Square, London, WC1B 3JN, England; *The Europa World Year Book.*

Statistical Office of the United Nations,

Publishing Service, New York, New York 10017 (800) 253-9646; *Statistical Yearbook.*

KOREA (REPUBLIC OF) - CONSUMER PRICES

Euromonitor International, Inc., 122 South Michigan Avenue, Suite 1200, Chicago, Illinois 60603 (800) 577-EURO; *World Marketing Data and Statistics.*

International Labour Office, I.L.O. Publications, 1828 L Street, N.W., Suite 801, Washington, D.C. 20036 (301) 638-3152; *Yearbook of Labour Statistics.*

KOREA (REPUBLIC OF) - CONSUMPTION EXPENDITURES

Korean Overseas Information Service, Ministry of Culture and Information, Seoul 110, Republic of Korea; *Statistical Data on Korea.*

KOREA (REPUBLIC OF) - COPPER - See (KOREA - REPUBLIC OF) - MINING AND MINERAL PRODUCTS

KOREA (REPUBLIC OF) - CORN PRODUCTION - See KOREA (REPUBLIC OF) - CROPS

KOREA (REPUBLIC OF) - CORPORATE TAXES - See KOREA (REPUBLIC OF) - TAXATION

KOREA (REPUBLIC OF) - COTTON - See KOREA (REPUBLIC OF) - CROPS

KOREA (REPUBLIC OF) - CROPS

Europa Publications Limited, 18 Bedford Square, London, WC1B 3JN, England; *The Europa World Year Book.*

Food and Agricultural Organization of the United Nations (FAO), Via delle Terme di Caracalla, 00100 Rome, Italy (Telephone Number in U.S. (202) 653-2400); *The State of Food and Agriculture;* and *Production Yearbook.*

M.E. Sharpe, 80 Business Park Drive, Armonk, New York 10504 (800) 541-6563; *The Illustrated Book of World Rankings.*

St. Martin's Press, Inc., 175 Fifth Avenue, New York, New York 10010 (800) 221-7945; *The Statesman's Year-Book.*

Statistical Office of the United Nations, Publishing Service, New York, New York 10017 (800) 253-9646; *Statistical Yearbook.*

United Nations Conference on Trade and Development, Central Statistical Service, Palais des Nations, Geneva, Switzerland (Telephone in U.S. (800) 253-9646); *UNCTAD Commodity Yearbook.*

KOREA (REPUBLIC OF) - CULTURAL

ASSETS

Korean Overseas Information Service, Ministry of Culture and Information, Seoul 110, Republic of Korea; *Statistical Data on Korea.*

KOREA (REPUBLIC OF) - CUSTOMS DUTIES

St. Martin's Press, Inc., 175 Fifth Avenue, New York, New York 10010 (800) 221-7945; *The Statesman's Year-Book.*

KOREA (REPUBLIC OF) - DAIRY PRODUCTS

Europa Publications Limited, 18 Bedford Square, London, WC1B 3JN, England; *The Europa World Year Book.*

Food and Agricultural Organization of the United Nations (FAO), Via delle Terme di Caracalla, 00100 Rome, Italy (Telephone Number in U.S. (202) 653-2400); *Production Yearbook;* and *The State of Food and Agriculture.*

M.E. Sharpe, 80 Business Park Drive, Armonk, New York 10504 (800) 541-6563; *The Illustrated Book of World Rankings.*

St. Martin's Press, Inc., 175 Fifth Avenue, New York, New York 10010 (800) 221-7945; *The Statesman's Year-Book.*

Statistical Office of the United Nations, Publishing Service, New York, New York 10017 (800) 253-9646; *Statistical Yearbook.*

KOREA (REPUBLIC OF) - DEATH RATES - See KOREA (REPUBLIC OF) - MORTALITY

KOREA (REPUBLIC OF) - DEFENSE EXPENDITURES - See KOREA (REPUBLIC OF) - MILITARY

KOREA (REPUBLIC OF) - DEMOGRAPHY

The Economist Intelligence Unit, 111 West 57th Street, New York, New York 10019 (800) 938-4685; *The World Market Atlas.*

The Economist Intelligence Unit (Asia) Limited, 10th Floor, Luk Kwok Centre, 72 Gloucester Road, Wanchai, Hong Kong (Phone Number in U.S. (800) 938-4685); *Asian Market Atlas.*

Euromonitor International, Inc., 122 South Michigan Avenue, Suite 1200, Chicago, Illinois 60603 (800) 577-EURO; *International Marketing Data and Statistics; World Marketing Data and Statistics;* and *The World Economic Factbook.*

M.E. Sharpe, 80 Business Park Drive, Armonk, New York 10504 (800) 541-6563; *The Illustrated Book of World Rankings.*

Statistical Office of the United Nations, Publishing Service, New York, New York 10017 (800) 253-9646; *Asia-Pacific in Figures;* and *Human Development Report.*

KOREA (REPUBLIC OF) - DEVELOPMENT ASSISTANCE

Statistical Office of the United Nations, Publishing Service, New York, New York 10017 (800) 253-9646; *Statistical Yearbook.*

KOREA (REPUBLIC OF) - DIAMOND PRODUCTION - See KOREA (REPUBLIC OF) - MINING AND MINERAL PRODUCTS

KOREA (REPUBLIC OF) - DISCOUNT RATES - See KOREA (REPUBLIC OF) - BANKING

KOREA (REPUBLIC OF) - DISEASES - See KOREA (REPUBLIC OF) - HEALTH

KOREA (REPUBLIC OF) - DIVORCE RATES

M.E. Sharpe, 80 Business Park Drive, Armonk, New York 10504 (800) 541-6563; *The Illustrated Book of World Rankings.*

Statistical Office of the United Nations, Publishing Service, New York, New York 10017 (800) 253-9646; *Demographic Yearbook;* and *Statistical Yearbook.*

KOREA (REPUBLIC OF) - DOGS

Korean Overseas Information Service, Ministry of Culture and Information, Seoul 110, Republic of Korea; *Statistical Data on Korea.*

KOREA (REPUBLIC OF) - DUCKS - See KOREA (REPUBLIC OF) - LIVESTOCK AND POULTRY

KOREA (REPUBLIC OF) - ECONOMY

Central Intelligence Agency, Washington, D.C. 20505 (703) 482-1100, www.cia.gov; *The World Factbook.*

Economist Intelligence Unit, 111 West 57th Street, New York, New York 10019 (800) 938-4685; *Korea (South) Country Report.*

Euromonitor International, Inc., 122 South Michigan Avenue, Suite 1200, Chicago, Illinois 60603 (800) 577-EURO; *International Marketing Data and Statistics; World Marketing Data and Statistics;* and *The World Economic Factbook.*

Europa Publications Limited, 18 Bedford Square, London, WC1B 3JN, England; *The Europa World Year Book.*

M.E. Sharpe, 80 Business Park Drive, Armonk, New York 10504 (800) 541-6563; *The Illustrated Book of World Rankings.*

St. Martin's Press, Inc., 175 Fifth Avenue, New York, New York 10010 (800) 221-7945; *The Statesman's Year-Book.*

Statistical Office of the United Nations, Publishing Service, New York, New York 10017 (800) 253-9646; *World Statistics Pocketbook.*

The World Bank, 1818 H Street, NW, Washington, D.C. 20433 (202) 477-1234; *The World Bank Atlas.*

KOREA (REPUBLIC OF) - EDUCATION

The Economist Intelligence Unit, 111 West 57th Street, New York, New York 10019 (800) 938-4685; *The World Market Atlas.*

The Economist Intelligence Unit (Asia) Limited, 10th Floor, Luk Kwok Centre, 72 Gloucester Road, Wanchai, Hong Kong (Phone Number in U.S. (800) 938-4685); *Asian Market Atlas.*

Euromonitor International, Inc., 122 South Michigan Avenue, Suite 1200, Chicago, Illinois 60603 (800) 577-EURO; *International Marketing Data and Statistics;* and *World Marketing Data and Statistics.*

Europa Publications Limited, 18 Bedford Square, London, WC1B 3JN, England; *The Europa World Year Book.*

Korean Overseas Information Service, Ministry of Culture and Information, Seoul 110, Republic of Korea; *Statistical Data on Korea.*

M.E. Sharpe, 80 Business Park Drive, Armonk, New York 10504 (800) 541-6563; *The Illustrated Book of World Rankings.*

St. Martin's Press, Inc., 175 Fifth Avenue, New York, New York 10010 (800) 221-7945; *The Statesman's Year-Book.*

Statistical Office of the United Nations, Publishing Service, New York, New York 10017 (800) 253-9646; *Asia-Pacific in Figures; Human Development Report;* and *Statistical Yearbook For Asia and the Pacific.*

United Nations Educational, Scientific and Cultural Organization (UNESCO), 7 Place de Fontenoy, F-75700 Paris, France (Telephone in U.S. (212) 963-5981); *Statistical Yearbook.*

The World Bank, 1818 H Street, NW, Washington, D.C. 20433 (202) 477-1234; *World Development Indicators.*

KOREA (REPUBLIC OF) - EGG PRODUCTION - See KOREA (REPUBLIC OF) - DAIRY PRODUCTS

KOREA (REPUBLIC OF) - EGGPLANT PRODUCTION - See KOREA (REPUBLIC OF) - CROPS

KOREA (REPUBLIC OF) - ELECTRICITY

Central Intelligence Agency, Washington, D.C. 20505 (703) 482-1100, www.cia.gov; *The World Factbook.*

Korean Overseas Information Service, Ministry of Culture and Information, Seoul 110, Republic of Korea; *Statistical Data on Korea.*

M.E. Sharpe, 80 Business Park Drive, Armonk, New York 10504 (800) 541-6563; *The Illustrated Book of World Rankings.*

St. Martin's Press, Inc., 175 Fifth Avenue, New York, New York 10010 (800) 221-7945; *The Statesman's Year-Book.*

Statistical Office of the United Nations, Publishing Service, New York, New York 10017 (800) 253-9646; *Human Development Report;* and *Statistical Yearbook.*

KOREA (REPUBLIC OF) - EMPLOYMENT

Euromonitor International, Inc., 122 South Michigan Avenue, Suite 1200, Chicago, Illinois 60603 (800) 577-EURO; *International Marketing Data and Statistics.*

International Labour Office, I.L.O. Publications, 1828 L Street, N.W., Suite 801, Washington, D.C. 20036 (301) 638-3152; *Yearbook of Labour Statistics.*

Korean Overseas Information Service, Ministry of Culture and Information, Seoul 110, Republic of Korea; *Statistical Data on Korea.*

M.E. Sharpe, 80 Business Park Drive, Armonk, New York 10504 (800) 541-6563; *The Illustrated Book of World Rankings.*

Statistical Office of the United Nations, Publishing Service, New York, New York 10017 (800) 253-9646; *Asia-Pacific in Figures;* and *Statistical Yearbook.*

KOREA (REPUBLIC OF) - ENERGY

Business Information Display, Incorporated, 4202 Sorrento Valley Boulevard, San Diego, California 92121; *World Energy Industry.*

Euromonitor International, Inc., 122 South Michigan Avenue, Suite 1200, Chicago, Illinois 60603 (800) 577-EURO; *International Marketing Data and Statistics; World Marketing Data and Statistics;* and *The World Economic Factbook.*

Food and Agricultural Organization of the United Nations (FAO), Via delle Terme di Caracalla, 00100 Rome, Italy (Telephone

Number in U.S. (202) 653-2400); *The State of Food and Agriculture.*

M.E. Sharpe, 80 Business Park Drive, Armonk, New York 10504 (800) 541-6563; *The Illustrated Book of World Rankings.*

St. Martin's Press, Inc., 175 Fifth Avenue, New York, New York 10010 (800) 221-7945; *The Statesman's Year-Book.*

Statistical Office of the United Nations, Publishing Service, New York, New York 10017 (800) 253-9646; *Asia-Pacific in Figures; Energy Statistics Yearbook; Human Development Report; Statistical Yearbook for Asia and the Pacific; World Statistics Pocketbook;* and *Statistical Yearbook.*

The World Bank, 1818 H Street, NW, Washington, D.C. 20433 (202) 477-1234; *The World Bank Atlas.*

KOREA (REPUBLIC OF) - ENVIRONMENT

Economist Intelligence Unit, 111 West 57th Street, New York, New York 10019 (800) 938-4685; *Korea (South) Country Report.*

Statistical Office of the United Nations, Publishing Service, New York, New York 10017 (800) 253-9646; *World Statistics Pocketbook.*

KOREA (REPUBLIC OF) - EXCHANGE RATES

Central Intelligence Agency, Washington, D.C. 20505 (703) 482-1100, www.cia.gov; *The World Factbook.*

The Economist Intelligence Unit (Asia) Limited, 10th Floor, Luk Kwok Centre, 72 Gloucester Road, Wanchai, Hong Kong (Phone Number in U.S. (800) 938-4685); *Asian Market Atlas.*

Euromonitor International, Inc., 122 South Michigan Avenue, Suite 1200, Chicago, Illinois 60603 (800) 577-EURO; *International Marketing Data and Statistics;* and *The World Economic Factbook.*

Europa Publications Limited, 18 Bedford Square, London, WC1B 3JN, England; *The Europa World Year Book.*

International Civil Aviation Organization, 999 University Street, Montreal, Quebec, Canada H3C 5H7 (514) 285-8219; *Civil Aviation Statistics of the World.*

Statistical Office of the United Nations, Publishing Service, New York, New York 10017 (800) 253-9646; *Statistical Yearbook;* and *World Statistics Pocketbook.*

Walden Publishing, Ltd., Two Market

Street, Saffron Walden Essex, CB10 1HZ, England; *The World of Information Asia and Pacific Review.*

KOREA (REPUBLIC OF) - EXPENDITURES PER HOUSEHOLD

Korean Overseas Information Service, Ministry of Culture and Information, Seoul 110, Republic of Korea; *Statistical Data on Korea.*

KOREA (REPUBLIC OF) - EXPORTS

Central Intelligence Agency, Washington, D.C. 20505 (703) 482-1100, www.cia.gov; *The World Factbook.*

The Economist Intelligence Unit, 111 West 57th Street, New York, New York 10019 (800) 938-4685; *Korea (South) Country Report; and The World Market Atlas.*

The Economist Intelligence Unit (Asia) Limited, 10th Floor, Luk Kwok Centre, 72 Gloucester Road, Wanchai, Hong Kong (Phone Number in U.S. (800) 938-4685); *Asian Market Atlas.*

Euromonitor International, Inc., 122 South Michigan Avenue, Suite 1200, Chicago, Illinois 60603 (800) 577-EURO; *International Marketing Data and Statistics;* and *The World Economic Factbook.*

Europa Publications Limited, 18 Bedford Square, London, WC1B 3JN, England; *The Europa World Year Book.*

Food and Agricultural Organization of the United Nations (FAO), Via delle Terme di Caracalla, 00100 Rome, Italy (Telephone Number in U.S. (202) 653-2400); *The State of Food and Agriculture.*

International Monetary Fund, 700 Nineteenth Street, NW, Washington, D.C. 20431 (202) 623-7000; *Direction of Trade Statistics.*

Korean Overseas Information Service, Ministry of Culture and Information, Seoul 110, Republic of Korea; *Statistical Data on Korea.*

St. Martin's Press, Inc., 175 Fifth Avenue, New York, New York 10010 (800) 221-7945; *The Statesman's Year-Book.*

United Nations Conference on Trade and Development (UNCTAD), New York, New York 10017 (800) 253-9646; *Handbook of International Trade and Development Statistics.*

Walden Publishing, Ltd., Two Market Street, Saffron Walden Essex, CB10 1HZ, England; *The World of Information Asia and Pacific Review.*

The World Bank, 1818 H Street, NW, Washington, D.C. 20433 (202) 477-1234; *World Development Indicators.*

KOREA (REPUBLIC OF) - EXTERNAL INDEBTEDNESS

The World Bank, 1818 H Street, NW, Washington, D.C. 20433 (202) 477-1234; *World Development Indicators.*

KOREA (REPUBLIC OF) - EXTERNAL TRADE

Euromonitor International, Inc., 122 South Michigan Avenue, Suite 1200, Chicago, Illinois 60603 (800) 577-EURO; *World Marketing Data and Statistics.*

Food and Agricultural Organization of the United Nations (FAO), Via delle Terme di Caracalla, 00100 Rome, Italy (Telephone Number in U.S. (202) 653-2400); *The State of Food and Agriculture;* and *Trade Yearbook.*

Statistical Office of the United Nations, Publishing Service, New York, New York 10017 (800) 253-9646; *Asia-Pacific in Figures; Statistical Yearbook;* and *Statistical Yearbook for Asia and the Pacific.*

KOREA (REPUBLIC OF) - FABRIC PRODUCTION - See KOREA (REPUBLIC OF) - TEXTILE INDUSTRY

KOREA (REPUBLIC OF) - FARM CROPS - See KOREA (REPUBLIC OF) - CROPS

KOREA (REPUBLIC OF) - FARM POPULATION

Korean Overseas Information Service, Ministry of Culture and Information, Seoul 110, Republic of Korea; *Statistical Data on Korea.*

KOREA (REPUBLIC OF) - FEMALE WORKING POPULATION - See KOREA (REPUBLIC OF) - EMPLOYMENT

KOREA (REPUBLIC OF) - FERTILITY RATES

Central Intelligence Agency, Washington, D.C. 20505 (703) 482-1100, www.cia.gov; *The World Factbook.*

The Economist Intelligence Unit (Asia) Limited, 10th Floor, Luk Kwok Centre, 72 Gloucester Road, Wanchai, Hong Kong (Phone Number in U.S. (800) 938-4685); *Asian Market Atlas.*

M.E. Sharpe, 80 Business Park Drive, Armonk, New York 10504 (800) 541-6563; *The Illustrated Book of World Rankings.*

Statistical Office of the United Nations, Publishing Service, New York, New York 10017 (800) 253-9646; *Human Development Report.*

The World Bank, 1818 H Street, NW, Washington, D.C. 20433 (202) 477-1234; *The World Bank Atlas;* and *World Development Indicators.*

KOREA (REPUBLIC OF) - FERTILIZER

Food and Agricultural Organization of the United Nations (FAO), Via delle Terme di Caracalla, 00100 Rome, Italy (Telephone Number in U.S. (202) 653-2400); *Fertilizer Yearbook;* and *The State of Food and Agriculture.*

Korean Overseas Information Service, Ministry of Culture and Information, Seoul 110, Republic of Korea; *Statistical Data on Korea.*

Statistical Office of the United Nations, Publishing Service, New York, New York 10017 (800) 253-9646; *Statistical Yearbook.*

KOREA (REPUBLIC OF) - FETAL MORTALITY - See KOREA (REPUBLIC OF) - MORTALITY

KOREA (REPUBLIC OF) - FIBRE PRODUCTION - See KOREA (REPUBLIC OF) - TEXTILE INDUSTRY

KOREA (REPUBLIC OF) - FILAMENT PRODUCTION - See KOREA (REPUBLIC OF) - TEXTILE INDUSTRY

KOREA (REPUBLIC OF) - FILM - See KOREA (REPUBLIC OF) - MOTION PICTURES

KOREA (REPUBLIC OF) - FINANCE

Economist Intelligence Unit, 111 West 57th Street, New York, New York 10019 (800) 938-4685; *Korea (South) Country Report.*

Europa Publications Limited, 18 Bedford Square, London, WC1B 3JN, England; *The Europa World Year Book.*

International Monetary Fund, 700 Nineteenth Street, NW, Washington, D.C. 20431 (202) 623-7000; *International Financial Statistics.*

M.E. Sharpe, 80 Business Park Drive, Armonk, New York 10504 (800) 541-6563; *The Illustrated Book of World Rankings.*

St. Martin's Press, Inc., 175 Fifth Avenue, New York, New York 10010 (800) 221-7945; *The Statesman's Year-Book.*

Statistical Office of the United Nations, Publishing Service, New York, New York 10017 (800) 253-9646; *Statistical Yearbook for Asia and the Pacific.*

KOREA (REPUBLIC OF) - FISHERIES

Europa Publications Limited, 18

Bedford Square, London, WC1B 3JN, England; *The Europa World Year Book.*

Food and Agricultural Organization of the United Nations (FAO), Via delle Terme di Caracalla, 00100 Rome, Italy (Telephone Number in U.S. (202) 653-2400); *The State of Food and Agriculture;* and *Yearbook of Fishery Statistics.*

Korean Overseas Information Service, Ministry of Culture and Information, Seoul 110, Republic of Korea; *Statistical Data on Korea.*

M.E. Sharpe, 80 Business Park Drive, Armonk, New York 10504 (800) 541-6563; *The Illustrated Book of World Rankings.*

St. Martin's Press, Inc., 175 Fifth Avenue, New York, New York 10010 (800) 221-7945; *The Statesman's Year-Book.*

Statistical Office of the United Nations, Publishing Service, New York, New York 10017 (800) 253-9646; *Statistical Yearbook.*

United Nations Conference on Trade and Development, Central Statistical Service, Palais des Nations, Geneva, Switzerland (Telephone in U.S. (800) 253-9646); *UNCTAD Commodity Yearbook.*

KOREA (REPUBLIC OF) - FLAX FIBRE PRODUCTION - See KOREA (REPUBLIC OF) - TEXTILE INDUSTRY

KOREA (REPUBLIC OF) - FLOUR PRODUCTION

Statistical Office of the United Nations, Publishing Service, New York, New York 10017 (800) 253-9646; *Statistical Yearbook.*

KOREA (REPUBLIC OF) - FOOD

Euromonitor International, Inc., 122 South Michigan Avenue, Suite 1200, Chicago, Illinois 60603 (800) 577-EURO; *Retail Trade International.*

Food and Agricultural Organization of the United Nations (FAO), Via delle Terme di Caracalla, 00100 Rome, Italy (Telephone Number in U.S. (202) 653-2400); *The State of Food and Agriculture;* and *Production Yearbook.*

Korean Overseas Information Service, Ministry of Culture and Information, Seoul 110, Republic of Korea; *Statistical Data on Korea.*

Statistical Office of the United Nations, Publishing Service, New York, New York 10017 (800) 253-9646; *Human Development Report;* and *Statistical Yearbook for Asia and the Pacific.*

United Nations Conference on Trade and Development, Central Statistical

Service, Palais des Nations, Geneva, Switzerland (Telephone in U.S. (800) 253-9646); *UNCTAD Commodity Yearbook.*

KOREA (REPUBLIC OF) - FOOTWEAR EXPENDITURES

Korean Overseas Information Service, Ministry of Culture and Information, Seoul 110, Republic of Korea; *Statistical Data on Korea.*

KOREA (REPUBLIC OF) - FOREIGN DEBT

St. Martin's Press, Inc., 175 Fifth Avenue, New York, New York 10010 (800) 221-7945; *The Statesman's Year-Book.*

Walden Publishing, Ltd., Two Market Street, Saffron Walden Essex, CB10 1HZ, England; *The World of Information Asia and Pacific Review.*

KOREA (REPUBLIC OF) - FOREIGN HOUSEHOLDS

Korean Overseas Information Service, Ministry of Culture and Information, Seoul 110, Republic of Korea; *Statistical Data on Korea.*

KOREA (REPUBLIC OF) - FOREIGN INVESTMENTS

Korean Overseas Information Service, Ministry of Culture and Information, Seoul 110, Republic of Korea; *Statistical Data on Korea.*

KOREA (REPUBLIC OF) - FOREIGN TRADE

Economist Intelligence Unit, 111 West 57th Street, New York, New York 10019 (800) 938-4685; *Korea (South) Country Report.*

The Economist Intelligence Unit (Asia) Limited, 10th Floor, Luk Kwok Centre, 72 Gloucester Road, Wanchai, Hong Kong (Phone Number in U.S. (800) 938-4685); *Asian Market Atlas.*

Euromonitor International, Inc., 122 South Michigan Avenue, Suite 1200, Chicago, Illinois 60603 (800) 577-EURO; *The World Economic Factbook.*

Europa Publications Limited, 18 Bedford Square, London, WC1B 3JN, England; *The Europa World Year Book.*

Food and Agricultural Organization of the United Nations (FAO), Via delle Terme di Caracalla, 00100 Rome, Italy (Telephone Number in U.S. (202) 653-2400); *The State of Food and Agriculture.*

M.E. Sharpe, 80 Business Park Drive, Armonk, New York 10504 (800) 541-6563; *The Illustrated Book of World Rankings.*

St. Martin's Press, Inc., 175 Fifth Avenue, New York, New York 10010 (800) 221-7945; *The Statesman's Year-Book*.

Statistical Office of the United Nations, Publishing Service, New York, New York 10017 (800) 253-9646; *International Trade Statistics Yearbook;* and *Statistical Yearbook*.

United Nations Conference on Trade and Development, Central Statistical Service, Palais des Nations, Geneva, Switzerland (Telephone in U.S. (800) 253-9646); *UNCTAD Commodity Yearbook*.

KOREA (REPUBLIC OF) - FORESTRY AND FOREST PRODUCTS

The Economist Intelligence Unit (Asia) Limited, 10th Floor, Luk Kwok Centre, 72 Gloucester Road, Wanchai, Hong Kong (Phone Number in U.S. (800) 938-4685); *Asian Market Atlas*.

Europa Publications Limited, 18 Bedford Square, London, WC1B 3JN, England; *The Europa World Year Book*.

Food and Agricultural Organization of the United Nations (FAO), Via delle Terme di Caracalla, 00100 Rome, Italy (Telephone Number in U.S. (202) 653-2400); *The State of Food and Agriculture;* and *Yearbook of Forest Products*.

Korean Overseas Information Service, Ministry of Culture and Information, Seoul 110, Republic of Korea; *Statistical Data on Korea*.

M.E. Sharpe, 80 Business Park Drive, Armonk, New York 10504 (800) 541-6563; *The Illustrated Book of World Rankings*.

St. Martin's Press, Inc., 175 Fifth Avenue, New York, New York 10010 (800) 221-7945; *The Statesman's Year-Book*.

Statistical Office of the United Nations, Publishing Service, New York, New York 10017 (800) 253-9646; *Statistical Yearbook*.

United Nations Conference on Trade and Development, Central Statistical Service, Palais des Nations, Geneva, Switzerland (Telephone in U.S. (800) 253-9646); *UNCTAD Commodity Yearbook*.

United Nations Educational, Scientific and Cultural Organization (UNESCO), 7 Place de Fontenoy, F-75700 Paris, France (Telephone in U.S. (212) 963-5981); *Statistical Yearbook*.

KOREA (REPUBLIC OF) - FURNITURE AND WOOD PRODUCTS EXPORTS AND IMPORTS

Statistical Office of the United Nations, Publishing Service, New York, New York

10017 (800) 253-9646; *International Trade Statistics Yearbook*.

KOREA (REPUBLIC OF) - FURNITURE EXPENDITURES

Korean Overseas Information Service, Ministry of Culture and Information, Seoul 110, Republic of Korea; *Statistical Data on Korea*.

KOREA (REPUBLIC OF) - GARLIC PRODUCTION - See KOREA (REPUBLIC OF) - CROPS

KOREA (REPUBLIC OF) - GAS PRODUCTION - See KOREA (REPUBLIC OF) - MINING AND MINERAL PRODUCTS

KOREA (REPUBLIC OF) - GENERAL INDUSTRIAL STATISTICS - See KOREA (REPUBLIC OF) - INDUSTRY

KOREA (REPUBLIC OF) - GENERAL MORTALITY - See KOREA (REPUBLIC OF) - MORTALITY

KOREA (REPUBLIC OF) - GEOGRAPHIC DATA

M.E. Sharpe, 80 Business Park Drive, Armonk, New York 10504 (800) 541-6563; *The Illustrated Book of World Rankings*.

KOREA (REPUBLIC OF) - GOATS - See KOREA (REPUBLIC OF) - LIVESTOCK AND POULTRY

KOREA (REPUBLIC OF) - GOLD HOLDINGS

Statistical Office of the United Nations, Publishing Service, New York, New York 10017 (800) 253-9646; *Statistical Yearbook*.

The World Bank, 1818 H Street, NW, Washington, D.C. 20433 (202) 477-1234; *World Development Indicators*.

KOREA (REPUBLIC OF) - GOLD PRODUCTION AND CONSUMPTION - See (JORDAN) - MINING AND MINERAL PRODUCTS

KOREA (REPUBLIC OF) - GOVERNMENT

Central Intelligence Agency, Washington, D.C. 20505 (703) 482-1100, www.cia.gov; *The World Factbook*.

Europa Publications Limited, 18 Bedford Square, London, WC1B 3JN, England; *The Europa World Year Book*.

St. Martin's Press, Inc., 175 Fifth Avenue, New York, New York 10010 (800) 221-7945; *The Statesman's Year-Book*.

Statistical Office of the United Nations, Publishing Service, New York, New York 10017 (800) 253-9646; *Asia-Pacific in Figures; National Accounts Statistics;* and

Statistical Yearbook.

The World Bank, 1818 H Street, NW, Washington, D.C. 20433 (202) 477-1234; *World Development Indicators*.

KOREA (REPUBLIC OF) - GRAIN PRODUCTION - See KOREA (REPUBLIC OF) - CROPS

KOREA (REPUBLIC OF) - GREEN PEPPER AND CHILIE PRODUCTION - See KOREA (REPUBLIC OF) - CROPS

KOREA (REPUBLIC OF) - GROSS DOMESTIC PRODUCT

The Economist Intelligence Unit, 111 West 57th Street, New York, New York 10019 (800) 938-4685; *Korea (South) Country Report;* and *The World Market Atlas*.

The Economist Intelligence Unit (Asia) Limited, 10th Floor, Luk Kwok Centre, 72 Gloucester Road, Wanchai, Hong Kong (Phone Number in U.S. (800) 938-4685); *Asian Market Atlas*.

Euromonitor International, Inc., 122 South Michigan Avenue, Suite 1200, Chicago, Illinois 60603 (800) 577-EURO; *International Marketing Data and Statistics;* and *The World Economic Factbook*.

Europa Publications Limited, 18 Bedford Square, London, WC1B 3JN, England; *The Europa World Year Book*.

M.E. Sharpe, 80 Business Park Drive, Armonk, New York 10504 (800) 541-6563; *The Illustrated Book of World Rankings*.

Statistical Office of the United Nations, Publishing Service, New York, New York 10017 (800) 253-9646; *Human Development Report; National Accounts Statistics;* and *Statistical Yearbook*.

The World Bank, 1818 H Street, NW, Washington, D.C. 20433 (202) 477-1234; *World Development Indicators*.

KOREA (REPUBLIC OF) - GROSS NATIONAL PRODUCT

Euromonitor International, Inc., 122 South Michigan Avenue, Suite 1200, Chicago, Illinois 60603 (800) 577-EURO; *International Marketing Data and Statistics*.

Europa Publications Limited, 18 Bedford Square, London, WC1B 3JN, England; *The Europa World Year Book*.

Korean Overseas Information Service, Ministry of Culture and Information, Seoul 110, Republic of Korea; *Statistical Data on Korea*.

St. Martin's Press, Inc., 175 Fifth

Avenue, New York, New York 10010 (800) 221-7945; *The Statesman's Year-Book.*

U.S. Arms Control and Disarmament Agency, 320 Twenty-first Street, NW, Washington, D.C. 20451 (202) 647-8677; *World Military Expenditures and Arms Transfers.*

Walden Publishing, Ltd., Two Market Street, Saffron Walden Essex, CB10 1HZ, England; *The World of Information Asia and Pacific Review.*

The World Bank, 1818 H Street, NW, Washington, D.C. 20433 (202) 477-1234; *The World Bank Atlas;* and *World Development Indicators.*

KOREA (REPUBLIC OF) - GROUNDNUT PRODUCTION - See KOREA (REPUBLIC OF) - CROPS

KOREA (REPUBLIC OF) - HEALTH

The Economist Intelligence Unit (Asia) Limited, 10th Floor, Luk Kwok Centre, 72 Gloucester Road, Wanchai, Hong Kong (Phone Number in U.S. (800) 938-4685); *Asian Market Atlas.*

Euromonitor International, Inc., 122 South Michigan Avenue, Suite 1200, Chicago, Illinois 60603 (800) 577-EURO; *World Marketing Data and Statistics.*

Korean Overseas Information Service, Ministry of Culture and Information, Seoul 110, Republic of Korea; *Statistical Data on Korea.*

M.E. Sharpe, 80 Business Park Drive, Armonk, New York 10504 (800) 541-6563; *The Illustrated Book of World Rankings.*

St. Martin's Press, Inc., 175 Fifth Avenue, New York, New York 10010 (800) 221-7945; *The Statesman's Year-Book.*

Statistical Office of the United Nations, Publishing Service, New York, New York 10017 (800) 253-9646; *Asia-Pacific in Figures; Human Development Report;* and *Statistical Yearbook.*

United Nations Children's Fund (UNICEF), 3 United Nations Plaza, New York, New York 10017 (800) 253-9646; *State of the World's Children.*

KOREA (REPUBLIC OF) - HEMP FIBRE PRODUCTION - See KOREA (REPUBLIC OF) - TEXTILE INDUSTRY

KOREA (REPUBLIC OF) - HIDE PRODUCTION - ALL TYPES

Food and Agricultural Organization of the United Nations (FAO), Via delle Terme di Caracalla, 00100 Rome, Italy (Telephone Number in U.S. (202) 653-2400);

Production Yearbook.

KOREA (REPUBLIC OF) - HIGHWAYS

Central Intelligence Agency, Washington, D.C. 20505 (703) 482-1100, www.cia.gov; *The World Factbook.*

The Economist Intelligence Unit (Asia) Limited, 10th Floor, Luk Kwok Centre, 72 Gloucester Road, Wanchai, Hong Kong (Phone Number in U.S. (800) 938-4685); *Asian Market Atlas.*

International Road Federation, 2600 Virginia Avenue, N.W., Washington, D.C. 20037 (202) 338-4641; *World Road Statistics.*

Korean Overseas Information Service, Ministry of Culture and Information, Seoul 110, Republic of Korea; *Statistical Data on Korea.*

St. Martin's Press, Inc., 175 Fifth Avenue, New York, New York 10010 (800) 221-7945; *The Statesman's Year-Book.*

KOREA (REPUBLIC OF) - HORSES - See KOREA (REPUBLIC OF) - LIVESTOCK AND POULTRY

KOREA (REPUBLIC OF) - HOURS OF WORK - See KOREA (REPUBLIC OF) - EMPLOYMENT

KOREA (REPUBLIC OF) - HOUSING AND HOUSING UNITS

Euromonitor International, Inc., 122 South Michigan Avenue, Suite 1200, Chicago, Illinois 60603 (800) 577-EURO; *World Marketing Data and Statistics.*

Korean Overseas Information Service, Ministry of Culture and Information, Seoul 110, Republic of Korea; *Statistical Data on Korea.*

M.E. Sharpe, 80 Business Park Drive, Armonk, New York 10504 (800) 541-6563; *The Illustrated Book of World Rankings.*

KOREA (REPUBLIC OF) - HYDROCHLORIC ACID PRODUCTION

Statistical Office of the United Nations, Publishing Service, New York, New York 10017 (800) 253-9646; *Statistical Yearbook.*

KOREA (REPUBLIC OF) - ILLITERATE POPULATION

Central Intelligence Agency, Washington, D.C. 20505 (703) 482-1100, www.cia.gov; *The World Factbook.*

The Economist Intelligence Unit (Asia) Limited, 10th Floor, Luk Kwok Centre, 72 Gloucester Road, Wanchai, Hong Kong (800) 938-4685; *The World Market Atlas.*

Euromonitor International, Inc., 122 South Michigan Avenue, Suite 1200, Chicago, Illinois 60603 (800) 577-EURO; *The World Economic Factbook.*

Statistical Office of the United Nations, Publishing Service, New York, New York 10017 (800) 253-9646; *Asia-Pacific in Figures;* and *Human Development Report.*

United Nations Educational, Scientific and Cultural Organization (UNESCO), 7 Place de Fontenoy, F-75700 Paris, France (Telephone in U.S. (212) 963-5981); *Statistical Yearbook.*

KOREA (REPUBLIC OF) - IMPORT MARKETS

Korean Overseas Information Service, Ministry of Culture and Information, Seoul 110, Republic of Korea; *Statistical Data on Korea.*

KOREA (REPUBLIC OF) - IMPORTS

Central Intelligence Agency, Washington, D.C. 20505 (703) 482-1100, www.cia.gov; *The World Factbook.*

The Economist Intelligence Unit, 111 West 57th Street, New York, New York 10019 (800) 938-4685; *Korea (South) Country Report;* and *The World Market Atlas.*

The Economist Intelligence Unit (Asia) Limited, 10th Floor, Luk Kwok Centre, 72 Gloucester Road, Wanchai, Hong Kong (Phone Number in U.S. (800) 938-4685); *Asian Market Atlas.*

Euromonitor International, Inc., 122 South Michigan Avenue, Suite 1200, Chicago, Illinois 60603 (800) 577-EURO; *International Marketing Data and Statistics;* and *The World Economic Factbook.*

Europa Publications Limited, 18 Bedford Square, London, WC1B 3JN, England; *The Europa World Year Book.*

Food and Agricultural Organization of the United Nations (FAO), Via delle Terme di Caracalla, 00100 Rome, Italy (Telephone Number in U.S. (202) 653-2400); *The State of Food and Agriculture.*

International Monetary Fund, 700 Nineteenth Street, NW, Washington, D.C. 20431 (202) 623-7000; *Direction of Trade Statistics.*

Korean Overseas Information Service, Ministry of Culture and Information, Seoul 110, Republic of Korea; *Statistical Data on Korea.*

St. Martin's Press, Inc., 175 Fifth Avenue, New York, New York 10010 (800) 221-7945; *The Statesman's Year-Book.*

United Nations Conference on Trade and Development (UNCTAD), New York, New York 10017 (800) 253-9646; *Handbook of International Trade and Development Statistics.*

Walden Publishing, Ltd., Two Market Street, Saffron Walden Essex, CB10 1HZ, England; *The World of Information Asia and Pacific Review.*

The World Bank, 1818 H Street, NW, Washington, D.C. 20433 (202) 477-1234; *World Development Indicators.*

KOREA (REPUBLIC OF) - INDUSTRIAL METALS PRODUCTION - See KOREA (REPUBLIC OF) - MINING AND MINERAL PRODUCTS

KOREA (REPUBLIC OF) - INDUSTRY

Central Intelligence Agency, Washington, D.C. 20505 (703) 482-1100, www.cia.gov; *The World Factbook.*

Economist Intelligence Unit, 111 West 57th Street, New York, New York 10019 (800) 938-4685; *Korea (South) Country Report.*

Euromonitor International, Inc., 122 South Michigan Avenue, Suite 1200, Chicago, Illinois 60603 (800) 577-EURO; *International Marketing Data and Statistics; World Marketing Data and Statistics;* and *The World Economic Factbook.*

Europa Publications Limited, 18 Bedford Square, London, WC1B 3JN, England; *The Europa World Year Book.*

International Labour Office, I.L.O. Publications,1828 L Street, N.W., Suite 801, Washington, D.C. 20036 (301) 638-3152 ; *Yearbook of Labour Statistics.*

M.E. Sharpe, 80 Business Park Drive, Armonk, New York 10504 (800) 541-6563; *The Illustrated Book of World Rankings.*

St. Martin's Press, Inc., 175 Fifth Avenue, New York, New York 10010 (800) 221-7945; *The Statesman's Year-Book.*

Statistical Office of the United Nations, Publishing Service, New York, New York 10017 (800) 253-9646; *Asia-Pacific in Figures; Industrial Statistics Yearbook; Statistical Yearbook;* and *Statistical Yearbook for Asia and the Pacific.*

The World Bank, 1818 H Street, NW, Washington, D.C. 20433 (202) 477-1234; *World Development Indicators.*

KOREA (REPUBLIC OF) - INFANT AND MATERNAL MORTALITY - See KOREA (REPUBLIC OF) - MORTALITY

KOREA (REPUBLIC OF) - INTERNAL TRADE

Statistical Office of the United Nations, Publishing Service, New York, New York 10017 (800) 253-9646; *Statistical Yearbook;* and *Statistical Yearbook for Asia and the Pacific.*

KOREA (REPUBLIC OF) - INTERNATIONAL RESERVES EXCLUDING GOLD

Statistical Office of the United Nations, Publishing Service, New York, New York 10017 (800) 253-9646; *Statistical Yearbook.*

The World Bank, 1818 H Street, NW, Washington, D.C. 20433 (202) 477-1234; *World Development Indicators.*

KOREA (REPUBLIC OF) - INVESTMENT

Korean Overseas Information Service, Ministry of Culture and Information, Seoul 110, Republic of Korea; *Statistical Data on Korea.*

KOREA (REPUBLIC OF) - IRON AND IRON ORE PRODUCTION - See KOREA (REPUBLIC OF) - MINING AND MINERAL PRODUCTS

KOREA (REPUBLIC OF) - IRRIGATION

Euromonitor International, Inc., 122 South Michigan Avenue, Suite 1200, Chicago, Illinois 60603 (800) 577-EURO; *International Marketing Data and Statistics.*

KOREA (REPUBLIC OF) - LABOR

Central Intelligence Agency, Washington, D.C. 20505 (703) 482-1100, www.cia.gov; *The World Factbook.*

The Economist Intelligence Unit (Asia) Limited, 10th Floor, Luk Kwok Centre, 72 Gloucester Road, Wanchai, Hong Kong (Phone Number in U.S. (800) 938-4685); *Asian Market Atlas.*

Euromonitor International, Inc., 122 South Michigan Avenue, Suite 1200, Chicago, Illinois 60603 (800) 577-EURO; *International Marketing Data and Statistics;* and *World Marketing Data and Statistics.*

Europa Publications Limited, 18 Bedford Square, London, WC1B 3JN, England; *The Europa World Year Book.*

Food and Agricultural Organization of the United Nations (FAO), Via delle Terme di Caracalla, 00100 Rome, Italy (Telephone Number in U.S. (202) 653-2400); *The State of Food and Agriculture.*

International Labour Office, I.L.O. Publications, 1828 L Street, N.W., Suite 801, Washington, D.C. 20036 (301) 638-3152; *Yearbook of Labour Statistics.*

M.E. Sharpe, 80 Business Park Drive, Armonk, New York 10504 (800) 541-6563;

The Illustrated Book of World Rankings.

St. Martin's Press, Inc., 175 Fifth Avenue, New York, New York 10010 (800) 221-7945; *The Statesman's Year-Book.*

Statistical Office of the United Nations, Publishing Service, New York, New York 10017 (800) 253-9646; *Human Development Report.*

The World Bank, 1818 H Street, NW, Washington, D.C. 20433 (202) 477-1234; *The World Bank Atlas;* and *World Development Indicators.*

KOREA (REPUBLIC OF) - LAND AREA

Korean Overseas Information Service, Ministry of Culture and Information, Seoul 110, Republic of Korea; *Statistical Data on Korea.*

KOREA (REPUBLIC OF) - LAND USE

Central Intelligence Agency, Washington, D.C. 20505 (703) 482-1100, www.cia.gov; *The World Factbook.*

Euromonitor International, Inc., 122 South Michigan Avenue, Suite 1200, Chicago, Illinois 60603 (800) 577-EURO; *International Marketing Data and Statistics.*

Food and Agricultural Organization of the United Nations (FAO), Via delle Terme di Caracalla, 00100 Rome, Italy (Telephone Number in U.S. (202) 653-2400); *Production Yearbook.*

KOREA (REPUBLIC OF) - LEAD AND LEAD ORE PRODUCTION - See KOREA (REPUBLIC OF) - MINING AND MINERAL PRODUCTS

KOREA (REPUBLIC OF) - LIBRARIES

M.E. Sharpe, 80 Business Park Drive, Armonk, New York 10504 (800) 541-6563; *The Illustrated Book of World Rankings.*

United Nations Educational, Scientific and Cultural Organization (UNESCO), 7 Place de Fontenoy, F-75700 Paris, France (Telephone in U.S. (212) 963-5981); *Statistical Yearbook.*

KOREA (REPUBLIC OF) - LIFE EXPECTANCY

Central Intelligence Agency, Washington, D.C. 20505 (703) 482-1100, www.cia.gov; *The World Factbook.*

The Economist Intelligence Unit (Asia) Limited, 10th Floor, Luk Kwok Centre, 72 Gloucester Road, Wanchai, Hong Kong (Phone Number in U.S. (800) 938-4685); *Asian Market Atlas.*

Euromonitor International, Inc., 122

South Michigan Avenue, Suite 1200, Chicago, Illinois 60603 (800) 577-EURO ; *The World Economic Factbook.*

Korean Overseas Information Service, Ministry of Culture and Information, Seoul 110, Republic of Korea; *Statistical Data on Korea.*

St. Martin's Press, Inc., 175 Fifth Avenue, New York, New York 10010 (800) 221-7945; *The Statesman's Year-Book.*

Statistical Office of the United Nations, Publishing Service, New York, New York 10017 (800) 253-9646; *Asia-Pacific in Figures; World Statistics Pocketbook;* and *Human Development Report.*

The World Bank, 1818 H Street, NW, Washington, D.C. 20433 (202) 477-1234; *The World Bank Atlas.*

KOREA (REPUBLIC OF) - LITERACY RATE

Euromonitor International, Inc., 122 South Michigan Avenue, Suite 1200, Chicago, Illinois 60603 (800) 577-EURO; *World Marketing Data and Statistics.*

KOREA (REPUBLIC OF) - LIVESTOCK AND POULTRY

Euromonitor International, Inc., 122 South Michigan Avenue, Suite 1200, Chicago, Illinois 60603 (800) 577-EURO; *International Marketing Data and Statistics.*

Europa Publications Limited, 18 Bedford Square, London, WC1B 3JN, England; *The Europa World Year Book.*

Food and Agricultural Organization of the United Nations (FAO), Via delle Terme di Caracalla, 00100 Rome, Italy (Telephone Number in U.S. (202) 653-2400); *Production Yearbook;* and *The State of Food and Agriculture.*

Korean Overseas Information Service, Ministry of Culture and Information, Seoul 110, Republic of Korea; *Statistical Data on Korea.*

M.E. Sharpe, 80 Business Park Drive, Armonk, New York 10504 (800) 541-6563; *The Illustrated Book of World Rankings.*

St. Martin's Press, Inc., 175 Fifth Avenue, New York, New York 10010 (800) 221-7945; *The Statesman's Year-Book.*

Statistical Office of the United Nations, Publishing Service, New York, New York 10017 (800) 253-9646; *Statistical Yearbook.*

United Nations Conference on Trade and Development, Central Statistical Service, Palais des Nations, Geneva, Switzerland (Telephone in U.S. (800) 253-9646); *UNCTAD Commodity Yearbook.*

KOREA (REPUBLIC OF) - LIVING LEVELS - See KOREA (REPUBLIC OF) - LIFE EXPECTANCY

KOREA (REPUBLIC OF) - MAIL - NUMBER OF PIECES SENT OR RECEIVED

Statistical Office of the United Nations, Publishing Service, New York, New York 10017 (800) 253-9646; *Statistical Yearbook.*

KOREA (REPUBLIC OF) - MANGANESE ORE PRODUCTION - See KOREA (REPUBLIC OF) - MINING AND MINERAL PRODUCTS

KOREA (REPUBLIC OF) - MANPOWER

Statistical Office of the United Nations, Publishing Service, New York, New York 10017 (800) 253-9646; *Statistical Yearbook for Asia and the Pacific.*

KOREA (REPUBLIC OF) - MANUFACTURING

M.E. Sharpe, 80 Business Park Drive, Armonk, New York 10504 (800) 541-6563; *The Illustrated Book of World Rankings.*

Statistical Office of the United Nations, Publishing Service, New York, New York 10017 (800) 253-9646; *Statistical Yearbook.*

The World Bank, 1818 H Street, NW, Washington, D.C. 20433 (202) 477-1234; *World Development Indicators.*

KOREA (REPUBLIC OF) - MARRIAGE RATES

Europa Publications Limited, 18 Bedford Square, London, WC1B 3JN, England; *The Europa World Year Book.*

M.E. Sharpe, 80 Business Park Drive, Armonk, New York 10504 (800) 541-6563; *The Illustrated Book of World Rankings.*

Statistical Office of the United Nations, Publishing Service, New York, New York 10017 (800) 253-9646; *Demographic Yearbook;* and *Statistical Yearbook.*

KOREA (REPUBLIC OF) - MEAT PRODUCTION - See KOREA (REPUBLIC OF) - LIVESTOCK AND POULTRY

KOREA (REPUBLIC OF) - MEDICAL CARE EXPENDITURES

Korean Overseas Information Service, Ministry of Culture and Information, Seoul 110, Republic of Korea; *Statistical Data on Korea.*

KOREA (REPUBLIC OF) - MEDICAL FACILITIES

Korean Overseas Information Service, Ministry of Culture and Information, Seoul 110, Republic of Korea; *Statistical Data on Korea.*

KOREA (REPUBLIC OF) - MERCHANT SHIPPING

Europa Publications Limited, 18 Bedford Square, London, WC1B 3JN, England; *The Europa World Year Book.*

St. Martin's Press, Inc., 175 Fifth Avenue, New York, New York 10010 (800) 221-7945; *The Statesman's Year-Book.*

Statistical Office of the United Nations, Publishing Service, New York, New York 10017 (800) 253-9646; *Statistical Yearbook.*

KOREA (REPUBLIC OF) - MILITARY

Central Intelligence Agency, Washington, D.C. 20505 (703) 482-1100, www.cia.gov; *The World Factbook.*

The Economist Intelligence Unit (Asia) Limited, 10th Floor, Luk Kwok Centre, 72 Gloucester Road, Wanchai, Hong Kong (Phone Number in U.S. (800) 938-4685); *Asian Market Atlas.*

Euromonitor International, Inc., 122 South Michigan Avenue, Suite 1200, Chicago, Illinois 60603 (800) 577-EURO; *World Marketing Data and Statistics.*

The International Institute for Strategic Studies, 23 Tavistock Street, London WC2E 7NQ, England 44 171 3797676; *The Military Balance.*

St. Martin's Press, Inc., 175 Fifth Avenue, New York, New York 10010 (800) 221-7945; *The Statesman's Year-Book.*

Statistical Office of the United Nations, Publishing Service, New York, New York 10017 (800) 253-9646; *Human Development Report.*

U.S. Arms Control and Disarmament Agency, 320 Twenty-first Street, NW, Washington, D.C. 20451 (202) 647-8677; *World Military Expenditures and Arms Transfers.*

KOREA (REPUBLIC OF) - MILK PRODUCTION - See KOREA (REPUBLIC OF) - DAIRY PRODUCTS

KOREA (REPUBLIC OF) - MILLET PRODUCTION - See KOREA (REPUBLIC OF) - CROPS

KOREA (REPUBLIC OF) - MINING AND MINERAL PRODUCTS

Europa Publications Limited, 18 Bedford Square, London, WC1B 3JN, England; *The Europa World Year Book.*

Korean Overseas Information Service, Ministry of Culture and Information, Seoul 110, Republic of Korea; *Statistical Data on Korea.*

M.E. Sharpe, 80 Business Park Drive, Armonk, New York 10504 (800) 541-6563; *The Illustrated Book of World Rankings*.

St. Martin's Press, Inc., 175 Fifth Avenue, New York, New York 10010 (800) 221-7945; *The Statesman's Year-Book*.

Statistical Office of the United Nations, Publishing Service, New York, New York 10017 (800) 253-9646; *Statistical Yearbook*.

United Nations Conference on Trade and Development, Central Statistical Service, Palais des Nations, Geneva, Switzerland (Telephone in U.S. (800) 253-9646); *UNCTAD Commodity Yearbook*.

KOREA (REPUBLIC OF) - MOLYBDENUM ORE PRODUCTION - See KOREA (REPUBLIC OF) - MINING AND MINERAL PRODUCTS

KOREA (REPUBLIC OF) - MONEY EXCHANGE RATE - See KOREA (REPUBLIC OF) - EXCHANGE RATES

KOREA (REPUBLIC OF) - MONEY RESERVES

Euromonitor International, Inc., 122 South Michigan Avenue, Suite 1200, Chicago, Illinois 60603 (800) 577-EURO; *International Marketing Data and Statistics*.

KOREA (REPUBLIC OF) - MONEY SUPPLY

Economist Intelligence Unit, 111 West 57th Street, New York, New York 10019 (800) 938-4685; *Korea (South) Country Report*.

Euromonitor International, Inc., 122 South Michigan Avenue, Suite 1200, Chicago, Illinois 60603 (800) 577-EURO; *International Marketing Data and Statistics*.

Europa Publications Limited, 18 Bedford Square, London, WC1B 3JN, England; *The Europa World Year Book*.

International Monetary Fund, 700 Nineteenth Street, NW, Washington, D.C. 20431 (202) 623-7000; *International Financial Statistics*.

Statistical Office of the United Nations, Publishing Service, New York, New York 10017; *Statistical Yearbook*.

The World Bank, 1818 H Street, NW, Washington, D.C. 20433 (202) 477-1234; *World Development Indicators*.

KOREA (REPUBLIC OF) - MORTALITY

Central Intelligence Agency, Washington, D.C. 20505 (703) 482-1100, www.cia.gov; *The World Factbook*.

The Economist Intelligence Unit (Asia)

Limited, 10th Floor, Luk Kwok Centre, 72 Gloucester Road, Wanchai, Hong Kong (Phone Number in U.S. (800) 938-4685); *Asian Market Atlas*.

Euromonitor International, Inc., 122 South Michigan Avenue, Suite 1200, Chicago, Illinois 60603 (800) 577-EURO; *International Marketing Data and Statistics; and The World Economic Factbook*.

Europa Publications Limited, 18 Bedford Square, London, WC1B 3JN, England; *The Europa World Year Book*.

St. Martin's Press, Inc., 175 Fifth Avenue, New York, New York 10010 (800) 221-7945; *The Statesman's Year-Book*.

Statistical Office of the United Nations, Publishing Service, New York, New York 10017 (800) 253-9646; *Asia-Pacific in Figures; Demographic Yearbook; Human Development Report; World Statistics Pocketbook; and Statistical Yearbook*.

United Nations Children's Fund (UNICEF), 3 United Nations Plaza, New York, New York 10017 (800) 253-9646; *State of the World's Children*.

The World Bank, 1818 H Street, NW, Washington, D.C. 20433 (202) 477-1234; *The World Bank Atlas; and World Development Indicators*.

KOREA (REPUBLIC OF) - MOTION PICTURES

Korean Overseas Information Service, Ministry of Culture and Information, Seoul 110, Republic of Korea; *Statistical Data on Korea*.

St. Martin's Press, Inc., 175 Fifth Avenue, New York, New York 10010 (800) 221-7945; *The Statesman's Year-Book*.

Statistical Office of the United Nations, Publishing Service, New York, New York 10017 (800) 253-9646; *Statistical Yearbook*.

United Nations Educational, Scientific and Cultural Organization (UNESCO), 7 Place de Fontenoy, F-75700 Paris, France (Telephone in U.S. (212) 963-5981); *Statistical Yearbook*.

KOREA (REPUBLIC OF) - MOTOR VEHICLE ASSEMBLY

Korean Overseas Information Service, Ministry of Culture and Information, Seoul 110, Republic of Korea; *Statistical Data on Korea*.

Statistical Office of the United Nations, Publishing Service, New York, New York 10017 (800) 253-9646; *Statistical Yearbook*.

KOREA (REPUBLIC OF) - MOTOR

VEHICLES IN USE

Europa Publications Limited, 18 Bedford Square, London, WC1B 3JN, England; *The Europa World Year Book*.

International Road Federation, 2600 Virginia Avenue, N.W., Washington, D.C. 20037 (202) 338-4641; *World Road Statistics*.

Korean Overseas Information Service, Ministry of Culture and Information, Seoul 110, Republic of Korea; *Statistical Data on Korea*.

Statistical Office of the United Nations, Publishing Service, New York, New York 10017 (800) 253-9646; *Statistical Yearbook*.

KOREA (REPUBLIC OF) - MUSEUMS

M.E. Sharpe, 80 Business Park Drive, Armonk, New York 10504 (800) 541-6563; *The Illustrated Book of World Rankings*.

United Nations Educational, Scientific and Cultural Organization (UNESCO), 7 Place de Fontenoy, F-75700 Paris, France (Telephone in U.S. (212) 963-5981); *Statistical Yearbook*.

KOREA (REPUBLIC OF) - NATALITY - See KOREA (REPUBLIC OF) - BIRTH RATES

KOREA (REPUBLIC OF) - NATIONAL ACCOUNTS

Europa Publications Limited, 18 Bedford Square, London, WC1B 3JN, England; *The Europa World Year Book*.

International Monetary Fund, 700 Nineteenth Street, NW, Washington, D.C. 20431 (202) 623-7000; *International Financial Statistics*.

Statistical Office of the United Nations, Publishing Service, New York, New York 10017 (800) 253-9646; *Asia-Pacific in Figures; National Accounts Statistics; Statistical Yearbook; and Statistical Yearbook for Asia and the Pacific*.

KOREA (REPUBLIC OF) - NATIONAL INCOME

Korean Overseas Information Service, Ministry of Culture and Information, Seoul 110, Republic of Korea; *Statistical Data on Korea*.

M.E. Sharpe, 80 Business Park Drive, Armonk, New York 10504 (800) 541-6563; *The Illustrated Book of World Rankings*.

Statistical Office of the United Nations, Publishing Service, New York, New York 10017 (800) 253-9646; *National Accounts Statistics; and Statistical Yearbook*.

KOREA (REPUBLIC OF) - NATIONAL PRODUCT

M.E. Sharpe, 80 Business Park Drive, Armonk, New York 10504 (800) 541-6563; *The Illustrated Book of World Rankings.*

Statistical Office of the United Nations, Publishing Service, New York, New York 10017 (800) 253-9646; *Statistical Yearbook.*

KOREA (REPUBLIC OF) - NATURAL GAS PRODUCTION - See KOREA (REPUBLIC OF) - MINING AND MINERAL PRODUCTS

KOREA (REPUBLIC OF) - NEWS AGENCIES

Korean Overseas Information Service, Ministry of Culture and Information, Seoul 110, Republic of Korea; *Statistical Data on Korea.*

KOREA (REPUBLIC OF) - NEWSPAPER PRODUCTION AND CONSUMPTION - See KOREA (REPUBLIC OF) - FORESTRY AND FOREST PRODUCTS

KOREA (REPUBLIC OF) - NEWSPRINT - See KOREA (REPUBLIC OF) - FORESTRY AND FOREST PRODUCTS

KOREA (REPUBLIC OF) - NICKEL ORE PRODUCTION AND CONSUMPTION - See KOREA (REPUBLIC OF) - MINING AND MINERAL PRODUCTS

KOREA (REPUBLIC OF) - OCCUPATIONS - See KOREA (REPUBLIC OF) - LABOR

KOREA (REPUBLIC OF) - PAPER - See KOREA (REPUBLIC OF) - FORESTRY AND FOREST PRODUCTS

KOREA (REPUBLIC OF) - PATENTS, TRADEMARKS AND SERVICE MARKS

Statistical Office of the United Nations, Publishing Service, New York, New York 10017 (800) 253-9646; *Statistical Yearbook.*

KOREA (REPUBLIC OF) - PEANUT PRODUCTION - See KOREA (REPUBLIC OF) - CROPS

KOREA (REPUBLIC OF) - PERIODICALS

Korean Overseas Information Service, Ministry of Culture and Information, Seoul 110, Republic of Korea; *Statistical Data on Korea.*

United Nations Educational, Scientific and Cultural Organization (UNESCO), 7 Place de Fontenoy, F-75700 Paris, France (Telephone in U.S. (212) 963-5981); *Statistical Yearbook.*

KOREA (REPUBLIC OF) - PESTICIDE USE

Food and Agricultural Organization of the United Nations (FAO), Via delle Terme di Caracalla, 00100 Rome, Italy (Telephone Number in U.S. (202) 653-2400); *The State of Food and Agriculture.*

KOREA (REPUBLIC OF) - PETROLEUM INDUSTRY

Food and Agricultural Organization of the United Nations (FAO), Via delle Terme di Caracalla, 00100 Rome, Italy (Telephone Number in U.S. (202) 653-2400); *The State of Food and Agriculture.*

M.E. Sharpe, 80 Business Park Drive, Armonk, New York 10504 (800) 541-6563; *The Illustrated Book of World Rankings.*

St. Martin's Press, Inc., 175 Fifth Avenue, New York, New York 10010 (800) 221-7945; *The Statesman's Year-Book.*

Statistical Office of the United Nations, Publishing Service, New York, New York 10017 (800) 253-9646; *Statistical Yearbook.*

United Nations Conference on Trade and Development, Central Statistical Service, Palais des Nations, Geneva, Switzerland (Telephone in U.S. (800) 253-9646); *UNCTAD Commodity Yearbook.*

KOREA (REPUBLIC OF) - PIG-IRON AND FERRO-ALLOY PRODUCTION - See KOREA (REPUBLIC OF) - MINING AND MINERAL PRODUCTS

KOREA (REPUBLIC OF) - PIGS - See KOREA (REPUBLIC OF) - LIVESTOCK AND POULTRY

KOREA (REPUBLIC OF) - PLASTICS AND RESIN PRODUCTION

Statistical Office of the United Nations, Publishing Service, New York, New York 10017 (800) 253-9646; *Statistical Yearbook.*

KOREA (REPUBLIC OF) - POPULATION

Central Intelligence Agency, Washington, D.C. 20505 (703) 482-1100, www.cia.gov; *The World Factbook.*

The Economist Intelligence Unit, 111 West 57th Street, New York, New York 10019 (800) 938-4685; *Korea (South) Country Report;* and *The World Market Atlas.*

The Economist Intelligence Unit (Asia) Limited, 10th Floor, Luk Kwok Centre, 72 Gloucester Road, Wanchai, Hong Kong (Phone Number in U.S. (800) 938-4685); *Asian Market Atlas.*

Euromonitor International, Inc., 122 South Michigan Avenue, Suite 1200, Chicago, Illinois 60603 (800) 577-EURO; *International Marketing Data and Statistics;* and *The World Economic Factbook.*

Europa Publications Limited, 18 Bedford Square, London, WC1B 3JN, England; *The Europa World Year Book.*

Food and Agricultural Organization of the United Nations (FAO), Via delle Terme di Caracalla, 00100 Rome, Italy (Telephone Number in U.S. (202) 653-2400); *Production Yearbook.*

International Labour Office, I.L.O. Publications, 1828 L Street, N.W., Suite 801, Washington, D.C. 20036 (301) 638-3152; *Yearbook of Labour Statistics.*

Korean Overseas Information Service, Ministry of Culture and Information, Seoul 110, Republic of Korea; *Statistical Data on Korea.*

M.E. Sharpe, 80 Business Park Drive, Armonk, New York 10504 (800) 541-6563; *The Illustrated Book of World Rankings.*

St. Martin's Press, Inc., 175 Fifth Avenue, New York, New York 10010 (800) 221-7945; *The Statesman's Year-Book.*

Statistical Office of the United Nations, Publishing Service, New York, New York 10017 (800) 253-9646; *Asia-Pacific in Figures; Demographic Yearbook; Human Development Report; Statistical Yearbook; World Statistics Pocketbook;* and *Statistical Yearbook for Asia and the Pacific.*

United Nations Educational, Scientific and Cultural Organization (UNESCO), 7 Place de Fontenoy, F-75700 Paris, France (Telephone in U.S. (212) 963-5981); *Statistical Yearbook.*

U.S. Arms Control and Disarmament Agency, 320 Twenty-first Street, NW, Washington, D.C. 20451 (202) 647-8677; *World Military Expenditures and Arms Transfers.*

Walden Publishing, Ltd., Two Market Street, Saffron Walden Essex, CB10 1HZ, England; *The World of Information Asia and Pacific Review.*

The World Bank, 1818 H Street, NW, Washington, D.C. 20433 (202) 477-1234; *The World Bank Atlas.*

KOREA (REPUBLIC OF) - POST OFFICES

Korean Overseas Information Service, Ministry of Culture and Information, Seoul 110, Republic of Korea; *Statistical Data on Korea.*

M.E. Sharpe, 80 Business Park Drive, Armonk, New York 10504 (800) 541-6563; *The Illustrated Book of World Rankings.*

St. Martin's Press, Inc., 175 Fifth Avenue, New York, New York 10010 (800) 221-7945; *The Statesman's Year-Book.*

KOREA (REPUBLIC OF) - POTATO PRODUCTION - See KOREA (REPUBLIC OF) - CROPS

KOREA (REPUBLIC OF) - PRECIPITATION

Korean Overseas Information Service, Ministry of Culture and Information, Seoul 110, Republic of Korea; *Statistical Data on Korea.*

KOREA (REPUBLIC OF) - PRICES

Food and Agricultural Organization of the United Nations (FAO), Via delle Terme di Caracalla, 00100 Rome, Italy (Telephone Number in U.S. (202) 653-2400); *Production Yearbook;* and *The State of Food and Agriculture.*

International Labour Office, I.L.O. Publications, 1828 L Street, N.W., Suite 801, Washington, D.C. 20036 (301) 638-3152; *Yearbook of Labour Statistics.*

M.E. Sharpe, 80 Business Park Drive, Armonk, New York 10504 (800) 541-6563; *The Illustrated Book of World Rankings.*

KOREA (REPUBLIC OF) - PRINTING AND WRITING PAPER - See KOREA (REPUBLIC OF) - FORESTRY AND FOREST PRODUCTS

KOREA (REPUBLIC OF) - PRODUCTION

M.E. Sharpe, 80 Business Park Drive, Armonk, New York 10504 (800) 541-6563; *The Illustrated Book of World Rankings.*

KOREA (REPUBLIC OF) - PRODUCTIVITY

Euromonitor International, Inc., 122 South Michigan Avenue, Suite 1200, Chicago, Illinois 60603 (800) 577-EURO; *International Marketing Data and Statistics.*

KOREA (REPUBLIC OF) - PUBLIC FINANCE - See KOREA (REPUBLIC OF) - FINANCE

KOREA (REPUBLIC OF) - RADIO BROADCASTING - See KOREA (REPUBLIC OF) - BROADCASTING

KOREA (REPUBLIC OF) - RADIO RECEIVERS

St. Martin's Press, Inc., 175 Fifth Avenue, New York, New York 10010 (800) 221-7945; *The Statesman's Year-Book.*

Statistical Office of the United Nations, Publishing Service, New York, New York 10017 (800) 253-9646; *Statistical Yearbook.*

KOREA (REPUBLIC OF) - RAILWAYS

Europa Publications Limited, 18 Bedford Square, London, WC1B 3JN, England; *The Europa World Year Book.*

Jane's Information Group, Sentinel House, 163 Brighton Road, Coulsdon, Surrey CR5 2NH, England (Telephone Number in U.S. (703) 683-3700); *Jane's World Railways.*

Korean Overseas Information Service, Ministry of Culture and Information, Seoul 110, Republic of Korea; *Statistical Data on Korea.*

St. Martin's Press, Inc., 175 Fifth Avenue, New York, New York 10010 (800) 221-7945; *The Statesman's Year-Book.*

Statistical Office of the United Nations, Publishing Service, New York, New York 10017 (800) 253-9646; *Statistical Yearbook.*

KOREA (REPUBLIC OF) - RAPESEED PRODUCTION - See KOREA (REPUBLIC OF) - CROPS

KOREA (REPUBLIC OF) - READING EXPENDITURES - EDUCATIONAL AND RECREATIONAL

Korean Overseas Information Service, Ministry of Culture and Information, Seoul 110, Republic of Korea; *Statistical Data on Korea.*

KOREA (REPUBLIC OF) - RELIGION

Central Intelligence Agency, Washington, D.C. 20505 (703) 482-1100, www.cia.gov; *The World Factbook.*

Korean Overseas Information Service, Ministry of Culture and Information, Seoul 110, Republic of Korea; *Statistical Data on Korea.*

M.E. Sharpe, 80 Business Park Drive, Armonk, New York 10504 (800) 541-6563; *The Illustrated Book of World Rankings.*

St. Martin's Press, Inc., 175 Fifth Avenue, New York, New York 10010 (800) 221-7945; *The Statesman's Year-Book.*

KOREA (REPUBLIC OF) - RENT PRICES

Europa Publications Limited, 18 Bedford Square, London, WC1B 3JN, England; *The Europa World Year Book.*

International Labour Office, I.L.O. Publications, 1828 L Street, N.W., Suite 801, Washington, D.C. 20036 (301) 638-3152; *Yearbook of Labour Statistics.*

KOREA (REPUBLIC OF) - RETAIL TRADE

Euromonitor International, Inc., 122 South Michigan Avenue, Suite 1200, Chicago, Illinois 60603 (800) 577-EURO; *Retail Trade International;* and *World Marketing Data and Statistics.*

Statistical Office of the United Nations, Publishing Service, New York, New York 10017 (800) 253-9646; *Statistical Yearbook.*

KOREA (REPUBLIC OF) - RICE PRODUCTION - See KOREA (REPUBLIC OF) - CROPS

KOREA (REPUBLIC OF) - ROADS - See KOREA (REPUBLIC OF) - HIGHWAYS

KOREA (REPUBLIC OF) - ROOT AND TUBER PRODUCTION - See KOREA (REPUBLIC OF) - CROPS

KOREA (REPUBLIC OF) - ROUNDWOOD PRODUCTION - See KOREA (REPUBLIC OF) - FORESTRY AND FOREST PRODUCTS

KOREA (REPUBLIC OF) - RUBBER PRODUCTION AND CONSUMPTION

M.E. Sharpe, 80 Business Park Drive, Armonk, New York 10504 (800) 541-6563; *The Illustrated Book of World Rankings.*

Statistical Office of the United Nations, Publishing Service, New York, New York 10017 (800) 253-9646; *Statistical Yearbook.*

KOREA (REPUBLIC OF) - SALT PRODUCTION - See KOREA (REPUBLIC OF) - MINING AND MINERAL PRODUCTS

KOREA (REPUBLIC OF) - SAWNWOOD PRODUCTION - See KOREA (REPUBLIC OF) - FORESTRY AND FOREST PRODUCTS

KOREA (REPUBLIC OF) - SCIENCE AND TECHNOLOGY - EXPENDITURE FOR RESEARCH - See KOREA (REPUBLIC OF) - SCIENTISTS, TECHNICIANS AND ENGINEERS

KOREA (REPUBLIC OF) - SCIENTISTS, TECHNICIANS AND ENGINEERS

Statistical Office of the United Nations, Publishing Service, New York, New York 10017 (800) 253-9646; *Statistical Yearbook.*

United Nations Educational, Scientific and Cultural Organization (UNESCO), 7 Place de Fontenoy, F-75700 Paris, France (Telephone in U.S. (212) 963-5981); *Statistical Yearbook.*

KOREA (REPUBLIC OF) - SENIOR CITIZENS

M.E. Sharpe, 80 Business Park Drive, Armonk, New York 10504 (800) 541-6563; *The Illustrated Book of World Rankings.*

KOREA (REPUBLIC OF) - SESAME SEED PRODUCTION - See KOREA (REPUBLIC OF) - CROPS

KOREA (REPUBLIC OF) - SHEEP - See KOREA (REPUBLIC OF) - LIVESTOCK AND POULTRY

KOREA (REPUBLIC OF) - SHIPBUILDING
CAPACITY

Korean Overseas Information Service,
Ministry of Culture and Information, Seoul
110, Republic of Korea; *Statistical Data on
Korea.*

KOREA (REPUBLIC OF) - SILVER
PRODUCTION AND CONSUMPTION - See
KOREA (REPUBLIC OF) - MINING AND
MINERAL PRODUCTS

KOREA (REPUBLIC OF) - SOCIAL DATA

M.E. Sharpe, 80 Business Park Drive,
Armonk, New York 10504 (800) 541-6563;
The Illustrated Book of World Rankings.

Statistical Office of the United Nations,
Publishing Service, New York, New York
10017 (800) 253-9646; *World Statistics
Pocketbook.*

KOREA (REPUBLIC OF) - SOCIAL
SECURITY

St. Martin's Press, Inc., 175 Fifth
Avenue, New York, New York 10010 (800)
221-7945; *The Statesman's Year-Book.*

Statistical Office of the United Nations,
Publishing Service, New York, New York
10017 (800) 253-9646; *National Accounts
Statistics.*

KOREA (REPUBLIC OF) - SOYBEAN
PRODUCTION - See KOREA (REPUBLIC
OF) - CROPS

KOREA (REPUBLIC OF) - STATE BUDGET
REVENUE AND EXPENDITURES

Euromonitor International, Inc., 122
South Michigan Avenue, Suite 1200,
Chicago, Illinois 60603 (800) 577-EURO;
International Marketing Data and Statistics.

KOREA (REPUBLIC OF) - STEEL - See
KOREA (REPUBLIC OF) - MINING AND
MINERAL PRODUCTS

KOREA (REPUBLIC OF) - STOCKS -
COMMODITY - MARKET PRICE -INDEX

Food and Agricultural Organization of
the United Nations (FAO), Via delle Terme
di Caracalla, 00100 Rome, Italy (Telephone
Number in U.S. (202) 653-2400); *The State
of Food and Agriculture.*

KOREA (REPUBLIC OF) - SUGAR
PRODUCTION AND CONSUMPTION - See
KOREA (REPUBLIC OF) - CROPS

KOREA (REPUBLIC OF) - SULPHURIC ACID
PRODUCTION - See (KOREA REPUBLIC
OF) - MINING AND MINERAL PRODUCTS

KOREA (REPUBLIC OF) - TAXATION

Europa Publications Limited, 18
Bedford Square, London, WC1B 3JN,
England; *The Europa World Year Book.*

International Road Federation, 2600
Virginia Avenue, N.W., Washington, D.C.
20037 (202) 338-4641; *World Road
Statistics.*

St. Martin's Press, Inc., 175 Fifth
Avenue, New York, New York 10010 (800)
221-7945; *The Statesman's Year-Book.*

The World Bank, 1818 H Street, NW,
Washington, D.C. 20433 (202) 477-1234;
World Development Indicators.

KOREA (REPUBLIC OF) - TELEGRAPH
SERVICE

Korean Overseas Information Service,
Ministry of Culture and Information, Seoul
110, Republic of Korea; *Statistical Data on
Korea.*

KOREA (REPUBLIC OF) - TELEPHONES IN
USE

American Telephone and Telegraph
Company, 26 Parsippany Road, Whippany,
New Jersey 07981 (800) 222-0300; *The
World's Telephones.*

Central Intelligence Agency,
Washington, D.C. 20505 (703) 482-1100,
www.cia.gov; *The World Factbook.*

The Economist Intelligence Unit (Asia)
Limited, 10th Floor, Luk Kwok Centre, 72
Gloucester Road, Wanchai, Hong Kong
(Phone Number in U.S. (800) 938-4685);
Asian Market Atlas.

Europa Publications Limited, 18
Bedford Square, London, WC1B 3JN,
England; *The Europa World Year Book.*

Korean Overseas Information Service,
Ministry of Culture and Information, Seoul
110, Republic of Korea; *Statistical Data on
Korea.*

St. Martin's Press, Inc., 175 Fifth
Avenue, New York, New York 10010 (800)
221-7945; *The Statesman's Year-Book.*

Statistical Office of the United Nations,
Publishing Service, New York, New York
10017 (800) 253-9646; *Statistical Yearbook;*
and *World Statistics Pocketbook.*

KOREA (REPUBLIC OF) - TELEVISION
BROADCASTING - See KOREA (REPUBLIC
OF) - BROADCASTING

KOREA (REPUBLIC OF) - TELEVISIONS IN
USE

The Economist Intelligence Unit (Asia)
Limited, 10th Floor, Luk Kwok Centre, 72
Gloucester Road, Wanchai, Hong Kong

(Phone Number in U.S. (800) 938-4685);
Asian Market Atlas.

Korean Overseas Information Service,
Ministry of Culture and Information, Seoul
110, Republic of Korea; *Statistical Data on
Korea.*

KOREA (REPUBLIC OF) - TEMPERATURE

Korean Overseas Information Service,
Ministry of Culture and Information, Seoul
110, Republic of Korea; *Statistical Data on
Korea.*

KOREA (REPUBLIC OF) - TEXTILE
INDUSTRY

Euromonitor International, Inc., 122
South Michigan Avenue, Suite 1200,
Chicago, Illinois 60603 (800) 577-EURO;
Retail Trade International.

Food and Agricultural Organization of
the United Nations (FAO), Via delle Terme
di Caracalla, 00100 Rome, Italy (Telephone
Number in U.S. (202) 653-2400);
Production Yearbook.

M.E. Sharpe, 80 Business Park Drive,
Armonk, New York 10504 (800) 541-6563;
The Illustrated Book of World Rankings.

St. Martin's Press, Inc., 175 Fifth
Avenue, New York, New York 10010 (800)
221-7945; *The Statesman's Year-Book.*

Statistical Office of the United Nations,
Publishing Service, New York, New York
10017 (800) 253-9646; *Statistical Yearbook.*

United Nations Conference on Trade
and Development, Central Statistical
Service, Palais des Nations, Geneva,
Switzerland (Telephone in U.S. (800) 253-
9646); *UNCTAD Commodity Yearbook.*

KOREA (REPUBLIC OF) - THEATRE

United Nations Educational, Scientific
and Cultural Organization (UNESCO), 7
Place de Fontenoy, F-75700 Paris, France
(Telephone in U.S. (212) 963-5981);
Statistical Yearbook.

KOREA (REPUBLIC OF) - TIN - See KOREA
(REPUBLIC OF) - MINING AND MINERAL
PRODUCTS

KOREA (REPUBLIC OF) - TIRE (MOTOR
VEHICLE) PRODUCTION

Statistical Office of the United Nations,
Publishing Service, New York, New York
10017 (800) 253-9646; *Statistical Yearbook.*

KOREA (REPUBLIC OF) - TOBACCO
PRODUCTION

M.E. Sharpe, 80 Business Park Drive,
Armonk, New York 10504 (800) 541-6563;

The Illustrated Book of World Rankings.

Statistical Office of the United Nations, Publishing Service, New York, New York 10017 (800) 253-9646; *Statistical Yearbook.*

KOREA (REPUBLIC OF) - TOURISM

Euromonitor International, Inc., 122 South Michigan Avenue, Suite 1200, Chicago, Illinois 60603 (800) 577-EURO; *The World Economic Factbook;* and *World Marketing Data and Statistics.*

Europa Publications Limited, 18 Bedford Square, London, WC1B 3JN, England; *The Europa World Year Book.*

Korean Overseas Information Service, Ministry of Culture and Information, Seoul 110, Republic of Korea; *Statistical Data on Korea.*

M.E. Sharpe, 80 Business Park Drive, Armonk, New York 10504 (800) 541-6563; *The Illustrated Book of World Rankings.*

St. Martin's Press, Inc., 175 Fifth Avenue, New York, New York 10010 (800) 221-7945; *The Statesman's Year-Book.*

Statistical Office of the United Nations, Publishing Service, New York, New York 10017 (800) 253-9646; *Statistical Yearbook.*

World Tourism Organization, Calle Capitan Haya 42, E-28020 Madrid, Spain; *Yearbook of Tourism Statistics.*

KOREA (REPUBLIC OF) - TRACTORS IN USE

Statistical Office of the United Nations, Publishing Service, New York, New York 10017 (800) 253-9646; *Statistical Yearbook.*

KOREA (REPUBLIC OF) - TRADE - See KOREA (REPUBLIC OF) - FOREIGN TRADE

KOREA (REPUBLIC OF) - TRADEMARKS AND SERVICE MARKS - See PATENTS, TRADEMARKS AND SERVICE MARKS

KOREA (REPUBLIC OF) - TRANSPORTATION AND COMMUNICATIONS

Central Intelligence Agency, Washington, D.C. 20505 (703) 482-1100, www.cia.gov; *The World Factbook.*

The Economist Intelligence Unit (Asia) Limited, 10th Floor, Luk Kwok Centre, 72 Gloucester Road, Wanchai, Hong Kong (Phone Number in U.S. (800) 938-4685); *Asian Market Atlas.*

Euromonitor International, Inc., 122 South Michigan Avenue, Suite 1200, Chicago, Illinois 60603 (800) 577-EURO; *International Marketing Data and Statistics;*

and *World Marketing Data and Statistics.*

Europa Publications Limited, 18 Bedford Square, London, WC1B 3JN, England; *The Europa World Year Book.*

Korean Overseas Information Service, Ministry of Culture and Information, Seoul 110, Republic of Korea; *Statistical Data on Korea.*

M.E. Sharpe, 80 Business Park Drive, Armonk, New York 10504 (800) 541-6563; *The Illustrated Book of World Rankings.*

St. Martin's Press, Inc., 175 Fifth Avenue, New York, New York 10010 (800) 221-7945; *The Statesman's Year-Book.*

Statistical Office of the United Nations, Publishing Service, New York, New York 10017 (800) 253-9646; *Human Development Report;* and *Statistical Yearbook for Asia and the Pacific.*

KOREA (REPUBLIC OF) - TUNGSTEN PRODUCTION AND CONSUMPTION - See KOREA (REPUBLIC OF) - MINING AND MINERAL PRODUCTS

KOREA (REPUBLIC OF) - UNEMPLOYMENT

Central Intelligence Agency, Washington, D.C. 20505 (703) 482-1100, www.cia.gov; *The World Factbook.*

Euromonitor International, Inc., 122 South Michigan Avenue, Suite 1200, Chicago, Illinois 60603 (800) 577-EURO; *International Marketing Data and Statistics.*

International Labour Office, I.L.O. Publications, 1828 L Street, N.W., Suite 801, Washington, D.C. 20036 (301) 638-3152; *Yearbook of Labour Statistics.*

Korean Overseas Information Service, Ministry of Culture and Information, Seoul 110, Republic of Korea; *Statistical Data on Korea.*

St. Martin's Press, Inc., 175 Fifth Avenue, New York, New York 10010 (800) 221-7945; *The Statesman's Year-Book.*

Statistical Office of the United Nations, Publishing Service, New York, New York 10017 (800) 253-9646; *Statistical Yearbook.*

KOREA (REPUBLIC OF) - UTILITY EXPENDITURES

Korean Overseas Information Service, Ministry of Culture and Information, Seoul 110, Republic of Korea; *Statistical Data on Korea.*

KOREA (REPUBLIC OF) - VITAL STATISTICS

Euromonitor International, Inc., 122

South Michigan Avenue, Suite 1200, Chicago, Illinois 60603 (800) 577-EURO; *International Marketing Data and Statistics.*

St. Martin's Press, Inc., 175 Fifth Avenue, New York, New York 10010 (800) 221-7945; *The Statesman's Year-Book.*

KOREA (REPUBLIC OF) - WAGES

International Labour Office, I.L.O. Publications, 1828 L Street, N.W., Suite 801, Washington, D.C. 20036 (301) 638-3152; *Yearbook of Labour Statistics.*

Statistical Office of the United Nations, Publishing Service, New York, New York 10017 (800) 253-9646; *Statistical Yearbook.*

KOREA (REPUBLIC OF) - WAGES AND PRICES

Statistical Office of the United Nations, Publishing Service, New York, New York 10017 (800) 253-9646; *Statistical Yearbook for Asia and the Pacific.*

KOREA (REPUBLIC OF) - WALNUT PRODUCTION - See KOREA (REPUBLIC OF) - CROPS

KOREA (REPUBLIC OF) - WATERMELON PRODUCTION - See KOREA (REPUBLIC OF) - CROPS

KOREA (REPUBLIC OF) - WEATHER - See KOREA (REPUBLIC OF) - CLIMATE

KOREA (REPUBLIC OF) - WHALING - See KOREA (REPUBLIC OF) - FISHERIES

KOREA (REPUBLIC OF) - WHEAT PRODUCTION AND PRICES - See KOREA (REPUBLIC OF) - CROPS

KOREA (REPUBLIC OF) - WHOLESALE PRICES - INDEX NUMBERS

Korean Overseas Information Service, Ministry of Culture and Information, Seoul 110, Republic of Korea; *Statistical Data on Korea.*

Statistical Office of the United Nations, Publishing Service, New York, New York 10017 (800) 253-9646; *Statistical Yearbook.*

KOREA (REPUBLIC OF) - WHOLESALE TRADE

Statistical Office of the United Nations, Publishing Service, New York, New York 10017 (800) 253-9646; *Statistical Yearbook.*

KOREA (REPUBLIC OF) - WINE PRODUCTION - See KOREA (REPUBLIC OF) - BEVERAGES

KOREA (REPUBLIC OF) - WOOD PULP PRODUCTION - See KOREA (REPUBLIC OF) - FORESTRY AND FOREST PRODUCTS

KOREA (REPUBLIC OF) - WOOL PRODUCTION AND CONSUMPTION - See KOREA (REPUBLIC OF) - TEXTILE INDUSTRY

KOREA (REPUBLIC OF) - YARN PRODUCTION - See KOREA (REPUBLIC OF) - TEXTILE INDUSTRY

KOREA (REPUBLIC OF) - ZINC AND ZINC ORE PRODUCTION AND CONSUMPTION - See KOREA (REPUBLIC OF) - MINING AND MINERAL PRODUCTS

KOREA (REPUBLIC OF) - ZOOS AND BOTANICAL GARDENS

United Nations Educational, Scientific and Cultural Organization (UNESCO), 7 Place de Fontenoy, F-75700 Paris, France (Telephone in U.S. (212) 963-5981); *Statistical Yearbook.*

KOREAN POPULATION

U.S. Department of Commerce, Bureau of the Census, Washington, D.C. 20233 (301) (301) 457-4100, www.census.gov; *Census of Population, General Population Characteristics, United States;* and press release.

Kuwait - National Statistical Office

Central Statistical Office, The Ministry of Planning, Post Office Box 26188, Safat, Kuwait 13123.

Kuwait - Primary Statistics Sources

Central Statistical Office, Post Office Box 26188, Safat, Kuwait; *Annual Statistical Abstract;* and *Monthly Digest of Statistics.*

KUWAIT - AGRICULTURE

Central Statistical Office, Ministry of Planning, Post Office Box 26188, Safat, Kuwait; *Annual Statistical Abstract - State of Kuwait.*

Economic Commission for Western Asia, Post Office Box 27, Baghdad, Iraq; *Statistical Abstract of Western Asia.*

Economist Intelligence Unit, 111 West 57th Street, New York, New York 10019 (800) 938-4685; *Kuwait Country Report.*

Euromonitor International, Inc., 122 South Michigan Avenue, Suite 1200, Chicago, Illinois 60603 (800) 577-EURO; *International Marketing Data and Statistics;* and *World Marketing Data and Statistics..*

Europa Publications Limited, 18

Bedford Square, London, WC1B 3JN, England; *The Europa World Year Book.*

Food and Agricultural Organization of the United Nations (FAO), Via delle Terme di Caracalla, 00100 Rome, Italy (Telephone Number in U.S. (202) 653-2400); *Production Yearbook; The State of Food and Agriculture;* and *Trade Yearbook.*

M.E. Sharpe, 80 Business Park Drive, Armonk, New York 10504 (800) 541-6563; *The Illustrated Book of World Rankings.*

St. Martin's Press, Inc., 175 Fifth Avenue, New York, New York 10010 (800) 221-7945; *The Statesman's Year-Book.*

Statistical Office of the United Nations, Publishing Service, New York, New York 10017 (800) 253-9646; *Statistical Yearbook.*

United Nations Conference on Trade and Development, Central Statistical Service, Palais des Nations, Geneva, Switzerland (Telephone in U.S. (800) 253-9646); *UNCTAD Commodity Yearbook.*

The World Bank, 1818 H Street, NW, Washington, D.C. 20433 (202) 477-1234; *World Development Indicators.*

KUWAIT - AIRLINE SERVICE

Economic Commission for Western Asia, Post Office Box 27, Baghdad, Iraq; *Statistical Abstract of Western Asia.*

Europa Publications Limited, 18 Bedford Square, London, WC1B 3JN, England; *The Europa World Year Book.*

International Civil Aviation Organization, 999 University Street, Montreal, Quebec, Canada H3C 5H7 (514) 285-8219; *Civil Aviation Statistics of the World.*

M.E. Sharpe, 80 Business Park Drive, Armonk, New York 10504 (800) 541-6563; *The Illustrated Book of World Rankings.*

St. Martin's Press, Inc., 175 Fifth Avenue, New York, New York 10010 (800) 221-7945; *The Statesman's Year-Book.*

Statistical Office of the United Nations, Publishing Service, New York, New York 10017 (800) 253-9646; *Statistical Yearbook.*

KUWAIT - AIRPORTS

Central Intelligence Agency, Washington, D.C. 20505 (703) 482-1100, www.cia.gov; *The World Factbook.*

KUWAIT - ALUMINUM PRODUCTION AND CONSUMPTION - See KUWAIT - MINING AND MINERAL PRODUCTS

KUWAIT - ANIMAL HEALTH

Food and Agricultural Organization of the United Nations (FAO), Via delle Terme di Caracalla, 00100 Rome, Italy (Telephone Number in U.S. (202) 653-2400); *Animal Health Yearbook.*

KUWAIT - AREA AND DENSITY OF POPULATION

Central Intelligence Agency, Washington, D.C. 20505 (703) 482-1100, www.cia.gov; *The World Factbook.*

Economic Commission for Western Asia, Post Office Box 27, Baghdad, Iraq; *Statistical Abstract of Western Asia.*

Euromonitor International, Inc., 122 South Michigan Avenue, Suite 1200, Chicago, Illinois 60603 (800) 577-EURO; *International Marketing Data and Statistics;* and *The World Economic Factbook.*

Europa Publications Limited, 18 Bedford Square, London, WC1B 3JN, England; *The Europa World Year Book.*

Food and Agricultural Organization of the United Nations (FAO), Via delle Terme di Caracalla, 00100 Rome, Italy (Telephone Number in U.S. (202) 653-2400); *The State of Food and Agriculture.*

M.E. Sharpe, 80 Business Park Drive, Armonk, New York 10504 (800) 541-6563; *The Illustrated Book of World Rankings.*

St. Martin's Press, Inc., 175 Fifth Avenue, New York, New York 10010 (800) 221-7945; *The Statesman's Year-Book.*

Statistical Office of the United Nations, Publishing Service, New York, New York 10017 (800) 253-9646; *Statistical Yearbook.*

United Nations Educational, Scientific and Cultural Organization (UNESCO), 7 Place de Fontenoy, F-75700 Paris, France (Telephone in U.S. (212) 963-5981); *Statistical Yearbook.*

The World Bank, 1818 H Street, NW, Washington, D.C. 20433 (202) 477-1234; *World Development Report.*

KUWAIT - ARMS EXPORTS AND IMPORTS - See KUWAIT - MILITARY

KUWAIT - BALANCE OF PAYMENTS

Economic Commission for Western Asia, Post Office Box 27, Baghdad, Iraq; *Statistical Abstract of Western Asia.*

The Economist Intelligence Unit, 111 West 57th Street, New York, New York 10019 (800) 938-4685; *The World Market Atlas.*

Europa Publications Limited, 18 Bedford Square, London, WC1B 3JN,

England; *The Europa World Year Book.*

International Monetary Fund, 700 Nineteenth Street, NW, Washington, D.C. 20431 (202) 623-7000; *Balance of Payments Yearbook.*

United Nations Conference on Trade and Development (UNCTAD), New York, New York 10017 (800) 253-9646; *Handbook of International Trade and Development Statistics.*

The World Bank, 1818 H Street, NW, Washington, D.C. 20433 (202) 477-1234; *World Development Report;* and *World Development Indicators.*

KUWAIT - BALANCE OF TRADE

Economic Commission for Western Asia, Post Office Box 27, Baghdad, Iraq; *Statistical Abstract of Western Asia.*

KUWAIT - BANKING

Central Statistical Office, Ministry of Planning, Post Office Box 26188, Safat, Kuwait; *Annual Statistical Abstract - State of Kuwait.*

Economic Commission for Western Asia, Post Office Box 27, Baghdad, Iraq; *Statistical Abstract of Western Asia.*

Euromonitor International, Inc., 122 South Michigan Avenue, Suite 1200, Chicago, Illinois 60603 (800) 577-EURO; *World Marketing Data and Statistics.*

Europa Publications Limited, 18 Bedford Square, London, WC1B 3JN, England; *The Europa World Year Book.*

International Monetary Fund, 700 Nineteenth Street, NW, Washington, D.C. 20431 (202) 623-7000; *International Financial Statistics.*

M.E. Sharpe, 80 Business Park Drive, Armonk, New York 10504 (800) 541-6563; *The Illustrated Book of World Rankings.*

St. Martin's Press, Inc., 175 Fifth Avenue, New York, New York 10010 (800) 221-7945; *The Statesman's Year-Book.*

KUWAIT - BARLEY PRODUCTION - See KUWAIT - CROPS

KUWAIT - BEER PRODUCTION - See KUWAIT - BEVERAGES

KUWAIT - BEVERAGES

M.E. Sharpe, 80 Business Park Drive, Armonk, New York 10504 (800) 541-6563; *The Illustrated Book of World Rankings.*

Statistical Office of the United Nations, Publishing Service, New York, New York

10017 (800) 253-9646; *Statistical Yearbook.*

KUWAIT - BIRTH RATES

Central Intelligence Agency, Washington, D.C. 20505 (703) 482-1100, www.cia.gov; *The World Factbook.*

Euromonitor International, Inc., 122 South Michigan Avenue, Suite 1200, Chicago, Illinois 60603 (800) 577-EURO; *International Marketing Data and Statistics;* and *The World Economic Factbook.*

Europa Publications Limited, 18 Bedford Square, London, WC1B 3JN, England; *The Europa World Year Book.*

M.E. Sharpe, 80 Business Park Drive, Armonk, New York 10504 (800) 541-6563; *The Illustrated Book of World Rankings.*

Statistical Office of the United Nations, Publishing Service, New York, New York 10017 (800) 253-9646; *Demographic Yearbook;* and *Statistical Yearbook.*

The World Bank, 1818 H Street, NW, Washington, D.C. 20433 (202) 477-1234; *World Development Indicators.*

World Health Organization, Office of Publications, 20 Avenue Appia, CH-1211 Geneva 27, Switzerland (Telephone Number in U.S. (518) 436-9686); *World Health Statistics Annual.*

KUWAIT - BOOK PRODUCTION

Europa Publications Limited, 18 Bedford Square, London, WC1B 3JN, England; *The Europa World Year Book.*

United Nations Educational, Scientific and Cultural Organization (UNESCO), 7 Place de Fontenoy, F-75700 Paris, France (Telephone in U.S. (212) 963-5981); *Statistical Yearbook.*

KUWAIT - BROADCASTING

Billboard Limited, Post Office Box 9027, 1006 AA Amsterdam, The Netherlands (Telephone Number in U.S. (212) 764-7300); *World Radio TV Handbook.*

Central Intelligence Agency, Washington, D.C. 20505 (703) 482-1100, www.cia.gov; *The World Factbook.*

Euromonitor International, Inc., 122 South Michigan Avenue, Suite 1200, Chicago, Illinois 60603 (800) 577-EURO; *World Marketing Data and Statistics.*

M.E. Sharpe, 80 Business Park Drive, Armonk, New York 10504 (800) 541-6563; *The Illustrated Book of World Rankings.*

St. Martin's Press, Inc., 175 Fifth Avenue, New York, New York 10010 (800)

221-7945; *The Statesman's Year-Book.*

KUWAIT - BUDGET

Central Intelligence Agency, Washington, D.C. 20505 (703) 482-1100, www.cia.gov; *The World Factbook.*

KUWAIT - CALORIE SUPPLY

Food and Agricultural Organization of the United Nations (FAO), Via delle Terme di Caracalla, 00100 Rome, Italy (Telephone Number in U.S. (202) 653-2400); *The State of Food and Agriculture.*

KUWAIT - CAPITAL REVENUE

International Monetary Fund, 700 Nineteenth Street, NW, Washington, D.C. 20431 (202) 623-7000; *Government Finance Statistics Yearbook.*

KUWAIT - CATTLE - See KUWAIT - LIVESTOCK AND POULTRY

KUWAIT - CAUSTIC SODA PRODUCTION - See KUWAIT - BEVERAGES

KUWAIT - CEMENT PRODUCTION - See KUWAIT - MINING AND MINERAL PRODUCTS

KUWAIT - CHEMICAL (ORGANIC) PRODUCTION - See KUWAIT - MINING AND MINERAL PRODUCTS

KUWAIT - CHICKENS - See KUWAIT - LIVESTOCK AND POULTRY

KUWAIT - CIGARETTE PRODUCTION - See KUWAIT - TOBACCO PRODUCTION

KUWAIT - CLIMATE

Central Statistical Office, Ministry of Planning, Post Office Box 26188, Safat, Kuwait; *Annual Statistical Abstract - State of Kuwait.*

M.E. Sharpe, 80 Business Park Drive, Armonk, New York 10504 (800) 541-6563; *The Illustrated Book of World Rankings.*

St. Martin's Press, Inc., 175 Fifth Avenue, New York, New York 10010 (800) 221-7945; *The Statesman's Year-Book.*

KUWAIT - COAL PRODUCTION - See KUWAIT - MINING AND MINERAL PRODUCTS

KUWAIT - COFFEE PRODUCTION AND CONSUMPTION - See KUWAIT - CROPS

KUWAIT - COMMERCE

St. Martin's Press, Inc., 175 Fifth Avenue, New York, New York 10010 (800) 221-7945; *The Statesman's Year-Book.*

KUWAIT - COMMUNICATIONS - See KUWAIT - TRANSPORTATION AND COMMUNICATIONS

KUWAIT - CONSTRUCTION INDUSTRY

M.E. Sharpe, 80 Business Park Drive, Armonk, New York 10504 (800) 541-6563; *The Illustrated Book of World Rankings.*

St. Martin's Press, Inc., 175 Fifth Avenue, New York, New York 10010 (800) 221-7945; *The Statesman's Year-Book.*

Statistical Office of the United Nations, Publishing Service, New York, New York 10017 (800) 253-9646; *Statistical Yearbook.*

KUWAIT - CONSUMER PRICE INDEX

Europa Publications Limited, 18 Bedford Square, London, WC1B 3JN, England; *The Europa World Year Book.*

Statistical Office of the United Nations, Publishing Service, New York, New York 10017 (800) 253-9646; *Statistical Yearbook.*

KUWAIT - CONSUMER PRICES

Euromonitor International, Inc., 122 South Michigan Avenue, Suite 1200, Chicago, Illinois 60603 (800) 577-EURO; *World Marketing Data and Statistics.*

International Labour Office, I.L.O. Publications, 1828 L Street, N.W., Suite 801, Washington, D.C. 20036 (301) 638-3152; *Yearbook of Labour Statistics.*

International Monetary Fund, 700 Nineteenth Street, NW, Washington, D.C. 20431 (202) 623-7000; *International Financial Statistics.*

KUWAIT - CONSUMPTION

The World Bank, 1818 H Street, NW, Washington, D.C. 20433 (202) 477-1234; *World Development Report.*

KUWAIT - COPPER PRODUCTION AND CONSUMPTION - See KUWAIT - MINING AND MINERAL PRODUCTS

KUWAIT - CORN PRODUCTION - See KUWAIT - CROPS

KUWAIT - CORPORATE TAXES - See KUWAIT - TAXATION

KUWAIT - COTTON PRODUCTION - See KUWAIT - CROPS

KUWAIT - CRIME

International Criminal Police Organization (INTERPOL), 50 quai Achille Lignon, F-69006 Lyon, France; *International Crime Statistics.*

Yale University Press, Yale Station, New Haven, Connecticut 06520 (800) 987-7323; *Violence and Crime in Cross-National Perspective.*

KUWAIT - CROPS

Europa Publications Limited, 18 Bedford Square, London, WC1B 3JN, England; *The Europa World Year Book.*

Food and Agricultural Organization of the United Nations (FAO), Via delle Terme di Caracalla, 00100 Rome, Italy (Telephone Number in U.S. (202) 653-2400); *The State of Food and Agriculture.*

M.E. Sharpe, 80 Business Park Drive, Armonk, New York 10504 (800) 541-6563; *The Illustrated Book of World Rankings.*

St. Martin's Press, Inc., 175 Fifth Avenue, New York, New York 10010 (800) 221-7945; *The Statesman's Year-Book.*

United Nations Conference on Trade and Development, Central Statistical Service, Palais des Nations, Geneva, Switzerland (Telephone in U.S. (800) 253-9646); *UNCTAD Commodity Yearbook.*

KUWAIT - CUSTOMS DUTIES

International Monetary Fund, 700 Nineteenth Street, NW, Washington, D.C. 20431 (202) 623-7000; *Government Finance Statistics Yearbook.*

KUWAIT - DAIRY PRODUCTS

Economic Commission for Western Asia, Post Office Box 27, Baghdad, Iraq; *Statistical Abstract of Western Asia.*

Europa Publications Limited, 18 Bedford Square, London, WC1B 3JN, England; *The Europa World Year Book.*

Food and Agricultural Organization of the United Nations (FAO), Via delle Terme di Caracalla, 00100 Rome, Italy (Telephone Number in U.S. (202) 653-2400); *The State of Food and Agriculture;* and *Production Yearbook.*

M.E. Sharpe, 80 Business Park Drive, Armonk, New York 10504 (800) 541-6563; *The Illustrated Book of World Rankings.*

St. Martin's Press, Inc., 175 Fifth Avenue, New York, New York 10010 (800) 221-7945; *The Statesman's Year-Book.*

KUWAIT - DEATH RATES - See KUWAIT - MORTALITY

KUWAIT - DEFENSE EXPENDITURES - See KUWAIT - MILITARY

KUWAIT - DEMOGRAPHY

The Economist Intelligence Unit, 111 West 57th Street, New York, New York 10019 (800) 938-4685; *The World Market Atlas.*

Euromonitor International, Inc., 122 South Michigan Avenue, Suite 1200, Chicago, Illinois 60603 (800) 577-EURO; *International Marketing Data and Statistics; World Marketing Data and Statistics;* and *The World Economic Factbook.*

M.E. Sharpe, 80 Business Park Drive, Armonk, New York 10504 (800) 541-6563; *The Illustrated Book of World Rankings.*

Statistical Office of the United Nations, Publishing Service, New York, New York 10017 (800) 253-9646; *Human Development Report.*

KUWAIT - DEVELOPMENT ASSISTANCE

Statistical Office of the United Nations, Publishing Service, New York, New York 10017 (800) 253-9646; *Statistical Yearbook.*

KUWAIT - DIAMOND PRODUCTION - See KUWAIT - MINING AND MINERAL PRODUCTS

KUWAIT - DIVORCE RATES

M.E. Sharpe, 80 Business Park Drive, Armonk, New York 10504 (800) 541-6563; *The Illustrated Book of World Rankings.*

Statistical Office of the United Nations, Publishing Service, New York, New York 10017 (800) 253-9646; *Demographic Yearbook;* and *Statistical Yearbook.*

KUWAIT - ECONOMY

Central Intelligence Agency, Washington, D.C. 20505 (703) 482-1100, www.cia.gov; *The World Factbook.*

Economist Intelligence Unit, 111 West 57th Street, New York, New York 10019 (800) 938-4685; *Kuwait Country Report.*

Euromonitor International, Inc., 122 South Michigan Avenue, Suite 1200, Chicago, Illinois 60603 (800) 577-EURO; *International Marketing Data and Statistics; World Marketing Data and Statistics;* and *The World Economic Factbook.*

Europa Publications Limited, 18 Bedford Square, London, WC1B 3JN, England; *The Europa World Year Book.*

M.E. Sharpe, 80 Business Park Drive, Armonk, New York 10504 (800) 541-6563; *The Illustrated Book of World Rankings.*

St. Martin's Press, Inc., 175 Fifth Avenue, New York, New York 10010 (800) 221-7945; *The Statesman's Year-Book.*

Statistical Office of the United Nations, Publishing Service, New York, New York 10017 (800) 253-9646; *World Statistics Pocketbook.*

The World Bank, 1818 H Street, NW, Washington, D.C. 20433 (202) 477-1234; *The World Bank Atlas;* and *World Development Report.*

KUWAIT - EDUCATION

Central Statistical Office, Ministry of Planning, Post Office Box 26188, Safat, Kuwait; *Annual Statistical Abstract - State of Kuwait.*

Economic Commission for Western Asia, Post Office Box 27, Baghdad, Iraq; *Statistical Abstract of Western Asia.*

The Economist Intelligence Unit, 111 West 57th Street, New York, New York 10019 (800) 938-4685; *The World Market Atlas.*

Euromonitor International, Inc., 122 South Michigan Avenue, Suite 1200, Chicago, Illinois 60603 (800) 577-EURO; *International Marketing Data and Statistics;* and *World Marketing Data and Statistics.*

Europa Publications Limited, 18 Bedford Square, London, WC1B 3JN, England; *The Europa World Year Book.*

International Monetary Fund, 700 Nineteenth Street, NW, Washington, D.C. 20431 (202) 623-7000; *Government Finance Statistics Yearbook.*

M.E. Sharpe, 80 Business Park Drive, Armonk, New York 10504 (800) 541-6563; *The Illustrated Book of World Rankings.*

St. Martin's Press, Inc., 175 Fifth Avenue, New York, New York 10010 (800) 221-7945; *The Statesman's Year-Book.*

Statistical Office of the United Nations, Publishing Service, New York, New York 10017 (800) 253-9646; *Human Development Report.*

United Nations Educational, Scientific and Cultural Organization (UNESCO), 7 Place de Fontenoy, F-75700 Paris, France (Telephone in U.S. (212) 963-5981); *Statistical Yearbook.*

The World Bank, 1818 H Street, NW, Washington, D.C. 20433 (202) 477-1234; *World Development Report;* and *World Development Indicators.*

KUWAIT - EGG PRODUCTION - See KUWAIT - DAIRY PRODUCTS

KUWAIT - ELECTRICITY

Central Intelligence Agency,

Washington, D.C. 20505 (703) 482-1100, www.cia.gov; *The World Factbook.*

M.E. Sharpe, 80 Business Park Drive, Armonk, New York 10504 (800) 541-6563; *The Illustrated Book of World Rankings.*

Penn Well Publishing Company, 1421 South Sheridan Road, Post Office Box 1260, Tulsa, Oklahoma 74101 (800) 752-9764; *International Energy Statistics Sourcebook.*

St. Martin's Press, Inc., 175 Fifth Avenue, New York, New York 10010 (800) 221-7945; *The Statesman's Year-Book.*

Statistical Office of the United Nations, Publishing Service, New York, New York 10017 (800) 253-9646; *Human Development Report;* and *Statistical Yearbook.*

KUWAIT - EMPLOYMENT

Economic Commission for Western Asia, Post Office Box 27, Baghdad, Iraq; *Statistical Abstract of Western Asia.*

Euromonitor International, Inc., 122 South Michigan Avenue, Suite 1200, Chicago, Illinois 60603 (800) 577-EURO; *International Marketing Data and Statistics.*

International Labour Office, I.L.O. Publications, 1828 L Street, N.W., Suite 801, Washington, D.C. 20036 (301) 638-3152; *Yearbook of Labour Statistics.*

M.E. Sharpe, 80 Business Park Drive, Armonk, New York 10504 (800) 541-6563; *The Illustrated Book of World Rankings.*

Statistical Office of the United Nations, Publishing Service, New York, New York 10017 (800) 253-9646; *Bulletin of Industrial Statistics for the Arab Countries;* and *Statistical Yearbook.*

KUWAIT - ENERGY

Business Information Display, Incorporated, 4202 Sorrento Valley Boulevard, San Diego, California 92121; *World Energy Industry.*

Economic Commission for Western Asia, Post Office Box 27, Baghdad, Iraq; *Statistical Abstract of Western Asia.*

Euromonitor International, Inc., 122 South Michigan Avenue, Suite 1200, Chicago, Illinois 60603 (800) 577-EURO; *International Marketing Data and Statistics; World Marketing Data and Statistics;* and *The World Economic Factbook.*

Food and Agricultural Organization of the United Nations (FAO), Via delle Terme di Caracalla, 00100 Rome, Italy (Telephone Number in U.S. (202) 653-2400); *The State of Food and Agriculture.*

M.E. Sharpe, 80 Business Park Drive, Armonk, New York 10504 (800) 541-6563; *The Illustrated Book of World Rankings.*

Penn Well Publishing Company, 1421 South Sheridan Road, Post Office Box 1260, Tulsa, Oklahoma 74101 (800) 752-9764; *International Energy Statistics Sourcebook.*

St. Martin's Press, Inc., 175 Fifth Avenue, New York, New York 10010 (800) 221-7945; *The Statesman's Year-Book.*

Statistical Office of the United Nations, Publishing Service, New York, New York 10017 (800) 253-9646; *Energy Statistics Yearbook; Human Development Report; World Statistics Pocketbook;* and *Statistical Yearbook.*

The World Bank, 1818 H Street, NW, Washington, D.C. 20433 (202) 477-1234; *The World Bank Atlas;* and *World Development Report.*

KUWAIT - ENVIRONMENT

Economist Intelligence Unit, 111 West 57th Street, New York, New York 10019 (800) 938-4685; *Kuwait Country Report.*

Statistical Office of the United Nations, Publishing Service, New York, New York 10017 (800) 253-9646; *World Statistics Pocketbook.*

KUWAIT - EXCHANGE RATE

Central Intelligence Agency, Washington, D.C. 20505 (703) 482-1100, www.cia.gov; *The World Factbook.*

Euromonitor International, Inc., 122 South Michigan Avenue, Suite 1200, Chicago, Illinois 60603 (800) 577-EURO; *International Marketing Data and Statistics;* and *The World Economic Factbook.*

Europa Publications Limited, 18 Bedford Square, London, WC1B 3JN, England; *The Europa World Year Book.*

International Civil Aviation Organization, 999 University Street, Montreal, Quebec, Canada H3C 5H7 (514) 285-8219; *Civil Aviation Statistics of the World.*

International Monetary Fund, 700 Nineteenth Street, NW, Washington, D.C. 20431 (202) 623-7000; *International Financial Statistics.*

Organization of Petroleum Exporting Countries, Obere Donaustrasse 93, 1020 Vienna 2, Austria; *OPEC Annual Statistical Bulletin.*

Statistical Office of the United Nations, Publishing Service, New York, New York 10017 (800) 253-9646; *Bulletin of Industrial*

Statistics for the Arab Countries; World Statistics Pocketbook; and Statistical Yearbook.

KUWAIT - EXPORTS

American Automobile Manufacturers Association, 1401 H Eye Street, NW, Suite 900, Washington, D.C. 20005 (202) 326-5500; World Motor Vehicle Data.

Central Intelligence Agency, Washington, D.C. 20505 (703) 482-1100, www.cia.gov; The World Factbook.

Economic Commission for Western Asia, Post Office Box 27, Baghdad, Iraq; Statistical Abstract of Western Asia.

The Economist Intelligence Unit, 111 West 57th Street, New York, New York 10019 (800) 938-4685; Kuwait Country Report; and The World Market Atlas.

Euromonitor International, Inc., 122 South Michigan Avenue, Suite 1200, Chicago, Illinois 60603 (800) 577-EURO ; International Marketing Data and Statistics; and The World Economic Factbook.

Europa Publications Limited, 18 Bedford Square, London, WC1B 3JN, England; The Europa World Year Book.

Food and Agricultural Organization of the United Nations (FAO), Via delle Terme di Caracalla, 00100 Rome, Italy (Telephone Number in U.S. (202) 653-2400); The State of Food and Agriculture.

International Monetary Fund, 700 Nineteenth Street, NW, Washington, D.C. 20431 (202) 623-7000; Direction of Trade Statistics,; and International Financial Statistics.

Organization of Petroleum Exporting Countries, Obere Donaustrasse 93, 1020 Vienna 2, Austria; OPEC Annual Statistical Bulletin.

St. Martin's Press, Inc., 175 Fifth Avenue, New York, New York 10010 (800) 221-7945; The Statesman's Year-Book.

Statistical Office of the United Nations, Publishing Service, New York, New York 10017 (800) 253-9646; Bulletin of Industrial Statistics for the Arab Countries.

United Nations Conference on Trade and Development (UNCTAD), New York, New York 10017 (800) 253-9646; Handbook of International Trade and Development Statistics.

The World Bank, 1818 H Street, NW, Washington, D.C. 20433 (202) 477-1234; World Development Report; and World Development Indicators.

KUWAIT - EXTERNAL INDEBTEDNESS

The World Bank, 1818 H Street, NW, Washington, D.C. 20433 (202) 477-1234; World Development Report; and World Development Indicators.

KUWAIT - EXTERNAL TRADE

Euromonitor International, Inc., 122 South Michigan Avenue, Suite 1200, Chicago, Illinois 60603 (800) 577-EURO; World Marketing Data and Statistics.

Food and Agricultural Organization of the United Nations (FAO), Via delle Terme di Caracalla, 00100 Rome, Italy (Telephone Number in U.S. (202) 653-2400); The State of Food and Agriculture; and Trade Yearbook.

Statistical Office of the United Nations, Publishing Service, New York, New York 10017 (800) 253-9646; Statistical Yearbook.

KUWAIT - FARM CROPS - See KUWAIT - CROPS

KUWAIT - FEMALE WORKING POPULATION - See KUWAIT - EMPLOYMENT

KUWAIT - FERTILITY RATES

Central Intelligence Agency, Washington, D.C. 20505 (703) 482-1100, www.cia.gov; The World Factbook.

M.E. Sharpe, 80 Business Park Drive, Armonk, New York 10504 (800) 541-6563; The Illustrated Book of World Rankings.

Statistical Office of the United Nations, Publishing Service, New York, New York 10017 (800) 253-9646; Human Development Report.

The World Bank, 1818 H Street, NW, Washington, D.C. 20433 (202) 477-1234; The World Bank Atlas; World Development Report; and World Development Indicators.

KUWAIT - FERTILIZER

Food and Agricultural Organization of the United Nations (FAO), Via delle Terme di Caracalla, 00100 Rome, Italy (Telephone Number in U.S. (202) 653-2400); Fertilizer Yearbook; and The State of Food and Agriculture.

Statistical Office of the United Nations, Publishing Service, New York, New York 10017 (800) 253-9646; Statistical Yearbook.

KUWAIT - FETAL MORTALITY - See KUWAIT - MORTALITY

KUWAIT - FINANCE

Central Statistical Office, Ministry of Planning, Post Office Box 26188, Safat, Kuwait; Annual Statistical Abstract - State of Kuwait.

Economic Commission for Western Asia, Post Office Box 27, Baghdad, Iraq; Statistical Abstract of Western Asia.

Economist Intelligence Unit, 111 West 57th Street, New York, New York 10019 (800) 938-4685; Kuwait Country Report.

Europa Publications Limited, 18 Bedford Square, London, WC1B 3JN, England; The Europa World Year Book.

International Monetary Fund, 700 Nineteenth Street, NW, Washington, D.C. 20431 (202) 623-7000; International Financial Statistics.

M.E. Sharpe, 80 Business Park Drive, Armonk, New York 10504 (800) 541-6563; The Illustrated Book of World Rankings.

St. Martin's Press, Inc., 175 Fifth Avenue, New York, New York 10010 (800) 221-7945; The Statesman's Year-Book.

KUWAIT - FISHERIES

Central Statistical Office, Ministry of Planning, Post Office Box 26188, Safat, Kuwait; Annual Statistical Abstract - State of Kuwait.

Economic Commission for Western Asia, Post Office Box 27, Baghdad, Iraq; Statistical Abstract of Western Asia.

Europa Publications Limited, 18 Bedford Square, London, WC1B 3JN, England; The Europa World Year Book.

Food and Agricultural Organization of the United Nations (FAO), Via delle Terme di Caracalla, 00100 Rome, Italy (Telephone Number in U.S. (202) 653-2400); The State of Food and Agriculture; and Yearbook of Fishery Statistics.

M.E. Sharpe, 80 Business Park Drive, Armonk, New York 10504 (800) 541-6563; The Illustrated Book of World Rankings.

St. Martin's Press, Inc., 175 Fifth Avenue, New York, New York 10010 (800) 221-7945; The Statesman's Year-Book.

Statistical Office of the United Nations, Publishing Service, New York, New York 10017 (800) 253-9646; Statistical Yearbook.

United Nations Conference on Trade and Development, Central Statistical Service, Palais des Nations, Geneva, Switzerland (Telephone in U.S. (800) 253-9646); UNCTAD Commodity Yearbook.

KUWAIT - FLOUR PRODUCTION

Statistical Office of the United Nations, Publishing Service, New York, New York 10017 (800) 253-9646; *Statistical Yearbook.*

KUWAIT - FOOD

Food and Agricultural Organization of the United Nations (FAO), Via delle Terme di Caracalla, 00100 Rome, Italy (Telephone Number in U.S. (202) 653-2400); *Production Yearbook;* and *The State of Food and Agriculture.*

Statistical Office of the United Nations, Publishing Service, New York, New York 10017 (800) 253-9646; *Human Development Report.*

United Nations Conference on Trade and Development, Central Statistical Service, Palais des Nations, Geneva, Switzerland (Telephone in U.S. (800) 253-9646); *UNCTAD Commodity Yearbook.*

KUWAIT - FOREIGN TRADE

Central Statistical Office, Ministry of Planning, Post Office Box 26188, Safat, Kuwait; *Annual Statistical Abstract - State of Kuwait.*

Economic Commission for Western Asia, Post Office Box 27, Baghdad, Iraq; *Statistical Abstract of Western Asia.*

Economist Intelligence Unit, 111 West 57th Street, New York, New York 10019 (800) 938-4685; *Kuwait Country Report.*

Euromonitor International, Inc., 122 South Michigan Avenue, Suite 1200, Chicago, Illinois 60603 (800) 577-EURO; *The World Economic Factbook.*

Europa Publications Limited, 18 Bedford Square, London, WC1B 3JN, England; *The Europa World Year Book.*

Food and Agricultural Organization of the United Nations (FAO), Via delle Terme di Caracalla, 00100 Rome, Italy (Telephone Number in U.S. (202) 653-2400); *The State of Food and Agriculture.*

International Monetary Fund, 700 Nineteenth Street, NW, Washington, D.C. 20431 (202) 623-7000; *International Financial Statistics.*

M.E. Sharpe, 80 Business Park Drive, Armonk, New York 10504 (800) 541-6563; *The Illustrated Book of World Rankings.*

St. Martin's Press, Inc., 175 Fifth Avenue, New York, New York 10010 (800) 221-7945; *The Statesman's Year-Book.*

Statistical Office of the United Nations, Publishing Service, New York, New York

10017 (800) 253-9646; *Bulletin of Industrial Statistics for the Arab Countries; International Trade Statstics Yearbook;* and *Statistical Yearbook.*

United Nations Conference on Trade and Development, Central Statistical Service, Palais des Nations, Geneva, Switzerland (Telephone in U.S. (800) 253-9646); *UNCTAD Commodity Yearbook.*

The World Bank, 1818 H Street, NW, Washington, D.C. 20433 (202) 477-1234; *World Development Report;* and *World Development Indicators.*

KUWAIT - FORESTRY AND FOREST PRODUCTS

Food and Agricultural Organization of the United Nations (FAO), Via delle Terme di Caracalla, 00100 Rome, Italy (Telephone Number in U.S. (202) 653-2400); *The State of Food and Agriculture;* and *Yearbook of Forest Products.*

M.E. Sharpe, 80 Business Park Drive, Armonk, New York 10504 (800) 541-6563; *The Illustrated Book of World Rankings.*

Statistical Office of the United Nations, Publishing Service, New York, New York 10017 (800) 253-9646; *Statistical Yearbook.*

United Nations Conference on Trade and Development, Central Statistical Service, Palais des Nations, Geneva, Switzerland (Telephone in U.S. (800) 253-9646); *UNCTAD Commodity Yearbook.*

United Nations Educational, Scientific and Cultural Organization (UNESCO), 7 Place de Fontenoy, F-75700 Paris, France (Telephone in U.S. (212) 963-5981); *Statistical Yearbook.*

The World Bank, 1818 H Street, NW, Washington, D.C. 20433 (202) 477-1234; *World Development Report.*

KUWAIT - GAS PRODUCTION - See KUWAIT - MINING AND MINERAL PRODUCTS

KUWAIT - GENERAL INDUSTRIAL STATISTICS - See KUWAIT - INDUSTRY

KUWAIT - GENERAL MORTALITY - See KUWAIT - MORTALITY

KUWAIT - GEOGRAPHIC DATA

M.E. Sharpe, 80 Business Park Drive, Armonk, New York 10504 (800) 541-6563; *The Illustrated Book of World Rankings.*

KUWAIT - GOATS - See (KUWAIT - LIVESTOCK AND POULTRY

KUWAIT - GOLD HOLDINGS

International Monetary Fund, 700 Nineteenth Street, NW, Washington, D.C. 20431 (202) 623-7000; *International Financial Statistics.*

Statistical Office of the United Nations, Publishing Service, New York, New York 10017 (800) 253-9646; *Statistical Yearbook.*

The World Bank, 1818 H Street, NW, Washington, D.C. 20433 (202) 477-1234; *World Development Indicators.*

KUWAIT - GOLD PRODUCTION - See KUWAIT - MINING AND MINERAL PRODUCTS

KUWAIT - GOVERNMENT

Central Intelligence Agency, Washington, D.C. 20505 (703) 482-1100, www.cia.gov; *The World Factbook.*

Economic Commission for Western Asia, Post Office Box 27, Baghdad, Iraq; *Statistical Abstract of Western Asia.*

Europa Publications Limited, 18 Bedford Square, London, WC1B 3JN, England; *The Europa World Year Book.*

International Monetary Fund, 700 Nineteenth Street, NW, Washington, D.C. 20431 (202) 623-7000; *Government Finance Statistics Yearbook;* and *International Financial Statistics.*

St. Martin's Press, Inc., 175 Fifth Avenue, New York, New York 10010 (800) 221-7945; *The Statesman's Year-Book.*

Statistical Office of the United Nations, Publishing Service, New York, New York 10017 (800) 253-9646; *National Accounts Statistics.*

The World Bank, 1818 H Street, NW, Washington, D.C. 20433 (202) 477-1234; *World Development Report;* and *World Development Indicators.*

KUWAIT - GRAIN PRODUCTION - See KUWAIT - CROPS

KUWAIT - GRANTS

International Monetary Fund, 700 Nineteenth Street, NW, Washington, D.C. 20431 (202) 623-7000; *Government Finance Statistics Yearbook.*

KUWAIT - GROSS DOMESTIC PRODUCT

Economic Commission for Western Asia, Post Office Box 27, Baghdad, Iraq; *Statistical Abstract of Western Asia.*

The Economist Intelligence Unit, 111 West 57th Street, New York, New York 10019 (800) 938-4685; *Kuwait Country Report;* and *The World Market Atlas.*

Euromonitor International, Inc., 122 South Michigan Avenue, Suite 1200, Chicago, Illinois 60603 (800) 577-EURO; *International Marketing Data and Statistics;* and *The World Economic Factbook.*

Europa Publications Limited, 18 Bedford Square, London, WC1B 3JN, England; *The Europa World Year Book.*

M.E. Sharpe, 80 Business Park Drive, Armonk, New York 10504 (800) 541-6563; *The Illustrated Book of World Rankings.*

Statistical Office of the United Nations, Publishing Service, New York, New York 10017 (800) 253-9646; *Bulletin of Industrial Statistics for the Arab Countries; Human Development Report; National Accounts Statistics;* and *Statistical Yearbook.*

The World Bank, 1818 H Street, NW, Washington, D.C. 20433 (202) 477-1234; *World Development Report;* and *World Development Indicators.*

KUWAIT - GROSS NATIONAL PRODUCT

Euromonitor International, Inc., 122 South Michigan Avenue, Suite 1200, Chicago, Illinois 60603 (800) 577-EURO; *International Marketing Data and Statistics.*

Organization of Petroleum Exporting Countries, Obere Donaustrasse 93, 1020 Vienna 2, Austria; *OPEC Annual Statistical Bulletin.*

St. Martin's Press, Inc., 175 Fifth Avenue, New York, New York 10010 (800) 221-7945; *The Statesman's Year-Book.*

U.S. Arms Control and Disarmament Agency, 320 Twenty-first Street, NW, Washington, D.C. 20451 (202) 647-8677; *World Military Expenditures and Arms Transfers.*

The World Bank, 1818 H Street, NW, Washington, D.C. 20433 (202) 477-1234; *The World Bank Atlas; World Development Report;* and *World Development Indicators.*

KUWAIT - HEALTH

Central Statistical Office, Ministry of Planning, Post Office Box 26188, Safat, Kuwait; *Annual Statistical Abstract - State of Kuwait.*

Economic Commission for Western Asia, Post Office Box 27, Baghdad, Iraq; *Statistical Abstract of Western Asia.*

Euromonitor International, Inc., 122 South Michigan Avenue, Suite 1200, Chicago, Illinois 60603 (800) 577-EURO; *World Marketing Data and Statistics.*

M.E. Sharpe, 80 Business Park Drive, Armonk, New York 10504 (800) 541-6563; *The Illustrated Book of World Rankings.*

St. Martin's Press, Inc., 175 Fifth Avenue, New York, New York 10010 (800) 221-7945; *The Statesman's Year-Book.*

Statistical Office of the United Nations, Publishing Service, New York, New York 10017 (800) 253-9646; *Human Development Report;* and *Statistical Yearbook.*

United Nations Children's Fund (UNICEF), 3 United Nations Plaza, New York, New York 10017 (800) 253-9646; *State of the World's Children.*

The World Bank, 1818 H Street, NW, Washington, D.C. 20433 (202) 477-1234; *World Development Report.*

KUWAIT - HEALTH EXPENDITURES

International Monetary Fund, 700 Nineteenth Street, NW, Washington, D.C. 20431 (202) 623-7000; *Government Finance Statistics Yearbook.*

KUWAIT - HIDE PRODUCTION

Food and Agricultural Organization of the United Nations (FAO), Via delle Terme di Caracalla, 00100 Rome, Italy (Telephone Number in U.S. (202) 653-2400); *Production Yearbook.*

KUWAIT - HIGHWAYS

Central Intelligence Agency, Washington, D.C. 20505 (703) 482-1100, www.cia.gov; *The World Factbook.*

Economic Commission for Western Asia, Post Office Box 27, Baghdad, Iraq; *Statistical Abstract of Western Asia.*

International Road Federation, 2600 Virginia Avenue, N.W., Washington, D.C. 20037 (202) 338-4641; *World Road Statistics.*

St. Martin's Press, Inc., 175 Fifth Avenue, New York, New York 10010 (800) 221-7945; *The Statesman's Year-Book.*

KUWAIT - HORSES - See KUWAIT - LIVESTOCK AND POULTRY

KUWAIT - HOURS OF WORK - See KUWAIT - EMPLOYMENT

KUWAIT - HOUSING AND HOUSING UNITS

Central Statistical Office, Ministry of Planning, Post Office Box 26188, Safat, Kuwait; *Annual Statistical Abstract - State of Kuwait.*

Euromonitor International, Inc., 122 South Michigan Avenue, Suite 1200, Chicago, Illinois 60603 (800) 577-EURO;

World Marketing Data and Statistics.

M.E. Sharpe, 80 Business Park Drive, Armonk, New York 10504 (800) 541-6563; *The Illustrated Book of World Rankings.*

KUWAIT - HOUSING EXPENDITURES

International Monetary Fund, 700 Nineteenth Street, NW, Washington, D.C. 20431 (202) 623-7000; *Government Finance Statistics Yearbook.*

KUWAIT - ILLITERATE POPULATION

Central Intelligence Agency, Washington, D.C. 20505 (703) 482-1100, www.cia.gov; *The World Factbook.*

The Economist Intelligence Unit, 111 West 57th Street, New York, New York 10019 (800) 938-4685; *The World Market Atlas.*

Euromonitor International, Inc., 122 South Michigan Avenue, Suite 1200, Chicago, Illinois 60603 (800) 577-EURO ; *The World Economic Factbook.*

Statistical Office of the United Nations, Publishing Service, New York, New York 10017 (800) 253-9646; *Human Development Report.*

United Nations Educational, Scientific and Cultural Organization (UNESCO), 7 Place de Fontenoy, F-75700 Paris, France (Telephone in U.S. (212) 963-5981); *Statistical Yearbook.*

KUWAIT - IMPORTS

American Automobile Manufacturers Association, 1401 H Street, NW, Suite 900, Washington, D.C. 20005 (202) 326-5500; *World Motor Vehicle Data.*

Central Intelligence Agency, Washington, D.C. 20505 (703) 482-1100, www.cia.gov; *The World Factbook.*

Economic Commission for Western Asia, Post Office Box 27, Baghdad, Iraq; *Statistical Abstract of Western Asia.*

The Economist Intelligence Unit, 111 West 57th Street, New York, New York 10019 (800) 938-4685; *Kuwait Country Report;* and *The World Market Atlas.*

Euromonitor International, Inc., 122 South Michigan Avenue, Suite 1200, Chicago, Illinois 60603 (800) 577-EURO; *International Marketing Data and Statistics;* and *The World Economic Factbook.*

Europa Publications Limited, 18 Bedford Square, London, WC1B 3JN, England; *The Europa World Year Book.*

Food and Agricultural Organization of

the United Nations (FAO), Via delle Terme di Caracalla, 00100 Rome, Italy (Telephone Number in U.S. (202) 653-2400); *The State of Food and Agriculture.*

International Monetary Fund, 700 Nineteenth Street, NW, Washington, D.C. 20431 (202) 623-7000; *Direction of Trade Statistics; International Financial Statistics;* and *Government Finance Statistics Yearbook.*

St. Martin's Press, Inc., 175 Fifth Avenue, New York, New York 10010 (800) 221-7945; *The Statesman's Year-Book.*

Statistical Office of the United Nations, Publishing Service, New York, New York 10017 (800) 253-9646; *Bulletin of Industrial Statistics for the Arab Countries.*

United Nations Conference on Trade and Development (UNCTAD), New York, New York 10017 (800) 253-9646; *Handbook of International Trade and Development Statistics.*

The World Bank, 1818 H Street, NW, Washington, D.C. 20433 (202) 477-1234; *World Development Report;* and *World Development Indicators.*

KUWAIT - INCOME TAXES - See KUWAIT - TAXATION

KUWAIT - INDUSTRY

Central Intelligence Agency, Washington, D.C. 20505 (703) 482-1100, www.cia.gov; *The World Factbook.*

Central Statistical Office, Ministry of Planning, Post Office Box 26188, Safat, Kuwait; *Annual Statistical Abstract - State of Kuwait.*

Economist Intelligence Unit, 111 West 57th Street, New York, New York 10019 (800) 938-4685; *Kuwait Country Report.*

Euromonitor International, Inc., 122 South Michigan Avenue, Suite 1200, Chicago, Illinois 60603 (800) 577-EURO; *International Marketing Data and Statistics; World Marketing Data and Statistics;* and *The World Economic Factbook.*

Europa Publications Limited, 18 Bedford Square, London, WC1B 3JN, England; *The Europa World Year Book.*

International Labour Office, I.L.O. Publications, 1828 L Street, N.W., Suite 801, Washington, D.C. 20036 (301) 638-3152; *Yearbook of Labour Statistics.*

M.E. Sharpe, 80 Business Park Drive, Armonk, New York 10504 (800) 541-6563; *The Illustrated Book of World Rankings.*

St. Martin's Press, Inc., 175 Fifth Avenue, New York, New York 10010 (800) 221-7945; *The Statesman's Year-Book.*

Statistical Office of the United Nations, Publishing Service, New York, New York 10017 (800) 253-9646; *Bulletin of Industrial Statistics for the Arab Countries;* and *Industrial Statistics Yearbook.*

The World Bank, 1818 H Street, NW, Washington, D.C. 20433 (202) 477-1234; *World Development Indicators.*

KUWAIT - INFANT AND MATERNAL MORTALITY - See KUWAIT - MORTALITY

KUWAIT - INTERNATIONAL LIQUIDITY

International Monetary Fund, 700 Nineteenth Street, NW, Washington, D.C. 20431 (202) 623-7000; *International Financial Statistics.*

KUWAIT - INTERNATIONAL RESERVES EXCLUDING GOLD

Statistical Office of the United Nations, Publishing Service, New York, New York 10017 (800) 253-9646; *Statistical Yearbook.*

The World Bank, 1818 H Street, NW, Washington, D.C. 20433 (202) 477-1234; *World Development Indicators.*

KUWAIT - IRON ORE PRODUCTION AND CONSUMPTION - See KUWAIT - MINING AND MINERAL PRODUCTS

KUWAIT - IRRIGATION

Euromonitor International, Inc., 122 South Michigan Avenue, Suite 1200, Chicago, Illinois 60603 (800) 577-EURO; *International Marketing Data and Statistics.*

KUWAIT - LABOR

Central Intelligence Agency, Washington, D.C. 20505 (703) 482-1100, www.cia.gov; *The World Factbook.*

Central Statistical Office, Ministry of Planning, Post Office Box 26188, Safat, Kuwait; *Annual Statistical Abstract - State of Kuwait.*

Economic Commission for Western Asia, Post Office Box 27, Baghdad, Iraq; *Statistical Abstract of Western Asia.*

Euromonitor International, Inc., 122 South Michigan Avenue, Suite 1200, Chicago, Illinois 60603 (800) 577-EURO; *International Marketing Data and Statistics;* and *World Marketing Data and Statistics..*

Europa Publications Limited, 18 Bedford Square, London, WC1B 3JN, England; *The Europa World Year Book.*

Food and Agricultural Organization of the United Nations (FAO), Via delle Terme di Caracalla, 00100 Rome, Italy (Telephone Number in U.S. (202) 653-2400); *The State of Food and Agriculture.*

International Labour Office, I.L.O. Publications, 1828 L Street, N.W., Suite 801, Washington, D.C. 20036 (301) 638-3152; *Yearbook of Labour Statistics.*

M.E. Sharpe, 80 Business Park Drive, Armonk, New York 10504 (800) 541-6563; *The Illustrated Book of World Rankings.*

St. Martin's Press, Inc., 175 Fifth Avenue, New York, New York 10010 (800) 221-7945; *The Statesman's Year-Book.*

Statistical Office of the United Nations, Publishing Service, New York, New York 10017 (800) 253-9646; *Human Development Report.*

The World Bank, 1818 H Street, NW, Washington, D.C. 20433 (202) 477-1234; *The World Bank Atlas; World Development Report;* and *World Development Indicators.*

KUWAIT - LAND USE

Central Intelligence Agency, Washington, D.C. 20505 (703) 482-1100, www.cia.gov; *The World Factbook.*

Economic Commission for Western Asia, Post Office Box 27, Baghdad, Iraq; *Statistical Abstract of Western Asia.*

Euromonitor International, Inc., 122 South Michigan Avenue, Suite 1200, Chicago, Illinois 60603 (800) 577-EURO; *International Marketing Data and Statistics.*

Food and Agricultural Organization of the United Nations (FAO), Via delle Terme di Caracalla, 00100 Rome, Italy (Telephone Number in U.S. (202) 653-2400); *Production Yearbook.*

The World Bank, 1818 H Street, NW, Washington, D.C. 20433 (202) 477-1234; *World Development Report.*

KUWAIT - LIBRARIES

M.E. Sharpe, 80 Business Park Drive, Armonk, New York 10504 (800) 541-6563; *The Illustrated Book of World Rankings.*

United Nations Educational, Scientific and Cultural Organization (UNESCO), 7 Place de Fontenoy, F-75700 Paris, France (Telephone in U.S. (212) 963-5981); *Statistical Yearbook.*

KUWAIT - LIFE EXPECTANCY

Central Intelligence Agency, Washington, D.C. 20505 (703) 482-1100, www.cia.gov; *The World Factbook.*

Euromonitor International, Inc., 122 South Michigan Avenue, Suite 1200, Chicago, Illinois 60603 (800) 577-EURO; *The World Economic Factbook.*

St. Martin's Press, Inc., 175 Fifth Avenue, New York, New York 10010 (800) 221-7945; *The Statesman's Year-Book.*

Statistical Office of the United Nations, Publishing Service, New York, New York 10017 (800) 253-9646; *Human Development Report;* and *World Statistics Pocketbook.*

The World Bank, 1818 H Street, NW, Washington, D.C. 20433 (202) 477-1234; *The World Bank Atlas;* and *World Development Report.*

KUWAIT - LITERACY RATE

Euromonitor International, Inc., 122 South Michigan Avenue, Suite 1200, Chicago, Illinois 60603 (800) 577-EURO; *World Marketing Data and Statistics.*

KUWAIT - LIVESTOCK AND POULTRY

Central Statistical Office, Ministry of Planning, Post Office Box 26188, Safat, Kuwait; *Annual Statistical Abstract - State of Kuwait.*

Economic Commission for Western Asia, Post Office Box 27, Baghdad, Iraq; *Statistical Abstract of Western Asia.*

Euromonitor International, Inc., 122 South Michigan Avenue, Suite 1200, Chicago, Illinois 60603 (800) 577-EURO; *International Marketing Data and Statistics.*

Europa Publications Limited, 18 Bedford Square, London, WC1B 3JN, England; *The Europa World Year Book.*

Food and Agricultural Organization of the United Nations (FAO), Via delle Terme di Caracalla, 00100 Rome, Italy (Telephone Number in U.S. (202) 653-2400); *Production Yearbook;* and *The State of Food and Agriculture.*

M.E. Sharpe, 80 Business Park Drive, Armonk, New York 10504 (800) 541-6563; *The Illustrated Book of World Rankings.*

St. Martin's Press, Inc., 175 Fifth Avenue, New York, New York 10010 (800) 221-7945; *The Statesman's Year-Book.*

Statistical Office of the United Nations, Publishing Service, New York, New York 10017 (800) 253-9646; *Statistical Yearbook.*

United Nations Conference on Trade and Development, Central Statistical Service, Palais des Nations, Geneva, Switzerland (Telephone in U.S. (800) 253-9646); *UNCTAD Commodity Yearbook.*

KUWAIT - LIVING LEVELS - See KUWAIT - LIFE EXPECTANCY

KUWAIT - MAIL - NUMBER OF PIECES SENT OR RECEIVED

Statistical Office of the United Nations, Publishing Service, New York, New York 10017 (800) 253-9646; *Statistical Yearbook.*

KUWAIT - MANUFACTURING

American Automobile Manufacturers Association, 1401 H Street, NW, Suite 900, Washington, D.C. 20005 (202) 326-5500; *World Motor Vehicle Data.*

M.E. Sharpe, 80 Business Park Drive, Armonk, New York 10504 (800) 541-6563; *The Illustrated Book of World Rankings.*

Statistical Office of the United Nations, Publishing Service, New York, New York 10017 (800) 253-9646; *Bulletin of Industrial Statistics for the Arab Countries;* and *Statistical Yearbook.*

The World Bank, 1818 H Street, NW, Washington, D.C. 20433 (202) 477-1234; *World Development Indicators.*

KUWAIT - MARRIAGE RATES

Europa Publications Limited, 18 Bedford Square, London, WC1B 3JN, England; *The Europa World Year Book.*

M.E. Sharpe, 80 Business Park Drive, Armonk, New York 10504 (800) 541-6563; *The Illustrated Book of World Rankings.*

Statistical Office of the United Nations, Publishing Service, New York, New York 10017 (800) 253-9646; *Demographic Yearbook;* and *Statistical Yearbook.*

KUWAIT - MEAT PRODUCTION - See KUWAIT - LIVESTOCK AND POULTRY

KUWAIT - MERCHANT SHIPPING

Economic Commission for Western Asia, Post Office Box 27, Baghdad, Iraq; *Statistical Abstract of Western Asia.*

Europa Publications Limited, 18 Bedford Square, London, WC1B 3JN, England; *The Europa World Year Book.*

Lloyd's Register of Shipping, 17 Battery Place, New York, New York 10004; *Register of Ships.*

Organization of Petroleum Exporting Countries, Obere Donaustrasse 93, 1020 Vienna 2, Austria; *OPEC Annual Statistical Bulletin.*

St. Martin's Press, Inc., 175 Fifth Avenue, New York, New York 10010 (800) 221-7945; *The Statesman's Year-Book.*

Statistical Office of the United Nations, Publishing Service, New York, New York 10017 (800) 253-9646; *Statistical Yearbook.*

U.S. Department of Transportation, Maritime Administration, 400 Seventh Street, SW, Washington, D.C. 20590 (202) 366-5807, www.marad.dot.gov; *A Statistical Analysis of the World's Merchant Fleets.*

KUWAIT - MILITARY

Central Intelligence Agency, Washington, D.C. 20505 (703) 482-1100, www.cia.gov; *The World Factbook.*

Euromonitor International, Inc., 122 South Michigan Avenue, Suite 1200, Chicago, Illinois 60603 (800) 577-EURO; *World Marketing Data and Statistics.*

The International Institute for Strategic Studies, 23 Tavistock Street, London WC2E 7NQ, England 44 171 3797676; *The Military Balance.*

International Monetary Fund, 700 Nineteenth Street, NW, Washington, D.C. 20431 (202) 623-7000; *Government Finance Statistics Yearbook.*

St. Martin's Press, Inc., 175 Fifth Avenue, New York, New York 10010 (800) 221-7945; *The Statesman's Year-Book.*

Statistical Office of the United Nations, Publishing Service, New York, New York 10017 (800) 253-9646; *Human Development Report.*

U.S. Arms Control and Disarmament Agency, 320 Twenty-first Street, NW, Washington, D.C. 20451 (202) 647-8677; *World Military Expenditures and Arms Transfers.*

KUWAIT - MILK PRODUCTION - See KUWAIT - DAIRY PRODUCTS

KUWAIT - MINING AND MINERAL PRODUCTS

Economic Commission for Western Asia, Post Office Box 27, Baghdad, Iraq; *Statistical Abstract of Western Asia.*

Europa Publications Limited, 18 Bedford Square, London, WC1B 3JN, England; *The Europa World Year Book.*

M.E. Sharpe, 80 Business Park Drive, Armonk, New York 10504 (800) 541-6563; *The Illustrated Book of World Rankings.*

Organization of Petroleum Exporting Countries, Obere Donaustrasse 93, 1020 Vienna 2, Austria; *OPEC Annual Statistical Bulletin.*

Penn Well Publishing Company, 1421 South Sheridan Road, Post Office Box 1260, Tulsa, Oklahoma 74101 (800) 752-9764; *International Energy Statistics Sourcebook.*

Statistical Office of the United Nations, Publishing Service, New York, New York 10017 (800) 253-9646; *Bulletin of Industrial Statistics for the Arab Countries;* and *Statistical Yearbook.*

United Nations Conference on Trade and Development, Central Statistical Service, Palais des Nations, Geneva, Switzerland (Telephone in U.S. (800) 253-9646); *UNCTAD Commodity Yearbook.*

United Nations Educational, Scientific and Cultural Organization (UNESCO), 7 Place de Fontenoy, F-75700 Paris, France (Telephone in U.S. (212) 963-5981); *Statistical Yearbook.*

KUWAIT - MONEY EXCHANGE RATES - See KUWAIT - EXCHANGE RATES

KUWAIT - MONEY RESERVES

Euromonitor International, Inc., 122 South Michigan Avenue, Suite 1200, Chicago, Illinois 60603 (800) 577-EURO; *International Marketing Data and Statistics.*

KUWAIT - MONEY SUPPLY

Economic Commission for Western Asia, Post Office Box 27, Baghdad, Iraq; *Statistical Abstract of Western Asia.*

Economist Intelligence Unit, 111 West 57th Street, New York, New York 10019 (800) 938-4685; *Kuwait Country Report.*

Euromonitor International, Inc., 122 South Michigan Avenue, Suite 1200, Chicago, Illinois 60603 (800) 577-EURO; *International Marketing Data and Statistics.*

Europa Publications Limited, 18 Bedford Square, London, WC1B 3JN, England; *The Europa World Year Book.*

International Monetary Fund, 700 Nineteenth Street, NW, Washington, D.C. 20431 (202) 623-7000; *International Financial Statistics.*

Statistical Office of the United Nations, Publishing Service, New York, New York 10017 (800) 253-9646; *Statistical Yearbook.*

The World Bank, 1818 H Street, NW, Washington, D.C. 20433 (202) 477-1234; *World Development Indicators.*

KUWAIT - MORTALITY

Central Intelligence Agency, Washington, D.C. 20505 (703) 482-1100, www.cia.gov; *The World Factbook.*

Euromonitor International, Inc., 122 South Michigan Avenue, Suite 1200, Chicago, Illinois 60603 (800) 577-EURO; *International Marketing Data and Statistics;* and *The World Economic Factbook.*

Europa Publications Limited, 18 Bedford Square, London, WC1B 3JN, England; *The Europa World Year Book.*

Statistical Office of the United Nations, Publishing Service, New York, New York 10017 (800) 253-9646; *Demographic Yearbook; Human Development Report; World Statistics Pocketbook;* and *Statistical Yearbook.*

United Nations Children's Fund (UNICEF), 3 United Nations Plaza, New York, New York 10017 (800) 253-9646; *State of the World's Children.*

The World Bank, 1818 H Street, NW, Washington, D.C. 20433 (202) 477-1234; *The World Bank Atlas; World Development Report;* and *World Development Indicators.*

World Health Organization, Office of Publications, 20 Avenue Appia, CH-1211 Geneva 27, Switzerland (Telephone Number in U.S. (518) 436-9686); *World Health Statistics Annual.*

KUWAIT - MOTION PICTURES

St. Martin's Press, Inc., 175 Fifth Avenue, New York, New York 10010 (800) 221-7945; *The Statesman's Year-Book.*

Statistical Office of the United Nations, Publishing Service, New York, New York 10017 (800) 253-9646; *Statistical Yearbook.*

KUWAIT - MOTOR VEHICLE PRODUCTION

American Automobile Manufacturers Association, 1401 H Street, NW, Suite 900, Washington, D.C. 20005 (202) 326-5500; *World Motor Vehicle Data.*

KUWAIT - MOTOR VEHICLE TAXES - See KUWAIT - TAXATION

KUWAIT - MOTOR VEHICLES IN USE

American Automobile Manufacturers Association, 1401 H Street, NW, Suite 900, Washington, D.C. 20005 (202) 326-5500; *World Motor Vehicle Data.*

Economic Commission for Western Asia, Post Office Box 27, Baghdad, Iraq; *Statistical Abstract of Western Asia.*

Europa Publications Limited, 18 Bedford Square, London, WC1B 3JN, England; *The Europa World Year Book.*

International Road Federation, 2600 Virginia Avenue, N.W., Washington, D.C.

20037 (202) 338-4641; *World Road Statistics.*

Statistical Office of the United Nations, Publishing Service, New York, New York 10017 (800) 253-9646; *Statistical Yearbook.*

KUWAIT - MUSEUMS

M.E. Sharpe, 80 Business Park Drive, Armonk, New York 10504 (800) 541-6563; *The Illustrated Book of World Rankings.*

United Nations Educational, Scientific and Cultural Organization (UNESCO), 7 Place de Fontenoy, F-75700 Paris, France (Telephone in U.S. (212) 963-5981); *Statistical Yearbook.*

KUWAIT - NATALITY - See KUWAIT - BIRTH RATES

KUWAIT - NATIONAL ACCOUNTS

Economic Commission for Western Asia, Post Office Box 27, Baghdad, Iraq; *Statistical Abstract of Western Asia.*

Europa Publications Limited, 18 Bedford Square, London, WC1B 3JN, England; *The Europa World Year Book.*

International Monetary Fund, 700 Nineteenth Street, NW, Washington, D.C. 20431 (202) 623-7000; *International Financial Statistics.*

Statistical Office of the United Nations, Publishing Service, New York, New York 10017 (800) 253-9646; *National Accounts Statistics;* and *Statistical Yearbook.*

KUWAIT - NATIONAL INCOME

Central Statistical Office, Ministry of Planning, Post Office Box 26188, Safat, Kuwait; *Annual Statistical Abstract - State of Kuwait.*

M.E. Sharpe, 80 Business Park Drive, Armonk, New York 10504 (800) 541-6563; *The Illustrated Book of World Rankings.*

Statistical Office of the United Nations, Publishing Service, New York, New York 10017 (800) 253-9646; *National Accounts Statistics;* and *Statistical Yearbook.*

KUWAIT - NATIONAL PRODUCT

M.E. Sharpe, 80 Business Park Drive, Armonk, New York 10504 (800) 541-6563; *The Illustrated Book of World Rankings.*

KUWAIT - NATURAL GAS PRODUCTION - See KUWAIT - MINING AND MINERAL PRODUCTS

KUWAIT - NEWSPAPER PRODUCTION - See KUWAIT - FORESTRY AND FOREST PRODUCTS

Switzerland (Telephone in U.S. (800) 253-9646); *UNCTAD Commodity Yearbook*.

KUWAIT - THEATRE

United Nations Educational, Scientific and Cultural Organization (UNESCO), 7 Place de Fontenoy, F-75700 Paris, France (Telephone in U.S. (212) 963-5981); *Statistical Yearbook*.

KUWAIT - TOBACCO PRODUCTION

M.E. Sharpe, 80 Business Park Drive, Armonk, New York 10504 (800) 541-6563; *The Illustrated Book of World Rankings*.

KUWAIT - TOURISM

Central Statistical Office, Ministry of Planning, Post Office Box 26188, Safat, Kuwait; *Annual Statistical Abstract - State of Kuwait*.

Economic Commission for Western Asia, Post Office Box 27, Baghdad, Iraq; *Statistical Abstract of Western Asia*.

Euromonitor International, Inc., 122 South Michigan Avenue, Suite 1200, Chicago, Illinois 60603 (800) 577-EURO; *The World Economic Factbook;* and *World Marketing Data and Statistics*.

M.E. Sharpe, 80 Business Park Drive, Armonk, New York 10504 (800) 541-6563; *The Illustrated Book of World Rankings*.

St. Martin's Press, Inc., 175 Fifth Avenue, New York, New York 10010 (800) 221-7945; *The Statesman's Year-Book*.

Statistical Office of the United Nations, Publishing Service, New York, New York 10017 (800) 253-9646; *Statistical Yearbook*.

KUWAIT - TRACTORS IN USE

Statistical Office of the United Nations, Publishing Service, New York, New York 10017 (800) 253-9646; *Statistical Yearbook*.

KUWAIT - TRADE - See KUWAIT - FOREIGN TRADE

KUWAIT - TRANSPORTATION AND COMMUNICATIONS

Central Intelligence Agency, Washington, D.C. 20505 (703) 482-1100, www.cia.gov; *The World Factbook*.

Central Statistical Office, Ministry of Planning, Post Office Box 26188, Safat, Kuwait; *Annual Statistical Abstract - State of Kuwait*.

Economic Commission for Western Asia, Post Office Box 27, Baghdad, Iraq; *Statistical Abstract of Western Asia*.

Euromonitor International, Inc., 122 South Michigan Avenue, Suite 1200, Chicago, Illinois 60603 (800) 577-EURO; *International Marketing Data and Statistics;* and *World Marketing Data and Statistics*.

Europa Publications Limited, 18 Bedford Square, London, WC1B 3JN, England; *The Europa World Year Book*.

M.E. Sharpe, 80 Business Park Drive, Armonk, New York 10504 (800) 541-6563; *The Illustrated Book of World Rankings*.

St. Martin's Press, Inc., 175 Fifth Avenue, New York, New York 10010 (800) 221-7945; *The Statesman's Year-Book*.

Statistical Office of the United Nations, Publishing Service, New York, New York 10017 (800) 253-9646; *Human Development Report*.

KUWAIT - UNEMPLOYMENT

Central Intelligence Agency, Washington, D.C. 20505 (703) 482-1100, www.cia.gov; *The World Factbook*.

Euromonitor International, Inc., 122 South Michigan Avenue, Suite 1200, Chicago, Illinois 60603 (800) 577-EURO; *International Marketing Data and Statistics*.

International Labour Office, I.L.O. Publications, 1828 L Street, N.W., Suite 801, Washington, D.C. 20036 (301) 638-3152; *Yearbook of Labour Statistics*.

St. Martin's Press, Inc., 175 Fifth Avenue, New York, New York 10010 (800) 221-7945; *The Statesman's Year-Book*.

KUWAIT - VITAL STATISTICS

Central Statistical Office, Ministry of Planning, Post Office Box 26188, Safat, Kuwait; *Annual Statistical Abstract - State of Kuwait*.

Euromonitor International, Inc., 122 South Michigan Avenue, Suite 1200, Chicago, Illinois 60603 (800) 577-EURO; *International Marketing Data and Statistics*.

Statistical Office of the United Nations, Publishing Service, New York, New York 10017 (800) 253-9646; *Statistical Yearbook*.

World Health Organization, Office of Publications, 20 Avenue Appia, CH-1211 Geneva 27, Switzerland (Telephone Number in U.S. (518) 436-9686); *World Health Statistics Annual*.

KUWAIT - WAGES

International Labour Office, I.L.O. Publications, 1828 L Street, N.W., Suite 801, Washington, D.C. 20036 (301) 638-3152; *Yearbook of Labour Statistics*.

KUWAIT - WEATHER - See KUWAIT - CLIMATE

KUWAIT - WELFARE EXPENDITURES

International Monetary Fund, 700 Nineteenth Street, NW, Washington, D.C. 20431 (202) 623-7000; *Government Finance Statistics Yearbook*.

KUWAIT - WHEAT PRODUCTION AND PRICES - See KUWAIT - CROPS

KUWAIT - WHOLESALE PRICES

International Monetary Fund, 700 Nineteenth Street, NW, Washington, D.C. 20431 (202) 623-7000; *International Financial Statistics*.

Statistical Office of the United Nations, Publishing Service, New York, New York 10017 (800) 253-9646; *Statistical Yearbook*.

KUWAIT - WINE PRODUCTION - See KUWAIT - BEVERAGES

KUWAIT - WOOL PRODUCTION - See KUWAIT - TEXTILE INDUSTRY

Kyrgyzstan - National Statistical Office

State Committee of Republic of Kyrgyzstan on Statistics, 374 Frunze Street, Bishkek 720884, Kyrgyzstan.

KYRGYZSTAN - ABORTIONS

Statistical Office of the United Nations, Publishing Service, New York, New York 10017 (800) 253-9646; *Trends in Europe and North America: The Statistical Yearbook of the Economic Commission for Europe*.

KYRGYZSTAN - AGRICULTURE

Academic International Press, Box 1111, Gulf Breeze, Florida 32562; *Russia and Eurasia Facts and Figures Annual*.

Business International Moscow, 23 Profsoyuznaya Ulitsa, 117859, Moscow (Telephone Number in U.S. (800) 938-4685); *The CIS Market Atlas*.

Economist Intelligence Unit, 111 West 57th Street, New York, New York 10019 (800) 938-4685; *Kyrgzstan Country Report*.

Euromonitor International, Inc., 122 South Michigan Avenue, Suite 1200, Chicago, Illinois 60603 (800) 577-EURO; *World Marketing Data and Statistics*.

Europa Publications Limited, 18 Bedford Square, London, WC1B 3JN, England; *The Europa World Year Book*.

Food and Agriculture Organization of the United Nations (FAO), Via delle Terme di Caracalla, 00100, Rome, Italy (Telephone Number in U.S. (202) 653-2400); *Production Yearbook; The State of Food and Agriculture;* and *Trade Yearbook.*

St. Martin's Press, Inc., 175 Fifth Avenue, New York, New York 10010 (800) 221-7945; *The Statesman's Year-Book.*

Statistical Office of the United Nations, Publishing Service, New York, New York 10017 (800) 253-9646; *Industrial Commodity Statistics Yearbook;* and *Statistical Yearbook.*

The World Bank, 1818 H Street, NW, Washington, D.C. 20433 (202) 477-1234; *Statistical Handbook: States of the Former USSR;* and *World Development Indicators.*

KYRGYZSTAN - AIRLINE SERVICE

Business International Moscow, 23 Profsoyuznaya Ulitsa, 117859, Moscow (Telephone Number in U.S. (800) 938-4685); *The CIS Market Atlas.*

International Civil Aviation Organization, 999 University Street, Montreal, Quebec, Canada H3C 5H7 (514) 285-8219; *Civil Aviation Statistics of the World.*

St. Martin's Press, Inc., 175 Fifth Avenue, New York, New York 10010 (800) 221-7945; *The Statesman's Year-Book.*

Statistical Office of the United Nations, Publishing Service, New York, New York 10017 (800) 253-9646; *Statistical Yearbook.*

KYRGYZSTAN - AIRPORTS

Central Intelligence Agency, Washington, D.C. 20505 (703) 482-1100, www.cia.gov; *The World Factbook.*

KYRGYZSTAN - ANIMAL HEALTH

Food and Agriculture Organization of the United Nations (FAO), Via delle Terme di Caracalla, 00100, Rome, Italy (Telephone Number in U.S. (202) 653-2400); *Animal Health Yearbook.*

KYRGYZSTAN - AREA AND DENSITY OF POPULATION

Academic International Press, Box 1111, Gulf Breeze, Florida 32562; *Russia and Eurasia Facts and Figures Annual.*

Business International Moscow, 23 Profsoyuznaya Ulitsa, 117859, Moscow (Telephone Number in U.S. (800) 938-4685); *The CIS Market Atlas.*

Central Intelligence Agency, Washington, D.C. 20505 (703) 482-1100,

www.cia.gov; *The World Factbook.*

Euromonitor International, Inc., 122 South Michigan Avenue, Suite 1200, Chicago, Illinois 60603 (800) 577-EURO; *The World Economic Factbook.*

Europa Publications Limited, 18 Bedford Square, London, WC1B 3JN, England; *The Europa World Year Book.*

St. Martin's Press, Inc., 175 Fifth Avenue, New York, New York 10010 (800) 221-7945; *The Statesman's Year-Book.*

Statistical Office of the United Nations, Publishing Service, New York, New York 10017 (800) 253-9646; *Statistical Yearbook;* and *Trends in Europe and North America: The Statistical Yearbook of the Economic Commission for Europe.*

United Nations Educational, Scientific and Cultural Organization (UNESCO), 7 Place de Fontenoy, F-75700 Paris, France (Telephone Number in U.S. (212) 963-5981); *Statistical Yearbook.*

The World Bank, 1818 H Street, NW, Washington, D.C. 20433 (202) 477-1234; *World Development Report.*

KYRGYZSTAN - BALANCE OF PAYMENTS

Europa Publications Limited, 18 Bedford Square, London, WC1B 3JN, England; *The Europa World Year Book.*

United Nations Conference on Trade and Development (UNCTAD), New York, New York 10017 (800) 253-9646; *Handbook of International Trade and Development Statistics.*

The World Bank, 1818 H Street, NW, Washington, D.C. 20433 (202) 477-1234; *World Development Report;* and *World Development Indicators.*

KYRGYZSTAN - BANKING

Business International Moscow, 23 Profsoyuznaya Ulitsa, 117859, Moscow (Telephone Number in U.S. (800) 938-4685); *The CIS Market Atlas.*

Euromonitor International, Inc., 122 South Michigan Avenue, Suite 1200, Chicago, Illinois 60603 (800) 577-EURO; *World Marketing Data and Statistics.*

St. Martin's Press, Inc., 175 Fifth Avenue, New York, New York 10010 (800) 221-7945; *The Statesman's Year-Book.*

KYRGYZSTAN - BEVERAGES

Statistical Office of the United Nations, Publishing Service, New York, New York 10017 (800) 253-9646; *Statistical Yearbook.*

KYRGYZSTAN - BIRTH RATES

Academic International Press, Box 1111, Gulf Breeze, Florida 32562; *Russia and Eurasia Facts and Figures Annual.*

Business International Moscow, 23 Profsoyuznaya Ulitsa, 117859, Moscow (Telephone Number in U.S. (800) 938-4685); *The CIS Market Atlas.*

Central Intelligence Agency, Washington, D.C. 20505 (703) 482-1100, www.cia.gov; *The World Factbook.*

Euromonitor International, Inc., 122 South Michigan Avenue, Suite 1200, Chicago, Illinois 60603 (800) 577-EURO; *International Marketing Data and Statistics;* and *The World Economic Factbook.*

Europa Publications Limited, 18 Bedford Square, London, WC1B 3JN, England; *The Europa World Year Book.*

St. Martin's Press, Inc., 175 Fifth Avenue, New York, New York 10010 (800) 221-7945; *The Statesman's Year-Book.*

Statistical Office of the United Nations, Publishing Service, New York, New York 10017 (800) 253-9646; *Statistical Yearbook.*

World Health Organization, Office of Publications, 20 Avenue Appia, CH-1211 Geneva 27, Switzerland (Telephone Number in U.S. (518) 436-9686); *World Health Statistics Annual.*

KYRGYZSTAN - BOOK PRODUCTION

Statistical Office of the United Nations, Publishing Service, New York, New York 10017 (800) 253-9646; *Trends in Europe and North America: The Statistical Yearbook of the Economic Commission for Europe.*

United Nations Educational, Scientific and Cultural Organization (UNESCO), 7 Place de Fontenoy, F-75700 Paris, France (Telephone Number in U.S. (212) 963-5981); *Statistical Yearbook.*

KYRGYZSTAN - BROADCASTING

Central Intelligence Agency, Washington, D.C. 20505 (703) 482-1100, www.cia.gov; *The World Factbook.*

Euromonitor International, Inc., 122 South Michigan Avenue, Suite 1200, Chicago, Illinois 60603 (800) 577-EURO; *World Marketing Data and Statistics.*

St. Martin's Press, Inc., 175 Fifth Avenue, New York, New York 10010 (800) 221-7945; *The Statesman's Year-Book.*

Statistical Office of the United Nations, Publishing Service, New York, New York 10017 (800) 253-9646; *Trends in Europe and*

North America: The Statistical Yearbook of the Economic Commission for Europe.

United Nations Educational, Scientific and Cultural Organization (UNESCO), 7 Place de Fontenoy, F-75700 Paris, France (Telephone Number in U.S. (212) 963-5981); *Statistical Yearbook.*

KYRGYZSTAN - BUDGET

Business International Moscow, 23 Profsoyuznaya Ulitsa, 117859, Moscow (Telephone Number in U.S. (800) 938-4685); *The CIS Market Atlas.*

Central Intelligence Agency, Washington, D.C. 20505 (703) 482-1100, www.cia.gov; *The World Factbook.*

KYRGYZSTAN - CAPITAL INVESTMENT

The World Bank, 1818 H Street, NW, Washington, D.C. 20433 (202) 477-1234; *Statistical Handbook: States of the Former USSR.*

KYRGYZSTAN - CATTLE - See KYRGYZSTAN - LIVESTOCK AND POULTRY

KYRGYZSTAN - CHEMICALS

Business International Moscow, 23 Profsoyuznaya Ulitsa, 117859, Moscow (Telephone Number in U.S. (800) 938-4685); *The CIS Market Atlas.*

KYRGYZSTAN - COAL PRODUCTION AND CONSUMPTION - See KYRGYZSTAN - MINING AND MINERAL PRODUCTS

KYRGYZSTAN - COMMERCE

St. Martin's Press, Inc., 175 Fifth Avenue, New York, New York 10010 (800) 221-7945; *The Statesman's Year-Book.*

KYRGYZSTAN - COMMUNICATIONS - See KYRGYZSTAN - TRANSPORTATION AND COMMUNICATIONS

KYRGYZSTAN - CONSTRUCTION INDUSTRY

Academic International Press, Box 1111, Gulf Breeze, Florida 32562; *Russia and Eurasia Facts and Figures Annual.*

Business International Moscow, 23 Profsoyuznaya Ulitsa, 117859, Moscow (Telephone Number in U.S. (800) 938-4685); *The CIS Market Atlas.*

Statistical Office of the United Nations, Publishing Service, New York, New York 10017 (800) 253-9646; *Statistical Yearbook.*

KYRGYZSTAN - CONSUMER PRICE INDEX

Statistical Office of the United Nations, Publishing Service, New York, New York

10017 (800) 253-9646; *Statistical Yearbook;* and *Trends in Europe and North America: The Statistical Yearbook of the Economic Commission for Europe.*

KYRGYZSTAN - CONSUMER PRICES

Euromonitor International, Inc., 122 South Michigan Avenue, Suite 1200, Chicago, Illinois 60603 (800) 577-EURO; *World Marketing Data and Statistics.*

KYRGYZSTAN - CONSUMER PRODUCTS

Business International Moscow, 23 Profsoyuznaya Ulitsa, 117859, Moscow (Telephone Number in U.S. (800) 938-4685); *The CIS Market Atlas.*

KYRGYZSTAN - CONSUMPTION

Business International Moscow, 23 Profsoyuznaya Ulitsa, 117859, Moscow (Telephone Number in U.S. (800) 938-4685); *The CIS Market Atlas.*

The World Bank, 1818 H Street, NW, Washington, D.C. 20433 (202) 477-1234; *Statistical Handbook: States of the Former USSR;* and *World Development Report.*

KYRGYZSTAN - COTTON PRODUCTION AND CONSUMPTION - See KYRGYZSTAN - CROPS

KYRGYZSTAN - CRIME

Academic International Press, Box 1111, Gulf Breeze, Florida 32562; *Russia and Eurasia Facts and Figures Annual.*

Statistical Office of the United Nations, Publishing Service, New York, New York 10017 (800) 253-9646; *Trends in Europe and North America: The Statistical Yearbook of the Economic Commission for Europe.*

KYRGYZSTAN - CROPS

Academic International Press, Box 1111, Gulf Breeze, Florida 32562; *Russia and Eurasia Facts and Figures Annual.*

Europa Publications Limited, 18 Bedford Square, London, WC1B 3JN, England; *The Europa World Year Book.*

Food and Agriculture Organization of the United Nations (FAO), Via delle Terme di Caracalla, 00100, Rome, Italy (Telephone Number in U.S. (202) 653-2400); *Production Yearbook; The State of Food and Agriculture;* and *Trade Yearbook.*

St. Martin's Press, Inc., 175 Fifth Avenue, New York, New York 10010 (800) 221-7945; *The Statesman's Year-Book.*

Statistical Office of the United Nations, Publishing Service, New York, New York 10017 (800) 253-9646; *Industrial*

Commodity Statistics Yearbook; and *Statistical Yearbook.*

The World Bank, 1818 H Street, NW, Washington, D.C. 20433 (202) 477-1234; *Statistical Handbook: States of the Former USSR.*

KYRGYZSTAN - DAIRY PRODUCTS

Europa Publications Limited, 18 Bedford Square, London, WC1B 3JN, England; *The Europa World Year Book.*

Food and Agriculture Organization of the United Nations (FAO), Via delle Terme di Caracalla, 00100, Rome, Italy (Telephone Number in U.S. (202) 653-2400); *Production Yearbook; The State of Food and Agriculture;* and *Trade Yearbook.*

St. Martin's Press, Inc., 175 Fifth Avenue, New York, New York 10010 (800) 221-7945; *The Statesman's Year-Book.*

Statistical Office of the United Nations, Publishing Service, New York, New York 10017 (800) 253-9646; *Industrial Commodity Statistics Yearbook;* and *Statistical Yearbook.*

KYRGYZSTAN - DEATH RATES - See KYRGYZSTAN - MORTALITY

KYRGYZSTAN - DEMOGRAPHY

Business International Moscow, 23 Profsoyuznaya Ulitsa, 117859, Moscow (Telephone Number in U.S. (800) 938-4685); *The CIS Market Atlas.*

Euromonitor International, Inc., 122 South Michigan Avenue, Suite 1200, Chicago, Illinois 60603 (800) 577-EURO; *International Marketing Data and Statistics; World Marketing Data and Statistics;* and *The World Economic Factbook.*

Statistical Office of the United Nations, Publishing Service, New York, New York 10017 (800) 253-9646; *Demographic Yearbook;* and *Human Development Report.*

The World Bank, 1818 H Street, NW, Washington, D.C. 20433 (202) 477-1234; *Statistical Handbook: States of the Former USSR.*

KYRGYZSTAN - DISEASES - See KYRGYZSTAN - HEALTH

KYRGYZSTAN - DIVORCE RATES

Academic International Press, Box 1111, Gulf Breeze, Florida 32562; *Russia and Eurasia Facts and Figures Annual.*

Statistical Office of the United Nations, Publishing Service, New York, New York 10017 (800) 253-9646; *Demographic*

Yearbook; Trends in Europe and North America: The Statistical Yearbook of the Economic Commission for Europe; and *Statistical Yearbook.*

KYRGYZSTAN - DOMESTIC INVESTMENT

Business International Moscow, 23 Profsoyuznaya Ulitsa, 117859, Moscow (Telephone Number in U.S. (800) 938-4685); *The CIS Market Atlas.*

KYRGYZSTAN - ECONOMY

Academic International Press, Box 1111, Gulf Breeze, Florida 32562; *Russia and Eurasia Facts and Figures Annual.*

Business International Moscow, 23 Profsoyuznaya Ulitsa, 117859, Moscow (Telephone Number in U.S. (800) 938-4685); *The CIS Market Atlas.*

Central Intelligence Agency, Washington, D.C. 20505 (703) 482-1100, www.cia.gov; *The World Factbook.*

Economist Intelligence Unit, 111 West 57th Street, New York, New York 10019 (800) 938-4685; *Kyrgyzstan Country Report.*

Euromonitor International, Inc., 122 South Michigan Avenue, Suite 1200, Chicago, Illinois 60603 (800) 577-EURO; *The World Economic Factbook;* and *World Marketing Data and Statistics.*

St. Martin's Press, Inc., 175 Fifth Avenue, New York, New York 10010 (800) 221-7945; *The Statesman's Year-Book.*

Statistical Office of the United Nations, Publishing Service, New York, New York 10017 (800) 253-9646; *World Statistics Pocketbook.*

The World Bank, 1818 H Street, NW, Washington, D.C. 20433 (202) 477-1234; *The World Bank Atlas;* and *World Development Report.*

KYRGYZSTAN - EDUCATION

Academic International Press, Box 1111, Gulf Breeze, Florida 32562; *Russia and Eurasia Facts and Figures Annual.*

Business International Moscow, 23 Profsoyuznaya Ulitsa, 117859, Moscow (Telephone Number in U.S. (800) 938-4685); *The CIS Market Atlas.*

Euromonitor International, Inc., 122 South Michigan Avenue, Suite 1200, Chicago, Illinois 60603 (800) 577-EURO; *International Marketing Data and Statistics;* and *World Marketing Data and Statistics.*

Europa Publications Limited, 18 Bedford Square, London, WC1B 3JN, England; *The Europa World Year Book.*

St. Martin's Press, Inc., 175 Fifth Avenue, New York, New York 10010 (800) 221-7945; *The Statesman's Year-Book.*

Statistical Office of the United Nations, Publishing Service, New York, New York 10017 (800) 253-9646; *Human Development Report;* and *Trends in Europe and North America: The Statistical Yearbook of the Economic Commission for Europe.*

United Nations Educational, Scientific and Cultural Organization (UNESCO), 7 Place de Fontenoy, F-75700 Paris, France (Telephone Number in U.S. (212) 963-5981); *Statistical Yearbook.*

The World Bank, 1818 H Street, NW, Washington, D.C. 20433 (202) 477-1234; *World Development Report.*

KYRGYZSTAN - ELECTRICITY

Academic International Press, Box 1111, Gulf Breeze, Florida 32562; *Russia and Eurasia Facts and Figures Annual.*

Business International Moscow, 23 Profsoyuznaya Ulitsa, 117859, Moscow (Telephone Number in U.S. (800) 938-4685); *The CIS Market Atlas.*

Central Intelligence Agency, Washington, D.C. 20505 (703) 482-1100, www.cia.gov; *The World Factbook.*

St. Martin's Press, Inc., 175 Fifth Avenue, New York, New York 10010 (800) 221-7945; *The Statesman's Year-Book.*

Statistical Office of the United Nations, Publishing Service, New York, New York 10017 (800) 253-9646; *Energy Statistics Yearbook; Human Development Report; Trends in Europe and North America: The Statistical Yearbook of the Economic Commission for Europe;* and *Statistical Yearbook.*

The World Bank, 1818 H Street, NW, Washington, D.C. 20433 (202) 477-1234; *Statistical Handbook: States of the Former USSR.*

KYRGYZSTAN - EMPLOYMENT

Euromonitor International, Inc., 122 South Michigan Avenue, Suite 1200, Chicago, Illinois 60603 (800) 577-EURO; *International Marketing Data and Statistics.*

Statistical Office of the United Nations, Publishing Service, New York, New York 10017 (800) 253-9646; *Statistical Yearbook;* and *Trends in Europe and North America: The Statistical Yearbook of the Economic Commission for Europe.*

The World Bank, 1818 H Street, NW, Washington, D.C. 20433 (202) 477-1234;

Statistical Handbook: States of the Former USSR.

KYRGYZSTAN - ENERGY

Academic International Press, Box 1111, Gulf Breeze, Florida 32562; *Russia and Eurasia Facts and Figures Annual.*

Business International Moscow, 23 Profsoyuznaya Ulitsa, 117859, Moscow (Telephone Number in U.S. (800) 938-4685); *The CIS Market Atlas.*

Euromonitor International, Inc., 122 South Michigan Avenue, Suite 1200, Chicago, Illinois 60603 (800) 577-EURO; *International Marketing Data and Statistics;* and *World Marketing Data and Statistics.*

St. Martin's Press, Inc., 175 Fifth Avenue, New York, New York 10010 (800) 221-7945; *The Statesman's Year-Book.*

Statistical Office of the United Nations, Publishing Service, New York, New York 10017 (800) 253-9646; *Energy Statistics Yearbook; Human Development Report; Trends in Europe and North America: The Statistical Yearbook of the Economic Commission for Europe; World Statistics Pocketbook;* and *Statistical Yearbook.*

The World Bank, 1818 H Street, NW, Washington, D.C. 20433 (202) 477-1234; *The World Bank Atlas; Statistical Handbook: States of the Former USSR;* and *World Development Report.*

KYRGYZSTAN - ENVIRONMENT

Business International Moscow, 23 Profsoyuznaya Ulitsa, 117859, Moscow (Telephone Number in U.S. (800) 938-4685); *The CIS Market Atlas.*

Economist Intelligence Unit, 111 West 57th Street, New York, New York 10019 (800) 938-4685; *Kyrgyzstan Country Report.*

Statistical Office of the United Nations, Publishing Service, New York, New York 10017 (800) 253-9646; *Statistical Yearbook; World Statistics Pocketbook;* and *Trends in Europe and North America: The Statistical Yearbook of the Economic Commission for Europe.*

KYRGYZSTAN - EXCHANGE RATES

Central Intelligence Agency, Washington, D.C. 20505 (703) 482-1100, www.cia.gov; *The World Factbook.*

Euromonitor International, Inc., 122 South Michigan Avenue, Suite 1200, Chicago, Illinois 60603 (800) 577-EURO; *International Marketing Data and Statistics.*

Europa Publications Limited, 18 Bedford Square, London, WC1B 3JN,

England; *The Europa World Year Book.*

Statistical Office of the United Nations, Publishing Service, New York, New York 10017 (800) 253-9646; *Statistical Yearbook; World Statistics Pocketbook;* and *Trends in Europe and North America: The Statistical Yearbook of the Economic Commission for Europe.*

Walden Publishing, Ltd., Two Market Street, Saffron Walden Essex, CB10 1HZ, England; *The World of Information Asia and Pacific Review.*

KYRGYZSTAN - EXPORTS

Academic International Press, Box 1111, Gulf Breeze, Florida 32562; *Russia and Eurasia Facts and Figures Annual.*

Business International Moscow, 23 Profsoyuznaya Ulitsa, 117859, Moscow (Telephone Number in U.S. (800) 938-4685); *The CIS Market Atlas.*

Central Intelligence Agency, Washington, D.C. 20505 (703) 482-1100, www.cia.gov; *The World Factbook.*

Economist Intelligence Unit, 111 West 57th Street, New York, New York 10019 (800) 938-4685; *Kyrgyzstan Country Report.*

Euromonitor International, Inc., 122 South Michigan Avenue, Suite 1200, Chicago, Illinois 60603 (800) 577-EURO; *International Marketing Data and Statistics.*

Europa Publications Limited, 18 Bedford Square, London, WC1B 3JN, England; *The Europa World Year Book.*

International Monetary Fund, 700 Nineteenth Street, NW, Washington, D.C. 20431 (202) 623-7000; *Direction of Trade Statistics.*

St. Martin's Press, Inc., 175 Fifth Avenue, New York, New York 10010 (800) 221-7945; *The Statesman's Year-Book.*

Statistical Office of the United Nations, Publishing Service, New York, New York 10017 (800) 253-9646; *International Trade Statistics Yearbook;* and *Trends in Europe and North America: The Statistical Yearbook of the Economic Commission for Europe.*

United Nations Conference on Trade and Development (UNCTAD), New York, New York 10017 (800) 253-9646; *Handbook of International Trade and Development Statistics.*

Walden Publishing, Ltd., Two Market Street, Saffron Walden Essex, CB10 1HZ, England; *The World of Information Asia and Pacific Review.*

The World Bank, 1818 H Street, NW, Washington, D.C. 20433 (202) 477-1234; *Statistical Handbook: States of the Former USSR; World Development Report;* and *World Development Indicators.*

KYRGYZSTAN - EXTERNAL DEBT

The World Bank, 1818 H Street, NW, Washington, D.C. 20433 (202) 477-1234; *World Development Indicators.*

KYRGYZSTAN - EXTERNAL INDEBTEDNESS

The World Bank, 1818 H Street, NW, Washington, D.C. 20433 (202) 477-1234; *World Development Report.*

KYRGYZSTAN - EXTERNAL TRADE

Academic International Press, Box 1111, Gulf Breeze, Florida 32562; *Russia and Eurasia Facts and Figures Annual.*

Euromonitor International, Inc., 122 South Michigan Avenue, Suite 1200, Chicago, Illinois 60603 (800) 577-EURO; *World Marketing Data and Statistics.*

Food and Agriculture Organization of the United Nations (FAO), Via delle Terme di Caracalla, 00100, Rome, Italy (Telephone Number in U.S. (202) 653-2400); *Trade Yearbook.*

Statistical Office of the United Nations, Publishing Service, New York, New York 10017 (800) 253-9646; *Statistical Yearbook.*

The World Bank, 1818 H Street, NW, Washington, D.C. 20433 (202) 477-1234; *Statistical Handbook: States of the Former USSR.*

KYRGYZSTAN - FABRIC PRODUCTION AND CONSUMPTION - See KYRGYZSTAN - TEXTILE INDUSTRY

KYRGYZSTAN - FERTILITY RATES

Central Intelligence Agency, Washington, D.C. 20505 (703) 482-1100, www.cia.gov; *The World Factbook.*

Statistical Office of the United Nations, Publishing Service, New York, New York 10017 (800) 253-9646; *Human Development Report;* and *Trends in Europe and North America: The Statistical Yearbook of the Economic Commission for Europe.*

The World Bank, 1818 H Street, NW, Washington, D.C. 20433 (202) 477-1234; *The World Bank Atlas; Statistical Handbook: States of the Former USSR; World Development Report;* and *World Development Indicators.*

World Health Organization, Office of Publications, 20 Avenue Appia, CH-1211

Geneva 27, Switzerland (Telephone Number in U.S. (518) 436-9686); *World Health Statistics Annual.*

KYRGYZSTAN - FERTILIZER

Food and Agriculture Organization of the United Nations (FAO), Via delle Terme di Caracalla, 00100, Rome, Italy (Telephone Number in U.S. (202) 653-2400); *Fertilizer Yearbook.*

Statistical Office of the United Nations, Publishing Service, New York, New York 10017 (800) 253-9646; *Industrial Commodity Statistics Yearbook;* and *Statistical Yearbook.*

KYRGYZSTAN - FINANCE

Economist Intelligence Unit, 111 West 57th Street, New York, New York 10019 (800) 938-4685; *Kyrgyzstan Country Report.*

Europa Publications Limited, 18 Bedford Square, London, WC1B 3JN, England; *The Europa World Year Book.*

St. Martin's Press, Inc., 175 Fifth Avenue, New York, New York 10010 (800) 221-7945; *The Statesman's Year-Book.*

The World Bank, 1818 H Street, NW, Washington, D.C. 20433 (202) 477-1234; *Statistical Handbook: States of the Former USSR.*

KYRGYZSTAN - FISHERIES

Food and Agriculture Organization of the United Nations (FAO), Via delle Terme di Caracalla, 00100, Rome, Italy (Telephone Number in U.S. (202) 653-2400); *The State of Food and Agriculture;* and *Yearbook of Fishery Statistics.*

Statistical Office of the United Nations, Publishing Service, New York, New York 10017 (800) 253-9646; *Industrial Commodity Statistics Yearbook;* and *Statistical Yearbook.*

KYRGYZSTAN - FOOD

Food and Agriculture Organization of the United Nations (FAO), Via delle Terme di Caracalla, 00100, Rome, Italy (Telephone Number in U.S. (202) 653-2400); *Production Yearbook; The State of Food and Agriculture;* and *Trade Yearbook.*

Statistical Office of the United Nations, Publishing Service, New York, New York 10017 (800) 253-9646; *Human Development Report;* and *Industrial Commodity Statistics Yearbook.*

KYRGYZSTAN - FOOTWEAR PRODUCTION AND CONSUMPTION - See KYRGYZSTAN - TEXTILE INDUSTRY

KYRGYZSTAN - FOREIGN DEBT

Walden Publishing, Ltd., Two Market Street, Saffron Walden Essex, CB10 1HZ, England; *The World of Information Asia and Pacific Review.*

KYRGYZSTAN - FOREIGN INVESTMENT

Business International Moscow, 23 Profsoyuznaya Ulitsa, 117859, Moscow (Telephone Number in U.S. (800) 938-4685); *The CIS Market Atlas.*

KYRGYZSTAN - FOREIGN TRADE

Business International Moscow, 23 Profsoyuznaya Ulitsa, 117859, Moscow (Telephone Number in U.S. (800) 938-4685); *The CIS Market Atlas.*

Economist Intelligence Unit, 111 West 57th Street, New York, New York 10019 (800) 938-4685; *Kyrgyzstan Country Report.*

Euromonitor International, Inc., 122 South Michigan Avenue, Suite 1200, Chicago, Illinois 60603 (800) 577-EURO; *The World Economic Factbook.*

Europa Publications Limited, 18 Bedford Square, London, WC1B 3JN, England; *The Europa World Year Book.*

Food and Agriculture Organization of the United Nations (FAO), Via delle Terme di Caracalla, 00100, Rome, Italy (Telephone Number in U.S. (202) 653-2400); *Trade Yearbook.*

International Monetary Fund, 700 Nineteenth Street, NW, Washington, D.C. 20431 (202) 623-7000; *Direction of Trade Statistics.*

St. Martin's Press, Inc., 175 Fifth Avenue, New York, New York 10010 (800) 221-7945; *The Statesman's Year-Book.*

Statistical Office of the United Nations, Publishing Service, New York, New York 10017 (800) 253-9646; *International Trade Statistics Yearbook;* and *Statistical Yearbook.*

The World Bank, 1818 H Street, NW, Washington, D.C. 20433 (202) 477-1234; *Statistical Handbook: States of the Former USSR; World Development Report;* and *World Development Indicators.*

KYRGYZSTAN - FORESTRY AND FOREST PRODUCTS

Academic International Press, Box 1111, Gulf Breeze, Florida 32562; *Russia and Eurasia Facts and Figures Annual.*

Business International Moscow, 23 Profsoyuznaya Ulitsa, 117859, Moscow (Telephone Number in U.S. (800) 938-

4685); *The CIS Market Atlas.*

Food and Agriculture Organization of the United Nations (FAO), Via delle Terme di Caracalla, 00100, Rome, Italy (Telephone Number in U.S. (202) 653-2400); *The State of Food and Agriculture;* and *Yearbook of Forest Products.*

Statistical Office of the United Nations, Publishing Service, New York, New York 10017 (800) 253-9646; *Industrial Commodity Statistics Yearbook; Trends in Europe and North America: The Statistical Yearbook of the Economic Commission for Europe;* and *Statistical Yearbook.*

United Nations Educational, Scientific and Cultural Organization (UNESCO), 7 Place de Fontenoy, F-75700 Paris, France (Telephone Number in U.S. (212) 963-5981); *Statistical Yearbook.*

The World Bank, 1818 H Street, NW, Washington, D.C. 20433 (202) 477-1234; *World Development Report.*

KYRGYZSTAN - GOATS - See KYRGYZSTAN - LIVESTOCK AND POULTRY

KYRGYZSTAN - GOVERNMENT

Academic International Press, Box 1111, Gulf Breeze, Florida 32562; *Russia and Eurasia Facts and Figures Annual.*

Central Intelligence Agency, Washington, D.C. 20505 (703) 482-1100, www.cia.gov; *The World Factbook.*

Europa Publications Limited, 18 Bedford Square, London, WC1B 3JN, England; *The Europa World Year Book.*

St. Martin's Press, Inc., 175 Fifth Avenue, New York, New York 10010 (800) 221-7945; *The Statesman's Year-Book.*

Statistical Office of the United Nations, Publishing Service, New York, New York 10017 (800) 253-9646; *National Accounts Statistics;* and *Statistical Yearbook.*

The World Bank, 1818 H Street, NW, Washington, D.C. 20433 (202) 477-1234; *Statistical Handbook: States of the Former USSR;* and *World Development Report.*

KYRGYZSTAN - GROSS DOMESTIC PRODUCT

Academic International Press, Box 1111, Gulf Breeze, Florida 32562; *Russia and Eurasia Facts and Figures Annual.*

Economist Intelligence Unit, 111 West 57th Street, New York, New York 10019 (800) 938-4685; *Kyrgyzstan Country Report.*

Euromonitor International, Inc., 122 South Michigan Avenue, Suite 1200,

Chicago, Illinois 60603 (800) 577-EURO; *International Marketing Data and Statistics;* and *The World Economic Factbook.*

Europa Publications Limited, 18 Bedford Square, London, WC1B 3JN, England; *The Europa World Year Book.*

Statistical Office of the United Nations, Publishing Service, New York, New York 10017 (800) 253-9646; *Human Development Report; National Accounts Statistics; Trends in Europe and North America: The Statistical Yearbook of the Economic Commission for Europe;* and *Statistical Yearbook.*

The World Bank, 1818 H Street, NW, Washington, D.C. 20433 (202) 477-1234; *Statistical Handbook: States of the Former USSR; World Development Report;* and *World Development Indicators.*

KYRGYZSTAN - GROSS NATIONAL PRODUCT

St. Martin's Press, Inc., 175 Fifth Avenue, New York, New York 10010 (800) 221-7945; *The Statesman's Year-Book.*

Walden Publishing, Ltd., Two Market Street, Saffron Walden Essex, CB10 1HZ, England; *The World of Information Asia and Pacific Review.*

The World Bank, 1818 H Street, NW, Washington, D.C. 20433 (202) 477-1234; The World Bank Atlas; *World Development Report;* and *World Development Indicators.*

KYRGYZSTAN - HEALTH

Academic International Press, Box 1111, Gulf Breeze, Florida 32562; *Russia and Eurasia Facts and Figures Annual.*

Business International Moscow, 23 Profsoyuznaya Ulitsa, 117859, Moscow (Telephone Number in U.S. (800) 938-4685); *The CIS Market Atlas.*

Euromonitor International, Inc., 122 South Michigan Avenue, Suite 1200, Chicago, Illinois 60603 (800) 577-EURO; *World Marketing Data and Statistics.*

St. Martin's Press, Inc., 175 Fifth Avenue, New York, New York 10010 (800) 221-7945; *The Statesman's Year-Book.*

Statistical Office of the United Nations, Publishing Service, New York, New York 10017 (800) 253-9646; *Human Development Report; Trends in Europe and North America: The Statistical Yearbook of the Economic Commission for Europe;* and *Statistical Yearbook.*

United Nations Children's Fund (UNICEF), 3 United Nations Plaza, New

York, New York 10017 (800) 253-9646; *State of the World's Children.*

The World Bank, 1818 H Street, NW, Washington, D.C. 20433 (202) 477-1234; *World Development Report.*

World Health Organization, Office of Publications, 20 Avenue Appia, CH-1211 Geneva 27, Switzerland (Telephone Number in U.S. (518) 436-9686); *World Health Statistics Annual.*

KYRGYZSTAN - HIGHWAYS

Academic International Press, Box 1111, Gulf Breeze, Florida 32562; *Russia and Eurasia Facts and Figures Annual.*

Business International Moscow, 23 Profsoyuznaya Ulitsa, 117859, Moscow (Telephone Number in U.S. (800) 938-4685); *The CIS Market Atlas.*

Central Intelligence Agency, Washington, D.C. 20505 (703) 482-1100, www.cia.gov; *The World Factbook.*

St. Martin's Press, Inc., 175 Fifth Avenue, New York, New York 10010 (800) 221-7945; *The Statesman's Year-Book.*

Statistical Office of the United Nations, Publishing Service, New York, New York 10017 (800) 253-9646; *Trends in Europe and North America: The Statistical Yearbook of the Economic Commission for Europe.*

KYRGYZSTAN - HOUSING AND HOUSING UNITS

Business International Moscow, 23 Profsoyuznaya Ulitsa, 117859, Moscow (Telephone Number in U.S. (800) 938-4685); *The CIS Market Atlas.*

Euromonitor International, Inc., 122 South Michigan Avenue, Suite 1200, Chicago, Illinois 60603 (800) 577-EURO; *World Marketing Data and Statistics.*

Statistical Office of the United Nations, Publishing Service, New York, New York 10017 (800) 253-9646; *Trends in Europe and North America: The Statistical Yearbook of the Economic Commission for Europe.*

KYRGYZSTAN - ILLITERATE POPULATION

Central Intelligence Agency, Washington, D.C. 20505 (703) 482-1100, www.cia.gov; *The World Factbook.*

Statistical Office of the United Nations, Publishing Service, New York, New York 10017 (800) 253-9646; *Human Development Report.*

United Nations Educational, Scientific and Cultural Organization (UNESCO), 7

Place de Fontenoy, F-75700 Paris, France (Telephone Number in U.S. (212) 963-5981); *Statistical Yearbook.*

KYRGYZSTAN - IMPORTS

Academic International Press, Box 1111, Gulf Breeze, Florida 32562; *Russia and Eurasia Facts and Figures Annual.*

Business International Moscow, 23 Profsoyuznaya Ulitsa, 117859, Moscow (Telephone Number in U.S. (800) 938-4685); *The CIS Market Atlas.*

Central Intelligence Agency, Washington, D.C. 20505 (703) 482-1100, www.cia.gov; *The World Factbook.*

Economist Intelligence Unit, 111 West 57th Street, New York, New York 10019 (800) 938-4685; *Kyrgyzstan Country Report.*

Euromonitor International, Inc., 122 South Michigan Avenue, Suite 1200, Chicago, Illinois 60603 (800) 577-EURO; *International Marketing Data and Statistics.*

Europa Publications Limited, 18 Bedford Square, London, WC1B 3JN, England; *The Europa World Year Book.*

International Monetary Fund, 700 Nineteenth Street, NW, Washington, D.C. 20431 (202) 623-7000; *Direction of Trade Statistics.*

St. Martin's Press, Inc., 175 Fifth Avenue, New York, New York 10010 (800) 221-7945; *The Statesman's Year-Book.*

Statistical Office of the United Nations, Publishing Service, New York, New York 10017 (800) 253-9646; *International Trade Statistics Yearbook;* and *Trends in Europe and North America: The Statistical Yearbook of the Economic Commission for Europe.*

United Nations Conference on Trade and Development (UNCTAD), New York, New York 10017 (800) 253-9646; *Handbook of International Trade and Development Statistics.*

Walden Publishing, Ltd., Two Market Street, Saffron Walden Essex, CB10 1HZ, England; *The World of Information Asia and Pacific Review.*

The World Bank, 1818 H Street, NW, Washington, D.C. 20433 (202) 477-1234; *Statistical Handbook: States of the Former USSR; World Development Report;* and *World Development Indicators.*

KYRGYZSTAN - INDUSTRY

Academic International Press, Box 1111, Gulf Breeze, Florida 32562; *Russia and Eurasia Facts and Figures Annual.*

Business International Moscow, 23 Profsoyuznaya Ulitsa, 117859, Moscow (Telephone Number in U.S. (800) 938-4685); *The CIS Market Atlas.*

Central Intelligence Agency, Washington, D.C. 20505 (703) 482-1100, www.cia.gov; *The World Factbook.*

Economist Intelligence Unit, 111 West 57th Street, New York, New York 10019 (800) 938-4685; *Kyrgyzstan Country Report.*

Euromonitor International, Inc., 122 South Michigan Avenue, Suite 1200, Chicago, Illinois 60603 (800) 577-EURO; *World Marketing Data and Statistics.*

Europa Publications Limited, 18 Bedford Square, London, WC1B 3JN, England; *The Europa World Year Book.*

St. Martin's Press, Inc., 175 Fifth Avenue, New York, New York 10010 (800) 221-7945; *The Statesman's Year-Book.*

Statistical Office of the United Nations, Publishing Service, New York, New York 10017 (800) 253-9646; *Industrial Commodity Statistics Yearbook; Trends in Europe and North America: The Statistical Yearbook of the Economic Commission for Europe;* and *Statistical Yearbook.*

The World Bank, 1818 H Street, NW, Washington, D.C. 20433 (202) 477-1234; *Statistical Handbook: States of the Former USSR;* and *World Development Indicators.*

KYRGYZSTAN - INFANT MORTALITY RATES - See KYRGYZSTAN - MORTALITY

KYRGYZSTAN - INTERNAL TRADE

Statistical Office of the United Nations, Publishing Service, New York, New York 10017 (800) 253-9646; *Statistical Yearbook.*

KYRGYZSTAN - LABOR

Academic International Press, Box 1111, Gulf Breeze, Florida 32562; *Russia and Eurasia Facts and Figures Annual.*

Business International Moscow, 23 Profsoyuznaya Ulitsa, 117859, Moscow (Telephone Number in U.S. (800) 938-4685); *The CIS Market Atlas.*

Central Intelligence Agency, Washington, D.C. 20505 (703) 482-1100, www.cia.gov; *The World Factbook.*

Euromonitor International, Inc., 122 South Michigan Avenue, Suite 1200, Chicago, Illinois 60603 (800) 577-EURO; *International Marketing Data and Statistics;* and *World Marketing Data and Statistics.*

Europa Publications Limited, 18 Bedford Square, London, WC1B 3JN,

England; *The Europa World Year Book*.

St. Martin's Press, Inc., 175 Fifth Avenue, New York, New York 10010 (800) 221-7945; *The Statesman's Year-Book*.

Statistical Office of the United Nations, Publishing Service, New York, New York 10017 (800) 253-9646; *Human Development Report;* and *Statistical Yearbook*.

The World Bank, 1818 H Street, NW, Washington, D.C. 20433 (202) 477-1234; *The World Bank Atlas; Statistical Handbook: States of the Former USSR; World Development Report;* and *World Development Indicators*.

KYRGYZSTAN - LAND USE

Central Intelligence Agency, Washington, D.C. 20505 (703) 482-1100, www.cia.gov; *The World Factbook*.

Euromonitor International, Inc., 122 South Michigan Avenue, Suite 1200, Chicago, Illinois 60603 (800) 577-EURO; *International Marketing Data and Statistics*.

Food and Agriculture Organization of the United Nations (FAO), Via delle Terme di Caracalla, 00100, Rome, Italy (Telephone Number in U.S. (202) 653-2400); *Production Yearbook*.

The World Bank, 1818 H Street, NW, Washington, D.C. 20433 (202) 477-1234; *World Development Report*.

KYRGYZSTAN - LIBRARIES

Statistical Office of the United Nations, Publishing Service, New York, New York 10017 (800) 253-9646; *Trends in Europe and North America: The Statistical Yearbook of the Economic Commission for Europe*.

United Nations Educational, Scientific and Cultural Organization (UNESCO), 7 Place de Fontenoy, F-75700 Paris, France (Telephone Number in U.S. (212) 963-5981); *Statistical Yearbook*.

KYRGYZSTAN - LIFE EXPECTANCY

Academic International Press, Box 1111, Gulf Breeze, Florida 32562; *Russia and Eurasia Facts and Figures Annual*.

Business International Moscow, 23 Profsoyuznaya Ulitsa, 117859, Moscow (Telephone Number in U.S. (800) 938-4685); *The CIS Market Atlas*.

Central Intelligence Agency, Washington, D.C. 20505 (703) 482-1100, www.cia.gov; *The World Factbook*.

Euromonitor International, Inc., 122 South Michigan Avenue, Suite 1200,

Chicago, Illinois 60603 (800) 577-EURO ; *The World Economic Factbook*.

Statistical Office of the United Nations, Publishing Service, New York, New York 10017 (800) 253-9646; *Demographic Yearbook; Trends in Europe and North America: The Statistical Yearbook of the Economic Commission for Europe; World Statistics Pocketbook;* and *Human Development Report*.

The World Bank, 1818 H Street, NW, Washington, D.C. 20433 (202) 477-1234; *The World Bank Atlas; World Development Report;* and *World Development Indicators*.

World Health Organization, Office of Publications, 20 Avenue Appia, CH-1211 Geneva 27, Switzerland (Telephone Number in U.S. (518) 436-9686); *World Health Statistics Annual*.

KYRGYZSTAN - LIVESTOCK AND POULTRY

Academic International Press, Box 1111, Gulf Breeze, Florida 32562; *Russia and Eurasia Facts and Figures Annual*.

Business International Moscow, 23 Profsoyuznaya Ulitsa, 117859, Moscow (Telephone Number in U.S. (800) 938-4685); *The CIS Market Atlas*.

Europa Publications Limited, 18 Bedford Square, London, WC1B 3JN, England; *The Europa World Year Book*.

Food and Agriculture Organization of the United Nations (FAO), Via delle Terme di Caracalla, 00100, Rome, Italy (Telephone Number in U.S. (202) 653-2400); *Production Yearbook; The State of Food and Agriculture;* and *Trade Yearbook*.

St. Martin's Press, Inc., 175 Fifth Avenue, New York, New York 10010 (800) 221-7945; *The Statesman's Year-Book*.

Statistical Office of the United Nations, Publishing Service, New York, New York 10017 (800) 253-9646; *Industrial Commodity Statistics Yearbook;* and *Statistical Yearbook*.

KYRGYZSTAN - MACHINERY

Statistical Office of the United Nations, Publishing Service, New York, New York 10017 (800) 253-9646; *Industrial Commodity Statistics Yearbook*.

KYRGYZSTAN - MAIL - NUMBER OF PIECES SENT OR RECEIVED

Statistical Office of the United Nations, Publishing Service, New York, New York 10017 (800) 253-9646; *Statistical Yearbook*.

KYRGYZSTAN - MANUFACTURING

Statistical Office of the United Nations, Publishing Service, New York, New York 10017 (800) 253-9646; *Industrial Commodity Statistics Yearbook;* and *Statistical Yearbook*.

The World Bank, 1818 H Street, NW, Washington, D.C. 20433 (202) 477-1234; *World Development Indicators*.

KYRGYZSTAN - MARRIAGE RATES

Academic International Press, Box 1111, Gulf Breeze, Florida 32562; *Russia and Eurasia Facts and Figures Annual*.

Europa Publications Limited, 18 Bedford Square, London, WC1B 3JN, England; *The Europa World Year Book*.

Statistical Office of the United Nations, Publishing Service, New York, New York 10017 (800) 253-9646; *Demographic Yearbook; Trends in Europe and North America: The Statistical Yearbook of the Economic Commission for Europe;* and *Statistical Yearbook*.

KYRGYZSTAN - MEAT PRODUCTION - See KYRGYZSTAN - LIVESTOCK AND POULTRY

KYRGYZSTAN - MERCHANT SHIPPING

Statistical Office of the United Nations, Publishing Service, New York, New York 10017 (800) 253-9646; *Statistical Yearbook*.

KYRGYZSTAN - MILITARY

Academic International Press, Box 1111, Gulf Breeze, Florida 32562; *Russia and Eurasia Facts and Figures Annual*.

Central Intelligence Agency, Washington, D.C. 20505 (703) 482-1100, www.cia.gov; *The World Factbook*.

Euromonitor International, Inc., 122 South Michigan Avenue, Suite 1200, Chicago, Illinois 60603 (800) 577-EURO; *World Marketing Data and Statistics*.

The International Institute for Strategic Studies, 23 Tavistock Street, London WC2E 7NQ, England 44 171 3797676; *The Military Balance*.

St. Martin's Press, Inc., 175 Fifth Avenue, New York, New York 10010 (800) 221-7945; *The Statesman's Year-Book*.

Statistical Office of the United Nations, Publishing Service, New York, New York 10017 (800) 253-9646; *Human Development Report*.

KYRGYZSTAN - MINING AND MINERAL PRODUCTS

Academic International Press, Box 1111, Gulf Breeze, Florida 32562; *Russia *and Eurasia Facts and Figures Annual.*

Business International Moscow, 23 Profsoyuznaya Ulitsa, 117859, Moscow (Telephone Number in U.S. (800) 938-4685); *The CIS Market Atlas.*

Europa Publications Limited, 18 Bedford Square, London, WC1B 3JN, England; *The Europa World Year Book.*

St. Martin's Press, Inc., 175 Fifth Avenue, New York, New York 10010 (800) 221-7945; *The Statesman's Year-Book.*

Statistical Office of the United Nations, Publishing Service, New York, New York 10017 (800) 253-9646; *Energy Statistics Yearbook; Industrial Commodity Statistics Yearbook;* and *Statistical Yearbook.*

KYRGYZSTAN - MONEY SUPPLY

Economist Intelligence Unit, 111 West 57th Street, New York, New York 10019 (800) 938-4685; *Kyrgyzstan Country Report.*

Europa Publications Limited, 18 Bedford Square, London, WC1B 3JN, England; *The Europa World Year Book.*

KYRGYZSTAN - MONUMENTS AND HISTORICAL SITES

United Nations Educational, Scientific and Cultural Organization (UNESCO), 7 Place de Fontenoy, F-75700 Paris, France (Telephone Number in U.S. (212) 963-5981); *Statistical Yearbook.*

KYRGYZSTAN - MORTALITY

Academic International Press, Box 1111, Gulf Breeze, Florida 32562; *Russia and Eurasia Facts and Figures Annual.*

Business International Moscow, 23 Profsoyuznaya Ulitsa, 117859, Moscow (Telephone Number in U.S. (800) 938-4685); *The CIS Market Atlas.*

Central Intelligence Agency, Washington, D.C. 20505 (703) 482-1100, www.cia.gov; *The World Factbook.*

Euromonitor International, Inc., 122 South Michigan Avenue, Suite 1200, Chicago, Illinois 60603 (800) 577-EURO; *International Marketing Data and Statistics;* and *The World Economic Factbook.*

Europa Publications Limited, 18 Bedford Square, London, WC1B 3JN, England; *The Europa World Year Book.*

St. Martin's Press, Inc., 175 Fifth Avenue, New York, New York 10010 (800) 221-7945; *The Statesman's Year-Book.*

Statistical Office of the United Nations, Publishing Service, New York, New York

10017 (800) 253-9646; *Demographic Yearbook; Human Development Report; Trends in Europe and North America: The Statistical Yearbook of the Economic Commission for Europe; World Statistics Pocketbook;* and *Statistical Yearbook.*

United Nations Children's Fund (UNICEF), 3 United Nations Plaza, New York, New York 10017 (800) 253-9646; *State of the World's Children.*

The World Bank, 1818 H Street, NW, Washington, D.C. 20433 (202) 477-1234; *The World Bank Atlas; World Development Report;* and *World Development Indicators.*

World Health Organization, Office of Publications, 20 Avenue Appia, CH-1211 Geneva 27, Switzerland (Telephone Number in U.S. (518) 436-9686); *World Health Statistics Annual.*

KYRGYZSTAN - MOTION PICTURES

Statistical Office of the United Nations, Publishing Service, New York, New York 10017 (800) 253-9646; *Statistical Yearbook.*

United Nations Educational, Scientific and Cultural Organization (UNESCO), 7 Place de Fontenoy, F-75700 Paris, France (Telephone Number in U.S. (212) 963-5981); *Statistical Yearbook.*

KYRGYZSTAN - MOTOR VEHICLES

Business International Moscow, 23 Profsoyuznaya Ulitsa, 117859, Moscow (Telephone Number in U.S. (800) 938-4685); *The CIS Market Atlas.*

Statistical Office of the United Nations, Publishing Service, New York, New York 10017 (800) 253-9646; *Statistical Yearbook.*

KYRGYZSTAN - MUSEUMS

United Nations Educational, Scientific and Cultural Organization (UNESCO), 7 Place de Fontenoy, F-75700 Paris, France (Telephone Number in U.S. (212) 963-5981); *Statistical Yearbook.*

KYRGYZSTAN - NATIONAL ACCOUNTS

Europa Publications Limited, 18 Bedford Square, London, WC1B 3JN, England; *The Europa World Year Book.*

Statistical Office of the United Nations, Publishing Service, New York, New York 10017 (800) 253-9646; *National Accounts Statistics;* and *Statistical Yearbook.*

The World Bank, 1818 H Street, NW, Washington, D.C. 20433 (202) 477-1234; *Statistical Handbook: States of the Former USSR.*

KYRGYZSTAN - NATIONAL INCOME

Business International Moscow, 23 Profsoyuznaya Ulitsa, 117859, Moscow (Telephone Number in U.S. (800) 938-4685); *The CIS Market Atlas.*

Statistical Office of the United Nations, Publishing Service, New York, New York 10017 (800) 253-9646; *Statistical Yearbook.*

KYRGYZSTAN - NATIONAL PRODUCT

Statistical Office of the United Nations, Publishing Service, New York, New York 10017 (800) 253-9646; *Statistical Yearbook.*

KYRGYZSTAN - PATENTS, TRADEMARKS AND SERVICE MARKS

Statistical Office of the United Nations, Publishing Service, New York, New York 10017 (800) 253-9646; *Statistical Yearbook.*

KYRGYZSTAN - PERIODICALS

United Nations Educational, Scientific and Cultural Organization (UNESCO), 7 Place de Fontenoy, F-75700 Paris, France (Telephone Number in U.S. (212) 963-5981); *Statistical Yearbook.*

KYRGYZSTAN - PETROLEUM INDUSTRY

Food and Agriculture Organization of the United Nations (FAO), Via delle Terme di Caracalla, 00100, Rome, Italy (Telephone Number in U.S. (202) 653-2400); *The State of Food and Agriculture.*

Statistical Office of the United Nations, Publishing Service, New York, New York 10017 (800) 253-9646; *Energy Statistics Yearbook; Industrial Commodity Statistics Yearbook; Trends in Europe and North America: The Statistical Yearbook of the Economic Commission for Europe;* and *Statistical Yearbook.*

KYRGYZSTAN - PIGS - See KYRGYZSTAN - LIVESTOCK AND POULTRY

KYRGYZSTAN - POPULATION

Academic International Press, Box 1111, Gulf Breeze, Florida 32562; *Russia and Eurasia Facts and Figures Annual.*

Business International Moscow, 23 Profsoyuznaya Ulitsa, 117859, Moscow (Telephone Number in U.S. (800) 938-4685); *The CIS Market Atlas.*

Central Intelligence Agency, Washington, D.C. 20505 (703) 482-1100, www.cia.gov; *The World Factbook.*

Economist Intelligence Unit, 111 West 57th Street, New York, New York 10019 (800) 938-4685; *Kyrgyzstan Country Report.*

Euromonitor International, Inc., 122 South Michigan Avenue, Suite 1200,

Chicago, Illinois 60603 (800) 577-EURO; *International Marketing Data and Statistics;* and *The World Economic Factbook.*

Europa Publications Limited, 18 Bedford Square, London, WC1B 3JN, England; *The Europa World Year Book.*

Food and Agriculture Organization of the United Nations (FAO), Via delle Terme di Caracalla, 00100, Rome, Italy (Telephone Number in U.S. (202) 653-2400); *Production Yearbook.*

St. Martin's Press, Inc., 175 Fifth Avenue, New York, New York 10010 (800) 221-7945; *The Statesman's Year-Book.*

Statistical Office of the United Nations, Publishing Service, New York, New York 10017 (800) 253-9646; *Demographic Yearbook; Human Development Report; Trends in Europe and North America: The Statistical Yearbook of the Economic Commission for Europe; World Statistics Pocketbook;* and *Statistical Yearbook.*

United Nations Educational, Scientific and Cultural Organization (UNESCO), 7 Place de Fontenoy, F-75700 Paris, France (Telephone Number in U.S. (212) 963-5981); *Statistical Yearbook.*

Walden Publishing, Ltd., Two Market Street, Saffron Walden Essex, CB10 1HZ, England; *The World of Information Asia and Pacific Review.*

The World Bank, 1818 H Street, NW, Washington, D.C. 20433 (202) 477-1234; *The World Bank Atlas; Statistical Handbook: States of the Former USSR; World Development Report;* and *World Development Indicators.*

World Health Organization, Office of Publications, 20 Avenue Appia, CH-1211 Geneva 27, Switzerland (Telephone Number in U.S. (518) 436-9686); *World Health Statistics Annual.*

KYRGYZSTAN - POST OFFICES

Statistical Office of the United Nations, Publishing Service, New York, New York 10017 (800) 253-9646; *Trends in Europe and North America: The Statistical Yearbook of the Economic Commission for Europe.*

KYRGYZSTAN - POULTRY - See KYRGYZSTAN - LIVESTOCK AND POULTRY

KYRGYZSTAN - PRICES

Food and Agriculture Organization of the United Nations (FAO), Via delle Terme di Caracalla, 00100, Rome, Italy (Telephone Number in U.S. (202) 653-2400); *Production Yearbook.*

The World Bank, 1818 H Street, NW, Washington, D.C. 20433 (202) 477-1234; *Statistical Handbook: States of the Former USSR.*

KYRGYZSTAN - PRODUCTION

The World Bank, 1818 H Street, NW, Washington, D.C. 20433 (202) 477-1234; *Statistical Handbook: States of the Former USSR.*

KYRGYZSTAN - PUBLIC FINANCE - See KYRGYZSTAN - FINANCE

KYRGYZSTAN - RADIO RECEIVER PRODUCTION

St. Martin's Press, Inc., 175 Fifth Avenue, New York, New York 10010 (800) 221-7945; *The Statesman's Year-Book.*

Statistical Office of the United Nations, Publishing Service, New York, New York 10017 (800) 253-9646; *National Accounts Statistics;* and *Statistical Yearbook.*

KYRGYZSTAN - RAILWAYS

Academic International Press, Box 1111, Gulf Breeze, Florida 32562; *Russia and Eurasia Facts and Figures Annual.*

Business International Moscow, 23 Profsoyuznaya Ulitsa, 117859, Moscow (Telephone Number in U.S. (800) 938-4685); *The CIS Market Atlas.*

St. Martin's Press, Inc., 175 Fifth Avenue, New York, New York 10010 (800) 221-7945; *The Statesman's Year-Book.*

Statistical Office of the United Nations, Publishing Service, New York, New York 10017 (800) 253-9646; *Statistical Yearbook;* and *Trends in Europe and North America: The Statistical Yearbook of the Economic Commission for Europe.*

KYRGYZSTAN - RELIGION

Academic International Press, Box 1111, Gulf Breeze, Florida 32562; *Russia and Eurasia Facts and Figures Annual.*

Central Intelligence Agency, Washington, D.C. 20505 (703) 482-1100, www.cia.gov; *The World Factbook.*

KYRGYZSTAN - RETAIL PRICE INDEX

Europa Publications Limited, 18 Bedford Square, London, WC1B 3JN, England; *The Europa World Year Book.*

KYRGYZSTAN - RETAIL TRADE

Business International Moscow, 23 Profsoyuznaya Ulitsa, 117859, Moscow (Telephone Number in U.S. (800) 938-4685); *The CIS Market Atlas.*

Euromonitor International, Inc., 122 South Michigan Avenue, Suite 1200, Chicago, Illinois 60603 (800) 577-EURO; *World Marketing Data and Statistics.*

Statistical Office of the United Nations, Publishing Service, New York, New York 10017 (800) 253-9646; *Statistical Yearbook.*

KYRGYZSTAN - ROADS - See KYRGYZSTAN - HIGHWAYS

KYRGYZSTAN - ROUNDWOOD PRODUCTION AND CONSUMPTION -See KYRGYZSTAN - FORESTRY AND FOREST PRODUCTS

KYRGYZSTAN - RUBBER PRODUCTION AND CONSUMPTION

Statistical Office of the United Nations, Publishing Service, New York, New York 10017 (800) 253-9646; *Statistical Yearbook.*

KYRGYZSTAN - SCIENTISTS, TECHNICIANS AND ENGINEERS

Statistical Office of the United Nations, Publishing Service, New York, New York 10017 (800) 253-9646; *Statistical Yearbook.*

KYRGYZSTAN - SHEEP - See KYRGYZSTAN - LIVESTOCK AND POULTRY

KYRGYZSTAN - SOCIAL DATA

Statistical Office of the United Nations, Publishing Service, New York, New York 10017 (800) 253-9646; *World Statistics Pocketbook.*

KYRGYZSTAN - SOCIAL SECURITY

Statistical Office of the United Nations, Publishing Service, New York, New York 10017 (800) 253-9646; *National Accounts Statistics.*

KYRGYZSTAN - STEEL - See KYRGYZSTAN - MINING AND MINERAL PRODUCTS

KYRGYZSTAN - TAXATION

Europa Publications Limited, 18 Bedford Square, London, WC1B 3JN, England; *The Europa World Year Book.*

KYRGYZSTAN - TELEPHONES IN USE

Academic International Press, Box 1111, Gulf Breeze, Florida 32562; *Russia and Eurasia Facts and Figures Annual.*

Central Intelligence Agency, Washington, D.C. 20505 (703) 482-1100, www.cia.gov; *The World Factbook.*

Statistical Office of the United Nations, Publishing Service, New York, New York 10017 (800) 253-9646; *Statistical Yearbook; World Statistics Pocketbook;* and *Trends in*

Europe and North America: The Statistical Yearbook of the Economic Commission for Europe.

KYRGYZSTAN - TEXTILE INDUSTRY

Business International Moscow, 23 Profsoyuznaya Ulitsa, 117859, Moscow (Telephone Number in U.S. (800) 938-4685); *The CIS Market Atlas.*

Statistical Office of the United Nations, Publishing Service, New York, New York 10017 (800) 253-9646; *Industrial Commodity Statistics Yearbook;* and *Statistical Yearbook.*

KYRGYZSTAN - THEATRE

United Nations Educational, Scientific and Cultural Organization (UNESCO), 7 Place de Fontenoy, F-75700 Paris, France (Telephone Number in U.S. (212) 963-5981); *Statistical Yearbook.*

KYRGYZSTAN - TIRE (MOTOR VEHICLE) PRODUCTION

Statistical Office of the United Nations, Publishing Service, New York, New York 10017 (800) 253-9646; *Statistical Yearbook.*

KYRGYZSTAN - TOBACCO PRODUCTION

Statistical Office of the United Nations, Publishing Service, New York, New York 10017 (800) 253-9646; *Statistical Yearbook.*

KYRGYZSTAN - TOURISM

Business International Moscow, 23 Profsoyuznaya Ulitsa, 117859, Moscow (Telephone Number in U.S. (800) 938-4685); *The CIS Market Atlas.*

Euromonitor International, Inc., 122 South Michigan Avenue, Suite 1200, Chicago, Illinois 60603 (800) 577-EURO; *The World Economic Factbook;* and *World Marketing Data and Statistics.*

Europa Publications Limited, 18 Bedford Square, London, WC1B 3JN, England; *The Europa World Year Book.*

Statistical Office of the United Nations, Publishing Service, New York, New York 10017 (800) 253-9646; *Statistical Yearbook;* and *Trends in Europe and North America: The Statistical Yearbook of the Economic Commission for Europe.*

KYRGYZSTAN - TRADEMARKS AND SERVICE MARKS - See KYRGYZSTAN - PATENTS, TRADEMARKS AND SERVICE MARKS

KYRGYZSTAN - TRANSPORTATION AND COMMUNICATIONS

Academic International Press, Box 1111, Gulf Breeze, Florida 32562; *Russia and Eurasia Facts and Figures Annual.*

Business International Moscow, 23 Profsoyuznaya Ulitsa, 117859, Moscow (Telephone Number in U.S. (800) 938-4685); *The CIS Market Atlas.*

Central Intelligence Agency, Washington, D.C. 20505 (703) 482-1100, www.cia.gov; *The World Factbook.*

Euromonitor International, Inc., 122 South Michigan Avenue, Suite 1200, Chicago, Illinois 60603 (800) 577-EURO; *International Marketing Data and Statistics;* and *World Marketing Data and Statistics.*

St. Martin's Press, Inc., 175 Fifth Avenue, New York, New York 10010 (800) 221-7945; *The Statesman's Year-Book.*

Statistical Office of the United Nations, Publishing Service, New York, New York 10017 (800) 253-9646; *Human Development Report;* and *Trends in Europe and North America: The Statistical Yearbook of the Economic Commission for Europe.*

KYRGYZSTAN - UNEMPLOYMENT

Central Intelligence Agency, Washington, D.C. 20505 (703) 482-1100, www.cia.gov; *The World Factbook.*

St. Martin's Press, Inc., 175 Fifth Avenue, New York, New York 10010 (800) 221-7945; *The Statesman's Year-Book.*

Statistical Office of the United Nations, Publishing Service, New York, New York 10017 (800) 253-9646; *Statistical Yearbook;* and *Trends in Europe and North America: The Statistical Yearbook of the Economic Commission for Europe.*

KYRGYZSTAN - VITAL STATISTICS

St. Martin's Press, Inc., 175 Fifth Avenue, New York, New York 10010 (800) 221-7945; *The Statesman's Year-Book.*

Statistical Office of the United Nations, Publishing Service, New York, New York 10017 (800) 253-9646; *Statistical Yearbook.*

World Health Organization, Office of Publications, 20 Avenue Appia, CH-1211 Geneva 27, Switzerland (Telephone Number in U.S. (518) 436-9686); *World Health Statistics Annual.*

KYRGYZSTAN - WAGES

Business International Moscow, 23 Profsoyuznaya Ulitsa, 117859, Moscow (Telephone Number in U.S. (800) 938-4685); *The CIS Market Atlas.*

Statistical Office of the United Nations, Publishing Service, New York, New York 10017 (800) 253-9646; *Statistical Yearbook.*

The World Bank, 1818 H Street, NW, Washington, D.C. 20433 (202) 477-1234; *Statistical Handbook: States of the Former USSR.*

KYRGYZSTAN - WELFARE

Academic International Press, Box 1111, Gulf Breeze, Florida 32562; *Russia and Eurasia Facts and Figures Annual.*

St. Martin's Press, Inc., 175 Fifth Avenue, New York, New York 10010 (800) 221-7945; *The Statesman's Year-Book.*

KYRGYZSTAN - WHOLESALE PRICES

Academic International Press, Box 1111, Gulf Breeze, Florida 32562; *Russia and Eurasia Facts and Figures Annual.*

Statistical Office of the United Nations, Publishing Service, New York, New York 10017 (800) 253-9646; *Statistical Yearbook.*

KYRGYZSTAN - WHOLESALE TRADE

Statistical Office of the United Nations, Publishing Service, New York, New York 10017 (800) 253-9646; *Statistical Yearbook.*

KYRGYZSTAN - WOOL PRODUCTION AND CONSUMPTION - See KYRGYZSTAN - TEXTILE INDUSTRY

L

LABOR FORCE EMPLOYMENT AND EARNINGS - See also individual industries or occupations

LABOR FORCE EMPLOYMENT AND EARNINGS - ACCIDENTS AND FATALITIES

National Safety Council, 1121 Spring Lake Drive, Itasca, Illinois 60143-3201 (630) 285-1121; *Accident Facts.*

U.S. Department of Labor, Bureau of Labor Statistics, Two Massachusetts Avenue, NE, Washington, D.C. 20212 (202) 691-5200, www.stats.bls.gov; *USDL News 98-336;* and *Occupational Injuries and Illnesses in the United States by Industry.*

LABOR FORCE EMPLOYMENT AND EARNINGS - AVERAGE PAY - STATES

U.S. Department of Labor, Bureau of Labor Statistics, Two Massachusetts Avenue, NE, Washington, D.C. 20212 (202) 691-5200, www.stats.bls.gov; *USDL News 99-171, Average Annual Pay by State and Industry.*

LABOR FORCE EMPLOYMENT AND EARNINGS - AVERAGE PAY - STATES - METRO AREAS

U.S. Department of Labor, Bureau of Labor Statistics, Two Massachusetts Avenue, NE, Washington, D.C. 20212 (202) 691-5200, www.stats.bls.gov; *USDL News 99-232, Average Annual Pay Levels in Metropolitan Areas.*

LABOR FORCE EMPLOYMENT AND EARNINGS - CITY GOVERNMENT

U.S. Department of Commerce, Bureau of the Census, Washington, D.C. 20233 (301) 457-4100, www.census.gov; *City Employment;* and unpublished data.

LABOR FORCE EMPLOYMENT AND EARNINGS - CIVILIAN LABOR FORCE - ADULT EDUCATION

U.S. Department of Education, National Center for Education Statistics, 555 New Jersey Avenue, NW, Washington, D.C. 20208-5574 (202) 219-1828, http://nces,ed.gov; *National Household Education Survey;* and *Adult Participation in Work-Related Courses.*

LABOR FORCE EMPLOYMENT AND EARNINGS - CIVILIAN LABOR FORCE - AMERICAN INDIAN, ESKIMO, ALEUT POPULATION

U.S. Department of Commerce, Bureau of the Census, Washington, D.C. 20233 (301) 457-4100, www.census.gov; *Current Population Reports;* and unpublished data.

LABOR FORCE EMPLOYMENT AND EARNINGS - CIVILIAN LABOR FORCE - ASIAN AND PACIFIC ISLANDER POPULATION

U.S. Department of Commerce, Bureau of the Census, Washington, D.C. 20233 (301) 457-4100, www.census.gov; *Current Population Reports;* and unpublished data.

LABOR FORCE EMPLOYMENT AND EARNINGS - CIVILIAN LABOR FORCE - BLACK POPULATION

U.S. Department of Commerce, Bureau of the Census, Washington, D.C. 20233 (301) 457-4100, www.census.gov; *Current Population Reports*, and unpublished data.

U.S. Department of Labor, Bureau of Labor Statistics, Two Massachusetts Avenue, NE, Washington, D.C. 20212 (202) 691-5200, www.stats.bls.gov; *Employment and Earnings; News; Monthly Labor Review;* Bulletin 2307; and unpublished data.

LABOR FORCE EMPLOYMENT AND EARNINGS - CIVILIAN LABOR FORCE - COMPUTER USE

U.S. Department of Education, National Center for Education Statistics, 555 New Jersey Avenue, NW, Washington, D.C. 20208-5574 (202) 219-1828, http://nces,ed.gov; *Digest of Education Statistics.*

LABOR FORCE EMPLOYMENT AND EARNINGS - CIVILIAN LABOR FORCE - DISPLACED WORKERS

U.S. Department of Labor, Bureau of Labor Statistics, 2 Massachusetts Avenue, NE, Washington, D.C. 20212 (202) 691-5200, www.stats.bls.gov; *News*, and unpublished data.

LABOR FORCE EMPLOYMENT AND EARNINGS - CIVILIAN LABOR FORCE - EDUCATIONAL ATTAINMENT

U.S. Department of Labor, Bureau of Labor Statistics, Two Massachusetts Avenue, NE, Washington, D.C. 20212 (202) 691-5200, www.stats.bls.gov; unpublished data.

LABOR FORCE EMPLOYMENT AND EARNINGS - CIVILIAN LABOR FORCE - EMPLOYED

U.S. Department of Labor, Bureau of Labor Statistics, Two Massachusetts Avenue, NE, Washington, D.C. 20212 (202) 691-5200, www.stats.bls.gov; *Employment and Earnings; Monthly Labor Review; Local Area Unemployment Statistics Program; News;* Bulletin 2307; and unpublished data.

LABOR FORCE EMPLOYMENT AND EARNINGS - CIVILIAN LABOR FORCE - FEMALE

U.S. Department of Labor, Bureau of Labor Statistics, Two Massachusetts Avenue, NE, Washington, D.C. 20212 (202) 691-5200, www.stats.bls.gov; *Employment and Earnings; News;* Bulletins 2217, 2340, 2307; and unpublished data

LABOR FORCE EMPLOYMENT AND EARNINGS - CIVILIAN LABOR FORCE - FEMALE - AGE OF CHILDREN

U.S. Department of Labor, Bureau of Labor Statistics, Two Massachusetts Avenue, NE, Washington, D.C. 20212 (202) 691-5200, www.stats.bls.gov; Bulletin 2307; and unpublished data.

LABOR FORCE EMPLOYMENT AND EARNINGS - CIVILIAN LABOR FORCE - FEMALE - MARITAL STATUS

U.S. Department of Labor, Bureau of Labor Statistics, Two Massachusetts Avenue, NE, Washington, D.C. 20212 (202) 691-5200, www.stats.bls.gov; Bulletins 2217, 2340, 2307; and unpublished data.

LABOR FORCE EMPLOYMENT AND EARNINGS - CIVILIAN LABOR FORCE - FEMALE - MULTIPLE JOB HOLDERS

U.S. Department of Labor, Bureau of Labor Statistics, Two Massachusetts Avenue, NE, Washington, D.C. 20212 (202) 691-5200, www.stats.bls.gov; *Employment and Earnings*; and unpublished data.

LABOR FORCE EMPLOYMENT AND EARNINGS - CIVILIAN LABOR FORCE - FULL TIME - PART TIME

U.S. Department of Labor, Bureau of Labor Statistics, Two Massachusetts Avenue, NE, Washington, D.C. 20212 (202) 691-5200, www.stats.bls.gov; *Employment and Earnings.*

LABOR FORCE EMPLOYMENT AND EARNINGS - CIVILIAN LABOR FORCE - FOREIGN-BORN POPULATION

U.S. Department of Commerce, Bureau of the Census, Washington, D.C. 20233 (301) 457-4100, www.census.gov; *Current Population Reports*; and Population Paper Listing PPL-92.

LABOR FORCE EMPLOYMENT AND EARNINGS - CIVILIAN LABOR FORCE - HIGH SCHOOL GRADUATES - DROPOUTS

U.S. Department of Labor, Bureau of Labor Statistics, Two Massachusetts Avenue, NE, Washington, D.C. 20212 (202) 691-5200, www.stats.bls.gov, *News;* Bulletin 2307; and unpublished data.

LABOR FORCE EMPLOYMENT AND EARNINGS - CIVILIAN LABOR FORCE - HISPANIC ORIGIN POPULATION

U.S. Department of Commerce, Bureau of the Census, Washington, D.C. 20233 (301) 457-4100, www.census.gov; *Current Population Reports;* and unpublished data.

U.S. Department of Labor, Bureau of Labor Statistics, Two Massachusetts Avenue, NE, Washington, D.C. 20212 (202) 691-5200, www.stats.bls.gov; *Employment and Earnings; Monthly Labor Review;* Bulletin 2307; and unpublished data.

LABOR FORCE EMPLOYMENT AND EARNINGS - CIVILIAN LABOR FORCE - METROPOLITAN AREAS

U.S. Department of Labor, Bureau of

Labor Statistics, Two Massachusetts Avenue, NE, Washington, D.C. 20212 (202) 691-5200, www.stats.bls.gov; *Local Area Unemployment Statistics Program.*

LABOR FORCE EMPLOYMENT AND EARNINGS - CIVILIAN LABOR FORCE - MINIMUM WAGE WORKERS

U.S. Department of Labor, Bureau of Labor Statistics, Two Massachusetts Avenue, NE, Washington, D.C. 20212 (202) 691-5200, www.stats.bls.gov; unpublished data.

LABOR FORCE EMPLOYMENT AND EARNINGS - CIVILIAN LABOR FORCE - MULTIPLE JOB HOLDERS

U.S. Department of Labor, Bureau of Labor Statistics, Two Massachusetts Avenue, NE, Washington, D.C. 20212 (202) 691-5200, www.stats.bls.gov; *Employment and Earnings*; and unpublished data.

LABOR FORCE EMPLOYMENT AND EARNINGS - CIVILIAN LABOR FORCE - NOT AT WORK

U.S. Department of Labor, Bureau of Labor Statistics, Two Massachusetts Avenue, NE, Washington, D.C. 20212 (202) 691-5200, www.stats.bls.gov; *Employment and Earnings;* and unpublished data.

LABOR FORCE EMPLOYMENT AND EARNINGS - CIVILIAN LABOR FORCE - PART TIME

U.S. Department of Labor, Bureau of Labor Statistics, Two Massachusetts Avenue, NE, Washington, D.C. 20212 (202) 691-5200, www.stats.bls.gov; *Employment and Earnings.*

LABOR FORCE EMPLOYMENT AND EARNINGS - CIVILIAN LABOR FORCE - PARTICIPATION RATES

U.S. Department of Labor, Bureau of Labor Statistics, Two Massachusetts Avenue, NE, Washington, D.C. 20212 (202) 691-5200, www.stats.bls.gov; *Employment and Earnings; Monthly Labor Review;* Bulletins 2307, 2217, 2340; unpublished data; and Internet site: "Local Area Unemployment Statistics, Geographic Profile," http://146.142.4.24/cgi-bin/survey/most?gp.

LABOR FORCE EMPLOYMENT AND EARNINGS - CIVILIAN LABOR FORCE - PARTICIPATION RATES - SELECTED COUNTRIES

Organization for Economic Cooperation and Development, 2 rue Andre-Pascal, 75 Paris 16, France (202) 785-6323; *Labor Force Statistics.*

U.S. Department of Labor, Bureau of

Labor Statistics, Two Massachusetts Avenue, NE, Washington, D.C. 20212 (202) 691-5200, www.stats.bls.gov; *Monthly Labor Review;* and *Comparative Labor Force Statistics for Ten Countries.*

LABOR FORCE EMPLOYMENT AND EARNINGS - CIVILIAN LABOR FORCE - PARTICIPATION RATES - WIVES, BY AGE OF YOUNGEST CHILD

U.S. Department of Labor, Bureau of Labor Statistics, Two Massachusetts Avenue, NE, Washington, D.C. 20212 (202) 691-5200, www.stats.bls.gov; Bulletin 2340 and unpublished data.

LABOR FORCE EMPLOYMENT AND EARNINGS - CIVILIAN LABOR FORCE - PROJECTIONS

U.S. Department of Labor, Bureau of Labor Statistics, Two Massachusetts Avenue, NE, Washington, D.C. 20212 (202) 691-5200, www.stats.bls.gov; Bulletin 2307; *Employment and Earnings; Monthly Labor Review;* and unpublished data.

LABOR FORCE EMPLOYMENT AND EARNINGS - CIVILIAN LABOR FORCE - RACE

U.S. Department of Commerce, Bureau of the Census, Washington, D.C. 20233 (301) 457-4100, www.census.gov; *Current Population Reports;* and unpublished data.

U.S. Department of Labor, Bureau of Labor Statistics, Two Massachusetts Avenue, NE, Washington, D.C. 20212 (202) 691-5200, www.stats.bls.gov; *Monthly Labor Review; Employment and Earnings; News;* Bulletin 2307; and unpublished data.

LABOR FORCE EMPLOYMENT AND EARNINGS - CIVILIAN LABOR FORCE - REASON NOT IN

U.S. Department of Labor, Bureau of Labor Statistics, Two Massachusetts Avenue, NE, Washington, D.C. 20212 (202) 691-5200, www.stats.bls.gov; *Employment and Earnings.*

LABOR FORCE EMPLOYMENT AND EARNINGS - CIVILIAN LABOR FORCE - SCHOOL ENROLLMENT - PERSONS 16 TO 24 YEARS OLD

U.S. Department of Labor, Bureau of Labor Statistics, Two Massachusetts Avenue, NE, Washington, D.C. 20212 (202) 691-5200, www.stats.bls.gov; Bulletin 2307; *News;* and unpublished data.

LABOR FORCE EMPLOYMENT AND EARNINGS - CIVILIAN LABOR FORCE - SELF-EMPLOYED WORKERS

U.S. Department of Labor, Bureau of Labor Statistics, Two Massachusetts

Avenue, NE, Washington, D.C. 20212 (202) 691-5200, www.stats.bls.gov; Bulletin 2307; *Employment and Earnings; News;* and unpublished data.

LABOR FORCE EMPLOYMENT AND EARNINGS - CIVILIAN LABOR FORCE - STATES

U.S. Department of Labor, Bureau of Labor Statistics, Two Massachusetts Avenue, NE, Washington, D.C. 20212 (202) 691-5200, www.stats.bls.gov; Internet site: "Local Area Unemployment Statistics, Geographic Profile," http://146.142.4.24/cgi-bin/surveymost?gp.

LABOR FORCE EMPLOYMENT AND EARNINGS - CIVILIAN LABOR FORCE - UNEMPLOYED

U.S. Department of Labor, Bureau of Labor Statistics, Two Massachusetts Avenue, NE, Washington, D.C. 20212 (202) 691-5200, www.stats.bls.gov; *Employment and Earnings; News;* Bulletin 2307; unpublished data; and Internet site: "Local Area Unemployment Statistics, Geographic Profile," http://146.142.4.24/cgi-bin/surveymost?gp

LABOR FORCE EMPLOYMENT AND EARNINGS - CIVILIAN LABOR FORCE - WOMEN WHO GAVE BIRTH IN PREVIOUS YEAR

U.S. Department of Commerce, Bureau of the Census, Washington, D.C. 20233 (301) 457-4100, www.census.gov; *Current Population Reports,* and unpublished data.

LABOR FORCE EMPLOYMENT AND EARNINGS - COMPUTER USE

U.S. Department of Education, National Center for Education Statistics, 555 New Jersey Avenue, NW, Washington, D.C. 20208-5574 (202) 219-1828, http://nces,ed.gov; *Digest of Education Statistics.*

LABOR FORCE EMPLOYMENT AND EARNINGS - DISABLED PERSONS

U.S. Department of Commerce, Bureau of the Census, Washington, D.C. 20233 (301) 457-4100, www.census.gov; unpublished data; and Internet site: http://www.census.gov/hhes/www/disable/dissipp.html.

LABOR FORCE EMPLOYMENT AND EARNINGS - DISPLACED WORKERS

U.S. Department of Labor, Bureau of Labor Statistics, Two Massachusetts Avenue, NE, Washington, D.C. 20212 (202) 691-5200, www.stats.bls.gov; *News.*

LABOR FORCE EMPLOYMENT AND EARNINGS - EARNINGS

U.S. Department of Commerce, Bureau of Economic Analysis, Fourteenth Street between Constitution Avenue and E Street, NW, Washington, D.C. 20230 (202) 606-9900; *The National Income and Product Accounts of the United States;* and *Survey of Current Business.*

U.S. Department of Commerce, Bureau of the Census, Washington, D.C. 20233 (301) 457-4100, www.census.gov; *Current Population Reports.*

U.S. Department of Labor, Bureau of Labor Statistics, Two Massachusetts Avenue, NE, Washington, D.C. 20212 (202) 691-5200, www.stats.bls.gov; *Productivity and Costs; Employment and Earnings; Average Annual Pay by State and Industry; Average Annual Pay Levels in Metropolitan Areas; Monthly Labor Review;* Bulletin 2307; and Internet sites: http://stats.bls.gov/ceshome.htm; http://stats.bls.gov/iprhome.htm.

LABOR FORCE EMPLOYMENT AND EARNINGS - EDUCATIONAL ATTAINMENT

U.S. Department of Commerce, Bureau of the Census, Washington, D.C. 20233 (301) 457-4100, www.census.gov; *Current Population Reports;* and unpublished data.

U.S. Department of Labor, Bureau of Labor Statistics, Two Massachusetts Avenue, NE, Washington, D.C. 20212 (202) 691-5200, www.stats.bls.gov; unpublished data.

LABOR FORCE EMPLOYMENT AND EARNINGS - ELDERLY

U.S. Department of Commerce, Bureau of the Census, Washington, D.C. 20233 (301) 457-4100, www.census.gov; *Current Population Reports;* and unpublished data.

U.S. Department of Labor, Bureau of Labor Statistics, Two Massachusetts Avenue, NE, Washington, D.C. 20212 (202) 691-5200, www.stats.bls.gov; *Employment and Earnings; Monthly Labor Review;* Bulletins 2217, 2307, 2340; and unpublished data.

LABOR FORCE EMPLOYMENT AND EARNINGS - EMPLOYEE BENEFITS

U.S. Department of Commerce, Bureau of the Census, Washington, D.C. 20233 (301) 457-4100, www.census.gov; unpublished data.

U.S. Department of Health and Human Services, National Center for Health Statistics, 3700 East-West Highway, Hyattsville, Maryland 20782 (301) 436-8500, www.cdc.gov/nchs, www.cdc.gov/nchs; *Employer-Sponsored Health Insurance, State and National Estimates.*

U.S. Department of Labor, Bureau of Labor Statistics, Two Massachusetts Avenue, NE, Washington, D.C. 20212 (202) 691-5200, www.stats.bls.gov; *News.*

LABOR FORCE EMPLOYMENT AND EARNINGS - EMPLOYEE BENEFITS - GOVERNMENT EMPLOYEES

U.S. Department of Labor, Bureau of Labor Statistics, Two Massachusetts Avenue, NE, Washington, D.C. 20212 (202) 691-5200, www.stats.bls.gov; *News,* and *Employer Costs for Employee Compensation.*

LABOR FORCE EMPLOYMENT AND EARNINGS - EMPLOYEE TRAINING

U.S. Department of Labor, Bureau of Labor Statistics, Two Massachusetts Avenue, NE, Washington, D.C. 20212 (202) 691-5200, www.stats.bls.gov; *Monthly Labor Review.*

U.S. Department of Education, National Center for Education Statistics, 555 New Jersey Avenue, NW, Washington, D.C. 20208-5574 (202) 219-1828, http://nces,ed.gov; *Adult Participation in Work-Related Courses.*

LABOR FORCE EMPLOYMENT AND EARNINGS - EMPLOYEES

U.S. Department of Labor, Bureau of Labor Statistics, Two Massachusetts Avenue, NE, Washington, D.C. 20212 (202) 691-5200, www.stats.bls.gov; *Employment and Earnings;* and Internet site: http://stats.bls.gov/ ceshome.htm.

LABOR FORCE EMPLOYMENT AND EARNINGS - EMPLOYEES - STATES

U.S. Department of Labor, Bureau of Labor Statistics, Two Massachusetts Avenue, NE, Washington, D.C. 20212 (202) 691-5200, www.stats.bls.gov; *Employment and Earnings.*

LABOR FORCE EMPLOYMENT AND EARNINGS - EMPLOYMENT COST INDEX

U.S. Department of Labor, Bureau of Labor Statistics, Two Massachusetts Avenue, NE, Washington, D.C. 20212 (202) 691-5200, www.stats.bls.gov; *News; Employment Cost Index; International Comparisons of Manufacturing Productivity and Unit Labor Cost Trends; New Release, USDL 98-376* and Internet site http://stats.bls.gov/ ecthome.htm.

LABOR FORCE EMPLOYMENT AND EARNINGS - EMPLOYMENT PROJECTIONS

U.S. Department of Labor, Bureau of Labor Statistics, Two Massachusetts Avenue, NE, Washington, D.C. 20212 (202)

691-5200, www.stats.bls.gov; *Monthly Labor Review.*

LABOR FORCE EMPLOYMENT AND EARNINGS - EMPLOYMENT TAXES AND CONTRIBUTIONS

Executive Office of the President, Office of Management and Budget, Executive Office Building, Washington, D.C. 20503 (202) 395-3080, www.whitehouse.gov/omb; *Historical Tables.*

LABOR FORCE EMPLOYMENT AND EARNINGS - FEMALE

U.S. Department of Commerce, Bureau of the Census, Washington, D.C. 20233 (301) 457-4100, www.census.gov; *Current Population Reports.*

U.S. Department of Labor, Bureau of Labor Statistics, Two Massachusetts Avenue, NE, Washington, D.C. 20212 (202) 691-5200, www.stats.bls.gov; *Employment and Earnings;* Bulletins 2217, 2307, and 2340; unpublished data; and Internet site: "Local Area Unemployment Statistics, Geographic Profile," http://146.142.4.24/cgi-surveymost?gp

LABOR FORCE EMPLOYMENT AND EARNINGS - FOREIGN COUNTRIES

Organisation for Economic Cooperation and Development (OECD), 2 rue Andre-Pascal, 75 Paris 16, France (Phone Number in U.S. (202) 785-6323); *OECD News Release, Standardized Unemployment Rates;* and *Labour Force Statistics.*

U.S. Department of Labor, Bureau of Labor Statistics, 2 Massachusetts Avenue, NE, Washington, D.C. 20212 (202) 691-5200, www.stats.bls.gov; *Comparative Labor Force Statistics for Ten Countries;* and *Monthly Labor Review.*

LABOR FORCE EMPLOYMENT AND EARNINGS - FOREIGN - OWNED FIRMS

U.S. Department of Commerce, Bureau of Economic Analysis, Fourteenth Street between Constitution Avenue and E Street, NW, Washington, D.C. 20230 (202) 606-9900, www.bea.doc.gov; *Survey of Current Business;* and *Foreign Direct Investment in the U.S., Operations of U.S. Affiliates of Foreign Companies.*

LABOR FORCE EMPLOYMENT AND EARNINGS - GOVERNMENT - See GOVERNMENT

LABOR FORCE EMPLOYMENT AND EARNINGS - HELP WANTED ADVERTISING

U.S. Department of Labor, Employment and Training Administration, 200 Constitution Avenue, NW, Washington, D.C. 20210 (202) 219-6871, www.doleta.gov; unpublished data.

LABOR FORCE EMPLOYMENT AND EARNINGS - HIGH SCHOOL GRADUATES AND DROPOUTS

U.S. Department of Labor, Bureau of Labor Statistics, Two Massachusetts Avenue, NE, Washington, D.C. 20212 (202) 691-5200, www.stats.bls.gov; Bulletin 2307; *News,* and unpublished data.

LABOR FORCE EMPLOYMENT AND EARNINGS - HISPANIC ORIGIN POPULATION

U.S. Department of Commerce, Bureau of the Census, Washington, D.C. 20233 (301) 457-4100, www.census.gov; *Current Population Reports.*

U.S. Department of Labor, Bureau of Labor Statistics, Two Massachusetts Avenue, NE, Washington, D.C. 20212 (202) 691-5200, www.stats.bls.gov; *Employment and Earnings; Monthly Labor Review;* Bulletin 2307 and unpublished data.

LABOR FORCE EMPLOYMENT AND EARNINGS - HOME-BASED BUSINESS

U.S. Department of Labor, Bureau of Labor Statistics, Two Massachusetts Avenue, NE, Washington, D.C. 20212 (202) 691-5200, www.stats.bls.gov; *News,* USDL 98-93

LABOR FORCE EMPLOYMENT AND EARNINGS - HOURS

U.S. Department of Labor, Bureau of Labor Statistics, Two Massachusetts Avenue, NE, Washington, D.C. 20212 (202) 691-5200, www.stats.bls.gov; *Employment and Earnings;* and Internet site: http://stats.bls.gov/ceshome.htm.

LABOR FORCE EMPLOYMENT AND EARNINGS - INDEXES OF COMPENSATION

U.S. Department of Labor, Bureau of Labor Statistics, Two Massachusetts Avenue, NE, Washington, D.C. 20212 (202) 691-5200, www.stats.bls.gov; *News, Productivity and Costs.*

LABOR FORCE EMPLOYMENT AND EARNINGS - INTERNET ACCESS

Mediamark Research, Inc., 708 Third Avenue, New York, New York 10017 (212) 599-0444; *Multimedia Audiences.*

LABOR FORCE EMPLOYMENT AND EARNINGS - INDEXES OF COMPENSATION

U.S. Department of Labor, Bureau of Labor Statistics, Two Massachusetts Avenue, NE, Washington, D.C. 20212 (202) 691-5200, www.stats.bls.gov; *News,* USDL 99-53; *News Release* USDL 98-376; and

Internet site: http://stats.bls.gov/iprhome.htm.

LABOR FORCE EMPLOYMENT AND EARNINGS - JOB OPENINGS AND PLACEMENTS

U.S. Department of Labor, Employment and Training Administration, 200 Constitution Avenue, NW, Washington, D.C. 20210 (202) 219-6871, www.doleta.gov; unpublished data.

LABOR FORCE EMPLOYMENT AND EARNINGS - MEDIA USERS

Time Warner, Time and Life Building, Rockefeller Center, New York, New York 10020 (212) 522-1212; *The Fortune Directories.*

LABOR FORCE EMPLOYMENT AND EARNINGS - METROPOLITAN AREAS

U.S. Department of Labor, Bureau of Labor Statistics, Two Massachusetts Avenue, NE, Washington, D.C. 20212 (202) 691-5200, www.stats.bls.gov; *Average Annual Pay Levels in Metropolitan Areas;* and *Local Area Unemployment Statistics Program.*

LABOR FORCE EMPLOYMENT AND EARNINGS - MINIMUM WAGE WORKERS

U.S. Department of Labor, Bureau of Labor Statistics, 200 Constitution Avenue, NW, Washington, D.C. 20210 (202) 691-5200, www.stats.bls.gov; unpublished data; and Internet site http://www.dol.gov/esa/public/minwage/main.htm.

LABOR FORCE EMPLOYMENT AND EARNINGS - OCCUPATIONAL GROUPS - See OCCUPATIONS and individual occupations

LABOR FORCE EMPLOYMENT AND EARNINGS - OCCUPATIONAL SAFETY

National Safety Council, 1121 Spring Lake Drive, Itasca, Illinois 60143-3201 (630) 285-1121; *Accident Facts.*

U.S. Department of Labor, Bureau of Labor Statistics, Two Massachusetts Avenue, NE, Washington, D.C. 20212 (202) 691-5200, www.stats.bls.gov; *Occupational Injuries and Illnesses in the United States by Industry.*

LABOR FORCE EMPLOYMENT AND EARNINGS - PERSONS WORKING AT HOME

U.S. Department of Labor, Bureau of Labor Statistics, Two Massachusetts Avenue, NE, Washington, D.C. 20212 (202) 691-5200, www.stats.bls.gov; *News,* USDL 98-93.

LABOR FORCE EMPLOYMENT AND EARNINGS - PRODUCTION WORKERS

U.S. Department of Commerce, Bureau of the Census, Washington, D.C. 20233 (301) 457-4100, www.census.gov; *Census of Manufactures;* and *Annual Survey of Manufactures.*

U.S. Department of Labor, Bureau of Labor Statistics, Two Massachusetts Avenue, NE, Washington, D.C. 20212 (202) 691-5200, www.stats.bls.gov; *Employment and Earnings;* and Internet site: http://stats.bls.gov/ ceshome.htm.

LABOR FORCE EMPLOYMENT AND EARNINGS - PRODUCTIVITY

Organisation for Economic Cooperation and Development (OECD), 2 rue Andre-Pascal, 75 Paris 16, France (Telephone Number in the United States (202) 785-6323); *Science, Technology and Industry Outlook.*

U.S. Department of Labor, Bureau of Labor Statistics, Two Massachusetts Avenue, NE, Washington, D.C. 20212 (202) 691-5200, www.stats.bls.gov; *Productivity and Costs; ; News,* USDL 99-53; *Employment and Earnings;* unpublished data; and Internet site http://stats.bls.gov/iprhome.htm.

LABOR FORCE EMPLOYMENT AND EARNINGS - SELF-EMPLOYED

U.S. Department of Labor, Bureau of Labor Statistics, Two Massachusetts Avenue, NE, Washington, D.C. 20212 (202) 691-5200, www.stats.bls.gov; *Bulletin 2307; Employment and Earnings; News* USDL 98-93; and unpublished data.

LABOR FORCE EMPLOYMENT AND EARNINGS - SOCIAL INSURANCE COVERAGE

Social Security Administration, 6400 Security Boulevard, Baltimore, Maryland 21235 (800) 772-1213, www.ssa.gov; *Annual Statistical Supplement to the Social Security Bulletin;* and unpublished data.

LABOR FORCE EMPLOYMENT AND EARNINGS - STATE DATA

U.S. Department of Labor, Bureau of Labor Statistics, Two Massachusetts Avenue, NE, Washington, D.C. 20212 (202) 691-5200, www.stats.bls.gov; Bulletin 2320; *Geographic Profile of Employment and Unemployment; Employment and Earnings; News, USDL 99-171;* and *Average Annual Pay By State and Industry.*

LABOR FORCE EMPLOYMENT AND EARNINGS - TENURE WITH EMPLOYER

U.S. Department of Labor, Bureau of

Labor Statistics, Two Massachusetts Avenue, NE, Washington, D.C. 20212 (202) 691-5200, www.stats.bls.gov; *News,* USDL 98-387; and unpublished data.

LABOR FORCE EMPLOYMENT AND EARNINGS - UNEMPLOYED WORKERS - See also UNEMPLOYMENT

LABOR FORCE EMPLOYMENT AND EARNINGS - UNEMPLOYED WORKERS - AGE

U.S. Department of Labor, Bureau of Labor Statistics, Two Massachusetts Avenue, NE, Washington, D.C. 20212 (202) 691-5200, www.stats.bls.gov; *Employment and Earnings; News,* USDL 99-75; and unpublished data.

LABOR FORCE EMPLOYMENT AND EARNINGS - UNEMPLOYED WORKERS - ASIAN AND PACIFIC ISLANDER POPULATION

U.S. Department of Labor, Bureau of Labor Statistics, Two Massachusetts Avenue, NE, Washington, D.C. 20212 (202) 691-5200, www.stats.bls.gov; *Current Population Reports;* and unpublished data.

LABOR FORCE EMPLOYMENT AND EARNINGS - UNEMPLOYED WORKERS - BLACK POPULATION

U.S. Department of Commerce, Bureau of the Census, Washington, D.C. 20233 (301) 457-4100, www.census.gov; *Current Population Reports,* and unpublished data.

U.S. Department of Labor, Bureau of Labor Statistics, Two Massachusetts Avenue, NE, Washington, D.C. 20212 (202) 691-5200, www.stats.bls.gov; *Employment and Earnings; News;* Bulletin 2307; and unpublished data.

LABOR FORCE EMPLOYMENT AND EARNINGS - UNEMPLOYED WORKERS - EDUCATIONAL ATTAINMENT

U.S. Department of Commerce, Bureau of the Census, Washington, D.C. 20233 (301) 457-4100, www.census.gov; *Current Population Reports;* and unpublished data.

U.S. Department of Labor, Bureau of Labor Statistics, Two Massachusetts Avenue, NE, Washington, D.C. 20212 (202) 691-5200, www.stats.bls.gov; unpublished data.

LABOR FORCE EMPLOYMENT AND EARNINGS - UNEMPLOYMENT WORKERS - FOREIGN-BORN POPULATION

U.S. Department of Commerce, Bureau of the Census, Washington, D.C. 20233 (301) 457-4100, www.census.gov; *Current Population Reports;* and Population Paper Listing PPL-92.

LABOR FORCE EMPLOYMENT AND EARNINGS - UNEMPLOYED WORKERS - FOREIGN COUNTRIES

Organisation for Economic Cooperation and Development (OECD), 2 rue Andre-Pascal, 75 Paris 16, France (Phone Number in U.S. (202) 785-6323); *OECD News Release, Standardized Unemployment Rates.*

U.S. Department of Labor, Bureau of Labor Statistics, Two Massachusetts Avenue, NE, Washington, D.C. 20212 (202) 691-5200, www.stats.bls.gov; *Comparative Labor Force Statistics for Ten Countries;* and *Monthly Labor Review.*

LABOR FORCE EMPLOYMENT AND EARNINGS - UNEMPLOYED WORKERS - HIGH SCHOOL GRADUATES AND DROPOUTS

U.S. Department of Labor, Bureau of Labor Statistics, Two Massachusetts Avenue, NE, Washington, D.C. 20212 (202) 691-5200, www.stats.bls.gov; *News;* Bulletin 2307; and unpublished data.

LABOR FORCE EMPLOYMENT AND EARNINGS - UNEMPLOYED WORKERS - HISPANIC ORIGIN POPULATION

U.S. Department of Commerce, Bureau of the Census, Washington, D.C. 20233 (301) 457-4100, www.census.gov; unpublished data.

U.S. Department of Labor, Bureau of Labor Statistics, Two Massachusetts Avenue, NE, Washington, D.C. 20212 (202) 691-5200, www.stats.bls.gov; *Employment and Earnings; Monthly Labor Review;* and unpublished data.

LABOR FORCE EMPLOYMENT AND EARNINGS - UNEMPLOYED WORKERS - INDUSTRY

U.S. Department of Labor, Bureau of Labor Statistics, Two Massachusetts Avenue, NE, Washington, D.C. 20212 (202) 691-5200, www.stats.bls.gov; *Employment and Earnings.*

LABOR FORCE EMPLOYMENT AND EARNINGS - UNEMPLOYED WORKERS - OCCUPATION

U.S. Department of Labor, Bureau of Labor Statistics, Two Massachusetts Avenue, NE, Washington, D.C. 20212 (202) 691-5200, www.stats.bls.gov; *Employment and Earnings.*

LABOR FORCE EMPLOYMENT AND EARNINGS - UNEMPLOYED WORKERS - RACE

U.S. Department of Commerce, Bureau of the Census, Washington, D.C. 20233

(301) 457-4100, www.census.gov; *Current Population Reports;* and unpublished data.

U.S. Department of Labor, Bureau of Labor Statistics, Two Massachusetts Avenue, NE, Washington, D.C. 20212 (202) 691-5200, www.stats.bls.gov; *Employment and Earnings,* Bulletin 2307 and unpublished data.

LABOR FORCE EMPLOYMENT AND EARNINGS - UNEMPLOYED WORKERS - REASON

U.S. Department of Labor, Bureau of Labor Statistics, Two Massachusetts Avenue, NE, Washington, D.C. 20212 (202) 691-5200, www.stats.bls.gov; *Employment and Earnings;* Bulletin 2307; and unpublished data.

LABOR FORCE EMPLOYMENT AND EARNINGS - UNEMPLOYED WORKERS - SEX

U.S. Department of Labor, Bureau of Labor Statistics, Two Massachusetts Avenue, NE, Washington, D.C. 20212 (202) 691-5200, www.stats.bls.gov; *Employment and Earnings; Monthly Labor Review; News;* Bulletin 2307; and unpublished data.

LABOR FORCE EMPLOYMENT AND EARNINGS - UNEMPLOYED WORKERS - STATES

U.S. Department of Labor, Bureau of Labor Statistics, Two Massachusetts Avenue, NE, Washington, D.C. 20212 (202) 691-5200, www.stats.bls.gov; *Geographic Profile of Employment and Unemployment.*

LABOR FORCE EMPLOYMENT AND EARNINGS - UNEMPLOYED WORKERS - UNION MEMBERSHIP

Bureau of National Affairs, 1231 25th Street, NW, Washington, D.C. 20037 (800) 372-1033, www.bns.com; *Union Membership and Earnings Data Book*; and Internet site: http://www.bna.com/bnaplus/databook.html.

U.S. Department of Labor, Bureau of Labor Statistics, Two Massachusetts Avenue, NE, Washington, D.C. 20212 (202) 691-5200, www.stats.bls.gov; *Employment and Earnings.*

LABOR FORCE EMPLOYMENT AND EARNINGS - WORK STOPPAGES

U.S. Department of Labor, Bureau of Labor Statistics, Two Massachusetts Avenue, NE, Washington, D.C. 20212 (202) 691-5200, www.stats.bls.gov; *Compensation and Working Conditions.*

LABOR FORCE EMPLOYMENT AND EARNINGS - WORKDAYS LOST

U.S. Department of Health and Human Services, National Center for Health Statistics, 3700 East-West Highway, Hyattsville, Maryland 20782 (301) 436-8500, www.cdc.gov/nchs; *Vital and Health Statistics;* and unpublished data.

LABOR FORCE EMPLOYMENT AND EARNINGS - YOUTH EMPLOYMENT PROGRAMS

The Congress of the U.S., Congressional Research Service, 10 First Street, SE, Washington, D.C. 20540 (202) 707-5700; *Cash and Noncash Benefits for Persons with Limited Income Eligibility Rules, Recipient and Expenditure Data.*

LABOR ORGANIZATIONS OR UNIONS

The Gale Group, 27500 Drake Road, Farmington Hills, Michigan 48331 (800) 877-4253; *Encyclopedia of Associations.*

LABOR ORGANIZATIONS OR UNIONS - EMPLOYEE BENEFIT COSTS

U.S. Department of Labor, Bureau of Labor Statistics, 2 Massachusetts Avenue, NE, Washington, D.C. 20212 (202) 691-5200, www.stats.bls.gov; *News, Employer Costs for Employee Compensation.*

LABOR ORGANIZATIONS OR UNIONS - MEMBERSHIP

Bureau of National Affairs, 1231 25th Street, NW, Washington, D.C. 20037 (800) 372-1033, www.bns.com; *Union Membership and Earnings Data Book*; and Internet site: http://www.bna.com/bnaplus/databook.html.

U.S. Department of Labor, Bureau of Labor Statistics, Two Massachusetts Avenue, NE, Washington, D.C. 20212 (202) 691-5200, www.stats.bls.gov; *Employment and Earnings.*

LABOR ORGANIZATIONS OR UNIONS - POLITICAL ACTION COMMITTEES (PAC)

Federal Election Commission, 999 E Street, NW, Washington, D.C. 20463 (800) 424-9530, www.fec.gov; *FEC Reports on Financial Activity, Final Report, Party and Non-Party Political Committees;* and press releases.

LABOR ORGANIZATIONS OR UNIONS - PUBLIC CONFIDENCE

Independent Sector, 1200 18th Street, Suite 200, Washington, D.C. 20036 (202) 467-6161; *Giving and Volunteering in the United States.*

LABOR STRIKES

U.S. Department of Labor, Bureau of Labor Statistics, Two Massachusetts

Avenue, NE, Washington, D.C. 20212 (202) 691-5200, www.stats.bls.gov; *Compensation and Working Conditions.*

LABORATORIES - MEDICAL AND DENTAL

U.S. Department of Commerce, Bureau of the Census, Washington, D.C. 20233 (301) 457-4100, www.census.gov; *Census of Service Industries.*

LACROSSE

The National Collegiate Athletic Association, 700 West Washington Street, Indianapolis, Indiana 46206 (317) 917-6222; *1997-98 Participation Study.*

LAMB AND MUTTON - See also MEAT and MEAT PRODUCTS

U.S. Department of Agriculture, Economic Research Service, 1800 M Street, NW, Washington, D.C. 20036 (202) 694-5050, www.ers.usda.gov; *Food Consumption, Prices, and Expenditures;* and *Livestock and Meat Statistics; Agricultural Outlook.*

LAMBS - See SHEEP AND LAMBS

LAND - See also FARMS and PUBLIC LANDS

LAND - AREA - CITIES

U.S. Department of Commerce, Bureau of the Census, Washington, D.C. 20233 (301) 457-4100, www.census.gov; *Census of Population and Housing, Population and Housing Unit Counts; General Population Characteristics*; and Internet site: http://www.census.gov/population/estimates/metro-city/scts/SC98TS-DR.txt.

LAND - AREA - COASTAL

U.S. Department of Commerce, Bureau of the Census, Washington, D.C. 20233 (301) 457-4100, www.census.gov; *Census of Population and Housing;* and unpublished data.

LAND - AREA - FOREIGN COUNTRIES

U.S. Department of Commerce, Bureau of the Census, Washington, D.C. 20233 (301) 457-4100, www.census.gov; International Data Base; and Internet site: http://www.census.gov/ipc/www/idbnew.htm.

LAND - AREA - NATIONAL PARKS

U.S. Department of the Interior, National Park Service, C Street between Eighteenth and Nineteenth Streets, NW, Washington, D.C. 20240 (202) 208-6843, www.nps.gov; *National Park Statistical Abstract;* and unpublished data.

LAND - AREA - OUTLYING AREAS

U.S. Department of Commerce, Bureau of the Census, Washington, D.C. 20233 (301) 457-4100, www.census.gov; *Census of Population and Housing;* and unpublished data from the TIGER/GICS computer file.

LAND - AREA - UNITED STATES

U.S. Department of Commerce, Bureau of the Census, Washington, D.C. 20233 (301) 457-4100, www.census.gov; *Census of Population and Housing; Census of Population and Housing, Population and Housing Unit Counts;* and unpublished data.

LAND - FARMLAND

U.S. Department of Agriculture, National Agricultural Statistics Service, Fourteenth Street and Independence Avenue, SW, Washington, D.C. 20250 (800) 727-9540, www.usda.gov/nass; *Farms and Land in Farms;* and *Census of Agriculture.*

LAND - FEDERAL LAND

General Services Administration, General Services Building, Eighteenth and F Streets, NW, Washington, D.C. 20405 (202) 708-5082, www.gsa.gov; *Inventory Report on Real Property Owned by the United States Throughout the World.*

LAND - FOREIGN INVESTORS

U.S. Department of Commerce, Bureau of Economic Analysis, Fourteenth Street between Constitution Avenue and E Street, NW, Washington, D.C. 20230 (202) 606-9900, www.bea.doc.gov; *Survey of Current Business; Foreign Direct Investment in the United States;* and *Operations of United States Affiliates of Foreign Companies.*

LAND - FOREST - AREA AND OWNERSHIP

U.S. Department of Agriculture, Forest Service, Post Office Box 96090, Washington, D.C. 20090 (202) 205-8333, www.fs.fed.us; *Forest Resources of the United States.*

LAND - PARKS

National Association of State Park Directors, 9894 East Holden Place, Tucson, Arizona 85748 (520) 298-4924; *Annual Information Exchange.*

U.S. Department of the Interior, National Park Service, C Street between Eighteenth and Nineteenth Streets, NW, Washington, D.C. 20240 (202) 208-6843, www.nps.gov; *National Park Service Abstract;* and unpublished data.

LANDFILLS - See also SOLID WASTE

Franklin Associates Limited, 4121 West 83rd Street, Suite 108, Prairie Village, Kansas 66208 (913) 649-2225; *Characterization of Municipal Solid Waste in the U.S.*

U.S. Department of Energy, Energy Information Administration, 1000 Independence Avenue, SW, Washington, D.C. 20585 (202) 586-8800, www.eia.doc.gov; *Emissions of Greenhouse Gases in the U.S.*

LANGUAGES SPOKEN AT HOME

Federal Interagency Forum on Child and Family Statistics, c/o National Maternal and Child Health Clearinghouse, 2070 Chain Bridge Road, Suite 450, Vienna, Virginia 22182 (703) 356-1964; *America's Children: Key National Indicators of Well-Being.*

U.S. Department of Commerce, Bureau of the Census, Washington, D.C. 20233 (301) 457-4100, www.census.gov; *Census of Population and Housing Data Paper Listing*, and Summary Tape File 3C.

Laos (People's Democratic Republic)--National Statistical Office

Ministry of Economy, Planning and Finance, Post Office Box 46, Vientiane, Laos.

Laos (People's Democratic Republic)--Primary Statistics Sources

Service National de la Statistique, Ministere du Plan et de la Cooperation, Post Office Box 46, Vientiane, Laos; *Bulletin de Statistiques* (Statistical Bulletin); and *Annuaire Statistique* (Statistical Yearbook).

LAOS (PEOPLE'S DEMOCRATIC REPUBLIC) - AGRICULTURE

Asian Development Bank, Post Office Box 789, 1099 Manila, Philippines; *Key Indicators of Developing Asian and Pacific Countries.*

Economist Intelligence Unit, 111 West 57th Street, New York, New York 10019 (800) 938-4685; *Laos Country Report.*

Euromonitor International, Inc., 122 South Michigan Avenue, Suite 1200, Chicago, Illinois 60603 (800) 577-EURO; *World Marketing Data and Statistics.*

Europa Publications Limited, 18 Bedford Square, London, WC1B 3JN, England; *The Europa World Year Book.*

Food and Agricultural Organization of the United Nations (FAO), Via delle Terme di Caracalla, 00100 Rome, Italy (Telephone Number in U.S. (202) 653-2400); *Production Yearbook; The State of Food and Agriculture;* and *Trade Yearbook.*

M.E. Sharpe, 80 Business Park Drive, Armonk, New York 10504 (800) 541-6563; *The Illustrated Book of World Rankings.*

St. Martin's Press, Inc., 175 Fifth Avenue, New York, New York 10010 (800) 221-7945; *The Statesman's Year-Book.*

Statistical Office of the United Nations, Publishing Service, New York, New York 10017 (800) 253-9646; *Asia-Pacific in Figures; Statistical Yearbook;* and *Statistical Yearbook for Asia and the Pacific.*

United Nations Conference on Trade and Development, Central Statistical Service, Palais des Nations, Geneva, Switzerland (Telephone in U.S. (800) 253-9646); *UNCTAD Commodity Yearbook.*

LAOS (PEOPLE'S DEMOCRATIC REPUBLIC) - AIRLINE SERVICE

The Economist Intelligence Unit (Asia) Limited, 10th Floor, Luk Kwok Centre, 72 Gloucester Road, Wanchai, Hong Kong (Phone Number in U.S. (800) 938-4685); *Asian Market Atlas.*

Europa Publications Limited, 18 Bedford Square, London, WC1B 3JN, England; *The Europa World Year Book.*

M.E. Sharpe, 80 Business Park Drive, Armonk, New York 10504 (800) 541-6563; *The Illustrated Book of World Rankings.*

St. Martin's Press, Inc., 175 Fifth Avenue, New York, New York 10010 (800) 221-7945; *The Statesman's Year-Book.*

Statistical Office of the United Nations, Publishing Service, New York, New York 10017 (800) 253-9646; *Statistical Yearbook.*

LAOS (PEOPLE'S DEMOCRATIC REPUBLIC) - AIRPORTS

Central Intelligence Agency, Washington, D.C. 20505 (703) 482-1100, www.cia.gov; *The World Factbook.*

LAOS (PEOPLE'S DEMOCRATIC REPUBLIC) - ALUMINUM PRODUCTION AND CONSUMPTION - See LAOS (PEOPLE'S DEMOCRATIC REPUBLIC) - MINING AND MINERAL PRODUCTS

LAOS (PEOPLE'S DEMOCRATIC REPUBLIC) - ANIMAL HEALTH

Food and Agricultural Organization of the United Nations (FAO), Via delle Terme di Caracalla, 00100 Rome, Italy (Telephone

Number in U.S. (202) 653-2400); *Animal Health Yearbook*.

LAOS (PEOPLE'S DEMOCRATIC REPUBLIC) - AREA AND DENSITY OF POPULATION

Central Intelligence Agency, Washington, D.C. 20505 (703) 351-2053; *The World Factbook*.

Euromonitor International, Inc., 122 South Michigan Avenue, Suite 1200, Chicago, Illinois 60603 (800) 577-EURO; *International Marketing Data and Statistics;* and *The World Economic Factbook*.

Europa Publications Limited, 18 Bedford Square, London, WC1B 3JN, England; *The Europa World Year Book*.

Food and Agricultural Organization of the United Nations (FAO), Via delle Terme di Caracalla, 00100 Rome, Italy (Telephone Number in U.S. (202) 653-2400); *The State of Food and Agriculture*.

M.E. Sharpe, 80 Business Park Drive, Armonk, New York 10504 (800) 541-6563; *The Illustrated Book of World Rankings*.

St. Martin's Press, Inc., 175 Fifth Avenue, New York, New York 10010 (800) 221-7945; *The Statesman's Year-Book*.

Statistical Office of the United Nations, Publishing Service, New York, New York 10017 (800) 253-9646; *Statistical Yearbook*.

United Nations Educational, Scientific and Cultural Organization (UNESCO), 7 Place de Fontenoy, F-75700 Paris, France (Telephone Number in U.S. (212) 963-5981); *Statistical Yearbook*.

The World Bank, 1818 H Street, NW, Washington, D.C. 20433 (202) 477-1234; *World Development Report*.

LAOS (PEOPLE'S DEMOCRATIC REPUBLIC) - ARMS EXPORTS AND IMPORTS - See LAOS (PEOPLE'S DEMOCRATIC REPUBLIC) - MILITARY

LAOS (PEOPLE'S DEMOCRATIC REPUBLIC) - BALANCE OF PAYMENTS

The Economist Intelligence Unit, 111 West 57th Street, New York, New York 10019 (800) 938-4685; *The World Market Atlas*.

Europa Publications Limited, 18 Bedford Square, London, WC1B 3JN, England; *The Europa World Year Book*.

United Nations Conference on Trade and Development (UNCTAD), New York, New York 10017 (800) 253-9646; *Handbook of International Trade and Development Statistics*.

The World Bank, 1818 H Street, NW, Washington, D.C. 20433 (202) 477-1234; *World Development Report*.

LAOS (PEOPLE'S DEMOCRATIC REPUBLIC) - BANKING

Asian Development Bank, Post Office Box 789, 1099 Manila, Philippines; *Key Indicators of Developing Asian and Pacific Countries*.

Euromonitor International, Inc., 122 South Michigan Avenue, Suite 1200, Chicago, Illinois 60603 (800) 577-EURO; *World Marketing Data and Statistics*.

Europa Publications Limited, 18 Bedford Square, London, WC1B 3JN, England; *The Europa World Year Book*.

M.E. Sharpe, 80 Business Park Drive, Armonk, New York 10504 (800) 541-6563; *The Illustrated Book of World Rankings*.

St. Martin's Press, Inc., 175 Fifth Avenue, New York, New York 10010 (800) 221-7945; *The Statesman's Year-Book*.

LAOS (PEOPLE'S DEMOCRATIC REPUBLIC) - BARLEY PRODUCTION - See LAOS (PEOPLE'S DEMOCRATIC REPUBLIC) - CROPS

LAOS (PEOPLE'S DEMOCRATIC REPUBLIC) - BEER PRODUCTION - See LAOS (PEOPLE'S DEMOCRATIC REPUBLIC) - BEVERAGES

LAOS (PEOPLE'S DEMOCRATIC REPUBLIC) - BEVERAGES

M.E. Sharpe, 80 Business Park Drive, Armonk, New York 10504 (800) 541-6563; *The Illustrated Book of World Rankings*.

LAOS (PEOPLE'S DEMOCRATIC REPUBLIC) - BIRTH RATES

Central Intelligence Agency, Washington, D.C. 20505 (703) 482-1100, www.cia.gov; *The World Factbook*.

The Economist Intelligence Unit (Asia) Limited, 10th Floor, Luk Kwok Centre, 72 Gloucester Road, Wanchai, Hong Kong (Phone Number in U.S. (800) 938-4685); *Asian Market Atlas*.

Euromonitor International, Inc., 122 South Michigan Avenue, Suite 1200, Chicago, Illinois 60603 (800) 577-EURO; *International Marketing Data and Statistics;* and *The World Economic Factbook*.

Europa Publications Limited, 18 Bedford Square, London, WC1B 3JN, England; *The Europa World Year Book*.

M.E. Sharpe, 80 Business Park Drive, Armonk, New York 10504 (800) 541-6563; *The Illustrated Book of World Rankings*.

St. Martin's Press, Inc., 175 Fifth Avenue, New York, New York 10010 (800) 221-7945; *The Statesman's Year-Book*.

Statistical Office of the United Nations, Publishing Service, New York, New York 10017 (800) 253-9646; *Asia-Pacific in Figures; Demographic Yearbook;* and *Statistical Yearbook*.

LAOS (PEOPLE'S DEMOCRATIC REPUBLIC) - BONDS

Asian Development Bank, Post Office Box 789, 1099 Manila, Philippines; *Key Indicators of Developing Asian and Pacific Countries*.

LAOS (PEOPLE'S DEMOCRATIC REPUBLIC) - BROADCASTING

Billboard Limited, Post Office Box 9027, 1006 AA Amsterdam, The Netherlands (Telephone Number in U.S. (212) 764-7300); *World Radio TV Handbook*.

Central Intelligence Agency, Washington, D.C. 20505 (703) 482-1100, www.cia.gov; *The World Factbook*.

The Economist Intelligence Unit (Asia) Limited, 10th Floor, Luk Kwok Centre, 72 Gloucester Road, Wanchai, Hong Kong (Phone Number in U.S. (800) 938-4685); *Asian Market Atlas*.

Euromonitor International, Inc., 122 South Michigan Avenue, Suite 1200, Chicago, Illinois 60603 (800) 577-EURO; *World Marketing Data and Statistics*.

M.E. Sharpe, 80 Business Park Drive, Armonk, New York 10504 (800) 541-6563; *The Illustrated Book of World Rankings*.

St. Martin's Press, Inc., 175 Fifth Avenue, New York, New York 10010 (800) 221-7945; *The Statesman's Year-Book*.

LAOS (PEOPLE'S DEMOCRATIC REPUBLIC) - BUDGET

Central Intelligence Agency, Washington, D.C. 20505 (703) 482-1100, www.cia.gov; *The World Factbook*.

LAOS (PEOPLE'S DEMOCRATIC REPUBLIC) - CALORIE SUPPLY

Asian Development Bank, Post Office Box 789, 1099 Manila, Philippines; *Key Indicators of Developing Asian and Pacific Countries*.

Food and Agricultural Organization of the United Nations (FAO), Via delle Terme di Caracalla, 00100 Rome, Italy (Telephone

Number in U.S. (202) 653-2400); *The State of Food and Agriculture.*

LAOS (PEOPLE'S DEMOCRATIC REPUBLIC) - CAPITAL INVESTMENT

Asian Development Bank, Post Office Box 789, 1099 Manila, Philippines; *Key Indicators of Developing Asian and Pacific Countries.*

LAOS (PEOPLE'S DEMOCRATIC REPUBLIC) - CAPITAL REVENUE

Asian Development Bank, Post Office Box 789, 1099 Manila, Philippines; *Key Indicators of Developing Asian and Pacific Countries.*

LAOS (PEOPLE'S DEMOCRATIC REPUBLIC) - CATTLE - See LAOS (PEOPLE'S DEMOCRATIC REPUBLIC) - LIVESTOCK AND POULTRY

LAOS (PEOPLE'S DEMOCRATIC REPUBLIC) - CEMENT PRODUCTION - See LAOS (PEOPLE'S DEMOCRATIC REPUBLIC) - MINING AND MINERAL PRODUCTS

LAOS (PEOPLE'S DEMOCRATIC REPUBLIC) - CHEMICAL (ORGANIC) PRODUCTION - See LAOS (PEOPLE'S DEMOCRATIC REPUBLIC) - MINING AND MINERAL PRODUCTS

LAOS (PEOPLE'S DEMOCRATIC REPUBLIC) - CHICKENS - See LAOS (PEOPLE'S DEMOCRATIC REPUBLIC) - LIVESTOCK AND POULTRY

LAOS (PEOPLE'S DEMOCRATIC REPUBLIC) - CIGARETTE PRODUCTION - See LAOS (PEOPLE'S DEMOCRATIC REPUBLIC) - TOBACCO PRODUCTION

LAOS (PEOPLE'S DEMOCRATIC REPUBLIC) - CLIMATE

M.E. Sharpe, 80 Business Park Drive, Armonk, New York 10504 (800) 541-6563; *The Illustrated Book of World Rankings.*

St. Martin's Press, Inc., 175 Fifth Avenue, New York, New York 10010 (800) 221-7945; *The Statesman's Year-Book.*

LAOS (PEOPLE'S DEMOCRATIC REPUBLIC) - COAL PRODUCTION - See LAOS (PEOPLE'S DEMOCRATIC REPUBLIC) - MINING AND MINERAL PRODUCTS

LAOS (PEOPLE'S DEMOCRATIC REPUBLIC) - COFFEE PRODUCTION AND CONSUMPTION - See LAOS (PEOPLE'S DEMOCRATIC REPUBLIC) - CROPS

LAOS (PEOPLE'S DEMOCRATIC REPUBLIC) - COMMERCE

St. Martin's Press, Inc., 175 Fifth Avenue, New York, New York 10010 (800) 221-7945; *The Statesman's Year-Book.*

LAOS (PEOPLE'S DEMOCRATIC REPUBLIC) - COMMUNICATIONS - See LAOS (PEOPLE'S DEMOCRATIC REPUBLIC) - TRANSPORTATION AND COMMUNICATIONS

LAOS (PEOPLE'S DEMOCRATIC REPUBLIC) - CONSTRUCTION INDUSTRY

M.E. Sharpe, 80 Business Park Drive, Armonk, New York 10504 (800) 541-6563; *The Illustrated Book of World Rankings.*

LAOS (PEOPLE'S DEMOCRATIC REPUBLIC) - CONSUMER PRICE INDEX

Asian Development Bank, Post Office Box 789, 1099 Manila, Philippines; *Key Indicators of Developing Asian and Pacific Countries.*

Europa Publications Limited, 18 Bedford Square, London, WC1B 3JN, England; *The Europa World Year Book.*

Statistical Office of the United Nations, Publishing Service, New York, New York 10017 (800) 253-9646; *Statistical Yearbook.*

LAOS (PEOPLE'S DEMOCRATIC REPUBLIC) - CONSUMER PRICES

Euromonitor International, Inc., 122 South Michigan Avenue, Suite 1200, Chicago, Illinois 60603 (800) 577-EURO; *World Marketing Data and Statistics.*

International Labour Office, I.L.O. Publications, 1828 L Street, N.W., Suite 801, Washington, D.C. (301) 638-3152; *Yearbook of Labour Statistics.*

LAOS (PEOPLE'S DEMOCRATIC REPUBLIC) - CONSUMPTION

The World Bank, 1818 H Street, NW, Washington, D.C. 20433 (202) 477-1234; *World Development Report.*

LAOS (PEOPLE'S DEMOCRATIC REPUBLIC) - COPPER - See LAOS (PEOPLE'S DEMOCRATIC REPUBLIC) - MINING AND MINERAL PRODUCTS

LAOS (PEOPLE'S DEMOCRATIC REPUBLIC) - CORN PRODUCTION See LAOS (PEOPLE'S DEMOCRATIC REPUBLIC) - CROPS

LAOS (PEOPLE'S DEMOCRATIC REPUBLIC) - COTTON PRODUCTION - See LAOS (PEOPLE'S DEMOCRATIC REPUBLIC) - CROPS

LAOS (PEOPLE'S DEMOCRATIC REPUBLIC) - CRIME

Yale University Press, Yale Station, New Haven, Connecticut 06520 (800) 987-7323; *Violence and Crime in Cross-National Perspective.*

LAOS (PEOPLE'S DEMOCRATIC REPUBLIC) - CROPS

Asian Development Bank, Post Office Box 789, 1099 Manila, Philippines; *Key Indicators of Developing Asian and Pacific Countries.*

Europa Publications Limited, 18 Bedford Square, London, WC1B 3JN, England; *The Europa World Year Book.*

Food and Agricultural Organization of the United Nations (FAO), Via delle Terme di Caracalla, 00100 Rome, Italy (Telephone Number in U.S. (202) 653-2400); *The State of Food and Agriculture;* and *Production Yearbook.*

M.E. Sharpe, 80 Business Park Drive, Armonk, New York 10504 (800) 541-6563; *The Illustrated Book of World Rankings.*

St. Martin's Press, Inc., 175 Fifth Avenue, New York, New York 10010 (800) 221-7945; *The Statesman's Year-Book.*

Statistical Office of the United Nations, Publishing Service, New York, New York 10017 (800) 253-9646; *Statistical Yearbook.*

United Nations Conference on Trade and Development, Central Statistical Service, Palais des Nations, Geneva, Switzerland (Telephone in U.S. (800) 253-9646); *UNCTAD Commodity Yearbook.*

LAOS (PEOPLE'S DEMOCRATIC REPUBLIC) - DAIRY PRODUCTS

Europa Publications Limited, 18 Bedford Square, London, WC1B 3JN, England; *The Europa World Year Book.*

Food and Agricultural Organization of the United Nations (FAO), Via delle Terme di Caracalla, 00100 Rome, Italy (Telephone Number in U.S. (202) 653-2400); *Production Yearbook;* and *The State of Food and Agriculture.*

M.E. Sharpe, 80 Business Park Drive, Armonk, New York 10504 (800) 541-6563; *The Illustrated Book of World Rankings.*

St. Martin's Press, Inc., 175 Fifth Avenue, New York, New York 10010 (800) 221-7945; *The Statesman's Year-Book.*

Statistical Office of the United Nations, Publishing Service, New York, New York 10017 (800) 253-9646; *Statistical Yearbook.*

LAOS (PEOPLE'S DEMOCRATIC REPUBLIC) - DEATH RATES - See LAOS (PEOPLE'S DEMOCRATIC REPUBLIC) - MORTALITY

LAOS (PEOPLE'S DEMOCRATIC
REPUBLIC) - DEFENSE EXPENDITURES -
See LAOS (PEOPLE'S DEMOCRATIC
REPUBLIC) - MILITARY

LAOS (PEOPLE'S DEMOCRATIC
REPUBLIC) - DEMOGRAPHY

The Economist Intelligence Unit, 111
West 57th Street, New York, New York
10019 (800) 938-4685; *The World Market
Atlas.*

The Economist Intelligence Unit (Asia)
Limited, 10th Floor, Luk Kwok Centre, 72
Gloucester Road, Wanchai, Hong Kong
(Phone Number in U.S. (800) 938-4685);
Asian Market Atlas.

Euromonitor International, Inc., 122
South Michigan Avenue, Suite 1200,
Chicago, Illinois 60603 (800) 577-EURO;
*International Marketing Data and Statistics;
World Marketing Data and Statistics;* and
The World Economic Factbook.

M.E. Sharpe, 80 Business Park Drive,
Armonk, New York 10504 (800) 541-6563;
The Illustrated Book of World Rankings.

Statistical Office of the United Nations,
Publishing Service, New York, New York
10017 (800) 253-9646; *Asia-Pacific in
Figures;* and *Human Development Report.*

LAOS (PEOPLE'S DEMOCRATIC
REPUBLIC) - DEVELOPMENT ASSISTANCE

Asian Development Bank, Post Office
Box 789, 1099 Manila, Philippines; *Key
Indicators of Developing Asian and Pacific
Countries.*

Statistical Office of the United Nations,
Publishing Service, New York, New York
10017 (800) 253-9646; *Statistical Yearbook.*

LAOS (PEOPLE'S DEMOCRATIC
REPUBLIC) - DIAMOND PRODUCTION -
See LAOS (PEOPLE'S DEMOCRATIC
REPUBLIC) - MINING AND MINERAL
PRODUCTS

LAOS (PEOPLE'S DEMOCRATIC
REPUBLIC) - DIVORCE

M.E. Sharpe, 80 Business Park Drive,
Armonk, New York 10504 (800) 541-6563;
The Illustrated Book of World Rankings.

Statistical Office of the United Nations,
Publishing Service, New York, New York
10017 (800) 253-9646; *Demographic
Yearbook.*

LAOS (PEOPLE'S DEMOCRATIC
REPUBLIC) - DUCKS - See LAOS (PEOPLE'S
DEMOCRATIC REPUBLIC) - LIVESTOCK
AND POULTRY

LAOS (PEOPLE'S DEMOCRATIC
REPUBLIC) - ECONOMY

Asian Development Bank, Post Office
Box 789, 1099 Manila, Philippines; *Key
Indicators of Developing Asian and Pacific
Countries.*

Central Intelligence Agency,
Washington, D.C. 20505 (703) 482-1100,
www.cia.gov; *The World Factbook.*

Economist Intelligence Unit, 111 West
57th Street, New York, New York 10019
(800) 938-4685; *Laos Country Report.*

Euromonitor International, Inc., 122
South Michigan Avenue, Suite 1200,
Chicago, Illinois 60603 (800) 577-EURO;
*International Marketing Data and Statistics;
World Marketing Data and Statistics;* and
The World Economic Factbook.

M.E. Sharpe, 80 Business Park Drive,
Armonk, New York 10504 (800) 541-6563;
The Illustrated Book of World Rankings.

St. Martin's Press, Inc., 175 Fifth
Avenue, New York, New York 10010 (800)
221-7945; *The Statesman's Year-Book.*

Statistical Office of the United Nations,
Publishing Service, New York, New York
10017 (800) 253-9646; *World Statistics
Pocketbook.*

The World Bank, 1818 H Street, NW,
Washington, D.C. 20433 (202) 477-1234;
The World Bank Atlas; and *World
Development Report.*

LAOS (PEOPLE'S DEMOCRATIC
REPUBLIC) - EDUCATION

The Economist Intelligence Unit, 111
West 57th Street, New York, New York
10019 (800) 938-4685; *The World Market
Atlas.*

The Economist Intelligence Unit (Asia)
Limited, 10th Floor, Luk Kwok Centre, 72
Gloucester Road, Wanchai, Hong Kong
(Phone Number in U.S. (800) 938-4685);
Asian Market Atlas.

Euromonitor International, Inc., 122
South Michigan Avenue, Suite 1200,
Chicago, Illinois 60603 (800) 577-EURO;
International Marketing Data and Statistics;
and *World Marketing Data and Statistics..*

Europa Publications Limited, 18
Bedford Square, London, WC1B 3JN,
England; *The Europa World Year Book.*

M.E. Sharpe, 80 Business Park Drive,
Armonk, New York 10504 (800) 541-6563;
The Illustrated Book of World Rankings.

St. Martin's Press, Inc., 175 Fifth
Avenue, New York, New York 10010 (800)
221-7945; *The Statesman's Year-Book.*

Statistical Office of the United Nations,
Publishing Service, New York, New York
10017 (800) 253-9646; *Asia-Pacific in
Figures;* and *Human Development Report.*

United Nations Educational, Scientific
and Cultural Organization (UNESCO), 7
Place de Fontenoy, F-75700 Paris, France
(Telephone Number in U.S. (212) 963-
5981); *Statistical Yearbook.*

The World Bank, 1818 H Street, NW,
Washington, D.C. 20433 (202) 477-1234;
World Development Report.

LAOS (PEOPLE'S DEMOCRATIC REPUBLIC)
- EGG PRODUCTION AND CONSUMPTION -
See LAOS (PEOPLE'S DEMOCRATIC
REPUBLIC) - DAIRY PRODUCTS

LAOS (PEOPLE'S DEMOCRATIC REPUBLIC)
- ELECTRICITY

Asian Development Bank, Post Office
Box 789, 1099 Manila, Philippines; *Key
Indicators of Developing Asian and Pacific
Countries.*

Central Intelligence Agency,
Washington, D.C. 20505 (703) 482-1100,
www.cia.gov; *The World Factbook.*

M.E. Sharpe, 80 Business Park Drive,
Armonk, New York 10504 (800) 541-6563;
The Illustrated Book of World Rankings.

St. Martin's Press, Inc., 175 Fifth
Avenue, New York, New York 10010 (800)
221-7945; *The Statesman's Year-Book.*

Statistical Office of the United Nations,
Publishing Service, New York, New York
10017 (800) 253-9646; *Human
Development Report;* and *Statistical
Yearbook.*

LAOS (PEOPLE'S DEMOCRATIC
REPUBLIC) - EMPLOYMENT

Euromonitor International, Inc., 122
South Michigan Avenue, Suite 1200,
Chicago, Illinois 60603 (800) 577-EURO;
International Marketing Data and Statistics.

International Labour Office,
I.L.O. Publications, 1828 L Street, N.W.,
Suite 801, Washington, D.C. (301) 638-3152;
Yearbook of Labour Statistics.

M.E. Sharpe, 80 Business Park Drive,
Armonk, New York 10504 (800) 541-6563;
The Illustrated Book of World Rankings.

Statistical Office of the United Nations,
Publishing Service, New York, New York
10017 (800) 253-9646; *Asia-Pacific in
Figures.*

LAOS (PEOPLE'S DEMOCRATIC REPUBLIC) - ENERGY

Euromonitor International, Inc., 122 South Michigan Avenue, Suite 1200, Chicago, Illinois 60603 (800) 577-EURO; *International Marketing Data and Statistics; World Marketing Data and Statistics;* and *The World Economic Factbook.*

Food and Agricultural Organization of the United Nations (FAO), Via delle Terme di Caracalla, 00100 Rome, Italy (Telephone Number in U.S. (202) 653-2400); *The State of Food and Agriculture.*

M.E. Sharpe, 80 Business Park Drive, Armonk, New York 10504 (800) 541-6563; *The Illustrated Book of World Rankings.*

St. Martin's Press, Inc., 175 Fifth Avenue, New York, New York 10010 (800) 221-7945; *The Statesman's Year-Book.*

Statistical Office of the United Nations, Publishing Service, New York, New York 10017 (800) 253-9646; *Asia-Pacific in Figures; Energy Statistics Yearbook; Human Development Report; Statistical Yearbook; World Statistics Pocketbook;* and *Statistical Yearbook for Asia and the Pacific.*

The World Bank, 1818 H Street, NW, Washington, D.C. 20433 (202) 477-1234; *The World Bank Atlas;* and *World Development Report.*

LAOS (PEOPLE'S DEMOCRATIC REPUBLIC) - ENVIRONMENT

Economist Intelligence Unit, 111 West 57th Street, New York, New York 10019 (800) 938-4685; *Laos Country Report.*

Statistical Office of the United Nations, Publishing Service, New York, New York 10017 (800) 253-9646; *World Statistics Pocketbook.*

LAOS (PEOPLE'S DEMOCRATIC REPUBLIC) - EXCHANGE RATES

Asian Development Bank, Post Office Box 789, 1099 Manila, Philippines; *Key Indicators of Developing Asian and Pacific Countries.*

The Economist Intelligence Unit (Asia) Limited, 10th Floor, Luk Kwok Centre, 72 Gloucester Road, Wanchai, Hong Kong (Phone Number in U.S. (800) 938-4685); *Asian Market Atlas.*

Euromonitor International, Inc., 122 South Michigan Avenue, Suite 1200, Chicago, Illinois 60603 (800) 577-EURO; *International Marketing Data and Statistics;* and *The World Economic Factbook.*

Europa Publications Limited, 18 Bedford Square, London, WC1B 3JN, England; *The Europa World Year Book.*

Statistical Office of the United Nations, Publishing Service, New York, New York 10017 (800) 253-9646; *Statistical Yearbook;* and *World Statistics Pocketbook.*

Walden Publishing, Ltd., Two Market Street, Saffron Walden Essex, CB10 1HZ, England; *The World of Information Asia and Pacific Review.*

LAOS (PEOPLE'S DEMOCRATIC REPUBLIC) - EXPORTS

Asian Development Bank, Post Office Box 789, 1099 Manila, Philippines; *Key Indicators of Developing Asian and Pacific Countries.*

Central Intelligence Agency, Washington, D.C. 20505 (703) 482-1100, www.cia.gov; *The World Factbook.*

The Economist Intelligence Unit, 111 West 57th Street, New York, New York 10019 (800) 938-4685; *Laos Country Report;* and *The World Market Atlas.*

The Economist Intelligence Unit (Asia) Limited, 10th Floor, Luk Kwok Centre, 72 Gloucester Road, Wanchai, Hong Kong (Phone Number in U.S. (800) 938-4685); *Asian Market Atlas.*

Euromonitor International, Inc., 122 South Michigan Avenue, Suite 1200, Chicago, Illinois 60603 (800) 577-EURO; *International Marketing Data and Statistics;* and *The World Economic Factbook.*

Europa Publications Limited, 18 Bedford Square, London, WC1B 3JN, England; *The Europa World Year Book.*

Food and Agricultural Organization of the United Nations (FAO), Via delle Terme di Caracalla, 00100 Rome, Italy (Telephone Number in U.S. (202) 653-2400); *The State of Food and Agriculture.*

International Monetary Fund, 700 Nineteenth Street, NW, Washington, D.C. 20431 (202) 623-7000; *Direction of Trade Statistics.*

St. Martin's Press, Inc., 175 Fifth Avenue, New York, New York 10010 (800) 221-7945; *The Statesman's Year-Book.*

United Nations Conference on Trade and Development (UNCTAD), New York, New York 10017 (800) 253-9646; *Handbook of International Trade and Development Statistics.*

Walden Publishing, Ltd., Two Market Street, Saffron Walden Essex, CB10 1HZ, England; *The World of Information Asia and Pacific Review.*

The World Bank, 1818 H Street, NW, Washington, D.C. 20433 (202) 477-1234; *World Development Report.*

LAOS (PEOPLE'S DEMOCRATIC REPUBLIC) - EXTERNAL INDEBTEDNESS

Asian Development Bank, Post Office Box 789, 1099 Manila, Philippines; *Key Indicators of Developing Asian and Pacific Countries.*

The World Bank, 1818 H Street, NW, Washington, D.C. 20433 (202) 477-1234; *World Development Report.*

LAOS (PEOPLE'S DEMOCRATIC REPUBLIC) - EXTERNAL TRADE

Asian Development Bank, Post Office Box 789, 1099 Manila, Philippines; *Key Indicators of Developing Asian and Pacific Countries.*

Euromonitor International, Inc., 122 South Michigan Avenue, Suite 1200, Chicago, Illinois 60603 (800) 577-EURO; *World Marketing Data and Statistics.*

Food and Agricultural Organization of the United Nations (FAO), Via delle Terme di Caracalla, 00100 Rome, Italy (Telephone Number in U.S. (202) 653-2400); *The State of Food and Agriculture;* and *Trade Yearbook.*

Statistical Office of the United Nations, Publishing Service, New York, New York 10017 (800) 253-9646; *Asia-Pacific in Figures;* and *Statistical Yearbook.*

LAOS (PEOPLE'S DEMOCRATIC REPUBLIC) - FARM CROPS - See LAOS (PEOPLE'S DEMOCRATIC REPUBLIC) - CROPS

LAOS (PEOPLE'S DEMOCRATIC REPUBLIC) - FEMALE WORKING POPULATION - See LAOS (PEOPLE'S DEMOCRATIC REPUBLIC) - EMPLOYMENT

LAOS (PEOPLE'S DEMOCRATIC REPUBLIC) - FERTILITY RATES

Central Intelligence Agency, Washington, D.C. 20505 (703) 482-1100, www.cia.gov; *The World Factbook.*

The Economist Intelligence Unit (Asia) Limited, 10th Floor, Luk Kwok Centre, 72 Gloucester Road, Wanchai, Hong Kong (Phone Number in U.S. (800) 938-4685); *Asian Market Atlas.*

M.E. Sharpe, 80 Business Park Drive, Armonk, New York 10504 (800) 541-6563; *The Illustrated Book of World Rankings.*

Statistical Office of the United Nations, Publishing Service, New York, New York 10017 (800) 253-9646; *Human Development Report.*

The World Bank, 1818 H Street, NW, Washington, D.C. 20433 (202) 477-1234; *The World Bank Atlas;* and *World Development Report.*

LAOS (PEOPLE'S DEMOCRATIC REPUBLIC) - FERTILIZER

Food and Agricultural Organization of the United Nations (FAO), Via delle Terme di Caracalla, 00100 Rome, Italy (Telephone Number in U.S. (202) 653-2400); *Fertilizer Yearbook.*

Statistical Office of the United Nations, Publishing Service, New York, New York 10017 (800) 253-9646; *Statistical Yearbook.*

LAOS (PEOPLE'S DEMOCRATIC REPUBLIC) - FETAL MORTALITY - See LAOS (PEOPLE'S DEMOCRATIC REPUBLIC) - MORTALITY

LAOS (PEOPLE'S DEMOCRATIC REPUBLIC) - FINANCE

Asian Development Bank, Post Office Box 789, 1099 Manila, Philippines; *Key Indicators of Developing Asian and Pacific Countries.*

Economist Intelligence Unit, 111 West 57th Street, New York, New York 10019 (800) 938-4685; *Laos Country Report.*

Europa Publications Limited, 18 Bedford Square, London, WC1B 3JN, England; *The Europa World Year Book.*

International Monetary Fund, 700 Nineteenth Street, NW, Washington, D.C. 20431 (202) 623-7000; *International Financial Statistics.*

M.E. Sharpe, 80 Business Park Drive, Armonk, New York 10504 (800) 541-6563; *The Illustrated Book of World Rankings.*

St. Martin's Press, Inc., 175 Fifth Avenue, New York, New York 10010 (800) 221-7945; *The Statesman's Year-Book.*

Statistical Office of the United Nations, Publishing Service, New York, New York 10017 (800) 253-9646; *Statistical Yearbook for Asia and the Pacific.*

LAOS (PEOPLE'S DEMOCRATIC REPUBLIC) - FISHERIES

Europa Publications Limited, 18 Bedford Square, London, WC1B 3JN, England; *The Europa World Year Book.*

Food and Agricultural Organization of the United Nations (FAO), Via delle Terme di Caracalla, 00100 Rome, Italy (Telephone Number in U.S. (202) 653-2400); *The State of Food and Agriculture;* and *Yearbook of Fishery Statistics.*

M.E. Sharpe, 80 Business Park Drive, Armonk, New York 10504 (800) 541-6563; *The Illustrated Book of World Rankings.*

Statistical Office of the United Nations, Publishing Service, New York, New York 10017 (800) 253-9646; *Statistical Yearbook.*

United Nations Conference on Trade and Development, Central Statistical Service, Palais des Nations, Geneva, Switzerland (Telephone in U.S. (800) 253-9646); *UNCTAD Commodity Yearbook.*

LAOS (PEOPLE'S DEMOCRATIC REPUBLIC) - FOOD

Food and Agricultural Organization of the United Nations (FAO), Via delle Terme di Caracalla, 00100 Rome, Italy (Telephone Number in U.S. (202) 653-2400); *The State of Food and Agriculture;* and *Production Yearbook.*

Statistical Office of the United Nations, Publishing Service, New York, New York 10017 (800) 253-9646; *Human Development Report;* and *Statistical Yearbook for Asia and the Pacific.*

United Nations Conference on Trade and Development, Central Statistical Service, Palais des Nations, Geneva, Switzerland (Telephone in U.S. (800) 253-9646); *UNCTAD Commodity Yearbook.*

LAOS (PEOPLE'S DEMOCRATIC REPUBLIC) - FOREIGN DEBT

Walden Publishing, Ltd., Two Market Street, Saffron Walden Essex, CB10 1HZ, England; *The World of Information Asia and Pacific Review.*

LAOS (PEOPLE'S DEMOCRATIC REPUBLIC) - FOREIGN TRADE

Asian Development Bank, Post Office Box 789, 1099 Manila, Philippines; *Key Indicators of Developing Asian and Pacific Countries.*

Economist Intelligence Unit, 111 West 57th Street, New York, New York 10019 (800) 938-4685; *Laos Country Report.*

The Economist Intelligence Unit (Asia) Limited, 10th Floor, Luk Kwok Centre, 72 Gloucester Road, Wanchai, Hong Kong (Phone Number in U.S. (800) 938-4685); *Asian Market Atlas.*

Euromonitor International, Inc., 122 South Michigan Avenue, Suite 1200, Chicago, Illinois 60603 (800) 577-EURO; *The World Economic Factbook.*

Europa Publications Limited, 18 Bedford Square, London, WC1B 3JN, England; *The Europa World Year Book.*

M.E. Sharpe, 80 Business Park Drive, Armonk, New York 10504 (800) 541-6563; *The Illustrated Book of World Rankings.*

Statistical Office of the United Nations, Publishing Service, New York, New York 10017 (800) 253-9646; *Statistical Yearbook.*

United Nations Conference on Trade and Development, Central Statistical Service, Palais des Nations, Geneva, Switzerland (Telephone in U.S. (800) 253-9646); *UNCTAD Commodity Yearbook.*

Food and Agricultural Organization of the United Nations (FAO), Via delle Terme di Caracalla, 00100 Rome, Italy (Telephone Number in U.S. (202) 653-2400); *The State of Food and Agriculture.*

M.E. Sharpe, 80 Business Park Drive, Armonk, New York 10504 (800) 541-6563; *The Illustrated Book of World Rankings.*

St. Martin's Press, Inc., 175 Fifth Avenue, New York, New York 10010 (800) 221-7945; *The Statesman's Year-Book.*

Statistical Office of the United Nations, Publishing Service, New York, New York 10017 (800) 253-9646; *International Trade Statistics;* and *Statistical Yearbook.*

United Nations Conference on Trade and Development, Central Statistical Service, Palais des Nations, Geneva, Switzerland (Telephone in U.S. (800) 253-9646); *UNCTAD Commodity Yearbook.*

The World Bank, 1818 H Street, NW, Washington, D.C. 20433 (202) 477-1234; *World Development Report.*

LAOS (PEOPLE'S DEMOCRATIC REPUBLIC) - FORESTRY AND FOREST PRODUCTS

The Economist Intelligence Unit (Asia) Limited, 10th Floor, Luk Kwok Centre, 72 Gloucester Road, Wanchai, Hong Kong (Phone Number in U.S. (800) 938-4685); *Asian Market Atlas.*

Europa Publications Limited, 18 Bedford Square, London, WC1B 3JN, England; *The Europa World Year Book.*

Food and Agricultural Organization of the United Nations (FAO), Via delle Terme di Caracalla, 00100 Rome, Italy (Telephone Number in U.S. (202) 653-2400); *The State of Food and Agriculture;* and *Yearbook of Forest Products.*

M.E. Sharpe, 80 Business Park Drive, Armonk, New York 10504 (800) 541-6563; *The Illustrated Book of World Rankings.*

St. Martin's Press, Inc., 175 Fifth Avenue, New York, New York 10010 (800) 221-7945; *The Statesman's Year-Book.*

Statistical Office of the United Nations, Publishing Service, New York, New York 10017 (800) 253-9646; *Statistical Yearbook.*

United Nations Conference on Trade and Development, Central Statistical Service, Palais des Nations, Geneva, Switzerland (Telephone in U.S. (800) 253-9646); *UNCTAD Commodity Yearbook.*

United Nations Educational, Scientific and Cultural Organization (UNESCO), 7 Place de Fontenoy, F-75700 Paris, France (Telephone Number in U.S. (212) 963-

5981); *Statistical Yearbook.*

The World Bank, 1818 H Street, NW, Washington, D.C. 20433 (202) 477-1234; *World Development Report.*

LAOS (PEOPLE'S DEMOCRATIC REPUBLIC) - GAS PRODUCTION - See LAOS (PEOPLE'S DEMOCRATIC REPUBLIC) - MINING AND MINERAL PRODUCTS

LAOS (PEOPLE'S DEMOCRATIC REPUBLIC) - GENERAL MORTALITY - See LAOS (PEOPLE'S DEMOCRATIC REPUBLIC) - MORTALITY

LAOS (PEOPLE'S DEMOCRATIC REPUBLIC) - GEOGRAPHIC DATA

M.E. Sharpe, 80 Business Park Drive, Armonk, New York 10504 (800) 541-6563; *The Illustrated Book of World Rankings.*

LAOS (PEOPLE'S DEMOCRATIC REPUBLIC) - GOLD PRODUCTION AND CONSUMPTION

M.E. Sharpe, 80 Business Park Drive, Armonk, New York 10504 (800) 541-6563; *The Illustrated Book of World Rankings.*

LAOS (PEOPLE'S DEMOCRATIC REPUBLIC) - GOVERNMENT

Asian Development Bank, Post Office Box 789, 1099 Manila, Philippines; *Key Indicators of Developing Asian and Pacific Countries.*

Central Intelligence Agency, Washington, D.C. 20505 (703) 482-1100, www.cia.gov; *The World Factbook.*

Europa Publications Limited, 18 Bedford Square, London, WC1B 3JN, England; *The Europa World Year Book.*

St. Martin's Press, Inc., 175 Fifth Avenue, New York, New York 10010 (800) 221-7945; *The Statesman's Year-Book.*

Statistical Office of the United Nations, Publishing Service, New York, New York 10017 (800) 253-9646; *Asia-Pacific in Figures; National Accounts Statistics;* and *Statistical Yearbook.*

The World Bank, 1818 H Street, NW, Washington, D.C. 20433 (202) 477-1234; *World Development Report.*

LAOS (PEOPLE'S DEMOCRATIC REPUBLIC) - GRAIN PRODUCTION - See LAOS (PEOPLE'S DEMOCRATIC REPUBLIC) - CROPS

LAOS (PEOPLE'S DEMOCRATIC REPUBLIC) - GROSS DOMESTIC PRODUCT

Asian Development Bank, Post Office Box 789, 1099 Manila, Philippines; *Key*

Indicators of Developing Asian and Pacific Countries.

The Economist Intelligence Unit, 111 West 57th Street, New York, New York 10019 (800) 938-4685; *Laos Country Report;* and *The World Market Atlas.*

The Economist Intelligence Unit (Asia) Limited, 10th Floor, Luk Kwok Centre, 72 Gloucester Road, Wanchai, Hong Kong (Phone Number in U.S. (800) 938-4685); *Asian Market Atlas.*

Euromonitor International, Inc., 122 South Michigan Avenue, Suite 1200, Chicago, Illinois 60603 (800) 577-EURO; *International Marketing Data and Statistics;* and *The World Economic Factbook.*

Europa Publications Limited, 18 Bedford Square, London, WC1B 3JN, England; *The Europa World Year Book.*

M.E. Sharpe, 80 Business Park Drive, Armonk, New York 10504 (800) 541-6563; *The Illustrated Book of World Rankings.*

Statistical Office of the United Nations, Publishing Service, New York, New York 10017 (800) 253-9646; *Human Development Report; National Accounts Statistics;* and *Statistical Yearbook.*

The World Bank, 1818 H Street, NW, Washington, D.C. 20433 (202) 477-1234; *World Development Report.*

LAOS (PEOPLE'S DEMOCRATIC REPUBLIC) - GROSS NATIONAL PRODUCT

Asian Development Bank, Post Office Box 789, 1099 Manila, Philippines; *Key Indicators of Developing Asian and Pacific Countries.*

Euromonitor International, Inc., 122 South Michigan Avenue, Suite 1200, Chicago, Illinois 60603 (800) 577-EURO; *International Marketing Data and Statistics.*

St. Martin's Press, Inc., 175 Fifth Avenue, New York, New York 10010 (800) 221-7945; *The Statesman's Year-Book.*

U.S. Arms Control and Disarmament Agency, 320 Twenty-first Street, NW, Washington, D.C. 20451 (202) 647-8677; *World Military Expenditures and Arms Transfers.*

Walden Publishing, Ltd., Two Market Street, Saffron Walden Essex, CB10 1HZ, England; *The World of Information Asia and Pacific Review.*

The World Bank, 1818 H Street, NW, Washington, D.C. 20433 (202) 477-1234; *The World Bank Atlas;* and *World Development Report.*

LAOS (PEOPLE'S DEMOCRATIC REPUBLIC) - GROUNDNUT PRODUCTION - See LAOS (PEOPLE'S DEMOCRATIC REPUBLIC) - CROPS

LAOS (PEOPLE'S DEMOCRATIC REPUBLIC) - HEALTH

The Economist Intelligence Unit (Asia) Limited, 10th Floor, Luk Kwok Centre, 72 Gloucester Road, Wanchai, Hong Kong (Phone Number in U.S. (800) 938-4685); *Asian Market Atlas.*

Euromonitor International, Inc., 122 South Michigan Avenue, Suite 1200, Chicago, Illinois 60603 (800) 577-EURO; *World Marketing Data and Statistics.*

M.E. Sharpe, 80 Business Park Drive, Armonk, New York 10504 (800) 541-6563; *The Illustrated Book of World Rankings.*

St. Martin's Press, Inc., 175 Fifth Avenue, New York, New York 10010 (800) 221-7945; *The Statesman's Year-Book.*

Statistical Office of the United Nations, Publishing Service, New York, New York 10017 (800) 253-9646; *Asia-Pacific in Figures; Human Development Report;* and *Statistical Yearbook.*

United Nations Children's Fund (UNICEF), 3 United Nations Plaza, New York, New York 10017 (800) 253-9646; *State of the World's Children.*

The World Bank, 1818 H Street, NW, Washington, D.C. 20433 (202) 477-1234; *World Development Report.*

LAOS (PEOPLE'S DEMOCRATIC REPUBLIC) - HIDE PRODUCTION

Food and Agricultural Organization of the United Nations (FAO), Via delle Terme di Caracalla, 00100 Rome, Italy (Telephone Number in U.S. (202) 653-2400); *Production Yearbook.*

LAOS (PEOPLE'S DEMOCRATIC REPUBLIC) - HIGHWAYS

Central Intelligence Agency, Washington, D.C. 20505 (703) 482-1100, www.cia.gov; *The World Factbook.*

The Economist Intelligence Unit (Asia) Limited, 10th Floor, Luk Kwok Centre, 72 Gloucester Road, Wanchai, Hong Kong (Phone Number in U.S. (800) 938-4685); *Asian Market Atlas.*

St. Martin's Press, Inc., 175 Fifth Avenue, New York, New York 10010 (800) 221-7945; *The Statesman's Year-Book.*

LAOS (PEOPLE'S DEMOCRATIC REPUBLIC) - HORSES - See LAOS (PEOPLE'S DEMOCRATIC REPUBLIC) - LIVESTOCK

AND POULTRY

LAOS (PEOPLE'S DEMOCRATIC REPUBLIC) - HOURS OF WORK - See LAOS (PEOPLE'S DEMOCRATIC REPUBLIC) - EMPLOYMENT

LAOS (PEOPLE'S DEMOCRATIC REPUBLIC) - HOUSING AND HOUSING UNITS

Euromonitor International, Inc., 122 South Michigan Avenue, Suite 1200, Chicago, Illinois 60603 (800) 577-EURO; *World Marketing Data and Statistics*.

M.E. Sharpe, 80 Business Park Drive, Armonk, New York 10504 (800) 541-6563; *The Illustrated Book of World Rankings*.

LAOS (PEOPLE'S DEMOCRATIC REPUBLIC) - ILLITERATE POPULATION

Central Intelligence Agency, Washington, D.C. 20505 (703) 482-1100, www.cia.gov; *The World Factbook*.

The Economist Intelligence Unit, 111 West 57th Street, New York, New York 10019 (800) 938-4685; *The World Market Atlas*.

Euromonitor International, Inc., 122 South Michigan Avenue, Suite 1200, Chicago, Illinois 60603 (800) 577-EURO; *The World Economic Factbook*.

St. Martin's Press, Inc., 175 Fifth Avenue, New York, New York 10010 (800) 221-7945; *The Statesman's Year-Book*.

Statistical Office of the United Nations, Publishing Service, New York, New York 10017 (800) 253-9646; *Asia-Pacific in Figures;* and *Human Development Report*.

United Nations Educational, Scientific and Cultural Organization (UNESCO), 7 Place de Fontenoy, F-75700 Paris, France (Telephone Number in U.S. (212) 963-5981); *Statistical Yearbook*.

LAOS (PEOPLE'S DEMOCRATIC REPUBLIC) - IMPORTS

Asian Development Bank, Post Office Box 789, 1099 Manila, Philippines; *Key Indicators of Developing Asian and Pacific Countries*.

Central Intelligence Agency, Washington, D.C. 20505 (703) 482-1100, www.cia.gov; *The World Factbook*.

The Economist Intelligence Unit, 111 West 57th Street, New York, New York 10019 (800) 938-4685; *Laos Country Report;* and *The World Market Atlas*.

The Economist Intelligence Unit (Asia) Limited, 10th Floor, Luk Kwok Centre, 72 Gloucester Road, Wanchai, Hong Kong (Phone Number in U.S. (800) 938-4685);

Asian Market Atlas.

Euromonitor International, Inc., 122 South Michigan Avenue, Suite 1200, Chicago, Illinois 60603 (800) 577-EURO; *International Marketing Data and Statistics;* and *The World Economic Factbook*.

Europa Publications Limited, 18 Bedford Square, London, WC1B 3JN, England; *The Europa World Year Book*.

Food and Agricultural Organization of the United Nations (FAO), Via delle Terme di Caracalla, 00100 Rome, Italy (Telephone Number in U.S. (202) 653-2400); *The State of Food and Agriculture*.

International Monetary Fund, 700 Nineteenth Street, NW, Washington, D.C. 20431 (202) 623-7000; *Direction of Trade Statistics*.

St. Martin's Press, Inc., 175 Fifth Avenue, New York, New York 10010 (800) 221-7945; *The Statesman's Year-Book*.

United Nations Conference on Trade and Development (UNCTAD), New York, New York 10017 (800) 253-9646; *Handbook of International Trade and Development Statistics*.

Walden Publishing, Ltd., Two Market Street, Saffron Walden Essex, CB10 1HZ, England; *The World of Information Asia and Pacific Review*.

The World Bank, 1818 H Street, NW, Washington, D.C. 20433 (202) 477-1234; *World Development Report*.

LAOS (PEOPLE'S DEMOCRATIC REPUBLIC) - INDUSTRY

Central Intelligence Agency, Washington, D.C. 20505 (703) 482-1100, www.cia.gov; *The World Factbook*.

Economist Intelligence Unit, 111 West 57th Street, New York, New York 10019 (800) 938-4685; *Laos Country Report*.

Euromonitor International, Inc., 122 South Michigan Avenue, Suite 1200, Chicago, Illinois 60603 (800) 577-EURO; *International Marketing Data and Statistics; World Marketing Data and Statistics;* and *The World Economic Factbook*.

Europa Publications Limited, 18 Bedford Square, London, WC1B 3JN, England; *The Europa World Year Book*.

International Labour Office, I.L.O. Publications, 1828 L Street, N.W., Suite 801, Washington, D.C. (301) 638-3152; *Yearbook of Labour Statistics*.

M.E. Sharpe, 80 Business Park Drive, Armonk, New York 10504 (800) 541-6563;

The Illustrated Book of World Rankings.

St. Martin's Press, Inc., 175 Fifth Avenue, New York, New York 10010 (800) 221-7945; *The Statesman's Year-Book*.

Statistical Office of the United Nations, Publishing Service, New York, New York 10017 (800) 253-9646; *Asia-Pacific in Figures;* and *Statistical Yearbook for Asia and the Pacific*.

LAOS (PEOPLE'S DEMOCRATIC REPUBLIC) - INFANT AND MATERNAL MORTALITY - See LAOS (PEOPLE'S DEMOCRATIC REPUBLIC) - MORTALITY

LAOS (PEOPLE'S DEMOCRATIC REPUBLIC) - INTERNAL TRADE

Statistical Office of the United Nations, Publishing Service, New York, New York 10017 (800) 253-9646; *Statistical Yearbook for Asia and the Pacific*.

LAOS (PEOPLE'S DEMOCRATIC REPUBLIC) - INTERNATIONAL RESERVES EXCLUDING GOLD

Asian Development Bank, Post Office Box 789, 1099 Manila, Philippines; *Key Indicators of Developing Asian and Pacific Countries*.

LAOS (PEOPLE'S DEMOCRATIC REPUBLIC) - INTERNATIONAL STATISTICS

Asian Development Bank, Post Office Box 789, 1099 Manila, Philippines; *Key Indicators of Developing Asian and Pacific Countries*.

LAOS (PEOPLE'S DEMOCRATIC REPUBLIC) - IRON ORE PRODUCTION AND CONSUMPTION - See LAOS (PEOPLE'S DEMOCRATIC REPUBLIC) - MINING AND MINERAL PRODUCTS

LAOS (PEOPLE'S DEMOCRATIC REPUBLIC) - IRRIGATION

Euromonitor International, Inc., 122 South Michigan Avenue, Suite 1200, Chicago, Illinois 60603 (800) 577-EURO; *International Marketing Data and Statistics*.

LAOS (PEOPLE'S DEMOCRATIC REPUBLIC) - LABOR

Central Intelligence Agency, Washington, D.C. 20505 (703) 482-1100, www.cia.gov; *The World Factbook*.

The Economist Intelligence Unit (Asia) Limited, 10th Floor, Luk Kwok Centre, 72 Gloucester Road, Wanchai, Hong Kong (Phone Number in U.S. (800) 938-4685); *Asian Market Atlas*.

Euromonitor International, Inc., 122 South Michigan Avenue, Suite 1200,

Chicago, Illinois 60603 (800) 577-EURO; *International Marketing Data and Statistics; and World Marketing Data and Statistics.*

Europa Publications Limited, 18 Bedford Square, London, WC1B 3JN, England; *The Europa World Year Book.*

Food and Agricultural Organization of the United Nations (FAO), Via delle Terme di Caracalla, 00100 Rome, Italy (Telephone Number in U.S. (202) 653-2400); *The State of Food and Agriculture.*

International Labour Office, I.L.O. Publications, 1828 L Street, N.W., Suite 801, Washington, D.C. (301) 638-3152; *Yearbook of Labour Statistics.*

M.E. Sharpe, 80 Business Park Drive, Armonk, New York 10504 (800) 541-6563; *The Illustrated Book of World Rankings.*

St. Martin's Press, Inc., 175 Fifth Avenue, New York, New York 10010 (800) 221-7945; *The Statesman's Year-Book.*

Statistical Office of the United Nations, Publishing Service, New York, New York 10017 (800) 253-9646; *Human Development Report.*

The World Bank, 1818 H Street, NW, Washington, D.C. 20433 (202) 477-1234; *The World Bank Atlas;* and *World Development Report.*

LAOS (PEOPLE'S DEMOCRATIC REPUBLIC) - LAND USE

Central Intelligence Agency, Washington, D.C. 20505 (703) 482-1100, www.cia.gov; *The World Factbook.*

Euromonitor International, Inc., 122 South Michigan Avenue, Suite 1200, Chicago, Illinois 60603 (800) 577-EURO; *International Marketing Data and Statistics.*

Food and Agricultural Organization of the United Nations (FAO), Via delle Terme di Caracalla, 00100 Rome, Italy (Telephone Number in U.S. (202) 653-2400); *Production Yearbook.*

The World Bank, 1818 H Street, NW, Washington, D.C. 20433 (202) 477-1234; *World Development Report.*

LAOS (PEOPLE'S DEMOCRATIC REPUBLIC) - LIBRARIES

M.E. Sharpe, 80 Business Park Drive, Armonk, New York 10504 (800) 541-6563; *The Illustrated Book of World Rankings.*

LAOS (PEOPLE'S DEMOCRATIC REPUBLIC) - LIFE EXPECTANCY

Central Intelligence Agency, Washington, D.C. 20505 (703) 482-1100,

www.cia.gov; *The World Factbook.*

The Economist Intelligence Unit (Asia) Limited, 10th Floor, Luk Kwok Centre, 72 Gloucester Road, Wanchai, Hong Kong (Phone Number in U.S. (800) 938-4685); *Asian Market Atlas.*

Euromonitor International, Inc., 122 South Michigan Avenue, Suite 1200, Chicago, Illinois 60603 (800) 577-EURO; *The World Economic Factbook.*

St. Martin's Press, Inc., 175 Fifth Avenue, New York, New York 10010 (800) 221-7945; *The Statesman's Year-Book.*

Statistical Office of the United Nations, Publishing Service, New York, New York 10017 (800) 253-9646; *Asia-Pacific in Figures; World Statistics Pocketbook;* and *Human Development Report.*

The World Bank, 1818 H Street, NW, Washington, D.C. 20433 (202) 477-1234; *The World Bank Atlas;* and *World Development Report.*

LAOS (PEOPLE'S DEMOCRATIC REPUBLIC) - LITERACY RATE

Euromonitor International, Inc., 122 South Michigan Avenue, Suite 1200, Chicago, Illinois 60603 (800) 577-EURO; *World Marketing Data and Statistics.*

LAOS (PEOPLE'S DEMOCRATIC REPUBLIC) - LIVESTOCK AND POULTRY

Euromonitor International, Inc., 122 South Michigan Avenue, Suite 1200, Chicago, Illinois 60603 (800) 577-EURO; *International Marketing Data and Statistics.*

Europa Publications Limited, 18 Bedford Square, London, WC1B 3JN, England; *The Europa World Year Book.*

Food and Agricultural Organization of the United Nations (FAO), Via delle Terme di Caracalla, 00100 Rome, Italy (Telephone Number in U.S. (202) 653-2400); *Production Yearbook;* and *The State of Food and Agriculture.*

M.E. Sharpe, 80 Business Park Drive, Armonk, New York 10504 (800) 541-6563; *The Illustrated Book of World Rankings.*

St. Martin's Press, Inc., 175 Fifth Avenue, New York, New York 10010 (800) 221-7945; *The Statesman's Year-Book.*

Statistical Office of the United Nations, Publishing Service, New York, New York 10017 (800) 253-9646; *Statistical Yearbook.*

United Nations Conference on Trade and Development, Central Statistical Service, Palais des Nations, Geneva, Switzerland (Telephone in U.S. (800) 253-

9646); *UNCTAD Commodity Yearbook.*

LAOS (PEOPLE'S DEMOCRATIC REPUBLIC) - LIVING LEVELS - See LAOS (PEOPLE'S DEMOCRATIC REPUBLIC) - LIFE EXPECTANCY

LAOS (PEOPLE'S DEMOCRATIC REPUBLIC) - MAIL - NUMBER OF ITEMS SENT AND RECEIVED

Statistical Office of the United Nations, Publishing Service, New York, New York 10017 (800) 253-9646; *Statistical Yearbook.*

LAOS (PEOPLE'S DEMOCRATIC REPUBLIC) - MANPOWER

Statistical Office of the United Nations, Publishing Service, New York, New York 10017 (800) 253-9646; *Statistical Yearbook for Asia and the Pacific.*

LAOS (PEOPLE'S DEMOCRATIC REPUBLIC) - MANUFACTURING

Asian Development Bank, Post Office Box 789, 1099 Manila, Philippines; *Key Indicators of Developing Asian and Pacific Countries.*

M.E. Sharpe, 80 Business Park Drive, Armonk, New York 10504 (800) 541-6563; *The Illustrated Book of World Rankings.*

LAOS (PEOPLE'S DEMOCRATIC REPUBLIC) - MARRIAGE RATES

M.E. Sharpe, 80 Business Park Drive, Armonk, New York 10504 (800) 541-6563; *The Illustrated Book of World Rankings.*

Statistical Office of the United Nations, Publishing Service, New York, New York 10017 (800) 253-9646; *Demographic Yearbook.*

LAOS (PEOPLE'S DEMOCRATIC REPUBLIC) - MEAT PRODUCTION - See LAOS (PEOPLE'S DEMOCRATIC REPUBLIC) - LIVESTOCK AND POULTRY

LAOS (PEOPLE'S DEMOCRATIC REPUBLIC) - MERCHANT SHIPPING

Europa Publications Limited, 18 Bedford Square, London, WC1B 3JN, England; *The Europa World Year Book.*

St. Martin's Press, Inc., 175 Fifth Avenue, New York, New York 10010 (800) 221-7945; *The Statesman's Year-Book.*

LAOS (PEOPLE'S DEMOCRATIC REPUBLIC) - MILITARY

Central Intelligence Agency, Washington, D.C. 20505 (703) 482-1100, www.cia.gov; *The World Factbook.*

The Economist Intelligence Unit (Asia)

Limited, 10th Floor, Luk Kwok Centre, 72 Gloucester Road, Wanchai, Hong Kong (Phone Number in U.S. (800) 938-4685); *Asian Market Atlas.*

Euromonitor International, Inc., 122 South Michigan Avenue, Suite 1200, Chicago, Illinois 60603 (800) 577-EURO; *World Marketing Data and Statistics.*

The International Institute for Strategic Studies, 23 Tavistock Street, London WC2E 7NQ, England 44 171 3797676; *The Military Balance.*

St. Martin's Press, Inc., 175 Fifth Avenue, New York, New York 10010 (800) 221-7945; *The Statesman's Year-Book.*

Statistical Office of the United Nations, Publishing Service, New York, New York 10017 (800) 253-9646; *Human Development Report.*

U.S. Arms Control and Disarmament Agency, 320 Twenty-first Street, NW, Washington, D.C. 20451 (202) 647-8677; *World Military Expenditures and Arms Transfers.*

LAOS (PEOPLE'S DEMOCRATIC REPUBLIC) - MINING AND MINERAL PRODUCTS

Asian Development Bank, Post Office Box 789, 1099 Manila, Philippines; *Key Indicators of Developing Asian and Pacific Countries.*

Europa Publications Limited, 18 Bedford Square, London, WC1B 3JN, England; *The Europa World Year Book.*

M.E. Sharpe, 80 Business Park Drive, Armonk, New York 10504 (800) 541-6563; *The Illustrated Book of World Rankings.*

St. Martin's Press, Inc., 175 Fifth Avenue, New York, New York 10010 (800) 221-7945; *The Statesman's Year-Book.*

Statistical Office of the United Nations, Publishing Service, New York, New York 10017 (800) 253-9646; *Statistical Yearbook.*

United Nations Conference on Trade and Development, Central Statistical Service, Palais des Nations, Geneva, Switzerland (Telephone in U.S. (800) 253-9646); *UNCTAD Commodity Yearbook.*

LAOS (PEOPLE'S DEMOCRATIC REPUBLIC) - MONEY EXCHANGE RATES

Euromonitor International, Inc., 122 South Michigan Avenue, Suite 1200, Chicago, Illinois 60603 (800) 577-EURO; *International Marketing Data and Statistics.*

Statistical Office of the United Nations, Publishing Service, New York, New York 10017 (800) 253-9646; *Statistical Yearbook.*

LAOS (PEOPLE'S DEMOCRATIC REPUBLIC) - MONEY RESERVES

Euromonitor International, Inc., 122 South Michigan Avenue, Suite 1200, Chicago, Illinois 60603 (800) 577-EURO; *International Marketing Data and Statistics.*

LAOS (PEOPLE'S DEMOCRATIC REPUBLIC) - MONEY SUPPLY

Asian Development Bank, Post Office Box 789, 1099 Manila, Philippines; *Key Indicators of Developing Asian and Pacific Countries.*

Economist Intelligence Unit, 111 West 57th Street, New York, New York 10019 (800) 938-4685; *Laos Country Report.*

Euromonitor International, Inc., 122 South Michigan Avenue, Suite 1200, Chicago, Illinois 60603 (800) 577-EURO; *International Marketing Data and Statistics.*

Europa Publications Limited, 18 Bedford Square, London, WC1B 3JN, England; *The Europa World Year Book.*

LAOS (PEOPLE'S DEMOCRATIC REPUBLIC) - MORTALITY

Central Intelligence Agency, Washington, D.C. 20505 (703) 482-1100, www.cia.gov; *The World Factbook.*

The Economist Intelligence Unit (Asia) Limited, 10th Floor, Luk Kwok Centre, 72 Gloucester Road, Wanchai, Hong Kong (Phone Number in U.S. (800) 938-4685); *Asian Market Atlas.*

Euromonitor International, Inc., 122 South Michigan Avenue, Suite 1200, Chicago, Illinois 60603 (800) 577-EURO; *International Marketing Data and Statistics;* and *The World Economic Factbook.*

Europa Publications Limited, 18 Bedford Square, London, WC1B 3JN, England; *The Europa World Year Book.*

St. Martin's Press, Inc., 175 Fifth Avenue, New York, New York 10010 (800) 221-7945; *The Statesman's Year-Book.*

Statistical Office of the United Nations, Publishing Service, New York, New York 10017 (800) 253-9646; *Asia-Pacific in Figures; Demographic Yearbook; Human Development Report; World Statistics Pocketbook;* and *Statistical Yearbook.*

United Nations Children's Fund (UNICEF), 3 United Nations Plaza, New York, New York 10017 (800) 253-9646; *State of the World's Children.*

The World Bank, 1818 H Street, NW, Washington, D.C. 20433 (202) 477-1234; *The World Bank Atlas;* and *World Development Report.*

LAOS (PEOPLE'S DEMOCRATIC REPUBLIC) - MOTOR VEHICLES IN USE

Europa Publications Limited, 18 Bedford Square, London, WC1B 3JN, England; *The Europa World Year Book.*

Statistical Office of the United Nations, Publishing Service, New York, New York 10017 (800) 253-9646; *Statistical Yearbook.*

LAOS (PEOPLE'S DEMOCRATIC REPUBLIC) - MUSEUMS

M.E. Sharpe, 80 Business Park Drive, Armonk, New York 10504 (800) 541-6563; *The Illustrated Book of World Rankings.*

LAOS (PEOPLE'S DEMOCRATIC REPUBLIC) - NATALITY - See LAOS (PEOPLE'S DEMOCRATIC REPUBLIC) - BIRTH RATES

LAOS (PEOPLE'S DEMOCRATIC REPUBLIC) - NATIONAL ACCOUNTS

Europa Publications Limited, 18 Bedford Square, London, WC1B 3JN, England; *The Europa World Year Book.*

Statistical Office of the United Nations, Publishing Service, New York, New York 10017 (800) 253-9646; *Asia-Pacific in Figures;* and *Statistical Yearbook.*

LAOS (PEOPLE'S DEMOCRATIC REPUBLIC) - NATIONAL INCOME

M.E. Sharpe, 80 Business Park Drive, Armonk, New York 10504 (800) 541-6563; *The Illustrated Book of World Rankings.*

Statistical Office of the United Nations, Publishing Service, New York, New York 10017 (800) 253-9646; *National Accounts Statistics;* and *Statistical Yearbook.*

LAOS (PEOPLE'S DEMOCRATIC REPUBLIC) - NATIONAL PRODUCT

M.E. Sharpe, 80 Business Park Drive, Armonk, New York 10504 (800) 541-6563; *The Illustrated Book of World Rankings.*

LAOS (PEOPLE'S DEMOCRATIC REPUBLIC) - NATURAL GAS - PRODUCTION - See LAOS (PEOPLE'S DEMOCRATIC REPUBLIC) - MINING AND MINERAL PRODUCTS

LAOS (PEOPLE'S DEMOCRATIC REPUBLIC) - NEWSPAPER CONSUMPTION AND PRODUCTION - See LAOS (PEOPLE'S DEMOCRATIC REPUBLIC) - FORESTRY AND FOREST PRODUCTS

LAOS (PEOPLE'S DEMOCRATIC REPUBLIC) - NEWSPRINT PRODUCTION AND CONSUMPTION - See LAOS (PEOPLE'S DEMOCRATIC REPUBLIC) - FORESTRY

AND FOREST PRODUCTS

LAOS (PEOPLE'S DEMOCRATIC REPUBLIC) - OCCUPATIONS - See LAOS (PEOPLE'S DEMOCRATIC REPUBLIC) - LABOR

LAOS (PEOPLE'S DEMOCRATIC REPUBLIC) - PAPER - See LAOS (PEOPLE'S DEMOCRATIC REPUBLIC) - FORESTRY AND FOREST PRODUCTS

LAOS (PEOPLE'S DEMOCRATIC REPUBLIC) - PATENTS, TRADEMARKS AND SERVICE MARKS

Statistical Office of the United Nations, Publishing Service, New York, New York 10017 (800) 253-9646; *Statistical Yearbook.*

LAOS (PEOPLE'S DEMOCRATIC REPUBLIC) - PEANUT PRODUCTION - See LAOS (PEOPLE'S DEMOCRATIC REPUBLIC) - CROPS

LAOS (PEOPLE'S DEMOCRATIC REPUBLIC) - PESTICIDE USE

Food and Agricultural Organization of the United Nations (FAO), Via delle Terme di Caracalla, 00100 Rome, Italy (Telephone Number in U.S. (202) 653-2400); *The State of Food and Agriculture.*

LAOS (PEOPLE'S DEMOCRATIC REPUBLIC) - PETROLEUM INDUSTRY

Asian Development Bank, Post Office Box 789, 1099 Manila, Philippines; *Key Indicators of Developing Asian and Pacific Countries.*

Food and Agricultural Organization of the United Nations (FAO), Via delle Terme di Caracalla, 00100 Rome, Italy (Telephone Number in U.S. (202) 653-2400); *The State of Food and Agriculture.*

M.E. Sharpe, 80 Business Park Drive, Armonk, New York 10504 (800) 541-6563; *The Illustrated Book of World Rankings.*

United Nations Conference on Trade and Development, Central Statistical Service, Palais des Nations, Geneva, Switzerland (Telephone in U.S. (800) 253-9646); *UNCTAD Commodity Yearbook.*

LAOS (PEOPLE'S DEMOCRATIC REPUBLIC) - PIGS - See LAOS (PEOPLE'S DEMOCRATIC REPUBLIC) - LIVESTOCK AND POULTRY

LAOS (PEOPLE'S DEMOCRATIC REPUBLIC) - POPULATION

Asian Development Bank, Post Office Box 789, 1099 Manila, Philippines; *Key Indicators of Developing Asian and Pacific Countries.*

Central Intelligence Agency,

Washington, D.C. 20505 (703) 482-1100, www.cia.gov; *The World Factbook.*

The Economist Intelligence Unit, 111 West 57th Street, New York, New York 10019 (800) 938-4685; *Laos Country Report;* and *The World Market Atlas.*

The Economist Intelligence Unit (Asia) Limited, 10th Floor, Luk Kwok Centre, 72 Gloucester Road, Wanchai, Hong Kong (Phone Number in U.S. (800) 938-4685); *Asian Market Atlas.*

Euromonitor International, Inc., 122 South Michigan Avenue, Suite 1200, Chicago, Illinois 60603 (800) 577-EURO; *International Marketing Data and Statistics;* and *The World Economic Factbook.*

Europa Publications Limited, 18 Bedford Square, London, WC1B 3JN, England; *The Europa World Year Book.*

Food and Agricultural Organization of the United Nations (FAO), Via delle Terme di Caracalla, 00100 Rome, Italy (Telephone Number in U.S. (202) 653-2400); *Production Yearbook.*

International Labour Office, I.L.O. Publications, 1828 L Street, N.W., Suite 801, Washington, D.C. (301) 638-3152; *Yearbook of Labour Statistics.*

M.E. Sharpe, 80 Business Park Drive, Armonk, New York 10504 (800) 541-6563; *The Illustrated Book of World Rankings.*

St. Martin's Press, Inc., 175 Fifth Avenue, New York, New York 10010 (800) 221-7945; *The Statesman's Year-Book.*

Statistical Office of the United Nations, Publishing Service, New York, New York 10017 (800) 253-9646; *Asia-Pacific in Figures; Demographic Yearbook; Human Development Report; Statistical Yearbook; World Statistics Pocketbook;* and *Statistical Yearbook for Asia and the Pacific.*

United Nations Educational, Scientific and Cultural Organization (UNESCO), 7 Place de Fontenoy, F-75700 Paris, France (Telephone Number in U.S. (212) 963-5981); *Statistical Yearbook.*

U.S. Arms Control and Disarmament Agency, 320 Twenty-first Street, NW, Washington, D.C. 20451 (202) 647-8677; *World Military Expenditures and Arms Transfers.*

Walden Publishing, Ltd., Two Market Street, Saffron Walden Essex, CB10 1HZ, England; *The World of Information Asia and Pacific Review.*

The World Bank, 1818 H Street, NW, Washington, D.C. 20433 (202) 477-1234; *The World Bank Atlas;* and *World*

Development Report.

World Health Organization, Office of Publications, 20 Avenue Appia, CH-1211 Geneva 27, Switzerland (Telephone Number in U.S. (518) 436-9686); *World Health Statistics Annual.*

LAOS (PEOPLE'S DEMOCRATIC REPUBLIC) - POST OFFICES

M.E. Sharpe, 80 Business Park Drive, Armonk, New York 10504 (800) 541-6563; *The Illustrated Book of World Rankings.*

LAOS (PEOPLE'S DEMOCRATIC REPUBLIC) - POTATO PRODUCTION - See LAOS (PEOPLE'S DEMOCRATIC REPUBLIC) - CROPS

LAOS (PEOPLE'S DEMOCRATIC REPUBLIC) - POULTRY MEAT - See LAOS (PEOPLE'S DEMOCRATIC REPUBLIC) - LIVESTOCK AND POULTRY

LAOS (PEOPLE'S DEMOCRATIC REPUBLIC) - PRICES

Asian Development Bank, Post Office Box 789, 1099 Manila, Philippines; *Key Indicators of Developing Asian and Pacific Countries.*

Food and Agricultural Organization of the United Nations (FAO), Via delle Terme di Caracalla, 00100 Rome, Italy (Telephone Number in U.S. (202) 653-2400); *Production Yearbook;* and *The State of Food and Agriculture.*

M.E. Sharpe, 80 Business Park Drive, Armonk, New York 10504 (800) 541-6563; *The Illustrated Book of World Rankings.*

LAOS (PEOPLE'S DEMOCRATIC REPUBLIC) - PRINTING AND WRITING PAPER - See LAOS (PEOPLE'S DEMOCRATIC REPUBLIC) - FORESTRY AND FOREST PRODUCTS

LAOS (PEOPLE'S DEMOCRATIC REPUBLIC) - PRODUCTION

M.E. Sharpe, 80 Business Park Drive, Armonk, New York 10504 (800) 541-6563; *The Illustrated Book of World Rankings.*

LAOS (PEOPLE'S DEMOCRATIC REPUBLIC) - PRODUCTIVITY

Euromonitor International, Inc., 122 South Michigan Avenue, Suite 1200, Chicago, Illinois 60603 (800) 577-EURO; *International Marketing Data and Statistics.*

LAOS (PEOPLE'S DEMOCRATIC REPUBLIC) - PUBLIC FINANCE - See LAOS (PEOPLE'S DEMOCRATIC REPUBLIC) - FINANCE

LAOS (PEOPLE'S DEMOCRATIC REPUBLIC) - RADIO BROADCASTING - See LAOS (PEOPLE'S DEMOCRATIC REPUBLIC) -

BROADCASTING

LAOS (PEOPLE'S DEMOCRATIC REPUBLIC) - RADIO RECEIVERS

St. Martin's Press, Inc., 175 Fifth Avenue, New York, New York 10010 (800) 221-7945; *The Statesman's Year-Book.*

LAOS (PEOPLE'S DEMOCRATIC REPUBLIC) - RAILWAYS

St. Martin's Press, Inc., 175 Fifth Avenue, New York, New York 10010 (800) 221-7945; *The Statesman's Year-Book.*

LAOS (PEOPLE'S DEMOCRATIC REPUBLIC) - RELIGION

Central Intelligence Agency, Washington, D.C. 20505 (703) 482-1100, www.cia.gov; *The World Factbook.*

M.E. Sharpe, 80 Business Park Drive, Armonk, New York 10504 (800) 541-6563; *The Illustrated Book of World Rankings.*

St. Martin's Press, Inc., 175 Fifth Avenue, New York, New York 10010 (800) 221-7945; *The Statesman's Year-Book.*

LAOS (PEOPLE'S DEMOCRATIC REPUBLIC) - RETAIL TRADE

Euromonitor International, Inc., 122 South Michigan Avenue, Suite 1200, Chicago, Illinois 60603 (800) 577-EURO; *World Marketing Data and Statistics.*

LAOS (PEOPLE'S DEMOCRATIC REPUBLIC) - RICE PRODUCTION - See LAOS (PEOPLE'S DEMOCRATIC REPUBLIC) - CROPS

LAOS (PEOPLE'S DEMOCRATIC REPUBLIC) - ROOT AND TUBER PRODUCTION - See LAOS (PEOPLE'S DEMOCRATIC REPUBLIC) - CROPS

LAOS (PEOPLE'S DEMOCRATIC REPUBLIC) - ROUNDWOOD PRODUCTION - See LAOS (PEOPLE'S DEMOCRATIC REPUBLIC) - FORESTRY AND FOREST PRODUCTS

LAOS (PEOPLE'S DEMOCRATIC REPUBLIC) - RUBBER PRODUCTION AND CONSUMPTION

M.E. Sharpe, 80 Business Park Drive, Armonk, New York 10504 (800) 541-6563; *The Illustrated Book of World Rankings.*

LAOS (PEOPLE'S DEMOCRATIC REPUBLIC) - SAWNWOOD PRODUCTION - See LAOS (PEOPLE'S DEMOCRATIC REPUBLIC) - FORESTRY AND FOREST PRODUCTS

LAOS (PEOPLE'S DEMOCRATIC REPUBLIC) - SCIENTISTS, TECHNICIANS

AND ENGINEERS

Statistical Office of the United Nations, Publishing Service, New York, New York 10017 (800) 253-9646; *Statistical Yearbook.*

United Nations Educational, Scientific and Cultural Organization (UNESCO), 7 Place de Fontenoy, F-75700 Paris, France (Telephone Number in U.S. (212) 963-5981); *Statistical Yearbook.*

LAOS (PEOPLE'S DEMOCRATIC REPUBLIC) - SENIOR CITIZENS

M.E. Sharpe, 80 Business Park Drive, Armonk, New York 10504 (800) 541-6563; *The Illustrated Book of World Rankings.*

LAOS (PEOPLE'S DEMOCRATIC REPUBLIC) - SHEEP - See LAOS (PEOPLE'S DEMOCRATIC REPUBLIC) - LIVESTOCK AND POULTRY

LAOS (PEOPLE'S DEMOCRATIC REPUBLIC) - SILVER PRODUCTION AND CONSUMPTION - See LAOS (PEOPLE'S DEMOCRATIC REPUBLIC) - MINING AND MINERAL PRODUCTS

LAOS (PEOPLE'S DEMOCRATIC REPUBLIC) - SOCIAL DATA

Asian Development Bank, Post Office Box 789, 1099 Manila, Philippines; *Key Indicators of Developing Asian and Pacific Countries.*

M.E. Sharpe, 80 Business Park Drive, Armonk, New York 10504 (800) 541-6563; *The Illustrated Book of World Rankings.*

Statistical Office of the United Nations, Publishing Service, New York, New York 10017 (800) 253-9646; *World Statistics Pocketbook.*

LAOS (PEOPLE'S DEMOCRATIC REPUBLIC) - SOCIAL SECURITY

Statistical Office of the United Nations, Publishing Service, New York, New York 10017 (800) 253-9646; *National Accounts Statistics.*

LAOS (PEOPLE'S DEMOCRATIC REPUBLIC) - SOYBEAN PRODUCTION - See LAOS (PEOPLE'S DEMOCRATIC REPUBLIC) - CROPS

LAOS (PEOPLE'S DEMOCRATIC REPUBLIC) - STATE BUDGET

Euromonitor International, Inc., 122 South Michigan Avenue, Suite 1200, Chicago, Illinois 60603 (800) 577-EURO; *International Marketing Data and Statistics.*

LAOS (PEOPLE'S DEMOCRATIC REPUBLIC) - STEEL - See LAOS (PEOPLE'S DEMOCRATIC REPUBLIC) - MINING AND

MINERAL PRODUCTS

LAOS (PEOPLE'S DEMOCRATIC REPUBLIC) - STOCKS - COMMODITY - MARKET PRICE - INDEX

Food and Agricultural Organization of the United Nations (FAO), Via delle Terme di Caracalla, 00100 Rome, Italy (Telephone Number in U.S. (202) 653-2400); *The State of Food and Agriculture.*

LAOS (PEOPLE'S DEMOCRATIC REPUBLIC) - SUGAR PRODUCTION - See LAOS (PEOPLE'S DEMOCRATIC REPUBLIC) - CROPS

LAOS (PEOPLE'S DEMOCRATIC REPUBLIC) - TAXATION

Europa Publications Limited, 18 Bedford Square, London, WC1B 3JN, England; *The Europa World Year Book.*

LAOS (PEOPLE'S DEMOCRATIC REPUBLIC) - TELEGRAPH SERVICE

American Telephone and Telegraph Company, 26 Parsippany Road, Whippany, New Jersey 07981 (800) 222-0300; *The World's Telephones.*

Statistical Office of the United Nations, Publishing Service, New York, New York 10017 (800) 253-9646; *Statistical Yearbook.*

LAOS (PEOPLE'S DEMOCRATIC REPUBLIC) - TELEPHONES IN USE

American Telephone and Telegraph Company, 26 Parsippany Road, Whippany, New Jersey 07981 (800) 222-0300; *The World's Telephones.*

Central Intelligence Agency, Washington, D.C. 20505 (703) 482-1100, www.cia.gov; *The World Factbook.*

The Economist Intelligence Unit (Asia) Limited, 10th Floor, Luk Kwok Centre, 72 Gloucester Road, Wanchai, Hong Kong (Phone Number in U.S. (800) 938-4685); *Asian Market Atlas.*

Europa Publications Limited, 18 Bedford Square, London, WC1B 3JN, England; *The Europa World Year Book.*

Statistical Office of the United Nations, Publishing Service, New York, New York 10017 (800) 253-9646; *Statistical Yearbook;* and *World Statistics Pocketbook.*

LAOS (PEOPLE'S DEMOCRATIC REPUBLIC) - TELEVISION

The Economist Intelligence Unit (Asia) Limited, 10th Floor, Luk Kwok Centre, 72 Gloucester Road, Wanchai, Hong Kong (Phone Number in U.S. (800) 938-4685); *Asian Market Atlas.*

LAOS (PEOPLE'S DEMOCRATIC REPUBLIC) - TELEVISION BROADCASTING - See LAOS (PEOPLE'S DEMOCRATIC REPUBLIC) - BROADCASTING

LAOS (PEOPLE'S DEMOCRATIC REPUBLIC) - TEXTILE INDUSTRY

M.E. Sharpe, 80 Business Park Drive, Armonk, New York 10504 (800) 541-6563; *The Illustrated Book of World Rankings.*

St. Martin's Press, Inc., 175 Fifth Avenue, New York, New York 10010 (800) 221-7945; *The Statesman's Year-Book.*

United Nations Conference on Trade and Development, Central Statistical Service, Palais des Nations, Geneva, Switzerland (Telephone in U.S. (800) 253-9646); *UNCTAD Commodity Yearbook.*

LAOS (PEOPLE'S DEMOCRATIC REPUBLIC) - TIN PRODUCTION - See LAOS (PEOPLE'S DEMOCRATIC REPUBLIC) - MINING AND MINERAL PRODUCTS

LAOS (PEOPLE'S DEMOCRATIC REPUBLIC) - TOBACCO PRODUCTION

M.E. Sharpe, 80 Business Park Drive, Armonk, New York 10504 (800) 541-6563; *The Illustrated Book of World Rankings.*

Statistical Office of the United Nations, Publishing Service, New York, New York 10017 (800) 253-9646; *Statistical Yearbook.*

LAOS (PEOPLE'S DEMOCRATIC REPUBLIC) - TOURISM

Euromonitor International, Inc., 122 South Michigan Avenue, Suite 1200, Chicago, Illinois 60603 (800) 577-EURO; *The World Economic Factbook;* and *World Marketing Data and Statistics.*

M.E. Sharpe, 80 Business Park Drive, Armonk, New York 10504 (800) 541-6563; *The Illustrated Book of World Rankings.*

LAOS (PEOPLE'S DEMOCRATIC REPUBLIC) - TRACTORS IN USE

Statistical Office of the United Nations, Publishing Service, New York, New York 10017 (800) 253-9646; *Statistical Yearbook.*

LAOS (PEOPLE'S DEMOCRATIC REPUBLIC) - TRADE - See LAOS (PEOPLE'S DEMOCRATIC REPUBLIC) - FOREIGN TRADE

LAOS (PEOPLE'S DEMOCRATIC REPUBLIC) - TRADEMARKS AND SERVICE MARKS - See LAOS (PEOPLE'S DEMOCRATIC REPUBLIC) - PATENTS, TRADEMARKS AND SERVICE MARKS

LAOS (PEOPLE'S DEMOCRATIC REPUBLIC) - TRANSPORTATION AND COMMUNICATIONS

Central Intelligence Agency, Washington, D.C. 20505 (703) 482-1100, www.cia.gov; *The World Factbook.*

The Economist Intelligence Unit (Asia) Limited, 10th Floor, Luk Kwok Centre, 72 Gloucester Road, Wanchai, Hong Kong (Phone Number in U.S. (800) 938-4685); *Asian Market Atlas.*

Euromonitor International, Inc., 122 South Michigan Avenue, Suite 1200, Chicago, Illinois 60603 (800) 577-EURO; *International Marketing Data and Statistics;* and *World Marketing Data and Statistics.*

Europa Publications Limited, 18 Bedford Square, London, WC1B 3JN, England; *The Europa World Year Book.*

M.E. Sharpe, 80 Business Park Drive, Armonk, New York 10504 (800) 541-6563; *The Illustrated Book of World Rankings.*

St. Martin's Press, Inc., 175 Fifth Avenue, New York, New York 10010 (800) 221-7945; *The Statesman's Year-Book.*

Statistical Office of the United Nations, Publishing Service, New York, New York 10017 (800) 253-9646; *Human Development Report;* and *Statistical Yearbook for Asia and the Pacific.*

LAOS (PEOPLE'S DEMOCRATIC REPUBLIC) - UNEMPLOYMENT

Central Intelligence Agency, Washington, D.C. 20505 (703) 482-1100, www.cia.gov; *The World Factbook.*

Euromonitor International, Inc., 122 South Michigan Avenue, Suite 1200, Chicago, Illinois 60603 (800) 577-EURO; *International Marketing Data and Statistics.*

International Labour Office, I.L.O. Publications, 1828 L Street, N.W., Suite 801, Washington, D.C. (301) 638-3152; *Yearbook of Labour Statistics.*

St. Martin's Press, Inc., 175 Fifth Avenue, New York, New York 10010 (800) 221-7945; *The Statesman's Year-Book.*

LAOS (PEOPLE'S DEMOCRATIC REPUBLIC) - VITAL STATISTICS

Euromonitor International, Inc., 122 South Michigan Avenue, Suite 1200, Chicago, Illinois 60603 (800) 577-EURO; *International Marketing Data and Statistics.*

St. Martin's Press, Inc., 175 Fifth Avenue, New York, New York 10010 (800) 221-7945; *The Statesman's Year-Book.*

Statistical Office of the United Nations, Publishing Service, New York, New York 10017 (800) 253-9646; *Statistical Yearbook.*

World Health Organization, Office of Publications, 20 Avenue Appia, CH-1211 Geneva 27, Switzerland (Telephone Number in U.S. (518) 436-9686); *World Health Statistics Annual.*

LAOS (PEOPLE'S DEMOCRATIC REPUBLIC) - WAGES

International Labour Office, I.L.O. Publications, 1828 L Street, N.W., Suite 801, Washington, D.C. (301) 638-3152; *Yearbook of Labour Statistics.*

Statistical Office of the United Nations, Publishing Service, New York, New York 10017 (800) 253-9646; *Statistical Yearbook for Asia and the Pacific.*

LAOS (PEOPLE'S DEMOCRATIC REPUBLIC) - WEATHER - See LAOS (PEOPLE'S DEMOCRATIC REPUBLIC) - CLIMATE

LAOS (PEOPLE'S DEMOCRATIC REPUBLIC) - WHEAT PRODUCTION - See LAOS (PEOPLE'S DEMOCRATIC REPUBLIC) - CROPS

LAOS (PEOPLE'S DEMOCRATIC REPUBLIC) - WHOLESALE PRICES -INDEX NUMBERS

Asian Development Bank, Post Office Box 789, 1099 Manila, Philippines; *Key Indicators of Developing Asian and Pacific Countries.*

LAOS (PEOPLE'S DEMOCRATIC REPUBLIC) - WINE PRODUCTION - See LAOS (PEOPLE'S DEMOCRATIC REPUBLIC) - BEVERAGES

LAOS (PEOPLE'S DEMOCRATIC REPUBLIC) - WOOL PRODUCTION - See LAOS (PEOPLE'S DEMOCRATIC REPUBLIC) - TEXTILE INDUSTRY

LAOTIAN POPULATION

U.S. Department of Commerce, Bureau of the Census, Washington, D.C. 20233 (301) 457-4100, www.census.gov; *Census of Population, General Population Characteristics, U.S.*

LARCENY - THEFT

U.S. Department of Justice, Bureau of Justice Statistics, 810 Seventh Street, NW, 2nd floor, Washington, D.C. 20531 (800) 732-3277, www.ojp.usdoj.gov/bjs; *Criminal Victimization.*

U.S. Department of Justice, Federal Bureau of Investigation, 935 Pennsylvania Avenue, NW, Washington, D.C. 20535 (202) 324-3691, www.fbi.gov; *Crime in the*

United States; and *Population-at-Risk Rates and Selected Crime Indicators.*

LARD

U.S. Department of Agriculture, Economic Research Service, 1800 M Street, NW, Washington, D.C. 20036 (202) 694-5050, www.ers.usda.gov; *Food Consumption, Prices and Expenditures;* and *Agricultural Outlook.*

LATEX - See RUBBER

Latvia--Primary Statistics Sources

Latvijas Republikas Valsts Statistikas Komiteja, Riga, Latvia; *Latvijas Statistikas Gadagramata.*

LATVIA - ABORTIONS

Statistical Office of the United Nations, Publishing Service, New York, New York 10017 (800) 253-9646; *Trends in Europe and North America: The Statistical Yearbook of the Economic Commission for Europe.*

LATVIA - AGRICULTURE

Academic International Press, Box 1111, Gulf Breeze, Florida 32562; *Russia and Eurasia Facts and Figures Annual.*

Business International Moscow, 23 Profsoyuznaya Ulitsa, 117859, Moscow (Telephone Number in U.S. (800) 938-4685); *The CIS Market Atlas.*

Economist Intelligence Unit, 111 West 57th Street, New York, New York 10019 (800) 938-4685; *Latvia Country Report.*

Euromonitor International, Inc., 122 South Michigan Avenue, Suite 1200, Chicago, Illinois 60603 (800) 577-EURO; *World Marketing Data and Statistics.*

Europa Publications Limited, 18 Bedford Square, London, WC1B 3JN, England; *The Europa World Year Book.*

Food and Agriculture Organization of the United Nations (FAO), Via delle Terme di Caracalla, 00100, Rome, Italy (Telephone Number in U.S. (202) 653-2400); *Production Yearbook; The State of Food and Agriculture;* and *Trade Yearbook.*

St. Martin's Press, Inc., 175 Fifth Avenue, New York, New York 10010 (800) 221-7945; *The Statesman's Year-Book.*

Statistical Office of the United Nations, Publishing Service, New York, New York 10017 (800) 253-9646; *Industrial Commodity Statistics Yearbook;* and *Statistical Yearbook.*

The World Bank, 1818 H Street, NW, Washington, D.C. 20433 (202) 477-1234; *Statistical Handbook: States of the Former USSR;* and *World Development Indicators.*

LATVIA - AIRLINE SERVICE

Business International Moscow, 23 Profsoyuznaya Ulitsa, 117859, Moscow (Telephone Number in U.S. (800) 938-4685); *The CIS Market Atlas.*

Europa Publications Limited, 18 Bedford Square, London, WC1B 3JN, England; *The Europa World Year Book.*

International Civil Aviation Organization, 999 University Street, Montreal, Quebec, Canada H3C 5H7 (514) 954-8219; *Civil Aviation Statistics of the World.*

St. Martin's Press, Inc., 175 Fifth Avenue, New York, New York 10010 (800) 221-7945; *The Statesman's Year-Book.*

Statistical Office of the United Nations, Publishing Service, New York, New York 10017 (800) 253-9646; *Statistical Yearbook.*

LATVIA - AIRPORTS

Central Intelligence Agency, Washington, D.C. 20505 (703) 482-1100, www.cia.gov; *The World Factbook.*

LATVIA - ANIMAL HEALTH

Food and Agriculture Organization of the United Nations (FAO), Via delle Terme di Caracalla, 00100, Rome, Italy (Telephone Number in U.S. (202) 653-2400); *Animal Health Yearbook.*

LATVIA - AREA AND DENSITY OF POPULATION

Academic International Press, Box 1111, Gulf Breeze, Florida 32562; *Russia and Eurasia Facts and Figures Annual.*

Business International Moscow, 23 Profsoyuznaya Ulitsa, 117859, Moscow (Telephone Number in U.S. (800) 938-4685); *The CIS Market Atlas.*

Central Intelligence Agency, Washington, D.C. 20505 (703) 482-1100, www.cia.gov; *The World Factbook.*

Euromonitor International, Inc., 122 South Michigan Avenue, Suite 1200, Chicago, Illinois 60603 (800) 577-EURO; *The World Economic Factbook.*

Europa Publications Limited, 18 Bedford Square, London, WC1B 3JN, England; *The Europa World Year Book.*

St. Martin's Press, Inc., 175 Fifth Avenue, New York, New York 10010 (800)

221-7945; *The Statesman's Year-Book.*

Statistical Office of the United Nations, Publishing Service, New York, New York 10017 (800) 253-9646; *Statistical Yearbook;* and *Trends in Europe and North America: The Statistical Yearbook of the Economic Commission for Europe.*

United Nations Educational, Scientific and Cultural Organization (UNESCO), 7 Place de Fontenoy, F-75700 Paris, France (Telephone Number in U.S. (212) 963-5981); *Statistical Yearbook.*

LATVIA - BALANCE OF PAYMENTS

Europa Publications Limited, 18 Bedford Square, London, WC1B 3JN, England; *The Europa World Year Book.*

United Nations Conference on Trade and Development (UNCTAD), New York, New York 10017 (800) 253-9646; *Handbook of International Trade and Development Statistics.*

The World Bank, 1818 H Street, NW, Washington, D.C. 20433 (202) 477-1234; *World Development Indicators.*

LATVIA - BANKING

Business International Moscow, 23 Profsoyuznaya Ulitsa, 117859, Moscow (Telephone Number in U.S. (800) 938-4685); *The CIS Market Atlas.*

Euromonitor International, Inc., 122 South Michigan Avenue, Suite 1200, Chicago, Illinois 60603 (800) 577-EURO; *World Marketing Data and Statistics.*

Europa Publications Limited, 18 Bedford Square, London, WC1B 3JN, England; *The Europa World Year Book.*

St. Martin's Press, Inc., 175 Fifth Avenue, New York, New York 10010 (800) 221-7945; *The Statesman's Year-Book.*

LATVIA - BEVERAGES

Statistical Office of the United Nations, Publishing Service, New York, New York 10017 (800) 253-9646; *Statistical Yearbook.*

LATVIA - BIRTH RATES

Academic International Press, Box 1111, Gulf Breeze, Florida 32562; *Russia and Eurasia Facts and Figures Annual.*

Business International Moscow, 23 Profsoyuznaya Ulitsa, 117859, Moscow (Telephone Number in U.S. (800) 938-4685); *The CIS Market Atlas.*

Central Intelligence Agency, Washington, D.C. 20505 (703) 482-1100, www.cia.gov; *The World Factbook.*

Euromonitor International, Inc., 122 South Michigan Avenue, Suite 1200, Chicago, Illinois 60603 (800) 577-EURO; *The World Economic Factbook.*

Europa Publications Limited, 18 Bedford Square, London, WC1B 3JN, England; *The Europa World Year Book.*

St. Martin's Press, Inc., 175 Fifth Avenue, New York, New York 10010 (800) 221-7945; *The Statesman's Year-Book.*

Statistical Office of the United Nations, Publishing Service, New York, New York 10017 (800) 253-9646; *Statistical Yearbook.*

World Health Organization, Office of Publications, 20 Avenue Appia, CH-1211 Geneva 27, Switzerland (Telephone Number in U.S. (518) 436-9686); *World Health Statistics Annual.*

LATVIA - BOOK PRODUCTION

Statistical Office of the United Nations, Publishing Service, New York, New York 10017 (800) 253-9646; *Trends in Europe and North America: The Statistical Yearbook of the Economic Commission for Europe.*

United Nations Educational, Scientific and Cultural Organization (UNESCO), 7 Place de Fontenoy, F-75700 Paris, France (Telephone Number in U.S. (212) 963-5981); *Statistical Yearbook.*

LATVIA - BROADCASTING

Central Intelligence Agency, Washington, D.C. 20505 (703) 482-1100, www.cia.gov; *The World Factbook.*

Euromonitor International, Inc., 122 South Michigan Avenue, Suite 1200, Chicago, Illinois 60603 (800) 577-EURO; *World Marketing Data and Statistics.*

St. Martin's Press, Inc., 175 Fifth Avenue, New York, New York 10010 (800) 221-7945; *The Statesman's Year-Book.*

Statistical Office of the United Nations, Publishing Service, New York, New York 10017 (800) 253-9646; *Trends in Europe and North America: The Statistical Yearbook of the Economic Commission for Europe.*

United Nations Educational, Scientific and Cultural Organization (UNESCO), 7 Place de Fontenoy, F-75700 Paris, France (Telephone Number in U.S. (212) 963-5981); *Statistical Yearbook.*

LATVIA - BUDGET

Business International Moscow, 23 Profsoyuznaya Ulitsa, 117859, Moscow (Telephone Number in U.S. (800) 938-4685); *The CIS Market Atlas.*

Central Intelligence Agency, Washington, D.C. 20505 (703) 482-1100, www.cia.gov; *The World Factbook.*

LATVIA - CAPITAL INVESTMENT

The World Bank, 1818 H Street, NW, Washington, D.C. 20433 (202) 477-1234; *Statistical Handbook: States of the Former USSR.*

LATVIA - CATTLE - See LATVIA - LIVESTOCK AND POULTRY

LATVIA - CHEMICALS

Business International Moscow, 23 Profsoyuznaya Ulitsa, 117859, Moscow (Telephone Number in U.S. (800) 938-4685); *The CIS Market Atlas.*

LATVIA - COAL PRODUCTION AND CONSUMPTION - See LATVIA - MINING AND MINERAL PRODUCTS

LATVIA - COMMERCE

St. Martin's Press, Inc., 175 Fifth Avenue, New York, New York 10010 (800) 221-7945; *The Statesman's Year-Book.*

LATVIA - COMMUNICATIONS - See LATVIA - TRANSPORTATION AND COMMUNICATIONS

LATVIA - CONSTRUCTION INDUSTRY

Academic International Press, Box 1111, Gulf Breeze, Florida 32562; *Russia and Eurasia Facts and Figures Annual.*

Business International Moscow, 23 Profsoyuznaya Ulitsa, 117859, Moscow (Telephone Number in U.S. (800) 938-4685); *The CIS Market Atlas.*

Statistical Office of the United Nations, Publishing Service, New York, New York 10017 (800) 253-9646; *Statistical Yearbook.*

LATVIA - CONSUMER PRICE INDEX

Europa Publications Limited, 18 Bedford Square, London, WC1B 3JN, England; *The Europa World Year Book.*

Statistical Office of the United Nations, Publishing Service, New York, New York 10017 (800) 253-9646; *Statistical Yearbook;* and *Trends in Europe and North America: The Statistical Yearbook of the Economic Commission for Europe.*

LATVIA - CONSUMER PRICES

Euromonitor International, Inc., 122 South Michigan Avenue, Suite 1200, Chicago, Illinois 60603 (800) 577-EURO; *World Marketing Data and Statistics.*

International Labour Office, I.L.O.

Publications, 1828 L Street, N.W., Suite 801, Washington, D.C. (301) 638-3152; *Yearbook of Labor Statistics.*

LATVIA - CONSUMER PRODUCTS

Business International Moscow, 23 Profsoyuznaya Ulitsa, 117859, Moscow (Telephone Number in U.S. (800) 938-4685); *The CIS Market Atlas.*

LATVIA - CONSUMPTION

Business International Moscow, 23 Profsoyuznaya Ulitsa, 117859, Moscow (Telephone Number in U.S. (800) 938-4685); *The CIS Market Atlas.*

The World Bank, 1818 H Street, NW, Washington, D.C. 20433 (202) 477-1234; *Statistical Handbook: States of the Former USSR.*

LATVIA - COTTON PRODUCTION AND CONSUMPTION - See LATVIA - TEXTILE INDUSTRY

LATVIA - CRIME

Academic International Press, Box 1111, Gulf Breeze, Florida 32562; *Russia and Eurasia Facts and Figures Annual.*

Statistical Office of the United Nations, Publishing Service, New York, New York 10017 (800) 253-9646; *Trends in Europe and North America: The Statistical Yearbook of the Economic Commission for Europe.*

LATVIA - CROPS

Academic International Press, Box 1111, Gulf Breeze, Florida 32562; *Russia and Eurasia Facts and Figures Annual.*

Europa Publications Limited, 18 Bedford Square, London, WC1B 3JN, England; *The Europa World Year Book.*

Food and Agriculture Organization of the United Nations (FAO), Via delle Terme di Caracalla, 00100, Rome, Italy (Telephone Number in U.S. (202) 653-2400); *Production Yearbook; The State of Food and Agriculture;* and *Trade Yearbook.*

St. Martin's Press, Inc., 175 Fifth Avenue, New York, New York 10010 (800) 221-7945; *The Statesman's Year-Book.*

Statistical Office of the United Nations, Publishing Service, New York, New York 10017 (800) 253-9646; *Industrial Commodity Statistics Yearbook;* and *Statistical Yearbook.*

The World Bank, 1818 H Street, NW, Washington, D.C. 20433 (202) 477-1234; *Statistical Handbook: States of the Former USSR.*

LATVIA - DAIRY PRODUCTS

Europa Publications Limited, 18 Bedford Square, London, WC1B 3JN, England; *The Europa World Year Book.*

Food and Agriculture Organization of the United Nations (FAO), Via delle Terme di Caracalla, 00100, Rome, Italy (Telephone Number in U.S. (202) 653-2400); *Production Yearbook; The State of Food and Agriculture;* and *Trade Yearbook.*

St. Martin's Press, Inc., 175 Fifth Avenue, New York, New York 10010 (800) 221-7945; *The Statesman's Year-Book.*

Statistical Office of the United Nations, Publishing Service, New York, New York 10017 (800) 253-9646; *Industrial Commodity Statistics Yearbook;* and *Statistical Yearbook.*

LATVIA - DEATH RATES - See LATVIA - MORTALITY

LATVIA - DEMOGRAPHY

Business International Moscow, 23 Profsoyuznaya Ulitsa, 117859, Moscow (Telephone Number in U.S. (800) 938-4685); *The CIS Market Atlas.*

The Economist Intelligence Unit, 111 West 57th Street, New York, New York 10019 (800) 938-4685; *The World Market Atlas.*

Euromonitor International, Inc., 122 South Michigan Avenue, Suite 1200, Chicago, Illinois 60603 (800) 577-EURO; *The World Economic Factbook;* and *World Marketing Data and Statistics.*

Statistical Office of the United Nations, Publishing Service, New York, New York 10017 (800) 253-9646; *Demographic Yearbook;* and *Human Development Report.*

The World Bank, 1818 H Street, NW, Washington, D.C. 20433 (202) 477-1234; *Statistical Handbook: States of the Former USSR.*

LATVIA - DISEASES - See LATVIA - HEALTH

LATVIA - DIVORCE RATES

Academic International Press, Box 1111, Gulf Breeze, Florida 32562; *Russia and Eurasia Facts and Figures Annual.*

Statistical Office of the United Nations, Publishing Service, New York, New York 10017 (800) 253-9646; *Demographic Yearbook; Trends in Europe and North America: The Statistical Yearbook of the Economic Commission for Europe;* and *Statistical Yearbook.*

LATVIA - DOMESTIC INVESTMENT

Business International Moscow, 23 Profsoyuznaya Ulitsa, 117859, Moscow (Telephone Number in U.S. (800) 938-4685); *The CIS Market Atlas.*

LATVIA - ECONOMY

Academic International Press, Box 1111, Gulf Breeze, Florida 32562; *Russia and Eurasia Facts and Figures Annual.*

Business International Moscow, 23 Profsoyuznaya Ulitsa, 117859, Moscow (Telephone Number in U.S. (800) 938-4685); *The CIS Market Atlas.*

Central Intelligence Agency, Washington, D.C. 20505 (703) 482-1100, www.cia.gov; *The World Factbook.*

Economist Intelligence Unit, 111 West 57th Street, New York, New York 10019 (800) 938-4685; *Latvia Country Report.*

Euromonitor International, Inc., 122 South Michigan Avenue, Suite 1200, Chicago, Illinois 60603 (800) 577-EURO; *The World Economic Factbook;* and *World Marketing Data and Statistics.*

St. Martin's Press, Inc., 175 Fifth Avenue, New York, New York 10010 (800) 221-7945; *The Statesman's Year-Book.*

The World Bank, 1818 H Street, NW, Washington, D.C. 20433 (202) 477-1234; *The World Bank Atlas.*

LATVIA - EDUCATION

Academic International Press, Box 1111, Gulf Breeze, Florida 32562; *Russia and Eurasia Facts and Figures Annual.*

Business International Moscow, 23 Profsoyuznaya Ulitsa, 117859, Moscow (Telephone Number in U.S. (800) 938-4685); *The CIS Market Atlas.*

The Economist Intelligence Unit, 111 West 57th Street, New York, New York 10019 (800) 938-4685; *The World Market Atlas.*

Euromonitor International, Inc., 122 South Michigan Avenue, Suite 1200, Chicago, Illinois 60603 (800) 577-EURO; *World Marketing Data and Statistics.*

Europa Publications Limited, 18 Bedford Square, London, WC1B 3JN, England; *The Europa World Year Book.*

St. Martin's Press, Inc., 175 Fifth Avenue, New York, New York 10010 (800) 221-7945; *The Statesman's Year-Book.*

Statistical Office of the United Nations, Publishing Service, New York, New York

10017 (800) 253-9646; *Human Development Report;* and *Trends in Europe and North America: The Statistical Yearbook of the Economic Commission for Europe.*

United Nations Educational, Scientific and Cultural Organization (UNESCO), 7 Place de Fontenoy, F-75700 Paris, France (Telephone Number in U.S. (212) 963-5981); *Statistical Yearbook.*

LATVIA - ELECTRICITY

Academic International Press, Box 1111, Gulf Breeze, Florida 32562; *Russia and Eurasia Facts and Figures Annual.*

Business International Moscow, 23 Profsoyuznaya Ulitsa, 117859, Moscow (Telephone Number in U.S. (800) 938-4685); *The CIS Market Atlas.*

Central Intelligence Agency, Washington, D.C. 20505 (703) 482-1100, www.cia.gov; *The World Factbook.*

St. Martin's Press, Inc., 175 Fifth Avenue, New York, New York 10010 (800) 221-7945; *The Statesman's Year-Book.*

Statistical Office of the United Nations, Publishing Service, New York, New York 10017 (800) 253-9646; *Energy Statistics Yearbook; Human Development Report; Trends in Europe and North America: The Statistical Yearbook · of the Economic Commission for Europe;* and *Statistical Yearbook.*

The World Bank, 1818 H Street, NW, Washington, D.C. 20433 (202) 477-1234; *Statistical Handbook: States of the Former USSR.*

LATVIA - EMPLOYMENT

International Labour Office, I.L.O. Publications, 1828 L Street, N.W., Suite 801, Washington, D.C. (301) 638-3152; *Yearbook of Labor Statistics.*

Statistical Office of the United Nations, Publishing Service, New York, New York 10017 (800) 253-9646; *Statistical Yearbook;* and *Trends in Europe and North America: The Statistical Yearbook of the Economic Commission for Europe.*

The World Bank, 1818 H Street, NW, Washington, D.C. 20433 (202) 477-1234; *Statistical Handbook: States of the Former USSR.*

LATVIA - ENERGY

Academic International Press, Box 1111, Gulf Breeze, Florida 32562; *Russia and Eurasia Facts and Figures Annual.*

Business International Moscow, 23

Profsoyuznaya Ulitsa, 117859, Moscow (Telephone Number in U.S. (800) 938-4685); *The CIS Market Atlas.*

Euromonitor International, Inc., 122 South Michigan Avenue, Suite 1200, Chicago, Illinois 60603 (800) 577-EURO; *The World Economic Factbook;* and *World Marketing Data and Statistics.*

St. Martin's Press, Inc., 175 Fifth Avenue, New York, New York 10010 (800) 221-7945; *The Statesman's Year-Book.*

Statistical Office of the United Nations, Publishing Service, New York, New York 10017 (800) 253-9646; *Energy Statistics Yearbook; Human Development Report; Trends in Europe and North America: The Statistical Yearbook of the Economic Commission for Europe;* and *Statistical Yearbook.*

The World Bank, 1818 H Street, NW, Washington, D.C. 20433 (202) 477-1234; *The World Bank Atlas;* and *Statistical Handbook: States of the Former USSR.*

LATVIA - ENVIRONMENT

Business International Moscow, 23 Profsoyuznaya Ulitsa, 117859, Moscow (Telephone Number in U.S. (800) 938-4685); *The CIS Market Atlas.*

Economist Intelligence Unit, 111 West 57th Street, New York, New York 10019 (800) 938-4685; *Latvia Country Report.*

Statistical Office of the United Nations, Publishing Service, New York, New York 10017 (800) 253-9646; *Statistical Yearbook;* and *Trends in Europe and North America: The Statistical Yearbook of the Economic Commission for Europe.*

LATVIA - EXCHANGE RATES

Central Intelligence Agency, Washington, D.C. 20505 (703) 482-1100, www.cia.gov; *The World Factbook.*

Euromonitor International, Inc., 122 South Michigan Avenue, Suite 1200, Chicago, Illinois 60603 (800) 577-EURO; *The World Economic Factbook.*

Europa Publications Limited, 18 Bedford Square, London, WC1B 3JN, England; *The Europa World Year Book.*

Statistical Office of the United Nations, Publishing Service, New York, New York 10017 (800) 253-9646; *Statistical Yearbook;* and *Trends in Europe and North America: The Statistical Yearbook of the Economic Commission for Europe.*

LATVIA - EXPORTS

Academic International Press, Box

1111, Gulf Breeze, Florida 32562; *Russia and Eurasia Facts and Figures Annual.*

Business International Moscow, 23 Profsoyuznaya Ulitsa, 117859, Moscow (Telephone Number in U.S. (800) 938-4685); *The CIS Market Atlas.*

Central Intelligence Agency, Washington, D.C. 20505 (703) 482-1100, www.cia.gov; *The World Factbook.*

The Economist Intelligence Unit, 111 West 57th Street, New York, New York 10019 (800) 938-4685; *Latvia Country Report;* and *The World Market Atlas.*

Euromonitor International, Inc., 122 South Michigan Avenue, Suite 1200, Chicago, Illinois 60603 (800) 577-EURO; *The World Economic Factbook.*

Europa Publications Limited, 18 Bedford Square, London, WC1B 3JN, England; *The Europa World Year Book.*

International Monetary Fund, 700 Nineteenth Street, NW, Washington, D.C. 20431 (202) 623-7000; *Direction of Trade Statistics.*

Statistical Office of the United Nations, Publishing Service, New York, New York 10017 (800) 253-9646; *International Trade Statistics Yearbook;* and *Trends in Europe and North America: The Statistical Yearbook of the Economic Commission for Europe.*

United Nations Conference on Trade and Development (UNCTAD), New York, New York 10017 (800) 253-9646; *Handbook of International Trade and Development Statistics.*

The World Bank, 1818 H Street, NW, Washington, D.C. 20433 (202) 477-1234; *World Development Indicators.*

LATVIA - EXTERNAL DEBT

The World Bank, 1818 H Street, NW, Washington, D.C. 20433 (202) 477-1234; *World Development Indicators.*

LATVIA - EXTERNAL TRADE

Academic International Press, Box 1111, Gulf Breeze, Florida 32562; *Russia and Eurasia Facts and Figures Annual.*

Euromonitor International, Inc., 122 South Michigan Avenue, Suite 1200, Chicago, Illinois 60603 (800) 577-EURO; *World Marketing Data and Statistics.*

Food and Agriculture Organization of the United Nations (FAO), Via delle Terme di Caracalla, 00100, Rome, Italy (Telephone Number in U.S. (202) 653-2400); *Trade Yearbook.*

Statistical Office of the United Nations, Publishing Service, New York, New York 10017 (800) 253-9646; *Statistical Yearbook.*

The World Bank, 1818 H Street, NW, Washington, D.C. 20433 (202) 477-1234; *Statistical Handbook: States of the Former USSR.*

LATVIA - FABRIC PRODUCTION AND CONSUMPTION - See LATVIA - TEXTILE INDUSTRY

LATVIA - FERTILITY RATES

Central Intelligence Agency, Washington, D.C. 20505 (703) 482-1100, www.cia.gov; *The World Factbook.*

Statistical Office of the United Nations, Publishing Service, New York, New York 10017 (800) 253-9646; *Human Development Report;* and *Trends in Europe and North America: The Statistical Yearbook of the Economic Commission for Europe.*

The World Bank, 1818 H Street, NW, Washington, D.C. 20433 (202) 477-1234; *The World Bank Atlas;* and *Statistical Handbook: States of the Former USSR;* and *World Development Indicators.*

World Health Organization, Office of Publications, 20 Avenue Appia, CH-1211 Geneva 27, Switzerland (Telephone Number in U.S. (518) 436-9686); *World Health Statistics Annual.*

LATVIA - FERTILIZER

Food and Agriculture Organization of the United Nations (FAO), Via delle Terme di Caracalla, 00100, Rome, Italy (Telephone Number in U.S. (202) 653-2400); *Fertilizer Yearbook.*

Statistical Office of the United Nations, Publishing Service, New York, New York 10017 (800) 253-9646; *Industrial Commodity Statistics Yearbook;* and *Statistical Yearbook.*

LATVIA - FINANCE

Economist Intelligence Unit, 111 West 57th Street, New York, New York 10019 (800) 938-4685; *Latvia Country Report.*

Europa Publications Limited, 18 Bedford Square, London, WC1B 3JN, England; *The Europa World Year Book.*

St. Martin's Press, Inc., 175 Fifth Avenue, New York, New York 10010 (800) 221-7945; *The Statesman's Year-Book.*

The World Bank, 1818 H Street, NW, Washington, D.C. 20433 (202) 477-1234; *Statistical Handbook: States of the Former USSR.*

LATVIA - FISHERIES

Europa Publications Limited, 18 Bedford Square, London, WC1B 3JN, England; *The Europa World Year Book.*

Food and Agriculture Organization of the United Nations (FAO), Via delle Terme di Caracalla, 00100, Rome, Italy (Telephone Number in U.S. (202) 653-2400); *The State of Food and Agriculture;* and *Yearbook of Fishery Statistics.*

Statistical Office of the United Nations, Publishing Service, New York, New York 10017 (800) 253-9646; *Industrial Commodity Statistics Yearbook;* and *Statistical Yearbook.*

LATVIA - FOOD

Food and Agriculture Organization of the United Nations (FAO), Via delle Terme di Caracalla, 00100, Rome, Italy (Telephone Number in U.S. (202) 653-2400); *Production Yearbook; The State of Food and Agriculture;* and *Trade Yearbook.*

Statistical Office of the United Nations, Publishing Service, New York, New York 10017 (800) 253-9646; *Human Development Report;* and *Industrial Commodity Statistics Yearbook.*

LATVIA - FOOTWEAR PRODUCTION AND CONSUMPTION - See LATVIA - TEXTILE INDUSTRY

LATVIA - FOREIGN INVESTMENT

Business International Moscow, 23 Profsoyuznaya Ulitsa, 117859, Moscow (Telephone Number in U.S. (800) 938-4685); *The CIS Market Atlas.*

LATVIA - FOREIGN TRADE

Business International Moscow, 23 Profsoyuznaya Ulitsa, 117859, Moscow (Telephone Number in U.S. (800) 938-4685); *The CIS Market Atlas.*

Economist Intelligence Unit, 111 West 57th Street, New York, New York 10019 (800) 938-4685; *Latvia Country Report.*

Euromonitor International, Inc., 122 South Michigan Avenue, Suite 1200, Chicago, Illinois 60603 (800) 577-EURO; *The World Economic Factbook.*

Europa Publications Limited, 18 Bedford Square, London, WC1B 3JN, England; *The Europa World Year Book.*

Food and Agriculture Organization of the United Nations (FAO), Via delle Terme di Caracalla, 00100, Rome, Italy (Telephone Number in U.S. (202) 653-2400); *Trade Yearbook.*

International Monetary Fund, 700 Nineteenth Street, NW, Washington, D.C. 20431 (202) 623-7000; *Direction of Trade Statistics.*

St. Martin's Press, Inc., 175 Fifth Avenue, New York, New York 10010 (800) 221-7945; *The Statesman's Year-Book.*

Statistical Office of the United Nations, Publishing Service, New York, New York 10017 (800) 253-9646; *International Trade Statistics Yearbook;* and *Statistical Yearbook.*

The World Bank, 1818 H Street, NW, Washington, D.C. 20433 (202) 477-1234; *Statistical Handbook: States of the Former USSR;* and *World Development Indicators.*

LATVIA - FORESTRY AND FOREST PRODUCTS

Academic International Press, Box 1111, Gulf Breeze, Florida 32562; *Russia and Eurasia Facts and Figures Annual.*

Business International Moscow, 23 Profsoyuznaya Ulitsa, 117859, Moscow (Telephone Number in U.S. (800) 938-4685); *The CIS Market Atlas.*

Europa Publications Limited, 18 Bedford Square, London, WC1B 3JN, England; *The Europa World Year Book.*

Food and Agriculture Organization of the United Nations (FAO), Via delle Terme di Caracalla, 00100, Rome, Italy (Telephone Number in U.S. (202) 653-2400); *The State of Food and Agriculture;* and *Yearbook of Forest Products.*

St. Martin's Press, Inc., 175 Fifth Avenue, New York, New York 10010 (800) 221-7945; *The Statesman's Year-Book.*

Statistical Office of the United Nations, Publishing Service, New York, New York 10017 (800) 253-9646; *Industrial Commodity Statistics Yearbook; Trends in Europe and North America: The Statistical Yearbook of the Economic Commission for Europe;* and *Statistical Yearbook.*

United Nations Educational, Scientific and Cultural Organization (UNESCO), 7 Place de Fontenoy, F-75700 Paris, France (Telephone Number in U.S. (212) 963-5981); *Statistical Yearbook.*

LATVIA - GOATS - See LATVIA - LIVESTOCK AND POULTRY

LATVIA - GOVERNMENT

Academic International Press, Box 1111, Gulf Breeze, Florida 32562; *Russia and Eurasia Facts and Figures Annual.*

Central Intelligence Agency,

Washington, D.C. 20505 (703) 482-1100, www.cia.gov; *The World Factbook.*

Europa Publications Limited, 18 Bedford Square, London, WC1B 3JN, England; *The Europa World Year Book.*

St. Martin's Press, Inc., 175 Fifth Avenue, New York, New York 10010 (800) 221-7945; *The Statesman's Year-Book.*

Statistical Office of the United Nations, Publishing Service, New York, New York 10017 (800) 253-9646; *National Accounts Statistics;* and *Statistical Yearbook.*

The World Bank, 1818 H Street, NW, Washington, D.C. 20433 (202) 477-1234; *Statistical Handbook: States of the Former USSR.*

LATVIA - GROSS DOMESTIC PRODUCT

Academic International Press, Box 1111, Gulf Breeze, Florida 32562; *Russia and Eurasia Facts and Figures Annual.*

The Economist Intelligence Unit, 111 West 57th Street, New York, New York 10019 (800) 938-4685; *Latvia Country Report;* and *The World Market Atlas.*

Euromonitor International, Inc., 122 South Michigan Avenue, Suite 1200, Chicago, Illinois 60603 (800) 577-EURO; *The World Economic Factbook.*

Europa Publications Limited, 18 Bedford Square, London, WC1B 3JN, England; *The Europa World Year Book.*

Statistical Office of the United Nations, Publishing Service, New York, New York 10017 (800) 253-9646; *Human Development Report; National Accounts Statistics; Trends in Europe and North America: The Statistical Yearbook of the Economic Commission for Europe;* and *Statistical Yearbook.*

The World Bank, 1818 H Street, NW, Washington, D.C. 20433 (202) 477-1234; *Statistical Handbook: States of the Former USSR;* and *World Development Indicators.*

LATVIA - GROSS NATIONAL PRODUCT

St. Martin's Press, Inc., 175 Fifth Avenue, New York, New York 10010 (800) 221-7945; *The Statesman's Year-Book.*

The World Bank, 1818 H Street, NW, Washington, D.C. 20433 (202) 477-1234; *The World Bank Atlas;* and *World Development Indicators.*

LATVIA - HEALTH

Academic International Press, Box 1111, Gulf Breeze, Florida 32562; *Russia and Eurasia Facts and Figures Annual.*

Business International Moscow, 23 Profsoyuznaya Ulitsa, 117859, Moscow (Telephone Number in U.S. (800) 938-4685); *The CIS Market Atlas.*

Euromonitor International, Inc., 122 South Michigan Avenue, Suite 1200, Chicago, Illinois 60603 (800) 577-EURO; *World Marketing Data and Statistics.*

St. Martin's Press, Inc., 175 Fifth Avenue, New York, New York 10010 (800) 221-7945; *The Statesman's Year-Book.*

Statistical Office of the United Nations, Publishing Service, New York, New York 10017 (800) 253-9646; *Human Development Report; Trends in Europe and North America: The Statistical Yearbook of the Economic Commission for Europe;* and *Statistical Yearbook.*

United Nations Children's Fund (UNICEF), 3 United Nations Plaza, New York, New York 10017 (800) 253-9646; *State of the World's Children.*

World Health Organization, Office of Publications, 20 Avenue Appia, CH-1211 Geneva 27, Switzerland (Telephone Number in U.S. (518) 436-9686); *World Health Statistics Annual.*

LATVIA - HIGHWAYS

Academic International Press, Box 1111, Gulf Breeze, Florida 32562; *Russia and Eurasia Facts and Figures Annual.*

Business International Moscow, 23 Profsoyuznaya Ulitsa, 117859, Moscow (Telephone Number in U.S. (800) 938-4685); *The CIS Market Atlas.*

Central Intelligence Agency, Washington, D.C. 20505 (703) 482-1100, www.cia.gov; *The World Factbook.*

St. Martin's Press, Inc., 175 Fifth Avenue, New York, New York 10010 (800) 221-7945; *The Statesman's Year-Book.*

Statistical Office of the United Nations, Publishing Service, New York, New York 10017 (800) 253-9646; *Annual Bulletin of Transport Statistics for Europe;* and *Trends in Europe and North America: The Statistical Yearbook of the Economic Commission for Europe.*

LATVIA - HOUSING AND HOUSING UNITS

Business International Moscow, 23 Profsoyuznaya Ulitsa, 117859, Moscow (Telephone Number in U.S. (800) 938-4685); *The CIS Market Atlas.*

Euromonitor International, Inc., 122 South Michigan Avenue, Suite 1200, Chicago, Illinois 60603 (800) 577-EURO; *World Marketing Data and Statistics.*

Statistical Office of the United Nations, Publishing Service, New York, New York 10017 (800) 253-9646; *Trends in Europe and North America: The Statistical Yearbook of the Economic Commission for Europe.*

LATVIA - ILLITERATE POPULATION

Central Intelligence Agency, Washington, D.C. 20505 (703) 482-1100, www.cia.gov; *The World Factbook.*

The Economist Intelligence Unit, 111 West 57th Street, New York, New York 10019 (800) 938-4685; *The World Market Atlas.*

Euromonitor International, Inc., 122 South Michigan Avenue, Suite 1200, Chicago, Illinois 60603 (800) 577-EURO; *The World Economic Factbook.*

Statistical Office of the United Nations, Publishing Service, New York, New York 10017 (800) 253-9646; *Human Development Report.*

United Nations Educational, Scientific and Cultural Organization (UNESCO), 7 Place de Fontenoy, F-75700 Paris, France (Telephone Number in U.S. (212) 963-5981); *Statistical Yearbook.*

LATVIA - IMPORTS

Academic International Press, Box 1111, Gulf Breeze, Florida 32562; *Russia and Eurasia Facts and Figures Annual.*

Business International Moscow, 23 Profsoyuznaya Ulitsa, 117859, Moscow (Telephone Number in U.S. (800) 938-4685); *The CIS Market Atlas.*

Central Intelligence Agency, Washington, D.C. 20505 (703) 482-1100, www.cia.gov; *The World Factbook.*

The Economist Intelligence Unit, 111 West 57th Street, New York, New York 10019 (800) 938-4685; *Latvia Country Report;* and *The World Market Atlas.*

Euromonitor International, Inc., 122 South Michigan Avenue, Suite 1200, Chicago, Illinois 60603 (800) 577-EURO; *The World Economic Factbook.*

Europa Publications Limited, 18 Bedford Square, London, WC1B 3JN, England; *The Europa World Year Book.*

International Monetary Fund, 700 Nineteenth Street, NW, Washington, D.C. 20431 (202) 623-7000; *Direction of Trade Statistics.*

Statistical Office of the United Nations, Publishing Service, New York, New York 10017 (800) 253-9646; *International Trade Statistics Yearbook;* and *Trends in Europe*

and *North America: The Statistical Yearbook of the Economic Commission for Europe.*

United Nations Conference on Trade and Development (UNCTAD), New York, New York 10017 (800) 253-9646; *Handbook of International Trade and Development Statistics.*

The World Bank, 1818 H Street, NW, Washington, D.C. 20433 (202) 477-1234; *Statistical Handbook: States of the Former USSR;* and *World Development Indicators.*

LATVIA - INDUSTRY

Academic International Press, Box 1111, Gulf Breeze, Florida 32562; *Russia and Eurasia Facts and Figures Annual.*

Business International Moscow, 23 Profsoyuznaya Ulitsa, 117859, Moscow (Telephone Number in U.S. (800) 938-4685); *The CIS Market Atlas.*

Central Intelligence Agency, Washington, D.C. 20505 (703) 482-1100, www.cia.gov; *The World Factbook.*

Economist Intelligence Unit, 111 West 57th Street, New York, New York 10019 (800) 938-4685; *Latvia Country Report.*

Euromonitor International, Inc., 122 South Michigan Avenue, Suite 1200, Chicago, Illinois 60603 (800) 577-EURO; *The World Economic Factbook;* and *World Marketing Data and Statistics.*

Europa Publications Limited, 18 Bedford Square, London, WC1B 3JN, England; *The Europa World Year Book.*

International Labour Office, I.L.O. Publications, 1828 L Street, N.W., Suite 801, Washington, D.C. (301) 638-3152; *Yearbook of Labor Statistics.*

St. Martin's Press, Inc., 175 Fifth Avenue, New York, New York 10010 (800) 221-7945; *The Statesman's Year-Book.*

Statistical Office of the United Nations, Publishing Service, New York, New York 10017 (800) 253-9646; *Industrial Commodity Statistics Yearbook; Trends in Europe and North America: The Statistical Yearbook of the Economic Commission for Europe;* and *Statistical Yearbook.*

The World Bank, 1818 H Street, NW, Washington, D.C. 20433 (202) 477-1234; *Statistical Handbook: States of the Former USSR;* and *World Development Indicators.*

LATVIA - INFANT MORTALITY RATES - See LATVIA - MORTALITY

LATVIA - INTERNAL TRADE

Statistical Office of the United Nations, Publishing Service, New York, New York 10017 (800) 253-9646; *Statistical Yearbook.*

LATVIA - LABOR

Academic International Press, Box 1111, Gulf Breeze, Florida 32562; *Russia and Eurasia Facts and Figures Annual.*

Business International Moscow, 23 Profsoyuznaya Ulitsa, 117859, Moscow (Telephone Number in U.S. (800) 938-4685); *The CIS Market Atlas.*

Central Intelligence Agency, Washington, D.C. 20505 (703) 482-1100, www.cia.gov; *The World Factbook.*

Euromonitor International, Inc., 122 South Michigan Avenue, Suite 1200, Chicago, Illinois 60603 (800) 577-EURO; *World Marketing Data and Statistics.*

Europa Publications Limited, 18 Bedford Square, London, WC1B 3JN, England; *The Europa World Year Book.*

International Labour Office, I.L.O. Publications, 1828 L Street, N.W., Suite 801, Washington, D.C. (301) 638-3152; *Yearbook of Labor Statistics.*

St. Martin's Press, Inc., 175 Fifth Avenue, New York, New York 10010 (800) 221-7945; *The Statesman's Year-Book.*

Statistical Office of the United Nations, Publishing Service, New York, New York 10017 (800) 253-9646; *Human Development Report;* and *Statistical Yearbook.*

The World Bank, 1818 H Street, NW, Washington, D.C. 20433 (202) 477-1234; *The World Bank Atlas; Statistical Handbook: States of the Former USSR;* and *World Development Indicators.*

LATVIA - LAND USE

Central Intelligence Agency, Washington, D.C. 20505 (703) 482-1100, www.cia.gov; *The World Factbook.*

Food and Agriculture Organization of the United Nations (FAO), Via delle Terme di Caracalla, 00100, Rome, Italy (Telephone Number in U.S. (202) 653-2400); *Production Yearbook.*

LATVIA - LIBRARIES

Statistical Office of the United Nations, Publishing Service, New York, New York 10017 (800) 253-9646; *Trends in Europe and North America: The Statistical Yearbook of the Economic Commission for Europe.*

United Nations Educational, Scientific

and Cultural Organization (UNESCO), 7 Place de Fontenoy, F-75700 Paris, France (Telephone Number in U.S. (212) 963-5981); *Statistical Yearbook.*

LATVIA - LIFE EXPECTANCY

Academic International Press, Box 1111, Gulf Breeze, Florida 32562; *Russia and Eurasia Facts and Figures Annual.*

Business International Moscow, 23 Profsoyuznaya Ulitsa, 117859, Moscow (Telephone Number in U.S. (800) 938-4685); *The CIS Market Atlas.*

Central Intelligence Agency, Washington, D.C. 20505 (703) 482-1100, www.cia.gov; *The World Factbook.*

Euromonitor International, Inc., 122 South Michigan Avenue, Suite 1200, Chicago, Illinois 60603 (800) 577-EURO; *The World Economic Factbook.*

St. Martin's Press, Inc., 175 Fifth Avenue, New York, New York 10010 (800) 221-7945; *The Statesman's Year-Book.*

Statistical Office of the United Nations, Publishing Service, New York, New York 10017 (800) 253-9646; *Demographic Yearbook; Trends in Europe and North America: The Statistical Yearbook of the Economic Commission for Europe;* and *Human Development Report.*

The World Bank, 1818 H Street, NW, Washington, D.C. 20433 (202) 477-1234; *The World Bank Atlas;* and *World Development Indicators.*

World Health Organization, Office of Publications, 20 Avenue Appia, CH-1211 Geneva 27, Switzerland (Telephone Number in U.S. (518) 436-9686); *World Health Statistics Annual.*

LATVIA - LITERACY RATE

Euromonitor International, Inc., 122 South Michigan Avenue, Suite 1200, Chicago, Illinois 60603 (800) 577-EURO; *World Marketing Data and Statistics.*

LATVIA - LIVESTOCK AND POULTRY

Academic International Press, Box 1111, Gulf Breeze, Florida 32562; *Russia and Eurasia Facts and Figures Annual.*

Business International Moscow, 23 Profsoyuznaya Ulitsa, 117859, Moscow (Telephone Number in U.S. (800) 938-4685); *The CIS Market Atlas.*

Europa Publications Limited, 18 Bedford Square, London, WC1B 3JN, England; *The Europa World Year Book.*

Food and Agriculture Organization of

the United Nations (FAO), Via delle Terme di Caracalla, 00100, Rome, Italy (Telephone Number in U.S. (202) 653-2400); *Production Yearbook; The State of Food and Agriculture;* and *Trade Yearbook.*

St. Martin's Press, Inc., 175 Fifth Avenue, New York, New York 10010 (800) 221-7945; *The Statesman's Year-Book.*

Statistical Office of the United Nations, Publishing Service, New York, New York 10017 (800) 253-9646; *Industrial Commodity Statistics Yearbook;* and *Statistical Yearbook.*

LATVIA - MACHINERY

Statistical Office of the United Nations, Publishing Service, New York, New York 10017 (800) 253-9646; *Industrial Commodity Statistics Yearbook.*

LATVIA - MAIL - NUMBER OF PIECES SENT OR RECEIVED

Statistical Office of the United Nations, Publishing Service, New York, New York 10017 (800) 253-9646; *Statistical Yearbook.*

LATVIA - MANUFACTURING

Statistical Office of the United Nations, Publishing Service, New York, New York 10017 (800) 253-9646; *Industrial Commodity Statistics Yearbook;* and *Statistical Yearbook.*

The World Bank, 1818 H Street, NW, Washington, D.C. 20433 (202) 477-1234; *World Development Indicators.*

LATVIA - MARRIAGE RATES

Academic International Press, Box 1111, Gulf Breeze, Florida 32562; *Russia and Eurasia Facts and Figures Annual.*

Europa Publications Limited, 18 Bedford Square, London, WC1B 3JN, England; *The Europa World Year Book.*

Statistical Office of the United Nations, Publishing Service, New York, New York 10017 (800) 253-9646; *Demographic Yearbook; Trends in Europe and North America: The Statistical Yearbook of the Economic Commission for Europe;* and *Statistical Yearbook.*

LATVIA - MEAT PRODUCTION - See LATVIA - LIVESTOCK AND POULTRY

LATVIA - MERCHANT SHIPPING

Europa Publications Limited, 18 Bedford Square, London, WC1B 3JN, England; *The Europa World Year Book.*

St. Martin's Press, Inc., 175 Fifth Avenue, New York, New York 10010 (800)

221-7945; *The Statesman's Year-Book.*

Statistical Office of the United Nations, Publishing Service, New York, New York 10017 (800) 253-9646; *Annual Bulletin of Transport Statistics for Europe;* and *Statistical Yearbook.*

LATVIA - MILITARY

Academic International Press, Box 1111, Gulf Breeze, Florida 32562; *Russia and Eurasia Facts and Figures Annual.*

Central Intelligence Agency, Washington, D.C. 20505 (703) 482-1100, www.cia.gov; *The World Factbook.*

Euromonitor International, Inc., 122 South Michigan Avenue, Suite 1200, Chicago, Illinois 60603 (800) 577-EURO; *World Marketing Data and Statistics.*

The International Institute for Strategic Studies, 23 Tavistock Street, London WC2E 7NQ, England 44 171 3797676; *The Military Balance.*

St. Martin's Press, Inc., 175 Fifth Avenue, New York, New York 10010 (800) 221-7945; *The Statesman's Year-Book.*

Statistical Office of the United Nations, Publishing Service, New York, New York 10017 (800) 253-9646; *Human Development Report.*

LATVIA - MINING AND MINERAL PRODUCTS

Academic International Press, Box 1111, Gulf Breeze, Florida 32562; *Russia and Eurasia Facts and Figures Annual.*

Business International Moscow, 23 Profsoyuznaya Ulitsa, 117859, Moscow (Telephone Number in U.S. (800) 938-4685); *The CIS Market Atlas.*

Europa Publications Limited, 18 Bedford Square, London, WC1B 3JN, England; *The Europa World Year Book.*

Statistical Office of the United Nations, Publishing Service, New York, New York 10017 (800) 253-9646; *Energy Statistics Yearbook; Industrial Commodity Statistics Yearbook;* and *Statistical Yearbook.*

LATVIA - MONEY SUPPLY

Economist Intelligence Unit, 111 West 57th Street, New York, New York 10019 (800) 938-4685; *Latvia Country Report.*

Europa Publications Limited, 18 Bedford Square, London, WC1B 3JN, England; *The Europa World Year Book.*

LATVIA - MONUMENTS AND HISTORICAL SITES

United Nations Educational, Scientific and Cultural Organization (UNESCO), 7 Place de Fontenoy, F-75700 Paris, France (Telephone Number in U.S. (212) 963-5981); *Statistical Yearbook.*

LATVIA - MORTALITY

Academic International Press, Box 1111, Gulf Breeze, Florida 32562; *Russia and Eurasia Facts and Figures Annual.*

Business International Moscow, 23 Profsoyuznaya Ulitsa, 117859, Moscow (Telephone Number in U.S. (800) 938-4685); *The CIS Market Atlas.*

Central Intelligence Agency, Washington, D.C. 20505 (703) 482-1100, www.cia.gov; *The World Factbook.*

Euromonitor International, Inc., 122 South Michigan Avenue, Suite 1200, Chicago, Illinois 60603 (800) 577-EURO; *The World Economic Factbook.*

Europa Publications Limited, 18 Bedford Square, London, WC1B 3JN, England; *The Europa World Year Book.*

St. Martin's Press, Inc., 175 Fifth Avenue, New York, New York 10010 (800) 221-7945; *The Statesman's Year-Book.*

Statistical Office of the United Nations, Publishing Service, New York, New York 10017 (800) 253-9646; *Demographic Yearbook; Human Development Report; Trends in Europe and North America: The Statistical Yearbook of the Economic Commission for Europe;* and *Statistical Yearbook.*

United Nations Children's Fund (UNICEF), 3 United Nations Plaza, New York, New York 10017 (800) 253-9646; *State of the World's Children.*

The World Bank, 1818 H Street, NW, Washington, D.C. 20433 (202) 477-1234; *The World Bank Atlas;* and *World Development Indicators.*

World Health Organization, Office of Publications, 20 Avenue Appia, CH-1211 Geneva 27, Switzerland (Telephone Number in U.S. (518) 436-9686); *World Health Statistics Annual.*

LATVIA - MOTION PICTURES

Statistical Office of the United Nations, Publishing Service, New York, New York 10017 (800) 253-9646; *Statistical Yearbook.*

United Nations Educational, Scientific and Cultural Organization (UNESCO), 7 Place de Fontenoy, F-75700 Paris, France (Telephone Number in U.S. (212) 963-5981); *Statistical Yearbook.*

LATVIA - MOTOR VEHICLES

Business International Moscow, 23 Profsoyuznaya Ulitsa, 117859, Moscow (Telephone Number in U.S. (800) 938-4685); *The CIS Market Atlas.*

Europa Publications Limited, 18 Bedford Square, London, WC1B 3JN, England; *The Europa World Year Book.*

Statistical Office of the United Nations, Publishing Service, New York, New York 10017 (800) 253-9646; *Statistical Yearbook.*

LATVIA - MUSEUMS

United Nations Educational, Scientific and Cultural Organization (UNESCO), 7 Place de Fontenoy, F-75700 Paris, France (Telephone Number in U.S. (212) 963-5981); *Statistical Yearbook.*

LATVIA - NATIONAL ACCOUNTS

Europa Publications Limited, 18 Bedford Square, London, WC1B 3JN, England; *The Europa World Year Book.*

Statistical Office of the United Nations, Publishing Service, New York, New York 10017 (800) 253-9646; *National Accounts Statistics Yearbook;* and *Statistical Yearbook.*

The World Bank, 1818 H Street, NW, Washington, D.C. 20433 (202) 477-1234; *Statistical Handbook: States of the Former USSR.*

LATVIA - NATIONAL INCOME

Business International Moscow, 23 Profsoyuznaya Ulitsa, 117859, Moscow (Telephone Number in U.S. (800) 938-4685); *The CIS Market Atlas.*

Statistical Office of the United Nations, Publishing Service, New York, New York 10017 (800) 253-9646; *National Accounts Statistics;* and *Statistical Yearbook.*

LATVIA - NATIONAL PRODUCT

Statistical Office of the United Nations, Publishing Service, New York, New York 10017 (800) 253-9646; *Statistical Yearbook.*

LATVIA - PATENTS, TRADEMARKS AND SERVICE MARKS

Statistical Office of the United Nations, Publishing Service, New York, New York 10017 (800) 253-9646; *Statistical Yearbook.*

LATVIA - PERIODICALS

United Nations Educational, Scientific and Cultural Organization (UNESCO), 7 Place de Fontenoy, F-75700 Paris, France (Telephone Number in U.S. (212) 963-

5981); *Statistical Yearbook.*

LATVIA - PETROLEUM INDUSTRY

Food and Agriculture Organization of the United Nations (FAO), Via delle Terme di Caracalla, 00100, Rome, Italy (Telephone Number in U.S. (202) 653-2400); *The State of Food and Agriculture.*

Statistical Office of the United Nations, Publishing Service, New York, New York 10017 (800) 253-9646; *Energy Statistics Yearbook; Industrial Commodity Statistics Yearbook; Trends in Europe and North America: The Statistical Yearbook of the Economic Commission for Europe;* and *Statistical Yearbook.*

LATVIA - PIGS - See LATVIA - LIVESTOCK AND POULTRY

LATVIA - POPULATION

Academic International Press, Box 1111, Gulf Breeze, Florida 32562; *Russia and Eurasia Facts and Figures Annual.*

Business International Moscow, 23 Profsoyuznaya Ulitsa, 117859, Moscow (Telephone Number in U.S. (800) 938-4685); *The CIS Market Atlas.*

Central Intelligence Agency, Washington, D.C. 20505 (703) 482-1100, www.cia.gov; *The World Factbook.*

The Economist Intelligence Unit, 111 West 57th Street, New York, New York 10019 (800) 938-4685; *Latvia Country Report;* and *The World Market Atlas.*

Euromonitor International, Inc., 122 South Michigan Avenue, Suite 1200, Chicago, Illinois 60603 (800) 577-EURO; *The World Economic Factbook.*

Europa Publications Limited, 18 Bedford Square, London, WC1B 3JN, England; *The Europa World Year Book.*

Food and Agriculture Organization of the United Nations (FAO), Via delle Terme di Caracalla, 00100, Rome, Italy (Telephone Number in U.S. (202) 653-2400); *Production Yearbook.*

International Labour Office, I.L.O. Publications, 1828 L Street, N.W., Suite 801, Washington, D.C. (301) 638-3152; *Yearbook of Labor Statistics.*

St. Martin's Press, Inc., 175 Fifth Avenue, New York, New York 10010 (800) 221-7945; *The Statesman's Year-Book.*

Statistical Office of the United Nations, Publishing Service, New York, New York 10017 (800) 253-9646; *Demographics Yearbook; Human Development Report; Trends in Europe and North America: The*

Statistical Yearbook of the Economic Commission for Europe; and *Statistical Yearbook.*

United Nations Educational, Scientific and Cultural Organization (UNESCO), 7 Place de Fontenoy, F-75700 Paris, France (Telephone Number in U.S. (212) 963-5981); *Statistical Yearbook.*

The World Bank, 1818 H Street, NW, Washington, D.C. 20433 (202) 477-1234; *The World Bank Atlas; Statistical Handbook: States of the Former USSR;* and *World Development Indicators.*

World Health Organization, Office of Publications, 20 Avenue Appia, CH-1211 Geneva 27, Switzerland (Telephone Number in U.S. (518) 436-9686); *World Health Statistics Annual.*

LATVIA - POST OFFICES

Statistical Office of the United Nations, Publishing Service, New York, New York 10017 (800) 253-9646; *Trends in Europe and North America: The Statistical Yearbook of the Economic Commission for Europe.*

LATVIA - POULTRY - See LATVIA - LIVESTOCK AND POULTRY

LATVIA - PRICES

Food and Agriculture Organization of the United Nations (FAO), Via delle Terme di Caracalla, 00100, Rome, Italy (Telephone Number in U.S. (202) 653-2400); *Production Yearbook.*

International Labour Office, I.L.O. Publications, 1828 L Street, N.W., Suite 801, Washington, D.C. (301) 638-3152; *Yearbook of Labor Statistics.*

The World Bank, 1818 H Street, NW, Washington, D.C. 20433 (202) 477-1234; *Statistical Handbook: States of the Former USSR.*

LATVIA - PRODUCTION

The World Bank, 1818 H Street, NW, Washington, D.C. 20433 (202) 477-1234; *Statistical Handbook: States of the Former USSR.*

LATVIA - PUBLIC FINANCE - See LATVIA - FINANCE

LATVIA - RADIO RECEIVER PRODUCTION

St. Martin's Press, Inc., 175 Fifth Avenue, New York, New York 10010 (800) 221-7945; *The Statesman's Year-Book.*

Statistical Office of the United Nations, Publishing Service, New York, New York 10017 (800) 253-9646; *Statistical Yearbook.*

LATVIA - RAILWAYS

Academic International Press, Box 1111, Gulf Breeze, Florida 32562; *Russia and Eurasia Facts and Figures Annual.*

Business International Moscow, 23 Profsoyuznaya Ulitsa, 117859, Moscow (Telephone Number in U.S. (800) 938-4685); *The CIS Market Atlas.*

Europa Publications Limited, 18 Bedford Square, London, WC1B 3JN, England; *The Europa World Year Book.*

St. Martin's Press, Inc., 175 Fifth Avenue, New York, New York 10010 (800) 221-7945; *The Statesman's Year-Book.*

Statistical Office of the United Nations, Publishing Service, New York, New York 10017 (800) 253-9646; *Annual Bulletin of Transport Statistics for Europe; Trends in Europe and North America: The Statistical Yearbook of the Economic Commission for Europe;* and *Statistical Yearbook.*

LATVIA - RELIGION

Academic International Press, Box 1111, Gulf Breeze, Florida 32562; *Russia and Eurasia Facts and Figures Annual.*

Central Intelligence Agency, Washington, D.C. 20505 (703) 482-1100, www.cia.gov; *The World Factbook.*

St. Martin's Press, Inc., 175 Fifth Avenue, New York, New York 10010 (800) 221-7945; *The Statesman's Year-Book.*

LATVIA - RENT PRICES

International Labour Office, I.L.O. Publications, 1828 L Street, N.W., Suite 801, Washington, D.C. (301) 638-3152; *Yearbook of Labor Statistics.*

LATVIA - RETAIL TRADE

Business International Moscow, 23 Profsoyuznaya Ulitsa, 117859, Moscow (Telephone Number in U.S. (800) 938-4685); *The CIS Market Atlas.*

Euromonitor International, Inc., 122 South Michigan Avenue, Suite 1200, Chicago, Illinois 60603 (800) 577-EURO; *World Marketing Data and Statistics.*

Statistical Office of the United Nations, Publishing Service, New York, New York 10017 (800) 253-9646; *Statistical Yearbook.*

LATVIA - ROADS - See LATVIA - HIGHWAYS

LATVIA - ROUNDWOOD PRODUCTION AND CONSUMPTION - See LATVIA - FORESTRY AND FOREST PRODUCTS

LATVIA - RUBBER PRODUCTION AND

CONSUMPTION

Statistical Office of the United Nations, Publishing Service, New York, New York 10017 (800) 253-9646; *Statistical Yearbook.*

LATVIA - SCIENTISTS, TECHNICIANS AND ENGINEERS

Statistical Office of the United Nations, Publishing Service, New York, New York 10017 (800) 253-9646; *Statistical Yearbook.*

LATVIA - SHEEP - See LATVIA - LIVESTOCK AND POULTRY

LATVIA - SOCIAL SECURITY

St. Martin's Press, Inc., 175 Fifth Avenue, New York, New York 10010 (800) 221-7945; *The Statesman's Year-Book.*

Statistical Office of the United Nations, Publishing Service, New York, New York 10017 (800) 253-9646; *National Accounts Statistics.*

LATVIA - STEEL PRODUCTION AND CONSUMPTION - See LATVIA - MINING AND MINERAL PRODUCTS

LATVIA - TAXATION

Europa Publications Limited, 18 Bedford Square, London, WC1B 3JN, England; *The Europa World Year Book.*

LATVIA - TELEPHONES IN USE

Academic International Press, Box 1111, Gulf Breeze, Florida 32562; *Russia and Eurasia Facts and Figures Annual.*

Central Intelligence Agency, Washington, D.C. 20505 (703) 482-1100, www.cia.gov; *The World Factbook.*

Europa Publications Limited, 18 Bedford Square, London, WC1B 3JN, England; *The Europa World Year Book.*

St. Martin's Press, Inc., 175 Fifth Avenue, New York, New York 10010 (800) 221-7945; *The Statesman's Year-Book.*

Statistical Office of the United Nations, Publishing Service, New York, New York 10017 (800) 253-9646; *Statistical Yearbook;* and *Trends in Europe and North America: The Statistical Yearbook of the Economic Commission for Europe.*

LATVIA - TEXTILE INDUSTRY

Business International Moscow, 23 Profsoyuznaya Ulitsa, 117859, Moscow (Telephone Number in U.S. (800) 938-4685); *The CIS Market Atlas.*

Statistical Office of the United Nations, Publishing Service, New York, New York

10017 (800) 253-9646; *Industrial Commodity Statistics Yearbook;* and *Statistical Yearbook.*

LATVIA - THEATRE

United Nations Educational, Scientific and Cultural Organization (UNESCO), 7 Place de Fontenoy, F-75700 Paris, France (Telephone Number in U.S. (212) 963-5981); *Statistical Yearbook.*

LATVIA - TIRE (MOTOR VEHICLE) PRODUCTION

Statistical Office of the United Nations, Publishing Service, New York, New York 10017 (800) 253-9646; *Statistical Yearbook.*

LATVIA - TOBACCO PRODUCTION

Statistical Office of the United Nations, Publishing Service, New York, New York 10017 (800) 253-9646; *Statistical Yearbook.*

LATVIA - TOURISM

Business International Moscow, 23 Profsoyuznaya Ulitsa, 117859, Moscow (Telephone Number in U.S. (800) 938-4685); *The CIS Market Atlas.*

Euromonitor International, Inc., 122 South Michigan Avenue, Suite 1200, Chicago, Illinois 60603 (800) 577-EURO; *The World Economic Factbook;* and *World Marketing Data and Statistics.*

Statistical Office of the United Nations, Publishing Service, New York, New York 10017 (800) 253-9646; *Statistical Yearbook;* and *Trends in Europe and North America: The Statistical Yearbook of the Economic Commission for Europe.*

LATVIA - TRADEMARKS AND SERVICE MARKS - See LATVIA - PATENTS, TRADEMARKS AND SERVICE MARKS

LATVIA - TRANSPORTATION AND COMMUNICATIONS

Academic International Press, Box 1111, Gulf Breeze, Florida 32562; *Russia and Eurasia Facts and Figures Annual.*

Business International Moscow, 23 Profsoyuznaya Ulitsa, 117859, Moscow (Telephone Number in U.S. (800) 938-4685); *The CIS Market Atlas.*

Central Intelligence Agency, Washington, D.C. 20505 (703) 482-1100, www.cia.gov; *The World Factbook.*

Euromonitor International, Inc., 122 South Michigan Avenue, Suite 1200, Chicago, Illinois 60603 (800) 577-EURO; *World Marketing Data and Statistics.*

Europa Publications Limited, 18

Bedford Square, London, WC1B 3JN, England; *The Europa World Year Book.*

St. Martin's Press, Inc., 175 Fifth Avenue, New York, New York 10010 (800) 221-7945; *The Statesman's Year-Book.*

Statistical Office of the United Nations, Publishing Service, New York, New York 10017 (800) 253-9646; *Annual Bulletin of Transport Statistics for Europe; Trends in Europe and North America: The Statistical Yearbook of the Economic Commission for Europe;* and *Human Development Report.*

LATVIA - UNEMPLOYMENT

Central Intelligence Agency, Washington, D.C. 20505 (703) 482-1100, www.cia.gov; *The World Factbook.*

International Labour Office, I.L.O. Publications, 1828 L Street, N.W., Suite 801, Washington, D.C. (301) 638-3152; *Yearbook of Labor Statistics.*

St. Martin's Press, Inc., 175 Fifth Avenue, New York, New York 10010 (800) 221-7945; *The Statesman's Year-Book.*

Statistical Office of the United Nations, Publishing Service, New York, New York 10017 (800) 253-9646; *Statistical Yearbook;* and *Trends in Europe and North America: The Statistical Yearbook of the Economic Commission for Europe.*

LATVIA - VITAL STATISTICS

St. Martin's Press, Inc., 175 Fifth Avenue, New York, New York 10010 (800) 221-7945; *The Statesman's Year-Book.*

Statistical Office of the United Nations, Publishing Service, New York, New York 10017 (800) 253-9646; *Statistical Yearbook.*

World Health Organization, Office of Publications, 20 Avenue Appia, CH-1211 Geneva 27, Switzerland (Telephone Number in U.S. (518) 436-9686); *World Health Statistics Annual.*

LATVIA - WAGES

Business International Moscow, 23 Profsoyuznaya Ulitsa, 117859, Moscow (Telephone Number in U.S. (800) 938-4685); *The CIS Market Atlas.*

International Labour Office, I.L.O. Publications, 1828 L Street, N.W., Suite 801, Washington, D.C. (301) 638-3152; *Yearbook of Labor Statistics.*

Statistical Office of the United Nations, Publishing Service, New York, New York 10017 (800) 253-9646; *Statistical Yearbook.*

The World Bank, 1818 H Street, NW, Washington, D.C. 20433 (202) 477-1234;

Statistical Handbook: States of the Former USSR.

LATVIA - WELFARE

Academic International Press, Box 1111, Gulf Breeze, Florida 32562; *Russia and Eurasia Facts and Figures Annual.*

LATVIA - WHOLESALE PRICES

Academic International Press, Box 1111, Gulf Breeze, Florida 32562; *Russia and Eurasia Facts and Figures Annual.*

Statistical Office of the United Nations, Publishing Service, New York, New York 10017 (800) 253-9646; *Statistical Yearbook.*

LATVIA - WHOLESALE TRADE

Statistical Office of the United Nations, Publishing Service, New York, New York 10017 (800) 253-9646; *Statistical Yearbook.*

LATVIA - WOOL PRODUCTION AND CONSUMPTION - See LATVIA - TEXTILE INDUSTRY

LAUNDRY - CLEANING AND GARMENT SERVICES - EARNINGS

U.S. Department of Commerce, Bureau of the Census, Washington, D.C. 20233 (301) 457-4100, www.census.gov; *Economic Census;* and *Census of Service Industries.*

U.S. Department of Labor, Bureau of Labor Statistics, Two Massachusetts Avenue, NE, Washington, D.C. 20212 (202) 691-5200, www.stats.bls.gov; *Employment and Earnings;* and Internet site: http://stats.bls.gov/ ceshome.htm.

LAUNDRY - CLEANING AND GARMENT SERVICES - EMPLOYEES

U.S. Department of Commerce, Bureau of the Census, Washington, D.C. 20233 (301) 457-4100, www.census.gov; *Economic Census;* and *Census of Service Industries.*

U.S. Department of Labor, Bureau of Labor Statistics, Two Massachusetts Avenue, NE, Washington, D.C. 20212 (202) 691-5200, www.stats.bls.gov; *Employment and Earnings;* and Internet site: http://www.stats.bls/ ceshome.htm.

LAUNDRY - CLEANING AND GARMENT SERVICES - ESTABLISHMENTS

U.S. Department of Commerce, Bureau of the Census, Washington, D.C. 20233 (301) 457-4100, www.census.gov; *Census of Service Industries;* and *Economic Census.*

LAUNDRY - CLEANING AND GARMENT

SERVICES - PRODUCTIVITY

U.S. Department of Labor, Bureau of Labor Statistics, Two Massachusetts Avenue, NE, Washington, D.C. 20212 (202) 691-5200, www.stats.bls.gov; *Productivity Measures for Selected Industries and Government Services;* and Internet site http://stats.bls.gov/iprhome.htm.

LAUNDRY - CLEANING AND GARMENT SERVICES - RECEIPTS

U.S. Department of Commerce, Bureau of the Census, Washington, D.C. 20233 (301) 457-4100, www.census.gov; *Current Business Reports; Service Annual Survey; Economic Census; Census of Service Industries;* and unpublished data.

LAW - DEGREES CONFERRED

U.S. Department of Education, National Center for Education Statistics, 555 New Jersey Avenue, NW, Washington, D.C. 20208-5574 (202) 219-1828, http://nces,ed.gov; *Digest of Education Statistics.*

LAW ENFORCEMENT - See also COURTS, CRIME and CORRECTIONAL INSTITUTIONS

LAW ENFORCEMENT - ARRESTS

U.S. Department of Justice, Federal Bureau of Investigation, 935 Pennsylvania Avenue, NW, Washington, D.C. 20535 (202) 324-3691, www.fbi.gov; *Crime in the United States.*

U.S. Department of Justice, National Institute of Justice, 633 Indiana Avenue, NW, Washington, D.C. 20531 (202) 307-0781, www.ojp.usdoj.gov/nij; *Drug Use Forecasting.*

LAW ENFORCEMENT - DRUG ENFORCEMENT

U.S. Department of Justice, Drug Enforcement Administration, 600-700 Army Navy Drive, Arlington, Virginia 22202 (202) 307-1000, www.usdoj.gov/dea; *Annual Report*; and unpublished data from Federal-wide Drug Seizure System.

U.S. Department of Justice, Federal Bureau of Investigation, 935 Pennsylvania Avenue, NW, Washington, D.C. 20535 (202) 324-3691, www.fbi.gov; *Crime in the United States.*

LAW ENFORCEMENT - EMPLOYEES

U.S. Department of Commerce, Bureau of the Census, Washington, D.C. 20233 (301) 457-4100, www.census.gov; Internet site: http://www.census.gov/pub/govs/www/apes.html.

LAW ENFORCEMENT - EXPENDITURES

U.S. Department of Commerce, Bureau of the Census, Washington, D.C. 20233 (301) 457-4100, www.census.gov; *Government Finances;* and Internet sites http://www.census.gov/pub/govs/www/index.htm; http://www.census.gov/ftp/pub/govs/www/state.html; http://www.census.gov/govs/www/st97.html; and http://www.census.gov/govs/www/estimate.html.

LAW ENFORCEMENT - HAND GUN CHECKS

U.S. Department of Justice, Bureau of Justice Statistics, 810 Seventh Street, NW, 2nd Floor, Washington, D.C. 20531 (800) 732-3277, www.ojp.usdoj.gov/bjs; *Presale Handgun Checks.*

LAW ENFORCEMENT - POLICE OFFICERS

U.S. Department of Commerce, Bureau of the Census, Washington, D.C. 20233 (301) 457-4100, www.census.gov; Internet site: http://www.census.gov/pub/pub/govs/www/apes.htm.

U.S. Department of Justice, Bureau of Justice Statistics, 810 Seventh Street, NW, 2nd Floor, Washington, D.C. 20531 (800) 732-3277, www.ojp.usdoj.gov/bjs; *Federal Law Enforcement Officers; Police Use of Force, National Collection of Data*; and *Census of State and Local Law Enforcement Agencies.*

U.S. Department of Justice, Federal Bureau of Investigation, 935 Pennsylvania Avenue, NW, Washington, D.C. 20535 (202) 324-3691, www.fbi.gov; *Law Enforcement Officers Killed and Assaulted.*

U.S. Department of Labor, Bureau of Labor Statistics, Two Massachusetts Avenue, NE, Washington, D.C. 20212 (202) 691-5200, www.stats.bls.gov; *Employment and Earnings;* and unpublished data.

LAW ENFORCEMENT - WIRETAPS

Administrative Office of the United States Courts, Thurgood Marshall Federal Judiciary Building, l Columbus Circle, NE, Washington, D.C. 20544 (202) 502-1455, www.uscourts.gov; *Report on Applications for Orders Authorizing or Approving the Interception of Wire, Oral or Electronic Communications.*

LAW ENFORCEMENT - WORKPLACE VIOLENCE

U.S. Department of Justice, Bureau of Justice Statistics, 810 Seventh Street, NW, 2nd Floor, Washington, D.C. 20531 (800) 732-3277, www.ojp.usdoj.gov/bjs; *Workplace Violence.*

LAWN CARE

The National Gardening Association, 180 Flynn Avenue, Burlington, Vermont 05401 (802) 863-1308; *National Gardening Survey.*

LAWYERS - See also LEGAL SERVICES

LAWYERS - EMPLOYMENT

U.S. Department of Labor, Bureau of Labor Statistics, Two Massachusetts Avenue, NE, Washington, D.C. 20212 (202) 691-5200, www.stats.bls.gov; *Employment and Earnings;* and unpublished data.

LEAD

U.S. Department of the Interior, Geological Survey, Office of Minerals Information, 12201 Sunrise Valley Drive, Reston, Virginia 22092 (703) 648-4000, www.minerals.usgs.gov; *Mineral Commodity Summaries.*

LEAD - AIR QUALITY

Environmental Protection Agency, 1200 Pennsylvania Avenue, NW, Washington, D.C. 20460 (888) 372-8255, www.epa.gov; *National Air Pollutant Emission Trends;* and *National Air Quality and Emissions Trends Report.*

LEAD - CONSUMPTION

U.S. Department of the Interior, Geological Survey, Office of Minerals Information, 12201 Sunrise Valley Drive, Reston, Virginia 22092 (703) 648-4000, www.minerals.usgs.gov; *Mineral Commodity Summaries.*

LEAD - EMPLOYMENT

U.S. Department of the Interior, Geological Survey, Office of Minerals Information, 12201 Sunrise Valley Drive, Reston, Virginia 22092 (703) 648-4000, www.minerals.usgs.gov; *Mineral Commodity Summaries.*

LEAD - FOREIGN TRADE

U.S. Department of the Interior, Geological Survey, Office of Minerals Information, 12201 Sunrise Valley Drive, Reston, Virginia 22092 (703) 648-4000, www.minerals.usgs.gov; *Mineral Commodity Summaries.*

LEAD - PRICES

U.S. Department of the Interior, Geological Survey, Office of Minerals Information, 12201 Sunrise Valley Drive, Reston, Virginia 22092 (703) 648-4000, www.minerals.usgs.gov; *Mineral Commodity Summaries;* and *Mineral Yearbook.*

LEAD - PRODUCTION AND VALUE

U.S. Department of the Interior, Geological Survey, Office of Minerals Information, 12201 Sunrise Valley Drive, Reston, Virginia 22092 (703) 648-4000, www.minerals.usgs.gov; *Annual Reports;* and *Mineral Commodity Summaries.*

LEAD - WATER QUALITY

U.S. Department of the Interior, Geological Survey, National Center, 12201 Sunrise Valley Drive, Reston, Virginia 22092 (703) 648-4000, www.usgs.gov; *Water-Data Report.*

LEAD - WORLD PRODUCTION

U.S. Department of the Interior, Geological Survey, Office of Minerals Information, 12201 Sunrise Valley Drive, Reston, Virginia 22092 (703) 648-4000, www.minerals.usgs.gov; *Annual Reports;* and *Mineral Commodity Summaries.*

LEATHER AND LEATHER PRODUCTS - MANUFACTURING - See also HIDES AND SKINS, and FOOTWEAR

LEATHER AND LEATHER PRODUCTS - MANUFACTURING - CAPITAL

U.S. Department of Commerce, Bureau of the Census, Washington, D.C. 20233 (301) 457-4100, www.census.gov; *Census of Manufactures;* and *Annual Survey of Manufactures.*

LEATHER AND LEATHER PRODUCTS - MANUFACTURING - EARNINGS

U.S. Department of Commerce, Bureau of the Census, Washington, D.C. 20233 (301) 457-4100, www.census.gov; *Census of Manufacturers; County Business Patterns;* and *Annual Survey of Manufactures.*

U.S. Department of Labor, Bureau of Labor Statistics, Two Massachusetts Avenue, NE, Washington, D.C. 20212 (202) 691-5200, www.stats.bls.gov; *Employment and Earnings;* and Internet site: http://stats.bls.gov/ ceshome.htm.

LEATHER AND LEATHER PRODUCTS - MANUFACTURING - EMPLOYEES

U.S. Department of Commerce, Bureau of the Census, Washington, D.C. 20233 (301) 457-4100, www.census.gov; *Census of Manufactures; County Business Patterns; Annual Survey of Manufactures;* and *1997 Economic Census, Core Business Statistics Series.*

U.S. Department of Labor, Bureau of Labor Statistics, Two Massachusetts Avenue, NE, Washington, D.C. 20212 (202) 691-5200, www.stats.bls.gov; *Employment and Earnings, Monthly Labor Review;* and Internet site: http://stats.bls.gov/ ceshome.htm.

LEATHER AND LEATHER PRODUCTS - MANUFACTURING - ENERGY CONSUMPTION

U.S. Department of Energy, Energy Information Administration, 1000 Independence Avenue, SW, Washington, D.C. 20585 (202) 586-8800, www.eia.doc.gov; *Manufacturing Energy Consumption.*

LEATHER AND LEATHER PRODUCTS - MANUFACTURING - ESTABLISHMENTS

U.S. Department of Commerce, Bureau of the Census, Washington, D.C. 20233 (301) 457-4100, www.census.gov; *County Business Patterns;* and *1997 Economic Census, Core Business Statistics Series.*

LEATHER AND LEATHER PRODUCTS - MANUFACTURING - FAILURES

The Dun and Bradstreet Corporation, One Diamond Hill Road, Murray Hill, New Jersey 07974 (908) 665-5000; *Business Failure Record.*

LEATHER AND LEATHER PRODUCTS - MANUFACTURING - FOREIGN TRADE

U.S. Department of Commerce, Bureau of the Census, Washington, D.C. 20233 (301) 457-4100, www.census.gov; *U.S. International Trade in Goods and Services.*

LEATHER AND LEATHER PRODUCTS - MANUFACTURING - GROSS DOMESTIC PRODUCT

U.S. Department of Commerce, Bureau of Economic Analysis, Fourteenth Street between Constitution Avenue and E Street, NW, Washington, D.C. 20230 (202) 606-9900, www.bea.doc.gov; *The National Income and Product Accounts of the United States;* and *Survey of Current Business.*

LEATHER AND LEATHER PRODUCTS - MANUFACTURING - OCCUPATIONAL SAFETY

U.S. Department of Labor, Bureau of Labor Statistics, Two Massachusetts Avenue, NE, Washington, D.C. 20212 (202) 691-5200, www.stats.bls.gov; *Occupational Injuries and Illnesses in the United States by Industry.*

LEATHER AND LEATHER PRODUCTS - MANUFACTURING - PRODUCTIVITY

Board of Governors of the Federal Reserve System, Twentieth Street and Constitution Avenue, NW, Washington, D.C. 20551 (202) 452-3000, www.bog.frb.fed.us; *Federal Reserve Bulletin;* and *Industrial Production and Capacity Utilization.*

LEATHER AND LEATHER PRODUCTS - MANUFACTURING - SHIPMENTS

U.S. Department of Commerce, Bureau of the Census, Washington, D.C. 20233 (301) 457-4100, www.census.gov; *Annual Survey of Manufactures;* and *Census of Manufactures.*

LEATHER AND LEATHER PRODUCTS - MANUFACTURING - TOXIC CHEMICAL RELEASES

Environmental Protection Agency, 1200 Pennsylvania Avenue, NW, Washington, D.C. 20460 (888) 372-8255, www.epa.gov; *Toxics Release Inventory.*

LEATHER AND LEATHER PRODUCTS - MANUFACTURING - VALUE ADDED

U.S. Department of Commerce, Bureau of the Census, Washington, D.C. 20233 (301) 457-4100, www.census.gov; *Census of Manufactures;* and *Annual Survey of Manufactures.*

Lebanon - National Statistical Office

Direction Central de la Statistique, Bir Hasan, Beirut, Lebanon.

Lebanon - Primary Statistics Sources

Direction Centrale de la Statistique, Ministere du Plan, Bir Hassan, Beirut, Lebanon; *Bulletin statistique mensuel* (Monthly Statistical Bulletin).

LEBANON - AGRICULTURE

Economic Commission for Western Asia, Post Office Box 27, Baghdad, Iraq; *Statistical Abstract of Western Asia.*

Economist Intelligence Unit, 111 West 57th Street, New York, New York 10019 (800) 938-4685; *Lebanon Country Report.*

Euromonitor International, Inc., 122 South Michigan Avenue, Suite 1200, Chicago, Illinois 60603 (800) 577-EURO; *International Marketing Data and Statistics;* and *World Marketing Data and Statistics.*

Europa Publications Limited, 18 Bedford Square, London, WC1B 3JN, England; *The Europa World Year Book.*

Food and Agricultural Organization of the United Nations (FAO), Via delle Terme di Caracalla, 00100 Rome, Italy (Telephone

Number in U.S. (202) 653-2400); *Production Yearbook; The State of Food and Agriculture;* and *Trade Yearbook.*

M.E. Sharpe, 80 Business Park Drive, Armonk, New York 10504 (800) 541-6563; *The Illustrated Book of World Rankings.*

St. Martin's Press, Inc., 175 Fifth Avenue, New York, New York 10010 (800) 221-7945; *The Statesman's Year-Book.*

Statistical Office of the United Nations, Publishing Service, New York, New York 10017 (800) 253-9646; *Statistical Yearbook.*

United Nations Conference on Trade and Development, Central Statistical Service, Palais des Nations, Geneva, Switzerland (Telephone in U.S. (800) 253-9646); *UNCTAD Commodity Yearbook.*

LEBANON - AIRLINE SERVICE

Economic Commission for Western Asia, Post Office Box 27, Baghdad, Iraq; *Statistical Abstract of Western Asia.*

Europa Publications Limited, 18 Bedford Square, London, WC1B 3JN, England; *The Europa World Year Book.*

International Civil Aviation Organization, 999 University Street, Montreal, Quebec, Canada H3C 5H7 (514) 954-8219; *Civil Aviation Statistics of the World.*

M.E. Sharpe, 80 Business Park Drive, Armonk, New York 10504 (800) 541-6563; *The Illustrated Book of World Rankings.*

St. Martin's Press, Inc., 175 Fifth Avenue, New York, New York 10010 (800) 221-7945; *The Statesman's Year-Book.*

Statistical Office of the United Nations, Publishing Service, New York, New York 10017 (800) 253-9646; *Statistical Yearbook.*

LEBANON - AIRPORTS

Central Intelligence Agency, Washington, D.C. 20505 (703) 482-1100, www.cia.gov; *The World Factbook.*

LEBANON - ALMOND PRODUCTION - See LEBANON - CROPS

LEBANON - ALUMINUM PRODUCTION AND CONSUMPTION - See LEBANON - MINING AND MINERAL PRODUCTS

LEBANON - ANIMAL HEALTH

Food and Agricultural Organization of the United Nations (FAO), Via delle Terme di Caracalla, 00100 Rome, Italy (Telephone Number in U.S. (202) 653-2400); *Animal Health Yearbook.*

LEBANON - AREA AND DENSITY OF POPULATION

Central Intelligence Agency, Washington, D.C. 20505 (703) 482-1100, www.cia.gov; *The World Factbook.*

Economic Commission for Western Asia, Post Office Box 27, Baghdad, Iraq; *Statistical Abstract of Western Asia.*

Euromonitor International, Inc., 122 South Michigan Avenue, Suite 1200, Chicago, Illinois 60603 (800) 577-EURO; *International Marketing Data and Statistics;* and *The World Economic Factbook.*

Europa Publications Limited, 18 Bedford Square, London, WC1B 3JN, England; *The Europa World Year Book.*

Food and Agricultural Organization of the United Nations (FAO), Via delle Terme di Caracalla, 00100 Rome, Italy (Telephone Number in U.S. (202) 653-2400); *The State of Food and Agriculture.*

M.E. Sharpe, 80 Business Park Drive, Armonk, New York 10504 (800) 541-6563; *The Illustrated Book of World Rankings.*

St. Martin's Press, Inc., 175 Fifth Avenue, New York, New York 10010 (800) 221-7945; *The Statesman's Year-Book.*

Statistical Office of the United Nations, Publishing Service, New York, New York 10017 (800) 253-9646; *Statistical Yearbook.*

United Nations Educational, Scientific and Cultural Organization (UNESCO), 7 Place de Fontenoy, F-75700 Paris, France (Telephone Number in U.S. (212) 963-5981); *Statistical Yearbook.*

LEBANON - ARMS EXPORTS AND IMPORTS - See LEBANON - MILITARY

LEBANON - BALANCE OF PAYMENTS

Economic Commission for Western Asia, Post Office Box 27, Baghdad, Iraq; *Statistical Abstract of Western Asia.*

The Economist Intelligence Unit, 111 West 57th Street, New York, New York 10019 (800) 938-4685; *The World Market Atlas.*

International Monetary Fund, 700 Nineteenth Street, NW, Washington, D.C. 20431 (202) 623-7000; *Balance of Payments Yearbook.*

LEBANON - BALANCE OF TRADE

Economic Commission for Western Asia, Post Office Box 27, Baghdad, Iraq; *Statistical Abstract of Western Asia.*

LEBANON - BANKING

Economic Commission for Western Asia, Post Office Box 27, Baghdad, Iraq; *Statistical Abstract of Western Asia.*

Euromonitor International, Inc., 122 South Michigan Avenue, Suite 1200, Chicago, Illinois 60603 (800) 577-EURO; *World Marketing Data and Statistics.*

Europa Publications Limited, 18 Bedford Square, London, WC1B 3JN, England; *The Europa World Year Book.*

International Monetary Fund, 700 Nineteenth Street, NW, Washington, D.C. 20431 (202) 623-7000; *International Financial Statistics.*

M.E. Sharpe, 80 Business Park Drive, Armonk, New York 10504 (800) 541-6563; *The Illustrated Book of World Rankings.*

St. Martin's Press, Inc., 175 Fifth Avenue, New York, New York 10010 (800) 221-7945; *The Statesman's Year-Book.*

LEBANON - BARLEY PRODUCTION - See LEBANON - CROPS

LEBANON - BEER PRODUCTION - See LEBANON - BEVERAGES

LEBANON - BEVERAGES

M.E. Sharpe, 80 Business Park Drive, Armonk, New York 10504 (800) 541-6563; *The Illustrated Book of World Rankings.*

Statistical Office of the United Nations, Publishing Service, New York, New York 10017 (800) 253-9646; *Statistical Yearbook.*

LEBANON - BIRTH RATES

Central Intelligence Agency, Washington, D.C. 20505 (703) 482-1100, www.cia.gov; *The World Factbook.*

Euromonitor International, Inc., 122 South Michigan Avenue, Suite 1200, Chicago, Illinois 60603 (800) 577-EURO; *International Marketing Data and Statistics;* and *The World Economic Factbook.*

Europa Publications Limited, 18 Bedford Square, London, WC1B 3JN, England; *The Europa World Year Book.*

M.E. Sharpe, 80 Business Park Drive, Armonk, New York 10504 (800) 541-6563; *The Illustrated Book of World Rankings.*

St. Martin's Press, Inc., 175 Fifth Avenue, New York, New York 10010 (800) 221-7945; *The Statesman's Year-Book.*

Statistical Office of the United Nations, Publishing Service, New York, New York 10017 (800) 253-9646; *Demographic Yearbook;* and *Statistical Yearbook.*

LEBANON - BROADCASTING

Billboard Limited, Post Office Box 9027, 1006 AA Amsterdam, The Netherlands (Telephone Number in U.S. (212) 764-7300); *World Radio TV Handbook.*

Central Intelligence Agency, Washington, D.C. 20505 (703) 482-1100, www.cia.gov; *The World Factbook.*

Euromonitor International, Inc., 122 South Michigan Avenue, Suite 1200, Chicago, Illinois 60603 (800) 577-EURO; *World Marketing Data and Statistics.*

M.E. Sharpe, 80 Business Park Drive, Armonk, New York 10504 (800) 541-6563; *The Illustrated Book of World Rankings.*

St. Martin's Press, Inc., 175 Fifth Avenue, New York, New York 10010 (800) 221-7945; *The Statesman's Year-Book.*

LEBANON - BUDGET

Central Intelligence Agency, Washington, D.C. 20505 (703) 482-1100, www.cia.gov; *The World Factbook.*

LEBANON - CABBAGE PRODUCTION - See LEBANON - CROPS

LEBANON - CALORIE SUPPLY

Food and Agricultural Organization of the United Nations (FAO), Via delle Terme di Caracalla, 00100 Rome, Italy (Telephone Number in U.S. (202) 653-2400); *The State of Food and Agriculture.*

LEBANON - CATTLE - See LEBANON - LIVESTOCK AND POULTRY

LEBANON - CAULIFLOWER PRODUCTION - See LEBANON - CROPS

LEBANON - CEMENT PRODUCTION - See LEBANON - MINING AND MINERAL PRODUCTS

LEBANON - CHEESE PRODUCTION AND CONSUMPTION - See LEBANON - DAIRY PRODUCTS

LEBANON - CHEMICAL (ORGANIC) PRODUCTION - See LEBANON -MINING AND MINERAL PRODUCTS

LEBANON - CHICK PEA PRODUCTION - See LEBANON - CROPS

LEBANON - CHICKENS - See LEBANON-LIVESTOCK AND POULTRY

LEBANON - CIGARETTE PRODUCTION - See LEBANON - TOBACCO PRODUCTION

LEBANON - CLIMATE

M.E. Sharpe, 80 Business Park Drive,

Armonk, New York 10504 (800) 541-6563; *The Illustrated Book of World Rankings.*

St. Martin's Press, Inc., 175 Fifth Avenue, New York, New York 10010 (800) 221-7945; *The Statesman's Year-Book.*

LEBANON - COAL PRODUCTION - See LEBANON - MINING AND MINERAL PRODUCTS

LEBANON - COFFEE PRODUCTION AND CONSUMPTION - See LEBANON - CROPS

LEBANON - COMMERCE

St. Martin's Press, Inc., 175 Fifth Avenue, New York, New York 10010 (800) 221-7945; *The Statesman's Year-Book.*

LEBANON - COMMUNICATIONS - See LEBANON - TRANSPORTATION AND COMMUNICATIONS

LEBANON - CONSTRUCTION INDUSTRY

M.E. Sharpe, 80 Business Park Drive, Armonk, New York 10504 (800) 541-6563; *The Illustrated Book of World Rankings.*

LEBANON - CONSUMER PRICE INDEX

Statistical Office of the United Nations, Publishing Service, New York, New York 10017 (800) 253-9646; *Statistical Yearbook.*

LEBANON - CONSUMER PRICES

Euromonitor International, Inc., 122 South Michigan Avenue, Suite 1200, Chicago, Illinois 60603 (800) 577-EURO; *World Marketing Data and Statistics.*

International Labour Office, I.L.O. Publications, 1828 L Street, N.W., Suite 801, Washington, D.C. (301) 638-3152; *Yearbook of Labour Statistics.*

LEBANON - COPPER PRODUCTION AND CONSUMPTION - See LEBANON - MINING AND MINERAL PRODUCTS

LEBANON - CORN PRODUCTION - See LEBANON - CROPS

LEBANON - CORPORATE TAXES - See LEBANON - TAXATION

LEBANON - COTTON PRODUCTION - See LEBANON - CROPS

LEBANON - CRIME

International Criminal Police Organization (INTERPOL), 50 quai Achille Lignon, F-69006 Lyon, France; *International Crime Statistics.*

Yale University Press, Yale Station, New Haven, Connecticut 06520 (800) 987-7323;

Violence and Crime in Cross-National Perspective.

LEBANON - CROPS

Europa Publications Limited, 18 Bedford Square, London, WC1B 3JN, England; *The Europa World Year Book.*

Food and Agricultural Organization of the United Nations (FAO), Via delle Terme di Caracalla, 00100 Rome, Italy (Telephone Number in U.S. (202) 653-2400); *Production Yearbook;* and *The State of Food and Agriculture.*

International Wheat Statistics, 23 Haymarket, London SW1Y 4SS, England; *World Wheat Statistics.*

M.E. Sharpe, 80 Business Park Drive, Armonk, New York 10504 (800) 541-6563; *The Illustrated Book of World Rankings.*

St. Martin's Press, Inc., 175 Fifth Avenue, New York, New York 10010 (800) 221-7945; *The Statesman's Year-Book.*

Statistical Office of the United Nations, Publishing Service, New York, New York 10017 (800) 253-9646; *Statistical Yearbook.*

United Nations Conference on Trade and Development, Central Statistical Service, Palais des Nations, Geneva, Switzerland (Telephone in U.S. (800) 253-9646); *UNCTAD Commodity Yearbook.*

LEBANON - DAIRY PRODUCTS

Economic Commission for Western Asia, Post Office Box 27, Baghdad, Iraq; *Statistical Abstract of Western Asia.*

Europa Publications Limited, 18 Bedford Square, London, WC1B 3JN, England; *The Europa World Year Book.*

Food and Agricultural Organization of the United Nations (FAO), Via delle Terme di Caracalla, 00100 Rome, Italy (Telephone Number in U.S. (202) 653-2400); *The State of Food and Agriculture;* and *Production Yearbook.*

M.E. Sharpe, 80 Business Park Drive, Armonk, New York 10504 (800) 541-6563; *The Illustrated Book of World Rankings.*

St. Martin's Press, Inc., 175 Fifth Avenue, New York, New York 10010 (800) 221-7945; *The Statesman's Year-Book.*

Statistical Office of the United Nations, Publishing Service, New York, New York 10017 (800) 253-9646; *Statistical Yearbook.*

LEBANON - DEATH RATES - See LEBANON - MORTALITY

LEBANON - DEFENSE EXPENDITURES - See

LEBANON - MILITARY

LEBANON - DEMOGRAPHY

The Economist Intelligence Unit, 111 West 57th Street, New York, New York 10019 (800) 938-4685; *The World Market Atlas.*

Euromonitor International, Inc., 122 South Michigan Avenue, Suite 1200, Chicago, Illinois 60603 (800) 577-EURO; *International Marketing Data and Statistics; World Marketing Data and Statistics;* and *The World Economic Factbook.*

M.E. Sharpe, 80 Business Park Drive, Armonk, New York 10504 (800) 541-6563; *The Illustrated Book of World Rankings.*

Statistical Office of the United Nations, Publishing Service, New York, New York 10017 (800) 253-9646; *Human Development Report.*

LEBANON - DEVELOPMENT ASSISTANCE

Statistical Office of the United Nations, Publishing Service, New York, New York 10017 (800) 253-9646; *Statistical Yearbook.*

LEBANON - DIAMOND PRODUCTION - See LEBANON - MINING AND MINERAL PRODUCTS

LEBANON - DIVORCE

M.E. Sharpe, 80 Business Park Drive, Armonk, New York 10504 (800) 541-6563; *The Illustrated Book of World Rankings.*

Statistical Office of the United Nations, Publishing Service, New York, New York 10017 (800) 253-9646; *Demographic Yearbook;* and *Statistical Yearbook.*

LEBANON - ECONOMY

Central Intelligence Agency, Washington, D.C. 20505 (703) 482-1100, www.cia.gov; *The World Factbook.*

Economist Intelligence Unit, 111 West 57th Street, New York, New York 10019 (800) 938-4685; *Lebanon Country Report.*

Euromonitor International, Inc., 122 South Michigan Avenue, Suite 1200, Chicago, Illinois 60603 (800) 577-EURO; *International Marketing Data and Statistics; World Marketing Data and Statistics;* and *The World Economic Factbook.*

M.E. Sharpe, 80 Business Park Drive, Armonk, New York 10504 (800) 541-6563; *The Illustrated Book of World Rankings.*

St. Martin's Press, Inc., 175 Fifth Avenue, New York, New York 10010 (800) 221-7945; *The Statesman's Year-Book.*

Statistical Office of the United Nations, Publishing Service, New York, New York 10017 (800) 253-9646; *World Statistics Pocketbook.*

The World Bank, 1818 H Street, NW, Washington, D.C. 20433 (202) 477-1234; *The World Bank Atlas.*

LEBANON - EDUCATION

Economic Commission for Western Asia, Post Office Box 27, Baghdad, Iraq; *Statistical Abstract of Western Asia.*

The Economist Intelligence Unit, 111 West 57th Street, New York, New York 10019 (800) 938-4685; *The World Market Atlas.*

Euromonitor International, Inc., 122 South Michigan Avenue, Suite 1200, Chicago, Illinois 60603 (800) 577-EURO; *International Marketing Data and Statistics;* and *World Marketing Data and Statistics.*

Europa Publications Limited, 18 Bedford Square, London, WC1B 3JN, England; *The Europa World Year Book.*

M.E. Sharpe, 80 Business Park Drive, Armonk, New York 10504 (800) 541-6563; *The Illustrated Book of World Rankings.*

St. Martin's Press, Inc., 175 Fifth Avenue, New York, New York 10010 (800) 221-7945; *The Statesman's Year-Book.*

Statistical Office of the United Nations, Publishing Service, New York, New York 10017 (800) 253-9646; *Human Development Report.*

United Nations Educational, Scientific and Cultural Organization (UNESCO), 7 Place de Fontenoy, F-75700 Paris, France (Telephone Number in U.S. (212) 963-5981); *Statistical Yearbook.*

LEBANON - EGG PRODUCTION AND CONSUMPTION - See LEBANON - DAIRY PRODUCTS

LEBANON - EGGPLANT PRODUCTION - See LEBANON - CROPS

LEBANON - ELECTRICITY

Central Intelligence Agency, Washington, D.C. 20505 (703) 482-1100, www.cia.gov; *The World Factbook.*

M.E. Sharpe, 80 Business Park Drive, Armonk, New York 10504 (800) 541-6563; *The Illustrated Book of World Rankings.*

St. Martin's Press, Inc., 175 Fifth Avenue, New York, New York 10010 (800) 221-7945; *The Statesman's Year-Book.*

Statistical Office of the United Nations,

Publishing Service, New York, New York 10017 (800) 253-9646; *Human Development Report;* and *Statistical Yearbook.*

LEBANON - EMPLOYMENT

Economic Commission for Western Asia, Post Office Box 27, Baghdad, Iraq; *Statistical Abstract of Western Asia.*

Euromonitor International, Inc., 122 South Michigan Avenue, Suite 1200, Chicago, Illinois 60603 (800) 577-EURO; *International Marketing Data and Statistics.*

International Labour Office, I.L.O. Publications, 1828 L Street, N.W., Suite 801, Washington, D.C. (301) 638-3152; *Yearbook of Labour Statistics.*

M.E. Sharpe, 80 Business Park Drive, Armonk, New York 10504 (800) 541-6563; *The Illustrated Book of World Rankings.*

Statistical Office of the United Nations, Publishing Service, New York, New York 10017 (800) 253-9646; *Bulletin of Industrial Statistics for the Arab Countries.*

LEBANON - ENERGY

Economic Commission for Western Asia, Post Office Box 27, Baghdad, Iraq; *Statistical Abstract of Western Asia.*

Euromonitor International, Inc., 122 South Michigan Avenue, Suite 1200, Chicago, Illinois 60603 (800) 577-EURO; *International Marketing Data and Statistics; World Marketing Data and Statistics;* and *The World Economic Factbook.*

Food and Agricultural Organization of the United Nations (FAO), Via delle Terme di Caracalla, 00100 Rome, Italy (Telephone Number in U.S. (202) 653-2400); *The State of Food and Agriculture.*

M.E. Sharpe, 80 Business Park Drive, Armonk, New York 10504 (800) 541-6563; *The Illustrated Book of World Rankings.*

St. Martin's Press, Inc., 175 Fifth Avenue, New York, New York 10010 (800) 221-7945; *The Statesman's Year-Book.*

Statistical Office of the United Nations, Publishing Service, New York, New York 10017 (800) 253-9646; *Energy Statistics Yearbook; Human Development Report; World Statistics Pocketbook;* and *Statistical Yearbook.*

The World Bank, 1818 H Street, NW, Washington, D.C. 20433 (202) 477-1234; *The World Bank Atlas.*

LEBANON - ENVIRONMENT

Economist Intelligence Unit, 111 West

57th Street, New York, New York 10019 (800) 938-4685; *Lebanon Country Report.*

Statistical Office of the United Nations, Publishing Service, New York, New York 10017 (800) 253-9646; *World Statistics Pocketbook.*

LEBANON - EXCHANGE RATES

Central Intelligence Agency, Washington, D.C. 20505 (703) 482-1100, www.cia.gov; *The World Factbook.*

Euromonitor International, Inc., 122 South Michigan Avenue, Suite 1200, Chicago, Illinois 60603 (800) 577-EURO; *International Marketing Data and Statistics;* and *The World Economic Factbook.*

Europa Publications Limited, 18 Bedford Square, London, WC1B 3JN, England; *The Europa World Year Book.*

International Civil Aviation Organization, 999 University Street, Montreal, Quebec, Canada H3C 5H7 (514) 954-8219; *Civil Aviation Statistics of the World.*

International Monetary Fund, 700 Nineteenth Street, NW, Washington, D.C. 20431 (202) 623-7000; *International Financial Statistics.*

Statistical Office of the United Nations, Publishing Service, New York, New York 10017 (800) 253-9646; *Bulletin of Industrial Statistics for the Arab Countries; World Statistics Pocketbook;* and *Statistical Yearbook.*

LEBANON - EXPORTS

Central Intelligence Agency, Washington, D.C. 20505 (703) 482-1100, www.cia.gov; *The World Factbook.*

Economic Commission for Western Asia, Post Office Box 27, Baghdad, Iraq; *Statistical Abstract of Western Asia.*

The Economist Intelligence Unit, 111 West 57th Street, New York, New York 10019 (800) 938-4685; *Lebanon Country Report;* and *The World Market Atlas.*

Euromonitor International, Inc., 122 South Michigan Avenue, Suite 1200, Chicago, Illinois 60603 (800) 577-EURO; *International Marketing Data and Statistics;* and *The World Economic Factbook.*

Europa Publications Limited, 18 Bedford Square, London, WC1B 3JN, England; *The Europa World Year Book.*

Food and Agricultural Organization of the United Nations (FAO), Via delle Terme di Caracalla, 00100 Rome, Italy (Telephone Number in U.S. (202) 653-2400); *The State*

of Food and Agriculture.

International Monetary Fund, 700 Nineteenth Street, NW, Washington, D.C. 20431 (202) 623-7000; *Direction of Trade Statistics.*

St. Martin's Press, Inc., 175 Fifth Avenue, New York, New York 10010 (800) 221-7945; *The Statesman's Year-Book.*

Statistical Office of the United Nations, Publishing Service, New York, New York 10017 (800) 253-9646; *Bulletin of Industrial Statistics for the Arab Countries.*

LEBANON - EXTERNAL TRADE

Euromonitor International, Inc., 122 South Michigan Avenue, Suite 1200, Chicago, Illinois 60603 (800) 577-EURO; *World Marketing Data and Statistics.*

Food and Agricultural Organization of the United Nations (FAO), Via delle Terme di Caracalla, 00100 Rome, Italy (Telephone Number in U.S. (202) 653-2400); *The State of Food and Agriculture;* and *Trade Yearbook.*

Statistical Office of the United Nations, Publishing Service, New York, New York 10017 (800) 253-9646; *Statistical Yearbook.*

LEBANON - FARM CROPS - See LEBANON - CROPS

LEBANON - FEMALE WORKING POPULATION - See LEBANON - EMPLOYMENT

LEBANON - FERTILITY RATES

Central Intelligence Agency, Washington, D.C. 20505 (703) 482-1100, www.cia.gov; *The World Factbook.*

M.E. Sharpe, 80 Business Park Drive, Armonk, New York 10504 (800) 541-6563; *The Illustrated Book of World Rankings.*

Statistical Office of the United Nations, Publishing Service, New York, New York 10017 (800) 253-9646; *Human Development Report.*

The World Bank, 1818 H Street, NW, Washington, D.C. 20433 (202) 477-1234; *The World Bank Atlas.*

LEBANON - FERTILIZER

Food and Agricultural Organization of the United Nations (FAO), Via delle Terme di Caracalla, 00100 Rome, Italy (Telephone Number in U.S. (202) 653-2400); *Fertilizer Yearbook;* and *The State of Food and Agriculture.*

Statistical Office of the United Nations, Publishing Service, New York, New York

10017 (800) 253-9646; *Statistical Yearbook.*

LEBANON - FETAL MORTALITY - See LEBANON - MORTALITY

LEBANON - FILM - See LEBANON - MOTION PICTURES

LEBANON - FINANCE

Economic Commission for Western Asia, Post Office Box 27, Baghdad, Iraq; *Statistical Abstract of Western Asia.*

Economist Intelligence Unit, 111 West 57th Street, New York, New York 10019 (800) 938-4685; *Lebanon Country Report.*

Europa Publications Limited, 18 Bedford Square, London, WC1B 3JN, England; *The Europa World Year Book.*

International Monetary Fund, 700 Nineteenth Street, NW, Washington, D.C. 20431 (202) 623-7000; *International Financial Statistics.*

M.E. Sharpe, 80 Business Park Drive, Armonk, New York 10504 (800) 541-6563; *The Illustrated Book of World Rankings.*

St. Martin's Press, Inc., 175 Fifth Avenue, New York, New York 10010 (800) 221-7945; *The Statesman's Year-Book.*

LEBANON - FISHERIES

Economic Commission for Western Asia, Post Office Box 27, Baghdad, Iraq; *Statistical Abstract of Western Asia.*

Europa Publications Limited, 18 Bedford Square, London, WC1B 3JN, England; *The Europa World Year Book.*

Food and Agricultural Organization of the United Nations (FAO), Via delle Terme di Caracalla, 00100 Rome, Italy (Telephone Number in U.S. (202) 653-2400); *The State of Food and Agriculture;* and *Yearbook of Fishery Statistics.*

M.E. Sharpe, 80 Business Park Drive, Armonk, New York 10504 (800) 541-6563; *The Illustrated Book of World Rankings.*

St. Martin's Press, Inc., 175 Fifth Avenue, New York, New York 10010 (800) 221-7945; *The Statesman's Year-Book.*

Statistical Office of the United Nations, Publishing Service, New York, New York 10017 (800) 253-9646; *Statistical Yearbook.*

United Nations Conference on Trade and Development, Central Statistical Service, Palais des Nations, Geneva, Switzerland (Telephone in U.S. (800) 253-9646); *UNCTAD Commodity Yearbook.*

LEBANON - FLOUR PRODUCTION

Statistical Office of the United Nations, Publishing Service, New York, New York 10017 (800) 253-9646; *Statistical Yearbook.*

LEBANON - FOOD

Food and Agricultural Organization of the United Nations (FAO), Via delle Terme di Caracalla, 00100 Rome, Italy (Telephone Number in U.S. (202) 653-2400); *The State of Food and Agriculture;* and *Production Yearbook.*

Statistical Office of the United Nations, Publishing Service, New York, New York 10017 (800) 253-9646; *Human Development Report.*

United Nations Conference on Trade and Development, Central Statistical Service, Palais des Nations, Geneva, Switzerland (Telephone in U.S. (800) 253-9646); *UNCTAD Commodity Yearbook.*

LEBANON - FOREIGN TRADE

Economic Commission for Western Asia, Post Office Box 27, Baghdad, Iraq; *Statistical Abstract of Western Asia.*

Economist Intelligence Unit, 111 West 57th Street, New York, New York 10019 (800) 938-4685; *Lebanon Country Report.*

Euromonitor International, Inc., 122 South Michigan Avenue, Suite 1200, Chicago, Illinois 60603 (800) 577-EURO; *The World Economic Factbook.*

Europa Publications Limited, 18 Bedford Square, London, WC1B 3JN, England; *The Europa World Year Book.*

Food and Agricultural Organization of the United Nations (FAO), Via delle Terme di Caracalla, 00100 Rome, Italy (Telephone Number in U.S. (202) 653-2400); *The State of Food and Agriculture.*

International Monetary Fund, 700 Nineteenth Street, NW, Washington, D.C. 20431 (202) 623-7000; *International Financial Statistics.*

M.E. Sharpe, 80 Business Park Drive, Armonk, New York 10504 (800) 541-6563; *The Illustrated Book of World Rankings.*

St. Martin's Press, Inc., 175 Fifth Avenue, New York, New York 10010 (800) 221-7945; *The Statesman's Year-Book.*

Statistical Office of the United Nations, Publishing Service, New York, New York 10017 (800) 253-9646; *Bulletin of Industrial Statistics for the Arab Countries; International Trade Statistics Yearbook;* and *Statistical Yearbook.*

United Nations Conference on Trade

and Development, Central Statistical Service, Palais des Nations, Geneva, Switzerland (Telephone in U.S. (800) 253-9646); *UNCTAD Commodity Yearbook.*

LEBANON - FORESTRY AND FOREST PRODUCTS

Europa Publications Limited, 18 Bedford Square, London, WC1B 3JN, England; *The Europa World Year Book.*

Food and Agricultural Organization of the United Nations (FAO), Via delle Terme di Caracalla, 00100 Rome, Italy (Telephone Number in U.S. (202) 653-2400); *The State of Food and Agriculture;* and *Yearbook of Forest Products.*

M.E. Sharpe, 80 Business Park Drive, Armonk, New York 10504 (800) 541-6563; *The Illustrated Book of World Rankings.*

St. Martin's Press, Inc., 175 Fifth Avenue, New York, New York 10010 (800) 221-7945; *The Statesman's Year-Book.*

Statistical Office of the United Nations, Publishing Service, New York, New York 10017 (800) 253-9646; *Statistical Yearbook.*

United Nations Educational, Scientific and Cultural Organization (UNESCO), 7 Place de Fontenoy, F-75700 Paris, France (Telephone Number in U.S. (212) 963-5981); *Statistical Yearbook.*

LEBANON - GARLIC PRODUCTION - See LEBANON - CROPS

LEBANON - GAS PRODUCTION - See LEBANON - MINING AND MINERAL PRODUCTS

LEBANON - GENERAL MORTALITY - See LEBANON - MORTALITY

LEBANON - GEOGRAPHIC DATA

M.E. Sharpe, 80 Business Park Drive, Armonk, New York 10504 (800) 541-6563; *The Illustrated Book of World Rankings.*

LEBANON - GOATS - See LEBANON - LIVESTOCK AND POULTRY

LEBANON - GOLD HOLDINGS

International Monetary Fund, 700 Nineteenth Street, NW, Washington, D.C. 20431 (202) 623-7000; *International Financial Statistics.*

Statistical Office of the United Nations, Publishing Service, New York, New York 10017 (800) 253-9646; *Statistical Yearbook.*

LEBANON - GOLD PRODUCTION AND CONSUMPTION - See LEBANON - MINING AND MINERAL PRODUCTS

LEBANON - GOVERNMENT

Central Intelligence Agency, Washington, D.C. 20505 (703) 482-1100, www.cia.gov; *The World Factbook.*

Economic Commission for Western Asia, Post Office Box 27, Baghdad, Iraq; *Statistical Abstract of Western Asia.*

Europa Publications Limited, 18 Bedford Square, London, WC1B 3JN, England; *The Europa World Year Book.*

International Monetary Fund, 700 Nineteenth Street, NW, Washington, D.C. 20431 (202) 623-7000; *International Financial Statistics.*

St. Martin's Press, Inc., 175 Fifth Avenue, New York, New York 10010 (800) 221-7945; *The Statesman's Year-Book.*

Statistical Office of the United Nations, Publishing Service, New York, New York 10017 (800) 253-9646; *National Accounts Statistics;* and *Statistical Yearbook.*

LEBANON - GRAIN PRODUCTION - See LEBANON - CROPS

LEBANON - GROSS DOMESTIC PRODUCT

Economic Commission for Western Asia, Post Office Box 27, Baghdad, Iraq; *Statistical Abstract of Western Asia.*

The Economist Intelligence Unit, 111 West 57th Street, New York, New York 10019 (800) 938-4685; *Lebanon Country Report;* and *The World Market Atlas.*

Euromonitor International, Inc., 122 South Michigan Avenue, Suite 1200, Chicago, Illinois 60603 (800) 577-EURO; *International Marketing Data and Statistics;* and *The World Economic Factbook.*

Europa Publications Limited, 18 Bedford Square, London, WC1B 3JN, England; *The Europa World Year Book.*

M.E. Sharpe, 80 Business Park Drive, Armonk, New York 10504 (800) 541-6563; *The Illustrated Book of World Rankings.*

Statistical Office of the United Nations, Publishing Service, New York, New York 10017 (800) 253-9646; *Bulletin of Industrial Statistics for the Arab Countries; Human Development Report; National Accounts Statistics;* and *Statistical Yearbook.*

LEBANON - GROSS NATIONAL PRODUCT

Euromonitor International, Inc., 122 South Michigan Avenue, Suite 1200, Chicago, Illinois 60603 (800) 577-EURO; *International Marketing Data and Statistics.*

U.S. Arms Control and Disarmament Agency, 320 Twenty-first Street, NW, Washington, D.C. 20451 (202) 647-8677; *World Military Expenditures and Arms Transfers.*

The World Bank, 1818 H Street, NW, Washington, D.C. 20433 (202) 477-1234; *The World Bank Atlas.*

LEBANON - GROUNDNUT PRODUCTION - See LEBANON - CROPS

LEBANON - HEALTH

Economic Commission for Western Asia, Post Office Box 27, Baghdad, Iraq; *Statistical Abstract of Western Asia.*

Euromonitor International, Inc., 122 South Michigan Avenue, Suite 1200, Chicago, Illinois 60603 (800) 577-EURO; *World Marketing Data and Statistics.*

M.E. Sharpe, 80 Business Park Drive, Armonk, New York 10504 (800) 541-6563; *The Illustrated Book of World Rankings.*

St. Martin's Press, Inc., 175 Fifth Avenue, New York, New York 10010 (800) 221-7945; *The Statesman's Year-Book.*

Statistical Office of the United Nations, Publishing Service, New York, New York 10017 (800) 253-9646; *Human Development Report;* and *Statistical Yearbook.*

United Nations Children's Fund (UNICEF), 3 United Nations Plaza, New York, New York 10017 (800) 253-9646; *State of the World's Children.*

LEBANON - HIDE PRODUCTION

Food and Agricultural Organization of the United Nations (FAO), Via delle Terme di Caracalla, 00100 Rome, Italy (Telephone Number in U.S. (202) 653-2400); *Production Yearbook.*

LEBANON - HIGHWAYS

Central Intelligence Agency, Washington, D.C. 20505 (703) 482-1100, www.cia.gov; *The World Factbook.*

Economic Commission for Western Asia, Post Office Box 27, Baghdad, Iraq; *Statistical Abstract of Western Asia.*

International Road Federation, 2600 Virginia Avenue, N.W., Washington, D.C. 20024 (202) 338-4641; *World Road Statistics.*

St. Martin's Press, Inc., 175 Fifth Avenue, New York, New York 10010 (800) 221-7945; *The Statesman's Year-Book.*

LEBANON - HORSES - See LEBANON - LIVESTOCK AND POULTRY

LEBANON - HOURS OF WORK - See LEBANON - EMPLOYMENT

LEBANON - HOUSING AND HOUSING UNITS

Euromonitor International, Inc., 122 South Michigan Avenue, Suite 1200, Chicago, Illinois 60603 (800) 577-EURO; *World Marketing Data and Statistics.*

M.E. Sharpe, 80 Business Park Drive, Armonk, New York 10504 (800) 541-6563; *The Illustrated Book of World Rankings.*

LEBANON - ILLITERATE POPULATION

Central Intelligence Agency, Washington, D.C. 20505 (703) 482-1100, www.cia.gov; *The World Factbook.*

The Economist Intelligence Unit, 111 West 57th Street, New York, New York 10019 (800) 938-4685; *The World Market Atlas.*

Euromonitor International, Inc., 122 South Michigan Avenue, Suite 1200, Chicago, Illinois 60603 (800) 577-EURO; *The World Economic Factbook.*

Statistical Office of the United Nations, Publishing Service, New York, New York 10017 (800) 253-9646; *Human Development Report.*

United Nations Educational, Scientific and Cultural Organization (UNESCO), 7 Place de Fontenoy, F-75700 Paris, France (Telephone Number in U.S. (212) 963-5981); *Statistical Yearbook.*

LEBANON - IMPORTS

Central Intelligence Agency, Washington, D.C. 20505 (703) 482-1100, www.cia.gov; *The World Factbook.*

Economic Commission for Western Asia, Post Office Box 27, Baghdad, Iraq; *Statistical Abstract of Western Asia.*

The Economist Intelligence Unit, 111 West 57th Street, New York, New York 10019 (800) 938-4685; *Lebanon Country Report;* and *The World Market Atlas.*

Euromonitor International, Inc., 122 South Michigan Avenue, Suite 1200, Chicago, Illinois 60603 (800) 577-EURO; *International Marketing Data and Statistics;* and *The World Economic Factbook.*

Europa Publications Limited, 18 Bedford Square, London, WC1B 3JN, England; *The Europa World Year Book.*

Food and Agricultural Organization of the United Nations (FAO), Via delle Terme di Caracalla, 00100 Rome, Italy (Telephone Number in U.S. (202) 653-2400); *The State*

of Food and Agriculture.

International Monetary Fund, 700 Nineteenth Street, NW, Washington, D.C. 20431 (202) 623-7000; *Direction of Trade Statistics.*

St. Martin's Press, Inc., 175 Fifth Avenue, New York, New York 10010 (800) 221-7945; *The Statesman's Year-Book.*

Statistical Office of the United Nations, Publishing Service, New York, New York 10017 (800) 253-9646; *Bulletin of Industrial Statistics for the Arab Countries.*

LEBANON - INDUSTRY

Central Intelligence Agency, Washington, D.C. 20505 (703) 482-1100, www.cia.gov; *The World Factbook.*

Economist Intelligence Unit, 111 West 57th Street, New York, New York 10019 (800) 938-4685; *Lebanon Country Report.*

Euromonitor International, Inc., 122 South Michigan Avenue, Suite 1200, Chicago, Illinois 60603 (800) 577-EURO; *International Marketing Data and Statistics; World Marketing Data and Statistics;* and *The World Economic Factbook.*

Europa Publications Limited, 18 Bedford Square, London, WC1B 3JN, England; *The Europa World Year Book.*

International Labour Office, I.L.O. Publications, 1828 L Street, N.W., Suite 801, Washington, D.C. (301) 638-3152; *Yearbook of Labour Statistics.*

M.E. Sharpe, 80 Business Park Drive, Armonk, New York 10504 (800) 541-6563; *The Illustrated Book of World Rankings.*

St. Martin's Press, Inc., 175 Fifth Avenue, New York, New York 10010 (800) 221-7945; *The Statesman's Year-Book.*

Statistical Office of the United Nations, Publishing Service, New York, New York 10017 (800) 253-9646; *Bulletin of Industrial Statistics for the Arab Countries;* and *Statistical Yearbook.*

LEBANON - INFANT AND MATERNAL MORTALITY - See LEBANON - MORTALITY

LEBANON - INTERNATIONAL LIQUIDITY

International Monetary Fund, 700 Nineteenth Street, NW, Washington, D.C. 20431 (202) 623-7000; *International Financial Statistics.*

LEBANON - INTERNATIONAL RESERVES EXCLUDING GOLD

Statistical Office of the United Nations, Publishing Service, New York, New York

10017 (800) 253-9646; *Statistical Yearbook.*

LEBANON - IRON ORE PRODUCTION AND CONSUMPTION - See LEBANON - MINING AND MINERAL PRODUCTS

LEBANON - IRRIGATION

Euromonitor International, Inc., 122 South Michigan Avenue, Suite 1200, Chicago, Illinois 60603 (800) 577-EURO; *International Marketing Data and Statistics.*

LEBANON - LABOR

Central Intelligence Agency, Washington, D.C. 20505 (703) 482-1100, www.cia.gov; *The World Factbook.*

Economic Commission for Western Asia, Post Office Box 27, Baghdad, Iraq; *Statistical Abstract of Western Asia.*

Euromonitor International, Inc., 122 South Michigan Avenue, Suite 1200, Chicago, Illinois 60603 (800) 577-EURO; *International Marketing Data and Statistics;* and *World Marketing Data and Statistics.*

Europa Publications Limited, 18 Bedford Square, London, WC1B 3JN, England; *The Europa World Year Book.*

Food and Agricultural Organization of the United Nations (FAO), Via delle Terme di Caracalla, 00100 Rome, Italy (Telephone Number in U.S. (202) 653-2400); *The State of Food and Agriculture.*

International Labour Office, I.L.O. Publications, 1828 L Street, N.W., Suite 801, Washington, D.C. (301) 638-3152; *Yearbook of Labour Statistics.*

M.E. Sharpe, 80 Business Park Drive, Armonk, New York 10504 (800) 541-6563; *The Illustrated Book of World Rankings.*

St. Martin's Press, Inc., 175 Fifth Avenue, New York, New York 10010 (800) 221-7945; *The Statesman's Year-Book.*

Statistical Office of the United Nations, Publishing Service, New York, New York 10017 (800) 253-9646; *Human Development Report.*

The World Bank, 1818 H Street, NW, Washington, D.C. 20433 (202) 477-1234; *The World Bank Atlas.*

LEBANON - LAND USE

Central Intelligence Agency, Washington, D.C. 20505 (703) 482-1100, www.cia.gov; *The World Factbook.*

Economic Commission for Western Asia, Post Office Box 27, Baghdad, Iraq; *Statistical Abstract of Western Asia.*

Euromonitor International, Inc., 122 South Michigan Avenue, Suite 1200, Chicago, Illinois 60603 (800) 577-EURO; *International Marketing Data and Statistics.*

Food and Agricultural Organization of the United Nations (FAO), Via delle Terme di Caracalla, 00100 Rome, Italy (Telephone Number in U.S. (202) 653-2400); *Production Yearbook.*

LEBANON - LIBRARIES

M.E. Sharpe, 80 Business Park Drive, Armonk, New York 10504 (800) 541-6563; *The Illustrated Book of World Rankings.*

LEBANON - LIFE EXPECTANCY

Central Intelligence Agency, Washington, D.C. 20505 (703) 482-1100, www.cia.gov; *The World Factbook.*

Euromonitor International, Inc., 122 South Michigan Avenue, Suite 1200, Chicago, Illinois 60603 (800) 577-EURO; *The World Economic Factbook.*

St. Martin's Press, Inc., 175 Fifth Avenue, New York, New York 10010 (800) 221-7945; *The Statesman's Year-Book.*

Statistical Office of the United Nations, Publishing Service, New York, New York 10017 (800) 253-9646; *Human Development Report;* and *World Statistics Pocketbook.*

The World Bank, 1818 H Street, NW, Washington, D.C. 20433 (202) 477-1234; *The World Bank Atlas.*

LEBANON - LITERACY RATE

Euromonitor International, Inc., 122 South Michigan Avenue, Suite 1200, Chicago, Illinois 60603 (800) 577-EURO; *World Marketing Data and Statistics.*

LEBANON - LIVESTOCK AND POULTRY

Economic Commission for Western Asia, Post Office Box 27, Baghdad, Iraq; *Statistical Abstract of Western Asia.*

Euromonitor International, Inc., 122 South Michigan Avenue, Suite 1200, Chicago, Illinois 60603 (800) 577-EURO; *International Marketing Data and Statistics.*

Europa Publications Limited, 18 Bedford Square, London, WC1B 3JN, England; *The Europa World Year Book.*

Food and Agricultural Organization of the United Nations (FAO), Via delle Terme di Caracalla, 00100 Rome, Italy (Telephone Number in U.S. (202) 653-2400); *Production Yearbook;* and *The State of Food and Agriculture.*

M.E. Sharpe, 80 Business Park Drive, Armonk, New York 10504 (800) 541-6563; *The Illustrated Book of World Rankings.*

St. Martin's Press, Inc., 175 Fifth Avenue, New York, New York 10010 (800) 221-7945; *The Statesman's Year-Book.*

Statistical Office of the United Nations, Publishing Service, New York, New York 10017 (800) 253-9646; *Statistical Yearbook.*

United Nations Conference on Trade and Development, Central Statistical Service, Palais des Nations, Geneva, Switzerland (Telephone in U.S. (800) 253-9646); *UNCTAD Commodity Yearbook.*

LEBANON - LIVING LEVELS - See LEBANON - LIFE EXPECTANCY

LEBANON - MANUFACTURING

M.E. Sharpe, 80 Business Park Drive, Armonk, New York 10504 (800) 541-6563; *The Illustrated Book of World Rankings.*

Statistical Office of the United Nations, Publishing Service, New York, New York 10017 (800) 253-9646; *Bulletin of Industrial Statistics for the Arab Countries.*

LEBANON - MARRIAGE RATES

M.E. Sharpe, 80 Business Park Drive, Armonk, New York 10504 (800) 541-6563; *The Illustrated Book of World Rankings.*

Statistical Office of the United Nations, Publishing Service, New York, New York 10017 (800) 253-9646; *Demographic Yearbook;* and *Statistical Yearbook.*

LEBANON - MEAT PRODUCTION - See LEBANON - LIVESTOCK AND POULTRY

LEBANON - MERCHANT SHIPPING

Economic Commission for Western Asia, Post Office Box 27, Baghdad, Iraq; *Statistical Abstract of Western Asia.*

Europa Publications Limited, 18 Bedford Square, London, WC1B 3JN, England; *The Europa World Year Book.*

Lloyd's Register of Shipping, 17 Battery Place, New York, New York 10004 (212) 425-8050; *Register of Ships.*

St. Martin's Press, Inc., 175 Fifth Avenue, New York, New York 10010 (800) 221-7945; *The Statesman's Year-Book.*

Statistical Office of the United Nations, Publishing Service, New York, New York 10017 (800) 253-9646; *Statistical Yearbook.*

U.S. Department of Transportation, Maritime Administration, 400 Seventh Street, SW, Washington, D.C. 20590 (202)

366-5807, www.marad.dot.gov; *A Statistical Analysis of the World's Merchant Fleets.*

LEBANON - MILITARY

Central Intelligence Agency, Washington, D.C. 20505 (703) 482-1100, www.cia.gov; *The World Factbook.*

Euromonitor International, Inc., 122 South Michigan Avenue, Suite 1200, Chicago, Illinois 60603 (800) 577-EURO; *World Marketing Data and Statistics.*

The International Institute for Strategic Studies, 23 Tavistock Street, London WC2E 7NQ, England 44 171 3797676; *The Military Balance.*

St. Martin's Press, Inc., 175 Fifth Avenue, New York, New York 10010 (800) 221-7945; *The Statesman's Year-Book.*

Statistical Office of the United Nations, Publishing Service, New York, New York 10017 (800) 253-9646; *Human Development Report.*

U.S. Arms Control and Disarmament Agency, 320 Twenty-first Street, NW, Washington, D.C. 20451 (202) 647-8677; *World Military Expenditures and Arms Transfers.*

LEBANON - MILK PRODUCTION - See LEBANON - DAIRY PRODUCTS

LEBANON - MINING AND MINERAL PRODUCTS

Economic Commission for Western Asia, Post Office Box 27, Baghdad, Iraq; *Statistical Abstract of Western Asia.*

Europa Publications Limited, 18 Bedford Square, London, WC1B 3JN, England; *The Europa World Year Book.*

M.E. Sharpe, 80 Business Park Drive, Armonk, New York 10504 (800) 541-6563; *The Illustrated Book of World Rankings.*

St. Martin's Press, Inc., 175 Fifth Avenue, New York, New York 10010 (800) 221-7945; *The Statesman's Year-Book.*

Statistical Office of the United Nations, Publishing Service, New York, New York 10017 (800) 253-9646; *Bulletin of Industrial Statistics for the Arab Countries;* and *Statistical Yearbook.*

United Nations Conference on Trade and Development, Central Statistical Service, Palais des Nations, Geneva, Switzerland (Telephone in U.S. (800) 253-9646); *UNCTAD Commodity Yearbook.*

LEBANON - MONEY EXCHANGE RATES -

See **LEBANON - EXCHANGE RATES**

LEBANON - MONEY RESERVES

Euromonitor International, Inc., 122 South Michigan Avenue, Suite 1200, Chicago, Illinois 60603 (800) 577-EURO; *International Marketing Data and Statistics.*

LEBANON - MONEY SUPPLY

Economic Commission for Western Asia, Post Office Box 27, Baghdad, Iraq; *Statistical Abstract of Western Asia.*

Economist Intelligence Unit, 111 West 57th Street, New York, New York 10019 (800) 938-4685; *Lebanon Country Report.*

Euromonitor International, Inc., 122 South Michigan Avenue, Suite 1200, Chicago, Illinois 60603 (800) 577-EURO; *International Marketing Data and Statistics.*

Europa Publications Limited, 18 Bedford Square, London, WC1B 3JN, England; *The Europa World Year Book.*

International Monetary Fund, 700 Nineteenth Street, NW, Washington, D.C. 20431 (202) 623-7000; *International Financial Statistics.*

Statistical Office of the United Nations, Publishing Service, New York, New York 10017 (800) 253-9646; *Statistical Yearbook.*

LEBANON - MORTALITY

Central Intelligence Agency, Washington, D.C. 20505 (703) 482-1100, www.cia.gov; *The World Factbook.*

Euromonitor International, Inc., 122 South Michigan Avenue, Suite 1200, Chicago, Illinois 60603 (800) 577-EURO; *International Marketing Data and Statistics; and The World Economic Factbook.*

Europa Publications Limited, 18 Bedford Square, London, WC1B 3JN, England; *The Europa World Year Book.*

St. Martin's Press, Inc., 175 Fifth Avenue, New York, New York 10010 (800) 221-7945; *The Statesman's Year-Book.*

Statistical Office of the United Nations, Publishing Service, New York, New York 10017 (800) 253-9646; *Demographic Yearbook; Human Development Report; World Statistics Pocketbook;* and *Statistical Yearbook.*

United Nations Children's Fund (UNICEF), 3 United Nations Plaza, New York, New York 10017 (800) 253-9646; *State of the World's Children.*

The World Bank, 1818 H Street, NW, Washington, D.C. 20433 (202) 477-1234;

The World Bank Atlas.

LEBANON - MOTION PICTURES

United Nations Educational, Scientific and Cultural Organization (UNESCO), 7 Place de Fontenoy, F-75700 Paris, France (Telephone Number in U.S. (212) 963-5981); *Statistical Yearbook.*

LEBANON - MOTOR VEHICLE TAXES - See LEBANON - TAXATION

LEBANON - MOTOR VEHICLES IN USE

Economic Commission for Western Asia, Post Office Box 27, Baghdad, Iraq; *Statistical Abstract of Western Asia.*

Europa Publications Limited, 18 Bedford Square, London, WC1B 3JN, England; *The Europa World Year Book.*

International Road Federation, 2600 Virginia Avenue, N.W., Washington, D.C. 20024 (202) 338-4641; *World Road Statistics.*

Statistical Office of the United Nations, Publishing Service, New York, New York 10017 (800) 253-9646; *Statistical Yearbook.*

LEBANON - MULES - See LEBANON - LIVESTOCK AND POULTRY

LEBANON - MUSEUMS

M.E. Sharpe, 80 Business Park Drive, Armonk, New York 10504 (800) 541-6563; *The Illustrated Book of World Rankings.*

United Nations Educational, Scientific and Cultural Organization (UNESCO), 7 Place de Fontenoy, F-75700 Paris, France (Telephone Number in U.S. (212) 963-5981); *Statistical Yearbook.*

LEBANON - NATALITY - See LEBANON - BIRTH RATES

LEBANON - NATIONAL ACCOUNTS

Economic Commission for Western Asia, Post Office Box 27, Baghdad, Iraq; *Statistical Abstract of Western Asia.*

Europa Publications Limited, 18 Bedford Square, London, WC1B 3JN, England; *The Europa World Year Book.*

Statistical Office of the United Nations, Publishing Service, New York, New York 10017 (800) 253-9646; *National Accounts Statistics;* and *Statistical Yearbook.*

LEBANON - NATIONAL INCOME

M.E. Sharpe, 80 Business Park Drive, Armonk, New York 10504 (800) 541-6563; *The Illustrated Book of World Rankings.*

Statistical Office of the United Nations, Publishing Service, New York, New York 10017 (800) 253-9646; *National Accounts Statistics;* and *Statistical Yearbook.*

LEBANON - NATIONAL PRODUCT

M.E. Sharpe, 80 Business Park Drive, Armonk, New York 10504 (800) 541-6563; *The Illustrated Book of World Rankings.*

LEBANON - NATURAL GAS - PRODUCTION - See LEBANON - MINING AND MINERAL PRODUCTS

LEBANON - NEWSPAPER PRODUCTION - See LEBANON - FORESTRY AND FORESTRY PRODUCTS

LEBANON - NEWSPRINT - See LEBANON - FORESTRY AND FOREST PRODUCTS

LEBANON - OATS PRODUCTION - See LEBANON - CROPS

LEBANON - OCCUPATIONS - See LEBANON - LABOR

LEBANON - PAPER - See LEBANON - FORESTRY AND FOREST PRODUCTS

LEBANON - PATENTS, TRADEMARKS AND SERVICE MARKS

Statistical Office of the United Nations, Publishing Service, New York, New York 10017 (800) 253-9646; *Statistical Yearbook.*

LEBANON - PEANUT PRODUCTION - See LEBANON - CROPS

LEBANON - PESTICIDE USE

Food and Agricultural Organization of the United Nations (FAO), Via delle Terme di Caracalla, 00100 Rome, Italy (Telephone Number in U.S. (202) 653-2400); *The State of Food and Agriculture.*

LEBANON - PETROLEUM INDUSTRY

Food and Agricultural Organization of the United Nations (FAO), Via delle Terme di Caracalla, 00100 Rome, Italy (Telephone Number in U.S. (202) 653-2400); *The State of Food and Agriculture.*

M.E. Sharpe, 80 Business Park Drive, Armonk, New York 10504 (800) 541-6563; *The Illustrated Book of World Rankings.*

St. Martin's Press, Inc., 175 Fifth Avenue, New York, New York 10010 (800) 221-7945; *The Statesman's Year-Book.*

Statistical Office of the United Nations, Publishing Service, New York, New York 10017 (800) 253-9646; *Statistical Yearbook.*

United Nations Conference on Trade and Development, Central Statistical Service, Palais des Nations, Geneva, Switzerland (Telephone in U.S. (800) 253-9646); *UNCTAD Commodity Yearbook.*

LEBANON - PIGS - See LEBANON - LIVESTOCK AND POULTRY

LEBANON - POPULATION

Central Intelligence Agency, Washington, D.C. 20505 (703) 482-1100, www.cia.gov; *The World Factbook.*

Economic Commission for Western Asia, Post Office Box 27, Baghdad, Iraq; *Statistical Abstract of Western Asia.*

The Economist Intelligence Unit, 111 West 57th Street, New York, New York 10019 (800) 938-4685; *Lebanon Country Report;* and *The World Market Atlas.*

Euromonitor International, Inc., 122 South Michigan Avenue, Suite 1200, Chicago, Illinois 60603 (800) 577-EURO; *International Marketing Data and Statistics;* and *The World Economic Factbook.*

Europa Publications Limited, 18 Bedford Square, London, WC1B 3JN, England; *The Europa World Year Book.*

Food and Agricultural Organization of the United Nations (FAO), Via delle Terme di Caracalla, 00100 Rome, Italy (Telephone Number in U.S. (202) 653-2400); *Production Yearbook.*

International Labour Office, I.L.O. Publications, 1828 L Street, N.W., Suite 801, Washington, D.C. (301) 638-3152; *Yearbook of Labour Statistics.*

M.E. Sharpe, 80 Business Park Drive, Armonk, New York 10504 (800) 541-6563; *The Illustrated Book of World Rankings.*

St. Martin's Press, Inc., 175 Fifth Avenue, New York, New York 10010 (800) 221-7945; *The Statesman's Year-Book.*

Statistical Office of the United Nations, Publishing Service, New York, New York 10017 (800) 253-9646; *Demographic Yearbook; Human Development Report; World Statistics Pocketbook;* and *Statistical Yearbook.*

United Nations Educational, Scientific and Cultural Organization (UNESCO), 7 Place de Fontenoy, F-75700 Paris, France (Telephone Number in U.S. (212) 963-5981); *Statistical Yearbook.*

U.S. Arms Control and Disarmament Agency, 320 Twenty-first Street, NW, Washington, D.C. 20451 (202) 647-8677; *World Military Expenditures and Arms Transfers.*

The World Bank, 1818 H Street, NW, Washington, D.C. 20433 (202) 477-1234; *The World Bank Atlas.*

World Health Organization, Office of Publications, 20 Avenue Appia, CH-1211 Geneva 27, Switzerland (Telephone Number in U.S. (518) 436-9686); *World Health Statistics Annual.*

LEBANON - POST OFFICES

M.E. Sharpe, 80 Business Park Drive, Armonk, New York 10504 (800) 541-6563; *The Illustrated Book of World Rankings.*

LEBANON - POTATO PRODUCTION - See LEBANON - CROPS

LEBANON - PRICES

Economic Commission for Western Asia, Post Office Box 27, Baghdad, Iraq; *Statistical Abstract of Western Asia.*

Food and Agricultural Organization of the United Nations (FAO), Via delle Terme di Caracalla, 00100 Rome, Italy (Telephone Number in U.S. (202) 653-2400); *Production Yearbook;* and *The State of Food and Agriculture.*

M.E. Sharpe, 80 Business Park Drive, Armonk, New York 10504 (800) 541-6563; *The Illustrated Book of World Rankings.*

LEBANON - PRINTING AND WRITING PAPER - See LEBANON - FORESTRY AND FOREST PRODUCTS

LEBANON - PRODUCTION

M.E. Sharpe, 80 Business Park Drive, Armonk, New York 10504 (800) 541-6563; *The Illustrated Book of World Rankings.*

LEBANON - PRODUCTIVITY

Euromonitor International, Inc., 122 South Michigan Avenue, Suite 1200, Chicago, Illinois 60603 (800) 577-EURO; *International Marketing Data and Statistics.*

LEBANON - PUBLIC FINANCE - See LEBANON - FINANCE

LEBANON - RADIO BROADCASTING - See LEBANON - BROADCASTING

LEBANON - RADIO RECEIVERS

St. Martin's Press, Inc., 175 Fifth Avenue, New York, New York 10010 (800) 221-7945; *The Statesman's Year-Book.*

LEBANON - RAILWAYS

Jane's Information Group, Sentinel House, 163 Brighton Road, Coulsdon, Surrey CR5 2NH, England (Telephone Number in U.S. (703) 683-3700); *Jane's World Railways.*

St. Martin's Press, Inc., 175 Fifth Avenue, New York, New York 10010 (800) 221-7945; *The Statesman's Year-Book.*

Statistical Office of the United Nations, Publishing Service, New York, New York 10017 (800) 253-9646; *Statistical Yearbook.*

LEBANON - RELIGION

Central Intelligence Agency, Washington, D.C. 20505 (703) 482-1100, www.cia.gov; *The World Factbook.*

M.E. Sharpe, 80 Business Park Drive, Armonk, New York 10504 (800) 541-6563; *The Illustrated Book of World Rankings.*

St. Martin's Press, Inc., 175 Fifth Avenue, New York, New York 10010 (800) 221-7945; *The Statesman's Year-Book.*

LEBANON - RETAIL TRADE

Euromonitor International, Inc., 122 South Michigan Avenue, Suite 1200, Chicago, Illinois 60603 (800) 577-EURO; *World Marketing Data and Statistics.*

LEBANON - RICE PRODUCTION - See LEBANON - CROPS

LEBANON - ROOT AND TUBER PRODUCTION - See LEBANON - CROPS

LEBANON - ROUNDWOOD PRODUCTION - See LEBANON - FORESTRY AND FOREST PRODUCTS

LEBANON - RUBBER PRODUCTION AND CONSUMPTION

M.E. Sharpe, 80 Business Park Drive, Armonk, New York 10504 (800) 541-6563; *The Illustrated Book of World Rankings.*

LEBANON - SALT PRODUCTION

Statistical Office of the United Nations, Publishing Service, New York, New York 10017 (800) 253-9646; *Statistical Yearbook.*

LEBANON - SAWNWOOD PRODUCTION - See LEBANON - FORESTRY AND FOREST PRODUCTS

LEBANON - SCIENTISTS, TECHNICIANS AND ENGINEERS

Statistical Office of the United Nations, Publishing Service, New York, New York 10017 (800) 253-9646; *Statistical Yearbook.*

United Nations Educational, Scientific and Cultural Organization (UNESCO), 7 Place de Fontenoy, F-75700 Paris, France (Telephone Number in U.S. (212) 963-5981); *Statistical Yearbook.*

LEBANON - SENIOR CITIZENS

M.E. Sharpe, 80 Business Park Drive, Armonk, New York 10504 (800) 541-6563; *The Illustrated Book of World Rankings.*

LEBANON - SHEEP - See LEBANON - LIVESTOCK AND POULTRY

LEBANON - SILVER PRODUCTION AND CONSUMPTION - See LEBANON - MINING AND MINERAL PRODUCTS

LEBANON - SOCIAL DATA

M.E. Sharpe, 80 Business Park Drive, Armonk, New York 10504 (800) 541-6563; *The Illustrated Book of World Rankings.*

Statistical Office of the United Nations, Publishing Service, New York, New York 10017 (800) 253-9646; *World Statistics Pocketbook.*

LEBANON - SOCIAL SECURITY

Statistical Office of the United Nations, Publishing Service, New York, New York 10017 (800) 253-9646; *National Accounts Statistics.*

LEBANON - STATE BUDGET

Euromonitor International, Inc., 122 South Michigan Avenue, Suite 1200, Chicago, Illinois 60603 (800) 577-EURO; *International Marketing Data and Statistics.*

LEBANON - STEEL - See LEBANON - MINING AND MINERAL PRODUCTS

LEBANON - STOCKS - COMMODITY - MARKET PRICE - INDEX

Food and Agricultural Organization of the United Nations (FAO), Via delle Terme di Caracalla, 00100 Rome, Italy (Telephone Number in U.S. (202) 653-2400); *The State of Food and Agriculture.*

LEBANON - SUGAR PRODUCTION AND CONSUMPTION - See LEBANON - CROPS

LEBANON - TAXATION

Europa Publications Limited, 18 Bedford Square, London, WC1B 3JN, England; *The Europa World Year Book.*

International Road Federation, 2600 Virginia Avenue, N.W., Washington, D.C. 20024 (202) 338-4641; *World Road Statistics.*

LEBANON - TELEPHONES IN USE

American Telephone and Telegraph Company, 26 Parsippany Road, Whippany, New Jersey 07981 (800) 222-0300; *The World's Telephones.*

Central Intelligence Agency, Washington, D.C. 20505 (703) 482-1100, www.cia.gov; *The World Factbook.*

St. Martin's Press, Inc., 175 Fifth Avenue, New York, New York 10010 (800) 221-7945; *The Statesman's Year-Book.*

Statistical Office of the United Nations, Publishing Service, New York, New York 10017 (800) 253-9646; *Statistical Yearbook; and World Statistics Pocketbook.*

LEBANON - TELEVISION BROADCASTING - See LEBANON - BROADCASTING

LEBANON - TEXTILE INDUSTRY

M.E. Sharpe, 80 Business Park Drive, Armonk, New York 10504 (800) 541-6563; *The Illustrated Book of World Rankings.*

Statistical Office of the United Nations, Publishing Service, New York, New York 10017 (800) 253-9646; *Statistical Yearbook.*

United Nations Conference on Trade and Development, Central Statistical Service, Palais des Nations, Geneva, Switzerland (Telephone in U.S. (800) 253-9646); *UNCTAD Commodity Yearbook.*

LEBANON - TOBACCO PRODUCTION

M.E. Sharpe, 80 Business Park Drive, Armonk, New York 10504 (800) 541-6563; *The Illustrated Book of World Rankings.*

Statistical Office of the United Nations, Publishing Service, New York, New York 10017 (800) 253-9646; *Statistical Yearbook.*

LEBANON - TOURISM

Economic Commission for Western Asia, Post Office Box 27, Baghdad, Iraq; *Statistical Abstract of Western Asia.*

Euromonitor International, Inc., 122 South Michigan Avenue, Suite 1200, Chicago, Illinois 60603 (800) 577-EURO; *The World Economic Factbook; and World Marketing Data and Statistics.*

M.E. Sharpe, 80 Business Park Drive, Armonk, New York 10504 (800) 541-6563; *The Illustrated Book of World Rankings.*

Statistical Office of the United Nations, Publishing Service, New York, New York 10017 (800) 253-9646; *Statistical Yearbook.*

LEBANON - TRACTORS IN USE

Statistical Office of the United Nations, Publishing Service, New York, New York 10017 (800) 253-9646; *Statistical Yearbook.*

LEBANON - TRADE - See LEBANON - FOREIGN TRADE

LEBANON - TRADEMARKS AND SERVICE MARKS - See LEBANON - PATENTS, TRADEMARKS AND SERVICE MARKS

LEBANON - TRANSPORTATION AND COMMUNICATIONS

Central Intelligence Agency, Washington, D.C. 20505 (703) 482-1100, www.cia.gov; *The World Factbook.*

Economic Commission for Western Asia, Post Office Box 27, Baghdad, Iraq; *Statistical Abstract of Western Asia.*

Euromonitor International, Inc., 122 South Michigan Avenue, Suite 1200, Chicago, Illinois 60603 (800) 577-EURO; *International Marketing Data and Statistics; and World Marketing Data and Statistics.*

Europa Publications Limited, 18 Bedford Square, London, WC1B 3JN, England; *The Europa World Year Book.*

M.E. Sharpe, 80 Business Park Drive, Armonk, New York 10504 (800) 541-6563; *The Illustrated Book of World Rankings.*

St. Martin's Press, Inc., 175 Fifth Avenue, New York, New York 10010 (800) 221-7945; *The Statesman's Year-Book.*

Statistical Office of the United Nations, Publishing Service, New York, New York 10017 (800) 253-9646; *Human Development Report.*

LEBANON - UNEMPLOYMENT

Central Intelligence Agency, Washington, D.C. 20505 (703) 482-1100, www.cia.gov; *The World Factbook.*

Euromonitor International, Inc., 122 South Michigan Avenue, Suite 1200, Chicago, Illinois 60603 (800) 577-EURO; *International Marketing Data and Statistics.*

International Labour Office, I.L.O. Publications, 1828 L Street, N.W., Suite 801, Washington, D.C. (301) 638-3152; *Yearbook of Labour Statistics.*

LEBANON - VITAL STATISTICS

Euromonitor International, Inc., 122 South Michigan Avenue, Suite 1200, Chicago, Illinois 60603 (800) 577-EURO; *International Marketing Data and Statistics.*

Statistical Office of the United Nations, Publishing Service, New York, New York 10017 (800) 253-9646; *Statistical Yearbook.*

World Health Organization, Office of Publications, 20 Avenue Appia, CH-1211 Geneva 27, Switzerland (Telephone Number in U.S. (518) 436-9686); *World Health Statistics Annual.*

LEBANON - WAGES

International Labour Office, I.L.O. Publications, 1828 L Street, N.W., Suite 801, Washington, D.C. (301) 638-3152; *Yearbook of Labour Statistics.*

LEBANON - WALNUT PRODUCTION - See LEBANON - CROPS

LEBANON - WATERMELON PRODUCTION - See LEBANON - CROPS

LEBANON - WEATHER - See LEBANON - CLIMATE

LEBANON - WHEAT PRODUCTION AND PRICES - See LEBANON - CROPS

LEBANON - WINE PRODUCTION - See LEBANON - BEVERAGES

LEBANON - WOOL PRODUCTION - See LEBANON - TEXTILE INDUSTRY

LEBANON - YARN PRODUCTION - See LEBANON - TEXTILE INDUSTRY

LEEWARD ISLANDS - AREA AND DENSITY OF POPULATION

St. Martin's Press, Inc., 175 Fifth Avenue, New York, New York 10010 (800) 221-7945; *The Statesman's Year-Book.*

LEEWARD ISLANDS - EXPORTS

International Monetary Fund, 700 Nineteenth Street, NW, Washington, D.C. 20431 (202) 623-7000; *Direction of Trade Statistics.*

LEEWARD ISLANDS - IMPORTS

International Monetary Fund, 700 Nineteenth Street, NW, Washington, D.C. 20431 (202) 623-7000; *Direction of Trade Statistics.*

LEEWARD ISLANDS - POPULATION

St. Martin's Press, Inc., 175 Fifth Avenue, New York, New York 10010 (800) 221-7945; *The Statesman's Year-Book.*

Statistical Office of the United Nations, Publishing Service, New York, New York 10017 (800) 253-9646; *Statistical Yearbook.*

LEGAL ASSISTANTS

U.S. Department of Labor, Bureau of Labor Statistics, Two Massachusetts Avenue, NE, Washington, D.C. 20212 (202) 691-5200, www.stats.bls.gov; *Employment and Earnings; and unpublished data.*

LEGAL SERVICES - EARNINGS

U.S. Department of Commerce, Bureau of the Census, Washington, D.C. 20233

(301) 457-4100, www.census.gov; *County Business Patterns;* and *Census of Service Industries.*

U.S. Department of Labor, Bureau of Labor Statistics, Two Massachusetts Avenue, NE, Washington, D.C. 20212 (202) 691-5200, www.stats.bls.gov; *Employment and Earnings;* and Internet site: http://stats.bls.gov/ ceshome.htm.

LEGAL SERVICES - EMPLOYEES

U.S. Department of Commerce, Bureau of the Census, Washington, D.C. 20233 (301) 457-4100, www.census.gov; *County Business Patterns;* and *Census of Service Industries.*

U.S. Department of Labor, Bureau of Labor Statistics, Two Massachusetts Avenue, NE, Washington, D.C. 20212 (202) 691-5200, www.stats.bls.gov; *Employment and Earnings; Monthly Labor Review;* unpublished data; and Internet site: http://stats.bls.gov/ ceshome.htm.

LEGAL SERVICES - ESTABLISHMENTS

U.S. Department of Commerce, Bureau of the Census, Washington, D.C. 20233 (301) 457-4100, www.census.gov; *County Business Patterns.*

LEGAL SERVICES - FINANCES

U.S. Department of Commerce, Bureau of the Census, Washington, D.C. 20233 (301) 457-4100, www.census.gov; *Census of Service Industries; Current Business Reports; Service Annual Survey;* and unpublished data.

LEGAL SERVICES - GROSS DOMESTIC PRODUCT

U.S. Department of Commerce, Bureau of Economic Analysis, Fourteenth Street between Constitution Avenue and E Street, NW, Washington, D.C. 20230 (202) 606-9900, www.bea.doc.gov; *Survey of Current Business.*

LEGAL SERVICES - OCCUPATIONAL SAFETY

U.S. Department of Labor, Bureau of Labor Statistics, Two Massachusetts Avenue, NE, Washington, D.C. 20212 (202) 691-5200, www.stats.bls.gov; *Occupational Injuries and Illnesses in the United States by Industry.*

LEGAL SERVICES - RECEIPTS

U.S. Department of Commerce, Bureau of the Census, Washington, D.C. 20233 (301) 457-4100, www.census.gov; *Current Business Reports; Service Annual Survey;* and *Census of Service Industries.*

LEGIONELLOSIS

U.S. Department of Health and Human Services, Centers for Disease Control and Prevention, 1600 Clifton Road, NE, Atlanta, Georgia 30333 (800) 311-3435, www.cdc.gov; *Summary of Notifiable Diseases, United States;* and *Morbidity and Weekly Report.*

LEGISLATURES - STATE PARTY COMPOSITION

Council of State Governments, Post Office Box 11910, Lexington, Kentucky 40578 (859) 244-8000; *State Elective Officials and the Legislatures.*

National Conference of State Legislatures, 1560 Broadway, Suite 700, Suite 2100, Denver, Colorado 80202 (303) 830-2200; *State Legislatures;* and unpublished data.

LEISURE ACTIVITIES - See RECREATION

LEMONS

U.S. Department of Agriculture, National Agricultural Statistics Service, Fourteenth Street and Independence Avenue, SW, Washington, D.C. 20250 (800) 727-9540; *Citrus Fruits.*

LENS EXTRACTION - INSERTION

U.S. Department of Health and Human Services, National Center for Health Statistics, 3700 East-West Highway, Hyattsville, Maryland 20782 (301) 436-8500, www.cdc.gov/nchs; *Advance Data, No. 296.*

LEPROSY

U.S. Department of Health and Human Services, Center for Disease Control and Prevention, 1600 Clifton Road, NE, Atlanta, Georgia 30333 (800) 639-3311, www.cdc.gov; *Summary of Notifiable Diseases, United States;* and *Morbidity and Mortality Weekly Report.*

Lesotho - National Statistical Office

Bureau of Statistics, Post Office Box 455, Maseru 100, Lesotho.

Lesotho - Primary Statistics Sources

Bureau of Statistics, Post Office Box 455, Maseru 100, Lesotho; *Quarterly Statistical Bulletin;* and *Lesotho Statistical Yearbook.*

LESOTHO - AGRICULTURE

Economist Intelligence Unit, 111 West 57th Street, New York, New York 10019 (800) 938-4685; *Lesotho Country Report.*

Euromonitor International, Inc., 122 South Michigan Avenue, Suite 1200, Chicago, Illinois 60603 (800) 577-EURO; *World Marketing Data and Statistics.*

Europa Publications Limited, 18 Bedford Square, London, WC1B 3JN, England; *The Europa World Year Book.*

Food and Agricultural Organization of the United Nations (FAO), Via delle Terme di Caracalla, 00100 Rome, Italy (Telephone Number in U.S. (202) 653-2400); *Production Yearbook; The State of Food and Agriculture;* and *Trade Yearbook.*

M.E. Sharpe, 80 Business Park Drive, Armonk, New York 10504 (800) 541-6563; *The Illustrated Book of World Rankings.*

St. Martin's Press, Inc., 175 Fifth Avenue, New York, New York 10010 (800) 221-7945; *The Statesman's Year-Book.*

Statistical Office of the United Nations, Publishing Service, New York, New York 10017 (800) 253-9646; *Statistical Yearbook;* and *Survey of Economic and Social Conditions in Africa.*

United Nations Conference on Trade and Development, Central Statistical Service, Palais des Nations, Geneva, Switzerland (Telephone in U.S. (800) 253-9646); *UNCTAD Commodity Yearbook.*

United Nations Economic Commission for Africa, Africa Hall, Post Office Box 3001, Addis Ababa, Ethiopia (Telephone Number in U.S. (800) 253-9646); *African Statistical Yearbook.*

The World Bank, 1818 H Street, NW, Washington, D.C. 20433 (202) 477-1234; *World Development Indicators.*

LESOTHO - AIRLINE SERVICE

Europa Publications Limited, 18 Bedford Square, London, WC1B 3JN, England; *The Europa World Year Book.*

International Civil Aviation Organization, 999 University Street, Montreal, Quebec, Canada H3C 5H7 (514) 954-8219; *Civil Aviation Statistics of the World.*

M.E. Sharpe, 80 Business Park Drive, Armonk, New York 10504 (800) 541-6563; *The Illustrated Book of World Rankings.*

St. Martin's Press, Inc., 175 Fifth Avenue, New York, New York 10010 (800) 221-7945; *The Statesman's Year-Book.*

United Nations Economic Commission

for Africa, Africa Hall, Post Office Box 3001, Addis Ababa, Ethiopia (Telephone Number in U.S. (800) 253-9646); *African Statistical Yearbook.*

LESOTHO - AIRPORTS

Central Intelligence Agency, Washington, D.C. 20505 (703) 482-1100, www.cia.gov; *The World Factbook.*

LESOTHO - ALUMINUM PRODUCTION AND CONSUMPTION - See LESOTHO - MINING AND MINERAL PRODUCTS

LESOTHO - ANIMAL HEALTH

Food and Agricultural Organization of the United Nations (FAO), Via delle Terme di Caracalla, 00100 Rome, Italy (Telephone Number in U.S. (202) 653-2400); *Animal Health Yearbook.*

LESOTHO - AREA AND DENSITY OF POPULATION

African Development Bank, 01 BP 1387, Abidjan 01, Cote d'Ivoire; *Selected Statistics on Regional Member Countries.*

Central Intelligence Agency, Washington, D.C. 20505 (703) 482-1100, www.cia.gov; *The World Factbook.*

Euromonitor International, Inc., 122 South Michigan Avenue, Suite 1200, Chicago, Illinois 60603 (800) 577-EURO; *The World Economic Factbook.*

Europa Publications Limited, 18 Bedford Square, London, WC1B 3JN, England; *The Europa World Year Book.*

Food and Agricultural Organization of the United Nations (FAO), Via delle Terme di Caracalla, 00100 Rome, Italy (Telephone Number in U.S. (202) 653-2400); *The State of Food and Agriculture.*

M.E. Sharpe, 80 Business Park Drive, Armonk, New York 10504 (800) 541-6563; *The Illustrated Book of World Rankings.*

St. Martin's Press, Inc., 175 Fifth Avenue, New York, New York 10010 (800) 221-7945; *The Statesman's Year-Book.*

Statistical Office of the United Nations, Publishing Service, New York, New York 10017 (800) 253-9646; *Statistical Yearbook;* and *Survey of Economic and Social Conditions in Africa.*

The World Bank, 1818 H Street, NW, Washington, D.C. 20433 (202) 477-1234; *World Development Report.*

LESOTHO - ARMS EXPORTS AND IMPORTS - See LESOTHO - MILITARY

LESOTHO - BALANCE OF PAYMENTS

African Development Bank, 01 BP 1387, Abidjan 01, Cote d'Ivoire; *Selected Statistics on Regional Member Countries.*

The Economist Intelligence Unit, 111 West 57th Street, New York, New York 10019 (800) 938-4685; *The World Market Atlas.*

Europa Publications Limited, 18 Bedford Square, London, WC1B 3JN, England; *The Europa World Year Book.*

International Monetary Fund, 700 Nineteenth Street, NW, Washington, D.C. 20431 (202) 623-7000; *Balance of Payments Yearbook.*

United Nations Conference on Trade and Development (UNCTAD), New York, New York 10017 (800) 253-9646; *Handbook of International Trade and Development Statistics.*

United Nations Economic Commission for Africa, Africa Hall, Post Office Box 3001, Addis Ababa, Ethiopia (Telephone Number in U.S. (800) 253-9646); *African Statistical Yearbook.*

The World Bank, 1818 H Street, NW, Washington, D.C. 20433 (202) 477-1234; *World Development Report;* and *World Development Indicators.*

LESOTHO - BANKING

Euromonitor International, Inc., 122 South Michigan Avenue, Suite 1200, Chicago, Illinois 60603 (800) 577-EURO; *World Marketing Data and Statistics.*

Europa Publications Limited, 18 Bedford Square, London, WC1B 3JN, England; *The Europa World Year Book.*

International Monetary Fund, 700 Nineteenth Street, NW, Washington, D.C. 20431 (202) 623-7000; *International Financial Statistics.*

M.E. Sharpe, 80 Business Park Drive, Armonk, New York 10504 (800) 541-6563; *The Illustrated Book of World Rankings.*

St. Martin's Press, Inc., 175 Fifth Avenue, New York, New York 10010 (800) 221-7945; *The Statesman's Year-Book.*

United Nations Economic Commission for Africa, Africa Hall, Post Office Box 3001, Addis Ababa, Ethiopia (Telephone Number in U.S. (800) 253-9646); *African Statistical Yearbook.*

LESOTHO - BARLEY PRODUCTION - See LESOTHO - CROPS

LESOTHO - BEER PRODUCTION - See LESOTHO - BEVERAGES

LESOTHO - BEVERAGES

M.E. Sharpe, 80 Business Park Drive, Armonk, New York 10504 (800) 541-6563; *The Illustrated Book of World Rankings.*

LESOTHO - BIRTH RATES

Central Intelligence Agency, Washington, D.C. 20505 (703) 482-1100, www.cia.gov; *The World Factbook.*

Euromonitor International, Inc., 122 South Michigan Avenue, Suite 1200, Chicago, Illinois 60603 (800) 577-EURO; *International Marketing Data and Statistics;* and *The World Economic Factbook.*

Europa Publications Limited, 18 Bedford Square, London, WC1B 3JN, England; *The Europa World Year Book.*

M.E. Sharpe, 80 Business Park Drive, Armonk, New York 10504 (800) 541-6563; *The Illustrated Book of World Rankings.*

Statistical Office of the United Nations, Publishing Service, New York, New York 10017 (800) 253-9646; *Demographic Yearbook; Statistical Yearbook;* and *Survey of Economic and Social Conditions in Africa.*

The World Bank, 1818 H Street, NW, Washington, D.C. 20433 (202) 477-1234; *World Development Indicators.*

LESOTHO - BROADCASTING

Billboard Limited, Post Office Box 9027, 1006 AA Amsterdam, The Netherlands (Telephone Number in U.S. (212) 764-7300); *World Radio TV Handbook.*

Central Intelligence Agency, Washington, D.C. 20505 (703) 482-1100, www.cia.gov; *The World Factbook.*

Euromonitor International, Inc., 122 South Michigan Avenue, Suite 1200, Chicago, Illinois 60603 (800) 577-EURO; *World Marketing Data and Statistics.*

M.E. Sharpe, 80 Business Park Drive, Armonk, New York 10504 (800) 541-6563; *The Illustrated Book of World Rankings.*

St. Martin's Press, Inc., 175 Fifth Avenue, New York, New York 10010 (800) 221-7945; *The Statesman's Year-Book.*

LESOTHO - BUDGET

Central Intelligence Agency, Washington, D.C. 20505 (703) 482-1100, www.cia.gov; *The World Factbook.*

LESOTHO - BUSINESS AND PROFESSIONAL LICENSES

International Monetary Fund, 700

Nineteenth Street, NW, Washington, D.C. 20431 (202) 623-7000; *Government Finance Statistics Yearbook.*

LESOTHO - CALORIE SUPPLY

African Development Bank, 01 BP 1387, Abidjan 01, Cote d'Ivoire; *Selected Statistics on Regional Member Countries.*

Food and Agricultural Organization of the United Nations (FAO), Via delle Terme di Caracalla, 00100 Rome, Italy (Telephone Number in U.S. (202) 653-2400); *The State of Food and Agriculture.*

LESOTHO - CAPITAL REVENUE

International Monetary Fund, 700 Nineteenth Street, NW, Washington, D.C. 20431 (202) 623-7000; *Government Finance Statistics Yearbook.*

LESOTHO - CATTLE - See LESOTHO - LIVESTOCK AND POULTRY

LESOTHO - CEMENT PRODUCTION - See LESOTHO - MINING AND MINERAL PRODUCTS

LESOTHO - CHEMICAL (ORGANIC) PRODUCTION - See LESOTHO - MINING AND MINERAL PRODUCTS

LESOTHO - CHICKENS - See LESOTHO - LIVESTOCK AND POULTRY

LESOTHO - CIGARETTE PRODUCTION - See LESOTHO - TOBACCO PRODUCTION

LESOTHO - CLIMATE

M.E. Sharpe, 80 Business Park Drive, Armonk, New York 10504 (800) 541-6563; *The Illustrated Book of World Rankings.*

St. Martin's Press, Inc., 175 Fifth Avenue, New York, New York 10010 (800) 221-7945; *The Statesman's Year-Book.*

LESOTHO - COAL PRODUCTION - See LESOTHO - MINING AND MINERAL PRODUCTS

LESOTHO - COFFEE PRODUCTION AND CONSUMPTION - See LESOTHO - CROPS

LESOTHO - COMMERCE

St. Martin's Press, Inc., 175 Fifth Avenue, New York, New York 10010 (800) 221-7945; *The Statesman's Year-Book.*

LESOTHO - COMMUNICATIONS - See LESOTHO - TRANSPORTATION AND COMMUNICATIONS

LESOTHO - CONSTRUCTION INDUSTRY

M.E. Sharpe, 80 Business Park Drive, Armonk, New York 10504 (800) 541-6563;

The Illustrated Book of World Rankings.

United Nations Economic Commission for Africa, Africa Hall, Post Office Box 3001, Addis Ababa, Ethiopia (Telephone Number in U.S. (800) 253-9646); *African Statistical Yearbook.*

World Intellectual Property Organization, 34 Chemin des Colombettes, CH-1211 Geneva 20, Switzerland; *Industrial Property Statistics.*

LESOTHO - CONSUMER PRICE INDEX

African Development Bank, 01 BP 1387, Abidjan 01, Cote d'Ivoire; *Selected Statistics on Regional Member Countries.*

Europa Publications Limited, 18 Bedford Square, London, WC1B 3JN, England; *The Europa World Year Book.*

Statistical Office of the United Nations, Publishing Service, New York, New York 10017 (800) 253-9646; *Statistical Yearbook;* and *Survey of Economic and Social Conditions in Africa.*

United Nations Economic Commission for Africa, Africa Hall, Post Office Box 3001, Addis Ababa, Ethiopia (Telephone Number in U.S. (800) 253-9646); *African Statistical Yearbook.*

LESOTHO - CONSUMER PRICES

Euromonitor International, Inc., 122 South Michigan Avenue, Suite 1200, Chicago, Illinois 60603 (800) 577-EURO; *World Marketing Data and Statistics.*

International Labour Office, I.L.O. Publications, 1828 L Street, N.W., Suite 801, Washington, D.C. (301) 638-3152; *Yearbook of Labour Statistics.*

International Monetary Fund, 700 Nineteenth Street, NW, Washington, D.C. 20431 (202) 623-7000; *International Financial Statistics.*

LESOTHO - CONSUMPTION

African Development Bank, 01 BP 1387, Abidjan 01, Cote d'Ivoire; *Selected Statistics on Regional Member Countries.*

Statistical Office of the United Nations, Publishing Service, New York, New York 10017 (800) 253-9646; *Survey of Economic and Social Conditions in Africa.*

The World Bank, 1818 H Street, NW, Washington, D.C. 20433 (202) 477-1234; *World Development Report.*

LESOTHO - COPPER PRODUCTION AND CONSUMPTION - See LESOTHO - MINING AND MINERAL PRODUCTS

LESOTHO - CORN PRODUCTION - See LESOTHO - CROPS

LESOTHO - CORPORATE TAXES - See LESOTHO - TAXATION

LESOTHO - COTTON PRODUCTION - See LESOTHO - CROPS

LESOTHO - CRIME

International Criminal Police Organization (INTERPOL), 50 quai Achille Lignon, F-69006 Lyon, France; *International Crime Statistics.*

LESOTHO - CROPS

Europa Publications Limited, 18 Bedford Square, London, WC1B 3JN, England; *The Europa World Year Book.*

Food and Agricultural Organization of the United Nations (FAO), Via delle Terme di Caracalla, 00100 Rome, Italy (Telephone Number in U.S. (202) 653-2400); *The State of Food and Agriculture.*

M.E. Sharpe, 80 Business Park Drive, Armonk, New York 10504 (800) 541-6563; *The Illustrated Book of World Rankings.*

St. Martin's Press, Inc., 175 Fifth Avenue, New York, New York 10010 (800) 221-7945; *The Statesman's Year-Book.*

Statistical Office of the United Nations, Publishing Service, New York, New York 10017 (800) 253-9646; *Statistical Yearbook.*

United Nations Conference on Trade and Development, Central Statistical Service, Palais des Nations, Geneva, Switzerland (Telephone in U.S. (800) 253-9646); *UNCTAD Commodity Yearbook.*

United Nations Economic Commission for Africa, Africa Hall, Post Office Box 3001, Addis Ababa, Ethiopia (Telephone Number in U.S. (800) 253-9646); *African Statistical Yearbook.*

LESOTHO - CUSTOMS DUTIES

International Monetary Fund, 700 Nineteenth Street, NW, Washington, D.C. 20431 (202) 623-7000; *Government Finance Statistics Yearbook.*

LESOTHO - DAIRY PRODUCTS

Europa Publications Limited, 18 Bedford Square, London, WC1B 3JN, England; *The Europa World Year Book.*

Food and Agricultural Organization of the United Nations (FAO), Via delle Terme di Caracalla, 00100 Rome, Italy (Telephone Number in U.S. (202) 653-2400); *The State of Food and Agriculture.*

M.E. Sharpe, 80 Business Park Drive, Armonk, New York 10504 (800) 541-6563; *The Illustrated Book of World Rankings.*

St. Martin's Press, Inc., 175 Fifth Avenue, New York, New York 10010 (800) 221-7945; *The Statesman's Year-Book.*

LESOTHO - DEATH RATES - See LESOTHO - MORTALITY

LESOTHO - DEFENSE EXPENDITURES - See LESOTHO - MILITARY

LESOTHO - DEMOGRAPHY

The Economist Intelligence Unit, 111 West 57th Street, New York, New York 10019 (800) 938-4685; *The World Market Atlas.*

Euromonitor International, Inc., 122 South Michigan Avenue, Suite 1200, Chicago, Illinois 60603 (800) 577-EURO; *International Marketing Data and Statistics; World Marketing Data and Statistics;* and *The World Economic Factbook.*

M.E. Sharpe, 80 Business Park Drive, Armonk, New York 10504 (800) 541-6563; *The Illustrated Book of World Rankings.*

Statistical Office of the United Nations, Publishing Service, New York, New York 10017 (800) 253-9646; *Human Development Report;* and *Survey of Economic and Social Conditions in Africa.*

LESOTHO - DEVELOPMENT ASSISTANCE

Statistical Office of the United Nations, Publishing Service, New York, New York 10017 (800) 253-9646; *Statistical Yearbook.*

LESOTHO - DIAMOND PRODUCTION - See LESOTHO - MINING AND MINERAL PRODUCTS

LESOTHO - DIVORCE

M.E. Sharpe, 80 Business Park Drive, Armonk, New York 10504 (800) 541-6563; *The Illustrated Book of World Rankings.*

Statistical Office of the United Nations, Publishing Service, New York, New York 10017 (800) 253-9646; *Demographic Yearbook.*

LESOTHO - ECONOMY

African Development Bank, 01 BP 1387, Abidjan 01, Cote d'Ivoire; *Selected Statistics on Regional Member Countries.*

Central Intelligence Agency, Washington, D.C. 20505 (703) 482-1100, www.cia.gov; *The World Factbook.*

Economist Intelligence Unit, 111 West 57th Street, New York, New York 10019

(800) 938-4685; *Lesotho Country Report.*

Euromonitor International, Inc., 122 South Michigan Avenue, Suite 1200, Chicago, Illinois 60603 (800) 577-EURO; *World Marketing Data and Statistics;* and *The World Economic Factbook.*

Europa Publications Limited, 18 Bedford Square, London, WC1B 3JN, England; *The Europa World Year Book.*

M.E. Sharpe, 80 Business Park Drive, Armonk, New York 10504 (800) 541-6563; *The Illustrated Book of World Rankings.*

St. Martin's Press, Inc., 175 Fifth Avenue, New York, New York 10010 (800) 221-7945; *The Statesman's Year-Book.*

Statistical Office of the United Nations, Publishing Service, New York, New York 10017 (800) 253-9646; *World Statistics Pocketbook.*

The World Bank, 1818 H Street, NW, Washington, D.C. 20433 (202) 477-1234; *The World Bank Atlas;* and *World Development Report.*

LESOTHO - EDUCATION

African Development Bank, 01 BP 1387, Abidjan 01, Cote d'Ivoire; *Selected Statistics on Regional Member Countries.*

The Economist Intelligence Unit, 111 West 57th Street, New York, New York 10019 (800) 938-4685; *The World Market Atlas.*

Euromonitor International, Inc., 122 South Michigan Avenue, Suite 1200, Chicago, Illinois 60603 (800) 577-EURO; *International Marketing Data and Statistics* and *World Marketing Data and Statistics..*

Europa Publications Limited, 18 Bedford Square, London, WC1B 3JN, England; *The Europa World Year Book.*

International Monetary Fund, 700 Nineteenth Street, NW, Washington, D.C. 20431 (202) 623-7000; *Government Finance Statistics Yearbook.*

M.E. Sharpe, 80 Business Park Drive, Armonk, New York 10504 (800) 541-6563; *The Illustrated Book of World Rankings.*

St. Martin's Press, Inc., 175 Fifth Avenue, New York, New York 10010 (800) 221-7945; *The Statesman's Year-Book.*

Statistical Office of the United Nations, Publishing Service, New York, New York 10017 (800) 253-9646; *Human Development Report;* and *Survey of Economic and Social Conditions in Africa.*

United Nations Economic Commission

for Africa, Africa Hall, Post Office Box 3001, Addis Ababa, Ethiopia (Telephone Number in U.S. (800) 253-9646); *African Statistical Yearbook.*

United Nations Educational, Scientific and Cultural Organization (UNESCO), 7 Place de Fontenoy, F-75700 Paris, France (Telephone Number in U.S. (212) 963-5981); *Statistical Yearbook.*

The World Bank, 1818 H Street, NW, Washington, D.C. 20433 (202) 477-1234; *World Development Report;* and *World Development Indicators.*

LESOTHO - EGG PRODUCTION AND CONSUMPTION - See LESOTHO - DAIRY PRODUCTS

LESOTHO - ELECTRICITY

Central Intelligence Agency, Washington, D.C. 20505 (703) 482-1100, www.cia.gov; *The World Factbook.*

St. Martin's Press, Inc., 175 Fifth Avenue, New York, New York 10010 (800) 221-7945; *The Statesman's Year-Book.*

Statistical Office of the United Nations, Publishing Service, New York, New York 10017 (800) 253-9646; *Human Development Report;* and *Survey of Economic and Social Conditions in Africa.*

United Nations Economic Commission for Africa, Africa Hall, Post Office Box 3001, Addis Ababa, Ethiopia (Telephone Number in U.S. (800) 253-9646); *African Statistical Yearbook.*

LESOTHO - EMPLOYMENT

Euromonitor International, Inc., 122 South Michigan Avenue, Suite 1200, Chicago, Illinois 60603 (800) 577-EURO; *International Marketing Data and Statistics.*

International Labour Office, I.L.O. Publications, 1828 L Street, N.W., Suite 801, Washington, D.C. (301) 638-3152; *Yearbook of Labour Statistics.*

M.E. Sharpe, 80 Business Park Drive, Armonk, New York 10504 (800) 541-6563; *The Illustrated Book of World Rankings.*

Statistical Office of the United Nations, Publishing Service, New York, New York 10017 (800) 253-9646; *Survey of Economic and Social Conditions in Africa.*

United Nations Economic Commission for Africa, Africa Hall, Post Office Box 3001, Addis Ababa, Ethiopia (Telephone Number in U.S. (800) 253-9646); *African Statistical Yearbook.*

LESOTHO - ENERGY

Euromonitor International, Inc., 122 South Michigan Avenue, Suite 1200, Chicago, Illinois 60603 (800) 577-EURO; *International Marketing Data and Statistics; World Marketing Data and Statistics;* and *The World Economic Factbook.*

Food and Agricultural Organization of the United Nations (FAO), Via delle Terme di Caracalla, 00100 Rome, Italy (Telephone Number in U.S. (202) 653-2400); *The State of Food and Agriculture.*

M.E. Sharpe, 80 Business Park Drive, Armonk, New York 10504 (800) 541-6563; *The Illustrated Book of World Rankings.*

St. Martin's Press, Inc., 175 Fifth Avenue, New York, New York 10010 (800) 221-7945; *The Statesman's Year-Book.*

Statistical Office of the United Nations, Publishing Service, New York, New York 10017 (800) 253-9646; *Energy Statistics Yearbook; World Statistics Pocketbook;* and *Human Development Report.*

United Nations Economic Commission for Africa, Africa Hall, Post Office Box 3001, Addis Ababa, Ethiopia (Telephone Number in U.S. (800) 253-9646); *African Statistical Yearbook.*

The World Bank, 1818 H Street, NW, Washington, D.C. 20433 (202) 477-1234; *The World Bank Atlas;* and *World Development Report.*

LESOTHO - ENVIRONMENT

Economist Intelligence Unit, 111 West 57th Street, New York, New York 10019 (800) 938-4685; *Lesotho Country Report.*

Statistical Office of the United Nations, Publishing Service, New York, New York 10017 (800) 253-9646; *World Statistics Pocketbook.*

LESOTHO - EXCHANGE RATES

African Development Bank, 01 BP 1387, Abidjan 01, Cote d'Ivoire; *Selected Statistics on Regional Member Countries.*

Central Intelligence Agency, Washington, D.C. 20505 (703) 482-1100, www.cia.gov; *The World Factbook.*

Euromonitor International, Inc., 122 South Michigan Avenue, Suite 1200, Chicago, Illinois 60603 (800) 577-EURO; *International Marketing Data and Statistics;* and *The World Economic Factbook.*

Europa Publications Limited, 18 Bedford Square, London, WC1B 3JN, England; *The Europa World Year Book.*

International Civil Aviation Organization, 999 University Street,

Montreal, Quebec, Canada H3C 5H7 (514) 954-8219; *Civil Aviation Statistics of the World.*

International Monetary Fund, 700 Nineteenth Street, NW, Washington, D.C. 20431 (202) 623-7000; *International Financial Statistics.*

Statistical Office of the United Nations, Publishing Service, New York, New York 10017 (800) 253-9646; *Statistical Yearbook;* and *World Statistics Pocketbook.*

LESOTHO - EXPORTS

African Development Bank, 01 BP 1387, Abidjan 01, Cote d'Ivoire; *Selected Statistics on Regional Member Countries.*

Central Intelligence Agency, Washington, D.C. 20505 (703) 482-1100, www.cia.gov; *The World Factbook.*

The Economist Intelligence Unit, 111 West 57th Street, New York, New York 10019 (800) 938-4685; *Lesotho Country Report;* and *The World Market Atlas.*

Euromonitor International, Inc., 122 South Michigan Avenue, Suite 1200, Chicago, Illinois 60603 (800) 577-EURO; *International Marketing Data and Statistics;* and *The World Economic Factbook.*

Europa Publications Limited, 18 Bedford Square, London, WC1B 3JN, England; *The Europa World Year Book.*

Food and Agricultural Organization of the United Nations (FAO), Via delle Terme di Caracalla, 00100 Rome, Italy (Telephone Number in U.S. (202) 653-2400); *The State of Food and Agriculture.*

International Monetary Fund, 700 Nineteenth Street, NW, Washington, D.C. 20431 (202) 623-7000; *Direction of Trade Statistics;* and *Government Finance Statistics Yearbook.*

St. Martin's Press, Inc., 175 Fifth Avenue, New York, New York 10010 (800) 221-7945; *The Statesman's Year-Book.*

Statistical Office of the United Nations, Publishing Service, New York, New York 10017 (800) 253-9646; *Survey of Economic and Social Conditions in Africa.*

United Nations Conference on Trade and Development (UNCTAD), New York, New York 10017 (800) 253-9646; *Handbook of International Trade and Development Statistics.*

United Nations Economic Commission for Africa, Africa Hall, Post Office Box 3001, Addis Ababa, Ethiopia (Telephone Number in U.S. (800) 253-9646); *African Statistical Yearbook.*

The World Bank, 1818 H Street, NW, Washington, D.C. 20433 (202) 477-1234; *World Development Report;* and *World Development Indicators.*

LESOTHO - EXTERNAL INDEBTEDNESS

African Development Bank, 01 BP 1387, Abidjan 01, Cote d'Ivoire; *Selected Statistics on Regional Member Countries.*

Statistical Office of the United Nations, Publishing Service, New York, New York 10017 (800) 253-9646; *Survey of Economic and Social Conditions in Africa.*

The World Bank, 1818 H Street, NW, Washington, D.C. 20433 (202) 477-1234; *World Development Report;* and *World Development Indicators.*

LESOTHO - EXTERNAL TRADE

African Development Bank, 01 BP 1387, Abidjan 01, Cote d'Ivoire; *Selected Statistics on Regional Member Countries.*

Euromonitor International, Inc., 122 South Michigan Avenue, Suite 1200, Chicago, Illinois 60603 (800) 577-EURO; *World Marketing Data and Statistics.*

Food and Agricultural Organization of the United Nations (FAO), Via delle Terme di Caracalla, 00100 Rome, Italy (Telephone Number in U.S. (202) 653-2400); *The State of Food and Agriculture;* and *Trade Yearbook.*

LESOTHO - FARM CROPS - See LESOTHO - CROPS

LESOTHO - FERTILITY RATES

Central Intelligence Agency, Washington, D.C. 20505 (703) 482-1100, www.cia.gov; *The World Factbook.*

M.E. Sharpe, 80 Business Park Drive, Armonk, New York 10504 (800) 541-6563; *The Illustrated Book of World Rankings.*

Statistical Office of the United Nations, Publishing Service, New York, New York 10017 (800) 253-9646; *Human Development Report;* and *Survey of Economic and Social Conditions in Africa.*

The World Bank, 1818 H Street, NW, Washington, D.C. 20433 (202) 477-1234; *The World Bank Atlas; World Development Report;* and *World Development Indicators.*

LESOTHO - FERTILIZER

Food and Agricultural Organization of the United Nations (FAO), Via delle Terme di Caracalla, 00100 Rome, Italy (Telephone Number in U.S. (202) 653-2400); *Fertilizer Yearbook;* and *The State of Food and Agriculture.*

Statistical Office of the United Nations, Publishing Service, New York, New York 10017 (800) 253-9646; *Statistical Yearbook.*

LESOTHO - FETAL MORTALITY - See LESOTHO - MORTALITY

LESOTHO - FINANCE

African Development Bank, 01 BP 1387, Abidjan 01, Cote d'Ivoire; *Selected Statistics on Regional Member Countries.*

Economist Intelligence Unit, 111 West 57th Street, New York, New York 10019 (800) 938-4685; *Lesotho Country Report.*

Europa Publications Limited, 18 Bedford Square, London, WC1B 3JN, England; *The Europa World Year Book.*

International Monetary Fund, 700 Nineteenth Street, NW, Washington, D.C. 20431 (202) 623-7000; *Government Finance Statistics Yearbook.*

M.E. Sharpe, 80 Business Park Drive, Armonk, New York 10504 (800) 541-6563; *The Illustrated Book of World Rankings.*

St. Martin's Press, Inc., 175 Fifth Avenue, New York, New York 10010 (800) 221-7945; *The Statesman's Year-Book.*

United Nations Economic Commission for Africa, Africa Hall, Post Office Box 3001, Addis Ababa, Ethiopia (Telephone Number in U.S. (800) 253-9646); *African Statistical Yearbook.*

LESOTHO - FISHERIES

Food and Agricultural Organization of the United Nations (FAO), Via delle Terme di Caracalla, 00100 Rome, Italy (Telephone Number in U.S. (202) 653-2400); *The State of Food and Agriculture;* and *Yearbook of Fishery Statistics.*

M.E. Sharpe, 80 Business Park Drive, Armonk, New York 10504 (800) 541-6563; *The Illustrated Book of World Rankings.*

Statistical Office of the United Nations, Publishing Service, New York, New York 10017 (800) 253-9646; *Survey of Economic and Social Conditions in Africa.*

United Nations Conference on Trade and Development, Central Statistical Service, Palais des Nations, Geneva, Switzerland (Telephone in U.S. (800) 253-9646); *UNCTAD Commodity Yearbook.*

United Nations Economic Commission for Africa, Africa Hall, Post Office Box 3001, Addis Ababa, Ethiopia (Telephone Number in U.S. (800) 253-9646); *African Statistical Yearbook.*

LESOTHO - FOOD

African Development Bank, 01 BP 1387, Abidjan 01, Cote d'Ivoire; *Selected Statistics on Regional Member Countries.*

Food and Agricultural Organization of the United Nations (FAO), Via delle Terme di Caracalla, 00100 Rome, Italy (Telephone Number in U.S. (202) 653-2400); *The State of Food and Agriculture;* and *Production Yearbook.*

Statistical Office of the United Nations, Publishing Service, New York, New York 10017 (800) 253-9646; *Human Development Report.*

LESOTHO - FOREIGN TRADE

Economist Intelligence Unit, 111 West 57th Street, New York, New York 10019 (800) 938-4685; *Lesotho Country Report.*

Euromonitor International, Inc., 122 South Michigan Avenue, Suite 1200, Chicago, Illinois 60603 (800) 577-EURO; *The World Economic Factbook.*

Europa Publications Limited, 18 Bedford Square, London, WC1B 3JN, England; *The Europa World Year Book.*

Food and Agricultural Organization of the United Nations (FAO), Via delle Terme di Caracalla, 00100 Rome, Italy (Telephone Number in U.S. (202) 653-2400); *The State of Food and Agriculture.*

M.E. Sharpe, 80 Business Park Drive, Armonk, New York 10504 (800) 541-6563; *The Illustrated Book of World Rankings.*

St. Martin's Press, Inc., 175 Fifth Avenue, New York, New York 10010 (800) 221-7945; *The Statesman's Year-Book.*

United Nations Conference on Trade and Development, Central Statistical Service, Palais des Nations, Geneva, Switzerland (Telephone in U.S. (800) 253-9646); *UNCTAD Commodity Yearbook.*

United Nations Economic Commission for Africa, Africa Hall, Post Office Box 3001, Addis Ababa, Ethiopia (Telephone Number in U.S. (800) 253-9646); *African Statistical Yearbook.*

The World Bank, 1818 H Street, NW, Washington, D.C. 20433 (202) 477-1234; *World Development Report;* and *World Development Indicators.*

LESOTHO - FORESTRY AND FOREST PRODUCTS

Europa Publications Limited, 18 Bedford Square, London, WC1B 3JN, England; *The Europa World Year Book.*

Food and Agricultural Organization of the United Nations (FAO), Via delle Terme

di Caracalla, 00100 Rome, Italy (Telephone Number in U.S. (202) 653-2400); *The State of Food and Agriculture;* and *Yearbook of Forest Products.*

M.E. Sharpe, 80 Business Park Drive, Armonk, New York 10504 (800) 541-6563; *The Illustrated Book of World Rankings.*

Statistical Office of the United Nations, Publishing Service, New York, New York 10017 (800) 253-9646; *Statistical Yearbook.*

United Nations Conference on Trade and Development, Central Statistical Service, Palais des Nations, Geneva, Switzerland (Telephone in U.S. (800) 253-9646); *UNCTAD Commodity Yearbook.*

United Nations Economic Commission for Africa, Africa Hall, Post Office Box 3001, Addis Ababa, Ethiopia (Telephone Number in U.S. (800) 253-9646); *African Statistical Yearbook.*

United Nations Educational, Scientific and Cultural Organization (UNESCO), 7 Place de Fontenoy, F-75700 Paris, France (Telephone Number in U.S. (212) 963-5981); *Statistical Yearbook.*

The World Bank, 1818 H Street, NW, Washington, D.C. 20433 (202) 477-1234; *World Development Report.*

LESOTHO - GAS PRODUCTION - See LESOTHO - MINING AND MINERAL PRODUCTS

LESOTHO - GENERAL MORTALITY - See LESOTHO - MORTALITY

LESOTHO - GEOGRAPHIC DATA

M.E. Sharpe, 80 Business Park Drive, Armonk, New York 10504 (800) 541-6563; *The Illustrated Book of World Rankings.*

LESOTHO - GOATS - See LESOTHO - LIVESTOCK AND POULTRY

LESOTHO - GOLD HOLDINGS

The World Bank, 1818 H Street, NW, Washington, D.C. 20433 (202) 477-1234; *World Development Indicators.*

LESOTHO - GOLD PRODUCTION AND CONSUMPTION - See LESOTHO - MINING AND MINERAL PRODUCTS

LESOTHO - GOVERNMENT

Central Intelligence Agency, Washington, D.C. 20505 (703) 482-1100, www.cia.gov; *The World Factbook.*

Europa Publications Limited, 18 Bedford Square, London, WC1B 3JN, England; *The Europa World Year Book.*

International Monetary Fund, 700 Nineteenth Street, NW, Washington, D.C. 20431 (202) 623-7000; *Government Finance Statistics Yearbook.*

St. Martin's Press, Inc., 175 Fifth Avenue, New York, New York 10010 (800) 221-7945; *The Statesman's Year-Book.*

Statistical Office of the United Nations, Publishing Service, New York, New York 10017 (800) 253-9646; *National Accounts Statistics;* and *Survey of Economic and Social Conditions in Africa.*

The World Bank, 1818 H Street, NW, Washington, D.C. 20433 (202) 477-1234; *World Development Report;* and *World Development Indicators.*

LESOTHO - GRAIN PRODUCTION - See LESOTHO - CROPS

LESOTHO - GRANTS

International Monetary Fund, 700 Nineteenth Street, NW, Washington, D.C. 20431 (202) 623-7000; *Government Finance Statistics Yearbook.*

LESOTHO - GROSS DOMESTIC PRODUCT

African Development Bank, 01 BP 1387, Abidjan 01, Cote d'Ivoire; *Selected Statistics on Regional Member Countries.*

The Economist Intelligence Unit, 111 West 57th Street, New York, New York 10019 (800) 938-4685; *Lesotho Country Report;* and *The World Market Atlas.*

Euromonitor International, Inc., 122 South Michigan Avenue, Suite 1200, Chicago, Illinois 60603 (800) 577-EURO; *International Marketing Data and Statistics;* and *The World Economic Factbook.*

Europa Publications Limited, 18 Bedford Square, London, WC1B 3JN, England; *The Europa World Year Book.*

M.E. Sharpe, 80 Business Park Drive, Armonk, New York 10504 (800) 541-6563; *The Illustrated Book of World Rankings.*

Statistical Office of the United Nations, Publishing Service, New York, New York 10017 (800) 253-9646; *Human Development Report; National Accounts Statistics; Statistical Yearbook;* and *Survey of Economic and Social Conditions in Africa.*

United Nations Economic Commission for Africa, Africa Hall, Post Office Box 3001, Addis Ababa, Ethiopia (Telephone Number in U.S. (800) 253-9646); *African Statistical Yearbook.*

The World Bank, 1818 H Street, NW, Washington, D.C. 20433 (202) 477-1234;

World Development Report; and *World Development Indicators.*

LESOTHO - GROSS NATIONAL PRODUCT

St. Martin's Press, Inc., 175 Fifth Avenue, New York, New York 10010 (800) 221-7945; *The Statesman's Year-Book.*

U.S. Arms Control and Disarmament Agency, 320 Twenty-first Street, NW, Washington, D.C. 20451 (202) 647-8677; *World Military Expenditures and Arms Transfers.*

The World Bank, 1818 H Street, NW, Washington, D.C. 20433 (202) 477-1234; *The World Bank Atlas; World Development Report;* and *World Development Indicators.*

LESOTHO - HEALTH

African Development Bank, 01 BP 1387, Abidjan 01, Cote d'Ivoire; *Selected Statistics on Regional Member Countries.*

Euromonitor International, Inc., 122 South Michigan Avenue, Suite 1200, Chicago, Illinois 60603 (800) 577-EURO; *World Marketing Data and Statistics.*

M.E. Sharpe, 80 Business Park Drive, Armonk, New York 10504 (800) 541-6563; *The Illustrated Book of World Rankings.*

St. Martin's Press, Inc., 175 Fifth Avenue, New York, New York 10010 (800) 221-7945; *The Statesman's Year-Book.*

Statistical Office of the United Nations, Publishing Service, New York, New York 10017 (800) 253-9646; *Human Development Report;* and *Statistical Yearbook.*

United Nations Children's Fund (UNICEF), 3 United Nations Plaza, New York, New York 10017 (800) 253-9646; *State of the World's Children.*

United Nations Economic Commission for Africa, Africa Hall, Post Office Box 3001, Addis Ababa, Ethiopia (Telephone Number in U.S. (800) 253-9646); *African Statistical Yearbook.*

The World Bank, 1818 H Street, NW, Washington, D.C. 20433 (202) 477-1234; *World Development Report.*

LESOTHO - HEALTH EXPENDITURES

International Monetary Fund, 700 Nineteenth Street, NW, Washington, D.C. 20431 (202) 623-7000; *Government Finance Statistics Yearbook.*

LESOTHO - HIDE PRODUCTION

Food and Agricultural Organization of the United Nations (FAO), Via delle Terme

di Caracalla, 00100 Rome, Italy (Telephone Number in U.S. (202) 653-2400); *Production Yearbook.*

LESOTHO - HIGHWAYS

Central Intelligence Agency, Washington, D.C. 20505 (703) 482-1100, www.cia.gov; *The World Factbook.*

International Road Federation, 2600 Virginia Avenue, N.W., Washington, D.C. 20024 (202) 338-4641; *World Road Statistics.*

St. Martin's Press, Inc., 175 Fifth Avenue, New York, New York 10010 (800) 221-7945; *The Statesman's Year-Book.*

Statistical Office of the United Nations, Publishing Service, New York, New York 10017 (800) 253-9646; *Survey of Economic and Social Conditions in Africa.*

United Nations Economic Commission for Africa, Africa Hall, Post Office Box 3001, Addis Ababa, Ethiopia (Telephone Number in U.S. (800) 253-9646); *African Statistical Yearbook.*

LESOTHO - HORSES - See LESOTHO - LIVESTOCK AND POULTRY

LESOTHO - HOURS OF WORK - See LESOTHO - EMPLOYMENT

LESOTHO - HOUSING

Euromonitor International, Inc., 122 South Michigan Avenue, Suite 1200, Chicago, Illinois 60603 (800) 577-EURO; *World Marketing Data and Statistics.*

International Monetary Fund, 700 Nineteenth Street, NW, Washington, D.C. 20431 (202) 623-7000; *Government Finance Statistics Yearbook.*

M.E. Sharpe, 80 Business Park Drive, Armonk, New York 10504 (800) 541-6563; *The Illustrated Book of World Rankings.*

LESOTHO - ILLITERATE POPULATION

Central Intelligence Agency, Washington, D.C. 20505 (703) 482-1100, www.cia.gov; *The World Factbook.*

The Economist Intelligence Unit, 111 West 57th Street, New York, New York 10019 (800) 938-4685; *The World Market Atlas.*

Euromonitor International, Inc., 122 South Michigan Avenue, Suite 1200, Chicago, Illinois 60603 (800) 577-EURO; *The World Economic Factbook.*

St. Martin's Press, Inc., 175 Fifth Avenue, New York, New York 10010 (800) 221-7945; *The Statesman's Year-Book.*

Statistical Office of the United Nations, Publishing Service, New York, New York 10017 (800) 253-9646; *Human Development Report.*

United Nations Educational, Scientific and Cultural Organization (UNESCO), 7 Place de Fontenoy, F-75700 Paris, France (Telephone Number in U.S. (212) 963-5981); *Statistical Yearbook.*

LESOTHO - IMPORTS

African Development Bank, 01 BP 1387, Abidjan 01, Cote d'Ivoire; *Selected Statistics on Regional Member Countries.*

Central Intelligence Agency, Washington, D.C. 20505 (703) 482-1100, www.cia.gov; *The World Factbook.*

The Economist Intelligence Unit, 111 West 57th Street, New York, New York 10019 (800) 938-4685; *Lesotho Country Report;* and *The World Market Atlas.*

Euromonitor International, Inc., 122 South Michigan Avenue, Suite 1200, Chicago, Illinois 60603 (800) 577-EURO; *International Marketing Data and Statistics;* and *The World Economic Factbook.*

Europa Publications Limited, 18 Bedford Square, London, WC1B 3JN, England; *The Europa World Year Book.*

Food and Agricultural Organization of the United Nations (FAO), Via delle Terme di Caracalla, 00100 Rome, Italy (Telephone Number in U.S. (202) 653-2400); *The State of Food and Agriculture.*

International Monetary Fund, 700 Nineteenth Street, NW, Washington, D.C. 20431 (202) 623-7000; *Direction of Trade Statistics;* and *Government Finance Statistics Yearbook.*

St. Martin's Press, Inc., 175 Fifth Avenue, New York, New York 10010 (800) 221-7945; *The Statesman's Year-Book.*

Statistical Office of the United Nations, Publishing Service, New York, New York 10017 (800) 253-9646; *Survey of Economic and Social Conditions in Africa.*

United Nations Conference on Trade and Development (UNCTAD), New York, New York 10017 (800) 253-9646; *Handbook of International Trade and Development Statistics.*

United Nations Economic Commission for Africa, Africa Hall, Post Office Box 3001, Addis Ababa, Ethiopia (Telephone Number in U.S. (800) 253-9646); *African Statistical Yearbook.*

The World Bank, 1818 H Street, NW,

Washington, D.C. 20433 (202) 477-1234; *World Development Report;* and *World Development Indicators.*

LESOTHO - INCOME TAXES - See LESOTHO - TAXATION

LESOTHO - INDUSTRY

Central Intelligence Agency, Washington, D.C. 20505 (703) 482-1100, www.cia.gov; *The World Factbook.*

Economist Intelligence Unit, 111 West 57th Street, New York, New York 10019 (800) 938-4685; *Lesotho Country Report.*

Euromonitor International, Inc., 122 South Michigan Avenue, Suite 1200, Chicago, Illinois 60603 (800) 577-EURO; *The World Economic Factbook;* and *World Marketing Data and Statistics.*

International Labour Office, I.L.O. Publications, 1828 L Street, N.W., Suite 801, Washington, D.C. (301) 638-3152; *Yearbook of Labour Statistics.*

M.E. Sharpe, 80 Business Park Drive, Armonk, New York 10504 (800) 541-6563; *The Illustrated Book of World Rankings.*

St. Martin's Press, Inc., 175 Fifth Avenue, New York, New York 10010 (800) 221-7945; *The Statesman's Year-Book.*

Statistical Office of the United Nations, Publishing Service, New York, New York 10017 (800) 253-9646; *Survey of Economic and Social Conditions in Africa.*

United Nations Economic Commission for Africa, Africa Hall, Post Office Box 3001, Addis Ababa, Ethiopia (Telephone Number in U.S. (800) 253-9646); *African Statistical Yearbook.*

The World Bank, 1818 H Street, NW, Washington, D.C. 20433 (202) 477-1234; *World Development Indicators.*

LESOTHO - INFANT AND MATERNAL MORTALITY - See LESOTHO - MORTALITY

LESOTHO - INTERNATIONAL LIQUIDITY

International Monetary Fund, 700 Nineteenth Street, NW, Washington, D.C. 20431 (202) 623-7000; *International Financial Statistics.*

LESOTHO - INTERNATIONAL RESERVES EXCLUDING GOLD

African Development Bank, 01 BP 1387, Abidjan 01, Cote d'Ivoire; *Selected Statistics on Regional Member Countries.*

Statistical Office of the United Nations, Publishing Service, New York, New York 10017 (800) 253-9646; *Statistical Yearbook.*

The World Bank, 1818 H Street, NW, Washington, D.C. 20433 (202) 477-1234; *World Development Indicators.*

LESOTHO - IRON ORE PRODUCTION AND CONSUMPTION - See LESOTHO - MINING AND MINERAL PRODUCTS

LESOTHO - LABOR

African Development Bank, 01 BP 1387, Abidjan 01, Cote d'Ivoire; *Selected Statistics on Regional Member Countries.*

Central Intelligence Agency, Washington, D.C. 20505 (703) 482-1100, www.cia.gov; *The World Factbook.*

Euromonitor International, Inc., 122 South Michigan Avenue, Suite 1200, Chicago, Illinois 60603 (800) 577-EURO; *International Marketing Data and Statistics;* and *World Marketing Data and Statistics.*

Europa Publications Limited, 18 Bedford Square, London, WC1B 3JN, England; *The Europa World Year Book.*

Food and Agricultural Organization of the United Nations (FAO), Via delle Terme di Caracalla, 00100 Rome, Italy (Telephone Number in U.S. (202) 653-2400); *The State of Food and Agriculture.*

International Labour Office, I.L.O. Publications, 1828 L Street, N.W., Suite 801, Washington, D.C. (301) 638-3152; *Yearbook of Labour Statistics.*

M.E. Sharpe, 80 Business Park Drive, Armonk, New York 10504 (800) 541-6563; *The Illustrated Book of World Rankings.*

St. Martin's Press, Inc., 175 Fifth Avenue, New York, New York 10010 (800) 221-7945; *The Statesman's Year-Book.*

Statistical Office of the United Nations, Publishing Service, New York, New York 10017 (800) 253-9646; *Human Development Report.*

The World Bank, 1818 H Street, NW, Washington, D.C. 20433 (202) 477-1234; *The World Bank Atlas; World Development Report;* and *World Development Indicators.*

LESOTHO - LAND USE

Central Intelligence Agency, Washington, D.C. 20505 (703) 482-1100, www.cia.gov; *The World Factbook.*

Euromonitor International, Inc., 122 South Michigan Avenue, Suite 1200, Chicago, Illinois 60603 (800) 577-EURO; *International Marketing Data and Statistics.*

Food and Agricultural Organization of the United Nations (FAO), Via delle Terme di Caracalla, 00100 Rome, Italy (Telephone

Number in U.S. (202) 653-2400); *Production Yearbook.*

The World Bank, 1818 H Street, NW, Washington, D.C. 20433 (202) 477-1234; *World Development Report.*

LESOTHO - LIBRARIES

M.E. Sharpe, 80 Business Park Drive, Armonk, New York 10504 (800) 541-6563; *The Illustrated Book of World Rankings.*

LESOTHO - LIFE EXPECTANCY

African Development Bank, 01 BP 1387, Abidjan 01, Cote d'Ivoire; *Selected Statistics on Regional Member Countries.*

Central Intelligence Agency, Washington, D.C. 20505 (703) 482-1100, www.cia.gov; *The World Factbook.*

Euromonitor International, Inc., 122 South Michigan Avenue, Suite 1200, Chicago, Illinois 60603 (800) 577-EURO; *The World Economic Factbook.*

Statistical Office of the United Nations, Publishing Service, New York, New York 10017 (800) 253-9646; *Human Development Report;* and *World Statistics Pocketbook.*

The World Bank, 1818 H Street, NW, Washington, D.C. 20433 (202) 477-1234; *The World Bank Atlas;* and *World Development Report.*

LESOTHO - LITERACY RATE

Euromonitor International, Inc., 122 South Michigan Avenue, Suite 1200, Chicago, Illinois 60603 (800) 577-EURO; *World Marketing Data and Statistics.*

Statistical Office of the United Nations, Publishing Service, New York, New York 10017 (800) 253-9646; *Survey of Economic and Social Conditions in Africa.*

LESOTHO - LIVESTOCK AND POULTRY

Europa Publications Limited, 18 Bedford Square, London, WC1B 3JN, England; *The Europa World Year Book.*

Food and Agricultural Organization of the United Nations (FAO), Via delle Terme di Caracalla, 00100 Rome, Italy (Telephone Number in U.S. (202) 653-2400); *Production Yearbook;* and *The State of Food and Agriculture.*

M.E. Sharpe, 80 Business Park Drive, Armonk, New York 10504 (800) 541-6563; *The Illustrated Book of World Rankings.*

St. Martin's Press, Inc., 175 Fifth Avenue, New York, New York 10010 (800) 221-7945; *The Statesman's Year-Book.*

Statistical Office of the United Nations, Publishing Service, New York, New York 10017 (800) 253-9646; *Statistical Yearbook;* and *Survey of Economic and Social Conditions in Africa.*

United Nations Conference on Trade and Development, Central Statistical Service, Palais des Nations, Geneva, Switzerland (Telephone in U.S. (800) 253-9646); *UNCTAD Commodity Yearbook.*

United Nations Economic Commission for Africa, Africa Hall, Post Office Box 3001, Addis Ababa, Ethiopia (Telephone Number in U.S. (800) 253-9646); *African Statistical Yearbook.*

LESOTHO - LIVING LEVELS - See LESOTHO - LIFE EXPECTANCY

LESOTHO - MAIL - NUMBER OF ITEMS SENT AND RECEIVED

Statistical Office of the United Nations, Publishing Service, New York, New York 10017 (800) 253-9646; *Statistical Yearbook.*

LESOTHO - MANUFACTURING

M.E. Sharpe, 80 Business Park Drive, Armonk, New York 10504 (800) 541-6563; *The Illustrated Book of World Rankings.*

Statistical Office of the United Nations, Publishing Service, New York, New York 10017 (800) 253-9646; *Survey of Economic and Social Conditions in Africa.*

United Nations Economic Commission for Africa, Africa Hall, Post Office Box 3001, Addis Ababa, Ethiopia (Telephone Number in U.S. (800) 253-9646); *African Statistical Yearbook.*

The World Bank, 1818 H Street, NW, Washington, D.C. 20433 (202) 477-1234; *World Development Indicators.*

LESOTHO - MARRIAGE RATES

M.E. Sharpe, 80 Business Park Drive, Armonk, New York 10504 (800) 541-6563; *The Illustrated Book of World Rankings.*

Statistical Office of the United Nations, Publishing Service, New York, New York 10017 (800) 253-9646; *Demographic Yearbook;* and *Statistical Yearbook.*

LESOTHO - MEAT PRODUCTION - See LESOTHO - LIVESTOCK AND POULTRY

LESOTHO - MERCHANT SHIPPING

United Nations Economic Commission for Africa, Africa Hall, Post Office Box 3001, Addis Ababa, Ethiopia (Telephone Number in U.S. (800) 253-9646); *African Statistical Yearbook.*

LESOTHO - MILITARY

Central Intelligence Agency, Washington, D.C. 20505 (703) 482-1100, www.cia.gov; *The World Factbook.*

Euromonitor International, Inc., 122 South Michigan Avenue, Suite 1200, Chicago, Illinois 60603 (800) 577-EURO; *World Marketing Data and Statistics.*

The International Institute for Strategic Studies, 23 Tavistock Street, London WC2E 7NQ, England 44 171 3797676; *The Military Balance.*

St. Martin's Press, Inc., 175 Fifth Avenue, New York, New York 10010 (800) 221-7945; *The Statesman's Year-Book.*

Statistical Office of the United Nations, Publishing Service, New York, New York 10017 (800) 253-9646; *Human Development Report.*

U.S. Arms Control and Disarmament Agency, 320 Twenty-first Street, NW, Washington, D.C. 20451 (202) 647-8677; *World Military Expenditures and Arms Transfers.*

LESOTHO - MILK PRODUCTION - See LESOTHO - DAIRY PRODUCTS

LESOTHO - MINING AND MINERAL PRODUCTS

Europa Publications Limited, 18 Bedford Square, London, WC1B 3JN, England; *The Europa World Year Book.*

M.E. Sharpe, 80 Business Park Drive, Armonk, New York 10504 (800) 541-6563; *The Illustrated Book of World Rankings.*

Statistical Office of the United Nations, Publishing Service, New York, New York 10017 (800) 253-9646; *Statistical Yearbook.*

United Nations Conference on Trade and Development, Central Statistical Service, Palais des Nations, Geneva, Switzerland (Telephone in U.S. (800) 253-9646); *UNCTAD Commodity Yearbook.*

United Nations Economic Commission for Africa, Africa Hall, Post Office Box 3001, Addis Ababa, Ethiopia (Telephone Number in U.S. (800) 253-9646); *African Statistical Yearbook.*

LESOTHO - MONEY EXCHANGE RATES - LESOTHO - EXCHANGE RATES

LESOTHO - MONEY SUPPLY

African Development Bank, 01 BP 1387, Abidjan 01, Cote d'Ivoire; *Selected Statistics on Regional Member Countries.*

Economist Intelligence Unit, 111 West

57th Street, New York, New York 10019 (800) 938-4685; *Lesotho Country Report.*

Europa Publications Limited, 18 Bedford Square, London, WC1B 3JN, England; *The Europa World Year Book.*

International Monetary Fund, 700 Nineteenth Street, NW, Washington, D.C. 20431 (202) 623-7000; *International Financial Statistics.*

LESOTHO - MORTALITY

Central Intelligence Agency, Washington, D.C. 20505 (703) 482-1100, www.cia.gov; *The World Factbook.*

Euromonitor International, Inc., 122 South Michigan Avenue, Suite 1200, Chicago, Illinois 60603 (800) 577-EURO; *International Marketing Data and Statistics;* and *The World Economic Factbook.*

Europa Publications Limited, 18 Bedford Square, London, WC1B 3JN, England; *The Europa World Year Book.*

Statistical Office of the United Nations, Publishing Service, New York, New York 10017 (800) 253-9646; *Demographic Yearbook; Human Development Report; Statistical Yearbook; World Statistics Pocketbook;* and *Survey of Economic and Social Conditions in Africa.*

United Nations Children's Fund (UNICEF), 3 United Nations Plaza, New York, New York 10017 (800) 253-9646; *State of the World's Children.*

The World Bank, 1818 H Street, NW, Washington, D.C. 20433 (202) 477-1234; *The World Bank Atlas;* and *World Development Report;* and *World Development Indicators.*

LESOTHO - MOTOR VEHICLE TAXES - See LESOTHO - TAXATION

LESOTHO - MOTOR VEHICLES IN USE

Europa Publications Limited, 18 Bedford Square, London, WC1B 3JN, England; *The Europa World Year Book.*

International Road Federation, 2600 Virginia Avenue, N.W., Washington, D.C. 20024 (202) 338-4641; *World Road Statistics.*

Statistical Office of the United Nations, Publishing Service, New York, New York 10017 (800) 253-9646; *Statistical Yearbook;* and *Survey of Economic and Social Conditions in Africa.*

LESOTHO - MULES - See LESOTHO - LIVESTOCK AND POULTRY

LESOTHO - MUSEUMS

M.E. Sharpe, 80 Business Park Drive, Armonk, New York 10504 (800) 541-6563; *The Illustrated Book of World Rankings.*

United Nations Educational, Scientific and Cultural Organization (UNESCO), 7 Place de Fontenoy, F-75700 Paris, France (Telephone Number in U.S. (212) 963-5981); *Statistical Yearbook.*

LESOTHO - NATALITY - See LESOTHO - BIRTH RATES

LESOTHO - NATIONAL ACCOUNTS

African Development Bank, 01 BP 1387, Abidjan 01, Cote d'Ivoire; *Selected Statistics on Regional Member Countries.*

Europa Publications Limited, 18 Bedford Square, London, WC1B 3JN, England; *The Europa World Year Book.*

Statistical Office of the United Nations, Publishing Service, New York, New York 10017 (800) 253-9646; *National Accounts Statistics;* and *Statistical Yearbook.*

United Nations Economic Commission for Africa, Africa Hall, Post Office Box 3001, Addis Ababa, Ethiopia (Telephone Number in U.S. (800) 253-9646); *African Statistical Yearbook.*

LESOTHO - NATIONAL INCOME

M.E. Sharpe, 80 Business Park Drive, Armonk, New York 10504 (800) 541-6563; *The Illustrated Book of World Rankings.*

Statistical Office of the United Nations, Publishing Service, New York, New York 10017 (800) 253-9646; *National Accounts Statistics;* and *Statistical Yearbook.*

LESOTHO - NATIONAL PRODUCT

M.E. Sharpe, 80 Business Park Drive, Armonk, New York 10504 (800) 541-6563; *The Illustrated Book of World Rankings.*

LESOTHO - NATURAL GAS - PRODUCTION - See LESOTHO - MINING AND MINERAL PRODUCTS

LESOTHO - NEWSPAPER PRODUCTION - See LESOTHO - FORESTRY AND FOREST PRODUCTS

LESOTHO - OCCUPATIONS - See LESOTHO - LABOR

LESOTHO - PATENTS, TRADEMARKS AND SERVICE MARKS

World Intellectual Property Organization, 34 Chemin des Colombettes, CH-1211 Geneva 20, Switzerland; *Industrial Property Statistics.*

LESOTHO - PEANUT PRODUCTION - See

LESOTHO - CROPS

LESOTHO - PESTICIDE USE

Food and Agricultural Organization of the United Nations (FAO), Via delle Terme di Caracalla, 00100 Rome, Italy (Telephone Number in U.S. (202) 653-2400); *The State of Food and Agriculture.*

LESOTHO - PETROLEUM INDUSTRY

Food and Agricultural Organization of the United Nations (FAO), Via delle Terme di Caracalla, 00100 Rome, Italy (Telephone Number in U.S. (202) 653-2400); *The State of Food and Agriculture.*

M.E. Sharpe, 80 Business Park Drive, Armonk, New York 10504 (800) 541-6563; *The Illustrated Book of World Rankings.*

United Nations Conference on Trade and Development, Central Statistical Service, Palais des Nations, Geneva, Switzerland (Telephone in U.S. (800) 253-9646); *UNCTAD Commodity Yearbook.*

LESOTHO - PIGS - See LESOTHO - LIVESTOCK AND POULTRY

LESOTHO - POPULATION

African Development Bank, 01 BP 1387, Abidjan 01, Cote d'Ivoire; *Selected Statistics on Regional Member Countries.*

Central Intelligence Agency, Washington, D.C. 20505 (703) 482-1100, www.cia.gov; *The World Factbook.*

The Economist Intelligence Unit, 111 West 57th Street, New York, New York 10019 (800) 938-4685; *Lesotho Country Report;* and *The World Market Atlas.*

Euromonitor International, Inc., 122 South Michigan Avenue, Suite 1200, Chicago, Illinois 60603 (800) 577-EURO; *International Marketing Data and Statistics;* and *The World Economic Factbook.*

Europa Publications Limited, 18 Bedford Square, London, WC1B 3JN, England; *The Europa World Year Book.*

Food and Agricultural Organization of the United Nations (FAO), Via delle Terme di Caracalla, 00100 Rome, Italy (Telephone Number in U.S. (202) 653-2400); *Production Yearbook.*

International Labour Office, I.L.O. Publications, 1828 L Street, N.W., Suite 801, Washington, D.C. (301) 638-3152; *Yearbook of Labour Statistics.*

M.E. Sharpe, 80 Business Park Drive, Armonk, New York 10504 (800) 541-6563; *The Illustrated Book of World Rankings.*

St. Martin's Press, Inc., 175 Fifth Avenue, New York, New York 10010 (800) 221-7945; *The Statesman's Year-Book.*

Statistical Office of the United Nations, Publishing Service, New York, New York 10017 (800) 253-9646; *Demographic Yearbook; Human Development Report; Statistical Yearbook; World Statistics Pocketbook;* and *Survey of Economic and Social Conditions in Africa.*

United Nations Educational, Scientific and Cultural Organization (UNESCO), 7 Place de Fontenoy, F-75700 Paris, France (Telephone Number in U.S. (212) 963-5981); *Statistical Yearbook.*

U.S. Arms Control and Disarmament Agency, 320 Twenty-first Street, NW, Washington, D.C. 20451 (202) 647-8677; *World Military Expenditures and Arms Transfers.*

The World Bank, 1818 H Street, NW, Washington, D.C. 20433 (202) 477-1234; *The World Bank Atlas;* and *World Development Report.*

World Health Organization, Office of Publications, 20 Avenue Appia, CH-1211 Geneva 27, Switzerland (Telephone Number in U.S. (518) 436-9686); *World Health Statistics Annual.*

LESOTHO - POST OFFICES

M.E. Sharpe, 80 Business Park Drive, Armonk, New York 10504 (800) 541-6563; *The Illustrated Book of World Rankings.*

LESOTHO - POTATO PRODUCTION - See LESOTHO - CROPS

LESOTHO - PRICES

Food and Agricultural Organization of the United Nations (FAO), Via delle Terme di Caracalla, 00100 Rome, Italy (Telephone Number in U.S. (202) 653-2400); *Production Yearbook;* and *The State of Food and Agriculture.*

International Labour Office, I.L.O. Publications, 1828 L Street, N.W., Suite 801, Washington, D.C. (301) 638-3152; *Yearbook of Labour Statistics.*

International Monetary Fund, 700 Nineteenth Street, NW, Washington, D.C. 20431 (202) 623-7000; *International Financial Statistics.*

M.E. Sharpe, 80 Business Park Drive, Armonk, New York 10504 (800) 541-6563; *The Illustrated Book of World Rankings.*

United Nations Economic Commission for Africa, Africa Hall, Post Office Box 3001, Addis Ababa, Ethiopia (Telephone Number in U.S. (800) 253-9646); *African Statistical Yearbook.*

LESOTHO - PRODUCTION

M.E. Sharpe, 80 Business Park Drive, Armonk, New York 10504 (800) 541-6563; *The Illustrated Book of World Rankings.*

LESOTHO - PROPERTY TAXES - See LESOTHO - TAXATION

LESOTHO - PUBLIC FINANCE - See LESOTHO - FINANCE

LESOTHO - RADIO BROADCASTING - See LESOTHO - BROADCASTING

LESOTHO - RADIO RECEIVERS

St. Martin's Press, Inc., 175 Fifth Avenue, New York, New York 10010 (800) 221-7945; *The Statesman's Year-Book.*

LESOTHO - RAILWAYS

St. Martin's Press, Inc., 175 Fifth Avenue, New York, New York 10010 (800) 221-7945; *The Statesman's Year-Book.*

Statistical Office of the United Nations, Publishing Service, New York, New York 10017 (800) 253-9646; *Survey of Economic and Social Conditions in Africa.*

United Nations Economic Commission for Africa, Africa Hall, Post Office Box 3001, Addis Ababa, Ethiopia (Telephone Number in U.S. (800) 253-9646); *African Statistical Yearbook.*

LESOTHO - RELIGION

Central Intelligence Agency, Washington, D.C. 20505 (703) 482-1100, www.cia.gov; *The World Factbook.*

M.E. Sharpe, 80 Business Park Drive, Armonk, New York 10504 (800) 541-6563; *The Illustrated Book of World Rankings.*

St. Martin's Press, Inc., 175 Fifth Avenue, New York, New York 10010 (800) 221-7945; *The Statesman's Year-Book.*

LESOTHO - RENT PRICES

International Labour Office, I.L.O. Publications, 1828 L Street, N.W., Suite 801, Washington, D.C. (301) 638-3152; *Yearbook of Labour Statistics.*

LESOTHO - RETAIL TRADE

Euromonitor International, Inc., 122 South Michigan Avenue, Suite 1200, Chicago, Illinois 60603 (800) 577-EURO; *World Marketing Data and Statistics.*

LESOTHO - RICE PRODUCTION - See LESOTHO - CROPS

LESOTHO - RUBBER PRODUCTION AND CONSUMPTION

M.E. Sharpe, 80 Business Park Drive, Armonk, New York 10504 (800) 541-6563; *The Illustrated Book of World Rankings.*

LESOTHO - SCIENTISTS, TECHNICIANS, AND ENGINEERS

United Nations Educational, Scientific and Cultural Organization (UNESCO), 7 Place de Fontenoy, F-75700 Paris, France (Telephone Number in U.S. (212) 963-5981); *Statistical Yearbook.*

LESOTHO - SENIOR CITIZENS

M.E. Sharpe, 80 Business Park Drive, Armonk, New York 10504 (800) 541-6563; *The Illustrated Book of World Rankings.*

LESOTHO - SHEEP - See LESOTHO - LIVESTOCK AND POULTRY

LESOTHO - SILVER PRODUCTION AND CONSUMPTION - See LESOTHO - MINING AND MINERAL PRODUCTS

LESOTHO - SOCIAL DATA

African Development Bank, 01 BP 1387, Abidjan 01, Cote d'Ivoire; *Selected Statistics on Regional Member Countries.*

M.E. Sharpe, 80 Business Park Drive, Armonk, New York 10504 (800) 541-6563; *The Illustrated Book of World Rankings.*

Statistical Office of the United Nations, Publishing Service, New York, New York 10017 (800) 253-9646; *World Statistics Pocketbook.*

LESOTHO - SOCIAL SECURITY

International Monetary Fund, 700 Nineteenth Street, NW, Washington, D.C. 20431 (202) 623-7000; *Government Finance Statistics Yearbook.*

Statistical Office of the United Nations, Publishing Service, New York, New York 10017 (800) 253-9646; *National Accounts Statistics.*

LESOTHO - STAMP TAXES AND DUTIES - See LESOTHO - TAXATION

LESOTHO - STEEL PRODUCTION - See LESOTHO - MINING AND MINERAL PRODUCTS

LESOTHO - STOCKS - COMMODITY - MARKET PRICE - INDEX

Food and Agricultural Organization of the United Nations (FAO), Via delle Terme di Caracalla, 00100 Rome, Italy (Telephone Number in U.S. (202) 653-2400); *The State of Food and Agriculture.*

LESOTHO - SUGAR PRODUCTION AND CONSUMPTION - See LESOTHO - CROPS

LESOTHO - TAXATION

Europa Publications Limited, 18 Bedford Square, London, WC1B 3JN, England; *The Europa World Year Book*.

International Monetary Fund, 700 Nineteenth Street, NW, Washington, D.C. 20431 (202) 623-7000; *Government Finance Statistics Yearbook*.

International Road Federation, 2600 Virginia Avenue, N.W., Washington, D.C. 20024 (202) 338-4641; *World Road Statistics*.

The World Bank, 1818 H Street, NW, Washington, D.C. 20433 (202) 477-1234; *World Development Indicators*.

LESOTHO - TELEPHONES IN USE

American Telephone and Telegraph Company, 26 Parsippany Road, Whippany, New Jersey 07981 (800) 222-0300; *The World's Telephones*.

Central Intelligence Agency, Washington, D.C. 20505 (703) 482-1100, www.cia.gov; *The World Factbook*.

Europa Publications Limited, 18 Bedford Square, London, WC1B 3JN, England; *The Europa World Year Book*.

St. Martin's Press, Inc., 175 Fifth Avenue, New York, New York 10010 (800) 221-7945; *The Statesman's Year-Book*.

Statistical Office of the United Nations, Publishing Service, New York, New York 10017 (800) 253-9646; *Statistical Yearbook;* and *World Statistics Pocketbook*.

LESOTHO - TELEVISION BROADCASTING - See LESOTHO - BROADCASTING

LESOTHO - TEXTILE INDUSTRY

M.E. Sharpe, 80 Business Park Drive, Armonk, New York 10504 (800) 541-6563; *The Illustrated Book of World Rankings*.

Statistical Office of the United Nations, Publishing Service, New York, New York 10017 (800) 253-9646; *Statistical Yearbook*.

United Nations Conference on Trade and Development, Central Statistical Service, Palais des Nations, Geneva, Switzerland (Telephone in U.S. (800) 253-9646); *UNCTAD Commodity Yearbook*.

LESOTHO - TOBACCO PRODUCTION

M.E. Sharpe, 80 Business Park Drive, Armonk, New York 10504 (800) 541-6563; *The Illustrated Book of World Rankings*.

LESOTHO - TOURISM

Euromonitor International, Inc., 122 South Michigan Avenue, Suite 1200, Chicago, Illinois 60603 (800) 577-EURO; *The World Economic Factbook;* and *World Marketing Data and Statistics*.

Europa Publications Limited, 18 Bedford Square, London, WC1B 3JN, England; *The Europa World Year Book*.

M.E. Sharpe, 80 Business Park Drive, Armonk, New York 10504 (800) 541-6563; *The Illustrated Book of World Rankings*.

St. Martin's Press, Inc., 175 Fifth Avenue, New York, New York 10010 (800) 221-7945; *The Statesman's Year-Book*.

United Nations Economic Commission for Africa, Africa Hall, Post Office Box 3001, Addis Ababa, Ethiopia (Telephone Number in U.S. (800) 253-9646); *African Statistical Yearbook*.

World Tourism Organization, Calle Capitan Haya 42, E-28020 Madrid, Spain; *Yearbook of Tourism Statistics*.

LESOTHO - TRACTORS IN USE

Statistical Office of the United Nations, Publishing Service, New York, New York 10017 (800) 253-9646; *Statistical Yearbook*.

LESOTHO - TRADE - See LESOTHO - FOREIGN TRADE

LESOTHO - TRADEMARKS AND SERVICE MARKS - See LESOTHO - PATENTS, TRADEMARKS AND SERVICE MARKS

LESOTHO - TRANSPORTATION AND COMMUNICATIONS

Central Intelligence Agency, Washington, D.C. 20505 (703) 482-1100, www.cia.gov; *The World Factbook*.

Euromonitor International, Inc., 122 South Michigan Avenue, Suite 1200, Chicago, Illinois 60603 (800) 577-EURO; *International Marketing Data and Statistics;* and *World Marketing Data and Statistics*.

Europa Publications Limited, 18 Bedford Square, London, WC1B 3JN, England; *The Europa World Year Book*.

M.E. Sharpe, 80 Business Park Drive, Armonk, New York 10504 (800) 541-6563; *The Illustrated Book of World Rankings*.

St. Martin's Press, Inc., 175 Fifth Avenue, New York, New York 10010 (800) 221-7945; *The Statesman's Year-Book*.

Statistical Office of the United Nations, Publishing Service, New York, New York 10017 (800) 253-9646; *Human*

Development Report.

United Nations Economic Commission for Africa, Africa Hall, Post Office Box 3001, Addis Ababa, Ethiopia (Telephone Number in U.S. (800) 253-9646); *African Statistical Yearbook*.

LESOTHO - UNEMPLOYMENT

Central Intelligence Agency, Washington, D.C. 20505 (703) 482-1100, www.cia.gov; *The World Factbook*.

International Labour Office, I.L.O. Publications,1828 L Street, N.W., Suite 801, Washington, D.C. (301) 638-3152; *Yearbook of Labour Statistics*.

LESOTHO - VITAL STATISTICS

Statistical Office of the United Nations, Publishing Service, New York, New York 10017 (800) 253-9646; *Statistical Yearbook*.

World Health Organization, Office of Publications, 20 Avenue Appia, CH-1211 Geneva 27, Switzerland (Telephone Number in U.S. (518) 436-9686); *World Health Statistics Annual*.

LESOTHO - WAGES

International Labour Office, I.L.O. Publications, 1828 L Street, N.W., Suite 801, Washington, D.C. (301) 638-3152; *Yearbook of Labour Statistics*.

LESOTHO - WEATHER - See LESOTHO - CLIMATE

LESOTHO - WELFARE EXPENDITURES

International Monetary Fund, 700 Nineteenth Street, NW, Washington, D.C. 20431 (202) 623-7000; *Government Finance Statistics Yearbook*.

LESOTHO - WHEAT PRODUCTION - See LESOTHO - CROPS

LESOTHO - WINE PRODUCTION - See LESOTHO - BEVERAGES

LESOTHO - WOOL PRODUCTION - See LESOTHO - TEXTILE INDUSTRY

LETTERS (POSTAL)

U.S. Postal Service, 475 L'Enfant Plaza West, SW, Washington, D.C. 20260-0010 (202) 268-2000, www.usps.gov; *United States Domestic Postage Rates: Recent History;* and unpublished data.

LETTUCE

U.S. Department of Agriculture, Economic Research Service, 1800 M Street, NW, Washington, D.C. 20036 (202) 694-5050, www.ers.usda.gov; *Farm Business*

Economic Report; Food Consumption, Prices, and Expenditures; and *Agricultural Outlook.*

U.S. Department of Agriculture, National Agricultural Statistics Service, Fourteenth Street and Independence Avenue, SW, Washington, D.C. 20250 (800) 727-9540, www.usda.gov/nass; *Agricultural Statistics;* and *Vegetables.*

U.S. Department of Labor, Bureau of Labor Statistics, Two Massachusetts Avenue, NE, Washington, D.C. 20212 (202) 691-5200, www.stats.bls.gov; *CPI Detail Report;* and *Monthly Labor Review.*

LEVERAGED BUY-OUTS

Thomson Financial Securities Data, 2 Gateway Center, Newark, New Jersey 07006 (973) 622-3100; *Merger and Corporate Transactions Database.*

Liberia - National Statistical Office

Bureau of Statistics, Ministry of Planning and Economic Affairs, Post Office Box 9016, Monrovia, Liberia.

Liberia - Primary Statistics Source

Ministry of Planning and Economic Affairs, P.O. Box 9016, Monrovia, Liberia; *Economic Survey of Liberia;* and *Quarterly Statistical Bulletin of Liberia.*

LIBERIA - AGRICULTURE

Economist Intelligence Unit, 111 West 57th Street, New York, New York 10019 (800) 938-4685; *Liberia Country Report.*

Euromonitor International, Inc., 122 South Michigan Avenue, Suite 1200, Chicago, Illinois 60603 (800) 577-EURO; *International Marketing Data and Statistics;* and *World Marketing Data and Statistics.*

Europa Publications Limited, 18 Bedford Square, London, WC1B 3JN, England; *The Europa World Year Book.*

Food and Agricultural Organization of the United Nations (FAO), Via delle Terme di Caracalla, 00100 Rome, Italy (Telephone Number in U.S. (202) 653-2400); *Production Yearbook; The State of Food and Agriculture;* and *Trade Yearbook.*

M.E. Sharpe, 80 Business Park Drive, Armonk, New York 10504 (800) 541-6563; *The Illustrated Book of World Rankings.*

St. Martin's Press, Inc., 175 Fifth

Avenue, New York, New York 10010 (800) 221-7945; *The Statesman's Year-Book.*

Statistical Office of the United Nations, Publishing Service, New York, New York 10017 (800) 253-9646; *Survey of Economic and Social Conditions in Africa;* and *Statistical Yearbook.*

United Nations Conference on Trade and Development, Central Statistical Service, Palais des Nations, Geneva, Switzerland (Telephone in U.S. (800) 253-9646); *UNCTAD Commodity Yearbook.*

United Nations Economic Commission for Africa, Africa Hall, Post Office Box 3001, Addis Ababa, Ethiopia (Telephone Number in U.S. (800) 253-9646); *African Statistical Yearbook.*

The World Bank, 1818 H Street, NW, Washington, D.C. 20433 (202) 477-1234; *World Development Indicators.*

LIBERIA - AIRLINE SERVICE

Europa Publications Limited, 18 Bedford Square, London, WC1B 3JN, England; *The Europa World Year Book.*

M.E. Sharpe, 80 Business Park Drive, Armonk, New York 10504 (800) 541-6563; *The Illustrated Book of World Rankings.*

St. Martin's Press, Inc., 175 Fifth Avenue, New York, New York 10010 (800) 221-7945; *The Statesman's Year-Book.*

United Nations Economic Commission for Africa, Africa Hall, Post Office Box 3001, Addis Ababa, Ethiopia (Telephone Number in U.S. (800) 253-9646); *African Statistical Yearbook.*

LIBERIA - AIRPORTS

Central Intelligence Agency, Washington, D.C. 20505 (703) 482-1100, www.cia.gov; *The World Factbook.*

LIBERIA - ALUMINUM PRODUCTION AND CONSUMPTION - See LIBERIA - MINING AND MINERAL PRODUCTS

LIBERIA - ANIMAL HEALTH

Food and Agricultural Organization of the United Nations (FAO), Via delle Terme di Caracalla, 00100 Rome, Italy (Telephone Number in U.S. (202) 653-2400); *Animal Health Yearbook.*

LIBERIA - AREA AND DENSITY OF POPULATION

African Development Bank, 01 BP 1387, Abidjan 01, Cote d'Ivoire; *Selected Statistics on Regional Member Countries.*

Central Intelligence Agency,

Washington, D.C. 20505 (703) 482-1100, www.cia.gov; *The World Factbook.*

Euromonitor International, Inc., 122 South Michigan Avenue, Suite 1200, Chicago, Illinois 60603 (800) 577-EURO; *International Marketing Data and Statistics;* and *The World Economic Factbook.*

Europa Publications Limited, 18 Bedford Square, London, WC1B 3JN, England; *The Europa World Year Book.*

Food and Agricultural Organization of the United Nations (FAO), Via delle Terme di Caracalla, 00100 Rome, Italy (Telephone Number in U.S. (202) 653-2400); *The State of Food and Agriculture.*

M.E. Sharpe, 80 Business Park Drive, Armonk, New York 10504 (800) 541-6563; *The Illustrated Book of World Rankings.*

St. Martin's Press, Inc., 175 Fifth Avenue, New York, New York 10010 (800) 221-7945; *The Statesman's Year-Book.*

Statistical Office of the United Nations, Publishing Service, New York, New York 10017 (800) 253-9646; *Statistical Yearbook;* and *Survey of Economic and Social Conditions in Africa.*

LIBERIA - ARMS EXPORTS AND IMPORTS - See LIBERIA - MILITARY

LIBERIA - BALANCE OF PAYMENTS

African Development Bank, 01 BP 1387, Abidjan 01, Cote d'Ivoire; *Selected Statistics on Regional Member Countries.*

The Economist Intelligence Unit, 111 West 57th Street, New York, New York 10019 (800) 938-4685; *The World Market Atlas.*

Europa Publications Limited, 18 Bedford Square, London, WC1B 3JN, England; *The Europa World Year Book.*

International Monetary Fund, 700 Nineteenth Street, NW, Washington, D.C. 20431 (202) 623-7000; *Balance of Payments Yearbook.*

United Nations Conference on Trade and Development (UNCTAD), New York, New York 10017 (800) 253-9646; *Handbook of International Trade and Development Statistics.*

United Nations Economic Commission for Africa, Africa Hall, Post Office Box 3001, Addis Ababa, Ethiopia (Telephone Number in U.S. (800) 253-9646); *African Statistical Yearbook.*

The World Bank, 1818 H Street, NW, Washington, D.C. 20433 (202) 477-1234;

World Development Indicators.

LIBERIA - BANKING

Euromonitor International, Inc., 122 South Michigan Avenue, Suite 1200, Chicago, Illinois 60603 (800) 577-EURO; *World Marketing Data and Statistics.*

Europa Publications Limited, 18 Bedford Square, London, WC1B 3JN, England; *The Europa World Year Book.*

International Monetary Fund, 700 Nineteenth Street, NW, Washington, D.C. 20431 (202) 623-7000; *Government Finance Statistics Yearbook;* and *International Financial Statistics.*

M.E. Sharpe, 80 Business Park Drive, Armonk, New York 10504 (800) 541-6563; *The Illustrated Book of World Rankings.*

St. Martin's Press, Inc., 175 Fifth Avenue, New York, New York 10010 (800) 221-7945; *The Statesman's Year-Book.*

United Nations Economic Commission for Africa, Africa Hall, Post Office Box 3001, Addis Ababa, Ethiopia (Telephone Number in U.S. (800) 253-9646); *African Statistical Yearbook.*

LIBERIA - BARLEY PRODUCTION - See LIBERIA - CROPS

LIBERIA - BEER PRODUCTION - See LIBERIA - BEVERAGES

LIBERIA - BEVERAGES

M.E. Sharpe, 80 Business Park Drive, Armonk, New York 10504 (800) 541-6563; *The Illustrated Book of World Rankings.*

Statistical Office of the United Nations, Publishing Service, New York, New York 10017 (800) 253-9646; *Statistical Yearbook.*

LIBERIA - BIRTH RATES

Central Intelligence Agency, Washington, D.C. 20505 (703) 482-1100, www.cia.gov; *The World Factbook.*

Euromonitor International, Inc., 122 South Michigan Avenue, Suite 1200, Chicago, Illinois 60603 (800) 577-EURO; *International Marketing Data and Statistics;* and *The World Economic Factbook.*

Europa Publications Limited, 18 Bedford Square, London, WC1B 3JN, England; *The Europa World Year Book.*

M.E. Sharpe, 80 Business Park Drive, Armonk, New York 10504 (800) 541-6563; *The Illustrated Book of World Rankings.*

Statistical Office of the United Nations, Publishing Service, New York, New York

10017 (800) 253-9646; *Demographic Yearbook; Statistical Yearbook;* and *Survey of Economic and Social Conditions in Africa.*

The World Bank, 1818 H Street, NW, Washington, D.C. 20433 (202) 477-1234; *World Development Indicators.*

LIBERIA - BONDS

International Monetary Fund, 700 Nineteenth Street, NW, Washington, D.C. 20431 (202) 623-7000; *Government Finance Statistics Yearbook.*

LIBERIA - BROADCASTING

Billboard Limited, Post Office Box 9027, 1006 AA Amsterdam, The Netherlands (Telephone Number in U.S. (212) 764-7300); *World Radio TV Handbook.*

Central Intelligence Agency, Washington, D.C. 20505 (703) 482-1100, www.cia.gov; *The World Factbook.*

Euromonitor International, Inc., 122 South Michigan Avenue, Suite 1200, Chicago, Illinois 60603 (800) 577-EURO; *World Marketing Data and Statistics.*

M.E. Sharpe, 80 Business Park Drive, Armonk, New York 10504 (800) 541-6563; *The Illustrated Book of World Rankings.*

St. Martin's Press, Inc., 175 Fifth Avenue, New York, New York 10010 (800) 221-7945; *The Statesman's Year-Book.*

United Nations Educational, Scientific and Cultural Organization (UNESCO), 7 Place de Fontenoy, F-75700 Paris, France (Telephone Number in U.S. (212) 963-5981); *Statistical Yearbook.*

LIBERIA - BUDGET

Central Intelligence Agency, Washington, D.C. 20505 (703) 482-1100, www.cia.gov; *The World Factbook.*

LIBERIA - BUSINESS AND PROFESSIONAL LICENSES

International Monetary Fund, 700 Nineteenth Street, NW, Washington, D.C. 20431 (202) 623-7000; *Government Finance Statistics Yearbook.*

LIBERIA - CALORIE SUPPLY

African Development Bank, 01 BP 1387, Abidjan 01, Cote d'Ivoire; *Selected Statistics on Regional Member Countries.*

Food and Agricultural Organization of the United Nations (FAO), Via delle Terme di Caracalla, 00100 Rome, Italy (Telephone Number in U.S. (202) 653-2400); *The State of Food and Agriculture.*

LIBERIA - CAPITAL REVENUE

International Monetary Fund, 700 Nineteenth Street, NW, Washington, D.C. 20431 (202) 623-7000; *Government Finance Statistics Yearbook.*

LIBERIA - CATTLE - See LIBERIA - LIVESTOCK AND POULTRY

LIBERIA - CEMENT PRODUCTION - See LIBERIA - MINING AND MINERAL PRODUCTS

LIBERIA - CHEMICAL (ORGANIC) PRODUCTION - See LIBERIA - MINING AND MINERAL PRODUCTS

LIBERIA - CHICKENS - See LIBERIA - LIVESTOCK AND POULTRY

LIBERIA - CIGARETTE PRODUCTION - See LIBERIA - TOBACCO PRODUCTION

LIBERIA - CLIMATE

M.E. Sharpe, 80 Business Park Drive, Armonk, New York 10504 (800) 541-6563; *The Illustrated Book of World Rankings.*

St. Martin's Press, Inc., 175 Fifth Avenue, New York, New York 10010 (800) 221-7945; *The Statesman's Year-Book.*

LIBERIA - COAL PRODUCTION - See LIBERIA - MINING AND MINERAL PRODUCTS

LIBERIA - COCOA (BEANS) PRODUCTION - See LIBERIA - CROPS

LIBERIA - COFFEE PRODUCTION AND CONSUMPTION - See LIBERIA - CROPS

LIBERIA - COMMERCE

St. Martin's Press, Inc., 175 Fifth Avenue, New York, New York 10010 (800) 221-7945; *The Statesman's Year-Book.*

LIBERIA - COMMUNICATIONS - See LIBERIA - TRANSPORTATION AND COMMUNICATIONS

LIBERIA - CONSTRUCTION INDUSTRY

M.E. Sharpe, 80 Business Park Drive, Armonk, New York 10504 (800) 541-6563; *The Illustrated Book of World Rankings.*

Statistical Office of the United Nations, Publishing Service, New York, New York 10017 (800) 253-9646; *Statistical Yearbook.*

United Nations Economic Commission for Africa, Africa Hall, Post Office Box 3001, Addis Ababa, Ethiopia (Telephone Number in U.S. (800) 253-9646); *African Statistical Yearbook.*

LIBERIA - CONSUMER PRICE INDEX

African Development Bank, 01 BP 1387, Abidjan 01, Cote d'Ivoire; *Selected Statistics on Regional Member Countries.*

Europa Publications Limited, 18 Bedford Square, London, WC1B 3JN, England; *The Europa World Year Book.*

Statistical Office of the United Nations, Publishing Service, New York, New York 10017 (800) 253-9646; *Statistical Yearbook;* and *Survey of Economic and Social Conditions in Africa.*

United Nations Economic Commission for Africa, Africa Hall, Post Office Box 3001, Addis Ababa, Ethiopia (Telephone Number in U.S. (800) 253-9646); *African Statistical Yearbook.*

LIBERIA - CONSUMER PRICES

Euromonitor International, Inc., 122 South Michigan Avenue, Suite 1200, Chicago, Illinois 60603 (800) 577-EURO; *World Marketing Data and Statistics.*

International Labour Office, I.L.O. Publications, 1828 L Street, N.W., Suite 801, Washington, D.C. (301) 638-3152; *Yearbook of Labour Statistics.*

International Monetary Fund, 700 Nineteenth Street, NW, Washington, D.C. 20431 (202) 623-7000; *International Financial Statistics.*

LIBERIA - CONSUMPTION

African Development Bank, 01 BP 1387, Abidjan 01, Cote d'Ivoire; *Selected Statistics on Regional Member Countries.*

International Rubber Study Group, York House, Eighth Floor, Empire Way, Wembley, London HA9 0PA, England; *Rubber Statistical Bulletin.*

Statistical Office of the United Nations, Publishing Service, New York, New York 10017 (800) 253-9646; *Survey of Economic and Social Conditions in Africa.*

LIBERIA - COPPER PRODUCTION AND CONSUMPTION - See LIBERIA - MINING AND MINERAL PRODUCTS

LIBERIA - CORN PRODUCTION - See LIBERIA - CROPS

LIBERIA - CORPORATE INCOME TAXES - See LIBERIA - TAXATION

LIBERIA - CORPORATE TAXES - See LIBERIA - TAXATION

LIBERIA - COTTON PRODUCTION - See LIBERIA - CROPS

LIBERIA - CROPS

Europa Publications Limited, 18 Bedford Square, London, WC1B 3JN, England; *The Europa World Year Book.*

Food and Agricultural Organization of the United Nations (FAO), Via delle Terme di Caracalla, 00100 Rome, Italy (Telephone Number in U.S. (202) 653-2400); *The State of Food and Agriculture.*

M.E. Sharpe, 80 Business Park Drive, Armonk, New York 10504 (800) 541-6563; *The Illustrated Book of World Rankings.*

St. Martin's Press, Inc., 175 Fifth Avenue, New York, New York 10010 (800) 221-7945; *The Statesman's Year-Book.*

Statistical Office of the United Nations, Publishing Service, New York, New York 10017 (800) 253-9646; *Statistical Yearbook.*

United Nations Conference on Trade and Development, Central Statistical Service, Palais des Nations, Geneva, Switzerland (Telephone in U.S. (800) 253-9646); *UNCTAD Commodity Yearbook.*

United Nations Economic Commission for Africa, Africa Hall, Post Office Box 3001, Addis Ababa, Ethiopia (Telephone Number in U.S. (800) 253-9646); *African Statistical Yearbook.*

LIBERIA - CUSTOMS DUTIES

International Monetary Fund, 700 Nineteenth Street, NW, Washington, D.C. 20431 (202) 623-7000; *Government Finance Statistics Yearbook.*

LIBERIA - DAIRY PRODUCTS

Europa Publications Limited, 18 Bedford Square, London, WC1B 3JN, England; *The Europa World Year Book.*

Food and Agricultural Organization of the United Nations (FAO), Via delle Terme di Caracalla, 00100 Rome, Italy (Telephone Number in U.S. (202) 653-2400); *Production Yearbook;* and *The State of Food and Agriculture.*

M.E. Sharpe, 80 Business Park Drive, Armonk, New York 10504 (800) 541-6563; *The Illustrated Book of World Rankings.*

St. Martin's Press, Inc., 175 Fifth Avenue, New York, New York 10010 (800) 221-7945; *The Statesman's Year-Book.*

LIBERIA - DEATH RATES - See LIBERIA - MORTALITY

LIBERIA - DEFENSE EXPENDITURES - See LIBERIA - MILITARY

LIBERIA - DEMOGRAPHY

The Economist Intelligence Unit, 111

West 57th Street, New York, New York 10019 (800) 938-4685; *The World Market Atlas.*

Euromonitor International, Inc., 122 South Michigan Avenue, Suite 1200, Chicago, Illinois 60603 (800) 577-EURO; *International Marketing Data and Statistics; World Marketing Data and Statistics;* and *The World Economic Factbook.*

M.E. Sharpe, 80 Business Park Drive, Armonk, New York 10504 (800) 541-6563; *The Illustrated Book of World Rankings.*

Statistical Office of the United Nations, Publishing Service, New York, New York 10017 (800) 253-9646; *Survey of Economic and Social Conditions in Africa.*

LIBERIA - DEVELOPMENT ASSISTANCE

Statistical Office of the United Nations, Publishing Service, New York, New York 10017 (800) 253-9646; *Statistical Yearbook.*

LIBERIA - DIAMONDS - See LIBERIA - MINING AND MINERAL PRODUCTS

LIBERIA - DIVORCE RATES

M.E. Sharpe, 80 Business Park Drive, Armonk, New York 10504 (800) 541-6563; *The Illustrated Book of World Rankings.*

Statistical Office of the United Nations, Publishing Service, New York, New York 10017 (800) 253-9646; *Demographic Yearbook;* and *Statistical Yearbook.*

LIBERIA - DUCKS - See LIBERIA - LIVESTOCK AND POULTRY

LIBERIA - ECONOMY

African Development Bank, 01 BP 1387, Abidjan 01, Cote d'Ivoire; *Selected Statistics on Regional Member Countries.*

Central Intelligence Agency, Washington, D.C. 20505 (703) 482-1100, www.cia.gov; *The World Factbook.*

Economist Intelligence Unit, 111 West 57th Street, New York, New York 10019 (800) 938-4685; *Liberia Country Report.*

Euromonitor International, Inc., 122 South Michigan Avenue, Suite 1200, Chicago, Illinois 60603 (800) 577-EURO; *International Marketing Data and Statistics; World Marketing Data and Statistics;* and *The World Economic Factbook.*

Europa Publications Limited, 18 Bedford Square, London, WC1B 3JN, England; *The Europa World Year Book.*

M.E. Sharpe, 80 Business Park Drive, Armonk, New York 10504 (800) 541-6563; *The Illustrated Book of World Rankings.*

St. Martin's Press, Inc., 175 Fifth Avenue, New York, New York 10010 (800) 221-7945; *The Statesman's Year-Book.*

Statistical Office of the United Nations, Publishing Service, New York, New York 10017 (800) 253-9646; *Foreign Trade Statistics for Africa;* and *World Statistics Pocketbook.*

The World Bank, 1818 H Street, NW, Washington, D.C. 20433 (202) 477-1234; *The World Bank Atlas.*

LIBERIA - EDUCATION

African Development Bank, 01 BP 1387, Abidjan 01, Cote d'Ivoire; *Selected Statistics on Regional Member Countries.*

The Economist Intelligence Unit, 111 West 57th Street, New York, New York 10019 (800) 938-4685; *The World Market Atlas.*

Euromonitor International, Inc., 122 South Michigan Avenue, Suite 1200, Chicago, Illinois 60603 (800) 577-EURO; *International Marketing Data and Statistics;* and *World Marketing Data and Statistics.*

Europa Publications Limited, 18 Bedford Square, London, WC1B 3JN, England; *The Europa World Year Book.*

International Monetary Fund, 700 Nineteenth Street, NW, Washington, D.C. 20431 (202) 623-7000; *Government Finance Statistics Yearbook.*

M.E. Sharpe, 80 Business Park Drive, Armonk, New York 10504 (800) 541-6563; *The Illustrated Book of World Rankings.*

St. Martin's Press, Inc., 175 Fifth Avenue, New York, New York 10010 (800) 221-7945; *The Statesman's Year-Book.*

Statistical Office of the United Nations, Publishing Service, New York, New York 10017 (800) 253-9646; *Survey of Economic and Social Conditions in Africa.*

United Nations Economic Commission for Africa, Africa Hall, Post Office Box 3001, Addis Ababa, Ethiopia (Telephone Number in U.S. (800) 253-9646); *African Statistical Yearbook.*

United Nations Educational, Scientific and Cultural Organization (UNESCO), 7 Place de Fontenoy, F-75700 Paris, France (Telephone Number in U.S. (212) 963-5981); *Statistical Yearbook.*

The World Bank, 1818 H Street, NW, Washington, D.C. 20433 (202) 477-1234; *World Development Indicators.*

LIBERIA - EGG PRODUCTION AND CONSUMPTION - See LIBERIA - DAIRY

PRODUCTS

LIBERIA - ELECTRICITY

Central Intelligence Agency, Washington, D.C. 20505 (703) 482-1100, www.cia.gov; *The World Factbook.*

M.E. Sharpe, 80 Business Park Drive, Armonk, New York 10504 (800) 541-6563; *The Illustrated Book of World Rankings.*

St. Martin's Press, Inc., 175 Fifth Avenue, New York, New York 10010 (800) 221-7945; *The Statesman's Year-Book.*

Statistical Office of the United Nations, Publishing Service, New York, New York 10017 (800) 253-9646; *Statistical Yearbook;* and *Survey of Economic and Social Conditions in Africa.*

United Nations Economic Commission for Africa, Africa Hall, Post Office Box 3001, Addis Ababa, Ethiopia (Telephone Number in U.S. (800) 253-9646); *African Statistical Yearbook.*

LIBERIA - EMPLOYMENT

Euromonitor International, Inc., 122 South Michigan Avenue, Suite 1200, Chicago, Illinois 60603 (800) 577-EURO; *International Marketing Data and Statistics.*

International Labour Office, I.L.O. Publications, 1828 L Street, N.W., Suite 801, Washington, D.C. (301) 638-3152; *Yearbook of Labour Statistics.*

M.E. Sharpe, 80 Business Park Drive, Armonk, New York 10504 (800) 541-6563; *The Illustrated Book of World Rankings.*

Statistical Office of the United Nations, Publishing Service, New York, New York 10017 (800) 253-9646; *Survey of Economic and Social Conditions in Africa.*

United Nations Economic Commission for Africa, Africa Hall, Post Office Box 3001, Addis Ababa, Ethiopia (Telephone Number in U.S. (800) 253-9646); *African Statistical Yearbook.*

LIBERIA - ENERGY

Euromonitor International, Inc., 122 South Michigan Avenue, Suite 1200, Chicago, Illinois 60603 (800) 577-EURO; *International Marketing Data and Statistics; World Marketing Data and Statistics;* and *The World Economic Factbook.*

Food and Agricultural Organization of the United Nations (FAO), Via delle Terme di Caracalla, 00100 Rome, Italy (Telephone Number in U.S. (202) 653-2400); *The State of Food and Agriculture.*

M.E. Sharpe, 80 Business Park Drive,

Armonk, New York 10504 (800) 541-6563; *The Illustrated Book of World Rankings.*

St. Martin's Press, Inc., 175 Fifth Avenue, New York, New York 10010 (800) 221-7945; *The Statesman's Year-Book.*

Statistical Office of the United Nations, Publishing Service, New York, New York 10017 (800) 253-9646; *Energy Statistics Yearbook; World Statistics Pocketbook;* and *Statistical Yearbook.*

United Nations Economic Commission for Africa, Africa Hall, Post Office Box 3001, Addis Ababa, Ethiopia (Telephone Number in U.S. (800) 253-9646); *African Statistical Yearbook.*

The World Bank, 1818 H Street, NW, Washington, D.C. 20433 (202) 477-1234; *The World Bank Atlas.*

LIBERIA - ENVIRONMENT

Economist Intelligence Unit, 111 West 57th Street, New York, New York 10019 (800) 938-4685; *Liberia Country Report.*

Statistical Office of the United Nations, Publishing Service, New York, New York 10017 (800) 253-9646; *World Statistics Pocketbook.*

LIBERIA - EXCHANGE RATES

African Development Bank, 01 BP 1387, Abidjan 01, Cote d'Ivoire; *Selected Statistics on Regional Member Countries.*

Central Intelligence Agency, Washington, D.C. 20505 (703) 482-1100, www.cia.gov; *The World Factbook.*

Euromonitor International, Inc., 122 South Michigan Avenue, Suite 1200, Chicago, Illinois 60603 (800) 577-EURO; *International Marketing Data and Statistics;* and *The World Economic Factbook.*

Europa Publications Limited, 18 Bedford Square, London, WC1B 3JN, England; *The Europa World Year Book.*

International Monetary Fund, 700 Nineteenth Street, NW, Washington, D.C. 20431 (202) 623-7000; *International Financial Statistics.*

Statistical Office of the United Nations, Publishing Service, New York, New York 10017 (800) 253-9646; *Foreign Trade Statistics for Africa; World Statistics Pocketbook;* and *Statistical Yearbook.*

LIBERIA - EXCISE TAXES - See LIBERIA - TAXATION

LIBERIA - EXPORTS

African Development Bank, 01 BP 1387,

Abidjan 01, Cote d'Ivoire; *Selected Statistics on Regional Member Countries.*

Central Intelligence Agency, Washington, D.C. 20505 (703) 482-1100, www.cia.gov; *The World Factbook.*

The Economist Intelligence Unit, 111 West 57th Street, New York, New York 10019 (800) 938-4685; *Liberia Country Report;* and *The World Market Atlas.*

Euromonitor International, Inc., 122 South Michigan Avenue, Suite 1200, Chicago, Illinois 60603 (800) 577-EURO; *International Marketing Data and Statistics; and The World Economic Factbook.*

Europa Publications Limited, 18 Bedford Square, London, WC1B 3JN, England; *The Europa World Year Book.*

Food and Agricultural Organization of the United Nations (FAO), Via delle Terme di Caracalla, 00100 Rome, Italy (Telephone Number in U.S. (202) 653-2400); *The State of Food and Agriculture.*

International Monetary Fund, 700 Nineteenth Street, NW, Washington, D.C. 20431 (202) 623-7000; *Direction of Trade Statistics; Government Finance Statistics Yearbook;* and *International Financial Statistics.*

International Rubber Study Group, York House, Eighth Floor, Empire Way, Wembley, London HA 9 0PA, England; *Rubber Statistical Bulletin.*

St. Martin's Press, Inc., 175 Fifth Avenue, New York, New York 10010 (800) 221-7945; *The Statesman's Year-Book.*

Statistical Office of the United Nations, Publishing Service, New York, New York 10017 (800) 253-9646; *Foreign Trade Statistics for Africa; and Survey of Economic and Social Conditions in Africa.*

United Nations Conference on Trade and Development (UNCTAD), New York, New York 10017 (800) 253-9646; *Handbook of International Trade and Development Statistics.*

United Nations Economic Commission for Africa, Africa Hall, Post Office Box 3001, Addis Ababa, Ethiopia (Telephone Number in U.S. (800) 253-9646); *African Statistical Yearbook.*

The World Bank, 1818 H Street, NW, Washington, D.C. 20433 (202) 477-1234; *World Development Indicators.*

LIBERIA - EXTERNAL INDEBTEDNESS

African Development Bank, 01 BP 1387, Abidjan 01, Cote d'Ivoire; *Selected Statistics on Regional Member Countries.*

Statistical Office of the United Nations, Publishing Service, New York, New York 10017 (800) 253-9646; *Survey of Economic and Social Conditions in Africa.*

The World Bank, 1818 H Street, NW, Washington, D.C. 20433 (202) 477-1234; *World Development Indicators.*

LIBERIA - EXTERNAL TRADE

African Development Bank, 01 BP 1387, Abidjan 01, Cote d'Ivoire; *Selected Statistics on Regional Member Countries.*

Euromonitor International, Inc., 122 South Michigan Avenue, Suite 1200, Chicago, Illinois 60603 (800) 577-EURO; *World Marketing Data and Statistics.*

Food and Agricultural Organization of the United Nations (FAO), Via delle Terme di Caracalla, 00100 Rome, Italy (Telephone Number in U.S. (202) 653-2400); *The State of Food and Agriculture;* and *Trade Yearbook.*

Statistical Office of the United Nations, Publishing Service, New York, New York 10017 (800) 253-9646; *Statistical Yearbook.*

LIBERIA - FARM CROPS - See LIBERIA - CROPS

LIBERIA - FEMALE WORKING POPULATION - See LIBERIA - EMPLOYMENT

LIBERIA - FERTILITY RATES

Central Intelligence Agency, Washington, D.C. 20505 (703) 482-1100, www.cia.gov; *The World Factbook.*

M.E. Sharpe, 80 Business Park Drive, Armonk, New York 10504 (800) 541-6563; *The Illustrated Book of World Rankings.*

Statistical Office of the United Nations, Publishing Service, New York, New York 10017 (800) 253-9646; *Survey of Economic and Social Conditions in Africa.*

The World Bank, 1818 H Street, NW, Washington, D.C. 20433 (202) 477-1234; *The World Bank Atlas;* and *World Development Indicators.*

LIBERIA - FERTILIZER

Food and Agricultural Organization of the United Nations (FAO), Via delle Terme di Caracalla, 00100 Rome, Italy (Telephone Number in U.S. (202) 653-2400); *Fertilizer Yearbook;* and *The State of Food and Agriculture.*

Statistical Office of the United Nations, Publishing Service, New York, New York 10017 (800) 253-9646; *Statistical Yearbook.*

LIBERIA - FETAL MORTALITY - See LIBERIA - MORTALITY

LIBERIA - FINANCE

African Development Bank, 01 BP 1387, Abidjan 01, Cote d'Ivoire; *Selected Statistics on Regional Member Countries.*

Economist Intelligence Unit, 111 West 57th Street, New York, New York 10019 (800) 938-4685; *Liberia Country Report.*

Europa Publications Limited, 18 Bedford Square, London, WC1B 3JN, England; *The Europa World Year Book.*

International Monetary Fund, 700 Nineteenth Street, NW, Washington, D.C. 20431 (202) 623-7000; *Government Finance Statistics Yearbook;* and *International Financial Statistics.*

M.E. Sharpe, 80 Business Park Drive, Armonk, New York 10504 (800) 541-6563; *The Illustrated Book of World Rankings.*

St. Martin's Press, Inc., 175 Fifth Avenue, New York, New York 10010 (800) 221-7945; *The Statesman's Year-Book.*

United Nations Economic Commission for Africa, Africa Hall, Post Office Box 3001, Addis Ababa, Ethiopia (Telephone Number in U.S. (800) 253-9646); *African Statistical Yearbook.*

LIBERIA - FISHERIES

Europa Publications Limited, 18 Bedford Square, London, WC1B 3JN, England; *The Europa World Year Book.*

Food and Agricultural Organization of the United Nations (FAO), Via delle Terme di Caracalla, 00100 Rome, Italy (Telephone Number in U.S. (202) 653-2400); *The State of Food and Agriculture.*

M.E. Sharpe, 80 Business Park Drive, Armonk, New York 10504 (800) 541-6563; *The Illustrated Book of World Rankings.*

St. Martin's Press, Inc., 175 Fifth Avenue, New York, New York 10010 (800) 221-7945; *The Statesman's Year-Book.*

Statistical Office of the United Nations, Publishing Service, New York, New York 10017 (800) 253-9646; *Statistical Yearbook; and Survey of Economic and Social Conditions in Africa.*

United Nations Conference on Trade and Development, Central Statistical Service, Palais des Nations, Geneva, Switzerland (Telephone in U.S. (800) 253-9646); *UNCTAD Commodity Yearbook.*

United Nations Economic Commission

for Africa, Africa Hall, Post Office Box 3001, Addis Ababa, Ethiopia (Telephone Number in U.S. (800) 253-9646); *African Statistical Yearbook.*

LIBERIA - FOOD

African Development Bank, 01 BP 1387, Abidjan 01, Cote d'Ivoire; *Selected Statistics on Regional Member Countries.*

Food and Agricultural Organization of the United Nations (FAO), Via delle Terme di Caracalla, 00100 Rome, Italy (Telephone Number in U.S. (202) 653-2400); *The State of Food and Agriculture;* and *Production Yearbook.*

United Nations Conference on Trade and Development, Central Statistical Service, Palais des Nations, Geneva, Switzerland (Telephone in U.S. (800) 253-9646); *UNCTAD Commodity Yearbook.*

LIBERIA - FOREIGN DEBT

International Monetary Fund, 700 Nineteenth Street, NW, Washington, D.C. 20431 (202) 623-7000; *Government Finance Statistics Yearbook.*

LIBERIA - FOREIGN TRADE

Economist Intelligence Unit, 111 West 57th Street, New York, New York 10019 (800) 938-4685; *Liberia Country Report.*

Euromonitor International, Inc., 122 South Michigan Avenue, Suite 1200, Chicago, Illinois 60603 (800) 577-EURO; *International Marketing Data and Statistics;* and *The World Economic Factbook.*

Europa Publications Limited, 18 Bedford Square, London, WC1B 3JN, England; *The Europa World Year Book.*

M.E. Sharpe, 80 Business Park Drive, Armonk, New York 10504 (800) 541-6563; *The Illustrated Book of World Rankings.*

St. Martin's Press, Inc., 175 Fifth Avenue, New York, New York 10010 (800) 221-7945; *The Statesman's Year-Book.*

Statistical Office of the United Nations, Publishing Service, New York, New York 10017 (800) 253-9646; *Foreign Trade Statistics for Africa; International Trade Statistics Yearbook;* and *Statistical Yearbook.*

United Nations Conference on Trade and Development, Central Statistical Service, Palais des Nations, Geneva, Switzerland (Telephone in U.S. (800) 253-9646); *UNCTAD Commodity Yearbook.*

United Nations Economic Commission for Africa, Africa Hall, Post Office Box 3001, Addis Ababa, Ethiopia (Telephone Number

in U.S. (800) 253-9646); *African Statistical Yearbook.*

The World Bank, 1818 H Street, NW, Washington, D.C. 20433 (202) 477-1234; *World Development Indicators.*

LIBERIA - FORESTRY AND FOREST PRODUCTS

Europa Publications Limited, 18 Bedford Square, London, WC1B 3JN, England; *The Europa World Year Book.*

Food and Agricultural Organization of the United Nations (FAO), Via delle Terme di Caracalla, 00100 Rome, Italy (Telephone Number in U.S. (202) 653-2400); *The State of Food and Agriculture;* and *Yearbook of Forest Products.*

M.E. Sharpe, 80 Business Park Drive, Armonk, New York 10504 (800) 541-6563; *The Illustrated Book of World Rankings.*

St. Martin's Press, Inc., 175 Fifth Avenue, New York, New York 10010 (800) 221-7945; *The Statesman's Year-Book.*

Statistical Office of the United Nations, Publishing Service, New York, New York 10017 (800) 253-9646; *Statistical Yearbook.*

United Nations Conference on Trade and Development, Central Statistical Service, Palais des Nations, Geneva, Switzerland (Telephone in U.S. (800) 253-9646); *UNCTAD Commodity Yearbook.*

United Nations Economic Commission for Africa, Africa Hall, Post Office Box 3001, Addis Ababa, Ethiopia (Telephone Number in U.S. (800) 253-9646); *African Statistical Yearbook.*

United Nations Educational, Scientific and Cultural Organization (UNESCO), 7 Place de Fontenoy, F-75700 Paris, France (Telephone Number in U.S. (212) 963-5981); *Statistical Yearbook.*

LIBERIA - GAS PRODUCTION - See LIBERIA - MINING AND MINERAL PRODUCTS

LIBERIA - GENERAL MORTALITY - See LIBERIA - MORTALITY

LIBERIA - GEOGRAPHIC DATA

M.E. Sharpe, 80 Business Park Drive, Armonk, New York 10504 (800) 541-6563; *The Illustrated Book of World Rankings.*

LIBERIA - GOATS - See LIBERIA - LIVESTOCK AND POULTRY

LIBERIA - GOLD HOLDINGS

Statistical Office of the United Nations, Publishing Service, New York, New York

10017 (800) 253-9646; *Statistical Yearbook.*

The World Bank, 1818 H Street, NW, Washington, D.C. 20433 (202) 477-1234; *World Development Indicators.*

LIBERIA - GOLD PRODUCTION AND CONSUMPTION - See LIBERIA -MINING AND MINERAL PRODUCTS

LIBERIA - GOVERNMENT

Central Intelligence Agency, Washington, D.C. 20505 (703) 482-1100, www.cia.gov; *The World Factbook.*

Europa Publications Limited, 18 Bedford Square, London, WC1B 3JN, England; *The Europa World Year Book.*

International Monetary Fund, 700 Nineteenth Street, NW, Washington, D.C. 20431 (202) 623-7000; *Government Finance Statistics Yearbook;* and *International Financial Statistics.*

St. Martin's Press, Inc., 175 Fifth Avenue, New York, New York 10010 (800) 221-7945; *The Statesman's Year-Book.*

Statistical Office of the United Nations, Publishing Service, New York, New York 10017 (800) 253-9646; *National Accounts Statistics; Statistical Yearbook;* and *Survey of Economic and Social Conditions in Africa.*

The World Bank, 1818 H Street, NW, Washington, D.C. 20433 (202) 477-1234; *World Development Indicators.*

LIBERIA - GRAIN PRODUCTION - See LIBERIA - CROPS

LIBERIA - GRANTS

International Monetary Fund, 700 Nineteenth Street, NW, Washington, D.C. 20431 (202) 623-7000; *Government Finance Statistics Yearbook.*

LIBERIA - GROSS DOMESTIC PRODUCT

African Development Bank, 01 BP 1387, Abidjan 01, Cote d'Ivoire; *Selected Statistics on Regional Member Countries.*

The Economist Intelligence Unit, 111 West 57th Street, New York, New York 10019 (800) 938-4685; *Liberia Country Report;* and *The World Market Atlas.*

Euromonitor International, Inc., 122 South Michigan Avenue, Suite 1200, Chicago, Illinois 60603 (800) 577-EURO; *International Marketing Data and Statistics;* and *The World Economic Factbook.*

Europa Publications Limited, 18 Bedford Square, London, WC1B 3JN, England; *The Europa World Year Book.*

M.E. Sharpe, 80 Business Park Drive, Armonk, New York 10504 (800) 541-6563; *The Illustrated Book of World Rankings*.

Statistical Office of the United Nations, Publishing Service, New York, New York 10017 (800) 253-9646; *National Accounts Statistics; Statistical Yearbook;* and *Survey of Economic and Social Conditions in Africa*.

United Nations Economic Commission for Africa, Africa Hall, Post Office Box 3001, Addis Ababa, Ethiopia (Telephone Number in U.S. (800) 253-9646); *African Statistical Yearbook*.

The World Bank, 1818 H Street, NW, Washington, D.C. 20433 (202) 477-1234; *World Development Indicators*.

LIBERIA - GROSS NATIONAL PRODUCT

Euromonitor International, Inc., 122 South Michigan Avenue, Suite 1200, Chicago, Illinois 60603 (800) 577-EURO; *International Marketing Data and Statistics*.

St. Martin's Press, Inc., 175 Fifth Avenue, New York, New York 10010 (800) 221-7945; *The Statesman's Year-Book*.

U.S. Arms Control and Disarmament Agency, 320 Twenty-first Street, NW, Washington, D.C. 20451 (202) 647-8677; *World Military Expenditures and Arms Transfers*.

The World Bank, 1818 H Street, NW, Washington, D.C. 20433 (202) 477-1234; *The World Bank Atlas;* and *World Development Indicators*.

LIBERIA - GROUNDNUT PRODUCTION - See LIBERIA - CROPS

LIBERIA - HEALTH

African Development Bank, 01 BP 1387, Abidjan 01, Cote d'Ivoire; *Selected Statistics on Regional Member Countries*.

Euromonitor International, Inc., 122 South Michigan Avenue, Suite 1200, Chicago, Illinois 60603 (800) 577-EURO; *World Marketing Data and Statistics*.

M.E. Sharpe, 80 Business Park Drive, Armonk, New York 10504 (800) 541-6563; *The Illustrated Book of World Rankings*.

St. Martin's Press, Inc., 175 Fifth Avenue, New York, New York 10010 (800) 221-7945; *The Statesman's Year-Book*.

Statistical Office of the United Nations, Publishing Service, New York, New York 10017 (800) 253-9646; *Statistical Yearbook*.

United Nations Children's Fund (UNICEF), 3 United Nations Plaza, New York, New York 10017 (800) 253-9646; *State of the World's Children*.

United Nations Economic Commission for Africa, Africa Hall, Post Office Box 3001, Addis Ababa, Ethiopia (Telephone Number in U.S. (800) 253-9646); *African Statistical Yearbook*.

LIBERIA - HEALTH EXPENDITURES

International Monetary Fund, 700 Nineteenth Street, NW, Washington, D.C. 20431 (202) 623-7000; *Government Finance Statistics Yearbook*.

LIBERIA - HIDE PRODUCTION

Food and Agricultural Organization of the United Nations (FAO), Via delle Terme di Caracalla, 00100 Rome, Italy (Telephone Number in U.S. (202) 653-2400); *Production Yearbook*.

LIBERIA - HIGHWAYS

Central Intelligence Agency, Washington, D.C. 20505 (703) 482-1100, www.cia.gov; *The World Factbook*.

International Road Federation, 2600 Virginia Avenue, N.W., Washington, D.C. 20024 (202) 338-4641; *World Road Statistics*.

St. Martin's Press, Inc., 175 Fifth Avenue, New York, New York 10010 (800) 221-7945; *The Statesman's Year-Book*.

Statistical Office of the United Nations, Publishing Service, New York, New York 10017 (800) 253-9646; *Survey of Economic and Social Conditions in Africa*.

United Nations Economic Commission for Africa, Africa Hall, Post Office Box 3001, Addis Ababa, Ethiopia (Telephone Number in U.S. (800) 253-9646); *African Statistical Yearbook*.

LIBERIA - HORSES - See LIBERIA - LIVESTOCK AND POULTRY

LIBERIA - HOURS OF WORK - See LIBERIA - EMPLOYMENT

LIBERIA - HOUSING

Euromonitor International, Inc., 122 South Michigan Avenue, Suite 1200, Chicago, Illinois 60603 (800) 577-EURO; *World Marketing Data and Statistics*.

M.E. Sharpe, 80 Business Park Drive, Armonk, New York 10504 (800) 541-6563; *The Illustrated Book of World Rankings*.

LIBERIA - HOUSING EXPENDITURES

International Monetary Fund, 700 Nineteenth Street, NW, Washington, D.C. 20431 (202) 623-7000; *Government Finance Statistics Yearbook*.

LIBERIA - ILLITERATE POPULATION

Central Intelligence Agency, Washington, D.C. 20505 (703) 482-1100, www.cia.gov; *The World Factbook*.

The Economist Intelligence Unit, 111 West 57th Street, New York, New York 10019 (800) 938-4685; *The World Market Atlas*.

Euromonitor International, Inc., 122 South Michigan Avenue, Suite 1200, Chicago, Illinois 60603 (800) 577-EURO; *The World Economic Factbook*.

United Nations Educational, Scientific and Cultural Organization (UNESCO), 7 Place de Fontenoy, F-75700 Paris, France (Telephone Number in U.S. (212) 963-5981); *Statistical Yearbook*.

LIBERIA - IMPORTS

African Development Bank, 01 BP 1387, Abidjan 01, Cote d'Ivoire; *Selected Statistics on Regional Member Countries*.

Central Intelligence Agency, Washington, D.C. 20505 (703) 482-1100, www.cia.gov; *The World Factbook*.

The Economist Intelligence Unit, 111 West 57th Street, New York, New York 10019 (800) 938-4685; *Liberia Country Report;* and *The World Market Atlas*.

Euromonitor International, Inc., 122 South Michigan Avenue, Suite 1200, Chicago, Illinois 60603 (800) 577-EURO; *International Marketing Data and Statistics;* and *The World Economic Factbook*.

Europa Publications Limited, 18 Bedford Square, London, WC1B 3JN, England; *The Europa World Year Book*.

Food and Agricultural Organization of the United Nations (FAO), Via delle Terme di Caracalla, 00100 Rome, Italy (Telephone Number in U.S. (202) 653-2400); *The State of Food and Agriculture*.

International Monetary Fund, 700 Nineteenth Street, NW, Washington, D.C. 20431 (202) 623-7000; *Direction of Trade Statistics; Government Finance Statistics Yearbook;* and *International Financial Statistics*.

International Rubber Study Group, York House, Eighth Floor, Empire Way, Wembley, London HA9 0PA, England; *Rubber Statistical Bulletin*.

St. Martin's Press, Inc., 175 Fifth Avenue, New York, New York 10010 (800) 221-7945; *The Statesman's Year-Book*.

Statistical Office of the United Nations, Publishing Service, New York, New York 10017 (800) 253-9646; *Foreign Trade Statistics for Africa;* and *Survey of Economic and Social Conditions in Africa.*

United Nations Conference on Trade and Development (UNCTAD), New York, New York 10017 (800) 253-9646; *Handbook of International Trade and Development Statistics.*

United Nations Economic Commission for Africa, Africa Hall, Post Office Box 3001, Addis Ababa, Ethiopia (Telephone Number in U.S. (800) 253-9646); *African Statistical Yearbook.*

The World Bank, 1818 H Street, NW, Washington, D.C. 20433 (202) 477-1234; *World Development Indicators.*

LIBERIA - INCOME TAXES - See LIBERIA - TAXATION

LIBERIA - INDUSTRY

Central Intelligence Agency, Washington, D.C. 20505 (703) 482-1100, www.cia.gov; *The World Factbook.*

Economist Intelligence Unit, 111 West 57th Street, New York, New York 10019 (800) 938-4685; *Liberia Country Report.*

Euromonitor International, Inc., 122 South Michigan Avenue, Suite 1200, Chicago, Illinois 60603 (800) 577-EURO; *International Marketing Data and Statistics; World Marketing Data and Statistics;* and *The World Economic Factbook.*

Europa Publications Limited, 18 Bedford Square, London, WC1B 3JN, England; *The Europa World Year Book.*

International Labour Office, I.L.O. Publications, 1828 L Street, N.W., Suite 801, Washington, D.C. (301) 638-3152; *Yearbook of Labour Statistics.*

M.E. Sharpe, 80 Business Park Drive, Armonk, New York 10504 (800) 541-6563; *The Illustrated Book of World Rankings.*

St. Martin's Press, Inc., 175 Fifth Avenue, New York, New York 10010 (800) 221-7945; *The Statesman's Year-Book.*

Statistical Office of the United Nations, Publishing Service, New York, New York 10017 (800) 253-9646; *Survey of Economic and Social Conditions in Africa.*

United Nations Economic Commission for Africa, Africa Hall, Post Office Box 3001, Addis Ababa, Ethiopia (Telephone Number in U.S. (800) 253-9646); *African Statistical Yearbook.*

The World Bank, 1818 H Street, NW,

Washington, D.C. 20433 (202) 477-1234; *World Development Indicators.*

World Intellectual Property Organization, 34 Chemin des Colombettes, CH-1211 Geneva 20, Switzerland; *Industrial Property Statistics.*

LIBERIA - INFANT AND MATERNAL MORTALITY - See LIBERIA - MORTALITY

LIBERIA - INTERNATIONAL LIQUIDITY

International Monetary Fund, 700 Nineteenth Street, NW, Washington, D.C. 20431 (202) 623-7000; *International Financial Statistics.*

LIBERIA - INTERNATIONAL RESERVES EXCLUDING GOLD

African Development Bank, 01 BP 1387, Abidjan 01, Cote d'Ivoire; *Selected Statistics on Regional Member Countries.*

Statistical Office of the United Nations, Publishing Service, New York, New York 10017 (800) 253-9646; *Statistical Yearbook.*

The World Bank, 1818 H Street, NW, Washington, D.C. 20433 (202) 477-1234; *World Development Indicators.*

LIBERIA - IRON ORE - See LIBERIA - MINING AND MINERAL PRODUCTS

LIBERIA - IRRIGATION

Euromonitor International, Inc., 122 South Michigan Avenue, Suite 1200, Chicago, Illinois 60603 (800) 577-EURO; *International Marketing Data and Statistics.*

LIBERIA - LABOR

African Development Bank, 01 BP 1387, Abidjan 01, Cote d'Ivoire; *Selected Statistics on Regional Member Countries.*

Central Intelligence Agency, Washington, D.C. 20505 (703) 482-1100, www.cia.gov; *The World Factbook.*

Euromonitor International, Inc., 122 South Michigan Avenue, Suite 1200, Chicago, Illinois 60603 (800) 577-EURO; *International Marketing Data and Statistics;* and *World Marketing Data and Statistics.*

Europa Publications Limited, 18 Bedford Square, London, WC1B 3JN, England; *The Europa World Year Book.*

Food and Agricultural Organization of the United Nations (FAO), Via delle Terme di Caracalla, 00100 Rome, Italy (Telephone Number in U.S. (202) 653-2400); *The State of Food and Agriculture.*

International Labour Office, I.L.O. Publications, 1828 L Street, N.W.,

Suite 801, Washington, D.C. (301) 638-3152; *Yearbook of Labour Statistics.*

M.E. Sharpe, 80 Business Park Drive, Armonk, New York 10504 (800) 541-6563; *The Illustrated Book of World Rankings.*

St. Martin's Press, Inc., 175 Fifth Avenue, New York, New York 10010 (800) 221-7945; *The Statesman's Year-Book.*

The World Bank, 1818 H Street, NW, Washington, D.C. 20433 (202) 477-1234; *The World Bank Atlas;* and *World Development Indicators.*

LIBERIA - LAND USE

Central Intelligence Agency, Washington, D.C. 20505 (703) 482-1100, www.cia.gov; *The World Factbook.*

Euromonitor International, Inc., 122 South Michigan Avenue, Suite 1200, Chicago, Illinois 60603 (800) 577-EURO; *International Marketing Data and Statistics.*

Food and Agricultural Organization of the United Nations (FAO), Via delle Terme di Caracalla, 00100 Rome, Italy (Telephone Number in U.S. (202) 653-2400); *Production Yearbook.*

LIBERIA - LIBRARIES

M.E. Sharpe, 80 Business Park Drive, Armonk, New York 10504 (800) 541-6563; *The Illustrated Book of World Rankings.*

LIBERIA - LIFE EXPECTANCY

African Development Bank, 01 BP 1387, Abidjan 01, Cote d'Ivoire; *Selected Statistics on Regional Member Countries.*

Central Intelligence Agency, Washington, D.C. 20505 (703) 482-1100, www.cia.gov; *The World Factbook.*

Euromonitor International, Inc., 122 South Michigan Avenue, Suite 1200, Chicago, Illinois 60603 (800) 577-EURO; *The World Economic Factbook.*

Statistical Office of the United Nations, Publishing Service, New York, New York 10017 (800) 253-9646; *World Statistics Pocketbook.*

The World Bank, 1818 H Street, NW, Washington, D.C. 20433 (202) 477-1234; *The World Bank Atlas.*

LIBERIA - LITERACY RATES

Euromonitor International, Inc., 122 South Michigan Avenue, Suite 1200, Chicago, Illinois 60603 (800) 577-EURO; *World Marketing Data and Statistics.*

Statistical Office of the United Nations,

Publishing Service, New York, New York 10017 (800) 253-9646; *Survey of Economic and Social Conditions in Africa.*

LIBERIA - LIVESTOCK AND POULTRY

Euromonitor International, Inc., 122 South Michigan Avenue, Suite 1200, Chicago, Illinois 60603 (800) 577-EURO; *International Marketing Data and Statistics.*

Europa Publications Limited, 18 Bedford Square, London, WC1B 3JN, England; *The Europa World Year Book.*

Food and Agricultural Organization of the United Nations (FAO), Via delle Terme di Caracalla, 00100 Rome, Italy (Telephone Number in U.S. (202) 653-2400); *Production Yearbook;* and *The State of Food and Agriculture.*

M.E. Sharpe, 80 Business Park Drive, Armonk, New York 10504 (800) 541-6563; *The Illustrated Book of World Rankings.*

St. Martin's Press, Inc., 175 Fifth Avenue, New York, New York 10010 (800) 221-7945; *The Statesman's Year-Book.*

Statistical Office of the United Nations, Publishing Service, New York, New York 10017 (800) 253-9646; *Statistical Yearbook;* and *Survey of Economic and Social Conditions in Africa.*

United Nations Conference on Trade and Development, Central Statistical Service, Palais des Nations, Geneva, Switzerland (Telephone in U.S. (800) 253-9646); *UNCTAD Commodity Yearbook.*

United Nations Economic Commission for Africa, Africa Hall, Post Office Box 3001, Addis Ababa, Ethiopia (Telephone Number in U.S. (800) 253-9646); *African Statistical Yearbook.*

LIBERIA - LIVING LEVELS - See LIBERIA - LIFE EXPECTANCY

LIBERIA - MAIL - NUMBER OF PIECES SENT OR RECEIVED

Statistical Office of the United Nations, Publishing Service, New York, New York 10017 (800) 253-9646; *Statistical Yearbook.*

LIBERIA - MANUFACTURING

M.E. Sharpe, 80 Business Park Drive, Armonk, New York 10504 (800) 541-6563; *The Illustrated Book of World Rankings.*

Statistical Office of the United Nations, Publishing Service, New York, New York 10017 (800) 253-9646; *Survey of Economic and Social Conditions in Africa.*

United Nations Economic Commission for Africa, Africa Hall, Post Office Box 3001,

Addis Ababa, Ethiopia (Telephone Number in U.S. (800) 253-9646); *African Statistical Yearbook.*

The World Bank, 1818 H Street, NW, Washington, D.C. 20433 (202) 477-1234; *World Development Indicators.*

LIBERIA - MARRIAGE RATES

M.E. Sharpe, 80 Business Park Drive, Armonk, New York 10504 (800) 541-6563; *The Illustrated Book of World Rankings.*

Statistical Office of the United Nations, Publishing Service, New York, New York 10017 (800) 253-9646; *Demographic Yearbook;* and *Statistical Yearbook.*

LIBERIA - MEAT PRODUCTION - See LIBERIA - LIVESTOCK AND POULTRY

LIBERIA - MERCHANT SHIPPING

Europa Publications Limited, 18 Bedford Square, London, WC1B 3JN, England; *The Europa World Year Book.*

Lloyd's Register of Shipping, 17 Battery Place, New York, New York 10004 (212) 425-8050; *Register of Ships.*

St. Martin's Press, Inc., 175 Fifth Avenue, New York, New York 10010 (800) 221-7945; *The Statesman's Year-Book.*

Statistical Office of the United Nations, Publishing Service, New York, New York 10017 (800) 253-9646; *Statistical Yearbook.*

United Nations Economic Commission for Africa, Africa Hall, Post Office Box 3001, Addis Ababa, Ethiopia (Telephone Number in U.S. (800) 253-9646); *African Statistical Yearbook.*

U.S. Department of Transportation, Maritime Administration, 400 Seventh Street, SW, Washington, D.C. 20590 (202) 366-5807, www.marad.dot.gov; *A Statistical Analysis of the World's Merchant Fleets.*

LIBERIA - MILITARY

Central Intelligence Agency, Washington, D.C. 20505 (703) 482-1100, www.cia.gov; *The World Factbook.*

Euromonitor International, Inc., 122 South Michigan Avenue, Suite 1200, Chicago, Illinois 60603 (800) 577-EURO; *World Marketing Data and Statistics.*

The International Institute for Strategic Studies, 23 Tavistock Street, London WC2E 7NQ, England 44 171 3797676; *The Military Balance.*

International Monetary Fund, 700 Nineteenth Street, NW, Washington, D.C. 20431 (202) 623-7000; *Government*

Finance Statistics Yearbook.

St. Martin's Press, Inc., 175 Fifth Avenue, New York, New York 10010 (800) 221-7945; *The Statesman's Year-Book.*

U.S. Arms Control and Disarmament Agency, 320 Twenty-first Street, NW, Washington, D.C. 20451 (202) 647-8677; *World Military Expenditures and Arms Transfers.*

LIBERIA - MILK PRODUCTION - See LIBERIA - DAIRY PRODUCTS

LIBERIA - MINING AND MINERAL PRODUCTS

Europa Publications Limited, 18 Bedford Square, London, WC1B 3JN, England; *The Europa World Year Book.*

International Monetary Fund, 700 Nineteenth Street, NW, Washington, D.C. 20431 (202) 623-7000; *International Financial Statistics.*

M.E. Sharpe, 80 Business Park Drive, Armonk, New York 10504 (800) 541-6563; *The Illustrated Book of World Rankings.*

St. Martin's Press, Inc., 175 Fifth Avenue, New York, New York 10010 (800) 221-7945; *The Statesman's Year-Book.*

Statistical Office of the United Nations, Publishing Service, New York, New York 10017 (800) 253-9646; *Statistical Yearbook.*

United Nations Conference on Trade and Development, Central Statistical Service, Palais des Nations, Geneva, Switzerland (Telephone in U.S. (800) 253-9646); *UNCTAD Commodity Yearbook.*

United Nations Economic Commission for Africa, Africa Hall, Post Office Box 3001, Addis Ababa, Ethiopia (Telephone Number in U.S. (800) 253-9646); *African Statistical Yearbook.*

LIBERIA - MONEY EXCHANGE RATES - See LIBERIA - EXCHANGE RATES

LIBERIA - MONEY RESERVES

Euromonitor International, Inc., 122 South Michigan Avenue, Suite 1200, Chicago, Illinois 60603 (800) 577-EURO; *International Marketing Data and Statistics.*

LIBERIA - MONEY SUPPLY

African Development Bank, 01 BP 1387, Abidjan 01, Cote d'Ivoire; *Selected Statistics on Regional Member Countries.*

Economist Intelligence Unit, 111 West 57th Street, New York, New York 10019 (800) 938-4685; *Liberia Country Report.*

Euromonitor International, Inc., 122 South Michigan Avenue, Suite 1200, Chicago, Illinois 60603 (800) 577-EURO; *International Marketing Data and Statistics.*

Europa Publications Limited, 18 Bedford Square, London, WC1B 3JN, England; *The Europa World Year Book.*

International Monetary Fund, 700 Nineteenth Street, NW, Washington, D.C. 20431 (202) 623-7000; *International Financial Statistics.*

The World Bank, 1818 H Street, NW, Washington, D.C. 20433 (202) 477-1234; *World Development Indicators.*

LIBERIA - MORTALITY

Central Intelligence Agency, Washington, D.C. 20505 (703) 482-1100, www.cia.gov; *The World Factbook.*

Euromonitor International, Inc., 122 South Michigan Avenue, Suite 1200, Chicago, Illinois 60603 (800) 577-EURO; *International Marketing Data and Statistics;* and *The World Economic Factbook.*

Europa Publications Limited, 18 Bedford Square, London, WC1B 3JN, England; *The Europa World Year Book.*

Statistical Office of the United Nations, Publishing Service, New York, New York 10017 (800) 253-9646; *Demographic Yearbook; Statistical Yearbook; World Statistics Pocketbook;* and *Survey of Economic and Social Conditions in Africa.*

United Nations Children's Fund (UNICEF), 3 United Nations Plaza, New York, New York 10017 (800) 253-9646; *State of the World's Children.*

The World Bank, 1818 H Street, NW, Washington, D.C. 20433 (202) 477-1234; *The World Bank Atlas;* and *World Development Indicators.*

LIBERIA - MOTOR VEHICLE TAXES - See LIBERIA - TAXATION

LIBERIA - MOTOR VEHICLES IN USE

Europa Publications Limited, 18 Bedford Square, London, WC1B 3JN, England; *The Europa World Year Book.*

International Road Federation, 2600 Virginia Avenue, N.W., Washington, D.C. 20037 (202) 338-4641; *World Road Statistics.*

Statistical Office of the United Nations, Publishing Service, New York, New York 10017 (800) 253-9646; *Statistical Yearbook;* and *Survey of Economic and Social Conditions in Africa.*

LIBERIA - MUSEUMS

M.E. Sharpe, 80 Business Park Drive, Armonk, New York 10504 (800) 541-6563; *The Illustrated Book of World Rankings.*

LIBERIA - NATALITY - See LIBERIA - BIRTH RATES

LIBERIA - NATIONAL ACCOUNTS

African Development Bank, 01 BP 1387, Abidjan 01, Cote d'Ivoire; *Selected Statistics on Regional Member Countries.*

Europa Publications Limited, 18 Bedford Square, London, WC1B 3JN, England; *The Europa World Year Book.*

Statistical Office of the United Nations, Publishing Service, New York, New York 10017 (800) 253-9646; *National Accounts Statistics;* and *Statistical Yearbook.*

United Nations Economic Commission for Africa, Africa Hall, Post Office Box 3001, Addis Ababa, Ethiopia (Telephone Number in U.S. (800) 253-9646); *African Statistical Yearbook.*

LIBERIA - NATIONAL INCOME

M.E. Sharpe, 80 Business Park Drive, Armonk, New York 10504 (800) 541-6563; *The Illustrated Book of World Rankings.*

Statistical Office of the United Nations, Publishing Service, New York, New York 10017 (800) 253-9646; *National Accounts Statistics;* and *Statistical Yearbook.*

LIBERIA - NATIONAL PRODUCT

M.E. Sharpe, 80 Business Park Drive, Armonk, New York 10504 (800) 541-6563; *The Illustrated Book of World Rankings.*

Statistical Office of the United Nations, Publishing Service, New York, New York 10017 (800) 253-9646; *Statistical Yearbook.*

LIBERIA - NATURAL GAS - PRODUCTION - See LIBERIA - MINING AND MINERAL PRODUCTS

LIBERIA - NATURAL RUBBER PRODUCTION

International Rubber Study Group, York House, Eighth Floor, Empire Way, Wembley, London HA9 0PA, England; *Rubber Statistical Bulletin.*

Statistical Office of the United Nations, Publishing Service, New York, New York 10017 (800) 253-9646; *Statistical Yearbook.*

LIBERIA - NEWSPAPER PRODUCTION - See LIBERIA - FORESTRY AND FOREST PRODUCTS

LIBERIA - NEWSPRINT - See LIBERIA - FORESTRY AND FOREST PRODUCTS

LIBERIA - OCCUPATIONS - See LIBERIA - LABOR

LIBERIA - PALM KERNEL PRODUCTION - See LIBERIA - CROPS

LIBERIA - PAPER - See LIBERIA - FORESTRY AND FOREST PRODUCTS

LIBERIA - PATENTS, TRADEMARKS AND SERVICE MARKS

World Intellectual Property Organization, 34 Chemin des Colombettes, CH-1211 Geneva 20, Switzerland; *Industrial Property Statistics.*

LIBERIA - PEANUT PRODUCTION - See LIBERIA - CROPS

LIBERIA - PESTICIDE USE

Food and Agricultural Organization of the United Nations (FAO), Via delle Terme di Caracalla, 00100 Rome, Italy (Telephone Number in U.S. (202) 653-2400); *The State of Food and Agriculture.*

LIBERIA - PETROLEUM INDUSTRY

Food and Agricultural Organization of the United Nations (FAO), Via delle Terme di Caracalla, 00100 Rome, Italy (Telephone Number in U.S. (202) 653-2400); *The State of Food and Agriculture.*

M.E. Sharpe, 80 Business Park Drive, Armonk, New York 10504 (800) 541-6563; *The Illustrated Book of World Rankings.*

Statistical Office of the United Nations, Publishing Service, New York, New York 10017 (800) 253-9646; *Statistical Yearbook.*

United Nations Conference on Trade and Development, Central Statistical Service, Palais des Nations, Geneva, Switzerland (Telephone in U.S. (800) 253-9646); *UNCTAD Commodity Yearbook.*

LIBERIA - PIGS - See LIBERIA - LIVESTOCK AND POULTRY

LIBERIA - POPULATION

African Development Bank, 01 BP 1387, Abidjan 01, Cote d'Ivoire; *Selected Statistics on Regional Member Countries.*

Central Intelligence Agency, Washington, D.C. 20505 (703) 482-1100, www.cia.gov; *The World Factbook.*

The Economist Intelligence Unit, 111 West 57th Street, New York, New York 10019 (800) 938-4685; *Liberia Country Report;* and *The World Market Atlas.*

Euromonitor International, Inc., 122 South Michigan Avenue, Suite 1200, Chicago, Illinois 60603 (800) 577-EURO; *International Marketing Data and Statistics;* and *The World Economic Factbook.*

Europa Publications Limited, 18 Bedford Square, London, WC1B 3JN, England; *The Europa World Year Book.*

Food and Agricultural Organization of the United Nations (FAO), Via delle Terme di Caracalla, 00100 Rome, Italy (Telephone Number in U.S. (202) 653-2400); *Production Yearbook.*

International Labour Office, I.L.O. Publications, 1828 L Street, N.W., Suite 801, Washington, D.C. 20036 (301) 638-3152; *Yearbook of Labour Statistics.*

M.E. Sharpe, 80 Business Park Drive, Armonk, New York 10504 (800) 541-6563; *The Illustrated Book of World Rankings.*

St. Martin's Press, Inc., 175 Fifth Avenue, New York, New York 10010 (800) 221-7945; *The Statesman's Year-Book.*

Statistical Office of the United Nations, Publishing Service, New York, New York 10017 (800) 253-9646; *Demographic Yearbook; Statistical Yearbook; World Statistics Pocketbook;* and *Survey of Economic and Social Conditions in Africa.*

United Nations Educational, Scientific and Cultural Organization (UNESCO), 7 Place de Fontenoy, F-75700 Paris, France (Telephone Number in U.S. (212) 963-5981); *Statistical Yearbook.*

U.S. Arms Control and Disarmament Agency, 320 Twenty-first Street, NW, Washington, D.C. 20451 (202) 647-8677; *World Military Expenditures and Arms Transfers.*

The World Bank, 1818 H Street, NW, Washington, D.C. 20433 (202) 477-1234; *The World Bank Atlas.*

World Health Organization, Office of Publications, 20 Avenue Appia, CH-1211 Geneva 27, Switzerland (Telephone Number in U.S. (518) 436-9686); *World Health Statistics Annual.*

LIBERIA - POST OFFICES

M.E. Sharpe, 80 Business Park Drive, Armonk, New York 10504 (800) 541-6563; *The Illustrated Book of World Rankings.*

LIBERIA - POTATO PRODUCTION - See LIBERIA - CROPS

LIBERIA - PRICES

Food and Agricultural Organization of the United Nations (FAO), Via delle Terme

di Caracalla, 00100 Rome, Italy (Telephone Number in U.S. (202) 653-2400); *Production Yearbook;* and *The State of Food and Agriculture.*

International Labour Office, I.L.O. Publications, 1828 L Street, N.W., Suite 801, Washington, D.C. 20036 (301) 638-3152; *Yearbook of Labour Statistics.*

International Monetary Fund, 700 Nineteenth Street, NW, Washington, D.C. 20431 (202) 623-7000; *International Financial Statistics.*

International Rubber Study Group, York House, Eighth Floor, Empire Way, Wembley, London HA9 0PA, England; *Rubber Statistical Bulletin.*

M.E. Sharpe, 80 Business Park Drive, Armonk, New York 10504 (800) 541-6563; *The Illustrated Book of World Rankings.*

United Nations Economic Commission for Africa, Africa Hall, Post Office Box 3001, Addis Ababa, Ethiopia (Telephone Number in U.S. (800) 253-9646); *African Statistical Yearbook.*

LIBERIA - PRINTING AND WRITING PAPER - See LIBERIA - FORESTRY AND FOREST PRODUCTS

LIBERIA - PRODUCTION

International Rubber Study Group, York House, Eighth Floor, Empire Way, Wembley, London HA9 0PA, England; *Rubber Statistical Bulletin.*

M.E. Sharpe, 80 Business Park Drive, Armonk, New York 10504 (800) 541-6563; *The Illustrated Book of World Rankings.*

LIBERIA - PRODUCTIVITY

Euromonitor International, Inc., 122 South Michigan Avenue, Suite 1200, Chicago, Illinois 60603 (800) 577-EURO; *International Marketing Data and Statistics.*

LIBERIA - PROPERTY TAXES - See LIBERIA - TAXATION

LIBERIA - PUBLIC FINANCE - See LIBERIA - FINANCE

LIBERIA - RADIO BROADCASTING - See LIBERIA - BROADCASTING

LIBERIA - RADIO RECEIVERS

St. Martin's Press, Inc., 175 Fifth Avenue, New York, New York 10010 (800) 221-7945; *The Statesman's Year-Book.*

LIBERIA - RAILWAYS

Jane's Information Group, Sentinel House, 163 Brighton Road, Coulsdon,

Surrey CR5 2NH, England (Telephone Number in U.S. (703) 683-3700); *Jane's World Railways.*

St. Martin's Press, Inc., 175 Fifth Avenue, New York, New York 10010 (800) 221-7945; *The Statesman's Year-Book.*

Statistical Office of the United Nations, Publishing Service, New York, New York 10017 (800) 253-9646; *Survey of Economic and Social Conditions in Africa.*

United Nations Economic Commission for Africa, Africa Hall, Post Office Box 3001, Addis Ababa, Ethiopia (Telephone Number in U.S. (800) 253-9646); *African Statistical Yearbook.*

LIBERIA - RELIGION

Central Intelligence Agency, Washington, D.C. 20505 (703) 482-1100, www.cia.gov; *The World Factbook.*

M.E. Sharpe, 80 Business Park Drive, Armonk, New York 10504 (800) 541-6563; *The Illustrated Book of World Rankings.*

St. Martin's Press, Inc., 175 Fifth Avenue, New York, New York 10010 (800) 221-7945; *The Statesman's Year-Book.*

LIBERIA - RENT PRICES

International Labour Office, I.L.O. Publications, 1828 L Street, N.W., Suite 801, Washington, D.C. 20036 (301) 638-3152; *Yearbook of Labour Statistics.*

LIBERIA - RETAIL TRADE

Euromonitor International, Inc., 122 South Michigan Avenue, Suite 1200, Chicago, Illinois 60603 (800) 577-EURO; *World Marketing Data and Statistics.*

LIBERIA - RICE PRODUCTION - See LIBERIA - CROPS

LIBERIA - ROOT AND TUBER PRODUCTION - See LIBERIA - CROPS

LIBERIA - ROUNDWOOD PRODUCTION - See LIBERIA - FORESTRY AND FOREST PRODUCTS

LIBERIA - RUBBER EXPORTS

International Monetary Fund, 700 Nineteenth Street, NW, Washington, D.C. 20431 (202) 623-7000; *International Financial Statistics.*

LIBERIA - RUBBER PRODUCTION AND CONSUMPTION

International Rubber Study Group, York House, Eighth Floor, Empire Way, Wembley, London HA9 0PA, England; *Rubber Statistical Bulletin.*

M.E. Sharpe, 80 Business Park Drive, Armonk, New York 10504 (800) 541-6563; *The Illustrated Book of World Rankings*.

Statistical Office of the United Nations, Publishing Service, New York, New York 10017 (800) 253-9646; *Statistical Yearbook*.

LIBERIA - SAWNWOOD PRODUCTION - See LIBERIA - FORESTRY AND FOREST PRODUCTS

LIBERIA - SCIENTISTS, TECHNICIANS AND ENGINEERS

United Nations Educational, Scientific and Cultural Organization (UNESCO), 7 Place de Fontenoy, F-75700 Paris, France (Telephone Number in U.S. (212) 963-5981); *Statistical Yearbook*.

LIBERIA - SENIOR CITIZENS

M.E. Sharpe, 80 Business Park Drive, Armonk, New York 10504 (800) 541-6563; *The Illustrated Book of World Rankings*.

LIBERIA - SHEEP - See LIBERIA - LIVESTOCK AND POULTRY

LIBERIA - SILVER PRODUCTION AND CONSUMPTION - See LIBERIA - MINING AND MINERAL PRODUCTS

LIBERIA - SOCIAL DATA

African Development Bank, 01 BP 1387, Abidjan 01, Cote d'Ivoire; *Selected Statistics on Regional Member Countries*.

M.E. Sharpe, 80 Business Park Drive, Armonk, New York 10504 (800) 541-6563; *The Illustrated Book of World Rankings*.

Statistical Office of the United Nations, Publishing Service, New York, New York 10017 (800) 253-9646; *World Statistics Pocketbook*.

LIBERIA - SOCIAL SECURITY

International Monetary Fund, 700 Nineteenth Street, NW, Washington, D.C. 20431 (202) 623-7000; *Government Finance Statistics Yearbook*.

Statistical Office of the United Nations, Publishing Service, New York, New York 10017 (800) 253-9646; *National Accounts Statistics*.

LIBERIA - STAMP TAXES AND DUTIES - See LIBERIA - TAXATION

LIBERIA - STATE BUDGET

Euromonitor International, Inc., 122 South Michigan Avenue, Suite 1200, Chicago, Illinois 60603 (800) 577-EURO; *International Marketing Data and Statistics*.

LIBERIA - STEEL - See LIBERIA - MINING AND MINERAL PRODUCTS

LIBERIA - STOCKS - COMMODITY - MARKET PRICE - INDEX

Food and Agricultural Organization of the United Nations (FAO), Via delle Terme di Caracalla, 00100 Rome, Italy (Telephone Number in U.S. (202) 653-2400); *The State of Food and Agriculture*.

LIBERIA - SUGAR PRODUCTION AND CONSUMPTION - See LIBERIA - CROPS

LIBERIA - TAXATION

Europa Publications Limited, 18 Bedford Square, London, WC1B 3JN, England; *The Europa World Year Book*.

International Monetary Fund, 700 Nineteenth Street, NW, Washington, D.C. 20431 (202) 623-7000; *Government Finance Statistics Yearbook*.

International Road Federation, 2600 Virginia Avenue, N.W., Washington, D.C. 20037 (202) 338-4641; *World Road Statistics*.

The World Bank, 1818 H Street, NW, Washington, D.C. 20433 (202) 477-1234; *World Development Indicators*.

LIBERIA - TELEPHONES IN USE

American Telephone and Telegraph Company, 26 Parsippany Road, Whippany, New Jersey 07981 (800) 222-0300; *The World's Telephones*.

Central Intelligence Agency, Washington, D.C. 20505 (703) 482-1100, www.cia.gov; *The World Factbook*.

Europa Publications Limited, 18 Bedford Square, London, WC1B 3JN, England; *The Europa World Year Book*.

St. Martin's Press, Inc., 175 Fifth Avenue, New York, New York 10010 (800) 221-7945; *The Statesman's Year-Book*.

Statistical Office of the United Nations, Publishing Service, New York, New York 10017 (800) 253-9646; *Statistical Yearbook;* and *World Statistics Pocketbook*.

LIBERIA - TELEVISION BROADCASTING - See LIBERIA - BROADCASTING

LIBERIA - TEXTILE INDUSTRY

M.E. Sharpe, 80 Business Park Drive, Armonk, New York 10504 (800) 541-6563; *The Illustrated Book of World Rankings*.

United Nations Conference on Trade and Development, Central Statistical Service, Palais des Nations, Geneva,

Switzerland (Telephone in U.S. (800) 253-9646); *UNCTAD Commodity Yearbook*.

LIBERIA - TIRE (MOTOR VEHICLE) PRODUCTION

International Rubber Study Group, York House, Eighth Floor, Empire Way, Wembley, London HA9 0PA, England; *Rubber Statistical Bulletin*.

LIBERIA - TOBACCO PRODUCTION

M.E. Sharpe, 80 Business Park Drive, Armonk, New York 10504 (800) 541-6563; *The Illustrated Book of World Rankings*.

Statistical Office of the United Nations, Publishing Service, New York, New York 10017 (800) 253-9646; *Statistical Yearbook*.

LIBERIA - TOURISM

Euromonitor International, Inc., 122 South Michigan Avenue, Suite 1200, Chicago, Illinois 60603 (800) 577-EURO; *The World Economic Factbook;* and *World Marketing Data and Statistics*.

M.E. Sharpe, 80 Business Park Drive, Armonk, New York 10504 (800) 541-6563; *The Illustrated Book of World Rankings*.

United Nations Economic Commission for Africa, Africa Hall, Post Office Box 3001, Addis Ababa, Ethiopia (Telephone Number in U.S. (800) 253-9646); *African Statistical Yearbook*.

LIBERIA - TRACTORS IN USE

Statistical Office of the United Nations, Publishing Service, New York, New York 10017 (800) 253-9646; *Statistical Yearbook*.

LIBERIA - TRADE - See LIBERIA - FOREIGN TRADE

LIBERIA - TRADEMARKS AND SERVICE MARKS - See LIBERIA - PATENTS, TRADEMARKS AND SERVICE MARKS

LIBERIA - TRANSPORTATION AND COMMUNICATIONS

Central Intelligence Agency, Washington, D.C. 20505 (703) 482-1100, www.cia.gov; *The World Factbook*.

Euromonitor International, Inc., 122 South Michigan Avenue, Suite 1200, Chicago, Illinois 60603 (800) 577-EURO; *International Marketing Data and Statistics;* and *World Marketing Data and Statistics*.

Europa Publications Limited, 18 Bedford Square, London, WC1B 3JN, England; *The Europa World Year Book*.

M.E. Sharpe, 80 Business Park Drive, Armonk, New York 10504 (800) 541-6563;

The Illustrated Book of World Rankings.

St. Martin's Press, Inc., 175 Fifth Avenue, New York, New York 10010 (800) 221-7945; *The Statesman's Year-Book.*

United Nations Economic Commission for Africa, Africa Hall, Post Office Box 3001, Addis Ababa, Ethiopia (Telephone Number in U.S. (800) 253-9646); *African Statistical Yearbook.*

LIBERIA - UNEMPLOYMENT

Central Intelligence Agency, Washington, D.C. 20505 (703) 482-1100, www.cia.gov; *The World Factbook.*

International Labour Office, I.L.O. Publications, 1828 L Street, N.W., Suite 801, Washington, D.C. 20036 (301) 638-3152; *Yearbook of Labour Statistics.*

Statistical Office of the United Nations, Publishing Service, New York, New York 10017 (800) 253-9646; *Statistical Yearbook.*

LIBERIA - VITAL STATISTICS

Euromonitor International, Inc., 122 South Michigan Avenue, Suite 1200, Chicago, Illinois 60603 (800) 577-EURO; *International Marketing Data and Statistics.*

Statistical Office of the United Nations, Publishing Service, New York, New York 10017 (800) 253-9646; *Statistical Yearbook.*

World Health Organization, Office of Publications, 20 Avenue Appia, CH-1211 Geneva 27, Switzerland (Telephone Number in U.S. (518) 436-9686); *World Health Statistics Annual.*

LIBERIA - WAGES

International Labour Office, I.L.O. Publications, 1828 L Street, N.W., Suite 801, Washington, D.C. 20036 (301) 638-3152; *Yearbook of Labour Statistics.*

LIBERIA - WEATHER - See LIBERIA - CLIMATE

LIBERIA - WELFARE EXPENDITURES

International Monetary Fund, 700 Nineteenth Street, NW, Washington, D.C. 20431 (202) 623-7000; *Government Finance Statistics Yearbook.*

LIBERIA - WHEAT PRODUCTION

M.E. Sharpe, 80 Business Park Drive, Armonk, New York 10504 (800) 541-6563; *The Illustrated Book of World Rankings.*

LIBERIA - WINE PRODUCTION - See LIBERIA - BEVERAGES

LIBERIA - WOOL PRODUCTION - See

LIBERIA - TEXTILE INDUSTRY

LIBRARIES AND LIBRARIANS

American Library Association, 50 East Huron, Chicago, Illinois 60611 (800) 545-2433; *The 1998 National Survey of U.S. Public Library Outlet Internet Connectivity: Final Report.*

R.R. Bowker Company, 121 Chanlon Road, New Providence, New Jersey 07974 (908) 464-6800; *The Bowker Annual: Library and Book Trade Almanac;* and *American Library Directory.*

U.S. Department of Education, National Center for Education Statistics,555 New Jersey Avenue, NW, Washington, D.C. 20208-5574 (202) 219-1828, http://nces,ed.gov; *Digest of Education Statistics; American Library Survey;* and *Public Libraries in the United States.*

LIBRARIES AND LIBRARIANS - DEGREES CONFERRED

U.S. Department of Education, National Center for Education Statistics, 555 New Jersey Avenue, NW, Washington, D.C. 20208-5574 (202) 219-1828, http://nces,ed.gov; *Digest of Education Statistics.*

LIBRARIES AND LIBRARIANS - EMPLOYEES

U.S. Department of Labor, Bureau of Labor Statistics, Two Massachusetts Avenue, NE, Washington, D.C. 20212 (202) 691-5200, www.stats.bls.gov; *Employment and Earnings;* and unpublished data.

LIBRARIES AND LIBRARIANS - GRANTS, FOUNDATIONS

The Foundation Center, 79 Fifth Avenue, New York, New York 10003 (212) 620-4230; *The Foundation Grants Index.*

LIBRARIES AND LIBRARIANS - INTERNET USE

American Library Association, 50 East Huron, Chicago, Illinois 60611 (800) 545-2433; *1998 National Survey of U.S. Public Library Outlet Internet Connectivity: Final Report.*

Libya - National Statistical Office

Central Statistical Office, Ministry of Development and Planning, Tripoli, Libya.

Libya - Primary Statistics Sources

Census and Statistical Department,

Secretariat of Planning, 40 Sharia Damascus, Tripoli, Libya; *Statistical Abstract of Libya;* and *Quarterly Bulletin of Statistics.*

LIBYA - AGRICULTURE

Economist Intelligence Unit, 111 West 57th Street, New York, New York 10019 (800) 938-4685; *Libya Country Report.*

Euromonitor International, Inc., 122 South Michigan Avenue, Suite 1200, Chicago, Illinois 60603 (800) 577-EURO; *International Marketing Data and Statistics;* and *World Marketing Data and Statistics.*

Europa Publications Limited, 18 Bedford Square, London, WC1B 3JN, England; *The Europa World Year Book.*

Federal Statistical Office, Gustav-Stresemann - Ring 11, D-6200, Wiesbaden, Germany; *Libyen.*

Food and Agricultural Organization of the United Nations (FAO), Via delle Terme di Caracalla, 00100 Rome, Italy (Telephone Number in U.S. (202) 653-2400); *Production Yearbook; The State of Food and Agriculture;* and *Trade Yearbook.*

M.E. Sharpe, 80 Business Park Drive, Armonk, New York 10504 (800) 541-6563; *The Illustrated Book of World Rankings.*

St. Martin's Press, Inc., 175 Fifth Avenue, New York, New York 10010 (800) 221-7945; *The Statesman's Year-Book.*

Statistical Office of the United Nations, Publishing Service, New York, New York 10017 (800) 253-9646; *Statistical Yearbook;* and *Survey of Economic and Social Conditions in Africa.*

United Nations Conference on Trade and Development, Central Statistical Service, Palais des Nations, Geneva, Switzerland (Telephone in U.S. (800) 253-9646); *UNCTAD Commodity Yearbook.*

United Nations Economic Commission for Africa, Africa Hall, Post Office Box 3001, Addis Ababa, Ethiopia (Telephone Number in U.S. (800) 253-9646); *African Statistical Yearbook.*

The World Bank, 1818 H Street, NW, Washington, D.C. 20433 (202) 477-1234; *World Development Indicators.*

LIBYA - AIRLINE SERVICE

Europa Publications Limited, 18 Bedford Square, London, WC1B 3JN, England; *The Europa World Year Book.*

M.E. Sharpe, 80 Business Park Drive, Armonk, New York 10504 (800) 541-6563; *The Illustrated Book of World Rankings.*

St. Martin's Press, Inc., 175 Fifth Avenue, New York, New York 10010 (800) 221-7945; *The Statesman's Year-Book.*

Statistical Office of the United Nations, Publishing Service, New York, New York 10017 (800) 253-9646; *Statistical Yearbook.*

United Nations Economic Commission for Africa, Africa Hall, Post Office Box 3001, Addis Ababa, Ethiopia (Telephone Number in U.S. (800) 253-9646); *African Statistical Yearbook.*

LIBYA - AIRPORTS

Central Intelligence Agency, Washington, D.C. 20505 (703) 482-1100, www.cia.gov; *The World Factbook.*

LIBYA - ALMOND PRODUCTION - See LIBYA - CROPS

LIBYA - ALUMINUM PRODUCTION AND CONSUMPTION - See LIBYA - MINING AND MINERAL PRODUCTS

LIBYA - ANIMAL HEALTH

Food and Agricultural Organization of the United Nations (FAO), Via delle Terme di Caracalla, 00100 Rome, Italy (Telephone Number in U.S. (202) 653-2400); *Animal Health Yearbook.*

LIBYA - AREA AND DENSITY OF POPULATION

African Development Bank, 01 BP 1387, Abidjan 01, Cote d'Ivoire; *Selected Statistics on Regional Member Countries.*

Central Intelligence Agency, Washington, D.C. 20505 (703) 482-1100, www.cia.gov; *The World Factbook.*

Euromonitor International, Inc., 122 South Michigan Avenue, Suite 1200, Chicago, Illinois 60603 (800) 577-EURO; *International Marketing Data and Statistics;* and *The World Economic Factbook.*

Europa Publications Limited, 18 Bedford Square, London, WC1B 3JN, England; *The Europa World Year Book.*

Federal Statistical Office, Gustav-Stresemann - Ring 11, D-6200, Wiesbaden, Germany; *Libyen.*

Food and Agricultural Organization of the United Nations (FAO), Via delle Terme di Caracalla, 00100 Rome, Italy (Telephone Number in U.S. (202) 653-2400); *The State of Food and Agriculture.*

M.E. Sharpe, 80 Business Park Drive, Armonk, New York 10504 (800) 541-6563; *The Illustrated Book of World Rankings.*

St. Martin's Press, Inc., 175 Fifth Avenue, New York, New York 10010 (800) 221-7945; *The Statesman's Year-Book.*

Statistical Office of the United Nations, Publishing Service, New York, New York 10017 (800) 253-9646; *Statistical Yearbook;* and *Survey of Economic and Social Conditions in Africa.*

United Nations Educational, Scientific and Cultural Organization (UNESCO), 7 Place de Fontenoy, F-75700 Paris, France (Telephone Number in U.S. (212) 963-5981); *Statistical Yearbook.*

LIBYA - ARMS EXPORTS AND IMPORTS - See LIBYA - MILITARY

LIBYA - BALANCE OF PAYMENTS

African Development Bank, 01 BP 1387, Abidjan 01, Cote d'Ivoire; *Selected Statistics on Regional Member Countries.*

The Economist Intelligence Unit, 111 West 57th Street, New York, New York 10019 (800) 938-4685; *The World Market Atlas.*

Europa Publications Limited, 18 Bedford Square, London, WC1B 3JN, England; *The Europa World Year Book.*

Federal Statistical Office, Gustav-Stresemann - Ring 11, D-6200, Wiesbaden, Germany; *Libyen.*

International Monetary Fund, 700 Nineteenth Street, NW, Washington, D.C. 20431 (202) 623-7000; *Balance of Payments Yearbook;* and *Balance of Payments Yearbook.*

United Nations Conference on Trade and Development (UNCTAD), New York, New York 10017 (800) 253-9646; *Handbook of International Trade and Development Statistics.*

United Nations Economic Commission for Africa, Africa Hall, Post Office Box 3001, Addis Ababa, Ethiopia (Telephone Number in U.S. (800) 253-9646); *African Statistical Yearbook.*

The World Bank, 1818 H Street, NW, Washington, D.C. 20433 (202) 477-1234; *World Development Indicators.*

LIBYA - BANKING

Euromonitor International, Inc., 122 South Michigan Avenue, Suite 1200, Chicago, Illinois 60603 (800) 577-EURO; *World Marketing Data and Statistics.*

Europa Publications Limited, 18 Bedford Square, London, WC1B 3JN, England; *The Europa World Year Book.*

International Monetary Fund, 700 Nineteenth Street, NW, Washington, D.C. 20431 (202) 623-7000; *International Financial Statistics.*

M.E. Sharpe, 80 Business Park Drive, Armonk, New York 10504 (800) 541-6563; *The Illustrated Book of World Rankings.*

St. Martin's Press, Inc., 175 Fifth Avenue, New York, New York 10010 (800) 221-7945; *The Statesman's Year-Book.*

Statistical Office of the United Nations, Publishing Service, New York, New York 10017 (800) 253-9646; *Statistical Yearbook.*

United Nations Economic Commission for Africa, Africa Hall, Post Office Box 3001, Addis Ababa, Ethiopia (Telephone Number in U.S. (800) 253-9646); *African Statistical Yearbook.*

LIBYA - BARLEY PRODUCTION - See LIBYA - CROPS

LIBYA - BEER PRODUCTION - See LIBYA - BEVERAGES

LIBYA - BEVERAGES

M.E. Sharpe, 80 Business Park Drive, Armonk, New York 10504 (800) 541-6563; *The Illustrated Book of World Rankings.*

Statistical Office of the United Nations, Publishing Service, New York, New York 10017 (800) 253-9646; *Statistical Yearbook.*

LIBYA - BIRTH RATES

Central Intelligence Agency, Washington, D.C. 20505 (703) 482-1100, www.cia.gov; *The World Factbook.*

Euromonitor International, Inc., 122 South Michigan Avenue, Suite 1200, Chicago, Illinois 60603 (800) 577-EURO; *International Marketing Data and Statistics;* and *The World Economic Factbook.*

Europa Publications Limited, 18 Bedford Square, London, WC1B 3JN, England; *The Europa World Year Book.*

M.E. Sharpe, 80 Business Park Drive, Armonk, New York 10504 (800) 541-6563; *The Illustrated Book of World Rankings.*

Statistical Office of the United Nations, Publishing Service, New York, New York 10017 (800) 253-9646; *Demographic Yearbook; Statistical Yearbook;* and *Survey of Economic and Social Conditions in Africa.*

The World Bank, 1818 H Street, NW, Washington, D.C. 20433 (202) 477-1234; *World Development Indicators.*

World Health Organization, Office of Publications, 20 Avenue Appia, CH-1211

Geneva 27, Switzerland (Telephone Number in U.S. (518) 436-9686); *World Health Statistics Annual.*

LIBYA - BOOK PRODUCTION

United Nations Educational, Scientific and Cultural Organization (UNESCO), 7 Place de Fontenoy, F-75700 Paris, France (Telephone Number in U.S. (212) 963-5981); *Statistical Yearbook.*

LIBYA - BROADCASTING

Billboard Limited, Post Office Box 9027, 1006 AA Amsterdam, The Netherlands (Telephone Number in U.S. (212) 764-7300); *World Radio TV Handbook.*

Central Intelligence Agency, Washington, D.C. 20505 (703) 482-1100, www.cia.gov; *The World Factbook.*

Euromonitor International, Inc., 122 South Michigan Avenue, Suite 1200, Chicago, Illinois 60603 (800) 577-EURO; *World Marketing Data and Statistics.*

M.E. Sharpe, 80 Business Park Drive, Armonk, New York 10504 (800) 541-6563; *The Illustrated Book of World Rankings.*

St. Martin's Press, Inc., 175 Fifth Avenue, New York, New York 10010 (800) 221-7945; *The Statesman's Year-Book.*

LIBYA - BUDGET

Central Intelligence Agency, Washington, D.C. 20505 (703) 482-1100, www.cia.gov; *The World Factbook.*

LIBYA - CALORIE SUPPLY

African Development Bank, 01 BP 1387, Abidjan 01, Cote d'Ivoire; *Selected Statistics on Regional Member Countries.*

Food and Agricultural Organization of the United Nations (FAO), Via delle Terme di Caracalla, 00100 Rome, Italy (Telephone Number in U.S. (202) 653-2400); *The State of Food and Agriculture.*

LIBYA - CATTLE - See LIBYA - LIVESTOCK AND POULTRY

LIBYA - CEMENT PRODUCTION - See LIBYA - MINING AND MINERAL PRODUCTS

LIBYA - CHEMICAL (ORGANIC) PRODUCTION - See LIBYA - MINING AND MINERAL PRODUCTS

LIBYA - CHICKENS - See LIBYA - LIVESTOCK AND POULTRY

LIBYA - CIGAR AND CIGARETTE PRODUCTION - See LIBYA - TOBACCO PRODUCTION

LIBYA - CLIMATE

M.E. Sharpe, 80 Business Park Drive, Armonk, New York 10504 (800) 541-6563; *The Illustrated Book of World Rankings.*

St. Martin's Press, Inc., 175 Fifth Avenue, New York, New York 10010 (800) 221-7945; *The Statesman's Year-Book.*

LIBYA - COAL PRODUCTION - See LIBYA - MINING AND MINERAL PRODUCTS

LIBYA - COFFEE PRODUCTION AND CONSUMPTION - See LIBYA - CROPS

LIBYA - COMMERCE

St. Martin's Press, Inc., 175 Fifth Avenue, New York, New York 10010 (800) 221-7945; *The Statesman's Year-Book.*

LIBYA - COMMUNICATIONS - See LIBYA - TRANSPORTATION AND COMMUNICATIONS

LIBYA - CONSTRUCTION INDUSTRY

M.E. Sharpe, 80 Business Park Drive, Armonk, New York 10504 (800) 541-6563; *The Illustrated Book of World Rankings.*

Statistical Office of the United Nations, Publishing Service, New York, New York 10017 (800) 253-9646; *Statistical Yearbook.*

United Nations Economic Commission for Africa, Africa Hall, Post Office Box 3001, Addis Ababa, Ethiopia (Telephone Number in U.S. (800) 253-9646); *African Statistical Yearbook.*

LIBYA - CONSUMER PRICE INDEX

African Development Bank, 01 BP 1387, Abidjan 01, Cote d'Ivoire; *Selected Statistics on Regional Member Countries.*

Europa Publications Limited, 18 Bedford Square, London, WC1B 3JN, England; *The Europa World Year Book.*

Statistical Office of the United Nations, Publishing Service, New York, New York 10017 (800) 253-9646; *Statistical Yearbook;* and *Survey of Economic and Social Conditions in Africa.*

United Nations Economic Commission for Africa, Africa Hall, Post Office Box 3001, Addis Ababa, Ethiopia (Telephone Number in U.S. (800) 253-9646); *African Statistical Yearbook.*

LIBYA - CONSUMER PRICES

Euromonitor International, Inc., 122 South Michigan Avenue, Suite 1200, Chicago, Illinois 60603 (800) 577-EURO; *World Marketing Data and Statistics.*

International Labour Office, I.L.O. Publications, 1828 L Street, N.W., Suite 801, Washington, D.C. 20036 (301) 638-3152; *Yearbook of Labour Statistics.*

International Monetary Fund, 700 Nineteenth Street, NW, Washington, D.C. 20431 (202) 623-7000; *International Financial Statistics.*

LIBYA - CONSUMPTION

African Development Bank, 01 BP 1387, Abidjan 01, Cote d'Ivoire; *Selected Statistics on Regional Member Countries.*

Statistical Office of the United Nations, Publishing Service, New York, New York 10017 (800) 253-9646; *Survey of Economic and Social Conditions in Africa.*

LIBYA - COPPER PRODUCTION AND CONSUMPTION - See LIBYA - MINING AND MINERAL PRODUCTS

LIBYA - CORN PRODUCTION - See LIBYA - CROPS

LIBYA - CORPORATE TAXES - See LIBYA - TAXATION

LIBYA - COTTON PRODUCTION - See LIBYA - CROPS

LIBYA - CRIME

International Criminal Police Organization (INTERPOL), 50 quai Achille Lignon, F-69006 Lyon, France; *International Crime Statistics.*

Yale University Press, Yale Station, New Haven, Connecticut 06520 (800) 987-7323; *Violence and Crime in Cross-National Perspective.*

LIBYA - CROPS

Europa Publications Limited, 18 Bedford Square, London, WC1B 3JN, England; *The Europa World Year Book.*

Food and Agricultural Organization of the United Nations (FAO), Via delle Terme di Caracalla, 00100 Rome, Italy (Telephone Number in U.S. (202) 653-2400); *Production Yearbook;* and *The State of Food and Agriculture.*

M.E. Sharpe, 80 Business Park Drive, Armonk, New York 10504 (800) 541-6563; *The Illustrated Book of World Rankings.*

St. Martin's Press, Inc., 175 Fifth Avenue, New York, New York 10010 (800) 221-7945; *The Statesman's Year-Book.*

Statistical Office of the United Nations, Publishing Service, New York, New York 10017 (800) 253-9646; *Statistical Yearbook.*

United Nations Conference on Trade and Development, Central Statistical Service, Palais des Nations, Geneva, Switzerland (Telephone in U.S. (800) 253-9646); *UNCTAD Commodity Yearbook.*

United Nations Economic Commission for Africa, Africa Hall, Post Office Box 3001, Addis Ababa, Ethiopia (Telephone Number in U.S. (800) 253-9646); *African Statistical Yearbook.*

LIBYA - DAIRY PRODUCTS

Europa Publications Limited, 18 Bedford Square, London, WC1B 3JN, England; *The Europa World Year Book.*

Food and Agricultural Organization of the United Nations (FAO), Via delle Terme di Caracalla, 00100 Rome, Italy (Telephone Number in U.S. (202) 653-2400); *The State of Food and Agriculture;* and *Production Yearbook.*

M.E. Sharpe, 80 Business Park Drive, Armonk, New York 10504 (800) 541-6563; *The Illustrated Book of World Rankings.*

St. Martin's Press, Inc., 175 Fifth Avenue, New York, New York 10010 (800) 221-7945; *The Statesman's Year-Book.*

Statistical Office of the United Nations, Publishing Service, New York, New York 10017 (800) 253-9646; *Statistical Yearbook.*

LIBYA - DEATH RATES - See LIBYA - MORTALITY

LIBYA - DEFENSE EXPENDITURES - See LIBYA - MILITARY

LIBYA - DEMOGRAPHY

The Economist Intelligence Unit, 111 West 57th Street, New York, New York 10019 (800) 938-4685; *The World Market Atlas.*

Euromonitor International, Inc., 122 South Michigan Avenue, Suite 1200, Chicago, Illinois 60603 (800) 577-EURO; *International Marketing Data and Statistics; World Marketing Data and Statistics;* and *The World Economic Factbook.*

Federal Statistical Office, Gustav-Stresemann - Ring 11, D-6200, Wiesbaden, Germany; *Libyen.*

M.E. Sharpe, 80 Business Park Drive, Armonk, New York 10504 (800) 541-6563; *The Illustrated Book of World Rankings.*

Statistical Office of the United Nations, Publishing Service, New York, New York 10017 (800) 253-9646; *Human Development Report;* and *Survey of Economic and Social Conditions in Africa.*

LIBYA - DEVELOPMENT ASSISTANCE

Statistical Office of the United Nations, Publishing Service, New York, New York 10017 (800) 253-9646; *Statistical Yearbook.*

LIBYA - DIAMOND PRODUCTION - See LIBYA - MINING AND MINERAL PRODUCTS

LIBYA - DISCOUNT RATES - See LIBYA - BANKING

LIBYA - DISEASE - See LIBYA - HEALTH

LIBYA - DIVORCE

M.E. Sharpe, 80 Business Park Drive, Armonk, New York 10504 (800) 541-6563; *The Illustrated Book of World Rankings.*

Statistical Office of the United Nations, Publishing Service, New York, New York 10017 (800) 253-9646; *Demographic Yearbook;* and *Statistical Yearbook.*

LIBYA - ECONOMY

African Development Bank, 01 BP 1387, Abidjan 01, Cote d'Ivoire; *Selected Statistics on Regional Member Countries.*

Central Intelligence Agency, Washington, D.C. 20505 (703) 482-1100, www.cia.gov; *The World Factbook.*

Economist Intelligence Unit, 111 West 57th Street, New York, New York 10019 (800) 938-4685; *Libya Country Report.*

Euromonitor International, Inc., 122 South Michigan Avenue, Suite 1200, Chicago, Illinois 60603 (800) 577-EURO; *International Marketing Data and Statistics; World Marketing Data and Statistics;* and *The World Economic Factbook.*

Federal Statistical Office, Gustav-Stresemann - Ring 11, D-6200, Wiesbaden, Germany; *Libyen.*

M.E. Sharpe, 80 Business Park Drive, Armonk, New York 10504 (800) 541-6563; *The Illustrated Book of World Rankings.*

St. Martin's Press, Inc., 175 Fifth Avenue, New York, New York 10010 (800) 221-7945; *The Statesman's Year-Book.*

Statistical Office of the United Nations, Publishing Service, New York, New York 10017 (800) 253-9646; *Foreign Trade Statistics for Africa;* and *World Statistics Pocketbook.*

The World Bank, 1818 H Street, NW, Washington, D.C. 20433 (202) 477-1234; *The World Bank Atlas.*

LIBYA - EDUCATION

African Development Bank, 01 BP 1387,

Abidjan 01, Cote d'Ivoire; *Selected Statistics on Regional Member Countries.*

The Economist Intelligence Unit, 111 West 57th Street, New York, New York 10019 (800) 938-4685; *The World Market Atlas.*

Euromonitor International, Inc., 122 South Michigan Avenue, Suite 1200, Chicago, Illinois 60603 (800) 577-EURO; *International Marketing Data and Statistics* and *World Marketing Data and Statistics.*

Europa Publications Limited, 18 Bedford Square, London, WC1B 3JN, England; *The Europa World Year Book.*

Federal Statistical Office, Gustav-Stresemann - Ring 11, D-6200, Wiesbaden, Germany; *Libyen.*

M.E. Sharpe, 80 Business Park Drive, Armonk, New York 10504 (800) 541-6563; *The Illustrated Book of World Rankings.*

St. Martin's Press, Inc., 175 Fifth Avenue, New York, New York 10010 (800) 221-7945; *The Statesman's Year-Book.*

Statistical Office of the United Nations, Publishing Service, New York, New York 10017 (800) 253-9646; *Human Development Report;* and *Survey of Economic and Social Conditions in Africa.*

United Nations Economic Commission for Africa, Africa Hall, Post Office Box 3001, Addis Ababa, Ethiopia (Telephone Number in U.S. (800) 253-9646); *African Statistical Yearbook.*

United Nations Educational, Scientific and Cultural Organization (UNESCO), 7 Place de Fontenoy, F-75700 Paris, France (Telephone Number in U.S. (212) 963-5981); *Statistical Yearbook.*

The World Bank, 1818 H Street, NW, Washington, D.C. 20433 (202) 477-1234; *World Development Indicators.*

LIBYA - EGG PRODUCTION AND CONSUMPTION - See LIBYA - DAIRY PRODUCTS

LIBYA - ELECTRICITY

Central Intelligence Agency, Washington, D.C. 20505 (703) 482-1100, www.cia.gov; *The World Factbook.*

M.E. Sharpe, 80 Business Park Drive, Armonk, New York 10504 (800) 541-6563; *The Illustrated Book of World Rankings.*

Penn Well Publishing Company, 1421 South Sheridan Road, Post Office Box 1260, Tulsa, Oklahoma 74101 (800) 752-9764; *International Energy Statistics Sourcebook.*

St. Martin's Press, Inc., 175 Fifth Avenue, New York, New York 10010 (800) 221-7945; *The Statesman's Year-Book.*

Statistical Office of the United Nations, Publishing Service, New York, New York 10017 (800) 253-9646; *Human Development Report; Statistical Yearbook;* and *Survey of Economic and Social Conditions in Africa.*

United Nations Economic Commission for Africa, Africa Hall, Post Office Box 3001, Addis Ababa, Ethiopia (Telephone Number in U.S. (800) 253-9646); *African Statistical Yearbook.*

LIBYA - EMPLOYMENT

Euromonitor International, Inc., 122 South Michigan Avenue, Suite 1200, Chicago, Illinois 60603 (800) 577-EURO; *International Marketing Data and Statistics.*

Federal Statistical Office, Gustav-Stresemann - Ring 11, D-6200, Wiesbaden, Germany; *Libyen.*

International Labour Office, I.L.O. Publications, 1828 L Street, N.W., Suite 801, Washington, D.C. 20036 (301) 638-3152; *Yearbook of Labour Statistics.*

M.E. Sharpe, 80 Business Park Drive, Armonk, New York 10504 (800) 541-6563; *The Illustrated Book of World Rankings.*

Statistical Office of the United Nations, Publishing Service, New York, New York 10017 (800) 253-9646; *Bulletin of Industrial Statistics for the Arab Countries; Statistical Yearbook;* and *Survey of Economic and Social Conditions in Africa.*

United Nations Economic Commission for Africa, Africa Hall, Post Office Box 3001, Addis Ababa, Ethiopia (Telephone Number in U.S. (800) 253-9646); *African Statistical Yearbook.*

LIBYA - ENERGY

Euromonitor International, Inc., 122 South Michigan Avenue, Suite 1200, Chicago, Illinois 60603 (800) 577-EURO; *International Marketing Data and Statistics; World Marketing Data and Statistics;* and *The World Economic Factbook.*

Food and Agricultural Organization of the United Nations (FAO), Via delle Terme di Caracalla, 00100 Rome, Italy (Telephone Number in U.S. (202) 653-2400); *The State of Food and Agriculture.*

M.E. Sharpe, 80 Business Park Drive, Armonk, New York 10504 (800) 541-6563; *The Illustrated Book of World Rankings.*

Penn Well Publishing Company, 1421 South Sheridan Road, Post Office Box 1260,

Tulsa, Oklahoma 74101 (800) 752-9764; *International Energy Statistics Sourcebook.*

St. Martin's Press, Inc., 175 Fifth Avenue, New York, New York 10010 (800) 221-7945; *The Statesman's Year-Book.*

Statistical Office of the United Nations, Publishing Service, New York, New York 10017 (800) 253-9646; *Energy Statistics Yearbook; Human Development Report; World Statistics Pocketbook;* and *Statistical Yearbook.*

United Nations Economic Commission for Africa, Africa Hall, Post Office Box 3001, Addis Ababa, Ethiopia (Telephone Number in U.S. (800) 253-9646); *African Statistical Yearbook.*

The World Bank, 1818 H Street, NW, Washington, D.C. 20433 (202) 477-1234; *The World Bank Atlas.*

LIBYA - ENVIRONMENT

Economist Intelligence Unit, 111 West 57th Street, New York, New York 10019 (800) 938-4685; *Libya Country Report.*

Statistical Office of the United Nations, Publishing Service, New York, New York 10017 (800) 253-9646; *World Statistics Pocketbook.*

LIBYA - EXCHANGE RATES

African Development Bank, 01 BP 1387, Abidjan 01, Cote d'Ivoire; *Selected Statistics on Regional Member Countries.*

Central Intelligence Agency, Washington, D.C. 20505 (703) 482-1100, www.cia.gov; *The World Factbook.*

Euromonitor International, Inc., 122 South Michigan Avenue, Suite 1200, Chicago, Illinois 60603 (800) 577-EURO; *International Marketing Data and Statistics;* and *The World Economic Factbook.*

Europa Publications Limited, 18 Bedford Square, London, WC1B 3JN, England; *The Europa World Year Book.*

International Monetary Fund, 700 Nineteenth Street, NW, Washington, D.C. 20431 (202) 623-7000; *International Financial Statistics.*

Organization of Petroleum Exporting Countries, Obere Donaustrasse 93, 1020 Vienna 2, Austria; *OPEC Annual Statistical Bulletin.*

Statistical Office of the United Nations, Publishing Service, New York, New York 10017 (800) 253-9646; *Bulletin of Industrial Statistics for the Arab Countries; Foreign Trade Statistics for Africa; World Statistics Pocketbook;* and *Statistical Yearbook.*

LIBYA - EXPORTS

African Development Bank, 01 BP 1387, Abidjan 01, Cote d'Ivoire; *Selected Statistics on Regional Member Countries.*

Central Intelligence Agency, Washington, D.C. 20505 (703) 482-1100, www.cia.gov; *The World Factbook.*

The Economist Intelligence Unit, 111 West 57th Street, New York, New York 10019 (800) 938-4685; *Libya Country Report;* and *The World Market Atlas.*

Euromonitor International, Inc., 122 South Michigan Avenue, Suite 1200, Chicago, Illinois 60603 (800) 577-EURO; *International Marketing Data and Statistics;* and *The World Economic Factbook.*

Europa Publications Limited, 18 Bedford Square, London, WC1B 3JN, England; *The Europa World Year Book.*

Food and Agricultural Organization of the United Nations (FAO), Via delle Terme di Caracalla, 00100 Rome, Italy (Telephone Number in U.S. (202) 653-2400); *The State of Food and Agriculture.*

International Monetary Fund, 700 Nineteenth Street, NW, Washington, D.C. 20431 (202) 623-7000; *Direction of Trade Statistics;* and *International Financial Statistics.*

Organization of Petroleum Exporting Countries, Obere Donaustrasse 93, 1020 Vienna 2, Austria; *OPEC Annual Statistical Bulletin.*

St. Martin's Press, Inc., 175 Fifth Avenue, New York, New York 10010 (800) 221-7945; *The Statesman's Year-Book.*

Statistical Office of the United Nations, Publishing Service, New York, New York 10017 (800) 253-9646; *Bulletin of Industrial Statistics for the Arab Countries; Foreign Trade Statistics for Africa;* and *Survey of Economic and Social Conditions in Africa.*

United Nations Conference on Trade and Development (UNCTAD), New York, New York 10017 (800) 253-9646; *Handbook of International Trade and Development Statistics.*

United Nations Economic Commission for Africa, Africa Hall, Post Office Box 3001, Addis Ababa, Ethiopia (Telephone Number in U.S. (800) 253-9646); *African Statistical Yearbook.*

The World Bank, 1818 H Street, NW, Washington, D.C. 20433 (202) 477-1234; *World Development Indicators.*

LIBYA - EXTERNAL INDEBTEDNESS

African Development Bank, 01 BP 1387, Abidjan 01, Cote d'Ivoire; *Selected Statistics on Regional Member Countries.*

Statistical Office of the United Nations, Publishing Service, New York, New York 10017 (800) 253-9646; *Survey of Economic and Social Conditions in Africa.*

The World Bank, 1818 H Street, NW, Washington, D.C. 20433 (202) 477-1234; *World Development Indicators.*

LIBYA - EXTERNAL TRADE

African Development Bank, 01 BP 1387, Abidjan 01, Cote d'Ivoire; *Selected Statistics on Regional Member Countries.*

Euromonitor International, Inc., 122 South Michigan Avenue, Suite 1200, Chicago, Illinois 60603 (800) 577-EURO; *World Marketing Data and Statistics.*

Food and Agricultural Organization of the United Nations (FAO), Via delle Terme di Caracalla, 00100 Rome, Italy (Telephone Number in U.S. (202) 653-2400); *The State of Food and Agriculture;* and *Trade Yearbook.*

Statistical Office of the United Nations, Publishing Service, New York, New York 10017 (800) 253-9646; *Statistical Yearbook.*

LIBYA - FARM CROPS - See LIBYA - CROPS

LIBYA - FEMALE WORKING POPULATION - See LIBYA - EMPLOYMENT

LIBYA - FERTILITY RATES

Central Intelligence Agency, Washington, D.C. 20505 (703) 482-1100, www.cia.gov; *The World Factbook.*

M.E. Sharpe, 80 Business Park Drive, Armonk, New York 10504 (800) 541-6563; *The Illustrated Book of World Rankings.*

Statistical Office of the United Nations, Publishing Service, New York, New York 10017 (800) 253-9646; *Human Development Report;* and *Survey of Economic and Social Conditions in Africa.*

The World Bank, 1818 H Street, NW, Washington, D.C. 20433 (202) 477-1234; *The World Bank Atlas;* and *World Development Indicators.*

LIBYA - FERTILIZER

Food and Agricultural Organization of the United Nations (FAO), Via delle Terme di Caracalla, 00100 Rome, Italy (Telephone Number in U.S. (202) 653-2400); *Fertilizer Yearbook;* and *The State of Food and Agriculture.*

Statistical Office of the United Nations, Publishing Service, New York, New York 10017 (800) 253-9646; *Statistical Yearbook.*

LIBYA - FETAL MORTALITY - See LIBYA - MORTALITY

LIBYA - FILM - See LIBYA - MOTION PICTURES

LIBYA - FINANCE

African Development Bank, 01 BP 1387, Abidjan 01, Cote d'Ivoire; *Selected Statistics on Regional Member Countries.*

Economist Intelligence Unit, 111 West 57th Street, New York, New York 10019 (800) 938-4685; *Libya Country Report.*

Europa Publications Limited, 18 Bedford Square, London, WC1B 3JN, England; *The Europa World Year Book.*

Federal Statistical Office, Gustav-Stresemann - Ring 11, D-6200, Wiesbaden, Germany; *Libyen.*

International Monetary Fund, 700 Nineteenth Street, NW, Washington, D.C. 20431 (202) 623-7000; *International Financial Statistics.*

M.E. Sharpe, 80 Business Park Drive, Armonk, New York 10504 (800) 541-6563; *The Illustrated Book of World Rankings.*

St. Martin's Press, Inc., 175 Fifth Avenue, New York, New York 10010 (800) 221-7945; *The Statesman's Year-Book.*

United Nations Economic Commission for Africa, Africa Hall, Post Office Box 3001, Addis Ababa, Ethiopia (Telephone Number in U.S. (800) 253-9646); *African Statistical Yearbook.*

LIBYA - FISHERIES

Europa Publications Limited, 18 Bedford Square, London, WC1B 3JN, England; *The Europa World Year Book.*

Federal Statistical Office, Gustav-Stresemann - Ring 11, D-6200, Wiesbaden, Germany; *Libyen.*

Food and Agricultural Organization of the United Nations (FAO), Via delle Terme di Caracalla, 00100 Rome, Italy (Telephone Number in U.S. (202) 653-2400); *The State of Food and Agriculture;* and *Yearbook of Fishery Statistics.*

M.E. Sharpe, 80 Business Park Drive, Armonk, New York 10504 (800) 541-6563; *The Illustrated Book of World Rankings.*

St. Martin's Press, Inc., 175 Fifth Avenue, New York, New York 10010 (800) 221-7945; *The Statesman's Year-Book.*

Statistical Office of the United Nations, Publishing Service, New York, New York 10017 (800) 253-9646; *Statistical Yearbook;* and *Survey of Economic and Social Conditions in Africa.*

United Nations Conference on Trade and Development, Central Statistical Service, Palais des Nations, Geneva, Switzerland (Telephone in U.S. (800) 253-9646); *UNCTAD Commodity Yearbook.*

United Nations Economic Commission for Africa, Africa Hall, Post Office Box 3001, Addis Ababa, Ethiopia (Telephone Number in U.S. (800) 253-9646); *African Statistical Yearbook.*

LIBYA - FLOUR PRODUCTION

Statistical Office of the United Nations, Publishing Service, New York, New York 10017 (800) 253-9646; *Statistical Yearbook.*

LIBYA - FOOD

African Development Bank, 01 BP 1387, Abidjan 01, Cote d'Ivoire; *Selected Statistics on Regional Member Countries.*

Food and Agricultural Organization of the United Nations (FAO), Via delle Terme di Caracalla, 00100 Rome, Italy (Telephone Number in U.S. (202) 653-2400); *The State of Food and Agriculture;* and *Production Yearbook.*

Statistical Office of the United Nations, Publishing Service, New York, New York 10017 (800) 253-9646; *Human Development Report.*

United Nations Conference on Trade and Development, Central Statistical Service, Palais des Nations, Geneva, Switzerland (Telephone in U.S. (800) 253-9646); *UNCTAD Commodity Yearbook.*

LIBYA - FOREIGN TRADE

Economist Intelligence Unit, 111 West 57th Street, New York, New York 10019 (800) 938-4685; *Libya Country Report.*

Euromonitor International, Inc., 122 South Michigan Avenue, Suite 1200, Chicago, Illinois 60603 (800) 577-EURO; *International Marketing Data and Statistics;* and *The World Economic Factbook.*

Europa Publications Limited, 18 Bedford Square, London, WC1B 3JN, England; *The Europa World Year Book.*

Federal Statistical Office, Gustav-Stresemann - Ring 11, D-6200, Wiesbaden, Germany; *Libyen.*

Food and Agricultural Organization of the United Nations (FAO), Via delle Terme di Caracalla, 00100 Rome, Italy (Telephone

Number in U.S. (202) 653-2400); *The State of Food and Agriculture.*

International Monetary Fund, 700 Nineteenth Street, NW, Washington, D.C. 20431 (202) 623-7000; *International Financial Statistics.*

M.E. Sharpe, 80 Business Park Drive, Armonk, New York 10504 (800) 541-6563; *The Illustrated Book of World Rankings.*

St. Martin's Press, Inc., 175 Fifth Avenue, New York, New York 10010 (800) 221-7945; *The Statesman's Year-Book.*

Statistical Office of the United Nations, Publishing Service, New York, New York 10017 (800) 253-9646; *Bulletin of Industrial Statistics for the Arab Countries; Foreign Trade Statistics for Africa; International Trade Statistics Yearbook;* and *Statistical Yearbook.*

United Nations Conference on Trade and Development, Central Statistical Service, Palais des Nations, Geneva, Switzerland (Telephone in U.S. (800) 253-9646); *UNCTAD Commodity Yearbook.*

United Nations Economic Commission for Africa, Africa Hall, Post Office Box 3001, Addis Ababa, Ethiopia (Telephone Number in U.S. (800) 253-9646); *African Statistical Yearbook.*

The World Bank, 1818 H Street, NW, Washington, D.C. 20433 (202) 477-1234; *World Development Indicators.*

LIBYA - FORESTRY AND FOREST PRODUCTS

Europa Publications Limited, 18 Bedford Square, London, WC1B 3JN, England; *The Europa World Year Book.*

Federal Statistical Office, Gustav-Stresemann - Ring 11, D-6200, Wiesbaden, Germany; *Libyen.*

Food and Agricultural Organization of the United Nations (FAO), Via delle Terme di Caracalla, 00100 Rome, Italy (Telephone Number in U.S. (202) 653-2400); *The State of Food and Agriculture;* and *Yearbook of Forest Products.*

M.E. Sharpe, 80 Business Park Drive, Armonk, New York 10504 (800) 541-6563; *The Illustrated Book of World Rankings.*

Statistical Office of the United Nations, Publishing Service, New York, New York 10017 (800) 253-9646; *Statistical Yearbook.*

United Nations Conference on Trade and Development, Central Statistical Service, Palais des Nations, Geneva, Switzerland (Telephone in U.S. (800) 253-9646); *UNCTAD Commodity Yearbook.*

United Nations Economic Commission for Africa, Africa Hall, Post Office Box 3001, Addis Ababa, Ethiopia (Telephone Number in U.S. (800) 253-9646); *African Statistical Yearbook.*

United Nations Educational, Scientific and Cultural Organization (UNESCO), 7 Place de Fontenoy, F-75700 Paris, France (Telephone Number in U.S. (212) 963-5981); *Statistical Yearbook.*

LIBYA - GAS - See LIBYA - MINING AND MINERAL PRODUCTS

LIBYA - GENERAL INDUSTRIAL STATISTICS - SEE LIBYA - INDUSTRY

LIBYA - GENERAL MORTALITY - See LIBYA - MORTALITY

LIBYA - GEOGRAPHIC DATA

M.E. Sharpe, 80 Business Park Drive, Armonk, New York 10504 (800) 541-6563; *The Illustrated Book of World Rankings.*

LIBYA - GOATS - See LIBYA - LIVESTOCK AND POULTRY

LIBYA - GOLD HOLDINGS

International Monetary Fund, 700 Nineteenth Street, NW, Washington, D.C. 20431 (202) 623-7000; *International Financial Statistics.*

Statistical Office of the United Nations, Publishing Service, New York, New York 10017 (800) 253-9646; *Statistical Yearbook.*

The World Bank, 1818 H Street, NW, Washington, D.C. 20433 (202) 477-1234; *World Development Indicators.*

LIBYA - GOLD PRODUCTION - See LIBYA - MINING AND MINERAL PRODUCTS

LIBYA - GOVERNMENT

Central Intelligence Agency, Washington, D.C. 20505 (703) 482-1100, www.cia.gov; *The World Factbook.*

International Monetary Fund, 700 Nineteenth Street, NW, Washington, D.C. 20431 (202) 623-7000; *International Financial Statistics.*

St. Martin's Press, Inc., 175 Fifth Avenue, New York, New York 10010 (800) 221-7945; *The Statesman's Year-Book.*

Statistical Office of the United Nations, Publishing Service, New York, New York 10017 (800) 253-9646; *National Accounts Statistics; Statistical Yearbook;* and *Survey of Economic and Social Conditions in Africa.*

The World Bank, 1818 H Street, NW,

Washington, D.C. 20433 (202) 477-1234; *World Development Indicators.*

LIBYA - GRAIN PRODUCTION - See LIBYA - CROPS

LIBYA - GREEN PEPPER AND CHILIE PRODUCTION - See LIBYA - CROPS

LIBYA - GROSS DOMESTIC PRODUCT

African Development Bank, 01 BP 1387, Abidjan 01, Cote d'Ivoire; *Selected Statistics on Regional Member Countries.*

The Economist Intelligence Unit, 111 West 57th Street, New York, New York 10019 (800) 938-4685; *Libya Country Report;* and *The World Market Atlas.*

Euromonitor International, Inc., 122 South Michigan Avenue, Suite 1200, Chicago, Illinois 60603 (800) 577-EURO; *International Marketing Data and Statistics;* and *The World Economic Factbook.*

Europa Publications Limited, 18 Bedford Square, London, WC1B 3JN, England; *The Europa World Year Book.*

M.E. Sharpe, 80 Business Park Drive, Armonk, New York 10504 (800) 541-6563; *The Illustrated Book of World Rankings.*

Statistical Office of the United Nations, Publishing Service, New York, New York 10017 (800) 253-9646; *Bulletin of Industrial Statistics for the Arab Countries; Human Development Report; National Accounts Statistics; Statistical Yearbook;* and *Survey of Economic and Social Conditions in Africa.*

The World Bank, 1818 H Street, NW, Washington, D.C. 20433 (202) 477-1234; *World Development Indicators.*

LIBYA - GROSS NATIONAL PRODUCT

Euromonitor International, Inc., 122 South Michigan Avenue, Suite 1200, Chicago, Illinois 60603 (800) 577-EURO; *International Marketing Data and Statistics.*

Europa Publications Limited, 18 Bedford Square, London, WC1B 3JN, England; *The Europa World Year Book.*

Organization of Petroleum Exporting Countries, Obere Donaustrasse 93, 1020 Vienna 2, Austria; *OPEC Annual Statistical Bulletin.*

St. Martin's Press, Inc., 175 Fifth Avenue, New York, New York 10010 (800) 221-7945; *The Statesman's Year-Book.*

United Nations Economic Commission for Africa, Africa Hall, Post Office Box 3001, Addis Ababa, Ethiopia (Telephone Number in U.S. (800) 253-9646); *African Statistical*

Yearbook.

U.S. Arms Control and Disarmament Agency, 320 Twenty-first Street, NW, Washington, D.C. 20451 (202) 647-8677; *World Military Expenditures and Arms Transfers.*

The World Bank, 1818 H Street, NW, Washington, D.C. 20433 (202) 477-1234; *The World Bank Atlas;* and *World Development Indicators.*

LIBYA - GROUNDNUTS PRODUCTION - See LIBYA - CROPS

LIBYA - HEALTH

African Development Bank, 01 BP 1387, Abidjan 01, Cote d'Ivoire; *Selected Statistics on Regional Member Countries.*

Euromonitor International, Inc., 122 South Michigan Avenue, Suite 1200, Chicago, Illinois 60603 (800) 577-EURO; *World Marketing Data and Statistics.*

Federal Statistical Office, Gustav-Stresemann - Ring 11, D-6200, Wiesbaden, Germany; *Libyen.*

M.E. Sharpe, 80 Business Park Drive, Armonk, New York 10504 (800) 541-6563; *The Illustrated Book of World Rankings.*

St. Martin's Press, Inc., 175 Fifth Avenue, New York, New York 10010 (800) 221-7945; *The Statesman's Year-Book.*

Statistical Office of the United Nations, Publishing Service, New York, New York 10017 (800) 253-9646; *Human Development Report;* and *Statistical Yearbook.*

United Nations Children's Fund (UNICEF), 3 United Nations Plaza, New York, New York 10017 (800) 253-9646; *State of the World's Children.*

United Nations Economic Commission for Africa, Africa Hall, Post Office Box 3001, Addis Ababa, Ethiopia (Telephone Number in U.S. (800) 253-9646); *African Statistical Yearbook.*

World Health Organization, Office of Publications, 20 Avenue Appia, CH-1211 Geneva 27, Switzerland (Telephone Number in U.S. (518) 436-9686); *World Health Statistics Annual.*

LIBYA - HIDE PRODUCTION

Food and Agricultural Organization of the United Nations (FAO), Via delle Terme di Caracalla, 00100 Rome, Italy (Telephone Number in U.S. (202) 653-2400); *Production Yearbook.*

LIBYA - HIGHWAYS

Central Intelligence Agency, Washington, D.C. 20505 (703) 482-1100, www.cia.gov; *The World Factbook.*

International Road Federation, 2600 Virginia Avenue, N.W., Washington, D.C. 20037 (202) 338-4641; *World Road Statistics.*

St. Martin's Press, Inc., 175 Fifth Avenue, New York, New York 10010 (800) 221-7945; *The Statesman's Year-Book.*

Statistical Office of the United Nations, Publishing Service, New York, New York 10017 (800) 253-9646; *Survey of Economic and Social Conditions in Africa.*

United Nations Economic Commission for Africa, Africa Hall, Post Office Box 3001, Addis Ababa, Ethiopia (Telephone Number in U.S. (800) 253-9646); *African Statistical Yearbook.*

LIBYA - HORSES - See LIBYA - LIVESTOCK AND POULTRY

LIBYA - HOURS OF WORK - See LIBYA - EMPLOYMENT

LIBYA - HOUSING AND HOUSING UNITS

Euromonitor International, Inc., 122 South Michigan Avenue, Suite 1200, Chicago, Illinois 60603 (800) 577-EURO; *World Marketing Data and Statistics.*

M.E. Sharpe, 80 Business Park Drive, Armonk, New York 10504 (800) 541-6563; *The Illustrated Book of World Rankings.*

LIBYA - ILLITERATE POPULATION

Central Intelligence Agency, Washington, D.C. 20505 (703) 482-1100, www.cia.gov; *The World Factbook.*

The Economist Intelligence Unit, 111 West 57th Street, New York, New York 10019 (800) 938-4685; *The World Market Atlas.*

Euromonitor International, Inc., 122 South Michigan Avenue, Suite 1200, Chicago, Illinois 60603 (800) 577-EURO; *The World Economic Factbook.*

Statistical Office of the United Nations, Publishing Service, New York, New York 10017 (800) 253-9646; *Human Development Report.*

United Nations Educational, Scientific and Cultural Organization (UNESCO), 7 Place de Fontenoy, F-75700 Paris, France (Telephone Number in U.S. (212) 963-5981); *Statistical Yearbook.*

LIBYA - IMPORTS

African Development Bank, 01 BP 1387,

Abidjan 01, Cote d'Ivoire; *Selected Statistics on Regional Member Countries.*

Central Intelligence Agency, Washington, D.C. 20505 (703) 482-1100, www.cia.gov; *The World Factbook.*

The Economist Intelligence Unit, 111 West 57th Street, New York, New York 10019 (800) 938-4685; *Libya Country Report;* and *The World Market Atlas.*

Euromonitor International, Inc., 122 South Michigan Avenue, Suite 1200, Chicago, Illinois 60603 (800) 577-EURO; *International Marketing Data and Statistics;* and *The World Economic Factbook.*

Europa Publications Limited, 18 Bedford Square, London, WC1B 3JN, England; *The Europa World Year Book.*

Food and Agricultural Organization of the United Nations (FAO), Via delle Terme di Caracalla, 00100 Rome, Italy (Telephone Number in U.S. (202) 653-2400); *The State of Food and Agriculture.*

International Monetary Fund, 700 Nineteenth Street, NW, Washington, D.C. 20431 (202) 623-7000; *Direction of Trade Statistics;* and *International Financial Statistics.*

St. Martin's Press, Inc., 175 Fifth Avenue, New York, New York 10010 (800) 221-7945; *The Statesman's Year-Book.*

Statistical Office of the United Nations, Publishing Service, New York, New York 10017 (800) 253-9646; *Bulletin of Industrial Statistics for the Arab Countries; Foreign Trade Statistics for Africa,* and *Survey of Economic and Social Conditions in Africa.*

United Nations Conference on Trade and Development (UNCTAD), New York, New York 10017 (800) 253-9646; *Handbook of International Trade and Development Statistics.*

United Nations Economic Commission for Africa, Africa Hall, Post Office Box 3001, Addis Ababa, Ethiopia (Telephone Number in U.S. (800) 253-9646); *African Statistical Yearbook.*

The World Bank, 1818 H Street, NW, Washington, D.C. 20433 (202) 477-1234; *World Development Indicators.*

LIBYA - INDUSTRY

Central Intelligence Agency, Washington, D.C. 20505 (703) 482-1100, www.cia.gov; *The World Factbook.*

Economist Intelligence Unit, 111 West 57th Street, New York, New York 10019 (800) 938-4685; *Libya Country Report.*

Euromonitor International, Inc., 122 South Michigan Avenue, Suite 1200, Chicago, Illinois 60603 (800) 577-EURO; *International Marketing Data and Statistics; World Marketing Data and Statistics;* and *The World Economic Factbook.*

Europa Publications Limited, 18 Bedford Square, London, WC1B 3JN, England; *The Europa World Year Book.*

Federal Statistical Office, Gustav-Stresemann - Ring 11, D-6200, Wiesbaden, Germany; *Libyen.*

International Labour Office, I.L.O. Publications, 1828 L Street, N.W., Suite 801, Washington, D.C. 20036 (301) 638-3152; *Yearbook of Labour Statistics.*

M.E. Sharpe, 80 Business Park Drive, Armonk, New York 10504 (800) 541-6563; *The Illustrated Book of World Rankings.*

St. Martin's Press, Inc., 175 Fifth Avenue, New York, New York 10010 (800) 221-7945; *The Statesman's Year-Book.*

Statistical Office of the United Nations, Publishing Service, New York, New York 10017 (800) 253-9646; *Bulletin of Industrial Statistics for the Arab Countries; Industrial Commodity Statistics Yearbook;* and *Survey of Economic and Social Conditions in Africa.*

United Nations Economic Commission for Africa, Africa Hall, Post Office Box 3001, Addis Ababa, Ethiopia (Telephone Number in U.S. (800) 253-9646); *African Statistical Yearbook.*

The World Bank, 1818 H Street, NW, Washington, D.C. 20433 (202) 477-1234; *World Development Indicators.*

LIBYA - INFANT AND MATERNAL MORTALITY - See LIBYA - MORTALITY

LIBYA - INTERNATIONAL RESERVES

International Monetary Fund, 700 Nineteenth Street, NW, Washington, D.C. 20431 (202) 623-7000; *International Financial Statistics.*

Statistical Office of the United Nations, Publishing Service, New York, New York 10017 (800) 253-9646; *Statistical Yearbook.*

LIBYA - INTERNATIONAL RESERVES EXCLUDING GOLD

African Development Bank, 01 BP 1387, Abidjan 01, Cote d'Ivoire; *Selected Statistics on Regional Member Countries.*

LIBYA - IRON ORE PRODUCTION - See LIBYA - MINING AND MINERAL PRODUCTS

LIBYA - IRRIGATION

Euromonitor International, Inc., 122 South Michigan Avenue, Suite 1200, Chicago, Illinois 60603 (800) 577-EURO; *International Marketing Data and Statistics.*

LIBYA - LABOR

African Development Bank, 01 BP 1387, Abidjan 01, Cote d'Ivoire; *Selected Statistics on Regional Member Countries.*

Central Intelligence Agency, Washington, D.C. 20505 (703) 482-1100, www.cia.gov; *The World Factbook.*

Euromonitor International, Inc., 122 South Michigan Avenue, Suite 1200, Chicago, Illinois 60603 (800) 577-EURO; *International Marketing Data and Statistics;* and *World Marketing Data and Statistics.*

Europa Publications Limited, 18 Bedford Square, London, WC1B 3JN, England; *The Europa World Year Book.*

Food and Agricultural Organization of the United Nations (FAO), Via delle Terme di Caracalla, 00100 Rome, Italy (Telephone Number in U.S. (202) 653-2400); *The State of Food and Agriculture.*

International Labour Office, I.L.O. Publications, 1828 L Street, N.W., Suite 801, Washington, D.C. 20036 (301) 638-3152; *Yearbook of Labour Statistics.*

M.E. Sharpe, 80 Business Park Drive, Armonk, New York 10504 (800) 541-6563; *The Illustrated Book of World Rankings.*

St. Martin's Press, Inc., 175 Fifth Avenue, New York, New York 10010 (800) 221-7945; *The Statesman's Year-Book.*

Statistical Office of the United Nations, Publishing Service, New York, New York 10017 (800) 253-9646; *Human Development Report.*

The World Bank, 1818 H Street, NW, Washington, D.C. 20433 (202) 477-1234; *The World Bank Atlas;* and *World Development Indicators.*

LIBYA - LAND USE

Central Intelligence Agency, Washington, D.C. 20505 (703) 482-1100, www.cia.gov; *The World Factbook.*

Euromonitor International, Inc., 122 South Michigan Avenue, Suite 1200, Chicago, Illinois 60603 (800) 577-EURO; *International Marketing Data and Statistics.*

Food and Agricultural Organization of the United Nations (FAO), Via delle Terme di Caracalla, 00100 Rome, Italy (Telephone Number in U.S. (202) 653-2400); *Production Yearbook.*

LIBYA - LIBRARIES

M.E. Sharpe, 80 Business Park Drive, Armonk, New York 10504 (800) 541-6563; *The Illustrated Book of World Rankings.*

LIBYA - LIFE EXPECTANCY

African Development Bank, 01 BP 1387, Abidjan 01, Cote d'Ivoire; *Selected Statistics on Regional Member Countries.*

Central Intelligence Agency, Washington, D.C. 20505 (703) 482-1100, www.cia.gov; *The World Factbook.*

Euromonitor International, Inc., 122 South Michigan Avenue, Suite 1200, Chicago, Illinois 60603 (800) 577-EURO; *The World Economic Factbook.*

Statistical Office of the United Nations, Publishing Service, New York, New York 10017 (800) 253-9646; *Human Development Report;* and *World Statistics Pocketbook.*

The World Bank, 1818 H Street, NW, Washington, D.C. 20433 (202) 477-1234; *The World Bank Atlas.*

LIBYA - LITERACY RATE

Euromonitor International, Inc., 122 South Michigan Avenue, Suite 1200, Chicago, Illinois 60603 (800) 577-EURO; *World Marketing Data and Statistics.*

Statistical Office of the United Nations, Publishing Service, New York, New York 10017 (800) 253-9646; *Survey of Economic and Social Conditions in Africa.*

LIBYA - LIVESTOCK AND POULTRY

Euromonitor International, Inc., 122 South Michigan Avenue, Suite 1200, Chicago, Illinois 60603 (800) 577-EURO; *International Marketing Data and Statistics.*

Europa Publications Limited, 18 Bedford Square, London, WC1B 3JN, England; *The Europa World Year Book.*

Food and Agricultural Organization of the United Nations (FAO), Via delle Terme di Caracalla, 00100 Rome, Italy (Telephone Number in U.S. (202) 653-2400); *Production Yearbook;* and *The State of Food and Agriculture.*

M.E. Sharpe, 80 Business Park Drive, Armonk, New York 10504 (800) 541-6563; *The Illustrated Book of World Rankings.*

St. Martin's Press, Inc., 175 Fifth Avenue, New York, New York 10010 (800) 221-7945; *The Statesman's Year-Book.*

Statistical Office of the United Nations, Publishing Service, New York, New York

10017 (800) 253-9646; *Statistical Yearbook;* and *Survey of Economic and Social Conditions in Africa.*

United Nations Conference on Trade and Development, Central Statistical Service, Palais des Nations, Geneva, Switzerland (Telephone in U.S. (800) 253-9646); *UNCTAD Commodity Yearbook.*

United Nations Economic Commission for Africa, Africa Hall, Post Office Box 3001, Addis Ababa, Ethiopia (Telephone Number in U.S. (800) 253-9646); *African Statistical Yearbook.*

LIBYA - LIVING LEVELS - See LIBYA - LIFE EXPECTANCY

LIBYA - MAIL - NUMBER OF PIECES SENT OR RECEIVED

Statistical Office of the United Nations, Publishing Service, New York, New York 10017 (800) 253-9646; *Statistical Yearbook.*

LIBYA - MANUFACTURING

M.E. Sharpe, 80 Business Park Drive, Armonk, New York 10504 (800) 541-6563; *The Illustrated Book of World Rankings.*

Statistical Office of the United Nations, Publishing Service, New York, New York 10017 (800) 253-9646; *Bulletin of Industrial Statistics for the Arab Countries; Statistical Yearbook;* and *Survey of Economic and Social Conditions in Africa.*

United Nations Economic Commission for Africa, Africa Hall, Post Office Box 3001, Addis Ababa, Ethiopia (Telephone Number in U.S. (800) 253-9646); *African Statistical Yearbook.*

The World Bank, 1818 H Street, NW, Washington, D.C. 20433 (202) 477-1234; *World Development Indicators.*

LIBYA - MARRIAGE RATES

Europa Publications Limited, 18 Bedford Square, London, WC1B 3JN, England; *The Europa World Year Book.*

M.E. Sharpe, 80 Business Park Drive, Armonk, New York 10504 (800) 541-6563; *The Illustrated Book of World Rankings.*

Statistical Office of the United Nations, Publishing Service, New York, New York 10017 (800) 253-9646; *Demographic Yearbook;* and *Statistical Yearbook.*

LIBYA - MEAT PRODUCTION - See LIBYA - LIVESTOCK AND POULTRY

LIBYA - MERCHANT SHIPPING

Europa Publications Limited, 18 Bedford Square, London, WC1B 3JN,

England; *The Europa World Year Book.*

Organization of Petroleum Exporting Countries, Obere Donaustrasse 93, 1020 Vienna 2, Austria; *OPEC Annual Statistical Bulletin.*

Statistical Office of the United Nations, Publishing Service, New York, New York 10017 (800) 253-9646; *Statistical Yearbook.*

United Nations Economic Commission for Africa, Africa Hall, Post Office Box 3001, Addis Ababa, Ethiopia (Telephone Number in U.S. (800) 253-9646); *African Statistical Yearbook.*

U.S. Department of Transportation, Maritime Administration, 400 Seventh Street, SW, Washington, D.C. 20590 (202) 366-5807, www.marad.dot.gov; *A Statistical Analysis of the World's Merchant Fleets.*

LIBYA - MILITARY

Central Intelligence Agency, Washington, D.C. 20505 (703) 482-1100, www.cia.gov; *The World Factbook.*

Euromonitor International, Inc., 122 South Michigan Avenue, Suite 1200, Chicago, Illinois 60603 (800) 577-EURO; *World Marketing Data and Statistics.*

The International Institute for Strategic Studies, 23 Tavistock Street, London WC2E 7NQ, England 44 171 3797676; *The Military Balance.*

St. Martin's Press, Inc., 175 Fifth Avenue, New York, New York 10010 (800) 221-7945; *The Statesman's Year-Book.*

Statistical Office of the United Nations, Publishing Service, New York, New York 10017 (800) 253-9646; *Human Development Report.*

U.S. Arms Control and Disarmament Agency, 320 Twenty-first Street, NW, Washington, D.C. 20451 (202) 647-8677; *World Military Expenditures and Arms Transfers.*

LIBYA - MILK PRODUCTION - See LIBYA - DAIRY PRODUCTS

LIBYA - MILLET PRODUCTION - See LIBYA - CROPS

LIBYA - MINING AND MINERAL PRODUCTS

Europa Publications Limited, 18 Bedford Square, London, WC1B 3JN, England; *The Europa World Year Book.*

M.E. Sharpe, 80 Business Park Drive, Armonk, New York 10504 (800) 541-6563; *The Illustrated Book of World Rankings.*

Organization of Petroleum Exporting

Countries, Obere Donaustrasse 93, 1020 Vienna 2, Austria; *OPEC Annual Statistical Bulletin.*

Penn Well Publishing Company, 1421 South Sheridan Road, Post Office Box 1260, Tulsa, Oklahoma 74101 (800) 752-9764; *International Energy Statistics Sourcebook.*

St. Martin's Press, Inc., 175 Fifth Avenue, New York, New York 10010 (800) 221-7945; *The Statesman's Year-Book.*

Statistical Office of the United Nations, Publishing Service, New York, New York 10017 (800) 253-9646; *Bulletin of Industrial Statistics for the Arab Countries;* and *Statistical Yearbook.*

United Nations Conference on Trade and Development, Central Statistical Service, Palais des Nations, Geneva, Switzerland (Telephone in U.S. (800) 253-9646); *UNCTAD Commodity Yearbook.*

United Nations Economic Commission for Africa, Africa Hall, Post Office Box 3001, Addis Ababa, Ethiopia (Telephone Number in U.S. (800) 253-9646); *African Statistical Yearbook.*

LIBYA - MONEY EXCHANGE RATES - See LIBYA - EXCHANGE RATES

LIBYA - MONEY RESERVES

Euromonitor International, Inc., 122 South Michigan Avenue, Suite 1200, Chicago, Illinois 60603 (800) 577-EURO; *International Marketing Data and Statistics.*

LIBYA - MONEY SUPPLY

African Development Bank, 01 BP 1387, Abidjan 01, Cote d'Ivoire; *Selected Statistics on Regional Member Countries.*

Economist Intelligence Unit, 111 West 57th Street, New York, New York 10019 (800) 938-4685; *Libya Country Report.*

Euromonitor International, Inc., 122 South Michigan Avenue, Suite 1200, Chicago, Illinois 60603 (800) 577-EURO; *International Marketing Data and Statistics.*

Europa Publications Limited, 18 Bedford Square, London, WC1B 3JN, England; *The Europa World Year Book.*

Federal Statistical Office, Gustav-Stresemann - Ring 11, D-6200, Wiesbaden, Germany; *Libyen.*

International Monetary Fund, 700 Nineteenth Street, NW, Washington, D.C. 20431 (202) 623-7000; *International Financial Statistics.*

Statistical Office of the United Nations, Publishing Service, New York, New York

10017 (800) 253-9646; *Statistical Yearbook.*

The World Bank, 1818 H Street, NW, Washington, D.C. 20433 (202) 477-1234; *World Development Indicators.*

LIBYA - MORTALITY

Central Intelligence Agency, Washington, D.C. 20505 (703) 482-1100, www.cia.gov; *The World Factbook.*

Euromonitor International, Inc., 122 South Michigan Avenue, Suite 1200, Chicago, Illinois 60603 (800) 577-EURO; *International Marketing Data and Statistics;* and *The World Economic Factbook.*

Europa Publications Limited, 18 Bedford Square, London, WC1B 3JN, England; *The Europa World Year Book.*

Statistical Office of the United Nations, Publishing Service, New York, New York 10017 (800) 253-9646; *Demographic Yearbook; Human Development Report; Statistical Yearbook; World Statistics Pocketbook;* and *Survey of Economic and Social Conditions in Africa.*

United Nations Children's Fund (UNICEF), 3 United Nations Plaza, New York, New York 10017 (800) 253-9646; *State of the World's Children.*

The World Bank, 1818 H Street, NW, Washington, D.C. 20433 (202) 477-1234; *The World Bank Atlas;* and *World Development Indicators.*

World Health Organization, Office of Publications, 20 Avenue Appia, CH-1211 Geneva 27, Switzerland (Telephone Number in U.S. (518) 436-9686); *World Health Statistics Annual.*

LIBYA - MOTION PICTURES

Statistical Office of the United Nations, Publishing Service, New York, New York 10017 (800) 253-9646; *Statistical Yearbook.*

United Nations Educational, Scientific and Cultural Organization (UNESCO), 7 Place de Fontenoy, F-75700 Paris, France (Telephone Number in U.S. (212) 963-5981); *Statistical Yearbook.*

LIBYA - MOTOR VEHICLE TAXES - See LIBYA - TAXATION

LIBYA - MOTOR VEHICLES IN USE

Europa Publications Limited, 18 Bedford Square, London, WC1B 3JN, England; *The Europa World Year Book.*

International Road Federation, 2600 Virginia Avenue, N.W., Washington, D.C. 20037 (202) 338-4641; *World Road*

Statistics.

Statistical Office of the United Nations, Publishing Service, New York, New York 10017 (800) 253-9646; *Statistical Yearbook;* and *Survey of Economic and Social Conditions in Africa.*

LIBYA - MULES - See LIBYA - LIVESTOCK AND POULTRY

LIBYA - MUSEUMS

M.E. Sharpe, 80 Business Park Drive, Armonk, New York 10504 (800) 541-6563; *The Illustrated Book of World Rankings.*

United Nations Educational, Scientific and Cultural Organization (UNESCO), 7 Place de Fontenoy, F-75700 Paris, France (Telephone Number in U.S. (212) 963-5981); *Statistical Yearbook.*

LIBYA - NATALITY - See LIBYA - BIRTH RATES

LIBYA - NATIONAL ACCOUNTS

African Development Bank, 01 BP 1387, Abidjan 01, Cote d'Ivoire; *Selected Statistics on Regional Member Countries.*

Europa Publications Limited, 18 Bedford Square, London, WC1B 3JN, England; *The Europa World Year Book.*

Federal Statistical Office, Gustav-Stresemann - Ring 11, D-6200, Wiesbaden, Germany; *Libyen.*

Statistical Office of the United Nations, Publishing Service, New York, New York 10017 (800) 253-9646; *National Accounts Statistics;* and *Statistical Yearbook.*

United Nations Economic Commission for Africa, Africa Hall, Post Office Box 3001, Addis Ababa, Ethiopia (Telephone Number in U.S. (800) 253-9646); *African Statistical Yearbook.*

LIBYA - NATIONAL INCOME

M.E. Sharpe, 80 Business Park Drive, Armonk, New York 10504 (800) 541-6563; *The Illustrated Book of World Rankings.*

Statistical Office of the United Nations, Publishing Service, New York, New York 10017 (800) 253-9646; *National Accounts Statistics;* and *Statistical Yearbook.*

LIBYA - NATIONAL PRODUCT

M.E. Sharpe, 80 Business Park Drive, Armonk, New York 10504 (800) 541-6563; *The Illustrated Book of World Rankings.*

Statistical Office of the United Nations, Publishing Service, New York, New York 10017 (800) 253-9646; *Statistical Yearbook.*

LIBYA - NATURAL GAS - See LIBYA - MINING AND MINERAL PRODUCTS

LIBYA - NEWSPAPER PRODUCTION - See LIBYA - FORESTRY AND FOREST PRODUCTS

LIBYA - NEWSPRINT - See LIBYA - FORESTRY AND FOREST PRODUCTS

LIBYA - OCCUPATIONS - See LIBYA - LABOR

LIBYA - PAPER - See LIBYA - FORESTRY AND FOREST PRODUCTS

LIBYA - PATENTS, TRADEMARKS AND SERVICE MARKS

Statistical Office of the United Nations, Publishing Service, New York, New York 10017 (800) 253-9646; *Statistical Yearbook.*

LIBYA - PEANUT PRODUCTION - See LIBYA - CROPS

LIBYA - PERIODICALS

United Nations Educational, Scientific and Cultural Organization (UNESCO), 7 Place de Fontenoy, F-75700 Paris, France (Telephone Number in U.S. (212) 963-5981); *Statistical Yearbook.*

LIBYA - PESTICIDE USE

Food and Agricultural Organization of the United Nations (FAO), Via delle Terme di Caracalla, 00100 Rome, Italy (Telephone Number in U.S. (202) 653-2400); *The State of Food and Agriculture.*

LIBYA - PETROLEUM INDUSTRY

Food and Agricultural Organization of the United Nations (FAO), Via delle Terme di Caracalla, 00100 Rome, Italy (Telephone Number in U.S. (202) 653-2400); *The State of Food and Agriculture.*

M.E. Sharpe, 80 Business Park Drive, Armonk, New York 10504 (800) 541-6563; *The Illustrated Book of World Rankings.*

Organization of Petroleum Exporting Countries, Obere Donaustrasse 93, 1020 Vienna 2, Austria; *OPEC Annual Statistical Bulletin.*

Penn Well Publishing Company, 1421 South Sheridan Road, Post Office Box 1260, Tulsa, Oklahoma 74101 (800) 752-9764; *International Energy Statistics Sourcebook.*

St. Martin's Press, Inc., 175 Fifth Avenue, New York, New York 10010 (800) 221-7945; *The Statesman's Year-Book.*

Statistical Office of the United Nations, Publishing Service, New York, New York

10017 (800) 253-9646; *Statistical Yearbook.*

United Nations Conference on Trade and Development, Central Statistical Service, Palais des Nations, Geneva, Switzerland (Telephone in U.S. (800) 253-9646); *UNCTAD Commodity Yearbook.*

LIBYA - PIGS - See LIBYA - LIVESTOCK AND POULTRY

LIBYA - PIPELINES FOR OIL AND PETROLEUM PRODUCTS

Organization of Petroleum Exporting Countries, Obere Donaustrasse 93, 1020 Vienna 2, Austria; *OPEC Annual Statistical Bulletin.*

LIBYA - POPULATION

African Development Bank, 01 BP 1387, Abidjan 01, Cote d'Ivoire; *Selected Statistics on Regional Member Countries.*

Central Intelligence Agency, Washington, D.C. 20505 (703) 482-1100, www.cia.gov; *The World Factbook.*

The Economist Intelligence Unit, 111 West 57th Street, New York, New York 10019 (800) 938-4685; *Libya Country Report;* and *The World Market Atlas.*

Euromonitor International, Inc., 122 South Michigan Avenue, Suite 1200, Chicago, Illinois 60603 (800) 577-EURO; *International Marketing Data and Statistics;* and *The World Economic Factbook.*

Europa Publications Limited, 18 Bedford Square, London, WC1B 3JN, England; *The Europa World Year Book.*

Federal Statistical Office, Gustav-Stresemann - Ring 11, D-6200, Wiesbaden, Germany; *Libyen.*

Food and Agricultural Organization of the United Nations (FAO), Via delle Terme di Caracalla, 00100 Rome, Italy (Telephone Number in U.S. (202) 653-2400); *Production Yearbook.*

International Labour Office, I.L.O. Publications, 1828 L Street, N.W., Suite 801, Washington, D.C. 20036 (301) 638-3152; *Yearbook of Labour Statistics.*

M.E. Sharpe, 80 Business Park Drive, Armonk, New York 10504 (800) 541-6563; *The Illustrated Book of World Rankings.*

St. Martin's Press, Inc., 175 Fifth Avenue, New York, New York 10010 (800) 221-7945; *The Statesman's Year-Book.*

Statistical Office of the United Nations, Publishing Service, New York, New York 10017 (800) 253-9646; *Demographic Yearbook; Human Development Report;*

Statistical Yearbook; World Statistics Pocketbook; and *Survey of Economic and Social Conditions in Africa.*

United Nations Educational, Scientific and Cultural Organization (UNESCO), 7 Place de Fontenoy, F-75700 Paris, France (Telephone Number in U.S. (212) 963-5981); *Statistical Yearbook.*

U.S. Arms Control and Disarmament Agency, 320 Twenty-first Street, NW, Washington, D.C. 20451 (202) 647-8677; *World Military Expenditures and Arms Transfers.*

The World Bank, 1818 H Street, NW, Washington, D.C. 20433 (202) 477-1234; *The World Bank Atlas.*

World Health Organization, Office of Publications, 20 Avenue Appia, CH-1211 Geneva 27, Switzerland (Telephone Number in U.S. (518) 436-9686); *World Health Statistics Annual.*

LIBYA - POST OFFICES

M.E. Sharpe, 80 Business Park Drive, Armonk, New York 10504 (800) 541-6563; *The Illustrated Book of World Rankings.*

LIBYA - POTATO PRODUCTION - See LIBYA - CROPS

LIBYA - PRICES

Federal Statistical Office, Gustav-Stresemann - Ring 11, D-6200, Wiesbaden, Germany; *Libyen.*

Food and Agricultural Organization of the United Nations (FAO), Via delle Terme di Caracalla, 00100 Rome, Italy (Telephone Number in U.S. (202) 653-2400); *Production Yearbook;* and *The State of Food and Agriculture.*

International Labour Office, I.L.O. Publications, 1828 L Street, N.W., Suite 801, Washington, D.C. 20036 (301) 638-3152; *Yearbook of Labour Statistics.*

International Monetary Fund, 700 Nineteenth Street, NW, Washington, D.C. 20431 (202) 623-7000; *International Financial Statistics.*

M.E. Sharpe, 80 Business Park Drive, Armonk, New York 10504 (800) 541-6563; *The Illustrated Book of World Rankings.*

United Nations Economic Commission for Africa, Africa Hall, Post Office Box 3001, Addis Ababa, Ethiopia (Telephone Number in U.S. (800) 253-9646); *African Statistical Yearbook.*

LIBYA - PRINTING AND WRITING PAPER - See LIBYA - FORESTRY AND FOREST PRODUCTS

LIBYA - PRODUCTION

M.E. Sharpe, 80 Business Park Drive, Armonk, New York 10504 (800) 541-6563; *The Illustrated Book of World Rankings.*

LIBYA - PRODUCTIVITY

Euromonitor International, Inc., 122 South Michigan Avenue, Suite 1200, Chicago, Illinois 60603 (800) 577-EURO; *International Marketing Data and Statistics.*

LIBYA - PUBLIC FINANCE - See LIBYA - FINANCE

LIBYA - RADIO BROADCASTING - See LIBYA - BROADCASTING

LIBYA - RADIO RECEIVERS

St. Martin's Press, Inc., 175 Fifth Avenue, New York, New York 10010 (800) 221-7945; *The Statesman's Year-Book.*

LIBYA - RAILWAYS

Jane's Information Group, Sentinel House, 163 Brighton Road, Coulsdon, Surrey CR5 2NH, England (Telephone Number in U.S. (703) 683-3700); *Jane's World Railways.*

United Nations Economic Commission for Africa, Africa Hall, Post Office Box 3001, Addis Ababa, Ethiopia (Telephone Number in U.S. (800) 253-9646); *African Statistical Yearbook.*

LIBYA - RELIGION

Central Intelligence Agency, Washington, D.C. 20505 (703) 482-1100, www.cia.gov; *The World Factbook.*

M.E. Sharpe, 80 Business Park Drive, Armonk, New York 10504 (800) 541-6563; *The Illustrated Book of World Rankings.*

St. Martin's Press, Inc., 175 Fifth Avenue, New York, New York 10010 (800) 221-7945; *The Statesman's Year-Book.*

LIBYA - RENT PRICES

International Labour Office, I.L.O. Publications, 1828 L Street, N.W., Suite 801, Washington, D.C. 20036 (301) 638-3152; *Yearbook of Labour Statistics.*

LIBYA - RETAIL TRADE

Euromonitor International, Inc., 122 South Michigan Avenue, Suite 1200, Chicago, Illinois 60603 (800) 577-EURO; *World Marketing Data and Statistics.*

LIBYA - RICE PRODUCTION - See LIBYA - CROPS

LIBYA - ROOT AND TUBER PRODUCTION - See LIBYA - CROPS

LIBYA - ROUNDWOOD PRODUCTION - See LIBYA - FORESTRY AND FOREST PRODUCTS

LIBYA - RUBBER PRODUCTION AND CONSUMPTION

M.E. Sharpe, 80 Business Park Drive, Armonk, New York 10504 (800) 541-6563; *The Illustrated Book of World Rankings.*

LIBYA - SALT PRODUCTION

Statistical Office of the United Nations, Publishing Service, New York, New York 10017 (800) 253-9646; *Statistical Yearbook.*

LIBYA - SAWNWOOD PRODUCTION - See LIBYA - FORESTRY AND FOREST PRODUCTS

LIBYA - SCIENTISTS, TECHNICIANS AND ENGINEERS

Statistical Office of the United Nations, Publishing Service, New York, New York 10017 (800) 253-9646; *Statistical Yearbook.*

United Nations Educational, Scientific and Cultural Organization (UNESCO), 7 Place de Fontenoy, F-75700 Paris, France (Telephone Number in U.S. (212) 963-5981); *Statistical Yearbook.*

LIBYA - SENIOR CITIZENS

M.E. Sharpe, 80 Business Park Drive, Armonk, New York 10504 (800) 541-6563; *The Illustrated Book of World Rankings.*

LIBYA - SHEEP - See LIBYA - LIVESTOCK AND POULTRY

LIBYA - SILVER PRODUCTION - See LIBYA - MINING AND MINERAL PRODUCTS

LIBYA - SOCIAL DATA

African Development Bank, 01 BP 1387, Abidjan 01, Cote d'Ivoire; *Selected Statistics on Regional Member Countries.*

M.E. Sharpe, 80 Business Park Drive, Armonk, New York 10504 (800) 541-6563; *The Illustrated Book of World Rankings.*

Statistical Office of the United Nations, Publishing Service, New York, New York 10017 (800) 253-9646; *World Statistics Pocketbook.*

LIBYA - SOCIAL SECURITY

Statistical Office of the United Nations, Publishing Service, New York, New York 10017 (800) 253-9646; *National Accounts Statistics.*

LIBYA - STATE BUDGET

Euromonitor International, Inc., 122 South Michigan Avenue, Suite 1200, Chicago, Illinois 60603 (800) 577-EURO; *International Marketing Data and Statistics.*

LIBYA - STEEL - See LIBYA - MINING AND MINERAL PRODUCTS

LIBYA - STOCKS - COMMODITY - MARKET PRICE - INDEX

Food and Agricultural Organization of the United Nations (FAO), Via delle Terme di Caracalla, 00100 Rome, Italy (Telephone Number in U.S. (202) 653-2400); *The State of Food and Agriculture.*

LIBYA - SUGAR PRODUCTION AND CONSUMPTION - See LIBYA - CROPS

LIBYA - TAXATION

International Road Federation, 2600 Virginia Avenue, N.W., Washington, D.C. 20037 (202) 338-4641; *World Road Statistics.*

The World Bank, 1818 H Street, NW, Washington, D.C. 20433 (202) 477-1234; *World Development Indicators.*

LIBYA - TELEPHONES IN USE

American Telephone and Telegraph Company, 26 Parsippany Road, Whippany, New Jersey 07981 (800) 222-0300; *The World's Telephones.*

Central Intelligence Agency, Washington, D.C. 20505 (703) 482-1100, www.cia.gov; *The World Factbook.*

Europa Publications Limited, 18 Bedford Square, London, WC1B 3JN, England; *The Europa World Year Book.*

St. Martin's Press, Inc., 175 Fifth Avenue, New York, New York 10010 (800) 221-7945; *The Statesman's Year-Book.*

Statistical Office of the United Nations, Publishing Service, New York, New York 10017 (800) 253-9646; *Statistical Yearbook;* and *World Statistics Pocketbook.*

LIBYA - TELEVISION BROADCASTING - See LIBYA - BROADCASTING

LIBYA - TEXTILE INDUSTRY

M.E. Sharpe, 80 Business Park Drive, Armonk, New York 10504 (800) 541-6563; *The Illustrated Book of World Rankings.*

St. Martin's Press, Inc., 175 Fifth Avenue, New York, New York 10010 (800) 221-7945; *The Statesman's Year-Book.*

United Nations Conference on Trade

and Development, Central Statistical Service, Palais des Nations, Geneva, Switzerland (Telephone in U.S. (800) 253-9646); *UNCTAD Commodity Yearbook.*

LIBYA - THEATRE

United Nations Educational, Scientific and Cultural Organization (UNESCO), 7 Place de Fontenoy, F-75700 Paris, France (Telephone Number in U.S. (212) 963-5981); *Statistical Yearbook.*

LIBYA - TOBACCO PRODUCTION

M.E. Sharpe, 80 Business Park Drive, Armonk, New York 10504 (800) 541-6563; *The Illustrated Book of World Rankings.*

Statistical Office of the United Nations, Publishing Service, New York, New York 10017 (800) 253-9646; *Statistical Yearbook.*

LIBYA - TOURISM

Euromonitor International, Inc., 122 South Michigan Avenue, Suite 1200, Chicago, Illinois 60603 (800) 577-EURO; *The World Economic Factbook;* and *World Marketing Data and Statistics.*

Federal Statistical Office, Gustav-Stresemann - Ring 11, D-6200, Wiesbaden, Germany; *Libyen.*

M.E. Sharpe, 80 Business Park Drive, Armonk, New York 10504 (800) 541-6563; *The Illustrated Book of World Rankings.*

Statistical Office of the United Nations, Publishing Service, New York, New York 10017 (800) 253-9646; *Statistical Yearbook.*

LIBYA - TRACTORS IN USE

Statistical Office of the United Nations, Publishing Service, New York, New York 10017 (800) 253-9646; *Statistical Yearbook.*

LIBYA - TRADE - See LIBYA - FOREIGN TRADE

LIBYA - TRADEMARKS AND SERVICE MARKS - See LIBYA - PATENTS, TRADEMARKS AND SERVICE MARKS

LIBYA - TRANSPORTATION AND COMMUNICATIONS

Central Intelligence Agency, Washington, D.C. 20505 (703) 482-1100, www.cia.gov; *The World Factbook.*

Euromonitor International, Inc., 122 South Michigan Avenue, Suite 1200, Chicago, Illinois 60603 (800) 577-EURO; *International Marketing Data and Statistics;* and *World Marketing Data and Statistics.*

Europa Publications Limited, 18 Bedford Square, London, WC1B 3JN,

England; *The Europa World Year Book.*

Federal Statistical Office, Gustav-Stresemann - Ring 11, D-6200, Wiesbaden, Germany; *Libyen.*

M.E. Sharpe, 80 Business Park Drive, Armonk, New York 10504 (800) 541-6563; *The Illustrated Book of World Rankings.*

St. Martin's Press, Inc., 175 Fifth Avenue, New York, New York 10010 (800) 221-7945; *The Statesman's Year-Book.*

Statistical Office of the United Nations, Publishing Service, New York, New York 10017 (800) 253-9646; *Human Development Report.*

United Nations Economic Commission for Africa, Africa Hall, Post Office Box 3001, Addis Ababa, Ethiopia (Telephone Number in U.S. (800) 253-9646); *African Statistical Yearbook.*

LIBYA - UNEMPLOYMENT

Central Intelligence Agency, Washington, D.C. 20505 (703) 482-1100, www.cia.gov; *The World Factbook.*

Euromonitor International, Inc., 122 South Michigan Avenue, Suite 1200, Chicago, Illinois 60603 (800) 577-EURO; *International Marketing Data and Statistics.*

International Labour Office, I.L.O. Publications, 1828 L Street, N.W., Suite 801, Washington, D.C. 20036 (301) 638-3152; *Yearbook of Labour Statistics.*

Statistical Office of the United Nations, Publishing Service, New York, New York 10017 (800) 253-9646; *Statistical Yearbook.*

LIBYA - VITAL STATISTICS

Euromonitor International, Inc., 122 South Michigan Avenue, Suite 1200, Chicago, Illinois 60603 (800) 577-EURO; *International Marketing Data and Statistics.*

Statistical Office of the United Nations, Publishing Service, New York, New York 10017 (800) 253-9646; *Statistical Yearbook.*

World Health Organization, Office of Publications, 20 Avenue Appia, CH-1211 Geneva 27, Switzerland (Telephone Number in U.S. (518) 436-9686); *World Health Statistics Annual.*

LIBYA - WAGES

Federal Statistical Office, Gustav-Stresemann - Ring 11, D-6200, Wiesbaden, Germany; *Libyen.*

International Labour Office, I.L.O. Publications, 1828 L Street, N.W., Suite 801, Washington, D.C. 20036 (301)

638-3152; *Yearbook of Labour Statistics.*

LIBYA - WATERMELON PRODUCTION - See LIBYA - CROPS

LIBYA - WEATHER - See LIBYA - CLIMATE

LIBYA - WHEAT PRODUCTION - See LIBYA - CROPS

LIBYA - WINE PRODUCTION - See LIBYA - BEVERAGES

LIBYA - WOOD PULP PRODUCTION - See LIBYA - FORESTRY AND FOREST PRODUCTS

LIBYA - WOOL PRODUCTION - See LIBYA - TEXTILE INDUSTRY

LICENSES, PERMITS, ETC. - TAXES

U.S. Department of Commerce, Bureau of the Census, Washington, D.C. 20233 (301) 457-4100, www.census.gov; *State Government Finances;* and Internet sites http://www.census.gov/ftp/pub/govs/www/state.html

Liechtenstein - National Statistical Office

Amt fur Volkswirtschaft des furstlichen Regierung, FL-9490 Vaduz, Liechtenstein.

Liechtenstein - Primary Statistics Source

Amt fur Volkswirtschaft des furstlichen Regierung, FL-9490 Vaduz, Liechtenstein *Statistisches Jahrbuch* (Statistical Yearbook).

LIECHTENSTEIN - AGRICULTURE

Euromonitor International, Inc., 122 South Michigan Avenue, Suite 1200, Chicago, Illinois 60603 (800) 577-EURO; *World Marketing Data and Statistics.*

Europa Publications Limited, 18 Bedford Square, London, WC1B 3JN, England; *The Europa World Year Book.*

Food and Agricultural Organization of the United Nations (FAO), Via delle Terme di Caracalla, 00100 Rome, Italy (Telephone Number in U.S. (202) 653-2400); *Production Yearbook; The State of Food and Agriculture;* and *Trade Yearbook.*

St. Martin's Press, Inc., 175 Fifth Avenue, New York, New York 10010 (800) 221-7945; *The Statesman's Year-Book.*

Statistical Office of the United Nations, Publishing Service, New York, New York 10017 (800) 253-9646; *Statistical Yearbook.*

LIECHTENSTEIN - AIRPORTS

Central Intelligence Agency, Washington, D.C. 20505 (703) 482-1100, www.cia.gov; *The World Factbook.*

LIECHTENSTEIN - AREA AND DENSITY OF POPULATION

Central Intelligence Agency, Washington, D.C. 20505 (703) 482-1100, www.cia.gov; *The World Factbook.*

Euromonitor International, Inc., 122 South Michigan Avenue, Suite 1200, Chicago, Illinois 60603 (800) 577-EURO; *The World Economic Factbook.*

Europa Publications Limited, 18 Bedford Square, London, WC1B 3JN, England; *The Europa World Year Book.*

Food and Agricultural Organization of the United Nations (FAO), Via delle Terme di Caracalla, 00100 Rome, Italy (Telephone Number in U.S. (202) 653-2400); *The State of Food and Agriculture.*

St. Martin's Press, Inc., 175 Fifth Avenue, New York, New York 10010 (800) 221-7945; *The Statesman's Year-Book.*

Statistical Office of the United Nations, Publishing Service, New York, New York 10017 (800) 253-9646; *Statistical Yearbook.*

United Nations Educational, Scientific and Cultural Organization (UNESCO), 7 Place de Fontenoy, F-75700 Paris, France (Telephone Number in U.S. (212) 963-5981); *Statistical Yearbook.*

LIECHTENSTEIN - BANKING

Euromonitor International, Inc., 122 South Michigan Avenue, Suite 1200, Chicago, Illinois 60603 (800) 577-EURO; *World Marketing Data and Statistics.*

St. Martin's Press, Inc., 175 Fifth Avenue, New York, New York 10010 (800) 221-7945; *The Statesman's Year-Book.*

LIECHTENSTEIN - BIRTH RATES

Central Intelligence Agency, Washington, D.C. 20505 (703) 482-1100, www.cia.gov; *The World Factbook.*

Euromonitor International, Inc., 122 South Michigan Avenue, Suite 1200, Chicago, Illinois 60603 (800) 577-EURO; *The World Economic Factbook.*

Europa Publications Limited, 18 Bedford Square, London, WC1B 3JN, England; *The Europa World Year Book.*

St. Martin's Press, Inc., 175 Fifth Avenue, New York, New York 10010 (800) 221-7945; *The Statesman's Year-Book.*

Statistical Office of the United Nations, Publishing Service, New York, New York 10017 (800) 253-9646; *Demographic Yearbook;* and *Statistical Yearbook.*

World Health Organization, Office of Publications, 20 Avenue Appia, CH-1211 Geneva 27, Switzerland (Telephone Number in U.S. (518) 436-9686); *World Health Statistics Annual.*

LIECHTENSTEIN - BROADCASTING

Central Intelligence Agency, Washington, D.C. 20505 (703) 482-1100, www.cia.gov; *The World Factbook.*

Euromonitor International, Inc., 122 South Michigan Avenue, Suite 1200, Chicago, Illinois 60603 (800) 577-EURO; *World Marketing Data and Statistics.*

St. Martin's Press, Inc., 175 Fifth Avenue, New York, New York 10010 (800) 221-7945; *The Statesman's Year-Book.*

LIECHTENSTEIN - BUDGET

Central Intelligence Agency, Washington, D.C. 20505 (703) 482-1100, www.cia.gov; *The World Factbook.*

LIECHTENSTEIN - CALORIE SUPPLY

Food and Agricultural Organization of the United Nations (FAO), Via delle Terme di Caracalla, 00100 Rome, Italy (Telephone Number in U.S. (202) 653-2400); *The State of Food and Agriculture.*

LIECHTENSTEIN - CATTLE - See LIECHTENSTEIN - LIVESTOCK AND POULTRY

LIECHTENSTEIN - CHEMICAL (ORGANIC) PRODUCTION - See LIECHTENSTEIN - MINING AND MINERAL PRODUCTS

LIECHTENSTEIN - COAL PRODUCTION - See LIECHTENSTEIN - MINING AND MINERAL PRODUCTS

LIECHTENSTEIN - COMMERCE

St. Martin's Press, Inc., 175 Fifth Avenue, New York, New York 10010 (800) 221-7945; *The Statesman's Year-Book.*

LIECHTENSTEIN - CONSUMER PRICES

Euromonitor International, Inc., 122 South Michigan Avenue, Suite 1200, Chicago, Illinois 60603 (800) 577-EURO; *World Marketing Data and Statistics.*

LIECHTENSTEIN - CORN PRODUCTION - See LIECHTENSTEIN - CROPS

LIECHTENSTEIN - CORPORATE TAXES - See LIECHTENSTEIN - TAXATION

LIECHTENSTEIN - CROPS

Europa Publications Limited, 18 Bedford Square, London, WC1B 3JN, England; *The Europa World Year Book.*

Food and Agricultural Organization of the United Nations (FAO), Via delle Terme di Caracalla, 00100 Rome, Italy (Telephone Number in U.S. (202) 653-2400); *The State of Food and Agriculture.*

St. Martin's Press, Inc., 175 Fifth Avenue, New York, New York 10010 (800) 221-7945; *The Statesman's Year-Book.*

Statistical Office of the United Nations, Publishing Service, New York, New York 10017 (800) 253-9646; *Statistical Yearbook.*

LIECHTENSTEIN - DAIRY PRODUCTS

Europa Publications Limited, 18 Bedford Square, London, WC1B 3JN, England; *The Europa World Year Book.*

Food and Agricultural Organization of the United Nations (FAO), Via delle Terme di Caracalla, 00100 Rome, Italy (Telephone Number in U.S. (202) 653-2400); *The State of Food and Agriculture.*

St. Martin's Press, Inc., 175 Fifth Avenue, New York, New York 10010 (800) 221-7945; *The Statesman's Year-Book.*

LIECHTENSTEIN - DEATH RATES - See LIECHTENSTEIN - MORTALITY

LIECHTENSTEIN - DEMOGRAPHY

Euromonitor International, Inc., 122 South Michigan Avenue, Suite 1200, Chicago, Illinois 60603 (800) 577-EURO; *The World Economic Factbook;* and *World Marketing Data and Statistics.*

LIECHTENSTEIN - DIVORCE RATES

Statistical Office of the United Nations, Publishing Service, New York, New York 10017 (800) 253-9646; *Demographic Yearbook;* and *Statistical Yearbook.*

LIECHTENSTEIN - ECONOMY

Central Intelligence Agency, Washington, D.C. 20505 (703) 482-1100, www.cia.gov; *The World Factbook.*

Euromonitor International, Inc., 122 South Michigan Avenue, Suite 1200, Chicago, Illinois 60603 (800) 577-EURO; *The World Economic Factbook;* and *World Marketing Data and Statistics.*

St. Martin's Press, Inc., 175 Fifth Avenue, New York, New York 10010 (800) 221-7945; *The Statesman's Year-Book.*

Statistical Office of the United Nations, Publishing Service, New York, New York 10017 (800) 253-9646; *World Statistics Pocketbook.*

LIECHTENSTEIN - EDUCATION

Euromonitor International, Inc., 122 South Michigan Avenue, Suite 1200, Chicago, Illinois 60603 (800) 577-EURO; *World Marketing Data and Statistics.*

Europa Publications Limited, 18 Bedford Square, London, WC1B 3JN, England; *The Europa World Year Book.*

St. Martin's Press, Inc., 175 Fifth Avenue, New York, New York 10010 (800) 221-7945; *The Statesman's Year-Book.*

United Nations Educational, Scientific and Cultural Organization (UNESCO), 7 Place de Fontenoy, F-75700 Paris, France (Telephone Number in U.S. (212) 963-5981); *Statistical Yearbook.*

LIECHTENSTEIN - EGG PRODUCTION AND CONSUMPTION - See LIECHTENSTEIN - DAIRY PRODUCTS

LIECHTENSTEIN - ELECTRICITY

Central Intelligence Agency, Washington, D.C. 20505 (703) 482-1100, www.cia.gov; *The World Factbook.*

St. Martin's Press, Inc., 175 Fifth Avenue, New York, New York 10010 (800) 221-7945; *The Statesman's Year-Book.*

LIECHTENSTEIN - ENERGY

Euromonitor International, Inc., 122 South Michigan Avenue, Suite 1200, Chicago, Illinois 60603 (800) 577-EURO; *The World Economic Factbook;* and *World Marketing Data and Statistics.*

Food and Agricultural Organization of the United Nations (FAO), Via delle Terme di Caracalla, 00100 Rome, Italy (Telephone Number in U.S. (202) 653-2400); *The State of Food and Agriculture.*

St. Martin's Press, Inc., 175 Fifth Avenue, New York, New York 10010 (800) 221-7945; *The Statesman's Year-Book.*

Statistical Office of the United Nations, Publishing Service, New York, New York 10017 (800) 253-9646; *World Statistics Pocketbook.*

LIECHTENSTEIN - ENVIRONMENT

Statistical Office of the United Nations, Publishing Service, New York, New York 10017 (800) 253-9646; *World Statistics Pocketbook.*

LIECHTENSTEIN - EXCHANGE RATES

Central Intelligence Agency, Washington, D.C. 20505 (703) 482-1100, www.cia.gov; *The World Factbook*.

Euromonitor International, Inc., 122 South Michigan Avenue, Suite 1200, Chicago, Illinois 60603 (800) 577-EURO; *The World Economic Factbook*.

Europa Publications Limited, 18 Bedford Square, London, WC1B 3JN, England; *The Europa World Year Book*.

Statistical Office of the United Nations, Publishing Service, New York, New York 10017 (800) 253-9646; *World Statistics Pocketbook*.

LIECHTENSTEIN - EXPORTS

Central Intelligence Agency, Washington, D.C. 20505 (703) 482-1100, www.cia.gov; *The World Factbook*.

Euromonitor International, Inc., 122 South Michigan Avenue, Suite 1200, Chicago, Illinois 60603 (800) 577-EURO; *The World Economic Factbook*.

Europa Publications Limited, 18 Bedford Square, London, WC1B 3JN, England; *The Europa World Year Book*.

Food and Agricultural Organization of the United Nations (FAO), Via delle Terme di Caracalla, 00100 Rome, Italy (Telephone Number in U.S. (202) 653-2400); *The State of Food and Agriculture*.

St. Martin's Press, Inc., 175 Fifth Avenue, New York, New York 10010 (800) 221-7945; *The Statesman's Year-Book*.

LIECHTENSTEIN - EXTERNAL TRADE

Euromonitor International, Inc., 122 South Michigan Avenue, Suite 1200, Chicago, Illinois 60603 (800) 577-EURO; *World Marketing Data and Statistics*.

Food and Agricultural Organization of the United Nations (FAO), Via delle Terme di Caracalla, 00100 Rome, Italy (Telephone Number in U.S. (202) 653-2400); *The State of Food and Agriculture;* and *Trade Yearbook*.

LIECHTENSTEIN - FARM CROPS - See LIECHTENSTEIN - CROPS

LIECHTENSTEIN - FERTILITY RATES

Central Intelligence Agency, Washington, D.C. 20505 (703) 482-1100, www.cia.gov; *The World Factbook*.

LIECHTENSTEIN - FERTILIZER

Food and Agricultural Organization of the United Nations (FAO), Via delle Terme di Caracalla, 00100 Rome, Italy (Telephone

Number in U.S. (202) 653-2400); *The State of Food and Agriculture*.

LIECHTENSTEIN - FETAL MORTALITY - See LIECHTENSTEIN - MORTALITY

LIECHTENSTEIN - FINANCE

Europa Publications Limited, 18 Bedford Square, London, WC1B 3JN, England; *The Europa World Year Book*.

St. Martin's Press, Inc., 175 Fifth Avenue, New York, New York 10010 (800) 221-7945; *The Statesman's Year-Book*.

LIECHTENSTEIN - FISHERIES

Food and Agricultural Organization of the United Nations (FAO), Via delle Terme di Caracalla, 00100 Rome, Italy (Telephone Number in U.S. (202) 653-2400); *The State of Food and Agriculture;* and *Yearbook of Fishery Statistics*.

LIECHTENSTEIN - FOOD

Food and Agricultural Organization of the United Nations (FAO), Via delle Terme di Caracalla, 00100 Rome, Italy (Telephone Number in U.S. (202) 653-2400); *The State of Food and Agriculture;* and *Production Yearbook*.

LIECHTENSTEIN - FOREIGN TRADE

Euromonitor International, Inc., 122 South Michigan Avenue, Suite 1200, Chicago, Illinois 60603 (800) 577-EURO; *The World Economic Factbook*.

Europa Publications Limited, 18 Bedford Square, London, WC1B 3JN, England; *The Europa World Year Book*.

Food and Agricultural Organization of the United Nations (FAO), Via delle Terme di Caracalla, 00100 Rome, Italy (Telephone Number in U.S. (202) 653-2400); *The State of Food and Agriculture*.

St. Martin's Press, Inc., 175 Fifth Avenue, New York, New York 10010 (800) 221-7945; *The Statesman's Year-Book*.

LIECHTENSTEIN - FORESTRY AND FOREST PRODUCTS

Europa Publications Limited, 18 Bedford Square, London, WC1B 3JN, England; *The Europa World Year Book*.

Food and Agricultural Organization of the United Nations (FAO), Via delle Terme di Caracalla, 00100 Rome, Italy (Telephone Number in U.S. (202) 653-2400); *The State of Food and Agriculture*.

Statistical Office of the United Nations, Publishing Service, New York, New York

10017 (800) 253-9646; *Statistical Yearbook*.

United Nations Educational, Scientific and Cultural Organization (UNESCO), 7 Place de Fontenoy, F-75700 Paris, France (Telephone Number in U.S. (212) 963-5981); *Statistical Yearbook*.

LIECHTENSTEIN - GENERAL MORTALITY - See LIECHTENSTEIN - MORTALITY

LIECHTENSTEIN - GOVERNMENT

Central Intelligence Agency, Washington, D.C. 20505 (703) 482-1100, www.cia.gov; *The World Factbook*.

Europa Publications Limited, 18 Bedford Square, London, WC1B 3JN, England; *The Europa World Year Book*.

St. Martin's Press, Inc., 175 Fifth Avenue, New York, New York 10010 (800) 221-7945; *The Statesman's Year-Book*.

LIECHTENSTEIN - GRAIN PRODUCTION - See LIECHTENSTEIN - CROPS

LIECHTENSTEIN - GROSS DOMESTIC PRODUCT

Euromonitor International, Inc., 122 South Michigan Avenue, Suite 1200, Chicago, Illinois 60603 (800) 577-EURO; *The World Economic Factbook*.

LIECHTENSTEIN - HEALTH

Euromonitor International, Inc., 122 South Michigan Avenue, Suite 1200, Chicago, Illinois 60603 (800) 577-EURO; *World Marketing Data and Statistics*.

St. Martin's Press, Inc., 175 Fifth Avenue, New York, New York 10010 (800) 221-7945; *The Statesman's Year-Book*.

LIECHTENSTEIN - HIGHWAYS

Central Intelligence Agency, Washington, D.C. 20505 (703) 482-1100, www.cia.gov; *The World Factbook*.

St. Martin's Press, Inc., 175 Fifth Avenue, New York, New York 10010 (800) 221-7945; *The Statesman's Year-Book*.

LIECHTENSTEIN - HOUSING AND HOUSING UNITS

Euromonitor International, Inc., 122 South Michigan Avenue, Suite 1200, Chicago, Illinois 60603 (800) 577-EURO; *World Marketing Data and Statistics*.

Statistical Office of the United Nations, Publishing Service, New York, New York 10017 (800) 253-9646; *Statistical Yearbook*.

LIECHTENSTEIN - ILLITERATE POPULATION

Central Intelligence Agency, Washington, D.C. 20505 (703) 482-1100, www.cia.gov; *The World Factbook.*

Euromonitor International, Inc., 122 South Michigan Avenue, Suite 1200, Chicago, Illinois 60603 (800) 577-EURO; *The World Economic Factbook.*

LIECHTENSTEIN - IMPORTS

Central Intelligence Agency, Washington, D.C. 20505 (703) 482-1100, www.cia.gov; *The World Factbook.*

Euromonitor International, Inc., 122 South Michigan Avenue, Suite 1200, Chicago, Illinois 60603 (800) 577-EURO; *The World Economic Factbook.*

Food and Agricultural Organization of the United Nations (FAO), Via delle Terme di Caracalla, 00100 Rome, Italy (Telephone Number in U.S. (202) 653-2400); *The State of Food and Agriculture.*

St. Martin's Press, Inc., 175 Fifth Avenue, New York, New York 10010 (800) 221-7945; *The Statesman's Year-Book.*

LIECHTENSTEIN - INDUSTRY

Central Intelligence Agency, Washington, D.C. 20505 (703) 482-1100, www.cia.gov; *The World Factbook.*

Euromonitor International, Inc., 122 South Michigan Avenue, Suite 1200, Chicago, Illinois 60603 (800) 577-EURO; *The World Economic Factbook;* and *World Marketing Data and Statistics.*

St. Martin's Press, Inc., 175 Fifth Avenue, New York, New York 10010 (800) 221-7945; *The Statesman's Year-Book.*

Statistical Office of the United Nations, Publishing Service, New York, New York 10017 (800) 253-9646; *Statistical Yearbook.*

LIECHTENSTEIN - INFANT AND MATERNAL MORTALITY - See LIECHTENSTEIN - MORTALITY

LIECHTENSTEIN - LABOR

Central Intelligence Agency, Washington, D.C. 20505 (703) 482-1100, www.cia.gov; *The World Factbook.*

Euromonitor International, Inc., 122 South Michigan Avenue, Suite 1200, Chicago, Illinois 60603 (800) 577-EURO; *World Marketing Data and Statistics.*

Europa Publications Limited, 18 Bedford Square, London, WC1B 3JN, England; *The Europa World Year Book.*

Food and Agricultural Organization of the United Nations (FAO), Via delle Terme

di Caracalla, 00100 Rome, Italy (Telephone Number in U.S. (202) 653-2400); *The State of Food and Agriculture.*

St. Martin's Press, Inc., 175 Fifth Avenue, New York, New York 10010 (800) 221-7945; *The Statesman's Year-Book.*

LIECHTENSTEIN - LAND USE

Central Intelligence Agency, Washington, D.C. 20505 (703) 482-1100, www.cia.gov; *The World Factbook.*

Food and Agricultural Organization of the United Nations (FAO), Via delle Terme di Caracalla, 00100 Rome, Italy (Telephone Number in U.S. (202) 653-2400); *Production Yearbook.*

LIECHTENSTEIN - LIBRARIES

United Nations Educational, Scientific and Cultural Organization (UNESCO), 7 Place de Fontenoy, F-75700 Paris, France (Telephone Number in U.S. (212) 963-5981); *Statistical Yearbook.*

LIECHTENSTEIN - LIFE EXPECTANCY

Central Intelligence Agency, Washington, D.C. 20505 (703) 482-1100, www.cia.gov; *The World Factbook.*

Euromonitor International, Inc., 122 South Michigan Avenue, Suite 1200, Chicago, Illinois 60603 (800) 577-EURO; *The World Economic Factbook.*

Statistical Office of the United Nations, Publishing Service, New York, New York 10017 (800) 253-9646; *World Statistics Pocketbook.*

LIECHTENSTEIN - LITERACY RATE

Euromonitor International, Inc., 122 South Michigan Avenue, Suite 1200, Chicago, Illinois 60603 (800) 577-EURO; *World Marketing Data and Statistics.*

LIECHTENSTEIN - LIVESTOCK AND POULTRY

Europa Publications Limited, 18 Bedford Square, London, WC1B 3JN, England; *The Europa World Year Book.*

Food and Agricultural Organization of the United Nations (FAO), Via delle Terme di Caracalla, 00100 Rome, Italy (Telephone Number in U.S. (202) 653-2400); *Production Yearbook;* and *The State of Food and Agriculture.*

St. Martin's Press, Inc., 175 Fifth Avenue, New York, New York 10010 (800) 221-7945; *The Statesman's Year-Book.*

Statistical Office of the United Nations, Publishing Service, New York, New York

10017 (800) 253-9646; *Statistical Yearbook.*

LIECHTENSTEIN - MAIL - PIECES SENT OR RECEIVED

Statistical Office of the United Nations, Publishing Service, New York, New York 10017 (800) 253-9646; *Statistical Yearbook.*

LIECHTENSTEIN - MARRIAGE RATES

Europa Publications Limited, 18 Bedford Square, London, WC1B 3JN, England; *The Europa World Year Book.*

Statistical Office of the United Nations, Publishing Service, New York, New York 10017 (800) 253-9646; *Demographic Yearbook;* and *Statistical Yearbook.*

LIECHTENSTEIN - MEAT PRODUCTION - See LIECHTENSTEIN - LIVESTOCK AND POULTRY

LIECHTENSTEIN - MILITARY

Central Intelligence Agency, Washington, D.C. 20505 (703) 482-1100, www.cia.gov; *The World Factbook.*

Euromonitor International, Inc., 122 South Michigan Avenue, Suite 1200, Chicago, Illinois 60603 (800) 577-EURO; *World Marketing Data and Statistics.*

LIECHTENSTEIN - MORTALITY

Central Intelligence Agency, Washington, D.C. 20505 (703) 482-1100, www.cia.gov; *The World Factbook.*

Euromonitor International, Inc., 122 South Michigan Avenue, Suite 1200, Chicago, Illinois 60603 (800) 577-EURO; *The World Economic Factbook.*

Europa Publications Limited, 18 Bedford Square, London, WC1B 3JN, England; *The Europa World Year Book.*

St. Martin's Press, Inc., 175 Fifth Avenue, New York, New York 10010 (800) 221-7945; *The Statesman's Year-Book.*

Statistical Office of the United Nations, Publishing Service, New York, New York 10017 (800) 253-9646; *Demographic Yearbook; World Statistics Pocketbook;* and *Statistical Yearbook.*

World Health Organization, Office of Publications, 20 Avenue Appia, CH-1211 Geneva 27, Switzerland (Telephone Number in U.S. (518) 436-9686); *World Health Statistics Annual.*

LIECHTENSTEIN - MOTION PICTURES

St. Martin's Press, Inc., 175 Fifth Avenue, New York, New York 10010 (800)

221-7945; *The Statesman's Year-Book.*

LIECHTENSTEIN - MOTOR VEHICLES IN USE

Europa Publications Limited, 18 Bedford Square, London, WC1B 3JN, England; *The Europa World Year Book.*

LIECHTENSTEIN - NATALITY - See LIECHTENSTEIN - BIRTH RATES

LIECHTENSTEIN - NEWSPAPER PRODUCTION - See LIECHTENSTEIN - FORESTRY AND FOREST PRODUCTS

LIECHTENSTEIN - OCCUPATIONS - See LIECHTENSTEIN - LABOR

LIECHTENSTEIN - PESTICIDE USE

Food and Agricultural Organization of the United Nations (FAO), Via delle Terme di Caracalla, 00100 Rome, Italy (Telephone Number in U.S. (202) 653-2400); *The State of Food and Agriculture.*

LIECHTENSTEIN - PETROLEUM INDUSTRY

Food and Agricultural Organization of the United Nations (FAO), Via delle Terme di Caracalla, 00100 Rome, Italy (Telephone Number in U.S. (202) 653-2400); *The State of Food and Agriculture.*

LIECHTENSTEIN - PIGS - See LIECHTENSTEIN - LIVESTOCK AND POULTRY

LIECHTENSTEIN - PATENTS, TRADEMARKS AND SERVICE MARKS

Statistical Office of the United Nations, Publishing Service, New York, New York 10017 (800) 253-9646; *Statistical Yearbook.*

LIECHTENSTEIN - POPULATION

Central Intelligence Agency, Washington, D.C. 20505 (703) 482-1100, www.cia.gov; *The World Factbook.*

Euromonitor International, Inc., 122 South Michigan Avenue, Suite 1200, Chicago, Illinois 60603 (800) 577-EURO; *The World Economic Factbook.*

Europa Publications Limited, 18 Bedford Square, London, WC1B 3JN, England; *The Europa World Year Book.*

Food and Agricultural Organization of the United Nations (FAO), Via delle Terme di Caracalla, 00100 Rome, Italy (Telephone Number in U.S. (202) 653-2400); *Production Yearbook.*

St. Martin's Press, Inc., 175 Fifth Avenue, New York, New York 10010 (800) 221-7945; *The Statesman's Year-Book.*

Statistical Office of the United Nations, Publishing Service, New York, New York 10017 (800) 253-9646; *Demographic Yearbook; World Statistics Pocketbook;* and *Statistical Yearbook.*

United Nations Educational, Scientific and Cultural Organization (UNESCO), 7 Place de Fontenoy, F-75700 Paris, France (Telephone Number in U.S. (212) 963-5981); *Statistical Yearbook.*

World Health Organization, Office of Publications, 20 Avenue Appia, CH-1211 Geneva 27, Switzerland (Telephone Number in U.S. (518) 436-9686); *World Health Statistics Annual.*

LIECHTENSTEIN - POST OFFICES

St. Martin's Press, Inc., 175 Fifth Avenue, New York, New York 10010 (800) 221-7945; *The Statesman's Year-Book.*

LIECHTENSTEIN - POTATO PRODUCTION - See LIECHTENSTEIN - CROPS

LIECHTENSTEIN - PRICES

Food and Agricultural Organization of the United Nations (FAO), Via delle Terme di Caracalla, 00100 Rome, Italy (Telephone Number in U.S. (202) 653-2400); *Production Yearbook;* and *The State of Food and Agriculture.*

LIECHTENSTEIN - RADIO RECEIVERS

St. Martin's Press, Inc., 175 Fifth Avenue, New York, New York 10010 (800) 221-7945; *The Statesman's Year-Book.*

LIECHTENSTEIN - RAILWAYS

St. Martin's Press, Inc., 175 Fifth Avenue, New York, New York 10010 (800) 221-7945; *The Statesman's Year-Book.*

LIECHTENSTEIN - RELIGION

Central Intelligence Agency, Washington, D.C. 20505 (703) 482-1100, www.cia.gov; *The World Factbook.*

St. Martin's Press, Inc., 175 Fifth Avenue, New York, New York 10010 (800) 221-7945; *The Statesman's Year-Book.*

LIECHTENSTEIN - RETAIL PRICE INDEX

Europa Publications Limited, 18 Bedford Square, London, WC1B 3JN, England; *The Europa World Year Book.*

LIECHTENSTEIN - RETAIL TRADE

Euromonitor International, Inc., 122 South Michigan Avenue, Suite 1200, Chicago, Illinois 60603 (800) 577-EURO; *World Marketing Data and Statistics.*

LIECHTENSTEIN - ROOT AND TUBER PRODUCTION

Food and Agricultural Organization of the United Nations (FAO), Via delle Terme di Caracalla, 00100 Rome, Italy (Telephone Number in U.S. (202) 653-2400); *Production Yearbook.*

LIECHTENSTEIN - SCIENTISTS, TECHNICIANS AND ENGINEERS

United Nations Educational, Scientific and Cultural Organization (UNESCO), 7 Place de Fontenoy, F-75700 Paris, France (Telephone Number in U.S. (212) 963-5981); *Statistical Yearbook.*

LIECHTENSTEIN - SHEEP - See LIECHTENSTEIN - LIVESTOCK AND POULTRY

LIECHTENSTEIN - SOCIAL DATA

Statistical Office of the United Nations, Publishing Service, New York, New York 10017 (800) 253-9646; *World Statistics Pocketbook.*

LIECHTENSTEIN - STOCKS - COMMODITY - MARKET PRICE - INDEX

Food and Agricultural Organization of the United Nations (FAO), Via delle Terme di Caracalla, 00100 Rome, Italy (Telephone Number in U.S. (202) 653-2400); *The State of Food and Agriculture.*

LIECHTENSTEIN - TAXATION

St. Martin's Press, Inc., 175 Fifth Avenue, New York, New York 10010 (800) 221-7945; *The Statesman's Year-Book.*

LIECHTENSTEIN - TELEPHONES IN USE

American Telephone and Telegraph Company, 26 Parsippany Road, Whippany, New Jersey 07981 (800) 222-0300; *The World's Telephones.*

Central Intelligence Agency, Washington, D.C. 20505 (703) 482-1100, www.cia.gov; *The World Factbook.*

Europa Publications Limited, 18 Bedford Square, London, WC1B 3JN, England; *The Europa World Year Book.*

St. Martin's Press, Inc., 175 Fifth Avenue, New York, New York 10010 (800) 221-7945; *The Statesman's Year-Book.*

Statistical Office of the United Nations, Publishing Service, New York, New York 10017 (800) 253-9646; *Statistical Yearbook;* and *World Statistics Pocketbook.*

LIECHTENSTEIN - TEXTILE INDUSTRY

St. Martin's Press, Inc., 175 Fifth

Avenue, New York, New York 10010 (800) 221-7945; *The Statesman's Year-Book.*

LIECHTENSTEIN - TOURISM

Euromonitor International, Inc., 122 South Michigan Avenue, Suite 1200, Chicago, Illinois 60603 (800) 577-EURO; *The World Economic Factbook;* and *World Marketing Data and Statistics.*

Europa Publications Limited, 18 Bedford Square, London, WC1B 3JN, England; *The Europa World Year Book.*

St. Martin's Press, Inc., 175 Fifth Avenue, New York, New York 10010 (800) 221-7945; *The Statesman's Year-Book.*

World Tourism Organization, Calle Capitan Haya 42, E-28020 Madrid, Spain; *Yearbook of Tourism Statistics.*

LIECHTENSTEIN - TRACTORS IN USE

Statistical Office of the United Nations, Publishing Service, New York, New York 10017 (800) 253-9646; *Statistical Yearbook.*

LIECHTENSTEIN - TRADE - See LIECHTENSTEIN - FOREIGN TRADE

LIECHTENSTEIN - TRADEMARKS AND SERVICE MARKS - See LIECHTENSTEIN - PATENTS, TRADEMARKS AND SERVICE MARKS

LIECHTENSTEIN - TRANSPORTATION AND COMMUNICATIONS

Central Intelligence Agency, Washington, D.C. 20505 (703) 482-1100, www.cia.gov; *The World Factbook.*

Euromonitor International, Inc., 122 South Michigan Avenue, Suite 1200, Chicago, Illinois 60603 (800) 577-EURO; *World Marketing Data and Statistics.*

Europa Publications Limited, 18 Bedford Square, London, WC1B 3JN, England; *The Europa World Year Book.*

St. Martin's Press, Inc., 175 Fifth Avenue, New York, New York 10010 (800) 221-7945; *The Statesman's Year-Book.*

LIECHTENSTEIN - UNEMPLOYMENT RATE

Central Intelligence Agency, Washington, D.C. 20505 (703) 482-1100, www.cia.gov; *The World Factbook.*

LIECHTENSTEIN - VITAL STATISTICS

Statistical Office of the United Nations, Publishing Service, New York, New York 10017 (800) 253-9646; *Statistical Yearbook.*

World Health Organization, Office of

Publications, 20 Avenue Appia, CH-1211 Geneva 27, Switzerland (Telephone Number in U.S. (518) 436-9686); *World Health Statistics Annual.*

LIFE EXPECTANCY

U.S. Department of Health and Human Services, National Center for Health Statistics, 3700 East-West Highway, Hyattsville, Maryland 20782 (301) 436-8500, www.cdc.gov/nchs; *Vital Statistics of the United States; National Vital Statistics Reports; U.S. Life Tables and Actuarial Tables; U.S. Decennial Life Tables for 1989-1991;* and unpublished data.

LIFE EXPECTANCY - FOREIGN COUNTRIES

U.S. Department of Commerce, Bureau of the Census, Washington, D.C. 20233 (301) 457-4100, www.census.gov; *International Data Base;* and Internet site: http://www.census.gov/ipc/www/idbnew.htm.

LIFE EXPECTANCY - PROJECTIONS

U.S. Department of Commerce, Bureau of the Census, Washington, D.C. 20233 (301) 457-4100, www.census.gov; *Vital Statistics of the United States;* and *National Vital Statistics Reports.*

LIFE INSURANCE

American Council of Life Insurance, 1001 Pennsylvania Avenue, NW, Washington, D.C. 20004 (202) 624-2000; *Life Insurance Fact Book;* and *Life Insurance Fact Book Update.*

LIFE INSURANCE - CAPITAL

American Council of Life Insurance, 1001 Pennsylvania Avenue, NW, Washington, D.C. 20004 (202) 624-2000; *Life Insurance Fact Book.*

LIFE INSURANCE - CASH VALUE

Board of Governors of the Federal Reserve System, 20th Street and Constitution Avenue, NW, Washington, D.C. 20551 (202) 452-3000, www.bog.frb.fed.us; *Federal Reserve Bulletin;* and unpublished data.

LIFE INSURANCE - CONSUMER EXPENDITURES

U.S. Department of Labor Statistics, Two Massachusetts Avenue, NE, Washington, D.C. 20212 (202) 691-5200, www.stats.bls.gov; *Consumer Expenditures in 1997;* and unpublished data.

LIFE INSURANCE - ESTABLISHMENTS

American Council of Life Insurance, 1001 Pennsylvania Avenue, NW, Washington, D.C. 20004 (202) 624-2000; *Life Insurance Fact Book.*

U.S. Department of Commerce, Bureau of the Census, Washington, D.C. 20233 (301) 457-4100, www.census.gov; *County Business Patterns.*

LIFE INSURANCE - FINANCES

American Council of Life Insurance, 1001 Pennsylvania Avenue, NW, Washington, D.C. 20004 (202) 624-2000; *Life Insurance Fact Book.*

Board of Governors of the Federal Reserve System, Twentieth Street and Constitution Avenue, NW, Washington, D.C. 20551 (202) 452-3000, www.bog.frb.fed.us; *Flow of Funds Accounts.*

LIFE INSURANCE - FLOW OF FUNDS

Board of Governors of the Federal Reserve System, Twentieth Street and Constitution Avenue, NW, Washington, D.C. 20551 (202) 452-3000, www.bog.frb.fed.us; *Flow of Funds Accounts.*

LIFE INSURANCE - IN FORCE

American Council of Life Insurance, 1001 Pennsylvania Avenue, NW, Washington, D.C. 20004 (202) 624-2000; *Life Insurance Fact Book.*

LIFE INSURANCE - INDIVIDUAL RETIREMENT ACCOUNTS

Investment Company Institute, 1401 H Street, 12th Floor, Washington, D.C. 20005 (202) 326-5800; *Mutual Fund Fact Book.*

LIFE INSURANCE - MORTGAGE LOANS OUTSTANDING

Board of Governors of the Federal Reserve System, Twentieth Street and Constitution Avenue, NW, Washington, D.C. 20551 (202) 452-3000, www.bog.frb.fed.us; *Federal Reserve Bulletin.*

LIFE INSURANCE - PURCHASES, POLICIES

American Council of Life Insurance, 1001 Pennsylvania Avenue, NW, Washington, D.C. 20004 (202) 624-2000; *Life Insurance Fact Book.*

LIFE INSURANCE - RESERVES

American Council of Life Insurance, 1001 Pennsylvania Avenue, NW, Washington, D.C. 20004 (202) 624-2000; *Life Insurance Fact Book.*

Board of Governors of the Federal Reserve System, Twentieth Street and Constitution Avenue, NW, Washington, D.C. 20551 (202) 452-3000. www.bog.frb.fed.us; *Flow of Funds Accounts.*

LIFE INSURANCE - SALES

American Council of Life Insurance, 1001 Pennsylvania Avenue, NW, Washington, D.C. 20004 (202) 624-2000; *Life Insurance Fact Book.*

LIFE SCIENCES

National Science Foundation, 4201 Wilson Boulevard, Arlington, Virginia 22230 (703) 306-1234, www.nsf.gov; *National Survey of Recent College Graduates;* and *Survey of Earned Doctorates, Selected Data on Science and Engineering Doctorate Awards.*

LIFE SCIENCES - DEGREES CONFERRED

National Science Foundation, 4201 Wilson Boulevard, Arlington, Virginia 22230 (703) 306-1234, www.nsf.gov; *National Survey of Recent College Graduates.*

U.S. Department of Education, National Center for Education Statistics, 555 New Jersey Avenue, NW, Washington, D.C. 20208-5574 (202) 219-1828, http://nces,ed.gov; *Digest of Education Statistics.*

LIFE SCIENCES - EMPLOYMENT

U.S. Department of Labor, Bureau of Labor Statistics, Two Massachusetts Avenue, NE, Washington, D.C. 20212 (202) 691-5200, www.stats.bls.gov; *Monthly Labor Review;* and unpublished data.

LIFE YEARS LOST

Institute for Health and Aging, University of California, San Francisco, San Francisco, California 94143 (415) 476-9483; unpublished data.

LIFETIME - AVERAGE

U.S. Department of Commerce, Bureau of the Census, Washington, D.C. 20233 (301) 457-4100, www.census.gov; *International Data Base;* and Internet site: http://www.census.gov/ipc/www/idbnew.html.

U.S. Department of Health and Human Services, National Center for Health Statistics, 3700 East-West Highway, Hyattsville, MD 20782 (301) 436-8500, www.cdc.gov/nchs; *U.S. Decennial Life Tables for 1989-1991.*

LIGHT AND POWER - See ELECTRIC LIGHT AND POWER INDUSTRY

LIME

U.S. Department of the Interior, Geological Survey, Office of Minerals Information, 12201 Sunrise Valley Drive, Reston, Virginia 22092 (703) 648-4000, www.minerals.usgs.gov; *Annual Reports;* and *Mineral Commodity Summaries.*

LIMES

U.S. Department of Agriculture, National Agricultural Statistics Service, Fourteenth Street between Constitution Avenue and E Street, NW, Washington, D.C. 20250 (800) 727-9540, www.usda.gov/nass; *Citrus Fruits.*

LIQUEFIED PETROLEUM GASES - CONSUMPTION

U.S. Department of Energy, Energy Information Administration, 1000 Independence Avenue, SW, Washington, D.C. 20585 (202) 586-8800, www.eia.doc.gov; *Petroleum Supply Annual.*

LIQUOR STORES - RETAIL - EARNINGS

U.S. Department of Commerce, Bureau of the Census, Washington, D.C. 20233 (301) 457-4100, www.census.gov; *County Business Patterns;* and *1997 Economic Census.*

LIQUOR STORES - RETAIL - EMPLOYEES

U.S. Department of Commerce, Bureau of the Census, Washington, D.C. 20233 (301) 457-4100, www.census.gov; *County Business Patterns;* and *1997 Economic Census.*

LIQUOR STORES - RETAIL - ESTABLISHMENTS

U.S. Department of Commerce, Bureau of the Census, Washington, D.C. 20233 (301) 457-4100, www.census.gov; *County Business Patterns;* and *1997 Economic Census.*

LIQUOR STORES - RETAIL - PRODUCTIVITY

U.S. Department of Labor, Bureau of Labor Statistics, Two Massachusetts Avenue, NE, Washington, D.C. 20212 (202) 691-5200, www.stats.bls.gov; Internet site http://stats.bls.gov/iprhome.htm.

LIQUOR STORES - RETAIL - SALES

U.S. Department of Agriculture, Economic Research Service, 1800 M Street, NW, Washington, D.C. 20036 (202) 694-5050, www.ers.usda.gov; *Food Consumption, Prices, and Expenditures;* and Internet site: http://www.econ.ag.gov.

U.S. Department of Commerce, Bureau

of the Census, Washington, D.C. 20233 (301) 457-4100, www.census.gov; *Current Business Repots, Annual Benchmark Report for Retail Trade; 1997 Economic Census;* and unpublished data.

LIQUORS AND BEVERAGES - ALCOHOLISM TREATMENT

U.S. Department of Health and Human Services, Substance Abuse and Mental Health Services Administration, 5600 Fishers Lane, Rockville, Maryland 20857 (800) 729-6686, www.samhsa.gov; *Uniform Facility Data Set: Annual Surveys.*

LIQUORS AND BEVERAGES - CONSUMPTION

U.S. Department of Agriculture, Economic Research Service, 1800 M Street, NW, Washington, D.C. 20036 (202) 694-5050, www.ers.usda.gov; *Food Consumption, Prices, and Expenditures;* and *Agricultural Outlook.*

U.S. Department of Health and Human Services, Substance Abuse and Mental Health Services Administration, 5600 Fishers Lane, Rockville, Maryland 20857 (800) 729-6686, www.samhsa.gov; *National Household Survey on Drug Abuse.*

LIQUORS AND BEVERAGES - GOVERNMENT REVENUES

U.S. Department of Commerce, Bureau of the Census, Washington, D.C. 20233 (301) 457-4100, www.census.gov; *Historical Statistics on Governmental Finances and Employment; Government Finances;* and Internet sites: http://census.gov/govs/www/index.html; http://census.gov/ftp/pub/govs/www/state.html; and http://www.census.gov/govs/www/estimate.html.

LIQUORS AND BEVERAGES - STATE LEGISLATION

National Safety Council, 1121 Spring Lake Drive, Itasca, Illinois 60143-3201 (630) 285-1121; *Accident Facts.*

LITERACY PROGRAMS

U.S. Department of Education, National Center for Education Statistics, 555 New Jersey Avenue, NW, Washington, D.C. 20208-5574 (202) 219-1828, http://nces,ed.gov; *Condition of Education, 1998.*

Lithuania - Primary Statistics Source

Lithuanian Department of Statistics, Vilnius, Lithuania; *Lithuania's Statistics Yearbook.*

LITHUANIA - AGRICULTURE

Academic International Press, Box 1111, Gulf Breeze, Florida 32562; *Russia and Eurasia Facts and Figures Annual.*

Business International Moscow, 23 Profsoyuznaya Ulitsa, 117859, Moscow (Telephone Number in U.S. (800) 938-4685); *The CIS Market Atlas.*

Economist Intelligence Unit, 111 West 57th Street, New York, New York 10019 (800) 938-4685; *Lithuania Country Report.*

Euromonitor International, Inc., 122 South Michigan Avenue, Suite 1200, Chicago, Illinois 60603 (800) 577-EURO; *World Marketing Data and Statistics.*

Europa Publications Limited, 18 Bedford Square, London, WC1B 3JN, England; *The Europa World Year Book.*

Food and Agriculture Organization of the United Nations (FAO), Via delle Terme di Caracalla, 00100, Rome, Italy (Telephone Number in U.S. (202) 653-2400); *Production Yearbook; The State of Food and Agriculture;* and *Trade Yearbook.*

St. Martin's Press, Inc., 175 Fifth Avenue, New York, New York 10010 (800) 221-7945; *The Statesman's Year-Book.*

Statistical Office of the United Nations, Publishing Service, New York, New York 10017 (800) 253-9646; *Industrial Commodity Statistics Yearbook;* and *Statistical Yearbook.*

The World Bank, 1818 H Street, NW, Washington, D.C. 20433 (202) 477-1234; *Statistical Handbook: States of the Former USSR;* and *World Development Indicators.*

LITHUANIA - AIRLINE SERVICE

Business International Moscow, 23 Profsoyuznaya Ulitsa, 117859, Moscow (Telephone Number in U.S. (800) 938-4685); *The CIS Market Atlas.*

Europa Publications Limited, 18 Bedford Square, London, WC1B 3JN, England; *The Europa World Year Book.*

International Civil Aviation Organization, 999 University Street, Montreal, Quebec, Canada H3C 5H7 (514) 954-8219; *Civil Aviation Statistics of the World.*

St. Martin's Press, Inc., 175 Fifth Avenue, New York, New York 10010 (800) 221-7945; *The Statesman's Year-Book.*

Statistical Office of the United Nations, Publishing Service, New York, New York 10017 (800) 253-9646; *Statistical Yearbook.*

LITHUANIA - AIRPORTS

Central Intelligence Agency, Washington, D.C. 20505 (703) 482-1100, www.cia.gov; *The World Factbook.*

LITHUANIA - ANIMAL HEALTH

Food and Agriculture Organization of the United Nations (FAO), Via delle Terme di Caracalla, 00100, Rome, Italy (Telephone Number in U.S. (202) 653-2400); *Animal Health Yearbook.*

LITHUANIA - AREA AND DENSITY OF POPULATION

Academic International Press, Box 1111, Gulf Breeze, Florida 32562; *Russia and Eurasia Facts and Figures Annual.*

Business International Moscow, 23 Profsoyuznaya Ulitsa, 117859, Moscow (Telephone Number in U.S. (800) 938-4685); *The CIS Market Atlas.*

Central Intelligence Agency, Washington, D.C. 20505 (703) 482-1100, www.cia.gov; *The World Factbook.*

Euromonitor International, Inc., 122 South Michigan Avenue, Suite 1200, Chicago, Illinois 60603 (800) 577-EURO; *The World Economic Factbook.*

Europa Publications Limited, 18 Bedford Square, London, WC1B 3JN, England; *The Europa World Year Book.*

St. Martin's Press, Inc., 175 Fifth Avenue, New York, New York 10010 (800) 221-7945; *The Statesman's Year-Book.*

Statistical Office of the United Nations, Publishing Service, New York, New York 10017 (800) 253-9646; *Statistical Yearbook.*

United Nations Educational, Scientific and Cultural Organization (UNESCO), 7 Place de Fontenoy, F-75700 Paris, France (Telephone Number in U.S. (212) 963-5981); *Statistical Yearbook.*

The World Bank, 1818 H Street, NW, Washington, D.C. 20433 (202) 477-1234; *World Development Report.*

LITHUANIA - BALANCE OF PAYMENTS

Europa Publications Limited, 18 Bedford Square, London, WC1B 3JN, England; *The Europa World Year Book.*

United Nations Conference on Trade and Development (UNCTAD), New York, New York 10017 (800) 253-9646; *Handbook of International Trade and Development Statistics.*

The World Bank, 1818 H Street, NW, Washington, D.C. 20433 (202) 477-1234;

World Development Report; and *World Development Indicators.*

LITHUANIA - BANKING

Business International Moscow, 23 Profsoyuznaya Ulitsa, 117859, Moscow (Telephone Number in U.S. (800) 938-4685); *The CIS Market Atlas.*

Euromonitor International, Inc., 122 South Michigan Avenue, Suite 1200, Chicago, Illinois 60603 (800) 577-EURO; *World Marketing Data and Statistics.*

St. Martin's Press, Inc., 175 Fifth Avenue, New York, New York 10010 (800) 221-7945; *The Statesman's Year-Book.*

LITHUANIA - BEVERAGES

Statistical Office of the United Nations, Publishing Service, New York, New York 10017 (800) 253-9646; *Statistical Yearbook.*

LITHUANIA - BIRTH RATES

Academic International Press, Box 1111, Gulf Breeze, Florida 32562; *Russia and Eurasia Facts and Figures Annual.*

Business International Moscow, 23 Profsoyuznaya Ulitsa, 117859, Moscow (Telephone Number in U.S. (800) 938-4685); *The CIS Market Atlas.*

Central Intelligence Agency, Washington, D.C. 20505 (703) 482-1100, www.cia.gov; *The World Factbook.*

Euromonitor International, Inc., 122 South Michigan Avenue, Suite 1200, Chicago, Illinois 60603 (800) 577-EURO; *The World Economic Factbook.*

Europa Publications Limited, 18 Bedford Square, London, WC1B 3JN, England; *The Europa World Year Book.*

St. Martin's Press, Inc., 175 Fifth Avenue, New York, New York 10010 (800) 221-7945; *The Statesman's Year-Book.*

Statistical Office of the United Nations, Publishing Service, New York, New York 10017 (800) 253-9646; *Statistical Yearbook.*

World Health Organization, Office of Publications, 20 Avenue Appia, CH-1211 Geneva 27, Switzerland (Telephone Number in U.S. (518) 436-9686); *World Health Statistics Annual.*

LITHUANIA - BOOK PRODUCTION

Europa Publications Limited, 18 Bedford Square, London, WC1B 3JN, England; *The Europa World Year Book.*

United Nations Educational, Scientific and Cultural Organization (UNESCO), 7

Place de Fontenoy, F-75700 Paris, France (Telephone Number in U.S. (212) 963-5981); *Statistical Yearbook.*

LITHUANIA - BROADCASTING

Central Intelligence Agency, Washington, D.C. 20505 (703) 482-1100, www.cia.gov; *The World Factbook.*

Euromonitor International, Inc., 122 South Michigan Avenue, Suite 1200, Chicago, Illinois 60603 (800) 577-EURO; *World Marketing Data and Statistics.*

St. Martin's Press, Inc., 175 Fifth Avenue, New York, New York 10010 (800) 221-7945; *The Statesman's Year-Book.*

United Nations Educational, Scientific and Cultural Organization (UNESCO), 7 Place de Fontenoy, F-75700 Paris, France (Telephone Number in U.S. (212) 963-5981); *Statistical Yearbook.*

LITHUANIA - BUDGET

Business International Moscow, 23 Profsoyuznaya Ulitsa, 117859, Moscow (Telephone Number in U.S. (800) 938-4685); *The CIS Market Atlas.*

Central Intelligence Agency, Washington, D.C. 20505 (703) 482-1100, www.cia.gov; *The World Factbook.*

LITHUANIA - CAPITAL INVESTMENT

The World Bank, 1818 H Street, NW, Washington, D.C. 20433 (202) 477-1234; *Statistical Handbook: States of the Former USSR.*

LITHUANIA - CATTLE - See LITHUANIA - LIVESTOCK AND POULTRY

LITHUANIA - CHEMICALS

Business International Moscow, 23 Profsoyuznaya Ulitsa, 117859, Moscow (Telephone Number in U.S. (800) 938-4685); *The CIS Market Atlas.*

LITHUANIA - COAL PRODUCTION AND CONSUMPTION - See LITHUANIA - MINING AND MINERAL PRODUCTS

LITHUANIA - COMMERCE

St. Martin's Press, Inc., 175 Fifth Avenue, New York, New York 10010 (800) 221-7945; *The Statesman's Year-Book.*

LITHUANIA - COMMUNICATIONS - See LITHUANIA - TRANSPORTATION AND COMMUNICATIONS

LITHUANIA - CONSTRUCTION INDUSTRY

Academic International Press, Box 1111, Gulf Breeze, Florida 32562; *Russia*

and Eurasia Facts and Figures Annual.

Business International Moscow, 23 Profsoyuznaya Ulitsa, 117859, Moscow (Telephone Number in U.S. (800) 938-4685); *The CIS Market Atlas.*

Statistical Office of the United Nations, Publishing Service, New York, New York 10017 (800) 253-9646; *Statistical Yearbook.*

LITHUANIA - CONSUMER PRICE INDEX

Europa Publications Limited, 18 Bedford Square, London, WC1B 3JN, England; *The Europa World Year Book.*

Statistical Office of the United Nations, Publishing Service, New York, New York 10017 (800) 253-9646; *Statistical Yearbook.*

LITHUANIA - CONSUMER PRICES

Euromonitor International, Inc., 122 South Michigan Avenue, Suite 1200, Chicago, Illinois 60603 (800) 577-EURO; *World Marketing Data and Statistics.*

International Labour Office, I.L.O. Publications, 1828 L Street, N.W., Suite 801, Washington, D.C. 20036 (301) 638-3152; *Yearbook of Labor Statistics.*

LITHUANIA - CONSUMER PRODUCTS

Business International Moscow, 23 Profsoyuznaya Ulitsa, 117859, Moscow (Telephone Number in U.S. (800) 938-4685); *The CIS Market Atlas.*

LITHUANIA - CONSUMPTION

Business International Moscow, 23 Profsoyuznaya Ulitsa, 117859, Moscow (Telephone Number in U.S. (800) 938-4685); *The CIS Market Atlas.*

The World Bank, 1818 H Street, NW, Washington, D.C. 20433 (202) 477-1234; *World Development Report;* and *Statistical Handbook: States of the Former USSR.*

LITHUANIA - COTTON PRODUCTION AND CONSUMPTION - See LITHUANIA - CROPS

LITHUANIA - CRIME

Academic International Press, Box 1111, Gulf Breeze, Florida 32562; *Russia and Eurasia Facts and Figures Annual.*

LITHUANIA - CROPS

Academic International Press, Box 1111, Gulf Breeze, Florida 32562; *Russia and Eurasia Facts and Figures Annual.*

Europa Publications Limited, 18 Bedford Square, London, WC1B 3JN, England; *The Europa World Year Book.*

Food and Agriculture Organization of the United Nations (FAO), Via delle Terme di Caracalla, 00100, Rome, Italy (Telephone Number in U.S. (202) 653-2400); *Production Yearbook; The State of Food and Agriculture;* and *Trade Yearbook.*

St. Martin's Press, Inc., 175 Fifth Avenue, New York, New York 10010 (800) 221-7945; *The Statesman's Year-Book.*

Statistical Office of the United Nations, Publishing Service, New York, New York 10017 (800) 253-9646; *Industrial Commodity Statistics Yearbook;* and *Statistical Yearbook.*

The World Bank, 1818 H Street, NW, Washington, D.C. 20433 (202) 477-1234; *Statistical Handbook: States of the Former USSR.*

LITHUANIA - DAIRY PRODUCTS

Europa Publications Limited, 18 Bedford Square, London, WC1B 3JN, England; *The Europa World Year Book.*

Food and Agriculture Organization of the United Nations (FAO), Via delle Terme di Caracalla, 00100, Rome, Italy (Telephone Number in U.S. (202) 653-2400); *Production Yearbook; The State of Food and Agriculture;* and *Trade Yearbook.*

St. Martin's Press, Inc., 175 Fifth Avenue, New York, New York 10010 (800) 221-7945; *The Statesman's Year-Book.*

Statistical Office of the United Nations, Publishing Service, New York, New York 10017 (800) 253-9646; *Industrial Commodity Statistics Yearbook;* and *Statistical Yearbook.*

LITHUANIA - DEATH RATES - See LITHUANIA - MORTALITY

LITHUANIA - DEMOGRAPHY

Business International Moscow, 23 Profsoyuznaya Ulitsa, 117859, Moscow (Telephone Number in U.S. (800) 938-4685); *The CIS Market Atlas.*

The Economist Intelligence Unit, 111 West 57th Street, New York, New York 10019 (800) 938-4685; *The World Market Atlas.*

Euromonitor International, Inc., 122 South Michigan Avenue, Suite 1200, Chicago, Illinois 60603 (800) 577-EURO; *The World Economic Factbook;* and *World Marketing Data and Statistics.*

Statistical Office of the United Nations, Publishing Service, New York, New York 10017 (800) 253-9646; *Demographic Yearbook;* and *Human Development*

Report.

The World Bank, 1818 H Street, NW, Washington, D.C. 20433 (202) 477-1234; *Statistical Handbook: States of the Former USSR.*

LITHUANIA - DISEASES - See LITHUANIA - HEALTH

LITHUANIA - DIVORCE RATES

Academic International Press, Box 1111, Gulf Breeze, Florida 32562; *Russia and Eurasia Facts and Figures Annual.*

Statistical Office of the United Nations, Publishing Service, New York, New York 10017 (800) 253-9646; *Demographic Yearbook;* and *Statistical Yearbook.*

LITHUANIA - DOMESTIC INVESTMENT

Business International Moscow, 23 Profsoyuznaya Ulitsa, 117859, Moscow (Telephone Number in U.S. (800) 938-4685); *The CIS Market Atlas.*

LITHUANIA - ECONOMY

Academic International Press, Box 1111, Gulf Breeze, Florida 32562; *Russia and Eurasia Facts and Figures Annual.*

Business International Moscow, 23 Profsoyuznaya Ulitsa, 117859, Moscow (Telephone Number in U.S. (800) 938-4685); *The CIS Market Atlas.*

Central Intelligence Agency, Washington, D.C. 20505 (703) 482-1100, www.cia.gov; *The World Factbook.*

Economist Intelligence Unit, 111 West 57th Street, New York, New York 10019 (800) 938-4685; *Lithuania Country Report.*

Euromonitor International, Inc., 122 South Michigan Avenue, Suite 1200, Chicago, Illinois 60603 (800) 577-EURO; *The World Economic Factbook;* and *World Marketing Data and Statistics.*

St. Martin's Press, Inc., 175 Fifth Avenue, New York, New York 10010 (800) 221-7945; *The Statesman's Year-Book.*

Statistical Office of the United Nations, Publishing Service, New York, New York 10017 (800) 253-9646; *World Statistics Pocketbook.*

The World Bank, 1818 H Street, NW, Washington, D.C. 20433 (202) 477-1234; *The World Bank Atlas; and World Development Report.*

LITHUANIA - EDUCATION

Academic International Press, Box 1111, Gulf Breeze, Florida 32562; *Russia*

and Eurasia Facts and Figures Annual.

Business International Moscow, 23 Profsoyuznaya Ulitsa, 117859, Moscow (Telephone Number in U.S. (800) 938-4685); *The CIS Market Atlas.*

The Economist Intelligence Unit, 111 West 57th Street, New York, New York 10019 (800) 938-4685; *The World Market Atlas.*

Euromonitor International, Inc., 122 South Michigan Avenue, Suite 1200, Chicago, Illinois 60603 (800) 577-EURO; *World Marketing Data and Statistics.*

Europa Publications Limited, 18 Bedford Square, London, WC1B 3JN, England; *The Europa World Year Book.*

International Labour Office, I.L.O. Publications, 1828 L Street, N.W., Suite 801, Washington, D.C. 20036 (301) 638-3152; *Yearbook of Labor Statistics.*

St. Martin's Press, Inc., 175 Fifth Avenue, New York, New York 10010 (800) 221-7945; *The Statesman's Year-Book.*

Statistical Office of the United Nations, Publishing Service, New York, New York 10017 (800) 253-9646; *Human Development Report.*

The World Bank, 1818 H Street, NW, Washington, D.C. 20433 (202) 477-1234; *World Development Report.*

LITHUANIA - ELECTRICITY

Academic International Press, Box 1111, Gulf Breeze, Florida 32562; *Russia and Eurasia Facts and Figures Annual.*

Business International Moscow, 23 Profsoyuznaya Ulitsa, 117859, Moscow (Telephone Number in U.S. (800) 938-4685); *The CIS Market Atlas.*

Central Intelligence Agency, Washington, D.C. 20505 (703) 482-1100, www.cia.gov; *The World Factbook.*

St. Martin's Press, Inc., 175 Fifth Avenue, New York, New York 10010 (800) 221-7945; *The Statesman's Year-Book.*

Statistical Office of the United Nations, Publishing Service, New York, New York 10017 (800) 253-9646; *Energy Statistics Yearbook; Human Development Report; and Statistical Yearbook.*

The World Bank, 1818 H Street, NW, Washington, D.C. 20433 (202) 477-1234; *Statistical Handbook: States of the Former USSR.*

LITHUANIA - EMPLOYMENT

International Labour Office, I.L.O. Publications, 1828 L Street, N.W., Suite 801, Washington, D.C. 20036 (301) 638-3152; *Yearbook of Labor Statistics.*

Statistical Office of the United Nations, Publishing Service, New York, New York 10017 (800) 253-9646; *Statistical Yearbook.*

The World Bank, 1818 H Street, NW, Washington, D.C. 20433 (202) 477-1234; *Statistical Handbook: States of the Former USSR.*

LITHUANIA - ENERGY

Academic International Press, Box 1111, Gulf Breeze, Florida 32562; *Russia and Eurasia Facts and Figures Annual.*

Business International Moscow, 23 Profsoyuznaya Ulitsa, 117859, Moscow (Telephone Number in U.S. (800) 938-4685); *The CIS Market Atlas.*

Euromonitor International, Inc., 122 South Michigan Avenue, Suite 1200, Chicago, Illinois 60603 (800) 577-EURO; *The World Economic Factbook; and World Marketing Data and Statistics.*

St. Martin's Press, Inc., 175 Fifth Avenue, New York, New York 10010 (800) 221-7945; *The Statesman's Year-Book.*

Statistical Office of the United Nations, Publishing Service, New York, New York 10017 (800) 253-9646; *Energy Statistics Yearbook; Human Development Report; World Statistics Pocketbook; and Statistical Yearbook.*

The World Bank, 1818 H Street, NW, Washington, D.C. 20433 (202) 477-1234; *The World Bank Atlas; World Development Report; and Statistical Handbook: States of the Former USSR.*

LITHUANIA - ENVIRONMENT

Business International Moscow, 23 Profsoyuznaya Ulitsa, 117859, Moscow (Telephone Number in U.S. (800) 938-4685); *The CIS Market Atlas.*

Economist Intelligence Unit, 111 West 57th Street, New York, New York 10019 (800) 938-4685; *Lithuania Country Report.*

Statistical Office of the United Nations, Publishing Service, New York, New York 10017 (800) 253-9646; *Statistical Yearbook; and World Statistics Pocketbook.*

LITHUANIA - EXCHANGE RATES

Central Intelligence Agency, Washington, D.C. 20505 (703) 482-1100, www.cia.gov; *The World Factbook.*

Euromonitor International, Inc., 122

South Michigan Avenue, Suite 1200, Chicago, Illinois 60603 (800) 577-EURO; *The World Economic Factbook.*

Europa Publications Limited, 18 Bedford Square, London, WC1B 3JN, England; *The Europa World Year Book.*

Statistical Office of the United Nations, Publishing Service, New York, New York 10017 (800) 253-9646; *Statistical Yearbook;* and *World Statistics Pocketbook.*

LITHUANIA - EXPORTS

Academic International Press, Box 1111, Gulf Breeze, Florida 32562; *Russia and Eurasia Facts and Figures Annual.*

Business International Moscow, 23 Profsoyuznaya Ulitsa, 117859, Moscow (Telephone Number in U.S. (800) 938-4685); *The CIS Market Atlas.*

Central Intelligence Agency, Washington, D.C. 20505 (703) 482-1100, www.cia.gov; *The World Factbook.*

The Economist Intelligence Unit, 111 West 57th Street, New York, New York 10019 (800) 938-4685; *Lithuania Country Report;* and *The World Market Atlas.*

Euromonitor International, Inc., 122 South Michigan Avenue, Suite 1200, Chicago, Illinois 60603 (800) 577-EURO; *The World Economic Factbook.*

Europa Publications Limited, 18 Bedford Square, London, WC1B 3JN, England; *The Europa World Year Book.*

International Monetary Fund, 700 Nineteenth Street, NW, Washington, D.C. 20431 (202) 623-7000; *Direction of Trade Statistics.*

St. Martin's Press, Inc., 175 Fifth Avenue, New York, New York 10010 (800) 221-7945; *The Statesman's Year-Book.*

Statistical Office of the United Nations, Publishing Service, New York, New York 10017 (800) 253-9646; *International Trade Statistics Yearbook.*

United Nations Conference on Trade and Development (UNCTAD), New York, New York 10017 (800) 253-9646; *Handbook of International Trade and Development Statistics.*

The World Bank, 1818 H Street, NW, Washington, D.C. 20433 - (202) 477-1234; *World Development Report; Statistical Handbook: States of the Former USSR;* and *World Development Indicators.*

LITHUANIA - EXTERNAL DEBT

The World Bank, 1818 H Street, NW,

Washington, D.C. 20433 (202) 477-1234; *World Development Indicators.*

LITHUANIA - EXTERNAL INDEBTEDNESS

The World Bank, 1818 H Street, NW, Washington, D.C. 20433 (202) 477-1234; *World Development Report.*

LITHUANIA - EXTERNAL TRADE

Academic International Press, Box 1111, Gulf Breeze, Florida 32562; *Russia and Eurasia Facts and Figures Annual.*

Euromonitor International, Inc., 122 South Michigan Avenue, Suite 1200, Chicago, Illinois 60603 (800) 577-EURO; *World Marketing Data and Statistics.*

Food and Agriculture Organization of the United Nations (FAO), Via delle Terme di Caracalla, 00100, Rome, Italy (Telephone Number in U.S. (202) 653-2400); *Trade Yearbook.*

Statistical Office of the United Nations, Publishing Service, New York, New York 10017 (800) 253-9646; *Statistical Yearbook.*

The World Bank, 1818 H Street, NW, Washington, D.C. 20433 (202) 477-1234; *Statistical Handbook: States of the Former USSR.*

LITHUANIA - FABRIC PRODUCTION AND CONSUMPTION - See LITHUANIA - TEXTILE INDUSTRY

LITHUANIA - FERTILITY RATES

Central Intelligence Agency, Washington, D.C. 20505 (703) 482-1100, www.cia.gov; *The World Factbook.*

Statistical Office of the United Nations, Publishing Service, New York, New York 10017 (800) 253-9646; *Human Development Report.*

The World Bank, 1818 H Street, NW, Washington, D.C. 20433 (202) 477-1234; *The World Bank Atlas; World Development Report; Statistical Handbook: States of the Former USSR;* and *World Development Indicators.*

World Health Organization, Office of Publications, 20 Avenue Appia, CH-1211 Geneva 27, Switzerland (Telephone Number in U.S. (518) 436-9686); *World Health Statistics Annual.*

LITHUANIA - FERTILIZER

Food and Agriculture Organization of the United Nations (FAO), Via delle Terme di Caracalla, 00100, Rome, Italy (Telephone Number in U.S. (202) 653-2400); *Fertilizer Yearbook.*

Statistical Office of the United Nations, Publishing Service, New York, New York 10017 (800) 253-9646; *Industrial Commodity Statistics Yearbook;* and *Statistical Yearbook.*

LITHUANIA - FINANCE

Economist Intelligence Unit, 111 West 57th Street, New York, New York 10019 (800) 938-4685; *Lithuania Country Report.*

Europa Publications Limited, 18 Bedford Square, London, WC1B 3JN, England; *The Europa World Year Book.*

St. Martin's Press, Inc., 175 Fifth Avenue, New York, New York 10010 (800) 221-7945; *The Statesman's Year-Book.*

The World Bank, 1818 H Street, NW, Washington, D.C. 20433 (202) 477-1234; *Statistical Handbook: States of the Former USSR.*

LITHUANIA - FISHERIES

Europa Publications Limited, 18 Bedford Square, London, WC1B 3JN, England; *The Europa World Year Book.*

Food and Agriculture Organization of the United Nations (FAO), Via delle Terme di Caracalla, 00100, Rome, Italy (Telephone Number in U.S. (202) 653-2400); *The State of Food and Agriculture;* and *Yearbook of Fishery Statistics.*

St. Martin's Press, Inc., 175 Fifth Avenue, New York, New York 10010 (800) 221-7945; *The Statesman's Year-Book.*

Statistical Office of the United Nations, Publishing Service, New York, New York 10017 (800) 253-9646; *Industrial Commodity Statistics Yearbook;* and *Statistical Yearbook.*

LITHUANIA - FOOD

Food and Agriculture Organization of the United Nations (FAO), Via delle Terme di Caracalla, 00100, Rome, Italy (Telephone Number in U.S. (202) 653-2400); *Production Yearbook; The State of Food and Agriculture;* and *Trade Yearbook.*

Statistical Office of the United Nations, Publishing Service, New York, New York 10017 (800) 253-9646; *Human Development Report;* and *Industrial Commodity Statistics Yearbook.*

LITHUANIA - FOOTWEAR PRODUCTION AND CONSUMPTION - See LITHUANIA - TEXTILE INDUSTRY

LITHUANIA - FOREIGN DEBT

St. Martin's Press, Inc., 175 Fifth Avenue, New York, New York 10010 (800)

221-7945; *The Statesman's Year-Book.*

LITHUANIA - FOREIGN INVESTMENT

Business International Moscow, 23 Profsoyuznaya Ulitsa, 117859, Moscow (Telephone Number in U.S. (800) 938-4685); *The CIS Market Atlas.*

LITHUANIA - FOREIGN TRADE

Business International Moscow, 23 Profsoyuznaya Ulitsa, 117859, Moscow (Telephone Number in U.S. (800) 938-4685); *The CIS Market Atlas.*

Economist Intelligence Unit, 111 West 57th Street, New York, New York 10019 (800) 938-4685; *Lithuania Country Report.*

Euromonitor International, Inc., 122 South Michigan Avenue, Suite 1200, Chicago, Illinois 60603 (800) 577-EURO; *The World Economic Factbook.*

Europa Publications Limited, 18 Bedford Square, London, WC1B 3JN, England; *The Europa World Year Book.*

Food and Agriculture Organization of the United Nations (FAO), Via delle Terme di Caracalla, 00100, Rome, Italy (Telephone Number in U.S. (202) 653-2400); *Trade Yearbook.*

International Monetary Fund, 700 Nineteenth Street, NW, Washington, D.C. 20431 (202) 623-7000; *Direction of Trade Statistics.*

St. Martin's Press, Inc., 175 Fifth Avenue, New York, New York 10010 (800) 221-7945; *The Statesman's Year-Book.*

Statistical Office of the United Nations, Publishing Service, New York, New York 10017 (800) 253-9646; *International Trade Statistics Yearbook;* and *Statistical Yearbook.*

The World Bank, 1818 H Street, NW, Washington, D.C. 20433 (202) 477-1234; *World Development Report; Statistical Handbook: States of the Former USSR;* and *World Development Indicators.*

LITHUANIA - FORESTRY AND FOREST PRODUCTS

Academic International Press, Box 1111, Gulf Breeze, Florida 32562; *Russia and Eurasia Facts and Figures Annual.*

Business International Moscow, 23 Profsoyuznaya Ulitsa, 117859, Moscow (Telephone Number in U.S. (800) 938-4685); *The CIS Market Atlas.*

Europa Publications Limited, 18 Bedford Square, London, WC1B 3JN, England; *The Europa World Year Book.*

Food and Agriculture Organization of the United Nations (FAO), Via delle Terme di Caracalla, 00100, Rome, Italy (Telephone Number in U.S. (202) 653-2400); *The State of Food and Agriculture;* and *Yearbook of Forest Products.*

International Labour Office, I.L.O. Publications, 1828 L Street, N.W., Suite 801, Washington, D.C. 20036 (301) 638-3152; *Yearbook of Labor Statistics.*

St. Martin's Press, Inc., 175 Fifth Avenue, New York, New York 10010 (800) 221-7945; *The Statesman's Year-Book.*

Statistical Office of the United Nations, Publishing Service, New York, New York 10017 (800) 253-9646; *Industrial Commodity Statistics Yearbook;* and *Statistical Yearbook.*

The World Bank, 1818 H Street, NW, Washington, D.C. 20433 (202) 477-1234; *World Development Report.*

LITHUANIA - GOATS - See LITHUANIA - LIVESTOCK AND POULTRY

LITHUANIA - GOVERNMENT

Academic International Press, Box 1111, Gulf Breeze, Florida 32562; *Russia and Eurasia Facts and Figures Annual.*

Central Intelligence Agency, Washington, D.C. 20505 (703) 482-1100, www.cia.gov; *The World Factbook.*

Europa Publications Limited, 18 Bedford Square, London, WC1B 3JN, England; *The Europa World Year Book.*

St. Martin's Press, Inc., 175 Fifth Avenue, New York, New York 10010 (800) 221-7945; *The Statesman's Year-Book.*

Statistical Office of the United Nations, Publishing Service, New York, New York 10017 (800) 253-9646; *National Accounts Statistics;* and *Statistical Yearbook.*

The World Bank, 1818 H Street, NW, Washington, D.C. 20433 (202) 477-1234; *World Development Report;* and *Statistical Handbook: States of the Former USSR.*

LITHUANIA - GROSS DOMESTIC PRODUCT

Academic International Press, Box 1111, Gulf Breeze, Florida 32562; *Russia and Eurasia Facts and Figures Annual.*

The Economist Intelligence Unit, 111 West 57th Street, New York, New York 10019 (800) 938-4685; *Lithuania Country Report;* and *The World Market Atlas.*

Euromonitor International, Inc., 122 South Michigan Avenue, Suite 1200, Chicago, Illinois 60603 (800) 577-EURO;

The World Economic Factbook.

Europa Publications Limited, 18 Bedford Square, London, WC1B 3JN, England; *The Europa World Year Book.*

Statistical Office of the United Nations, Publishing Service, New York, New York 10017 (800) 253-9646; *Human Development Report; National Accounts Statistics;* and *Statistical Yearbook.*

The World Bank, 1818 H Street, NW, Washington, D.C. 20433 (202) 477-1234; *World Development Report;* and *Statistical Handbook: States of the Former USSR;* and *World Development Indicators.*

LITHUANIA - GROSS NATIONAL PRODUCT

St. Martin's Press, Inc., 175 Fifth Avenue, New York, New York 10010 (800) 221-7945; *The Statesman's Year-Book.*

The World Bank, 1818 H Street, NW, Washington, D.C. 20433 (202) 477-1234; *The World Bank Atlas; World Development Report;* and *World Development Indicators.*

LITHUANIA - HEALTH

Academic International Press, Box 1111, Gulf Breeze, Florida 32562; *Russia and Eurasia Facts and Figures Annual.*

Business International Moscow, 23 Profsoyuznaya Ulitsa, 117859, Moscow (Telephone Number in U.S. (800) 938-4685); *The CIS Market Atlas.*

Euromonitor International, Inc., 122 South Michigan Avenue, Suite 1200, Chicago, Illinois 60603 (800) 577-EURO; *World Marketing Data and Statistics.*

St. Martin's Press, Inc., 175 Fifth Avenue, New York, New York 10010 (800) 221-7945; *The Statesman's Year-Book.*

Statistical Office of the United Nations, Publishing Service, New York, New York 10017 (800) 253-9646; *Human Development Report;* and *Statistical Yearbook.*

United Nations Children's Fund (UNICEF), 3 United Nations Plaza, New York, New York 10017 (800) 253-9646; *State of the World's Children.*

The World Bank, 1818 H Street, NW, Washington, D.C. 20433 (202) 477-1234; *World Development Report.*

World Health Organization, Office of Publications, 20 Avenue Appia, CH-1211 Geneva 27, Switzerland (Telephone Number in U.S. (518) 436-9686); *World Health Statistics Annual.*

LITHUANIA - HIGHWAYS

Academic International Press, Box 1111, Gulf Breeze, Florida 32562; *Russia and Eurasia Facts and Figures Annual.*

Business International Moscow, 23 Profsoyuznaya Ulitsa, 117859, Moscow (Telephone Number in U.S. (800) 938-4685); *The CIS Market Atlas.*

Central Intelligence Agency, Washington, D.C. 20505 (703) 482-1100, www.cia.gov; *The World Factbook.*

St. Martin's Press, Inc., 175 Fifth Avenue, New York, New York 10010 (800) 221-7945; *The Statesman's Year-Book.*

Statistical Office of the United Nations, Publishing Service, New York, New York 10017 (800) 253-9646; *Annual Bulletin of Transport Statistics for Europe.*

LITHUANIA - HOUSING AND HOUSING UNITS

Business International Moscow, 23 Profsoyuznaya Ulitsa, 117859, Moscow (Telephone Number in U.S. (800) 938-4685); *The CIS Market Atlas.*

Euromonitor International, Inc., 122 South Michigan Avenue, Suite 1200, Chicago, Illinois 60603 (800) 577-EURO; *World Marketing Data and Statistics.*

LITHUANIA - ILLITERATE POPULATION

Central Intelligence Agency, Washington, D.C. 20505 (703) 482-1100, www.cia.gov; *The World Factbook.*

The Economist Intelligence Unit, 111 West 57th Street, New York, New York 10019 (800) 938-4685; *The World Market Atlas.*

Euromonitor International, Inc., 122 South Michigan Avenue, Suite 1200, Chicago, Illinois 60603 (800) 577-EURO; *The World Economic Factbook.*

International Labour Office, I.L.O. Publications, 1828 L Street, N.W., Suite 801, Washington, D.C. 20036 (301) 638-3152; *Yearbook of Labor Statistics.*

Statistical Office of the United Nations, Publishing Service, New York, New York 10017 (800) 253-9646; *Human Development Report.*

LITHUANIA - IMPORTS

Academic International Press, Box 1111, Gulf Breeze, Florida 32562; *Russia and Eurasia Facts and Figures Annual.*

Business International Moscow, 23 Profsoyuznaya Ulitsa, 117859, Moscow (Telephone Number in U.S. (800) 938-4685); *The CIS Market Atlas.*

Central Intelligence Agency, Washington, D.C. 20505 (703) 482-1100, www.cia.gov; *The World Factbook.*

The Economist Intelligence Unit, 111 West 57th Street, New York, New York 10019 (800) 938-4685; *Lithuania Country Report;* and *The World Market Atlas.*

Euromonitor International, Inc., 122 South Michigan Avenue, Suite 1200, Chicago, Illinois 60603 (800) 577-EURO; *The World Economic Factbook.*

Europa Publications Limited, 18 Bedford Square, London, WC1B 3JN, England; *The Europa World Year Book.*

International Monetary Fund, 700 Nineteenth Street, NW, Washington, D.C. 20431 (202) 623-7000; *Direction of Trade Statistics.*

St. Martin's Press, Inc., 175 Fifth Avenue, New York, New York 10010 (800) 221-7945; *The Statesman's Year-Book.*

Statistical Office of the United Nations, Publishing Service, New York, New York 10017 (800) 253-9646; *International Trade Statistics Yearbook.*

United Nations Conference on Trade and Development (UNCTAD), New York, New York 10017 (800) 253-9646; *Handbook of International Trade and Development Statistics.*

The World Bank, 1818 H Street, NW, Washington, D.C. 20433 (202) 477-1234; *World Development Report; Statistical Handbook: States of the Former USSR;* and *World Development Indicators.*

LITHUANIA - INDUSTRY

Academic International Press, Box 1111, Gulf Breeze, Florida 32562; *Russia and Eurasia Facts and Figures Annual.*

Business International Moscow, 23 Profsoyuznaya Ulitsa, 117859, Moscow (Telephone Number in U.S. (800) 938-4685); *The CIS Market Atlas.*

Central Intelligence Agency, Washington, D.C. 20505 (703) 482-1100, www.cia.gov; *The World Factbook.*

Economist Intelligence Unit, 111 West 57th Street, New York, New York 10019 (800) 938-4685; *Lithuania Country Report.*

Euromonitor International, Inc., 122 South Michigan Avenue, Suite 1200, Chicago, Illinois 60603 (800) 577-EURO; *The World Economic Factbook;* and *World Marketing Data and Statistics.*

Europa Publications Limited, 18 Bedford Square, London, WC1B 3JN, England; *The Europa World Year Book.*

International Labour Office, I.L.O. Publications, 1828 L Street, N.W., Suite 801, Washington, D.C. 20036 (301) 638-3152; *Yearbook of Labor Statistics.*

St. Martin's Press, Inc., 175 Fifth Avenue, New York, New York 10010 (800) 221-7945; *The Statesman's Year-Book.*

Statistical Office of the United Nations, Publishing Service, New York, New York 10017 (800) 253-9646; *Industrial Commodity Statistics Yearbook;* and *Statistical Yearbook.*

The World Bank, 1818 H Street, NW, Washington, D.C. 20433 (202) 477-1234; *Statistical Handbook: States of the Former USSR;* and *World Development Indicators.*

World Intellectual Property Organization, 34 Chemin des Colombettes, CH-1211 Geneva 20, Switzerland; *Industrial Property Statistics.*

LITHUANIA - INFANT MORTALITY RATES - See LITHUANIA - MORTALITY

LITHUANIA - INTERNAL TRADE

Statistical Office of the United Nations, Publishing Service, New York, New York 10017 (800) 253-9646; *Statistical Yearbook.*

LITHUANIA - LABOR

Academic International Press, Box 1111, Gulf Breeze, Florida 32562; *Russia and Eurasia Facts and Figures Annual.*

Business International Moscow, 23 Profsoyuznaya Ulitsa, 117859, Moscow (Telephone Number in U.S. (800) 938-4685); *The CIS Market Atlas.*

Central Intelligence Agency, Washington, D.C. 20505 (703) 482-1100, www.cia.gov; *The World Factbook.*

Euromonitor International, Inc., 122 South Michigan Avenue, Suite 1200, Chicago, Illinois 60603 (800) 577-EURO; *World Marketing Data and Statistics.*

Europa Publications Limited, 18 Bedford Square, London, WC1B 3JN, England; *The Europa World Year Book.*

International Labour Office, I.L.O. Publications, 1828 L Street, N.W., Suite 801, Washington, D.C. 20036 (301) 638-3152; *Yearbook of Labor Statistics.*

St. Martin's Press, Inc., 175 Fifth Avenue, New York, New York 10010 (800) 221-7945; *The Statesman's Year-Book.*

Statistical Office of the United Nations, Publishing Service, New York, New York 10017 (800) 253-9646; *Human Development Report;* and *Statistical Yearbook.*

The World Bank, 1818 H Street, NW, Washington, D.C. 20433 (202) 477-1234; *The World Bank Atlas; World Development Report; Statistical Handbook: States of the Former USSR;* and *World Development Indicators.*

LITHUANIA - LAND USE

Central Intelligence Agency, Washington, D.C. 20505 (703) 482-1100, www.cia.gov; *The World Factbook.*

Food and Agriculture Organization of the United Nations (FAO), Via delle Terme di Caracalla, 00100, Rome, Italy (Telephone Number in U.S. (202) 653-2400); *Production Yearbook.*

The World Bank, 1818 H Street, NW, Washington, D.C. 20433 (202) 477-1234; *World Development Report.*

LITHUANIA - LIBRARIES

International Labour Office, I.L.O. Publications, 1828 L Street, N.W., Suite 801, Washington, D.C. 20036 (301) 638-3152; *Yearbook of Labor Statistics.*

LITHUANIA - LIFE EXPECTANCY

Academic International Press, Box 1111, Gulf Breeze, Florida 32562; *Russia and Eurasia Facts and Figures Annual.*

Business International Moscow, 23 Profsoyuznaya Ulitsa, 117859, Moscow (Telephone Number in U.S. (800) 938-4685); *The CIS Market Atlas.*

Central Intelligence Agency, Washington, D.C. 20505 (703) 482-1100, www.cia.gov; *The World Factbook.*

Euromonitor International, Inc., 122 South Michigan Avenue, Suite 1200, Chicago, Illinois 60603 (800) 577-EURO; *The World Economic Factbook.*

St. Martin's Press, Inc., 175 Fifth Avenue, New York, New York 10010 (800) 221-7945; *The Statesman's Year-Book.*

Statistical Office of the United Nations, Publishing Service, New York, New York 10017 (800) 253-9646; *Demographic Yearbook; World Statistics Pocketbook;* and *Human Development Report.*

The World Bank, 1818 H Street, NW, Washington, D.C. 20433 (202) 477-1234; *The World Bank Atlas; World Development Report;* and *World Development Indicators.*

World Health Organization, Office of Publications, 20 Avenue Appia, CH-1211 Geneva 27, Switzerland (Telephone Number in U.S. (518) 436-9686); *World Health Statistics Annual.*

LITHUANIA - LITERACY RATE

Euromonitor International, Inc., 122 South Michigan Avenue, Suite 1200, Chicago, Illinois 60603 (800) 577-EURO; *World Marketing Data and Statistics.*

LITHUANIA - LIVESTOCK AND POULTRY

Academic International Press, Box 1111, Gulf Breeze, Florida 32562; *Russia and Eurasia Facts and Figures Annual.*

Business International Moscow, 23 Profsoyuznaya Ulitsa, 117859, Moscow (Telephone Number in U.S. (800) 938-4685); *The CIS Market Atlas.*

Europa Publications Limited, 18 Bedford Square, London, WC1B 3JN, England; *The Europa World Year Book.*

Food and Agriculture Organization of the United Nations (FAO), Via delle Terme di Caracalla, 00100, Rome, Italy (Telephone Number in U.S. (202) 653-2400); *Production Yearbook; The State of Food and Agriculture;* and *Trade Yearbook.*

St. Martin's Press, Inc., 175 Fifth Avenue, New York, New York 10010 (800) 221-7945; *The Statesman's Year-Book.*

Statistical Office of the United Nations, Publishing Service, New York, New York 10017 (800) 253-9646; *Industrial Commodity Statistics Yearbook;* and *Statistical Yearbook.*

LITHUANIA - MACHINERY

Statistical Office of the United Nations, Publishing Service, New York, New York 10017 (800) 253-9646; *Industrial Commodity Statistics Yearbook.*

LITHUANIA - MAIL - NUMBER OF PIECES SENT OR RECEIVED

Statistical Office of the United Nations, Publishing Service, New York, New York 10017 (800) 253-9646; *Statistical Yearbook.*

LITHUANIA - MANUFACTURING

Statistical Office of the United Nations, Publishing Service, New York, New York 10017 (800) 253-9646; *Industrial Commodity Statistics Yearbook;* and *Statistical Yearbook.*

The World Bank, 1818 H Street, NW, Washington, D.C. 20433 (202) 477-1234; *World Development Indicators.*

LITHUANIA - MARRIAGE RATES

Academic International Press, Box 1111, Gulf Breeze, Florida 32562; *Russia and Eurasia Facts and Figures Annual.*

Europa Publications Limited, 18 Bedford Square, London, WC1B 3JN, England; *The Europa World Year Book.*

Statistical Office of the United Nations, Publishing Service, New York, New York 10017 (800) 253-9646; *Demographic Yearbook;* and *Statistical Yearbook.*

LITHUANIA - MEAT PRODUCTION - See LITHUANIA - LIVESTOCK AND POULTRY

LITHUANIA - MERCHANT SHIPPING

Europa Publications Limited, 18 Bedford Square, London, WC1B 3JN, England; *The Europa World Year Book.*

Statistical Office of the United Nations, Publishing Service, New York, New York 10017 (800) 253-9646; *Annual Bulletin of Transport Statistics for Europe;* and *Statistical Yearbook.*

LITHUANIA - MILITARY

Academic International Press, Box 1111, Gulf Breeze, Florida 32562; *Russia and Eurasia Facts and Figures Annual.*

Central Intelligence Agency, Washington, D.C. 20505 (703) 482-1100, www.cia.gov; *The World Factbook.*

Euromonitor International, Inc., 122 South Michigan Avenue, Suite 1200, Chicago, Illinois 60603 (800) 577-EURO; *World Marketing Data and Statistics.*

The International Institute for Strategic Studies, 23 Tavistock Street, London WC2E 7NQ, England 44 171 3797676; *The Military Balance.*

St. Martin's Press, Inc., 175 Fifth Avenue, New York, New York 10010 (800) 221-7945; *The Statesman's Year-Book.*

Statistical Office of the United Nations, Publishing Service, New York, New York 10017 (800) 253-9646; *Human Development Report.*

LITHUANIA - MINING AND MINERAL PRODUCTS

Academic International Press, Box 1111, Gulf Breeze, Florida 32562; *Russia and Eurasia Facts and Figures Annual.*

Business International Moscow, 23 Profsoyuznaya Ulitsa, 117859, Moscow (Telephone Number in U.S. (800) 938-4685); *The CIS Market Atlas.*

Europa Publications Limited, 18 Bedford Square, London, WC1B 3JN, England; *The Europa World Year Book.*

St. Martin's Press, Inc., 175 Fifth Avenue, New York, New York 10010 (800) 221-7945; *The Statesman's Year-Book.*

Statistical Office of the United Nations, Publishing Service, New York, New York 10017 (800) 253-9646; *Energy Statistics Yearbook; Industrial Commodity Statistics Yearbook;* and *Statistical Yearbook.*

LITHUANIA - MONEY SUPPLY

Economist Intelligence Unit, 111 West 57th Street, New York, New York 10019 (800) 938-4685; *Lithuania Country Report.*

Europa Publications Limited, 18 Bedford Square, London, WC1B 3JN, England; *The Europa World Year Book.*

LITHUANIA - MONUMENTS AND HISTORICAL SITES

United Nations Educational, Scientific and Cultural Organization (UNESCO), 7 Place de Fontenoy, F-75700 Paris, France (Telephone Number in U.S. (212) 963-5981); *Statistical Yearbook.*

LITHUANIA - MORTALITY

Academic International Press, Box 1111, Gulf Breeze, Florida 32562; *Russia and Eurasia Facts and Figures Annual.*

Business International Moscow, 23 Profsoyuznaya Ulitsa, 117859, Moscow (Telephone Number in U.S. (800) 938-4685); *The CIS Market Atlas.*

Central Intelligence Agency, Washington, D.C. 20505 (703) 482-1100, www.cia.gov; *The World Factbook.*

Euromonitor International, Inc., 122 South Michigan Avenue, Suite 1200, Chicago, Illinois 60603 (800) 577-EURO; *The World Economic Factbook.*

Europa Publications Limited, 18 Bedford Square, London, WC1B 3JN, England; *The Europa World Year Book.*

St. Martin's Press, Inc., 175 Fifth Avenue, New York, New York 10010 (800) 221-7945; *The Statesman's Year-Book.*

Statistical Office of the United Nations, Publishing Service, New York, New York 10017 (800) 253-9646; *Demographic Yearbook; Human Development Report; World Statistics Pocketbook;* and *Statistical Yearbook.*

United Nations Children's Fund (UNICEF), 3 United Nations Plaza, New York, New York 10017 (800) 253-9646; *State of the World's Children.*

The World Bank, 1818 H Street, NW, Washington, D.C. 20433 (202) 477-1234; *The World Bank Atlas; World Development Report;* and *World Development Indicators.*

World Health Organization, Office of Publications, 20 Avenue Appia, CH-1211 Geneva 27, Switzerland (Telephone Number in U.S. (518) 436-9686); *World Health Statistics Annual.*

LITHUANIA - MOTION PICTURES

International Labour Office, I.L.O. Publications, 1828 L Street, N.W., Suite 801, Washington, D.C. 20036 (301) 638-3152; *Yearbook of Labor Statistics.*

Statistical Office of the United Nations, Publishing Service, New York, New York 10017 (800) 253-9646; *Statistical Yearbook.*

United Nations Educational, Scientific and Cultural Organization (UNESCO), 7 Place de Fontenoy, F-75700 Paris, France (Telephone Number in U.S. (212) 963-5981); *Statistical Yearbook.*

LITHUANIA - MOTOR VEHICLE PRODUCTION

Europa Publications Limited, 18 Bedford Square, London, WC1B 3JN, England; *The Europa World Year Book.*

Statistical Office of the United Nations, Publishing Service, New York, New York 10017 (800) 253-9646; *Statistical Yearbook.*

LITHUANIA - MOTOR VEHICLES

Business International Moscow, 23 Profsoyuznaya Ulitsa, 117859, Moscow (Telephone Number in U.S. (800) 938-4685); *The CIS Market Atlas.*

LITHUANIA - NATIONAL ACCOUNTS

Europa Publications Limited, 18 Bedford Square, London, WC1B 3JN, England; *The Europa World Year Book.*

Statistical Office of the United Nations, Publishing Service, New York, New York 10017 (800) 253-9646; *National Accounts Statistics;* and *Statistical Yearbook.*

The World Bank, 1818 H Street, NW, Washington, D.C. 20433 (202) 477-1234; *Statistical Handbook: States of the Former USSR.*

LITHUANIA - NATIONAL INCOME

Business International Moscow, 23 Profsoyuznaya Ulitsa, 117859, Moscow (Telephone Number in U.S. (800) 938-4685); *The CIS Market Atlas.*

Statistical Office of the United Nations, Publishing Service, New York, New York 10017 (800) 253-9646; *National Accounts Statistics;* and *Statistical Yearbook.*

LITHUANIA - NATIONAL PRODUCT

Statistical Office of the United Nations, Publishing Service, New York, New York 10017 (800) 253-9646; *Statistical Yearbook.*

LITHUANIA - PATENTS, TRADEMARKS AND SERVICE MARKS

Statistical Office of the United Nations, Publishing Service, New York, New York 10017 (800) 253-9646; *Statistical Yearbook.*

World Intellectual Property Organization, 34 Chemin des Colombettes, CH-1211 Geneva 20, Switzerland; *Industrial Property Statistics.*

LITHUANIA - PERIODICALS

United Nations Educational, Scientific and Cultural Organization (UNESCO), 7 Place de Fontenoy, F-75700 Paris, France (Telephone Number in U.S. (212) 963-5981); *Statistical Yearbook.*

LITHUANIA - PETROLEUM INDUSTRY

Food and Agriculture Organization of the United Nations (FAO), Via delle Terme di Caracalla, 00100, Rome, Italy (Telephone Number in U.S. (202) 653-2400); *The State of Food and Agriculture.*

St. Martin's Press, Inc., 175 Fifth Avenue, New York, New York 10010 (800) 221-7945; *The Statesman's Year-Book.*

Statistical Office of the United Nations, Publishing Service, New York, New York 10017 (800) 253-9646; *Energy Statistics Yearbook; Industrial Commodity Statistics Yearbook;* and *Statistical Yearbook.*

LITHUANIA - PIGS - See LITHUANIA - LIVESTOCK AND POULTRY

LITHUANIA - POPULATION

Academic International Press, Box 1111, Gulf Breeze, Florida 32562; *Russia and Eurasia Facts and Figures Annual.*

Business International Moscow, 23 Profsoyuznaya Ulitsa, 117859, Moscow (Telephone Number in U.S. (800) 938-4685); *The CIS Market Atlas.*

Central Intelligence Agency, Washington, D.C. 20505 (703) 482-1100, www.cia.gov; *The World Factbook.*

The Economist Intelligence Unit, 111 West 57th Street, New York, New York 10019 (800) 938-4685; *Lithuania Country Report;* and *The World Market Atlas.*

Euromonitor International, Inc., 122 South Michigan Avenue, Suite 1200, Chicago, Illinois 60603 (800) 577-EURO; *The World Economic Factbook.*

Europa Publications Limited, 18 Bedford Square, London, WC1B 3JN, England; *The Europa World Year Book.*

Food and Agriculture Organization of the United Nations (FAO), Via delle Terme di Caracalla, 00100, Rome, Italy (Telephone Number in U.S. (202) 653-2400); *Production Yearbook.*

International Labour Office, I.L.O. Publications, 1828 L Street, N.W., Suite 801, Washington, D.C. 20036 (301) 638-3152; *Yearbook of Labor Statistics.*

St. Martin's Press, Inc., 175 Fifth Avenue, New York, New York 10010 (800) 221-7945; *The Statesman's Year-Book.*

Statistical Office of the United Nations, Publishing Service, New York, New York 10017 (800) 253-9646; *Demographic Yearbook; Human Development Report; World Statistics Pocketbook;* and *Statistical Yearbook.*

United Nations Educational, Scientific and Cultural Organization (UNESCO), 7 Place de Fontenoy, F-75700 Paris, France (Telephone Number in U.S. (212) 963-5981); *Statistical Yearbook.*

The World Bank, 1818 H Street, NW, Washington, D.C. 20433 (202) 477-1234; *The World Bank Atlas; World Development Report; Statistical Handbook: States of the Former USSR;* and *World Development Indicators.*

World Health Organization, Office of Publications, 20 Avenue Appia, CH-1211 Geneva 27, Switzerland (Telephone Number in U.S. (518) 436-9686); *World Health Statistics Annual.*

LITHUANIA - POULTRY - See
LITHUANIA - LIVESTOCK AND POULTRY

LITHUANIA - PRICES

Food and Agriculture Organization of the United Nations (FAO), Via delle Terme di Caracalla, 00100, Rome, Italy (Telephone Number in U.S. (202) 653-2400); *Production Yearbook.*

International Labour Office, I.L.O. Publications, 1828 L Street, N.W., Suite 801, Washington, D.C. 20036 (301) 638-3152; *Yearbook of Labor Statistics.*

The World Bank, 1818 H Street, NW, Washington, D.C. 20433 (202) 477-1234; *Statistical Handbook: States of the Former USSR.*

LITHUANIA - PRODUCTION

The World Bank, 1818 H Street, NW, Washington, D.C. 20433 (202) 477-1234; *Statistical Handbook: States of the Former USSR.*

LITHUANIA - PUBLIC FINANCE - See
LITHUANIA - FINANCE

LITHUANIA - RADIO RECEIVER PRODUCTION

St. Martin's Press, Inc., 175 Fifth Avenue, New York, New York 10010 (800) 221-7945; *The Statesman's Year-Book.*

Statistical Office of the United Nations, Publishing Service, New York, New York 10017 (800) 253-9646; *Statistical Yearbook.*

LITHUANIA - RAILWAYS

Academic International Press, Box 1111, Gulf Breeze, Florida 32562; *Russia and Eurasia Facts and Figures Annual.*

Business International Moscow, 23 Profsoyuznaya Ulitsa, 117859, Moscow (Telephone Number in U.S. (800) 938-4685); *The CIS Market Atlas.*

Europa Publications Limited, 18 Bedford Square, London, WC1B 3JN, England; *The Europa World Year Book.*

St. Martin's Press, Inc., 175 Fifth Avenue, New York, New York 10010 (800) 221-7945; *The Statesman's Year-Book.*

Statistical Office of the United Nations, Publishing Service, New York, New York 10017 (800) 253-9646; *Annual Bulletin of Transport Statistics for Europe;* and *Statistical Yearbook.*

LITHUANIA - RELIGION

Academic International Press, Box 1111, Gulf Breeze, Florida 32562; *Russia and Eurasia Facts and Figures Annual.*

Central Intelligence Agency, Washington, D.C. 20505 (703) 482-1100, www.cia.gov; *The World Factbook.*

St. Martin's Press, Inc., 175 Fifth Avenue, New York, New York 10010 (800) 221-7945; *The Statesman's Year-Book.*

LITHUANIA - RENT PRICES

International Labour Office, I.L.O. Publications, 1828 L Street, N.W., Suite 801, Washington, D.C. 20036 (301) 638-3152; *Yearbook of Labor Statistics.*

LITHUANIA - RETAIL TRADE

Business International Moscow, 23

Profsoyuznaya Ulitsa, 117859, Moscow (Telephone Number in U.S. (800) 938-4685); *The CIS Market Atlas.*

Euromonitor International, Inc., 122 South Michigan Avenue, Suite 1200, Chicago, Illinois 60603 (800) 577-EURO; *World Marketing Data and Statistics.*

Statistical Office of the United Nations, Publishing Service, New York, New York 10017 (800) 253-9646; *Statistical Yearbook.*

LITHUANIA - ROADS - See LITHUANIA - HIGHWAYS

LITHUANIA - ROUNDWOOD PRODUCTION AND CONSUMPTION - See LITHUANIA - FORESTRY AND FOREST PRODUCTS

LITHUANIA - RUBBER PRODUCTION AND CONSUMPTION

Statistical Office of the United Nations, Publishing Service, New York, New York 10017 (800) 253-9646; *Statistical Yearbook.*

LITHUANIA - SCIENTISTS, TECHNICIANS AND ENGINEERS

Statistical Office of the United Nations, Publishing Service, New York, New York 10017 (800) 253-9646; *Statistical Yearbook.*

LITHUANIA - SHEEP - See LITHUANIA - LIVESTOCK AND POULTRY

LITHUANIA - SOCIAL DATA

Statistical Office of the United Nations, Publishing Service, New York, New York 10017 (800) 253-9646; *World Statistics Pocketbook.*

LITHUANIA - SOCIAL SECURITY

Statistical Office of the United Nations, Publishing Service, New York, New York 10017 (800) 253-9646; *National Accounts Statistics.*

LITHUANIA - STEEL PRODUCTION AND CONSUMPTION - See LITHUANIA - MINING AND MINERAL PRODUCTS

LITHUANIA - TAXATION

Europa Publications Limited, 18 Bedford Square, London, WC1B 3JN, England; *The Europa World Year Book.*

LITHUANIA - TELEPHONES IN USE

Academic International Press, Box 1111, Gulf Breeze, Florida 32562; *Russia and Eurasia Facts and Figures Annual.*

Central Intelligence Agency, Washington, D.C. 20505 (703) 482-1100, www.cia.gov; *The World Factbook.*

St. Martin's Press, Inc., 175 Fifth Avenue, New York, New York 10010 (800) 221-7945; *The Statesman's Year-Book.*

Statistical Office of the United Nations, Publishing Service, New York, New York 10017 (800) 253-9646; *Statistical Yearbook;* and *World Statistics Pocketbook.*

LITHUANIA - TEXTILE INDUSTRY

Business International Moscow, 23 Profsoyuznaya Ulitsa, 117859, Moscow (Telephone Number in U.S. (800) 938-4685); *The CIS Market Atlas.*

St. Martin's Press, Inc., 175 Fifth Avenue, New York, New York 10010 (800) 221-7945; *The Statesman's Year-Book.*

Statistical Office of the United Nations, Publishing Service, New York, New York 10017 (800) 253-9646; *Industrial Commodity Statistics Yearbook;* and *Statistical Yearbook.*

LITHUANIA - THEATRE

United Nations Educational, Scientific and Cultural Organization (UNESCO), 7 Place de Fontenoy, F-75700 Paris, France (Telephone Number in U.S. (212) 963-5981); *Statistical Yearbook.*

LITHUANIA - TIRE (MOTOR VEHICLE) PRODUCTION

Statistical Office of the United Nations, Publishing Service, New York, New York 10017 (800) 253-9646; *Statistical Yearbook.*

LITHUANIA - TOBACCO PRODUCTION

Statistical Office of the United Nations, Publishing Service, New York, New York 10017 (800) 253-9646; *Statistical Yearbook.*

LITHUANIA - TOURISM

Business International Moscow, 23 Profsoyuznaya Ulitsa, 117859, Moscow (Telephone Number in U.S. (800) 938-4685); *The CIS Market Atlas.*

Euromonitor International, Inc., 122 South Michigan Avenue, Suite 1200, Chicago, Illinois 60603 (800) 577-EURO; *The World Economic Factbook;* and *World Marketing Data and Statistics.*

Statistical Office of the United Nations, Publishing Service, New York, New York 10017 (800) 253-9646; *Statistical Yearbook.*

LITHUANIA - TRADEMARKS AND SERVICE MARKS - See LITHUANIA - PATENTS, TRADEMARKS AND SERVICE MARKS

LITHUANIA - TRANSPORTATION AND COMMUNICATIONS

Academic International Press, Box 1111, Gulf Breeze, Florida 32562; *Russia and Eurasia Facts and Figures Annual.*

Business International Moscow, 23 Profsoyuznaya Ulitsa, 117859, Moscow (Telephone Number in U.S. (800) 938-4685); *The CIS Market Atlas.*

Central Intelligence Agency, Washington, D.C. 20505 (703) 482-1100, www.cia.gov; *The World Factbook.*

Euromonitor International, Inc., 122 South Michigan Avenue, Suite 1200, Chicago, Illinois 60603 (800) 577-EURO; *World Marketing Data and Statistics.*

Europa Publications Limited, 18 Bedford Square, London, WC1B 3JN, England; *The Europa World Year Book.*

St. Martin's Press, Inc., 175 Fifth Avenue, New York, New York 10010 (800) 221-7945; *The Statesman's Year-Book.*

Statistical Office of the United Nations, Publishing Service, New York, New York 10017 (800) 253-9646; *Annual Bulletin of Transport Statistics for Europe;* and *Human Development Report.*

LITHUANIA - UNEMPLOYMENT

Central Intelligence Agency, Washington, D.C. 20505 (703) 482-1100, www.cia.gov; *The World Factbook.*

International Labour Office, I.L.O. Publications, 1828 L Street, N.W., Suite 801, Washington, D.C. 20036 (301) 638-3152; *Yearbook of Labor Statistics.*

Statistical Office of the United Nations, Publishing Service, New York, New York 10017 (800) 253-9646; *Statistical Yearbook.*

LITHUANIA - VITAL STATISTICS

St. Martin's Press, Inc., 175 Fifth Avenue, New York, New York 10010 (800) 221-7945; *The Statesman's Year-Book.*

Statistical Office of the United Nations, Publishing Service, New York, New York 10017 (800) 253-9646; *Statistical Yearbook.*

World Health Organization, Office of Publications, 20 Avenue Appia, CH-1211 Geneva 27, Switzerland (Telephone Number in U.S. (518) 436-9686); *World Health Statistics Annual.*

LITHUANIA - WAGES

Business International Moscow, 23 Profsoyuznaya Ulitsa, 117859, Moscow (Telephone Number in U.S. (800) 938-4685); *The CIS Market Atlas.*

International Labour Office, I.L.O.

Publications, 1828 L Street, N.W., Suite 801, Washington, D.C. 20036 (301) 638-3152; *Yearbook of Labor Statistics.*

Statistical Office of the United Nations, Publishing Service, New York, New York 10017 (800) 253-9646; *Statistical Yearbook.*

The World Bank, 1818 H Street, NW, Washington, D.C. 20433 (202) 477-1234; *Statistical Handbook: States of the Former USSR.*

LITHUANIA - WELFARE

Academic International Press, Box 1111, Gulf Breeze, Florida 32562; *Russia and Eurasia Facts and Figures Annual.*

LITHUANIA - WHOLESALE PRICES

Academic International Press, Box 1111, Gulf Breeze, Florida 32562; *Russia and Eurasia Facts and Figures Annual.*

Statistical Office of the United Nations, Publishing Service, New York, New York 10017 (800) 253-9646; *Statistical Yearbook.*

LITHUANIA - WHOLESALE TRADE

Statistical Office of the United Nations, Publishing Service, New York, New York 10017 (800) 253-9646; *Statistical Yearbook.*

LITHUANIA - WOOL PRODUCTION AND CONSUMPTION - See LITHUANIA - TEXTILE INDUSTRY

LIVESTOCK AND LIVESTOCK PRODUCTS - See also ANIMALS - DOMESTIC, and Individual Classes

LIVESTOCK AND LIVESTOCK PRODUCTS - COMMODITY FUTURES TRADING

Commodity Research Bureau, Inc., 30 South Wacker Drive, Chicago Illinois 60606 (312) 454-1801; *CRB Commodity Index Report.*

LIVESTOCK AND LIVESTOCK PRODUCTS - CONSUMPTION

U.S. Department of Agriculture, Economic Research Service, 1800 M Street, NW, Washington, D.C. 20036 (202) 694-5050, www.ers.usda.gov; *Data; Food Consumption, Prices, and Expenditures;* and *Agricultural Outlook.*

LIVESTOCK AND LIVESTOCK PRODUCTS - FARM MARKETINGS - SALES

U.S. Department of Agriculture, Economic Research Service, 1800 M Street, NW, Washington, D.C. 20036 (202) 694-5050, www.ers.usda.gov; *Farm Business Economic Report.*

LIVESTOCK AND LIVESTOCK PRODUCTS - FARM OUTPUT AND MARKETING INDEXES

Executive Office of the President, Council of Economic Advisers, Old Executive Office Building, Washington, D.C. 20502 (202) 395-5084,www.whitehouse.gov/cea; *Economic Report of the President.*

U.S. Department of Agriculture, Economic Research Service,1800 M Street, NW, Washington, D.C. 20036 (202) 694-5050, www.ers.usda.gov; *Agricultural Outlook.*

LIVESTOCK AND LIVESTOCK PRODUCTS - FOREIGN TRADE

U.S. Department of Agriculture, Economic Research Service, 1800 M Street, NW, Washington, D.C. 20036 (202) 694-5050, www.ers.usda.gov; *Agricultural Statistics; Foreign Agricultural Trade of the United States; Livestock and Meat Statistics; Agricultural Outlook; Food Consumption, Prices, and Expenditures; U.S. Agricultural Trade Update;* and *Annual Data.*

U.S. Department of Commerce, Bureau of the Census, Washington, D.C. 20233 (301) 457-4100, www.census.gov; *U.S. International Trade Goods and Services.*

LIVESTOCK AND LIVESTOCK PRODUCTS - NUMBER AND VALUE ON FARMS

U.S. Department of Agriculture, National Agricultural Statistics Service, Fourteenth Street and Independence Avenue, SW, Washington, D.C. 20250 (800) 727-9540, www.usda.gov/nass; *Meat Animals - Production, Disposition, and Income;* and *Agricultural Statistics.*

LIVESTOCK AND LIVESTOCK PRODUCTS - PRICES

U.S. Department of Agriculture, National Agricultural Statistics Service, Fourteenth Street and Independence Avenue, SW, Washington, D.C. 20250 (800) 727-9540, www.usda.gov/nass; *Agricultural Prices: Annual Summary; Meat Animals - Production, Disposition, and Income;* and *Agricultural Statistics.*

LIVESTOCK AND LIVESTOCK PRODUCTS - PRODUCTION

Executive Office of the President, Council of Economic Advisers, Old Executive Office Building, Washington, D.C. 20502 (202) 395-5084, www.whitehouse.gov/cea; *Economic Report of the President.*

U.S. Department of Agriculture, Economic Research Service, 1800 M Street, NW, Washington, D.C. 20036 (202) 694-5050, www.ers.usda.gov; *Agricultural Statistics; Agricultural Outlook; Meat Animals - Production, Disposition and Income; Food Consumption, Prices, Expenditures;* and *Annual Data.*

LIVESTOCK AND LIVESTOCK PRODUCTS - PURCHASES

U.S. Department of Agriculture, Economic Research Service, 1800 M Street, NW, Washington, D.C. 20036 (202) 694-5050, www.ers.usda.gov; *Farm Business Economic Report.*

LIVESTOCK AND LIVESTOCK PRODUCTS - SUPPLY

U.S. Department of Agriculture, Economic Research Service, 1800 M Street, NW, Washington, D.C. 20036 (202) 694-5050, www.ers.usda.gov; *Agricultural Outlook;* and *Food Consumption, Prices, and Expenditures.*

LIVESTOCK AND LIVESTOCK PRODUCTS - VALUE ON FARMS

U.S. Department of Agriculture, National Agricultural Statistics Service, Fourteenth Street and Independence Avenue, SW, Washington, D.C. 20250 20250 (800) 727-9540, www.usda.gov/nass; *Agricultural Statistics;* and *Meat Animals - Production, Disposition, and Income.*

LIVING COST - See CONSUMER PRICE INDEXES and PRICES

LOANS AND MORTGAGES - See also DEBT

LOANS AND MORTGAGES - AUTOMOBILE LOANS

Board of Governors of the Federal Reserve System, Twentieth Street and Constitution Avenue, NW, Washington, D.C. 20551 (202) 452-3000. www.bog.frb.fed.us; *Federal Reserve Bulletin;* and *Annual Statistical Digest.*

LOANS AND MORTGAGES - BANKS - COMMERCIAL

Board of Governors of the Federal Reserve System, 20th Street and Constitution Avenue, NW, Washington, D.C. 20551 (202) 452-3000. www.bog.frb.fed.us; *Federal Reserve Bulletin;* and *Delinquency Rates All Banks, SA;* Internet site: http://www.bog.frb.fed.us/releases/chargeoff/delallsa.txt.

Federal Deposit Insurance Corporation, 550 Seventeenth Street, NW, Washington, D.C. 20429 (202) 393-8400, www.fdic.gov; *Annual Report; The FDIC Quarterly Banking Profile;* and *Statistics on Banking.*

LOANS AND MORTGAGES - COMMERCIAL PAPER

Board of Governors of the Federal Reserve System, 20th Street and Constitution Avenue, NW, Washington, D.C. 20551 (202) 452-3000. www.bog.frb.fed.us; *Federal Reserve Bulletin.*

LOANS AND MORTGAGES - CONSUMER CREDIT

Board of Governors of the Federal Reserve System, Twentieth Street and Constitution Avenue, NW, Washington, D.C. 20551 (202)452-3000, www.bog.frb.fed.us; *Federal Reserve Bulletin; Annual Statistical Digest;* and Internet site: http://www.bog.frb.fed.us/releases/chargeoff/delallsa.txt.

LOANS AND MORTGAGES - CREDIT MARKET - FLOW OF FUNDS

Board of Governors of the Federal Reserve System, Twentieth Street and Constitution Avenue, NW, Washington, D.C. 20551 (202) 452-3000. www.bog.frb.fed.us; *Flow of Funds Accounts.*

LOANS AND MORTGAGES - CREDIT UNIONS

Board of Governors of the Federal Reserve System, 20th Street and Constitution Avenue, NW, Washington, D.C. 20551 (202) 452-3000. www.bog.frb.fed.us; *Federal Reserve Bulletin.*

National Credit Union Administration, 1775 Duke Street, Alexandria, Virginia 22314 (703) 518-6300; *Annual Report of the National Credit Union Administration;* and unpublished data.

LOANS AND MORTGAGES - DELINQUENCY RATES

American Bankers Association, 1120 Connecticut Avenue, NW, Washington, D.C. 20036 (202) 663-5000; *Consumer Credit Delinquency Bulletin.*

Board of Governors of the Federal Reserve System, 20th Street and Constitution Avenue, NW, Washington, D.C. 20551 (202) 452-3000, www.bog.frb.fed.us; *Delinquency Rates All Banks, SA;* and Internet site: http://bog.frb.fed.us/releases/chargeoff/delallsa.txt.

Mortgage Bankers Association of America, 1125 Fifteenth Street, NW, Washington, D.C. 20005 (202) 861-6500; *National Delinquency Survey.*

LOANS AND MORTGAGES - DIRECT LOANS

Executive Office of the President, Office of Management and Budget, Executive

Office Building, Washington, D.C. 20503 (202) 395-3080, www.whitehouse.gov/omb; *Analytical Perspectives.*

LOANS AND MORTGAGES - FARM - See FARM MORTGAGE LOANS

LOANS AND MORTGAGES - FEDERAL HOUSING ADMINISTRATION

Mortgage Bankers Association of America, 1125 Fifteenth Street, NW, Washington, D.C. 20005 (202) 861-6500; *National Delinquency Survey.*

LOANS AND MORTGAGES - FINANCE COMPANY

Board of Governors of the Federal Reserve System, 20th Street and Constitution Avenue, NW, Washington, D.C. 20551 (202) 452-3000, www.bog.frb.fed.us; *Federal Reserve Bulletin.*

LOANS AND MORTGAGES - FORECLOSURE RATES

Mortgage Bankers Association of America, 1125 Fifteenth Street, NW, Washington, D.C. 20005 (202) 861-6500; *National Delinquency Survey.*

LOANS AND MORTGAGES - FOREIGN COUNTRIES

Board of Governors of the Federal Reserve System, Federal Financial Institutions Examination Council, Twentieth Street and Constitution Avenue, NW, Washington, D.C. 20551 (202) 452-3000, www.bog.frb.fed.us; statistical release.

LOANS AND MORTGAGES - GUARANTEED LOANS

Executive Office of the President, Office of Management and Budget, Executive Office Building, Washington, D.C. 20503 (202) 395-3080, www.whitehouse.gov/omb; *Analytical Perspectives.*

LOANS AND MORTGAGES - HOME MORTGAGE/EQUITY LOANS

Board of Governors of the Federal Reserve System, Twentieth Street and Constitution Avenue, NW, Washington, D.C. 20551 (202) 452-3000, www.bog.frb.fed.us; *Federal Reserve Bulletin; Delinquency Rates All Banks, SA;* and Internet site: http://www.bog.frb.fed.us/releases/chargeoff/delallsa.txt.

LOANS AND MORTGAGES - INSTALLMENT LOANS

Board of Governors of the Federal Reserve System, Twentieth Street and Constitution Avenue, NW, Washington,

D.C. 20551 (202) 452-3000, www.bog.frb.fed.us; *Federal Reserve Bulletin;* and unpublished data.

LOANS AND MORTGAGES - INTEREST RATES

Board of Governors of the Federal Reserve System, Twentieth Street and Constitution Avenue, NW, Washington, D.C. 20551 (202) 452-3000, www.bog.frb.fed.us; *Federal Reserve Bulletin;* and *Annual Statistical Digest.*

Federal Housing Finance Board, 1777 F Street NW, Washington, D.C. 20006 (202) 408-2500, www.fhfb.gov; *Rates and Terms on Conventional Home Mortgages, Annual Summary.*

LOANS AND MORTGAGES - LIFE INSURANCE

American Council of Life Insurance, 1001 Pennsylvania Avenue, NW, Washington, D.C. 20004 (202) 624-2000; *Life Insurance Fact Book.*

LOANS AND MORTGAGES - MINORITY - OPERATED SMALL BUSINESSES

Small Business Administration, 409 Third Street, SW, Washington, D.C. 20416 (800) UASK-SBA, www.sbaonline.sba.gov; unpublished data.

LOANS AND MORTGAGES - MORTGAGE-BACKED SECURITIES

Bond Market Association, 40 Broad Street, 12th Floor, New York, New York 10004-2373 (212) 809-7000.

LOANS AND MORTGAGES - MORTGAGE COMPANIES

U.S. Department of Housing and Urban Development, 451 Seventh Street, SW, Washington, D.C. 20410 (800) 998-9999, www.hud.gov; monthly and quarterly press releases based on the *Survey of Mortgage Lending Activity.*

LOANS AND MORTGAGES - MORTGAGE POOLS

Board of Governors of the Federal Reserve System, 20th Street and Constitution Avenue, NW, Washington, D.C. 20551 (202) 452-3000, www.bog.frb.fed.us; *Flow of Funds Accounts.*

LOANS AND MORTGAGES - MORTGAGES

Board of Governors of the Federal Reserve System, Twentieth Street and Constitution Avenue, NW, Washington, D.C. 20551 (202) 452-3000, www.bog.frb.fed.us (202) 452-3000,

www.bog.frb.fed.us; *Federal Reserve Bulletin; Flow of Funds Accounts;* and *Balance Sheets for the U.S. Economy.*

LOANS AND MORTGAGES - PERSONAL LOANS

Board of Governors of the Federal Reserve System, Twentieth Street and Constitution Avenue, NW, Washington, D.C. 20551 (202) 452-3000, www.bog.frb.fed.us; *Federal Reserve Bulletin;* and *Annual Statistical Digest.*

LOANS AND MORTGAGES - SAVINGS INSTITUTIONS

Board of Governors of the Federal Reserve System, Twentieth Street and Constitution Avenue, NW, Washington, D.C. 20551 (202) 452-3000, www.bog.frb.fed.us; *Federal Reserve Bulletin.*

National Credit Union Administration, 1775 Duke Street, Alexandria, Virginia 22314 (703) 518-6300; *Annual Report of the National Credit Union Administration;* and unpublished data.

LOANS AND MORTGAGES - VETERANS ADMINISTRATION

Mortgage Bankers Association of America, 1125 Fifteenth Street, NW, Washington, D.C. 20005 (202) 861-6500; *National Delinquency Survey.*

U.S. Department of Veterans Affairs, 810 Vermont Avenue, NW, Washington, D.C. 20420 (202) 273-5700; *Annual Report of the Secretary of Veterans Affairs;* and unpublished data.

LOBSTERS

U.S. Department of Commerce, National Oceanic and Atmospheric Administration, National Marine Fisheries Service, 1335 East-West Highway, Silver Spring, Maryland 20910 (301) 713-2239, www.nmfs.noass.gov; *Fisheries of the United States.*

LOCAL AND SUBURBAN TRANSIT - See PASSENGER TRANSIT INDUSTRY

LOCAL GOVERNMENT - See Individual Governmental Units and STATE AND LOCAL GOVERNMENT

LOCOMOTIVES (RAILROAD)

Association of American Railroads, American Railroads Building, 50 F Street, NW, Washington, D.C. 20001 (202) 639-2100; *Railroad Facts; Statistics of Railroads of Class I;* and *Analysis of Class I Railroads.*

LODGING INDUSTRIES - See HOTELS AND OTHER LODGING PLACES

LOTTERIES

TLF Publications, Inc., Boyds, Maryland 20841 (301) 540-0123; *LaFleur's Fiscal Lottery Special Report;* and *LaFleur's Lottery World Government Profit Report.*

LOUISIANA - See STATE DATA (FOR INDIVIDUAL STATES)

Louisiana - Primary Statistics Source

Division of Business and Economic Research, University of New Orleans, New Orleans, Louisiana 70148 (504) 286-6248; *Statistical Abstract of Louisiana.*

Louisiana - State Data Centers

Office of the Data Base Commission, Post Office Box 94095, 105 North Third Street, Baton Rouge, Louisiana 70802, Ms. Karen Paterson (225) 219-4025.

Center for Business and Economic Research, Northeast Louisiana University, Monroe, Louisiana 71209, Dr. Jerry Wall (318) 342-1215.

Division of Business and Economic Research, Northeast Louisiana University, Monroe, Louisiana 71209-0101, Mr. Jerry Wall, Ph.D. (318) 342-1215.

Division of Business and Economic Research, University of New Orleans, Lake Front, New Orleans, Louisiana 70148, Pat Conner (504) 280-7326.

Division of Business Research, Louisiana Tech University, Post Office Box 10318, Ruston, Louisiana 71272, Ms. Vickie Blue (318) 257-3701

Reference Department, Louisiana State Library, Post Office Box 131, Baton Rouge, Louisiana 70821, Ms. Virginia Smith (504) 342-4914.

The Louisiana Population Data Center, Department of Sociology, Room 126, Stubbs Hall, Louisiana State University, Baton Rouge, Louisiana 70803-5411, Mr. Andrew Deseran (504) 388-1113.

LOW BIRTHRATE

U.S. Department of Health and Human Services, National Center for Health Statistics, 3700 East-West Highway, Hyattsville, Maryland 20782 (301) 436-8500, www.cdc.gov/nchs; *Vital Statistics of the United States; National Vital Statistics*

Report; and unpublished data.

LSD

U.S. Department of Health and Human Services, Substance Abuse and Mental Health Services Administration, 5600 Fishers Lane, Rockville, Maryland 20857 (800) 729-6686, www.samhsa.gov; *National Household Survey on Drug Abuse.*

LUMBER - CONSUMPTION

U.S. Department of Agriculture, Forest Service, Post Office Box 96090, Washington, D.C. 20090 (202) 205-8333, www.fs.fed.us; *Timber Demand and Technology Assessment;* and *Agricultural Statistics.*

LUMBER - FOREIGN TRADE

U.S. Department of Agriculture, Forest Service, Post Office Box 96090, Washington, D.C. 20090 (202) 205-8333, www.fs.fed.us; *Timber Demand and Technology Assessment;* and *Agricultural Statistics.*

LUMBER - PRICES

U.S. Department of Labor, Bureau of Labor Statistics, Two Massachusetts Avenue, NE, Washington, D.C. 20212 (202) 691-5200, www.stats.bls.gov; *Producer Price Indexes.*

LUMBER - PRODUCTION

U.S. Department of Agriculture, Forest Service, Post Office Box 96090, Washington, D.C. 20090 (202) 205-8333, www.fs.fed.us; *Timber Demand and Technology Assessment.*

LUMBER - RAILROAD CAR LOADINGS

Association of American Railroads, 50 F Street, NW, Washington, D.C. 20001 (202) 639-2100; *Weekly Railroad Traffic;* and *Freight Commodity Statistics.*

U.S. Department of Agriculture, Forest Service, Post Office Box 96090, Washington, D.C. 20090 (202) 205-8333, www.fs.fed.us; *Timber Demand and Technology Assessment;* and *Agricultural Statistics.*

LUMBER - WATERBORNE COMMERCE

U.S. Department of the Army, Corps of Engineers, The Pentagon, Washington, D.C. 20310 (202) 545-6700, www.usace.army. mil; *Waterborne Commerce of the United States.*

LUMBER AND WOOD PRODUCTS - MANUFACTURING - EARNINGS

U.S. Department of Commerce, Bureau

of Economic Analysis, Fourteenth Street between Constitution Avenue and E Street, NW, Washington, D.C. 20230 (202) 606-9900, www.bea.doc.gov; *Survey of Current Business;* and *Foreign Direct Investment in the United States, Operations of U.S. Affiliates of Foreign Companies..*

U.S. Department of Commerce, Bureau of the Census, Washington, D.C. 20233 (301) 457-4100, www.census.gov; *Census of Manufactures;* and *Annual Survey of Manufactures.*

U.S. Department of Labor, Bureau of Labor Statistics, Two Massachusetts Avenue, NE, Washington, D.C. 20212 (202) 691-5200, www.stats.bls.gov; *Employment and Earnings;* and Internet site: http://stats.bls.gov/ceshome. htm.

LUMBER AND WOOD PRODUCTS - MANUFACTURING - EMPLOYEES

U.S. Department of Commerce, Bureau of Economic Analysis, Fourteenth Street between Constitution Avenue and E Street, NW, Washington, D.C. 20230 (202) 606-9900, www.bea.doc.gov; *Foreign Direct Investment in the U.S., Operations of U.S. Affiliates of Foreign Companies;* and *Survey of Current Business.*

U.S. Department of Commerce, Bureau of the Census, Washington, D.C. 20233 (301) 457-4100, www.census.gov; *Census of Manufactures;* and *Annual Survey of Manufactures.*

U.S. Department of Labor, Bureau of Labor Statistics, Two Massachusetts Avenue, NE, Washington, D.C. 20212 (202) 691-5200, www.stats.bls.gov; *Employment and Earnings; Monthly Labor Review;* and Internet site: http://stats.bls.gov/ ceshome.htm.

LUMBER AND WOOD PRODUCTS - MANUFACTURING - ENERGY CONSUMPTION

U.S. Department of Energy, Energy Information Administration, 1000 Independence Avenue, SW, Washington, D.C. 20585 (202) 586-8800, www.eia.doc.gov; *Manufacturing Energy Consumption.*

LUMBER AND WOOD PRODUCTS - MANUFACTURING - ESTABLISHMENTS

U.S. Department of Commerce, Bureau of Economic Analysis, Fourteenth Street between Constitution Avenue and E Street, NW, Washington, D.C. 20230 (202) 606-9900, www.bea.doc.gov; *Survey of Current Business;* and *Foreign Direct Investment in the U.S., Operations of U.S. Affiliates of Foreign Companies.*

U.S. Department of Commerce, Bureau of the Census, Washington, D.C. 20233 (301) 457-4100, www.census.gov; *Census of Manufactures; Annual Survey of Manufactures;* and *Final Industry Series.*

LUMBER AND WOOD PRODUCTS - MANUFACTURING - FAILURES

Dun and Bradstreet Corporation, 299 Park Avenue, 24th Floor, New York, New York 10171 (212) 593-6800; *Business Failure Record.*

LUMBER AND WOOD PRODUCTS - MANUFACTURING - FOREIGN TRADE

U.S. Department of Commerce, Bureau of the Census, Washington, D.C. 20233 (301) 457-4100, www.census.gov; *U.S. International Trade in Goods and Services.*

LUMBER AND WOOD PRODUCTS - MANUFACTURING - GROSS DOMESTIC PRODUCT

U.S. Department of Commerce, Bureau of Economic Analysis, Fourteenth Street between Constitution Avenue and E Streets, NW, Washington, D.C. 20230 (202) 606-9900, www.bea.doc.gov; *Survey of Current Business.*

LUMBER AND WOOD PRODUCTS - MANUFACTURING - MERGERS AND ACQUISITIONS

Thomson Financial Securities Data, 2 Gateway Center, Newark, New Jersey 07006 (973) 622-3100; *Merger and Corporate Transactions Database.*

LUMBER AND WOOD PRODUCTS - MANUFACTURING - OCCUPATIONAL SAFETY

U.S. Department of Labor, Bureau of Labor Statistics, Two Massachusetts Avenue, NE, Washington, D.C. 20212 (202) 691-5200, www.stats.bls.gov; *Occupational Injuries and Illnesses in the United States by Industry.*

LUMBER AND WOOD PRODUCTS - MANUFACTURING - PRICES

U.S. Department of Labor, Bureau of Labor Statistics, Two Massachusetts Avenue, NE, Washington, D.C. 20212 (202) 691-5200, www.stats.bls.gov; *Producer Price Indexes.*

LUMBER AND WOOD PRODUCTS - MANUFACTURING - PRODUCTIVITY

U.S. Department of Labor, Bureau of Labor Statistics, Two Massachusetts Avenue, NE, Washington, D.C. 20212 (202) 691-5200, www.stats.bls.gov; Internet site http://stats.bls.gov/iprhome.htm.

LUMBER AND WOOD PRODUCTS - MANUFACTURING - RAILROAD CAR LOADINGS

Association of American Railroads, American Railroads Building, 50 F Street, NW, Washington, D.C. 20001 (202) 639-2333; *Freight Commodity Statistics;* and *Weekly Railroad Traffic.*

LUMBER AND WOOD PRODUCTS - MANUFACTURING - SHIPMENTS

U.S. Department of Commerce, Bureau of the Census, Washington, D.C. 20233 (301) 457-4100, www.census.gov; *Census of Manufactures; Annual Survey of Manufactures;* and *Final Industry Series.*

LUMBER AND WOOD PRODUCTS - MANUFACTURING - TOXIC CHEMICAL RELEASES

Environmental Protection Agency, 1200 Pennsylvania Avenue, NW, Washington, D.C. 20460 (888) 372-8255, www.epa.gov; *Toxics Release Inventory.*

LUMBER AND WOOD PRODUCTS - MANUFACTURING - VALUE ADDED

U.S. Department of Commerce, Bureau of the Census, Washington, D.C. 20233 (301) 457-4100, www.census.gov; *Census of Manufactures;* and *Annual Survey of Manufactures.*

Luxembourg - National Statistical Office

Service Central de la Statistique et des Etudes Economiques, 19-21 Boulevard Royal, B.P. 304, L-2013, Luxembourg.

Luxembourg - Primary Statistics Sources

STATEC, 19-21 Boulevard Royal, B.P. 304, L-2013, Luxembourg; *Annuaire Statistique du Luxembourg* (Statistical Yearbook for Luxembourg), and *Bulletin du STATEC* (STATEC Bulletin).

LUXEMBOURG - ABORTIONS

European Commission Office of Press and Public Affairs, 2100 M Street, NW, Washington, D.C. 20037 (202) 862-9500; *Demographic Statistics.*

LUXEMBOURG - AGRICULTURE

Economist Intelligence Unit, 111 West 57th Street, New York, New York 10019 (800) 938-4685; *Luxembourg Country Report.*

Euromonitor International, Inc., 122 South Michigan Avenue, Suite 1200,

Chicago, Illinois 60603 (800) 577-EURO; *World Marketing Data and Statistics.*

Europa Publications Limited, 18 Bedford Square, London, WC1B 3JN, England; *The Europa World Year Book.*

European Commission Office of Press and Public Affairs, 2100 M Street, NW, Washington, D.C. 20037 (202) 862-9500; *Agriculture: Statistical Yearbook, Basic Statistics of the Community, Eurostatistics: Data for Short-Term Economic Analysis, Regions: Statistical Yearbook.*

Food and Agricultural Organization of the United Nations (FAO), Via delle Terme di Caracalla, 00100 Rome, Italy (Telephone Number in U.S. (202) 653-2400); *Production Yearbook; The State of Food and Agriculture;* and *Trade Yearbook.*

Organisation for Economic Co-operation and Development (OECD), 2 rue Andre-Pascal, 75 Paris 16, France (Telephone in U.S. (202) 785-6323); *Economic Accounts for Agriculture; Indicators of Industrial Activity, Industrial Structure Statistics;* and *OECD Economic Surveys: Belgium - Luxembourg.*

St. Martin's Press, Inc., 175 Fifth Avenue, New York, New York 10010 (800) 221-7945; *The Statesman's Year-Book.*

Statistical Office of the United Nations, Publishing Service, New York, New York 10017 (800) 253-9646; *Statistical Yearbook.*

United Nations Conference on Trade and Development, Central Statistical Service, Palais des Nations, Geneva, Switzerland (Telephone in U.S. (800) 253-9646); *UNCTAD Commodity Yearbook.*

The World Bank, 1818 H Street, NW, Washington, D.C. 20433 (202) 477-1234; *World Development Indicators.*

LUXEMBOURG - AIRLINE SERVICE

Europa Publications Limited, 18 Bedford Square, London, WC1B 3JN, England; *The Europa World Year Book.*

European Commission Office of Press and Public Affairs, 2100 M Street, NW, Washington, D.C. 20037 (202) 862-9500; *Basic Statistics of the Community; Regions: Statistical Yearbook;* and *Transport Annual Statistics.*

International Civil Aviation Organization, 999 University Street, Montreal, Quebec, Canada H3C 5H7 (514) 954-8219; *Civil Aviation Statistics of the World.*

Organisation for Economic Co-operation and Development (OECD), 2 rue Andre-Pascal, 75 Paris 16, France

(Telephone in U.S. (202) 785-6323); *Tourism Policy and International Tourism in OECD Member Countries.*

St. Martin's Press, Inc., 175 Fifth Avenue, New York, New York 10010 (800) 221-7945; *The Statesman's Year-Book.*

Statistical Office of the United Nations, Publishing Service, New York, New York 10017 (800) 253-9646; *Statistical Yearbook.*

LUXEMBOURG - AIRPORTS

Central Intelligence Agency, Washington, D.C. 20505 (703) 482-1100, www.cia.gov; *The World Factbook.*

LUXEMBOURG - ALMOND PRODUCTION - See LUXEMBOURG - CROPS

LUXEMBOURG - ALUMINUM PRODUCTION AND CONSUMPTION - See LUXEMBOURG - MINING AND MINERAL PRODUCTS

LUXEMBOURG - ANIMAL FEEDINGSTUFFS

Organisation for Economic Co-operation and Development (OECD), 2 rue Andre-Pascal, 75 Paris 16, France (Telephone in U.S. (202) 785-6323); *Foreign Trade by Commodities.*

LUXEMBOURG - ANIMAL HEALTH

Food and Agricultural Organization of the United Nations (FAO), Via delle Terme di Caracalla, 00100 Rome, Italy (Telephone Number in U.S. (202) 653-2400); *Animal Health Yearbook.*

LUXEMBOURG - ANTIMONY AND ANTIMONY ORE PRODUCTION AND CONSUMPTION - See LUXEMBOURG - MINING AND MINERAL PRODUCTS

LUXEMBOURG - APPLE PRODUCTION - See LUXEMBOURG - CROPS

LUXEMBOURG - AREA AND DENSITY OF POPULATION

Central Intelligence Agency, Washington, D.C. 20505 (703) 482-1100, www.cia.gov; *The World Factbook.*

Euromonitor International, Inc., 122 South Michigan Avenue, Suite 1200, Chicago, Illinois 60603 (800) 577-EURO; *The World Economic Factbook.*

Europa Publications Limited, 18 Bedford Square, London, WC1B 3JN, England; *The Europa World Year Book.*

European Commission Office of Press and Public Affairs, 2100 M Street, NW,

Washington, D.C. 20037 (202) 862-9500; *Basic Statistics of the Community;* and *Demographic Statistics.*

Food and Agricultural Organization of the United Nations (FAO), Via delle Terme di Caracalla, 00100 Rome, Italy (Telephone Number in U.S. (202) 653-2400); *The State of Food and Agriculture.*

St. Martin's Press, Inc., 175 Fifth Avenue, New York, New York 10010 (800) 221-7945; *The Statesman's Year-Book.*

Statistical Office of the United Nations, Publishing Service, New York, New York 10017 (800) 253-9646; *Statistical Yearbook.*

LUXEMBOURG - ARMS EXPORTS AND IMPORTS - See - LUXEMBOURG - MILITARY

LUXEMBOURG - ARSENIC PRODUCTION AND CONSUMPTION - See LUXEMBOURG - MINING AND MINERAL PRODUCTS

LUXEMBOURG - BALANCE OF PAYMENTS

Europa Publications Limited, 18 Bedford Square, London, WC1B 3JN, England; *The Europa World Year Book.*

European Commission Office of Press and Public Affairs, 2100 M Street, NW, Washington, D.C. 20037 (202) 862-9500; *ACP: Basic Statistics; Basic Statistics of the Community; Energy Statistics Yearbook;* and *Eurostatistics: Data for Short-Term Economic Analysis.*

Organisation for Economic Co-operation and Development (OECD), 2 rue Andre-Pascal, 75 Paris 16, France (Telephone in U.S. (202) 785-6323); *Economic Outlook; Geographical Distribution of Financial Flows to Developing Countries;* and *OECD Economic Surveys: Belgium -Luxembourg.*

United Nations Conference on Trade and Development (UNCTAD), New York, New York 10017 (800) 253-9646; *Handbook of International Trade and Development Statistics.*

The World Bank, 1818 H Street, NW, Washington, D.C. 20433 (202) 477-1234; *World Development Indicators.*

LUXEMBOURG - BANANA PRODUCTION - See LUXEMBOURG - CROPS

LUXEMBOURG - BANKING

Euromonitor International, Inc., 122 South Michigan Avenue, Suite 1200, Chicago, Illinois 60603 (800) 577-EURO; *World Marketing Data and Statistics.*

Europa Publications Limited, 18 Bedford Square, London, WC1B 3JN, England; *The Europa World Year Book.*

European Commission Office of Press and Public Affairs, 2100 M Street, NW, Washington, D.C. 20037 (202) 862-9500; *ACP: Basic Statistics;* and *Eurostatistics: Data for Short-Term Economic Analysis.*

International Monetary Fund, 700 Nineteenth Street, NW, Washington, D.C. 20431 (202) 623-7000; *International Financial Statistics.*

Organisation for Economic Co-operation and Development (OECD), 2 rue Andre-Pascal, 75 Paris 16, France (Telephone in U.S. (202) 785-6323); *Economic Outlook; Financial Market Trends;* and *OECD Economic Surveys: Belgium - Luxembourg.*

St. Martin's Press, Inc., 175 Fifth Avenue, New York, New York 10010 (800) 221-7945; *The Statesman's Year-Book.*

LUXEMBOURG - BARLEY PRODUCTION - See LUXEMBOURG - CROPS

LUXEMBOURG - BAUXITE PRODUCTION AND CONSUMPTION - See LUXEMBOURG - MINING AND MINERAL PRODUCTS

LUXEMBOURG - BEER PRODUCTION - See LUXEMBOURG - BEVERAGES

LUXEMBOURG - BEVERAGES

European Commission Office of Press and Public Affairs, 2100 M Street, NW, Washington, D.C. 20037 (202) 862-9500; *Basic Statistics of the Community.*

Organisation for Economic Co-operation and Development (OECD), 2 rue Andre-Pascal, 75 Paris 16, France (Telephone in U.S. (202) 785-6323); *Indicators of Industrial Activity.*

Statistical Office of the United Nations, Publishing Service, New York, New York 10017 (800) 253-9646; *Statistical Yearbook.*

LUXEMBOURG - BIRTH RATES

Central Intelligence Agency, Washington, D.C. 20505 (703) 482-1100, www.cia.gov; *The World Factbook.*

Euromonitor International, Inc., 122 South Michigan Avenue, Suite 1200, Chicago, Illinois 60603 (800) 577-EURO; *The World Economic Factbook.*

Europa Publications Limited, 18 Bedford Square, London, WC1B 3JN, England; *The Europa World Year Book.*

European Commission Office of Press and Public Affairs, 2100 M Street, NW, Washington, D.C. 20037 (202) 862-9500; *Basic Statistics of the Community;* and *Demographic Statistics.*

Organisation for Economic Co-operation and Development (OECD), 2 rue Andre-Pascal, 75 Paris 16, France (Telephone in U.S. (202) 785-6323); *Labor Force Statistics.*

St. Martin's Press, Inc., 175 Fifth Avenue, New York, New York 10010 (800) 221-7945; *The Statesman's Year-Book.*

Statistical Office of the United Nations, Publishing Service, New York, New York 10017 (800) 253-9646; *Demographic Yearbook;* and *Statistical Yearbook.*

The World Bank, 1818 H Street, NW, Washington, D.C. 20433 (202) 477-1234; *World Development Indicators.*

World Health Organization, Office of Publications, 20 Avenue Appia, CH-1211 Geneva 27, Switzerland (Telephone Number in U.S. (518) 436-9686); *World Health Statistics Annual.*

LUXEMBOURG - BISMUTH PRODUCTION AND CONSUMPTION - See LUXEMBOURG - MINING AND MINERAL PRODUCTS

LUXEMBOURG - BONDS

European Commission Office of Press and Public Affairs, 2100 M Street, NW, Washington, D.C. 20037 (202) 862-9500; *Basic Statistics of the Community.*

Organisation for Economic Co-operation and Development (OECD), 2 rue Andre-Pascal, 75 Paris 16, France (Telephone in U.S. (202) 785-6323); *Financial Market Trends.*

Statistical Office of the United Nations, Publishing Service, New York, New York 10017 (800) 253-9646; *Statistical Yearbook.*

LUXEMBOURG - BOOK PRODUCTION

Euromonitor International, Inc., 122 South Michigan Avenue, Suite 1200, Chicago, Illinois 60603 (800) 577-EURO; *European Marketing Data and Statistics.*

Europa Publications Limited, 18 Bedford Square, London, WC1B 3JN, England; *The Europa World Year Book.*

Organisation for Economic Co-operation and Development (OECD), 2 rue Andre-Pascal, 75 Paris 16, France (Telephone in U.S. (202) 785-6323); *Indicators of Industrial Activity.*

United Nations Educational, Scientific and Cultural Organization (UNESCO), 7 Place de Fontenoy, F-75700 Paris, France (Telephone Number in U.S. (212) 963-5981); *Statistical Yearbook.*

LUXEMBOURG - BROADCASTING

Billboard Limited, Post Office Box 9027, 1006 AA Amsterdam, The Netherlands (Telephone Number in U.S. (212) 764-7300); *World Radio TV Handbook.*

Central Intelligence Agency, Washington, D.C. 20505 (703) 482-1100, www.cia.gov; *The World Factbook.*

Euromonitor International, Inc., 122 South Michigan Avenue, Suite 1200, Chicago, Illinois 60603 (800) 577-EURO; *World Marketing Data and Statistics.*

European Commission Office of Press and Public Affairs, 2100 M Street, NW, Washington, D.C. 20037 (202) 862-9500; *Basic Statistics of the Community.*

St. Martin's Press, Inc., 175 Fifth Avenue, New York, New York 10010 (800) 221-7945; *The Statesman's Year-Book.*

United Nations Educational, Scientific and Cultural Organization (UNESCO), 7 Place de Fontenoy, F-75700 Paris, France (Telephone Number in U.S. (212) 963-5981); *Statistical Yearbook.*

LUXEMBOURG - BUDGET

Central Intelligence Agency, Washington, D.C. 20505 (703) 482-1100, www.cia.gov; *The World Factbook.*

LUXEMBOURG - BUSINESS

European Commission Office of Press and Public Affairs, 2100 M Street, NW, Washington, D.C. 20037 (202) 862-9500; *Basic Statistics of the Community.*

LUXEMBOURG - BUSINESS AND PROFESSIONAL LICENSES

International Monetary Fund, 700 Nineteenth Street, NW, Washington, D.C. 20431 (202) 623-7000; *Government Finance Statistics Yearbook.*

LUXEMBOURG - BUTTER - See LUXEMBOURG - DAIRY PRODUCTS

LUXEMBOURG - CABBAGE PRODUCTION - See LUXEMBOURG - CROPS

LUXEMBOURG - CADMIUM PRODUCTION AND CONSUMPTION - See LUXEMBOURG - MINING AND MINERAL PRODUCTS

LUXEMBOURG - CALORIE SUPPLY

Food and Agricultural Organization of the United Nations (FAO), Via delle Terme di Caracalla, 00100 Rome, Italy (Telephone Number in U.S. (202) 653-2400); *The State of Food and Agriculture.*

LUXEMBOURG - CAPITAL INVESTMENT

Organisation for Economic Co-operation and Development (OECD), 2 rue Andre-Pascal, 75 Paris 16, France (Telephone in U.S. (202) 785-6323); *Economic Outlook;* and *Financial Market Trends.*

LUXEMBOURG - CAPITAL REVENUE

International Monetary Fund, 700 Nineteenth Street, NW, Washington, D.C. 20431 (202) 623-7000; *Government Finance Statistics Yearbook.*

Organisation for Economic Co-operation and Development (OECD), 2 rue Andre-Pascal, 75 Paris 16, France (Telephone in U.S. (202) 785-6323); *Economic Outlook;* and *Financial Market Trends.*

LUXEMBOURG - CASHEW NUT PRODUCTION - See LUXEMBOURG - CROPS

LUXEMBOURG - CASTOR BEAN PRODUCTION - See LUXEMBOURG - CROPS

LUXEMBOURG - CATTLE - See LUXEMBOURG - LIVESTOCK AND POULTRY

LUXEMBOURG - CAULIFLOWER PRODUCTION - See LUXEMBOURG - CROPS

LUXEMBOURG - CAUSTIC SODA PRODUCTION - See LUXEMBOURG - BEVERAGES

LUXEMBOURG - CEMENT PRODUCTION - See LUXEMBOURG - MINING AND MINERAL PRODUCTS

LUXEMBOURG - CEREAL PRODUCTION - See LUXEMBOURG - CROPS

LUXEMBOURG - CHEESE - See LUXEMBOURG - DAIRY PRODUCTS

LUXEMBOURG - CHEMICAL INDUSTRY

European Commission Office of Press and Public Affairs, 2100 M Street, NW, Washington, D.C. 20037 (202) 862-9500; *Industrial Production: Quarterly Statistics.*

LUXEMBOURG - CHEMICAL (ORGANIC) PRODUCTION - See LUXEMBOURG - MINING AND MINERAL PRODUCTS

LUXEMBOURG - CHESTNUT PRODUCTION - See LUXEMBOURG - CROPS

LUXEMBOURG - CHICKENS - See LUXEMBOURG - LIVESTOCK AND POULTRY

LUXEMBOURG - CHROMITE PRODUCTION AND CONSUMPTION - See

LUXEMBOURG - MINING AND MINERAL PRODUCTS

LUXEMBOURG - CHROMIUM ORE PRODUCTION AND CONSUMPTION - See LUXEMBOURG - MINING AND MINERAL PRODUCTS

LUXEMBOURG - CLASS STRUCTURE

European Commission Office of Press and Public Affairs, 2100 M Street, NW, Washington, D.C. 20037 (202) 862-9500; *Basic Statistics of the Community;* and *Labor Force Sample Survey.*

LUXEMBOURG - CLIMATE

St. Martin's Press, Inc., 175 Fifth Avenue, New York, New York 10010 (800) 221-7945; *The Statesman's Year-Book.*

LUXEMBOURG - CLOTHING - See LUXEMBOURG - TEXTILE INDUSTRY

LUXEMBOURG - COAL PRODUCTION - See LUXEMBOURG - MINING AND MINERAL PRODUCTS

LUXEMBOURG - COBALT PRODUCTION AND CONSUMPTION - See LUXEMBOURG - MINING AND MINERAL PRODUCTS

LUXEMBOURG - COCOA (BEANS) PRODUCTION - See LUXEMBOURG - CROPS

LUXEMBOURG - COFFEE - See LUXEMBOURG - CROPS

LUXEMBOURG - COKE AND COKE OVEN ORE PRODUCTION AND CONSUMPTION - See LUXEMBOURG - MINING AND MINERAL PRODUCTS

LUXEMBOURG - COMMERCE

St. Martin's Press, Inc., 175 Fifth Avenue, New York, New York 10010 (800) 221-7945; *The Statesman's Year-Book.*

LUXEMBOURG - COMMUNICATIONS - See LUXEMBOURG - TRANSPORTATION AND COMMUNICATIONS

LUXEMBOURG - CONSTRUCTION\ INDUSTRY

European Commission Office of Press and Public Affairs, 2100 M Street, NW, Washington, D.C. 20037 (202) 862-9500; *Basic Statistics of the Community;* and *Labor Force Sample Survey.*

Organisation for Economic Co-operation and Development (OECD), 2 rue Andre-Pascal, 75 Paris 16, France (Telephone in U.S. (202) 785-6323); *Industrial Structure Statistics; The Iron and Steel Industry; Main Economic Indicators - Historical Statistics;* and *OECD Economic*

Surveys: Belgium - Luxembourg.

Statistical Office of the United Nations, Publishing Service, New York, New York 10017 (800) 253-9646; *Statistical Yearbook.*

LUXEMBOURG - CONSUMER PRICE INDEX

Europa Publications Limited, 18 Bedford Square, London, WC1B 3JN, England; *The Europa World Year Book.*

European Commission Office of Press and Public Affairs, 2100 M Street, NW, Washington, D.C. 20037 (202) 862-9500; *Basic Statistics of the Community;* and *Money and Finance.*

Organisation for Economic Co-operation and Development (OECD), 2 rue Andre-Pascal, 75 Paris 16, France (Telephone in U.S. (202) 785-6323); *Economic Outlook.*

Statistical Office of the United Nations, Publishing Service, New York, New York 10017 (800) 253-9646; *Statistical Yearbook.*

LUXEMBOURG - CONSUMER PRICES

Euromonitor International, Inc., 122 South Michigan Avenue, Suite 1200, Chicago, Illinois 60603 (800) 577-EURO; *European Marketing Data and Statistics; Basic Statistics of the Community; Eurostatistics: Data for Short-Term Economic Analysis;* and *World Marketing Data and Statistics.*

International Labour Office, I.L.O. Publications, 1828 L Street, N.W., Suite 801, Washington, D.C. 20036 (301) 638-3152; *Yearbook of Labour Statistics.*

International Monetary Fund, 700 Nineteenth Street, NW, Washington, D.C. 20431 (202) 623-7000; *International Financial Statistics.*

Organisation for Economic Co-operation and Development (OECD), 2 rue Andre-Pascal, 75 Paris 16, France (Telephone in U.S. (202) 785-6323); *Economic Outlook;* and *Main Economic Indicators - Historical Statistics.*

LUXEMBOURG - CONSUMPTION

European Commission Office of Press and Public Affairs, 2100 M Street, NW, Washington, D.C. 20037 (202) 862-9500; *Basic Statistics of the Community.*

International Iron and Steel Institute, 120, rue Colonel Bourg, B-1140 Brussels, Belgium; *Steel Statistical Yearbook.*

Organisation for Economic Co-operation and Development (OECD), 2 rue Andre-Pascal, 75 Paris 16, France (Telephone in U.S. (202) 785-6323); *The*

Footwear, Raw Hides and Skins, and Leather Industry in OECD Countries; The Iron and Steel Industry; Meat Balances in OECD Member Countries; The Non-Ferrous Metals Industry; The Pulp and Paper Industry; and *Textile Industry in OECD Countries.*

LUXEMBOURG - COPPER AND COPPER ORE PRODUCTION AND CONSUMPTION - See LUXEMBOURG - MINING AND MINERAL PRODUCTS

LUXEMBOURG - CORN PRODUCTION - See LUXEMBOURG - CROPS

LUXEMBOURG - CORPORATE TAXES - SEE LUXEMBOURG - TAXATION

LUXEMBOURG - COTTON - See LUXEMBOURG - CROPS

LUXEMBOURG - CRIME

International Criminal Police Organization (INTERPOL), 50 quai Achille Lignon, F-69006 Lyon, France; *International Crime Statistics.*

Yale University Press, Yale Station, New Haven, Connecticut 06520 (800) 987-7323; *Violence and Crime in Cross-National Perspective.*

LUXEMBOURG - CROPS

Commodity Research Bureau, Incorporated, 30 South Wacker Drive, Chicago Illinois 60606 (312) 454-1801; *Commodity Year Book.*

Euromonitor International, Inc., 122 South Michigan Avenue, Suite 1200, Chicago, Illinois 60603 (800) 577-EURO; *European Marketing Data and Statistics;* and *Basic Statistics of the Community.*

Europa Publications Limited, 18 Bedford Square, London, WC1B 3JN, England; *The Europa World Year Book.*

European Commission Office of Press and Public Affairs, 2100 M Street, NW, Washington, D.C. 20037 (202) 862-9500; *ACP: Basic Statistics; Agriculture: Statistical Yearbook; Basic Statistics of the Community; Crop Production: Quarterly Statistics; Eurostatistics: Data for Short-Term Economic Analysis;* and *Regions: Statistical Yearbook.*

Food and Agricultural Organization of the United Nations (FAO), Via delle Terme di Caracalla, 00100 Rome, Italy (Telephone Number in U.S. (202) 653-2400); *Production Yearbook;* and *The State of Food and Agriculture.*

International Wheat Statistics, 28 Haymarket, London SW1Y 4SS, England; *World Wheat Statistics.*

Organisation for Economic Co-operation and Development (OECD), 2 rue Andre-Pascal, 75 Paris 16, France (Telephone Number in U.S. (202) 785-6323); *Economic Accounts for Agriculture; Foreign Trade by Commodities;* and *Textile Industry in OECD Countries.*

St. Martin's Press, Inc., 175 Fifth Avenue, New York, New York 10010 (800) 221-7945; *The Statesman's Year-Book.*

Statistical Office of the United Nations, Publishing Service, New York, New York 10017 (800) 253-9646; *Statistical Yearbook.*

United Nations Conference on Trade and Development, Central Statistical Service, Palais des Nations, Geneva, Switzerland (Telephone in U.S. (800) 253-9646); *UNCTAD Commodity Yearbook.*

LUXEMBOURG - CUSTOMS DUTIES

European Commission Office of Press and Public Affairs, 2100 M Street, NW, Washington, D.C. 20037 (202) 862-9500; *Basic Statistics of the Community.*

Organisation for Economic Co-operation and Development (OECD), 2 rue Andre-Pascal, 75 Paris 16, France (Telephone in U.S. (202) 785-6323); *The Non-Ferrous Metals Industry.*

LUXEMBOURG - DAIRY PRODUCTS

. Commodity Research Bureau, Incorporated, 30 South Wacker Drive, Chicago Illinois 60606 (312) 454-1801; *Commodity Year Book.*

Europa Publications Limited, 18 Bedford Square, London, WC1B 3JN, England; *The Europa World Year Book.*

European Commission Office of Press and Public Affairs, 2100 M Street, NW, Washington, D.C. 20037 (202) 862-9500; *Basic Statistics of the Community;* and *Eurostatistics: Data for Short-Term Economic Analysis.*

Food and Agricultural Organization of the United Nations (FAO), Via delle Terme di Caracalla, 00100 Rome, Italy (Telephone Number in U.S. (202) 653-2400); *Production Yearbook;* and *The State of Food and Agriculture.*

Organisation for Economic Co-operation and Development (OECD), 2 rue Andre-Pascal, 75 Paris 16, France (Telephone in U.S. (202) 785-6323); *Economic Accounts for Agriculture;* and *Milk, Milk Products, and Egg Balances in OECD Member Countries.*

St. Martin's Press, Inc., 175 Fifth Avenue, New York, New York 10010 (800) 221-7945; *The Statesman's Year-Book.*

Statistical Office of the United Nations, Publishing Service, New York, New York 10017 (800) 253-9646; *Statistical Yearbook.*

LUXEMBOURG - DEATH RATES - See LUXEMBOURG - MORTALITY

LUXEMBOURG - DEFENSE EXPENDITURES - See LUXEMBOURG - MILITARY

LUXEMBOURG - DEMOGRAPHY

The Economist Intelligence Unit, 111 West 57th Street, New York, New York 10019 (800) 938-4685; *The World Market Atlas.*

Euromonitor International, Inc., 122 South Michigan Avenue, Suite 1200, Chicago, Illinois 60603 (800) 577-EURO; *The World Economic Factbook;* and *World Marketing Data and Statistics.*

European Commission Office of Press and Public Affairs, 2100 M Street, NW, Washington, D.C. 20037 (202) 862-9500; *Basic Statistics of the Community; Demographic Statistics; Employment and Unemployment;* and *Regions: Statistical Yearbook.*

Statistical Office of the United Nations, Publishing Service, New York, New York 10017 (800) 253-9646; *Human Development Report.*

LUXEMBOURG - DEVELOPMENT ASSISTANCE

European Commission Office of Press and Public Affairs, 2100 M Street, NW, Washington, D.C. 20037 (202) 862-9500; *ACP: Basic Statistics;* and *Basic Statistics of the Community;* and *Government Financing of Research and Development.*

Organisation for Economic Co-operation and Development (OECD), 2 rue Andre-Pascal, 75 Paris 16, France (Telephone in U.S. (202) 785-6323); *Geographical Distribution of Financial Flows to Developing Countries.*

LUXEMBOURG - DIAMONDS - See LUXEMBOURG - MINING AND MINERAL PRODUCTS

LUXEMBOURG - DISCOUNT RATES - See LUXEMBOURG - BANKING

LUXEMBOURG - DISEASES - See LUXEMBOURG - HEALTH

LUXEMBOURG - DIVORCE

European Commission Office of Press and Public Affairs, 2100 M Street, NW, Washington, D.C. 20037 (202) 862-9500; *Demographic Statistics.*

Statistical Office of the United Nations, Publishing Service, New York, New York 10017 (800) 253-9646; *Demographic Yearbook;* and *Statistical Yearbook.*

LUXEMBOURG - DOMESTIC PRODUCT

European Commission Office of Press and Public Affairs, 2100 M Street, NW, Washington, D.C. 20037 (202) 862-9500; *Basic Statistics of the Community.*

LUXEMBOURG - DUCKS - See LUXEMBOURG - LIVESTOCK AND POULTRY

LUXEMBOURG - ECONOMY

Central Intelligence Agency, Washington, D.C. 20505 (703) 482-1100, www.cia.gov; *The World Factbook.*

Economist Intelligence Unit, 111 West 57th Street, New York, New York 10019 (800) 938-4685; *Luxembourg Country Report.*

Euromonitor International, Inc., 122 South Michigan Avenue, Suite 1200, Chicago, Illinois 60603 (800) 577-EURO; *European Marketing Data and Statistics; World Marketing Data and Statistics;* and *The World Economic Factbook.*

European Commission Office of Press and Public Affairs, 2100 M Street, NW, Washington, D.C. 20037 (202) 862-9500; *ACP: Basic Statistics; Basic Statistics of the Community; Energy Statistics Yearbook; Labor Force Sample Survey;* and *Money and Finance.*

Organisation for Economic Co-operation and Development (OECD), 2 rue Andre-Pascal, 75 Paris 16, France (Telephone in U.S. (202) 785-6323); *Economic Outlook; Geographical Distribution of Financial Flows to Developing Countries; Main Economic Indicators - Historical Statistics; OECD Economic Surveys: Belgium - Luxembourg;* and *OECD Employment Outlook.*

St. Martin's Press, Inc., 175 Fifth Avenue, New York, New York 10010 (800) 221-7945; *The Statesman's Year-Book.*

Statistical Office of the United Nations, Publishing Service, New York, New York 10017 (800) 253-9646; *World Statistics Pocketbook.*

The World Bank, 1818 H Street, NW, Washington, D.C. 20433 (202) 477-1234; *The World Bank Atlas.*

LUXEMBOURG - EDUCATION

The Economist Intelligence Unit, 111 West 57th Street, New York, New York 10019 (800) 938-4685; *The World Market*

Atlas.

Euromonitor International, Inc., 122 South Michigan Avenue, Suite 1200, Chicago, Illinois 60603 (800) 577-EURO; *European Marketing Data and Statistics;* and *World Marketing Data and Statistics.*

Europa Publications Limited, 18 Bedford Square, London, WC1B 3JN, England; *The Europa World Year Book.*

European Commission Office of Press and Public Affairs, 2100 M Street, NW, Washington, D.C. 20037 (202) 862-9500; *Basic Statistics of the Community;* and *Regions: Statistical Yearbook.*

International Monetary Fund, 700 Nineteenth Street, NW, Washington, D.C. 20431 (202) 623-7000; *Government Finance Statistics Yearbook.*

Organisation for Economic Co-operation and Development (OECD), 2 rue Andre-Pascal, 75 Paris 16, France (Telephone Number in U.S. (202) 785-6323), *Education in OECD Countries.*

St. Martin's Press, Inc., 175 Fifth Avenue, New York, New York 10010 (800) 221-7945; *The Statesman's Year-Book.*

Statistical Office of the United Nations, Publishing Service, New York, New York 10017 (800) 253-9646; *Human Development Report.*

United Nations Educational, Scientific and Cultural Organization (UNESCO), 7 Place de Fontenoy, F-75700 Paris, France (Telephone Number in U.S. (212) 963-5981); *Statistical Yearbook.*

The World Bank, 1818 H Street, NW, Washington, D.C. 20433 (202) 477-1234; *World Development Indicators.*

LUXEMBOURG - EGG PRODUCTION AND CONSUMPTION - See LUXEMBOURG - DAIRY PRODUCTS

LUXEMBOURG - ELECTRICITY

Central Intelligence Agency, Washington, D.C. 20505 (703) 482-1100, www.cia.gov; *The World Factbook.*

European Commission Office of Press and Public Affairs, 2100 M Street, NW, Washington, D.C. 20037 (202) 862-9500; *Basic Statistics of the Community; Coal Information; Energy: Monthly Statistics; Energy Statistics Yearbook; Eurostatistics: Data for Short-Term Economic Analysis; Industrial Structure Statistics;* and *Regions: Statistical Yearbook.*

Organisation for Economic Co-operation and Development (OECD), 2 rue

Andre-Pascal, 75 Paris 16, France (Telephone in U.S. (202) 785-6323); *Energy Statistics of OECD Countries;* and *Indicators of Industrial Activity.*

St. Martin's Press, Inc., 175 Fifth Avenue, New York, New York 10010 (800) 221-7945; *The Statesman's Year-Book.*

Statistical Office of the United Nations, Publishing Service, New York, New York 10017 (800) 253-9646; *Human Development Report;* and *Statistical Yearbook.*

LUXEMBOURG - EMPLOYMENT

Euromonitor International, Inc., 122 South Michigan Avenue, Suite 1200, Chicago, Illinois 60603 (800) 577-EURO; *European Marketing Data and Statistics.*

European Commission Office of Press and Public Affairs, 2100 M Street, NW, Washington, D.C. 20037 (202) 862-9500; *Earnings in Agriculture; Basic Statistics of the Community; Employment and Unemployment; Eurostatistics: Data for Short-Term Economic Analysis; Iron and Steel: Statistical Yearbook; Labor Force Sample Survey;* and *Transport Annual Statistics.*

International Labour Office, I.L.O. Publications, 1828 L Street, N.W., Suite 801, Washington, D.C. 20036 (301) 638-3152; *Yearbook of Labour Statistics.*

Organisation for Economic Co-operation and Development (OECD), 2 rue Andre-Pascal, 75 Paris 16, France (Telephone in U.S. (202) 785-6323); *Economic Outlook; The Iron and Steel Industry; OECD Economic Surveys: Belgium - Luxembourg; OECD Employment Outlook;* and *Textile Industry in OECD Countries.*

Statistical Office of the United Nations, Publishing Service, New York, New York 10017 (800) 253-9646; *Statistical Yearbook.*

LUXEMBOURG - ENERGY

Euromonitor International, Inc., 122 South Michigan Avenue, Suite 1200, Chicago, Illinois 60603 (800) 577-EURO; *Basic Statistics of the Community; European Marketing Data and Statistics; Labor Force Sample Survey; World Marketing Data and Statistics;* and *The World Economic Factbook.*

European Commission Office of Press and Public Affairs, 2100 M Street, NW, Washington, D.C. 20037 (202) 862-9500; *Basic Statistics of the Community; Energy: Monthly Statistics; Energy Statistics Yearbook; Regions: Statistical Yearbook;* and *Transport Annual Statistics.*

Food and Agricultural Organization of

the United Nations (FAO), Via delle Terme di Caracalla, 00100 Rome, Italy (Telephone Number in U.S. (202) 653-2400); *The State of Food and Agriculture.*

Organisation for Economic Co-operation and Development (OECD), 2 rue Andre-Pascal, 75 Paris 16, France (Telephone in U.S. (202) 785-6323); *Coal Information; Energy Statistics of OECD Countries; OECD Environmental Data;* and *Oil and Gas Information.*

St. Martin's Press, Inc., 175 Fifth Avenue, New York, New York 10010 (800) 221-7945; *The Statesman's Year-Book.*

Statistical Office of the United Nations, Publishing Service, New York, New York 10017 (800) 253-9646; *Energy Statistics Yearbook; Human Development Report; World Statistics Pocketbook;* and *Statistical Yearbook.*

The World Bank, 1818 H Street, NW, Washington, D.C. 20433 (202) 477-1234; *The World Bank Atlas.*

LUXEMBOURG - ENGINEERING AND METAL PRODUCTS

European Commission Office of Press and Public Affairs, 2100 M Street, NW, Washington, D.C. 20037 (202) 862-9500; *Basic Statistics of the Community;* and *Industrial Production: Quarterly Statistics.*

LUXEMBOURG - ENVIRONMENT

Economist Intelligence Unit, 111 West 57th Street, New York, New York 10019 (800) 938-4685; *Luxembourg Country Report.*

Statistical Office of the United Nations, Publishing Service, New York, New York 10017 (800) 253-9646; *World Statistics Pocketbook.*

LUXEMBOURG - EXCHANGE RATES

Central Intelligence Agency, Washington, D.C. 20505 (703) 482-1100, www.cia.gov; *The World Factbook.*

Euromonitor International, Inc., 122 South Michigan Avenue, Suite 1200, Chicago, Illinois 60603 (800) 577-EURO; *The World Economic Factbook.*

Europa Publications Limited, 18 Bedford Square, London, WC1B 3JN, England; *The Europa World Year Book.*

European Commission Office of Press and Public Affairs, 2100 M Street, NW, Washington, D.C. 20037 (202) 862-9500; *Basic Statistics of the Community; Eurostatistics: Data for Short-Term Economic Analysis;* and *Money and Finance.*

International Civil Aviation Organization, 999 University Street, Montreal, Quebec, Canada H3C 5H7 (514) 954-8219; *Civil Aviation Statistics of the World.*

International Monetary Fund, 700 Nineteenth Street, NW, Washington, D.C. 20431 (202) 623-7000; *International Financial Statistics.*

Organisation for Economic Co-operation and Development (OECD), 2 rue Andre-Pascal, 75 Paris 16, France (Telephone in U.S. (202) 785-6323); *Economic Outlook; Financial Market Trends; Revenue Statistics of OECD Member Countries;* and *Tourism Policy and International Tourism in OECD Member Countries.*

Statistical Office of the United Nations, Publishing Service, New York, New York 10017 (800) 253-9646; *Statistical Yearbook;* and *World Statistics Pocketbook.*

LUXEMBOURG - EXCISE TAXES - See LUXEMBOURG - TAXATION

LUXEMBOURG - EXPORTS

American Automobile Manufacturers Association, 1401 H Street, NW, Suite 900, Washington, D.C. 20005 (202) 326-5500; *World Motor Vehicle Data.*

Central Intelligence Agency, Washington, D.C. 20505 (703) 482-1100, www.cia.gov; *The World Factbook.*

The Economist Intelligence Unit, 111 West 57th Street, New York, New York 10019 (800) 938-4685; *Luxembourg Country Report;* and *The World Market Atlas.*

Euromonitor International, Inc., 122 South Michigan Avenue, Suite 1200, Chicago, Illinois 60603 (800) 577-EURO; *The World Economic Factbook.*

Europa Publications Limited, 18 Bedford Square, London, WC1B 3JN, England; *The Europa World Year Book.*

European Commission Office of Press and Public Affairs, 2100 M Street, NW, Washington, D.C. 20037 (202) 862-9500; *Basic Statistics of the Community; Energy: Monthly Statistics; Energy Statistics Yearbook; Eurostatistics: Data for Short-Term Economic Analysis; External Trade: Monthly Statistics; External Trade: Statistical Yearbook;* and *Fisheries: Yearly Statistics.*

Food and Agricultural Organization of the United Nations (FAO), Via delle Terme di Caracalla, 00100 Rome, Italy (Telephone Number in U.S. (202) 653-2400); *The State of Food and Agriculture.*

International Iron and Steel Institute, 120, rue Colonel Bourg, B-1140 Brussels, Belgium; *Steel Statistical Yearbook.*

Organisation for Economic Co-operation and Development (OECD), 2 rue Andre-Pascal, 75 Paris 16, France (Telephone in U.S. (202) 785-6323); *Economic Outlook; The Footwear, Raw Hides and Skins, and Leather Industry in OECD Countries; Foreign Trade by Commodities; Geographical Distribution of Financial Flows to Developing Countries; Industrial Structure Statistics; The Iron and Steel Industry; Milk, Milk Products, and Egg Balances in OECD Member Countries; OECD Economic Surveys: Belgium - Luxembourg;* and *The Pulp and Paper Industry.*

United Nations Conference on Trade and Development (UNCTAD), New York, New York 10017 (800) 253-9646; *Handbook of International Trade and Development Statistics.*

The World Bank, 1818 H Street, NW, Washington, D.C. 20433 (202) 477-1234; *World Development Indicators.*

LUXEMBOURG - EXTERNAL FINANCING

Organisation for Economic Co-operation and Development (OECD), 2 rue Andre-Pascal, 75 Paris 16, France (Telephone in U.S. (202) 785-6323); *Economic Outlook, Financial Market Trends.*

LUXEMBOURG - EXTERNAL INDEBTEDNESS

Organisation for Economic Co-operation and Development (OECD), 2 rue Andre-Pascal, 75 Paris 16, France (Telephone in U.S. (202) 785-6323); *Financial Market Trends;* and *Geographical Distribution of Financial Flows to Developing Countries.*

The World Bank, 1818 H Street, NW, Washington, D.C. 20433 (202) 477-1234; *World Development Indicators.*

LUXEMBOURG - EXTERNAL TRADE

Euromonitor International, Inc., 122 South Michigan Avenue, Suite 1200, Chicago, Illinois 60603 (800) 577-EURO; *World Marketing Data and Statistics.*

European Commission Office of Press and Public Affairs, 2100 M Street, NW, Washington, D.C. 20037 (202) 862-9500; *ACP: Basic Statistics; Basic Statistics of the Community; Eurostatistics: Data for Short-Term Economic Analysis; External Trade: Monthly Statistics;* and *External Trade: Statistical Yearbook.*

Food and Agricultural Organization of

the United Nations (FAO), Via delle Terme di Caracalla, 00100 Rome, Italy (Telephone Number in U.S. (202) 653-2400); *The State of Food and Agriculture;* and *Trade Yearbook.*

Statistical Office of the United Nations, Publishing Service, New York, New York 10017 (800) 253-9646; *Statistical Yearbook.*

LUXEMBOURG - FABRIC PRODUCTION - See LUXEMBOURG - TEXTILE INDUSTRY

LUXEMBOURG - FARM CROPS - See LUXEMBOURG - CROPS

LUXEMBOURG - FEMALE WORKING POPULATION - See LUXEMBOURG - EMPLOYMENT

LUXEMBOURG - FERTILITY RATES

Central Intelligence Agency, Washington, D.C. 20505 (703) 482-1100, www.cia.gov; *The World Factbook.*

European Commission Office of Press and Public Affairs, 2100 M Street, NW, Washington, D.C. 20037 (202) 862-9500; *Demographic Statistics.*

Statistical Office of the United Nations, Publishing Service, New York, New York 10017 (800) 253-9646; *Human Development Report.*

The World Bank, 1818 H Street, NW, Washington, D.C. 20433 (202) 477-1234; *The World Bank Atlas;* and *World Development Indicators.*

LUXEMBOURG - FERTILIZER

European Commission Office of Press and Public Affairs, 2100 M Street, NW, Washington, D.C. 20037 (202) 862-9500; *Basic Statistics of the Community.*

Food and Agricultural Organization of the United Nations (FAO), Via delle Terme di Caracalla, 00100 Rome, Italy (Telephone Number in U.S. (202) 653-2400); *Fertilizer Yearbook,* and *State of Food and Agriculture.*

Organisation for Economic Co-operation and Development (OECD), 2 rue Andre-Pascal, 75 Paris 16, France (Telephone in U.S. (202) 785-6323); *Economic Accounts for Agriculture;* and *Foreign Trade by Commodities.*

Statistical Office of the United Nations, Publishing Service, New York, New York 10017 (800) 253-9646; *Statistical Yearbook.*

LUXEMBOURG - FETAL MORTALITY - See LUXEMBOURG - MORTALITY

LUXEMBOURG - FIBRE PRODUCTION - See LUXEMBOURG - TEXTILE INDUSTRY

LUXEMBOURG - FILAMENT
PRODUCTION - See LUXEMBOURG -
TEXTILE INDUSTRY

LUXEMBOURG - FINANCE

Economist Intelligence Unit, 111 West 57th Street, New York, New York 10019 (800) 938-4685; *Luxembourg Country Report.*

Europa Publications Limited, 18 Bedford Square, London, WC1B 3JN, England; *The Europa World Year Book.*

European Commission Office of Press and Public Affairs, 2100 M Street, NW, Washington, D.C. 20037 (202) 862-9500; *ACP: Basic Statistics; Basic Statistics of the Community;* and *Eurostatistics: Data for Short-Term Economic Analysis.*

International Monetary Fund, 700 Nineteenth Street, NW, Washington, D.C. 20431 (202) 623-7000; *International Financial Statistics.*

Organisation for Economic Co-operation and Development (OECD), 2 rue Andre-Pascal, 75 Paris 16, France (Telephone in U.S. (202) 785-6323); *Economic Outlook; Financial Market Trends; Geographical Distribution of Financial Flows to Developing Countries; OECD Financial Statistics;* and *Revenue Statistics of OECD Member Countries.*

St. Martin's Press, Inc., 175 Fifth Avenue, New York, New York 10010 (800) 221-7945; *The Statesman's Year-Book.*

LUXEMBOURG - FISHERIES

Euromonitor International, Inc., 122 South Michigan Avenue, Suite 1200, Chicago, Illinois 60603 (800) 577-EURO; *European Marketing Data and Statistics.*

European Commission Office of Press and Public Affairs, 2100 M Street, NW, Washington, D.C. 20037 (202) 862-9500; *Agriculture: Statistical Yearbook; Basic Statistics of the Community;* and *Fisheries: Yearly Statistics.*

Food and Agricultural Organization of the United Nations (FAO), Via delle Terme di Caracalla, 00100 Rome, Italy (Telephone Number in U.S. (202) 653-2400); *The State of Food and Agriculture;* and *Yearbook of Fishery Statistics.*

Organisation for Economic Co-operation and Development (OECD), 2 rue Andre-Pascal, 75 Paris 16, France (Telephone in U.S. (202) 785-6323); *Fisheries: Yearly Statistics; Foreign Trade by Commodities;* and *Industrial Structure Statistics.*

United Nations Conference on Trade and Development, Central Statistical Service, Palais des Nations, Geneva, Switzerland (Telephone in U.S. (800) 253-9646); *UNCTAD Commodity Yearbook.*

LUXEMBOURG - FLAX AND FLAX FIBRE PRODUCTION - See LUXEMBOURG - TEXTILE INDUSTRY

LUXEMBOURG - FLOUR PRODUCTION

European Commission Office of Press and Public Affairs, 2100 M Street, NW, Washington, D.C. 20037 (202) 862-9500; *Basic Statistics of the Community.*

Statistical Office of the United Nations, Publishing Service, New York, New York 10017 (800) 253-9646; *Statistical Yearbook.*

LUXEMBOURG - FOOD

Euromonitor International, Inc., 122 South Michigan Avenue, Suite 1200, Chicago, Illinois 60603 (800) 577-EURO; *Retail Trade International.*

European Commission Office of Press and Public Affairs, 2100 M Street, NW, Washington, D.C. 20037 (202) 862-9500; *Basic Statistics of the Community.*

Food and Agricultural Organization of the United Nations (FAO), Via delle Terme di Caracalla, 00100 Rome, Italy (Telephone Number in U.S. (202) 653-2400); *Production Yearbook;* and *The State of Food and Agriculture.*

Organisation for Economic Co-operation and Development (OECD), 2 rue Andre-Pascal, 75 Paris 16, France (Telephone in U.S. (202) 785-6323); *Foreign Trade by Commodities.*

Statistical Office of the United Nations, Publishing Service, New York, New York 10017 (800) 253-9646; *Human Development Report.*

United Nations Conference on Trade and Development, Central Statistical Service, Palais des Nations, Geneva, Switzerland (Telephone in U.S. (800) 253-9646); *UNCTAD Commodity Yearbook.*

LUXEMBOURG - FOOTWEAR - PRODUCTION INDEX

Organisation for Economic Co-operation and Development (OECD), 2 rue Andre-Pascal, 75 Paris 16, France (Telephone in U.S. (202) 785-6323); *Indicators of Industrial Activity.*

LUXEMBOURG - FOREIGN DEBT

Organisation for Economic Co-operation and Development (OECD), 2 rue Andre-Pascal, 75 Paris 16, France

(Telephone in U.S. (202) 785-6323); *Economic Outlook.*

St. Martin's Press, Inc., 175 Fifth Avenue, New York, New York 10010 (800) 221-7945; *The Statesman's Year-Book.*

LUXEMBOURG - FOREIGN INDEBTEDNESS

Organisation for Economic Co-operation and Development (OECD), 2 rue Andre-Pascal, 75 Paris 16, France (Telephone in U.S. (202) 785-6323); *Economic Outlook;* and *Financial Market Trends.*

LUXEMBOURG - FOREIGN OFFICIAL RESERVES

European Commission Office of Press and Public Affairs, 2100 M Street, NW, Washington, D.C. 20037 (202) 862-9500; *Money and Finance.*

LUXEMBOURG - FOREIGN TRADE

Economist Intelligence Unit, 111 West 57th Street, New York, New York 10019 (800) 938-4685; *Luxembourg Country Report.*

Euromonitor International, Inc., 122 South Michigan Avenue, Suite 1200, Chicago, Illinois 60603 (800) 577-EURO; *European Marketing Data and Statistics;* and *The World Economic Factbook.*

Europa Publications Limited, 18 Bedford Square, London, WC1B 3JN, England; *The Europa World Year Book.*

European Commission Office of Press and Public Affairs, 2100 M Street, NW, Washington, D.C. 20037 (202) 862-9500; *Basic Statistics of the Community; Energy Statistics Yearbook;* and *Iron and Steel: Statistical Yearbook.*

Food and Agricultural Organization of the United Nations (FAO), Via delle Terme di Caracalla, 00100 Rome, Italy (Telephone Number in U.S. (202) 653-2400); *The State of Food and Agriculture.*

International Iron and Steel Institute, 120, rue Colonel Bourg, B-1140 Brussels, Belgium; *Steel Statistical Yearbook.*

Organisation for Economic Co-operation and Development (OECD), 2 rue Andre-Pascal, 75 Paris 16, France (Telephone in U.S. (202) 785-6323); *Economic Outlook; The Footwear, Raw Hides and Skins, and Leather Industry in OECD Countries; Foreign Trade by Commodities; Maritime Transport; Meat Balances in OECD Member Countries;* and *OECD Economic Surveys: Belgium - Luxembourg.*

St. Martin's Press, Inc., 175 Fifth Avenue, New York, New York 10010 (800) 221-7945; *The Statesman's Year-Book.*

Statistical Office of the United Nations, Publishing Service, New York, New York 10017 (800) 253-9646; *Statistical Yearbook.*

United Nations Conference on Trade and Development, Central Statistical Service, Palais des Nations, Geneva, Switzerland (Telephone in U.S. (800) 253-9646); *UNCTAD Commodity Yearbook.*

The World Bank, 1818 H Street, NW, Washington, D.C. 20433 (202) 477-1234; *World Development Indicators.*

LUXEMBOURG - FORESTRY AND FOREST PRODUCTS

Euromonitor International, Inc., 122 South Michigan Avenue, Suite 1200, Chicago, Illinois 60603 (800) 577-EURO; *European Marketing Data and Statistics.*

Europa Publications Limited, 18 Bedford Square, London, WC1B 3JN, England; *The Europa World Year Book.*

European Commission Office of Press and Public Affairs, 2100 M Street, NW, Washington, D.C. 20037 (202) 862-9500; *Agriculture: Statistical Yearbook; Basic Statistics of the Community;* and *Industrial Production: Quarterly Statistics.*

Food and Agricultural Organization of the United Nations (FAO), Via delle Terme di Caracalla, 00100 Rome, Italy (Telephone Number in U.S. (202) 653-2400); *The State of Food and Agriculture.*

Organisation for Economic Co-operation and Development (OECD), 2 rue Andre-Pascal, 75 Paris 16, France (Telephone in U.S. (202) 785-6323); *Foreign Trade by Commodities; Indicators of Industrial Activity; Industrial Structure Statistics;* and *The Pulp and Paper Industry.*

St. Martin's Press, Inc., 175 Fifth Avenue, New York, New York 10010 (800) 221-7945; *The Statesman's Year-Book.*

Statistical Office of the United Nations, Publishing Service, New York, New York 10017 (800) 253-9646; *Statistical Yearbook.*

United Nations Conference on Trade and Development, Central Statistical Service, Palais des Nations, Geneva, Switzerland (Telephone in U.S. (800) 253-9646); *UNCTAD Commodity Yearbook.*

United Nations Educational, Scientific and Cultural Organization (UNESCO), 7 Place de Fontenoy, F-75700 Paris, France (Telephone Number in U.S. (212) 963-5981); *Statistical Yearbook.*

LUXEMBOURG - FRUIT PRODUCTION - See LUXEMBOURG - CROPS

LUXEMBOURG - FURNITURE AND WOOD PRODUCTS - EXPORTS AND IMPORTS

European Commission Office of Press and Public Affairs, 2100 M Street, NW, Washington, D.C. 20037 (202) 862-9500; *Basic Statistics of the Community.*

Organisation for Economic Co-operation and Development (OECD), 2 rue Andre-Pascal, 75 Paris 16, France (Telephone in U.S. (202) 785-6323); *Foreign Trade by Commodities;* and *Industrial Structure Statistics.*

LUXEMBOURG - GARLIC PRODUCTION - See LUXEMBOURG - CROPS

LUXEMBOURG - GAS - See LUXEMBOURG - MINING AND MINERAL PRODUCTS

LUXEMBOURG - GENERAL INDUSTRIAL STATISTICS - See LUXEMBOURG - INDUSTRY

LUXEMBOURG - GENERAL MORTALITY - See LUXEMBOURG - MORTALITY

LUXEMBOURG - GEOGRAPHIC DATA

European Commission Office of Press and Public Affairs, 2100 M Street, NW, Washington, D.C. 20037 (202) 862-9500; *Basic Statistics of the Community.*

LUXEMBOURG - GLASS AND GLASS PRODUCTS - PRODUCTION INDEX - See LUXEMBOURG - MINING AND MINERAL PRODUCTS

LUXEMBOURG - GOATS - See LUXEMBOURG - LIVESTOCK AND POULTRY

LUXEMBOURG - GOLD HOLDINGS

The World Bank, 1818 H Street, NW, Washington, D.C. 20433 (202) 477-1234; *World Development Indicators.*

LUXEMBOURG - GOLD PRODUCTION AND CONSUMPTION - See LUXEMBOURG - MINING AND MINERAL PRODUCTS

LUXEMBOURG - GOVERNMENT

Central Intelligence Agency, Washington, D.C. 20505 (703) 482-1100, www.cia.gov; *The World Factbook.*

Europa Publications Limited, 18 Bedford Square, London, WC1B 3JN, England; *The Europa World Year Book.*

European Commission Office of Press and Public Affairs, 2100 M Street, NW, Washington, D.C. 20037 (202) 862-9500; *Basic Statistics of the Community;*

Government Financing of Research and Development; and *Money and Finances.*

International Monetary Fund, 700 Nineteenth Street, NW, Washington, D.C. 20431 (202) 623-7000; *Government Finance Statistics Yearbook.*

Organisation for Economic Co-operation and Development (OECD), 2 rue Andre-Pascal, 75 Paris 16, France (Telephone in U.S. (202) 785-6323); *Economic Outlook;* and *Revenue Statistics of OECD Member Countries.*

St. Martin's Press, Inc., 175 Fifth Avenue, New York, New York 10010 (800) 221-7945; *The Statesman's Year-Book.*

Statistical Office of the United Nations, Publishing Service, New York, New York 10017 (800) 253-9646; *National Accounts Statistics.*

The World Bank, 1818 H Street, NW, Washington, D.C. 20433 (202) 477-1234; *World Development Indicators.*

LUXEMBOURG - GRAIN PRODUCTION - See LUXEMBOURG - CROPS

LUXEMBOURG - GRANTS

International Monetary Fund, 700 Nineteenth Street, NW, Washington, D.C. 20431 (202) 623-7000; *Government Finance Statistics Yearbook.*

Organisation for Economic Co-operation and Development (OECD), 2 rue Andre-Pascal, 75 Paris 16, France (Telephone in U.S. (202) 785-6323); *Geographical Distribution of Financial Flows to Developing Countries.*

LUXEMBOURG - GREEN PEPPER AND CHILIE PRODUCTION - See LUXEMBOURG - CROPS

LUXEMBOURG - GROSS DOMESTIC PRODUCT

The Economist Intelligence Unit, 111 West 57th Street, New York, New York 10019 (800) 938-4685; *Luxembourg Country Report;* and *The World Market Atlas.*

Euromonitor International, Inc., 122 South Michigan Avenue, Suite 1200, Chicago, Illinois 60603 (800) 577-EURO; *The World Economic Factbook.*

European Commission Office of Press and Public Affairs, 2100 M Street, NW, Washington, D.C. 20037 (202) 862-9500; *Basic Statistics of the Community; Eurostatistics: Data for Short-Term Economic Analysis; Government Financing of Research and Development; Iron and Steel: Statistical Yearbook;* and *Money and Finance.*

Organisation for Economic Co-operation and Development (OECD), 2 rue Andre-Pascal, 75 Paris 16, France (Telephone in U.S. (202) 785-6323); *Economic Outlook; Geographical Distribution of Financial Flows to Developing Countries;* and *Revenue Statistics of OECD Member Countries.*

St. Martin's Press, Inc., 175 Fifth Avenue, New York, New York 10010 (800) 221-7945; *The Statesman's Year-Book.*

Statistical Office of the United Nations, Publishing Service, New York, New York 10017 (800) 253-9646; *Human Development Report; National Accounts Statistics;* and *Statistical Yearbook.*

The World Bank, 1818 H Street, NW, Washington, D.C. 20433 (202) 477-1234; *World Development Indicators.*

LUXEMBOURG - GROSS INDUSTRIAL PRODUCT - GROWTH RATES

European Commission Office of Press and Public Affairs, 2100 M Street, NW, Washington, D.C. 20037 (202) 862-9500; *Government Financing of Research and Development.*

LUXEMBOURG - GROSS NATIONAL PRODUCT

European Commission Office of Press and Public Affairs, 2100 M Street, NW, Washington, D.C. 20037 (202) 862-9500; *ACP: Basic Statistics;* and *Basic Statistics of the Community.*

Organisation for Economic Co-operation and Development (OECD), 2 rue Andre-Pascal, 75 Paris 16, France (Telephone in U.S. (202) 785-6323); *Economic Outlook;* and *Geographical Distribution of Financial Flows to Developing Countries.*

U.S. Arms Control and Disarmament Agency, 320 Twenty-first Street, NW, Washington, D.C. 20451 (202) 647-8677; *World Military Expenditures and Arms Transfers.*

The World Bank, 1818 H Street, NW, Washington, D.C. 20433 (202) 477-1234; *The World Bank Atlas;* and *World Development Indicators.*

LUXEMBOURG - GROUNDNUT PRODUCTION - See LUXEMBOURG - CROPS

LUXEMBOURG - HAY PRODUCTION - See LUXEMBOURG - CROPS

LUXEMBOURG - HAZELNUT PRODUCTION - See LUXEMBOURG - CROPS

LUXEMBOURG - HEALTH

Euromonitor International, Inc., 122 South Michigan Avenue, Suite 1200, Chicago, Illinois 60603 (800) 577-EURO; *World Marketing Data and Statistics.*

European Commission Office of Press and Public Affairs, 2100 M Street, NW, Washington, D.C. 20037 (202) 862-9500; *Basic Statistics of the Community;* and *Regions: Statistical Yearbook.*

Organisation for Economic Co-operation and Development (OECD), 2 rue Andre-Pascal, 75 Paris 16, France (Telephone Number in U.S. (202) 785-6323); *OECD Health Systems: Facts and Trends.*

St. Martin's Press, Inc., 175 Fifth Avenue, New York, New York 10010 (800) 221-7945; *The Statesman's Year-Book.*

Statistical Office of the United Nations, Publishing Service, New York, New York 10017 (800) 253-9646; *Human Development Report;* and *Statistical Yearbook.*

World Health Organization, Office of Publications, 20 Avenue Appia, CH-1211 Geneva 27, Switzerland (Telephone Number in U.S. (518) 436-9686); *World Health Statistics Annual.*

LUXEMBOURG - HEALTH EXPENDITURES

International Monetary Fund, 700 Nineteenth Street, NW, Washington, D.C. 20431 (202) 623-7000; *Government Finance Statistics Yearbook.*

LUXEMBOURG - HEMP FIBRE PRODUCTION - See LUXEMBOURG - TEXTILE INDUSTRY

LUXEMBOURG - HIDE PRODUCTION

Food and Agricultural Organization of the United Nations (FAO), Via delle Terme di Caracalla, 00100 Rome, Italy (Telephone Number in U.S. (202) 653-2400); *Production Yearbook.*

Organisation for Economic Co-operation and Development (OECD), 2 rue Andre-Pascal, 75 Paris 16, France (Telephone in U.S. (202) 785-6323); *The Footwear, Raw Hides and Skins, and Leather Industry in OECD Countries; Foreign Trade by Commodities;* and *Indicators of Industrial Activity.*

LUXEMBOURG - HIGHWAYS

Central Intelligence Agency, Washington, D.C. 20505 (703) 482-1100, www.cia.gov; *The World Factbook.*

European Commission Office of Press and Public Affairs, 2100 M Street, NW, Washington, D.C. 20037 (202) 862-9500; *Basic Statistics of the Community;* and *Transport Annual Statistics.*

International Road Federation, 2600 Virginia Avenue, N.W., Washington, D.C. 20037 (202) 338-4641; *World Road Statistics.*

St. Martin's Press, Inc., 175 Fifth Avenue, New York, New York 10010 (800) 221-7945; *The Statesman's Year-Book.*

Statistical Office of the United Nations, Publishing Service, New York, New York 10017 (800) 253-9646; *Annual Bulletin of Transport Statistics for Europe.*

LUXEMBOURG - HOPS PRODUCTION - See LUXEMBOURG - CROPS

LUXEMBOURG - HORSES - See LUXEMBOURG - LIVESTOCK AND POULTRY

LUXEMBOURG - HOURS OF WORK - See LUXEMBOURG - EMPLOYMENT

LUXEMBOURG - HOUSING AND HOUSING UNITS

Euromonitor International, Inc., 122 South Michigan Avenue, Suite 1200, Chicago, Illinois 60603 (800) 577-EURO; *World Marketing Data and Statistics.*

European Commission Office of Press and Public Affairs, 2100 M Street, NW, Washington, D.C. 20037 (202) 862-9500; *Basic Statistics of the Community; Labor Force Sample Survey;* and *Regions: Statistical Yearbook.*

LUXEMBOURG - HOUSING CONSTRUCTION - See LUXEMBOURG - CONSTRUCTION INDUSTRY

LUXEMBOURG - HOUSING EXPENDITURES

European Commission Office of Press and Public Affairs, 2100 M Street, NW, Washington, D.C. 20037 (202) 862-9500; *Basic Statistics of the Community.*

International Monetary Fund, 700 Nineteenth Street, NW, Washington, D.C. 20431 (202) 623-7000; *Government Finance Statistics Yearbook.*

LUXEMBOURG - HYDROCHLORIC ACID PRODUCTION

European Commission Office of Press and Public Affairs, 2100 M Street, NW, Washington, D.C. 20037 (202) 862-9500; *Basic Statistics of the Community.*

LUXEMBOURG - ILLITERATE POPULATION

Central Intelligence Agency, Washington, D.C. 20505 (703) 482-1100, www.cia.gov; *The World Factbook*.

The Economist Intelligence Unit, 111 West 57th Street, New York, New York 10019 (800) 938-4685; *The World Market Atlas*.

Euromonitor International, Inc., 122 South Michigan Avenue, Suite 1200, Chicago, Illinois 60603 (800) 577-EURO; *The World Economic Factbook*.

Statistical Office of the United Nations, Publishing Service, New York, New York 10017 (800) 253-9646; *Human Development Report*.

LUXEMBOURG - IMPORTS

American Automobile Manufacturers Association, 1401 H Street, NW, Suite 900, Washington, D.C. 20005 (202) 326-5500; *World Motor Vehicle Data*.

Central Intelligence Agency, Washington, D.C. 20505 (703) 482-1100, www.cia.gov; *The World Factbook*.

The Economist Intelligence Unit, 111 West 57th Street, New York, New York 10019 (800) 938-4685; *Luxembourg Country Report;* and *The World Market Atlas*.

Euromonitor International, Inc., 122 South Michigan Avenue, Suite 1200, Chicago, Illinois 60603 (800) 577-EURO; *The World Economic Factbook*.

Europa Publications Limited, 18 Bedford Square, London, WC1B 3JN, England; *The Europa World Year Book*.

European Commission Office of Press and Public Affairs, 2100 M Street, NW, Washington, D.C. 20037 (202) 862-9500; *Basic Statistics of the Community; Energy: Monthly Statistics; Energy Statistics Yearbook; Eurostatistics: Data for Short-Term Economic Analysis; External Trade: Monthly Statistics; External Trade: Statistical Yearbook;* and *Fisheries: Yearly Statistics*.

Food and Agricultural Organization of the United Nations (FAO), Via delle Terme di Caracalla, 00100 Rome, Italy (Telephone Number in U.S. (202) 653-2400); *The State of Food and Agriculture*.

International Iron and Steel Institute, 120, rue Colonel Bourg, B-1140 Brussels, Belgium; *Steel Statistical Yearbook*.

Organisation for Economic Co-operation and Development (OECD), 2 rue Andre-Pascal, 75 Paris 16, France (Telephone in U.S. (202) 785-6323); *Economic Outlook; The Footwear, Raw Hides and Skins, and Leather Industry in*

OECD Countries; Industrial Structure Statistics; The Iron and Steel Industry; Milk, Milk Products, and Egg Balances in OECD Member Countries; OECD Economic Surveys: Belgium - Luxembourg; and *The Pulp and Paper Industry*.

United Nations Conference on Trade and Development (UNCTAD), New York, New York 10017 (800) 253-9646; *Handbook of International Trade and Development Statistics*.

The World Bank, 1818 H Street, NW, Washington, D.C. 20433 (202) 477-1234; *World Development Indicators*.

LUXEMBOURG - INCOME TAXES - See LUXEMBOURG - TAXATION

LUXEMBOURG - INDUSTRIAL METALS PRODUCTION - See LUXEMBOURG - MINING AND MINERAL PRODUCTS

LUXEMBOURG - INDUSTRY

Central Intelligence Agency, Washington, D.C. 20505 (703) 482-1100, www.cia.gov; *The World Factbook*.

Economist Intelligence Unit, 111 West 57th Street, New York, New York 10019 (800) 938-4685; *Luxembourg Country Report*.

Euromonitor International, Inc., 122 South Michigan Avenue, Suite 1200, Chicago, Illinois 60603 (800) 577-EURO; *The World Economic Factbook;* and *World Marketing Data and Statistics*.

Europa Publications Limited, 18 Bedford Square, London, WC1B 3JN, England; *The Europa World Year Book*.

European Commission Office of Press and Public Affairs, 2100 M Street, NW, Washington, D.C. 20037 (202) 862-9500; *Basic Statistics of the Community; Employment and Unemployment; Eurostatistics: Data for Short-Term Economic Analysis;* and *Labor Force Sample Survey*.

International Labour Office, I.L.O. Publications, 1828 L Street, N.W., Suite 801, Washington, D.C. 20036 (301) 638-3152; *Yearbook of Labour Statistics*.

Organisation for Economic Co-operation and Development (OECD), 2 rue Andre-Pascal, 75 Paris 16, France (Telephone in U.S. (202) 785-6323); *Economic Outlook; Industrial Structure Statistics;* and *Main Economic Indicators - Historical Statistics*.

St. Martin's Press, Inc., 175 Fifth Avenue, New York, New York 10010 (800) 221-7945; *The Statesman's Year-Book*.

Statistical Office of the United Nations, Publishing Service, New York, New York 10017 (800) 253-9646; *Industrial Commodity Statistics Yearbook;* and *Statistical Yearbook*.

The World Bank, 1818 H Street, NW, Washington, D.C. 20433 (202) 477-1234; *World Development Indicators*.

World Intellectual Property Organization, 34 Chemin des Colombettes, CH-1211 Geneva 20, Switzerland; *Industrial Property Statistics*.

LUXEMBOURG - INFANT AND MATERNAL MORTALITY - See LUXEMBOURG - MORTALITY

LUXEMBOURG - INTEREST RATES

European Commission Office of Press and Public Affairs, 2100 M Street, NW, Washington, D.C. 20037 (202) 862-9500; *Money and Finance*.

Organisation for Economic Co-operation and Development (OECD), 2 rue Andre-Pascal, 75 Paris 16, France (Telephone in U.S. (202) 785-6323); *Economic Outlook; Financial Market Trends;* and *OECD Financial Statistics*.

LUXEMBOURG - INTERNAL TRADE

European Commission Office of Press and Public Affairs, 2100 M Street, NW, Washington, D.C. 20037 (202) 862-9500; *Basic Statistics of the Community*.

LUXEMBOURG - INTERNATIONAL FINANCE

European Commission Office of Press and Public Affairs, 2100 M Street, NW, Washington, D.C. 20037 (202) 862-9500; *Basic Statistics of the Community*.

Organisation for Economic Co-operation and Development (OECD), 2 rue Andre-Pascal, 75 Paris 16, France (Telephone in U.S. (202) 785-6323); *Economic Outlook;* and *Financial Market Trends*.

LUXEMBOURG - INTERNATIONAL LIQUIDITY

International Monetary Fund, 700 Nineteenth Street, NW, Washington, D.C. 20431 (202) 623-7000; *International Financial Statistics*.

Organisation for Economic Co-operation and Development (OECD), 2 rue Andre-Pascal, 75 Paris 16, France (Telephone in U.S. (202) 785-6323); *Economic Outlook;* and *Financial Market Trends*.

LUXEMBOURG - INTERNATIONAL

RESERVES EXCLUDING GOLD

Statistical Office of the United Nations, Publishing Service, New York, New York 10017 (800) 253-9646; *Statistical Yearbook.*

The World Bank, 1818 H Street, NW, Washington, D.C. 20433 (202) 477-1234; *World Development Indicators.*

LUXEMBOURG - INTERNATIONAL STATISTICS

Organisation for Economic Co-operation and Development (OECD), 2 rue Andre-Pascal, 75 Paris 16, France (Telephone in U.S. (202) 785-6323); *Financial Market Trends;* and *Tourism Policy and International Tourism in OECD Member Countries.*

LUXEMBOURG - INVESTMENTS

Organisation for Economic Co-operation and Development (OECD), 2 rue Andre-Pascal, 75 Paris 16, France (Telephone in U.S. (202) 785-6323); *Economic Outlook; Financial Market Trends; Industrial Structure Statistics; The Iron and Steel Industry;* and *Textile Industry in OECD Countries.*

LUXEMBOURG - IRON ORE - See LUXEMBOURG - MINING AND MINERAL PRODUCTS

LUXEMBOURG - JUTE PRODUCTION - See LUXEMBOURG - CROPS

LUXEMBOURG - LABOR

Central Intelligence Agency, Washington, D.C. 20505 (703) 482-1100, www.cia.gov; *The World Factbook.*

Euromonitor International, Inc., 122 South Michigan Avenue, Suite 1200, Chicago, Illinois 60603 (800) 577-EURO; *World Marketing Data and Statistics.*

Europa Publications Limited, 18 Bedford Square, London, WC1B 3JN, England; *The Europa World Year Book.*

European Commission Office of Press and Public Affairs, 2100 M Street, NW, Washington, D.C. 20037 (202) 862-9500; *Basic Statistics of the Community; Labor Force Sample Survey;* and *Regions: Statistical Yearbook.*

Food and Agricultural Organization of the United Nations (FAO), Via delle Terme di Caracalla, 00100 Rome, Italy (Telephone Number in U.S. (202) 653-2400); *The State of Food and Agriculture.*

International Labour Office, I.L.O. Publications, 1828 L Street, N.W., Suite 801, Washington, D.C. 20036 (301) 638-3152; *Yearbook of Labour Statistics.*

Organisation for Economic Co-operation and Development (OECD), 2 rue Andre-Pascal, 75 Paris 16, France (Telephone in U.S. (202) 785-6323); *Economic Outlook; The Iron and Steel Industry; Labor Force Statistics; Main Economic Indicators - Historical Statistics; Maritime Transport; OECD Economic Surveys: Belgium - Luxembourg; OECD Employment Outlook;* and *Textile Industry in OECD Countries.*

St. Martin's Press, Inc., 175 Fifth Avenue, New York, New York 10010 (800) 221-7945; *The Statesman's Year-Book.*

Statistical Office of the United Nations, Publishing Service, New York, New York 10017 (800) 253-9646; *Human Development Report.*

The World Bank, 1818 H Street, NW, Washington, D.C. 20433 (202) 477-1234; *The World Bank Atlas;* and *World Development Indicators.*

LUXEMBOURG - LAND USE

Central Intelligence Agency, Washington, D.C. 20505 (703) 482-1100, www.cia.gov; *The World Factbook.*

Euromonitor International, Inc., 122 South Michigan Avenue, Suite 1200, Chicago, Illinois 60603 (800) 577-EURO; *European Marketing Data and Statistics.*

European Commission Office of Press and Public Affairs, 2100 M Street, NW, Washington, D.C. 20037 (202) 862-9500; *Agriculture: Statistical Yearbook; Basic Statistics of the Community; Crop Production: Quarterly Statistics;* and *Regions: Statistical Yearbook.*

Food and Agricultural Organization of the United Nations (FAO), Via delle Terme di Caracalla, 00100 Rome, Italy (Telephone Number in U.S. (202) 653-2400); *Production Yearbook.*

LUXEMBOURG - LEAD AND LEAD ORE PRODUCTION AND CONSUMPTION - See LUXEMBOURG - MINING AND MINERAL PRODUCTS

LUXEMBOURG - LEATHER - PRODUCTION INDEX

Organisation for Economic Co-operation and Development (OECD), 2 rue Andre-Pascal, 75 Paris 16, France (Telephone in U.S. (202) 785-6323); *Indicators of Industrial Activity.*

LUXEMBOURG - LEATHER AND FOOTWEAR EXPORTS AND IMPORTS

European Commission Office of Press and Public Affairs, 2100 M Street, NW, Washington, D.C. 20037 (202) 862-9500;

Basic Statistics of the Community.

Organisation for Economic Co-operation and Development (OECD), 2 rue Andre-Pascal, 75 Paris 16, France (Telephone in U.S. (202) 785-6323); *The Footwear, Raw Hides and Skins, and Leather Industry in OECD Countries.*

LUXEMBOURG - LIBRARIES

Euromonitor International, Inc., 122 South Michigan Avenue, Suite 1200, Chicago, Illinois 60603 (800) 577-EURO; *European Marketing Data and Statistics.*

LUXEMBOURG - LIFE EXPECTANCY

Central Intelligence Agency, Washington, D.C. 20505 (703) 482-1100, www.cia.gov; *The World Factbook.*

Euromonitor International, Inc., 122 South Michigan Avenue, Suite 1200, Chicago, Illinois 60603 (800) 577-EURO; *The World Economic Factbook.*

Organisation for Economic Co-operation and Development (OECD), 2 rue Andre-Pascal, 75 Paris 16, France (Telephone in U.S. (202) 785-6323); *Economic Outlook.*

Statistical Office of the United Nations, Publishing Service, New York, New York 10017 (800) 253-9646; *Human Development Report;* and *World Statistics Pocketbook*

The World Bank, 1818 H Street, NW, Washington, D.C. 20433 (202) 477-1234; *The World Bank Atlas.*

LUXEMBOURG - LIGNITE PRODUCTION - See LUXEMBOURG - MINING AND MINERAL PRODUCTS

LUXEMBOURG - LITERACY RATE

Euromonitor International, Inc., 122 South Michigan Avenue, Suite 1200, Chicago, Illinois 60603 (800) 577-EURO; *World Marketing Data and Statistics.*

LUXEMBOURG - LIVESTOCK AND POULTRY

Commodity Research Bureau, Incorporated, 30 South Wacker Drive, Chicago Illinois 60606 (312) 454-1801; *Commodity Year Book.*

Euromonitor International, Inc., 122 South Michigan Avenue, Suite 1200, Chicago, Illinois 60603 (800) 577-EURO; *European Marketing Data and Statistics.*

Europa Publications Limited, 18 Bedford Square, London, WC1B 3JN, England; *The Europa World Year Book.*

European Commission Office of Press

and Public Affairs, 2100 M Street, NW, Washington, D.C. 20037 (202) 862-9500; *Agriculture: Statistical Yearbook; Basic Statistics of the Community; Eurostatistics: Data for Short-Term Economic Analysis;* and *Regions: Statistical Yearbook.*

Food and Agricultural Organization of the United Nations (FAO), Via delle Terme di Caracalla, 00100 Rome, Italy (Telephone Number in U.S. (202) 653-2400); *Production Yearbook;* and *The State of Food and Agriculture.*

Organisation for Economic Co-operation and Development (OECD), 2 rue Andre-Pascal, 75 Paris 16, France (Telephone in U.S. (202) 785-6323); *Economic Accounts for Agriculture;* and *Meat Balances in OECD Member Countries.*

St. Martin's Press, Inc., 175 Fifth Avenue, New York, New York 10010 (800) 221-7945; *The Statesman's Year-Book.*

United Nations Conference on Trade and Development, Central Statistical Service, Palais des Nations, Geneva, Switzerland (Telephone in U.S. (800) 253-9646); *UNCTAD Commodity Yearbook.*

LUXEMBOURG - LIVING LEVELS - See LUXEMBOURG - LIFE EXPECTANCY

LUXEMBOURG - MACHINERY - PRODUCTION INDEX

Organisation for Economic Co-operation and Development (OECD), 2 rue Andre-Pascal, 75 Paris 16, France (Telephone in U.S. (202) 785-6323); *Indicators of Industrial Activity.*

LUXEMBOURG - MAGNESIUM PRODUCTION AND CONSUMPTION - See LUXEMBOURG - MINING AND MINERAL PRODUCTS

LUXEMBOURG - MAIL - NUMBER OF PIECES SENT OR RECEIVED

European Commission Office of Press and Public Affairs, 2100 M Street, NW, Washington, D.C. 20037 (202) 862-9500; *Transport Annual Statistics.*

Statistical Office of the United Nations, Publishing Service, New York, New York 10017 (800) 253-9646; *Statistical Yearbook.*

LUXEMBOURG - MAIN ECONOMIC INDICATORS - See LUXEMBOURG - ECONOMY

LUXEMBOURG - MANGANESE PRODUCTION AND CONSUMPTION -See LUXEMBOURG - MINING AND MINERAL PRODUCTS

LUXEMBOURG - MANUFACTURING

American Automobile Manufacturers Association, 1401 H Street, NW, Suite 900, Washington, D.C. 20005 (202) 326-5500; *World Motor Vehicle Data.*

European Commission Office of Press and Public Affairs, 2100 M Street, NW, Washington, D.C. 20037 (202) 862-9500; *Basic Statistics of the Community; Eurostatistics: Data for Short-Term Economic Analysis; Industrial Production: Quarterly Statistics;* and *Labor Force Sample Survey.*

Organisation for Economic Co-operation and Development (OECD), 2 rue Andre-Pascal, 75 Paris 16, France (Telephone in U.S. (202) 785-6323); *Indicators of Industrial Activity;* and *OECD Economic Surveys: Belgium - Luxembourg.*

Statistical Office of the United Nations, Publishing Service, New York, New York 10017 (800) 253-9646; *Statistical Yearbook.*

The World Bank, 1818 H Street, NW, Washington, D.C. 20433 (202) 477-1234; *World Development Indicators.*

LUXEMBOURG - MARRIAGE RATES

Europa Publications Limited, 18 Bedford Square, London, WC1B 3JN, England; *The Europa World Year Book.*

European Commission Office of Press and Public Affairs, 2100 M Street, NW, Washington, D.C. 20037 (202) 862-9500; *Basic Statistics of the Community.*

Statistical Office of the United Nations, Publishing Service, New York, New York 10017 (800) 253-9646; *Demographic Yearbook;* and *Statistical Yearbook.*

LUXEMBOURG - MEAT PRODUCTION - See LUXEMBOURG - LIVESTOCK AND POULTRY

LUXEMBOURG - MERCHANT SHIPPING

European Commission Office of Press and Public Affairs, 2100 M Street, NW, Washington, D.C. 20037 (202) 862-9500; *Basic Statistics of the Community; Fisheries: Yearly Statistics; Transport Annual Statistics;* and *Regions: Statistical Yearbook.*

Organisation for Economic Co-operation and Development (OECD), 2 rue Andre-Pascal, 75 Paris 16, France (Telephone in U.S. (202) 785-6323); *Maritime Transport.*

St. Martin's Press, Inc., 175 Fifth Avenue, New York, New York 10010 (800) 221-7945; *The Statesman's Year-Book.*

Statistical Office of the United Nations, Publishing Service, New York, New York

10017 (800) 253-9646; *Annual Bulletin of Transport Statistics for Europe.*

LUXEMBOURG - MERCURY PRODUCTION AND CONSUMPTION - See LUXEMBOURG - MINING AND MINERAL PRODUCTS

LUXEMBOURG - MILITARY

Central Intelligence Agency, Washington, D.C. 20505 (703) 482-1100, www.cia.gov; *The World Factbook.*

Euromonitor International, Inc., 122 South Michigan Avenue, Suite 1200, Chicago, Illinois 60603 (800) 577-EURO; *World Marketing Data and Statistics.*

European Commission Office of Press and Public Affairs, 2100 M Street, NW, Washington, D.C. 20037 (202) 862-9500; *Government Financing of Research and Development.*

The International Institute for Strategic Studies, 23 Tavistock Street, London WC2E 7NQ, England 44 171 3797676; *The Military Balance.*

International Monetary Fund, 700 Nineteenth Street, NW, Washington, D.C. 20431 (202) 623-7000; *Government Finance Statistics Yearbook.*

St. Martin's Press, Inc., 175 Fifth Avenue, New York, New York 10010 (800) 221-7945; *The Statesman's Year-Book.*

Statistical Office of the United Nations, Publishing Service, New York, New York 10017 (800) 253-9646; *Human Development Report.*

U.S. Arms Control and Disarmament Agency, 320 Twenty-first Street, NW, Washington, D.C. 20451 (202) 647-8677; *World Military Expenditures and Arms Transfers.*

LUXEMBOURG - MILK PRODUCTION - LUXEMBOURG - DAIRY PRODUCTS

LUXEMBOURG - MILLET PRODUCTION - See LUXEMBOURG - CROPS

LUXEMBOURG - MINING AND MINERAL PRODUCTS

Commodity Research Bureau, Incorporated, 30 South Wacker Drive, Chicago Illinois 60606 (312) 454-1801; *Commodity Year Book.*

Europa Publications Limited, 18 Bedford Square, London, WC1B 3JN, England; *The Europa World Year Book.*

European Commission Office of Press and Public Affairs, 2100 M Street, NW, Washington, D.C. 20037 (202) 862-9500; *ACP: Basic Statistics; Basic Statistics of the*

Community; Energy: Monthly Statistics; Energy Statistics Yearbook; Eurostatistics: Data for Short-Term Economic Analysis; Industrial Production: Quarterly Statistics; Iron and Steel: Statistical Yearbook; and *Regions: Statistical Yearbook.*

International Iron and Steel Institute, 120, rue Colonel Bourg, B-1140 Brussels, Belgium; *Steel Statistical Yearbook.*

Organisation for Economic Co-operation and Development (OECD), 2 rue Andre-Pascal, 75 Paris 16, France (Telephone in U.S. (202) 785-6323); *Coal Information; Energy Statistics of OECD Countries; Foreign Trade by Commodities; Indicators of Industrial Activity; Industrial Structure Statistics; The Iron and Steel Industry; The Non-Ferrous Metals Industry;* and *OECD Economic Surveys: Belgium - Luxembourg.*

St. Martin's Press, Inc., 175 Fifth Avenue, New York, New York 10010 (800) 221-7945; *The Statesman's Year-Book.*

Statistical Office of the United Nations, Publishing Service, New York, New York 10017 (800) 253-9646; *Statistical Yearbook.*

United Nations Conference on Trade and Development, Central Statistical Service, Palais des Nations, Geneva, Switzerland (Telephone in U.S. (800) 253-9646); *UNCTAD Commodity Yearbook.*

LUXEMBOURG - MOLYBDENUM AND MOLYBDENUM ORE PRODUCTION AND CONSUMPTION - See LUXEMBOURG - MINING AND MINERAL PRODUCTS

LUXEMBOURG - MONEY AND CREDIT

Organisation for Economic Co-operation and Development (OECD), 2 rue Andre-Pascal, 75 Paris 16, France (Telephone in U.S. (202) 785-6323); *OECD Economic Surveys: Belgium - Luxembourg.*

LUXEMBOURG - MONEY EXCHANGE RATE - See LUXEMBOURG - EXCHANGE RATES

LUXEMBOURG - MONEY RATES - MARKET

European Commission Office of Press and Public Affairs, 2100 M Street, NW, Washington, D.C. 20037 (202) 862-9500; *Basic Statistics of the Community.*

Organisation for Economic Co-operation and Development (OECD), 2 rue Andre-Pascal, 75 Paris 16, France (Telephone in U.S. (202) 785-6323); *Economic Outlook;* and *Financial Market Trends.*

LUXEMBOURG - MONEY RESERVES

European Commission Office of Press

and Public Affairs, 2100 M Street, NW, Washington, D.C. 20037 (202) 862-9500; *Basic Statistics of the Community.*

Organisation for Economic Co-operation and Development (OECD), 2 rue Andre-Pascal, 75 Paris 16, France (Telephone in U.S. (202) 785-6323); *Economic Outlook;* and *Financial Market Trends.*

LUXEMBOURG - MONEY SUPPLY

Economist Intelligence Unit, 111 West 57th Street, New York, New York 10019 (800) 938-4685; *Luxembourg Country Report.*

European Commission Office of Press and Public Affairs, 2100 M Street, NW, Washington, D.C. 20037 (202) 862-9500; *Basic Statistics of the Community; Eurostatistics: Data for Short-Term Economic Analysis;* and *Money and Finance.*

Organisation for Economic Co-operation and Development (OECD), 2 rue Andre-Pascal, 75 Paris 16, France (Telephone in U.S. (202) 785-6323); *Economic Outlook.*

The World Bank, 1818 H Street, NW, Washington, D.C. 20433 (202) 477-1234; *World Development Indicators.*

LUXEMBOURG - MORTALITY

Central Intelligence Agency, Washington, D.C. 20505 (703) 482-1100, www.cia.gov; *The World Factbook.*

Euromonitor International, Inc., 122 South Michigan Avenue, Suite 1200, Chicago, Illinois 60603 (800) 577-EURO; *The World Economic Factbook.*

Europa Publications Limited, 18 Bedford Square, London, WC1B 3JN, England; *The Europa World Year Book.*

European Commission Office of Press and Public Affairs, 2100 M Street, NW, Washington, D.C. 20037 (202) 862-9500; *Basic Statistics of the Community;* and *Demographic Statistics.*

St. Martin's Press, Inc., 175 Fifth Avenue, New York, New York 10010 (800) 221-7945; *The Statesman's Year-Book.*

Statistical Office of the United Nations, Publishing Service, New York, New York 10017 (800) 253-9646; *Demographic Yearbook; Human Development Report; World Statistics Pocketbook;* and *Statistical Yearbook.*

The World Bank, 1818 H Street, NW, Washington, D.C. 20433 (202) 477-1234; *The World Bank Atlas;* and *World*

Development Indicators.

World Health Organization, Office of Publications, 20 Avenue Appia, CH-1211 Geneva 27, Switzerland (Telephone Number in U.S. (518) 436-9686); *World Health Statistics Annual.*

LUXEMBOURG - MOTION PICTURES

St. Martin's Press, Inc., 175 Fifth Avenue, New York, New York 10010 (800) 221-7945; *The Statesman's Year-Book.*

Statistical Office of the United Nations, Publishing Service, New York, New York 10017 (800) 253-9646; *Statistical Yearbook.*

LUXEMBOURG - MOTOR VEHICLE PRODUCTION

American Automobile Manufacturers Association, 1401 H Street, NW, Suite 900, Washington, D.C. 20005 (202) 326-5500; *World Motor Vehicle Data.*

Europa Publications Limited, 18 Bedford Square, London, WC1B 3JN, England; *The Europa World Year Book.*

European Commission Office of Press and Public Affairs, 2100 M Street, NW, Washington, D.C. 20037 (202) 862-9500; *Basic Statistics of the Community;* and *Eurostatistics: Data for Short-Term Economic Analysis.*

Organisation for Economic Co-operation and Development (OECD), 2 rue Andre-Pascal, 75 Paris 16, France (Telephone in U.S. (202) 785-6323); *Foreign Trade by Commodities;* and *Indicators of Industrial Activity.*

LUXEMBOURG - MOTOR VEHICLE TAXES - See LUXEMBOURG - TAXATION

LUXEMBOURG - MOTOR VEHICLES IN USE

American Automobile Manufacturers Association, 1401 H Street, NW, Suite 900, Washington, D.C. 20005 (202) 326-5500; *World Motor Vehicle Data.*

European Commission Office of Press and Public Affairs, 2100 M Street, NW, Washington, D.C. 20037 (202) 862-9500; *Basic Statistics of the Community;* and *Transport Annual Statistics.*

International Road Federation, 2600 Virginia Avenue, N.W., Washington, D.C. 20037 (202) 338-4641; *World Road Statistics.*

Statistical Office of the United Nations, Publishing Service, New York, New York 10017 (800) 253-9646; *Statistical Yearbook.*

LUXEMBOURG - MULES - See LUXEMBOURG - LIVESTOCK AND

POULTRY

LUXEMBOURG - MUSEUMS

Euromonitor International, Inc., 122 South Michigan Avenue, Suite 1200, Chicago, Illinois 60603 (800) 577-EURO; *European Marketing Data and Statistics.*

United Nations Educational, Scientific and Cultural Organization (UNESCO), 7 Place de Fontenoy, F-75700 Paris, France (Telephone Number in U.S. (212) 963-5981); *Statistical Yearbook.*

LUXEMBOURG - NATALITY - See LUXEMBOURG - BIRTH RATES

LUXEMBOURG - NATIONAL ACCOUNTS

Europa Publications Limited, 18 Bedford Square, London, WC1B 3JN, England; *The Europa World Year Book.*

European Commission Office of Press and Public Affairs, 2100 M Street, NW, Washington, D.C. 20037 (202) 862-9500; *Basic Statistics of the Community;* and *Eurostatistics: Data for Short-Term Economic Analysis.*

Organisation for Economic Co-operation and Development (OECD), 2 rue Andre-Pascal, 75 Paris 16, France (Telephone in U.S. (202) 785-6323); *Economic Outlook.*

Statistical Office of the United Nations, Publishing Service, New York, New York 10017 (800) 253-9646; *National Accounts Statistics;* and *Statistical Yearbook.*

LUXEMBOURG - NATIONAL INCOME

Organisation for Economic Co-operation and Development (OECD), 2 rue Andre-Pascal, 75 Paris 16, France (Telephone in U.S. (202) 785-6323); *Economic Outlook.*

Statistical Office of the United Nations, Publishing Service, New York, New York 10017 (800) 253-9646; *National Accounts Statistics;* and *Statistical Yearbook.*

LUXEMBOURG - NATIONAL PRODUCT

European Commission Office of Press and Public Affairs, 2100 M Street, NW, Washington, D.C. 20037 (202) 862-9500; *Basic Statistics of the Community.*

Organisation for Economic Co-operation and Development (OECD), 2 rue Andre-Pascal, 75 Paris 16, France (Telephone in U.S. (202) 785-6323); *Economic Outlook.*

Statistical Office of the United Nations, Publishing Service, New York, New York 10017 (800) 253-9646; *Statistical Yearbook.*

LUXEMBOURG - NATURAL GAS PRODUCTION - See LUXEMBOURG - MINING AND MINERAL PRODUCTS

LUXEMBOURG - NATURAL RUBBER PRODUCTION

European Commission Office of Press and Public Affairs, 2100 M Street, NW, Washington, D.C. 20037 (202) 862-9500; *Basic Statistics of the Community.*

LUXEMBOURG - NEWSPAPER PRODUCTION - See LUXEMBOURG - FORESTRY AND FOREST PRODUCTS

LUXEMBOURG - NEWSPRINT EXPORTS AND IMPORTS - See FORESTRY AND FOREST PRODUCTS

LUXEMBOURG - NICKEL AND NICKEL ORE PRODUCTION AND CONSUMPTION - See LUXEMBOURG - MINING AND MINERAL PRODUCTS

LUXEMBOURG - NITRIC ACID PRODUCTION - See LUXEMBOURG - MINING AND MINERAL PRODUCTS

LUXEMBOURG - OATS PRODUCTION - See LUXEMBOURG - CROPS

LUXEMBOURG - OCCUPATIONS - See LUXEMBOURG - LABOR FORCE

LUXEMBOURG - OIL PRODUCING CROPS

European Commission Office of Press and Public Affairs, 2100 M Street, NW, Washington, D.C. 20037 (202) 862-9500; *Basic Statistics of the Community.*

Organisation for Economic Co-operation and Development (OECD), 2 rue Andre-Pascal, 75 Paris 16, France (Telephone in U.S. (202) 785-6323); *Foreign Trade by Commodities.*

LUXEMBOURG - ONION PRODUCTION - See LUXEMBOURG - CROPS

LUXEMBOURG - PALM KERNEL PRODUCTION - See LUXEMBOURG - CROPS

LUXEMBOURG - PAPER - See LUXEMBOURG - FORESTRY AND FOREST PRODUCTS

LUXEMBOURG - PATENTS, TRADEMARKS AND SERVICE MARKS

Statistical Office of the United Nations, Publishing Service, New York, New York 10017 (800) 253-9646; *Statistical Yearbook.*

World Intellectual Property Organization, 34 Chemin des Colombettes, CH-1211 Geneva 20, Switzerland; *Industrial Property Statistics.*

LUXEMBOURG - PEANUT PRODUCTION - See LUXEMBOURG - CROPS

LUXEMBOURG - PEPPER PRODUCTION - See LUXEMBOURG - CROPS

LUXEMBOURG - PERIODICALS

United Nations Educational, Scientific and Cultural Organization (UNESCO), 7 Place de Fontenoy, F-75700 Paris, France (Telephone Number in U.S. (212) 963-5981); *Statistical Yearbook.*

LUXEMBOURG - PESTICIDE USE

Food and Agricultural Organization of the United Nations (FAO), Via delle Terme di Caracalla, 00100 Rome, Italy (Telephone Number in U.S. (202) 653-2400); *The State of Food and Agriculture.*

LUXEMBOURG - PETROLEUM INDUSTRY

European Commission Office of Press and Public Affairs, 2100 M Street, NW, Washington, D.C. 20037 (202) 862-9500; *ACP: Basic Statistics; Basic Statistics of the Community;* and *Energy Statistics Yearbook.*

Euromonitor International, Inc., 122 South Michigan Avenue, Suite 1200, Chicago, Illinois 60603 (800) 577-EURO; *European Marketing Data and Statistics.*

Food and Agricultural Organization of the United Nations (FAO), Via delle Terme di Caracalla, 00100 Rome, Italy (Telephone Number in U.S. (202) 653-2400); *The State of Food and Agriculture.*

Organisation for Economic Co-operation and Development (OECD), 2 rue Andre-Pascal, 75 Paris 16, France (Telephone in U.S. (202) 785-6323); *Energy Statistics of OECD Countries; Foreign Trade by Commodities; Indicators of Industrial Activity;* and *Oil and Gas Information.*

United Nations Conference on Trade and Development, Central Statistical Service, Palais des Nations, Geneva, Switzerland (Telephone in U.S. (800) 253-9646); *UNCTAD Commodity Yearbook.*

LUXEMBOURG - PHOSPHATE AND PHOSPHATE ROCK PRODUCTION - See LUXEMBOURG - MINING AND MINERAL PRODUCTS

LUXEMBOURG - PIG-IRON AND FERRO-ALLOY PRODUCTION - See LUXEMBOURG - MINING AND MINERAL PRODUCTS

LUXEMBOURG - PIGS - See LUXEMBOURG - LIVESTOCK AND POULTRY

LUXEMBOURG - PIPELINES FOR OIL AND

PETROLEUM PRODUCTS

European Commission Office of Press and Public Affairs, 2100 M Street, NW, Washington, D.C. 20037 (202) 862-9500; *Transport Annual Statistics.*

LUXEMBOURG - PLASTIC AND RESIN PRODUCTION

European Commission Office of Press and Public Affairs, 2100 M Street, NW, Washington, D.C. 20037 (202) 862-9500; *Basic Statistics of the Community.*

Organisation for Economic Co-operation and Development (OECD), 2 rue Andre-Pascal, 75 Paris 16, France (Telephone in U.S. (202) 785-6323); *Foreign Trade by Commodities.*

LUXEMBOURG - PLATINUM PRODUCTION - See LUXEMBOURG - MINING AND MINERAL PRODUCTS

LUXEMBOURG - POPULATION

Central Intelligence Agency, Washington, D.C. 20505 (703) 482-1100, www.cia.gov; *The World Factbook.*

The Economist Intelligence Unit, 111 West 57th Street, New York, New York 10019 (800) 938-4685; *Luxembourg Country Report;* and *The World Market Atlas.*

Euromonitor International, Inc., 122 South Michigan Avenue, Suite 1200, Chicago, Illinois 60603 (800) 577-EURO; *European Marketing Data and Statistics;* and *The World Economic Factbook.*

Europa Publications Limited, 18 Bedford Square, London, WC1B 3JN, England; *The Europa World Year Book.*

European Commission Office of Press and Public Affairs, 2100 M Street, NW, Washington, D.C. 20037 (202) 862-9500; *ACP: Basic Statistics; Basic Statistics of the Community; Demographic Statistics; Employment and Unemployment; Fisheries: Yearly Statistics; Iron and Steel: Statistical Yearbook; Labor Force Sample Survey;* and *Regions: Statistical Yearbook.*

Food and Agricultural Organization of the United Nations (FAO), Via delle Terme di Caracalla, 00100 Rome, Italy (Telephone Number in U.S. (202) 653-2400); *Production Yearbook.*

International Labour Office, I.L.O. Publications, 1828 L Street, N.W., Suite 801, Washington, D.C. 20036 (301) 638-3152; *Yearbook of Labour Statistics.*

St. Martin's Press, Inc., 175 Fifth Avenue, New York, New York 10010 (800) 221-7945; *The Statesman's Year-Book.*

Statistical Office of the United Nations, Publishing Service, New York, New York 10017 (800) 253-9646; *Demographic Yearbook; Human Development Report; World Statistics Pocketbook;* and *Statistical Yearbook.*

United Nations Educational, Scientific and Cultural Organization (UNESCO), 7 Place de Fontenoy, F-75700 Paris, France (Telephone Number in U.S. (212) 963-5981); *Statistical Yearbook.*

U.S. Arms Control and Disarmament Agency, 320 Twenty-first Street, NW, Washington, D.C. 20451 (202) 647-8677; *World Military Expenditures and Arms Transfers.*

The World Bank, 1818 H Street, NW, Washington, D.C. 20433 (202) 477-1234; *The World Bank Atlas.*

World Health Organization, Office of Publications, 20 Avenue Appia, CH-1211 Geneva 27, Switzerland (Telephone Number in U.S. (518) 436-9686); *World Health Statistics Annual.*

LUXEMBOURG - POST OFFICES

St. Martin's Press, Inc., 175 Fifth Avenue, New York, New York 10010 (800) 221-7945; *The Statesman's Year-Book.*

LUXEMBOURG - POTATO PRODUCTION - See LUXEMBOURG - CROPS

LUXEMBOURG - POULTRY - See LUXEMBOURG - LIVESTOCK AND POULTRY

LUXEMBOURG - POWER PRODUCTION INDUSTRY

European Commission Office of Press and Public Affairs, 2100 M Street, NW, Washington, D.C. 20037 (202) 862-9500; *Basic Statistics of the Community.*

Statistical Office of the United Nations, Publishing Service, New York, New York 10017 (800) 253-9646; *Statistical Yearbook.*

LUXEMBOURG - PRICES

European Commission Office of Press and Public Affairs, 2100 M Street, NW, Washington, D.C. 20037 (202) 862-9500; *Basic Statistics of the Community;* and *Eurostatistics: Data for Short-Term Economic Analysis.*

Food and Agricultural Organization of the United Nations (FAO), Via delle Terme di Caracalla, 00100 Rome, Italy (Telephone Number in U.S. (202) 653-2400); *Production Yearbook;* and *The State of Food and Agriculture.*

International Labour Office,

I.L.O. Publications, 1828 L Street, N.W., Suite 801, Washington, D.C. 20036 (301) 638-3152; *Yearbook of Labour Statistics.*

International Monetary Fund, 700 Nineteenth Street, NW, Washington, D.C. 20431 (202) 623-7000; *International Financial Statistics.*

Organisation for Economic Co-operation and Development (OECD), 2 rue Andre-Pascal, 75 Paris 16, France (Telephone in U.S. (202) 785-6323); *Economic Outlook; The Footwear, Raw Hides and Skins, and Leather Industry in OECD Countries; Indicators of Industrial Activity; The Iron and Steel Industry;* and *The Pulp and Paper Industry.*

LUXEMBOURG - PRINTING AND WRITING PAPER - See LUXEMBOURG - FORESTRY AND FOREST PRODUCTS

LUXEMBOURG - PRODUCTION

American Automobile Manufacturers Association, 1401 H Street, NW, Suite 900, Washington, D.C. 20005 (202) 326-5500; *World Motor Vehicle Data.*

European Commission Office of Press and Public Affairs, 2100 M Street, NW, Washington, D.C. 20037 (202) 862-9500; *Basic Statistics of the Community; Eurostatistics: Data for Short-Term Economic Analysis;* and *Fisheries: Yearly Statistics.*

International Iron and Steel Institute, 120, rue Colonel Bourg, B-1140 Brussels, Belgium; *Steel Statistical Yearbook.*

Organisation for Economic Co-operation and Development (OECD), 2 rue Andre-Pascal, 75 Paris 16, France (Telephone in U.S. (202) 785-6323); *Economic Outlook; The Footwear, Raw Hides and Skins, and Leather Industry in OECD Countries; Indicators of Industrial Activity; Industrial Structure Statistics; The Iron and Steel Industry; Meat Balances in OECD Member Countries; The Non-Ferrous Metals Industry; The Pulp and Paper Industry;* and *Textile Industry in OECD Countries.*

LUXEMBOURG - PRODUCTIVITY

European Commission Office of Press and Public Affairs, 2100 M Street, NW, Washington, D.C. 20037 (202) 862-9500; *Basic Statistics of the Community.*

Organisation for Economic Co-operation and Development (OECD), 2 rue Andre-Pascal, 75 Paris 16, France (Telephone in U.S. (202) 785-6323); *Economic Outlook.*

LUXEMBOURG - PROPERTY TAXES - See LUXEMBOURG - TAXATION

LUXEMBOURG - PUBLIC CONSUMPTION FUND

European Commission Office of Press and Public Affairs, 2100 M Street, NW, Washington, D.C. 20037 (202) 862-9500; *Basic Statistics of the Community.*

Organisation for Economic Co-operation and Development (OECD), 2 rue Andre-Pascal, 75 Paris 16, France (Telephone in U.S. (202) 785-6323); *Revenue Statistics of OECD Member Countries.*

LUXEMBOURG - PUBLIC EXPENDITURES

European Commission Office of Press and Public Affairs, 2100 M Street, NW, Washington, D.C. 20037 (202) 862-9500; *Basic Statistics of the Community.*

Organisation for Economic Co-operation and Development (OECD), 2 rue Andre-Pascal, 75 Paris 16, France (Telephone in U.S. (202) 785-6323); *Revenue Statistics of OECD Member Countries.*

LUXEMBOURG - PUBLIC FINANCE - See LUXEMBOURG - FINANCE

LUXEMBOURG - PUBLIC HEALTH - See LUXEMBOURG - HEALTH

LUXEMBOURG - PUBLIC REVENUES

Organisation for Economic Co-operation and Development (OECD), 2 rue Andre-Pascal, 75 Paris 16, France (Telephone in U.S. (202) 785-6323); *Revenue Statistics of OECD Member Countries.*

LUXEMBOURG - RADIO BROADCASTING - See LUXEMBOURG - BROADCASTING

LUXEMBOURG - RADIO RECEIVERS

St. Martin's Press, Inc., 175 Fifth Avenue, New York, New York 10010 (800) 221-7945; *The Statesman's Year-Book.*

LUXEMBOURG - RAILWAYS

Euromonitor International, Inc., 122 South Michigan Avenue, Suite 1200, Chicago, Illinois 60603 (800) 577-EURO; *European Marketing Data and Statistics.*

Europa Publications Limited, 18 Bedford Square, London, WC1B 3JN, England; *The Europa World Year Book.*

European Commission Office of Press and Public Affairs, 2100 M Street, NW, Washington, D.C. 20037 (202) 862-9500; *Basic Statistics of the Community; Regions: Statistical Yearbook;* and *Transport Annual Statistics.*

Jane's Information Group, Sentinel House, 163 Brighton Road, Coulsdon, Surrey CR5 2NH, England (Telephone Number in U.S. (703) 683-3700); *Jane's World Railways.*

St. Martin's Press, Inc., 175 Fifth Avenue, New York, New York 10010 (800) 221-7945; *The Statesman's Year-Book.*

Statistical Office of the United Nations, Publishing Service, New York, New York 10017 (800) 253-9646; *Annual Bulletin of Transport Statistics for Europe;* and *Statistical Yearbook.*

LUXEMBOURG - RANCHING

European Commission Office of Press and Public Affairs, 2100 M Street, NW, Washington, D.C. 20037 (202) 862-9500; *Basic Statistics of the Community.*

LUXEMBOURG - RAPESEED PRODUCTION - See LUXEMBOURG - CROPS

LUXEMBOURG - RELIGION

Central Intelligence Agency, Washington, D.C. 20505 (703) 482-1100, www.cia.gov; *The World Factbook.*

St. Martin's Press, Inc., 175 Fifth Avenue, New York, New York 10010 (800) 221-7945; *The Statesman's Year-Book.*

LUXEMBOURG - RETAIL TRADE

Euromonitor International, Inc., 122 South Michigan Avenue, Suite 1200, Chicago, Illinois 60603 (800) 577-EURO; *Retail Trade International;* and *World Marketing Data and Statistics.*

European Commission Office of Press and Public Affairs, 2100 M Street, NW, Washington, D.C. 20037 (202) 862-9500; *Basic Statistics of the Community;* and *Eurostatistics: Data for Short-Term Economic Analysis.*

Statistical Office of the United Nations, Publishing Service, New York, New York 10017 (800) 253-9646; *Statistical Yearbook.*

LUXEMBOURG - RICE PRODUCTION - See LUXEMBOURG - CROPS

LUXEMBOURG - ROOT AND TUBER PRODUCTION - See LUXEMBOURG - CROPS

LUXEMBOURG - ROUNDWOOD PRODUCTION - See LUXEMBOURG - FORESTRY AND FOREST PRODUCTS

LUXEMBOURG - RUBBER PRODUCTION AND CONSUMPTION

European Commission Office of Press and Public Affairs, 2100 M Street, NW, Washington, D.C. 20037 (202) 862-9500; *Basic Statistics of the Community.*

Organisation for Economic Co-operation and Development (OECD), 2 rue Andre-Pascal, 75 Paris 16, France (Telephone in U.S. (202) 785-6323); *Foreign Trade by Commodities.*

Statistical Office of the United Nations, Publishing Service, New York, New York 10017 (800) 253-9646; *Statistical Yearbook.*

LUXEMBOURG - RYE PRODUCTION - See LUXEMBOURG - CROPS

LUXEMBOURG - SAFFLOWER SEED PRODUCTION - See LUXEMBOURG - CROPS

LUXEMBOURG - SALT PRODUCTION

International Monetary Fund, 700 Nineteenth Street, NW, Washington, D.C. 20431 (202) 623-7000; *International Financial Statistics.*

Organisation for Economic Co-operation and Development (OECD), 2 rue Andre-Pascal, 75 Paris 16, France (Telephone in U.S. (202) 785-6323); *Indicators of Industrial Activity.*

LUXEMBOURG - SAVINGS ACCOUNT DEPOSITS - See LUXEMBOURG - BANKING

LUXEMBOURG - SAWNWOOD PRODUCTION - See LUXEMBOURG - FORESTRY AND FOREST PRODUCTS

LUXEMBOURG - SCIENCE AND TECHNOLOGY - EXPENDITURE FOR RESEARCH - See LUXEMBOURG - SCIENTISTS, TECHNICIANS AND ENGINEERS

LUXEMBOURG - SCIENTISTS, TECHNICIANS AND ENGINEERS

European Commission Office of Press and Public Affairs, 2100 M Street, NW, Washington, D.C. 20037 (202) 862-9500; *Basic Statistics of the Community.*

LUXEMBOURG - SESAME SEED PRODUCTION - See LUXEMBOURG - CROPS

LUXEMBOURG - SHEEP - See LUXEMBOURG - LIVESTOCK AND POULTRY

LUXEMBOURG - SHIPBUILDING - PRODUCTION INDEX

Organisation for Economic Co-operation and Development (OECD), 2 rue Andre-Pascal, 75 Paris 16, France (Telephone in U.S. (202) 785-6323);

Indicators of Industrial Activity.

LUXEMBOURG - SILVER PRODUCTION AND CONSUMPTION - See LUXEMBOURG - MINING AND MINERAL PRODUCTS

LUXEMBOURG - SISAL PRODUCTION - See LUXEMBOURG - CROPS

LUXEMBOURG - SOCIAL DATA

European Commission Office of Press and Public Affairs, 2100 M Street, NW, Washington, D.C. 20037 (202) 862-9500; *ACP: Basic Statistics, Basic Statistics of the Community.*

Statistical Office of the United Nations, Publishing Service, New York, New York 10017 (800) 253-9646; *World Statistics Pocketbook.*

LUXEMBOURG - SOCIAL SECURITY

European Commission Office of Press and Public Affairs, 2100 M Street, NW, Washington, D.C. 20037 (202) 862-9500; *Basic Statistics of the Community.*

Organisation for Economic Co-operation and Development (OECD), 2 rue Andre-Pascal, 75 Paris 16, France (Telephone in U.S. (202) 785-6323); *Revenue Statistics of OECD Member Countries.*

Statistical Office of the United Nations, Publishing Service, New York, New York 10017 (800) 253-9646; *National Accounts Statistics.*

LUXEMBOURG - SOCIOECONOMIC DATA

European Commission Office of Press and Public Affairs, 2100 M Street, NW, Washington, D.C. 20037 (202) 862-9500; *Basic Statistics of the Community.*

Organisation for Economic Co-operation and Development (OECD), 2 rue Andre-Pascal, 75 Paris 16, France (Telephone in U.S. (202) 785-6323); *Economic Outlook.*

LUXEMBOURG - SOYBEAN PRODUCTION - See LUXEMBOURG - CROPS

LUXEMBOURG - STAMP TAXES AND DUTIES - See LUXEMBOURG - TAXATION

LUXEMBOURG - STEEL - See LUXEMBOURG - MINING AND MINERAL PRODUCTS

LUXEMBOURG - STOCKS - COMMODITY - MARKET PRICE - INDEX

Food and Agricultural Organization of the United Nations (FAO), Via delle Terme di Caracalla, 00100 Rome, Italy (Telephone

Number in U.S. (202) 653-2400); *The State of Food and Agriculture.*

LUXEMBOURG - STRAW PRODUCTION - See LUXEMBOURG - CROPS

LUXEMBOURG - SUGAR - See LUXEMBOURG - CROPS

LUXEMBOURG - SUGARBEET PRODUCTION - See LUXEMBOURG - CROPS

LUXEMBOURG - SULPHUR AND SULPHURIC ACID PRODUCTION - See LUXEMBOURG - MINING AND MINERAL PRODUCTS

LUXEMBOURG - SUNFLOWER PRODUCTION - See LUXEMBOURG - CROPS

LUXEMBOURG - TAXATION

Europa Publications Limited, 18 Bedford Square, London, WC1B 3JN, England; *The Europa World Year Book.*

European Commission Office of Press and Public Affairs, 2100 M Street, NW, Washington, D.C. 20037 (202) 862-9500; *Basic Statistics of the Community.*

International Monetary Fund, 700 Nineteenth Street, NW, Washington, D.C. 20431 (202) 623-7000; *Government Finance Statistics Yearbook.*

International Road Federation, 2600 Virginia Avenue, N.W., Washington, D.C. 20037 (202) 338-4641; *World Road Statistics.*

Organisation for Economic Co-operation and Development (OECD), 2 rue Andre-Pascal, 75 Paris 16, France (Telephone in U.S. (202) 785-6323); *Revenue Statistics of OECD Member Countries.*

The World Bank, 1818 H Street, NW, Washington, D.C. 20433 (202) 477-1234; *World Development Indicators.*

LUXEMBOURG - TEA PRODUCTION - See LUXEMBOURG - CROPS

LUXEMBOURG - TELEGRAPH SERVICE

European Commission Office of Press and Public Affairs, 2100 M Street, NW, Washington, D.C. 20037 (202) 862-9500; *Transport Annual Statistics.*

Statistical Office of the United Nations, Publishing Service, New York, New York 10017 (800) 253-9646; *Statistical Yearbook.*

LUXEMBOURG - TELEPHONES IN USE

American Telephone and Telegraph

Company, 26 Parsippany Road, Whippany, New Jersey 07981 (800) 222-0300; *The World's Telephones.*

Central Intelligence Agency, Washington, D.C. 20505 (703) 482-1100, www.cia.gov; *The World Factbook.*

Europa Publications Limited, 18 Bedford Square, London, WC1B 3JN, England; *The Europa World Year Book.*

European Commission Office of Press and Public Affairs, 2100 M Street, NW, Washington, D.C. 20037 (202) 862-9500; *Transport Annual Statistics.*

St. Martin's Press, Inc., 175 Fifth Avenue, New York, New York 10010 (800) 221-7945; *The Statesman's Year-Book.*

Statistical Office of the United Nations, Publishing Service, New York, New York 10017 (800) 253-9646; *Statistical Yearbook;* and *World Statistics Pocketbook.*

LUXEMBOURG - TELEVISION BROADCASTING - See LUXEMBOURG - BROADCASTING

LUXEMBOURG - TELEVISION RECEIVER PRODUCTION

European Commission Office of Press and Public Affairs, 2100 M Street, NW, Washington, D.C. 20037 (202) 862-9500; *Basic Statistics of the Community.*

LUXEMBOURG - TEXTILE INDUSTRY

Euromonitor International, Inc., 122 South Michigan Avenue, Suite 1200, Chicago, Illinois 60603 (800) 577-EURO; *Retail Trade International.*

European Commission Office of Press and Public Affairs, 2100 M Street, NW, Washington, D.C. 20037 (202) 862-9500; *Basic Statistics of the Community; Eurostatistics: Data for Short-Term Economic Analysis;* and *Industrial Production: Quarterly Statistics.*

Food and Agricultural Organization of the United Nations (FAO), Via delle Terme di Caracalla, 00100 Rome, Italy (Telephone Number in U.S. (202) 653-2400); *Production Yearbook.*

Organisation for Economic Co-operation and Development (OECD), 2 rue Andre-Pascal, 75 Paris 16, France (Telephone in U.S. (202) 785-6323); *Economic Accounts for Agriculture; Indicators of Industrial Activity; Industrial Structure Statistics; Foreign Trade by Commodities;* and *Textile Industry in OECD Countries.*

United Nations Conference on Trade and Development, Central Statistical

Service, Palais des Nations, Geneva, Switzerland (Telephone in U.S. (800) 253-9646); *UNCTAD Commodity Yearbook*.

LUXEMBOURG - THEATRE

United Nations Educational, Scientific and Cultural Organization (UNESCO), 7 Place de Fontenoy, F-75700 Paris, France (Telephone Number in U.S. (212) 963-5981); *Statistical Yearbook*.

LUXEMBOURG - TIMBER - RESOURCE FORESTS - See LUXEMBOURG - FORESTRY AND FOREST PRODUCTS

LUXEMBOURG - TIN - See LUXEMBOURG - MINING AND MINERAL PRODUCTS

LUXEMBOURG - TIRE (MOTOR VEHICLE) PRODUCTION

Statistical Office of the United Nations, Publishing Service, New York, New York 10017 (800) 253-9646; *Statistical Yearbook*.

LUXEMBOURG - TOBACCO PRODUCTION

Euromonitor International, Inc., 122 South Michigan Avenue, Suite 1200, Chicago, Illinois 60603 (800) 577-EURO; *European Marketing Data and Statistics*.

European Commission Office of Press and Public Affairs, 2100 M Street, NW, Washington, D.C. 20037 (202) 862-9500; *Basic Statistics of the Community*; and *Industrial Production: Quarterly Statistics*.

Organisation for Economic Co-operation and Development (OECD), 2 rue Andre-Pascal, 75 Paris 16, France (Telephone in U.S. (202) 785-6323); *Foreign Trade by Commodities; Indicators of Industrial Activity;* and *Industrial Structure Statistics*.

LUXEMBOURG - TOURISM

Euromonitor International, Inc., 122 South Michigan Avenue, Suite 1200, Chicago, Illinois 60603 (800) 577-EURO; *European Marketing Data and Statistics; World Marketing Data and Statistics;* and *The World Economic Factbook*.

Europa Publications Limited, 18 Bedford Square, London, WC1B 3JN, England; *The Europa World Year Book*.

European Commission Office of Press and Public Affairs, 2100 M Street, NW, Washington, D.C. 20037 (202) 862-9500; *Transport Annual Statistics*.

Organisation for Economic Co-operation and Development (OECD), 2 rue Andre-Pascal, 75 Paris 16, France (Telephone in U.S. (202) 785-6323); *Tourism Policy and International Tourism in OECD Member Countries*.

St. Martin's Press, Inc., 175 Fifth Avenue, New York, New York 10010 (800) 221-7945; *The Statesman's Year-Book*.

Statistical Office of the United Nations, Publishing Service, New York, New York 10017 (800) 253-9646; *Statistical Yearbook*.

World Tourism Organization, Calle Capitan Haya 42, E-28020 Madrid, Spain; *Yearbook of Tourism Statistics*.

LUXEMBOURG - TRACTORS IN USE

European Commission Office of Press and Public Affairs, 2100 M Street, NW, Washington, D.C. 20037 (202) 862-9500; *Transport Annual Statistics*.

Statistical Office of the United Nations, Publishing Service, New York, New York 10017 (800) 253-9646; *Statistical Yearbook*.

LUXEMBOURG - TRADE - See LUXEMBOURG - FOREIGN TRADE
LUXEMBOURG - TRADEMARKS AND SERVICE MARKS - See LUXEMBOURG - PATENTS, TRADEMARKS AND SERVICE MARKS

LUXEMBOURG - TRANSPORTATION AND COMMUNICATIONS

Central Intelligence Agency, Washington, D.C. 20505 (703) 482-1100, www.cia.gov; *The World Factbook*.

Euromonitor International, Inc., 122 South Michigan Avenue, Suite 1200, Chicago, Illinois 60603 (800) 577-EURO; *World Marketing Data and Statistics*.

Europa Publications Limited, 18 Bedford Square, London, WC1B 3JN, England; *The Europa World Year Book*.

European Commission Office of Press and Public Affairs, 2100 M Street, NW, Washington, D.C. 20037 (202) 862-9500; *Basic Statistics of the Community; Energy Statistics Yearbook; Regions: Statistical Yearbook;* and *Transport Annual Statistics*.

St. Martin's Press, Inc., 175 Fifth Avenue, New York, New York 10010 (800) 221-7945; *The Statesman's Year-Book*.

Statistical Office of the United Nations, Publishing Service, New York, New York 10017 (800) 253-9646; *Human Development Report*.

LUXEMBOURG - TUNGSTEN PRODUCTION AND CONSUMPTION - See LUXEMBOURG - MINING AND MINERAL PRODUCTS

LUXEMBOURG - TURKEYS - See LUXEMBOURG - LIVESTOCK AND POULTRY

LUXEMBOURG - UNEMPLOYMENT

Central Intelligence Agency, Washington, D.C. 20505 (703) 482-1100, www.cia.gov; *The World Factbook*.

Euromonitor International, Inc., 122 South Michigan Avenue, Suite 1200, Chicago, Illinois 60603 (800) 577-EURO; *European Marketing Data and Statistics*.

European Commission Office of Press and Public Affairs, 2100 M Street, NW, Washington, D.C. 20037 (202) 862-9500; *Basic Statistics of the Community; Employment and Unemployment; Eurostatistics: Data for Short-Term Economic Analysis; Labor Force Sample Survey;* and *Regions: Statistical Yearbook*.

International Labour Office, I.L.O. Publications, 1828 L Street, N.W., Suite 801, Washington, D.C. 20036 (301) 638-3152; *Yearbook of Labour Statistics*.

Organisation for Economic Co-operation and Development (OECD), 2 rue Andre-Pascal, 75 Paris 16, France (Telephone in U.S. (202) 785-6323); *Economic Outlook; Labor Force Statistics; OECD Economic Surveys: Belgium - Luxembourg;* and *OECD Employment Outlook*.

Statistical Office of the United Nations, Publishing Service, New York, New York 10017 (800) 253-9646; *Statistical Yearbook*.

LUXEMBOURG - URANIUM PRODUCTION AND CONSUMPTION - See LUXEMBOURG - MINING AND MINERAL PRODUCTS

LUXEMBOURG - VANADIUM AND VANADIUM ORE PRODUCTION AND CONSUMPTION - See LUXEMBOURG - MINING AND MINERAL PRODUCTS

LUXEMBOURG - VITAL STATISTICS

Euromonitor International, Inc., 122 South Michigan Avenue, Suite 1200, Chicago, Illinois 60603 (800) 577-EURO; *European Marketing Data and Statistics*.

European Commission Office of Press and Public Affairs, 2100 M Street, NW, Washington, D.C. 20037 (202) 862-9500; *Basic Statistics of the Community*.

St. Martin's Press, Inc., 175 Fifth Avenue, New York, New York 10010 (800) 221-7945; *The Statesman's Year-Book*.

Statistical Office of the United Nations, Publishing Service, New York, New York 10017 (800) 253-9646; *Statistical Yearbook*.

World Health Organization, Office of Publications, 20 Avenue Appia, CH-1211

Geneva 27, Switzerland (Telephone Number in U.S. (518) 436-9686); *World Health Statistics Annual.*

LUXEMBOURG - WAGES

Euromonitor International, Inc., 122 South Michigan Avenue, Suite 1200, Chicago, Illinois 60603 (800) 577-EURO; *European Marketing Data and Statistics.*

European Commission Office of Press and Public Affairs, 2100 M Street, NW, Washington, D.C. 20037 (202) 862-9500; *Basic Statistics of the Community; Earnings in Agriculture;* and *Eurostatistics: Data for Short-Term Economic Analysis.*

International Labour Office, I.L.O. Publications, 1828 L Street, N.W., Suite 801, Washington, D.C. 20036 (301) 638-3152; *Yearbook of Labour Statistics.*

Organisation for Economic Co-operation and Development (OECD), 2 rue Andre-Pascal, 75 Paris 16, France (Telephone in U.S. (202) 785-6323); *Economic Outlook;* and *Industrial Structure Statistics.*

Statistical Office of the United Nations, Publishing Service, New York, New York 10017 (800) 253-9646; *Statistical Yearbook.*

LUXEMBOURG - WALNUT PRODUCTION - See LUXEMBOURG - CROPS

LUXEMBOURG - WATERWAYS IN USE
European Commission Office of Press and Public Affairs, 2100 M Street, NW, Washington, D.C. 20037 (202) 862-9500; *Basic Statistics of the Community;* and *Transport Annual Statistics.*

Organisation for Economic Co-operation and Development (OECD), 2 rue Andre-Pascal, 75 Paris 16, France (Telephone in U.S. (202) 785-6323); *Maritime Transport.*

Statistical Office of the United Nations, Publishing Service, New York, New York 10017 (800) 253-9646; *Annual Bulletin of Transport Statistics for Europe.*

LUXEMBOURG - WEATHER - See LUXEMBOURG - CLIMATE

LUXEMBOURG - WELFARE

European Commission Office of Press and Public Affairs, 2100 M Street, NW, Washington, D.C. 20037 (202) 862-9500; *Basic Statistics of the Community.*

LUXEMBOURG - WELFARE EXPENDITURES

European Commission Office of Press and Public Affairs, 2100 M Street, NW, Washington, D.C. 20037 (202) 862-9500; *Basic Statistics of the Community.*

International Monetary Fund, 700 Nineteenth Street, NW, Washington, D.C. 20431 (202) 623-7000; *Government Finance Statistics Yearbook.*

LUXEMBOURG - WHEAT PRODUCTION AND CONSUMPTION - See LUXEMBOURG - CROPS

LUXEMBOURG - WHOLESALE PRICES

European Commission Office of Press and Public Affairs, 2100 M Street, NW, Washington, D.C. 20037 (202) 862-9500; *Basic Statistics of the Community.*

Statistical Office of the United Nations, Publishing Service, New York, New York 10017 (800) 253-9646; *Statistical Yearbook.*

LUXEMBOURG - WINE PRODUCTION - See LUXEMBOURG - BEVERAGES

LUXEMBOURG - WOOD AND WOOD PULP - See LUXEMBOURG - FORESTRY AND FOREST PRODUCTS

LUXEMBOURG - WOOL - INDUSTRIAL CONSUMPTION - See LUXEMBOURG - TEXTILE INDUSTRY

LUXEMBOURG - WOOL PRODUCTION - See LUXEMBOURG - TEXTILE INDUSTRY

LUXEMBOURG - YARN PRODUCTION - See LUXEMBOURG - TEXTILE INDUSTRY

LUXEMBOURG - ZINC AND ZINC ORE PRODUCTION AND CONSUMPTION - See LUXEMBOURG - MINING AND MINERAL PRODUCTS

LYME DISEASE

U.S. Department of Health and Human Services, Centers for Disease Control and Prevention, 1600 Clifton Road, NE, Atlanta, Georgia 30333 (480) 311-3435, www.cdc.gov; *Summary of Notifiable Diseases, U.S.; Morbidity and Mortality Weekly Report.*

M

MACADAMIA NUTS

U.S. Department of Agriculture, National Agricultural Statistics Service, Fourteenth Street and Independence Avenue, SW, Washington, D.C. 20250 (800) 727-9540, www.usda.gov/nass; *Noncitrus Fruits and Nuts.*

Macau - National Statistical Office

Direccao de Servicos de Estatistica e Lensos, Post Office Box 3022, Macau.

Macau - Primary Statistics Source

Reparticao Provincial dos Servicos de Estatistica, Macau, Macau; *Anuario Estatistico* (Statistical Yearbook); and *Boletim Mensal de Estatistica* (Monthly Bulletin of Statistics).

MACAU - AGRICULTURE

Economist Intelligence Unit, 111 West 57th Street, New York, New York 10019 (800) 938-4685; *Macau Country Report.*

Euromonitor International, Inc., 122 South Michigan Avenue, Suite 1200, Chicago, Illinois 60603 (800) 577-EURO; *World Marketing Data and Statistics.*

Europa Publications Limited, 18 Bedford Square, London, WC1B 3JN, England; *The Europa World Year Book.*

Food and Agricultural Organization of the United Nations (FAO), Via delle Terme di Caracalla, 00100 Rome, Italy (Telephone Number in U.S. (202) 653-2400); *Production Yearbook; The State of Food and Agriculture;* and *Trade Yearbook.*

United Nations Conference on Trade and Development, Central Statistical Service, Palais des Nations, Geneva, Switzerland (Telephone in U.S. (800) 253-9646); *UNCTAD Commodity Yearbook.*

MACAU - AIRPORTS

Central Intelligence Agency, Washington, D.C. 20505 (703) 482-1100, www.cia.gov; *The World Factbook.*

MACAU - ANIMAL HEALTH

Food and Agricultural Organization of the United Nations (FAO), Via delle Terme di Caracalla, 00100 Rome, Italy (Telephone Number in U.S. (202) 653-2400); *Animal Health Yearbook.*

MACAU - AREA AND DENSITY OF POPULATION

Central Intelligence Agency, Washington, D.C. 20505 (703) 482-1100, www.cia.gov; *The World Factbook.*

Euromonitor International, Inc., 122 South Michigan Avenue, Suite 1200, Chicago, Illinois 60603 (800) 577-EURO; *The World Economic Factbook.*

Europa Publications Limited, 18 Bedford Square, London, WC1B 3JN, England; *The Europa World Year Book.*

Food and Agricultural Organization of the United Nations (FAO), Via delle Terme di Caracalla, 00100 Rome, Italy (Telephone Number in U.S. (202) 653-2400); *The State of Food and Agriculture.*

St. Martin's Press, Inc., 175 Fifth Avenue, New York, New York 10010 (800) 221-7945; *The Statesman's Year-Book.*

Statistical Office of the United Nations, Publishing Service, New York, New York 10017 (800) 253-9646; *Statistical Yearbook.*

MACAU - BANKING

Euromonitor International, Inc., 122 South Michigan Avenue, Suite 1200, Chicago, Illinois 60603 (800) 577-EURO; *World Marketing Data and Statistics.*

St. Martin's Press, Inc., 175 Fifth Avenue, New York, New York 10010 (800) 221-

7945; *The Statesman's Year-Book.*

MACAU - BEVERAGES

Statistical Office of the United Nations, Publishing Service, New York, New York 10017 (800) 253-9646; *Statistical Yearbook.*

MACAU - BIRTH RATES

Central Intelligence Agency, Washington, D.C. 20505 (703) 482-1100, www.cia.gov; *The World Factbook.*

The Economist Intelligence Unit (Asia) Limited, 10th Floor, Luk Kwok Centre, 72 Gloucester Road, Wanchai, Hong Kong (Phone Number in U.S. (800) 938-4685); *Asian Market Atlas.*

Euromonitor International, Inc., 122 South Michigan Avenue, Suite 1200, Chicago, Illinois 60603 (800) 577-EURO; *International Marketing Data and Statistics;* and *The World Economic Factbook.*

Europa Publications Limited, 18 Bedford Square, London, WC1B 3JN, England; *The Europa World Year Book.*

St. Martin's Press, Inc., 175 Fifth Avenue, New York, New York 10010 (800) 221-7945; *The Statesman's Year-Book.*

Statistical Office of the United Nations, Publishing Service, New York, New York 10017 (800) 253-9646; *Demographic Yearbook;* and *Statistical Yearbook.*

World Health Organization, Office of Publications, 20 Avenue Appia, CH-1211 Geneva 27, Switzerland (Telephone Number in U.S. (518) 436-9686); *World Health Statistics Annual.*

MACAU - BROADCASTING

Billboard Limited, Post Office Box 9027, 1006 AA Amsterdam, The Netherlands (Telephone Number in U.S. (212) 764-7300); *World Radio TV Handbook.*

Central Intelligence Agency,

Washington, D.C. 20505 (703) 482-1100, www.cia.gov; *The World Factbook.*

The Economist Intelligence Unit (Asia) Limited, 10th Floor, Luk Kwok Centre, 72 Gloucester Road, Wanchai, Hong Kong (Phone Number in U.S. (800) 938-4685); *Asian Market Atlas.*

Euromonitor International, Inc., 122 South Michigan Avenue, Suite 1200, Chicago, Illinois 60603 (800) 577-EURO; *World Marketing Data and Statistics.*

St. Martin's Press, Inc., 175 Fifth Avenue, New York, New York 10010 (800) 221-7945; *The Statesman's Year-Book.*

MACAU - BUDGET

Central Intelligence Agency, Washington, D.C. 20505 (703) 482-1100, www.cia.gov; *The World Factbook.*

MACAU - CALORIE SUPPLY

Food and Agricultural Organization of the United Nations (FAO), Via delle Terme di Caracalla, 00100 Rome, Italy (Telephone Number in U.S. (202) 653-2400); *The State of Food and Agriculture.*

MACAU - CHEMICAL (ORGANIC) PRODUCTION - See MACAU - MINING AND MINERAL PRODUCTS

MACAU - COAL PRODUCTION - See MACAU - MINING AND MINERAL PRODUCTS

MACAU - COMMERCE

St. Martin's Press, Inc., 175 Fifth Avenue, New York, New York 10010 (800) 221-7945; *The Statesman's Year-Book.*

MACAU - CONSTRUCTION INDUSTRY

St. Martin's Press, Inc., 175 Fifth Avenue, New York, New York 10010 (800) 221-7945; *The Statesman's Year-Book.*

Statistical Office of the United Nations, Publishing Service, New York, New York 10017 (800) 253-9646; *Statistical Yearbook.*

MACAU - CONSUMER PRICE INDEX

Europa Publications Limited, 18 Bedford Square, London, WC1B 3JN, England; *The Europa World Year Book.*

MACAU - CONSUMER PRICES

Euromonitor International, Inc., 122 South Michigan Avenue, Suite 1200, Chicago, Illinois 60603 (800) 577-EURO; *World Marketing Data and Statistics.*

MACAU - CORN PRODUCTION - See MACAU - CROPS

MACAU - CORPORATE TAXES - See MACAU - TAXATION

MACAU - CROPS

Food and Agricultural Organization of the United Nations (FAO), Via delle Terme di Caracalla, 00100 Rome, Italy (Telephone Number in U.S. (202) 653-2400); *The State of Food and Agriculture.*

United Nations Conference on Trade and Development, Central Statistical Service, Palais des Nations, Geneva, Switzerland (Telephone in U.S. (800) 253-9646); *UNCTAD Commodity Yearbook.*

MACAU - DAIRY PRODUCTS

Food and Agricultural Organization of the United Nations (FAO), Via delle Terme di Caracalla, 00100 Rome, Italy (Telephone Number in U.S. (202) 653-2400); *The State of Food and Agriculture.*

MACAU - DEATH RATES - See MACAU - MORTALITY

MACAU - DEMOGRAPHY

The Economist Intelligence Unit, 111 West 57th Street, New York, New York 10019 (800) 938-4685; *The World Market Atlas.*

The Economist Intelligence Unit (Asia) Limited, 10th Floor, Luk Kwok Centre, 72 Gloucester Road, Wanchai, Hong Kong (Phone Number in U.S. (800) 938-4685); *Asian Market Atlas.*

Euromonitor International, Inc., 122 South Michigan Avenue, Suite 1200, Chicago, Illinois 60603 (800) 577-EURO; *International Marketing Data and Statistics; World Marketing Data and Statistics;* and *The World Economic Factbook.*

MACAU - DEVELOPMENT ASSISTANCE

Statistical Office of the United Nations, Publishing Service, New York, New York 10017 (800) 253-9646; *Statistical Yearbook.*

MACAU - DIVORCE

Statistical Office of the United Nations, Publishing Service, New York, New York 10017 (800) 253-9646; *Demographic Yearbook.*

MACAU - ECONOMY

Central Intelligence Agency, Washington, D.C. 20505 (703) 482-1100, www.cia.gov; *The World Factbook.*

Economist Intelligence Unit, 111 West 57th Street, New York, New York 10019 (800) 938-4685; *Macau Country Report.*

Euromonitor International, Inc., 122 South Michigan Avenue, Suite 1200, Chicago, Illinois 60603 (800) 577-EURO; *The World Economic Factbook;* and *World Marketing Data and Statistics.*

Europa Publications Limited, 18 Bedford Square, London, WC1B 3JN, England; *The Europa World Year Book.*

St. Martin's Press, Inc., 175 Fifth Avenue, New York, New York 10010 (800) 221-7945; *The Statesman's Year-Book.*

Statistical Office of the United Nations, Publishing Service, New York, New York 10017 (800) 253-9646; *World Statistics Pocketbook.*

The World Bank, 1818 H Street, NW, Washington, D.C. 20433 (202) 477-1234; *The World Bank Atlas.*

MACAU - EDUCATION

The Economist Intelligence Unit, 111 West 57th Street, New York, New York 10019 (800) 938-4685; *The World Market Atlas.*

The Economist Intelligence Unit (Asia) Limited, 10th Floor, Luk Kwok Centre, 72 Gloucester Road, Wanchai, Hong Kong (Phone Number in U.S. (800) 938-4685); *Asian Market Atlas.*

Euromonitor International, Inc., 122 South Michigan Avenue, Suite 1200, Chicago, Illinois 60603 (800) 577-EURO; *International Marketing Data and Statistics;* and *World Marketing Data and Statistics.*

Europa Publications Limited, 18 Bedford Square, London, WC1B 3JN, England; *The Europa World Year Book.*

St. Martin's Press, Inc., 175 Fifth Avenue, New York, New York 10010 (800) 221-7945; *The Statesman's Year-Book.*

United Nations Educational, Scientific and Cultural Organization (UNESCO), 7 Place de Fontenoy, F-75700 Paris, France (Telephone Number in U.S. (212) 963-5981); *Statistical Yearbook.*

MACAU - EGG PRODUCTION AND CONSUMPTION - See MACAU - DAIRY PRODUCTS

MACAU - ELECTRICITY

Central Intelligence Agency, Washington, D.C. 20505 (703) 482-1100, www.cia.gov; *The World Factbook.*

Statistical Office of the United Nations, Publishing Service, New York, New York 10017 (800) 253-9646; *Statistical Yearbook.*

United Nations Educational, Scientific and Cultural Organization (UNESCO), 7 Place de Fontenoy, F-75700 Paris, France (Telephone Number in U.S. (212) 963-5981); *Statistical Yearbook.*

MACAU - EMPLOYMENT

Euromonitor International, Inc., 122 South Michigan Avenue, Suite 1200, Chicago, Illinois 60603 (800) 577-EURO; *International Marketing Data and Statistics.*

MACAU - ENERGY

Euromonitor International, Inc., 122 South Michigan Avenue, Suite 1200, Chicago, Illinois 60603 (800) 577-EURO; *International Marketing Data and Statistics; World Marketing Data and Statistics;* and *The World Economic Factbook.*

Food and Agricultural Organization of the United Nations (FAO), Via delle Terme di Caracalla, 00100 Rome, Italy (Telephone Number in U.S. (202) 653-2400); *The State of Food and Agriculture.*

Statistical Office of the United Nations, Publishing Service, New York, New York 10017 (800) 253-9646; *Energy Statistics Yearbook; World Statistics Pocketbook;* and *Statistical Yearbook.*

The World Bank, 1818 H Street, NW, Washington, D.C. 20433 (202) 477-1234; *The World Bank Atlas.*

MACAU - ENVIRONMENT

Economist Intelligence Unit, 111 West 57th Street, New York, New York 10019 (800) 938-4685; *Macau Country Report.*

Statistical Office of the United Nations, Publishing Service, New York, New York 10017 (800) 253-9646; *World Statistics Pocketbook.*

MACAU - EXCHANGE RATES

Central Intelligence Agency, Washington, D.C. 20505 (703) 482-1100, www.cia.gov; *The World Factbook.*

The Economist Intelligence Unit (Asia) Limited, 10th Floor, Luk Kwok Centre, 72 Gloucester Road, Wanchai, Hong Kong (Phone Number in U.S. (800) 938-4685); *Asian Market Atlas.*

Euromonitor International, Inc., 122 South Michigan Avenue, Suite 1200, Chicago, Illinois 60603 (800) 577-EURO; *International Marketing Data and Statistics;* and *The World Economic Factbook.*

Europa Publications Limited, 18 Bedford Square, London, WC1B 3JN, England; *The Europa World Year Book.*

Statistical Office of the United Nations, Publishing Service, New York, New York 10017 (800) 253-9646; *World Statistics Pocketbook.*

Walden Publishing Ltd., Two Market Street, Saffron Walden Essex, CB10 1HZ, England; *The World of Information Asia and Pacific Review.*

MACAU - EXPORTS

Central Intelligence Agency, Washington, D.C. 20505 (703) 482-1100, www.cia.gov; *The World Factbook.*

The Economist Intelligence Unit, 111 West 57th Street, New York, New York 10019 (800) 938-4685; *Macau Country Report;* and *The World Market Atlas.*

The Economist Intelligence Unit (Asia) Limited, 10th Floor, Luk Kwok Centre, 72 Gloucester Road, Wanchai, Hong Kong (Phone Number in U.S. (800) 938-4685); *Asian Market Atlas.*

Euromonitor International, Inc., 122 South Michigan Avenue, Suite 1200, Chicago, Illinois 60603 (800) 577-EURO; *International Marketing Data and Statistics;* and *The World Economic Factbook.*

Europa Publications Limited, 18 Bedford Square, London, WC1B 3JN, England; *The Europa World Year Book.*

Food and Agricultural Organization of the United Nations (FAO), Via delle Terme di Caracalla, 00100 Rome, Italy (Telephone Number in U.S. (202) 653-2400); *The State of Food and Agriculture.*

International Monetary Fund, 700 Nineteenth Street, NW, Washington, D.C. 20431 (202) 623-7000; *Direction of Trade Statistics.*

St. Martin's Press, Inc., 175 Fifth Avenue, New York, New York 10010 (800) 221-7945; *The Statesman's Year-Book.* istics.

Walden Publishing Ltd., Two Market Street, Saffron Walden Essex, CB10 1HZ, England; *The World of Information Asia and Pacific Review.*

MACAU - EXTERNAL TRADE

Euromonitor International, Inc., 122 South Michigan Avenue, Suite 1200, Chicago, Illinois 60603 (800) 577-EURO; *World Marketing Data and Statistics.*

Food and Agricultural Organization of the United Nations (FAO), Via delle Terme di Caracalla, 00100 Rome, Italy (Telephone Number in U.S. (202) 653-2400); *The State of Food and Agriculture;* and *Trade Yearbook.*

Statistical Office of the United Nations, Publishing Service, New York, New York 10017 (800) 253-9646; *World Statistics Pocketbook.*

Walden Publishing Ltd., Two Market Street, Saffron Walden Essex, CB10 1HZ, England; *The World of Information Asia and Pacific Review.*

MACAU - FARM CROPS - See MACAU - CROPS

MACAU - FERTILITY RATES

Central Intelligence Agency, Washington, D.C. 20505 (703) 482-1100, www.cia.gov; *The World Factbook.*

The World Bank, 1818 H Street, NW, Washington, D.C. 20433 (202) 477-1234; *The World Bank Atlas.*

MACAU - FERTILIZER

The Economist Intelligence Unit (Asia) Limited, 10th Floor, Luk Kwok Centre, 72 Gloucester Road, Wanchai, Hong Kong (Phone Number in U.S. (800) 938-4685); *Asian Market Atlas.*

Food and Agricultural Organization of the United Nations (FAO), Via delle Terme di Caracalla, 00100 Rome, Italy (Telephone Number in U.S. (202) 653-2400); *Fertilizer Yearbook;* and *The State of Food and Agriculture.*

Statistical Office of the United Nations, Publishing Service, New York, New York 10017 (800) 253-9646; *Statistical Yearbook.*

MACAU - FETAL MORTALITY - See MACAU - MORTALITY

MACAU - FINANCE

Economist Intelligence Unit, 111 West 57th Street, New York, New York 10019 (800) 938-4685; *Macau Country Report.*

Europa Publications Limited, 18 Bedford Square, London, WC1B 3JN, England; *The Europa World Year Book.*

St. Martin's Press, Inc., 175 Fifth Avenue, New York, New York 10010 (800) 221-7945; *The Statesman's Year-Book.*

MACAU - FISHERIES

Europa Publications Limited, 18 Bedford Square, London, WC1B 3JN, England; *The Europa World Year Book.*

Food and Agricultural Organization of the United Nations (FAO), Via delle Terme di Caracalla, 00100 Rome, Italy (Telephone Number in U.S. (202) 653-2400); *The State of Food and Agriculture;* and *Yearbook of Fishery Statistics.*

Statistical Office of the United Nations, Publishing Service, New York, New York 10017 (800) 253-9646; *Statistical Yearbook.*

United Nations Conference on Trade

and Development, Central Statistical Service, Palais des Nations, Geneva, Switzerland (Telephone in U.S. (800) 253-9646); *UNCTAD Commodity Yearbook*.

MACAU - FOOD

Food and Agricultural Organization of the United Nations (FAO), Via delle Terme di Caracalla, 00100 Rome, Italy (Telephone Number in U.S. (202) 653-2400); *Production Yearbook;* and *The State of Food and Agriculture*.

United Nations Conference on Trade and Development, Central Statistical Service, Palais des Nations, Geneva, Switzerland (Telephone in U.S. (800) 253-9646); *UNCTAD Commodity Yearbook*.

MACAU - FOREIGN DEBT

Walden Publishing Ltd., Two Market Street, Saffron Walden Essex, CB10 1HZ, England; *The World of Information Asia and Pacific Review*.

MACAU - FOREIGN TRADE

Economist Intelligence Unit, 111 West 57th Street, New York, New York 10019 (800) 938-4685; *Macau Country Report*.

The Economist Intelligence Unit (Asia) Limited, 10th Floor, Luk Kwok Centre, 72 Gloucester Road, Wanchai, Hong Kong (Phone Number in U.S. (800) 938-4685); *Asian Market Atlas*.

Euromonitor International, Inc., 122 South Michigan Avenue, Suite 1200, Chicago, Illinois 60603 (800) 577-EURO; *The World Economic Factbook*.

Europa Publications Limited, 18 Bedford Square, London, WC1B 3JN, England; *The Europa World Year Book*.

Food and Agricultural Organization of the United Nations (FAO), Via delle Terme di Caracalla, 00100 Rome, Italy (Telephone Number in U.S. (202) 653-2400); *The State of Food and Agriculture*.

St. Martin's Press, Inc., 175 Fifth Avenue, New York, New York 10010 (800) 221-7945; *The Statesman's Year-Book*.

Statistical Office of the United Nations, Publishing Service, New York, New York 10017 (800) 253-9646; *International Trade Statistics Yearbook;* and *Statistical Yearbook*.

United Nations Conference on Trade and Development, Central Statistical Service, Palais des Nations, Geneva, Switzerland (Telephone in U.S. (800) 253-9646); *UNCTAD Commodity Yearbook*.

MACAU - FORESTRY AND FOREST PRODUCTS

The Economist Intelligence Unit (Asia) Limited, 10th Floor, Luk Kwok Centre, 72 Gloucester Road, Wanchai, Hong Kong (Phone Number in U.S. (800) 938-4685); *Asian Market Atlas*.

Food and Agricultural Organization of the United Nations (FAO), Via delle Terme di Caracalla, 00100 Rome, Italy (Telephone Number in U.S. (202) 653-2400); *The State of Food and Agriculture;* and *Yearbook of Forest Products*.

Statistical Office of the United Nations, Publishing Service, New York, New York 10017 (800) 253-9646; *Statistical Yearbook*.

United Nations Conference on Trade and Development, Central Statistical Service, Palais des Nations, Geneva, Switzerland (Telephone in U.S. (800) 253-9646); *UNCTAD Commodity Yearbook*.

United Nations Educational, Scientific and Cultural Organization (UNESCO), 7 Place de Fontenoy, F-75700 Paris, France (Telephone Number in U.S. (212) 963-5981); *Statistical Yearbook*.

MACAU - GENERAL INDUSTRIAL STATISTICS - See MACAU - INDUSTRY

MACAU - GENERAL MORTALITY - See MACAU - MORTALITY

MACAU - GOVERNMENT

Central Intelligence Agency, Washington, D.C. 20505 (703) 482-1100, www.cia.gov; *The World Factbook*.

Europa Publications Limited, 18 Bedford Square, London, WC1B 3JN, England; *The Europa World Year Book*.

St. Martin's Press, Inc., 175 Fifth Avenue, New York, New York 10010 (800) 221-7945; *The Statesman's Year-Book*.

MACAU - GRAIN PRODUCTION - See MACAU - CROPS

MACAU - GROSS DOMESTIC PRODUCT

The Economist Intelligence Unit, 111 West 57th Street, New York, New York 10019 (800) 938-4685; *Macau Country Report;* and *The World Market Atlas*.

The Economist Intelligence Unit (Asia) Limited, 10th Floor, Luk Kwok Centre, 72 Gloucester Road, Wanchai, Hong Kong (Phone Number in U.S. (800) 938-4685); *Asian Market Atlas*.

Euromonitor International, Inc., 122 South Michigan Avenue, Suite 1200, Chicago, Illinois 60603 (800) 577-EURO;

International Marketing Data and Statistics; and *The World Economic Factbook*.

Europa Publications Limited, 18 Bedford Square, London, WC1B 3JN, England; *The Europa World Year Book*.

MACAU - GROSS NATIONAL PRODUCT

Walden Publishing Ltd., Two Market Street, Saffron Walden Essex, CB10 1HZ, England; *The World of Information Asia and Pacific Review*.

The World Bank, 1818 H Street, NW, Washington, D.C. 20433 (202) 477-1234; *The World Bank Atlas*.

MACAU - HEALTH

The Economist Intelligence Unit (Asia) Limited, 10th Floor, Luk Kwok Centre, 72 Gloucester Road, Wanchai, Hong Kong (Phone Number in U.S. (800) 938-4685); *Asian Market Atlas*.

Euromonitor International, Inc., 122 South Michigan Avenue, Suite 1200, Chicago, Illinois 60603 (800) 577-EURO; *World Marketing Data and Statistics*.

St. Martin's Press, Inc., 175 Fifth Avenue, New York, New York 10010 (800) 221-7945; *The Statesman's Year-Book*.

Statistical Office of the United Nations, Publishing Service, New York, New York 10017 (800) 253-9646; *Statistical Yearbook*.

MACAU - HIDE PRODUCTION

Food and Agricultural Organization of the United Nations (FAO), Via delle Terme di Caracalla, 00100 Rome, Italy (Telephone Number in U.S. (202) 653-2400); *Production Yearbook*.

MACAU - HIGHWAYS

Central Intelligence Agency, Washington, D.C. 20505 (703) 482-1100, www.cia.gov; *The World Factbook*.

The Economist Intelligence Unit (Asia) Limited, 10th Floor, Luk Kwok Centre, 72 Gloucester Road, Wanchai, Hong Kong (Phone Number in U.S. (800) 938-4685); *Asian Market Atlas*.

St. Martin's Press, Inc., 175 Fifth Avenue, New York, New York 10010 (800) 221-7945; *The Statesman's Year-Book*.

MACAU - HOUSING AND HOUSING UNITS

Euromonitor International, Inc., 122 South Michigan Avenue, Suite 1200, Chicago, Illinois 60603 (800) 577-EURO; *World Marketing Data and Statistics*.

MACAU - ILLITERATE POPULATION

Central Intelligence Agency, Washington, D.C. 20505 (703) 482-1100, www.cia.gov; *The World Factbook*.

The Economist Intelligence Unit, 111 West 57th Street, New York, New York 10019 (800) 938-4685; *The World Market Atlas*.

Euromonitor International, Inc., 122 South Michigan Avenue, Suite 1200, Chicago, Illinois 60603 (800) 577-EURO; *The World Economic Factbook*.

United Nations Educational, Scientific and Cultural Organization (UNESCO), 7 Place de Fontenoy, F-75700 Paris, France (Telephone Number in U.S. (212) 963-5981); *Statistical Yearbook*.

MACAU - IMPORTS

Central Intelligence Agency, Washington, D.C. 20505 (703) 482-1100, www.cia.gov; *The World Factbook*.

The Economist Intelligence Unit, 111 West 57th Street, New York, New York 10019 (800) 938-4685; *Macau Country Report;* and *The World Market Atlas*.

The Economist Intelligence Unit (Asia) Limited, 10th Floor, Luk Kwok Centre, 72 Gloucester Road, Wanchai, Hong Kong (Phone Number in U.S. (800) 938-4685); *Asian Market Atlas*.

Euromonitor International, Inc., 122 South Michigan Avenue, Suite 1200, Chicago, Illinois 60603 (800) 577-EURO; *International Marketing Data and Statistics;* and *The World Economic Factbook*.

Europa Publications Limited, 18 Bedford Square, London, WC1B 3JN, England; *The Europa World Year Book*.

Food and Agricultural Organization of the United Nations (FAO), Via delle Terme di Caracalla, 00100 Rome, Italy (Telephone Number in U.S. (202) 653-2400); *The State of Food and Agriculture*.

International Monetary Fund, 700 Nineteenth Street, NW, Washington, D.C. 20431 (202) 623-7000; *Direction of Trade Statistics*.

St. Martin's Press, Inc., 175 Fifth Avenue, New York, New York 10010 (800) 221-7945; *The Statesman's Year-Book*.

Walden Publishing Ltd., Two Market Street, Saffron Walden Essex, CB10 1HZ, England; *The World of Information Asia and Pacific Review*.

MACAU - INDUSTRY

Central Intelligence Agency, Washington, D.C. 20505 (703) 482-1100, www.cia.gov; *The World Factbook*.

Economist Intelligence Unit, 111 West 57th Street, New York, New York 10019 (800) 938-4685; *Macau Country Report*.

Euromonitor International, Inc., 122 South Michigan Avenue, Suite 1200, Chicago, Illinois 60603 (800) 577-EURO; *The World Economic Factbook;* and *World Marketing Data and Statistics*.

Europa Publications Limited, 18 Bedford Square, London, WC1B 3JN, England; *The Europa World Year Book*.

St. Martin's Press, Inc., 175 Fifth Avenue, New York, New York 10010 (800) 221-7945; *The Statesman's Year-Book*.

Statistical Office of the United Nations, Publishing Service, New York, New York 10017 (800) 253-9646; *Industrial Commodity Statistics Yearbook*.

World Intellectual Property Organization, 34 Chemin des Colombettes, CH-1211 Geneva 20, Switzerland; *Industrial Property Statistics*.

MACAU - INFANT AND MATERNAL MORTALITY - See MACAU - MORTALITY

MACAU - LABOR

Central Intelligence Agency, Washington, D.C. 20505 (703) 482-1100, www.cia.gov; *The World Factbook*.

The Economist Intelligence Unit (Asia) Limited, 10th Floor, Luk Kwok Centre, 72 Gloucester Road, Wanchai, Hong Kong (Phone Number in U.S. (800) 938-4685); *Asian Market Atlas*.

Euromonitor International, Inc., 122 South Michigan Avenue, Suite 1200, Chicago, Illinois 60603 (800) 577-EURO; *International Marketing Data and Statistics;* and *World Marketing Data and Statistics*.

Europa Publications Limited, 18 Bedford Square, London, WC1B 3JN, England; *The Europa World Year Book*.

Food and Agricultural Organization of the United Nations (FAO), Via delle Terme di Caracalla, 00100 Rome, Italy (Telephone Number in U.S. (202) 653-2400); *The State of Food and Agriculture*.

St. Martin's Press, Inc., 175 Fifth Avenue, New York, New York 10010 (800) 221-7945; *The Statesman's Year-Book*.

The World Bank, 1818 H Street, NW, Washington, D.C. 20433 (202) 477-1234;

The World Bank Atlas.

MACAU - LAND USE

Central Intelligence Agency, Washington, D.C. 20505 (703) 482-1100, www.cia.gov; *The World Factbook*.

Euromonitor International, Inc., 122 South Michigan Avenue, Suite 1200, Chicago, Illinois 60603 (800) 577-EURO; *International Marketing Data and Statistics*.

Food and Agricultural Organization of the United Nations (FAO), Via delle Terme di Caracalla, 00100 Rome, Italy (Telephone Number in U.S. (202) 653-2400); *Production Yearbook*.

MACAU - LIFE EXPECTANCY

Central Intelligence Agency, Washington, D.C. 20505 (703) 482-1100, www.cia.gov; *The World Factbook*.

Euromonitor International, Inc., 122 South Michigan Avenue, Suite 1200, Chicago, Illinois 60603 (800) 577-EURO; *The World Economic Factbook*.

Statistical Office of the United Nations, Publishing Service, New York, New York 10017 (800) 253-9646; *World Statistics Pocketbook*.

The World Bank, 1818 H Street, NW, Washington, D.C. 20433 (202) 477-1234; *The World Bank Atlas*.

MACAU - LITERACY RATE

Euromonitor International, Inc., 122 South Michigan Avenue, Suite 1200, Chicago, Illinois 60603 (800) 577-EURO; *World Marketing Data and Statistics*.

MACAU - LIVESTOCK AND POULTRY

Europa Publications Limited, 18 Bedford Square, London, WC1B 3JN, England; *The Europa World Year Book*.

Food and Agricultural Organization of the United Nations (FAO), Via delle Terme di Caracalla, 00100 Rome, Italy (Telephone Number in U.S. (202) 653-2400); *Production Yearbook;* and *The State of Food and Agriculture*.

United Nations Conference on Trade and Development, Central Statistical Service, Palais des Nations, Geneva, Switzerland (Telephone in U.S. (800) 253-9646); *UNCTAD Commodity Yearbook*.

MACAU - MAIL - PIECES SENT OR RECEIVED

Statistical Office of the United Nations, Publishing Service, New York, New York 10017 (800) 253-9646; *Statistical Yearbook*.

MACAU - MANUFACTURING

Statistical Office of the United Nations, Publishing Service, New York, New York 10017 (800) 253-9646; *Statistical Yearbook.*

MACAU - MARRIAGE RATES

Europa Publications Limited, 18 Bedford Square, London, WC1B 3JN, England; *The Europa World Year Book.*

Statistical Office of the United Nations, Publishing Service, New York, New York 10017 (800) 253-9646; *Demographic Yearbook.*

MACAU - MEAT PRODUCTION - See MACAU - LIVESTOCK AND POULTRY

MACAU - MERCHANT SHIPPING

Europa Publications Limited, 18 Bedford Square, London, WC1B 3JN, England; *The Europa World Year Book.*

St. Martin's Press, Inc., 175 Fifth Avenue, New York, New York 10010 (800) 221-7945; *The Statesman's Year-Book.*

Statistical Office of the United Nations, Publishing Service, New York, New York 10017 (800) 253-9646; *Statistical Yearbook.*

MACAU - MILITARY

Central Intelligence Agency, Washington, D.C. 20505 (703) 482-1100, www.cia.gov; *The World Factbook.*

The Economist Intelligence Unit (Asia) Limited, 10th Floor, Luk Kwok Centre, 72 Gloucester Road, Wanchai, Hong Kong (Phone Number in U.S. (800) 938-4685); *Asian Market Atlas.*

Euromonitor International, Inc., 122 South Michigan Avenue, Suite 1200, Chicago, Illinois 60603 (800) 577-EURO; *World Marketing Data and Statistics.*

MACAU - MINING AND MINERAL PRODUCTS

United Nations Conference on Trade and Development, Central Statistical Service, Palais des Nations, Geneva, Switzerland (Telephone in U.S. (800) 253-9646); *UNCTAD Commodity Yearbook.*

MACAU - MONEY SUPPLY

Economist Intelligence Unit, 111 West 57th Street, New York, New York 10019 (800) 938-4685; *Macau Country Report.*

Europa Publications Limited, 18 Bedford Square, London, WC1B 3JN, England; *The Europa World Year Book.*

MACAU - MORTALITY

Central Intelligence Agency, Washington, D.C. 20505 (703) 482-1100, www.cia.gov; *The World Factbook.*

The Economist Intelligence Unit (Asia) Limited, 10th Floor, Luk Kwok Centre, 72 Gloucester Road, Wanchai, Hong Kong (Phone Number in U.S. (800) 938-4685); *Asian Market Atlas.*

Euromonitor International, Inc., 122 South Michigan Avenue, Suite 1200, Chicago, Illinois 60603 (800) 577-EURO; *International Marketing Data and Statistics;* and *The World Economic Factbook.*

Europa Publications Limited, 18 Bedford Square, London, WC1B 3JN, England; *The Europa World Year Book.*

St. Martin's Press, Inc., 175 Fifth Avenue, New York, New York 10010 (800) 221-7945; *The Statesman's Year-Book.*

Statistical Office of the United Nations, Publishing Service, New York, New York 10017 (800) 253-9646; *Demographic Yearbook; World Statistics Pocketbook;* and *Statistical Yearbook.*

The World Bank, 1818 H Street, NW, Washington, D.C. 20433 (202) 477-1234; *The World Bank Atlas.*

World Health Organization, Office of Publications, 20 Avenue Appia, CH-1211 Geneva 27, Switzerland (Telephone Number in U.S. (518) 436-9686); *World Health Statistics Annual.*

MACAU - MOTION PICTURES

Statistical Office of the United Nations, Publishing Service, New York, New York 10017 (800) 253-9646; *Statistical Yearbook.*

MACAU - MOTOR VEHICLES IN USE

Europa Publications Limited, 18 Bedford Square, London, WC1B 3JN, England; *The Europa World Year Book.*

Statistical Office of the United Nations, Publishing Service, New York, New York 10017 (800) 253-9646; *Statistical Yearbook.*

MACAU - NATALITY - See MACAU - BIRTH RATES

MACAU - NEWSPAPER PRODUCTION - See MACAU - FORESTRY AND FOREST PRODUCTS

MACAU - NEWSPRINT - See MACAU - FORESTRY AND FOREST PRODUCTS

MACAU - OCCUPATIONS - See MACAU - LABOR

MACAU - PAPER - See MACAU - FORESTRY AND FOREST PRODUCTS

MACAU - PATENTS, TRADEMARKS AND SERVICE MARKS

World Intellectual Property Organization, 34 Chemin des Colombettes, CH-1211 Geneva 20, Switzerland; *Industrial Property Statistics.*

MACAU - PESTICIDE USE

Food and Agricultural Organization of the United Nations (FAO), Via delle Terme di Caracalla, 00100 Rome, Italy (Telephone Number in U.S. (202) 653-2400); *The State of Food and Agriculture.*

MACAU - PETROLEUM INDUSTRY

Food and Agricultural Organization of the United Nations (FAO), Via delle Terme di Caracalla, 00100 Rome, Italy (Telephone Number in U.S. (202) 653-2400); *The State of Food and Agriculture.*

United Nations Conference on Trade and Development, Central Statistical Service, Palais des Nations, Geneva, Switzerland (Telephone in U.S. (800) 253-9646); *UNCTAD Commodity Yearbook.*

MACAU - POPULATION

Central Intelligence Agency, Washington, D.C. 20505 (703) 482-1100, www.cia.gov; *The World Factbook.*

The Economist Intelligence Unit, 111 West 57th Street, New York, New York 10019 (800) 938-4685; *Macau Country Report;* and *The World Market Atlas.*

The Economist Intelligence Unit (Asia) Limited, 10th Floor, Luk Kwok Centre, 72 Gloucester Road, Wanchai, Hong Kong (Phone Number in U.S. (800) 938-4685); *Asian Market Atlas.*

Euromonitor International, Inc., 122 South Michigan Avenue, Suite 1200, Chicago, Illinois 60603 (800) 577-EURO; *International Marketing Data and Statistics;* and *The World Economic Factbook.*

Europa Publications Limited, 18 Bedford Square, London, WC1B 3JN, England; *The Europa World Year Book.*

Food and Agricultural Organization of the United Nations (FAO), Via delle Terme di Caracalla, 00100 Rome, Italy (Telephone Number in U.S. (202) 653-2400); *Production Yearbook.*

St. Martin's Press, Inc., 175 Fifth Avenue, New York, New York 10010 (800) 221-7945; *The Statesman's Year-Book.*

Statistical Office of the United Nations, Publishing Service, New York, New York 10017 (800) 253-9646; *Demographic Yearbook; World Statistics Pocketbook;* and

Statistical Yearbook.

Walden Publishing Ltd., Two Market Street, Saffron Walden Essex, CB10 1HZ, England; *The World of Information Asia and Pacific Review.*

The World Bank, 1818 H Street, NW, Washington, D.C. 20433 (202) 477-1234; *The World Bank Atlas.*

World Health Organization, Office of Publications, 20 Avenue Appia, CH-1211 Geneva 27, Switzerland (Telephone Number in U.S. (518) 436-9686); *World Health Statistics Annual.*

MACAU - PRICES

Food and Agricultural Organization of the United Nations (FAO), Via delle Terme di Caracalla, 00100 Rome, Italy (Telephone Number in U.S. (202) 653-2400); *Production Yearbook;* and *The State of Food and Agriculture.*

MACAU - PRINTING AND WRITING PAPER - See MACAU - FORESTRY AND FOREST PRODUCTS

MACAU - RADIO BROADCASTING - See MACAU - BROADCASTING

MACAU - RADIO RECEIVERS

St. Martin's Press, Inc., 175 Fifth Avenue, New York, New York 10010 (800) 221-7945; *The Statesman's Year-Book.*

MACAU - RELIGION

Central Intelligence Agency, Washington, D.C. 20505 (703) 482-1100, www.cia.gov; *The World Factbook.*

St. Martin's Press, Inc., 175 Fifth Avenue, New York, New York 10010 (800) 221-7945; *The Statesman's Year-Book.*

MACAU - RETAIL TRADE

Euromonitor International, Inc., 122 South Michigan Avenue, Suite 1200, Chicago, Illinois 60603 (800) 577-EURO; *World Marketing Data and Statistics.*

MACAU - ROUNDWOOD PRODUCTION - See MACAU - FORESTRY AND FOREST PRODUCTS

MACAU - SAWNWOOD PRODUCTION - See MACAU - FORESTRY AND FOREST PRODUCTS

MACAU - SOCIAL DATA

Statistical Office of the United Nations, Publishing Service, New York, New York 10017 (800) 253-9646; *World Statistics Pocketbook.*

MACAU - STOCKS - COMMODITY - MARKET PRICE - INDEX

Food and Agricultural Organization of the United Nations (FAO), Via delle Terme di Caracalla, 00100 Rome, Italy (Telephone Number in U.S. (202) 653-2400); *The State of Food and Agriculture.*

MACAU - TELEPHONES IN USE

American Telephone and Telegraph Company, 26 Parsippany Road, Whippany, New Jersey 07981 (800) 222-0300; *The World's Telephones.*

Central Intelligence Agency, Washington, D.C. 20505 (703) 482-1100, www.cia.gov; *The World Factbook.*

The Economist Intelligence Unit (Asia) Limited, 10th Floor, Luk Kwok Centre, 72 Gloucester Road, Wanchai, Hong Kong (Phone Number in U.S. (800) 938-4685); *Asian Market Atlas.*

Europa Publications Limited, 18 Bedford Square, London, WC1B 3JN, England; *The Europa World Year Book.*

St. Martin's Press, Inc., 175 Fifth Avenue, New York, New York 10010 (800) 221-7945; *The Statesman's Year-Book.*

Statistical Office of the United Nations, Publishing Service, New York, New York 10017 (800) 253-9646; *Statistical Yearbook;* and *World Statistics Pocketbook.*

MACAU - TELEVISION BROADCASTING - See MACAU - BROADCASTING

MACAU - TEXTILE INDUSTRY

St. Martin's Press, Inc., 175 Fifth Avenue, New York, New York 10010 (800) 221-7945; *The Statesman's Year-Book.*

United Nations Conference on Trade and Development, Central Statistical Service, Palais des Nations, Geneva, Switzerland (Telephone in U.S. (800) 253-9646); *UNCTAD Commodity Yearbook.*

MACAU - TOURISM

Euromonitor International, Inc., 122 South Michigan Avenue, Suite 1200, Chicago, Illinois 60603 (800) 577-EURO; *The World Economic Factbook;* and *World Marketing Data and Statistics.*

Europa Publications Limited, 18 Bedford Square, London, WC1B 3JN, England; *The Europa World Year Book.*

St. Martin's Press, Inc., 175 Fifth Avenue, New York, New York 10010 (800) 221-7945; *The Statesman's Year-Book.*

Statistical Office of the United Nations,

Publishing Service, New York, New York 10017 (800) 253-9646; *Statistical Yearbook.*

World Tourism Organization, Calle Capitan Haya 42, E-28020 Madrid, Spain; *Yearbook of Tourism Statistics.*

MACAU - TRADE - See MACAU - FOREIGN TRADE

MACAU - TRADEMARKS AND SERVICE MARKS - See MACAU - PATENTS, TRADEMARKS AND SERVICE MARKS

MACAU - TRANSPORTATION AND COMMUNICATIONS

Central Intelligence Agency, Washington, D.C. 20505 (703) 482-1100, www.cia.gov; *The World Factbook.*

The Economist Intelligence Unit (Asia) Limited, 10th Floor, Luk Kwok Centre, 72 Gloucester Road, Wanchai, Hong Kong (Phone Number in U.S. (800) 938-4685); *Asian Market Atlas.*

Euromonitor International, Inc., 122 South Michigan Avenue, Suite 1200, Chicago, Illinois 60603 (800) 577-EURO; *International Marketing Data and Statistics;* and *World Marketing Data and Statistics.*

Europa Publications Limited, 18 Bedford Square, London, WC1B 3JN, England; *The Europa World Year Book.*

St. Martin's Press, Inc., 175 Fifth Avenue, New York, New York 10010 (800) 221-7945; *The Statesman's Year-Book.*

MACAU - UNEMPLOYMENT RATE

Central Intelligence Agency, Washington, D.C. 20505 (703) 482-1100, www.cia.gov; *The World Factbook.*

MACAU - VITAL STATISTICS

St. Martin's Press, Inc., 175 Fifth Avenue, New York, New York 10010 (800) 221-7945; *The Statesman's Year-Book.*

Statistical Office of the United Nations, Publishing Service, New York, New York 10017 (800) 253-9646; *Statistical Yearbook.*

World Health Organization, Office of Publications, 20 Avenue Appia, CH-1211 Geneva 27, Switzerland (Telephone Number in U.S. (518) 436-9686); *World Health Statistics Annual.*

MACAU - WINE PRODUCTION - See MACAU - BEVERAGES

MACEDONIA - ABORTIONS

Statistical Office of the United Nations, Publishing Service, New York, New York 10017 (800) 253-9646; *Trends in Europe and*

North America: The Statistical Yearbook of the Economic Commission for Europe.

MACEDONIA - AGRICULTURE

Economist Intelligence Unit, 111 West 57th Street, New York, New York 10019 (800) 938-4685; *Macedonia Country Report.*

Euromonitor International, Inc., 122 South Michigan Avenue, Suite 1200, Chicago, Illinois 60603 (800) 577-EURO; *World Marketing Data and Statistics.*

Europa Publications Limited, 18 Bedford Square, London, WC1B 3JN, England; *The Europa World Year Book.*

Food and Agriculture Organization of the United Nations (FAO), Via delle Terme di Caracalla, 00100, Rome, Italy (Telephone Number in U.S. (202) 653-2400); *Production Yearbook; The State of Food and Agriculture;* and *Trade Yearbook.*

St. Martin's Press, Inc., 175 Fifth Avenue, New York, New York 10010 (800) 221-7945; *The Statesman's Year-Book.*

Statistical Office of the United Nations, Publishing Service, New York, New York 10017 (800) 253-9646; *Industrial Commodity Statistics Yearbook;* and *Statistical Yearbook.*

MACEDONIA - AIRLINE SERVICE

Europa Publications Limited, 18 Bedford Square, London, WC1B 3JN, England; *The Europa World Year Book.*

International Civil Aviation Organization, 999 University Street, Montreal, Quebec, Canada H3C 5H7 (514) 954-8219; *Civil Aviation Statistics of the World.*

St. Martin's Press, Inc., 175 Fifth Avenue, New York, New York 10010 (800) 221-7945; *The Statesman's Year-Book.*

Statistical Office of the United Nations, Publishing Service, New York, New York 10017 (800) 253-9646; *Statistical Yearbook.*

MACEDONIA - AIRPORTS

Central Intelligence Agency, Washington, D.C. 20505 (703) 482-1100, www.cia.gov; *The World Factbook.*

MACEDONIA - ANIMAL HEALTH

Food and Agriculture Organization of the United Nations (FAO), Via delle Terme di Caracalla, 00100, Rome, Italy (Telephone Number in U.S. (202) 653-2400); *Animal Health Yearbook.*

MACEDONIA - AREA AND DENSITY OF POPULATION

Central Intelligence Agency, Washington, D.C. 20505 (703) 482-1100, www.cia.gov; *The World Factbook.*

Euromonitor International, Inc., 122 South Michigan Avenue, Suite 1200, Chicago, Illinois 60603 (800) 577-EURO; *The World Economic Factbook.*

Europa Publications Limited, 18 Bedford Square, London, WC1B 3JN, England; *The Europa World Year Book.*

St. Martin's Press, Inc., 175 Fifth Avenue, New York, New York 10010 (800) 221-7945; *The Statesman's Year-Book.*

Statistical Office of the United Nations, Publishing Service, New York, New York 10017 (800) 253-9646; *Statistical Yearbook;* and *Trends in Europe and North America: The Statistical Yearbook of the Economic Commission for Europe.*

United Nations Educational, Scientific and Cultural Organization (UNESCO), 7 Place de Fontenoy, F-75700 Paris, France (Telephone Number in U.S. (212) 963-5981); *Statistical Yearbook.*

The World Bank, 1818 H Street, NW, Washington, D.C. 20433 (202) 477-1234; *World Development Report.*

MACEDONIA - BALANCE OF PAYMENTS

The World Bank, 1818 H Street, NW, Washington, D.C. 20433 (202) 477-1234; *World Development Report.*

MACEDONIA - BANKING

Euromonitor International, Inc., 122 South Michigan Avenue, Suite 1200, Chicago, Illinois 60603 (800) 577-EURO; *World Marketing Data and Statistics.*

St. Martin's Press, Inc., 175 Fifth Avenue, New York, New York 10010 (800) 221-7945; *The Statesman's Year-Book.*

MACEDONIA - BEVERAGES

Statistical Office of the United Nations, Publishing Service, New York, New York 10017 (800) 253-9646; *Statistical Yearbook.*

MACEDONIA - BIRTH RATES

Central Intelligence Agency, Washington, D.C. 20505 (703) 482-1100, www.cia.gov; *The World Factbook.*

Euromonitor International, Inc., 122 South Michigan Avenue, Suite 1200, Chicago, Illinois 60603 (800) 577-EURO; *The World Economic Factbook.*

St. Martin's Press, Inc., 175 Fifth Avenue, New York, New York 10010 (800) 221-7945; *The Statesman's Year-Book.*

Statistical Office of the United Nations, Publishing Service, New York, New York 10017 (800) 253-9646; *Statistical Yearbook.*

MACEDONIA - BOOK PRODUCTION

Statistical Office of the United Nations, Publishing Service, New York, New York 10017 (800) 253-9646; *Trends in Europe and North America: The Statistical Yearbook of the Economic Commission for Europe.*

St. Martin's Press, Inc., 175 Fifth Avenue, New York, New York 10010 (800) 221-7945; *The Statesman's Year-Book.*

United Nations Educational, Scientific and Cultural Organization (UNESCO), 7 Place de Fontenoy, F-75700 Paris, France (Telephone Number in U.S. (212) 963-5981); *Statistical Yearbook.*

MACEDONIA - BROADCASTING

Central Intelligence Agency, Washington, D.C. 20505 (703) 482-1100, www.cia.gov; *The World Factbook.*

Euromonitor International, Inc., 122 South Michigan Avenue, Suite 1200, Chicago, Illinois 60603 (800) 577-EURO; *World Marketing Data and Statistics.*

St. Martin's Press, Inc., 175 Fifth Avenue, New York, New York 10010 (800) 221-7945; *The Statesman's Year-Book.*

Statistical Office of the United Nations, Publishing Service, New York, New York 10017 (800) 253-9646; *Trends in Europe and North America: The Statistical Yearbook of the Economic Commission for Europe.*

United Nations Educational, Scientific and Cultural Organization (UNESCO), 7 Place de Fontenoy, F-75700 Paris, France (Telephone Number in U.S. (212) 963-5981); *Statistical Yearbook.*

MACEDONIA - BUDGET

Central Intelligence Agency, Washington, D.C. 20505 (703) 482-1100, www.cia.gov; *The World Factbook.*

MACEDONIA - CLIMATE

St. Martin's Press, Inc., 175 Fifth Avenue, New York, New York 10010 (800) 221-7945; *The Statesman's Year-Book.*

MACEDONIA - COMMERCE

St. Martin's Press, Inc., 175 Fifth Avenue, New York, New York 10010 (800) 221-7945; *The Statesman's Year-Book.*

MACEDONIA - CONSTRUCTION INDUSTRY

Statistical Office of the United Nations, Publishing Service, New York, New York

10017 (800) 253-9646; *Statistical Yearbook.*

MACEDONIA - CONSUMER PRICE INDEX

Statistical Office of the United Nations, Publishing Service, New York, New York 10017 (800) 253-9646; *Statistical Yearbook;* and *Trends in Europe and North America: The Statistical Yearbook of the Economic Commission for Europe.*

MACEDONIA - CONSUMER PRICES

Euromonitor International, Inc., 122 South Michigan Avenue, Suite 1200, Chicago, Illinois 60603 (800) 577-EURO; *World Marketing Data and Statistics.*

MACEDONIA - CONSUMPTION

The World Bank, 1818 H Street, NW, Washington, D.C. 20433 (202) 477-1234; *World Development Report.*

MACEDONIA - CRIME

Statistical Office of the United Nations, Publishing Service, New York, New York 10017 (800) 253-9646; *Trends in Europe and North America: The Statistical Yearbook of the Economic Commission for Europe.*

MACEDONIA - CROPS

Europa Publications Limited, 18 Bedford Square, London, WC1B 3JN, England; *The Europa World Year Book.*

Food and Agriculture Organization of the United Nations (FAO), Via delle Terme di Caracalla, 00100, Rome, Italy (Telephone Number in U.S. (202) 653-2400); *Production Yearbook; The State of Food and Agriculture;* and *Trade Yearbook.*

St. Martin's Press, Inc., 175 Fifth Avenue, New York, New York 10010 (800) 221-7945; *The Statesman's Year-Book.*

Statistical Office of the United Nations, Publishing Service, New York, New York 10017 (800) 253-9646; *Industrial Commodity Statistics Yearbook;* and *Statistical Yearbook.*

MACEDONIA - DAIRY PRODUCTS

Europa Publications Limited, 18 Bedford Square, London, WC1B 3JN, England; *The Europa World Year Book.*

Food and Agriculture Organization of the United Nations (FAO), Via delle Terme di Caracalla, 00100, Rome, Italy (Telephone Number in U.S. (202) 653-2400); *Production Yearbook; The State of Food and Agriculture;* and *Trade Yearbook.*

St. Martin's Press, Inc., 175 Fifth Avenue, New York, New York 10010 (800) 221-7945; *The Statesman's Year-Book.*

Statistical Office of the United Nations, Publishing Service, New York, New York 10017 (800) 253-9646; *Industrial Commodity Statistics Yearbook;* and *Statistical Yearbook.*

MACEDONIA - DEATH RATES - See MACEDONIA - MORTALITY

MACEDONIA - DEMOGRAPHY

Euromonitor International, Inc., 122 South Michigan Avenue, Suite 1200, Chicago, Illinois 60603 (800) 577-EURO; *The World Economic Factbook;* and *World Marketing Data and Statistics.*

Statistical Office of the United Nations, Publishing Service, New York, New York 10017 (800) 253-9646; *Demographic Yearbook;* and *Human Development Report.*

MACEDONIA - DIVORCE RATES

Statistical Office of the United Nations, Publishing Service, New York, New York 10017 (800) 253-9646; *Demographic Yearbook; Trends in Europe and North America: The Statistical Yearbook of the Economic Commission for Europe;* and *Statistical Yearbook.*

MACEDONIA - ECONOMY

Central Intelligence Agency, Washington, D.C. 20505 (703) 482-1100, www.cia.gov; *The World Factbook.*

Economist Intelligence Unit, 111 West 57th Street, New York, New York 10019 (800) 938-4685; *Macedonia Country Report.*

Euromonitor International, Inc., 122 South Michigan Avenue, Suite 1200, Chicago, Illinois 60603 (800) 577-EURO; *The World Economic Factbook;* and *World Marketing Data and Statistics.*

St. Martin's Press, Inc., 175 Fifth Avenue, New York, New York 10010 (800) 221-7945; *The Statesman's Year-Book.*

Statistical Office of the United Nations, Publishing Service, New York, New York 10017 (800) 253-9646; *International Trade Statistics Yearbook;* and *World Statistics Pocketbook.*

The World Bank, 1818 H Street, NW, Washington, D.C. 20433 (202) 477-1234; *The World Bank Atlas;* and *World Development Report.*

MACEDONIA - EDUCATION

Euromonitor International, Inc., 122 South Michigan Avenue, Suite 1200, Chicago, Illinois 60603 (800) 577-EURO; *World Marketing Data and Statistics.*

St. Martin's Press, Inc., 175 Fifth Avenue, New York, New York 10010 (800) 221-7945; *The Statesman's Year-Book.*

Statistical Office of the United Nations, Publishing Service, New York, New York 10017 (800) 253-9646; *Human Development Report;* and *Trends in Europe and North America: The Statistical Yearbook of the Economic Commission for Europe.*

United Nations Educational, Scientific and Cultural Organization (UNESCO), 7 Place de Fontenoy, F-75700 Paris, France (Telephone Number in U.S. (212) 963-5981); *Statistical Yearbook.*

The World Bank, 1818 H Street, NW, Washington, D.C. 20433 (202) 477-1234; *World Development Report.*

MACEDONIA - ELECTRICITY

Central Intelligence Agency, Washington, D.C. 20505 (703) 482-1100, www.cia.gov; *The World Factbook.*

St. Martin's Press, Inc., 175 Fifth Avenue, New York, New York 10010 (800) 221-7945; *The Statesman's Year-Book.*

Statistical Office of the United Nations, Publishing Service, New York, New York 10017 (800) 253-9646; *Energy Statistics Yearbook; Human Development Report; Trends in Europe and North America: The Statistical Yearbook of the Economic Commission for Europe;* and *Statistical Yearbook.*

MACEDONIA - EMPLOYMENT

Statistical Office of the United Nations, Publishing Service, New York, New York 10017 (800) 253-9646; *Statistical Yearbook;* and *Trends in Europe and North America: The Statistical Yearbook of the Economic Commission for Europe.*

MACEDONIA - ENERGY

Euromonitor International, Inc., 122 South Michigan Avenue, Suite 1200, Chicago, Illinois 60603 (800) 577-EURO; *The World Economic Factbook;* and *World Marketing Data and Statistics.*

St. Martin's Press, Inc., 175 Fifth Avenue, New York, New York 10010 (800) 221-7945; *The Statesman's Year-Book.*

Statistical Office of the United Nations, Publishing Service, New York, New York 10017 (800) 253-9646; *Energy Statistics Yearbook; Human Development Report; Trends in Europe and North America: The Statistical Yearbook of the Economic Commission for Europe; World Statistics Pocketbook;* and *Statistical Yearbook.*

The World Bank, 1818 H Street, NW, Washington, D.C. 20433 (202) 477-1234; *The World Bank Atlas;* and *World Development Report.*

MACEDONIA - ENVIRONMENT

Economist Intelligence Unit, 111 West 57th Street, New York, New York 10019 (800) 938-4685; *Macedonia Country Report.*

Statistical Office of the United Nations, Publishing Service, New York, New York 10017 (800) 253-9646; *Statistical Yearbook; World Statistics Pocketbook;* and *Trends in Europe and North America: The Statistical Yearbook of the Economic Commission for Europe.*

MACEDONIA - EXCHANGE RATES

Central Intelligence Agency, Washington, D.C. 20505 (703) 482-1100, www.cia.gov; *The World Factbook.*

Euromonitor International, Inc., 122 South Michigan Avenue, Suite 1200, Chicago, Illinois 60603 (800) 577-EURO; *The World Economic Factbook.*

Europa Publications Limited, 18 Bedford Square, London, WC1B 3JN, England; *The Europa World Year Book.*

Statistical Office of the United Nations, Publishing Service, New York, New York 10017 (800) 253-9646; *Statistical Yearbook; World Statistics Pocketbook;* and *Trends in Europe and North America: The Statistical Yearbook of the Economic Commission for Europe.*

MACEDONIA - EXPORTS

Central Intelligence Agency, Washington, D.C. 20505 (703) 482-1100, www.cia.gov; *The World Factbook.*

Economist Intelligence Unit, 111 West 57th Street, New York, New York 10019 (800) 938-4685; *Macedonia Country Report.*

Euromonitor International, Inc., 122 South Michigan Avenue, Suite 1200, Chicago, Illinois 60603 (800) 577-EURO; *The World Economic Factbook.*

Europa Publications Limited, 18 Bedford Square, London, WC1B 3JN, England; *The Europa World Year Book.*

St. Martin's Press, Inc., 175 Fifth Avenue, New York, New York 10010 (800) 221-7945; *The Statesman's Year-Book.*

Statistical Office of the United Nations, Publishing Service, New York, New York 10017 (800) 253-9646; *Trends in Europe and North America: The Statistical Yearbook of the Economic Commission for Europe.*

The World Bank, 1818 H Street, NW, Washington, D.C. 20433 (202) 477-1234; *World Development Report.*

MACEDONIA - EXTERNAL INDEBTEDNESS

The World Bank, 1818 H Street, NW, Washington, D.C. 20433 (202) 477-1234; *World Development Report.*

MACEDONIA - EXTERNAL TRADE

Euromonitor International, Inc., 122 South Michigan Avenue, Suite 1200, Chicago, Illinois 60603 (800) 577-EURO; *World Marketing Data and Statistics.*

Food and Agriculture Organization of the United Nations (FAO), Via delle Terme di Caracalla, 00100, Rome, Italy (Telephone Number in U.S. (202) 653-2400); *Trade Yearbook.*

Statistical Office of the United Nations, Publishing Service, New York, New York 10017 (800) 253-9646; *Statistical Yearbook.*

MACEDONIA - FERTILITY RATES

Central Intelligence Agency, Washington, D.C. 20505 (703) 482-1100, www.cia.gov; *The World Factbook.*

Statistical Office of the United Nations, Publishing Service, New York, New York 10017 (800) 253-9646; *Human Development Report;* and *Trends in Europe and North America: The Statistical Yearbook of the Economic Commission for Europe.*

The World Bank, 1818 H Street, NW, Washington, D.C. 20433 (202) 477-1234; *The World Bank Atlas;* and *World Development Report.*

MACEDONIA - FERTILIZER

Food and Agriculture Organization of the United Nations (FAO), Via delle Terme di Caracalla, 00100, Rome, Italy (Telephone Number in U.S. (202) 653-2400); *Fertilizer Yearbook.*

Statistical Office of the United Nations, Publishing Service, New York, New York 10017 (800) 253-9646; *Industrial Commodity Statistics Yearbook;* and *Statistical Yearbook.*

MACEDONIA - FINANCE

Economist Intelligence Unit, 111 West 57th Street, New York, New York 10019 (800) 938-4685; *Macedonia Country Report.*

Europa Publications Limited, 18 Bedford Square, London, WC1B 3JN, England; *The Europa World Year Book.*

St. Martin's Press, Inc., 175 Fifth

Avenue, New York, New York 10010 (800) 221-7945; *The Statesman's Year-Book.*

MACEDONIA - FISHERIES

Food and Agriculture Organization of the United Nations (FAO), Via delle Terme di Caracalla, 00100, Rome, Italy (Telephone Number in U.S. (202) 653-2400); *The State of Food and Agriculture;* and *Yearbook of Fishery Statistics.*

Statistical Office of the United Nations, Publishing Service, New York, New York 10017 (800) 253-9646; *Industrial Commodity Statistics Yearbook;* and *Statistical Yearbook.*

MACEDONIA - FOOD

Food and Agriculture Organization of the United Nations (FAO), Via delle Terme di Caracalla, 00100, Rome, Italy (Telephone Number in U.S. (202) 653-2400); *The State of Food and Agriculture;* and *Trade Yearbook.*

Statistical Office of the United Nations, Publishing Service, New York, New York 10017 (800) 253-9646; *Human Development Report;* and *Industrial Commodity Statistics Yearbook.*

MACEDONIA - FOREIGN DEBT

St. Martin's Press, Inc., 175 Fifth Avenue, New York, New York 10010 (800) 221-7945; *The Statesman's Year-Book.*

MACEDONIA - FOREIGN TRADE

Economist Intelligence Unit, 111 West 57th Street, New York, New York 10019 (800) 938-4685; *Macedonia Country Report.*

Euromonitor International, Inc., 122 South Michigan Avenue, Suite 1200, Chicago, Illinois 60603 (800) 577-EURO; *The World Economic Factbook.*

Europa Publications Limited, 18 Bedford Square, London, WC1B 3JN, England; *The Europa World Year Book.*

Food and Agriculture Organization of the United Nations (FAO), Via delle Terme di Caracalla, 00100, Rome, Italy (Telephone Number in U.S. (202) 653-2400); *Trade Yearbook.*

St. Martin's Press, Inc., 175 Fifth Avenue, New York, New York 10010 (800) 221-7945; *The Statesman's Year-Book.*

Statistical Office of the United Nations, Publishing Service, New York, New York 10017 (800) 253-9646; *International Trade Statistics Yearbook;* and *Statistical Yearbook.*

The World Bank, 1818 H Street, NW,

Washington, D.C. 20433 (202) 477-1234; *World Development Report*.

MACEDONIA - FORESTRY AND FOREST PRODUCTS

Europa Publications Limited, 18 Bedford Square, London, WC1B 3JN, England; *The Europa World Year Book*.

Food and Agriculture Organization of the United Nations (FAO), Via delle Terme di Caracalla, 00100, Rome, Italy (Telephone Number in U.S. (202) 653-2400); *The State of Food and Agriculture;* and *Yearbook of Forest Products*.

St. Martin's Press, Inc., 175 Fifth Avenue, New York, New York 10010 (800) 221-7945; *The Statesman's Year-Book*.

Statistical Office of the United Nations, Publishing Service, New York, New York 10017 (800) 253-9646; *Industrial Commodity Statistics Yearbook; Trends in Europe and North America: The Statistical Yearbook of the Economic Commission for Europe;* and *Statistical Yearbook*.

United Nations Educational, Scientific and Cultural Organization (UNESCO), 7 Place de Fontenoy, F-75700 Paris, France (Telephone Number in U.S. (212) 963-5981); *Statistical Yearbook*.

The World Bank, 1818 H Street, NW, Washington, D.C. 20433 (202) 477-1234; *World Development Report*.

MACEDONIA - GOVERNMENT

Central Intelligence Agency, Washington, D.C. 20505 (703) 482-1100, www.cia.gov; *The World Factbook*.

St. Martin's Press, Inc., 175 Fifth Avenue, New York, New York 10010 (800) 221-7945; *The Statesman's Year-Book*.

Statistical Office of the United Nations, Publishing Service, New York, New York 10017 (800) 253-9646; *Statistical Yearbook*.

The World Bank, 1818 H Street, NW, Washington, D.C. 20433 (202) 477-1234; *World Development Report*.

MACEDONIA - GROSS DOMESTIC PRODUCT

Economist Intelligence Unit, 111 West 57th Street, New York, New York 10019 (800) 938-4685; *Macedonia Country Report*.

Euromonitor International, Inc., 122 South Michigan Avenue, Suite 1200, Chicago, Illinois 60603 (800) 577-EURO; *The World Economic Factbook*.

Statistical Office of the United Nations, Publishing Service, New York, New York 10017 (800) 253-9646; *Human Development*

Report; National Accounts Statistics; Trends in Europe and North America: The Statistical Yearbook of the Economic Commission for Europe; and *Statistical Yearbook*.

The World Bank, 1818 H Street, NW, Washington, D.C. 20433 (202) 477-1234; *World Development Report*.

MACEDONIA - GROSS NATIONAL PRODUCT

The World Bank, 1818 H Street, NW, Washington, D.C. 20433 (202) 477-1234; *The World Bank Atlas;* and *World Development Report*.

MACEDONIA - HEALTH

Euromonitor International, Inc., 122 South Michigan Avenue, Suite 1200, Chicago, Illinois 60603 (800) 577-EURO; *World Marketing Data and Statistics*.

St. Martin's Press, Inc., 175 Fifth Avenue, New York, New York 10010 (800) 221-7945; *The Statesman's Year-Book*.

Statistical Office of the United Nations, Publishing Service, New York, New York 10017 (800) 253-9646; *Human Development Report;* and *Trends in Europe and North America: The Statistical Yearbook of the Economic Commission for Europe*.

United Nations Children's Fund (UNICEF), 3 United Nations Plaza, New York, New York 10017 (800) 253-9646; *State of the World's Children*.

The World Bank, 1818 H Street, NW, Washington, D.C. 20433 (202) 477-1234; *World Development Report*.

MACEDONIA - HIGHWAYS

Central Intelligence Agency, Washington, D.C. 20505 (703) 482-1100, www.cia.gov; *The World Factbook*.

St. Martin's Press, Inc., 175 Fifth Avenue, New York, New York 10010 (800) 221-7945; *The Statesman's Year-Book*.

Statistical Office of the United Nations, Publishing Service, New York, New York 10017 (800) 253-9646; *Trends in Europe and North America: The Statistical Yearbook of the Economic Commission for Europe*.

MACEDONIA - HOUSING AND HOUSING UNITS

Euromonitor International, Inc., 122 South Michigan Avenue, Suite 1200, Chicago, Illinois 60603 (800) 577-EURO; *World Marketing Data and Statistics*.

Statistical Office of the United Nations,

Publishing Service, New York, New York 10017 (800) 253-9646; *Trends in Europe and North America: The Statistical Yearbook of the Economic Commission for Europe*.

MACEDONIA - ILLITERATE POPULATION

Central Intelligence Agency, Washington, D.C. 20505 (703) 482-1100, www.cia.gov; *The World Factbook*.

Euromonitor International, Inc., 122 South Michigan Avenue, Suite 1200, Chicago, Illinois 60603 (800) 577-EURO; *The World Economic Factbook*.

Statistical Office of the United Nations, Publishing Service, New York, New York 10017 (800) 253-9646; *Human Development Report*.

United Nations Educational, Scientific and Cultural Organization (UNESCO), 7 Place de Fontenoy, F-75700 Paris, France (Telephone Number in U.S. (212) 963-5981); *Statistical Yearbook*.

MACEDONIA - IMPORTS

Central Intelligence Agency, Washington, D.C. 20505 (703) 482-1100, www.cia.gov; *The World Factbook*.

Economist Intelligence Unit, 111 West 57th Street, New York, New York 10019 (800) 938-4685; *Macedonia Country Report*.

Euromonitor International, Inc., 122 South Michigan Avenue, Suite 1200, Chicago, Illinois 60603 (800) 577-EURO; *The World Economic Factbook*.

Europa Publications Limited, 18 Bedford Square, London, WC1B 3JN, England; *The Europa World Year Book*.

St. Martin's Press, Inc., 175 Fifth Avenue, New York, New York 10010 (800) 221-7945; *The Statesman's Year-Book*.

Statistical Office of the United Nations, Publishing Service, New York, New York 10017 (800) 253-9646; *Trends in Europe and North America: The Statistical Yearbook of the Economic Commission for Europe*.

The World Bank, 1818 H Street, NW, Washington, D.C. 20433 (202) 477-1234; *World Development Report*.

MACEDONIA - INDUSTRY

Central Intelligence Agency, Washington, D.C. 20505 (703) 482-1100, www.cia.gov; *The World Factbook*.

Economist Intelligence Unit, 111 West 57th Street, New York, New York 10019 (800) 938-4685; *Macedonia Country Report*.

Euromonitor International, Inc., 122 South Michigan Avenue, Suite 1200, Chicago, Illinois 60603 (800) 577-EURO; *The World Economic Factbook;* and *World Marketing Data and Statistics.*

Europa Publications Limited, 18 Bedford Square, London, WC1B 3JN, England; *The Europa World Year Book.*

St. Martin's Press, Inc., 175 Fifth Avenue, New York, New York 10010 (800) 221-7945; *The Statesman's Year-Book.*

Statistical Office of the United Nations, Publishing Service, New York, New York 10017 (800) 253-9646; *Industrial Commodity Statistics Yearbook; International Trade Statistics Yearbook; Trends in Europe and North America: The Statistical Yearbook of the Economic Commission for Europe;* and *Statistical Yearbook.*

MACEDONIA - INTERNAL TRADE

Statistical Office of the United Nations, Publishing Service, New York, New York 10017 (800) 253-9646; *Statistical Yearbook.*

MACEDONIA - LABOR

Central Intelligence Agency, Washington, D.C. 20505 (703) 482-1100, www.cia.gov; *The World Factbook.*

Euromonitor International, Inc., 122 South Michigan Avenue, Suite 1200, Chicago, Illinois 60603 (800) 577-EURO; *World Marketing Data and Statistics.*

St. Martin's Press, Inc., 175 Fifth Avenue, New York, New York 10010 (800) 221-7945; *The Statesman's Year-Book.*

Statistical Office of the United Nations, Publishing Service, New York, New York 10017 (800) 253-9646; *Human Development Report;* and *Statistical Yearbook.*

The World Bank, 1818 H Street, NW, Washington, D.C. 20433 (202) 477-1234; *The World Bank Atlas;* and *World Development Report.*

MACEDONIA - LAND USE

Central Intelligence Agency, Washington, D.C. 20505 (703) 482-1100, www.cia.gov; *The World Factbook.*

Food and Agriculture Organization of the United Nations (FAO), Via delle Terme di Caracalla, 00100, Rome, Italy (Telephone Number in U.S. (202) 653-2400); *Production Yearbook.*

The World Bank, 1818 H Street, NW, Washington, D.C. 20433 (202) 477-1234; *World Development Report.*

MACEDONIA - LIBRARIES

Statistical Office of the United Nations, Publishing Service, New York, New York 10017 (800) 253-9646; *Trends in Europe and North America: The Statistical Yearbook of the Economic Commission for Europe.*

United Nations Educational, Scientific and Cultural Organization (UNESCO), 7 Place de Fontenoy, F-75700 Paris, France (Telephone Number in U.S. (212) 963-5981); *Statistical Yearbook.*

MACEDONIA - LIFE EXPECTANCY

Central Intelligence Agency, Washington, D.C. 20505 (703) 482-1100, www.cia.gov; *The World Factbook.*

Euromonitor International, Inc., 122 South Michigan Avenue, Suite 1200, Chicago, Illinois 60603 (800) 577-EURO; *The World Economic Factbook.*

St. Martin's Press, Inc., 175 Fifth Avenue, New York, New York 10010 (800) 221-7945; *The Statesman's Year-Book.*

Statistical Office of the United Nations, Publishing Service, New York, New York 10017 (800) 253-9646; *Demographic Yearbook; Trends in Europe and North America: The Statistical Yearbook of the Economic Commission for Europe; World Statistics Pocketbook;* and *Human Development Report.*

The World Bank, 1818 H Street, NW, Washington, D.C. 20433 (202) 477-1234; *The World Bank Atlas;* and *World Development Report.*

MACEDONIA - LITERACY RATE

Euromonitor International, Inc., 122 South Michigan Avenue, Suite 1200, Chicago, Illinois 60603 (800) 577-EURO; *World Marketing Data and Statistics.*

MACEDONIA - LIVESTOCK AND POULTRY

Europa Publications Limited, 18 Bedford Square, London, WC1B 3JN, England; *The Europa World Year Book.*

Food and Agriculture Organization of the United Nations (FAO), Via delle Terme di Caracalla, 00100, Rome, Italy (Telephone Number in U.S. (202) 653-2400); *Production Yearbook; The State of Food and Agriculture;* and *Trade Yearbook.*

St. Martin's Press, Inc., 175 Fifth Avenue, New York, New York 10010 (800) 221-7945; *The Statesman's Year-Book.*

Statistical Office of the United Nations, Publishing Service, New York, New York 10017 (800) 253-9646; *Industrial Commodity Statistics Yearbook;* and *Statistical Yearbook.*

MACEDONIA - MACHINERY

Statistical Office of the United Nations, Publishing Service, New York, New York 10017 (800) 253-9646; *Industrial Commodity Statistics Yearbook.*

MACEDONIA - MAIL - NUMBER OF PIECES SENT OR RECEIVED

Statistical Office of the United Nations, Publishing Service, New York, New York 10017 (800) 253-9646; *Statistical Yearbook.*

MACEDONIA - MANUFACTURING

Statistical Office of the United Nations, Publishing Service, New York, New York 10017 (800) 253-9646; *Industrial Commodity Statistics Yearbook;* and *Statistical Yearbook.*

MACEDONIA - MARRIAGE RATES

Statistical Office of the United Nations, Publishing Service, New York, New York 10017 (800) 253-9646; *Demographic Yearbook; Trends in Europe and North America: The Statistical Yearbook of the Economic Commission for Europe;* and *Statistical Yearbook.*

MACEDONIA - MERCHANT SHIPPING

Statistical Office of the United Nations, Publishing Service, New York, New York 10017 (800) 253-9646; *Statistical Yearbook.*

MACEDONIA - MILITARY

Central Intelligence Agency, Washington, D.C. 20505 (703) 482-1100, www.cia.gov; *The World Factbook.*

Euromonitor International, Inc., 122 South Michigan Avenue, Suite 1200, Chicago, Illinois 60603 (800) 577-EURO; *World Marketing Data and Statistics.*

The International Institute for Strategic Studies, 23 Tavistock Street, London WC2E 7NQ, England; *The Military Balance.*

St. Martin's Press, Inc., 175 Fifth Avenue, New York, New York 10010 (800) 221-7945; *The Statesman's Year-Book.*

Statistical Office of the United Nations, Publishing Service, New York, New York 10017 (800) 253-9646; *Human Development Report.*

MACEDONIA - MINING AND MINERAL PRODUCTS

Europa Publications Limited, 18 Bedford Square, London, WC1B 3JN, England; *The Europa World Year Book.*

St. Martin's Press, Inc., 175 Fifth Avenue, New York, New York 10010 (800)

221-7945; *The Statesman's Year-Book.*

Statistical Office of the United Nations, Publishing Service, New York, New York 10017 (800) 253-9646; *Energy Statistics Yearbook; Industrial Commodity Statistics Yearbook;* and *Statistical Yearbook.*

MACEDONIA - MONEY SUPPLY

Economist Intelligence Unit, 111 West 57th Street, New York, New York 10019 (800) 938-4685; *Macedonia Country Report.*

MACEDONIA - MONUMENTS AND HISTORICAL SITES

United Nations Educational, Scientific and Cultural Organization (UNESCO), 7 Place de Fontenoy, F-75700 Paris, France (Telephone Number in U.S. (212) 963-5981); *Statistical Yearbook.*

MACEDONIA - MORTALITY

Central Intelligence Agency, Washington, D.C. 20505 (703) 482-1100, www.cia.gov; *The World Factbook.*

Euromonitor International, Inc., 122 South Michigan Avenue, Suite 1200, Chicago, Illinois 60603 (800) 577-EURO; *The World Economic Factbook.*

St. Martin's Press, Inc., 175 Fifth Avenue, New York, New York 10010 (800) 221-7945; *The Statesman's Year-Book.*

Statistical Office of the United Nations, Publishing Service, New York, New York 10017 (800) 253-9646; *Demographic Yearbook; Human Development Report; Trends in Europe and North America: The Statistical Yearbook of the Economic Commission for Europe; World Statistics Pocketbook;* and *Statistical Yearbook.*

United Nations Children's Fund (UNICEF), 3 United Nations Plaza, New York, New York 10017 (800) 253-9646; *State of the World's Children.*

The World Bank, 1818 H Street, NW, Washington, D.C. 20433 (202) 477-1234; *The World Bank Atlas;* and *World Development Report.*

MACEDONIA - MOTION PICTURES

St. Martin's Press, Inc., 175 Fifth Avenue, New York, New York 10010 (800) 221-7945; *The Statesman's Year-Book.*

Statistical Office of the United Nations, Publishing Service, New York, New York 10017 (800) 253-9646; *Statistical Yearbook.*

United Nations Educational, Scientific and Cultural Organization (UNESCO), 7 Place de Fontenoy, F-75700 Paris, France (Telephone Number in U.S. (212) 963-5981);

Statistical Yearbook.

MACEDONIA - MOTOR VEHICLE PRODUCTION

Statistical Office of the United Nations, Publishing Service, New York, New York 10017 (800) 253-9646; *Statistical Yearbook.*

MACEDONIA - MUSEUMS

United Nations Educational, Scientific and Cultural Organization (UNESCO), 7 Place de Fontenoy, F-75700 Paris, France (Telephone Number in U.S. (212) 963-5981); *Statistical Yearbook.*

MACEDONIA - NATIONAL ACCOUNTS

Statistical Office of the United Nations, Publishing Service, New York, New York 10017 (800) 253-9646; *National Accounts Statistics;* and *Statistical Yearbook.*

MACEDONIA - NATIONAL INCOME

Statistical Office of the United Nations, Publishing Service, New York, New York 10017 (800) 253-9646; *Statistical Yearbook.*

MACEDONIA - NATIONAL PRODUCT

Statistical Office of the United Nations, Publishing Service, New York, New York 10017 (800) 253-9646; *Statistical Yearbook.*

MACEDONIA - PATENTS, TRADEMARKS AND SERVICE MARKS

Statistical Office of the United Nations, Publishing Service, New York, New York 10017 (800) 253-9646; *Statistical Yearbook.*

MACEDONIA - PERIODICALS

United Nations Educational, Scientific and Cultural Organization (UNESCO), 7 Place de Fontenoy, F-75700 Paris, France (Telephone Number in U.S. (212) 963-5981); *Statistical Yearbook.*

MACEDONIA - PETROLEUM INDUSTRY

Food and Agriculture Organization of the United Nations (FAO), Via delle Terme di Caracalla, 00100, Rome, Italy (Telephone Number in U.S. (202) 653-2400); *The State of Food and Agriculture.*

Statistical Office of the United Nations, Publishing Service, New York, New York 10017 (800) 253-9646; *Energy Statistics Yearbook; Industrial Commodity Statistics Yearbook; Trends in Europe and North America: The Statistical Yearbook of the Economic Commission for Europe;* and *Statistical Yearbook.*

MACEDONIA - POPULATION

Central Intelligence Agency,

Washington, D.C. 20505 (703) 482-1100, www.cia.gov; *The World Factbook.*

Economist Intelligence Unit, 111 West 57th Street, New York, New York 10019 (800) 938-4685; *Macedonia Country Report.*

Euromonitor International, Inc., 122 South Michigan Avenue, Suite 1200, Chicago, Illinois 60603 (800) 577-EURO; *The World Economic Factbook.*

Europa Publications Limited, 18 Bedford Square, London, WC1B 3JN, England; *The Europa World Year Book.*

Food and Agriculture Organization of the United Nations (FAO), Via delle Terme di Caracalla, 00100, Rome, Italy (Telephone Number in U.S. (202) 653-2400); *Production Yearbook.*

St. Martin's Press, Inc., 175 Fifth Avenue, New York, New York 10010 (800) 221-7945; *The Statesman's Year-Book.*

Statistical Office of the United Nations, Publishing Service, New York, New York 10017 (800) 253-9646; *Demographic Yearbook; Human Development Report; Trends in Europe and North America: The Statistical Yearbook of the Economic Commission for Europe; World Statistics Pocketbook;* and *Statistical Yearbook.*

United Nations Educational, Scientific and Cultural Organization (UNESCO), 7 Place de Fontenoy, F-75700 Paris, France (Telephone Number in U.S. (212) 963-5981); *Statistical Yearbook.*

The World Bank, 1818 H Street, NW, Washington, D.C. 20433 (202) 477-1234; *The World Bank Atlas;* and *World Development Report.*

MACEDONIA - POST OFFICES

St. Martin's Press, Inc., 175 Fifth Avenue, New York, New York 10010 (800) 221-7945; *The Statesman's Year-Book.*

Statistical Office of the United Nations, Publishing Service, New York, New York 10017 (800) 253-9646; *Trends in Europe and North America: The Statistical Yearbook of the Economic Commission for Europe.*

MACEDONIA - PRICES

Food and Agriculture Organization of the United Nations (FAO), Via delle Terme di Caracalla, 00100, Rome, Italy (Telephone Number in U.S. (202) 653-2400); *Production Yearbook.*

MACEDONIA - RADIO RECEIVERS

St. Martin's Press, Inc., 175 Fifth Avenue, New York, New York 10010 (800) 221-7945; *The Statesman's Year-Book.*

Statistical Office of the United Nations, Publishing Service, New York, New York 10017 (800) 253-9646; *Statistical Yearbook.*

MACEDONIA - RAILWAYS

Europa Publications Limited, 18 Bedford Square, London, WC1B 3JN, England; *The Europa World Year Book.*

St. Martin's Press, Inc., 175 Fifth Avenue, New York, New York 10010 (800) 221-7945; *The Statesman's Year-Book.*

Statistical Office of the United Nations, Publishing Service, New York, New York 10017 (800) 253-9646; *Statistical Yearbook; and Trends in Europe and North America: The Statistical Yearbook of the Economic Commission for Europe.*

MACEDONIA - RELIGION

Central Intelligence Agency, Washington, D.C. 20505 (703) 482-1100, www.cia.gov; *The World Factbook.*

St. Martin's Press, Inc., 175 Fifth Avenue, New York, New York 10010 (800) 221-7945; *The Statesman's Year-Book.*

MACEDONIA - RETAIL TRADE

Euromonitor International, Inc., 122 South Michigan Avenue, Suite 1200, Chicago, Illinois 60603 (800) 577-EURO; *World Marketing Data and Statistics.*

Statistical Office of the United Nations, Publishing Service, New York, New York 10017 (800) 253-9646; *Statistical Yearbook.*

MACEDONIA - ROADS - See MACEDONIA - HIGHWAYS

MACEDONIA - RUBBER PRODUCTION AND CONSUMPTION

Statistical Office of the United Nations, Publishing Service, New York, New York 10017 (800) 253-9646; *Statistical Yearbook.*

MACEDONIA - SCIENTISTS, TECHNICIANS AND ENGINEERS

Statistical Office of the United Nations, Publishing Service, New York, New York 10017 (800) 253-9646; *Statistical Yearbook.*

MACEDONIA - SOCIAL DATA

Statistical Office of the United Nations, Publishing Service, New York, New York 10017 (800) 253-9646; *World Statistics Pocketbook.*

MACEDONIA - TELEPHONES IN USE

Central Intelligence Agency, Washington, D.C. 20505 (703) 482-1100, www.cia.gov; *The World Factbook.*

Europa Publications Limited, 18 Bedford Square, London, WC1B 3JN, England; *The Europa World Year Book.*

St. Martin's Press, Inc., 175 Fifth Avenue, New York, New York 10010 (800) 221-7945; *The Statesman's Year-Book.*

Statistical Office of the United Nations, Publishing Service, New York, New York 10017 (800) 253-9646; *Statistical Yearbook; World Statistics Pocketbook; and Trends in Europe and North America: The Statistical Yearbook of the Economic Commission for Europe.*

MACEDONIA - TEXTILE INDUSTRY

Statistical Office of the United Nations, Publishing Service, New York, New York 10017 (800) 253-9646; *Industrial Commodity Statistics Yearbook; and Statistical Yearbook.*

MACEDONIA - THEATRE

United Nations Educational, Scientific and Cultural Organization (UNESCO), 7 Place de Fontenoy, F-75700 Paris, France (Telephone Number in U.S. (212) 963-5981); *Statistical Yearbook.*

MACEDONIA - TIRE (MOTOR VEHICLE) PRODUCTION

Statistical Office of the United Nations, Publishing Service, New York, New York 10017 (800) 253-9646; *Statistical Yearbook.*

MACEDONIA - TOBACCO PRODUCTION

Statistical Office of the United Nations, Publishing Service, New York, New York 10017 (800) 253-9646; *Statistical Yearbook.*

MACEDONIA - TOURISM

Euromonitor International, Inc., 122 South Michigan Avenue, Suite 1200, Chicago, Illinois 60603 (800) 577-EURO; *The World Economic Factbook; and World Marketing Data and Statistics.*

St. Martin's Press, Inc., 175 Fifth Avenue, New York, New York 10010 (800) 221-7945; *The Statesman's Year-Book.*

Statistical Office of the United Nations, Publishing Service, New York, New York 10017 (800) 253-9646; *Statistical Yearbook; and Trends in Europe and North America: The Statistical Yearbook of the Economic Commission for Europe.*

MACEDONIA - TRADEMARKS AND SERVICE MARKS - See MACEDONIA - PATENTS, TRADEMARKS AND SERVICE MARKS

MACEDONIA - TRANSPORTATION AND COMMUNICATIONS

Central Intelligence Agency, Washington, D.C. 20505 (703) 482-1100, www.cia.gov; *The World Factbook.*

Euromonitor International, Inc., 122 South Michigan Avenue, Suite 1200, Chicago, Illinois 60603 (800) 577-EURO; *World Marketing Data and Statistics.*

Europa Publications Limited, 18 Bedford Square, London, WC1B 3JN, England; *The Europa World Year Book.*

St. Martin's Press, Inc., 175 Fifth Avenue, New York, New York 10010 (800) 221-7945; *The Statesman's Year-Book.*

Statistical Office of the United Nations, Publishing Service, New York, New York 10017 (800) 253-9646; *Human Development Report; and Trends in Europe and North America: The Statistical Yearbook of the Economic Commission for Europe.*

MACEDONIA - UNEMPLOYMENT

Central Intelligence Agency, Washington, D.C. 20505 (703) 482-1100, www.cia.gov; *The World Factbook.*

St. Martin's Press, Inc., 175 Fifth Avenue, New York, New York 10010 (800) 221-7945; *The Statesman's Year-Book.*

Statistical Office of the United Nations, Publishing Service, New York, New York 10017 (800) 253-9646; *Statistical Yearbook; and Trends in Europe and North America: The Statistical Yearbook of the Economic Commission for Europe.*

MACEDONIA - VITAL STATISTICS

St. Martin's Press, Inc., 175 Fifth Avenue, New York, New York 10010 (800) 221-7945; *The Statesman's Year-Book.*

Statistical Office of the United Nations, Publishing Service, New York, New York 10017 (800) 253-9646; *Statistical Yearbook.*

MACEDONIA - WAGES

Statistical Office of the United Nations, Publishing Service, New York, New York 10017 (800) 253-9646; *Statistical Yearbook.*

MACEDONIA - WELFARE

St. Martin's Press, Inc., 175 Fifth Avenue, New York, New York 10010 (800) 221-7945; *The Statesman's Year-Book.*

MACEDONIA - WHOLESALE PRICES

Statistical Office of the United Nations, Publishing Service, New York, New York 10017 (800) 253-9646; *Statistical Yearbook.*

MACEDONIA - WHOLESALE TRADE

Statistical Office of the United Nations, Publishing Service, New York, New York 10017 (800) 253-9646; *Statistical Yearbook.*

MACHINE TOOLS

Association for Manufacturing Technology, 7901 Westpark Drive, McLean, Virginia 22102 (800) 544-3597; *U.S. Machine Tool Consumption Report.*

U.S. Department of Commerce, Bureau of the Census, Washington, D.C. 20233 (301) 457-4100, www.census.gov; *Annual Benchmark Report for Wholesale Trade;* and unpublished data.

U.S. Department of Labor, Bureau of Labor Statistics, Two Massachusetts Avenue, NE, Washington, D.C. 20212 (202) 691-5200, www.stats.bls.gov; Internet site: http://stats.bls.gov/ iprhome.htm.

MACHINERY - See Individual Types and INDUSTRIAL MACHINERY AND EQUIPMENT

MACKEREL - PACIFIC

U.S. Department of Commerce, National Oceanic and Atmospheric Administration, National Marine Fisheries Service, 1315 East-West Highway, Silver Spring, Maryland 20910 (301) 713-2239, www.nmfs.noaa.gov; *Fisheries of the United States.*

Madagascar - National Statistical Office

Direction Generale de la Banque des Donnes d L'Etat, BP 485, Antananarivo, Madagascar.

Madagascar - Primary Statistics Source

Institut National de la Statistique et de la Recherche Economique, BP 38, Antananarivo, Madagascar; *Bulletin mensuel de statistique.* (Monthly bulletin of statistics).

MADAGASCAR - AGRICULTURE

Economist Intelligence Unit, 111 West 57th Street, New York, New York 10019 (800) 938-4685; *Madagascar Country Report.*

Euromonitor International, Inc., 122 South Michigan Avenue, Suite 1200, Chicago, Illinois 60603 (800) 577-EURO; *International Marketing Data and Statistics;* and *World Marketing Data and Statistics.*

Europa Publications Limited, 18 Bedford Square, London, WC1B 3JN, England; *The Europa World Year Book.*

Food and Agricultural Organization of the United Nations (FAO), Via delle Terme di Caracalla, 00100 Rome, Italy (Telephone Number in U.S. (202) 653-2400); *Production Yearbook; The State of Food and Agriculture;* and *Trade Yearbook.*

M.E. Sharpe, 80 Business Park Drive, Armonk, New York 10504 (800) 541-6563; *The Illustrated Book of World Rankings.*

St. Martin's Press, Inc., 175 Fifth Avenue, New York, New York 10010 (800) 221-7945; *The Statesman's Year-Book.*

Statistical Office of the United Nations, Publishing Service, New York, New York 10017 (800) 253-9646; *Statistical Yearbook;* and *Survey of Economic and Social Conditions in Africa.*

United Nations Conference on Trade and Development, Central Statistical Service, Palais des Nations, Geneva, Switzerland (Telephone in U.S. (800) 253-9646); *UNCTAD Commodity Yearbook.*

United Nations Economic Commission for Africa, Africa Hall, Post Office Box 3001, Addis Ababa, Ethiopia (Telephone Number in U.S. (800) 253-9646); *African Statistical Yearbook.*

The World Bank, 1818 H Street, NW, Washington, D.C. 20433 (202) 477-1234; *World Development Indicators.*

MADAGASCAR - AIRLINE SERVICE

Europa Publications Limited, 18 Bedford Square, London, WC1B 3JN, England; *The Europa World Year Book.*

International Civil Aviation Organization, 999 University Street, Montreal, Quebec, Canada H3C 5H7 (514) 954-8219; *Civil Aviation Statistics of the World.*

M.E. Sharpe, 80 Business Park Drive, Armonk, New York 10504 (800) 541-6563; *The Illustrated Book of World Rankings.*

St. Martin's Press, Inc., 175 Fifth Avenue, New York, New York 10010 (800) 221-7945; *The Statesman's Year-Book.*

Statistical Office of the United Nations, Publishing Service, New York, New York 10017 (800) 253-9646; *Statistical Yearbook.*

United Nations Economic Commission for Africa, Africa Hall, Post Office Box 3001, Addis Ababa, Ethiopia (Telephone Number in U.S. (800) 253-9646); *African Statistical Yearbook.*

MADAGASCAR - AIRPORTS

Central Intelligence Agency, Washington, D.C. 20505 (703) 482-1100, www.cia.gov; *The World Factbook.*

MADAGASCAR - ALUMINUM PRODUCTION AND CONSUMPTION - See MADAGASCAR - MINING AND MINERAL PRODUCTS

MADAGASCAR - ANIMAL HEALTH

Food and Agricultural Organization of the United Nations (FAO), Via delle Terme di Caracalla, 00100 Rome, Italy (Telephone Number in U.S. (202) 653-2400); *Animal Health Yearbook.*

MADAGASCAR - AREA AND DENSITY OF POPULATION

African Development Bank, 01 BP 1387, Abidjan 01, Cote d'Ivoire; *Selected Statistics on Regional Member Countries.*

Central Intelligence Agency, Washington, D.C. 20505 (703) 482-1100, www.cia.gov; *The World Factbook.*

Euromonitor International, Inc., 122 South Michigan Avenue, Suite 1200, Chicago, Illinois 60603 (800) 577-EURO; *International Marketing Data and Statistics;* and *The World Economic Factbook.*

Europa Publications Limited, 18 Bedford Square, London, WC1B 3JN, England; *The Europa World Year Book.*

Food and Agricultural Organization of the United Nations (FAO), Via delle Terme di Caracalla, 00100 Rome, Italy (Telephone Number in U.S. (202) 653-2400); *The State of Food and Agriculture.*

M.E. Sharpe, 80 Business Park Drive, Armonk, New York 10504 (800) 541-6563; *The Illustrated Book of World Rankings.*

St. Martin's Press, Inc., 175 Fifth Avenue, New York, New York 10010 (800) 221-7945; *The Statesman's Year-Book.*

Statistical Office of the United Nations, Publishing Service, New York, New York 10017 (800) 253-9646; *Statistical Yearbook;* and *Survey of Economic and Social Conditions in Africa.*

The World Bank, 1818 H Street, NW, Washington, D.C. 20433 (202) 477-1234; *World Development Report.*

MADAGASCAR - ARMS EXPORTS AND IMPORTS - See MADAGASCAR - MILITARY

MADAGASCAR - BALANCE OF PAYMENTS

African Development Bank, 01 BP 1387, Abidjan 01, Cote d'Ivoire; *Selected Statistics on Regional Member Countries.*

The Economist Intelligence Unit, 111 West 57th Street, New York, New York 10019 (800) 938-4685; *The World Market Atlas.*

Europa Publications Limited, 18 Bedford Square, London, WC1B 3JN, England; *The Europa World Year Book*.

International Monetary Fund, 700 Nineteenth Street, NW, Washington, D.C. 20431 (202) 623-7000; *Balance of Payments Yearbook*.

United Nations Conference on Trade and Development (UNCTAD), New York, New York 10017 (800) 253-9646; *Handbook of International Trade and Development Statistics*.

United Nations Economic Commission for Africa, Africa Hall, Post Office Box 3001, Addis Ababa, Ethiopia (Telephone Number in U.S. (800) 253-9646); *African Statistical Yearbook*.

The World Bank, 1818 H Street, NW, Washington, D.C. 20433 (202) 477-1234; *World Development Report*; and *World Development Indicators*.

MADAGASCAR - BANKING

Euromonitor International, Inc., 122 South Michigan Avenue, Suite 1200, Chicago, Illinois 60603 (800) 577-EURO; *World Marketing Data and Statistics*.

Europa Publications Limited, 18 Bedford Square, London, WC1B 3JN, England; *The Europa World Year Book*.

International Monetary Fund, 700 Nineteenth Street, NW, Washington, D.C. 20431 (202) 623-7000; *International Financial Statistics*.

M.E. Sharpe, 80 Business Park Drive, Armonk, New York 10504 (800) 541-6563; *The Illustrated Book of World Rankings*.

St. Martin's Press, Inc., 175 Fifth Avenue, New York, New York 10010 (800) 221-7945; *The Statesman's Year-Book*.

United Nations Economic Commission for Africa, Africa Hall, Post Office Box 3001, Addis Ababa, Ethiopia (Telephone Number in U.S. (800) 253-9646); *African Statistical Yearbook*.

MADAGASCAR - BARLEY PRODUCTION - See MADAGASCAR - CROPS

MADAGASCAR - BEER PRODUCTION - See MADAGASCAR - BEVERAGES

MADAGASCAR - BEVERAGES

M.E. Sharpe, 80 Business Park Drive, Armonk, New York 10504 (800) 541-6563; *The Illustrated Book of World Rankings*.

Statistical Office of the United Nations, Publishing Service, New York, New York 10017 (800) 253-9646; *Statistical Yearbook*.

MADAGASCAR - BIRTH RATES

Central Intelligence Agency, Washington, D.C. 20505 (703) 482-1100, www.cia.gov; *The World Factbook*.

Euromonitor International, Inc., 122 South Michigan Avenue, Suite 1200, Chicago, Illinois 60603 (800) 577-EURO; *International Marketing Data and Statistics*; and *The World Economic Factbook*.

Europa Publications Limited, 18 Bedford Square, London, WC1B 3JN, England; *The Europa World Year Book*.

M.E. Sharpe, 80 Business Park Drive, Armonk, New York 10504 (800) 541-6563; *The Illustrated Book of World Rankings*.

St. Martin's Press, Inc., 175 Fifth Avenue, New York, New York 10010 (800) 221-7945; *The Statesman's Year-Book*.

Statistical Office of the United Nations, Publishing Service, New York, New York 10017 (800) 253-9646; *Demographic Yearbook; Statistical Yearbook;* and *Survey of Economic and Social Conditions in Africa*.

The World Bank, 1818 H Street, NW, Washington, D.C. 20433 (202) 477-1234; *World Development Indicators*.

MADAGASCAR - BONDS

International Monetary Fund, 700 Nineteenth Street, NW, Washington, D.C. 20431 (202) 623-7000; *Government Finance Statistics Yearbook*.

MADAGASCAR - BOOK PRODUCTION

Europa Publications Limited, 18 Bedford Square, London, WC1B 3JN, England; *The Europa World Year Book*.

United Nations Educational, Scientific and Cultural Organization (UNESCO), 7 Place de Fontenoy, F-75700 Paris, France (Telephone Number in U.S. (212) 963-5981); *Statistical Yearbook*.

MADAGASCAR - BROADCASTING

Billboard Limited, Post Office Box 9027, 1006 AA Amsterdam, The Netherlands (Telephone Number in U.S. (212) 764-7300); *World Radio TV Handbook*.

Central Intelligence Agency, Washington, D.C. 20505 (703) 482-1100, www.cia.gov; *The World Factbook*.

Euromonitor International, Inc., 122 South Michigan Avenue, Suite 1200, Chicago, Illinois 60603 (800) 577-EURO; *World Marketing Data and Statistics*.

M.E. Sharpe, 80 Business Park Drive,

Armonk, New York 10504 (800) 541-6563; *The Illustrated Book of World Rankings*.

St. Martin's Press, Inc., 175 Fifth Avenue, New York, New York 10010 (800) 221-7945; *The Statesman's Year-Book*.

United Nations Educational, Scientific and Cultural Organization (UNESCO), 7 Place de Fontenoy, F-75700 Paris, France (Telephone Number in U.S. (212) 963-5981); *Statistical Yearbook*.

MADAGASCAR - BUDGET

Central Intelligence Agency, Washington, D.C. 20505 (703) 482-1100, www.cia.gov; *The World Factbook*.

MADAGASCAR - BUSINESS AND PROFESSIONAL LICENSES

International Monetary Fund, 700 Nineteenth Street, NW, Washington, D.C. 20431 (202) 623-7000; *Government Finance Statistics Yearbook*.

MADAGASCAR - CALORIE SUPPLY

African Development Bank, 01 BP 1387, Abidjan 01, Cote d'Ivoire; *Selected Statistics on Regional Member Countries*.

Food and Agricultural Organization of the United Nations (FAO), Via delle Terme di Caracalla, 00100 Rome, Italy (Telephone Number in U.S. (202) 653-2400); *The State of Food and Agriculture*.

MADAGASCAR - CAPITAL REVENUE

International Monetary Fund, 700 Nineteenth Street, NW, Washington, D.C. 20431 (202) 623-7000; *Government Finance Statistics Yearbook*.

MADAGASCAR - CASHEW NUT PRODUCTION - See MADAGASCAR - CROPS

MADAGASCAR - CASTOR BEAN PRODUCTION - See MADAGASCAR - CROPS

MADAGASCAR - CATTLE - See MADAGASCAR - LIVESTOCK AND POULTRY

MADAGASCAR - CEMENT PRODUCTION - See MADAGASCAR - MINING AND MINERAL PRODUCTS

MADAGASCAR - CHEMICAL (ORGANIC) PRODUCTION - See MADAGASCAR - MINING AND MINERAL PRODUCTS

MADAGASCAR - CHICKENS - See MADAGASCAR - LIVESTOCK AND POULTRY

MADAGASCAR - CHROMIUM ORE

PRODUCTION - See MADAGASCAR - MINING AND MINERAL PRODUCTS

MADAGASCAR - CIGARETTE PRODUCTION - See MADAGASCAR - TOBACCO PRODUCTION

MADAGASCAR - CLIMATE

M.E. Sharpe, 80 Business Park Drive, Armonk, New York 10504 (800) 541-6563; *The Illustrated Book of World Rankings.*

St. Martin's Press, Inc., 175 Fifth Avenue, New York, New York 10010 (800) 221-7945; *The Statesman's Year-Book.*

MADAGASCAR - CLOVES EXPORTS

International Monetary Fund, 700 Nineteenth Street, NW, Washington, D.C. 20431 (202) 623-7000; *International Financial Statistics.*

MADAGASCAR - COAL PRODUCTION - See MADAGASCAR - MINING AND MINERAL PRODUCTS

MADAGASCAR - COCOA PRODUCTION

Statistical Office of the United Nations, Publishing Service, New York, New York 10017 (800) 253-9646; *Statistical Yearbook.*

MADAGASCAR - COFFEE - See MADAGASCAR - CROPS

MADAGASCAR - COMMERCE

St. Martin's Press, Inc., 175 Fifth Avenue, New York, New York 10010 (800) 221-7945; *The Statesman's Year-Book.*

MADAGASCAR - COMMUNICATIONS - See MADAGASCAR - TRANSPORTATION AND COMMUNICATIONS

MADAGASCAR - CONSTRUCTION INDUSTRY

M.E. Sharpe, 80 Business Park Drive, Armonk, New York 10504 (800) 541-6563; *The Illustrated Book of World Rankings.*

Statistical Office of the United Nations, Publishing Service, New York, New York 10017 (800) 253-9646; *Statistical Yearbook.*

United Nations Economic Commission for Africa, Africa Hall, Post Office Box 3001, Addis Ababa, Ethiopia (Telephone Number in U.S. (800) 253-9646); *African Statistical Yearbook.*

MADAGASCAR - CONSUMER PRICE INDEX

African Development Bank, 01 BP 1387, Abidjan 01, Cote d'Ivoire; *Selected Statistics on Regional Member Countries.*

Europa Publications Limited, 18 Bedford Square, London, WC1B 3JN, England; *The Europa World Year Book.*

Statistical Office of the United Nations, Publishing Service, New York, New York 10017 (800) 253-9646; *Statistical Yearbook;* and *Survey of Economic and Social Conditions in Africa.*

United Nations Economic Commission for Africa, Africa Hall, Post Office Box 3001, Addis Ababa, Ethiopia (Telephone Number in U.S. (800) 253-9646); *African Statistical Yearbook.*

MADAGASCAR - CONSUMER PRICES

Euromonitor International, Inc., 122 South Michigan Avenue, Suite 1200, Chicago, Illinois 60603 (800) 577-EURO; *World Marketing Data and Statistics.*

International Labour Office, I.L.O. Publications, 1828 L Street, N.W., Suite 801, Washington, D.C. 20036 (301) 638-3152; *Yearbook of Labour Statistics.*

International Monetary Fund, 700 Nineteenth Street, NW, Washington, D.C. 20431 (202) 623-7000; *International Financial Statistics.*

MADAGASCAR - CONSUMPTION

African Development Bank, 01 BP 1387, Abidjan 01, Cote d'Ivoire; *Selected Statistics on Regional Member Countries.*

Statistical Office of the United Nations, Publishing Service, New York, New York 10017 (800) 253-9646; *Survey of Economic and Social Conditions in Africa.*

The World Bank, 1818 H Street, NW, Washington, D.C. 20433 (202) 477-1234; *World Development Report.*

MADAGASCAR - COPPER PRODUCTION - See MADAGASCAR - MINING AND MINERAL PRODUCTS

MADAGASCAR - CORN PRODUCTION - See MADAGASCAR - CROPS

MADAGASCAR - CORPORATE TAXES - See MADAGASCAR - TAXATION

MADAGASCAR - COTTON PRODUCTION AND CONSUMPTION - See MADAGASCAR - CROPS

MADAGASCAR - CRIME

Yale University Press, Yale Station, New Haven, Connecticut 06520 (800) 987-7323; *Violence and Crime in Cross-National Perspective.*

MADAGASCAR - CROPS

Europa Publications Limited, 18

Bedford Square, London, WC1B 3JN, England; *The Europa World Year Book.*

Food and Agricultural Organization of the United Nations (FAO), Via delle Terme di Caracalla, 00100 Rome, Italy (Telephone Number in U.S. (202) 653-2400); *Production Yearbook;* and *The State of Food and Agriculture.*

International Monetary Fund, 700 Nineteenth Street, NW, Washington, D.C. 20431 (202) 623-7000; *International Financial Statistics.*

M.E. Sharpe, 80 Business Park Drive, Armonk, New York 10504 (800) 541-6563; *The Illustrated Book of World Rankings.*

St. Martin's Press, Inc., 175 Fifth Avenue, New York, New York 10010 (800) 221-7945; *The Statesman's Year-Book.*

Statistical Office of the United Nations, Publishing Service, New York, New York 10017 (800) 253-9646; *Statistical Yearbook.*

United Nations Conference on Trade and Development, Central Statistical Service, Palais des Nations, Geneva, Switzerland (Telephone in U.S. (800) 253-9646); *UNCTAD Commodity Yearbook.*

United Nations Economic Commission for Africa, Africa Hall, Post Office Box 3001, Addis Ababa, Ethiopia (Telephone Number in U.S. (800) 253-9646); *African Statistical Yearbook.*

MADAGASCAR - CUSTOMS DUTIES

International Monetary Fund, 700 Nineteenth Street, NW, Washington, D.C. 20431 (202) 623-7000; *Government Finance Statistics Yearbook.*

MADAGASCAR - DAIRY PRODUCTS

Europa Publications Limited, 18 Bedford Square, London, WC1B 3JN, England; *The Europa World Year Book.*

Food and Agricultural Organization of the United Nations (FAO), Via delle Terme di Caracalla, 00100 Rome, Italy (Telephone Number in U.S. (202) 653-2400); *Production Yearbook;* and *The State of Food and Agriculture.*

M.E. Sharpe, 80 Business Park Drive, Armonk, New York 10504 (800) 541-6563; *The Illustrated Book of World Rankings.*

St. Martin's Press, Inc., 175 Fifth Avenue, New York, New York 10010 (800) 221-7945; *The Statesman's Year-Book.*

Statistical Office of the United Nations, Publishing Service, New York, New York 10017 (800) 253-9646; *Statistical Yearbook.*

MADAGASCAR - DEATH RATES - See MADAGASCAR - MORTALITY

MADAGASCAR - DEFENSE EXPENDITURES - See MADAGASCAR - MILITARY

MADAGASCAR - DEMOGRAPHY

Euromonitor International, Inc., 122 South Michigan Avenue, Suite 1200, Chicago, Illinois 60603 (800) 577-EURO; *International Marketing Data and Statistics; World Marketing Data and Statistics;* and *The World Economic Factbook.*

M.E. Sharpe, 80 Business Park Drive, Armonk, New York 10504 (800) 541-6563; *The Illustrated Book of World Rankings.*

Statistical Office of the United Nations, Publishing Service, New York, New York 10017 (800) 253-9646; *Human Development Report;* and *Survey of Economic and Social Conditions in Africa.*

MADAGASCAR - DEVELOPMENT ASSISTANCE

Statistical Office of the United Nations, Publishing Service, New York, New York 10017 (800) 253-9646; *Statistical Yearbook.*

MADAGASCAR - DIAMOND PRODUCTION - See MADAGASCAR - MINING AND MINERAL PRODUCTS

MADAGASCAR - DISEASES - See MADAGASCAR - HEALTH

MADAGASCAR - DIVORCE

M.E. Sharpe, 80 Business Park Drive, Armonk, New York 10504 (800) 541-6563; *The Illustrated Book of World Rankings.*

Statistical Office of the United Nations, Publishing Service, New York, New York 10017 (800) 253-9646; *Demographic Yearbook.*

MADAGASCAR - DUCKS

Food and Agricultural Organization of the United Nations (FAO), Via delle Terme di Caracalla, 00100 Rome, Italy (Telephone Number in U.S. (202) 653-2400); *Production Yearbook.*

MADAGASCAR - ECONOMY

African Development Bank, 01 BP 1387, Abidjan 01, Cote d'Ivoire; *Selected Statistics on Regional Member Countries.*

Central Intelligence Agency, Washington, D.C. 20505 (703) 482-1100, www.cia.gov; *The World Factbook.*

Economist Intelligence Unit, 111 West 57th Street, New York, New York 10019 (800) 938-4685; *Madagascar Country Report.*

Euromonitor International, Inc., 122 South Michigan Avenue, Suite 1200, Chicago, Illinois 60603 (800) 577-EURO; *International Marketing Data and Statistics; World Marketing Data and Statistics;* and *The World Economic Factbook.*

Europa Publications Limited, 18 Bedford Square, London, WC1B 3JN, England; *The Europa World Year Book.*

M.E. Sharpe, 80 Business Park Drive, Armonk, New York 10504 (800) 541-6563; *The Illustrated Book of World Rankings.*

St. Martin's Press, Inc., 175 Fifth Avenue, New York, New York 10010 (800) 221-7945; *The Statesman's Year-Book.*

Statistical Office of the United Nations, Publishing Service, New York, New York 10017 (800) 253-9646; *Foreign Trade Statistics for Africa;* and *World Statistics Pocketbook.*

The World Bank, 1818 H Street, NW, Washington, D.C. 20433 (202) 477-1234; *The World Bank Atlas;* and *World Development Report.*

MADAGASCAR - EDUCATION

African Development Bank, 01 BP 1387, Abidjan 01, Cote d'Ivoire; *Selected Statistics on Regional Member Countries.*

The Economist Intelligence Unit, 111 West 57th Street, New York, New York 10019 (800) 938-4685; *The World Market Atlas.*

Euromonitor International, Inc., 122 South Michigan Avenue, Suite 1200, Chicago, Illinois 60603 (800) 577-EURO; *International Marketing Data and Statistics;* and *World Marketing Data and Statistics.*

Europa Publications Limited, 18 Bedford Square, London, WC1B 3JN, England; *The Europa World Year Book.*

International Monetary Fund, 700 Nineteenth Street, NW, Washington, D.C. 20431 (202) 623-7000; *Government Finance Statistics Yearbook.*

M.E. Sharpe, 80 Business Park Drive, Armonk, New York 10504 (800) 541-6563; *The Illustrated Book of World Rankings.*

St. Martin's Press, Inc., 175 Fifth Avenue, New York, New York 10010 (800) 221-7945; *The Statesman's Year-Book.*

Statistical Office of the United Nations, Publishing Service, New York, New York 10017 (800) 253-9646; *Human Development Report; Statistical Yearbook;*

and *Survey of Economic and Social Conditions in Africa.*

United Nations Economic Commission for Africa, Africa Hall, Post Office Box 3001, Addis Ababa, Ethiopia (Telephone Number in U.S. (800) 253-9646); *African Statistical Yearbook.*

United Nations Educational, Scientific and Cultural Organization (UNESCO), 7 Place de Fontenoy, F-75700 Paris, France (Telephone Number in U.S. (212) 963-5981); *Statistical Yearbook.*

The World Bank, 1818 H Street, NW, Washington, D.C. 20433 (202) 477-1234; *World Development Report;* and *World Development Indicators.*

MADAGASCAR - EGG PRODUCTION AND CONSUMPTION - See MADAGASCAR - DAIRY PRODUCTS

MADAGASCAR - ELECTRICITY

Central Intelligence Agency, Washington, D.C. 20505 (703) 482-1100, www.cia.gov; *The World Factbook.*

M.E. Sharpe, 80 Business Park Drive, Armonk, New York 10504 (800) 541-6563; *The Illustrated Book of World Rankings.*

St. Martin's Press, Inc., 175 Fifth Avenue, New York, New York 10010 (800) 221-7945; *The Statesman's Year-Book.*

Statistical Office of the United Nations, Publishing Service, New York, New York 10017 (800) 253-9646; *Human Development Report; Statistical Yearbook;* and *Survey of Economic and Social Conditions in Africa.*

United Nations Economic Commission for Africa, Africa Hall, Post Office Box 3001, Addis Ababa, Ethiopia (Telephone Number in U.S. (800) 253-9646); *African Statistical Yearbook.*

MADAGASCAR - EMPLOYMENT

Euromonitor International, Inc., 122 South Michigan Avenue, Suite 1200, Chicago, Illinois 60603 (800) 577-EURO; *International Marketing Data and Statistics.*

International Labour Office, I.L.O. Publications, 1828 L Street, N.W., Suite 801, Washington, D.C. 20036 (301) 638-3152; *Yearbook of Labour Statistics.*

M.E. Sharpe, 80 Business Park Drive, Armonk, New York 10504 (800) 541-6563; *The Illustrated Book of World Rankings.*

Statistical Office of the United Nations, Publishing Service, New York, New York 10017 (800) 253-9646; *Statistical Yearbook;*

and *Survey of Economic and Social Conditions in Africa.*

United Nations Economic Commission for Africa, Africa Hall, Post Office Box 3001, Addis Ababa, Ethiopia (Telephone Number in U.S. (800) 253-9646); *African Statistical Yearbook.*

MADAGASCAR - ENERGY

Euromonitor International, Inc., 122 South Michigan Avenue, Suite 1200, Chicago, Illinois 60603 (800) 577-EURO; *International Marketing Data and Statistics; World Marketing Data and Statistics;* and *The World Economic Factbook.*

Food and Agricultural Organization of the United Nations (FAO), Via delle Terme di Caracalla, 00100 Rome, Italy (Telephone Number in U.S. (202) 653-2400); *The State of Food and Agriculture.*

M.E. Sharpe, 80 Business Park Drive, Armonk, New York 10504 (800) 541-6563; *The Illustrated Book of World Rankings.*

St. Martin's Press, Inc., 175 Fifth Avenue, New York, New York 10010 (800) 221-7945; *The Statesman's Year-Book.*

Statistical Office of the United Nations, Publishing Service, New York, New York 10017 (800) 253-9646; *Energy Statistics Yearbook; Human Development Report; World Statistics Pocketbook;* and *Statistical Yearbook.*

United Nations Economic Commission for Africa, Africa Hall, Post Office Box 3001, Addis Ababa, Ethiopia (Telephone Number in U.S. (800) 253-9646); *African Statistical Yearbook.*

The World Bank, 1818 H Street, NW, Washington, D.C. 20433 (202) 477-1234; *The World Bank Atlas;* and *World Development Report.*

MADAGASCAR - ENVIRONMENT

Economist Intelligence Unit, 111 West 57th Street, New York, New York 10019 (800) 938-4685; *Madagascar Country Report.*

Statistical Office of the United Nations, Publishing Service, New York, New York 10017 (800) 253-9646; *World Statistics Pocketbook.*

MADAGASCAR - EXCHANGE RATES

African Development Bank, 01 BP 1387, Abidjan 01, Cote d'Ivoire; *Selected Statistics on Regional Member Countries.*

Central Intelligence Agency, Washington, D.C. 20505 (703) 482-1100, www.cia.gov; *The World Factbook.*

Euromonitor International, Inc., 122 South Michigan Avenue, Suite 1200, Chicago, Illinois 60603 (800) 577-EURO; *International Marketing Data and Statistics;* and *The World Economic Factbook.*

Europa Publications Limited, 18 Bedford Square, London, WC1B 3JN, England; *The Europa World Year Book.*

International Civil Aviation Organization, 999 University Street, Montreal, Quebec, Canada H3C 5H7 (514) 954-8219; *Civil Aviation Statistics of the World.*

International Monetary Fund, 700 Nineteenth Street, NW, Washington, D.C. 20431 (202) 623-7000; *International Financial Statistics.*

Statistical Office of the United Nations, Publishing Service, New York, New York 10017 (800) 253-9646; *Foreign Trade Statistics for Africa; World Statistics Pocketbook;* and *Statistical Yearbook.*

MADAGASCAR - EXCISE TAXES - See MADAGASCAR - TAXATION

MADAGASCAR - EXPORTS

African Development Bank, 01 BP 1387, Abidjan 01, Cote d'Ivoire; *Selected Statistics on Regional Member Countries.*

Central Intelligence Agency, Washington, D.C. 20505 (703) 482-1100, www.cia.gov; *The World Factbook.*

The Economist Intelligence Unit, 111 West 57th Street, New York, New York 10019 (800) 938-4685; *Madagascar Country Report;* and *The World Market Atlas.*

Euromonitor International, Inc., 122 South Michigan Avenue, Suite 1200, Chicago, Illinois 60603 (800) 577-EURO; *International Marketing Data and Statistics;* and *The World Economic Factbook.*

Europa Publications Limited, 18 Bedford Square, London, WC1B 3JN, England; *The Europa World Year Book.*

Food and Agricultural Organization of the United Nations (FAO), Via delle Terme di Caracalla, 00100 Rome, Italy (Telephone Number in U.S. (202) 653-2400); *The State of Food and Agriculture.*

International Monetary Fund, 700 Nineteenth Street, NW, Washington, D.C. 20431 (202) 623-7000; *Direction of Trade Statistics; Government Finance Statistics Yearbook;* and *International Financial Statistics.*

St. Martin's Press, Inc., 175 Fifth Avenue, New York, New York 10010 (800) 221-7945; *The Statesman's Year-Book.*

Statistical Office of the United Nations, Publishing Service, New York, New York 10017 (800) 253-9646; *Foreign Trade Statistics for Africa;* and *Survey of Economic and Social Conditions in Africa.*

United Nations Conference on Trade and Development (UNCTAD), New York, New York 10017 (800) 253-9646; *Handbook of International Trade and Development Statistics.*

United Nations Economic Commission for Africa, Africa Hall, Post Office Box 3001, Addis Ababa, Ethiopia (Telephone Number in U.S. (800) 253-9646); *African Statistical Yearbook.*

The World Bank, 1818 H Street, NW, Washington, D.C. 20433 (202) 477-1234; *World Development Report;* and *World Development Indicators.*

MADAGASCAR - EXTERNAL INDEBTEDNESS

African Development Bank, 01 BP 1387, Abidjan 01, Cote d'Ivoire; *Selected Statistics on Regional Member Countries.*

Statistical Office of the United Nations, Publishing Service, New York, New York 10017 (800) 253-9646; *Survey of Economic and Social Conditions in Africa.*

The World Bank, 1818 H Street, NW, Washington, D.C. 20433 (202) 477-1234; *World Development Report;* and *World Development Indicators.*

MADAGASCAR - EXTERNAL TRADE

African Development Bank, 01 BP 1387, Abidjan 01, Cote d'Ivoire; *Selected Statistics on Regional Member Countries.*

Euromonitor International, Inc., 122 South Michigan Avenue, Suite 1200, Chicago, Illinois 60603 (800) 577-EURO; *World Marketing Data and Statistics.*

Food and Agricultural Organization of the United Nations (FAO), Via delle Terme di Caracalla, 00100 Rome, Italy (Telephone Number in U.S. (202) 653-2400); *The State of Food and Agriculture;* and *Trade Yearbook.*

Statistical Office of the United Nations, Publishing Service, New York, New York 10017 (800) 253-9646; *Statistical Yearbook.*

MADAGASCAR - FABRIC PRODUCTION - See MADAGASCAR - TEXTILE INDUSTRY

MADAGASCAR - FARM CROPS - See MADAGASCAR - CROPS

MADAGASCAR - FEMALE WORKING POPULATION - See MADAGASCAR -

EMPLOYMENT

MADAGASCAR - FERTILITY RATES

Central Intelligence Agency, Washington, D.C. 20505 (703) 482-1100, www.cia.gov; *The World Factbook*.

M.E. Sharpe, 80 Business Park Drive, Armonk, New York 10504 (800) 541-6563; *The Illustrated Book of World Rankings*.

Statistical Office of the United Nations, Publishing Service, New York, New York 10017 (800) 253-9646; *Human Development Report;* and *Survey of Economic and Social Conditions in Africa*.

The World Bank, 1818 H Street, NW, Washington, D.C. 20433 (202) 477-1234; *The World Bank Atlas; World Development Report;* and *World Development Indicators*.

MADAGASCAR - FERTILIZER

Food and Agricultural Organization of the United Nations (FAO), Via delle Terme di Caracalla, 00100 Rome, Italy (Telephone Number in U.S. (202) 653-2400); *The State of Food and Agriculture*.

Statistical Office of the United Nations, Publishing Service, New York, New York 10017 (800) 253-9646; *Statistical Yearbook*.

MADAGASCAR - FETAL MORTALITY - See MADAGASCAR - MORTALITY

MADAGASCAR - FINANCE

African Development Bank, 01 BP 1387, Abidjan 01, Cote d'Ivoire; *Selected Statistics on Regional Member Countries*.

Economist Intelligence Unit, 111 West 57th Street, New York, New York 10019 (800) 938-4685; *Madagascar Country Report*.

Europa Publications Limited, 18 Bedford Square, London, WC1B 3JN, England; *The Europa World Year Book*.

International Monetary Fund, 700 Nineteenth Street, NW, Washington, D.C. 20431 (202) 623-7000; *Government Finance Statistics Yearbook*.

M.E. Sharpe, 80 Business Park Drive, Armonk, New York 10504 (800) 541-6563; *The Illustrated Book of World Rankings*.

St. Martin's Press, Inc., 175 Fifth Avenue, New York, New York 10010 (800) 221-7945; *The Statesman's Year-Book*.

United Nations Economic Commission for Africa, Africa Hall, Post Office Box 3001, Addis Ababa, Ethiopia (Telephone Number in U.S. (800) 253-9646); *African Statistical Yearbook*.

MADAGASCAR - FISHERIES

Europa Publications Limited, 18 Bedford Square, London, WC1B 3JN, England; *The Europa World Year Book*.

Food and Agricultural Organization of the United Nations (FAO), Via delle Terme di Caracalla, 00100 Rome, Italy (Telephone Number in U.S. (202) 653-2400); *The State of Food and Agriculture;* and *Yearbook of Fishery Statistics*.

M.E. Sharpe, 80 Business Park Drive, Armonk, New York 10504 (800) 541-6563; *The Illustrated Book of World Rankings*.

St. Martin's Press, Inc., 175 Fifth Avenue, New York, New York 10010 (800) 221-7945; *The Statesman's Year-Book*.

Statistical Office of the United Nations, Publishing Service, New York, New York 10017 (800) 253-9646; *Statistical Yearbook;* and *Survey of Economic and Social Conditions in Africa*.

United Nations Conference on Trade and Development, Central Statistical Service, Palais des Nations, Geneva, Switzerland (Telephone in U.S. (800) 253-9646); *UNCTAD Commodity Yearbook*.

United Nations Economic Commission for Africa, Africa Hall, Post Office Box 3001, Addis Ababa, Ethiopia (Telephone Number in U.S. (800) 253-9646); *African Statistical Yearbook*.

MADAGASCAR - FOOD

African Development Bank, 01 BP 1387, Abidjan 01, Cote d'Ivoire; *Selected Statistics on Regional Member Countries*.

Food and Agricultural Organization of the United Nations (FAO), Via delle Terme di Caracalla, 00100 Rome, Italy (Telephone Number in U.S. (202) 653-2400); *Production Yearbook;* and *The State of Food and Agriculture*.

Statistical Office of the United Nations, Publishing Service, New York, New York 10017 (800) 253-9646; *Human Development Report*.

United Nations Conference on Trade and Development, Central Statistical Service, Palais des Nations, Geneva, Switzerland (Telephone in U.S. (800) 253-9646); *UNCTAD Commodity Yearbook*.

MADAGASCAR - FOREIGN DEBT

Europa Publications Limited, 18 Bedford Square, London, WC1B 3JN, England; *The Europa World Year Book*.

International Monetary Fund, 700 Nineteenth Street, NW, Washington, D.C. 20431 (202) 623-7000; *Government Finance Statistics Yearbook*.

MADAGASCAR - FOREIGN TRADE

Economist Intelligence Unit, 111 West 57th Street, New York, New York 10019 (800) 938-4685; *Madagascar Country Report*.

Euromonitor International, Inc., 122 South Michigan Avenue, Suite 1200, Chicago, Illinois 60603 (800) 577-EURO; *International Marketing Data and Statistics;* and *The World Economic Factbook*.

Food and Agricultural Organization of the United Nations (FAO), Via delle Terme di Caracalla, 00100 Rome, Italy (Telephone Number in U.S. (202) 653-2400); *The State of Food and Agriculture*.

M.E. Sharpe, 80 Business Park Drive, Armonk, New York 10504 (800) 541-6563; *The Illustrated Book of World Rankings*.

St. Martin's Press, Inc., 175 Fifth Avenue, New York, New York 10010 (800) 221-7945; *The Statesman's Year-Book*.

Statistical Office of the United Nations, Publishing Service, New York, New York 10017 (800) 253-9646; *Foreign Trade Statistics for Africa; International Trade Statistics Yearbook;* and *Statistical Yearbook*.

United Nations Conference on Trade and Development, Central Statistical Service, Palais des Nations, Geneva, Switzerland (Telephone in U.S. (800) 253-9646); *UNCTAD Commodity Yearbook*.

United Nations Economic Commission for Africa, Africa Hall, Post Office Box 3001, Addis Ababa, Ethiopia (Telephone Number in U.S. (800) 253-9646); *African Statistical Yearbook*.

The World Bank, 1818 H Street, NW, Washington, D.C. 20433 (202) 477-1234; *World Development Report;* and *World Development Indicators*.

MADAGASCAR - FORESTRY AND FOREST PRODUCTS

Europa Publications Limited, 18 Bedford Square, London, WC1B 3JN, England; *The Europa World Year Book*.

Food and Agricultural Organization of the United Nations (FAO), Via delle Terme di Caracalla, 00100 Rome, Italy (Telephone Number in U.S. (202) 653-2400); *The State of Food and Agriculture;* and *Yearbook of Forest Products*.

M.E. Sharpe, 80 Business Park Drive, Armonk, New York 10504 (800) 541-6563; *The Illustrated Book of World Rankings*.

St. Martin's Press, Inc., 175 Fifth Avenue, New York, New York 10010 (800) 221-7945; *The Statesman's Year-Book.*

Statistical Office of the United Nations, Publishing Service, New York, New York 10017 (800) 253-9646; *Statistical Yearbook.*

United Nations Conference on Trade and Development, Central Statistical Service, Palais des Nations, Geneva, Switzerland (Telephone in U.S. (800) 253-9646); *UNCTAD Commodity Yearbook.*

United Nations Economic Commission for Africa, Africa Hall, Post Office Box 3001, Addis Ababa, Ethiopia (Telephone Number in U.S. (800) 253-9646); *African Statistical Yearbook.*

United Nations Educational, Scientific and Cultural Organization (UNESCO), 7 Place de Fontenoy, F-75700 Paris, France (Telephone Number in U.S. (212) 963-5981); *Statistical Yearbook.*

The World Bank, 1818 H Street, NW, Washington, D.C. 20433 (202) 477-1234; *World Development Report.*

MADAGASCAR - GAS PRODUCTION - See MADAGASCAR - MINING AND MINERAL PRODUCTS

MADAGASCAR - GENERAL INDUSTRIAL STATISTICS - See MADAGASCAR - INDUSTRY

MADAGASCAR - GENERAL MORTALITY - See MADAGASCAR - MORTALITY

MADAGASCAR - GEOGRAPHIC DATA

M.E. Sharpe, 80 Business Park Drive, Armonk, New York 10504 (800) 541-6563; *The Illustrated Book of World Rankings.*

MADAGASCAR - GOATS - See MADAGASCAR - LIVESTOCK AND POULTRY

MADAGASCAR - GOLD HOLDINGS

Statistical Office of the United Nations, Publishing Service, New York, New York 10017 (800) 253-9646; *Statistical Yearbook.*

The World Bank, 1818 H Street, NW, Washington, D.C. 20433 (202) 477-1234; *World Development Indicators.*

MADAGASCAR - GOLD PRODUCTION AND CONSUMPTION - See MADAGASCAR - MINING AND MINERAL PRODUCTS

MADAGASCAR - GOVERNMENT

Central Intelligence Agency, Washington, D.C. 20505 (703) 482-1100, www.cia.gov; *The World Factbook.*

Europa Publications Limited, 18 Bedford

Square, London, WC1B 3JN, England; *The Europa World Year Book.*

International Monetary Fund, 700 Nineteenth Street, NW, Washington, D.C. 20431 (202) 623-7000; *Government Finance Statistics Yearbook;* and *International Financial Statistics.*

St. Martin's Press, Inc., 175 Fifth Avenue, New York, New York 10010 (800) 221-7945; *The Statesman's Year-Book.*

Statistical Office of the United Nations, Publishing Service, New York, New York 10017 (800) 253-9646; *National Accounts Statistics;* and *Survey of Economic and Social Conditions in Africa.*

The World Bank, 1818 H Street, NW, Washington, D.C. 20433 (202) 477-1234; *World Development Report;* and *World Development Indicators.*

MADAGASCAR - GRAIN PRODUCTION - See MADAGASCAR - CROPS

MADAGASCAR - GRANTS

International Monetary Fund, 700 Nineteenth Street, NW, Washington, D.C. 20431 (202) 623-7000; *Government Finance Statistics Yearbook.*

MADAGASCAR - GROSS DOMESTIC PRODUCT

African Development Bank, 01 BP 1387, Abidjan 01, Cote d'Ivoire; *Selected Statistics on Regional Member Countries.*

The Economist Intelligence Unit, 111 West 57th Street, New York, New York 10019 (800) 938-4685; *Madagascar Country Report;* and *The World Market Atlas.*

Euromonitor International, Inc., 122 South Michigan Avenue, Suite 1200, Chicago, Illinois 60603 (800) 577-EURO; *International Marketing Data and Statistics;* and *The World Economic Factbook.*

Europa Publications Limited, 18 Bedford Square, London, WC1B 3JN, England; *The Europa World Year Book.*

M.E. Sharpe, 80 Business Park Drive, Armonk, New York 10504 (800) 541-6563; *The Illustrated Book of World Rankings.*

Statistical Office of the United Nations, Publishing Service, New York, New York 10017 (800) 253-9646; *Human Development Report; National Accounts Statistics; Statistical Yearbook;* and *Survey of Economic and Social Conditions in Africa.*

United Nations Economic Commission for Africa, Africa Hall, Post Office Box 3001, Addis Ababa, Ethiopia (Telephone Number

in U.S. (800) 253-9646); *African Statistical Yearbook.*

The World Bank, 1818 H Street, NW, Washington, D.C. 20433 (202) 477-1234; *World Development Report;* and *World Development Indicators.*

MADAGASCAR - GROSS NATIONAL PRODUCT

Euromonitor International, Inc., 122 South Michigan Avenue, Suite 1200, Chicago, Illinois 60603 (800) 577-EURO; *International Marketing Data and Statistics.*

St. Martin's Press, Inc., 175 Fifth Avenue, New York, New York 10010 (800) 221-7945; *The Statesman's Year-Book.*

U.S. Arms Control and Disarmament Agency, 320 Twenty-first Street, NW, Washington, D.C. 20451 (202) 647-8677; *World Military Expenditures and Arms Transfers.*

The World Bank, 1818 H Street, NW, Washington, D.C. 20433 (202) 477-1234; *The World Bank Atlas; World Development Report;* and *World Development Indicators.*

MADAGASCAR - GROUNDNUT PRODUCTION - See MADAGASCAR - CROPS

MADAGASCAR - HEALTH

African Development Bank, 01 BP 1387, Abidjan 01, Cote d'Ivoire; *Selected Statistics on Regional Member Countries.*

Euromonitor International, Inc., 122 South Michigan Avenue, Suite 1200, Chicago, Illinois 60603 (800) 577-EURO; *World Marketing Data and Statistics.*

M.E. Sharpe, 80 Business Park Drive, Armonk, New York 10504 (800) 541-6563; *The Illustrated Book of World Rankings.*

St. Martin's Press, Inc., 175 Fifth Avenue, New York, New York 10010 (800) 221-7945; *The Statesman's Year-Book.*

Statistical Office of the United Nations, Publishing Service, New York, New York 10017 (800) 253-9646; *Human Development Report;* and *Statistical Yearbook.*

United Nations Children's Fund (UNICEF), 3 United Nations Plaza, New York, New York 10017 (800) 253-9646; *State of the World's Children.*

United Nations Economic Commission for Africa, Africa Hall, Post Office Box 3001, Addis Ababa, Ethiopia (Telephone Number in U.S. (800) 253-9646); *African Statistical Yearbook.*

The World Bank, 1818 H Street, NW, Washington, D.C. 20433 (202) 477-1234; *World Development Report.*

World Health Organization, Office of Publications, 20 Avenue Appia, CH-1211 Geneva 27, Switzerland (Telephone Number in U.S. (518) 436-9686); *World Health Statistics Annual.*

MADAGASCAR - HEALTH EXPENDITURES

Food and Agricultural Organization of the United Nations (FAO), Via delle Terme di Caracalla, 00100 Rome, Italy (Telephone Number in U.S. (202) 653-2400); *Production Yearbook.*

MADAGASCAR - HIDE PRODUCTION

Food and Agricultural Organization of the United Nations (FAO), Via delle Terme di Caracalla, 00100 Rome, Italy (Telephone Number in U.S. (202) 653-2400); *Production Yearbook.*

MADAGASCAR - HIGHWAYS

Central Intelligence Agency, Washington, D.C. 20505 (703) 482-1100, www.cia.gov; *The World Factbook.*

International Road Federation, 2600 Virginia Avenue, N.W., Washington, D.C. 20037 (202) 338-4641; *World Road Statistics.*

St. Martin's Press, Inc., 175 Fifth Avenue, New York, New York 10010 (800) 221-7945; *The Statesman's Year-Book.*

Statistical Office of the United Nations, Publishing Service, New York, New York 10017 (800) 253-9646; *Survey of Economic and Social Conditions in Africa.*

United Nations Economic Commission for Africa, Africa Hall, Post Office Box 3001, Addis Ababa, Ethiopia (Telephone Number in U.S. (800) 253-9646); *African Statistical Yearbook.*

MADAGASCAR - HORSES - See MADAGASCAR - LIVESTOCK AND POULTRY

MADAGASCAR - HOURS OF WORK - See MADAGASCAR - EMPLOYMENT

MADAGASCAR - HOUSING AND HOUSING UNITS

Euromonitor International, Inc., 122 South Michigan Avenue, Suite 1200, Chicago, Illinois 60603 (800) 577-EURO; *World Marketing Data and Statistics.*

MADAGASCAR - HOUSING EXPENDITURES

International Monetary Fund, 700 Nineteenth Street, NW, Washington, D.C.

20431 (202) 623-7000; *Government Finance Statistics Yearbook.*

M.E. Sharpe, 80 Business Park Drive, Armonk, New York 10504 (800) 541-6563; *The Illustrated Book of World Rankings.*

MADAGASCAR - ILLITERATE POPULATION

Central Intelligence Agency, Washington, D.C. 20505 (703) 482-1100, www.cia.gov; *The World Factbook.*

The Economist Intelligence Unit, 111 West 57th Street, New York, New York 10019 (800) 938-4685; *The World Market Atlas.*

Euromonitor International, Inc., 122 South Michigan Avenue, Suite 1200, Chicago, Illinois 60603 (800) 577-EURO; *The World Economic Factbook.*

Statistical Office of the United Nations, Publishing Service, New York, New York 10017 (800) 253-9646; *Human Development Report.*

United Nations Educational, Scientific and Cultural Organization (UNESCO), 7 Place de Fontenoy, F-75700 Paris, France (Telephone Number in U.S. (212) 963-5981); *Statistical Yearbook.*

MADAGASCAR - IMPORTS

African Development Bank, 01 BP 1387, Abidjan 01, Cote d'Ivoire; *Selected Statistics on Regional Member Countries.*

Central Intelligence Agency, Washington, D.C. 20505 (703) 482-1100, www.cia.gov; *The World Factbook.*

The Economist Intelligence Unit, 111 West 57th Street, New York, New York 10019 (800) 938-4685; *Madagascar Country Report;* and *The World Market Atlas.*

Euromonitor International, Inc., 122 South Michigan Avenue, Suite 1200, Chicago, Illinois 60603 (800) 577-EURO; *International Marketing Data and Statistics;* and *The World Economic Factbook.*

Europa Publications Limited, 18 Bedford Square, London, WC1B 3JN, England; *The Europa World Year Book.*

Food and Agricultural Organization of the United Nations (FAO), Via delle Terme di Caracalla, 00100 Rome, Italy (Telephone Number in U.S. (202) 653-2400); *The State of Food and Agriculture.*

International Monetary Fund, 700 Nineteenth Street, NW, Washington, D.C. 20431 (202) 623-7000; *Direction of Trade Statistics; Government Finance Statistics Yearbook;* and *International Financial*

Statistics.

St. Martin's Press, Inc., 175 Fifth Avenue, New York, New York 10010 (800) 221-7945; *The Statesman's Year-Book.*

Statistical Office of the United Nations, Publishing Service, New York, New York 10017 (800) 253-9646; *Foreign Trade Statistics for Africa;* and *Survey of Economic and Social Conditions in Africa.*

United Nations Conference on Trade and Development (UNCTAD), New York, New York 10017 (800) 253-9646; *Handbook of International Trade and Development Statistics.*

United Nations Economic Commission for Africa, Africa Hall, Post Office Box 3001, Addis Ababa, Ethiopia (Telephone Number in U.S. (800) 253-9646); *African Statistical Yearbook.*

The World Bank, 1818 H Street, NW, Washington, D.C. 20433 (202) 477-1234; *World Development Report;* and *World Development Indicators.*

MADAGASCAR - INCOME TAXES - See MADAGASCAR - TAXATION

MADAGASCAR - INDUSTRY

Central Intelligence Agency, Washington, D.C. 20505 (703) 482-1100, www.cia.gov; *The World Factbook.*

Economist Intelligence Unit, 111 West 57th Street, New York, New York 10019 (800) 938-4685; *Madagascar Country Report.*

Euromonitor International, Inc., 122 South Michigan Avenue, Suite 1200, Chicago, Illinois 60603 (800) 577-EURO; *International Marketing Data and Statistics; World Marketing Data and Statistics;* and *The World Economic Factbook.*

Europa Publications Limited, 18 Bedford Square, London, WC1B 3JN, England; *The Europa World Year Book.*

International Labour Office, I.L.O. Publications, 1828 L Street, N.W., Suite 801, Washington, D.C. 20036 (301) 638-3152; *Yearbook of Labour Statistics.*

M.E. Sharpe, 80 Business Park Drive, Armonk, New York 10504 (800) 541-6563; *The Illustrated Book of World Rankings.*

St. Martin's Press, Inc., 175 Fifth Avenue, New York, New York 10010 (800) 221-7945; *The Statesman's Year-Book.*

Statistical Office of the United Nations, Publishing Service, New York, New York 10017 (800) 253-9646; *Industrial Commodity Statistics Yearbook;* and *Survey* of Economic and Social Conditions in Africa.

United Nations Economic Commission for Africa, Africa Hall, Post Office Box 3001, Addis Ababa, Ethiopia (Telephone Number in U.S. (800) 253-9646); African Statistical Yearbook.

The World Bank, 1818 H Street, NW, Washington, D.C. 20433 (202) 477-1234; World Development Indicators.

MADAGASCAR - INFANT AND MATERNAL MORTALITY - See MADAGASCAR - MORTALITY

MADAGASCAR - INTERNATIONAL LIQUIDITY

International Monetary Fund, 700 Nineteenth Street, NW, Washington, D.C. 20431 (202) 623-7000; International Financial Statistics.

MADAGASCAR - INTERNATIONAL RESERVES EXCLUDING GOLD

African Development Bank, 01 BP 1387, Abidjan 01, Cote d'Ivoire; Selected Statistics on Regional Member Countries.

Statistical Office of the United Nations, Publishing Service, New York, New York 10017 (800) 253-9646; Statistical Yearbook.

The World Bank, 1818 H Street, NW, Washington, D.C. 20433 (202) 477-1234; World Development Indicators.

MADAGASCAR - IRON ORE PRODUCTION AND CONSUMPTION - See MADAGASCAR - MINING AND MINERAL PRODUCTS

MADAGASCAR - IRRIGATION

Euromonitor International, Inc., 122 South Michigan Avenue, Suite 1200, Chicago, Illinois 60603 (800) 577-EURO; International Marketing Data and Statistics.

MADAGASCAR - JUTE PRODUCTION - See MADAGASCAR - CROPS

MADAGASCAR - LABOR

African Development Bank, 01 BP 1387, Abidjan 01, Cote d'Ivoire; Selected Statistics on Regional Member Countries.

Central Intelligence Agency, Washington, D.C. 20505 (703) 482-1100, www.cia.gov; The World Factbook.

Euromonitor International, Inc., 122 South Michigan Avenue, Suite 1200, Chicago, Illinois 60603 (800) 577-EURO; International Marketing Data and Statistics; and World Marketing Data and Statistics.

Europa Publications Limited, 18 Bedford Square, London, WC1B 3JN, England; The

Europa World Year Book.

Food and Agricultural Organization of the United Nations (FAO), Via delle Terme di Caracalla, 00100 Rome, Italy (Telephone Number in U.S. (202) 653-2400); The State of Food and Agriculture.

International Labour Office, I.L.O. Publications, 1828 L Street, N.W., Suite 801, Washington, D.C. 20036 (301) 638-3152; Yearbook of Labour Statistics.

M.E. Sharpe, 80 Business Park Drive, Armonk, New York 10504 (800) 541-6563; The Illustrated Book of World Rankings.

St. Martin's Press, Inc., 175 Fifth Avenue, New York, New York 10010 (800) 221-7945; The Statesman's Year-Book.

Statistical Office of the United Nations, Publishing Service, New York, New York 10017 (800) 253-9646; Human Development Report.

The World Bank, 1818 H Street, NW, Washington, D.C. 20433 (202) 477-1234; The World Bank Atlas; World Development Report; and World Development Indicators.

MADAGASCAR - LAND USE

Central Intelligence Agency, Washington, D.C. 20505 (703) 482-1100, www.cia.gov; The World Factbook.

Euromonitor International, Inc., 122 South Michigan Avenue, Suite 1200, Chicago, Illinois 60603 (800) 577-EURO; International Marketing Data and Statistics.

Food and Agricultural Organization of the United Nations (FAO), Via delle Terme di Caracalla, 00100 Rome, Italy (Telephone Number in U.S. (202) 653-2400); Production Yearbook.

The World Bank, 1818 H Street, NW, Washington, D.C. 20433 (202) 477-1234; World Development Report.

MADAGASCAR - LIBRARIES

M.E. Sharpe, 80 Business Park Drive, Armonk, New York 10504 (800) 541-6563; The Illustrated Book of World Rankings.

United Nations Educational, Scientific and Cultural Organization (UNESCO), 7 Place de Fontenoy, F-75700 Paris, France (Telephone Number in U.S. (212) 963-5981); Statistical Yearbook.

MADAGASCAR - LIFE EXPECTANCY

African Development Bank, 01 BP 1387, Abidjan 01, Cote d'Ivoire; Selected Statistics on Regional Member Countries.

Central Intelligence Agency, Washington, D.C. 20505 (703) 482-1100, www.cia.gov; The World Factbook.

Euromonitor International, Inc., 122 South Michigan Avenue, Suite 1200, Chicago, Illinois 60603 (800) 577-EURO; The World Economic Factbook.

St. Martin's Press, Inc., 175 Fifth Avenue, New York, New York 10010 (800) 221-7945; The Statesman's Year-Book.

Statistical Office of the United Nations, Publishing Service, New York, New York 10017 (800) 253-9646; Human Development Report; and World Statistics Pocketbook.

The World Bank, 1818 H Street, NW, Washington, D.C. 20433 (202) 477-1234; The World Bank Atlas; and World Development Report.

MADAGASCAR - LIGNITE PRODUCTION - See MADAGASCAR - MINING AND MINERAL PRODUCTS

MADAGASCAR - LITERACY RATE

Euromonitor International, Inc., 122 South Michigan Avenue, Suite 1200, Chicago, Illinois 60603 (800) 577-EURO; World Marketing Data and Statistics.

Statistical Office of the United Nations, Publishing Service, New York, New York 10017 (800) 253-9646; Survey of Economic and Social Conditions in Africa.

MADAGASCAR - LIVESTOCK AND POULTRY

Euromonitor International, Inc., 122 South Michigan Avenue, Suite 1200, Chicago, Illinois 60603 (800) 577-EURO; International Marketing Data and Statistics.

Europa Publications Limited, 18 Bedford Square, London, WC1B 3JN, England; The Europa World Year Book.

Food and Agricultural Organization of the United Nations (FAO), Via delle Terme di Caracalla, 00100 Rome, Italy (Telephone Number in U.S. (202) 653-2400); Production Yearbook; and The State of Food and Agriculture.

M.E. Sharpe, 80 Business Park Drive, Armonk, New York 10504 (800) 541-6563; The Illustrated Book of World Rankings.

St. Martin's Press, Inc., 175 Fifth Avenue, New York, New York 10010 (800) 221-7945; The Statesman's Year-Book.

Statistical Office of the United Nations, Publishing Service, New York, New York 10017 (800) 253-9646; Statistical Yearbook;

and *Survey of Economic and Social Conditions in Africa.*

United Nations Conference on Trade and Development, Central Statistical Service, Palais des Nations, Geneva, Switzerland (Telephone in U.S. (800) 253-9646); *UNCTAD Commodity Yearbook.*

United Nations Economic Commission for Africa, Africa Hall, Post Office Box 3001, Addis Ababa, Ethiopia (Telephone Number in U.S. (800) 253-9646); *African Statistical Yearbook.*

MADAGASCAR - LIVING LEVELS - See MADAGASCAR - LIFE EXPECTANCY

MADAGASCAR - MAIL TRAFFIC - NUMBER OF ITEMS SENT AND RECEIVED

Statistical Office of the United Nations, Publishing Service, New York, New York 10017 (800) 253-9646; *Statistical Yearbook.*

MADAGASCAR - MANUFACTURING

M.E. Sharpe, 80 Business Park Drive, Armonk, New York 10504 (800) 541-6563; *The Illustrated Book of World Rankings.*

Statistical Office of the United Nations, Publishing Service, New York, New York 10017 (800) 253-9646; *Statistical Yearbook;* and *Survey of Economic and Social Conditions in Africa.*

United Nations Economic Commission for Africa, Africa Hall, Post Office Box 3001, Addis Ababa, Ethiopia (Telephone Number in U.S. (800) 253-9646); *African Statistical Yearbook.*

The World Bank, 1818 H Street, NW, Washington, D.C. 20433 (202) 477-1234; *World Development Indicators.*

MADAGASCAR - MARRIAGE RATES

M.E. Sharpe, 80 Business Park Drive, Armonk, New York 10504 (800) 541-6563; *The Illustrated Book of World Rankings.*

Statistical Office of the United Nations, Publishing Service, New York, New York 10017 (800) 253-9646; *Demographic Yearbook.*

MADAGASCAR - MEAT PRODUCTION - See MADAGASCAR - LIVESTOCK AND POULTRY

MADAGASCAR - MERCHANT SHIPPING

Europa Publications Limited, 18 Bedford Square, London, WC1B 3JN, England; *The Europa World Year Book.*

St. Martin's Press, Inc., 175 Fifth Avenue, New York, New York 10010 (800) 221-7945; *The Statesman's Year-Book.*

Statistical Office of the United Nations, Publishing Service, New York, New York 10017 (800) 253-9646; *Statistical Yearbook.*

United Nations Economic Commission for Africa, Africa Hall, Post Office Box 3001, Addis Ababa, Ethiopia (Telephone Number in U.S. (800) 253-9646); *African Statistical Yearbook.*

MADAGASCAR - MILITARY

Central Intelligence Agency, Washington, D.C. 20505 (703) 482-1100, www.cia.gov; *The World Factbook.*

Euromonitor International, Inc., 122 South Michigan Avenue, Suite 1200, Chicago, Illinois 60603 (800) 577-EURO; *World Marketing Data and Statistics.*

The International Institute for Strategic Studies, 23 Tavistock Street, London WC2E 7NQ, England; *The Military Balance.*

International Monetary Fund, 700 Nineteenth Street, NW, Washington, D.C. 20431 (202) 623-7000; *Government Finance Statistics Yearbook.*

St. Martin's Press, Inc., 175 Fifth Avenue, New York, New York 10010 (800) 221-7945; *The Statesman's Year-Book.*

Statistical Office of the United Nations, Publishing Service, New York, New York 10017 (800) 253-9646; *Human Development Report.*

U.S. Arms Control and Disarmament Agency, 320 Twenty-first Street, NW, Washington, D.C. 20451 (202) 647-8677; *World Military Expenditures and Arms Transfers.*

MADAGASCAR - MILK PRODUCTION - See MADAGASCAR - DAIRY PRODUCTS

MADAGASCAR - MINING AND MINERAL PRODUCTS

Europa Publications Limited, 18 Bedford Square, London, WC1B 3JN, England; *The Europa World Year Book.*

M.E. Sharpe, 80 Business Park Drive, Armonk, New York 10504 (800) 541-6563; *The Illustrated Book of World Rankings.*

Statistical Office of the United Nations, Publishing Service, New York, New York 10017 (800) 253-9646; *Statistical Yearbook.*

United Nations Conference on Trade and Development, Central Statistical Service, Palais des Nations, Geneva, Switzerland (Telephone in U.S. (800) 253-9646); *UNCTAD Commodity Yearbook.*

United Nations Economic Commission for Africa, Africa Hall, Post Office Box 3001, Addis Ababa, Ethiopia (Telephone Number in U.S. (800) 253-9646); *African Statistical Yearbook.*

MADAGASCAR - MONEY EXCHANGE RATES - See MADAGASCAR - EXCHANGE RATES

MADAGASCAR - MONEY RESERVES

Euromonitor International, Inc., 122 South Michigan Avenue, Suite 1200, Chicago, Illinois 60603 (800) 577-EURO; *International Marketing Data and Statistics.*

International Monetary Fund, 700 Nineteenth Street, NW, Washington, D.C. 20431 (202) 623-7000; *International Financial Statistics.*

Statistical Office of the United Nations, Publishing Service, New York, New York 10017 (800) 253-9646; *Statistical Yearbook.*

MADAGASCAR - MONEY SUPPLY

African Development Bank, 01 BP 1387, Abidjan 01, Cote d'Ivoire; *Selected Statistics on Regional Member Countries.*

Economist Intelligence Unit, 111 West 57th Street, New York, New York 10019 (800) 938-4685; *Madagascar Country Report.*

Europa Publications Limited, 18 Bedford Square, London, WC1B 3JN, England; *The Europa World Year Book.*

The World Bank, 1818 H Street, NW, Washington, D.C. 20433 (202) 477-1234; *World Development Indicators.*

MADAGASCAR - MORTALITY

Central Intelligence Agency, Washington, D.C. 20505 (703) 482-1100, www.cia.gov; *The World Factbook.*

Euromonitor International, Inc., 122 South Michigan Avenue, Suite 1200, Chicago, Illinois 60603 (800) 577-EURO; *International Marketing Data and Statistics;* and *The World Economic Factbook.*

Europa Publications Limited, 18 Bedford Square, London, WC1B 3JN, England; *The Europa World Year Book.*

St. Martin's Press, Inc., 175 Fifth Avenue, New York, New York 10010 (800) 221-7945; *The Statesman's Year-Book.*

Statistical Office of the United Nations, Publishing Service, New York, New York 10017 (800) 253-9646; *Demographic Yearbook; Human Development Report; Statistical Yearbook; World Statistics Pocketbook;* and *Survey of Economic and Social Conditions in Africa.*

United Nations Children's Fund (UNICEF), 3 United Nations Plaza, New York, New York 10017 (800) 253-9646; *State of the World's Children.*

The World Bank, 1818 H Street, NW, Washington, D.C. 20433 (202) 477-1234; *The World Bank Atlas; World Development Report;* and *World Development Indicators.*

World Health Organization, Office of Publications, 20 Avenue Appia, CH-1211 Geneva 27, Switzerland (Telephone Number in U.S. (518) 436-9686); *World Health Statistics Annual.*

MADAGASCAR - MOTOR VEHICLE PRODUCTION

Statistical Office of the United Nations, Publishing Service, New York, New York 10017 (800) 253-9646; *Statistical Yearbook.*

MADAGASCAR - MOTOR VEHICLE TAXES - See MADAGASCAR - TAXATION

MADAGASCAR - MOTOR VEHICLES IN USE

Europa Publications Limited, 18 Bedford Square, London, WC1B 3JN, England; *The Europa World Year Book.*

International Road Federation, 2600 Virginia Avenue, N.W., Washington, D.C. 20037 (202) 338-4641; *World Road Statistics.*

Statistical Office of the United Nations, Publishing Service, New York, New York 10017 (800) 253-9646; *Statistical Yearbook;* and *Survey of Economic and Social Conditions in Africa.*

MADAGASCAR - MUSEUMS

M.E. Sharpe, 80 Business Park Drive, Armonk, New York 10504 (800) 541-6563; *The Illustrated Book of World Rankings.*

United Nations Educational, Scientific and Cultural Organization (UNESCO), 7 Place de Fontenoy, F-75700 Paris, France (Telephone Number in U.S. (212) 963-5981); *Statistical Yearbook.*

MADAGASCAR - NATALITY - See MADAGASCAR - BIRTH RATES

MADAGASCAR - NATIONAL ACCOUNTS

African Development Bank, 01 BP 1387, Abidjan 01, Cote d'Ivoire; *Selected Statistics on Regional Member Countries.*

Europa Publications Limited, 18 Bedford Square, London, WC1B 3JN, England; *The Europa World Year Book.*

Statistical Office of the United Nations, Publishing Service, New York, New York 10017 (800) 253-9646; *National Account Statistics.*

United Nations Economic Commission for Africa, Africa Hall, Post Office Box 3001, Addis Ababa, Ethiopia (Telephone Number in U.S. (800) 253-9646); *African Statistical Yearbook.*

MADAGASCAR - NATIONAL INCOME

M.E. Sharpe, 80 Business Park Drive, Armonk, New York 10504 (800) 541-6563; *The Illustrated Book of World Rankings.*

Statistical Office of the United Nations, Publishing Service, New York, New York 10017 (800) 253-9646; *National Accounts Statistics;* and *Statistical Yearbook.*

MADAGASCAR - NATIONAL PRODUCT

M.E. Sharpe, 80 Business Park Drive, Armonk, New York 10504 (800) 541-6563; *The Illustrated Book of World Rankings.*

MADAGASCAR - NATURAL GAS - PRODUCTION - See MADAGASCAR - MINING AND MINERAL PRODUCTS

MADAGASCAR - NEWSPAPER PRODUCTION - See MADAGASCAR - FORESTRY AND FOREST PRODUCTS

MADAGASCAR - NEWSPRINT PRODUCTION AND CONSUMPTION - See MADAGASCAR - FORESTRY AND FOREST PRODUCTS

MADAGASCAR - OCCUPATIONS - See MADAGASCAR - LABOR

MADAGASCAR - PALM OIL AND PALM KERNEL PRODUCTION - See MADAGASCAR - CROPS

MADAGASCAR - PAPER - See MADAGASCAR - FORESTRY AND FOREST PRODUCTS

MADAGASCAR - PEANUT PRODUCTION - See MADAGASCAR - CROPS

MADAGASCAR - PERIODICALS

United Nations Educational, Scientific and Cultural Organization (UNESCO), 7 Place de Fontenoy, F-75700 Paris, France (Telephone Number in U.S. (212) 963-5981); *Statistical Yearbook.*

MADAGASCAR - PESTICIDE USE

Food and Agricultural Organization of the United Nations (FAO), Via delle Terme di Caracalla, 00100 Rome, Italy (Telephone Number in U.S. (202) 653-2400); *The State of Food and Agriculture.*

MADAGASCAR - PETROLEUM INDUSTRY

Food and Agricultural Organization of the United Nations (FAO), Via delle Terme

di Caracalla, 00100 Rome, Italy (Telephone Number in U.S. (202) 653-2400); *The State of Food and Agriculture.*

M.E. Sharpe, 80 Business Park Drive, Armonk, New York 10504 (800) 541-6563; *The Illustrated Book of World Rankings.*

St. Martin's Press, Inc., 175 Fifth Avenue, New York, New York 10010 (800) 221-7945; *The Statesman's Year-Book.*

Statistical Office of the United Nations, Publishing Service, New York, New York 10017 (800) 253-9646; *Statistical Yearbook.*

United Nations Conference on Trade and Development, Central Statistical Service, Palais des Nations, Geneva, Switzerland (Telephone in U.S. (800) 253-9646); *UNCTAD Commodity Yearbook.*

MADAGASCAR - PIGS - See MADAGASCAR - LIVESTOCK AND POULTRY

MADAGASCAR - POPULATION

African Development Bank, 01 BP 1387, Abidjan 01, Cote d'Ivoire; *Selected Statistics on Regional Member Countries.*

Central Intelligence Agency, Washington, D.C. 20505 (703) 482-1100, www.cia.gov; *The World Factbook.*

The Economist Intelligence Unit, 111 West 57th Street, New York, New York 10019 (800) 938-4685; *Madagascar Country Report;* and *The World Market Atlas.*

Euromonitor International, Inc., 122 South Michigan Avenue, Suite 1200, Chicago, Illinois 60603 (800) 577-EURO; *International Marketing Data and Statistics;* and *The World Economic Factbook.*

Europa Publications Limited, 18 Bedford Square, London, WC1B 3JN, England; *The Europa World Year Book.*

Food and Agricultural Organization of the United Nations (FAO), Via delle Terme di Caracalla, 00100 Rome, Italy (Telephone Number in U.S. (202) 653-2400); *Production Yearbook.*

International Labour Office, I.L.O. Publications, 1828 L Street, N.W., Suite 801, Washington, D.C. 20036 (301) 638-3152; *Yearbook of Labour Statistics.*

M.E. Sharpe, 80 Business Park Drive, Armonk, New York 10504 (800) 541-6563; *The Illustrated Book of World Rankings.*

St. Martin's Press, Inc., 175 Fifth Avenue, New York, New York 10010 (800) 221-7945; *The Statesman's Year-Book.*

Statistical Office of the United Nations, Publishing Service, New York, New York

10017 (800) 253-9646; *Demographic Yearbook; Human Development Report; Statistical Yearbook; World Statistics Pocketbook;* and *Survey of Economic and Social Conditions in Africa.*

U.S. Arms Control and Disarmament Agency, 320 Twenty-first Street, NW, Washington, D.C. 20451 (202) 647-8677; *World Military Expenditures and Arms Transfers.*

The World Bank, 1818 H Street, NW, Washington, D.C. 20433 (202) 477-1234; *The World Bank Atlas;* and *World Development Report.*

World Health Organization, Office of Publications, 20 Avenue Appia, CH-1211 Geneva 27, Switzerland (Telephone Number in U.S. (518) 436-9686); *World Health Statistics Annual.*

MADAGASCAR - POST OFFICES

St. Martin's Press, Inc., 175 Fifth Avenue, New York, New York 10010 (800) 221-7945; *The Statesman's Year-Book.*

MADAGASCAR - POTATO PRODUCTION - See MADAGASCAR - CROPS

MADAGASCAR - PRICES

Food and Agricultural Organization of the United Nations (FAO), Via delle Terme di Caracalla, 00100 Rome, Italy (Telephone Number in U.S. (202) 653-2400); *Production Yearbook;* and *The State of Food and Agriculture.*

International Labour Office, I.L.O. Publications, 1828 L Street, N.W., Suite 801, Washington, D.C. 20036 (301) 638-3152; *Yearbook of Labour Statistics.*

M.E. Sharpe, 80 Business Park Drive, Armonk, New York 10504 (800) 541-6563; *The Illustrated Book of World Rankings.*

United Nations Economic Commission for Africa, Africa Hall, Post Office Box 3001, Addis Ababa, Ethiopia (Telephone Number in U.S. (800) 253-9646); *African Statistical Yearbook.*

MADAGASCAR - PRINTING AND WRITING PAPER - See MADAGASCAR - FORESTRY AND FOREST PRODUCTS

MADAGASCAR - PRODUCTION

M.E. Sharpe, 80 Business Park Drive, Armonk, New York 10504 (800) 541-6563; *The Illustrated Book of World Rankings.*

MADAGASCAR - PRODUCTIVITY

Euromonitor International, Inc., 122 South Michigan Avenue, Suite 1200, Chicago, Illinois 60603 (800) 577-EURO;

International Marketing Data and Statistics.

MADAGASCAR - PROPERTY TAXES

International Monetary Fund, 700 Nineteenth Street, NW, Washington, D.C. 20431 (202) 623-7000; *Government Finance Statistics Yearbook.*

MADAGASCAR - PUBLIC FINANCE - See MADAGASCAR - FINANCE

MADAGASCAR - RADIO BROADCAST-ING - See MADAGASCAR - BROADCASTING

MADAGASCAR - RADIO RECEIVERS

St. Martin's Press, Inc., 175 Fifth Avenue, New York, New York 10010 (800) 221-7945; *The Statesman's Year-Book.*

MADAGASCAR - RAILWAY USE

Statistical Office of the United Nations, Publishing Service, New York, New York 10017 (800) 253-9646; *Statistical Yearbook;* and *Survey of Economic and Social Conditions in Africa.*

MADAGASCAR - RAILWAYS

Europa Publications Limited, 18 Bedford Square, London, WC1B 3JN, England; *The Europa World Year Book.*

Jane's Information Group, Sentinel House, 163 Brighton Road, Coulsdon, Surrey CR5 2NH, England (Telephone Number in U.S. (703) 683-3700); *Jane's World Railways.*

St. Martin's Press, Inc., 175 Fifth Avenue, New York, New York 10010 (800) 221-7945; *The Statesman's Year-Book.*

United Nations Economic Commission for Africa, Africa Hall, Post Office Box 3001, Addis Ababa, Ethiopia (Telephone Number in U.S. (800) 253-9646); *African Statistical Yearbook.*

MADAGASCAR - RELIGION

Central Intelligence Agency, Washington, D.C. 20505 (703) 482-1100, www.cia.gov; *The World Factbook.*

M.E. Sharpe, 80 Business Park Drive, Armonk, New York 10504 (800) 541-6563; *The Illustrated Book of World Rankings.*

St. Martin's Press, Inc., 175 Fifth Avenue, New York, New York 10010 (800) 221-7945; *The Statesman's Year-Book.*

MADAGASCAR - RETAIL TRADE

Euromonitor International, Inc., 122 South Michigan Avenue, Suite 1200, Chicago, Illinois 60603 (800) 577-EURO;

World Marketing Data and Statistics.

MADAGASCAR - RICE PRODUCTION - See MADAGASCAR - CROPS

MADAGASCAR - ROOT AND TUBER PRODUCTION - See MADAGASCAR - CROPS

MADAGASCAR - ROUNDWOOD PRODUCTION - See MADAGASCAR - FORESTRY AND FOREST PRODUCTS

MADAGASCAR - RUBBER PRODUCTION AND CONSUMPTION

M.E. Sharpe, 80 Business Park Drive, Armonk, New York 10504 (800) 541-6563; *The Illustrated Book of World Rankings.*

MADAGASCAR - SALT PRODUCTION

Statistical Office of the United Nations, Publishing Service, New York, New York 10017 (800) 253-9646; *Statistical Yearbook.*

MADAGASCAR - SAWNWOOD PRODUCTION - See MADAGASCAR - FORESTRY AND FOREST PRODUCTS

MADAGASCAR - SCIENCE AND TECHNOLOGY - EXPENDITURE FOR RESEARCH - See MADAGASCAR - SCIENTISTS, TECHNICIANS AND ENGINEERS

MADAGASCAR - SCIENTISTS, TECHNICIANS AND ENGINEERS

Statistical Office of the United Nations, Publishing Service, New York, New York 10017 (800) 253-9646; *Statistical Yearbook.*

MADAGASCAR - SENIOR CITIZENS

M.E. Sharpe, 80 Business Park Drive, Armonk, New York 10504 (800) 541-6563; *The Illustrated Book of World Rankings.*

MADAGASCAR - SHEEP - See MADAGASCAR - LIVESTOCK AND POULTRY

MADAGASCAR - SILVER PRODUCTION AND CONSUMPTION - See MADAGASCAR - MINING AND MINERAL PRODUCTS

MADAGASCAR - SISAL PRODUCTION - See MADAGASCAR - CROPS

MADAGASCAR - SOCIAL DATA

African Development Bank, 01 BP 1387, Abidjan 01, Cote d'Ivoire; *Selected Statistics on Regional Member Countries.*

M.E. Sharpe, 80 Business Park Drive, Armonk, New York 10504 (800) 541-6563; *The Illustrated Book of World Rankings.*

Statistical Office of the United Nations, Publishing Service, New York, New York 10017 (800) 253-9646; *World Statistics Pocketbook.*

MADAGASCAR - SOCIAL SECURITY

International Monetary Fund, 700 Nineteenth Street, NW, Washington, D.C. 20431 (202) 623-7000; *Government Finance Statistics Yearbook.*

Statistical Office of the United Nations, Publishing Service, New York, New York 10017 (800) 253-9646; *National Accounts Statistics.*

MADAGASCAR - STAMP
TAXES AND DUTIES - See
MADAGASCAR - TAXATION

MADAGASCAR - STATE BUDGET

Euromonitor International, Inc., 122 South Michigan Avenue, Suite 1200, Chicago, Illinois 60603 (800) 577-EURO; *International Marketing Data and Statistics.*

MADAGASCAR - STEEL - See
MADAGASCAR - MINING AND
MINERAL PRODUCTS

MADAGASCAR - STOCKS -
COMMODITY - MARKET PRICE - INDEX

Food and Agricultural Organization of the United Nations (FAO), Via delle Terme di Caracalla, 00100 Rome, Italy (Telephone Number in U.S. (202) 653-2400); *The State of Food and Agriculture.*

MADAGASCAR - SUGAR PRODUCTION AND CONSUMPTION - See MADAGASCAR - CROPS

MADAGASCAR - TAXATION

Europa Publications Limited, 18 Bedford Square, London, WC1B 3JN, England; *The Europa World Year Book.*

International Monetary Fund, 700 Nineteenth Street, NW, Washington, D.C. 20431 (202) 623-7000; *Government Finance Statistics Yearbook.*

International Road Federation, 2600 Virginia Avenue, N.W., Washington, D.C. 20037 (202) 338-4641; *World Road Statistics.*

The World Bank, 1818 H Street, NW, Washington, D.C. 20433 (202) 477-1234; *World Development Indicators.*

MADAGASCAR - TELEGRAPH SERVICE

Statistical Office of the United Nations, Publishing Service, New York, New York 10017 (800) 253-9646; *Statistical Yearbook.*

MADAGASCAR - TELEPHONES IN USE

American Telephone and Telegraph Company, 26 Parsippany Road, Whippany, New Jersey 07981 (800) 222-0300; *The World's Telephones.*

Central Intelligence Agency, Washington, D.C. 20505 (703) 482-1100, www.cia.gov; *The World Factbook.*

Europa Publications Limited, 18 Bedford Square, London, WC1B 3JN, England; *The Europa World Year Book.*

St. Martin's Press, Inc., 175 Fifth Avenue, New York, New York 10010 (800) 221-7945; *The Statesman's Year-Book.*

Statistical Office of the United Nations, Publishing Service, New York, New York 10017 (800) 253-9646; *Statistical Yearbook;* and *World Statistics Pocketbook.*

MADAGASCAR - TELEVISION BROADCASTING - See MADAGASCAR - BROADCASTING

MADAGASCAR - TEXTILE INDUSTRY

M.E. Sharpe, 80 Business Park Drive, Armonk, New York 10504 (800) 541-6563; *The Illustrated Book of World Rankings.*

Statistical Office of the United Nations, Publishing Service, New York, New York 10017 (800) 253-9646; *Statistical Yearbook.*

United Nations Conference on Trade and Development, Central Statistical Service, Palais des Nations, Geneva, Switzerland (Telephone in U.S. (800) 253-9646); *UNCTAD Commodity Yearbook.*

MADAGASCAR - THEATRE

United Nations Educational, Scientific and Cultural Organization (UNESCO), 7 Place de Fontenoy, F-75700 Paris, France (Telephone Number in U.S. (212) 963-5981); *Statistical Yearbook.*

MADAGASCAR - TOBACCO PRODUCTION

M.E. Sharpe, 80 Business Park Drive, Armonk, New York 10504 (800) 541-6563; *The Illustrated Book of World Rankings.*

Statistical Office of the United Nations, Publishing Service, New York, New York 10017 (800) 253-9646; *Statistical Yearbook.*

MADAGASCAR - TOURISM

Euromonitor International, Inc., 122 South Michigan Avenue, Suite 1200, Chicago, Illinois 60603 (800) 577-EURO ; *The World Economic Factbook;* and *World Marketing Data and Stations.*

Europa Publications Limited, 18 Bedford Square, London, WC1B 3JN,

England; *The Europa World Year Book.*

M.E. Sharpe, 80 Business Park Drive, Armonk, New York 10504 (800) 541-6563; *The Illustrated Book of World Rankings.*

St. Martin's Press, Inc., 175 Fifth Avenue, New York, New York 10010 (800) 221-7945; *The Statesman's Year-Book.*

Statistical Office of the United Nations, Publishing Service, New York, New York 10017 (800) 253-9646; *Statistical Yearbook.*

United Nations Economic Commission for Africa, Africa Hall, Post Office Box 3001, Addis Ababa, Ethiopia (Telephone Number in U.S. (800) 253-9646); *African Statistical Yearbook.*

World Tourism Organization, Calle Capitan Haya 42, E-28020 Madrid, Spain; *Yearbook of Tourism Statistics.*

MADAGASCAR - TRACTORS IN USE

Statistical Office of the United Nations, Publishing Service, New York, New York 10017 (800) 253-9646; *Statistical Yearbook.*

MADAGASCAR - TRADE - See
MADAGASCAR - FOREIGN TRADE

MADAGASCAR - TRANSPORTATION AND COMMUNICATIONS

Central Intelligence Agency, Washington, D.C. 20505 (703) 482-1100, www.cia.gov; *The World Factbook.*

Euromonitor International, Inc., 122 South Michigan Avenue, Suite 1200, Chicago, Illinois 60603 (800) 577-EURO; *International Marketing Data and Statistics;* and *World Marketing Data and Statistics.*

Europa Publications Limited, 18 Bedford Square, London, WC1B 3JN, England; *The Europa World Year Book.*

M.E. Sharpe, 80 Business Park Drive, Armonk, New York 10504 (800) 541-6563; *The Illustrated Book of World Rankings.*

St. Martin's Press, Inc., 175 Fifth Avenue, New York, New York 10010 (800) 221-7945; *The Statesman's Year-Book.*

Statistical Office of the United Nations, Publishing Service, New York, New York 10017 (800) 253-9646; *Human Development Report.*

United Nations Economic Commission for Africa, Africa Hall, Post Office Box 3001, Addis Ababa, Ethiopia (Telephone Number in U.S. (800) 253-9646); *African Statistical Yearbook.*

MADAGASCAR - UNEMPLOYMENT

Central Intelligence Agency, Washington, D.C. 20505 (703) 482-1100, www.cia.gov; *The World Factbook.*

Euromonitor International, Inc., 122 South Michigan Avenue, Suite 1200, Chicago, Illinois 60603 (800) 577-EURO; *International Marketing Data and Statistics.*

International Labour Office, I.L.O. Publications, 1828 L Street, N.W., Suite 801, Washington, D.C. 20036 (301) 638-3152; *Yearbook of Labour Statistics.*

Statistical Office of the United Nations, Publishing Service, New York, New York 10017 (800) 253-9646; *Statistical Yearbook.*

MADAGASCAR - VANILLA EXPORTS

International Monetary Fund, 700 Nineteenth Street, NW, Washington, D.C. 20431 (202) 623-7000; *International Financial Statistics.*

MADAGASCAR - VITAL STATISTICS

Euromonitor International, Inc., 122 South Michigan Avenue, Suite 1200, Chicago, Illinois 60603 (800) 577-EURO; *International Marketing Data and Statistics.*

St. Martin's Press, Inc., 175 Fifth Avenue, New York, New York 10010 (800) 221-7945; *The Statesman's Year-Book.*

Statistical Office of the United Nations, Publishing Service, New York, New York 10017 (800) 253-9646; *Statistical Yearbook.*

World Health Organization, Office of Publications, 20 Avenue Appia, CH-1211 Geneva 27, Switzerland (Telephone Number in U.S. (518) 436-9686); *World Health Statistics Annual.*

MADAGASCAR - WAGES

International Labour Office, I.L.O. Publications, 1828 L Street, N.W., Suite 801, Washington, D.C. 20036 (301) 638-3152; *Yearbook of Labour Statistics.*

MADAGASCAR - WEATHER - See MADAGASCAR - CLIMATE

MADAGASCAR - WELFARE EXPENDITURES

International Monetary Fund, 700 Nineteenth Street, NW, Washington, D.C. 20431 (202) 623-7000; *Government Finance Statistics Yearbook.*

MADAGASCAR - WHEAT PRODUCTION

M.E. Sharpe, 80 Business Park Drive, Armonk, New York 10504 (800) 541-6563; *The Illustrated Book of World Rankings.*

MADAGASCAR - WINE PRODUCTION - See MADAGASCAR - BEVERAGES

MADAGASCAR - WOOL PRODUCTION - See MADAGASCAR - TEXTILE INDUSTRY

MADAGASCAR - YARN PRODUCTION - See MADAGASCAR - TEXTILE INDUSTRY

MAGAZINES - ADVERTISING EXPENDITURES

McCann-Erickson, Inc., 750 Third Avenue, New York, New York 10017; compiled for Crain Communications, Incorporated, 740 North Rush Street, Chicago, Illinois 60611 (212) 649-5200; in *Advertising Age.*

Publishers Information Bureau, 9019 Third Avenue, New York, New York 10022 (212) 872-3700; unpublished data compiled by Competitive Media Reporting.

MAGAZINES - PRICES

Library Journal, 249 West 17th Street, New York, New York 10011 (212) 463-6819; *Library Journal.*

MAGAZINES - READING AND RECEIPTS

Veronis, Suhler and Associates, 350 Park Avenue, New York, New York 10022 (212) 935-4990; *Communications Industry Forecast Report.*

MAGAZINES - SALES - MAIL ORDER

Richard D. Irwin, Inc., 1333 Burr Ridge Parkway, Burr Ridge, Illinois 60521 (708) 789-4000; *Portable Mail Order Industry Statistics*; data extracted from *Annual Guides to Mail Order Sales*, Marketing Logistics, Inc., 1460 Cloverdale Avenue, Highland Park, Illinois 60035 (847) 831-1575.

MAGNESIUM

U.S. Department of the Interior, Geological Survey, Office of Minerals Information, 12201 Sunrise Valley Drive, Reston, Virginia 22092 (703) 648-4000, www.minerals.usgs.gov; *Annual Reports;* and *Mineral Commodity Summaries.*

MAIL

U.S. Postal Service, 475 L'Enfant Plaza West, SW, Washington, D.C. 20260 (202) 268-2000, www.usps.gov; *Annual Report of the Postmaster General; Comprehensive Statement on Postal Operations; U.S. Domestic Postage Rate: Recent History;* and unpublished data.

MAINE - See also STATE DATA (FOR INDIVIDUAL STATES)

Maine - Primary Statistics Source

Maine Department of Economic and Community Development, State House Station 59, Augusta, Maine 04333 (207) 287-3153; *Maine: A Statistical Summary.*

Maine - State Data Centers

Maine State Planning Office, State House Station #38, Augusta, Maine 04333-0038, Mr. Eric VonMagnus, Census Information Officer (207) 287-2989.

MALARIA

U.S. Department of Health and Human Services, Centers for Disease Control and Prevention, 1600 Clifton Road, NE, Atlanta, Georgia 30333 (800) 311-3435, www.cdc.gov; *Summary of Notifiable Diseases;* and *Morbidity and Mortality Weekly Report.*

Malawi - National Statistical Office

National Statistical Office, Post Office Box 333, Zomba, Malawi.

Malawi - Primary Statistics Source

National Statistical Office, Post Office Box 333, Zomba, Malawi; *Malawi Statistical Yearbook;* and *Monthly Bulletin of Statistics.*

MALAWI - AGRICULTURE

Economist Intelligence Unit, 111 West 57th Street, New York, New York 10019 (800) 938-4685; *Malawi Country Report.*

Euromonitor International, Inc., 122 South Michigan Avenue, Suite 1200, Chicago, Illinois 60603 (800) 577-EURO; *International Marketing Data and Statistics;* and *World Marketing Data and Statistics.*

Europa Publications Limited, 18 Bedford Square, London, WC1B 3JN, England; *The Europa World Year Book.*

Food and Agricultural Organization of the United Nations (FAO), Via delle Terme di Caracalla, 00100 Rome, Italy (Telephone Number in U.S. (202) 653-2400); *Production Yearbook; The State of Food and Agriculture;* and *Trade Yearbook.*

M.E. Sharpe, 80 Business Park Drive, Armonk, New York 10504 (800) 541-6563; *The Illustrated Book of World Rankings.*

St. Martin's Press, Inc., 175 Fifth Avenue, New York, New York 10010 (800) 221-7945; *The Statesman's Year-Book.*

Statistical Office of the United Nations, Publishing Service, New York, New York 10017 (800) 253-9646; *Statistical Yearbook; and Survey of Economic and Social Conditions in Africa.*

United Nations Conference on Trade and Development, Central Statistical Service, Palais des Nations, Geneva, Switzerland (Telephone in U.S. (800) 253-9646); *UNCTAD Commodity Yearbook.*

United Nations Economic Commission for Africa, Africa Hall, Post Office Box 3001, Addis Ababa, Ethiopia (Telephone Number in U.S. (800) 253-9646); *African Statistical Yearbook.*

The World Bank, 1818 H Street, NW, Washington, D.C. 20433 (202) 477-1234; *World Development Indicators.*

MALAWI - AIRLINE SERVICE

Europa Publications Limited, 18 Bedford Square, London, WC1B 3JN, England; *The Europa World Year Book.*

International Civil Aviation Organization, 999 University Street, Montreal, Quebec, Canada H3C 5H7 (514) 954-8219; *Civil Aviation Statistics of the World.*

M.E. Sharpe, 80 Business Park Drive, Armonk, New York 10504 (800) 541-6563; *The Illustrated Book of World Rankings.*

St. Martin's Press, Inc., 175 Fifth Avenue, New York, New York 10010 (800) 221-7945; *The Statesman's Year-Book.*

Statistical Office of the United Nations, Publishing Service, New York, New York 10017 (800) 253-9646; *Statistical Yearbook.*

United Nations Economic Commission for Africa, Africa Hall, Post Office Box 3001, Addis Ababa, Ethiopia (Telephone Number in U.S. (800) 253-9646); *African Statistical Yearbook.*

MALAWI - AIRPORTS

Central Intelligence Agency, Washington, D.C. 20505 (703) 482-1100, www.cia.gov; *The World Factbook.*

MALAWI - ALUMINUM PRODUCTION AND CONSUMPTION - See MALAWI - MINING AND MINERAL PRODUCTS

MALAWI - ANIMAL HEALTH

Food and Agricultural Organization of the United Nations (FAO), Via delle Terme di Caracalla, 00100 Rome, Italy (Telephone Number in U.S. (202) 653-2400); *Animal Health Yearbook.*

MALAWI - AREA AND DENSITY OF POPULATION

African Development Bank, 01 BP 1387, Abidjan 01, Cote d'Ivoire; *Selected Statistics on Regional Member Countries.*

Central Intelligence Agency, Washington, D.C. 20505 (703) 482-1100, www.cia.gov; *The World Factbook.*

Euromonitor International, Inc., 122 South Michigan Avenue, Suite 1200, Chicago, Illinois 60603 (800) 577-EURO; *International Marketing Data and Statistics; and The World Economic Factbook.*

Europa Publications Limited, 18 Bedford Square, London, WC1B 3JN, England; *The Europa World Year Book.*

Food and Agricultural Organization of the United Nations (FAO), Via delle Terme di Caracalla, 00100 Rome, Italy (Telephone Number in U.S. (202) 653-2400); *The State of Food and Agriculture.*

M.E. Sharpe, 80 Business Park Drive, Armonk, New York 10504 (800) 541-6563; *The Illustrated Book of World Rankings.*

St. Martin's Press, Inc., 175 Fifth Avenue, New York, New York 10010 (800) 221-7945; *The Statesman's Year-Book.*

Statistical Office of the United Nations, Publishing Service, New York, New York 10017 (800) 253-9646; *Statistical Yearbook; and Survey of Economic and Social Conditions in Africa.*

The World Bank, 1818 H Street, NW, Washington, D.C. 20433 (202) 477-1234; *World Development Report.*

MALAWI - ARMS EXPORTS AND IMPORTS - See MALAWI - MILITARY

MALAWI - BALANCE OF PAYMENTS

African Development Bank, 01 BP 1387, Abidjan 01, Cote d'Ivoire; *Selected Statistics on Regional Member Countries.*

The Economist Intelligence Unit, 111 West 57th Street, New York, New York 10019 (800) 938-4685; *The World Market Atlas.*

Europa Publications Limited, 18 Bedford Square, London, WC1B 3JN, England; *The Europa World Year Book.*

International Monetary Fund, 700 Nineteenth Street, NW, Washington, D.C. 20431 (202) 623-7000; *Balance of Payments Yearbook; and International Financial Statistics.*

United Nations Conference on Trade and Development (UNCTAD), New York, New York 10017 (800) 253-9646; *Handbook of International Trade and Development Statistics.*

United Nations Economic Commission for Africa, Africa Hall, Post Office Box 3001, Addis Ababa, Ethiopia (Telephone Number in U.S. (800) 253-9646); *African Statistical Yearbook.*

The World Bank, 1818 H Street, NW, Washington, D.C. 20433 (202) 477-1234; *World Development Report; and World Development Indicators.*

MALAWI - BANKING

Asian Development Bank, Post Office Box 789, 1099 Manila, Philippines; *Key Indicators of Developing Asian and Pacific Countries.*

Euromonitor International, Inc., 122 South Michigan Avenue, Suite 1200, Chicago, Illinois 60603 (800) 577-EURO; *World Marketing Data and Statistics.*

Europa Publications Limited, 18 Bedford Square, London, WC1B 3JN, England; *The Europa World Year Book.*

International Monetary Fund, 700 Nineteenth Street, NW, Washington, D.C. 20431 (202) 623-7000; *International Financial Statistics.*

M.E. Sharpe, 80 Business Park Drive, Armonk, New York 10504 (800) 541-6563; *The Illustrated Book of World Rankings.*

St. Martin's Press, Inc., 175 Fifth Avenue, New York, New York 10010 (800) 221-7945; *The Statesman's Year-Book.*

United Nations Economic Commission for Africa, Africa Hall, Post Office Box 3001, Addis Ababa, Ethiopia (Telephone Number in U.S. (800) 253-9646); *African Statistical Yearbook.*

MALAWI - BARLEY PRODUCTION - See MALAWI - CROPS

MALAWI - BEER PRODUCTION - See MALAWI - BEVERAGES

MALAWI - BEVERAGES

M.E. Sharpe, 80 Business Park Drive, Armonk, New York 10504 (800) 541-6563; *The Illustrated Book of World Rankings.*

Statistical Office of the United Nations, Publishing Service, New York, New York 10017 (800) 253-9646; *Statistical Yearbook.*

MALAWI - BIRTH RATES

Central Intelligence Agency,

Washington, D.C. 20505 (703) 482-1100, www.cia.gov; *The World Factbook.*

Euromonitor International, Inc., 122 South Michigan Avenue, Suite 1200, Chicago, Illinois 60603 (800) 577-EURO; *International Marketing Data and Statistics;* and *The World Economic Factbook.*

Europa Publications Limited, 18 Bedford Square, London, WC1B 3JN, England; *The Europa World Year Book.*

M.E. Sharpe, 80 Business Park Drive, Armonk, New York 10504 (800) 541-6563; *The Illustrated Book of World Rankings.*

Statistical Office of the United Nations, Publishing Service, New York, New York 10017 (800) 253-9646; *Demographic Yearbook; Statistical Yearbook;* and *Survey of Economic and Social Conditions in Africa.*

The World Bank, 1818 H Street, NW, Washington, D.C. 20433 (202) 477-1234; *World Development Indicators.*

MALAWI - BOOK PRODUCTION

Europa Publications Limited, 18 Bedford Square, London, WC1B 3JN, England; *The Europa World Year Book.*

United Nations Educational, Scientific and Cultural Organization (UNESCO), 7 Place de Fontenoy, F-75700 Paris, France (Telephone Number in U.S. (212) 963-5981); *Statistical Yearbook.*

MALAWI - BROADCASTING

Billboard Limited, Post Office Box 9027, 1006 AA Amsterdam, The Netherlands (Telephone Number in U.S. (212) 764-7300); *World Radio TV Handbook.*

Central Intelligence Agency, Washington, D.C. 20505 (703) 482-1100, www.cia.gov; *The World Factbook.*

Euromonitor International, Inc., 122 South Michigan Avenue, Suite 1200, Chicago, Illinois 60603 (800) 577-EURO; *World Marketing Data and Statistics.*

M.E. Sharpe, 80 Business Park Drive, Armonk, New York 10504 (800) 541-6563; *The Illustrated Book of World Rankings.*

St. Martin's Press, Inc., 175 Fifth Avenue, New York, New York 10010 (800) 221-7945; *The Statesman's Year-Book.*

MALAWI - BUDGET

Central Intelligence Agency, Washington, D.C. 20505 (703) 482-1100, www.cia.gov; *The World Factbook.*

MALAWI - BUSINESS AND PROFESSIONAL LICENSES

International Monetary Fund, 700 Nineteenth Street, NW, Washington, D.C. 20431 (202) 623-7000; *Government Finance Statistics Yearbook.*

MALAWI - CABBAGE PRODUCTION - See MALAWI - CROPS

MALAWI - CALORIE SUPPLY

African Development Bank, 01 BP 1387, Abidjan 01, Cote d'Ivoire; *Selected Statistics on Regional Member Countries.*

Food and Agricultural Organization of the United Nations (FAO), Via delle Terme di Caracalla, 00100 Rome, Italy (Telephone Number in U.S. (202) 653-2400); *The State of Food and Agriculture.*

MALAWI - CAPITAL REVENUE

International Monetary Fund, 700 Nineteenth Street, NW, Washington, D.C. 20431 (202) 623-7000; *Government Finance Statistics Yearbook.*

MALAWI - CATTLE - See MALAWI - LIVESTOCK AND POULTRY

MALAWI - CEMENT PRODUCTION - See MALAWI - MINING AND MINERAL PRODUCTS

MALAWI - CHEMICAL (ORGANIC) PRODUCTION - See MALAWI - MINING AND MINERAL PRODUCTS

MALAWI - CHICKENS - See MALAWI - LIVESTOCK AND POULTRY

MALAWI - CIGARETTE PRODUCTION - See MALAWI - TOBACCO PRODUCTION

MALAWI - CLIMATE

M.E. Sharpe, 80 Business Park Drive, Armonk, New York 10504 (800) 541-6563; *The Illustrated Book of World Rankings.*

St. Martin's Press, Inc., 175 Fifth Avenue, New York, New York 10010 (800) 221-7945; *The Statesman's Year-Book.*

MALAWI - COAL PRODUCTION - See MALAWI - MINING AND MINERAL PRODUCTS

MALAWI - COFFEE PRODUCTION AND CONSUMPTION - See MALAWI - CROPS

MALAWI - COMMERCE

St. Martin's Press, Inc., 175 Fifth Avenue, New York, New York 10010 (800) 221-7945; *The Statesman's Year-Book.*

MALAWI - COMMUNICATIONS - See MALAWI - TRANSPORTATION AND COMMUNICATIONS

MALAWI - CONSTRUCTION INDUSTRY

M.E. Sharpe, 80 Business Park Drive, Armonk, New York 10504 (800) 541-6563; *The Illustrated Book of World Rankings.*

Statistical Office of the United Nations, Publishing Service, New York, New York 10017 (800) 253-9646; *Statistical Yearbook.*

United Nations Economic Commission for Africa, Africa Hall, Post Office Box 3001, Addis Ababa, Ethiopia (Telephone Number in U.S. (800) 253-9646); *African Statistical Yearbook.*

MALAWI - CONSUMER PRICE INDEX

African Development Bank, 01 BP 1387, Abidjan 01, Cote d'Ivoire; *Selected Statistics on Regional Member Countries.*

Europa Publications Limited, 18 Bedford Square, London, WC1B 3JN, England; *The Europa World Year Book.*

Statistical Office of the United Nations, Publishing Service, New York, New York 10017 (800) 253-9646; *Statistical Yearbook;* and *Survey of Economic and Social Conditions in Africa.*

United Nations Economic Commission for Africa, Africa Hall, Post Office Box 3001, Addis Ababa, Ethiopia (Telephone Number in U.S. (800) 253-9646); *African Statistical Yearbook.*

MALAWI - CONSUMER PRICES

Euromonitor International, Inc., 122 South Michigan Avenue, Suite 1200, Chicago, Illinois 60603 (800) 577-EURO; *World Marketing Data and Statistics.*

International Labour Office, I.L.O. Publications, 1828 L Street, N.W., Suite 801, Washington, D.C. 20036 (301) 638-3152; *Yearbook of Labour Statistics.*

International Monetary Fund, 700 Nineteenth Street, NW, Washington, D.C. 20431 (202) 623-7000; *International Financial Statistics.*

MALAWI - CONSUMPTION

African Development Bank, 01 BP 1387, Abidjan 01, Cote d'Ivoire; *Selected Statistics on Regional Member Countries.*

Statistical Office of the United Nations, Publishing Service, New York, New York 10017 (800) 253-9646; *Survey of Economic and Social Conditions in Africa.*

The World Bank, 1818 H Street, NW, Washington, D.C. 20433 (202) 477-1234; *World Development Report.*

MALAWI - COPPER PRODUCTION AND

CONSUMPTION - See MALAWI - MINING AND MINERAL PRODUCTS

MALAWI - CORN PRODUCTION - See MALAWI - CROPS

MALAWI - CORPORATE TAXES - See MALAWI - TAXATION

MALAWI - COTTON PRODUCTION - See MALAWI - CROPS

MALAWI - CRIME

International Criminal Police Organization (INTERPOL), 26 rue Armengaud, 92210 Saint Cloud, France; *International Crime Statistics.*

Yale University Press, Yale Station, New Haven, Connecticut 06520 (800) 987-7323; *Violence and Crime in Cross-National Perspective.*

MALAWI - CROPS

Commodity Research Bureau, 30 South Wacker Drive, Chicago Illinois 60606 (312) 454-1801; *Commodity Yearbook.*

Europa Publications Limited, 18 Bedford Square, London, WC1B 3JN, England; *The Europa World Year Book.*

Food and Agricultural Organization of the United Nations (FAO), Via delle Terme di Caracalla, 00100 Rome, Italy (Telephone Number in U.S. (202) 653-2400); *Production Yearbook;* and *The State of Food and Agriculture.*

International Monetary Fund, 700 Nineteenth Street, NW, Washington, D.C. 20431 (202) 623-7000; *International Financial Statistics.*

M.E. Sharpe, 80 Business Park Drive, Armonk, New York 10504 (800) 541-6563; *The Illustrated Book of World Rankings.*

St. Martin's Press, Inc., 175 Fifth Avenue, New York, New York 10010 (800) 221-7945; *The Statesman's Year-Book.*

Statistical Office of the United Nations, Publishing Service, New York, New York 10017 (800) 253-9646; *Statistical Yearbook.*

United Nations Conference on Trade and Development, Central Statistical Service, Palais des Nations, Geneva, Switzerland (Telephone in U.S. (800) 253-9646); *UNCTAD Commodity Yearbook.*

United Nations Economic Commission for Africa, Africa Hall, Post Office Box 3001, Addis Ababa, Ethiopia (Telephone Number in U.S. (800) 253-9646); *African Statistical Yearbook.*

MALAWI - CUSTOMS DUTIES

International Monetary Fund, 700 Nineteenth Street, NW, Washington, D.C. 20431 (202) 623-7000; *Government Finance Statistics Yearbook.*

MALAWI - DAIRY PRODUCTS

Europa Publications Limited, 18 Bedford Square, London, WC1B 3JN, England; *The Europa World Year Book.*

Food and Agricultural Organization of the United Nations (FAO), Via delle Terme di Caracalla, 00100 Rome, Italy (Telephone Number in U.S. (202) 653-2400); *The State of Food and Agriculture.*

M.E. Sharpe, 80 Business Park Drive, Armonk, New York 10504 (800) 541-6563; *The Illustrated Book of World Rankings.*

St. Martin's Press, Inc., 175 Fifth Avenue, New York, New York 10010 (800) 221-7945; *The Statesman's Year-Book.*

Statistical Office of the United Nations, Publishing Service, New York, New York 10017 (800) 253-9646; *Statistical Yearbook.*

MALAWI - DEATH RATES - See MALAWI - MORTALITY

MALAWI - DEFENSE EXPENDITURES - See MALAWI - MILITARY

MALAWI - DEMOGRAPHY

The Economist Intelligence Unit, 111 West 57th Street, New York, New York 10019 (800) 938-4685; *The World Market Atlas.*

Euromonitor International, Inc., 122 South Michigan Avenue, Suite 1200, Chicago, Illinois 60603 (800) 577-EURO; *International Marketing Data and Statistics; World Marketing Data and Statistics;* and *The World Economic Factbook.*

M.E. Sharpe, 80 Business Park Drive, Armonk, New York 10504 (800) 541-6563; *The Illustrated Book of World Rankings.*

Statistical Office of the United Nations, Publishing Service, New York, New York 10017 (800) 253-9646; *Human Development Report;* and *Survey of Economic and Social Conditions in Africa.*

MALAWI - DEVELOPMENT ASSISTANCE

Statistical Office of the United Nations, Publishing Service, New York, New York 10017 (800) 253-9646; *Statistical Yearbook.*

MALAWI - DIAMOND PRODUCTION - See MALAWI - MINING AND MINERAL PRODUCTS

MALAWI - DISEASES - See MALAWI - HEALTH

MALAWI - DIVORCE

M.E. Sharpe, 80 Business Park Drive, Armonk, New York 10504 (800) 541-6563; *The Illustrated Book of World Rankings.*

Statistical Office of the United Nations, Publishing Service, New York, New York 10017 (800) 253-9646; *Demographic Yearbook.*

MALAWI - ECONOMY

African Development Bank, 01 BP 1387, Abidjan 01, Cote d'Ivoire; *Selected Statistics on Regional Member Countries.*

Central Intelligence Agency, Washington, D.C. 20505 (703) 482-1100, www.cia.gov; *The World Factbook.*

Economist Intelligence Unit, 111 West 57th Street, New York, New York 10019 (800) 938-4685; *Malawi Country Report.*

Euromonitor International, Inc., 122 South Michigan Avenue, Suite 1200, Chicago, Illinois 60603 (800) 577-EURO; *International Marketing Data and Statistics; World Marketing Data and Statistics;* and *The World Economic Factbook.*

Europa Publications Limited, 18 Bedford Square, London, WC1B 3JN, England; *The Europa World Year Book.*

M.E. Sharpe, 80 Business Park Drive, Armonk, New York 10504 (800) 541-6563; *The Illustrated Book of World Rankings.*

St. Martin's Press, Inc., 175 Fifth Avenue, New York, New York 10010 (800) 221-7945; *The Statesman's Year-Book.*

Statistical Office of the United Nations, Publishing Service, New York, New York 10017 (800) 253-9646; *World Statistics Pocketbook.*

The World Bank, 1818 H Street, NW, Washington, D.C. 20433 (202) 477-1234; *The World Bank Atlas;* and *World Development Report.*

MALAWI - EDUCATION

African Development Bank, 01 BP 1387, Abidjan 01, Cote d'Ivoire; *Selected Statistics on Regional Member Countries.*

The Economist Intelligence Unit, 111 West 57th Street, New York, New York 10019 (800) 938-4685; *The World Market Atlas.*

Euromonitor International, Inc., 122 South Michigan Avenue, Suite 1200, Chicago, Illinois 60603 (800) 577-EURO; *International Marketing Data and Statistics;* and *World Marketing Data and Statistics.*

Europa Publications Limited, 18 Bedford Square, London, WC1B 3JN, England; *The Europa World Year Book*.

International Monetary Fund, 700 Nineteenth Street, NW, Washington, D.C. 20431 (202) 623-7000; *Government Finance Statistics Yearbook*.

M.E. Sharpe, 80 Business Park Drive, Armonk, New York 10504 (800) 541-6563; *The Illustrated Book of World Rankings*.

St. Martin's Press, Inc., 175 Fifth Avenue, New York, New York 10010 (800) 221-7945; *The Statesman's Year-Book*.

Statistical Office of the United Nations, Publishing Service, New York, New York 10017 (800) 253-9646; *Human Development Report;* and *Survey of Economic and Social Conditions in Africa*.

United Nations Economic Commission for Africa, Africa Hall, Post Office Box 3001, Addis Ababa, Ethiopia (Telephone Number in U.S. (800) 253-9646); *African Statistical Yearbook*.

United Nations Educational, Scientific and Cultural Organization (UNESCO), 7 Place de Fontenoy, F-75700 Paris, France (Telephone Number in U.S. (212) 963-5981); *Statistical Yearbook*.

The World Bank, 1818 H Street, NW, Washington, D.C. 20433 (202) 477-1234; *World Development Report;* and *World Development Indicators*.

MALAWI - EGG PRODUCTION AND CONSUMPTION - See MALAWI - DAIRY PRODUCTS

MALAWI - ELECTRICITY

Central Intelligence Agency, Washington, D.C. 20505 (703) 482-1100, www.cia.gov; *The World Factbook*.

M.E. Sharpe, 80 Business Park Drive, Armonk, New York 10504 (800) 541-6563; *The Illustrated Book of World Rankings*.

St. Martin's Press, Inc., 175 Fifth Avenue, New York, New York 10010 (800) 221-7945; *The Statesman's Year-Book*.

Statistical Office of the United Nations, Publishing Service, New York, New York 10017 (800) 253-9646; *Human Development Report; Statistical Yearbook;* and *Survey of Economic and Social Conditions in Africa*.

United Nations Economic Commission for Africa, Africa Hall, Post Office Box 3001, Addis Ababa, Ethiopia (Telephone Number in U.S. (800) 253-9646); *African Statistical Yearbook*.

MALAWI - EMPLOYMENT

Euromonitor International, Inc., 122 South Michigan Avenue, Suite 1200, Chicago, Illinois 60603 (800) 577-EURO; *International Marketing Data and Statistics*.

International Labour Office, I.L.O. Publications, 1828 L Street, N.W., Suite 801, Washington, D.C. 20036 (301) 638-3152; *Yearbook of Labour Statistics*.

M.E. Sharpe, 80 Business Park Drive, Armonk, New York 10504 (800) 541-6563; *The Illustrated Book of World Rankings*.

Statistical Office of the United Nations, Publishing Service, New York, New York 10017 (800) 253-9646; *Statistical Yearbook;* and *Survey of Economic and Social Conditions in Africa*.

United Nations Economic Commission for Africa, Africa Hall, Post Office Box 3001, Addis Ababa, Ethiopia (Telephone Number in U.S. (800) 253-9646); *African Statistical Yearbook*.

MALAWI - ENERGY

Euromonitor International, Inc., 122 South Michigan Avenue, Suite 1200, Chicago, Illinois 60603 (800) 577-EURO; *International Marketing Data and Statistics; World Marketing Data and Statistics;* and *The World Economic Factbook*.

Food and Agricultural Organization of the United Nations (FAO), Via delle Terme di Caracalla, 00100 Rome, Italy (Telephone Number in U.S. (202) 653-2400); *The State of Food and Agriculture*.

M.E. Sharpe, 80 Business Park Drive, Armonk, New York 10504 (800) 541-6563; *The Illustrated Book of World Rankings*.

St. Martin's Press, Inc., 175 Fifth Avenue, New York, New York 10010 (800) 221-7945; *The Statesman's Year-Book*.

Statistical Office of the United Nations, Publishing Service, New York, New York 10017 (800) 253-9646; *Energy Statistics Yearbook; Human Development Report; World Statistics Pocketbook;* and *Statistical Yearbook*.

United Nations Economic Commission for Africa, Africa Hall, Post Office Box 3001, Addis Ababa, Ethiopia (Telephone Number in U.S. (800) 253-9646); *African Statistical Yearbook*.

The World Bank, 1818 H Street, NW, Washington, D.C. 20433 (202) 477-1234; *The World Bank Atlas;* and *World Development Report*.

MALAWI - ENVIRONMENT

Economist Intelligence Unit, 111 West

57th Street, New York, New York 10019 (800) 938-4685; *Malawi Country Report*.

Statistical Office of the United Nations, Publishing Service, New York, New York 10017 (800) 253-9646; *World Statistics Pocketbook*.

MALAWI - EXCHANGE RATES

African Development Bank, 01 BP 1387, Abidjan 01, Cote d'Ivoire; *Selected Statistics on Regional Member Countries*.

Central Intelligence Agency, Washington, D.C. 20505 (703) 482-1100, www.cia.gov; *The World Factbook*.

Euromonitor International, Inc., 122 South Michigan Avenue, Suite 1200, Chicago, Illinois 60603 (800) 577-EURO; *International Marketing Data and Statistics;* and *The World Economic Factbook*.

Europa Publications Limited, 18 Bedford Square, London, WC1B 3JN, England; *The Europa World Year Book*.

International Civil Aviation Organization, 999 University Street, Montreal, Quebec, Canada H3C 5H7 (514) 954-8219; *Civil Aviation Statistics of the World*.

International Monetary Fund, 700 Nineteenth Street, NW, Washington, D.C. 20431 (202) 623-7000; *International Financial Statistics*.

Statistical Office of the United Nations, Publishing Service, New York, New York 10017 (800) 253-9646; *Statistical Yearbook;* and *World Statistics Pocketbook*.

MALAWI - EXCISE TAXES - See MALAWI - TAXATION

MALAWI - EXPORTS

African Development Bank, 01 BP 1387, Abidjan 01, Cote d'Ivoire; *Selected Statistics on Regional Member Countries*.

Central Intelligence Agency, Washington, D.C. 20505 (703) 482-1100, www.cia.gov; *The World Factbook*.

The Economist Intelligence Unit, 111 West 57th Street, New York, New York 10019 (800) 938-4685; *Malawi Country Report;* and *The World Market Atlas*.

Euromonitor International, Inc., 122 South Michigan Avenue, Suite 1200, Chicago, Illinois 60603 (800) 577-EURO; *International Marketing Data and Statistics;* and *The World Economic Factbook*.

Europa Publications Limited, 18 Bedford Square, London, WC1B 3JN, England; *The Europa World Year Book*.

Food and Agricultural Organization of the United Nations (FAO), Via delle Terme di Caracalla, 00100 Rome, Italy (Telephone Number in U.S. (202) 653-2400); *The State of Food and Agriculture.*

International Monetary Fund, 700 Nineteenth Street, NW, Washington, D.C. 20431 (202) 623-7000; *Direction of Trade Statistics;* and *International Financial Statistics.*

St. Martin's Press, Inc., 175 Fifth Avenue, New York, New York 10010 (800) 221-7945; *The Statesman's Year-Book.*

Statistical Office of the United Nations, Publishing Service, New York, New York 10017 (800) 253-9646; *Survey of Economic and Social Conditions in Africa.*

United Nations Conference on Trade and Development (UNCTAD), New York, New York 10017 (800) 253-9646; *Handbook of International Trade and Development Statistics.*

United Nations Economic Commission for Africa, Africa Hall, Post Office Box 3001, Addis Ababa, Ethiopia (Telephone Number in U.S. (800) 253-9646); *African Statistical Yearbook.*

The World Bank, 1818 H Street, NW, Washington, D.C. 20433 (202) 477-1234; *World Development Report;* and *World Development Indicators.*

MALAWI - EXTERNAL INDEBTEDNESS

African Development Bank, 01 BP 1387, Abidjan 01, Cote d'Ivoire; *Selected Statistics on Regional Member Countries.*

Statistical Office of the United Nations, Publishing Service, New York, New York 10017 (800) 253-9646; *Survey of Economic and Social Conditions in Africa.*

The World Bank, 1818 H Street, NW, Washington, D.C. 20433 (202) 477-1234; *World Development Report;* and *World Development Indicators.*

MALAWI - EXTERNAL TRADE

African Development Bank, 01 BP 1387, Abidjan 01, Cote d'Ivoire; *Selected Statistics on Regional Member Countries.*

Euromonitor International, Inc., 122 South Michigan Avenue, Suite 1200, Chicago, Illinois 60603 (800) 577-EURO; *World Marketing Data and Statistics.*

Food and Agricultural Organization of the United Nations (FAO), Via delle Terme di Caracalla, 00100 Rome, Italy (Telephone Number in U.S. (202) 653-2400); *The State of Food and Agriculture;* and *Trade Yearbook.*

Statistical Office of the United Nations, Publishing Service, New York, New York 10017 (800) 253-9646; *Statistical Yearbook.*

MALAWI - FARM CROPS - See MALAWI - CROPS

MALAWI - FEMALE WORKING POPULATION - See MALAWI - EMPLOYMENT

MALAWI - FERTILITY RATES

Central Intelligence Agency, Washington, D.C. 20505 (703) 482-1100, www.cia.gov; *The World Factbook.*

M.E. Sharpe, 80 Business Park Drive, Armonk, New York 10504 (800) 541-6563; *The Illustrated Book of World Rankings.*

Statistical Office of the United Nations, Publishing Service, New York, New York 10017 (800) 253-9646; *Human Development Report;* and *Survey of Economic and Social Conditions in Africa.*

The World Bank, 1818 H Street, NW, Washington, D.C. 20433 (202) 477-1234; *The World Bank Atlas; World Development Report;* and *World Development Indicators.*

MALAWI - FERTILIZER

Food and Agricultural Organization of the United Nations (FAO), Via delle Terme di Caracalla, 00100 Rome, Italy (Telephone Number in U.S. (202) 653-2400); *Fertilizer Yearbook;* and *The State of Food and Agriculture.*

Statistical Office of the United Nations, Publishing Service, New York, New York 10017 (800) 253-9646; *Statistical Yearbook.*

MALAWI - FETAL MORTALITY - See MALAWI - MORTALITY

MALAWI - FINANCE

African Development Bank, 01 BP 1387, Abidjan 01, Cote d'Ivoire; *Selected Statistics on Regional Member Countries.*

Economist Intelligence Unit, 111 West 57th Street, New York, New York 10019 (800) 938-4685; *Malawi Country Report.*

Europa Publications Limited, 18 Bedford Square, London, WC1B 3JN, England; *The Europa World Year Book.*

International Monetary Fund, 700 Nineteenth Street, NW, Washington, D.C. 20431 (202) 623-7000; *International Financial Statistics.*

M.E. Sharpe, 80 Business Park Drive, Armonk, New York 10504 (800) 541-6563; *The Illustrated Book of World Rankings.*

St. Martin's Press, Inc., 175 Fifth Avenue, New York, New York 10010 (800) 221-7945; *The Statesman's Year-Book.*

United Nations Economic Commission for Africa, Africa Hall, Post Office Box 3001, Addis Ababa, Ethiopia (Telephone Number in U.S. (800) 253-9646); *African Statistical Yearbook.*

MALAWI - FISHERIES

Europa Publications Limited, 18 Bedford Square, London, WC1B 3JN, England; *The Europa World Year Book.*

Food and Agricultural Organization of the United Nations (FAO), Via delle Terme di Caracalla, 00100 Rome, Italy (Telephone Number in U.S. (202) 653-2400); *The State of Food and Agriculture;* and *Yearbook of Fishery Statistics.*

M.E. Sharpe, 80 Business Park Drive, Armonk, New York 10504 (800) 541-6563; *The Illustrated Book of World Rankings.*

St. Martin's Press, Inc., 175 Fifth Avenue, New York, New York 10010 (800) 221-7945; *The Statesman's Year-Book.*

Statistical Office of the United Nations, Publishing Service, New York, New York 10017 (800) 253-9646; *Statistical Yearbook;* and *Survey of Economic and Social Conditions in Africa.*

United Nations Conference on Trade and Development, Central Statistical Service, Palais des Nations, Geneva, Switzerland (Telephone in U.S. (800) 253-9646); *UNCTAD Commodity Yearbook.*

United Nations Economic Commission for Africa, Africa Hall, Post Office Box 3001, Addis Ababa, Ethiopia (Telephone Number in U.S. (800) 253-9646); *African Statistical Yearbook.*

MALAWI - FOOD

African Development Bank, 01 BP 1387, Abidjan 01, Cote d'Ivoire; *Selected Statistics on Regional Member Countries.*

Food and Agricultural Organization of the United Nations (FAO), Via delle Terme di Caracalla, 00100 Rome, Italy (Telephone Number in U.S. (202) 653-2400); *Production Yearbook;* and *The State of Food and Agriculture.*

Statistical Office of the United Nations, Publishing Service, New York, New York 10017 (800) 253-9646; *Human Development Report.*

United Nations Conference on Trade and Development, Central Statistical Service, Palais des Nations, Geneva, Switzerland (Telephone in U.S. (800) 253-

9646); *UNCTAD Commodity Yearbook.*

MALAWI - FOREIGN DEBT

International Monetary Fund, 700 Nineteenth Street, NW, Washington, D.C. 20431 (202) 623-7000; *Government Finance Statistics Yearbook.*

MALAWI - FOREIGN TRADE

Economist Intelligence Unit, 111 West 57th Street, New York, New York 10019 (800) 938-4685; *Malawi Country Report.*

Euromonitor International, Inc., 122 South Michigan Avenue, Suite 1200, Chicago, Illinois 60603 (800) 577-EURO; *International Marketing Data and Statistics;* and *The World Economic Factbook.*

Europa Publications Limited, 18 Bedford Square, London, WC1B 3JN, England; *The Europa World Year Book.*

Food and Agricultural Organization of the United Nations (FAO), Via delle Terme di Caracalla, 00100 Rome, Italy (Telephone Number in U.S. (202) 653-2400); *The State of Food and Agriculture.*

M.E. Sharpe, 80 Business Park Drive, Armonk, New York 10504 (800) 541-6563; *The Illustrated Book of World Rankings.*

St. Martin's Press, Inc., 175 Fifth Avenue, New York, New York 10010 (800) 221-7945; *The Statesman's Year-Book.*

Statistical Office of the United Nations, Publishing Service, New York, New York 10017 (800) 253-9646; *International Trade Statistics Yearbook;* and *Statistical Yearbook.*

United Nations Conference on Trade and Development, Central Statistical Service, Palais des Nations, Geneva, Switzerland (Telephone in U.S. (800) 253-9646); *UNCTAD Commodity Yearbook.*

United Nations Economic Commission for Africa, Africa Hall, Post Office Box 3001, Addis Ababa, Ethiopia (Telephone Number in U.S. (800) 253-9646); *African Statistical Yearbook.*

The World Bank, 1818 H Street, NW, Washington, D.C. 20433 (202) 477-1234; *World Development Report;* and *World Development Indicators.*

MALAWI - FORESTRY AND FOREST PRODUCTS

Europa Publications Limited, 18 Bedford Square, London, WC1B 3JN, England; *The Europa World Year Book.*

Food and Agricultural Organization of the United Nations (FAO), Via delle Terme di Caracalla, 00100 Rome, Italy (Telephone Number in U.S. (202) 653-2400); *The State of Food and Agriculture;* and *Yearbook of Forest Products.*

M.E. Sharpe, 80 Business Park Drive, Armonk, New York 10504 (800) 541-6563; *The Illustrated Book of World Rankings.*

St. Martin's Press, Inc., 175 Fifth Avenue, New York, New York 10010 (800) 221-7945; *The Statesman's Year-Book.*

Statistical Office of the United Nations, Publishing Service, New York, New York 10017 (800) 253-9646; *Statistical Yearbook.*

United Nations Conference on Trade and Development, Central Statistical Service, Palais des Nations, Geneva, Switzerland (Telephone in U.S. (800) 253-9646); *UNCTAD Commodity Yearbook.*

United Nations Economic Commission for Africa, Africa Hall, Post Office Box 3001, Addis Ababa, Ethiopia (Telephone Number in U.S. (800) 253-9646); *African Statistical Yearbook.*

United Nations Educational, Scientific and Cultural Organization (UNESCO), 7 Place de Fontenoy, F-75700 Paris, France (Telephone Number in U.S. (212) 963-5981); *Statistical Yearbook.*

The World Bank, 1818 H Street, NW, Washington, D.C. 20433 (202) 477-1234; *World Development Report.*

MALAWI - GAS PRODUCTION - See MALAWI - MINING AND MINERAL PRODUCTS

MALAWI - GENERAL INDUSTRIAL STATISTICS - See MALAWI - INDUSTRY

MALAWI - GENERAL MORTALITY - See MALAWI - MORTALITY

MALAWI - GEOGRAPHIC DATA

M.E. Sharpe, 80 Business Park Drive, Armonk, New York 10504 (800) 541-6563; *The Illustrated Book of World Rankings.*

MALAWI - GOATS - See MALAWI - LIVESTOCK AND POULTRY

MALAWI - GOLD HOLDINGS

International Monetary Fund, 700 Nineteenth Street, NW, Washington, D.C. 20431 (202) 623-7000; *International Financial Statistics.*

Statistical Office of the United Nations, Publishing Service, New York, New York 10017 (800) 253-9646; *Statistical Yearbook.*

The World Bank, 1818 H Street, NW, Washington, D.C. 20433 (202) 477-1234; *World Development Indicators.*

MALAWI - GOLD PRODUCTION AND CONSUMPTION - See MALAWI - MINING AND MINERAL PRODUCTS

MALAWI - GOVERNMENT

Central Intelligence Agency, Washington, D.C. 20505 (703) 482-1100, www.cia.gov; *The World Factbook.*

Europa Publications Limited, 18 Bedford Square, London, WC1B 3JN, England; *The Europa World Year Book.*

International Monetary Fund, 700 Nineteenth Street, NW, Washington, D.C. 20431 (202) 623-7000; *Government Finance Statistics Yearbook;* and *International Financial Statistics.*

St. Martin's Press, Inc., 175 Fifth Avenue, New York, New York 10010 (800) 221-7945; *The Statesman's Year-Book.*

Statistical Office of the United Nations, Publishing Service, New York, New York 10017 (800) 253-9646; *National Accounts Statistics; Statistical Yearbook;* and *Survey of Economic and Social Conditions in Africa.*

The World Bank, 1818 H Street, NW, Washington, D.C. 20433 (202) 477-1234; *World Development Report;* and *World Development Indicators.*

MALAWI - GRAIN PRODUCTION - See MALAWI - CROPS

MALAWI - GRANTS

International Monetary Fund, 700 Nineteenth Street, NW, Washington, D.C. 20431 (202) 623-7000; *Government Finance Statistics Yearbook.*

MALAWI - GROSS DOMESTIC PRODUCT

African Development Bank, 01 BP 1387, Abidjan 01, Cote d'Ivoire; *Selected Statistics on Regional Member Countries.*

The Economist Intelligence Unit, 111 West 57th Street, New York, New York 10019 (800) 938-4685; *Malawi Country Report;* and *The World Market Atlas.*

Euromonitor International, Inc., 122 South Michigan Avenue, Suite 1200, Chicago, Illinois 60603 (800) 577-EURO; *International Marketing Data and Statistics;* and *The World Economic Factbook.*

Europa Publications Limited, 18 Bedford Square, London, WC1B 3JN, England; *The Europa World Year Book.*

M.E. Sharpe, 80 Business Park Drive, Armonk, New York 10504 (800) 541-6563;

The Illustrated Book of World Rankings.

Statistical Office of the United Nations, Publishing Service, New York, New York 10017 (800) 253-9646; *Human Development Report; National Accounts Statistics; Statistical Yearbook;* and *Survey of Economic and Social Conditions in Africa.*

United Nations Economic Commission for Africa, Africa Hall, Post Office Box 3001, Addis Ababa, Ethiopia (Telephone Number in U.S. (800) 253-9646); *African Statistical Yearbook.*

The World Bank, 1818 H Street, NW, Washington, D.C. 20433 (202) 477-1234; *World Development Report;* and *World Development Indicators.*

MALAWI - GROSS NATIONAL PRODUCT

Euromonitor International, Inc., 122 South Michigan Avenue, Suite 1200, Chicago, Illinois 60603 (800) 577-EURO; *International Marketing Data and Statistics.*

St. Martin's Press, Inc., 175 Fifth Avenue, New York, New York 10010 (800) 221-7945; *The Statesman's Year-Book.*

U.S. Arms Control and Disarmament Agency, 320 Twenty-first Street, NW, Washington, D.C. 20451 (202) 647-8677; *World Military Expenditures and Arms Transfers.*

The World Bank, 1818 H Street, NW, Washington, D.C. 20433 (202) 477-1234; *The World Bank Atlas; World Development Report;* and *World Development Indicators.*

MALAWI - GROUNDNUTS EXPORTS - See MALAWI - CROPS

MALAWI - HEALTH

African Development Bank, 01 BP 1387, Abidjan 01, Cote d'Ivoire; *Selected Statistics on Regional Member Countries.*

Euromonitor International, Inc., 122 South Michigan Avenue, Suite 1200, Chicago, Illinois 60603 (800) 577-EURO; *World Marketing Data and Statistics.*

M.E. Sharpe, 80 Business Park Drive, Armonk, New York 10504 (800) 541-6563; *The Illustrated Book of World Rankings.*

St. Martin's Press, Inc., 175 Fifth Avenue, New York, New York 10010 (800) 221-7945; *The Statesman's Year-Book.*

Statistical Office of the United Nations, Publishing Service, New York, New York 10017 (800) 253-9646; *Human Development Report;* and *Statistical Yearbook.*

United Nations Children's Fund (UNICEF), 3 United Nations Plaza, New York, New York 10017 (800) 253-9646; *State of the World's Children.*

United Nations Economic Commission for Africa, Africa Hall, Post Office Box 3001, Addis Ababa, Ethiopia (Telephone Number in U.S. (800) 253-9646); *African Statistical Yearbook.*

The World Bank, 1818 H Street, NW, Washington, D.C. 20433 (202) 477-1234; *World Development Report.*

World Health Organization, Office of Publications, 20 Avenue Appia, CH-1211 Geneva 27, Switzerland (Telephone Number in U.S. (518) 436-9686); *World Health Statistics Annual.*

MALAWI - HEALTH EXPENDITURES

International Monetary Fund, 700 Nineteenth Street, NW, Washington, D.C. 20431 (202) 623-7000; *Government Finance Statistics Yearbook.*

MALAWI - HIDE PRODUCTION

Food and Agricultural Organization of the United Nations (FAO), Via delle Terme di Caracalla, 00100 Rome, Italy (Telephone Number in U.S. (202) 653-2400); *Production Yearbook.*

MALAWI - HIGHWAYS

Central Intelligence Agency, Washington, D.C. 20505 (703) 482-1100, www.cia.gov; *The World Factbook.*

International Road Federation, 2600 Virginia Avenue, N.W., Washington, D.C. 20037 (202) 338-4641, ; *World Road Statistics.*

St. Martin's Press, Inc., 175 Fifth Avenue, New York, New York 10010 (800) 221-7945; *The Statesman's Year-Book.*

Statistical Office of the United Nations, Publishing Service, New York, New York 10017 (800) 253-9646; *Survey of Economic and Social Conditions in Africa.*

United Nations Economic Commission for Africa, Africa Hall, Post Office Box 3001, Addis Ababa, Ethiopia (Telephone Number in U.S. (800) 253-9646); *African Statistical Yearbook.*

MALAWI - HORSES - See MALAWI - LIVESTOCK AND POULTRY

MALAWI - HOURS OF WORK - See MALAWI - EMPLOYMENT

MALAWI - HOUSING AND HOUSING UNITS

Euromonitor International, Inc., 122 South Michigan Avenue, Suite 1200, Chicago, Illinois 60603 (800) 577-EURO;

World Marketing Data and Statistics.

M.E. Sharpe, 80 Business Park Drive, Armonk, New York 10504 (800) 541-6563; *The Illustrated Book of World Rankings.*

MALAWI - HOUSING EXPENDITURES

International Monetary Fund, 700 Nineteenth Street, NW, Washington, D.C. 20431 (202) 623-7000; *Government Finance Statistics Yearbook.*

MALAWI - ILLITERATE POPULATION

Central Intelligence Agency, Washington, D.C. 20505 (703) 482-1100, www.cia.gov; *The World Factbook.*

The Economist Intelligence Unit, 111 West 57th Street, New York, New York 10019 (800) 938-4685; *The World Market Atlas.*

Euromonitor International, Inc., 122 South Michigan Avenue, Suite 1200, Chicago, Illinois 60603 (800) 577-EURO; *The World Economic Factbook.*

Statistical Office of the United Nations, Publishing Service, New York, New York 10017 (800) 253-9646; *Human Development Report.*

United Nations Educational, Scientific and Cultural Organization (UNESCO), 7 Place de Fontenoy, F-75700 Paris, France (Telephone Number in U.S. (212) 963-5981); *Statistical Yearbook.*

MALAWI - IMPORTS

African Development Bank, 01 BP 1387, Abidjan 01, Cote d'Ivoire; *Selected Statistics on Regional Member Countries.*

Central Intelligence Agency, Washington, D.C. 20505 (703) 482-1100, www.cia.gov; *The World Factbook.*

The Economist Intelligence Unit, 111 West 57th Street, New York, New York 10019 (800) 938-4685; *Malawi Country Report;* and *The World Market Atlas.*

Euromonitor International, Inc., 122 South Michigan Avenue, Suite 1200, Chicago, Illinois 60603 (800) 577-EURO; *International Marketing Data and Statistics;* and *The World Economic Factbook.*

Europa Publications Limited, 18 Bedford Square, London, WC1B 3JN, England; *The Europa World Year Book.*

Food and Agricultural Organization of the United Nations (FAO), Via delle Terme di Caracalla, 00100 Rome, Italy (Telephone Number in U.S. (202) 653-2400); *The State of Food and Agriculture.*

International Monetary Fund, 700 Nineteenth Street, NW, Washington, D.C. 20431 (202) 623-7000; *Direction of Trade Statistics; Government Finance Statistics Yearbook;* and *International Financial Statistics.*

St. Martin's Press, Inc., 175 Fifth Avenue, New York, New York 10010 (800) 221-7945; *The Statesman's Year-Book.*

Statistical Office of the United Nations, Publishing Service, New York, New York 10017 (800) 253-9646; *Survey of Economic and Social Conditions in Africa.*

United Nations Conference on Trade and Development (UNCTAD), New York, New York 10017 (800) 253-9646; *Handbook of International Trade and Development Statistics.*

United Nations Economic Commission for Africa, Africa Hall, Post Office Box 3001, Addis Ababa, Ethiopia (Telephone Number in U.S. (800) 253-9646); *African Statistical Yearbook.*

The World Bank, 1818 H Street, NW, Washington, D.C. 20433 (202) 477-1234; *World Development Report;* and *World Development Indicators.*

MALAWI - INCOME TAXES - See MALAWI - TAXATION

MALAWI - INDUSTRY

Central Intelligence Agency, Washington, D.C. 20505 (703) 482-1100, www.cia.gov; *The World Factbook.*

Economist Intelligence Unit, 111 West 57th Street, New York, New York 10019 (800) 938-4685; *Malawi Country Report.*

Euromonitor International, Inc., 122 South Michigan Avenue, Suite 1200, Chicago, Illinois 60603 (800) 577-EURO; *International Marketing Data and Statistics; World Marketing Data and Statistics;* and *The World Economic Factbook.*

Europa Publications Limited, 18 Bedford Square, London, WC1B 3JN, England; *The Europa World Year Book.*

International Labour Office, I.L.O. Publications, 1828 L Street, N.W., Suite 801, Washington, D.C. 20036 (301) 638-3152; *Yearbook of Labour Statistics.*

M.E. Sharpe, 80 Business Park Drive, Armonk, New York 10504 (800) 541-6563; *The Illustrated Book of World Rankings.*

St. Martin's Press, Inc., 175 Fifth Avenue, New York, New York 10010 (800) 221-7945; *The Statesman's Year-Book.*

Statistical Office of the United Nations,

Publishing Service, New York, New York 10017 (800) 253-9646; *Industrial Commodity Statistics Yearbook; Statistical Yearbook;* and *Survey of Economic and Social Conditions in Africa.*

United Nations Economic Commission for Africa, Africa Hall, Post Office Box 3001, Addis Ababa, Ethiopia (Telephone Number in U.S. (800) 253-9646); *African Statistical Yearbook.*

The World Bank, 1818 H Street, NW, Washington, D.C. 20433 (202) 477-1234; *World Development Indicators.*

World Intellectual Property Organization, 34 Chemin des Colombettes, CH-1211 Geneva 20, Switzerland; *Industrial Property Statistics.*

MALAWI - INFANT AND MATERNAL MORTALITY - See MALAWI - MORTALITY

MALAWI - INTERNATIONAL LIQUIDITY

International Monetary Fund, 700 Nineteenth Street, NW, Washington, D.C. 20431 (202) 623-7000; *International Financial Statistics.*

MALAWI - INTERNATIONAL RESERVES EXCLUDING GOLD

African Development Bank, 01 BP 1387, Abidjan 01, Cote d'Ivoire; *Selected Statistics on Regional Member Countries.*

Statistical Office of the United Nations, Publishing Service, New York, New York 10017 (800) 253-9646; *Statistical Yearbook.*

The World Bank, 1818 H Street, NW, Washington, D.C. 20433 (202) 477-1234; *World Development Indicators.*

MALAWI - IRON ORE PRODUCTION AND CONSUMPTION - See MALAWI - MINING AND MINERAL PRODUCTS

MALAWI - IRRIGATION

Euromonitor International, Inc., 122 South Michigan Avenue, Suite 1200, Chicago, Illinois 60603 (800) 577-EURO; *International Marketing Data and Statistics.*

MALAWI - LABOR

African Development Bank, 01 BP 1387, Abidjan 01, Cote d'Ivoire; *Selected Statistics on Regional Member Countries.*

Central Intelligence Agency, Washington, D.C. 20505 (703) 482-1100, www.cia.gov; *The World Factbook.*

Euromonitor International, Inc., 122 South Michigan Avenue, Suite 1200, Chicago, Illinois 60603 (800) 577-EURO;

International Marketing Data and Statistics; and *World Marketing Data and Statistics.*

Europa Publications Limited, 18 Bedford Square, London, WC1B 3JN, England; *The Europa World Year Book.*

M.E. Sharpe, 80 Business Park Drive, Armonk, New York 10504 (800) 541-6563; *The Illustrated Book of World Rankings.*

Food and Agricultural Organization of the United Nations (FAO), Via delle Terme di Caracalla, 00100 Rome, Italy (Telephone Number in U.S. (202) 653-2400); *The State of Food and Agriculture.*

International Labour Office, I.L.O. Publications, 1828 L Street, N.W., Suite 801, Washington, D.C. 20036 (301) 638-3152; *Yearbook of Labour Statistics.*

St. Martin's Press, Inc., 175 Fifth Avenue, New York, New York 10010 (800) 221-7945; *The Statesman's Year-Book.*

Statistical Office of the United Nations, Publishing Service, New York, New York 10017 (800) 253-9646; *Human Development Report.*

The World Bank, 1818 H Street, NW, Washington, D.C. 20433 (202) 477-1234; *The World Bank Atlas; World Development Report;* and *World Development Indicators.*

MALAWI - LAND USE

Central Intelligence Agency, Washington, D.C. 20505 (703) 482-1100, www.cia.gov; *The World Factbook.*

Euromonitor International, Inc., 122 South Michigan Avenue, Suite 1200, Chicago, Illinois 60603 (800) 577-EURO; *International Marketing Data and Statistics.*

Food and Agricultural Organization of the United Nations (FAO), Via delle Terme di Caracalla, 00100 Rome, Italy (Telephone Number in U.S. (202) 653-2400); *Production Yearbook.*

The World Bank, 1818 H Street, NW, Washington, D.C. 20433 (202) 477-1234; *World Development Report.*

MALAWI - LIBRARIES

M.E. Sharpe, 80 Business Park Drive, Armonk, New York 10504 (800) 541-6563; *The Illustrated Book of World Rankings.*

United Nations Educational, Scientific and Cultural Organization (UNESCO), 7 Place de Fontenoy, F-75700 Paris, France (Telephone Number in U.S. (212) 963-5981); *Statistical Yearbook.*

MALAWI - LIFE EXPECTANCY

African Development Bank, 01 BP 1387, Abidjan 01, Cote d'Ivoire; *Selected Statistics on Regional Member Countries.*

Central Intelligence Agency, Washington, D.C. 20505 (703) 482-1100, www.cia.gov; *The World Factbook.*

Euromonitor International, Inc., 122 South Michigan Avenue, Suite 1200, Chicago, Illinois 60603 (800) 577-EURO; *The World Economic Factbook.*

Statistical Office of the United Nations, Publishing Service, New York, New York 10017 (800) 253-9646; *Human Development Report;* and *World Statistics Pocketbook.*

The World Bank, 1818 H Street, NW, Washington, D.C. 20433 (202) 477-1234; *The World Bank Atlas;* and *World Development Report.*

MALAWI - LITERACY RATE

Euromonitor International, Inc., 122 South Michigan Avenue, Suite 1200, Chicago, Illinois 60603 (800) 577-EURO; *World Marketing Data and Statistics.*

Statistical Office of the United Nations, Publishing Service, New York, New York 10017 (800) 253-9646; *Survey of Economic and Social Conditions in Africa.*

MALAWI - LIVESTOCK AND POULTRY

Euromonitor International, Inc., 122 South Michigan Avenue, Suite 1200, Chicago, Illinois 60603 (800) 577-EURO; *International Marketing Data and Statistics.*

Europa Publications Limited, 18 Bedford Square, London, WC1B 3JN, England; *The Europa World Year Book.*

Food and Agricultural Organization of the United Nations (FAO), Via delle Terme di Caracalla, 00100 Rome, Italy (Telephone Number in U.S. (202) 653-2400); *Production Yearbook;* and *The State of Food and Agriculture.*

M.E. Sharpe, 80 Business Park Drive, Armonk, New York 10504 (800) 541-6563; *The Illustrated Book of World Rankings.*

St. Martin's Press, Inc., 175 Fifth Avenue, New York, New York 10010 (800) 221-7945; *The Statesman's Year-Book.*

Statistical Office of the United Nations, Publishing Service, New York, New York 10017 (800) 253-9646; *Survey of Economic and Social Conditions in Africa.*

United Nations Conference on Trade and Development, Central Statistical Service, Palais des Nations, Geneva, Switzerland (Telephone in U.S. (800) 253-9646); *UNCTAD Commodity Yearbook.*

United Nations Economic Commission for Africa, Africa Hall, Post Office Box 3001, Addis Ababa, Ethiopia (Telephone Number in U.S. (800) 253-9646); *African Statistical Yearbook.*

MALAWI - LIVING LEVELS - See MALAWI - LIFE EXPECTANCY

MALAWI - MANUFACTURING

M.E. Sharpe, 80 Business Park Drive, Armonk, New York 10504 (800) 541-6563; *The Illustrated Book of World Rankings.*

Statistical Office of the United Nations, Publishing Service, New York, New York 10017 (800) 253-9646; *Statistical Yearbook;* and *Survey of Economic and Social Conditions in Africa.*

United Nations Economic Commission for Africa, Africa Hall, Post Office Box 3001, Addis Ababa, Ethiopia (Telephone Number in U.S. (800) 253-9646); *African Statistical Yearbook.*

The World Bank, 1818 H Street, NW, Washington, D.C. 20433 (202) 477-1234; *World Development Indicators.*

MALAWI - MARRIAGE RATES

M.E. Sharpe, 80 Business Park Drive, Armonk, New York 10504 (800) 541-6563; *The Illustrated Book of World Rankings.*

Statistical Office of the United Nations, Publishing Service, New York, New York 10017 (800) 253-9646; *Demographic Yearbook.*

MALAWI - MEAT PRODUCTION - See MALAWI - LIVESTOCK AND POULTRY

MALAWI - MERCHANT SHIPPING

Europa Publications Limited, 18 Bedford Square, London, WC1B 3JN, England; *The Europa World Year Book.*

St. Martin's Press, Inc., 175 Fifth Avenue, New York, New York 10010 (800) 221-7945; *The Statesman's Year-Book*

United Nations Economic Commission for Africa, Africa Hall, Post Office Box 3001, Addis Ababa, Ethiopia (Telephone Number in U.S. (800) 253-9646); *African Statistical Yearbook.*

MALAWI - MILITARY

Central Intelligence Agency, Washington, D.C. 20505 (703) 482-1100, www.cia.gov; *The World Factbook.*

Euromonitor International, Inc., 122 South Michigan Avenue, Suite 1200,

Chicago, Illinois 60603 (800) 577-EURO; *World Marketing Data and Statistics.*

The International Institute for Strategic Studies, 23 Tavistock Street, London WC2E 7NQ, England; *The Military Balance.*

International Monetary Fund, 700 Nineteenth Street, NW, Washington, D.C. 20431 (202) 623-7000; *Government Finance Statistics Yearbook.*

St. Martin's Press, Inc., 175 Fifth Avenue, New York, New York 10010 (800) 221-7945; *The Statesman's Year-Book.*

Statistical Office of the United Nations, Publishing Service, New York, New York 10017 (800) 253-9646; *Human Development Report.*

U.S. Arms Control and Disarmament Agency, 320 Twenty-first Street, NW, Washington, D.C. 20451 (202) 647-8677; *World Military Expenditures and Arms Transfers.*

MALAWI - MILK PRODUCTION - See MALAWI - DAIRY PRODUCTS

MALAWI - MINING AND MINERAL PRODUCTS

Europa Publications Limited, 18 Bedford Square, London, WC1B 3JN, England; *The Europa World Year Book.*

M.E. Sharpe, 80 Business Park Drive, Armonk, New York 10504 (800) 541-6563; *The Illustrated Book of World Rankings.*

St. Martin's Press, Inc., 175 Fifth Avenue, New York, New York 10010 (800) 221-7945; *The Statesman's Year-Book.*

Statistical Office of the United Nations, Publishing Service, New York, New York 10017 (800) 253-9646; *Statistical Yearbook.*

United Nations Conference on Trade and Development, Central Statistical Service, Palais des Nations, Geneva, Switzerland (Telephone in U.S. (800) 253-9646); *UNCTAD Commodity Yearbook.*

United Nations Economic Commission for Africa, Africa Hall, Post Office Box 3001, Addis Ababa, Ethiopia (Telephone Number in U.S. (800) 253-9646); *African Statistical Yearbook.*

MALAWI - MONEY EXCHANGE RATE - See MALAWI - EXCHANGE RATES

MALAWI - MONEY RESERVES

Euromonitor International, Inc., 122 South Michigan Avenue, Suite 1200, Chicago, Illinois 60603 (800) 577-EURO; *International Marketing Data and Statistics.*

MALAWI - MONEY SUPPLY

African Development Bank, 01 BP 1387, Abidjan 01, Cote d'Ivoire; *Selected Statistics on Regional Member Countries.*

Economist Intelligence Unit, 111 West 57th Street, New York, New York 10019 (800) 938-4685; *Malawi Country Report.*

Euromonitor International, Inc., 122 South Michigan Avenue, Suite 1200, Chicago, Illinois 60603 (800) 577-EURO; *International Marketing Data and Statistics.*

Europa Publications Limited, 18 Bedford Square, London, WC1B 3JN, England; *The Europa World Year Book.*

International Monetary Fund, 700 Nineteenth Street, NW, Washington, D.C. 20431 (202) 623-7000; *International Financial Statistics.*

Statistical Office of the United Nations, Publishing Service, New York, New York 10017 (800) 253-9646; *Statistical Yearbook.*

The World Bank, 1818 H Street, NW, Washington, D.C. 20433 (202) 477-1234; *World Development Indicators.*

MALAWI - MORTALITY

Central Intelligence Agency, Washington, D.C. 20505 (703) 482-1100, www.cia.gov; *The World Factbook.*

Euromonitor International, Inc., 122 South Michigan Avenue, Suite 1200, Chicago, Illinois 60603 (800) 577-EURO; *International Marketing Data and Statistics;* and *The World Economic Factbook.*

Europa Publications Limited, 18 Bedford Square, London, WC1B 3JN, England; *The Europa World Year Book.*

Statistical Office of the United Nations, Publishing Service, New York, New York 10017 (800) 253-9646; *Demographic Yearbook; Human Development Report; World Statistics Pocketbook; Statistical Yearbook;* and *Survey of Economic and Social Conditions in Africa.*

United Nations Children's Fund (UNICEF), 3 United Nations Plaza, New York, New York 10017 (800) 253-9646; *State of the World's Children.*

The World Bank, 1818 H Street, NW, Washington, D.C. 20433 (202) 477-1234; *The World Bank Atlas; World Development Report;* and *World Development Indicators.*

World Health Organization, Office of Publications, 20 Avenue Appia, CH-1211 Geneva 27, Switzerland (Telephone Number in U.S. (518) 436-9686); *World Health*

Statistics Annual.

MALAWI - MOTION PICTURES

Statistical Office of the United Nations, Publishing Service, New York, New York 10017 (800) 253-9646; *Statistical Yearbook.*

MALAWI - MOTOR VEHICLE TAXES - See MALAWI - TAXATION

MALAWI - MOTOR VEHICLES IN USE

Europa Publications Limited, 18 Bedford Square, London, WC1B 3JN, England; *The Europa World Year Book.*

International Road Federation, 2600 Virginia Avenue, N.W., Washington, D.C. 20037 (202) 338-4641; *World Road Statistics.*

Statistical Office of the United Nations, Publishing Service, New York, New York 10017 (800) 253-9646; *Statistical Yearbook;* and *Survey of Economic and Social Conditions in Africa.*

MALAWI - MUSEUMS

M.E. Sharpe, 80 Business Park Drive, Armonk, New York 10504 (800) 541-6563; *The Illustrated Book of World Rankings.*

United Nations Educational, Scientific and Cultural Organization (UNESCO), 7 Place de Fontenoy, F-75700 Paris, France (Telephone Number in U.S. (212) 963-5981); *Statistical Yearbook.*

MALAWI - NATALITY - See MALAWI - BIRTH RATES

MALAWI - NATIONAL ACCOUNTS

African Development Bank, 01 BP 1387, Abidjan 01, Cote d'Ivoire; *Selected Statistics on Regional Member Countries.*

Europa Publications Limited, 18 Bedford Square, London, WC1B 3JN, England; *The Europa World Year Book.*

International Monetary Fund, 700 Nineteenth Street, NW, Washington, D.C. 20431 (202) 623-7000; *International Financial Statistics.*

Statistical Office of the United Nations, Publishing Service, New York, New York 10017 (800) 253-9646; *National Account Statistics;* and *Statistical Yearbook.*

United Nations Economic Commission for Africa, Africa Hall, Post Office Box 3001, Addis Ababa, Ethiopia (Telephone Number in U.S. (800) 253-9646); *African Statistical Yearbook.*

MALAWI - NATIONAL INCOME

M.E. Sharpe, 80 Business Park Drive, Armonk, New York 10504 (800) 541-6563; *The Illustrated Book of World Rankings.*

Statistical Office of the United Nations, Publishing Service, New York, New York 10017 (800) 253-9646; *National Accounts Statistics;* and *Statistical Yearbook.*

MALAWI - NATIONAL PRODUCT

M.E. Sharpe, 80 Business Park Drive, Armonk, New York 10504 (800) 541-6563; *The Illustrated Book of World Rankings.*

Statistical Office of the United Nations, Publishing Service, New York, New York 10017 (800) 253-9646; *Statistical Yearbook.*

MALAWI - NATURAL GAS PRODUCTION - See MALAWI - MINING AND MINERAL PRODUCTS

MALAWI - NEWSPAPER PRODUCTION - See MALAWI - FORESTRY AND FORESTRY PRODUCTS

MALAWI - NEWSPRINT - See MALAWI - FORESTRY AND FOREST PRODUCTS

MALAWI - OCCUPATIONS - See MALAWI - LABOR

MALAWI - PAPER - See MALAWI - FORESTRY AND FOREST PRODUCTS

MALAWI - PATENTS, TRADEMARKS AND SERVICE MARKS

Statistical Office of the United Nations, Publishing Service, New York, New York 10017 (800) 253-9646; *Statistical Yearbook.*

World Intellectual Property Organization, 34 Chemin des Colombettes, CH-1211 Geneva 20, Switzerland; *Industrial Property Statistics.*

MALAWI - PEANUT PRODUCTION - See MALAWI - CROPS

MALAWI - PERIODICALS

United Nations Educational, Scientific and Cultural Organization (UNESCO), 7 Place de Fontenoy, F-75700 Paris, France (Telephone Number in U.S. (212) 963-5981); *Statistical Yearbook.*

MALAWI - PESTICIDE USE

Food and Agricultural Organization of the United Nations (FAO), Via delle Terme di Caracalla, 00100 Rome, Italy (Telephone Number in U.S. (202) 653-2400); *The State of Food and Agriculture.*

MALAWI - PETROLEUM INDUSTRY

Food and Agricultural Organization of

the United Nations (FAO), Via delle Terme di Caracalla, 00100 Rome, Italy (Telephone Number in U.S. (202) 653-2400); *The State of Food and Agriculture.*

M.E. Sharpe, 80 Business Park Drive, Armonk, New York 10504 (800) 541-6563; *The Illustrated Book of World Rankings.*

United Nations Conference on Trade and Development, Central Statistical Service, Palais des Nations, Geneva, Switzerland (Telephone in U.S. (800) 253-9646); *UNCTAD Commodity Yearbook.*

MALAWI - PIGS - See MALAWI - LIVESTOCK AND POULTRY

MALAWI - POPULATION

African Development Bank, 01 BP 1387, Abidjan 01, Cote d'Ivoire; *Selected Statistics on Regional Member Countries.*

Central Intelligence Agency, Washington, D.C. 20505 (703) 482-1100, www.cia.gov; *The World Factbook.*

The Economist Intelligence Unit, 111 West 57th Street, New York, New York 10019 (800) 938-4685; *Malawi Country Report;* and *The World Market Atlas.*

Euromonitor International, Inc., 122 South Michigan Avenue, Suite 1200, Chicago, Illinois 60603 (800) 577-EURO; *International Marketing Data and Statistics;* and *The World Economic Factbook.*

Europa Publications Limited, 18 Bedford Square, London, WC1B 3JN, England; *The Europa World Year Book.*

Food and Agricultural Organization of the United Nations (FAO), Via delle Terme di Caracalla, 00100 Rome, Italy (Telephone Number in U.S. (202) 653-2400); *Production Yearbook.*

International Labour Office, I.L.O. Publications, 1828 L Street, N.W., Suite 801, Washington, D.C. 20036 (301) 638-3152; *Yearbook of Labour Statistics.*

M.E. Sharpe, 80 Business Park Drive, Armonk, New York 10504 (800) 541-6563; *The Illustrated Book of World Rankings.*

St. Martin's Press, Inc., 175 Fifth Avenue, New York, New York 10010 (800) 221-7945; *The Statesman's Year-Book.*

Statistical Office of the United Nations, Publishing Service, New York, New York 10017 (800) 253-9646; *Demographic Yearbook; Human Development Report; Statistical Yearbook; World Statistics Pocketbook;* and *Survey of Economic and Social Conditions in Africa.*

U.S. Arms Control and Disarmament

Agency, 320 Twenty-first Street, NW, Washington, D.C. 20451 (202) 647-8677; *World Military Expenditures and Arms Transfers.*

The World Bank, 1818 H Street, NW, Washington, D.C. 20433 (202) 477-1234; *The World Bank Atlas;* and *World Development Report.*

World Health Organization, Office of Publications, 20 Avenue Appia, CH-1211 Geneva 27, Switzerland (Telephone Number in U.S. (518) 436-9686); *World Health Statistics Annual.*

MALAWI - POST OFFICES

M.E. Sharpe, 80 Business Park Drive, Armonk, New York 10504 (800) 541-6563; *The Illustrated Book of World Rankings.*

MALAWI - POTATO PRODUCTION - See MALAWI - CROPS

MALAWI - POWER PRODUCTION INDUSTRY - ESTABLISHMENTS, PAYROLLS, VALUE ADDED, ETC.

Statistical Office of the United Nations, Publishing Service, New York, New York 10017 (800) 253-9646; *Statistical Yearbook.*

MALAWI - PRICES

Food and Agricultural Organization of the United Nations (FAO), Via delle Terme di Caracalla, 00100 Rome, Italy (Telephone Number in U.S. (202) 653-2400); *Production Yearbook;* and *The State of Food and Agriculture.*

International Labour Office, I.L.O. Publications, 1828 L Street, N.W., Suite 801, Washington, D.C. 20036 (301) 638-3152; *Yearbook of Labour Statistics.*

M.E. Sharpe, 80 Business Park Drive, Armonk, New York 10504 (800) 541-6563; *The Illustrated Book of World Rankings.*

United Nations Economic Commission for Africa, Africa Hall, Post Office Box 3001, Addis Ababa, Ethiopia (Telephone Number in U.S. (800) 253-9646); *African Statistical Yearbook.*

MALAWI - PRINTING AND WRITING PAPER CONSUMPTION - See MALAWI - FORESTRY AND FOREST PRODUCTS

MALAWI - PRODUCTION

M.E. Sharpe, 80 Business Park Drive, Armonk, New York 10504 (800) 541-6563; *The Illustrated Book of World Rankings.*

MALAWI - PRODUCTIVITY

Euromonitor International, Inc., 122 South Michigan Avenue, Suite 1200,

Chicago, Illinois 60603 (800) 577-EURO; *International Marketing Data and Statistics.*

MALAWI - PROPERTY TAXES

International Monetary Fund, 700 Nineteenth Street, NW, Washington, D.C. 20431 (202) 623-7000; *Government Finance Statistics Yearbook.*

MALAWI - PUBLIC FINANCE - See MALAWI - FINANCE

MALAWI - RADIO BROADCASTING - See MALAWI - BROADCASTING

MALAWI - RADIO RECEIVERS

St. Martin's Press, Inc., 175 Fifth Avenue, New York, New York 10010 (800) 221-7945; *The Statesman's Year-Book.*

Statistical Office of the United Nations, Publishing Service, New York, New York 10017 (800) 253-9646; *Statistical Yearbook.*

MALAWI - RAILWAYS

Europa Publications Limited, 18 Bedford Square, London, WC1B 3JN, England; *The Europa World Year Book.*

Jane's Information Group, Sentinel House, 163 Brighton Road, Coulsdon, Surrey CR5 2NH, England (Telephone Number in U.S. (703) 683-3700); *Jane's World Railways.*

St. Martin's Press, Inc., 175 Fifth Avenue, New York, New York 10010 (800) 221-7945; *The Statesman's Year-Book.*

Statistical Office of the United Nations, Publishing Service, New York, New York 10017 (800) 253-9646; *Statistical Yearbook;* and *Survey of Economic and Social Conditions in Africa.*

United Nations Economic Commission for Africa, Africa Hall, Post Office Box 3001, Addis Ababa, Ethiopia (Telephone Number in U.S. (800) 253-9646); *African Statistical Yearbook.*

MALAWI - RELIGION

Central Intelligence Agency, Washington, D.C. 20505 (703) 482-1100, www.cia.gov; *The World Factbook.*

M.E. Sharpe, 80 Business Park Drive, Armonk, New York 10504 (800) 541-6563; *The Illustrated Book of World Rankings.*

St. Martin's Press, Inc., 175 Fifth Avenue, New York, New York 10010 (800) 221-7945; *The Statesman's Year-Book.*

MALAWI - RETAIL TRADE

Euromonitor International, Inc., 122 South Michigan Avenue, Suite 1200, Chicago, Illinois 60603 (800) 577-EURO; *World Marketing Data and Statistics.*

Statistical Office of the United Nations, Publishing Service, New York, New York 10017 (800) 253-9646; *Statistical Yearbook.*

MALAWI - RICE PRODUCTION - See MALAWI - CROPS

MALAWI - ROOT AND TUBER PRODUCTION - See MALAWI - CROPS

MALAWI - ROUNDWOOD PRODUCTION - See MALAWI - FORESTRY AND FOREST PRODUCTS

MALAWI - RUBBER PRODUCTION AND CONSUMPTION

M.E. Sharpe, 80 Business Park Drive, Armonk, New York 10504 (800) 541-6563; *The Illustrated Book of World Rankings.*

MALAWI - SAWNWOOD PRODUCTION - See FORESTRY AND FOREST PRODUCTS

MALAWI - SCIENTISTS, TECHNICIANS AND ENGINEERS

United Nations Educational, Scientific and Cultural Organization (UNESCO), 7 Place de Fontenoy, F-75700 Paris, France (Telephone Number in U.S. (212) 963-5981); *Statistical Yearbook.*

MALAWI - SENIOR CITIZENS

M.E. Sharpe, 80 Business Park Drive, Armonk, New York 10504 (800) 541-6563; *The Illustrated Book of World Rankings.*

MALAWI - SHEEP - See MALAWI - LIVESTOCK AND POULTRY

MALAWI - SILVER PRODUCTION AND CONSUMPTION - See MALAWI - MINING AND MINERAL PRODUCTS

MALAWI - SISAL PRODUCTION - See MALAWI - CROPS

MALAWI - SOCIAL DATA

African Development Bank, 01 BP 1387, Abidjan 01, Cote d'Ivoire; *Selected Statistics on Regional Member Countries.*

M.E. Sharpe, 80 Business Park Drive, Armonk, New York 10504 (800) 541-6563; *The Illustrated Book of World Rankings.*

Statistical Office of the United Nations, Publishing Service, New York, New York 10017 (800) 253-9646; *World Statistics Pocketbook.*

MALAWI - SOCIAL SECURITY

International Monetary Fund, 700 Nineteenth Street, NW, Washington, D.C. 20431 (202) 623-7000; *Government Finance Statistics Yearbook.*

Statistical Office of the United Nations, Publishing Service, New York, New York 10017 (800) 253-9646; *National Accounts Statistics.*

MALAWI - STAMP TAXES AND DUTIES - See MALAWI - TAXATION

MALAWI - STATE BUDGET

Euromonitor International, Inc., 122 South Michigan Avenue, Suite 1200, Chicago, Illinois 60603 (800) 577-EURO; *International Marketing Data and Statistics.*

MALAWI - STEEL - See MALAWI - MINING AND MINERAL PRODUCTS

MALAWI - STOCKS - COMMODITY - MARKET PRICE - INDEX

Food and Agricultural Organization of the United Nations (FAO), Via delle Terme di Caracalla, 00100 Rome, Italy (Telephone Number in U.S. (202) 653-2400); *The State of Food and Agriculture.*

MALAWI - SUGAR - See MALAWI - CROPS

MALAWI - TAXATION

Europa Publications Limited, 18 Bedford Square, London, WC1B 3JN, England; *The Europa World Year Book.*

International Monetary Fund, 700 Nineteenth Street, NW, Washington, D.C. 20431 (202) 623-7000; *Government Finance Statistics.*

International Road Federation, 2600 Virginia Avenue, N.W., Washington, D.C. 20037 (202) 338-4641; *World Road Statistics.*

The World Bank, 1818 H Street, NW, Washington, D.C. 20433 (202) 477-1234; *World Development Indicators.*

MALAWI - TEA - See MALAWI - CROPS

MALAWI - TELEPHONES IN USE

American Telephone and Telegraph Company, 26 Parsippany Road, Whippany, New Jersey 07981 (800) 222-0300; *The World's Telephones.*

Central Intelligence Agency, Washington, D.C. 20505 (703) 482-1100, www.cia.gov; *The World Factbook.*

Europa Publications Limited, 18 Bedford Square, London, WC1B 3JN, England; *The Europa World Year Book.*

St. Martin's Press, Inc., 175 Fifth Avenue, New York, New York 10010 (800) 221-7945; *The Statesman's Year-Book.*

Statistical Office of the United Nations, Publishing Service, New York, New York 10017 (800) 253-9646; *World Statistics Pocketbook.*

MALAWI - TELEVISION BROADCASTING - See MALAWI - BROADCASTING

MALAWI - TEXTILE INDUSTRY

M.E. Sharpe, 80 Business Park Drive, Armonk, New York 10504 (800) 541-6563; *The Illustrated Book of World Rankings.*

United Nations Conference on Trade and Development, Central Statistical Service, Palais des Nations, Geneva, Switzerland (Telephone in U.S. (800) 253-9646); *UNCTAD Commodity Yearbook.*

MALAWI - TOBACCO EXPORTS

International Monetary Fund, 700 Nineteenth Street, NW, Washington, D.C. 20431 (202) 623-7000; *International Financial Statistics.*

M.E. Sharpe, 80 Business Park Drive, Armonk, New York 10504 (800) 541-6563; *The Illustrated Book of World Rankings.*

Statistical Office of the United Nations, Publishing Service, New York, New York 10017 (800) 253-9646; *Statistical Yearbook.*

MALAWI - TOBACCO PRODUCTION

M.E. Sharpe, 80 Business Park Drive, Armonk, New York 10504 (800) 541-6563; *The Illustrated Book of World Rankings.*

Statistical Office of the United Nations, Publishing Service, New York, New York 10017 (800) 253-9646; *Statistical Yearbook.*

MALAWI - TOURISM

Euromonitor International, Inc., 122 South Michigan Avenue, Suite 1200, Chicago, Illinois 60603 (800) 577-EURO; *The World Economic Factbook;* and *World Marketing Data and Statistics.*

Europa Publications Limited, 18 Bedford Square, London, WC1B 3JN, England; *The Europa World Year Book.*

M.E. Sharpe, 80 Business Park Drive, Armonk, New York 10504 (800) 541-6563; *The Illustrated Book of World Rankings.*

St. Martin's Press, Inc., 175 Fifth Avenue, New York, New York 10010 (800) 221-7945; *The Statesman's Year-Book.*

Statistical Office of the United Nations, Publishing Service, New York, New York

10017 (800) 253-9646; *Statistical Yearbook.*

United Nations Economic Commission for Africa, Africa Hall, Post Office Box 3001, Addis Ababa, Ethiopia (Telephone Number in U.S. (800) 253-9646); *African Statistical Yearbook.*

World Tourism Organization, Calle Capitan Haya 42, E-28020 Madrid, Spain; *Yearbook of Tourism Statistics.*

MALAWI - TRACTORS IN USE

Statistical Office of the United Nations, Publishing Service, New York, New York 10017 (800) 253-9646; *Statistical Yearbook.*

MALAWI - TRADE - See MALAWI - FOREIGN TRADE

MALAWI - TRADEMARKS AND SERVICE MARKS - See MALAWI - PATENTS, TRADEMARKS AND SERVICE MARKS

MALAWI - TRANSPORTATION AND COMMUNICATIONS

Central Intelligence Agency, Washington, D.C. 20505 (703) 482-1100, www.cia.gov; *The World Factbook.*

Euromonitor International, Inc., 122 South Michigan Avenue, Suite 1200, Chicago, Illinois 60603 (800) 577-EURO; *International Marketing Data and Statistics;* and *World Marketing Data and Statistics.*

Europa Publications Limited, 18 Bedford Square, London, WC1B 3JN, England; *The Europa World Year Book.*

M.E. Sharpe, 80 Business Park Drive, Armonk, New York 10504 (800) 541-6563; *The Illustrated Book of World Rankings.*

St. Martin's Press, Inc., 175 Fifth Avenue, New York, New York 10010 (800) 221-7945; *The Statesman's Year-Book.*

Statistical Office of the United Nations, Publishing Service, New York, New York 10017 (800) 253-9646; *Human Development Report.*

United Nations Economic Commission for Africa, Africa Hall, Post Office Box 3001, Addis Ababa, Ethiopia (Telephone Number in U.S. (800) 253-9646); *African Statistical Yearbook.*

MALAWI - UNEMPLOYMENT

Central Intelligence Agency, Washington, D.C. 20505 (703) 482-1100, www.cia.gov; *The World Factbook.*

Euromonitor International, Inc., 122 South Michigan Avenue, Suite 1200, Chicago, Illinois 60603 (800) 577-EURO;

International Marketing Data and Statistics.

International Labour Office, I.L.O. Publications, 1828 L Street, N.W., Suite 801, Washington, D.C. 20036 (301) 638-3152; *Yearbook of Labour Statistics.*

MALAWI - VITAL STATISTICS

Euromonitor International, Inc., 122 South Michigan Avenue, Suite 1200, Chicago, Illinois 60603 (800) 577-EURO; *International Marketing Data and Statistics.*

Statistical Office of the United Nations, Publishing Service, New York, New York 10017 (800) 253-9646; *Statistical Yearbook.*

World Health Organization, Office of Publications, 20 Avenue Appia, CH-1211 Geneva 27, Switzerland (Telephone Number in U.S. (518) 436-9686); *World Health Statistics Annual.*

MALAWI - WAGES

International Labour Office, I.L.O. Publications, 1828 L Street, N.W., Suite 801, Washington, D.C. 20036 (301) 638-3152; *Yearbook of Labour Statistics.*

Statistical Office of the United Nations, Publishing Service, New York, New York 10017 (800) 253-9646; *Statistical Yearbook.*

MALAWI - WEATHER - See MALAWI - CLIMATE

MALAWI - WELFARE EXPENDITURES

International Monetary Fund, 700 Nineteenth Street, NW, Washington, D.C. 20431 (202) 623-7000; *Government Finance Statistics Yearbook.*

MALAWI - WHEAT PRODUCTION

M.E. Sharpe, 80 Business Park Drive, Armonk, New York 10504 (800) 541-6563; *The Illustrated Book of World Rankings.*

Statistical Office of the United Nations, Publishing Service, New York, New York 10017 (800) 253-9646; *Statistical Yearbook.*

MALAWI - WHOLESALE TRADE

Statistical Office of the United Nations, Publishing Service, New York, New York 10017 (800) 253-9646; *Statistical Yearbook.*

MALAWI - WINE PRODUCTION - See MALAWI - BEVERAGES

MALAWI - WOOL PRODUCTION - See MALAWI - TEXTILE INDUSTRY

Malaysia - National

Statistical Office

Department of Statistics, Jalan Cenderasari, Kuala Lumpur, Malaysia.

Malaysia - Primary Statistics Source

Department of Statistics, Jalan Cenderasari, Kuala Lumpur, Malaysia; *Buku Tahunan Perangkaan* (Yearbook of Statistics).

MALAYSIA - AGRICULTURE

Asian Development Bank, Post Office Box 789, 1099 Manila, Philippines; *Key Indicators of Developing Asian and Pacific Countries.*

Euromonitor International, Inc., 122 South Michigan Avenue, Suite 1200, Chicago, Illinois 60603 (800) 577-EURO; *World Marketing Data and Statistics.*

Europa Publications Limited, 18 Bedford Square, London, WC1B 3JN, England; *The Europa World Year Book.*

Food and Agricultural Organization of the United Nations (FAO), Via delle Terme di Caracalla, 00100 Rome, Italy (Telephone Number in U.S. (202) 653-2400); *Production Yearbook; The State of Food and Agriculture;* and *Trade Yearbook.*

M.E. Sharpe, 80 Business Park Drive, Armonk, New York 10504 (800) 541-6563; *The Illustrated Book of World Rankings.*

St. Martin's Press, Inc., 175 Fifth Avenue, New York, New York 10010 (800) 221-7945; *The Statesman's Year-Book.*

Statistical Office of the United Nations, Publishing Service, New York, New York 10017 (800) 253-9646; *Asia-Pacific in Figures; Statistical Yearbook;* and *Statistical Yearbook for Asia and the Pacific.*

United Nations Conference on Trade and Development, Central Statistical Service, Palais des Nations, Geneva, Switzerland (Telephone in U.S. (800) 253-9646); *UNCTAD Commodity Yearbook.*

The World Bank, 1818 H Street, NW, Washington, D.C. 20433 (202) 477-1234; *World Development Indicators.*

MALAYSIA - AIRLINE SERVICE

The Economist Intelligence Unit (Asia) Limited, 10th Floor, Luk Kwok Centre, 72 Gloucester Road, Wanchai, Hong Kong (Phone Number in U.S. (800) 938-4685); *Asian Market Atlas.*

Europa Publications Limited, 18

Bedford Square, London, WC1B 3JN, England; *The Europa World Year Book*.

International Civil Aviation Organization, 999 University Street, Montreal, Quebec, Canada H3C 5H7 (514) 954-8219; *Civil Aviation Statistics of the World*.

M.E. Sharpe, 80 Business Park Drive, Armonk, New York 10504 (800) 541-6563; *The Illustrated Book of World Rankings*.

St. Martin's Press, Inc., 175 Fifth Avenue, New York, New York 10010 (800) 221-7945; *The Statesman's Year-Book*.

Statistical Office of the United Nations, Publishing Service, New York, New York 10017 (800) 253-9646; *Statistical Yearbook*.

MALAYSIA - AIRPORTS

Central Intelligence Agency, Washington, D.C. 20505 (703) 482-1100, www.cia.gov; *The World Factbook*.

MALAYSIA - ALUMINUM PRODUCTION AND CONSUMPTION - See MALAYSIA - MINING AND MINERAL PRODUCTS

MALAYSIA - ANIMAL HEALTH

Food and Agricultural Organization of the United Nations (FAO), Via delle Terme di Caracalla, 00100 Rome, Italy (Telephone Number in U.S. (202) 653-2400); *Animal Health Yearbook*.

MALAYSIA - ANTIMONY AND ANTIMONY ORE CONSUMPTION AND PRODUCTION - See MALAYSIA - MINING AND MINERAL PRODUCTS

MALAYSIA - AREA AND DENSITY OF POPULATION

Central Intelligence Agency, Washington, D.C. 20505 (703) 482-1100, www.cia.gov; *The World Factbook*.

Euromonitor International, Inc., 122 South Michigan Avenue, Suite 1200, Chicago, Illinois 60603 (800) 577-EURO; *International Marketing Data and Statistics*; and *The World Economic Factbook*.

Europa Publications Limited, 18 Bedford Square, London, WC1B 3JN, England; *The Europa World Year Book*.

Food and Agricultural Organization of the United Nations (FAO), Via delle Terme di Caracalla, 00100 Rome, Italy (Telephone Number in U.S. (202) 653-2400); *The State of Food and Agriculture*.

M.E. Sharpe, 80 Business Park Drive, Armonk, New York 10504 (800) 541-6563; *The Illustrated Book of World Rankings*.

St. Martin's Press, Inc., 175 Fifth Avenue,

New York, New York 10010 (800) 221-7945; *The Statesman's Year-Book*.

Statistical Office of the United Nations, Publishing Service, New York, New York 10017 (800) 253-9646; *Statistical Yearbook*.

The World Bank, 1818 H Street, NW, Washington, D.C. 20433 (202) 477-1234; *World Development Report*.

MALAYSIA - ARMS EXPORTS AND IMPORTS - See MALAYSIA - MILITARY

MALAYSIA - ARSENIC PRODUCTION AND CONSUMPTION - See MALAYSIA - MINING AND MINERAL PRODUCTS

MALAYSIA - BALANCE OF PAYMENTS

The Economist Intelligence Unit, 111 West 57th Street, New York, New York 10019 (800) 938-4685; *The World Market Atlas*.

Europa Publications Limited, 18 Bedford Square, London, WC1B 3JN, England; *The Europa World Year Book*.

International Monetary Fund, 700 Nineteenth Street, NW, Washington, D.C. 20431 (202) 623-7000; *Balance of Payments Yearbook*; and *International Financial Statistics*.

United Nations Conference on Trade and Development (UNCTAD), New York, New York 10017 (800) 253-9646; *Handbook of International Trade and Development Statistics*.

The World Bank, 1818 H Street, NW, Washington, D.C. 20433 (202) 477-1234; *World Development Report*; and *World Development Indicators*.

MALAYSIA - BANKING

Asian Development Bank, Post Office Box 789, 1099 Manila, Philippines; *Key Indicators of Developing Asian and Pacific Countries*.

Euromonitor International, Inc., 122 South Michigan Avenue, Suite 1200, Chicago, Illinois 60603 (800) 577-EURO; *World Marketing Data and Statistics*.

Europa Publications Limited, 18 Bedford Square, London, WC1B 3JN, England; *The Europa World Year Book*.

International Monetary Fund, 700 Nineteenth Street, NW, Washington, D.C. 20431 (202) 623-7000; *International Financial Statistics*.

M.E. Sharpe, 80 Business Park Drive, Armonk, New York 10504 (800) 541-6563; *The Illustrated Book of World Rankings*.

St. Martin's Press, Inc., 175 Fifth Avenue, New York, New York 10010 (800) 221-7945; *The Statesman's Year-Book*.

MALAYSIA - BARLEY PRODUCTION - See MALAYSIA - CROPS

MALAYSIA - BAUXITE PRODUCTION AND CONSUMPTION - See MALAYSIA - MINING AND MINERAL PRODUCTS

MALAYSIA - BEER PRODUCTION - See MALAYSIA - BEVERAGES

MALAYSIA - BEVERAGES

M.E. Sharpe, 80 Business Park Drive, Armonk, New York 10504 (800) 541-6563; *The Illustrated Book of World Rankings*.

MALAYSIA - BIRTH RATES

Central Intelligence Agency, Washington, D.C. 20505 (703) 482-1100, www.cia.gov; *The World Factbook*.

The Economist Intelligence Unit (Asia) Limited, 10th Floor, Luk Kwok Centre, 72 Gloucester Road, Wanchai, Hong Kong (Phone Number in U.S. (800) 938-4685); *Asian Market Atlas*.

Euromonitor International, Inc., 122 South Michigan Avenue, Suite 1200, Chicago, Illinois 60603 (800) 577-EURO; *International Marketing Data and Statistics*; and *The World Economic Factbook*.

Europa Publications Limited, 18 Bedford Square, London, WC1B 3JN, England; *The Europa World Year Book*.

M.E. Sharpe, 80 Business Park Drive, Armonk, New York 10504 (800) 541-6563; *The Illustrated Book of World Rankings*.

St. Martin's Press, Inc., 175 Fifth Avenue, New York, New York 10010 (800) 221-7945; *The Statesman's Year-Book*.

Statistical Office of the United Nations, Publishing Service, New York, New York 10017 (800) 253-9646; *Asia-Pacific in Figures*; *Demographic Yearbook*; and *Statistical Yearbook*.

The World Bank, 1818 H Street, NW, Washington, D.C. 20433 (202) 477-1234; *World Development Indicators*.

World Health Organization, Office of Publications, 20 Avenue Appia, CH-1211 Geneva 27, Switzerland (Telephone Number in U.S. (518) 436-9686); *World Health Statistics Annual*.

MALAYSIA - BISMUTH PRODUCTION AND CONSUMPTION - See MALAYSIA - MINING AND MINERAL PRODUCTS

MALAYSIA - BONDS

Asian Development Bank, Post Office Box 789, 1099 Manila, Philippines; *Key Indicators of Developing Asian and Pacific Countries.*

International Monetary Fund, 700 Nineteenth Street, NW, Washington, D.C. 20431 (202) 623-7000; *Government Finance Statistics Yearbook.*

MALAYSIA - BOOK PRODUCTION

Europa Publications Limited, 18 Bedford Square, London, WC1B 3JN, England; *The Europa World Year Book.*

United Nations Educational, Scientific and Cultural Organization (UNESCO), 7 Place de Fontenoy, F-75700 Paris, France (Telephone Number in U.S. (212) 963-5981); *Statistical Yearbook.*

MALAYSIA - BROADCASTING

Billboard Limited, Post Office Box 9027, 1006 AA Amsterdam, The Netherlands (Telephone Number in U.S. (212) 764-7300); *World Radio TV Handbook.*

Central Intelligence Agency, Washington, D.C. 20505 (703) 482-1100, www.cia.gov; *The World Factbook.*

The Economist Intelligence Unit (Asia) Limited, 10th Floor, Luk Kwok Centre, 72 Gloucester Road, Wanchai, Hong Kong (Phone Number in U.S. (800) 938-4685); *Asian Market Atlas.*

Euromonitor International, Inc., 122 South Michigan Avenue, Suite 1200, Chicago, Illinois 60603 (800) 577-EURO; *World Marketing Data and Statistics.*

M.E. Sharpe, 80 Business Park Drive, Armonk, New York 10504 (800) 541-6563; *The Illustrated Book of World Rankings.*

St. Martin's Press, Inc., 175 Fifth Avenue, New York, New York 10010 (800) 221-7945; *The Statesman's Year-Book.*

United Nations Educational, Scientific and Cultural Organization (UNESCO), 7 Place de Fontenoy, F-75700 Paris, France (Telephone Number in U.S. (212) 963-5981); *Statistical Yearbook.*

MALAYSIA - BUDGET

Central Intelligence Agency, Washington, D.C. 20505 (703) 482-1100, www.cia.gov; *The World Factbook.*

MALAYSIA - BUSINESS AND PROFESSIONAL LICENSES

International Monetary Fund, 700 Nineteenth Street, NW, Washington, D.C. 20431 (202) 623-7000; *Government Finance Statistics Yearbook.*

MALAYSIA - CADMIUM PRODUCTION AND CONSUMPTION - See - MALAYSIA -MINING AND MINERAL PRODUCTS

MALAYSIA - CALORIE SUPPLY

Asian Development Bank, Post Office Box 789, 1099 Manila, Philippines; *Key Indicators of Developing Asian and Pacific Countries.*

Food and Agricultural Organization of the United Nations (FAO), Via delle Terme di Caracalla, 00100 Rome, Italy (Telephone Number in U.S. (202) 653-2400); *The State of Food and Agriculture.*

MALAYSIA - CAPITAL INVESTMENT

Asian Development Bank, Post Office Box 789, 1099 Manila, Philippines; *Key Indicators of Developing Asian and Pacific Countries.*

MALAYSIA - CAPITAL REVENUE

Asian Development Bank, Post Office Box 789, 1099 Manila, Philippines; *Key Indicators of Developing Asian and Pacific Countries.*

International Monetary Fund, 700 Nineteenth Street, NW, Washington, D.C. 20431 (202) 623-7000; *Government Finance Statistics Yearbook.*

MALAYSIA - CASHEW NUT PRODUCTION - See MALAYSIA - CROPS

MALAYSIA - CATTLE - See MALAYSIA - LIVESTOCK AND POULTRY

MALAYSIA - CEMENT PRODUCTION - See MALAYSIA - MINING AND MINERAL PRODUCTS

MALAYSIA - CHICKENS - See MALAYSIA - LIVESTOCK AND POULTRY

MALAYSIA - CHROMITE PRODUCTION AND CONSUMPTION - See MALAYSIA - MINING AND MINERAL PRODUCTS

MALAYSIA - CHROMIUM ORE PRODUCTION AND CONSUMPTION -See MALAYSIA - MINING AND MINERAL PRODUCTS

MALAYSIA - CIGAR AND CIGARETTE PRODUCTION - See MALAYSIA - TOBACCO PRODUCTION

MALAYSIA - CLIMATE

M.E. Sharpe, 80 Business Park Drive, Armonk, New York 10504 (800) 541-6563; *The Illustrated Book of World Rankings.*

St. Martin's Press, Inc., 175 Fifth Avenue, New York, New York 10010 (800) 221-7945; *The Statesman's Year-Book.*

MALAYSIA - COAL PRODUCTION - See MALAYSIA - MINING AND MINERAL PRODUCTS

MALAYSIA - COBALT PRODUCTION AND CONSUMPTION - See MALAYSIA - MINING AND MINERAL PRODUCTS

MALAYSIA - COCOA PRODUCTION

Statistical Office of the United Nations, Publishing Service, New York, New York 10017 (800) 253-9646; *Statistical Yearbook.*

MALAYSIA - COFFEE PRODUCTION AND CONSUMPTION - See MALAYSIA - CROPS

MALAYSIA - COKE AND COKE OVEN ORE PRODUCTION AND CONSUMPTION - See MALAYSIA - MINING AND MINERAL PRODUCTS

MALAYSIA - COMMERCE

St. Martin's Press, Inc., 175 Fifth Avenue, New York, New York 10010 (800) 221-7945; *The Statesman's Year-Book.*

MALAYSIA - COMMUNICATIONS - See MALAYSIA - TRANSPORTATION AND COMMUNICATIONS

MALAYSIA - CONSTRUCTION INDUSTRY

M.E. Sharpe, 80 Business Park Drive, Armonk, New York 10504 (800) 541-6563; *The Illustrated Book of World Rankings.*

Statistical Office of the United Nations, Publishing Service, New York, New York 10017 (800) 253-9646; *Statistical Yearbook.*

MALAYSIA - CONSUMER PRICE INDEX

Asian Development Bank, Post Office Box 789, 1099 Manila, Philippines; *Key Indicators of Developing Asian and Pacific Countries.*

Europa Publications Limited, 18 Bedford Square, London, WC1B 3JN, England; *The Europa World Year Book.*

Statistical Office of the United Nations, Publishing Service, New York, New York 10017 (800) 253-9646; *Statistical Yearbook.*

MALAYSIA - CONSUMER PRICES

Euromonitor International, Inc., 122 South Michigan Avenue, Suite 1200, Chicago, Illinois 60603 (800) 577-EURO; *World Marketing Data and Statistics.*

International Labour Office, I.L.O. Publications, 1828 L Street, N.W., Suite 801, Washington, D.C. 20036 (301) 638-3152; *Yearbook of Labour Statistics.*

International Monetary Fund, 700

Nineteenth Street, NW, Washington, D.C. 20431 (202) 623-7000; *International Financial Statistics.*

MALAYSIA - CONSUMPTION

International Rubber Study Group, York House, Eighth Floor, Empire Way, Wembley, London HA9 0PA, England; *Rubber Statistical Bulletin.*

The World Bank, 1818 H Street, NW, Washington, D.C. 20433 (202) 477-1234; *World Development Report.*

MALAYSIA - COPPER AND COPPER ORE PRODUCTION AND CONSUMPTION - See MALAYSIA - MINING AND MINERAL PRODUCTS

MALAYSIA - CORN PRODUCTION - See MALAYSIA - CROPS

MALAYSIA - CORPORATE TAXES - See MALAYSIA - TAXATION

MALAYSIA - COTTON PRODUCTION - See MALAYSIA - CROPS

MALAYSIA - CRIME

International Criminal Police Organization (INTERPOL), 26 rue Armengaud, 92210 Saint Cloud, France; *International Crime Statistics.*

Yale University Press, Yale Station, New Haven, Connecticut 06520 (800) 987-7323; *Violence and Crime in Cross-National Perspective.*

MALAYSIA - CROPS

Asian Development Bank, Post Office Box 789, 1099 Manila, Philippines; *Key Indicators of Developing Asian and Pacific Countries.*

Europa Publications Limited, 18 Bedford Square, London, WC1B 3JN, England; *The Europa World Year Book.*

Food and Agricultural Organization of the United Nations (FAO), Via delle Terme di Caracalla, 00100 Rome, Italy (Telephone Number in U.S. (202) 653-2400); *Production Yearbook;* and *The State of Food and Agriculture.*

International Monetary Fund, 700 Nineteenth Street, NW, Washington, D.C. 20431 (202) 623-7000; *International Financial Statistics.*

M.E. Sharpe, 80 Business Park Drive, Armonk, New York 10504 (800) 541-6563; *The Illustrated Book of World Rankings.*

St. Martin's Press, Inc., 175 Fifth Avenue, New York, New York 10010 (800) 221-7945; *The Statesman's Year-Book.*

Statistical Office of the United Nations, Publishing Service, New York, New York 10017 (800) 253-9646; *Statistical Yearbook.*

United Nations Conference on Trade and Development, Central Statistical Service, Palais des Nations, Geneva, Switzerland (Telephone in U.S. (800) 253-9646); *UNCTAD Commodity Yearbook.*

MALAYSIA - CUSTOMS DUTIES

International Monetary Fund, 700 Nineteenth Street, NW, Washington, D.C. 20431 (202) 623-7000; *Government Finance Statistics Yearbook.*

St. Martin's Press, Inc., 175 Fifth Avenue, New York, New York 10010 (800) 221-7945; *The Statesman's Year-Book.*

MALAYSIA - DAIRY PRODUCTS

Europa Publications Limited, 18 Bedford Square, London, WC1B 3JN, England; *The Europa World Year Book.*

Food and Agricultural Organization of the United Nations (FAO), Via delle Terme di Caracalla, 00100 Rome, Italy (Telephone Number in U.S. (202) 653-2400); *Production Yearbook;* and *The State of Food and Agriculture.*

M.E. Sharpe, 80 Business Park Drive, Armonk, New York 10504 (800) 541-6563; *The Illustrated Book of World Rankings.*

St. Martin's Press, Inc., 175 Fifth Avenue, New York, New York 10010 (800) 221-7945; *The Statesman's Year-Book.*

Statistical Office of the United Nations, Publishing Service, New York, New York 10017 (800) 253-9646; *Statistical Yearbook.*

MALAYSIA - DEATH RATES - See MALAYSIA - MORTALITY

MALAYSIA - DEFENSE EXPENDITURES - See MALAYSIA - MILITARY

MALAYSIA - DEMOGRAPHY

The Economist Intelligence Unit, 111 West 57th Street, New York, New York 10019 (800) 938-4685; *The World Market Atlas.*

The Economist Intelligence Unit (Asia) Limited, 10th Floor, Luk Kwok Centre, 72 Gloucester Road, Wanchai, Hong Kong (Phone Number in U.S. (800) 938-4685); *Asian Market Atlas.*

Euromonitor International, Inc., 122 South Michigan Avenue, Suite 1200, Chicago, Illinois 60603 (800) 577-EURO; *International Marketing Data and Statistics; World Marketing Data and Statistics;* and *The World Economic Factbook.*

M.E. Sharpe, 80 Business Park Drive, Armonk, New York 10504 (800) 541-6563; *The Illustrated Book of World Rankings.*

Statistical Office of the United Nations, Publishing Service, New York, New York 10017 (800) 253-9646; *Asia-Pacific in Figures;* and *Human Development Report.*

MALAYSIA - DEVELOPMENT ASSISTANCE

Asian Development Bank, Post Office Box 789, 1099 Manila, Philippines; *Key Indicators of Developing Asian and Pacific Countries.*

Statistical Office of the United Nations, Publishing Service, New York, New York 10017 (800) 253-9646; *Statistical Yearbook.*

MALAYSIA - DIAMOND PRODUCTION - See MALAYSIA - MINING AND MINERAL PRODUCTS

MALAYSIA - DISEASES - See MALAYSIA - HEALTH

MALAYSIA - DIVORCE

M.E. Sharpe, 80 Business Park Drive, Armonk, New York 10504 (800) 541-6563; *The Illustrated Book of World Rankings.*

Statistical Office of the United Nations, Publishing Service, New York, New York 10017 (800) 253-9646; *Demographic Yearbook;* and *Statistical Yearbook.*

MALAYSIA - DUCKS

Food and Agricultural Organization of the United Nations (FAO), Via delle Terme di Caracalla, 00100 Rome, Italy (Telephone Number in U.S. (202) 653-2400); *Production Yearbook.*

MALAYSIA - ECONOMY

Asian Development Bank, Post Office Box 789, 1099 Manila, Philippines; *Key Indicators of Developing Asian and Pacific Countries.*

Central Intelligence Agency, Washington, D.C. 20505 (703) 482-1100, www.cia.gov; *The World Factbook.*

Euromonitor International, Inc., 122 South Michigan Avenue, Suite 1200, Chicago, Illinois 60603 (800) 577-EURO; *International Marketing Data and Statistics; World Marketing Data and Statistics;* and *The World Economic Factbook.*

Europa Publications Limited, 18 Bedford Square, London, WC1B 3JN, England; *The Europa World Year Book.*

M.E. Sharpe, 80 Business Park Drive,

Armonk, New York 10504 (800) 541-6563; *The Illustrated Book of World Rankings.*

St. Martin's Press, Inc., 175 Fifth Avenue, New York, New York 10010 (800) 221-7945; *The Statesman's Year-Book.*

Statistical Office of the United Nations, Publishing Service, New York, New York 10017 (800) 253-9646; *World Statistics Pocketbook.*

The World Bank, 1818 H Street, NW, Washington, D.C. 20433 (202) 477-1234; *The World Bank Atlas;* and *World Development Report.*

MALAYSIA - EDUCATION

The Economist Intelligence Unit, 111 West 57th Street, New York, New York 10019 (800) 938-4685; *The World Market Atlas.*

The Economist Intelligence Unit (Asia) Limited, 10th Floor, Luk Kwok Centre, 72 Gloucester Road, Wanchai, Hong Kong (Phone Number in U.S. (800) 938-4685); *Asian Market Atlas.*

Euromonitor International, Inc., 122 South Michigan Avenue, Suite 1200, Chicago, Illinois 60603 (800) 577-EURO; *International Marketing Data and Statistics;* and *World Marketing Data and Statistics.*

Europa Publications Limited, 18 Bedford Square, London, WC1B 3JN, England; *The Europa World Year Book.*

M.E. Sharpe, 80 Business Park Drive, Armonk, New York 10504 (800) 541-6563; *The Illustrated Book of World Rankings.*

St. Martin's Press, Inc., 175 Fifth Avenue, New York, New York 10010 (800) 221-7945; *The Statesman's Year-Book.*

Statistical Office of the United Nations, Publishing Service, New York, New York 10017 (800) 253-9646; *Asia-Pacific in Figures; Human Development Report;* and *Statistical Yearbook for Asia and the Pacific*

United Nations Educational, Scientific and Cultural Organization (UNESCO), 7 Place de Fontenoy, F-75700 Paris, France (Telephone Number in U.S. (212) 963-5981); *Statistical Yearbook.*

The World Bank, 1818 H Street, NW, Washington, D.C. 20433 (202) 477-1234; *World Development Report;* and *World Development Indicators.*

MALAYSIA - EGG PRODUCTION AND CONSUMPTION - See MALAYSIA - DAIRY PRODUCTS

MALAYSIA - ELECTRICITY

Asian Development Bank, Post Office Box 789, 1099 Manila, Philippines; *Key Indicators of Developing Asian and Pacific Countries.*

Central Intelligence Agency, Washington, D.C. 20505 (703) 482-1100, www.cia.gov; *The World Factbook.*

M.E. Sharpe, 80 Business Park Drive, Armonk, New York 10504 (800) 541-6563; *The Illustrated Book of World Rankings.*

Penn Well Publishing Company, 1421 South Sheridan Road, Post Office Box 1260, Tulsa, Oklahoma 74101 (800) 752-9764; *International Energy Statistics Sourcebook.*

St. Martin's Press, Inc., 175 Fifth Avenue, New York, New York 10010 (800) 221-7945; *The Statesman's Year-Book.*

Statistical Office of the United Nations, Publishing Service, New York, New York 10017 (800) 253-9646; *Electric Power in Asia and the Pacific; Human Development Report;* and *Statistical Yearbook.*

MALAYSIA - EMPLOYMENT

Euromonitor International, Inc., 122 South Michigan Avenue, Suite 1200, Chicago, Illinois 60603 (800) 577-EURO; *International Marketing Data and Statistics.*

International Labour Office, I.L.O. Publications, 1828 L Street, N.W., Suite 801, Washington, D.C. 20036 (301) 638-3152; *Yearbook of Labour Statistics.*

M.E. Sharpe, 80 Business Park Drive, Armonk, New York 10504 (800) 541-6563; *The Illustrated Book of World Rankings.*

Statistical Office of the United Nations, Publishing Service, New York, New York 10017 (800) 253-9646; *Asia-Pacific in Figures;* and *Statistical Yearbook.*

MALAYSIA - ENERGY

Euromonitor International, Inc., 122 South Michigan Avenue, Suite 1200, Chicago, Illinois 60603 (800) 577-EURO; *International Marketing Data and Statistics; World Marketing Data and Statistics;* and *The World Economic Factbook.*

Food and Agricultural Organization of the United Nations (FAO), Via delle Terme di Caracalla, 00100 Rome, Italy (Telephone Number in U.S. (202) 653-2400); *The State of Food and Agriculture.*

M.E. Sharpe, 80 Business Park Drive, Armonk, New York 10504 (800) 541-6563; *The Illustrated Book of World Rankings.*

Penn Well Publishing Company, 1421 South Sheridan Road, Post Office Box 1260, Tulsa, Oklahoma 74101 (800) 752-9764;

International Energy Statistics Sourcebook.

St. Martin's Press, Inc., 175 Fifth Avenue, New York, New York 10010 (800) 221-7945; *The Statesman's Year-Book.*

Statistical Office of the United Nations, Publishing Service, New York, New York 10017 (800) 253-9646; *Asia-Pacific in Figures; Energy Statistics Yearbook; Human Development Report; Statistical Yearbook; World Statistics Pocketbook;* and *Statistical Yearbook for Asia and the Pacific.*

The World Bank, 1818 H Street, NW, Washington, D.C. 20433 (202) 477-1234; *The World Bank Atlas;* and *World Development Report.*

MALAYSIA - ENVIRONMENT

Statistical Office of the United Nations, Publishing Service, New York, New York 10017 (800) 253-9646; *World Statistics Pocketbook.*

MALAYSIA - EXCHANGE RATES

Asian Development Bank, Post Office Box 789, 1099 Manila, Philippines; *Key Indicators of Developing Asian and Pacific Countries.*

Central Intelligence Agency, Washington, D.C. 20505 (703) 482-1100, www.cia.gov; *The World Factbook.*

The Economist Intelligence Unit (Asia) Limited, 10th Floor, Luk Kwok Centre, 72 Gloucester Road, Wanchai, Hong Kong (Phone Number in U.S. (800) 938-4685); *Asian Market Atlas.*

Euromonitor International, Inc., 122 South Michigan Avenue, Suite 1200, Chicago, Illinois 60603 (800) 577-EURO; *International Marketing Data and Statistics;* and *The World Economic Factbook.*

Europa Publications Limited, 18 Bedford Square, London, WC1B 3JN, England; *The Europa World Year Book.*

International Civil Aviation Organization, 999 University Street, Montreal, Quebec, Canada H3C 5H7 (514) 954-8219; *Civil Aviation Statistics of the World.*

International Monetary Fund, 700 Nineteenth Street, NW, Washington, D.C. 20431 (202) 623-7000; *International Financial Statistics.*

Statistical Office of the United Nations, Publishing Service, New York, New York 10017 (800) 253-9646; *Statistical Yearbook;* and *World Statistics Pocketbook.*

Walden Publishing Ltd., Two Market Street, Saffron Walden Essex, CB10 1HZ,

England; *The World of Information Asia and Pacific Review*.

MALAYSIA - EXCISE TAXES - See MALAYSIA - TAXATION

MALAYSIA - EXPORTS

American Automobile Manufacturers Association, 1401 H Street, NW, Suite 900, Washington, D.C. 20005 (202) 326-5500; *World Motor Vehicle Data*.

Asian Development Bank, Post Office Box 789, 1099 Manila, Philippines; *Key Indicators of Developing Asian and Pacific Countries*.

Central Intelligence Agency, Washington, D.C. 20505 (703) 482-1100, www.cia.gov; *The World Factbook*.

The Economist Intelligence Unit, 111 West 57th Street, New York, New York 10019 (800) 938-4685; *The World Market Atlas*.

The Economist Intelligence Unit (Asia) Limited, 10th Floor, Luk Kwok Centre, 72 Gloucester Road, Wanchai, Hong Kong (Phone Number in U.S. (800) 938-4685); *Asian Market Atlas*.

Euromonitor International, Inc., 122 South Michigan Avenue, Suite 1200, Chicago, Illinois 60603 (800) 577-EURO; *International Marketing Data and Statistics;* and *The World Economic Factbook*.

Europa Publications Limited, 18 Bedford Square, London, WC1B 3JN, England; *The Europa World Year Book*.

Food and Agricultural Organization of the United Nations (FAO), Via delle Terme di Caracalla, 00100 Rome, Italy (Telephone Number in U.S. (202) 653-2400); *The State of Food and Agriculture*.

International Monetary Fund, 700 Nineteenth Street, NW, Washington, D.C. 20431 (202) 623-7000; *Direction of Trade Statistics; Government Finance Statistics Yearbook;* and *International Financial Statistics*.

International Rubber Study Group, York House, Eighth Floor, Empire Way, Wembley, London HA9 0PA, England; *Rubber Statistical Bulletin*.

St. Martin's Press, Inc., 175 Fifth Avenue, New York, New York 10010 (800) 221-7945; *The Statesman's Year-Book*.

Statistical Office of the United Nations, Publishing Service, New York, New York 10017 (800) 253-9646; *Foreign Trade Statistics of Asia and the Pacific*.

United Nations Conference on Trade and Development (UNCTAD), New York, New York 10017 (800) 253-9646; *Handbook of International Trade and Development Statistics*.

Walden Publishing Ltd., Two Market Street, Saffron Walden Essex, CB10 1HZ, England; *The World of Information Asia and Pacific Review*.

The World Bank, 1818 H Street, NW, Washington, D.C. 20433 (202) 477-1234; *World Development Report;* and *World Development Indicators*.

MALAYSIA - EXTERNAL FINANCING

Asian Development Bank, Post Office Box 789, 1099 Manila, Philippines; *Key Indicators of Developing Asian and Pacific Countries*.

MALAYSIA - EXTERNAL INDEBTEDNESS

Asian Development Bank, Post Office Box 789, 1099 Manila, Philippines; *Key Indicators of Developing Asian and Pacific Countries*.

The World Bank, 1818 H Street, NW, Washington, D.C. 20433 (202) 477-1234; *World Development Report;* and *World Development Indicators*.

MALAYSIA - EXTERNAL TRADE

Asian Development Bank, Post Office Box 789, 1099 Manila, Philippines; *Key Indicators of Developing Asian and Pacific Countries*.

Euromonitor International, Inc., 122 South Michigan Avenue, Suite 1200, Chicago, Illinois 60603 (800) 577-EURO; *World Marketing Data and Statistics*.

Food and Agricultural Organization of the United Nations (FAO), Via delle Terme di Caracalla, 00100 Rome, Italy (Telephone Number in U.S. (202) 653-2400); *The State of Food and Agriculture;* and *Trade Yearbook*.

Statistical Office of the United Nations, Publishing Service, New York, New York 10017 (800) 253-9646; *Asia-Pacific in Figures; Statistical Yearbook;* and *Statistical Yearbook for Asia and the Pacific*.

MALAYSIA - FABRIC PRODUCTION - See MALAYSIA - TEXTILE INDUSTRY

MALAYSIA - FARM CROPS - See MALAYSIA - CROPS

MALAYSIA - FEMALE WORKING POPULATION - See MALAYSIA - EMPLOYMENT

MALAYSIA - FERTILITY RATES

Central Intelligence Agency, Washington, D.C. 20505 (703) 482-1100, www.cia.gov; *The World Factbook*.

The Economist Intelligence Unit (Asia) Limited, 10th Floor, Luk Kwok Centre, 72 Gloucester Road, Wanchai, Hong Kong (Phone Number in U.S. (800) 938-4685); *Asian Market Atlas*.

M.E. Sharpe, 80 Business Park Drive, Armonk, New York 10504 (800) 541-6563; *The Illustrated Book of World Rankings*.

Statistical Office of the United Nations, Publishing Service, New York, New York 10017 (800) 253-9646; *Human Development Report*.

The World Bank, 1818 H Street, NW, Washington, D.C. 20433 (202) 477-1234; *The World Bank Atlas;* and *World Development Report*.

MALAYSIA - FERTILIZER

Food and Agricultural Organization of the United Nations (FAO), Via delle Terme di Caracalla, 00100 Rome, Italy (Telephone Number in U.S. (202) 653-2400); *The State of Food and Agriculture*.

Statistical Office of the United Nations, Publishing Service, New York, New York 10017 (800) 253-9646; *Statistical Yearbook*.

The World Bank, 1818 H Street, NW, Washington, D.C. 20433 (202) 477-1234; *World Development Indicators*.

MALAYSIA - FETAL MORTALITY - See MALAYSIA - MORTALITY

MALAYSIA - FIBRE PRODUCTION - See MALAYSIA - TEXTILE INDUSTRY

MALAYSIA - FILMS - See MALAYSIA - MOTION PICTURES

MALAYSIA - FINANCE

Asian Development Bank, Post Office Box 789, 1099 Manila, Philippines; *Key Indicators of Developing Asian and Pacific Countries*.

Europa Publications Limited, 18 Bedford Square, London, WC1B 3JN, England; *The Europa World Year Book*.

International Monetary Fund, 700 Nineteenth Street, NW, Washington, D.C. 20431 (202) 623-7000; *International Financial Statistics*.

M.E. Sharpe, 80 Business Park Drive, Armonk, New York 10504 (800) 541-6563; *The Illustrated Book of World Rankings*.

St. Martin's Press, Inc., 175 Fifth Avenue, New York, New York 10010 (800)

221-7945; *The Statesman's Year-Book.*

Statistical Office of the United Nations, Publishing Service, New York, New York 10017 (800) 253-9646; *Statistical Yearbook for Asia and the Pacific.*

MALAYSIA - FISHERIES

Europa Publications Limited, 18 Bedford Square, London, WC1B 3JN, England; *The Europa World Year Book.*

Food and Agricultural Organization of the United Nations (FAO), Via delle Terme di Caracalla, 00100 Rome, Italy (Telephone Number in U.S. (202) 653-2400); *The State of Food and Agriculture;* and *Yearbook of Fishery Statistics.*

M.E. Sharpe, 80 Business Park Drive, Armonk, New York 10504 (800) 541-6563; *The Illustrated Book of World Rankings.*

St. Martin's Press, Inc., 175 Fifth Avenue, New York, New York 10010 (800) 221-7945; *The Statesman's Year-Book.*

Statistical Office of the United Nations, Publishing Service, New York, New York 10017 (800) 253-9646; *Statistical Yearbook.*

United Nations Conference on Trade and Development, Central Statistical Service, Palais des Nations, Geneva, Switzerland (Telephone in U.S. (800) 253-9646); *UNCTAD Commodity Yearbook.*

MALAYSIA - FLOUR PRODUCTION

Statistical Office of the United Nations, Publishing Service, New York, New York 10017 (800) 253-9646; *Statistical Yearbook.*

MALAYSIA - FOOD

Euromonitor International, Inc., 122 South Michigan Avenue, Suite 1200, Chicago, Illinois 60603 (800) 577-EURO; *Retail Trade International.*

Food and Agricultural Organization of the United Nations (FAO), Via delle Terme di Caracalla, 00100 Rome, Italy (Telephone Number in U.S. (202) 653-2400); *Production Yearbook;* and *The State of Food and Agriculture.*

Statistical Office of the United Nations, Publishing Service, New York, New York 10017 (800) 253-9646; *Human Development Report;* and *Statistical Yearbook for Asia and the Pacific.*

United Nations Conference on Trade and Development, Central Statistical Service, Palais des Nations, Geneva, Switzerland (Telephone in U.S. (800) 253-9646); *UNCTAD Commodity Yearbook.*

MALAYSIA - FOREIGN DEBT

International Monetary Fund, 700 Nineteenth Street, NW, Washington, D.C. 20431 (202) 623-7000; *Government Finance Statistics Yearbook.*

Walden Publishing Ltd., Two Market Street, Saffron Walden Essex, CB10 1HZ, England; *The World of Information Asia and Pacific Review.*

MALAYSIA - FOREIGN TRADE

Asian Development Bank, Post Office Box 789, 1099 Manila, Philippines; *Key Indicators of Developing Asian and Pacific Countries.*

The Economist Intelligence Unit (Asia) Limited, 10th Floor, Luk Kwok Centre, 72 Gloucester Road, Wanchai, Hong Kong (Phone Number in U.S. (800) 938-4685); *Asian Market Atlas.*

Euromonitor International, Inc., 122 South Michigan Avenue, Suite 1200, Chicago, Illinois 60603 (800) 577-EURO; *International Marketing Data and Statistics;* and *The World Economic Factbook.*

Europa Publications Limited, 18 Bedford Square, London, WC1B 3JN, England; *The Europa World Year Book.*

Food and Agricultural Organization of the United Nations (FAO), Via delle Terme di Caracalla, 00100 Rome, Italy (Telephone Number in U.S. (202) 653-2400); *The State of Food and Agriculture.*

International Monetary Fund, 700 Nineteenth Street, NW, Washington, D.C. 20431 (202) 623-7000; *International Financial Statistics.*

M.E. Sharpe, 80 Business Park Drive, Armonk, New York 10504 (800) 541-6563; *The Illustrated Book of World Rankings.*

St. Martin's Press, Inc., 175 Fifth Avenue, New York, New York 10010 (800) 221-7945; *The Statesman's Year-Book.*

Statistical Office of the United Nations, Publishing Service, New York, New York 10017 (800) 253-9646; *International Trade Statistics Yearbook;* and *Statistical Yearbook.*

United Nations Conference on Trade and Development, Central Statistical Service, Palais des Nations, Geneva, Switzerland (Telephone in U.S. (800) 253-9646); *UNCTAD Commodity Yearbook.*

The World Bank, 1818 H Street, NW, Washington, D.C. 20433 (202) 477-1234; *World Development Report;* and *World Development Indicators.*

MALAYSIA - FORESTRY AND FOREST PRODUCTS

American Forest and Paper Association, 1111 Nineteenth Street, NW, Washington, D.C. 20036 (202) 463-2700; *Wood Pulp and Fiber Statistics.*

The Economist Intelligence Unit (Asia) Limited, 10th Floor, Luk Kwok Centre, 72 Gloucester Road, Wanchai, Hong Kong (Phone Number in U.S. (800) 938-4685); *Asian Market Atlas.*

Europa Publications Limited, 18 Bedford Square, London, WC1B 3JN, England; *The Europa World Year Book.*

Food and Agricultural Organization of the United Nations (FAO), Via delle Terme di Caracalla, 00100 Rome, Italy (Telephone Number in U.S. (202) 653-2400); *The State of Food and Agriculture;* and *Yearbook of Forest Products.*

International Monetary Fund, 700 Nineteenth Street, NW, Washington, D.C. 20431 (202) 623-7000; *International Financial Statistics.*

M.E. Sharpe, 80 Business Park Drive, Armonk, New York 10504 (800) 541-6563; *The Illustrated Book of World Rankings.*

St. Martin's Press, Inc., 175 Fifth Avenue, New York, New York 10010 (800) 221-7945; *The Statesman's Year-Book.*

Statistical Office of the United Nations, Publishing Service, New York, New York 10017 (800) 253-9646; *Statistical Yearbook.*

United Nations Conference on Trade and Development, Central Statistical Service, Palais des Nations, Geneva, Switzerland (Telephone in U.S. (800) 253-9646); *UNCTAD Commodity Yearbook.*

United Nations Educational, Scientific and Cultural Organization (UNESCO), 7 Place de Fontenoy, F-75700 Paris, France (Telephone Number in U.S. (212) 963-5981); *Statistical Yearbook.*

The World Bank, 1818 H Street, NW, Washington, D.C. 20433 (202) 477-1234; *World Development Report.*

MALAYSIA - GAS PRODUCTION - See MALAYSIA - MINING AND MINERAL PRODUCTS

MALAYSIA - GENERAL INDUSTRIAL STATISTICS - See MALAYSIA - INDUSTRY

MALAYSIA - GENERAL MORTALITY - See MALAYSIA - MORTALITY

MALAYSIA - GEOGRAPHIC DATA

M.E. Sharpe, 80 Business Park Drive, Armonk, New York 10504 (800) 541-6563; *The Illustrated Book of World Rankings.*

MALAYSIA - GOATS - See MALAYSIA - LIVESTOCK AND POULTRY

MALAYSIA - GOLD HOLDINGS

Statistical Office of the United Nations, Publishing Service, New York, New York 10017 (800) 253-9646; *Statistical Yearbook.*

The World Bank, 1818 H Street, NW, Washington, D.C. 20433 (202) 477-1234; *World Development Indicators.*

MALAYSIA - GOLD PRODUCTION AND CONSUMPTION - See MALAYSIA - MINING AND MINERAL PRODUCTS

MALAYSIA - GOVERNMENT

Asian Development Bank, Post Office Box 789, 1099 Manila, Philippines; *Key Indicators of Developing Asian and Pacific Countries.*

Central Intelligence Agency, Washington, D.C. 20505 (703) 482-1100, www.cia.gov; *The World Factbook.*

Europa Publications Limited, 18 Bedford Square, London, WC1B 3JN, England; *The Europa World Year Book.*

International Monetary Fund, 700 Nineteenth Street, NW, Washington, D.C. 20431 (202) 623-7000; *Government Finance Statistics Yearbook;* and *International Financial Statistics.*

St. Martin's Press, Inc., 175 Fifth Avenue, New York, New York 10010 (800) 221-7945; *The Statesman's Year-Book.*

Statistical Office of the United Nations, Publishing Service, New York, New York 10017 (800) 253-9646; *Asia-Pacific in Figures; National Accounts Statistics;* and *Statistical Yearbook.*

The World Bank, 1818 H Street, NW, Washington, D.C. 20433 (202) 477-1234; *World Development Report;* and *World Development Indicators.*

MALAYSIA - GRAIN PRODUCTION - See MALAYSIA - CROPS

MALAYSIA - GRANTS

International Monetary Fund, 700 Nineteenth Street, NW, Washington, D.C. 20431 (202) 623-7000; *Government Finance Statistics Yearbook.*

MALAYSIA - GROSS DOMESTIC PRODUCT

Asian Development Bank, Post Office Box 789, 1099 Manila, Philippines; *Key Indicators of Developing Asian and Pacific Countries.*

The Economist Intelligence Unit, 111 West 57th Street, New York, New York 10019 (800) 938-4685; *The World Market Atlas.*

The Economist Intelligence Unit (Asia) Limited, 10th Floor, Luk Kwok Centre, 72 Gloucester Road, Wanchai, Hong Kong (Phone Number in U.S. (800) 938-4685); *Asian Market Atlas.*

Euromonitor International, Inc., 122 South Michigan Avenue, Suite 1200, Chicago, Illinois 60603 (800) 577-EURO; *International Marketing Data and Statistics;* and *The World Economic Factbook.*

Europa Publications Limited, 18 Bedford Square, London, WC1B 3JN, England; *The Europa World Year Book.*

M.E. Sharpe, 80 Business Park Drive, Armonk, New York 10504 (800) 541-6563; *The Illustrated Book of World Rankings.*

Statistical Office of the United Nations, Publishing Service, New York, New York 10017 (800) 253-9646; *Human Development Report; National Accounts Statistics;* and *Statistical Yearbook.*

The World Bank, 1818 H Street, NW, Washington, D.C. 20433 (202) 477-1234; *World Development Report;* and *World Development Indicators.*

MALAYSIA - GROSS NATIONAL PRODUCT

Asian Development Bank, Post Office Box 789, 1099 Manila, Philippines; *Key Indicators of Developing Asian and Pacific Countries.*

Euromonitor International, Inc., 122 South Michigan Avenue, Suite 1200, Chicago, Illinois 60603 (800) 577-EURO; *International Marketing Data and Statistics.*

Europa Publications Limited, 18 Bedford Square, London, WC1B 3JN, England; *The Europa World Year Book.*

St. Martin's Press, Inc., 175 Fifth Avenue, New York, New York 10010 (800) 221-7945; *The Statesman's Year-Book.*

U.S. Arms Control and Disarmament Agency, 320 Twenty-first Street, NW, Washington, D.C. 20451 (202) 647-8677; *World Military Expenditures and Arms Transfers.*

Walden Publishing Ltd., Two Market Street, Saffron Walden Essex, CB10 1HZ, England; *The World of Information Asia and Pacific Review.*

The World Bank, 1818 H Street, NW, Washington, D.C. 20433 (202) 477-1234; *The World Bank Atlas; World Development Report;* and *World Development Indicators.*

MALAYSIA - GROUNDNUT PRODUCTION - See MALAYSIA - CROPS

MALAYSIA - HEALTH

The Economist Intelligence Unit (Asia) Limited, 10th Floor, Luk Kwok Centre, 72 Gloucester Road, Wanchai, Hong Kong (Phone Number in U.S. (800) 938-4685); *Asian Market Atlas.*

Euromonitor International, Inc., 122 South Michigan Avenue, Suite 1200, Chicago, Illinois 60603 (800) 577-EURO; *World Marketing Data and Statistics.*

M.E. Sharpe, 80 Business Park Drive, Armonk, New York 10504 (800) 541-6563; *The Illustrated Book of World Rankings.*

St. Martin's Press, Inc., 175 Fifth Avenue, New York, New York 10010 (800) 221-7945; *The Statesman's Year-Book.*

Statistical Office of the United Nations, Publishing Service, New York, New York 10017 (800) 253-9646; *Asia-Pacific in Figures; Human Development Report;* and *Statistical Yearbook.*

United Nations Children's Fund (UNICEF), 3 United Nations Plaza, New York, New York 10017 (800) 253-9646; *State of the World's Children.*

The World Bank, 1818 H Street, NW, Washington, D.C. 20433 (202) 477-1234; *World Development Report.*

World Health Organization, Office of Publications, 20 Avenue Appia, CH-1211 Geneva 27, Switzerland (Telephone Number in U.S. (518) 436-9686); *World Health Statistics Annual.*

MALAYSIA - HIDE PRODUCTION

Food and Agricultural Organization of the United Nations (FAO), Via delle Terme di Caracalla, 00100 Rome, Italy (Telephone Number in U.S. (202) 653-2400); *Production Yearbook.*

MALAYSIA - HIGHWAYS

Central Intelligence Agency, Washington, D.C. 20505 (703) 482-1100, www.cia.gov; *The World Factbook.*

The Economist Intelligence Unit (Asia) Limited, 10th Floor, Luk Kwok Centre, 72 Gloucester Road, Wanchai, Hong Kong (Phone Number in U.S. (800) 938-4685); *Asian Market Atlas.*

International Road Federation, 2600 Virginia Avenue, N.W., Washington, D.C. 20037 (202) 338-4641; *World Road*

Statistics.

St. Martin's Press, Inc., 175 Fifth Avenue, New York, New York 10010 (800) 221-7945; *The Statesman's Year-Book.*

MALAYSIA - HORSES - See MALAYSIA - LIVESTOCK AND POULTRY

MALAYSIA - HOURS OF WORK - See MALAYSIA - EMPLOYMENT

MALAYSIA - HOUSING AND HOUSING UNITS

Euromonitor International, Inc., 122 South Michigan Avenue, Suite 1200, Chicago, Illinois 60603 (800) 577-EURO; *World Marketing Data and Statistics.*

MALAYSIA - HOUSING EXPENDITURES

International Monetary Fund, 700 Nineteenth Street, NW, Washington, D.C. 20431 (202) 623-7000; *Government Finance Statistics Yearbook.*

M.E. Sharpe, 80 Business Park Drive, Armonk, New York 10504 (800) 541-6563; *The Illustrated Book of World Rankings.*

MALAYSIA - ILLITERATE POPULATION

Central Intelligence Agency, Washington, D.C. 20505 (703) 482-1100, www.cia.gov; *The World Factbook.*

The Economist Intelligence Unit, 111 West 57th Street, New York, New York 10019 (800) 938-4685; *The World Market Atlas.*

Euromonitor International, Inc., 122 South Michigan Avenue, Suite 1200, Chicago, Illinois 60603 (800) 577-EURO; *The World Economic Factbook.*

Statistical Office of the United Nations, Publishing Service, New York, New York 10017 (800) 253-9646; *Asia-Pacific in Figures;* and *Human Development Report.*

United Nations Educational, Scientific and Cultural Organization (UNESCO), 7 Place de Fontenoy, F-75700 Paris, France (Telephone Number in U.S. (212) 963-5981); *Statistical Yearbook.*

MALAYSIA - IMPORTS

American Automobile Manufacturers Association, 1401 H Street, NW, Suite 900, Washington, D.C. 20005 (202) 326-5500; *World Motor Vehicle Data.*

Asian Development Bank, Post Office Box 789, 1099 Manila, Philippines; *Key Indicators of Developing Asian and Pacific Countries.*

Central Intelligence Agency, Washington, D.C. 20505 (703) 482-1100,

www.cia.gov; *The World Factbook.*

The Economist Intelligence Unit, 111 West 57th Street, New York, New York 10019 (800) 938-4685; *The World Market Atlas.*

The Economist Intelligence Unit (Asia) Limited, 10th Floor, Luk Kwok Centre, 72 Gloucester Road, Wanchai, Hong Kong (Phone Number in U.S. (800) 938-4685); *Asian Market Atlas.*

Euromonitor International, Inc., 122 South Michigan Avenue, Suite 1200, Chicago, Illinois 60603 (800) 577-EURO; *International Marketing Data and Statistics;* and *The World Economic Factbook.*

Europa Publications Limited, 18 Bedford Square, London, WC1B 3JN, England; *The Europa World Year Book.*

Food and Agricultural Organization of the United Nations (FAO), Via delle Terme di Caracalla, 00100 Rome, Italy (Telephone Number in U.S. (202) 653-2400); *The State of Food and Agriculture.*

International Monetary Fund, 700 Nineteenth Street, NW, Washington, D.C. 20431 (202) 623-7000; *Direction of Trade Statistics; Government Finance Statistics Yearbook;* and *International Financial Statistics.*

International Rubber Study Group, York House, Eighth Floor, Empire Way, Wembley, London HA9 0PA, England; *Rubber Statistical Bulletin.*

St. Martin's Press, Inc., 175 Fifth Avenue, New York, New York 10010 (800) 221-7945; *The Statesman's Year-Book.*

Statistical Office of the United Nations, Publishing Service, New York, New York 10017 (800) 253-9646; *Foreign Trade Statistics of Asia and the Pacific.*

United Nations Conference on Trade and Development (UNCTAD), New York, New York 10017 (800) 253-9646; *Handbook of International Trade and Development Statistics.*

Walden Publishing Ltd., Two Market Street, Saffron Walden Essex, CB10 1HZ, England; *The World of Information Asia and Pacific Review.*

The World Bank, 1818 H Street, NW, Washington, D.C. 20433 (202) 477-1234; *World Development Report;* and *World Development Indicators.*

MALAYSIA - INCOME TAXES - See MALAYSIA - TAXATION

MALAYSIA - INDUSTRIAL METALS PRODUCTION - See MALAYSIA -MINING

AND MINERAL PRODUCTS

MALAYSIA - INDUSTRY

Central Intelligence Agency, Washington, D.C. 20505 (703) 482-1100, www.cia.gov; *The World Factbook.*

Euromonitor International, Inc., 122 South Michigan Avenue, Suite 1200, Chicago, Illinois 60603 (800) 577-EURO; *International Marketing Data and Statistics; World Marketing Data and Statistics;* and *The World Economic Factbook.*

Europa Publications Limited, 18 Bedford Square, London, WC1B 3JN, England; *The Europa World Year Book.*

International Labour Office, I.L.O. Publications, 1828 L Street, N.W., Suite 801, Washington, D.C. 20036 (301) 638-3152; *Yearbook of Labour Statistics.*

M.E. Sharpe, 80 Business Park Drive, Armonk, New York 10504 (800) 541-6563; *The Illustrated Book of World Rankings.*

St. Martin's Press, Inc., 175 Fifth Avenue, New York, New York 10010 (800) 221-7945; *The Statesman's Year-Book.*

Statistical Office of the United Nations, Publishing Service, New York, New York 10017 (800) 253-9646; *Asia-Pacific in Figures; Industrial Statistics Yearbook;* and *Statistical Yearbook for Asia and the Pacific.*

The World Bank, 1818 H Street, NW, Washington, D.C. 20433 (202) 477-1234; *World Development Indicators.*

World Intellectual Property Organization, 34 Chemin des Colombettes, CH-1211 Geneva 20, Switzerland; *Industrial Property Statistics.*

MALAYSIA - INFANT AND MATERNAL MORTALITY - See MALAYSIA - MORTALITY

MALAYSIA - INTERNAL TRADE

Statistical Office of the United Nations, Publishing Service, New York, New York 10017 (800) 253-9646; *Statistical Yearbook for Asia and the Pacific.*

MALAYSIA - INTERNATIONAL LIQUIDITY

International Monetary Fund, 700 Nineteenth Street, NW, Washington, D.C. 20431 (202) 623-7000; *International Financial Statistics.*

MALAYSIA - INTERNATIONAL RESERVES EXCLUDING GOLD

Asian Development Bank, Post Office Box 789, 1099 Manila, Philippines; *Key Indicators of Developing Asian and Pacific*

Countries.

Statistical Office of the United Nations, Publishing Service, New York, New York 10017 (800) 253-9646; *Statistical Yearbook.*

The World Bank, 1818 H Street, NW, Washington, D.C. 20433 (202) 477-1234; *World Development Indicators.*

MALAYSIA - INTERNATIONAL STATISTICS

Asian Development Bank, Post Office Box 789, 1099 Manila, Philippines; *Key Indicators of Developing Asian and Pacific Countries.*

MALAYSIA - INVESTMENTS

International Monetary Fund, 700 Nineteenth Street, NW, Washington, D.C. 20431 (202) 623-7000; *International Financial Statistics.*

MALAYSIA - IRON ORE PRODUCTION AND CONSUMPTION - See MALAYSIA - MINING AND MINERAL PRODUCTS

MALAYSIA - IRRIGATION

Euromonitor International, Inc., 122 South Michigan Avenue, Suite 1200, Chicago, Illinois 60603 (800) 577-EURO; *International Marketing Data and Statistics.*

MALAYSIA - LABOR

Central Intelligence Agency, Washington, D.C. 20505 (703) 482-1100, www.cia.gov; *The World Factbook.*

The Economist Intelligence Unit (Asia) Limited, 10th Floor, Luk Kwok Centre, 72 Gloucester Road, Wanchai, Hong Kong (Phone Number in U.S. (800) 938-4685); *Asian Market Atlas.*

Euromonitor International, Inc., 122 South Michigan Avenue, Suite 1200, Chicago, Illinois 60603 (800) 577-EURO; *International Marketing Data and Statistics; and World Marketing Data and Statistics.*

Europa Publications Limited, 18 Bedford Square, London, WC1B 3JN, England; *The Europa World Year Book.*

Food and Agricultural Organization of the United Nations (FAO), Via delle Terme di Caracalla, 00100 Rome, Italy (Telephone Number in U.S. (202) 653-2400); *The State of Food and Agriculture.*

International Labour Office, I.L.O. Publications, 1828 L Street, N.W., Suite 801, Washington, D.C. 20036 (301) 638-3152; *Yearbook of Labour Statistics.*

M.E. Sharpe, 80 Business Park Drive, Armonk, New York 10504 (800) 541-6563; *The Illustrated Book of World Rankings.*

St. Martin's Press, Inc., 175 Fifth Avenue, New York, New York 10010 (800) 221-7945; *The Statesman's Year-Book.*

Statistical Office of the United Nations, Publishing Service, New York, New York 10017 (800) 253-9646; *Human Development Report.*

The World Bank, 1818 H Street, NW, Washington, D.C. 20433 (202) 477-1234; *The World Bank Atlas; World Development Report; and World Development Indicators.*

MALAYSIA - LAND USE

Central Intelligence Agency, Washington, D.C. 20505 (703) 482-1100, www.cia.gov; *The World Factbook.*

Euromonitor International, Inc., 122 South Michigan Avenue, Suite 1200, Chicago, Illinois 60603 (800) 577-EURO; *International Marketing Data and Statistics.*

Food and Agricultural Organization of the United Nations (FAO), Via delle Terme di Caracalla, 00100 Rome, Italy (Telephone Number in U.S. (202) 653-2400); *Production Yearbook.*

The World Bank, 1818 H Street, NW, Washington, D.C. 20433 (202) 477-1234; *World Development Report.*

MALAYSIA - LEAD AND LEAD ORE PRODUCTION AND CONSUMPTION - See MALAYSIA - MINING AND MINERAL PRODUCTS

MALAYSIA - LIBRARIES

M.E. Sharpe, 80 Business Park Drive, Armonk, New York 10504 (800) 541-6563; *The Illustrated Book of World Rankings.*

United Nations Educational, Scientific and Cultural Organization (UNESCO), 7 Place de Fontenoy, F-75700 Paris, France (Telephone Number in U.S. (212) 963-5981); *Statistical Yearbook.*

MALAYSIA - LIFE EXPECTANCY

Central Intelligence Agency, Washington, D.C. 20505 (703) 482-1100, www.cia.gov; *The World Factbook.*

The Economist Intelligence Unit (Asia) Limited, 10th Floor, Luk Kwok Centre, 72 Gloucester Road, Wanchai, Hong Kong (Phone Number in U.S. (800) 938-4685); *Asian Market Atlas.*

Euromonitor International, Inc., 122 South Michigan Avenue, Suite 1200, Chicago, Illinois 60603 (800) 577-EURO; *The World Economic Factbook.*

St. Martin's Press, Inc., 175 Fifth Avenue, New York, New York 10010 (800) 221-7945; *The Statesman's Year-Book.*

Statistical Office of the United Nations, Publishing Service, New York, New York 10017 (800) 253-9646; *Asia-Pacific in Figures; World Statistics Pocketbook; and Human Development Report.*

The World Bank, 1818 H Street, NW, Washington, D.C. 20433 (202) 477-1234; *The World Bank Atlas; and World Development Report.*

MALAYSIA - LITERACY RATE

Euromonitor International, Inc., 122 South Michigan Avenue, Suite 1200, Chicago, Illinois 60603 (800) 577-EURO; *World Marketing Data and Statistics.*

MALAYSIA - LIVESTOCK AND POULTRY

Euromonitor International, Inc., 122 South Michigan Avenue, Suite 1200, Chicago, Illinois 60603 (800) 577-EURO; *International Marketing Data and Statistics.*

Europa Publications Limited, 18 Bedford Square, London, WC1B 3JN, England; *The Europa World Year Book.*

Food and Agricultural Organization of the United Nations (FAO), Via delle Terme di Caracalla, 00100 Rome, Italy (Telephone Number in U.S. (202) 653-2400); *Production Yearbook; and The State of Food and Agriculture.*

M.E. Sharpe, 80 Business Park Drive, Armonk, New York 10504 (800) 541-6563; *The Illustrated Book of World Rankings.*

St. Martin's Press, Inc., 175 Fifth Avenue, New York, New York 10010 (800) 221-7945; *The Statesman's Year-Book.*

Statistical Office of the United Nations, Publishing Service, New York, New York 10017 (800) 253-9646; *Statistical Yearbook.*

United Nations Conference on Trade and Development, Central Statistical Service, Palais des Nations, Geneva, Switzerland (Telephone in U.S. (800) 253-9646); *UNCTAD Commodity Yearbook.*

MALAYSIA - LIVING LEVELS - See MALAYSIA - LIFE EXPECTANCY

MALAYSIA - MAGNESIUM PRODUCTION AND CONSUMPTION - See MALAYSIA - MINING AND MINERAL PRODUCTS

MALAYSIA - MAIL - NUMBER OF ITEMS SENT OR RECEIVED

Statistical Office of the United Nations,

Publishing Service, New York, New York 10017 (800) 253-9646; *Statistical Yearbook.*

MALAYSIA - MANGANESE PRODUCTION AND CONSUMPTION - See MALAYSIA - MINING AND MINERAL PRODUCTS

MALAYSIA - MANPOWER

Statistical Office of the United Nations, Publishing Service, New York, New York 10017 (800) 253-9646; *Statistical Yearbook for Asia and the Pacific.*

MALAYSIA - MANUFACTURING

American Automobile Manufacturers Association, 1401 H Street, NW, Suite 900, Washington, D.C. 20005 (202) 326-5500; *World Motor Vehicle Data.*

Asian Development Bank, Post Office Box 789, 1099 Manila, Philippines; *Key Indicators of Developing Asian and Pacific Countries.*

M.E. Sharpe, 80 Business Park Drive, Armonk, New York 10504 (800) 541-6563; *The Illustrated Book of World Rankings.*

Statistical Office of the United Nations, Publishing Service, New York, New York 10017 (800) 253-9646; *Statistical Yearbook.*

The World Bank, 1818 H Street, NW, Washington, D.C. 20433 (202) 477-1234; *World Development Indicators.*

MALAYSIA - MARRIAGE RATES

M.E. Sharpe, 80 Business Park Drive, Armonk, New York 10504 (800) 541-6563; *The Illustrated Book of World Rankings.*

Statistical Office of the United Nations, Publishing Service, New York, New York 10017 (800) 253-9646; *Demographic Yearbook;* and *Statistical Yearbook.*

MALAYSIA - MEAT PRODUCTION - See MALAYSIA - LIVESTOCK AND POULTRY

MALAYSIA - MERCHANT SHIPPING

Europa Publications Limited, 18 Bedford Square, London, WC1B 3JN, England; *The Europa World Year Book.*

Lloyd's Register of Shipping, 17 Battery Place, New York, New York 10004 (212) 425-8050; *Register of Ships.*

St. Martin's Press, Inc., 175 Fifth Avenue, New York, New York 10010 (800) 221-7945; *The Statesman's Year-Book.*

Statistical Office of the United Nations, Publishing Service, New York, New York 10017 (800) 253-9646; *Statistical Yearbook.*

U.S. Department of Transportation,

Maritime Administration, 400 Seventh Street, SW, Washington, D.C. 20590 (202) 366-5807, www.marad.dot.gov; *A Statistical Analysis of the World's Merchant Fleets.*

MALAYSIA - MERCURY PRODUCTION AND CONSUMPTION - See MALAYSIA - MINING AND MINERAL PRODUCTS

MALAYSIA - MILITARY

Central Intelligence Agency, Washington, D.C. 20505 (703) 482-1100, www.cia.gov; *The World Factbook.*

The Economist Intelligence Unit (Asia) Limited, 10th Floor, Luk Kwok Centre, 72 Gloucester Road, Wanchai, Hong Kong (Phone Number in U.S. (800) 938-4685); *Asian Market Atlas.*

Euromonitor International, Inc., 122 South Michigan Avenue, Suite 1200, Chicago, Illinois 60603 (800) 577-EURO; *World Marketing Data and Statistics.*

The International Institute for Strategic Studies, 23 Tavistock Street, London WC2E 7NQ, England; *The Military Balance.*

St. Martin's Press, Inc., 175 Fifth Avenue, New York, New York 10010 (800) 221-7945; *The Statesman's Year-Book.*

Statistical Office of the United Nations, Publishing Service, New York, New York 10017 (800) 253-9646; *Human Development Report.*

U.S. Arms Control and Disarmament Agency, 320 Twenty-first Street, NW, Washington, D.C. 20451 (202) 647-8677; *World Military Expenditures and Arms Transfers.*

MALAYSIA - MILK PRODUCTION - See MALAYSIA - DAIRY PRODUCTS

MALAYSIA - MINING AND MINERAL PRODUCTS

Asian Development Bank, Post Office Box 789, 1099 Manila, Philippines; *Key Indicators of Developing Asian and Pacific Countries.*

Commodity Research Bureau, 30 South Wacker Drive, Chicago Illinois 60606 (312) 454-1801; *Commodity Yearbook.*

Europa Publications Limited, 18 Bedford Square, London, WC1B 3JN, England; *The Europa World Year Book.*

International Monetary Fund, 700 Nineteenth Street, NW, Washington, D.C. 20431 (202) 623-7000; *International Financial Statistics.*

M.E. Sharpe, 80 Business Park Drive,

Armonk, New York 10504 (800) 541-6563; *The Illustrated Book of World Rankings.*

Penn Well Publishing Company, 1421 South Sheridan Road, Post Office Box 1260, Tulsa, Oklahoma 74101 (800) 752-9764; *International Energy Statistics Sourcebook.*

St. Martin's Press, Inc., 175 Fifth Avenue, New York, New York 10010 (800) 221-7945; *The Statesman's Year-Book.*

Statistical Office of the United Nations, Publishing Service, New York, New York 10017 (800) 253-9646; *Statistical Yearbook.*

United Nations Conference on Trade and Development, Central Statistical Service, Palais des Nations, Geneva, Switzerland (Telephone in U.S. (800) 253-9646); *UNCTAD Commodity Yearbook.*

MALAYSIA - MOLYBDENUM AND MOLYBDENUM ORE PRODUCTION AND CONSUMPTION - See MALAYSIA - MINING AND MINERAL PRODUCTS

MALAYSIA - MONEY EXCHANGE RATES - See MALAYSIA - EXCHANGE RATES

MALAYSIA - MONEY RESERVES

Euromonitor International, Inc., 122 South Michigan Avenue, Suite 1200, Chicago, Illinois 60603 (800) 577-EURO; *International Marketing Data and Statistics.*

MALAYSIA - MONEY SUPPLY

Asian Development Bank, Post Office Box 789, 1099 Manila, Philippines; *Key Indicators of Developing Asian and Pacific Countries.*

Euromonitor International, Inc., 122 South Michigan Avenue, Suite 1200, Chicago, Illinois 60603 (800) 577-EURO; *International Marketing Data and Statistics.*

Europa Publications Limited, 18 Bedford Square, London, WC1B 3JN, England; *The Europa World Year Book.*

International Monetary Fund, 700 Nineteenth Street, NW, Washington, D.C. 20431 (202) 623-7000; *International Financial Statistics.*

Statistical Office of the United Nations, Publishing Service, New York, New York 10017 (800) 253-9646; *Statistical Yearbook.*

The World Bank, 1818 H Street, NW, Washington, D.C. 20433 (202) 477-1234; *World Development Indicators.*

MALAYSIA - MONUMENTS AND HISTORICAL SITES

United Nations Educational, Scientific and Cultural Organization (UNESCO), 7 Place de Fontenoy, F-75700 Paris, France (Telephone Number in U.S. (212) 963-5981); *Statistical Yearbook.*

MALAYSIA - MORTALITY

Central Intelligence Agency, Washington, D.C. 20505 (703) 482-1100, www.cia.gov; *The World Factbook.*

The Economist Intelligence Unit (Asia) Limited, 10th Floor, Luk Kwok Centre, 72 Gloucester Road, Wanchai, Hong Kong (Phone Number in U.S. (800) 938-4685); *Asian Market Atlas.*

Euromonitor International, Inc., 122 South Michigan Avenue, Suite 1200, Chicago, Illinois 60603 (800) 577-EURO; *International Marketing Data and Statistics;* and *The World Economic Factbook.*

Europa Publications Limited, 18 Bedford Square, London, WC1B 3JN, England; *The Europa World Year Book.*

St. Martin's Press, Inc., 175 Fifth Avenue, New York, New York 10010 (800) 221-7945; *The Statesman's Year-Book.*

Statistical Office of the United Nations, Publishing Service, New York, New York 10017 (800) 253-9646; *Asia-Pacific in Figures; Human Development Report; Demographic Yearbook; World Statistics Pocketbook;* and *Statistical Yearbook.*

United Nations Children's Fund (UNICEF), 3 United Nations Plaza, New York, New York 10017 (800) 253-9646; *State of the World's Children.*

The World Bank, 1818 H Street, NW, Washington, D.C. 20433 (202) 477-1234; *The World Bank Atlas; World Development Report;* and *World Development Indicators.*

World Health Organization, Office of Publications, 20 Avenue Appia, CH-1211 Geneva 27, Switzerland (Telephone Number in U.S. (518) 436-9686); *World Health Statistics Annual.*

MALAYSIA - MOTION PICTURES

Statistical Office of the United Nations, Publishing Service, New York, New York 10017 (800) 253-9646; *Statistical Yearbook.*

United Nations Educational, Scientific and Cultural Organization (UNESCO), 7 Place de Fontenoy, F-75700 Paris, France (Telephone Number in U.S. (212) 963-5981); *Statistical Yearbook.*

MALAYSIA - MOTOR VEHICLE PRODUCTION

American Automobile Manufacturers Association, 1401 H Street, NW, Suite 900,

Washington, D.C. 20005 (202) 326-5500; *World Motor Vehicle Data.*

Europa Publications Limited, 18 Bedford Square, London, WC1B 3JN, England; *The Europa World Year Book.*

Statistical Office of the United Nations, Publishing Service, New York, New York 10017 (800) 253-9646; *Statistical Yearbook.*

MALAYSIA - MOTOR VEHICLE TAXES - See MALAYSIA - TAXATION

MALAYSIA - MOTOR VEHICLES IN USE

American Automobile Manufacturers Association, 1401 H Street, NW, Suite 900, Washington, D.C. 20005 (202) 326-5500; *World Motor Vehicle Data.*

International Road Federation, 2600 Virginia Avenue, N.W., Washington, D.C. 20037 (202) 338-4641; *World Road Statistics.*

Statistical Office of the United Nations, Publishing Service, New York, New York 10017 (800) 253-9646; *Statistical Yearbook.*

MALAYSIA - MUSEUMS

M.E. Sharpe, 80 Business Park Drive, Armonk, New York 10504 (800) 541-6563; *The Illustrated Book of World Rankings.*

United Nations Educational, Scientific and Cultural Organization (UNESCO), 7 Place de Fontenoy, F-75700 Paris, France (Telephone Number in U.S. (212) 963-5981); *Statistical Yearbook.*

MALAYSIA - NATALITY - See MALAYSIA - BIRTH RATES

MALAYSIA - NATIONAL ACCOUNTS

Europa Publications Limited, 18 Bedford Square, London, WC1B 3JN, England; *The Europa World Year Book.*

International Monetary Fund, 700 Nineteenth Street, NW, Washington, D.C. 20431 (202) 623-7000; *International Financial Statistics.*

Statistical Office of the United Nations, Publishing Service, New York, New York 10017 (800) 253-9646; *Asia-Pacific in Figures; National Account Statistics; Statistical Yearbook;* and *Statistical Yearbook for Asia and the Pacific.*

MALAYSIA - NATIONAL INCOME

M.E. Sharpe, 80 Business Park Drive, Armonk, New York 10504 (800) 541-6563; *The Illustrated Book of World Rankings.*

Statistical Office of the United Nations, Publishing Service, New York, New York

10017 (800) 253-9646; *National Accounts Statistics;* and *Statistical Yearbook.*

MALAYSIA - NATIONAL PRODUCT

M.E. Sharpe, 80 Business Park Drive, Armonk, New York 10504 (800) 541-6563; *The Illustrated Book of World Rankings.*

Statistical Office of the United Nations, Publishing Service, New York, New York 10017 (800) 253-9646; *Statistical Yearbook.*

MALAYSIA - NATURAL GAS PRODUCTION - See MALAYSIA - MINING AND MINERAL PRODUCTS

MALAYSIA - NATURAL RUBBER PRODUCTION

International Rubber Study Group, York House, Eighth Floor, Empire Way, Wembley, London HA9 0PA, England; *Rubber Statistical Bulletin.*

Statistical Office of the United Nations, Publishing Service, New York, New York 10017 (800) 253-9646; *Statistical Yearbook.*

MALAYSIA - NEWSPAPER PRODUCTION - See MALAYSIA - FORESTRY AND FOREST PRODUCTS

MALAYSIA - NEWSPRINT - See MALAYSIA - FORESTRY AND FOREST PRODUCTS

MALAYSIA - NICKEL AND NICKEL ORE PRODUCTION AND CONSUMPTION - See MALAYSIA - MINING AND MINERAL PRODUCTS

MALAYSIA - PALM OIL AND PALM KERNELS PRODUCTION - See MALAYSIA - CROPS

MALAYSIA - PAPER - See MALAYSIA - FORESTRY AND FOREST PRODUCTS

MALAYSIA - PATENTS, TRADEMARKS AND SERVICE MARKS

Statistical Office of the United Nations, Publishing Service, New York, New York 10017 (800) 253-9646; *Statistical Yearbook.*

World Intellectual Property Organization, 34 Chemin des Colombettes, CH-1211 Geneva 20, Switzerland; *Industrial Property Statistics.*

MALAYSIA - PEANUT PRODUCTION - See MALAYSIA - MALAYSIA - CROPS

MALAYSIA - PERIODICALS

United Nations Educational, Scientific and Cultural Organization (UNESCO), 7 Place de Fontenoy, F-75700 Paris, France (Telephone Number in U.S. (212) 963-5981); *Statistical Yearbook.*

MALAYSIA - PESTICIDE USE

Food and Agricultural Organization of the United Nations (FAO), Via delle Terme di Caracalla, 00100 Rome, Italy (Telephone Number in U.S. (202) 653-2400); *The State of Food and Agriculture.*

MALAYSIA - PETROLEUM INDUSTRY

Asian Development Bank, Post Office Box 789, 1099 Manila, Philippines; *Key Indicators of Developing Asian and Pacific Countries.*

Food and Agricultural Organization of the United Nations (FAO), Via delle Terme di Caracalla, 00100 Rome, Italy (Telephone Number in U.S. (202) 653-2400); *The State of Food and Agriculture.*

International Monetary Fund, 700 Nineteenth Street, NW, Washington, D.C. 20431 (202) 623-7000; *International Financial Statistics.*

M.E. Sharpe, 80 Business Park Drive, Armonk, New York 10504 (800) 541-6563; *The Illustrated Book of World Rankings.*

Penn Well Publishing Company, 1421 South Sheridan Road, Post Office Box 1260, Tulsa, Oklahoma 74101 (800) 752-9764; *International Energy Statistics Sourcebook.*

St. Martin's Press, Inc., 175 Fifth Avenue, New York, New York 10010 (800) 221-7945; *The Statesman's Year-Book.*

Statistical Office of the United Nations, Publishing Service, New York, New York 10017 (800) 253-9646; *Statistical Yearbook.*

United Nations Conference on Trade and Development, Central Statistical Service, Palais des Nations, Geneva, Switzerland (Telephone in U.S. (800) 253-9646); *UNCTAD Commodity Yearbook.*

MALAYSIA - PIGS - See MALAYSIA - LIVESTOCK AND POULTRY

MALAYSIA - PLATINUM PRODUCTION - See MALAYSIA - MINING AND MINERAL PRODUCTS

MALAYSIA - POPULATION

Asian Development Bank, Post Office Box 789, 1099 Manila, Philippines; *Key Indicators of Developing Asian and Pacific Countries.*

Central Intelligence Agency, Washington, D.C. 20505 (703) 482-1100, www.cia.gov; *The World Factbook.*

The Economist Intelligence Unit, 111 West 57th Street, New York, New York 10019 (800) 938-4685; *The World Market Atlas.*

The Economist Intelligence Unit (Asia) Limited, 10th Floor, Luk Kwok Centre, 72 Gloucester Road, Wanchai, Hong Kong (Phone Number in U.S. (800) 938-4685); *Asian Market Atlas.*

Euromonitor International, Inc., 122 South Michigan Avenue, Suite 1200, Chicago, Illinois 60603 (800) 577-EURO; *International Marketing Data and Statistics;* and *The World Economic Factbook.*

Europa Publications Limited, 18 Bedford Square, London, WC1B 3JN, England; *The Europa World Year Book.*

Food and Agricultural Organization of the United Nations (FAO), Via delle Terme di Caracalla, 00100 Rome, Italy (Telephone Number in U.S. (202) 653-2400); *Production Yearbook.*

International Labour Office, I.L.O. Publications, 1828 L Street, N.W., Suite 801, Washington, D.C. 20036 (301) 638-3152; *Yearbook of Labour Statistics.*

M.E. Sharpe, 80 Business Park Drive, Armonk, New York 10504 (800) 541-6563; *The Illustrated Book of World Rankings.*

St. Martin's Press, Inc., 175 Fifth Avenue, New York, New York 10010 (800) 221-7945; *The Statesman's Year-Book.*

Statistical Office of the United Nations, Publishing Service, New York, New York 10017 (800) 253-9646; *Asia-Pacific in Figures; Demographic Yearbook; Human Development Report; Statistical Yearbook; World Statistics Pocketbook;* and *Statistical Yearbook for Asia and the Pacific.*

U.S. Arms Control and Disarmament Agency, 320 Twenty-first Street, NW, Washington, D.C. 20451 (202) 647-8677; *World Military Expenditures and Arms Transfers.*

Walden Publishing Ltd., Two Market Street, Saffron Walden Essex, CB10 1HZ, England; *The World of Information Asia and Pacific Review.*

The World Bank, 1818 H Street, NW, Washington, D.C. 20433 (202) 477-1234; *The World Bank Atlas;* and *World Development Report.*

World Health Organization, Office of Publications, 20 Avenue Appia, CH-1211 Geneva 27, Switzerland (Telephone Number in U.S. (518) 436-9686); *World Health Statistics Annual.*

MALAYSIA - POST OFFICES

M.E. Sharpe, 80 Business Park Drive, Armonk, New York 10504 (800) 541-6563; *The Illustrated Book of World Rankings.*

St. Martin's Press, Inc., 175 Fifth Avenue, New York, New York 10010 (800) 221-7945; *The Statesman's Year-Book.*

MALAYSIA - POTATO PRODUCTION - See MALAYSIA - CROPS

MALAYSIA - POWER PRODUCTION INDUSTRY - ESTABLISHMENTS, PAYROLLS, VALUE ADDED, ETC.

Statistical Office of the United Nations, Publishing Service, New York, New York 10017 (800) 253-9646; *Electric Power in Asia and the Pacific.*

MALAYSIA - PRICES

Asian Development Bank, Post Office Box 789, 1099 Manila, Philippines; *Key Indicators of Developing Asian and Pacific Countries.*

Food and Agricultural Organization of the United Nations (FAO), Via delle Terme di Caracalla, 00100 Rome, Italy (Telephone Number in U.S. (202) 653-2400); *Production Yearbook;* and *The State of Food and Agriculture.*

International Labour Office, I.L.O. Publications, 1828 L Street, N.W., Suite 801, Washington, D.C. 20036 (301) 638-3152; *Yearbook of Labour Statistics.*

International Monetary Fund, 700 Nineteenth Street, NW, Washington, D.C. 20431 (202) 623-7000; *International Financial Statistics.*

International Rubber Study Group, York House, Eighth Floor, Empire Way, Wembley, London HA9 0PA, England; *Rubber Statistical Bulletin.*

M.E. Sharpe, 80 Business Park Drive, Armonk, New York 10504 (800) 541-6563; *The Illustrated Book of World Rankings.*

MALAYSIA - PRINTING AND WRITING PAPER - See MALAYSIA - FORESTRY AND FOREST PRODUCTS

MALAYSIA - PRODUCTION

American Automobile Manufacturers Association, 1401 H Street, NW, Suite 900, Washington, D.C. 20005 (202) 326-5500; *World Motor Vehicle Data.*

International Rubber Study Group, York House, Eighth Floor, Empire Way, Wembley, London HA9 0PA, England; *Rubber Statistical Bulletin.*

M.E. Sharpe, 80 Business Park Drive, Armonk, New York 10504 (800) 541-6563; *The Illustrated Book of World Rankings.*

MALAYSIA - PRODUCTIVITY

Euromonitor International, Inc., 122 South Michigan Avenue, Suite 1200, Chicago, Illinois 60603 (800) 577-EURO; *International Marketing Data and Statistics.*

MALAYSIA - PROPERTY TAXES - See MALAYSIA - TAXATION

MALAYSIA - PUBLIC FINANCE - See MALAYSIA - FINANCE

MALAYSIA - RADIO BROADCASTING - See MALAYSIA - BROADCASTING

MALAYSIA - RADIO RECEIVERS

St. Martin's Press, Inc., 175 Fifth Avenue, New York, New York 10010 (800) 221-7945; *The Statesman's Year-Book.*

MALAYSIA - RAILWAY USE

Statistical Office of the United Nations, Publishing Service, New York, New York 10017 (800) 253-9646; *Statistical Yearbook.*

MALAYSIA - RAILWAYS

Europa Publications Limited, 18 Bedford Square, London, WC1B 3JN, England; *The Europa World Year Book.*

Jane's Information Group, Sentinel House, 163 Brighton Road, Coulsdon, Surrey CR5 2NH, England (Telephone Number in U.S. (703) 683-3700); *Jane's World Railways.*

St. Martin's Press, Inc., 175 Fifth Avenue, New York, New York 10010 (800) 221-7945; *The Statesman's Year-Book.*

MALAYSIA - RELIGION

Central Intelligence Agency, Washington, D.C. 20505 (703) 482-1100, www.cia.gov; *The World Factbook.*

M.E. Sharpe, 80 Business Park Drive, Armonk, New York 10504 (800) 541-6563; *The Illustrated Book of World Rankings.*

St. Martin's Press, Inc., 175 Fifth Avenue, New York, New York 10010 (800) 221-7945; *The Statesman's Year-Book.*

MALAYSIA - RETAIL TRADE

Euromonitor International, Inc., 122 South Michigan Avenue, Suite 1200, Chicago, Illinois 60603 (800) 577-EURO; *World Marketing Data and Statistics;* and *Retail Trade International.*

Statistical Office of the United Nations, Publishing Service, New York, New York 10017 (800) 253-9646; *Statistical Yearbook.*

MALAYSIA - RICE PRODUCTION - See MALAYSIA - CROPS

MALAYSIA - ROOT AND TUBER PRODUCTION - See MALAYSIA - CROPS

MALAYSIA - ROUNDWOOD PRODUCTION - See MALAYSIA - FORESTRY AND FOREST PRODUCTS

MALAYSIA - RUBBER PRODUCTION AND CONSUMPTION

Commodity Research Bureau, 30 South Wacker Drive, Chicago Illinois 60606 (312) 454-1801; *Commodity Yearbook.*

International Rubber Study Group, York House, Eighth Floor, Empire Way, Wembley, London HA9 0PA, England; *International Financial Statistics;* and *Rubber Statistical Bulletin.*

M.E. Sharpe, 80 Business Park Drive, Armonk, New York 10504 (800) 541-6563; *The Illustrated Book of World Rankings.*

MALAYSIA - SAWNWOOD PRODUCTION - See MALAYSIA - FORESTRY AND FOREST PRODUCTS

MALAYSIA - SCIENTISTS, TECHNICIANS AND ENGINEERS

Statistical Office of the United Nations, Publishing Service, New York, New York 10017 (800) 253-9646; *Statistical Yearbook.*

MALAYSIA - SENIOR CITIZENS

M.E. Sharpe, 80 Business Park Drive, Armonk, New York 10504 (800) 541-6563; *The Illustrated Book of World Rankings.*

MALAYSIA - SHEEP - See MALAYSIA - LIVESTOCK AND POULTRY

MALAYSIA - SILVER PRODUCTION AND CONSUMPTION - See MALAYSIA - MINING AND MINERAL PRODUCTS

MALAYSIA - SOCIAL DATA

Asian Development Bank, Post Office Box 789, 1099 Manila, Philippines; *Key Indicators of Developing Asian and Pacific Countries.*

M.E. Sharpe, 80 Business Park Drive, Armonk, New York 10504 (800) 541-6563; *The Illustrated Book of World Rankings.*

Statistical Office of the United Nations, Publishing Service, New York, New York 10017 (800) 253-9646; *World Statistics Pocketbook.*

MALAYSIA - SOCIAL SECURITY

St. Martin's Press, Inc., 175 Fifth Avenue, New York, New York 10010 (800) 221-7945; *The Statesman's Year-Book.*

Statistical Office of the United Nations,

Publishing Service, New York, New York 10017 (800) 253-9646; *National Accounts Statistics.*

MALAYSIA - SOYBEAN PRODUCTION - See MALAYSIA - CROPS

MALAYSIA - STAMP TAXES AND DUTIES - See MALAYSIA - TAXATION

MALAYSIA - STATE BUDGET

Euromonitor International, Inc., 122 South Michigan Avenue, Suite 1200, Chicago, Illinois 60603 (800) 577-EURO; *International Marketing Data and Statistics.*

MALAYSIA - STEEL - See MALAYSIA - MINING AND MINERAL PRODUCTS

MALAYSIA - STOCKS - COMMODITY - MARKET PRICE - INDEX

Food and Agricultural Organization of the United Nations (FAO), Via delle Terme di Caracalla, 00100 Rome, Italy (Telephone Number in U.S. (202) 653-2400); *The State of Food and Agriculture.*

MALAYSIA - SUGAR PRODUCTION AND CONSUMPTION - See MALAYSIA - CROPS

MALAYSIA - TAXATION

Europa Publications Limited, 18 Bedford Square, London, WC1B 3JN, England; *The Europa World Year Book.*

International Monetary Fund, 700 Nineteenth Street, NW, Washington, D.C. 20431 (202) 623-7000; *Government Finance Statistics Yearbook.*

International Road Federation, 2600 Virginia Avenue, N.W., Washington, D.C. 20037 (202) 338-4641; *World Road Statistics.*

St. Martin's Press, Inc., 175 Fifth Avenue, New York, New York 10010 (800) 221-7945; *The Statesman's Year-Book.*

The World Bank, 1818 H Street, NW, Washington, D.C. 20433 (202) 477-1234; *World Development Indicators.*

MALAYSIA - TEA PRODUCTION - See MALAYSIA - CROPS

MALAYSIA - TELEGRAPH SERVICE

Statistical Office of the United Nations, Publishing Service, New York, New York 10017 (800) 253-9646; *Statistical Yearbook.*

MALAYSIA - TELEPHONES IN USE

American Telephone and Telegraph Company, 26 Parsippany Road, Whippany, New Jersey 07981 (800) 222-0300; *The*

World's Telephones.

Central Intelligence Agency, Washington, D.C. 20505 (703) 482-1100, www.cia.gov; *The World Factbook.*

The Economist Intelligence Unit (Asia) Limited, 10th Floor, Luk Kwok Centre, 72 Gloucester Road, Wanchai, Hong Kong (Phone Number in U.S. (800) 938-4685); *Asian Market Atlas.*

Europa Publications Limited, 18 Bedford Square, London, WC1B 3JN, England; *The Europa World Year Book.*

St. Martin's Press, Inc., 175 Fifth Avenue, New York, New York 10010 (800) 221-7945; *The Statesman's Year-Book.*

Statistical Office of the United Nations, Publishing Service, New York, New York 10017 (800) 253-9646; *Statistical Yearbook;* and *World Statistics Pocketbook.*

MALAYSIA - TELEVISION BROADCASTING - See MALAYSIA - BROADCASTING

MALAYSIA - TELEVISION RECEIVER PRODUCTION

Statistical Office of the United Nations, Publishing Service, New York, New York 10017 (800) 253-9646; *Statistical Yearbook.*

MALAYSIA - TEXTILE INDUSTRY

American Forest and Paper Association, 1111 Nineteenth Street, NW, Washington, D.C. 20036 (202) 463-2700; *Wood Pulp and Fiber Statistics.*

Euromonitor International, Inc., 122 South Michigan Avenue, Suite 1200, Chicago, Illinois 60603 (800) 577-EURO; *Retail Trade International.*

M.E. Sharpe, 80 Business Park Drive, Armonk, New York 10504 (800) 541-6563; *The Illustrated Book of World Rankings.*

Statistical Office of the United Nations, Publishing Service, New York, New York 10017 (800) 253-9646; *Statistical Yearbook.*

United Nations Conference on Trade and Development, Central Statistical Service, Palais des Nations, Geneva, Switzerland (Telephone in U.S. (800) 253-9646); *UNCTAD Commodity Yearbook.*

MALAYSIA - THEATRE

United Nations Educational, Scientific and Cultural Organization (UNESCO), 7 Place de Fontenoy, F-75700 Paris, France (Telephone Number in U.S. (212) 963-5981); *Statistical Yearbook.*

MALAYSIA - TIN - See MALAYSIA - MINING

AND MINERAL PRODUCTS

MALAYSIA - TIRE (MOTOR VEHICLE) PRODUCTION

International Rubber Study Group, York House, Eighth Floor, Empire Way, Wembley, London HA9 0PA, England; *Rubber Statistical Bulletin.*

Statistical Office of the United Nations, Publishing Service, New York, New York 10017 (800) 253-9646; *Statistical Yearbook.*

MALAYSIA - TOBACCO PRODUCTION

M.E. Sharpe, 80 Business Park Drive, Armonk, New York 10504 (800) 541-6563; *The Illustrated Book of World Rankings.*

Statistical Office of the United Nations, Publishing Service, New York, New York 10017 (800) 253-9646; *Statistical Yearbook.*

MALAYSIA - TOURISM

Euromonitor International, Inc., 122 South Michigan Avenue, Suite 1200, Chicago, Illinois 60603 (800) 577-EURO; *The World Economic Factbook;* and *World Marketing Data and Statistics.*

Europa Publications Limited, 18 Bedford Square, London, WC1B 3JN, England; *The Europa World Year Book.*

M.E. Sharpe, 80 Business Park Drive, Armonk, New York 10504 (800) 541-6563; *The Illustrated Book of World Rankings.*

St. Martin's Press, Inc., 175 Fifth Avenue, New York, New York 10010 (800) 221-7945; *The Statesman's Year-Book.*

Statistical Office of the United Nations, Publishing Service, New York, New York 10017 (800) 253-9646; *Statistical Yearbook.*

World Tourism Organization, Calle Capitan Haya 42, E-28020 Madrid, Spain; *Yearbook of Tourism Statistics.*

MALAYSIA - TRACTORS IN USE

Statistical Office of the United Nations, Publishing Service, New York, New York 10017 (800) 253-9646; *Statistical Yearbook.*

MALAYSIA - TRADE - See MALAYSIA - FOREIGN TRADE

MALAYSIA - TRADEMARKS AND SERVICE MARKS - See MALAYSIA - PATENTS, TRADEMARKS AND SERVICE MARKS

MALAYSIA - TRANSPORTATION AND COMMUNICATIONS

Central Intelligence Agency, Washington, D.C. 20505 (703) 482-1100, www.cia.gov; *The World Factbook.*

The Economist Intelligence Unit (Asia) Limited, 10th Floor, Luk Kwok Centre, 72 Gloucester Road, Wanchai, Hong Kong (Phone Number in U.S. (800) 938-4685); *Asian Market Atlas.*

Euromonitor International, Inc., 122 South Michigan Avenue, Suite 1200, Chicago, Illinois 60603 (800) 577-EURO; *International Marketing Data and Statistics;* and *World Marketing Data and Statistics.*

Europa Publications Limited, 18 Bedford Square, London, WC1B 3JN, England; *The Europa World Year Book.*

M.E. Sharpe, 80 Business Park Drive, Armonk, New York 10504 (800) 541-6563; *The Illustrated Book of World Rankings.*

St. Martin's Press, Inc., 175 Fifth Avenue, New York, New York 10010 (800) 221-7945; *The Statesman's Year-Book.*

Statistical Office of the United Nations, Publishing Service, New York, New York 10017 (800) 253-9646; *Human Development Report;* and *Statistical Yearbook for Asia and the Pacific.*

MALAYSIA - TUNGSTEN PRODUCTION AND CONSUMPTION - See MALAYSIA - MINING AND MINERAL PRODUCTS

MALAYSIA - UNEMPLOYMENT

Central Intelligence Agency, Washington, D.C. 20505 (703) 482-1100, www.cia.gov; *The World Factbook.*

Euromonitor International, Inc., 122 South Michigan Avenue, Suite 1200, Chicago, Illinois 60603 (800) 577-EURO; *International Marketing Data and Statistics.*

International Labour Office, I.L.O. Publications, 1828 L Street, N.W., Suite 801, Washington, D.C. 20036 (301) 638-3152; *Yearbook of Labour Statistics.*

St. Martin's Press, Inc., 175 Fifth Avenue, New York, New York 10010 (800) 221-7945; *The Statesman's Year-Book.*

Statistical Office of the United Nations, Publishing Service, New York, New York 10017 (800) 253-9646; *Statistical Yearbook.*

MALAYSIA - URANIUM PRODUCTION AND CONSUMPTION - See MALAYSIA - MINING AND MINERAL PRODUCTS

MALAYSIA - UTILITIES

Statistical Office of the United Nations, Publishing Service, New York, New York 10017 (800) 253-9646; *Electric Power in Asia and the Pacific.*

MALAYSIA - VANADIUM AND VANADIUM

ORE PRODUCTION - See MALAYSIA - MINING AND MINERAL PRODUCTS

MALAYSIA - VITAL STATISTICS

St. Martin's Press, Inc., 175 Fifth Avenue, New York, New York 10010 (800) 221-7945; *The Statesman's Year-Book.*

Statistical Office of the United Nations, Publishing Service, New York, New York 10017 (800) 253-9646; *Statistical Yearbook.*

World Health Organization, Office of Publications, 20 Avenue Appia, CH-1211 Geneva 27, Switzerland (Telephone Number in U.S. (518) 436-9686); *World Health Statistics Annual.*

MALAYSIA - WAGES

International Labour Office, I.L.O. Publications, 1828 L Street, N.W., Suite 801, Washington, D.C. 20036 (301) 638-3152; *Yearbook of Labour Statistics.*

MALAYSIA - WAGES AND PRICES

Statistical Office of the United Nations, Publishing Service, New York, New York 10017 (800) 253-9646; *Statistical Yearbook for Asia and the Pacific.*

MALAYSIA - WATERMELON PRODUCTION - See MALAYSIA - CROPS

MALAYSIA - WEATHER

M.E. Sharpe, 80 Business Park Drive, Armonk, New York 10504 (800) 541-6563; *The Illustrated Book of World Rankings.*

MALAYSIA - WHEAT PRODUCTION - See MALAYSIA - CROPS

MALAYSIA - WHOLESALE PRICES - INDEX NUMBERS

Asian Development Bank, Post Office Box 789, 1099 Manila, Philippines; *Key Indicators of Developing Asian and Pacific Countries.*

MALAYSIA - WHOLESALE TRADE

Statistical Office of the United Nations, Publishing Service, New York, New York 10017 (800) 253-9646; *Statistical Yearbook.*

MALAYSIA - WINE PRODUCTION - See MALAYSIA - BEVERAGES

MALAYSIA - WOOD - See MALAYSIA - FORESTRY AND FOREST PRODUCTS

MALAYSIA - WOOL PRODUCTION - See MALAYSIA - TEXTILE INDUSTRY

MALAYSIA - YARN PRODUCTION - See MALAYSIA - TEXTILE INDUSTRY

MALAYSIA - ZINC AND ZINC ORE PRODUCTION AND CONSUMPTION - See MALAYSIA - MINING AND MINERAL PRODUCTS

MALAYSIA - ZOOS AND BOTANICAL GARDENS

United Nations Educational, Scientific and Cultural Organization (UNESCO), 7 Place de Fontenoy, F-75700 Paris, France (Telephone Number in U.S. (212) 963-5981); *Statistical Yearbook.*

Maldives - National Statistical Office

Ministry of Planning and Environment, Male 20-05, Republic of Maldives.

Maldives - Primary Statistics Source

Ministry of Planning and Development, Maldives; *Statistical Year Book of Maldives.*

MALDIVES - AGRICULTURE

Asian Development Bank, Post Office Box 789, 1099 Manila, Philippines; *Key Indicators of Developing Asian and Pacific Countries.*

Euromonitor International, Inc., 122 South Michigan Avenue, Suite 1200, Chicago, Illinois 60603 (800) 577-EURO; *World Marketing Data and Statistics.*

Europa Publications Limited, 18 Bedford Square, London, WC1B 3JN, England; *The Europa World Year Book.*

Food and Agricultural Organization of the United Nations (FAO), Via delle Terme di Caracalla, 00100 Rome, Italy (Telephone Number in U.S. (202) 653-2400); *Production Yearbook; The State of Food and Agriculture;* and *Trade Yearbook.*

St. Martin's Press, Inc., 175 Fifth Avenue, New York, New York 10010 (800) 221-7945; *The Statesman's Year-Book.*

Statistical Office of the United Nations, Publishing Service, New York, New York 10017 (800) 253-9646; *Asia-Pacific in Figures;* and *Statistical Yearbook for Asia and the Pacific.*

United Nations Conference on Trade and Development, Central Statistical Service, Palais des Nations, Geneva, Switzerland (Telephone in U.S. (800) 253-9646); *UNCTAD Commodity Yearbook.*

MALDIVES - AIRLINE SERVICE

St. Martin's Press, Inc., 175 Fifth Avenue, New York, New York 10010 (800) 221-7945; *The Statesman's Year-Book.*

MALDIVES - AIRPORTS

Central Intelligence Agency, Washington, D.C. 20505 (703) 482-1100, www.cia.gov; *The World Factbook.*

MALDIVES - AREA AND DENSITY OF POPULATION

Central Intelligence Agency, Washington, D.C. 20505 (703) 482-1100, www.cia.gov; *The World Factbook.*

Euromonitor International, Inc., 122 South Michingan Avenue, Suite 1200, Chicago, Illinois 60603 (800) 577-EURO; *The World Economic Factbook.*

Europa Publications Limited, 18 Bedford Square, London, WC1B 3JN, England; *The Europa World Year Book.*

Food and Agricultural Organization of the United Nations (FAO), Via delle Terme di Caracalla, 00100 Rome, Italy (Telephone Number in U.S. (202) 653-2400); *The State of Food and Agriculture.*

St. Martin's Press, Inc., 175 Fifth Avenue, New York, New York 10010 (800) 221-7945; *The Statesman's Year-Book.*

Statistical Office of the United Nations, Publishing Service, New York, New York 10017 (800) 253-9646; *Statistical Yearbook.*

MALDIVES - BALANCE OF PAYMENTS

Europa Publications Limited, 18 Bedford Square, London, WC1B 3JN, England; *The Europa World Year Book.*

United Nations Conference on Trade and Development (UNCTAD), New York, New York 10017 (800) 253-9646; *Handbook of International Trade and Development Statistics.*

MALDIVES - BANKING

Asian Development Bank, Post Office Box 789, 1099 Manila, Philippines; *Key Indicators of Developing Asian and Pacific Countries.*

Euromonitor International, Inc., 122 South Michigan Avenue, Suite 1200, Chicago, Illinois 60603 (800) 577-EURO; *World Marketing Data and Statistics.*

Europa Publications Limited, 18 Bedford Square, London, WC1B 3JN, England; *The Europa World Year Book.*

MALDIVES - BIRTH RATES

Central Intelligence Agency,

Washington, D.C. 20505 (703) 482-1100, www.cia.gov; *The World Factbook.*

Euromonitor International, Inc., 122 South Michingan Avenue, Suite 1200, Chicago, Illinois 60603 (800) 577-EURO; *International Marketing Data and Statistics;* and *The World Economic Factbook.*

Europa Publications Limited, 18 Bedford Square, London, WC1B 3JN, England; *The Europa World Year Book.*

Statistical Office of the United Nations, Publishing Service, New York, New York 10017 (800) 253-9646; *Asia-Pacific in Figures; Demographic Yearbook;* and *Statistical Yearbook.*

World Health Organization, Office of Publications, 20 Avenue Appia, CH-1211 Geneva 27, Switzerland (Telephone Number in U.S. (518) 436-9686); *World Health Statistics Annual.*

MALDIVES - BONDS

Asian Development Bank, Post Office Box 789, 1099 Manila, Philippines; *Key Indicators of Developing Asian and Pacific Countries.*

MALDIVES - BROADCASTING

Billboard Limited, Post Office Box 9027, 1006 AA Amsterdam, The Netherlands (Telephone Number in U.S. (212) 764-7300); *World Radio TV Handbook.*

Central Intelligence Agency, Washington, D.C. 20505 (703) 482-1100, www.cia.gov; *The World Factbook.*

Euromonitor International, Inc., 122 South Michigan Avenue, Suite 1200, Chicago, Illinois 60603 (800) 577-EURO; *World Marketing Data and Statistics.*

St. Martin's Press, Inc., 175 Fifth Avenue, New York, New York 10010 (800) 221-7945; *The Statesman's Year-Book.*

United Nations Educational, Scientific and Cultural Organization (UNESCO), 7 Place de Fontenoy, F-75700 Paris, France (Telephone Number in U.S. (212) 963-5981); *Statistical Yearbook.*

MALDIVES - BUDGET

Central Intelligence Agency, Washington, D.C. 20505 (703) 482-1100, www.cia.gov; *The World Factbook.*

MALDIVES - CALORIE SUPPLY

Asian Development Bank, Post Office Box 789, 1099 Manila, Philippines; *Key Indicators of Developing Asian and Pacific Countries.*

Food and Agricultural Organization of the United Nations (FAO), Via delle Terme di Caracalla, 00100 Rome, Italy (Telephone Number in U.S. (202) 653-2400); *The State of Food and Agriculture.*

MALDIVES - CAPITAL INVESTMENT

Asian Development Bank, Post Office Box 789, 1099 Manila, Philippines; *Key Indicators of Developing Asian and Pacific Countries.*

MALDIVES - CAPITAL REVENUE

Asian Development Bank, Post Office Box 789, 1099 Manila, Philippines; *Key Indicators of Developing Asian and Pacific Countries.*

MALDIVES - CLIMATE

St. Martin's Press, Inc., 175 Fifth Avenue, New York, New York 10010 (800) 221-7945; *The Statesman's Year-Book.*

MALDIVES - COMMERCE

St. Martin's Press, Inc., 175 Fifth Avenue, New York, New York 10010 (800) 221-7945; *The Statesman's Year-Book.*

MALDIVES - COMMUNICATION

Statistical Office of the United Nations, Publishing Service, New York, New York 10017 (800) 253-9646; *Statistical Yearbook for Asia and the Pacific.*

MALDIVES - CONSUMER PRICE INDEX

Asian Development Bank, Post Office Box 789, 1099 Manila, Philippines; *Key Indicators of Developing Asian and Pacific Countries.*

MALDIVES - CONSUMER PRICES

Euromonitor International, Inc., 122 South Michigan Avenue, Suite 1200, Chicago, Illinois 60603 (800) 577-EURO; *World Marketing Data and Statistics.*

MALDIVES - CORN PRODUCTION - See MALDIVES - CROPS

MALDIVES - CROPS

Asian Development Bank, Post Office Box 789, 1099 Manila, Philippines; *Key Indicators of Developing Asian and Pacific Countries.*

Europa Publications Limited, 18 Bedford Square, London, WC1B 3JN, England; *The Europa World Year Book.*

Food and Agricultural Organization of the United Nations (FAO), Via delle Terme di Caracalla, 00100 Rome, Italy (Telephone Number in U.S. (202) 653-2400);

Production Yearbook; and *The State of Food and Agriculture.*

St. Martin's Press, Inc., 175 Fifth Avenue, New York, New York 10010 (800) 221-7945; *The Statesman's Year-Book.*

United Nations Conference on Trade and Development, Central Statistical Service, Palais des Nations, Geneva, Switzerland (Telephone in U.S. (800) 253-9646); *UNCTAD Commodity Yearbook.*

MALDIVES - CUSTOMS DUTIES

St. Martin's Press, Inc., 175 Fifth Avenue, New York, New York 10010 (800) 221-7945; *The Statesman's Year-Book.*

MALDIVES - DAIRY PRODUCTS

Food and Agricultural Organization of the United Nations (FAO), Via delle Terme di Caracalla, 00100 Rome, Italy (Telephone Number in U.S. (202) 653-2400); *The State of Food and Agriculture.*

MALDIVES - DEATH RATES - See MALDIVES - MORTALITY

MALDIVES - DEMOGRAPHY

Euromonitor International, Inc., 122 South Michingan Avenue, Suite 1200, Chicago, Illinois 60603 (800) 577-EURO; *International Marketing Data and Statistics; World Marketing Data and Statistics;* and *The World Economic Factbook.*

Statistical Office of the United Nations, Publishing Service, New York, New York 10017 (800) 253-9646; *Asia-Pacific in Figures;* and *Human Development Report.*

MALDIVES - DEVELOPMENT ASSISTANCE

Asian Development Bank, Post Office Box 789, 1099 Manila, Philippines; *Key Indicators of Developing Asian and Pacific Countries.*

Statistical Office of the United Nations, Publishing Service, New York, New York 10017 (800) 253-9646; *Statistical Yearbook.*

MALDIVES - DIVORCE RATES

Statistical Office of the United Nations, Publishing Service, New York, New York 10017 (800) 253-9646; *Demographic Yearbook; Statistical Yearbook;* and *Statistical Yearbook for Asia and the Pacific.*

MALDIVES - ECONOMY

Asian Development Bank, Post Office Box 789, 1099 Manila, Philippines; *Key Indicators of Developing Asian and Pacific Countries.*

Central Intelligence Agency, Washington, D.C. 20505 (703) 482-1100, www.cia.gov; *The World Factbook*.

Euromonitor International, Inc., 122 South Michingan Avenue, Suite 1200, Chicago, Illinois 60603 (800) 577-EURO; *The World Economic Factbook;* and *World Marketing Data and Statistics*.

Europa Publications Limited, 18 Bedford Square, London, WC1B 3JN, England; *The Europa World Year Book*.

St. Martin's Press, Inc., 175 Fifth Avenue, New York, New York 10010 (800) 221-7945; *The Statesman's Year-Book*.

Statistical Office of the United Nations, Publishing Service, New York, New York 10017 (800) 253-9646; *World Statistics Pocketbook*.

The World Bank, 1818 H Street, NW, Washington, D.C. 20433 (202) 477-1234; *The World Bank Atlas*.

MALDIVES - EDUCATION

Euromonitor International, Inc., 122 South Michingan Avenue, Suite 1200, Chicago, Illinois 60603 (800) 577-EURO; *International Marketing Data and Statistics;* and *World Marketing Data and Statistics*.

Europa Publications Limited, 18 Bedford Square, London, WC1B 3JN, England; *The Europa World Year Book*.

St. Martin's Press, Inc., 175 Fifth Avenue, New York, New York 10010 (800) 221-7945; *The Statesman's Year-Book*.

Statistical Office of the United Nations, Publishing Service, New York, New York 10017 (800) 253-9646; *Asia-Pacific in Figures; Human Development Report;* and *Statistical Yearbook for Asia and the Pacific*.

United Nations Educational, Scientific and Cultural Organization (UNESCO), 7 Place de Fontenoy, F-75700 Paris, France (Telephone Number in U.S. (212) 963-5981); *Statistical Yearbook*.

MALDIVES - EGG PRODUCTION - See MALDIVES - DAIRY PRODUCTS

MALDIVES - ELECTRICITY

Asian Development Bank, Post Office Box 789, 1099 Manila, Philippines; *Key Indicators of Developing Asian and Pacific Countries*.

Central Intelligence Agency, Washington, D.C. 20505 (703) 482-1100, www.cia.gov; *The World Factbook*.

St. Martin's Press, Inc., 175 Fifth Avenue, New York, New York 10010 (800) 221-7945;

The Statesman's Year-Book.

Statistical Office of the United Nations, Publishing Service, New York, New York 10017 (800) 253-9646; *Human Development Report*.

MALDIVES - EMPLOYMENT

Euromonitor International, Inc., 122 South Michingan Avenue, Suite 1200, Chicago, Illinois 60603 (800) 577-EURO; *International Marketing Data and Statistics*.

Statistical Office of the United Nations, Publishing Service, New York, New York 10017 (800) 253-9646; *Asia-Pacific in Figures*.

MALDIVES - ENERGY

Euromonitor International, Inc., 122 South Michingan Avenue, Suite 1200, Chicago, Illinois 60603 (800) 577-EURO; *International Marketing Data and Statistics; World Marketing Data and Statistics;* and *The World Economic Factbook*.

Food and Agricultural Organization of the United Nations (FAO), Via delle Terme di Caracalla, 00100 Rome, Italy (Telephone Number in U.S. (202) 653-2400); *The State of Food and Agriculture*.

St. Martin's Press, Inc., 175 Fifth Avenue, New York, New York 10010 (800) 221-7945; *The Statesman's Year-Book*.

Statistical Office of the United Nations, Publishing Service, New York, New York 10017 (800) 253-9646; *Asia-Pacific in Figures; Human Development Report; World Statistics Pocketbook;* and *Statistical Yearbook for Asia and the Pacific*.

The World Bank, 1818 H Street, NW, Washington, D.C. 20433 (202) 477-1234; *The World Bank Atlas*.

MALDIVES - ENVIRONMENT

Statistical Office of the United Nations, Publishing Service, New York, New York 10017 (800) 253-9646; *World Statistics Pocketbook*.

MALDIVES - EXCHANGE RATES

Asian Development Bank, Post Office Box 789, 1099 Manila, Philippines; *Key Indicators of Developing Asian and Pacific Countries*.

Central Intelligence Agency, Washington, D.C. 20505 (703) 482-1100, www.cia.gov; *The World Factbook*.

Euromonitor International, Inc., 122 South Michingan Avenue, Suite 1200, Chicago, Illinois 60603 (800) 577-EURO; *International Marketing Data and Statistics;*

and *The World Economic Factbook*.

Europa Publications Limited, 18 Bedford Square, London, WC1B 3JN, England; *The Europa World Year Book*.

Statistical Office of the United Nations, Publishing Service, New York, New York 10017 (800) 253-9646; *Statistical Yearbook;* and *World Statistics Pocketbook*.

Walden Publishing Ltd., Two Market Street, Saffron Walden Essex, CB10 1HZ, England; *The World of Information Asia and Pacific Review*.

MALDIVES - EXPORTS

Asian Development Bank, Post Office Box 789, 1099 Manila, Philippines; *Key Indicators of Developing Asian and Pacific Countries*.

Central Intelligence Agency, Washington, D.C. 20505 (703) 482-1100, www.cia.gov; *The World Factbook*.

Euromonitor International, Inc., 122 South Michingan Avenue, Suite 1200, Chicago, Illinois 60603 (800) 577-EURO; *International Marketing Data and Statistics;* and *The World Economic Factbook*.

Europa Publications Limited, 18 Bedford Square, London, WC1B 3JN, England; *The Europa World Year Book*.

Food and Agricultural Organization of the United Nations (FAO), Via delle Terme di Caracalla, 00100 Rome, Italy (Telephone Number in U.S. (202) 653-2400); *The State of Food and Agriculture*.

International Monetary Fund, 700 Nineteenth Street, NW, Washington, D.C. 20431 (202) 623-7000; *Direction of Trade Statistics*.

St. Martin's Press, Inc., 175 Fifth Avenue, New York, New York 10010 (800) 221-7945; *The Statesman's Year-Book*.

United Nations Conference on Trade and Development (UNCTAD), New York, New York 10017 (800) 253-9646, *Handbook of International Trade and Development Statistics*.

Walden Publishing Ltd., Two Market Street, Saffron Walden Essex, CB10 1HZ, England; *The World of Information Asia and Pacific Review*.

MALDIVES - EXTERNAL FINANCING

Asian Development Bank, Post Office Box 789, 1099 Manila, Philippines; *Key Indicators of Developing Asian and Pacific Countries*.

MALDIVES - EXTERNAL INDEBTEDNESS

Asian Development Bank, Post Office Box 789, 1099 Manila, Philippines; *Key Indicators of Developing Asian and Pacific Countries.*

MALDIVES - EXTERNAL TRADE

Asian Development Bank, Post Office Box 789, 1099 Manila, Philippines; *Key Indicators of Developing Asian and Pacific Countries.*

Euromonitor International, Inc., 122 South Michigan Avenue, Suite 1200, Chicago, Illinois 60603 (800) 577-EURO; *World Marketing Data and Statistics.*

Food and Agricultural Organization of the United Nations (FAO), Via delle Terme di Caracalla, 00100 Rome, Italy (Telephone Number in U.S. (202) 653-2400); *The State of Food and Agriculture; and Trade Yearbook.*

Statistical Office of the United Nations, Publishing Service, New York, New York 10017 (800) 253-9646; *Asia-Pacific in Figures; and Statistical Yearbook for Asia and the Pacific.*

MALDIVES - FARM CROPS - See
MALDIVES - CROPS

MALDIVES - FERTILITY RATE

Central Intelligence Agency, Washington, D.C. 20505 (703) 482-1100, www.cia.gov; *The World Factbook.*

Statistical Office of the United Nations, Publishing Service, New York, New York 10017 (800) 253-9646; *Human Development Report.*

The World Bank, 1818 H Street, NW, Washington, D.C. 20433 (202) 477-1234; *The World Bank Atlas.*

MALDIVES - FERTILIZER

Food and Agricultural Organization of the United Nations (FAO), Via delle Terme di Caracalla, 00100 Rome, Italy (Telephone Number in U.S. (202) 653-2400); *The State of Food and Agriculture.*

MALDIVES - FETAL MORTALITY - MALDIVES - MORTALITY

MALDIVES - FINANCE

Asian Development Bank, Post Office Box 789, 1099 Manila, Philippines; *Key Indicators of Developing Asian and Pacific Countries.*

Europa Publications Limited, 18 Bedford Square, London, WC1B 3JN, England; *The Europa World Year Book.*

St. Martin's Press, Inc., 175 Fifth Avenue, New York, New York 10010 (800) 221-7945; *The Statesman's Year-Book.*

Statistical Office of the United Nations, Publishing Service, New York, New York 10017 (800) 253-9646; *Statistical Yearbook for Asia and the Pacific.*

MALDIVES - FISHERIES

Europa Publications Limited, 18 Bedford Square, London, WC1B 3JN, England; *The Europa World Year Book.*

Food and Agricultural Organization of the United Nations (FAO), Via delle Terme di Caracalla, 00100 Rome, Italy (Telephone Number in U.S. (202) 653-2400); *The State of Food and Agriculture; and Yearbook of Fishery Statistics.*

St. Martin's Press, Inc., 175 Fifth Avenue, New York, New York 10010 (800) 221-7945; *The Statesman's Year-Book.*

Statistical Office of the United Nations, Publishing Service, New York, New York 10017 (800) 253-9646; *Statistical Yearbook.*

United Nations Conference on Trade and Development, Central Statistical Service, Palais des Nations, Geneva, Switzerland (Telephone in U.S. (800) 253-9646); *UNCTAD Commodity Yearbook.*

MALDIVES - FOOD

Food and Agricultural Organization of the United Nations (FAO), Via delle Terme di Caracalla, 00100 Rome, Italy (Telephone Number in U.S. (202) 653-2400); *Production Yearbook; and The State of Food and Agriculture.*

Statistical Office of the United Nations, Publishing Service, New York, New York 10017 (800) 253-9646; *Human Development Report; and Statistical Yearbook for Asia and the Pacific.*

United Nations Conference on Trade and Development, Central Statistical Service, Palais des Nations, Geneva, Switzerland (Telephone in U.S. (800) 253-9646); *UNCTAD Commodity Yearbook.*

MALDIVES - FOREIGN DEBT

Walden Publishing Ltd., Two Market Street, Saffron Walden Essex, CB10 1HZ, England; *The World of Information Asia and Pacific Review.*

MALDIVES - FOREIGN TRADE

Asian Development Bank, Post Office Box 789, 1099 Manila, Philippines; *Key Indicators of Developing Asian and Pacific Countries.*

Euromonitor International, Inc., 122 South Michigan Avenue, Suite 1200, Chicago, Illinois 60603 (800) 577-EURO; *The World Economic Factbook.*

Europa Publications Limited, 18 Bedford Square, London, WC1B 3JN, England; *The Europa World Year Book.*

Food and Agricultural Organization of the United Nations (FAO), Via delle Terme di Caracalla, 00100 Rome, Italy (Telephone Number in U.S. (202) 653-2400); *The State of Food and Agriculture.*

St. Martin's Press, Inc., 175 Fifth Avenue, New York, New York 10010 (800) 221-7945; *The Statesman's Year-Book.*

United Nations Conference on Trade and Development, Central Statistical Service, Palais des Nations, Geneva, Switzerland (Telephone in U.S. (800) 253-9646); *UNCTAD Commodity Yearbook.*

MALDIVES - FORESTRY AND FOREST PRODUCTS

Food and Agricultural Organization of the United Nations (FAO), Via delle Terme di Caracalla, 00100 Rome, Italy (Telephone Number in U.S. (202) 653-2400); *The State of Food and Agriculture.*

Statistical Office of the United Nations, Publishing Service, New York, New York 10017 (800) 253-9646; *Statistical Yearbook.*

United Nations Conference on Trade and Development, Central Statistical Service, Palais des Nations, Geneva, Switzerland (Telephone in U.S. (800) 253-9646); *UNCTAD Commodity Yearbook.*

MALDIVES - GENERAL MORTALITY - See MALDIVES - MORTALITY

MALDIVES - GOVERNMENT

Asian Development Bank, Post Office Box 789, 1099 Manila, Philippines; *Key Indicators of Developing Asian and Pacific Countries.*

Central Intelligence Agency, Washington, D.C. 20505 (703) 482-1100, www.cia.gov; *The World Factbook.*

Europa Publications Limited, 18 Bedford Square, London, WC1B 3JN, England; *The Europa World Year Book.*

St. Martin's Press, Inc., 175 Fifth Avenue, New York, New York 10010 (800) 221-7945; *The Statesman's Year-Book.*

Statistical Office of the United Nations, Publishing Service, New York, New York 10017 (800) 253-9646; *Asia-Pacific in Figures; and National Accounts Statistics.*

MALDIVES - GRAIN PRODUCTION - See MALDIVES - CROPS

MALDIVES - GROSS DOMESTIC PRODUCT

Asian Development Bank, Post Office Box 789, 1099 Manila, Philippines; *Key Indicators of Developing Asian and Pacific Countries.*

Euromonitor International, Inc., 122 South Michigan Avenue, Suite 1200, Chicago, Illinois 60603 (800) 577-EURO; *International Marketing Data and Statistics;* and *The World Economic Factbook.*

Europa Publications Limited, 18 Bedford Square, London, WC1B 3JN, England; *The Europa World Year Book.*

Statistical Office of the United Nations, Publishing Service, New York, New York 10017 (800) 253-9646; *Human Development Report; National Accounts Statistics;* and *Statistical Yearbook.*

MALDIVES - GROSS NATIONAL PRODUCT

Asian Development Bank, Post Office Box 789, 1099 Manila, Philippines; *Key Indicators of Developing Asian and Pacific Countries.*

St. Martin's Press, Inc., 175 Fifth Avenue, New York, New York 10010 (800) 221-7945; *The Statesman's Year-Book.*

Statistical Office of the United Nations, Publishing Service, New York, New York 10017 (800) 253-9646; *National Accounts Statistics.*

Walden Publishing Ltd., Two Market Street, Saffron Walden Essex, CB10 1HZ, England; *The World of Information Asia and Pacific Review.*

The World Bank, 1818 H Street, NW, Washington, D.C. 20433 (202) 477-1234; *The World Bank Atlas.*

MALDIVES - HEALTH

Euromonitor International, Inc., 122 South Michigan Avenue, Suite 1200, Chicago, Illinois 60603 (800) 577-EURO; *World Marketing Data and Statistics.*

St. Martin's Press, Inc., 175 Fifth Avenue, New York, New York 10010 (800) 221-7945; *The Statesman's Year-Book.*

Statistical Office of the United Nations, Publishing Service, New York, New York 10017 (800) 253-9646; *Asia-Pacific in Figures; Human Development Report;* and *Statistical Yearbook.*

MALDIVES - HIGHWAYS

Central Intelligence Agency,

Washington, D.C. 20505 (703) 482-1100, www.cia.gov; *The World Factbook.*

St. Martin's Press, Inc., 175 Fifth Avenue, New York, New York 10010 (800) 221-7945; *The Statesman's Year-Book.*

MALDIVES - HOUSING AND HOUSING UNITS

Euromonitor International, Inc., 122 South Michigan Avenue, Suite 1200, Chicago, Illinois 60603 (800) 577-EURO; *World Marketing Data and Statistics.*

MALDIVES - ILLITERATE POPULATION

Central Intelligence Agency, Washington, D.C. 20505 (703) 482-1100, www.cia.gov; *The World Factbook.*

Euromonitor International, Inc., 122 South Michigan Avenue, Suite 1200, Chicago, Illinois 60603 (800) 577-EURO; *The World Economic Factbook.*

Statistical Office of the United Nations, Publishing Service, New York, New York 10017 (800) 253-9646; *Asia-Pacific in Figures;* and *Human Development Report.*

United Nations Educational, Scientific and Cultural Organization (UNESCO), 7 Place de Fontenoy, F-75700 Paris, France (Telephone Number in U.S. (212) 963-5981); *Statistical Yearbook.*

MALDIVES - IMPORTS

Asian Development Bank, Post Office Box 789, 1099 Manila, Philippines; *Key Indicators of Developing Asian and Pacific Countries.*

Central Intelligence Agency, Washington, D.C. 20505 (703) 482-1100, www.cia.gov; *The World Factbook.*

Euromonitor International, Inc., 122 South Michigan Avenue, Suite 1200, Chicago, Illinois 60603 (800) 577-EURO; *International Marketing Data and Statistics;* and *The World Economic Factbook.*

Europa Publications Limited, 18 Bedford Square, London, WC1B 3JN, England; *The Europa World Year Book.*

Food and Agricultural Organization of the United Nations (FAO), Via delle Terme di Caracalla, 00100 Rome, Italy (Telephone Number in U.S. (202) 653-2400); *The State of Food and Agriculture.*

International Monetary Fund, 700 Nineteenth Street, NW, Washington, D.C. 20431 (202) 623-7000; *Direction of Trade Statistics.*

St. Martin's Press, Inc., 175 Fifth Avenue, New York, New York 10010 (800)

221-7945; *The Statesman's Year-Book.*

United Nations Conference on Trade and Development (UNCTAD), New York, New York 10017 (800) 253-9646, *Handbook of International Trade and Development Statistics.*

Walden Publishing Ltd., Two Market Street, Saffron Walden Essex, CB10 1HZ, England; *The World of Information Asia and Pacific Review.*

MALDIVES - INDUSTRY

Central Intelligence Agency, Washington, D.C. 20505 (703) 482-1100, www.cia.gov; *The World Factbook.*

Euromonitor International, Inc., 122 South Michigan Avenue, Suite 1200, Chicago, Illinois 60603 (800) 577-EURO; *The World Economic Factbook;* and *World Marketing Data and Statistics.*

Europa Publications Limited, 18 Bedford Square, London, WC1B 3JN, England; *The Europa World Year Book.*

St. Martin's Press, Inc., 175 Fifth Avenue, New York, New York 10010 (800) 221-7945; *The Statesman's Year-Book.*

Statistical Office of the United Nations, Publishing Service, New York, New York 10017 (800) 253-9646; *Asia-Pacific in Figures;* and *Statistical Yearbook for Asia and the Pacific.*

MALDIVES - INFANT AND MATERNAL MORTALITY - See MALDIVES - MORTALITY

MALDIVES - INTERNAL TRADE

Statistical Office of the United Nations, Publishing Service, New York, New York 10017 (800) 253-9646; *Statistical Yearbook for Asia and the Pacific.*

MALDIVES - INTERNATIONAL RESERVES EXCLUDING GOLD

Asian Development Bank, Post Office Box 789, 1099 Manila, Philippines; *Key Indicators of Developing Asian and Pacific Countries.*

MALDIVES - INTERNATIONAL STATISTICS

Asian Development Bank, Post Office Box 789, 1099 Manila, Philippines; *Key Indicators of Developing Asian and Pacific Countries.*

MALDIVES - LABOR

Central Intelligence Agency, Washington, D.C. 20505 (703) 482-1100, www.cia.gov; *The World Factbook.*

Euromonitor International, Inc., 122

South Michigan Avenue, Suite 1200, Chicago, Illinois 60603 (800) 577-EURO; *International Marketing Data and Statistics;* and *World Marketing Data and Statistics.*

Europa Publications Limited, 18 Bedford Square, London, WC1B 3JN, England; *The Europa World Year Book.*

Food and Agricultural Organization of the United Nations (FAO), Via delle Terme di Caracalla, 00100 Rome, Italy (Telephone Number in U.S. (202) 653-2400); *The State of Food and Agriculture.*

St. Martin's Press, Inc., 175 Fifth Avenue, New York, New York 10010 (800) 221-7945; *The Statesman's Year-Book.*

Statistical Office of the United Nations, Publishing Service, New York, New York 10017 (800) 253-9646; *Human Development Report.*

The World Bank, 1818 H Street, NW, Washington, D.C. 20433 (202) 477-1234; *The World Bank Atlas.*

MALDIVES - LAND USE

Central Intelligence Agency, Washington, D.C. 20505 (703) 482-1100, www.cia.gov; *The World Factbook.*

Euromonitor International, Inc., 122 South Michingan Avenue, Suite 1200, Chicago, Illinois 60603 (800) 577-EURO; *International Marketing Data and Statistics.*

Food and Agricultural Organization of the United Nations (FAO), Via delle Terme di Caracalla, 00100 Rome, Italy (Telephone Number in U.S. (202) 653-2400); *Production Yearbook.*

MALDIVES - LIFE EXPECTANCY

Central Intelligence Agency, Washington, D.C. 20505 (703) 482-1100, www.cia.gov; *The World Factbook.*

Euromonitor International, Inc., 122 South Michingan Avenue, Suite 1200, Chicago, Illinois 60603 (800) 577-EURO; *The World Economic Factbook.*

Statistical Office of the United Nations, Publishing Service, New York, New York 10017 (800) 253-9646; *Asia-Pacific in Figures;* and *Human Development Report;* and *World Statistics Pocketbook.*

The World Bank, 1818 H Street, NW, Washington, D.C. 20433 (202) 477-1234; *The World Bank Atlas.*

MALDIVES - LITERACY RATE

Euromonitor International, Inc., 122 South Michigan Avenue, Suite 1200, Chicago, Illinois 60603 (800) 577-EURO;

World Marketing Data and Statistics.

MALDIVES - LIVESTOCK AND POULTRY

Food and Agricultural Organization of the United Nations (FAO), Via delle Terme di Caracalla, 00100 Rome, Italy (Telephone Number in U.S. (202) 653-2400); *Production Yearbook;* and *The State of Food and Agriculture.*

United Nations Conference on Trade and Development, Central Statistical Service, Palais des Nations, Geneva, Switzerland (Telephone in U.S. (800) 253-9646); *UNCTAD Commodity Yearbook.*

MALDIVES - MAIL - NUMBER OF ITEMS SENT AND RECEIVED

Statistical Office of the United Nations, Publishing Service, New York, New York 10017 (800) 253-9646; *Statistical Yearbook.*

MALDIVES - MANPOWER

Statistical Office of the United Nations, Publishing Service, New York, New York 10017 (800) 253-9646; *Statistical Yearbook for Asia and the Pacific.*

MALDIVES - MANUFACTURING

Asian Development Bank, Post Office Box 789, 1099 Manila, Philippines; *Key Indicators of Developing Asian and Pacific Countries.*

MALDIVES - MARRIAGE RATES

Statistical Office of the United Nations, Publishing Service, New York, New York 10017 (800) 253-9646; *Demographic Yearbook;* and *Statistical Yearbook.*

MALDIVES - MEAT PRODUCTION - See MALDIVES - LIVESTOCK AND POULTRY

MALDIVES - MERCHANT SHIPPING

Europa Publications Limited, 18 Bedford Square, London, WC1B 3JN, England; *The Europa World Year Book.*

St. Martin's Press, Inc., 175 Fifth Avenue, New York, New York 10010 (800) 221-7945; *The Statesman's Year-Book.*

Statistical Office of the United Nations, Publishing Service, New York, New York 10017 (800) 253-9646; *Statistical Yearbook.*

U.S. Department of Transportation, Maritime Administration, 400 Seventh Street, SW, Washington, D.C. 20590 (202) 366-5807, www.marad.dot.gov; *A Statistical Analysis of the World's Merchant Fleets.*

MALDIVES - MILITARY

Central Intelligence Agency, Washington, D.C. 20505 (703) 482-1100, www.cia.gov; *The World Factbook.*

Euromonitor International, Inc., 122 South Michigan Avenue, Suite 1200, Chicago, Illinois 60603 (800) 577-EURO; *World Marketing Data and Statistics.*

Statistical Office of the United Nations, Publishing Service, New York, New York 10017 (800) 253-9646; *Human Development Report.*

MALDIVES - MINING AND MINERAL PRODUCTS

Asian Development Bank, Post Office Box 789, 1099 Manila, Philippines; *Key Indicators of Developing Asian and Pacific Countries.*

St. Martin's Press, Inc., 175 Fifth Avenue, New York, New York 10010 (800) 221-7945; *The Statesman's Year-Book.*

United Nations Conference on Trade and Development, Central Statistical Service, Palais des Nations, Geneva, Switzerland (Telephone in U.S. (800) 253-9646); *UNCTAD Commodity Yearbook.*

MALDIVES - MONEY EXCHANGE RATES - EXCHANGE RATES

MALDIVES - MONEY SUPPLY

Asian Development Bank, Post Office Box 789, 1099 Manila, Philippines; *Key Indicators of Developing Asian and Pacific Countries.*

Europa Publications Limited, 18 Bedford Square, London, WC1B 3JN, England; *The Europa World Year Book.*

MALDIVES - MORTALITY

Central Intelligence Agency, Washington, D.C. 20505 (703) 482-1100, www.cia.gov; *The World Factbook.*

Euromonitor International, Inc., 122 South Michigan Avenue, Suite 1200, Chicago, Illinois 60603 (800) 577-EURO; *International Marketing Data and Statistics;* and *The World Economic Factbook.*

Europa Publications Limited, 18 Bedford Square, London, WC1B 3JN, England; *The Europa World Year Book.*

Statistical Office of the United Nations, Publishing Service, New York, New York 10017 (800) 253-9646; *Asia-Pacific in Figures; Demographic Yearbook; Human Development Report; World Statistics Pocketbook;* and *Statistical Yearbook.*

The World Bank, 1818 H Street, NW, Washington, D.C. 20433 (202) 477-1234;

The World Bank Atlas.

World Health Organization, Office of Publications, 20 Avenue Appia, CH-1211 Geneva 27, Switzerland (Telephone Number in U.S. (518) 436-9686); *World Health Statistics Annual.*

MALDIVES - MOTOR VEHICLES IN USE

Europa Publications Limited, 18 Bedford Square, London, WC1B 3JN, England; *The Europa World Year Book.*

MALDIVES - MUSEUMS

United Nations Educational, Scientific and Cultural Organization (UNESCO), 7 Place de Fontenoy, F-75700 Paris, France (Telephone Number in U.S. (212) 963-5981); *Statistical Yearbook.*

MALDIVES - NATALITY - See MALDIVES - BIRTH RATES

MALDIVES - NATIONAL ACCOUNTS

Statistical Office of the United Nations, Publishing Service, New York, New York 10017 (800) 253-9646; *Asia-Pacific in Figures;* and *Statistical Yearbook for Asia and the Pacific.*

MALDIVES - NEWSPAPER - See MALDIVES - FORESTRY AND FOREST PRODUCTS

MALDIVES - PERIODICALS

United Nations Educational, Scientific and Cultural Organization (UNESCO), 7 Place de Fontenoy, F-75700 Paris, France (Telephone Number in U.S. (212) 963-5981); *Statistical Yearbook.*

MALDIVES - PESTICIDE USE

Food and Agricultural Organization of the United Nations (FAO), Via delle Terme di Caracalla, 00100 Rome, Italy (Telephone Number in U.S. (202) 653-2400); *The State of Food and Agriculture.*

MALDIVES - PETROLEUM INDUSTRY

Asian Development Bank, Post Office Box 789, 1099 Manila, Philippines; *Key Indicators of Developing Asian and Pacific Countries.*

Food and Agricultural Organization of the United Nations (FAO), Via delle Terme di Caracalla, 00100 Rome, Italy (Telephone Number in U.S. (202) 653-2400); *The State of Food and Agriculture.*

United Nations Conference on Trade and Development, Central Statistical Service, Palais des Nations, Geneva, Switzerland (Telephone in U.S. (800) 253-9646); *UNCTAD Commodity Yearbook.*

MALDIVES - POPULATION

Asian Development Bank, Post Office Box 789, 1099 Manila, Philippines; *Key Indicators of Developing Asian and Pacific Countries.*

Central Intelligence Agency, Washington, D.C. 20505 (703) 482-1100, www.cia.gov; *The World Factbook.*

Euromonitor International, Inc., 122 South Michigan Avenue, Suite 1200, Chicago, Illinois 60603 (800) 577-EURO; *International Marketing Data and Statistics;* and *The World Economic Factbook.*

Europa Publications Limited, 18 Bedford Square, London, WC1B 3JN, England; *The Europa World Year Book.*

Food and Agricultural Organization of the United Nations (FAO), Via delle Terme di Caracalla, 00100 Rome, Italy (Telephone Number in U.S. (202) 653-2400); *Production Yearbook.*

St. Martin's Press, Inc., 175 Fifth Avenue, New York, New York 10010 (800) 221-7945; *The Statesman's Year-Book.*

Statistical Office of the United Nations, Publishing Service, New York, New York 10017 (800) 253-9646; *Asia-Pacific in Figures; Demographic Yearbook; Human Development Report; Statistical Yearbook; World Statistics Pocketbook;* and *Statistical Yearbook for Asia and the Pacific.*

Walden Publishing Ltd., Two Market Street, Saffron Walden Essex, CB10 1HZ, England; *The World of Information Asia and Pacific Review.*

The World Bank, 1818 H Street, NW, Washington, D.C. 20433 (202) 477-1234; *The World Bank Atlas.*

MALDIVES - PRICES

Asian Development Bank, Post Office Box 789, 1099 Manila, Philippines; *Key Indicators of Developing Asian and Pacific Countries.*

Food and Agricultural Organization of the United Nations (FAO), Via delle Terme di Caracalla, 00100 Rome, Italy (Telephone Number in U.S. (202) 653-2400); *Production Yearbook;* and *The State of Food and Agriculture.*

MALDIVES - RADIO BROADCASTING - See MALDIVES - BROADCASTING

MALDIVES - RADIO RECEIVERS

St. Martin's Press, Inc., 175 Fifth Avenue, New York, New York 10010 (800) 221-7945; *The Statesman's Year-Book.*

MALDIVES - RELIGION

Central Intelligence Agency, Washington, D.C. 20505 (703) 482-1100, www.cia.gov; *The World Factbook.*

St. Martin's Press, Inc., 175 Fifth Avenue, New York, New York 10010 (800) 221-7945; *The Statesman's Year-Book.*

MALDIVES - RETAIL TRADE

Euromonitor International, Inc., 122 South Michigan Avenue, Suite 1200, Chicago, Illinois 60603 (800) 577-EURO; *World Marketing Data and Statistics.*

MALDIVES - RICE PRODUCTION - See MALDIVES - CROPS

MALDIVES - ROOT AND TUBER PRODUCTION - See MALDIVES - CROPS

MALDIVES - SOCIAL DATA

Asian Development Bank, Post Office Box 789, 1099 Manila, Philippines; *Key Indicators of Developing Asian and Pacific Countries.*

Statistical Office of the United Nations, Publishing Service, New York, New York 10017 (800) 253-9646; *World Statistics Pocketbook.*

MALDIVES - SOCIAL SECURITY

Statistical Office of the United Nations, Publishing Service, New York, New York 10017 (800) 253-9646; *National Accounts Statistics.*

MALDIVES - STOCKS - COMMODITY - MARKET PRICE - INDEX

Food and Agricultural Organization of the United Nations (FAO), Via delle Terme di Caracalla, 00100 Rome, Italy (Telephone Number in U.S. (202) 653-2400); *The State of Food and Agriculture.*

MALDIVES - TAXATION

Europa Publications Limited, 18 Bedford Square, London, WC1B 3JN, England; *The Europa World Year Book.*

MALDIVES - TELEPHONES IN USE

American Telephone and Telegraph Company, 26 Parsippany Road, Whippany, New Jersey 07981 (800) 222-0300; *The World's Telephones.*

Central Intelligence Agency, Washington, D.C. 20505 (703) 482-1100, www.cia.gov; *The World Factbook.*

St. Martin's Press, Inc., 175 Fifth Avenue, New York, New York 10010 (800) 221-7945; *The Statesman's Year-Book.*

Statistical Office of the United Nations, Publishing Service, New York, New York 10017 (800) 253-9646; *World Statistics Pocketbook.*

United Nations Educational, Scientific and Cultural Organization (UNESCO), 7 Place de Fontenoy, F-75700 Paris, France (Telephone Number in U.S. (212) 963-5981); *Statistical Yearbook.*

MALDIVES - TEXTILE INDUSTRY

St. Martin's Press, Inc., 175 Fifth Avenue, New York, New York 10010 (800) 221-7945; *The Statesman's Year-Book.*

United Nations Conference on Trade and Development, Central Statistical Service, Palais des Nations, Geneva, Switzerland (Telephone in U.S. (800) 253-9646); *UNCTAD Commodity Yearbook.*

MALDIVES - TOURISM

Euromonitor International, Inc., 122 South Michigan Avenue, Suite 1200, Chicago, Illinois 60603 (800) 577-EURO; *The World Economic Factbook;* and *World Marketing Data and Statistics.*

Europa Publications Limited, 18 Bedford Square, London, WC1B 3JN, England; *The Europa World Year Book.*

St. Martin's Press, Inc., 175 Fifth Avenue, New York, New York 10010 (800) 221-7945; *The Statesman's Year-Book.*

World Tourism Organization, Calle Capitan Haya 42, E-28020 Madrid, Spain; *Yearbook of Tourism Statistics.*

MALDIVES - TRADE - See MALDIVES - FOREIGN TRADE

MALDIVES - TRANSPORTATION AND COMMUNICATIONS

Central Intelligence Agency, Washington, D.C. 20505 (703) 482-1100, www.cia.gov; *The World Factbook.*

Euromonitor International, Inc., 122 South Michingan Avenue, Suite 1200, Chicago, Illinois 60603 (800) 577-EURO; *International Marketing Data and Statistics;* and *World Marketing Data and Statistics.*

Europa Publications Limited, 18 Bedford Square, London, WC1B 3JN, England; *The Europa World Year Book.*

St. Martin's Press, Inc., 175 Fifth Avenue, New York, New York 10010 (800) 221-7945; *The Statesman's Year-Book.*

Statistical Office of the United Nations, Publishing Service, New York, New York 10017 (800) 253-9646; *Human Development Report;* and *Statistical Yearbook for Asia and the Pacific.*

MALDIVES - UNEMPLOYMENT RATE

Central Intelligence Agency, Washington, D.C. 20505 (703) 482-1100, www.cia.gov; *The World Factbook.*

MALDIVES - VITAL STATISTICS

Statistical Office of the United Nations, Publishing Service, New York, New York 10017 (800) 253-9646; *Statistical Yearbook.*

World Health Organization, Office of Publications, 20 Avenue Appia, CH-1211 Geneva 27, Switzerland (Telephone Number in U.S. (518) 436-9686); *World Health Statistics Annual.*

MALDIVES - WAGES AND PRICES

Statistical Office of the United Nations, Publishing Service, New York, New York 10017 (800) 253-9646; *Statistical Yearbook for Asia and the Pacific.*

MALDIVES - WHOLESALE PRICES - INDEX NUMBERS

Asian Development Bank, Post Office Box 789, 1099 Manila, Philippines; *Key Indicators of Developing Asian and Pacific Countries.*

MALE HOUSEHOLDER - See HOUSEHOLDS OR FAMILIES

Mali - National Statistical Office

Direction Nationale de L'Informatique, Ministere du Plan, B.P. 12, Bamako, Mali.

Mali- Primary Statistics Sources

Direction Nationale de la Statistique, BP12, Bamako, Mali; *Annuaire Statistique du Mali* (Statistical Yearbook of Mali); and *Bulletin Mensuel de Statistique* (Monthly bulletin of statistics).

MALI - AGRICULTURE

Economist Intelligence Unit, 111 West 57th Street, New York, New York 10019 (800) 938-4685; *Mali Country Report.*

Euromonitor International, Inc., 122 South Michingan Avenue, Suite 1200, Chicago, Illinois 60603 (800) 577-EURO; *International Marketing Data and Statistics;* and *World Marketing Data and Statistics.*

Europa Publications Limited, 18 Bedford Square, London, WC1B 3JN, England; *The Europa World Year Book.*

Food and Agricultural Organization of the United Nations (FAO), Via delle Terme di Caracalla, 00100 Rome, Italy (Telephone Number in U.S. (202) 653-2400); *The State of Food and Agriculture;* and *Trade Yearbook.*

M.E. Sharpe, 80 Business Park Drive, Armonk, New York 10504 (800) 541-6563; *The Illustrated Book of World Rankings.*

St. Martin's Press, Inc., 175 Fifth Avenue, New York, New York 10010 (800) 221-7945; *The Statesman's Year-Book.*

Statistical Office of the United Nations, Publishing Service, New York, New York 10017 (800) 253-9646; *Statistical Yearbook;* and *Survey of Economic and Social Conditions in Africa.*

United Nations Conference on Trade and Development, Central Statistical Service, Palais des Nations, Geneva, Switzerland (Telephone in U.S. (800) 253-9646); *UNCTAD Commodity Yearbook.*

United Nations Economic Commission for Africa, Africa Hall, Post Office Box 3001, Addis Ababa, Ethiopia (Telephone Number in U.S. (800) 253-9646); *African Statistical Yearbook.*

The World Bank, 1818 H Street, NW, Washington, D.C. 20433 (202) 477-1234; *World Development Indicators.*

MALI - AIRLINE SERVICE

Europa Publications Limited, 18 Bedford Square, London, WC1B 3JN, England; *The Europa World Year Book.*

M.E. Sharpe, 80 Business Park Drive, Armonk, New York 10504 (800) 541-6563; *The Illustrated Book of World Rankings.*

St. Martin's Press, Inc., 175 Fifth Avenue, New York, New York 10010 (800) 221-7945; *The Statesman's Year-Book.*

Statistical Office of the United Nations, Publishing Service, New York, New York 10017 (800) 253-9646; *Statistical Yearbook.*

United Nations Economic Commission for Africa, Africa Hall, Post Office Box 3001, Addis Ababa, Ethiopia (Telephone Number in U.S. (800) 253-9646); *African Statistical Yearbook.*

MALI - AIRPORTS

Central Intelligence Agency, Washington, D.C. 20505 (703) 482-1100, www.cia.gov; *The World Factbook.*

MALI - ALUMINUM PRODUCTION AND CONSUMPTION - See MALI - MINING AND MINERAL PRODUCTS

MALI - ANIMAL HEALTH

Food and Agricultural Organization of the United Nations (FAO), Via delle Terme di Caracalla, 00100 Rome, Italy (Telephone Number in U.S. (202) 653-2400); *Animal Health Yearbook.*

MALI - AREA AND DENSITY OF POPULATION

African Development Bank, 01 BP 1387, Abidjan 01, Cote d'Ivoire; *Selected Statistics on Regional Member Countries.*

Central Intelligence Agency, Washington, D.C. 20505 (703) 482-1100, www.cia.gov; *The World Factbook.*

Euromonitor International, Inc., 122 South Michingan Avenue, Suite 1200, Chicago, Illinois 60603 (800) 577-EURO; *International Marketing Data and Statistics;* and *The World Economic Factbook.*

Europa Publications Limited, 18 Bedford Square, London, WC1B 3JN, England; *The Europa World Year Book.*

Food and Agricultural Organization of the United Nations (FAO), Via delle Terme di Caracalla, 00100 Rome, Italy (Telephone Number in U.S. (202) 653-2400); *The State of Food and Agriculture.*

M.E. Sharpe, 80 Business Park Drive, Armonk, New York 10504 (800) 541-6563; *The Illustrated Book of World Rankings.*

St. Martin's Press, Inc., 175 Fifth Avenue, New York, New York 10010 (800) 221-7945; *The Statesman's Year-Book.*

Statistical Office of the United Nations, Publishing Service, New York, New York 10017 (800) 253-9646; *Statistical Yearbook;* and *Survey of Economic and Social Conditions in Africa.*

The World Bank, 1818 H Street, NW, Washington, D.C. 20433 (202) 477-1234; *World Development Report.*

MALI - ARMS EXPORTS AND IMPORTS - See MALI - MILITARY

MALI - BALANCE OF PAYMENTS

African Development Bank, 01 BP 1387, Abidjan 01, Cote d'Ivoire; *Selected Statistics on Regional Member Countries.*

The Economist Intelligence Unit, 111 West 57th Street, New York, New York 10019 (800) 938-4685; *The World Market Atlas.*

Europa Publications Limited, 18 Bedford Square, London, WC1B 3JN, England; *The Europa World Year Book.*

International Monetary Fund, 700 Nineteenth Street, NW, Washington, D.C. 20431 (202) 623-7000; *Balance of Payments Yearbook.*

United Nations Economic Commission for Africa, Africa Hall, Post Office Box 3001, Addis Ababa, Ethiopia (Telephone Number in U.S. (800) 253-9646); *African Statistical Yearbook.*

United Nations Conference on Trade and Development (UNCTAD), New York, New York 10017 (800) 253-9646, *Handbook of International Trade and Development Statistics.*

The World Bank, 1818 H Street, NW, Washington, D.C. 20433 (202) 477-1234; *World Development Report;* and *World Development Indicators.*

MALI - BANKING

Euromonitor International, Inc., 122 South Michigan Avenue, Suite 1200, Chicago, Illinois 60603 (800) 577-EURO; *World Marketing Data and Statistics.*

Europa Publications Limited, 18 Bedford Square, London, WC1B 3JN, England; *The Europa World Year Book.*

International Monetary Fund, 700 Nineteenth Street, NW, Washington, D.C. 20431 (202) 623-7000; *International Financial Statistics.*

M.E. Sharpe, 80 Business Park Drive, Armonk, New York 10504 (800) 541-6563; *The Illustrated Book of World Rankings.*

St. Martin's Press, Inc., 175 Fifth Avenue, New York, New York 10010 (800) 221-7945; *The Statesman's Year-Book.*

United Nations Economic Commission for Africa, Africa Hall, Post Office Box 3001, Addis Ababa, Ethiopia (Telephone Number in U.S. (800) 253-9646); *African Statistical Yearbook.*

MALI - BARLEY PRODUCTION - See MALI - CROPS

MALI - BEER PRODUCTION - See MALI - BEVERAGES

MALI - BEVERAGES

M.E. Sharpe, 80 Business Park Drive, Armonk, New York 10504 (800) 541-6563; *The Illustrated Book of World Rankings.*

Statistical Office of the United Nations, Publishing Service, New York, New York 10017 (800) 253-9646; *Statistical Yearbook.*

MALI - BIRTH RATES

Central Intelligence Agency,

Washington, D.C. 20505 (703) 482-1100, www.cia.gov; *The World Factbook.*

Euromonitor International, Inc., 122 South Michingan Avenue, Suite 1200, Chicago, Illinois 60603 (800) 577-EURO; *International Marketing Data and Statistics;* and *The World Economic Factbook.*

Europa Publications Limited, 18 Bedford Square, London, WC1B 3JN, England; *The Europa World Year Book.*

M.E. Sharpe, 80 Business Park Drive, Armonk, New York 10504 (800) 541-6563; *The Illustrated Book of World Rankings.*

St. Martin's Press, Inc., 175 Fifth Avenue, New York, New York 10010 (800) 221-7945; *The Statesman's Year-Book.*

Statistical Office of the United Nations, Publishing Service, New York, New York 10017 (800) 253-9646; *Demographic Yearbook; Statistical Yearbook;* and *Survey of Economic and Social Conditions in Africa.*

The World Bank, 1818 H Street, NW, Washington, D.C. 20433 (202) 477-1234; *World Development Indicators.*

MALI - BONDS

International Monetary Fund, 700 Nineteenth Street, NW, Washington, D.C. 20431 (202) 623-7000; *Government Finance Statistics Yearbook.*

MALI - BOOK PRODUCTION

Europa Publications Limited, 18 Bedford Square, London, WC1B 3JN, England; *The Europa World Year Book.*

United Nations Educational, Scientific and Cultural Organization (UNESCO), 7 Place de Fontenoy, F-75700 Paris, France (Telephone Number in U.S. (212) 963-5981); *Statistical Yearbook.*

MALI - BROADCASTING

Billboard Limited, Post Office Box 9027, 1006 AA Amsterdam, The Netherlands (Telephone Number in U.S. (212) 764-7300); *World Radio TV Handbook.*

Central Intelligence Agency, Washington, D.C. 20505 (703) 482-1100, www.cia.gov; *The World Factbook.*

Euromonitor International, Inc., 122 South Michingan Avenue, Suite 1200, Chicago, Illinois 60603 (800) 577-EURO; *World Marketing Data and Statistics.*

M.E. Sharpe, 80 Business Park Drive, Armonk, New York 10504 (800) 541-6563; *The Illustrated Book of World Rankings.*

St. Martin's Press, Inc., 175 Fifth Avenue, New York, New York 10010 (800) 221-7945; *The Statesman's Year-Book.*

MALI - BUDGET

Europa Publications Limited, 18 Bedford Square, London, WC1B 3JN, England; *The Europa World Year Book.*

MALI - BUSINESS AND PROPERTY TAXES

International Monetary Fund, 700 Nineteenth Street, NW, Washington, D.C. 20431 (202) 623-7000; *Government Finance Statistics Yearbook.*

MALI - BUTTER PRODUCTION - See MALI - DAIRY PRODUCTS

MALI - CALORIE SUPPLY

African Development Bank, 01 BP 1387, Abidjan 01, Cote d'Ivoire; *Selected Statistics on Regional Member Countries.*

Food and Agricultural Organization of the United Nations (FAO), Via delle Terme di Caracalla, 00100 Rome, Italy (Telephone Number in U.S. (202) 653-2400); *The State of Food and Agriculture.*

MALI - CAPITAL REVENUE

International Monetary Fund, 700 Nineteenth Street, NW, Washington, D.C. 20431 (202) 623-7000; *Government Finance Statistics Yearbook.*

MALI - CATTLE - See MALI - LIVESTOCK AND POULTRY

MALI - CEMENT PRODUCTION - See MALI - MINING AND MINERAL PRODUCTS

MALI - CHEMICAL (ORGANIC) PRODUCTION - See MALI - MINING AND MINERAL PRODUCTS

MALI - CHICKENS - See MALI - LIVESTOCK AND POULTRY

MALI - CLIMATE

M.E. Sharpe, 80 Business Park Drive, Armonk, New York 10504 (800) 541-6563; *The Illustrated Book of World Rankings.*

St. Martin's Press, Inc., 175 Fifth Avenue, New York, New York 10010 (800) 221-7945; *The Statesman's Year-Book.*

MALI - COAL PRODUCTION - See MALI - MINING AND MINERAL PRODUCTS

MALI - COFFEE PRODUCTION - See MALI - CROPS

MALI - COMMERCE

St. Martin's Press, Inc., 175 Fifth Avenue,

New York, New York 10010 (800) 221-7945; *The Statesman's Year-Book.*

MALI - COMMUNICATIONS - See MALI - TRANSPORTATION AND COMMUNICATIONS

MALI - CONSTRUCTION INDUSTRY

M.E. Sharpe, 80 Business Park Drive, Armonk, New York 10504 (800) 541-6563; *The Illustrated Book of World Rankings.*

United Nations Economic Commission for Africa, Africa Hall, Post Office Box 3001, Addis Ababa, Ethiopia (Telephone Number in U.S. (800) 253-9646); *African Statistical Yearbook.*

MALI - CONSUMER PRICE INDEX

African Development Bank, 01 BP 1387, Abidjan 01, Cote d'Ivoire; *Selected Statistics on Regional Member Countries.*

Europa Publications Limited, 18 Bedford Square, London, WC1B 3JN, England; *The Europa World Year Book.*

Statistical Office of the United Nations, Publishing Service, New York, New York 10017 (800) 253-9646; *Statistical Yearbook;* and *Survey of Economic and Social Conditions in Africa.*

United Nations Economic Commission for Africa, Africa Hall, Post Office Box 3001, Addis Ababa, Ethiopia (Telephone Number in U.S. (800) 253-9646); *African Statistical Yearbook.*

MALI - CONSUMER PRICES

Euromonitor International, Inc., 122 South Michigan Avenue, Suite 1200, Chicago, Illinois 60603 (800) 577-EURO; *World Marketing Data and Statistics.*

International Labour Office, I.L.O. Publications, 1828 L Street, N.W., Suite 801, Washington, D.C. 20036 (301) 638-3152; *Yearbook of Labour Statistics.*

MALI - CONSUMPTION

African Development Bank, 01 BP 1387, Abidjan 01, Cote d'Ivoire; *Selected Statistics on Regional Member Countries.*

Statistical Office of the United Nations, Publishing Service, New York, New York 10017 (800) 253-9646; *Survey of Economic and Social Conditions in Africa.*

The World Bank, 1818 H Street, NW, Washington, D.C. 20433 (202) 477-1234; *World Development Report.*

MALI - COPPER PRODUCTION - See MALI - MINING AND MINERAL PRODUCTS

MALI - CORN PRODUCTION - See MALI - CROPS

MALI - CORPORATE TAXES - See MALI - TAXATION

MALI - COTTON - See MALI - CROPS

MALI - CROPS

Central Intelligence Agency, Washington, D.C. 20505 (703) 482-1100, www.cia.gov; *The World Factbook.*

Europa Publications Limited, 18 Bedford Square, London, WC1B 3JN, England; *The Europa World Year Book.*

Food and Agricultural Organization of the United Nations (FAO), Via delle Terme di Caracalla, 00100 Rome, Italy (Telephone Number in U.S. (202) 653-2400); *Production Yearbook;* and *The State of Food and Agriculture.*

International Monetary Fund, 700 Nineteenth Street, NW, Washington, D.C. 20431 (202) 623-7000; *International Financial Statistics.*

M.E. Sharpe, 80 Business Park Drive, Armonk, New York 10504 (800) 541-6563; *The Illustrated Book of World Rankings.*

St. Martin's Press, Inc., 175 Fifth Avenue, New York, New York 10010 (800) 221-7945; *The Statesman's Year-Book.*

Statistical Office of the United Nations, Publishing Service, New York, New York 10017 (800) 253-9646; *Statistical Yearbook.*

United Nations Economic Commission for Africa, Africa Hall, Post Office Box 3001, Addis Ababa, Ethiopia (Telephone Number in U.S. (800) 253-9646); *African Statistical Yearbook.*

MALI - CUSTOMS DUTIES

International Monetary Fund, 700 Nineteenth Street, NW, Washington, D.C. 20431 (202) 623-7000; *Government Finance Statistics Yearbook.*

St. Martin's Press, Inc., 175 Fifth Avenue, New York, New York 10010 (800) 221-7945; *The Statesman's Year-Book.*

MALI - DAIRY PRODUCTS

Europa Publications Limited, 18 Bedford Square, London, WC1B 3JN, England; *The Europa World Year Book.*

Food and Agricultural Organization of the United Nations (FAO), Via delle Terme di Caracalla, 00100 Rome, Italy (Telephone Number in U.S. (202) 653-2400); *Production Yearbook;* and *The State of Food and Agriculture.*

M.E. Sharpe, 80 Business Park Drive, Armonk, New York 10504 (800) 541-6563; *The Illustrated Book of World Rankings.*

St. Martin's Press, Inc., 175 Fifth Avenue, New York, New York 10010 (800) 221-7945; *The Statesman's Year-Book.*

Statistical Office of the United Nations, Publishing Service, New York, New York 10017 (800) 253-9646; *Statistical Yearbook.*

MALI - DEATH RATES - See MALI - MORTALITY

MALI - DEFENSE EXPENDITURES

International Monetary Fund, 700 Nineteenth Street, NW, Washington, D.C. 20431 (202) 623-7000; *Government Finance Statistics Yearbook.*

U.S. Arms Control and Disarmament Agency, 320 Twenty-first Street, NW, Washington, D.C. 20451 (202) 647-8677; *World Military Expenditures and Arms Transfers.*

MALI - DEMOGRAPHY

The Economist Intelligence Unit, 111 West 57th Street, New York, New York 10019 (800) 938-4685; *The World Market Atlas.*

Euromonitor International, Inc., 122 South Michigan Avenue, Suite 1200, Chicago, Illinois 60603 (800) 577-EURO; *International Marketing Data and Statistics; World Marketing Data and Statistics; and The World Economic Factbook.*

M.E. Sharpe, 80 Business Park Drive, Armonk, New York 10504 (800) 541-6563; *The Illustrated Book of World Rankings.*

Statistical Office of the United Nations, Publishing Service, New York, New York 10017 (800) 253-9646; *Human Development Report; and Survey of Economic and Social Conditions in Africa.*

MALI - DEVELOPMENT ASSISTANCE

Statistical Office of the United Nations, Publishing Service, New York, New York 10017 (800) 253-9646; *Statistical Yearbook.*

MALI - DIAMOND PRODUCTION - See MALI - MINING AND MINERAL PRODUCTS

MALI - DISEASES - See MALI - HEALTH

MALI - DIVORCE

M.E. Sharpe, 80 Business Park Drive, Armonk, New York 10504 (800) 541-6563; *The Illustrated Book of World Rankings.*

Statistical Office of the United Nations, Publishing Service, New York, New York

10017 (800) 253-9646; *Demographic Yearbook.*

MALI - ECONOMY

African Development Bank, 01 BP 1387, Abidjan 01, Cote d'Ivoire; *Selected Statistics on Regional Member Countries.*

Central Intelligence Agency, Washington, D.C. 20505 (703) 482-1100, www.cia.gov; *The World Factbook.*

Economist Intelligence Unit, 111 West 57th Street, New York, New York 10019 (800) 938-4685; *Mali Country Report.*

Euromonitor International, Inc., 122 South Michigan Avenue, Suite 1200, Chicago, Illinois 60603 (800) 577-EURO; *International Marketing Data and Statistics; World Marketing Data and Statistics; and The World Economic Factbook.*

Europa Publications Limited, 18 Bedford Square, London, WC1B 3JN, England; *The Europa World Year Book.*

M.E. Sharpe, 80 Business Park Drive, Armonk, New York 10504 (800) 541-6563; *The Illustrated Book of World Rankings.*

St. Martin's Press, Inc., 175 Fifth Avenue, New York, New York 10010 (800) 221-7945; *The Statesman's Year-Book.*

Statistical Office of the United Nations, Publishing Service, New York, New York 10017 (800) 253-9646; *World Statistics Pocketbook.*

The World Bank, 1818 H Street, NW, Washington, D.C. 20433 (202) 477-1234; *The World Bank Atlas; and World Development Report.*

MALI - EDUCATION

African Development Bank, 01 BP 1387, Abidjan 01, Cote d'Ivoire; *Selected Statistics on Regional Member Countries.*

The Economist Intelligence Unit, 111 West 57th Street, New York, New York 10019 (800) 938-4685; *The World Market Atlas.*

Euromonitor International, Inc., 122 South Michingan Avenue, Suite 1200, Chicago, Illinois 60603 (800) 577-EURO; *International Marketing Data and Statistics; and World Marketing Data and Statistics.*

Europa Publications Limited, 18 Bedford Square, London, WC1B 3JN, England; *The Europa World Year Book.*

International Monetary Fund, 700 Nineteenth Street, NW, Washington, D.C. 20431 (202) 623-7000; *Government Finance Statistics Yearbook.*

M.E. Sharpe, 80 Business Park Drive, Armonk, New York 10504 (800) 541-6563; *The Illustrated Book of World Rankings.*

St. Martin's Press, Inc., 175 Fifth Avenue, New York, New York 10010 (800) 221-7945; *The Statesman's Year-Book.*

Statistical Office of the United Nations, Publishing Service, New York, New York 10017 (800) 253-9646; *Human Development Report; and Survey of Economic and Social Conditions in Africa.*

United Nations Economic Commission for Africa, Africa Hall, Post Office Box 3001, Addis Ababa, Ethiopia (Telephone Number in U.S. (800) 253-9646); *African Statistical Yearbook.*

United Nations Educational, Scientific and Cultural Organization (UNESCO), 7 Place de Fontenoy, F-75700 Paris, France (Telephone Number in U.S. (212) 963-5981); *Statistical Yearbook.*

The World Bank, 1818 H Street, NW, Washington, D.C. 20433 (202) 477-1234; *World Development Report; and World Development Indicators.*

MALI - EGG PRODUCTION - See MALI - DAIRY PRODUCTS

MALI - ELECTRICITY

Central Intelligence Agency, Washington, D.C. 20505 (703) 482-1100, www.cia.gov; *The World Factbook.*

M.E. Sharpe, 80 Business Park Drive, Armonk, New York 10504 (800) 541-6563; *The Illustrated Book of World Rankings.*

St. Martin's Press, Inc., 175 Fifth Avenue, New York, New York 10010 (800) 221-7945; *The Statesman's Year-Book.*

Statistical Office of the United Nations, Publishing Service, New York, New York 10017 (800) 253-9646; *Human Development Report; Statistical Yearbook; and Survey of Economic and Social Conditions in Africa.*

United Nations Economic Commission for Africa, Africa Hall, Post Office Box 3001, Addis Ababa, Ethiopia (Telephone Number in U.S. (800) 253-9646); *African Statistical Yearbook.*

MALI - EMPLOYMENT

Euromonitor International, Inc., 122 South Michingan Avenue, Suite 1200, Chicago, Illinois 60603 (800) 577-EURO; *International Marketing Data and Statistics.*

International Labour Office, I.L.O. Publications, 1828 L Street, N.W., Suite 801, Washington, D.C. 20036 (301)

638-3152; *Yearbook of Labour Statistics.*

M.E. Sharpe, 80 Business Park Drive, Armonk, New York 10504 (800) 541-6563; *The Illustrated Book of World Rankings.*

Statistical Office of the United Nations, Publishing Service, New York, New York 10017 (800) 253-9646; *Statistical Yearbook;* and *Survey of Economic and Social Conditions in Africa.*

United Nations Economic Commission for Africa, Africa Hall, Post Office Box 3001, Addis Ababa, Ethiopia (Telephone Number in U.S. (800) 253-9646); *African Statistical Yearbook.*

MALI - ENERGY

Euromonitor International, Inc., 122 South Michigan Avenue, Suite 1200, Chicago, Illinois 60603 (800) 577-EURO; *International Marketing Data and Statistics; World Marketing Data and Statistics;* and *The World Economic Factbook.*

M.E. Sharpe, 80 Business Park Drive, Armonk, New York 10504 (800) 541-6563; *The Illustrated Book of World Rankings.*

St. Martin's Press, Inc., 175 Fifth Avenue, New York, New York 10010 (800) 221-7945; *The Statesman's Year-Book.*

Statistical Office of the United Nations, Publishing Service, New York, New York 10017 (800) 253-9646; *Energy Statistics Yearbook; Human Development Report; World Statistics Pocketbook;* and *Statistical Yearbook.*

United Nations Economic Commission for Africa, Africa Hall, Post Office Box 3001, Addis Ababa, Ethiopia (Telephone Number in U.S. (800) 253-9646); *African Statistical Yearbook.*

The World Bank, 1818 H Street, NW, Washington, D.C. 20433 (202) 477-1234; *The World Bank Atlas;* and *World Development Report.*

MALI - ENVIRONMENT

Economist Intelligence Unit, 111 West 57th Street, New York, New York 10019 (800) 938-4685; *Mali Country Report.*

Statistical Office of the United Nations, Publishing Service, New York, New York 10017 (800) 253-9646; *World Statistics Pocketbook.*

MALI - EXCHANGE RATES

African Development Bank, 01 BP 1387, Abidjan 01, Cote d'Ivoire; *Selected Statistics on Regional Member Countries.*

Central Intelligence Agency,

Washington, D.C. 20505 (703) 482-1100, www.cia.gov; *The World Factbook.*

Euromonitor International, Inc., 122 South Michigan Avenue, Suite 1200, Chicago, Illinois 60603 (800) 577-EURO; *International Marketing Data and Statistics;* and *The World Economic Factbook.*

Europa Publications Limited, 18 Bedford Square, London, WC1B 3JN, England; *The Europa World Year Book.*

International Monetary Fund, 700 Nineteenth Street, NW, Washington, D.C. 20431 (202) 623-7000; *International Financial Statistics.*

Statistical Office of the United Nations, Publishing Service, New York, New York 10017 (800) 253-9646; *Statistical Yearbook;* and *World Statistics Pocketbook.*

MALI - EXCISE TAXES - See MALI - TAXATION

MALI - EXPORTS

African Development Bank, 01 BP 1387, Abidjan 01, Cote d'Ivoire; *Selected Statistics on Regional Member Countries.*

Central Intelligence Agency, Washington, D.C. 20505 (703) 482-1100, www.cia.gov; *The World Factbook.*

The Economist Intelligence Unit, 111 West 57th Street, New York, New York 10019 (800) 938-4685; *Mali Country Report;* and *The World Market Atlas.*

Euromonitor International, Inc., 122 South Michigan Avenue, Suite 1200, Chicago, Illinois 60603 (800) 577-EURO; *International Marketing Data and Statistics;* and *The World Economic Factbook.*

Europa Publications Limited, 18 Bedford Square, London, WC1B 3JN, England; *The Europa World Year Book.*

Food and Agricultural Organization of the United Nations (FAO), Via delle Terme di Caracalla, 00100 Rome, Italy (Telephone Number in U.S. (202) 653-2400); *The State of Food and Agriculture.*

International Monetary Fund, 700 Nineteenth Street, NW, Washington, D.C. 20431 (202) 623-7000; *Direction of Trade Statistics; Government Finance Statistics Yearbook;* and *International Financial Statistics.*

St. Martin's Press, Inc., 175 Fifth Avenue, New York, New York 10010 (800) 221-7945; *The Statesman's Year-Book.*

Statistical Office of the United Nations, Publishing Service, New York, New York 10017 (800) 253-9646; *Survey of Economic*

and Social Conditions in Africa.

United Nations Conference on Trade and Development (UNCTAD), New York, New York 10017 (800) 253-9646, *Handbook of International Trade and Development Statistics.*

United Nations Economic Commission for Africa, Africa Hall, Post Office Box 3001, Addis Ababa, Ethiopia (Telephone Number in U.S. (800) 253-9646); *African Statistical Yearbook.*

The World Bank, 1818 H Street, NW, Washington, D.C. 20433 (202) 477-1234; *World Development Report;* and *World Development Indicators.*

MALI - EXTERNAL INDEBTEDNESS

African Development Bank, 01 BP 1387, Abidjan 01, Cote d'Ivoire; *Selected Statistics on Regional Member Countries.*

Statistical Office of the United Nations, Publishing Service, New York, New York 10017 (800) 253-9646; *Survey of Economic and Social Conditions in Africa.*

The World Bank, 1818 H Street, NW, Washington, D.C. 20433 (202) 477-1234; *World Development Report;* and *World Development Indicators.*

MALI - EXTERNAL TRADE

African Development Bank, 01 BP 1387, Abidjan 01, Cote d'Ivoire; *Selected Statistics on Regional Member Countries.*

Euromonitor International, Inc., 122 South Michigan Avenue, Suite 1200, Chicago, Illinois 60603 (800) 577-EURO; *World Marketing Data and Statistics.*

Food and Agricultural Organization of the United Nations (FAO), Via delle Terme di Caracalla, 00100 Rome, Italy (Telephone Number in U.S. (202) 653-2400); *The State of Food and Agriculture;* and *Trade Yearbook.*

Statistical Office of the United Nations, Publishing Service, New York, New York 10017 (800) 253-9646; *Statistical Yearbook.*

MALI - FARM CROPS - See MALI - CROPS

MALI - FEMALE WORKING POPULATION - See MALI - EMPLOYMENT

MALI - FERTILITY RATES

Central Intelligence Agency, Washington, D.C. 20505 (703) 482-1100, www.cia.gov; *The World Factbook.*

M.E. Sharpe, 80 Business Park Drive, Armonk, New York 10504 (800) 541-6563; *The Illustrated Book of World Rankings.*

Statistical Office of the United Nations, Publishing Service, New York, New York 10017 (800) 253-9646; *Human Development Report;* and *Survey of Economic and Social Conditions in Africa.*

The World Bank, 1818 H Street, NW, Washington, D.C. 20433 (202) 477-1234; *The World Bank Atlas; World Development Report;* and *World Development Indicators.*

MALI - FERTILIZER

Food and Agricultural Organization of the United Nations (FAO), Via delle Terme di Caracalla, 00100 Rome, Italy (Telephone Number in U.S. (202) 653-2400); *Fertilizer Yearbook;* and *The State of Food and Agriculture.*

Statistical Office of the United Nations, Publishing Service, New York, New York 10017 (800) 253-9646; *Statistical Yearbook.*

MALI - FETAL MORTALITY - See MALI - MORTALITY

MALI - FINANCE

African Development Bank, 01 BP 1387, Abidjan 01, Cote d'Ivoire; *Selected Statistics on Regional Member Countries.*

Economist Intelligence Unit, 111 West 57th Street, New York, New York 10019 (800) 938-4685; *Mali Country Report.*

Europa Publications Limited, 18 Bedford Square, London, WC1B 3JN, England; *The Europa World Year Book.*

International Monetary Fund, 700 Nineteenth Street, NW, Washington, D.C. 20431 (202) 623-7000; *Government Finance Statistics Yearbook;* and *International Financial Statistics.*

M.E. Sharpe, 80 Business Park Drive, Armonk, New York 10504 (800) 541-6563; *The Illustrated Book of World Rankings.*

St. Martin's Press, Inc., 175 Fifth Avenue, New York, New York 10010 (800) 221-7945; *The Statesman's Year-Book.*

United Nations Economic Commission for Africa, Africa Hall, Post Office Box 3001, Addis Ababa, Ethiopia (Telephone Number in U.S. (800) 253-9646); *African Statistical Yearbook.*

MALI - FISHERIES

Europa Publications Limited, 18 Bedford Square, London, WC1B 3JN, England; *The Europa World Year Book.*

Food and Agricultural Organization of the United Nations (FAO), Via delle Terme di Caracalla, 00100 Rome, Italy (Telephone Number in U.S. (202) 653-2400); *The State*

of Food and Agriculture; and *Yearbook of Fishery Statistics.*

M.E. Sharpe, 80 Business Park Drive, Armonk, New York 10504 (800) 541-6563; *The Illustrated Book of World Rankings.*

St. Martin's Press, Inc., 175 Fifth Avenue, New York, New York 10010 (800) 221-7945; *The Statesman's Year-Book.*

Statistical Office of the United Nations, Publishing Service, New York, New York 10017 (800) 253-9646; *Statistical Yearbook;* and *Survey of Economic and Social Conditions in Africa.*

United Nations Conference on Trade and Development, Central Statistical Service, Palais des Nations, Geneva, Switzerland (Telephone in U.S. (800) 253-9646); *UNCTAD Commodity Yearbook.*

United Nations Economic Commission for Africa, Africa Hall, Post Office Box 3001, Addis Ababa, Ethiopia (Telephone Number in U.S. (800) 253-9646); *African Statistical Yearbook.*

MALI - FOOD

African Development Bank, 01 BP 1387, Abidjan 01, Cote d'Ivoire; *Selected Statistics on Regional Member Countries.*

Food and Agricultural Organization of the United Nations (FAO), Via delle Terme di Caracalla, 00100 Rome, Italy (Telephone Number in U.S. (202) 653-2400); *Production Yearbook;* and *The State of Food and Agriculture.*

Statistical Office of the United Nations, Publishing Service, New York, New York 10017 (800) 253-9646; *Human Development Report.*

United Nations Conference on Trade and Development, Central Statistical Service, Palais des Nations, Geneva, Switzerland (Telephone in U.S. (800) 253-9646); *UNCTAD Commodity Yearbook.*

MALI - FOREIGN TRADE

Economist Intelligence Unit, 111 West 57th Street, New York, New York 10019 (800) 938-4685; *Mali Country Report.*

Euromonitor International, Inc., 122 South Michingan Avenue, Suite 1200, Chicago, Illinois 60603 (800) 577-EURO; *International Marketing Data and Statistics;* and *The World Economic Factbook.*

Europa Publications Limited, 18 Bedford Square, London, WC1B 3JN, England; *The Europa World Year Book.*

Food and Agricultural Organization of the United Nations (FAO), Via delle Terme

di Caracalla, 00100 Rome, Italy (Telephone Number in U.S. (202) 653-2400); *The State of Food and Agriculture.*

International Monetary Fund, 700 Nineteenth Street, NW, Washington, D.C. 20431 (202) 623-7000; *International Financial Statistics.*

M.E. Sharpe, 80 Business Park Drive, Armonk, New York 10504 (800) 541-6563; *The Illustrated Book of World Rankings.*

St. Martin's Press, Inc., 175 Fifth Avenue, New York, New York 10010 (800) 221-7945; *The Statesman's Year-Book.*

Statistical Office of the United Nations, Publishing Service, New York, New York 10017 (800) 253-9646; *Statistical Yearbook;* and *International Trade Statistics Yearbook.*

United Nations Conference on Trade and Development, Central Statistical Service, Palais des Nations, Geneva, Switzerland (Telephone in U.S. (800) 253-9646); *UNCTAD Commodity Yearbook.*

United Nations Economic Commission for Africa, Africa Hall, Post Office Box 3001, Addis Ababa, Ethiopia (Telephone Number in U.S. (800) 253-9646); *African Statistical Yearbook.*

The World Bank, 1818 H Street, NW, Washington, D.C. 20433 (202) 477-1234; *World Development Report;* and *World Development Indicators.*

MALI - FORESTRY AND FOREST PRODUCTS

Europa Publications Limited, 18 Bedford Square, London, WC1B 3JN, England; *The Europa World Year Book.*

Food and Agricultural Organization of the United Nations (FAO), Via delle Terme di Caracalla, 00100 Rome, Italy (Telephone Number in U.S. (202) 653-2400); *The State of Food and Agriculture;* and *Yearbook of Forest Products.*

M.E. Sharpe, 80 Business Park Drive, Armonk, New York 10504 (800) 541-6563; *The Illustrated Book of World Rankings.*

St. Martin's Press, Inc., 175 Fifth Avenue, New York, New York 10010 (800) 221-7945; *The Statesman's Year-Book.*

Statistical Office of the United Nations, Publishing Service, New York, New York 10017 (800) 253-9646; *Statistical Yearbook.*

United Nations Conference on Trade and Development, Central Statistical Service, Palais des Nations, Geneva, Switzerland (Telephone in U.S. (800) 253-9646); *UNCTAD Commodity Yearbook.*

United Nations Economic Commission for Africa, Africa Hall, Post Office Box 3001, Addis Ababa, Ethiopia (Telephone Number in U.S. (800) 253-9646); *African Statistical Yearbook*.

United Nations Educational, Scientific and Cultural Organization (UNESCO), 7 Place de Fontenoy, F-75700 Paris, France (Telephone Number in U.S. (212) 963-5981); *Statistical Yearbook*.

The World Bank, 1818 H Street, NW, Washington, D.C. 20433 (202) 477-1234; *World Development Report*.

MALI - GAS PRODUCTION - See MALI - MINING AND MINERAL PRODUCTS

MALI - GENERAL MORTALITY - See MALI - MORTALITY

MALI - GEOGRAPHIC DATA

M.E. Sharpe, 80 Business Park Drive, Armonk, New York 10504 (800) 541-6563; *The Illustrated Book of World Rankings*.

MALI - GOATS - See MALI - LIVESTOCK AND POULTRY

MALI - GOLD HOLDINGS

International Monetary Fund, 700 Nineteenth Street, NW, Washington, D.C. 20431 (202) 623-7000; *International Financial Statistics*.

Statistical Office of the United Nations, Publishing Service, New York, New York 10017 (800) 253-9646; *Statistical Yearbook*.

The World Bank, 1818 H Street, NW, Washington, D.C. 20433 (202) 477-1234; *World Development Indicators*.

MALI - GOLD PRODUCTION AND CONSUMPTION - See MALI - MINING AND MINERAL PRODUCTS

MALI - GOVERNMENT

Central Intelligence Agency, Washington, D.C. 20505 (703) 482-1100, www.cia.gov; *The World Factbook*.

Europa Publications Limited, 18 Bedford Square, London, WC1B 3JN, England; *The Europa World Year Book*.

International Monetary Fund, 700 Nineteenth Street, NW, Washington, D.C. 20431 (202) 623-7000; *Government Finance Statistics Yearbook;* and *International Financial Statistics*.

St. Martin's Press, Inc., 175 Fifth Avenue, New York, New York 10010 (800) 221-7945; *The Statesman's Year-Book*.

Statistical Office of the United Nations,

Publishing Service, New York, New York 10017 (800) 253-9646; *National Accounts Statistics;* and *Survey of Economic and Social Conditions in Africa*.

The World Bank, 1818 H Street, NW, Washington, D.C. 20433 (202) 477-1234; *World Development Report;* and *World Development Indicators*.

MALI - GRAIN PRODUCTION - See MALI - CROPS

MALI - GRANTS

International Monetary Fund, 700 Nineteenth Street, NW, Washington, D.C. 20431 (202) 623-7000; *Government Finance Statistics Yearbook*.

MALI - GROSS DOMESTIC PRODUCT

African Development Bank, 01 BP 1387, Abidjan 01, Cote d'Ivoire; *Selected Statistics on Regional Member Countries*.

The Economist Intelligence Unit, 111 West 57th Street, New York, New York 10019 (800) 938-4685; *Mali Country Report;* and *The World Market Atlas*.

Euromonitor International, Inc., 122 South Michigan Avenue, Suite 1200, Chicago, Illinois 60603 (800) 577-EURO; *International Marketing Data and Statistics;* and *The World Economic Factbook*.

Europa Publications Limited, 18 Bedford Square, London, WC1B 3JN, England; *The Europa World Year Book*.

International Monetary Fund, 700 Nineteenth Street, NW, Washington, D.C. 20431 (202) 623-7000; *International Financial Statistics*.

M.E. Sharpe, 80 Business Park Drive, Armonk, New York 10504 (800) 541-6563; *The Illustrated Book of World Rankings*.

Statistical Office of the United Nations, Publishing Service, New York, New York 10017 (800) 253-9646; *Human Development Report; National Accounts Statistics; Statistical Yearbook;* and *Survey of Economic and Social Conditions in Africa*.

United Nations Economic Commission for Africa, Africa Hall, Post Office Box 3001, Addis Ababa, Ethiopia (Telephone Number in U.S. (800) 253-9646); *African Statistical Yearbook*.

The World Bank, 1818 H Street, NW, Washington, D.C. 20433 (202) 477-1234; *World Development Report;* and *World Development Indicators*.

MALI - GROSS NATIONAL PRODUCT

Euromonitor International, Inc., 122 South Michigan Avenue, Suite 1200, Chicago, Illinois 60603 (800) 577-EURO; *International Marketing Data and Statistics*.

St. Martin's Press, Inc., 175 Fifth Avenue, New York, New York 10010 (800) 221-7945; *The Statesman's Year-Book*.

U.S. Arms Control and Disarmament Agency, 320 Twenty-first Street, NW, Washington, D.C. 20451 (202) 647-8677; *World Military Expenditures and Arms Transfers*.

The World Bank, 1818 H Street, NW, Washington, D.C. 20433 (202) 477-1234; *The World Bank Atlas; World Development Report;* and *World Development Indicators*.

MALI - GROUNDNUTS - See MALI - CROPS

MALI - HEALTH

African Development Bank, 01 BP 1387, Abidjan 01, Cote d'Ivoire; *Selected Statistics on Regional Member Countries*.

Euromonitor International, Inc., 122 South Michigan Avenue, Suite 1200, Chicago, Illinois 60603 (800) 577-EURO; *World Marketing Data and Statistics*.

M.E. Sharpe, 80 Business Park Drive, Armonk, New York 10504 (800) 541-6563; *The Illustrated Book of World Rankings*.

St. Martin's Press, Inc., 175 Fifth Avenue, New York, New York 10010 (800) 221-7945; *The Statesman's Year-Book*.

Statistical Office of the United Nations, Publishing Service, New York, New York 10017 (800) 253-9646; *Human Development Report;* and *Statistical Yearbook*.

United Nations Children's Fund (UNICEF), 3 United Nations Plaza, New York, New York 10017 (800) 253-9646; *State of the World's Children*.

United Nations Economic Commission for Africa, Africa Hall, Post Office Box 3001, Addis Ababa, Ethiopia (Telephone Number in U.S. (800) 253-9646); *African Statistical Yearbook*.

The World Bank, 1818 H Street, NW, Washington, D.C. 20433 (202) 477-1234; *World Development Report*.

World Health Organization, Office of Publications, 20 Avenue Appia, CH-1211 Geneva 27, Switzerland (Telephone Number in U.S. (518) 436-9686); *World Health Statistics Annual*.

MALI - HEALTH EXPENDITURES

International Monetary Fund, 700 Nineteenth Street, NW, Washington, D.C. 20431 (202) 623-7000; *Government Finance Statistics Yearbook.*

MALI - HIDE PRODUCTION

Food and Agricultural Organization of the United Nations (FAO), Via delle Terme di Caracalla, 00100 Rome, Italy (Telephone Number in U.S. (202) 653-2400); *Production Yearbook.*

MALI - HIGHWAYS

Central Intelligence Agency, Washington, D.C. 20505 (703) 482-1100, www.cia.gov; *The World Factbook.*

International Road Federation, 2600 Virginia Avenue, N.W., Washington, D.C. 20037 (202) 338-4641; *World Road Statistics.*

St. Martin's Press, Inc., 175 Fifth Avenue, New York, New York 10010 (800) 221-7945; *The Statesman's Year-Book.*

Statistical Office of the United Nations, Publishing Service, New York, New York 10017 (800) 253-9646; *Survey of Economic and Social Conditions in Africa.*

United Nations Economic Commission for Africa, Africa Hall, Post Office Box 3001, Addis Ababa, Ethiopia (Telephone Number in U.S. (800) 253-9646); *African Statistical Yearbook.*

MALI - HORSES - See MALI - LIVESTOCK AND POULTRY

MALI - HOURS OF WORK - See MALI - EMPLOYMENT

MALI - HOUSING AND HOUSING UNITS

Euromonitor International, Inc., 122 South Michigan Avenue, Suite 1200, Chicago, Illinois 60603 (800) 577-EURO; *World Marketing Data and Statistics.*

MALI - HOUSING EXPENDITURES

International Monetary Fund, 700 Nineteenth Street, NW, Washington, D.C. 20431 (202) 623-7000; *Government Finance Statistics Yearbook.*

M.E. Sharpe, 80 Business Park Drive, Armonk, New York 10504 (800) 541-6563; *The Illustrated Book of World Rankings.*

MALI - ILLITERATE POPULATION

Central Intelligence Agency, Washington, D.C. 20505 (703) 482-1100, www.cia.gov; *The World Factbook.*

The Economist Intelligence Unit, 111 West 57th Street, New York, New York 10019 (800) 938-4685; *The World Market Atlas.*

Euromonitor International, Inc., 122 South Michigan Avenue, Suite 1200, Chicago, Illinois 60603 (800) 577-EURO; *The World Economic Factbook.*

St. Martin's Press, Inc., 175 Fifth Avenue, New York, New York 10010 (800) 221-7945; *The Statesman's Year-Book.*

Statistical Office of the United Nations, Publishing Service, New York, New York 10017 (800) 253-9646; *Human Development Report.*

United Nations Educational, Scientific and Cultural Organization (UNESCO), 7 Place de Fontenoy, F-75700 Paris, France (Telephone Number in U.S. (212) 963-5981); *Statistical Yearbook.*

MALI - IMPORTS

African Development Bank, 01 BP 1387, Abidjan 01, Cote d'Ivoire; *Selected Statistics on Regional Member Countries.*

Central Intelligence Agency, Washington, D.C. 20505 (703) 482-1100, www.cia.gov; *The World Factbook.*

The Economist Intelligence Unit, 111 West 57th Street, New York, New York 10019 (800) 938-4685; *Mali Country Report;* and *The World Market Atlas.*

Euromonitor International, Inc., 122 South Michigan Avenue, Suite 1200, Chicago, Illinois 60603 (800) 577-EURO; *International Marketing Data and Statistics;* and *The World Economic Factbook.*

Europa Publications Limited, 18 Bedford Square, London, WC1B 3JN, England; *The Europa World Year Book.*

Food and Agricultural Organization of the United Nations (FAO), Via delle Terme di Caracalla, 00100 Rome, Italy (Telephone Number in U.S. (202) 653-2400); *The State of Food and Agriculture.*

International Monetary Fund, 700 Nineteenth Street, NW, Washington, D.C. 20431 (202) 623-7000; *Direction of Trade Statistics; Government Finance Statistics Yearbook;* and *International Financial Statistics.*

St. Martin's Press, Inc., 175 Fifth Avenue, New York, New York 10010 (800) 221-7945; *The Statesman's Year-Book.*

Statistical Office of the United Nations, Publishing Service, New York, New York 10017 (800) 253-9646; *Survey of Economic and Social Conditions in Africa.*

United Nations Conference on Trade and Development (UNCTAD), New York, New York 10017 (800) 253-9646; *Handbook of International Trade and Development Statistics.*

United Nations Economic Commission for Africa, Africa Hall, Post Office Box 3001, Addis Ababa, Ethiopia (Telephone Number in U.S. (800) 253-9646); *African Statistical Yearbook.*

The World Bank, 1818 H Street, NW, Washington, D.C. 20433 (202) 477-1234; *World Development Report;* and *World Development Indicators.*

MALI - INCOME TAXES - See MALI - TAXATION

MALI - INDUSTRY

Central Intelligence Agency, Washington, D.C. 20505 (703) 482-1100, www.cia.gov; *The World Factbook.*

Economist Intelligence Unit, 111 West 57th Street, New York, New York 10019 (800) 938-4685; *Mali Country Report.*

Euromonitor International, Inc., 122 South Michigan Avenue, Suite 1200, Chicago, Illinois 60603 (800) 577-EURO; *International Marketing Data and Statistics; World Marketing Data and Statistics;* and *The World Economic Factbook.*

Europa Publications Limited, 18 Bedford Square, London, WC1B 3JN, England; *The Europa World Year Book.*

International Labour Office, I.L.O. Publications, 1828 L Street, N.W., Suite 801, Washington, D.C. 20036 (301) 638-3152; *Yearbook of Labour Statistics.*

M.E. Sharpe, 80 Business Park Drive, Armonk, New York 10504 (800) 541-6563; *The Illustrated Book of World Rankings.*

St. Martin's Press, Inc., 175 Fifth Avenue, New York, New York 10010 (800) 221-7945; *The Statesman's Year-Book.*

Statistical Office of the United Nations, Publishing Service, New York, New York 10017 (800) 253-9646; *Survey of Economic and Social Conditions in Africa.*

United Nations Economic Commission for Africa, Africa Hall, Post Office Box 3001, Addis Ababa, Ethiopia (Telephone Number in U.S. (800) 253-9646); *African Statistical Yearbook.*

The World Bank, 1818 H Street, NW, Washington, D.C. 20433 (202) 477-1234; *World Development Indicators.*

MALI - INFANT AND MATERNAL MORTALITY - See MALI - MORTALITY

MALI - INTERNATIONAL LIQUIDITY

International Monetary Fund, 700 Nineteenth Street, NW, Washington, D.C. 20431 (202) 623-7000; *International Financial Statistics*.

MALI - INTERNATIONAL RESERVES EXCLUDING GOLD

African Development Bank, 01 BP 1387, Abidjan 01, Cote d'Ivoire; *Selected Statistics on Regional Member Countries*.

Statistical Office of the United Nations, Publishing Service, New York, New York 10017 (800) 253-9646; *Statistical Yearbook*.

The World Bank, 1818 H Street, NW, Washington, D.C. 20433 (202) 477-1234; *World Development Indicators*.

MALI - IRON ORE PRODUCTION AND CONSUMPTION - See MALI - MINING AND MINERAL PRODUCTS

MALI - IRRIGATION

Euromonitor International, Inc., 122 South Michigan Avenue, Suite 1200, Chicago, Illinois 60603 (800) 577-EURO; *International Marketing Data and Statistics*.

MALI - JUTE PRODUCTION - See MALI - CROPS

MALI - LABOR

African Development Bank, 01 BP 1387, Abidjan 01, Cote d'Ivoire; *Selected Statistics on Regional Member Countries*.

Central Intelligence Agency, Washington, D.C. 20505 (703) 482-1100, www.cia.gov; *The World Factbook*.

Euromonitor International, Inc., 122 South Michigan Avenue, Suite 1200, Chicago, Illinois 60603 (800) 577-EURO; *International Marketing Data and Statistics;* and *World Marketing Data and Statistics*.

Europa Publications Limited, 18 Bedford Square, London, WC1B 3JN, England; *The Europa World Year Book*.

Food and Agricultural Organization of the United Nations (FAO), Via delle Terme di Caracalla, 00100 Rome, Italy (Telephone Number in U.S. (202) 653-2400); *The State of Food and Agriculture*.

International Labour Office, I.L.O. Publications, 1828 L Street, N.W., Suite 801, Washington, D.C. 20036 (301) 638-3152; *Yearbook of Labour Statistics*.

M.E. Sharpe, 80 Business Park Drive, Armonk, New York 10504 (800) 541-6563; *The Illustrated Book of World Rankings*.

St. Martin's Press, Inc., 175 Fifth Avenue, New York, New York 10010 (800) 221-7945; *The Statesman's Year-Book*.

Statistical Office of the United Nations, Publishing Service, New York, New York 10017 (800) 253-9646; *Human Development Report*.

The World Bank, 1818 H Street, NW, Washington, D.C. 20433 (202) 477-1234; *The World Bank Atlas; World Development Report;* and *World Development Indicators*.

MALI - LAND USE

Central Intelligence Agency, Washington, D.C. 20505 (703) 482-1100, www.cia.gov; *The World Factbook*.

Euromonitor International, Inc., 122 South Michigan Avenue, Suite 1200, Chicago, Illinois 60603 (800) 577-EURO; *International Marketing Data and Statistics*.

Food and Agricultural Organization of the United Nations (FAO), Via delle Terme di Caracalla, 00100 Rome, Italy (Telephone Number in U.S. (202) 653-2400); *Production Yearbook*.

The World Bank, 1818 H Street, NW, Washington, D.C. 20433 (202) 477-1234; *World Development Report*.

MALI - LIBRARIES

M.E. Sharpe, 80 Business Park Drive, Armonk, New York 10504 (800) 541-6563; *The Illustrated Book of World Rankings*.

United Nations Educational, Scientific and Cultural Organization (UNESCO), 7 Place de Fontenoy, F-75700 Paris, France (Telephone Number in U.S. (212) 963-5981); *Statistical Yearbook*.

MALI - LIFE EXPECTANCY

African Development Bank, 01 BP 1387, Abidjan 01, Cote d'Ivoire; *Selected Statistics on Regional Member Countries*.

Central Intelligence Agency, Washington, D.C. 20505 (703) 482-1100, www.cia.gov; *The World Factbook*.

Euromonitor International, Inc., 122 South Michigan Avenue, Suite 1200, Chicago, Illinois 60603 (800) 577-EURO; *The World Economic Factbook*.

St. Martin's Press, Inc., 175 Fifth Avenue, New York, New York 10010 (800) 221-7945; *The Statesman's Year-Book*.

Statistical Office of the United Nations, Publishing Service, New York, New York 10017 (800) 253-9646; *Human Development Report;* and *World Statistics*

Pocketbook.

The World Bank, 1818 H Street, NW, Washington, D.C. 20433 (202) 477-1234; *The World Bank Atlas;* and *World Development Report*.

MALI - LITERACY RATE

Euromonitor International, Inc., 122 South Michigan Avenue, Suite 1200, Chicago, Illinois 60603 (800) 577-EURO; *World Marketing Data and Statistics*.

Statistical Office of the United Nations, Publishing Service, New York, New York 10017 (800) 253-9646; *Survey of Economic and Social Conditions in Africa*.

MALI - LIVESTOCK AND POULTRY

Euromonitor International, Inc., 122 South Michigan Avenue, Suite 1200, Chicago, Illinois 60603 (800) 577-EURO; *International Marketing Data and Statistics*.

Europa Publications Limited, 18 Bedford Square, London, WC1B 3JN, England; *The Europa World Year Book*.

Food and Agricultural Organization of the United Nations (FAO), Via delle Terme di Caracalla, 00100 Rome, Italy (Telephone Number in U.S. (202) 653-2400); *Production Yearbook;* and *The State of Food and Agriculture*.

M.E. Sharpe, 80 Business Park Drive, Armonk, New York 10504 (800) 541-6563; *The Illustrated Book of World Rankings*.

St. Martin's Press, Inc., 175 Fifth Avenue, New York, New York 10010 (800) 221-7945; *The Statesman's Year-Book*.

Statistical Office of the United Nations, Publishing Service, New York, New York 10017 (800) 253-9646; *Statistical Yearbook;* and *Survey of Economic and Social Conditions in Africa*.

United Nations Conference on Trade and Development, Central Statistical Service, Palais des Nations, Geneva, Switzerland (Telephone in U.S. (800) 253-9646); *UNCTAD Commodity Yearbook*.

United Nations Economic Commission for Africa, Africa Hall, Post Office Box 3001, Addis Ababa, Ethiopia (Telephone Number in U.S. (800) 253-9646); *African Statistical Yearbook*.

MALI - LIVING LEVELS - See MALI - LIFE EXPECTANCY

MALI - MAIL - NUMBER OF ITEMS SENT OR RECEIVED

Statistical Office of the United Nations,

Publishing Service, New York, New York 10017 (800) 253-9646; *Statistical Yearbook*.

MALI - MANUFACTURING

M.E. Sharpe, 80 Business Park Drive, Armonk, New York 10504 (800) 541-6563; *The Illustrated Book of World Rankings*.

Statistical Office of the United Nations, Publishing Service, New York, New York 10017 (800) 253-9646; *Survey of Economic and Social Conditions in Africa*.

United Nations Economic Commission for Africa, Africa Hall, Post Office Box 3001, Addis Ababa, Ethiopia (Telephone Number in U.S. (800) 253-9646); *African Statistical Yearbook*.

The World Bank, 1818 H Street, NW, Washington, D.C. 20433 (202) 477-1234; *World Development Indicators*.

MALI - MARRIAGE RATES

M.E. Sharpe, 80 Business Park Drive, Armonk, New York 10504 (800) 541-6563; *The Illustrated Book of World Rankings*.

Statistical Office of the United Nations, Publishing Service, New York, New York 10017 (800) 253-9646; *Demographic Yearbook*.

MALI - MEAT PRODUCTION - See MALI - LIVESTOCK AND POULTRY

MALI - MERCHANT SHIPPING

Europa Publications Limited, 18 Bedford Square, London, WC1B 3JN, England; *The Europa World Year Book*.

St. Martin's Press, Inc., 175 Fifth Avenue, New York, New York 10010 (800) 221-7945; *The Statesman's Year-Book*.

United Nations Economic Commission for Africa, Africa Hall, Post Office Box 3001, Addis Ababa, Ethiopia (Telephone Number in U.S. (800) 253-9646); *African Statistical Yearbook*.

MALI - MILITARY

Central Intelligence Agency, Washington, D.C. 20505 (703) 482-1100, www.cia.gov; *The World Factbook*.

Euromonitor International, Inc., 122 South Michigan Avenue, Suite 1200, Chicago, Illinois 60603 (800) 577-EURO; *World Marketing Data and Statistics*.

The International Institute for Strategic Studies, 23 Tavistock Street, London WC2E 7NQ, England; *The Military Balance*.

M.E. Sharpe, 80 Business Park Drive, Armonk, New York 10504 (800) 541-6563;

The Illustrated Book of World Rankings.

St. Martin's Press, Inc., 175 Fifth Avenue, New York, New York 10010 (800) 221-7945; *The Statesman's Year-Book*.

Statistical Office of the United Nations, Publishing Service, New York, New York 10017 (800) 253-9646; *Human Development Report*.

U.S. Arms Control and Disarmament Agency, 320 Twenty-first Street, NW, Washington, D.C. 20451 (202) 647-8677; *World Military Expenditures and Arms Transfers*.

MALI - MILK PRODUCTION - See MALI - DAIRY PRODUCTS

MALI - MILLET PRODUCTION - See MALI - CROPS

MALI - MINING AND MINERAL PRODUCTS

Europa Publications Limited, 18 Bedford Square, London, WC1B 3JN, England; *The Europa World Year Book*.

M.E. Sharpe, 80 Business Park Drive, Armonk, New York 10504 (800) 541-6563; *The Illustrated Book of World Rankings*.

St. Martin's Press, Inc., 175 Fifth Avenue, New York, New York 10010 (800) 221-7945; *The Statesman's Year-Book*.

Statistical Office of the United Nations, Publishing Service, New York, New York 10017 (800) 253-9646; *Statistical Yearbook*.

United Nations Conference on Trade and Development, Central Statistical Service, Palais des Nations, Geneva, Switzerland (Telephone in U.S. (800) 253-9646); *UNCTAD Commodity Yearbook*.

United Nations Economic Commission for Africa, Africa Hall, Post Office Box 3001, Addis Ababa, Ethiopia (Telephone Number in U.S. (800) 253-9646); *African Statistical Yearbook*.

MALI - MONEY EXCHANGE RATES - See MALI - EXCHANGE RATES

MALI - MONEY RESERVES

Euromonitor International, Inc., 122 South Michigan Avenue, Suite 1200, Chicago, Illinois 60603 (800) 577-EURO; *International Marketing Data and Statistics*.

MALI - MONEY SUPPLY

African Development Bank, 01 BP 1387, Abidjan 01, Cote d'Ivoire; *Selected Statistics on Regional Member Countries*.

Economist Intelligence Unit, 111 West

57th Street, New York, New York 10019 (800) 938-4685; *Mali Country Report*.

Euromonitor International, Inc., 122 South Michigan Avenue, Suite 1200, Chicago, Illinois 60603 (800) 577-EURO; *International Marketing Data and Statistics*.

Europa Publications Limited, 18 Bedford Square, London, WC1B 3JN, England; *The Europa World Year Book*.

International Monetary Fund, 700 Nineteenth Street, NW, Washington, D.C. 20431 (202) 623-7000; *International Financial Statistics*.

Statistical Office of the United Nations, Publishing Service, New York, New York 10017 (800) 253-9646; *Statistical Yearbook*.

The World Bank, 1818 H Street, NW, Washington, D.C. 20433 (202) 477-1234; *World Development Indicators*.

MALI - MORTALITY

Central Intelligence Agency, Washington, D.C. 20505 (703) 482-1100, www.cia.gov; *The World Factbook*.

Euromonitor International, Inc., 122 South Michigan Avenue, Suite 1200, Chicago, Illinois 60603 (800) 577-EURO; *International Marketing Data and Statistics; and The World Economic Factbook*.

Europa Publications Limited, 18 Bedford Square, London, WC1B 3JN, England; *The Europa World Year Book*.

St. Martin's Press, Inc., 175 Fifth Avenue, New York, New York 10010 (800) 221-7945; *The Statesman's Year-Book*.

Statistical Office of the United Nations, Publishing Service, New York, New York 10017 (800) 253-9646; *Demographic Yearbook; Human Development Report; Statistical Yearbook; World Statistics Pocketbook; and Survey of Economic and Social Conditions in Africa*.

United Nations Children's Fund (UNICEF), 3 United Nations Plaza, New York, New York 10017 (800) 253-9646; *State of the World's Children*.

The World Bank, 1818 H Street, NW, Washington, D.C. 20433 (202) 477-1234; *The World Bank Atlas; World Development Report; and World Development Indicators*.

World Health Organization, Office of Publications, 20 Avenue Appia, CH-1211 Geneva 27, Switzerland (Telephone Number in U.S. (518) 436-9686); *World Health Statistics Annual*.

MALI - MOTOR VEHICLE TAXES - See

MALI - TAXATION

MALI - MOTOR VEHICLES IN USE

Europa Publications Limited, 18 Bedford Square, London, WC1B 3JN, England; *The Europa World Year Book.*

International Road Federation, 2600 Virginia Avenue, N.W., Washington, D.C. 20037 (202) 338-4641; *World Road Statistics.*

Statistical Office of the United Nations, Publishing Service, New York, New York 10017 (800) 253-9646; *Statistical Yearbook;* and *Survey of Economic and Social Conditions in Africa.*

MALI - MUSEUMS

M.E. Sharpe, 80 Business Park Drive, Armonk, New York 10504 (800) 541-6563; *The Illustrated Book of World Rankings.*

Statistical Office of the United Nations, Publishing Service, New York, New York 10017 (800) 253-9646; *Statistical Yearbook.*

MALI - NATALITY - See MALI - BIRTH RATES

MALI - NATIONAL ACCOUNTS

African Development Bank, 01 BP 1387, Abidjan 01, Cote d'Ivoire; *Selected Statistics on Regional Member Countries.*

Europa Publications Limited, 18 Bedford Square, London, WC1B 3JN, England; *The Europa World Year Book.*

International Monetary Fund, 700 Nineteenth Street, NW, Washington, D.C. 20431 (202) 623-7000; *International Financial Statistics.*

Statistical Office of the United Nations, Publishing Service, New York, New York 10017 (800) 253-9646; *National Account Statistics;* and *Statistical Yearbook.*

United Nations Economic Commission for Africa, Africa Hall, Post Office Box 3001, Addis Ababa, Ethiopia (Telephone Number in U.S. (800) 253-9646); *African Statistical Yearbook.*

MALI - NATIONAL INCOME

M.E. Sharpe, 80 Business Park Drive, Armonk, New York 10504 (800) 541-6563; *The Illustrated Book of World Rankings.*

Statistical Office of the United Nations, Publishing Service, New York, New York 10017 (800) 253-9646; *National Accounts Statistics;* and *Statistical Yearbook.*

MALI - NATIONAL PRODUCT

M.E. Sharpe, 80 Business Park Drive, Armonk, New York 10504 (800) 541-6563;

The Illustrated Book of World Rankings.

MALI - NATURAL GAS - PRODUCTION - See MALI - MINING AND MINERAL PRODUCTS

MALI - NEWSPAPER PRODUCTION - See MALI - FORESTRY AND FOREST PRODUCTS

MALI - NEWSPRINT - See MALI - FORESTRY AND FOREST PRODUCTS

MALI - OCCUPATIONS - See MALI - LABOR

MALI - PAPER - See MALI - FORESTRY AND FOREST PRODUCTS

MALI - PEANUT PRODUCTION - See MALI - CROPS

MALI - PERIODICALS

United Nations Educational, Scientific and Cultural Organization (UNESCO), 7 Place de Fontenoy, F-75700 Paris, France (Telephone Number in U.S. (212) 963-5981); *Statistical Yearbook.*

MALI - PESTICIDE USE

Food and Agricultural Organization of the United Nations (FAO), Via delle Terme di Caracalla, 00100 Rome, Italy (Telephone Number in U.S. (202) 653-2400); *The State of Food and Agriculture.*

MALI - PETROLEUM INDUSTRY

Food and Agricultural Organization of the United Nations (FAO), Via delle Terme di Caracalla, 00100 Rome, Italy (Telephone Number in U.S. (202) 653-2400); *The State of Food and Agriculture.*

M.E. Sharpe, 80 Business Park Drive, Armonk, New York 10504 (800) 541-6563; *The Illustrated Book of World Rankings.*

United Nations Conference on Trade and Development, Central Statistical Service, Palais des Nations, Geneva, Switzerland (Telephone in U.S. (800) 253-9646); *UNCTAD Commodity Yearbook.*

MALI - PIGS - See MALI - LIVESTOCK AND POULTRY

MALI - POPULATION

African Development Bank, 01 BP 1387, Abidjan 01, Cote d'Ivoire; *Selected Statistics on Regional Member Countries.*

Central Intelligence Agency, Washington, D.C. 20505 (703) 482-1100, www.cia.gov; *The World Factbook.*

The Economist Intelligence Unit, 111 West 57th Street, New York, New York 10019 (800) 938-4685; *Mali Country Report;*

and *The World Market Atlas.*

Euromonitor International, Inc., 122 South Michigan Avenue, Suite 1200, Chicago, Illinois 60603 (800) 577-EURO; *International Marketing Data and Statistics;* and *The World Economic Factbook.*

Europa Publications Limited, 18 Bedford Square, London, WC1B 3JN, England; *The Europa World Year Book.*

Food and Agricultural Organization of the United Nations (FAO), Via delle Terme di Caracalla, 00100 Rome, Italy (Telephone Number in U.S. (202) 653-2400); *Production Yearbook.*

International Labour Office, I.L.O. Publications, 1828 L Street, N.W., Suite 801, Washington, D.C. 20036 (301) 638-3152; *Yearbook of Labour Statistics.*

M.E. Sharpe, 80 Business Park Drive, Armonk, New York 10504 (800) 541-6563; *The Illustrated Book of World Rankings.*

St. Martin's Press, Inc., 175 Fifth Avenue, New York, New York 10010 (800) 221-7945; *The Statesman's Year-Book.*

Statistical Office of the United Nations, Publishing Service, New York, New York 10017 (800) 253-9646; *Demographic Yearbook; Human Development Report; Statistical Yearbook; World Statistics Pocketbook;* and *Survey of Economic and Social Conditions in Africa.*

U.S. Arms Control and Disarmament Agency, 320 Twenty-first Street, NW, Washington, D.C. 20451 (202) 647-8677; *World Military Expenditures and Arms Transfers.*

The World Bank, 1818 H Street, NW, Washington, D.C. 20433 (202) 477-1234; *The World Bank Atlas;* and *World Development Report.*

World Health Organization, Office of Publications, 20 Avenue Appia, CH-1211 Geneva 27, Switzerland (Telephone Number in U.S. (518) 436-9686); *World Health Statistics Annual.*

MALI - POST OFFICES

M.E. Sharpe, 80 Business Park Drive, Armonk, New York 10504 (800) 541-6563; *The Illustrated Book of World Rankings.*

MALI - POTATO PRODUCTION - See MALI - CROPS

MALI - PRICES

Food and Agricultural Organization of the United Nations (FAO), Via delle Terme di Caracalla, 00100 Rome, Italy (Telephone Number in U.S. (202) 653-2400); *The State*

of Food and Agriculture; and *Trade Yearbook.*

International Labour Office, I.L.O. Publications, 1828 L Street, N.W., Suite 801, Washington, D.C. 20036 (301) 638-3152; *Yearbook of Labour Statistics.*

M.E. Sharpe, 80 Business Park Drive, Armonk, New York 10504 (800) 541-6563; *The Illustrated Book of World Rankings.*

United Nations Economic Commission for Africa, Africa Hall, Post Office Box 3001, Addis Ababa, Ethiopia (Telephone Number in U.S. (800) 253-9646); *African Statistical Yearbook.*

MALI - PRINTING AND WRITING PAPER - See MALI - FORESTRY AND FOREST PRODUCTS

MALI - PRODUCTION

M.E. Sharpe, 80 Business Park Drive, Armonk, New York 10504 (800) 541-6563; *The Illustrated Book of World Rankings.*

MALI - PRODUCTIVITY

Euromonitor International, Inc., 122 South Michigan Avenue, Suite 1200, Chicago, Illinois 60603 (800) 577-EURO; *International Marketing Data and Statistics.*

MALI - PROPERTY TAXES - See MALI - TAXATION

MALI - PUBLIC FINANCE - See MALI - FINANCE

MALI - RADIO BROADCASTING - See MALI - BROADCASTING

MALI - RADIO RECEIVERS

St. Martin's Press, Inc., 175 Fifth Avenue, New York, New York 10010 (800) 221-7945; *The Statesman's Year-Book.*

MALI - RAILWAYS

Europa Publications Limited, 18 Bedford Square, London, WC1B 3JN, England; *The Europa World Year Book.*

Jane's Information Group, Sentinel House, 163 Brighton Road, Coulsdon, Surrey CR5 2NH, England (Telephone Number in U.S. (703) 683-3700); *Jane's World Railways.*

St. Martin's Press, Inc., 175 Fifth Avenue, New York, New York 10010 (800) 221-7945; *The Statesman's Year-Book.*

Statistical Office of the United Nations, Publishing Service, New York, New York 10017 (800) 253-9646; *Statistical Yearbook;* and *Survey of Economic and Social Conditions in Africa.*

United Nations Economic Commission for Africa, Africa Hall, Post Office Box 3001, Addis Ababa, Ethiopia (Telephone Number in U.S. (800) 253-9646); *African Statistical Yearbook.*

MALI - RELIGION

Central Intelligence Agency, Washington, D.C. 20505 (703) 482-1100, www.cia.gov; *The World Factbook.*

M.E. Sharpe, 80 Business Park Drive, Armonk, New York 10504 (800) 541-6563; *The Illustrated Book of World Rankings.*

St. Martin's Press, Inc., 175 Fifth Avenue, New York, New York 10010 (800) 221-7945; *The Statesman's Year-Book.*

MALI - RETAIL TRADE

Euromonitor International, Inc., 122 South Michigan Avenue, Suite 1200, Chicago, Illinois 60603 (800) 577-EURO; *World Marketing Data and Statistics.*

MALI - RICE PRODUCTION - See MALI - CROPS

MALI - ROOT AND TUBER PRODUCTION - See MALI - CROPS

MALI - ROUNDWOOD PRODUCTION - See MALI - FORESTRY AND FOREST PRODUCTS

MALI - RUBBER PRODUCTION

M.E. Sharpe, 80 Business Park Drive, Armonk, New York 10504 (800) 541-6563; *The Illustrated Book of World Rankings.*

MALI - SALT PRODUCTION - See MALI - MINING AND MINERAL PRODUCTS

MALI - SAWNWOOD PRODUCTION - See MALI - FORESTRY AND FOREST PRODUCTS

MALI - SENIOR CITIZENS

M.E. Sharpe, 80 Business Park Drive, Armonk, New York 10504 (800) 541-6563; *The Illustrated Book of World Rankings.*

MALI - SHEEP - See MALI - LIVESTOCK AND POULTRY

MALI - SILVER PRODUCTION AND CONSUMPTION - See MALI - MINING AND MINERAL PRODUCTS

MALI - SOCIAL DATA

African Development Bank, 01 BP 1387, Abidjan 01, Cote d'Ivoire; *Selected Statistics on Regional Member Countries.*

M.E. Sharpe, 80 Business Park Drive, Armonk, New York 10504 (800) 541-6563;

The Illustrated Book of World Rankings.

Statistical Office of the United Nations, Publishing Service, New York, New York 10017 (800) 253-9646; *World Statistics Pocketbook.*

MALI - SOCIAL SECURITY

International Monetary Fund, 700 Nineteenth Street, NW, Washington, D.C. 20431 (202) 623-7000; *Government Finance Statistics Yearbook.*

Statistical Office of the United Nations, Publishing Service, New York, New York 10017 (800) 253-9646; *National Accounts Statistics.*

MALI - STAMP TAXES AND DUTIES - See MALI - TAXATION

MALI - STATE BUDGET

Euromonitor International, Inc., 122 South Michigan Avenue, Suite 1200, Chicago, Illinois 60603 (800) 577-EURO; *International Marketing Data and Statistics.*

MALI - STEEL PRODUCTION - See MALI - MINING AND MINERAL PRODUCTS

MALI - STOCKS - COMMODITY - MARKET PRICE - INDEX

Food and Agricultural Organization of the United Nations (FAO), Via delle Terme di Caracalla, 00100 Rome, Italy (Telephone Number in U.S. (202) 653-2400); *The State of Food and Agriculture.*

MALI - SUGAR PRODUCTION - See MALI - CROPS

MALI - TAXATION

Europa Publications Limited, 18 Bedford Square, London, WC1B 3JN, England; *The Europa World Year Book.*

International Monetary Fund, 700 Nineteenth Street, NW, Washington, D.C. 20431 (202) 623-7000; *Government Finance Statistics Yearbook.*

International Road Federation, 2600 Virginia Avenue, N.W., Washington, D.C. 20037 (202) 338-4641; *World Road Statistics.*

The World Bank, 1818 H Street, NW, Washington, D.C. 20433 (202) 477-1234; *World Development Indicators.*

MALI - TELEPHONES IN USE

American Telephone and Telegraph Company, 26 Parsippany Road, Whippany, New Jersey 07981 (800) 222-0300; *The World's Telephones.*

Central Intelligence Agency, Washington, D.C. 20505 (703) 482-1100, www.cia.gov; *The World Factbook.*

Europa Publications Limited, 18 Bedford Square, London, WC1B 3JN, England; *The Europa World Year Book.*

St. Martin's Press, Inc., 175 Fifth Avenue, New York, New York 10010 (800) 221-7945; *The Statesman's Year-Book.*

Statistical Office of the United Nations, Publishing Service, New York, New York 10017 (800) 253-9646; *Statistical Yearbook;* and *World Statistics Pocketbook.*

MALI - TELEVISION BROADCASTING - See MALI - BROADCASTING

MALI - TEXTILE INDUSTRY

M.E. Sharpe, 80 Business Park Drive, Armonk, New York 10504 (800) 541-6563; *The Illustrated Book of World Rankings.*

United Nations Conference on Trade and Development, Central Statistical Service, Palais des Nations, Geneva, Switzerland (Telephone in U.S. (800) 253-9646); *UNCTAD Commodity Yearbook.*

MALI - TOBACCO PRODUCTION

M.E. Sharpe, 80 Business Park Drive, Armonk, New York 10504 (800) 541-6563; *The Illustrated Book of World Rankings.*

Statistical Office of the United Nations, Publishing Service, New York, New York 10017 (800) 253-9646; *Statistical Yearbook.*

MALI - TOURISM

Euromonitor International, Inc., 122 South Michigan Avenue, Suite 1200, Chicago, Illinois 60603 (800) 577-EURO; *The World Economic Factbook;* and *World Marketing Data and Statistics.*

Europa Publications Limited, 18 Bedford Square, London, WC1B 3JN, England; *The Europa World Year Book.*

M.E. Sharpe, 80 Business Park Drive, Armonk, New York 10504 (800) 541-6563; *The Illustrated Book of World Rankings.*

St. Martin's Press, Inc., 175 Fifth Avenue, New York, New York 10010 (800) 221-7945; *The Statesman's Year-Book.*

Statistical Office of the United Nations, Publishing Service, New York, New York 10017 (800) 253-9646; *Statistical Yearbook.*

United Nations Economic Commission for Africa, Africa Hall, Post Office Box 3001, Addis Ababa, Ethiopia (Telephone Number in U.S. (800) 253-9646); *African Statistical Yearbook.*

World Tourism Organization, Calle Capitan Haya 42, E-28020 Madrid, Spain; *Yearbook of Tourism Statistics.*

MALI - TRACTORS IN USE

Statistical Office of the United Nations, Publishing Service, New York, New York 10017 (800) 253-9646; *Statistical Yearbook.*

MALI - TRADE - See MALI - FOREIGN TRADE

MALI - TRANSPORTATION AND COMMUNICATIONS

Central Intelligence Agency, Washington, D.C. 20505 (703) 482-1100, www.cia.gov; *The World Factbook.*

Euromonitor International, Inc., 122 South Michigan Avenue, Suite 1200, Chicago, Illinois 60603 (800) 577-EURO; *International Marketing Data and Statistics;* and *World Marketing Data and Statistics.*

Europa Publications Limited, 18 Bedford Square, London, WC1B 3JN, England; *The Europa World Year Book.*

M.E. Sharpe, 80 Business Park Drive, Armonk, New York 10504 (800) 541-6563; *The Illustrated Book of World Rankings.*

St. Martin's Press, Inc., 175 Fifth Avenue, New York, New York 10010 (800) 221-7945; *The Statesman's Year-Book.*

Statistical Office of the United Nations, Publishing Service, New York, New York 10017 (800) 253-9646; *Human Development Report.*

United Nations Economic Commission for Africa, Africa Hall, Post Office Box 3001, Addis Ababa, Ethiopia (Telephone Number in U.S. (800) 253-9646); *African Statistical Yearbook.*

MALI - TRAVEL FARES ABROAD

International Monetary Fund, 700 Nineteenth Street, NW, Washington, D.C. 20431 (202) 623-7000; *Government Finance Statistics Yearbook.*

MALI - UNEMPLOYMENT

Central Intelligence Agency, Washington, D.C. 20505 (703) 482-1100, www.cia.gov; *The World Factbook.*

Euromonitor International, Inc., 122 South Michigan Avenue, Suite 1200, Chicago, Illinois 60603 (800) 577-EURO; *International Marketing Data and Statistics.*

International Labour Office, I.L.O. Publications, 1828 L Street, N.W., Suite 801, Washington, D.C. 20036 (301)

638-3152; *Yearbook of Labour Statistics.*

Statistical Office of the United Nations, Publishing Service, New York, New York 10017 (800) 253-9646; *Statistical Yearbook.*

MALI - VITAL STATISTICS

Euromonitor International, Inc., 122 South Michigan Avenue, Suite 1200, Chicago, Illinois 60603 (800) 577-EURO; *International Marketing Data and Statistics.*

St. Martin's Press, Inc., 175 Fifth Avenue, New York, New York 10010 (800) 221-7945; *The Statesman's Year-Book.*

Statistical Office of the United Nations, Publishing Service, New York, New York 10017 (800) 253-9646; *Statistical Yearbook.*

World Health Organization, Office of Publications, 20 Avenue Appia, CH-1211 Geneva 27, Switzerland (Telephone Number in U.S. (518) 436-9686); *World Health Statistics Annual.*

MALI - WAGES

International Labour Office, I.L.O. Publications, 1828 L Street, N.W., Suite 801, Washington, D.C. 20036 (301) 638-3152; *Yearbook of Labour Statistics.*

Statistical Office of the United Nations, Publishing Service, New York, New York 10017 (800) 253-9646; *Statistical Yearbook.*

MALI - WEATHER - See MALI - CLIMATE

MALI - WELFARE EXPENDITURES

International Monetary Fund, 700 Nineteenth Street, NW, Washington, D.C. 20431 (202) 623-7000; *Government Finance Statistics Yearbook.*

MALI - WHEAT PRODUCTION - See MALI - CROPS

MALI - WINE PRODUCTION - See MALI - BEVERAGES

MALI - WOOL PRODUCTION - See MALI - TEXTILE INDUSTRY

MALT BEVERAGES - See also BEVERAGES

U.S. Department of Agriculture, Economic Research Service, 1800 M Street, NW, Washington, D.C. 20036 (202) 694-5050, www.ers.usda.gov; *Food Consumption, Prices, and Expenditures; U.S. Agricultural Trade Update; Agricultural Outlook;* and *Foreign Agricultural Trade of the United States.*

U.S. Department of the Treasury, Bureau of Alcohol, Tobacco and Firearms,

650 Massachusetts Avenue, NW, Washington, D.C. 20226 (202) 927-8500, www.atf.treas.gov; *Alcohol and Tobacco Summary Statistics.*

MALT BEVERAGES - BEER

U.S. Department of Agriculture, Economic Research Service, 1800 M Street, NW, Washington, D.C. 20036 (202) 694-5050, www.ers.usda.gov; *Food Consumption, Prices, and Expenditures; U.S. Agricultural Trade Update; Agricultural Outlook;* and *Foreign Agricultural Trade of the United States.*

U.S. Department of Labor, Bureau of Labor Statistics, Two Massachusetts Avenue, NE, Washington, D.C. 20212 (202) 691-5200, www.stats.bls.gov; *Monthly Labor Review;* and *CPI Detailed Report.*

Malta - National Statistical Office

Central Office of Statistics, Auberge D'Italie, Valletta, Malta.

Malta - Primary Statistics Sources

Central Office of Statistics, Auberge D'Italie, Valletta, Malta; *Annual Abstract of Statistics* and *Quarterly Digest of Statistics.*

MALTA - ABORTIONS

Statistical Office of the United Nations, Publishing Service, New York, New York 10017 (800) 253-9646; *Trends in Europe and North America: The Statistical Yearbook of the Economic Commission for Europe.*

MALTA - AGRICULTURE

Economist Intelligence Unit, 111 West 57th Street, New York, New York 10019 (800) 938-4685; *Malta Country Report.*

Euromonitor International, Inc., 122 South Michigan Avenue, Suite 1200, Chicago, Illinois 60603 (800) 577-EURO; *World Marketing Data and Statistics.*

Europa Publications Limited, 18 Bedford Square, London, WC1B 3JN, England; *The Europa World Year Book.*

Food and Agricultural Organization of the United Nations (FAO), Via delle Terme di Caracalla, 00100 Rome, Italy (Telephone Number in U.S. (202) 653-2400); *Production Yearbook; The State of Food and Agriculture;* and *Trade Yearbook.*

St. Martin's Press, Inc., 175 Fifth Avenue, New York, New York 10010 (800) 221-7945; *The Statesman's Year-Book.*

Statistical Office of the United Nations, Publishing Service, New York, New York 10017 (800) 253-9646; *Statistical Yearbook.*

United Nations Conference on Trade and Development, Central Statistical Service, Palais des Nations, Geneva, Switzerland (Telephone in U.S. (800) 253-9646); *UNCTAD Commodity Yearbook.*

The World Bank, 1818 H Street, NW, Washington, D.C. 20433 (202) 477-1234; *World Development Indicators.*

MALTA - AIRLINE SERVICE

Europa Publications Limited, 18 Bedford Square, London, WC1B 3JN, England; *The Europa World Year Book.*

International Civil Aviation Organization, 999 University Street, Montreal, Quebec, Canada H3C 5H7 (514) 954-8219; *Civil Aviation Statistics of the World.*

St. Martin's Press, Inc., 175 Fifth Avenue, New York, New York 10010 (800) 221-7945; *The Statesman's Year-Book.*

Statistical Office of the United Nations, Publishing Service, New York, New York 10017 (800) 253-9646; *Statistical Yearbook.*

MALTA - AIRPORTS

Central Intelligence Agency, Washington, D.C. 20505 (703) 482-1100, www.cia.gov; *The World Factbook.*

MALTA - ANIMAL HEALTH

Food and Agricultural Organization of the United Nations (FAO), Via delle Terme di Caracalla, 00100 Rome, Italy (Telephone Number in U.S. (202) 653-2400); *Animal Health Yearbook.*

MALTA - AREA AND DENSITY OF POPULATION

Central Intelligence Agency, Washington, D.C. 20505 (703) 482-1100, www.cia.gov; *The World Factbook.*

Euromonitor International, Inc., 122 South Michingan Avenue, Suite 1200, Chicago, Illinois 60603 (800) 577-EURO; *The World Economic Factbook.*

Europa Publications Limited, 18 Bedford Square, London, WC1B 3JN, England; *The Europa World Year Book.*

Food and Agricultural Organization of the United Nations (FAO), Via delle Terme di Caracalla, 00100 Rome, Italy (Telephone Number in U.S. (202) 653-2400); *The State of Food and Agriculture.*

St. Martin's Press, Inc., 175 Fifth

Avenue, New York, New York 10010 (800) 221-7945; *The Statesman's Year-Book.*

Statistical Office of the United Nations, Publishing Service, New York, New York 10017 (800) 253-9646; *Statistical Yearbook;* and *Trends in Europe and North America: The Statistical Yearbook of the Economic Commission for Europe.*

MALTA - ARMS EXPORTS AND IMPORTS - See MALTA - MILITARY

MALTA - BALANCE OF PAYMENTS

Europa Publications Limited, 18 Bedford Square, London, WC1B 3JN, England; *The Europa World Year Book.*

International Monetary Fund, 700 Nineteenth Street, NW, Washington, D.C. 20431 (202) 623-7000; *Balance of Payments Yearbook.*

United Nations Conference on Trade and Development (UNCTAD), New York, New York 10017 (800) 253-9646, *Handbook of International Trade and Development Statistics.*

The World Bank, 1818 H Street, NW, Washington, D.C. 20433 (202) 477-1234; *World Development Indicators.*

MALTA - BANKING

Euromonitor International, Inc., 122 South Michigan Avenue, Suite 1200, Chicago, Illinois 60603 (800) 577-EURO; *World Marketing Data and Statistics.*

Europa Publications Limited, 18 Bedford Square, London, WC1B 3JN, England; *The Europa World Year Book.*

International Monetary Fund, 700 Nineteenth Street, NW, Washington, D.C. 20431 (202) 623-7000; *International Financial Statistics.*

St. Martin's Press, Inc., 175 Fifth Avenue, New York, New York 10010 (800) 221-7945; *The Statesman's Year-Book.*

MALTA - BARLEY PRODUCTION - See MALTA - CROPS

MALTA - BEER PRODUCTION - See MALTA - BEVERAGES

MALTA - BEVERAGES

Statistical Office of the United Nations, Publishing Service, New York, New York 10017 (800) 253-9646; *Statistical Yearbook.*

MALTA - BIRTH RATES

Central Intelligence Agency, Washington, D.C. 20505 (703) 482-1100, www.cia.gov; *The World Factbook.*

Euromonitor International, Inc., 122 South Michigan Avenue, Suite 1200, Chicago, Illinois 60603 (800) 577-EURO; *The World Economic Factbook.*

Europa Publications Limited, 18 Bedford Square, London, WC1B 3JN, England; *The Europa World Year Book.*

St. Martin's Press, Inc., 175 Fifth Avenue, New York, New York 10010 (800) 221-7945; *The Statesman's Year-Book.*

Statistical Office of the United Nations, Publishing Service, New York, New York 10017 (800) 253-9646; *Demographic Yearbook;* and *Statistical Yearbook.*

The World Bank, 1818 H Street, NW, Washington, D.C. 20433 (202) 477-1234; *World Development Indicators.*

World Health Organization, Office of Publications, 20 Avenue Appia, CH-1211 Geneva 27, Switzerland (Telephone Number in U.S. (518) 436-9686); *World Health Statistics Annual.*

MALTA - BONDS

International Monetary Fund, 700 Nineteenth Street, NW, Washington, D.C. 20431 (202) 623-7000; *Government Finance Statistics Yearbook.*

MALTA - BOOK PRODUCTION

Euromonitor International, Inc., 122 South Michigan Avenue, Suite 1200, Chicago, Illinois 60603 (800) 577-EURO; *European Marketing Data and Statistics.*

Europa Publications Limited, 18 Bedford Square, London, WC1B 3JN, England; *The Europa World Year Book.*

Statistical Office of the United Nations, Publishing Service, New York, New York 10017 (800) 253-9646; *Trends in Europe and North America: The Statistical Yearbook of the Economic Commission for Europe.*

United Nations Educational, Scientific and Cultural Organization (UNESCO), 7 Place de Fontenoy, F-75700 Paris, France (Telephone Number in U.S. (212) 963-5981); *Statistical Yearbook.*

MALTA - BROADCASTING

Billboard Limited, Post Office Box 9027, 1006 AA Amsterdam, The Netherlands (Telephone Number in U.S. (212) 764-7300); *World Radio TV Handbook.*

Central Intelligence Agency, Washington, D.C. 20505 (703) 482-1100, www.cia.gov; *The World Factbook.*

Euromonitor International, Inc., 122 South Michigan Avenue, Suite 1200,

Chicago, Illinois 60603 (800) 577-EURO; *World Marketing Data and Statistics.*

Europa Publications Limited, 18 Bedford Square, London, WC1B 3JN, England; *The Europa World Year Book.*

St. Martin's Press, Inc., 175 Fifth Avenue, New York, New York 10010 (800) 221-7945; *The Statesman's Year-Book.*

Statistical Office of the United Nations, Publishing Service, New York, New York 10017 (800) 253-9646; *Trends in Europe and North America: The Statistical Yearbook of the Economic Commission for Europe.*

United Nations Educational, Scientific and Cultural Organization (UNESCO), 7 Place de Fontenoy, F-75700 Paris, France (Telephone Number in U.S. (212) 963-5981); *Statistical Yearbook.*

MALTA - BUDGET

Central Intelligence Agency, Washington, D.C. 20505 (703) 482-1100, www.cia.gov; *The World Factbook.*

MALTA - BUSINESS AND PROFESSIONAL LICENSES

International Monetary Fund, 700 Nineteenth Street, NW, Washington, D.C. 20431 (202) 623-7000; *Government Finance Statistics Yearbook.*

MALTA - CALORIE SUPPLY

Food and Agricultural Organization of the United Nations (FAO), Via delle Terme di Caracalla, 00100 Rome, Italy (Telephone Number in U.S. (202) 653-2400); *The State of Food and Agriculture.*

MALTA - CAPITAL REVENUE

International Monetary Fund, 700 Nineteenth Street, NW, Washington, D.C. 20431 (202) 623-7000; *Government Finance Statistics Yearbook.*

MALTA - CATTLE - See MALTA - LIVESTOCK AND POULTRY

MALTA - CEREAL PRODUCTION - See MALTA - CROPS

MALTA - CIGARETTE PRODUCTION - See MALTA - TOBACCO PRODUCTION

MALTA - CLIMATE

St. Martin's Press, Inc., 175 Fifth Avenue, New York, New York 10010 (800) 221-7945; *The Statesman's Year-Book.*

MALTA - COMMERCE

St. Martin's Press, Inc., 175 Fifth Avenue, New York, New York 10010 (800)

221-7945; *The Statesman's Year-Book.*

MALTA - CONSTRUCTION INDUSTRY

St. Martin's Press, Inc., 175 Fifth Avenue, New York, New York 10010 (800) 221-7945; *The Statesman's Year-Book.*

Statistical Office of the United Nations, Publishing Service, New York, New York 10017 (800) 253-9646; *Statistical Yearbook.*

MALTA - CONSUMER PRICE INDEX

Statistical Office of the United Nations, Publishing Service, New York, New York 10017 (800) 253-9646; *Statistical Yearbook;* and *Trends in Europe and North America: The Statistical Yearbook of the Economic Commission for Europe.*

MALTA - CONSUMER PRICES

Euromonitor International, Inc., 122 South Michigan Avenue, Suite 1200, Chicago, Illinois 60603 (800) 577-EURO; *European Marketing Data and Statistics;* and *World Marketing Data and Statistics.*

International Labour Office, I.L.O. Publications, 1828 L Street, N.W., Suite 801, Washington, D.C. 20036 (301) 638-3152; *Yearbook of Labour Statistics.*

International Monetary Fund, 700 Nineteenth Street, NW, Washington, D.C. 20431 (202) 623-7000; *International Financial Statistics.*

MALTA - CORN PRODUCTION - See MALTA - CROPS

MALTA - CORPORATE TAXES - See MALTA - TAXATION

MALTA - COTTON - See MALTA - CROPS

MALTA - CRIME

International Criminal Police Organization (INTERPOL), 50 quai Achille Lignon, F-69006 Lyon, France; *International Crime Statistics.*

Statistical Office of the United Nations, Publishing Service, New York, New York 10017 (800) 253-9646; *Trends in Europe and North America: The Statistical Yearbook of the Economic Commission for Europe.*

Yale University Press, Yale Station, New Haven, Connecticut 06520 (800) 987-7323; *Violence and Crime in Cross-National Perspective.*

MALTA - CROPS

Euromonitor International, Inc., 122 South Michigan Avenue, Suite 1200, Chicago, Illinois 60603 (800) 577-EURO;

European Marketing Data and Statistics.

Europa Publications Limited, 18 Bedford Square, London, WC1B 3JN, England; *The Europa World Year Book.*

Food and Agricultural Organization of the United Nations (FAO), Via delle Terme di Caracalla, 00100 Rome, Italy (Telephone Number in U.S. (202) 653-2400); *Production Yearbook;* and *The State of Food and Agriculture.*

St. Martin's Press, Inc., 175 Fifth Avenue, New York, New York 10010 (800) 221-7945; *The Statesman's Year-Book.*

Statistical Office of the United Nations, Publishing Service, New York, New York 10017 (800) 253-9646; *Statistical Yearbook.*

United Nations Conference on Trade and Development, Central Statistical Service, Palais des Nations, Geneva, Switzerland (Telephone in U.S. (800) 253-9646); *UNCTAD Commodity Yearbook.*

MALTA - CUSTOMS DUTIES

International Monetary Fund, 700 Nineteenth Street, NW, Washington, D.C. 20431 (202) 623-7000; *Government Finance Statistics Yearbook.*

St. Martin's Press, Inc., 175 Fifth Avenue, New York, New York 10010 (800) 221-7945; *The Statesman's Year-Book.*

MALTA - DAIRY PRODUCTS

Europa Publications Limited, 18 Bedford Square, London, WC1B 3JN, England; *The Europa World Year Book.*

Food and Agricultural Organization of the United Nations (FAO), Via delle Terme di Caracalla, 00100 Rome, Italy (Telephone Number in U.S. (202) 653-2400); *Production Yearbook* and *The State of Food and Agriculture.*

St. Martin's Press, Inc., 175 Fifth Avenue, New York, New York 10010 (800) 221-7945; *The Statesman's Year-Book.*

Statistical Office of the United Nations, Publishing Service, New York, New York 10017 (800) 253-9646; *Statistical Yearbook.*

MALTA - DEATH RATES - See MALTA - MORTALITY

MALTA - DEFENSE EXPENDITURES - See MALTA - MILITARY

MALTA - DEMOGRAPHY

Euromonitor International, Inc., 122 South Michigan Avenue, Suite 1200, Chicago, Illinois 60603 (800) 577-EURO; *The World Economic Factbook;* and *World*

Marketing Data and Statistics.

Statistical Office of the United Nations, Publishing Service, New York, New York 10017 (800) 253-9646; *Human Development Report.*

MALTA - DIVORCE RATES

Statistical Office of the United Nations, Publishing Service, New York, New York 10017 (800) 253-9646; *Demographic Yearbook;* and *Trends in Europe and North America: The Statistical Yearbook of the Economic Commission for Europe.*

MALTA - DUCKS - See MALTA - LIVESTOCK AND POULTRY

MALTA - ECONOMY

Central Intelligence Agency, Washington, D.C. 20505 (703) 482-1100, www.cia.gov; *The World Factbook.*

Economist Intelligence Unit, 111 West 57th Street, New York, New York 10019 (800) 938-4685; *Malta Country Report.*

Euromonitor International, Inc., 122 South Michigan Avenue, Suite 1200, Chicago, Illinois 60603 (800) 577-EURO; *European Marketing Data and Statistics; World Marketing Data and Statistics;* and *The World Economic Factbook.*

Europa Publications Limited, 18 Bedford Square, London, WC1B 3JN, England; *The Europa World Year Book.*

St. Martin's Press, Inc., 175 Fifth Avenue, New York, New York 10010 (800) 221-7945; *The Statesman's Year-Book.*

Statistical Office of the United Nations, Publishing Service, New York, New York 10017 (800) 253-9646; *World Statistics Pocketbook.*

The World Bank, 1818 H Street, NW, Washington, D.C. 20433 (202) 477-1234; *The World Bank Atlas.*

MALTA - EDUCATION

Euromonitor International, Inc., 122 South Michigan Avenue, Suite 1200, Chicago, Illinois 60603 (800) 577-EURO; *European Marketing Data and Statistics;* and *World Marketing Data and Statistics.*

Europa Publications Limited, 18 Bedford Square, London, WC1B 3JN, England; *The Europa World Year Book.*

International Monetary Fund, 700 Nineteenth Street, NW, Washington, D.C. 20431 (202) 623-7000; *Government Finance Statistics Yearbook.*

St. Martin's Press, Inc., 175 Fifth

Avenue, New York, New York 10010 (800) 221-7945; *The Statesman's Year-Book.*

Statistical Office of the United Nations, Publishing Service, New York, New York 10017 (800) 253-9646; *Human Development Report;* and *Trends in Europe and North America: The Statistical Yearbook of the Economic Commission for Europe.*

United Nations Educational, Scientific and Cultural Organization (UNESCO), 7 Place de Fontenoy, F-75700 Paris, France (Telephone Number in U.S. (212) 963-5981); *Statistical Yearbook.*

The World Bank, 1818 H Street, NW, Washington, D.C. 20433 (202) 477-1234; *World Development Indicators.*

MALTA - EGG PRODUCTION AND CONSUMPTION - See MALTA - DAIRY PRODUCTS

MALTA - ELECTRICITY

Central Intelligence Agency, Washington, D.C. 20505 (703) 482-1100, www.cia.gov; *The World Factbook.*

St. Martin's Press, Inc., 175 Fifth Avenue, New York, New York 10010 (800) 221-7945; *The Statesman's Year-Book.*

Statistical Office of the United Nations, Publishing Service, New York, New York 10017 (800) 253-9646; *Human Development Report; Trends in Europe and North America: The Statistical Yearbook of the Economic Commission for Europe;* and *Statistical Yearbook.*

MALTA - EMPLOYMENT

Euromonitor International, Inc., 122 South Michigan Avenue, Suite 1200, Chicago, Illinois 60603 (800) 577-EURO; *European Marketing Data and Statistics.*

International Labour Office, I.L.O. Publications, 1828 L Street, N.W., Suite 801, Washington, D.C. 20036 (301) 638-3152; *Yearbook of Labour Statistics.*

Statistical Office of the United Nations, Publishing Service, New York, New York 10017 (800) 253-9646; *Statistical Yearbook;* and *Trends in Europe and North America: The Statistical Yearbook of the Economic Commission for Europe.*

MALTA - ENERGY

Euromonitor International, Inc., 122 South Michigan Avenue, Suite 1200, Chicago, Illinois 60603 (800) 577-EURO; *European Marketing Data and Statistics; World Marketing Data and Statistics;* and *The World Economic Factbook.*

Food and Agricultural Organization of the United Nations (FAO), Via delle Terme di Caracalla, 00100 Rome, Italy (Telephone Number in U.S. (202) 653-2400); *The State of Food and Agriculture.*

St. Martin's Press, Inc., 175 Fifth Avenue, New York, New York 10010 (800) 221-7945; *The Statesman's Year-Book.*

Statistical Office of the United Nations, Publishing Service, New York, New York 10017 (800) 253-9646; *Energy Statistics Yearbook; Human Development Report; Trends in Europe and North America: The Statistical Yearbook of the Economic Commission for Europe; World Statistics Pocketbook;* and *Statistical Yearbook.*

The World Bank, 1818 H Street, NW, Washington, D.C. 20433 (202) 477-1234; *The World Bank Atlas.*

MALTA - ENVIRONMENT

Economist Intelligence Unit, 111 West 57th Street, New York, New York 10019 (800) 938-4685; *Malta Country Report.*

Statistical Office of the United Nations, Publishing Service, New York, New York 10017 (800) 253-9646; *Trends in Europe and North America: The Statistical Yearbook of the Economic Commission for Europe;* and *World Statistics Pocketbook.*

MALTA - EXCHANGE RATES

Central Intelligence Agency, Washington, D.C. 20505 (703) 482-1100, www.cia.gov; *The World Factbook.*

Euromonitor International, Inc., 122 South Michingan Avenue, Suite 1200, Chicago, Illinois 60603 (800) 577-EURO; *The World Economic Factbook.*

Europa Publications Limited, 18 Bedford Square, London, WC1B 3JN, England; *The Europa World Year Book.*

International Civil Aviation Organization, 999 University Street, Montreal, Quebec, Canada H3C 5H7 (514) 954-8219; *Civil Aviation Statistics of the World.*

International Monetary Fund, 700 Nineteenth Street, NW, Washington, D.C. 20431 (202) 623-7000; *International Financial Statistics.*

Statistical Office of the United Nations, Publishing Service, New York, New York 10017 (800) 253-9646; *Statistical Yearbook; World Statistics Pocketbook;* and *Trends in Europe and North America: The Statistical Yearbook of the Economic Commission for Europe.*

MALTA - EXCISE TAXES - See MALTA - TAXATION

MALTA - EXPORTS

Central Intelligence Agency, Washington, D.C. 20505 (703) 482-1100, www.cia.gov; *The World Factbook.*

Economist Intelligence Unit, 111 West 57th Street, New York, New York 10019 (800) 938-4685; *Malta Country Report.*

Euromonitor International, Inc., 122 South Michingan Avenue, Suite 1200, Chicago, Illinois 60603 (800) 577-EURO; *The World Economic Factbook.*

Europa Publications Limited, 18 Bedford Square, London, WC1B 3JN, England; *The Europa World Year Book.*

Food and Agricultural Organization of the United Nations (FAO), Via delle Terme di Caracalla, 00100 Rome, Italy (Telephone Number in U.S. (202) 653-2400); *The State of Food and Agriculture.*

International Monetary Fund, 700 Nineteenth Street, NW, Washington, D.C. 20431 (202) 623-7000; *Direction of Trade Statistics.*

St. Martin's Press, Inc., 175 Fifth Avenue, New York, New York 10010 (800) 221-7945; *The Statesman's Year-Book.*

Statistical Office of the United Nations, Publishing Service, New York, New York 10017 (800) 253-9646; *Trends in Europe and North America: The Statistical Yearbook of the Economic Commission for Europe.*

United Nations Conference on Trade and Development (UNCTAD), New York, New York 10017 (800) 253-9646; *Handbook of International Trade and Development Statistics.*

The World Bank, 1818 H Street, NW, Washington, D.C. 20433 (202) 477-1234; *World Development Indicators.*

MALTA - EXTERNAL INDEBTEDNESS

The World Bank, 1818 H Street, NW, Washington, D.C. 20433 (202) 477-1234; *World Development Indicators.*

MALTA - EXTERNAL TRADE

Euromonitor International, Inc., 122 South Michigan Avenue, Suite 1200, Chicago, Illinois 60603 (800) 577-EURO; *World Marketing Data and Statistics.*

Food and Agricultural Organization of the United Nations (FAO), Via delle Terme di Caracalla, 00100 Rome, Italy (Telephone Number in U.S. (202) 653-2400); *The State of Food and Agriculture;* and *Trade Yearbook.*

Statistical Office of the United Nations,

Publishing Service, New York, New York 10017 (800) 253-9646; *Statistical Yearbook.*

MALTA - FARM CROPS - See MALTA - CROPS

MALTA - FERTILITY RATES

Central Intelligence Agency, Washington, D.C. 20505 (703) 482-1100, www.cia.gov; *The World Factbook.*

Statistical Office of the United Nations, Publishing Service, New York, New York 10017 (800) 253-9646; *Human Development Report;* and *Trends in Europe and North America: The Statistical Yearbook of the Economic Commission for Europe.*

The World Bank, 1818 H Street, NW, Washington, D.C. 20433 (202) 477-1234; *The World Bank Atlas;* and *World Development Indicators.*

MALTA - FERTILIZER

Food and Agricultural Organization of the United Nations (FAO), Via delle Terme di Caracalla, 00100 Rome, Italy (Telephone Number in U.S. (202) 653-2400); *Fertilizer Yearbook;* and *The State of Food and Agriculture.*

Statistical Office of the United Nations, Publishing Service, New York, New York 10017 (800) 253-9646; *Statistical Yearbook.*

MALTA - FETAL MORTALITY - See MALTA - MORTALITY

MALTA - FINANCE

Economist Intelligence Unit, 111 West 57th Street, New York, New York 10019 (800) 938-4685; *Malta Country Report.*

Europa Publications Limited, 18 Bedford Square, London, WC1B 3JN, England; *The Europa World Year Book.*

St. Martin's Press, Inc., 175 Fifth Avenue, New York, New York 10010 (800) 221-7945; *The Statesman's Year-Book.*

MALTA - FISHERIES

Euromonitor International, Inc., 122 South Michigan Avenue, Suite 1200, Chicago, Illinois 60603 (800) 577-EURO; *European Marketing Data and Statistics.*

Europa Publications Limited, 18 Bedford Square, London, WC1B 3JN, England; *The Europa World Year Book.*

Food and Agricultural Organization of the United Nations (FAO), Via delle Terme di Caracalla, 00100 Rome, Italy (Telephone Number in U.S. (202) 653-2400); *The State*

of Food and Agriculture; and Yearbook of Fishery Statistics.

International Monetary Fund, 700 Nineteenth Street, NW, Washington, D.C. 20431 (202) 623-7000; Government Finance Statistics Yearbook; and International Financial Statistics.

St. Martin's Press, Inc., 175 Fifth Avenue, New York, New York 10010 (800) 221-7945; The Statesman's Year-Book.

Statistical Office of the United Nations, Publishing Service, New York, New York 10017 (800) 253-9646; Statistical Yearbook.

United Nations Conference on Trade and Development, Central Statistical Service, Palais des Nations, Geneva, Switzerland (Telephone in U.S. (800) 253-9646); UNCTAD Commodity Yearbook.

MALTA - FLOUR PRODUCTION

Statistical Office of the United Nations, Publishing Service, New York, New York 10017 (800) 253-9646; Statistical Yearbook.

MALTA - FOOD

Food and Agricultural Organization of the United Nations (FAO), Via delle Terme di Caracalla, 00100 Rome, Italy (Telephone Number in U.S. (202) 653-2400); Production Yearbook; and The State of Food and Agriculture.

Statistical Office of the United Nations, Publishing Service, New York, New York 10017 (800) 253-9646; Human Development Report.

United Nations Conference on Trade and Development, Central Statistical Service, Palais des Nations, Geneva, Switzerland (Telephone in U.S. (800) 253-9646); UNCTAD Commodity Yearbook.

MALTA - FOREIGN DEBT

International Monetary Fund, 700 Nineteenth Street, NW, Washington, D.C. 20431 (202) 623-7000; Government Finance Statistics Yearbook.

MALTA - FOREIGN TRADE

Economist Intelligence Unit, 111 West 57th Street, New York, New York 10019 (800) 938-4685; Malta Country Report.

Euromonitor International, Inc., 122 South Michingan Avenue, Suite 1200, Chicago, Illinois 60603 (800) 577-EURO; European Marketing Data and Statistics; and The World Economic Factbook.

Europa Publications Limited, 18 Bedford Square, London, WC1B 3JN, England; The Europa World Year Book.

Food and Agricultural Organization of the United Nations (FAO), Via delle Terme di Caracalla, 00100 Rome, Italy (Telephone Number in U.S. (202) 653-2400); The State of Food and Agriculture.

International Monetary Fund, 700 Nineteenth Street, NW, Washington, D.C. 20431 (202) 623-7000; International Financial Statistics.

St. Martin's Press, Inc., 175 Fifth Avenue, New York, New York 10010 (800) 221-7945; The Statesman's Year-Book.

Statistical Office of the United Nations, Publishing Service, New York, New York 10017 (800) 253-9646; International Trade Statistics Yearbook; and Statistical Yearbook.

United Nations Conference on Trade and Development, Central Statistical Service, Palais des Nations, Geneva, Switzerland (Telephone in U.S. (800) 253-9646); UNCTAD Commodity Yearbook.

The World Bank, 1818 H Street, NW, Washington, D.C. 20433 (202) 477-1234; World Development Indicators.

MALTA - FORESTRY AND FOREST PRODUCTS

Euromonitor International, Inc., 122 South Michingan Avenue, Suite 1200, Chicago, Illinois 60603 (800) 577-EURO; European Marketing Data and Statistics.

Food and Agricultural Organization of the United Nations (FAO), Via delle Terme di Caracalla, 00100 Rome, Italy (Telephone Number in U.S. (202) 653-2400); The State of Food and Agriculture; and Yearbook of Forest Products.

Statistical Office of the United Nations, Publishing Service, New York, New York 10017 (800) 253-9646; Statistical Yearbook; and Trends in Europe and North America: The Statistical Yearbook of the Economic Commission for Europe.

United Nations Conference on Trade and Development, Central Statistical Service, Palais des Nations, Geneva, Switzerland (Telephone in U.S. (800) 253-9646); UNCTAD Commodity Yearbook.

United Nations Educational, Scientific and Cultural Organization (UNESCO), 7 Place de Fontenoy, F-75700 Paris, France (Telephone Number in U.S. (212) 963-5981); Statistical Yearbook.

MALTA - GAS PRODUCTION - See MALTA - MINING AND MINERAL PRODUCTS

MALTA - GENERAL INDUSTRIAL STATISTICS - See MALTA - INDUSTRY

MALTA - GENERAL MORTALITY - See MALTA - MORTALITY

MALTA - GOLD HOLDINGS

International Monetary Fund, 700 Nineteenth Street, NW, Washington, D.C. 20431 (202) 623-7000; International Financial Statistics.

Statistical Office of the United Nations, Publishing Service, New York, New York 10017 (800) 253-9646; Statistical Yearbook.

The World Bank, 1818 H Street, NW, Washington, D.C. 20433 (202) 477-1234; World Development Indicators.

MALTA - GOVERNMENT

Central Intelligence Agency, Washington, D.C. 20505 (703) 482-1100, www.cia.gov; The World Factbook.

Europa Publications Limited, 18 Bedford Square, London, WC1B 3JN, England; The Europa World Year Book.

International Monetary Fund, 700 Nineteenth Street, NW, Washington, D.C. 20431 (202) 623-7000; Government Finance Statistics Yearbook; and International Financial Statistics.

St. Martin's Press, Inc., 175 Fifth Avenue, New York, New York 10010 (800) 221-7945; The Statesman's Year-Book.

Statistical Office of the United Nations, Publishing Service, New York, New York 10017 (800) 253-9646; National Accounts Statistics.

The World Bank, 1818 H Street, NW, Washington, D.C. 20433 (202) 477-1234; World Development Indicators.

MALTA - GRAIN PRODUCTION - See MALTA - CROPS

MALTA - GRANTS

International Monetary Fund, 700 Nineteenth Street, NW, Washington, D.C. 20431 (202) 623-7000; Government Finance Statistics Yearbook.

MALTA - GROSS DOMESTIC PRODUCT

Economist Intelligence Unit, 111 West 57th Street, New York, New York 10019 (800) 938-4685; Malta Country Report.

Euromonitor International, Inc., 122 South Michingan Avenue, Suite 1200, Chicago, Illinois 60603 (800) 577-EURO; The World Economic Factbook.

Europa Publications Limited, 18 Bedford Square, London, WC1B 3JN,

England; *The Europa World Year Book.*

Statistical Office of the United Nations, Publishing Service, New York, New York 10017 (800) 253-9646; *Human Development Report; National Accounts Statistics; Trends in Europe and North America: The Statistical Yearbook of the Economic Commission for Europe;* and *Statistical Yearbook.*

The World Bank, 1818 H Street, NW, Washington, D.C. 20433 (202) 477-1234; *World Development Indicators.*

MALTA - GROSS NATIONAL PRODUCT

St. Martin's Press, Inc., 175 Fifth Avenue, New York, New York 10010 (800) 221-7945; *The Statesman's Year-Book.*

U.S. Arms Control and Disarmament Agency, 320 Twenty-first Street, NW, Washington, D.C. 20451 (202) 647-8677; *World Military Expenditures and Arms Transfers.*

The World Bank, 1818 H Street, NW, Washington, D.C. 20433 (202) 477-1234; *The World Bank Atlas;* and *World Development Indicators.*

MALTA - HEALTH

Euromonitor International, Inc., 122 South Michigan Avenue, Suite 1200, Chicago, Illinois 60603 (800) 577-EURO; *World Marketing Data and Statistics.*

St. Martin's Press, Inc., 175 Fifth Avenue, New York, New York 10010 (800) 221-7945; *The Statesman's Year-Book.*

Statistical Office of the United Nations, Publishing Service, New York, New York 10017 (800) 253-9646; *Human Development Report; Trends in Europe and North America: The Statistical Yearbook of the Economic Commission for Europe;* and *Statistical Yearbook.*

MALTA - HEALTH EXPENDITURES

International Monetary Fund, 700 Nineteenth Street, NW, Washington, D.C. 20431 (202) 623-7000; *Government Finance Statistics Yearbook.*

MALTA - HIDE PRODUCTION

Food and Agricultural Organization of the United Nations (FAO), Via delle Terme di Caracalla, 00100 Rome, Italy (Telephone Number in U.S. (202) 653-2400); *Production Yearbook.*

Statistical Office of the United Nations, Publishing Service, New York, New York 10017 (800) 253-9646; *Statistical Yearbook.*

MALTA - HIGHWAYS

Central Intelligence Agency, Washington, D.C. 20505 (703) 482-1100, www.cia.gov; *The World Factbook.*

International Road Federation, 2600 Virginia Avenue, N.W., Washington, D.C. 20037 (202) 338-4641; *World Road Statistics.*

St. Martin's Press, Inc., 175 Fifth Avenue, New York, New York 10010 (800) 221-7945; *The Statesman's Year-Book.*

Statistical Office of the United Nations, Publishing Service, New York, New York 10017 (800) 253-9646; *Annual Bulletin of Transport Statistics for Europe;* and *Trends in Europe and North America: The Statistical Yearbook of the Economic Commission for Europe.*

MALTA - HORSES - See MALTA - LIVESTOCK AND POULTRY

MALTA - HOURS OF WORK - See MALTA - EMPLOYMENT

MALTA - HOUSING AND HOUSING UNITS

Euromonitor International, Inc., 122 South Michigan Avenue, Suite 1200, Chicago, Illinois 60603 (800) 577-EURO; *World Marketing Data and Statistics.*

Statistical Office of the United Nations, Publishing Service, New York, New York 10017 (800) 253-9646; *Trends in Europe and North America: The Statistical Yearbook of the Economic Commission for Europe.*

MALTA - HOUSING EXPENDITURES

International Monetary Fund, 700 Nineteenth Street, NW, Washington, D.C. 20431 (202) 623-7000; *Government Finance Statistics Yearbook.*

MALTA - ILLITERATE POPULATION

Central Intelligence Agency, Washington, D.C. 20505 (703) 482-1100, www.cia.gov; *The World Factbook.*

Euromonitor International, Inc., 122 South Michigan Avenue, Suite 1200, Chicago, Illinois 60603 (800) 577-EURO; *The World Economic Factbook.*

Statistical Office of the United Nations, Publishing Service, New York, New York 10017 (800) 253-9646; *Human Development Report.*

United Nations Educational, Scientific and Cultural Organization (UNESCO), 7 Place de Fontenoy, F-75700 Paris, France (Telephone Number in U.S. (212) 963-5981); *Statistical Yearbook.*

MALTA - IMPORTS

Central Intelligence Agency, Washington, D.C. 20505 (703) 482-1100, www.cia.gov; *The World Factbook.*

Economist Intelligence Unit, 111 West 57th Street, New York, New York 10019 (800) 938-4685; *Malta Country Report.*

Euromonitor International, Inc., 122 South Michigan Avenue, Suite 1200, Chicago, Illinois 60603 (800) 577-EURO; *The World Economic Factbook.*

Europa Publications Limited, 18 Bedford Square, London, WC1B 3JN, England; *The Europa World Year Book.*

Food and Agricultural Organization of the United Nations (FAO), Via delle Terme di Caracalla, 00100 Rome, Italy (Telephone Number in U.S. (202) 653-2400); *The State of Food and Agriculture.*

International Monetary Fund, 700 Nineteenth Street, NW, Washington, D.C. 20431 (202) 623-7000; *Direction of Trade Statistics;* and *Government Finance Statistics Yearbook.*

St. Martin's Press, Inc., 175 Fifth Avenue, New York, New York 10010 (800) 221-7945; *The Statesman's Year-Book.*

Statistical Office of the United Nations, Publishing Service, New York, New York 10017 (800) 253-9646; *Trends in Europe and North America: The Statistical Yearbook of the Economic Commission for Europe.*

United Nations Conference on Trade and Development (UNCTAD), New York, New York 10017 (800) 253-9646; *Handbook of International Trade and Development Statistics.*

The World Bank, 1818 H Street, NW, Washington, D.C. 20433 (202) 477-1234; *World Development Indicators.*

MALTA - INCOME TAXES - See MALTA - TAXATION

MALTA - INDUSTRY

Central Intelligence Agency, Washington, D.C. 20505 (703) 482-1100, www.cia.gov; *The World Factbook.*

Economist Intelligence Unit, 111 West 57th Street, New York, New York 10019 (800) 938-4685; *Malta Country Report.*

Euromonitor International, Inc., 122 South Michigan Avenue, Suite 1200, Chicago, Illinois 60603 (800) 577-EURO; *The World Economic Factbook;* and *World Marketing Data and Statistics.*

International Labour Office, I.L.O. Publications, 1828 L Street, N.W.,

Suite 801, Washington, D.C. 20036 (301) 638-3152; *Yearbook of Labour Statistics.*

St. Martin's Press, Inc., 175 Fifth Avenue, New York, New York 10010 (800) 221-7945; *The Statesman's Year-Book.*

Statistical Office of the United Nations, Publishing Service, New York, New York 10017 (800) 253-9646; *Industrial Statistics Yearbook; Trends in Europe and North America: The Statistical Yearbook of the Economic Commission for Europe;* and *Statistical Yearbook.*

The World Bank, 1818 H Street, NW, Washington, D.C. 20433 (202) 477-1234; *World Development Indicators.*

World Intellectual Property Organization, 34 Chemin des Colombettes, CH-1211 Geneva 20, Switzerland; *Industrial Property Statistics.*

MALTA - INFANT AND MATERNAL MORTALITY - See MALTA - MORTALITY

MALTA - INTERNATIONAL LIQUIDITY

International Monetary Fund, 700 Nineteenth Street, NW, Washington, D.C. 20431 (202) 623-7000; *International Financial Statistics.*

MALTA - INTERNATIONAL RESERVES EXCLUDING GOLD

Statistical Office of the United Nations, Publishing Service, New York, New York 10017 (800) 253-9646; *Statistical Yearbook.*

The World Bank, 1818 H Street, NW, Washington, D.C. 20433 (202) 477-1234; *World Development Indicators.*

MALTA - LABOR

Central Intelligence Agency, Washington, D.C. 20505 (703) 482-1100, www.cia.gov; *The World Factbook.*

Euromonitor International, Inc., 122 South Michigan Avenue, Suite 1200, Chicago, Illinois 60603 (800) 577-EURO; *World Marketing Data and Statistics.*

Europa Publications Limited, 18 Bedford Square, London, WC1B 3JN, England; *The Europa World Year Book.*

Food and Agricultural Organization of the United Nations (FAO), Via delle Terme di Caracalla, 00100 Rome, Italy (Telephone Number in U.S. (202) 653-2400); *The State of Food and Agriculture.*

International Labour Office, I.L.O. Publications, 1828 L Street, N.W., Suite 801, Washington, D.C. 20036 (301) 638-3152; *Yearbook of Labour Statistics.*

St. Martin's Press, Inc., 175 Fifth Avenue, New York, New York 10010 (800) 221-7945; *The Statesman's Year-Book.*

Statistical Office of the United Nations, Publishing Service, New York, New York 10017 (800) 253-9646; *Human Development Report.*

The World Bank, 1818 H Street, NW, Washington, D.C. 20433 (202) 477-1234; *The World Bank Atlas;* and *World Development Indicators.*

MALTA - LAND USE

Central Intelligence Agency, Washington, D.C. 20505 (703) 482-1100, www.cia.gov; *The World Factbook.*

Euromonitor International, Inc., 122 South Michigan Avenue, Suite 1200, Chicago, Illinois 60603 (800) 577-EURO; *European Marketing Data and Statistics.*

Food and Agricultural Organization of the United Nations (FAO), Via delle Terme di Caracalla, 00100 Rome, Italy (Telephone Number in U.S. (202) 653-2400); *Production Yearbook.*

MALTA - LIBRARIES

Euromonitor International, Inc., 122 South Michigan Avenue, Suite 1200, Chicago, Illinois 60603 (800) 577-EURO; *European Marketing Data and Statistics.*

Statistical Office of the United Nations, Publishing Service, New York, New York 10017 (800) 253-9646; *Trends in Europe and North America: The Statistical Yearbook of the Economic Commission for Europe.*

United Nations Educational, Scientific and Cultural Organization (UNESCO), 7 Place de Fontenoy, F-75700 Paris, France (Telephone Number in U.S. (212) 963-5981); *Statistical Yearbook.*

MALTA - LIFE EXPECTANCY

Central Intelligence Agency, Washington, D.C. 20505 (703) 482-1100, www.cia.gov; *The World Factbook.*

Euromonitor International, Inc., 122 South Michigan Avenue, Suite 1200, Chicago, Illinois 60603 (800) 577-EURO; *The World Economic Factbook.*

Statistical Office of the United Nations, Publishing Service, New York, New York 10017 (800) 253-9646; *Human Development Report; World Statistics Pocketbook;* and *Trends in Europe and North America: The Statistical Yearbook of the Economic Commission for Europe.*

The World Bank, 1818 H Street, NW, Washington, D.C. 20433 (202) 477-1234; *The World Bank Atlas.*

MALTA - LITERACY RATE

Euromonitor International, Inc., 122 South Michigan Avenue, Suite 1200, Chicago, Illinois 60603 (800) 577-EURO; *World Marketing Data and Statistics.*

MALTA - LIVESTOCK AND POULTRY

Euromonitor International, Inc., 122 South Michigan Avenue, Suite 1200, Chicago, Illinois 60603 (800) 577-EURO; *European Marketing Data and Statistics.*

Europa Publications Limited, 18 Bedford Square, London, WC1B 3JN, England; *The Europa World Year Book.*

Food and Agricultural Organization of the United Nations (FAO), Via delle Terme di Caracalla, 00100 Rome, Italy (Telephone Number in U.S. (202) 653-2400); *Production Yearbook;* and *The State of Food and Agriculture.*

St. Martin's Press, Inc., 175 Fifth Avenue, New York, New York 10010 (800) 221-7945; *The Statesman's Year-Book.*

Statistical Office of the United Nations, Publishing Service, New York, New York 10017 (800) 253-9646; *Statistical Yearbook.*

United Nations Conference on Trade and Development, Central Statistical Service, Palais des Nations, Geneva, Switzerland (Telephone in U.S. (800) 253-9646); *UNCTAD Commodity Yearbook.*

MALTA - LIVING LEVELS - See MALTA - LIFE EXPECTANCY

MALTA - MAIL - NUMBER OF ITEMS SENT AND RECEIVED

Statistical Office of the United Nations, Publishing Service, New York, New York 10017 (800) 253-9646; *Statistical Yearbook.*

MALTA - MANUFACTURING

Statistical Office of the United Nations, Publishing Service, New York, New York 10017 (800) 253-9646; *Statistical Yearbook.*

The World Bank, 1818 H Street, NW, Washington, D.C. 20433 (202) 477-1234; *World Development Indicators.*

MALTA - MARRIAGE RATES

Statistical Office of the United Nations, Publishing Service, New York, New York 10017 (800) 253-9646; *Demographic Yearbook; Trends in Europe and North America: The Statistical Yearbook of the Economic Commission for Europe;* and *Statistical Yearbook.*

MALTA - MEAT PRODUCTION - See
MALTA - LIVESTOCK AND POULTRY

MALTA - MERCHANT SHIPPING

Europa Publications Limited, 18 Bedford
Square, London, WC1B 3JN, England; *The
Europa World Year Book.*

Lloyd's Register of Shipping, 17 Battery
Place, New York, New York 10004 (212)
425-8050; *Register of Ships.*

St. Martin's Press, Inc., 175 Fifth Avenue,
New York, New York 10010 (800) 221-7945;
The Statesman's Year-Book.

Statistical Office of the United Nations,
Publishing Service, New York, New York
10017 (800) 253-9646; *Statistical Yearbook.*

U.S. Department of Transportation,
Maritime Administration, 400 Seventh Street,
SW, Washington, D.C. 20590 (202) 366-5807,
www.marad.dot.gov; *A Statistical Analysis
of the World's Merchant Fleets.*

MALTA - METAL PRODUCTS - See MALTA -
MINING AND MINERAL PRODUCTS

MALTA - MILITARY

Central Intelligence Agency,
Washington, D.C. 20505 (703) 482-1100,
www.cia.gov; *The World Factbook.*

Euromonitor International, Inc., 122
South Michigan Avenue, Suite 1200,
Chicago, Illinois 60603 (800) 577-EURO;
World Marketing Data and Statistics.

The International Institute for Strategic
Studies, 23 Tavistock Street, London WC2E
7NQ, England; *The Military Balance.*

International Monetary Fund, 700
Nineteenth Street, NW, Washington,
D.C. 20431 (202) 623-7000; *Government
Finance Statistics Yearbook.*

St. Martin's Press, Inc., 175 Fifth Avenue,
New York, New York 10010 (800) 221-7945;
The Statesman's Year-Book.

Statistical Office of the United Nations,
Publishing Service, New York, New York
10017 (800) 253-9646; *Human Development
Report.*

U.S. Arms Control and Disarmament
Agency, 320 Twenty-first Street, NW,
Washington, D.C. 20451 (202) 647-8677;
*World Military Expenditures and Arms
Transfers.*

MALTA - MILK PRODUCTION - See MALTA -
DAIRY PRODUCTS

MALTA - MINING AND MINERAL PRODUCTS

Statistical Office of the United Nations,

Publishing Service, New York, New York
10017 (800) 253-9646; *Statistical Yearbook.*

United Nations Conference on Trade
and Development, Central Statistical
Service, Palais des Nations, Geneva,
Switzerland (Telephone in U.S. (800) 253-
9646); *UNCTAD Commodity Yearbook.*

MALTA - MONEY EXCHANGE RATES - See
MALTA - EXCHANGE RATES

MALTA - MONEY SUPPLY

Economist Intelligence Unit, 111 West
57th Street, New York, New York 10019
(800) 938-4685; *Malta Country Report.*

Europa Publications Limited, 18
Bedford Square, London, WC1B 3JN,
England; *The Europa World Year Book.*

International Monetary Fund, 700
Nineteenth Street, NW, Washington,
D.C. 20431 (202) 623-7000; *International
Financial Statistics.*

Statistical Office of the United Nations,
Publishing Service, New York, New York
10017 (800) 253-9646; *Statistical Yearbook.*

The World Bank, 1818 H Street, NW,
Washington, D.C. 20433 (202) 477-1234;
World Development Indicators.

MALTA - MONUMENTS AND HISTORICAL
SITES

United Nations Educational, Scientific
and Cultural Organization (UNESCO), 7
Place de Fontenoy, F-75700 Paris, France
(Telephone Number in U.S. (212) 963-
5981); *Statistical Yearbook.*

MALTA - MORTALITY

Central Intelligence Agency,
Washington, D.C. 20505 (703) 482-1100,
www.cia.gov; *The World Factbook.*

Euromonitor International, Inc., 122
South Michingan Avenue, Suite 1200,
Chicago, Illinois 60603 (800) 577-EURO;
The World Economic Factbook.

Europa Publications Limited, 18
Bedford Square, London, WC1B 3JN,
England; *The Europa World Year Book.*

St. Martin's Press, Inc., 175 Fifth
Avenue, New York, New York 10010 (800)
221-7945; *The Statesman's Year-Book.*

Statistical Office of the United Nations,
Publishing Service, New York, New York
10017 (800) 253-9646; *Demographic
Yearbook; Human Development Report;
Trends in Europe and North America: The
Statistical Yearbook of the Economic
Commission for Europe; World Statistics
Pocketbook;* and *Statistical Yearbook.*

The World Bank, 1818 H Street, NW,
Washington, D.C. 20433 (202) 477-1234;
The World Bank Atlas; and *World
Development Indicators.*

World Health Organization, Office of
Publications, 20 Avenue Appia, CH-1211
Geneva 27, Switzerland (Telephone
Number in U.S. (518) 436-9686); *World
Health Statistics Annual.*

MALTA - MOTION PICTURES

St. Martin's Press, Inc., 175 Fifth
Avenue, New York, New York 10010 (800)
221-7945; *The Statesman's Year-Book.*

Statistical Office of the United Nations,
Publishing Service, New York, New York
10017 (800) 253-9646; *Statistical Yearbook.*

MALTA - MOTOR VEHICLE TAXES - See
MALTA - TAXATION

MALTA - MOTOR VEHICLES IN USE

Europa Publications Limited, 18
Bedford Square, London, WC1B 3JN,
England; *The Europa World Year Book.*

International Road Federation, 2600
Virginia Avenue, N.W., Washington, D.C.
20037 (202) 338-4641; *World Road
Statistics.*

Statistical Office of the United Nations,
Publishing Service, New York, New York
10017 (800) 253-9646; *Statistical Yearbook.*

MALTA - MULES - See MALTA - LIVESTOCK
AND POULTRY

MALTA - MUSEUMS

Euromonitor International, Inc., 122
South Michingan Avenue, Suite 1200,
Chicago, Illinois 60603 (800) 577-EURO;
European Marketing Data and Statistics.

United Nations Educational, Scientific
and Cultural Organization (UNESCO), 7
Place de Fontenoy, F-75700 Paris, France
(Telephone Number in U.S. (212) 963-
5981); *Statistical Yearbook.*

MALTA - NATALITY - See MALTA - BIRTH
RATES

MALTA - NATIONAL ACCOUNTS

Statistical Office of the United Nations,
Publishing Service, New York, New York
10017 (800) 253-9646; *National Account
Statistics;* and *Statistical Yearbook.*

MALTA - NATIONAL INCOME

Statistical Office of the United Nations,
Publishing Service, New York, New York

10017 (800) 253-9646; *National Accounts Statistics;* and *Statistical Yearbook.*

MALTA - NATIONAL PRODUCT

Statistical Office of the United Nations, Publishing Service, New York, New York 10017 (800) 253-9646; *Statistical Yearbook.*

MALTA - NEWSPAPER PRODUCTION - See MALTA - FORESTRY AND FOREST PRODUCTS

MALTA - PATENTS, TRADEMARKS AND SERVICE MARKS

Statistical Office of the United Nations, Publishing Service, New York, New York 10017 (800) 253-9646; *Statistical Yearbook.*

World Intellectual Property Organization, 34 Chemin des Colombettes, CH-1211 Geneva 20, Switzerland; *Industrial Property Statistics.*

MALTA - PERIODICALS

United Nations Educational, Scientific and Cultural Organization (UNESCO), 7 Place de Fontenoy, F-75700 Paris, France (Telephone Number in U.S. (212) 963-5981); *Statistical Yearbook.*

MALTA - PESTICIDE USE

Food and Agricultural Organization of the United Nations (FAO), Via delle Terme di Caracalla, 00100 Rome, Italy (Telephone Number in U.S. (202) 653-2400); *The State of Food and Agriculture.*

MALTA - PETROLEUM INDUSTRY

Euromonitor International, Inc., 122 South Michingan Avenue, Suite 1200, Chicago, Illinois 60603 (800) 577-EURO; *European Marketing Data and Statistics.*

Food and Agricultural Organization of the United Nations (FAO), Via delle Terme di Caracalla, 00100 Rome, Italy (Telephone Number in U.S. (202) 653-2400); *The State of Food and Agriculture.*

St. Martin's Press, Inc., 175 Fifth Avenue, New York, New York 10010 (800) 221-7945; *The Statesman's Year-Book.*

Statistical Office of the United Nations, Publishing Service, New York, New York 10017 (800) 253-9646; *Trends in Europe and North America: The Statistical Yearbook of the Economic Commission for Europe.*

United Nations Conference on Trade and Development, Central Statistical Service, Palais des Nations, Geneva, Switzerland (Telephone in U.S. (800) 253-9646); *UNCTAD Commodity Yearbook.*

MALTA - PIGS - See MALTA - LIVESTOCK

AND POULTRY

MALTA - POPULATION

Central Intelligence Agency, Washington, D.C. 20505 (703) 482-1100, www.cia.gov; *The World Factbook.*

Economist Intelligence Unit, 111 West 57th Street, New York, New York 10019 (800) 938-4685; *Malta Country Report.*

Euromonitor International, Inc., 122 South Michingan Avenue, Suite 1200, Chicago, Illinois 60603 (800) 577-EURO; *European Marketing Data and Statistics;* and *The World Economic Factbook.*

Europa Publications Limited, 18 Bedford Square, London, WC1B 3JN, England; *The Europa World Year Book.*

Food and Agricultural Organization of the United Nations (FAO), Via delle Terme di Caracalla, 00100 Rome, Italy (Telephone Number in U.S. (202) 653-2400); *Production Yearbook.*

International Labour Office, I.L.O. Publications, 1828 L Street, N.W., Suite 801, Washington, D.C. 20036 (301) 638-3152; *Yearbook of Labour Statistics.*

St. Martin's Press, Inc., 175 Fifth Avenue, New York, New York 10010 (800) 221-7945; *The Statesman's Year-Book.*

Statistical Office of the United Nations, Publishing Service, New York, New York 10017 (800) 253-9646; *Demographic Yearbook; Human Development Report; Trends in Europe and North America: The Statistical Yearbook of the Economic Commission for Europe; World Statistics Pocketbook;* and *Statistical Yearbook.*

U.S. Arms Control and Disarmament Agency, 320 Twenty-first Street, NW, Washington, D.C. 20451 (202) 647-8677; *World Military Expenditures and Arms Transfers.*

The World Bank, 1818 H Street, NW, Washington, D.C. 20433 (202) 477-1234; *The World Bank Atlas.*

World Health Organization, Office of Publications, 20 Avenue Appia, CH-1211 Geneva 27, Switzerland (Telephone Number in U.S. (518) 436-9686); *World Health Statistics Annual.*

MALTA - POST OFFICES

Statistical Office of the United Nations, Publishing Service, New York, New York 10017 (800) 253-9646; *Trends in Europe and North America: The Statistical Yearbook of the Economic Commission for Europe.*

MALTA - POTATO PRODUCTION - See

MALTA - CROPS

MALTA - PRICES

Food and Agricultural Organization of the United Nations (FAO), Via delle Terme di Caracalla, 00100 Rome, Italy (Telephone Number in U.S. (202) 653-2400); *Production Yearbook;* and *The State of Food and Agriculture.*

International Labour Office, I.L.O. Publications, 1828 L Street, N.W., Suite 801, Washington, D.C. 20036 (301) 638-3152; *Yearbook of Labour Statistics.*

International Monetary Fund, 700 Nineteenth Street, NW, Washington, D.C. 20431 (202) 623-7000; *International Financial Statistics.*

MALTA - PROPERTY TAXES

International Monetary Fund, 700 Nineteenth Street, NW, Washington, D.C. 20431 (202) 623-7000; *Government Finance Statistics Yearbook.*

MALTA - RADIO BROADCASTING - See MALTA - BROADCASTING

MALTA - RADIO RECEIVERS

St. Martin's Press, Inc., 175 Fifth Avenue, New York, New York 10010 (800) 221-7945; *The Statesman's Year-Book.*

MALTA - RAILWAY USE

Euromonitor International, Inc., 122 South Michingan Avenue, Suite 1200, Chicago, Illinois 60603 (800) 577-EURO; *European Marketing Data and Statistics.*

Statistical Office of the United Nations, Publishing Service, New York, New York 10017 (800) 253-9646; *Trends in Europe and North America: The Statistical Yearbook of the Economic Commission for Europe.*

MALTA - RELIGION

Central Intelligence Agency, Washington, D.C. 20505 (703) 482-1100, www.cia.gov; *The World Factbook.*

St. Martin's Press, Inc., 175 Fifth Avenue, New York, New York 10010 (800) 221-7945; *The Statesman's Year-Book.*

MALTA - RENT PRICES

International Labour Office, I.L.O. Publications, 1828 L Street, N.W., Suite 801, Washington, D.C. 20036 (301) 638-3152; *Yearbook of Labour Statistics.*

MALTA - RETAIL PRICE INDEX

Europa Publications Limited, 18 Bedford Square, London, WC1B 3JN,

England; *The Europa World Year Book.*

MALTA - RETAIL TRADE

Euromonitor International, Inc., 122 South Michigan Avenue, Suite 1200, Chicago, Illinois 60603 (800) 577-EURO; *World Marketing Data and Statistics.*

MALTA - ROOT AND TUBER PRODUCTION - See MALTA - CROPS

MALTA - ROUNDWOOD PRODUCTION - See MALTA - FORESTRY AND FOREST PRODUCTS

MALTA - SALT PRODUCTION - See MALTA - MINING AND MINERAL PRODUCTS

MALTA - SAWNWOOD PRODUCTION - See MALTA - FORESTRY AND FOREST PRODUCTS

MALTA - SCIENCE AND TECHNOLOGY - EXPENDITURE FOR RESEARCH - See MALTA - SCIENTISTS, TECHNICIANS AND ENGINEERS

MALTA - SCIENTISTS, TECHNICIANS AND ENGINEERS

Statistical Office of the United Nations, Publishing Service, New York, New York 10017 (800) 253-9646; *Statistical Yearbook.*

MALTA - SHEEP - See MALTA - LIVESTOCK AND POULTRY

MALTA - SOCIAL DATA

Statistical Office of the United Nations, Publishing Service, New York, New York 10017 (800) 253-9646; *World Statistics Pocketbook.*

MALTA - SOCIAL SECURITY

International Monetary Fund, 700 Nineteenth Street, NW, Washington, D.C. 20431 (202) 623-7000; *Government Finance Statistics Yearbook.*

St. Martin's Press, Inc., 175 Fifth Avenue, New York, New York 10010 (800) 221-7945; *The Statesman's Year-Book.*

Statistical Office of the United Nations, Publishing Service, New York, New York 10017 (800) 253-9646; *National Accounts Statistics.*

MALTA - STAMP TAXES AND DUTIES - See MALTA - TAXATION

MALTA - STOCKS - COMMODITY - MARKET PRICE - INDEX

Food and Agricultural Organization of the United Nations (FAO), Via delle Terme di Caracalla, 00100 Rome, Italy (Telephone Number in U.S. (202) 653-2400); *The State*

of Food and Agriculture.

MALTA - TAXATION

Europa Publications Limited, 18 Bedford Square, London, WC1B 3JN, England; *The Europa World Year Book.*

International Monetary Fund, 700 Nineteenth Street, NW, Washington, D.C. 20431 (202) 623-7000; *Government Finance Statistics Yearbook.*

International Road Federation, 2600 Virginia Avenue, N.W., Washington, D.C. 20037 (202) 338-4641; *World Road Statistics.*

St. Martin's Press, Inc., 175 Fifth Avenue, New York, New York 10010 (800) 221-7945; *The Statesman's Year-Book.*

The World Bank, 1818 H Street, NW, Washington, D.C. 20433 (202) 477-1234; *World Development Indicators.*

MALTA - TELEGRAPH SERVICE

Statistical Office of the United Nations, Publishing Service, New York, New York 10017 (800) 253-9646; *Statistical Yearbook.*

MALTA - TELEPHONES IN USE

American Telephone and Telegraph Company, 26 Parsippany Road, Whippany, New Jersey 07981 (800) 222-0300; *The World's Telephones.*

Central Intelligence Agency, Washington, D.C. 20505 (703) 482-1100, www.cia.gov; *The World Factbook.*

Europa Publications Limited, 18 Bedford Square, London, WC1B 3JN, England; *The Europa World Year Book.*

St. Martin's Press, Inc., 175 Fifth Avenue, New York, New York 10010 (800) 221-7945; *The Statesman's Year-Book.*

Statistical Office of the United Nations, Publishing Service, New York, New York 10017 (800) 253-9646; *Statistical Yearbook; World Statistics Pocketbook;* and *Trends in Europe and North America: The Statistical Yearbook of the Economic Commission for Europe.*

MALTA - TELEVISION BROADCASTING - See MALTA - BROADCASTING

MALTA - TEXTILE INDUSTRY

St. Martin's Press, Inc., 175 Fifth Avenue, New York, New York 10010 (800) 221-7945; *The Statesman's Year-Book.*

United Nations Conference on Trade and Development, Central Statistical Service, Palais des Nations, Geneva,

Switzerland (Telephone in U.S. (800) 253-9646); *UNCTAD Commodity Yearbook.*

MALTA - TOBACCO PRODUCTION

Euromonitor International, Inc., 122 South Michingan Avenue, Suite 1200, Chicago, Illinois 60603 (800) 577-EURO; *European Marketing Data and Statistics.*

Statistical Office of the United Nations, Publishing Service, New York, New York 10017 (800) 253-9646; *Statistical Yearbook.*

MALTA - TOURISM

Euromonitor International, Inc., 122 South Michingan Avenue, Suite 1200, Chicago, Illinois 60603 (800) 577-EURO; *European Marketing Data and Statistics; World Marketing Data and Statistics;* and *The World Economic Factbook.*

Europa Publications Limited, 18 Bedford Square, London, WC1B 3JN, England; *The Europa World Year Book.*

St. Martin's Press, Inc., 175 Fifth Avenue, New York, New York 10010 (800) 221-7945; *The Statesman's Year-Book.*

Statistical Office of the United Nations, Publishing Service, New York, New York 10017 (800) 253-9646; *Statistical Yearbook;* and *Trends in Europe and North America: The Statistical Yearbook of the Economic Commission for Europe.*

World Tourism Organization, Calle Capitan Haya 42, E-28020 Madrid, Spain; *Yearbook of Tourism Statistics.*

MALTA - TRACTORS IN USE

Statistical Office of the United Nations, Publishing Service, New York, New York 10017 (800) 253-9646; *Statistical Yearbook.*

MALTA - TRADE - See MALTA - FOREIGN TRADE

MALTA - TRADEMARKS AND SERVICE MARKS - See MALTA - PATENTS, TRADEMARKS AND SERVICE MARKS

MALTA - TRANSPORTATION AND COMMUNICATIONS

Central Intelligence Agency, Washington, D.C. 20505 (703) 482-1100, www.cia.gov; *The World Factbook.*

Euromonitor International, Inc., 122 South Michigan Avenue, Suite 1200, Chicago, Illinois 60603 (800) 577-EURO; *World Marketing Data and Statistics.*

Europa Publications Limited, 18 Bedford Square, London, WC1B 3JN, England; *The Europa World Year Book.*

St. Martin's Press, Inc., 175 Fifth Avenue, New York, New York 10010 (800) 221-7945; *The Statesman's Year-Book*.

Statistical Office of the United Nations, Publishing Service, New York, New York 10017 (800) 253-9646; *Human Development Report;* and *Trends in Europe and North America: The Statistical Yearbook of the Economic Commission for Europe.*

MALTA - TURKEYS - See MALTA - LIVESTOCK AND POULTRY

MALTA - UNEMPLOYMENT

Central Intelligence Agency, Washington, D.C. 20505 (703) 482-1100, www.cia.gov; *The World Factbook.*

Euromonitor International, Inc., 122 South Michigan Avenue, Suite 1200, Chicago, Illinois 60603 (800) 577-EURO; *European Marketing Data and Statistics.*

International Labour Office, I.L.O. Publications, 1828 L Street, N.W., Suite 801, Washington, D.C. 20036 (301) 638-3152; *Yearbook of Labour Statistics.*

St. Martin's Press, Inc., 175 Fifth Avenue, New York, New York 10010 (800) 221-7945; *The Statesman's Year-Book.*

Statistical Office of the United Nations, Publishing Service, New York, New York 10017 (800) 253-9646; *Statistical Yearbook;* and *Trends in Europe and North America: The Statistical Yearbook of the Economic Commission for Europe.*

MALTA - VITAL STATISTICS

St. Martin's Press, Inc., 175 Fifth Avenue, New York, New York 10010 (800) 221-7945; *The Statesman's Year-Book.*

Statistical Office of the United Nations, Publishing Service, New York, New York 10017 (800) 253-9646; *Statistical Yearbook.*

World Health Organization, Office of Publications, 20 Avenue Appia, CH-1211 Geneva 27, Switzerland (Telephone Number in U.S. (518) 436-9686); *World Health Statistics Annual.*

MALTA - WAGES

Euromonitor International, Inc., 122 South Michigan Avenue, Suite 1200, Chicago, Illinois 60603 (800) 577-EURO; *European Marketing Data and Statistics.*

International Labour Office, I.L.O. Publications, 1828 L Street, N.W., Suite 801, Washington, D.C. 20036 (301) 638-3152; *Yearbook of Labour Statistics.*

MALTA - WELFARE EXPENDITURES

International Monetary Fund, 700 Nineteenth Street, NW, Washington, D.C. 20431 (202) 623-7000; *Government Finance Statistics Yearbook.*

MALTA - WHEAT PRODUCTION - See MALTA - CROPS

MALTA - WINE PRODUCTION - See MALTA - BEVERAGES

MALTA - ZOOS AND BOTANICAL GARDENS

United Nations Educational, Scientific and Cultural Organization (UNESCO), 7 Place de Fontenoy, F-75700 Paris, France (Telephone Number in U.S. (212) 963-5981); *Statistical Yearbook.*

MANAGED CARE - HEALTH PLANS

U.S. Department of Health and Human Services, Health Care Financing Administration, 200 Independence Avenue, SW, Washington, D.C. 20201 (202) 690-6145, www.hcfa.gov; *Managed Care Trends; Managed Care State Enrollment;* and Internet sites: http://www.hcfa.gov/medicaid/trends97.htm; and http://www.hcfa.gov/medicaid/mcsten97.htm.

U.S. Department of Health and Human Services, National Center for Health Statistics, 3700 East-West Highway, Hyattsville, MD 20782 (301) 436-8500, www.cdc.gov/nchs; *Employer-Sponsored Health Insurance, State and National Estimates.*

MANAGERS - See PROPRIETORS, ETC.

MANGANESE

U.S. Department of Defense, Defense Logistics Agency, 8725 John J. Kingman road, Fort Belvoir, Virginia 22060 (7093) 767-6666; *Statistical Supplement, Stockpile Report to the Congress.*

U.S. Department of the Interior, Geological Survey, Office of Minerals Information, 12201 Sunrise Valley Drive, Reston, Virginia 22092 (703) 648-4000, www.minerals.usgs.gov; *Mineral Commodity Summaries.*

MANGANIFEROUS ORE

U.S. Department of the Interior, Geological Survey, Office of Minerals Information, 12201 Sunrise Valley Drive, Reston, Virginia 22092 (703) 648-4000, www.minerals.usgs.gov; *Mineral Commodity Summaries.*

MAN-MADE FIBERS AND FABRICS - See also Specific Items and FOREIGN TRADE

MANUFACTURED PRODUCTS - See also Individual Products

MANUFACTURED PRODUCTS - EXPORTS - UNITED STATES AS COMPARED TO WORLD

U.S. Department of Commerce, International Trade Administration, Office of Trade and Economic Analysis, Fourteenth Street between Constitution Avenue and E Street, NW, Washington, D.C. 20230 (202) 482-3809, www.ita.doc.gov/tradestats; *United Nations Commodity Trade Statistics; Statistical Yearbook of the Republic of China;* and unpublished data.

MANUFACTURED PRODUCTS - PRODUCTION INDEXES

Board of Governors of the Federal Reserve System, Twentieth Street and Constitution Avenue, NW, Washington, D.C. 20551 (202) 452-3000, www.bog.frb.fed.us; *Federal Reserve Bulletin;* and *Industrial Production and Capacity Utilization.*

MANUFACTURERS' EXCISE TAXES

U.S. Department of the Treasury, Bureau of Alcohol, Tobacco and Firearms, 650 Massachusetts Avenue, NW, Washington, D.C. 20226 (202) 927-8500, www.atf.treas.gov; *Alcohol and Tobacco Tax Collections.*

U.S. Department of the Treasury, Internal Revenue Service, 1111 Constitution Avenue, NW, Washington, D.C. 20224 (202) 874-0410, www.irs.ustreas.gov; *Annual Report.*

MANUFACTURING INDUSTRY - See also Individual Industries

MANUFACTURING INDUSTRY - CAPITAL

Board of Governors of the Federal Reserve System, Twentieth Street and Constitution Avenue, NW, Washington, D.C. 20551 (202) 452-3000, www.bog.frb.fed.us; *Federal Reserve Bulletin;* and *Annual Statistical Digest.*

Executive Office of the President, Council of Economic Advisers, Old Executive Office Building, Washington, D.C. 20502 (202) 395-5084, www.whitehouse.gov/cea; *Economic Report of the President.*

U.S. Department of Commerce, Bureau of the Census, Washington, D.C. 20233 (301) 457-4100, www.census.gov; *Quarterly Financial Report for Manufacturing, Mining and Trade Corporations.*

U.S. Department of Commerce, Bureau of Economic Analysis, Fourteenth Street between Constitution and E Streets, NW, Washington, D.C. 20230 (202) 606-9900, www.bea.doc.gov; *National Income and*

Product Accounts; and *Survey of Current Business.*

MANUFACTURING INDUSTRY - COMPANIES EXPORTING

U.S. Department of Commerce, Bureau of the Census, Washington, D.C. 20233 (301) 457-4100, www.census.gov; *A Profile of U.S. Exporting Companies.*

MANUFACTURING INDUSTRY - EARNINGS

U.S. Department of Commerce, Bureau of Economic Analysis, Fourteenth Street between Constitution Avenue and E Street, NW, Washington, D.C. 20230 (202) 606-9900, www.bea.doc.gov; *The National Income and Product Accounts of the United States;* and *Survey of Current Business.*

U.S. Department of Commerce, Bureau of the Census, Washington, D.C. 20233 (301) 457-4100, www.census.gov; *Census of Manufactures; Annual Survey of Manufactures; County Business Patterns; 1997 Economic Census, Core Business Statistics Series; Statistics of U.S. Businesses;* and *Economic Census of Outlying Areas.*

U.S. Department of Labor, Bureau of Labor Statistics, Two Massachusetts Avenue, NE, Washington, D.C. 20212 (202) 691-5200, www.stats.bls.gov; *Employment and Earnings;* and Internet site: http://stats.bls.gov/ceshome.htm.

MANUFACTURING INDUSTRY - ECONOMIC INDICATORS

The Conference Board, 845 Third Avenue, New York, New York 10022 (212) 887-8500; *Business Cycle Indicators.*

MANUFACTURING INDUSTRY - EMPLOYEES

U.S. Department of Commerce, Bureau of the Census, Washington, D.C. 20233 (301) 457-4100, www.census.gov; *Annual Survey of Manufactures; Census of Manufactures; County Business Patterns; Economic Census of Outlying Areas; 1997 Economic Census: Advance Summary Statistics for the U.S. 1997 NAICS Basis; Statistics of U.S. Businesses;* and *Exports from Manufacturing Establishments.*

U.S. Department of Labor, Bureau of Labor Statistics, Two Massachusetts Avenue, NE, Washington, D.C. 20212 (202) 691-5200, www.stats.bls.gov; *News; Employment and Earnings; Monthly Labor Review;* unpublished data: and Internet site: http://stats.bls.gov/ceshome.htm.

U.S. Department of the Treasury, Internal Revenue Service, 1111 Constitution Avenue, NW, Washington, D.C. 20224 (202) 874-0410, www.irs.ustreas.gov; *Statistics of Income;* various publications.

MANUFACTURING INDUSTRY - ENERGY CONSUMPTION

U.S. Department of Energy, Energy Information Administration, 1000 Independence Avenue, SW, Washington, D.C. 20585 (202) 586-1185; *Manufacturing Energy Consumption.*

MANUFACTURING INDUSTRY - ESTABLISHMENTS

Time Warner, Time and Life Building, Rockefeller Center, New York, New York 10020 (212) 522-1212; *Fortune.*

U.S. Department of Commerce, Bureau of the Census, Washington, D.C. 20233 (301) 457-4100, www.census.gov; *Annual Survey of Manufactures; County Business Patterns; Census of Manufactures; 1997 Economic Census: Advance Summary Statistics for the U.S. 1997 NAICS Basis; Statistics of U.S. Businesses;* and *Economic Census of Outlying Areas.*

U.S. Department of Labor, Bureau of Labor Statistics, Two Massachusetts Avenue, NW, Washington, D.C. 20212 (202) 691-5200, www.stats.bls.gov; *Employment and Earnings.*

MANUFACTURING INDUSTRY - FAILURES

Dun and Bradstreet Corporation, 299 Park Avenue, 24th Floor, New York, New York 10171 (212) 593-6800; *Business Failure Record.*

MANUFACTURING INDUSTRY - FINANCES

Executive Office of the President, Council of Economic Advisers, Old Executive Office Building, Washington, D.C. 20502 (202)395-5084, www.whitehouse.gov/cea; *Economic Report of the President.*

Puerto Rico Planning Board, San Juan, Puerto Rico; *Economic Report of the Governor.*

U.S. Department of Commerce, Bureau of the Census, Washington, D.C. 20233 (301) 457-4100, www.census.gov; *Quarterly Financial Report for Manufacturing, Mining and Trade Corporations.*

U.S. Department of the Treasury, Internal Revenue Service, 1111 Constitution Avenue, NW, Washington, D.C. 20224 (202) 874-0410, www.irs.ustreas.gov; *Statistics of Income, Corporation Income Tax Returns; Statistics of Income, Partnership Returns;* and *Statistics of Income Bulletin.*

MANUFACTURING INDUSTRY - FOREIGN COUNTRIES

U.S. Department of Labor, Bureau of Labor Statistics, Two Massachusetts

Avenue, NE, Washington, D.C. 20212 (202) 691-5200, www.stats.bls.gov; *News Release USDL-98-376;* and *International Comparisons of Manufacturing Productivity and Unit Labor Cost Trends.*

MANUFACTURING INDUSTRY - FOREIGN INVESTMENTS IN UNITED STATES

U.S. Department of Commerce, Bureau of Economic Analysis, Fourteenth Street between Constitution Avenue and E Street, NW, Washington, D.C. 20230 (202) 606-9900, www.bea.doc.gov; *Survey of Current Business.*

MANUFACTURING INDUSTRY - FORM OF ORGANIZATION

U.S. Department of Commerce, Bureau of the Census, Washington, D.C. 20233 (301) 457-4100, www.census.gov; *Census of Manufactures;* and *Annual Survey of Manufactures.*

MANUFACTURING INDUSTRY - GROSS DOMESTIC PRODUCT

Puerto Rico Planning Board, San Juan, Puerto Rico; *Economic Report of the Governor.*

U.S. Department of Commerce, Bureau of Economic Analysis, Fourteenth Street between Constitution Avenue and E Street, NW, Washington, D.C. 20230 (202) 606-9900, www.bea.doc.gov; *Survey of Current Business.*

MANUFACTURING INDUSTRY - HEALTH INSURANCE COVERAGE - EMPLOYEES

U.S. Department of Health and Human Services, National Center for Health Statistics; 3700 East-West Highway, Hyattsville, Maryland 20782 (301) 436-8500, www.cdc.gov/nchs; *Employer-Sponsored Health Insurance, State and National Estimates.*

MANUFACTURING INDUSTRY - INVENTORIES

U.S. Department of Commerce, Bureau of the Census, Washington, D.C. 20233 (301) 457-4100, www.census.gov; *Current Industrial Reports, Manufacturers' Shipments, Inventories and Orders.*

MANUFACTURING INDUSTRY - INVESTMENT ABROAD

U.S. Department of Commerce, Bureau of Economic Analysis, Fourteenth Street between Constitution Avenue and E Street, NW, Washington, D.C. 20230 (202) 606-9900, www.bea.doc.gov; *Survey of Current Business.*

MANUFACTURING INDUSTRY - MULTINATIONAL COMPANIES

U.S. Department of Commerce, Bureau of Economic Analysis, Fourteenth Street between Constitution and E Streets, NW, Washington, D.C. 20230 (202) 606-9900, www.bea.doc.gov; *Survey of Current Business*.

MANUFACTURING INDUSTRY - OCCUPATIONAL SAFETY

National Safety Council, 1121 Spring Lake Drive, Itasca, Illinois 60143-3201 (630) 285-1121; *Accident Facts*.

U.S. Department of Labor, Bureau of Labor Statistics, Two Massachusetts Avenue, NE, Washington, D.C. 20212 (202) 691-5200, www.stats.bls.gov; *Occupational Injuries and Illnesses in the United States by Industry*.

MANUFACTURING INDUSTRY - OUTLYING AREAS OF UNITED STATES

U.S. Department of Commerce, Bureau of the Census, Washington, D.C. 20233 (301) 457-4100, www.census.gov; *Economic Census of Outlying Areas;* and *County Business Patterns*.

MANUFACTURING INDUSTRY - PRODUCTIVITY

Board of Governors of the Federal Reserve System, Twentieth Street and Constitution Avenue, NW, Washington, D.C. 20551 (202) 452-3000, www.bog.frb.fed.us; *Federal Reserve Bulletin; Capacity Utilization in Manufacturing, Mining, Utilities, and Industrial Materials;* and *Industrial Production and Capacity Utilization*.

U.S. Department of Labor, Bureau of Labor Statistics, Two Massachusetts Avenue, NE, Washington, D.C. 20212 (202) 691-5200, www.stats.bls.gov; *News USDL 99-53; Productivity and Cost;* and Internet site: http://stats.bls.gov/ iprhome.htm.

MANUFACTURING INDUSTRY - PRODUCTIVITY - FOREIGN COUNTRIES

Organization for Economic Cooperation and Development, 2 rue Andre-Pascal, 75 Paris 16, France (Telephone Number in U.S. (202) 785-6323); *Science, Technology and Industry Outlook*.

U.S. Department of Labor, Bureau of Labor Statistics, Two Massachusetts Avenue, NE, Washington, D.C. 20212 (202) 691-5200, www.stats.bls.gov; *International Comparisons of Manufacturing Productivity and Unit Labor Trends*.

MANUFACTURING INDUSTRY - PROFITS

Executive Office of the President, Council of Economic Advisers, Old Executive Office Building, Washington, D.C.

20502 (202) 395-5084, www.whitehouse. gov.cea; *Economic Report of the President*.

U.S. Department of Commerce, Bureau of Economic Analysis, Fourteenth Street between Constitution Avenue and E Street, NW, Washington, D.C. 20230 (202) 606-9900, www.bea.doc.gov; *Survey of Current Business;* and *National Income and Product Accounts of the United States*.

U.S. Department of Commerce, Bureau of the Census, Washington, D.C. 20233 (301) 457-4100, www.census.gov; *Quarterly Financial Report for Manufacturing, Mining, and Trade Corporations*.

U.S. Department of the Treasury, Internal Revenue Service, 1111 Constitution Avenue, NW, Washington, D.C. 20224 (202) 874-0410, www.irs.ustreas.gov; *Statistics of Income*, various publications; and *Statistics of Income, Corporation Income Tax Return*.

MANUFACTURING INDUSTRY - SALES, SHIPMENTS, RECEIPTS

Executive Office of the President, Council of Economic Advisers, Old Executive Office Building, Washington, D.C. 20502 (202) 395-5084, www.whitehouse. gov/cea; *Economic Report of the President*.

Time Warner, Time and Life Building, Rockefeller Center, New York, New York 10020 (212) 522-1212; *Fortune*.

U.S. Department of Commerce, Bureau of the Census, Washington, D.C. 20233 (301) 457-4100, www.census.gov; *1997 Economic Census: Advance Summary Statistics for the U.S. 1997 NAICS Basis; Quarterly Financial Report for Manufacturing, Mining, and Trade Corporations; Current Business Reports; Current Industrial Reports, Manufactures' Shipments, Inventories, and Orders; Census of Manufactures; Annual Survey of Manufactures;* and *Statistics of U.S. Businesses*.

U.S. Department of the Treasury, Internal Revenue Service, 1111 Constitution Avenue, NW, Washington, D.C. 20224 (202) 874-0410, www.irs.ustreas.gov; *Statistics of Income*, various publications; and *Statistics of Income, Corporation Income Tax Returns*.

MANUFACTURING INDUSTRY - TOXIC CHEMICAL RELEASES

Environmental Protection Agency, 1200 Pennsylvania Avenue, NW, Washington, D.C. 20460 (888) 372-8255, www.epa.gov; *Toxics Release Inventory*.

MANUFACTURING INDUSTRY - UNION MEMBERSHIP

U.S. Department of Labor, Bureau of Labor Statistics, Two Massachusetts Avenue, NE, Washington, D.C. 20212 (202) 691-5200, www.stats.bls.gov; *Employment and Earnings*.

MANUFACTURING INDUSTRY - VALUE ADDED

U.S. Department of Commerce, Bureau of the Census, Washington, D.C. 20233 (301) 457-4100, www.census.gov; *Annual Survey of Manufactures;* and *Census of Manufactures*.

U.S. Department of Labor, Bureau of Labor Statistics, Two Massachusetts Avenue, NW, Washington, D.C. 20212 (202) 691-5200, www.stats.bls.gov; *Employment and Earnings*.

MARGARINE

U.S. Department of Agriculture, Economic Research Service, 1800 M Street, NW, Washington, D.C. 20036 (202) 694-5050, www.ers.usda.gov; *Food Consumption, Prices, and Expenditures;* and *Agricultural Outlook*.

U.S. Department of Labor, Bureau of Labor Statistics, Two Massachusetts Avenue, NE, Washington, D.C. 20212 (202) 691-5200, www.stats.bls.gov; *CPI Detailed Report;* and *Monthly Labor Review*.

MARIHUANA - See also: DRUGS (ILLEGAL)

MARIHUANA - ARRESTS, SEIZURES

U.S. Department of Justice, Drug Enforcement Administration, 600-700 Army Navy Drive, Arlington, Virginia 22202 (202) 307-1000, www.usdoj.gov/dea; unpublished data from Federal-wide Drug Seizure System.

U.S. Department of Justice, Federal Bureau of Investigation, 935 Pennsylvania Avenue, NW, Washington, D.C. 20535 (202) 324-3691, www.fbi.gov; *Crime in the United States*.

MARIHUANA - USE

U.S. Department of Health and Human Services, Substance Abuse and Mental Health Services Administration, 5600 Fishers Lane, Rockville, Maryland 20857 (800) 729-6686, www.samhsa.gov; *National Household Survey on Drug Abuse*.

MARINE CORPS

U.S. Department of Defense, Office of the Secretary, The Pentagon, Washington, D.C. 20301 (703) 545-6700; *Selected Manpower Statistics*.

MARITAL STATUS OF POPULATION

U.S. Department of Commerce, Bureau of the Census, Washington, D.C. 20233 (301) 457-4100, www.census.gov; *Current Population Reports; Marital Status and Living Arrangements: March 1998;* and unpublished data.

MARITAL STATUS OF POPULATION - BLACK POPULATION

U.S. Department of Commerce, Bureau of the Census, Washington, D.C. 20233 (301) 457-4100, www.census.gov; *Current Population Reports;* and unpublished data.

MARITAL STATUS OF POPULATION - BY PRESENCE OF CHILDREN

U.S. Department of Commerce, Bureau of the Census, Washington, D.C. 20233 (301) 457-4100, www.census.gov; *Current Population Reports;* and unpublished data.

MARITAL STATUS OF POPULATION - COHABITATION EXPERIENCE

U.S. Department of Health and Human Services, National Center for Health Statistics, 3700 East-West Highway, Hyattsville, Maryland 20782 (301) 436-8500, www.cdc.gov/nchs; *Fertility, Family Planning, and Women's Health: New Data from the 1995 National Survey of Family Growth, Vital and Health Statistics.*

MARITAL STATUS OF POPULATION - COMPUTER USE

Mediamark Research, Inc., 708 Third Avenue, New York, New York 10017 (212) 599-0444; Internet site: www.mediamark.com

MARITAL STATUS OF POPULATION - COUPLES WITH OR WITHOUT OWN HOUSEHOLD

U.S. Department of Commerce, Bureau of the Census, Washington, D.C. 20233 (301) 457-4100, www.census.gov; *Current Population Reports;* and unpublished data.

MARITAL STATUS OF POPULATION - ELDERLY

U.S. Department of Commerce, Bureau of the Census, Washington, D.C. 20233 (301) 457-4100, www.census.gov; *Current Population Reports;* and unpublished data.

MARITAL STATUS OF POPULATION - EMPLOYED PERSONS

U.S. Department of Labor, Bureau of Labor Statistics, Two Massachusetts Avenue, NE, Washington, D.C. 20212 (202) 691-5200, www.stats.bls.gov; *Employment and Earnings;* and unpublished data.

MARITAL STATUS OF POPULATION -

FEMALE HOUSEHOLDER

U.S. Department of Commerce, Bureau of the Census, Washington, D.C. 20233 (301) 457-4100, www.census.gov; *Current Population Reports;* and unpublished data.

MARITAL STATUS OF POPULATION - HISPANIC ORIGIN POPULATION

U.S. Department of Commerce, Bureau of the Census, Washington, D.C. 20233 (301) 457-4100, www.census.gov; *Current Population Reports;* and unpublished data.

MARITAL STATUS OF POPULATION - HOUSEHOLDER STATUS

U.S. Department of Commerce, Bureau of the Census, Washington, D.C. 20233 (301) 457-4100, www.census.gov; *Current Population Reports*; unpublished data.

MARITAL STATUS OF POPULATION - INTERNET USE

Mediamark Research, Inc., 708 Third Avenue, New York, New York 10017 (212) 599-0444; *Cyberstats;* and Internet site: http://www.mediamark.com.

MARITAL STATUS OF POPULATION - LABOR FORCE - PARTICIPATION RATES

U.S. Department of Labor, Bureau of Labor Statistics, Two Massachusetts Avenue, NE, Washington, D.C. 20212 (202) 691-5200, www.stats.bls.gov; Bulletins 2307, 2217 and 2340; and unpublished data.

MARITAL STATUS OF POPULATION - NONFAMILY HOUSEHOLDER

U.S. Department of Commerce, Bureau of the Census, Washington, D.C. 20233 (301) 457-4100, www.census.gov; *Current Population Reports.*

MARITAL STATUS OF POPULATION - OUTLYING AREAS

U.S. Department of Commerce, Bureau of the Census, Washington, D.C. 20233 (301) 457-4100, www.census.gov; *Census of Population and Housing.*

MARITAL STATUS OF POPULATION - UNMARRIED COUPLES

U.S. Department of Commerce, Bureau of the Census, Washington, D.C. 20233 (301) 457-4100, www.census.gov; *Current Population Reports.*

MARITAL STATUS OF POPULATION - WOMEN IN THE LABOR FORCE

U.S. Department of Labor, Bureau of Labor Statistics, Two Massachusetts Avenue, NE, Washington, D.C. 20212 (202) 691-5200, www.stats.bls.gov; Bulletin 2307;

and unpublished data.

MARITAL STATUS OF POPULATION - WORK SCHEDULES

U.S. Department of Labor, Bureau of Labor Statistics, Two Massachusetts Avenue, NE, Washington, D.C. 20212 (202) 691-5200, www.stats.bls.gov; *Employment and Earnings*; and unpublished data.

MARRIAGE AND DIVORCE - See also MARITAL STATUS

U.S. Department of Commerce, Bureau of the Census, Washington, D.C. 20233 (301) 457-4100, www.census.gov; *Current Population Reports.*

U.S. Department of Health and Human Services, National Center for Health Statistics, 3700 East-West Highway, Hyattsville, Maryland 20782 (301) 436-8500, www.cdc.gov/nchs; *Vital Statistics of the United States; National Vital Statistics Report;* and unpublished data.

MARRIAGE AND DIVORCE - MEDIAN AGE AT MARRIAGE

U.S. Department of Health and Human Services, National Center for Health Statistics, 3700 East-West Highway, Hyattsville, Maryland 20782 (301) 436-8500, www.cdc.gov/nchs; *Vital Statistics of the United States; National Vital Statistics Report;* and unpublished data.

MARRIAGE AND DIVORCE - OUTLYING AREAS OF UNITED STATES

U.S. Department of Health and Human Services, National Center for Health Statistics, 3700 East-West Highway, Hyattsville, Maryland 20782 (301) 436-8500, www.cdc.gov/nchs; *Vital Statistics of the United States.*

MARRIAGE AND DIVORCE - REMARRIAGES

U.S. Department of Commerce, Bureau of the Census, Washington, D.C. 20233 (301) 457-4100, www.census.gov; *Current Population Reports.*

U.S. Department of Health and Human Services, National Center for Health Statistics, 3700 East-West Highway, Hyattsville, Maryland 20782 (301) 436-8500, www.cdc.gov/nchs; *Vital Statistics of the United States; Advance Data from Vital and Health Statistics; National Vital Statistics Report;* and unpublished data.

MARRIED COUPLES - See HOUSEHOLDS OR FAMILIES

MARRIED PERSONS - See MARITAL STATUS

Marshall Islands (Republic of) - National Statistical Office

Office of Planning and Statistics, Majuro, Republic of the Marshall Islands 96960.

MARSHALL ISLANDS - AGRICULTURE

Europa Publications Limited, 18 Bedford Square, London, WC1B 3JN, England; *The Europa World Year Book.*

Food and Agriculture Organization of the United Nations (FAO), Via delle Terme di Caracalla, 00100, Rome, Italy (Telephone Number in U.S. (202) 653-2400); *Production Yearbook;* and *Trade Yearbook.*

St. Martin's Press, Inc., 175 Fifth Avenue, New York, New York 10010 (800) 221-7945; *The Statesman's Year-Book.*

Statistical Office of the United Nations, Publishing Service, New York, New York 10017 (800) 253-9646; *Asia-Pacific in Figures;* and *Statistical Yearbook.*

MARSHALL ISLANDS - AIRLINE SERVICE

Europa Publications Limited, 18 Bedford Square, London, WC1B 3JN, England; *The Europa World Year Book.*

St. Martin's Press, Inc., 175 Fifth Avenue, New York, New York 10010 (800) 221-7945; *The Statesman's Year-Book.*

Statistical Office of the United Nations, Publishing Service, New York, New York 10017 (800) 253-9646; *Statistical Yearbook.*

MARSHALL ISLANDS - AIRPORTS

Central Intelligence Agency, Washington, D.C. 20505 (703) 482-1100, www.cia.gov; *The World Factbook.*

MARSHALL ISLANDS - ANIMAL HEALTH

Food and Agriculture Organization of the United Nations (FAO), Via delle Terme di Caracalla, 00100, Rome, Italy (Telephone Number in U.S. (202) 653-2400); *Animal Health Yearbook.*

MARSHALL ISLANDS - AREA AND DENSITY OF POPULATION

Central Intelligence Agency, Washington, D.C. 20505 (703) 482-1100, www.cia.gov; *The World Factbook.*

Europa Publications Limited, 18 Bedford Square, London, WC1B 3JN, England; *The Europa World Year Book.*

St. Martin's Press, Inc., 175 Fifth Avenue,

New York, New York 10010 (800) 221-7945; *The Statesman's Year-Book.*

Statistical Office of the United Nations, Publishing Service, New York, New York 10017 (800) 253-9646; *Statistical Yearbook.*

MARSHALL ISLANDS - BEVERAGES

Statistical Office of the United Nations, Publishing Service, New York, New York 10017 (800) 253-9646; *Statistical Yearbook.*

MARSHALL ISLANDS - BIRTH RATES

Central Intelligence Agency, Washington, D.C. 20505 (703) 482-1100, www.cia.gov; *The World Factbook.*

Europa Publications Limited, 18 Bedford Square, London, WC1B 3JN, England; *The Europa World Year Book.*

Statistical Office of the United Nations, Publishing Service, New York, New York 10017 (800) 253-9646; *Asia-Pacific in Figures;* and *Statistical Yearbook.*

MARSHALL ISLANDS - BROADCASTING

Billboard Limited, Post Office Box 9027, 1006 AA Amsterdam, The Netherlands (Telephone Number in U.S. (212) 764-7300); *World Radio TV Handbook.*

Central Intelligence Agency, Washington, D.C. 20505 (703) 482-1100, www.cia.gov; *The World Factbook.*

St. Martin's Press, Inc., 175 Fifth Avenue, New York, New York 10010 (800) 221-7945; *The Statesman's Year-Book.*

MARSHALL ISLANDS - BUDGET

Central Intelligence Agency, Washington, D.C. 20505 (703) 482-1100, www.cia.gov; *The World Factbook.*

MARSHALL ISLANDS - CLIMATE

St. Martin's Press, Inc., 175 Fifth Avenue, New York, New York 10010 (800) 221-7945; *The Statesman's Year-Book.*

MARSHALL ISLANDS - COMMERCE

St. Martin's Press, Inc., 175 Fifth Avenue, New York, New York 10010 (800) 221-7945; *The Statesman's Year-Book.*

MARSHALL ISLANDS - CONSTRUCTION INDUSTRY

Statistical Office of the United Nations, Publishing Service, New York, New York 10017 (800) 253-9646; *Statistical Yearbook.*

MARSHALL ISLANDS - CONSUMER PRICE INDEX

Statistical Office of the United Nations, Publishing Service, New York, New York 10017 (800) 253-9646; *Statistical Yearbook.*

MARSHALL ISLANDS - CROPS

Europa Publications Limited, 18 Bedford Square, London, WC1B 3JN, England; *The Europa World Year Book.*

Food and Agriculture Organization of the United Nations (FAO), Via delle Terme di Caracalla, 00100, Rome, Italy (Telephone Number in U.S. (202) 653-2400); *Production Yearbook;* and *Trade Yearbook.*

St. Martin's Press, Inc., 175 Fifth Avenue, New York, New York 10010 (800) 221-7945; *The Statesman's Year-Book.*

Statistical Office of the United Nations, Publishing Service, New York, New York 10017 (800) 253-9646; *Industrial Commodity Statistics Yearbook;* and *Statistical Yearbook.*

MARSHALL ISLANDS - DAIRY PRODUCTS

Food and Agriculture Organization of the United Nations (FAO), Via delle Terme di Caracalla, 00100, Rome, Italy (Telephone Number in U.S. (202) 653-2400); *Production Yearbook;* and *Trade Yearbook.*

Statistical Office of the United Nations, Publishing Service, New York, New York 10017 (800) 253-9646; *Industrial Commodity Statistics Yearbook;* and *Statistical Yearbook.*

MARSHALL ISLANDS - DEMOGRAPHY

Statistical Office of the United Nations, Publishing Service, New York, New York 10017 (800) 253-9646; *Asia-Pacific in Figures;* and *Demographic Yearbook.*

MARSHALL ISLANDS - DIVORCE RATES

Statistical Office of the United Nations, Publishing Service, New York, New York 10017 (800) 253-9646; *Demographic Yearbook;* and *Statistical Yearbook.*

MARSHALL ISLANDS - ECONOMY

Central Intelligence Agency, Washington, D.C. 20505 (703) 482-1100, www.cia.gov; *The World Factbook.*

St. Martin's Press, Inc., 175 Fifth Avenue, New York, New York 10010 (800) 221-7945; *The Statesman's Year-Book.*

Statistical Office of the United Nations, Publishing Service, New York, New York 10017 (800) 253-9646; *World Statistics Pocketbook.*

The World Bank, 1818 H Street, NW, Washington, D.C. 20433 (202) 477-1234;

The World Bank Atlas.

MARSHALL ISLANDS - EDUCATION

Europa Publications Limited, 18 Bedford Square, London, WC1B 3JN, England; *The Europa World Year Book.*

St. Martin's Press, Inc., 175 Fifth Avenue, New York, New York 10010 (800) 221-7945; *The Statesman's Year-Book.*

Statistical Office of the United Nations, Publishing Service, New York, New York 10017 (800) 253-9646; *Asia-Pacific in Figures.*

MARSHALL ISLANDS - ELECTRICITY

Central Intelligence Agency, Washington, D.C. 20505 (703) 482-1100, www.cia.gov; *The World Factbook.*

Statistical Office of the United Nations, Publishing Service, New York, New York 10017 (800) 253-9646; *Energy Statistics Yearbook;* and *Statistical Yearbook.*

MARSHALL ISLANDS - EMPLOYMENT

Statistical Office of the United Nations, Publishing Service, New York, New York 10017 (800) 253-9646; *Asia-Pacific in Figures;* and *Statistical Yearbook.*

MARSHALL ISLANDS - ENERGY

Statistical Office of the United Nations, Publishing Service, New York, New York 10017 (800) 253-9646; *Asia-Pacific in Figures; Energy Statistics Yearbook; World Statistics Pocketbook;* and *Statistical Yearbook.*

The World Bank, 1818 H Street, NW, Washington, D.C. 20433 (202) 477-1234; *The World Bank Atlas.*

MARSHALL ISLANDS - ENVIRONMENT

Statistical Office of the United Nations, Publishing Service, New York, New York 10017 (800) 253-9646; *Statistical Yearbook;* and *World Statistics Pocketbook.*

MARSHALL ISLANDS - EXCHANGE RATES

Central Intelligence Agency, Washington, D.C. 20505 (703) 482-1100, www.cia.gov; *The World Factbook.*

Europa Publications Limited, 18 Bedford Square, London, WC1B 3JN, England; *The Europa World Year Book.*

Statistical Office of the United Nations, Publishing Service, New York, New York 10017 (800) 253-9646; *Statistical Yearbook;* and *World Statistics Pocketbook.*

Walden Publishing Ltd., Two Market Street, Saffron Walden Essex, CB10 1HZ, England; *The World of Information Asia and Pacific Review.*

MARSHALL ISLANDS - EXPORTS

Central Intelligence Agency, Washington, D.C. 20505 (703) 482-1100, www.cia.gov; *The World Factbook.*

Europa Publications Limited, 18 Bedford Square, London, WC1B 3JN, England; *The Europa World Year Book.*

St. Martin's Press, Inc., 175 Fifth Avenue, New York, New York 10010 (800) 221-7945; *The Statesman's Year-Book.*

Statistical Office of the United Nations, Publishing Service, New York, New York 10017 (800) 253-9646; *International Trade Statistics Yearbook.*

Walden Publishing Ltd., Two Market Street, Saffron Walden Essex, CB10 1HZ, England; *The World of Information Asia and Pacific Review.*

MARSHALL ISLANDS - EXTERNAL TRADE

Food and Agriculture Organization of the United Nations (FAO), Via delle Terme di Caracalla, 00100, Rome, Italy (Telephone Number in U.S. (202) 653-2400); *Trade Yearbook.*

Statistical Office of the United Nations, Publishing Service, New York, New York 10017 (800) 253-9646; *Asia-Pacific in Figures;* and *Statistical Yearbook.*

MARSHALL ISLANDS - FERTILITY RATES

Central Intelligence Agency, Washington, D.C. 20505 (703) 482-1100, www.cia.gov; *The World Factbook.*

The World Bank, 1818 H Street, NW, Washington, D.C. 20433 (202) 477-1234; *The World Bank Atlas.*

MARSHALL ISLANDS - FERTILIZER

Food and Agriculture Organization of the United Nations (FAO), Via delle Terme di Caracalla, 00100, Rome, Italy (Telephone Number in U.S. (202) 653-2400); *Fertilizer Yearbook.*

Statistical Office of the United Nations, Publishing Service, New York, New York 10017 (800) 253-9646; *Industrial Commodity Statistics Yearbook;* and *Statistical Yearbook.*

MARSHALL ISLANDS - FINANCE

Europa Publications Limited, 18 Bedford Square, London, WC1B 3JN, England; *The Europa World Year Book.*

MARSHALL ISLANDS - FISHERIES

Europa Publications Limited, 18 Bedford Square, London, WC1B 3JN, England; *The Europa World Year Book.*

Food and Agriculture Organization of the United Nations (FAO), Via delle Terme di Caracalla, 00100, Rome, Italy (Telephone Number in U.S. (202) 653-2400); *Yearbook of Fishery Statistics.*

Statistical Office of the United Nations, Publishing Service, New York, New York 10017 (800) 253-9646; *Industrial Commodity Statistics Yearbook;* and *Statistical Yearbook.*

MARSHALL ISLANDS - FOOD

Food and Agriculture Organization of the United Nations (FAO), Via delle Terme di Caracalla, 00100, Rome, Italy (Telephone Number in U.S. (202) 653-2400); *Production Yearbook;* and *Trade Yearbook.*

Statistical Office of the United Nations, Publishing Service, New York, New York 10017 (800) 253-9646; *Industrial Commodity Statistics Yearbook.*

MARSHALL ISLANDS - FOREIGN DEBT

Walden Publishing Ltd., Two Market Street, Saffron Walden Essex, CB10 1HZ, England; *The World of Information Asia and Pacific Review.*

MARSHALL ISLANDS - FOREIGN TRADE

Europa Publications Limited, 18 Bedford Square, London, WC1B 3JN, England; *The Europa World Year Book.*

Food and Agriculture Organization of the United Nations (FAO), Via delle Terme di Caracalla, 00100, Rome, Italy (Telephone Number in U.S. (202) 653-2400); *Trade Yearbook.*

Statistical Office of the United Nations, Publishing Service, New York, New York 10017 (800) 253-9646; *International Trade Statistics Yearbook;* and *Statistical Yearbook.*

MARSHALL ISLANDS - FORESTRY AND FOREST PRODUCTS

Food and Agriculture Organization of the United Nations (FAO), Via delle Terme di Caracalla, 00100, Rome, Italy (Telephone Number in U.S. (202) 653-2400); *Yearbook of Forest Products.*

Statistical Office of the United Nations, Publishing Service, New York, New York 10017 (800) 253-9646; *Industrial Commodity Statistics Yearbook;* and *Statistical Yearbook.*

MARSHALL ISLANDS - GOVERNMENT

Central Intelligence Agency, Washington, D.C. 20505 (703) 482-1100, www.cia.gov; *The World Factbook*.

Europa Publications Limited, 18 Bedford Square, London, WC1B 3JN, England; *The Europa World Year Book*.

St. Martin's Press, Inc., 175 Fifth Avenue, New York, New York 10010 (800) 221-7945; *The Statesman's Year-Book*.

Statistical Office of the United Nations, Publishing Service, New York, New York 10017 (800) 253-9646; *Asia-Pacific in Figures;* and *Statistical Yearbook*.

MARSHALL ISLANDS - GROSS DOMESTIC PRODUCT

Statistical Office of the United Nations, Publishing Service, New York, New York 10017 (800) 253-9646; *National Accounts Statistics;* and *Statistical Yearbook*.

MARSHALL ISLANDS - GROSS NATIONAL PRODUCT

Walden Publishing Ltd., Two Market Street, Saffron Walden Essex, CB10 1HZ, England; *The World of Information Asia and Pacific Review*.

The World Bank, 1818 H Street, NW, Washington, D.C. 20433 (202) 477-1234; *The World Bank Atlas*.

MARSHALL ISLANDS - HEALTH

St. Martin's Press, Inc., 175 Fifth Avenue, New York, New York 10010 (800) 221-7945; *The Statesman's Year-Book*.

Statistical Office of the United Nations, Publishing Service, New York, New York 10017 (800) 253-9646; *Asia-Pacific in Figures;* and *Statistical Yearbook*.

MARSHALL ISLANDS - HIGHWAYS

Central Intelligence Agency, Washington, D.C. 20505 (703) 482-1100, www.cia.gov; *The World Factbook*.

MARSHALL ISLANDS - ILLITERATE POPULATION

Central Intelligence Agency, Washington, D.C. 20505 (703) 482-1100, www.cia.gov; *The World Factbook*.

Statistical Office of the United Nations, Publishing Service, New York, New York 10017 (800) 253-9646; *Asia-Pacific in Figures*.

MARSHALL ISLANDS - IMPORTS

Central Intelligence Agency,

Washington, D.C. 20505 (703) 482-1100, www.cia.gov; *The World Factbook*.

Europa Publications Limited, 18 Bedford Square, London, WC1B 3JN, England; *The Europa World Year Book*.

St. Martin's Press, Inc., 175 Fifth Avenue, New York, New York 10010 (800) 221-7945; *The Statesman's Year-Book*.

Statistical Office of the United Nations, Publishing Service, New York, New York 10017 (800) 253-9646; *International Trade Statistics Yearbook*.

Walden Publishing Ltd., Two Market Street, Saffron Walden Essex, CB10 1HZ, England; *The World of Information Asia and Pacific Review*.

MARSHALL ISLANDS - INDUSTRY

Central Intelligence Agency, Washington, D.C. 20505 (703) 482-1100, www.cia.gov; *The World Factbook*.

Statistical Office of the United Nations, Publishing Service, New York, New York 10017 (800) 253-9646; *Asia-Pacific in Figures; Industrial Commodity Statistics Yearbook;* and *Statistical Yearbook*.

MARSHALL ISLANDS - INTERNAL TRADE

Statistical Office of the United Nations, Publishing Service, New York, New York 10017 (800) 253-9646; *Statistical Yearbook*.

MARSHALL ISLANDS - LABOR

Central Intelligence Agency, Washington, D.C. 20505 (703) 482-1100, www.cia.gov; *The World Factbook*.

Statistical Office of the United Nations, Publishing Service, New York, New York 10017 (800) 253-9646; *Statistical Yearbook*.

The World Bank, 1818 H Street, NW, Washington, D.C. 20433 (202) 477-1234; *The World Bank Atlas*.

MARSHALL ISLANDS - LAND USE

Central Intelligence Agency, Washington, D.C. 20505 (703) 482-1100, www.cia.gov; *The World Factbook*.

Food and Agriculture Organization of the United Nations (FAO), Via delle Terme di Caracalla, 00100, Rome, Italy (Telephone Number in U.S. (202) 653-2400); *Production Yearbook*.

MARSHALL ISLANDS - LIFE EXPECTANCY

Central Intelligence Agency, Washington, D.C. 20505 (703) 482-1100, www.cia.gov; *The World Factbook*.

Statistical Office of the United Nations, Publishing Service, New York, New York 10017 (800) 253-9646; *Asia-Pacific in Figures; World Statistics Pocketbook;* and *Demographic Yearbook*.

The World Bank, 1818 H Street, NW, Washington, D.C. 20433 (202) 477-1234; *The World Bank Atlas*.

MARSHALL ISLANDS - LIVESTOCK AND POULTRY

Europa Publications Limited, 18 Bedford Square, London, WC1B 3JN, England; *The Europa World Year Book*.

Food and Agriculture Organization of the United Nations (FAO), Via delle Terme di Caracalla, 00100, Rome, Italy (Telephone Number in U.S. (202) 653-2400); *Production Yearbook;* and *Trade Yearbook*.

Statistical Office of the United Nations, Publishing Service, New York, New York 10017 (800) 253-9646; *Industrial Commodity Statistics Yearbook;* and *Statistical Yearbook*.

MARSHALL ISLANDS - MACHINERY

Statistical Office of the United Nations, Publishing Service, New York, New York 10017 (800) 253-9646; *Industrial Commodity Statistics Yearbook*.

MARSHALL ISLANDS - MAIL - NUMBER OF PIECES SENT OR RECEIVED

Statistical Office of the United Nations, Publishing Service, New York, New York 10017 (800) 253-9646; *Statistical Yearbook*.

MARSHALL ISLANDS - MANUFACTURING

Statistical Office of the United Nations, Publishing Service, New York, New York 10017 (800) 253-9646; *Industrial Commodity Statistics Yearbook;* and *Statistical Yearbook*.

MARSHALL ISLANDS - MARRIAGE RATES

Statistical Office of the United Nations, Publishing Service, New York, New York 10017 (800) 253-9646; *Demographic Yearbook;* and *Statistical Yearbook*.

MARSHALL ISLANDS - MERCHANT SHIPPING

Europa Publications Limited, 18 Bedford Square, London, WC1B 3JN, England; *The Europa World Year Book*.

Statistical Office of the United Nations, Publishing Service, New York, New York 10017 (800) 253-9646; *Statistical Yearbook*.

MARSHALL ISLANDS - MILITARY

Central Intelligence Agency, Washington, D.C. 20505 (703) 482-1100, www.cia.gov; *The World Factbook.*

St. Martin's Press, Inc., 175 Fifth Avenue, New York, New York 10010 (800) 221-7945; *The Statesman's Year-Book.*

MARSHALL ISLANDS - MINING AND MINERAL PRODUCTS

St. Martin's Press, Inc., 175 Fifth Avenue, New York, New York 10010 (800) 221-7945; *The Statesman's Year-Book.*

Statistical Office of the United Nations, Publishing Service, New York, New York 10017 (800) 253-9646; *Energy Statistics Yearbook; Industrial Commodity Statistics Yearbook;* and *Statistical Yearbook.*

MARSHALL ISLANDS - MORTALITY

Central Intelligence Agency, Washington, D.C. 20505 (703) 482-1100, www.cia.gov; *The World Factbook.*

Europa Publications Limited, 18 Bedford Square, London, WC1B 3JN, England; *The Europa World Year Book.*

Statistical Office of the United Nations, Publishing Service, New York, New York 10017 (800) 253-9646; *Asia-Pacific in Figures; Demographic Yearbook; World Statistics Pocketbook;* and *Statistical Yearbook.*

The World Bank, 1818 H Street, NW, Washington, D.C. 20433 (202) 477-1234; *The World Bank Atlas.*

MARSHALL ISLANDS - MOTION PICTURES

Statistical Office of the United Nations, Publishing Service, New York, New York 10017 (800) 253-9646; *Statistical Yearbook.*

MARSHALL ISLANDS - MOTOR VEHICLE PRODUCTION

Europa Publications Limited, 18 Bedford Square, London, WC1B 3JN, England; *The Europa World Year Book.*

Statistical Office of the United Nations, Publishing Service, New York, New York 10017 (800) 253-9646; *Statistical Yearbook.*

MARSHALL ISLANDS - NATIONAL ACCOUNTS

Statistical Office of the United Nations, Publishing Service, New York, New York 10017 (800) 253-9646; *Asia-Pacific in Figures; National Accounts Statistics;* and *Statistical Yearbook.*

MARSHALL ISLANDS - NATIONAL INCOME

Statistical Office of the United Nations,

Publishing Service, New York, New York 10017 (800) 253-9646; *Statistical Yearbook.*

MARSHALL ISLANDS - NATIONAL PRODUCT

Statistical Office of the United Nations, Publishing Service, New York, New York 10017 (800) 253-9646; *Statistical Yearbook.*

MARSHALL ISLANDS - PATENTS, TRADEMARKS AND SERVICE MARKS

Statistical Office of the United Nations, Publishing Service, New York, New York 10017 (800) 253-9646; *Statistical Yearbook.*

MARSHALL ISLANDS - PETROLEUM INDUSTRY

Statistical Office of the United Nations, Publishing Service, New York, New York 10017 (800) 253-9646; *Energy Statistics Yearbook; Industrial Commodity Statistics Yearbook;* and *Statistical Yearbook.*

MARSHALL ISLANDS - POPULATION

Central Intelligence Agency, Washington, D.C. 20505 (703) 482-1100, www.cia.gov; *The World Factbook.*

Europa Publications Limited, 18 Bedford Square, London, WC1B 3JN, England; *The Europa World Year Book.*

Food and Agriculture Organization of the United Nations (FAO), Via delle Terme di Caracalla, 00100, Rome, Italy (Telephone Number in U.S. (202) 653-2400); *Production Yearbook.*

St. Martin's Press, Inc., 175 Fifth Avenue, New York, New York 10010 (800) 221-7945; *The Statesman's Year-Book.*

Statistical Office of the United Nations, Publishing Service, New York, New York 10017 (800) 253-9646; *Asia-Pacific in Figures; Demographic Yearbook; World Statistics Pocketbook;* and *Statistical Yearbook.*

Walden Publishing Ltd., Two Market Street, Saffron Walden Essex, CB10 1HZ, England; *The World of Information Asia and Pacific Review.*

The World Bank, 1818 H Street, NW, Washington, D.C. 20433 (202) 477-1234; *The World Bank Atlas.*

MARSHALL ISLANDS - PRICES

Food and Agriculture Organization of the United Nations (FAO), Via delle Terme di Caracalla, 00100, Rome, Italy (Telephone Number in U.S. (202) 653-2400); *Production Yearbook.*

MARSHALL ISLANDS - RADIO

RECEIVERS

St. Martin's Press, Inc., 175 Fifth Avenue, New York, New York 10010 (800) 221-7945; *The Statesman's Year-Book.*

Statistical Office of the United Nations, Publishing Service, New York, New York 10017 (800) 253-9646; *Statistical Yearbook.*

MARSHALL ISLANDS - RAILWAYS

Statistical Office of the United Nations, Publishing Service, New York, New York 10017 (800) 253-9646; *Statistical Yearbook.*

MARSHALL ISLANDS - RELIGION

Central Intelligence Agency, Washington, D.C. 20505 (703) 482-1100, www.cia.gov; *The World Factbook.*

St. Martin's Press, Inc., 175 Fifth Avenue, New York, New York 10010 (800) 221-7945; *The Statesman's Year-Book.*

MARSHALL ISLANDS - RETAIL TRADE

Statistical Office of the United Nations, Publishing Service, New York, New York 10017 (800) 253-9646; *Statistical Yearbook.*

MARSHALL ISLANDS - RUBBER PRODUCTION AND CONSUMPTION

Statistical Office of the United Nations, Publishing Service, New York, New York 10017 (800) 253-9646; *Statistical Yearbook.*

MARSHALL ISLANDS - SCIENTISTS, TECHNICIANS AND ENGINEERS

Statistical Office of the United Nations, Publishing Service, New York, New York 10017 (800) 253-9646; *Statistical Yearbook.*

MARSHALL ISLANDS - SOCIAL DATA

Statistical Office of the United Nations, Publishing Service, New York, New York 10017 (800) 253-9646; *World Statistics Pocketbook.*

MARSHALL ISLANDS - TELEPHONES IN USE

Central Intelligence Agency, Washington, D.C. 20505 (703) 482-1100, www.cia.gov; *The World Factbook.*

St. Martin's Press, Inc., 175 Fifth Avenue, New York, New York 10010 (800) 221-7945; *The Statesman's Year-Book.*

Statistical Office of the United Nations, Publishing Service, New York, New York 10017 (800) 253-9646; *Statistical Yearbook;* and *World Statistics Pocketbook.*

MARSHALL ISLANDS - TEXTILE INDUSTRY

Statistical Office of the United Nations, Publishing Service, New York, New York 10017 (800) 253-9646; *Industrial Commodity Statistics Yearbook;* and *Statistical Yearbook.*

MARSHALL ISLANDS - TIRE (MOTOR VEHICLE) PRODUCTION

Statistical Office of the United Nations, Publishing Service, New York, New York 10017 (800) 253-9646; *Statistical Yearbook.*

MARSHALL ISLANDS - TOBACCO PRODUCTION

Statistical Office of the United Nations, Publishing Service, New York, New York 10017 (800) 253-9646; *Statistical Yearbook.*

MARSHALL ISLANDS - TOURISM

Statistical Office of the United Nations, Publishing Service, New York, New York 10017 (800) 253-9646; *Statistical Yearbook.*

World Tourism Organization, Calle Capitan Haya 42, E-28020 Madrid, Spain; *Yearbook of Tourism Statistics.*

MARSHALL ISLANDS - TRADEMARKS AND SERVICE MARKS - See MARSHALL ISLANDS - PATENTS, TRADEMARKS AND SERVICE MARKS

MARSHALL ISLANDS - TRANSPORTATION AND COMMUNICATIONS

Central Intelligence Agency, Washington, D.C. 20505 (703) 482-1100, www.cia.gov; *The World Factbook.*

Europa Publications Limited, 18 Bedford Square, London, WC1B 3JN, England; *The Europa World Year Book.*

St. Martin's Press, Inc., 175 Fifth Avenue, New York, New York 10010 (800) 221-7945; *The Statesman's Year-Book.*

MARSHALL ISLANDS - UNEMPLOYMENT RATE

Central Intelligence Agency, Washington, D.C. 20505 (703) 482-1100, www.cia.gov; *The World Factbook.*

MARSHALL ISLANDS - VITAL STATISTICS

Statistical Office of the United Nations, Publishing Service, New York, New York 10017 (800) 253-9646; *Statistical Yearbook.*

MARSHALL ISLANDS - WAGES

Statistical Office of the United Nations, Publishing Service, New York, New York 10017 (800) 253-9646; *Statistical Yearbook.*

MARSHALL ISLANDS - WHOLESALE PRICES

Statistical Office of the United Nations, Publishing Service, New York, New York 10017 (800) 253-9646; *Statistical Yearbook.*

MARSHALL ISLANDS - WHOLESALE TRADE

Statistical Office of the United Nations, Publishing Service, New York, New York 10017 (800) 253-9646; *Statistical Yearbook.*

MARTIAL ARTS

National Sporting Goods Association, 1601 Feehanville Drive, Suite 300, Mount Prospect, Illinois 60056 (847) 296-6742; *Sports Participation in 1998.*

Martinique - Primary Statistics Sources

Institut National de la Statistique et des Etudes Economiques, BP 863, 97175 Pointe-a-Pitre, France: *Annuaire statistique de la Martinique* (Statistical Yearbook of Martinique); *Bulletin Statistique* (Statistical bulletin); and *Tableaux Economiques Regionaux, Martinique.*

MARTINIQUE - AGRICULTURE

Euromonitor International, Inc., 122 South Michigan Avenue, Suite 1200, Chicago, Illinois 60603 (800) 577-EURO; *World Marketing Data and Statistics.*

Europa Publications Limited, 18 Bedford Square, London, WC1B 3JN, England; *The Europa World Year Book.*

Food and Agricultural Organization of the United Nations (FAO), Via delle Terme di Caracalla, 00100 Rome, Italy (Telephone Number in U.S. (202) 653-2400); *Production Yearbook;* and *The State of Food and Agriculture.*

St. Martin's Press, Inc., 175 Fifth Avenue, New York, New York 10010 (800) 221-7945; *The Statesman's Year-Book.*

Statistical Office of the United Nations, Publishing Service, New York, New York 10017 (800) 253-9646; *Statistical Yearbook.*

United Nations Conference on Trade and Development, Central Statistical Service, Palais des Nations, Geneva, Switzerland (Telephone in U.S. (800) 253-9646); *UNCTAD Commodity Yearbook.*

MARTINIQUE - AIRLINE SERVICE

Europa Publications Limited, 18 Bedford Square, London, WC1B 3JN, England; *The Europa World Year Book.*

St. Martin's Press, Inc., 175 Fifth Avenue, New York, New York 10010 (800) 221-7945; *The Statesman's Year-Book.*

MARTINIQUE - AIRPORTS

Central Intelligence Agency, Washington, D.C. 20505 (703) 482-1100, www.cia.gov; *The World Factbook.*

MARTINIQUE - AREA AND DENSITY OF POPULATION

Central Intelligence Agency, Washington, D.C. 20505 (703) 482-1100, www.cia.gov; *The World Factbook.*

Euromonitor International, Inc., 122 South Michigan Avenue, Suite 1200, Chicago, Illinois 60603 (800) 577-EURO; *The World Economic Factbook.*

Europa Publications Limited, 18 Bedford Square, London, WC1B 3JN, England; *The Europa World Year Book.*

Food and Agricultural Organization of the United Nations (FAO), Via delle Terme di Caracalla, 00100 Rome, Italy (Telephone Number in U.S. (202) 653-2400); *The State of Food and Agriculture.*

St. Martin's Press, Inc., 175 Fifth Avenue, New York, New York 10010 (800) 221-7945; *The Statesman's Year-Book.*

Statistical Office of the United Nations, Publishing Service, New York, New York 10017 (800) 253-9646; *Statistical Yearbook.*

MARTINIQUE - BANKING

Euromonitor International, Inc., 122 South Michigan Avenue, Suite 1200, Chicago, Illinois 60603 (800) 577-EURO; *World Marketing Data and Statistics.*

St. Martin's Press, Inc., 175 Fifth Avenue, New York, New York 10010 (800) 221-7945; *The Statesman's Year-Book.*

MARTINIQUE - BIRTH RATES

Central Intelligence Agency, Washington, D.C. 20505 (703) 482-1100, www.cia.gov; *The World Factbook.*

Euromonitor International, Inc., 122 South Michigan Avenue, Suite 1200, Chicago, Illinois 60603 (800) 577-EURO; *International Marketing Data and Statistics;* and *The World Economic Factbook.*

Europa Publications Limited, 18 Bedford Square, London, WC1B 3JN, England; *The Europa World Year Book.*

St. Martin's Press, Inc., 175 Fifth Avenue, New York, New York 10010 (800) 221-7945; *The Statesman's Year-Book.*

Statistical Office of the United Nations, Publishing Service, New York, New York

10017 (800) 253-9646; *Demographic Yearbook;* and *Statistical Yearbook.*

World Health Organization, Office of Publications, 20 Avenue Appia, CH-1211 Geneva 27, Switzerland (Telephone Number in U.S. (518) 436-9686); *World Health Statistics Annual.*

MARTINIQUE - BOOK PRODUCTION

United Nations Educational, Scientific and Cultural Organization (UNESCO), 7 Place de Fontenoy, F-75700 Paris, France (Telephone Number in U.S. (212) 963-5981); *Statistical Yearbook.*

MARTINIQUE - BROADCASTING

Billboard Limited, Post Office Box 9027, 1006 AA Amsterdam, The Netherlands (Telephone Number in U.S. (212) 764-7300); *World Radio TV Handbook.*

Central Intelligence Agency, Washington, D.C. 20505 (703) 482-1100, www.cia.gov; *The World Factbook.*

Euromonitor International, Inc., 122 South Michigan Avenue, Suite 1200, Chicago, Illinois 60603 (800) 577-EURO; *World Marketing Data and Statistics.*

St. Martin's Press, Inc., 175 Fifth Avenue, New York, New York 10010 (800) 221-7945; *The Statesman's Year-Book.*

MARTINIQUE - BUDGET

Central Intelligence Agency, Washington, D.C. 20505 (703) 482-1100, www.cia.gov; *The World Factbook.*

MARTINIQUE - CALORIE SUPPLY

Food and Agricultural Organization of the United Nations (FAO), Via delle Terme di Caracalla, 00100 Rome, Italy (Telephone Number in U.S. (202) 653-2400); *The State of Food and Agriculture.*

MARTINIQUE - CATTLE - See MARTINIQUE - LIVESTOCK AND POULTRY

MARTINIQUE - CHEMICAL (ORGANIC) PRODUCTION - See MARTINIQUE - MINING AND MINERAL PRODUCTS

MARTINIQUE - CLIMATE

St. Martin's Press, Inc., 175 Fifth Avenue, New York, New York 10010 (800) 221-7945; *The Statesman's Year-Book.*

MARTINIQUE - COAL PRODUCTION - See MARTINIQUE - MINING AND MINERAL PRODUCTS

MARTINIQUE - COCOA PRODUCTION

Statistical Office of the United Nations,

Publishing Service, New York, New York 10017 (800) 253-9646; *Statistical Yearbook.*

MARTINIQUE - COMMERCE

St. Martin's Press, Inc., 175 Fifth Avenue, New York, New York 10010 (800) 221-7945; *The Statesman's Year-Book.*

MARTINIQUE - CONSTRUCTION INDUSTRY

Statistical Office of the United Nations, Publishing Service, New York, New York 10017 (800) 253-9646; *Statistical Yearbook.*

MARTINIQUE - CONSUMER PRICE INDEX

Europa Publications Limited, 18 Bedford Square, London, WC1B 3JN, England; *The Europa World Year Book.*

Statistical Office of the United Nations, Publishing Service, New York, New York 10017 (800) 253-9646; *Statistical Yearbook.*

MARTINIQUE - CONSUMER PRICES

Euromonitor International, Inc., 122 South Michigan Avenue, Suite 1200, Chicago, Illinois 60603 (800) 577-EURO; *World Marketing Data and Statistics.*

International Labour Office, I.L.O. Publications, 1828 L Street, N.W., Suite 801, Washington, D.C. 20036 (301) 638-3152; *Yearbook of Labour Statistics.*

MARTINIQUE - CORN PRODUCTION - See MARTINIQUE - CROPS

MARTINIQUE - CROPS

Europa Publications Limited, 18 Bedford Square, London, WC1B 3JN, England; *The Europa World Year Book.*

Food and Agricultural Organization of the United Nations (FAO), Via delle Terme di Caracalla, 00100 Rome, Italy (Telephone Number in U.S. (202) 653-2400); *Production Yearbook;* and *The State of Food and Agriculture.*

St. Martin's Press, Inc., 175 Fifth Avenue, New York, New York 10010 (800) 221-7945; *The Statesman's Year-Book.*

United Nations Conference on Trade and Development, Central Statistical Service, Palais des Nations, Geneva, Switzerland (Telephone in U.S. (800) 253-9646); *UNCTAD Commodity Yearbook.*

MARTINIQUE - DAIRY PRODUCTS

Europa Publications Limited, 18 Bedford Square, London, WC1B 3JN, England; *The Europa World Year Book.*

Food and Agricultural Organization of the United Nations (FAO), Via delle Terme

di Caracalla, 00100 Rome, Italy (Telephone Number in U.S. (202) 653-2400); *The State of Food and Agriculture.*

St. Martin's Press, Inc., 175 Fifth Avenue, New York, New York 10010 (800) 221-7945; *The Statesman's Year-Book.*

MARTINIQUE - DEATH RATES - See MARTINIQUE - MORTALITY

MARTINIQUE - DEMOGRAPHY

Euromonitor International, Inc., 122 South Michigan Avenue, Suite 1200, Chicago, Illinois 60603 (800) 577-EURO; *International Marketing Data and Statistics; World Marketing Data and Statistics;* and *The World Economic Factbook.*

MARTINIQUE - DEVELOPMENT ASSISTANCE

Statistical Office of the United Nations, Publishing Service, New York, New York 10017 (800) 253-9646; *Statistical Yearbook.*

MARTINIQUE - DISEASE - See MARTINIQUE - HEALTH

MARTINIQUE - DIVORCE

Statistical Office of the United Nations, Publishing Service, New York, New York 10017 (800) 253-9646; *Demographic Yearbook;* and *Statistical Yearbook.*

MARTINIQUE - DUCKS - See MARTINIQUE - LIVESTOCK AND POULTRY

MARTINIQUE - ECONOMY

Central Intelligence Agency, Washington, D.C. 20505 (703) 482-1100, www.cia.gov; *The World Factbook.*

Euromonitor International, Inc., 122 South Michigan Avenue, Suite 1200, Chicago, Illinois 60603 (800) 577-EURO; *The World Economic Factbook;* and *World Marketing Data and Statistics.*

Europa Publications Limited, 18 Bedford Square, London, WC1B 3JN, England; *The Europa World Year Book.*

St. Martin's Press, Inc., 175 Fifth Avenue, New York, New York 10010 (800) 221-7945; *The Statesman's Year-Book.*

Statistical Office of the United Nations, Publishing Service, New York, New York 10017 (800) 253-9646; *World Statistics Pocketbook.*

The World Bank, 1818 H Street, NW, Washington, D.C. 20433 (202) 477-1234; *The World Bank Atlas.*

MARTINIQUE - EDUCATION

Euromonitor International, Inc., 122 South Michigan Avenue, Suite 1200, Chicago, Illinois 60603 (800) 577-EURO; *International Marketing Data and Statistics;* and *World Marketing Data and Statistics.*

Europa Publications Limited, 18 Bedford Square, London, WC1B 3JN, England; *The Europa World Year Book.*

St. Martin's Press, Inc., 175 Fifth Avenue, New York, New York 10010 (800) 221-7945; *The Statesman's Year-Book.*

MARTINIQUE - EGG PRODUCTION AND CONSUMPTION - See MARTINIQUE - DAIRY PRODUCTS

MARTINIQUE - ELECTRICITY

Central Intelligence Agency, Washington, D.C. 20505 (703) 482-1100, www.cia.gov; *The World Factbook.*

St. Martin's Press, Inc., 175 Fifth Avenue, New York, New York 10010 (800) 221-7945; *The Statesman's Year-Book.*

Statistical Office of the United Nations, Publishing Service, New York, New York 10017 (800) 253-9646; *Statistical Yearbook.*

MARTINIQUE - EMPLOYMENT

Euromonitor International, Inc., 122 South Michigan Avenue, Suite 1200, Chicago, Illinois 60603 (800) 577-EURO; *International Marketing Data and Statistics.*

International Labour Office, I.L.O. Publications, 1828 L Street, N.W., Suite 801, Washington, D.C. 20036 (301) 638-3152; *Yearbook of Labour Statistics.*

MARTINIQUE - ENERGY

Euromonitor International, Inc., 122 South Michigan Avenue, Suite 1200, Chicago, Illinois 60603 (800) 577-EURO; *International Marketing Data and Statistics; World Marketing Data and Statistics;* and *The World Economic Factbook.*

Food and Agricultural Organization of the United Nations (FAO), Via delle Terme di Caracalla, 00100 Rome, Italy (Telephone Number in U.S. (202) 653-2400); *The State of Food and Agriculture.*

St. Martin's Press, Inc., 175 Fifth Avenue, New York, New York 10010 (800) 221-7945; *The Statesman's Year-Book.*

Statistical Office of the United Nations, Publishing Service, New York, New York 10017 (800) 253-9646; *Energy Statistics Yearbook; World Statistics Pocketbook;* and *Statistical Yearbook.*

The World Bank, 1818 H Street, NW, Washington, D.C. 20433 (202) 477-1234;

The World Bank Atlas.

MARTINIQUE - ENVIRONMENT

Statistical Office of the United Nations, Publishing Service, New York, New York 10017 (800) 253-9646; *World Statistics Pocketbook.*

MARTINIQUE - EXCHANGE RATES

Central Intelligence Agency, Washington, D.C. 20505 (703) 482-1100, www.cia.gov; *The World Factbook.*

Euromonitor International, Inc., 122 South Michigan Avenue, Suite 1200, Chicago, Illinois 60603 (800) 577-EURO; *International Marketing Data and Statistics;* and *The World Economic Factbook.*

Europa Publications Limited, 18 Bedford Square, London, WC1B 3JN, England; *The Europa World Year Book.*

Statistical Office of the United Nations, Publishing Service, New York, New York 10017 (800) 253-9646; *World Statistics Pocketbook.*

MARTINIQUE - EXPORTS

Central Intelligence Agency, Washington, D.C. 20505 (703) 482-1100, www.cia.gov; *The World Factbook.*

Euromonitor International, Inc., 122 South Michigan Avenue, Suite 1200, Chicago, Illinois 60603 (800) 577-EURO; *International Marketing Data and Statistics;* and *The World Economic Factbook.*

Europa Publications Limited, 18 Bedford Square, London, WC1B 3JN, England; *The Europa World Year Book.*

Food and Agricultural Organization of the United Nations (FAO), Via delle Terme di Caracalla, 00100 Rome, Italy (Telephone Number in U.S. (202) 653-2400); *The State of Food and Agriculture.*

International Monetary Fund, 700 Nineteenth Street, NW, Washington, D.C. 20431 (202) 623-7000; *Direction of Trade Statistics.*

St. Martin's Press, Inc., 175 Fifth Avenue, New York, New York 10010 (800) 221-7945; *The Statesman's Year-Book.*

MARTINIQUE - EXTERNAL TRADE

Euromonitor International, Inc., 122 South Michigan Avenue, Suite 1200, Chicago, Illinois 60603 (800) 577-EURO; *World Marketing Data and Statistics.*

Food and Agricultural Organization of the United Nations (FAO), Via delle Terme di Caracalla, 00100 Rome, Italy (Telephone

Number in U.S. (202) 653-2400); *The State of Food and Agriculture;* and *Trade Yearbook.*

Statistical Office of the United Nations, Publishing Service, New York, New York 10017 (800) 253-9646; *Statistical Yearbook.*

MARTINIQUE - FARM CROPS - See MARTINIQUE - CROPS

MARTINIQUE - FERTILITY RATES

Central Intelligence Agency, Washington, D.C. 20505 (703) 482-1100, www.cia.gov; *The World Factbook.*

The World Bank, 1818 H Street, NW, Washington, D.C. 20433 (202) 477-1234; *The World Bank Atlas.*

MARTINIQUE - FERTILIZER

Food and Agricultural Organization of the United Nations (FAO), Via delle Terme di Caracalla, 00100 Rome, Italy (Telephone Number in U.S. (202) 653-2400); *Fertilizer Yearbook;* and *The State of Food and Agriculture.*

Statistical Office of the United Nations, Publishing Service, New York, New York 10017 (800) 253-9646; *Statistical Yearbook.*

MARTINIQUE - FETAL MORTALITY - See MARTINIQUE - MORTALITY

MARTINIQUE - FINANCE

Europa Publications Limited, 18 Bedford Square, London, WC1B 3JN, England; *The Europa World Year Book.*

MARTINIQUE - FISHERIES

Europa Publications Limited, 18 Bedford Square, London, WC1B 3JN, England; *The Europa World Year Book.*

Food and Agricultural Organization of the United Nations (FAO), Via delle Terme di Caracalla, 00100 Rome, Italy (Telephone Number in U.S. (202) 653-2400); *The State of Food and Agriculture;* and *Yearbook of Fishery Statistics.*

St. Martin's Press, Inc., 175 Fifth Avenue, New York, New York 10010 (800) 221-7945; *The Statesman's Year-Book.*

Statistical Office of the United Nations, Publishing Service, New York, New York 10017 (800) 253-9646; *Statistical Yearbook.*

United Nations Conference on Trade and Development, Central Statistical Service, Palais des Nations, Geneva, Switzerland (Telephone in U.S. (800) 253-9646); *UNCTAD Commodity Yearbook.*

MARTINIQUE - FOOD

Food and Agricultural Organization of the United Nations (FAO), Via delle Terme di Caracalla, 00100 Rome, Italy (Telephone Number in U.S. (202) 653-2400); *Production Yearbook;* and *The State of Food and Agriculture.*

United Nations Conference on Trade and Development, Central Statistical Service, Palais des Nations, Geneva, Switzerland (Telephone in U.S. (800) 253-9646); *UNCTAD Commodity Yearbook.*

MARTINIQUE - FOREIGN TRADE

Euromonitor International, Inc., 122 South Michigan Avenue, Suite 1200, Chicago, Illinois 60603 (800) 577-EURO; *The World Economic Factbook.*

Europa Publications Limited, 18 Bedford Square, London, WC1B 3JN, England; *The Europa World Year Book.*

Food and Agricultural Organization of the United Nations (FAO), Via delle Terme di Caracalla, 00100 Rome, Italy (Telephone Number in U.S. (202) 653-2400); *The State of Food and Agriculture.*

St. Martin's Press, Inc., 175 Fifth Avenue, New York, New York 10010 (800) 221-7945; *The Statesman's Year-Book.*

Statistical Office of the United Nations, Publishing Service, New York, New York 10017 (800) 253-9646; *International Trade Statistics Yearbook;* and *Statistical Yearbook.*

United Nations Conference on Trade and Development, Central Statistical Service, Palais des Nations, Geneva, Switzerland (Telephone in U.S. (800) 253-9646); *UNCTAD Commodity Yearbook.*

MARTINIQUE - FORESTRY AND FOREST PRODUCTS

Europa Publications Limited, 18 Bedford Square, London, WC1B 3JN, England; *The Europa World Year Book.*

Food and Agricultural Organization of the United Nations (FAO), Via delle Terme di Caracalla, 00100 Rome, Italy (Telephone Number in U.S. (202) 653-2400); *The State of Food and Agriculture;* and *Yearbook of Forest Products.*

St. Martin's Press, Inc., 175 Fifth Avenue, New York, New York 10010 (800) 221-7945; *The Statesman's Year-Book.*

Statistical Office of the United Nations, Publishing Service, New York, New York 10017 (800) 253-9646; *Statistical Yearbook.*

United Nations Conference on Trade and Development, Central Statistical Service, Palais des Nations, Geneva,

Switzerland (Telephone in U.S. (800) 253-9646); *UNCTAD Commodity Yearbook.*

United Nations Educational, Scientific and Cultural Organization (UNESCO), 7 Place de Fontenoy, F-75700 Paris, France (Telephone Number in U.S. (212) 963-5981); *Statistical Yearbook.*

MARTINIQUE - GENERAL MORTALITY - See MARTINIQUE - MORTALITY

MARTINIQUE - GOVERNMENT

Central Intelligence Agency, Washington, D.C. 20505 (703) 482-1100, www.cia.gov; *The World Factbook.*

Europa Publications Limited, 18 Bedford Square, London, WC1B 3JN, England; *The Europa World Year Book.*

St. Martin's Press, Inc., 175 Fifth Avenue, New York, New York 10010 (800) 221-7945; *The Statesman's Year-Book.*

Statistical Office of the United Nations, Publishing Service, New York, New York 10017 (800) 253-9646; *National Accounts Statistics.*

MARTINIQUE - GRAIN PRODUCTION - See MARTINIQUE - CROPS

MARTINIQUE - GROSS DOMESTIC PRODUCT

Euromonitor International, Inc., 122 South Michigan Avenue, Suite 1200, Chicago, Illinois 60603 (800) 577-EURO; *International Marketing Data and Statistics;* and *The World Economic Factbook.*

Europa Publications Limited, 18 Bedford Square, London, WC1B 3JN, England; *The Europa World Year Book.*

Statistical Office of the United Nations, Publishing Service, New York, New York 10017 (800) 253-9646; *National Accounts Statistics;* and *Statistical Yearbook.*

MARTINIQUE - GROSS NATIONAL PRODUCT

The World Bank, 1818 H Street, NW, Washington, D.C. 20433 (202) 477-1234; *The World Bank Atlas.*

MARTINIQUE - HEALTH

Euromonitor International, Inc., 122 South Michigan Avenue, Suite 1200, Chicago, Illinois 60603 (800) 577-EURO; *World Marketing Data and Statistics.*

St. Martin's Press, Inc., 175 Fifth Avenue, New York, New York 10010 (800) 221-7945; *The Statesman's Year-Book.*

Statistical Office of the United Nations,

Publishing Service, New York, New York 10017 (800) 253-9646; *Statistical Yearbook.*

World Health Organization, Office of Publications, 20 Avenue Appia, CH-1211 Geneva 27, Switzerland (Telephone Number in U.S. (518) 436-9686); *World Health Statistics Annual.*

MARTINIQUE - HIDE PRODUCTION

Food and Agricultural Organization of the United Nations (FAO), Via delle Terme di Caracalla, 00100 Rome, Italy (Telephone Number in U.S. (202) 653-2400); *Production Yearbook.*

MARTINIQUE - HIGHWAYS

Central Intelligence Agency, Washington, D.C. 20505 (703) 482-1100, www.cia.gov; *The World Factbook.*

St. Martin's Press, Inc., 175 Fifth Avenue, New York, New York 10010 (800) 221-7945; *The Statesman's Year-Book.*

MARTINIQUE - HORSES - See MARTINIQUE - LIVESTOCK AND POULTRY

MARTINIQUE - HOURS OF WORK - See MARTINIQUE - EMPLOYMENT

MARTINIQUE - HOUSING AND HOUSING UNITS

Euromonitor International, Inc., 122 South Michigan Avenue, Suite 1200, Chicago, Illinois 60603 (800) 577-EURO; *World Marketing Data and Statistics.*

MARTINIQUE - ILLITERATE POPULATION

Central Intelligence Agency, Washington, D.C. 20505 (703) 482-1100, www.cia.gov; *The World Factbook.*

Euromonitor International, Inc., 122 South Michigan Avenue, Suite 1200, Chicago, Illinois 60603 (800) 577-EURO; *The World Economic Factbook.*

United Nations Educational, Scientific and Cultural Organization (UNESCO), 7 Place de Fontenoy, F-75700 Paris, France (Telephone Number in U.S. (212) 963-5981); *Statistical Yearbook.*

MARTINIQUE - IMPORTS

Central Intelligence Agency, Washington, D.C. 20505 (703) 482-1100, www.cia.gov; *The World Factbook.*

Euromonitor International, Inc., 122 South Michigan Avenue, Suite 1200, Chicago, Illinois 60603 (800) 577-EURO; *International Marketing Data and Statistics;* and *The World Economic Factbook.*

Europa Publications Limited, 18 Bedford Square, London, WC1B 3JN, England; *The Europa World Year Book.*

Food and Agricultural Organization of the United Nations (FAO), Via delle Terme di Caracalla, 00100 Rome, Italy (Telephone Number in U.S. (202) 653-2400); *The State of Food and Agriculture.*

International Monetary Fund, 700 Nineteenth Street, NW, Washington, D.C. 20431 (202) 623-7000; *Direction of Trade Statistics.*

St. Martin's Press, Inc., 175 Fifth Avenue, New York, New York 10010 (800) 221-7945; *The Statesman's Year-Book.*

MARTINIQUE - INDUSTRY

Central Intelligence Agency, Washington, D.C. 20505 (703) 482-1100, www.cia.gov; *The World Factbook.*

Euromonitor International, Inc., 122 South Michigan Avenue, Suite 1200, Chicago, Illinois 60603 (800) 577-EURO; *The World Economic Factbook;* and *World Marketing Data and Statistics.*

Europa Publications Limited, 18 Bedford Square, London, WC1B 3JN, England; *The Europa World Year Book.*

International Labour Office, I.L.O. Publications, 1828 L Street, N.W., Suite 801, Washington, D.C. 20036 (301) 638-3152; *Yearbook of Labour Statistics.*

St. Martin's Press, Inc., 175 Fifth Avenue, New York, New York 10010 (800) 221-7945; *The Statesman's Year-Book.*

MARTINIQUE - INFANT AND MATERNAL MORTALITY - See MARTINIQUE - MORTALITY

MARTINIQUE - LABOR

Central Intelligence Agency, Washington, D.C. 20505 (703) 482-1100, www.cia.gov; *The World Factbook.*

Euromonitor International, Inc., 122 South Michigan Avenue, Suite 1200, Chicago, Illinois 60603 (800) 577-EURO; *International Marketing Data and Statistics;* and *World Marketing Data and Statistics.*

Europa Publications Limited, 18 Bedford Square, London, WC1B 3JN, England; *The Europa World Year Book.*

Food and Agricultural Organization of the United Nations (FAO), Via delle Terme di Caracalla, 00100 Rome, Italy (Telephone Number in U.S. (202) 653-2400); *The State of Food and Agriculture.*

International Labour Office,

I.L.O. Publications, 1828 L Street, N.W., Suite 801, Washington, D.C. 20036 (301) 638-3152; *Yearbook of Labour Statistics.*

St. Martin's Press, Inc., 175 Fifth Avenue, New York, New York 10010 (800) 221-7945; *The Statesman's Year-Book.*

The World Bank, 1818 H Street, NW, Washington, D.C. 20433 (202) 477-1234; *The World Bank Atlas.*

MARTINIQUE - LAND USE

Central Intelligence Agency, Washington, D.C. 20505 (703) 482-1100, www.cia.gov; *The World Factbook.*

Euromonitor International, Inc., 122 South Michigan Avenue, Suite 1200, Chicago, Illinois 60603 (800) 577-EURO; *International Marketing Data and Statistics.*

Food and Agricultural Organization of the United Nations (FAO), Via delle Terme di Caracalla, 00100 Rome, Italy (Telephone Number in U.S. (202) 653-2400); *Production Yearbook.*

MARTINIQUE - LIFE EXPECTANCY

Central Intelligence Agency, Washington, D.C. 20505 (703) 482-1100, www.cia.gov; *The World Factbook.*

Euromonitor International, Inc., 122 South Michigan Avenue, Suite 1200, Chicago, Illinois 60603 (800) 577-EURO; *The World Economic Factbook.*

Statistical Office of the United Nations, Publishing Service, New York, New York 10017 (800) 253-9646; *World Statistics Pocketbook.*

The World Bank, 1818 H Street, NW, Washington, D.C. 20433 (202) 477-1234; *The World Bank Atlas.*

MARTINIQUE - LITERACY RATE

Euromonitor International, Inc., 122 South Michigan Avenue, Suite 1200, Chicago, Illinois 60603 (800) 577-EURO; *World Marketing Data and Statistics.*

MARTINIQUE - LIVESTOCK AND POULTRY

Europa Publications Limited, 18 Bedford Square, London, WC1B 3JN, England; *The Europa World Year Book.*

Food and Agricultural Organization of the United Nations (FAO), Via delle Terme di Caracalla, 00100 Rome, Italy (Telephone Number in U.S. (202) 653-2400); *Production Yearbook;* and *The State of Food and Agriculture.*

St. Martin's Press, Inc., 175 Fifth Avenue, New York, New York 10010 (800)

221-7945; *The Statesman's Year-Book.*

Statistical Office of the United Nations, Publishing Service, New York, New York 10017 (800) 253-9646; *Statistical Yearbook.*

United Nations Conference on Trade and Development, Central Statistical Service, Palais des Nations, Geneva, Switzerland (Telephone in U.S. (800) 253-9646); *UNCTAD Commodity Yearbook.*

MARTINIQUE - MARRIAGE RATES

Europa Publications Limited, 18 Bedford Square, London, WC1B 3JN, England; *The Europa World Year Book.*

Statistical Office of the United Nations, Publishing Service, New York, New York 10017 (800) 253-9646; *Demographic Yearbook;* and *Statistical Yearbook.*

MARTINIQUE - MEAT PRODUCTION - See MARTINIQUE - LIVESTOCK AND POULTRY

MARTINIQUE - MERCHANT SHIPPING

Europa Publications Limited, 18 Bedford Square, London, WC1B 3JN, England; *The Europa World Year Book.*

St. Martin's Press, Inc., 175 Fifth Avenue, New York, New York 10010 (800) 221-7945; *The Statesman's Year-Book.*

Statistical Office of the United Nations, Publishing Service, New York, New York 10017 (800) 253-9646; *Statistical Yearbook.*

MARTINIQUE - MILITARY

Central Intelligence Agency, Washington, D.C. 20505 (703) 482-1100, www.cia.gov; *The World Factbook.*

Euromonitor International, Inc., 122 South Michigan Avenue, Suite 1200, Chicago, Illinois 60603 (800) 577-EURO; *World Marketing Data and Statistics.*

MARTINIQUE - MINING AND MINERALS

St. Martin's Press, Inc., 175 Fifth Avenue, New York, New York 10010 (800) 221-7945; *The Statesman's Year-Book.*

Statistical Office of the United Nations, Publishing Service, New York, New York 10017 (800) 253-9646; *Energy Statistics Yearbook; Industrial Commodity Statistics Yearbook;* and *Statistical Yearbook.*

United Nations Conference on Trade and Development, Central Statistical Service, Palais des Nations, Geneva, Switzerland (Telephone in U.S. (800) 253-9646); *UNCTAD Commodity Yearbook.*

MARTINIQUE - MONEY SUPPLY

Europa Publications Limited, 18 Bedford Square, London, WC1B 3JN, England; *The Europa World Year Book.*

MARTINIQUE - MORTALITY

Central Intelligence Agency, Washington, D.C. 20505 (703) 482-1100, www.cia.gov; *The World Factbook.*

Euromonitor International, Inc., 122 South Michigan Avenue, Suite 1200, Chicago, Illinois 60603 (800) 577-EURO; *International Marketing Data and Statistics;* and *The World Economic Factbook.*

Europa Publications Limited, 18 Bedford Square, London, WC1B 3JN, England; *The Europa World Year Book.*

St. Martin's Press, Inc., 175 Fifth Avenue, New York, New York 10010 (800) 221-7945; *The Statesman's Year-Book.*

Statistical Office of the United Nations, Publishing Service, New York, New York 10017 (800) 253-9646; *Demographic Yearbook; World Statistics Pocketbook;* and *Statistical Yearbook.*

The World Bank, 1818 H Street, NW, Washington, D.C. 20433 (202) 477-1234; *The World Bank Atlas.*

World Health Organization, Office of Publications, 20 Avenue Appia, CH-1211 Geneva 27, Switzerland (Telephone Number in U.S. (518) 436-9686); *World Health Statistics Annual.*

MARTINIQUE - MOTOR VEHICLES IN USE

Europa Publications Limited, 18 Bedford Square, London, WC1B 3JN, England; *The Europa World Year Book.*

Statistical Office of the United Nations, Publishing Service, New York, New York 10017 (800) 253-9646; *Statistical Yearbook.*

MARTINIQUE - NATALITY - See MARTINIQUE - BIRTH RATES

MARTINIQUE - NATIONAL ACCOUNTS

Statistical Office of the United Nations, Publishing Service, New York, New York 10017 (800) 253-9646; *Statistical Yearbook;* and *National Account Statistics.*

MARTINIQUE - NATIONAL INCOME

Statistical Office of the United Nations, Publishing Service, New York, New York 10017 (800) 253-9646; *National Accounts Statistics;* and *Statistical Yearbook.*

MARTINIQUE - NEWSPAPER PRODUCTION - See MARTINIQUE - FORESTRY AND FOREST PRODUCTS

MARTINIQUE - NEWSPRINT - See MARTINIQUE - FORESTRY AND FOREST PRODUCTS

MARTINIQUE - OCCUPATIONS - See MARTINIQUE - LABOR

MARTINIQUE - PAPER CONSUMPTION - See MARTINIQUE - FORESTRY AND FOREST PRODUCTS

MARTINIQUE - PERIODICALS

United Nations Educational, Scientific and Cultural Organization (UNESCO), 7 Place de Fontenoy, F-75700 Paris, France (Telephone Number in U.S. (212) 963-5981); *Statistical Yearbook.*

MARTINIQUE - PESTICIDE USE

Food and Agricultural Organization of the United Nations (FAO), Via delle Terme di Caracalla, 00100 Rome, Italy (Telephone Number in U.S. (202) 653-2400); *The State of Food and Agriculture.*

MARTINIQUE - PETROLEUM INDUSTRY

Food and Agricultural Organization of the United Nations (FAO), Via delle Terme di Caracalla, 00100 Rome, Italy (Telephone Number in U.S. (202) 653-2400); *The State of Food and Agriculture.*

St. Martin's Press, Inc., 175 Fifth Avenue, New York, New York 10010 (800) 221-7945; *The Statesman's Year-Book.*

Statistical Office of the United Nations, Publishing Service, New York, New York 10017 (800) 253-9646; *Statistical Yearbook.*

United Nations Conference on Trade and Development, Central Statistical Service, Palais des Nations, Geneva, Switzerland (Telephone in U.S. (800) 253-9646); *UNCTAD Commodity Yearbook.*

MARTINIQUE - PIGS - SEE MARTINIQUE - LIVESTOCK AND POULTRY

MARTINIQUE - POPULATION

Central Intelligence Agency, Washington, D.C. 20505 (703) 482-1100, www.cia.gov; *The World Factbook.*

Euromonitor International, Inc., 122 South Michigan Avenue, Suite 1200, Chicago, Illinois 60603 (800) 577-EURO; *International Marketing Data and Statistics;* and *The World Economic Factbook.*

Europa Publications Limited, 18 Bedford Square, London, WC1B 3JN, England; *The Europa World Year Book.*

Food and Agricultural Organization of the United Nations (FAO), Via delle Terme di Caracalla, 00100 Rome, Italy (Telephone

Number in U.S. (202) 653-2400); *Production Yearbook.*

International Labour Office, I.L.O. Publications, 1828 L Street, N.W., Suite 801, Washington, D.C. 20036 (301) 638-3152; *Yearbook of Labour Statistics.*

St. Martin's Press, Inc., 175 Fifth Avenue, New York, New York 10010 (800) 221-7945; *The Statesman's Year-Book.*

Statistical Office of the United Nations, Publishing Service, New York, New York 10017 (800) 253-9646; *Demographic Yearbook; World Statistics Pocketbook;* and *Statistical Yearbook.*

The World Bank, 1818 H Street, NW, Washington, D.C. 20433 (202) 477-1234; *The World Bank Atlas.*

World Health Organization, Office of Publications, 20 Avenue Appia, CH-1211 Geneva 27, Switzerland (Telephone Number in U.S. (518) 436-9686); *World Health Statistics Annual.*

MARTINIQUE - POST OFFICES

St. Martin's Press, Inc., 175 Fifth Avenue, New York, New York 10010 (800) 221-7945; *The Statesman's Year-Book.*

MARTINIQUE - PRICES

Food and Agricultural Organization of the United Nations (FAO), Via delle Terme di Caracalla, 00100 Rome, Italy (Telephone Number in U.S. (202) 653-2400); *Production Yearbook;* and *The State of Food and Agriculture.*

International Labour Office, I.L.O. Publications, 1828 L Street, N.W., Suite 801, Washington, D.C. 20036 (301) 638-3152; *Yearbook of Labour Statistics.*

MARTINIQUE - PRINTING AND WRITING PAPER - See MARTINIQUE FORESTRY AND FOREST PRODUCTS

MARTINIQUE - RADIO RECEIVERS

St. Martin's Press, Inc., 175 Fifth Avenue, New York, New York 10010 (800) 221-7945; *The Statesman's Year-Book.*

MARTINIQUE - RELIGION

Central Intelligence Agency, Washington, D.C. 20505 (703) 482-1100, www.cia.gov; *The World Factbook.*

St. Martin's Press, Inc., 175 Fifth Avenue, New York, New York 10010 (800) 221-7945; *The Statesman's Year-Book.*

MARTINIQUE - RENT PRICES

International Labour Office,

I.L.O. Publications, 1828 L Street, N.W., Suite 801, Washington, D.C. 20036 (301) 638-3152; *Yearbook of Labour Statistics.*

MARTINIQUE - RETAIL TRADE

Euromonitor International, Inc., 122 South Michigan Avenue, Suite 1200, Chicago, Illinois 60603 (800) 577-EURO; *World Marketing Data and Statistics.*

MARTINIQUE - ROOT AND TUBER PRODUCTION - See MARTINIQUE - CROPS

MARTINIQUE - ROUNDWOOD PRODUCTION - See MARTINIQUE - FORESTRY AND FOREST PRODUCTS

MARTINIQUE - SALT PRODUCTION - See MARTINIQUE - MINING AND MINERAL PRODUCTS

MARTINIQUE - SAWNWOOD PRODUCTION - See MARTINIQUE - FORESTRY AND FOREST PRODUCTS

MARTINIQUE - SHEEP - See MARTINIQUE - LIVESTOCK AND POULTRY

MARTINIQUE - SOCIAL DATA

Statistical Office of the United Nations, Publishing Service, New York, New York 10017 (800) 253-9646; *World Statistics Pocketbook.*

MARTINIQUE - SOCIAL SECURITY

Statistical Office of the United Nations, Publishing Service, New York, New York 10017 (800) 253-9646; *National Accounts Statistics.*

MARTINIQUE - STOCKS - COMMODITY - MARKET PRICE - INDEX

Food and Agricultural Organization of the United Nations (FAO), Via delle Terme di Caracalla, 00100 Rome, Italy (Telephone Number in U.S. (202) 653-2400); *The State of Food and Agriculture.*

MARTINIQUE - SUGAR PRODUCTION AND CONSUMPTION - See MARTINIQUE - CROPS

MARTINIQUE - TELEPHONES IN USE

American Telephone and Telegraph Company, 26 Parsippany Road, Whippany, New Jersey 07981 (800) 222-0300; *The World's Telephones.*

Central Intelligence Agency, Washington, D.C. 20505 (703) 482-1100, www.cia.gov; *The World Factbook.*

Europa Publications Limited, 18 Bedford Square, London, WC1B 3JN, England; *The Europa World Year Book.*

St. Martin's Press, Inc., 175 Fifth Avenue,

New York, New York 10010 (800) 221-7945; *The Statesman's Year-Book.*

Statistical Office of the United Nations, Publishing Service, New York, New York 10017 (800) 253-9646; *Statistical Yearbook;* and *World Statistics Pocketbook.*

MARTINIQUE - TEXTILE INDUSTRY

United Nations Conference on Trade and Development, Central Statistical Service, Palais des Nations, Geneva, Switzerland (Telephone in U.S. (800) 253-9646); *UNCTAD Commodity Yearbook.*

MARTINIQUE - TOURISM

Euromonitor International, Inc., 122 South Michigan Avenue, Suite 1200, Chicago, Illinois 60603 (800) 577-EURO; *The World Economic Factbook;* and *World Marketing Data and Statistics.*

Europa Publications Limited, 18 Bedford Square, London, WC1B 3JN, England; *The Europa World Year Book.*

St. Martin's Press, Inc., 175 Fifth Avenue, New York, New York 10010 (800) 221-7945; *The Statesman's Year-Book.*

World Tourism Organization, Calle Capitan Haya 42, E-28020 Madrid, Spain; *Yearbook of Tourism Statistics.*

MARTINIQUE - TRACTORS IN USE

Statistical Office of the United Nations, Publishing Service, New York, New York 10017 (800) 253-9646; *Statistical Yearbook.*

MARTINIQUE - TRADE - See MARTINIQUE - FOREIGN TRADE

MARTINIQUE - TRANSPORTATION AND COMMUNICATIONS

Central Intelligence Agency, Washington, D.C. 20505 (703) 482-1100, www.cia.gov; *The World Factbook.*

Euromonitor International, Inc., 122 South Michigan Avenue, Suite 1200, Chicago, Illinois 60603 (800) 577-EURO; *International Marketing Data and Statistics;* and *World Marketing Data and Statistics.*

Europa Publications Limited, 18 Bedford Square, London, WC1B 3JN, England; *The Europa World Year Book.*

St. Martin's Press, Inc., 175 Fifth Avenue, New York, New York 10010 (800) 221-7945; *The Statesman's Year-Book.*

MARTINIQUE - TURKEYS - See MARTINIQUE - LIVESTOCK AND POULTRY

MARTINIQUE - UNEMPLOYMENT

Central Intelligence Agency, Washington, D.C. 20505 (703) 482-1100, www.cia.gov; *The World Factbook.*

International Labour Office, I.L.O. Publications, 1828 L Street, N.W., Suite 801, Washington, D.C. 20036 (301) 638-3152; *Yearbook of Labour Statistics.*

St. Martin's Press, Inc., 175 Fifth Avenue, New York, New York 10010 (800) 221-7945; *The Statesman's Year-Book.*

MARTINIQUE - VITAL STATISTICS

St. Martin's Press, Inc., 175 Fifth Avenue, New York, New York 10010 (800) 221-7945; *The Statesman's Year-Book.*

Statistical Office of the United Nations, Publishing Service, New York, New York 10017 (800) 253-9646; *Statistical Yearbook.*

World Health Organization, Office of Publications, 20 Avenue Appia, CH-1211 Geneva 27, Switzerland (Telephone Number in U.S. (518) 436-9686); *World Health Statistics Annual.*

MARTINIQUE - WAGES

International Labour Office, I.L.O. Publications, 1828 L Street, N.W., Suite 801, Washington, D.C. 20036 (301) 638-3152; *Yearbook of Labour Statistics.*

MARYLAND - See also STATE DATA (FOR INDIVIDUAL STATES)

Maryland - Primary Statistics Source

Department of Economic and Employment Development, 217 East Redwood Street, Baltimore, Maryland 21202 (410) 333-6953; *Maryland Statistical Abstract.*

Maryland - State Data Centers

Maryland Department of State Planning, 301 West Preston Street, Baltimore, Maryland 21201, Ms. Jane Traynham (410) 225-4450.

Enoch Pratt Free Library, State Library Resource Center, 400 Cathedral Street, Baltimore, Maryland 21201, Mr. Jeff Korman (410) 396-1789.

Maryland Small Business Development Center, 7100 Baltimore Avenue, Suite 401, Baltimore, Maryland 20740, Ms. Lora Brown (301) 403-8300.

McKeldin Library, Government Documents, Governments Document Section, University of Maryland, College

Park, Maryland 20742, Ms. Marianne Ryan (301) 405-9169.

MASSACHUSETTS - See also STATE DATA (FOR INDIVIDUAL STATES)

Massachusetts - Primary Statistics Source

Massachusetts Institute for Social and Economic Research, 128 Thompson Hall, University of Massachusetts, Amherst, Massachusetts 01003 (413) 545-3460; *Projected Total Population and Age Distribution for 2000 and 2005: Massachusetts Cities and Towns.*

Massachusetts - State Data Centers

Massachusetts Institute for Social and Economic Research, University of Massachusetts, 128 Thompson Hall, Amherst, Massachusetts 01003, Mr. Stephen Coelen, Ph.D., Director (413) 545-3460, John Gaviglio (413) 545-3460..

Massachusetts Institute for Social and Economic Research, Post Office Box 219, The State House, Boston, Massachusetts 02133-0219, Mr. William Murray (617) 727-4537.

Cape Cod Community Library, Library/Learning Resource Center, 2240 Iyanough Road, West Barnstable, Massachusetts 02668, Ms. Jean Marie Fraser (508) 362-2131.

University of Massachusetts, Documents Library, 100 Morrissey Boulevard, Boston, Massachusetts 02125, Ms. Frances Schlisinger (617) 287-5935.

MATERNAL AND CHILD HEALTH SERVICES - EXPENDITURES FOR

Social Security Administration, 6400 Security Boulevard, Baltimore, Maryland 21235 (800) 772-1213, www.ssa.gov; *Social Security Bulletin;* and unpublished data.

U.S. Department of Health and Human Services, Health Care Financing Administration, 200 Independence Avenue, SW, Washington, D.C. 20201 (202) 690-6145, www.hcfa.gov; *Health Care Financing Review.*

MATERNITY LEAVE

U.S. Department of Health and Human Services, National Center for Health Statistics, 3700 East-West Highway, Hyattsville, MD 20782 (301) 436-8500, www.cdc.gov/nchs; *Fertility, Family Planning, and Women's Health: New Data from the 1995 National Survey of Family Growth, Vital and Health Statistics.*

MATHEMATICS - DEGREES CONFERRED

National Science Foundation, 4201 Wilson Boulevard, Arlington, Virginia 22230 (703) 366-1234, www.nsf.gov; *Survey of Earned Doctorates, Selected Data on Science and Engineering Doctorate Awards;* and *National Survey of Recent College Graduates.*

U.S. Department of Commerce, Bureau of the Census, Washington, D.C. 20233 9301) 457-4100, www.census.gov; unpublished data.

U.S. Department of Education, National Center for Education Statistics; 555 New Jersey Avenue, NW, Washington, D.C. 20208-5574 (202) 219-1828, http://nces.ed.gov; *Digest of Education Statistics.*

MATHEMATICS - EMPLOYMENT

U.S. Department of Labor, Bureau of Labor Statistics, Two Massachusetts Avenue, NE, Washington, D.C. 20212 (202) 691-5200, www.stats.bls.gov; *Monthly Labor Review*; and unpublished data.

MATHEMATICS - SALARY OFFERS

National Association of Colleges and Employers, 62 Highland Avenue, Bethlehem, Pennsylvania 18017 (800) 544-5272; *Salary Survey: A Study of Beginning Offers.*

Mauritania - National Statistical Office

Direction de la Statistique et des Etudes Economiques (Department of Statistics and Economic Research), BP 240, Nouakchott, Mauritania.

Mauritania - Primary Statistics Sources

Direction de la Statistique, BP 240, Nouakchott, Mauritania; *Annuaire Statistique* (Statistical Yearbook); and *Bulletin Mensuel Statistique* (Monthly bulletin of statistics).

MAURITANIA - AGRICULTURE

Economist Intelligence Unit, 111 West 57th Street, New York, New York 10019 (800) 938-4685; *Mauritania Country Report.*

Euromonitor International, Inc., 122 South Michigan Avenue, Suite 1200, Chicago, Illinois 60603 (800) 577-EURO; *International Marketing Data and Statistics;* and *World Marketing Data and Statistics.*

Europa Publications Limited, 18 Bedford Square, London, WC1B 3JN, England; *The Europa World Year Book.*

Federal Statistical Office, Gustav-Stresemann - Ring 11, D-6200, Wiesbaden, Germany; *Mauretanien.*

Food and Agricultural Organization of the United Nations (FAO), Via delle Terme di Caracalla, 00100 Rome, Italy (Telephone Number in U.S. (202) 653-2400); *Production Yearbook; The State of Food and Agriculture;* and *Trade Yearbook.*

M.E. Sharpe, 80 Business Park Drive, Armonk, New York 10504 (800) 541-6563; *The Illustrated Book of World Rankings.*

St. Martin's Press, Inc., 175 Fifth Avenue, New York, New York 10010 (800) 221-7945; *The Statesman's Year-Book.*

Statistical Office of the United Nations, Publishing Service, New York, New York 10017 (800) 253-9646; *Survey of Economic and Social Conditions in Africa.*

United Nations Conference on Trade and Development, Central Statistical Service, Palais des Nations, Geneva, Switzerland (Telephone in U.S. (800) 253-9646); *UNCTAD Commodity Yearbook.*

United Nations Economic Commission for Africa, Africa Hall, Post Office Box 3001, Addis Ababa, Ethiopia (Telephone Number in U.S. (800) 253-9646); *African Statistical Yearbook.*

The World Bank, 1818 H Street, NW, Washington, D.C. 20433 (202) 477-1234; *World Development Indicators.*

MAURITANIA - AIRLINE SERVICE

Europa Publications Limited, 18 Bedford Square, London, WC1B 3JN, England; *The Europa World Year Book.*

International Civil Aviation Organization, 999 University Street, Montreal, Quebec, Canada H3C 5H7 (514) 954-8219; *Civil Aviation Statistics of the World.*

M.E. Sharpe, 80 Business Park Drive, Armonk, New York 10504 (800) 541-6563; *The Illustrated Book of World Rankings.*

St. Martin's Press, Inc., 175 Fifth Avenue, New York, New York 10010 (800) 221-7945; *The Statesman's Year-Book.*

Statistical Office of the United Nations, Publishing Service, New York, New York 10017 (800) 253-9646; *Statistical Yearbook.*

United Nations Economic Commission for Africa, Africa Hall, Post Office Box 3001, Addis Ababa, Ethiopia (Telephone Number in U.S. (800) 253-9646); *African Statistical Yearbook.*

MAURITANIA - AIRPORTS

Central Intelligence Agency, Washington, D.C. 20505 (703) 482-1100, www.cia.gov; *The World Factbook.*

MAURITANIA - ALUMINUM PRODUCTION AND CONSUMPTION - See MAURITANIA - MINING AND MINERAL PRODUCTS

MAURITANIA - ANIMAL HEALTH

Food and Agricultural Organization of the United Nations (FAO), Via delle Terme di Caracalla, 00100 Rome, Italy (Telephone Number in U.S. (202) 653-2400); *Animal Health Yearbook.*

MAURITANIA - AREA AND DENSITY OF POPULATION

African Development Bank, 01 BP 1387, Abidjan 01, Cote d'Ivoire; *Selected Statistics on Regional Member Countries.*

Central Intelligence Agency, Washington, D.C. 20505 (703) 482-1100, www.cia.gov; *The World Factbook.*

Euromonitor International, Inc., 122 South Michigan Avenue, Suite 1200, Chicago, Illinois 60603 (800) 577-EURO; *International Marketing Data and Statistics;* and *The World Economic Factbook.*

Europa Publications Limited, 18 Bedford Square, London, WC1B 3JN, England; *The Europa World Year Book.*

Federal Statistical Office, Gustav-Stresemann - Ring 11, D-6200, Wiesbaden, Germany; *Mauretanien.*

Food and Agricultural Organization of the United Nations (FAO), Via delle Terme di Caracalla, 00100 Rome, Italy (Telephone Number in U.S. (202) 653-2400); *The State of Food and Agriculture.*

M.E. Sharpe, 80 Business Park Drive, Armonk, New York 10504 (800) 541-6563; *The Illustrated Book of World Rankings.*

St. Martin's Press, Inc., 175 Fifth Avenue, New York, New York 10010 (800) 221-7945; *The Statesman's Year-Book.*

Statistical Office of the United National, Publishing Service, New York, New York 10017 (800) 253-9646; *Survey of Economic and Social Conditions in Africa.*

The World Bank, 1818 H Street, NW, Washington, D.C. 20433 (202) 477-1234; *World Development Report.*

MAURITANIA - ARMS EXPORTS AND IMPORTS - See MAURITANIA - MILITARY

MAURITANIA - BALANCE OF PAYMENTS

African Development Bank, 01 BP 1387, Abidjan 01, Cote d'Ivoire; *Selected Statistics on Regional Member Countries.*

The Economist Intelligence Unit, 111 West 57th Street, New York, New York 10019 (800) 938-4685; *The World Market Atlas.*

Europa Publications Limited, 18 Bedford Square, London, WC1B 3JN, England; *The Europa World Year Book.*

Federal Statistical Office, Gustav-Stresemann - Ring 11, D-6200, Wiesbaden, Germany; *Mauretanien.*

International Monetary Fund, 700 Nineteenth Street, NW, Washington, D.C. 20431 (202) 623-7000; *Balance of Payments Yearbook.*

United Nations Conference on Trade and Development (UNCTAD), New York, New York 10017 (800) 253-9646, *Handbook of International Trade and Development Statistics.*

United Nations Economic Commission for Africa, Africa Hall, Post Office Box 3001, Addis Ababa, Ethiopia (Telephone Number in U.S. (800) 253-9646); *African Statistical Yearbook.*

The World Bank, 1818 H Street, NW, Washington, D.C. 20433 (202) 477-1234; *World Development Report;* and *World Development Indicators.*

MAURITANIA - BANKING

Euromonitor International, Inc., 122 South Michigan Avenue, Suite 1200, Chicago, Illinois 60603 (800) 577-EURO; *World Marketing Data and Statistics.*

Europa Publications Limited, 18 Bedford Square, London, WC1B 3JN, England; *The Europa World Year Book.*

International Monetary Fund, 700 Nineteenth Street, NW, Washington, D.C. 20431 (202) 623-7000; *International Financial Statistics.*

M.E. Sharpe, 80 Business Park Drive, Armonk, New York 10504 (800) 541-6563; *The Illustrated Book of World Rankings.*

St. Martin's Press, Inc., 175 Fifth Avenue, New York, New York 10010 (800) 221-7945; *The Statesman's Year-Book.*

Statistical Office of the United Nations, Publishing Service, New York, New York 10017 (800) 253-9646; *Statistical Yearbook.*

United Nations Economic Commission for Africa, Africa Hall, Post Office Box 3001,

Addis Ababa, Ethiopia (Telephone Number in U.S. (800) 253-9646); *African Statistical Yearbook.*

MAURITANIA - BARLEY PRODUCTION - See MAURITANIA - CROPS

MAURITANIA - BEER PRODUCTION - See MAURITANIA - BEVERAGES

MAURITANIA - BEVERAGES

M.E. Sharpe, 80 Business Park Drive, Armonk, New York 10504 (800) 541-6563; *The Illustrated Book of World Rankings.*

MAURITANIA - BIRTH RATES

Central Intelligence Agency, Washington, D.C. 20505 (703) 482-1100, www.cia.gov; *The World Factbook.*

Euromonitor International, Inc., 122 South Michigan Avenue, Suite 1200, Chicago, Illinois 60603 (800) 577-EURO; *International Marketing Data and Statistics;* and *The World Economic Factbook.*

Europa Publications Limited, 18 Bedford Square, London, WC1B 3JN, England; *The Europa World Year Book.*

M.E. Sharpe, 80 Business Park Drive, Armonk, New York 10504 (800) 541-6563; *The Illustrated Book of World Rankings.*

St. Martin's Press, Inc., 175 Fifth Avenue, New York, New York 10010 (800) 221-7945; *The Statesman's Year-Book.*

Statistical Office of the United Nations, Publishing Service, New York, New York 10017 (800) 253-9646; *Demographic Yearbook; Statistical Yearbook;* and *Survey of Economic and Social Conditions in Africa.*

The World Bank, 1818 H Street, NW, Washington, D.C. 20433 (202) 477-1234; *World Development Indicators.*

MAURITANIA - BOOK PRODUCTION

United Nations Educational, Scientific and Cultural Organization (UNESCO), 7 Place de Fontenoy, F-75700 Paris, France (Telephone Number in U.S. (212) 963-5981); *Statistical Yearbook.*

MAURITANIA - BROADCASTING

Billboard Limited, Post Office Box 9027, 1006 AA Amsterdam, The Netherlands (Telephone Number in U.S. (212) 764-7300); *World Radio TV Handbook.*

Central Intelligence Agency, Washington, D.C. 20505 (703) 482-1100, www.cia.gov; *The World Factbook.*

Euromonitor International, Inc., 122 South Michigan Avenue, Suite 1200, Chicago, Illinois 60603 (800) 577-EURO; *World Marketing Data and Statistics.*

M.E. Sharpe, 80 Business Park Drive, Armonk, New York 10504 (800) 541-6563; *The Illustrated Book of World Rankings.*

St. Martin's Press, Inc., 175 Fifth Avenue, New York, New York 10010 (800) 221-7945; *The Statesman's Year-Book.*

MAURITANIA - BUDGET

Central Intelligence Agency, Washington, D.C. 20505 (703) 482-1100, www.cia.gov; *The World Factbook.*

MAURITANIA - BUSINESS AND PROFESSIONAL LICENSES

International Monetary Fund, 700 Nineteenth Street, NW, Washington, D.C. 20431 (202) 623-7000; *Government Finance Statistics Yearbook.*

MAURITANIA - CALORIE SUPPLY

African Development Bank, 01 BP 1387, Abidjan 01, Cote d'Ivoire; *Selected Statistics on Regional Member Countries.*

Food and Agricultural Organization of the United Nations (FAO), Via delle Terme di Caracalla, 00100 Rome, Italy (Telephone Number in U.S. (202) 653-2400); *The State of Food and Agriculture.*

MAURITANIA - CAPITAL REVENUE

International Monetary Fund, 700 Nineteenth Street, NW, Washington, D.C. 20431 (202) 623-7000; *Government Finance Statistics Yearbook.*

MAURITANIA - CATTLE - See MAURITANIA - LIVESTOCK AND POULTRY

MAURITANIA - CEMENT PRODUCTION - See MAURITANIA - MINING AND MINERAL PRODUCTS

MAURITANIA - CHEESE PRODUCTION AND CONSUMPTION - See MAURITANIA - DAIRY PRODUCTS

MAURITANIA - CHEMICAL (ORGANIC) PRODUCTION - See MAURITANIA - MINING AND MINERAL PRODUCTS

MAURITANIA - CHICKENS - See MAURITANIA - LIVESTOCK AND POULTRY

MAURITANIA - CIGARETTE PRODUCTION - See MAURITANIA - TOBACCO PRODUCTION

MAURITANIA - CLIMATE

M.E. Sharpe, 80 Business Park Drive,

Armonk, New York 10504 (800) 541-6563; *The Illustrated Book of World Rankings.*

St. Martin's Press, Inc., 175 Fifth Avenue, New York, New York 10010 (800) 221-7945; *The Statesman's Year-Book.*

MAURITANIA - COAL PRODUCTION - See MAURITANIA - MINING AND MINERAL PRODUCTS

MAURITANIA - COFFEE PRODUCTION AND CONSUMPTION - See MAURITANIA - CROPS

MAURITANIA - COMMERCE

St. Martin's Press, Inc., 175 Fifth Avenue, New York, New York 10010 (800) 221-7945; *The Statesman's Year-Book.*

MAURITANIA - COMMUNICATIONS - See MAURITANIA - TRANSPORTATION AND COMMUNICATIONS

MAURITANIA - CONSTRUCTION INDUSTRY

M.E. Sharpe, 80 Business Park Drive, Armonk, New York 10504 (800) 541-6563; *The Illustrated Book of World Rankings.*

United Nations Economic Commission for Africa, Africa Hall, Post Office Box 3001, Addis Ababa, Ethiopia (Telephone Number in U.S. (800) 253-9646); *African Statistical Yearbook.*

MAURITANIA - CONSUMER PRICE INDEX

African Development Bank, 01 BP 1387, Abidjan 01, Cote d'Ivoire; *Selected Statistics on Regional Member Countries.*

Europa Publications Limited, 18 Bedford Square, London, WC1B 3JN, England; *The Europa World Year Book.*

Statistical Office of the United Nations, Publishing Service, New York, New York 10017 (800) 253-9646; *Statistical Yearbook;* and *Survey of Economic and Social Conditions in Africa.*
United Nations Economic Commission for Africa, Africa Hall, Post Office Box 3001, Addis Ababa, Ethiopia (Telephone Number in U.S. (800) 253-9646); *African Statistical Yearbook.*

MAURITANIA - CONSUMER PRICES

Euromonitor International, Inc., 122 South Michigan Avenue, Suite 1200, Chicago, Illinois 60603 (800) 577-EURO; *World Marketing Data and Statistics.*

International Labour Office, I.L.O. Publications, 1828 L Street, N.W., Suite 801, Washington, D.C. 20036 (301) 638-3152; *Yearbook of Labour Statistics.*

International Monetary Fund, 700 Nineteenth Street, NW, Washington, D.C. 20431 (202) 623-7000; *International Financial Statistics.*

MAURITANIA - CONSUMPTION

African Development Bank, 01 BP 1387, Abidjan 01, Cote d'Ivoire; *Selected Statistics on Regional Member Countries.*

Statistical Office of the United Nations, Publishing Service, New York, New York 10017 (800) 253-9646; *Survey of Economic and Social Conditions in Africa.*

The World Bank, 1818 H Street, NW, Washington, D.C. 20433 (202) 477-1234; *World Development Report.*

MAURITANIA - COPPER AND COPPER ORE PRODUCTION AND CONSUMPTION - See MAURITANIA - MINING AND MINERAL PRODUCTS

MAURITANIA - CORN PRODUCTION - See MAURITANIA - CROPS

MAURITANIA - CORPORATE TAXES - See MAURITANIA - TAXATION

MAURITANIA - COTTON - See MAURITANIA - CROPS

MAURITANIA - CRIME

Yale University Press, Yale Station, New Haven, Connecticut 06520 (800) 987-7323; *Violence and Crime in Cross-National Perspective.*

MAURITANIA - CROPS

Europa Publications Limited, 18 Bedford Square, London, WC1B 3JN, England; *The Europa World Year Book.*

Food and Agricultural Organization of the United Nations (FAO), Via delle Terme di Caracalla, 00100 Rome, Italy (Telephone Number in U.S. (202) 653-2400); *Production Yearbook;* and *The State of Food and Agriculture.*

M.E. Sharpe, 80 Business Park Drive, Armonk, New York 10504 (800) 541-6563; *The Illustrated Book of World Rankings.*

St. Martin's Press, Inc., 175 Fifth Avenue, New York, New York 10010 (800) 221-7945; *The Statesman's Year-Book.*

Statistical Office of the United Nations, Publishing Service, New York, New York 10017 (800) 253-9646; *Statistical Yearbook.*

United Nations Conference on Trade and Development, Central Statistical Service, Palais des Nations, Geneva, Switzerland (Telephone in U.S. (800) 253-9646); *UNCTAD Commodity Yearbook.*

United Nations Economic Commission for Africa, Africa Hall, Post Office Box 3001, Addis Ababa, Ethiopia (Telephone Number in U.S. (800) 253-9646); *African Statistical Yearbook*.

MAURITANIA - DAIRY PRODUCTS

Europa Publications Limited, 18 Bedford Square, London, WC1B 3JN, England; *The Europa World Year Book*.

Food and Agricultural Organization of the United Nations (FAO), Via delle Terme di Caracalla, 00100 Rome, Italy (Telephone Number in U.S. (202) 653-2400); *Production Yearbook;* and *The State of Food and Agriculture*.

M.E. Sharpe, 80 Business Park Drive, Armonk, New York 10504 (800) 541-6563; *The Illustrated Book of World Rankings*.

Statistical Office of the United Nations, Publishing Service, New York, New York 10017 (800) 253-9646; *Statistical Yearbook*.

MAURITANIA - DEATH RATES - See MAURITANIA - MORTALITY

MAURITANIA - DEFENSE EXPENDITURES

International Monetary Fund, 700 Nineteenth Street, NW, Washington, D.C. 20431 (202) 623-7000; *Government Finance Statistics Yearbook*.

U.S. Arms Control and Disarmament Agency, 320 Twenty-first Street, NW, Washington, D.C. 20451 (202) 647-8677; *World Military Expenditures and Arms Transfers*.

MAURITANIA - DEMOGRAPHY

Euromonitor International, Inc., 122 South Michigan Avenue, Suite 1200, Chicago, Illinois 60603 (800) 577-EURO; *International Marketing Data and Statistics; World Marketing Data and Statistics;* and *The World Economic Factbook*.

Federal Statistical Office, Gustav-Stresemann - Ring 11, D-6200, Wiesbaden, Germany; *Mauretanien*.

M.E. Sharpe, 80 Business Park Drive, Armonk, New York 10504 (800) 541-6563; *The Illustrated Book of World Rankings*.

Statistical Office of the United Nations, Publishing Service, New York, New York 10017 (800) 253-9646; *Human Development Report;* and *Survey of Economic and Social Conditions in Africa*.

MAURITANIA - DEVELOPMENT ASSISTANCE

Statistical Office of the United Nations, Publishing Service, New York, New York

10017 (800) 253-9646; *Statistical Yearbook*.

MAURITANIA - DIAMOND PRODUCTION - See MAURITANIA - MINING AND MINERAL PRODUCTS

MAURITANIA - DISCOUNT RATES - See MAURITANIA - BANKING

MAURITANIA - DIVORCE

M.E. Sharpe, 80 Business Park Drive, Armonk, New York 10504 (800) 541-6563; *The Illustrated Book of World Rankings*.

Statistical Office of the United Nations, Publishing Service, New York, New York 10017 (800) 253-9646; *Demographic Yearbook*.

MAURITANIA - ECONOMY

African Development Bank, 01 BP 1387, Abidjan 01, Cote d'Ivoire; *Selected Statistics on Regional Member Countries*.

Central Intelligence Agency, Washington, D.C. 20505 (703) 482-1100, www.cia.gov; *The World Factbook*.

Economist Intelligence Unit, 111 West 57th Street, New York, New York 10019 (800) 938-4685; *Mauritania Country Report*.

Euromonitor International, Inc., 122 South Michigan Avenue, Suite 1200, Chicago, Illinois 60603 (800) 577-EURO; *International Marketing Data and Statistics; World Marketing Data and Statistics;* and *The World Economic Factbook*.

Europa Publications Limited, 18 Bedford Square, London, WC1B 3JN, England; *The Europa World Year Book*.

Federal Statistical Office, Gustav-Stresemann - Ring 11, D-6200, Wiesbaden, Germany; *Mauretanien*.

M.E. Sharpe, 80 Business Park Drive, Armonk, New York 10504 (800) 541-6563; *The Illustrated Book of World Rankings*.

St. Martin's Press, Inc., 175 Fifth Avenue, New York, New York 10010 (800) 221-7945; *The Statesman's Year-Book*.

Statistical Office of the United Nations, Publishing Service, New York, New York 10017 (800) 253-9646; *Foreign Trade Statistics for Africa;* and *World Statistics Pocketbook*

The World Bank, 1818 H Street, NW, Washington, D.C. 20433 (202) 477-1234; *The World Bank Atlas;* and *World Development Report*.

MAURITANIA - EDUCATION

African Development Bank, 01 BP 1387,

Abidjan 01, Cote d'Ivoire; *Selected Statistics on Regional Member Countries*.

The Economist Intelligence Unit, 111 West 57th Street, New York, New York 10019 (800) 938-4685; *The World Market Atlas*.

Euromonitor International, Inc., 122 South Michigan Avenue, Suite 1200, Chicago, Illinois 60603 (800) 577-EURO; *International Marketing Data and Statistics;* and *World Marketing Data and Statistics*.

Europa Publications Limited, 18 Bedford Square, London, WC1B 3JN, England; *The Europa World Year Book*.

Federal Statistical Office, Gustav-Stresemann - Ring 11, D-6200, Wiesbaden, Germany; *Mauretanien*.

International Monetary Fund, 700 Nineteenth Street, NW, Washington, D.C. 20431 (202) 623-7000; *Government Finance Statistics Yearbook*.

M.E. Sharpe, 80 Business Park Drive, Armonk, New York 10504 (800) 541-6563; *The Illustrated Book of World Rankings*.

St. Martin's Press, Inc., 175 Fifth Avenue, New York, New York 10010 (800) 221-7945; *The Statesman's Year-Book*.

Statistical Office of the United Nations, Publishing Service, New York, New York 10017 (800) 253-9646; *Human Development Report;* and *Survey of Economic and Social Conditions in Africa*.

United Nations Economic Commission for Africa, Africa Hall, Post Office Box 3001, Addis Ababa, Ethiopia (Telephone Number in U.S. (800) 253-9646); *African Statistical Yearbook*.

United Nations Educational, Scientific and Cultural Organization (UNESCO), 7 Place de Fontenoy, F-75700 Paris, France (Telephone Number in U.S. (212) 963-5981); *Statistical Yearbook*.

The World Bank, 1818 H Street, NW, Washington, D.C. 20433 (202) 477-1234; *World Development Report;* and *World Development Indicators*.

MAURITANIA - EGG PRODUCTION AND CONSUMPTION - See MAURITANIA - DAIRY PRODUCTS

MAURITANIA - ELECTRICITY

Central Intelligence Agency, Washington, D.C. 20505 (703) 482-1100, www.cia.gov; *The World Factbook*.

M.E. Sharpe, 80 Business Park Drive, Armonk, New York 10504 (800) 541-6563; *The Illustrated Book of World Rankings*.

St. Martin's Press, Inc., 175 Fifth Avenue, New York, New York 10010 (800) 221-7945; *The Statesman's Year-Book.*

Statistical Office of the United Nations, Publishing Service, New York, New York 10017 (800) 253-9646; *Human Development Report; Statistical Yearbook; and Survey of Economic and Social Conditions in Africa.*

United Nations Economic Commission for Africa, Africa Hall, Post Office Box 3001, Addis Ababa, Ethiopia (Telephone Number in U.S. (800) 253-9646); *African Statistical Yearbook.*

MAURITANIA - EMPLOYMENT

Euromonitor International, Inc., 122 South Michigan Avenue, Suite 1200, Chicago, Illinois 60603 (800) 577-EURO; *International Marketing Data and Statistics.*

Federal Statistical Office, Gustav-Stresemann - Ring 11, D-6200, Wiesbaden, Germany; *Mauretanien.*

International Labour Office, I.L.O. Publications, 1828 L Street, N.W., Suite 801, Washington, D.C. 20036 (301) 638-3152; *Yearbook of Labour Statistics.*

M.E. Sharpe, 80 Business Park Drive, Armonk, New York 10504 (800) 541-6563; *The Illustrated Book of World Rankings.*

Statistical Office of the United Nations, Publishing Service, New York, New York 10017 (800) 253-9646; *Bulletin of Industrial Statistics for the Arab Countries; and Survey of Economic and Social Conditions in Africa.*

United Nations Economic Commission for Africa, Africa Hall, Post Office Box 3001, Addis Ababa, Ethiopia (Telephone Number in U.S. (800) 253-9646); *African Statistical Yearbook.*

MAURITANIA - ENERGY

Euromonitor International, Inc., 122 South Michigan Avenue, Suite 1200, Chicago, Illinois 60603 (800) 577-EURO; *International Marketing Data and Statistics; World Marketing Data and Statistics; and The World Economic Factbook.*

Food and Agricultural Organization of the United Nations (FAO), Via delle Terme di Caracalla, 00100 Rome, Italy (Telephone Number in U.S. (202) 653-2400); *The State of Food and Agriculture.*

M.E. Sharpe, 80 Business Park Drive, Armonk, New York 10504 (800) 541-6563; *The Illustrated Book of World Rankings.*

St. Martin's Press, Inc., 175 Fifth Avenue, New York, New York 10010 (800) 221-7945; *The Statesman's Year-Book.*

Statistical Office of the United Nations, Publishing Service, New York, New York 10017 (800) 253-9646; *Energy Statistics Yearbook; Human Development Report; World Statistics Pocketbook; and Statistical Yearbook.*

United Nations Economic Commission for Africa, Africa Hall, Post Office Box 3001, Addis Ababa, Ethiopia (Telephone Number in U.S. (800) 253-9646); *African Statistical Yearbook.*

The World Bank, 1818 H Street, NW, Washington, D.C. 20433 (202) 477-1234; *The World Bank Atlas; and World Development Report.*

MAURITANIA - ENVIRONMENT

Economist Intelligence Unit, 111 West 57th Street, New York, New York 10019 (800) 938-4685; *Mauritania Country Report.*

Statistical Office of the United Nations, Publishing Service, New York, New York 10017 (800) 253-9646; *World Statistics Pocketbook.*

MAURITANIA - EXCHANGE RATES

African Development Bank, 01 BP 1387, Abidjan 01, Cote d'Ivoire; *Selected Statistics on Regional Member Countries.*

Central Intelligence Agency, Washington, D.C. 20505 (703) 482-1100, www.cia.gov; *The World Factbook.*

Euromonitor International, Inc., 122 South Michigan Avenue, Suite 1200, Chicago, Illinois 60603 (800) 577-EURO; *International Marketing Data and Statistics; and The World Economic Factbook.*

Europa Publications Limited, 18 Bedford Square, London, WC1B 3JN, England; *The Europa World Year Book.*

International Civil Aviation Organization, 999 University Street, Montreal, Quebec, Canada H3C 5H7 (514) 954-8219; *Civil Aviation Statistics of the World.*

International Monetary Fund, 700 Nineteenth Street, NW, Washington, D.C. 20431 (202) 623-7000; *International Financial Statistics.*

Statistical Office of the United Nations, Publishing Service, New York, New York 10017 (800) 253-9646; *Bulletin of Industrial Statistics for the Arab Countries; Foreign Trade Statistics for Africa; World Statistics Pocketbook; and Statistical Yearbook.*

MAURITANIA - EXCISE TAXES - See MAURITANIA - TAXATION

MAURITANIA - EXPORTS

African Development Bank, 01 BP 1387, Abidjan 01, Cote d'Ivoire; *Selected Statistics on Regional Member Countries.*

Central Intelligence Agency, Washington, D.C. 20505 (703) 482-1100, www.cia.gov; *The World Factbook.*

The Economist Intelligence Unit, 111 West 57th Street, New York, New York 10019 (800) 938-4685; *Mauritania Country Report; and The World Market Atlas.*

Euromonitor International, Inc., 122 South Michigan Avenue, Suite 1200, Chicago, Illinois 60603 (800) 577-EURO; *International Marketing Data and Statistics; and The World Economic Factbook.*

Europa Publications Limited, 18 Bedford Square, London, WC1B 3JN, England; *The Europa World Year Book.*

Food and Agricultural Organization of the United Nations (FAO), Via delle Terme di Caracalla, 00100 Rome, Italy (Telephone Number in U.S. (202) 653-2400); *The State of Food and Agriculture.*

International Monetary Fund, 700 Nineteenth Street, NW, Washington, D.C. 20431 (202) 623-7000; *Direction of Trade Statistics; Government Finance Statistics Yearbook; and International Financial Statistics.*

St. Martin's Press, Inc., 175 Fifth Avenue, New York, New York 10010 (800) 221-7945; *The Statesman's Year-Book.*

Statistical Office of the United Nations, Publishing Service, New York, New York 10017 (800) 253-9646; *Bulletin of Industrial Statistics for the Arab Countries; Foreign Trade Statistics for Africa; and Survey of Economic and Social Conditions in Africa.*

United Nations Conference on Trade and Development (UNCTAD), New York, New York 10017 (800) 253-9646, *Handbook of International Trade and Development Statistics.*

United Nations Economic Commission for Africa, Africa Hall, Post Office Box 3001, Addis Ababa, Ethiopia (Telephone Number in U.S. (800) 253-9646); *African Statistical Yearbook.*

The World Bank, 1818 H Street, NW, Washington, D.C. 20433 (202) 477-1234; *World Development Report; and World Development Indicators.*

MAURITANIA - EXTERNAL INDEBTEDNESS

African Development Bank, 01 BP 1387, Abidjan 01, Cote d'Ivoire; *Selected Statistics on Regional Member Countries.*

Statistical Office of the United Nations, Publishing Service, New York, New York 10017 (800) 253-9646; *Survey of Economic and Social Conditions in Africa.*

The World Bank, 1818 H Street, NW, Washington, D.C. 20433 (202) 477-1234; *World Development Report;* and *World Development Indicators.*

MAURITANIA - EXTERNAL TRADE

African Development Bank, 01 BP 1387, Abidjan 01, Cote d'Ivoire; *Selected Statistics on Regional Member Countries.*

Euromonitor International, Inc., 122 South Michigan Avenue, Suite 1200, Chicago, Illinois 60603 (800) 577-EURO; *World Marketing Data and Statistics.*

Food and Agricultural Organization of the United Nations (FAO), Via delle Terme di Caracalla, 00100 Rome, Italy (Telephone Number in U.S. (202) 653-2400); *The State of Food and Agriculture;* and *Trade Yearbook.*

Statistical Office of the United Nations, Publishing Service, New York, New York 10017 (800) 253-9646; *Statistical Yearbook.*

MAURITANIA - FARM CROPS - See MAURITANIA - CROPS

MAURITANIA - FEMALE WORKING POPULATION - See MAURITANIA - EMPLOYMENT

MAURITANIA - FERTILITY RATES

Central Intelligence Agency, Washington, D.C. 20505 (703) 482-1100, www.cia.gov; *The World Factbook.*

M.E. Sharpe, 80 Business Park Drive, Armonk, New York 10504 (800) 541-6563; *The Illustrated Book of World Rankings.*

Statistical Office of the United Nations, Publishing Service, New York, New York 10017 (800) 253-9646; *Human Development Report;* and *Survey of Economic and Social Conditions in Africa.*

The World Bank, 1818 H Street, NW, Washington, D.C. 20433 (202) 477-1234; *The World Bank Atlas; World Development Report;* and *World Development Indicators.*

MAURITANIA - FERTILIZER

Food and Agricultural Organization of the United Nations (FAO), Via delle Terme di Caracalla, 00100 Rome, Italy (Telephone Number in U.S. (202) 653-2400); *Fertilizer Yearbook;* and *The State of Food and Agriculture.*

Statistical Office of the United Nations, Publishing Service, New York, New York 10017 (800) 253-9646; *Statistical Yearbook.*

MAURITANIA - FETAL MORTALITY - See MAURITANIA - MORTALITY

MAURITANIA - FINANCE

African Development Bank, 01 BP 1387, Abidjan 01, Cote d'Ivoire; *Selected Statistics on Regional Member Countries.*

Economist Intelligence Unit, 111 West 57th Street, New York, New York 10019 (800) 938-4685; *Mauritania Country Report.*

Europa Publications Limited, 18 Bedford Square, London, WC1B 3JN, England; *The Europa World Year Book.*

Federal Statistical Office, Gustav-Stresemann - Ring 11, D-6200, Wiesbaden, Germany; *Mauretanien.*

International Monetary Fund, 700 Nineteenth Street, NW, Washington, D.C. 20431 (202) 623-7000; *Government Finance Statistics Yearbook;* and *International Financial Statistics.*

M.E. Sharpe, 80 Business Park Drive, Armonk, New York 10504 (800) 541-6563; *The Illustrated Book of World Rankings.*

St. Martin's Press, Inc., 175 Fifth Avenue, New York, New York 10010 (800) 221-7945; *The Statesman's Year-Book.*

Statistical Office of the United Nations, Publishing Service, New York, New York 10017 (800) 253-9646; *Statistical Yearbook;* and *Survey of Economic and Social Conditions in Africa.*

United Nations Economic Commission for Africa, Africa Hall, Post Office Box 3001, Addis Ababa, Ethiopia (Telephone Number in U.S. (800) 253-9646); *African Statistical Yearbook.*

MAURITANIA - FISHERIES

Europa Publications Limited, 18 Bedford Square, London, WC1B 3JN, England; *The Europa World Year Book.*

Federal Statistical Office, Gustav-Stresemann - Ring 11, D-6200, Wiesbaden, Germany; *Mauretanien.*

Food and Agricultural Organization of the United Nations (FAO), Via delle Terme di Caracalla, 00100 Rome, Italy (Telephone Number in U.S. (202) 653-2400); *The State of Food and Agriculture;* and *Yearbook of Fishery Statistics.*

International Monetary Fund, 700 Nineteenth Street, NW, Washington, D.C. 20431 (202) 623-7000; *International*

Financial Statistics.

M.E. Sharpe, 80 Business Park Drive, Armonk, New York 10504 (800) 541-6563; *The Illustrated Book of World Rankings.*

St. Martin's Press, Inc., 175 Fifth Avenue, New York, New York 10010 (800) 221-7945; *The Statesman's Year-Book.*

United Nations Conference on Trade and Development, Central Statistical Service, Palais des Nations, Geneva, Switzerland (Telephone in U.S. (800) 253-9646); *UNCTAD Commodity Yearbook.*

United Nations Economic Commission for Africa, Africa Hall, Post Office Box 3001, Addis Ababa, Ethiopia (Telephone Number in U.S. (800) 253-9646); *African Statistical Yearbook.*

MAURITANIA - FOOD

African Development Bank, 01 BP 1387, Abidjan 01, Cote d'Ivoire; *Selected Statistics on Regional Member Countries.*

Food and Agricultural Organization of the United Nations (FAO), Via delle Terme di Caracalla, 00100 Rome, Italy (Telephone Number in U.S. (202) 653-2400); *Production Yearbook;* and *The State of Food and Agriculture.*

Statistical Office of the United Nations, Publishing Service, New York, New York 10017 (800) 253-9646; *Human Development Report.*

United Nations Conference on Trade and Development, Central Statistical Service, Palais des Nations, Geneva, Switzerland (Telephone in U.S. (800) 253-9646); *UNCTAD Commodity Yearbook.*

MAURITANIA - FOREIGN DEBT

International Monetary Fund, 700 Nineteenth Street, NW, Washington, D.C. 20431 (202) 623-7000; *Government Finance Statistics Yearbook.*

MAURITANIA - FOREIGN TRADE

Economist Intelligence Unit, 111 West 57th Street, New York, New York 10019 (800) 938-4685; *Mauritania Country Report.*

Euromonitor International, Inc., 122 South Michigan Avenue, Suite 1200, Chicago, Illinois 60603 (800) 577-EURO; *International Marketing Data and Statistics;* and *The World Economic Factbook.*

Europa Publications Limited, 18 Bedford Square, London, WC1B 3JN, England; *The Europa World Year Book.*

Federal Statistical Office, Gustav-Stresemann - Ring 11, D-6200, Wiesbaden,

Germany; *Mauretanien*.

Food and Agricultural Organization of the United Nations (FAO), Via delle Terme di Caracalla, 00100 Rome, Italy (Telephone Number in U.S. (202) 653-2400); *The State of Food and Agriculture*.

M.E. Sharpe, 80 Business Park Drive, Armonk, New York 10504 (800) 541-6563; *The Illustrated Book of World Rankings*.

St. Martin's Press, Inc., 175 Fifth Avenue, New York, New York 10010 (800) 221-7945; *The Statesman's Year-Book*.

Statistical Office of the United Nations, Publishing Service, New York, New York 10017 (800) 253-9646; *Bulletin of Industrial Statistics for the Arab Countries; Foreign Trade Statistics for Africa; International Trade Statistics Yearbook;* and *Statistical Yearbook*.

United Nations Economic Commission for Africa, Africa Hall, Post Office Box 3001, Addis Ababa, Ethiopia (Telephone Number in U.S. (800) 253-9646); *African Statistical Yearbook*.

The World Bank, 1818 H Street, NW, Washington, D.C. 20433 (202) 477-1234; *World Development Report;* and *World Development Indicators*.

MAURITANIA - FORESTRY AND FOREST PRODUCTS

Europa Publications Limited, 18 Bedford Square, London, WC1B 3JN, England; *The Europa World Year Book*.

Federal Statistical Office, Gustav-Stresemann - Ring 11, D-6200, Wiesbaden, Germany; *Mauretanien*.

Food and Agricultural Organization of the United Nations (FAO), Via delle Terme di Caracalla, 00100 Rome, Italy (Telephone Number in U.S. (202) 653-2400); *The State of Food and Agriculture;* and *Yearbook of Forest Products*.

M.E. Sharpe, 80 Business Park Drive, Armonk, New York 10504 (800) 541-6563; *The Illustrated Book of World Rankings*.

St. Martin's Press, Inc., 175 Fifth Avenue, New York, New York 10010 (800) 221-7945; *The Statesman's Year-Book*.

Statistical Office of the United Nations, Publishing Service, New York, New York 10017 (800) 253-9646; *Statistical Yearbook*.

United Nations Conference on Trade and Development, Central Statistical Service, Palais des Nations, Geneva, Switzerland (Telephone in U.S. (800) 253-9646); *UNCTAD Commodity Yearbook*.

United Nations Economic Commission for Africa, Africa Hall, Post Office Box 3001, Addis Ababa, Ethiopia (Telephone Number in U.S. (800) 253-9646); *African Statistical Yearbook*.

The World Bank, 1818 H Street, NW, Washington, D.C. 20433 (202) 477-1234; *World Development Report*.

MAURITANIA - GAS PRODUCTION - See MAURITANIA - MINING AND MINERAL PRODUCTS

MAURITANIA - GENERAL MORTALITY - See MAURITANIA - MORTALITY

MAURITANIA - GEOGRAPHIC DATA

M.E. Sharpe, 80 Business Park Drive, Armonk, New York 10504 (800) 541-6563; *The Illustrated Book of World Rankings*.

MAURITANIA - GOATS - See MAURITANIA - LIVESTOCK AND POULTRY

MAURITANIA - GOLD HOLDINGS

International Monetary Fund, 700 Nineteenth Street, NW, Washington, D.C. 20431 (202) 623-7000; *International Financial Statistics*.

Statistical Office of the United Nations, Publishing Service, New York, New York 10017 (800) 253-9646; *Statistical Yearbook*.

The World Bank, 1818 H Street, NW, Washington, D.C. 20433 (202) 477-1234; *World Development Indicators*.

MAURITANIA - GOLD PRODUCTION AND CONSUMPTION - See MAURITANIA - MINING AND MINERAL PRODUCTS

MAURITANIA - GOVERNMENT

Central Intelligence Agency, Washington, D.C. 20505 (703) 482-1100, www.cia.gov; *The World Factbook*.

Europa Publications Limited, 18 Bedford Square, London, WC1B 3JN, England; *The Europa World Year Book*.

International Monetary Fund, 700 Nineteenth Street, NW, Washington, D.C. 20431 (202) 623-7000; *Government Finance Statistics Yearbook*.

St. Martin's Press, Inc., 175 Fifth Avenue, New York, New York 10010 (800) 221-7945; *The Statesman's Year-Book*.

Statistical Office of the United Nations, Publishing Service, New York, New York 10017 (800) 253-9646; *National Accounts Statistics;* and *Survey of Economic and Social Conditions in Africa*.

The World Bank, 1818 H Street, NW,

Washington, D.C. 20433 (202) 477-1234; *World Development Report;* and *World Development Indicators*.

MAURITANIA - GRAIN PRODUCTION - See MAURITANIA - CROPS

MAURITANIA - GRANTS

International Monetary Fund, 700 Nineteenth Street, NW, Washington, D.C. 20431 (202) 623-7000; *Government Finance Statistics Yearbook*.

MAURITANIA - GROSS DOMESTIC PRODUCT

African Development Bank, 01 BP 1387, Abidjan 01, Cote d'Ivoire; *Selected Statistics on Regional Member Countries*.

The Economist Intelligence Unit, 111 West 57th Street, New York, New York 10019 (800) 938-4685; *Mauritania Country Report;* and *The World Market Atlas*.

Euromonitor International, Inc., 122 South Michigan Avenue, Suite 1200, Chicago, Illinois 60603 (800) 577-EURO; *International Marketing Data and Statistics;* and *The World Economic Factbook*.

Europa Publications Limited, 18 Bedford Square, London, WC1B 3JN, England; *The Europa World Year Book*.

M.E. Sharpe, 80 Business Park Drive, Armonk, New York 10504 (800) 541-6563; *The Illustrated Book of World Rankings*.

Statistical Office of the United Nations, Publishing Service, New York, New York 10017 (800) 253-9646; *Bulletin of Industrial Statistics for the Arab Countries; Human Development Report; National Accounts Statistics; Statistical Yearbook;* and *Survey of Economic and Social Conditions in Africa*.

United Nations Economic Commission for Africa, Africa Hall, Post Office Box 3001, Addis Ababa, Ethiopia (Telephone Number in U.S. (800) 253-9646); *African Statistical Yearbook*.

The World Bank, 1818 H Street, NW, Washington, D.C. 20433 (202) 477-1234; *World Development Report;* and *World Development Indicators*.

MAURITANIA - GROSS NATIONAL PRODUCT

Euromonitor International, Inc., 122 South Michigan Avenue, Suite 1200, Chicago, Illinois 60603 (800) 577-EURO; *International Marketing Data and Statistics*.

St. Martin's Press, Inc., 175 Fifth Avenue, New York, New York 10010 (800)

221-7945; *The Statesman's Year-Book.*

U.S. Arms Control and Disarmament Agency, 320 Twenty-first Street, NW, Washington, D.C. 20451 (202) 647-8677; *World Military Expenditures and Arms Transfers.*

The World Bank, 1818 H Street, NW, Washington, D.C. 20433 (202) 477-1234; *The World Bank Atlas; World Development Report;* and *World Development Indicators.*

MAURITANIA - GROUNDNUT PRODUCTION - See MAURITANIA - CROPS

MAURITANIA - HEALTH

African Development Bank, 01 BP 1387, Abidjan 01, Cote d'Ivoire; *Selected Statistics on Regional Member Countries.*

Euromonitor International, Inc., 122 South Michigan Avenue, Suite 1200, Chicago, Illinois 60603 (800) 577-EURO; *World Marketing Data and Statistics.*

Federal Statistical Office, Gustav-Stresemann - Ring 11, D-6200, Wiesbaden, Germany; *Mauretanien.*

M.E. Sharpe, 80 Business Park Drive, Armonk, New York 10504 (800) 541-6563; *The Illustrated Book of World Rankings.*

St. Martin's Press, Inc., 175 Fifth Avenue, New York, New York 10010 (800) 221-7945; *The Statesman's Year-Book.*

Statistical Office of the United Nations, Publishing Service, New York, New York 10017 (800) 253-9646; *Human Development Report;* and *Statistical Yearbook.*

United Nations Children's Fund (UNICEF), 3 United Nations Plaza, New York, New York 10017 (800) 253-9646; *State of the World's Children.*

United Nations Economic Commission for Africa, Africa Hall, Post Office Box 3001, Addis Ababa, Ethiopia (Telephone Number in U.S. (800) 253-9646); *African Statistical Yearbook.*

The World Bank, 1818 H Street, NW, Washington, D.C. 20433 (202) 477-1234; *World Development Report.*

MAURITANIA - HEALTH EXPENDITURES

International Monetary Fund, 700 Nineteenth Street, NW, Washington, D.C. 20431 (202) 623-7000; *Government Finance Statistics Yearbook.*

MAURITANIA - HIDE PRODUCTION

Food and Agricultural Organization of the United Nations (FAO), Via delle Terme di Caracalla, 00100 Rome, Italy (Telephone Number in U.S. (202) 653-2400); *Production Yearbook.*

MAURITANIA - HIGHWAYS

Central Intelligence Agency, Washington, D.C. 20505 (703) 482-1100, www.cia.gov; *The World Factbook.*

International Road Federation, 2600 Virginia Avenue, N.W., Washington, D.C. 20037 (202) 338-4641; *World Road Statistics.*

St. Martin's Press, Inc., 175 Fifth Avenue, New York, New York 10010 (800) 221-7945; *The Statesman's Year-Book.*

Statistical Office of the United Nations, Publishing Service, New York, New York 10017 (800) 253-9646; *Survey of Economic and Social Conditions in Africa.*

United Nations Economic Commission for Africa, Africa Hall, Post Office Box 3001, Addis Ababa, Ethiopia (Telephone Number in U.S. (800) 253-9646); *African Statistical Yearbook.*

MAURITANIA - HORSES - See MAURITANIA - LIVESTOCK AND POULTRY

MAURITANIA - HOURS OF WORK - See MAURITANIA - EMPLOYMENT

MAURITANIA - HOUSING AND HOUSING UNITS

Euromonitor International, Inc., 122 South Michigan Avenue, Suite 1200, Chicago, Illinois 60603 (800) 577-EURO; *World Marketing Data and Statistics.*

MAURITANIA - HOUSING EXPENDITURES

International Monetary Fund, 700 Nineteenth Street, NW, Washington, D.C. 20431 (202) 623-7000; *Government Finance Statistics Yearbook.*

M.E. Sharpe, 80 Business Park Drive, Armonk, New York 10504 (800) 541-6563; *The Illustrated Book of World Rankings.*

MAURITANIA - ILLITERATE POPULATION

Central Intelligence Agency, Washington, D.C. 20505 (703) 482-1100, www.cia.gov; *The World Factbook.*

The Economist Intelligence Unit, 111 West 57th Street, New York, New York 10019 (800) 938-4685; *The World Market Atlas.*

Euromonitor International, Inc., 122 South Michigan Avenue, Suite 1200, Chicago, Illinois 60603 (800) 577-EURO; *The World Economic Factbook.*

Statistical Office of the United Nations, Publishing Service, New York, New York 10017 (800) 253-9646; *Human Development Report.*

United Nations Educational, Scientific and Cultural Organization (UNESCO), 7 Place de Fontenoy, F-75700 Paris, France (Telephone Number in U.S. (212) 963-5981); *Statistical Yearbook.*

MAURITANIA - INDUSTRY

Federal Statistical Office, Gustav-Stresemann - Ring 11, D-6200, Wiesbaden, Germany; *Mauretanien.*

M.E. Sharpe, 80 Business Park Drive, Armonk, New York 10504 (800) 541-6563; *The Illustrated Book of World Rankings.*

MAURITANIA - IMPORTS

African Development Bank, 01 BP 1387, Abidjan 01, Cote d'Ivoire; *Selected Statistics on Regional Member Countries.*

Central Intelligence Agency, Washington, D.C. 20505 (703) 482-1100, www.cia.gov; *The World Factbook.*

The Economist Intelligence Unit, 111 West 57th Street, New York, New York 10019 (800) 938-4685; *Mauritania Country Report;* and *The World Market Atlas.*

Euromonitor International, Inc., 122 South Michigan Avenue, Suite 1200, Chicago, Illinois 60603 (800) 577-EURO; *International Marketing Data and Statistics;* and *The World Economic Factbook.*

Europa Publications Limited, 18 Bedford Square, London, WC1B 3JN, England; *The Europa World Year Book.*

Food and Agricultural Organization of the United Nations (FAO), Via delle Terme di Caracalla, 00100 Rome, Italy (Telephone Number in U.S. (202) 653-2400); *The State of Food and Agriculture.*

International Monetary Fund, 700 Nineteenth Street, NW, Washington, D.C. 20431 (202) 623-7000; *Direction of Trade Statistics; Government Finance Statistics Yearbook;* and *International Financial Statistics.*

St. Martin's Press, Inc., 175 Fifth Avenue, New York, New York 10010 (800) 221-7945; *The Statesman's Year-Book.*

Statistical Office of the United Nations, Publishing Service, New York, New York 10017 (800) 253-9646; *Bulletin of Industrial Statistics for the Arab Countries; Foreign Trade Statistics for Africa; Foreign Trade Statistics for Africa;* and *Survey of Economic and Social Conditions in Africa.*

United Nations Conference on Trade and Development (UNCTAD), New York, New York 10017 (800) 253-9646, *Handbook of International Trade and Development Statistics.*

United Nations Economic Commission for Africa, Africa Hall, Post Office Box 3001, Addis Ababa, Ethiopia (Telephone Number in U.S. (800) 253-9646); *African Statistical Yearbook.*

The World Bank, 1818 H Street, NW, Washington, D.C. 20433 (202) 477-1234; *World Development Report;* and *World Development Indicators.*

MAURITANIA - INCOME TAXES - See MAURITANIA - TAXATION

MAURITANIA - INDUSTRY

Central Intelligence Agency, Washington, D.C. 20505 (703) 482-1100, www.cia.gov; *The World Factbook.*

Economist Intelligence Unit, 111 West 57th Street, New York, New York 10019 (800) 938-4685; *Mauritania Country Report.*

Euromonitor International, Inc., 122 South Michigan Avenue, Suite 1200, Chicago, Illinois 60603 (800) 577-EURO; *The World Economic Factbook;* and *World Marketing Data and Statistics.*

Europa Publications Limited, 18 Bedford Square, London, WC1B 3JN, England; *The Europa World Year Book.*

International Labour Office, I.L.O. Publications, 1828 L Street, N.W., Suite 801, Washington, D.C. 20036 (301) 638-3152; *Yearbook of Labour Statistics.*

St. Martin's Press, Inc., 175 Fifth Avenue, New York, New York 10010 (800) 221-7945; *The Statesman's Year-Book.*

Statistical Office of the United Nations, Publishing Service, New York, New York 10017 (800) 253-9646; *Bulletin of Industrial Statistics for the Arab Countries;* and *Survey of Economic and Social Conditions in Africa.*

United Nations Economic Commission for Africa, Africa Hall, Post Office Box 3001, Addis Ababa, Ethiopia (Telephone Number in U.S. (800) 253-9646); *African Statistical Yearbook.*

The World Bank, 1818 H Street, NW, Washington, D.C. 20433 (202) 477-1234; *World Development Indicators.*

MAURITANIA - INFANT AND MATERNAL MORTALITY - See MAURITANIA - MORTALITY

MAURITANIA - INTERNATIONAL LIQUIDITY

International Monetary Fund, 700 Nineteenth Street, NW, Washington, D.C. 20431 (202) 623-7000; *International Financial Statistics.*

MAURITANIA - INTERNATIONAL RESERVES EXCLUDING GOLD

African Development Bank, 01 BP 1387, Abidjan 01, Cote d'Ivoire; *Selected Statistics on Regional Member Countries.*

Statistical Office of the United Nations, Publishing Service, New York, New York 10017 (800) 253-9646; *Statistical Yearbook.*

The World Bank, 1818 H Street, NW, Washington, D.C. 20433 (202) 477-1234; *World Development Indicators.*

MAURITANIA - IRON AND IRON ORE - See MAURITANIA - MINING AND MINERAL PRODUCTS

MAURITANIA - IRRIGATION

Euromonitor International, Inc., 122 South Michigan Avenue, Suite 1200, Chicago, Illinois 60603 (800) 577-EURO; *International Marketing Data and Statistics.*

MAURITANIA - LABOR

African Development Bank, 01 BP 1387, Abidjan 01, Cote d'Ivoire; *Selected Statistics on Regional Member Countries.*

Central Intelligence Agency, Washington, D.C. 20505 (703) 482-1100, www.cia.gov; *The World Factbook.*

Euromonitor International, Inc., 122 South Michigan Avenue, Suite 1200, Chicago, Illinois 60603 (800) 577-EURO; *International Marketing Data and Statistics;* and *World Marketing Data and Statistics.*

Europa Publications Limited, 18 Bedford Square, London, WC1B 3JN, England; *The Europa World Year Book.*

Food and Agricultural Organization of the United Nations (FAO), Via delle Terme di Caracalla, 00100 Rome, Italy (Telephone Number in U.S. (202) 653-2400); *The State of Food and Agriculture.*

International Labour Office, I.L.O. Publications, 1828 L Street, N.W., Suite 801, Washington, D.C. 20036 (301) 638-3152; *Yearbook of Labour Statistics.*

M.E. Sharpe, 80 Business Park Drive, Armonk, New York 10504 (800) 541-6563; *The Illustrated Book of World Rankings.*

St. Martin's Press, Inc., 175 Fifth Avenue, New York, New York 10010 (800) 221-7945; *The Statesman's Year-Book.*

Statistical Office of the United Nations, Publishing Service, New York, New York 10017 (800) 253-9646; *Human Development Report.*

The World Bank, 1818 H Street, NW, Washington, D.C. 20433 (202) 477-1234; *The World Bank Atlas; World Development Report;* and *World Development Indicators.*

MAURITANIA - LAND USE

Central Intelligence Agency, Washington, D.C. 20505 (703) 482-1100, www.cia.gov; *The World Factbook.*

Euromonitor International, Inc., 122 South Michigan Avenue, Suite 1200, Chicago, Illinois 60603 (800) 577-EURO; *International Marketing Data and Statistics.*

Food and Agricultural Organization of the United Nations (FAO), Via delle Terme di Caracalla, 00100 Rome, Italy (Telephone Number in U.S. (202) 653-2400); *Production Yearbook.*

The World Bank, 1818 H Street, NW, Washington, D.C. 20433 (202) 477-1234; *World Development Report.*

MAURITANIA - LIBRARIES

M.E. Sharpe, 80 Business Park Drive, Armonk, New York 10504 (800) 541-6563; *The Illustrated Book of World Rankings.*

United Nations Educational, Scientific and Cultural Organization (UNESCO), 7 Place de Fontenoy, F-75700 Paris, France (Telephone Number in U.S. (212) 963-5981); *Statistical Yearbook.*

MAURITANIA - LIFE EXPECTANCY

African Development Bank, 01 BP 1387, Abidjan 01, Cote d'Ivoire; *Selected Statistics on Regional Member Countries.*

Central Intelligence Agency, Washington, D.C. 20505 (703) 482-1100, www.cia.gov; *The World Factbook.*

Euromonitor International, Inc., 122 South Michigan Avenue, Suite 1200, Chicago, Illinois 60603 (800) 577-EURO; *The World Economic Factbook.*

St. Martin's Press, Inc., 175 Fifth Avenue, New York, New York 10010 (800) 221-7945; *The Statesman's Year-Book.*

Statistical Office of the United Nations, Publishing Service, New York, New York 10017 (800) 253-9646; *Human Development Report;* and *World Statistics Pocketbook.*

The World Bank, 1818 H Street, NW, Washington, D.C. 20433 (202) 477-1234;

The World Bank Atlas; and *World Development Report.*

MAURITANIA - LITERACY RATE

Euromonitor International, Inc., 122 South Michigan Avenue, Suite 1200, Chicago, Illinois 60603 (800) 577-EURO; *World Marketing Data and Statistics.*

Statistical Office of the United Nations, Publishing Service, New York, New York 10017 (800) 253-9646; *Survey of Economic and Social Conditions in Africa.*

MAURITANIA - LIVESTOCK AND POULTRY

Euromonitor International, Inc., 122 South Michigan Avenue, Suite 1200, Chicago, Illinois 60603 (800) 577-EURO; *International Marketing Data and Statistics.*

Europa Publications Limited, 18 Bedford Square, London, WC1B 3JN, England; *The Europa World Year Book.*

Food and Agricultural Organization of the United Nations (FAO), Via delle Terme di Caracalla, 00100 Rome, Italy (Telephone Number in U.S. (202) 653-2400); *Production Yearbook;* and *The State of Food and Agriculture.*

M.E. Sharpe, 80 Business Park Drive, Armonk, New York 10504 (800) 541-6563; *The Illustrated Book of World Rankings.*

Statistical Office of the United Nations, Publishing Service, New York, New York 10017 (800) 253-9646; *Statistical Yearbook;* and *Survey of Economic and Social Conditions in Africa.*

United Nations Conference on Trade and Development, Central Statistical Service, Palais des Nations, Geneva, Switzerland (Telephone in U.S. (800) 253-9646); *UNCTAD Commodity Yearbook.*

United Nations Economic Commission for Africa, Africa Hall, Post Office Box 3001, Addis Ababa, Ethiopia (Telephone Number in U.S. (800) 253-9646); *African Statistical Yearbook.*

MAURITANIA - LIVING LEVELS - See MAURITANIA - LIFE EXPECTANCY

MAURITANIA - MAIL - NUMBER OF ITEMS SENT OR RECEIVED

Statistical Office of the United Nations, Publishing Service, New York, New York 10017 (800) 253-9646; *Statistical Yearbook.*

MAURITANIA - MANUFACTURING

M.E. Sharpe, 80 Business Park Drive, Armonk, New York 10504 (800) 541-6563; *The Illustrated Book of World Rankings.*

Statistical Office of the United Nations, Publishing Service, New York, New York 10017 (800) 253-9646; *Bulletin of Industrial Statistics for the Arab Countries;* and *Survey of Economic and Social Conditions in Africa.*

United Nations Economic Commission for Africa, Africa Hall, Post Office Box 3001, Addis Ababa, Ethiopia (Telephone Number in U.S. (800) 253-9646); *African Statistical Yearbook.*

The World Bank, 1818 H Street, NW, Washington, D.C. 20433 (202) 477-1234; *World Development Indicators.*

MAURITANIA - MARRIAGE

M.E. Sharpe, 80 Business Park Drive, Armonk, New York 10504 (800) 541-6563; *The Illustrated Book of World Rankings.*

Statistical Office of the United Nations, Publishing Service, New York, New York 10017 (800) 253-9646; *Demographic Yearbook.*

MAURITANIA - MEAT PRODUCTION - See MAURITANIA - LIVESTOCK AND POULTRY

MAURITANIA - MERCHANT SHIPPING

Europa Publications Limited, 18 Bedford Square, London, WC1B 3JN, England; *The Europa World Year Book.*

Lloyd's Register of Shipping, 17 Battery Place, New York, New York 10004 (212) 425-8050; *Register of Ships.*

St. Martin's Press, Inc., 175 Fifth Avenue, New York, New York 10010 (800) 221-7945; *The Statesman's Year-Book.*

Statistical Office of the United Nations, Publishing Service, New York, New York 10017 (800) 253-9646; *Statistical Yearbook.*

United Nations Economic Commission for Africa, Africa Hall, Post Office Box 3001, Addis Ababa, Ethiopia (Telephone Number in U.S. (800) 253-9646); *African Statistical Yearbook.*

MAURITANIA - MILITARY

Central Intelligence Agency, Washington, D.C. 20505 (703) 482-1100, www.cia.gov; *The World Factbook.*

Euromonitor International, Inc., 122 South Michigan Avenue, Suite 1200, Chicago, Illinois 60603 (800) 577-EURO; *World Marketing Data and Statistics.*

The International Institute for Strategic Studies, 23 Tavistock Street, London WC2E 7NQ, England; *The Military Balance.*

St. Martin's Press, Inc., 175 Fifth

Avenue, New York, New York 10010 (800) 221-7945; *The Statesman's Year-Book.*

Statistical Office of the United Nations, Publishing Service, New York, New York 10017 (800) 253-9646; *Human Development Report.*

U.S. Arms Control and Disarmament Agency, 320 Twenty-first Street, NW, Washington, D.C. 20451 (202) 647-8677; *World Military Expenditures and Arms Transfers.*

MAURITANIA - MILK PRODUCTION - See MAURITANIA - DAIRY PRODUCTS

MAURITANIA - MILLET PRODUCTION - See MAURITANIA - CROPS

MAURITANIA - MINING AND MINERAL PRODUCTS

Europa Publications Limited, 18 Bedford Square, London, WC1B 3JN, England; *The Europa World Year Book.*

International Monetary Fund, 700 Nineteenth Street, NW, Washington, D.C. 20431 (202) 623-7000; *International Financial Statistics.*

M.E. Sharpe, 80 Business Park Drive, Armonk, New York 10504 (800) 541-6563; *The Illustrated Book of World Rankings.*

St. Martin's Press, Inc., 175 Fifth Avenue, New York, New York 10010 (800) 221-7945; *The Statesman's Year-Book.*

Statistical Office of the United Nations, Publishing Service, New York, New York 10017 (800) 253-9646; *Bulletin of Industrial Statistics for the Arab Countries;* and *Statistical Yearbook.*

United Nations Conference on Trade and Development, Central Statistical Service, Palais des Nations, Geneva, Switzerland (Telephone in U.S. (800) 253-9646); *UNCTAD Commodity Yearbook.*

United Nations Economic Commission for Africa, Africa Hall, Post Office Box 3001, Addis Ababa, Ethiopia (Telephone Number in U.S. (800) 253-9646); *African Statistical Yearbook.*

MAURITANIA - MONEY EXCHANGE RATES - See MAURITANIA - EXCHANGE RATES

MAURITANIA - MONEY RESERVES

Euromonitor International, Inc., 122 South Michigan Avenue, Suite 1200, Chicago, Illinois 60603 (800) 577-EURO; *International Marketing Data and Statistics.*

MAURITANIA - MONEY SUPPLY

African Development Bank, 01 BP 1387, Abidjan 01, Cote d'Ivoire; *Selected Statistics on Regional Member Countries.*

Economist Intelligence Unit, 111 West 57th Street, New York, New York 10019 (800) 938-4685; *Mauritania Country Report.*

Euromonitor International, Inc., 122 South Michigan Avenue, Suite 1200, Chicago, Illinois 60603 (800) 577-EURO; *International Marketing Data and Statistics.*

Europa Publications Limited, 18 Bedford Square, London, WC1B 3JN, England; *The Europa World Year Book.*

Federal Statistical Office, Gustav-Stresemann - Ring 11, D-6200, Wiesbaden, Germany; *Mauretanien.*

International Monetary Fund, 700 Nineteenth Street, NW, Washington, D.C. 20431 (202) 623-7000; *International Financial Statistics.*

Statistical Office of the United Nations, Publishing Service, New York, New York 10017 (800) 253-9646; *Statistical Yearbook.*

The World Bank, 1818 H Street, NW, Washington, D.C. 20433 (202) 477-1234; *World Development Indicators.*

MAURITANIA - MORTALITY

Central Intelligence Agency, Washington, D.C. 20505 (703) 482-1100, www.cia.gov; *The World Factbook.*

Euromonitor International, Inc., 122 South Michigan Avenue, Suite 1200, Chicago, Illinois 60603 (800) 577-EURO; *International Marketing Data and Statistics;* and *The World Economic Factbook.*

Europa Publications Limited, 18 Bedford Square, London, WC1B 3JN, England; *The Europa World Year Book.*

St. Martin's Press, Inc., 175 Fifth Avenue, New York, New York 10010 (800) 221-7945; *The Statesman's Year-Book.*
Statistical Office of the United Nations, Publishing Service, New York, New York 10017 (800) 253-9646; *Demographic Yearbook; Human Development Report; Statistical Yearbook; World Statistics Pocketbook;* and *Survey of Economic and Social Conditions in Africa.*

United Nations Children's Fund (UNICEF), 3 United Nations Plaza, New York, New York 10017 (800) 253-9646; *State of the World's Children.*

The World Bank, 1818 H Street, NW, Washington, D.C. 20433 (202) 477-1234; *The World Bank Atlas; World Development Report;* and *World Development Indicators.*

MAURITANIA - MOTOR VEHICLE TAXES - See MAURITANIA - TAXATION

MAURITANIA - MOTOR VEHICLES IN USE

Europa Publications Limited, 18 Bedford Square, London, WC1B 3JN, England; *The Europa World Year Book.*

International Road Federation, 2600 Virginia Avenue, N.W., Washington, D.C. 20037 (202) 338-4641; *World Road Statistics.*

Statistical Office of the United Nations, Publishing Service, New York, New York 10017 (800) 253-9646; *Statistical Yearbook;* and *Survey of Economic and Social Conditions in Africa.*

MAURITANIA - MUSEUMS

M.E. Sharpe, 80 Business Park Drive, Armonk, New York 10504 (800) 541-6563; *The Illustrated Book of World Rankings.*

United Nations Educational, Scientific and Cultural Organization (UNESCO), 7 Place de Fontenoy, F-75700 Paris, France (Telephone Number in U.S. (212) 963-5981); *Statistical Yearbook.*

MAURITANIA - NATALITY - See MAURITANIA - BIRTH RATES

MAURITANIA - NATIONAL ACCOUNTS

African Development Bank, 01 BP 1387, Abidjan 01, Cote d'Ivoire; *Selected Statistics on Regional Member Countries.*

Europa Publications Limited, 18 Bedford Square, London, WC1B 3JN, England; *The Europa World Year Book.*

Federal Statistical Office, Gustav-Stresemann - Ring 11, D-6200, Wiesbaden, Germany; *Mauretanien.*

Statistical Office of the United Nations, Publishing Service, New York, New York 10017 (800) 253-9646; *National Account Statistics;* and *Statistical Yearbook.*

United Nations Economic Commission for Africa, Africa Hall, Post Office Box 3001, Addis Ababa, Ethiopia (Telephone Number in U.S. (800) 253-9646); *African Statistical Yearbook.*

MAURITANIA - NATIONAL INCOME

M.E. Sharpe, 80 Business Park Drive, Armonk, New York 10504 (800) 541-6563; *The Illustrated Book of World Rankings.*

Statistical Office of the United Nations, Publishing Service, New York, New York 10017 (800) 253-9646; *National Accounts Statistics;* and *Statistical Yearbook.*

MAURITANIA - NATIONAL PRODUCT

M.E. Sharpe, 80 Business Park Drive, Armonk, New York 10504 (800) 541-6563; *The Illustrated Book of World Rankings.*

MAURITANIA - NATURAL GAS - PRODUCTION - See MAURITANIA - MINING AND MINERAL PRODUCTS

MAURITANIA - NEWSPAPER PRODUCTION - See MAURITANIA - FORESTRY AND FOREST PRODUCTS

MAURITANIA - OCCUPATIONS - See MAURITANIA - LABOR

MAURITANIA - PEANUT PRODUCTION - See MAURITANIA - CROPS

MAURITANIA - PESTICIDE USE

Food and Agricultural Organization of the United Nations (FAO), Via delle Terme di Caracalla, 00100 Rome, Italy (Telephone Number in U.S. (202) 653-2400); *The State of Food and Agriculture.*

MAURITANIA - PETROLEUM INDUSTRY

Food and Agricultural Organization of the United Nations (FAO), Via delle Terme di Caracalla, 00100 Rome, Italy (Telephone Number in U.S. (202) 653-2400); *The State of Food and Agriculture.*

M.E. Sharpe, 80 Business Park Drive, Armonk, New York 10504 (800) 541-6563; *The Illustrated Book of World Rankings.*

United Nations Conference on Trade and Development, Central Statistical Service, Palais des Nations, Geneva, Switzerland (Telephone in U.S. (800) 253-9646); *UNCTAD Commodity Yearbook.*

MAURITANIA - PIGS - See MAURITANIA - LIVESTOCK AND POULTRY

MAURITANIA - POPULATION

African Development Bank, 01 BP 1387, Abidjan 01, Cote d'Ivoire; *Selected Statistics on Regional Member Countries.*

Central Intelligence Agency, Washington, D.C. 20505 (703) 482-1100, www.cia.gov; *The World Factbook.*

The Economist Intelligence Unit, 111 West 57th Street, New York, New York 10019 (800) 938-4685; *Mauritania Country Report;* and *The World Market Atlas.*

Euromonitor International, Inc., 122 South Michigan Avenue, Suite 1200, Chicago, Illinois 60603 (800) 577-EURO; *International Marketing Data and Statistics;* and *The World Economic Factbook.*

Europa Publications Limited, 18

Bedford Square, London, WC1B 3JN, England; *The Europa World Year Book.*

Federal Statistical Office, Gustav-Stresemann - Ring 11, D-6200, Wiesbaden, Germany; *Mauretanien.*

Food and Agricultural Organization of the United Nations (FAO), Via delle Terme di Caracalla, 00100 Rome, Italy (Telephone Number in U.S. (202) 653-2400); *Production Yearbook.*

International Labour Office, I.L.O. Publications, 1828 L Street, N.W., Suite 801, Washington, D.C. 20036 (301) 638-3152; *Yearbook of Labour Statistics.*

M.E. Sharpe, 80 Business Park Drive, Armonk, New York 10504 (800) 541-6563; *The Illustrated Book of World Rankings.*

St. Martin's Press, Inc., 175 Fifth Avenue, New York, New York 10010 (800) 221-7945; *The Statesman's Year-Book.*

Statistical Office of the United Nations, Publishing Service, New York, New York 10017; *Demographic Yearbook; Human Development Report; Statistical Yearbook; World Statistics Pocketbook;* and *Survey of Economic and Social Conditions in Africa.*

U.S. Arms Control and Disarmament Agency, 320 Twenty-first Street, NW, Washington, D.C. 20451 (202) 647-8677; *World Military Expenditures and Arms Transfers.*

The World Bank, 1818 H Street, NW, Washington, D.C. 20433 (202) 477-1234; *The World Bank Atlas;* and *World Development Report.*

World Health Organization, Office of Publications, 20 Avenue Appia, CH-1211 Geneva 27, Switzerland (Telephone in U.S. (518) 436-9686); *World Health Statistics Annual.*

MAURITANIA - POST OFFICES

M.E. Sharpe, 80 Business Park Drive, Armonk, New York 10504 (800) 541-6563; *The Illustrated Book of World Rankings.*

MAURITANIA - POTATO PRODUCTION - See MAURITANIA - CROPS

MAURITANIA - PRICES

Federal Statistical Office, Gustav-Stresemann - Ring 11, D-6200, Wiesbaden, Germany; *Mauretanien.*

Food and Agricultural Organization of the United Nations (FAO), Via delle Terme di Caracalla, 00100 Rome, Italy (Telephone Number in U.S. (202) 653-2400); *Production Yearbook;* and *The State of Food and Agriculture.*

International Labour Office, I.L.O. Publications, 1828 L Street, NW, Suite 801, Washington, D.C. 20036 (301) 638-3152; *Yearbook of Labour Statistics.*

International Monetary Fund, 700 Nineteenth Street, NW, Washington, D.C. 20431 (202) 623-7000; *International Financial Statistics.*

M.E. Sharpe, 80 Business Park Drive, Armonk, New York 10504 (800) 541-6563; *The Illustrated Book of World Rankings.*

United Nations Economic Commission for Africa, Africa Hall, Post Office Box 3001, Addis Ababa, Ethiopia (Telephone Number in U.S. (800) 253-9646); *African Statistical Yearbook.*

MAURITANIA - PRODUCTION

M.E. Sharpe, 80 Business Park Drive, Armonk, New York 10504 (800) 541-6563; *The Illustrated Book of World Rankings.*

MAURITANIA - PRODUCTIVITY

Euromonitor International, Inc., 122 South Michigan Avenue, Suite 1200, Chicago, Illinois 60603 (800) 577-EURO; *International Marketing Data and Statistics.*

MAURITANIA - PROPERTY TAXES - See MAURITANIA - TAXATION

MAURITANIA - PUBLIC FINANCE - See MAURITANIA - FINANCE

MAURITANIA - RADIO BROADCASTING - See MAURITANIA - BROADCASTING

MAURITANIA - RADIO RECEIVERS

St. Martin's Press, Inc., 175 Fifth Avenue, New York, New York 10010 (800) 221-7945; *The Statesman's Year-Book.*

MAURITANIA - RAILWAYS

Europa Publications Limited, 18 Bedford Square, London, WC1B 3JN, England; *The Europa World Year Book.*

Jane's Information Group, Sentinel House, 163 Brighton Road, Coulsdon, Surrey CR5 2NH, England (Telephone Number in U.S. (703) 683-3700); *Jane's World Railways.*

St. Martin's Press, Inc., 175 Fifth Avenue, New York, New York 10010 (800) 221-7945; *The Statesman's Year-Book.*

Statistical Office of the United Nations, Publishing Service, New York, New York 10017 (800) 253-9646; *Statistical Yearbook;* and *Survey of Economic and Social Conditions in Africa.*

United Nations Economic Commission for Africa, Africa Hall, Post Office Box 3001, Addis Ababa, Ethiopia (Telephone Number in U.S. (800) 253-9646); *African Statistical Yearbook.*

MAURITANIA - RELIGION

Central Intelligence Agency, Washington, D.C. 20505 (703) 482-1100, www.cia.gov; *The World Factbook.*

M.E. Sharpe, 80 Business Park Drive, Armonk, New York 10504 (800) 541-6563; *The Illustrated Book of World Rankings.*

St. Martin's Press, Inc., 175 Fifth Avenue, New York, New York 10010 (800) 221-7945; *The Statesman's Year-Book.*

MAURITANIA - RETAIL TRADE

Euromonitor International, Inc., 122 South Michigan Avenue, Suite 1200, Chicago, Illinois 60603 (800) 577-EURO; *World Marketing Data and Statistics.*

Statistical Office of the United Nations, Publishing Service, New York, New York 10017 (800) 253-9646; *Statistical Yearbook.*

MAURITANIA - RICE PRODUCTION - See MAURITANIA - CROPS

MAURITANIA - ROOT AND TUBER PRODUCTION - See MAURITANIA - CROPS

MAURITANIA - ROUNDWOOD PRODUCTION - See MAURITANIA - FORESTRY AND FOREST PRODUCTS

MAURITANIA - RUBBER PRODUCTION AND CONSUMPTION

M.E. Sharpe, 80 Business Park Drive, Armonk, New York 10504 (800) 541-6563; *The Illustrated Book of World Rankings.*

MAURITANIA - SAWNWOOD PRODUCTION - See MAURITANIA - FORESTRY AND FOREST PRODUCTS

MAURITANIA - SENIOR CITIZENS

M.E. Sharpe, 80 Business Park Drive, Armonk, New York 10504 (800) 541-6563; *The Illustrated Book of World Rankings.*

MAURITANIA - SHEEP - See MAURITANIA - LIVESTOCK AND POULTRY

MAURITANIA - SILVER PRODUCTION AND CONSUMPTION - See MAURITANIA - MINING AND MINERAL PRODUCTS

MAURITANIA - SOCIAL DATA

African Development Bank, 01 BP 1387, Abidjan 01, Cote d'Ivoire; *Selected Statistics on Regional Member Countries.*

M.E. Sharpe, 80 Business Park Drive, Armonk, New York 10504 (800) 541-6563; *The Illustrated Book of World Rankings.*

Statistical Office of the United Nations, Publishing Service, New York, New York 10017 (800) 253-9646; *World Statistics Pocketbook.*

MAURITANIA - SOCIAL SECURITY

International Monetary Fund, 700 Nineteenth Street, NW, Washington, D.C. 20431 (202) 623-7000; *Government Finance Statistics Yearbook.*

Statistical Office of the United Nations, Publishing Service, New York, New York 10017 (800) 253-9646; *National Accounts Statistics.*

MAURITANIA - STAMP TAXES AND DUTIES - See MAURITANIA - TAXATION

MAURITANIA - STATE BUDGET

Euromonitor International, Inc., 122 South Michigan Avenue, Suite 1200, Chicago, Illinois 60603 (800) 577-EURO; *International Marketing Data and Statistics.*

MAURITANIA - STEEL PRODUCTION - See MAURITANIA - MINING AND MINERAL PRODUCTS

MAURITANIA - STOCKS - COMMODITY - MARKET PRICE - INDEX

Food and Agricultural Organization of the United Nations (FAO), Via delle Terme di Caracalla, 00100 Rome, Italy (Telephone Number in U.S. (202) 653-2400); *The State of Food and Agriculture.*

MAURITANIA - SUGAR PRODUCTION AND CONSUMPTION - See MAURITANIA - CROPS

MAURITANIA - TAXATION

Europa Publications Limited, 18 Bedford Square, London, WC1B 3JN, England; *The Europa World Year Book.*

International Monetary Fund, 700 Nineteenth Street, NW, Washington, D.C. 20431 (202) 623-7000; *Government Finance Statistics Yearbook.*

International Road Federation, 2600 Virginia Avenue, NW, Washington, D.C. 20037 (202) 338-4641; *World Road Statistics.*

The World Bank, 1818 H Street, NW, Washington, D.C. 20433 (202) 477-1234; *World Development Indicators.*

MAURITANIA - TELEPHONES IN USE

American Telephone and Telegraph Company, 26 Parsippany Road, Whippany, New Jersey 07981 (800) 222-0300; *The World's Telephones.*

Central Intelligence Agency, Washington, D.C. 20505 (703) 482-1100, www.cia.gov; *The World Factbook.*

Europa Publications Limited, 18 Bedford Square, London, WC1B 3JN, England; *The Europa World Year Book.*

St. Martin's Press, Inc., 175 Fifth Avenue, New York, New York 10010 (800) 221-7945; *The Statesman's Year-Book.*

Statistical Office of the United Nations, Publishing Service, New York, New York 10017 (800) 253-9646; *World Statistics Pocketbook.*

MAURITANIA - TELEVISION

M.E. Sharpe, 80 Business Park Drive, Armonk, New York 10504 (800) 541-6563; *The Illustrated Book of World Rankings.*

MAURITANIA - TEXTILE INDUSTRY

United Nations Conference on Trade and Development, Central Statistical Service, Palais des Nations, Geneva, Switzerland (Telephone in U.S. (800) 253-9646); *UNCTAD Commodity Yearbook.*

MAURITANIA - TOBACCO PRODUCTION

M.E. Sharpe, 80 Business Park Drive, Armonk, New York 10504 (800) 541-6563; *The Illustrated Book of World Rankings.*

MAURITANIA - TOURISM

Euromonitor International, Inc., 122 South Michigan Avenue, Suite 1200, Chicago, Illinois 60603 (800) 577-EURO; *The World Economic Factbook;* and *World Marketing Data and Statistics.*

Europa Publications Limited, 18 Bedford Square, London, WC1B 3JN, England; *The Europa World Year Book.*

Federal Statistical Office, Gustav-Stresemann - Ring 11, D-6200, Wiesbaden, Germany; *Mauretanien.*

M.E. Sharpe, 80 Business Park Drive, Armonk, New York 10504 (800) 541-6563; *The Illustrated Book of World Rankings.*

St. Martin's Press, Inc., 175 Fifth Avenue, New York, New York 10010 (800) 221-7945; *The Statesman's Year-Book.*

Statistical Office of the United Nations, Publishing Service, New York, New York 10017 (800) 253-9646; *Statistical Yearbook.*

United Nations Economic Commission for Africa, Africa Hall, Post Office Box 3001, Addis Ababa, Ethiopia (Telephone Number in U.S. (800) 253-9646); *African Statistical Yearbook.*

World Tourism Organization, Calle Capitan Haya 42, E-28020 Madrid, Spain; *Yearbook of Tourism Statistics.*

MAURITANIA - TRADE - See MAURITANIA - FOREIGN TRADE

MAURITANIA - TRANSPORTATION AND COMMUNICATIONS

Central Intelligence Agency, Washington, D.C. 20505 (703) 482-1100, www.cia.gov; *The World Factbook.*

Euromonitor International, Inc., 122 South Michigan Avenue, Suite 1200, Chicago, Illinois 60603 (800) 577-EURO; *International Marketing Data and Statistics;* and *World Marketing Data and Statistics..*

Europa Publications Limited, 18 Bedford Square, London, WC1B 3JN, England; *The Europa World Year Book.*

Federal Statistical Office, Gustav-Stresemann - Ring 11, D-6200, Wiesbaden, Germany; *Mauretanien.*

M.E. Sharpe, 80 Business Park Drive, Armonk, New York 10504 (800) 541-6563; *The Illustrated Book of World Rankings.*

St. Martin's Press, Inc., 175 Fifth Avenue, New York, New York 10010 (800) 221-7945; *The Statesman's Year-Book.*

Statistical Office of the United Nations, Publishing Service, New York, New York 10017 (800) 253-9646; *Human Development Report.*

United Nations Economic Commission for Africa, Africa Hall, Post Office Box 3001, Addis Ababa, Ethiopia (Telephone Number in U.S. (800) 253-9646); *African Statistical Yearbook.*

MAURITANIA - UNEMPLOYMENT

Central Intelligence Agency, Washington, D.C. 20505 (703) 482-1100, www.cia.gov; *The World Factbook.*

Euromonitor International, Inc., 122 South Michigan Avenue, Suite 1200, Chicago, Illinois 60603 (800) 577-EURO; *International Marketing Data and Statistics.*

International Labour Office, I.L.O. Publications, 1828 L Street, NW, Suite 801, Washington, D.C. 20036 (301) 638-3152; *Yearbook of Labour Statistics.*

MAURITANIA - VITAL STATISTICS

Euromonitor International, Inc., 122 South Michigan Avenue, Suite 1200, Chicago, Illinois 60603 (800) 577-EURO;

International Marketing Data and Statistics.

St. Martin's Press, Inc., 175 Fifth Avenue, New York, New York 10010 (800) 221-7945; *The Statesman's Year-Book.*

Statistical Office of the United Nations, Publishing Service, New York, New York 10017 (800) 253-9646; *Statistical Yearbook.*

World Health Organization, Office of Publications, 20 Avenue Appia, CH-1211 Geneva 27, Switzerland (Telephone in U.S. (518) 436-9686); *World Health Statistics Annual.*

MAURITANIA - WAGES

Federal Statistical Office, Gustav-Stresemann - Ring 11, D-6200, Wiesbaden, Germany; *Mauretanien.*

International Labour Office, I.L.O. Publications, 1828 L Street, NW, Suite 801, Washington, D.C. 20036 (301) 638-3152; *Yearbook of Labour Statistics.*

MAURITANIA - WATERMELON PRODUCTION - See MAURITANIA - CROPS

MAURITANIA - WEATHER - See MAURITANIA - CLIMATE

MAURITANIA - WELFARE EXPENDITURES

International Monetary Fund, 700 Nineteenth Street, NW, Washington, D.C. 20431 (202) 623-7000; *Government Finance Statistics Yearbook.*

MAURITANIA - WHEAT PRODUCTION - See MAURITANIA - CROPS

MAURITANIA - WINE PRODUCTION - See MAURITANIA - BEVERAGES

MAURITANIA - WOOL PRODUCTION

M.E. Sharpe, 80 Business Park Drive, Armonk, New York 10504 (800) 541-6563; *The Illustrated Book of World Rankings.*

Mauritius - National Statistical Office

Central Statistical Office, Ministry of Economic Planning and Development, Royal Road, Port Louis, Mauritius.

Mauritius - Primary Statistics Source

Central Statistical Office, Government Printer, Port Louis, Mauritius; *Annual Digest of Statistics.*

MAURITIUS - AGRICULTURE

Economist Intelligence Unit, 111 West 57th Street, New York, New York 10019 (800) 938-4685; *Mauritius Country Report.*

Euromonitor International, Inc., 122 South Michigan Avenue, Suite 1200, Chicago, Illinois 60603 (800) 577-EURO; *World Marketing Data and Statistics.*

Europa Publications Limited, 18 Bedford Square, London, WC1B 3JN, England; *The Europa World Year Book.*

Federal Statistical Office, Gustav-Stresemann - Ring 11, D-6200, Wiesbaden, Germany; *Mauritius.*

Food and Agricultural Organization of the United Nations (FAO), Via delle Terme di Caracalla, 00100 Rome, Italy (Telephone Number in U.S. (202) 653-2400); The State of Food and Agriculture; *Survey of Economic and Social Conditions in Africa;* and *Trade Yearbook.*

M.E. Sharpe, 80 Business Park Drive, Armonk, New York 10504 (800) 541-6563; *The Illustrated Book of World Rankings.*

St. Martin's Press, Inc., 175 Fifth Avenue, New York, New York 10010 (800) 221-7945; *The Statesman's Year-Book.*

Statistical Office of the United Nations, Publishing Service, New York, New York 10017 (800) 253-9646; *Statistical Yearbook;* and *Survey of Economic and Social Conditions in Africa.*

United Nations Conference on Trade and Development, Central Statistical Service, Palais des Nations, Geneva, Switzerland (Telephone in U.S. (800) 253-9646); *UNCTAD Commodity Yearbook.*

United Nations Economic Commission for Africa, Africa Hall, Post Office Box 3001, Addis Ababa, Ethiopia (Telephone Number in U.S. (800) 253-9646); *African Statistical Yearbook.*

The World Bank, 1818 H Street, NW, Washington, D.C. 20433 (202) 477-1234; *World Development Indicators.*

MAURITIUS - AIRLINE SERVICE

Europa Publications Limited, 18 Bedford Square, London, WC1B 3JN, England; *The Europa World Year Book.*

International Civil Aviation Organization, 999 University Street, Montreal, Quebec, Canada H3C 5H7 (514) 954-8219; *Civil Aviation Statistics of the World.*

M.E. Sharpe, 80 Business Park Drive, Armonk, New York 10504 (800) 541-6563; *The Illustrated Book of World Rankings.*

St. Martin's Press, Inc., 175 Fifth Avenue, New York, New York 10010 (800) 221-7945; *The Statesman's Year-Book.*

United Nations Economic Commission for Africa, Africa Hall, Post Office Box 3001, Addis Ababa, Ethiopia (Telephone Number in U.S. (800) 253-9646); *African Statistical Yearbook.*

MAURITIUS - AIRPORTS

Central Intelligence Agency, Washington, D.C. 20505 (703) 482-1100, www.cia.gov; *The World Factbook.*

MAURITIUS - ALUMINUM PRODUCTION AND CONSUMPTION - See MAURITIUS - MINING AND MINERAL PRODUCTS

MAURITIUS - ANIMAL HEALTH

Food and Agricultural Organization of the United Nations (FAO), Via delle Terme di Caracalla, 00100 Rome, Italy (Telephone Number in U.S. (202) 653-2400); *Animal Health Yearbook.*

MAURITIUS - AREA AND DENSITY OF POPULATION

African Development Bank, 01 BP 1387, Abidjan 01, Cote d'Ivoire; *Selected Statistics on Regional Member Countries.*

Central Intelligence Agency, Washington, D.C. 20505 (703) 482-1100, www.cia.gov; *The World Factbook.*

Euromonitor International, Inc., 122 South Michigan Avenue, Suite 1200, Chicago, Illinois 60603 (800) 577-EURO; *The World Economic Factbook.*

Europa Publications Limited, 18 Bedford Square, London, WC1B 3JN, England; *The Europa World Year Book.*

Federal Statistical Office, Gustav-Stresemann - Ring 11, D-6200, Wiesbaden, Germany; *Mauritius.*

Food and Agricultural Organization of the United Nations (FAO), Via delle Terme di Caracalla, 00100 Rome, Italy (Telephone Number in U.S. (202) 653-2400); The State of Food and Agriculture.

M.E. Sharpe, 80 Business Park Drive, Armonk, New York 10504 (800) 541-6563; *The Illustrated Book of World Rankings.*

St. Martin's Press, Inc., 175 Fifth Avenue, New York, New York 10010 (800) 221-7945; *The Statesman's Year-Book.*

Statistical Office of the United Nations, Publishing Service, New York, New York 10017 (800) 253-9646; *Statistical Yearbook;* and *Survey of Economic and Social Conditions in Africa.*

The World Bank, 1818 H Street, NW, Washington, D.C. 20433 (202) 477-1234; *World Development Report*.

MAURITIUS - ARMS EXPORTS AND IMPORTS - See MAURITIUS - MILITARY

MAURITIUS - BALANCE OF PAYMENTS

African Development Bank, 01 BP 1387, Abidjan 01, Cote d'Ivoire; *Selected Statistics on Regional Member Countries*.

Europa Publications Limited, 18 Bedford Square, London, WC1B 3JN, England; *The Europa World Year Book*.

Federal Statistical Office, Gustav-Stresemann - Ring 11, D-6200, Wiesbaden, Germany; *Mauritius*.

International Monetary Fund, 700 Nineteenth Street, NW, Washington, D.C. 20431 (202) 623-7000; Balance of Payments Yearbook.

United Nations Conference on Trade and Development (UNCTAD), New York, New York 10017 (800) 253-9646; *Handbook of International Trade and Development Statistics*.

United Nations Economic Commission for Africa, Africa Hall, Post Office Box 3001, Addis Ababa, Ethiopia (Telephone Number in U.S. (800) 253-9646); *African Statistical Yearbook*.

The World Bank, 1818 H Street, NW, Washington, D.C. 20433 (202) 477-1234; *World Development Report;* and *World Development Indicators*.

MAURITIUS - BANKING

Euromonitor International, Inc., 122 South Michigan Avenue, Suite 1200, Chicago, Illinois 60603 (800) 577-EURO; *World Marketing Data and Statistics*.

Europa Publications Limited, 18 Bedford Square, London, WC1B 3JN, England; *The Europa World Year Book*.

International Monetary Fund, 700 Nineteenth Street, NW, Washington, D.C. 20431 (202) 623-7000; *Government Finance Statistics Yearbook*.

M.E. Sharpe, 80 Business Park Drive, Armonk, New York 10504 (800) 541-6563; *The Illustrated Book of World Rankings*.

St. Martin's Press, Inc., 175 Fifth Avenue, New York, New York 10010 (800) 221-7945; *The Statesman's Year-Book*.

Statistical Office of the United Nations, Publishing Service, New York, New York 10017 (800) 253-9646; *Statistical Yearbook*.

United Nations Economic Commission for Africa, Africa Hall, Post Office Box 3001, Addis Ababa, Ethiopia (Telephone Number in U.S. (800) 253-9646); *African Statistical Yearbook*.

MAURITIUS - BARLEY PRODUCTION - See MAURITIUS - CROPS

MAURITIUS - BEER PRODUCTION - See MAURITIUS - BEVERAGES

MAURITIUS - BEVERAGES

M.E. Sharpe, 80 Business Park Drive, Armonk, New York 10504 (800) 541-6563; *The Illustrated Book of World Rankings*.

Statistical Office of the United Nations, Publishing Service, New York, New York 10017 (800) 253-9646; *Statistical Yearbook*.

MAURITIUS - BIRTH RATES

Central Intelligence Agency, Washington, D.C. 20505 (703) 482-1100, www.cia.gov; *The World Factbook*.

Euromonitor International, Inc., 122 South Michigan Avenue, Suite 1200, Chicago, Illinois 60603 (800) 577-EURO; *International Marketing Data and Statistics;* and *The World Economic Factbook*.

Europa Publications Limited, 18 Bedford Square, London, WC1B 3JN, England; *The Europa World Year Book*.

M.E. Sharpe, 80 Business Park Drive, Armonk, New York 10504 (800) 541-6563; *The Illustrated Book of World Rankings*.

St. Martin's Press, Inc., 175 Fifth Avenue, New York, New York 10010 (800) 221-7945; *The Statesman's Year-Book*.

Statistical Office of the United Nations, Publishing Service, New York, New York 10017 (800) 253-9646; *Demographic Yearbook, Statistical Yearbook;* and *Survey of Economic and Social Conditions in Africa*.

The World Bank, 1818 H Street, NW, Washington, D.C. 20433 (202) 477-1234; *World Development Indicators*.

World Health Organization, Office of Publications, 20 Avenue Appia, CH-1211 Geneva 27, Switzerland (Telephone in U.S. (518) 436-9686); *World Health Statistics Annual*.

MAURITIUS - BONDS

International Monetary Fund, 700 Nineteenth Street, NW, Washington, D.C. 20431 (202) 623-7000; *Government Finance Statistics Yearbook*.

MAURITIUS - BOOK PRODUCTION

Europa Publications Limited, 18 Bedford Square, London, WC1B 3JN, England; *The Europa World Year Book*.

United Nations Educational, Scientific and Cultural Organization (UNESCO), 7 Place de Fontenoy, F-75700 Paris, France; *Statistical Yearbook*.

MAURITIUS - BROADCASTING

Billboard Limited, Post Office Box 9027, 1006 AA Amsterdam, The Netherlands (Telephone Number in U.S. (212) 764-7300); *World Radio TV Handbook*.

Central Intelligence Agency, Washington, D.C. 20505 (703) 482-1100, www.cia.gov; *The World Factbook*.

Euromonitor International, Inc., 122 South Michigan Avenue, Suite 1200, Chicago, Illinois 60603 (800) 577-EURO; *World Marketing Data and Statistics*.

M.E. Sharpe, 80 Business Park Drive, Armonk, New York 10504 (800) 541-6563; *The Illustrated Book of World Rankings*.

St. Martin's Press, Inc., 175 Fifth Avenue, New York, New York 10010 (800) 221-7945; *The Statesman's Year-Book*.

MAURITIUS - BUDGET

Central Intelligence Agency, Washington, D.C. 20505 (703) 482-1100, www.cia.gov; *The World Factbook*.

MAURITIUS - BUSINESS AND PROFESSIONAL LICENSES

International Monetary Fund, 700 Nineteenth Street, NW, Washington, D.C. 20431 (202) 623-7000; *Government Finance Statistics Yearbook*.

MAURITIUS - CALORIE SUPPLY

African Development Bank, 01 BP 1387, Abidjan 01, Cote d'Ivoire; *Selected Statistics on Regional Member Countries*.

Food and Agricultural Organization of the United Nations (FAO), Via delle Terme di Caracalla, 00100 Rome, Italy (Telephone Number in U.S. (202) 653-2400); *The State of Food and Agriculture*.

MAURITIUS - CAPITAL REVENUE

International Monetary Fund, 700 Nineteenth Street, NW, Washington, D.C. 20431 (202) 623-7000; *Government Finance Statistics Yearbook*.

MAURITIUS - CATTLE - See MAURITIUS - LIVESTOCK AND POULTRY

MAURITIUS - CEMENT PRODUCTION - See MAURITIUS - MINING AND MINERAL

PRODUCTS

MAURITIUS - CHEMICAL (ORGANIC) PRODUCTION - See MAURITIUS - MINING AND MINERAL PRODUCTS

MAURITIUS - CHICKENS - See MAURITIUS - LIVESTOCK AND POULTRY

MAURITIUS - CIGARETTE PRODUCTION - See MAURITIUS - TOBACCO PRODUCTION

MAURITIUS - CLIMATE

M.E. Sharpe, 80 Business Park Drive, Armonk, New York 10504 (800) 541-6563; *The Illustrated Book of World Rankings.*

St. Martin's Press, Inc., 175 Fifth Avenue, New York, New York 10010 (800) 221-7945; *The Statesman's Year-Book.*

MAURITIUS - CLOTHING EXPORTS AND IMPORTS - See MAURITIUS - TEXTILE INDUSTRY

MAURITIUS - COAL PRODUCTION - See MAURITIUS - MINING AND MINERAL PRODUCTS

MAURITIUS - COFFEE PRODUCTION AND CONSUMPTION - See MAURITIUS - CROPS

MAURITIUS - COMMERCE

St. Martin's Press, Inc., 175 Fifth Avenue, New York, New York 10010 (800) 221-7945; *The Statesman's Year-Book.*

MAURITIUS - COMMUNICATIONS - See MAURITIUS - TRANSPORTATION AND COMMUNICATIONS

MAURITIUS - CONSTRUCTION INDUSTRY

M.E. Sharpe, 80 Business Park Drive, Armonk, New York 10504 (800) 541-6563; *The Illustrated Book of World Rankings.*

Statistical Office of the United Nations, Publishing Service, New York, New York 10017 (800) 253-9646; *Statistical Yearbook.*

United Nations Economic Commission for Africa, Africa Hall, Post Office Box 3001, Addis Ababa, Ethiopia (Telephone Number in U.S. (800) 253-9646); *African Statistical Yearbook.*

MAURITIUS - CONSUMER PRICE INDEX

African Development Bank, 01 BP 1387, Abidjan 01, Cote d'Ivoire; *Selected Statistics on Regional Member Countries.*

Europa Publications Limited, 18 Bedford Square, London, WC1B 3JN, England; *The Europa World Year Book.*

Statistical Office of the United Nations, Publishing Service, New York, New York 10017 (800) 253-9646; *Statistical Yearbook;* and *Survey of Economic and Social Conditions in Africa.*

United Nations Economic Commission for Africa, Africa Hall, Post Office Box 3001, Addis Ababa, Ethiopia (Telephone Number in U.S. (800) 253-9646); *African Statistical Yearbook.*

MAURITIUS - CONSUMER PRICES

Euromonitor International, Inc., 122 South Michigan Avenue, Suite 1200, Chicago, Illinois 60603 (800) 577-EURO; *World Marketing Data and Statistics.*

International Labour Office, I.L.O. Publications, 1828 L Street, NW, Suite 801, Washington, D.C. 20036 (301) 638-3152; *Yearbook of Labour Statistics.*

International Monetary Fund, 700 Nineteenth Street, NW, Washington, D.C. 20431 (202) 623-7000; *International Financial Statistics.*

MAURITIUS - CONSUMPTION

African Development Bank, 01 BP 1387, Abidjan 01, Cote d'Ivoire; *Selected Statistics on Regional Member Countries.*

Statistical Office of the United Nations, Publishing Service, New York, New York 10017 (800) 253-9646; *Survey of Economic and Social Conditions in Africa.*

The World Bank, 1818 H Street, NW, Washington, D.C. 20433 (202) 477-1234; *World Development Report.*

MAURITIUS - COPPER PRODUCTION AND CONSUMPTION - See MAURITIUS - MINING AND MINERAL PRODUCTS

MAURITIUS - CORN PRODUCTION - See MAURITIUS - CROPS

MAURITIUS - CORPORATE TAXES - See MAURITIUS - TAXATION

MAURITIUS - COTTON PRODUCTION - See MAURITIUS - CROPS

MAURITIUS - CRIME

Yale University Press, Yale Station, New Haven, Connecticut 06520 (800) 987-7323; *Violence and Crime in Cross-National Perspective.*

MAURITIUS - CROPS

Europa Publications Limited, 18 Bedford Square, London, WC1B 3JN, England; *The Europa World Year Book.*

Food and Agricultural Organization of

the United Nations (FAO), Via delle Terme di Caracalla, 00100 Rome, Italy (Telephone Number in U.S. (202) 653-2400); *Production Yearbook;* and *The State of Food and Agriculture.*

International Monetary Fund, 700 Nineteenth Street, NW, Washington, D.C. 20431 (202) 623-7000; *International Financial Statistics.*

M.E. Sharpe, 80 Business Park Drive, Armonk, New York 10504 (800) 541-6563; *The Illustrated Book of World Rankings.*

St. Martin's Press, Inc., 175 Fifth Avenue, New York, New York 10010 (800) 221-7945; *The Statesman's Year-Book.*

Statistical Office of the United Nations, Publishing Service, New York, New York 10017 (800) 253-9646; *Statistical Yearbook.*

United Nations Conference on Trade and Development, Central Statistical Service, Palais des Nations, Geneva, Switzerland (Telephone in U.S. (800) 253-9646); *UNCTAD Commodity Yearbook.*

United Nations Economic Commission for Africa, Africa Hall, Post Office Box 3001, Addis Ababa, Ethiopia (Telephone Number in U.S. (800) 253-9646); *African Statistical Yearbook.*

MAURITIUS - CUSTOMS DUTIES

International Monetary Fund, 700 Nineteenth Street, NW, Washington, D.C. 20431 (202) 623-7000; *Government Finance Statistics Yearbook.*

St. Martin's Press, Inc., 175 Fifth Avenue, New York, New York 10010 (800) 221-7945; *The Statesman's Year-Book.*

MAURITIUS - DAIRY PRODUCTS

Europa Publications Limited, 18 Bedford Square, London, WC1B 3JN, England; *The Europa World Year Book.*

Food and Agricultural Organization of the United Nations (FAO), Via delle Terme di Caracalla, 00100 Rome, Italy (Telephone Number in U.S. (202) 653-2400); *The State of Food and Agriculture.*

M.E. Sharpe, 80 Business Park Drive, Armonk, New York 10504 (800) 541-6563; *The Illustrated Book of World Rankings.*

St. Martin's Press, Inc., 175 Fifth Avenue, New York, New York 10010 (800) 221-7945; *The Statesman's Year-Book.*

MAURITIUS - DEATH RATES - See MAURITIUS - MORTALITY

MAURITIUS - DEFENSE EXPENDITURES - See MAURITIUS - MILITARY

MAURITIUS - DEMOGRAPHY

Euromonitor International, Inc., 122 South Michigan Avenue, Suite 1200, Chicago, Illinois 60603 (800) 577-EURO; *International Marketing Data and Statistics; World Marketing Data and Statistics;* and *The World Economic Factbook.*

Federal Statistical Office, Gustav-Stresemann - Ring 11, D-6200, Wiesbaden, Germany; *Mauritius.*

M.E. Sharpe, 80 Business Park Drive, Armonk, New York 10504 (800) 541-6563; *The Illustrated Book of World Rankings.*

Statistical Office of the United Nations, Publishing Service, New York, New York 10017 (800) 253-9646; *Human Development Report;* and *Survey of Economic and Social Conditions in Africa.*

MAURITIUS - DEVELOPMENT ASSISTANCE

Statistical Office of the United Nations, Publishing Service, New York, New York 10017 (800) 253-9646; *Statistical Yearbook.*

MAURITIUS - DIAMOND PRODUCTION - See MAURITIUS - MINING AND MINERAL PRODUCTS

MAURITIUS - DISCOUNT RATES - See MAURITIUS - BANKING

MAURITIUS - DISEASE - See MAURITIUS - HEALTH

MAURITIUS - DIVORCE

M.E. Sharpe, 80 Business Park Drive, Armonk, New York 10504 (800) 541-6563; *The Illustrated Book of World Rankings.*

Statistical Office of the United Nations, Publishing Service, New York, New York 10017 (800) 253-9646; *Demographic Yearbook.*

MAURITIUS - DUCKS - See MAURITIUS - LIVESTOCK AND POULTRY

MAURITIUS - ECONOMY

African Development Bank, 01 BP 1387, Abidjan 01, Cote d'Ivoire; *Selected Statistics on Regional Member Countries.*

Central Intelligence Agency, Washington, D.C. 20505 (703) 482-1100, www.cia.gov; *The World Factbook.*

Economist Intelligence Unit, 111 West 57th Street, New York, New York 10019 (800) 938-4685; *Mauritius Country Report.*

Euromonitor International, Inc., 122 South Michigan Avenue, Suite 1200, Chicago, Illinois 60603 (800) 577-EURO;

The World Economic Factbook; and *World Marketing Data and Statistics.*

Federal Statistical Office, Gustav-Stresemann - Ring 11, D-6200, Wiesbaden, Germany; *Mauritius.*

M.E. Sharpe, 80 Business Park Drive, Armonk, New York 10504 (800) 541-6563; *The Illustrated Book of World Rankings.*

St. Martin's Press, Inc., 175 Fifth Avenue, New York, New York 10010 (800) 221-7945; The Statesman's Year-Book.

Statistical Office of the United Nations, Publishing Service, New York, New York 10017; *Foreign Trade Statistics for Africa;* and *World Statistics Pocketbook.*

The World Bank, 1818 H Street, NW, Washington, D.C. 20433 (202) 477-1234; *The World Bank Atlas;* and *World Development Report.*

MAURITIUS - EDUCATION

African Development Bank, 01 BP 1387, Abidjan 01, Cote d'Ivoire; *Selected Statistics on Regional Member Countries.*

Euromonitor International, Inc., 122 South Michigan Avenue, Suite 1200, Chicago, Illinois 60603 (800) 577-EURO; *International Marketing Data and Statistics;* and *World Marketing Data and Statistics.*

Europa Publications Limited, 18 Bedford Square, London, WC1B 3JN, England; *The Europa World Year Book.*

Federal Statistical Office, Gustav-Stresemann - Ring 11, D-6200, Wiesbaden, Germany; *Mauritius.*

International Monetary Fund, 700 Nineteenth Street, NW, Washington, D.C. 20431 (202) 623-7000; Government Finance Statistics Yearbook.

M.E. Sharpe, 80 Business Park Drive, Armonk, New York 10504 (800) 541-6563; *The Illustrated Book of World Rankings.*

St. Martin's Press, Inc., 175 Fifth Avenue, New York, New York 10010 (800) 221-7945; *The Statesman's Year-Book.*

Statistical Office of the United Nations, Publishing Service, New York, New York 10017 (800) 253-9646; *Human Development Report;* and *Survey of Economic and Social Conditions in Africa.*

United Nations Economic Commission for Africa, Africa Hall, Post Office Box 3001, Addis Ababa, Ethiopia (Telephone Number in U.S. (800) 253-9646); *African Statistical Yearbook.*

United Nations Educational, Scientific

and Cultural Organization (UNESCO), 7 Place de Fontenoy, F-75700 Paris, France (Telephone Number in U.S. (212) 963-5981); *Statistical Yearbook.*

The World Bank, 1818 H Street, NW, Washington, D.C. 20433 (202) 477-1234; *World Development Report;* and *World Development Indicators.*

MAURITIUS - EGG PRODUCTION AND CONSUMPTION - See MAURITIUS - DAIRY PRODUCTS

MAURITIUS - ELECTRICITY

Central Intelligence Agency, Washington, D.C. 20505 (703) 482-1100, www.cia.gov; *The World Factbook.*

M.E. Sharpe, 80 Business Park Drive, Armonk, New York 10504 (800) 541-6563; *The Illustrated Book of World Rankings.*

St. Martin's Press, Inc., 175 Fifth Avenue, New York, New York 10010 (800) 221-7945; *The Statesman's Year-Book.*

Statistical Office of the United Nations, Publishing Service, New York, New York 10017 (800) 253-9646; *Human Development Report; Statistical Yearbook;* and *Survey of Economic and Social Conditions in Africa.*

United Nations Economic Commission for Africa, Africa Hall, Post Office Box 3001, Addis Ababa, Ethiopia (Telephone Number in U.S. (800) 253-9646); *African Statistical Yearbook.*

MAURITIUS - EMPLOYMENT

Euromonitor International, Inc., 122 South Michigan Avenue, Suite 1200, Chicago, Illinois 60603 (800) 577-EURO; *International Marketing Data and Statistics.*

Federal Statistical Office, Gustav-Stresemann - Ring 11, D-6200, Wiesbaden, Germany; *Mauritius.*

International Labour Office, I.L.O. Publications, 1828 L Street, NW, Suite 801, Washington, D.C. 20036 (301) 638-3152; Yearbook of Labour Statistics.

M.E. Sharpe, 80 Business Park Drive, Armonk, New York 10504 (800) 541-6563; *The Illustrated Book of World Rankings.*

Statistical Office of the United Nations, Publishing Service, New York, New York 10017 (800) 253-9646; *Statistical Yearbook;* and *Survey of Economic and Social Conditions in Africa.*

United Nations Economic Commission for Africa, Africa Hall, Post Office Box 3001, Addis Ababa, Ethiopia (Telephone Number in U.S. (800) 253-9646); *African Statistical*

Yearbook.

MAURITIUS - ENERGY

Euromonitor International, Inc., 122 South Michigan Avenue, Suite 1200, Chicago, Illinois 60603 (800) 577-EURO; *International Marketing Data and Statistics; World Marketing Data and Statistics;* and *The World Economic Factbook.*

Food and Agricultural Organization of the United Nations (FAO), Via delle Terme di Caracalla, 00100 Rome, Italy (Telephone Number in U.S. (202) 653-2400); *The State of Food and Agriculture.*

M.E. Sharpe, 80 Business Park Drive, Armonk, New York 10504 (800) 541-6563; *The Illustrated Book of World Rankings.*

St. Martin's Press, Inc., 175 Fifth Avenue, New York, New York 10010 (800) 221-7945; *The Statesman's Year-Book.*

Statistical Office of the United Nations, Publishing Service, New York, New York 10017 (800) 253-9646; *Energy Statistics Yearbook; Human Development Report; World Statistics Pocketbook;* and *Statistical Yearbook.*

United Nations Economic Commission for Africa, Africa Hall, Post Office Box 3001, Addis Ababa, Ethiopia (Telephone Number in U.S. (800) 253-9646); *African Statistical Yearbook.*

The World Bank, 1818 H Street, NW, Washington, D.C. 20433 (202) 477-1234; *The World Bank Atlas;* and *World Development Report.*

MAURITIUS - ENVIRONMENT

Economist Intelligence Unit, 111 West 57th Street, New York, New York 10019 (800) 938-4685; *Mauritius Country Report.*

Statistical Office of the United Nations, Publishing Service, New York, New York 10017 (800) 253-9646; *World Statistics Pocketbook.*

MAURITIUS - EXCHANGE RATES

African Development Bank, 01 BP 1387, Abidjan 01, Cote d'Ivoire; *Selected Statistics on Regional Member Countries.*

Central Intelligence Agency, Washington, D.C. 20505 (703) 482-1100, www.cia.gov; *The World Factbook.*

Euromonitor International, Inc., 122 South Michigan Avenue, Suite 1200, Chicago, Illinois 60603 (800) 577-EURO; *International Marketing Data and Statistics;* and *The World Economic Factbook.*

Europa Publications Limited, 18 Bedford

Square, London, WC1B 3JN, England; *The Europa World Year Book.*

International Civil Aviation Organization, 999 University Street, Montreal, Quebec, Canada H3C 5H7 (514) 954-8219; *Civil Aviation Statistics of the World.*

International Monetary Fund, 700 Nineteenth Street, NW, Washington, D.C. 20431 (202) 623-7000; *International Financial Statistics.*

Statistical Office of the United Nations, Publishing Service, New York, New York 10017 ((800) 253-9646; *Foreign Trade Statistics for Africa; World Statistics Pocketbook;* and *Statistical Yearbook.*

MAURITIUS - EXCISE TAXES - See MAURITIUS - TAXATION

MAURITIUS - EXPORTS

African Development Bank, 01 BP 1387, Abidjan 01, Cote d'Ivoire; *Selected Statistics on Regional Member Countries.*

Central Intelligence Agency, Washington, D.C. 20505 (703) 482-1100, www.cia.gov; *The World Factbook.*

Economist Intelligence Unit, 111 West 57th Street, New York, New York 10019 (800) 938-4685; *Mauritius Country Report.*

Euromonitor International, Inc., 122 South Michigan Avenue, Suite 1200, Chicago, Illinois 60603 (800) 577-EURO; *International Marketing Data and Statistics;* and *The World Economic Factbook.*

Europa Publications Limited, 18 Bedford Square, London, WC1B 3JN, England; *The Europa World Year Book.*

Food and Agricultural Organization of the United Nations (FAO), Via delle Terme di Caracalla, 00100 Rome, Italy (Telephone Number in U.S. (202) 653-2400); *The State of Food and Agriculture.*

International Monetary Fund, 700 Nineteenth Street, NW, Washington, D.C. 20431 (202) 623-7000; *Direction of Trade Statistics; Government Finance Statistics Yearbook;* and *International Financial Statistics.*

St. Martin's Press, Inc., 175 Fifth Avenue, New York, New York 10010 (800) 221-7945; *The Statesman's Year-Book.*

Statistical Office of the United Nations, Publishing Service, New York, New York 10017 (800) 253-9646; *Foreign Trade Statistics for Africa;* and *Survey of Economic and Social Conditions in Africa.*

United Nations Conference on Trade

and Development (UNCTAD), New York, New York 10017 (800) 253-9646; *Handbook of International Trade and Development Statistics.*

United Nations Economic Commission for Africa, Africa Hall, Post Office Box 3001, Addis Ababa, Ethiopia (Telephone Number in U.S. (800) 253-9646); *African Statistical Yearbook.*

The World Bank, 1818 H Street, NW, Washington, D.C. 20433 (202) 477-1234; *World Development Report;* and *World Development Indicators.*

MAURITIUS - EXTERNAL INDEBTEDNESS

African Development Bank, 01 BP 1387, Abidjan 01, Cote d'Ivoire; *Selected Statistics on Regional Member Countries.*

Statistical Office of the United Nations, Publishing Service, New York, New York 10017 (800) 253-9646; *Survey of Economic and Social Conditions in Africa.*

The World Bank, 1818 H Street, NW, Washington, D.C. 20433 (202) 477-1234; *World Development Report;* and *World Development Indicators.*

MAURITIUS - EXTERNAL TRADE

African Development Bank, 01 BP 1387, Abidjan 01, Cote d'Ivoire; *Selected Statistics on Regional Member Countries.*

Euromonitor International, Inc., 122 South Michigan Avenue, Suite 1200, Chicago, Illinois 60603 (800) 577-EURO; *World Marketing Data and Statistics.*

Food and Agricultural Organization of the United Nations (FAO), Via delle Terme di Caracalla, 00100 Rome, Italy (Telephone Number in U.S. (202) 653-2400); *The State of Food and Agriculture;* and *Trade Yearbook.*

Statistical Office of the United Nations, Publishing Service, New York, New York 10017 (800) 253-9646; *Statistical Yearbook.*

MAURITIUS - FARM CROPS - See MAURITIUS - CROPS

MAURITIUS - FERTILITY RATES

Central Intelligence Agency, Washington, D.C. 20505 (703) 482-1100, www.cia.gov; *The World Factbook.*

M.E. Sharpe, 80 Business Park Drive, Armonk, New York 10504 (800) 541-6563; *The Illustrated Book of World Rankings.*

Statistical Office of the United Nations, Publishing Service, New York, New York 10017 (800) 253-9646; *Human Development Report;* and *Survey of*

Economic and Social Conditions in Africa.

The World Bank, 1818 H Street, NW, Washington, D.C. 20433 (202) 477-1234; *The World Bank Atlas; World Development Report;* and *World Development Indicators.*

MAURITIUS - FERTILIZER

Food and Agricultural Organization of the United Nations (FAO), Via delle Terme di Caracalla, 00100 Rome, Italy (Telephone Number in U.S. (202) 653-2400); *Fertilizer Yearbook;* and *The State of Food and Agriculture.*

Statistical Office of the United Nations, Publishing Service, New York, New York 10017 (800) 253-9646; *Statistical Yearbook.*

MAURITIUS - FETAL MORTALITY - See MAURITIUS - MORTALITY

MAURITIUS - FINANCE

African Development Bank, 01 BP 1387, Abidjan 01, Cote d'Ivoire; *Selected Statistics on Regional Member Countries.*

Economist Intelligence Unit, 111 West 57th Street, New York, New York 10019 (800) 938-4685; *Mauritius Country Report.*

Europa Publications Limited, 18 Bedford Square, London, WC1B 3JN, England; *The Europa World Year Book.*

Federal Statistical Office, Gustav-Stresemann - Ring 11, D-6200, Wiesbaden, Germany; *Mauritius.*

International Monetary Fund, 700 Nineteenth Street, NW, Washington, D.C. 20431 (202) 623-7000; International Financial Statistics.

M.E. Sharpe, 80 Business Park Drive, Armonk, New York 10504 (800) 541-6563; *The Illustrated Book of World Rankings.*

St. Martin's Press, Inc., 175 Fifth Avenue, New York, New York 10010 (800) 221-7945; *The Statesman's Year-Book.*

United Nations Economic Commission for Africa, Africa Hall, Post Office Box 3001, Addis Ababa, Ethiopia (Telephone Number in U.S. (800) 253-9646); *African Statistical Yearbook.*

MAURITIUS - FISHERIES

Europa Publications Limited, 18 Bedford Square, London, WC1B 3JN, England; *The Europa World Year Book.*

Federal Statistical Office, Gustav-Stresemann - Ring 11, D-6200, Wiesbaden, Germany; *Mauritius.*

Food and Agricultural Organization of

the United Nations (FAO), Via delle Terme di Caracalla, 00100 Rome, Italy (Telephone Number in U.S. (202) 653-2400); The State of Food and Agriculture; and *Yearbook of Fishery Statistics.*

M.E. Sharpe, 80 Business Park Drive, Armonk, New York 10504 (800) 541-6563; *The Illustrated Book of World Rankings.*

St. Martin's Press, Inc., 175 Fifth Avenue, New York, New York 10010 (800) 221-7945; *The Statesman's Year-Book.*

Statistical Office of the United Nations, Publishing Service, New York, New York 10017 (800) 253-9646; *Statistical Yearbook;* and *Survey of Economic and Social Conditions in Africa.*

United Nations Conference on Trade and Development, Central Statistical Service, Palais des Nations, Geneva, Switzerland (Telephone in U.S. (800) 253-9646); *UNCTAD Commodity Yearbook.*

United Nations Economic Commission for Africa, Africa Hall, Post Office Box 3001, Addis Ababa, Ethiopia (Telephone Number in U.S. (800) 253-9646); *African Statistical Yearbook.*

MAURITIUS - FOOD

African Development Bank, 01 BP 1387, Abidjan 01, Cote d'Ivoire; *Selected Statistics on Regional Member Countries.*

Food and Agricultural Organization of the United Nations (FAO), Via delle Terme di Caracalla, 00100 Rome, Italy (Telephone Number in U.S. (202) 653-2400); *Production Yearbook;* and *The State of Food and Agriculture.*

Statistical Office of the United Nations, Publishing Service, New York, New York 10017 (800) 253-9646; *Human Development Report.*

MAURITIUS - FOREIGN DEBT

International Monetary Fund, 700 Nineteenth Street, NW, Washington, D.C. 20431 (202) 623-7000; *Government Finance Statistics Yearbook.*

MAURITIUS - FOREIGN TRADE

Economist Intelligence Unit, 111 West 57th Street, New York, New York 10019 (800) 938-4685; *Mauritius Country Report.*

Euromonitor International, Inc., 122 South Michigan Avenue, Suite 1200, Chicago, Illinois 60603 (800) 577-EURO; *The World Economic Factbook.*

Europa Publications Limited, 18 Bedford Square, London, WC1B 3JN, England; *The Europa World Year Book.*

Federal Statistical Office, Gustav-Stresemann - Ring 11, D-6200, Wiesbaden, Germany; *Mauritius.*

Food and Agricultural Organization of the United Nations (FAO), Via delle Terme di Caracalla, 00100 Rome, Italy (Telephone Number in U.S. (202) 653-2400); The State of Food and Agriculture.

International Monetary Fund, 700 Nineteenth Street, NW, Washington, D.C. 20431 (202) 623-7000; *International Financial Statistics.*

M.E. Sharpe, 80 Business Park Drive, Armonk, New York 10504 (800) 541-6563; *The Illustrated Book of World Rankings.*

St. Martin's Press, Inc., 175 Fifth Avenue, New York, New York 10010 (800) 221-7945; *The Statesman's Year-Book.*

Statistical Office of the United Nations, Publishing Service, New York, New York 10017 (800) 253-9646; *Foreign Trade Statistics for Africa; International Trade Statistics Yearbook;* and *Statistical Yearbook.*

United Nations Conference on Trade and Development, Central Statistical Service, Palais des Nations, Geneva, Switzerland (Telephone in U.S. (800) 253-9646); *UNCTAD Commodity Yearbook.*

United Nations Economic Commission for Africa, Africa Hall, Post Office Box 3001, Addis Ababa, Ethiopia (Telephone Number in U.S. (800) 253-9646); *African Statistical Yearbook.*

The World Bank, 1818 H Street, NW, Washington, D.C. 20433 (202) 477-1234; *World Development Report;* and *World Development Indicators.*

MAURITIUS - FORESTRY AND FOREST PRODUCTS

Europa Publications Limited, 18 Bedford Square, London, WC1B 3JN, England; *The Europa World Year Book.*

Federal Statistical Office, Gustav-Stresemann - Ring 11, D-6200, Wiesbaden, Germany; *Mauritius.*

Food and Agricultural Organization of the United Nations (FAO), Via delle Terme di Caracalla, 00100 Rome, Italy (Telephone Number in U.S. (202) 653-2400); The State of Food and Agriculture; and *Yearbook of Forest Products.*

M.E. Sharpe, 80 Business Park Drive, Armonk, New York 10504 (800) 541-6563; *The Illustrated Book of World Rankings.*

St. Martin's Press, Inc., 175 Fifth Avenue, New York, New York 10010 (800)

221-7945; *The Statesman's Year-Book.*

Statistical Office of the United Nations, Publishing Service, New York, New York 10017 (800) 253-9646; *Statistical Yearbook.*

United Nations Economic Commission for Africa, Africa Hall, Post Office Box 3001, Addis Ababa, Ethiopia (Telephone Number in U.S. (800) 253-9646); *African Statistical Yearbook.*

United Nations Educational, Scientific and Cultural Organization (UNESCO), 7 Place de Fontenoy, F-75700 Paris, France (Telephone Number in U.S. (212) 963-5981); *Statistical Yearbook.*

The World Bank, 1818 H Street, NW, Washington, D.C. 20433 (202) 477-1234; *World Development Report.*

MAURITIUS - GAS PRODUCTION - See MAURITIUS - MINING AND MINERAL PRODUCTS

MAURITIUS - GENERAL INDUSTRIAL STATISTICS - See MAURITIUS - INDUSTRY

MAURITIUS - GENERAL MORTALITY - See MAURITIUS - MORTALITY

MAURITIUS - GEOGRAPHIC DATA

M.E. Sharpe, 80 Business Park Drive, Armonk, New York 10504 (800) 541-6563; *The Illustrated Book of World Rankings.*

MAURITIUS - GOATS - See MAURITIUS - LIVESTOCK AND POULTRY

MAURITIUS - GOLD HOLDINGS

International Monetary Fund, 700 Nineteenth Street, NW, Washington, D.C. 20431 (202) 623-7000; *International Financial Statistics.*

Statistical Office of the United Nations, Publishing Service, New York, New York 10017 (800) 253-9646; *Statistical Yearbook.*

The World Bank, 1818 H Street, NW, Washington, D.C. 20433 (202) 477-1234; *World Development Indicators.*

MAURITIUS - GOLD PRODUCTION AND CONSUMPTION - See MAURITIUS - MINING AND MINERAL PRODUCTS

MAURITIUS - GOVERNMENT

Central Intelligence Agency, Washington, D.C. 20505 (703) 482-1100, www.cia.gov; *The World Factbook.*

International Monetary Fund, 700 Nineteenth Street, NW, Washington, D.C. 20431 (202) 623-7000; *Government Finance Statistics Yearbook;* and

International Financial Statistics.

St. Martin's Press, Inc., 175 Fifth Avenue, New York, New York 10010 (800) 221-7945; *The Statesman's Year-Book.*

Statistical Office of the United Nations, Publishing Service, New York, New York 10017 (800) 253-9646; *National Accounts Statistics;* and *Survey of Economic and Social Conditions in Africa.*

The World Bank, 1818 H Street, NW, Washington, D.C. 20433 (202) 477-1234; *World Development Report;* and *World Development Indicators.*

MAURITIUS - GRAIN PRODUCTION - See MAURITIUS - CROPS

MAURITIUS - GRANTS

International Monetary Fund, 700 Nineteenth Street, NW, Washington, D.C. 20431 (202) 623-7000; *Government Finance Statistics Yearbook.*

MAURITIUS - GROSS DOMESTIC PRODUCT

African Development Bank, 01 BP 1387, Abidjan 01, Cote d'Ivoire; *Selected Statistics on Regional Member Countries.*

Economist Intelligence Unit, 111 West 57th Street, New York, New York 10019 (800) 938-4685; *Mauritius Country Report.*

Euromonitor International, Inc., 122 South Michigan Avenue, Suite 1200, Chicago, Illinois 60603 (800) 577-EURO; *International Marketing Data and Statistics;* and *The World Economic Factbook.*

Europa Publications Limited, 18 Bedford Square, London, WC1B 3JN, England; *The Europa World Year Book.*

M.E. Sharpe, 80 Business Park Drive, Armonk, New York 10504 (800) 541-6563; *The Illustrated Book of World Rankings.*

Statistical Office of the United Nations, Publishing Service, New York, New York 10017 (800) 253-9646; *Human Development Report; National Accounts Statistics; Statistical Yearbook;* and *Survey of Economic and Social Conditions in Africa.*

United Nations Economic Commission for Africa, Africa Hall, Post Office Box 3001, Addis Ababa, Ethiopia (Telephone Number in U.S. (800) 253-9646); *African Statistical Yearbook.*

The World Bank, 1818 H Street, NW, Washington, D.C. 20433 (202) 477-1234; *World Development Report;* and *World Development Indicators.*

MAURITIUS - GROSS NATIONAL PRODUCT

St. Martin's Press, Inc., 175 Fifth Avenue, New York, New York 10010 (800) 221-7945; *The Statesman's Year-Book.*

U.S. Arms Control and Disarmament Agency, 320 Twenty-first Street, NW, Washington, D.C. 20451 (202) 647-8677; *World Military Expenditures and Arms Transfers.*

The World Bank, 1818 H Street, NW, Washington, D.C. 20433 (202) 477-1234; *The World Bank Atlas; World Development Report;* and *World Development Indicators.*

MAURITIUS - GROUNDNUT PRODUCTION - See MAURITIUS - CROPS

MAURITIUS - HEALTH

African Development Bank, 01 BP 1387, Abidjan 01, Cote d'Ivoire; *Selected Statistics on Regional Member Countries.*

Euromonitor International, Inc., 122 South Michigan Avenue, Suite 1200, Chicago, Illinois 60603 (800) 577-EURO; *World Marketing Data and Statistics.*

Federal Statistical Office, Gustav-Stresemann - Ring 11, D-6200, Wiesbaden, Germany; *Mauritius.*

M.E. Sharpe, 80 Business Park Drive, Armonk, New York 10504 (800) 541-6563; *The Illustrated Book of World Rankings.*

St. Martin's Press, Inc., 175 Fifth Avenue, New York, New York 10010 (800) 221-7945; The Statesman's Year-Book.

Statistical Office of the United Nations, Publishing Service, New York, New York 10017 (800) 253-9646; *Human Development Report;* and *Statistical Yearbook.*

United Nations Children's Fund (UNICEF), 3 United Nations Plaza, New York, New York 10017 (800) 253-9646; *State of the World's Children.*

United Nations Economic Commission for Africa, Africa Hall, Post Office Box 3001, Addis Ababa, Ethiopia (Telephone Number in U.S. (800) 253-9646); *African Statistical Yearbook.*

The World Bank, 1818 H Street, NW, Washington, D.C. 20433 (202) 477-1234; *World Development Report.*

World Health Organization, Office of Publications, 20 Avenue Appia, CH-1211 Geneva 27, Switzerland (Telephone in U.S. (518) 436-9686); *World Health Statistics Annual.*

MAURITIUS - HIDE PRODUCTION

Food and Agricultural Organization of the United Nations (FAO), Via delle Terme di Caracalla, 00100 Rome, Italy (Telephone Number in U.S. (202) 653-2400); *Production Yearbook.*

MAURITIUS - HIGHWAYS

Central Intelligence Agency, Washington, D.C. 20505 (703) 482-1100, www.cia.gov; *The World Factbook.*

St. Martin's Press, Inc., 175 Fifth Avenue, New York, New York 10010 (800) 221-7945; *The Statesman's Year-Book.*

Statistical Office of the United Nations, Publishing Service, New York, New York 10017 (800) 253-9646; *Survey of Economic and Social Conditions in Africa.*

United Nations Economic Commission for Africa, Africa Hall, Post Office Box 3001, Addis Ababa, Ethiopia (Telephone Number in U.S. (800) 253-9646); *African Statistical Yearbook.*

MAURITIUS - HORSES - See MAURITIUS - LIVESTOCK AND POULTRY

MAURITIUS - HOURS OF WORK - See MAURITIUS - EMPLOYMENT

MAURITIUS - HOUSING AND HOUSING UNITS

Euromonitor International, Inc., 122 South Michigan Avenue, Suite 1200, Chicago, Illinois 60603 (800) 577-EURO; *World Marketing Data and Statistics.*

MAURITIUS - HOUSING EXPENDITURES

International Monetary Fund, 700 Nineteenth Street, NW, Washington, D.C. 20431 (202) 623-7000; *Government Finance Statistics Yearbook.*

M.E. Sharpe, 80 Business Park Drive, Armonk, New York 10504 (800) 541-6563; *The Illustrated Book of World Rankings.*

MAURITIUS - ILLITERATE POPULATION

Central Intelligence Agency, Washington, D.C. 20505 (703) 482-1100, www.cia.gov; *The World Factbook.*

Euromonitor International, Inc., 122 South Michigan Avenue, Suite 1200, Chicago, Illinois 60603 (800) 577-EURO; *The World Economic Factbook.*

Statistical Office of the United Nations, Publishing Service, New York, New York 10017 (800) 253-9646; *Human Development Report.*

United Nations Educational, Scientific and Cultural Organization (UNESCO), 7 Place de Fontenoy, F-75700 Paris, France (Telephone Number in U.S. (212) 963-5981); *Statistical Yearbook.*

MAURITIUS - IMPORTS

African Development Bank, 01 BP 1387, Abidjan 01, Cote d'Ivoire; *Selected Statistics on Regional Member Countries.*

Central Intelligence Agency, Washington, D.C. 20505 (703) 482-1100, www.cia.gov; *The World Factbook.*

Economist Intelligence Unit, 111 West 57th Street, New York, New York 10019 (800) 938-4685; *Mauritius Country Report.*

Euromonitor International, Inc., 122 South Michigan Avenue, Suite 1200, Chicago, Illinois 60603 (800) 577-EURO; *International Marketing Data and Statistics;* and *The World Economic Factbook.*

Europa Publications Limited, 18 Bedford Square, London, WC1B 3JN, England; *The Europa World Year Book.*

Food and Agricultural Organization of the United Nations (FAO), Via delle Terme di Caracalla, 00100 Rome, Italy (Telephone Number in U.S. (202) 653-2400); *The State of Food and Agriculture.*

International Monetary Fund, 700 Nineteenth Street, NW, Washington, D.C. 20431 (202) 623-7000; *Direction of Trade Statistics; Government Finance Statistics Yearbook;* and *International Financial Statistics.*

St. Martin's Press, Inc., 175 Fifth Avenue, New York, New York 10010 (800) 221-7945; *The Statesman's Year-Book.*

Statistical Office of the United Nations, Publishing Service, New York, New York 10017 (800) 253-9646; *Foreign Trade Statistics for Africa;* and *Survey of Economic and Social Conditions in Africa.*

United Nations Conference on Trade and Development (UNCTAD), New York, New York 10017 (800) 253-9646; *Handbook of International Trade and Development Statistics.*

United Nations Economic Commission for Africa, Africa Hall, Post Office Box 3001, Addis Ababa, Ethiopia (Telephone Number in U.S. (800) 253-9646); *African Statistical Yearbook.*

The World Bank, 1818 H Street, NW, Washington, D.C. 20433 (202) 477-1234; *World Development Report;* and *World Development Indicators.*

MAURITIUS - INCOME TAXES - See

MAURITIUS - TAXATION

MAURITIUS - INDUSTRY

Central Intelligence Agency, Washington, D.C. 20505 (703) 482-1100, www.cia.gov; *The World Factbook.*

Economist Intelligence Unit, 111 West 57th Street, New York, New York 10019 (800) 938-4685; *Mauritius Country Report.*

Euromonitor International, Inc., 122 South Michigan Avenue, Suite 1200, Chicago, Illinois 60603 (800) 577-EURO; *The World Economic Factbook;* and *World Marketing Data and Statistics.*

Europa Publications Limited, 18 Bedford Square, London, WC1B 3JN, England; *The Europa World Year Book.*

Federal Statistical Office, Gustav-Stresemann - Ring 11, D-6200, Wiesbaden, Germany; *Mauritius.*

International Labour Office, I.L.O. Publications, 1828 L Street, NW, Suite 801, Washington, D.C. 20036 (301) 638-3152; Yearbook of Labour Statistics.

M.E. Sharpe, 80 Business Park Drive, Armonk, New York 10504 (800) 541-6563; *The Illustrated Book of World Rankings.*

St. Martin's Press, Inc., 175 Fifth Avenue, New York, New York 10010 (800) 221-7945; *The Statesman's Year-Book.*

Statistical Office of the United Nations, Publishing Service, New York, New York 10017 (800) 253-9646; *Industrial Commodity Statistics Yearbook;* and *Survey of Economic and Social Conditions in Africa.*

United Nations Economic Commission for Africa, Africa Hall, Post Office Box 3001, Addis Ababa, Ethiopia (Telephone Number in U.S. (800) 253-9646); *African Statistical Yearbook.*

The World Bank, 1818 H Street, NW, Washington, D.C. 20433 (202) 477-1234; *World Development Indicators.*

World Intellectual Property Organization, 34 Chemin des Colombettes, CH-1211 Geneva 20, Switzerland; *Industrial Property Statistics.*

MAURITIUS - INFANT AND MATERNAL MORTALITY - See MAURITIUS - MORTALITY

MAURITIUS - INTERNATIONAL LIQUIDITY

International Monetary Fund, 700 Nineteenth Street, NW, Washington, D.C. 20431 (202) 623-7000; *International*

Financial Statistics.

MAURITIUS - INTERNATIONAL RESERVES EXCLUDING GOLD

African Development Bank, 01 BP 1387, Abidjan 01, Cote d'Ivoire; *Selected Statistics on Regional Member Countries.*

Statistical Office of the United Nations, Publishing Service, New York, New York 10017 (800) 253-9646; *Statistical Yearbook.*

The World Bank, 1818 H Street, NW, Washington, D.C. 20433 (202) 477-1234; *World Development Indicators.*

MAURITIUS - IRON ORE PRODUCTION AND CONSUMPTION - See MAURITIUS - MINING AND MINERAL PRODUCTS

MAURITIUS - LABOR

African Development Bank, 01 BP 1387, Abidjan 01, Cote d'Ivoire; *Selected Statistics on Regional Member Countries.*

Central Intelligence Agency, Washington, D.C. 20505 (703) 482-1100, www.cia.gov; *The World Factbook.*

Euromonitor International, Inc., 122 South Michigan Avenue, Suite 1200, Chicago, Illinois 60603 (800) 577-EURO; *International Marketing Data and Statistics;* and *World Marketing Data and Statistics.*

Europa Publications Limited, 18 Bedford Square, London, WC1B 3JN, England; *The Europa World Year Book.*

Food and Agricultural Organization of the United Nations (FAO), Via delle Terme di Caracalla, 00100 Rome, Italy (Telephone Number in U.S. (202) 653-2400); *The State of Food and Agriculture.*

International Labour Office, I.L.O. Publications, 1828 L Street, NW, Suite 801, Washington, D.C. 20036 (301) 638-3152; *Yearbook of Labour Statistics.*

M.E. Sharpe, 80 Business Park Drive, Armonk, New York 10504 (800) 541-6563; *The Illustrated Book of World Rankings.*

St. Martin's Press, Inc., 175 Fifth Avenue, New York, New York 10010 (800) 221-7945; *The Statesman's Year-Book.*

Statistical Office of the United Nations, Publishing Service, New York, New York 10017 (800) 253-9646; *Human Development Report.*

The World Bank, 1818 H Street, NW, Washington, D.C. 20433 (202) 477-1234; *The World Bank Atlas; World Development Report;* and *World Development Indicators.*

MAURITIUS - LAND USE

Central Intelligence Agency, Washington, D.C. 20505 (703) 482-1100, www.cia.gov; *The World Factbook.*

Euromonitor International, Inc., 122 South Michigan Avenue, Suite 1200, Chicago, Illinois 60603 (800) 577-EURO; *International Marketing Data and Statistics.*

Food and Agricultural Organization of the United Nations (FAO), Via delle Terme di Caracalla, 00100 Rome, Italy (Telephone Number in U.S. (202) 653-2400); *Production Yearbook.*

The World Bank, 1818 H Street, NW, Washington, D.C. 20433 (202) 477-1234; *World Development Report.*

MAURITIUS - LIBRARIES

M.E. Sharpe, 80 Business Park Drive, Armonk, New York 10504 (800) 541-6563; *The Illustrated Book of World Rankings.*

United Nations Educational, Scientific and Cultural Organization (UNESCO), 7 Place de Fontenoy, F-75700 Paris, France (Telephone Number in U.S. (212) 963-5981); *Statistical Yearbook.*

MAURITIUS - LIFE EXPECTANCY

African Development Bank, 01 BP 1387, Abidjan 01, Cote d'Ivoire; *Selected Statistics on Regional Member Countries.*

Central Intelligence Agency, Washington, D.C. 20505 (703) 482-1100, www.cia.gov; *The World Factbook.*

Euromonitor International, Inc., 122 South Michigan Avenue, Suite 1200, Chicago, Illinois 60603 (800) 577-EURO; *The World Economic Factbook.*

Statistical Office of the United Nations, Publishing Service, New York, New York 10017 (800) 253-9646; *Human Development Report;* and *World Statistics Pocketbook.*

The World Bank, 1818 H Street, NW, Washington, D.C. 20433 (202) 477-1234; *The World Bank Atlas;* and *World Development Report.*

MAURITIUS - LITERACY RATE

Euromonitor International, Inc., 122 South Michigan Avenue, Suite 1200, Chicago, Illinois 60603 (800) 577-EURO; *World Marketing Data and Statistics.*

Statistical Office of the United Nations, Publishing Service, New York, New York 10017 (800) 253-9646; *Survey of Economic and Social Conditions in Africa.*

MAURITIUS - LIVESTOCK AND POULTRY

Europa Publications Limited, 18 Bedford Square, London, WC1B 3JN, England; *The Europa World Year Book.*

Food and Agricultural Organization of the United Nations (FAO), Via delle Terme di Caracalla, 00100 Rome, Italy (Telephone Number in U.S. (202) 653-2400); *Production Yearbook;* and *The State of Food and Agriculture.*

M.E. Sharpe, 80 Business Park Drive, Armonk, New York 10504 (800) 541-6563; *The Illustrated Book of World Rankings.*

St. Martin's Press, Inc., 175 Fifth Avenue, New York, New York 10010 (800) 221-7945; *The Statesman's Year-Book.*

Statistical Office of the United Nations, Publishing Service, New York, New York 10017 (800) 253-9646; *Survey of Economic and Social Conditions in Africa.*

United Nations Conference on Trade and Development, Central Statistical Service, Palais des Nations, Geneva, Switzerland (Telephone in U.S. (800) 253-9646); *UNCTAD Commodity Yearbook.*

United Nations Economic Commission for Africa, Africa Hall, Post Office Box 3001, Addis Ababa, Ethiopia (Telephone Number in U.S. (800) 253-9646); *African Statistical Yearbook.*

MAURITIUS - LIVING LEVELS - See MAURITIUS - LIFE EXPECTANCY

MAURITIUS - MAIL - PIECES SENT OR RECEIVED

Statistical Office of the United Nations, Publishing Service, New York, New York 10017 (800) 253-9646; *Statistical Yearbook.*

MAURITIUS - MANUFACTURING

M.E. Sharpe, 80 Business Park Drive, Armonk, New York 10504 (800) 541-6563; *The Illustrated Book of World Rankings.*

Statistical Office of the United Nations, Publishing Service, New York, New York 10017 (800) 253-9646; *Statistical Yearbook;* and *Survey of Economic and Social Conditions in Africa.*

United Nations Economic Commission for Africa, Africa Hall, Post Office Box 3001, Addis Ababa, Ethiopia (Telephone Number in U.S. (800) 253-9646); *African Statistical Yearbook.*

The World Bank, 1818 H Street, NW, Washington, D.C. 20433 (202) 477-1234; *World Development Indicators.*

MAURITIUS - MARRIAGE RATES

Europa Publications Limited, 18

Bedford Square, London, WC1B 3JN, England; *The Europa World Year Book.*

M.E. Sharpe, 80 Business Park Drive, Armonk, New York 10504 (800) 541-6563; *The Illustrated Book of World Rankings.*

Statistical Office of the United Nations, Publishing Service, New York, New York 10017 (800) 253-9646; *Demographic Yearbook.*

MAURITIUS - MEAT PRODUCTION - See - MAURITIUS - LIVESTOCK AND POULTRY

MAURITIUS - MERCHANT SHIPPING

Europa Publications Limited, 18 Bedford Square, London, WC1B 3JN, England; *The Europa World Year Book.*

Lloyd's Register of Shipping, 17 Battery Place, New York, New York 10004 (212) 425-8050; *Register of Ships.*

St. Martin's Press, Inc., 175 Fifth Avenue, New York, New York 10010 (800) 221-7945; *The Statesman's Year-Book.*

Statistical Office of the United Nations, Publishing Service, New York, New York 10017 (800) 253-9646; *Statistical Yearbook.*

United Nations Economic Commission for Africa, Africa Hall, Post Office Box 3001, Addis Ababa, Ethiopia (Telephone Number in U.S. (800) 253-9646); *African Statistical Yearbook.*

U.S. Department of Transportation, Maritime Administration, 400 Seventh Street, SW, Washington, D.C. 20590 (202) 366-5807, www.marad.dot.gov; *A Statistical Analysis of the World's Merchant Fleets.*

MAURITIUS - MILITARY

Central Intelligence Agency, Washington, D.C. 20505 (703) 482-1100, www.cia.gov; *The World Factbook.*

Euromonitor International, Inc., 122 South Michigan Avenue, Suite 1200, Chicago, Illinois 60603 (800) 577-EURO; *World Marketing Data and Statistics.*

International Monetary Fund, 700 Nineteenth Street, NW, Washington, D.C. 20431 (202) 623-7000; *Government Finance Statistics Yearbook.*

M.E. Sharpe, 80 Business Park Drive, Armonk, New York 10504 (800) 541-6563; *The Illustrated Book of World Rankings.*

St. Martin's Press, Inc., 175 Fifth Avenue, New York, New York 10010 (800) 221-7945; *The Statesman's Year-Book.*

Statistical Office of the United Nations, Publishing Service, New York, New York

10017 (800) 253-9646; *Human Development Report.*

U.S. Arms Control and Disarmament Agency, 320 Twenty-first Street, NW, Washington, D.C. 20451 (202) 647-8677; *World Military Expenditures and Arms Transfers.*

MAURITIUS - MINING AND MINERAL PRODUCTS

Europa Publications Limited, 18 Bedford Square, London, WC1B 3JN, England; *The Europa World Year Book.*

M.E. Sharpe, 80 Business Park Drive, Armonk, New York 10504 (800) 541-6563; *The Illustrated Book of World Rankings.*

Statistical Office of the United Nations, Publishing Service, New York, New York 10017 (800) 253-9646; *Statistical Yearbook.*

United Nations Conference on Trade and Development, Central Statistical Service, Palais des Nations, Geneva, Switzerland (Telephone in U.S. (800) 253-9646); *UNCTAD Commodity Yearbook.*

United Nations Economic Commission for Africa, Africa Hall, Post Office Box 3001, Addis Ababa, Ethiopia (Telephone Number in U.S. (800) 253-9646); *African Statistical Yearbook.*

MAURITIUS - MONEY EXCHANGE RATE - See MAURITIUS - EXCHANGE RATES

MAURITIUS - MONEY SUPPLY

African Development Bank, 01 BP 1387, Abidjan 01, Cote d'Ivoire; *Selected Statistics on Regional Member Countries.*

Economist Intelligence Unit, 111 West 57th Street, New York, New York 10019 (800) 938-4685; *Mauritius Country Report.*

Europa Publications Limited, 18 Bedford Square, London, WC1B 3JN, England; *The Europa World Year Book.*

Federal Statistical Office, Gustav-Stresemann - Ring 11, D-6200, Wiesbaden, Germany; *Mauritius.*

International Monetary Fund, 700 Nineteenth Street, NW, Washington, D.C. 20431 (202) 623-7000; *International Financial Statistics.*

The World Bank, 1818 H Street, NW, Washington, D.C. 20433 (202) 477-1234; *World Development Indicators.*

MAURITIUS - MONUMENTS AND HISTORICAL SITES

United Nations Educational, Scientific

and Cultural Organization (UNESCO), 7 Place de Fontenoy, F-75700 Paris, France (Telephone Number in U.S. (212) 963-5981); *Statistical Yearbook.*

MAURITIUS - MORTALITY

Central Intelligence Agency, Washington, D.C. 20505 (703) 482-1100, www.cia.gov; *The World Factbook.*

Euromonitor International, Inc., 122 South Michigan Avenue, Suite 1200, Chicago, Illinois 60603 (800) 577-EURO; *International Marketing Data and Statistics;* and *The World Economic Factbook.*

Europa Publications Limited, 18 Bedford Square, London, WC1B 3JN, England; *The Europa World Year Book.*

St. Martin's Press, Inc., 175 Fifth Avenue, New York, New York 10010 (800) 221-7945; *The Statesman's Year-Book.*

Statistical Office of the United Nations, Publishing Service, New York, New York 10017 (800) 253-9646; *Demographic Yearbook; Human Development Report; Statistical Yearbook; World Statistics Pocketbook;* and *Survey of Economic and Social Conditions in Africa.*

United Nations Children's Fund (UNICEF), 3 United Nations Plaza, New York, New York 10017 (800) 253-9646; *State of the World's Children.*

The World Bank, 1818 H Street, NW, Washington, D.C. 20433 (202) 477-1234; *The World Bank Atlas; World Development Report;* and *World Development Indicators.*

World Health Organization, Office of Publications, 20 Avenue Appia, CH-1211 Geneva 27, Switzerland (Telephone in U.S. (518) 436-9686); *World Health Statistics Annual.*

MAURITIUS - MOTION PICTURES

St. Martin's Press, Inc., 175 Fifth Avenue, New York, New York 10010 (800) 221-7945; *The Statesman's Year-Book.*

Statistical Office of the United Nations, Publishing Service, New York, New York 10017 (800) 253-9646; *Statistical Yearbook.*

MAURITIUS - MOTOR VEHICLE TAXES - See MAURITIUS - TAXATION

MAURITIUS - MOTOR VEHICLES IN USE

Europa Publications Limited, 18 Bedford Square, London, WC1B 3JN, England; *The Europa World Year Book.*

Statistical Office of the United Nations, Publishing Service, New York, New York 10017 (800) 253-9646; *Statistical Yearbook;*

and *Survey of Economic and Social Conditions in Africa.*

MAURITIUS - MUSEUMS

M.E. Sharpe, 80 Business Park Drive, Armonk, New York 10504 (800) 541-6563; *The Illustrated Book of World Rankings.*

United Nations Educational, Scientific and Cultural Organization (UNESCO), 7 Place de Fontenoy, F-75700 Paris, France (Telephone Number in U.S. (212) 963-5981); *Statistical Yearbook.*

MAURITIUS - NATALITY - See MAURITIUS - BIRTH RATES

MAURITIUS - NATIONAL ACCOUNTS

African Development Bank, 01 BP 1387, Abidjan 01, Cote d'Ivoire; *Selected Statistics on Regional Member Countries.*

Europa Publications Limited, 18 Bedford Square, London, WC1B 3JN, England; *The Europa World Year Book.*

Federal Statistical Office, Gustav-Stresemann - Ring 11, D-6200, Wiesbaden, Germany; *Mauritius.*

International Monetary Fund, 700 Nineteenth Street, NW, Washington, D.C. 20431 (202) 623-7000; *International Financial Statistics.*

Statistical Office of the United Nations, Publishing Service, New York, New York 10017 (800) 253-9646; *National Account Statistics;* and *Statistical Yearbook.*

United Nations Economic Commission for Africa, Africa Hall, Post Office Box 3001, Addis Ababa, Ethiopia (Telephone Number in U.S. (800) 253-9646); *African Statistical Yearbook.*

MAURITIUS - NATIONAL INCOME

M.E. Sharpe, 80 Business Park Drive, Armonk, New York 10504 (800) 541-6563; *The Illustrated Book of World Rankings.*

Statistical Office of the United Nations, Publishing Service, New York, New York 10017 (800) 253-9646; *National Accounts Statistics;* and *Statistical Yearbook.*

MAURITIUS - NATIONAL PRODUCT

M.E. Sharpe, 80 Business Park Drive, Armonk, New York 10504 (800) 541-6563; *The Illustrated Book of World Rankings.*

Statistical Office of the United Nations, Publishing Service, New York, New York 10017 (800) 253-9646; *Statistical Yearbook.*

MAURITIUS - NATURAL GAS - PRODUCTION - See MAURITIUS - MINING AND MINERAL PRODUCTS

MAURITIUS - NEWSPAPER PRODUCTION - See MAURITIUS - FORESTRY AND FOREST PRODUCTS

MAURITIUS - NEWSPRINT - See MAURITIUS - FORESTRY AND FOREST PRODUCTS

MAURITIUS - OCCUPATIONS - See MAURITIUS - LABOR

MAURITIUS - PAPER - See MAURITIUS - FORESTRY AND FOREST PRODUCTS

MAURITIUS - PATENTS, TRADEMARKS AND SERVICE MARKS

Statistical Office of the United Nations, Publishing Service, New York, New York 10017 (800) 253-9646; *Statistical Yearbook.*

World Intellectual Property Organization, 34 Chemin des Colombettes, CH-1211 Geneva 20, Switzerland; *Industrial Property Statistics.*

MAURITIUS - PEANUT PRODUCTION - See MAURITIUS - CROPS

MAURITIUS - PERIODICALS

United Nations Educational, Scientific and Cultural Organization (UNESCO), 7 Place de Fontenoy, F-75700 Paris, France (Telephone Number in U.S. (212) 963-5981); *Statistical Yearbook.*

MAURITIUS - PESTICIDE USE

Food and Agricultural Organization of the United Nations (FAO), Via delle Terme di Caracalla, 00100 Rome, Italy (Telephone Number in U.S. (202) 653-2400); *The State of Food and Agriculture.*

MAURITIUS - PETROLEUM INDUSTRY

Food and Agricultural Organization of the United Nations (FAO), Via delle Terme di Caracalla, 00100 Rome, Italy (Telephone Number in U.S. (202) 653-2400); *The State of Food and Agriculture.*

M.E. Sharpe, 80 Business Park Drive, Armonk, New York 10504 (800) 541-6563; *The Illustrated Book of World Rankings.*

MAURITIUS - PIGS - See MAURITIUS - LIVESTOCK AND POULTRY

MAURITIUS - POPULATION

African Development Bank, 01 BP 1387, Abidjan 01, Cote d'Ivoire; *Selected Statistics on Regional Member Countries.*

Central Intelligence Agency, Washington, D.C. 20505 (703) 482-1100, www.cia.gov; *The World Factbook.*

Economist Intelligence Unit, 111 West 57th Street, New York, New York 10019 (800) 938-4685; *Mauritius Country Report.*

Euromonitor International, Inc., 122 South Michigan Avenue, Suite 1200, Chicago, Illinois 60603 (800) 577-EURO; *International Marketing Data and Statistics;* and *The World Economic Factbook.*

Europa Publications Limited, 18 Bedford Square, London, WC1B 3JN, England; *The Europa World Year Book.*

Federal Statistical Office, Gustav-Stresemann - Ring 11, D-6200, Wiesbaden, Germany; *Mauritius.*

Food and Agricultural Organization of the United Nations (FAO), Via delle Terme di Caracalla, 00100 Rome, Italy (Telephone Number in U.S. (202) 653-2400); *Production Yearbook.*

International Labour Office, I.L.O. Publications, 1828 L Street, NW, Suite 801, Washington, D.C. 20036 (301) 638-3152; *Yearbook of Labour Statistics.*

M.E. Sharpe, 80 Business Park Drive, Armonk, New York 10504 (800) 541-6563; *The Illustrated Book of World Rankings.*

St. Martin's Press, Inc., 175 Fifth Avenue, New York, New York 10010 (800) 221-7945; *The Statesman's Year-Book.*

Statistical Office of the United Nations, Publishing Service, New York, New York 10017 (800) 253-9646; *Demographic Yearbook; Human Development Report; Statistical Yearbook; World Statistics Pocketbook;* and *Survey of Economic and Social Conditions in Africa.*

U.S. Arms Control and Disarmament Agency, 320 Twenty-first Street, NW, Washington, D.C. 20451 (202) 647-8677; *World Military Expenditures and Arms Transfers.*

The World Bank, 1818 H Street, NW, Washington, D.C. 20433 (202) 477-1234; *The World Bank Atlas;* and *World Development Report.*

World Health Organization, Office of Publications, 20 Avenue Appia, CH-1211 Geneva 27, Switzerland (Telephone in U.S. (518) 436-9686); *World Health Statistics Annual.*

MAURITIUS - POST OFFICES

MAURITIUS - POTATO PRODUCTION - See MAURITIUS - CROPS

MAURITIUS - POWER PRODUCTION INDUSTRY - ESTABLISHMENTS, PAYROLLS, VALUE ADDED, ETC.

Statistical Office of the United Nations, Publishing Service, New York, New York 10017 (800) 253-9646; *Statistical Yearbook.*

MAURITIUS - PRICES

Federal Statistical Office, Gustav-Stresemann - Ring 11, D-6200, Wiesbaden, Germany; *Mauritius.*

Food and Agricultural Organization of the United Nations (FAO), Via delle Terme di Caracalla, 00100 Rome, Italy (Telephone Number in U.S. (202) 653-2400); Production Yearbook; and *The State of Food and Agriculture.*

International Labour Office, I.L.O. Publications, 1828 L Street, NW, Suite 801, Washington, D.C. 20036 (301) 638-3152; *Yearbook of Labour Statistics.*

International Monetary Fund, 700 Nineteenth Street, NW, Washington, D.C. 20431 (202) 623-7000; *International Financial Statistics.*

M.E. Sharpe, 80 Business Park Drive, Armonk, New York 10504 (800) 541-6563; *The Illustrated Book of World Rankings.*

United Nations Economic Commission for Africa, Africa Hall, Post Office Box 3001, Addis Ababa, Ethiopia (Telephone Number in U.S. (800) 253-9646); *African Statistical Yearbook.*

MAURITIUS - PRINTING AND WRITING PAPER - See MAURITIUS - FORESTRY AND FOREST PRODUCTS

MAURITIUS - PRODUCTION

M.E. Sharpe, 80 Business Park Drive, Armonk, New York 10504 (800) 541-6563; *The Illustrated Book of World Rankings.*

MAURITIUS - PROPERTY TAXES

International Monetary Fund, 700 Nineteenth Street, NW, Washington, D.C. 20431 (202) 623-7000; *Government Finance Statistics Yearbook.*

MAURITIUS - PUBLIC FINANCE - See MAURITIUS - FINANCE

MAURITIUS - RADIO BROADCASTING - See MAURITIUS - BROADCASTING

MAURITIUS - RADIO RECEIVERS

St. Martin's Press, Inc., 175 Fifth Avenue, New York, New York 10010 (800) 221-7945; *The Statesman's Year-Book.*

MAURITIUS - RAILWAY USE

United Nations Economic Commission for Africa, Africa Hall, Post Office Box 3001,

Addis Ababa, Ethiopia (Telephone Number in U.S. (800) 253-9646); *African Statistical Yearbook.*

MAURITIUS - RELIGION

Central Intelligence Agency, Washington, D.C. 20505 (703) 482-1100, www.cia.gov; *The World Factbook.*

M.E. Sharpe, 80 Business Park Drive, Armonk, New York 10504 (800) 541-6563; *The Illustrated Book of World Rankings.*

St. Martin's Press, Inc., 175 Fifth Avenue, New York, New York 10010 (800) 221-7945; *The Statesman's Year-Book.*

MAURITIUS - RENT PRICES

International Labour Office, I.L.O. Publications, 1828 L Street, NW, Suite 801, Washington, D.C. 20036 (301) 638-3152; *Yearbook of Labour Statistics.*

MAURITIUS - RETAIL TRADE

Euromonitor International, Inc., 122 South Michigan Avenue, Suite 1200, Chicago, Illinois 60603 (800) 577-EURO; *World Marketing Data and Statistics.*

Statistical Office of the United Nations, Publishing Service, New York, New York 10017 (800) 253-9646; *Statistical Yearbook.*

MAURITIUS - RICE PRODUCTION - See MAURITIUS - CROPS

MAURITIUS - ROOT AND TUBER PRODUCTION - See MAURITIUS - CROPS

MAURITIUS - ROUNDWOOD PRODUCTION - See MAURITIUS - FORESTRY AND FOREST PRODUCTS

MAURITIUS - RUBBER PRODUCTION

M.E. Sharpe, 80 Business Park Drive, Armonk, New York 10504 (800) 541-6563; *The Illustrated Book of World Rankings.*

MAURITIUS - SALT PRODUCTION - See MAURITIUS - MINING AND MINERAL PRODUCTS

MAURITIUS - SCIENCE AND TECHNOLOGY - EXPENDITURE FOR RESEARCH - See MAURITIUS - SCIENTISTS, ENGINEERS AND TECHNICIANS

MAURITIUS - SCIENTISTS, ENGINEERS AND TECHNICIANS

Statistical Office of the United Nations, Publishing Service, New York, New York 10017 (800) 253-9646; *Statistical Yearbook.*

United Nations Educational, Scientific and Cultural Organization (UNESCO), 7

Place de Fontenoy, F-75700 Paris, France (Telephone Number in U.S. (212) 963-5981); *Statistical Yearbook.*

MAURITIUS - SENIOR CITIZENS

M.E. Sharpe, 80 Business Park Drive, Armonk, New York 10504 (800) 541-6563; *The Illustrated Book of World Rankings.*

MAURITIUS - SHEEP - See MAURITIUS - LIVESTOCK AND POULTRY

MAURITIUS - SILVER PRODUCTION AND CONSUMPTION - See MAURITIUS - MINING AND MINERAL PRODUCTS

MAURITIUS - SOCIAL DATA

African Development Bank, 01 BP 1387, Abidjan 01, Cote d'Ivoire; *Selected Statistics on Regional Member Countries.*

M.E. Sharpe, 80 Business Park Drive, Armonk, New York 10504 (800) 541-6563; *The Illustrated Book of World Rankings.*

Statistical Office of the United Nations, Publishing Service, New York, New York 10017 (800) 253-9646; *World Statistics Pocketbook.*

MAURITIUS - SOCIAL SECURITY

Statistical Office of the United Nations, Publishing Service, New York, New York 10017 (800) 253-9646; *National Accounts Statistics.*

MAURITIUS - STAMP TAXES AND DUTIES - See MAURITIUS - TAXATION

MAURITIUS - STEEL PRODUCTION - See MAURITIUS - MINING AND MINERAL PRODUCTS

MAURITIUS - STOCKS - COMMODITY - MARKET PRICE - INDEX

Food and Agricultural Organization of the United Nations (FAO), Via delle Terme di Caracalla, 00100 Rome, Italy (Telephone Number in U.S. (202) 653-2400); *The State of Food and Agriculture.*

MAURITIUS - SUGAR - See MAURITIUS - CROPS

MAURITIUS - TAX REVENUE - See MAURITIUS - TAXATION

MAURITIUS - TAXATION

Europa Publications Limited, 18 Bedford Square, London, WC1B 3JN, England; *The Europa World Year Book.*

International Monetary Fund, 700 Nineteenth Street, NW, Washington, D.C. 20431 (202) 623-7000; *Government Finance Statistics Yearbook.*

St. Martin's Press, Inc., 175 Fifth Avenue, New York, New York 10010 (800) 221-7945; *The Statesman's Year-Book.*

The World Bank, 1818 H Street, NW, Washington, D.C. 20433 (202) 477-1234; *World Development Indicators.*

MAURITIUS - TEA PRODUCTION - See MAURITIUS - CROPS

MAURITIUS - TELEPHONES IN USE

American Telephone and Telegraph Company, 26 Parsippany Road, Whippany, New Jersey 07981 (800) 222-0300; *The World's Telephones.*

Central Intelligence Agency, Washington, D.C. 20505 (703) 482-1100, www.cia.gov; *The World Factbook.*

Europa Publications Limited, 18 Bedford Square, London, WC1B 3JN, England; *The Europa World Year Book.*

St. Martin's Press, Inc., 175 Fifth Avenue, New York, New York 10010 (800) 221-7945; *The Statesman's Year-Book.*

Statistical Office of the United Nations, Publishing Service, New York, New York 10017 (800) 253-9646; *Statistical Yearbook; and World Statistics Pocketbook.*

MAURITIUS - TELEVISION BROADCASTING - See MAURITIUS - BROADCASTING

MAURITIUS - TEXTILE INDUSTRY

M.E. Sharpe, 80 Business Park Drive, Armonk, New York 10504 (800) 541-6563; *The Illustrated Book of World Rankings.*

St. Martin's Press, Inc., 175 Fifth Avenue, New York, New York 10010 (800) 221-7945; *The Statesman's Year-Book.*

Statistical Office of the United Nations, Publishing Service, New York, New York 10017 (800) 253-9646; *Statistical Yearbook.*

United Nations Conference on Trade and Development, Central Statistical Service, Palais des Nations, Geneva, Switzerland (Telephone in U.S. (800) 253-9646); *UNCTAD Commodity Yearbook.*

MAURITIUS - TOBACCO PRODUCTION

M.E. Sharpe, 80 Business Park Drive, Armonk, New York 10504 (800) 541-6563; *The Illustrated Book of World Rankings.*

Statistical Office of the United Nations, Publishing Service, New York, New York 10017 (800) 253-9646; *Statistical Yearbook.*

MAURITIUS - TOURISM

Euromonitor International, Inc., 122 South Michigan Avenue, Suite 1200, Chicago, Illinois 60603 (800) 577-EURO; *The World Economic Factbook; and World Marketing Data and Statistics.*

Europa Publications Limited, 18 Bedford Square, London, WC1B 3JN, England; *The Europa World Year Book.*

Federal Statistical Office, Gustav-Stresemann - Ring 11, D-6200, Wiesbaden, Germany; *Mauritius.*

M.E. Sharpe, 80 Business Park Drive, Armonk, New York 10504 (800) 541-6563; *The Illustrated Book of World Rankings.*

St. Martin's Press, Inc., 175 Fifth Avenue, New York, New York 10010 (800) 221-7945; *The Statesman's Year-Book.*

Statistical Office of the United Nations, Publishing Service, New York, New York 10017 (800) 253-9646; *Statistical Yearbook.*

United Nations Economic Commission for Africa, Africa Hall, Post Office Box 3001, Addis Ababa, Ethiopia (Telephone Number in U.S. (800) 253-9646); *African Statistical Yearbook.*

MAURITIUS - TRACTORS IN USE

Statistical Office of the United Nations, Publishing Service, New York, New York 10017 (800) 253-9646; *Statistical Yearbook.*

MAURITIUS - TRADE - See MAURITIUS - FOREIGN TRADE

MAURITIUS - TRADEMARKS AND SERVICE MARKS - See MAURITIUS - PATENTS, TRADEMARKS AND SERVICE MARKS

MAURITIUS - TRANSPORTATION AND COMMUNICATIONS

Central Intelligence Agency, Washington, D.C. 20505 (703) 482-1100, www.cia.gov; *The World Factbook.*

Euromonitor International, Inc., 122 South Michigan Avenue, Suite 1200, Chicago, Illinois 60603 (800) 577-EURO; *International Marketing Data and Statistics; and World Marketing Data and Statistics.*

Europa Publications Limited, 18 Bedford Square, London, WC1B 3JN, England; *The Europa World Year Book.*

Federal Statistical Office, Gustav-Stresemann - Ring 11, D-6200, Wiesbaden, Germany; *Mauritius.*

M.E. Sharpe, 80 Business Park Drive, Armonk, New York 10504 (800) 541-6563; *The Illustrated Book of World Rankings.*

St. Martin's Press, Inc., 175 Fifth

Avenue, New York, New York 10010 (800) 221-7945; *The Statesman's Year-Book.*

Statistical Office of the United Nations, Publishing Service, New York, New York 10017 (800) 253-9646; *Human Development Report.*

United Nations Economic Commission for Africa, Africa Hall, Post Office Box 3001, Addis Ababa, Ethiopia (Telephone Number in U.S. (800) 253-9646); *African Statistical Yearbook.*

MAURITIUS - TURKEYS - See MAURITIUS - LIVESTOCK AND POULTRY

MAURITIUS - UNEMPLOYMENT

Central Intelligence Agency, Washington, D.C. 20505 (703) 482-1100, www.cia.gov; *The World Factbook.*

International Labour Office, I.L.O. Publications, 1828 L Street, NW, Suite 801, Washington, D.C. 20036 (301) 638-3152; *Yearbook of Labour Statistics.*

St. Martin's Press, Inc., 175 Fifth Avenue, New York, New York 10010 (800) 221-7945; *The Statesman's Year-Book.*

Statistical Office of the United Nations, Publishing Service, New York, New York 10017 (800) 253-9646; *Statistical Yearbook.*

MAURITIUS - VITAL STATISTICS

St. Martin's Press, Inc., 175 Fifth Avenue, New York, New York 10010 (800) 221-7945; *The Statesman's Year-Book.*

Statistical Office of the United Nations, Publishing Service, New York, New York 10017 (800) 253-9646; *Statistical Yearbook.*

World Health Organization, Office of Publications, 20 Avenue Appia, CH-1211 Geneva 27, Switzerland (Telephone in U.S. (518) 436-9686); *World Health Statistics Annual.*

MAURITIUS - WAGES

Federal Statistical Office, Gustav-Stresemann - Ring 11, D-6200, Wiesbaden, Germany; *Mauritius.*

International Labour Office, I.L.O. Publications, 1828 L Street, NW, Suite 801, Washington, D.C. 20036 (301) 638-3152; *Yearbook of Labour Statistics.*

MAURITIUS - WAGES IN MANUFACTURING

Statistical Office of the United Nations, Publishing Service, New York, New York 10017 (800) 253-9646; *Statistical Yearbook.*

MAURITIUS - WEATHER - See

MAURITIUS - CLIMATE

MAURITIUS - WHEAT PRODUCTION - See MAURITIUS - CROPS

MAURITIUS - WHOLESALE TRADE

Statistical Office of the United Nations, Publishing Service, New York, New York 10017 (800) 253-9646; *Statistical Yearbook.*

MAURITIUS - WINE PRODUCTION - See MAURITIUS - BEVERAGES

MAURITIUS - WOOL PRODUCTION - See MAURITIUS - TEXTILE INDUSTRY

MAURITIUS - YARN PRODUCTION - See MAURITIUS - TEXTILE INDUSTRY

MAYOTTE - AGRICULTURE

Europa Publications Limited, 18 Bedford Square, London, WC1B 3JN, England; *The Europa World Year Book.*

MAYOTTE - AIRLINE SERVICE

Europa Publications Limited, 18 Bedford Square, London, WC1B 3JN, England; *The Europa World Year Book.*

MAYOTTE - AREA

Europa Publications Limited, 18 Bedford Square, London, WC1B 3JN, England; *The Europa World Year Book.*

MAYOTTE - ECONOMY

The World Bank, 1818 H Street, NW, Washington, D.C. 20433 (202) 477-1234; *The World Bank Atlas.*

MAYOTTE - EDUCATION

Europa Publications Limited, 18 Bedford Square, London, WC1B 3JN, England; *The Europa World Year Book.*

MAYOTTE - ENERGY

The World Bank, 1818 H Street, NW, Washington, D.C. 20433 (202) 477-1234; *The World Bank Atlas.*

MAYOTTE - EXCHANGE RATES

Europa Publications Limited, 18 Bedford Square, London, WC1B 3JN, England; *The Europa World Year Book.*

MAYOTTE - EXPORTS

Europa Publications Limited, 18 Bedford Square, London, WC1B 3JN, England; *The Europa World Year Book.*

MAYOTTE - FERTILITY

The World Bank, 1818 H Street, NW,

Washington, D.C. 20433 (202) 477-1234; *The World Bank Atlas.*

MAYOTTE - FINANCE

Europa Publications Limited, 18 Bedford Square, London, WC1B 3JN, England; *The Europa World Year Book.*

MAYOTTE - FISHERIES

Europa Publications Limited, 18 Bedford Square, London, WC1B 3JN, England; *The Europa World Year Book.*

MAYOTTE - FOREIGN TRADE

Europa Publications Limited, 18 Bedford Square, London, WC1B 3JN, England; *The Europa World Year Book.*

MAYOTTE - GOVERNMENT

Europa Publications Limited, 18 Bedford Square, London, WC1B 3JN, England; *The Europa World Year Book.*

MAYOTTE - GROSS NATIONAL PRODUCTS

The World Bank, 1818 H Street, NW, Washington, D.C. 20433 (202) 477-1234; *The World Bank Atlas.*

MAYOTTE - IMPORTS

Europa Publications Limited, 18 Bedford Square, London, WC1B 3JN, England; *The Europa World Year Book.*

MAYOTTE - LABOR

The World Bank, 1818 H Street, NW, Washington, D.C. 20433 (202) 477-1234; *The World Bank Atlas.*

MAYOTTE - LIFE EXPECTANCY

The World Bank, 1818 H Street, NW, Washington, D.C. 20433 (202) 477-1234; *The World Bank Atlas.*

MAYOTTE - LIVESTOCK AND POULTRY

Europa Publications Limited, 18 Bedford Square, London, WC1B 3JN, England; *The Europa World Year Book.*

MAYOTTE - MONEY SUPPLY

Europa Publications Limited, 18 Bedford Square, London, WC1B 3JN, England; *The Europa World Year Book.*

MAYOTTE - MORTALITY

Europa Publications Limited, 18 Bedford Square, London, WC1B 3JN, England; *The Europa World Year Book.*

The World Bank, 1818 H Street, NW, Washington, D.C. 20433 (202) 477-1234;

The World Bank Atlas.

MAYOTTE - POPULATION

Europa Publications Limited, 18 Bedford Square, London, WC1B 3JN, England; *The Europa World Year Book.*

The World Bank, 1818 H Street, NW, Washington, D.C. 20433 (202) 477-1234; *The World Bank Atlas.*

MAYOTTE - TRANSPORTATION

Europa Publications Limited, 18 Bedford Square, London, WC1B 3JN, England; *The Europa World Year Book.*

MEASLES

U.S. Department of Health and Human Services, Centers for Disease Control and Prevention, 1600 Clifton Road, NE, Atlanta, Georgia 30333 (800) 311-3435, www.cdc.gov; *Summary of Notifiable Diseases, U.S. Morbidity and Mortality Weekly Report.*

MEASURING, ANALYZING, AND CONTROLLING INSTRUMENTS - See INSTRUMENTS AND RELATED PRODUCTS - MANUFACTURING

MEAT AND MEAT PRODUCTS - See also FOOD AND KINDRED PRODUCTS and Individual Meats

MEAT AND MEAT PRODUCTS - CONSUMER EXPENDITURES

U.S. Department of Labor, Bureau of Labor Statistics, Two Massachusetts Avenue, NE, Washington, D.C. 20212 (202) 691-5200, www.stats.bls.gov; *Consumer Expenditures in 1997;* and unpublished data.

MEAT AND MEAT PRODUCTS - CONSUMPTION

U.S. Department of Agriculture, Center for Nutrition and Promotion, 1120 Twentieth Street, NW, North Lobby Suite 200, Washington, D.C. 20036 (202) 418-2312, www.usda.gov/cnpp; unpublished data.

U.S. Department of Agriculture, Economic Research Service, 1800 M Street, NW, Washington, D.C. 20036 (202) 694-5050, www.ers.usda.gov; *Food Consumption, Prices and Expenditures;* and *Agricultural Outlook.*

U.S. Department of Agriculture, Foreign Agricultural Service, Fourteenth Street and Independence Avenue, SW, Washington, D.C. 20250 (202) 720-7115, www.fas.usda.gov; *Livestock and Poultry: World Markets and Trade;* and *Meat Animals-Production, Disposition,* and

Income; and Agricultural Outlook.

MEAT AND MEAT PRODUCTS - EXPENDITURES

U.S. Department of Agriculture, Economic Research Service, 1800 M Street, NW, Washington, D.C. 20036 (202) 694-5050, www.ers.usda.gov; *Food Cost Review; Food Review;* and *Agricultural Statistics.*

MEAT AND MEAT PRODUCTS - EXPENDITURES - FOOD AT HOME

U.S. Department of Labor, Bureau of Labor Statistics, Two Massachusetts Avenue, NE, Washington, D.C. 20212 (202) 691-5200, www.stats.bls.gov; *Consumer Expenditures in 1997.*

MEAT AND MEAT PRODUCTS - FOREIGN TRADE

U.S. Department of Agriculture, Economic Research Service, 1800 M Street, NW, Washington, D.C. 20036 (202) 694-5050, www.ers.usda.gov; *Food Consumption, Prices, and Expenditures; Foreign Agricultural Trade of the United States; Agricultural Statistics; Agricultural Outlook; U.S. Agricultural Update*; and unpublished data.

U.S. Department of Commerce, Bureau of the Census, Washington, D.C. 20233 (301) 457-4100, www.census.gov; *U.S. International Trade in Goods and Services.*

MEAT AND MEAT PRODUCTS - PRICE INDEXES

U.S. Department of Labor, Bureau of Labor Statistics, Two Massachusetts Avenue, NE, Washington, D.C. 20212 (202) 691-5200, www.stats.bls.gov; *CPI Detailed Report;* and *Monthly Labor Review.*

MEAT AND MEAT PRODUCTS - PRODUCTION

Food and Agriculture Organization of the United Nations (FAO), Via delle Terme di Caracalla, 00100 Rome, Italy (Telephone Number in U.S. (202) 653-2400); *FAOSTAT Database.*

U.S. Department of Agriculture, Economic Research Service, 1800 M Street, NW, Washington, D.C. 20036 (202) 694-5050, www.ers.usda.gov; *Agricultural Outlook;* and *Food Consumption, Prices, and Expenditures.*

MEAT AND MEAT PRODUCTS - SUPPLY

U.S. Department of Agriculture, Economic Research Service, 1800 M Street, NW, Washington, D.C. 20036 (202) 694-5050, www.ers.usda.gov; *Agricultural Outlook;* and *Food Consumption, Prices,*

and Expenditures.

MEDIA - See also individual medium

Editor and Publisher Company, 11 West 19th Street, New York, New York 10011 (212) 675-4380; *Editor and Publisher International Year Book.*

Independent Sector, 1200 18th Street, NW, Suite 200, Washington, D.C. 20036 (202) 467-6161; *Giving and Volunteering in the United States.*

Mediamark Research Incorporation, 708 Third Avenue, New York, New York 10017 (212) 599-0444; *Multimedia Audiences.*

Radio Advertising Bureau, 304 Park Avenue, South, New York, New York 10010 (212) 387-2100; *Radio Facts; Radio Marketing Guide;* and *Fact Book for Advertisers.*

Television Bureau of Advertising, Inc., 3 East 54th Street, New York, New York 10022 (212) 486-1111; *Trends in Television.*

U.S. Department of Commerce, Bureau of the Census, Washington, D.C. 20233 (301) 457-4100, www.census.gov; *Census of Housing.*

Veronis, Suhler and Associates, 350 Park Avenue, New York, New York 10022 (212) 935-4990; *Communications Industry Report.*

Warren Publishing, 2115 Ward Court, NW, Washington, D.C. 20037 (202) 872-9200; *Television and Cable Factbook.*

MEDICAID - COVERAGE - RECIPIENTS

U.S. Department of Commerce, Bureau of the Census, Washington, D.C. 20233 (301) 457-4100, www.census.gov; *Current Population Reports;* unpublished data; and Internet site: http://ferret.bls.census.gov/macro/031998/noncash/1001.htm.

U.S. Department of Health and Human Services, Health Care Financing Administration, 200 Independence Avenue, SW, Washington, D.C. 20201 (202) 690-6145, www.hcfa.gov; *Health Care Financing Review; Statistical Report on Medical Care: Eligibles, Recipients, Payments and Services;* unpublished data; and Internet sites: http://www.hcfa.gov/medicaid/trends97.htm; and "Managed Care State Enrollment," http://www.hcfa.gov/medicaid/mcsten97.htm

U.S. Library of Congress, Congressional Research Service, 10 First Street, SE, Washington, D.C. 20540 (202) 707-5000, www.loc.gov; *Cash and Non-Cash Benefits for Persons With Limited Income: Eligibility*

Rules, Recipient and Expenditure Data.

MEDICAID - EXPENDITURES

Social Security Administration, 6400 Security Boulevard, Baltimore, Maryland 21235 (800) 772-1213, www.ssa.gov; *Social Security Bulletin;* and unpublished data.

U.S. Department of Health and Human Services, Health Care Financing Administration, 200 Independence Avenue, SW, Washington, D.C. 20201 (202) 690-6145, www.hcfa.gov; Internet sites: "National Health Expenditures Table 5," http://www.hcfa.gov/stats/nhe-oact/tables/t13.htm; "National Health Expenditures Table 5," http://www.hcfa.gov/stats/nhe-oact/tables/t14.htm; http://hcfa,gov/stats/NHE-Proj/tables/t01.htm; and http://www.hcfa.gov/stats/NHE-Proj/tables/to2A.htm.

U.S. Library of Congress, Congressional Research Service, 10 First Street, SE, Washington, D.C. 20540 (202) 707-5000, www.loc.gov; *Cash and Non-Cash Benefits for Persons with Limited Income: Eligibility Rules, Recipient and Expenditure Data.*

MEDICAID - NURSING HOMES

U.S. Department of Health and Human Services, Health Care Financing Administration, 200 Independence Avenue, SW, Washington, D.C. 20201 (800) 690-6145, www.hcfa.gov; *Statistical Report on Medical Care: Eligibles, Recipients, Payments, and Servcies.*

U.S. Department of Health and Human Services, National Center for Health Statistics, 3700 East-West Highway, Hyattsville, MD 20782 (301) 436-8500; *Advanced Data, No. 280 and 289.*

MEDICAID - STATE DATA

U.S. Department of Health and Human Services, Health Care Financing Administration, 200 Independence Avenue, SW, Washington, D.C. 20201 (202) 690-6145, www.hcfa.gov; *Statistical Report on Medical Care: Eligibles, Recipients, Payments and Services.*

MEDICAL CARE - See also HEALTH AND HEALTH SERVICES

MEDICAL CARE - BUDGET OUTLAYS

Executive Office of the President, Office of Management and Budget, Executive Office Building, Washington, D.C. 20503 (202) 395-3080, www.whitehosue.gov/omb; *Historical Tables.*

MEDICAL CARE - EXPENDITURES FOR

Social Security Administration, 6400 Security Boulevard, Baltimore, Maryland

21235 (800) 772-1213, www.ssa.gov; *Social Security Bulletin;* and unpublished data.

U.S. Department of Commerce, Bureau of Economic Analysis, 14th Street between Constitution Avenue and E Street, NW, Washington, D.C. 20230 (202) 606-9900, www.bea.doc.gov; *National Income and Product Accounts of the United States*; and *Survey of Current Business.*

U.S. Department of Health and Human Services, Health Care Financing Administration, 200 Independence Avenue, SW, Washington, D.C. 20201 (202) 690-6145, www.hcfa.gov; *Health Care Financing Review;* and unpublished data.

U.S. Department of Labor, Bureau of Labor Statistics, Two Massachusetts Avenue, NE, Washington, D.C. 20212 (202) 691-5200, www.stats.bls.gov; *Consumer Expenditures in 1995;* and unpublished data.

U.S. Library of Congress, 101 Independence Avenue, SE, Washington, D.C. 20540 (202) 707-5000, www.loc.gov; *Cash and Noncast Benefits for Persons With Limited Income: Eligibility Rules, Recipient, and Expenditure Data.*

MEDICAL CARE - HOSPITAL VISITS

U.S. Department of Health and Human Services, National Center for Health Statistics, 3700 East-West Highway, Hyattsville, Maryland 20782 (301) 436-8500, www.cdc.gov/nchs; *Advance Data, No. 304*; and unpublished data.

MEDICAL CARE - INSURANCE BENEFITS

Health Insurance Association of America, 555 13th Street, NW, Suite 600, Washington, D.C. 20004 (202) 824-1600; *Source Book of Health Insurance Data.*

U.S. Department of Health and Human Services, Health Care Financing Administration, 200 Independence Avenue, SW, Washington, D.C. 20201 (202) 690-6145, www.hcfa.gov; *Health Care Financing Review.*

MEDICAL CARE - INSURANCE BENEFITS - EXPENDITURES FOR

U.S. Department of Health and Human Services, Health Care Financing Administration, 200 Independence Avenue, SW, Washington, D.C. 20201 (202) 690-6145, www.hcfa.gov; *Health Care Financing Review.*

MEDICAL CARE - PRICE INDEXES - CONSUMER

U.S. Department of Labor, Bureau of Labor Statistics, Two Massachusetts Avenue, NE, Washington, D.C. 20212 (202) 691-5200, www.stats.bls.gov; *Consumer Price Index*

Detailed Report; Monthly Labor Review; and *Handbook of Labor Statistics.*

MEDICAL CARE - PRICE INDEXES - CONSUMER - FIXED-WEIGHTED

U.S. Department of Commerce, Bureau of Economic Analysis, Fourteenth Street between Constitution Avenue and E Street, NW, Washington, D.C. 20230 (202) 606-9900, www.bea.doc.gov; *The National Income and Product Accounts of the United States*; and *Survey of Current Business.*

MEDICAL CARE - PRODUCTS AND SHIPMENTS

U.S. Department of Commerce, Bureau of the Census, Washington, D.C. 20233 (301) 457-4100, www.census.gov; *Current Industrial Reports; Manufacturers' Shipments, Inventories and Orders*; and monthly press releases.

MEDICAL CARE - REIMBURSEMENTS

U.S. Department of Health and Human Services, Health Care Financing Administration, 200 Independence Avenue, SW, Washington, D.C. 20201 (202) 690-6145, www.hcfa.gov; unpublished data.

MEDICAL RESEARCH

U.S. Department of Health and Human Services, Health Care Financing Administration, 200 Independence Avenue, SW, Washington, D.C. 20201 (202) 690-6145, www.hcfa.gov; *Health Care Financing Review.*

MEDICAL SCHOOLS

U.S. Department of Education, National Center for Education Statistics, 555 New Jersey Avenue, NW, Washington, D.C. 20208-5574 (202) 219-1828, http://nces.ed.gov; *Digest of Education Statistics.*

U.S. Department of Health and Human Services, National Center for Health Statistics, 3700 East-West Highway, Hyattsville, Maryland 20782 (301) 436-8500, www.cdc.gov/nchs; *Health, United States.*

MEDICAL SCHOOLS - FOREIGN GRADUATES

American Medical Association, 515 North State Street, Chicago, Illinois 60610 (312) 464-5000; *Physician Characteristics and Distribution in the U.S.*

MEDICAL SCHOOLS - NUMBER - STUDENTS - GRADUATES

U.S. Department of Education, National Center for Education Statistics, 555 New Jersey Avenue, NW, Washington, D.C. 20208-5574 (202) 219-1828,

http://nces.ed.gov; *Digest of Education Statistics.*

U.S. Department of Health and Human Services, National Center for Health Statistics, 3700 East-West Highway, Hyattsville, Maryland 20782 (301) 436-8500, www.cdc.gov/nchs; *Health, United States.*

MEDICAL SCIENCES - EMPLOYMENT

U.S. Department of Labor, Bureau of Labor Statistics, Two Massachusetts Avenue, NE, Washington, D.C. 20212 (202) 691-5200, www.stats.bls.gov; *Monthly Labor Review; Employment and Earnings;* and unpublished data.

MEDICAL SERVICES - See HEALTH SERVICES

MEDICARE - BENEFIT PAYMENTS EXPENDITURES

Social Security Administration, 6400 Security Boulevard, Baltimore, Maryland 21235 (800) 772-1213, www.ssa.gov; *Social Security Bulletin;* and unpublished data.

U.S. Department of Health and Human Services, Health Care Financing Administration, 200 Independence Avenue, SW, Washington, D.C. 20201 (202) 690-6145, www.hcfa.gov; *Medicare Program Statistics; Health Care Review;* and unpublished data.

MEDICARE - CONTRIBUTIONS

U.S. Department of Health and Human Services, Health Care Financing Administration, 200 Independence Avenue, SW, Washington, D.C. 20201 (202) 690-6145, www.hcfa.gov; *Annual Report of the Board of Trustees of the Federal Hospital Insurance Trust Fund*; and *Annual Report of the Board of Trustees of the Federal Supplementary Medical Insurance Trust Fund.*

MEDICARE - HOSPITAL VISITS

U.S. Department of Health and Human Services, National Center for Health Statistics, 3700 East-West Highway, Hyattsville, Maryland 20782 (301) 436-8500, www.cdc.gov/nchs; *Advance Data;* and unpublished data.

MEDICARE - NURSING HOMES

U.S. Department of Health and Human Services, National Center for Health Statistics, 3700 East-West Highway, Hyattsville, Maryland 20782 (301) 436-8500, www.cdc.gov/nchs; *Advance Data, No. 280 and 289.*

MEDICARE - STATE DATA

U.S. Department of Health and Human

Services, Health Care Financing Administration, 200 Independence Avenue, SW, Washington, D.C. 20210 (202) 690-6145, www.hcfa.gov; unpublished data.

MEDICARE - TRUST FUNDS

U.S. Department of Health and Human Services, Health Care Financing Administration, 200 Independence Avenue, SW, Washington, D.C. 20201 (202) 690-6145, www.hcfa.gov; *Annual Report of the Board of Trustees of the Federal Hospital Insurance Trust Fund*; and *Annual Report of the Board of Trustees of the Federal Supplementary Medical Insurance Trust Fund.*

MEDICARE - UTILIZATION AND CHARGES

U.S. Department of Health and Human Services, Health Care Financing Administration, 200 Independence Avenue, SW, Washington, D.C. 20201 (202) 690-6145, www.hcfa.gov; *Medicare Program Statistics;* and unpublished data.

MEDICINES - See DRUGS AND MEDICINES

MELONS

U.S. Department of Agriculture, Economic Research Service, 1800 M Street, NW, Washington, D.C. 20036 (202) 694-5050, www.ers.usda.gov; *Agricultural Outlook; Agricultural Statistics; Farm Business Economic Report; Food Consumption, Prices, and Expenditures;* and *Vegetables.*

MEMBERS OF CONGRESS - See CONGRESS, UNITED STATES

MEMBERSHIP ORGANIZATIONS - EARNINGS

U.S. Department of Commerce, Bureau of the Census, Washington, D.C. 20233 (301) 457-4100, www.census.gov; *Census of Service Industries;* and *County Business Patterns.*

U.S. Department of Labor, Bureau of Labor Statistics, Two Massachusetts Avenue, NE, Washington, D.C. 20212 (202) 691-5200, www.stats.bls.gov; *Employment and Earnings;* and Internet site: http://stats.bls.gov/ceshome. htm.

MEMBERSHIP ORGANIZATIONS - EMPLOYEES

U.S. Department of Commerce, Bureau of the Census, Washington, D.C. 20233 (301) 457-4100, www.census.gov; *Census of Service Industries;* and *County Business Patterns.*

U.S. Department of Labor, Bureau of Labor Statistics, Two Massachusetts Avenue, NE, Washington, D.C. 20212 (202) 691-5200,

www.stats.bls.gov; *Monthly Labor Review; Employment and Earnings;* and Internet site: http://stats.bls. gov/ceshome.

MEMBERSHIP ORGANIZATIONS - ESTABLISHMENTS

U.S. Department of Commerce, Bureau of the Census, Washington, D.C. 20233 (301) 457-4100, www.census.gov; *Census of Service Industries;* and *County Business Patterns.*

MEMBERSHIP ORGANIZATIONS - FINANCES

U.S. Department of Commerce, Bureau of the Census, Washington, D.C. 20233 (301) 457-4100, www.census.gov; *Census of Service Industries;* and *Current Business Reports, Service Annual Survey.*

MEMBERSHIP ORGANIZATIONS - GROSS NATIONAL PRODUCT

U.S. Department of Commerce, Bureau of Economic Analysis, Fourteenth Street between Constitution Avenue and E Street, NW, Washington, D.C. 20230 (202) 606-9900, www.bea.doc.gov; *Survey of Current Business.*

MENHADEN

U.S. Department of Commerce, National Oceanic and Atmospheric Administration, National Marine Fisheries Service, 1315 East-West Highway, Silver Spring, Maryland 20910 (301) 713-2239, www.nmfs.noaa. gov; *Fisheries of the United States.*

MENINGITIS

U.S. Department of Health and Human Services, Centers for Disease Control and Prevention, 1600 Clifton Road, NE, Atlanta, Georgia 30333 (800) 311-3435, www.cdc.gov; *Summary of Notifiable Diseases, U.S. Morbidity and Mortality Weekly Report.*

U.S. Department of Health and Human Services, National Center for Health Statistics, 3700 East-West Highway, Hyattsville, Maryland 20782 (301) 436-8500, www.cdc.gov/nchs; *Vital Statistics of the U.S.; National Vital Statistics Report;* and unpublished data.

MENTAL HOSPITALS

American Hospital Association, One North Franklin, Suite 27, Chicago, Illinois 60606 (800) 242-2626; *Hospital Statistics.*

U.S. Department of Health and Human Services, Substance Abuse and Mental Health Services Administration, 5600 Fishers Lane, Rockville, Maryland 20857

(800) 729-6686, www.samhsa.gov; unpublished data.

MERCHANDISE - See FOREIGN TRADE and GENERAL MERCHANDISE STORES

MERCHANT VESSELS

Shipbuilders Council of America, 1600 Wilson Boulevard, Suite 100, Arlington, Virginia 22209 (703) 351-6734; unpublished data.

U.S. Department of Transportation, Maritime Administration, 400 Seventh Street, SW, Washington, D.C. 20590 (202) 366-5807, www.marad.dot.gov; unpublished data.

MERCHANT VESSELS - EMPLOYMENT AND WAGE SCALE

U.S. Department of Transportation, Maritime Administration, 400 Seventh Street, SW, Washington, D.C. 20590 (202) 366-5807, www.marad.dot.gov; *United States Merchant Marine Data Sheet;* and unpublished data.

MERCHANT VESSELS - FOREIGN COUNTRIES

U.S. Department of Transportation, Maritime Administration, 400 Seventh Street, SW, Washington, D.C. 20590 (202) 366-5807, www.marad.dot.gov; *Merchant Fleets of the World;* and unpublished data.

MERCHANT VESSELS - NUMBER

Lloyd's Register of Shipping, 17 Battery Place, New York, New York 10004 (212) 425-8050, *World Fleet Statistics.*

U.S. Department of Transportation, Maritime Administration, 400 Seventh Street, SW, Washington, D.C. 20590 (202) 366-5807, www.marad.dot.gov; unpublished data.

MERCHANT VESSELS - NUMBER - LOST

Lloyd's Register of Shipping, 17 Battery Place, New York, New York 10004 (212) 425-8050; *Casualty Return.*

MERCHANT VESSELS - NUMBER - TONNAGE

U.S. Department of Transportation, Maritime Administration, 400 Seventh Street, SW, Washington, D.C. 20590 (202) 366-5807, www.marad.dot.gov; unpublished data.

MERCHANT VESSELS - NUMBER - WORLD

Statistical Office of the United Nations, Publishing Service, New York, New York 10017 (800) 253-9646; *Monthly Bulletin of Statistics.*

U.S. Department of Transportation, Maritime Administration, 400 Seventh Street, SW, Washington, D.C. 20590 (202) 366-5807, www.marad.dot.gov; *Merchant Fleets of the World;* and unpublished data.

MERCURY

U.S. Department of the Interior, Geological Survey, Office of Minerals Information, 12201 Sunrise Valley Drive, Reston, Virginia 22092 (703) 648-4000, www.minerals.usgs.gov; *Annual Reports;* and *Mineral Commodity Summaries.*

MERGERS AND ACQUISITIONS

Thomson Financial Securities Data, Two Gateway Center, Newark, New Jersey 07006 (973) 622-3100; *Merger and Corporate Transactions Database.*

METAL INDUSTRIES - PRIMARY - MANUFACTURING - See also IRON AND STEEL

METAL INDUSTRIES - PRIMARY - MANUFACTURING - CAPITAL

U.S. Department of Commerce, Bureau of Economic Analysis, Fourteenth Street between Constitution Avenue and E Street, NW, Washington, D.C. 20230 (202) 606-9900, www.bea.doc.gov; *Survey of Current Business.*

METAL INDUSTRIES - PRIMARY - MANUFACTURING - EARNINGS

U.S. Department of the Census, Washington, D.C. 20233 (301) 457-4100, www.census.gov; *Census of Manufactures;* and *Annual Survey of Manufactures.*

U.S. Department of Labor, Bureau of Labor Statistics, Two Massachusetts Avenue, NE, Washington, D.C. 20212 (202) 691-5200, www.stats.bls.gov; *Employment and Wages, Annual Averages; Employment and Earnings;* and Bulletins 2445, 2481 and 2483.

METAL INDUSTRIES - PRIMARY - MANUFACTURING - EMPLOYEES

U.S. Department of Commerce, Bureau of the Census, Washington, D.C. 20233 (301) 457-4100, www.census.gov; *Census of Manufactures;* and *Annual Survey of Manufactures.*

U.S. Department of Labor, Bureau of Labor Statistics, Two Massachusetts Avenue, NE, Washington, D.C. 20212 (202) 691-5200, www.stats.bls.gov; *Employment and Earnings;* and Internet site: http://stats.bls.gov/ceshome. htm.

METAL INDUSTRIES - PRIMARY MANUFACTURING - ENERGY CONSUMPTION

U.S. Department of Energy, Energy Information Administration, 1000 Independence Avenue, SW, Washington, D.C. 20585 (202) 586-1185; *Manufacturing Energy Consumption.*

METAL INDUSTRIES - PRIMARY - MANUFACTURING - FINANCE

American Iron and Steel Institute, 1101 Seventeenth Street, NW, Washington, D.C. 20036 (202) 452-7100; *Annual Statistical Report.*

METAL INDUSTRIES - PRIMARY - MANUFACTURING - FOREIGN TRADE

American Iron and Steel Institute, 1101 Seventeenth Street, NW, Washington, D.C. 20036 (202) 452-7100; *U.S. International Trade in Goods and Services.*

U.S. Department of Commerce, Bureau of the Census, Washington, D.C. 20233 (301) 457-4100, www.census.gov; *Census of Manufactures; Annual Survey of Manufactures; U.S. Merchandise Trade;* and *Exports from Manufacturing Establishments.*

METAL INDUSTRIES - PRIMARY - MANUFACTURING - GROSS DOMESTIC PRODUCT

U.S. Department of Commerce, Bureau of Economic Analysis, Fourteenth Street between Constitution Avenue and E Street, NW, Washington, D.C. 20230 (202) 606-9900, www.bea.doc.gov; *Survey of Current Business.*

METAL INDUSTRIES - PRIMARY - MANUFACTURING - MERGERS AND ACQUISITIONS

Thomson Financial Securities Data, Two Gateway Center, Newark, New Jersey 07006 (973) 622-3100; *Merger and Corporate Transactions Database.*

METAL INDUSTRIES - PRIMARY - MANUFACTURING - MULTINATIONAL COMPANIES

U.S. Department of Commerce, Bureau of Economic Analysis, Fourteenth Street between Constitution Avenue and E Street, NW, Washington, D.C. 20230 (202) 606-9900, www.bea.doc.gov; *Survey of Current Business.*

METAL INDUSTRIES - PRIMARY - MANUFACTURING - OCCUPATIONAL SAFETY

U.S. Department of Labor, Bureau of Labor Statistics, Two Massachusetts Avenue, NE, Washington, D.C. 20212 (202) 691-5200, www.stats.bls.gov; *Occupational Injuries and Illnesses in the United States by Industry.*

METAL INDUSTRIES - PRIMARY - MANUFACTURING - PATENTS

U.S. Department of Commerce, Patent and Trademark Office, 2121 Crystal Drive, Arlington, Virginia 22202 (703) 305-8341, www.uspto.gov; *Patenting Trends in the U.S., State Country Report.*

METAL INDUSTRIES - PRIMARY - MANUFACTURING - PRODUCTIVITY

Board of Governors of the Federal Reserve System, Twentieth Street and Constitution Avenue, NW, Washington, D.C. 20551 (202) 452-3000, www.bog.frb.fed.us; *Federal Reserve Bulletin;* and *Industrial Production and Capacity Utilization.*

U.S. Department of Labor, Bureau of Labor Statistics, Two Massachusetts Avenue, NE, Washington, D.C. 20212 (202) 691-5200, www.stats.bls.gov; Internet site http://stats.bls.gov/iprhome.htm.

METAL INDUSTRIES - PRIMARY - MANUFACTURING - PROFITS

Forbes, Incorporated, 60 Fifth Avenue, New York, New York 10011 (212) 691-6130; *Forbes Annual Report on American Industry.*

Time Warner, Time and Life Building, Rockefeller Center, New York, New York 10019 (212) 522-1212; *The Fortune Directories.*

U.S. Department of Commerce, Bureau of Economic Analysis, Fourteenth Street between Constitution Avenue and E Street, NW, Washington, D.C. 20230 (202) 606-9900, www.bea.doc.gov; *Survey of the Current Business.*

U.S. Department of Commerce, Bureau of the Census, Washington, D.C. 20233 (301) 457-4100, www.census.gov; *Quarterly Financial Report for Manufacturing, Mining and Trade Corporations.*

METAL INDUSTRIES - PRIMARY MANUFACTURING - RESEARCH AND DEVELOPMENT

National Science Foundation 4201 Wilson Boulevard, Arlington, Virginia 22230 (703) 306-1234, www.nsf.gov; *Research and Development in Industry.*

METAL INDUSTRIES - PRIMARY - MANUFACTURING - SHIPMENTS

American Iron and Steel Institute, 1101 Seventeenth Street, NW, Washington, D.C. 20036 (202) 452-7100; *Annual Statistical Report.*

U.S. Department of Commerce, Bureau

of the Census, Washington, D.C. 20233 (301) 457-4100, www.census.gov; *Census of Manufactures; Annual Survey of Manufactures; Manufacturing Profiles; Current Industrial Reports; Manufactures' Shipments, Inventories, and Orders;* and Internet site: http://www.census.gov/ftp/pub/industrymq35w97a.txt.

METAL INDUSTRIES - PRIMARY MANUFACTURING - TOXIC CHEMICAL RELEASES

Environmental Protection Agency, 1200 Pennsylvania Avenue, NW, Washington, D.C. 20460 (888) 372-8255, www.epa.gov; *Toxics Release Inventory.*

METAL INDUSTRIES - PRIMARY - MANUFACTURING - VALUE ADDED

U.S. Department of Commerce, Bureau of the Census, Washington, D.C. 20233 (301) 457-4100, www.census.gov; *Census of Manufactures;* and *Annual Survey of Manufactures.*

METAL MINING INDUSTRY - CAPITAL

U.S. Department of Labor, Bureau of Labor Statistics, Two Massachusetts Avenue, NW, Washington, D.C. 20212 (202) 691-5200, www.stats.bls.gov; *Employment and Earnings;* and Bulletin 2370.

METAL MINING INDUSTRY - EARNINGS

U.S. Department of Labor, Bureau of Labor Statistics, Two Massachusetts Avenue, NE, Washington, D.C. 20212 (202) 691-5200, www.stats.bls.gov; *Employment and Earnings;* Bulletins 2370; and Internet site: http://stats.bls.gov/ceshome.htm.

METAL MINING INDUSTRY - EMPLOYEES

U.S. Department of Labor, Bureau of Labor Statistics, Two Massachusetts Avenue, NE, Washington, D.C. 20212 (202) 691-5200, www.stats.bls.gov; *Employment and Earnings;* Bulletin 2370; and Internet site: http://stats.bls.gov/ceshome.htm.

METAL MINING INDUSTRY - ESTABLISHMENTS

U.S. Department of Labor, Bureau of Labor Statistics, Two Massachusetts Avenue, NW, Washington, D.C. 20212 (202) 691-5200, www.stats.bls.gov; *Employment and Earnings;* and Bulletin 2370.

METAL MINING INDUSTRY - OCCUPATIONAL SAFETY

U.S. Department of Labor, Bureau of Labor Statistics, Two Massachusetts Avenue, NE, Washington, D.C. 20212 (202) 691-5200, www.stats.bls.gov; *Occupational Injuries and Illnesses in the U.S. by Industry.*

METAL MINING INDUSTRY - PRODUCTION INDEXES

Board of Governors of the Federal Reserve System, Twentieth Street and Constitution Avenue, NW, Washington, D.C. 20551 (202) 452-3000, www.bog.frb.fed.us; *Federal Reserve Bulletin;* and *Industrial Production and Capacity Utilization.*

METAL MINING INDUSTRY - PRODUCTIVITY

U.S. Department of Labor, Bureau of Labor Statistics, Two Massachusetts Avenue, NE, Washington, D.C. 20212 (202) 691-5200, www.stats.bls.gov; Internet site: http://stats.bls.gov/ iprhome.htm.

METAL MINING INDUSTRY - SHIPMENTS

U.S. Department of Labor, Bureau of Labor Statistics, Two Massachusetts Avenue, NW, Washington, D.C. 20212 (202) 691-5200, www.stats.bls.gov; *Employment and Earnings;* and Bulletin 2370.

METAL MINING INDUSTRY - VALUE ADDED

U.S. Department of Labor, Bureau of Labor Statistics, Two Massachusetts Avenue, NW, Washington, D.C. 20212 (202) 691-5200, www.stats.bls.gov; *Employment and Earnings;* and Bulletin 2370.

METAL WORKING MACHINERY

U.S. Department of Commerce, Bureau of the Census, Washington, D.C. 20233 (301) 457-4100, www.census.gov; *Census of Manufactures; Annual Survey of Manufactures; Manufacturing Profiles;* and Internet site: http://www.census.gov/ftp/pub/industrymq35w97a.txt.

U.S. Department of Labor, Bureau of Labor Statistics, Two Massachusetts Avenue, NE, Washington, D.C. 20212 (202) 691-5200, www.stats.bls.gov; *Employment and Earnings;* and Internet site: http://stats.bls.gov/ceshome.htm.

METALS

U.S. Department of the Interior, Geological Survey, Office of Minerals Information, 12201 Sunrise Valley Drive, Reston, Virginia 22092 (703) 648-4000, www.minerals.usgs.gov; *Annual Reports;* and *Mineral Commodity Summaries.*

METALS - FOREIGN TRADE

U.S. Department of Commerce, Bureau of the Census, Washington, D.C. 20233 (301) 457-4100, www.census.gov; *U.S. International Trade in Goods and Services.*

METALS - PRODUCTION AND VALUE

U.S. Department of the Interior, Geological Survey, Office of Minerals Information, 12201 Sunrise Valley Drive, Reston, Virginia 22092 (703) 648-4000, www.minerals.usgs.gov; *Annual Reports;* and *Mineral Commodity Summaries.*

METALS - PRODUCTION AND VALUE - INDEXES OF PRODUCTION

Board of Governors of the Federal Reserve System, Twentieth Street and Constitution Avenue, NW, Washington, D.C. 20551 (202) 452-3000, www.bog.frb.fed.us; *Federal Reserve Bulletin;* and *Industrial Production and Capacity Utilization.*

METALS - RAILROAD CAR LOADINGS OF

Association of American Railroads, American Railroads Building, 50 F Street, NW, Washington, D.C. 20001 (202) 639-2100; *Freight Commodity Statistics;* and *Weekly Railroad Traffic.*

METALS - SPOT MARKET PRICE INDEXES

Commodity Research Bureau, 30 South Wacker Drive, Chicago Illinois 60606 (312) 454-1801; *CRB Bureau Commodity Index Report.*

METALS - STRATEGIC AND CRITICAL MATERIALS

U.S. Department of Defense, Defense Logistics Agency, 8725 John J. Kingman Road, Fort Belvoir, Virginia 22060 (703) 767-6666; *Statistical Supplement, Stockpile Report to the Congress.*

METALS - WORLD PRODUCTION

U.S. Department of the Interior, Geological Survey, Office of Minerals Information, 12201 Sunrise Valley Drive, Reston, Virginia 22092 (703) 648-4000, www.minerals.usgs.gov; *Annual Reports;* and *Mineral Commodity Summaries.*

METHANE GASES

U.S. Department of Energy, Energy Information Administration 1000 Independence Avenue, SW, Washington, D.C. 20585 (202) 586-1185; *Emissions of Greenhouse Gases in the U.S.*

METROPOLITAN AREAS - AIRLINE MARKETS

Air Transport Association of America, 1301 Pennsylvania Avenue, NW, Suite 1100, Washington, D.C. 20004-7017 (202) 626-4000; *Air Transport.*

METROPOLITAN AREAS - AMERICAN INDIAN, ESKIMO, ALEUT

U.S. Department of Commerce, Bureau

STATISTICS SOURCES, Twenty-sixth Edition - 2003

of the Census, Washington, D.C. 20233 (301) 457-4100, www.census.gov; unpublished data.

METROPOLITAN AREAS - ASIAN, PACIFIC ISLANDER

U.S. Department of Commerce, Bureau of the Census, Washington, D.C. 20233 (301) 457-4100, www.census.gov; unpublished data.

METROPOLITAN AREAS - BLACK

U.S. Department of Commerce, Bureau of the Census, Washington, D.C. 20233 (301) 457-4100, www.census.gov; unpublished data.

METROPOLITAN AREAS - CIVILIAN LABOR FORCE

U.S. Department of Labor, Bureau of Labor Statistics, Two Massachusetts Avenue, NE, Washington, D.C. 20212 (202) 691-5200, www.stats.bls.gov; *Local Area Unemployment Statistics Program.*

METROPOLITAN AREAS - CONSUMER EXPENDITURES

U.S. Department of Labor, Bureau of Labor Statistics, Two Massachusetts Avenue, NE, Washington, D.C. 20212 (202) 691-5200, www.stats.bls.gov; *Consumer Expenditures.*

METROPOLITAN AREAS - CONSUMER PRICE INDEX

Association for Applied Community Researchers, Post Office Box 407, Arlington, Virginia 22210 (703) 522-4980; *Cost of Living Index.*

METROPOLITAN AREAS - EARNINGS

U.S. Department of Labor, Bureau of Labor Statistics, Two Massachusetts Avenue, NE, Washington, D.C. 20212 (202) 691-5200, www.stats.bls.gov; *Average Annual Pay Levels in Metropolitan Areas;* and *News, USDL 99-232.*

METROPOLITAN AREAS - HISPANIC ORIGIN

U.S. Department of Commerce, Bureau of the Census, Washington, D.C. 20233 (301) 457-4100, www.census.gov; unpublished data.

METROPOLITAN AREAS - HOUSEHOLDS

U.S. Department of Commerce, Bureau of the Census, Washington, D.C. 20233 (301) 457-4100, www.census.gov; *Census of Population and Housing, Supplementary Reports; Census of Population and Housing, Population and Housing Unit Counts;* computer diskette PE-23; and unpublished data.

METROPOLITAN AREAS - HOUSING - PRICES

National Association of Realtors, 430 North Michigan Avenue, Chicago, Illinois 60611 (800) 874-6500; *Real Estate Outlook: Market Trends and Insights.*

METROPOLITAN AREAS - INCOME

U.S. Department of Commerce, Bureau of Economic Analysis, Fourteenth Street between Constitution Avenue and E Street, NW, Washington, D.C. 20230 (202) 606-9900, www.bea.doc.gov; *Survey of Current Business.*

METROPOLITAN AREAS - LAND AREA

U.S. Department of Commerce, Bureau of the Census, Washington, D.C. 20233 (301) 457-4100, www.census.gov; *Census of Population and Housing; Supplementary Reports, Metropolitan Areas as Defined by the Office of Management and Budget; Census of Population and Housing, Population and Housing Unit Counts;* unpublished data; and Internet site: http://www.census.gov/population/estimates/metro-city/ma96-05.txt.

METROPOLITAN AREAS - POPULATION

U.S. Department of Commerce, Bureau of the Census, Washington, D.C. 20233 (301) 457-4100, www.census.gov; *Census of Population; Supplementary Reports, Metropolitan Areas as Defined by the Office of Management and Budget; Census of Population and Housing, Population and Housing Unit Counts;* unpublished data; and Internet site: http://www.census.gov/population/estimates/metro-city/ma96-05.txt.

MEXICAN ORIGIN POPULATION

U.S. Department of Commerce, Bureau of the Census, Washington, D.C. 20233 (301) 457-4100, www.census.gov; *Census of Population, General Population Characterization, United States;* and unpublished data.

MEXICAN ORIGIN POPULATION - BIRTHS AND BIRTH RATES

U.S. Department of Health and Human Services, National Center for Health Statistics, 3700 East-West Highway, Hyattsville, Maryland 20782 (301) 436-8500, www.cdc.gov/nchs; *Vital Statistics of the United States;* and *National Vital Statistics Report.*

MEXICAN ORIGIN POPULATION - EDUCATIONAL ATTAINMENT

U.S. Department of Commerce, Bureau of the Census, Washington, D.C. 20233

(301) 457-4100, www.census.gov; *Census of Population, U.S. Summary; Current Population Reports;* and unpublished data.

MEXICAN ORIGIN POPULATION - LABOR FORCE

U.S. Department of Labor, Bureau of Labor Statistics, Two Massachusetts Avenue, NE, Washington, D.C. 20212 (202) 691-5200, www.stats.bls.gov; *Employment and Earnings;* and Bulletin 2307.

Mexico - National Statistical Office

Instituto Nacional de Estadistica Geografia e Informatica, Patriotismo No. 711, PH, CP 03810 Mexico, DF, Mexico.

Mexico - Primary Statistics Sources

Instituto Nacional de Estadistica, Geografia e Informatica, CP 03810, Mexico; *Annuario Estadistico de los Estados Unidos Mexicanos;* and *Agenda estadistica.*

MEXICO - AGRICULTURE

The Economist Intelligence Unit, 111 West 57th Street, New York, New York 10019 (800) 938-4685; *Mexico Country Report;* and *The New Latin America Market Atlas.*

Euromonitor International, Inc., 122 South Michigan Avenue, Suite 1200, Chicago, Illinois 60603 (800) 577-EURO; *International Marketing Data and Statistics;* and *World Marketing Data and Statistics.*

Europa Publications Limited, 18 Bedford Square, London, WC1B 3JN, England; *The Europa World Year Book.*

Food and Agricultural Organization of the United Nations (FAO), Via delle Terme di Caracalla, 00100 Rome, Italy (Telephone Number in U.S. (202) 653-2400); *The State of Food and Agriculture.*

Inter-American Development Bank, 1300 New York Avenue, NW, Washington, D.C. 20577 (202) 872-1445; *Economic and Social Progress in Latin America.*

M.E. Sharpe, 80 Business Park Drive, Armonk, New York 10504 (800) 541-6563; *The Illustrated Book of World Rankings.*

St. Martin's Press, Inc., 175 Fifth Avenue, New York, New York 10010 (800) 221-7945; *The Statesman's Year-Book.*

Statistical Office of the United Nations, Publishing Service, New York, New York 10017 (800) 253-9646; *Statistical Yearbook for Latin America and the Caribbean;* and

Statistical Yearbook.

U.C.L.A. Latin American Center Publications, University of California, Los Angeles, California 90024 (310) 825-6634; *Statistical Abstract of Latin America.*

United Nations Conference on Trade and Development, Central Statistical Service, Palais des Nations, Geneva, Switzerland (Telephone in U.S. (800) 253-9646); *UNCTAD Commodity Yearbook.*

The World Bank, 1818 H Street, NW, Washington, D.C. 20433 (202) 477-1234; *World Development Indicators.*

MEXICO - AIRLINE SERVICE

The Economist Intelligence Unit, 111 West 57th Street, New York, New York 10019 (800) 938-4685; *The New Latin America Market Atlas.*

Europa Publications Limited, 18 Bedford Square, London, WC1B 3JN, England; *The Europa World Year Book.*

International Civil Aviation Organization, 999 University Street, Montreal, Quebec, Canada H3C 5H7 (514) 954-8219; *Civil Aviation Statistics of the World.*

M.E. Sharpe, 80 Business Park Drive, Armonk, New York 10504 (800) 541-6563; *The Illustrated Book of World Rankings.*

St. Martin's Press, Inc., 175 Fifth Avenue, New York, New York 10010 (800) 221-7945; *The Statesman's Year-Book.*

Statistical Office of the United Nations, Publishing Service, New York, New York 10017 (800) 253-9646; *Statistical Yearbook.*

MEXICO - AIRPORTS

Central Intelligence Agency, Washington, D.C. 20505 (703) 482-1100, www.cia.gov; *The World Factbook.*

MEXICO - ALUMINUM PRODUCTION AND CONSUMPTION - See MEXICO - MINING AND MINERAL PRODUCTS

MEXICO - ANIMAL FEEDINGSTUFFS OF AQUATIC ANIMAL ORIGIN

Statistical Office of the United Nations, Publishing Service, New York, New York 10017 (800) 253-9646; *Statistical Yearbook.*

MEXICO - ANIMAL HEALTH

Food and Agricultural Organization of the United Nations (FAO), Via delle Terme di Caracalla, 00100 Rome, Italy (Telephone Number in U.S. (202) 653-2400); *Animal Health Yearbook.*

MEXICO - ANTIMONY AND ANTIMONY ORE

PRODUCTION AND CONSUMPTION - See MEXICO - MINING AND MINERAL PRODUCTS

MEXICO - APPLES - See MEXICO - CROPS

MEXICO - AREA AND DENSITY OF POPULATION

Central Intelligence Agency, Washington, D.C. 20505 (703) 482-1100, www.cia.gov; *The World Factbook.*

Euromonitor International, Inc., 122 South Michigan Avenue, Suite 1200, Chicago, Illinois 60603 (800) 577-EURO; *International Marketing Data and Statistics;* and *The World Economic Factbook.*

Europa Publications Limited, 18 Bedford Square, London, WC1B 3JN, England; *The Europa World Year Book.*

Food and Agricultural Organization of the United Nations (FAO), Via delle Terme di Caracalla, 00100 Rome, Italy (Telephone Number in U.S. (202) 653-2400); *The State of Food and Agriculture.*

Inter-American Development Bank, 1300 New York Avenue, NW, Washington, D.C. 20577 (202) 872-1445; *Economic and Social Progress in Latin America.*

M.E. Sharpe, 80 Business Park Drive, Armonk, New York 10504 (800) 541-6563; *The Illustrated Book of World Rankings.*

Statistical Office of the United Nations, Publishing Service, New York, New York 10017 (800) 253-9646; *Statistical Yearbook.*

United Nations Educational, Scientific and Cultural Organization (UNESCO), 7 Place de Fontenoy, F-75700 Paris, France (Telephone Number in U.S. (212) 963-5981); *Statistical Yearbook.*

The World Bank, 1818 H Street, NW, Washington, D.C. 20433 (202) 477-1234; *World Development Report.*

MEXICO - ARMS EXPORTS AND IMPORTS - See MEXICO - MILITARY

MEXICO - ARSENIC PRODUCTION AND CONSUMPTION - See MEXICO - MINING AND MINERAL PRODUCTS

MEXICO - BALANCE OF PAYMENTS

The Economist Intelligence Unit, 111 West 57th Street, New York, New York 10019 (800) 938-4685; *The New Latin America Market Atlas;* and *The World Market Atlas.*

Europa Publications Limited, 18 Bedford Square, London, WC1B 3JN, England; *The Europa World Year Book.*

Inter-American Development Bank, 1300 New York Avenue, NW, Washington, D.C. 20577 (202) 872-1445; *Economic and Social Progress in Latin America.*

International Monetary Fund, 700 Nineteenth Street, NW, Washington, D.C. 20431 (202) 623-7000; *Balance of Payments Yearbook;* and *International Financial Statistics.*

Organization of American States (OAS), General Secretariat, Washington, D.C. 20006 (202) 458-3533; *Statistical Bulletin of the OAS.*

Statistical Office of the United Nations, Publishing Service, New York, New York 10017 (800) 253-9646; *Economic Survey of Latin America and the Caribbean;* and *Statistical Yearbook for Latin America and the Caribbean.*

U.C.L.A. Latin American Center Publications, University of California, Los Angeles, California 90024 (310) 825-6634; *Statistical Abstract of Latin America.*

United Nations Conference on Trade and Development (UNCTAD), New York, New York 10017 (800) 253-9646; *Handbook of International Trade and Development Statistics.*

The World Bank, 1818 H Street, NW, Washington, D.C. 20433 (202) 477-1234; *World Development Report;* and *World Development Indicators.*

MEXICO - BANANA PRODUCTION - See MEXICO - CROPS

MEXICO - BANKING

Euromonitor International, Inc., 122 South Michigan Avenue, Suite 1200, Chicago, Illinois 60603 (800) 577-EURO; *World Marketing Data and Statistics.*

Europa Publications Limited, 18 Bedford Square, London, WC1B 3JN, England; *The Europa World Year Book.*

Inter-American Development Bank, 1300 New York Avenue, NW, Washington, D.C. 20577 (202) 872-1445; *Economic and Social Progress in Latin America.*

International Monetary Fund, 700 Nineteenth Street, NW, Washington, D.C. 20431 (202) 623-7000; *International Financial Statistics.*

M.E. Sharpe, 80 Business Park Drive, Armonk, New York 10504 (800) 541-6563; *The Illustrated Book of World Rankings.*

Organization of American States (OAS), General Secretariat, Washington, D.C. 20006 (202) 458-3533; *Statistical Bulletin of the OAS.*

St. Martin's Press, Inc., 175 Fifth Avenue, New York, New York 10010 (800) 221-7945; *The Statesman's Year-Book.*

Statistical Office of the United Nations, Publishing Service, New York, New York 10017 (800) 253-9646; *Statistical Yearbook; and Statistical Yearbook for Latin America and the Caribbean.*

MEXICO - BARLEY PRODUCTION - See MEXICO - CROPS

MEXICO - BAUXITE PRODUCTION AND CONSUMPTION - See MEXICO - MINING AND MINERAL PRODUCTS

MEXICO - BEER PRODUCTION - See MEXICO - BEVERAGES

MEXICO - BEVERAGES

M.E. Sharpe, 80 Business Park Drive, Armonk, New York 10504 (800) 541-6563; *The Illustrated Book of World Rankings.*

Statistical Office of the United Nations, Publishing Service, New York, New York 10017 (800) 253-9646; *Statistical Yearbook.*

MEXICO - BIRTH RATES

Central Intelligence Agency, Washington, D.C. 20505 (703) 482-1100, www.cia.gov; *The World Factbook.*

Euromonitor International, Inc., 122 South Michigan Avenue, Suite 1200, Chicago, Illinois 60603 (800) 577-EURO; *International Marketing Data and Statistics; and The World Economic Factbook.*

Europa Publications Limited, 18 Bedford Square, London, WC1B 3JN, England; *The Europa World Year Book.*

M.E. Sharpe, 80 Business Park Drive, Armonk, New York 10504 (800) 541-6563; *The Illustrated Book of World Rankings.*

St. Martin's Press, Inc., 175 Fifth Avenue, New York, New York 10010 (800) 221-7945; *The Statesman's Year-Book.*

Statistical Office of the United Nations, Publishing Service, New York, New York 10017 (800) 253-9646; *Demographic Yearbook; Statistical Yearbook; and Statistical Yearbook for Latin America and the Caribbean.*

The World Bank, 1818 H Street, NW, Washington, D.C. 20433 (202) 477-1234; *World Development Indicators.*

World Health Organization, Office of Publications, 20 Avenue Appia, CH-1211 Geneva 27, Switzerland (Telephone in U.S. (518) 436-9686); *World Health Statistics Annual.*

MEXICO - BISMUTH PRODUCTION AND CONSUMPTION - See MEXICO - MINING AND MINERAL PRODUCTS

MEXICO - BONDS

Inter-American Development Bank, 1300 New York Avenue, NW, Washington, D.C. 20577 (202) 872-1445; *Economic and Social Progress in Latin America.*

International Monetary Fund, 700 Nineteenth Street, NW, Washington, D.C. 20431 (202) 623-7000; *Government Finance Statistics Yearbook.*

Europa Publications Limited, 18 Bedford Square, London, WC1B 3JN, England; *The Europa World Year Book.*

MEXICO - BROADCASTING

Billboard Limited, Post Office Box 9027, 1006 AA Amsterdam, The Netherlands (Telephone Number in U.S. (212) 764-7300); *World Radio TV Handbook.*

Central Intelligence Agency, Washington, D.C. 20505 (703) 482-1100, www.cia.gov; *The World Factbook.*

Euromonitor International, Inc., 122 South Michigan Avenue, Suite 1200, Chicago, Illinois 60603 (800) 577-EURO; *World Marketing Data and Statistics.*

M.E. Sharpe, 80 Business Park Drive, Armonk, New York 10504 (800) 541-6563; *The Illustrated Book of World Rankings.*

St. Martin's Press, Inc., 175 Fifth Avenue, New York, New York 10010 (800) 221-7945; *The Statesman's Year-Book.*

United Nations Educational, Scientific and Cultural Organization (UNESCO), 7 Place de Fontenoy, F-75700 Paris, France (Telephone Number in U.S. (212) 963-5981); *Statistical Yearbook.*

MEXICO - BUDGET

Central Intelligence Agency, Washington, D.C. 20505 (703) 482-1100, www.cia.gov; *The World Factbook.*

MEXICO - BUSINESS

Inter-American Development Bank, 1300 New York Avenue, NW, Washington, D.C. 20577 (202) 872-1445; *Economic and Social Progress in Latin America.*

MEXICO - BUSINESS AND PROFESSIONAL LICENSES

International Monetary Fund, 700 Nineteenth Street, NW, Washington, D.C. 20431 (202) 623-7000; *Government Finance Statistics Yearbook.*

MEXICO - BUTTER PRODUCTION - See MEXICO - DAIRY PRODUCTS

MEXICO - CADMIUM PRODUCTION AND CONSUMPTION - See MEXICO - MINING AND MINERAL PRODUCTS

MEXICO - CALORIE SUPPLY

Food and Agricultural Organization of the United Nations (FAO), Via delle Terme di Caracalla, 00100 Rome, Italy (Telephone Number in U.S. (202) 653-2400); *The State of Food and Agriculture.*

Statistical Office of the United Nations, Publishing Service, New York, New York 10017 (800) 253-9646; *Statistical Yearbook for Latin America and the Caribbean.*

MEXICO - CAPITAL INVESTMENT

Inter-American Development Bank, 1300 New York Avenue, NW, Washington, D.C. 20577 (202) 872-1445; *Economic and Social Progress in Latin America.*

MEXICO - CAPITAL REVENUE

Inter-American Development Bank, 1300 New York Avenue, NW, Washington, D.C. 20577 (202) 872-1445; *Economic and Social Progress in Latin America.*

International Monetary Fund, 700 Nineteenth Street, NW, Washington, D.C. 20431 (202) 623-7000; *Government Finance Statistics Yearbook.*

MEXICO - CASTOR BEAN PRODUCTION - See MEXICO - CROPS

MEXICO - CATTLE - See MEXICO - LIVESTOCK AND POULTRY

MEXICO - CAUSTIC SODA PRODUCTION - See MEXICO - BEVERAGES

MEXICO - CEMENT PRODUCTION - See MEXICO - MINING AND MINERAL PRODUCTS

MEXICO - CHEESE PRODUCTION AND CONSUMPTION - See MEXICO - DAIRY PRODUCTS

MEXICO - CHEMICAL (ORGANIC) PRODUCTION - See MEXICO - MINING AND MINERAL PRODUCTS

MEXICO - CHICK PEA PRODUCTION - See MEXICO - CROPS

MEXICO - CHICKENS - See MEXICO - LIVESTOCK AND POULTRY

MEXICO - CHROMITE PRODUCTION AND CONSUMPTION - See MEXICO - MINING AND MINERAL PRODUCTS

MEXICO - CHROMIUM ORE PRODUCTION

AND CONSUMPTION - See MEXICO - MINING AND MINERAL PRODUCTS

MEXICO - CIGARETTE PRODUCTION - See MEXICO - TOBACCO PRODUCTION

MEXICO - CLIMATE

M.E. Sharpe, 80 Business Park Drive, Armonk, New York 10504 (800) 541-6563; *The Illustrated Book of World Rankings.*

St. Martin's Press, Inc., 175 Fifth Avenue, New York, New York 10010 (800) 221-7945; *The Statesman's Year-Book.*

MEXICO - COAL PRODUCTION - See MEXICO - MINING AND MINERAL PRODUCTS

MEXICO - COBALT PRODUCTION AND CONSUMPTION - See MEXICO - MINING AND MINERAL PRODUCTS

MEXICO - COCOA (BEANS) PRODUCTION - See MEXICO - CROPS

MEXICO - COFFEE - See MEXICO - CROPS

MEXICO - COKE, COKE OVEN COKE AND COKE OVEN ORE PRODUCTION AND CONSUMPTION - See MEXICO - MINING AND MINERAL PRODUCTS

MEXICO - COMMERCE

St. Martin's Press, Inc., 175 Fifth Avenue, New York, New York 10010 (800) 221-7945; *The Statesman's Year-Book.*

MEXICO - COMMUNICATIONS - See MEXICO - TRANSPORTATION AND COMMUNICATIONS

MEXICO - CONSTRUCTION INDUSTRY

The Economist Intelligence Unit, 111 West 57th Street, New York, New York 10019 (800) 938-4685; *The New Latin America Market Atlas.*

Inter-American Development Bank, 1300 New York Avenue, NW, Washington, D.C. 20577 (202) 872-1445; *Economic and Social Progress in Latin America.*

M.E. Sharpe, 80 Business Park Drive, Armonk, New York 10504 (800) 541-6563; *The Illustrated Book of World Rankings.*

Statistical Office of the United Nations, Publishing Service, New York, New York 10017 (800) 253-9646; *Statistical Yearbook.*

U.C.L.A. Latin American Center Publications, University of California, Los Angeles, California 90024 (310) 825-6634; *Statistical Abstract of Latin America.*

MEXICO - CONSUMER PRICE INDEX

Europa Publications Limited, 18 Bedford Square, London, WC1B 3JN, England; *The Europa World Year Book.*

Statistical Office of the United Nations, Publishing Service, New York, New York 10017 (800) 253-9646; *Statistical Yearbook.*

MEXICO - CONSUMER PRICES

The Economist Intelligence Unit, 111 West 57th Street, New York, New York 10019 (800) 938-4685; *The New Latin America Market Atlas.*

Euromonitor International, Inc., 122 South Michigan Avenue, Suite 1200, Chicago, Illinois 60603 (800) 577-EURO; *World Marketing Data and Statistics.*

International Labour Office, I.L.O. Publications, 1828 L Street, NW, Suite 801, Washington, D.C. 20036 (301) 638-3152; *Yearbook of Labour Statistics.*

International Monetary Fund, 700 Nineteenth Street, NW, Washington, D.C. 20431 (202) 623-7000; *International Financial Statistics.*

Organization of American States (OAS), General Secretariat, Washington, D.C. 20006 (202) 458-3533; *Statistical Bulletin of the OAS.*

U.C.L.A. Latin American Center Publications, University of California, Los Angeles, California 90024 (310) 825-6634; *Statistical Abstract of Latin America.*

MEXICO - CONSUMPTION

The Economist Intelligence Unit, 111 West 57th Street, New York, New York 10019 (800) 938-4685; *The New Latin America Market Atlas.*

Inter-American Development Bank, 1300 New York Avenue, NW, Washington, D.C. 20577 (202) 872-1445; *Economic and Social Progress in Latin America.*

International Lead and Zinc Study Group, Metro House, 58 St. James's Street, London SW1A 1LD England; *Lead and Zinc Statistics.*

Statistical Office of the United Nations, Publishing Service, New York, New York 10017 (800) 253-9646; *Statistical Yearbook for Latin America and the Caribbean.*

The World Bank, 1818 H Street, NW, Washington, D.C. 20433 (202) 477-1234; *World Development Report.*

MEXICO - COOPERATIVES

U.C.L.A. Latin American Center Publications, University of California, Los Angeles, California 90024 (310) 825-6634;

Statistical Abstract of Latin America.

MEXICO - COPPER AND COPPER ORE PRODUCTION AND CONSUMPTION - See MEXICO - MINING AND MINERAL PRODUCTS

MEXICO - CORN PRODUCTION - See MEXICO - CROPS

MEXICO - CORPORATE INCOME TAXES - See MEXICO - TAXATION

MEXICO - CORPORATE TAXES - See MEXICO - TAXATION

MEXICO - COTTON - See MEXICO - CROPS

MEXICO - CRIME

Yale University Press, Yale Station, New Haven, Connecticut 06520 (800) 987-7323; *Violence and Crime in Cross-National Perspective.*

MEXICO - CROPS

Commodity Research Bureau, 30 South Wacker Drive, Chicago Illinois 60606 (312) 454-1801; *Commodity Year Book.*

The Economist Intelligence Unit, 111 West 57th Street, New York, New York 10019 (800) 938-4685; *The New Latin America Market Atlas.*

Europa Publications Limited, 18 Bedford Square, London, WC1B 3JN, England; *The Europa World Year Book.*

Food and Agricultural Organization of the United Nations (FAO), Via delle Terme di Caracalla, 00100 Rome, Italy (Telephone Number in U.S. (202) 653-2400); *Production Yearbook;* and *The State of Food and Agriculture.*

International Lead and Zinc Study Group, Metro House, 58 St. James's Street, London SW1A 1LD England; *Lead and Zinc Statistics.*

International Monetary Fund, 700 Nineteenth Street, NW, Washington, D.C. 20431 (202) 623-7000; *International Financial Statistics.*

M.E. Sharpe, 80 Business Park Drive, Armonk, New York 10504 (800) 541-6563; *The Illustrated Book of World Rankings.*

Organization of American States (OAS), General Secretariat, Washington, D.C. 20006 (202) 458-3533; *Statistical Bulletin of the OAS.*

St. Martin's Press, Inc., 175 Fifth Avenue, New York, New York 10010 (800) 221-7945; *The Statesman's Year-Book.*

Statistical Office of the United Nations,

Publishing Service, New York, New York 10017 (800) 253-9646; *Statistical Yearbook.*

U.C.L.A. Latin American Center Publications, University of California, Los Angeles, California 90024 (310) 825-6634; *Statistical Abstract of Latin America.*

United Nations Conference on Trade and Development, Central Statistical Service, Palais des Nations, Geneva, Switzerland (Telephone in U.S. (800) 253-9646); *UNCTAD Commodity Yearbook.*

MEXICO - CUSTOMS DUTIES

Inter-American Development Bank, 1300 New York Avenue, NW, Washington, D.C. 20577 (202) 872-1445; *Economic and Social Progress in Latin America.*

International Monetary Fund, 700 Nineteenth Street, NW, Washington, D.C. 20431 (202) 623-7000; *Government Finance Statistics Yearbook.*

MEXICO - DAIRY PRODUCTS

Europa Publications Limited, 18 Bedford Square, London, WC1B 3JN, England; *The Europa World Year Book.*

Food and Agricultural Organization of the United Nations (FAO), Via delle Terme di Caracalla, 00100 Rome, Italy (Telephone Number in U.S. (202) 653-2400); *The State of Food and Agriculture.*

M.E. Sharpe, 80 Business Park Drive, Armonk, New York 10504 (800) 541-6563; *The Illustrated Book of World Rankings.*

St. Martin's Press, Inc., 175 Fifth Avenue, New York, New York 10010 (800) 221-7945; *The Statesman's Year-Book.*

Statistical Office of the United Nations, Publishing Service, New York, New York 10017 (800) 253-9646; *Statistical Yearbook.*

U.C.L.A. Latin American Center Publications, University of California, Los Angeles, California 90024 (310) 825-6634; *Statistical Abstract of Latin America.*

MEXICO - DEATH RATES - See MEXICO - MORTALITY

MEXICO - DEBT

The Economist Intelligence Unit, 111 West 57th Street, New York, New York 10019 (800) 938-4685; *The New Latin America Market Atlas.*

MEXICO - DEFENSE

The Economist Intelligence Unit, 111 West 57th Street, New York, New York 10019 (800) 938-4685; *The New Latin America Market Atlas.*

MEXICO - DEFENSE EXPENDITURES - See MEXICO - MILITARY

MEXICO - DEMOGRAPHY

The Economist Intelligence Unit, 111 West 57th Street, New York, New York 10019 (800) 938-4685; *The World Market Atlas.*

Euromonitor International, Inc., 122 South Michigan Avenue, Suite 1200, Chicago, Illinois 60603 (800) 577-EURO; *International Marketing Data and Statistics; World Marketing Data and Statistics;* and *The World Economic Factbook.*

M.E. Sharpe, 80 Business Park Drive, Armonk, New York 10504 (800) 541-6563; *The Illustrated Book of World Rankings.*

Statistical Office of the United Nations, Publishing Service, New York, New York 10017 (800) 253-9646; *Human Development Report.*

MEXICO - DEVELOPMENT ASSISTANCE

Inter-American Development Bank, 1300 New York Avenue, NW, Washington, D.C. 20577 (202) 872-1445; *Economic and Social Progress in Latin America.*

Statistical Office of the United Nations, Publishing Service, New York, New York 10017 (800) 253-9646; *Statistical Yearbook.*

MEXICO - DIAMOND PRODUCTION - See MEXICO - MINING AND MINERAL PRODUCTS

MEXICO - DISCOUNT RATES - See MEXICO - BANKING

MEXICO - DISEASES - See MEXICO - HEALTH

MEXICO - DIVORCE

M.E. Sharpe, 80 Business Park Drive, Armonk, New York 10504 (800) 541-6563; *The Illustrated Book of World Rankings.*

Statistical Office of the United Nations, Publishing Service, New York, New York 10017 (800) 253-9646; *Demographic Yearbook;* and *Statistical Yearbook.*

MEXICO - DUCKS - See MEXICO - LIVESTOCK AND POULTRY

MEXICO - ECONOMY

Central Intelligence Agency, Washington, D.C. 20505 (703) 482-1100, www.cia.gov; *The World Factbook.*

Economist Intelligence Unit, 111 West 57th Street, New York, New York 10019 (800) 938-4685; *Mexico Country Report.*

Euromonitor International, Inc., 122 South Michigan Avenue, Suite 1200, Chicago, Illinois 60603 (800) 577-EURO; *The World Economic Factbook;* and *World Marketing Data and Statistics.*

Europa Publications Limited, 18 Bedford Square, London, WC1B 3JN, England; *The Europa World Year Book.*

Inter-American Development Bank, 1300 New York Avenue, NW, Washington, D.C. 20577 (202) 872-1445; *Economic and Social Progress in Latin America;* and *International Marketing Data and Statistics.*

M.E. Sharpe, 80 Business Park Drive, Armonk, New York 10504 (800) 541-6563; *The Illustrated Book of World Rankings.*

Organization of American States (OAS), General Secretariat, Washington, D.C. 20006 (202) 458-3533; *Statistical Bulletin of the OAS.*

St. Martin's Press, Inc., 175 Fifth Avenue, New York, New York 10010 (800) 221-7945; *The Statesman's Year-Book.*

Statistical Office of the United Nations, Publishing Service, New York, New York 10017 (800) 253-9646; *Economic Survey for Latin America and the Caribbean;* and *World Statistics Pocketbook.*

U.C.L.A. Latin American Center Publications, University of California, Los Angeles, California 90024 (310) 825-6634; *Statistical Abstract of Latin America.*

The World Bank, 1818 H Street, NW, Washington, D.C. 20433 (202) 477-1234; *The World Bank Atlas;* and *World Development Report.*

MEXICO - EDUCATION

The Economist Intelligence Unit, 111 West 57th Street, New York, New York 10019 (800) 938-4685; *The New Latin America Market Atlas;* and *The World Market Atlas.*

Euromonitor International, Inc., 122 South Michigan Avenue, Suite 1200, Chicago, Illinois 60603 (800) 577-EURO; *International Marketing Data and Statistics;* and *World Marketing Data and Statistics.*

Europa Publications Limited, 18 Bedford Square, London, WC1B 3JN, England; *The Europa World Year Book.*

International Monetary Fund, 700 Nineteenth Street, NW, Washington, D.C. 20431 (202) 623-7000; *Government Finance Statistics Yearbook.*

M.E. Sharpe, 80 Business Park Drive, Armonk, New York 10504 (800) 541-6563; *The Illustrated Book of World Rankings.*

St. Martin's Press, Inc., 175 Fifth Avenue, New York, New York 10010 (800) 221-7945; *The Statesman's Year-Book.*

Statistical Office of the United Nations, Publishing Service, New York, New York 10017 (800) 253-9646; *Human Development Report.*

U.C.L.A. Latin American Center Publications, University of California, Los Angeles, California 90024 (310) 825-6634; *Statistical Abstract of Latin America.*

United Nations Educational, Scientific and Cultural Organization (UNESCO), 7 Place de Fontenoy, F-75700 Paris, France (Telephone Number in U.S. (212) 963-5981); *Statistical Yearbook.*

The World Bank, 1818 H Street, NW, Washington, D.C. 20433 (202) 477-1234; *World Development Report;* and *World Development Indicators.*

MEXICO - EGG PRODUCTION AND CONSUMPTION - See MEXICO - DAIRY PRODUCTS

MEXICO - EGGPLANT PRODUCTION - See MEXICO - CROPS

MEXICO - ELECTRICITY

Central Intelligence Agency, Washington, D.C. 20505 (703) 482-1100, www.cia.gov; *The World Factbook.*

The Economist Intelligence Unit, 111 West 57th Street, New York, New York 10019 (800) 938-4685; *The New Latin America Market Atlas.*

Inter-American Development Bank, 1300 New York Avenue, NW, Washington, D.C. 20577 (202) 872-1445; *Economic and Social Progress in Latin America.*

M.E. Sharpe, 80 Business Park Drive, Armonk, New York 10504 (800) 541-6563; *The Illustrated Book of World Rankings.*

Penn Well Publishing Company, 1421 South Sheridan Road, Post Office Box 1260, Tulsa, Oklahoma 74101 (800) 752-9764; *International Energy Statistics Sourcebook.*

St. Martin's Press, Inc., 175 Fifth Avenue, New York, New York 10010 (800) 221-7945; *The Statesman's Year-Book.*

Statistical Office of the United Nations, Publishing Service, New York, New York 10017 (800) 253-9646; *Human Development Report;* and *Statistical Yearbook.*

MEXICO - EMPLOYMENT

Euromonitor International, Inc., 122 South Michigan Avenue, Suite 1200, Chicago, Illinois 60603 (800) 577-EURO;

International Marketing Data and Statistics.

International Labour Office, I.L.O. Publications, 1828 L Street, NW, Suite 801, Washington, D.C. 20036 (301) 638-3152; *Yearbook of Labour Statistics.*

M.E. Sharpe, 80 Business Park Drive, Armonk, New York 10504 (800) 541-6563; *The Illustrated Book of World Rankings.*

Statistical Office of the United Nations, Publishing Service, New York, New York 10017 (800) 253-9646; *Statistical Yearbook;* and *Statistical Yearbook for Latin America and the Caribbean.*

U.C.L.A. Latin American Center Publications, University of California, Los Angeles, California 90024 (310) 825-6634; *Statistical Abstracts of Latin America.*

MEXICO - ENERGY

The Economist Intelligence Unit, 111 West 57th Street, New York, New York 10019 (800) 938-4685; *The New Latin America Market Atlas.*

Euromonitor International, Inc., 122 South Michigan Avenue, Suite 1200, Chicago, Illinois 60603 (800) 577-EURO; *International Marketing Data and Statistics; World Marketing Data and Statistics;* and *The World Economic Factbook.*

Food and Agricultural Organization of the United Nations (FAO), Via delle Terme di Caracalla, 00100 Rome, Italy (Telephone Number in U.S. (202) 653-2400); *The State of Food and Agriculture.*

M.E. Sharpe, 80 Business Park Drive, Armonk, New York 10504 (800) 541-6563; *The Illustrated Book of World Rankings.*

Penn Well Publishing Company, 1421 South Sheridan Road, Post Office Box 1260, Tulsa, Oklahoma 74101 (800) 752-9764; *International Energy Statistics Sourcebook.*

St. Martin's Press, Inc., 175 Fifth Avenue, New York, New York 10010 (800) 221-7945; *The Statesman's Year-Book.*

Statistical Office of the United Nations, Publishing Service, New York, New York 10017 (800) 253-9646; *Energy Statistics Yearbook; Human Development Report; Statistical Yearbook; World Statistics Pocketbook;* and *Statistical Yearbook for Latin America and the Caribbean.*

U.C.L.A. Latin American Center Publications, University of California, Los Angeles, California 90024 (310) 825-6634; *Statistical Abstract of Latin America.*

The World Bank, 1818 H Street, NW, Washington, D.C. 20433 (202) 477-1234;

The World Bank Atlas; and *World Development Report.*

MEXICO - ENVIRONMENT

Economist Intelligence Unit, 111 West 57th Street, New York, New York 10019 (800) 938-4685; *Mexico Country Report.*

Statistical Office of the United Nations, Publishing Service, New York, New York 10017 (800) 253-9646; *World Statistics Pocketbook.*

MEXICO - EXCHANGE RATES

Central Intelligence Agency, Washington, D.C. 20505 (703) 482-1100, www.cia.gov; *The World Factbook.*

Euromonitor International, Inc., 122 South Michigan Avenue, Suite 1200, Chicago, Illinois 60603 (800) 577-EURO; *International Marketing Data and Statistics;* and *The World Economic Factbook.*

Europa Publications Limited, 18 Bedford Square, London, WC1B 3JN, England; *The Europa World Year Book.*

Inter-American Development Bank, 1300 New York Avenue, NW, Washington, D.C. 20577 (202) 872-1445; *Economic and Social Progress in Latin America.*

International Civil Aviation Organization, 999 University Street, Montreal, Quebec, Canada H3C 5H7 (514) 954-8219; *Civil Aviation Statistics of the World.*

International Monetary Fund, 700 Nineteenth Street, NW, Washington, D.C. 20431 (202) 623-7000; *International Financial Statistics.*

Organization of American States (OAS), General Secretariat, Washington, D.C. 20006 (202) 458-3533; *Statistical Bulletin of the OAS.*

Statistical Office of the United Nations, Publishing Service, New York, New York 10017 (800) 253-9646; *Statistical Yearbook;* and *World Statistics Pocketbook.*

U.C.L.A. Latin American Center Publications, University of California, Los Angeles, California 90024 (310) 825-6634; *Statistical Abstract of Latin America.*

MEXICO - EXCISE TAXES - See MEXICO - TAXATION

MEXICO - EXPORTS

American Automobile Manufacturers Association, 1401 H Street, NW, Suite 900, Washington, D.C. 20005 (202) 326-5500; *World Motor Vehicle Data.*

Central Intelligence Agency, Washington, D.C. 20505 (703) 482-1100, www.cia.gov; *The World Factbook.*

The Economist Intelligence Unit, 111 West 57th Street, New York, New York 10019 (800) 938-4685; *The New Latin America Market Atlas; Mexico Country Report;* and *The World Market Atlas.*

Euromonitor International, Inc., 122 South Michigan Avenue, Suite 1200, Chicago, Illinois 60603 (800) 577-EURO; *International Marketing Data and Statistics;* and *The World Economic Factbook.*

Europa Publications Limited, 18 Bedford Square, London, WC1B 3JN, England; *The Europa World Year Book.*

Food and Agricultural Organization of the United Nations (FAO), Via delle Terme di Caracalla, 00100 Rome, Italy (Telephone Number in U.S. (202) 653-2400); *The State of Food and Agriculture.*

Inter-American Development Bank, 1300 New York Avenue, NW, Washington, D.C. 20577 (202) 872-1445; *Economic and Social Progress in Latin America.*

International Lead and Zinc Study Group, Metro House, 58 St. James's Street, London SW1A 1LD England; *Lead and Zinc Statistics.*

International Monetary Fund, 700 Nineteenth Street, NW, Washington, D.C. 20431 (202) 623-7000; *Direction of Trade Statistics; Government Finance Statistics Yearbook;* and *International Financial Statistics.*

Organization of American States (OAS), General Secretariat, Washington, D.C. 20006 (202) 458-3533; *Statistical Bulletin of the OAS.*

St. Martin's Press, Inc., 175 Fifth Avenue, New York, New York 10010 (800) 221-7945; *The Statesman's Year-Book.*

United Nations Conference on Trade and Development (UNCTAD), New York, New York 10017 (800) 253-9646; *Handbook of International Trade and Development Statistics.*

The World Bank, 1818 H Street, NW, Washington, D.C. 20433 (202) 477-1234; *World Development Report;* and *World Development Indicators.*

MEXICO - EXTERNAL FINANCING

Inter-American Development Bank, 1300 New York Avenue, NW, Washington, D.C. 20577 (202) 872-1445; *Economic and Social Progress in Latin America.*

Statistical Office of the United Nations, Publishing Service, New York, New York 10017 (800) 253-9646; *Statistical Yearbook for Latin America and the Caribbean.*

MEXICO - EXTERNAL INDEBTEDNESS

Inter-American Development Bank, 1300 New York Avenue, NW, Washington, D.C. 20577 (202) 872-1445; *Economic and Social Progress in Latin America.*

Statistical Office of the United Nations, Publishing Service, New York, New York 10017 (800) 253-9646; *Statistical Yearbook for Latin America and the Caribbean.*

The World Bank, 1818 H Street, NW, Washington, D.C. 20433 (202) 477-1234; *World Development Report;* and *World Development Indicators.*

MEXICO - EXTERNAL TRADE

Euromonitor International, Inc., 122 South Michigan Avenue, Suite 1200, Chicago, Illinois 60603 (800) 577-EURO; *World Marketing Data and Statistics.*

Food and Agricultural Organization of the United Nations (FAO), Via delle Terme di Caracalla, 00100 Rome, Italy (Telephone Number in U.S. (202) 653-2400); *The State of Food and Agriculture;* and *Trade Yearbook.*

Inter-American Development Bank, 1300 New York Avenue, NW, Washington, D.C. 20577 (202) 872-1445; *Economic and Social Progress in Latin America.*

Statistical Office of the United Nations, Publishing Service, New York, New York 10017 (800) 253-9646; *Statistical Yearbook;* and *Statistical Yearbook for Latin America and the Caribbean.*

MEXICO - FABRIC PRODUCTION - See MEXICO - TEXTILE INDUSTRY

MEXICO - FAMILY PLANNING

U.C.L.A. Latin American Center Publications, University of California, Los Angeles, California 90024 (310) 825-6634; *Statistical Abstract of Latin America.*

MEXICO - FARM CROPS - See MEXICO - CROPS

MEXICO - FEMALE WORKING POPULATION - See MEXICO - EMPLOYMENT

MEXICO - FERTILITY RATES

Central Intelligence Agency, Washington, D.C. 20505 (703) 482-1100, www.cia.gov; *The World Factbook.*

M.E. Sharpe, 80 Business Park Drive,

Armonk, New York 10504 (800) 541-6563; *The Illustrated Book of World Rankings.*

Statistical Office of the United Nations, Publishing Service, New York, New York 10017 (800) 253-9646; *Human Development Report.*

The World Bank, 1818 H Street, NW, Washington, D.C. 20433 (202) 477-1234; *The World Bank Atlas; World Development Report;* and *World Development Indicators.*

MEXICO - FERTILIZER

The Economist Intelligence Unit, 111 West 57th Street, New York, New York 10019 (800) 938-4685; *The New Latin America Market Atlas.*

Food and Agricultural Organization of the United Nations (FAO), Via delle Terme di Caracalla, 00100 Rome, Italy (Telephone Number in U.S. (202) 653-2400); *Fertilizer Yearbook;* and *The State of Food and Agriculture.*

Statistical Office of the United Nations, Publishing Service, New York, New York 10017 (800) 253-9646; *Statistical Yearbook.*

MEXICO - FETAL MORTALITY - See MEXICO - MORTALITY

MEXICO - FIBRE PRODUCTION - See MEXICO - TEXTILE INDUSTRY

MEXICO - FILAMENT PRODUCTION - See MEXICO - TEXTILE INDUSTRY

MEXICO - FILM - See MEXICO - MOTION PICTURES

MEXICO - FINANCE

Economist Intelligence Unit, 111 West 57th Street, New York, New York 10019 (800) 938-4685; *Mexico Country Report.*

Europa Publications Limited, 18 Bedford Square, London, WC1B 3JN, England; *The Europa World Year Book.*

Inter-American Development Bank, 1300 New York Avenue, NW, Washington, D.C. 20577 (202) 872-1445; *Economic and Social Progress in Latin America.*

International Monetary Fund, 700 Nineteenth Street, NW, Washington, D.C. 20431 (202) 623-7000; *Government Finance Statistics Yearbook;* and *International Financial Statistics.*

M.E. Sharpe, 80 Business Park Drive, Armonk, New York 10504 (800) 541-6563; *The Illustrated Book of World Rankings.*

Organization of American States (OAS), General Secretariat, Washington, D.C. 20006 (202) 458-3533; *Statistical*

Bulletin of the OAS.

St. Martin's Press, Inc., 175 Fifth Avenue, New York, New York 10010 (800) 221-7945; *The Statesman's Year-Book.*

U.C.L.A. Latin American Center Publications, University of California, Los Angeles, California 90024 (310) 825-6634; *Statistical Abstract of Latin America.*

MEXICO - FISHERIES

Europa Publications Limited, 18 Bedford Square, London, WC1B 3JN, England; *The Europa World Year Book.*

Food and Agricultural Organization of the United Nations (FAO), Via delle Terme di Caracalla, 00100 Rome, Italy (Telephone Number in U.S. (202) 653-2400); *The State of Food and Agriculture;* and *Yearbook of Fishery Statistics.*

Inter-American Development Bank, 1300 New York Avenue, NW, Washington, D.C. 20577 (202) 872-1445; *Economic and Social Progress in Latin America.*

M.E. Sharpe, 80 Business Park Drive, Armonk, New York 10504 (800) 541-6563; *The Illustrated Book of World Rankings.*

St. Martin's Press, Inc., 175 Fifth Avenue, New York, New York 10010 (800) 221-7945; *The Statesman's Year-Book.*

Statistical Office of the United Nations, Publishing Service, New York, New York 10017 (800) 253-9646; *Statistical Yearbook.*

U.C.L.A. Latin American Center Publications, University of California, Los Angeles, California 90024 (310) 825-6634; *Statistical Abstract of Latin America.*

United Nations Conference on Trade and Development, Central Statistical Service, Palais des Nations, Geneva, Switzerland (Telephone in U.S. (800) 253-9646); *UNCTAD Commodity Yearbook.*

MEXICO - FLOUR PRODUCTION

Commodity Research Bureau, 30 South Wacker Drive, Chicago Illinois 60606 (312) 454-1801; *Commodity Year Book.*

Statistical Office of the United Nations, Publishing Service, New York, New York 10017 (800) 253-9646; *Statistical Yearbook.*

MEXICO - FOOD

Euromonitor International, Inc., 122 South Michigan Avenue, Suite 1200, Chicago, Illinois 60603 (800) 577-EURO; *Retail Trade International.*

Food and Agricultural Organization of the United Nations (FAO), Via delle Terme

di Caracalla, 00100 Rome, Italy (Telephone Number in U.S. (202) 653-2400); *Production Yearbook;* and *The State of Food and Agriculture.*

Statistical Office of the United Nations, Publishing Service, New York, New York 10017 (800) 253-9646; *Human Development Report.*

United Nations Conference on Trade and Development, Central Statistical Service, Palais des Nations, Geneva, Switzerland (Telephone in U.S. (800) 253-9646); *UNCTAD Commodity Yearbook.*

MEXICO - FOREIGN AID

Inter-American Development Bank, 1300 New York Avenue, NW, Washington, D.C. 20577 (202) 872-1445; *Economic and Social Progress in Latin America.*

MEXICO - FOREIGN DEBT

The Economist Intelligence Unit, 111 West 57th Street, New York, New York 10019 (800) 938-4685; *The New Latin America Market Atlas.*

Inter-American Development Bank, 1300 New York Avenue, NW, Washington, D.C. 20577 (202) 872-1445; *Economic and Social Progress in Latin America.*

MEXICO - FOREIGN INDEBTEDNESS

Inter-American Development Bank, 1300 New York Avenue, NW, Washington, D.C. 20577 (202) 872-1445; *Economic and Social Progress in Latin America.*

Statistical Office of the United Nations, Publishing Service, New York, New York 10017 (800) 253-9646; *Economic Survey of Latin America and the Caribbean.*

MEXICO - FOREIGN INVESTMENT

The Economist Intelligence Unit, 111 West 57th Street, New York, New York 10019 (800) 938-4685; *The New Latin America Market Atlas.*

MEXICO - FOREIGN TRADE

The Economist Intelligence Unit, 111 West 57th Street, New York, New York 10019 (800) 938-4685; *Mexico Country Report;* and *The New Latin America Market Atlas.*

Euromonitor International, Inc., 122 South Michigan Avenue, Suite 1200, Chicago, Illinois 60603 (800) 577-EURO; *International Marketing Data and Statistics;* and *The World Economic Factbook.*

Europa Publications Limited, 18 Bedford Square, London, WC1B 3JN, England; *The Europa World Year Book.*

Food and Agricultural Organization of the United Nations (FAO), Via delle Terme di Caracalla, 00100 Rome, Italy (Telephone Number in U.S. (202) 653-2400); *The State of Food and Agriculture.*

Inter-American Development Bank, 1300 New York Avenue, NW, Washington, D.C. 20577 (202) 872-1445; *Economic and Social Progress in Latin America.*

International Monetary Fund, 700 Nineteenth Street, NW, Washington, D.C. 20431 (202) 623-7000; *International Financial Statistics.*

M.E. Sharpe, 80 Business Park Drive, Armonk, New York 10504 (800) 541-6563; *The Illustrated Book of World Rankings.*

St. Martin's Press, Inc., 175 Fifth Avenue, New York, New York 10010 (800) 221-7945; *The Statesman's Year-Book.*

Statistical Office of the United Nations, Publishing Service, New York, New York 10017 (800) 253-9646; *Economic Survey of Latin America and the Caribbean; International Trade Statistics Yearbook;* and *Statistical Yearbook.*

U.C.L.A. Latin American Center Publications, University of California, Los Angeles, California 90024 (310) 825-6634; *Statistical Abstract of Latin America.*

The World Bank, 1818 H Street, NW, Washington, D.C. 20433 (202) 477-1234; *World Development Report;* and *World Development Indicators.*

MEXICO - FORESTRY AND FOREST PRODUCTS

American Forest and Paper Association, 1111 Nineteenth Street, NW, Washington, D.C. 20036 (202) 463-2700; *Wood Pulp and Fiber Statistics.*

The Economist Intelligence Unit, 111 West 57th Street, New York, New York 10019 (800) 938-4685; *The New Latin America Market Atlas.*

Europa Publications Limited, 18 Bedford Square, London, WC1B 3JN, England; *The Europa World Year Book.*

Food and Agricultural Organization of the United Nations (FAO), Via delle Terme di Caracalla, 00100 Rome, Italy (Telephone Number in U.S. (202) 653-2400); *The State of Food and Agriculture;* and *Yearbook of Forest Products.*

Inter-American Development Bank, 1300 New York Avenue, NW, Washington, D.C. 20577 (202) 872-1445; *Economic and Social Progress in Latin America.*

M.E. Sharpe, 80 Business Park Drive,

Armonk, New York 10504 (800) 541-6563; *The Illustrated Book of World Rankings.*

St. Martin's Press, Inc., 175 Fifth Avenue, New York, New York 10010 (800) 221-7945; *The Statesman's Year-Book.*

Statistical Office of the United Nations, Publishing Service, New York, New York 10017 (800) 253-9646; *Statistical Yearbook.*

U.C.L.A. Latin American Center Publications, University of California, Los Angeles, California 90024 (310) 825-6634; *Statistical Abstract of Latin America.*

United Nations Educational, Scientific and Cultural Organization (UNESCO), 7 Place de Fontenoy, F-75700 Paris, France (Telephone Number in U.S. (212) 963-5981); *Statistical Yearbook.*

The World Bank, 1818 H Street, NW, Washington, D.C. 20433 (202) 477-1234; *World Development Report.*

MEXICO - GARLIC PRODUCTION - See MEXICO - CROPS

MEXICO - GAS - See MEXICO - MINING AND MINERAL PRODUCTS

MEXICO - GENERAL INDUSTRIAL STATISTICS - See MEXICO - INDUSTRY

MEXICO - GENERAL MORTALITY - See MEXICO - MORTALITY

MEXICO - GEOGRAPHIC DATA

M.E. Sharpe, 80 Business Park Drive, Armonk, New York 10504 (800) 541-6563; *The Illustrated Book of World Rankings.*

U.C.L.A. Latin American Center Publications, University of California, Los Angeles, California 90024 (310) 825-6634; *Statistical Abstract of Latin America.*

MEXICO - GOATS - See MEXICO - LIVESTOCK AND POULTRY

MEXICO - GOLD HOLDINGS

International Monetary Fund, 700 Nineteenth Street, NW, Washington, D.C. 20431 (202) 623-7000; *International Financial Statistics.*

Statistical Office of the United Nations, Publishing Service, New York, New York 10017 (800) 253-9646; *Statistical Yearbook.*

The World Bank, 1818 H Street, NW, Washington, D.C. 20433 (202) 477-1234; *World Development Indicators.*

MEXICO - GOLD PRODUCTION AND CONSUMPTION - See MEXICO - MINING AND MINERAL PRODUCTS

MEXICO - GOLD RESERVES

The Economist Intelligence Unit, 111 West 57th Street, New York, New York 10019 (800) 938-4685; *The New Latin America Market Atlas.*

MEXICO - GOVERNMENT

Central Intelligence Agency, Washington, D.C. 20505 (703) 482-1100, www.cia.gov; *The World Factbook.*

Europa Publications Limited, 18 Bedford Square, London, WC1B 3JN, England; *The Europa World Year Book.*

Inter-American Development Bank, 1300 New York Avenue, NW, Washington, D.C. 20577 (202) 872-1445; *Economic and Social Progress in Latin America.*

International Monetary Fund, 700 Nineteenth Street, NW, Washington, D.C. 20431 (202) 623-7000; *Government Finance Statistics Yearbook;* and *International Financial Statistics.*

St. Martin's Press, Inc., 175 Fifth Avenue, New York, New York 10010 (800) 221-7945; *The Statesman's Year-Book.*

Statistical Office of the United Nations, Publishing Service, New York, New York 10017 (800) 253-9646; *National Accounts Statistics.*

The World Bank, 1818 H Street, NW, Washington, D.C. 20433 (202) 477-1234; *World Development Report;* and *World Development Indicators.*

MEXICO - GRAIN PRODUCTION - See MEXICO - CROPS

MEXICO - GRANTS

International Monetary Fund, 700 Nineteenth Street, NW, Washington, D.C. 20431 (202) 623-7000; *Government Finance Statistics Yearbook.*

MEXICO - GREEN PEPPER AND CHILIE PRODUCTION - See MEXICO - CROPS

MEXICO - GROSS DOMESTIC PRODUCT

The Economist Intelligence Unit, 111 West 57th Street, New York, New York 10019 (800) 938-4685; *The New Latin America Market Atlas; Mexico Country Report;* and *The World Market Atlas.*

Euromonitor International, Inc., 122 South Michigan Avenue, Suite 1200, Chicago, Illinois 60603 (800) 577-EURO; *International Marketing Data and Statistics;* and *The World Economic Factbook.*

Europa Publications Limited, 18 Bedford Square, London, WC1B 3JN,

England; *The Europa World Year Book.*

Inter-American Development Bank, 1300 New York Avenue, NW, Washington, D.C. 20577 (202) 872-1445; *Economic and Social Progress in Latin America.*

M.E. Sharpe, 80 Business Park Drive, Armonk, New York 10504 (800) 541-6563; *The Illustrated Book of World Rankings.*

Organization of American States (OAS), General Secretariat, Washington, D.C. 20006 (202) 458-3533; *Statistical Bulletin of the OAS.*

Statistical Office of the United Nations, Publishing Service, New York, New York 10017 (800) 253-9646; *Human Development Report; National Accounts Statistics; Statistical Yearbook;* and *Statistical Yearbook for Latin America and the Caribbean.*

U.C.L.A. Latin American Center Publications, University of California, Los Angeles, California 90024 (310) 825-6634; *Statistical Abstract of Latin America.*

The World Bank, 1818 H Street, NW, Washington, D.C. 20433 (202) 477-1234; *World Development Report;* and *World Development Indicators.*

MEXICO - GROSS NATIONAL PRODUCT

Euromonitor International, Inc., 122 South Michigan Avenue, Suite 1200, Chicago, Illinois 60603 (800) 577-EURO; *International Marketing Data and Statistics.*

Inter-American Development Bank, 1300 New York Avenue, NW, Washington, D.C. 20577 (202) 872-1445; *Economic and Social Progress in Latin America.*

St. Martin's Press, Inc., 175 Fifth Avenue, New York, New York 10010 (800) 221-7945; *The Statesman's Year-Book.*

U.S. Arms Control and Disarmament Agency, 320 Twenty-first Street, NW, Washington, D.C. 20451 (202) 647-8677; *World Military Expenditures and Arms Transfers.*

The World Bank, 1818 H Street, NW, Washington, D.C. 20433 (202) 477-1234; *The World Bank Atlas; World Development Report;* and *World Development Indicators.*

MEXICO - GROUNDNUT PRODUCTION - See MEXICO - CROPS

MEXICO - HEALTH

The Economist Intelligence Unit, 111 West 57th Street, New York, New York 10019 (800) 938-4685; *The New Latin America Market Atlas.*

Euromonitor International, Inc., 122 South Michigan Avenue, Suite 1200, Chicago, Illinois 60603 (800) 577-EURO; *World Marketing Data and Statistics.*

M.E. Sharpe, 80 Business Park Drive, Armonk, New York 10504 (800) 541-6563; *The Illustrated Book of World Rankings.*

St. Martin's Press, Inc., 175 Fifth Avenue, New York, New York 10010 (800) 221-7945; *The Statesman's Year-Book.*

Statistical Office of the United Nations, Publishing Service, New York, New York 10017 (800) 253-9646; *Human Development Report; Statistical Yearbook.* and *Statistical Yearbook for Latin America and the Caribbean.*

U.C.L.A. Latin American Center Publications, University of California, Los Angeles, California 90024 (310) 825-6634; *Statistical Abstract of Latin America.*

United Nations Children's Fund (UNICEF), 3 United Nations Plaza, New York, New York 10017 (800) 253-9646; *State of the World's Children.*

The World Bank, 1818 H Street, NW, Washington, D.C. 20433 (202) 477-1234; *World Development Report.*

World Health Organization, Office of Publications, 20 Avenue Appia, CH-1211 Geneva 27, Switzerland (Telephone in U.S. (518) 436-9686); *World Health Statistics Annual.*

MEXICO - HIDE PRODUCTION

Commodity Research Bureau, 30 South Wacker Drive, Chicago Illinois 60606 (312) 454-1801; *Commodity Year Book.*

Food and Agricultural Organization of the United Nations (FAO), Via delle Terme di Caracalla, 00100 Rome, Italy (Telephone Number in U.S. (202) 653-2400); *Production Yearbook.*

MEXICO - HIGHWAYS

Central Intelligence Agency, Washington, D.C. 20505 (703) 482-1100, www.cia.gov; *The World Factbook.*

The Economist Intelligence Unit, 111 West 57th Street, New York, New York 10019 (800) 938-4685; *The New Latin America Market Atlas.*

International Road Federation, 2600 Virginia Avenue, NW, Washington, D.C. 20037 (202) 338-4641; *World Road Statistics.*

St. Martin's Press, Inc., 175 Fifth Avenue, New York, New York 10010 (800) 221-7945; *The Statesman's Year-Book.*

MEXICO - HONEY PRODUCTION

Commodity Research Bureau, 30 South Wacker Drive, Chicago Illinois 60606 (312) 454-1801; *Commodity Year Book.*

MEXICO - HORSES - See MEXICO - LIVESTOCK AND POULTRY

MEXICO - HOURS OF WORK - See MEXICO - EMPLOYMENT

MEXICO - HOUSING AND HOUSING UNITS

Euromonitor International, Inc., 122 South Michigan Avenue, Suite 1200, Chicago, Illinois 60603 (800) 577-EURO; *World Marketing Data and Statistics.*

M.E. Sharpe, 80 Business Park Drive, Armonk, New York 10504 (800) 541-6563; *The Illustrated Book of World Rankings.*

U.C.L.A. Latin American Center Publications, University of California, Los Angeles, California 90024 (310) 825-6634; *Statistical Abstract of Latin America.*

MEXICO - HYDROCHLORIC ACID PRODUCTION

Statistical Office of the United Nations, Publishing Service, New York, New York 10017 (800) 253-9646; *Statistical Yearbook.*

MEXICO - ILLITERACY RATES

The Economist Intelligence Unit, 111 West 57th Street, New York, New York 10019 (800) 938-4685; *The New Latin America Market Atlas.*

MEXICO - ILLITERATE POPULATION

Central Intelligence Agency, Washington, D.C. 20505 (703) 482-1100, www.cia.gov; *The World Factbook.*

The Economist Intelligence Unit, 111 West 57th Street, New York, New York 10019 (800) 938-4685; *The World Market Atlas.*

Euromonitor International, Inc., 122 South Michigan Avenue, Suite 1200, Chicago, Illinois 60603 (800) 577-EURO; *The World Economic Factbook.*

St. Martin's Press, Inc., 175 Fifth Avenue, New York, New York 10010 (800) 221-7945; *The Statesman's Year-Book.*

Statistical Office of the United Nations, Publishing Service, New York, New York 10017 (800) 253-9646; *Human Development Report.*

United Nations Educational, Scientific and Cultural Organization (UNESCO), 7 Place de Fontenoy, F-75700 Paris, France (Telephone Number in U.S. (212) 963-

5981); *Statistical Yearbook.*

MEXICO - IMMIGRATION

U.C.L.A. Latin American Center Publications, University of California, Los Angeles, California 90024 (310) 825-6634; *Statistical Abstract of Latin America.*

MEXICO - IMPORTS

American Automobile Manufacturers Association, 1401 H Street, NW, Suite 900, Washington, D.C. 20005 (202) 326-5500; *World Motor Vehicle Data.*

Central Intelligence Agency, Washington, D.C. 20505 (703) 482-1100, www.cia.gov; *The World Factbook.*

The Economist Intelligence Unit, 111 West 57th Street, New York, New York 10019 (800) 938-4685; *The New Latin America Market Atlas; Mexico Country Report;* and *The World Market Atlas.*

Euromonitor International, Inc., 122 South Michigan Avenue, Suite 1200, Chicago, Illinois 60603 (800) 577-EURO; *International Marketing Data and Statistics;* and *The World Economic Factbook.*

Europa Publications Limited, 18 Bedford Square, London, WC1B 3JN, England; *The Europa World Year Book.*

Food and Agricultural Organization of the United Nations (FAO), Via delle Terme di Caracalla, 00100 Rome, Italy (Telephone Number in U.S. (202) 653-2400); *The State of Food and Agriculture.*

Inter-American Development Bank, 1300 New York Avenue, NW, Washington, D.C. 20577 (202) 872-1445; *Economic and Social Progress in Latin America.*

International Lead and Zinc Study Group, Metro House, 58 St. James's Street, London SW1A 1LD England; *Lead and Zinc Statistics.*

International Monetary Fund, 700 Nineteenth Street, NW, Washington, D.C. 20431 (202) 623-7000; *Direction of Trade Statistics; Government Finance Statistics Yearbook;* and *International Financial Statistics.*

Organization of American States (OAS), General Secretariat, Washington, D.C. 20006 (202) 458-3533; *Statistical Bulletin of the OAS.*

St. Martin's Press, Inc., 175 Fifth Avenue, New York, New York 10010 (800) 221-7945; *The Statesman's Year-Book.*

United Nations Conference on Trade and Development (UNCTAD), New York, New York 10017 (800) 253-9646; *Handbook* of International Trade and Development Statistics.

The World Bank, 1818 H Street, NW, Washington, D.C. 20433 (202) 477-1234; *World Development Report;* and *World Development Indicators.*

MEXICO - INCOME DISTRIBUTION

Statistical Office of the United Nations, Publishing Service, New York, New York 10017 (800) 253-9646; *Statistical Yearbook for Latin America and the Caribbean.*

U.C.L.A. Latin American Center Publications, University of California, Los Angeles, California 90024 (310) 825-6634; *Statistical Abstract of Latin America.*

MEXICO - INCOME TAXES - See MEXICO - TAXATION

MEXICO - INDUSTRIAL METALS PRODUCTION - See MEXICO - MINING AND MINERAL PRODUCTS

MEXICO - INDUSTRY

Central Intelligence Agency, Washington, D.C. 20505 (703) 482-1100, www.cia.gov; *The World Factbook.*

Economist Intelligence Unit, 111 West 57th Street, New York, New York 10019 (800) 938-4685; *Mexico Country Report.*

Euromonitor International, Inc., 122 South Michigan Avenue, Suite 1200, Chicago, Illinois 60603 (800) 577-EURO; *International Marketing Data and Statistics; World Marketing Data and Statistics;* and *The World Economic Factbook.*

Europa Publications Limited, 18 Bedford Square, London, WC1B 3JN, England; *The Europa World Year Book.*

International Labour Office, I.L.O. Publications, 1828 L Street, NW, Suite 801, Washington, D.C. 20036 (301) 638-3152; *Yearbook of Labour Statistics.*

M.E. Sharpe, 80 Business Park Drive, Armonk, New York 10504 (800) 541-6563; *The Illustrated Book of World Rankings.*

St. Martin's Press, Inc., 175 Fifth Avenue, New York, New York 10010 (800) 221-7945; *The Statesman's Year-Book.*

Statistical Office of the United Nations, Publishing Service, New York, New York 10017 (800) 253-9646; *Economic Survey of Latin America and the Caribbean; Industrial Commodity Statistics Yearbook;* and *Statistical Yearbook.*

U.C.L.A. Latin American Center Publications, University of California, Los Angeles, California 90024 (310) 825-6634;

Statistical Abstract of Latin America.

The World Bank, 1818 H Street, NW, Washington, D.C. 20433 (202) 477-1234; *World Development Indicators.*

World Intellectual Property Organization, 34 Chemin des Colombettes, CH-1211 Geneva 20, Switzerland; *Industrial Property Statistics.*

MEXICO - INFANT AND MATERNAL MORTALITY - See MEXICO - MORTALITY

MEXICO - INFLATIONARY FACTORS

Statistical Office of the United Nations, Publishing Service, New York, New York 10017 (800) 253-9646; *Economic Survey of Latin America and the Caribbean.*

MEXICO - INTEREST RATES

Inter-American Development Bank, 1300 New York Avenue, NW, Washington, D.C. 20577 (202) 872-1445; *Economic and Social Progress in Latin America.*

Organization of American States (OAS), General Secretariat, Washington, D.C. 20006 (202) 458-3533; *Statistical Bulletin of the OAS.*

MEXICO - INTERNATIONAL FINANCE

Inter-American Development Bank, 1300 New York Avenue, NW, Washington, D.C. 20577 (202) 872-1445; *Economic and Social Progress in Latin America.*

U.C.L.A. Latin American Center Publications, University of California, Los Angeles, California 90024 (310) 825-6634; *Statistical Abstract of Latin America.*

MEXICO - INTERNATIONAL LIQUIDITY

Inter-American Development Bank, 1300 New York Avenue, NW, Washington, D.C. 20577 (202) 872-1445; *Economic and Social Progress in Latin America.*

International Monetary Fund, 700 Nineteenth Street, NW, Washington, D.C. 20431 (202) 623-7000; *International Financial Statistics.*

MEXICO - INTERNATIONAL RESERVES

Organization of American States (OAS), General Secretariat, Washington, D.C. 20006 (202) 458-3533; *Statistical Bulletin of the OAS.*

MEXICO - INTERNATIONAL RESERVES EXCLUDING GOLD

Inter-American Development Bank, 1300 New York Avenue, NW, Washington, D.C. 20577 (202) 872-1445; *Economic and Social Progress in Latin America.*

Statistical Office of the United Nations, Publishing Service, New York, New York 10017 (800) 253-9646; *Statistical Yearbook.*

The World Bank, 1818 H Street, NW, Washington, D.C. 20433 (202) 477-1234; *World Development Indicators.*

MEXICO - INTERNATIONAL STATISTICS

Inter-American Development Bank, 1300 New York Avenue, NW, Washington, D.C. 20577 (202) 872-1445; *Economic and Social Progress in Latin America.*

U.C.L.A. Latin American Center Publications, University of California, Los Angeles, California 90024 (310) 825-6634; *Statistical Abstract of Latin America.*

MEXICO - INVESTMENTS

Inter-American Development Bank, 1300 New York Avenue, NW, Washington, D.C. 20577 (202) 872-1445; *Economic and Social Progress in Latin America.*

International Monetary Fund, 700 Nineteenth Street, NW, Washington, D.C. 20431 (202) 623-7000; *International Financial Statistics.*

Statistical Office of the United Nations, Publishing Service, New York, New York 10017 (800) 253-9646; *Statistical Yearbook for Latin America and the Caribbean.*

MEXICO - IRON ORE PRODUCTION AND CONSUMPTION - See MEXICO - MINING AND MINERAL PRODUCTS

MEXICO - IRRIGATION

Euromonitor International, Inc., 122 South Michigan Avenue, Suite 1200, Chicago, Illinois 60603 (800) 577-EURO; *International Marketing Data and Statistics.*

Inter-American Development Bank, 1300 New York Avenue, NW, Washington, D.C. 20577 (202) 872-1445; *Economic and Social Progress in Latin America.*

MEXICO - LABOR

Central Intelligence Agency, Washington, D.C. 20505 (703) 482-1100, www.cia.gov; *The World Factbook.*

The Economist Intelligence Unit, 111 West 57th Street, New York, New York 10019 (800) 938-4685; *The New Latin America Market Atlas.*

Euromonitor International, Inc., 122 South Michigan Avenue, Suite 1200, Chicago, Illinois 60603 (800) 577-EURO; *International Marketing Data and Statistics;* and *World Marketing Data and Statistics.*

Europa Publications Limited, 18 Bedford Square, London, WC1B 3JN, England; *The Europa World Year Book*.

Food and Agricultural Organization of the United Nations (FAO), Via delle Terme di Caracalla, 00100 Rome, Italy (Telephone Number in U.S. (202) 653-2400); *The State of Food and Agriculture*.

International Labour Office, I.L.O. Publications,1828 L Street, NW, Suite 801, Washington, D.C. 20036 (301) 638-3152; *Yearbook of Labour Statistics*.

M.E. Sharpe, 80 Business Park Drive, Armonk, New York 10504 (800) 541-6563; *The Illustrated Book of World Rankings*.

St. Martin's Press, Inc., 175 Fifth Avenue, New York, New York 10010 (800) 221-7945; *The Statesman's Year-Book*.

Statistical Office of the United Nations, Publishing Service, New York, New York 10017 (800) 253-9646; *Human Development Report*.

The World Bank, 1818 H Street, NW, Washington, D.C. 20433 (202) 477-1234; *The World Bank Atlas; World Development Report;* and *World Development Indicators*.

MEXICO - LAND AREA

The Economist Intelligence Unit, 111 West 57th Street, New York, New York 10019 (800) 938-4685; *The New Latin America Market Atlas*.

MEXICO - LAND USE

Central Intelligence Agency, Washington, D.C. 20505 (703) 482-1100, www.cia.gov; *The World Factbook*.

Euromonitor International, Inc., 122 South Michigan Avenue, Suite 1200, Chicago, Illinois 60603 (800) 577-EURO; *International Marketing Data and Statistics*.

Food and Agricultural Organization of the United Nations (FAO), Via delle Terme di Caracalla, 00100 Rome, Italy (Telephone Number in U.S. (202) 653-2400); *Production Yearbook*.

Inter-American Development Bank, 1300 New York Avenue, NW, Washington, D.C. 20577 (202) 872-1445; *Economic and Social Progress in Latin America*.

The World Bank, 1818 H Street, NW, Washington, D.C. 20433 (202) 477-1234; *World Development Report*.

MEXICO - LEAD AND LEAD ORE PRODUCTION AND CONSUMPTION - See MEXICO - MINING AND MINERAL PRODUCTS

MEXICO - LIBRARIES

M.E. Sharpe, 80 Business Park Drive, Armonk, New York 10504 (800) 541-6563; *The Illustrated Book of World Rankings*.

United Nations Educational, Scientific and Cultural Organization (UNESCO), 7 Place de Fontenoy, F-75700 Paris, France (Telephone Number in U.S. (212) 963-5981); *Statistical Yearbook*.

MEXICO - LIFE EXPECTANCY RATE

Central Intelligence Agency, Washington, D.C. 20505 (703) 482-1100, www.cia.gov; *The World Factbook*.

The Economist Intelligence Unit, 111 West 57th Street, New York, New York 10019 (800) 938-4685; *The New Latin America Market Atlas*.

Euromonitor International, Inc., 122 South Michigan Avenue, Suite 1200, Chicago, Illinois 60603 (800) 577-EURO; *The World Economic Factbook*.

Statistical Office of the United Nations, Publishing Service, New York, New York 10017 (800) 253-9646; *Human Development Report; World Statistics Pocketbook;* and *Statistical Yearbook for Latin America and the Caribbean*.

The World Bank, 1818 H Street, NW, Washington, D.C. 20433 (202) 477-1234; *The World Bank Atlas;* and *World Development Report*.

MEXICO - LITERACY RATE

Euromonitor International, Inc., 122 South Michigan Avenue, Suite 1200, Chicago, Illinois 60603 (800) 577-EURO; *World Marketing Data and Statistics*.

MEXICO - LIVESTOCK AND POULTRY

Commodity Research Bureau, 30 South Wacker Drive, Chicago Illinois 60606 (312) 454-1801; *Commodity Year Book*.

Euromonitor International, Inc., 122 South Michigan Avenue, Suite 1200, Chicago, Illinois 60603 (800) 577-EURO; *International Marketing Data and Statistics*.

Europa Publications Limited, 18 Bedford Square, London, WC1B 3JN, England; *The Europa World Year Book*.

Food and Agricultural Organization of the United Nations (FAO), Via delle Terme di Caracalla, 00100 Rome, Italy (Telephone Number in U.S. (202) 653-2400); *Production Yearbook;* and *The State of Food and Agriculture*.

M.E. Sharpe, 80 Business Park Drive,

Armonk, New York 10504 (800) 541-6563; *The Illustrated Book of World Rankings*.

St. Martin's Press, Inc., 175 Fifth Avenue, New York, New York 10010 (800) 221-7945; *The Statesman's Year-Book*.

Statistical Office of the United Nations, Publishing Service, New York, New York 10017 (800) 253-9646; *Statistical Yearbook*.

United Nations Conference on Trade and Development, Central Statistical Service, Palais des Nations, Geneva, Switzerland (Telephone in U.S. (800) 253-9646); *UNCTAD Commodity Yearbook*.

MEXICO - LIVING LEVELS - See MEXICO - LIFE EXPECTANCY

MEXICO - MAGNESIUM PRODUCTION AND CONSUMPTION - See MEXICO - MINING AND MINERAL PRODUCTS

MEXICO - MAIL - NUMBER OF PIECES SENT OR RECEIVED

Statistical Office of the United Nations, Publishing Service, New York, New York 10017 (800) 253-9646; *Statistical Yearbook*.

MEXICO - MAIN ECONOMIC INDICATORS - See MEXICO - ECONOMY

MEXICO - MAIN INDICATORS - See MEXICO - ECONOMY

MEXICO - MANGANESE AND MANGANESE ORE PRODUCTION - See MEXICO - MINING AND MINERAL PRODUCTS

MEXICO - MANUFACTURING

American Automobile Manufacturers Association, 1401 H Street, NW, Suite 900, Washington, D.C. 20005 (202) 326-5500; *World Motor Vehicle Data*.

The Economist Intelligence Unit, 111 West 57th Street, New York, New York 10019 (800) 938-4685; *The New Latin America Market Atlas*.

Inter-American Development Bank, 1300 New York Avenue, NW, Washington, D.C. 20577 (202) 872-1445; *Economic and Social Progress in Latin America*.

M.E. Sharpe, 80 Business Park Drive, Armonk, New York 10504 (800) 541-6563; *The Illustrated Book of World Rankings*.

Organization of American States (OAS), General Secretariat, Washington, D.C. 20006 (202) 458-3533; *Statistical Bulletin of the OAS*.

Statistical Office of the United Nations, Publishing Service, New York, New York 10017 (800) 253-9646; *Statistical Yearbook;* and *Statistical Yearbook for Latin America* and the Caribbean.

The World Bank, 1818 H Street, NW, Washington, D.C. 20433 (202) 477-1234; *World Development Indicators.*

MEXICO - MARRIAGE RATES

Europa Publications Limited, 18 Bedford Square, London, WC1B 3JN, England; *The Europa World Year Book.*

M.E. Sharpe, 80 Business Park Drive, Armonk, New York 10504 (800) 541-6563; *The Illustrated Book of World Rankings.*

Statistical Office of the United Nations, Publishing Service, New York, New York 10017 (800) 253-9646; *Demographic Yearbook;* and *Statistical Yearbook.*

MEXICO - MEAT PRODUCTION - See MEXICO - LIVESTOCK AND POULTRY

MEXICO - MEDICAL PERSONNEL

U.C.L.A. Latin American Center Publications, University of California, Los Angeles, California 90024 (310) 825-6634; *Statistical Abstract of Latin America.*

MEXICO - MERCHANT SHIPPING

Europa Publications Limited, 18 Bedford Square, London, WC1B 3JN, England; *The Europa World Year Book.*

Lloyd's Register of Shipping, 17 Battery Place, New York, New York 10004 (212) 425-8050; *Register of Ships.*

St. Martin's Press, Inc., 175 Fifth Avenue, New York, New York 10010 (800) 221-7945; *The Statesman's Year-Book.*

Statistical Office of the United Nations, Publishing Service, New York, New York 10017 (800) 253-9646; *Statistical Yearbook.*

U.S. Department of Transportation, Maritime Administration, 400 Seventh Street, SW, Washington, D.C. 20590 (202) 366-5807, www.marad.dot.gov; *A Statistical Analysis of the World's Merchant Fleets.*

MEXICO - MERCURY PRODUCTION AND CONSUMPTION - See MEXICO - MINING AND MINERAL PRODUCTS

MEXICO - MILK PRODUCTION - See MEXICO - DAIRY PRODUCTS

MEXICO - MILITARY

Central Intelligence Agency, Washington, D.C. 20505 (703) 482-1100, www.cia.gov; *The World Factbook.*

The Economist Intelligence Unit, 111 West 57th Street, New York, New York 10019 (800) 938-4685; *The New Latin America Market Atlas.*

Euromonitor International, Inc., 122 South Michigan Avenue, Suite 1200, Chicago, Illinois 60603 (800) 577-EURO; *World Marketing Data and Statistics.*

The International Institute for Strategic Studies, 23 Tavistock Street, London WC2E 7NQ, England; *The Military Balance.*

International Monetary Fund, 700 Nineteenth Street, NW, Washington, D.C. 20431 (202) 623-7000; *Government Finance Statistics Yearbook.*

St. Martin's Press, Inc., 175 Fifth Avenue, New York, New York 10010 (800) 221-7945; *The Statesman's Year-Book.*

Statistical Office of the United Nations, Publishing Service, New York, New York 10017 (800) 253-9646; *Human Development Report.*

U.C.L.A. Latin American Center Publications, University of California, Los Angeles, California 90024 (310) 825-6634; *Statistical Abstract of Latin America.*

U.S. Arms Control and Disarmament Agency, 320 Twenty-first Street, NW, Washington, D.C. 20451 (202) 647-8677; *World Military Expenditures and Arms Transfers.*

MEXICO - MILK PRODUCTION - See MEXICO - DAIRY PRODUCTS

MEXICO - MINING AND MINERAL PRODUCTS

Commodity Research Bureau, 30 South Wacker Drive, Chicago Illinois 60606 (312) 454-1801; *Commodity Year Book.*

The Economist Intelligence Unit, 111 West 57th Street, New York, New York 10019 (800) 938-4685; *The New Latin America Market Atlas.*

Europa Publications Limited, 18 Bedford Square, London, WC1B 3JN, England; *The Europa World Year Book.*

Inter-American Development Bank, 1300 New York Avenue, NW, Washington, D.C. 20577 (202) 872-1445; *Economic and Social Progress in Latin America.*

International Lead and Zinc Study Group, Metro House, 58 St. James's Street, London SW1A 1LD England; *Lead and Zinc Statistics.*

M.E. Sharpe, 80 Business Park Drive, Armonk, New York 10504 (800) 541-6563; *The Illustrated Book of World Rankings.*

Penn Well Publishing Company, 1421 South Sheridan Road, Post Office Box 1260,

Tulsa, Oklahoma 74101 (800) 752-9764; *International Energy Statistics Sourcebook.*

St. Martin's Press, Inc., 175 Fifth Avenue, New York, New York 10010 (800) 221-7945; *The Statesman's Year-Book.*

Statistical Office of the United Nations, Publishing Service, New York, New York 10017 (800) 253-9646; *Statistical Yearbook;* and *Statistical Yearbook for Latin America and the Caribbean.*

U.C.L.A. Latin American Center Publications, University of California, Los Angeles, California 90024 (310) 825-6634; *Statistical Abstract of Latin America.*

United Nations Conference on Trade and Development, Central Statistical Service, Palais des Nations, Geneva, Switzerland (Telephone in U.S. (800) 253-9646); *UNCTAD Commodity Yearbook.*

MEXICO - MOLASSES PRODUCTION - See MEXICO - CROPS

MEXICO - MOLYBDENUM AND MOLYBDENUM ORE PRODUCTION AND CONSUMPTION - See MEXICO - MINING AND MINERAL PRODUCTS

MEXICO - MONEY EXCHANGE RATE - See MEXICO - EXCHANGE RATES

MEXICO - MONEY RATES - MARKET

Inter-American Development Bank, 1300 New York Avenue, NW, Washington, D.C. 20577 (202) 872-1445; *Economic and Social Progress in Latin America.*

MEXICO - MONEY RESERVES

Euromonitor International, Inc., 122 South Michigan Avenue, Suite 1200, Chicago, Illinois 60603 (800) 577-EURO; *International Marketing Data and Statistics.*

Inter-American Development Bank, 1300 New York Avenue, NW, Washington, D.C. 20577 (202) 872-1445; *Economic and Social Progress in Latin America.*

MEXICO - MONEY SUPPLY

Economist Intelligence Unit, 111 West 57th Street, New York, New York 10019 (800) 938-4685; *Mexico Country Report.*

Euromonitor International, Inc., 122 South Michigan Avenue, Suite 1200, Chicago, Illinois 60603 (800) 577-EURO; *International Marketing Data and Statistics.*

Europa Publications Limited, 18 Bedford Square, London, WC1B 3JN, England; *The Europa World Year Book.*

Inter-American Development Bank, 1300 New York Avenue, NW, Washington, D.C. 20577 (202) 872-1445; *Economic and Social Progress in Latin America.*

International Monetary Fund, 700 Nineteenth Street, NW, Washington, D.C. 20431 (202) 623-7000; *International Financial Statistics.*

Statistical Office of the United Nations, Publishing Service, New York, New York 10017 (800) 253-9646; *Statistical Yearbook.*

U.C.L.A. Latin American Center Publications, University of California, Los Angeles, California 90024 (310) 825-6634; *Statistical Abstract of Latin America.*

The World Bank, 1818 H Street, NW, Washington, D.C. 20433 (202) 477-1234; *World Development Indicators.*

MEXICO - MONUMENTS AND HISTORICAL SITES

United Nations Educational, Scientific and Cultural Organization (UNESCO), 7 Place de Fontenoy, F-75700 Paris, France (Telephone Number in U.S. (212) 963-5981); *Statistical Yearbook.*

MEXICO - MORTALITY

Central Intelligence Agency, Washington, D.C. 20505 (703) 482-1100, www.cia.gov; *The World Factbook.*

The Economist Intelligence Unit, 111 West 57th Street, New York, New York 10019 (800) 938-4685; *The New Latin America Market Atlas.*

Euromonitor International, Inc., 122 South Michigan Avenue, Suite 1200, Chicago, Illinois 60603 (800) 577-EURO; *International Marketing Data and Statistics;* and *The World Economic Factbook.*

Europa Publications Limited, 18 Bedford Square, London, WC1B 3JN, England; *The Europa World Year Book.*

St. Martin's Press, Inc., 175 Fifth Avenue, New York, New York 10010 (800) 221-7945; *The Statesman's Year-Book.*

Statistical Office of the United Nations, Publishing Service, New York, New York 10017 (800) 253-9646; *Demographic Yearbook; Human Development Report; World Statistics Pocketbook;* and *Statistical Yearbook.*

United Nations Children's Fund (UNICEF), 3 United Nations Plaza, New York, New York 10017 (800) 253-9646; *State of the World's Children.*

The World Bank, 1818 H Street, NW, Washington, D.C. 20433 (202) 477-1234; *The*

World Bank Atlas; and *World Development Report;* and *World Development Indicators.*

World Health Organization, Office of Publications, 20 Avenue Appia, CH-1211 Geneva 27, Switzerland (Telephone in U.S. (518) 436-9686); *World Health Statistics Annual.*

MEXICO - MOTION PICTURES

St. Martin's Press, Inc., 175 Fifth Avenue, New York, New York 10010 (800) 221-7945; *The Statesman's Year-Book.*

Statistical Office of the United Nations, Publishing Service, New York, New York 10017 (800) 253-9646; *Statistical Yearbook.*

United Nations Educational, Scientific and Cultural Organization (UNESCO), 7 Place de Fontenoy, F-75700 Paris, France (Telephone Number in U.S. (212) 963-5981); *Statistical Yearbook.*

MEXICO - MOTOR VEHICLE PRODUCTION

American Automobile Manufacturers Association, 1401 H Street, NW, Suite 900, Washington, D.C. 20005 (202) 326-5500; *World Motor Vehicle Data.*

Europa Publications Limited, 18 Bedford Square, London, WC1B 3JN, England; *The Europa World Year Book.*

MEXICO - MOTOR VEHICLE PRODUCTION AND ASSEMBLY

Statistical Office of the United Nations, Publishing Service, New York, New York 10017 (800) 253-9646; *Statistical Yearbook.*

MEXICO - MOTOR VEHICLE TAXES - See MEXICO - TAXATION

MEXICO - MOTOR VEHICLES

The Economist Intelligence Unit, 111 West 57th Street, New York, New York 10019 (800) 938-4685; *The New Latin America Market Atlas.*

MEXICO - MOTOR VEHICLES IN USE

American Automobile Manufacturers Association, 1401 H Street, NW, Suite 900, Washington, D.C. 20005 (202) 326-5500; *World Motor Vehicle Data.*

International Road Federation, 2600 Virginia Avenue, NW, Washington, D.C. 20037 (202) 338-4641; *World Road Statistics.*

Statistical Office of the United Nations, Publishing Service, New York, New York 10017 (800) 253-9646; *Statistical Yearbook.*

MEXICO - MULES - See MEXICO -

LIVESTOCK AND POULTRY

MEXICO - MUSEUMS

M.E. Sharpe, 80 Business Park Drive, Armonk, New York 10504 (800) 541-6563; *The Illustrated Book of World Rankings.*

United Nations Educational, Scientific and Cultural Organization (UNESCO), 7 Place de Fontenoy, F-75700 Paris, France (Telephone Number in U.S. (212) 963-5981); *Statistical Yearbook.*

MEXICO - NATALITY - See MEXICO - BIRTH RATES

MEXICO - NATIONAL ACCOUNTS

Europa Publications Limited, 18 Bedford Square, London, WC1B 3JN, England; *The Europa World Year Book.*

Inter-American Development Bank, 1300 New York Avenue, NW, Washington, D.C. 20577 (202) 872-1445; *Economic and Social Progress in Latin America.*

International Monetary Fund, 700 Nineteenth Street, NW, Washington, D.C. 20431 (202) 623-7000; *International Financial Statistics.*

Organization of American States (OAS), General Secretariat, Washington, D.C. 20006 (202) 458-3533; *Statistical Bulletin of the OAS.*

Statistical Office of the United Nations, Publishing Service, New York, New York 10017 (800) 253-9646; *Statistical Yearbook.*

MEXICO - NATIONAL INCOME

Inter-American Development Bank, 1300 New York Avenue, NW, Washington, D.C. 20577 (202) 872-1445; *Economic and Social Progress in Latin America.*

M.E. Sharpe, 80 Business Park Drive, Armonk, New York 10504 (800) 541-6563; *The Illustrated Book of World Rankings.*

Statistical Office of the United Nations, Publishing Service, New York, New York 10017 (800) 253-9646; *National Account Statistics; Statistical Yearbook;* and *Statistical Yearbook for Latin America and the Caribbean.*

U.C.L.A. Latin American Center Publications, University of California, Los Angeles, California 90024 (310) 825-6634; *Statistical Abstract of Latin America.*

MEXICO - NATIONAL PRODUCT

M.E. Sharpe, 80 Business Park Drive, p Armonk, New York 10504 (800) 541-6563; *The Illustrated Book of World Rankings.*

Statistical Office of the United Nations, Publishing Service, New York, New York 10017 (800) 253-9646; *Statistical Yearbook.*

MEXICO - NATURAL GAS

Commodity Research Bureau, 30 South Wacker Drive, Chicago Illinois 60606 (312) 454-1801; *Commodity Year Book.*

Inter-American Development Bank, 1300 New York Avenue, NW, Washington, D.C. 20577 (202) 872-1445; *Economic and Social Progress in Latin America.*

Statistical Office of the United Nations, Publishing Service, New York, New York 10017 (800) 253-9646; *Statistical Yearbook.*

MEXICO - NATURAL GAS - PRODUCTION - See MEXICO - MINING AND MINERAL PRODUCTS

MEXICO - NEWSPAPER PRODUCTION - See MEXICO - FORESTRY AND FOREST PRODUCTION

MEXICO - NEWSPRINT - See MEXICO - FORESTRY AND FOREST PRODUCTS

MEXICO - NICKEL AND NICKEL ORE PRODUCTION AND CONSUMPTION - See MEXICO - MINING AND MINERAL PRODUCTS

MEXICO - NITRIC ACID PRODUCTION - See MEXICO - MINING AND MINERAL PRODUCTS

MEXICO - NUTRITION

Statistical Office of the United Nations, Publishing Service, New York, New York 10017 (800) 253-9646; *Statistical Yearbook for Latin America and the Caribbean.*

MEXICO - OATS PRODUCTION - See MEXICO - CROPS

MEXICO - OCCUPATIONS - See MEXICO - LABOR

MEXICO - ONION PRODUCTION - See MEXICO - CROPS

MEXICO - ORANGE PRODUCTION - See MEXICO - CROPS

MEXICO - PALM KERNELS PRODUCTION - See MEXICO - CROPS

MEXICO - PAPER - See MEXICO - FORESTRY AND FOREST PRODUCTS

MEXICO - PATENTS, TRADEMARKS AND SERVICE MARKS

Statistical Office of the United Nations, Publishing Service, New York, New York 10017 (800) 253-9646; *Statistical Yearbook.*

World Intellectual Property Organization, 34 Chemin des Colombettes, CH-1211 Geneva 20, Switzerland; *Industrial Property Statistics.*

MEXICO - PEANUT PRODUCTION - See MEXICO - CROPS

MEXICO - PERIODICALS

United Nations Educational, Scientific and Cultural Organization (UNESCO), 7 Place de Fontenoy, F-75700 Paris, France (Telephone Number in U.S. (212) 963-5981); *Statistical Yearbook.*

MEXICO - PESTICIDE USE

Food and Agricultural Organization of the United Nations (FAO), Via delle Terme di Caracalla, 00100 Rome, Italy (Telephone Number in U.S. (202) 653-2400); *The State of Food and Agriculture.*

MEXICO - PETROLEUM INDUSTRY

Commodity Research Bureau, 30 South Wacker Drive, Chicago Illinois 60606 (312) 454-1801; *Commodity Year Book.*

The Economist Intelligence Unit, 111 West 57th Street, New York, New York 10019 (800) 938-4685; *The New Latin America Market Atlas.*

Food and Agricultural Organization of the United Nations (FAO), Via delle Terme di Caracalla, 00100 Rome, Italy (Telephone Number in U.S. (202) 653-2400); *The State of Food and Agriculture.*

Inter-American Development Bank, 1300 New York Avenue, NW, Washington, D.C. 20577 (202) 872-1445; *Economic and Social Progress in Latin America.*

International Monetary Fund, 700 Nineteenth Street, NW, Washington, D.C. 20431 (202) 623-7000; *International Financial Statistics.*

M.E. Sharpe, 80 Business Park Drive, Armonk, New York 10504 (800) 541-6563; *The Illustrated Book of World Rankings.*

Organization of American States (OAS), General Secretariat, Washington, D.C. 20006 (202) 458-3533; *Statistical Bulletin of the OAS.*

Penn Well Publishing Company, 1421 South Sheridan Road, Post Office Box 1260, Tulsa, Oklahoma 74101 (800) 752-9764; *International Energy Statistics Sourcebook.*

St. Martin's Press, Inc., 175 Fifth Avenue, New York, New York 10010 (800) 221-7945; *The Statesman's Year-Book.*

Statistical Office of the United Nations,

Publishing Service, New York, New York 10017 (800) 253-9646; *Statistical Yearbook.*

United Nations Conference on Trade and Development, Central Statistical Service, Palais des Nations, Geneva, Switzerland (Telephone in U.S. (800) 253-9646); *UNCTAD Commodity Yearbook.*

MEXICO - PHOSPHATE ROCK PRODUCTION - See MEXICO - MINING AND MINERAL PRODUCTS

MEXICO - PIG-IRON AND FERRO-ALLOY PRODUCTION - See MEXICO - MINING AND MINERAL PRODUCTS

MEXICO - PIGS - See MEXICO - LIVESTOCK AND POULTRY

MEXICO - PLASTICS AND RESINS PRODUCTION

Statistical Office of the United Nations, Publishing Service, New York, New York 10017 (800) 253-9646; *Statistical Yearbook.*

MEXICO - PLATINUM PRODUCTION - See MEXICO - MINING AND MINERAL PRODUCTS

MEXICO - POLITICAL DATA

U.C.L.A. Latin American Center Publications, University of California, Los Angeles, California 90024 (310) 825-6634; *Statistical Abstract of Latin America.*

MEXICO - POPULATION

Central Intelligence Agency, Washington, D.C. 20505 (703) 482-1100, www.cia.gov; *The World Factbook.*

The Economist Intelligence Unit, 111 West 57th Street, New York, New York 10019 (800) 938-4685; *The New Latin America Market Atlas; Mexico Country Report;* and *The World Market Atlas.*

Euromonitor International, Inc., 122 South Michigan Avenue, Suite 1200, Chicago, Illinois 60603 (800) 577-EURO; *International Marketing Data and Statistics;* and *The World Economic Factbook.*

Europa Publications Limited, 18 Bedford Square, London, WC1B 3JN, England; *The Europa World Year Book.*

Food and Agricultural Organization of the United Nations (FAO), Via delle Terme di Caracalla, 00100 Rome, Italy (Telephone Number in U.S. (202) 653-2400); *Production Yearbook.*

Inter-American Development Bank, 1300 New York Avenue, NW, Washington, D.C. 20577 (202) 872-1445; *Economic and Social Progress in Latin America.*

International Labour Office, I.L.O. Publications, 1828 L Street, NW, Suite 801, Washington, D.C. 20036 (301) 638-3152; *Yearbook of Labour Statistics.*

M.E. Sharpe, 80 Business Park Drive, Armonk, New York 10504 (800) 541-6563; *The Illustrated Book of World Rankings.*

Organization of American States, (OAS), General Secretariat, Washington, D.C. 20006 (202) 458-3533; *Statistical Bulletin of the OAS.*

St. Martin's Press, Inc., 175 Fifth Avenue, New York, New York 10010 (800) 221-7945; *The Statesman's Year-Book.*

Statistical Office of the United Nations, Publishing Service, New York, New York 10017 (800) 253-9646; *Demographic Yearbook; Human Development Report; Statistical Yearbook; World Statistics Pocketbook;* and *Statistical Yearbook for Latin America and the Caribbean.*

U.C.L.A. Latin American Center Publications, University of California, Los Angeles, California 90024 (310) 825-6634; *Statistical Abstract of Latin America.*

U.S. Arms Control and Disarmament Agency, 320 Twenty-first Street, NW, Washington, D.C. 20451 (202) 647-8677; *World Military Expenditures and Arms Transfers.*

The World Bank, 1818 H Street, NW, Washington, D.C. 20433 (202) 477-1234; *The World Bank Atlas;* and *World Development Report.*

World Health Organization, Office of Publications, 20 Avenue Appia, CH-1211 Geneva 27, Switzerland (Telephone in U.S. (518) 436-9686); *World Health Statistics Annual.*

MEXICO - POST OFFICES

M.E. Sharpe, 80 Business Park Drive, Armonk, New York 10504 (800) 541-6563; *The Illustrated Book of World Rankings.*

MEXICO - POTATO PRODUCTION - See MEXICO - CROPS

MEXICO - PRICES

Food and Agricultural Organization of the United Nations (FAO), Via delle Terme di Caracalla, 00100 Rome, Italy (Telephone Number in U.S. (202) 653-2400); *Production Yearbook;* and *The State of Food and Agriculture.*

International Labour Office, I.L.O. Publications, 1828 L Street, NW, Suite 801, Washington, D.C. 20036 (301) 638-3152; *Yearbook of Labour Statistics.*

International Lead and Zinc Study Group, Metro House, 58 St. James's Street, London SW1A 1LD England; *Lead and Zinc Statistics.*

International Monetary Fund, 700 Nineteenth Street, NW, Washington, D.C. 20431 (202) 623-7000; *International Financial Statistics.*

M.E. Sharpe, 80 Business Park Drive, Armonk, New York 10504 (800) 541-6563; *The Illustrated Book of World Rankings.*

Statistical Office of the United Nations, Publishing Service, New York, New York 10017 (800) 253-9646; *Economic Survey of Latin America and the Caribbean;* and *Statistical Yearbook for Latin America and the Caribbean.*

MEXICO - PRINTING AND WRITING PAPER - See MEXICO - FORESTRY AND FOREST PRODUCTS

MEXICO - PRODUCTION

American Automobile Manufacturers Association, 1401 H Street, NW, Suite 900, Washington, D.C. 20005 (202) 326-5500; *World Motor Vehicle Data.*

International Lead and Zinc Study Group, Metro House, 58 St. James's Street, London SW1A 1LD England; *Lead and Zinc Statistics.*

M.E. Sharpe, 80 Business Park Drive, Armonk, New York 10504 (800) 541-6563; *The Illustrated Book of World Rankings.*

MEXICO - PRODUCTIVITY

Euromonitor International, Inc., 122 South Michigan Avenue, Suite 1200, Chicago, Illinois 60603 (800) 577-EURO; *International Marketing Data and Statistics.*

MEXICO - PROPERTY TAXES

Inter-American Development Bank, 1300 New York Avenue, NW, Washington, D.C. 20577 (202) 872-1445; *Economic and Social Progress in Latin America.*

International Monetary Fund, 700 Nineteenth Street, NW, Washington, D.C. 20431 (202) 623-7000; *Government Finance Statistics Yearbook.*

MEXICO - PUBLIC CONSUMPTION FUND

Inter-American Development Bank, 1300 New York Avenue, NW, Washington, D.C. 20577 (202) 872-1445; *Economic and Social Progress in Latin America.*

MEXICO - PUBLIC EXPENDITURE

Inter-American Development Bank,

1300 New York Avenue, NW, Washington, D.C. 20577 (202) 872-1445; *Economic and Social Progress in Latin America.*

Organization of American States (OAS), General Secretariat, Washington, D.C. 20006 (202) 458-3533; *Statistical Bulletin of the OAS.*

Statistical Office of the United Nations, Publishing Service, New York, New York 10017 (800) 253-9646; *Statistical Yearbook for Latin America and the Caribbean.*

MEXICO - PUBLIC FINANCE - See MEXICO - BANKING

MEXICO - PUBLIC REVENUE

Inter-American Development Bank, 1300 New York Avenue, NW, Washington, D.C. 20577 (202) 872-1445; *Economic and Social Progress in Latin America.*

Organization of American States (OAS), General Secretariat, Washington, D.C. 20006 (202) 458-3533; *Statistical Bulletin of the OAS.*

MEXICO - RADIO BROADCASTING - See MEXICO - BROADCASTING

MEXICO - RADIO RECEIVERS

St. Martin's Press, Inc., 175 Fifth Avenue, New York, New York 10010 (800) 221-7945; *The Statesman's Year-Book.*

Statistical Office of the United Nations, Publishing Service, New York, New York 10017 (800) 253-9646; *Statistical Yearbook.*

MEXICO - RAILWAY USE

Statistical Office of the United Nations, Publishing Service, New York, New York 10017 (800) 253-9646; *Statistical Yearbook.*

MEXICO - RAILWAYS

The Economist Intelligence Unit, 111 West 57th Street, New York, New York 10019 (800) 938-4685; *The New Latin America Market Atlas.*

Europa Publications Limited, 18 Bedford Square, London, WC1B 3JN, England; *The Europa World Year Book.*

Jane's Information Group, Sentinel House, 163 Brighton Road, Coulsdon, Surrey CR5 2NH, England (Telephone Number in U.S. (703) 683-3700); *Jane's World Railways.*

St. Martin's Press, Inc., 175 Fifth Avenue, New York, New York 10010 (800) 221-7945; *The Statesman's Year-Book.*

MEXICO - RANCHING

U.C.L.A. Latin American Center Publications, University of California, Los Angeles, California 90024 (310) 825-6634; *Statistical Abstract of Latin America.*

MEXICO - RAPESEED PRODUCTION - See MEXICO - CROPS

MEXICO - RELIGION

Central Intelligence Agency, Washington, D.C. 20505 (703) 482-1100, www.cia.gov; *The World Factbook.*

M.E. Sharpe, 80 Business Park Drive, Armonk, New York 10504 (800) 541-6563; *The Illustrated Book of World Rankings.*

St. Martin's Press, Inc., 175 Fifth Avenue, New York, New York 10010 (800) 221-7945; *The Statesman's Year-Book.*

U.C.L.A. Latin American Center Publications, University of California, Los Angeles, California 90024 (310) 825-6634; *Statistical Abstract of Latin America.*

MEXICO - RENT PRICES

International Labour Office, I.L.O. Publications, 1828 L Street, NW, Suite 801, Washington, D.C. 20036 (301) 638-3152; *Yearbook of Labour Statistics.*

MEXICO - RESERVES EXCLUDING GOLD

The Economist Intelligence Unit, 111 West 57th Street, New York, New York 10019 (800) 938-4685; *The New Latin America Market Atlas.*

MEXICO - RETAIL TRADE

Euromonitor International, Inc., 122 South Michigan Avenue, Suite 1200, Chicago, Illinois 60603 (800) 577-EURO; *World Marketing Data and Statistics;* and *Retail Trade International..*

Inter-American Development Bank, 1300 New York Avenue, NW, Washington, D.C. 20577 (202) 872-1445; *Economic and Social Progress in Latin America.*

Statistical Office of the United Nations, Publishing Service, New York, New York 10017 (800) 253-9646; *Statistical Yearbook.*

MEXICO - RICE PRODUCTION - See MEXICO - CROPS

MEXICO - ROOT AND TUBER PRODUCTION - See MEXICO - CROPS

MEXICO - ROUNDWOOD PRODUCTION - See MEXICO - FORESTRY AND FOREST PRODUCTS

MEXICO - RUBBER PRODUCTION AND CONSUMPTION

M.E. Sharpe, 80 Business Park Drive, Armonk, New York 10504 (800) 541-6563; *The Illustrated Book of World Rankings.*

Statistical Office of the United Nations, Publishing Service, New York, New York 10017 (800) 253-9646; *Statistical Yearbook.*

MEXICO - SAFFLOWER SEED PRODUCTION - See MEXICO - CROPS

MEXICO - SALT PRODUCTION - See MEXICO - MINING AND MINERAL PRODUCTS

MEXICO - SAWNWOOD PRODUCTION - See MEXICO - FORESTRY AND FOREST PRODUCTS

MEXICO - SCIENCE AND TECHNOLOGY

U.C.L.A. Latin American Center Publications, University of California, Los Angeles, California 90024 (310) 825-6634; *Statistical Abstract of Latin America.*

MEXICO - SCIENCE AND TECHNOLOGY - EXPENDITURE FOR RESEARCH - See MEXICO - SCIENTISTS, TECHNICIANS AND ENGINEERS

MEXICO - SCIENTISTS, TECHNICIANS AND ENGINEERS

Statistical Office of the United Nations, Publishing Service, New York, New York 10017 (800) 253-9646; *Statistical Yearbook.*

MEXICO - SENIOR CITIZENS

M.E. Sharpe, 80 Business Park Drive, Armonk, New York 10504 (800) 541-6563; *The Illustrated Book of World Rankings.*

MEXICO - SESAME SEED PRODUCTION - See MEXICO - CROPS

MEXICO - SHEEP - See MEXICO - LIVESTOCK AND POULTRY

MEXICO - SHRIMP EXPORTS

International Monetary Fund, 700 Nineteenth Street, NW, Washington, D.C. 20431 (202) 623-7000; *International Financial Statistics.*

MEXICO - SILVER PRODUCTION AND CONSUMPTION - See MEXICO - MINING AND MINERAL PRODUCTS

MEXICO - SOCIAL DATA

M.E. Sharpe, 80 Business Park Drive, Armonk, New York 10504 (800) 541-6563; *The Illustrated Book of World Rankings.*

Statistical Office of the United Nations, Publishing Service, New York, New York 10017 (800) 253-9646; *World Statistics*

Pocketbook.

U.C.L.A. Latin American Center Publications, University of California, Los Angeles, California 90024 (310) 825-6634; *Statistical Abstract of Latin America.*

MEXICO - SOCIAL SECURITY

Inter-American Development Bank, 1300 New York Avenue, NW, Washington, D.C. 20577 (202) 872-1445; *Economic and Social Progress in Latin America.*

International Monetary Fund, 700 Nineteenth Street, NW, Washington, D.C. 20431 (202) 623-7000; *Government Finance Statistics Yearbook.*

St. Martin's Press, Inc., 175 Fifth Avenue, New York, New York 10010 (800) 221-7945; *The Statesman's Year-Book.*

Statistical Office of the United Nations, Publishing Service, New York, New York 10017 (800) 253-9646; *National Accounts Statistics.*

MEXICO - SOCIOECONOMIC DATA

Inter-American Development Bank, 1300 New York Avenue, NW, Washington, D.C. 20577 (202) 872-1445; *Economic and Social Progress in Latin America.*

U.C.L.A. Latin American Center Publications, University of California, Los Angeles, California 90024 (310) 825-6634; *Statistical Abstract of Latin America.*

MEXICO - SOYBEAN PRODUCTION - See MEXICO - CROPS

MEXICO - STAMP TAXES AND DUTIES - See MEXICO - TAXATION

MEXICO - STATE BUDGET REVENUE AND EXPENDITURES

Euromonitor International, Inc., 122 South Michigan Avenue, Suite 1200, Chicago, Illinois 60603 (800) 577-EURO; *International Marketing Data and Statistics.*

Inter-American Development Bank, 1300 New York Avenue, NW, Washington, D.C. 20577 (202) 872-1445; *Economic and Social Progress in Latin America.*

MEXICO - STEEL - See MEXICO - MINING AND MINERAL PRODUCTS

MEXICO - STOCKS - COMMODITY - MARKET PRICE - INDEX

Food and Agricultural Organization of the United Nations (FAO), Via delle Terme di Caracalla, 00100 Rome, Italy (Telephone Number in U.S. (202) 653-2400); *The State of Food and Agriculture.*

International Lead and Zinc Study Group, Metro House, 58 St. James's Street, London SW1A 1LD England; *Lead and Zinc Statistics*.

MEXICO - SUGAR - See MEXICO - CROPS

MEXICO - SULPHUR AND SULPHURIC ACID PRODUCTION - See MEXICO - MINING AND MINERAL PRODUCTS

MEXICO - TAXATION

Europa Publications Limited, 18 Bedford Square, London, WC1B 3JN, England; *The Europa World Year Book*.

Inter-American Development Bank, 1300 New York Avenue, NW, Washington, D.C. 20577 (202) 872-1445; *Economic and Social Progress in Latin America*.

International Monetary Fund, 700 Nineteenth Street, NW, Washington, D.C. 20431 (202) 623-7000; *Government Finance Statistics Yearbook*.

International Road Federation, 2600 Virginia Avenue, NW, Washington, D.C. 20037 (202) 338-4641; *World Road Statistics*.

Statistical Office of the United Nations, Publishing Service, New York, New York 10017 (800) 253-9646; *Statistical Yearbook for Latin America and the Caribbean*.

The World Bank, 1818 H Street, NW, Washington, D.C. 20433 (202) 477-1234; *World Development Indicators*.

MEXICO - TELEGRAPH SERVICE

Statistical Office of the United Nations, Publishing Service, New York, New York 10017 (800) 253-9646; *Statistical Yearbook*.

MEXICO - TELEPHONES IN USE

American Telephone and Telegraph Company, 26 Parsippany Road, Whippany, New Jersey 07981 (800) 222-0300; *The World's Telephones*.

Central Intelligence Agency, Washington, D.C. 20505 (703) 482-1100, www.cia.gov; *The World Factbook*.

The Economist Intelligence Unit, 111 West 57th Street, New York, New York 10019 (800) 938-4685; *The New Latin America Market Atlas*.

Europa Publications Limited, 18 Bedford Square, London, WC1B 3JN, England; *The Europa World Year Book*.

St. Martin's Press, Inc., 175 Fifth Avenue, New York, New York 10010 (800) 221-7945; *The Statesman's Year-Book*.

Statistical Office of the United Nations,

Publishing Service, New York, New York 10017 (800) 253-9646; *Statistical Yearbook;* and *World Statistics Pocketbook*.

MEXICO - TELEVISION BROADCASTING - See MEXICO - BROADCASTING

MEXICO - TELEVISION RECEIVER PRODUCTION

Statistical Office of the United Nations, Publishing Service, New York, New York 10017 (800) 253-9646; *Statistical Yearbook*.

MEXICO - TEXTILE INDUSTRY

American Forest and Paper Association, 1111 Nineteenth Street, NW, Washington, D.C. 20036 (202) 463-2700; *Wood Pulp and Fiber Statistics*.

Euromonitor International, Inc., 122 South Michigan Avenue, Suite 1200, Chicago, Illinois 60603 (800) 577-EURO; *Retail Trade International*.

M.E. Sharpe, 80 Business Park Drive, Armonk, New York 10504 (800) 541-6563; *The Illustrated Book of World Rankings*.

Statistical Office of the United Nations, Publishing Service, New York, New York 10017 (800) 253-9646; *Statistical Yearbook*.

United Nations Conference on Trade and Development, Central Statistical Service, Palais des Nations, Geneva, Switzerland (Telephone in U.S. (800) 253-9646); *UNCTAD Commodity Yearbook*.

MEXICO - THEATRE

United Nations Educational, Scientific and Cultural Organization (UNESCO), 7 Place de Fontenoy, F-75700 Paris, France (Telephone Number in U.S. (212) 963-5981); *Statistical Yearbook*.

MEXICO - TIN - See MEXICO - MINING AND MINERAL PRODUCTS

MEXICO - TIRE (MOTOR VEHICLE) PRODUCTION

Statistical Office of the United Nations, Publishing Service, New York, New York 10017 (800) 253-9646; *Statistical Yearbook*.

MEXICO - TOBACCO PRODUCTION

M.E. Sharpe, 80 Business Park Drive, Armonk, New York 10504 (800) 541-6563; *The Illustrated Book of World Rankings*.

Statistical Office of the United Nations, Publishing Service, New York, New York 10017 (800) 253-9646; *Statistical Yearbook*.

U.C.L.A. Latin American Center Publications, University of California, Los

Angeles, California 90024 (310) 825-6634; *Statistical Abstract of Latin America*.

MEXICO - TOURISM

The Economist Intelligence Unit, 111 West 57th Street, New York, New York 10019 (800) 938-4685; *The New Latin America Market Atlas*.

Euromonitor International, Inc., 122 South Michigan Avenue, Suite 1200, Chicago, Illinois 60603 (800) 577-EURO; *The World Economic Factbook;* and *World Marketing Data and Statistics*.

Europa Publications Limited, 18 Bedford Square, London, WC1B 3JN, England; *The Europa World Year Book*.

M.E. Sharpe, 80 Business Park Drive, Armonk, New York 10504 (800) 541-6563; *The Illustrated Book of World Rankings*.

Organization of American States (OAS), General Secretariat, Washington, D.C. 20006 (202) 458-3533; *Statistical Bulletin of the OAS*.

St. Martin's Press, Inc., 175 Fifth Avenue, New York, New York 10010 (800) 221-7945; *The Statesman's Year-Book*.

Statistical Office of the United Nations, Publishing Service, New York, New York 10017 (800) 253-9646; *Statistical Yearbook*.

U.C.L.A. Latin American Center Publications, University of California, Los Angeles, California 90024 (310) 825-6634; *Statistical Abstract of Latin America*.

World Tourism Organization, Calle Capitan Haya 42, E-28020 Madrid, Spain; *Yearbook of Tourism Statistics*.

MEXICO - TRACTORS IN USE

The Economist Intelligence Unit, 111 West 57th Street, New York, New York 10019 (800) 938-4685; *The New Latin America Market Atlas*.

Statistical Office of the United Nations, Publishing Service, New York, New York 10017 (800) 253-9646; *Statistical Yearbook*.

MEXICO - TRADE - See MEXICO - FOREIGN TRADE

MEXICO - TRADEMARKS AND SERVICE MARKS - See MEXICO - PATENTS, TRADEMARKS AND SERVICE MARKS

MEXICO - TRANSPORTATION AND COMMUNICATIONS

Central Intelligence Agency, Washington, D.C. 20505 (703) 482-1100, www.cia.gov; *The World Factbook*.

The Economist Intelligence Unit, 111 West 57th Street, New York, New York 10019 (800) 938-4685; *The New Latin America Market Atlas.*

Euromonitor International, Inc., 122 South Michigan Avenue, Suite 1200, Chicago, Illinois 60603 (800) 577-EURO; *International Marketing Data and Statistics;* and. *World Marketing Data and Statistics.*

Europa Publications Limited, 18 Bedford Square, London, WC1B 3JN, England; *The Europa World Year Book.*

Inter-American Development Bank, 1300 New York Avenue, NW, Washington, D.C. 20577 (202) 872-1445; *Economic and Social Progress in Latin America.*

M.E. Sharpe, 80 Business Park Drive, Armonk, New York 10504 (800) 541-6563; *The Illustrated Book of World Rankings.*

St. Martin's Press, Inc., 175 Fifth Avenue, New York, New York 10010 (800) 221-7945; *The Statesman's Year-Book.*

Statistical Office of the United Nations, Publishing Service, New York, New York 10017 (800) 253-9646; *Human Development Report.*

U.C.L.A. Latin American Center Publications, University of California, Los Angeles, California 90024 (310) 825-6634; *Statistical Abstract of Latin America.*

MEXICO - TUNGSTEN PRODUCTION AND CONSUMPTION - See MEXICO - MINING AND MINERAL PRODUCTS

MEXICO - TURKEYS - See MEXICO - LIVESTOCK AND POULTRY

MEXICO - UNEMPLOYMENT

Central Intelligence Agency, Washington, D.C. 20505 (703) 482-1100, www.cia.gov; *The World Factbook.*

The Economist Intelligence Unit, 111 West 57th Street, New York, New York 10019 (800) 938-4685; *The New Latin America Market Atlas.*

Euromonitor International, Inc., 122 South Michigan Avenue, Suite 1200, Chicago, Illinois 60603 (800) 577-EURO; *International Marketing Data and Statistics.*

International Labour Office, I.L.O. Publications, 1828 L Street, NW, Suite 801, Washington, D.C. 20036 (301) 638-3152; *Yearbook of Labour Statistics.*

Organization of American States (OAS), General Secretariat, Washington, D.C. 20006 (202) 458-3533; *Statistical Bulletin of the OAS.*

U.C.L.A. Latin American Center Publications, University of California, Los Angeles, California 90024 (310) 825-6634; *Statistical Abstract of Latin America.*

MEXICO - URANIUM PRODUCTION AND CONSUMPTION - See MEXICO - MINING AND MINERAL PRODUCTS

MEXICO - UTILITIES

U.C.L.A. Latin American Center Publications, University of California, Los Angeles, California 90024 (310) 825-6634; *Statistical Abstract of Latin America.*

MEXICO - VANADIUM AND VANADIUM ORE PRODUCTION AND CONSUMPTION - See MEXICO - MINING AND MINERAL PRODUCTS

MEXICO - VITAL STATISTICS

Euromonitor International, Inc., 122 South Michigan Avenue, Suite 1200, Chicago, Illinois 60603 (800) 577-EURO; *International Marketing Data and Statistics.*

St. Martin's Press, Inc., 175 Fifth Avenue, New York, New York 10010 (800) 221-7945; *The Statesman's Year-Book.*

Statistical Office of the United Nations, Publishing Service, New York, New York 10017 (800) 253-9646; *Statistical Yearbook.*

World Health Organization, Office of Publications, 20 Avenue Appia, CH-1211 Geneva 27, Switzerland (Telephone in U.S. (518) 436-9686); *World Health Statistics Annual.*

MEXICO - WAGES

International Labour Office, I.L.O. Publications, 1828 L Street, NW, Suite 801, Washington, D.C. 20036 (301) 638-3152; *Yearbook of Labour Statistics.*

Organization of American States (OAS), General Secretariat, Washington, D.C. 20006 (202) 458-3533; *Statistical Bulletin of the OAS.*

Statistical Office of the United Nations, Publishing Service, New York, New York 10017 (800) 253-9646; *Statistical Yearbook.*

U.C.L.A. Latin American Center Publications, University of California, Los Angeles, California 90024 (310) 825-6634; *Statistical Abstract of Latin America.*

MEXICO - WALNUT PRODUCTION - See MEXICO - CROPS

MEXICO - WATERMELON PRODUCTION - See MEXICO - CROPS

MEXICO - WEATHER - See MEXICO - CLIMATE

MEXICO - WELFARE

Inter-American Development Bank, 1300 New York Avenue, NW, Washington, D.C. 20577 (202) 872-1445; *Economic and Social Progress in Latin America.*

International Monetary Fund, 700 Nineteenth Street, NW, Washington, D.C. 20431 (202) 623-7000; *Government Finance Statistics Yearbook.*

MEXICO - WHEAT PRODUCTION - See MEXICO - CROPS

MEXICO - WHOLESALE PRICES

Inter-American Development Bank, 1300 New York Avenue, NW, Washington, D.C. 20577 (202) 872-1445; *Economic and Social Progress in Latin America.*

International Monetary Fund, 700 Nineteenth Street, NW, Washington, D.C. 20431 (202) 623-7000; *International Financial Statistics.*

Organization of American States (OAS), General Secretariat, Washington, D.C. 20006 (202) 458-3533; *Statistical Bulletin of the OAS.*

Statistical Office of the United Nations, Publishing Service, New York, New York 10017 (800) 253-9646; *Statistical Yearbook.*

MEXICO - WHOLESALE TRADE

Inter-American Development Bank, 1300 New York Avenue, NW, Washington, D.C. 20577 (202) 872-1445; *Economic and Social Progress in Latin America.*

Statistical Office of the United Nations, Publishing Service, New York, New York 10017 (800) 253-9646; *Statistical Yearbook.*

MEXICO - WINE PRODUCTION - See MEXICO - BEVERAGES

MEXICO - WOOD AND WOOD PULP - See MEXICO - FORESTRY AND FOREST PRODUCTS

MEXICO - WOOL PRODUCTION AND CONSUMPTION - See MEXICO TEXTILE INDUSTRY

MEXICO - YARN PRODUCTION - See MEXICO - TEXTILE INDUSTRY

MEXICO - ZINC AND ZINC ORE PRODUCTION AND CONSUMPTION - See MEXICO - MINING AND MINERAL PRODUCTS

MICA

U.S. Department of the Interior, Geological Survey, Office of Minerals Information, 12201 Sunrise Valley Drive,

Reston, Virginia 22092 (703) 648-4000, www.minerals.usgs.gov; *Annual Reports;* and *Mineral Commodity Summaries.*

MICA - FOREIGN TRADE (SHEET)

U.S. Department of the Interior, Geological Survey, Office of Minerals Information, 12201 Sunrise Valley Drive, Reston, Virginia 22092 (703) 648-4000, www.minerals.usgs.gov; *Mineral Commodity Summaries.*

MICA - PRODUCTION AND VALUE

U.S. Department of the Interior, Geological Survey, Office of Minerals Information, 12201 Sunrise Valley Drive, Reston, Virginia 22092 (703) 648-4000, www.minerals.usgs.gov; *Annual Reports;* and *Mineral Commodity Summaries.*

MICA - SCRAP AND FLAKE

U.S. Department of the Interior, Geological Survey, Office of Minerals Information, 12201 Sunrise Valley Drive, Reston, Virginia 22092 (703) 648-4000, www.minerals.usgs.gov; *Mineral Commodity Summaries.*

MICA - WORLD PRODUCTION

U.S. Department of the Interior, Geological Survey, Office of Minerals Information, 12201 Sunrise Valley Drive, Reston, Virginia 22092 (703) 648-4000, www.minerals.usgs.gov; *Mineral Commodity Summaries.*

MICHIGAN - See also STATE DATA (FOR INDIVIDUAL STATES)

Michigan - Primary Statistics Source

School of Business Administration, Bureau of Business Research, Wayne State University, Detroit, Michigan 48202 (313) 872-4311; *Michigan Statistical Abstract.*

Michigan - State Data Centers

Michigan Information Center, Office of State Budget, Department of Management and Budget, 111 S. Capitol, G.W. Romney Building, Lansing, Michigan 48913, Ms. Carolyn Lauer (517) 373-7910.

Michigan Economic Development Corporation, Victor Office Center, 4th Floor, Lansing, Michigan 48913, Mr. Tom Nicholas.

Michigan Metropolitan Information Center, Center for Urban Studies, Wayne State University, Faculty/Administration Building, 656 West Kirby, Detroit, Michigan 40802, Kurt Metzger (313) 577-8996.

The Library of Michigan, Government Documents Service, Post Office Box 30007, 717 West Allegan Street, Lansing, Michigan 48909-7507, Ms. Ann Marie Sanders (517) 373-9489.

MICROCOMPUTERS - See COMPUTERS

Micronesia (Federated States of) - National Statistical Office

Office of Planning and Statistics, Post Office Box PS4, National Government Federated States of Micronesia, Palikir, Pohnpei FM 96941.

MICRONESIA (FEDERATED STATES OF) - AGRICULTURE

Europa Publications Limited, 18 Bedford Square, London, WC1B 3JN, England; *The Europa World Year Book.*

Food and Agriculture Organization of the United Nations (FAO), Via delle Terme de Caracalla, 00100, Rome, Italy (Telephone Number in U.S. (202) 653-2400); *Production Yearbook;* and *Trade Yearbook.*

St. Martin's Press, Inc., 175 Fifth Avenue, New York, New York 10010 (800) 221-7945; *The Statesman's Year-Book.*

Statistical Office of the United Nations, Publishing Service, New York, New York 10017 (800) 253-9646; *Asia-Pacific in Figures; Industrial Commodity Statistics Yearbook;* and *Statistical Yearbook.*

MICRONESIA (FEDERATED STATES OF) - AIRLINE SERVICE

St. Martin's Press, Inc., 175 Fifth Avenue, New York, New York 10010 (800) 221-7945; *The Statesman's Year-Book.*

Statistical Office of the United Nations, Publishing Service, New York, New York 10017 (800) 253-9646; *Statistical Yearbook.*

MICRONESIA (FEDERATED STATES OF) - AIRPORTS

Central Intelligence Agency, Washington, D.C. 20505 (703) 482-1100, www.cia.gov; *The World Factbook.*

MICRONESIA (FEDERATED STATES OF) - ANIMAL HEALTH

Food and Agriculture Organization of the United Nations (FAO), Via delle Terme de Caracalla, 00100, Rome, Italy (Telephone Number in U.S. (202) 653-2400); *Animal Health Yearbook.*

MICRONESIA (FEDERATED STATES OF) -

AREA AND DENSITY OF POPULATION

Central Intelligence Agency, Washington, D.C. 20505 (703) 482-1100, www.cia.gov; *The World Factbook.*

Europa Publications Limited, 18 Bedford Square, London, WC1B 3JN, England; *The Europa World Year Book.*

St. Martin's Press, Inc., 175 Fifth Avenue, New York, New York 10010 (800) 221-7945; *The Statesman's Year-Book.*

Statistical Office of the United Nations, Publishing Service, New York, New York 10017 (800) 253-9646; *Statistical Yearbook.*

MICRONESIA (FEDERATED STATES OF) - BEVERAGES

Statistical Office of the United Nations, Publishing Service, New York, New York 10017 (800) 253-9646; *Statistical Yearbook.*

MICRONESIA (FEDERATED STATES OF) - BIRTH RATES

Central Intelligence Agency, Washington, D.C. 20505 (703) 482-1100, www.cia.gov; *The World Factbook.*

Europa Publications Limited, 18 Bedford Square, London, WC1B 3JN, England; *The Europa World Year Book.*

Statistical Office of the United Nations, Publishing Service, New York, New York 10017 (800) 253-9646; *Asia-Pacific in Figures;* and *Statistical Yearbook.*

MICRONESIA (FEDERATED STATES OF) - BROADCASTING

Billboard Limited, Post Office Box 9027, 1006 AA Amsterdam, The Netherlands (Telephone Number in U.S. (212) 764-7300); *World Radio TV Handbook.*

Central Intelligence Agency, Washington, D.C. 20505 (703) 482-1100, www.cia.gov; *The World Factbook.*

St. Martin's Press, Inc., 175 Fifth Avenue, New York, New York 10010 (800) 221-7945; *The Statesman's Year-Book.*

MICRONESIA (FEDERATED STATES OF) - BUDGET

Central Intelligence Agency, Washington, D.C. 20505 (703) 482-1100, www.cia.gov; *The World Factbook.*

MICRONESIA (FEDERATED STATES OF) - CLIMATE

St. Martin's Press, Inc., 175 Fifth Avenue, New York, New York 10010 (800) 221-7945; *The Statesman's Year-Book.*

MICRONESIA (FEDERATED STATES OF) - COMMERCE

St. Martin's Press, Inc., 175 Fifth Avenue, New York, New York 10010 (800) 221-7945; *The Statesman's Year-Book.*

MICRONESIA (FEDERATED STATES OF) - CONSTRUCTION INDUSTRY

Statistical Office of the United Nations, Publishing Service, New York, New York 10017 (800) 253-9646; *Statistical Yearbook.*

MICRONESIA (FEDERATED STATES OF) - CONSUMER PRICE INDEX

Statistical Office of the United Nations, Publishing Service, New York, New York 10017 (800) 253-9646; *Statistical Yearbook.*

MICRONESIA (FEDERATED STATES OF) - CROPS

Food and Agriculture Organization of the United Nations (FAO), Via delle Terme de Caracalla, 00100, Rome, Italy (Telephone Number in U.S. (202) 653-2400); *Production Yearbook;* and *Trade Yearbook.*

St. Martin's Press, Inc., 175 Fifth Avenue, New York, New York 10010 (800) 221-7945; *The Statesman's Year-Book.*

Statistical Office of the United Nations, Publishing Service, New York, New York 10017 (800) 253-9646; *Industrial Commodity Statistics Yearbook;* and *Statistical Yearbook.*

MICRONESIA (FEDERATED STATES OF) - DAIRY PRODUCTS

Food and Agriculture Organization of the United Nations (FAO), Via delle Terme de Caracalla, 00100, Rome, Italy (Telephone Number in U.S. (202) 653-2400); *Production Yearbook;* and *Trade Yearbook.*

Statistical Office of the United Nations, Publishing Service, New York, New York 10017 (800) 253-9646; *Industrial Commodity Statistics Yearbook;* and *Statistical Yearbook.*

MICRONESIA (FEDERATED STATES OF) - DEMOGRAPHY

Statistical Office of the United Nations, Publishing Service, New York, New York 10017 (800) 253-9646; *Asia-Pacific in Figures;* and *Demographic Yearbook.*

MICRONESIA (FEDERATED STATES OF) - DIVORCE RATES

Statistical Office of the United Nations, Publishing Service, New York, New York 10017 (800) 253-9646; *Demographic Yearbook;* and *Statistical Yearbook.*

MICRONESIA (FEDERATED STATES OF) - ECONOMY

Central Intelligence Agency, Washington, D.C. 20505 (703) 482-1100, www.cia.gov; *The World Factbook.*

St. Martin's Press, Inc., 175 Fifth Avenue, New York, New York 10010 (800) 221-7945; *The Statesman's Year-Book.*

Statistical Office of the United Nations, Publishing Service, New York, New York 10017 (800) 253-9646; *World Statistics Pocketbook.*

The World Bank, 1818 H Street, NW, Washington, D.C. 20433 (202) 477-1234; *The World Bank Atlas.*

MICRONESIA (FEDERATED STATES OF) - EDUCATION

Europa Publications Limited, 18 Bedford Square, London, WC1B 3JN, England; *The Europa World Year Book.*

St. Martin's Press, Inc., 175 Fifth Avenue, New York, New York 10010 (800) 221-7945; *The Statesman's Year-Book.*

Statistical Office of the United Nations, Publishing Service, New York, New York 10017 (800) 253-9646; *Asia-Pacific in Figures.*

MICRONESIA (FEDERATED STATES OF) - ELECTRICITY

Central Intelligence Agency, Washington, D.C. 20505 (703) 482-1100, www.cia.gov; *The World Factbook.*

Statistical Office of the United Nations, Publishing Service, New York, New York 10017 (800) 253-9646; *Energy Statistics Yearbook;* and *Statistical Yearbook.*

MICRONESIA (FEDERATED STATES OF) - EMPLOYMENT

Statistical Office of the United Nations, Publishing Service, New York, New York 10017 (800) 253-9646; *Asia-Pacific in Figures;* and *Statistical Yearbook.*

MICRONESIA (FEDERATED STATES OF) - ENERGY

Statistical Office of the United Nations, Publishing Service, New York, New York 10017 (800) 253-9646; *Asia-Pacific in Figures; Energy Statistics Yearbook; World Statistics Pocketbook;* and *Statistical Yearbook.*

The World Bank, 1818 H Street, NW, Washington, D.C. 20433 (202) 477-1234; *The World Bank Atlas.*

MICRONESIA (FEDERATED STATES OF) -

ENVIRONMENT

Statistical Office of the United Nations, Publishing Service, New York, New York 10017 (800) 253-9646; *Statistical Yearbook;* and *World Statistics Pocketbook.*

MICRONESIA (FEDERATED STATES OF) - EXCHANGE RATES

Central Intelligence Agency, Washington, D.C. 20505 (703) 482-1100, www.cia.gov; *The World Factbook.*

Europa Publications Limited, 18 Bedford Square, London, WC1B 3JN, England; *The Europa World Year Book.*

Statistical Office of the United Nations, Publishing Service, New York, New York 10017 (800) 253-9646; *Statistical Yearbook;* and *World Statistics Pocketbook.*

MICRONESIA (FEDERATED STATES OF) - EXPORTS

Central Intelligence Agency, Washington, D.C. 20505 (703) 482-1100, www.cia.gov; *The World Factbook.*

Europa Publications Limited, 18 Bedford Square, London, WC1B 3JN, England; *The Europa World Year Book.*

St. Martin's Press, Inc., 175 Fifth Avenue, New York, New York 10010 (800) 221-7945; *The Statesman's Year-Book.*

Statistical Office of the United Nations, Publishing Service, New York, New York 10017 (800) 253-9646; *International Trade Statistics Yearbook.*

MICRONESIA (FEDERATED STATES OF) - EXTERNAL TRADE

Food and Agriculture Organization of the United Nations (FAO), Via delle Terme de Caracalla, 00100, Rome, Italy (Telephone Number in U.S. (202) 653-2400); *Trade Yearbook.*

Statistical Office of the United Nations, Publishing Service, New York, New York 10017 (800) 253-9646; *Asia-Pacific in Figures;* and *Statistical Yearbook.*

MICRONESIA (FEDERATED STATES OF) - FERTILITY RATES

Central Intelligence Agency, Washington, D.C. 20505 (703) 482-1100, www.cia.gov; *The World Factbook.*

The World Bank, 1818 H Street, NW, Washington, D.C. 20433 (202) 477-1234; *The World Bank Atlas.*

MICRONESIA (FEDERATED STATES OF) - FERTILIZER

Food and Agriculture Organization of the United Nations (FAO), Via delle Terme de Caracalla, 00100, Rome, Italy (Telephone Number in U.S. (202) 653-2400); *Fertilizer Yearbook.*

Statistical Office of the United Nations, Publishing Service, New York, New York 10017 (800) 253-9646; *Industrial Commodity Statistics Yearbook;* and *Statistical Yearbook.*

MICRONESIA (FEDERATED STATES OF) - FINANCE

Europa Publications Limited, 18 Bedford Square, London, WC1B 3JN, England; *The Europa World Year Book.*

MICRONESIA (FEDERATED STATES OF) - FISHERIES

Europa Publications Limited, 18 Bedford Square, London, WC1B 3JN, England; *The Europa World Year Book.*

Food and Agriculture Organization of the United Nations (FAO), Via delle Terme de Caracalla, 00100, Rome, Italy (Telephone Number in U.S. (202) 653-2400); *Yearbook of Fishery Statistics.*

St. Martin's Press, Inc., 175 Fifth Avenue, New York, New York 10010 (800) 221-7945; *The Statesman's Year-Book.*

Statistical Office of the United Nations, Publishing Service, New York, New York 10017 (800) 253-9646; *Industrial Commodity Statistics Yearbook;* and *Statistical Yearbook.*

MICRONESIA (FEDERATED STATES OF) - FOOD

Food and Agriculture Organization of the United Nations (FAO), Via delle Terme de Caracalla, 00100, Rome, Italy (Telephone Number in U.S. (202) 653-2400); *Production Yearbook;* and *Trade Yearbook.*

Statistical Office of the United Nations, Publishing Service, New York, New York 10017 (800) 253-9646; *Industrial Commodity Statistics Yearbook.*

MICRONESIA (FEDERATED STATES OF) - FOREIGN TRADE

Europa Publications Limited, 18 Bedford Square, London, WC1B 3JN, England; *The Europa World Year Book.*

Food and Agriculture Organization of the United Nations (FAO), Via delle Terme de Caracalla, 00100, Rome, Italy (Telephone Number in U.S. (202) 653-2400); *Trade Yearbook.*

Statistical Office of the United Nations, Publishing Service, New York, New York

10017 (800) 253-9646; *International Trade Statistics Yearbook;* and *Statistical Yearbook.*

MICRONESIA (FEDERATED STATES OF) - FORESTRY AND FOREST PRODUCTS

Food and Agriculture Organization of the United Nations (FAO), Via delle Terme de Caracalla, 00100, Rome, Italy (Telephone Number in U.S. (202) 653-2400); *Yearbook of Forest Products.*

Statistical Office of the United Nations, Publishing Service, New York, New York 10017 (800) 253-9646; *Industrial Commodity Statistics Yearbook;* and *Statistical Yearbook.*

MICRONESIA (FEDERATED STATES OF) - GOVERNMENT

Central Intelligence Agency, Washington, D.C. 20505 (703) 482-1100, www.cia.gov; *The World Factbook.*

St. Martin's Press, Inc., 175 Fifth Avenue, New York, New York 10010 (800) 221-7945; *The Statesman's Year-Book.*

Statistical Office of the United Nations, Publishing Service, New York, New York 10017 (800) 253-9646; *Asia-Pacific in Figures;* and *Statistical Yearbook.*

MICRONESIA (FEDERATED STATES OF) - GROSS DOMESTIC PRODUCT

Statistical Office of the United Nations, Publishing Service, New York, New York 10017 (800) 253-9646; *Statistical Yearbook.*

MICRONESIA (FEDERATED STATES OF) - GROSS NATIONAL PRODUCT

St. Martin's Press, Inc., 175 Fifth Avenue, New York, New York 10010 (800) 221-7945; *The Statesman's Year-Book.*

Statistical Office of the United Nations, Publishing Service, New York, New York 10017 (800) 253-9646; *National Accounts Statistics.*

The World Bank, 1818 H Street, NW, Washington, D.C. 20433 (202) 477-1234; *The World Bank Atlas.*

MICRONESIA (FEDERATED STATES OF) - HEALTH

St. Martin's Press, Inc., 175 Fifth Avenue, New York, New York 10010 (800) 221-7945; *The Statesman's Year-Book.*

Statistical Office of the United Nations, Publishing Service, New York, New York 10017 (800) 253-9646; *Asia-Pacific in Figures;* and *Statistical Yearbook.*

MICRONESIA (FEDERATED STATES OF) -

HIGHWAYS

Central Intelligence Agency, Washington, D.C. 20505 (703) 482-1100, www.cia.gov; *The World Factbook.*

St. Martin's Press, Inc., 175 Fifth Avenue, New York, New York 10010 (800) 221-7945; *The Statesman's Year-Book.*

MICRONESIA (FEDERATED STATES OF) - ILLITERATE POPULATION

Central Intelligence Agency, Washington, D.C. 20505 (703) 482-1100, www.cia.gov; *The World Factbook.*

Statistical Office of the United Nations, Publishing Service, New York, New York 10017 (800) 253-9646; *Asia-Pacific in Figures.*

MICRONESIA (FEDERATED STATES OF) - IMPORTS

Central Intelligence Agency, Washington, D.C. 20505 (703) 482-1100, www.cia.gov; *The World Factbook.*

Europa Publications Limited, 18 Bedford Square, London, WC1B 3JN, England; *The Europa World Year Book.*

St. Martin's Press, Inc., 175 Fifth Avenue, New York, New York 10010 (800) 221-7945; *The Statesman's Year-Book.*

Statistical Office of the United Nations, Publishing Service, New York, New York 10017 (800) 253-9646; *International Trade Statistics Yearbook.*

MICRONESIA (FEDERATED STATES OF) - INDUSTRY

Central Intelligence Agency, Washington, D.C. 20505 (703) 482-1100, www.cia.gov; *The World Factbook.*

Statistical Office of the United Nations, Publishing Service, New York, New York 10017 (800) 253-9646; *Asia-Pacific in Figures; Industrial Commodity Statistics Yearbook;* and *Statistical Yearbook.*

MICRONESIA (FEDERATED STATES OF) - INTERNAL TRADE

Statistical Office of the United Nations, Publishing Service, New York, New York 10017 (800) 253-9646; *Statistical Yearbook.*

MICRONESIA (FEDERATED STATES OF) - LABOR

Central Intelligence Agency, Washington, D.C. 20505 (703) 482-1100, www.cia.gov; *The World Factbook.*

Europa Publications Limited, 18 Bedford Square, London, WC1B 3JN,

England; *The Europa World Year Book*.

Statistical Office of the United Nations, Publishing Service, New York, New York 10017 (800) 253-9646; *Statistical Yearbook*.

The World Bank, 1818 H Street, NW, Washington, D.C. 20433 (202) 477-1234; *The World Bank Atlas*.

MICRONESIA (FEDERATED STATES OF) - LAND USE

Central Intelligence Agency, Washington, D.C. 20505 (703) 482-1100, www.cia.gov; *The World Factbook*.

Food and Agriculture Organization of the United Nations (FAO), Via delle Terme de Caracalla, 00100, Rome, Italy (Telephone Number in U.S. (202) 653-2400); *Production Yearbook*.

MICRONESIA (FEDERATED STATES OF) - LIFE EXPECTANCY

Central Intelligence Agency, Washington, D.C. 20505 (703) 482-1100, www.cia.gov; *The World Factbook*.

Statistical Office of the United Nations, Publishing Service, New York, New York 10017 (800) 253-9646; *Asia-Pacific in Figures; World Statistics Pocketbook;* and *Demographic Yearbook*.

The World Bank, 1818 H Street, NW, Washington, D.C. 20433 (202) 477-1234; *The World Bank Atlas*.

MICRONESIA (FEDERATED STATES OF) - LIVESTOCK AND POULTRY

Europa Publications Limited, 18 Bedford Square, London, WC1B 3JN, England; *The Europa World Year Book*.

Food and Agriculture Organization of the United Nations (FAO), Via delle Terme de Caracalla, 00100, Rome, Italy (Telephone Number in U.S. (202) 653-2400); *Production Yearbook;* and *Trade Yearbook*.

Statistical Office of the United Nations, Publishing Service, New York, New York 10017 (800) 253-9646; *Industrial Commodity Statistics Yearbook;* and *Statistical Yearbook*.

MICRONESIA (FEDERATED STATES OF) - MACHINERY

Statistical Office of the United Nations, Publishing Service, New York, New York 10017 (800) 253-9646; *Industrial Commodity Statistics Yearbook*.

MICRONESIA (FEDERATED STATES OF) - MAIL - NUMBER OF PIECES SENT OR RECEIVED

Statistical Office of the United Nations, Publishing Service, New York, New York 10017 (800) 253-9646; *Statistical Yearbook*.

MICRONESIA (FEDERATED STATES OF) - MANUFACTURING

Statistical Office of the United Nations, Publishing Service, New York, New York 10017 (800) 253-9646; *Industrial Commodity Statistics Yearbook;* and *Statistical Yearbook*.

MICRONESIA (FEDERATED STATES OF) - MARRIAGE RATES

Statistical Office of the United Nations, Publishing Service, New York, New York 10017 (800) 253-9646; *Demographic Yearbook;* and *Statistical Yearbook*.

MICRONESIA (FEDERATED STATES OF) - MERCHANT SHIPPING

Europa Publications Limited, 18 Bedford Square, London, WC1B 3JN, England; *The Europa World Year Book*.

Statistical Office of the United Nations, Publishing Service, New York, New York 10017 (800) 253-9646; *Statistical Yearbook*.

MICRONESIA (FEDERATED STATES OF) - MILITARY

Central Intelligence Agency, Washington, D.C. 20505 (703) 482-1100, www.cia.gov; *The World Factbook*.

MICRONESIA (FEDERATED STATES OF) - MINING AND MINERAL PRODUCTS

Europa Publications Limited, 18 Bedford Square, London, WC1B 3JN, England; *The Europa World Year Book*.

Statistical Office of the United Nations, Publishing Service, New York, New York 10017 (800) 253-9646; *Energy Statistics Yearbook; Industrial Commodity Statistics Yearbook;* and *Statistical Yearbook*.

MICRONESIA (FEDERATED STATES OF) - MORTALITY

Central Intelligence Agency, Washington, D.C. 20505 (703) 482-1100, www.cia.gov; *The World Factbook*.

Europa Publications Limited, 18 Bedford Square, London, WC1B 3JN, England; *The Europa World Year Book*.

Statistical Office of the United Nations, Publishing Service, New York, New York 10017 (800) 253-9646; *Asia-Pacific in Figures; Demographic Yearbook; World Statistics Pocketbook;* and *Statistical Yearbook*.

The World Bank, 1818 H Street, NW,

Washington, D.C. 20433 (202) 477-1234; *The World Bank Atlas*.

MICRONESIA (FEDERATED STATES OF) - MOTION PICTURES

Statistical Office of the United Nations, Publishing Service, New York, New York 10017 (800) 253-9646; *Statistical Yearbook*.

MICRONESIA (FEDERATED STATES OF) - MOTOR VEHICLE PRODUCTION

Statistical Office of the United Nations, Publishing Service, New York, New York 10017 (800) 253-9646; *Statistical Yearbook*.

MICRONESIA (FEDERATED STATES OF) - NATIONAL ACCOUNTS

Statistical Office of the United Nations, Publishing Service, New York, New York 10017 (800) 253-9646; *Asia-Pacific in Figures; National Accounts Statistics;* and *Statistical Yearbook*.

MICRONESIA (FEDERATED STATES OF) - NATIONAL INCOME

Statistical Office of the United Nations, Publishing Service, New York, New York 10017 (800) 253-9646; *Statistical Yearbook*.

MICRONESIA (FEDERATED STATES OF) - NATIONAL PRODUCT

Statistical Office of the United Nations, Publishing Service, New York, New York 10017 (800) 253-9646; *Statistical Yearbook*.

MICRONESIA (FEDERATED STATES OF) - PATENTS

Statistical Office of the United Nations, Publishing Service, New York, New York 10017 (800) 253-9646; *Statistical Yearbook*.

MICRONESIA (FEDERATED STATES OF) - PETROLEUM INDUSTRY

Statistical Office of the United Nations, Publishing Service, New York, New York 10017 (800) 253-9646; *Energy Statistics Yearbook; Industrial Commodity Statistics Yearbook;* and *Statistical Yearbook*.

MICRONESIA (FEDERATED STATES OF) - POPULATION

Central Intelligence Agency, Washington, D.C. 20505 (703) 482-1100, www.cia.gov; *The World Factbook*.

Europa Publications Limited, 18 Bedford Square, London, WC1B 3JN, England; *The Europa World Year Book*.

Food and Agriculture Organization of the United Nations (FAO), Via delle Terme de Caracalla, 00100, Rome, Italy (Telephone Number in U.S. (202) 653-

2400); *Production Yearbook.*

St. Martin's Press, Inc., 175 Fifth Avenue, New York, New York 10010 (800) 221-7945; *The Statesman's Year-Book.*

Statistical Office of the United Nations, Publishing Service, New York, New York 10017 (800) 253-9646; *Asia-Pacific in Figures; Demographic Yearbook; World Statistics Pocketbook;* and *Statistical Yearbook.*

The World Bank, 1818 H Street, NW, Washington, D.C. 20433 (202) 477-1234; *The World Bank Atlas.*

MICRONESIA (FEDERATED STATES OF) - PRICES

Food and Agriculture Organization of the United Nations (FAO), Via delle Terme de Caracalla, 00100, Rome, Italy (Telephone Number in U.S. (202) 653-2400); *Production Yearbook.*

MICRONESIA (FEDERATED STATES OF) - RADIO RECEIVERS

St. Martin's Press, Inc., 175 Fifth Avenue, New York, New York 10010 (800) 221-7945; *The Statesman's Year-Book.*

Statistical Office of the United Nations, Publishing Service, New York, New York 10017 (800) 253-9646; *Statistical Yearbook.*

MICRONESIA (FEDERATED STATES OF) - RAILWAYS

Statistical Office of the United Nations, Publishing Service, New York, New York 10017 (800) 253-9646; *Statistical Yearbook.*

MICRONESIA (FEDERATED STATES OF) - RELIGION

Central Intelligence Agency, Washington, D.C. 20505 (703) 482-1100, www.cia.gov; *The World Factbook.*

St. Martin's Press, Inc., 175 Fifth Avenue, New York, New York 10010 (800) 221-7945; *The Statesman's Year-Book.*

MICRONESIA (FEDERATED STATES OF) - RETAIL TRADE

Statistical Office of the United Nations, Publishing Service, New York, New York 10017 (800) 253-9646; *Statistical Yearbook.*

MICRONESIA (FEDERATED STATES OF) -See MICRONESIA (FEDERATED STATES OF) - HIGHWAYS

MICRONESIA (FEDERATED STATES OF) - RUBBER PRODUCTION AND CONSUMPTION

Statistical Office of the United Nations,

Publishing Service, New York, New York 10017 (800) 253-9646; *Statistical Yearbook.*

MICRONESIA (FEDERATED STATES OF) - SCIENTISTS, TECHNICIANS AND ENGINEERS

Statistical Office of the United Nations, Publishing Service, New York, New York 10017 (800) 253-9646; *Statistical Yearbook.*

MICRONESIA (FEDERATED STATES OF) - SOCIAL DATA

Statistical Office of the United Nations, Publishing Service, New York, New York 10017 (800) 253-9646; *World Statistics Pocketbook.*

MICRONESIA (FEDERATED STATES OF) - TELEPHONES IN USE

Central Intelligence Agency, Washington, D.C. 20505 (703) 482-1100, www.cia.gov; *The World Factbook.*

St. Martin's Press, Inc., 175 Fifth Avenue, New York, New York 10010 (800) 221-7945; *The Statesman's Year-Book.*

Statistical Office of the United Nations, Publishing Service, New York, New York 10017 (800) 253-9646; *Statistical Yearbook; and World Statistics Pocketbook.*

MICRONESIA (FEDERATED STATES OF) - TEXTILE INDUSTRY

Statistical Office of the United Nations, Publishing Service, New York, New York 10017 (800) 253-9646; *Industrial Commodity Statistics Yearbook;* and *Statistical Yearbook.*

MICRONESIA (FEDERATED STATES OF) - TIRE (MOTOR VEHICLE) PRODUCTION

Statistical Office of the United Nations, Publishing Service, New York, New York 10017 (800) 253-9646; *Statistical Yearbook.*

MICRONESIA (FEDERATED STATES OF) - TOBACCO PRODUCTION

Statistical Office of the United Nations, Publishing Service, New York, New York 10017 (800) 253-9646; *Statistical Yearbook.*

MICRONESIA (FEDERATED STATES OF) - TOURISM

Europa Publications Limited, 18 Bedford Square, London, WC1B 3JN, England; *The Europa World Year Book.*

St. Martin's Press, Inc., 175 Fifth Avenue, New York, New York 10010 (800) 221-7945; *The Statesman's Year-Book.*

Statistical Office of the United Nations, Publishing Service, New York, New York

10017 (800) 253-9646; *Statistical Yearbook.*

MICRONESIA (FEDERATED STATES OF) - TRADEMARKS AND SERVICE MARKS - See PATENTS, TRADEMARKS AND SERVICE MARKS

MICRONESIA (FEDERATED STATES OF) - TRANSPORTATION AND COMMUNICATIONS

Central Intelligence Agency, Washington, D.C. 20505 (703) 482-1100, www.cia.gov; *The World Factbook.*

Europa Publications Limited, 18 Bedford Square, London, WC1B 3JN, England; *The Europa World Year Book.*

St. Martin's Press, Inc., 175 Fifth Avenue, New York, New York 10010 (800) 221-7945; *The Statesman's Year-Book.*

MICRONESIA (FEDERATED STATES OF) - UNEMPLOYMENT

Central Intelligence Agency, Washington, D.C. 20505 (703) 482-1100, www.cia.gov; *The World Factbook.*

Statistical Office of the United Nations, Publishing Service, New York, New York 10017 (800) 253-9646; *Statistical Yearbook.*

MICRONESIA (FEDERATED STATES OF) - VITAL STATISTICS

Statistical Office of the United Nations, Publishing Service, New York, New York 10017 (800) 253-9646; *Statistical Yearbook.*

MICRONESIA (FEDERATED STATES OF) - WAGES

Statistical Office of the United Nations, Publishing Service, New York, New York 10017 (800) 253-9646; *Statistical Yearbook.*

MICRONESIA (FEDERATED STATES OF) - WHOLESALE PRICES

Statistical Office of the United Nations, Publishing Service, New York, New York 10017 (800) 253-9646; *Statistical Yearbook.*

MICRONESIA (FEDERATED STATES OF) - WHOLESALE TRADE

Statistical Office of the United Nations, Publishing Service, New York, New York 10017 (800) 253-9646; *Statistical Yearbook.*

MIDWAY ISLANDS - AGRICULTURE

Food and Agricultural Organization of the United Nations (FAO), Via delle Terme di Caracalla, 00100 Rome, Italy (Telephone Number in U.S. (202) 653-2400); *Production Yearbook; The State of Food and Agriculture;* and *Trade Yearbook.*

MIDWAY ISLANDS - AIRPORTS

Central Intelligence Agency, Washington, D.C. 20505 (703) 482-1100, www.cia.gov; *The World Factbook.*

MIDWAY ISLANDS - AREA AND DENSITY OF POPULATION

Central Intelligence Agency, Washington, D.C. 20505 (703) 482-1100, www.cia.gov; *The World Factbook.*

Food and Agricultural Organization of the United Nations (FAO), Via delle Terme di Caracalla, 00100 Rome, Italy (Telephone Number in U.S. (202) 653-2400); *The State of Food and Agriculture.*

St. Martin's Press, Inc., 175 Fifth Avenue, New York, New York 10010 (800) 221-7945; *The Statesman's Year-Book.*

Statistical Office of the United Nations, Publishing Service, New York, New York 10017 (800) 253-9646; *Statistical Yearbook.*

MIDWAY ISLANDS - BIRTH RATES

Central Intelligence Agency, Washington, D.C. 20505 (703) 482-1100, www.cia.gov; *The World Factbook.*

Statistical Office of the United Nations, Publishing Service, New York, New York 10017 (800) 253-9646; *Demographic Yearbook.*

MIDWAY ISLANDS - BROADCASTING

Billboard Limited, Post Office Box 9027, 1006 AA Amsterdam, The Netherlands (Telephone Number in U.S. (212) 764-7300); *World Radio TV Handbook.*

Central Intelligence Agency, Washington, D.C. 20505 (703) 482-1100, www.cia.gov; *The World Factbook.*

MIDWAY ISLANDS - BUDGET

Central Intelligence Agency, Washington, D.C. 20505 (703) 482-1100, www.cia.gov; *The World Factbook.*

MIDWAY ISLANDS - CALORIE SUPPLY

Food and Agricultural Organization of the United Nations (FAO), Via delle Terme di Caracalla, 00100 Rome, Italy (Telephone Number in U.S. (202) 653-2400); *The State of Food and Agriculture.*

MIDWAY ISLANDS - CORN - See MIDWAY ISLANDS - CROPS

MIDWAY ISLANDS - CROPS

Food and Agricultural Organization of the United Nations (FAO), Via delle Terme di Caracalla, 00100 Rome, Italy (Telephone

Number in U.S. (202) 653-2400); *The State of Food and Agriculture.*

MIDWAY ISLANDS - DAIRY PRODUCTS

Food and Agricultural Organization of the United Nations (FAO), Via delle Terme di Caracalla, 00100 Rome, Italy (Telephone Number in U.S. (202) 653-2400); *The State of Food and Agriculture.*

MIDWAY ISLANDS - DIVORCE

Statistical Office of the United Nations, Publishing Service, New York, New York 10017 (800) 253-9646; *Demographic Yearbook.*

MIDWAY ISLANDS - ECONOMY

Central Intelligence Agency, Washington, D.C. 20505 (703) 482-1100, www.cia.gov; *The World Factbook.*

MIDWAY ISLANDS - EGG PRODUCTION - See MIDWAY ISLANDS - DAIRY PRODUCTS

MIDWAY ISLANDS - ELECTRICITY

Central Intelligence Agency, Washington, D.C. 20505 (703) 482-1100, www.cia.gov; *The World Factbook.*

MIDWAY ISLANDS - ENERGY

Food and Agricultural Organization of the United Nations (FAO), Via delle Terme di Caracalla, 00100 Rome, Italy (Telephone Number in U.S. (202) 653-2400); *The State of Food and Agriculture.*

MIDWAY ISLANDS - EXCHANGE RATES

Central Intelligence Agency, Washington, D.C. 20505 (703) 482-1100, www.cia.gov; *The World Factbook.*

MIDWAY ISLANDS - EXPORTS

Central Intelligence Agency, Washington, D.C. 20505 (703) 482-1100, www.cia.gov; *The World Factbook.*

Food and Agricultural Organization of the United Nations (FAO), Via delle Terme di Caracalla, 00100 Rome, Italy (Telephone Number in U.S. (202) 653-2400); *The State of Food and Agriculture.*

MIDWAY ISLANDS - EXTERNAL TRADE

Food and Agricultural Organization of the United Nations (FAO), Via delle Terme di Caracalla, 00100 Rome, Italy (Telephone Number in U.S. (202) 653-2400); *The State of Food and Agriculture;* and *Trade Yearbook.*

MIDWAY ISLANDS - FARM CROPS - See MIDWAY ISLANDS - CROPS

MIDWAY ISLANDS - FERTILITY RATES

Central Intelligence Agency, Washington, D.C. 20505 (703) 482-1100, www.cia.gov; *The World Factbook.*

MIDWAY ISLANDS - FERTILIZER

Food and Agricultural Organization of the United Nations (FAO), Via delle Terme di Caracalla, 00100 Rome, Italy (Telephone Number in U.S. (202) 653-2400); *The State of Food and Agriculture.*

MIDWAY ISLANDS - FETAL MORTALITY - See MIDWAY ISLANDS - MORTALITY

MIDWAY ISLANDS - FISHERIES

Food and Agricultural Organization of the United Nations (FAO), Via delle Terme di Caracalla, 00100 Rome, Italy (Telephone Number in U.S. (202) 653-2400); *The State of Food and Agriculture;* and *Yearbook of Fishery Statistics.*

MIDWAY ISLANDS - FOOD

Food and Agricultural Organization of the United Nations (FAO), Via delle Terme di Caracalla, 00100 Rome, Italy (Telephone Number in U.S. (202) 653-2400); *Production Yearbook;* and *The State of Food and Agriculture.*

MIDWAY ISLANDS - FOREIGN TRADE

Food and Agricultural Organization of the United Nations (FAO), Via delle Terme di Caracalla, 00100 Rome, Italy (Telephone Number in U.S. (202) 653-2400); *The State of Food and Agriculture.*

MIDWAY ISLANDS - FORESTRY AND FOREST PRODUCTS

Food and Agricultural Organization of the United Nations (FAO), Via delle Terme di Caracalla, 00100 Rome, Italy (Telephone Number in U.S. (202) 653-2400); *The State of Food and Agriculture.*

MIDWAY ISLANDS - GENERAL MORTALITY - See MIDWAY ISLANDS - MORTALITY

MIDWAY ISLANDS - GOVERNMENT

Central Intelligence Agency, Washington, D.C. 20505 (703) 482-1100, www.cia.gov; *The World Factbook.*

MIDWAY ISLANDS - GRAIN PRODUCTION - See MIDWAY ISLANDS -CROPS

MIDWAY ISLANDS - HIGHWAYS

Central Intelligence Agency, Washington, D.C. 20505 (703) 482-1100, www.cia.gov; *The World Factbook.*

MIDWAY ISLANDS - ILLITERATE POPULATION

Central Intelligence Agency, Washington, D.C. 20505 (703) 482-1100, www.cia.gov; *The World Factbook.*

MIDWAY ISLANDS - IMPORTS

Central Intelligence Agency, Washington, D.C. 20505 (703) 482-1100, www.cia.gov; *The World Factbook.*

Food and Agricultural Organization of the United Nations (FAO), Via delle Terme di Caracalla, 00100 Rome, Italy (Telephone Number in U.S. (202) 653-2400); *The State of Food and Agriculture.*

MIDWAY ISLANDS - INDUSTRY

Central Intelligence Agency, Washington, D.C. 20505 (703) 482-1100, www.cia.gov; *The World Factbook.*

MIDWAY ISLANDS - INFANT AND MATERNAL MORTALITY - See MIDWAY ISLANDS - MORTALITY

MIDWAY ISLANDS - LABOR

Central Intelligence Agency, Washington, D.C. 20505 (703) 482-1100, www.cia.gov; *The World Factbook.*

Food and Agricultural Organization of the United Nations (FAO), Via delle Terme di Caracalla, 00100 Rome, Italy (Telephone Number in U.S. (202) 653-2400); *The State of Food and Agriculture.*

MIDWAY ISLANDS - LAND USE

Central Intelligence Agency, Washington, D.C. 20505 (703) 482-1100, www.cia.gov; *The World Factbook.*

Food and Agricultural Organization of the United Nations (FAO), Via delle Terme di Caracalla, 00100 Rome, Italy (Telephone Number in U.S. (202) 653-2400); *Production Yearbook.*

MIDWAY ISLANDS - LIFE EXPECTANCY

Central Intelligence Agency, Washington, D.C. 20505 (703) 482-1100, www.cia.gov; *The World Factbook.*

MIDWAY ISLANDS - LIVESTOCK AND POULTRY

Food and Agricultural Organization of the United Nations (FAO), Via delle Terme di Caracalla, 00100 Rome, Italy (Telephone Number in U.S. (202) 653-2400); *Production Yearbook;* and *The State of Food and Agriculture.*

MIDWAY ISLANDS - MARRIAGE RATES

Statistical Office of the United Nations, Publishing Service, New York, New York 10017 (800) 253-9646; *Demographic Yearbook.*

MIDWAY ISLANDS - MEAT PRODUCTION - See MIDWAY ISLANDS - LIVESTOCK AND POULTRY

MIDWAY ISLANDS - MILITARY

Central Intelligence Agency, Washington, D.C. 20505 (703) 482-1100, www.cia.gov; *The World Factbook.*

MIDWAY ISLANDS - MORTALITY

Central Intelligence Agency, Washington, D.C. 20505 (703) 482-1100, www.cia.gov; *The World Factbook.*

Statistical Office of the United Nations, Publishing Service, New York, New York 10017 (800) 253-9646; *Demographic Yearbook.*

MIDWAY ISLANDS - NATALITY - See MIDWAY ISLANDS - BIRTH RATES

MIDWAY ISLANDS - PESTICIDE USE

Food and Agricultural Organization of the United Nations (FAO), Via delle Terme di Caracalla, 00100 Rome, Italy (Telephone Number in U.S. (202) 653-2400); *The State of Food and Agriculture.*

MIDWAY ISLANDS - PETROLEUM INDUSTRY

Food and Agricultural Organization of the United Nations (FAO), Via delle Terme di Caracalla, 00100 Rome, Italy (Telephone Number in U.S. (202) 653-2400); *The State of Food and Agriculture.*

MIDWAY ISLANDS - POPULATION

Central Intelligence Agency, Washington, D.C. 20505 (703) 482-1100, www.cia.gov; *The World Factbook.*

Food and Agricultural Organization of the United Nations (FAO), Via delle Terme di Caracalla, 00100 Rome, Italy (Telephone Number in U.S. (202) 653-2400); *Production Yearbook.*

St. Martin's Press, Inc., 175 Fifth Avenue, New York, New York 10010 (800) 221-7945; *The Statesman's Year-Book.*

Statistical Office of the United Nations, Publishing Service, New York, New York 10017 (800) 253-9646; *Demographic Yearbook;* and *Statistical Yearbook.*

World Health Organization, Office of Publications, 20 Avenue Appia, CH-1211 Geneva 27, Switzerland (Telephone in U.S. (518) 436-9686); *World Health Statistics*

Annual.

MIDWAY ISLANDS - PRICES

Food and Agricultural Organization of the United Nations (FAO), Via delle Terme di Caracalla, 00100 Rome, Italy (Telephone Number in U.S. (202) 653-2400); *Production Yearbook;* and *The State of Food and Agriculture.*

MIDWAY ISLANDS - RELIGION

Central Intelligence Agency, Washington, D.C. 20505 (703) 482-1100, www.cia.gov; *The World Factbook.*

MIDWAY ISLANDS - STOCKS - COMMODITY - MARKET PRICE - INDEX

Food and Agricultural Organization of the United Nations (FAO), Via delle Terme di Caracalla, 00100 Rome, Italy (Telephone Number in U.S. (202) 653-2400); *The State of Food and Agriculture.*

MIDWAY ISLANDS - TELEPHONES IN USE

American Telephone and Telegraph Company, 26 Parsippany Road, Whippany, New Jersey 07981 (800) 222-0300; *The World's Telephones.*

Central Intelligence Agency, Washington, D.C. 20505 (703) 482-1100, www.cia.gov; *The World Factbook.*

MIDWAY ISLANDS - TRADE - See MIDWAY ISLANDS - FOREIGN TRADE

MIDWAY ISLANDS - TRANSPORTATION AND COMMUNICATIONS

Central Intelligence Agency, Washington, D.C. 20505 (703) 482-1100, www.cia.gov; *The World Factbook.*

MIDWAY ISLANDS - UNEMPLOYMENT RATE

Central Intelligence Agency, Washington, D.C. 20505 (703) 482-1100, www.cia.gov; *The World Factbook.*

MIDWAY ISLANDS - VITAL STATISTICS

World Health Organization, Office of Publications, 20 Avenue Appia, CH-1211 Geneva 27, Switzerland (Telephone in U.S. (518) 436-9686); *World Health Statistics Annual.*

MIGRATION

U.S. Department of Commerce, Bureau of the Census, Washington, D.C. 20233 (301) 457-4100, www.census.gov; *Current Population Reports; Census of Population, General Population Characteristics, U.S.,* and unpublished data.

MILITARY BASES

U.S. Department of Defense, The Pentagon, Washington, D.C. 20301 (703) 545-6700; *Selected Manpower Statistics*.

MILITARY EXPENDITURES - WORLDWIDE

U.S. Arms Control and Disarmament Agency, 320 Twenty-first Street, NW, Washington, D.C. 20541 (202) 647-8677; *World Military Expenditures and Arms Transfers*.

MILITARY EXPENDITURES - WORLDWIDE - FOREIGN COUNTRIES

U.S. Arms Control and Disarmament Agency, 320 Twenty-first Street, NW, Washington, D.C. 20541 (202) 647-8677; *World Military Expenditures and Arms Transfers*.

MILITARY OUTLAYS

Executive Office of the President, Office of Management and Budget, Executive Office Building, Washington, D.C. 20503 (202) 395-3080, www.whitehouse.gov/omb; *Historical Tables*.

MILITARY SCIENCES - DEGREES CONFERRED

U.S. Department of Education, National Center for Education Statistics, 555 New Jersey Avenue, NW, Washington, D.C. 20208-5574 (202) 219-1828, http://nces.ed.gov; *Digest of Educational Statistics*.

MILITARY SERVICES - BASIC PAY

U.S. Department of Commerce, Bureau of the Census, Washington, D.C. 20233 (301) 457-4100, www.census.gov; *Current Population Reports; Census of Population, General Population Characteristics, U.S.*, and unpublished data.

U.S. Department of Defense, The Pentagon, Washington, D.C. 20301 (703) 545-6700; *Selected Manpower* Statistics.

MILITARY SERVICES - CASUALTIES

The President's Commission on Veterans' Pensions, The White House Office, 1600 Pennsylvania Avenue, NW, Washington, D.C. 20500 (202) 233-4000; *Veterans' Benefits in the United States*.

U.S. Department of Defense, Office of the Secretary, The Pentagon, Washington, D.C. 20301 (703) 545-6700; unpublished data.

MILITARY SERVICES - CONSTRUCTION - VALUE OF BUILDINGS

U.S. Department of Commerce, Bureau

of the Census, Washington, D.C. 20233 (301) 457-4100, www.census.gov; *Current Construction Reports, Value of Construction*.

MILITARY SERVICES - CONTRACT AWARDS

U.S. Department of Defense, Office of the Secretary, The Pentagon, Washington, D.C. 20301 (703) 545-6700; *Prime Contract Awards;* and *Atlas/Data Abstract for the United States and Selected Areas*.

MILITARY SERVICES - EXPENDITURES

Executive Office of the President, Office of Management and Budget, Executive Office Building, Washington, D.C. 20503 (202) 395-3080, www.whitehouse.gov/omb; *Historical Tables*.

U.S. Department of Defense, Office of the Secretary, The Pentagon, Washington, D.C. 20301 (703) 545-6700; *Atlas/Data Abstract for the U.S. and Selected Areas*.

MILITARY SERVICES - NATIONAL GUARD

U.S. National Guard Bureau, The Pentagon, Washington, D.C. 20301 (202) 443-5100; *Annual Review of the Chief, National Guard Bureau;* and unpublished data.

MILITARY SERVICES - PAY GRADES

U.S. Department of Commerce, Bureau of the Census, Washington, D.C. 20233 (301) 457-4100, www.census.gov; *Current Population Reports; Census of Population, General Population Characteristics, U.S.*, and unpublished data.

U.S. Department of Defense, The Pentagon, Washington, D.C. 20350 (703) 545-6700; *Selected Manpower Statistics*.

MILITARY SERVICES - PAYROLL

U.S. Department of Defense, Office of the Secretary, The Pentagon, Washington, D.C. 20301 (703) 545-6700; *Atlas/State Data Abstract for the United States and Selected Areas*.

MILITARY SERVICES - PERSONNEL

U.S. Department of Defense, Office of the Secretary, The Pentagon, Washington, D.C. 20301 (703) 545-6700; *Selected Manpower Statistics;* and *Atlas/State Data Abstract for the United States and Selected Areas*.

MILITARY SERVICES - PERSONNEL - FOREIGN COUNTRIES

U.S. Department of Defense, Office of the Secretary, The Pentagon, Washington, D.C. 20301 (703) 545-6700; *Selected Manpower Statistics*.

MILITARY SERVICES - PERSONNEL - RANK

U.S. Department of Defense, the Pentagon, Washington, D.C. 20350 (703) 545-6700; *Selected Manpower Statistics*.

MILITARY SERVICES - PUBLIC CONFIDENCE

Independent Sector, 1200 18th Street, NW, Suite 200, Washington, D.C. 20036 (202) 467-6161; *Giving and Volunteering in the United States*.

MILITARY SERVICES - RESERVES - BY BRANCH

U.S. Department of Defense, Office of the Secretary, The Pentagon, Washington, D.C. 20301 (703) 545-6700; *Official Guard and Manpower Strengths and Statistics*.

MILITARY SERVICES - RESERVES - BY BRANCH - COSTS - BY BRANCH

U.S. Department of Defense, Office of the Secretary, The Pentagon, Washington, D.C. 20301 (703) 545-6700; unpublished data.

MILITARY SERVICES - RESERVES - BY BRANCH - SEX AND RACE

U.S. Department of Defense, The Pentagon, Washington, D.C. 20350 (703) 545-6700; *Official Guard and Reserve Manpower Strengths and Statistics*.

MILITARY SERVICES - RETIREES

Employee Benefit Research Institute, 2121 K Street, NW, Suite 600, Washington, D.C. 20037 (202) 659-0670; *EBRI Databook on Employee Benefits*.

U.S. Department of Commerce, Bureau of the Census, Washington, D.C. 20233 (301) 457-4100, www.census.gov; Internet site http://ferret.bls.census.gov/macro/031998/faminc/09000.html.

U.S. Department of Defense, Office of the Secretary, The Pentagon, Washington, D.C. 20301 (703) 545-6700; *Selected Manpower Statistics*.

MILITARY SERVICES - RETIREMENT SYSTEM

Employment Benefit Research Institute, 2121 K Street, NW, Suite 600, Washington, D.C. 20037 (202) 659-0670; *EBRI Databook on Employee Benefits*.

MILITARY SERVICES - SELECTIVE SERVICE - INDUCTEES

U.S. Department of Defense, Office of the Secretary, The Pentagon, Washington, D.C. 20301 (703) 545-6700; *Selected Manpower Statistics*.

MILITARY SERVICES - SELECTIVE SERVICE - INDUCTEES - BY WAR

The President's Commission on Veteran's Pensions, The White House, 1600 Pennsylvania Avenue, NW, Washington, D.C. 20500 (202) 233-4000; *Veteran's Benefits in the United States.*

U.S. Department of Defense, The Pentagon, Washington, D.C. 20301 (703) 545-6700; unpublished data.

MILK - CREAM AND OTHER DAIRY PRODUCTS - CONSUMPTION

U.S. Department of Agriculture, Economic Research Service, 1800 M Street, NW, Washington, D.C. 20036 (202) 694-5050, www.ers.usda.gov; *Food Consumption, Prices, and Expenditures; Agricultural Outlook;* and unpublished data.

MILK - PRICES

U.S. Department of Labor, Bureau of Labor Statistics, Two Massachusetts Avenue, NE, Washington, D.C. 20212 (202) 691-5200, www.stats.bls.gov; *CPI Detailed Report.*

MILK - PRODUCTION

U.S. Department of Agriculture, Economic Research Service, 1800 M Street, NW, Washington, D.C. 20036 (202) 694-5050, www.ers.usda.gov; *Agricultural Outlook.*

U.S. Department of Agriculture, National Agricultural Statistics Service, Fourteenth Street and Independence Avenue, SW, Washington, D.C. 20250; *Dairy Products;* and *Milk* (800) 727-9540, www.usda.gov/nass *Production, Disposition, and Income.*

MILK - SALES

U.S. Department of Agriculture, National Agricultural Statistics Service, Fourteenth Street and Independence Avenue, SW, Washington, D.C. 20250 (800) 727-9540, www.usda.gov/nass; *Dairy Products;* and *Milk Production, Disposition, and Income.*

MILO - See SORGHUM FOR GRAIN

MINERAL FUELS

U.S. Department of Energy, Energy Information Administration, Washington, D.C. 20585 (202) 586-8800; *Annual Energy Review.*

MINERALS AND MINERAL PRODUCTS - See also MINING and Individual Minerals

MINERALS AND MINERAL PRODUCTS - FOREIGN TRADE

U.S. Department of Commerce, Bureau of the Census, Washington, D.C. 20233 (301) 457-4100, www.census.gov; import and export data.

U.S. Department of the Interior, Geological Survey, Office of Minerals Information, 12201 Sunrise Valley Drive, Reston, Virginia 22092 (703) 648-4000, www.minerals.usgs.gov; *Mineral Commodity Summaries.*

MINERALS AND MINERAL PRODUCTS - FOREIGN TRADE - WATERBORNE COMMERCE

U.S. Department of the Army, Corps of Engineers, The Pentagon, Washington, D.C. 20301 (202) 545-6700; *Waterborne Commerce of the United States.*

MINERALS AND MINERAL PRODUCTS - IMPORTS AS PERCENT OF CONSUMPTION

U.S. Department of Commerce, Bureau of the Census, Washington, D.C. 20233 (301) 457-4100, www.census.gov; import and export data.

U.S. Department of the Interior, Geological Survey, Office of Minerals Information, 12201 Sunrise Valley Drive, Reston, Virginia 22092 (703) 648-4000, www.minerals.usgs.gov; *Mineral Commodity Summaries.*

MINERALS AND MINERAL PRODUCTS - PRICE INDEXES

U.S. Department of Labor, Bureau of Labor Statistics, Two Massachusetts Avenue, NE, Washington, D.C. 20212 (202) 691-5200, www.stats.bls.gov; *News;* and *U.S. Import and Export Price Indexes.*

MINERALS AND MINERAL PRODUCTS - PRICES

U.S. Department of the Interior, Geological Survey, Office of Minerals Information, 12201 Sunrise Valley Drive, Reston, Virginia 22092 (703) 648-4000, www.minerals.usgs.gov; *Mineral Commodity Summaries;* and *Annual Reports.*

MINERALS AND MINERAL PRODUCTS - PRODUCTION AND VALUE

Board of Governors of the Federal Reserve System, Twentieth Street and Constitution Avenue, NW, Washington, D.C. 20551 (202) 452-3000, www.bog.frb.fed.us; *Federal Reserve Bulletin;* and *Industrial Production and Capacity Utilization.*

U.S. Department of the Interior, Geological Survey, Office of Minerals Information, 12201 Sunrise Valley Drive, Reston, Virginia 22092 (703) 648-4000, www.minerals.usgs.gov; *Annual Reports;*

and *Mineral Commodities Summaries.*

MINERALS AND MINERAL PRODUCTS - PRODUCTION AND VALUE - FOREIGN COUNTRIES

U.S. Department of Energy, Energy Information Administration, 1000 Independence Avenue, SW, Washington, D.C. 20585 (202) 586-5000; *International Energy Annual.*

MINERALS AND MINERAL PRODUCTS - STRATEGIC AND CRITICAL MATERIALS

U.S. Department of Defense, Defense Logistics Agency, 8725 John J. Kingman Road, Fort Belvoir, Virginia 22060 (703) 767-6666; *Statistical Supplement, Stockpile Report to the Congress.*

MINERALS AND MINERAL PRODUCTS - WORLD PRODUCTION

U.S. Department of Energy, Energy Information Administration, 1000 Independence Avenue, SW, Washington, D.C. 20585 (202) 586-5000; *Annual Reports;* and *Mineral Commodities Summaries.*

MINING AND QUARRYING OF NON-METALLIC MINERALS (EXCEPT FUELS) - CAPITAL

U.S. Department of Commerce, Bureau of the Census, Washington, D.C. 20233 (301) 457-4100, www.census.gov; *Census of Mineral Industries;* and *1997 Economic Census, Core Business Statistics Series.*

MINING AND QUARRYING OF NON-METALLIC MINERALS (EXCEPT FUELS) - EARNINGS

U.S. Department of Commerce, Bureau of the Census, Washington, D.C. 20233 (301) 457-4100, www.census.gov; *County Business Patterns; 1997 Census, Core Business Statistics Serices;* and *Census of Mineral Industries.*

U.S. Department of Labor, Bureau of Labor Statistics, Two Massachusetts Avenue, NE, Washington, D.C. 20212 (202) 691-5200, www.stats.bls.gov; *Employment and Earnings;* and Internet site: http://stats.bls.gov/ceshome.htm.

MINING AND QUARRYING OF NON-METALLIC MINERALS (EXCEPT FUELS) - EMPLOYEES

U.S. Department of Commerce, Bureau of the Census, Washington, D.C. 20233 (301) 457-4100, www.census.gov; *County Business Patterns; 1997 Census, Core Business Statistics Series;* and *Census of Mineral Industries.*

U.S. Department of Labor, Bureau of Labor Statistics, Two Massachusetts

Avenue, NE, Washington, D.C. 20212 (202) 691-5200, www.stats.bls.gov; *Employment and Earnings;* and Internet Site: http://stats.bls.gov/ ceshome.htm.

MINING AND QUARRYING OF NON-METALLIC MINERALS (EXCEPT FUELS) - ESTABLISHMENTS

U.S. Department of Commerce, Bureau of the Census, Washington, D.C. 20233 (301) 457-4100, www.census.gov; *Census of Mineral Industries; 1997 Economic Census Core Business Statistics Series;* and *County Business Patterns.*

MINING AND QUARRYING OF NON-METALLIC MINERALS (EXCEPT FUELS) - GROSS DOMESTIC PRODUCT

U.S. Department of Commerce, Bureau of Economic Analysis, Fourteenth Street between Constitution Avenue and E Street, NW, Washington, D.C. 20230 (202) 606-9900, www.bea.doc.gov; *Survey of Current Business.*

MINING AND QUARRYING OF NON-METALLIC MINERALS (EXCEPT FUELS) - OCCUPATIONAL SAFETY

U.S. Department of Labor, Bureau of Labor Statistics, Two Massachusetts Avenue, NE, Washington, D.C. 20212 (202) 691-5200, www.stats.bls.gov; *Occupational Injuries and Illnesses in the United States by Industry.*

MINING AND QUARRYING OF NON-METALLIC MINERALS (EXCEPT FUELS) - PRODUCTIVITY

U.S. Department of Labor, Bureau of Labor Statistics, Two Massachusetts Avenue, NE, Washington, D.C. 20212 (202) 691-5200, www.stats.bls.gov; Internet site http://stats.bls.gov/iprhome.htm.

MINING AND QUARRYING OF NON-METALLIC MINERALS (EXCEPT FUELS) - SHIPMENTS, RECEIPTS

U.S. Department of Commerce, Bureau of the Census, Washington, D.C. 20233 (301) 457-4100, www.census.gov; *1997 Economic Census, Core Business Statistics Series*; and *Census of Mineral Industries.*

MINING AND QUARRYING OF NON-METALLIC MINERALS (EXCEPT FUELS) - VALUE ADDED

U.S. Department of Commerce, Bureau of the Census, Washington, D.C. 20233 (301) 457-4100, www.census.gov; *Census of Mineral Industries;* and *1997 Economic Census, Core Business Statistics Series.*

MINING INDUSTRY - See also MINERALS AND MINERAL PRODUCTS and Individual Minerals

MINING INDUSTRY - ASSETS

Time Warner, Time and Life Building, Rockefeller Center, New York, New York 10019 (212) 522-1212; *The Fortune Directories.*

U.S. Department of the Treasury, Internal Revenue Service, 1111 Constitution Avenue, NW, Washington, D.C. 20224 (202)874-0410, www.irs.ustreas.gov; *Statistics of Income, Corporation Income Tax Returns.*

MINING INDUSTRY - CAPITAL

U.S. Department of Commerce, Bureau of Economic Analysis, Fourteenth Street between Constitution Avenue and E Street, NW, Washington, D.C. 20230 (202) 606-9900, www.bea.doc.gov; *Survey of Current Business.*

MINING INDUSTRY - CAPITAL - EXPENDITURES

U.S. Department of Commerce, Bureau of the Census, Washington, D.C. 20233 (301) 457-4100, www.census.gov; *Census of Mineral Industries;* and *1997 Economic Census, Core Business Statistics Series.*

U.S. Department of Labor, Bureau of Labor Statistics, Two Massachusetts Avenue, NE, Washington, D.C. 20212 (202) 691-5200, www.stats.bls.gov; *Employment and Earnings*; and Bulletin 2370.

MINING INDUSTRY - EARNINGS

U.S. Department of Commerce, Bureau of Economic Analysis, Fourteenth Street between Constitution Avenue and E Street, NW, Washington, D.C. 20230 (202) 606-9900, www.bea.doc.gov; *The National Income and Product Accounts of the United States;* and *Survey of Current Business.*

U.S. Department of Commerce, Bureau of the Census, Washington, D.C. 20233 (301) 457-4100, www.census.gov; *Census of Mineral Industries; Statistics of U.S. Businesses; 1997 Economic Census, Core Business Statistics Series;* and *County Business Patterns.*

U.S. Department of Labor, Bureau of Labor Statistics, Two Massachusetts Avenue, NE, Washington, D.C. 20212 (202) 691-5200, www.stats.bls.gov; *Employment and Earnings;* and Bulletins 2370; and Internet site: http://stats/ bls.gov/ceshome.htm.

MINING INDUSTRY - EMPLOYEES

U.S. Department of Commerce, Bureau of the Census, Washington, D.C. 20233 (301) 457-4100, www.census.gov; *Census of Mineral Industries; County Business Patterns; Statistics of U.S. Businesses; 1997*

Economic Census: Advance Summary Statistics for the U.S.; and *Census of Mineral Industries.*

U.S. Department of Labor, Bureau of Labor Statistics, Two Massachusetts Avenue, NE, Washington, D.C. 20212 (202) 691-5200, www.stats.bls.gov; *Employment and Earnings; Monthly Labor Review;* Bulletins 2370; unpublished data; and Internet site: http:// stats.bls.gov/ceshome.htm.

MINING INDUSTRY - ESTABLISHMENTS

U.S. Department of Commerce, Bureau of the Census, Washington, D.C. 20233 (301) 457-4100, www.census.gov; *Census of Mineral Industries; 1997 Economic Census: Advance Summary Statistics for the U.S. 1997 NAICS Basis; Statistics of U.S. Businesses; 1997 Economic Census, Core Business Statistics Series;* and *County Business Patterns.*

MINING INDUSTRY - FAILURES

Dun and Bradstreet Corporation, 299 Park Avenue, 24th Floor, New York, New York 10171 (212) 593-6800; *Business Failure Record.*

MINING INDUSTRY - FINANCES

Time Warner, Time and Life Building, Rockefeller Center, New York, New York 10019 (212) 522-1212; *The Fortune Directories.*

U.S. Department of Commerce, Bureau of the Census, Washington, D.C. 20233 (301) 457-4100, www.census.gov; *Census of Mineral Industries.*

U.S. Department of the Treasury, Internal Revenue Service, 1111 Constitution Avenue, NW, Washington, D.C. 20224 (202) 874-0410, www.irs.ustreas.gov; *Statistics of Income,* various publications; *Statistics of Income, Corporation Income Tax Returns; Statistics of Income Bulletin and Partnership Returns;* and unpublished data.

MINING INDUSTRY - FOREIGN INVESTMENTS IN THE UNITED STATES

U.S. Department of Commerce, Bureau of Economic Analysis, Fourteenth Street between Constitution Avenue and E Street, NW, Washington, D.C. 20230 (202) 606-9900, www.bea.doc.gov; *Survey of Current Business;* and *Foreign Direct Investment in the United States, Operations of U.S. Affiliates of Foreign Countries;* and *Foreign Direct Investment in the U.S., Benchmark Survey.*

MINING INDUSTRY - GROSS DOMESTIC PRODUCT

U.S. Department of Commerce, Bureau

of Economic Analysis, Fourteenth Street between Constitution Avenue and E Street, NW, Washington, D.C. 20230 (202) 606-9900, www.bea.doc.gov; *Survey of Current Business.*

MINING INDUSTRY - HEALTH INSURANCE COVERAGE - EMPLOYEES

U.S. Department of Health and Human Services, National Center for Health Statistics, 3700 East-West Highway, Hyattsville, Maryland 20782 (301) 436-8500, www.cdc.gov/nchs; *Employer-Sponsored Health Insurance, State and National Estimates.*

MINING INDUSTRY - MERGERS AND ACQUISITIONS

Thomson Financial Securities Data, Two Gateway Center, Newark, New Jersey 07006 (973) 622-3100; *Merger and Corporate Transactions Database.*

MINING INDUSTRY - OCCUPATIONAL SAFETY

National Safety Council, 1121 Spring Lake Drive, Itasca, Illinois 60143-3201 (630) 285-1121; *Accident Facts.*

U.S. Department of Labor, Bureau of Labor Statistics, Two Massachusetts Avenue, NE, Washington, D.C. 20212 (202) 691-5200, www.stats.bls.gov; *Occupational Injuries and Illnesses in the United States by Industry.*

MINING INDUSTRY - PRODUCTIVITY

U.S. Department of Labor, Bureau of Labor Statistics, Two Massachusetts Avenue, NE, Washington, D.C. 20212 (202) 691-5200, www.stats.bls.gov; Internet site http://stats.bls.gov/iprhome.htm.

MINING INDUSTRY - PROFITS

Time Warner, Time and Life Building, Rockefeller Center, New York, New York 10019 (212) 522-1212; *The Fortune Directories.*

U.S. Department of the Treasury, Internal Revenue Service, 1111 Constitution Avenue, NW, Washington, D.C. 20224 (202) 874-0410, www.irs.ustreas.us; *Statistics of Income; Statistics of Income Bulletin and Partnership Returns; Statistics of Income, Corporation Income Tax Returns;* and *Statistics of Income Bulletin.*

MINING INDUSTRY - RECEIPTS

Time Warner, Time and Life Building, Rockefeller Center, New York, New York 10019 (212) 522-1212; *The Fortune Directories.*

U.S. Department of Commerce, Bureau

of the Census, Washington, D.C. 20233 (301) 457-4100, www.census.gov; *Census of Mineral Industries; 1997 Economic Census: Advance Summary Statistics for the U.S. NAICS Basis; 1997 Economic Census, Core Business Statistics Series;* and *Statistics of U.S. Businesses.*

U.S. Department of the Treasury, Internal Revenue Service, 1111 Constitution Avenue, NW, Washington, D.C. 20224 (202) 874-0410, www.irs.ustreas.us; *Statistics of Income,* various publications; and unpublished data.

MINING INDUSTRY - SHIPMENTS

U.S. Department of Commerce, Bureau of the Census, Washington, D.C. 20233 (301) 457-4100, www.census.gov; *Census of Mineral Industries; 1997 Economic Census: Advance Summary Statistics for the U.S. 1997 NAICS Basis; Manufacturing Profiles, 1995;* and Internet site: http://census.gov/ftp/pub/industry/1/ma35f97.pdf.

U.S. Department of Labor, Bureau of Labor Statistics, Two Massachusetts Avenue, NE. Washington, D.C. 20212 (202) 691-5200, www.stats.bls.gov; *Employment and Earnings*; and Bulletin 2370.

MINING INDUSTRY - UNION MEMBERSHIP

U.S. Department of Labor, Bureau of Labor Statistics, Two Massachusetts Avenue, NE, Washington, D.C. 20212 (202) 691-5200, www.stats.bls.gov; *Employment and Earnings.*

MINING INDUSTRY - VALUE ADDED

U.S. Department of Commerce, Bureau of the Census, Washington, D.C. 20233 (301) 457-4100, www.census.gov; *Census of Mineral Industries;* and *1997 Economic Census, Core Business Statistics Series.*

MINING MACHINERY

U.S. Department of Commerce, Bureau of the Census, Washington, D.C. 20233 (301) 457-4100, www.census.gov; *Manufacturing Profiles;* and Internet site: http://www.census.gov/ftp/pub/industry/1/ma35f97.pdf.

MINNESOTA - See also STATE DATA (FOR INDIVIDUAL STATES)

Minnesota - Primary Statistics Sources

Department of Trade and Economic Development, Business Development and Analysis Division, 500 Metro Square Building, St. Paul, Minnesota 55101 (612) 296-8283; *Compare Minnesota: An*

Economic and Statistical Factbook; and *Economic Report to the Governor: State of Minnesota.*

Office of State Demographer, State Planning Agency, 300 Centennial Building, St. Paul, Minnesota 55155 (612) 296-2557; *Minnesota Population and Household Estimates.*

Minnesota - State Data Centers

Education Resource Center, Department of Education, 501 Capitol Square Building, St. Paul, Minnesota 55101, Patricia Tupper (612) 296-6684.

Headwaters Regional Data Commission, 403 Fourth Street, NW, Box 906, Bemiji, Minnesota 56601, Tim Flathers, (218) 751-3108.

Machine Readable Data Center, University of Minnesota, Two Wilson Library, 309 Nineteenth Avenue, South, Minneapolis, Minnesota 55455, Wendy Treadwell (612) 624-4389.

State Demographer's Office, Minnesota Planning, 300 Centennial Office Building, 658 Cedar Street, St. Paul, Minnesota 55155, Mr. David Birkholz (651) 296-2557.

MISSISSIPPI - See also STATE DATA (FOR INDIVIDUAL STATES)

Mississippi - Primary Statistics Source

Mississippi State University, College of Business and Industry, Division of Research, Mississippi State, Mississippi 39762 (601) 325-3817; *Mississippi Statistical Abstract.*

Mississippi - State Data Centers

Center for Population Studies, University of Mississippi, Leavell Hall, Room 101, University, Mississippi 38677, Ms. Rachel McNeely, Manager (662) 915-7288.

Industry Resource Bureau, Mississippi Department of Economics and Community Development, 1200 Walter Silas Building, Post Office Box 849, Jackson, Mississippi 39205, Deloise Tate (601) 359-3593.

Southern Mississippi Planning and Development District, 2015A 15th Street, Gulfport, Mississippi 39501-2021, Leslie Newcomb, Exec. Director, (228) 868-2311.

MISSISSIPPI RIVER TRAFFIC

U.S. Department of the Army, Corps of

Engineers, The Pentagon, Washington, D.C. 20301 (202) 545-6700; *Waterborne Commerce of the United States.*

MISSOURI - See also STATE DATA (FOR INDIVIDUAL STATES)

Missouri - Primary Statistics Source

Business and Public Administration Research Center, University of Missouri, Columbia, Missouri 65211 (314) 882-4805; *Statistical Abstract for Missouri.*

Missouri - State Data Centers

Missouri State Data Center, Missouri State Library, Office of the Secretary of State, 600 West Main Street, Post Office Box 387, Jefferson City, Missouri 65102, Ms. Debra Pitts (573) 526-7648.

Center for Economic Information, University of Missouri-Kansas City, 207 Haag Hall, Kansas City, M issouri 64131, Mr. Peter Eaton (816) 235-2832.

Geographic Resources Center, University of Missouri-Columbia, 17 Stewart Hall, Columbia, Missouri 65211, Mr. Tim Haithcoat (573) 882-2324.

Office of Administration, 124 Capitol Building, Post Office Box 809, Jefferson City, Missouri 65102, Mr. Ryan Burson (573) 751-2345.

Office of Social and Economic Data Analysis, University of Missouri-Columbia, 602 Clark Hall, Columbia, Missouri 65211, Ms. Evelyn J. Cleveland (573) 882-7396.

Small Business Research Information Center, University of Missouri-Rolla, 104 Nagogami Terrace, Rolla, Missouri 65409-1340, Ms. Cathy Frank (573) 341-6584.

MOBILE HOMES

U.S. Department of Commerce, Bureau of the Census, Washington, D.C. 20233 (301) 457-4100, www.census.gov; *Current Construction Reports;* and *American Housing Survey in the U.S.*

MOBILE HOMES - CAPITAL STOCKS

U.S. Department of Commerce, Bureau of Economic Analysis, Fourteenth Street between Constitution Avenue and E Street, NW, Washington, D.C. 20230 (202) 606-9900, www.bea.doc.gov; *Survey of Current Business.*

MOBILITY STATUS OF POPULATION

U.S. Department of Commerce, Bureau

of the Census, Washington, D.C. 20233 (301) 457-4100, www.census.gov; *Current Population Reports.*

MOLDOVA - ABORTIONS

Statistical Office of the United Nations, Publishing Service, New York, New York 10017 (800) 253-9646; *Trends in Europe and North America: The Statistical Yearbook of the Economic Commission for Europe.*

MOLDOVA - AGRICULTURE

Academic International Press, Box 1111, Gulf Breeze, Florida 32562; *Russia and Eurasia Facts and Figures Annual.*

Business International Moscow, 23 Profsoyuznaya Ulitsa, 117859, Moscow (Telephone Number in U.S. (800) 938-4685); *The CIS Market Atlas.*

Economist Intelligence Unit, 111 West 57th Street, New York, New York 10019 (800) 938-4685; *Moldova Country Report.*

Euromonitor International, Inc., 122 South Michigan Avenue, Suite 1200, Chicago, Illinois 60603 (800) 577-EURO; *World Marketing Data and Statistics.*

Europa Publications Limited, 18 Bedford Square, London, WC1B 3JN, England; *The Europa World Year Book.*

Food and Agriculture Organization of the United Nations (FAO), Via delle Terme de Caracalla, 00100, Rome, Italy (Telephone Number in U.S. (202) 653-2400); *Production Yearbook; The State of Food and Agriculture;* and *Trade Yearbook.*

St. Martin's Press, Inc., 175 Fifth Avenue, New York, New York 10010 (800) 221-7945; *The Statesman's Year-Book.*

Statistical Office of the United Nations, Publishing Service, New York, New York 10017 (800) 253-9646; *Industrial Commodity Statistics Yearbook;* and *Statistical Yearbook.*

The World Bank, 1818 H Street, NW, Washington, D.C. 20433 (202) 477-1234; *Statistical Handbook: States of the Former USSR;* and *World Development Indicators.*

MOLDOVA - AIRLINE SERVICE

Business International Moscow, 23 Profsoyuznaya Ulitsa, 117859, Moscow (Telephone Number in U.S. (800) 938-4685); *The CIS Market Atlas.*

International Civil Aviation Organization, 999 University Street, Montreal, Quebec, Canada H3C 5H7 (514) 954-8219; *Civil Aviation Statistics of the World.*

St. Martin's Press, Inc., 175 Fifth Avenue, New York, New York 10010 (800) 221-7945; *The Statesman's Year-Book.*

Statistical Office of the United Nations, Publishing Service, New York, New York 10017 (800) 253-9646; *Statistical Yearbook.*

MOLDOVA - ANIMAL HEALTH

Food and Agriculture Organization of the United Nations (FAO), Via delle Terme di Caracalla, 00100, Rome, Italy (Telephone Number in U.S. (202) 653-2400); *Animal Health Yearbook.*

MOLDOVA - AREA AND DENSITY OF POPULATION

Academic International Press, Box 1111, Gulf Breeze, Florida 32562; *Russia and Eurasia Facts and Figures Annual.*

Business International Moscow, 23 Profsoyuznaya Ulitsa, 117859, Moscow (Telephone Number in U.S. (800) 938-4685); *The CIS Market Atlas.*

Euromonitor International, Inc., 122 South Michigan Avenue, Suite 1200, Chicago, Illinois 60603 (800) 577-EURO; *The World Economic Factbook.*

Europa Publications Limited, 18 Bedford Square, London, WC1B 3JN, England; *The Europa World Year Book.*

St. Martin's Press, Inc., 175 Fifth Avenue, New York, New York 10010 (800) 221-7945; *The Statesman's Year-Book.*

Statistical Office of the United Nations, Publishing Service, New York, New York 10017 (800) 253-9646; *Statistical Yearbook;* and *Trends in Europe and North America: The Statistical Yearbook of the Economic Commission for Europe.*

United Nations Educational, Scientific and Cultural Organization (UNESCO), 7 Place de Fontenoy, F-75700 Paris, France (Telephone Number in U.S. (212) 963-5981); *Statistical Yearbook.*

The World Bank, 1818 H Street, NW, Washington, D.C. 20433 (202) 477-1234; *World Development Report.*

MOLDOVA - BALANCE OF PAYMENTS

United Nations Conference on Trade and Development (UNCTAD), New York, New York 10017 (800) 253-9646; *Handbook of International Trade and Development Statistics.*

The World Bank, 1818 H Street, NW, Washington, D.C. 20433 (202) 477-1234; *World Development Report;* and *World Development Indicators.*

MOLDOVA - BANKING

Business International Moscow, 23 Profsoyuznaya Ulitsa, 117859, Moscow (Telephone Number in U.S. (800) 938-4685); *The CIS Market Atlas.*

Euromonitor International, Inc., 122 South Michigan Avenue, Suite 1200, Chicago, Illinois 60603 (800) 577-EURO; *World Marketing Data and Statistics.*

Europa Publications Limited, 18 Bedford Square, London, WC1B 3JN, England; *The Europa World Year Book*.

St. Martin's Press, Inc., 175 Fifth Avenue, New York, New York 10010 (800) 221-7945; *The Statesman's Year-Book.*

MOLDOVA - BEVERAGES

Statistical Office of the United Nations, Publishing Service, New York, New York 10017 (800) 253-9646; *Statistical Yearbook.*

MOLDOVA - BIRTH RATES

Academic International Press, Box 1111, Gulf Breeze, Florida 32562; *Russia and Eurasia Facts and Figures Annual.*

Business International Moscow, 23 Profsoyuznaya Ulitsa, 117859, Moscow (Telephone Number in U.S. (800) 938-4685); *The CIS Market Atlas.*

Euromonitor International, Inc.,122 South Michigan Avenue, Suite 1200, Chicago, Illinois 60603 (800) 577-EURO; *The World Economic Factbook.*

Europa Publications Limited, 18 Bedford Square, London, WC1B 3JN, England; *The Europa World Year Book*.

Statistical Office of the United Nations, Publishing Service, New York, New York 10017 (800) 253-9646; *Statistical Yearbook.*

St. Martin's Press, Inc., 175 Fifth Avenue, New York, New York 10010 (800) 221-7945; *The Statesman's Year-Book.*

World Health Organization, Office of Publications, 20 Avenue Appia, CH-1211 Geneva 27, Switzerland (Telephone Number in U.S. (518) 436-9686); *World Health Statistics Annual.*

MOLDOVA - BOOK PRODUCTION

Statistical Office of the United Nations, Publishing Service, New York, New York 10017 (800) 253-9646; *Trends in Europe and North America: The Statistical Yearbook of the Economic Commission for Europe.*

United Nations Educational, Scientific and Cultural Organization (UNESCO), 7 Place de Fontenoy, F-75700 Paris, France (Telephone Number in U.S. (212) 963-5981); *Statistical Yearbook.*

MOLDOVA - BROADCASTING

Euromonitor International, Inc., 122 South Michigan Avenue, Suite 1200, Chicago, Illinois 60603 (800) 577-EURO; *World Marketing Data and Statistics.*

St. Martin's Press, Inc., 175 Fifth Avenue, New York, New York 10010 (800) 221-7945; *The Statesman's Year-Book.*

Statistical Office of the United Nations, Publishing Service, New York, New York 10017 (800) 253-9646; *Trends in Europe and North America: The Statistical Yearbook of the Economic Commission for Europe.*

United Nations Educational, Scientific and Cultural Organization (UNESCO), 7 Place de Fontenoy, F-75700 Paris, France (Telephone Number in U.S. (212) 963-5981); *Statistical Yearbook.*

MOLDOVA - BUDGET

Business International Moscow, 23 Profsoyuznaya Ulitsa, 117859, Moscow (Telephone Number in U.S. (800) 938-4685); *The CIS Market Atlas.*

MOLDOVA - CAPITAL INVESTMENT

The World Bank, 1818 H Street, NW, Washington, D.C. 20433 (202) 477-1234; *Statistical Handbook: States of the Former USSR.*

MOLDOVA - CATTLE - See MOLDOVA - LIVESTOCK AND POULTRY

MOLDOVA - CHEMICALS

Business International Moscow, 23 Profsoyuznaya Ulitsa, 117859, Moscow (Telephone Number in U.S. (800) 938-4685); *The CIS Market Atlas.*

MOLDOVA - COAL PRODUCTION AND CONSUMPTION - See MOLDOVA - MINING AND MINERAL PRODUCTS

MOLDOVA - COMMERCE

St. Martin's Press, Inc., 175 Fifth Avenue, New York, New York 10010 (800) 221-7945; *The Statesman's Year-Book.*

MOLDOVA - COMMUNICATIONS - See MOLDOVA - TRANSPORTATION AND COMMUNICATIONS

MOLDOVA - CONSTRUCTION INDUSTRY

Academic International Press, Box 1111, Gulf Breeze, Florida 32562; *Russia and Eurasia Facts and Figures Annual.*

Business International Moscow, 23

Profsoyuznaya Ulitsa, 117859, Moscow (Telephone Number in U.S. (800) 938-4685); *The CIS Market Atlas.*

Statistical Office of the United Nations, Publishing Service, New York, New York 10017 (800) 253-9646; *Statistical Yearbook.*

MOLDOVA - CONSUMER PRICE INDEX

Europa Publications Limited, 18 Bedford Square, London, WC1B 3JN, England; *The Europa World Year Book*.

Statistical Office of the United Nations, Publishing Service, New York, New York 10017 (800) 253-9646; *Statistical Yearbook;* and *Trends in Europe and North America: The Statistical Yearbook of the Economic Commission for Europe.*

MOLDOVA - CONSUMER PRICES

Euromonitor International, Inc., 122 South Michigan Avenue, Suite 1200, Chicago, Illinois 60603 (800) 577-EURO; *World Marketing Data and Statistics.*

International Labour Office, I.L.O. Publications, 1828 L Street, NW, Suite 801, Washington, D.C. 20036 (301) 638-3152; *Yearbook of Labour Statistics.*

MOLDOVA - CONSUMER PRODUCTS

Business International Moscow, 23 Profsoyuznaya Ulitsa, 117859, Moscow (Telephone Number in U.S. (800) 938-4685); *The CIS Market Atlas.*

MOLDOVA - CONSUMPTION

Business International Moscow, 23 Profsoyuznaya Ulitsa, 117859, Moscow (Telephone Number in U.S. (800) 938-4685); *The CIS Market Atlas.*

The World Bank, 1818 H Street, NW, Washington, D.C. 20433 (202) 477-1234; *World Development Report;* and *Statistical Handbook: States of the Former USSR.*

MOLDOVA - COTTON PRODUCTION AND CONSUMPTION - See MOLDOVA - TEXTILE INDUSTRY

MOLDOVA - CRIME

Academic International Press, Box 1111, Gulf Breeze, Florida 32562; *Russia and Eurasia Facts and Figures Annual.*

Statistical Office of the United Nations, Publishing Service, New York, New York 10017 (800) 253-9646; *Trends in Europe and North America: The Statistical Yearbook of the Economic Commission for Europe.*

MOLDOVA - CROPS

Academic International Press, Box

1111, Gulf Breeze, Florida 32562; *Russia and Eurasia Facts and Figures Annual.*

Europa Publications Limited, 18 Bedford Square, London, WC1B 3JN, England; *The Europa World Year Book.*

Food and Agriculture Organization of the United Nations (FAO), Via delle Terme de Caracalla, 00100, Rome, Italy (Telephone Number in U.S. (202) 653-2400); *Production Yearbook; The State of Food and Agriculture;* and *Trade Yearbook.*

St. Martin's Press, Inc., 175 Fifth Avenue, New York, New York 10010 (800) 221-7945; *The Statesman's Year-Book.*

Statistical Office of the United Nations, Publishing Service, New York, New York 10017 (800) 253-9646; *Industrial Commodity Statistics Yearbook;* and *Statistical Yearbook.*

The World Bank, 1818 H Street, NW, Washington, D.C. 20433 (202) 477-1234; *Statistical Handbook: States of the Former USSR.*

MOLDOVA - DAIRY PRODUCTS

Europa Publications Limited, 18 Bedford Square, London, WC1B 3JN, England; *The Europa World Year Book.*

Food and Agriculture Organization of the United Nations (FAO), Via delle Terme de Caracalla, 00100, Rome, Italy (Telephone Number in U.S. (202) 653-2400); *Production Yearbook; The State of Food and Agriculture;* and *Trade Yearbook.*

St. Martin's Press, Inc., 175 Fifth Avenue, New York, New York 10010 (800) 221-7945; *The Statesman's Year-Book.*

Statistical Office of the United Nations, Publishing Service, New York, New York 10017 (800) 253-9646; *Industrial Commodity Statistics Yearbook;* and *Statistical Yearbook.*

MOLDOVA - DEATH RATES - See MOLDOVA - MORTALITY

MOLDOVA - DEMOGRAPHY

Business International Moscow, 23 Profsoyuznaya Ulitsa, 117859, Moscow (Telephone Number in U.S. (800) 938-4685); *The CIS Market Atlas.*

Euromonitor International, Inc., 122 South Michigan Avenue, Suite 1200, Chicago, Illinois 60603 (800) 577-EURO; *The World Economic Factbook;* and *World Marketing Data and Statistics.*

Statistical Office of the United Nations, Publishing Service, New York, New York 10017 (800) 253-9646; *Demographic*

Yearbook; and *Human Development Report.*

The World Bank, 1818 H Street, NW, Washington, D.C. 20433 (202) 477-1234; *Statistical Handbook: States of the Former USSR.*

MOLDOVA - DISEASES - See MOLDOVA - HEALTH

MOLDOVA - DIVORCE RATES

Academic International Press, Box 1111, Gulf Breeze, Florida 32562; *Russia and Eurasia Facts and Figures Annual.*

Statistical Office of the United Nations, Publishing Service, New York, New York 10017 (800) 253-9646; *Demographic Yearbook; Trends in Europe and North America: The Statistical Yearbook of the Economic Commission for Europe;* and *Statistical Yearbook.*

MOLDOVA - DOMESTIC INVESTMENT

Business International Moscow, 23 Profsoyuznaya Ulitsa, 117859, Moscow (Telephone Number in U.S. (800) 938-4685); *The CIS Market Atlas.*

MOLDOVA - ECONOMY

Academic International Press, Box 1111, Gulf Breeze, Florida 32562; *Russia and Eurasia Facts and Figures Annual.*

Business International Moscow, 23 Profsoyuznaya Ulitsa, 117859, Moscow (Telephone Number in U.S. (800) 938-4685); *The CIS Market Atlas.*

Economist Intelligence Unit, 111 West 57th Street, New York, New York 10019 (800) 938-4685; *Moldova Country Report.*

Euromonitor International, Inc., 122 South Michigan Avenue, Suite 1200, Chicago, Illinois 60603 (800) 577-EURO; *The World Economic Factbook;* and *World Marketing Data and Statistics.*

St. Martin's Press, Inc., 175 Fifth Avenue, New York, New York 10010 (800) 221-7945; *The Statesman's Year-Book.*

Statistical Office of the United Nations, Publishing Service, New York, New York 10017 (800) 253-9646; *World Statistics Pocketbook.*

The World Bank, 1818 H Street, NW, Washington, D.C. 20433 (202) 477-1234; *The World Bank Atlas;* and *World Development Report.*

MOLDOVA - EDUCATION

Academic International Press, Box 1111, Gulf Breeze, Florida 32562; *Russia*

and Eurasia Facts and Figures Annual.

Business International Moscow, 23 Profsoyuznaya Ulitsa, 117859, Moscow (Telephone Number in U.S. (800) 938-4685); *The CIS Market Atlas.*

Euromonitor International, Inc., 122 South Michigan Avenue, Suite 1200, Chicago, Illinois 60603 (800) 577-EURO; *World Marketing Data and Statistics.*

Europa Publications Limited, 18 Bedford Square, London, WC1B 3JN, England; *The Europa World Year Book.*

St. Martin's Press, Inc., 175 Fifth Avenue, New York, New York 10010 (800) 221-7945; *The Statesman's Year-Book.*

Statistical Office of the United Nations, Publishing Service, New York, New York 10017 (800) 253-9646; *Human Development Report;* and *Trends in Europe and North America: The Statistical Yearbook of the Economic Commission for Europe.*

United Nations Educational, Scientific and Cultural Organization (UNESCO), 7 Place de Fontenoy, F-75700 Paris, France (Telephone Number in U.S. (212) 963-5981); *Statistical Yearbook.*

The World Bank, 1818 H Street, NW, Washington, D.C. 20433 (202) 477-1234; *World Development Report.*

MOLDOVA - ELECTRICITY

Academic International Press, Box 1111, Gulf Breeze, Florida 32562; *Russia and Eurasia Facts and Figures Annual.*

Business International Moscow, 23 Profsoyuznaya Ulitsa, 117859, Moscow (Telephone Number in U.S. (800) 938-4685); *The CIS Market Atlas.*

St. Martin's Press, Inc., 175 Fifth Avenue, New York, New York 10010 (800) 221-7945; *The Statesman's Year-Book.*

Statistical Office of the United Nations, Publishing Service, New York, New York 10017 (800) 253-9646; *Energy Statistics Yearbook; Human Development Report; Trends in Europe and North America: The Statistical Yearbook of the Economic Commission for Europe;* and *Statistical Yearbook.*

The World Bank, 1818 H Street, NW, Washington, D.C. 20433 (202) 477-1234; *Statistical Handbook: States of the Former USSR.*

MOLDOVA - EMPLOYMENT

International Labour Office, I.L.O. Publications, 1828 L Street, NW, Suite 801,

Washington, D.C. 20036 (301) 638-3152; *Yearbook of Labour Statistics.*

Statistical Office of the United Nations, Publishing Service, New York, New York 10017 (800) 253-9646; *Statistical Yearbook;* and *Trends in Europe and North America: The Statistical Yearbook of the Economic Commission for Europe.*

The World Bank, 1818 H Street, NW, Washington, D.C. 20433 (202) 477-1234; *Statistical Handbook: States of the Former USSR.*

MOLDOVA - ENERGY

Academic International Press, Box 1111, Gulf Breeze, Florida 32562; *Russia and Eurasia Facts and Figures Annual.*

Business International Moscow, 23 Profsoyuznaya Ulitsa, 117859, Moscow (Telephone Number in U.S. (800) 938-4685); *The CIS Market Atlas.*

Euromonitor International, Inc., 122 South Michigan Avenue, Suite 1200, Chicago, Illinois 60603 (800) 577-EURO; *The World Economic Factbook;* and *World Marketing Data and Statistics.*

St. Martin's Press, Inc., 175 Fifth Avenue, New York, New York 10010 (800) 221-7945; *The Statesman's Year-Book.*

Statistical Office of the United Nations, Publishing Service, New York, New York 10017 (800) 253-9646; *Energy Statistics Yearbook; Human Development Report; Trends in Europe and North America: The Statistical Yearbook of the Economic Commission for Europe; World Statistics Pocketbook;* and *Statistical Yearbook.*

The World Bank, 1818 H Street, NW, Washington, D.C. 20433 (202) 477-1234; *The World Bank Atlas; World Development Report;* and *Statistical Handbook: States of the Former USSR.*

MOLDOVA - ENVIRONMENT

Business International Moscow, 23 Profsoyuznaya Ulitsa, 117859, Moscow (Telephone Number in U.S. (800) 938-4685); *The CIS Market Atlas.*

Economist Intelligence Unit, 111 West 57th Street, New York, New York 10019 (800) 938-4685; *Moldova Country Report.*

Statistical Office of the United Nations, Publishing Service, New York, New York 10017 (800) 253-9646; *Statistical Yearbook; World Statistics Pocketbook;* and *Trends in Europe and North America: The Statistical Yearbook of the Economic Commission for Europe.*

MOLDOVA - EXCHANGE RATES

Euromonitor International, Inc., 122 South Michigan Avenue, Suite 1200, Chicago, Illinois 60603 (800) 577-EURO; *The World Economic Factbook.*

Europa Publications Limited, 18 Bedford Square, London, WC1B 3JN, England; *The Europa World Year Book.*

Statistical Office of the United Nations, Publishing Service, New York, New York 10017 (800) 253-9646; *Statistical Yearbook; World Statistics Pocketbook;* and *Trends in Europe and North America: The Statistical Yearbook of the Economic Commission for Europe.*

MOLDOVA - EXPORTS

Academic International Press, Box 1111, Gulf Breeze, Florida 32562; *Russia and Eurasia Facts and Figures Annual.*

Business International Moscow, 23 Profsoyuznaya Ulitsa, 117859, Moscow (Telephone Number in U.S. (800) 938-4685); *The CIS Market Atlas.*

Economist Intelligence Unit, 111 West 57th Street, New York, New York 10019 (800) 938-4685; *Moldova Country Report.*

Euromonitor International, Inc., 122 South Michigan Avenue, Suite 1200, Chicago, Illinois 60603 (800) 577-EURO; *The World Economic Factbook.*

Europa Publications Limited, 18 Bedford Square, London, WC1B 3JN, England; *The Europa World Year Book.*

International Monetary Fund, 700 Nineteenth Street, NW, Washington, D.C. 20431 (202) 623-7000; *Direction of Trade Statistics.*

St. Martin's Press, Inc., 175 Fifth Avenue, New York, New York 10010 (800) 221-7945; *The Statesman's Year-Book.*

Statistical Office of the United Nations, Publishing Service, New York, New York 10017 (800) 253-9646; *International Trade Statistics Yearbook;* and *Trends in Europe and North America: The Statistical Yearbook of the Economic Commission for Europe.*

United Nations Conference on Trade and Development (UNCTAD), New York, New York 10017 (800) 253-9646; *Handbook of International Trade and Development Statistics.*

The World Bank, 1818 H Street, NW, Washington, D.C. 20433 (202) 477-1234; *World Development Report; Statistical Handbook: States of the Former USSR;* and *World Development Indicators.*

MOLDOVA - EXTERNAL DEBT

The World Bank, 1818 H Street, NW, Washington, D.C. 20433 (202) 477-1234; *World Development Indicators.*

MOLDOVA - EXTERNAL INDEBTEDNESS

The World Bank, 1818 H Street, NW, Washington, D.C. 20433 (202) 477-1234; *World Development Report.*

MOLDOVA - EXTERNAL TRADE

Academic International Press, Box 1111, Gulf Breeze, Florida 32562; *Russia and Eurasia Facts and Figures Annual.*

Euromonitor International, Inc., 122 South Michigan Avenue, Suite 1200, Chicago, Illinois 60603 (800) 577-EURO; *World Marketing Data and Statistics.*

Food and Agriculture Organization of the United Nations (FAO), Via delle Terme de Caracalla, 00100, Rome, Italy (Telephone Number in U.S. (202) 653-2400); *Trade Yearbook.*

Statistical Office of the United Nations, Publishing Service, New York, New York 10017 (800) 253-9646; *Statistical Yearbook.*

The World Bank, 1818 H Street, NW, Washington, D.C. 20433 (202) 477-1234; *Statistical Handbook: States of the Former USSR.*

MOLDOVA - FABRIC PRODUCTION AND CONSUMPTION - See MOLDOVA - TEXTILE INDUSTRY

MOLDOVA - FERTILITY RATES

Statistical Office of the United Nations, Publishing Service, New York, New York 10017 (800) 253-9646; *Human Development Report;* and *Trends in Europe and North America: The Statistical Yearbook of the Economic Commission for Europe.*

The World Bank, 1818 H Street, NW, Washington, D.C. 20433 (202) 477-1234; *The World Bank Atlas; World Development Report; Statistical Handbook: States of the Former USSR;* and *World Development Indicators.*

World Health Organization, Office of Publications, 20 Avenue Appia, CH-1211 Geneva 27, Switzerland (Telephone Number in U.S. (518) 436-9686); *World Health Statistics Annual.*

MOLDOVA - FERTILIZER

Food and Agriculture Organization of the United Nations (FAO), Via delle Terme de Caracalla, 00100, Rome, Italy (Telephone Number in U.S. (202) 653-2400); *Fertilizer Yearbook.*

Statistical Office of the United Nations, Publishing Service, New York, New York 10017 (800) 253-9646; *Industrial Commodity Statistics Yearbook;* and *Statistical Yearbook.*

MOLDOVA - FINANCE

Economist Intelligence Unit, 111 West 57th Street, New York, New York 10019 (800) 938-4685; *Moldova Country Report.*

Europa Publications Limited, 18 Bedford Square, London, WC1B 3JN, England; *The Europa World Year Book.*

St. Martin's Press, Inc., 175 Fifth Avenue, New York, New York 10010 (800) 221-7945; *The Statesman's Year-Book.*

The World Bank, 1818 H Street, NW, Washington, D.C. 20433 (202) 477-1234; *Statistical Handbook: States of the Former USSR.*

MOLDOVA - FISHERIES

Food and Agriculture Organization of the United Nations (FAO), Via delle Terme de Caracalla, 00100, Rome, Italy (Telephone Number in U.S. (202) 653-2400); *The State of Food and Agriculture;* and *Yearbook of Fishery Statistics.*

St. Martin's Press, Inc., 175 Fifth Avenue, New York, New York 10010 (800) 221-7945; *The Statesman's Year-Book.*

Statistical Office of the United Nations, Publishing Service, New York, New York 10017 (800) 253-9646; *Industrial Commodity Statistics Yearbook;* and *Statistical Yearbook.*

MOLDOVA - FOOD

Food and Agriculture Organization of the United Nations (FAO), Via delle Terme de Caracalla, 00100, Rome, Italy (Telephone Number in U.S. (202) 653-2400); *Production Yearbook; The State of Food and Agriculture;* and *Trade Yearbook.*

Statistical Office of the United Nations, Publishing Service, New York, New York 10017 (800) 253-9646; *Human Development Report;* and *Industrial Commodity Statistics Yearbook.*

MOLDOVA - FOOTWEAR PRODUCTION AND CONSUMPTION - See MOLDOVA - TEXTILE INDUSTRY

MOLDOVA - FOREIGN INVESTMENT

Business International Moscow, 23 Profsoyuznaya Ulitsa, 117859, Moscow (Telephone Number in U.S. (800) 938-4685); *The CIS Market Atlas.*

MOLDOVA - FOREIGN TRADE

Business International Moscow, 23 Profsoyuznaya Ulitsa, 117859, Moscow (Telephone Number in U.S. (800) 938-4685); *The CIS Market Atlas.*

Economist Intelligence Unit, 111 West 57th Street, New York, New York 10019 (800) 938-4685; *Moldova Country Report.*

Euromonitor International, Inc., 122 South Michigan Avenue, Suite 1200, Chicago, Illinois 60603 (800) 577-EURO; *The World Economic Factbook.*

Europa Publications Limited, 18 Bedford Square, London, WC1B 3JN, England; *The Europa World Year Book.*

Food and Agriculture Organization of the United Nations (FAO), Via delle Terme de Caracalla, 00100, Rome, Italy (Telephone Number in U.S. (202) 653-2400); *Trade Yearbook.*

International Monetary Fund, 700 Nineteenth Street, NW, Washington, D.C. 20431 (202) 623-7000; *Direction of Trade Statistics.*

St. Martin's Press, Inc., 175 Fifth Avenue, New York, New York 10010 (800) 221-7945; *The Statesman's Year-Book.*

Statistical Office of the United Nations, Publishing Service, New York, New York 10017 (800) 253-9646; *International Trade Statistics Yearbook;* and *Statistical Yearbook.*

The World Bank, 1818 H Street, NW, Washington, D.C. 20433 (202) 477-1234; *World Development Report; Statistical Handbook: States of the Former USSR;* and *World Development Indicators.*

MOLDOVA - FORESTRY AND FOREST PRODUCTS

Academic International Press, Box 1111, Gulf Breeze, Florida 32562; *Russia and Eurasia Facts and Figures Annual.*

Business International Moscow, 23 Profsoyuznaya Ulitsa, 117859, Moscow (Telephone Number in U.S. (800) 938-4685); *The CIS Market Atlas.*

Food and Agriculture Organization of the United Nations (FAO), Via delle Terme de Caracalla, 00100, Rome, Italy (Telephone Number in U.S. (202) 653-2400); *The State of Food and Agriculture;* and *Yearbook of Forest Products.*

Statistical Office of the United Nations, Publishing Service, New York, New York 10017 (800) 253-9646; *Industrial Commodity Statistics Yearbook; Trends in Europe and North America: The Statistical Yearbook of the Economic Commission for Europe;* and *Statistical Yearbook.*

United Nations Educational, Scientific and Cultural Organization (UNESCO), 7 Place de Fontenoy, F-75700 Paris, France (Telephone Number in U.S. (212) 963-5981); *Statistical Yearbook.*

The World Bank, 1818 H Street, NW, Washington, D.C. 20433 (202) 477-1234; *World Development Report.*

MOLDOVA - GOATS - See MOLDOVA - LIVESTOCK AND POULTRY

MOLDOVA - GOVERNMENT

Academic International Press, Box 1111, Gulf Breeze, Florida 32562; *Russia and Eurasia Facts and Figures Annual.*

Europa Publications Limited, 18 Bedford Square, London, WC1B 3JN, England; *The Europa World Year Book.*

St. Martin's Press, Inc., 175 Fifth Avenue, New York, New York 10010 (800) 221-7945; *The Statesman's Year-Book.*

Statistical Office of the United Nations, Publishing Service, New York, New York 10017 (800) 253-9646; *Statistical Yearbook.*

The World Bank, 1818 H Street, NW, Washington, D.C. 20433 (202) 477-1234; *World Development Report;* and *Statistical Handbook: States of the Former USSR.*

MOLDOVA - GROSS DOMESTIC PRODUCT

Academic International Press, Box 1111, Gulf Breeze, Florida 32562; *Russia and Eurasia Facts and Figures Annual.*

Economist Intelligence Unit, 111 West 57th Street, New York, New York 10019 (800) 938-4685; *Moldova Country Report.*

Euromonitor International, Inc., 122 South Michigan Avenue, Suite 1200, Chicago, Illinois 60603 (800) 577-EURO; *The World Economic Factbook.*

Statistical Office of the United Nations, Publishing Service, New York, New York 10017 (800) 253-9646; *Human Development Report; National Accounts Statistics; Trends in Europe and North America: The Statistical Yearbook of the Economic Commission for Europe;* and *Statistical Yearbook.*

The World Bank, 1818 H Street, NW, Washington, D.C. 20433 (202) 477-1234; *World Development Report; Statistical Handbook: States of the Former USSR;* and *World Development Indicators.*

MOLDOVA - GROSS NATIONAL PRODUCT

St. Martin's Press, Inc., 175 Fifth Avenue, New York, New York 10010 (800)

221-7945; *The Statesman's Year-Book.*

The World Bank, 1818 H Street, NW, Washington, D.C. 20433 (202) 477-1234; *The World Bank Atlas; World Development Report;* and *World Development Indicators.*

MOLDOVA - HEALTH

Academic International Press, Box 1111, Gulf Breeze, Florida 32562; *Russia and Eurasia Facts and Figures Annual.*

Business International Moscow, 23 Profsoyuznaya Ulitsa, 117859, Moscow (Telephone Number in U.S. (800) 938-4685); *The CIS Market Atlas.*

Euromonitor International, Inc., 122 South Michigan Avenue, Suite 1200, Chicago, Illinois 60603 (800) 577-EURO; *World Marketing Data and Statistics.*

St. Martin's Press, Inc., 175 Fifth Avenue, New York, New York 10010 (800) 221-7945; *The Statesman's Year-Book.*

Statistical Office of the United Nations, Publishing Service, New York, New York 10017 (800) 253-9646; *Human Development Report; Trends in Europe and North America: The Statistical Yearbook of the Economic Commission for Europe;* and *Statistical Yearbook.*

United Nations Children's Fund (UNICEF), 3 United Nations Plaza, New York, New York 10017 (800) 253-9646; *State of the World's Children.*

The World Bank, 1818 H Street, NW, Washington, D.C. 20433 (202) 477-1234; *World Development Report.*

World Health Organization, Office of Publications, 20 Avenue Appia, CH-1211 Geneva 27, Switzerland (Telephone Number in U.S. (518) 436-9686); *World Health Statistics Annual.*

MOLDOVA - HIGHWAYS

Academic International Press, Box 1111, Gulf Breeze, Florida 32562; *Russia and Eurasia Facts and Figures Annual.*

Business International Moscow, 23 Profsoyuznaya Ulitsa, 117859, Moscow (Telephone Number in U.S. (800) 938-4685); *The CIS Market Atlas.*

Statistical Office of the United Nations, Publishing Service, New York, New York 10017 (800) 253-9646; *Annual Bulletin of Transport Statistics for Europe;* and *Trends in Europe and North America: The Statistical Yearbook of the Economic Commission for Europe.*

St. Martin's Press, Inc., 175 Fifth Avenue, New York, New York 10010 (800) 221-7945;

The Statesman's Year-Book.

MOLDOVA - HOUSING AND HOUSING UNITS

Business International Moscow, 23 Profsoyuznaya Ulitsa, 117859, Moscow (Telephone Number in U.S. (800) 938-4685); *The CIS Market Atlas.*

Euromonitor International, Inc., 122 South Michigan Avenue, Suite 1200, Chicago, Illinois 60603 (800) 577-EURO; *World Marketing Data and Statistics.*

Statistical Office of the United Nations, Publishing Service, New York, New York 10017 (800) 253-9646; *Trends in Europe and North America: The Statistical Yearbook of the Economic Commission for Europe.*

MOLDOVA - ILLITERATE POPULATION

Euromonitor International, Inc., 122 South Michigan Avenue, Suite 1200, Chicago, Illinois 60603 (800) 577-EURO; *The World Economic Factbook.*

Statistical Office of the United Nations, Publishing Service, New York, New York 10017 (800) 253-9646; *Human Development Report.*

United Nations Educational, Scientific and Cultural Organization (UNESCO), 7 Place de Fontenoy, F-75700 Paris, France (Telephone Number in U.S. (212) 963-5981); *Statistical Yearbook.*

MOLDOVA - IMPORTS

Academic International Press, Box 1111, Gulf Breeze, Florida 32562; *Russia and Eurasia Facts and Figures Annual.*

Business International Moscow, 23 Profsoyuznaya Ulitsa, 117859, Moscow (Telephone Number in U.S. (800) 938-4685); *The CIS Market Atlas.*

Economist Intelligence Unit, 111 West 57th Street, New York, New York 10019 (800) 938-4685; *Moldova Country Report.*

Euromonitor International, Inc., 122 South Michigan Avenue, Suite 1200, Chicago, Illinois 60603 (800) 577-EURO; *The World Economic Factbook.*

Europa Publications Limited, 18 Bedford Square, London, WC1B 3JN, England; *The Europa World Year Book.*

International Monetary Fund, 700 Nineteenth Street, NW, Washington, D.C. 20431 (202) 623-7000; *Direction of Trade Statistics.*

St. Martin's Press, Inc., 175 Fifth Avenue, New York, New York 10010 (800) 221-7945; *The Statesman's Year-Book.*

Statistical Office of the United Nations, Publishing Service, New York, New York 10017 (800) 253-9646; *International Trade Statistics Yearbook;* and *Trends in Europe and North America: The Statistical Yearbook of the Economic Commission for Europe.*

United Nations Conference on Trade and Development (UNCTAD), New York, New York 10017 (800) 253-9646; *Handbook of International Trade and Development Statistics.*

The World Bank, 1818 H Street, NW, Washington, D.C. 20433 (202) 477-1234; *World Development Report; Statistical Handbook: States of the Former USSR;* and *World Development Indicators.*

MOLDOVA - INDUSTRY

Academic International Press, Box 1111, Gulf Breeze, Florida 32562; *Russia and Eurasia Facts and Figures Annual.*

Business International Moscow, 23 Profsoyuznaya Ulitsa, 117859, Moscow (Telephone Number in U.S. (800) 938-4685); *The CIS Market Atlas.*

Economist Intelligence Unit, 111 West 57th Street, New York, New York 10019 (800) 938-4685; *Moldova Country Report.*

Euromonitor International, Inc., 122 South Michigan Avenue, Suite 1200, Chicago, Illinois 60603 (800) 577-EURO; *The World Economic Factbook;* and *World Marketing Data and Statistics.*

Europa Publications Limited, 18 Bedford Square, London, WC1B 3JN, England; *The Europa World Year Book.*

International Labour Office, I.L.O. Publications, 1828 L Street, NW, Suite 801, Washington, D.C. 20036 (301) 638-3152; *Yearbook of Labour Statistics.*

St. Martin's Press, Inc., 175 Fifth Avenue, New York, New York 10010 (800) 221-7945; *The Statesman's Year-Book.*

Statistical Office of the United Nations, Publishing Service, New York, New York 10017 (800) 253-9646; *Industrial Commodity Statistics Yearbook; Trends in Europe and North America: The Statistical Yearbook of the Economic Commission for Europe;* and *Statistical Yearbook.*

The World Bank, 1818 H Street, NW, Washington, D.C. 20433 (202) 477-1234; *Statistical Handbook: States of the Former USSR;* and *World Development Indicators.*

MOLDOVA - INFANT MORTALITY RATE - See MOLDOVA - MORTALITY

MOLDOVA - INTERNAL TRADE

Statistical Office of the United Nations, Publishing Service, New York, New York 10017 (800) 253-9646; *Statistical Yearbook.*

MOLDOVA - LABOR

Academic International Press, Box 1111, Gulf Breeze, Florida 32562; *Russia and Eurasia Facts and Figures Annual.*

Business International Moscow, 23 Profsoyuznaya Ulitsa, 117859, Moscow (Telephone Number in U.S. (800) 938-4685); *The CIS Market Atlas.*

Euromonitor International, Inc., 122 South Michigan Avenue, Suite 1200, Chicago, Illinois 60603 (800) 577-EURO; *World Marketing Data and Statistics.*

Europa Publications Limited, 18 Bedford Square, London, WC1B 3JN, England; *The Europa World Year Book.*

International Labour Office, I.L.O. Publications, 1828 L Street, NW, Suite 801, Washington, D.C. 20036 (301) 638-3152; *Yearbook of Labour Statistics.*

St. Martin's Press, Inc., 175 Fifth Avenue, New York, New York 10010 (800) 221-7945; *The Statesman's Year-Book.*

Statistical Office of the United Nations, Publishing Service, New York, New York 10017 (800) 253-9646; *Human Development Report;* and *Statistical Yearbook.*

The World Bank, 1818 H Street, NW, Washington, D.C. 20433 (202) 477-1234; *The World Bank Atlas; World Development Report; Statistical Handbook: States of the Former USSR;* and *World Development Indicators.*

MOLDOVA - LAND USE

Food and Agriculture Organization of the United Nations (FAO), Via delle Terme de Caracalla, 00100, Rome, Italy (Telephone Number in U.S. (202) 653-2400); *Production Yearbook.*

The World Bank, 1818 H Street, NW, Washington, D.C. 20433 (202) 477-1234; *World Development Report.*

MOLDOVA - LIBRARIES

Statistical Office of the United Nations, Publishing Service, New York, New York 10017 (800) 253-9646; *Trends in Europe and North America: The Statistical Yearbook of the Economic Commission for Europe.*

United Nations Educational, Scientific and Cultural Organization (UNESCO), 7 Place de Fontenoy, F-75700 Paris, France (Telephone Number in U.S. (212) 963-5981); *Statistical Yearbook.*

MOLDOVA - LIFE EXPECTANCY

Academic International Press, Box 1111, Gulf Breeze, Florida 32562; *Russia and Eurasia Facts and Figures Annual.*

Business International Moscow, 23 Profsoyuznaya Ulitsa, 117859, Moscow (Telephone Number in U.S. (800) 938-4685); *The CIS Market Atlas.*

Euromonitor International, Inc., 122 South Michigan Avenue, Suite 1200, Chicago, Illinois 60603 (800) 577-EURO; *The World Economic Factbook.*

Statistical Office of the United Nations, Publishing Service, New York, New York 10017 (800) 253-9646; *Demographic Yearbook; Trends in Europe and North America: The Statistical Yearbook of the Economic Commission for Europe; World Statistics Pocketbook;* and *Human Development Report.*

The World Bank, 1818 H Street, NW, Washington, D.C. 20433 (202) 477-1234; *The World Bank Atlas; World Development Report;* and *World Development Indicators.*

World Health Organization, Office of Publications, 20 Avenue Appia, CH-1211 Geneva 27, Switzerland (Telephone Number in U.S. (518) 436-9686); *World Health Statistics Annual.*

MOLDOVA - LITERACY RATE

Euromonitor International, Inc., 122 South Michigan Avenue, Suite 1200, Chicago, Illinois 60603 (800) 577-EURO; *World Marketing Data and Statistics.*

MOLDOVA - LIVESTOCK AND POULTRY

Academic International Press, Box 1111, Gulf Breeze, Florida 32562; *Russia and Eurasia Facts and Figures Annual.*

Business International Moscow, 23 Profsoyuznaya Ulitsa, 117859, Moscow (Telephone Number in U.S. (800) 938-4685); *The CIS Market Atlas.*

Europa Publications Limited, 18 Bedford Square, London, WC1B 3JN, England; *The Europa World Year Book.*

Food and Agriculture Organization of the United Nations (FAO), Via delle Terme de Caracalla, 00100, Rome, Italy (Telephone Number in U.S. (202) 653-2400); *Production Yearbook; The State of Food and Agriculture;* and *Trade Yearbook.*

St. Martin's Press, Inc., 175 Fifth Avenue, New York, New York 10010 (800) 221-7945; *The Statesman's Year-Book.*

Statistical Office of the United Nations, Publishing Service, New York, New York

10017 (800) 253-9646; *Industrial Commodity Statistics Yearbook;* and *Statistical Yearbook.*

MOLDOVA - MACHINERY

Statistical Office of the United Nations, Publishing Service, New York, New York 10017 (800) 253-9646; *Industrial Commodity Statistics Yearbook.*

MOLDOVA - MAIL - NUMBER OF PIECES SENT OR RECEIVED

Statistical Office of the United Nations, Publishing Service, New York, New York 10017 (800) 253-9646; *Statistical Yearbook.*

MOLDOVA - MANUFACTURING

Statistical Office of the United Nations, Publishing Service, New York, New York 10017 (800) 253-9646; *Industrial Commodity Statistics Yearbook;* and *Statistical Yearbook.*

The World Bank, 1818 H Street, NW, Washington, D.C. 20433 (202) 477-1234; *World Development Indicators.*

MOLDOVA - MARRIAGE RATES

Academic International Press, Box 1111, Gulf Breeze, Florida 32562; *Russia and Eurasia Facts and Figures Annual.*

Europa Publications Limited, 18 Bedford Square, London, WC1B 3JN, England; *The Europa World Year Book.*

Statistical Office of the United Nations, Publishing Service, New York, New York 10017 (800) 253-9646; *Demographic Yearbook; Trends in Europe and North America: The Statistical Yearbook of the Economic Commission for Europe;* and *Statistical Yearbook.*

MOLDOVA - MEAT PRODUCTION - See MOLDOVA - LIVESTOCK AND POULTRY

MOLDOVA - MERCHANT SHIPPING

Statistical Office of the United Nations, Publishing Service, New York, New York 10017 (800) 253-9646; *Annual Bulletin of Transport Statistics for Europe;* and *Statistical Yearbook.*

MOLDOVA - MILITARY

Academic International Press, Box 1111, Gulf Breeze, Florida 32562; *Russia and Eurasia Facts and Figures Annual.*

Euromonitor International, Inc., 122 South Michigan Avenue, Suite 1200, Chicago, Illinois 60603 (800) 577-EURO; *World Marketing Data and Statistics.*

The International Institute for Strategic Studies, 23 Tavistock Street, London WC2E 7NQ, England; *The Military Balance.*

St. Martin's Press, Inc., 175 Fifth Avenue, New York, New York 10010 (800) 221-7945; *The Statesman's Year-Book.*

Statistical Office of the United Nations, Publishing Service, New York, New York 10017 (800) 253-9646; *Human Development Report.*

MOLDOVA - MINING AND MINERAL PRODUCTS

Academic International Press, Box 1111, Gulf Breeze, Florida 32562; *Russia and Eurasia Facts and Figures Annual.*

Business International Moscow, 23 Profsoyuznaya Ulitsa, 117859, Moscow (Telephone Number in U.S. (800) 938-4685); *The CIS Market Atlas.*

St. Martin's Press, Inc., 175 Fifth Avenue, New York, New York 10010 (800) 221-7945; *The Statesman's Year-Book.*

Statistical Office of the United Nations, Publishing Service, New York, New York 10017 (800) 253-9646; *Energy Statistics Yearbook; Industrial Commodity Statistics Yearbook;* and *Statistical Yearbook.*

MOLDOVA - MONEY SUPPLY

Economist Intelligence Unit, 111 West 57th Street, New York, New York 10019 (800) 938-4685; *Moldova Country Report.*

Europa Publications Limited, 18 Bedford Square, London, WC1B 3JN, England; *The Europa World Year Book.*

MOLDOVA - MONUMENTS AND HISTORICAL SITES

United Nations Educational, Scientific and Cultural Organization (UNESCO), 7 Place de Fontenoy, F-75700 Paris, France (Telephone Number in U.S. (212) 963-5981); *Statistical Yearbook.*

MOLDOVA - MORTALITY

Academic International Press, Box 1111, Gulf Breeze, Florida 32562; *Russia and Eurasia Facts and Figures Annual.*

Business International Moscow, 23 Profsoyuznaya Ulitsa, 117859, Moscow (Telephone Number in U.S. (800) 938-4685); *The CIS Market Atlas.*

Euromonitor International, Inc., 122 South Michigan Avenue, Suite 1200, Chicago, Illinois 60603 (800) 577-EURO; *The World Economic Factbook.*

Europa Publications Limited, 18 Bedford Square, London, WC1B 3JN, England; *The Europa World Year Book.*

St. Martin's Press, Inc., 175 Fifth Avenue, New York, New York 10010 (800) 221-7945; *The Statesman's Year-Book.*

Statistical Office of the United Nations, Publishing Service, New York, New York 10017 (800) 253-9646; *Demographic Yearbook; Human Development Report; Trends in Europe and North America: The Statistical Yearbook of the Economic Commission for Europe; World Statistics Pocketbook;* and *Statistical Yearbook.*

United Nations Children's Fund (UNICEF), 3 United Nations Plaza, New York, New York 10017 (800) 253-9646; *State of the World's Children.*

The World Bank, 1818 H Street, NW, Washington, D.C. 20433 (202) 477-1234; *The World Bank Atlas; World Development Report;* and *World Development Indicators.*

World Health Organization, Office of Publications, 20 Avenue Appia, CH-1211 Geneva 27, Switzerland (Telephone Number in U.S. (518) 436-9686); *World Health Statistics Annual.*

MOLDOVA - MOTION PICTURES

Statistical Office of the United Nations, Publishing Service, New York, New York 10017 (800) 253-9646; *Statistical Yearbook.*

United Nations Educational, Scientific and Cultural Organization (UNESCO), 7 Place de Fontenoy, F-75700 Paris, France (Telephone Number in U.S. (212) 963-5981); *Statistical Yearbook.*

MOLDOVA - MOTOR VEHICLES

Business International Moscow, 23 Profsoyuznaya Ulitsa, 117859, Moscow (Telephone Number in U.S. (800) 938-4685); *The CIS Market Atlas.*

Europa Publications Limited, 18 Bedford Square, London, WC1B 3JN, England; *The Europa World Year Book.*

Statistical Office of the United Nations, Publishing Service, New York, New York 10017 (800) 253-9646; *Statistical Yearbook.*

MOLDOVA - MUSEUMS

United Nations Educational, Scientific and Cultural Organization (UNESCO), 7 Place de Fontenoy, F-75700 Paris, France (Telephone Number in U.S. (212) 963-5981); *Statistical Yearbook.*

MOLDOVA - NATIONAL ACCOUNTS

Europa Publications Limited, 18 Bedford Square, London, WC1B 3JN, England; *The Europa World Year Book.*

Statistical Office of the United Nations, Publishing Service, New York, New York 10017 (800) 253-9646; *National Accounts Statistics;* and *Statistical Yearbook.*

The World Bank, 1818 H Street, NW, Washington, D.C. 20433 (202) 477-1234; *Statistical Handbook: States of the Former USSR.*

MOLDOVA - NATIONAL INCOME

Business International Moscow, 23 Profsoyuznaya Ulitsa, 117859, Moscow (Telephone Number in U.S. (800) 938-4685); *The CIS Market Atlas.*

Statistical Office of the United Nations, Publishing Service, New York, New York 10017 (800) 253-9646; *Statistical Yearbook.*

MOLDOVA - NATIONAL PRODUCT

Statistical Office of the United Nations, Publishing Service, New York, New York 10017 (800) 253-9646; *Statistical Yearbook.*

MOLDOVA - PATENTS, TRADEMARKS AND SERVICE MARKS

Statistical Office of the United Nations, Publishing Service, New York, New York 10017 (800) 253-9646; *Statistical Yearbook.*

MOLDOVA - PERIODICALS

United Nations Educational, Scientific and Cultural Organization (UNESCO), 7 Place de Fontenoy, F-75700 Paris, France (Telephone Number in U.S. (212) 963-5981); *Statistical Yearbook.*

MOLDOVA - PETROLEUM INDUSTRY

Food and Agriculture Organization of the United Nations (FAO), Via delle Terme de Caracalla, 00100, Rome, Italy (Telephone Number in U.S. (202) 653-2400); *The State of Food and Agriculture.*

Statistical Office of the United Nations, Publishing Service, New York, New York 10017 (800) 253-9646; *Energy Statistics Yearbook; Industrial Commodity Statistics Yearbook; Trends in Europe and North America: The Statistical Yearbook of the Economic Commission for Europe;* and *Statistical Yearbook.*

MOLDOVA - PIGS - See MOLDOVA - LIVESTOCK AND POULTRY

MOLDOVA - POPULATION

Academic International Press, Box 1111, Gulf Breeze, Florida 32562; *Russia and Eurasia Facts and Figures Annual.*

Business International Moscow, 23

Profsoyuznaya Ulitsa, 117859, Moscow (Telephone Number in U.S. (800) 938-4685); *The CIS Market Atlas.*

Economist Intelligence Unit, 111 West 57th Street, New York, New York 10019 (800) 938-4685; *Moldova Country Report.*

Euromonitor International, Inc., 122 South Michigan Avenue, Suite 1200, Chicago, Illinois 60603 (800) 577-EURO; *World Development Report;* and *The World Economic Factbook.*

Europa Publications Limited, 18 Bedford Square, London, WC1B 3JN, England; *The Europa World Year Book.*

Food and Agriculture Organization of the United Nations (FAO), Via delle Terme de Caracalla, 00100, Rome, Italy (Telephone Number in U.S. (202) 653-2400); *Production Yearbook.*

International Labour Office, I.L.O. Publications, 1828 L Street, NW, Suite 801, Washington, D.C. 20036 (301) 638-3152; *Yearbook of Labour Statistics.*

St. Martin's Press, Inc., 175 Fifth Avenue, New York, New York 10010 (800) 221-7945; *The Statesman's Year-Book.*

Statistical Office of the United Nations, Publishing Service, New York, New York 10017 (800) 253-9646; *Demographic Yearbook; Human Development Report; Trends in Europe and North America: The Statistical Yearbook of the Economic Commission for Europe; World Statistics Pocketbook;* and *Statistical Yearbook.*

United Nations Educational, Scientific and Cultural Organization (UNESCO), 7 Place de Fontenoy, F-75700 Paris, France (Telephone Number in U.S. (212) 963-5981); *Statistical Yearbook.*

The World Bank, 1818 H Street, NW, Washington, D.C. 20433 (202) 477-1234; *The World Bank Atlas; World Development Report; Statistical Handbook: States of the Former USSR;* and *World Development Indicators.*

World Health Organization, Office of Publications, 20 Avenue Appia, CH-1211 Geneva 27, Switzerland (Telephone Number in U.S. (518) 436-9686); *World Health Statistics Annual.*

MOLDOVA - POST OFFICES

Statistical Office of the United Nations, Publishing Service, New York, New York 10017 (800) 253-9646; *Trends in Europe and North America: The Statistical Yearbook of the Economic Commission for Europe.*

MOLDOVA - POULTRY - See MOLDOVA - LIVESTOCK AND POULTRY

Business International Moscow, 23 Profsoyuznaya Ulitsa, 117859, Moscow (Telephone Number in U.S. (800) 938-4685); *The CIS Market Atlas.*

MOLDOVA - PRICES

Food and Agriculture Organization of the United Nations (FAO), Via delle Terme de Caracalla, 00100, Rome, Italy (Telephone Number in U.S. (202) 653-2400); *Production Yearbook.*

International Labour Office, I.L.O. Publications, 1828 L Street, NW, Suite 801, Washington, D.C. 20036 (301) 638-3152; *Yearbook of Labour Statistics.*

The World Bank, 1818 H Street, NW, Washington, D.C. 20433 (202) 477-1234; *Statistical Handbook: States of the Former USSR.*

MOLDOVA - PRODUCTION

The World Bank, 1818 H Street, NW, Washington, D.C. 20433 (202) 477-1234; *Statistical Handbook: States of the Former USSR.*

MOLDOVA - PUBLIC FINANCE - See MOLDOVA - FINANCE

MOLDOVA - RADIO RECEIVER PRODUCTION

Statistical Office of the United Nations, Publishing Service, New York, New York 10017 (800) 253-9646; *Statistical Yearbook.*

MOLDOVA - RADIO RECEIVERS

St. Martin's Press, Inc., 175 Fifth Avenue, New York, New York 10010 (800) 221-7945; *The Statesman's Year-Book.*

MOLDOVA - RAILWAYS

Academic International Press, Box 1111, Gulf Breeze, Florida 32562; *Russia and Eurasia Facts and Figures Annual.*

Business International Moscow, 23 Profsoyuznaya Ulitsa, 117859, Moscow (Telephone Number in U.S. (800) 938-4685); *The CIS Market Atlas.*

Statistical Office of the United Nations, Publishing Service, New York, New York 10017 (800) 253-9646; *Annual Bulletin of Transport Statistics for Europe; Trends in Europe and North America: The Statistical Yearbook of the Economic Commission for Europe;* and *Statistical Yearbook.*

St. Martin's Press, Inc., 175 Fifth Avenue, New York, New York 10010 (800) 221-7945; *The Statesman's Year-Book.*

MOLDOVA - RELIGION

Academic International Press, Box 1111, Gulf Breeze, Florida 32562; *Russia and Eurasia Facts and Figures Annual.*

MOLDOVA - RENT PRICES

International Labour Office, I.L.O. Publications, 1828 L Street, NW, Suite 801, Washington, D.C. 20036 (301) 638-3152; *Yearbook of Labour Statistics.*

MOLDOVA - RETAIL TRADE

Business International Moscow, 23 Profsoyuznaya Ulitsa, 117859, Moscow (Telephone Number in U.S. (800) 938-4685); *The CIS Market Atlas.*

Euromonitor International, Inc., 122 South Michigan Avenue, Suite 1200, Chicago, Illinois 60603 (800) 577-EURO; *World Marketing Data and Statistics.*

Statistical Office of the United Nations, Publishing Service, New York, New York 10017 (800) 253-9646; *Statistical Yearbook.*

MOLDOVA - ROADS - See MOLDOVA - HIGHWAYS

MOLDOVA - ROUNDWOOD PRODUCTION AND CONSUMPTION - See MOLDOVA - FORESTRY AND FOREST PRODUCTS

MOLDOVA - RUBBER PRODUCTION AND CONSUMPTION

Statistical Office of the United Nations, Publishing Service, New York, New York 10017 (800) 253-9646; *Statistical Yearbook.*

MOLDOVA - SCIENTISTS, TECHNICIANS AND ENGINEERS

Statistical Office of the United Nations, Publishing Service, New York, New York 10017 (800) 253-9646; *Statistical Yearbook.*

MOLDOVA - SHEEP - See MOLDOVA - LIVESTOCK AND POULTRY

MOLDOVA - SOCIAL DATA

Statistical Office of the United Nations, Publishing Service, New York, New York 10017 (800) 253-9646; *World Statistics Pocketbook.*

MOLDOVA - STEEL PRODUCTION AND CONSUMPTION - See MOLDOVA - MINING AND MINERAL PRODUCTS

MOLDOVA - TAXATION

Europa Publications Limited, 18 Bedford Square, London, WC1B 3JN, England; *The Europa World Year Book.*

MOLDOVA - TELEPHONES IN USE

Academic International Press, Box

1111, Gulf Breeze, Florida 32562; *Russia and Eurasia Facts and Figures Annual.*

Statistical Office of the United Nations, Publishing Service, New York, New York 10017 (800) 253-9646; *Statistical Yearbook; World Statistics Pocketbook;* and *Trends in Europe and North America: The Statistical Yearbook of the Economic Commission for Europe.*

MOLDOVA - TEXTILE INDUSTRY

Business International Moscow, 23 Profsoyuznaya Ulitsa, 117859, Moscow (Telephone Number in U.S. (800) 938-4685); *The CIS Market Atlas.*

St. Martin's Press, Inc., 175 Fifth Avenue, New York, New York 10010 (800) 221-7945; *The Statesman's Year-Book.*

Statistical Office of the United Nations, Publishing Service, New York, New York 10017 (800) 253-9646; *Industrial Commodity Statistics Yearbook;* and *Statistical Yearbook.*

MOLDOVA - THEATRE

United Nations Educational, Scientific and Cultural Organization (UNESCO), 7 Place de Fontenoy, F-75700 Paris, France (Telephone Number in U.S. (212) 963-5981); *Statistical Yearbook.*

MOLDOVA - TIRE (MOTOR VEHICLE) PRODUCTION

Statistical Office of the United Nations, Publishing Service, New York, New York 10017 (800) 253-9646; *Statistical Yearbook.*

MOLDOVA - TOBACCO PRODUCTION

Statistical Office of the United Nations, Publishing Service, New York, New York 10017 (800) 253-9646; *Statistical Yearbook.*

MOLDOVA - TOURISM

Business International Moscow, 23 Profsoyuznaya Ulitsa, 117859, Moscow (Telephone Number in U.S. (800) 938-4685); *The CIS Market Atlas.*

Euromonitor International, Inc., 122 South Michigan Avenue, Suite 1200, Chicago, Illinois 60603 (800) 577-EURO; *The World Economic Factbook;* and *World Marketing Data and Statistics.*

Statistical Office of the United Nations, Publishing Service, New York, New York 10017 (800) 253-9646; *Statistical Yearbook;* and *Trends in Europe and North America: The Statistical Yearbook of the Economic Commission for Europe.*

MOLDOVA - TRADEMARKS AND SERVICE MARKS - See MOLDOVA - PATENTS, TRADEMARKS AND SERVICE MARKS

MOLDOVA - TRANSPORTATION AND COMMUNICATIONS

Academic International Press, Box 1111, Gulf Breeze, Florida 32562; *Russia and Eurasia Facts and Figures Annual.*

Business International Moscow, 23 Profsoyuznaya Ulitsa, 117859, Moscow (Telephone Number in U.S. (800) 938-4685); *The CIS Market Atlas.*

Euromonitor International, Inc., 122 South Michigan Avenue, Suite 1200, Chicago, Illinois 60603 (800) 577-EURO; *World Marketing Data and Statistics.*

Europa Publications Limited, 18 Bedford Square, London, WC1B 3JN, England; *The Europa World Year Book.*

Statistical Office of the United Nations, Publishing Service, New York, New York 10017 (800) 253-9646; *Annual Bulletin of Transport Statistics for Europe; Trends in Europe and North America: The Statistical Yearbook of the Economic Commission for Europe;* and *Human Development Report.*

St. Martin's Press, Inc., 175 Fifth Avenue, New York, New York 10010 (800) 221-7945; *The Statesman's Year-Book.*

MOLDOVA - UNEMPLOYMENT

International Labour Office, I.L.O. Publications, 1828 L Street, NW, Suite 801, Washington, D.C. 20036 (301) 638-3152; *Yearbook of Labour Statistics.*

St. Martin's Press, Inc., 175 Fifth Avenue, New York, New York 10010 (800) 221-7945; *The Statesman's Year-Book.*

Statistical Office of the United Nations, Publishing Service, New York, New York 10017 (800) 253-9646; *Statistical Yearbook;* and *Trends in Europe and North America: The Statistical Yearbook of the Economic Commission for Europe.*

MOLDOVA - VITAL STATISTICS

St. Martin's Press, Inc., 175 Fifth Avenue, New York, New York 10010 (800) 221-7945; *The Statesman's Year-Book.*

Statistical Office of the United Nations, Publishing Service, New York, New York 10017 (800) 253-9646; *Statistical Yearbook.*

World Health Organization, Office of Publications, 20 Avenue Appia, CH-1211 Geneva 27, Switzerland (Telephone Number in U.S. (518) 436-9686); *World Health Statistics Annual.*

MOLDOVA - WAGES

Business International Moscow, 23 Profsoyuznaya Ulitsa, 117859, Moscow (Telephone Number in U.S. (800) 938-4685); *The CIS Market Atlas.*

International Labour Office, I.L.O. Publications, 1828 L Street, NW, Suite 801, Washington, D.C. 20036 (301) 638-3152; *Yearbook of Labour Statistics.*

Statistical Office of the United Nations, Publishing Service, New York, New York 10017 (800) 253-9646; *Statistical Yearbook.*

The World Bank, 1818 H Street, NW, Washington, D.C. 20433 (202) 477-1234; *Statistical Handbook: States of the Former USSR.*

MOLDOVA - WELFARE

Academic International Press, Box 1111, Gulf Breeze, Florida 32562; *Russia and Eurasia Facts and Figures Annual.*

St. Martin's Press, Inc., 175 Fifth Avenue, New York, New York 10010 (800) 221-7945; *The Statesman's Year-Book.*

MOLDOVA - WHOLESALE PRICES

Academic International Press, Box 1111, Gulf Breeze, Florida 32562; *Russia and Eurasia Facts and Figures Annual.*

Statistical Office of the United Nations, Publishing Service, New York, New York 10017 (800) 253-9646; *Statistical Yearbook.*

MOLDOVA - WHOLESALE TRADE

Statistical Office of the United Nations, Publishing Service, New York, New York 10017 (800) 253-9646; *Statistical Yearbook.*

MOLDOVA - WOOL PRODUCTION AND CONSUMPTION - See MOLDOVA - TEXTILE INDUSTRY

MOLYBDENUM

U.S. Department of the Interior, Bureau of the Mines, 810 Seventh Street, NW, Washington, D.C. 20241 (202) 501-9649; *Annual Reports;* and *Mineral Commodity Summaries.*

Monaco - National Statistical Office

Services des Statistiques, et des Etudes Economiques, rue des Iris, Monte Carlo, Monaco.

Monaco - Primary Statistics Source

Services des Statistiques et des Etudes Economiques, 4 rue des Iris, Monte Carlo, Monaco; *Statistiques annuelles,* (Annual Statistics).

MONACO - ABORTIONS

Statistical Office of the United Nations, Publishing Service, New York, New York 10017 (800) 253-9646; *Trends in Europe and North America: The Statistical Yearbook of the Economic Commission for Europe.*

MONACO - AGRICULTURE

Euromonitor International, Inc., 122 South Michigan Avenue, Suite 1200, Chicago, Illinois 60603 (800) 577-EURO; *World Marketing Data and Statistics.*

Food and Agricultural Organization of the United Nations (FAO), Via delle Terme di Caracalla, 00100 Rome, Italy (Telephone Number in U.S. (202) 653-2400); *Production Yearbook; The State of Food and Agriculture;* and *Trade Yearbook.*

M.E. Sharpe, 80 Business Park Drive, Armonk, New York 10504 (800) 541-6563; *The Illustrated Book of World Rankings.*

Statistical Office of the United Nations, Publishing Service, New York, New York 10017 (800) 253-9646; *Industrial Commodity Statistics Yearbook;* and *Statistical Yearbook.*

MONACO - AIRLINE SERVICE

M.E. Sharpe, 80 Business Park Drive, Armonk, New York 10504 (800) 541-6563; *The Illustrated Book of World Rankings.*

Statistical Office of the United Nations, Publishing Service, New York, New York 10017 (800) 253-9646; *Statistical Yearbook.*

St. Martin's Press, Inc., 175 Fifth Avenue, New York, New York 10010 (800) 221-7945; *The Statesman's Year-Book.*

MONACO - AIRPORTS

Central Intelligence Agency, Washington, D.C. 20505 (703) 482-1100, www.cia.gov; *The World Factbook.*

MONACO - ALUMINUM PRODUCTION AND CONSUMPTION - See MONACO - MINING AND MINERAL PRODUCTS

MONACO - ANIMAL HEALTH

Food and Agriculture Organization of the United Nations (FAO), Via delle Terme di Caracalla, 00100, Rome, Italy (Telephone Number in U.S. (202) 653-2400); *Animal Health Yearbook.*

MONACO - AREA AND DENSITY OF POPULATION

Central Intelligence Agency, Washington, D.C. 20505 (703) 482-1100, www.cia.gov; *The World Factbook.*

Euromonitor International, Inc., 122 South Michigan Avenue, Suite 1200, Chicago, Illinois 60603 (800) 577-EURO; *The World Economic Factbook.*

Europa Publications Limited, 18 Bedford Square, London, WC1B 3JN, England; *The Europa World Year Book.*

Food and Agricultural Organization of the United Nations (FAO), Via delle Terme di Caracalla, 00100 Rome, Italy (Telephone Number in U.S. (202) 653-2400); *The State of Food and Agriculture.*

M.E. Sharpe, 80 Business Park Drive, Armonk, New York 10504 (800) 541-6563; *The Illustrated Book of World Rankings.*

St. Martin's Press, Inc., 175 Fifth Avenue, New York, New York 10010 (800) 221-7945; *The Statesman's Year-Book.*

Statistical Office of the United Nations, Publishing Service, New York, New York 10017 (800) 253-9646; *Statistical Yearbook;* and *Trends in Europe and North America: The Statistical Yearbook of the Economic Commission for Europe.*

United Nations Educational, Scientific and Cultural Organization (UNESCO), 7 Place de Fontenoy, F-75700 Paris, France (Telephone Number in U.S. (212) 963-5981); *Statistical Yearbook.*

MONACO - BANKING

Euromonitor International, Inc., 122 South Michigan Avenue, Suite 1200, Chicago, Illinois 60603 (800) 577-EURO; *World Marketing Data and Statistics.*

M.E. Sharpe, 80 Business Park Drive, Armonk, New York 10504 (800) 541-6563; *The Illustrated Book of World Rankings.*

St. Martin's Press, Inc., 175 Fifth Avenue, New York, New York 10010 (800) 221-7945; *The Statesman's Year-Book.*

MONACO - BARLEY PRODUCTION - See MONACO - CROPS

MONACO - BEER PRODUCTION - See MONACO - BEVERAGES

MONACO - BEVERAGES

M.E. Sharpe, 80 Business Park Drive, Armonk, New York 10504 (800) 541-6563; *The Illustrated Book of World Rankings.*

Statistical Office of the United Nations, Publishing Service, New York, New York 10017 (800) 253-9646; *Statistical Yearbook.*

MONACO - BIRTH RATES

Central Intelligence Agency, Washington, D.C. 20505 (703) 482-1100, www.cia.gov; *The World Factbook.*

Euromonitor International, Inc., 122 South Michigan Avenue, Suite 1200, Chicago, Illinois 60603 (800) 577-EURO; *The World Economic Factbook.*

Europa Publications Limited, 18 Bedford Square, London, WC1B 3JN, England; *The Europa World Year Book.*

M.E. Sharpe, 80 Business Park Drive, Armonk, New York 10504 (800) 541-6563; *The Illustrated Book of World Rankings.*

Statistical Office of the United Nations, Publishing Service, New York, New York 10017 (800) 253-9646; *Demographic Yearbook;* and *Statistical Yearbook.*

World Health Organization, Office of Publications, 20 Avenue Appia, CH-1211 Geneva 27, Switzerland (Telephone Number in U.S. (518) 436-9686); *World Health Statistics Annual.*

MONACO - BOOK PRODUCTION

Statistical Office of the United Nations, Publishing Service, New York, New York 10017 (800) 253-9646; *Trends in Europe and North America: The Statistical Yearbook of the Economic Commission for Europe.*

United Nations Educational, Scientific and Cultural Organization (UNESCO), 7 Place de Fontenoy, F-75700 Paris, France (Telephone Number in U.S. (212) 963-5981); *Statistical Yearbook.*

MONACO - BROADCASTING

Billboard Limited, Post Office Box 9027, 1006 AA Amsterdam, The Netherlands (Telephone Number in U.S. (212) 764-7300); *World Radio TV Handbook.*

Central Intelligence Agency, Washington, D.C. 20505 (703) 482-1100, www.cia.gov; *The World Factbook.*

Euromonitor International, Inc., 122 South Michigan Avenue, Suite 1200, Chicago, Illinois 60603 (800) 577-EURO; *World Marketing Data and Statistics.*

M.E. Sharpe, 80 Business Park Drive, Armonk, New York 10504 (800) 541-6563; *The Illustrated Book of World Rankings.*

St. Martin's Press, Inc., 175 Fifth Avenue, New York, New York 10010 (800) 221-7945; *The Statesman's Year-Book.*

Statistical Office of the United Nations, Publishing Service, New York, New York 10017 (800) 253-9646; *Trends in Europe and*

North America: The Statistical Yearbook of the Economic Commission for Europe.

United Nations Educational, Scientific and Cultural Organization (UNESCO), 7 Place de Fontenoy, F-75700 Paris, France (Telephone Number in U.S. (212) 963-5981); *Statistical Yearbook.*

MONACO - BUDGET

Central Intelligence Agency, Washington, D.C. 20505 (703) 482-1100, www.cia.gov; *The World Factbook.*

MONACO - CALORIE SUPPLY

Food and Agricultural Organization of the United Nations (FAO), Via delle Terme di Caracalla, 00100 Rome, Italy (Telephone Number in U.S. (202) 653-2400); *The State of Food and Agriculture.*

MONACO - CATTLE - See MONACO - LIVESTOCK AND POULTRY

MONACO - CEMENT PRODUCTION - See MONACO - MINING AND MINERAL PRODUCTS

MONACO - CIGARETTE PRODUCTION - See MONACO - TOBACCO PRODUCTION

MONACO - CLIMATE

M.E. Sharpe, 80 Business Park Drive, Armonk, New York 10504 (800) 541-6563; *The Illustrated Book of World Rankings.*

St. Martin's Press, Inc., 175 Fifth Avenue, New York, New York 10010 (800) 221-7945; *The Statesman's Year-Book.*

MONACO - COAL PRODUCTION - See MONACO - MINING AND MINERAL PRODUCTS

MONACO - COFFEE PRODUCTION - See MONACO - CROPS

MONACO - COMMERCE

St. Martin's Press, Inc., 175 Fifth Avenue, New York, New York 10010 (800) 221-7945; *The Statesman's Year-Book.*

MONACO - CONSTRUCTION INDUSTRY

M.E. Sharpe, 80 Business Park Drive, Armonk, New York 10504 (800) 541-6563; *The Illustrated Book of World Rankings.*

Statistical Office of the United Nations, Publishing Service, New York, New York 10017 (800) 253-9646; *Statistical Yearbook.*

MONACO - CONSUMER PRICE INDEX

Statistical Office of the United Nations, Publishing Service, New York, New York 10017 (800) 253-9646; *Statistical Yearbook;*

and *Trends in Europe and North America: The Statistical Yearbook of the Economic Commission for Europe.*

MONACO - CONSUMER PRICES

Euromonitor International, Inc., 122 South Michigan Avenue, Suite 1200, Chicago, Illinois 60603 (800) 577-EURO; *World Marketing Data and Statistics.*

MONACO - COPPER PRODUCTION AND CONSUMPTION - See MONACO - MINING AND MINERAL PRODUCTS

MONACO - CORN PRODUCTION - See MONACO - CROPS

MONACO - COTTON PRODUCTION - See MONACO - CROPS

MONACO - CRIME

International Criminal Police Organization (INTERPOL), 50 qui Achille Lignon, F-69006 Lyon, France; *International Crime Statistics.*

Statistical Office of the United Nations, Publishing Service, New York, New York 10017 (800) 253-9646; *Trends in Europe and North America: The Statistical Yearbook of the Economic Commission for Europe.*

Yale University Press, Yale Station, New Haven, Connecticut 06520 (800) 987-7323; *Violence and Crime in Cross-National Perspective.*

MONACO - CROPS

Food and Agricultural Organization of the United Nations (FAO), Via delle Terme di Caracalla, 00100 Rome, Italy (Telephone Number in U.S. (202) 653-2400); *Production Yearbook; The State of Food and Agriculture;* and *Trade Yearbook.*

M.E. Sharpe, 80 Business Park Drive, Armonk, New York 10504 (800) 541-6563; *The Illustrated Book of World Rankings.*

Statistical Office of the United Nations, Publishing Service, New York, New York 10017 (800) 253-9646; *Industrial Commodity Statistics Yearbook;* and *Statistical Yearbook.*

MONACO - DAIRY PRODUCTS

Food and Agricultural Organization of the United Nations (FAO), Via delle Terme di Caracalla, 00100 Rome, Italy (Telephone Number in U.S. (202) 653-2400); *Production Yearbook; The State of Food and Agriculture;* and *Trade Yearbook.*

M.E. Sharpe, 80 Business Park Drive, Armonk, New York 10504 (800) 541-6563; *The Illustrated Book of World Rankings.*

Statistical Office of the United Nations,

Publishing Service, New York, New York 10017 (800) 253-9646; *Industrial Commodity Statistics Yearbook;* and *Statistical Yearbook.*

MONACO - DEATH RATES - See MONACO - MORTALITY

MONACO - DEMOGRAPHY

Euromonitor International, Inc., 122 South Michigan Avenue, Suite 1200, Chicago, Illinois 60603 (800) 577-EURO; *The World Economic Factbook;* and *World Marketing Data and Statistics.*

M.E. Sharpe, 80 Business Park Drive, Armonk, New York 10504 (800) 541-6563; *The Illustrated Book of World Rankings.*

Statistical Office of the United Nations, Publishing Service, New York, New York 10017 (800) 253-9646; *Demographic Yearbook.*

MONACO - DIAMOND PRODUCTION - See MONACO - MINING AND MINERAL PRODUCTS

MONACO - DIVORCE RATES

M.E. Sharpe, 80 Business Park Drive, Armonk, New York 10504 (800) 541-6563; *The Illustrated Book of World Rankings.*

Statistical Office of the United Nations, Publishing Service, New York, New York 10017 (800) 253-9646; *Demographic Yearbook; Trends in Europe and North America: The Statistical Yearbook of the Economic Commission for Europe;* and *Statistical Yearbook.*

MONACO - ECONOMY

Central Intelligence Agency, Washington, D.C. 20505 (703) 482-1100, www.cia.gov; *The World Factbook.*

Euromonitor International, Inc., 122 South Michigan Avenue, Suite 1200, Chicago, Illinois 60603 (800) 577-EURO; *The World Economic Factbook;* and *World Marketing Data and Statistics.*

M.E. Sharpe, 80 Business Park Drive, Armonk, New York 10504 (800) 541-6563; *The Illustrated Book of World Rankings.*

St. Martin's Press, Inc., 175 Fifth Avenue, New York, New York 10010 (800) 221-7945; *The Statesman's Year-Book.*

Statistical Office of the United Nations, Publishing Service, New York, New York 10017 (800) 253-9646; *World Statistics Pocketbook.*

MONACO - EDUCATION

Euromonitor International, Inc., 122

South Michigan Avenue, Suite 1200, Chicago, Illinois 60603 (800) 577-EURO; *World Marketing Data and Statistics.*

Europa Publications Limited, 18 Bedford Square, London, WC1B 3JN, England; *The Europa World Year Book.*

M.E. Sharpe, 80 Business Park Drive, Armonk, New York 10504 (800) 541-6563; *The Illustrated Book of World Rankings.*

St. Martin's Press, Inc., 175 Fifth Avenue, New York, New York 10010 (800) 221-7945; *The Statesman's Year-Book.*

Statistical Office of the United Nations, Publishing Service, New York, New York 10017 (800) 253-9646; *Trends in Europe and North America: The Statistical Yearbook of the Economic Commission for Europe.*

United Nations Educational, Scientific and Cultural Organization (UNESCO), 7 Place de Fontenoy, F-75700 Paris, France (Telephone Number in U.S. (212) 963-5981); *Statistical Yearbook.*

MONACO - EGG PRODUCTION AND CONSUMPTION - See MONACO - DAIRY PRODUCTS

MONACO - ELECTRICITY

Central Intelligence Agency, Washington, D.C. 20505 (703) 482-1100, www.cia.gov; *The World Factbook.*

M.E. Sharpe, 80 Business Park Drive, Armonk, New York 10504 (800) 541-6563; *The Illustrated Book of World Rankings.*

Statistical Office of the United Nations, Publishing Service, New York, New York 10017 (800) 253-9646; *Energy Statistics Yearbook; Trends in Europe and North America: The Statistical Yearbook of the Economic Commission for Europe;* and *Statistical Yearbook.*

MONACO - EMPLOYMENT

M.E. Sharpe, 80 Business Park Drive, Armonk, New York 10504 (800) 541-6563; *The Illustrated Book of World Rankings.*

Statistical Office of the United Nations, Publishing Service, New York, New York 10017 (800) 253-9646; *Statistical Yearbook;* and *Trends in Europe and North America: The Statistical Yearbook of the Economic Commission for Europe.*

MONACO - ENERGY

Euromonitor International, Inc., 122 South Michigan Avenue, Suite 1200, Chicago, Illinois 60603 (800) 577-EURO; *The World Economic Factbook;* and *World Marketing Data and Statistics.*

Food and Agricultural Organization of the United Nations (FAO), Via delle Terme di Caracalla, 00100 Rome, Italy (Telephone Number in U.S. (202) 653-2400); *The State of Food and Agriculture.*

M.E. Sharpe, 80 Business Park Drive, Armonk, New York 10504 (800) 541-6563; *The Illustrated Book of World Rankings.*

Statistical Office of the United Nations, Publishing Service, New York, New York 10017 (800) 253-9646; *Energy Statistics Yearbook; Trends in Europe and North America: The Statistical Yearbook of the Economic Commission for Europe; World Statistics Pocketbook;* and *Statistical Yearbook.*

MONACO - ENVIRONMENT

Statistical Office of the United Nations, Publishing Service, New York, New York 10017 (800) 253-9646; *Statistical Yearbook; World Statistics Pocketbook;* and *Trends in Europe and North America: The Statistical Yearbook of the Economic Commission for Europe.*

MONACO - EXCHANGE RATES

Central Intelligence Agency, Washington, D.C. 20505 (703) 482-1100, www.cia.gov; *The World Factbook.*

Euromonitor International, Inc., 122 South Michigan Avenue, Suite 1200, Chicago, Illinois 60603 (800) 577-EURO; *The World Economic Factbook.*

Europa Publications Limited, 18 Bedford Square, London, WC1B 3JN, England; *The Europa World Year Book.*

Statistical Office of the United Nations, Publishing Service, New York, New York 10017 (800) 253-9646; *Statistical Yearbook; World Statistics Pocketbook;* and *Trends in Europe and North America: The Statistical Yearbook of the Economic Commission for Europe.*

MONACO - EXPORTS

Central Intelligence Agency, Washington, D.C. 20505 (703) 482-1100, www.cia.gov; *The World Factbook.*

Euromonitor International, Inc., 122 South Michigan Avenue, Suite 1200, Chicago, Illinois 60603 (800) 577-EURO; *The World Economic Factbook.*

Europa Publications Limited, 18 Bedford Square, London, WC1B 3JN, England; *The Europa World Year Book.*

Food and Agricultural Organization of the United Nations (FAO), Via delle Terme di Caracalla, 00100 Rome, Italy (Telephone Number in U.S. (202) 653-2400); *The State of Food and Agriculture.*

Statistical Office of the United Nations, Publishing Service, New York, New York 10017 (800) 253-9646; *International Trade Statistics Yearbook;* and *Trends in Europe and North America: The Statistical Yearbook of the Economic Commission for Europe.*

MONACO - EXTERNAL TRADE

Euromonitor International, Inc., 122 South Michigan Avenue, Suite 1200, Chicago, Illinois 60603 (800) 577-EURO; *World Marketing Data and Statistics.*

Food and Agricultural Organization of the United Nations (FAO), Via delle Terme di Caracalla, 00100 Rome, Italy (Telephone Number in U.S. (202) 653-2400); *The State of Food and Agriculture;* and *Trade Yearbook.*

Statistical Office of the United Nations, Publishing Service, New York, New York 10017 (800) 253-9646; *Statistical Yearbook.*

MONACO - FARM CROPS - See MONACO - CROPS

MONACO - FERTILITY RATES

Central Intelligence Agency, Washington, D.C. 20505 (703) 482-1100, www.cia.gov; *The World Factbook.*

M.E. Sharpe, 80 Business Park Drive, Armonk, New York 10504 (800) 541-6563; *The Illustrated Book of World Rankings.*

Statistical Office of the United Nations, Publishing Service, New York, New York 10017 (800) 253-9646; *Trends in Europe and North America: The Statistical Yearbook of the Economic Commission for Europe.*

MONACO - FERTILIZER

Food and Agriculture Organization of the United Nations (FAO), Via delle Terme de Caracalla, 00100, Rome, Italy (Telephone Number in U.S. (202) 653-2400); *Fertilizer Yearbook;* and *The State of Food and Agriculture.*

Statistical Office of the United Nations, Publishing Service, New York, New York 10017 (800) 253-9646; *Industrial Commodity Statistics Yearbook;* and *Statistical Yearbook.*

MONACO - FETAL MORTALITY - See MONACO - MORTALITY

MONACO - FINANCE

Europa Publications Limited, 18 Bedford Square, London, WC1B 3JN, England; *The Europa World Year Book.*

M.E. Sharpe, 80 Business Park Drive, Armonk, New York 10504 (800) 541-6563; *The Illustrated Book of World Rankings*.

St. Martin's Press, Inc., 175 Fifth Avenue, New York, New York 10010 (800) 221-7945; *The Statesman's Year-Book*.

MONACO - FISHERIES

Food and Agricultural Organization of the United Nations (FAO), Via delle Terme di Caracalla, 00100 Rome, Italy (Telephone Number in U.S. (202) 653-2400); *The State of Food and Agriculture;* and *Yearbook of Fishery Statistics*.

M.E. Sharpe, 80 Business Park Drive, Armonk, New York 10504 (800) 541-6563; *The Illustrated Book of World Rankings*.

Statistical Office of the United Nations, Publishing Service, New York, New York 10017 (800) 253-9646; *Industrial Commodity Statistics Yearbook;* and *Statistical Yearbook*.

MONACO - FOOD

Food and Agricultural Organization of the United Nations (FAO), Via delle Terme di Caracalla, 00100 Rome, Italy (Telephone Number in U.S. (202) 653-2400); *Production Yearbook; The State of Food and Agriculture;* and *Trade Yearbook*.

Statistical Office of the United Nations, Publishing Service, New York, New York 10017 (800) 253-9646; *Industrial Commodity Statistics Yearbook*.

MONACO - FOREIGN TRADE

Euromonitor International, Inc., 122 South Michigan Avenue, Suite 1200, Chicago, Illinois 60603 (800) 577-EURO; *The World Economic Factbook*.

Europa Publications Limited, 18 Bedford Square, London, WC1B 3JN, England; *The Europa World Year Book*.

Food and Agricultural Organization of the United Nations (FAO), Via delle Terme di Caracalla, 00100 Rome, Italy (Telephone Number in U.S. (202) 653-2400); *The State of Food and Agriculture;* and *Trade Yearbook*.

M.E. Sharpe, 80 Business Park Drive, Armonk, New York 10504 (800) 541-6563; *The Illustrated Book of World Rankings*.

Statistical Office of the United Nations, Publishing Service, New York, New York 10017 (800) 253-9646; *International Trade Statistics Yearbook;* and *Statistical Yearbook*.

MONACO - FORESTRY AND FOREST PRODUCTS

Food and Agricultural Organization of the United Nations (FAO), Via delle Terme di Caracalla, 00100 Rome, Italy (Telephone Number in U.S. (202) 653-2400); *The State of Food and Agriculture;* and *Yearbook of Forest Products*.

M.E. Sharpe, 80 Business Park Drive, Armonk, New York 10504 (800) 541-6563; *The Illustrated Book of World Rankings*.

Statistical Office of the United Nations, Publishing Service, New York, New York 10017 (800) 253-9646; *Industrial Commodity Statistics Yearbook; Trends in Europe and North America: The Statistical Yearbook of the Economic Commission for Europe;* and *Statistical Yearbook*.

United Nations Educational, Scientific and Cultural Organization (UNESCO), 7 Place de Fontenoy, F-75700 Paris, France (Telephone Number in U.S. (212) 963-5981); *Statistical Yearbook*.

MONACO - GAS PRODUCTION - See MONACO - MINING AND MINERAL PRODUCTS

MONACO - GENERAL MORTALITY - See MONACO - MORTALITY

MONACO - GEOGRAPHIC DATA

M.E. Sharpe, 80 Business Park Drive, Armonk, New York 10504 (800) 541-6563; *The Illustrated Book of World Rankings*.

MONACO - GOLD PRODUCTION AND CONSUMPTION - See MONACO - MINING AND MINERAL PRODUCTS

MONACO - GOVERNMENT

Central Intelligence Agency, Washington, D.C. 20505 (703) 482-1100, www.cia.gov; *The World Factbook*.

Europa Publications Limited, 18 Bedford Square, London, WC1B 3JN, England; *The Europa World Year Book*.

St. Martin's Press, Inc., 175 Fifth Avenue, New York, New York 10010 (800) 221-7945; *The Statesman's Year-Book*.

Statistical Office of the United Nations, Publishing Service, New York, New York 10017 (800) 253-9646; *Statistical Yearbook*.

MONACO - GRAIN PRODUCTION - See MONACO - CROPS

MONACO - GROSS DOMESTIC PRODUCT

Euromonitor International, Inc., 122 South Michigan Avenue, Suite 1200, Chicago, Illinois 60603 (800) 577-EURO; *The World Economic Factbook*.

M.E. Sharpe, 80 Business Park Drive,

Armonk, New York 10504 (800) 541-6563; *The Illustrated Book of World Rankings*.

Statistical Office of the United Nations, Publishing Service, New York, New York 10017 (800) 253-9646; *National Accounts Statistics; Trends in Europe and North America: The Statistical Yearbook of the Economic Commission for Europe;* and *Statistical Yearbook*.

MONACO - HEALTH

Euromonitor International, Inc., 122 South Michigan Avenue, Suite 1200, Chicago, Illinois 60603 (800) 577-EURO; *World Marketing Data and Statistics*.

M.E. Sharpe, 80 Business Park Drive, Armonk, New York 10504 (800) 541-6563; *The Illustrated Book of World Rankings*.

St. Martin's Press, Inc., 175 Fifth Avenue, New York, New York 10010 (800) 221-7945; *The Statesman's Year-Book*.

Statistical Office of the United Nations, Publishing Service, New York, New York 10017 (800) 253-9646; *Statistical Yearbook;* and *Trends in Europe and North America: The Statistical Yearbook of the Economic Commission for Europe*.

MONACO - HEALTH AND MEDICAL SERVICES

Statistical Office of the United Nations, Publishing Service, New York, New York 10017 (800) 253-9646; *Statistical Yearbook*.

MONACO - HIGHWAYS

Central Intelligence Agency, Washington, D.C. 20505 (703) 482-1100, www.cia.gov; *The World Factbook*.

St. Martin's Press, Inc., 175 Fifth Avenue, New York, New York 10010 (800) 221-7945; *The Statesman's Year-Book*.

Statistical Office of the United Nations, Publishing Service, New York, New York 10017 (800) 253-9646; *Trends in Europe and North America: The Statistical Yearbook of the Economic Commission for Europe*.

MONACO - HORSES - See MONACO - LIVESTOCK AND POULTRY

MONACO - HOUSING

Euromonitor International, Inc., 122 South Michigan Avenue, Suite 1200, Chicago, Illinois 60603 (800) 577-EURO; *World Marketing Data and Statistics*.

M.E. Sharpe, 80 Business Park Drive, Armonk, New York 10504 (800) 541-6563; *The Illustrated Book of World Rankings*.

Statistical Office of the United Nations,

Publishing Service, New York, New York 10017 (800) 253-9646; *Trends in Europe and North America: The Statistical Yearbook of the Economic Commission for Europe.*

MONACO - ILLITERATE POPULATION

Central Intelligence Agency, Washington, D.C. 20505 (703) 482-1100, www.cia.gov; *The World Factbook.*

Euromonitor International, Inc., 122 South Michigan Avenue, Suite 1200, Chicago, Illinois 60603 (800) 577-EURO; *The World Economic Factbook.*

United Nations Educational, Scientific and Cultural Organization (UNESCO), 7 Place de Fontenoy, F-75700 Paris, France (Telephone Number in U.S. (212) 963-5981); *Statistical Yearbook.*

MONACO - IMPORTS

Central Intelligence Agency, Washington, D.C. 20505 (703) 482-1100, www.cia.gov; *The World Factbook.*

Euromonitor International, Inc., 122 South Michigan Avenue, Suite 1200, Chicago, Illinois 60603 (800) 577-EURO; *The World Economic Factbook.*

Europa Publications Limited, 18 Bedford Square, London, WC1B 3JN, England; *The Europa World Year Book.*

Food and Agricultural Organization of the United Nations (FAO), Via delle Terme di Caracalla, 00100 Rome, Italy (Telephone Number in U.S. (202) 653-2400); *The State of Food and Agriculture.*

Statistical Office of the United Nations, Publishing Service, New York, New York 10017 (800) 253-9646; *International Trade Statistics Yearbook;* and *Trends in Europe and North America: The Statistical Yearbook of the Economic Commission for Europe.*

MONACO - INDUSTRY

Central Intelligence Agency, Washington, D.C. 20505 (703) 482-1100, www.cia.gov; *The World Factbook.*

Euromonitor International, Inc., 122 South Michigan Avenue, Suite 1200, Chicago, Illinois 60603 (800) 577-EURO; *The World Economic Factbook;* and *World Marketing Data and Statistics.*

M.E. Sharpe, 80 Business Park Drive, Armonk, New York 10504 (800) 541-6563; *The Illustrated Book of World Rankings.*

St. Martin's Press, Inc., 175 Fifth Avenue, New York, New York 10010 (800) 221-7945; *The Statesman's Year-Book.*

Statistical Office of the United Nations,

Publishing Service, New York, New York 10017 (800) 253-9646; *Industrial Commodity Statistics Yearbook; Trends in Europe and North America: The Statistical Yearbook of the Economic Commission for Europe;* and *Statistical Yearbook.*

World Intellectual Property Organization, 34 Chemin des Colombettes, CH-1211 Geneva 20, Switzerland; *Industrial Property Statistics.*

MONACO - INFANT AND MATERNAL MORTALITY - See MONACO - MORTALITY

MONACO - INTERNAL TRADE

Statistical Office of the United Nations, Publishing Service, New York, New York 10017 (800) 253-9646; *Statistical Yearbook.*

MONACO - IRON ORE PRODUCTION AND CONSUMPTION - See MONACO - MINING AND MINERAL PRODUCTS

MONACO - LABOR

Central Intelligence Agency, Washington, D.C. 20505 (703) 482-1100, www.cia.gov; *The World Factbook.*

Euromonitor International, Inc., 122 South Michigan Avenue, Suite 1200, Chicago, Illinois 60603 (800) 577-EURO; *World Marketing Data and Statistics.*

Food and Agricultural Organization of the United Nations (FAO), Via delle Terme di Caracalla, 00100 Rome, Italy (Telephone Number in U.S. (202) 653-2400); *The State of Food and Agriculture.*

M.E. Sharpe, 80 Business Park Drive, Armonk, New York 10504 (800) 541-6563; *The Illustrated Book of World Rankings.*

St. Martin's Press, Inc., 175 Fifth Avenue, New York, New York 10010 (800) 221-7945; *The Statesman's Year-Book.*

Statistical Office of the United Nations, Publishing Service, New York, New York 10017 (800) 253-9646; *Statistical Yearbook.*

MONACO - LAND USE

Central Intelligence Agency, Washington, D.C. 20505 (703) 482-1100, www.cia.gov; *The World Factbook.*

Food and Agricultural Organization of the United Nations (FAO), Via delle Terme di Caracalla, 00100 Rome, Italy (Telephone Number in U.S. (202) 653-2400); *Production Yearbook.*

MONACO - LIBRARIES

M.E. Sharpe, 80 Business Park Drive, Armonk, New York 10504 (800) 541-6563; *The Illustrated Book of World Rankings.*

Statistical Office of the United Nations, Publishing Service, New York, New York 10017 (800) 253-9646; *Trends in Europe and North America: The Statistical Yearbook of the Economic Commission for Europe.*

United Nations Educational, Scientific and Cultural Organization (UNESCO), 7 Place de Fontenoy, F-75700 Paris, France (Telephone Number in U.S. (212) 963-5981); *Statistical Yearbook.*

MONACO - LIFE EXPECTANCY

Central Intelligence Agency, Washington, D.C. 20505 (703) 482-1100, www.cia.gov; *The World Factbook.*

Euromonitor International, Inc., 122 South Michigan Avenue, Suite 1200, Chicago, Illinois 60603 (800) 577-EURO; *The World Economic Factbook.*

Statistical Office of the United Nations, Publishing Service, New York, New York 10017 (800) 253-9646; *Demographic Yearbook; World Statistics Pocketbook;* and *Trends in Europe and North America: The Statistical Yearbook of the Economic Commission for Europe.*

MONACO - LITERACY RATE

Euromonitor International, Inc., 122 South Michigan Avenue, Suite 1200, Chicago, Illinois 60603 (800) 577-EURO; *World Marketing Data and Statistics.*

MONACO - LIVESTOCK AND POULTRY

Food and Agricultural Organization of the United Nations (FAO), Via delle Terme di Caracalla, 00100 Rome, Italy (Telephone Number in U.S. (202) 653-2400); *Production Yearbook; The State of Food and Agriculture;* and *Trade Yearbook.*

M.E. Sharpe, 80 Business Park Drive, Armonk, New York 10504 (800) 541-6563; *The Illustrated Book of World Rankings.*

Statistical Office of the United Nations, Publishing Service, New York, New York 10017 (800) 253-9646; *Industrial Commodity Statistics Yearbook;* and *Statistical Yearbook.*

MONACO - MACHINERY

Statistical Office of the United Nations, Publishing Service, New York, New York 10017 (800) 253-9646; *Industrial Commodity Statistics Yearbook.*

MONACO - MAIL - NUMBER OF PIECES SENT OR RECEIVED

Statistical Office of the United Nations, Publishing Service, New York, New York 10017 (800) 253-9646; *Statistical Yearbook.*

MONACO - MANUFACTURING

M.E. Sharpe, 80 Business Park Drive, Armonk, New York 10504 (800) 541-6563; *The Illustrated Book of World Rankings.*

Statistical Office of the United Nations, Publishing Service, New York, New York 10017 (800) 253-9646; *Industrial Commodity Statistics Yearbook;* and *Statistical Yearbook.*

MONACO - MARRIAGE RATES

Europa Publications Limited, 18 Bedford Square, London, WC1B 3JN, England; *The Europa World Year Book.*

M.E. Sharpe, 80 Business Park Drive, Armonk, New York 10504 (800) 541-6563; *The Illustrated Book of World Rankings.*

Statistical Office of the United Nations, Publishing Service, New York, New York 10017 (800) 253-9646; *Demographic Yearbook; Trends in Europe and North America: The Statistical Yearbook of the Economic Commission for Europe;* and *Statistical Yearbook.*

MONACO - MEAT PRODUCTION - See MONACO - LIVESTOCK AND POULTRY

MONACO - MERCHANT SHIPPING

St. Martin's Press, Inc., 175 Fifth Avenue, New York, New York 10010 (800) 221-7945; *The Statesman's Year-Book.*

Statistical Office of the United Nations, Publishing Service, New York, New York 10017 (800) 253-9646; *Statistical Yearbook.*

MONACO - MILK PRODUCTION - See MONACO - DAIRY PRODUCTS

MONACO - MILITARY

Central Intelligence Agency, Washington, D.C. 20505 (703) 482-1100, www.cia.gov; *The World Factbook.*

Euromonitor International, Inc., 122 South Michigan Avenue, Suite 1200, Chicago, Illinois 60603 (800) 577-EURO; *World Marketing Data and Statistics.*

MONACO - MINING AND MINERAL PRODUCTS

M.E. Sharpe, 80 Business Park Drive, Armonk, New York 10504 (800) 541-6563; *The Illustrated Book of World Rankings.*

Statistical Office of the United Nations, Publishing Service, New York, New York 10017 (800) 253-9646; *Energy Statistics Yearbook; Industrial Commodity Statistics Yearbook;* and *Statistical Yearbook.*

MONACO - MONUMENTS AND HISTORICAL

SITES

United Nations Educational, Scientific and Cultural Organization (UNESCO), 7 Place de Fontenoy, F-75700 Paris, France (Telephone Number in U.S. (212) 963-5981); *Statistical Yearbook.*

MONACO - MORTALITY

Central Intelligence Agency, Washington, D.C. 20505 (703) 482-1100, www.cia.gov; *The World Factbook.*

Euromonitor International, Inc., 122 South Michigan Avenue, Suite 1200, Chicago, Illinois 60603 (800) 577-EURO; *The World Economic Factbook.*

Europa Publications Limited, 18 Bedford Square, London, WC1B 3JN, England; *The Europa World Year Book.*

Statistical Office of the United Nations, Publishing Service, New York, New York 10017 (800) 253-9646; *Demographic Yearbook; Trends in Europe and North America: The Statistical Yearbook of the Economic Commission for Europe; World Statistics Pocketbook;* and *Statistical Yearbook.*

World Health Organization, Office of Publications, 20 Avenue Appia, CH-1211 Geneva 27, Switzerland (Telephone Number in U.S. (518) 436-9686); *World Health Statistics Annual.*

MONACO - MOTION PICTURES

St. Martin's Press, Inc., 175 Fifth Avenue, New York, New York 10010 (800) 221-7945; *The Statesman's Year-Book.*

Statistical Office of the United Nations, Publishing Service, New York, New York 10017 (800) 253-9646; *Statistical Yearbook.*

United Nations Educational, Scientific and Cultural Organization (UNESCO), 7 Place de Fontenoy, F-75700 Paris, France (Telephone Number in U.S. (212) 963-5981); *Statistical Yearbook.*

MONACO - MOTOR VEHICLE PRODUCTION

Europa Publications Limited, 18 Bedford Square, London, WC1B 3JN, England; *The Europa World Year Book.*

Statistical Office of the United Nations, Publishing Service, New York, New York 10017 (800) 253-9646; *Statistical Yearbook.*

MONACO - MUSEUMS

M.E. Sharpe, 80 Business Park Drive, Armonk, New York 10504 (800) 541-6563; *The Illustrated Book of World Rankings.*

United Nations Educational, Scientific and Cultural Organization (UNESCO), 7 Place de Fontenoy, F-75700 Paris, France (Telephone Number in U.S. (212) 963-5981); *Statistical Yearbook.*

MONACO - NATALITY - See MONACO - BIRTH RATES

MONACO - NATIONAL ACCOUNTS

Statistical Office of the United Nations, Publishing Service, New York, New York 10017 (800) 253-9646; *National Accounts Statistics;* and *Statistical Yearbook.*

MONACO - NATIONAL INCOME

M.E. Sharpe, 80 Business Park Drive, Armonk, New York 10504 (800) 541-6563; *The Illustrated Book of World Rankings.*

Statistical Office of the United Nations, Publishing Service, New York, New York 10017 (800) 253-9646; *Statistical Yearbook.*

MONACO - NATIONAL PRODUCT

M.E. Sharpe, 80 Business Park Drive, Armonk, New York 10504 (800) 541-6563; *The Illustrated Book of World Rankings.*

Statistical Office of the United Nations, Publishing Service, New York, New York 10017 (800) 253-9646; *Statistical Yearbook.*

MONACO - NATURAL GAS - PRODUCTION - See MONACO - MINING AND MINERAL PRODUCTS

MONACO - NEWSPAPER PRODUCTION - See MONACO - FORESTRY AND FOREST PRODUCTS

MONACO - PATENTS, TRADEMARKS AND SERVICE MARKS

Statistical Office of the United Nations, Publishing Service, New York, New York 10017 (800) 253-9646; *Statistical Yearbook.*

World Intellectual Property Organization, 34 Chemin des Colombettes, CH-1211 Geneva 20, Switzerland; *Industrial Property Statistics.*

MONACO - PEANUT PRODUCTION - See MONACO - CROPS

MONACO - PERIODICALS

United Nations Educational, Scientific and Cultural Organization (UNESCO), 7 Place de Fontenoy, F-75700 Paris, France (Telephone Number in U.S. (212) 963-5981); *Statistical Yearbook.*

MONACO - PESTICIDE USE

Food and Agricultural Organization of the United Nations (FAO), Via delle Terme

di Caracalla, 00100 Rome, Italy (Telephone Number in U.S. (202) 653-2400); *The State of Food and Agriculture*.

MONACO - PETROLEUM INDUSTRY

Food and Agricultural Organization of the United Nations (FAO), Via delle Terme di Caracalla, 00100 Rome, Italy (Telephone Number in U.S. (202) 653-2400); *The State of Food and Agriculture*.

M.E. Sharpe, 80 Business Park Drive, Armonk, New York 10504 (800) 541-6563; *The Illustrated Book of World Rankings*.

Statistical Office of the United Nations, Publishing Service, New York, New York 10017 (800) 253-9646; *Energy Statistics Yearbook; Industrial Commodity Statistics Yearbook; Trends in Europe and North America: The Statistical Yearbook of the Economic Commission for Europe; and Statistical Yearbook*.

MONACO - PIGS - See MONACO - LIVESTOCK AND POULTRY

MONACO - POPULATION

Central Intelligence Agency, Washington, D.C. 20505 (703) 482-1100, www.cia.gov; *The World Factbook*.

Euromonitor International, Inc., 122 South Michigan Avenue, Suite 1200, Chicago, Illinois 60603 (800) 577-EURO; *The World Economic Factbook*.

Europa Publications Limited, 18 Bedford Square, London, WC1B 3JN, England; *The Europa World Year Book*.

Food and Agricultural Organization of the United Nations (FAO), Via delle Terme di Caracalla, 00100 Rome, Italy (Telephone Number in U.S. (202) 653-2400); *Production Yearbook*.

International Labour Office, I.L.O. Publications, 1828 L Street, NW, Suite 801, Washington, D.C. 20036 (301) 638-3152; *Yearbook of Labour Statistics*.

M.E. Sharpe, 80 Business Park Drive, Armonk, New York 10504 (800) 541-6563; *The Illustrated Book of World Rankings*.

St. Martin's Press, Inc., 175 Fifth Avenue, New York, New York 10010 (800) 221-7945; *The Statesman's Year-Book*.

Statistical Office of the United Nations, Publishing Service, New York, New York 10017 (800) 253-9646; *Demographic Yearbook; Trends in Europe and North America: The Statistical Yearbook of the Economic Commission for Europe; World Statistics Pocketbook; and Statistical Yearbook*.

United Nations Educational, Scientific and Cultural Organization (UNESCO), 7 Place de Fontenoy, F-75700 Paris, France (Telephone Number in U.S. (212) 963-5981); *Statistical Yearbook*.

World Health Organization, Office of Publications, 20 Avenue Appia, CH-1211 Geneva 27, Switzerland (Telephone Number in U.S. (518) 436-9686); *World Health Statistics Annual*.

MONACO - POST OFFICES

M.E. Sharpe, 80 Business Park Drive, Armonk, New York 10504 (800) 541-6563; *The Illustrated Book of World Rankings*.

St. Martin's Press, Inc., 175 Fifth Avenue, New York, New York 10010 (800) 221-7945; *The Statesman's Year-Book*.

Statistical Office of the United Nations, Publishing Service, New York, New York 10017 (800) 253-9646; *Trends in Europe and North America: The Statistical Yearbook of the Economic Commission for Europe*.

MONACO - POTATO PRODUCTION - See MONACO - CROPS

MONACO - PRICES

Food and Agricultural Organization of the United Nations (FAO), Via delle Terme di Caracalla, 00100 Rome, Italy (Telephone Number in U.S. (202) 653-2400); *Production Yearbook; and The State of Food and Agriculture*.

M.E. Sharpe, 80 Business Park Drive, Armonk, New York 10504 (800) 541-6563; *The Illustrated Book of World Rankings*.

MONACO - PRODUCTION

M.E. Sharpe, 80 Business Park Drive, Armonk, New York 10504 (800) 541-6563; *The Illustrated Book of World Rankings*.

MONACO - PUBLIC FINANCE - See MONACO - FINANCE

MONACO - RADIO BROADCASTING - See MONACO - BROADCASTING

MONACO - RADIO RECEIVER PRODUCTION

Statistical Office of the United Nations, Publishing Service, New York, New York 10017 (800) 253-9646; *Statistical Yearbook*.

MONACO - RADIO RECEIVERS

St. Martin's Press, Inc., 175 Fifth Avenue, New York, New York 10010 (800) 221-7945; *The Statesman's Year-Book*.

MONACO - RAILWAYS

St. Martin's Press, Inc., 175 Fifth Avenue, New York, New York 10010 (800) 221-7945; *The Statesman's Year-Book*.

Statistical Office of the United Nations, Publishing Service, New York, New York 10017 (800) 253-9646; *Statistical Yearbook; and Trends in Europe and North America: The Statistical Yearbook of the Economic Commission for Europe*.

MONACO - RELIGION

Central Intelligence Agency, Washington, D.C. 20505 (703) 482-1100, www.cia.gov; *The World Factbook*.

M.E. Sharpe, 80 Business Park Drive, Armonk, New York 10504 (800) 541-6563; *The Illustrated Book of World Rankings*.

St. Martin's Press, Inc., 175 Fifth Avenue, New York, New York 10010 (800) 221-7945; *The Statesman's Year-Book*.

MONACO - RETAIL TRADE

Euromonitor International, Inc., 122 South Michigan Avenue, Suite 1200, Chicago, Illinois 60603 (800) 577-EURO; *World Marketing Data and Statistics*.

Statistical Office of the United Nations, Publishing Service, New York, New York 10017 (800) 253-9646; *Statistical Yearbook*.

MONACO - RICE PRODUCTION - See MONACO - CROPS

MONACO - RUBBER PRODUCTION AND CONSUMPTION

M.E. Sharpe, 80 Business Park Drive, Armonk, New York 10504 (800) 541-6563; *The Illustrated Book of World Rankings*.

Statistical Office of the United Nations, Publishing Service, New York, New York 10017 (800) 253-9646; *Statistical Yearbook*.

MONACO - SCIENTISTS, TECHNICIANS AND ENGINEERS

Statistical Office of the United Nations, Publishing Service, New York, New York 10017 (800) 253-9646; *Statistical Yearbook*.

MONACO - SENIOR CITIZENS

M.E. Sharpe, 80 Business Park Drive, Armonk, New York 10504 (800) 541-6563; *The Illustrated Book of World Rankings*.

MONACO - SHEEP - See MONACO - LIVESTOCK AND POULTRY

MONACO - SILVER PRODUCTION AND CONSUMPTION - See MONACO - MINING AND MINERAL PRODUCTS

MONACO - SOCIAL DATA

M.E. Sharpe, 80 Business Park Drive, Armonk, New York 10504 (800) 541-6563; *The Illustrated Book of World Rankings.*

Statistical Office of the United Nations, Publishing Service, New York, New York 10017 (800) 253-9646; *World Statistics Pocketbook.*

MONACO - STEEL PRODUCTION - See MONACO - MINING AND MINERAL PRODUCTS

MONACO - STOCKS - COMMODITY - MARKET PRICE - INDEX

Food and Agricultural Organization of the United Nations (FAO), Via delle Terme di Caracalla, 00100 Rome, Italy (Telephone Number in U.S. (202) 653-2400); *The State of Food and Agriculture.*

MONACO - SUGAR PRODUCTION AND CONSUMPTION - See MONACO - CROPS

MONACO - TELEGRAPH SERVICE

Statistical Office of the United Nations, Publishing Service, New York, New York 10017 (800) 253-9646; *Statistical Yearbook.*

MONACO - TELEPHONES IN USE

American Telephone and Telegraph Company, 26 Parsippany Road, Whippany, New Jersey 07981 (800) 222-0300; *The World's Telephones.*

Central Intelligence Agency, Washington, D.C. 20505 (703) 482-1100, www.cia.gov; *The World Factbook.*

Europa Publications Limited, 18 Bedford Square, London, WC1B 3JN, England; *The Europa World Year Book.*

St. Martin's Press, Inc., 175 Fifth Avenue, New York, New York 10010 (800) 221-7945; *The Statesman's Year-Book.*

Statistical Office of the United Nations, Publishing Service, New York, New York 10017 (800) 253-9646; *Statistical Yearbook; World Statistics Pocketbook;* and *Trends in Europe and North America: The Statistical Yearbook of the Economic Commission for Europe.*

MONACO - TELEVISION BROADCASTING - See MONACO - BROADCASTING

MONACO - TEXTILE INDUSTRY

M.E. Sharpe, 80 Business Park Drive, Armonk, New York 10504 (800) 541-6563; *The Illustrated Book of World Rankings.*

Statistical Office of the United Nations, Publishing Service, New York, New York 10017 (800) 253-9646; *Industrial Commodity*

Statistics Yearbook; and *Statistical Yearbook.*

MONACO - THEATRE

United Nations Educational, Scientific and Cultural Organization (UNESCO), 7 Place de Fontenoy, F-75700 Paris, France (Telephone Number in U.S. (212) 963-5981); *Statistical Yearbook.*

MONACO - TIRE (MOTOR VEHICLE) PRODUCTION

Statistical Office of the United Nations, Publishing Service, New York, New York 10017 (800) 253-9646; *Statistical Yearbook.*

MONACO - TOBACCO PRODUCTION

M.E. Sharpe, 80 Business Park Drive, Armonk, New York 10504 (800) 541-6563; *The Illustrated Book of World Rankings.*

Statistical Office of the United Nations, Publishing Service, New York, New York 10017 (800) 253-9646; *Statistical Yearbook.*

MONACO - TOURISM

Euromonitor International, Inc., 122 South Michigan Avenue, Suite 1200, Chicago, Illinois 60603 (800) 577-EURO; *The World Economic Factbook;* and *World Marketing Data and Statistics.*

Europa Publications Limited, 18 Bedford Square, London, WC1B 3JN, England; *The Europa World Year Book.*

M.E. Sharpe, 80 Business Park Drive, Armonk, New York 10504 (800) 541-6563; *The Illustrated Book of World Rankings.*

St. Martin's Press, Inc., 175 Fifth Avenue, New York, New York 10010 (800) 221-7945; *The Statesman's Year-Book.*

Statistical Office of the United Nations, Publishing Service, New York, New York 10017 (800) 253-9646; *Statistical Yearbook;* and *Trends in Europe and North America: The Statistical Yearbook of the Economic Commission for Europe.*

World Tourism Organization, Calle Capitan Haya 42, E-28020 Madrid, Spain; *Yearbook of Tourism Statistics.*

MONACO - TRADE - See MONACO - FOREIGN TRADE

MONACO - TRADEMARKS AND SERVICE MARKS - See MONACO - PATENTS, TRADEMARKS AND SERVICE MARKS

MONACO - TRANSPORTATION AND COMMUNICATIONS

Central Intelligence Agency, Washington, D.C. 20505 (703) 482-1100,

www.cia.gov; *The World Factbook.*

Euromonitor International, Inc., 122 South Michigan Avenue, Suite 1200, Chicago, Illinois 60603 (800) 577-EURO; *World Marketing Data and Statistics.*

Europa Publications Limited, 18 Bedford Square, London, WC1B 3JN, England; *The Europa World Year Book.*

M.E. Sharpe, 80 Business Park Drive, Armonk, New York 10504 (800) 541-6563; *The Illustrated Book of World Rankings.*

St. Martin's Press, Inc., 175 Fifth Avenue, New York, New York 10010 (800) 221-7945; *The Statesman's Year-Book.*

Statistical Office of the United Nations, Publishing Service, New York, New York 10017 (800) 253-9646; *Trends in Europe and North America: The Statistical Yearbook of the Economic Commission for Europe.*

MONACO - UNEMPLOYMENT

Central Intelligence Agency, Washington, D.C. 20505 (703) 482-1100, www.cia.gov; *The World Factbook.*

Statistical Office of the United Nations, Publishing Service, New York, New York 10017 (800) 253-9646; *Statistical Yearbook;* and *Trends in Europe and North America: The Statistical Yearbook of the Economic Commission for Europe.*

MONACO - VITAL STATISTICS

Statistical Office of the United Nations, Publishing Service, New York, New York 10017 (800) 253-9646; *Statistical Yearbook.*

World Health Organization, Office of Publications, 20 Avenue Appia, CH-1211 Geneva 27, Switzerland (Telephone Number in U.S. (518) 436-9686); *World Health Statistics Annual.*

MONACO - WAGES

Statistical Office of the United Nations, Publishing Service, New York, New York 10017 (800) 253-9646; *Statistical Yearbook.*

MONACO - WEATHER - See MONACO - CLIMATE

MONACO - WHEAT PRODUCTION - See MONACO - CROPS

MONACO - WHOLESALE PRICES

Statistical Office of the United Nations, Publishing Service, New York, New York 10017 (800) 253-9646; *Statistical Yearbook.*

MONACO - WHOLESALE TRADE

Statistical Office of the United Nations,

Publishing Service, New York, New York 10017 (800) 253-9646; *Statistical Yearbook.*

MONACO - WINE PRODUCTION - See MONACO - BEVERAGES

MONACO - WOOL PRODUCTION - See MONACO - TEXTILE INDUSTRY

MONACO - ZOOS AND BOTANICAL GARDENS

United Nations Educational, Scientific and Cultural Organization (UNESCO), 7 Place de Fontenoy, F-75700 Paris, France (Telephone Number in U.S. (212) 963-5981); *Statistical Yearbook.*

MONETARY SYSTEM AND BANKS - FLOW OF FUNDS

Board of Governors of the Federal Reserve System, Twentieth Street and Constitution Avenue, NW, Washington, D.C. 20551 (202) 452-3000, www.bog.frb.fed.us; *Flow of Funds Accounts.*

MONEY MARKET ACCOUNTS - FUNDS

Board of Governors of the Federal Reserve System, Twentieth Street and Constitution Avenue, NW, Washington, D.C. 20551 (202) 452-3000, www.bog.frb.fed.us; *Flow of Funds Accounts.*

MONEY MARKET ACCOUNTS - FUNDS - FAMILIES USING

Board of Governors of the Federal Reserve System, Twentieth Street and Constitution Avenue, NW, Washington, D.C. 20551 (202) 452-3000, www.bog.frb.fed.us; *Flow of Funds Accounts;* and *Federal Reserve Bulletin.*

MONEY MARKET RATES

Board of Governors of the Federal Reserve System, Twentieth Street and Constitution Avenue, NW, Washington, D.C. 20551 (202) 452-3000, www.bog.frb.fed.us; *Federal Reserve Bulletin;* and *Annual Statistical Digest.*

MONEY SUPPLY - STOCK

Board of Governors of the Federal Reserve System, Twentieth Street and Constitution Avenue, NW, Washington, D.C. 20551 (202) 452-3000, www.bog.frb.fed.us; *Federal Reserve Bulletin;* and *Money Stock, Liquid Assets, and Debt Measures, Federal Reserve Statistical Release.*

Mongolia - National Statistical Office

Central Statistical Office, Ulan Bator, Mongolia.

Mongolia - Primary Statistics Source

Central Statistical Office, Ulan Bator, Mongolia; *National Economy of the MPR for 60 Years.*

MONGOLIA - AGRICULTURE

Economist Intelligence Unit, 111 West 57th Street, New York, New York 10019 (800) 938-4685; *Mongolia Country Report.*

Euromonitor International, Inc., 122 South Michigan Avenue, Suite 1200, Chicago, Illinois 60603 (800) 577-EURO; *World Marketing Data and Statistics.*

Europa Publications Limited, 18 Bedford Square, London, WC1B 3JN, England; *The Europa World Year Book.*

Food and Agricultural Organization of the United Nations (FAO), Via delle Terme di Caracalla, 00100 Rome, Italy (Telephone Number in U.S. (202) 653-2400); *Production Yearbook; The State of Food and Agriculture; The State of Food and Agriculture;* and *Trade Yearbook.*

M.E. Sharpe, 80 Business Park Drive, Armonk, New York 10504 (800) 541-6563; *The Illustrated Book of World Rankings.*

St. Martin's Press, Inc., 175 Fifth Avenue, New York, New York 10010 (800) 221-7945; *The Statesman's Year-Book.*

Statistical Office of the United Nations, Publishing Service, New York, New York 10017 (800) 253-9646; *Asia-Pacific in Figures; Statistical Yearbook;* and *Statistical Yearbook for Asia and the Pacific.*

United Nations Conference on Trade and Development, Central Statistical Service, Palais des Nations, Geneva, Switzerland (Telephone in U.S. (800) 253-9646); *UNCTAD Commodity Yearbook.*

MONGOLIA - AIRLINE SERVICE

The Economist Intelligence Unit (Asia) Limited, 10th Floor, Luk Kwok Centre, 72 Gloucester Road, Wanchai, Hong Kong (Phone Number in U.S. (800) 938-4685); *Asian Market Atlas.*

Europa Publications Limited, 18 Bedford Square, London, WC1B 3JN, England; *The Europa World Year Book.*

M.E. Sharpe, 80 Business Park Drive, Armonk, New York 10504 (800) 541-6563; *The Illustrated Book of World Rankings.*

St. Martin's Press, Inc., 175 Fifth Avenue, New York, New York 10010 (800) 221-7945; *The Statesman's Year-Book.*

MONGOLIA - AIRPORTS

Central Intelligence Agency, Washington, D.C. 20505 (703) 482-1100, www.cia.gov; *The World Factbook.*

MONGOLIA - ALUMINUM PRODUCTION AND CONSUMPTION - See MONGOLIA - MINING AND MINERAL PRODUCTS

MONGOLIA - ANIMAL HEALTH

Food and Agricultural Organization of the United Nations (FAO), Via delle Terme di Caracalla, 00100 Rome, Italy (Telephone Number in U.S. (202) 653-2400); *Animal Health Yearbook.*

MONGOLIA - AREA AND DENSITY OF POPULATION

Central Intelligence Agency, Washington, D.C. 20505 (703) 482-1100, www.cia.gov; *The World Factbook.*

Euromonitor International, Inc., 122 South Michigan Avenue, Suite 1200, Chicago, Illinois 60603 (800) 577-EURO; *The World Economic Factbook.*

Europa Publications Limited, 18 Bedford Square, London, WC1B 3JN, England; *The Europa World Year Book.*

Food and Agricultural Organization of the United Nations (FAO), Via delle Terme di Caracalla, 00100 Rome, Italy (Telephone Number in U.S. (202) 653-2400); *The State of Food and Agriculture.*

M.E. Sharpe, 80 Business Park Drive, Armonk, New York 10504 (800) 541-6563; *The Illustrated Book of World Rankings.*

St. Martin's Press, Inc., 175 Fifth Avenue, New York, New York 10010 (800) 221-7945; *The Statesman's Year-Book.*

Statistical Office of the United Nations, Publishing Service, New York, New York 10017 (800) 253-9646; *Statistical Yearbook.*

The World Bank, 1818 H Street, NW, Washington, D.C. 20433 (202) 477-1234; *World Development Report.*

MONGOLIA - ARMS EXPORTS AND IMPORTS - See MONGOLIA - MILITARY

MONGOLIA - BALANCE OF PAYMENTS

United Nations Conference on Trade and Development (UNCTAD), New York, New York 10017 (800) 253-9646; *Handbook of International Trade and Development Statistics.*

The World Bank, 1818 H Street, NW, Washington, D.C. 20433 (202) 477-1234;

World Development Report.

MONGOLIA - BANKING

Euromonitor International, Inc., 122 South Michigan Avenue, Suite 1200, Chicago, Illinois 60603 (800) 577-EURO; *World Marketing Data and Statistics.*

M.E. Sharpe, 80 Business Park Drive, Armonk, New York 10504 (800) 541-6563; *The Illustrated Book of World Rankings.*

St. Martin's Press, Inc., 175 Fifth Avenue, New York, New York 10010 (800) 221-7945; *The Statesman's Year-Book.*

MONGOLIA - BARLEY PRODUCTION - See MONGOLIA - CROPS

MONGOLIA - BEER PRODUCTION - See MONGOLIA - BEVERAGES

MONGOLIA - BEVERAGES

M.E. Sharpe, 80 Business Park Drive, Armonk, New York 10504 (800) 541-6563; *The Illustrated Book of World Rankings.*

Statistical Office of the United Nations, Publishing Service, New York, New York 10017 (800) 253-9646; *Statistical Yearbook.*

MONGOLIA - BIRTH RATES

Central Intelligence Agency, Washington, D.C. 20505 (703) 482-1100, www.cia.gov; *The World Factbook.*

The Economist Intelligence Unit (Asia) Limited, 10th Floor, Luk Kwok Centre, 72 Gloucester Road, Wanchai, Hong Kong (Phone Number in U.S. (800) 938-4685); *Asian Market Atlas.*

Euromonitor International, Inc., 122 South Michigan Avenue, Suite 1200, Chicago, Illinois 60603 (800) 577-EURO; *International Marketing Data and Statistics;* and *The World Economic Factbook.*

Europa Publications Limited, 18 Bedford Square, London, WC1B 3JN, England; *The Europa World Year Book.*

M.E. Sharpe, 80 Business Park Drive, Armonk, New York 10504 (800) 541-6563; *The Illustrated Book of World Rankings.*

St. Martin's Press, Inc., 175 Fifth Avenue, New York, New York 10010 (800) 221-7945; *The Statesman's Year-Book.*

Statistical Office of the United Nations, Publishing Service, New York, New York 10017 (800) 253-9646; *Asia-Pacific in Figures; Demographic Yearbook;* and *Statistical Yearbook.*

MONGOLIA - BOOK PRODUCTION

Europa Publications Limited, 18 Bedford Square, London, WC1B 3JN, England; *The Europa World Year Book.*

St. Martin's Press, Inc., 175 Fifth Avenue, New York, New York 10010 (800) 221-7945; *The Statesman's Year-Book.*

MONGOLIA - BROADCASTING

Billboard Limited, Post Office Box 9027, 1006 AA Amsterdam, The Netherlands (Telephone Number in U.S. (212) 764-7300); *World Radio TV Handbook.*

Central Intelligence Agency, Washington, D.C. 20505 (703) 482-1100, www.cia.gov; *The World Factbook.*

Euromonitor International, Inc., 122 South Michigan Avenue, Suite 1200, Chicago, Illinois 60603 (800) 577-EURO; *World Marketing Data and Statistics.*

St. Martin's Press, Inc., 175 Fifth Avenue, New York, New York 10010 (800) 221-7945; *The Statesman's Year-Book.*

MONGOLIA - BUDGET

Central Intelligence Agency, Washington, D.C. 20505 (703) 482-1100, www.cia.gov; *The World Factbook.*

MONGOLIA - BUILDING CONSTRUCTION

Statistical Office of the United Nations, Publishing Service, New York, New York 10017 (800) 253-9646; *Statistical Yearbook.*

MONGOLIA - BUTTER PRODUCTION - See MONGOLIA - DAIRY PRODUCTS

MONGOLIA - CALORIE SUPPLY

Food and Agricultural Organization of the United Nations (FAO), Via delle Terme di Caracalla, 00100 Rome, Italy (Telephone Number in U.S. (202) 653-2400); *The State of Food and Agriculture.*

MONGOLIA - CATTLE - See MONGOLIA - LIVESTOCK AND POULTRY

MONGOLIA - CEMENT PRODUCTION - See MONGOLIA - MINING AND MINERAL PRODUCTS

MONGOLIA - CHEESE PRODUCTION AND CONSUMPTION - See MONGOLIA - DAIRY PRODUCTS

MONGOLIA - CIGARETTE PRODUCTION - See MONGOLIA - TOBACCO PRODUCTION

MONGOLIA - CLIMATE

M.E. Sharpe, 80 Business Park Drive, Armonk, New York 10504 (800) 541-6563; *The Illustrated Book of World Rankings.*

St. Martin's Press, Inc., 175 Fifth Avenue, New York, New York 10010 (800) 221-7945; *The Statesman's Year-Book.*

MONGOLIA - COAL PRODUCTION - See MONGOLIA - MINING AND MINERAL PRODUCTS

MONGOLIA - COFFEE PRODUCTION AND CONSUMPTION - See MONGOLIA - CROPS

MONGOLIA - COMMERCE

St. Martin's Press, Inc., 175 Fifth Avenue, New York, New York 10010 (800) 221-7945; *The Statesman's Year-Book.*

MONGOLIA - COMMUNICATIONS - See MONGOLIA - TRANSPORTATION AND COMMUNICATIONS

MONGOLIA - CONSTRUCTION INDUSTRY

M.E. Sharpe, 80 Business Park Drive, Armonk, New York 10504 (800) 541-6563; *The Illustrated Book of World Rankings.*

St. Martin's Press, Inc., 175 Fifth Avenue, New York, New York 10010 (800) 221-7945; *The Statesman's Year-Book.*

Statistical Office of the United Nations, Publishing Service, New York, New York 10017 (800) 253-9646; *Statistical Yearbook.*

MONGOLIA - CONSUMER PRICES

Euromonitor International, Inc., 122 South Michigan Avenue, Suite 1200, Chicago, Illinois 60603 (800) 577-EURO; *World Marketing Data and Statistics.*

MONGOLIA - CONSUMPTION

The World Bank, 1818 H Street, NW, Washington, D.C. 20433 (202) 477-1234; *World Development Report.*

MONGOLIA - COPPER PRODUCTION AND CONSUMPTION - See MONGOLIA - MINING AND MINERAL PRODUCTS

MONGOLIA - CORN PRODUCTION - See MONGOLIA - CROPS

MONGOLIA - COTTON PRODUCTION - See MONGOLIA - CROPS

MONGOLIA - CROPS

The Economist Intelligence Unit (Asia) Limited, 10th Floor, Luk Kwok Centre, 72 Gloucester Road, Wanchai, Hong Kong (Phone Number in U.S. (800) 938-4685); *Asian Market Atlas.*

Europa Publications Limited, 18 Bedford Square, London, WC1B 3JN, England; *The Europa World Year Book.*

Food and Agricultural Organization of

the United Nations (FAO), Via delle Terme di Caracalla, 00100 Rome, Italy (Telephone Number in U.S. (202) 653-2400); *Production Yearbook;* and *The State of Food and Agriculture.*

M.E. Sharpe, 80 Business Park Drive, Armonk, New York 10504 (800) 541-6563; *The Illustrated Book of World Rankings.*

St. Martin's Press, Inc., 175 Fifth Avenue, New York, New York 10010 (800) 221-7945; *The Statesman's Year-Book.*

Statistical Office of the United Nations, Publishing Service, New York, New York 10017 (800) 253-9646; *Statistical Yearbook.*

United Nations Conference on Trade and Development, Central Statistical Service, Palais des Nations, Geneva, Switzerland (Telephone in U.S. (800) 253-9646); *UNCTAD Commodity Yearbook.*

MONGOLIA - CUSTOMS DUTIES

St. Martin's Press, Inc., 175 Fifth Avenue, New York, New York 10010 (800) 221-7945; *The Statesman's Year-Book.*

MONGOLIA - DAIRY PRODUCTS

Europa Publications Limited, 18 Bedford Square, London, WC1B 3JN, England; *The Europa World Year Book.*

Food and Agricultural Organization of the United Nations (FAO), Via delle Terme di Caracalla, 00100 Rome, Italy (Telephone Number in U.S. (202) 653-2400); *Production Yearbook;* and *The State of Food and Agriculture.*

M.E. Sharpe, 80 Business Park Drive, Armonk, New York 10504 (800) 541-6563; *The Illustrated Book of World Rankings.*

St. Martin's Press, Inc., 175 Fifth Avenue, New York, New York 10010 (800) 221-7945; *The Statesman's Year-Book.*

Statistical Office of the United Nations, Publishing Service, New York, New York 10017 (800) 253-9646; *Statistical Yearbook.*

MONGOLIA - DEATH RATES - See MONGOLIA - MORTALITY

MONGOLIA - DEFENSE EXPENDITURES - See MONGOLIA - MILITARY

MONGOLIA - DEMOGRAPHY

The Economist Intelligence Unit (Asia) Limited, 10th Floor, Luk Kwok Centre, 72 Gloucester Road, Wanchai, Hong Kong (Phone Number in U.S. (800) 938-4685); *Asian Market Atlas.*

Euromonitor International, Inc., 122 South Michigan Avenue, Suite 1200,

Chicago, Illinois 60603 (800) 577-EURO; *International Marketing Data and Statistics;* and *The World Economic Factbook.*

M.E. Sharpe, 80 Business Park Drive, Armonk, New York 10504 (800) 541-6563; *The Illustrated Book of World Rankings.*

Statistical Office of the United Nations, Publishing Service, New York, New York 10017 (800) 253-9646; *Asia-Pacific in Figure;* and *Human Development Report.*

MONGOLIA - DIAMOND PRODUCTION - See MONGOLIA - MINING AND MINERAL PRODUCTS

MONGOLIA - DIVORCE RATES

M.E. Sharpe, 80 Business Park Drive, Armonk, New York 10504 (800) 541-6563; *The Illustrated Book of World Rankings.*

Statistical Office of the United Nations, Publishing Service, New York, New York 10017 (800) 253-9646; *Demographic Yearbook.*

MONGOLIA - ECONOMY

Central Intelligence Agency, Washington, D.C. 20505 (703) 482-1100, www.cia.gov; *The World Factbook.*

Economist Intelligence Unit, 111 West 57th Street, New York, New York 10019 (800) 938-4685; *Mongolia Country Report.*

Euromonitor International, Inc., 122 South Michigan Avenue, Suite 1200, Chicago, Illinois 60603 (800) 577-EURO; *The World Economic Factbook;* and *World Marketing Data and Statistics.*

Europa Publications Limited, 18 Bedford Square, London, WC1B 3JN, England; *The Europa World Year Book.*

M.E. Sharpe, 80 Business Park Drive, Armonk, New York 10504 (800) 541-6563; *The Illustrated Book of World Rankings.*

St. Martin's Press, Inc., 175 Fifth Avenue, New York, New York 10010 (800) 221-7945; *The Statesman's Year-Book.*

Statistical Office of the United Nations, Publishing Service, New York, New York 10017 (800) 253-9646; *World Statistics Pocketbook.*

The World Bank, 1818 H Street, NW, Washington, D.C. 20433 (202) 477-1234; *The World Bank Atlas;* and *World Development Report.*

MONGOLIA - EDUCATION

The Economist Intelligence Unit (Asia) Limited, 10th Floor, Luk Kwok Centre, 72 Gloucester Road, Wanchai, Hong Kong

(Phone Number in U.S. (800) 938-4685); *Asian Market Atlas.*

Euromonitor International, Inc., 122 South Michigan Avenue, Suite 1200, Chicago, Illinois 60603 (800) 577-EURO; *International Marketing Data and Statistics;* and *World Marketing Data and Statistics.*

Europa Publications Limited, 18 Bedford Square, London, WC1B 3JN, England; *The Europa World Year Book.*

M.E. Sharpe, 80 Business Park Drive, Armonk, New York 10504 (800) 541-6563; *The Illustrated Book of World Rankings.*

St. Martin's Press, Inc., 175 Fifth Avenue, New York, New York 10010 (800) 221-7945; *The Statesman's Year-Book.*

Statistical Office of the United Nations, Publishing Service, New York, New York 10017 (800) 253-9646; *Asia-Pacific in Figures; Human Development Report;* and *Statistical Yearbook for Asia and the Pacific.*

United Nations Educational, Scientific and Cultural Organization (UNESCO), 7 Place de Fontenoy, F-75700 Paris, France (Telephone Number in U.S. (212) 963-5981); *Statistical Yearbook.*

The World Bank, 1818 H Street, NW, Washington, D.C. 20433 (202) 477-1234; *World Development Report.*

MONGOLIA - EGG PRODUCTION AND CONSUMPTION - See MONGOLIA - DAIRY PRODUCTS

MONGOLIA - ELECTRICITY

Central Intelligence Agency, Washington, D.C. 20505 (703) 482-1100, www.cia.gov; *The World Factbook.*

M.E. Sharpe, 80 Business Park Drive, Armonk, New York 10504 (800) 541-6563; *The Illustrated Book of World Rankings.*

St. Martin's Press, Inc., 175 Fifth Avenue, New York, New York 10010 (800) 221-7945; *The Statesman's Year-Book.*

Statistical Office of the United Nations, Publishing Service, New York, New York 10017 (800) 253-9646; *Electric Power in Asia and the Pacific; Human Development Report;* and *Statistical Yearbook.*

MONGOLIA - EMPLOYMENT

Euromonitor International, Inc., 122 South Michigan Avenue, Suite 1200, Chicago, Illinois 60603 (800) 577-EURO; *International Marketing Data and Statistics.*

M.E. Sharpe, 80 Business Park Drive, Armonk, New York 10504 (800) 541-6563;

The Illustrated Book of World Rankings.

Statistical Office of the United Nations, Publishing Service, New York, New York 10017 (800) 253-9646; *Asia-Pacific in Figures;* and *Statistical Yearbook.*

MONGOLIA - ENERGY

Euromonitor International, Inc., 122 South Michigan Avenue, Suite 1200, Chicago, Illinois 60603 (800) 577-EURO; *International Marketing Data and Statistics; The World Economic Factbook;* and *World Marketing Data and Statistics.*

Food and Agricultural Organization of the United Nations (FAO), Via delle Terme di Caracalla, 00100 Rome, Italy (Telephone Number in U.S. (202) 653-2400); *The State of Food and Agriculture.*

M.E. Sharpe, 80 Business Park Drive, Armonk, New York 10504 (800) 541-6563; *The Illustrated Book of World Rankings.*

St. Martin's Press, Inc., 175 Fifth Avenue, New York, New York 10010 (800) 221-7945; *The Statesman's Year-Book.*

Statistical Office of the United Nations, Publishing Service, New York, New York 10017 (800) 253-9646; *Asia-Pacific in Figures; Energy Statistics Yearbook; Human Development Report; World Statistics Pocketbook;* and *Statistical Yearbook.*

The World Bank, 1818 H Street, NW, Washington, D.C. 20433 (202) 477-1234; *The World Bank Atlas;* and *World Development Report.*

MONGOLIA - ENVIRONMENT

Economist Intelligence Unit, 111 West 57th Street, New York, New York 10019 (800) 938-4685; *Mongolia Country Report.*

MONGOLIA - EXCHANGE RATES

Central Intelligence Agency, Washington, D.C. 20505 (703) 482-1100, www.cia.gov; *The World Factbook.*

The Economist Intelligence Unit (Asia) Limited, 10th Floor, Luk Kwok Centre, 72 Gloucester Road, Wanchai, Hong Kong (Phone Number in U.S. (800) 938-4685); *Asian Market Atlas.*

Euromonitor International, Inc., 122 South Michigan Avenue, Suite 1200, Chicago, Illinois 60603 (800) 577-EURO; *International Marketing Data and Statistics;* and *The World Economic Factbook.*

Europa Publications Limited, 18 Bedford Square, London, WC1B 3JN, England; *The Europa World Year Book.*

Statistical Office of the United Nations,

Publishing Service, New York, New York 10017 (800) 253-9646; *Statistical Yearbook;* and *World Statistics Pocketbook.*

Walden Publishing Ltd., Two Market Street, Saffron Walden Essex, CB10 1HZ, England; *The World of Information Asia and Pacific Review.*

MONGOLIA - EXPORTS

Central Intelligence Agency, Washington, D.C. 20505 (703) 482-1100, www.cia.gov; *The World Factbook.*

Economist Intelligence Unit, 111 West 57th Street, New York, New York 10019 (800) 938-4685; *Mongolia Country Report.*

The Economist Intelligence Unit (Asia) Limited, 10th Floor, Luk Kwok Centre, 72 Gloucester Road, Wanchai, Hong Kong (Phone Number in U.S. (800) 938-4685); *Asian Market Atlas.*

Euromonitor International, Inc., 122 South Michigan Avenue, Suite 1200, Chicago, Illinois 60603 (800) 577-EURO; *International Marketing Data and Statistics;* and *The World Economic Factbook.*

Europa Publications Limited, 18 Bedford Square, London, WC1B 3JN, England; *The Europa World Year Book.*

Food and Agricultural Organization of the United Nations (FAO), Via delle Terme di Caracalla, 00100 Rome, Italy (Telephone Number in U.S. (202) 653-2400); *The State of Food and Agriculture.*

International Monetary Fund, 700 Nineteenth Street, NW, Washington, D.C. 20431 (202) 623-7000; *Direction of Trade Statistics.*

St. Martin's Press, Inc., 175 Fifth Avenue, New York, New York 10010 (800) 221-7945; *The Statesman's Year-Book.*

United Nations Conference on Trade and Development (UNCTAD), New York, New York 10017 (800) 253-9646; *Handbook of International Trade and Development Statistics.*

Walden Publishing Ltd., Two Market Street, Saffron Walden Essex, CB10 1HZ, England; *The World of Information Asia and Pacific Review.*

The World Bank, 1818 H Street, NW, Washington, D.C. 20433 (202) 477-1234; *World Development Report.*

MONGOLIA - EXTERNAL INDEBTEDNESS

The World Bank, 1818 H Street, NW, Washington, D.C. 20433 (202) 477-1234; *World Development Report.*

MONGOLIA - EXTERNAL TRADE

Euromonitor International, Inc., 122 South Michigan Avenue, Suite 1200, Chicago, Illinois 60603 (800) 577-EURO; *World Marketing Data and Statistics.*

Food and Agricultural Organization of the United Nations (FAO), Via delle Terme di Caracalla, 00100 Rome, Italy (Telephone Number in U.S. (202) 653-2400); *The State of Food and Agriculture;* and *Trade Yearbook.*

Statistical Office of the United Nations, Publishing Service, New York, New York 10017 (800) 253-9646; *Asia-Pacific in Figures;* and *Statistical Yearbook for Asia and the Pacific.*

MONGOLIA - FARM CROPS - See MONGOLIA - CROPS

MONGOLIA - FERTILITY RATES

Central Intelligence Agency, Washington, D.C. 20505 (703) 482-1100, www.cia.gov; *The World Factbook.*

M.E. Sharpe, 80 Business Park Drive, Armonk, New York 10504 (800) 541-6563; *The Illustrated Book of World Rankings.*

Statistical Office of the United Nations, Publishing Service, New York, New York 10017 (800) 253-9646; *Human Development Report.*

The World Bank, 1818 H Street, NW, Washington, D.C. 20433 (202) 477-1234; *The World Bank Atlas;* and *World Development Report.*

MONGOLIA - FERTILIZER

Food and Agricultural Organization of the United Nations (FAO), Via delle Terme di Caracalla, 00100 Rome, Italy (Telephone Number in U.S. (202) 653-2400); *Fertilizer Yearbook;* and *The State of Food and Agriculture.*

Statistical Office of the United Nations, Publishing Service, New York, New York 10017 (800) 253-9646; *Statistical Yearbook.*

MONGOLIA - FETAL MORTALITY - See MONGOLIA - MORTALITY

MONGOLIA - FINANCE

Economist Intelligence Unit, 111 West 57th Street, New York, New York 10019 (800) 938-4685; *Mongolia Country Report.*

Europa Publications Limited, 18 Bedford Square, London, WC1B 3JN, England; *The Europa World Year Book.*

M.E. Sharpe, 80 Business Park Drive, Armonk, New York 10504 (800) 541-6563;

The Illustrated Book of World Rankings.

St. Martin's Press, Inc., 175 Fifth Avenue, New York, New York 10010 (800) 221-7945; *The Statesman's Year-Book.*

Statistical Office of the United Nations, Publishing Service, New York, New York 10017 (800) 253-9646; *Statistical Yearbook for Asia and the Pacific.*

MONGOLIA - FISHERIES

Europa Publications Limited, 18 Bedford Square, London, WC1B 3JN, England; *The Europa World Year Book.*

Food and Agricultural Organization of the United Nations (FAO), Via delle Terme di Caracalla, 00100 Rome, Italy (Telephone Number in U.S. (202) 653-2400); *The State of Food and Agriculture;* and *Yearbook of Fishery Statistics.*

M.E. Sharpe, 80 Business Park Drive, Armonk, New York 10504 (800) 541-6563; *The Illustrated Book of World Rankings.*

United Nations Conference on Trade and Development, Central Statistical Service, Palais des Nations, Geneva, Switzerland (Telephone in U.S. (800) 253-9646); *UNCTAD Commodity Yearbook.*

MONGOLIA - FLAX PRODUCTION - See MONGOLIA - TEXTILE INDUSTRY

MONGOLIA - FLOUR PRODUCTION

Statistical Office of the United Nations, Publishing Service, New York, New York 10017 (800) 253-9646; *Statistical Yearbook.*

MONGOLIA - FOOD

Food and Agricultural Organization of the United Nations (FAO), Via delle Terme di Caracalla, 00100 Rome, Italy (Telephone Number in U.S. (202) 653-2400); *Production Yearbook;* and *The State of Food and Agriculture.*

Statistical Office of the United Nations, Publishing Service, New York, New York 10017 (800) 253-9646; *Human Development Report;* and *Statistical Yearbook for Asia and the Pacific.*

United Nations Conference on Trade and Development, Central Statistical Service, Palais des Nations, Geneva, Switzerland (Telephone in U.S. (800) 253-9646); *UNCTAD Commodity Yearbook.*

MONGOLIA - FOREIGN DEBT

St. Martin's Press, Inc., 175 Fifth Avenue, New York, New York 10010 (800) 221-7945; *The Statesman's Year-Book.*

Walden Publishing Ltd., Two Market Street, Saffron Walden Essex, CB10 1HZ, England; *The World of Information Asia and Pacific Review.*

MONGOLIA - FOREIGN TRADE

Economist Intelligence Unit, 111 West 57th Street, New York, New York 10019 (800) 938-4685; *Mongolia Country Report.*

The Economist Intelligence Unit (Asia) Limited, 10th Floor, Luk Kwok Centre, 72 Gloucester Road, Wanchai, Hong Kong (Phone Number in U.S. (800) 938-4685); *Asian Market Atlas.*

Euromonitor International, Inc., 122 South Michigan Avenue, Suite 1200, Chicago, Illinois 60603 (800) 577-EURO; *The World Economic Factbook.*

Europa Publications Limited, 18 Bedford Square, London, WC1B 3JN, England; *The Europa World Year Book.*

Food and Agricultural Organization of the United Nations (FAO), Via delle Terme di Caracalla, 00100 Rome, Italy (Telephone Number in U.S. (202) 653-2400); *The State of Food and Agriculture.*

M.E. Sharpe, 80 Business Park Drive, Armonk, New York 10504 (800) 541-6563; *The Illustrated Book of World Rankings.*

St. Martin's Press, Inc., 175 Fifth Avenue, New York, New York 10010 (800) 221-7945; *The Statesman's Year-Book.*

Statistical Office of the United Nations, Publishing Service, New York, New York 10017 (800) 253-9646; *Statistical Yearbook.*

United Nations Conference on Trade and Development, Central Statistical Service, Palais des Nations, Geneva, Switzerland (Telephone in U.S. (800) 253-9646); *UNCTAD Commodity Yearbook.*

The World Bank, 1818 H Street, NW, Washington, D.C. 20433 (202) 477-1234; *World Development Report.*

MONGOLIA - FORESTRY AND FOREST PRODUCTS

The Economist Intelligence Unit (Asia) Limited, 10th Floor, Luk Kwok Centre, 72 Gloucester Road, Wanchai, Hong Kong (Phone Number in U.S. (800) 938-4685); *Asian Market Atlas.*

Europa Publications Limited, 18 Bedford Square, London, WC1B 3JN, England; *The Europa World Year Book.*

Food and Agricultural Organization of the United Nations (FAO), Via delle Terme di Caracalla, 00100 Rome, Italy (Telephone Number in U.S. (202) 653-2400); *The State of Food and Agriculture;* and *Yearbook of Forest Products.*

M.E. Sharpe, 80 Business Park Drive, Armonk, New York 10504 (800) 541-6563; *The Illustrated Book of World Rankings.*

St. Martin's Press, Inc., 175 Fifth Avenue, New York, New York 10010 (800) 221-7945; *The Statesman's Year-Book.*

Statistical Office of the United Nations, Publishing Service, New York, New York 10017 (800) 253-9646; *Statistical Yearbook.*

United Nations Conference on Trade and Development, Central Statistical Service, Palais des Nations, Geneva, Switzerland (Telephone in U.S. (800) 253-9646); *UNCTAD Commodity Yearbook.*

United Nations Educational, Scientific and Cultural Organization (UNESCO), 7 Place de Fontenoy, F-75700 Paris, France (Telephone Number in U.S. (212) 963-5981); *Statistical Yearbook.*

The World Bank, 1818 H Street, NW, Washington, D.C. 20433 (202) 477-1234; *World Development Report.*

MONGOLIA - GAS PRODUCTION - See MONGOLIA - MINING AND MINERAL PRODUCTS

MONGOLIA - GENERAL INDUSTRIAL STATISTICS - See MONGOLIA - INDUSTRY

MONGOLIA - GENERAL MORTALITY - See MONGOLIA - MORTALITY

MONGOLIA - GEOGRAPHIC DATA

M.E. Sharpe, 80 Business Park Drive, Armonk, New York 10504 (800) 541-6563; *The Illustrated Book of World Rankings.*

MONGOLIA - GOLD PRODUCTION AND CONSUMPTION - See MONGOLIA - MINING AND MINERAL PRODUCTS

MONGOLIA - GOVERNMENT

Central Intelligence Agency, Washington, D.C. 20505 (703) 482-1100, www.cia.gov; *The World Factbook.*

Europa Publications Limited, 18 Bedford Square, London, WC1B 3JN, England; *The Europa World Year Book.*

St. Martin's Press, Inc., 175 Fifth Avenue, New York, New York 10010 (800) 221-7945; *The Statesman's Year-Book.*

Statistical Office of the United Nations, Publishing Service, New York, New York 10017 (800) 253-9646; *Asia-Pacific in Figures;* and *National Accounts Statistics.*

The World Bank, 1818 H Street, NW, Washington, D.C. 20433 (202) 477-1234; *World Development Report.*

MONGOLIA - GRAIN PRODUCTION - See MONGOLIA - CROPS

MONGOLIA - GROSS DOMESTIC PRODUCT

Economist Intelligence Unit, 111 West 57th Street, New York, New York 10019 (800) 938-4685; *Mongolia Country Report.*

The Economist Intelligence Unit (Asia) Limited, 10th Floor, Luk Kwok Centre, 72 Gloucester Road, Wanchai, Hong Kong (Phone Number in U.S. (800) 938-4685); *Asian Market Atlas.*

Euromonitor International, Inc., 122 South Michigan Avenue, Suite 1200, Chicago, Illinois 60603 (800) 577-EURO; *International Marketing Data and Statistics;* and *The World Economic Factbook.*

M.E. Sharpe, 80 Business Park Drive, Armonk, New York 10504 (800) 541-6563; *The Illustrated Book of World Rankings.*

Statistical Office of the United Nations, Publishing Service, New York, New York 10017 (800) 253-9646; *Human Development Report;* and *National Accounts Statistics.*

The World Bank, 1818 H Street, NW, Washington, D.C. 20433 (202) 477-1234; *World Development Report.*

MONGOLIA - GROSS NATIONAL PRODUCT

St. Martin's Press, Inc., 175 Fifth Avenue, New York, New York 10010 (800) 221-7945; *The Statesman's Year-Book.*

U.S. Arms Control and Disarmament Agency, 320 Twenty-first Street, NW, Washington, D.C. 20451 (202) 647-8677; *World Military Expenditures and Arms Transfers.*

Walden Publishing Ltd., Two Market Street, Saffron Walden Essex, CB10 1HZ, England; *The World of Information Asia and Pacific Review.*

The World Bank, 1818 H Street, NW, Washington, D.C. 20433 (202) 477-1234; *The World Bank Atlas;* and *World Development Report.*

MONGOLIA - HEALTH

The Economist Intelligence Unit (Asia) Limited, 10th Floor, Luk Kwok Centre, 72 Gloucester Road, Wanchai, Hong Kong (Phone Number in U.S. (800) 938-4685); *Asian Market Atlas.*

Euromonitor International, Inc., 122 South Michigan Avenue, Suite 1200, Chicago, Illinois 60603 (800) 577-EURO;

World Marketing Data and Statistics.

M.E. Sharpe, 80 Business Park Drive, Armonk, New York 10504 (800) 541-6563; *The Illustrated Book of World Rankings.*

St. Martin's Press, Inc., 175 Fifth Avenue, New York, New York 10010 (800) 221-7945; *The Statesman's Year-Book.*

Statistical Office of the United Nations, Publishing Service, New York, New York 10017 (800) 253-9646; *Asia-Pacific in Figures; Human Development Report;* and *Statistical Yearbook.*

United Nations Children's Fund (UNICEF), 3 United Nations Plaza, New York, New York 10017 (800) 253-9646; *State of the World's Children.*

The World Bank, 1818 H Street, NW, Washington, D.C. 20433 (202) 477-1234; *World Development Report.*

MONGOLIA - HEALTH AND MEDICAL SERVICES

Statistical Office of the United Nations, Publishing Service, New York, New York 10017 (800) 253-9646; *Statistical Yearbook.*

MONGOLIA - HIDE PRODUCTION

Food and Agricultural Organization of the United Nations (FAO), Via delle Terme di Caracalla, 00100 Rome, Italy (Telephone Number in U.S. (202) 653-2400); *Production Yearbook.*

MONGOLIA - HIGHWAYS

Central Intelligence Agency, Washington, D.C. 20505 (703) 482-1100, www.cia.gov; *The World Factbook.*

The Economist Intelligence Unit (Asia) Limited, 10th Floor, Luk Kwok Centre, 72 Gloucester Road, Wanchai, Hong Kong (Phone Number in U.S. (800) 938-4685); *Asian Market Atlas.*

St. Martin's Press, Inc., 175 Fifth Avenue, New York, New York 10010 (800) 221-7945; *The Statesman's Year-Book.*

MONGOLIA - HORSES - See MONGOLIA - LIVESTOCK AND POULTRY

MONGOLIA - HOUSING AND HOUSING INDUSTRY

Euromonitor International, Inc., 122 South Michigan Avenue, Suite 1200, Chicago, Illinois 60603 (800) 577-EURO; *World Marketing Data and Statistics.*

MONGOLIA - HOUSING CONSTRUCTION - See MONGOLIA - CONSTRUCTION INDUSTRY

MONGOLIA - ILLITERATE POPULATION

Central Intelligence Agency, Washington, D.C. 20505 (703) 482-1100, www.cia.gov; *The World Factbook.*

Euromonitor International, Inc., 122 South Michigan Avenue, Suite 1200, Chicago, Illinois 60603 (800) 577-EURO; *The World Economic Factbook.*

Statistical Office of the United Nations, Publishing Service, New York, New York 10017 (800) 253-9646; *Asia-Pacific in Figures;* and *Human Development Report.*

United Nations Educational, Scientific and Cultural Organization (UNESCO), 7 Place de Fontenoy, F-75700 Paris, France (Telephone Number in U.S. (212) 963-5981); *Statistical Yearbook.*

MONGOLIA - IMPORTS

Central Intelligence Agency, Washington, D.C. 20505 (703) 482-1100, www.cia.gov; *The World Factbook.*

Economist Intelligence Unit, 111 West 57th Street, New York, New York 10019 (800) 938-4685; *Mongolia Country Report.*

The Economist Intelligence Unit (Asia) Limited, 10th Floor, Luk Kwok Centre, 72 Gloucester Road, Wanchai, Hong Kong (Phone Number in U.S. (800) 938-4685); *Asian Market Atlas.*

Euromonitor International, Inc., 122 South Michigan Avenue, Suite 1200, Chicago, Illinois 60603 (800) 577-EURO; *International Marketing Data and Statistics;* and *The World Economic Factbook.*

Europa Publications Limited, 18 Bedford Square, London, WC1B 3JN, England; *The Europa World Year Book.*

Food and Agricultural Organization of the United Nations (FAO), Via delle Terme di Caracalla, 00100 Rome, Italy (Telephone Number in U.S. (202) 653-2400); *The State of Food and Agriculture.*

International Monetary Fund, 700 Nineteenth Street, NW, Washington, D.C. 20431 (202) 623-7000; *Direction of Trade Statistics.*

St. Martin's Press, Inc., 175 Fifth Avenue, New York, New York 10010 (800) 221-7945; *The Statesman's Year-Book.*

United Nations Conference on Trade and Development (UNCTAD), New York, New York 10017 (800) 253-9646; *Handbook of International Trade and Development Statistics.*

Walden Publishing Ltd., Two Market Street, Saffron Walden Essex, CB10 1HZ,

England; *The World of Information Asia and Pacific Review.*

The World Bank, 1818 H Street, NW, Washington, D.C. 20433 (202) 477-1234; *World Development Report.*

MONGOLIA - INDUSTRY

Central Intelligence Agency, Washington, D.C. 20505 (703) 482-1100, www.cia.gov; *The World Factbook.*

Economist Intelligence Unit, 111 West 57th Street, New York, New York 10019 (800) 938-4685; *Mongolia Country Report.*

Euromonitor International, Inc., 122 South Michigan Avenue, Suite 1200, Chicago, Illinois 60603 (800) 577-EURO; *The World Economic Factbook;* and *World Marketing Data and Statistics.*

Europa Publications Limited, 18 Bedford Square, London, WC1B 3JN, England; *The Europa World Year Book.*

M.E. Sharpe, 80 Business Park Drive, Armonk, New York 10504 (800) 541-6563; *The Illustrated Book of World Rankings.*

St. Martin's Press, Inc., 175 Fifth Avenue, New York, New York 10010 (800) 221-7945; *The Statesman's Year-Book.*

Statistical Office of the United Nations, Publishing Service, New York, New York 10017 (800) 253-9646; *Asia-Pacific in Figures; Industrial Commodity Statistics Yearbook; Statistical Yearbook;* and *Statistical Yearbook for Asia and the Pacific.*

World Intellectual Property Organization, 34 Chemin des Colombettes, CH-1211 Geneva 20, Switzerland; *Industrial Property Statistics.*

MONGOLIA - INFANT AND MATERNAL MORTALITY - See MONGOLIA - MORTALITY

MONGOLIA - INTERNAL TRADE

Statistical Office of the United Nations, Publishing Service, New York, New York 10017 (800) 253-9646; *Statistical Yearbook for Asia and the Pacific.*

MONGOLIA - IRON ORE PRODUCTION AND CONSUMPTION - See MONGOLIA - MINING AND MINERAL PRODUCTS

MONGOLIA - LABOR

Central Intelligence Agency, Washington, D.C. 20505 (703) 482-1100, www.cia.gov; *The World Factbook.*

The Economist Intelligence Unit (Asia) Limited, 10th Floor, Luk Kwok Centre, 72 Gloucester Road, Wanchai, Hong Kong (Phone Number in U.S. (800) 938-4685);

Asian Market Atlas.

Euromonitor International, Inc., 122 South Michigan Avenue, Suite 1200, Chicago, Illinois 60603 (800) 577-EURO; *International Marketing Data and Statistics;* and *World Marketing Data and Statistics.*

Europa Publications Limited, 18 Bedford Square, London, WC1B 3JN, England; *The Europa World Year Book.*

Food and Agricultural Organization of the United Nations (FAO), Via delle Terme di Caracalla, 00100 Rome, Italy (Telephone Number in U.S. (202) 653-2400); *The State of Food and Agriculture.*

M.E. Sharpe, 80 Business Park Drive, Armonk, New York 10504 (800) 541-6563; *The Illustrated Book of World Rankings.*

St. Martin's Press, Inc., 175 Fifth Avenue, New York, New York 10010 (800) 221-7945; *The Statesman's Year-Book.*

Statistical Office of the United Nations, Publishing Service, New York, New York 10017 (800) 253-9646; *Human Development Report.*

The World Bank, 1818 H Street, NW, Washington, D.C. 20433 (202) 477-1234; *The World Bank Atlas;* and *World Development Report.*

MONGOLIA - LAND USE

Central Intelligence Agency, Washington, D.C. 20505 (703) 482-1100, www.cia.gov; *The World Factbook.*

Euromonitor International, Inc., 122 South Michigan Avenue, Suite 1200, Chicago, Illinois 60603 (800) 577-EURO; *International Marketing Data and Statistics.*

Food and Agricultural Organization of the United Nations (FAO), Via delle Terme di Caracalla, 00100 Rome, Italy (Telephone Number in U.S. (202) 653-2400); *Production Yearbook.*

The World Bank, 1818 H Street, NW, Washington, D.C. 20433 (202) 477-1234; *World Development Report.*

MONGOLIA - LIBRARIES

M.E. Sharpe, 80 Business Park Drive, Armonk, New York 10504 (800) 541-6563; *The Illustrated Book of World Rankings.*

MONGOLIA - LIFE EXPECTANCY

Central Intelligence Agency, Washington, D.C. 20505 (703) 482-1100, www.cia.gov; *The World Factbook.*

The Economist Intelligence Unit (Asia) Limited, 10th Floor, Luk Kwok Centre, 72

Gloucester Road, Wanchai, Hong Kong (Phone Number in U.S. (800) 938-4685); *Asian Market Atlas.*

Euromonitor International, Inc., 122 South Michigan Avenue, Suite 1200, Chicago, Illinois 60603 (800) 577-EURO; *The World Economic Factbook.*

St. Martin's Press, Inc., 175 Fifth Avenue, New York, New York 10010 (800) 221-7945; *The Statesman's Year-Book.*

Statistical Office of the United Nations, Publishing Service, New York, New York 10017 (800) 253-9646; *Asia-Pacific in Figures; World Statistics Pocketbook;* and *Human Development Report.*

The World Bank, 1818 H Street, NW, Washington, D.C. 20433 (202) 477-1234; *The World Bank Atlas;* and *World Development Report.*

MONGOLIA - LIGNITE PRODUCTION - See MONGOLIA - MINING AND MINERAL PRODUCTS

MONGOLIA - LITERACY RATE

Euromonitor International, Inc., 122 South Michigan Avenue, Suite 1200, Chicago, Illinois 60603 (800) 577-EURO; *World Marketing Data and Statistics.*

MONGOLIA - LIVESTOCK AND POULTRY

Europa Publications Limited, 18 Bedford Square, London, WC1B 3JN, England; *The Europa World Year Book.*

Food and Agricultural Organization of the United Nations (FAO), Via delle Terme di Caracalla, 00100 Rome, Italy (Telephone Number in U.S. (202) 653-2400); *Production Yearbook;* and *The State of Food and Agriculture.*

M.E. Sharpe, 80 Business Park Drive, Armonk, New York 10504 (800) 541-6563; *The Illustrated Book of World Rankings.*

St. Martin's Press, Inc., 175 Fifth Avenue, New York, New York 10010 (800) 221-7945; *The Statesman's Year-Book.*

Statistical Office of the United Nations, Publishing Service, New York, New York 10017 (800) 253-9646; *Statistical Yearbook.*

United Nations Conference on Trade and Development, Central Statistical Service, Palais des Nations, Geneva, Switzerland (Telephone in U.S. (800) 253-9646); *UNCTAD Commodity Yearbook.*

MONGOLIA - LIVING LEVELS - See MONGOLIA - LIFE EXPECTANCY

MONGOLIA - MANPOWER

Statistical Office of the United Nations, Publishing Service, New York, New York 10017 (800) 253-9646; *Statistical Yearbook for Asia and the Pacific.*

MONGOLIA - MANUFACTURING

M.E. Sharpe, 80 Business Park Drive, Armonk, New York 10504 (800) 541-6563; *The Illustrated Book of World Rankings.*

Statistical Office of the United Nations, Publishing Service, New York, New York 10017 (800) 253-9646; *Statistical Yearbook.*

MONGOLIA - MARRIAGE

Europa Publications Limited, 18 Bedford Square, London, WC1B 3JN, England; *The Europa World Year Book.*

M.E. Sharpe, 80 Business Park Drive, Armonk, New York 10504 (800) 541-6563; *The Illustrated Book of World Rankings.*

Statistical Office of the United Nations, Publishing Service, New York, New York 10017 (800) 253-9646; *Demographic Yearbook.*

MONGOLIA - MEAT PRODUCTION - See MONGOLIA - LIVESTOCK AND POULTRY

MONGOLIA - MERCHANT SHIPPING

Europa Publications Limited, 18 Bedford Square, London, WC1B 3JN, England; *The Europa World Year Book.*

St. Martin's Press, Inc., 175 Fifth Avenue, New York, New York 10010 (800) 221-7945; *The Statesman's Year-Book.*

MONGOLIA - MILITARY

Central Intelligence Agency, Washington, D.C. 20505 (703) 482-1100, www.cia.gov; *The World Factbook.*

The Economist Intelligence Unit (Asia) Limited, 10th Floor, Luk Kwok Centre, 72 Gloucester Road, Wanchai, Hong Kong (Phone Number in U.S. (800) 938-4685); *Asian Market Atlas.*

Euromonitor International, Inc., 122 South Michigan Avenue, Suite 1200, Chicago, Illinois 60603 (800) 577-EURO; *World Marketing Data and Statistics.*

The International Institute for Strategic Studies, 23 Tavistock Street, London WC2E 7NQ, England; *The Military Balance.*

St. Martin's Press, Inc., 175 Fifth Avenue, New York, New York 10010 (800) 221-7945; *The Statesman's Year-Book.*

Statistical Office of the United Nations, Publishing Service, New York, New York 10017 (800) 253-9646; *Human Development Report.*

U.S. Arms Control and Disarmament Agency, 320 Twenty-first Street, NW, Washington, D.C. 20451 (202) 647-8677; *World Military Expenditures and Arms Transfers.*

MONGOLIA - MILK PRODUCTION - See MONGOLIA - DAIRY PRODUCTS

MONGOLIA - MINING AND MINERAL PRODUCTS

Europa Publications Limited, 18 Bedford Square, London, WC1B 3JN, England; *The Europa World Year Book.*

M.E. Sharpe, 80 Business Park Drive, Armonk, New York 10504 (800) 541-6563; *The Illustrated Book of World Rankings.*

St. Martin's Press, Inc., 175 Fifth Avenue, New York, New York 10010 (800) 221-7945; *The Statesman's Year-Book.*

Statistical Office of the United Nations, Publishing Service, New York, New York 10017 (800) 253-9646; *Statistical Yearbook.*

United Nations Conference on Trade and Development, Central Statistical Service, Palais des Nations, Geneva, Switzerland (Telephone in U.S. (800) 253-9646); *UNCTAD Commodity Yearbook.*

MONGOLIA - MONEY EXCHANGE RATE - See MONGOLIA - EXCHANGE RATES

MONGOLIA MONEY SUPPLY

Economist Intelligence Unit, 111 West 57th Street, New York, New York 10019 (800) 938-4685; *Mongolia Country Report.*

MONGOLIA - MORTALITY

Central Intelligence Agency, Washington, D.C. 20505 (703) 482-1100, www.cia.gov; *The World Factbook.*

The Economist Intelligence Unit (Asia) Limited, 10th Floor, Luk Kwok Centre, 72 Gloucester Road, Wanchai, Hong Kong (Phone Number in U.S. (800) 938-4685); *Asian Market Atlas.*

Euromonitor International, Inc., 122 South Michigan Avenue, Suite 1200, Chicago, Illinois 60603 (800) 577-EURO; *International Marketing Data and Statistics;* and *The World Economic Factbook.*

Europa Publications Limited, 18 Bedford Square, London, WC1B 3JN, England; *The Europa World Year Book.*

St. Martin's Press, Inc., 175 Fifth Avenue, New York, New York 10010 (800) 221-7945; *The Statesman's Year-Book.*

Statistical Office of the United Nations, Publishing Service, New York, New York 10017 (800) 253-9646; *Asia-Pacific in Figures; Demographic Yearbook; Human Development Report; World Statistics Pocketbook;* and *Statistical Yearbook.*

United Nations Children's Fund (UNICEF), 3 United Nations Plaza, New York, New York 10017 (800) 253-9646; *State of the World's Children.*

The World Bank, 1818 H Street, NW, Washington, D.C. 20433 (202) 477-1234; *The World Bank Atlas;* and *World Development Report.*

MONGOLIA - MOTION PICTURES

St. Martin's Press, Inc., 175 Fifth Avenue, New York, New York 10010 (800) 221-7945; *The Statesman's Year-Book.*

Statistical Office of the United Nations, Publishing Service, New York, New York 10017 (800) 253-9646; *Statistical Yearbook.*

MONGOLIA - MUSEUMS

M.E. Sharpe, 80 Business Park Drive, Armonk, New York 10504 (800) 541-6563; *The Illustrated Book of World Rankings.*

United Nations Educational, Scientific and Cultural Organization (UNESCO), 7 Place de Fontenoy, F-75700 Paris, France (Telephone Number in U.S. (212) 963-5981); *Statistical Yearbook.*

MONGOLIA - NATALITY - See MONGOLIA - BIRTH RATES

MONGOLIA - NATIONAL ACCOUNTS

Europa Publications Limited, 18 Bedford Square, London, WC1B 3JN, England; *The Europa World Year Book.*

Statistical Office of the United Nations, Publishing Service, New York, New York 10017 (800) 253-9646; *Asia-Pacific in Figures; National Account Statistics;* and *Statistical Yearbook.*

MONGOLIA - NATIONAL INCOME

M.E. Sharpe, 80 Business Park Drive, Armonk, New York 10504 (800) 541-6563; *The Illustrated Book of World Rankings.*

Statistical Office of the United Nations, Publishing Service, New York, New York 10017 (800) 253-9646; *National Accounts Statistics.*

MONGOLIA - NATIONAL PRODUCT

M.E. Sharpe, 80 Business Park Drive, Armonk, New York 10504 (800) 541-6563; *The Illustrated Book of World Rankings.*

Statistical Office of the United Nations, Publishing Service, New York, New York 10017 (800) 253-9646; *Statistical Yearbook.*

MONGOLIA - NATURAL GAS - PRODUCTION - See MONGOLIA - MINING AND MINERAL PRODUCTS

MONGOLIA - NET MATERIAL PRODUCT - AVERAGE ANNUAL GROWTH

Statistical Office of the United Nations, Publishing Service, New York, New York 10017 (800) 253-9646; *Statistical Yearbook.*

MONGOLIA - NEWSPAPER PRODUCTION - See MONGOLIA - FORESTRY AND FOREST PRODUCTS

MONGOLIA - NEWSPRINT - See MONGOLIA - FORESTRY AND FOREST PRODUCTS

MONGOLIA - OATS PRODUCTION - See MONGOLIA - CROPS

MONGOLIA - PAPER - See MONGOLIA - FORESTRY AND FOREST PRODUCTS

MONGOLIA - PATENTS, TRADEMARKS AND SERVICE MARKS

World Intellectual Property Organization, 34 Chemin des Colombettes, CH-1211 Geneva 20, Switzerland; *Industrial Property Statistics.*

MONGOLIA - PEANUT PRODUCTION - See MONGOLIA - CROPS

MONGOLIA - PESTICIDE USE

Food and Agricultural Organization of the United Nations (FAO), Via delle Terme di Caracalla, 00100 Rome, Italy (Telephone Number in U.S. (202) 653-2400); *The State of Food and Agriculture.*

MONGOLIA - PETROLEUM INDUSTRY

Food and Agricultural Organization of the United Nations (FAO), Via delle Terme di Caracalla, 00100 Rome, Italy (Telephone Number in U.S. (202) 653-2400); *The State of Food and Agriculture.*

M.E. Sharpe, 80 Business Park Drive, Armonk, New York 10504 (800) 541-6563; *The Illustrated Book of World Rankings.*

Statistical Office of the United Nations, Publishing Service, New York, New York 10017 (800) 253-9646; *Statistical Yearbook.*

United Nations Conference on Trade and Development, Central Statistical Service, Palais des Nations, Geneva, Switzerland (Telephone in U.S. (800) 253-9646); *UNCTAD Commodity Yearbook.*

MONGOLIA - PIGS - See MONGOLIA -

LIVESTOCK AND POULTRY

MONGOLIA - POPULATION

Central Intelligence Agency, Washington, D.C. 20505 (703) 482-1100, www.cia.gov; *The World Factbook.*

Economist Intelligence Unit, 111 West 57th Street, New York, New York 10019 (800) 938-4685; *Mongolia Country Report.*

The Economist Intelligence Unit (Asia) Limited, 10th Floor, Luk Kwok Centre, 72 Gloucester Road, Wanchai, Hong Kong (Phone Number in U.S. (800) 938-4685); *Asian Market Atlas.*

Euromonitor International, Inc., 122 South Michigan Avenue, Suite 1200, Chicago, Illinois 60603 (800) 577-EURO; *International Marketing Data and Statistics;* and *The World Economic Factbook.*

Europa Publications Limited, 18 Bedford Square, London, WC1B 3JN, England; *The Europa World Year Book.*

Food and Agricultural Organization of the United Nations (FAO), Via delle Terme di Caracalla, 00100 Rome, Italy (Telephone Number in U.S. (202) 653-2400); *Production Yearbook.*

M.E. Sharpe, 80 Business Park Drive, Armonk, New York 10504 (800) 541-6563; *The Illustrated Book of World Rankings.*

St. Martin's Press, Inc., 175 Fifth Avenue, New York, New York 10010 (800) 221-7945; *The Statesman's Year-Book.*

Statistical Office of the United Nations, Publishing Service, New York, New York 10017 (800) 253-9646; *Asia-Pacific in Figures; Demographic Yearbook; Human Development Report; Statistical Yearbook; World Statistics Pocketbook;* and *Statistical Yearbook for Asia and the Pacific.*

U.S. Arms Control and Disarmament Agency, 320 Twenty-first Street, NW, Washington, D.C. 20451 (202) 647-8677; *World Military Expenditures and Arms Transfers.*

Walden Publishing Ltd., Two Market Street, Saffron Walden Essex, CB10 1HZ, England; *The World of Information Asia and Pacific Review.*

The World Bank, 1818 H Street, NW, Washington, D.C. 20433 (202) 477-1234; *The World Bank Atlas;* and *World Development Report.*

World Health Organization, Office of Publications, 20 Avenue Appia, CH-1211 Geneva 27, Switzerland (Telephone Number in U.S. (518) 436-9686); *World*

Health Statistics Annual.

MONGOLIA - POST OFFICES

M.E. Sharpe, 80 Business Park Drive, Armonk, New York 10504 (800) 541-6563; *The Illustrated Book of World Rankings.*

St. Martin's Press, Inc., 175 Fifth Avenue, New York, New York 10010 (800) 221-7945; *The Statesman's Year-Book.*

MONGOLIA - POTATO PRODUCTION - See MONGOLIA - CROPS

MONGOLIA - POWER PRODUCTION INDUSTRY - ESTABLISHMENTS, PAYROLLS, VALUE ADDED, ETC.

Statistical Office of the United Nations, Publishing Service, New York, New York 10017 (800) 253-9646; *Electric Power in Asia and the Pacific.*

MONGOLIA - PRICES

Food and Agricultural Organization of the United Nations (FAO), Via delle Terme di Caracalla, 00100 Rome, Italy (Telephone Number in U.S. (202) 653-2400); *Production Yearbook;* and *The State of Food and Agriculture.*

M.E. Sharpe, 80 Business Park Drive, Armonk, New York 10504 (800) 541-6563; *The Illustrated Book of World Rankings.*

MONGOLIA - PRINTING AND WRITING PAPER - See MONGOLIA - FORESTRY AND FOREST PRODUCTS

MONGOLIA - PRODUCTION

M.E. Sharpe, 80 Business Park Drive, Armonk, New York 10504 (800) 541-6563; *The Illustrated Book of World Rankings.*

MONGOLIA - PUBLIC FINANCE - See MONGOLIA - FINANCE

MONGOLIA - RADIO

The Economist Intelligence Unit (Asia) Limited, 10th Floor, Luk Kwok Centre, 72 Gloucester Road, Wanchai, Hong Kong (Phone Number in U.S. (800) 938-4685); *Asian Market Atlas.*

M.E. Sharpe, 80 Business Park Drive, Armonk, New York 10504 (800) 541-6563; *The Illustrated Book of World Rankings.*

MONGOLIA - RADIO RECEIVERS

St. Martin's Press, Inc., 175 Fifth Avenue, New York, New York 10010 (800) 221-7945; *The Statesman's Year-Book.*

MONGOLIA - RAILWAYS

Europa Publications Limited, 18 Bedford Square, London, WC1B 3JN, England; *The Europa World Year Book*.

St. Martin's Press, Inc., 175 Fifth Avenue, New York, New York 10010 (800) 221-7945; *The Statesman's Year-Book*.

Statistical Office of the United Nations, Publishing Service, New York, New York 10017 (800) 253-9646; *Statistical Yearbook*.

MONGOLIA - RELIGION

Central Intelligence Agency, Washington, D.C. 20505 (703) 482-1100, www.cia.gov; *The World Factbook*.

M.E. Sharpe, 80 Business Park Drive, Armonk, New York 10504 (800) 541-6563; *The Illustrated Book of World Rankings*.

St. Martin's Press, Inc., 175 Fifth Avenue, New York, New York 10010 (800) 221-7945; *The Statesman's Year-Book*.

MONGOLIA - RETAIL TRADE

Euromonitor International, Inc., 122 South Michigan Avenue, Suite 1200, Chicago, Illinois 60603 (800) 577-EURO; *World Marketing Data and Statistics*.

Statistical Office of the United Nations, Publishing Service, New York, New York 10017 (800) 253-9646; *Statistical Yearbook*.

MONGOLIA - RICE PRODUCTION - See MONGOLIA - CROPS

MONGOLIA - ROOT AND TUBER PRODUCTION - See MONGOLIA - CROPS

MONGOLIA - ROUNDWOOD PRODUCTION - See MONGOLIA - FORESTRY AND FOREST PRODUCTS

MONGOLIA - RUBBER PRODUCTION AND CONSUMPTION

M.E. Sharpe, 80 Business Park Drive, Armonk, New York 10504 (800) 541-6563; *The Illustrated Book of World Rankings*.

MONGOLIA - SALT PRODUCTION - See MONGOLIA - MINING AND MINERAL PRODUCTS

MONGOLIA - SAWNWOOD PRODUCTION - See MONGOLIA - FORESTRY AND FOREST PRODUCTS

MONGOLIA - SCIENCE AND TECHNOLOGY - EXPENDITURE FOR RESEARCH - See MONGOLIA - SCIENTISTS, TECHNICIANS AND ENGINEERS

MONGOLIA - SCIENTISTS, TECHNICIANS AND ENGINEERS

Statistical Office of the United Nations,

Publishing Service, New York, New York 10017 (800) 253-9646; *Statistical Yearbook*.

MONGOLIA - SENIOR CITIZENS

M.E. Sharpe, 80 Business Park Drive, Armonk, New York 10504 (800) 541-6563; *The Illustrated Book of World Rankings*.

MONGOLIA - SHEEP - See MONGOLIA - LIVESTOCK AND POULTRY

MONGOLIA - SILVER PRODUCTION AND CONSUMPTION - See MONGOLIA - MINING AND MINERAL PRODUCTS

MONGOLIA - SOCIAL DATA

M.E. Sharpe, 80 Business Park Drive, Armonk, New York 10504 (800) 541-6563; *The Illustrated Book of World Rankings*.

Statistical Office of the United Nations, Publishing Service, New York, New York 10017 (800) 253-9646; *World Statistics Pocketbook*.

MONGOLIA - SOCIAL SECURITY

Statistical Office of the United Nations, Publishing Service, New York, New York 10017 (800) 253-9646; *National Accounts Statistics*.

MONGOLIA - STEEL - See MONGOLIA - MINING AND MINERAL PRODUCTS

MONGOLIA - STOCKS - COMMODITY - MARKET PRICE - INDEX

Food and Agricultural Organization of the United Nations (FAO), Via delle Terme di Caracalla, 00100 Rome, Italy (Telephone Number in U.S. (202) 653-2400); *The State of Food and Agriculture*.

MONGOLIA - SUGAR PRODUCTION AND CONSUMPTION - See MONGOLIA - CROPS

MONGOLIA - TAXATION

Europa Publications Limited, 18 Bedford Square, London, WC1B 3JN, England; *The Europa World Year Book*.

St. Martin's Press, Inc., 175 Fifth Avenue, New York, New York 10010 (800) 221-7945; *The Statesman's Year-Book*.

MONGOLIA - TELEPHONES IN USE

American Telephone and Telegraph Company, 26 Parsippany Road, Whippany, New Jersey 07981 (800) 222-0300; *The World's Telephones*.

Central Intelligence Agency, Washington, D.C. 20505 (703) 482-1100, www.cia.gov; *The World Factbook*.

The Economist Intelligence Unit (Asia) Limited, 10th Floor, Luk Kwok Centre, 72 Gloucester Road, Wanchai, Hong Kong (Phone Number in U.S. (800) 938-4685); *Asian Market Atlas*.

Europa Publications Limited, 18 Bedford Square, London, WC1B 3JN, England; *The Europa World Year Book*.

St. Martin's Press, Inc., 175 Fifth Avenue, New York, New York 10010 (800) 221-7945; *The Statesman's Year-Book*.

Statistical Office of the United Nations, Publishing Service, New York, New York 10017 (800) 253-9646; *Statistical Yearbook*; and *World Statistics Pocketbook*.

MONGOLIA - TELEVISION

The Economist Intelligence Unit (Asia) Limited, 10th Floor, Luk Kwok Centre, 72 Gloucester Road, Wanchai, Hong Kong (Phone Number in U.S. (800) 938-4685); *Asian Market Atlas*.

M.E. Sharpe, 80 Business Park Drive, Armonk, New York 10504 (800) 541-6563; *The Illustrated Book of World Rankings*.

MONGOLIA - TELEVISION BROADCASTING - See MONGOLIA - BROADCASTING

MONGOLIA - TEXTILE INDUSTRY

M.E. Sharpe, 80 Business Park Drive, Armonk, New York 10504 (800) 541-6563; *The Illustrated Book of World Rankings*.

Statistical Office of the United Nations, Publishing Service, New York, New York 10017 (800) 253-9646; *Statistical Yearbook*.

United Nations Conference on Trade and Development, Central Statistical Service, Palais des Nations, Geneva, Switzerland (Telephone in U.S. (800) 253-9646); *UNCTAD Commodity Yearbook*.

MONGOLIA - TIMBER - See MONGOLIA - FORESTRY AND FOREST PRODUCTS

MONGOLIA - TOBACCO PRODUCTION

M.E. Sharpe, 80 Business Park Drive, Armonk, New York 10504 (800) 541-6563; *The Illustrated Book of World Rankings*.

MONGOLIA - TOURISM

Euromonitor International, Inc., 122 South Michigan Avenue, Suite 1200, Chicago, Illinois 60603 (800) 577-EURO; *The World Economic Factbook;* and *World Marketing Data and Statistics*.

M.E. Sharpe, 80 Business Park Drive, Armonk, New York 10504 (800) 541-6563; *The Illustrated Book of World Rankings*.

St. Martin's Press, Inc., 175 Fifth Avenue, New York, New York 10010 (800) 221-7945; *The Statesman's Year-Book.*

World Tourism Organization, Calle Capitan Haya 42, E-28020 Madrid, Spain; *Yearbook of Tourism Statistics.*

MONGOLIA - TRACTORS IN USE

Statistical Office of the United Nations, Publishing Service, New York, New York 10017 (800) 253-9646; *Statistical Yearbook.*

MONGOLIA - TRADE - See MONGOLIA - FOREIGN TRADE

MONGOLIA - TRADEMARKS AND SERVICE MARKS - See MONGOLIA - PATENTS, TRADEMARKS AND SERVICE MARKS

MONGOLIA - TRANSPORTATION AND COMMUNICATIONS

Central Intelligence Agency, Washington, D.C. 20505 (703) 482-1100, www.cia.gov; *The World Factbook.*

The Economist Intelligence Unit (Asia) Limited, 10th Floor, Luk Kwok Centre, 72 Gloucester Road, Wanchai, Hong Kong (Phone Number in U.S. (800) 938-4685); *Asian Market Atlas.*

Euromonitor International, Inc., 122 South Michigan Avenue, Suite 1200, Chicago, Illinois 60603 (800) 577-EURO; *International Marketing Data and Statistics;* and *World Marketing Data and Statistics.*

Europa Publications Limited, 18 Bedford Square, London, WC1B 3JN, England; *The Europa World Year Book.*

M.E. Sharpe, 80 Business Park Drive, Armonk, New York 10504 (800) 541-6563; *The Illustrated Book of World Rankings.*

St. Martin's Press, Inc., 175 Fifth Avenue, New York, New York 10010 (800) 221-7945; *The Statesman's Year-Book.*

Statistical Office of the United Nations, Publishing Service, New York, New York 10017 (800) 253-9646; *Human Development Report;* and *Statistical Yearbook for Asia and the Pacific.*

MONGOLIA - UNEMPLOYMENT

Central Intelligence Agency, Washington, D.C. 20505 (703) 482-1100, www.cia.gov; *The World Factbook.*

MONGOLIA - UTILITIES

Statistical Office of the United Nations, Publishing Service, New York, New York 10017 (800) 253-9646; *Electric Power in Asia and the Pacific.*

MONGOLIA - VITAL STATISTICS

St. Martin's Press, Inc., 175 Fifth Avenue, New York, New York 10010 (800) 221-7945; *The Statesman's Year-Book.*

Statistical Office of the United Nations, Publishing Service, New York, New York 10017 (800) 253-9646; *Statistical Yearbook.*

World Health Organization, Office of Publications, 20 Avenue Appia, CH-1211 Geneva 27, Switzerland (Telephone Number in U.S. (518) 436-9686); *World Health Statistics Annual.*

MONGOLIA - WAGES AND PRICES

Statistical Office of the United Nations, Publishing Service, New York, New York 10017 (800) 253-9646; *Statistical Yearbook for Asia and the Pacific.*

MONGOLIA - WEATHER - See MONGOLIA - CLIMATE

MONGOLIA - WHEAT PRODUCTION - See MONGOLIA - CROPS

MONGOLIA - WHOLESALE TRADE

Statistical Office of the United Nations, Publishing Service, New York, New York 10017 (800) 253-9646; *Statistical Yearbook.*

MONGOLIA - WINE PRODUCTION - See MONGOLIA - BEVERAGES

MONGOLIA - WOOL PRODUCTION - See MONGOLIA - TEXTILE INDUSTRY

MONITORS

U.S. Department of Commerce, Bureau of the Census, Washington, D.C. 20233 (301) 457-4100, www.census.gov; *County Business Patterns.*

MONTANA - See also STATE DATA (FOR INDIVIDUAL STATES)

Montana - Primary Statistics Source

Montana Department of Commerce, Census and Economic Information Center, 1424 Ninth Avenue, Helena, Montana 59620 (406) 444-2896; Statistical Reports from the Montana County Database.

Montana - State Data Centers

Census and Economic Information Center, Montana Department of Commerce, Post Office Box 200505, 1424 Ninth Avenue, Helena, Montana 59620-0505, Mr. Alan B. Cox (406) 444-4393.

Bureau of Business and Economic Research, University of Montana, Missoula, Montana 59812, Mr. Jim Sylvester (406) 243-5113.

Montana State Library, 1515 East 6th Avenue, Helena, Montana 59620, Mr. Don Cornish (406) 444-5351.

Natural Resource Center, 1515 East 6th Avenue, Post Office Box 201800, Helena, Montana 59620-1800, Velda Welch (406) 444-3345.

Research and Analysis Bureau, Job Service Division, Montana Department of Labor and Industry, Post Office Box 1728, Helena, Montana 59624, Ms. Cathy Shenkle (406) 444-2430.

MONTENEGRO - See YUGOSLAVIA

Montserrat - National Statistical Office

Statistics Office, Chief Statistician, Government Headquarters, Plymouth, Montserrat.

Montserrat - Primary Statistics Source

Statistics Office, P.O. Box 292, Plymouth, Montserrat; *Statistical Digest.*

MONTSERRAT - AGRICULTURE

Europa Publications Limited, 18 Bedford Square, London, WC1B 3JN, England; *The Europa World Year Book.*

Food and Agricultural Organization of the United Nations (FAO), Via delle Terme di Caracalla, 00100 Rome, Italy (Telephone Number in U.S. (202) 653-2400); *Production Yearbook; The State of Food and Agriculture;* and *Trade Yearbook.*

St. Martin's Press, Inc., 175 Fifth Avenue, New York, New York 10010 (800) 221-7945; *The Statesman's Year-Book.*

Statistical Office of the United Nations, Publishing Service, New York, New York 10017 (800) 253-9646; *Statistical Yearbook.*

United Nations Conference on Trade and Development, Central Statistical Service, Palais des Nations, Geneva, Switzerland (Telephone in U.S. (800) 253-9646); *UNCTAD Commodity Yearbook.*

MONTSERRAT - AIRLINE SERVICE

Europa Publications Limited, 18 Bedford Square, London, WC1B 3JN, England; *The Europa World Year Book.*

St. Martin's Press, Inc., 175 Fifth Avenue, New York, New York 10010 (800) 221-7945; *The Statesman's Year-Book.*

MONTSERRAT - AIRPORTS

Central Intelligence Agency, Washington, D.C. 20505 (703) 482-1100, www.cia.gov; *The World Factbook.*

MONTSERRAT - AREA AND DENSITY OF POPULATION

Central Intelligence Agency, Washington, D.C. 20505 (703) 482-1100, www.cia.gov; *The World Factbook.*

Europa Publications Limited, 18 Bedford Square, London, WC1B 3JN, England; *The Europa World Year Book.*

Food and Agricultural Organization of the United Nations (FAO), Via delle Terme di Caracalla, 00100 Rome, Italy (Telephone Number in U.S. (202) 653-2400); *The State of Food and Agriculture.*

St. Martin's Press, Inc., 175 Fifth Avenue, New York, New York 10010 (800) 221-7945; *The Statesman's Year-Book.*

Statistical Office of the United Nations, Publishing Service, New York, New York 10017 (800) 253-9646; *Statistical Yearbook.*

MONTSERRAT - BALANCE OF PAYMENTS

Europa Publications Limited, 18 Bedford Square, London, WC1B 3JN, England; *The Europa World Year Book.*

MONTSERRAT - BANKING

St. Martin's Press, Inc., 175 Fifth Avenue, New York, New York 10010 (800) 221-7945; *The Statesman's Year-Book.*

MONTSERRAT - BIRTH RATES

Central Intelligence Agency, Washington, D.C. 20505 (703) 482-1100, www.cia.gov; *The World Factbook.*

Europa Publications Limited, 18 Bedford Square, London, WC1B 3JN, England; *The Europa World Year Book.*

Statistical Office of the United Nations, Publishing Service, New York, New York 10017 (800) 253-9646; *Demographic Yearbook;* and *Statistical Yearbook.*

World Health Organization, Office of Publications, 20 Avenue Appia, CH-1211 Geneva 27, Switzerland (Telephone Number in U.S. (518) 436-9686); *World Health Statistics Annual.*

MONTSERRAT - BROADCASTING

Billboard Limited, Post Office Box 9027, 1006 AA Amsterdam, The Netherlands (Telephone Number in U.S. (212) 764-7300); *World Radio TV Handbook.*

Central Intelligence Agency, Washington, D.C. 20505 (703) 482-1100, www.cia.gov; *The World Factbook.*

St. Martin's Press, Inc., 175 Fifth Avenue, New York, New York 10010 (800) 221-7945; *The Statesman's Year-Book.*

MONTSERRAT - BUDGET

Central Intelligence Agency, Washington, D.C. 20505 (703) 482-1100, www.cia.gov; *The World Factbook.*

MONTSERRAT - CALORIE SUPPLY

Food and Agricultural Organization of the United Nations (FAO), Via delle Terme di Caracalla, 00100 Rome, Italy (Telephone Number in U.S. (202) 653-2400); *The State of Food and Agriculture.*

MONTSERRAT - CATTLE - See MONTSERRAT - LIVESTOCK AND POULTRY

MONTSERRAT - CLIMATE

St. Martin's Press, Inc., 175 Fifth Avenue, New York, New York 10010 (800) 221-7945; *The Statesman's Year-Book.*

MONTSERRAT - COMMERCE

St. Martin's Press, Inc., 175 Fifth Avenue, New York, New York 10010 (800) 221-7945; *The Statesman's Year-Book.*

MONTSERRAT - CONSUMER PRICE INDEX

Europa Publications Limited, 18 Bedford Square, London, WC1B 3JN, England; *The Europa World Year Book.*

Statistical Office of the United Nations, Publishing Service, New York, New York 10017 (800) 253-9646; *Statistical Yearbook.*

MONTSERRAT - CONSUMER PRICES

International Labour Office, I.L.O. Publications, 1828 L Street, NW, Suite 801, Washington, D.C. 20036 (301) 638-3152; *Yearbook of Labour Statistics.*

MONTSERRAT - CORN PRODUCTION - See MONTSERRAT - CROPS

MONTSERRAT - CORPORATE TAXES - See MONTSERRAT - TAXATION

MONTSERRAT - CROPS

Food and Agricultural Organization of the United Nations (FAO), Via delle Terme di Caracalla, 00100 Rome, Italy (Telephone Number in U.S. (202) 653-2400); *The State of Food and Agriculture.*

St. Martin's Press, Inc., 175 Fifth Avenue, New York, New York 10010 (800) 221-7945; *The Statesman's Year-Book.*

United Nations Conference on Trade and Development, Central Statistical Service, Palais des Nations, Geneva, Switzerland (Telephone in U.S. (800) 253-9646); *UNCTAD Commodity Yearbook.*

MONTSERRAT - CUSTOMS DUTIES

St. Martin's Press, Inc., 175 Fifth Avenue, New York, New York 10010 (800) 221-7945; *The Statesman's Year-Book.*

MONTSERRAT - DAIRY PRODUCTS

Food and Agricultural Organization of the United Nations (FAO), Via delle Terme di Caracalla, 00100 Rome, Italy (Telephone Number in U.S. (202) 653-2400); *The State of Food and Agriculture.*

St. Martin's Press, Inc., 175 Fifth Avenue, New York, New York 10010 (800) 221-7945; *The Statesman's Year-Book.*

MONTSERRAT - DEATH RATES - See MONTSERRAT - MORTALITY

MONTSERRAT - DISEASES - See MONTSERRAT - HEALTH

MONTSERRAT - DIVORCE

Statistical Office of the United Nations, Publishing Service, New York, New York 10017 (800) 253-9646; *Demographic Yearbook;* and *Statistical Yearbook.*

MONTSERRAT - ECONOMY

Central Intelligence Agency, Washington, D.C. 20505 (703) 482-1100, www.cia.gov; *The World Factbook.*

Europa Publications Limited, 18 Bedford Square, London, WC1B 3JN, England; *The Europa World Year Book.*

St. Martin's Press, Inc., 175 Fifth Avenue, New York, New York 10010 (800) 221-7945; *The Statesman's Year-Book.*

MONTSERRAT - EDUCATION

Europa Publications Limited, 18 Bedford Square, London, WC1B 3JN, England; *The Europa World Year Book.*

St. Martin's Press, Inc., 175 Fifth Avenue, New York, New York 10010 (800) 221-7945; *The Statesman's Year-Book.*

United Nations Educational, Scientific and Cultural Organization (UNESCO), 7 Place de Fontenoy, F-75700 Paris, France (Telephone Number in U.S. (212) 963-

5981); *Statistical Yearbook.*

MONTSERRAT - EGG PRODUCTION AND CONSUMPTION - See MONTSERRAT - DAIRY PRODUCTS

MONTSERRAT - ELECTRICITY

Central Intelligence Agency, Washington, D.C. 20505 (703) 482-1100, www.cia.gov; *The World Factbook.*

St. Martin's Press, Inc., 175 Fifth Avenue, New York, New York 10010 (800) 221-7945; *The Statesman's Year-Book.*

MONTSERRAT - EMPLOYMENT

International Labour Office, I.L.O. Publications, 1828 L Street, NW, Suite 801, Washington, D.C. 20036 (301) 638-3152; *Yearbook of Labour Statistics.*

MONTSERRAT - ENERGY

Food and Agricultural Organization of the United Nations (FAO), Via delle Terme di Caracalla, 00100 Rome, Italy (Telephone Number in U.S. (202) 653-2400); *The State of Food and Agriculture.*

St. Martin's Press, Inc., 175 Fifth Avenue, New York, New York 10010 (800) 221-7945; *The Statesman's Year-Book.*

Statistical Office of the United Nations, Publishing Service, New York, New York 10017 (800) 253-9646; *Statistical Yearbook.*

MONTSERRAT - EXCHANGE RATES

Central Intelligence Agency, Washington, D.C. 20505 (703) 482-1100, www.cia.gov; *The World Factbook.*

Europa Publications Limited, 18 Bedford Square, London, WC1B 3JN, England; *The Europa World Year Book.*

MONTSERRAT - EXPORTS

Central Intelligence Agency, Washington, D.C. 20505 (703) 482-1100, www.cia.gov; *The World Factbook.*

Europa Publications Limited, 18 Bedford Square, London, WC1B 3JN, England; *The Europa World Year Book.*

Food and Agricultural Organization of the United Nations (FAO), Via delle Terme di Caracalla, 00100 Rome, Italy (Telephone Number in U.S. (202) 653-2400); *The State of Food and Agriculture.*

St. Martin's Press, Inc., 175 Fifth Avenue, New York, New York 10010 (800) 221-7945; *The Statesman's Year-Book.*

MONTSERRAT - EXTERNAL TRADE

Food and Agricultural Organization of the United Nations (FAO), Via delle Terme di Caracalla, 00100 Rome, Italy (Telephone Number in U.S. (202) 653-2400); *The State of Food and Agriculture;* and *Trade Yearbook.*

MONTSERRAT - FARM CROPS - See MONTSERRAT - CROPS

MONTSERRAT - FERTILITY RATES

Central Intelligence Agency, Washington, D.C. 20505 (703) 482-1100, www.cia.gov; *The World Factbook.*

MONTSERRAT - FERTILIZER

Food and Agricultural Organization of the United Nations (FAO), Via delle Terme di Caracalla, 00100 Rome, Italy (Telephone Number in U.S. (202) 653-2400); *The State of Food and Agriculture.*

MONTSERRAT - FETAL MORTALITY - See MONTSERRAT - MORTALITY

MONTSERRAT - FINANCE

Europa Publications Limited, 18 Bedford Square, London, WC1B 3JN, England; *The Europa World Year Book.*

St. Martin's Press, Inc., 175 Fifth Avenue, New York, New York 10010 (800) 221-7945; *The Statesman's Year-Book.*

MONTSERRAT - FISHERIES

Europa Publications Limited, 18 Bedford Square, London, WC1B 3JN, England; *The Europa World Year Book.*

Food and Agricultural Organization of the United Nations (FAO), Via delle Terme di Caracalla, 00100 Rome, Italy (Telephone Number in U.S. (202) 653-2400); *The State of Food and Agriculture;* and *Yearbook of Fishery Statistics.*

St. Martin's Press, Inc., 175 Fifth Avenue, New York, New York 10010 (800) 221-7945; *The Statesman's Year-Book.*

United Nations Conference on Trade and Development, Central Statistical Service, Palais des Nations, Geneva, Switzerland (Telephone in U.S. (800) 253-9646); *UNCTAD Commodity Yearbook.*

MONTSERRAT - FOOD

Food and Agricultural Organization of the United Nations (FAO), Via delle Terme di Caracalla, 00100 Rome, Italy (Telephone Number in U.S. (202) 653-2400); *Production Yearbook;* and *The State of Food and Agriculture.*

United Nations Conference on Trade and Development, Central Statistical

Service, Palais des Nations, Geneva, Switzerland (Telephone in U.S. (800) 253-9646); *UNCTAD Commodity Yearbook.*

MONTSERRAT - FOREIGN TRADE

Food and Agricultural Organization of the United Nations (FAO), Via delle Terme di Caracalla, 00100 Rome, Italy (Telephone Number in U.S. (202) 653-2400); *The State of Food and Agriculture.*

St. Martin's Press, Inc., 175 Fifth Avenue, New York, New York 10010 (800) 221-7945; *The Statesman's Year-Book.*

Statistical Office of the United Nations, Publishing Service, New York, New York 10017 (800) 253-9646; *International Trade Statistics Yearbook.*

United Nations Conference on Trade and Development, Central Statistical Service, Palais des Nations, Geneva, Switzerland (Telephone in U.S. (800) 253-9646); *UNCTAD Commodity Yearbook.*

MONTSERRAT - FORESTRY AND FOREST PRODUCTS

Food and Agricultural Organization of the United Nations (FAO), Via delle Terme di Caracalla, 00100 Rome, Italy (Telephone Number in U.S. (202) 653-2400); *The State of Food and Agriculture.*

Statistical Office of the United Nations, Publishing Service, New York, New York 10017 (800) 253-9646; *Statistical Yearbook.*

United Nations Conference on Trade and Development, Central Statistical Service, Palais des Nations, Geneva, Switzerland (Telephone in U.S. (800) 253-9646); *UNCTAD Commodity Yearbook.*

MONTSERRAT - GENERAL MORTALITY - See MONTSERRAT - MORTALITY

MONTSERRAT - GOVERNMENT

Central Intelligence Agency, Washington, D.C. 20505 (703) 482-1100, www.cia.gov; *The World Factbook.*

Europa Publications Limited, 18 Bedford Square, London, WC1B 3JN, England; *The Europa World Year Book.*

St. Martin's Press, Inc., 175 Fifth Avenue, New York, New York 10010 (800) 221-7945; *The Statesman's Year-Book.*

Statistical Office of the United Nations, Publishing Service, New York, New York 10017 (800) 253-9646; *National Accounts Statistics.*

MONTSERRAT - GRAIN PRODUCTION - See MONTSERRAT - CROPS

MONTSERRAT - GROSS DOMESTIC PRODUCT

Europa Publications Limited, 18 Bedford Square, London, WC1B 3JN, England; *The Europa World Year Book.*

Statistical Office of the United Nations, Publishing Service, New York, New York 10017 (800) 253-9646; *National Accounts Statistics;* and *Statistical Yearbook.*

MONTSERRAT - GROSS NATIONAL PRODUCT

St. Martin's Press, Inc., 175 Fifth Avenue, New York, New York 10010 (800) 221-7945; *The Statesman's Year-Book.*

MONTSERRAT - HEALTH

St. Martin's Press, Inc., 175 Fifth Avenue, New York, New York 10010 (800) 221-7945; *The Statesman's Year-Book.*

Statistical Office of the United Nations, Publishing Service, New York, New York 10017 (800) 253-9646; *Statistical Yearbook.*

World Health Organization, Office of Publications, 20 Avenue Appia, CH-1211 Geneva 27, Switzerland (Telephone Number in U.S. (518) 436-9686); *World Health Statistics Annual.*

MONTSERRAT - HEALTH AND MEDICAL SERVICES

Statistical Office of the United Nations, Publishing Service, New York, New York 10017 (800) 253-9646; *Statistical Yearbook.*

MONTSERRAT - HIDE PRODUCTION

Food and Agricultural Organization of the United Nations (FAO), Via delle Terme di Caracalla, 00100 Rome, Italy (Telephone Number in U.S. (202) 653-2400); *Production Yearbook.*

MONTSERRAT - HIGHWAYS

Central Intelligence Agency, Washington, D.C. 20505 (703) 482-1100, www.cia.gov; *The World Factbook.*

St. Martin's Press, Inc., 175 Fifth Avenue, New York, New York 10010 (800) 221-7945; *The Statesman's Year-Book.*

MONTSERRAT - HOURS OF WORK - See MONTSERRAT - EMPLOYMENT

MONTSERRAT - ILLITERATE POPULATION

Central Intelligence Agency, Washington, D.C. 20505 (703) 482-1100, www.cia.gov; *The World Factbook.*

United Nations Educational, Scientific

and Cultural Organization (UNESCO), 7 Place de Fontenoy, F-75700 Paris, France (Telephone Number in U.S. (212) 963-5981); *Statistical Yearbook.*

MONTSERRAT - IMPORTS

Central Intelligence Agency, Washington, D.C. 20505 (703) 482-1100, www.cia.gov; *The World Factbook.*

Europa Publications Limited, 18 Bedford Square, London, WC1B 3JN, England; *The Europa World Year Book.*

Food and Agricultural Organization of the United Nations (FAO), Via delle Terme di Caracalla, 00100 Rome, Italy (Telephone Number in U.S. (202) 653-2400); *The State of Food and Agriculture.*

St. Martin's Press, Inc., 175 Fifth Avenue, New York, New York 10010 (800) 221-7945; *The Statesman's Year-Book.*

MONTSERRAT - INDUSTRY

Central Intelligence Agency, Washington, D.C. 20505 (703) 482-1100, www.cia.gov; *The World Factbook.*

Europa Publications Limited, 18 Bedford Square, London, WC1B 3JN, England; *The Europa World Year Book.*

International Labour Office, I.L.O. Publications, 1828 L Street, NW, Suite 801, Washington, D.C. 20036 (301) 638-3152; *Yearbook of Labour Statistics.*

St. Martin's Press, Inc., 175 Fifth Avenue, New York, New York 10010 (800) 221-7945; *The Statesman's Year-Book.*

MONTSERRAT - INFANT AND MATERNAL MORTALITY - See MONTSERRAT - MORALITY

MONTSERRAT - LABOR

Central Intelligence Agency, Washington, D.C. 20505 (703) 482-1100, www.cia.gov; *The World Factbook.*

Food and Agricultural Organization of the United Nations (FAO), Via delle Terme di Caracalla, 00100 Rome, Italy (Telephone Number in U.S. (202) 653-2400); *The State of Food and Agriculture.*

International Labour Office, I.L.O. Publications, 1828 L Street, NW, Suite 801, Washington, D.C. 20036 (301) 638-3152; *Yearbook of Labour Statistics.*

St. Martin's Press, Inc., 175 Fifth Avenue, New York, New York 10010 (800) 221-7945; *The Statesman's Year-Book.*

MONTSERRAT - LAND USE

Central Intelligence Agency, Washington, D.C. 20505 (703) 482-1100, www.cia.gov; *The World Factbook.*

Food and Agricultural Organization of the United Nations (FAO), Via delle Terme di Caracalla, 00100 Rome, Italy (Telephone Number in U.S. (202) 653-2400); *Production Yearbook.*

MONTSERRAT - LIFE EXPECTANCY

Central Intelligence Agency, Washington, D.C. 20505 (703) 482-1100, www.cia.gov; *The World Factbook.*

MONTSERRAT - LIVESTOCK AND POULTRY

Europa Publications Limited, 18 Bedford Square, London, WC1B 3JN, England; *The Europa World Year Book.*

Food and Agricultural Organization of the United Nations (FAO), Via delle Terme di Caracalla, 00100 Rome, Italy (Telephone Number in U.S. (202) 653-2400); *Production Yearbook;* and *The State of Food and Agriculture.*

St. Martin's Press, Inc., 175 Fifth Avenue, New York, New York 10010 (800) 221-7945; *The Statesman's Year-Book.*

Statistical Office of the United Nations, Publishing Service, New York, New York 10017 (800) 253-9646; *Statistical Yearbook.*

United Nations Conference on Trade and Development, Central Statistical Service, Palais des Nations, Geneva, Switzerland (Telephone in U.S. (800) 253-9646); *UNCTAD Commodity Yearbook.*

MONTSERRAT - MAIL - NUMBER OF ITEMS SENT AND RECEIVED

Statistical Office of the United Nations, Publishing Service, New York, New York 10017 (800) 253-9646; *Statistical Yearbook.*

MONTSERRAT - MARRIAGE RATES

Statistical Office of the United Nations, Publishing Service, New York, New York 10017 (800) 253-9646; *Demographic Yearbook;* and *Statistical Yearbook.*

MONTSERRAT - MEAT PRODUCTION - See MONTSERRAT - LIVESTOCK AND POULTRY

MONTSERRAT - MERCHANT SHIPPING

Europa Publications Limited, 18 Bedford Square, London, WC1B 3JN, England; *The Europa World Year Book.*

St. Martin's Press, Inc., 175 Fifth Avenue, New York, New York 10010 (800) 221-7945; *The Statesman's Year-Book.*

Statistical Office of the United Nations,

Publishing Service, New York, New York 10017 (800) 253-9646; *Statistical Yearbook.*

MONTSERRAT - MILITARY

Central Intelligence Agency, Washington, D.C. 20505 (703) 482-1100, www.cia.gov; *The World Factbook.*

MONTSERRAT - MINING AND MINERAL PRODUCTS

United Nations Conference on Trade and Development, Central Statistical Service, Palais des Nations, Geneva, Switzerland (Telephone in U.S. (800) 253-9646); *UNCTAD Commodity Yearbook.*

MONTSERRAT - MORTALITY

Central Intelligence Agency, Washington, D.C. 20505 (703) 482-1100, www.cia.gov; *The World Factbook.*

Europa Publications Limited, 18 Bedford Square, London, WC1B 3JN, England; *The Europa World Year Book.*

Statistical Office of the United Nations, Publishing Service, New York, New York 10017 (800) 253-9646; *Demographic Yearbook;* and *Statistical Yearbook.*

World Health Organization, Office of Publications, 20 Avenue Appia, CH-1211 Geneva 27, Switzerland (Telephone Number in U.S. (518) 436-9686); *World Health Statistics Annual.*

MONTSERRAT - MOTOR VEHICLES IN USE

Europa Publications Limited, 18 Bedford Square, London, WC1B 3JN, England; *The Europa World Year Book.*

MONTSERRAT - NATALITY - See MONTSERRAT - BIRTH RATES

MONTSERRAT - NATIONAL ACCOUNTS

Statistical Office of the United Nations, Publishing Service, New York, New York 10017 (800) 253-9646; *Statistical Yearbook;* and *National Account Statistics.*

MONTSERRAT - NATIONAL INCOME

Statistical Office of the United Nations, Publishing Service, New York, New York 10017 (800) 253-9646; *National Accounts Statistics;* and *Statistical Yearbook.*

MONTSERRAT - NEWSPAPER PRODUCTION - See MONTSERRAT - FORESTRY AND FOREST PRODUCTS

MONTSERRAT - OCCUPATIONS - See MONTSERRAT - LABOR

MONTSERRAT - PERIODICALS

United Nations Educational, Scientific and Cultural Organization (UNESCO), 7 Place de Fontenoy, F-75700 Paris, France (Telephone Number in U.S. (212) 963-5981); *Statistical Yearbook.*

MONTSERRAT - PESTICIDE USE

Food and Agricultural Organization of the United Nations (FAO), Via delle Terme di Caracalla, 00100 Rome, Italy (Telephone Number in U.S. (202) 653-2400); *The State of Food and Agriculture.*

MONTSERRAT - PETROLEUM INDUSTRY

Food and Agricultural Organization of the United Nations (FAO), Via delle Terme di Caracalla, 00100 Rome, Italy (Telephone Number in U.S. (202) 653-2400); *The State of Food and Agriculture.*

United Nations Conference on Trade and Development, Central Statistical Service, Palais des Nations, Geneva, Switzerland (Telephone in U.S. (800) 253-9646); *UNCTAD Commodity Yearbook.*

MONTSERRAT - PIGS - See MONTSERRAT - LIVESTOCK AND POULTRY

MONTSERRAT - POPULATION

Central Intelligence Agency, Washington, D.C. 20505 (703) 482-1100, www.cia.gov; *The World Factbook.*

Europa Publications Limited, 18 Bedford Square, London, WC1B 3JN, England; *The Europa World Year Book.*

Food and Agricultural Organization of the United Nations (FAO), Via delle Terme di Caracalla, 00100 Rome, Italy (Telephone Number in U.S. (202) 653-2400); *Production Yearbook.*

International Labour Office, I.L.O. Publications, 1828 L Street, NW, Suite 801, Washington, D.C. 20036 (301) 638-3152; *Yearbook of Labour Statistics.*

St. Martin's Press, Inc., 175 Fifth Avenue, New York, New York 10010 (800) 221-7945; *The Statesman's Year-Book.*

Statistical Office of the United Nations, Publishing Service, New York, New York 10017 (800) 253-9646; *Demographic Yearbook;* and *Statistical Yearbook.*

World Health Organization, Office of Publications, 20 Avenue Appia, CH-1211 Geneva 27, Switzerland (Telephone Number in U.S. (518) 436-9686); *World Health Statistics Annual.*

MONTSERRAT - PRICES

Food and Agricultural Organization of

the United Nations (FAO), Via delle Terme di Caracalla, 00100 Rome, Italy (Telephone Number in U.S. (202) 653-2400); *Production Yearbook;* and *The State of Food and Agriculture.*

International Labour Office, I.L.O. Publications, 1828 L Street, NW, Suite 801, Washington, D.C. 20036 (301) 638-3152; *Yearbook of Labour Statistics.*

MONTSERRAT - RADIO RECEIVERS

St. Martin's Press, Inc., 175 Fifth Avenue, New York, New York 10010 (800) 221-7945; *The Statesman's Year-Book.*

MONTSERRAT - RELIGION

Central Intelligence Agency, Washington, D.C. 20505 (703) 482-1100, www.cia.gov; *The World Factbook.*

St. Martin's Press, Inc., 175 Fifth Avenue, New York, New York 10010 (800) 221-7945; *The Statesman's Year-Book.*

MONTSERRAT - ROUNDWOOD PRODUCTION - See MONTSERRAT - FORESTRY AND FOREST PRODUCTS

MONTSERRAT - SHEEP - See MONTSERRAT - LIVESTOCK AND POULTRY

MONTSERRAT - SOCIAL SECURITY

Statistical Office of the United Nations, Publishing Service, New York, New York 10017 (800) 253-9646; *National Accounts Statistics.*

MONTSERRAT - STOCKS - COMMODITY - MARKET PRICE - INDEX

Food and Agricultural Organization of the United Nations (FAO), Via delle Terme di Caracalla, 00100 Rome, Italy (Telephone Number in U.S. (202) 653-2400); *The State of Food and Agriculture.*

MONTSERRAT - TELEPHONES IN USE

American Telephone and Telegraph Company, 26 Parsippany Road, Whippany, New Jersey 07981 (800) 222-0300; *The World's Telephones.*

Central Intelligence Agency, Washington, D.C. 20505 (703) 482-1100, www.cia.gov; *The World Factbook.*

Europa Publications Limited, 18 Bedford Square, London, WC1B 3JN, England; *The Europa World Year Book.*

St. Martin's Press, Inc., 175 Fifth Avenue, New York, New York 10010 (800) 221-7945; *The Statesman's Year-Book.*

Statistical Office of the United Nations, Publishing Service, New York, New York

10017 (800) 253-9646; *Statistical Yearbook.*

MONTSERRAT - TEXTILE INDUSTRY

St. Martin's Press, Inc., 175 Fifth Avenue, New York, New York 10010 (800) 221-7945; *The Statesman's Year-Book.*

United Nations Conference on Trade and Development, Central Statistical Service, Palais des Nations, Geneva, Switzerland (Telephone in U.S. (800) 253-9646); *UNCTAD Commodity Yearbook.*

MONTSERRAT - THEATRE

United Nations Educational, Scientific and Cultural Organization (UNESCO), 7 Place de Fontenoy, F-75700 Paris, France (Telephone Number in U.S. (212) 963-5981); *Statistical Yearbook.*

MONTSERRAT - TOURISM

Europa Publications Limited, 18 Bedford Square, London, WC1B 3JN, England; *The Europa World Year Book.*

St. Martin's Press, Inc., 175 Fifth Avenue, New York, New York 10010 (800) 221-7945; *The Statesman's Year-Book.*

World Tourism Organization, Calle Capitan Haya 42, E-28020 Madrid, Spain; *Yearbook of Tourism Statistics.*

MONTSERRAT - TRACTORS IN USE

Statistical Office of the United Nations, Publishing Service, New York, New York 10017 (800) 253-9646; *Statistical Yearbook.*

MONTSERRAT - TRADE - See
MONTSERRAT - FOREIGN TRADE

MONTSERRAT - TRANSPORTATION AND COMMUNICATIONS

Central Intelligence Agency, Washington, D.C. 20505 (703) 482-1100, www.cia.gov; *The World Factbook.*

Europa Publications Limited, 18 Bedford Square, London, WC1B 3JN, England; *The Europa World Year Book.*

St. Martin's Press, Inc., 175 Fifth Avenue, New York, New York 10010 (800) 221-7945; *The Statesman's Year-Book.*

MONTSERRAT - UNEMPLOYMENT

Central Intelligence Agency, Washington, D.C. 20505 (703) 482-1100, www.cia.gov; *The World Factbook.*

International Labour Office, I.L.O. Publications, 1828 L Street, NW, Suite 801, Washington, D.C. 20036 (301) 638-3152; *Yearbook of Labour Statistics.*

MONTSERRAT - VITAL STATISTICS

Statistical Office of the United Nations, Publishing Service, New York, New York 10017 (800) 253-9646; *Statistical Yearbook.*

World Health Organization, Office of Publications, 20 Avenue Appia, CH-1211 Geneva 27, Switzerland (Telephone Number in U.S. (518) 436-9686); *World Health Statistics Annual.*

MONTSERRAT - WAGES

International Labour Office, I.L.O. Publications, 1828 L Street, NW, Suite 801, Washington, D.C. 20036 (301) 638-3152; *Yearbook of Labour Statistics.*

Morocco - National Statistical Offices

Direction de la Statistique, BP 178, Rabat, Morocco.

Office des Changes, Division des Etudes et de la Balance des Paiements, Place Moulay Hassan, BP 71, Rabat, Morocco.

Morocco - Primary Statistics Sources

Direction de la Statistique, BP 178, Rabat, Morocco; *Annuaire Statistique du Maroc* (Statistical Yearbook of Morocco); and *Bulletin Mensuel de Statistique* (Monthly Bulletin of Statistics).

MOROCCO - AGRICULTURE

Economist Intelligence Unit, 111 West 57th Street, New York, New York 10019 (800) 938-4685; *Morocco Country Report.*

Euromonitor International, Inc., 122 South Michigan Avenue, Suite 1200, Chicago, Illinois 60603 (800) 577-EURO; *International Marketing Data and Statistics;* and *World Marketing Data and Statistics.*

Europa Publications Limited, 18 Bedford Square, London, WC1B 3JN, England; *The Europa World Year Book.*

Federal Statistical Office, Gustav-Stresemann - Ring 11, D-6200, Wiesbaden, Germany; *Morokko.*

Food and Agricultural Organization of the United Nations (FAO), Via delle Terme di Caracalla, 00100 Rome, Italy (Telephone Number in U.S. (202) 653-2400); *Production Yearbook;* and *The State of Food and Agriculture.*

M.E. Sharpe, 80 Business Park Drive, Armonk, New York 10504 (800) 541-6563;

The Illustrated Book of World Rankings.

St. Martin's Press, Inc., 175 Fifth Avenue, New York, New York 10010 (800) 221-7945; *The Statesman's Year-Book.*

Statistical Office of the United Nations, Publishing Service, New York, New York 10017 (800) 253-9646; *Statistical Yearbook;* and *Survey of Economic and Social Conditions in Africa.*

United Nations Conference on Trade and Development, Central Statistical Service, Palais des Nations, Geneva, Switzerland (Telephone in U.S. (800) 253-9646); *UNCTAD Commodity Yearbook.*

United Nations Economic Commission for Africa, Africa Hall, Post Office Box 3001, Addis Ababa, Ethiopia (Telephone Number in U.S. (800) 253-9646); *African Statistical Yearbook.*

The World Bank, 1818 H Street, NW, Washington, D.C. 20433 (202) 477-1234; *World Development Indicators.*

MOROCCO - AIRLINE SERVICE

Europa Publications Limited, 18 Bedford Square, London, WC1B 3JN, England; *The Europa World Year Book.*

International Civil Aviation Organization, 999 University Street, Montreal, Quebec, Canada H3C 5H7 (514) 954-8219; *Civil Aviation Statistics of the World.*

M.E. Sharpe, 80 Business Park Drive, Armonk, New York 10504 (800) 541-6563; *The Illustrated Book of World Rankings.*

St. Martin's Press, Inc., 175 Fifth Avenue, New York, New York 10010 (800) 221-7945; *The Statesman's Year-Book.*

Statistical Office of the United Nations, Publishing Service, New York, New York 10017 (800) 253-9646; *Statistical Yearbook.*

United Nations Economic Commission for Africa, Africa Hall, Post Office Box 3001, Addis Ababa, Ethiopia (Telephone Number in U.S. (800) 253-9646); *African Statistical Yearbook.*

MOROCCO - AIRPORTS

Central Intelligence Agency, Washington, D.C. 20505 (703) 482-1100, www.cia.gov; *The World Factbook.*

MOROCCO - ALMOND PRODUCTION - See MOROCCO - CROPS

MOROCCO - ALUMINUM PRODUCTION AND CONSUMPTION - See MOROCCO - MINING AND MINERAL PRODUCTS

MOROCCO - ANIMAL FEEDINGSTUFFS OF AQUATIC ANIMAL ORIGIN

Statistical Office of the United Nations, Publishing Service, New York, New York 10017 (800) 253-9646; *Statistical Yearbook.*

MOROCCO - ANIMAL HEALTH

Food and Agricultural Organization of the United Nations (FAO), Via delle Terme di Caracalla, 00100 Rome, Italy (Telephone Number in U.S. (202) 653-2400); *Animal Health Yearbook.*

MOROCCO - ANTIMONY AND ANTIMONY ORE PRODUCTION AND CONSUMPTION - See MOROCCO - MINING AND MINERAL PRODUCTS

MOROCCO - AREA AND DENSITY OF POPULATION

African Development Bank, 01 BP 1387, Abidjan 01, Cote d'Ivoire; *Selected Statistics on Regional Member Countries.*

Central Intelligence Agency, Washington, D.C. 20505 (703) 482-1100, www.cia.gov; *The World Factbook.*

Euromonitor International, Inc., 122 South Michigan Avenue, Suite 1200, Chicago, Illinois 60603 (800) 577-EURO; *International Marketing Data and Statistics;* and *The World Economic Factbook.*

Europa Publications Limited, 18 Bedford Square, London, WC1B 3JN, England; *The Europa World Year Book.*

Federal Statistical Office, Gustav-Stresemann - Ring 11, D-6200, Wiesbaden, Germany; *Morokko.*

Food and Agricultural Organization of the United Nations (FAO), Via delle Terme di Caracalla, 00100 Rome, Italy (Telephone Number in U.S. (202) 653-2400); *The State of Food and Agriculture.*

M.E. Sharpe, 80 Business Park Drive, Armonk, New York 10504 (800) 541-6563; *The Illustrated Book of World Rankings.*

St. Martin's Press, Inc., 175 Fifth Avenue, New York, New York 10010 (800) 221-7945; *The Statesman's Year-Book.*

Statistical Office of the United Nations, Publishing Service, New York, New York 10017 (800) 253-9646; *Statistical Yearbook;* and *Survey of Economic and Social Conditions in Africa.*

The World Bank, 1818 H Street, NW, Washington, D.C. 20433 (202) 477-1234; *World Development Report.*

MOROCCO - ARMS EXPORTS AND IMPORTS - See MOROCCO - MILITARY

MOROCCO - ARTICHOKE PRODUCTION

Food and Agricultural Organization of the United Nations (FAO), Via delle Terme di Caracalla, 00100 Rome, Italy (Telephone Number in U.S. (202) 653-2400); *Production Yearbook.*

MOROCCO - BALANCE OF PAYMENTS

African Development Bank, 01 BP 1387, Abidjan 01, Cote d'Ivoire; *Selected Statistics on Regional Member Countries.*

The Economist Intelligence Unit, 111 West 57th Street, New York, New York 10019 (800) 938-4685; *The World Market Atlas.*

Europa Publications Limited, 18 Bedford Square, London, WC1B 3JN, England; *The Europa World Year Book.*

Federal Statistical Office, Gustav-Stresemann - Ring 11, D-6200, Wiesbaden, Germany; *Morokko.*

International Monetary Fund, 700 Nineteenth Street, NW, Washington, D.C. 20431 (202) 623-7000; *Balance of Payments Yearbook;* and *International Financial Statistics.*

United Nations Conference on Trade and Development (UNCTAD), New York, New York 10017 (800) 253-9646; *Handbook of International Trade and Development Statistics.*

United Nations Economic Commission for Africa, Africa Hall, Post Office Box 3001, Addis Ababa, Ethiopia (Telephone Number in U.S. (800) 253-9646); *African Statistical Yearbook.*

The World Bank, 1818 H Street, NW, Washington, D.C. 20433 (202) 477-1234; *World Development Report;* and *World Development Indicators.*

MOROCCO - BANKING

Euromonitor International, Inc., 122 South Michigan Avenue, Suite 1200, Chicago, Illinois 60603 (800) 577-EURO; *World Marketing Data and Statistics.*

Europa Publications Limited, 18 Bedford Square, London, WC1B 3JN, England; *The Europa World Year Book.*

International Monetary Fund, 700 Nineteenth Street, NW, Washington, D.C. 20431 (202) 623-7000; *Government Finance Statistics Yearbook;* and *International Financial Statistics.*

M.E. Sharpe, 80 Business Park Drive, Armonk, New York 10504 (800) 541-6563; *The Illustrated Book of World Rankings.*

St. Martin's Press, Inc., 175 Fifth Avenue, New York, New York 10010 (800) 221-7945; *The Statesman's Year-Book.*

Statistical Office of the United Nations, Publishing Service, New York, New York 10017 (800) 253-9646; *Statistical Yearbook.*

United Nations Economic Commission for Africa, Africa Hall, Post Office Box 3001, Addis Ababa, Ethiopia (Telephone Number in U.S. (800) 253-9646); *African Statistical Yearbook.*

MOROCCO - BARLEY PRODUCTION - See MOROCCO - CROPS

MOROCCO - BEER PRODUCTION - See MOROCCO - BEVERAGES

MOROCCO - BEVERAGES

M.E. Sharpe, 80 Business Park Drive, Armonk, New York 10504 (800) 541-6563; *The Illustrated Book of World Rankings.*

Statistical Office of the United Nations, Publishing Service, New York, New York 10017 (800) 253-9646; *Statistical Yearbook.*

MOROCCO - BIRTH RATES

Central Intelligence Agency, Washington, D.C. 20505 (703) 482-1100, www.cia.gov; *The World Factbook.*

Euromonitor International, Inc., 122 South Michigan Avenue, Suite 1200, Chicago, Illinois 60603 (800) 577-EURO; *International Marketing Data and Statistics;* and *The World Economic Factbook.*

Europa Publications Limited, 18 Bedford Square, London, WC1B 3JN, England; *The Europa World Year Book.*

M.E. Sharpe, 80 Business Park Drive, Armonk, New York 10504 (800) 541-6563; *The Illustrated Book of World Rankings.*

St. Martin's Press, Inc., 175 Fifth Avenue, New York, New York 10010 (800) 221-7945; *The Statesman's Year-Book.*

Statistical Office of the United Nations, Publishing Service, New York, New York 10017 (800) 253-9646; *Demographic Yearbook; Statistical Yearbook;* and *Survey of Economic and Social Conditions in Africa.*

The World Bank, 1818 H Street, NW, Washington, D.C. 20433 (202) 477-1234; *World Development Indicators.*

MOROCCO - BONDS

International Monetary Fund, 700 Nineteenth Street, NW, Washington, D.C. 20431 (202) 623-7000; *Government Finance Statistics Yearbook.*

MOROCCO - BOOK PRODUCTION

St. Martin's Press, Inc., 175 Fifth Avenue, New York, New York 10010 (800) 221-7945; *The Statesman's Year-Book*.

MOROCCO - BROADCASTING

Billboard Limited, Post Office Box 9027, 1006 AA Amsterdam, The Netherlands (Telephone Number in U.S. (212) 764-7300); *World Radio TV Handbook*.

Central Intelligence Agency, Washington, D.C. 20505 (703) 482-1100, www.cia.gov; *The World Factbook*.

Euromonitor International, Inc., 122 South Michigan Avenue, Suite 1200, Chicago, Illinois 60603 (800) 577-EURO; *World Marketing Data and Statistics*.

Europa Publications Limited, 18 Bedford Square, London, WC1B 3JN, England; *The Europa World Year Book*.

M.E. Sharpe, 80 Business Park Drive, Armonk, New York 10504 (800) 541-6563; *The Illustrated Book of World Rankings*.

St. Martin's Press, Inc., 175 Fifth Avenue, New York, New York 10010 (800) 221-7945; *The Statesman's Year-Book*.

United Nations Educational, Scientific and Cultural Organization (UNESCO), 7 Place de Fontenoy, F-75700 Paris, France (Telephone Number in U.S. (212) 963-5981); *Statistical Yearbook*.

MOROCCO - BUDGET

Central Intelligence Agency, Washington, D.C. 20505 (703) 482-1100, www.cia.gov; *The World Factbook*.

MOROCCO - BUILDING CONSTRUCTION

Statistical Office of the United Nations, Publishing Service, New York, New York 10017 (800) 253-9646; *Statistical Yearbook*.

MOROCCO - BUSINESS AND PROFESSIONAL LICENSES

International Monetary Fund, 700 Nineteenth Street, NW, Washington, D.C. 20431 (202) 623-7000; *Government Finance Statistics Yearbook*.

MOROCCO - BUTTER PRODUCTION - See MOROCCO - DAIRY PRODUCTS

MOROCCO - CALORIE SUPPLY

African Development Bank, 01 BP 1387, Abidjan 01, Cote d'Ivoire; *Selected Statistics on Regional Member Countries*.

Food and Agricultural Organization of the United Nations (FAO), Via delle Terme di Caracalla, 00100 Rome, Italy (Telephone Number in U.S. (202) 653-2400); *The State of Food and Agriculture*.

MOROCCO - CAPITAL REVENUE

International Monetary Fund, 700 Nineteenth Street, NW, Washington, D.C. 20431 (202) 623-7000; *Government Finance Statistics Yearbook*.

MOROCCO - CATTLE - See MOROCCO - LIVESTOCK AND POULTRY

MOROCCO - CEMENT PRODUCTION - See MOROCCO - MINING AND MINERAL PRODUCTS

MOROCCO - CHEESE PRODUCTION - See MOROCCO - DAIRY PRODUCTS

MOROCCO - CHEMICAL (ORGANIC) PRODUCTION - See MOROCCO - MINING AND MINERAL PRODUCTS

MOROCCO - CHICK PEA PRODUCTION - See MOROCCO - CROPS

MOROCCO - CIGAR PRODUCTION - See MOROCCO - TOBACCO PRODUCTION

MOROCCO - CIGARETTE PRODUCTION - See MOROCCO - TOBACCO PRODUCTION

MOROCCO - CLIMATE

M.E. Sharpe, 80 Business Park Drive, Armonk, New York 10504 (800) 541-6563; *The Illustrated Book of World Rankings*.

St. Martin's Press, Inc., 175 Fifth Avenue, New York, New York 10010 (800) 221-7945; *The Statesman's Year-Book*.

MOROCCO - COAL PRODUCTION - See MOROCCO - MINING AND MINERAL PRODUCTS

MOROCCO - COBALT PRODUCTION AND CONSUMPTION - See MOROCCO - MINING AND MINERAL PRODUCTS

MOROCCO - COFFEE PRODUCTION AND CONSUMPTION - See MOROCCO - CROPS

MOROCCO - COMMERCE

St. Martin's Press, Inc., 175 Fifth Avenue, New York, New York 10010 (800) 221-7945; *The Statesman's Year-Book*.

MOROCCO - COMMUNICATIONS - See MOROCCO - TRANSPORTATION AND COMMUNICATIONS

MOROCCO - CONSTRUCTION INDUSTRY

M.E. Sharpe, 80 Business Park Drive, Armonk, New York 10504 (800) 541-6563; *The Illustrated Book of World Rankings*.

Statistical Office of the United Nations, Publishing Service, New York, New York 10017 (800) 253-9646; *Statistical Yearbook*.

United Nations Economic Commission for Africa, Africa Hall, Post Office Box 3001, Addis Ababa, Ethiopia (Telephone Number in U.S. (800) 253-9646); *African Statistical Yearbook*.

MOROCCO - CONSUMER PRICE INDEX

African Development Bank, 01 BP 1387, Abidjan 01, Cote d'Ivoire; *Selected Statistics on Regional Member Countries*.

Europa Publications Limited, 18 Bedford Square, London, WC1B 3JN, England; *The Europa World Year Book*.

Statistical Office of the United Nations, Publishing Service, New York, New York 10017 (800) 253-9646; *Statistical Yearbook*; and *Survey of Economic and Social Conditions in Africa*.

United Nations Economic Commission for Africa, Africa Hall, Post Office Box 3001, Addis Ababa, Ethiopia (Telephone Number in U.S. (800) 253-9646); *African Statistical Yearbook*.

MOROCCO - CONSUMER PRICES

Euromonitor International, Inc., 122 South Michigan Avenue, Suite 1200, Chicago, Illinois 60603 (800) 577-EURO; *World Marketing Data and Statistics*.

International Monetary Fund, 700 Nineteenth Street, NW, Washington, D.C. 20431 (202) 623-7000; *International Financial Statistics*.

MOROCCO - CONSUMPTION

African Development Bank, 01 BP 1387, Abidjan 01, Cote d'Ivoire; *Selected Statistics on Regional Member Countries*.

International Lead and Zinc Study Group, Metro House, 58 St. James's Street, London SW1A 1LD England; *Lead and Zinc Statistics*.

Statistical Office of the United Nations, Publishing Service, New York, New York 10017 (800) 253-9646; *Survey of Economic and Social Conditions in Africa*.

The World Bank, 1818 H Street, NW, Washington, D.C. 20433 (202) 477-1234; *World Development Report*.

MOROCCO - COPPER AND COPPER ORE PRODUCTION AND CONSUMPTION - See MOROCCO - MINING AND MINERAL PRODUCTS

MOROCCO - CORN PRODUCTION - See

MOROCCO - CROPS

MOROCCO - CORPORATE TAXES - See MOROCCO - TAXATION

MOROCCO - COTTON - See MOROCCO - CROPS

MOROCCO - CRIME

International Criminal Police Organization (INTERPOL), 50 quai Achille Lignon, F-69006 Lyon, France; *International Crime Statistics.*

Yale University Press, Yale Station, New Haven, Connecticut 06520 (800) 987-7323; *Violence and Crime in Cross-National Perspective.*

MOROCCO - CROPS

Commodity Research Bureau, 30 South Wacker Drive, Chicago Illinois 60606 (312) 454-1801; *Commodity Year Book.*

Europa Publications Limited, 18 Bedford Square, London, WC1B 3JN, England; *The Europa World Year Book.*

Food and Agricultural Organization of the United Nations (FAO), Via delle Terme di Caracalla, 00100 Rome, Italy (Telephone Number in U.S. (202) 653-2400); *Production Yearbook;* and *The State of Food and Agriculture.*

International Monetary Fund, 700 Nineteenth Street, NW, Washington, D.C. 20431 (202) 623-7000; *International Financial Statistics.*

M.E. Sharpe, 80 Business Park Drive, Armonk, New York 10504 (800) 541-6563; *The Illustrated Book of World Rankings.*

St. Martin's Press, Inc., 175 Fifth Avenue, New York, New York 10010 (800) 221-7945; *The Statesman's Year-Book.*

Statistical Office of the United Nations, Publishing Service, New York, New York 10017 (800) 253-9646; *Statistical Yearbook.*

United Nations Conference on Trade and Development, Central Statistical Service, Palais des Nations, Geneva, Switzerland (Telephone in U.S. (800) 253-9646); *UNCTAD Commodity Yearbook.*

United Nations Economic Commission for Africa, Africa Hall, Post Office Box 3001, Addis Ababa, Ethiopia (Telephone Number in U.S. (800) 253-9646); *African Statistical Yearbook.*

MOROCCO - CUSTOMS DUTIES

International Monetary Fund, 700 Nineteenth Street, NW, Washington, D.C. 20431 (202) 623-7000; *Government*

Finance Statistics Yearbook.

St. Martin's Press, Inc., 175 Fifth Avenue, New York, New York 10010 (800) 221-7945; *The Statesman's Year-Book.*

MOROCCO - DAIRY PRODUCTS

Europa Publications Limited, 18 Bedford Square, London, WC1B 3JN, England; *The Europa World Year Book.*

Food and Agricultural Organization of the United Nations (FAO), Via delle Terme di Caracalla, 00100 Rome, Italy (Telephone Number in U.S. (202) 653-2400); *Production Yearbook;* and *The State of Food and Agriculture.*

M.E. Sharpe, 80 Business Park Drive, Armonk, New York 10504 (800) 541-6563; *The Illustrated Book of World Rankings.*

St. Martin's Press, Inc., 175 Fifth Avenue, New York, New York 10010 (800) 221-7945; *The Statesman's Year-Book.*

Statistical Office of the United Nations, Publishing Service, New York, New York 10017 (800) 253-9646; *Statistical Yearbook.*

MOROCCO - DEATH RATES - See MOROCCO - MORTALITY

MOROCCO - DEFENSE EXPENDITURES - See MOROCCO - MILITARY

MOROCCO - DEMOGRAPHY

The Economist Intelligence Unit, 111 West 57th Street, New York, New York 10019 (800) 938-4685; *The World Market Atlas.*

Euromonitor International, Inc., 122 South Michigan Avenue, Suite 1200, Chicago, Illinois 60603 (800) 577-EURO; *International Marketing Data and Statistics; The World Economic Factbook;* and *World Marketing Data and Statistics.*

Federal Statistical Office, Gustav-Stresemann - Ring 11, D-6200, Wiesbaden, Germany; *Morokko.*

M.E. Sharpe, 80 Business Park Drive, Armonk, New York 10504 (800) 541-6563; *The Illustrated Book of World Rankings.*

Statistical Office of the United Nations, Publishing Service, New York, New York 10017 (800) 253-9646; *Human Development Report;* and *Survey of Economic and Social Conditions in Africa.*

MOROCCO - DEVELOPMENT ASSISTANCE

Statistical Office of the United Nations, Publishing Service, New York, New York 10017 (800) 253-9646; *Statistical Yearbook.*

MOROCCO - DIAMOND PRODUCTION - See MOROCCO - MINING AND MINERAL PRODUCTS

MOROCCO - DIVORCE

M.E. Sharpe, 80 Business Park Drive, Armonk, New York 10504 (800) 541-6563; *The Illustrated Book of World Rankings.*

Statistical Office of the United Nations, Publishing Service, New York, New York 10017 (800) 253-9646; *Demographic Yearbook.*

MOROCCO - ECONOMY

African Development Bank, 01 BP 1387, Abidjan 01, Cote d'Ivoire; *Selected Statistics on Regional Member Countries.*

Central Intelligence Agency, Washington, D.C. 20505 (703) 482-1100, www.cia.gov; *The World Factbook.*

Economist Intelligence Unit, 111 West 57th Street, New York, New York 10019 (800) 938-4685; *Morocco Country Report.*

Euromonitor International, Inc., 122 South Michigan Avenue, Suite 1200, Chicago, Illinois 60603 (800) 577-EURO; *International Marketing Data and Statistics; The World Economic Factbook;* and *World Marketing Data and Statistics.*

Europa Publications Limited, 18 Bedford Square, London, WC1B 3JN, England; *The Europa World Year Book.*

Federal Statistical Office, Gustav-Stresemann - Ring 11, D-6200, Wiesbaden, Germany; *Morokko.*

M.E. Sharpe, 80 Business Park Drive, Armonk, New York 10504 (800) 541-6563; *The Illustrated Book of World Rankings.*

St. Martin's Press, Inc., 175 Fifth Avenue, New York, New York 10010 (800) 221-7945; *The Statesman's Year-Book.*

Statistical Office of the United Nations, Publishing Service, New York, New York 10017 (800) 253-9646; *Foreign Trade Statistics for Africa;* and *World Statistics Pocketbook.*

The World Bank, 1818 H Street, NW, Washington, D.C. 20433 (202) 477-1234; *The World Bank Atlas;* and *World Development Report.*

MOROCCO - EDUCATION

African Development Bank, 01 BP 1387, Abidjan 01, Cote d'Ivoire; *Selected Statistics on Regional Member Countries.*

The Economist Intelligence Unit, 111 West 57th Street, New York, New York

10019 (800) 938-4685; *The World Market Atlas.*

Euromonitor International, Inc., 122 South Michigan Avenue, Suite 1200, Chicago, Illinois 60603 (800) 577-EURO; *International Marketing Data and Statistics; and World Marketing Data and Statistics.*

Europa Publications Limited, 18 Bedford Square, London, WC1B 3JN, England; *The Europa World Year Book.*

Federal Statistical Office, Gustav-Stresemann - Ring 11, D-6200, Wiesbaden, Germany; *Morokko.*

International Monetary Fund, 700 Nineteenth Street, NW, Washington, D.C. 20431 (202) 623-7000; *Government Finance Statistics Yearbook.*

M.E. Sharpe, 80 Business Park Drive, Armonk, New York 10504 (800) 541-6563; *The Illustrated Book of World Rankings.*

St. Martin's Press, Inc., 175 Fifth Avenue, New York, New York 10010 (800) 221-7945; *The Statesman's Year-Book.*

Statistical Office of the United Nations, Publishing Service, New York, New York 10017 (800) 253-9646; *Human Development Report;* and *Survey of Economic and Social Conditions in Africa.*

United Nations Economic Commission for Africa, Africa Hall, Post Office Box 3001, Addis Ababa, Ethiopia (Telephone Number in U.S. (800) 253-9646); *African Statistical Yearbook.*

United Nations Educational, Scientific and Cultural Organization (UNESCO), 7 Place de Fontenoy, F-75700 Paris, France (Telephone Number in U.S. (212) 963-5981); *Statistical Yearbook.*

The World Bank, 1818 H Street, NW, Washington, D.C. 20433 (202) 477-1234; *World Development Report;* and *World Development Indicators.*

MOROCCO - EGG PRODUCTION AND CONSUMPTION - See MOROCCO - DAIRY PRODUCTS

MOROCCO - ELECTRICITY

Central Intelligence Agency, Washington, D.C. 20505 (703) 482-1100, www.cia.gov; *The World Factbook.*

M.E. Sharpe, 80 Business Park Drive, Armonk, New York 10504 (800) 541-6563; *The Illustrated Book of World Rankings.*

Penn Well Publishing Company, 1421 South Sheridan Road, Post Office Box 1260, Tulsa, Oklahoma 74101 (800) 752-9764; *International Energy Statistics Sourcebook.*

St. Martin's Press, Inc., 175 Fifth Avenue, New York, New York 10010 (800) 221-7945; *The Statesman's Year-Book.*

Statistical Office of the United Nations, Publishing Service, New York, New York 10017 (800) 253-9646; *Human Development Report; Statistical Yearbook;* and *Survey of Economic and Social Conditions in Africa.*

United Nations Economic Commission for Africa, Africa Hall, Post Office Box 3001, Addis Ababa, Ethiopia (Telephone Number in U.S. (800) 253-9646); *African Statistical Yearbook.*

MOROCCO - EMPLOYMENT

Euromonitor International, Inc., 122 South Michigan Avenue, Suite 1200, Chicago, Illinois 60603 (800) 577-EURO; *International Marketing Data and Statistics.*

Federal Statistical Office, Gustav-Stresemann - Ring 11, D-6200, Wiesbaden, Germany; *Morokko.*

M.E. Sharpe, 80 Business Park Drive, Armonk, New York 10504 (800) 541-6563; *The Illustrated Book of World Rankings.*

Statistical Office of the United Nations, Publishing Service, New York, New York 10017 (800) 253-9646; *Bulletin of Industrial Statistics for the Arab Countries;* and *Survey of Economic and Social Conditions in Africa.*

United Nations Economic Commission for Africa, Africa Hall, Post Office Box 3001, Addis Ababa, Ethiopia (Telephone Number in U.S. (800) 253-9646); *African Statistical Yearbook.*

MOROCCO - ENERGY

Euromonitor International, Inc., 122 South Michigan Avenue, Suite 1200, Chicago, Illinois 60603 (800) 577-EURO; *International Marketing Data and Statistics; The World Economic Factbook;* and *World Marketing Data and Statistics.*

Food and Agricultural Organization of the United Nations (FAO), Via delle Terme di Caracalla, 00100 Rome, Italy (Telephone Number in U.S. (202) 653-2400); *The State of Food and Agriculture.*

M.E. Sharpe, 80 Business Park Drive, Armonk, New York 10504 (800) 541-6563; *The Illustrated Book of World Rankings.*

Penn Well Publishing Company, 1421 South Sheridan Road, Post Office Box 1260, Tulsa, Oklahoma 74101 (800) 752-9764; *International Energy Statistics Sourcebook.*

St. Martin's Press, Inc., 175 Fifth Avenue, New York, New York 10010 (800)

221-7945; *The Statesman's Year-Book.*

Statistical Office of the United Nations, Publishing Service, New York, New York 10017 (800) 253-9646; *Energy Statistics Yearbook; Human Development Report; World Statistics Pocketbook;* and *Statistical Yearbook.*

United Nations Economic Commission for Africa, Africa Hall, Post Office Box 3001, Addis Ababa, Ethiopia (Telephone Number in U.S. (800) 253-9646); *African Statistical Yearbook.*

The World Bank, 1818 H Street, NW, Washington, D.C. 20433 (202) 477-1234; *The World Bank Atlas;* and *World Development Report.*

MOROCCO - ENVIRONMENT

Economist Intelligence Unit, 111 West 57th Street, New York, New York 10019 (800) 938-4685; *Morocco Country Report.*

Statistical Office of the United Nations, Publishing Service, New York, New York 10017 (800) 253-9646; *World Statistics Pocketbook.*

MOROCCO - EXCHANGE RATES

African Development Bank, 01 BP 1387, Abidjan 01, Cote d'Ivoire; *Selected Statistics on Regional Member Countries.*

Central Intelligence Agency, Washington, D.C. 20505 (703) 482-1100, www.cia.gov; *The World Factbook.*

Euromonitor International, Inc., 122 South Michigan Avenue, Suite 1200, Chicago, Illinois 60603 (800) 577-EURO; *International Marketing Data and Statistics;* and *The World Economic Factbook.*

Europa Publications Limited, 18 Bedford Square, London, WC1B 3JN, England; *The Europa World Year Book.*

International Civil Aviation Organization, 999 University Street, Montreal, Quebec, Canada H3C 5H7 (514) 954-8219; *Civil Aviation Statistics of the World.*

International Monetary Fund, 700 Nineteenth Street, NW, Washington, D.C. 20431 (202) 623-7000; *International Financial Statistics.*

Statistical Office of the United Nations, Publishing Service, New York, New York 10017 (800) 253-9646; *Bulletin of Industrial Statistics for the Arab Countries; Foreign Trade Statistics for Africa; World Statistics Pocketbook;* and *Statistical Yearbook.*

MOROCCO - EXCISE TAXES - See MOROCCO - TAXATION

MOROCCO - EXPORTS

African Development Bank, 01 BP 1387, Abidjan 01, Cote d'Ivoire; *Selected Statistics on Regional Member Countries.*

American Automobile Manufacturers Association, 1401 H Eye Street, NW, Suite 900, Washington, D.C. 20005 (202) 326-5500; *World Motor Vehicle Data.*

Central Intelligence Agency, Washington, D.C. 20505 (703) 482-1100, www.cia.gov; *The World Factbook.*

Economist Intelligence Unit, 111 West 57th Street, New York, New York 10019 (800) 938-4685; *Morocco Country Report.*

The Economist Intelligence Unit (Asia) Limited, 10th Floor, Luk Kwok Centre, 72 Gloucester Road, Wanchai, Hong Kong (Phone Number in U.S. (800) 938-4685); *Asian Market Atlas.*

Euromonitor International, Inc., 122 South Michigan Avenue, Suite 1200, Chicago, Illinois 60603 (800) 577-EURO; *International Marketing Data and Statistics;* and *The World Economic Factbook.*

Europa Publications Limited, 18 Bedford Square, London, WC1B 3JN, England; *The Europa World Year Book.*

Food and Agricultural Organization of the United Nations (FAO), Via delle Terme di Caracalla, 00100 Rome, Italy (Telephone Number in U.S. (202) 653-2400); *The State of Food and Agriculture.*

International Lead and Zinc Study Group, Metro House, 58 St. James's Street, London SW1A 1LD England; *Lead and Zinc Statistics.*

International Monetary Fund, 700 Nineteenth Street, NW, Washington, D.C. 20431 (202) 623-7000; *Direction of Trade Statistics; Government Finance Statistics Yearbook;* and *International Financial Statistics.*

St. Martin's Press, Inc., 175 Fifth Avenue, New York, New York 10010 (800) 221-7945; *The Statesman's Year-Book.*

Statistical Office of the United Nations, Publishing Service, New York, New York 10017 (800) 253-9646; *Bulletin of Industrial Statistics for the Arab Countries; Foreign Trade Statistics for Africa;* and *Survey of Economic and Social Conditions in Africa.*

United Nations Conference on Trade and Development (UNCTAD), New York, New York 10017 (800) 253-9646; *Handbook of International Trade and Development Statistics.*

United Nations Economic Commission for Africa, Africa Hall, Post Office Box 3001, Addis Ababa, Ethiopia (Telephone Number in U.S. (800) 253-9646); *African Statistical Yearbook.*

The World Bank, 1818 H Street, NW, Washington, D.C. 20433 (202) 477-1234; *World Development Report;* and *World Development Indicators.*

MOROCCO - EXTERNAL INDEBTEDNESS

African Development Bank, 01 BP 1387, Abidjan 01, Cote d'Ivoire; *Selected Statistics on Regional Member Countries.*

Statistical Office of the United Nations, Publishing Service, New York, New York 10017 (800) 253-9646; *Survey of Economic and Social Conditions in Africa.*

The World Bank, 1818 H Street, NW, Washington, D.C. 20433 (202) 477-1234; *World Development Report;* and *World Development Indicators.*

MOROCCO - EXTERNAL TRADE

African Development Bank, 01 BP 1387, Abidjan 01, Cote d'Ivoire; *Selected Statistics on Regional Member Countries.*

Euromonitor International, Inc., 122 South Michigan Avenue, Suite 1200, Chicago, Illinois 60603 (800) 577-EURO; *World Marketing Data and Statistics.*

Food and Agricultural Organization of the United Nations (FAO), Via delle Terme di Caracalla, 00100 Rome, Italy (Telephone Number in U.S. (202) 653-2400); *The State of Food and Agriculture;* and *Trade Yearbook.*

Statistical Office of the United Nations, Publishing Service, New York, New York 10017 (800) 253-9646; *Statistical Yearbook.*

MOROCCO - FABRIC PRODUCTION - See MOROCCO - TEXTILE INDUSTRY

MOROCCO - FARM CROPS - See MOROCCO - CROPS

MOROCCO - FEMALE WORKING POPULATION - See MOROCCO - EMPLOYMENT

MOROCCO - FERTILITY RATES

Central Intelligence Agency, Washington, D.C. 20505 (703) 482-1100, www.cia.gov; *The World Factbook.*

M.E. Sharpe, 80 Business Park Drive, Armonk, New York 10504 (800) 541-6563; *The Illustrated Book of World Rankings.*

Statistical Office of the United Nations, Publishing Service, New York, New York 10017 (800) 253-9646; *Human Development Report;* and *Survey of Economic and Social Conditions in Africa.*

The World Bank, 1818 H Street, NW, Washington, D.C. 20433 (202) 477-1234; *The World Bank Atlas; World Development Report;* and *World Development Indicators.*

MOROCCO - FERTILIZER

Food and Agricultural Organization of the United Nations (FAO), Via delle Terme di Caracalla, 00100 Rome, Italy (Telephone Number in U.S. (202) 653-2400); *Fertilizer Yearbook;* and *The State of Food and Agriculture.*

Statistical Office of the United Nations, Publishing Service, New York, New York 10017 (800) 253-9646; *Statistical Yearbook.*

MOROCCO - FETAL MORTALITY - See MOROCCO - MORTALITY

MOROCCO - FINANCE

African Development Bank, 01 BP 1387, Abidjan 01, Cote d'Ivoire; *Selected Statistics on Regional Member Countries.*

Economist Intelligence Unit, 111 West 57th Street, New York, New York 10019 (800) 938-4685; *Morocco Country Report.*

Europa Publications Limited, 18 Bedford Square, London, WC1B 3JN, England; *The Europa World Year Book.*

Federal Statistical Office, Gustav-Stresemann - Ring 11, D-6200, Wiesbaden, Germany; *Morokko.*

Food and Agricultural Organization of the United Nations (FAO), Via delle Terme di Caracalla, 00100 Rome, Italy (Telephone Number in U.S. (202) 653-2400); *The State of Food and Agriculture;* and *Yearbook of Fishery Statistics.*

International Monetary Fund, 700 Nineteenth Street, NW, Washington, D.C. 20431 (202) 623-7000; *Government Finance Statistics Yearbook;* and *International Financial Statistics.*

M.E. Sharpe, 80 Business Park Drive, Armonk, New York 10504 (800) 541-6563; *The Illustrated Book of World Rankings.*

St. Martin's Press, Inc., 175 Fifth Avenue, New York, New York 10010 (800) 221-7945; *The Statesman's Year-Book.*

Statistical Office of the United Nations, Publishing Service, New York, New York 10017 (800) 253-9646; *Statistical Yearbook;* and *Survey of Economic and Social Conditions in Africa.*

United Nations Economic Commission for Africa, Africa Hall, Post Office Box 3001,

Addis Ababa, Ethiopia (Telephone Number in U.S. (800) 253-9646); *African Statistical Yearbook.*

MOROCCO - FISHERIES

Europa Publications Limited, 18 Bedford Square, London, WC1B 3JN, England; *The Europa World Year Book.*

Federal Statistical Office, Gustav-Stresemann - Ring 11, D-6200, Wiesbaden, Germany; *Morokko.*

St. Martin's Press, Inc., 175 Fifth Avenue, New York, New York 10010 (800) 221-7945; *The Statesman's Year-Book.*

United Nations Conference on Trade and Development, Central Statistical Service, Palais des Nations, Geneva, Switzerland (Telephone in U.S. (800) 253-9646); *UNCTAD Commodity Yearbook.*

United Nations Economic Commission for Africa, Africa Hall, Post Office Box 3001, Addis Ababa, Ethiopia (Telephone Number in U.S. (800) 253-9646); *African Statistical Yearbook.*

MOROCCO - FLOUR PRODUCTION

Statistical Office of the United Nations, Publishing Service, New York, New York 10017 (800) 253-9646; *Statistical Yearbook.*

MOROCCO - FOOD

African Development Bank, 01 BP 1387, Abidjan 01, Cote d'Ivoire; *Selected Statistics on Regional Member Countries.*

Food and Agricultural Organization of the United Nations (FAO), Via delle Terme di Caracalla, 00100 Rome, Italy (Telephone Number in U.S. (202) 653-2400); *Production Yearbook;* and *The State of Food and Agriculture.*

Statistical Office of the United Nations, Publishing Service, New York, New York 10017 (800) 253-9646; *Human Development Report.*

United Nations Conference on Trade and Development, Central Statistical Service, Palais des Nations, Geneva, Switzerland (Telephone in U.S. (800) 253-9646); *UNCTAD Commodity Yearbook.*

MOROCCO - FOREIGN DEBT

International Monetary Fund, 700 Nineteenth Street, NW, Washington, D.C. 20431 (202) 623-7000; *Government Finance Statistics Yearbook.*

St. Martin's Press, Inc., 175 Fifth Avenue, New York, New York 10010 (800) 221-7945; *The Statesman's Year-Book.*

MOROCCO - FOREIGN TRADE

Economist Intelligence Unit, 111 West 57th Street, New York, New York 10019 (800) 938-4685; *Morocco Country Report.*

Euromonitor International, Inc., 122 South Michigan Avenue, Suite 1200, Chicago, Illinois 60603 (800) 577-EURO; *International Marketing Data and Statistics;* and *The World Economic Factbook.*

Europa Publications Limited, 18 Bedford Square, London, WC1B 3JN, England; *The Europa World Year Book.*

Federal Statistical Office, Gustav-Stresemann - Ring 11, D-6200, Wiesbaden, Germany; *Morokko.*

Food and Agricultural Organization of the United Nations (FAO), Via delle Terme di Caracalla, 00100 Rome, Italy (Telephone Number in U.S. (202) 653-2400); *The State of Food and Agriculture.*

International Monetary Fund, 700 Nineteenth Street, NW, Washington, D.C. 20431 (202) 623-7000; *International Financial Statistics.*

M.E. Sharpe, 80 Business Park Drive, Armonk, New York 10504 (800) 541-6563; *The Illustrated Book of World Rankings.*

St. Martin's Press, Inc., 175 Fifth Avenue, New York, New York 10010 (800) 221-7945; *The Statesman's Year-Book.*

Statistical Office of the United Nations, Publishing Service, New York, New York 10017 (800) 253-9646; *Bulletin of Industrial Statistics for the Arab Countries; Foreign Trade Statistics for Africa; International Trade Statistics Yearbook;* and *Statistical Yearbook.*

United Nations Conference on Trade and Development, Central Statistical Service, Palais des Nations, Geneva, Switzerland (Telephone in U.S. (800) 253-9646); *UNCTAD Commodity Yearbook.*

United Nations Economic Commission for Africa, Africa Hall, Post Office Box 3001, Addis Ababa, Ethiopia (Telephone Number in U.S. (800) 253-9646); *African Statistical Yearbook.*

The World Bank, 1818 H Street, NW, Washington, D.C. 20433 (202) 477-1234; *World Development Report;* and *World Development Indicators.*

MOROCCO - FORESTRY AND FOREST PRODUCTS

Europa Publications Limited, 18 Bedford Square, London, WC1B 3JN, England; *The Europa World Year Book.*

Federal Statistical Office, Gustav-Stresemann - Ring 11, D-6200, Wiesbaden, Germany; *Morokko.*

Food and Agricultural Organization of the United Nations (FAO), Via delle Terme di Caracalla, 00100 Rome, Italy (Telephone Number in U.S. (202) 653-2400); *The State of Food and Agriculture;* and *Yearbook of Forest Products.*

M.E. Sharpe, 80 Business Park Drive, Armonk, New York 10504 (800) 541-6563; *The Illustrated Book of World Rankings.*

St. Martin's Press, Inc., 175 Fifth Avenue, New York, New York 10010 (800) 221-7945; *The Statesman's Year-Book.*

Statistical Office of the United Nations, Publishing Service, New York, New York 10017 (800) 253-9646; *Statistical Yearbook.*

United Nations Conference on Trade and Development, Central Statistical Service, Palais des Nations, Geneva, Switzerland (Telephone in U.S. (800) 253-9646); *UNCTAD Commodity Yearbook.*

United Nations Economic Commission for Africa, Africa Hall, Post Office Box 3001, Addis Ababa, Ethiopia (Telephone Number in U.S. (800) 253-9646); *African Statistical Yearbook.*

United Nations Educational, Scientific and Cultural Organization (UNESCO), 7 Place de Fontenoy, F-75700 Paris, France (Telephone Number in U.S. (212) 963-5981); *Statistical Yearbook.*

The World Bank, 1818 H Street, NW, Washington, D.C. 20433 (202) 477-1234; *World Development Report.*

MOROCCO - FRUIT EXPORTS

International Monetary Fund, 700 Nineteenth Street, NW, Washington, D.C. 20431 (202) 623-7000; *International Financial Statistics.*

MOROCCO - GAS PRODUCTION - See MOROCCO - MINING AND MINERAL PRODUCTS

MOROCCO - GENERAL MORTALITY - See MOROCCO - MORTALITY

MOROCCO - GEOGRAPHIC DATA

M.E. Sharpe, 80 Business Park Drive, Armonk, New York 10504 (800) 541-6563; *The Illustrated Book of World Rankings.*

MOROCCO - GOATS - See MOROCCO - LIVESTOCK AND POULTRY

MOROCCO - GOLD HOLDINGS

International Monetary Fund, 700

Nineteenth Street, NW, Washington, D.C. 20431 (202) 623-7000; *International Financial Statistics.*

Statistical Office of the United Nations, Publishing Service, New York, New York 10017 (800) 253-9646; *Statistical Yearbook.*

The World Bank, 1818 H Street, NW, Washington, D.C. 20433 (202) 477-1234; *World Development Indicators.*

MOROCCO - GOLD PRODUCTION AND CONSUMPTION - See MOROCCO - MINING AND MINERAL PRODUCTS

MOROCCO - GOVERNMENT

Central Intelligence Agency, Washington, D.C. 20505 (703) 482-1100, www.cia.gov; *The World Factbook.*

Europa Publications Limited, 18 Bedford Square, London, WC1B 3JN, England; *The Europa World Year Book.*

International Monetary Fund, 700 Nineteenth Street, NW, Washington, D.C. 20431 (202) 623-7000; *Government Finance Statistics Yearbook;* and *International Financial Statistics.*

St. Martin's Press, Inc., 175 Fifth Avenue, New York, New York 10010 (800) 221-7945; *The Statesman's Year-Book.*

Statistical Office of the United Nations, Publishing Service, New York, New York 10017 (800) 253-9646; *National Accounts Statistics;* and *Survey of Economic and Social Conditions in Africa.*

The World Bank, 1818 H Street, NW, Washington, D.C. 20433 (202) 477-1234; *World Development Report;* and *World Development Indicators.*

MOROCCO - GRAIN PRODUCTION - See MOROCCO - CROPS

MOROCCO - GRANTS

International Monetary Fund, 700 Nineteenth Street, NW, Washington, D.C. 20431 (202) 623-7000; *Government Finance Statistics Yearbook.*

MOROCCO - GROSS DOMESTIC PRODUCT

African Development Bank, 01 BP 1387, Abidjan 01, Cote d'Ivoire; *Selected Statistics on Regional Member Countries.*

Economist Intelligence Unit, 111 West 57th Street, New York, New York 10019 (800) 938-4685; *Morocco Country Report.*

Euromonitor International, Inc., 122 South Michigan Avenue, Suite 1200, Chicago, Illinois 60603 (800) 577-EURO; *International Marketing Data and Statistics;*

and *The World Economic Factbook.*

Europa Publications Limited, 18 Bedford Square, London, WC1B 3JN, England; *The Europa World Year Book.*

M.E. Sharpe, 80 Business Park Drive, Armonk, New York 10504 (800) 541-6563; *The Illustrated Book of World Rankings.*

Statistical Office of the United Nations, Publishing Service, New York, New York 10017 (800) 253-9646; *Bulletin of Industrial Statistics for the Arab Countries; Human Development Report; National Accounts Statistics; Statistical Yearbook;* and *Survey of Economic and Social Conditions in Africa.*

United Nations Economic Commission for Africa, Africa Hall, Post Office Box 3001, Addis Ababa, Ethiopia (Telephone Number in U.S. (800) 253-9646); *African Statistical Yearbook.*

The World Bank, 1818 H Street, NW, Washington, D.C. 20433 (202) 477-1234; *World Development Report;* and *World Development Indicators.*

MOROCCO - GROSS NATIONAL PRODUCT

Euromonitor International, Inc., 122 South Michigan Avenue, Suite 1200, Chicago, Illinois 60603 (800) 577-EURO; *International Marketing Data and Statistics.*

St. Martin's Press, Inc., 175 Fifth Avenue, New York, New York 10010 (800) 221-7945; *The Statesman's Year-Book.*

U.S. Arms Control and Disarmament Agency, 320 Twenty-first Street, NW, Washington, D.C. 20451 (202) 647-8677; *World Military Expenditures and Arms Transfers.*

The World Bank, 1818 H Street, NW, Washington, D.C. 20433 (202) 477-1234; *The World Bank Atlas; World Development Report;* and *World Development Indicators.*

MOROCCO - GROUNDNUT PRODUCTION - See MOROCCO - CROPS

MOROCCO - HEALTH

African Development Bank, 01 BP 1387, Abidjan 01, Cote d'Ivoire; *Selected Statistics on Regional Member Countries.*

Euromonitor International, Inc., 122 South Michigan Avenue, Suite 1200, Chicago, Illinois 60603 (800) 577-EURO; *World Marketing Data and Statistics.*

Federal Statistical Office, Gustav-Stresemann - Ring 11, D-6200, Wiesbaden, Germany; *Morokko.*

M.E. Sharpe, 80 Business Park Drive, Armonk, New York 10504 (800) 541-6563; *The Illustrated Book of World Rankings.*

St. Martin's Press, Inc., 175 Fifth Avenue, New York, New York 10010 (800) 221-7945; *The Statesman's Year-Book.*

Statistical Office of the United Nations, Publishing Service, New York, New York 10017 (800) 253-9646; *Human Development Report;* and *Statistical Yearbook.*

United Nations Children's Fund (UNICEF), 3 United Nations Plaza, New York, New York 10017 (800) 253-9646; *State of the World's Children.*

United Nations Economic Commission for Africa, Africa Hall, Post Office Box 3001, Addis Ababa, Ethiopia (Telephone Number in U.S. (800) 253-9646); *African Statistical Yearbook.*

The World Bank, 1818 H Street, NW, Washington, D.C. 20433 (202) 477-1234; *World Development Report.*

MOROCCO - HEALTH AND MEDICAL SERVICES

Statistical Office of the United Nations, Publishing Service, New York, New York 10017 (800) 253-9646; *Statistical Yearbook.*

MOROCCO - HEALTH EXPENDITURES

International Monetary Fund, 700 Nineteenth Street, NW, Washington, D.C. 20431 (202) 623-7000; *Government Finance Statistics Yearbook.*

MOROCCO - HIDE PRODUCTION

Food and Agricultural Organization of the United Nations (FAO), Via delle Terme di Caracalla, 00100 Rome, Italy (Telephone Number in U.S. (202) 653-2400); *Production Yearbook.*

MOROCCO - HIGHWAYS

Central Intelligence Agency, Washington, D.C. 20505 (703) 482-1100, www.cia.gov; *The World Factbook.*

St. Martin's Press, Inc., 175 Fifth Avenue, New York, New York 10010 (800) 221-7945; *The Statesman's Year-Book.*

Statistical Office of the United Nations, Publishing Service, New York, New York 10017 (800) 253-9646; *Survey of Economic and Social Conditions in Africa.*

United Nations Economic Commission for Africa, Africa Hall, Post Office Box 3001, Addis Ababa, Ethiopia (Telephone Number in U.S. (800) 253-9646); *African Statistical Yearbook.*

MOROCCO - HORSES - See MOROCCO - LIVESTOCK AND POULTRY

MOROCCO - HOURS OF WORK - See MOROCCO - EMPLOYMENT

MOROCCO - HOUSING AND HOUSING UNITS

Euromonitor International, Inc., 122 South Michigan Avenue, Suite 1200, Chicago, Illinois 60603 (800) 577-EURO; *World Marketing Data and Statistics.*

MOROCCO - HOUSING EXPENDITURES

International Monetary Fund, 700 Nineteenth Street, NW, Washington, D.C. 20431 (202) 623-7000; *Government Finance Statistics Yearbook.*

M.E. Sharpe, 80 Business Park Drive, Armonk, New York 10504 (800) 541-6563; *The Illustrated Book of World Rankings.*

MOROCCO - ILLITERATE POPULATION

Central Intelligence Agency, Washington, D.C. 20505 (703) 482-1100, www.cia.gov; *The World Factbook.*

Euromonitor International, Inc., 122 South Michigan Avenue, Suite 1200, Chicago, Illinois 60603 (800) 577-EURO; *The World Economic Factbook.*

Statistical Office of the United Nations, Publishing Service, New York, New York 10017 (800) 253-9646; *Human Development Report.*

United Nations Educational, Scientific and Cultural Organization (UNESCO), 7 Place de Fontenoy, F-75700 Paris, France (Telephone Number in U.S. (212) 963-5981); *Statistical Yearbook.*

MOROCCO - IMPORTS

African Development Bank, 01 BP 1387, Abidjan 01, Cote d'Ivoire; *Selected Statistics on Regional Member Countries.*

American Automobile Manufacturers Association, 1401 H Street, NW, Suite 900, Washington, D.C. 20005 (202) 326-5500; *World Motor Vehicle Data.*

Central Intelligence Agency, Washington, D.C. 20505 (703) 482-1100, www.cia.gov; *The World Factbook.*

The Economist Intelligence Unit, 111 West 57th Street, New York, New York 10019 (800) 938-4685; *Morocco Country Report;* and *The World Market Atlas.*

Euromonitor International, Inc., 122 South Michigan Avenue, Suite 1200, Chicago, Illinois 60603 (800) 577-EURO; *International Marketing Data and Statistics;*

and *The World Economic Factbook.*

Europa Publications Limited, 18 Bedford Square, London, WC1B 3JN, England; *The Europa World Year Book.*

Food and Agricultural Organization of the United Nations (FAO), Via delle Terme di Caracalla, 00100 Rome, Italy (Telephone Number in U.S. (202) 653-2400); *The State of Food and Agriculture.*

International Lead and Zinc Study Group, Metro House, 58 St. James's Street, London SW1A 1LD England; *Lead and Zinc Statistics.*

International Monetary Fund, 700 Nineteenth Street, NW, Washington, D.C. 20431 (202) 623-7000; *Direction of Trade Statistics; Government Finance Statistics Yearbook;* and *International Financial Statistics.*

St. Martin's Press, Inc., 175 Fifth Avenue, New York, New York 10010 (800) 221-7945; *The Statesman's Year-Book.*

Statistical Office of the United Nations, Publishing Service, New York, New York 10017 (800) 253-9646; *Bulletin of Industrial Statistics for the Arab Countries; Foreign Trade Statistics for Africa;* and *Survey of Economic and Social Conditions in Africa.*

United Nations Conference on Trade and Development (UNCTAD), New York, New York 10017 (800) 253-9646; *Handbook of International Trade and Development Statistics.*

United Nations Economic Commission for Africa, Africa Hall, Post Office Box 3001, Addis Ababa, Ethiopia (Telephone Number in U.S. (800) 253-9646); *African Statistical Yearbook.*

The World Bank, 1818 H Street, NW, Washington, D.C. 20433 (202) 477-1234; *World Development Report;* and *World Development Indicators.*

MOROCCO - INCOME TAXES - See MOROCCO - TAXATION

MOROCCO - INDIVIDUAL INCOME TAXES

International Monetary Fund, 700 Nineteenth Street, NW, Washington, D.C. 20431 (202) 623-7000; *Government Finance Statistics Yearbook.*

MOROCCO - INDUSTRIAL METALS PRODUCTION - See MOROCCO - MINING AND MINERAL PRODUCTS

MOROCCO - INDUSTRY

Central Intelligence Agency, Washington, D.C. 20505 (703) 482-1100, www.cia.gov; *The World Factbook.*

Economist Intelligence Unit, 111 West 57th Street, New York, New York 10019 (800) 938-4685; *Morocco Country Report.*

Euromonitor International, Inc., 122 South Michigan Avenue, Suite 1200, Chicago, Illinois 60603 (800) 577-EURO; *International Marketing Data and Statistics; The World Economic Factbook;* and *World Marketing Data and Statistics.*

Europa Publications Limited, 18 Bedford Square, London, WC1B 3JN, England; *The Europa World Year Book.*

Federal Statistical Office, Gustav-Stresemann - Ring 11, D-6200, Wiesbaden, Germany; *Morokko.*

M.E. Sharpe, 80 Business Park Drive, Armonk, New York 10504 (800) 541-6563; *The Illustrated Book of World Rankings.*

St. Martin's Press, Inc., 175 Fifth Avenue, New York, New York 10010 (800) 221-7945; *The Statesman's Year-Book.*

Statistical Office of the United Nations, Publishing Service, New York, New York 10017 (800) 253-9646; *Bulletin of Industrial Statistics for the Arab Countries; Statistical Yearbook;* and *Survey of Economic and Social Conditions in Africa.*

United Nations Economic Commission for Africa, Africa Hall, Post Office Box 3001, Addis Ababa, Ethiopia (Telephone Number in U.S. (800) 253-9646); *African Statistical Yearbook.*

The World Bank, 1818 H Street, NW, Washington, D.C. 20433 (202) 477-1234; *World Development Indicators.*

World Intellectual Property Organization, 34 Chemin des Colombettes, CH-1211 Geneva 20, Switzerland; *Industrial Property Statistics.*

MOROCCO - INFANT AND MATERNAL MORTALITY - See MOROCCO - MORTALITY

MOROCCO - INTERNATIONAL LIQUIDITY

International Monetary Fund, 700 Nineteenth Street, NW, Washington, D.C. 20431 (202) 623-7000; *International Financial Statistics.*

MOROCCO - INTERNATIONAL RESERVES EXCLUDING GOLD

African Development Bank, 01 BP 1387, Abidjan 01, Cote d'Ivoire; *Selected Statistics on Regional Member Countries.*

Statistical Office of the United Nations, Publishing Service, New York, New York 10017 (800) 253-9646; *Statistical Yearbook.*

The World Bank, 1818 H Street, NW, Washington, D.C. 20433 (202) 477-1234; *World Development Indicators.*

MOROCCO - INVESTMENTS

International Monetary Fund, 700 Nineteenth Street, NW, Washington, D.C. 20431 (202) 623-7000; *International Financial Statistics.*

MOROCCO - IRON ORE PRODUCTION AND CONSUMPTION - See MOROCCO - MINING AND MINERAL PRODUCTS

MOROCCO - IRRIGATION

Euromonitor International, Inc., 122 South Michigan Avenue, Suite 1200, Chicago, Illinois 60603 (800) 577-EURO; *International Marketing Data and Statistics*

MOROCCO - LABOR

African Development Bank, 01 BP 1387, Abidjan 01, Cote d'Ivoire; *Selected Statistics on Regional Member Countries.*

Central Intelligence Agency, Washington, D.C. 20505 (703) 482-1100, www.cia.gov; *The World Factbook.*

Euromonitor International, Inc., 122 South Michigan Avenue, Suite 1200, Chicago, Illinois 60603 (800) 577-EURO; *International Marketing Data and Statistics; and World Marketing Data and Statistics.*

Food and Agricultural Organization of the United Nations (FAO), Via delle Terme di Caracalla, 00100 Rome, Italy (Telephone Number in U.S. (202) 653-2400); *The State of Food and Agriculture.*

M.E. Sharpe, 80 Business Park Drive, Armonk, New York 10504 (800) 541-6563; *The Illustrated Book of World Rankings.*

St. Martin's Press, Inc., 175 Fifth Avenue, New York, New York 10010 (800) 221-7945; *The Statesman's Year-Book.*

Statistical Office of the United Nations, Publishing Service, New York, New York 10017 (800) 253-9646; *Human Development Report.*

The World Bank, 1818 H Street, NW, Washington, D.C. 20433 (202) 477-1234; *The World Bank Atlas; World Development Report; and World Development Indicators.*

MOROCCO - LAND USE

Central Intelligence Agency, Washington, D.C. 20505 (703) 482-1100, www.cia.gov; *The World Factbook.*

Euromonitor International, Inc., 122 South Michigan Avenue, Suite 1200, Chicago, Illinois 60603 (800) 577-EURO;

International Marketing Data and Statistics.

Food and Agricultural Organization of the United Nations (FAO), Via delle Terme di Caracalla, 00100 Rome, Italy (Telephone Number in U.S. (202) 653-2400); *Production Yearbook.*

The World Bank, 1818 H Street, NW, Washington, D.C. 20433 (202) 477-1234; *World Development Report.*

MOROCCO - LEAD AND LEAD ORE PRODUCTION AND CONSUMPTION - See MOROCCO - MINING AND MINERAL PRODUCTS

MOROCCO - LIBRARIES

M.E. Sharpe, 80 Business Park Drive, Armonk, New York 10504 (800) 541-6563; *The Illustrated Book of World Rankings.*

United Nations Educational, Scientific and Cultural Organization (UNESCO), 7 Place de Fontenoy, F-75700 Paris, France (Telephone Number in U.S. (212) 963-5981); *Statistical Yearbook.*

MOROCCO - LIFE EXPECTANCY

African Development Bank, 01 BP 1387, Abidjan 01, Cote d'Ivoire; *Selected Statistics on Regional Member Countries.*

Central Intelligence Agency, Washington, D.C. 20505 (703) 482-1100, www.cia.gov; *The World Factbook.*

Euromonitor International, Inc., 122 South Michigan Avenue, Suite 1200, Chicago, Illinois 60603 (800) 577-EURO; *The World Economic Factbook.*

Statistical Office of the United Nations, Publishing Service, New York, New York 10017 (800) 253-9646; *Human Development Report; and World Statistics Pocketbook.*

The World Bank, 1818 H Street, NW, Washington, D.C. 20433 (202) 477-1234; *The World Bank Atlas; and World Development Report.*

MOROCCO - LITERACY RATE

Euromonitor International, Inc., 122 South Michigan Avenue, Suite 1200, Chicago, Illinois 60603 (800) 577-EURO; *World Marketing Data and Statistics.*

Statistical Office of the United Nations, Publishing Service, New York, New York 10017 (800) 253-9646; *Survey of Economic and Social Conditions in Africa.*

MOROCCO - LIVESTOCK AND POULTRY

Euromonitor International, Inc., 122 South Michigan Avenue, Suite 1200, Chicago, Illinois 60603 (800) 577-EURO; *International Marketing Data and Statistics.*

Europa Publications Limited, 18 Bedford Square, London, WC1B 3JN, England; *The Europa World Year Book.*

Food and Agricultural Organization of the United Nations (FAO), Via delle Terme di Caracalla, 00100 Rome, Italy (Telephone Number in U.S. (202) 653-2400); *Production Yearbook; and The State of Food and Agriculture.*

M.E. Sharpe, 80 Business Park Drive, Armonk, New York 10504 (800) 541-6563; *The Illustrated Book of World Rankings.*

St. Martin's Press, Inc., 175 Fifth Avenue, New York, New York 10010 (800) 221-7945; *The Statesman's Year-Book.*

Statistical Office of the United Nations, Publishing Service, New York, New York 10017 (800) 253-9646; *Statistical Yearbook; and Survey of Economic and Social Conditions in Africa.*

United Nations Conference on Trade and Development, Central Statistical Service, Palais des Nations, Geneva, Switzerland (Telephone in U.S. (800) 253-9646); *UNCTAD Commodity Yearbook.*

United Nations Economic Commission for Africa, Africa Hall, Post Office Box 3001, Addis Ababa, Ethiopia (Telephone Number in U.S. (800) 253-9646); *African Statistical Yearbook.*

MOROCCO - LIVING LEVELS - See MOROCCO - LIFE EXPECTANCY

MOROCCO - MAIL - NUMBER OF PIECES SENT OR RECEIVED

Statistical Office of the United Nations, Publishing Service, New York, New York 10017 (800) 253-9646; *Statistical Yearbook.*

MOROCCO - MANGANESE AND MANGANESE ORE PRODUCTION AND CONSUMPTION - See MOROCCO - MINING AND MINERAL PRODUCTS

MOROCCO - MANUFACTURING

American Automobile Manufacturers Association, 1401 H Street, NW, Suite 900, Washington, D.C. 20005 (202) 326-5500; *World Motor Vehicle Data.*

International Monetary Fund, 700 Nineteenth Street, NW, Washington, D.C. 20431 (202) 623-7000; *International Financial Statistics.*

M.E. Sharpe, 80 Business Park Drive, Armonk, New York 10504 (800) 541-6563;

The Illustrated Book of World Rankings.

Statistical Office of the United Nations, Publishing Service, New York, New York 10017 (800) 253-9646; *Bulletin of Industrial Statistics for the Arab Countries; Statistical Yearbook;* and *Survey of Economic and Social Conditions in Africa.*

United Nations Economic Commission for Africa, Africa Hall, Post Office Box 3001, Addis Ababa, Ethiopia (Telephone Number in U.S. (800) 253-9646); *African Statistical Yearbook.*

The World Bank, 1818 H Street, NW, Washington, D.C. 20433 (202) 477-1234; *World Development Indicators.*

MOROCCO - MARRIAGE

M.E. Sharpe, 80 Business Park Drive, Armonk, New York 10504 (800) 541-6563; *The Illustrated Book of World Rankings.*

Statistical Office of the United Nations, Publishing Service, New York, New York 10017 (800) 253-9646; *Demographic Yearbook.*

MOROCCO - MEAT PRODUCTION - See MOROCCO - LIVESTOCK AND POULTRY

MOROCCO - MERCHANT SHIPPING

Europa Publications Limited, 18 Bedford Square, London, WC1B 3JN, England; *The Europa World Year Book.*

Lloyd's Register of Shipping, 17 Battery Place, New York, New York 10004 (212) 425-8050; *Register of Ships.*

St. Martin's Press, Inc., 175 Fifth Avenue, New York, New York 10010 (800) 221-7945; *The Statesman's Year-Book.*

Statistical Office of the United Nations, Publishing Service, New York, New York 10017 (800) 253-9646; *Statistical Yearbook.*

United Nations Economic Commission for Africa, Africa Hall, Post Office Box 3001, Addis Ababa, Ethiopia (Telephone Number in U.S. (800) 253-9646); *African Statistical Yearbook.*

U.S. Department of Transportation, Maritime Administration, 400 Seventh Street, SW, Washington, D.C. 20590 (202) 366-5807, www.marad.dot.gov; *A Statistical Analysis of the World's Merchant Fleets.*

MOROCCO - MILITARY

Central Intelligence Agency, Washington, D.C. 20505 (703) 482-1100, www.cia.gov; *The World Factbook.*

Euromonitor International, Inc., 122 South Michigan Avenue, Suite 1200,

Chicago, Illinois 60603 (800) 577-EURO; *World Marketing Data and Statistics.*

The International Institute for Strategic Studies, 23 Tavistock Street, London WC2E 7NQ, England; *The Military Balance.*

International Monetary Fund, 700 Nineteenth Street, NW, Washington, D.C. 20431 (202) 623-7000; *Government Finance Statistics Yearbook.*

St. Martin's Press, Inc., 175 Fifth Avenue, New York, New York 10010 (800) 221-7945; *The Statesman's Year-Book.*

Statistical Office of the United Nations, Publishing Service, New York, New York 10017 (800) 253-9646; *Human Development Report.*

U.S. Arms Control and Disarmament Agency, 320 Twenty-first Street, NW, Washington, D.C. 20451 (202) 647-8677; *World Military Expenditures and Arms Transfers.*

MOROCCO - MILK PRODUCTION - See MOROCCO - DAIRY PRODUCTS

MOROCCO - MILLET PRODUCTION - See MOROCCO - CROPS

MOROCCO - MINING AND MINERAL PRODUCTS

Commodity Research Bureau, 30 South Wacker Drive, Chicago Illinois 60606 (312) 454-1801; *Commodity Year Book.*

Europa Publications Limited, 18 Bedford Square, London, WC1B 3JN, England; *The Europa World Year Book.*

International Lead and Zinc Study Group, Metro House, 58 St. James's Street, London SW1A 1LD England; *Lead and Zinc Statistics.*

M.E. Sharpe, 80 Business Park Drive, Armonk, New York 10504 (800) 541-6563; *The Illustrated Book of World Rankings.*

Penn Well Publishing Company, 1421 South Sheridan Road, Post Office Box 1260, Tulsa, Oklahoma 74101 (800) 752-9764; *International Energy Statistics Sourcebook.*

St. Martin's Press, Inc., 175 Fifth Avenue, New York, New York 10010 (800) 221-7945; *The Statesman's Year-Book.*

Statistical Office of the United Nations, Publishing Service, New York, New York 10017 (800) 253-9646; *Bulletin of Industrial Statistics for the Arab Countries;* and *Statistical Yearbook.*

United Nations Conference on Trade and Development, Central Statistical Service, Palais des Nations, Geneva,

Switzerland (Telephone in U.S. (800) 253-9646); *UNCTAD Commodity Yearbook.*

United Nations Economic Commission for Africa, Africa Hall, Post Office Box 3001, Addis Ababa, Ethiopia (Telephone Number in U.S. (800) 253-9646); *African Statistical Yearbook.*

MOROCCO - MONEY EXCHANGE RATE - See MOROCCO - EXCHANGE RATES

MOROCCO - MONEY RESERVES

Euromonitor International, Inc., 122 South Michigan Avenue, Suite 1200, Chicago, Illinois 60603 (800) 577-EURO; *International Marketing Data and Statistics.*

MOROCCO - MONEY SUPPLY

African Development Bank, 01 BP 1387, Abidjan 01, Cote d'Ivoire; *Selected Statistics on Regional Member Countries.*

Economist Intelligence Unit, 111 West 57th Street, New York, New York 10019 (800) 938-4685; *Morocco Country Report.*

Euromonitor International, Inc., 122 South Michigan Avenue, Suite 1200, Chicago, Illinois 60603 (800) 577-EURO; *International Marketing Data and Statistics.*

Europa Publications Limited, 18 Bedford Square, London, WC1B 3JN, England; *The Europa World Year Book.*

Federal Statistical Office, Gustav-Stresemann - Ring 11, D-6200, Wiesbaden, Germany; *Morokko.*

International Monetary Fund, 700 Nineteenth Street, NW, Washington, D.C. 20431 (202) 623-7000; *International Financial Statistics.*

Statistical Office of the United Nations, Publishing Service, New York, New York 10017 (800) 253-9646; *Statistical Yearbook.*

The World Bank, 1818 H Street, NW, Washington, D.C. 20433 (202) 477-1234; *World Development Indicators.*

MOROCCO - MORTALITY

Central Intelligence Agency, Washington, D.C. 20505 (703) 482-1100, www.cia.gov; *The World Factbook.*

Euromonitor International, Inc., 122 South Michigan Avenue, Suite 1200, Chicago, Illinois 60603 (800) 577-EURO; *International Marketing Data and Statistics;* and *The World Economic Factbook.*

Europa Publications Limited, 18 Bedford Square, London, WC1B 3JN,

England; *The Europa World Year Book.*

St. Martin's Press, Inc., 175 Fifth Avenue, New York, New York 10010 (800) 221-7945; *The Statesman's Year-Book.*

Statistical Office of the United Nations, Publishing Service, New York, New York 10017 (800) 253-9646; *Demographic Yearbook; Human Development Report; Statistical Yearbook; World Statistics Pocketbook;* and *Survey of Economic and Social Conditions in Africa.*

United Nations Children's Fund (UNICEF), 3 United Nations Plaza, New York, New York 10017 (800) 253-9646; *State of the World's Children.*

The World Bank, 1818 H Street, NW, Washington, D.C. 20433 (202) 477-1234; *The World Bank Atlas; World Development Report;* and *World Development Indicators.*

MOROCCO - MOTION PICTURES

St. Martin's Press, Inc., 175 Fifth Avenue, New York, New York 10010 (800) 221-7945; *The Statesman's Year-Book.*

Statistical Office of the United Nations, Publishing Service, New York, New York 10017 (800) 253-9646; *Statistical Yearbook.*

MOROCCO - MOTOR VEHICLE ASSEMBLY

Statistical Office of the United Nations, Publishing Service, New York, New York 10017 (800) 253-9646; *Statistical Yearbook.*

MOROCCO - MOTOR VEHICLE PRODUCTION

American Automobile Manufacturers Association, 1620 Eye Street, NW, Suite 900, Washington, D.C. 20005 (202) 326-5500; *World Motor Vehicle Data.*

Europa Publications Limited, 18 Bedford Square, London, WC1B 3JN, England; *The Europa World Year Book.*

MOROCCO - MOTOR VEHICLE TAXES - See MOROCCO - TAXATION

MOROCCO - MOTOR VEHICLES IN USE

American Automobile Manufacturers Association, 1401 H Street, NW, Suite 900, Washington, D.C. 20005 (202) 326-5500; *World Motor Vehicle Data.*

Statistical Office of the United Nations, Publishing Service, New York, New York 10017 (800) 253-9646; *Statistical Yearbook;* and *Survey of Economic and Social Conditions in Africa.*

MOROCCO - MULES - See MOROCCO - LIVESTOCK AND POULTRY

MOROCCO - MUSEUMS

M.E. Sharpe, 80 Business Park Drive, Armonk, New York 10504 (800) 541-6563; *The Illustrated Book of World Rankings.*

MOROCCO - NATALITY - See MOROCCO - BIRTH RATES

MOROCCO - NATIONAL ACCOUNTS

African Development Bank, 01 BP 1387, Abidjan 01, Cote d'Ivoire; *Selected Statistics on Regional Member Countries.*

Federal Statistical Office, Gustav-Stresemann - Ring 11, D-6200, Wiesbaden, Germany; *Morokko.*

Europa Publications Limited, 18 Bedford Square, London, WC1B 3JN, England; *The Europa World Year Book.*

International Monetary Fund, 700 Nineteenth Street, NW, Washington, D.C. 20431 (202) 623-7000; *International Financial Statistics.*

Statistical Office of the United Nations, Publishing Service, New York, New York 10017 (800) 253-9646; *Statistical Yearbook.*

United Nations Economic Commission for Africa, Africa Hall, Post Office Box 3001, Addis Ababa, Ethiopia (Telephone Number in U.S. (800) 253-9646); *African Statistical Yearbook.*

MOROCCO - NATIONAL INCOME

M.E. Sharpe, 80 Business Park Drive, Armonk, New York 10504 (800) 541-6563; *The Illustrated Book of World Rankings.*

Statistical Office of the United Nations, Publishing Service, New York, New York 10017 (800) 253-9646; *National Accounts Statistics;* and *Statistical Yearbook.*

MOROCCO - NATIONAL PRODUCT

M.E. Sharpe, 80 Business Park Drive, Armonk, New York 10504 (800) 541-6563; *The Illustrated Book of World Rankings.*

Statistical Office of the United Nations, Publishing Service, New York, New York 10017 (800) 253-9646; *Statistical Yearbook.*

MOROCCO - NATURAL GAS - PRODUCTION - See MOROCCO - MINING AND MINERAL PRODUCTS

MOROCCO - NEWSPAPER PRODUCTION - See MOROCCO - FORESTRY AND FOREST PRODUCTS

MOROCCO - NEWSPRINT - See MOROCCO - FORESTRY AND FOREST PRODUCTS

MOROCCO - NICKEL AND NICKEL ORE PRODUCTION AND CONSUMPTION - See MOROCCO - MINING AND MINERAL PRODUCTS

MOROCCO - OATS PRODUCTION - See MOROCCO - CROPS

MOROCCO - OCCUPATIONS - See MOROCCO - LABOR

MOROCCO - ORANGES - See MOROCCO - CROPS

MOROCCO - PAPER - See MOROCCO - FORESTRY AND FOREST PRODUCTS

MOROCCO - PATENTS, TRADEMARKS AND SERVICE MARKS

Statistical Office of the United Nations, Publishing Service, New York, New York 10017 (800) 253-9646; *Statistical Yearbook.*

World Intellectual Property Organization, 34 Chemin des Colombettes, CH-1211 Geneva 20, Switzerland; *Industrial Property Statistics.*

MOROCCO - PEANUT PRODUCTION - See MOROCCO - CROPS

MOROCCO - PERIODICALS

United Nations Educational, Scientific and Cultural Organization (UNESCO), 7 Place de Fontenoy, F-75700 Paris, France (Telephone Number in U.S. (212) 963-5981); *Statistical Yearbook.*

MOROCCO - PESTICIDE USE

Food and Agricultural Organization of the United Nations (FAO), Via delle Terme di Caracalla, 00100 Rome, Italy (Telephone Number in U.S. (202) 653-2400); *The State of Food and Agriculture.*

MOROCCO - PETROLEUM INDUSTRY

Food and Agricultural Organization of the United Nations (FAO), Via delle Terme di Caracalla, 00100 Rome, Italy (Telephone Number in U.S. (202) 653-2400); *The State of Food and Agriculture.*

M.E. Sharpe, 80 Business Park Drive, Armonk, New York 10504 (800) 541-6563; *The Illustrated Book of World Rankings.*

Penn Well Publishing Company, 1421 South Sheridan Road, Post Office Box 1260, Tulsa, Oklahoma 74101 (800) 752-9764; *International Energy Statistics Sourcebook.*

Statistical Office of the United Nations, Publishing Service, New York, New York 10017 (800) 253-9646; *Statistical Yearbook.*

United Nations Conference on Trade and Development, Central Statistical

Service, Palais des Nations, Geneva, Switzerland (Telephone in U.S. (800) 253-9646); *UNCTAD Commodity Yearbook*.

MOROCCO - PHOSPHATE EXPORTS

International Monetary Fund, 700 Nineteenth Street, NW, Washington, D.C. 20431 (202) 623-7000; *International Financial Statistics*.

MOROCCO - PHOSPHATE ROCK PRODUCTION - See MOROCCO - MINING AND MINERAL PRODUCTS

MOROCCO - PIG-IRON AND FERRO-ALLOY PRODUCTION - See MOROCCO - MINING AND MINERAL PRODUCTS

MOROCCO - PIGS - See MOROCCO - LIVESTOCK AND POULTRY

MOROCCO - POPULATION

African Development Bank, 01 BP 1387, Abidjan 01, Cote d'Ivoire; *Selected Statistics on Regional Member Countries*.

Central Intelligence Agency, Washington, D.C. 20505 (703) 482-1100, www.cia.gov; *The World Factbook*.

The Economist Intelligence Unit, 111 West 57th Street, New York, New York 10019 (800) 938-4685; *Morocco Country Report;* and *The World Market Atlas*.

Euromonitor International, Inc., 122 South Michigan Avenue, Suite 1200, Chicago, Illinois 60603 (800) 577-EURO; *International Marketing Data and Statistics;* and *The World Economic Factbook*.

Europa Publications Limited, 18 Bedford Square, London, WC1B 3JN, England; *The Europa World Year Book*.

Federal Statistical Office, Gustav-Stresemann - Ring 11, D-6200, Wiesbaden, Germany; *Morokko*.

Food and Agricultural Organization of the United Nations (FAO), Via delle Terme di Caracalla, 00100 Rome, Italy (Telephone Number in U.S. (202) 653-2400); *Production Yearbook*.

M.E. Sharpe, 80 Business Park Drive, Armonk, New York 10504 (800) 541-6563; *The Illustrated Book of World Rankings*.

St. Martin's Press, Inc., 175 Fifth Avenue, New York, New York 10010 (800) 221-7945; *The Statesman's Year-Book*.

Statistical Office of the United Nations, Publishing Service, New York, New York 10017 (800) 253-9646; *Demographic Yearbook; Human Development Report; Statistical Yearbook; World Statistics Pocketbook;* and *Survey of Economic and Social Conditions in Africa*.

U.S. Arms Control and Disarmament Agency, 320 Twenty-first Street, NW, Washington, D.C. 20451 (202) 647-8677; *World Military Expenditures and Arms Transfers*.

The World Bank, 1818 H Street, NW, Washington, D.C. 20433 (202) 477-1234; *The World Bank Atlas;* and *World Development Report*.

World Health Organization, Office of Publications, 20 Avenue Appia, CH-1211 Geneva 27, Switzerland (Telephone Number in U.S. (518) 436-9686); *World Health Statistics Annual*.

MOROCCO - POST OFFICES

M.E. Sharpe, 80 Business Park Drive, Armonk, New York 10504 (800) 541-6563; *The Illustrated Book of World Rankings*.

St. Martin's Press, Inc., 175 Fifth Avenue, New York, New York 10010 (800) 221-7945; *The Statesman's Year-Book*.

MOROCCO - POTATO PRODUCTION - See MOROCCO - CROPS

MOROCCO - PRICES

Federal Statistical Office, Gustav-Stresemann - Ring 11, D-6200, Wiesbaden, Germany; *Morokko*.

Food and Agricultural Organization of the United Nations (FAO), Via delle Terme di Caracalla, 00100 Rome, Italy (Telephone Number in U.S. (202) 653-2400); *Production Yearbook;* and *The State of Food and Agriculture*.

International Lead and Zinc Study Group, Metro House, 58 St. James's Street, London SW1A 1LD England; *Lead and Zinc Statistics*.

International Monetary Fund, 700 Nineteenth Street, NW, Washington, D.C. 20431 (202) 623-7000; *International Financial Statistics*.

M.E. Sharpe, 80 Business Park Drive, Armonk, New York 10504 (800) 541-6563; *The Illustrated Book of World Rankings*.

United Nations Economic Commission for Africa, Africa Hall, Post Office Box 3001, Addis Ababa, Ethiopia (Telephone Number in U.S. (800) 253-9646); *African Statistical Yearbook*.

MOROCCO - PRINTING AND WRITING PAPER - See MOROCCO - FORESTRY AND FOREST PRODUCTS

MOROCCO - PRODUCTION

American Automobile Manufacturers Association, 1401 H Street, NW, Suite 900, Washington, D.C. 20005 (202) 326-5500; *World Motor Vehicle Data*.

International Lead and Zinc Study Group, Metro House, 58 St. James's Street, London SW1A 1LD England; *Lead and Zinc Statistics*.

M.E. Sharpe, 80 Business Park Drive, Armonk, New York 10504 (800) 541-6563; *The Illustrated Book of World Rankings*.

MOROCCO - PRODUCTIVITY

International Monetary Fund, 700 Nineteenth Street, NW, Washington, D.C. 20431 (202) 623-7000; *International Financial Statistics*.

MOROCCO - PROPERTY TAXES

International Monetary Fund, 700 Nineteenth Street, NW, Washington, D.C. 20431 (202) 623-7000; *Government Finance Statistics Yearbook*.

MOROCCO - PUBLIC FINANCE - See MOROCCO - FINANCE

MOROCCO - RADIO BROADCASTING - See MOROCCO - BROADCASTING

MOROCCO - RADIO RECEIVERS

St. Martin's Press, Inc., 175 Fifth Avenue, New York, New York 10010 (800) 221-7945; *The Statesman's Year-Book*.

MOROCCO - RAILWAY USE

Statistical Office of the United Nations, Publishing Service, New York, New York 10017 (800) 253-9646; *Statistical Yearbook*.

MOROCCO - RAILWAYS

Europa Publications Limited, 18 Bedford Square, London, WC1B 3JN, England; *The Europa World Year Book*.

Jane's Information Group, Sentinel House, 163 Brighton Road, Coulsdon, Surrey CR5 2NH, England (Telephone Number in U.S. (703) 683-3700); *Jane's World Railways*.

St. Martin's Press, Inc., 175 Fifth Avenue, New York, New York 10010 (800) 221-7945; *The Statesman's Year-Book*.

United Nations Economic Commission for Africa, Africa Hall, Post Office Box 3001, Addis Ababa, Ethiopia (Telephone Number in U.S. (800) 253-9646); *African Statistical Yearbook*.

MOROCCO - RELIGION

Central Intelligence Agency,

Washington, D.C. 20505 (703) 482-1100, www.cia.gov; *The World Factbook.*

M.E. Sharpe, 80 Business Park Drive, Armonk, New York 10504 (800) 541-6563; *The Illustrated Book of World Rankings.*

St. Martin's Press, Inc., 175 Fifth Avenue, New York, New York 10010 (800) 221-7945; *The Statesman's Year-Book.*

MOROCCO - RETAIL TRADE

Euromonitor International, Inc., 122 South Michigan Avenue, Suite 1200, Chicago, Illinois 60603 (800) 577-EURO; *World Marketing Data and Statistics.*

MOROCCO - RICE PRODUCTION - See MOROCCO - CROPS

MOROCCO - ROOT AND TUBER PRODUCTION - See MOROCCO - CROPS

MOROCCO - RUBBER PRODUCTION AND CONSUMPTION

M.E. Sharpe, 80 Business Park Drive, Armonk, New York 10504 (800) 541-6563; *The Illustrated Book of World Rankings.*

MOROCCO - SAFFLOWER SEED PRODUCTION - See MOROCCO - CROPS

MOROCCO - SALT PRODUCTION - See MOROCCO - MINING AND MINERAL PRODUCTS

MOROCCO - SAWNWOOD PRODUCTION - See MOROCCO - FORESTRY AND FOREST PRODUCTS

MOROCCO - SENIOR CITIZENS

M.E. Sharpe, 80 Business Park Drive, Armonk, New York 10504 (800) 541-6563; *The Illustrated Book of World Rankings.*

MOROCCO - SHEEP - See MOROCCO - LIVESTOCK AND POULTRY

MOROCCO - SILVER PRODUCTION AND CONSUMPTION - See MOROCCO - MINING AND MINERAL PRODUCTS

MOROCCO - SISAL PRODUCTION - See MOROCCO - CROPS

MOROCCO - SOCIAL DATA

African Development Bank, 01 BP 1387, Abidjan 01, Cote d'Ivoire; *Selected Statistics on Regional Member Countries.*

M.E. Sharpe, 80 Business Park Drive, Armonk, New York 10504 (800) 541-6563; *The Illustrated Book of World Rankings.*

Statistical Office of the United Nations, Publishing Service, New York, New York 10017 (800) 253-9646; *World Statistics Pocketbook.*

MOROCCO - SOCIAL SECURITY

International Monetary Fund, 700 Nineteenth Street, NW, Washington, D.C. 20431 (202) 623-7000; *Government Finance Statistics Yearbook.*

Statistical Office of the United Nations, Publishing Service, New York, New York 10017 (800) 253-9646; *National Accounts Statistics.*

MOROCCO - STAMP TAXES AND DUTIES - See MOROCCO - TAXATION

MOROCCO - STATE BUDGET

Euromonitor International, Inc., 122 South Michigan Avenue, Suite 1200, Chicago, Illinois 60603 (800) 577-EURO; *International Marketing Data and Statistics.*

MOROCCO - STEEL - See MOROCCO - MINING AND MINERAL PRODUCTS

MOROCCO - STOCKS - COMMODITY - MARKET PRICE - INDEX

Food and Agricultural Organization of the United Nations (FAO), Via delle Terme di Caracalla, 00100 Rome, Italy (Telephone Number in U.S. (202) 653-2400); *The State of Food and Agriculture.*

International Lead and Zinc Study Group, Metro House, 58 St. James's Street, London SW1A 1LD England; *Lead and Zinc Statistics.*

MOROCCO - SUGAR PRODUCTION AND CONSUMPTION - See MOROCCO - CROPS

MOROCCO - SULPHURIC ACID PRODUCTION - See MOROCCO - MINING AND MINERAL PRODUCTS

MOROCCO - TAX REVENUE - See MOROCCO - TAXATION

MOROCCO - TAXATION

Europa Publications Limited, 18 Bedford Square, London, WC1B 3JN, England; *The Europa World Year Book.*

International Monetary Fund, 700 Nineteenth Street, NW, Washington, D.C. 20431 (202) 623-7000; *Government Finance Statistics Yearbook.*

The World Bank, 1818 H Street, NW, Washington, D.C. 20433 (202) 477-1234; *World Development Indicators.*

MOROCCO - TEA CONSUMPTION - See MOROCCO - CROPS

MOROCCO - TELEGRAPH SERVICE

Pocketbook.

St. Martin's Press, Inc., 175 Fifth Avenue, New York, New York 10010 (800) 221-7945; *The Statesman's Year-Book.*

Statistical Office of the United Nations, Publishing Service, New York, New York 10017 (800) 253-9646; *Statistical Yearbook.*

MOROCCO - TELEPHONES IN USE

American Telephone and Telegraph Company, 26 Parsippany Road, Whippany, New Jersey 07981 (800) 222-0300; *The World's Telephones.*

Central Intelligence Agency, Washington, D.C. 20505 (703) 482-1100, www.cia.gov; *The World Factbook.*

Europa Publications Limited, 18 Bedford Square, London, WC1B 3JN, England; *The Europa World Year Book.*

Statistical Office of the United Nations, Publishing Service, New York, New York 10017 (800) 253-9646; *Statistical Yearbook;* and *World Statistics Pocketbook.*

MOROCCO - TELEVISION BROADCASTING - See MOROCCO - BROADCASTING

MOROCCO - TEXTILE INDUSTRY

M.E. Sharpe, 80 Business Park Drive, Armonk, New York 10504 (800) 541-6563; *The Illustrated Book of World Rankings.*

St. Martin's Press, Inc., 175 Fifth Avenue, New York, New York 10010 (800) 221-7945; *The Statesman's Year-Book.*

Statistical Office of the United Nations, Publishing Service, New York, New York 10017 (800) 253-9646; *Statistical Yearbook.*

United Nations Conference on Trade and Development, Central Statistical Service, Palais des Nations, Geneva, Switzerland (Telephone in U.S. (800) 253-9646); *UNCTAD Commodity Yearbook.*

MOROCCO - TIN - See MOROCCO - MINING AND MINERAL PRODUCTS

MOROCCO - TIRE (MOTOR VEHICLE) PRODUCTION

Statistical Office of the United Nations, Publishing Service, New York, New York 10017 (800) 253-9646; *Statistical Yearbook.*

MOROCCO - TOBACCO PRODUCTION

M.E. Sharpe, 80 Business Park Drive, Armonk, New York 10504 (800) 541-6563; *The Illustrated Book of World Rankings.*

Statistical Office of the United Nations, Publishing Service, New York, New York 10017 (800) 253-9646; *Statistical Yearbook.*

MOROCCO - TOBACCO PRODUCTS

Statistical Office of the United Nations, Publishing Service, New York, New York 10017 (800) 253-9646; *Statistical Yearbook*.

MOROCCO - TOURISM

Euromonitor International, Inc., 122 South Michigan Avenue, Suite 1200, Chicago, Illinois 60603 (800) 577-EURO; *The World Economic Factbook;* and *World Marketing Data and Statistics*.

Europa Publications Limited, 18 Bedford Square, London, WC1B 3JN, England; *The Europa World Year Book*.

Federal Statistical Office, Gustav-Stresemann - Ring 11, D-6200, Wiesbaden, Germany; *Morokko*.

M.E. Sharpe, 80 Business Park Drive, Armonk, New York 10504 (800) 541-6563; *The Illustrated Book of World Rankings*.

Statistical Office of the United Nations, Publishing Service, New York, New York 10017 (800) 253-9646; *Statistical Yearbook*.

United Nations Economic Commission for Africa, Africa Hall, Post Office Box 3001, Addis Ababa, Ethiopia (Telephone Number in U.S. (800) 253-9646); *African Statistical Yearbook*.

World Tourism Organization, Calle Capitan Haya 42, E-28020 Madrid, Spain; *Yearbook of Tourism Statistics*.

MOROCCO - TRACTORS IN USE

Statistical Office of the United Nations, Publishing Service, New York, New York 10017 (800) 253-9646; *Statistical Yearbook*.

MOROCCO - TRADE - See MOROCCO - FOREIGN TRADE

MOROCCO - TRADEMARKS AND SERVICE MARKS - See MOROCCO - PATENTS, TRADEMARKS AND SERVICE MARKS

MOROCCO - TRANSPORTATION AND COMMUNICATIONS

Central Intelligence Agency, Washington, D.C. 20505 (703) 351-2053; *The World Factbook*.

Euromonitor International, Inc., 122 South Michigan Avenue, Suite 1200, Chicago, Illinois 60603 (800) 577-EURO; *International Marketing Data and Statistics; and World Marketing Data and Statistics*.

Europa Publications Limited, 18 Bedford Square, London, WC1B 3JN, England; *The Europa World Year Book*.

Federal Statistical Office, Gustav-

Stresemann - Ring 11, D-6200, Wiesbaden, Germany; *Morokko*.

M.E. Sharpe, 80 Business Park Drive, Armonk, New York 10504 (800) 541-6563; *The Illustrated Book of World Rankings*.

St. Martin's Press, Inc., 175 Fifth Avenue, New York, New York 10010 (800) 221-7945; *The Statesman's Year-Book*.

Statistical Office of the United Nations, Publishing Service, New York, New York 10017 (800) 253-9646; *Human Development Report*.

United Nations Economic Commission for Africa, Africa Hall, Post Office Box 3001, Addis Ababa, Ethiopia (Telephone Number in U.S. (800) 253-9646); *African Statistical Yearbook*.

MOROCCO - UNEMPLOYMENT

Central Intelligence Agency, Washington, D.C. 20505 (703) 482-1100, www.cia.gov; *The World Factbook*.

Euromonitor International, Inc., 122 South Michigan Avenue, Suite 1200, Chicago, Illinois 60603 (800) 577-EURO; *International Marketing Data and Statistics*.

Statistical Office of the United Nations, Publishing Service, New York, New York 10017 (800) 253-9646; *Statistical Yearbook*.

MOROCCO - VITAL STATISTICS

Euromonitor International, Inc., 122 South Michigan Avenue, Suite 1200, Chicago, Illinois 60603 (800) 577-EURO; *International Marketing Data and Statistics*.

St. Martin's Press, Inc., 175 Fifth Avenue, New York, New York 10010 (800) 221-7945; *The Statesman's Year-Book*.

Statistical Office of the United Nations, Publishing Service, New York, New York 10017 (800) 253-9646; *Statistical Yearbook*.

World Health Organization, Office of Publications, 20 Avenue Appia, CH-1211 Geneva 27, Switzerland (Telephone Number in U.S. (518) 436-9686); *World Health Statistics Annual*.

MOROCCO - WAGES IN MANUFACTURING

Federal Statistical Office, Gustav-Stresemann - Ring 11, D-6200, Wiesbaden, Germany; *Morokko*.

Statistical Office of the United Nations, Publishing Service, New York, New York 10017 (800) 253-9646; *Statistical Yearbook*.

MOROCCO - WALNUT PRODUCTION - See MOROCCO - CROPS

MOROCCO - WATERMELON PRODUCTION - See MOROCCO - CROPS

MOROCCO - WEATHER - See MOROCCO - CLIMATE

MOROCCO - WELFARE EXPENDITURES

International Monetary Fund, 700 Nineteenth Street, NW, Washington, D.C. 20431 (202) 623-7000; *Government Finance Statistics Yearbook*.

MOROCCO - WHEAT PRODUCTION - See MOROCCO - CROPS

MOROCCO - WHOLESALE PRICES - INDEX NUMBERS

Statistical Office of the United Nations, Publishing Service, New York, New York 10017 (800) 253-9646; *Statistical Yearbook*.

MOROCCO - WINE PRODUCTION - See MOROCCO - BEVERAGES

MOROCCO - WOOD PULP PRODUCTION - See MOROCCO - FORESTRY AND FOREST PRODUCTS

MOROCCO - WOOL PRODUCTION - See MOROCCO - TEXTILE INDUSTRY

MOROCCO - YARN PRODUCTION - See MOROCCO - TEXTILE INDUSTRY

MOROCCO - ZINC AND ZINC ORE PRODUCTION AND CONSUMPTION - See MOROCCO - MINING AND MINERAL PRODUCTS

MORTALITY COSTS

Institute for Health and Aging, University of California, San Francisco, San Francisco, California 94143 (415) 476-9483; unpublished data.

MORTGAGE POOLS AND TRUSTS

Board of Governors of the Federal Reserve System, Twentieth Street and Constitution Avenue, NW, Washington, D.C. 20551 (202) 452-3000, www.bog.frb.fed.us; *Federal Reserve Bulletin;* and *Flow of Funds Accounts*.

MORTGAGES - See LOANS AND MORTGAGES

MOTION PICTURES INDUSTRY - EARNINGS

U.S. Department of Commerce, Bureau of the Census, Washington, D.C. 20233 (301) 457-4100, www.census.gov; *Census of Service Industries;* and *County Business Patterns*.

U.S. Department of Labor, Bureau of Labor Statistics, Two Massachusetts Avenue, NE, Washington, D.C. 20212 (202)

691-5200, www.stats.bls.gov; *Employment and Earnings;* and Internet site: http://stats.bls.gov/ ceshome.htm.

MOTION PICTURES INDUSTRY - EMPLOYEES

U.S. Department of Commerce, Bureau of the Census, Washington, D.C. 20233 (301) 457-4100, www.census.gov; *County Business Patterns;* and *Census of Service Industries.*

U.S. Department of Labor, Bureau of Labor Statistics, Two Massachusetts Avenue, NE, Washington, D.C. 20212 (202) 691-5200, www.stats.bls.gov; *Employment and Earnings;* and Internet site: http://stats.bls.gov/ ceshome.htm.

MOTION PICTURES INDUSTRY - ESTABLISHMENTS

U.S. Department of Commerce, Bureau of the Census, Washington, D.C. 20233 (301) 457-4100, www.census.gov; *County Business* Patterns; and *Census of Service Industries.*

MOTION PICTURES INDUSTRY - GROSS DOMESTIC PRODUCT

U.S. Department of Commerce, Bureau of Economic Analysis, Fourteenth Street between Constitution Avenue and E Street, NW, Washington, D.C. 20230 (202) 606-9900, www.bea.doc.gov; *Survey of Current Business.*

MOTION PICTURES INDUSTRY - MERGERS AND ACQUISITIONS

Thompson Financial Securities Data, Two Gateway Center, Newark, New Jersey 07006 (973) 622-3100; *Merger and Corporate Transactions Database.*

MOTION PICTURES INDUSTRY - PRODUCTIVITY

U.S. Department of Labor, Bureau of Labor Statistics, Two Massachusetts Avenue, NE, Washington, D.C. 20212 (202) 691-5200, www.stats.bls.gov; Internet site: http://stats.bls.gov/ iprhome.htm.

MOTION PICTURES INDUSTRY - RECEIPTS

U.S. Department of Commerce, Bureau of the Census, Washington, D.C. 20233 (301) 457-4100, www.census.gov; *Current Business Reports, Service Annual Survey; Census of Service Industries;* and unpublished data.

MOTOR FREIGHT TRANSPORTATION AND WAREHOUSING - See TRUCKING AND WAREHOUSING

MOTOR FUEL

U.S. Department of Transportation, Federal Highway Administration, 400 Seventh Street, SW, Washington, D.C. 20590 (202) 366-0660, www.fhwa.dot.gov; *Highway Statistics.*

MOTOR FUEL - ADVERTISING EXPENDITURES

Television Bureau of Advertising, Inc., 3 East 54th Street, New York, New York 10022 (212) 486-1111; data compiled by Competitive Media Reporting, 11 West 42nd Street, New York, New York 10036 (212) 789-1400.

MOTOR FUEL - CONSUMPTION - CIVIL AVIATION

U.S. Department of Transportation, Federal Aviation Administration, 800 Independence Avenue, SW, Washington, D.C. 20591 (202) 367-3484, www.faa.gov; *FAA Statistical Handbook of Aviation;* unpublished data; and Internet site http://api.hq.faa.gov/ apohome.htm.

MOTOR FUEL - CONSUMPTION - MOTOR VEHICLES

U.S. Department of Transportation, Federal Highway Administration, 400 Seventh Street, SW, Washington, D.C. 20590 (202) 366-0660, www.fhwa.dot.gov; *Highway Statistics.*

MOTOR FUEL - TAXES

U.S. Department of Commerce, Bureau of the Census, Washington, D.C. 20233 (301) 457-4100, www.census.gov; *State Government Finances;* and Internet site http://www.census.gov/ftp/pub/govs/www/ state.html.

MOTOR FUEL - TAXES - STATES

U.S. Department of Transportation, Federal Highway Administration, 400 Seventh Street, SW, Washington, D.C. 20590 (202) 366-0660, www.fhwa.dot.gov; *Highway Statistics.*

MOTOR HOMES

American Automobile Manufacturers Association, 1401 H Street, NW, Suite 900, Washington, D.C. 20005 (202) 326-5500; *Motor Vehicle Facts and Figures.*

Recreation Vehicle Industry Association, Post Office Box 2999, 1896 Preston White Drive, Reston, Virginia 22090 (703) 620-6003; *RVIA Industry Profile 1997.*

MOTOR VEHICLE DEALERS - RETAIL - EARNINGS

U.S. Department of Commerce, Bureau of the Census, Washington, D.C. 20233 (301) 457-4100, www.census.gov; *County*

Business Patterns; and 1997 Economic Census.

MOTOR VEHICLE DEALERS - RETAIL - EMPLOYEES

U.S. Department of Commerce, Bureau of the Census, Washington, D.C. 20233 (301) 457-4100, www.census.gov; *1997 Economic Census;* and *County Business Patterns.*

MOTOR VEHICLE DEALERS - RETAIL - ESTABLISHMENTS

U.S. Department of Commerce, Bureau of the Census, Washington, D.C. 20233 (301) 457-4100, www.census.gov; *1997 Economic Census;* and *County Business Patterns.*

MOTOR VEHICLE DEALERS - RETAIL - FINANCES

National Automobile Dealers Association, 8400 Westpark Drive, McLean, Virginia 22102 (703) 827-7000; *NADA Data.*

MOTOR VEHICLE DEALERS - RETAIL - FRANCHISES

National Automobile Dealers Association, 8400 Westpark Drive, McLean, Virginia 22102 (703) 827-7000; *NADA Data.*

MOTOR VEHICLE DEALERS - RETAIL - INVENTORIES

National Automobile Dealers Association, 8400 Westpark Drive, McLean, Virginia 22102 (703) 827-7000; *NADA Data.*

U.S. Department of Commerce, Bureau of the Census, Washington, D.C. 20233 (301) 457-4100, www.census.gov; *Current Business Reports, Annual Benchmark Report for Retail Trade;* and unpublished data.

MOTOR VEHICLE DEALERS - RETAIL - PRODUCTIVITY

U.S. Department of Labor, Bureau of Labor Statistics, Washington, D.C. 20210 (202) 523-1327; Internet site http://stats.bls.gov/iprhome.html.

MOTOR VEHICLE DEALERS - RETAIL - PROFITS

National Automobile Dealers Association, 8400 Westpark Drive, McLean, Virginia 22102 (703) 827-7000; *NADA Data.*

MOTOR VEHICLE DEALERS - RETAIL - SALES

Market Statistics, 355 Pack Avenue, South, New York, New York 10010 (212) 592-6250; *The Survey of Buying Power Data Service.*

National Automobile Dealers Association, 8400 Westpark Drive, McLean, Virginia 22102 (703) 827-7000; *NADA Data.*

U.S. Department of Commerce, Bureau of the Census, Washington, D.C. 20233 (301) 457-4100, www.census.gov; *; Current Business Reports, Annual Benchmark Report for Retail Trade; County Business Patterns; 1997 Economic Census;* and unpublished data.

MOTOR VEHICLES - ACCIDENTS/DEATHS

National Safety Council, 1121 Spring Lake Drive, Itasca, Illinois 60143-3201 (630) 285-1121; *Accident Facts.*

U.S. Department of Health and Human Services, National Center for Health Statistics, 3700 East-West Highway, Hyattsville, Maryland 20782 (301) 436-8500, www.cdc.gov/nchs; *National Vital Statistics Report; Vital Statistics of the United States;* and unpublished data.

U.S. Department of Transportation, Bureau of Transportation Statistics, 400 Seventh Street, SW, Washington, D.C. 20590 (800) 853-1351, www.bts.gov; *National Transportation Statistics.*

U.S. Department of Transportation, Federal Highway Administration, 400 Seventh Street, SW, Washington, D.C. 20201 (202) 366-0660, www.fhwa.dot.gov; *Fatal Accident Reporting System.*

MOTOR VEHICLES - ACCIDENTS/DEATHS - FOREIGN COUNTRIES

U.S. Department of Health and Human Services, National Center for Health Statistics, 3700 East-West Highway, Hyattsville, Maryland 20782 (301) 436-8500, www.cdc.gov/nchs; *Advance Data, No. 303.*

World Health Organization, Office of Publications, 20 Avenue Appia, CH-1211 Geneva 27, Switzerland (Telephone Number in U.S. (518) 436-9686); *World Health Statistics Annual.*

MOTOR VEHICLES - ADVERTISING EXPENDITURES

Television Bureau of Advertising, Inc., 3 East 54th Street, New York, New York 10022 (212) 486-1111; from data compiled by Competitive Media Reporting, 11 West 42nd Street, New York 10036 (212) 789-1400.

MOTOR VEHICLES - AIR POLLUTANT EMISSIONS

Environmental Protection Agency, 1200 Pennsylvania Avenue, NW, Washington, D.C. 20460 (888) 372-8255, www.epa.gov; *National Air Pollutant Emission Trends.*

MOTOR VEHICLES - ALTERNATIVE FUELED VEHICLES IN USE

U.S. Department of Energy, Energy Information Administration, 1000 Independence Avenue, SW, Washington, D.C. 20585 (202) 586-1185; *Alternatives to Traditional Transportation Fuels.*

MOTOR VEHICLES - COMMON CARRIERS

American Public Transportation Association, 1201 New York, NW, Suite 400, Washington, D.C. 20005 (202) 898-4000; *Transit Fact Book;* and Internet site: http://www.apta.com/pubs/stats/index.htm.

Eno Transportation Foundation, One Farragut Square, South, Suite 500, Washington, D.C. 20006 (202) 879-4700; *Transportation in America.*

U.S. Department of Commerce, Bureau of the Census, Washington, D.C. 20233 (301) 457-4100, www.census.gov; *Current Business Reports, 1997 Transportation Annual Survey.*

U.S. Department of Transportation, Bureau of Transportation Statistics, 400 Seventh Street, SW, Washington, D.C. 20590 (800) 853-1351, www.bts.gov; *Selected Earnings Data, Class I Motor Carriers of Passengers.*

MOTOR VEHICLES - CONSUMER EXPENDITURES

U.S. Department of Labor, Bureau of Labor Statistics, Two Massachusetts Avenue, NE, Washington, D.C. 20212 (202) 691-5200, www.stats.bls.gov; *Consumer Expenditures in 1997;* and unpublished data.

MOTOR VEHICLES - DRIVERS LICENSES

U.S. Department of Transportation, Federal Highway Administration, 400 Seventh Street, SW, Washington, D.C. 20590 (202) 366-0660, www.fhwa.dot.gov; *Selected Highway Statistics and Charts,* and *Highway Statistics.*

MOTOR VEHICLES - ENGINES

U.S. Department of Commerce, Bureau of the Census, Washington, D.C. 20233 (301) 457-4100, www.census.gov; *Manufacturing Profiles.*

MOTOR VEHICLES - EXPENDITURE PER NEW CAR

American Automobile Manufacturers Association, 1401 H Street, NW, Suite 900, Washington, D.C. 20005 (202) 326-5500; *Motor Vehicle Facts and Figures.*

U.S. Department of Commerce, Bureau of the Economic Analysis, Fourteenth Street

between Constitution Avenue and E Street, NW, Washington, D.C. 20230 (202) 606-9900, www.bea.doc.gov; *Survey of Current Business.*

MOTOR VEHICLES - FARM EXPENDITURES

U.S. Department of Agriculture, Economic Research Service, 1800 M Street, NW, Washington, D.C. 20036 (202) 694-5050, www.ers.usda.gov; *Agricultural Statistics;* and *Farm Business Economic Report.*

MOTOR VEHICLES - FOREIGN COUNTRIES

U.S. Department of Transportation, Federal Highway Administration, 400 Seventh Street, SW, Washington, D.C. 20590 (202) 366-0660, www.fhwa.dot.gov; *Highway Statistics.*

MOTOR VEHICLES - FOREIGN TRADE

American Automobile Manufacturers Association, 1401 H Street, NW, Suite 900, Washington, D.C. 20005 (202) 326-5500; *Motor Vehicle Facts and Figures;* and *World Motor Vehicle Data Book.*

MOTOR VEHICLES - FUEL CONSUMED

U.S. Department of Transportation, Federal Highway Administration, 400 Seventh Street, SW, Washington, D.C. 20590 (202) 366-0660, www.fhwa.dot.gov; *Highway Statistics.*

MOTOR VEHICLES - IMPORTS

American Automobile Manufacturers Association, 1401 H Street, NW, Suite 900, Washington, D.C. 20005 (202) 326-5500; *Motor Vehicle Facts and Figures.*

U.S. Department of Commerce, Bureau of the Economic Analysis, Fourteenth Street between Constitution Avenue and E Street, NW, Washington, D.C. 20230 (202) 606-9900, www.bea.doc.gov; *Survey of Current Business.*

MOTOR VEHICLES - INSURANCE

Insurance Information Institute, 110 William Street, New York, New York 10038 (212) 669-9200; *The Fact Book, Property/Casualty Insurance Facts.*

MOTOR VEHICLES - MILES OF TRAVEL

U.S. Department of Transportation, Federal Highway Administration, 400 Seventh Street, Washington, D.C. 20590 (202) 366-0660, www.fhwa.dot.gov; *Highway Statistics;* and *Selected Highway Statistics and Charts.*

MOTOR VEHICLES - MOTOR VEHICLES IN USE

American Automobile Manufacturers Association, 1401 H Street, NW, Washington, D.C. 20005 (202) 326-5500; *Motor Vehicle Facts and Figures*, and *World Motor Vehicle Data Book*.

MOTOR VEHICLES - NATIONAL INCOME ACCOUNTS

U.S. Department of Commerce, Bureau of Economic Analysis, Fourteenth Street between Constitution Avenue and E Street, NW, Washington, D.C. 20230 (202) 606-9900, www.bea.doc.gov; *The National Income and Product Accounts of the United States;* and *Survey of Current Business.*

MOTOR VEHICLES - OWNERSHIP

U.S. Department of Commerce, Bureau of the Census, Washington, D.C. 20233 (301) 457-4100, www.census.gov; *Current Housing Reports;* and *American Housing Survey in the United States.*

MOTOR VEHICLES - PASSENGER OUTLAYS

Eno Transportation Foundation, One Farragut Square, South, Suite 500, Washington, D.C. 20006 (202) 879-4700; *Transportation in America.*

MOTOR VEHICLES - PRICE INDEXES - CONSUMER

U.S. Department of Labor, Bureau of Labor Statistics, Two Massachusetts Avenue, NE, Washington, D.C. 20212 (202) 691-5200, www.stats.bls.gov; *Monthly Labor Review;* and *Consumer Price Indexes Detailed Report.*

MOTOR VEHICLES - PRICE INDEXES - CONSUMER - FIXED WEIGHT

U.S. Department of Commerce, Bureau of Economic Analysis, Fourteenth Street between Constitution Avenue and E Street, NW, Washington, D.C. 20230 (202) 606-9900, www.bea.doc.gov; *The National Income and Product Accounts of the U.S.;* and *Survey of Current Business.*

MOTOR VEHICLES - PRODUCTION

American Automobile Manufacturers Association, 1401 H Street, NW, Suite 900, Washington, D.C. 20005 (202) 326-5500; *Motor Vehicle Facts and Figures;* and *World Motor Vehicle Data Book.*

MOTOR VEHICLES - RAILROAD CAR LOADINGS

Association of American Railroads, American Railroads Building, 50 F Street, NW, Washington, D.C. 20001 (202) 639-2100; *Weekly Railroad Traffic.*

MOTOR VEHICLES - RECALLED FOR SAFETY DEFECTS

U.S. Department of Transportation, National Highway Traffic Safety Administration, 400 Seventh Street, SW, Washington, D.C. 20590 (202) 366-8892, www.nhtsa.dot.gov; *Motor Vehicles Recall Campaigns.*

MOTOR VEHICLES - RECREATIONAL VEHICLES

American Automobile Manufacturers Association, 1401 H Street, NW, Suite 900, Washington, D.C. 20005 (202) 326-5500; *Motor Vehicle Facts and Figures.*

Recreation Vehicle Industry Association, Post Office Box 2999, 1896 Preston White Drive, Reston, Virginia 22090 (703) 620-6003; *RVIA Industry Profile 1997.*

MOTOR VEHICLES - REGISTRATIONS

U.S. Department of Transportation, Federal Highway Administration, 400 Seventh Street, SW, Washington, D.C. 20590 (202) 366-0660, www.fhwa.dot.gov; *Highway Statistics* and *Selected Highway Statistics and Charts.*

MOTOR VEHICLES - SALES

American Automobile Manufacturers Association, 1401 H Street, NW, Suite 900, Washington, D.C. 20005 (202) 326-5500; *Motor Vehicle Facts and Figures.*

U.S. Department of Commerce, Bureau of the Economic Analysis, Fourteenth Street between Constitution Avenue and E Street, NW, Washington, D.C. 20230 (202) 606-9900, www.bea.doc.gov; *Survey of Current Business.*

MOTOR VEHICLES - SERVICE AND REPAIR SHOPS - See AUTOMOTIVE REPAIR, SERVICES AND PARKING

MOTOR VEHICLES - TAXES - LICENSES AND MOTOR FUEL

U.S. Department of Commerce, Bureau of the Census, Washington, D.C. 20233 (301) 457-4100, www.census.gov; *State Government Finances;* and Internet site http://www.census.gov/ftp/pub/govs/www/state.html.

U.S. Department of Transportation, Federal Highway Administration, 400 Seventh Street, SW, Washington, D.C. 20590 (202) 366-0660, www.fhwa.dot.gov; *Highway Statistics.*

MOTOR VEHICLES - THEFT

U.S. Department of Justice, Bureau of Justice Statistics, 810 Seventh Street, NW, 2nd Floor, Washington, D.C. 20531 (800) 732-3277, www.ojp.usdoj.gov/bjs; *Criminal Victimization.*

U.S. Department of Justice, Federal Bureau of Investigation, 935 Pennsylvania Avenue, NW, Washington, D.C. 20535 (202) 324-3691, www.fbi.gov; *Crime in the United States;* and *Population-at-Risk Rates and Selected Crime Indicators.*

MOTOR VEHICLES - TIRES AND BATTERIES

Rubber Manufacturers Association, Inc., 1400 K Street, NW, Washington, D.C. 20005 (202) 682-4800; *RMA Monthly Tire Report.*

MOTOR VEHICLES - TRUCKS

U.S. Department of Transportation, Federal Highway Administration, 400 Seventh Street, Washington, D.C. 20590 (202) 366-0660, www.fhwa.dot.gov; *Highway Statistics;* and *Highway Statistics Summary.*

MOTOR VEHICLES AND EQUIPMENT - MANUFACTURING - CAPITAL

U.S. Department of Commerce, Bureau of Economic Analysis, Fourteenth Street between Constitution Avenue and E Street, NW, Washington, D.C. 20230 (202) 606-9900, www.bea.doc.gov; *Survey of Current Business.*

MOTOR VEHICLES AND EQUIPMENT - MANUFACTURING - EARNINGS

U.S. Department of Commerce, Bureau of the Census, Washington, D.C. 20233 (301) 457-4100, www.census.gov; *Census of Manufactures;* and *Annual Survey of Manufactures.*

U.S. Department of Labor, Bureau of Labor Statistics, Two Massachusetts Avenue, NE, Washington, D.C. 20212 (202) 691-5200, www.stats.bls.gov; *Employment and Earnings;* and Internet site: http://stats.bls.gov/ ceshome.htm..

MOTOR VEHICLES AND EQUIPMENT - MANUFACTURING - EMPLOYEES

U.S. Department of Commerce, Bureau of the Census, Washington, D.C. 20233 (301) 457-4100, www.census.gov; *Census of Manufactures;* and *Annual Survey of Manufactures.*

U.S. Department of Labor, Bureau of Labor Statistics, Two Massachusetts Avenue, NE, Washington, D.C. 20212 (202) 691-5200, www.stats.bls.gov; *Monthly Labor Review; Employment and Earnings;* and Internet site: http://stats.bls.gov/ceshome.htm.

MOTOR VEHICLES AND EQUIPMENT - MANUFACTURING - FOREIGN TRADE

U.S. Department of Commerce, Bureau of the Census, Washington, D.C. 20233 (301) 457-4100, www.census.gov; *U.S.*

International Trade in Goods and Services.

MOTOR VEHICLES AND EQUIPMENT - MANUFACTURING - GROSS DOMESTIC PRODUCT

U.S. Department of Commerce, Bureau of Economic Analysis, Fourteenth Street between Constitution Avenue and E Street, NW, Washington, D.C. 20230 (202) 606-9900, www.bea.doc.gov; *The National Income and Product Accounts of the United States;* and *Survey of Current Business.*

MOTOR VEHICLES AND EQUIPMENT - MANUFACTURING - INVENTORIES

U.S. Department of Commerce, Bureau of the Census, Washington, D.C. 20233 (301) 457-4100, www.census.gov; *Current Industrial Reports, Manufactures Shipments, Inventories, and Orders.*

MOTOR VEHICLES AND EQUIPMENT - MANUFACTURING - OCCUPATIONAL SAFETY

U.S. Department of Labor, Bureau of Labor Statistics, Two Massachusetts Avenue, NE, Washington, D.C. 20212 (202) 691-5200, www.stats.bls.gov; *Occupational Injuries and Illnesses in the United States by Industry.*

MOTOR VEHICLES AND EQUIPMENT - MANUFACTURING - PRODUCTIVITY

Board of Governors of the Federal Reserve System, Twentieth Street and Constitution Avenue, NW, Washington, D.C. 20551 (202) 452-3000, www.bog.frb.fed.us; *Federal Reserve Bulletin;* and *Industrial Production and Capacity Utilization.*

U.S. Department of Labor, Bureau of Labor Statistics, Two Massachusetts Avenue, NE, Washington, D.C. 20212 (202) 691-5200, www.stats.bls.gov; Internet site http://stats.bls.gov/iprhome.htm.

MOTOR VEHICLES AND EQUIPMENT - MANUFACTURING - PROFITS

Executive Office of the President, Council of Economic Advisers, Old Executive Office Building, Washington, D.C. 20502 (202) 395-5084, www.whitehouse.gov/cea; *Economic Report of the President.*

Forbes, Incorporated, 60 Fifth Avenue, New York, New York 10011 (212) 691-6130; *Forbes Annual Report on American Industry.*

Time Warner, Time and Life Building, Rockefeller Center, New York, New York 10020 (212) 522-1212; *The Fortune Directories.*

U.S. Department of Commerce, Bureau of the Census, Washington, D.C. 20233 (301) 457-4100, www.census.gov; *Quarterly*

Financial Report for Manufacturing, Mining and Trade Corporations.

MOTOR VEHICLES AND EQUIPMENT - MANUFACTURING - RESEARCH AND DEVELOPMENT

National Science Foundation, 4201 Wilson Boulevard, Arlington, Virginia 22230 (703) 306-1234, www.nsf.gov; *Research and Development in Industry.*

MOTOR VEHICLES AND EQUIPMENT - MANUFACTURING - SALES, SHIPMENTS, RECEIPTS

American Iron and Steel Institute, 1101 17th Street, NW, Washington, D.C. 20036 (202) 452-7100; *Annual Statistical Report.*

Forbes, Inc., 60 Fifth Avenue, New York, New York 10011 (212) 691-6130; *Forbes Annual Report on American Industry.*

Statistical Office of the United Nations, Publishing Service, New York, New York 10017 (800) 253-9646; *Monthly Bulletin of Statistics.*

U.S. Department of Commerce, Bureau of the Census, Washington, D.C. 20233 (301) 457-4100, www.census.gov; *Census of Manufactures; Annual Survey of Manufactures; Current Industrial Reports, Manufactures' Shipments, Inventories and Orders; Exports from Manufacturing Establishments;* and *Manufacturing Profiles*

MOTOR VEHICLES AND EQUIPMENT - MANUFACTURING - VALUE ADDED

U.S. Department of Commerce, Bureau of the Census, Washington, D.C. 20233 (301) 457-4100, www.census.gov; *Census of Manufactures;* and *Annual Survey of Manufactures.*

MOTORCYCLES

National Safety Council, 1121 Spring Lake Drive, Itasca, Illinois 60143-3201 (630) 285-1121; *Accident Facts.*

U.S. Department of Commerce, Bureau of the Census, Washington, D.C. 20233 (301) 457-4100, www.census.gov; *U.S. International Trade in Goods and Services.*

U.S. Department of Transportation, Federal Highway Administration, 400 Seventh Street, SW, Washington, D.C. 20590 (202) 366-0660, www.fhwa.dot.gov; *Highway Statistics;* and *Selected Highway Statistics and Charts.*

MOTORCYCLES - ACCIDENTS AND DEATHS

National Safety Council, 1121 Spring Lake Drive, Itasca, Illinois 60143-3201 (630) 285-1121; *Accident Facts.*

MOTORCYCLES - FOREIGN COUNTRIES

U.S. Department of Transportation, Federal Highway Administration, 400 Seventh Street, SW, Washington, D.C. 20590 (202) 366-0660, www.fhwa.dot.gov; *Highway Statistics.*

MOTORCYCLES - FOREIGN TRADE

U.S. Department of Commerce, Bureau of the Census, Washington, D.C. 20233 (301) 457-4100, www.census.gov; *U.S. International Trade in Goods and Services.*

MOTORCYCLES - HELMET LAW

National Safety Council, 1121 Spring Lake Drive, Itasca, Illinois 60143-3201 (630) 285-1121; *Accident Facts.*

MOUNTAIN BIKING

National Sporting Goods Association, 1601 Feehanville Drive, Suite 300, Mount Prospect, Illinois 60056 (847) 296-6742; *Sports Participation in 1998.*

MOVIE THEATERS

U.S. Department of Commerce, Bureau of the Census, Washington, D.C. 20233 (301) 457-4100, www.census.gov; *Current Business Report, Service Annual Survey.*

Veronis, Suhler and Associates, Inc., 350 Park Avenue, New York, New York 10022 (212) 935-4990; *Communications Industry Report.*

Mozambique - National Statistical Office

National Directorate of Statistics, Ministerio do Plano, Av Ahmed Sekou Toure 21, CP 493, Maputo, Mozambique.

Mozambique - Primary Statistics Sources

Direccao Nacional de Estatistica, CP 493, Maputo, Mozambique; *Anuario estatistico* (Statistical Yearbook); and *Boletim Mensal de estatistics* (Monthly Bulletin of Statistics).

MOZAMBIQUE - AGRICULTURE

Economist Intelligence Unit, 111 West 57th Street, New York, New York 10019 (800) 938-4685; *Mozambique Country Report.*

Euromonitor International, Inc., 122 South Michigan Avenue, Suite 1200, Chicago, Illinois 60603 (800) 577-EURO; *International Marketing Data and Statistics;* and *World Marketing Data and Statistics.*

Europa Publications Limited, 18 Bedford Square, London, WC1B 3JN, England; *The Europa World Year Book*.

Federal Statistical Office, Gustav-Stresemann - Ring 11, D-6200, Wiesbaden, Germany; *Mosambik*.

Food and Agricultural Organization of the United Nations (FAO), Via delle Terme di Caracalla, 00100 Rome, Italy (Telephone Number in U.S. (202) 653-2400); *Production Yearbook; The State of Food and Agriculture;* and *Trade Yearbook*.

M.E. Sharpe, 80 Business Park Drive, Armonk, New York 10504 (800) 541-6563; *The Illustrated Book of World Rankings*.

St. Martin's Press, Inc., 175 Fifth Avenue, New York, New York 10010 (800) 221-7945; *The Statesman's Year-Book*.

Statistical Office of the United Nations, Publishing Service, New York, New York 10017 (800) 253-9646; *Statistical Yearbook;* and *Survey of Economic and Social Conditions in Africa*.

United Nations Conference on Trade and Development, Central Statistical Service, Palais des Nations, Geneva, Switzerland (Telephone in U.S. (800) 253-9646); *UNCTAD Commodity Yearbook*.

United Nations Economic Commission for Africa, Africa Hall, Post Office Box 3001, Addis Ababa, Ethiopia (Telephone Number in U.S. (800) 253-9646); *African Statistical Yearbook*.

The World Bank, 1818 H Street, NW, Washington, D.C. 20433 (202) 477-1234; *World Development Indicators*.

MOZAMBIQUE - AIRLINE SERVICE

Europa Publications Limited, 18 Bedford Square, London, WC1B 3JN, England; *The Europa World Year Book*.

M.E. Sharpe, 80 Business Park Drive, Armonk, New York 10504 (800) 541-6563; *The Illustrated Book of World Rankings*.

St. Martin's Press, Inc., 175 Fifth Avenue, New York, New York 10010 (800) 221-7945; *The Statesman's Year-Book*.

United Nations Economic Commission for Africa, Africa Hall, Post Office Box 3001, Addis Ababa, Ethiopia (Telephone Number in U.S. (800) 253-9646); *African Statistical Yearbook*.

MOZAMBIQUE - AIRPORTS

Central Intelligence Agency, Washington, D.C. 20505 (703) 482-1100, www.cia.gov; *The World Factbook*.

MOZAMBIQUE - ALUMINUM PRODUCTION AND CONSUMPTION - See MOZAMBIQUE - MINING AND MINERAL PRODUCTS

MOZAMBIQUE - ANIMAL HEALTH

Food and Agricultural Organization of the United Nations (FAO), Via delle Terme di Caracalla, 00100 Rome, Italy (Telephone Number in U.S. (202) 653-2400); *Animal Health Yearbook*.

MOZAMBIQUE - AREA AND DENSITY OF POPULATION

African Development Bank, 01 BP 1387, Abidjan 01, Cote d'Ivoire; *Selected Statistics on Regional Member Countries*.

Central Intelligence Agency, Washington, D.C. 20505 (703) 482-1100, www.cia.gov; *The World Factbook*.

Euromonitor International, Inc., 122 South Michigan Avenue, Suite 1200, Chicago, Illinois 60603 (800) 577-EURO; *International Marketing Data and Statistics;* and *The World Economic Factbook*.

Europa Publications Limited, 18 Bedford Square, London, WC1B 3JN, England; *The Europa World Year Book*.

Federal Statistical Office, Gustav-Stresemann - Ring 11, D-6200, Wiesbaden, Germany; *Mosambik*.

Food and Agricultural Organization of the United Nations (FAO), Via delle Terme di Caracalla, 00100 Rome, Italy (Telephone Number in U.S. (202) 653-2400); *The State of Food and Agriculture*.

M.E. Sharpe, 80 Business Park Drive, Armonk, New York 10504 (800) 541-6563; *The Illustrated Book of World Rankings*.

St. Martin's Press, Inc., 175 Fifth Avenue, New York, New York 10010 (800) 221-7945; *The Statesman's Year-Book*.

Statistical Office of the United Nations, Publishing Service, New York, New York 10017 (800) 253-9646; *Statistical Yearbook;* and *Survey of Economic and Social Conditions in Africa*.

The World Bank, 1818 H Street, NW, Washington, D.C. 20433 (202) 477-1234; *World Development Report*.

MOZAMBIQUE - ARMS EXPORTS AND IMPORTS - See MOZAMBIQUE - MILITARY

MOZAMBIQUE - BALANCE OF PAYMENTS

African Development Bank, 01 BP 1387, Abidjan 01, Cote d'Ivoire; *Selected Statistics on Regional Member Countries*.

The Economist Intelligence Unit, 111 West 57th Street, New York, New York 10019 (800) 938-4685; *The World Market Atlas*.

Europa Publications Limited, 18 Bedford Square, London, WC1B 3JN, England; *The Europa World Year Book*.

Federal Statistical Office, Gustav-Stresemann - Ring 11, D-6200, Wiesbaden, Germany; *Mosambik*.

United Nations Conference on Trade and Development (UNCTAD), New York, New York 10017 (800) 253-9646; *Handbook of International Trade and Development Statistics*.

The World Bank, 1818 H Street, NW, Washington, D.C. 20433 (202) 477-1234; *World Development Report;* and *World Development Indicators*.

MOZAMBIQUE - BANKING

Euromonitor International, Inc., 122 South Michigan Avenue, Suite 1200, Chicago, Illinois 60603 (800) 577-EURO; *World Marketing Data and Statistics*.

Europa Publications Limited, 18 Bedford Square, London, WC1B 3JN, England; *The Europa World Year Book*.

M.E. Sharpe, 80 Business Park Drive, Armonk, New York 10504 (800) 541-6563; *The Illustrated Book of World Rankings*.

St. Martin's Press, Inc., 175 Fifth Avenue, New York, New York 10010 (800) 221-7945; *The Statesman's Year-Book*.

MOZAMBIQUE - BARLEY PRODUCTION - See MOZAMBIQUE - CROPS

MOZAMBIQUE - BAUXITE PRODUCTION AND CONSUMPTION - See MOZAMBIQUE - MINING AND MINERAL PRODUCTS

MOZAMBIQUE - BEER PRODUCTION - See MOZAMBIQUE - BEVERAGES

MOZAMBIQUE - BEVERAGES

M.E. Sharpe, 80 Business Park Drive, Armonk, New York 10504 (800) 541-6563; *The Illustrated Book of World Rankings*.

Statistical Office of the United Nations, Publishing Service, New York, New York 10017 (800) 253-9646; *Statistical Yearbook*.

MOZAMBIQUE - BIRTH RATES

Central Intelligence Agency, Washington, D.C. 20505 (703) 482-1100, www.cia.gov; *The World Factbook*.

Euromonitor International, Inc., 122 South Michigan Avenue, Suite 1200,

Chicago, Illinois 60603 (800) 577-EURO; *International Marketing Data and Statistics;* and *The World Economic Factbook.*

Europa Publications Limited, 18 Bedford Square, London, WC1B 3JN, England; *The Europa World Year Book.*

M.E. Sharpe, 80 Business Park Drive, Armonk, New York 10504 (800) 541-6563; *The Illustrated Book of World Rankings.*

Statistical Office of the United Nations, Publishing Service, New York, New York 10017 (800) 253-9646; *Demographic Yearbook; Statistical Yearbook;* and *Survey of Economic and Social Conditions in Africa.*

The World Bank, 1818 H Street, NW, Washington, D.C. 20433 (202) 477-1234; *World Development Indicators.*

MOZAMBIQUE - BOOK PRODUCTION

Europa Publications Limited, 18 Bedford Square, London, WC1B 3JN, England; *The Europa World Year Book.*

MOZAMBIQUE - BROADCASTING

Billboard Limited, Post Office Box 9027, 1006 AA Amsterdam, The Netherlands (Telephone Number in U.S. (212) 764-7300); *World Radio TV Handbook.*

Central Intelligence Agency, Washington, D.C. 20505 (703) 482-1100, www.cia.gov; *The World Factbook.*

Euromonitor International, Inc., 122 South Michigan Avenue, Suite 1200, Chicago, Illinois 60603 (800) 577-EURO; *World Marketing Data and Statistics.*

M.E. Sharpe, 80 Business Park Drive, Armonk, New York 10504 (800) 541-6563; *The Illustrated Book of World Rankings.*

St. Martin's Press, Inc., 175 Fifth Avenue, New York, New York 10010 (800) 221-7945; *The Statesman's Year-Book.*

MOZAMBIQUE - BUDGET

Central Intelligence Agency, Washington, D.C. 20505 (703) 482-1100, www.cia.gov; *The World Factbook.*

MOZAMBIQUE - CALORIE SUPPLY

African Development Bank, 01 BP 1387, Abidjan 01, Cote d'Ivoire; *Selected Statistics on Regional Member Countries.*

Food and Agricultural Organization of the United Nations (FAO), Via delle Terme di Caracalla, 00100 Rome, Italy (Telephone Number in U.S. (202) 653-2400); *The State of Food and Agriculture.*

MOZAMBIQUE - CASHEW NUT

PRODUCTION - See MOZAMBIQUE -CROPS

MOZAMBIQUE - CASTOR BEAN PRODUCTION - See MOZAMBIQUE - CROPS

MOZAMBIQUE - CATTLE - See MOZAMBIQUE - LIVESTOCK AND POULTRY

MOZAMBIQUE - CEMENT PRODUCTION - See MOZAMBIQUE - MINING AND MINERAL PRODUCTS

MOZAMBIQUE - CHEMICAL (ORGANIC) PRODUCTION - See MOZAMBIQUE - MINING AND MINERAL PRODUCTS

MOZAMBIQUE - CHICKENS - See MOZAMBIQUE - LIVESTOCK AND POULTRY

MOZAMBIQUE - CIGARETTE PRODUCTION - See MOZAMBIQUE - TOBACCO PRODUCTION

MOZAMBIQUE - CLIMATE

M.E. Sharpe, 80 Business Park Drive, Armonk, New York 10504 (800) 541-6563; *The Illustrated Book of World Rankings.*

St. Martin's Press, Inc., 175 Fifth Avenue, New York, New York 10010 (800) 221-7945; *The Statesman's Year-Book.*

MOZAMBIQUE - COAL PRODUCTION - See MOZAMBIQUE - MINING AND MINERAL PRODUCTS

MOZAMBIQUE - COFFEE PRODUCTION AND CONSUMPTION - See MOZAMBIQUE - CROPS

MOZAMBIQUE - COMMERCE

St. Martin's Press, Inc., 175 Fifth Avenue, New York, New York 10010 (800) 221-7945; *The Statesman's Year-Book.*

MOZAMBIQUE - COMMUNICATIONS - See MOZAMBIQUE - TRANSPORTATION AND COMMUNICATIONS

MOZAMBIQUE - CONSTRUCTION INDUSTRY

M.E. Sharpe, 80 Business Park Drive, Armonk, New York 10504 (800) 541-6563; *The Illustrated Book of World Rankings.*

Statistical Office of the United Nations, Publishing Service, New York, New York 10017 (800) 253-9646; *Statistical Yearbook.*

United Nations Economic Commission for Africa, Africa Hall, Post Office Box 3001, Addis Ababa, Ethiopia (Telephone Number in U.S. (800) 253-9646); *African Statistical Yearbook.*

MOZAMBIQUE - CONSUMER PRICE INDEX

African Development Bank, 01 BP 1387, Abidjan 01, Cote d'Ivoire; *Selected Statistics on Regional Member Countries.*

Europa Publications Limited, 18 Bedford Square, London, WC1B 3JN, England; *The Europa World Year Book.*

Statistical Office of the United Nations, Publishing Service, New York, New York 10017 (800) 253-9646; *Statistical Yearbook;* and *Survey of Economic and Social Conditions in Africa.*

MOZAMBIQUE - CONSUMER PRICES

International Labour Office, I.L.O. Publications, 1828 L Street, NW., Suite 801, Washington, D.C. 20036 (301) 638-3152; *Yearbook of Labour Statistics.*

MOZAMBIQUE - CONSUMER PRICES

Euromonitor International, Inc., 122 South Michigan Avenue, Suite 1200, Chicago, Illinois 60603 (800) 577-EURO; *World Marketing Data and Statistics.*

MOZAMBIQUE - CONSUMPTION

African Development Bank, 01 BP 1387, Abidjan 01, Cote d'Ivoire; *Selected Statistics on Regional Member Countries.*

Statistical Office of the United Nations, Publishing Service, New York, New York 10017 (800) 253-9646; *Survey of Economic and Social Conditions in Africa.*

The World Bank, 1818 H Street, NW, Washington, D.C. 20433 (202) 477-1234; *World Development Report.*

MOZAMBIQUE - COPPER AND COPPER ORE PRODUCTION AND CONSUMPTION - See MOZAMBIQUE - MINING AND MINERAL PRODUCTS

MOZAMBIQUE - CORN PRODUCTION - See MOZAMBIQUE - CROPS

MOZAMBIQUE - CORPORATE TAXES - See MOZAMBIQUE - TAXATION

MOZAMBIQUE - COTTON - See MOZAMBIQUE - CROPS

MOZAMBIQUE - CROPS

Commodity Research Bureau, 30 South Wacker Drive, Chicago Illinois 60606 (312) 454-1801; *Commodity Year Book.*

Europa Publications Limited, 18 Bedford Square, London, WC1B 3JN, England; *The Europa World Year Book.*

Food and Agricultural Organization of the United Nations (FAO), Via delle Terme

di Caracalla, 00100 Rome, Italy (Telephone Number in U.S. (202) 653-2400); *Production Yearbook;* and *The State of Food and Agriculture.*

M.E. Sharpe, 80 Business Park Drive, Armonk, New York 10504 (800) 541-6563; *The Illustrated Book of World Rankings.*

St. Martin's Press, Inc., 175 Fifth Avenue, New York, New York 10010 (800) 221-7945; *The Statesman's Year-Book.*

Statistical Office of the United Nations, Publishing Service, New York, New York 10017 (800) 253-9646; *Statistical Yearbook.*

United Nations Conference on Trade and Development, Central Statistical Service, Palais des Nations, Geneva, Switzerland (Telephone in U.S. (800) 253-9646); *UNCTAD Commodity Yearbook.*

United Nations Economic Commission for Africa, Africa Hall, Post Office Box 3001, Addis Ababa, Ethiopia (Telephone Number in U.S. (800) 253-9646); *African Statistical Yearbook.*

MOZAMBIQUE - CUSTOMS DUTIES

St. Martin's Press, Inc., 175 Fifth Avenue, New York, New York 10010 (800) 221-7945; *The Statesman's Year-Book.*

MOZAMBIQUE - DAIRY PRODUCTS

Europa Publications Limited, 18 Bedford Square, London, WC1B 3JN, England; *The Europa World Year Book.*

Food and Agricultural Organization of the United Nations (FAO), Via delle Terme di Caracalla, 00100 Rome, Italy (Telephone Number in U.S. (202) 653-2400); *Production Yearbook;* and *The State of Food and Agriculture.*

M.E. Sharpe, 80 Business Park Drive, Armonk, New York 10504 (800) 541-6563; *The Illustrated Book of World Rankings.*

St. Martin's Press, Inc., 175 Fifth Avenue, New York, New York 10010 (800) 221-7945; *The Statesman's Year-Book.*

Statistical Office of the United Nations, Publishing Service, New York, New York 10017 (800) 253-9646; *Statistical Yearbook.*

MOZAMBIQUE - DEATH RATES - See MOZAMBIQUE - MORTALITY

MOZAMBIQUE - DEFENSE EXPENDITURES - See MOZAMBIQUE - MILITARY

MOZAMBIQUE - DEMOGRAPHY

The Economist Intelligence Unit, 111 West 57th Street, New York, New York

10019 (800) 938-4685; *The World Market Atlas.*

Euromonitor International, Inc., 122 South Michigan Avenue, Suite 1200, Chicago, Illinois 60603 (800) 577-EURO; *International Marketing Data and Statistics; The World Economic Factbook;* and *World Marketing Data and Statistics.*

Federal Statistical Office, Gustav-Stresemann - Ring 11, D-6200, Wiesbaden, Germany; *Mosambik.*

M.E. Sharpe, 80 Business Park Drive, Armonk, New York 10504 (800) 541-6563; *The Illustrated Book of World Rankings.*

Statistical Office of the United Nations, Publishing Service, New York, New York 10017 (800) 253-9646; *Human Development Report;* and *Survey of Economic and Social Conditions in Africa.*

MOZAMBIQUE - DEVELOPMENT ASSISTANCE

Statistical Office of the United Nations, Publishing Service, New York, New York 10017 (800) 253-9646; *Statistical Yearbook.*

MOZAMBIQUE - DIAMOND PRODUCTION - See MOZAMBIQUE - MINING AND MINERAL PRODUCTS

MOZAMBIQUE - DISEASES - See MOZAMBIQUE - HEALTH

MOZAMBIQUE - DIVORCE RATES

M.E. Sharpe, 80 Business Park Drive, Armonk, New York 10504 (800) 541-6563; *The Illustrated Book of World Rankings.*

Statistical Office of the United Nations, Publishing Service, New York, New York 10017 (800) 253-9646; *Demographic Yearbook.*

MOZAMBIQUE - DUCKS - See MOZAMBIQUE - LIVESTOCK AND POULTRY

MOZAMBIQUE - ECONOMY

African Development Bank, 01 BP 1387, Abidjan 01, Cote d'Ivoire; *Selected Statistics on Regional Member Countries.*

Central Intelligence Agency, Washington, D.C. 20505 (703) 482-1100, www.cia.gov; *The World Factbook.*

Economist Intelligence Unit, 111 West 57th Street, New York, New York 10019 (800) 938-4685; *Mozambique Country Report.*

Euromonitor International, Inc., 122 South Michigan Avenue, Suite 1200, Chicago, Illinois 60603 (800) 577-EURO;

International Marketing Data and Statistics; The World Economic Factbook; and *World Marketing Data and Statistics.*

Europa Publications Limited, 18 Bedford Square, London, WC1B 3JN, England; *The Europa World Year Book.*

Federal Statistical Office, Gustav-Stresemann - Ring 11, D-6200, Wiesbaden, Germany; *Mosambik.*

M.E. Sharpe, 80 Business Park Drive, Armonk, New York 10504 (800) 541-6563; *The Illustrated Book of World Rankings.*

St. Martin's Press, Inc., 175 Fifth Avenue, New York, New York 10010 (800) 221-7945; *The Statesman's Year-Book.*

Statistical Office of the United Nations, Publishing Service, New York, New York 10017 (800) 253-9646; *Human Development Report; World Statistics Pocketbook;* and *Foreign Trade Statistics for Africa.*

The World Bank, 1818 H Street, NW, Washington, D.C. 20433 (202) 477-1234; *The World Bank Atlas;* and *World Development Report.*

MOZAMBIQUE - EDUCATION

African Development Bank, 01 BP 1387, Abidjan 01, Cote d'Ivoire; *Selected Statistics on Regional Member Countries.*

The Economist Intelligence Unit, 111 West 57th Street, New York, New York 10019 (800) 938-4685; *The World Market Atlas.*

Euromonitor International, Inc., 122 South Michigan Avenue, Suite 1200, Chicago, Illinois 60603 (800) 577-EURO; (Telephone Number in U.S. (312) 922-1115); *International Marketing Data and Statistics;* and *World Marketing Data and Statistics.*

Europa Publications Limited, 18 Bedford Square, London, WC1B 3JN, England; *The Europa World Year Book.*

Federal Statistical Office, Gustav-Stresemann - Ring 11, D-6200, Wiesbaden, Germany; *Mosambik.*

M.E. Sharpe, 80 Business Park Drive, Armonk, New York 10504 (800) 541-6563; *The Illustrated Book of World Rankings.*

St. Martin's Press, Inc., 175 Fifth Avenue, New York, New York 10010 (800) 221-7945; *The Statesman's Year-Book.*

Statistical Office of the United Nations, Publishing Service, New York, New York 10017 (800) 253-9646; *Human Development Report;* and *Survey of*

Economic and Social Conditions in Africa.

United Nations Economic Commission for Africa, Africa Hall, Post Office Box 3001, Addis Ababa, Ethiopia (Telephone Number in U.S. (800) 253-9646); *African Statistical Yearbook.*

The World Bank, 1818 H Street, NW, Washington, D.C. 20433 (202) 477-1234; *World Development Report;* and *World Development Indicators.*

MOZAMBIQUE - EGG PRODUCTION - See MOZAMBIQUE - DAIRY PRODUCTS

MOZAMBIQUE - ELECTRICITY

Central Intelligence Agency, Washington, D.C. 20505 (703) 482-1100, www.cia.gov; *The World Factbook.*

M.E. Sharpe, 80 Business Park Drive, Armonk, New York 10504 (800) 541-6563; *The Illustrated Book of World Rankings.*

St. Martin's Press, Inc., 175 Fifth Avenue, New York, New York 10010 (800) 221-7945; *The Statesman's Year-Book.*

Statistical Office of the United Nations, Publishing Service, New York, New York 10017 (800) 253-9646; *Human Development Report; Statistical Yearbook;* and *Survey of Economic and Social Conditions in Africa.*

United Nations Economic Commission for Africa, Africa Hall, Post Office Box 3001, Addis Ababa, Ethiopia (Telephone Number in U.S. (800) 253-9646); *African Statistical Yearbook.*

MOZAMBIQUE - EMPLOYMENT

Euromonitor International, Inc., 122 South Michigan Avenue, Suite 1200, Chicago, Illinois 60603 (800) 577-EURO; *International Marketing Data and Statistics.*

Federal Statistical Office, Gustav-Stresemann - Ring 11, D-6200, Wiesbaden, Germany; *Mosambik.*

International Labour Office, I.L.O. Publications, 1828 L Street, NW., Suite 801, Washington, D.C. 20036 (301) 638-3152; *Yearbook of Labour Statistics.*

M.E. Sharpe, 80 Business Park Drive, Armonk, New York 10504 (800) 541-6563; *The Illustrated Book of World Rankings.*

Statistical Office of the United Nations, Publishing Service, New York, New York 10017 (800) 253-9646; *Statistical Yearbook;* and *Survey of Economic and Social Conditions in Africa.*

United Nations Economic Commission for Africa, Africa Hall, Post Office Box 3001, Addis Ababa, Ethiopia (Telephone Number

in U.S. (800) 253-9646); *African Statistical Yearbook.*

MOZAMBIQUE - ENERGY

Euromonitor International, Inc., 122 South Michigan Avenue, Suite 1200, Chicago, Illinois 60603 (800) 577-EURO; *International Marketing Data and Statistics; The World Economic Factbook;* and *World Marketing Data and Statistics.*

Food and Agricultural Organization of the United Nations (FAO), Via delle Terme di Caracalla, 00100 Rome, Italy (Telephone Number in U.S. (202) 653-2400); *The State of Food and Agriculture.*

M.E. Sharpe, 80 Business Park Drive, Armonk, New York 10504 (800) 541-6563; *The Illustrated Book of World Rankings.*

St. Martin's Press, Inc., 175 Fifth Avenue, New York, New York 10010 (800) 221-7945; *The Statesman's Year-Book.*

Statistical Office of the United Nations, Publishing Service, New York, New York 10017 (800) 253-9646; *Energy Statistics Yearbook; Human Development Report; World Statistics Pocketbook;* and *Statistical Yearbook.*

United Nations Economic Commission for Africa, Africa Hall, Post Office Box 3001, Addis Ababa, Ethiopia (Telephone Number in U.S. (800) 253-9646); *African Statistical Yearbook.*

The World Bank, 1818 H Street, NW, Washington, D.C. 20433 (202) 477-1234; *The World Bank Atlas;* and *World Development Report.*

MOZAMBIQUE - ENVIRONMENT

Economist Intelligence Unit, 111 West 57th Street, New York, New York 10019 (800) 938-4685; *Mozambique Country Report.*

Statistical Office of the United Nations, Publishing Service, New York, New York 10017 (800) 253-9646; *World Statistics Pocketbook.*

MOZAMBIQUE - EXCHANGE RATES

African Development Bank, 01 BP 1387, Abidjan 01, Cote d'Ivoire; *Selected Statistics on Regional Member Countries.*

Central Intelligence Agency, Washington, D.C. 20505 (703) 482-1100, www.cia.gov; *The World Factbook.*

Euromonitor International, Inc., 122 South Michigan Avenue, Suite 1200, Chicago, Illinois 60603 (800) 577-EURO; *International Marketing Data and Statistics;* and *The World Economic Factbook.*

Europa Publications Limited, 18 Bedford Square, London, WC1B 3JN, England; *The Europa World Year Book.*

Statistical Office of the United Nations, Publishing Service, New York, New York 10017 (800) 253-9646; *Foreign Trade Statistics for Africa; World Statistics Pocketbook;* and *Statistical Yearbook.*

MOZAMBIQUE - EXPORTS

African Development Bank, 01 BP 1387, Abidjan 01, Cote d'Ivoire; *Selected Statistics on Regional Member Countries.*

Central Intelligence Agency, Washington, D.C. 20505 (703) 482-1100, www.cia.gov; *The World Factbook.*

The Economist Intelligence Unit, 111 West 57th Street, New York, New York 10019 (800) 938-4685; *Mozambique Country Report;* and *The World Market Atlas.*

Euromonitor International, Inc., 122 South Michigan Avenue, Suite 1200, Chicago, Illinois 60603 (800) 577-EURO; *International Marketing Data and Statistics;* and *The World Economic Factbook*

Europa Publications Limited, 18 Bedford Square, London, WC1B 3JN, England; *The Europa World Year Book.*

Food and Agricultural Organization of the United Nations (FAO), Via delle Terme di Caracalla, 00100 Rome, Italy (Telephone Number in U.S. (202) 653-2400); *The State of Food and Agriculture.*

International Monetary Fund, 700 Nineteenth Street, NW, Washington, D.C. 20431 (202) 623-7000; *Direction of Trade Statistics.*

St. Martin's Press, Inc., 175 Fifth Avenue, New York, New York 10010 (800) 221-7945; *The Statesman's Year-Book.*

Statistical Office of the United Nations, Publishing Service, New York, New York 10017 (800) 253-9646; *Foreign Trade Statistics for Africa;* and *Survey of Economic and Social Conditions in Africa.*

United Nations Conference on Trade and Development (UNCTAD), New York, New York 10017 (800) 253-9646; *Handbook of International Trade and Development Statistics.*

United Nations Economic Commission for Africa, Africa Hall, Post Office Box 3001, Addis Ababa, Ethiopia (Telephone Number in U.S. (800) 253-9646); *African Statistical Yearbook.*

The World Bank, 1818 H Street, NW, Washington, D.C. 20433 (202) 477-1234;

World Development Report; and *World Development Indicators.*

MOZAMBIQUE - EXTERNAL INDEBTEDNESS

African Development Bank, 01 BP 1387, Abidjan 01, Cote d'Ivoire; *Selected Statistics on Regional Member Countries.*

Statistical Office of the United Nations, Publishing Service, New York, New York 10017 (800) 253-9646; *Survey of Economic and Social Conditions in Africa.*

The World Bank, 1818 H Street, NW, Washington, D.C. 20433 (202) 477-1234; *World Development Report.*

MOZAMBIQUE - EXTERNAL TRADE

African Development Bank, 01 BP 1387, Abidjan 01, Cote d'Ivoire; *Selected Statistics on Regional Member Countries.*

Euromonitor International, Inc., 122 South Michigan Avenue, Suite 1200, Chicago, Illinois 60603 (800) 577-EURO; *World Marketing Data and Statistics.*

Food and Agricultural Organization of the United Nations (FAO), Via delle Terme di Caracalla, 00100 Rome, Italy (Telephone Number in U.S. (202) 653-2400); *The State of Food and Agriculture;* and *Trade Yearbook.*

Statistical Office of the United Nations, Publishing Service, New York, New York 10017 (800) 253-9646; *Statistical Yearbook.*

The World Bank, 1818 H Street, NW, Washington, D.C. 20433 (202) 477-1234; *World Development Indicators.*

MOZAMBIQUE - FABRIC PRODUCTION - See MOZAMBIQUE - TEXTILE INDUSTRY

MOZAMBIQUE - FARM CROPS - See MOZAMBIQUE - CROPS

MOZAMBIQUE - FEMALE WORKING POPULATION - See MOZAMBIQUE - EMPLOYMENT

MOZAMBIQUE - FERTILITY RATES

Central Intelligence Agency, Washington, D.C. 20505 (703) 482-1100, www.cia.gov; *The World Factbook.*

M.E. Sharpe, 80 Business Park Drive, Armonk, New York 10504 (800) 541-6563; *The Illustrated Book of World Rankings.*

Statistical Office of the United Nations, Publishing Service, New York, New York 10017 (800) 253-9646; *Human Development Report;* and *Survey of Economic and Social Conditions in Africa.*

The World Bank, 1818 H Street, NW, Washington, D.C. 20433 (202) 477-1234; *The World Bank Atlas; World Development Report;* and *World Development Indicators.*

MOZAMBIQUE - FERTILIZER PRICES

Food and Agricultural Organization of the United Nations (FAO), Via delle Terme di Caracalla, 00100 Rome, Italy (Telephone Number in U.S. (202) 653-2400); *The State of Food and Agriculture.*

MOZAMBIQUE - FERTILIZER PRODUCTION AND CONSUMPTION

Food and Agricultural Organization of the United Nations (FAO), Via delle Terme di Caracalla, 00100 Rome, Italy (Telephone Number in U.S. (202) 653-2400); *Fertilizer Yearbook.*

Statistical Office of the United Nations, Publishing Service, New York, New York 10017 (800) 253-9646; *Statistical Yearbook.*

MOZAMBIQUE - FETAL MORTALITY - See MOZAMBIQUE - MORTALITY

MOZAMBIQUE - FINANCE

African Development Bank, 01 BP 1387, Abidjan 01, Cote d'Ivoire; *Selected Statistics on Regional Member Countries.*

Economist Intelligence Unit, 111 West 57th Street, New York, New York 10019 (800) 938-4685; *Mozambique Country Report.*

Europa Publications Limited, 18 Bedford Square, London, WC1B 3JN, England; *The Europa World Year Book.*

Federal Statistical Office, Gustav-Stresemann - Ring 11, D-6200, Wiesbaden, Germany; *Mosambik.*

M.E. Sharpe, 80 Business Park Drive, Armonk, New York 10504 (800) 541-6563; *The Illustrated Book of World Rankings.*

St. Martin's Press, Inc., 175 Fifth Avenue, New York, New York 10010 (800) 221-7945; *The Statesman's Year-Book.*

MOZAMBIQUE - FISHERIES

Europa Publications Limited, 18 Bedford Square, London, WC1B 3JN, England; *The Europa World Year Book.*

Federal Statistical Office, Gustav-Stresemann - Ring 11, D-6200, Wiesbaden, Germany; *Mosambik.*

Food and Agricultural Organization of the United Nations (FAO), Via delle Terme di Caracalla, 00100 Rome, Italy (Telephone Number in U.S. (202) 653-2400); *The State of Food and Agriculture;* and *Yearbook of Fishery Statistics.*

M.E. Sharpe, 80 Business Park Drive, Armonk, New York 10504 (800) 541-6563; *The Illustrated Book of World Rankings.*

St. Martin's Press, Inc., 175 Fifth Avenue, New York, New York 10010 (800) 221-7945; *The Statesman's Year-Book.*

Statistical Office of the United Nations, Publishing Service, New York, New York 10017 (800) 253-9646; *Statistical Yearbook;* and *Survey of Economic and Social Conditions in Africa.*

United Nations Conference on Trade and Development, Central Statistical Service, Palais des Nations, Geneva, Switzerland (Telephone in U.S. (800) 253-9646); *UNCTAD Commodity Yearbook.*

United Nations Economic Commission for Africa, Africa Hall, Post Office Box 3001, Addis Ababa, Ethiopia (Telephone Number in U.S. (800) 253-9646); *African Statistical Yearbook.*

MOZAMBIQUE - FLOUR PRODUCTION

Statistical Office of the United Nations, Publishing Service, New York, New York 10017 (800) 253-9646; *Statistical Yearbook.*

MOZAMBIQUE - FOOD

African Development Bank, 01 BP 1387, Abidjan 01, Cote d'Ivoire; *Selected Statistics on Regional Member Countries.*

Food and Agricultural Organization of the United Nations (FAO), Via delle Terme di Caracalla, 00100 Rome, Italy (Telephone Number in U.S. (202) 653-2400); *Production Yearbook;* and *The State of Food and Agriculture.*

Statistical Office of the United Nations, Publishing Service, New York, New York 10017 (800) 253-9646; *Human Development Report.*

United Nations Conference on Trade and Development, Central Statistical Service, Palais des Nations, Geneva, Switzerland (Telephone in U.S. (800) 253-9646); *UNCTAD Commodity Yearbook.*

MOZAMBIQUE - FOREIGN DEBT

St. Martin's Press, Inc., 175 Fifth Avenue, New York, New York 10010 (800) 221-7945; *The Statesman's Year-Book.*

MOZAMBIQUE - FOREIGN TRADE

Economist Intelligence Unit, 111 West 57th Street, New York, New York 10019 (800) 938-4685; *Mozambique Country Report.*

Euromonitor International, Inc., 122 South Michigan Avenue, Suite 1200, Chicago, Illinois 60603 (800) 577-EURO; *International Marketing Data and Statistics;* and *The World Economic Factbook.*

Europa Publications Limited, 18 Bedford Square, London, WC1B 3JN, England; *The Europa World Year Book.*

Federal Statistical Office, Gustav-Stresemann - Ring 11, D-6200, Wiesbaden, Germany; *Mosambik.*

Food and Agricultural Organization of the United Nations (FAO), Via delle Terme di Caracalla, 00100 Rome, Italy (Telephone Number in U.S. (202) 653-2400); *The State of Food and Agriculture.*

M.E. Sharpe, 80 Business Park Drive, Armonk, New York 10504 (800) 541-6563; *The Illustrated Book of World Rankings.*

St. Martin's Press, Inc., 175 Fifth Avenue, New York, New York 10010 (800) 221-7945; *The Statesman's Year-Book.*

Statistical Office of the United Nations, Publishing Service, New York, New York 10017 (800) 253-9646; *Foreign Trade Statistics for Africa; International Trade Statistics Yearbook;* and *Statistical Yearbook.*

United Nations Conference on Trade and Development, Central Statistical Service, Palais des Nations, Geneva, Switzerland (Telephone in U.S. (800) 253-9646); *UNCTAD Commodity Yearbook.*

United Nations Economic Commission for Africa, Africa Hall, Post Office Box 3001, Addis Ababa, Ethiopia (Telephone Number in U.S. (800) 253-9646); *African Statistical Yearbook.*

The World Bank, 1818 H Street, NW, Washington, D.C. 20433 (202) 477-1234; *World Development Report;* and *World Development Indicators.*

MOZAMBIQUE - FORESTRY AND FOREST PRODUCTS

Europa Publications Limited, 18 Bedford Square, London, WC1B 3JN, England; *The Europa World Year Book.*

Federal Statistical Office, Gustav-Stresemann - Ring 11, D-6200, Wiesbaden, Germany; *Mosambik.*

Food and Agricultural Organization of the United Nations (FAO), Via delle Terme di Caracalla, 00100 Rome, Italy (Telephone Number in U.S. (202) 653-2400); *The State of Food and Agriculture;* and *Yearbook of Forest Products.*

M.E. Sharpe, 80 Business Park Drive,

Armonk, New York 10504 (800) 541-6563; *The Illustrated Book of World Rankings.*

St. Martin's Press, Inc., 175 Fifth Avenue, New York, New York 10010 (800) 221-7945; *The Statesman's Year-Book.*

Statistical Office of the United Nations, Publishing Service, New York, New York 10017 (800) 253-9646; *Statistical Yearbook.*

United Nations Conference on Trade and Development, Central Statistical Service, Palais des Nations, Geneva, Switzerland (Telephone in U.S. (800) 253-9646); *UNCTAD Commodity Yearbook.*

United Nations Economic Commission for Africa, Africa Hall, Post Office Box 3001, Addis Ababa, Ethiopia (Telephone Number in U.S. (800) 253-9646); *African Statistical Yearbook.*

United Nations Educational, Scientific and Cultural Organization (UNESCO), 7 Place de Fontenoy, F-75700 Paris, France (Telephone Number in U.S. (212) 963-5981); *Statistical Yearbook.*

The World Bank, 1818 H Street, NW, Washington, D.C. 20433 (202) 477-1234; *World Development Report.*

MOZAMBIQUE - GAS PRODUCTION - See MOZAMBIQUE - MINING AND MINERAL PRODUCTS

MOZAMBIQUE - GENERAL MORTALITY - See MOZAMBIQUE - MORTALITY

MOZAMBIQUE - GEOGRAPHIC DATA

M.E. Sharpe, 80 Business Park Drive, Armonk, New York 10504 (800) 541-6563; *The Illustrated Book of World Rankings.*

MOZAMBIQUE - GOATS - See MOZAMBIQUE - LIVESTOCK AND POULTRY

MOZAMBIQUE - GOLD PRODUCTION AND CONSUMPTION - See MOZAMBIQUE - MINING AND MINERAL PRODUCTS

MOZAMBIQUE - GOVERNMENT

Central Intelligence Agency, Washington, D.C. 20505 (703) 482-1100, www.cia.gov; *The World Factbook.*

Europa Publications Limited, 18 Bedford Square, London, WC1B 3JN, England; *The Europa World Year Book.*

St. Martin's Press, Inc., 175 Fifth Avenue, New York, New York 10010 (800) 221-7945; *The Statesman's Year-Book.*

Statistical Office of the United Nations, Publishing Service, New York, New York 10017 (800) 253-9646; *National Accounts*

Statistics; and *Survey of Economic and Social Conditions in Africa.*

The World Bank, 1818 H Street, NW, Washington, D.C. 20433 (202) 477-1234; *World Development Report;* and *World Development Indicators.*

MOZAMBIQUE - GRAIN PRODUCTION

Food and Agricultural Organization of the United Nations (FAO), Via delle Terme di Caracalla, 00100 Rome, Italy (Telephone Number in U.S. (202) 653-2400); *The State of Food and Agriculture.*

MOZAMBIQUE - GROSS DOMESTIC PRODUCT

African Development Bank, 01 BP 1387, Abidjan 01, Cote d'Ivoire; *Selected Statistics on Regional Member Countries.*

The Economist Intelligence Unit, 111 West 57th Street, New York, New York 10019 (800) 938-4685; *Mozambique Country Report;* and *The World Market Atlas.*

Euromonitor International, Inc., 122 South Michigan Avenue, Suite 1200, Chicago, Illinois 60603 (800) 577-EURO; *International Marketing Data and Statistics;* and *The World Economic Factbook.*

Europa Publications Limited, 18 Bedford Square, London, WC1B 3JN, England; *The Europa World Year Book.*

M.E. Sharpe, 80 Business Park Drive, Armonk, New York 10504 (800) 541-6563; *The Illustrated Book of World Rankings.*

St. Martin's Press, Inc., 175 Fifth Avenue, New York, New York 10010 (800) 221-7945; *The Statesman's Year-Book.*

Statistical Office of the United Nations, Publishing Service, New York, New York 10017 (800) 253-9646; *Human Development Report; National Accounts Statistics; Statistical Yearbook;* and *Survey of Economic and Social Conditions in Africa.*

United Nations Economic Commission for Africa, Africa Hall, Post Office Box 3001, Addis Ababa, Ethiopia (Telephone Number in U.S. (800) 253-9646); *African Statistical Yearbook.*

The World Bank, 1818 H Street, NW, Washington, D.C. 20433 (202) 477-1234; *World Development Report;* and *World Development Indicators.*

MOZAMBIQUE - GROSS NATIONAL PRODUCT

Euromonitor International, Inc., 122 South Michigan Avenue, Suite 1200,

Chicago, Illinois 60603 (800) 577-EURO; *International Marketing Data and Statistics.*

U.S. Arms Control and Disarmament Agency, 320 Twenty-first Street, NW, Washington, D.C. 20451 (202) 647-8677; *World Military Expenditures and Arms Transfers.*

The World Bank, 1818 H Street, NW, Washington, D.C. 20433 (202) 477-1234; *The World Bank Atlas; World Development Report;* and *World Development Indicators.*

MOZAMBIQUE - GROUNDNUT PRODUCTION - See MOZAMBIQUE - CROPS

MOZAMBIQUE - HEALTH

African Development Bank, 01 BP 1387, Abidjan 01, Cote d'Ivoire; *Selected Statistics on Regional Member Countries.*

Euromonitor International, Inc., 122 South Michigan Avenue, Suite 1200, Chicago, Illinois 60603 (800) 577-EURO; *World Marketing Data and Statistics.*

Federal Statistical Office, Gustav-Stresemann - Ring 11, D-6200, Wiesbaden, Germany; *Mosambik.*

M.E. Sharpe, 80 Business Park Drive, Armonk, New York 10504 (800) 541-6563; *The Illustrated Book of World Rankings.*

St. Martin's Press, Inc., 175 Fifth Avenue, New York, New York 10010 (800) 221-7945; *The Statesman's Year-Book.*

Statistical Office of the United Nations, Publishing Service, New York, New York 10017 (800) 253-9646; *Human Development Report;* and *Statistical Yearbook.*

United Nations Children's Fund (UNICEF), 3 United Nations Plaza, New York, New York 10017 (800) 253-9646; *State of the World's Children.*

United Nations Economic Commission for Africa, Africa Hall, Post Office Box 3001, Addis Ababa, Ethiopia (Telephone Number in U.S. (800) 253-9646); *African Statistical Yearbook.*

The World Bank, 1818 H Street, NW, Washington, D.C. 20433 (202) 477-1234; *World Development Report.*

World Health Organization, Office of Publications, 20 Avenue Appia, CH-1211 Geneva 27, Switzerland (Telephone Number in U.S. (518) 436-9686); *World Health Statistics Annual.*

MOZAMBIQUE - HEALTH AND MEDICAL SERVICES

Statistical Office of the United Nations, Publishing Service, New York, New York 10017 (800) 253-9646; *Statistical Yearbook.*

MOZAMBIQUE - HIDE PRODUCTION

Food and Agricultural Organization of the United Nations (FAO), Via delle Terme di Caracalla, 00100 Rome, Italy (Telephone Number in U.S. (202) 653-2400); *Production Yearbook.*

MOZAMBIQUE - HIGHWAYS

Central Intelligence Agency, Washington, D.C. 20505 (703) 482-1100, www.cia.gov; *The World Factbook.*

St. Martin's Press, Inc., 175 Fifth Avenue, New York, New York 10010 (800) 221-7945; *The Statesman's Year-Book.*

Statistical Office of the United Nations, Publishing Service, New York, New York 10017 (800) 253-9646; *Survey of Economic and Social Conditions in Africa.*

United Nations Economic Commission for Africa, Africa Hall, Post Office Box 3001, Addis Ababa, Ethiopia (Telephone Number in U.S. (800) 253-9646); *African Statistical Yearbook.*

MOZAMBIQUE - HORSES - See MOZAMBIQUE - LIVESTOCK AND POULTRY

MOZAMBIQUE - HOURS OF WORK - See MOZAMBIQUE - EMPLOYMENT

MOZAMBIQUE - HOUSING AND HOUSING UNITS

Euromonitor International, Inc., 122 South Michigan Avenue, Suite 1200, Chicago, Illinois 60603 (800) 577-EURO; *World Marketing Data and Statistics.*

M.E. Sharpe, 80 Business Park Drive, Armonk, New York 10504 (800) 541-6563; *The Illustrated Book of World Rankings.*

MOZAMBIQUE - ILLITERATE POPULATION

Central Intelligence Agency, Washington, D.C. 20505 (703) 482-1100, www.cia.gov; *The World Factbook.*

The Economist Intelligence Unit, 111 West 57th Street, New York, New York 10019 (800) 938-4685; *The World Market Atlas.*

Euromonitor International, Inc., 122 South Michigan Avenue, Suite 1200, Chicago, Illinois 60603 (800) 577-EURO; *The World Economic Factbook.*

St. Martin's Press, Inc., 175 Fifth Avenue, New York, New York 10010 (800) 221-7945; *The Statesman's Year-Book.*

Statistical Office of the United Nations, Publishing Service, New York, New York 10017 (800) 253-9646; *Human Development Report.*

United Nations Educational, Scientific and Cultural Organization (UNESCO), 7 Place de Fontenoy, F-75700 Paris, France (Telephone Number in U.S. (212) 963-5981; *Statistical Yearbook.*

MOZAMBIQUE - IMPORTS

African Development Bank, 01 BP 1387, Abidjan 01, Cote d'Ivoire; *Selected Statistics on Regional Member Countries.*

Central Intelligence Agency, Washington, D.C. 20505 (703) 482-1100, www.cia.gov; *The World Factbook.*

The Economist Intelligence Unit, 111 West 57th Street, New York, New York 10019 (800) 938-4685; *Mozambique Country Report;* and *The World Market Atlas.*

Euromonitor International, Inc., 122 South Michigan Avenue, Suite 1200, Chicago, Illinois 60603 (800) 577-EURO; *International Marketing Data and Statistics;* and *The World Economic Factbook.*

Europa Publications Limited, 18 Bedford Square, London, WC1B 3JN, England; *The Europa World Year Book.*

Food and Agricultural Organization of the United Nations (FAO), Via delle Terme di Caracalla, 00100 Rome, Italy (Telephone Number in U.S. (202) 653-2400); *The State of Food and Agriculture.*

International Monetary Fund, 700 Nineteenth Street, NW, Washington, D.C. 20431 (202) 623-7000; *Direction of Trade Statistics.*

St. Martin's Press, Inc., 175 Fifth Avenue, New York, New York 10010 (800) 221-7945; *The Statesman's Year-Book.*

Statistical Office of the United Nations, Publishing Service, New York, New York 10017 (800) 253-9646; *Foreign Trade Statistics for Africa;* and *Survey of Economic and Social Conditions in Africa.*

United Nations Conference on Trade and Development (UNCTAD), New York, New York 10017 (800) 253-9646; *Handbook of International Trade and Development Statistics.*

United Nations Economic Commission for Africa, Africa Hall, Post Office Box 3001, Addis Ababa, Ethiopia (Telephone Number in U.S. (800) 253-9646); *African Statistical Yearbook.*

The World Bank, 1818 H Street, NW,

Washington, D.C. 20433 (202) 477-1234; *World Development Report;* and *World Development Indicators.*

MOZAMBIQUE - INDUSTRIAL ACIDS PRODUCTION

Central Intelligence Agency, Washington, D.C. 20505 (703) 482-1100, www.cia.gov; *The World Factbook.*

Statistical Office of the United Nations, Publishing Service, New York, New York 10017 (800) 253-9646; *Statistical Yearbook.*

MOZAMBIQUE - INDUSTRY

Economist Intelligence Unit, 111 West 57th Street, New York, New York 10019 (800) 938-4685; *Mozambique Country Report.*

Euromonitor International, Inc., 122 South Michigan Avenue, Suite 1200, Chicago, Illinois 60603 (800) 577-EURO; *International Marketing Data and Statistics; The World Economic Factbook;* and *World Marketing Data and Statistics.*

Europa Publications Limited, 18 Bedford Square, London, WC1B 3JN, England; *The Europa World Year Book.*

Federal Statistical Office, Gustav-Stresemann - Ring 11, D-6200, Wiesbaden, Germany; *Mosambik.*

International Labour Office, I.L.O. Publications, 1828 L Street, NW., Suite 801, Washington, D.C. 20036 (301) 638-3152; *Yearbook of Labour Statistics.*

M.E. Sharpe, 80 Business Park Drive, Armonk, New York 10504 (800) 541-6563; *The Illustrated Book of World Rankings.*

St. Martin's Press, Inc., 175 Fifth Avenue, New York, New York 10010 (800) 221-7945; *The Statesman's Year-Book.*

Statistical Office of the United Nations, Publishing Service, New York, New York 10017 (800) 253-9646; *Statistical Yearbook;* and *Survey of Economic and social Conditions in Africa.*

United Nations Economic Commission for Africa, Africa Hall, Post Office Box 3001, Addis Ababa, Ethiopia (Telephone Number in U.S. (800) 253-9646); *African Statistical Yearbook.*

The World Bank, 1818 H Street, NW, Washington, D.C. 20433 (202) 477-1234; *World Development Indicators.*

MOZAMBIQUE - INFANT AND MATERNAL MORTALITY - See MOZAMBIQUE - MORTALITY

MOZAMBIQUE - INTERNATIONAL RESERVES EXCLUDING GOLD

African Development Bank, 01 BP 1387, Abidjan 01, Cote d'Ivoire; *Selected Statistics on Regional Member Countries.*

The World Bank, 1818 H Street, NW, Washington, D.C. 20433 (202) 477-1234; *World Development Indicators.*

MOZAMBIQUE - IRON ORE PRODUCTION AND CONSUMPTION - See MOZAMBIQUE - MINING AND MINERAL PRODUCTS

MOZAMBIQUE - IRRIGATION

Euromonitor International, Inc., 122 South Michigan Avenue, Suite 1200, Chicago, Illinois 60603 (800) 577-EURO; *International Marketing Data and Statistics.*

MOZAMBIQUE - JUTE PRODUCTION - See MOZAMBIQUE - CROPS

MOZAMBIQUE - LABOR

African Development Bank, 01 BP 1387, Abidjan 01, Cote d'Ivoire; *Selected Statistics on Regional Member Countries.*

Central Intelligence Agency, Washington, D.C. 20505 (703) 482-1100, www.cia.gov; *The World Factbook.*

Euromonitor International, Inc., 122 South Michigan Avenue, Suite 1200, Chicago, Illinois 60603 (800) 577-EURO; *International Marketing Data and Statistics;* and *World Marketing Data and Statistics.*

Europa Publications Limited, 18 Bedford Square, London, WC1B 3JN, England; *The Europa World Year Book.*

Food and Agricultural Organization of the United Nations (FAO), Via delle Terme di Caracalla, 00100 Rome, Italy (Telephone Number in U.S. (202) 653-2400); *The State of Food and Agriculture.*

International Labour Office, I.L.O. Publications, 1828 L Street, NW., Suite 801, Washington, D.C. 20036 (301) 638-3152; *Yearbook of Labour Statistics.*

M.E. Sharpe, 80 Business Park Drive, Armonk, New York 10504 (800) 541-6563; *The Illustrated Book of World Rankings.*

St. Martin's Press, Inc., 175 Fifth Avenue, New York, New York 10010 (800) 221-7945; *The Statesman's Year-Book.*

Statistical Office of the United Nations, Publishing Service, New York, New York 10017 (800) 253-9646; *Human Development Report.*

The World Bank, 1818 H Street, NW, Washington, D.C. 20433 (202) 477-1234; *The World Bank Atlas; World Development Report;* and *World Development Indicators.*

MOZAMBIQUE - LAND USE

Central Intelligence Agency, Washington, D.C. 20505 (703) 482-1100, www.cia.gov; *The World Factbook.*

Euromonitor International, Inc., 122 South Michigan Avenue, Suite 1200, Chicago, Illinois 60603 (800) 577-EURO; *International Marketing Data and Statistics.*

Food and Agricultural Organization of the United Nations (FAO), Via delle Terme di Caracalla, 00100 Rome, Italy (Telephone Number in U.S. (202) 653-2400); *Production Yearbook.*

The World Bank, 1818 H Street, NW, Washington, D.C. 20433 (202) 477-1234; *World Development Report.*

MOZAMBIQUE - LIBRARIES

M.E. Sharpe, 80 Business Park Drive, Armonk, New York 10504 (800) 541-6563; *The Illustrated Book of World Rankings.*

United Nations Educational, Scientific and Cultural Organization (UNESCO), 7 Place de Fontenoy, F-75700 Paris, France (Telephone Number in U.S. (212) 963-5981); *Statistical Yearbook.*

MOZAMBIQUE - LIFE EXPECTANCY

African Development Bank, 01 BP 1387, Abidjan 01, Cote d'Ivoire; *Selected Statistics on Regional Member Countries.*

Central Intelligence Agency, Washington, D.C. 20505 (703) 482-1100, www.cia.gov; *The World Factbook.*

Euromonitor International, Inc., 122 South Michigan Avenue, Suite 1200, Chicago, Illinois 60603 (800) 577-EURO; *The World Economic Factbook.*

Statistical Office of the United Nations, Publishing Service, New York, New York 10017 (800) 253-9646; *Human Development Report;* and *World Statistics Pocketbook.*

The World Bank, 1818 H Street, NW, Washington, D.C. 20433 (202) 477-1234; *The World Bank Atlas;* and *World Development Report.*

MOZAMBIQUE - LIGNITE PRODUCTION - See MOZAMBIQUE - MINING AND MINERAL PRODUCTS

MOZAMBIQUE - LITERACY RATE

Euromonitor International, Inc., 122 South Michigan Avenue, Suite 1200, Chicago, Illinois 60603 (800) 577-EURO; *World Marketing Data and Statistics.*

Statistical Office of the United Nations, Publishing Service, New York, New York 10017 (800) 253-9646; *Survey of Economic and Social Conditions in Africa.*

MOZAMBIQUE - LIVESTOCK AND POULTRY

Euromonitor International, Inc., 122 South Michigan Avenue, Suite 1200, Chicago, Illinois 60603 (800) 577-EURO; *International Marketing Data and Statistics.*

Europa Publications Limited, 18 Bedford Square, London, WC1B 3JN, England; *The Europa World Year Book.*

Food and Agricultural Organization of the United Nations (FAO), Via delle Terme di Caracalla, 00100 Rome, Italy (Telephone Number in U.S. (202) 653-2400); *Production Yearbook;* and *The State of Food and Agriculture.*

M.E. Sharpe, 80 Business Park Drive, Armonk, New York 10504 (800) 541-6563; *The Illustrated Book of World Rankings.*

St. Martin's Press, Inc., 175 Fifth Avenue, New York, New York 10010 (800) 221-7945; *The Statesman's Year-Book.*

Statistical Office of the United Nations, Publishing Service, New York, New York 10017 (800) 253-9646; *Statistical Yearbook;* and *Survey of Economic and Social Conditions in Africa.*

United Nations Conference on Trade and Development, Central Statistical Service, Palais des Nations, Geneva, Switzerland (Telephone in U.S. (800) 253-9646); *UNCTAD Commodity Yearbook.*

United Nations Economic Commission for Africa, Africa Hall, Post Office Box 3001, Addis Ababa, Ethiopia (Telephone Number in U.S. (800) 253-9646); *African Statistical Yearbook.*

MOZAMBIQUE - LIVING LEVELS - See MOZAMBIQUE - LIFE EXPECTANCY

MOZAMBIQUE - MAIL - NUMBER OF ITEMS SENT AND RECEIVED

Statistical Office of the United Nations, Publishing Service, New York, New York 10017 (800) 253-9646; *Statistical Yearbook.*

MOZAMBIQUE - MANUFACTURING

M.E. Sharpe, 80 Business Park Drive, Armonk, New York 10504 (800) 541-6563; *The Illustrated Book of World Rankings.*

Statistical Office of the United Nations, Publishing Service, New York, New York 10017 (800) 253-9646; *Statistical Yearbook;* and *Survey of Economic and Social Conditions in Africa.*

United Nations Economic Commission for Africa, Africa Hall, Post Office Box 3001, Addis Ababa, Ethiopia (Telephone Number in U.S. (800) 253-9646); *African Statistical Yearbook.*

The World Bank, 1818 H Street, NW, Washington, D.C. 20433 (202) 477-1234; *World Development Indicators.*

MOZAMBIQUE - MARRIAGE RATES

M.E. Sharpe, 80 Business Park Drive, Armonk, New York 10504 (800) 541-6563; *The Illustrated Book of World Rankings.*

Statistical Office of the United Nations, Publishing Service, New York, New York 10017 (800) 253-9646; *Demographic Yearbook.*

MOZAMBIQUE - MEAT PRODUCTION - See MOZAMBIQUE - LIVESTOCK AND POULTRY

MOZAMBIQUE - MERCHANT SHIPPING

Europa Publications Limited, 18 Bedford Square, London, WC1B 3JN, England; *The Europa World Year Book.*

St. Martin's Press, Inc., 175 Fifth Avenue, New York, New York 10010 (800) 221-7945; *The Statesman's Year-Book.*

Statistical Office of the United Nations, Publishing Service, New York, New York 10017 (800) 253-9646; *Statistical Yearbook.*

United Nations Economic Commission for Africa, Africa Hall, Post Office Box 3001, Addis Ababa, Ethiopia (Telephone Number in U.S. (800) 253-9646); *African Statistical Yearbook.*

U.S. Department of Transportation, Maritime Administration, 400 Seventh Street, SW, Washington, D.C. 20590 (202) 366-5807, www.marad.dot.gov; *A Statistical Analysis of the World's Merchant Fleets.*

MOZAMBIQUE - MILITARY

Central Intelligence Agency, Washington, D.C. 20505 (703) 482-1100, www.cia.gov; *The World Factbook.*

Euromonitor International, Inc., 122 South Michigan Avenue, Suite 1200, Chicago, Illinois 60603 (800) 577-EURO; *World Marketing Data and Statistics.*

The International Institute for Strategic Studies, 23 Tavistock Street, London WC2E 7NQ, England; *The Military Balance.*

St. Martin's Press, Inc., 175 Fifth Avenue, New York, New York 10010 (800) 221-7945; *The Statesman's Year-Book.*

Statistical Office of the United Nations, Publishing Service, New York, New York 10017 (800) 253-9646; *Human Development Report.*

U.S. Arms Control and Disarmament Agency, 320 Twenty-first Street, NW, Washington, D.C. 20451 (202) 647-8677; *World Military Expenditures and Arms Transfers.*

MOZAMBIQUE - MILK PRODUCTION - See MOZAMBIQUE - DAIRY PRODUCTS

MOZAMBIQUE - MILLET PRODUCTION - See MOZAMBIQUE - CROPS

MOZAMBIQUE - MINING AND MINERAL PRODUCTS

Europa Publications Limited, 18 Bedford Square, London, WC1B 3JN, England; *The Europa World Year Book.*

M.E. Sharpe, 80 Business Park Drive, Armonk, New York 10504 (800) 541-6563; *The Illustrated Book of World Rankings.*

St. Martin's Press, Inc., 175 Fifth Avenue, New York, New York 10010 (800) 221-7945; *The Statesman's Year-Book.*

Statistical Office of the United Nations, Publishing Service, New York, New York 10017 (800) 253-9646; *Statistical Yearbook.*

United Nations Conference on Trade and Development, Central Statistical Service, Palais des Nations, Geneva, Switzerland (Telephone in U.S. (800) 253-9646); *UNCTAD Commodity Yearbook.*

United Nations Economic Commission for Africa, Africa Hall, Post Office Box 3001, Addis Ababa, Ethiopia (Telephone Number in U.S. (800) 253-9646); *African Statistical Yearbook.*

The World Bank, 1818 H Street, NW, Washington, D.C. 20433 (202) 477-1234; *World Development Indicators.*

MOZAMBIQUE - MONEY EXCHANGE RATES - See MOZAMBIQUE - EXCHANGE RATES

MOZAMBIQUE - MONEY RESERVES

Euromonitor International, Inc., 122 South Michigan Avenue, Suite 1200, Chicago, Illinois 60603 (800) 577-EURO; *International Marketing Data and Statistics.*

MOZAMBIQUE - MONEY SUPPLY

African Development Bank, 01 BP 1387, Abidjan 01, Cote d'Ivoire; *Selected Statistics on Regional Member Countries.*

Economist Intelligence Unit, 111 West

57th Street, New York, New York 10019 (800) 938-4685; *Mozambique Country Report.*

Euromonitor International, Inc., 122 South Michigan Avenue, Suite 1200, Chicago, Illinois 60603 (800) 577-EURO; *International Marketing Data and Statistics.*

Europa Publications Limited, 18 Bedford Square, London, WC1B 3JN, England; *The Europa World Year Book.*

Federal Statistical Office, Gustav-Stresemann - Ring 11, D-6200, Wiesbaden, Germany; *Mosambik.*

The World Bank, 1818 H Street, NW, Washington, D.C. 20433 (202) 477-1234; *World Development Indicators.*

MOZAMBIQUE - MORTALITY

Central Intelligence Agency, Washington, D.C. 20505 (703) 482-1100, www.cia.gov; *The World Factbook.*

Euromonitor International, Inc., 122 South Michigan Avenue, Suite 1200, Chicago, Illinois 60603 (800) 577-EURO; *International Marketing Data and Statistics;* and *The World Economic Factbook.*

Europa Publications Limited, 18 Bedford Square, London, WC1B 3JN, England; *The Europa World Year Book.*

Statistical Office of the United Nations, Publishing Service, New York, New York 10017 (800) 253-9646; *Demographic Yearbook; Human Development Report; Statistical Yearbook; World Statistics Pocketbook;* and *Survey of Economic and Social Conditions in Africa.*

United Nations Children's Fund (UNICEF), 3 United Nations Plaza, New York, New York 10017 (800) 253-9646; *State of the World's Children.*

The World Bank, 1818 H Street, NW, Washington, D.C. 20433 (202) 477-1234; *The World Bank Atlas; World Development Report;* and *World Development Indicators.*

World Health Organization, Office of Publications, 20 Avenue Appia, CH-1211 Geneva 27, Switzerland (Telephone Number in U.S. (518) 436-9686); *World Health Statistics Annual.*

MOZAMBIQUE - MOTION PICTURES

St. Martin's Press, Inc., 175 Fifth Avenue, New York, New York 10010 (800) 221-7945; *The Statesman's Year-Book.*

MOZAMBIQUE - MOTOR VEHICLES IN USE

Europa Publications Limited, 18 Bedford Square, London, WC1B 3JN, England; *The Europa World Year Book.*

Statistical Office of the United Nations, Publishing Service, New York, New York 10017 (800) 253-9646; *Statistical Yearbook;* and *Survey of Economic and Social Conditions in Africa.*

MOZAMBIQUE - MUSEUMS

M.E. Sharpe, 80 Business Park Drive, Armonk, New York 10504 (800) 541-6563; *The Illustrated Book of World Rankings.*

MOZAMBIQUE - NATALITY - See MOZAMBIQUE - BIRTH RATES

MOZAMBIQUE - NATIONAL ACCOUNTS

African Development Bank, 01 BP 1387, Abidjan 01, Cote d'Ivoire; *Selected Statistics on Regional Member Countries.*

Europa Publications Limited, 18 Bedford Square, London, WC1B 3JN, England; *The Europa World Year Book.*

Federal Statistical Office, Gustav-Stresemann - Ring 11, D-6200, Wiesbaden, Germany; *Mosambik.*

Statistical Office of the United Nations, Publishing Service, New York, New York 10017 (800) 253-9646; *Statistical Yearbook.*

United Nations Economic Commission for Africa, Africa Hall, Post Office Box 3001, Addis Ababa, Ethiopia (Telephone Number in U.S. (800) 253-9646); *African Statistical Yearbook.*

MOZAMBIQUE - NATIONAL INCOME

M.E. Sharpe, 80 Business Park Drive, Armonk, New York 10504 (800) 541-6563; *The Illustrated Book of World Rankings.*

Statistical Office of the United Nations, Publishing Service, New York, New York 10017 (800) 253-9646; *National Accounts Statistics.*

MOZAMBIQUE - NATIONAL PRODUCT

M.E. Sharpe, 80 Business Park Drive, Armonk, New York 10504 (800) 541-6563; *The Illustrated Book of World Rankings.*

MOZAMBIQUE - NATURAL GAS - PRODUCTION - See MOZAMBIQUE - MINING AND MINERAL PRODUCTS

MOZAMBIQUE - NEWSPAPER PRODUCTION - See MOZAMBIQUE - FORESTRY AND FOREST PRODUCTS

MOZAMBIQUE - NEWSPRINT - See MOZAMBIQUE - FORESTRY AND FOREST PRODUCTS

MOZAMBIQUE - OCCUPATIONS - See MOZAMBIQUE - LABOR

MOZAMBIQUE - PAPER - See MOZAMBIQUE - FORESTRY AND FOREST PRODUCTS

MOZAMBIQUE - PEANUT PRODUCTION - See MOZAMBIQUE - CROPS

MOZAMBIQUE - PESTICIDE USE

Food and Agricultural Organization of the United Nations (FAO), Via delle Terme di Caracalla, 00100 Rome, Italy (Telephone Number in U.S. (202) 653-2400); *The State of Food and Agriculture.*

MOZAMBIQUE - PETROLEUM INDUSTRY

Food and Agricultural Organization of the United Nations (FAO), Via delle Terme di Caracalla, 00100 Rome, Italy (Telephone Number in U.S. (202) 653-2400); *The State of Food and Agriculture.*

M.E. Sharpe, 80 Business Park Drive, Armonk, New York 10504 (800) 541-6563; *The Illustrated Book of World Rankings.*

Statistical Office of the United Nations, Publishing Service, New York, New York 10017 (800) 253-9646; *Statistical Yearbook.*

United Nations Conference on Trade and Development, Central Statistical Service, Palais des Nations, Geneva, Switzerland (Telephone in U.S. (800) 253-9646); *UNCTAD Commodity Yearbook.*

MOZAMBIQUE - PIGS - See MOZAMBIQUE - LIVESTOCK AND POULTRY

MOZAMBIQUE - POPULATION

African Development Bank, 01 BP 1387, Abidjan 01, Cote d'Ivoire; *Selected Statistics on Regional Member Countries.*

Central Intelligence Agency, Washington, D.C. 20505 (703) 482-1100, www.cia.gov; *The World Factbook.*

The Economist Intelligence Unit, 111 West 57th Street, New York, New York 10019 (800) 938-4685; *Mozambique Country Report;* and *The World Market Atlas.*

Euromonitor International, Inc., 122 South Michigan Avenue, Suite 1200, Chicago, Illinois 60603 (800) 577-EURO; *International Marketing Data and Statistics;* and *The World Economic Factbook.*

Europa Publications Limited, 18 Bedford Square, London, WC1B 3JN, England; *The Europa World Year Book.*

Federal Statistical Office, Gustav-Stresemann - Ring 11, D-6200, Wiesbaden, Germany; *Mosambik.*

Food and Agricultural Organization of

the United Nations (FAO), Via delle Terme di Caracalla, 00100 Rome, Italy (Telephone Number in U.S. (202) 653-2400); *Production Yearbook.*

International Labour Office, I.L.O. Publications, 1828 L Street, NW., Suite 801, Washington, D.C. 20036 (301) 638-3152; *Yearbook of Labour Statistics.*

M.E. Sharpe, 80 Business Park Drive, Armonk, New York 10504 (800) 541-6563; *The Illustrated Book of World Rankings.*

St. Martin's Press, Inc., 175 Fifth Avenue, New York, New York 10010 (800) 221-7945; *The Statesman's Year-Book.*

Statistical Office of the United Nations, Publishing Service, New York, New York 10017 (800) 253-9646; *Demographic Yearbook; Human Development Report; Statistical Yearbook; World Statistics Pocketbook;* and *Survey of Economic and Social Conditions in Africa.*

U.S. Arms Control and Disarmament Agency, 320 Twenty-first Street, NW, Washington, D.C. 20451 (202) 647-8677; *World Military Expenditures and Arms Transfers.*

The World Bank, 1818 H Street, NW, Washington, D.C. 20433 (202) 477-1234; *The World Bank Atlas;* and *World Development Report.*

World Health Organization, Office of Publications, 20 Avenue Appia, CH-1211 Geneva 27, Switzerland (Telephone Number in U.S. (518) 436-9686); *World Health Statistics Annual.*

MOZAMBIQUE - POST OFFICES

M.E. Sharpe, 80 Business Park Drive, Armonk, New York 10504 (800) 541-6563; *The Illustrated Book of World Rankings.*

MOZAMBIQUE - POTATO PRODUCTION - See MOZAMBIQUE - CROPS

MOZAMBIQUE - POWER PRODUCTION INDUSTRY

Statistical Office of the United Nations, Publishing Service, New York, New York 10017 (800) 253-9646; *Statistical Yearbook.*

MOZAMBIQUE - PRICES

Federal Statistical Office, Gustav-Stresemann - Ring 11, D-6200, Wiesbaden, Germany; *Mosambik.*

Food and Agricultural Organization of the United Nations (FAO), Via delle Terme di Caracalla, 00100 Rome, Italy (Telephone Number in U.S. (202) 653-2400); *Production Yearbook;* and *The State of Food and Agriculture.*

International Labour Office, I.L.O. Publications, 1828 L Street, NW., Suite 801, Washington, D.C. 20036 (301) 638-3152; *Yearbook of Labour Statistics.*

M.E. Sharpe, 80 Business Park Drive, Armonk, New York 10504 (800) 541-6563; *The Illustrated Book of World Rankings.*

MOZAMBIQUE - PRODUCTION

M.E. Sharpe, 80 Business Park Drive, Armonk, New York 10504 (800) 541-6563; *The Illustrated Book of World Rankings.*

MOZAMBIQUE - PRODUCTIVITY

Euromonitor International, Inc., 122 South Michigan Avenue, Suite 1200, Chicago, Illinois 60603 (800) 577-EURO; *International Marketing Data and Statistics.*

MOZAMBIQUE - PUBLIC FINANCE - See MOZAMBIQUE - FINANCE

MOZAMBIQUE - RADIO BROADCASTING - See MOZAMBIQUE - BROADCASTING

MOZAMBIQUE - RADIO RECEIVER PRODUCTION

Statistical Office of the United Nations, Publishing Service, New York, New York 10017 (800) 253-9646; *Statistical Yearbook.*

MOZAMBIQUE - RADIO RECEIVERS

St. Martin's Press, Inc., 175 Fifth Avenue, New York, New York 10010 (800) 221-7945; *The Statesman's Year-Book.*

MOZAMBIQUE - RAILWAY USE

Europa Publications Limited, 18 Bedford Square, London, WC1B 3JN, England; *The Europa World Year Book.*

Statistical Office of the United Nations, Publishing Service, New York, New York 10017 (800) 253-9646; *Statistical Yearbook;* and *Survey of Economic and Social Conditions in Africa.*

MOZAMBIQUE - RAILWAYS

Jane's Information Group, Sentinel House, 163 Brighton Road, Coulsdon, Surrey CR5 2NH, England (Telephone Number in U.S. (703) 683-3700); *Jane's World Railways.*

St. Martin's Press, Inc., 175 Fifth Avenue, New York, New York 10010 (800) 221-7945; *The Statesman's Year-Book.*

United Nations Economic Commission for Africa, Africa Hall, Post Office Box 3001, Addis Ababa, Ethiopia (Telephone Number in U.S. (800) 253-9646); *African Statistical Yearbook.*

MOZAMBIQUE - RELIGION

Central Intelligence Agency, Washington, D.C. 20505 (703) 482-1100, www.cia.gov; *The World Factbook.*

M.E. Sharpe, 80 Business Park Drive, Armonk, New York 10504 (800) 541-6563; *The Illustrated Book of World Rankings.*

St. Martin's Press, Inc., 175 Fifth Avenue, New York, New York 10010 (800) 221-7945; *The Statesman's Year-Book.*

MOZAMBIQUE - RENT PRICES

International Labour Office, I.L.O. Publications, 1828 L Street, NW., Suite 801, Washington, D.C. 20036 (301) 638-3152; *Yearbook of Labour Statistics.*

MOZAMBIQUE - RETAIL TRADE

Euromonitor International, Inc., 122 South Michigan Avenue, Suite 1200, Chicago, Illinois 60603 (800) 577-EURO; *World Marketing Data and Statistics.*

MOZAMBIQUE - RICE PRODUCTION - See MOZAMBIQUE - CROPS

MOZAMBIQUE - ROOT AND TUBER PRODUCTION - See MOZAMBIQUE - CROPS

MOZAMBIQUE - ROUNDWOOD PRODUCTION - See MOZAMBIQUE - FORESTRY AND FOREST PRODUCTS

MOZAMBIQUE - RUBBER PRODUCTION AND CONSUMPTION

M.E. Sharpe, 80 Business Park Drive, Armonk, New York 10504 (800) 541-6563; *The Illustrated Book of World Rankings.*

MOZAMBIQUE - SALT PRODUCTION - See MOZAMBIQUE - MINING AND MINERAL PRODUCTS

MOZAMBIQUE - SAWNWOOD PRODUCTION - See MOZAMBIQUE - FORESTRY AND FOREST PRODUCTS

MOZAMBIQUE - SENIOR CITIZENS

M.E. Sharpe, 80 Business Park Drive, Armonk, New York 10504 (800) 541-6563; *The Illustrated Book of World Rankings.*

MOZAMBIQUE - SESAME SEED PRODUCTION - See MOZAMBIQUE CROPS

MOZAMBIQUE - SHEEP - See MOZAMBIQUE - LIVESTOCK AND POULTRY

MOZAMBIQUE - SILVER PRODUCTION AND CONSUMPTION - See MOZAMBIQUE - MINING AND MINERAL PRODUCTS

MOZAMBIQUE - SISAL PRODUCTION - See MOZAMBIQUE - CROPS

MOZAMBIQUE - SOCIAL DATA

African Development Bank, 01 BP 1387, Abidjan 01, Cote d'Ivoire; *Selected Statistics on Regional Member Countries.*

M.E. Sharpe, 80 Business Park Drive, Armonk, New York 10504 (800) 541-6563; *The Illustrated Book of World Rankings.*

Statistical Office of the United Nations, Publishing Service, New York, New York 10017 (800) 253-9646; *World Statistics Pocketbook.*

MOZAMBIQUE - SOCIAL SECURITY

Statistical Office of the United Nations, Publishing Service, New York, New York 10017 (800) 253-9646; *National Accounts Statistics.*

MOZAMBIQUE - STATE BUDGET

Euromonitor International, Inc., 122 South Michigan Avenue, Suite 1200, Chicago, Illinois 60603 (800) 577-EURO; *International Marketing Data and Statistics.*

MOZAMBIQUE - STEEL - See MOZAMBIQUE - MINING AND MINERAL PRODUCTS

MOZAMBIQUE - STOCKS - COMMODITY - MARKET PRICE - INDEX

Food and Agricultural Organization of the United Nations (FAO), Via delle Terme di Caracalla, 00100 Rome, Italy (Telephone Number in U.S. (202) 653-2400); *The State of Food and Agriculture.*

MOZAMBIQUE - SUGAR PRODUCTION AND CONSUMPTION - See MOZAMBIQUE - CROPS

MOZAMBIQUE - SULPHURIC ACID - See MOZAMBIQUE - MINING AND MINERAL PRODUCTS

MOZAMBIQUE - TAX REVENUE - See MOZAMBIQUE - TAXATION

MOZAMBIQUE - TAXATION

Europa Publications Limited, 18 Bedford Square, London, WC1B 3JN, England; *The Europa World Year Book.*

The World Bank, 1818 H Street, NW, Washington, D.C. 20433 (202) 477-1234; *World Development Indicators.*

MOZAMBIQUE - TEA PRODUCTION - See MOZAMBIQUE - CROPS

MOZAMBIQUE - TELEPHONES IN USE

American Telephone and Telegraph Company, 26 Parsippany Road, Whippany, New Jersey 07981 (800) 222-0300; *The World's Telephones.*

Central Intelligence Agency, Washington, D.C. 20505 (703) 482-1100, www.cia.gov; *The World Factbook.*

Europa Publications Limited, 18 Bedford Square, London, WC1B 3JN, England; *The Europa World Year Book.*

St. Martin's Press, Inc., 175 Fifth Avenue, New York, New York 10010 (800) 221-7945; *The Statesman's Year-Book.*

Statistical Office of the United Nations, Publishing Service, New York, New York 10017 (800) 253-9646; *Statistical Yearbook;* and *World Statistics Pocketbook.*

MOZAMBIQUE - TELEVISION BROADCASTING - See MOZAMBIQUE - BROADCASTING

MOZAMBIQUE - TEXTILE INDUSTRY

M.E. Sharpe, 80 Business Park Drive, Armonk, New York 10504 (800) 541-6563; *The Illustrated Book of World Rankings.*

Statistical Office of the United Nations, Publishing Service, New York, New York 10017 (800) 253-9646; *Statistical Yearbook.*

United Nations Conference on Trade and Development, Central Statistical Service, Palais des Nations, Geneva, Switzerland (Telephone in U.S. (800) 253-9646); *UNCTAD Commodity Yearbook.*

MOZAMBIQUE - TOBACCO PRODUCTION

M.E. Sharpe, 80 Business Park Drive, Armonk, New York 10504 (800) 541-6563; *The Illustrated Book of World Rankings.*

Statistical Office of the United Nations, Publishing Service, New York, New York 10017 (800) 253-9646; *Statistical Yearbook.*

MOZAMBIQUE - TOURISM

Euromonitor International, Inc., 122 South Michigan Avenue, Suite 1200, Chicago, Illinois 60603 (800) 577-EURO; *The World Economic Factbook;* and *World Marketing Data and Statistics.*

Federal Statistical Office, Gustav-Stresemann - Ring 11, D-6200, Wiesbaden, Germany; *Mosambik.*

M.E. Sharpe, 80 Business Park Drive, Armonk, New York 10504 (800) 541-6563; *The Illustrated Book of World Rankings.*

United Nations Economic Commission for Africa, Africa Hall, Post Office Box 3001, Addis Ababa, Ethiopia (Telephone Number in U.S. (800) 253-9646); *African Statistical Yearbook.*

MOZAMBIQUE - TRACTORS IN USE

Statistical Office of the United Nations, Publishing Service, New York, New York 10017 (800) 253-9646; *Statistical Yearbook.*

MOZAMBIQUE - TRADE - See MOZAMBIQUE - FOREIGN TRADE

MOZAMBIQUE - TRANSPORTATION AND COMMUNICATIONS

Central Intelligence Agency, Washington, D.C. 20505 (703) 482-1100, www.cia.gov; *The World Factbook.*

Euromonitor International, Inc., 122 South Michigan Avenue, Suite 1200, Chicago, Illinois 60603 (800) 577-EURO; *International Marketing Data and Statistics;* and *World Marketing Data and Statistics.*

Europa Publications Limited, 18 Bedford Square, London, WC1B 3JN, England; *The Europa World Year Book.*

Federal Statistical Office, Gustav-Stresemann - Ring 11, D-6200, Wiesbaden, Germany; *Mosambik.*

M.E. Sharpe, 80 Business Park Drive, Armonk, New York 10504 (800) 541-6563; *The Illustrated Book of World Rankings.*

St. Martin's Press, Inc., 175 Fifth Avenue, New York, New York 10010 (800) 221-7945; *The Statesman's Year-Book.*

Statistical Office of the United Nations, Publishing Service, New York, New York 10017 (800) 253-9646; *Human Development Report.*

United Nations Economic Commission for Africa, Africa Hall, Post Office Box 3001, Addis Ababa, Ethiopia (Telephone Number in U.S. (800) 253-9646); *African Statistical Yearbook.*

MOZAMBIQUE - UNEMPLOYMENT

Central Intelligence Agency, Washington, D.C. 20505 (703) 482-1100, www.cia.gov; *The World Factbook.*

International Labour Office, I.L.O. Publications, 1828 L Street, NW., Suite 801, Washington, D.C. 20036 (301) 638-3152; *Yearbook of Labour Statistics.*

Statistical Office of the United Nations, Publishing Service, New York, New York 10017 (800) 253-9646; *Statistical Yearbook.*

MOZAMBIQUE - VITAL STATISTICS

Euromonitor International, Inc., 122 South Michigan Avenue, Suite 1200,

Chicago, Illinois 60603 (800) 577-EURO; *International Marketing Data and Statistics.*

Statistical Office of the United Nations, Publishing Service, New York, New York 10017 (800) 253-9646; *Statistical Yearbook.*

World Health Organization, Office of Publications, 20 Avenue Appia, CH-1211 Geneva 27, Switzerland (Telephone Number in U.S. (518) 436-9686); *World Health Statistics Annual.*

MOZAMBIQUE - WAGES

Federal Statistical Office, Gustav-Stresemann - Ring 11, D-6200, Wiesbaden, Germany; *Mosambik.*

International Labour Office, I.L.O. Publications, 1828 L Street, NW., Suite 801, Washington, D.C. 20036 (301) 638-3152; *Yearbook of Labour Statistics.*

MOZAMBIQUE - WEATHER - See MOZAMBIQUE - CLIMATE

MOZAMBIQUE - WHEAT PRODUCTION - See MOZAMBIQUE - CROPS

MOZAMBIQUE - WINE PRODUCTION - See MOZAMBIQUE - BEVERAGES

MOZAMBIQUE - WOOL PRODUCTION - See MOZAMBIQUE - TEXTILE INDUSTRY

MOZAMBIQUE - YARN PRODUCTION - See MOZAMBIQUE - TEXTILE INDUSTRY

MULLET - CATCH

U.S. Department of Commerce, National Oceanic and Atmospheric Administration, National Marine Fisheries Service, 1315 East-West Highway, Silver Spring, Maryland 20910 (301) 713-2239, www.nmfs.noaa.gov; *Fisheries of the United States.*

MULTINATIONAL COMPANIES

U.S. Department of Commerce, Bureau of Economic Analysis, Fourteenth Street between Constitution Avenue and E Street, NW, Washington, D.C. 20230 (202) 606-9900, www.bea.doc.gov; *Survey of Current Business.*

MULTIPLE BIRTHS

U.S. Department of Health and Human Services, National Center for Health Statistics, 3700 East-West Highway, Hyattsville, Maryland 20782 (301) 436-8500, www.cdc.gov/nchs; *Advance Report of Natality Statistics*; and *National Vital Statistics.*

MULTIPLE JOBHOLDERS

U.S. Department of Labor, Bureau of Labor Statistics, Two Massachusetts Avenue,

NE, Washington, D.C. 20212 (202) 691-5200, www.stats.bls.gov; *Employment and Earnings*; and unpublished data.

MUMPS

U.S. Department of Health and Human Services, Centers for Disease Control and Prevention, 1600 Clifton Road, NE, Atlanta, Georgia 30333 (800) 311-3435, www.cdc.gov; *Summary of Notifiable Diseases;* and *United States Morbidity and Mortality Weekly Report.*

MUNICIPAL AND STATE BONDS

Board of Governors of the Federal Reserve System, Twentieth Street and Constitution Avenue, NW, Washington, D.C. 20551 (202) 452-3000, www.bog.frb.fed.us; *Federal Reserve Bulletin.*

MUNICIPAL WASTE

Franklin Associates Limited, 4121 West Eighty-third Street, Suite 108, Prairie Village, Kansas 66208 (913) 649-2225; *Characterization of Municipal Solid Waste in the United States.*

MUNICIPAL WASTE - FOREIGN COUNTRIES

Organisation for Economic Co-operation and Development (OECD), 2 rue Andre-Pascal, 75 Paris 16, France (Telephone Number in U.S. (202) 785-6323); *Toward Sustainable Development: Environmental Indicators;* and *OECD in Figures.*

MUNICIPALITIES - See CITIES and METROPOLITAN AREAS

MURDERS

U.S. Department of Health and Human Services, National Center for Health Statistics, 3700 East West Highway, Hyattsville, Maryland 20783 (301) 436-8500, www.cdc.gov/nchs; *Vital Statistics of the United States;* and unpublished data.

U.S. Department of Justice, Federal Bureau of Investigation, 935 Pennsylvania Avenue, NW, Washington, D.C. 20535 (202) 324-3691, www.fbi.gov; *Crime in the United States.*

MUSEUMS

National Endowment for the Arts, 1100 Pennsylvania Avenue, NW, Washington, D.C. 20506 (202) 682-5400, www.arts.gov; *Annual Report.*

National Endowment for the Humanities, 1100 Pennsylvania Avenue, NW, Washington, D.C. 20506 (202) 606-8400, www.neh.fed.us; *Annual Report.*

MUSEUMS - BOTANICAL - ZOOLOGICAL GARDENS - EARNINGS

U.S. Department of Commerce, Bureau of the Census, Washington, D.C. 20233 (301) 457-4100, www.census.gov; *1997 Economic Census.*

MUSEUMS - BOTANICAL - ZOOLOGICAL GARDENS - EMPLOYEES

U.S. Department of Commerce, Bureau of the Census, Washington, D.C. 20233 (301) 457-4100, www.census.gov; *Census of Service Industries,* and *1997 Economic Census.*

MUSEUMS - BOTANICAL - ZOOLOGICAL GARDENS - ESTABLISHMENTS

U.S. Department of Commerce, Bureau of the Census, Washington, D.C. 20233 (301) 457-4100, www.census.gov; *Census of Service Industries;* and *1997 Economic Survey.*

MUSEUMS - BOTANICAL - ZOOLOGICAL GARDENS - FEDERAL AID

U.S. National Endowment for the Arts, 1100 Pennsylvania Avenue, NW, Washington, D.C. 20506 (202) 682-5400, www.arts.gov; *Annual Report.*

U.S. National Endowment for the Humanities, 1100 Pennsylvania Avenue, NW, Washington, D.C. 20506 (202) 606-8400, www.neh.fed.us; *Annual Report.*

MUSEUMS - BOTANICAL - ZOOLOGICAL GARDENS - FINANCES

U.S. Department of Commerce, Bureau of the Census, Washington, D.C. 20233 (301) 457-4100, www.census.gov; *Current Business Reports, Service Annual Survey.*

U.S. National Endowment for the Arts, 1100 Pennsylvania Avenue, NW, Washington, D.C. 20506 (202) 682-5400, www.arts.gov; *Annual Report.*

U.S. National Endowment for the Humanities, 1100 Pennsylvania Avenue, NW, Washington, D.C. 20506 (202) 606-8400, www.neh.fed.us; *Annual Report.*

MUSEUMS - BOTANICAL - ZOOLOGICAL GARDENS - OCCUPATIONAL SAFETY

U.S. Department of Labor, Bureau of Labor Statistics, Two Massachusetts Avenue, NE, Washington, D.C. 20212 (202) 691-5200, www.stats.bls.gov; *Occupational Injuries and Illnesses in the United States by Industry.*

MUSEUMS - BOTANICAL - ZOOLOGICAL GARDENS - RECEIPTS

U.S. Department of Commerce, Bureau

of the Census, Washington, D.C. 20233 (301) 457-4100, www.census.gov; *Census of Service Industries; 1997 Economic Census; Current Business Reports, Service Annual Survey;* and unpublished data.

MUSHROOMS

U.S. Department of Agriculture, Economic Research Service, 1800 M Street, NW, Washington, D.C. 20036 (202) 694-5050, www.ers.usda.gov; *Farm Business Economic Report.*

U.S. Department of Agriculture, National Agricultural Statistics Service, Fourteenth Street and Independence Avenue, SW, Washington, D.C. 20250 (800) 727-9540, www.usda.gov/nass; *Vegetables;* and *Agricultural Statistics.*

MUSIC - LISTENING AND EXPENDITURES

National Endowment for the Arts, 1100 Pennsylvania Avenue, NW, Washington, D.C. 20506 (202) 682-5400, www.arts.gov; *Survey of Public Participation in the Arts.*

Recording Industry Association of America, 1020 19th Street, NW, Suite 200, Washington, D.C. 20036 (202) 775-0101; *Top Ten Fact Book*; and *1998 Consumer Profile.*

Veronis, Suhler and Associates, 350 Park Avenue, New York, New York 10022 (212) 935-4990; *Communications Industry Report.*

MUSIC - INDUSTRY RECEIPTS

Recording Industry Association of America, 1020 19th Street, NW, Suite 200, Washington, D.C. 20036 (202) 775-0101; Internet site http://www.riaa.com.

Veronis, Suhler and Associates, 350 Park Avenue, New York, New York 10022 (212) 935-4990; *Communications Industry Report.*

MUSICIANS AND COMPOSERS

U.S. Department of Labor, Bureau of Labor Statistics, Two Massachusetts Avenue, NE, Washington, D.C. 20212 (202) 691-5200, www.stats.bls.gov; *Employment and Earnings;* and unpublished data.

MUSLIM POPULATION - See RELIGION

MUTTON - See also MEAT AND MEAT PRODUCTS

MUTTON

U.S. Department of Agriculture, Economic Research Service, 1800 M Street, NW, Washington, D.C. 20036 (202) 694-5050, www.ers.usda.gov; *Food Consumption, Prices, and Expenditures;* and *Agricultural Outlook.*

MUTUAL FUNDS

Access Research, Inc., 8 Griffin Road North, Windsor, Connecticut 06095 (860) 688-8821; *Marketplace Update.*

Board of Governors of the Federal Reserve System, Twentieth Street and Constitution Avenue, NW, Washington, D.C. 20551 (202) 452-3000, www.bog.frb.fed.us; *Flow of Funds; Federal Reserve Bulletin;* and unpublished data.

Investment Company Institute, 1401 H Street, NW, Washington, D.C. 20005 (202) 326-5800; *Mutual Fund Fact Book;* and *Fundamentals, Investment Company Institute Research in Brief.*

Securities and Exchange Commission, 450 Fifth Street, NW, Washington, D.C. 20549 (202) 942-4040, www.sec.gov; *Annual Report.*

Myanmar - National Statistical Office

Central Statistical Organization, Ministry of Planning and Finance, Six Storeyed Building, Strand Road, Yangon, Myanmar.

Myanmar - Primary Statistics Sources

Central Statistical and Economics Department, New Secretariat, Yangon, Myanmar; *Statistical Yearbook.*

Central Statistical Organization, Six Storeyed Building, Strand Road, Yangon, Myanmar; *Statistical Yearbook; Statistical Pocketbook;* and *Quarterly Bulletin of Statistics.*

MYANMAR - AGRICULTURE

Asian Development Bank, Post Office Box 789, Manila, 1099 Manila, Philippines; *Key Indicators of Developing Asian and Pacific Countries.*

Economist Intelligence Unit, 111 West 57th Street, New York, New York 10019 (800) 938-4685; *Myanmar Country Report.*

Euromonitor International, Inc., 122 South Michigan Avenue, Suite 1200, Chicago, Illinois 60603 (800) 577-EURO; *International Marketing Data and Statistics;* and *World Marketing Data and Statistics.*

Europa Publications Limited, 18 Bedford Square, London, WC1B 3JN, England; *The Europa World Year Book.*

Federal Statistical Office, Gustav - Stresemann - Ring 11, D-6200 Wiesbaden, Germany; *Myanmar.*

Food and Agricultural Organization of the United Nations (FAO), Via delle Terme di Caracalla, 00100 Rome, Italy (Telephone Number in U.S. (202) 653-2400); *Production Yearbook; The State of Food and Agriculture;* and *Trade Yearbook.*

M.E. Sharpe, 80 Business Park Drive, Armonk, New York 10504 (800) 541-6563; *The Illustrated Book of World Rankings.*

St. Martin's Press, Inc., 175 Fifth Avenue, New York, New York 10010 (800) 221-7945; *The Statesman's Year-Book.*

Statistical Office of the United Nations, Publishing Service, New York, New York 10017 (800) 253-9646; *Asia-Pacific in Figures;* and *Statistical Yearbook.*

United Nations Conference on Trade and Development, Central Statistical Service, Palais des Nations, Geneva, Switzerland (Telephone in U.S. (800) 253-9646); *UNCTAD Commodity Yearbook.*

MYANMAR - AIRLINE SERVICE

The Economist Intelligence Unit (Asia) Limited, 10th Floor, Luk Kwok Centre, 72 Gloucester Road, Wanchai, Hong Kong (Phone Number in U.S. (800) 938-4685); *Asian Market Atlas.*

Europa Publications Limited, 18 Bedford Square, London, WC1B 3JN, England; *The Europa World Year Book.*

International Civil Aviation Organization, 999 University Street, Montreal, Quebec, Canada H3C 5H7 (514) 954-8219; *Civil Aviation Statistics of the World.*

M.E. Sharpe, 80 Business Park Drive, Armonk, New York 10504 (800) 541-6563; *The Illustrated Book of World Rankings.*

St. Martin's Press, Inc., 175 Fifth Avenue, New York, New York 10010 (800) 221-7945; *The Statesman's Year-Book.*

Statistical Office of the United Nations, Publishing Service, New York, New York 10017 (800) 253-9646; *Statistical Yearbook.*

MYANMAR - AIRPORTS

Central Intelligence Agency, Washington, D.C. 20505 (703) 482-1100, www.cia.gov; *The World Factbook.*

MYANMAR - ALUMINUM PRODUCTION AND CONSUMPTION - See MYANMAR - MINING AND MINERAL PRODUCTS

MYANMAR - ANIMAL HEALTH

Food and Agricultural Organization of the United Nations (FAO), Via delle Terme di Caracalla, 00100, Rome, Italy (Telephone

Number in U.S. (202) 653-2400); *Animal Health Yearbook.*

MYANMAR - ANTIMONY PRODUCTION -See MYANMAR - MINING AND MINERAL PRODUCTS

MYANMAR - AREA AND DENSITY OF POPULATION

Central Intelligence Agency, Washington, D.C. 20505 (703) 482-1100, www.cia.gov; *The World Factbook.*

Euromonitor International, Inc., 122 South Michigan Avenue, Suite 1200, Chicago, Illinois 60603 (800) 577-EURO; *International Marketing Data and Statistics;* and *The World Economic Factbook.*

Europa Publications Limited, 18 Bedford Square, London, WC1B 3JN, England; *The Europa World Year Book.*

Federal Statistical Office, Gustav - Stresemann - Ring 11, D-6200 Wiesbaden, Germany; *Myanmar.*

Food and Agricultural Organization of the United Nations (FAO), Via delle Terme di Caracalla, 00100 Rome, Italy (Telephone Number in U.S. (202) 653-2400); *The State of Food and Agriculture.*

M.E. Sharpe, 80 Business Park Drive, Armonk, New York 10504 (800) 541-6563; *The Illustrated Book of World Rankings.*

St. Martin's Press, Inc., 175 Fifth Avenue, New York, New York 10010 (800) 221-7945; *The Statesman's Year-Book.*

Statistical Office of the United Nations, Publishing Service, New York, New York 10017 (800) 253-9646; *Statistical Yearbook.*

The World Bank, 1818 H Street, NW, Washington, D.C. 20433 (202) 477-1234; *World Development Report.*

MYANMAR - ARMS EXPORTS AND IMPORTS - See MYANMAR - MILITARY

MYANMAR - BALANCE OF PAYMENTS

The Economist Intelligence Unit, 111 West 57th Street, New York, New York 10019 (800) 938-4685; *The World Market Atlas.*

Europa Publications Limited, 18 Bedford Square, London, WC1B 3JN, England; *The Europa World Year Book.*

Federal Statistical Office, Gustav - Stresemann - Ring 11, D-6200 Wiesbaden, Germany; *Myanmar.*

International Monetary Fund, 700 Nineteenth Street, NW, Washington, D.C. 20431 (202) 623-7000; *International Financial Statistics.*

United Nations Conference on Trade and Development (UNCTAD), New York, New York 10017 (800) 253-9646; *Handbook of International Trade and Development Statistics.*

The World Bank, 1818 H Street, NW, Washington, D.C. 20433 (202) 477-1234; *World Development Report.*

MYANMAR - BANKING

Asian Development Bank, Post Office Box 789, Manila, 1099 Manila, Philippines; *Key Indicators of Developing Asian and Pacific Countries.*

Euromonitor International, Inc., 122 South Michigan Avenue, Suite 1200, Chicago, Illinois 60603 (800) 577-EURO; *World Marketing Data and Statistics.*

Europa Publications Limited, 18 Bedford Square, London, WC1B 3JN, England; *The Europa World Year Book.*

International Monetary Fund, 700 Nineteenth Street, NW, Washington, D.C. 20431 (202) 623-7000; *International Financial Statistics.*

M.E. Sharpe, 80 Business Park Drive, Armonk, New York 10504 (800) 541-6563; *The Illustrated Book of World Rankings.*

St. Martin's Press, Inc., 175 Fifth Avenue, New York, New York 10010 (800) 221-7945; *The Statesman's Year-Book.*

MYANMAR - BARLEY PRODUCTION - See MYANMAR - CROPS

MYANMAR - BEER PRODUCTION - See MYANMAR - BEVERAGES

M.E. Sharpe, 80 Business Park Drive, Armonk, New York 10504 (800) 541-6563; *The Illustrated Book of World Rankings.*

Statistical Office of the United Nations, Publishing Service, New York, New York 10017 (800) 253-9646; *Statistical Yearbook.*

MYANMAR - BIRTH RATES

Central Intelligence Agency, Washington, D.C. 20505 (703) 482-1100, www.cia.gov; *The World Factbook.*

The Economist Intelligence Unit (Asia) Limited, 10th Floor, Luk Kwok Centre, 72 Gloucester Road, Wanchai, Hong Kong (Phone Number in U.S. (800) 938-4685); *Asian Market Atlas.*

Euromonitor International, Inc., 122 South Michigan Avenue, Suite 1200, Chicago, Illinois 60603 (800) 577-EURO; *International Marketing Data and Statistics;*

and *The World Economic Factbook.*

Europa Publications Limited, 18 Bedford Square, London, WC1B 3JN, England; *The Europa World Year Book.*

M.E. Sharpe, 80 Business Park Drive, Armonk, New York 10504 (800) 541-6563; *The Illustrated Book of World Rankings.*

St. Martin's Press, Inc., 175 Fifth Avenue, New York, New York 10010 (800) 221-7945; *The Statesman's Year-Book.*

Statistical Office of the United Nations, Publishing Service, New York, New York 10017 (800) 253-9646; *Asia-Pacific in Figures; Demographic Yearbook;* and *Statistical Yearbook.*

MYANMAR - BONDS

Asian Development Bank, Post Office Box 789, Manila, 1099 Manila, Philippines; *Key Indicators of Developing Asian and Pacific Countries.*

MYANMAR - BROADCASTING

Billboard Limited, Post Office Box 9027, 1006 AA Amsterdam, The Netherlands (Telephone Number in U.S. (212) 764-7300); *World Radio TV Handbook.*

Central Intelligence Agency, Washington, D.C. 20505 (703) 482-1100, www.cia.gov; *The World Factbook.*

The Economist Intelligence Unit (Asia) Limited, 10th Floor, Luk Kwok Centre, 72 Gloucester Road, Wanchai, Hong Kong (Phone Number in U.S. (800) 938-4685); *Asian Market Atlas.*

Euromonitor International, Inc., 122 South Michigan Avenue, Suite 1200, Chicago, Illinois 60603 (800) 577-EURO; *World Marketing Data and Statistics.*

M.E. Sharpe, 80 Business Park Drive, Armonk, New York 10504 (800) 541-6563; *The Illustrated Book of World Rankings.*

St. Martin's Press, Inc., 175 Fifth Avenue, New York, New York 10010 (800) 221-7945; *The Statesman's Year-Book.*

MYANMAR - BUDGET

Central Intelligence Agency, Washington, D.C. 20505 (703) 482-1100, www.cia.gov; *The World Factbook.*

MYANMAR - BUTTER PRODUCTION - See MYANMAR - DAIRY PRODUCTS

MYANMAR - CALORIE SUPPLY

Asian Development Bank, Post Office Box 789, Manila, 1099 Manila, Philippines;

Key Indicators of Developing Asian and Pacific Countries.

Food and Agricultural Organization of the United Nations (FAO), Via delle Terme di Caracalla, 00100 Rome, Italy (Telephone Number in U.S. (202) 653-2400); *The State of Food and Agriculture.*

MYANMAR - CAPITAL INVESTMENT

Asian Development Bank, Post Office Box 789, Manila, 1099 Manila, Philippines; *Key Indicators of Developing Asian and Pacific Countries.*

MYANMAR - CAPITAL REVENUE

Asian Development Bank, Post Office Box 789, Manila, 1099 Manila, Philippines; *Key Indicators of Developing Asian and Pacific Countries.*

MYANMAR - CATTLE - See MYANMAR - LIVESTOCK AND POULTRY

MYANMAR - CEMENT PRODUCTION - See MYANMAR - MINING AND MINERAL PRODUCTS

MYANMAR - CHEESE PRODUCTION AND CONSUMPTION - See MYANMAR - DAIRY PRODUCTS

MYANMAR - CHEMICAL (ORGANIC) PRODUCTION - See MYANMAR - MINING AND MINERAL PRODUCTS

MYANMAR - CHICK PEA PRODUCTION - See MYANMAR - CROPS

MYANMAR - CHICKENS - See MYANMAR - LIVESTOCK AND POULTRY

MYANMAR - CIGAR AND CIGARETTE PRODUCTION - See MYANMAR - TOBACCO PRODUCTION

MYANMAR - CLIMATE

M.E. Sharpe, 80 Business Park Drive, Armonk, New York 10504 (800) 541-6563; *The Illustrated Book of World Rankings.*

St. Martin's Press, Inc., 175 Fifth Avenue, New York, New York 10010 (800) 221-7945; *The Statesman's Year-Book.*

MYANMAR - COAL PRODUCTION - See MYANMAR - MINING AND MINERAL PRODUCTS

MYANMAR - COFFEE PRODUCTION AND CONSUMPTION - See MYANMAR - CROPS

MYANMAR - COMMERCE

St. Martin's Press, Inc., 175 Fifth Avenue, New York, New York 10010 (800) 221-7945; *The Statesman's Year-Book.*

MYANMAR - COMMUNICATIONS - See MYANMAR - TRANSPORTATION AND COMMUNICATIONS

MYANMAR - CONSTRUCTION INDUSTRY

M.E. Sharpe, 80 Business Park Drive, Armonk, New York 10504 (800) 541-6563; *The Illustrated Book of World Rankings.*

Statistical Office of the United Nations, Publishing Service, New York, New York 10017 (800) 253-9646; *Statistical Yearbook.*

MYANMAR - CONSUMER PRICE INDEX

Asian Development Bank, Post Office Box 789, Manila, 1099 Manila, Philippines; *Key Indicators of Developing Asian and Pacific Countries.*

Europa Publications Limited, 18 Bedford Square, London, WC1B 3JN, England; *The Europa World Year Book.*

Federal Statistical Office, Gustav - Stresemann - Ring 11, D-6200 Wiesbaden, Germany; *Myanmar.*

Statistical Office of the United Nations, Publishing Service, New York, New York 10017 (800) 253-9646; *Statistical Yearbook.*

MYANMAR - CONSUMER PRICES

Euromonitor International, Inc., 122 South Michigan Avenue, Suite 1200, Chicago, Illinois 60603 (800) 577-EURO; *World Marketing Data and Statistics.*

Federal Statistical Office, Gustav - Stresemann - Ring 11, D-6200 Wiesbaden, Germany; *Myanmar.*

International Labour Office, I.L.O. Publications, 1828 L Street, NW., Suite 801, Washington, D.C. 20036 (301) 638-3152; *Yearbook of Labour Statistics.*

International Monetary Fund, 700 Nineteenth Street, NW, Washington, D.C. 20431 (202) 623-7000; *International Financial Statistics.*

MYANMAR - CONSUMPTION

International Rubber Study Group, York House, Eighth Floor, Empire Way, Wembley, London HA9 0PA, England; *Rubber Statistical Bulletin.*

The World Bank, 1818 H Street, NW, Washington, D.C. 20433 (202) 477-1234; *World Development Report.*

MYANMAR - COPPER AND COPPER ORE PRODUCTION AND CONSUMPTION - See MYANMAR - MINING AND MINERAL PRODUCTS

MYANMAR - CORN PRODUCTION - See

MYANMAR - CROPS

MYANMAR - CORPORATE TAXES - See MYANMAR - TAXATION

MYANMAR - COTTON - See MYANMAR - CROPS

MYANMAR - CRIME

International Criminal Police Organization (INTERPOL), 50 quai Achille Lignon, F-69006 Lyon, France; *International Crime Statistics.*

Yale University Press, Yale Station, New Haven, Connecticut 06520 (800) 987-7323; *Violence and Crime in Cross-National Perspective.*

MYANMAR - CROPS

Asian Development Bank, Post Office Box 789, Manila, 1099 Manila, Philippines; *Key Indicators of Developing Asian and Pacific Countries.*

Commodity Research Bureau, 30 South Wacker Drive, Chicago Illinois 60606 (312) 454-1801; *Commodity Year Book.*

Europa Publications Limited, 18 Bedford Square, London, WC1B 3JN, England; *The Europa World Year Book.*

Food and Agricultural Organization of the United Nations (FAO), Via delle Terme di Caracalla, 00100 Rome, Italy (Telephone Number in U.S. (202) 653-2400); *Production Yearbook;* and *The State of Food and Agriculture.*

International Monetary Fund, 700 Nineteenth Street, NW, Washington, D.C. 20431 (202) 623-7000; *International Financial Statistics.*

M.E. Sharpe, 80 Business Park Drive, Armonk, New York 10504 (800) 541-6563; *The Illustrated Book of World Rankings.*

St. Martin's Press, Inc., 175 Fifth Avenue, New York, New York 10010 (800) 221-7945; *The Statesman's Year-Book.*

Statistical Office of the United Nations, Publishing Service, New York, New York 10017 (800) 253-9646; *Statistical Yearbook.*

United Nations Conference on Trade and Development, Central Statistical Service, Palais des Nations, Geneva, Switzerland (Telephone in U.S. (800) 253-9646); *UNCTAD Commodity Yearbook.*

MYANMAR - CUSTOMS DUTIES

St. Martin's Press, Inc., 175 Fifth Avenue, New York, New York 10010 (800) 221-7945; *The Statesman's Year-Book.*

MYANMAR - DAIRY PRODUCTS

Europa Publications Limited, 18 Bedford Square, London, WC1B 3JN, England; *The Europa World Year Book.*

Food and Agricultural Organization of the United Nations (FAO), Via delle Terme di Caracalla, 00100 Rome, Italy (Telephone Number in U.S. (202) 653-2400); *Production Yearbook; and The State of Food and Agriculture.*

M.E. Sharpe, 80 Business Park Drive, Armonk, New York 10504 (800) 541-6563; *The Illustrated Book of World Rankings.*

St. Martin's Press, Inc., 175 Fifth Avenue, New York, New York 10010 (800) 221-7945; *The Statesman's Year-Book.*

Statistical Office of the United Nations, Publishing Service, New York, New York 10017 (800) 253-9646; *Statistical Yearbook.*

MYANMAR - DEATH RATES - See MYANMAR - MORTALITY

MYANMAR - DEFENSE EXPENDITURES - See MYANMAR - MILITARY

MYANMAR - DEMOGRAPHY

The Economist Intelligence Unit, 111 West 57th Street, New York, New York 10019 (800) 938-4685; *The World Market Atlas.*

The Economist Intelligence Unit (Asia) Limited, 10th Floor, Luk Kwok Centre, 72 Gloucester Road, Wanchai, Hong Kong (Phone Number in U.S. (800) 938-4685); *Asian Market Atlas.*

Euromonitor International, Inc., 122 South Michigan Avenue, Suite 1200, Chicago, Illinois 60603 (800) 577-EURO; *International Marketing Data and Statistics; The World Economic Factbook; and World Marketing Data and Statistics.*

Federal Statistical Office, Gustav - Stresemann - Ring 11, D-6200 Wiesbaden, Germany; *Myanmar.*

M.E. Sharpe, 80 Business Park Drive, Armonk, New York 10504 (800) 541-6563; *The Illustrated Book of World Rankings.*

Statistical Office of the United Nations, Publishing Service, New York, New York 10017 (800) 253-9646; *Asia-Pacific in Figures; and Human Development Report.*

MYANMAR - DEVELOPMENT ASSISTANCE

Asian Development Bank, Post Office Box 789, Manila, 1099 Manila, Philippines; *Key Indicators of Developing Asian and Pacific Countries.*

Statistical Office of the United Nations, Publishing Service, New York, New York 10017 (800) 253-9646; *Statistical Yearbook.*

MYANMAR - DIAMOND PRODUCTION - See MYANMAR - MINING AND MINERAL PRODUCTS

MYANMAR - DISEASES - See MYANMAR - HEALTH

MYANMAR - DIVORCE

M.E. Sharpe, 80 Business Park Drive, Armonk, New York 10504 (800) 541-6563; *The Illustrated Book of World Rankings.*

Statistical Office of the United Nations, Publishing Service, New York, New York 10017 (800) 253-9646; *Demographic Yearbook.*

MYANMAR - DUCKS - See MYANMAR - LIVESTOCK AND POULTRY

MYANMAR - ECONOMY

Asian Development Bank, Post Office Box 789, Manila, 1099 Manila, Philippines; *Key Indicators of Developing Asian and Pacific Countries.*

Central Intelligence Agency, Washington, D.C. 20505 (703) 482-1100, www.cia.gov; *The World Factbook.*

Economist Intelligence Unit, 111 West 57th Street, New York, New York 10019 (800) 938-4685; *Myanmar Country Report.*

Euromonitor International, Inc., 122 South Michigan Avenue, Suite 1200, Chicago, Illinois 60603 (800) 577-EURO; *International Marketing Data and Statistics; The World Economic Factbook; and World Marketing Data and Statistics.*

Europa Publications Limited, 18 Bedford Square, London, WC1B 3JN, England; *The Europa World Year Book.*

Federal Statistical Office, Gustav - Stresemann - Ring 11, D-6200 Wiesbaden, Germany; *Myanmar.*

M.E. Sharpe, 80 Business Park Drive, Armonk, New York 10504 (800) 541-6563; *The Illustrated Book of World Rankings.*

St. Martin's Press, Inc., 175 Fifth Avenue, New York, New York 10010 (800) 221-7945; *The Statesman's Year-Book.*

Statistical Office of the United Nations, Publishing Service, New York, New York 10017 (800) 253-9646; *World Statistics Pocketbook.*

The World Bank, 1818 H Street, NW, Washington, D.C. 20433 (202) 477-1234; *The World Bank Atlas; and World Development Report.*

MYANMAR - EDUCATION

The Economist Intelligence Unit, 111 West 57th Street, New York, New York 10019 (800) 938-4685; *The World Market Atlas.*

The Economist Intelligence Unit (Asia) Limited, 10th Floor, Luk Kwok Centre, 72 Gloucester Road, Wanchai, Hong Kong (Phone Number in U.S. (800) 938-4685); *Asian Market Atlas.*

Euromonitor International, Inc., 122 South Michigan Avenue, Suite 1200, Chicago, Illinois 60603 (800) 577-EURO; *International Marketing Data and Statistics.*

Europa Publications Limited, 18 Bedford Square, London, WC1B 3JN, England; *The Europa World Year Book.*

Federal Statistical Office, Gustav - Stresemann - Ring 11, D-6200 Wiesbaden, Germany; *Myanmar.*

M.E. Sharpe, 80 Business Park Drive, Armonk, New York 10504 (800) 541-6563; *The Illustrated Book of World Rankings.*

St. Martin's Press, Inc., 175 Fifth Avenue, New York, New York 10010 (800) 221-7945; *The Statesman's Year-Book.*

Statistical Office of the United Nations, Publishing Service, New York, New York 10017 (800) 253-9646; *Asia-Pacific in Figures; Human Development Report; and Statistical Yearbook for Asia and the Pacific.*

United Nations Educational, Scientific and Cultural Organization (UNESCO), 7 Place de Fontenoy, F-75700 Paris, France (Telephone Number in U.S. (212) 963-5981); *Statistical Yearbook.*

The World Bank, 1818 H Street, NW, Washington, D.C. 20433 (202) 477-1234; *World Development Report.*

MYANMAR - EGG PRODUCTION AND CONSUMPTION - See MYANMAR - DAIRY PRODUCTS

MYANMAR - ELECTRICITY

Asian Development Bank, Post Office Box 789, Manila, 1099 Manila, Philippines; *Key Indicators of Developing Asian and Pacific Countries.*

Central Intelligence Agency, Washington, D.C. 20505 (703) 482-1100, www.cia.gov; *The World Factbook.*

M.E. Sharpe, 80 Business Park Drive, Armonk, New York 10504 (800) 541-6563; *The Illustrated Book of World Rankings.*

Penn Well Publishing Company, 1421 South Sheridan Road, Post Office Box 1260, Tulsa, Oklahoma 74101 (800) 752-9764; *International Energy Statistics Sourcebook.*

St. Martin's Press, Inc., 175 Fifth Avenue, New York, New York 10010 (800) 221-7945; *The Statesman's Year-Book.*

Statistical Office of the United Nations, Publishing Service, New York, New York 10017 (800) 253-9646; *Electric Power in Asia and the Pacific; Human Development Report;* and *Statistical Yearbook.*

MYANMAR - EMPLOYMENT

Euromonitor International, Inc., 122 South Michigan Avenue, Suite 1200, Chicago, Illinois 60603 (800) 577-EURO; *International Marketing Data and Statistics.*

Federal Statistical Office, Gustav - Stresemann - Ring 11, D-6200 Wiesbaden, Germany; *Myanmar.*

International Labour Office, I.L.O. Publications, 1828 L Street, NW., Suite 801, Washington, D.C. 20036 (301) 638-3152; *Yearbook of Labour Statistics.*

M.E. Sharpe, 80 Business Park Drive, Armonk, New York 10504 (800) 541-6563; *The Illustrated Book of World Rankings.*

Statistical Office of the United Nations, Publishing Service, New York, New York 10017 (800) 253-9646; *Asia-Pacific in Figures;* and *Statistical Yearbook.*

MYANMAR - ENERGY

Euromonitor International, Inc., 122 South Michigan Avenue, Suite 1200, Chicago, Illinois 60603 (800) 577-EURO; *International Marketing Data and Statistics; The World Economic Factbook;* and *World Marketing Data and Statistics.*

M.E. Sharpe, 80 Business Park Drive, Armonk, New York 10504 (800) 541-6563; *The Illustrated Book of World Rankings.*

Penn Well Publishing Company, 1421 South Sheridan Road, Post Office Box 1260, Tulsa, Oklahoma 74101 (800) 752-9764; *International Energy Statistics Sourcebook.*

St. Martin's Press, Inc., 175 Fifth Avenue, New York, New York 10010 (800) 221-7945; *The Statesman's Year-Book.*

Statistical Office of the United Nations, Publishing Service, New York, New York 10017 (800) 253-9646; *Asia-Pacific in Figures; Energy Statistics Yearbook; Human Development Report; Statistical Yearbook; World Statistics Pocketbook*; and *Statistical Yearbook for Asia and the Pacific.*

The World Bank, 1818 H Street, NW, Washington, D.C. 20433 (202) 477-1234; *The World Bank Atlas;* and *World Development Report.*

MYANMAR - ENVIRONMENT

Economist Intelligence Unit, 111 West 57th Street, New York, New York 10019 (800) 938-4685; *Myanmar Country Report.*

Statistical Office of the United Nations, Publishing Service, New York, New York 10017 (800) 253-9646; *World Statistics Pocketbook.*

MYANMAR - EXCHANGE RATES

Asian Development Bank, Post Office Box 789, Manila, 1099 Manila, Philippines; *Key Indicators of Developing Asian and Pacific Countries.*

Central Intelligence Agency, Washington, D.C. 20505 (703) 482-1100, www.cia.gov; *The World Factbook.*

The Economist Intelligence Unit (Asia) Limited, 10th Floor, Luk Kwok Centre, 72 Gloucester Road, Wanchai, Hong Kong (Phone Number in U.S. (800) 938-4685); *Asian Market Atlas.*

Euromonitor International, Inc., 122 South Michigan Avenue, Suite 1200, Chicago, Illinois 60603 (800) 577-EURO; *International Marketing Data and Statistics;* and *The World Economic Factbook.*

Europa Publications Limited, 18 Bedford Square, London, WC1B 3JN, England; *The Europa World Year Book.*

International Civil Aviation Organization, 999 University Street, Montreal, Quebec, Canada H3C 5H7 (514) 954-8219; *Civil Aviation Statistics of the World.*

International Monetary Fund, 700 Nineteenth Street, NW, Washington, D.C. 20431 (202) 623-7000; *International Financial Statistics.*

Statistical Office of the United Nations, Publishing Service, New York, New York 10017 (800) 253-9646; *Statistical Yearbook;* and *World Statistics Pocketbook.*

Walden Publishing Ltd., Two Market Street, Saffron Walden Essex, CB10 1HZ, England; *The World of Information Asia and Pacific Review.*

MYANMAR - EXPORTS

Asian Development Bank, Post Office Box 789, Manila, 1099 Manila, Philippines; *Key Indicators of Developing Asian and Pacific Countries.*

Central Intelligence Agency, Washington, D.C. 20505 (703) 482-1100, www.cia.gov; *The World Factbook.*

The Economist Intelligence Unit, 111 West 57th Street, New York, New York 10019 (800) 938-4685; *Myanmar Country Report;* and *The World Market Atlas.*

The Economist Intelligence Unit (Asia) Limited, 10th Floor, Luk Kwok Centre, 72 Gloucester Road, Wanchai, Hong Kong (Phone Number in U.S. (800) 938-4685); *Asian Market Atlas.*

Euromonitor International, Inc., 122 South Michigan Avenue, Suite 1200, Chicago, Illinois 60603 (800) 577-EURO; *International Marketing Data and Statistics;* and *The World Economic Factbook.*

Europa Publications Limited, 18 Bedford Square, London, WC1B 3JN, England; *The Europa World Year Book.*

Food and Agricultural Organization of the United Nations (FAO), Via delle Terme di Caracalla, 00100 Rome, Italy (Telephone Number in U.S. (202) 653-2400); *The State of Food and Agriculture.*

International Monetary Fund, 700 Nineteenth Street, NW, Washington, D.C. 20431 (202) 623-7000; *Direction of Trade Statistics;* and *International Financial Statistics.*

International Rubber Study Group, York House, Eighth Floor, Empire Way, Wembley, London HA9 0PA, England; *Rubber Statistical Bulletin.*

St. Martin's Press, Inc., 175 Fifth Avenue, New York, New York 10010 (800) 221-7945; *The Statesman's Year-Book.*

United Nations Conference on Trade and Development (UNCTAD), New York, New York 10017 (800) 253-9646; *Handbook of International Trade and Development Statistics.*

Walden Publishing Ltd., Two Market Street, Saffron Walden Essex, CB10 1HZ, England; *The World of Information Asia and Pacific Review.*

The World Bank, 1818 H Street, NW, Washington, D.C. 20433 (202) 477-1234; *World Development Report.*

MYANMAR - EXTERNAL FINANCING

Asian Development Bank, Post Office Box 789, Manila, 1099 Manila, Philippines; *Key Indicators of Developing Asian and Pacific Countries.*

MYANMAR - EXTERNAL INDEBTEDNESS

Asian Development Bank, Post Office

Box 789, Manila, 1099 Manila, Philippines; *Key Indicators of Developing Asian and Pacific Countries.*

The World Bank, 1818 H Street, NW, Washington, D.C. 20433 (202) 477-1234; *World Development Report.*

MYANMAR - EXTERNAL TRADE

Asian Development Bank, Post Office Box 789, Manila, 1099 Manila, Philippines; *Key Indicators of Developing Asian and Pacific Countries.*

Euromonitor International, Inc., 122 South Michigan Avenue, Suite 1200, Chicago, Illinois 60603 (800) 577-EURO; *World Marketing Data and Statistics.*

Food and Agricultural Organization of the United Nations (FAO), Via delle Terme di Caracalla, 00100 Rome, Italy (Telephone Number in U.S. (202) 653-2400); *The State of Food and Agriculture;* and *Trade Yearbook.*

Statistical Office of the United Nations, Publishing Service, New York, New York 10017 (800) 253-9646; *Asia-Pacific in Figures;* and *Statistical Yearbook for Asia and the Pacific.*

MYANMAR - FABRIC PRODUCTION - See MYANMAR - TEXTILE INDUSTRY

MYANMAR - FARM CROPS - See MYANMAR - CROPS

MYANMAR - FEMALE WORKING POPULATION - See MYANMAR - EMPLOYMENT

MYANMAR - FERTILITY RATES

Central Intelligence Agency, Washington, D.C. 20505 (703) 482-1100, www.cia.gov; *The World Factbook.*

The Economist Intelligence Unit (Asia) Limited, 10th Floor, Luk Kwok Centre, 72 Gloucester Road, Wanchai, Hong Kong (Phone Number in U.S. (800) 938-4685); *Asian Market Atlas.*

M.E. Sharpe, 80 Business Park Drive, Armonk, New York 10504 (800) 541-6563; *The Illustrated Book of World Rankings.*

Statistical Office of the United Nations, Publishing Service, New York, New York 10017 (800) 253-9646; *Human Development Report.*

The World Bank, 1818 H Street, NW, Washington, D.C. 20433 (202) 477-1234; *The World Bank Atlas;* and *World Development Report.*

MYANMAR - FERTILIZER

Food and Agricultural Organization of the United Nations (FAO), Via delle Terme di Caracalla, 00100 Rome, Italy (Telephone Number in U.S. (202) 653-2400); *The State of Food and Agriculture.*

Statistical Office of the United Nations, Publishing Service, New York, New York 10017 (800) 253-9646; *Statistical Yearbook.*

MYANMAR - FETAL MORTALITY - See MYANMAR - MORTALITY

MYANMAR - FILMS PRODUCED - LONG - See MYANMAR - MOTION PICTURES

MYANMAR - FINANCE

Economist Intelligence Unit, 111 West 57th Street, New York, New York 10019 (800) 938-4685; *Myanmar Country Report.*

Europa Publications Limited, 18 Bedford Square, London, WC1B 3JN, England; *The Europa World Year Book.*

Federal Statistical Office, Gustav - Stresemann - Ring 11, D-6200 Wiesbaden, Germany; *Myanmar.*

International Monetary Fund, 700 Nineteenth Street, NW, Washington, D.C. 20431 (202) 623-7000; *International Financial Statistics.*

M.E. Sharpe, 80 Business Park Drive, Armonk, New York 10504 (800) 541-6563; *The Illustrated Book of World Rankings.*

St. Martin's Press, Inc., 175 Fifth Avenue, New York, New York 10010 (800) 221-7945; *The Statesman's Year-Book.*

Statistical Office of the United Nations, Publishing Service, New York, New York 10017 (800) 253-9646; *Statistical Yearbook for Asia and the Pacific.*

MYANMAR - FISHERIES

Europa Publications Limited, 18 Bedford Square, London, WC1B 3JN, England; *The Europa World Year Book.*

Federal Statistical Office, Gustav - Stresemann - Ring 11, D-6200 Wiesbaden, Germany; *Myanmar.*

Food and Agricultural Organization of the United Nations (FAO), Via delle Terme di Caracalla, 00100 Rome, Italy (Telephone Number in U.S. (202) 653-2400); *The State of Food and Agriculture;* and *Yearbook of Fishery Statistics.*

M.E. Sharpe, 80 Business Park Drive, Armonk, New York 10504 (800) 541-6563; *The Illustrated Book of World Rankings.*

St. Martin's Press, Inc., 175 Fifth

Avenue, New York, New York 10010 (800) 221-7945; *The Statesman's Year-Book.*

Statistical Office of the United Nations, Publishing Service, New York, New York 10017 (800) 253-9646; *Statistical Yearbook.*

United Nations Conference on Trade and Development, Central Statistical Service, Palais des Nations, Geneva, Switzerland (Telephone in U.S. (800) 253-9646); *UNCTAD Commodity Yearbook.*

MYANMAR - FLOUR PRODUCTION

Statistical Office of the United Nations, Publishing Service, New York, New York 10017 (800) 253-9646; *Statistical Yearbook.*

MYANMAR - FOOD

Food and Agricultural Organization of the United Nations (FAO), Via delle Terme di Caracalla, 00100 Rome, Italy (Telephone Number in U.S. (202) 653-2400); *Production Yearbook;* and *The State of Food and Agriculture.*

Statistical Office of the United Nations, Publishing Service, New York, New York 10017 (800) 253-9646; *Human Development Report;* and *Statistical Yearbook for Asia and the Pacific.*

United Nations Conference on Trade and Development, Central Statistical Service, Palais des Nations, Geneva, Switzerland (Telephone in U.S. (800) 253-9646); *UNCTAD Commodity Yearbook.*

MYANMAR - FOREIGN DEBT

St. Martin's Press, Inc., 175 Fifth Avenue, New York, New York 10010 (800) 221-7945; *The Statesman's Year-Book.*

Walden Publishing Ltd., Two Market Street, Saffron Walden Essex, CB10 1HZ, England; *The World of Information Asia and Pacific Review.*

MYANMAR - FOREIGN TRADE

Asian Development Bank, Post Office Box 789, Manila, 1099 Manila, Philippines; *Key Indicators of Developing Asian and Pacific Countries.*

Economist Intelligence Unit, 111 West 57th Street, New York, New York 10019 (800) 938-4685; *Myanmar Country Report.*

The Economist Intelligence Unit (Asia) Limited, 10th Floor, Luk Kwok Centre, 72 Gloucester Road, Wanchai, Hong Kong (Phone Number in U.S. (800) 938-4685); *Asian Market Atlas.*

Euromonitor International, Inc., 122 South Michigan Avenue, Suite 1200, Chicago, Illinois 60603 (800) 577-EURO;

International Marketing Data and Statistics; and *The World Economic Factbook.*

Europa Publications Limited, 18 Bedford Square, London, WC1B 3JN, England; *The Europa World Year Book.*

Federal Statistical Office, Gustav - Stresemann - Ring 11, D-6200 Wiesbaden, Germany; *Myanmar.*

Food and Agricultural Organization of the United Nations (FAO), Via delle Terme di Caracalla, 00100 Rome, Italy (Telephone Number in U.S. (202) 653-2400); *The State of Food and Agriculture.*

M.E. Sharpe, 80 Business Park Drive, Armonk, New York 10504 (800) 541-6563; *The Illustrated Book of World Rankings.*

Organisation for Economic Co-operation and Development (OECD), 2 rue Andre-Pascal, 75 Paris 16, France (Telephone Number in U.S. (202) 785-6323); *Trade by Commodities.*

St. Martin's Press, Inc., 175 Fifth Avenue, New York, New York 10010 (800) 221-7945; *The Statesman's Year-Book.*

Statistical Office of the United Nations, Publishing Service, New York, New York 10017 (800) 253-9646; *International Trade Statistics Yearbook;* and *Statistical Yearbook.*

United Nations Conference on Trade and Development, Central Statistical Service, Palais des Nations, Geneva, Switzerland (Telephone in U.S. (800) 253-9646); *UNCTAD Commodity Yearbook.*

The World Bank, 1818 H Street, NW, Washington, D.C. 20433 (202) 477-1234; *World Development Report.*

MYANMAR - FORESTRY AND FOREST PRODUCTS

The Economist Intelligence Unit (Asia) Limited, 10th Floor, Luk Kwok Centre, 72 Gloucester Road, Wanchai, Hong Kong (Phone Number in U.S. (800) 938-4685); *Asian Market Atlas.*

Europa Publications Limited, 18 Bedford Square, London, WC1B 3JN, England; *The Europa World Year Book.*

Federal Statistical Office, Gustav - Stresemann - Ring 11, D-6200 Wiesbaden, Germany; *Myanmar.*

Food and Agricultural Organization of the United Nations (FAO), Via delle Terme di Caracalla, 00100 Rome, Italy (Telephone Number in U.S. (202) 653-2400); *The State of Food and Agriculture;* and *Yearbook of Forest Products.*

M.E. Sharpe, 80 Business Park Drive, Armonk, New York 10504 (800) 541-6563; *The Illustrated Book of World Rankings.*

St. Martin's Press, Inc., 175 Fifth Avenue, New York, New York 10010 (800) 221-7945; *The Statesman's Year-Book.*

Statistical Office of the United Nations, Publishing Service, New York, New York 10017 (800) 253-9646; *Statistical Yearbook.*

United Nations Educational, Scientific and Cultural Organization (UNESCO), 7 Place de Fontenoy, F-75700 Paris, France (Telephone Number in U.S. (212) 963-5981); *Statistical Yearbook.*

The World Bank, 1818 H Street, NW, Washington, D.C. 20433 (202) 477-1234; *World Development Report.*

MYANMAR - GARLIC PRODUCTION - See MYANMAR - CROPS

MYANMAR - GAS PRODUCTION - See MYANMAR - MINING AND MINERAL PRODUCTS

MYANMAR - GENERAL INDUSTRIAL STATISTICS - See MYANMAR - INDUSTRY

MYANMAR - GENERAL MORTALITY - See MYANMAR - MORTALITY

MYANMAR - GEOGRAPHIC DATA

Federal Statistical Office, Gustav - Stresemann - Ring 11, D-6200 Wiesbaden, Germany; *Myanmar.*

M.E. Sharpe, 80 Business Park Drive, Armonk, New York 10504 (800) 541-6563; *The Illustrated Book of World Rankings.*

MYANMAR - GOATS - See MYANMAR - LIVESTOCK AND POULTRY

MYANMAR - GOLD HOLDINGS

International Monetary Fund, 700 Nineteenth Street, NW, Washington, D.C. 20431 (202) 623-7000; *International Financial Statistics.*

Statistical Office of the United Nations, Publishing Service, New York, New York 10017 (800) 253-9646; *Statistical Yearbook.*

MYANMAR - GOLD PRODUCTION AND CONSUMPTION - See MYANMAR - MINING AND MINERAL PRODUCTS

MYANMAR - GOVERNMENT

Asian Development Bank, Post Office Box 789, Manila, 1099 Manila, Philippines; *Key Indicators of Developing Asian and Pacific Countries.*

Central Intelligence Agency, Washington, D.C. 20505 (703) 482-1100, www.cia.gov; *The World Factbook.*

Europa Publications Limited, 18 Bedford Square, London, WC1B 3JN, England; *The Europa World Year Book.*

International Monetary Fund, 700 Nineteenth Street, NW, Washington, D.C. 20431 (202) 623-7000; *International Financial Statistics.*

St. Martin's Press, Inc., 175 Fifth Avenue, New York, New York 10010 (800) 221-7945; *The Statesman's Year-Book.*

Statistical Office of the United Nations, Publishing Service, New York, New York 10017 (800) 253-9646; *Asia-Pacific in Figures; National Accounts Statistics;* and *Statistical Yearbook.*

The World Bank, 1818 H Street, NW, Washington, D.C. 20433 (202) 477-1234; *World Development Report.*

MYANMAR - GRAIN PRODUCTION

Food and Agricultural Organization of the United Nations (FAO), Via delle Terme di Caracalla, 00100 Rome, Italy (Telephone Number in U.S. (202) 653-2400); *The State of Food and Agriculture.*

MYANMAR - GROSS DOMESTIC PRODUCT

Asian Development Bank, Post Office Box 789, Manila, 1099 Manila, Philippines; *Key Indicators of Developing Asian and Pacific Countries.*

The Economist Intelligence Unit, 111 West 57th Street, New York, New York 10019 (800) 938-4685; *Myanmar Country Report;* and *The World Market Atlas.*

The Economist Intelligence Unit (Asia) Limited, 10th Floor, Luk Kwok Centre, 72 Gloucester Road, Wanchai, Hong Kong (Phone Number in U.S. (800) 938-4685); *Asian Market Atlas.*

Euromonitor International, Inc., 122 South Michigan Avenue, Suite 1200, Chicago, Illinois 60603 (800) 577-EURO; *International Marketing Data and Statistics;* and *The World Economic Factbook.*

Europa Publications Limited, 18 Bedford Square, London, WC1B 3JN, England; *The Europa World Year Book.*

M.E. Sharpe, 80 Business Park Drive, Armonk, New York 10504 (800) 541-6563; *The Illustrated Book of World Rankings.*

Statistical Office of the United Nations, Publishing Service, New York, New York 10017 (800) 253-9646; *Human Development Report; National Accounts Statistics;* and *Statistical Yearbook.*

The World Bank, 1818 H Street, NW, Washington, D.C. 20433 (202) 477-1234; *World Development Report.*

MYANMAR - GROSS NATIONAL PRODUCT

Asian Development Bank, Post Office Box 789, Manila, 1099 Manila, Philippines; *Key Indicators of Developing Asian and Pacific Countries.*

Euromonitor International, Inc., 122 South Michigan Avenue, Suite 1200, Chicago, Illinois 60603 (800) 577-EURO; *International Marketing Data and Statistics.*

U.S. Arms Control and Disarmament Agency, 320 Twenty-first Street, NW, Washington, D.C. 20451 (202) 647-8677; *World Military Expenditures and Arms Transfers.*

Walden Publishing Ltd., Two Market Street, Saffron Walden Essex, CB10 1HZ, England; *The World of Information Asia and Pacific Review.*

The World Bank, 1818 H Street, NW, Washington, D.C. 20433 (202) 477-1234; *The World Bank Atlas;* and *World Development Report.*

MYANMAR - GROUNDNUTS PRODUCTION - See MYANMAR - CROPS

MYANMAR - HEALTH

The Economist Intelligence Unit (Asia) Limited, 10th Floor, Luk Kwok Centre, 72 Gloucester Road, Wanchai, Hong Kong (Phone Number in U.S. (800) 938-4685); *Asian Market Atlas.*

Euromonitor International, Inc., 122 South Michigan Avenue, Suite 1200, Chicago, Illinois 60603 (800) 577-EURO; *World Marketing Data and Statistics.*

Federal Statistical Office, Gustav - Stresemann - Ring 11, D-6200 Wiesbaden, Germany; *Myanmar.*

M.E. Sharpe, 80 Business Park Drive, Armonk, New York 10504 (800) 541-6563; *The Illustrated Book of World Rankings.*

St. Martin's Press, Inc., 175 Fifth Avenue, New York, New York 10010 (800) 221-7945; *The Statesman's Year-Book.*

Statistical Office of the United Nations, Publishing Service, New York, New York 10017 (800) 253-9646; *Asia-Pacific in Figures; Human Development Report;* and *Statistical Yearbook.*

United Nations Children's Fund (UNICEF), 3 United Nations Plaza, New York, New York 10017 (800) 253-9646; *State of the World's Children.*

The World Bank, 1818 H Street, NW, Washington, D.C. 20433 (202) 477-1234; *World Development Report.*

World Health Organization, Office of Publications, 20 Avenue Appia, CH-1211 Geneva 27, Switzerland (Telephone Number in U.S. (518) 436-9686); *World Health Statistics Annual.*

MYANMAR - HEALTH AND MEDICAL SERVICES

Federal Statistical Office, Gustav - Stresemann - Ring 11, D-6200 Wiesbaden, Germany; *Myanmar.*

Statistical Office of the United Nations, Publishing Service, New York, New York 10017 (800) 253-9646; *Statistical Yearbook.*

MYANMAR - HIDE PRODUCTION

Food and Agricultural Organization of the United Nations (FAO), Via delle Terme di Caracalla, 00100 Rome, Italy (Telephone Number in U.S. (202) 653-2400); *Production Yearbook.*

MYANMAR - HIGHWAYS

Central Intelligence Agency, Washington, D.C. 20505 (703) 482-1100, www.cia.gov; *The World Factbook.*

The Economist Intelligence Unit (Asia) Limited, 10th Floor, Luk Kwok Centre, 72 Gloucester Road, Wanchai, Hong Kong (Phone Number in U.S. (800) 938-4685); *Asian Market Atlas.*

International Road Federation, 2600 Virginia Avenue, NW., Washington, D.C. 20037 (202) 338-4641; *World Road Statistics.*

St. Martin's Press, Inc., 175 Fifth Avenue, New York, New York 10010 (800) 221-7945; *The Statesman's Year-Book.*

MYANMAR - HORSES - See MYANMAR - LIVESTOCK AND POULTRY

MYANMAR - HOURS OF WORK - See MYANMAR - EMPLOYMENT

MYANMAR - HOUSING AND HOUSING UNITS

Euromonitor International, Inc., 122 South Michigan Avenue, Suite 1200, Chicago, Illinois 60603 (800) 577-EURO; *World Marketing Data and Statistics.*

M.E. Sharpe, 80 Business Park Drive, Armonk, New York 10504 (800) 541-6563; *The Illustrated Book of World Rankings.*

MYANMAR - ILLITERATE POPULATION

Central Intelligence Agency,

Washington, D.C. 20505 (703) 482-1100, www.cia.gov; *The World Factbook.*

The Economist Intelligence Unit, 111 West 57th Street, New York, New York 10019 (800) 938-4685; *The World Market Atlas.*

Euromonitor International, Inc., 122 South Michigan Avenue, Suite 1200, Chicago, Illinois 60603 (800) 577-EURO; *The World Economic Factbook.*

Statistical Office of the United Nations, Publishing Service, New York, New York 10017 (800) 253-9646; *Asia-Pacific in Figures;* and *Human Development Report.*

United Nations Educational, Scientific and Cultural Organization (UNESCO), 7 Place de Fontenoy, F-75700 Paris, France (Telephone Number in U.S. (212) 963-5981); *Statistical Yearbook.*

MYANMAR - IMPORTS

Asian Development Bank, Post Office Box 789, Manila, 1099 Manila, Philippines; *Key Indicators of Developing Asian and Pacific Countries.*

Central Intelligence Agency, Washington, D.C. 20505 (703) 482-1100, www.cia.gov; *The World Factbook.*

The Economist Intelligence Unit, 111 West 57th Street, New York, New York 10019 (800) 938-4685; *Myanmar Country Report;* and *The World Market Atlas.*

The Economist Intelligence Unit (Asia) Limited, 10th Floor, Luk Kwok Centre, 72 Gloucester Road, Wanchai, Hong Kong (Phone Number in U.S. (800) 938-4685); *Asian Market Atlas.*

Euromonitor International, Inc., 122 South Michigan Avenue, Suite 1200, Chicago, Illinois 60603 (800) 577-EURO; *International Marketing Data and Statistics;* and *The World Economic Factbook.*

Europa Publications Limited, 18 Bedford Square, London, WC1B 3JN, England; *The Europa World Year Book.*

Food and Agricultural Organization of the United Nations (FAO), Via delle Terme di Caracalla, 00100 Rome, Italy (Telephone Number in U.S. (202) 653-2400); *The State of Food and Agriculture.*

International Monetary Fund, 700 Nineteenth Street, NW, Washington, D.C. 20431 (202) 623-7000; *Direction of Trade Statistics;* and *International Financial Statistics.*

International Rubber Study Group, York House, Eighth Floor, Empire Way, Wembley, London HA9 0PA, England;

Rubber Statistical Bulletin.

St. Martin's Press, Inc., 175 Fifth Avenue, New York, New York 10010 (800) 221-7945; *The Statesman's Year-Book.*

United Nations Conference on Trade and Development (UNCTAD), New York, New York 10017 (800) 253-9646; *Handbook of International Trade and Development Statistics.*

Walden Publishing Ltd., Two Market Street, Saffron Walden Essex, CB10 1HZ, England; *The World of Information Asia and Pacific Review.*

The World Bank, 1818 H Street, NW, Washington, D.C. 20433 (202) 477-1234; *World Development Report.*

MYANMAR - IMPORTS FROM OTHER DEVELOPING COUNTRIES

Asian Development Bank, Post Office Box 789, Manila, 1099 Manila, Philippines; *Key Indicators of Developing Asian and Pacific Countries.*

MYANMAR - INDUSTRIAL METALS PRODUCTION - See MYANMAR -MINING AND MINERAL PRODUCTS

MYANMAR - INDUSTRY

Central Intelligence Agency, Washington, D.C. 20505 (703) 482-1100, www.cia.gov; *The World Factbook.*

Economist Intelligence Unit, 111 West 57th Street, New York, New York 10019 (800) 938-4685; *Myanmar Country Report.*

Euromonitor International, Inc., 122 South Michigan Avenue, Suite 1200, Chicago, Illinois 60603 (800) 577-EURO; *International Marketing Data and Statistics; The World Economic Factbook;* and *World Marketing Data and Statistics.*

Europa Publications Limited, 18 Bedford Square, London, WC1B 3JN, England; *The Europa World Year Book.*

Federal Statistical Office, Gustav - Stresemann - Ring 11, D-6200 Wiesbaden, Germany; *Myanmar.*

International Labour Office, I.L.O. Publications, 1828 L Street, NW., Suite 801, Washington, D.C. 20036 (301) 638-3152; *Yearbook of Labour Statistics.*

M.E. Sharpe, 80 Business Park Drive, Armonk, New York 10504 (800) 541-6563; *The Illustrated Book of World Rankings.*

Statistical Office of the United Nations, Publishing Service, New York, New York 10017 (800) 253-9646; *Asia-Pacific in Figures;* and *Statistical Yearbook for Asia*

and the Pacific.

MYANMAR - INFANT AND MATERNAL MORTALITY - See MYANMAR - MORTALITY

MYANMAR - INTERNAL TRADE

Statistical Office of the United Nations, Publishing Service, New York, New York 10017 (800) 253-9646; *Statistical Yearbook for Asia and the Pacific.*

MYANMAR - INTERNATIONAL LIQUIDITY

International Monetary Fund, 700 Nineteenth Street, NW, Washington, D.C. 20431 (202) 623-7000; *International Financial Statistics.*

MYANMAR - INTERNATIONAL RESERVES EXCLUDING GOLD

Asian Development Bank, Post Office Box 789, Manila, 1099 Manila, Philippines; *Key Indicators of Developing Asian and Pacific Countries.*

Statistical Office of the United Nations, Publishing Service, New York, New York 10017 (800) 253-9646; *Statistical Yearbook.*

MYANMAR - INTERNATIONAL STATISTICS

Asian Development Bank, Post Office Box 789, Manila, 1099 Manila, Philippines; *Key Indicators of Developing Asian and Pacific Countries.*

MYANMAR - INVESTMENTS

International Monetary Fund, 700 Nineteenth Street, NW, Washington, D.C. 20431 (202) 623-7000; *International Financial Statistics.*

MYANMAR - IRON ORE PRODUCTION AND CONSUMPTION - See MYANMAR - MINING AND MINERAL PRODUCTS

MYANMAR - IRRIGATION

Euromonitor International, Inc., 122 South Michigan Avenue, Suite 1200, Chicago, Illinois 60603 (800) 577-EURO; *International Marketing Data and Statistics.*

MYANMAR - JUTE PRODUCTION - See MYANMAR - CROPS

MYANMAR - LABOR

Central Intelligence Agency, Washington, D.C. 20505 (703) 482-1100, www.cia.gov; *The World Factbook.*

The Economist Intelligence Unit (Asia) Limited, 10th Floor, Luk Kwok Centre, 72 Gloucester Road, Wanchai, Hong Kong (Phone Number in U.S. (800) 938-4685); *Asian Market Atlas.*

Euromonitor International, Inc., 122 South Michigan Avenue, Suite 1200, Chicago, Illinois 60603 (800) 577-EURO; *International Marketing Data and Statistics;* and *World Marketing Data and Statistics.*

Europa Publications Limited, 18 Bedford Square, London, WC1B 3JN, England; *The Europa World Year Book.*

Food and Agricultural Organization of the United Nations (FAO), Via delle Terme di Caracalla, 00100 Rome, Italy (Telephone Number in U.S. (202) 653-2400); *The State of Food and Agriculture.*

International Labour Office, I.L.O. Publications, 1828 L Street, NW., Suite 801, Washington, D.C. 20036 (301) 638-3152; *Yearbook of Labour Statistics.*

M.E. Sharpe, 80 Business Park Drive, Armonk, New York 10504 (800) 541-6563; *The Illustrated Book of World Rankings.*

St. Martin's Press, Inc., 175 Fifth Avenue, New York, New York 10010 (800) 221-7945; *The Statesman's Year-Book.*

Statistical Office of the United Nations, Publishing Service, New York, New York 10017 (800) 253-9646; *Human Development Report.*

The World Bank, 1818 H Street, NW, Washington, D.C. 20433 (202) 477-1234; *The World Bank Atlas;* and *World Development Report.*

MYANMAR - LAND USE

Central Intelligence Agency, Washington, D.C. 20505 (703) 482-1100, www.cia.gov; *The World Factbook.*

Euromonitor International, Inc., 122 South Michigan Avenue, Suite 1200, Chicago, Illinois 60603 (800) 577-EURO; *International Marketing Data and Statistics.*

Food and Agricultural Organization of the United Nations (FAO), Via delle Terme di Caracalla, 00100 Rome, Italy (Telephone Number in U.S. (202) 653-2400); *Production Yearbook.*

The World Bank, 1818 H Street, NW, Washington, D.C. 20433 (202) 477-1234; *World Development Report.*

MYANMAR - LEAD AND LEAD ORE PRODUCTION AND CONSUMPTION - See MYANMAR - MINING AND MINERAL PRODUCTS

MYANMAR - LIBRARIES

M.E. Sharpe, 80 Business Park Drive, Armonk, New York 10504 (800) 541-6563; *The Illustrated Book of World Rankings.*

MYANMAR - LIFE EXPECTANCY

Central Intelligence Agency, Washington, D.C. 20505 (703) 482-1100, www.cia.gov; *The World Factbook.*

The Economist Intelligence Unit (Asia) Limited, 10th Floor, Luk Kwok Centre, 72 Gloucester Road, Wanchai, Hong Kong (Phone Number in U.S. (800) 938-4685); *Asian Market Atlas.*

Euromonitor International, Inc., 122 South Michigan Avenue, Suite 1200, Chicago, Illinois 60603 (800) 577-EURO; *The World Economic Factbook.*

St. Martin's Press, Inc., 175 Fifth Avenue, New York, New York 10010 (800) 221-7945; *The Statesman's Year-Book.*

Statistical Office of the United Nations, Publishing Service, New York, New York 10017 (800) 253-9646; *Asia-Pacific in Figures; World Statistics Pocketbook;* and *Human Development Report.*

The World Bank, 1818 H Street, NW, Washington, D.C. 20433 (202) 477-1234; *The World Bank Atlas;* and *World Development Report.*

MYANMAR - LIGNITE PRODUCTION - See MYANMAR - MINING AND MINERAL PRODUCTS

MYANMAR - LITERACY RATE

Euromonitor International, Inc., 122 South Michigan Avenue, Suite 1200, Chicago, Illinois 60603 (800) 577-EURO; *World Marketing Data and Statistics.*

MYANMAR - LIVESTOCK AND POULTRY

Euromonitor International, Inc., 122 South Michigan Avenue, Suite 1200, Chicago, Illinois 60603 (800) 577-EURO; *International Marketing Data and Statistics.*

Europa Publications Limited, 18 Bedford Square, London, WC1B 3JN, England; *The Europa World Year Book.*

Food and Agricultural Organization of the United Nations (FAO), Via delle Terme di Caracalla, 00100 Rome, Italy (Telephone Number in U.S. (202) 653-2400); *Production Yearbook;* and *The State of Food and Agriculture.*

M.E. Sharpe, 80 Business Park Drive, Armonk, New York 10504 (800) 541-6563; *The Illustrated Book of World Rankings.*

Statistical Office of the United Nations, Publishing Service, New York, New York 10017 (800) 253-9646; *Statistical Yearbook.*

United Nations Conference on Trade and Development, Central Statistical Service, Palais des Nations, Geneva, Switzerland (Telephone in U.S. (800) 253-9646); *UNCTAD Commodity Yearbook.*

MYANMAR - LIVING LEVELS - See MYANMAR - LIFE EXPECTANCY

MYANMAR - MAIL - NUMBER OF PIECES SENT OR RECEIVED

Statistical Office of the United Nations, Publishing Service, New York, New York 10017 (800) 253-9646; *Statistical Yearbook.*

MYANMAR - MANPOWER

Statistical Office of the United Nations, Publishing Service, New York, New York 10017 (800) 253-9646; *Statistical Yearbook for Asia and the Pacific.*

MYANMAR - MANUFACTURING

Asian Development Bank, Post Office Box 789, Manila, 1099 Manila, Philippines; *Key Indicators of Developing Asian and Pacific Countries.*

M.E. Sharpe, 80 Business Park Drive, Armonk, New York 10504 (800) 541-6563; *The Illustrated Book of World Rankings.*

Statistical Office of the United Nations, Publishing Service, New York, New York 10017 (800) 253-9646; *Statistical Yearbook.*

MYANMAR - MARRIAGE RATES

M.E. Sharpe, 80 Business Park Drive, Armonk, New York 10504 (800) 541-6563; *The Illustrated Book of World Rankings.*

Statistical Office of the United Nations, Publishing Service, New York, New York 10017 (800) 253-9646; *Demographic Yearbook.*

MYANMAR - MEAT PRODUCTION - See MYANMAR - LIVESTOCK AND POULTRY

MYANMAR - MERCHANT SHIPPING

Europa Publications Limited, 18 Bedford Square, London, WC1B 3JN, England; *The Europa World Year Book.*

Lloyd's Register of Shipping, 17 Battery Place, New York, New York 10004 (212) 425-8050; *Register of Ships.*

St. Martin's Press, Inc., 175 Fifth Avenue, New York, New York 10010 (800) 221-7945; *The Statesman's Year-Book.*

Statistical Office of the United Nations, Publishing Service, New York, New York 10017 (800) 253-9646; *Statistical Yearbook.*

U.S. Department of Transportation, Maritime Administration, 400 Seventh Street, SW, Washington, D.C. 20590 (202) 366-5807, www.marad.dot.gov; *A Statistical Analysis of the World's Merchant Fleets.*

MYANMAR - MILITARY

Central Intelligence Agency, Washington, D.C. 20505 (703) 482-1100, www.cia.gov; *The World Factbook.*

The Economist Intelligence Unit (Asia) Limited, 10th Floor, Luk Kwok Centre, 72 Gloucester Road, Wanchai, Hong Kong (Phone Number in U.S. (800) 938-4685); *Asian Market Atlas.*

Euromonitor International, Inc., 122 South Michigan Avenue, Suite 1200, Chicago, Illinois 60603 (800) 577-EURO; *World Marketing Data and Statistics.*

The International Institute for Strategic Studies, 23 Tavistock Street, London WC2E 7NQ, England; *The Military Balance.*

St. Martin's Press, Inc., 175 Fifth Avenue, New York, New York 10010 (800) 221-7945; *The Statesman's Year-Book.*

Statistical Office of the United Nations, Publishing Service, New York, New York 10017 (800) 253-9646; *Human Development Report.*

U.S. Arms Control and Disarmament Agency, 320 Twenty-first Street, NW, Washington, D.C. 20451 (202) 647-8677; *World Military Expenditures and Arms Transfers.*

MYANMAR - MILK PRODUCTION - See MYANMAR - DAIRY PRODUCTS

MYANMAR - MILLET PRODUCTION - See MYANMAR - CROPS

MYANMAR - MINING AND MINERAL PRODUCTS

Asian Development Bank, Post Office Box 789, Manila, 1099 Manila, Philippines; *Key Indicators of Developing Asian and Pacific Countries.*

Europa Publications Limited, 18 Bedford Square, London, WC1B 3JN, England; *The Europa World Year Book.*

M.E. Sharpe, 80 Business Park Drive, Armonk, New York 10504 (800) 541-6563; *The Illustrated Book of World Rankings.*

Penn Well Publishing Company, 1421 South Sheridan Road, Post Office Box 1260, Tulsa, Oklahoma 74101 (800) 752-9764; *International Energy Statistics Sourcebook.*

St. Martin's Press, Inc., 175 Fifth Avenue, New York, New York 10010 (800) 221-7945; *The Statesman's Year-Book.*

Statistical Office of the United Nations,

Publishing Service, New York, New York 10017 (800) 253-9646; *Statistical Yearbook.*

United Nations Conference on Trade and Development, Central Statistical Service, Palais des Nations, Geneva, Switzerland (Telephone in U.S. (800) 253-9646); *UNCTAD Commodity Yearbook.*

MYANMAR - MONEY EXCHANGE RATE -See MYANMAR - EXCHANGE RATES

MYANMAR - MONEY RESERVES

Euromonitor International, Inc., 122 South Michigan Avenue, Suite 1200, Chicago, Illinois 60603 (800) 577-EURO; *International Marketing Data and Statistics.*

MYANMAR - MONEY SUPPLY

Asian Development Bank, Post Office Box 789, Manila, 1099 Manila, Philippines; *Key Indicators of Developing Asian and Pacific Countries.*

Economist Intelligence Unit, 111 West 57th Street, New York, New York 10019 (800) 938-4685; *Myanmar Country Report.*

Euromonitor International, Inc., 122 South Michigan Avenue, Suite 1200, Chicago, Illinois 60603 (800) 577-EURO; *International Marketing Data and Statistics.*

Europa Publications Limited, 18 Bedford Square, London, WC1B 3JN, England; *The Europa World Year Book.*

Federal Statistical Office, Gustav - Stresemann - Ring 11, D-6200 Wiesbaden, Germany; *Myanmar.*

International Monetary Fund, 700 Nineteenth Street, NW, Washington, D.C. 20431 (202) 623-7000; *International Financial Statistics.*

Statistical Office of the United Nations, Publishing Service, New York, New York 10017 (800) 253-9646; *Statistical Yearbook.*

MYANMAR - MORTALITY

Central Intelligence Agency, Washington, D.C. 20505 (703) 482-1100, www.cia.gov; *The World Factbook.*

The Economist Intelligence Unit (Asia) Limited, 10th Floor, Luk Kwok Centre, 72 Gloucester Road, Wanchai, Hong Kong (Phone Number in U.S. (800) 938-4685); *Asian Market Atlas.*

Euromonitor International, Inc., 122 South Michigan Avenue, Suite 1200, Chicago, Illinois 60603 (800) 577-EURO; *International Marketing Data and Statistics;* and *The World Economic Factbook.*

Europa Publications Limited, 18 Bedford

Square, London, WC1B 3JN, England; *The Europa World Year Book.*

St. Martin's Press, Inc., 175 Fifth Avenue, New York, New York 10010 (800) 221-7945; *The Statesman's Year-Book.*

Statistical Office of the United Nations, Publishing Service, New York, New York 10017 (800) 253-9646; *Asia-Pacific in Figures; Demographic Yearbook; Human Development Report; World Statistics Pocketbook;* and *Statistical Yearbook.*

United Nations Children's Fund (UNICEF), 3 United Nations Plaza, New York, New York 10017 (800) 253-9646; *State of the World's Children.*

The World Bank, 1818 H Street, NW, Washington, D.C. 20433 (202) 477-1234; *The World Bank Atlas;* and *World Development Report.*

World Health Organization, Office of Publications, 20 Avenue Appia, CH-1211 Geneva 27, Switzerland (Telephone Number in U.S. (518) 436-9686); *World Health Statistics Annual.*

MYANMAR - MOTION PICTURES

Statistical Office of the United Nations, Publishing Service, New York, New York 10017 (800) 253-9646; *Statistical Yearbook.*

United Nations Educational, Scientific and Cultural Organization (UNESCO), 7 Place de Fontenoy, F-75700 Paris, France (Telephone Number in U.S. (212) 963-5981); *Statistical Yearbook.*

MYANMAR - MOTOR VEHICLE PRODUCTION AND ASSEMBLY

Statistical Office of the United Nations, Publishing Service, New York, New York 10017 (800) 253-9646; *Statistical Yearbook.*

MYANMAR - MOTOR VEHICLE TAXES - See MYANMAR - TAXATION

MYANMAR - MOTOR VEHICLES IN USE

International Road Federation, 2600 Virginia Avenue, NW., Washington, D.C. 20037 (202) 338-4641; *World Road Statistics.*

Statistical Office of the United Nations, Publishing Service, New York, New York 10017 (800) 253-9646; *Statistical Yearbook.*

MYANMAR - MULES - See MYANMAR - LIVESTOCK AND POULTRY

MYANMAR - MUSEUMS

M.E. Sharpe, 80 Business Park Drive, Armonk, New York 10504 (800) 541-6563; *The Illustrated Book of World Rankings.*

United Nations Educational, Scientific and Cultural Organization (UNESCO), 7 Place de Fontenoy, F-75700 Paris, France (Telephone Number in U.S. (212) 963-5981); *Statistical Yearbook.*

MYANMAR - NATALITY - See MYANMAR - BIRTH RATES

MYANMAR - NATIONAL ACCOUNTS

Europa Publications Limited, 18 Bedford Square, London, WC1B 3JN, England; *The Europa World Year Book.*

Federal Statistical Office, Gustav - Stresemann - Ring 11, D-6200 Wiesbaden, Germany; *Myanmar.*

Statistical Office of the United Nations, Publishing Service, New York, New York 10017 (800) 253-9646; *Asia-Pacific in Figures; National Accounts Statistics;* and *Statistical Yearbook.*

MYANMAR - NATIONAL INCOME

M.E. Sharpe, 80 Business Park Drive, Armonk, New York 10504 (800) 541-6563; *The Illustrated Book of World Rankings.*

Statistical Office of the United Nations, Publishing Service, New York, New York 10017 (800) 253-9646; *National Accounts Statistics;* and *Statistical Yearbook.*

MYANMAR - NATIONAL PRODUCT

M.E. Sharpe, 80 Business Park Drive, Armonk, New York 10504 (800) 541-6563; *The Illustrated Book of World Rankings.*

Statistical Office of the United Nations, Publishing Service, New York, New York 10017 (800) 253-9646; *Statistical Yearbook.*

MYANMAR - NATURAL GAS - PRODUCTION - See MYANMAR - MINING AND MINERAL PRODUCTS

MYANMAR - NATURAL RUBBER PRODUCTION

International Rubber Study Group, York House, Eighth Floor, Empire Way, Wembley, London HA9 0PA, England; *Rubber Statistical Bulletin.*

Statistical Office of the United Nations, Publishing Service, New York, New York 10017 (800) 253-9646; *Statistical Yearbook.*

MYANMAR - NEWSPAPER PRODUCTION - See MYANMAR - FORESTRY AND FOREST PRODUCTS

MYANMAR - NEWSPRINT - See MYANMAR - FORESTRY AND FOREST PRODUCTS

MYANMAR - NICKEL ORE PRODUCTION AND CONSUMPTION - See MYANMAR -

MINING AND MINERAL PRODUCTS

MYANMAR - OCCUPATIONS - See MYANMAR - LABOR FORCE

MYANMAR - OILCAKES EXPORTS

International Monetary Fund, 700 Nineteenth Street, NW, Washington, D.C. 20431 (202) 623-7000; *International Financial Statistics.*

MYANMAR - PAPER - See MYANMAR - FORESTRY AND FOREST PRODUCTS

MYANMAR - PEANUT PRODUCTION - See MYANMAR - CROPS

MYANMAR - PERIODICALS

United Nations Educational, Scientific and Cultural Organization (UNESCO), 7 Place de Fontenoy, F-75700 Paris, France (Telephone Number in U.S. (212) 963-5981); *Statistical Yearbook.*

MYANMAR - PESTICIDE USE

Food and Agricultural Organization of the United Nations (FAO), Via delle Terme di Caracalla, 00100 Rome, Italy (Telephone Number in U.S. (202) 653-2400); *The State of Food and Agriculture.*

MYANMAR - PETROLEUM INDUSTRY

Asian Development Bank, Post Office Box 789, Manila, 1099 Manila, Philippines; *Key Indicators of Developing Asian and Pacific Countries.*

Food and Agricultural Organization of the United Nations (FAO), Via delle Terme di Caracalla, 00100 Rome, Italy (Telephone Number in U.S. (202) 653-2400); *The State of Food and Agriculture.*

M.E. Sharpe, 80 Business Park Drive, Armonk, New York 10504 (800) 541-6563; *The Illustrated Book of World Rankings.*

Penn Well Publishing Company, 1421 South Sheridan Road, Post Office Box 1260, Tulsa, Oklahoma 74101 (800) 752-9764; *International Energy Statistics Sourcebook.*

St. Martin's Press, Inc., 175 Fifth Avenue, New York, New York 10010 (800) 221-7945; *The Statesman's Year-Book.*

Statistical Office of the United Nations, Publishing Service, New York, New York 10017 (800) 253-9646; *Statistical Yearbook.*

United Nations Conference on Trade and Development, Central Statistical Service, Palais des Nations, Geneva, Switzerland (Telephone in U.S. (800) 253-9646); *UNCTAD Commodity Yearbook.*

MYANMAR - PIGS - See MYANMAR -

LIVESTOCK AND POULTRY

MYANMAR - POPULATION

Asian Development Bank, Post Office Box 789, Manila, 1099 Manila, Philippines; *Key Indicators of Developing Asian and Pacific Countries.*

Central Intelligence Agency, Washington, D.C. 20505 (703) 482-1100, www.cia.gov; *The World Factbook.*

The Economist Intelligence Unit, 111 West 57th Street, New York, New York 10019 (800) 938-4685; *Myanmar Country Report;* and *The World Market Atlas.*

The Economist Intelligence Unit (Asia) Limited, 10th Floor, Luk Kwok Centre, 72 Gloucester Road, Wanchai, Hong Kong (Phone Number in U.S. (800) 938-4685); *Asian Market Atlas.*

Euromonitor International, Inc., 122 South Michigan Avenue, Suite 1200, Chicago, Illinois 60603 (800) 577-EURO; *International Marketing Data and Statistics;* and *The World Economic Factbook.*

Europa Publications Limited, 18 Bedford Square, London, WC1B 3JN, England; *The Europa World Year Book.*

Federal Statistical Office, Gustav - Stresemann - Ring 11, D-6200 Wiesbaden, Germany; *Myanmar.*

Food and Agricultural Organization of the United Nations (FAO), Via delle Terme di Caracalla, 00100 Rome, Italy (Telephone Number in U.S. (202) 653-2400); *Production Yearbook.*

International Labour Office, I.L.O. Publications, 1828 L Street, NW., Suite 801, Washington, D.C. 20036 (301) 638-3152; *Yearbook of Labour Statistics.*

M.E. Sharpe, 80 Business Park Drive, Armonk, New York 10504 (800) 541-6563; *The Illustrated Book of World Rankings.*

St. Martin's Press, Inc., 175 Fifth Avenue, New York, New York 10010 (800) 221-7945; *The Statesman's Year-Book.*

Statistical Office of the United Nations, Publishing Service, New York, New York 10017 (800) 253-9646; *Asia-Pacific in Figures; Demographic Yearbook; Human Development Report; Statistical Yearbook; World Statistics Pocketbook;* and *Statistical Yearbook for Asia and the Pacific.*

United Nations Educational, Scientific and Cultural Organization (UNESCO), 7 Place de Fontenoy, F-75700 Paris, France (Telephone Number in U.S. (212) 963-5981); *Statistical Yearbook.*

U.S. Arms Control and Disarmament Agency, 320 Twenty-first Street, NW, Washington, D.C. 20451 (202) 647-8677; *World Military Expenditures and Arms Transfers.*

Walden Publishing Ltd., Two Market Street, Saffron Walden Essex, CB10 1HZ, England; *The World of Information Asia and Pacific Review.*

The World Bank, 1818 H Street, NW, Washington, D.C. 20433 (202) 477-1234; *The World Bank Atlas;* and *World Development Report.*

World Health Organization, Office of Publications, 20 Avenue Appia, CH-1211 Geneva 27, Switzerland (Telephone Number in U.S. (518) 436-9686); *World Health Statistics Annual.*

MYANMAR - POST OFFICES

M.E. Sharpe, 80 Business Park Drive, Armonk, New York 10504 (800) 541-6563; *The Illustrated Book of World Rankings.*

St. Martin's Press, Inc., 175 Fifth Avenue, New York, New York 10010 (800) 221-7945; *The Statesman's Year-Book.*

MYANMAR - POTATO PRODUCTION - See MYANMAR - CROPS

MYANMAR - POWER PRODUCTION INDUSTRY - ESTABLISHMENTS, PAYROLLS, VALUE ADDED, ETC.

Statistical Office of the United Nations, Publishing Service, New York, New York 10017 (800) 253-9646; *Electric Power in Asia and the Pacific.*

MYANMAR - PRICES

Asian Development Bank, Post Office Box 789, Manila, 1099 Manila, Philippines; *Key Indicators of Developing Asian and Pacific Countries.*

Federal Statistical Office, Gustav - Stresemann - Ring 11, D-6200 Wiesbaden, Germany; *Myanmar.*

Food and Agricultural Organization of the United Nations (FAO), Via delle Terme di Caracalla, 00100 Rome, Italy (Telephone Number in U.S. (202) 653-2400); *Production Yearbook;* and *The State of Food and Agriculture.*

International Labour Office, I.L.O. Publications, 1828 L Street, NW., Suite 801, Washington, D.C. 20036 (301) 638-3152; *Yearbook of Labour Statistics.*

International Monetary Fund, 700 Nineteenth Street, NW, Washington, D.C. 20431 (202) 623-7000; *International Financial Statistics.*

International Rubber Study Group, York House, Eighth Floor, Empire Way, Wembley, London HA9 0PA, England; *Rubber Statistical Bulletin.*

M.E. Sharpe, 80 Business Park Drive, Armonk, New York 10504 (800) 541-6563; *The Illustrated Book of World Rankings.*

MYANMAR - PRINTING AND WRITING PAPER - See MYANMAR - FORESTRY AND FOREST PRODUCTS

MYANMAR - PRODUCTION

International Rubber Study Group, York House, Eighth Floor, Empire Way, Wembley, London HA9 0PA, England; *Rubber Statistical Bulletin.*

M.E. Sharpe, 80 Business Park Drive, Armonk, New York 10504 (800) 541-6563; *The Illustrated Book of World Rankings.*

MYANMAR - PRODUCTIVITY

Euromonitor International, Inc., 122 South Michigan Avenue, Suite 1200, Chicago, Illinois 60603 (800) 577-EURO; *International Marketing Data and Statistics.*

MYANMAR - PUBLIC FINANCE - See MYANMAR - FINANCE

MYANMAR - RADIO BROADCASTING - See MYANMAR - BROADCASTING

MYANMAR - RADIO RECEIVER PRODUCTION

Statistical Office of the United Nations, Publishing Service, New York, New York 10017 (800) 253-9646; *Statistical Yearbook.*

MYANMAR - RADIO RECEIVERS

St. Martin's Press, Inc., 175 Fifth Avenue, New York, New York 10010 (800) 221-7945; *The Statesman's Year-Book.*

MYANMAR - RAILWAYS

Europa Publications Limited, 18 Bedford Square, London, WC1B 3JN, England; *The Europa World Year Book.*

St. Martin's Press, Inc., 175 Fifth Avenue, New York, New York 10010 (800) 221-7945; *The Statesman's Year-Book.*

Statistical Office of the United Nations, Publishing Service, New York, New York 10017 (800) 253-9646; *Statistical Yearbook.*

MYANMAR - RAPESEED PRODUCTION - See MYANMAR - CROPS

MYANMAR - RELIGION

Central Intelligence Agency, Washington, D.C. 20505 (703) 482-1100,

www.cia.gov; *The World Factbook.*

M.E. Sharpe, 80 Business Park Drive, Armonk, New York 10504 (800) 541-6563; *The Illustrated Book of World Rankings.*

St. Martin's Press, Inc., 175 Fifth Avenue, New York, New York 10010 (800) 221-7945; *The Statesman's Year-Book.*

MYANMAR - RENT PRICES

International Labour Office, I.L.O. Publications, 1828 L Street, NW., Suite 801, Washington, D.C. 20036 (301) 638-3152; *Yearbook of Labour Statistics.*

MYANMAR - RETAIL TRADE

Euromonitor International, Inc., 122 South Michigan Avenue, Suite 1200, Chicago, Illinois 60603 (800) 577-EURO; *World Marketing Data and Statistics.*

MYANMAR - RICE - See MYANMAR - CROPS

MYANMAR - ROOT AND TUBER PRODUCTION - See MYANMAR - CROPS

MYANMAR - ROUNDWOOD PRODUCTION - See MYANMAR - FORESTRY AND FOREST PRODUCTS

MYANMAR - RUBBER PRODUCTION AND CONSUMPTION

International Rubber Study Group, York House, Eighth Floor, Empire Way, Wembley, London HA9 0PA, England; *Rubber Statistical Bulletin.*

M.E. Sharpe, 80 Business Park Drive, Armonk, New York 10504 (800) 541-6563; *The Illustrated Book of World Rankings.*

Statistical Office of the United Nations, Publishing Service, New York, New York 10017 (800) 253-9646; *Statistical Yearbook.*

MYANMAR - SALT PRODUCTION - See MYANMAR - MINING AND MINERAL PRODUCTS

MYANMAR - SAWNWOOD PRODUCTION - See MYANMAR - FORESTRY AND FOREST PRODUCTS

MYANMAR - SCIENCE AND TECHNOLOGY - EXPENDITURE FOR RESEARCH - See MYANMAR - SCIENTISTS, TECHNOLOGISTS AND ENGINEERS

MYANMAR - SCIENTISTS, TECHNOLOGISTS AND ENGINEERS

Statistical Office of the United Nations, Publishing Service, New York, New York 10017 (800) 253-9646; *Statistical Yearbook.*

MYANMAR - SENIOR CITIZENS

M.E. Sharpe, 80 Business Park Drive, Armonk, New York 10504 (800) 541-6563; *The Illustrated Book of World Rankings.*

MYANMAR - SESAME SEED PRODUCTION - See MYANMAR - CROPS

MYANMAR - SHEEP - See MYANMAR - LIVESTOCK AND POULTRY

MYANMAR - SILVER PRODUCTION AND CONSUMPTION - See MYANMAR - MINING AND MINERAL PRODUCTS

MYANMAR - SOCIAL DATA

Asian Development Bank, Post Office Box 789, Manila, 1099 Manila, Philippines; *Key Indicators of Developing Asian and Pacific Countries.*

M.E. Sharpe, 80 Business Park Drive, Armonk, New York 10504 (800) 541-6563; *The Illustrated Book of World Rankings.*

MYANMAR - SOCIAL SECURITY

Statistical Office of the United Nations, Publishing Service, New York, New York 10017 (800) 253-9646; *National Accounts Statistics.*

MYANMAR - SOYBEAN PRODUCTION - See MYANMAR - CROPS

MYANMAR - STATE BUDGET

Euromonitor International, Inc., 122 South Michigan Avenue, Suite 1200, Chicago, Illinois 60603 (800) 577-EURO; *International Marketing Data and Statistics.*

MYANMAR - STEEL - See MYANMAR - MINING AND MINERAL PRODUCTS

MYANMAR - STOCKS - COMMODITY - MARKET PRICE - INDEX

Food and Agricultural Organization of the United Nations (FAO), Via delle Terme di Caracalla, 00100 Rome, Italy (Telephone Number in U.S. (202) 653-2400); *The State of Food and Agriculture.*

MYANMAR - SUGAR PRODUCTION AND CONSUMPTION - See MYANMAR - CROPS

MYANMAR - TAXATION

Europa Publications Limited, 18 Bedford Square, London, WC1B 3JN, England; *The Europa World Year Book.*

International Road Federation, 2600 Virginia Avenue, NW., Washington, D.C. 20037 (202) 338-4641; *World Road Statistics.*

MYANMAR - TEAK EXPORTS

International Monetary Fund, 700

Nineteenth Street, NW, Washington, D.C. 20431 (202) 623-7000; *International Financial Statistics.*

MYANMAR - TELEGRAPH SERVICE

Statistical Office of the United Nations, Publishing Service, New York, New York 10017 (800) 253-9646; *Statistical Yearbook.*

MYANMAR - TELEPHONES IN USE

American Telephone and Telegraph Company, 26 Parsippany Road, Whippany, New Jersey 07981 (800) 222-0300; *The World's Telephones.*

Central Intelligence Agency, Washington, D.C. 20505 (703) 482-1100, www.cia.gov; *The World Factbook.*

The Economist Intelligence Unit (Asia) Limited, 10th Floor, Luk Kwok Centre, 72 Gloucester Road, Wanchai, Hong Kong (Phone Number in U.S. (800) 938-4685); *Asian Market Atlas.*

Europa Publications Limited, 18 Bedford Square, London, WC1B 3JN, England; *The Europa World Year Book.*

St. Martin's Press, Inc., 175 Fifth Avenue, New York, New York 10010 (800) 221-7945; *The Statesman's Year-Book.*

Statistical Office of the United Nations, Publishing Service, New York, New York 10017 (800) 253-9646; *Statistical Yearbook;* and *World Statistics Pocketbook.*

MYANMAR - TELEVISION BROADCASTING - See MYANMAR - BROADCASTING

MYANMAR - TEXTILE INDUSTRY

M.E. Sharpe, 80 Business Park Drive, Armonk, New York 10504 (800) 541-6563; *The Illustrated Book of World Rankings.*

Statistical Office of the United Nations, Publishing Service, New York, New York 10017 (800) 253-9646; *Statistical Yearbook.*

United Nations Conference on Trade and Development, Central Statistical Service, Palais des Nations, Geneva, Switzerland (Telephone in U.S. (800) 253-9646); *UNCTAD Commodity Yearbook.*

MYANMAR - TIN PRODUCTION - See MYANMAR - MINING AND MINERAL PRODUCTS

MYANMAR - TIRE (MOTOR VEHICLE) PRODUCTION

International Rubber Study Group, York House, Eighth Floor, Empire Way, Wembley, London HA9 0PA, England; *Rubber Statistical Bulletin.*

MYANMAR - TOBACCO PRODUCTION

M.E. Sharpe, 80 Business Park Drive, Armonk, New York 10504 (800) 541-6563; *The Illustrated Book of World Rankings.*

Statistical Office of the United Nations, Publishing Service, New York, New York 10017 (800) 253-9646; *Statistical Yearbook.*

MYANMAR - TOURISM

Euromonitor International, Inc., 122 South Michigan Avenue, Suite 1200, Chicago, Illinois 60603 (800) 577-EURO; *The World Economic Factbook;* and *World Marketing Data and Statistics.*

Europa Publications Limited, 18 Bedford Square, London, WC1B 3JN, England; *The Europa World Year Book.*

Federal Statistical Office, Gustav - Stresemann - Ring 11, D-6200 Wiesbaden, Germany; *Myanmar.*

M.E. Sharpe, 80 Business Park Drive, Armonk, New York 10504 (800) 541-6563; *The Illustrated Book of World Rankings.*

St. Martin's Press, Inc., 175 Fifth Avenue, New York, New York 10010 (800) 221-7945; *The Statesman's Year-Book*

MYANMAR - TRACTORS IN USE

Statistical Office of the United Nations, Publishing Service, New York, New York 10017 (800) 253-9646; *Statistical Yearbook.*

MYANMAR - TRADE - See MYANMAR - FOREIGN TRADE

MYANMAR - TRANSPORTATION AND COMMUNICATIONS

Central Intelligence Agency, Washington, D.C. 20505 (703) 482-1100, www.cia.gov; *The World Factbook.*

The Economist Intelligence Unit (Asia) Limited, 10th Floor, Luk Kwok Centre, 72 Gloucester Road, Wanchai, Hong Kong (Phone Number in U.S. (800) 938-4685); *Asian Market Atlas.*

Euromonitor International, Inc., 122 South Michigan Avenue, Suite 1200, Chicago, Illinois 60603 (800) 577-EURO; *International Marketing Data and Statistics;* and *World Marketing Data and Statistics.*

Europa Publications Limited, 18 Bedford Square, London, WC1B 3JN, England; *The Europa World Year Book.*

Federal Statistical Office, Gustav - Stresemann - Ring 11, D-6200 Wiesbaden, Germany; *Myanmar.*

M.E. Sharpe, 80 Business Park Drive,

Armonk, New York 10504 (800) 541-6563; *The Illustrated Book of World Rankings.*

St. Martin's Press, Inc., 175 Fifth Avenue, New York, New York 10010 (800) 221-7945; *The Statesman's Year-Book.*

Statistical Office of the United Nations, Publishing Service, New York, New York 10017 (800) 253-9646; *Human Development Report;* and *Statistical Yearbook for Asia and the Pacific.*

MYANMAR - TUNGSTEN PRODUCTION AND CONSUMPTION

Statistical Office of the United Nations, Publishing Service, New York, New York 10017 (800) 253-9646; *Statistical Yearbook.*

MYANMAR - TURKEYS - See MYANMAR - LIVESTOCK AND POULTRY

MYANMAR - UNEMPLOYMENT

Central Intelligence Agency, Washington, D.C. 20505 (703) 482-1100, www.cia.gov; *The World Factbook.*

Euromonitor International, Inc., 122 South Michigan Avenue, Suite 1200, Chicago, Illinois 60603 (800) 577-EURO; *International Marketing Data and Statistics.*

International Labour Office, I.L.O. Publications, 1828 L Street, NW., Suite 801, Washington, D.C. 20036 (301) 638-3152; *Yearbook of Labour Statistics.*

Statistical Office of the United Nations, Publishing Service, New York, New York 10017 (800) 253-9646; *Statistical Yearbook.*

MYANMAR - UTILITIES

Statistical Office of the United Nations, Publishing Service, New York, New York 10017 (800) 253-9646; *Electric Power in Asia and the Pacific.*

MYANMAR - VITAL STATISTICS

Euromonitor International, Inc., 122 South Michigan Avenue, Suite 1200, Chicago, Illinois 60603 (800) 577-EURO; *International Marketing Data and Statistics.*

St. Martin's Press, Inc., 175 Fifth Avenue, New York, New York 10010 (800) 221-7945; *The Statesman's Year-Book.*

Statistical Office of the United Nations, Publishing Service, New York, New York 10017 (800) 253-9646; *Statistical Yearbook.*

World Health Organization, Office of Publications, 20 Avenue Appia, CH-1211 Geneva 27, Switzerland (Telephone Number in U.S. (518) 436-9686); *World Health Statistics Annual.*

MYANMAR - WAGES

Federal Statistical Office, Gustav - Stresemann - Ring 11, D-6200 Wiesbaden, Germany; *Myanmar.*

International Labour Office, I.L.O. Publications, 1828 L Street, NW., Suite 801, Washington, D.C. 20036 (301) 638-3152; *Yearbook of Labour Statistics.*

Statistical Office of the United Nations, Publishing Service, New York, New York 10017 (800) 253-9646; *Statistical Yearbook for Asia and the Pacific.*

MYANMAR - WEATHER - See MYANMAR - CLIMATE

MYANMAR - WHEAT PRODUCTION - See MYANMAR - CROPS

MYANMAR - WHOLESALE PRICES - INDEX NUMBERS

Asian Development Bank, Post Office Box 789, Manila, 1099 Manila, Philippines; *Key Indicators of Developing Asian and Pacific Countries.*

MYANMAR - WINE PRODUCTION - See MYANMAR - BEVERAGES

MYANMAR - WOOL PRODUCTION - See MYANMAR - TEXTILE INDUSTRY

MYANMAR - YARN PRODUCTION - See MYANMAR - TEXTILE INDUSTRY

MYANMAR - ZINC ORE PRODUCTION AND CONSUMPTION - See MYANMAR - MINING AND MINERAL PRODUCTS

MYRINGOTOMY

U.S. Department of Health and Human Services, National Center for Health Statistics, 3700 East-West Highway, Hyattsville, Maryland 20782 (301) 436-8500, www.cdc.gov/nchs; *Advance Data, No. 296.*

N

Namibia - National Statistical Office

Central Statistical Office, National Planning Commission, Sixth Floor, Government Offices, Private Bag 13356, Windhoek, Namibia.

NAMIBIA - AGRICULTURE

Economist Intelligence Unit, 111 West 57th Street, New York, New York 10019 (800) 938-4685; *Namibia Country Report.*

Euromonitor International, Inc., 122 South Michigan Avenue, Suite 1200, Chicago, Illinois 60603 (800) 577-EURO; *World Marketing Data and Statistics.*

Europa Publications Limited, 18 Bedford Square, London, WC1B 3JN, England; *The Europa World Year Book.*

Food and Agricultural Organization of the United Nations (FAO) Via delle Terme di Caracalla, 00100 Rome, Italy (Telephone Number in U.S. (202) 653-2400); *The State of Food and Agriculture; and Trade Yearbook.*

St. Martin's Press, Inc., 175 Fifth Avenue, New York, New York 10010 (800) 221-7945; *The Statesman's Year-Book.*

Statistical Office of the United Nations, Publishing Service, New York, New York 10017 (800) 253-9646; *Industrial Commodity Statistics Yearbook; and Statistical Yearbook.*

United Nations Conference on Trade and Development, Central Statistical Service, Palais des Nations, Geneva, Switzerland (Telephone in U.S. (800) 253-9646); *UNCTAD Commodity Yearbook.*

United Nations Economic Commission for Africa, Africa Hall, Post Office Box 3001, Addis Ababa, Ethiopia (Telephone Number in U.S. (800) 253-9646); *African Statistical Yearbook.*

NAMIBIA - AIRLINE SERVICE

Europa Publications Limited, 18 Bedford Square, London, WC1B 3JN, England; *The Europa World Year Book.*

St. Martin's Press, Inc., 175 Fifth Avenue, New York, New York 10010 (800) 221-7945; *The Statesman's Year-Book.*

Statistical Office of the United Nations, Publishing Service, New York, New York 10017 (800) 253-9646; *Statistical Yearbook.*

NAMIBIA - AIRPORTS

Central Intelligence Agency, Washington, D.C. 20505 (703) 482-1100, www.cia.gov; *The World Factbook.*

NAMIBIA - ANIMAL HEALTH

Food and Agricultural Organization of the United Nations (FAO), Via delle Terme di Caracalla, 00100 Rome, Italy (Telephone Number in U.S. (202) 653-2400); *Animal Health Yearbook.*

NAMIBIA - AREA AND DENSITY OF POPULATION

Central Intelligence Agency, Washington, D.C. 20505 (703) 482-1100, www.cia.gov; *The World Factbook.*

Euromonitor International, Inc., 122 South Michigan Avenue, Suite 1200, Chicago, Illinois 60603 (800) 577-EURO; *The World Economic Factbook.*

Europa Publications Limited, 18 Bedford Square, London, WC1B 3JN, England; *The Europa World Year Book.*

Food and Agricultural Organization of the United Nations (FAO) Via delle Terme di Caracalla, 00100 Rome, Italy (Telephone Number in U.S. (202) 653-2400); *The State of Food and Agriculture.*

St. Martin's Press, Inc., 175 Fifth Avenue, New York, New York 10010 (800) 221-7945; *The Statesman's Year-Book.*

Statistical Office of the United Nations, Publishing Service, New York, New York 10017 (800) 253-9646; *Statistical Yearbook.*

United Nations Educational, Scientific and Cultural Organization (UNESCO), 7 Place de Fontenoy, F-75700 Paris, France (Telephone Number in U.S. (212) 963-5981); *Statistical Yearbook.*

The World Bank, 1818 H Street, NW, Washington, D.C. 20433 (202) 477-1234; *World Development Report.*

NAMIBIA - BALANCE OF PAYMENTS

The Economist Intelligence Unit, 111 West 57th Street, New York, New York 10019 (800) 938-4685; *The World Market Atlas.*

Europa Publications Limited, 18 Bedford Square, London, WC1B 3JN, England; *The Europa World Year Book.*

United Nations Conference on Trade and Development (UNCTAD), New York, New York 10017 (800) 253-9646; *Handbook of International Trade and Development Statistics.*

The World Bank, 1818 H Street, NW, Washington, D.C. 20433 (202) 477-1234; *World Development Report.*

NAMIBIA - BANKING

Euromonitor International, Inc., 122 South Michigan Avenue, Suite 1200, Chicago, Illinois 60603 (800) 577-EURO; *World Marketing Data and Statistics.*

St. Martin's Press, Inc., 175 Fifth Avenue, New York, New York 10010 (800) 221-7945; *The Statesman's Year-Book.*

NAMIBIA - BEER PRODUCTION - See NAMIBIA - BEVERAGES

NAMIBIA - BEVERAGES

Statistical Office of the United Nations, Publishing Service, New York, New York

10017 (800) 253-9646; *Statistical Yearbook.*

NAMIBIA - BIRTH RATES

Central Intelligence Agency, Washington, D.C. 20505 (703) 482-1100, www.cia.gov; *The World Factbook.*

Euromonitor International, Inc., 122 South Michigan Avenue, Suite 1200, Chicago, Illinois 60603 (800) 577-EURO; *International Marketing Data and Statistics;* and *The World Economic Factbook.*

Europa Publications Limited, 18 Bedford Square, London, WC1B 3JN, England; *The Europa World Year Book.*

Statistical Office of the United Nations, Publishing Service, New York, New York 10017 (800) 253-9646; *Demographic Yearbook;* and *Statistical Yearbook.*

NAMIBIA - BOOK PRODUCTION

Europa Publications Limited, 18 Bedford Square, London, WC1B 3JN, England; *The Europa World Year Book.*

United Nations Educational, Scientific and Cultural Organization (UNESCO), 7 Place de Fontenoy, F-75700 Paris, France (Telephone Number in U.S. (212) 963-5981); *Statistical Yearbook.*

NAMIBIA - BROADCASTING

Billboard Limited, Post Office Box 9027, 1006 AA Amsterdam, The Netherlands (Telephone Number in U.S. (212) 764-7300); *World Radio TV Handbook.*

Central Intelligence Agency, Washington, D.C. 20505 (703) 482-1100, www.cia.gov; *The World Factbook.*

Euromonitor International, Inc., 122 South Michigan Avenue, Suite 1200, Chicago, Illinois 60603 (800) 577-EURO; *World Marketing Data and Statistics.*

St. Martin's Press, Inc., 175 Fifth Avenue, New York, New York 10010 (800) 221-7945; *The Statesman's Year-Book.*

United Nations Educational, Scientific and Cultural Organization (UNESCO), 7 Place de Fontenoy, F-75700 Paris, France (Telephone Number in U.S. (212) 963-5981); *Statistical Yearbook.*

NAMIBIA - BUDGET

Central Intelligence Agency, Washington, D.C. 20505 (703) 482-1100, www.cia.gov; *The World Factbook.*

NAMIBIA - BUTTER PRODUCTION - See NAMIBIA - DAIRY PRODUCTS

NAMIBIA - CALORIE SUPPLY

Food and Agricultural Organization of the United Nations (FAO) Via delle Terme di Caracalla, 00100 Rome, Italy (Telephone Number in U.S. (202) 653-2400); *The State of Food and Agriculture.*

NAMIBIA - CATTLE - See NAMIBIA - LIVESTOCK AND POULTRY

NAMIBIA - CLIMATE

St. Martin's Press, Inc., 175 Fifth Avenue, New York, New York 10010 (800) 221-7945; *The Statesman's Year-Book.*

NAMIBIA - COMMERCE

St. Martin's Press, Inc., 175 Fifth Avenue, New York, New York 10010 (800) 221-7945; *The Statesman's Year-Book.*

NAMIBIA - CONSTRUCTION INDUSTRY

Statistical Office of the United Nations, Publishing Service, New York, New York 10017 (800) 253-9646; *Statistical Yearbook.*

United Nations Economic Commission for Africa, Africa Hall, Post Office Box 3001, Addis Ababa, Ethiopia (Telephone Number in U.S. (800) 253-9646); *African Statistical Yearbook.*

NAMIBIA - CONSUMER PRICE INDEX

Europa Publications Limited, 18 Bedford Square, London, WC1B 3JN, England; *The Europa World Year Book.*

Statistical Office of the United Nations, Publishing Service, New York, New York 10017 (800) 253-9646; *Statistical Yearbook.*

NAMIBIA - CONSUMER PRICES

Euromonitor International, Inc., 122 South Michigan Avenue, Suite 1200, Chicago, Illinois 60603 (800) 577-EURO; *World Marketing Data and Statistics.*

NAMIBIA - CONSUMPTION

The World Bank, 1818 H Street, NW, Washington, D.C. 20433 (202) 477-1234; *World Development Report.*

NAMIBIA - COPPER AND COPPER ORE PRODUCTION AND CONSUMPTION - See NAMIBIA - MINING AND MINERAL PRODUCTS

NAMIBIA - CORN PRODUCTION - See NAMIBIA - CROPS

NAMIBIA - CROPS

Europa Publications Limited, 18 Bedford Square, London, WC1B 3JN, England; *The Europa World Year Book.*

Food and Agricultural Organization of

the United Nations (FAO) Via delle Terme di Caracalla, 00100 Rome, Italy (Telephone Number in U.S. (202) 653-2400); *The State of Food and Agriculture;* and *Production Yearbook.*

St. Martin's Press, Inc., 175 Fifth Avenue, New York, New York 10010 (800) 221-7945; *The Statesman's Year-Book.*

Statistical Office of the United Nations, Publishing Service, New York, New York 10017 (800) 253-9646; *Industrial Commodity Statistics Yearbook;* and *Statistical Yearbook.*

United Nations Conference on Trade and Development, Central Statistical Service, Palais des Nations, Geneva, Switzerland (Telephone in U.S. (800) 253-9646); *UNCTAD Commodity Yearbook.*

United Nations Economic Commission for Africa, Africa Hall, Post Office Box 3001, Addis Ababa, Ethiopia (Telephone Number in U.S. (800) 253-9646); *African Statistical Yearbook.*

NAMIBIA - DAIRY PRODUCTS

Europa Publications Limited, 18 Bedford Square, London, WC1B 3JN, England; *The Europa World Year Book.*

Food and Agricultural Organization of the United Nations (FAO) Via delle Terme di Caracalla, 00100 Rome, Italy (Telephone Number in U.S. (202) 653-2400); *The State of Food and Agriculture.*

St. Martin's Press, Inc., 175 Fifth Avenue, New York, New York 10010 (800) 221-7945; *The Statesman's Year-Book.*

Statistical Office of the United Nations, Publishing Service, New York, New York 10017 (800) 253-9646; *Industrial Commodity Statistics Yearbook;* and *Statistical Yearbook.*

NAMIBIA - DEATH RATES - See NAMIBIA - MORTALITY

NAMIBIA - DEMOGRAPHY

The Economist Intelligence Unit, 111 West 57th Street, New York, New York 10019 (800) 938-4685; *The World Market Atlas.*

Euromonitor International, Inc., 122 South Michigan Avenue, Suite 1200, Chicago, Illinois 60603 (800) 577-EURO; *International Marketing Data and Statistics; The World Economic Factbook;* and *World Marketing Data and Statistics.*

Statistical Office of the United Nations, Publishing Service, New York, New York 10017 (800) 253-9646; *Demographic Yearbook;* and *Human Development*

Report.

NAMIBIA - DIAMOND PRODUCTION - See NAMIBIA - MINING AND MINERAL PRODUCTS

NAMIBIA - DIVORCE

Statistical Office of the United Nations, Publishing Service, New York, New York 10017 (800) 253-9646; *Demographic Yearbook;* and *Statistical Yearbook.*

NAMIBIA - ECONOMY

Central Intelligence Agency, Washington, D.C. 20505 (703) 482-1100, www.cia.gov; *The World Factbook.*

Economist Intelligence Unit, 111 West 57th Street, New York, New York 10019 (800) 938-4685; *Namibia Country Report.*

Euromonitor International, Inc., 122 South Michigan Avenue, Suite 1200, Chicago, Illinois 60603 (800) 577-EURO; *The World Economic Factbook;* and *World Marketing Data and Statistics.*

Europa Publications Limited, 18 Bedford Square, London, WC1B 3JN, England; *The Europa World Year Book.*

St. Martin's Press, Inc., 175 Fifth Avenue, New York, New York 10010 (800) 221-7945; *The Statesman's Year-Book.*

Statistical Office of the United Nations, Publishing Service, New York, New York 10017 (800) 253-9646; *World Statistics Pocketbook.*

The World Bank, 1818 H Street, NW, Washington, D.C. 20433 (202) 477-1234; *The World Bank Atlas;* and *World Development Report.*

NAMIBIA - EDUCATION

The Economist Intelligence Unit, 111 West 57th Street, New York, New York 10019 (800) 938-4685; *The World Market Atlas.*

Euromonitor International, Inc., 122 South Michigan Avenue, Suite 1200, Chicago, Illinois 60603 (800) 577-EURO; *International Marketing Data and Statistics;* and *World Marketing Data and Statistics.*

Europa Publications Limited, 18 Bedford Square, London, WC1B 3JN, England; *The Europa World Year Book.*

St. Martin's Press, Inc., 175 Fifth Avenue, New York, New York 10010 (800) 221-7945; *The Statesman's Year-Book.*

Statistical Office of the United Nations, Publishing Service, New York, New York 10017 (800) 253-9646; *Human*

Development Report.

United Nations Economic Commission for Africa, Africa Hall, Post Office Box 3001, Addis Ababa, Ethiopia (Telephone Number in U.S. (800) 253-9646); *African Statistical Yearbook.*

United Nations Educational, Scientific and Cultural Organization (UNESCO), 7 Place de Fontenoy, F-75700 Paris, France (Telephone Number in U.S. (212) 963-5981); *Statistical Yearbook.*

The World Bank, 1818 H Street, NW, Washington, D.C. 20433 (202) 477-1234; *World Development Report.*

NAMIBIA - EGG PRODUCTION AND CONSUMPTION - See NAMIBIA - DAIRY PRODUCTS

NAMIBIA - ELECTRICITY

Central Intelligence Agency, Washington, D.C. 20505 (703) 482-1100, www.cia.gov; *The World Factbook.*

St. Martin's Press, Inc., 175 Fifth Avenue, New York, New York 10010 (800) 221-7945; *The Statesman's Year-Book.*

Statistical Office of the United Nations, Publishing Service, New York, New York 10017 (800) 253-9646; *Energy Statistics Yearbook; Human Development Report;* and *Statistical Yearbook.*

United Nations Economic Commission for Africa, Africa Hall, Post Office Box 3001, Addis Ababa, Ethiopia (Telephone Number in U.S. (800) 253-9646); *African Statistical Yearbook.*

NAMIBIA - EMPLOYMENT

Euromonitor International, Inc., 122 South Michigan Avenue, Suite 1200, Chicago, Illinois 60603 (800) 577-EURO; *International Marketing Data and Statistics.*

Statistical Office of the United Nations, Publishing Service, New York, New York 10017 (800) 253-9646; *Statistical Yearbook.*

United Nations Economic Commission for Africa, Africa Hall, Post Office Box 3001, Addis Ababa, Ethiopia (Telephone Number in U.S. (800) 253-9646); *African Statistical Yearbook.*

NAMIBIA - ENERGY

Euromonitor International, Inc., 122 South Michigan Avenue, Suite 1200, Chicago, Illinois 60603 (800) 577-EURO; *International Marketing Data and Statistics; The World Economic Factbook;* and *World Marketing Data and Statistics.*

Food and Agricultural Organization of

the United Nations (FAO) Via delle Terme di Caracalla, 00100 Rome, Italy (Telephone Number in U.S. (202) 653-2400); *The State of Food and Agriculture.*

St. Martin's Press, Inc., 175 Fifth Avenue, New York, New York 10010 (800) 221-7945; *The Statesman's Year-Book.*

Statistical Office of the United Nations, Publishing Service, New York, New York 10017 (800) 253-9646; *Energy Statistics Yearbook; Human Development Report; World Statistics Pocketbook;* and *Statistical Yearbook.*

United Nations Economic Commission for Africa, Africa Hall, Post Office Box 3001, Addis Ababa, Ethiopia (Telephone Number in U.S. (800) 253-9646); *African Statistical Yearbook.*

The World Bank, 1818 H Street, NW, Washington, D.C. 20433 (202) 477-1234; *The World Bank Atlas;* and *World Development Report.*

NAMIBIA - ENVIRONMENT

Economist Intelligence Unit, 111 West 57th Street, New York, New York 10019 (800) 938-4685; *Namibia Country Report.*

Statistical Office of the United Nations, Publishing Service, New York, New York 10017 (800) 253-9646; *Statistical Yearbook;* and *World Statistics Pocketbook.*

NAMIBIA - EXCHANGE RATES

Central Intelligence Agency, Washington, D.C. 20505 (703) 482-1100, www.cia.gov; *The World Factbook.*

Euromonitor International, Inc., 122 South Michigan Avenue, Suite 1200, Chicago, Illinois 60603 (800) 577-EURO; *International Marketing Data and Statistics;* and *The World Economic Factbook.*

Europa Publications Limited, 18 Bedford Square, London, WC1B 3JN, England; *The Europa World Year Book.*

Statistical Office of the United Nations, Publishing Service, New York, New York 10017 (800) 253-9646; *Statistical Yearbook;* and *World Statistics Pocketbook.*

NAMIBIA - EXPORTS

Central Intelligence Agency, Washington, D.C. 20505 (703) 482-1100, www.cia.gov; *The World Factbook.*

The Economist Intelligence Unit, 111 West 57th Street, New York, New York 10019 (800) 938-4685; *Namibia Country Report;* and *The World Market Atlas.*

Euromonitor International, Inc., 122

South Michigan Avenue, Suite 1200, Chicago, Illinois 60603 (800) 577-EURO; *International Marketing Data and Statistics;* and *The World Economic Factbook.*

Europa Publications Limited, 18 Bedford Square, London, WC1B 3JN, England; *The Europa World Year Book.*

Food and Agricultural Organization of the United Nations (FAO) Via delle Terme di Caracalla, 00100 Rome, Italy (Telephone Number in U.S. (202) 653-2400); *The State of Food and Agriculture.*

International Monetary Fund, 700 Nineteenth Street, NW, Washington, D.C. 20431 (202) 623-7000; *Direction of Trade Statistics.*

St. Martin's Press, Inc., 175 Fifth Avenue, New York, New York 10010 (800) 221-7945; *The Statesman's Year-Book.*

Statistical Office of the United Nations, Publishing Service, New York, New York 10017 (800) 253-9646; *International Trade Statistics Yearbook.*

United Nations Conference on Trade and Development (UNCTAD), New York, New York 10017 (800) 253-9646; *Handbook of International Trade and Development Statistics.*

The World Bank, 1818 H Street, NW, Washington, D.C. 20433 (202) 477-1234; *World Development Report.*

NAMIBIA - EXTERNAL INDEBTEDNESS

The World Bank, 1818 H Street, NW, Washington, D.C. 20433 (202) 477-1234; *World Development Report.*

NAMIBIA - EXTERNAL TRADE

Euromonitor International, Inc., 122 South Michigan Avenue, Suite 1200, Chicago, Illinois 60603 (800) 577-EURO; *World Marketing Data and Statistics.*

Food and Agricultural Organization of the United Nations (FAO) Via delle Terme di Caracalla, 00100 Rome, Italy (Telephone Number in U.S. (202) 653-2400); *The State of Food and Agriculture;* and *Trade Yearbook.*

Statistical Office of the United Nations, Publishing Service, New York, New York 10017 (800) 253-9646; *Statistical Yearbook.*

NAMIBIA - FARM CROPS - See NAMIBIA - CROPS

NAMIBIA - FERTILITY RATES

Central Intelligence Agency, Washington, D.C. 20505 (703) 482-1100, www.cia.gov; *The World Factbook.*

Statistical Office of the United Nations, Publishing Service, New York, New York 10017 (800) 253-9646; *Human Development Report.*

The World Bank, 1818 H Street, NW, Washington, D.C. 20433 (202) 477-1234; *The World Bank Atlas;* and *World Development Report.*

NAMIBIA - FERTILIZER

Food and Agricultural Organization of the United Nations (FAO) Via delle Terme di Caracalla, 00100 Rome, Italy (Telephone Number in U.S. (202) 653-2400); *The State of Food and Agriculture.*

Statistical Office of the United Nations, Publishing Service, New York, New York 10017 (800) 253-9646; *Industrial Commodity Statistics Yearbook;* and *Statistical Yearbook.*

NAMIBIA - FETAL MORTALITY - See NAMIBIA - MORTALITY

NAMIBIA - FINANCE

Economist Intelligence Unit, 111 West 57th Street, New York, New York 10019 (800) 938-4685; *Namibia Country Report.*

Europa Publications Limited, 18 Bedford Square, London, WC1B 3JN, England; *The Europa World Year Book.*

St. Martin's Press, Inc., 175 Fifth Avenue, New York, New York 10010 (800) 221-7945; *The Statesman's Year-Book.*

NAMIBIA - FISHERIES

Europa Publications Limited, 18 Bedford Square, London, WC1B 3JN, England; *The Europa World Year Book.*

Food and Agricultural Organization of the United Nations (FAO) Via delle Terme di Caracalla, 00100 Rome, Italy (Telephone Number in U.S. (202) 653-2400); *The State of Food and Agriculture;* and *Yearbook of Fishery Statistics.*

St. Martin's Press, Inc., 175 Fifth Avenue, New York, New York 10010 (800) 221-7945; *The Statesman's Year-Book.*

Statistical Office of the United Nations, Publishing Service, New York, New York 10017 (800) 253-9646; *Industrial Commodity Statistics Yearbook;* and *Statistical Yearbook.*

United Nations Conference on Trade and Development, Central Statistical Service, Palais des Nations, Geneva, Switzerland (Telephone in U.S. (800) 253-9646); *UNCTAD Commodity Yearbook.*

United Nations Economic Commission for Africa, Africa Hall, Post Office Box 3001, Addis Ababa, Ethiopia (Telephone Number in U.S. (800) 253-9646); *African Statistical Yearbook.*

NAMIBIA - FOOD

Food and Agricultural Organization of the United Nations (FAO), Via delle Terme di Caracalla, 00100 Rome, Italy (Telephone Number in U.S. (202) 653-2400); *Production Yearbook;* and *The State of Food and Agriculture.*

Statistical Office of the United Nations, Publishing Service, New York, New York 10017 (800) 253-9646; *Human Development Report;* and *Industrial Commodity Statistics Yearbook.*

United Nations Conference on Trade and Development, Central Statistical Service, Palais des Nations, Geneva, Switzerland (Telephone in U.S. (800) 253-9646); *UNCTAD Commodity Yearbook.*

NAMIBIA - FOREIGN TRADE

Economist Intelligence Unit, 111 West 57th Street, New York, New York 10019 (800) 938-4685; *Namibia Country Report.*

Euromonitor International, Inc., 122 South Michigan Avenue, Suite 1200, Chicago, Illinois 60603 (800) 577-EURO; *The World Economic Factbook.*

St. Martin's Press, Inc., 175 Fifth Avenue, New York, New York 10010 (800) 221-7945; *The Statesman's Year-Book.*

Statistical Office of the United Nations, Publishing Service, New York, New York 10017 (800) 253-9646; *International Trade Statistics Yearbook;* and *Statistical Yearbook.*

United Nations Conference on Trade and Development, Central Statistical Service, Palais des Nations, Geneva, Switzerland (Telephone in U.S. (800) 253-9646); *UNCTAD Commodity Yearbook.*

The World Bank, 1818 H Street, NW, Washington, D.C. 20433 (202) 477-1234; *World Development Report.*

NAMIBIA - FORESTRY AND FOREST PRODUCTS

Food and Agricultural Organization of the United Nations (FAO) Via delle Terme di Caracalla, 00100 Rome, Italy (Telephone Number in U.S. (202) 653-2400); *The State of Food and Agriculture.*

St. Martin's Press, Inc., 175 Fifth Avenue, New York, New York 10010 (800) 221-7945; *The Statesman's Year-Book.*

Statistical Office of the United Nations, Publishing Service, New York, New York 10017 (800) 253-9646; *Industrial Commodity Statistics Yearbook;* and *Statistical Yearbook.*

United Nations Conference on Trade and Development, Central Statistical Service, Palais des Nations, Geneva, Switzerland (Telephone in U.S. (800) 253-9646); *UNCTAD Commodity Yearbook.*

United Nations Economic Commission for Africa, Africa Hall, Post Office Box 3001, Addis Ababa, Ethiopia (Telephone Number in U.S. (800) 253-9646); *African Statistical Yearbook.*

United Nations Educational, Scientific and Cultural Organization (UNESCO), 7 Place de Fontenoy, F-75700 Paris, France (Telephone Number in U.S. (212) 963-5981); *Statistical Yearbook.*

The World Bank, 1818 H Street, NW, Washington, D.C. 20433 (202) 477-1234; *World Development Report.*

NAMIBIA - GENERAL MORTALITY - See NAMIBIA - MORTALITY

NAMIBIA - GOVERNMENT

Central Intelligence Agency, Washington, D.C. 20505 (703) 482-1100, www.cia.gov; *The World Factbook.*

Europa Publications Limited, 18 Bedford Square, London, WC1B 3JN, England; *The Europa World Year Book.*

St. Martin's Press, Inc., 175 Fifth Avenue, New York, New York 10010 (800) 221-7945; *The Statesman's Year-Book.*

Statistical Office of the United Nations, Publishing Service, New York, New York 10017 (800) 253-9646; *Statistical Yearbook.*

The World Bank, 1818 H Street, NW, Washington, D.C. 20433 (202) 477-1234; *World Development Report.*

NAMIBIA - GRAIN PRODUCTION - See NAMIBIA - CROPS

NAMIBIA - GROSS DOMESTIC PRODUCT

The Economist Intelligence Unit, 111 West 57th Street, New York, New York 10019 (800) 938-4685; *Namibia Country Report;* and *The World Market Atlas.*

Euromonitor International, Inc., 122 South Michigan Avenue, Suite 1200, Chicago, Illinois 60603 (800) 577-EURO; *International Marketing Data and Statistics;* and *The World Economic Factbook.*

Europa Publications Limited, 18 Bedford Square, London, WC1B 3JN,

England; *The Europa World Year Book.*

Statistical Office of the United Nations, Publishing Service, New York, New York 10017 (800) 253-9646; *Human Development Report; National Accounts Statistics;* and *Statistical Yearbook.*

United Nations Economic Commission for Africa, Africa Hall, Post Office Box 3001, Addis Ababa, Ethiopia (Telephone Number in U.S. (800) 253-9646); *African Statistical Yearbook.*

The World Bank, 1818 H Street, NW, Washington, D.C. 20433 (202) 477-1234; *World Development Report.*

NAMIBIA - GROSS NATIONAL PRODUCT

Europa Publications Limited, 18 Bedford Square, London, WC1B 3JN, England; *The Europa World Year Book.*

St. Martin's Press, Inc., 175 Fifth Avenue, New York, New York 10010 (800) 221-7945; *The Statesman's Year-Book.*

The World Bank, 1818 H Street, NW, Washington, D.C. 20433 (202) 477-1234; *The World Bank Atlas;* and *World Development Report.*

NAMIBIA - HEALTH

Euromonitor International, Inc., 122 South Michigan Avenue, Suite 1200, Chicago, Illinois 60603 (800) 577-EURO; *World Marketing Data and Statistics.*

St. Martin's Press, Inc., 175 Fifth Avenue, New York, New York 10010 (800) 221-7945; *The Statesman's Year-Book.*

Statistical Office of the United Nations, Publishing Service, New York, New York 10017 (800) 253-9646; *Human Development Report;* and *Statistical Yearbook.*

United Nations Children's Fund (UNICEF), 3 United Nations Plaza, New York, New York 10017 (800) 253-9646; *State of the World's Children.*

United Nations Economic Commission for Africa, Africa Hall, Post Office Box 3001, Addis Ababa, Ethiopia (Telephone Number in U.S. (800) 253-9646); *African Statistical Yearbook.*

The World Bank, 1818 H Street, NW, Washington, D.C. 20433 (202) 477-1234; *World Development Report.*

NAMIBIA - HIDE PRODUCTION

Food and Agricultural Organization of the United Nations (FAO), Via delle Terme di Caracalla, 00100 Rome, Italy (Telephone Number in U.S. (202) 653-2400);

Production Yearbook.

NAMIBIA - HIGHWAYS

Central Intelligence Agency, Washington, D.C. 20505 (703) 482-1100, www.cia.gov; *The World Factbook.*

St. Martin's Press, Inc., 175 Fifth Avenue, New York, New York 10010 (800) 221-7945; *The Statesman's Year-Book.*

NAMIBIA - HORSES - See NAMIBIA - LIVESTOCK AND POULTRY

NAMIBIA - HOUSING AND HOUSING UNITS

Euromonitor International, Inc., 122 South Michigan Avenue, Suite 1200, Chicago, Illinois 60603 (800) 577-EURO; *World Marketing Data and Statistics.*

NAMIBIA - ILLITERATE POPULATION

Central Intelligence Agency, Washington, D.C. 20505 (703) 482-1100, www.cia.gov; *The World Factbook.*

The Economist Intelligence Unit, 111 West 57th Street, New York, New York 10019 (800) 938-4685; *The World Market Atlas.*

Euromonitor International, Inc., 122 South Michigan Avenue, Suite 1200, Chicago, Illinois 60603 (800) 577-EURO; *The World Economic Factbook.*

Statistical Office of the United Nations, Publishing Service, New York, New York 10017 (800) 253-9646; *Human Development Report.*

United Nations Educational, Scientific and Cultural Organization (UNESCO), 7 Place de Fontenoy, F-75700 Paris, France (Telephone Number in U.S. (212) 963-5981); *Statistical Yearbook.*

NAMIBIA - IMPORTS

Central Intelligence Agency, Washington, D.C. 20505 (703) 482-1100, www.cia.gov; *The World Factbook.*

The Economist Intelligence Unit, 111 West 57th Street, New York, New York 10019 (800) 938-4685; *Namibia Country Report;* and *The World Market Atlas.*

Euromonitor International, Inc., 122 South Michigan Avenue, Suite 1200, Chicago, Illinois 60603 (800) 577-EURO; *International Marketing Data and Statistics;* and *The World Economic Factbook.*

Europa Publications Limited, 18 Bedford Square, London, WC1B 3JN, England; *The Europa World Year Book.*

Food and Agricultural Organization of

the United Nations (FAO) Via delle Terme di Caracalla, 00100 Rome, Italy (Telephone Number in U.S. (202) 653-2400); *The State of Food and Agriculture.*

International Monetary Fund, 700 Nineteenth Street, NW, Washington, D.C. 20431 (202) 623-7000; *Direction of Trade Statistics.*

St. Martin's Press, Inc., 175 Fifth Avenue, New York, New York 10010 (800) 221-7945; *The Statesman's Year-Book.*

Statistical Office of the United Nations, Publishing Service, New York, New York 10017 (800) 253-9646; *International Trade Statistics Yearbook;* and *Statistical Yearbook.*

United Nations Conference on Trade and Development (UNCTAD), New York, New York 10017 (800) 253-9646; *Handbook of International Trade and Development Statistics.*

The World Bank, 1818 H Street, NW, Washington, D.C. 20433 (202) 477-1234; *World Development Report.*

NAMIBIA - INDUSTRY

Central Intelligence Agency, Washington, D.C. 20505 (703) 482-1100, www.cia.gov; *The World Factbook.*

Economist Intelligence Unit, 111 West 57th Street, New York, New York 10019 (800) 938-4685; *Namibia Country Report.*

Euromonitor International, Inc., 122 South Michigan Avenue, Suite 1200, Chicago, Illinois 60603 (800) 577-EURO; *The World Economic Factbook;* and *World Marketing Data and Statistics.*

Europa Publications Limited, 18 Bedford Square, London, WC1B 3JN, England; *The Europa World Year Book.*

St. Martin's Press, Inc., 175 Fifth Avenue, New York, New York 10010 (800) 221-7945; *The Statesman's Year-Book.*

Statistical Office of the United Nations, Publishing Service, New York, New York 10017 (800) 253-9646; *Industrial Commodity Statistics Yearbook;* and *Statistical Yearbook.*

United Nations Economic Commission for Africa, Africa Hall, Post Office Box 3001, Addis Ababa, Ethiopia (Telephone Number in U.S. (800) 253-9646); *African Statistical Yearbook.*

World Intellectual Property Organization, 34 Chemin des Colombettes, CH-1211 Geneva 20, Switzerland; *Industrial Property Statistics.*

NAMIBIA - INFANT AND MATERNAL MORTALITY - See NAMIBIA - MORTALITY

NAMIBIA - INTERNAL TRADE

Statistical Office of the United Nations, Publishing Service, New York, New York 10017 (800) 253-9646; *Statistical Yearbook.*

NAMIBIA - LABOR

Central Intelligence Agency, Washington, D.C. 20505 (703) 482-1100, www.cia.gov; *The World Factbook.*

Euromonitor International, Inc., 122 South Michigan Avenue, Suite 1200, Chicago, Illinois 60603 (800) 577-EURO; *International Marketing Data and Statistics;* and *World Marketing Data and Statistics.*

Food and Agricultural Organization of the United Nations (FAO) Via delle Terme di Caracalla, 00100 Rome, Italy (Telephone Number in U.S. (202) 653-2400); *The State of Food and Agriculture.*

St. Martin's Press, Inc., 175 Fifth Avenue, New York, New York 10010 (800) 221-7945; *The Statesman's Year-Book.*

Statistical Office of the United Nations, Publishing Service, New York, New York 10017 (800) 253-9646; *Human Development Report;* and *Statistical Yearbook.*

The World Bank, 1818 H Street, NW, Washington, D.C. 20433 (202) 477-1234; *The World Bank Atlas;* and *World Development Report.*

NAMIBIA - LAND USE

Central Intelligence Agency, Washington, D.C. 20505 (703) 482-1100, www.cia.gov; *The World Factbook.*

Euromonitor International, Inc., 122 South Michigan Avenue, Suite 1200, Chicago, Illinois 60603 (800) 577-EURO; *International Marketing Data and Statistics.*

Food and Agricultural Organization of the United Nations (FAO), Via delle Terme di Caracalla, 00100 Rome, Italy (Telephone Number in U.S. (202) 653-2400); *Production Yearbook.*

The World Bank, 1818 H Street, NW, Washington, D.C. 20433 (202) 477-1234; *World Development Report.*

NAMIBIA - LEAD AND LEAD ORE PRODUCTION AND CONSUMPTION - See NAMIBIA - MINING AND MINERAL PRODUCTS

NAMIBIA - LIBRARIES

United Nations Educational, Scientific

and Cultural Organization (UNESCO), 7 Place de Fontenoy, F-75700 Paris, France (Telephone Number in U.S. (212) 963-5981); *Statistical Yearbook.*

NAMIBIA - LIFE EXPECTANCY

Central Intelligence Agency, Washington, D.C. 20505 (703) 482-1100, www.cia.gov; *The World Factbook.*

Euromonitor International, Inc., 122 South Michigan Avenue, Suite 1200, Chicago, Illinois 60603 (800) 577-EURO; *The World Economic Factbook.*

Statistical Office of the United Nations, Publishing Service, New York, New York 10017 (800) 253-9646; *Demographic Yearbook; World Statistics Pocketbook;* and *Human Development Report.*

The World Bank, 1818 H Street, NW, Washington, D.C. 20433 (202) 477-1234; *The World Bank Atlas;* and *World Development Report.*

NAMIBIA - LITERACY RATE

Euromonitor International, Inc., 122 South Michigan Avenue, Suite 1200, Chicago, Illinois 60603 (800) 577-EURO; *World Marketing Data and Statistics.*

NAMIBIA - LIVESTOCK AND POULTRY

Europa Publications Limited, 18 Bedford Square, London, WC1B 3JN, England; *The Europa World Year Book.*

Food and Agricultural Organization of the United Nations (FAO), Via delle Terme di Caracalla, 00100 Rome, Italy (Telephone Number in U.S. (202) 653-2400); *Production Yearbook;* and *The State of Food and Agriculture.*

St. Martin's Press, Inc., 175 Fifth Avenue, New York, New York 10010 (800) 221-7945; *The Statesman's Year-Book.*

Statistical Office of the United Nations, Publishing Service, New York, New York 10017 (800) 253-9646; *Industrial Commodity Statistics Yearbook;* and *Statistical Yearbook.*

United Nations Conference on Trade and Development, Central Statistical Service, Palais des Nations, Geneva, Switzerland (Telephone in U.S. (800) 253-9646); *UNCTAD Commodity Yearbook.*

United Nations Economic Commission for Africa, Africa Hall, Post Office Box 3001, Addis Ababa, Ethiopia (Telephone Number in U.S. (800) 253-9646); *African Statistical Yearbook.*

NAMIBIA - LIVING LEVELS - See NAMIBIA - LIFE EXPECTANCY

NAMIBIA - MACHINERY

Statistical Office of the United Nations, Publishing Service, New York, New York 10017 (800) 253-9646; *Industrial Commodity Statistics Yearbook.*

NAMIBIA - MAIL - NUMBER OF PIECES SENT OR RECEIVED

Statistical Office of the United Nations, Publishing Service, New York, New York 10017 (800) 253-9646; *Statistical Yearbook.*

NAMIBIA - MANGANESE ORE PRODUCTION AND CONSUMPTION -See NAMIBIA - MINING AND MINERAL PRODUCTS

NAMIBIA - MANUFACTURING

Statistical Office of the United Nations, Publishing Service, New York, New York 10017 (800) 253-9646; *Industrial Commodity Statistics Yearbook;* and *Statistical Yearbook.*

United Nations Economic Commission for Africa, Africa Hall, Post Office Box 3001, Addis Ababa, Ethiopia (Telephone Number in U.S. (800) 253-9646); *African Statistical Yearbook.*

NAMIBIA - MARRIAGE RATES

Statistical Office of the United Nations, Publishing Service, New York, New York 10017 (800) 253-9646; *Demographic Yearbook;* and *Statistical Yearbook.*

NAMIBIA - MEAT PRODUCTION - ALL TYPES OF MEAT AND POULTRY

Food and Agricultural Organization of the United Nations (FAO), Via delle Terme di Caracalla, 00100 Rome, Italy (Telephone Number in U.S. (202) 653-2400); *Production Yearbook;* and *The State of Food and Agriculture.*

Statistical Office of the United Nations, Publishing Service, New York, New York 10017 (800) 253-9646; *Statistical Yearbook.*

NAMIBIA - MERCHANT SHIPPING

Europa Publications Limited, 18 Bedford Square, London, WC1B 3JN, England; *The Europa World Year Book.*

St. Martin's Press, Inc., 175 Fifth Avenue, New York, New York 10010 (800) 221-7945; *The Statesman's Year-Book.*

Statistical Office of the United Nations, Publishing Service, New York, New York 10017 (800) 253-9646; *Statistical Yearbook.*

NAMIBIA - MILITARY

Central Intelligence Agency,

Washington, D.C. 20505 (703) 482-1100, www.cia.gov; *The World Factbook.*

Euromonitor International, Inc., 122 South Michigan Avenue, Suite 1200, Chicago, Illinois 60603 (800) 577-EURO; *World Marketing Data and Statistics.*

The International Institute for Strategic Studies, 23 Tavistock Street, London WC2E 7NQ, England; *The Military Balance.*

St. Martin's Press, Inc., 175 Fifth Avenue, New York, New York 10010 (800) 221-7945; *The Statesman's Year-Book.*

Statistical Office of the United Nations, Publishing Service, New York, New York 10017 (800) 253-9646; *Human Development Report.*

NAMIBIA - MILK PRODUCTION - See NAMIBIA - DAIRY PRODUCTS

NAMIBIA - MILLET PRODUCTION - See NAMIBIA - CROPS

NAMIBIA - MINING AND MINERAL PRODUCTS

Commodity Research Bureau, Inc., 30 South Wacker Drive, Chicago Illinois 60606 (312) 454-1801; *Commodity Year Book.*

Europa Publications Limited, 18 Bedford Square, London, WC1B 3JN, England; *The Europa World Year Book.*

St. Martin's Press, Inc., 175 Fifth Avenue, New York, New York 10010 (800) 221-7945; *The Statesman's Year-Book.*

Statistical Office of the United Nations, Publishing Service, New York, New York 10017 (800) 253-9646; *Energy Statistics Yearbook; Industrial Commodity Statistics Yearbook;* and *Statistical Yearbook.*

United Nations Conference on Trade and Development, Central Statistical Service, Palais des Nations, Geneva, Switzerland (Telephone in U.S. (800) 253-9646); *UNCTAD Commodity Yearbook.*

United Nations Economic Commission for Africa, Africa Hall, Post Office Box 3001, Addis Ababa, Ethiopia (Telephone Number in U.S. (800) 253-9646); *African Statistical Yearbook.*

NAMIBIA - MONEY SUPPLY

Economist Intelligence Unit, 111 West 57th Street, New York, New York 10019 (800) 938-4685; *Namibia Country Report.*

Europa Publications Limited, 18 Bedford Square, London, WC1B 3JN, England; *The Europa World Year Book.*

NAMIBIA - MONUMENTS AND HISTORICAL

SITES

United Nations Educational, Scientific and Cultural Organization (UNESCO), 7 Place de Fontenoy, F-75700 Paris, France (Telephone Number in U.S. (212) 963-5981); *Statistical Yearbook.*

NAMIBIA - MORTALITY

Central Intelligence Agency, Washington, D.C. 20505 (703) 482-1100, www.cia.gov; *The World Factbook.*

Euromonitor International, Inc., 122 South Michigan Avenue, Suite 1200, Chicago, Illinois 60603 (800) 577-EURO; *International Marketing Data and Statistics; The World Economic Factbook;* and *World Marketing Data and Statistics.*

Europa Publications Limited, 18 Bedford Square, London, WC1B 3JN, England; *The Europa World Year Book.*

Statistical Office of the United Nations, Publishing Service, New York, New York 10017 (800) 253-9646; *Demographic Yearbook; Human Development Report; World Statistics Pocketbook;* and *Statistical Yearbook.*

The World Bank, 1818 H Street, NW, Washington, D.C. 20433 (202) 477-1234; *The World Bank Atlas;* and *World Development Report.*

NAMIBIA - MOTION PICTURES

Statistical Office of the United Nations, Publishing Service, New York, New York 10017 (800) 253-9646; *Statistical Yearbook.*

United Nations Educational, Scientific and Cultural Organization (UNESCO), 7 Place de Fontenoy, F-75700 Paris, France (Telephone Number in U.S. (212) 963-5981); *Statistical Yearbook.*

NAMIBIA - MOTOR VEHICLE PRODUCTION

Europa Publications Limited, 18 Bedford Square, London, WC1B 3JN, England; *The Europa World Year Book.*

Statistical Office of the United Nations, Publishing Service, New York, New York 10017 (800) 253-9646; *Statistical Yearbook.*

NAMIBIA - MULES - See NAMIBIA - LIVESTOCK AND POULTRY

NAMIBIA - MUSEUMS

United Nations Educational, Scientific and Cultural Organization (UNESCO), 7 Place de Fontenoy, F-75700 Paris, France (Telephone Number in U.S. (212) 963-5981); *Statistical Yearbook.*

NAMIBIA - NATALITY - See NAMIBIA -

BIRTH RATES

NAMIBIA - NATIONAL ACCOUNTS

Europa Publications Limited, 18 Bedford Square, London, WC1B 3JN, England; *The Europa World Year Book.*

Statistical Office of the United Nations, Publishing Service, New York, New York 10017 (800) 253-9646; *National Accounts Statistics;* and *Statistical Yearbook.*

United Nations Economic Commission for Africa, Africa Hall, Post Office Box 3001, Addis Ababa, Ethiopia (Telephone Number in U.S. (800) 253-9646); *African Statistical Yearbook.*

NAMIBIA - NATIONAL INCOME

Statistical Office of the United Nations, Publishing Service, New York, New York 10017 (800) 253-9646; *Statistical Yearbook.*

NAMIBIA - NATIONAL PRODUCT

Statistical Office of the United Nations, Publishing Service, New York, New York 10017 (800) 253-9646; *Statistical Yearbook.*

NAMIBIA - NEWSPAPER PRODUCTION - See NAMIBIA - FORESTRY AND FOREST PRODUCTS

NAMIBIA - PATENTS, TRADEMARKS AND SERVICE MARKS

Statistical Office of the United Nations, Publishing Service, New York, New York 10017 (800) 253-9646; *Statistical Yearbook.*

World Intellectual Property Organization, 34 Chemin des Colombettes, CH-1211 Geneva 20, Switzerland; *Industrial Property Statistics.*

NAMIBIA - PERIODICALS

United Nations Educational, Scientific and Cultural Organization (UNESCO), 7 Place de Fontenoy, F-75700 Paris, France (Telephone Number in U.S. (212) 963-5981); *Statistical Yearbook.*

NAMIBIA - PESTICIDE USE

Food and Agricultural Organization of the United Nations (FAO) Via delle Terme di Caracalla, 00100 Rome, Italy (Telephone Number in U.S. (202) 653-2400); *The State of Food and Agriculture.*

NAMIBIA - PETROLEUM INDUSTRY

Food and Agricultural Organization of the United Nations (FAO) Via delle Terme di Caracalla, 00100 Rome, Italy (Telephone Number in U.S. (202) 653-2400); *The State of Food and Agriculture.*

Statistical Office of the United Nations, Publishing Service, New York, New York 10017 (800) 253-9646; *Energy Statistics Yearbook; Industrial Commodity Statistics Yearbook;* and *Statistical Yearbook.*

United Nations Conference on Trade and Development, Central Statistical Service, Palais des Nations, Geneva, Switzerland (Telephone in U.S. (800) 253-9646); *UNCTAD Commodity Yearbook.*

NAMIBIA - PIGS - See NAMIBIA - LIVESTOCK AND POULTRY

NAMIBIA - POPULATION

Central Intelligence Agency, Washington, D.C. 20505 (703) 482-1100, www.cia.gov; *The World Factbook.*

The Economist Intelligence Unit, 111 West 57th Street, New York, New York 10019 (800) 938-4685; *Namibia Country Report;* and *The World Market Atlas.*

Euromonitor International, Inc., 122 South Michigan Avenue, Suite 1200, Chicago, Illinois 60603 (800) 577-EURO; *International Marketing Data and Statistics;* and *The World Economic Factbook.*

Europa Publications Limited, 18 Bedford Square, London, WC1B 3JN, England; *The Europa World Year Book.*

Food and Agricultural Organization of the United Nations (FAO), Via delle Terme di Caracalla, 00100 Rome, Italy (Telephone Number in U.S. (202) 653-2400); *Production Yearbook.*

St. Martin's Press, Inc., 175 Fifth Avenue, New York, New York 10010 (800) 221-7945; *The Statesman's Year-Book.*

Statistical Office of the United Nations, Publishing Service, New York, New York 10017 (800) 253-9646; *Demographic Yearbook; Human Development Report; World Statistics Pocketbook;* and *Statistical Yearbook.*

United Nations Educational, Scientific and Cultural Organization (UNESCO), 7 Place de Fontenoy, F-75700 Paris, France (Telephone Number in U.S. (212) 963-5981); *Statistical Yearbook.*

The World Bank, 1818 H Street, NW, Washington, D.C. 20433 (202) 477-1234; *The World Bank Atlas;* and *World Development Report.*

World Health Organization, Office of Publications, 20 Avenue Appia, CH-1211 Geneva 27, Switzerland (Telephone Number in U.S. (518) 436-9686); *World Health Statistics Annual.*

NAMIBIA - POST OFFICES

St. Martin's Press, Inc., 175 Fifth Avenue, New York, New York 10010 (800) 221-7945; *The Statesman's Year-Book.*

NAMIBIA - PRICES

Food and Agricultural Organization of the United Nations (FAO), Via delle Terme di Caracalla, 00100 Rome, Italy (Telephone Number in U.S. (202) 653-2400); *Production Yearbook;* and *The State of Food and Agriculture.*

NAMIBIA - RADIO BROADCASTING - See NAMIBIA - BROADCASTING

NAMIBIA - RADIO RECEIVERS

St. Martin's Press, Inc., 175 Fifth Avenue, New York, New York 10010 (800) 221-7945; *The Statesman's Year-Book.*

Statistical Office of the United Nations, Publishing Service, New York, New York 10017 (800) 253-9646; *Statistical Yearbook.*

NAMIBIA - RAILWAYS

St. Martin's Press, Inc., 175 Fifth Avenue, New York, New York 10010 (800) 221-7945; *The Statesman's Year-Book.*

Statistical Office of the United Nations, Publishing Service, New York, New York 10017 (800) 253-9646; *Statistical Yearbook.*

NAMIBIA - RELIGION

Central Intelligence Agency, Washington, D.C. 20505 (703) 482-1100, www.cia.gov; *The World Factbook.*

St. Martin's Press, Inc., 175 Fifth Avenue, New York, New York 10010 (800) 221-7945; *The Statesman's Year-Book.*

NAMIBIA - RETAIL TRADE

Euromonitor International, Inc., 122 South Michigan Avenue, Suite 1200, Chicago, Illinois 60603 (800) 577-EURO; *World Marketing Data and Statistics.*

Statistical Office of the United Nations, Publishing Service, New York, New York 10017 (800) 253-9646; *Statistical Yearbook.*

NAMIBIA - ROOT AND TUBER PRODUCTION - See NAMIBIA - CROPS

NAMIBIA - RUBBER PRODUCTION AND CONSUMPTION

Statistical Office of the United Nations, Publishing Service, New York, New York 10017 (800) 253-9646; *Statistical Yearbook.*

NAMIBIA - SALT PRODUCTION - See NAMIBIA - MINING AND MINERAL PRODUCTS

NAMIBIA - SCIENTISTS, TECHNICIANS AND ENGINEERS

Statistical Office of the United Nations, Publishing Service, New York, New York 10017 (800) 253-9646; *Statistical Yearbook.*

NAMIBIA - SHEEP - See NAMIBIA - LIVESTOCK AND POULTRY

NAMIBIA - SILVER PRODUCTION AND CONSUMPTION - See NAMIBIA - MINING AND MINERAL PRODUCTS

NAMIBIA - SOCIAL DATA

Statistical Office of the United Nations, Publishing Service, New York, New York 10017 (800) 253-9646; *World Statistics Pocketbook.*

NAMIBIA - STOCKS - COMMODITY - MARKET PRICE - INDEX

Food and Agricultural Organization of the United Nations (FAO) Via delle Terme di Caracalla, 00100 Rome, Italy (Telephone Number in U.S. (202) 653-2400); *The State of Food and Agriculture.*

NAMIBIA - TAXATION

Europa Publications Limited, 18 Bedford Square, London, WC1B 3JN, England; *The Europa World Year Book.*

NAMIBIA - TELEPHONES IN USE

American Telephone and Telegraph Company, 26 Parsippany Road, Whippany, New Jersey 07981 (800) 222-0300; *The World's Telephones.*

Central Intelligence Agency, Washington, D.C. 20505 (703) 482-1100, www.cia.gov; *The World Factbook.*

St. Martin's Press, Inc., 175 Fifth Avenue, New York, New York 10010 (800) 221-7945; *The Statesman's Year-Book.*

Statistical Office of the United Nations, Publishing Service, New York, New York 10017 (800) 253-9646; *Statistical Yearbook;* and *World Statistics Pocketbook.*

NAMIBIA - TELEVISION BROADCASTING - See NAMIBIA - BROADCASTING

NAMIBIA - TEXTILE INDUSTRY

St. Martin's Press, Inc., 175 Fifth Avenue, New York, New York 10010 (800) 221-7945; *The Statesman's Year-Book.*

Statistical Office of the United Nations, Publishing Service, New York, New York 10017 (800) 253-9646; *Industrial Commodity Statistics Yearbook;* and *Statistical Yearbook.*

United Nations Conference on Trade and Development, Central Statistical Service, Palais des Nations, Geneva, Switzerland (Telephone in U.S. (800) 253-9646); *UNCTAD Commodity Yearbook.*

NAMIBIA - THEATRE

United Nations Educational, Scientific and Cultural Organization (UNESCO), 7 Place de Fontenoy, F-75700 Paris, France (Telephone Number in U.S. (212) 963-5981); *Statistical Yearbook.*

NAMIBIA - TIN PRODUCTION - See NAMIBIA - MINING AND MINERAL PRODUCTS

NAMIBIA - TIRE (MOTOR VEHICLE) PRODUCTION

Statistical Office of the United Nations, Publishing Service, New York, New York 10017 (800) 253-9646; *Statistical Yearbook.*

NAMIBIA - TOBACCO PRODUCTION

Statistical Office of the United Nations, Publishing Service, New York, New York 10017 (800) 253-9646; *Statistical Yearbook.*

NAMIBIA - TOURISM

Euromonitor International, Inc., 122 South Michigan Avenue, Suite 1200, Chicago, Illinois 60603 (800) 577-EURO; *The World Economic Factbook;* and *World Marketing Data and Statistics.*

St. Martin's Press, Inc., 175 Fifth Avenue, New York, New York 10010 (800) 221-7945; *The Statesman's Year-Book.*

Statistical Office of the United Nations, Publishing Service, New York, New York 10017 (800) 253-9646; *Statistical Yearbook.*

NAMIBIA - TRACTORS IN USE

Statistical Office of the United Nations, Publishing Service, New York, New York 10017 (800) 253-9646; *Statistical Yearbook.*

NAMIBIA - TRADE

Food and Agricultural Organization of the United Nations (FAO) Via delle Terme di Caracalla, 00100 Rome, Italy (Telephone Number in U.S. (202) 653-2400); *The State of Food and Agriculture.*

NAMIBIA - TRADEMARKS AND SERVICE MARKS - See NAMIBIA - PATENTS, TRADEMARKS AND SERVICE MARKS

NAMIBIA - TRANSPORTATION AND COMMUNICATIONS

Central Intelligence Agency, Washington, D.C. 20505 (703) 482-1100, www.cia.gov; *The World Factbook.*

Euromonitor International, Inc., 122 South Michigan Avenue, Suite 1200, Chicago, Illinois 60603 (800) 577-EURO; *International Marketing Data and Statistics;* and *World Marketing Data and Statistics.*

Europa Publications Limited, 18 Bedford Square, London, WC1B 3JN, England; *The Europa World Year Book.*

St. Martin's Press, Inc., 175 Fifth Avenue, New York, New York 10010 (800) 221-7945; *The Statesman's Year-Book.*

Statistical Office of the United Nations, Publishing Service, New York, New York 10017 (800) 253-9646; *Human Development Report.*

NAMIBIA - TUNGSTEN PRODUCTION AND CONSUMPTION - See NAMIBIA - MINING AND MINERAL PRODUCTS

NAMIBIA - UNEMPLOYMENT

Central Intelligence Agency, Washington, D.C. 20505 (703) 482-1100, www.cia.gov; *The World Factbook.*

St. Martin's Press, Inc., 175 Fifth Avenue, New York, New York 10010 (800) 221-7945; *The Statesman's Year-Book.*

Statistical Office of the United Nations, Publishing Service, New York, New York 10017 (800) 253-9646; *Statistical Yearbook.*

NAMIBIA - URANIUM PRODUCTION AND CONSUMPTION - See NAMIBIA - MINING AND MINERAL PRODUCTS

NAMIBIA - VANADIUM ORE PRODUCTION AND CONSUMPTION - See NAMIBIA - MINING AND MINERAL PRODUCTS

NAMIBIA - VITAL STATISTICS

Statistical Office of the United Nations, Publishing Service, New York, New York 10017 (800) 253-9646; *Statistical Yearbook.*

World Health Organization, Office of Publications, 20 Avenue Appia, CH-1211 Geneva 27, Switzerland (Telephone Number in U.S. (518) 436-9686); *World Health Statistics Annual.*

NAMIBIA - WAGES

Statistical Office of the United Nations, Publishing Service, New York, New York 10017 (800) 253-9646; *Statistical Yearbook.*

NAMIBIA - WHEAT PRODUCTION - See NAMIBIA - CROPS

NAMIBIA - WHOLESALE PRICES

Statistical Office of the United Nations, Publishing Service, New York, New York 10017 (800) 253-9646; *Statistical Yearbook.*

NAMIBIA - WHOLESALE TRADE

Statistical Office of the United Nations, Publishing Service, New York, New York 10017 (800) 253-9646; *Statistical Yearbook.*

NAMIBIA - ZINC ORE PRODUCTION AND CONSUMPTION - See NAMIBIA - MINING AND MINERAL PRODUCTS

NATIONAL AERONAUTICS AND SPACE ADMINISTRATION

National Science Foundation, 4201 Wilson Boulevard, Arlington, Virginia 22230 (703) 306-1234, www.nsf.gov; *Federal Funds for Research and Development.*

NATIONAL AERONAUTICS AND SPACE ADMINISTRATION - BUDGET

National Aeronautics and Space Administration, 300 E Street, SW, Washington, D.C. 20546 (202) 358-1000, www.nasa.gov; Internet site http://ifmp.nasa.gov/codeb/budget/1000html/myb.htm.

NATIONAL AERONAUTICS AND SPACE ADMINISTRATION - EXPENDITURES - RESEARCH AND DEVELOPMENT

National Science Foundation, 4201 Wilson Boulevard, Arlington, Virginia 22230 (703) 306-1234, www.nsf.gov; *National Patterns of Research and Development Resources.*

NATIONAL AERONAUTICS AND SPACE ADMINISTRATION - EXPENDITURES - SPACE PROGRAM

National Aeronautics and Space Administration, 300 E Street, SW, Washington, D.C. 20546 (202) 358-1000, www.nasa.gov; *NASA Pocket Statistics*; and Internet site: http://ifmp.nasa.gov/codeb/budget/1000html/myb.htm.

NATIONAL AERONAUTICS AND SPACE ADMINISTRATION - SPACE LAUNCHES

The Congress of the U.S., Congressional Research Service, 101 Independence Avenue, SE, Washington, D.C. 20540 (202) 707-5700; *Space Activities of the United States, CIS and Other Launching Countries Organization;* and Internet site: http://www.ksc.nasa.gov/shuttle/missions/missions.htm.

National Aeronautics and Space Administration, 300 E Street, SW, Washington, D.C. 20546 (202) 358-1000, www.nasa.gov; Internet site: http://www.ksc.nasa.gov/shuttle/missions/missions/htm.

NATIONAL ASSOCIATION OF SECURITIES DEALERS (NASDAQ)

National Association of Securities Dealers, 1735 K Street, NW, Washington, D.C. 20006 (202) 728-8000; *Fact Book.*

NATIONAL ASSOCIATION OF SECURITIES DEALERS (NASDAQ) - STOCK INDICES

Global Financial Data, 784 Fremont Villas, Los Angeles, California 90042 (310) 642-4659; unpublished data; and Internet sites: "GFD Standard and Poor's Sectors," http://www.globalfindata.com/tbspect.htm; "U.S. Stock Capitalization Indices," http://ww.globalfindata.com/tbcap.htm; "Global Financial Data Dow Jones Industrial Average," http://www.globalfindata.com/tbdjia.htm.

NATIONAL BANKS - See BANKS

NATIONAL COLLEGIATE ATHLETIC ASSOCIATION - SPORT PARTICIPATION

National Collegiate Athletic Association, 700 West Washington Street, Indianapolis, Indiana 46206 (317) 917-6222; *1997-1998 Participation Study.*

NATIONAL DEBT - See DEBT

NATIONAL DEFENSE - See also Individual Military Services

NATIONAL DEFENSE - CONTRACT AWARDS AND PAYROLLS

U.S. Department of Defense, Office of the Secretary, The Pentagon, Washington, D.C. 20301 (703) 545-6700; *Atlas/Data Abstract for the United States and Selected Areas.*

NATIONAL DEFENSE - EMPLOYMENT - DEFENSE-RELATED INDUSTRIES

U.S. Department of Labor, Bureau of Labor Statistics, Two Massachusetts Avenue, NE, Washington, D.C. 20212 (202) 691-5200, www.stats.bls.gov; *Monthly Labor Review.*

NATIONAL DEFENSE - EXPENDITURES - WORLD

U.S. Arms Control and Disarmament Agency, 320 Twenty-first Street, NW, Washington, D.C. 20451 (202) 647-8677; *World Military Expenditures and Arms Transfers.*

NATIONAL DEFENSE - FEDERAL EMPLOYMENT AND PAYROLLS

U.S. Department of Commerce, Bureau of the Census, Washington, D.C. 20233 (301) 457-4100, www.census.gov; Internet site http://www.census.gov/pub/govs/www/apes.html.

NATIONAL DEFENSE - FEDERAL OUTLAYS

Executive Office of the President, Office of Management and Budget, Executive Office Building, Washington, D.C. 20503 (202) 395-3080,www.whitehouse.gov/omb; *The Budget of the United States Government;* and *Historical Tables.*

NATIONAL DEFENSE - MILITARY FORCES

U.S. Department of Defense, Office of the Secretary, The Pentagon, Washington, D.C. 20301 (703) 545-6700; *Selected Manpower Statistics.*

U.S. Department of Transportation, United States Coast Guard, 2100 Second Street, SW, Washington, D.C. 20593 (202) 267-2229, www.uscg.mil; *Annual Report of the Secretary of Transportation.*

NATIONAL DEFENSE - MILITARY FORCES - BRANCH OF SERVICE

U.S. Department of Defense, Office of the Secretary, The Pentagon, Washington, D.C. 20301 (703) 545-6700; *Selected Manpower Statistics.*

NATIONAL DEFENSE - MILITARY FORCES - FOREIGN COUNTRIES

U.S. Arms Control and Disarmament Agency, 320 Twenty-first Street, NW, Washington, D.C. 20451 (202) 647-8677; *World Military Expenditures and Arms Transfers.*

NATIONAL DEFENSE - OUTLAYS

Executive Office of the President, Office of Management and Budget, Executive Office Building, Washington, D.C. 20503 (202) 395-3080, www.whitehouse.gov/omb; *Historical Tables.*

NATIONAL DEFENSE - READY RESERVES

U.S. Department of Defense, The Pentagon, Washington, D.C. 20301-1155 (703) 545-6700; *Official Guard and Reserve Manpower Strengths and Statistics.*

NATIONAL DEFENSE - WORLDWIDE MILITARY EXPENDITURES

U.S. Arms Control and Disarmament Agency, 320 Twenty-first Street, NW, Washington, D.C. 20451 (202) 647-8677; *World Military Expenditures and Arms Transfers.*

NATIONAL FORESTS - See FORESTS

NATIONAL GUARD

U.S. National Guard, The Pentagon, Washington, D.C. 20301 (202) 433-5100; *Annual Review of the Chief, National Guard Bureau;* and unpublished data.

NATIONAL INCOME - See also GROSS DOMESTIC PRODUCT

U.S. Department of Commerce, Bureau of Economic Analysis, Fourteenth Street between Constitution Avenue and E Street, NW, Washington, D.C. 20230 (202) 606-9900, www.bea.doc.gov; *The National Income and Product Accounts of the United States;* and *Survey of Current Business.*

NATIONAL NONPROFIT ASSOCIATIONS - NUMBER, BY TYPE

The Gale Group, 27500 Drake Road, Farmington Hills, Michigan 48331 (800) 877-4253; *Encyclopedia of Associations.*

NATO COUNTRIES - MILITARY EXPENDITURES

U.S. Arms Control and Disarmament Agency, 320 Twenty-first Street, NW, Washington, D.C. 20451 (202) 647-8677; *World Military Expenditures and Arms Transfers.*

NATURAL GAS - CONSUMPTION

U.S. Department of Energy, Energy Information Administration, 1000 Independence Avenue, SW, Washington, D.C. 20585 (202) 586-1185; *Annual Energy Outlook; State Energy Data Report; Household Energy Consumption and Expenditures; Monthly Energy Review; International Energy Annual; International Energy Outlook;* and *Commercial Buildings Energy Consumption and Expenditures.*

NATURAL GAS - EXPENDITURES

U.S. Department of Energy, Energy Information Administration, 1000 Independence Avenue, SW, Washington, D.C. 20585 (202) 586-1185; *State Energy Price and Expenditure Report; Household Energy Consumption and Expenditures;* and *Commercial Buildings Energy Consumption and Expenditures.*

NATURAL GAS - FOREIGN TRADE

U.S. Department of Commerce, Bureau of the Census, Washington, D.C. 20233 (301) 457-4100, www.census.gov; *U.S. Merchandise Trade.*

U.S. Department of Energy, Energy Information Administration, 1000 Independence Avenue, SW, Washington, D.C. 20586 (202) 586-1185; *Annual Energy Outlook; Annual Energy Review;* and *U.S. International Trade in Goods and Services.*

NATURAL GAS - PLANT LIQUIDS

U.S. Department of Energy, Energy Information Administration, 1000 Independence Avenue, SW, Washington, D.C. 20585 (202) 586-1185; *U.S. Crude Oil, Natural Gas, and Natural Gas Liquids Reserves, Annual Report.*

NATURAL GAS - PLANT LIQUIDS - PRODUCTION

U.S. Department of Energy, Energy Information Administration, 1000 Independence Avenue, SW, Washington, D.C. 20585 (202) 586-1185; *Energy Data Reports; Natural Gas Annual;* and *Natural Gas Monthly.*

NATURAL GAS - PLANT LIQUIDS - RESERVES

U.S. Department of Energy, Energy Information Administration, 1000 Independence Avenue, SW, Washington, D.C. 20585 (202) 586-1185; *U.S. Crude Oil, Natural Gas, and Natural Gas Liquids Reserves, Annual Report.*

NATURAL GAS - PLANT LIQUIDS - SUPPLY

U.S. Department of Energy, Energy Information Administration, 1000 Independence Avenue, SW, Washington, D.C. 20585 (202) 586-1185; *Annual Energy Review, Petroleum Supply Annual; U.S. Crude Oil, Natural Gas, and Natural Gas Liquids Reserves;* and *Monthly Energy Review.*

NATURAL GAS - PLANT LIQUIDS - VALUE

U.S. Department of Energy, Energy Information Administration, 1000 Independence Avenue, SW, Washington, D.C. 20585 (202) 586-1185; *Petroleum Supply Annual; Petroleum Marketing Annual; Natural Gas Annual;* and *Natural Gas Monthly.*

NATURAL GAS - PRICES

U.S. Department of Energy, Energy Information Administration, 1000 Independence Avenue, SW, Washington, D.C. 20585 (202) 586-5000; *Annual Energy Review; International Energy Annual; Natural Gas Annual, Vol. I & II;* and *Monthly Energy Review.*

U.S. Department of Labor, Bureau of Labor Statistics, Two Massachusetts Avenue, NE, Washington, D.C. 20212 (202) 691-5200, www.stats.bls.gov; *Monthly Labor Review; CPI Detailed Report;* and *Producer Price Indexes.*

NATURAL GAS - PRODUCTION

U. S. Department of Energy, Energy Information Administration 1000 Independence Avenue, SW, Washington, D.C. 20585 (202) 586-5000; *Annual Energy Review; Annual Energy Outlook; Monthly Energy Review; Petroleum Supply Annual; Natural Gas Annual;* and *Natural Gas Monthly.*

NATURAL GAS - PRODUCTION - WORLD

U. S. Department of Energy, Energy Information Administration 1000 Independence Avenue, SW, Washington, D.C. 20585 (202) 586-5000; *Annual Energy Review; International Energy Annual; Natural Gas Annual, Vol. I & II;* and *Monthly Energy Review.*

NATURAL GAS - RESERVES

U. S. Department of Energy, Energy Information Administration 1000 Independence Avenue, SW, Washington, D.C. 20585 (202) 586-5000; *U.S. Crude Oil, Natural Gas, and Natural Gas Liquids Reserves, Annual Report.*

NATURAL RESOURCES - FEDERAL OUTLAYS

Executive Office of the President, Office of Management and Budget, Executive Office Building, Washington, D.C. 20503 (202) 395-3080, www.whitehouse.gov/omb; *Historical Tables.*

NATURAL RESOURCES - GOVERNMENTAL FINANCES

U.S. Department of Commerce, Bureau of the Census, Washington, D.C. 20233 (301) 457-4100, www.census.gov; unpublished data; and Internet site: http://www.census.gov/pub/govs/www/index. html.

NATURAL RESOURCES - GOVERNMENTAL FINANCES - AID TO STATE AND LOCAL GOVERNMENTS

Executive Office of the President, Office of Management and Budget, Executive Office Building, Washington, D.C. 20503 (202) 395-3080, www,whitehosue.gov/omb; *Historical Tables;* and *Budget of the United States Government.*

NATURAL RESOURCES - GOVERNMENTAL FINANCES - GOVERNMENT EMPLOYMENT AND PAYROLLS

U.S. Department of Commerce, Bureau of the Census, Washington, D.C. 20233 (301) 457-4100, www.census.gov; Internet site: http://www.census.gov/pub/govs/www/apes.html.

NATURAL RESOURCES - GOVERNMENTAL FINANCES - GOVERNMENTAL REVENUE

U.S. Department of Commerce, Bureau of the Census, Washington, D.C. 20233 (301) 457-4100, www.census.gov; Internet site: http://www.census.gov/pub/govs/www/index.html.

NATURAL RESOURCES -
GOVERNMENTAL FINANCES -
STATE AND LOCAL GOVERNMENTS

U.S. Department of Commerce, Bureau
of the Census, Washington, D.C. 20233
(301) 457-4100, www.census.gov;
Governmental Finances; and Internet site
http://www.census.gov/govs/www/
estimate/.html.

NATURAL RESOURCES -
GOVERNMENTAL FINANCES -
STATE GOVERNMENTS

National Association of State Budget
Officers, Hall of the States, 444 North
Capitol Street, NW, Washington, D.C.
20001 (202) 624-5382; *Fiscal Survey of the
States;* and *State Expenditure Report.*

U.S. Department of Commerce, Bureau
of the Census, Washington, D.C. 20233
(301) 457-4100, www.census.gov; *State
Government Finances;* and Internet site
http://www.census.gov/ftp/pub/govs/www/
state.html.

NATURE STUDY (RECREATION)

U.S. Department of Agriculture, Forest
Service, Fourteenth Street and
Independence Avenue, SW, Washington,
D.C. 20250 (202) 720-5237,
www.fsa.usda.gov; *Annual Report.*

Nauru - National Statistical Office

Department of Island Development and
Industry, Government Offices, Yaren
District, Republic of Nauru, Central Pacific.

NAURU - AGRICULTURE

Euromonitor International, Inc., 122
South Michigan Avenue, Suite 1200,
Chicago, Illinois 60603 (800) 577-EURO;
World Marketing Data and Statistics.

Europa Publications Limited, 18
Bedford Square, London, WC1B 3JN,
England; *The Europa World Year Book.*

Food and Agricultural Organization of
the United Nations (FAO) Via delle Terme
di Caracalla, 00100 Rome, Italy (Telephone
Number in U.S. (202) 653-2400);
*Production Yearbook; The State of Food
and Agriculture;* and *Trade Yearbook.*

M.E. Sharpe, 80 Business Park Drive,
Armonk, New York 10504 (800) 541-6563;
The Illustrated Book of World Rankings.

Statistical Office of the United Nations,
Publishing Service, New York, New York
10017 (800) 253-9646; *Asia-Pacific in
Figures;* and *Statistical Yearbook for Asia
and the Pacific.*

United Nations Conference on Trade
and Development, Central Statistical
Service, Palais des Nations, Geneva,
Switzerland (Telephone in U.S. (800) 253-
9646); *UNCTAD Commodity Yearbook.*

NAURU - AIRLINE SERVICE

M.E. Sharpe, 80 Business Park Drive,
Armonk, New York 10504 (800) 541-6563;
The Illustrated Book of World Rankings.

St. Martin's Press, Inc., 175 Fifth Avenue,
New York, New York 10010 (800) 221-7945;
The Statesman's Year-Book.

NAURU - AIRPORTS

Central Intelligence Agency,
Washington, D.C. 20505 (703) 482-1100,
www.cia.gov; *The World Factbook.*

NAURU - ALUMINUM PRODUCTION AND
CONSUMPTION - See NAURU - MINING
AND MINERAL PRODUCTS

NAURU - AREA AND DENSITY OF
POPULATION

Central Intelligence Agency,
Washington, D.C. 20505 (703) 482-1100,
www.cia.gov; *The World Factbook.*

Euromonitor International, Inc., 122
South Michigan Avenue, Suite 1200,
Chicago, Illinois 60603 (800) 577-EURO;
The World Economic Factbook.

Europa Publications Limited, 18
Bedford Square, London, WC1B 3JN,
England; *The Europa World Year Book.*

Food and Agricultural Organization of
the United Nations (FAO) Via delle Terme
di Caracalla, 00100 Rome, Italy (Telephone
Number in U.S. (202) 653-2400); *The State
of Food and Agriculture.*

M.E. Sharpe, 80 Business Park Drive,
Armonk, New York 10504 (800) 541-6563;
The Illustrated Book of World Rankings.

St. Martin's Press, Inc., 175 Fifth Avenue,
New York, New York 10010 (800) 221-7945;
The Statesman's Year-Book.

Statistical Office of the United Nations,
Publishing Service, New York, New York
10017 (800) 253-9646; *Statistical Yearbook.*

United Nations Educational, Scientific
and Cultural Organization (UNESCO), 7
Place de Fontenoy, F-75700 Paris, France
(Telephone Number in U.S. (212) 963-
5981); *Statistical Yearbook.*

NAURU - BANKING

Euromonitor International, Inc., 122

South Michigan Avenue, Suite 1200,
Chicago, Illinois 60603 (800) 577-EURO;
World Marketing Data and Statistics.

M.E. Sharpe, 80 Business Park Drive,
Armonk, New York 10504 (800) 541-6563;
The Illustrated Book of World Rankings.

NAURU - BARLEY PRODUCTION - See
NAURU - CROPS

NAURU - BEER PRODUCTION - See
NAURU - BEVERAGES

NAURU - BEVERAGES

M.E. Sharpe, 80 Business Park Drive,
Armonk, New York 10504 (800) 541-6563;
The Illustrated Book of World Rankings.

NAURU - BIRTH RATES

Central Intelligence Agency,
Washington, D.C. 20505 (703) 482-1100,
www.cia.gov; *The World Factbook.*

Euromonitor International, Inc., 122
South Michigan Avenue, Suite 1200,
Chicago, Illinois 60603 (800) 577-EURO;
International Marketing Data and Statistics;
and *The World Economic Factbook.*

Europa Publications Limited, 18
Bedford Square, London, WC1B 3JN,
England; *The Europa World Year Book.*

M.E. Sharpe, 80 Business Park Drive,
Armonk, New York 10504 (800) 541-6563;
The Illustrated Book of World Rankings.

St. Martin's Press, Inc., 175 Fifth
Avenue, New York, New York 10010 (800)
221-7945; *The Statesman's Year-Book.*

Statistical Office of the United Nations,
Publishing Service, New York, New York
10017 (800) 253-9646; *Asia-Pacific in
Figures; Demographic Yearbook;* and
Statistical Yearbook.

World Health Organization, Office of
Publications, 20 Avenue Appia, CH-1211
Geneva 27, Switzerland (Telephone
Number in U.S. (518) 436-9686); *World
Health Statistics Annual.*

NAURU - BROADCASTING

Billboard Limited, Post Office Box 9027,
1006 AA Amsterdam, The Netherlands
(Telephone Number in U.S. (212) 764-
7300); *World Radio TV Handbook.*

Central Intelligence Agency,
Washington, D.C. 20505 (703) 482-1100,
www.cia.gov; *The World Factbook.*

Euromonitor International, Inc., 122
South Michigan Avenue, Suite 1200,
Chicago, Illinois 60603 (800) 577-EURO;
World Marketing Data and Statistics.

M.E. Sharpe, 80 Business Park Drive, Armonk, New York 10504 (800) 541-6563; *The Illustrated Book of World Rankings.*

St. Martin's Press, Inc., 175 Fifth Avenue, New York, New York 10010 (800) 221-7945; *The Statesman's Year-Book.*

NAURU - BUDGET

Central Intelligence Agency, Washington, D.C. 20505 (703) 482-1100, www.cia.gov; *The World Factbook.*

NAURU - CALORIE SUPPLY

Food and Agricultural Organization of the United Nations (FAO) Via delle Terme di Caracalla, 00100 Rome, Italy (Telephone Number in U.S. (202) 653-2400); *The State of Food and Agriculture.*

NAURU - CATTLE - See NAURU - LIVESTOCK AND POULTRY

NAURU - CEMENT PRODUCTION - See NAURU - MINING AND MINERAL PRODUCTS

NAURU - CIGARETTE PRODUCTION - See NAURU - TOBACCO PRODUCTION

NAURU - CLIMATE

M.E. Sharpe, 80 Business Park Drive, Armonk, New York 10504 (800) 541-6563; *The Illustrated Book of World Rankings.*

St. Martin's Press, Inc., 175 Fifth Avenue, New York, New York 10010 (800) 221-7945; *The Statesman's Year-Book.*

NAURU - CLOTHING EXPORTS AND IMPORTS - See NAURU - TEXTILE INDUSTRY

NAURU - COAL PRODUCTION - See NAURU - MINING AND MINERAL PRODUCTS

NAURU - COFFEE PRODUCTION AND CONSUMPTION - See NAURU CROPS

NAURU - COMMERCE

St. Martin's Press, Inc., 175 Fifth Avenue, New York, New York 10010 (800) 221-7945; *The Statesman's Year-Book.*

NAURU - COMMUNICATIONS - See NAURU - TRANSPORTATION AND COMMUNICATIONS

NAURU - CONSTRUCTION

M.E. Sharpe, 80 Business Park Drive, Armonk, New York 10504 (800) 541-6563; *The Illustrated Book of World Rankings.*

NAURU - CONSUMER PRICES

Euromonitor International, Inc., 122 South Michigan Avenue, Suite 1200, Chicago, Illinois 60603 (800) 577-EURO; *World Marketing Data and Statistics.*

NAURU - CONSUMPTION

South Pacific Commission, Post Box D5, Noumea Cedex, New Caledonia; *Statistical Bulletin of the South Pacific: Retail Price Indexes.*

NAURU - COPPER PRODUCTION AND CONSUMPTION - See NAURU -MINING AND MINERAL PRODUCTS

NAURU - CORN PRODUCTION - See NAURU - CROPS

NAURU - COTTON PRODUCTION - See NAURU - CROPS

NAURU - CROPS

Europa Publications Limited, 18 Bedford Square, London, WC1B 3JN, England; *The Europa World Year Book.*

Food and Agricultural Organization of the United Nations (FAO) Via delle Terme di Caracalla, 00100 Rome, Italy (Telephone Number in U.S. (202) 653-2400); *The State of Food and Agriculture.*

M.E. Sharpe, 80 Business Park Drive, Armonk, New York 10504 (800) 541-6563; *The Illustrated Book of World Rankings.*

United Nations Conference on Trade and Development, Central Statistical Service, Palais des Nations, Geneva, Switzerland (Telephone in U.S. (800) 253-9646); *UNCTAD Commodity Yearbook.*

NAURU - DAIRY PRODUCTS

Food and Agricultural Organization of the United Nations (FAO) Via delle Terme di Caracalla, 00100 Rome, Italy (Telephone Number in U.S. (202) 653-2400); *The State of Food and Agriculture.*

M.E. Sharpe, 80 Business Park Drive, Armonk, New York 10504 (800) 541-6563; *The Illustrated Book of World Rankings.*

NAURU - DEATH RATES - See NAURU - MORTALITY

NAURU - DEMOGRAPHY

Euromonitor International, Inc., 122 South Michigan Avenue, Suite 1200, Chicago, Illinois 60603 (800) 577-EURO; *International Marketing Data and Statistics; The World Economic Factbook;* and *World Marketing Data and Statistics.*

M.E. Sharpe, 80 Business Park Drive, Armonk, New York 10504 (800) 541-6563; *The Illustrated Book of World Rankings.*

Statistical Office of the United Nations, Publishing Service, New York, New York 10017 (800) 253-9646; *Asia-Pacific in Figures.*

NAURU - DIAMOND PRODUCTION - See NAURU - MINING AND MINERAL PRODUCTS

NAURU - DIVORCE

M.E. Sharpe, 80 Business Park Drive, Armonk, New York 10504 (800) 541-6563; *The Illustrated Book of World Rankings.*

Statistical Office of the United Nations, Publishing Service, New York, New York 10017 (800) 253-9646; *Demographic Yearbook.*

NAURU - ECONOMY

Central Intelligence Agency, Washington, D.C. 20505 (703) 482-1100, www.cia.gov; *The World Factbook.*

Euromonitor International, Inc., 122 South Michigan Avenue, Suite 1200, Chicago, Illinois 60603 (800) 577-EURO; *The World Economic Factbook;* and *World Marketing Data and Statistics.*

Europa Publications Limited, 18 Bedford Square, London, WC1B 3JN, England; *The Europa World Year Book.*

M.E. Sharpe, 80 Business Park Drive, Armonk, New York 10504 (800) 541-6563; *The Illustrated Book of World Rankings.*

St. Martin's Press, Inc., 175 Fifth Avenue, New York, New York 10010 (800) 221-7945; *The Statesman's Year-Book.*

Statistical Office of the United Nations, Publishing Service, New York, New York 10017 (800) 253-9646; *World Statistics Pocketbook.*

NAURU - EDUCATION

Euromonitor International, Inc., 122 South Michigan Avenue, Suite 1200, Chicago, Illinois 60603 (800) 577-EURO; *International Marketing Data and Statistics;* and *World Marketing Data and Statistics.*

Europa Publications Limited, 18 Bedford Square, London, WC1B 3JN, England; *The Europa World Year Book.*

M.E. Sharpe, 80 Business Park Drive, Armonk, New York 10504 (800) 541-6563; *The Illustrated Book of World Rankings.*

St. Martin's Press, Inc., 175 Fifth Avenue, New York, New York 10010 (800) 221-7945; *The Statesman's Year-Book.*

Statistical Office of the United Nations, Publishing Service, New York, New York

10017 (800) 253-9646; *Asia-Pacific in Figures;* and *Statistical Yearbook for Asia and the Pacific.*

United Nations Educational, Scientific and Cultural Organization (UNESCO), 7 Place de Fontenoy, F-75700 Paris, France (Telephone Number in U.S. (212) 963-5981); *Statistical Yearbook.*

NAURU - EGG PRODUCTION AND CONSUMPTION - See NAURU - DAIRY PRODUCTS

NAURU - ELECTRICITY

Central Intelligence Agency, Washington, D.C. 20505 (703) 482-1100, www.cia.gov; *The World Factbook.*

M.E. Sharpe, 80 Business Park Drive, Armonk, New York 10504 (800) 541-6563; *The Illustrated Book of World Rankings.*

Statistical Office of the United Nations, Publishing Service, New York, New York 10017 (800) 253-9646; *Statistical Yearbook.*

NAURU - EMPLOYMENT

Euromonitor International, Inc., 122 South Michigan Avenue, Suite 1200, Chicago, Illinois 60603 (800) 577-EURO; *International Marketing Data and Statistics.*

M.E. Sharpe, 80 Business Park Drive, Armonk, New York 10504 (800) 541-6563; *The Illustrated Book of World Rankings.*

Statistical Office of the United Nations, Publishing Service, New York, New York 10017 (800) 253-9646; *Asia-Pacific in Figures.*

NAURU - ENERGY

Euromonitor International, Inc., 122 South Michigan Avenue, Suite 1200, Chicago, Illinois 60603 (800) 577-EURO; *International Marketing Data and Statistics; The World Economic Factbook;* and *World Marketing Data and Statistics.*

Food and Agricultural Organization of the United Nations (FAO) Via delle Terme di Caracalla, 00100 Rome, Italy (Telephone Number in U.S. (202) 653-2400); *The State of Food and Agriculture.*

M.E. Sharpe, 80 Business Park Drive, Armonk, New York 10504 (800) 541-6563; *The Illustrated Book of World Rankings.*

Statistical Office of the United Nations, Publishing Service, New York, New York 10017 (800) 253-9646; *Asia-Pacific in Figures; Statistical Yearbook; World Statistics Pocketbook;* and *Statistical Yearbook for Asia and the Pacific.*

NAURU - ENVIRONMENT

Statistical Office of the United Nations, Publishing Service, New York, New York 10017 (800) 253-9646; *World Statistics Pocketbook.*

NAURU - EXCHANGE RATES

Central Intelligence Agency, Washington, D.C. 20505 (703) 482-1100, www.cia.gov; *The World Factbook.*

Euromonitor International, Inc., 122 South Michigan Avenue, Suite 1200, Chicago, Illinois 60603 (800) 577-EURO; *International Marketing Data and Statistics;* and *The World Economic Factbook.*

Europa Publications Limited, 18 Bedford Square, London, WC1B 3JN, England; *The Europa World Year Book.*

Statistical Office of the United Nations, Publishing Service, New York, New York 10017 (800) 253-9646; *World Statistics Pocketbook.*

Walden Publishing Ltd., Two Market Street, Saffron Walden Essex, CB10 1HZ, England; *The World of Information Asia and Pacific Review.*

NAURU - EXPORTS

Central Intelligence Agency, Washington, D.C. 20505 (703) 482-1100, www.cia.gov; *The World Factbook.*

Euromonitor International, Inc., 122 South Michigan Avenue, Suite 1200, Chicago, Illinois 60603 (800) 577-EURO; *International Marketing Data and Statistics;* and *The World Economic Factbook.*

Europa Publications Limited, 18 Bedford Square, London, WC1B 3JN, England; *The Europa World Year Book.*

Food and Agricultural Organization of the United Nations (FAO) Via delle Terme di Caracalla, 00100 Rome, Italy (Telephone Number in U.S. (202) 653-2400); *The State of Food and Agriculture.*

International Monetary Fund, 700 Nineteenth Street, NW, Washington, D.C. 20431 (202) 623-7000; *Direction of Trade Statistics.*

St. Martin's Press, Inc., 175 Fifth Avenue, New York, New York 10010 (800) 221-7945; *The Statesman's Year-Book.*

South Pacific Commission, Post Box D5, Noumea Cedex, New Caledonia; *Statistical Bulletin of the South Pacific: Overseas Trade.*

Walden Publishing Ltd., Two Market Street, Saffron Walden Essex, CB10 1HZ, England; *The World of Information Asia and Pacific Review.*

NAURU - EXTERNAL TRADE

Euromonitor International, Inc., 122 South Michigan Avenue, Suite 1200, Chicago, Illinois 60603 (800) 577-EURO; *World Marketing Data and Statistics.*

Food and Agricultural Organization of the United Nations (FAO) Via delle Terme di Caracalla, 00100 Rome, Italy (Telephone Number in U.S. (202) 653-2400); *The State of Food and Agriculture;* and *Trade Yearbook.*

Statistical Office of the United Nations, Publishing Service, New York, New York 10017 (800) 253-9646; *Asia-Pacific in Figures;* and *Statistical Yearbook for Asia and the Pacific.*

NAURU - FARM CROPS - See NAURU - CROPS

NAURU - FERTILITY RATES

Central Intelligence Agency, Washington, D.C. 20505 (703) 482-1100, www.cia.gov; *The World Factbook.*

M.E. Sharpe, 80 Business Park Drive, Armonk, New York 10504 (800) 541-6563; *The Illustrated Book of World Rankings.*

NAURU - FERTILIZER

Food and Agricultural Organization of the United Nations (FAO) Via delle Terme di Caracalla, 00100 Rome, Italy (Telephone Number in U.S. (202) 653-2400); *The State of Food and Agriculture.*

NAURU - FETAL MORTALITY - See NAURU - MORTALITY

NAURU - FINANCE

Europa Publications Limited, 18 Bedford Square, London, WC1B 3JN, England; *The Europa World Year Book.*

M.E. Sharpe, 80 Business Park Drive, Armonk, New York 10504 (800) 541-6563; *The Illustrated Book of World Rankings.*

St. Martin's Press, Inc., 175 Fifth Avenue, New York, New York 10010 (800) 221-7945; *The Statesman's Year-Book.*

Statistical Office of the United Nations, Publishing Service, New York, New York 10017 (800) 253-9646; *Statistical Yearbook for Asia and the Pacific.*

NAURU - FISHERIES

Europa Publications Limited, 18 Bedford Square, London, WC1B 3JN, England; *The Europa World Year Book.*

Food and Agricultural Organization of the United Nations (FAO) Via delle Terme

di Caracalla, 00100 Rome, Italy (Telephone Number in U.S. (202) 653-2400); *The State of Food and Agriculture;* and *Yearbook of Fishery Statistics.*

M.E. Sharpe, 80 Business Park Drive, Armonk, New York 10504 (800) 541-6563; *The Illustrated Book of World Rankings.*

United Nations Conference on Trade and Development, Central Statistical Service, Palais des Nations, Geneva, Switzerland (Telephone in U.S. (800) 253-9646); *UNCTAD Commodity Yearbook.*

NAURU - FOOD

Food and Agricultural Organization of the United Nations (FAO), Via delle Terme di Caracalla, 00100 Rome, Italy (Telephone Number in U.S. (202) 653-2400); *Production Yearbook;* and *The State of Food and Agriculture.*

South Pacific Commission, Post Box D5, Noumea Cedex, New Caledonia; *Statistical Bulletin of the South Pacific: Retail Price Indexes.*

Statistical Office of the United Nations, Publishing Service, New York, New York 10017 (800) 253-9646; *Statistical Yearbook for Asia and the Pacific.*

United Nations Conference on Trade and Development, Central Statistical Service, Palais des Nations, Geneva, Switzerland (Telephone in U.S. (800) 253-9646); *UNCTAD Commodity Yearbook.*

NAURU - FOREIGN DEBT

Walden Publishing Ltd., Two Market Street, Saffron Walden Essex, CB10 1HZ, England; *The World of Information Asia and Pacific Review.*

NAURU - FOREIGN TRADE

Euromonitor International, Inc., 122 South Michigan Avenue, Suite 1200, Chicago, Illinois 60603 (800) 577-EURO; *The World Economic Factbook.*

Europa Publications Limited, 18 Bedford Square, London, WC1B 3JN, England; *The Europa World Year Book.*

Food and Agricultural Organization of the United Nations (FAO) Via delle Terme di Caracalla, 00100 Rome, Italy (Telephone Number in U.S. (202) 653-2400); *The State of Food and Agriculture.*

M.E. Sharpe, 80 Business Park Drive, Armonk, New York 10504 (800) 541-6563; *The Illustrated Book of World Rankings.*

South Pacific Commission, Post Box D5, Noumea Cedex, New Caledonia; *Statistical Bulletin of the South Pacific:*

Overseas Trade.

St. Martin's Press, Inc., 175 Fifth Avenue, New York, New York 10010 (800) 221-7945; *The Statesman's Year-Book.*

United Nations Conference on Trade and Development, Central Statistical Service, Palais des Nations, Geneva, Switzerland (Telephone in U.S. (800) 253-9646); *UNCTAD Commodity Yearbook.*

NAURU - FORESTRY AND FOREST PRODUCTS

Food and Agricultural Organization of the United Nations (FAO) Via delle Terme di Caracalla, 00100 Rome, Italy (Telephone Number in U.S. (202) 653-2400); *The State of Food and Agriculture.*

M.E. Sharpe, 80 Business Park Drive, Armonk, New York 10504 (800) 541-6563; *The Illustrated Book of World Rankings.*

United Nations Conference on Trade and Development, Central Statistical Service, Palais des Nations, Geneva, Switzerland (Telephone in U.S. (800) 253-9646); *UNCTAD Commodity Yearbook.*

NAURU - GAS PRODUCTION - See NAURU - MINING AND MINERAL PRODUCTS

NAURU - GENERAL MORTALITY - See NAURU - MORTALITY

NAURU - GEOGRAPHIC DATA

M.E. Sharpe, 80 Business Park Drive, Armonk, New York 10504 (800) 541-6563; *The Illustrated Book of World Rankings.*

NAURU - GOLD PRODUCTION AND CONSUMPTION - See NAURU - MINING AND MINERAL PRODUCTS

NAURU - GOVERNMENT

Central Intelligence Agency, Washington, D.C. 20505 (703) 482-1100, www.cia.gov; *The World Factbook.*

Europa Publications Limited, 18 Bedford Square, London, WC1B 3JN, England; *The Europa World Year Book.*

St. Martin's Press, Inc., 175 Fifth Avenue, New York, New York 10010 (800) 221-7945; *The Statesman's Year-Book.*

Statistical Office of the United Nations, Publishing Service, New York, New York 10017 (800) 253-9646; *Asia-Pacific in Figures.*

NAURU - GRAIN PRODUCTION - See NAURU - CROPS

NAURU - GROSS DOMESTIC PRODUCT

Euromonitor International, Inc., 122 South Michigan Avenue, Suite 1200, Chicago, Illinois 60603 (800) 577-EURO; *International Marketing Data and Statistics;* and *The World Economic Factbook.*

M.E. Sharpe, 80 Business Park Drive, Armonk, New York 10504 (800) 541-6563; *The Illustrated Book of World Rankings.*

NAURU - GROSS NATIONAL PRODUCT

St. Martin's Press, Inc., 175 Fifth Avenue, New York, New York 10010 (800) 221-7945; *The Statesman's Year-Book.*

Walden Publishing Ltd., Two Market Street, Saffron Walden Essex, CB10 1HZ, England; *The World of Information Asia and Pacific Review.*

NAURU - HEALTH

Euromonitor International, Inc., 122 South Michigan Avenue, Suite 1200, Chicago, Illinois 60603 (800) 577-EURO; *World Marketing Data and Statistics.*

M.E. Sharpe, 80 Business Park Drive, Armonk, New York 10504 (800) 541-6563; *The Illustrated Book of World Rankings.*

South Pacific Commission, Post Box D5, Noumea Cedex, New Caledonia; *Statistical Bulletin of the South Pacific: Retail Price Indexes.*

Statistical Office of the United Nations, Publishing Service, New York, New York 10017 (800) 253-9646; *Asia-Pacific in Figures;* and *Statistical Yearbook.*

NAURU - HIGHWAYS

Central Intelligence Agency, Washington, D.C. 20505 (703) 482-1100, www.cia.gov; *The World Factbook.*

NAURU - HORSES - See NAURU - LIVESTOCK AND POULTRY

NAURU - HOUSING AND HOUSING UNITS

Euromonitor International, Inc., 122 South Michigan Avenue, Suite 1200, Chicago, Illinois 60603 (800) 577-EURO; *World Marketing Data and Statistics.*

M.E. Sharpe, 80 Business Park Drive, Armonk, New York 10504 (800) 541-6563; *The Illustrated Book of World Rankings.*

South Pacific Commission, Post Box D5, Noumea Cedex, New Caledonia; *Statistical Bulletin of the South Pacific: Retail Price Indexes.*

NAURU - HOUSING EXPENDITURES

South Pacific Commission, Post Box D5, Noumea Cedex, New Caledonia;

Statistical Bulletin of the South Pacific: Retail Price Indexes.

NAURU - ILLITERATE POPULATION

Central Intelligence Agency, Washington, D.C. 20505 (703) 482-1100, www.cia.gov; *The World Factbook.*

Euromonitor International, Inc., 122 South Michigan Avenue, Suite 1200, Chicago, Illinois 60603 (800) 577-EURO; *The World Economic Factbook.*

Statistical Office of the United Nations, Publishing Service, New York, New York 10017 (800) 253-9646; *Asia-Pacific in Figures.*

NAURU - IMPORTS

Central Intelligence Agency, Washington, D.C. 20505 (703) 482-1100, www.cia.gov; *The World Factbook.*

Euromonitor International, Inc., 122 South Michigan Avenue, Suite 1200, Chicago, Illinois 60603 (800) 577-EURO; *International Marketing Data and Statistics;* and *The World Economic Factbook.*

Europa Publications Limited, 18 Bedford Square, London, WC1B 3JN, England; *The Europa World Year Book.*

Food and Agricultural Organization of the United Nations (FAO) Via delle Terme di Caracalla, 00100 Rome, Italy (Telephone Number in U.S. (202) 653-2400); *The State of Food and Agriculture.*

International Monetary Fund, 700 Nineteenth Street, NW, Washington, D.C. 20431 (202) 623-7000; *Direction of Trade Statistics.*

South Pacific Commission, Post Box D5, Noumea Cedex, New Caledonia; *Statistical Bulletin of the South Pacific: Overseas Trade.*

St. Martin's Press, Inc., 175 Fifth Avenue, New York, New York 10010 (800) 221-7945; *The Statesman's Year-Book.*

Walden Publishing Ltd., Two Market Street, Saffron Walden Essex, CB10 1HZ, England; *The World of Information Asia and Pacific Review.*

NAURU - INDUSTRY

Central Intelligence Agency, Washington, D.C. 20505 (703) 482-1100, www.cia.gov; *The World Factbook.*

Euromonitor International, Inc., 122 South Michigan Avenue, Suite 1200, Chicago, Illinois 60603 (800) 577-EURO; *The World Economic Factbook;* and *World Marketing Data and Statistics.*

M.E. Sharpe, 80 Business Park Drive, Armonk, New York 10504 (800) 541-6563; *The Illustrated Book of World Rankings.*

St. Martin's Press, Inc., 175 Fifth Avenue, New York, New York 10010 (800) 221-7945; *The Statesman's Year-Book.*

Statistical Office of the United Nations, Publishing Service, New York, New York 10017 (800) 253-9646; *Asia-Pacific in Figures;* and *Statistical Yearbook for Asia and the Pacific.*

NAURU - INFANT AND MATERNAL MORTALITY - See NAURU - MORTALITY

NAURU - INTERNAL TRADE

Statistical Office of the United Nations, Publishing Service, New York, New York 10017 (800) 253-9646; *Statistical Yearbook for Asia and the Pacific.*

NAURU - IRON ORE PRODUCTION AND CONSUMPTION - See NAURU - MINING AND MINERAL PRODUCTS

NAURU - LABOR

Central Intelligence Agency, Washington, D.C. 20505 (703) 482-1100, www.cia.gov; *The World Factbook.*

Euromonitor International, Inc., 122 South Michigan Avenue, Suite 1200, Chicago, Illinois 60603 (800) 577-EURO; *International Marketing Data and Statistics;* and *World Marketing Data and Statistics.*

Food and Agricultural Organization of the United Nations (FAO) Via delle Terme di Caracalla, 00100 Rome, Italy (Telephone Number in U.S. (202) 653-2400); *The State of Food and Agriculture.*

M.E. Sharpe, 80 Business Park Drive, Armonk, New York 10504 (800) 541-6563; *The Illustrated Book of World Rankings.*

St. Martin's Press, Inc., 175 Fifth Avenue, New York, New York 10010 (800) 221-7945; *The Statesman's Year-Book.*

NAURU - LAND USE

Central Intelligence Agency, Washington, D.C. 20505 (703) 482-1100, www.cia.gov; *The World Factbook.*

Euromonitor International, Inc., 122 South Michigan Avenue, Suite 1200, Chicago, Illinois 60603 (800) 577-EURO; *International Marketing Data and Statistics.*

Food and Agricultural Organization of the United Nations (FAO), Via delle Terme di Caracalla, 00100 Rome, Italy (Telephone Number in U.S. (202) 653-2400); *Production Yearbook.*

NAURU - LIBRARIES

M.E. Sharpe, 80 Business Park Drive, Armonk, New York 10504 (800) 541-6563; *The Illustrated Book of World Rankings.*

NAURU - LIFE EXPECTANCY

Central Intelligence Agency, Washington, D.C. 20505 (703) 482-1100, www.cia.gov; *The World Factbook.*

Euromonitor International, Inc., 122 South Michigan Avenue, Suite 1200, Chicago, Illinois 60603 (800) 577-EURO; *The World Economic Factbook.*

Statistical Office of the United Nations, Publishing Service, New York, New York 10017 (800) 253-9646; *Asia-Pacific in Figures;* and *World Statistics Pocketbook.*

NAURU - LITERACY RATE

Euromonitor International, Inc., 122 South Michigan Avenue, Suite 1200, Chicago, Illinois 60603 (800) 577-EURO; *World Marketing Data and Statistics.*

NAURU - LIVESTOCK AND POULTRY

Europa Publications Limited, 18 Bedford Square, London, WC1B 3JN, England; *The Europa World Year Book.*

Food and Agricultural Organization of the United Nations (FAO), Via delle Terme di Caracalla, 00100 Rome, Italy (Telephone Number in U.S. (202) 653-2400); *Production Yearbook;* and *The State of Food and Agriculture.*

M.E. Sharpe, 80 Business Park Drive, Armonk, New York 10504 (800) 541-6563; *The Illustrated Book of World Rankings.*

United Nations Conference on Trade and Development, Central Statistical Service, Palais des Nations, Geneva, Switzerland (Telephone in U.S. (800) 253-9646); *UNCTAD Commodity Yearbook.*

NAURU - MANPOWER

Statistical Office of the United Nations, Publishing Service, New York, New York 10017 (800) 253-9646; *Statistical Yearbook for Asia and the Pacific.*

NAURU - MANUFACTURING

M.E. Sharpe, 80 Business Park Drive, Armonk, New York 10504 (800) 541-6563; *The Illustrated Book of World Rankings.*

NAURU - MARRIAGE RATES

M.E. Sharpe, 80 Business Park Drive, Armonk, New York 10504 (800) 541-6563; *The Illustrated Book of World Rankings.*

Statistical Office of the United Nations, Publishing Service, New York, New York 10017 (800) 253-9646; *Demographic Yearbook;* and *Statistical Yearbook.*

NAURU - MEAT PRODUCTION - ALL TYPES OF MEAT AND POULTRY

Food and Agricultural Organization of the United Nations (FAO) Via delle Terme di Caracalla, 00100 Rome, Italy (Telephone Number in U.S. (202) 653-2400); *The State of Food and Agriculture.*

M.E. Sharpe, 80 Business Park Drive, Armonk, New York 10504 (800) 541-6563; *The Illustrated Book of World Rankings.*

NAURU - MERCHANT SHIPPING

Europa Publications Limited, 18 Bedford Square, London, WC1B 3JN, England; *The Europa World Year Book.*

St. Martin's Press, Inc., 175 Fifth Avenue, New York, New York 10010 (800) 221-7945; *The Statesman's Year-Book.*

Statistical Office of the United Nations, Publishing Service, New York, New York 10017 (800) 253-9646; *Statistical Yearbook.*

U.S. Department of Transportation, Maritime Administration, 400 Seventh Street, SW, Washington, D.C. 20590 (202) 366-5807, www.marad.dot.gov; *A Statistical Analysis of the World's Merchant Fleets.*

NAURU - MILK PRODUCTION - See NAURU - DAIRY PRODUCTS

NAURU - MILITARY

Central Intelligence Agency, Washington, D.C. 20505 (703) 482-1100, www.cia.gov; *The World Factbook.*

Euromonitor International, Inc., 122 South Michigan Avenue, Suite 1200, Chicago, Illinois 60603 (800) 577-EURO; *World Marketing Data and Statistics.*

NAURU - MINING AND MINERAL PRODUCTS

Europa Publications Limited, 18 Bedford Square, London, WC1B 3JN, England; *The Europa World Year Book.*

M.E. Sharpe, 80 Business Park Drive, Armonk, New York 10504 (800) 541-6563; *The Illustrated Book of World Rankings.*

Statistical Office of the United Nations, Publishing Service, New York, New York 10017 (800) 253-9646; *Statistical Yearbook.*

United Nations Conference on Trade and Development, Central Statistical Service, Palais des Nations, Geneva,

Switzerland (Telephone in U.S. (800) 253-9646); *UNCTAD Commodity Yearbook.*

NAURU - MORTALITY

Central Intelligence Agency, Washington, D.C. 20505 (703) 482-1100, www.cia.gov; *The World Factbook.*

Euromonitor International, Inc., 122 South Michigan Avenue, Suite 1200, Chicago, Illinois 60603 (800) 577-EURO; *International Marketing Data and Statistics;* and *The World Economic Factbook.*

Europa Publications Limited, 18 Bedford Square, London, WC1B 3JN, England; *The Europa World Year Book.*

St. Martin's Press, Inc., 175 Fifth Avenue, New York, New York 10010 (800) 221-7945; *The Statesman's Year-Book.*

Statistical Office of the United Nations, Publishing Service, New York, New York 10017 (800) 253-9646; *Asia-Pacific in Figures; Demographic Yearbook; World Statistics Pocketbook;* and *Statistical Yearbook.*

World Health Organization, Office of Publications, 20 Avenue Appia, CH-1211 Geneva 27, Switzerland (Telephone Number in U.S. (518) 436-9686); *World Health Statistics Annual.*

NAURU - MOTION PICTURES

St. Martin's Press, Inc., 175 Fifth Avenue, New York, New York 10010 (800) 221-7945; *The Statesman's Year-Book.*

Statistical Office of the United Nations, Publishing Service, New York, New York 10017 (800) 253-9646; *Statistical Yearbook.*

NAURU - MOTOR VEHICLES IN USE

Europa Publications Limited, 18 Bedford Square, London, WC1B 3JN, England; *The Europa World Year Book.*

NAURU - MUSEUMS

M.E. Sharpe, 80 Business Park Drive, Armonk, New York 10504 (800) 541-6563; *The Illustrated Book of World Rankings.*

NAURU - NATALITY - See NAURU - BIRTH RATES

NAURU - NATIONAL ACCOUNTS

Statistical Office of the United Nations, Publishing Service, New York, New York 10017 (800) 253-9646; *Asia-Pacific in Figures;* and *Statistical Yearbook for Asia and the Pacific.*

NAURU - NATIONAL INCOME

M.E. Sharpe, 80 Business Park Drive, Armonk, New York 10504 (800) 541-6563; *The Illustrated Book of World Rankings.*

NAURU - NATIONAL PRODUCT

M.E. Sharpe, 80 Business Park Drive, Armonk, New York 10504 (800) 541-6563; *The Illustrated Book of World Rankings.*

NAURU - NATURAL GAS PRODUCTION - See NAURU - MINING AND MINERAL PRODUCTS

NAURU - PEANUT PRODUCTION - See NAURU - CROPS

NAURU - PERIODICALS

United Nations Educational, Scientific and Cultural Organization (UNESCO), 7 Place de Fontenoy, F-75700 Paris, France (Telephone Number in U.S. (212) 963-5981); *Statistical Yearbook.*

NAURU - PESTICIDE USE

Food and Agricultural Organization of the United Nations (FAO) Via delle Terme di Caracalla, 00100 Rome, Italy (Telephone Number in U.S. (202) 653-2400); *The State of Food and Agriculture.*

NAURU - PETROLEUM INDUSTRY

Food and Agricultural Organization of the United Nations (FAO) Via delle Terme di Caracalla, 00100 Rome, Italy (Telephone Number in U.S. (202) 653-2400); *The State of Food and Agriculture.*

M.E. Sharpe, 80 Business Park Drive, Armonk, New York 10504 (800) 541-6563; *The Illustrated Book of World Rankings.*

United Nations Conference on Trade and Development, Central Statistical Service, Palais des Nations, Geneva, Switzerland (Telephone in U.S. (800) 253-9646); *UNCTAD Commodity Yearbook.*

NAURU - PHOSPHATE ROCK PRODUCTION - See NAURU - MINING AND MINERAL PRODUCTS

NAURU - PIGS - See NAURU - LIVESTOCK AND POULTRY

NAURU - POPULATION

Central Intelligence Agency, Washington, D.C. 20505 (703) 482-1100, www.cia.gov; *The World Factbook.*

Euromonitor International, Inc., 122 South Michigan Avenue, Suite 1200, Chicago, Illinois 60603 (800) 577-EURO; *International Marketing Data and Statistics;* and *The World Economic Factbook.*

Europa Publications Limited, 18 Bedford Square, London, WC1B 3JN, England; *The Europa World Year Book.*

Food and Agricultural Organization of the United Nations (FAO), Via delle Terme di Caracalla, 00100 Rome, Italy (Telephone Number in U.S. (202) 653-2400); *Production Yearbook.*

M.E. Sharpe, 80 Business Park Drive, Armonk, New York 10504 (800) 541-6563; *The Illustrated Book of World Rankings.*

St. Martin's Press, Inc., 175 Fifth Avenue, New York, New York 10010 (800) 221-7945; *The Statesman's Year-Book.*

Statistical Office of the United Nations, Publishing Service, New York, New York 10017 (800) 253-9646; *Asia-Pacific in Figures; Demographic Yearbook; Statistical Yearbook; World Statistics Pocketbook; and Statistical Yearbook for Asia and the Pacific.*

United Nations Educational, Scientific and Cultural Organization (UNESCO), 7 Place de Fontenoy, F-75700 Paris, France (Telephone Number in U.S. (212) 963-5981); *Statistical Yearbook.*

Walden Publishing Ltd., Two Market Street, Saffron Walden Essex, CB10 1HZ, England; *The World of Information Asia and Pacific Review.*

World Health Organization, Office of Publications, 20 Avenue Appia, CH-1211 Geneva 27, Switzerland (Telephone Number in U.S. (518) 436-9686); *World Health Statistics Annual.*

NAURU - POST OFFICES

M.E. Sharpe, 80 Business Park Drive, Armonk, New York 10504 (800) 541-6563; *The Illustrated Book of World Rankings.*

NAURU - POTATO PRODUCTION - See NAURU - CROPS

NAURU - PRICES

Food and Agricultural Organization of the United Nations (FAO), Via delle Terme di Caracalla, 00100 Rome, Italy (Telephone Number in U.S. (202) 653-2400); *Production Yearbook; and The State of Food and Agriculture.*

M.E. Sharpe, 80 Business Park Drive, Armonk, New York 10504 (800) 541-6563; *The Illustrated Book of World Rankings.*

South Pacific Commission, Post Box D5, Noumea Cedex, New Caledonia; *Statistical Bulletin of the South Pacific: Overseas Trade; and Statistical Bulletin of the South Pacific: Retail Price Indexes.*

NAURU - PRODUCTION

M.E. Sharpe, 80 Business Park Drive, Armonk, New York 10504 (800) 541-6563; *The Illustrated Book of World Rankings.*

NAURU - PUBLIC FINANCE - See NAURU - FINANCE

NAURU - RADIO BROADCASTING - See NAURU - BROADCASTING

NAURU - RADIO RECEIVERS

St. Martin's Press, Inc., 175 Fifth Avenue, New York, New York 10010 (800) 221-7945; *The Statesman's Year-Book.*

NAURU - RELIGION

Central Intelligence Agency, Washington, D.C. 20505 (703) 482-1100, www.cia.gov; *The World Factbook.*

M.E. Sharpe, 80 Business Park Drive, Armonk, New York 10504 (800) 541-6563; *The Illustrated Book of World Rankings.*

St. Martin's Press, Inc., 175 Fifth Avenue, New York, New York 10010 (800) 221-7945; *The Statesman's Year-Book.*

NAURU - RETAIL TRADE

Euromonitor International, Inc., 122 South Michigan Avenue, Suite 1200, Chicago, Illinois 60603 (800) 577-EURO; *World Marketing Data and Statistics.*

NAURU - RICE PRODUCTION - See NAURU - CROPS

NAURU - RUBBER PRODUCTION AND CONSUMPTION

M.E. Sharpe, 80 Business Park Drive, Armonk, New York 10504 (800) 541-6563; *The Illustrated Book of World Rankings.*

NAURU - SENIOR CITIZENS

M.E. Sharpe, 80 Business Park Drive, Armonk, New York 10504 (800) 541-6563; *The Illustrated Book of World Rankings.*

NAURU - SHEEP - See NAURU - LIVESTOCK AND POULTRY

NAURU - SILVER PRODUCTION AND CONSUMPTION - See NAURU - MINING AND MINERAL PRODUCTS

NAURU - SOCIAL DATA

Statistical Office of the United Nations, Publishing Service, New York, New York 10017 (800) 253-9646; *World Statistics Pocketbook.*

NAURU - SOCIAL PRODUCTION

M.E. Sharpe, 80 Business Park Drive, Armonk, New York 10504 (800) 541-6563; *The Illustrated Book of World Rankings.*

NAURU - STEEL PRODUCTION - See NAURU - MINING AND MINERAL PRODUCTS

NAURU - STOCKS - COMMODITY - MARKET PRICE - INDEX

Food and Agricultural Organization of the United Nations (FAO) Via delle Terme di Caracalla, 00100 Rome, Italy (Telephone Number in U.S. (202) 653-2400); *The State of Food and Agriculture.*

NAURU - SUGAR PRODUCTION AND CONSUMPTION - See NAURU - CROPS

NAURU - TELEPHONES IN USE

American Telephone and Telegraph Company, 26 Parsippany Road, Whippany, New Jersey 07981 (800) 222-0300; *The World's Telephones.*

Central Intelligence Agency, Washington, D.C. 20505 (703) 482-1100, www.cia.gov; *The World Factbook.*

Europa Publications Limited, 18 Bedford Square, London, WC1B 3JN, England; *The Europa World Year Book.*

St. Martin's Press, Inc., 175 Fifth Avenue, New York, New York 10010 (800) 221-7945; *The Statesman's Year-Book.*

Statistical Office of the United Nations, Publishing Service, New York, New York 10017 (800) 253-9646; *World Statistics Pocketbook.*

NAURU - TELEVISION BROADCASTING - See NAURU - BROADCASTING

NAURU - TEXTILE INDUSTRY

M.E. Sharpe, 80 Business Park Drive, Armonk, New York 10504 (800) 541-6563; *The Illustrated Book of World Rankings.*

South Pacific Commission, Post Box D5, Noumea Cedex, New Caledonia; *Statistical Bulletin of the South Pacific: Retail Price Indexes.*

United Nations Conference on Trade and Development, Central Statistical Service, Palais des Nations, Geneva, Switzerland (Telephone in U.S. (800) 253-9646); *UNCTAD Commodity Yearbook.*

NAURU - TOBACCO PRODUCTION

M.E. Sharpe, 80 Business Park Drive, Armonk, New York 10504 (800) 541-6563; *The Illustrated Book of World Rankings.*

South Pacific Commission, Post Box

D5, Noumea Cedex, New Caledonia; *Statistical Bulletin of the South Pacific: Retail Price Indexes.*

NAURU - TOURISM

Euromonitor International, Inc., 122 South Michigan Avenue, Suite 1200, Chicago, Illinois 60603 (800) 577-EURO; *The World Economic Factbook;* and *World Marketing Data and Statistics.*

M.E. Sharpe, 80 Business Park Drive, Armonk, New York 10504 (800) 541-6563; *The Illustrated Book of World Rankings.*

NAURU - TRADE - See NAURU - FOREIGN TRADE

NAURU - TRANSPORTATION AND COMMUNICATIONS

Central Intelligence Agency, Washington, D.C. 20505 (703) 482-1100, www.cia.gov; *The World Factbook.*

Euromonitor International, Inc., 122 South Michigan Avenue, Suite 1200, Chicago, Illinois 60603 (800) 577-EURO; *International Marketing Data and Statistics;* and *World Marketing Data and Statistics.*

Europa Publications Limited, 18 Bedford Square, London, WC1B 3JN, England; *The Europa World Year Book.*

M.E. Sharpe, 80 Business Park Drive, Armonk, New York 10504 (800) 541-6563; *The Illustrated Book of World Rankings.*

South Pacific Commission, Post Box D5, Noumea Cedex, New Caledonia; *Statistical Bulletin of the South Pacific: Retail Price Indexes.*

St. Martin's Press, Inc., 175 Fifth Avenue, New York, New York 10010 (800) 221-7945; *The Statesman's Year-Book.*

Statistical Office of the United Nations, Publishing Service, New York, New York 10017 (800) 253-9646; *Statistical Yearbook for Asia and the Pacific.*

NAURU - UNEMPLOYMENT RATE

Central Intelligence Agency, Washington, D.C. 20505 (703) 482-1100, www.cia.gov; *The World Factbook.*

NAURU - VITAL STATISTICS

St. Martin's Press, Inc., 175 Fifth Avenue, New York, New York 10010 (800) 221-7945; *The Statesman's Year-Book.*

Statistical Office of the United Nations, Publishing Service, New York, New York 10017 (800) 253-9646; *Statistical Yearbook.*

World Health Organization, Office of

Publications, 20 Avenue Appia, CH-1211 Geneva 27, Switzerland (Telephone Number in U.S. (518) 436-9686); *World Health Statistics Annual.*

NAURU - WAGES AND PRICES

Statistical Office of the United Nations, Publishing Service, New York, New York 10017 (800) 253-9646; *Statistical Yearbook for Asia and the Pacific.*

NAURU - WEATHER - See NAURU - CLIMATE

NAURU - WHEAT PRODUCTION - See NAURU - CROPS

NAURU - WINE PRODUCTION - See NAURU - BEVERAGES

NAURU - WOOL PRODUCTION - See NAURU - TEXTILE INDUSTRY

NAVY

U.S. Department of Defense, Office of the Secretary, The Pentagon, Washington, D.C. 20301 (703) 545-6700; *Selected Manpower Statistics.*

NEBRASKA - See also STATE DATA (FOR INDIVIDUAL STATES)

Nebraska - Primary Statistics Source

Department of Economic Development, Division of Research, Box 94666, 301 Centennial Mall South, Lincoln, Nebraska 68509 (402) 471-3784; *Nebraska Statistical Handbook.*

Nebraska - State Data Centers

Center for Public Affairs Research, Nebraska State Data Center, Annex 26, University of Nebraska at Omaha, Omaha, Nebraska 68182-0001, Mr. Jerome Deichert (402) 554-2134.

Federal Documents Librarian, Nebraska Library Commission, The Atrium, 1200 North Street, Suite 120, Lincoln, Nebraska 68508-2006, Ms. Lori Sailors (402) 471-2045.

Nebraska Department of Administration Services, Information Management Services, 301 Centennial Mail S., Lower Level, Post Office Box 95045, Lincoln, Nebraska 68509-5045, Mr. Jerry Douglas (402) 471-4855.

Nebraska Department of Labor, 550 South 16th Street, Post Office Box 94600, Lincoln, Nebraska 68509-4600, Mr. Phillip Baker (402) 471-2600.

Nebraska Natural Resources Commission, 301 Centennial Mall South, Post Office Box 94876, Lincoln, Nebraska 68509-4876, Mahendra Bansal (402) 471-3964.

Policy Research Office, Post Office Box 94601, State Capitol, Room 1319, Lincoln, Nebraska 68509-4601, Ms. Lauren Hill (402) 471-2414.

NECTARINES

U.S. Department of Agriculture, Economic Research Service, 1800 M Street, NW, Washington, D.C. 20036 (202) 694-5050, www.ers.usda.gov; *Food Consumption, Prices, and Expenditures;* and *Agricultural Outlook.*

U.S. Department of Agriculture, National Agricultural Statistics Service, Fourteenth Street and Independence Avenue, SW, Washington, D.C. 20250 (800) 727-9540, www.usda.gov/nass; *Citrus Fruits.*

NEONATAL DEATHS - See also DEATHS AND DEATH RATES

NEONATAL DEATHS

U.S. Department of Health and Human Services, National Center for Health Statistics, 3700 East-West Highway, Hyattsville, Maryland 20782 (301) 436-8500, www.cdc.gov/nchs; *Vital Statistics of the United States; National Vital Statistics Report;* and unpublished data.

Nepal - National Statistical Office

Central Bureau of Statistics, National Planning Commission Secretariat, Ramshah Path, Thapathali, Kathmandu, Nepal.

Nepal - Primary Statistics Sources

Central Bureau of Statistics, National Planning Commission Secretariat, Ramshah Path, Thapathali, Kathmandu, Nepal; *Statistical Pocket Book;* and *Statistical Yearbook of Nepal.*

Consultancy Services Division, Nepal Industrial Development Corporation, Kathmandu, Nepal; *Statistical Abstract.*

Economic Planning Section, Program Office, US AID, Kathmandu, Nepal; *Economic Data Papers - Nepal.*

NEPAL - AGRICULTURE

Asian Development Bank, Post Office Box 789, 1099 Manila, Philippines; *Key*

Indicators of Developing Asian and Pacific Countries.

Economist Intelligence Unit, 111 West 57th Street, New York, New York 10019 (800) 938-4685; *Nepal Country Report.*

Euromonitor International, Inc., 122 South Michigan Avenue, Suite 1200, Chicago, Illinois 60603 (800) 577-EURO; *International Marketing Data and Statistics;* and *World Marketing Data and Statistics.*

Europa Publications Limited, 18 Bedford Square, London, WC1B 3JN, England; *The Europa World Year Book.*

Food and Agricultural Organization of the United Nations (FAO) Via delle Terme di Caracalla, 00100 Rome, Italy (Telephone Number in U.S. (202) 653-2400); *Production Yearbook; The State of Food and Agriculture;* and *Trade Yearbook.*

M.E. Sharpe, 80 Business Park Drive, Armonk, New York 10504 (800) 541-6563; *The Illustrated Book of World Rankings.*

St. Martin's Press, Inc., 175 Fifth Avenue, New York, New York 10010 (800) 221-7945; *The Statesman's Year-Book.*

Statistical Office of the United Nations, Publishing Service, New York, New York 10017 (800) 253-9646; *Asia-Pacific in Figures; Statistical Yearbook;* and *Statistical Yearbook for Asia and the Pacific.*

United Nations Conference on Trade and Development, Central Statistical Service, Palais des Nations, Geneva, Switzerland (Telephone in U.S. (800) 253-9646); *UNCTAD Commodity Yearbook.*

The World Bank, 1818 H Street, NW, Washington, D.C. 20433 (202) 477-1234; *World Tables.*

NEPAL - AIRLINE SERVICE

The Economist Intelligence Unit (Asia) Limited, 10th Floor, Luk Kwok Centre, 72 Gloucester Road, Wanchai, Hong Kong (Phone Number in U.S. (800) 938-4685); *Asian Market Atlas.*

Europa Publications Limited, 18 Bedford Square, London, WC1B 3JN, England; *The Europa World Year Book.*

International Civil Aviation Organization, 999 University Street, Montreal, Quebec, Canada H3C 5H7 (514) 954-8219; *Civil Aviation Statistics of the World.*

M.E. Sharpe, 80 Business Park Drive, Armonk, New York 10504 (800) 541-6563; *The Illustrated Book of World Rankings.*

St. Martin's Press, Inc., 175 Fifth Avenue, New York, New York 10010 (800) 221-7945; *The Statesman's Year-Book.*

NEPAL - AIRPORTS

Central Intelligence Agency, Washington, D.C. 20505 (703) 482-1100, www.cia.gov; *The World Factbook.*

NEPAL - ALUMINUM PRODUCTION AND CONSUMPTION - See NEPAL - MINING AND MINERAL PRODUCTS

NEPAL - ANIMAL HEALTH

Food and Agricultural Organization of the United Nations (FAO), Via delle Terme di Caracalla, 00100 Rome, Italy (Telephone Number in U.S. (202) 653-2400); *Animal Health Yearbook.*

NEPAL - AREA AND DENSITY OF POPULATION

Central Intelligence Agency, Washington, D.C. 20505 (703) 482-1100, www.cia.gov; *The World Factbook.*

Euromonitor International, Inc., 122 South Michigan Avenue, Suite 1200, Chicago, Illinois 60603 (800) 577-EURO; *International Marketing Data and Statistics;* and *The World Economic Factbook.*

Europa Publications Limited, 18 Bedford Square, London, WC1B 3JN, England; *The Europa World Year Book.*

Food and Agricultural Organization of the United Nations (FAO) Via delle Terme di Caracalla, 00100 Rome, Italy (Telephone Number in U.S. (202) 653-2400); *The State of Food and Agriculture.*

M.E. Sharpe, 80 Business Park Drive, Armonk, New York 10504 (800) 541-6563; *The Illustrated Book of World Rankings.*

St. Martin's Press, Inc., 175 Fifth Avenue, New York, New York 10010 (800) 221-7945; *The Statesman's Year-Book.*

Statistical Office of the United Nations, Publishing Service, New York, New York 10017 (800) 253-9646; *Statistical Yearbook.*

United Nations Educational, Scientific and Cultural Organization (UNESCO), 7 Place de Fontenoy, F-75700 Paris, France (Telephone Number in U.S. (212) 963-5981); *Statistical Yearbook.*

The World Bank, 1818 H Street, NW, Washington, D.C. 20433 (202) 477-1234; *World Development Report.*

NEPAL - ARMS EXPORTS AND IMPORTS - See NEPAL - MILITARY

NEPAL - BALANCE OF PAYMENTS

The Economist Intelligence Unit, 111 West 57th Street, New York, New York 10019 (800) 938-4685; *The World Market Atlas.*

Europa Publications Limited, 18 Bedford Square, London, WC1B 3JN, England; *The Europa World Year Book.*

International Monetary Fund, 700 Nineteenth Street, NW, Washington, D.C. 20431 (202) 623-7000; *Balance of Payments Yearbook.*

United Nations Conference on Trade and Development (UNCTAD), New York, New York 10017 (800) 253-9646; *Handbook of International Trade and Development Statistics.*

The World Bank, 1818 H Street, NW, Washington, D.C. 20433 (202) 477-1234; *World Development Report;* and *World Tables.*

NEPAL - BANKING

Asian Development Bank, Post Office Box 789, 1099 Manila, Philippines; *Key Indicators of Developing Asian and Pacific Countries.*

Euromonitor International, Inc., 122 South Michigan Avenue, Suite 1200, Chicago, Illinois 60603 (800) 577-EURO; *World Marketing Data and Statistics.*

Europa Publications Limited, 18 Bedford Square, London, WC1B 3JN, England; *The Europa World Year Book.*

International Monetary Fund, 700 Nineteenth Street, NW, Washington, D.C. 20431 (202) 623-7000; *Government Finance Statistics Yearbook.*

M.E. Sharpe, 80 Business Park Drive, Armonk, New York 10504 (800) 541-6563; *The Illustrated Book of World Rankings.*

St. Martin's Press, Inc., 175 Fifth Avenue, New York, New York 10010 (800) 221-7945; *The Statesman's Year-Book.*

NEPAL - BARLEY PRODUCTION - See NEPAL - CROPS

NEPAL - BEER PRODUCTION - See NEPAL - BEVERAGES

NEPAL - BEVERAGES

M.E. Sharpe, 80 Business Park Drive, Armonk, New York 10504 (800) 541-6563; *The Illustrated Book of World Rankings.*

Statistical Office of the United Nations, Publishing Service, New York, New York 10017 (800) 253-9646; *Statistical Yearbook.*

NEPAL - BIRTH RATES

Central Intelligence Agency, Washington, D.C. 20505 (703) 482-1100, www.cia.gov; *The World Factbook*.

The Economist Intelligence Unit (Asia) Limited, 10th Floor, Luk Kwok Centre, 72 Gloucester Road, Wanchai, Hong Kong (Phone Number in U.S. (800) 938-4685); *Asian Market Atlas*.

Euromonitor International, Inc., 122 South Michigan Avenue, Suite 1200, Chicago, Illinois 60603 (800) 577-EURO; *International Marketing Data and Statistics;* and *The World Economic Factbook*.

Europa Publications Limited, 18 Bedford Square, London, WC1B 3JN, England; *The Europa World Year Book*.

M.E. Sharpe, 80 Business Park Drive, Armonk, New York 10504 (800) 541-6563; *The Illustrated Book of World Rankings*.

St. Martin's Press, Inc., 175 Fifth Avenue, New York, New York 10010 (800) 221-7945; *The Statesman's Year-Book*.

Statistical Office of the United Nations, Publishing Service, New York, New York 10017 (800) 253-9646; *Asia-Pacific in Figures; Demographic Yearbook;* and *Statistical Yearbook*.

The World Bank, 1818 H Street, NW, Washington, D.C. 20433 (202) 477-1234; *World Tables*.

NEPAL - BONDS

Asian Development Bank, Post Office Box 789, 1099 Manila, Philippines; *Key Indicators of Developing Asian and Pacific Countries*.

International Monetary Fund, 700 Nineteenth Street, NW, Washington, D.C. 20431 (202) 623-7000; *Government Finance Statistics Yearbook*.

NEPAL - BOOK PRODUCTION

United Nations Educational, Scientific and Cultural Organization (UNESCO), 7 Place de Fontenoy, F-75700 Paris, France (Telephone Number in U.S. (212) 963-5981); *Statistical Yearbook*.

NEPAL - BROADCASTING

Billboard Limited, Post Office Box 9027, 1006 AA Amsterdam, The Netherlands (Telephone Number in U.S. (212) 764-7300); *World Radio TV Handbook*.

Central Intelligence Agency, Washington, D.C. 20505 (703) 482-1100, www.cia.gov; *The World Factbook*.

The Economist Intelligence Unit (Asia) Limited, 10th Floor, Luk Kwok Centre, 72 Gloucester Road, Wanchai, Hong Kong (Phone Number in U.S. (800) 938-4685); *Asian Market Atlas*.

Euromonitor International, Inc., 122 South Michigan Avenue, Suite 1200, Chicago, Illinois 60603 (800) 577-EURO; *World Marketing Data and Statistics*.

M.E. Sharpe, 80 Business Park Drive, Armonk, New York 10504 (800) 541-6563; *The Illustrated Book of World Rankings*.

St. Martin's Press, Inc., 175 Fifth Avenue, New York, New York 10010 (800) 221-7945; *The Statesman's Year-Book*.

United Nations Educational, Scientific and Cultural Organization (UNESCO), 7 Place de Fontenoy, F-75700 Paris, France (Telephone Number in U.S. (212) 963-5981); *Statistical Yearbook*.

NEPAL - BUDGET

Central Intelligence Agency, Washington, D.C. 20505 (703) 482-1100, www.cia.gov; *The World Factbook*.

NEPAL - BUSINESS AND PROFESSIONAL LICENSES

International Monetary Fund, 700 Nineteenth Street, NW, Washington, D.C. 20431 (202) 623-7000; *Government Finance Statistics Yearbook*.

NEPAL - BUTTER PRODUCTION - See NEPAL - DAIRY PRODUCTS

NEPAL - CALORIE SUPPLY

Asian Development Bank, Post Office Box 789, 1099 Manila, Philippines; *Key Indicators of Developing Asian and Pacific Countries*.

Food and Agricultural Organization of the United Nations (FAO) Via delle Terme di Caracalla, 00100 Rome, Italy (Telephone Number in U.S. (202) 653-2400); *The State of Food and Agriculture*.

NEPAL - CAPITAL INVESTMENT

Asian Development Bank, Post Office Box 789, 1099 Manila, Philippines; *Key Indicators of Developing Asian and Pacific Countries*.

NEPAL - CAPITAL REVENUE

Asian Development Bank, Post Office Box 789, 1099 Manila, Philippines; *Key Indicators of Developing Asian and Pacific Countries*.

International Monetary Fund, 700 Nineteenth Street, NW, Washington, D.C.

20431 (202) 623-7000; *Government Finance Statistics Yearbook*.

NEPAL - CATTLE - See NEPAL - LIVESTOCK AND POULTRY

NEPAL - CEMENT PRODUCTION - See NEPAL - MINING AND MINERAL PRODUCTS

NEPAL - CHEESE PRODUCTION AND CONSUMPTION - See NEPAL - DAIRY PRODUCTS

NEPAL - CHICK PEA PRODUCTION - See NEPAL - CROPS

NEPAL - CHICKENS - See NEPAL - LIVESTOCK AND POULTRY

NEPAL - CIGARETTE PRODUCTION - See NEPAL - TOBACCO PRODUCTION

NEPAL - CLIMATE

M.E. Sharpe, 80 Business Park Drive, Armonk, New York 10504 (800) 541-6563; *The Illustrated Book of World Rankings*.

St. Martin's Press, Inc., 175 Fifth Avenue, New York, New York 10010 (800) 221-7945; *The Statesman's Year-Book*.

NEPAL - COAL PRODUCTION - See NEPAL - MINING AND MINERAL PRODUCTS

NEPAL - COFFEE PRODUCTION AND CONSUMPTION - See NEPAL - CROPS

NEPAL - COMMERCE

St. Martin's Press, Inc., 175 Fifth Avenue, New York, New York 10010 (800) 221-7945; *The Statesman's Year-Book*.

NEPAL - COMMUNICATIONS - See NEPAL - TRANSPORTATION AND COMMUNICATIONS

NEPAL - CONSTRUCTION

M.E. Sharpe, 80 Business Park Drive, Armonk, New York 10504 (800) 541-6563; *The Illustrated Book of World Rankings*.

NEPAL - CONSUMER PRICE INDEX

Asian Development Bank, Post Office Box 789, 1099 Manila, Philippines; *Key Indicators of Developing Asian and Pacific Countries*.

Europa Publications Limited, 18 Bedford Square, London, WC1B 3JN, England; *The Europa World Year Book*.

Statistical Office of the United Nations, Publishing Service, New York, New York 10017 (800) 253-9646; *Statistical Yearbook*.

NEPAL - CONSUMER PRICES

Euromonitor International, Inc., 122 South Michigan Avenue, Suite 1200, Chicago, Illinois 60603 (800) 577-EURO; *World Marketing Data and Statistics.*

International Labour Office, I.L.O. Publications, 1828 L Street, NW., Suite 801, Washington, D.C. 20036 (301) 638-3152; *Yearbook of Labour Statistics.*

NEPAL - CONSUMPTION

The World Bank, 1818 H Street, NW, Washington, D.C. 20433 (202) 477-1234; *World Development Report.*

NEPAL - COPPER PRODUCTION AND CONSUMPTION - See NEPAL -MINING AND MINERAL PRODUCTS

NEPAL - CORN PRODUCTION - See NEPAL - CROPS

NEPAL - CORPORATE TAXES - See NEPAL - TAXATION

NEPAL - COTTON PRODUCTION - See NEPAL - CROPS

NEPAL - CRIME

Yale University Press, Yale Station, New Haven, Connecticut 06520 (800) 987-7323; *Violence and Crime in Cross-National Perspective.*

NEPAL - CROPS

Asian Development Bank, Post Office Box 789, 1099 Manila, Philippines; *Key Indicators of Developing Asian and Pacific Countries.*

Europa Publications Limited, 18 Bedford Square, London, WC1B 3JN, England; *The Europa World Year Book.*

Food and Agricultural Organization of the United Nations (FAO), Via delle Terme di Caracalla, 00100 Rome, Italy (Telephone Number in U.S. (202) 653-2400); *Production Yearbook;* and *The State of Food and Agriculture.*

M.E. Sharpe, 80 Business Park Drive, Armonk, New York 10504 (800) 541-6563; *The Illustrated Book of World Rankings.*

St. Martin's Press, Inc., 175 Fifth Avenue, New York, New York 10010 (800) 221-7945; *The Statesman's Year-Book.*

Statistical Office of the United Nations, Publishing Service, New York, New York 10017 (800) 253-9646; *Statistical Yearbook.*

United Nations Conference on Trade and Development, Central Statistical Service, Palais des Nations, Geneva,

Switzerland (Telephone in U.S. (800) 253-9646); *UNCTAD Commodity Yearbook.*

NEPAL - CUSTOMS DUTIES

International Monetary Fund, 700 Nineteenth Street, NW, Washington, D.C. 20431 (202) 623-7000; *Government Finance Statistics Yearbook.*

St. Martin's Press, Inc., 175 Fifth Avenue, New York, New York 10010 (800) 221-7945; *The Statesman's Year-Book.*

NEPAL - DAIRY PRODUCTS

Europa Publications Limited, 18 Bedford Square, London, WC1B 3JN, England; *The Europa World Year Book.*

Food and Agricultural Organization of the United Nations (FAO) Via delle Terme di Caracalla, 00100 Rome, Italy (Telephone Number in U.S. (202) 653-2400); *The State of Food and Agriculture.*

M.E. Sharpe, 80 Business Park Drive, Armonk, New York 10504 (800) 541-6563; *The Illustrated Book of World Rankings.*

St. Martin's Press, Inc., 175 Fifth Avenue, New York, New York 10010 (800) 221-7945; *The Statesman's Year-Book.*

Statistical Office of the United Nations, Publishing Service, New York, New York 10017 (800) 253-9646; *Statistical Yearbook.*

NEPAL - DEATH RATES - See NEPAL - MORTALITY

NEPAL - DEFENSE EXPENDITURES - See NEPAL - MILITARY

NEPAL - DEMOGRAPHY

The Economist Intelligence Unit, 111 West 57th Street, New York, New York 10019 (800) 938-4685; *The World Market Atlas.*

The Economist Intelligence Unit (Asia) Limited, 10th Floor, Luk Kwok Centre, 72 Gloucester Road, Wanchai, Hong Kong (Phone Number in U.S. (800) 938-4685); *Asian Market Atlas.*

Euromonitor International, Inc., 122 South Michigan Avenue, Suite 1200, Chicago, Illinois 60603 (800) 577-EURO; *International Marketing Data and Statistics; The World Economic Factbook;* and *World Marketing Data and Statistics.*

M.E. Sharpe, 80 Business Park Drive, Armonk, New York 10504 (800) 541-6563; *The Illustrated Book of World Rankings.*

Statistical Office of the United Nations, Publishing Service, New York, New York 10017 (800) 253-9646; *Asia-Pacific in*

Figures; and *Human Development Report.*

NEPAL - DEVELOPMENT ASSISTANCE

Asian Development Bank, Post Office Box 789, 1099 Manila, Philippines; *Key Indicators of Developing Asian and Pacific Countries.*

Statistical Office of the United Nations, Publishing Service, New York, New York 10017 (800) 253-9646; *Statistical Yearbook.*

NEPAL - DIAMOND PRODUCTION - See NEPAL - MINING AND MINERAL PRODUCTS

NEPAL - DIVORCE

M.E. Sharpe, 80 Business Park Drive, Armonk, New York 10504 (800) 541-6563; *The Illustrated Book of World Rankings.*

Statistical Office of the United Nations, Publishing Service, New York, New York 10017 (800) 253-9646; *Demographic Yearbook.*

NEPAL - ECONOMY

Asian Development Bank, Post Office Box 789, 1099 Manila, Philippines; *Key Indicators of Developing Asian and Pacific Countries.*

Central Intelligence Agency, Washington, D.C. 20505 (703) 482-1100, www.cia.gov; *The World Factbook.*

Economist Intelligence Unit, 111 West 57th Street, New York, New York 10019 (800) 938-4685; *Nepal Country Report.*

Euromonitor International, Inc., 122 South Michigan Avenue, Suite 1200, Chicago, Illinois 60603 (800) 577-EURO; *International Marketing Data and Statistics; The World Economic Factbook;* and *World Marketing Data and Statistics.*

Europa Publications Limited, 18 Bedford Square, London, WC1B 3JN, England; *The Europa World Year Book.*

M.E. Sharpe, 80 Business Park Drive, Armonk, New York 10504 (800) 541-6563; *The Illustrated Book of World Rankings.*

St. Martin's Press, Inc., 175 Fifth Avenue, New York, New York 10010 (800) 221-7945; *The Statesman's Year-Book.*

Statistical Office of the United Nations, Publishing Service, New York, New York 10017 (800) 253-9646; *World Statistics Pocketbook.*

The World Bank, 1818 H Street, NW, Washington, D.C. 20433 (202) 477-1234; *The World Bank Atlas;* and *World Development Report.*

NEPAL - EDUCATION

The Economist Intelligence Unit, 111 West 57th Street, New York, New York 10019 (800) 938-4685; *The World Market Atlas.*

The Economist Intelligence Unit (Asia) Limited, 10th Floor, Luk Kwok Centre, 72 Gloucester Road, Wanchai, Hong Kong (Phone Number in U.S. (800) 938-4685); *Asian Market Atlas.*

Euromonitor International, Inc., 122 South Michigan Avenue, Suite 1200, Chicago, Illinois 60603 (800) 577-EURO; *International Marketing Data and Statistics;* and *World Marketing Data and Statistics.*

Europa Publications Limited, 18 Bedford Square, London, WC1B 3JN, England; *The Europa World Year Book.*

International Monetary Fund, 700 Nineteenth Street, NW, Washington, D.C. 20431 (202) 623-7000; *Government Finance Statistics Yearbook.*

M.E. Sharpe, 80 Business Park Drive, Armonk, New York 10504 (800) 541-6563; *The Illustrated Book of World Rankings.*

St. Martin's Press, Inc., 175 Fifth Avenue, New York, New York 10010 (800) 221-7945; *The Statesman's Year-Book.*

Statistical Office of the United Nations, Publishing Service, New York, New York 10017 (800) 253-9646; *Asia-Pacific in Figures; Human Development Report;* and *Statistical Yearbook for Asia and the Pacific.*

United Nations Educational, Scientific and Cultural Organization (UNESCO), 7 Place de Fontenoy, F-75700 Paris, France (Telephone Number in U.S. (212) 963-5981); *Statistical Yearbook.*

The World Bank, 1818 H Street, NW, Washington, D.C. 20433 (202) 477-1234; *World Development Report;* and *World Tables.*

NEPAL - EGG PRODUCTION AND CONSUMPTION - See NEPAL - DAIRY PRODUCTS

NEPAL - ELECTRICITY

Asian Development Bank, Post Office Box 789, 1099 Manila, Philippines; *Key Indicators of Developing Asian and Pacific Countries.*

Central Intelligence Agency, Washington, D.C. 20505 (703) 482-1100, www.cia.gov; *The World Factbook.*

M.E. Sharpe, 80 Business Park Drive, Armonk, New York 10504 (800) 541-6563;

The Illustrated Book of World Rankings.

St. Martin's Press, Inc., 175 Fifth Avenue, New York, New York 10010 (800) 221-7945; *The Statesman's Year-Book.*

Statistical Office of the United Nations, Publishing Service, New York, New York 10017 (800) 253-9646; *Electric Power in Asia and the Pacific; Human Development Report;* and *Statistical Yearbook.*

NEPAL - EMPLOYMENT

Euromonitor International, Inc., 122 South Michigan Avenue, Suite 1200, Chicago, Illinois 60603 (800) 577-EURO; *International Marketing Data and Statistics.*

International Labour Office, I.L.O. Publications, 1828 L Street, NW., Suite 801, Washington, D.C. 20036 (301) 638-3152; *Yearbook of Labour Statistics.*

M.E. Sharpe, 80 Business Park Drive, Armonk, New York 10504 (800) 541-6563; *The Illustrated Book of World Rankings.*

Statistical Office of the United Nations, Publishing Service, New York, New York 10017 (800) 253-9646; *Asia-Pacific in Figures.*

NEPAL - ENERGY

Euromonitor International, Inc., 122 South Michigan Avenue, Suite 1200, Chicago, Illinois 60603 (800) 577-EURO; *International Marketing Data and Statistics; The World Economic Factbook;* and *World Marketing Data and Statistics.*

Food and Agricultural Organization of the United Nations (FAO) Via delle Terme di Caracalla, 00100 Rome, Italy (Telephone Number in U.S. (202) 653-2400); *The State of Food and Agriculture.*

M.E. Sharpe, 80 Business Park Drive, Armonk, New York 10504 (800) 541-6563; *The Illustrated Book of World Rankings.*

St. Martin's Press, Inc., 175 Fifth Avenue, New York, New York 10010 (800) 221-7945; *The Statesman's Year-Book.*

Statistical Office of the United Nations, Publishing Service, New York, New York 10017 (800) 253-9646; *Asia-Pacific in Figures; Energy Statistics Yearbook; Human Development Report; Statistical Yearbook; World Statistics Pocketbook;* and *Statistical Yearbook for Asia and the Pacific.*

The World Bank, 1818 H Street, NW, Washington, D.C. 20433 (202) 477-1234; *The World Bank Atlas;* and *World Development Report.*

NEPAL - ENVIRONMENT

Economist Intelligence Unit, 111 West 57th Street, New York, New York 10019 (800) 938-4685; *Nepal Country Report.*

Statistical Office of the United Nations, Publishing Service, New York, New York 10017 (800) 253-9646; *World Statistics Pocketbook.*

NEPAL - EXCHANGE RATES

Asian Development Bank, Post Office Box 789, 1099 Manila, Philippines; *Key Indicators of Developing Asian and Pacific Countries.*

Central Intelligence Agency, Washington, D.C. 20505 (703) 482-1100, www.cia.gov; *The World Factbook.*

The Economist Intelligence Unit (Asia) Limited, 10th Floor, Luk Kwok Centre, 72 Gloucester Road, Wanchai, Hong Kong (Phone Number in U.S. (800) 938-4685); *Asian Market Atlas.*

Euromonitor International, Inc., 122 South Michigan Avenue, Suite 1200, Chicago, Illinois 60603 (800) 577-EURO; *International Marketing Data and Statistics;* and *The World Economic Factbook.*

Europa Publications Limited, 18 Bedford Square, London, WC1B 3JN, England; *The Europa World Year Book.*

International Civil Aviation Organization, 999 University Street, Montreal, Quebec, Canada H3C 5H7 (514) 954-8219; *Civil Aviation Statistics of the World.*

Statistical Office of the United Nations, Publishing Service, New York, New York 10017 (800) 253-9646; *Statistical Yearbook;* and *World Statistics Pocketbook.*

Walden Publishing Ltd., Two Market Street, Saffron Walden Essex, CB10 1HZ, England; *The World of Information Asia and Pacific Review.*

NEPAL - EXCISE TAXES - See NEPAL - TAXATION

NEPAL - EXPORTS

Asian Development Bank, Post Office Box 789, 1099 Manila, Philippines; *Key Indicators of Developing Asian and Pacific Countries.*

Central Intelligence Agency, Washington, D.C. 20505 (703) 482-1100, www.cia.gov; *The World Factbook.*

The Economist Intelligence Unit, 111 West 57th Street, New York, New York 10019 (800) 938-4685; *Nepal Country Report; and The World Market Atlas.*

The Economist Intelligence Unit (Asia) Limited, 10th Floor, Luk Kwok Centre, 72 Gloucester Road, Wanchai, Hong Kong (Phone Number in U.S. (800) 938-4685); *Asian Market Atlas.*

Euromonitor International, Inc., 122 South Michigan Avenue, Suite 1200, Chicago, Illinois 60603 (800) 577-EURO; *International Marketing Data and Statistics;* and *The World Economic Factbook.*

Europa Publications Limited, 18 Bedford Square, London, WC1B 3JN, England; *The Europa World Year Book.*

Food and Agricultural Organization of the United Nations (FAO) Via delle Terme di Caracalla, 00100 Rome, Italy (Telephone Number in U.S. (202) 653-2400); *The State of Food and Agriculture.*

International Monetary Fund, 700 Nineteenth Street, NW, Washington, D.C. 20431 (202) 623-7000; *Direction of Trade Statistics;* and *Government Finance Statistics Yearbook.*

St. Martin's Press, Inc., 175 Fifth Avenue, New York, New York 10010 (800) 221-7945; *The Statesman's Year-Book.*

United Nations Conference on Trade and Development (UNCTAD), New York, New York 10017 (800) 253-9646; *Handbook of International Trade and Development Statistics.*

Walden Publishing Ltd., Two Market Street, Saffron Walden Essex, CB10 1HZ, England; *The World of Information Asia and Pacific Review.*

The World Bank, 1818 H Street, NW, Washington, D.C. 20433 (202) 477-1234; *World Development Report;* and *World Tables.*

NEPAL - EXTERNAL FINANCING

Asian Development Bank, Post Office Box 789, 1099 Manila, Philippines; *Key Indicators of Developing Asian and Pacific Countries.*

NEPAL - EXTERNAL INDEBTEDNESS

Asian Development Bank, Post Office Box 789, 1099 Manila, Philippines; *Key Indicators of Developing Asian and Pacific Countries.*

The World Bank, 1818 H Street, NW, Washington, D.C. 20433 (202) 477-1234; *World Development Report;* and *World Tables.*

NEPAL - EXTERNAL TRADE

Asian Development Bank, Post Office Box 789, 1099 Manila, Philippines; *Key*

Indicators of Developing Asian and Pacific Countries.

Euromonitor International, Inc., 122 South Michigan Avenue, Suite 1200, Chicago, Illinois 60603 (800) 577-EURO; *World Marketing Data and Statistics.*

Food and Agricultural Organization of the United Nations (FAO) Via delle Terme di Caracalla, 00100 Rome, Italy (Telephone Number in U.S. (202) 653-2400); *The State of Food and Agriculture;* and *Trade Yearbook.*

Statistical Office of the United Nations, Publishing Service, New York, New York 10017 (800) 253-9646; *Asia-Pacific in Figures;* and *Statistical Yearbook for Asia and the Pacific.*

NEPAL - FARM CROPS - See NEPAL - CROPS

NEPAL - FEMALE WORKING POPULATION - See NEPAL - EMPLOYMENT

NEPAL - FERTILITY RATES

Central Intelligence Agency, Washington, D.C. 20505 (703) 482-1100, www.cia.gov; *The World Factbook.*

The Economist Intelligence Unit (Asia) Limited, 10th Floor, Luk Kwok Centre, 72 Gloucester Road, Wanchai, Hong Kong (Phone Number in U.S. (800) 938-4685); *Asian Market Atlas.*

M.E. Sharpe, 80 Business Park Drive, Armonk, New York 10504 (800) 541-6563; *The Illustrated Book of World Rankings.*

Statistical Office of the United Nations, Publishing Service, New York, New York 10017 (800) 253-9646; *Human Development Report.*

The World Bank, 1818 H Street, NW, Washington, D.C. 20433 (202) 477-1234; *The World Bank Atlas; World Development Report;* and *World Tables.*

NEPAL - FERTILIZER

Food and Agricultural Organization of the United Nations (FAO) Via delle Terme di Caracalla, 00100 Rome, Italy (Telephone Number in U.S. (202) 653-2400); *The State of Food and Agriculture.*

Statistical Office of the United Nations, Publishing Service, New York, New York 10017 (800) 253-9646; *Statistical Yearbook.*

NEPAL - FETAL MORTALITY - See NEPAL - MORTALITY

NEPAL - FINANCE

Asian Development Bank, Post Office Box 789, 1099 Manila, Philippines; *Key Indicators of Developing Asian and Pacific Countries.*

Economist Intelligence Unit, 111 West 57th Street, New York, New York 10019 (800) 938-4685; *Nepal Country Report.*

Europa Publications Limited, 18 Bedford Square, London, WC1B 3JN, England; *The Europa World Year Book.*

International Monetary Fund, 700 Nineteenth Street, NW, Washington, D.C. 20431 (202) 623-7000; *Government Finance Statistics Yearbook;* and *International Financial Statistics.*

M.E. Sharpe, 80 Business Park Drive, Armonk, New York 10504 (800) 541-6563; *The Illustrated Book of World Rankings.*

St. Martin's Press, Inc., 175 Fifth Avenue, New York, New York 10010 (800) 221-7945; *The Statesman's Year-Book.*

Statistical Office of the United Nations, Publishing Service, New York, New York 10017 (800) 253-9646; *Statistical Yearbook for Asia and the Pacific.*

NEPAL - FISHERIES

Europa Publications Limited, 18 Bedford Square, London, WC1B 3JN, England; *The Europa World Year Book.*

Food and Agricultural Organization of the United Nations (FAO) Via delle Terme di Caracalla, 00100 Rome, Italy (Telephone Number in U.S. (202) 653-2400); *The State of Food and Agriculture;* and *Yearbook of Fishery Statistics.*

M.E. Sharpe, 80 Business Park Drive, Armonk, New York 10504 (800) 541-6563; *The Illustrated Book of World Rankings.*

Statistical Office of the United Nations, Publishing Service, New York, New York 10017 (800) 253-9646; *Statistical Yearbook.*

United Nations Conference on Trade and Development, Central Statistical Service, Palais des Nations, Geneva, Switzerland (Telephone in U.S. (800) 253-9646); *UNCTAD Commodity Yearbook.*

NEPAL - FOOD

Food and Agricultural Organization of the United Nations (FAO), Via delle Terme di Caracalla, 00100 Rome, Italy (Telephone Number in U.S. (202) 653-2400); *Production Yearbook;* and *The State of Food and Agriculture.*

Statistical Office of the United Nations, Publishing Service, New York, New York 10017 (800) 253-9646; *Human*

Development Report; and *Statistical Yearbook for Asia and the Pacific.*

United Nations Conference on Trade and Development, Central Statistical Service, Palais des Nations, Geneva, Switzerland (Telephone in U.S. (800) 253-9646); *UNCTAD Commodity Yearbook.*

NEPAL - FOREIGN DEBT

International Monetary Fund, 700 Nineteenth Street, NW, Washington, D.C. 20431 (202) 623-7000; *Government Finance Statistics Yearbook.*

St. Martin's Press, Inc., 175 Fifth Avenue, New York, New York 10010 (800) 221-7945; *The Statesman's Year-Book.*

Walden Publishing Ltd., Two Market Street, Saffron Walden Essex, CB10 1HZ, England; *The World of Information Asia and Pacific Review.*

NEPAL - FOREIGN TRADE

Asian Development Bank, Post Office Box 789, 1099 Manila, Philippines; *Key Indicators of Developing Asian and Pacific Countries.*

Economist Intelligence Unit, 111 West 57th Street, New York, New York 10019 (800) 938-4685; *Nepal Country Report.*

The Economist Intelligence Unit (Asia) Limited, 10th Floor, Luk Kwok Centre, 72 Gloucester Road, Wanchai, Hong Kong (Phone Number in U.S. (800) 938-4685); *Asian Market Atlas.*

Euromonitor International, Inc., 122 South Michigan Avenue, Suite 1200, Chicago, Illinois 60603 (800) 577-EURO; *International Marketing Data and Statistics;* and *The World Economic Factbook.*

Europa Publications Limited, 18 Bedford Square, London, WC1B 3JN, England; *The Europa World Year Book.*

Food and Agricultural Organization of the United Nations (FAO) Via delle Terme di Caracalla, 00100 Rome, Italy (Telephone Number in U.S. (202) 653-2400); *The State of Food and Agriculture.*

M.E. Sharpe, 80 Business Park Drive, Armonk, New York 10504 (800) 541-6563; *The Illustrated Book of World Rankings.*

St. Martin's Press, Inc., 175 Fifth Avenue, New York, New York 10010 (800) 221-7945; *The Statesman's Year-Book.*

Statistical Office of the United Nations, Publishing Service, New York, New York 10017 (800) 253-9646; *International Trade Statistics Yearbook.*

The World Bank, 1818 H Street, NW, Washington, D.C. 20433 (202) 477-1234; *World Development Report;* and *World Tables.*

NEPAL - FORESTRY AND FOREST PRODUCTS

The Economist Intelligence Unit (Asia) Limited, 10th Floor, Luk Kwok Centre, 72 Gloucester Road, Wanchai, Hong Kong (Phone Number in U.S. (800) 938-4685); *Asian Market Atlas.*

Europa Publications Limited, 18 Bedford Square, London, WC1B 3JN, England; *The Europa World Year Book.*

Food and Agricultural Organization of the United Nations (FAO) Via delle Terme di Caracalla, 00100 Rome, Italy (Telephone Number in U.S. (202) 653-2400); *The State of Food and Agriculture;* and *Yearbook of Forest Products.*

M.E. Sharpe, 80 Business Park Drive, Armonk, New York 10504 (800) 541-6563; *The Illustrated Book of World Rankings.*

St. Martin's Press, Inc., 175 Fifth Avenue, New York, New York 10010 (800) 221-7945; *The Statesman's Year-Book.*

Statistical Office of the United Nations, Publishing Service, New York, New York 10017 (800) 253-9646; *Statistical Yearbook.*

United Nations Conference on Trade and Development, Central Statistical Service, Palais des Nations, Geneva, Switzerland (Telephone in U.S. (800) 253-9646); *UNCTAD Commodity Yearbook.*

United Nations Educational, Scientific and Cultural Organization (UNESCO), 7 Place de Fontenoy, F-75700 Paris, France (Telephone Number in U.S. (212) 963-5981); *Statistical Yearbook.*

The World Bank, 1818 H Street, NW, Washington, D.C. 20433 (202) 477-1234; *World Development Report.*

NEPAL - GAS PRODUCTION - See NEPAL - MINING AND MINERAL PRODUCTS

NEPAL - GENERAL MORTALITY - See NEPAL - MORTALITY

NEPAL - GEOGRAPHIC DATA

M.E. Sharpe, 80 Business Park Drive, Armonk, New York 10504 (800) 541-6563; *The Illustrated Book of World Rankings.*

NEPAL - GOATS - See NEPAL - LIVESTOCK AND POULTRY

NEPAL - GOLD HOLDINGS

Statistical Office of the United Nations,

Publishing Service, New York, New York 10017 (800) 253-9646; *Statistical Yearbook.*

The World Bank, 1818 H Street, NW, Washington, D.C. 20433 (202) 477-1234; *World Tables.*

NEPAL - GOLD PRODUCTION AND CONSUMPTION - See NEPAL - MINING AND MINERAL PRODUCTS

NEPAL - GOVERNMENT

Asian Development Bank, Post Office Box 789, 1099 Manila, Philippines; *Key Indicators of Developing Asian and Pacific Countries.*

Central Intelligence Agency, Washington, D.C. 20505 (703) 482-1100, www.cia.gov; *The World Factbook.*

Europa Publications Limited, 18 Bedford Square, London, WC1B 3JN, England; *The Europa World Year Book.*

International Monetary Fund, 700 Nineteenth Street, NW, Washington, D.C. 20431 (202) 623-7000; *Government Finance Statistics Yearbook.*

St. Martin's Press, Inc., 175 Fifth Avenue, New York, New York 10010 (800) 221-7945; *The Statesman's Year-Book.*

Statistical Office of the United Nations, Publishing Service, New York, New York 10017 (800) 253-9646; *Asia-Pacific in Figures;* and *National Accounts Statistics.*

The World Bank, 1818 H Street, NW, Washington, D.C. 20433 (202) 477-1234; *World Development Report;* and *World Tables.*

NEPAL - GRAIN PRODUCTION - See NEPAL - CROPS

NEPAL - GRANTS

International Monetary Fund, 700 Nineteenth Street, NW, Washington, D.C. 20431 (202) 623-7000; *Government Finance Statistics Yearbook.*

NEPAL - GROSS DOMESTIC PRODUCT

Asian Development Bank, Post Office Box 789, 1099 Manila, Philippines; *Key Indicators of Developing Asian and Pacific Countries.*

The Economist Intelligence Unit, 111 West 57th Street, New York, New York 10019 (800) 938-4685; *Nepal Country Report;* and *The World Market Atlas.*

The Economist Intelligence Unit (Asia) Limited, 10th Floor, Luk Kwok Centre, 72 Gloucester Road, Wanchai, Hong Kong (Phone Number in U.S. (800) 938-4685);

Asian Market Atlas.

Euromonitor International, Inc., 122 South Michigan Avenue, Suite 1200, Chicago, Illinois 60603 (800) 577-EURO; *International Marketing Data and Statistics;* and *The World Economic Factbook.*

Europa Publications Limited, 18 Bedford Square, London, WC1B 3JN, England; *The Europa World Year Book.*

M.E. Sharpe, 80 Business Park Drive, Armonk, New York 10504 (800) 541-6563; *The Illustrated Book of World Rankings.*

Statistical Office of the United Nations, Publishing Service, New York, New York 10017 (800) 253-9646; *Human Development Report; National Accounts Statistics;* and *Statistical Yearbook.*

The World Bank, 1818 H Street, NW, Washington, D.C. 20433 (202) 477-1234; *World Development Report;* and *World Tables.*

NEPAL - GROSS NATIONAL PRODUCT

Asian Development Bank, Post Office Box 789, 1099 Manila, Philippines; *Key Indicators of Developing Asian and Pacific Countries.*

Euromonitor International, Inc., 122 South Michigan Avenue, Suite 1200, Chicago, Illinois 60603 (800) 577-EURO; *International Marketing Data and Statistics.*

Europa Publications Limited, 18 Bedford Square, London, WC1B 3JN, England; *The Europa World Year Book.*

St. Martin's Press, Inc., 175 Fifth Avenue, New York, New York 10010 (800) 221-7945; *The Statesman's Year-Book.*

U.S. Arms Control and Disarmament Agency, 320 Twenty-first Street, NW, Washington, D.C. 20451 (202) 647-8677; *World Military Expenditures and Arms Transfers.*

Walden Publishing Ltd., Two Market Street, Saffron Walden Essex, CB10 1HZ, England; *The World of Information Asia and Pacific Review.*

The World Bank, 1818 H Street, NW, Washington, D.C. 20433 (202) 477-1234; *The World Bank Atlas; World Development Report;* and *World Tables.*

NEPAL - HEALTH

The Economist Intelligence Unit (Asia) Limited, 10th Floor, Luk Kwok Centre, 72 Gloucester Road, Wanchai, Hong Kong (Phone Number in U.S. (800) 938-4685); *Asian Market Atlas.*

Euromonitor International, Inc., 122 South Michigan Avenue, Suite 1200, Chicago, Illinois 60603 (800) 577-EURO; *World Marketing Data and Statistics.*

M.E. Sharpe, 80 Business Park Drive, Armonk, New York 10504 (800) 541-6563; *The Illustrated Book of World Rankings.*

St. Martin's Press, Inc., 175 Fifth Avenue, New York, New York 10010 (800) 221-7945; *The Statesman's Year-Book.*

Statistical Office of the United Nations, Publishing Service, New York, New York 10017 (800) 253-9646; *Asia-Pacific in Figures; Human Development Report;* and *Statistical Yearbook.*

United Nations Children's Fund (UNICEF), 3 United Nations Plaza, New York, New York 10017 (800) 253-9646; *State of the World's Children.*

The World Bank, 1818 H Street, NW, Washington, D.C. 20433 (202) 477-1234; *World Development Report.*

NEPAL - HEALTH

International Monetary Fund, 700 Nineteenth Street, NW, Washington, D.C. 20431 (202) 623-7000; *Government Finance Statistics Yearbook.*

The World Bank, 1818 H Street, NW, Washington, D.C. 20433 (202) 477-1234; *World Development Report.*

NEPAL - HIDE PRODUCTION

Food and Agricultural Organization of the United Nations (FAO), Via delle Terme di Caracalla, 00100 Rome, Italy (Telephone Number in U.S. (202) 653-2400); *Production Yearbook.*

NEPAL - HIGHWAYS

Central Intelligence Agency, Washington, D.C. 20505 (703) 482-1100, www.cia.gov; *The World Factbook.*

The Economist Intelligence Unit (Asia) Limited, 10th Floor, Luk Kwok Centre, 72 Gloucester Road, Wanchai, Hong Kong (Phone Number in U.S. (800) 938-4685); *Asian Market Atlas.*

International Road Federation, 2600 Virginia Avenue, NW., Washington, D.C. 20037 (202) 338-4641; *World Road Statistics.*

St. Martin's Press, Inc., 175 Fifth Avenue, New York, New York 10010 (800) 221-7945; *The Statesman's Year-Book.*

NEPAL - HORSES - See NEPAL - LIVESTOCK AND POULTRY

NEPAL - HOURS OF WORK - See NEPAL - EMPLOYMENT

NEPAL - HOUSING AND HOUSING UNITS

Euromonitor International, Inc., 122 South Michigan Avenue, Suite 1200, Chicago, Illinois 60603 (800) 577-EURO; *World Marketing Data and Statistics.*

M.E. Sharpe, 80 Business Park Drive, Armonk, New York 10504 (800) 541-6563; *The Illustrated Book of World Rankings.*

NEPAL - HOUSING EXPENDITURES

International Monetary Fund, 700 Nineteenth Street, NW, Washington, D.C. 20431 (202) 623-7000; *Government Finance Statistics Yearbook.*

NEPAL - ILLITERATE POPULATION

Central Intelligence Agency, Washington, D.C. 20505 (703) 482-1100, www.cia.gov; *The World Factbook.*

Euromonitor International, Inc., 122 South Michigan Avenue, Suite 1200, Chicago, Illinois 60603 (800) 577-EURO; *The World Economic Factbook.*

St. Martin's Press, Inc., 175 Fifth Avenue, New York, New York 10010 (800) 221-7945; *The Statesman's Year-Book.*

Statistical Office of the United Nations, Publishing Service, New York, New York 10017 (800) 253-9646; *Asia-Pacific in Figures;* and *Human Development Report.*

United Nations Educational, Scientific and Cultural Organization (UNESCO), 7 Place de Fontenoy, F-75700 Paris, France (Telephone Number in U.S. (212) 963-5981); *Statistical Yearbook.*

NEPAL - IMPORTS

Asian Development Bank, Post Office Box 789, 1099 Manila, Philippines; *Key Indicators of Developing Asian and Pacific Countries.*

Central Intelligence Agency, Washington, D.C. 20505 (703) 482-1100, www.cia.gov; *The World Factbook.*

The Economist Intelligence Unit, 111 West 57th Street, New York, New York 10019 (800) 938-4685; *Nepal Country Report;* and *The World Market Atlas.*

The Economist Intelligence Unit (Asia) Limited, 10th Floor, Luk Kwok Centre, 72 Gloucester Road, Wanchai, Hong Kong (Phone Number in U.S. (800) 938-4685); *Asian Market Atlas.*

Euromonitor International, Inc., 122 South Michigan Avenue, Suite 1200,

Chicago, Illinois 60603 (800) 577-EURO; *International Marketing Data and Statistics;* and *The World Economic Factbook.*

Europa Publications Limited, 18 Bedford Square, London, WC1B 3JN, England; *The Europa World Year Book.*

Food and Agricultural Organization of the United Nations (FAO) Via delle Terme di Caracalla, 00100 Rome, Italy (Telephone Number in U.S. (202) 653-2400); *The State of Food and Agriculture.*

International Monetary Fund, 700 Nineteenth Street, NW, Washington, D.C. 20431 (202) 623-7000; *Direction of Trade Statistics;* and *Government Finance Statistics Yearbook.*

St. Martin's Press, Inc., 175 Fifth Avenue, New York, New York 10010 (800) 221-7945; *The Statesman's Year-Book.*

United Nations Conference on Trade and Development (UNCTAD), New York, New York 10017 (800) 253-9646; *Handbook of International Trade and Development Statistics.*

Walden Publishing Ltd., Two Market Street, Saffron Walden Essex, CB10 1HZ, England; *The World of Information Asia and Pacific Review.*

The World Bank, 1818 H Street, NW, Washington, D.C. 20433 (202) 477-1234; *World Development Report;* and *World Tables.*

NEPAL - INCOME TAXES - See NEPAL - TAXATION

NEPAL - INDUSTRY

Central Intelligence Agency, Washington, D.C. 20505 (703) 482-1100, www.cia.gov; *The World Factbook.*

Economist Intelligence Unit, 111 West 57th Street, New York, New York 10019 (800) 938-4685; *Nepal Country Report.*

Euromonitor International, Inc., 122 South Michigan Avenue, Suite 1200, Chicago, Illinois 60603 (800) 577-EURO; *International Marketing Data and Statistics; The World Economic Factbook;* and *World Marketing Data and Statistics.*

Europa Publications Limited, 18 Bedford Square, London, WC1B 3JN, England; *The Europa World Year Book.*

International Labour Office, I.L.O. Publications, 1828 L Street, NW., Suite 801, Washington, D.C. 20036 (301) 638-3152; *Yearbook of Labour Statistics.*

M.E. Sharpe, 80 Business Park Drive, Armonk, New York 10504 (800) 541-6563;

The Illustrated Book of World Rankings.

St. Martin's Press, Inc., 175 Fifth Avenue, New York, New York 10010 (800) 221-7945; *The Statesman's Year-Book.*

Statistical Office of the United Nations, Publishing Service, New York, New York 10017 (800) 253-9646; *Asia-Pacific in Figures.*

Statistical Office of the United Nations, Publishing Service, New York, New York 10017 (800) 253-9646; *Statistical Yearbook for Asia and the Pacific.*

The World Bank, 1818 H Street, NW, Washington, D.C. 20433 (202) 477-1234; *World Tables.*

World Intellectual Property Organization, 34 Chemin des Colombettes, CH-1211 Geneva 20, Switzerland; *Industrial Property Statistics.*

NEPAL - INFANT AND MATERNAL MORTALITY

The Economist Intelligence Unit (Asia) Limited, 10th Floor, Luk Kwok Centre, 72 Gloucester Road, Wanchai, Hong Kong (Phone Number in U.S. (800) 938-4685); *Asian Market Atlas.*

Statistical Office of the United Nations, Publishing Service, New York, New York 10017 (800) 253-9646; *Demographic Yearbook.*

The World Bank, 1818 H Street, NW, Washington, D.C. 20433 (202) 477-1234; *World Tables.*

NEPAL - INTERNAL TRADE

Statistical Office of the United Nations, Publishing Service, New York, New York 10017 (800) 253-9646; *Statistical Yearbook for Asia and the Pacific.*

NEPAL - INTERNATIONAL RESERVES EXCLUDING GOLD

Asian Development Bank, Post Office Box 789, 1099 Manila, Philippines; *Key Indicators of Developing Asian and Pacific Countries.*

Statistical Office of the United Nations, Publishing Service, New York, New York 10017 (800) 253-9646; *Statistical Yearbook.*

The World Bank, 1818 H Street, NW, Washington, D.C. 20433 (202) 477-1234; *World Tables.*

NEPAL - INTERNATIONAL STATISTICS

Asian Development Bank, Post Office Box 789, 1099 Manila, Philippines; *Key Indicators of Developing Asian and Pacific*

Countries.

NEPAL - IRON ORE PRODUCTION AND CONSUMPTION - See NEPAL - MINING AND MINERAL PRODUCTS

NEPAL - IRRIGATION

Euromonitor International, Inc., 122 South Michigan Avenue, Suite 1200, Chicago, Illinois 60603 (800) 577-EURO; *International Marketing Data and Statistics.*

NEPAL - JUTE PRODUCTION - See NEPAL - CROPS

NEPAL - LABOR

Central Intelligence Agency, Washington, D.C. 20505 (703) 482-1100, www.cia.gov; *The World Factbook.*

The Economist Intelligence Unit (Asia) Limited, 10th Floor, Luk Kwok Centre, 72 Gloucester Road, Wanchai, Hong Kong (Phone Number in U.S. (800) 938-4685); *Asian Market Atlas.*

Euromonitor International, Inc., 122 South Michigan Avenue, Suite 1200, Chicago, Illinois 60603 (800) 577-EURO; *International Marketing Data and Statistics;* and *World Marketing Data and Statistics.*

Food and Agricultural Organization of the United Nations (FAO) Via delle Terme di Caracalla, 00100 Rome, Italy (Telephone Number in U.S. (202) 653-2400); *The State of Food and Agriculture.*

International Labour Office, I.L.O. Publications, 1828 L Street, NW., Suite 801, Washington, D.C. 20036 (301) 638-3152; *Yearbook of Labour Statistics.*

M.E. Sharpe, 80 Business Park Drive, Armonk, New York 10504 (800) 541-6563; *The Illustrated Book of World Rankings.*

St. Martin's Press, Inc., 175 Fifth Avenue, New York, New York 10010 (800) 221-7945; *The Statesman's Year-Book.*

Statistical Office of the United Nations, Publishing Service, New York, New York 10017 (800) 253-9646; *Human Development Report.*

The World Bank, 1818 H Street, NW, Washington, D.C. 20433 (202) 477-1234; *The World Bank Atlas; World Development Report;* and *World Tables.*

NEPAL - LAND USE

Central Intelligence Agency, Washington, D.C. 20505 (703) 482-1100, www.cia.gov; *The World Factbook.*

Euromonitor International, Inc., 122 South Michigan Avenue, Suite 1200,

Chicago, Illinois 60603 (800) 577-EURO; *International Marketing Data and Statistics.*

Food and Agricultural Organization of the United Nations (FAO), Via delle Terme di Caracalla, 00100 Rome, Italy (Telephone Number in U.S. (202) 653-2400); *Production Yearbook.*

The World Bank, 1818 H Street, NW, Washington, D.C. 20433 (202) 477-1234; *World Development Report.*

NEPAL - LIBRARIES

M.E. Sharpe, 80 Business Park Drive, Armonk, New York 10504 (800) 541-6563; *The Illustrated Book of World Rankings.*

NEPAL - LIFE EXPECTANCY

Central Intelligence Agency, Washington, D.C. 20505 (703) 482-1100, www.cia.gov; *The World Factbook.*

The Economist Intelligence Unit (Asia) Limited, 10th Floor, Luk Kwok Centre, 72 Gloucester Road, Wanchai, Hong Kong (Phone Number in U.S. (800) 938-4685); *Asian Market Atlas.*

Euromonitor International, Inc., 122 South Michigan Avenue, Suite 1200, Chicago, Illinois 60603 (800) 577-EURO; *The World Economic Factbook.*

St. Martin's Press, Inc., 175 Fifth Avenue, New York, New York 10010 (800) 221-7945; *The Statesman's Year-Book.*

Statistical Office of the United Nations, Publishing Service, New York, New York 10017 (800) 253-9646; *Asia-Pacific in Figures; World Statistics Pocketbook;* and *Human Development Report.*

The World Bank, 1818 H Street, NW, Washington, D.C. 20433 (202) 477-1234; *The World Bank Atlas;* and *World Development Report.*

NEPAL - LITERACY RATE

Euromonitor International, Inc., 122 South Michigan Avenue, Suite 1200, Chicago, Illinois 60603 (800) 577-EURO; *World Marketing Data and Statistics.*

NEPAL - LIVESTOCK AND POULTRY

Euromonitor International, Inc., 122 South Michigan Avenue, Suite 1200, Chicago, Illinois 60603 (800) 577-EURO; *International Marketing Data and Statistics.*

Europa Publications Limited, 18 Bedford Square, London, WC1B 3JN, England; *The Europa World Year Book.*

Food and Agricultural Organization of the United Nations (FAO), Via delle Terme

di Caracalla, 00100 Rome, Italy (Telephone Number in U.S. (202) 653-2400); *Production Yearbook;* and *The State of Food and Agriculture.*

M.E. Sharpe, 80 Business Park Drive, Armonk, New York 10504 (800) 541-6563; *The Illustrated Book of World Rankings.*

St. Martin's Press, Inc., 175 Fifth Avenue, New York, New York 10010 (800) 221-7945; *The Statesman's Year-Book.*

Statistical Office of the United Nations, Publishing Service, New York, New York 10017 (800) 253-9646; *Statistical Yearbook.*

United Nations Conference on Trade and Development, Central Statistical Service, Palais des Nations, Geneva, Switzerland (Telephone in U.S. (800) 253-9646); *UNCTAD Commodity Yearbook.*

NEPAL - LIVING LEVELS - See NEPAL - LIFE EXPECTANCY

NEPAL - MANPOWER

Statistical Office of the United Nations, Publishing Service, New York, New York 10017 (800) 253-9646; *Statistical Yearbook for Asia and the Pacific.*

NEPAL - MANUFACTURING

Asian Development Bank, Post Office Box 789, 1099 Manila, Philippines; *Key Indicators of Developing Asian and Pacific Countries.*

M.E. Sharpe, 80 Business Park Drive, Armonk, New York 10504 (800) 541-6563; *The Illustrated Book of World Rankings.*

The World Bank, 1818 H Street, NW, Washington, D.C. 20433 (202) 477-1234; *World Tables.*

NEPAL - MARRIAGE RATES

M.E. Sharpe, 80 Business Park Drive, Armonk, New York 10504 (800) 541-6563; *The Illustrated Book of World Rankings.*

Statistical Office of the United Nations, Publishing Service, New York, New York 10017 (800) 253-9646; *Demographic Yearbook.*

NEPAL - MEAT PRODUCTION - ALL TYPES OF MEAT AND POULTRY

Food and Agricultural Organization of the United Nations (FAO) Via delle Terme di Caracalla, 00100 Rome, Italy (Telephone Number in U.S. (202) 653-2400); *The State of Food and Agriculture.*

M.E. Sharpe, 80 Business Park Drive, Armonk, New York 10504 (800) 541-6563; *The Illustrated Book of World Rankings.*

Statistical Office of the United Nations, Publishing Service, New York, New York 10017 (800) 253-9646; *Statistical Yearbook.*

NEPAL - MILITARY

Central Intelligence Agency, Washington, D.C. 20505 (703) 482-1100, www.cia.gov; *The World Factbook.*

The Economist Intelligence Unit (Asia) Limited, 10th Floor, Luk Kwok Centre, 72 Gloucester Road, Wanchai, Hong Kong (Phone Number in U.S. (800) 938-4685); *Asian Market Atlas.*

Euromonitor International, Inc., 122 South Michigan Avenue, Suite 1200, Chicago, Illinois 60603 (800) 577-EURO; *World Marketing Data and Statistics.*

The International Institute for Strategic Studies, 23 Tavistock Street, London WC2E 7NQ, England; *The Military Balance.*

International Monetary Fund, 700 Nineteenth Street, NW, Washington, D.C. 20431 (202) 623-7000; *Government Finance Statistics Yearbook.*

St. Martin's Press, Inc., 175 Fifth Avenue, New York, New York 10010 (800) 221-7945; *The Statesman's Year-Book.*

Statistical Office of the United Nations, Publishing Service, New York, New York 10017 (800) 253-9646; *Human Development Report.*

U.S. Arms Control and Disarmament Agency, 320 Twenty-first Street, NW, Washington, D.C. 20451 (202) 647-8677; *World Military Expenditures and Arms Transfers.*

NEPAL - MILK PRODUCTION - See NEPAL - DAIRY PRODUCTS

NEPAL - MILLET PRODUCTION - See NEPAL - CROPS

NEPAL - MINING AND MINERAL PRODUCTS

Asian Development Bank, Post Office Box 789, 1099 Manila, Philippines; *Key Indicators of Developing Asian and Pacific Countries.*

M.E. Sharpe, 80 Business Park Drive, Armonk, New York 10504 (800) 541-6563; *The Illustrated Book of World Rankings.*

United Nations Conference on Trade and Development, Central Statistical Service, Palais des Nations, Geneva, Switzerland (Telephone in U.S. (800) 253-9646); *UNCTAD Commodity Yearbook.*

NEPAL - MONEY EXCHANGE RATE - See NEPAL - EXCHANGE RATES

NEPAL - MONEY RESERVES

Euromonitor International, Inc., 122 South Michigan Avenue, Suite 1200, Chicago, Illinois 60603 (800) 577-EURO; *International Marketing Data and Statistics.*

NEPAL - MONEY SUPPLY

Asian Development Bank, Post Office Box 789, 1099 Manila, Philippines; *Key Indicators of Developing Asian and Pacific Countries.*

Economist Intelligence Unit, 111 West 57th Street, New York, New York 10019 (800) 938-4685; *Nepal Country Report.*

Euromonitor International, Inc., 122 South Michigan Avenue, Suite 1200, Chicago, Illinois 60603 (800) 577-EURO; *International Marketing Data and Statistics.*

Europa Publications Limited, 18 Bedford Square, London, WC1B 3JN, England; *The Europa World Year Book.*

Statistical Office of the United Nations, Publishing Service, New York, New York 10017 (800) 253-9646; *Statistical Yearbook.*

The World Bank, 1818 H Street, NW, Washington, D.C. 20433 (202) 477-1234; *World Tables.*

NEPAL - MORTALITY

Central Intelligence Agency, Washington, D.C. 20505 (703) 482-1100, www.cia.gov; *The World Factbook.*

The Economist Intelligence Unit (Asia) Limited, 10th Floor, Luk Kwok Centre, 72 Gloucester Road, Wanchai, Hong Kong (Phone Number in U.S. (800) 938-4685); *Asian Market Atlas.*

Euromonitor International, Inc., 122 South Michigan Avenue, Suite 1200, Chicago, Illinois 60603 (800) 577-EURO; *International Marketing Data and Statistics;* and *The World Economic Factbook.*

Europa Publications Limited, 18 Bedford Square, London, WC1B 3JN, England; *The Europa World Year Book.*

St. Martin's Press, Inc., 175 Fifth Avenue, New York, New York 10010 (800) 221-7945; *The Statesman's Year-Book.*

Statistical Office of the United Nations, Publishing Service, New York, New York 10017 (800) 253-9646; *Asia-Pacific in Figures; Demographic Yearbook; Human Development Report; World Statistics Pocketbook;* and *Statistical Yearbook.*

United Nations Children's Fund (UNICEF), 3 United Nations Plaza, New York, New York 10017 (800) 253-9646; *State of the World's Children.*

The World Bank, 1818 H Street, NW, Washington, D.C. 20433 (202) 477-1234; *The World Bank Atlas;* and *World Development Report.*

NEPAL - MOTOR VEHICLE TAXES - See NEPAL - TAXATION

NEPAL - MOTOR VEHICLES IN USE

Europa Publications Limited, 18 Bedford Square, London, WC1B 3JN, England; *The Europa World Year Book.*

International Road Federation, 2600 Virginia Avenue, NW., Washington, D.C. 20037 (202) 338-4641; *World Road Statistics.*

Statistical Office of the United Nations, Publishing Service, New York, New York 10017 (800) 253-9646; *Statistical Yearbook.*

NEPAL - MUSEUMS

M.E. Sharpe, 80 Business Park Drive, Armonk, New York 10504 (800) 541-6563; *The Illustrated Book of World Rankings.*

NEPAL - NATALITY - See NEPAL - BIRTH RATES

NEPAL - NATIONAL ACCOUNTS

Europa Publications Limited, 18 Bedford Square, London, WC1B 3JN, England; *The Europa World Year Book.*

Statistical Office of the United Nations, Publishing Service, New York, New York 10017 (800) 253-9646; *Asia-Pacific in Figures; National Accounts Statistics; Statistical Yearbook;* and *Statistical Yearbook for Asia and the Pacific.*

NEPAL - NATIONAL INCOME

M.E. Sharpe, 80 Business Park Drive, Armonk, New York 10504 (800) 541-6563; *The Illustrated Book of World Rankings.*

Statistical Office of the United Nations, Publishing Service, New York, New York 10017 (800) 253-9646; *National Accounts Statistics;* and *Statistical Yearbook.*

NEPAL - NATIONAL PRODUCT

M.E. Sharpe, 80 Business Park Drive, Armonk, New York 10504 (800) 541-6563; *The Illustrated Book of World Rankings.*

Statistical Office of the United Nations, Publishing Service, New York, New York 10017 (800) 253-9646; *Statistical Yearbook.*

NEPAL - NATURAL GAS PRODUCTION - See NEPAL - MINING AND MINERAL PRODUCTS

NEPAL - NEWSPAPER PRODUCTION - See NEPAL - FORESTRY AND FOREST PRODUCTS

NEPAL - PATENTS, TRADEMARKS AND SERVICE MARKS

Statistical Office of the United Nations, Publishing Service, New York, New York 10017 (800) 253-9646; *Statistical Yearbook.*

World Intellectual Property Organization, 34 Chemin des Colombettes, CH-1211 Geneva 20, Switzerland; *Industrial Property Statistics.*

NEPAL - PEANUT PRODUCTION - See NEPAL - CROPS

NEPAL - PERIODICALS

United Nations Educational, Scientific and Cultural Organization (UNESCO), 7 Place de Fontenoy, F-75700 Paris, France (Telephone Number in U.S. (212) 963-5981); *Statistical Yearbook.*

NEPAL - PESTICIDE USE

Food and Agricultural Organization of the United Nations (FAO) Via delle Terme di Caracalla, 00100 Rome, Italy (Telephone Number in U.S. (202) 653-2400); *The State of Food and Agriculture.*

NEPAL - PETROLEUM INDUSTRY

Asian Development Bank, Post Office Box 789, 1099 Manila, Philippines; *Key Indicators of Developing Asian and Pacific Countries.*

Food and Agricultural Organization of the United Nations (FAO) Via delle Terme di Caracalla, 00100 Rome, Italy (Telephone Number in U.S. (202) 653-2400); *The State of Food and Agriculture.*

M.E. Sharpe, 80 Business Park Drive, Armonk, New York 10504 (800) 541-6563; *The Illustrated Book of World Rankings.*

United Nations Conference on Trade and Development, Central Statistical Service, Palais des Nations, Geneva, Switzerland (Telephone in U.S. (800) 253-9646); *UNCTAD Commodity Yearbook.*

NEPAL - PIGS - See NEPAL - LIVESTOCK AND POULTRY

NEPAL - POPULATION

Asian Development Bank, Post Office Box 789, 1099 Manila, Philippines; *Key Indicators of Developing Asian and Pacific Countries.*

Central Intelligence Agency, Washington, D.C. 20505 (703) 482-1100, www.cia.gov; *The World Factbook.*

The Economist Intelligence Unit, 111 West 57th Street, New York, New York 10019 (800) 938-4685; *Nepal Country Report;* and *The World Market Atlas.*

The Economist Intelligence Unit (Asia) Limited, 10th Floor, Luk Kwok Centre, 72 Gloucester Road, Wanchai, Hong Kong (Phone Number in U.S. (800) 938-4685); *Asian Market Atlas.*

Euromonitor International, Inc., 122 South Michigan Avenue, Suite 1200, Chicago, Illinois 60603 (800) 577-EURO; *International Marketing Data and Statistics;* and *The World Economic Factbook.*

Europa Publications Limited, 18 Bedford Square, London, WC1B 3JN, England; *The Europa World Year Book.*

Food and Agricultural Organization of the United Nations (FAO), Via delle Terme di Caracalla, 00100 Rome, Italy (Telephone Number in U.S. (202) 653-2400); *Production Yearbook.*

International Labour Office, I.L.O. Publications, 1828 L Street, NW., Suite 801, Washington, D.C. 20036 (301) 638-3152 ; *Yearbook of Labour Statistics.*

M.E. Sharpe, 80 Business Park Drive, Armonk, New York 10504 (800) 541-6563; *The Illustrated Book of World Rankings.*

St. Martin's Press, Inc., 175 Fifth Avenue, New York, New York 10010 (800) 221-7945; *The Statesman's Year-Book.*

Statistical Office of the United Nations, Publishing Service, New York, New York 10017 (800) 253-9646; *Asia-Pacific in Figures; Demographic Yearbook; Human Development Report; Statistical Yearbook; World Statistics Pocketbook;* and *Statistical Yearbook for Asia and the Pacific.*

United Nations Educational, Scientific and Cultural Organization (UNESCO), 7 Place de Fontenoy, F-75700 Paris, France (Telephone Number in U.S. (212) 963-5981); *Statistical Yearbook.*

U.S. Arms Control and Disarmament Agency, 320 Twenty-first Street, NW, Washington, D.C. 20451 (202) 647-8677; *World Military Expenditures and Arms Transfers.*

Walden Publishing Ltd., Two Market Street, Saffron Walden Essex, CB10 1HZ, England; *The World of Information Asia and Pacific Review.*

The World Bank, 1818 H Street, NW, Washington, D.C. 20433 (202) 477-1234; *The World Bank Atlas;* and *World Development Report.*

World Health Organization, Office of Publications, 20 Avenue Appia, CH-1211 Geneva 27, Switzerland (Telephone Number in U.S. (518) 436-9686); *World Health Statistics Annual.*

NEPAL - POST OFFICES

M.E. Sharpe, 80 Business Park Drive, Armonk, New York 10504 (800) 541-6563; *The Illustrated Book of World Rankings.*

St. Martin's Press, Inc., 175 Fifth Avenue, New York, New York 10010 (800) 221-7945; *The Statesman's Year-Book.*

NEPAL - POTATO PRODUCTION - See NEPAL - CROPS

NEPAL - POWER PRODUCTION INDUSTRY - ESTABLISHMENTS, PAYROLLS, VALUE ADDED, ETC.

Statistical Office of the United Nations, Publishing Service, New York, New York 10017 (800) 253-9646; *Electric Power in Asia and the Pacific.*

NEPAL - PRICES

Asian Development Bank, Post Office Box 789, 1099 Manila, Philippines; *Key Indicators of Developing Asian and Pacific Countries.*

Food and Agricultural Organization of the United Nations (FAO), Via delle Terme di Caracalla, 00100 Rome, Italy (Telephone Number in U.S. (202) 653-2400); *Production Yearbook;* and *The State of Food and Agriculture.*

International Labour Office, I.L.O. Publications, 1828 L Street, NW., Suite 801, Washington, D.C. 20036 (301) 638-3152; *Yearbook of Labour Statistics.*

M.E. Sharpe, 80 Business Park Drive, Armonk, New York 10504 (800) 541-6563; *The Illustrated Book of World Rankings.*

NEPAL - PRODUCTION

M.E. Sharpe, 80 Business Park Drive, Armonk, New York 10504 (800) 541-6563; *The Illustrated Book of World Rankings.*

NEPAL - PRODUCTIVITY

Euromonitor International, Inc., 122 South Michigan Avenue, Suite 1200, Chicago, Illinois 60603 (800) 577-EURO; *International Marketing Data and Statistics.*

NEPAL - PROPERTY TAXES - See NEPAL - TAXATION

NEPAL - PUBLIC FINANCE - See NEPAL - FINANCE

NEPAL - RADIO BROADCASTING - See

NEPAL - BROADCASTING

NEPAL - RADIO RECEIVERS

St. Martin's Press, Inc., 175 Fifth Avenue, New York, New York 10010 (800) 221-7945; *The Statesman's Year-Book.*

NEPAL - RAILWAYS

Jane's Information Group, Sentinel House, 163 Brighton Road, Coulsdon, Surrey CR5 2NH, England (Telephone Number in U.S. (703) 683-3700); *Jane's World Railways.*

St. Martin's Press, Inc., 175 Fifth Avenue, New York, New York 10010 (800) 221-7945; *The Statesman's Year-Book.*

NEPAL - RELIGION

Central Intelligence Agency, Washington, D.C. 20505 (703) 482-1100, www.cia.gov; *The World Factbook.*

M.E. Sharpe, 80 Business Park Drive, Armonk, New York 10504 (800) 541-6563; *The Illustrated Book of World Rankings.*

St. Martin's Press, Inc., 175 Fifth Avenue, New York, New York 10010 (800) 221-7945; *The Statesman's Year-Book.*

NEPAL - RENT PRICES

International Labour Office, I.L.O. Publications, 1828 L Street, NW., Suite 801, Washington, D.C. 20036 (301) 638-3152; *Yearbook of Labour Statistics.*

NEPAL - RETAIL TRADE

Euromonitor International, Inc., 122 South Michigan Avenue, Suite 1200, Chicago, Illinois 60603 (800) 577-EURO; *World Marketing Data and Statistics.*

NEPAL - RICE PRODUCTION - See NEPAL - CROPS

NEPAL - ROOT AND TUBER PRODUCTION - See NEPAL - CROPS

NEPAL - ROUNDWOOD PRODUCTION - See NEPAL - FORESTRY AND FOREST PRODUCTS

NEPAL - RUBBER PRODUCTION AND CONSUMPTION

M.E. Sharpe, 80 Business Park Drive, Armonk, New York 10504 (800) 541-6563; *The Illustrated Book of World Rankings.*

NEPAL - SAWNWOOD PRODUCTION - See NEPAL - FORESTRY AND FOREST PRODUCTS

NEPAL - SENIOR CITIZENS

M.E. Sharpe, 80 Business Park Drive, Armonk, New York 10504 (800) 541-6563; *The Illustrated Book of World Rankings.*

NEPAL - SHEEP - See NEPAL - LIVESTOCK AND POULTRY

NEPAL - SILVER PRODUCTION AND CONSUMPTION - See NEPAL - MINING AND MINERAL PRODUCTS

NEPAL - SOCIAL DATA

Asian Development Bank, Post Office Box 789, 1099 Manila, Philippines; *Key Indicators of Developing Asian and Pacific Countries.*

M.E. Sharpe, 80 Business Park Drive, Armonk, New York 10504 (800) 541-6563; *The Illustrated Book of World Rankings.*

Statistical Office of the United Nations, Publishing Service, New York, New York 10017 (800) 253-9646; *World Statistics Pocketbook.*

NEPAL - SOCIAL SECURITY

International Monetary Fund, 700 Nineteenth Street, NW, Washington, D.C. 20431 (202) 623-7000; *Government Finance Statistics Yearbook.*

Statistical Office of the United Nations, Publishing Service, New York, New York 10017 (800) 253-9646; *National Accounts Statistics.*

NEPAL - STATE BUDGET REVENUE AND EXPENDITURES

Euromonitor International, Inc., 122 South Michigan Avenue, Suite 1200, Chicago, Illinois 60603 (800) 577-EURO; *International Marketing Data and Statistics.*

NEPAL - STEEL PRODUCTION - See NEPAL - MINING AND MINERAL PRODUCTS

NEPAL - STOCKS - COMMODITY - MARKET PRICE - INDEX

Food and Agricultural Organization of the United Nations (FAO) Via delle Terme di Caracalla, 00100 Rome, Italy (Telephone Number in U.S. (202) 653-2400); *The State of Food and Agriculture.*

NEPAL - SUGAR PRODUCTION AND CONSUMPTION - See NEPAL - CROPS

NEPAL - TAX REVENUES - SEE NEPAL - TAXATION

NEPAL - TAXATION

Europa Publications Limited, 18 Bedford Square, London, WC1B 3JN, England; *The Europa World Year Book.*

International Monetary Fund, 700 Nineteenth Street, NW, Washington, D.C. 20431 (202) 623-7000; *Government Finance Statistics Yearbook.*

International Road Federation, 2600 Virginia Avenue, NW., Washington, D.C. 20037 (202) 338-4641; *World Road Statistics.*

The World Bank, 1818 H Street, NW, Washington, D.C. 20433 (202) 477-1234; *World Development Indicators.*

NEPAL - TELEPHONES IN USE

American Telephone and Telegraph Company, 26 Parsippany Road, Whippany, New Jersey 07981 (800) 222-0300; *The World's Telephones.*

Central Intelligence Agency, Washington, D.C. 20505 (703) 482-1100, www.cia.gov; *The World Factbook.*

The Economist Intelligence Unit (Asia) Limited, 10th Floor, Luk Kwok Centre, 72 Gloucester Road, Wanchai, Hong Kong (Phone Number in U.S. (800) 938-4685); *Asian Market Atlas.*

Europa Publications Limited, 18 Bedford Square, London, WC1B 3JN, England; *The Europa World Year Book.*

St. Martin's Press, Inc., 175 Fifth Avenue, New York, New York 10010 (800) 221-7945; *The Statesman's Year-Book.*

Statistical Office of the United Nations, Publishing Service, New York, New York 10017 (800) 253-9646; *Statistical Yearbook;* and *World Statistics Pocketbook.*

NEPAL - TELEVISION BROADCASTING - See NEPAL - BROADCASTING

NEPAL - TEXTILE INDUSTRY

M.E. Sharpe, 80 Business Park Drive, Armonk, New York 10504 (800) 541-6563; *The Illustrated Book of World Rankings.*

St. Martin's Press, Inc., 175 Fifth Avenue, New York, New York 10010 (800) 221-7945; *The Statesman's Year-Book.*

United Nations Conference on Trade and Development, Central Statistical Service, Palais des Nations, Geneva, Switzerland (Telephone in U.S. (800) 253-9646); *UNCTAD Commodity Yearbook.*

NEPAL - THEATRE

United Nations Educational, Scientific and Cultural Organization (UNESCO), 7 Place de Fontenoy, F-75700 Paris, France (Telephone Number in U.S. (212) 963-5981); *Statistical Yearbook.*

NEPAL - TOBACCO PRODUCTION

M.E. Sharpe, 80 Business Park Drive, Armonk, New York 10504 (800) 541-6563; *The Illustrated Book of World Rankings.*

Statistical Office of the United Nations, Publishing Service, New York, New York 10017 (800) 253-9646; *Statistical Yearbook.*

NEPAL - TOURISM

Euromonitor International, Inc., 122 South Michigan Avenue, Suite 1200, Chicago, Illinois 60603 (800) 577-EURO; *The World Economic Factbook.*

Europa Publications Limited, 18 Bedford Square, London, WC1B 3JN, England; *The Europa World Year Book.*

M.E. Sharpe, 80 Business Park Drive, Armonk, New York 10504 (800) 541-6563; *The Illustrated Book of World Rankings.*

St. Martin's Press, Inc., 175 Fifth Avenue, New York, New York 10010 (800) 221-7945; *The Statesman's Year-Book.*

Statistical Office of the United Nations, Publishing Service, New York, New York 10017 (800) 253-9646; *Statistical Yearbook.*

World Tourism Organization, Calle Capitan Haya 42, E-28020 Madrid, Spain; *Yearbook of Tourism Statistics.*

NEPAL - TRACTORS IN USE

Statistical Office of the United Nations, Publishing Service, New York, New York 10017 (800) 253-9646; *Statistical Yearbook.*

NEPAL - TRADE - See NEPAL - FOREIGN TRADE

NEPAL - TRADEMARKS AND SERVICE MARKS - See NEPAL - PATENTS, TRADEMARKS AND SERVICE MARKS

NEPAL - TRANSPORTATION AND COMMUNICATIONS

The Economist Intelligence Unit (Asia) Limited, 10th Floor, Luk Kwok Centre, 72 Gloucester Road, Wanchai, Hong Kong (Phone Number in U.S. (800) 938-4685); *Asian Market Atlas.*

Euromonitor International, Inc., 122 South Michigan Avenue, Suite 1200, Chicago, Illinois 60603 (800) 577-EURO; *International Marketing Data and Statistics;* and *World Marketing Data and Statistics.*

Europa Publications Limited, 18 Bedford Square, London, WC1B 3JN, England; *The Europa World Year Book.*

M.E. Sharpe, 80 Business Park Drive, Armonk, New York 10504 (800) 541-6563;

The Illustrated Book of World Rankings.

St. Martin's Press, Inc., 175 Fifth Avenue, New York, New York 10010 (800) 221-7945; *The Statesman's Year-Book.*

Statistical Office of the United Nations, Publishing Service, New York, New York 10017 (800) 253-9646; *Human Development Report;* and *Statistical Yearbook for Asia and the Pacific.*

NEPAL - UNEMPLOYMENT

Euromonitor International, Inc., 122 South Michigan Avenue, Suite 1200, Chicago, Illinois 60603 (800) 577-EURO; *International Marketing Data and Statistics.*

International Labour Office, I.L.O. Publications, 1828 L Street, NW., Suite 801, Washington, D.C. 20036 (301) 638-3152; *Yearbook of Labour Statistics.*

NEPAL - UTILITIES

Statistical Office of the United Nations, Publishing Service, New York, New York 10017 (800) 253-9646; *Electric Power in Asia and the Pacific.*

NEPAL - VITAL STATISTICS

Euromonitor International, Inc., 122 South Michigan Avenue, Suite 1200, Chicago, Illinois 60603 (800) 577-EURO; *International Marketing Data and Statistics.*

International Labour Office, I.L.O. Publications, 1828 L Street, NW., Suite 801, Washington, D.C. 20036 (301) 638-3152; *Yearbook of Labour Statistics.*

St. Martin's Press, Inc., 175 Fifth Avenue, New York, New York 10010 (800) 221-7945; *The Statesman's Year-Book.*

Statistical Office of the United Nations, Publishing Service, New York, New York 10017 (800) 253-9646; *Statistical Yearbook.*

World Health Organization, Office of Publications, 20 Avenue Appia, CH-1211 Geneva 27, Switzerland (Telephone Number in U.S. (518) 436-9686); *World Health Statistics Annual.*

NEPAL - WAGES AND PRICES

Statistical Office of the United Nations, Publishing Service, New York, New York 10017 (800) 253-9646; *Statistical Yearbook for Asia and the Pacific.*

NEPAL - WEATHER - See NEPAL - CLIMATE

NEPAL - WELFARE

International Monetary Fund, 700 Nineteenth Street, NW, Washington, D.C. 20431 (202) 623-7000; *Government*

Finance Statistics Yearbook.

NEPAL - WHEAT PRODUCTION AND PRICES - See NEPAL - CROPS

NEPAL - WHOLESALE PRICES

Asian Development Bank, Post Office Box 789, 1099 Manila, Philippines; *Key Indicators of Developing Asian and Pacific Countries.*

NEPAL - WINE PRODUCTION - See NEPAL - BEVERAGES

NEPAL - WOOL PRODUCTION - See NEPAL - TEXTILE INDUSTRY

Netherlands - National Statistical Office

Netherlands Central Bureau of Statistics, 428 Prises Beatrix laan, 2270 AZ Voorburg, The Hague, Netherlands.

Netherlands - Primary Statistics Sources

Netherlands Central Bureau of Statistics, 428 Prises Beatrix laan, 2270 AZ Voorburg, The Hague, Netherlands; *Statistical Pocketbook;* and *Statistical Yearbook of the Netherlands.*

NETHERLANDS - ABORTIONS

European Community Information Service, 2100 M Street, NW, Washington, D.C. 20037 (202) 862-9500; *Demographic Statistics.*

Statistical Office of the United Nations, Publishing Service, New York, New York 10017 (800) 253-9646; *Trends in Europe and North America: The Statistical Yearbook of the Economic Commission for Europe.*

United Nations Conference on Trade and Development, Central Statistical Service, Palais des Nations, Geneva, Switzerland (Telephone in U.S. (800) 253-9646); *UNCTAD Commodity Yearbook.*

NETHERLANDS - AGRICULTURE

Economist Intelligence Unit, 111 West 57th Street, New York, New York 10019 (800) 938-4685; *Netherlands Country Report.*

Euromonitor International, Inc., 122 South Michigan Avenue, Suite 1200, Chicago, Illinois 60603 (800) 577-EURO; *World Marketing Data and Statistics.*

Europa Publications Limited, 18 Bedford Square, London, WC1B 3JN, England; *The Europa World Year Book.*

European Commission Office of Press and Public Affairs, 2100 M Street, NW, Washington, D.C. 20037 (202) 862-9500; *Agriculture: Statistical Yearbook; Basic Statistics of the Community; Eurostatistics: Data for Short-term Economic Analysis; Labor Force Sample Survey;* and *Regions: Statistical Yearbook.*

Food and Agricultural Organization of the United Nations (FAO) Via delle Terme di Caracalla, 00100 Rome, Italy (Telephone Number in U.S. (202) 653-2400); *Production Yearbook; The State of Food and Agriculture;* and *Trade Yearbook.*

M.E. Sharpe, 80 Business Park Drive, Armonk, New York 10504 (800) 541-6563; *The Illustrated Book of World Rankings.*

Netherlands Central Bureau of Statistics, Staatsuitgeverij, The Hague, Netherlands; *Industrial Structure Statistics;* and *Statistical Yearbook of the Netherlands.*

Organisation for Economic Co-operation and Development (OECD), 2 rue Andre-Pascal, 75 Paris 16, France (Telephone Number in U.S. (202) 785-6323); *Economic Accounts for Agriculture; Indicators of Industrial Activity;* and *OECD Economic Surveys: Netherlands.*

St. Martin's Press, Inc., 175 Fifth Avenue, New York, New York 10010 (800) 221-7945; *The Statesman's Year-Book.*

Statistical Office of the United Nations, Publishing Service, New York, New York 10017 (800) 253-9646; *Statistical Yearbook.*

The World Bank, 1818 H Street, NW, Washington, D.C. 20433 (202) 477-1234; *World Development Indicators.*

NETHERLANDS - AIRLINE SERVICE

Europa Publications Limited, 18 Bedford Square, London, WC1B 3JN, England; *The Europa World Year Book.*

European Commission Office of Press and Public Affairs, 2100 M Street, NW, Washington, D.C. 20037 (202) 862-9500; *Basic Statistics of the Community; Regions: Statistical Yearbook;* and *Transport Annual Statistics.*

International Civil Aviation Organization, 999 University Street, Montreal, Quebec, Canada H3C 5H7 (514) 954-8219; *Civil Aviation Statistics of the World.*

M.E. Sharpe, 80 Business Park Drive, Armonk, New York 10504 (800) 541-6563; *The Illustrated Book of World Rankings.*

Organisation for Economic Co-operation and Development (OECD), 2 rue Andre-Pascal, 75 Paris 16, France

(Telephone Number in U.S. (202) 785-6323); *Tourism Policy and International Tourism in OECD Member Countries.*

St. Martin's Press, Inc., 175 Fifth Avenue, New York, New York 10010 (800) 221-7945; *The Statesman's Year-Book.*

Statistical Office of the United Nations, Publishing Service, New York, New York 10017 (800) 253-9646; *Statistical Yearbook.*

NETHERLANDS - AIRPORT

Central Intelligence Agency, Washington, D.C. 20505 (703) 482-1100, www.cia.gov; *The World Factbook.*

NETHERLANDS - ALMOND PRODUCTION - See NETHERLANDS - CROPS

NETHERLANDS - ALUMINUM PRODUCTION AND CONSUMPTION - See NETHERLANDS - MINING AND MINERAL PRODUCTS

NETHERLANDS - ANIMAL FEEDINGSTUFFS

Organisation for Economic Co-operation and Development (OECD), 2 rue Andre-Pascal, 75 Paris 16, France (Telephone Number in U.S. (202) 785-6323); *Foreign Trade by Commodities.*

Statistical Office of the United Nations, Publishing Service, New York, New York 10017 (800) 253-9646; *Statistical Yearbook.*

NETHERLANDS - ANIMAL HEALTH

Food and Agricultural Organization of the United Nations (FAO), Via delle Terme di Caracalla, 00100 Rome, Italy (Telephone Number in U.S. (202) 653-2400); *Animal Health Yearbook.*

NETHERLANDS - ANTIMONY AND ANTIMONY ORE PRODUCTION AND CONSUMPTION - See NETHERLANDS - MINING AND MINERAL PRODUCTS

NETHERLANDS - APPLES - See NETHERLANDS - CROPS

NETHERLANDS - AREA AND DENSITY OF POPULATION

Central Intelligence Agency, Washington, D.C. 20505 (703) 482-1100, www.cia.gov; *The World Factbook.*

Euromonitor International, Inc., 122 South Michigan Avenue, Suite 1200, Chicago, Illinois 60603 (800) 577-EURO; *The World Economic Factbook.*

Europa Publications Limited, 18 Bedford Square, London, WC1B 3JN, England; *The Europa World Year Book.*

European Commission Office of Press

and Public Affairs, 2100 M Street, NW, Washington, D.C. 20037 (202) 862-9500; *Basic Statistics of the Community;* and *Demographic Statistics.*

Food and Agricultural Organization of the United Nations (FAO) Via delle Terme di Caracalla, 00100 Rome, Italy (Telephone Number in U.S. (202) 653-2400); *The State of Food and Agriculture.*

Netherlands Central Bureau of Statistics, Staatsuitgeverij, The Hague, Netherlands; *Statistical Yearbook of the Netherlands.*

St. Martin's Press, Inc., 175 Fifth Avenue, New York, New York 10010 (800) 221-7945; *The Statesman's Year-Book.*

Statistical Office of the United Nations, Publishing Service, New York, New York 10017 (800) 253-9646; *Statistical Yearbook;* and *Trends in Europe and North America: The Statistical Yearbook of the Economic Commission for Europe.*

United Nations Educational, Scientific and Cultural Organization (UNESCO), 7 Place de Fontenoy, F-75700 Paris, France (Telephone Number in U.S. (212) 963-5981); *Statistical Yearbook.*

The World Bank, 1818 H Street, NW, Washington, D.C. 20433 (202) 477-1234; *World Development Report.*

NETHERLANDS - ARMS EXPORTS AND IMPORTS - See NETHERLANDS - MILITARY

NETHERLANDS - ARSENIC PRODUCTION AND CONSUMPTION - See NETHERLANDS - MINING AND MINERAL PRODUCTS

NETHERLANDS - BALANCE OF PAYMENTS

The Economist Intelligence Unit, 111 West 57th Street, New York, New York 10019 (800) 938-4685; *The World Market Atlas.*

Europa Publications Limited, 18 Bedford Square, London, WC1B 3JN, England; *The Europa World Year Book.*

European Commission Office of Press and Public Affairs, 2100 M Street, NW, Washington, D.C. 20037 (202) 862-9500; *ACP: Basic Statistics; Basic Statistics of the Community; Energy Statistics Yearbook;* and *Eurostatistics: Data for Short-term Economic Analysis.*

International Monetary Fund, 700 Nineteenth Street, NW, Washington, D.C. 20431 (202) 623-7000; *Balance of Payments Yearbook;* and *International Financial Statistics.*

Netherlands Central Bureau of Statistics, Staatsuitgeverij, The Hague, Netherlands; *Statistical Yearbook of the Netherlands.*

Organisation for Economic Co-operation and Development (OECD), 2 rue Andre-Pascal, 75 Paris 16, France (Telephone Number in U.S. (202) 785-6323); *Economic Outlook; Geographical Distribution of Financial Flows to Developing Countries; Main Economic Indicators - Historical Statistics;* and *OECD Economic Surveys: Netherlands.*

United Nations Conference on Trade and Development (UNCTAD), New York, New York 10017 (800) 253-9646; *Handbook of International Trade and Development Statistics.*

The World Bank, 1818 H Street, NW, Washington, D.C. 20433 (202) 477-1234; *World Development Report;* and *World Development Indicators.*

NETHERLANDS - BANANA PRODUCTION - See NETHERLANDS - CROPS

NETHERLANDS - BANKING

Euromonitor International, Inc., 122 South Michigan Avenue, Suite 1200, Chicago, Illinois 60603 (800) 577-EURO; *World Marketing Data and Statistics.*

Europa Publications Limited, 18 Bedford Square, London, WC1B 3JN, England; *The Europa World Year Book.*

European Commission Office of Press and Public Affairs, 2100 M Street, NW, Washington, D.C. 20037 (202) 862-9500; *ACP: Basic Statistics,* and *Eurostatistics: Data for Short-term Economic Analysis.*

International Monetary Fund, 700 Nineteenth Street, NW, Washington, D.C. 20431 (202) 623-7000; *Government Finance Statistics Yearbook;* and *International Financial Statistics.*

M.E. Sharpe, 80 Business Park Drive, Armonk, New York 10504 (800) 541-6563; *The Illustrated Book of World Rankings.*

Netherlands Central Bureau of Statistics, Staatsuitgeverij, The Hague, Netherlands; *Statistical Yearbook of the Netherlands.*

Organisation for Economic Co-operation and Development (OECD), 2 rue Andre-Pascal, 75 Paris 16, France (Telephone Number in U.S. (202) 785-6323); *Economic Outlook; Financial Market Trends;* and *OECD Economic Surveys: Netherlands.*

St. Martin's Press, Inc., 175 Fifth Avenue, New York, New York 10010 (800)

221-7945; *The Statesman's Year-Book.*

Statistical Office of the United Nations, Publishing Service, New York, New York 10017 (800) 253-9646; *Statistical Yearbook.*

NETHERLANDS - BARLEY PRODUCTION - See NETHERLANDS - CROPS

NETHERLANDS - BAUXITE PRODUCTION AND CONSUMPTION - See NETHERLANDS - MINING AND MINERAL PRODUCTS

NETHERLANDS - BEER PRODUCTION - See NETHERLANDS - BEVERAGES

NETHERLANDS - BEVERAGES

European Commission Office of Press and Public Affairs, 2100 M Street, NW, Washington, D.C. 20037 (202) 862-9500; *Basic Statistics of the Community.*

M.E. Sharpe, 80 Business Park Drive, Armonk, New York 10504 (800) 541-6563; *The Illustrated Book of World Rankings.*

Organisation for Economic Co-operation and Development (OECD), 2 rue Andre-Pascal, 75 Paris 16, France (Telephone Number in U.S. (202) 785-6323); *Indicators of Industrial Activity.*

Statistical Office of the United Nations, Publishing Service, New York, New York 10017 (800) 253-9646; *Statistical Yearbook.*

NETHERLANDS - BIRTH RATES

Central Intelligence Agency, Washington, D.C. 20505 (703) 482-1100, www.cia.gov; *The World Factbook.*

Euromonitor International, Inc., 122 South Michigan Avenue, Suite 1200, Chicago, Illinois 60603 (800) 577-EURO; *The World Economic Factbook.*

European Commission Office of Press and Public Affairs, 2100 M Street, NW, Washington, D.C. 20037 (202) 862-9500; *Basic Statistics of the Community; and Demographic Statistics.*

M.E. Sharpe, 80 Business Park Drive, Armonk, New York 10504 (800) 541-6563; *The Illustrated Book of World Rankings.*

St. Martin's Press, Inc., 175 Fifth Avenue, New York, New York 10010 (800) 221-7945; *The Statesman's Year-Book.*

Statistical Office of the United Nations, Publishing Service, New York, New York 10017 (800) 253-9646; *Demographic Yearbook; and Statistical Yearbook.*

The World Bank, 1818 H Street, NW, Washington, D.C. 20433 (202) 477-1234; *World Development Indicators.*

World Health Organization, Office of Publications, 20 Avenue Appia, CH-1211 Geneva 27, Switzerland (Telephone Number in U.S. (518) 436-9686); *World Health Statistics Annual.*

NETHERLANDS - BISMUTH PRODUCTION AND CONSUMPTION - See NETHERLANDS - MINING AND MINERAL PRODUCTS

NETHERLANDS - BONDS

European Commission Office of Press and Public Affairs, 2100 M Street, NW, Washington, D.C. 20037 (202) 862-9500; *Basic Statistics of the Community.*

International Monetary Fund, 700 Nineteenth Street, NW, Washington, D.C. 20431 (202) 623-7000; *Government Finance Statistics Yearbook.*

Organisation for Economic Co-operation and Development (OECD), 2 rue Andre-Pascal, 75 Paris 16, France (Telephone Number in U.S. (202) 785-6323); *Financial Market Trends.*

Statistical Office of the United Nations, Publishing Service, New York, New York 10017 (800) 253-9646; *Statistical Yearbook.*

NETHERLANDS - BOOK PRODUCTION

Euromonitor International, Inc., 122 South Michigan Avenue, Suite 1200, Chicago, Illinois 60603 (800) 577-EURO; *European Marketing Data and Statistics.*

Europa Publications Limited, 18 Bedford Square, London, WC1B 3JN, England; *The Europa World Year Book.*

Food and Agricultural Organization of the United Nations (FAO) Via delle Terme di Caracalla, 00100 Rome, Italy (Telephone Number in U.S. (202) 653-2400); *The State of Food and Agriculture.*

St. Martin's Press, Inc., 175 Fifth Avenue, New York, New York 10010 (800) 221-7945; *The Statesman's Year-Book.*

Statistical Office of the United Nations, Publishing Service, New York, New York 10017 (800) 253-9646; *Trends in Europe and North America: The Statistical Yearbook of the Economic Commission for Europe.*

United Nations Educational, Scientific and Cultural Organization (UNESCO), 7 Place de Fontenoy, F-75700 Paris, France (Telephone Number in U.S. (212) 963-5981); *Statistical Yearbook.*

NETHERLANDS - BROADCASTING

Billboard Limited, Post Office Box 9027, 1006 AA Amsterdam, The Netherlands (Telephone Number in U.S. (212) 764-

7300); *World Radio TV Handbook.*

Central Intelligence Agency, Washington, D.C. 20505 (703) 482-1100, www.cia.gov; *The World Factbook.*

Euromonitor International, Inc., 122 South Michigan Avenue, Suite 1200, Chicago, Illinois 60603 (800) 577-EURO; *World Marketing Data and Statistics.*

European Commission Office of Press and Public Affairs, 2100 M Street, NW, Washington, D.C. 20037 (202) 862-9500; *Basic Statistics of the Community.*

M.E. Sharpe, 80 Business Park Drive, Armonk, New York 10504 (800) 541-6563; *The Illustrated Book of World Rankings.*

St. Martin's Press, Inc., 175 Fifth Avenue, New York, New York 10010 (800) 221-7945; *The Statesman's Year-Book.*

Statistical Office of the United Nations, Publishing Service, New York, New York 10017 (800) 253-9646; *Trends in Europe and North America: The Statistical Yearbook of the Economic Commission for Europe.*

United Nations Educational, Scientific and Cultural Organization (UNESCO), 7 Place de Fontenoy, F-75700 Paris, France (Telephone Number in U.S. (212) 963-5981); *Statistical Yearbook.*

NETHERLANDS - BUDGET

Central Intelligence Agency, Washington, D.C. 20505 (703) 482-1100, www.cia.gov; *The World Factbook.*

NETHERLANDS - BUSINESS

European Commission Office of Press and Public Affairs, 2100 M Street, NW, Washington, D.C. 20037 (202) 862-9500; *Basic Statistics of the Community.*

Organisation for Economic Co-operation and Development (OECD), 2 rue Andre-Pascal, 75 Paris 16, France (Telephone Number in U.S. (202) 785-6323); *Main Economic Indicators - Historical Statistics.*

NETHERLANDS - BUTTER - See NETHERLANDS - DAIRY PRODUCTS

NETHERLANDS - CABBAGE PRODUCTION - See NETHERLANDS - CROPS

NETHERLANDS - CADMIUM PRODUCTION AND CONSUMPTION - See NETHERLANDS - MINING AND MINERAL PRODUCTS

NETHERLANDS - CALORIE SUPPLY

Food and Agricultural Organization of

the United Nations (FAO) Via delle Terme di Caracalla, 00100 Rome, Italy (Telephone Number in U.S. (202) 653-2400); *The State of Food and Agriculture.*

NETHERLANDS - CAPITAL INVESTMENT

Organisation for Economic Co-operation and Development (OECD), 2 rue Andre-Pascal, 75 Paris 16, France (Telephone Number in U.S. (202) 785-6323); *Economic Outlook;* and *Financial Market Trends.*

NETHERLANDS - CAPITAL REVENUE

International Monetary Fund, 700 Nineteenth Street, NW, Washington, D.C. 20431 (202) 623-7000; *Government Finance Statistics Yearbook.*

Organisation for Economic Co-operation and Development (OECD), 2 rue Andre-Pascal, 75 Paris 16, France (Telephone Number in U.S. (202) 785-6323); *Economic Outlook;* and *Financial Market Trends.*

NETHERLANDS - CASHEW NUT PRODUCTION - See NETHERLANDS - CROPS

NETHERLANDS - CASTOR BEAN PRODUCTION - See NETHERLANDS - CROPS

NETHERLANDS - CATTLE - See NETHERLANDS - LIVESTOCK AND POULTRY

NETHERLANDS - CAULIFLOWER PRODUCTION - See NETHERLANDS - CROPS

NETHERLANDS - CAUSTIC SODA PRODUCTION - See NETHERLANDS - BEVERAGES

NETHERLANDS - CEMENT PRODUCTION - See NETHERLANDS - MINING AND MINERAL PRODUCTS

NETHERLANDS - CEREAL PRODUCTION - See NETHERLANDS - CROPS

NETHERLANDS - CHEESE - See NETHERLANDS - DAIRY PRODUCTS

NETHERLANDS - CHEMICAL INDUSTRY

European Commission Office of Press and Public Affairs, 2100 M Street, NW, Washington, D.C. 20037 (202) 862-9500; *Industrial Production: Quarterly Statistics.*

NETHERLANDS - CHEMICAL (ORGANIC) PRODUCTION - See NETHERLANDS - MINING AND MINERAL PRODUCTS

NETHERLANDS - CHESTNUT

PRODUCTION - See NETHERLANDS - CROPS

NETHERLANDS - CHICKENS - See NETHERLANDS - LIVESTOCK AND POULTRY

NETHERLANDS - CHROMITE PRODUCTION AND CONSUMPTION - See NETHERLANDS - MINING AND MINERAL PRODUCTS

NETHERLANDS - CHROMIUM ORE PRODUCTION AND CONSUMPTION - See NETHERLANDS - MINING AND MINERAL PRODUCTS

NETHERLANDS - CIGAR PRODUCTION - See NETHERLANDS - TOBACCO PRODUCTION

NETHERLANDS - CIGARETTE PRODUCTION - See NETHERLANDS - TOBACCO PRODUCTION

NETHERLANDS - CLASS STRUCTURE

European Commission Office of Press and Public Affairs, 2100 M Street, NW, Washington, D.C. 20037 (202) 862-9500; *Basic Statistics of the Community;* and *Labor Force Sample Survey.*

NETHERLANDS - CLIMATE

M.E. Sharpe, 80 Business Park Drive, Armonk, New York 10504 (800) 541-6563; *The Illustrated Book of World Rankings.*

Netherlands Central Bureau of Statistics, Staatsuitgeverij, The Hague, Netherlands; *Statistical Yearbook of the Netherlands.*

St. Martin's Press, Inc., 175 Fifth Avenue, New York, New York 10010 (800) 221-7945; *The Statesman's Year-Book.*

NETHERLANDS - CLOTHING - PRODUCTION INDEX - See NETHERLANDS - TEXTILE INDUSTRY

NETHERLANDS - CLOTHING EXPORTS AND IMPORTS - See NETHERLANDS - TEXTILE INDUSTRY

NETHERLANDS - COAL PRODUCTION - See NETHERLANDS - MINING AND MINERAL PRODUCTS

NETHERLANDS - COBALT PRODUCTION AND CONSUMPTION - See NETHERLANDS - MINING AND MINERAL PRODUCTS

NETHERLANDS - COCOA (BEANS) PRODUCTION - See NETHERLANDS - CROPS

NETHERLANDS - COFFEE - See

NETHERLANDS - CROPS

NETHERLANDS - COKE AND COKE OVEN COKE PRODUCTION AND CONSUMPTION - See NETHERLANDS - MINING AND MINERAL PRODUCTS

NETHERLANDS - COKE OVEN ORE PRODUCTION AND CONSUMPTION - See NETHERLANDS - MINING AND MINERAL PRODUCTS

NETHERLANDS - COMMERCE

St. Martin's Press, Inc., 175 Fifth Avenue, New York, New York 10010 (800) 221-7945; *The Statesman's Year-Book.*

NETHERLANDS - COMMERCE EMPLOYMENT - MALE AND FEMALE - See NETHERLANDS - EMPLOYMENT

NETHERLANDS - COMMUNICATION EMPLOYMENT - MALE AND FEMALE - See NETHERLANDS - EMPLOYMENT

NETHERLANDS - COMMUNICATIONS - See NETHERLANDS - TRANSPORTATION AND COMMUNICATIONS

NETHERLANDS - CONSTRUCTION INDUSTRY

European Commission Office of Press and Public Affairs, 2100 M Street, NW, Washington, D.C. 20037 (202) 862-9500; *Basic Statistics of the Community.*

M.E. Sharpe, 80 Business Park Drive, Armonk, New York 10504 (800) 541-6563; *The Illustrated Book of World Rankings.*

Organisation for Economic Co-operation and Development (OECD), 2 rue Andre-Pascal, 75 Paris 16, France (Telephone Number in U.S. (202) 785-6323); *Industrial Structure Statistics; The Iron and Steel Industry; Main Economic Indicators - Historical Statistics;* and *OECD Economic Surveys: Netherlands.*

St. Martin's Press, Inc., 175 Fifth Avenue, New York, New York 10010 (800) 221-7945; *The Statesman's Year-Book.*

Statistical Office of the United Nations, Publishing Service, New York, New York 10017 (800) 253-9646; *Statistical Yearbook.*

NETHERLANDS - CONSUMER PRICE INDEX

Europa Publications Limited, 18 Bedford Square, London, WC1B 3JN, England; *The Europa World Year Book.*

European Commission Office of Press and Public Affairs, 2100 M Street, NW, Washington, D.C. 20037 (202) 862-9500; *Basic Statistics of the Community.*

Organisation for Economic Co-

operation and Development (OECD), 2 rue Andre-Pascal, 75 Paris 16, France (Telephone Number in U.S. (202) 785-6323); *Economic Outlook.*

Statistical Office of the United Nations, Publishing Service, New York, New York 10017 (800) 253-9646; *Statistical Yearbook;* and *Trends in Europe and North America: The Statistical Yearbook of the Economic Commission for Europe.*

NETHERLANDS - CONSUMER PRICES

Euromonitor International, Inc., 122 South Michigan Avenue, Suite 1200, Chicago, Illinois 60603 (800) 577-EURO; *European Marketing Data and Statistics;* and *World Marketing Data and Statistics.*

European Commission Office of Press and Public Affairs, 2100 M Street, NW, Washington, D.C. 20037 (202) 862-9500; *Basic Statistics of the Community; Eurostatistics: Data for Short-term Economic Analysis;* and *Money and Finance.*

International Labour Office, I.L.O. Publications, 1828 L Street, NW., Suite 801, Washington, D.C. 20036 (301) 638-3152; *Yearbook of Labour Statistics.*

International Monetary Fund, 700 Nineteenth Street, NW, Washington, D.C. 20431 (202) 623-7000; *International Financial Statistics.*

Organisation for Economic Co-operation and Development (OECD), 2 rue Andre-Pascal, 75 Paris 16, France (Telephone Number in U.S. (202) 785-6323); *Economic Outlook.*

NETHERLANDS - CONSUMPTION

European Commission Office of Press and Public Affairs, 2100 M Street, NW, Washington, D.C. 20037 (202) 862-9500; *Basic Statistics of the Community.*

International Iron and Steel Institute, 120, rue Colonel Bourg, B-1140 Brussels, Belgium; *Steel Statistical Yearbook.*

International Lead and Zinc Study Group, Metro House, 58 St. James's Street, London SW1A 1LD England; *Lead and Zinc Statistics.*

International Rubber Study Group, York House, Eighth Floor, Empire Way, Wembley, London HA9 0PA, England; *Rubber Statistical Bulletin.*

Organisation for Economic Co-operation and Development (OECD), 2 rue Andre-Pascal, 75 Paris 16, France (Telephone Number in U.S. (202) 785-6323); *The Footwear, Raw Hides and Skins, and Leather Industry in OECD*

Countries; *The Iron and Steel Industry; Meat Balances in OECD Member Countries; The Non-Ferrous Metals Industry; The Pulp and Paper Industry;* and *Textile Industry in OECD Countries.*

The World Bank, 1818 H Street, NW, Washington, D.C. 20433 (202) 477-1234; *World Development Report.*

NETHERLANDS - COPPER AND COPPER ORE PRODUCTION AND CONSUMPTION - See NETHERLANDS - MINING AND MINERAL PRODUCTS

NETHERLANDS - CORN PRODUCTION - See NETHERLANDS - CROPS

NETHERLANDS - CORPORATE INCOME TAXES - See NETHERLANDS - TAXATION

NETHERLANDS - CORPORATE TAXES - See NETHERLANDS - TAXATION

NETHERLANDS - COTTON - See NETHERLANDS - CROPS

NETHERLANDS - CRIME

International Criminal Police Organization (INTERPOL), 50 quai Achille Lignon, F-69006 Lyon, France; *International Crime Statistics.*

Statistical Office of the United Nations, Publishing Service, New York, New York 10017 (800) 253-9646; *Trends in Europe and North America: The Statistical Yearbook of the Economic Commission for Europe.*

Yale University Press, Yale Station, New Haven, Connecticut 06520 (800) 987-7323; *Violence and Crime in Cross-National Perspective.*

NETHERLANDS - CROPS

Commodity Research Bureau, Inc., 30 South Wacker Drive, Chicago Illinois 60606 (312) 454-1801; *Commodity Year Book.*

Euromonitor International, Inc., 122 South Michigan Avenue, Suite 1200, Chicago, Illinois 60603 (800) 577-EURO; *European Marketing Data and Statistics.*

Europa Publications Limited, 18 Bedford Square, London, WC1B 3JN, England; *The Europa World Year Book.*

European Commission Office of Press and Public Affairs, 2100 M Street, NW, Washington, D.C. 20037 (202) 862-9500; *ACP: Basic Statistics; Agriculture: Statistical Yearbook; Basic Statistics of the Community; Crop Production: Quarterly Statistics; Eurostatistics: Data for Short-term Economic Analysis;* and *Regions: Statistical Yearbook.*

Food and Agricultural Organization of

the United Nations (FAO), Via delle Terme di Caracalla, 00100 Rome, Italy (Telephone Number in U.S. (202) 653-2400); *Production Yearbook;* and *The State of Food and Agriculture.*

M.E. Sharpe, 80 Business Park Drive, Armonk, New York 10504 (800) 541-6563; *The Illustrated Book of World Rankings.*

Organisation for Economic Co-operation and Development (OECD), 2 rue Andre-Pascal, 75 Paris 16, France (Telephone Number in U.S. (202) 785-6323); *Economic Accounts for Agriculture; Foreign Trade by Commodities; Milk, Milk Products, and Egg Balances in OECD Member Countries;* and *Textile Industry in OECD Countries.*

St. Martin's Press, Inc., 175 Fifth Avenue, New York, New York 10010 (800) 221-7945; *The Statesman's Year-Book.*

Statistical Office of the United Nations, Publishing Service, New York, New York 10017 (800) 253-9646; *Statistical Yearbook.*

United Nations Conference on Trade and Development, Central Statistical Service, Palais des Nations, Geneva, Switzerland (Telephone in U.S. (800) 253-9646); *UNCTAD Commodity Yearbook.*

NETHERLANDS - CUSTOMS DUTIES

European Commission Office of Press and Public Affairs, 2100 M Street, NW, Washington, D.C. 20037 (202) 862-9500; *Basic Statistics of the Community.*

International Monetary Fund, 700 Nineteenth Street, NW, Washington, D.C. 20431 (202) 623-7000; *Government Finance Statistics Yearbook.*

Organisation for Economic Co-operation and Development (OECD), 2 rue Andre-Pascal, 75 Paris 16, France (Telephone Number in U.S. (202) 785-6323); *The Non-Ferrous Metals Industry.*

St. Martin's Press, Inc., 175 Fifth Avenue, New York, New York 10010 (800) 221-7945; *The Statesman's Year-Book.*

NETHERLANDS - DAIRY PRODUCTS

Commodity Research Bureau, Inc., 30 South Wacker Drive, Chicago, Illinois 60606 (312) 454-1801; *Commodity Year Book.*

Europa Publications Limited, 18 Bedford Square, London, WC1B 3JN, England; *The Europa World Year Book.*

European Commission Office of Press and Public Affairs, 2100 M Street, NW, Washington, D.C. 20037 (202) 862-9500; *Basic Statistics of the Community;* and *Eurostatistics: Data for Short-term*

Economic Analysis.

Food and Agricultural Organization of the United Nations (FAO) Via delle Terme di Caracalla, 00100 Rome, Italy (Telephone Number in U.S. (202) 653-2400); *The State of Food and Agriculture.*

M.E. Sharpe, 80 Business Park Drive, Armonk, New York 10504 (800) 541-6563; *The Illustrated Book of World Rankings.*

Organisation for Economic Co-operation and Development (OECD), 2 rue Andre-Pascal, 75 Paris 16, France (Telephone Number in U.S. (202) 785-6323); *Economic Accounts for Agriculture;* and *Milk, Milk Products, and Egg Balances in OECD Member Countries.*

St. Martin's Press, Inc., 175 Fifth Avenue, New York, New York 10010 (800) 221-7945; *The Statesman's Year-Book.*

Statistical Office of the United Nations, Publishing Service, New York, New York 10017 (800) 253-9646; *Statistical Yearbook.*

NETHERLANDS - DEATH RATES - See NETHERLANDS - MORTALITY

NETHERLANDS - DEFENSE EXPENDITURES - See NETHERLANDS - MILITARY

NETHERLANDS - DEMOGRAPHY

The Economist Intelligence Unit, 111 West 57th Street, New York, New York 10019 (800) 938-4685; *The World Market Atlas.*

Euromonitor International, Inc., 122 South Michigan Avenue, Suite 1200, Chicago, Illinois 60603 (800) 577-EURO; *The World Economic Factbook;* and *World Marketing Data and Statistics.*

European Commission Office of Press and Public Affairs, 2100 M Street, NW, Washington, D.C. 20037 (202) 862-9500; *Basic Statistics of the Community; Demographic Statistics; Employment and Unemployment;* and *Regions: Statistical Yearbook.*

M.E. Sharpe, 80 Business Park Drive, Armonk, New York 10504 (800) 541-6563; *The Illustrated Book of World Rankings.*

Statistical Office of the United Nations, Publishing Service, New York, New York 10017 (800) 253-9646; *Human Development Report.*

NETHERLANDS - DEVELOPMENT ASSISTANCE

European Commission Office of Press and Public Affairs, 2100 M Street, NW, Washington, D.C. 20037 (202) 862-9500;

ACP: Basic Statistics; Basic Statistics of the Community; and *Government Financing of Research and Development.*

Organisation for Economic Co-operation and Development (OECD), 2 rue Andre-Pascal, 75 Paris 16, France (Telephone Number in U.S. (202) 785-6323); *Geographical Distribution of Financial Flows to Developing Countries.*

Statistical Office of the United Nations, Publishing Service, New York, New York 10017 (800) 253-9646; *Statistical Yearbook.*

NETHERLANDS - DIAMOND EXPORTS - See NETHERLANDS - MINING AND MINERAL PRODUCTS

NETHERLANDS - DIAMOND PRODUCTION - See NETHERLANDS - MINING AND MINERAL PRODUCTS

NETHERLANDS - DISCOUNT RATES - See NETHERLANDS - BANKING

NETHERLANDS - DISEASE - See NETHERLANDS - HEALTH

NETHERLANDS - DIVORCE RATES

European Commission Office of Press and Public Affairs, 2100 M Street, NW, Washington, D.C. 20037 (202) 862-9500; *Demographic Statistics;* and *Eurostat Review.*

M.E. Sharpe, 80 Business Park Drive, Armonk, New York 10504 (800) 541-6563; *The Illustrated Book of World Rankings.*

Statistical Office of the United Nations, Publishing Service, New York, New York 10017 (800) 253-9646; *Demographic Yearbook; Trends in Europe and North America: The Statistical Yearbook of the Economic Commission for Europe;* and *Statistical Yearbook.*

NETHERLANDS - DOMESTIC PRODUCT

European Commission Office of Press and Public Affairs, 2100 M Street, NW, Washington, D.C. 20037 (202) 862-9500; *Basic Statistics of the Community.*

NETHERLANDS - DUCKS - See NETHERLANDS - LIVESTOCK AND POULTRY

NETHERLANDS - ECONOMY

Central Intelligence Agency, Washington, D.C. 20505 (703) 482-1100, www.cia.gov; *The World Factbook.*

Economist Intelligence Unit, 111 West 57th Street, New York, New York 10019 (800) 938-4685; *Netherlands Country Report.*

Euromonitor International, Inc., 122 South Michigan Avenue, Suite 1200, Chicago, Illinois 60603 (800) 577-EURO; *European Marketing Data and Statistics; The World Economic Factbook;* and *World Marketing Data and Statistics.*

Europa Publications Limited, 18 Bedford Square, London, WC1B 3JN, England; *The Europa World Year Book.*

European Commission Office of Press and Public Affairs, 2100 M Street, NW, Washington, D.C. 20037 (202) 862-9500; *ACP: Basic Statistics; Basic Statistics of the Community; Energy Statistics Yearbook; Labor Force Sample Survey;* and *Money and Finance.*

M.E. Sharpe, 80 Business Park Drive, Armonk, New York 10504 (800) 541-6563; *The Illustrated Book of World Rankings.*

Organisation for Economic Co-operation and Development (OECD), 2 rue Andre-Pascal, 75 Paris 16, France (Telephone Number in U.S. (202) 785-6323); *Economic Outlook; Geographical Distribution of Financial Flows to Developing Countries; OECD Economic Surveys: Netherlands;* and *OECD Employment Outlook.*

St. Martin's Press, Inc., 175 Fifth Avenue, New York, New York 10010 (800) 221-7945; *The Statesman's Year-Book.*

Statistical Office of the United Nations, Publishing Service, New York, New York 10017 (800) 253-9646; *World Statistics Pocketbook.*

The World Bank, 1818 H Street, NW, Washington, D.C. 20433 (202) 477-1234; *The World Bank Atlas;* and *World Development Report.*

NETHERLANDS - EDUCATION

The Economist Intelligence Unit, 111 West 57th Street, New York, New York 10019 (800) 938-4685; *The World Market Atlas.*

Euromonitor International, Inc., 122 South Michigan Avenue, Suite 1200, Chicago, Illinois 60603 (800) 577-EURO; *European Marketing Data and Statistics;* and *World Marketing Data and Statistics.*

Europa Publications Limited, 18 Bedford Square, London, WC1B 3JN, England; *The Europa World Year Book.*

European Commission Office of Press and Public Affairs, 2100 M Street, NW, Washington, D.C. 20037 (202) 862-9500; *Basic Statistics of the Community;* and *Regions: Statistical Yearbook.*

International Monetary Fund, 700

Nineteenth Street, NW, Washington, D.C. 20431 (202) 623-7000; *Government Finance Statistics Yearbook.*

M.E. Sharpe, 80 Business Park Drive, Armonk, New York 10504 (800) 541-6563; *The Illustrated Book of World Rankings.*

Netherlands Central Bureau of Statistics, Staatsuitgeverij, The Hague, Netherlands; *Statistical Yearbook of the Netherlands.*

Organisation for Economic Co-operation and Development (OECD), 2 rue Andre-Pascal, 75 Paris 16, France (Telephone Number in U.S. (202) 785-6323); *Education in OECD Countries.*

St. Martin's Press, Inc., 175 Fifth Avenue, New York, New York 10010 (800) 221-7945; *The Statesman's Year-Book.*

Statistical Office of the United Nations, Publishing Service, New York, New York 10017 (800) 253-9646; *Human Development Report; and Trends in Europe and North America: The Statistical Yearbook of the Economic Commission for Europe.*

United Nations Educational, Scientific and Cultural Organization (UNESCO), 7 Place de Fontenoy, F-75700 Paris, France (Telephone Number in U.S. (212) 963-5981); *Statistical Yearbook.*

The World Bank, 1818 H Street, NW, Washington, D.C. 20433 (202) 477-1234; *World Development Report; and World Development Indicators.*

NETHERLANDS - EGG PRODUCTION AND CONSUMPTION - See NETHERLANDS - DAIRY PRODUCTS

NETHERLANDS - ELECTRICITY

Central Intelligence Agency, Washington, D.C. 20505 (703) 482-1100, www.cia.gov; *The World Factbook.*

European Commission Office of Press and Public Affairs, 2100 M Street, NW, Washington, D.C. 20037 (202) 862-9500; *Basic Statistics of the Community; Energy: Monthly Statistics; Energy Statistics Yearbook; Eurostatistics: Data for Short-term Economic Analysis; and Regions: Statistical Yearbook.*

M.E. Sharpe, 80 Business Park Drive, Armonk, New York 10504 (800) 541-6563; *The Illustrated Book of World Rankings.*

Organisation for Economic Co-operation and Development (OECD), 2 rue Andre-Pascal, 75 Paris 16, France (Telephone Number in U.S. (202) 785-6323); *Coal Information; Energy Statistics of OECD Countries; Indicators of Industrial Activity; Industrial Structure Statistics; and Regions: Statistical Yearbook.*

Penn Well Publishing Company, 1421 South Sheridan Road, Post Office Box 1260, Tulsa, Oklahoma 74101 (800) 752-9764; *International Energy Statistics Sourcebook.*

St. Martin's Press, Inc., 175 Fifth Avenue, New York, New York 10010 (800) 221-7945; *The Statesman's Year-Book.*

Statistical Office of the United Nations, Publishing Service, New York, New York 10017 (800) 253-9646; *Human Development Report; Trends in Europe and North America: The Statistical Yearbook of the Economic Commission for Europe; and Statistical Yearbook.*

NETHERLANDS - EMPLOYMENT

Euromonitor International, Inc., 122 South Michigan Avenue, Suite 1200, Chicago, Illinois 60603 (800) 577-EURO; *European Marketing Data and Statistics.*

European Commission Office of Press and Public Affairs, 2100 M Street, NW, Washington, D.C. 20037 (202) 862-9500; *Basic Statistics of the Community; Earnings in Agriculture; Employment and Unemployment; Eurostatistics: Data for Short-term Economic Analysis; Iron and Steel: Statistical Yearbook; Labor Force Sample Survey; and Transport Annual Statistics.*

International Labour Office, I.L.O. Publications, 1828 L Street, NW., Suite 801, Washington, D.C. 20036 (301) 638-3152; *Yearbook of Labour Statistics.*

M.E. Sharpe, 80 Business Park Drive, Armonk, New York 10504 (800) 541-6563; *The Illustrated Book of World Rankings.*

Organisation for Economic Co-operation and Development (OECD), 2 rue Andre-Pascal, 75 Paris 16, France (Telephone Number in U.S. (202) 785-6323); *Economic Outlook; The Iron and Steel Industry; OECD Economic Surveys: Netherlands; OECD Employment Outlook; and Textile Industry in OECD Countries.*

Statistical Office of the United Nations, Publishing Service, New York, New York 10017 (800) 253-9646; *Statistical Yearbook; and Trends in Europe and North America: The Statistical Yearbook of the Economic Commission for Europe.*

NETHERLANDS - ENERGY

Euromonitor International, Inc., 122 South Michigan Avenue, Suite 1200, Chicago, Illinois 60603 (800) 577-EURO; *European Marketing Data and Statistics; The World Economic Factbook; and World Marketing Data and Statistics.*

European Commission Office of Press and Public Affairs, 2100 M Street, NW, Washington, D.C. 20037 (202) 862-9500; *Basic Statistics of the Community; Energy: Monthly Statistics; Energy Statistics Yearbook; and Transport Annual Statistics.*

Food and Agricultural Organization of the United Nations (FAO) Via delle Terme di Caracalla, 00100 Rome, Italy (Telephone Number in U.S. (202) 653-2400); *The State of Food and Agriculture.*

M.E. Sharpe, 80 Business Park Drive, Armonk, New York 10504 (800) 541-6563; *The Illustrated Book of World Rankings.*

Organisation for Economic Co-operation and Development (OECD), 2 rue Andre-Pascal, 75 Paris 16, France (Telephone Number in U.S. (202) 785-6323); *Coal Information; Energy Statistics for OECD Countries; OECD Environmental Data; and Oil and Gas Information.*

Penn Well Publishing Company, 1421 South Sheridan Road, Post Office Box 1260, Tulsa, Oklahoma 74101 (800) 752-9764; *International Energy Statistics Sourcebook.*

St. Martin's Press, Inc., 175 Fifth Avenue, New York, New York 10010 (800) 221-7945; *The Statesman's Year-Book.*

Statistical Office of the United Nations, Publishing Service, New York, New York 10017 (800) 253-9646; *Energy Statistics Yearbook; Human Development Report; Trends in Europe and North America: The Statistical Yearbook of the Economic Commission for Europe; World Statistics Pocketbook; and Statistical Yearbook.*

The World Bank, 1818 H Street, NW, Washington, D.C. 20433 (202) 477-1234; *The World Bank Atlas; and World Development Report.*

NETHERLANDS - ENGINEERING AND METAL PRODUCTS - EXPORTS AND IMPORTS

European Commission Office of Press and Public Affairs, 2100 M Street, NW, Washington, D.C. 20037 (202) 862-9500; *Basic Statistics of the Community; Energy: Monthly Statistics; and Industrial Production: Quarterly Statistics.*

NETHERLANDS - ENVIRONMENT

Economist Intelligence Unit, 111 West 57th Street, New York, New York 10019 (800) 938-4685; *Netherlands Country Report.*

Organisation for Economic Co-operation and Development (OECD), 2 rue Andre-Pascal, 75 Paris 16, France (Telephone Number in U.S. (202) 785-6323); *OECD Environmental Data.*

Statistical Office of the United Nations, Publishing Service, New York, New York 10017 (800) 253-9646; *Trends in Europe and North America: The Statistical Yearbook of the Economic Commission for Europe;* and *World Statistics Pocketbook.*

NETHERLANDS - EXCHANGE RATES

Central Intelligence Agency, Washington, D.C. 20505 (703) 482-1100, www.cia.gov; *The World Factbook.*

Euromonitor International, Inc., 122 South Michigan Avenue, Suite 1200, Chicago, Illinois 60603 (800) 577-EURO; *The World Economic Factbook.*

Europa Publications Limited, 18 Bedford Square, London, WC1B 3JN, England; *The Europa World Year Book.*

European Commission Office of Press and Public Affairs, 2100 M Street, NW, Washington, D.C. 20037 (202) 862-9500; *Basic Statistics of the Community; Eurostatistics: Data for Short-term Economic Analysis;* and *Money and Finance.*

International Civil Aviation Organization, 999 University Street, Montreal, Quebec, Canada H3C 5H7 (514) 954-8219; *Civil Aviation Statistics of the World.*

International Monetary Fund, 700 Nineteenth Street, NW, Washington, D.C. 20431 (202) 623-7000; *International Financial Statistics.*

Organisation for Economic Co-operation and Development (OECD), 2 rue Andre-Pascal, 75 Paris 16, France (Telephone Number in U.S. (202) 785-6323); *Economic Outlook; Financial Market Trends; Revenue Statistics of OECD Member Countries;* and *Tourism Policy and International Tourism in OECD Member Countries.*

Statistical Office of the United Nations, Publishing Service, New York, New York 10017 (800) 253-9646; *Statistical Yearbook; World Statistics Pocketbook;* and *Trends in Europe and North America: The Statistical Yearbook of the Economic Commission for Europe.*

NETHERLANDS - EXCISE TAXES - See NETHERLANDS - TAXATION

NETHERLANDS - EXPORTS

Central Intelligence Agency, Washington, D.C. 20505 (703) 482-1100, www.cia.gov; *The World Factbook.*

The Economist Intelligence Unit, 111 West 57th Street, New York, New York 10019 (800) 938-4685; *Netherlands Country Report;* and *The World Market Atlas.*

Euromonitor International, Inc., 122 South Michigan Avenue, Suite 1200, Chicago, Illinois 60603 (800) 577-EURO; *The World Economic Factbook.*

Europa Publications Limited, 18 Bedford Square, London, WC1B 3JN, England; *The Europa World Year Book.*

European Commission Office of Press and Public Affairs, 2100 M Street, NW, Washington, D.C. 20037 (202) 862-9500; *Basic Statistics of the Community; Energy Statistics Yearbook; Eurostatistics: Data for Short-term Economic Analysis; External Trade: Statistical Yearbook; External Trade: Monthly Statistics;* and *Fisheries: Yearly Statistics.*

Food and Agricultural Organization of the United Nations (FAO) Via delle Terme di Caracalla, 00100 Rome, Italy (Telephone Number in U.S. (202) 653-2400); *The State of Food and Agriculture.*

International Iron and Steel Institute, 120, rue Colonel Bourg, B-1140 Brussels, Belgium; *Steel Statistical Yearbook.*

International Lead and Zinc Study Group, Metro House, 58 St. James's Street, London SW1A 1LD England; *Lead and Zinc Statistics.*

International Monetary Fund, 700 Nineteenth Street, NW, Washington, D.C. 20431 (202) 623-7000; *Direction of Trade Statistics;* and *International Financial Statistics.*

International Rubber Study Group, York House, Eighth Floor, Empire Way, Wembley, London HA9 0PA, England; *Rubber Statistical Bulletin.*

Organisation for Economic Co-operation and Development (OECD), 2 rue Andre-Pascal, 75 Paris 16, France (Telephone Number in U.S. (202) 785-6323); *Economic Outlook; The Footwear, Raw Hides and Skins, and Leather Industry in OECD Countries; Foreign Trade by Commodities; Geographical Distribution of Financial Flows to Developing Countries; Industrial Structure Statistics; The Iron and Steel Industry; Milk, Milk Products, and Egg Balances in OECD Member Countries; OECD Economic Surveys: Netherlands; The Pulp and Paper Industry;* and *Review of Fisheries in OECD Member Countries.*

St. Martin's Press, Inc., 175 Fifth Avenue, New York, New York 10010 (800) 221-7945; *The Statesman's Year-Book.*

Statistical Office of the United Nations, Publishing Service, New York, New York 10017 (800) 253-9646; *Trends in Europe and North America: The Statistical Yearbook of* the Economic Commission for Europe.

United Nations Conference on Trade and Development (UNCTAD), New York, New York 10017 (800) 253-9646; *Handbook of International Trade and Development Statistics.*

The World Bank, 1818 H Street, NW, Washington, D.C. 20433 (202) 477-1234; *World Development Report;* and *World Development Indicators.*

NETHERLANDS - EXTERNAL FINANCING

Organisation for Economic Co-operation and Development (OECD), 2 rue Andre-Pascal, 75 Paris 16, France (Telephone Number in U.S. (202) 785-6323); *Economic Outlook;* and *Financial Market Trends.*

NETHERLANDS - EXTERNAL INDEBTEDNESS

Organisation for Economic Co-operation and Development (OECD), 2 rue Andre-Pascal, 75 Paris 16, France (Telephone Number in U.S. (202) 785-6323); *Financial Market Trends;* and *Geographical Distribution of Financial Flows to Developing Countries.*

The World Bank, 1818 H Street, NW, Washington, D.C. 20433 (202) 477-1234; *World Development Report;* and *World Development Indicators.*

NETHERLANDS - EXTERNAL TRADE

Euromonitor International, Inc., 122 South Michigan Avenue, Suite 1200, Chicago, Illinois 60603 (800) 577-EURO; *World Marketing Data and Statistics.*

European Commission Office of Press and Public Affairs, 2100 M Street, NW, Washington, D.C. 20037 (202) 862-9500; *ACP: Basic Statistics; Basic Statistics of the Community; Eurostatistics: Data for Short-term Economic Analysis; External Trade: Statistical Yearbook;* and *External Trade: Monthly Statistics.*

Food and Agricultural Organization of the United Nations (FAO) Via delle Terme di Caracalla, 00100 Rome, Italy (Telephone Number in U.S. (202) 653-2400); *The State of Food and Agriculture;* and *Trade Yearbook.*

Statistical Office of the United Nations, Publishing Service, New York, New York 10017 (800) 253-9646; *Statistical Yearbook.*

NETHERLANDS - FABRIC PRODUCTION - See NETHERLANDS - TEXTILE INDUSTRY

NETHERLANDS - FARM CROPS - See NETHERLANDS - CROPS

NETHERLANDS - FEMALE WORKING POPULATION - See NETHERLANDS - EMPLOYMENT

NETHERLANDS - FERTILITY RATES

Central Intelligence Agency, Washington, D.C. 20505 (703) 482-1100, www.cia.gov; *The World Factbook.*

European Commission Office of Press and Public Affairs, 2100 M Street, NW, Washington, D.C. 20037 (202) 862-9500; *Demographic Statistics.*

M.E. Sharpe, 80 Business Park Drive, Armonk, New York 10504 (800) 541-6563; *The Illustrated Book of World Rankings.*

Statistical Office of the United Nations, Publishing Service, New York, New York 10017 (800) 253-9646; *Human Development Report;* and *Trends in Europe and North America: The Statistical Yearbook of the Economic Commission for Europe.*

The World Bank, 1818 H Street, NW, Washington, D.C. 20433 (202) 477-1234; *The World Bank Atlas; World Development Report;* and *World Development Indicators.*

NETHERLANDS - FERTILIZER

European Commission Office of Press and Public Affairs, 2100 M Street, NW, Washington, D.C. 20037 (202) 862-9500; *Basic Statistics of the Community.*

Food and Agricultural Organization of the United Nations (FAO), Via delle Terme di Caracalla, 00100 Rome, Italy (Telephone Number in U.S. (202) 653-2400); *Fertilizer Yearbook;* and *The State of Food and Agriculture.*

Organisation for Economic Co-operation and Development (OECD), 2 rue Andre-Pascal, 75 Paris 16, France (Telephone Number in U.S. (202) 785-6323); *Economic Accounts for Agriculture;* and *Foreign Trade by Commodities.*

Statistical Office of the United Nations, Publishing Service, New York, New York 10017 (800) 253-9646; *Statistical Yearbook.*

NETHERLANDS - FETAL MORTALITY - See NETHERLANDS - MORTALITY

NETHERLANDS - FIBRE PRODUCTION - See NETHERLANDS - TEXTILE INDUSTRY

NETHERLANDS - FILAMENT PRODUCTION - See NETHERLANDS - TEXTILE INDUSTRY

NETHERLANDS - FILMS - See NETHERLANDS - MOTION PICTURES

NETHERLANDS - FINANCE

Economist Intelligence Unit, 111 West 57th Street, New York, New York 10019 (800) 938-4685; *Netherlands Country Report.*

European Commission Office of Press and Public Affairs, 2100 M Street, NW, Washington, D.C. 20037 (202) 862-9500; *ACP: Basic Statistics;* and *Basic Statistics of the Community; Eurostatistics: Data for Short-term Economic Analysis;* and *Money and Finance.*

International Monetary Fund, 700 Nineteenth Street, NW, Washington, D.C. 20431 (202) 623-7000; *Government Finance Statistics Yearbook;* and *International Financial Statistics.*

M.E. Sharpe, 80 Business Park Drive, Armonk, New York 10504 (800) 541-6563; *The Illustrated Book of World Rankings.*

Netherlands Central Bureau of Statistics, Staatsuitgeverij, The Hague, Netherlands; *Statistical Yearbook of the Netherlands.*

Organisation for Economic Co-operation and Development (OECD), 2 rue Andre-Pascal, 75 Paris 16, France (Telephone Number in U.S. (202) 785-6323); *Economic Outlook; Financial Market Trends; Geographical Distribution of Financial Flows to Developing Countries; OECD Financial Statistics;* and *Revenue Statistics of OECD Member Countries.*

St. Martin's Press, Inc., 175 Fifth Avenue, New York, New York 10010 (800) 221-7945; *The Statesman's Year-Book.*

NETHERLANDS - FISHERIES

Euromonitor International, Inc., 122 South Michigan Avenue, Suite 1200, Chicago, Illinois 60603 (800) 577-EURO; *European Marketing Data and Statistics.*

Europa Publications Limited, 18 Bedford Square, London, WC1B 3JN, England; *The Europa World Year Book.*

European Commission Office of Press and Public Affairs, 2100 M Street, NW, Washington, D.C. 20037 (202) 862-9500; *Agriculture: Statistical Yearbook;* and *Fisheries: Yearly Statistics.*

Food and Agricultural Organization of the United Nations (FAO) Via delle Terme di Caracalla, 00100 Rome, Italy (Telephone Number in U.S. (202) 653-2400); *The State of Food and Agriculture.*

M.E. Sharpe, 80 Business Park Drive, Armonk, New York 10504 (800) 541-6563; *The Illustrated Book of World Rankings.*

Netherlands Central Bureau of Statistics, Staatsuitgeverij, The Hague,

Netherlands; *Statistical Yearbook of the Netherlands.*

Organisation for Economic Co-operation and Development (OECD), 2 rue Andre-Pascal, 75 Paris 16, France (Telephone Number in U.S. (202) 785-6323); *Foreign Trade by Commodities; Industrial Structure Statistics;* and *Review of Fisheries in OECD Member Countries.*

St. Martin's Press, Inc., 175 Fifth Avenue, New York, New York 10010 (800) 221-7945; *The Statesman's Year-Book.*

Statistical Office of the United Nations, Publishing Service, New York, New York 10017 (800) 253-9646; *Statistical Yearbook.*

United Nations Conference on Trade and Development, Central Statistical Service, Palais des Nations, Geneva, Switzerland (Telephone in U.S. (800) 253-9646); *UNCTAD Commodity Yearbook.*

NETHERLANDS - FLAX AND FLAX FIBRE PRODUCTION - See NETHERLANDS - TEXTILE INDUSTRY

NETHERLANDS - FLOUR PRODUCTION

European Commission Office of Press and Public Affairs, 2100 M Street, NW, Washington, D.C. 20037 (202) 862-9500; *Basic Statistics of the Community.*

Statistical Office of the United Nations, Publishing Service, New York, New York 10017 (800) 253-9646; *Statistical Yearbook.*

NETHERLANDS - FOOD

Euromonitor International, Inc., 122 South Michigan Avenue, Suite 1200, Chicago, Illinois 60603 (800) 577-EURO; *Retail Trade International.*

European Commission Office of Press and Public Affairs, 2100 M Street, NW, Washington, D.C. 20037 (202) 862-9500; *Basic Statistics of the Community.*

Food and Agricultural Organization of the United Nations (FAO), Via delle Terme di Caracalla, 00100 Rome, Italy (Telephone Number in U.S. (202) 653-2400); *Production Yearbook;* and *The State of Food and Agriculture.*

Organisation for Economic Co-operation and Development (OECD), 2 rue Andre-Pascal, 75 Paris 16, France (Telephone Number in U.S. (202) 785-6323); *Food Consumption Statistics;* and *Foreign Trade by Commodities.*

Statistical Office of the United Nations, Publishing Service, New York, New York 10017 (800) 253-9646; *Human Development Report.*

United Nations Conference on Trade and Development, Central Statistical Service, Palais des Nations, Geneva, Switzerland (Telephone in U.S. (800) 253-9646); *UNCTAD Commodity Yearbook.*

NETHERLANDS - FOOTWEAR - PRODUCTION INDEX

Organisation for Economic Co-operation and Development (OECD), 2 rue Andre-Pascal, 75 Paris 16, France (Telephone Number in U.S. (202) 785-6323); *Indicators of Industrial Activity.*

NETHERLANDS - FOREIGN DEBT

International Monetary Fund, 700 Nineteenth Street, NW, Washington, D.C. 20431 (202) 623-7000; *Government Finance Statistics Yearbook.*

Organisation for Economic Co-operation and Development (OECD), 2 rue Andre-Pascal, 75 Paris 16, France (Telephone Number in U.S. (202) 785-6323); *Economic Outlook.*

St. Martin's Press, Inc., 175 Fifth Avenue, New York, New York 10010 (800) 221-7945; *The Statesman's Year-Book.*

NETHERLANDS - FOREIGN FINANCE

Organisation for Economic Co-operation and Development (OECD), 2 rue Andre-Pascal, 75 Paris 16, France (Telephone Number in U.S. (202) 785-6323); *Economic Outlook; Financial Market Trends;* and *Main Economic Indicators - Historical Statistics.*

NETHERLANDS - FOREIGN INDEBTEDNESS

Organisation for Economic Co-operation and Development (OECD), 2 rue Andre-Pascal, 75 Paris 16, France (Telephone Number in U.S. (202) 785-6323); *Economic Outlook;* and *Financial Market Trends.*

NETHERLANDS - FOREIGN OFFICIAL RESERVES

European Commission Office of Press and Public Affairs, 2100 M Street, NW, Washington, D.C. 20037 (202) 862-9500; *Money and Finance.*

NETHERLANDS - FOREIGN TRADE

Economist Intelligence Unit, 111 West 57th Street, New York, New York 10019 (800) 938-4685; *Netherlands Country Report.*

Euromonitor International, Inc., 122 South Michigan Avenue, Suite 1200, Chicago, Illinois 60603 (800) 577-EURO; *European Marketing Data and Statistics;*

and *The World Economic Factbook.*

Europa Publications Limited, 18 Bedford Square, London, WC1B 3JN, England; *The Europa World Year Book.*

European Commission Office of Press and Public Affairs, 2100 M Street, NW, Washington, D.C. 20037 (202) 862-9500; *Basic Statistics of the Community; Energy Statistics Yearbook;* and *Iron and Steel: Statistical Yearbook.*

Food and Agricultural Organization of the United Nations (FAO) Via delle Terme di Caracalla, 00100 Rome, Italy (Telephone Number in U.S. (202) 653-2400); *The State of Food and Agriculture.*

International Iron and Steel Institute, 120, rue Colonel Bourg, B-1140 Brussels, Belgium; *Steel Statistical Yearbook.*

M.E. Sharpe, 80 Business Park Drive, Armonk, New York 10504 (800) 541-6563; *The Illustrated Book of World Rankings.*

Netherlands Central Bureau of Statistics, Staatsuitgeverij, The Hague, Netherlands; *Statistical Yearbook of the Netherlands.*

Organisation for Economic Co-operation and Development (OECD), 2 rue Andre-Pascal, 75 Paris 16, France (Telephone Number in U.S. (202) 785-6323); *Economic Outlook; The Footwear, Raw Hides and Skins, and Leather Industry in OECD Countries; Foreign Trade by Commodities; Main Economic Indicators - Historical Statistics; Maritime Transport; Meat Balances in OECD Member Countries;* and *OECD Economic Surveys: Netherlands.*

St. Martin's Press, Inc., 175 Fifth Avenue, New York, New York 10010 (800) 221-7945; *The Statesman's Year-Book.*

Statistical Office of the United Nations, Publishing Service, New York, New York 10017 (800) 253-9646; *International Trade Statistics Yearbook;* and *Statistical Yearbook.*

United Nations Conference on Trade and Development, Central Statistical Service, Palais des Nations, Geneva, Switzerland (Telephone in U.S. (800) 253-9646); *UNCTAD Commodity Yearbook.*

The World Bank, 1818 H Street, NW, Washington, D.C. 20433 (202) 477-1234; *World Development Report;* and *World Development Indicators.*

World Bureau of Metal Statistics, 27-A High Street, Ware, Herts. SG12 9BA, England; *World Metal Statistics.*

NETHERLANDS - FORESTRY AND FOREST

PRODUCTS

American Forest and Paper Association, 1111 Nineteenth Street, NW, Suite 800, Washington, D.C. 20036 (202) 463-2700; *Wood Pulp and Fiber Statistics.*

Euromonitor International, Inc., 122 South Michigan Avenue, Suite 1200, Chicago, Illinois 60603 (800) 577-EURO; *European Marketing Data and Statistics.*

European Commission Office of Press and Public Affairs, 2100 M Street, NW, Washington, D.C. 20037 (202) 862-9500; *Agriculture: Statistical Yearbook; Basic Statistics of the Community;* and *Industrial Production: Quarterly Statistics.*

Food and Agricultural Organization of the United Nations (FAO) Via delle Terme di Caracalla, 00100 Rome, Italy (Telephone Number in U.S. (202) 653-2400); *The State of Food and Agriculture;* and *Yearbook of Forest Products.*

M.E. Sharpe, 80 Business Park Drive, Armonk, New York 10504 (800) 541-6563; *The Illustrated Book of World Rankings.*

Organisation for Economic Co-operation and Development (OECD), 2 rue Andre-Pascal, 75 Paris 16, France (Telephone Number in U.S. (202) 785-6323); *Foreign Trade by Commodities; Indicators of Industrial Activity; Industrial Structure Statistics;* and *The Pulp and Paper Industry.*

St. Martin's Press, Inc., 175 Fifth Avenue, New York, New York 10010 (800) 221-7945; *The Statesman's Year-Book.*

Statistical Office of the United Nations, Publishing Service, New York, New York 10017 (800) 253-9646; *Statistical Yearbook;* and *Trends in Europe and North America: The Statistical Yearbook of the Economic Commission for Europe.*

United Nations Conference on Trade and Development, Central Statistical Service, Palais des Nations, Geneva, Switzerland (Telephone in U.S. (800) 253-9646); *UNCTAD Commodity Yearbook.*

United Nations Educational, Scientific and Cultural Organization (UNESCO), 7 Place de Fontenoy, F-75700 Paris, France (Telephone Number in U.S. (212) 963-5981); *Statistical Yearbook.*

The World Bank, 1818 H Street, NW, Washington, D.C. 20433 (202) 477-1234; *World Development Report.*

NETHERLANDS - FRUIT PRODUCTION

European Commission Office of Press and Public Affairs, 2100 M Street, NW, Washington, D.C. 20037 (202) 862-9500;

Basic Statistics of the Community.

Organisation for Economic Co-operation and Development (OECD), 2 rue Andre-Pascal, 75 Paris 16, France (Telephone Number in U.S. (202) 785-6323); *Economic Accounts for Agriculture;* and *Foreign Trade by Commodities.*

NETHERLANDS - FURNITURE AND WOOD PRODUCTS - EXPORTS AND IMPORTS

European Commission Office of Press and Public Affairs, 2100 M Street, NW, Washington, D.C. 20037 (202) 862-9500; *Basic Statistics of the Community.*

Organisation for Economic Co-operation and Development (OECD), 2 rue Andre-Pascal, 75 Paris 16, France (Telephone Number in U.S. (202) 785-6323); *Foreign Trade by Commodities;* and *Industrial Structure Statistics.*

NETHERLANDS - GARLIC PRODUCTION - See NETHERLANDS - CROPS

NETHERLANDS - GAS - See NETHERLANDS - MINING AND MINERAL PRODUCTS

NETHERLANDS - GENERAL INDUSTRIAL STATISTICS - See NETHERLANDS - INDUSTRY

NETHERLANDS - GENERAL MORTALITY - See NETHERLANDS - MORTALITY

NETHERLANDS - GEOGRAPHIC DATA

European Commission Office of Press and Public Affairs, 2100 M Street, NW, Washington, D.C. 20037 (202) 862-9500; *Basic Statistics of the Community.*

M.E. Sharpe, 80 Business Park Drive, Armonk, New York 10504 (800) 541-6563; *The Illustrated Book of World Rankings.*

NETHERLANDS - GLASS AND GLASS PRODUCTS - PRODUCTION INDEX - See NETHERLANDS - MINING AND MINERAL PRODUCTS

NETHERLANDS - GOATS - See NETHERLANDS - LIVESTOCK AND POULTRY

NETHERLANDS - GOLD HOLDINGS

International Monetary Fund, 700 Nineteenth Street, NW, Washington, D.C. 20431 (202) 623-7000; *International Financial Statistics.*

Statistical Office of the United Nations, Publishing Service, New York, New York 10017 (800) 253-9646; *Statistical Yearbook.*

The World Bank, 1818 H Street, NW,

Washington, D.C. 20433 (202) 477-1234; *World Development Indicators.*

NETHERLANDS - GOLD PRODUCTION AND CONSUMPTION - See NETHERLANDS - MINING AND MINERAL PRODUCTS

NETHERLANDS - GOVERNMENT

Central Intelligence Agency, Washington, D.C. 20505 (703) 482-1100, www.cia.gov; *The World Factbook.*

Europa Publications Limited, 18 Bedford Square, London, WC1B 3JN, England; *The Europa World Year Book.*

European Commission Office of Press and Public Affairs, 2100 M Street, NW, Washington, D.C. 20037 (202) 862-9500; *Basic Statistics of the Community; Government Financing of Research and Development;* and *Money and Finance.*

International Monetary Fund, 700 Nineteenth Street, NW, Washington, D.C. 20431 (202) 623-7000; *Government Finance Statistics Yearbook;* and *International Financial Statistics.*

Organisation for Economic Co-operation and Development (OECD), 2 rue Andre-Pascal, 75 Paris 16, France (Telephone Number in U.S. (202) 785-6323); *Economic Outlook;* and *Revenue Statistics of OECD Member Countries.*

St. Martin's Press, Inc., 175 Fifth Avenue, New York, New York 10010 (800) 221-7945; *The Statesman's Year-Book.*

Statistical Office of the United Nations, Publishing Service, New York, New York 10017 (800) 253-9646; *National Accounts Statistics;* and *Statistical Yearbook.*

The World Bank, 1818 H Street, NW, Washington, D.C. 20433 (202) 477-1234; *World Development Report;* and *World Development Indicators.*

NETHERLANDS - GRAIN PRODUCTION

European Commission Office of Press and Public Affairs, 2100 M Street, NW, Washington, D.C. 20037 (202) 862-9500; *Basic Statistics of the Community.*

Food and Agricultural Organization of the United Nations (FAO) Via delle Terme di Caracalla, 00100 Rome, Italy (Telephone Number in U.S. (202) 653-2400); *The State of Food and Agriculture.*

Organisation for Economic Co-operation and Development (OECD), 2 rue Andre-Pascal, 75 Paris 16, France (Telephone Number in U.S. (202) 785-6323); *Economic Accounts for Agriculture.*

NETHERLANDS - GRANTS

International Monetary Fund, 700 Nineteenth Street, NW, Washington, D.C. 20431 (202) 623-7000; *Government Finance Statistics Yearbook.*

Organisation for Economic Co-operation and Development (OECD), 2 rue Andre-Pascal, 75 Paris 16, France (Telephone Number in U.S. (202) 785-6323); *Geographical Distribution of Financial Flows to Developing Countries.*

NETHERLANDS - GREEN PEPPER AND CHILIE PRODUCTION - See NETHERLANDS - CROPS

NETHERLANDS - GROSS DOMESTIC PRODUCT

The Economist Intelligence Unit, 111 West 57th Street, New York, New York 10019 (800) 938-4685; *Netherlands Country Report;* and *The World Market Atlas.*

Euromonitor International, Inc., 122 South Michigan Avenue, Suite 1200, Chicago, Illinois 60603 (800) 577-EURO; *The World Economic Factbook.*

Europa Publications Limited, 18 Bedford Square, London, WC1B 3JN, England; *The Europa World Year Book.*

European Commission Office of Press and Public Affairs, 2100 M Street, NW, Washington, D.C. 20037 (202) 862-9500; *Basic Statistics of the Community; Eurostatistics: Data for Short-term Economic Analysis; Government Financing of Research and Development; Iron and Steel: Statistical Yearbook;* and *Money and Finance.*

M.E. Sharpe, 80 Business Park Drive, Armonk, New York 10504 (800) 541-6563; *The Illustrated Book of World Rankings.*

Organisation for Economic Co-operation and Development (OECD), 2 rue Andre-Pascal, 75 Paris 16, France (Telephone Number in U.S. (202) 785-6323); *Economic Outlook; Geographical Distribution of Financial Flows to Developing Countries;* and *Revenue Statistics of OECD Member Countries.*

Statistical Office of the United Nations, Publishing Service, New York, New York 10017 (800) 253-9646; *Human Development Report; National Accounts Statistics; Trends in Europe and North America: The Statistical Yearbook of the Economic Commission for Europe;* and *Statistical Yearbook.*

The World Bank, 1818 H Street, NW, Washington, D.C. 20433 (202) 477-1234; *World Development Report;* and *World Development Indicators.*

NETHERLANDS - GROSS INDUSTRIAL

PRODUCT

European Commission Office of Press and Public Affairs, 2100 M Street, NW, Washington, D.C. 20037 (202) 862-9500; *Government Financing of Research and Development.*

The World Bank, 1818 H Street, NW, Washington, D.C. 20433 (202) 477-1234; *World Development Report.*

NETHERLANDS - GROSS NATIONAL PRODUCT

Europa Publications Limited, 18 Bedford Square, London, WC1B 3JN, England; *The Europa World Year Book.*

European Commission Office of Press and Public Affairs, 2100 M Street, NW, Washington, D.C. 20037 (202) 862-9500; *ACP: Basic Statistics;* and *Basic Statistics of the Community.*

Organisation for Economic Co-operation and Development (OECD), 2 rue Andre-Pascal, 75 Paris 16, France (Telephone Number in U.S. (202) 785-6323); *Economic Outlook;* and *Geographical Distribution of Financial Flows to Developing Countries.*

St. Martin's Press, Inc., 175 Fifth Avenue, New York, New York 10010 (800) 221-7945; *The Statesman's Year-Book.*

U.S. Arms Control and Disarmament Agency, 320 Twenty-first Street, NW, Washington, D.C. 20451 (202) 647-8677; *World Military Expenditures and Arms Transfers.*

The World Bank, 1818 H Street, NW, Washington, D.C. 20433 (202) 477-1234; *The World Bank Atlas;* and *World Development Indicators.*

NETHERLANDS - GROUNDNUT PRODUCTION - See **NETHERLANDS - CROPS**

NETHERLANDS - HAY PRODUCTION - See **NETHERLANDS - CROPS**

NETHERLANDS - HAZELNUT PRODUCTION - See **NETHERLANDS - CROPS**

NETHERLANDS - HEALTH

Euromonitor International, Inc., 122 South Michigan Avenue, Suite 1200, Chicago, Illinois 60603 (800) 577-EURO; *World Marketing Data and Statistics.*

European Commission Office of Press and Public Affairs, 2100 M Street, NW, Washington, D.C. 20037 (202) 862-9500; *Basic Statistics of the Community;* and *Regions: Statistical Yearbook.*

M.E. Sharpe, 80 Business Park Drive, Armonk, New York 10504 (800) 541-6563; *The Illustrated Book of World Rankings.*

Netherlands Central Bureau of Statistics, Staatsuitgeverij, The Hague, Netherlands; *Statistical Yearbook of the Netherlands.*

Organisation for Economic Co-operation and Development (OECD), 2 rue Andre-Pascal, 75 Paris 16, France (Telephone Number in the U.S. (785-6323); *OECD Health Systems: Facts and Trends.*

St. Martin's Press, Inc., 175 Fifth Avenue, New York, New York 10010 (800) 221-7945; *The Statesman's Year-Book.*

Statistical Office of the United Nations, Publishing Service, New York, New York 10017 (800) 253-9646; *Human Development Report; Trends in Europe and North America: The Statistical Yearbook of the Economic Commission for Europe;* and *Statistical Yearbook.*

United Nations Children's Fund (UNICEF), 3 United Nations Plaza, New York, New York 10017 (800) 253-9646; *State of the World's Children.*

The World Bank, 1818 H Street, NW, Washington, D.C. 20433 (202) 477-1234; *World Development Report.*

World Health Organization, Office of Publications, 20 Avenue Appia, CH-1211 Geneva 27, Switzerland (Telephone Number in U.S. (518) 436-9686); *World Health Statistics Annual.*

NETHERLANDS - HEALTH EXPENDITURES

International Monetary Fund, 700 Nineteenth Street, NW, Washington, D.C. 20431 (202) 623-7000; *Government Finance Statistics Yearbook.*

NETHERLANDS - HEMP FIBRE PRODUCTION - See **NETHERLANDS - TEXTILE INDUSTRY**

NETHERLANDS - HIDE PRODUCTION

Food and Agricultural Organization of the United Nations (FAO), Via delle Terme di Caracalla, 00100 Rome, Italy (Telephone Number in U.S. (202) 653-2400); *Production Yearbook.*

Organisation for Economic Co-operation and Development (OECD), 2 rue Andre-Pascal, 75 Paris 16, France (Telephone Number in U.S. (202) 785-6323); *The Footwear, Raw Hides and Skins, and Leather Industry in OECD Countries; Foreign Trade by Commodities;* and *Indicators of Industrial Activity.*

NETHERLANDS - HIGHWAYS

Central Intelligence Agency, Washington, D.C. 20505 (703) 482-1100, www.cia.gov; *The World Factbook.*

European Commission Office of Press and Public Affairs, 2100 M Street, NW, Washington, D.C. 20037 (202) 862-9500; *Basic Statistics of the Community;* and *Transport Annual Statistics.*

International Road Federation, 2600 Virginia Avenue, NW., Washington, D.C. 20037 (202) 338-4641; *World Road Statistics.*

St. Martin's Press, Inc., 175 Fifth Avenue, New York, New York 10010 (800) 221-7945; *The Statesman's Year-Book.*

Statistical Office of the United Nations, Publishing Service, New York, New York 10017 (800) 253-9646; *Annual Bulletin of Transport Statistics for Europe;* and *Trends in Europe and North America: The Statistical Yearbook of the Economic Commission for Europe.*

NETHERLANDS - HOME FINANCE

Organisation for Economic Co-operation and Development (OECD), 2 rue Andre-Pascal, 75 Paris 16, France (Telephone Number in U.S. (202) 785-6323); *Main Economic Indicators - Historical Statistics.*

NETHERLANDS - HOPS PRODUCTION - See **NETHERLANDS - CROPS**

NETHERLANDS - HORSES - See **NETHERLANDS - LIVESTOCK AND POULTRY**

NETHERLANDS - HOURS OF WORK - See **NETHERLANDS - EMPLOYMENT**

NETHERLANDS - HOUSING AND HOUSING UNITS

Euromonitor International, Inc., 122 South Michigan Avenue, Suite 1200, Chicago, Illinois 60603 (800) 577-EURO; *World Marketing Data and Statistics.*

European Commission Office of Press and Public Affairs, 2100 M Street, NW, Washington, D.C. 20037 (202) 862-9500; *Basic Statistics of the Community; Labor Force Sample Survey;* and *Regions: Statistical Yearbook.*

M.E. Sharpe, 80 Business Park Drive, Armonk, New York 10504 (800) 541-6563; *The Illustrated Book of World Rankings.*

Statistical Office of the United Nations, Publishing Service, New York, New York 10017 (800) 253-9646; *Trends in Europe and North America: The Statistical Yearbook of the Economic Commission for Europe.*

NETHERLANDS - HOUSING
CONSTRUCTION - See NETHERLANDS -
CONSTRUCTION INDUSTRY

NETHERLANDS - HOUSING
EXPENDITURES

European Commission Office of Press
and Public Affairs, 2100 M Street, NW,
Washington, D.C. 20037 (202) 862-9500;
Basic Statistics of the Community.

International Monetary Fund, 700
Nineteenth Street, NW, Washington, D.C.
20431 (202) 623-7000; *Government
Finance Statistics Yearbook.*

Netherlands Central Bureau of
Statistics, Staatsuitgeverij, The Hague,
Netherlands; *Statistical Yearbook of the
Netherlands.*

NETHERLANDS - HYDROCHLORIC ACID
PRODUCTION

European Commission Office of Press
and Public Affairs, 2100 M Street, NW,
Washington, D.C. 20037 (202) 862-9500;
Basic Statistics of the Community.

Statistical Office of the United Nations,
Publishing Service, New York, New York
10017 (800) 253-9646; *Statistical Yearbook.*

NETHERLANDS - ILLITERATE
POPULATION

Central Intelligence Agency,
Washington, D.C. 20505 (703) 482-1100,
www.cia.gov; *The World Factbook.*

The Economist Intelligence Unit, 111
West 57th Street, New York, New York
10019 (800) 938-4685; *The World Market
Atlas.*

Euromonitor International, Inc., 122
South Michigan Avenue, Suite 1200,
Chicago, Illinois 60603 (800) 577-EURO;
The World Economic Factbook.

Statistical Office of the United Nations,
Publishing Service, New York, New York
10017 (800) 253-9646; *Human
Development Report.*

NETHERLANDS - IMPORTS

Central Intelligence Agency,
Washington, D.C. 20505 (703) 482-1100,
www.cia.gov; *The World Factbook.*

The Economist Intelligence Unit, 111
West 57th Street, New York, New York
10019 (800) 938-4685; *Netherlands Country
Report;* and *The World Market Atlas.*

Europa Publications Limited, 18
Bedford Square, London, WC1B 3JN,
England; *The Europa World Year Book.*

European Commission Office of Press
and Public Affairs, 2100 M Street, NW,
Washington, D.C. 20037 (202) 862-9500;
*Basic Statistics of the Community, Energy:
Monthly Statistics, Energy Statistics
Yearbook, Eurostatistics: Data for Short-
term Economic Analysis, External Trade:
Statistical Yearbook, External Trade:
Monthly Statistics; Fisheries: Yearly
Statistics;* and *The World Economic
Factbook.*

Food and Agricultural Organization of
the United Nations (FAO) Via delle Terme
di Caracalla, 00100 Rome, Italy (Telephone
Number in U.S. (202) 653-2400; *The State
of Food and Agriculture.*

International Iron and Steel Institute,
120, rue Colonel Bourg, B-1140 Brussels,
Belgium; *Steel Statistical Yearbook.*

International Lead and Zinc Study
Group, Metro House, 58 St. James's Street,
London SW1A 1LD England; *Lead and Zinc
Statistics.*

International Monetary Fund, 700
Nineteenth Street, NW, Washington, D.C.
20431 (202) 623-7000; *Direction of Trade
Statistics; Government Finance Statistics
Yearbook;* and *International Financial
Statistics.*

International Rubber Study Group, York
House, Eighth Floor, Empire Way,
Wembley, London HA9 0PA, England;
Rubber Statistical Bulletin.

Organisation for Economic Co-
operation and Development (OECD), 2 rue
Andre-Pascal, 75 Paris 16, France
(Telephone Number in U.S. (202) 785-
6323); *Economic Outlook; The Footwear,
Raw Hides and Skins, and Leather Industry
in OECD Countries; Industrial Structure
Statistics; The Iron and Steel Industry; Milk,
Milk Products, and Egg Balances in OECD
Member Countries; OECD Economic
Surveys: Netherlands; The Pulp and Paper
Industry;* and *Review of Fisheries in OECD
Member Countries.*

St. Martin's Press, Inc., 175 Fifth Avenue,
New York, New York 10010 (800) 221-7945;
The Statesman's Year-Book.

Statistical Office of the United Nations,
Publishing Service, New York, New York
10017 (800) 253-9646; *Trends in Europe and
North America: The Statistical Yearbook of
the Economic Commission for Europe.*

United Nations Conference on Trade
and Development (UNCTAD), New York,
New York 10017 (800) 253-9646; *Handbook
of International Trade and Development
Statistics.*

The World Bank, 1818 H Street, NW,
Washington, D.C. 20433 (202) 477-1234;

World Development Report; and *World
Development Indicators.*

NETHERLANDS - INCOME TAXES - See
NETHERLANDS - TAXATION

NETHERLANDS - INDUSTRIAL METALS
PRODUCTION - See NETHERLANDS -
MINING AND MINERAL PRODUCTS

NETHERLANDS - INDUSTRY

Central Intelligence Agency,
Washington, D.C. 20505 (703) 482-1100,
www.cia.gov; *The World Factbook.*

Economist Intelligence Unit, 111 West
57th Street, New York, New York 10019
(800) 938-4685; *Netherlands Country
Report.*

Euromonitor International, Inc., 122
South Michigan Avenue, Suite 1200,
Chicago, Illinois 60603 (800) 577-EURO;
The World Economic Factbook; and *World
Marketing Data and Statistics.*

Europa Publications Limited, 18
Bedford Square, London, WC1B 3JN,
England; *The Europa World Year Book.*

European Commission Office of Press
and Public Affairs, 2100 M Street, NW,
Washington, D.C. 20037 (202) 862-9500;
*Basic Statistics of the Community;
Employment and Unemployment;
Eurostatistics: Data for Short-term
Economic Analysis;* and *Labor Force
Sample Survey.*

International Labour Office,
I.L.O. Publications, 1828 L Street, NW.,
Suite 801, Washington, D.C. 20036 (301)
638-3152; *Yearbook of Labour Statistics.*

M.E. Sharpe, 80 Business Park Drive,
Armonk, New York 10504 (800) 541-6563;
The Illustrated Book of World Rankings.

Organisation for Economic Co-
operation and Development (OECD), 2 rue
Andre-Pascal, 75 Paris 16, France
(Telephone Number in U.S. (202) 785-
6323); *Economic Outlook; Industrial
Structure Statistics; Main Economic
Indicators - Historical Statistics;* and *OECD
Environmental Data.*

St. Martin's Press, Inc., 175 Fifth
Avenue, New York, New York 10010 (800)
221-7945; *The Statesman's Year-Book.*

Statistical Office of the United Nations,
Publishing Service, New York, New York
10017 (800) 253-9646; *Industrial
Commodity Statistics Yearbook; Trends in
Europe and North America: The Statistical
Yearbook of the Economic Commission for
Europe;* and *Statistical Yearbook.*

The World Bank, 1818 H Street, NW,

Washington, D.C. 20433 (202) 477-1234; *World Development Indicators.*

World Intellectual Property Organization, 34 Chemin des Colombettes, CH-1211 Geneva 20, Switzerland; *Industrial Property Statistics.*

NETHERLANDS - INFANT AND MATERNAL MORTALITY - See NETHERLANDS - MORTALITY

NETHERLANDS - INTEREST RATES

European Commission Office of Press and Public Affairs, 2100 M Street, NW, Washington, D.C. 20037 (202) 862-9500; *Money and Finance.*

Organisation for Economic Co-operation and Development (OECD), 2 rue Andre-Pascal, 75 Paris 16, France (Telephone Number in U.S. (202) 785-6323); *Economic Outlook; Financial Market Trends; Main Economic Indicators - Historical Statistics;* and *OECD Financial Statistics.*

NETHERLANDS - INTERNAL TRADE

European Commission Office of Press and Public Affairs, 2100 M Street, NW, Washington, D.C. 20037 (202) 862-9500; *Basic Statistics of the Community.*

Organisation for Economic Co-operation and Development (OECD), 2 rue Andre-Pascal, 75 Paris 16, France (Telephone Number in U.S. (202) 785-6323); *Main Economic Indicators - Historical Statistics.*

Statistical Office of the United Nations, Publishing Service, New York, New York 10017 (800) 253-9646; *Statistical Yearbook.*

NETHERLANDS - INTERNATIONAL FINANCE

European Commission Office of Press and Public Affairs, 2100 M Street, NW, Washington, D.C. 20037 (202) 862-9500; *Basic Statistics of the Community.*

Organisation for Economic Co-operation and Development (OECD), 2 rue Andre-Pascal, 75 Paris 16, France (Telephone Number in U.S. (202) 785-6323); *Economic Outlook;* and *Financial Market Trends.*

NETHERLANDS - INTERNATIONAL LIQUIDITY

International Monetary Fund, 700 Nineteenth Street, NW, Washington, D.C. 20431 (202) 623-7000; *International Financial Statistics.*

Organisation for Economic Co-operation and Development (OECD), 2 rue

Andre-Pascal, 75 Paris 16, France (Telephone Number in U.S. (202) 785-6323); *Economic Outlook;* and *Financial Market Trends.*

NETHERLANDS - INTERNATIONAL RESERVES EXCLUDING GOLD

Statistical Office of the United Nations, Publishing Service, New York, New York 10017 (800) 253-9646; *Statistical Yearbook.*

The World Bank, 1818 H Street, NW, Washington, D.C. 20433 (202) 477-1234; *World Development Indicators.*

NETHERLANDS - INTERNATIONAL STATISTICS

Organisation for Economic Co-operation and Development (OECD), 2 rue Andre-Pascal, 75 Paris 16, France (Telephone Number in U.S. (202) 785-6323); *Financial Market Trends;* and *Tourism Policy and International Tourism in OECD Member Countries.*

NETHERLANDS - INVESTMENTS

International Monetary Fund, 700 Nineteenth Street, NW, Washington, D.C. 20431 (202) 623-7000; *International Financial Statistics.*

Organisation for Economic Co-operation and Development (OECD), 2 rue Andre-Pascal, 75 Paris 16, France (Telephone Number in U.S. (202) 785-6323); *Economic Outlook; Financial Market Trends; Industrial Structure Statistics; The Iron and Steel Industry;* and *Textile Industry in OECD Countries.*

NETHERLANDS - IRON ORE PRODUCTION AND CONSUMPTION - See NETHERLANDS - MINING AND MINERAL PRODUCTS

NETHERLANDS - JUTE PRODUCTION - See NETHERLANDS - CROPS

NETHERLANDS - LABOR

Central Intelligence Agency, Washington, D.C. 20505 (703) 482-1100, www.cia.gov; *The World Factbook.*

Euromonitor International, Inc., 122 South Michigan Avenue, Suite 1200, Chicago, Illinois 60603 (800) 577-EURO; *World Marketing Data and Statistics.*

European Commission Office of Press and Public Affairs, 2100 M Street, NW, Washington, D.C. 20037 (202) 862-9500; *Basic Statistics of the Community; Labor Force Sample Survey;* and *Regions: Statistical Yearbook.*

Food and Agricultural Organization of the United Nations (FAO) Via delle Terme

di Caracalla, 00100 Rome, Italy (Telephone Number in U.S. (202) 653-2400); *The State of Food and Agriculture.*

International Labour Office, I.L.O. Publications, 1828 L Street, NW., Suite 801, Washington, D.C. 20036 (301) 638-3152; *Yearbook of Labour Statistics.*

M.E. Sharpe, 80 Business Park Drive, Armonk, New York 10504 (800) 541-6563; *The Illustrated Book of World Rankings.*

Netherlands Central Bureau of Statistics, Staatsuitgeverij, The Hague, Netherlands; *Statistical Yearbook of the Netherlands.*

Organisation for Economic Co-operation and Development (OECD), 2 rue Andre-Pascal, 75 Paris 16, France (Telephone Number in U.S. (202) 785-6323); *Economic Outlook; Main Economic Indicators - Historical Statistics; OECD Economic Surveys: Netherlands;* and *OECD Employment Outlook.*

St. Martin's Press, Inc., 175 Fifth Avenue, New York, New York 10010 (800) 221-7945; *The Statesman's Year-Book.*

Statistical Office of the United Nations, Publishing Service, New York, New York 10017 (800) 253-9646; *Human Development Report.*

The World Bank, 1818 H Street, NW, Washington, D.C. 20433 (202) 477-1234; *The World Bank Atlas; World Development Report;* and *World Development Indicators.*

NETHERLANDS - LAND USE

Central Intelligence Agency, Washington, D.C. 20505 (703) 482-1100, www.cia.gov; *The World Factbook.*

Euromonitor International, Inc., 122 South Michigan Avenue, Suite 1200, Chicago, Illinois 60603 (800) 577-EURO; *European Marketing Data and Statistics.*

European Commission Office of Press and Public Affairs, 2100 M Street, NW, Washington, D.C. 20037 (202) 862-9500; *Agriculture: Statistical Yearbook; Basic Statistics of the Community; Crop Production: Quarterly Statistics;* and *Regions: Statistical Yearbook.*

Food and Agricultural Organization of the United Nations (FAO), Via delle Terme di Caracalla, 00100 Rome, Italy (Telephone Number in U.S. (202) 653-2400); *Production Yearbook.*

The World Bank, 1818 H Street, NW, Washington, D.C. 20433 (202) 477-1234; *World Development Report.*

NETHERLANDS - LEAD AND LEAD ORE

PRODUCTION AND CONSUMPTION - See NETHERLANDS - MINING AND MINERAL PRODUCTS

NETHERLANDS - LEATHER AND FOOTWEAR EXPORTS AND IMPORTS

European Commission Office of Press and Public Affairs, 2100 M Street, NW, Washington, D.C. 20037 (202) 862-9500; *Basic Statistics of the Community*.

Organisation for Economic Co-operation and Development (OECD), 2 rue Andre-Pascal, 75 Paris 16, France (Telephone Number in U.S. (202) 785-6323); *The Footwear, Raw Hides and Skins, and Leather Industry in OECD Countries*.

NETHERLANDS - LEATHER PRODUCTION INDEX

Organisation for Economic Co-operation and Development (OECD), 2 rue Andre-Pascal, 75 Paris 16, France (Telephone Number in U.S. (202) 785-6323); *Indicators of Industrial Activity*.

NETHERLANDS - LIBRARIES

Euromonitor International, Inc., 122 South Michigan Avenue, Suite 1200, Chicago, Illinois 60603 (800) 577-EURO; *European Marketing Data and Statistics*.

M.E. Sharpe, 80 Business Park Drive, Armonk, New York 10504 (800) 541-6563; *The Illustrated Book of World Rankings*.

Statistical Office of the United Nations, Publishing Service, New York, New York 10017 (800) 253-9646; *Trends in Europe and North America: The Statistical Yearbook of the Economic Commission for Europe*.

NETHERLANDS - LIFE EXPECTANCY

Central Intelligence Agency, Washington, D.C. 20505 (703) 482-1100, www.cia.gov; *The World Factbook*.

Euromonitor International, Inc., 122 South Michigan Avenue, Suite 1200, Chicago, Illinois 60603 (800) 577-EURO; *The World Economic Factbook*.

Organisation for Economic Co-operation and Development (OECD), 2 rue Andre-Pascal, 75 Paris 16, France (Telephone Number in U.S. (202) 785-6323); *Economic Outlook*.

Statistical Office of the United Nations, Publishing Service, New York, New York 10017 (800) 253-9646; *Human Development Report; World Statistics Pocketbook;* and *Trends in Europe and North America: The Statistical Yearbook of the Economic Commission for Europe*.

The World Bank, 1818 H Street, NW, Washington, D.C. 20433 (202) 477-1234; *The World Bank Atlas;* and *World Development Report*.

NETHERLANDS - LIGNITE PRODUCTION - See NETHERLANDS - MINING AND MINERAL PRODUCTS

NETHERLANDS - LITERACY RATE

Euromonitor International, Inc., 122 South Michigan Avenue, Suite 1200, Chicago, Illinois 60603 (800) 577-EURO; *World Marketing Data and Statistics*.

NETHERLANDS - LIVESTOCK AND POULTRY

Euromonitor International, Inc., 122 South Michigan Avenue, Suite 1200, Chicago, Illinois 60603 (800) 577-EURO; *European Marketing Data and Statistics*.

Europa Publications Limited, 18 Bedford Square, London, WC1B 3JN, England; *The Europa World Year Book*.

European Commission Office of Press and Public Affairs, 2100 M Street, NW, Washington, D.C. 20037 (202) 862-9500; *Agriculture: Statistical Yearbook; Basic Statistics of the Community; Eurostatistics: Data for Short-term Economic Analysis;* and *Regions: Statistical Yearbook*.

Food and Agricultural Organization of the United Nations (FAO), Via delle Terme di Caracalla, 00100 Rome, Italy (Telephone Number in U.S. (202) 653-2400); *Production Yearbook;* and *The State of Food and Agriculture*.

M.E. Sharpe, 80 Business Park Drive, Armonk, New York 10504 (800) 541-6563; *The Illustrated Book of World Rankings*.

Organisation for Economic Co-operation and Development (OECD), 2 rue Andre-Pascal, 75 Paris 16, France (Telephone Number in U.S. (202) 785-6323); *Economic Accounts for Agriculture;* and *Meat Balances in OECD Member Countries*.

St. Martin's Press, Inc., 175 Fifth Avenue, New York, New York 10010 (800) 221-7945; *The Statesman's Year-Book*.

Statistical Office of the United Nations, Publishing Service, New York, New York 10017 (800) 253-9646; *Statistical Yearbook*.

United Nations Conference on Trade and Development, Central Statistical Service, Palais des Nations, Geneva, Switzerland (Telephone in U.S. (800) 253-9646); *UNCTAD Commodity Yearbook*.

NETHERLANDS - LIVING LEVELS - See NETHERLANDS - LIFE EXPECTANCY

NETHERLANDS - MACHINERY - PRODUCTION INDEX

Organisation for Economic Co-operation and Development (OECD), 2 rue Andre-Pascal, 75 Paris 16, France (Telephone Number in U.S. (202) 785-6323); *Indicators of Industrial Activity*.

NETHERLANDS - MAGNESIUM PRODUCTION AND CONSUMPTION - See NETHERLANDS - MINING AND MINERAL PRODUCTS

NETHERLANDS - MAIL - NUMBER OF PIECES SENT OR RECEIVED

European Commission Office of Press and Public Affairs, 2100 M Street, NW, Washington, D.C. 20037 (202) 862-9500; *Transport Annual Statistics*.

Statistical Office of the United Nations, Publishing Service, New York, New York 10017 (800) 253-9646; *Statistical Yearbook*.

NETHERLANDS - MAIN ECONOMIC INDICATORS - See NETHERLANDS - ECONOMY

NETHERLANDS - MANGANESE PRODUCTION AND CONSUMPTION -See NETHERLANDS - MINING AND MINERAL PRODUCTS

NETHERLANDS - MANUFACTURING

American Automobile Manufacturers Association, 1401 H Street, NW, Suite 900, Washington, D.C. 20005 (202) 326-5500; *World Motor Vehicle Data*.

European Commission Office of Press and Public Affairs, 2100 M Street, NW, Washington, D.C. 20037 (202) 862-9500; *Basic Statistics of the Community; Eurostatistics: Data for Short-term Economic Analysis; Industrial Production: Quarterly Statistics;* and *Labor Force Sample Survey*.

M.E. Sharpe, 80 Business Park Drive, Armonk, New York 10504 (800) 541-6563; *The Illustrated Book of World Rankings*.

Netherlands Central Bureau of Statistics, Staatsuitgeverij, The Hague, Netherlands; *Statistical Yearbook of the Netherlands*.

Organisation for Economic Co-operation and Development (OECD), 2 rue Andre-Pascal, 75 Paris 16, France (Telephone Number in U.S. (202) 785-6323); *Foreign Trade by Commodities; Indicators of Industrial Activity; Industrial Structure Statistics;* and *OECD Economic Surveys: Netherlands*.

Statistical Office of the United Nations, Publishing Service, New York, New York

10017 (800) 253-9646; *Statistical Yearbook.*

The World Bank, 1818 H Street, NW, Washington, D.C. 20433 (202) 477-1234; *World Development Indicators.*

NETHERLANDS - MARRIAGE RATES

Europa Publications Limited, 18 Bedford Square, London, WC1B 3JN, England; *The Europa World Year Book.*

European Commission Office of Press and Public Affairs, 2100 M Street, NW, Washington, D.C. 20037 (202) 862-9500; *Basic Statistics of the Community.*

M.E. Sharpe, 80 Business Park Drive, Armonk, New York 10504 (800) 541-6563; *The Illustrated Book of World Rankings.*

Statistical Office of the United Nations, Publishing Service, New York, New York 10017 (800) 253-9646; *Demographic Yearbook; Trends in Europe and North America: The Statistical Yearbook of the Economic Commission for Europe;* and *Statistical Yearbook.*

NETHERLANDS - MEAT PRODUCTION - See NETHERLANDS - LIVESTOCK AND POULTRY

NETHERLANDS - MERCHANT SHIPPING

Europa Publications Limited, 18 Bedford Square, London, WC1B 3JN, England; *The Europa World Year Book.*

European Commission Office of Press and Public Affairs, 2100 M Street, NW, Washington, D.C. 20037 (202) 862-9500; *Basic Statistics of the Community; Fisheries: Yearly Statistics; Regions: Statistical Yearbook;* and *Transport Annual Statistics.*

Lloyd's Register of Shipping, 17 Battery Place, New York, New York 10004 (212) 425-8050; *Register of Ships.*

Organisation for Economic Co-operation and Development (OECD), 2 rue Andre-Pascal, 75 Paris 16, France (Telephone Number in U.S. (202) 785-6323); *Maritime Transport.*

St. Martin's Press, Inc., 175 Fifth Avenue, New York, New York 10010 (800) 221-7945; *The Statesman's Year-Book.*

Statistical Office of the United Nations, Publishing Service, New York, New York 10017 (800) 253-9646; *Statistical Yearbook;* and *Annual Bulletin of Transport Statistics for Europe.*

U.S. Department of Transportation, Maritime Administration, 400 Seventh Street, SW, Washington, D.C. 20590 (202) 366-5807, www.marad.dot.gov; *A Statistical*

Analysis of the World's Merchant Fleets.

NETHERLANDS - MERCURY PRODUCTION AND CONSUMPTION - See NETHERLANDS - MINING AND MINERAL PRODUCTS

NETHERLANDS - MILITARY

Central Intelligence Agency, Washington, D.C. 20505 (703) 482-1100, www.cia.gov; *The World Factbook.*

Euromonitor International, Inc., 122 South Michigan Avenue, Suite 1200, Chicago, Illinois 60603 (800) 577-EURO; *World Marketing Data and Statistics.*

European Commission Office of Press and Public Affairs, 2100 M Street, NW, Washington, D.C. 20037 (202) 862-9500; *Government Financing of Research and Development.*

The International Institute for Strategic Studies, 23 Tavistock Street, London WC2E 7NQ, England; *The Military Balance.*

International Monetary Fund, 700 Nineteenth Street, NW, Washington, D.C. 20431 (202) 623-7000; *Government Finance Statistics Yearbook.*

St. Martin's Press, Inc., 175 Fifth Avenue, New York, New York 10010 (800) 221-7945; *The Statesman's Year-Book.*

Statistical Office of the United Nations, Publishing Service, New York, New York 10017 (800) 253-9646; *Human Development Report.*

U.S. Arms Control and Disarmament Agency, 320 Twenty-first Street, NW, Washington, D.C. 20451 (202) 647-8677; *World Military Expenditures and Arms Transfers.*

NETHERLANDS - MILK PRODUCTION - See NETHERLANDS - DAIRY PRODUCTS

NETHERLANDS - MILLET PRODUCTION - See NETHERLANDS - CROPS

NETHERLANDS - MINING AND MINERAL PRODUCTS

Commodity Research Bureau, Inc., 30 South Wacker Drive, Chicago, Illinois 60606 (312) 454-1801; *Commodity Year Book.*

Europa Publications Limited, 18 Bedford Square, London, WC1B 3JN, England; *The Europa World Year Book.*

European Commission Office of Press and Public Affairs, 2100 M Street, NW, Washington, D.C. 20037 (202) 862-9500; *ACP: Basic Statistics; Basic Statistics of the Community; Energy: Monthly Statistics; Energy Statistics Yearbook; Eurostatistics:*

Data for Short-term Economic Analysis; Industrial Production: Quarterly Statistics; Iron and Steel: Statistical Yearbook; and *Regions: Statistical Yearbook.*

International Iron and Steel Institute, 120, rue Colonel Bourg, B-1140 Brussels, Belgium; *Steel Statistical Yearbook.*

International Lead and Zinc Study Group, Metro House, 58 St. James's Street, London SW1A 1LD England; *Lead and Zinc Statistics.*

M.E. Sharpe, 80 Business Park Drive, Armonk, New York 10504 (800) 541-6563; *The Illustrated Book of World Rankings.*

Organisation for Economic Co-operation and Development (OECD), 2 rue Andre-Pascal, 75 Paris 16, France (Telephone Number in U.S. (202) 785-6323); *Coal Information; Energy Statistics of OECD Countries; Foreign Trade by Commodities; Indicators of Industrial Activity; Industrial Structure Statistics; The Iron and Steel Industry; The Non-Ferrous Metals Industry;* and *OECD Economic Surveys: Netherlands.*

Penn Well Publishing Company, 1421 South Sheridan Road, Post Office Box 1260, Tulsa, Oklahoma 74101 (800) 752-9764; *International Energy Statistics Sourcebook.*

St. Martin's Press, Inc., 175 Fifth Avenue, New York, New York 10010 (800) 221-7945; *The Statesman's Year-Book.*

Statistical Office of the United Nations, Publishing Service, New York, New York 10017 (800) 253-9646; *Statistical Yearbook.*

United Nations Conference on Trade and Development, Central Statistical Service, Palais des Nations, Geneva, Switzerland (Telephone in U.S. (800) 253-9646); *UNCTAD Commodity Yearbook.*

World Bureau of Metal Statistics, 27-A High Street, Ware, Herts. SG12 9BA, England; *World Metal Statistics.*

NETHERLANDS - MOLYBDENUM AND MOLYBDENUM ORE PRODUCTION AND CONSUMPTION - See NETHERLANDS - MINING AND MINERAL PRODUCTS

NETHERLANDS - MONEY AND CREDIT

Organization for Economic Co-operation and Development (OECD), 2 rue Andre-Pascal, 75 Paris 16, France (Telephone Number in U.S. (202) 785-6232); *OECD Economic Surveys: Netherlands.*

NETHERLANDS - MONEY EXCHANGE RATE - See NETHERLANDS - EXCHANGE RATES

NETHERLANDS - MONEY RATES - MARKET

European Commission Office of Press and Public Affairs, 2100 M Street, NW, Washington, D.C. 20037 (202) 862-9500; *Basic Statistics of the Community*.

Organisation for Economic Co-operation and Development (OECD), 2 rue Andre-Pascal, 75 Paris 16, France (Telephone Number in U.S. (202) 785-6323); *Economic Outlook, and Financial Market Trends*.

Statistical Office of the United Nations, Publishing Service, New York, New York 10017 (800) 253-9646; *Statistical Yearbook*.

NETHERLANDS - MONEY RESERVES

European Commission Office of Press and Public Affairs, 2100 M Street, NW, Washington, D.C. 20037 (202) 862-9500; *Basic Statistics of the Community*.

Organisation for Economic Co-operation and Development (OECD), 2 rue Andre-Pascal, 75 Paris 16, France (Telephone Number in U.S. (202) 785-6323); *Economic Outlook; and Financial Market Trends*.

NETHERLANDS - MONEY SUPPLY

Economist Intelligence Unit, 111 West 57th Street, New York, New York 10019 (800) 938-4685; *Netherlands Country Report*.

Europa Publications Limited, 18 Bedford Square, London, WC1B 3JN, England; *The Europa World Year Book*.

European Commission Office of Press and Public Affairs, 2100 M Street, NW, Washington, D.C. 20037 (202) 862-9500; *Basic Statistics of the Community; Eurostatistics: Data for Short-term Economic Analysis; and Money and Finance*.

International Monetary Fund, 700 Nineteenth Street, NW, Washington, D.C. 20431 (202) 623-7000; *International Financial Statistics*.

Netherlands Central Bureau of Statistics, Staatsuitgeverij, The Hague, Netherlands; *Statistical Yearbook of the Netherlands*.

Organisation for Economic Co-operation and Development (OECD), 2 rue Andre-Pascal, 75 Paris 16, France (Telephone Number in U.S. (202) 785-6323); *Economic Outlook*.

Statistical Office of the United Nations, Publishing Service, New York, New York 10017 (800) 253-9646; *Statistical Yearbook*.

The World Bank, 1818 H Street, NW, Washington, D.C. 20433 (202) 477-1234; *World Development Indicators*.

NETHERLANDS - MORTALITY

Central Intelligence Agency, Washington, D.C. 20505 (703) 482-1100, www.cia.gov; *The World Factbook*.

Euromonitor International, Inc., 122 South Michigan Avenue, Suite 1200, Chicago, Illinois 60603 (800) 577-EURO; *The World Economic Factbook*.

Europa Publications Limited, 18 Bedford Square, London, WC1B 3JN, England; *The Europa World Year Book*.

European Commission Office of Press and Public Affairs, 2100 M Street, NW, Washington, D.C. 20037 (202) 862-9500; *Basic Statistics of the Community; and Demographic Statistics*.

St. Martin's Press, Inc., 175 Fifth Avenue, New York, New York 10010 (800) 221-7945; *The Statesman's Year-Book*.

Statistical Office of the United Nations, Publishing Service, New York, New York 10017 (800) 253-9646; *Demographic Yearbook; Human Development Report; Trends in Europe and North America: The Statistical Yearbook of the Economic Commission for Europe; World Statistics Pocketbook; and Statistical Yearbook*.

United Nations Children's Fund (UNICEF), 3 United Nations Plaza, New York, New York 10017 (800) 253-9646; *State of the World's Children*.

The World Bank, 1818 H Street, NW, Washington, D.C. 20433 (202) 477-1234; *The World Bank Atlas; World Development Report; and World Development Indicators*.

World Health Organization, Office of Publications, 20 Avenue Appia, CH-1211 Geneva 27, Switzerland (Telephone Number in U.S. (518) 436-9686); *World Health Statistics Annual*.

NETHERLANDS - MOTION PICTURES

St. Martin's Press, Inc., 175 Fifth Avenue, New York, New York 10010 (800) 221-7945; *The Statesman's Year-Book*.

Statistical Office of the United Nations, Publishing Service, New York, New York 10017 (800) 253-9646; *Statistical Yearbook*.

United Nations Educational, Scientific and Cultural Organization (UNESCO), 7 Place de Fontenoy, F-75700 Paris, France (Telephone Number in U.S. (212) 963-5981); *Statistical Yearbook*.

NETHERLANDS - MOTOR VEHICLE PRODUCTION

American Automobile Manufacturers Association, 1401 H Eye Street, NW, Suite 900, Washington, D.C. 20005 (202) 326-5500; *World Motor Vehicle Data*.

Europa Publications Limited, 18 Bedford Square, London, WC1B 3JN, England; *The Europa World Year Book*.

European Commission Office of Press and Public Affairs, 2100 M Street, NW, Washington, D.C. 20037 (202) 862-9500; *Basic Statistics of the Community; and Eurostatistics: Data for Short-term Economic Analysis*.

Organisation for Economic Co-operation and Development (OECD), 2 rue Andre-Pascal, 75 Paris 16, France (Telephone Number in U.S. (202) 785-6323); *Foreign Trade by Commodities; and Indicators of Industrial Activity*.

NETHERLANDS - MOTOR VEHICLE PRODUCTION AND ASSEMBLY

Statistical Office of the United Nations, Publishing Service, New York, New York 10017 (800) 253-9646; *Statistical Yearbook*.

NETHERLANDS - MOTOR VEHICLE TAXES - See NETHERLANDS - TAXATION

NETHERLANDS - MOTOR VEHICLES IN USE

American Automobile Manufacturers Association, 1401 H Street, NW, Suite 900, Washington, D.C. 20005 (202) 326-5500; *World Motor Vehicle Data*.

European Commission Office of Press and Public Affairs, 2100 M Street, NW, Washington, D.C. 20037 (202) 862-9500; *Basic Statistics of the Community; and Transport Annual Statistics*.

International Road Federation, 2600 Virginia Avenue, NW., Washington, D.C. 20037 (202) 338-4641; *World Road Statistics*.

Statistical Office of the United Nations, Publishing Service, New York, New York 10017 (800) 253-9646; *Statistical Yearbook*.

NETHERLANDS - MULES - See NETHERLANDS - LIVESTOCK AND POULTRY

NETHERLANDS - MUSEUMS

Euromonitor International, Inc., 122 South Michigan Avenue, Suite 1200, Chicago, Illinois 60603 (800) 577-EURO; *European Marketing Data and Statistics*.

M.E. Sharpe, 80 Business Park Drive, Armonk, New York 10504 (800) 541-6563;

The Illustrated Book of World Rankings.

United Nations Educational, Scientific and Cultural Organization (UNESCO), 7 Place de Fontenoy, F-75700 Paris, France (Telephone Number in U.S. (212) 963-5981); *Statistical Yearbook.*

NETHERLANDS - NATALITY - See NETHERLANDS - BIRTH RATES

NETHERLANDS - NATIONAL ACCOUNTS

Europa Publications Limited, 18 Bedford Square, London, WC1B 3JN, England; *The Europa World Year Book.*

European Commission Office of Press and Public Affairs, 2100 M Street, NW, Washington, D.C. 20037 (202) 862-9500; *Basic Statistics of the Community;* and *Eurostatistics: Data for Short-term Economic Analysis.*

Netherlands Central Bureau of Statistics, Staatsuitgeverij, The Hague, Netherlands; *Statistical Yearbook of the Netherlands.*

Organisation for Economic Co-operation and Development (OECD), 2 rue Andre-Pascal, 75 Paris 16, France (Telephone Number in U.S. (202) 785-6323); *Economic Outlook.*

Statistical Office of the United Nations, Publishing Service, New York, New York 10017 (800) 253-9646; *National Accounts Statistics;* and *Statistical Yearbook.*

NETHERLANDS - NATIONAL INCOME

M.E. Sharpe, 80 Business Park Drive, Armonk, New York 10504 (800) 541-6563; *The Illustrated Book of World Rankings.*

Organisation for Economic Co-operation and Development (OECD), 2 rue Andre-Pascal, 75 Paris 16, France (Telephone Number in U.S. (202) 785-6323); *Economic Outlook.*

Statistical Office of the United Nations, Publishing Service, New York, New York 10017 (800) 253-9646; *National Accounts Statistics;* and *Statistical Yearbook.*

NETHERLANDS - NATIONAL PRODUCT

European Commission Office of Press and Public Affairs, 2100 M Street, NW, Washington, D.C. 20037 (202) 862-9500; *Basic Statistics of the Community.*

M.E. Sharpe, 80 Business Park Drive, Armonk, New York 10504 (800) 541-6563; *The Illustrated Book of World Rankings.*

Organisation for Economic Co-operation and Development (OECD), 2 rue Andre-Pascal, 75 Paris 16, France

(Telephone Number in U.S. (202) 785-6323); *Economic Outlook;* and *Main Economic Indicators - Historical Statistics.*

Statistical Office of the United Nations, Publishing Service, New York, New York 10017 (800) 253-9646; *Statistical Yearbook.*

NETHERLANDS - NATURAL GAS PRODUCTION - See NETHERLANDS - MINING AND MINERAL PRODUCTS

NETHERLANDS - NATURAL RUBBER PRODUCTION

European Commission Office of Press and Public Affairs, 2100 M Street, NW, Washington, D.C. 20037 (202) 862-9500; *Basic Statistics of the Community.*

International Rubber Study Group, York House, Eighth Floor, Empire Way, Wembley, London HA9 0PA, England; *Rubber Statistical Bulletin.*

NETHERLANDS - NEWSPAPER PRODUCTION - See NETHERLANDS - FORESTRY AND FOREST PRODUCTS

NETHERLANDS - NEWSPRINT - See NETHERLANDS - FORESTRY AND FOREST PRODUCTS

NETHERLANDS - NICKEL AND NICKEL ORE PRODUCTION AND CONSUMPTION - See NETHERLANDS - MINING AND MINERAL PRODUCTS

NETHERLANDS - NITRIC ACID PRODUCTION - See NETHERLANDS - MINING AND MINERAL PRODUCTS

NETHERLANDS - OATS PRODUCTION - See NETHERLANDS - CROPS

NETHERLANDS - OCCUPATIONS - See NETHERLANDS - LABOR FORCE

NETHERLANDS - OIL PRODUCING CROPS

European Commission Office of Press and Public Affairs, 2100 M Street, NW, Washington, D.C. 20037 (202) 862-9500; *Basic Statistics of the Community.*

Organisation for Economic Co-operation and Development (OECD), 2 rue Andre-Pascal, 75 Paris 16, France (Telephone Number in U.S. (202) 785-6323); *Foreign Trade by Commodities.*

NETHERLANDS - ONION PRODUCTION - See NETHERLANDS - CROPS

NETHERLANDS - PALM KERNEL PRODUCTION - See NETHERLANDS - CROPS

NETHERLANDS - PAPER - See NETHERLANDS - FORESTRY AND FOREST PRODUCTS

NETHERLANDS - PATENTS, TRADEMARKS AND SERVICE MARKS

Statistical Office of the United Nations, Publishing Service, New York, New York 10017 (800) 253-9646; *Statistical Yearbook.*

World Intellectual Property Organization, 34 Chemin des Colombettes, CH-1211 Geneva 20, Switzerland; *Industrial Property Statistics.*

NETHERLANDS - PEANUT PRODUCTION - See NETHERLANDS - CROPS

NETHERLANDS - PEPPER PRODUCTION - See NETHERLANDS - CROPS

NETHERLANDS - PESTICIDE USE

Food and Agricultural Organization of the United Nations (FAO) Via delle Terme di Caracalla, 00100 Rome, Italy (Telephone Number in U.S. (202) 653-2400); *The State of Food and Agriculture.*

NETHERLANDS - PETROLEUM INDUSTRY

Euromonitor International, Inc., 122 South Michigan Avenue, Suite 1200, Chicago, Illinois 60603 (800) 577-EURO; *European Marketing Data and Statistics.*

European Commission Office of Press and Public Affairs, 2100 M Street, NW, Washington, D.C. 20037 (202) 862-9500; *ACP: Basic Statistics; Basic Statistics of the Community;* and *Energy Statistics Yearbook.*

Food and Agricultural Organization of the United Nations (FAO) Via delle Terme di Caracalla, 00100 Rome, Italy (Telephone Number in U.S. (202) 653-2400); *The State of Food and Agriculture.*

M.E. Sharpe, 80 Business Park Drive, Armonk, New York 10504 (800) 541-6563; *The Illustrated Book of World Rankings.*

Organisation for Economic Co-operation and Development (OECD), 2 rue Andre-Pascal, 75 Paris 16, France (Telephone Number in U.S. (202) 785-6323); *Energy Statistics of OECD Countries; Foreign Trade by Commodities; Indicators of Industrial Activity;* and *Oil and Gas Information.*

Penn Well Publishing Company, 1421 South Sheridan Road, Post Office Box 1260, Tulsa, Oklahoma 74101 (800) 752-9764; *International Energy Statistics Sourcebook.*

St. Martin's Press, Inc., 175 Fifth Avenue, New York, New York 10010 (800) 221-7945; *The Statesman's Year-Book.*

Statistical Office of the United Nations,

Publishing Service, New York, New York 10017 (800) 253-9646; *Statistical Yearbook;* and *Trends in Europe and North America: The Statistical Yearbook of the Economic Commission for Europe.*

United Nations Conference on Trade and Development, Central Statistical Service, Palais des Nations, Geneva, Switzerland (Telephone in U.S. (800) 253-9646); *UNCTAD Commodity Yearbook.*

NETHERLANDS - PHOSPHATE ROCK PRODUCTION - See NETHERLANDS - MINING AND MINERAL PRODUCTS

NETHERLANDS - PHOSPHATES PRODUCTION - See NETHERLANDS - MINING AND MINERAL PRODUCTS

NETHERLANDS - PIG IRON AND FERRO-ALLOY PRODUCTION - See NETHERLANDS - MINING AND MINERAL PRODUCTS

NETHERLANDS - PIGS - See NETHERLANDS - LIVESTOCK AND POULTRY

NETHERLANDS - PIPELINES FOR OIL AND PETROLEUM PRODUCTS

European Commission Office of Press and Public Affairs, 2100 M Street, NW, Washington, D.C. 20037 (202) 862-9500; *Transport Annual Statistics.*

Statistical Office of the United Nations, Publishing Service, New York, New York 10017 (800) 253-9646; *Annual Bulletin of Transport Statistics for Europe.*

NETHERLANDS - PLASTIC AND RESIN PRODUCTION

Commodity Research Bureau, Inc., 30 South Wacker Drive, Chicago, Illinois 60606 (312) 454-1801; *Commodity Year Book.*

European Commission Office of Press and Public Affairs, 2100 M Street, NW, Washington, D.C. 20037 (202) 862-9500; *Basic Statistics of the Community.*

Organisation for Economic Co-operation and Development (OECD), 2 rue Andre-Pascal, 75 Paris 16, France (Telephone Number in U.S. (202) 785-6323); *Foreign Trade by Commodities.*

Statistical Office of the United Nations, Publishing Service, New York, New York 10017 (800) 253-9646; *Statistical Yearbook.*

NETHERLANDS - PLATINUM PRODUCTION - See NETHERLANDS - MINING AND MINERAL PRODUCTS

NETHERLANDS - POPULATION

Central Intelligence Agency,

Washington, D.C. 20505 (703) 482-1100, www.cia.gov; *The World Factbook.*

The Economist Intelligence Unit, 111 West 57th Street, New York, New York 10019 (800) 938-4685; *Netherlands Country Report;* and *The World Market Atlas.*

Euromonitor International, Inc., 122 South Michigan Avenue, Suite 1200, Chicago, Illinois 60603 (800) 577-EURO; *European Marketing Data and Statistics;* and *The World Economic Factbook.*

Europa Publications Limited, 18 Bedford Square, London, WC1B 3JN, England; *The Europa World Year Book.*

European Commission Office of Press and Public Affairs, 2100 M Street, NW, Washington, D.C. 20037 (202) 862-9500; *ACP: Basic Statistics; Basic Statistics of the Community; Demographic Statistics; Employment and Unemployment; Fisheries: Yearly Statistics; Iron and Steel: Statistical Yearbook; Labor Force Sample Survey;* and *Regions: Statistical Yearbook.*

Food and Agricultural Organization of the United Nations (FAO), Via delle Terme di Caracalla, 00100 Rome, Italy (Telephone Number in U.S. (202) 653-2400); *Production Yearbook.*

International Labour Office, I.L.O. Publications, 1828 L Street, NW., Suite 801, Washington, D.C. 20036 (301) 638-3152; *Yearbook of Labour Statistics.*

M.E. Sharpe, 80 Business Park Drive, Armonk, New York 10504 (800) 541-6563; *The Illustrated Book of World Rankings.*

Netherlands Central Bureau of Statistics, Staatsuitgeverij, The Hague, Netherlands; *Statistical Yearbook of the Netherlands.*

St. Martin's Press, Inc., 175 Fifth Avenue, New York, New York 10010 (800) 221-7945; *The Statesman's Year-Book.*

Statistical Office of the United Nations, Publishing Service, New York, New York 10017 (800) 253-9646; *Demographic Yearbook; Human Development Report; Trends in Europe and North America: The Statistical Yearbook of the Economic Commission for Europe; World Statistics Pocketbook;* and *Statistical Yearbook.*

United Nations Educational, Scientific and Cultural Organization (UNESCO), 7 Place de Fontenoy, F-75700 Paris, France (Telephone Number in U.S. (212) 963-5981); *Statistical Yearbook.*

U.S. Arms Control and Disarmament Agency, 320 Twenty-first Street, NW, Washington, D.C. 20451 (202) 647-8677; *World Military Expenditures and Arms*

Transfers.

The World Bank, 1818 H Street, NW, Washington, D.C. 20433 (202) 477-1234; *The World Bank Atlas;* and *World Development Report.*

NETHERLANDS - POST OFFICES

M.E. Sharpe, 80 Business Park Drive, Armonk, New York 10504 (800) 541-6563; *The Illustrated Book of World Rankings.*

Statistical Office of the United Nations, Publishing Service, New York, New York 10017 (800) 253-9646; *Trends in Europe and North America: The Statistical Yearbook of the Economic Commission for Europe.*

NETHERLANDS - POTATO PRODUCTION - See NETHERLANDS - CROPS

NETHERLANDS - POWER PRODUCTION INDUSTRY

European Commission Office of Press and Public Affairs, 2100 M Street, NW, Washington, D.C. 20037 (202) 862-9500; *Basic Statistics of the Community.*

Statistical Office of the United Nations, Publishing Service, New York, New York 10017 (800) 253-9646; *Statistical Yearbook.*

NETHERLANDS - PRICES

European Commission Office of Press and Public Affairs, 2100 M Street, NW, Washington, D.C. 20037 (202) 862-9500; *Basic Statistics of the Community;* and *Eurostatistics: Data for Short-term Economic Analysis.*

Food and Agricultural Organization of the United Nations (FAO), Via delle Terme di Caracalla, 00100 Rome, Italy (Telephone Number in U.S. (202) 653-2400); *Production Yearbook;* and *The State of Food and Agriculture.*

International Labour Office, I.L.O. Publications, 1828 L Street, NW., Suite 801, Washington, D.C. 20036 (301) 638-3152; *Yearbook of Labour Statistics.*

International Lead and Zinc Study Group, Metro House, 58 St. James's Street, London SW1A 1LD England; *Lead and Zinc Statistics.*

International Monetary Fund, 700 Nineteenth Street, NW, Washington, D.C. 20431 (202) 623-7000; *International Financial Statistics.*

International Rubber Study Group, York House, Eighth Floor, Empire Way, Wembley, London HA9 0PA, England; *Rubber Statistical Bulletin.*

M.E. Sharpe, 80 Business Park Drive, Armonk, New York 10504 (800) 541-6563; *The Illustrated Book of World Rankings.*

Netherlands Central Bureau of Statistics, Staatsuitgeverij, The Hague, Netherlands; *Statistical Yearbook of the Netherlands.*

Organisation for Economic Co-operation and Development (OECD), 2 rue Andre-Pascal, 75 Paris 16, France (Telephone Number in U.S. (202) 785-6323); *Economic Outlook; The Footwear, Raw Hides and Skins, and Leather Industry in OECD Countries; Indicators of Industrial Activity; The Iron and Steel Industry; Main Economic Indicators - Historical Statistics; and The Pulp and Paper Industry.*

World Bureau of Metal Statistics, 27-A High Street, Ware, Herts. SG12 9BA, England; *World Metal Statistics.*

NETHERLANDS - PRINTING AND WRITING PAPER - See NETHERLANDS - FORESTRY AND FOREST PRODUCTS

NETHERLANDS - PRODUCTION

American Automobile Manufacturers Association, 1401 H Street, NW, Suite 900, Washington, D.C. 20005 (202) 326-5500; *World Motor Vehicle Data.*

European Commission Office of Press and Public Affairs, 2100 M Street, NW, Washington, D.C. 20037 (202) 862-9500; *Basic Statistics of the Community; Eurostatistics: Data for Short-term Economic Analysis; and Fisheries: Yearly Statistics.*

International Iron and Steel Institute, 120, rue Colonel Bourg, B-1140 Brussels, Belgium; *Steel Statistical Yearbook.*

International Lead and Zinc Study Group, Metro House, 58 St. James's Street, London SW1A 1LD England; *Lead and Zinc Statistics.*

International Rubber Study Group, York House, Eighth Floor, Empire Way, Wembley, London HA9 0PA, England; *Rubber Statistical Bulletin.*

M.E. Sharpe, 80 Business Park Drive, Armonk, New York 10504 (800) 541-6563; *The Illustrated Book of World Rankings.*

Organisation for Economic Co-operation and Development (OECD), 2 rue Andre-Pascal, 75 Paris 16, France (Telephone Number in U.S. (202) 785-6323); *Economic Outlook; The Footwear, Raw Hides and Skins, and Leather Industry in OECD Countries; Indicators of Industrial Activity; Industrial Structure Statistics; The Iron and Steel Industry; Meat Balances in OECD Member Countries; Milk, Milk*

Products, and Egg Balances in OECD Member Countries; The Non-Ferrous Metals Industry; The Pulp and Paper Industry; and Textile Industry in OECD Countries.

NETHERLANDS - PRODUCTIVITY

European Commission Office of Press and Public Affairs, 2100 M Street, NW, Washington, D.C. 20037 (202) 862-9500; *Basic Statistics of the Community.*

Organisation for Economic Co-operation and Development (OECD), 2 rue Andre-Pascal, 75 Paris 16, France (Telephone Number in U.S. (202) 785-6323); *Economic Outlook.*

NETHERLANDS - PROPERTY TAXES - See NETHERLANDS - TAXATION

NETHERLANDS - PUBLIC CONSUMPTION FUND

European Commission Office of Press and Public Affairs, 2100 M Street, NW, Washington, D.C. 20037 (202) 862-9500; *Basic Statistics of the Community.*

Organisation for Economic Co-operation and Development (OECD), 2 rue Andre-Pascal, 75 Paris 16, France (Telephone Number in U.S. (202) 785-6323); *Revenue Statistics of OECD Member Countries.*

NETHERLANDS - PUBLIC EXPENDITURES

European Commission Office of Press and Public Affairs, 2100 M Street, NW, Washington, D.C. 20037 (202) 862-9500; *Basic Statistics of the Community.*

Organisation for Economic Co-operation and Development (OECD), 2 rue Andre-Pascal, 75 Paris 16, France (Telephone Number in U.S. (202) 785-6323); *Revenue Statistics of OECD Member Countries.*

NETHERLANDS - PUBLIC FINANCE - See NETHERLANDS - FINANCE

NETHERLANDS - PUBLIC HEALTH - See NETHERLANDS - HEALTH

NETHERLANDS - PUBLIC REVENUES

Organisation for Economic Co-operation and Development (OECD), 2 rue Andre-Pascal, 75 Paris 16, France (Telephone Number in U.S. (202) 785-6323); *Revenue Statistics of OECD Member Countries.*

NETHERLANDS - RADIO BROADCASTING - See NETHERLANDS - BROADCASTING

NETHERLANDS - RADIO RECEIVERS

St. Martin's Press, Inc., 175 Fifth Avenue, New York, New York 10010 (800) 221-7945; *The Statesman's Year-Book.*

NETHERLANDS - RAILWAYS

Euromonitor International, Inc., 122 South Michigan Avenue, Suite 1200, Chicago, Illinois 60603 (800) 577-EURO; *European Marketing Data and Statistics.*

Europa Publications Limited, 18 Bedford Square, London, WC1B 3JN, England; *The Europa World Year Book.*

European Commission Office of Press and Public Affairs, 2100 M Street, NW, Washington, D.C. 20037 (202) 862-9500; *Basic Statistics of the Community; Regions: Statistical Yearbook; and Transport Annual Statistics.*

Jane's Information Group, Sentinel House, 163 Brighton Road, Coulsdon, Surrey CR5 2NH, England (Telephone Number in U.S. (703) 683-3700); *Jane's World Railways.*

St. Martin's Press, Inc., 175 Fifth Avenue, New York, New York 10010 (800) 221-7945; *The Statesman's Year-Book.*

Statistical Office of the United Nations, Publishing Service, New York, New York 10017 (800) 253-9646; *Annual Bulletin of Transport Statistics for Europe; Trends in Europe and North America: The Statistical Yearbook of the Economic Commission for Europe; and Statistical Yearbook.*

NETHERLANDS - RANCHING

European Commission Office of Press and Public Affairs, 2100 M Street, NW, Washington, D.C. 20037 (202) 862-9500; *Basic Statistics of the Community.*

NETHERLANDS - RAPESEED PRODUCTION - See NETHERLANDS - CROPS

NETHERLANDS - RELIGION

Central Intelligence Agency, Washington, D.C. 20505 (703) 482-1100, www.cia.gov; *The World Factbook.*

M.E. Sharpe, 80 Business Park Drive, Armonk, New York 10504 (800) 541-6563; *The Illustrated Book of World Rankings.*

St. Martin's Press, Inc., 175 Fifth Avenue, New York, New York 10010 (800) 221-7945; *The Statesman's Year-Book.*

NETHERLANDS - RENT PRICES

International Labour Office, I.L.O. Publications, 1828 L Street, NW., Suite 801, Washington, D.C. 20036 (301) 638-3152; *Yearbook of Labour Statistics.*

NETHERLANDS - RETAIL TRADE

Euromonitor International, Inc., 122 South Michigan Avenue, Suite 1200, Chicago, Illinois 60603 (800) 577-EURO; *Retail Trade International;* and *World Marketing Data and Statistics.*

European Commission Office of Press and Public Affairs, 2100 M Street, NW, Washington, D.C. 20037 (202) 862-9500; *Basic Statistics of the Community;* and *Eurostatistics: Data for Short-term Economic Analysis.*

Statistical Office of the United Nations, Publishing Service, New York, New York 10017 (800) 253-9646; *Statistical Yearbook.*

NETHERLANDS - RICE PRODUCTION - See NETHERLANDS - CROPS

NETHERLANDS - ROOT AND TUBER PRODUCTION - See NETHERLANDS - CROPS

NETHERLANDS - ROUNDWOOD PRODUCTION - See NETHERLANDS - FORESTRY AND FOREST PRODUCTS

NETHERLANDS - RUBBER PRODUCTION AND CONSUMPTION

European Commission Office of Press and Public Affairs, 2100 M Street, NW, Washington, D.C. 20037 (202) 862-9500; *Basic Statistics of the Community.*

International Rubber Study Group, York House, Eighth Floor, Empire Way, Wembley, London HA9 0PA, England; *Rubber Statistical Bulletin.*

M.E. Sharpe, 80 Business Park Drive, Armonk, New York 10504 (800) 541-6563; *The Illustrated Book of World Rankings.*

Organisation for Economic Co-operation and Development (OECD), 2 rue Andre-Pascal, 75 Paris 16, France (Telephone Number in U.S. (202) 785-6323); *Foreign Trade by Commodities.*

Statistical Office of the United Nations, Publishing Service, New York, New York 10017 (800) 253-9646; *Statistical Yearbook.*

NETHERLANDS - RYE PRODUCTION - See NETHERLANDS - CROPS

NETHERLANDS - SAFFLOWER SEED PRODUCTION - See NETHERLANDS - CROPS

NETHERLANDS - SALES

Organisation for Economic Co-operation and Development (OECD), 2 rue Andre-Pascal, 75 Paris 16, France (Telephone Number in U.S. (202) 785-6323); *Main Economic Indicators -*

Historical Statistics.

NETHERLANDS - SALT PRODUCTION - See NETHERLANDS - MINING AND MINERAL PRODUCTS

NETHERLANDS - SAVINGS ACCOUNT DEPOSITS - See NETHERLANDS - BANKING

NETHERLANDS - SAWNWOOD PRODUCTION - See NETHERLANDS - FORESTRY AND FOREST PRODUCTS

NETHERLANDS - SCIENCE AND TECHNOLOGY - See NETHERLANDS - SCIENTISTS, TECHNICIANS AND ENGINEERS

NETHERLANDS - SCIENCE AND TECHNOLOGY - EXPENDITURE FOR RESEARCH - See NETHERLANDS - SCIENTISTS, TECHNICIANS AND ENGINEERS

NETHERLANDS - SCIENTISTS, TECHNICIANS AND ENGINEERS

European Commission Office of Press and Public Affairs, 2100 M Street, NW, Washington, D.C. 20037 (202) 862-9500; *Basic Statistics of the Community.*

Netherlands Central Bureau of Statistics, Staatsuitgeverij, The Hague, Netherlands; *Statistical Yearbook of the Netherlands.*

Statistical Office of the United Nations, Publishing Service, New York, New York 10017 (800) 253-9646; *Statistical Yearbook.*

NETHERLANDS - SENIOR CITIZENS

M.E. Sharpe, 80 Business Park Drive, Armonk, New York 10504 (800) 541-6563; *The Illustrated Book of World Rankings.*

NETHERLANDS - SERVICES INDUSTRY EMPLOYMENT - MALE AND FEMALE

European Commission Office of Press and Public Affairs, 2100 M Street, NW, Washington, D.C. 20037 (202) 862-9500; *Basic Statistics of the Community; Employment and Unemployment;* and *Labor Force Sample Survey.*

Organisation for Economic Co-operation and Development (OECD), 2 rue Andre-Pascal, 75 Paris 16, France (Telephone Number in U.S. (202) 785-6323); *OECD Employment Outlook.*

NETHERLANDS - SESAME SEED PRODUCTION - See NETHERLANDS - CROPS

NETHERLANDS - SHEEP - See NETHERLANDS - LIVESTOCK AND POULTRY

NETHERLANDS - SHIPBUILDING - PRODUCTION INDEX

Organisation for Economic Co-operation and Development (OECD), 2 rue Andre-Pascal, 75 Paris 16, France (Telephone Number in U.S. (202) 785-6323); *Indicators of Industrial Activity.*

NETHERLANDS - SILVER PRODUCTION AND CONSUMPTION - See NETHERLANDS - MINING AND MINERAL PRODUCTS

NETHERLANDS - SISAL PRODUCTION - See NETHERLANDS - CROPS

NETHERLANDS - SOCIAL DATA

European Commission Office of Press and Public Affairs, 2100 M Street, NW, Washington, D.C. 20037 (202) 862-9500; *ACP: Basic Statistics, Basic Statistics of the Community.*

M.E. Sharpe, 80 Business Park Drive, Armonk, New York 10504 (800) 541-6563; *The Illustrated Book of World Rankings.*

Statistical Office of the United Nations, Publishing Service, New York, New York 10017 (800) 253-9646; *World Statistics Pocketbook.*

NETHERLANDS - SOCIAL SECURITY

European Commission Office of Press and Public Affairs, 2100 M Street, NW, Washington, D.C. 20037 (202) 862-9500; *Basic Statistics of the Community.*

International Monetary Fund, 700 Nineteenth Street, NW, Washington, D.C. 20431 (202) 623-7000; *Government Finance Statistics Yearbook.*

Organisation for Economic Co-operation and Development (OECD), 2 rue Andre-Pascal, 75 Paris 16, France (Telephone Number in U.S. (202) 785-6323); *Revenue Statistics of OECD Member Countries.*

St. Martin's Press, Inc., 175 Fifth Avenue, New York, New York 10010 (800) 221-7945; *The Statesman's Year-Book.*

Statistical Office of the United Nations, Publishing Service, New York, New York 10017 (800) 253-9646; *National Accounts Statistics.*

NETHERLANDS - SOCIOECONOMIC DATA

European Commission Office of Press and Public Affairs, 2100 M Street, NW, Washington, D.C. 20037 (202) 862-9500; *Basic Statistics of the Community.*

Organisation for Economic Co-

operation and Development (OECD), 2 rue Andre-Pascal, 75 Paris 16, France (Telephone Number in U.S. (202) 785-6323); *Economic Outlook*.

NETHERLANDS - SOYBEAN PRODUCTION

European Commission Office of Press and Public Affairs, 2100 M Street, NW, Washington, D.C. 20037 (202) 862-9500; *Basic Statistics of the Community*.

NETHERLANDS - STAMP TAXES AND DUTIES - See NETHERLANDS - TAXATION

NETHERLANDS - STEEL - See NETHERLANDS - MINING AND MINERAL PRODUCTS

NETHERLANDS - STOCKS - COMMODITY - MARKET PRICE - INDEXES

Food and Agricultural Organization of the United Nations (FAO) Via delle Terme di Caracalla, 00100 Rome, Italy (Telephone Number in U.S. (202) 653-2400); *The State of Food and Agriculture*.

International Lead and Zinc Study Group, Metro House, 58 St. James's Street, London SW1A 1LD England; *Lead and Zinc Statistics*.

Statistical Office of the United Nations, Publishing Service, New York, New York 10017 (800) 253-9646; *Statistical Yearbook*.

World Bureau of Metal Statistics, 27-A High Street, Ware, Herts. SG12 9BA, England; *World Metal Statistics*.

NETHERLANDS - STRAW PRODUCTION - See NETHERLANDS - CROPS

NETHERLANDS - SUGAR - See SUGAR - NETHERLANDS - CROPS

NETHERLANDS - SUGAR PRODUCTION AND CONSUMPTION

European Commission Office of Press and Public Affairs, 2100 M Street, NW, Washington, D.C. 20037 (202) 862-9500; *ACP: Basic Statistics;* and *Basic Statistics of the Community*.

M.E. Sharpe, 80 Business Park Drive, Armonk, New York 10504 (800) 541-6563; *The Illustrated Book of World Rankings*.

Statistical Office of the United Nations, Publishing Service, New York, New York 10017 (800) 253-9646; *Statistical Yearbook*.

NETHERLANDS - SUGARBEET PRODUCTION

European Commission Office of Press and Public Affairs, 2100 M Street, NW,

Washington, D.C. 20037 (202) 862-9500; *Basic Statistics of the Community*.

NETHERLANDS - SULPHUR PRODUCTION - See NETHERLANDS - MINING AND MINERAL PRODUCTS

NETHERLANDS - SULPHURIC ACID - See NETHERLANDS - MINING AND MINERAL PRODUCTS

NETHERLANDS - SULPHURIC ACID PRODUCTION - See NETHERLANDS - MINING AND MINERAL PRODUCTS

NETHERLANDS - SUNFLOWER PRODUCTION - See NETHERLANDS - CROPS

NETHERLANDS - TAXATION

Europa Publications Limited, 18 Bedford Square, London, WC1B 3JN, England; *The Europa World Year Book*.

European Commission Office of Press and Public Affairs, 2100 M Street, NW, Washington, D.C. 20037 (202) 862-9500; *Basic Statistics of the Community*.

International Monetary Fund, 700 Nineteenth Street, NW, Washington, D.C. 20431 (202) 623-7000; *Government Finance Statistics Yearbook*.

International Road Federation, 2600 Virginia Avenue, NW., Washington, D.C. 20037 (202) 338-4641; *World Road Statistics*.

Netherlands Central Bureau of Statistics, Staatsuitgeverij, The Hague, Netherlands; *Statistical Yearbook of the Netherlands*.

Organisation for Economic Co-operation and Development (OECD), 2 rue Andre-Pascal, 75 Paris 16, France (Telephone Number in U.S. (202) 785-6323); *Revenue Statistics of OECD Member Countries*.

The World Bank, 1818 H Street, NW, Washington, D.C. 20433 (202) 477-1234; *World Development Indicators*.

NETHERLANDS - TAX REVENUE - See NETHERLANDS - TAXATION

NETHERLANDS - TEA PRODUCTION AND CONSUMPTION - See NETHERLANDS - CROPS

NETHERLANDS - TELEGRAPH SERVICE

NETHERLANDS - TELEPHONES IN USE

American Telephone and Telegraph Company, 26 Parsippany Road, Whippany, New Jersey 07981 (800) 222-0300; *The World's Telephones*.

Central Intelligence Agency, Washington, D.C. 20505 (703) 482-1100, www.cia.gov; *The World Factbook*.

Europa Publications Limited, 18 Bedford Square, London, WC1B 3JN, England; *The Europa World Year Book*.

European Commission Office of Press and Public Affairs, 2100 M Street, NW, Washington, D.C. 20037 (202) 862-9500; *Basic Statistics of the Community;* and *Transport Annual Statistics*.

St. Martin's Press, Inc., 175 Fifth Avenue, New York, New York 10010 (800) 221-7945; *The Statesman's Year-Book*.

Statistical Office of the United Nations, Publishing Service, New York, New York 10017 (800) 253-9646; *Statistical Yearbook; World Statistics Pocketbook;* and *Trends in Europe and North America: The Statistical Yearbook of the Economic Commission for Europe*.

World Health Organization, Office of Publications, 20 Avenue Appia, CH-1211 Geneva 27, Switzerland (Telephone Number in U.S. (518) 436-9686); *World Health Statistics Annual*.

NETHERLANDS - TELEVISION BROADCASTING - See NETHERLANDS - BROADCASTING

NETHERLANDS - TELEVISION RECEIVER PRODUCTION

European Commission Office of Press and Public Affairs, 2100 M Street, NW, Washington, D.C. 20037 (202) 862-9500; *Basic Statistics of the Community*.

NETHERLANDS - TEXTILE INDUSTRY

American Forest and Paper Association, 1111 Nineteenth Street, NW, Suite 800, Washington, D.C. 20036 (202) 463-2700; *Wood Pulp and Fiber Statistics*.

European Commission Office of Press and Public Affairs, 2100 M Street, NW, Washington, D.C. 20037 (202) 862-9500; *Basic Statistics of the Community; Eurostatistics: Data for Short-term Economic Analysis;* and *Industrial Production: Quarterly Statistics*.

Euromonitor International, Inc., 122 South Michigan Avenue, Suite 1200, Chicago, Illinois 60603 (800) 577-EURO; *Retail Trade International*.

Food and Agricultural Organization of the United Nations (FAO), Via delle Terme di Caracalla, 00100 Rome, Italy (Telephone Number in U.S. (202) 653-2400); *Production Yearbook*.

M.E. Sharpe, 80 Business Park Drive,

Armonk, New York 10504 (800) 541-6563; *The Illustrated Book of World Rankings.*

Organisation for Economic Co-operation and Development (OECD), 2 rue Andre-Pascal, 75 Paris 16, France (Telephone Number in U.S. (202) 785-6323); *Economic Accounts for Agriculture; Foreign Trade by Commodities; Indicators of Industrial Activity; Industrial Structure Statistics;* and *Textile Industry in OECD Countries.*

St. Martin's Press, Inc., 175 Fifth Avenue, New York, New York 10010 (800) 221-7945; *The Statesman's Year-Book.*

Statistical Office of the United Nations, Publishing Service, New York, New York 10017 (800) 253-9646; *Statistical Yearbook.*

United Nations Conference on Trade and Development, Central Statistical Service, Palais des Nations, Geneva, Switzerland (Telephone in U.S. (800) 253-9646); *UNCTAD Commodity Yearbook.*

NETHERLANDS - THEATRE

United Nations Educational, Scientific and Cultural Organization (UNESCO), 7 Place de Fontenoy, F-75700 Paris, France (Telephone Number in U.S. (212) 963-5981); *Statistical Yearbook.*

NETHERLANDS - TIMBER - See NETHERLANDS - FORESTRY AND FOREST PRODUCTS

NETHERLANDS - TIN - See NETHERLANDS - MINING AND MINERAL PRODUCTS

NETHERLANDS - TIRE (MOTOR VEHICLE) PRODUCTION

International Rubber Study Group, York House, Eighth Floor, Empire Way, Wembley, London HA9 0PA, England; *Rubber Statistical Bulletin.*

NETHERLANDS - TOBACCO PRODUCTION

Euromonitor International, Inc., 122 South Michigan Avenue, Suite 1200, Chicago, Illinois 60603 (800) 577-EURO; *European Marketing Data and Statistics.*

European Commission Office of Press and Public Affairs, 2100 M Street, NW, Washington, D.C. 20037 (202) 862-9500; *Basic Statistics of the Community;* and *Industrial Production: Quarterly Statistics.*

M.E. Sharpe, 80 Business Park Drive, Armonk, New York 10504 (800) 541-6563; *The Illustrated Book of World Rankings.*

Organisation for Economic Co-operation and Development (OECD), 2 rue Andre-Pascal, 75 Paris 16, France

(Telephone Number in U.S. (202) 785-6323); *Foreign Trade by Commodities; Indicators of Industrial Activity;* and *Industrial Structure Statistics.*

Statistical Office of the United Nations, Publishing Service, New York, New York 10017 (800) 253-9646; *Statistical Yearbook.*

NETHERLANDS - TOURISM

Euromonitor International, Inc., 122 South Michigan Avenue, Suite 1200, Chicago, Illinois 60603 (800) 577-EURO; *European Marketing Data and Statistics; The World Economic Factbook;* and *World Marketing Data and Statistics.*

Europa Publications Limited, 18 Bedford Square, London, WC1B 3JN, England; *The Europa World Year Book.*

European Commission Office of Press and Public Affairs, 2100 M Street, NW, Washington, D.C. 20037 (202) 862-9500; *Transport Annual Statistics.*

M.E. Sharpe, 80 Business Park Drive, Armonk, New York 10504 (800) 541-6563; *The Illustrated Book of World Rankings.*

Organisation for Economic Co-operation and Development (OECD), 2 rue Andre-Pascal, 75 Paris 16, France (Telephone Number in U.S. (202) 785-6323); *Tourism Policy and International Tourism in OECD Member Countries.*

St. Martin's Press, Inc., 175 Fifth Avenue, New York, New York 10010 (800) 221-7945; *The Statesman's Year-Book.*

Statistical Office of the United Nations, Publishing Service, New York, New York 10017 (800) 253-9646; *Statistical Yearbook;* and *Trends in Europe and North America: The Statistical Yearbook of the Economic Commission for Europe.*

World Tourism Organization, Calle Capitan Haya 42, E-28020 Madrid, Spain; *Yearbook of Tourism Statistics.*

NETHERLANDS - TRACTORS IN USE

Statistical Office of the United Nations, Publishing Service, New York, New York 10017 (800) 253-9646; *Statistical Yearbook.*

NETHERLANDS - TRADE - See NETHERLANDS - FOREIGN TRADE

NETHERLANDS - TRADEMARKS AND SERVICE MARKS - See NETHERLANDS - PATENTS, TRADEMARKS AND SERVICE MARKS

NETHERLANDS - TRANSPORTATION AND COMMUNICATIONS

Central Intelligence Agency,

Washington, D.C. 20505 (703) 482-1100, www.cia.gov; *The World Factbook.*

Euromonitor International, Inc., 122 South Michigan Avenue, Suite 1200, Chicago, Illinois 60603 (800) 577-EURO; *World Marketing Data and Statistics.*

Europa Publications Limited, 18 Bedford Square, London, WC1B 3JN, England; *The Europa World Year Book.*

European Commission Office of Press and Public Affairs, 2100 M Street, NW, Washington, D.C. 20037 (202) 862-9500; *Basic Statistics of the Community; Energy Statistics Yearbook; Regions: Statistical Yearbook;* and *Transport Annual Statistics.*

M.E. Sharpe, 80 Business Park Drive, Armonk, New York 10504 (800) 541-6563; *The Illustrated Book of World Rankings.*

Netherlands Central Bureau of Statistics, Staatsuitgeverij, The Hague, Netherlands; *Statistical Yearbook of the Netherlands.*

St. Martin's Press, Inc., 175 Fifth Avenue, New York, New York 10010 (800) 221-7945; *The Statesman's Year-Book.*

Statistical Office of the United Nations, Publishing Service, New York, New York 10017 (800) 253-9646; *Human Development Report;* and *Trends in Europe and North America: The Statistical Yearbook of the Economic Commission for Europe.*

NETHERLANDS - TRANSPORTATION EMPLOYMENT - MALE AND FEMALE - See NETHERLANDS - EMPLOYMENT

NETHERLANDS - TUNGSTEN PRODUCTION AND CONSUMPTION - See NETHERLANDS - MINING AND MINERAL PRODUCTS

NETHERLANDS - TURKEYS - See NETHERLANDS - LIVESTOCK AND POULTRY

NETHERLANDS - UNEMPLOYMENT

Central Intelligence Agency, Washington, D.C. 20505 (703) 482-1100, www.cia.gov; *The World Factbook.*

Euromonitor International, Inc., 122 South Michigan Avenue, Suite 1200, Chicago, Illinois 60603 (800) 577-EURO; *European Marketing Data and Statistics.*

European Commission Office of Press and Public Affairs, 2100 M Street, NW, Washington, D.C. 20037 (202) 862-9500; *Basic Statistics of the Community; Employment and Unemployment; Eurostatistics: Data for Short-term Economic Analysis; Labor Force Sample Survey;* and *Regions: Statistical Yearbook.*

International Labour Office, I.L.O. Publications, 1828 L Street, NW, Suite 801, Washington, D.C. 20036 (301) 638-3152; *Yearbook of Labour Statistics.*

Organisation for Economic Co-operation and Development (OECD), 2 rue Andre-Pascal, 75 Paris 16, France (Telephone Number in U.S. (202) 785-6323); *Economic Outlook; OECD Economic Surveys: Netherlands;* and *OECD Employment Outlook.*

St. Martin's Press, Inc., 175 Fifth Avenue, New York, New York 10010 (800) 221-7945; *The Statesman's Year-Book.*

Statistical Office of the United Nations, Publishing Service, New York, New York 10017 (800) 253-9646; *Statistical Yearbook; and Trends in Europe and North America: The Statistical Yearbook of the Economic Commission for Europe.*

NETHERLANDS - URANIUM PRODUCTION AND CONSUMPTION - See NETHERLANDS - MINING AND MINERAL PRODUCTS

NETHERLANDS - UTILITIES

European Commission Office of Press and Public Affairs, 2100 M Street, NW, Washington, D.C. 20037 (202) 862-9500; *Basic Statistics of the Community.*

NETHERLANDS - VANADIUM AND VANADIUM ORE PRODUCTION AND CONSUMPTION - See NETHERLANDS - MINING AND MINERAL PRODUCTS

NETHERLANDS - VITAL STATISTICS

European Commission Office of Press and Public Affairs, 2100 M Street, NW, Washington, D.C. 20037 (202) 862-9500; *Basic Statistics of the Community.*

St. Martin's Press, Inc., 175 Fifth Avenue, New York, New York 10010 (800) 221-7945; *The Statesman's Year-Book.*

Statistical Office of the United Nations, Publishing Service, New York, New York 10017 (800) 253-9646; *Statistical Yearbook.*

NETHERLANDS - WAGES

Euromonitor International, Inc., 122 South Michigan Avenue, Suite 1200, Chicago, Illinois 60603 (800) 577-EURO; *European Marketing Data and Statistics.*

European Commission Office of Press and Public Affairs, 2100 M Street, NW, Washington, D.C. 20037 (202) 862-9500; *Basic Statistics of the Community; Earnings in Agriculture;* and *Eurostatistics: Data for Short-term Economic Analysis.*

International Labour Office,

I.L.O. Publications, 1828 L Street, NW, Suite 801, Washington, D.C. 20036 (301) 638-3152; *Yearbook of Labour Statistics.*

Organisation for Economic Co-operation and Development (OECD), 2 rue Andre-Pascal, 75 Paris 16, France (Telephone Number in U.S. (202) 785-6323); *Economic Outlook; Industrial Structure Statistics;* and *Main Economic Indicators - Historical Statistics.*

Statistical Office of the United Nations, Publishing Service, New York, New York 10017 (800) 253-9646; *Statistical Yearbook.*

NETHERLANDS - WALNUT PRODUCTION - See NETHERLANDS - CROPS

NETHERLANDS - WATERWAYS IN USE

European Commission Office of Press and Public Affairs, 2100 M Street, NW, Washington, D.C. 20037 (202) 862-9500; *Basic Statistics of the Community;* and *Transport Annual Statistics.*

Organisation for Economic Co-operation and Development (OECD), 2 rue Andre-Pascal, 75 Paris 16, France (Telephone Number in U.S. (202) 785-6323); *Maritime Transport.*

Statistical Office of the United Nations, Publishing Service, New York, New York 10017 (800) 253-9646; *Annual Bulletin of Transport Statistics for Europe.*

NETHERLANDS - WEATHER - See NETHERLANDS - CLIMATE

NETHERLANDS - WELFARE

European Commission Office of Press and Public Affairs, 2100 M Street, NW, Washington, D.C. 20037 (202) 862-9500; *Basic Statistics of the Community.*

International Monetary Fund, 700 Nineteenth Street, NW, Washington, D.C. 20431 (202) 623-7000; *Government Finance Statistics Yearbook.*

NETHERLANDS - WHEAT PRODUCTION AND PRICES - See NETHERLANDS CROPS

NETHERLANDS - WHOLESALE PRICES

European Commission Office of Press and Public Affairs, 2100 M Street, NW, Washington, D.C. 20037 (202) 862-9500; *Basic Statistics of the Community.*

Statistical Office of the United Nations, Publishing Service, New York, New York 10017 (800) 253-9646; *Statistical Yearbook.*

NETHERLANDS - WHOLESALE TRADE

European Commission Office of Press

and Public Affairs, 2100 M Street, NW, Washington, D.C. 20037 (202) 862-9500; *Basic Statistics of the Community.*

Statistical Office of the United Nations, Publishing Service, New York, New York 10017 (800) 253-9646; *Statistical Yearbook.*

NETHERLANDS - WINE PRODUCTION - See NETHERLANDS - BEVERAGES

NETHERLANDS - WOOD AND WOOD PULP - See NETHERLANDS - FORESTRY AND FOREST PRODUCTS

NETHERLANDS - WOOL - INDUSTRIAL CONSUMPTION - See NETHERLANDS - TEXTILE INDUSTRY

NETHERLANDS - WOOL PRODUCTION - See NETHERLANDS - TEXTILE INDUSTRY

NETHERLANDS - YARN PRODUCTION - See NETHERLANDS - TEXTILE INDUSTRY

NETHERLANDS - ZINC AND ZINC ORE PRODUCTION AND CONSUMPTION - See NETHERLANDS - MINING AND MINERAL PRODUCTS

NETHERLANDS - ZINC (SLAB) CONSUMPTION - See NETHERLANDS - MINING AND MINERAL PRODUCTS

Netherlands Antilles - National Statistical Office

Central Bureau of Statistics, Willemstad, Curacao, Netherlands Antilles.

Netherlands Antilles - Primary Statistics Source

Central Bureau of Statistics, Willemstad, Curacao, Netherlands Antilles; *Statistisch jaarboek: Nederlandse Antillen* (Statistical Yearbook: Netherlands Antilles).

NETHERLANDS ANTILLES - AGRICULTURE

Economist Intelligence Unit, 111 West 57th Street, New York, New York 10019 (800) 938-4685; *Netherlands Antilles Country Report.*

Euromonitor International, Inc., 122 South Michigan Avenue, Suite 1200, Chicago, Illinois 60603 (800) 577-EURO; *World Marketing Data and Statistics.*

Europa Publications Limited, 18 Bedford Square, London, WC1B 3JN, England; *The Europa World Year Book.*

Food and Agricultural Organization of the United Nations (FAO) Via delle Terme di Caracalla, 00100 Rome, Italy (Telephone Number in U.S. (202) 653-2400);

Production Yearbook; The State of Food and Agriculture; and *Trade Yearbook.*

St. Martin's Press, Inc., 175 Fifth Avenue, New York, New York 10010 (800) 221-7945; *The Statesman's Year-Book.*

Statistical Office of the United Nations, Publishing Service, New York, New York 10017 (800) 253-9646; *Statistical Yearbook.*

United Nations Conference on Trade and Development, Central Statistical Service, Palais des Nations, Geneva, Switzerland (Telephone in U.S. (800) 253-9646); *UNCTAD Commodity Yearbook.*

NETHERLANDS ANTILLES - AIRLINE SERVICE

St. Martin's Press, Inc., 175 Fifth Avenue, New York, New York 10010 (800) 221-7945; *The Statesman's Year-Book.*

NETHERLANDS ANTILLES - AIRPORTS

Central Intelligence Agency, Washington, D.C. 20505 (703) 482-1100, www.cia.gov; *The World Factbook.*

NETHERLANDS ANTILLES - AREA AND DENSITY OF POPULATION

Central Intelligence Agency, Washington, D.C. 20505 (703) 482-1100, www.cia.gov; *The World Factbook.*

Euromonitor International, Inc., 122 South Michigan Avenue, Suite 1200, Chicago, Illinois 60603 (800) 577-EURO; *The World Economic Factbook.*

Europa Publications Limited, 18 Bedford Square, London, WC1B 3JN, England; *The Europa World Year Book.*

Food and Agricultural Organization of the United Nations (FAO) Via delle Terme di Caracalla, 00100 Rome, Italy (Telephone Number in U.S. (202) 653-2400); *The State of Food and Agriculture.*

St. Martin's Press, Inc., 175 Fifth Avenue, New York, New York 10010 (800) 221-7945; *The Statesman's Year-Book.*

Statistical Office of the United Nations, Publishing Service, New York, New York 10017 (800) 253-9646; *Statistical Yearbook.*
United Nations Educational, Scientific and Cultural Organization (UNESCO), 7 Place de Fontenoy, F-75700 Paris, France (Telephone Number in U.S. (212) 963-5981); *Statistical Yearbook.*

NETHERLANDS ANTILLES - BALANCE OF PAYMENTS

The Economist Intelligence Unit, 111 West 57th Street, New York, New York 10019 (800) 938-4685; *The World Market*

Atlas.

Europa Publications Limited, 18 Bedford Square, London, WC1B 3JN, England; *The Europa World Year Book.*

International Monetary Fund, 700 Nineteenth Street, NW, Washington, D.C. 20431 (202) 623-7000; *Balance of Payments Yearbook.*

NETHERLANDS ANTILLES - BANKING

Euromonitor International, Inc., 122 South Michigan Avenue, Suite 1200, Chicago, Illinois 60603 (800) 577-EURO; *World Marketing Data and Statistics.*

Europa Publications Limited, 18 Bedford Square, London, WC1B 3JN, England; *The Europa World Year Book.*

International Monetary Fund, 700 Nineteenth Street, NW, Washington, D.C. 20431 (202) 623-7000; *Government Finance Statistics Yearbook;* and *International Financial Statistics.*

St. Martin's Press, Inc., 175 Fifth Avenue, New York, New York 10010 (800) 221-7945; *The Statesman's Year-Book.*

NETHERLANDS ANTILLES - BEER PRODUCTION - See NETHERLANDS ANTILLES - BEVERAGES

NETHERLANDS ANTILLES - BEVERAGES

Statistical Office of the United Nations, Publishing Service, New York, New York 10017 (800) 253-9646; *Statistical Yearbook.*

NETHERLANDS ANTILLES - BIRTH RATES

Central Intelligence Agency, Washington, D.C. 20505 (703) 482-1100, www.cia.gov; *The World Factbook.*

Euromonitor International, Inc., 122 South Michigan Avenue, Suite 1200, Chicago, Illinois 60603 (800) 577-EURO; *International Marketing Data and Statistics;* and *The World Economic Factbook.*

Europa Publications Limited, 18 Bedford Square, London, WC1B 3JN, England; *The Europa World Year Book.*

St. Martin's Press, Inc., 175 Fifth Avenue, New York, New York 10010 (800) 221-7945; *The Statesman's Year-Book.*

Statistical Office of the United Nations, Publishing Service, New York, New York 10017 (800) 253-9646; *Demographic Yearbook;* and *Statistical Yearbook.*

NETHERLANDS ANTILLES - BONDS

International Monetary Fund, 700 Nineteenth Street, NW, Washington, D.C.

20431 (202) 623-7000; *Government Finance Statistics Yearbook.*

NETHERLANDS ANTILLES - BOOK PRODUCTION

Europa Publications Limited, 18 Bedford Square, London, WC1B 3JN, England; *The Europa World Year Book.*

United Nations Educational, Scientific and Cultural Organization (UNESCO), 7 Place de Fontenoy, F-75700 Paris, France (Telephone Number in U.S. (212) 963-5981); *Statistical Yearbook.*

NETHERLANDS ANTILLES - BROADCASTING

Billboard Limited, Post Office Box 9027, 1006 AA Amsterdam, The Netherlands (Telephone Number in U.S. (212) 764-7300); *World Radio TV Handbook.*

Central Intelligence Agency, Washington, D.C. 20505 (703) 482-1100, www.cia.gov; *The World Factbook.*

Euromonitor International, Inc., 122 South Michigan Avenue, Suite 1200, Chicago, Illinois 60603 (800) 577-EURO; *World Marketing Data and Statistics.*

Europa Publications Limited, 18 Bedford Square, London, WC1B 3JN, England; *The Europa World Year Book.*

St. Martin's Press, Inc., 175 Fifth Avenue, New York, New York 10010 (800) 221-7945; *The Statesman's Year-Book.*

NETHERLANDS ANTILLES - BUDGET

Central Intelligence Agency, Washington, D.C. 20505 (703) 482-1100, www.cia.gov; *The World Factbook.*

NETHERLANDS ANTILLES - CALORIE SUPPLY

Food and Agricultural Organization of the United Nations (FAO) Via delle Terme di Caracalla, 00100 Rome, Italy (Telephone Number in U.S. (202) 653-2400); *The State of Food and Agriculture.*

NETHERLANDS ANTILLES - CAPITAL REVENUE

International Monetary Fund, 700 Nineteenth Street, NW, Washington, D.C. 20431 (202) 623-7000; *Government Finance Statistics Yearbook.*

NETHERLANDS ANTILLES - CATTLE - See NETHERLANDS ANTILLES - LIVESTOCK AND POULTRY

NETHERLANDS ANTILLES - CHEMICAL (ORGANIC) PRODUCTION - See NETHERLANDS ANTILLES - MINING AND

MINERAL PRODUCTS

NETHERLANDS ANTILLES - CLIMATE

St. Martin's Press, Inc., 175 Fifth Avenue, New York, New York 10010 (800) 221-7945; *The Statesman's Year-Book.*

NETHERLANDS ANTILLES - COAL PRODUCTION - See NETHERLANDS ANTILLES - MINING AND MINERAL PRODUCTS

NETHERLANDS ANTILLES - COMMERCE

St. Martin's Press, Inc., 175 Fifth Avenue, New York, New York 10010 (800) 221-7945; *The Statesman's Year-Book.*

NETHERLANDS ANTILLES - CONSTRUCTION INDUSTRY

Statistical Office of the United Nations, Publishing Service, New York, New York 10017 (800) 253-9646; *Statistical Yearbook.*

NETHERLANDS ANTILLES - CONSUMER PRICE INDEX

Europa Publications Limited, 18 Bedford Square, London, WC1B 3JN, England; *The Europa World Year Book.*

Statistical Office of the United Nations, Publishing Service, New York, New York 10017 (800) 253-9646; *Statistical Yearbook.*

NETHERLANDS ANTILLES - CONSUMER PRICES

Euromonitor International, Inc., 122 South Michigan Avenue, Suite 1200, Chicago, Illinois 60603 (800) 577-EURO; *World Marketing Data and Statistics.*

International Labour Office, I.L.O. Publications, 1828 L Street, NW, Suite 801, Washington, D.C. 20036 (301) 638-3152; *Yearbook of Labour Statistics.*

International Monetary Fund, 700 Nineteenth Street, NW, Washington, D.C. 20431 (202) 623-7000; *International Financial Statistics.*

NETHERLANDS ANTILLES - CORN PRODUCTION - See NETHERLANDS ANTILLES - CROPS

NETHERLANDS ANTILLES - CORPORATE TAXES - See NETHERLANDS ANTILLES - TAXATION

NETHERLANDS ANTILLES - CRIME

Yale University Press, Yale Station, New Haven, Connecticut 06520 (800) 987-7323; *Violence and Crime in Cross-National Perspective.*

NETHERLANDS ANTILLES - CROPS

Food and Agricultural Organization of the United Nations (FAO) Via delle Terme di Caracalla, 00100 Rome, Italy (Telephone Number in U.S. (202) 653-2400); *The State of Food and Agriculture.*

United Nations Conference on Trade and Development, Central Statistical Service, Palais des Nations, Geneva, Switzerland (Telephone in U.S. (800) 253-9646); *UNCTAD Commodity Yearbook.*

NETHERLANDS ANTILLES - CUSTOMS DUTIES

International Monetary Fund, 700 Nineteenth Street, NW, Washington, D.C. 20431 (202) 623-7000; *Government Finance Statistics Yearbook.*

St. Martin's Press, Inc., 175 Fifth Avenue, New York, New York 10010 (800) 221-7945; *The Statesman's Year-Book.*

NETHERLANDS ANTILLES - DAIRY PRODUCTS

Food and Agricultural Organization of the United Nations (FAO) Via delle Terme di Caracalla, 00100 Rome, Italy (Telephone Number in U.S. (202) 653-2400); *The State of Food and Agriculture.*

NETHERLANDS ANTILLES - DEATH RATES - See NETHERLANDS ANTILLES -MORTALITY

NETHERLANDS ANTILLES - DEFENSE EXPENDITURES - See NETHERLANDS ANTILLES - MILITARY

NETHERLANDS ANTILLES - DEMOGRAPHY

The Economist Intelligence Unit, 111 West 57th Street, New York, New York 10019 (800) 938-4685; *The World Market Atlas.*

Euromonitor International, Inc., 122 South Michigan Avenue, Suite 1200, Chicago, Illinois 60603 (800) 577-EURO; *International Marketing Data and Statistics; The World Economic Factbook;* and *World Marketing Data and Statistics.*

NETHERLANDS ANTILLES - DEVELOPMENT ASSISTANCE

Statistical Office of the United Nations, Publishing Service, New York, New York 10017 (800) 253-9646; *Statistical Yearbook.*

NETHERLANDS ANTILLES - DIVORCE RATES

Statistical Office of the United Nations, Publishing Service, New York, New York 10017 (800) 253-9646; *Demographic Yearbook;* and *Statistical Yearbook.*

NETHERLANDS ANTILLES - ECONOMY

Central Intelligence Agency, Washington, D.C. 20505 (703) 482-1100, www.cia.gov; *The World Factbook.*

Economist Intelligence Unit, 111 West 57th Street, New York, New York 10019 (800) 938-4685; *Netherlands Antilles Country Report.*

Euromonitor International, Inc., 122 South Michigan Avenue, Suite 1200, Chicago, Illinois 60603 (800) 577-EURO; *The World Economic Factbook;* and *World Marketing Data and Statistics.*

Europa Publications Limited, 18 Bedford Square, London, WC1B 3JN, England; *The Europa World Year Book.*

St. Martin's Press, Inc., 175 Fifth Avenue, New York, New York 10010 (800) 221-7945; *The Statesman's Year-Book.*

Statistical Office of the United Nations, Publishing Service, New York, New York 10017 (800) 253-9646; *World Statistics Pocketbook.*

The World Bank, 1818 H Street, NW, Washington, D.C. 20433 (202) 477-1234; *The World Bank Atlas.*

NETHERLANDS ANTILLES - EDUCATION

The Economist Intelligence Unit, 111 West 57th Street, New York, New York 10019 (800) 938-4685; *The World Market Atlas.*

Euromonitor International, Inc., 122 South Michigan Avenue, Suite 1200, Chicago, Illinois 60603 (800) 577-EURO; *International Marketing Data and Statistics;* and *World Marketing Data and Statistics.*

Europa Publications Limited, 18 Bedford Square, London, WC1B 3JN, England; *The Europa World Year Book.*

International Monetary Fund, 700 Nineteenth Street, NW, Washington, D.C. 20431 (202) 623-7000; *Government Finance Statistics Yearbook.*

St. Martin's Press, Inc., 175 Fifth Avenue, New York, New York 10010 (800) 221-7945; *The Statesman's Year-Book.*

United Nations Educational, Scientific and Cultural Organization (UNESCO), 7 Place de Fontenoy, F-75700 Paris, France (Telephone Number in U.S. (212) 963-5981); *Statistical Yearbook.*

NETHERLANDS ANTILLES - EGG PRODUCTION AND CONSUMPTION - See NETHERLANDS ANTILLES - DAIRY PRODUCTS

NETHERLANDS ANTILLES - ELECTRICITY

Central Intelligence Agency, Washington, D.C. 20505 (703) 482-1100, www.cia.gov; *The World Factbook.*

St. Martin's Press, Inc., 175 Fifth Avenue, New York, New York 10010 (800) 221-7945; *The Statesman's Year-Book.*

Statistical Office of the United Nations, Publishing Service, New York, New York 10017 (800) 253-9646; *Statistical Yearbook.*

NETHERLANDS ANTILLES - EMPLOYMENT

Euromonitor International, Inc., 122 South Michigan Avenue, Suite 1200, Chicago, Illinois 60603 (800) 577-EURO; *International Marketing Data and Statistics.*

International Labour Office, I.L.O. Publications, 1828 L Street, NW, Suite 801, Washington, D.C. 20036 (301) 638-3152; *Yearbook of Labour Statistics.*

NETHERLANDS ANTILLES - ENERGY

Euromonitor International, Inc., 122 South Michigan Avenue, Suite 1200, Chicago, Illinois 60603 (800) 577-EURO; *International Marketing Data and Statistics; The World Economic Factbook;* and *World Marketing Data and Statistics.*

Food and Agricultural Organization of the United Nations (FAO) Via delle Terme di Caracalla, 00100 Rome, Italy (Telephone Number in U.S. (202) 653-2400); *The State of Food and Agriculture.*

St. Martin's Press, Inc., 175 Fifth Avenue, New York, New York 10010 (800) 221-7945; *The Statesman's Year-Book.*

Statistical Office of the United Nations, Publishing Service, New York, New York 10017 (800) 253-9646; *Energy Statistics Yearbook; World Statistics Pocketbook;* and *Statistical Yearbook.*

The World Bank, 1818 H Street, NW, Washington, D.C. 20433 (202) 477-1234; *The World Bank Atlas.*

NETHERLANDS ANTILLES - ENVIRONMENT

Economist Intelligence Unit, 111 West 57th Street, New York, New York 10019 (800) 938-4685; *Netherlands Antilles Country Report.*

Statistical Office of the United Nations, Publishing Service, New York, New York 10017 (800) 253-9646; *World Statistics Pocketbook.*

NETHERLANDS ANTILLES - EXCHANGE RATES

Central Intelligence Agency, Washington, D.C. 20505 (703) 482-1100,

www.cia.gov; *The World Factbook.*

Euromonitor International, Inc., 122 South Michigan Avenue, Suite 1200, Chicago, Illinois 60603 (800) 577-EURO; *International Marketing Data and Statistics;* and *The World Economic Factbook.*

Europa Publications Limited, 18 Bedford Square, London, WC1B 3JN, England; *The Europa World Year Book.*

International Monetary Fund, 700 Nineteenth Street, NW, Washington, D.C. 20431 (202) 623-7000; *International Financial Statistics.*

Statistical Office of the United Nations, Publishing Service, New York, New York 10017 (800) 253-9646; *World Statistics Pocketbook.*

NETHERLANDS ANTILLES - EXCISE TAXES - See NETHERLANDS ANTILLES -TAXATION

NETHERLANDS ANTILLES - EXPORTS

Central Intelligence Agency, Washington, D.C. 20505 (703) 482-1100, www.cia.gov; *The World Factbook.*

The Economist Intelligence Unit, 111 West 57th Street, New York, New York 10019 (800) 938-4685; *Netherlands Antilles Country Report;* and *The World Market Atlas.*

Euromonitor International, Inc., 122 South Michigan Avenue, Suite 1200, Chicago, Illinois 60603 (800) 577-EURO; *International Marketing Data and Statistics;* and *The World Economic Factbook.*

Europa Publications Limited, 18 Bedford Square, London, WC1B 3JN, England; *The Europa World Year Book.*

Food and Agricultural Organization of the United Nations (FAO) Via delle Terme di Caracalla, 00100 Rome, Italy (Telephone Number in U.S. (202) 653-2400); *The State of Food and Agriculture.*

International Monetary Fund, 700 Nineteenth Street, NW, Washington, D.C. 20431 (202) 623-7000; *Direction of Trade Statistics.*

St. Martin's Press, Inc., 175 Fifth Avenue, New York, New York 10010 (800) 221-7945; *The Statesman's Year-Book.*

NETHERLANDS ANTILLES - EXTERNAL TRADE

Euromonitor International, Inc., 122 South Michigan Avenue, Suite 1200, Chicago, Illinois 60603 (800) 577-EURO; *World Marketing Data and Statistics.*

Food and Agricultural Organization of

the United Nations (FAO) Via delle Terme di Caracalla, 00100 Rome, Italy (Telephone Number in U.S. (202) 653-2400); *The State of Food and Agriculture;* and *Trade Yearbook.*

Statistical Office of the United Nations, Publishing Service, New York, New York 10017 (800) 253-9646; *Statistical Yearbook.*

NETHERLANDS ANTILLES - FARM CROPS - See NETHERLANDS ANTILLES -CROPS

NETHERLANDS ANTILLES - FERTILITY RATES

Central Intelligence Agency, Washington, D.C. 20505 (703) 482-1100, www.cia.gov; *The World Factbook.*

The World Bank, 1818 H Street, NW, Washington, D.C. 20433 (202) 477-1234; *The World Bank Atlas.*

NETHERLANDS ANTILLES - FERTILIZER

Food and Agricultural Organization of the United Nations (FAO) Via delle Terme di Caracalla, 00100 Rome, Italy (Telephone Number in U.S. (202) 653-2400); *The State of Food and Agriculture.*

Statistical Office of the United Nations, Publishing Service, New York, New York 10017 (800) 253-9646; *Statistical Yearbook.*

NETHERLANDS ANTILLES - FETAL MORTALITY - See NETHERLANDS ANTILLES - MORTALITY

NETHERLANDS ANTILLES - FINANCE

Economist Intelligence Unit, 111 West 57th Street, New York, New York 10019 (800) 938-4685; *Netherlands Antilles Country Report.*

Europa Publications Limited, 18 Bedford Square, London, WC1B 3JN, England; *The Europa World Year Book.*

International Monetary Fund, 700 Nineteenth Street, NW, Washington, D.C. 20431 (202) 623-7000; *Government Finance Statistics Yearbook.*

St. Martin's Press, Inc., 175 Fifth Avenue, New York, New York 10010 (800) 221-7945; *The Statesman's Year-Book.*

NETHERLANDS ANTILLES - FISHERIES

Europa Publications Limited, 18 Bedford Square, London, WC1B 3JN, England; *The Europa World Year Book.*

Food and Agricultural Organization of the United Nations (FAO) Via delle Terme di Caracalla, 00100 Rome, Italy (Telephone Number in U.S. (202) 653-2400); *The State of Food and Agriculture;* and *Yearbook of*

Fishery Statistics.

St. Martin's Press, Inc., 175 Fifth Avenue, New York, New York 10010 (800) 221-7945; *The Statesman's Year-Book.*

Statistical Office of the United Nations, Publishing Service, New York, New York 10017 (800) 253-9646; *Statistical Yearbook.*

United Nations Conference on Trade and Development, Central Statistical Service, Palais des Nations, Geneva, Switzerland (Telephone in U.S. (800) 253-9646); *UNCTAD Commodity Yearbook.*

NETHERLANDS ANTILLES - FOOD

Food and Agricultural Organization of the United Nations (FAO), Via delle Terme di Caracalla, 00100 Rome, Italy (Telephone Number in U.S. (202) 653-2400); *Production Yearbook;* and *The State of Food and Agriculture.*

United Nations Conference on Trade and Development, Central Statistical Service, Palais des Nations, Geneva, Switzerland (Telephone in U.S. (800) 253-9646); *UNCTAD Commodity Yearbook.*

NETHERLANDS ANTILLES - FOREIGN DEBT

International Monetary Fund, 700 Nineteenth Street, NW, Washington, D.C. 20431 (202) 623-7000; *Government Finance Statistics Yearbook.*

NETHERLANDS ANTILLES - FOREIGN TRADE

Economist Intelligence Unit, 111 West 57th Street, New York, New York 10019 (800) 938-4685; *Netherlands Antilles Country Report.*

Euromonitor International, Inc., 122 South Michigan Avenue, Suite 1200, Chicago, Illinois 60603 (800) 577-EURO; *The World Economic Factbook.*

Europa Publications Limited, 18 Bedford Square, London, WC1B 3JN, England; *The Europa World Year Book.*

Food and Agricultural Organization of the United Nations (FAO) Via delle Terme di Caracalla, 00100 Rome, Italy (Telephone Number in U.S. (202) 653-2400); *The State of Food and Agriculture.*

St. Martin's Press, Inc., 175 Fifth Avenue, New York, New York 10010 (800) 221-7945; *The Statesman's Year-Book.*

Statistical Office of the United Nations, Publishing Service, New York, New York 10017 (800) 253-9646; *International Trade Statistics Yearbook;* and *Statistical Yearbook.*

United Nations Conference on Trade and Development, Central Statistical Service, Palais des Nations, Geneva, Switzerland (Telephone in U.S. (800) 253-9646); *UNCTAD Commodity Yearbook.*

NETHERLANDS ANTILLES - FORESTRY AND FOREST PRODUCTS

Food and Agricultural Organization of the United Nations (FAO) Via delle Terme di Caracalla, 00100 Rome, Italy (Telephone Number in U.S. (202) 653-2400); *The State of Food and Agriculture;* and *Yearbook of Forest Products.*

Statistical Office of the United Nations, Publishing Service, New York, New York 10017 (800) 253-9646; *Statistical Yearbook.*

United Nations Conference on Trade and Development, Central Statistical Service, Palais des Nations, Geneva, Switzerland (Telephone in U.S. (800) 253-9646); *UNCTAD Commodity Yearbook.*

United Nations Educational, Scientific and Cultural Organization (UNESCO), 7 Place de Fontenoy, F-75700 Paris, France (Telephone Number in U.S. (212) 963-5981); *Statistical Yearbook.*

NETHERLANDS ANTILLES - GENERAL MORTALITY - See NETHERLANDS ANTILLES - MORTALITY

NETHERLANDS ANTILLES - GOLD HOLDINGS

International Monetary Fund, 700 Nineteenth Street, NW, Washington, D.C. 20431 (202) 623-7000; *International Financial Statistics.*

NETHERLANDS ANTILLES - GOVERNMENT

Central Intelligence Agency, Washington, D.C. 20505 (703) 482-1100, www.cia.gov; *The World Factbook.*

International Monetary Fund, 700 Nineteenth Street, NW, Washington, D.C. 20431 (202) 623-7000; *Government Finance Statistics Yearbook.*

St. Martin's Press, Inc., 175 Fifth Avenue, New York, New York 10010 (800) 221-7945; *The Statesman's Year-Book.*

Statistical Office of the United Nations, Publishing Service, New York, New York 10017 (800) 253-9646; *National Accounts Statistics.*

NETHERLANDS ANTILLES - GRAIN PRODUCTION - See NETHERLANDS ANTILLES - CROPS

NETHERLANDS ANTILLES - GRANTS

International Monetary Fund, 700 Nineteenth Street, NW, Washington, D.C. 20431 (202) 623-7000; *Government Finance Statistics Yearbook.*

NETHERLANDS ANTILLES - GROSS DOMESTIC PRODUCT

The Economist Intelligence Unit, 111 West 57th Street, New York, New York 10019 (800) 938-4685; *Netherlands Antilles Country Report;* and *The World Market Atlas.*

Euromonitor International, Inc., 122 South Michigan Avenue, Suite 1200, Chicago, Illinois 60603 (800) 577-EURO; *International Marketing Data and Statistics;* and *The World Economic Factbook.*

Europa Publications Limited, 18 Bedford Square, London, WC1B 3JN, England; *The Europa World Year Book.*

Statistical Office of the United Nations, Publishing Service, New York, New York 10017 (800) 253-9646; *National Accounts Statistics;* and *Statistical Yearbook.*

NETHERLANDS ANTILLES - GROSS NATIONAL PRODUCT

The World Bank, 1818 H Street, NW, Washington, D.C. 20433 (202) 477-1234; *The World Bank Atlas.*

NETHERLANDS ANTILLES - HEALTH

Euromonitor International, Inc., 122 South Michigan Avenue, Suite 1200, Chicago, Illinois 60603 (800) 577-EURO; *World Marketing Data and Statistics.*

St. Martin's Press, Inc., 175 Fifth Avenue, New York, New York 10010 (800) 221-7945; *The Statesman's Year-Book.*

Statistical Office of the United Nations, Publishing Service, New York, New York 10017 (800) 253-9646; *Statistical Yearbook.*

NETHERLANDS ANTILLES - HEALTH EXPENDITURES

International Monetary Fund, 700 Nineteenth Street, NW, Washington, D.C. 20431 (202) 623-7000; *Government Finance Statistics Yearbook.*

NETHERLANDS ANTILLES - HIDE PRODUCTION

Food and Agricultural Organization of the United Nations (FAO), Via delle Terme di Caracalla, 00100 Rome, Italy (Telephone Number in U.S. (202) 653-2400); *Production Yearbook.*

NETHERLANDS ANTILLES - HIGHWAYS

Central Intelligence Agency,

Washington, D.C. 20505 (703) 482-1100, www.cia.gov; *The World Factbook.*

St. Martin's Press, Inc., 175 Fifth Avenue, New York, New York 10010 (800) 221-7945; *The Statesman's Year-Book.*

NETHERLANDS ANTILLES - HOURS OF WORK - See NETHERLANDS ANTILLES - EMPLOYMENT

NETHERLANDS ANTILLES - HOUSING AND HOUSING UNITS

Euromonitor International, Inc., 122 South Michigan Avenue, Suite 1200, Chicago, Illinois 60603 (800) 577-EURO; *World Marketing Data and Statistics.*

NETHERLANDS ANTILLES - HOUSING EXPENDITURES

International Monetary Fund, 700 Nineteenth Street, NW, Washington, D.C. 20431 (202) 623-7000; *Government Finance Statistics Yearbook.*

NETHERLANDS ANTILLES - ILLITERATE POPULATION

Central Intelligence Agency, Washington, D.C. 20505 (703) 482-1100, www.cia.gov; *The World Factbook.*

The Economist Intelligence Unit, 111 West 57th Street, New York, New York 10019 (800) 938-4685; *The World Market Atlas.*

Euromonitor International, Inc., 122 South Michigan Avenue, Suite 1200, Chicago, Illinois 60603 (800) 577-EURO; *The World Economic Factbook.*

United Nations Educational, Scientific and Cultural Organization (UNESCO), 7 Place de Fontenoy, F-75700 Paris, France (Telephone Number in U.S. (212) 963-5981); *Statistical Yearbook.*

NETHERLANDS ANTILLES - IMPORTS

Central Intelligence Agency, Washington, D.C. 20505 (703) 482-1100, www.cia.gov; *The World Factbook.*

The Economist Intelligence Unit, 111 West 57th Street, New York, New York 10019 (800) 938-4685; *Netherlands Antilles Country Report;* and *The World Market Atlas.*

Euromonitor International, Inc., 122 South Michigan Avenue, Suite 1200, Chicago, Illinois 60603 (800) 577-EURO; *International Marketing Data and Statistics;* and *The World Economic Factbook.*

Europa Publications Limited, 18 Bedford Square, London, WC1B 3JN, England; *The Europa World Year Book.*

Food and Agricultural Organization of the United Nations (FAO) Via delle Terme di Caracalla, 00100 Rome, Italy (Telephone Number in U.S. (202) 653-2400); *The State of Food and Agriculture.*

International Monetary Fund, 700 Nineteenth Street, NW, Washington, D.C. 20431 (202) 623-7000; *Direction of Trade Statistics;* and *Government Finance Statistics Yearbook.*

St. Martin's Press, Inc., 175 Fifth Avenue, New York, New York 10010 (800) 221-7945; *The Statesman's Year-Book.*

NETHERLANDS ANTILLES - INCOME TAXES - See NETHERLANDS ANTILLES -TAXATION

NETHERLANDS ANTILLES - INDUSTRY

Central Intelligence Agency, Washington, D.C. 20505 (703) 482-1100, www.cia.gov; *The World Factbook.*

Economist Intelligence Unit, 111 West 57th Street, New York, New York 10019 (800) . 938-4685; *Netherlands Antilles Country Report.*

Euromonitor International, Inc., 122 South Michigan Avenue, Suite 1200, Chicago, Illinois 60603 (800) 577-EURO; *The World Economic Factbook;* and *World Marketing Data and Statistics.*

Europa Publications Limited, 18 Bedford Square, London, WC1B 3JN, England; *The Europa World Year Book.*

International Labour Office, I.L.O. Publications, 1828 L Street, NW, Suite 801, Washington, D.C. 20036 (301) 638-3152; *Yearbook of Labour Statistics.*

St. Martin's Press, Inc., 175 Fifth Avenue, New York, New York 10010 (800) 221-7945; *The Statesman's Year-Book.*

NETHERLANDS ANTILLES - INFANT AND MATERNAL MORTALITY - See NETHERLANDS ANTILLES - MORTALITY

NETHERLANDS ANTILLES - INTERNATIONAL LIQUIDITY

International Monetary Fund, 700 Nineteenth Street, NW, Washington, D.C. 20431 (202) 623-7000; *International Financial Statistics.*

NETHERLANDS ANTILLES - INTERNATIONAL RESERVES EXCLUDING GOLD

Statistical Office of the United Nations, Publishing Service, New York, New York 10017 (800) 253-9646; *Statistical Yearbook.*

NETHERLANDS ANTILLES - LABOR

Central Intelligence Agency, Washington, D.C. 20505 (703) 482-1100, www.cia.gov; *The World Factbook.*

Euromonitor International, Inc., 122 South Michigan Avenue, Suite 1200, Chicago, Illinois 60603 (800) 577-EURO; *International Marketing Data and Statistics;* and *World Marketing Data and Statistics.*

Europa Publications Limited, 18 Bedford Square, London, WC1B 3JN, England; *The Europa World Year Book.*

Food and Agricultural Organization of the United Nations (FAO) Via delle Terme di Caracalla, 00100 Rome, Italy (Telephone Number in U.S. (202) 653-2400); *The State of Food and Agriculture.*

International Labour Office, I.L.O. Publications, 1828 L Street, NW, Suite 801, Washington, D.C. 20036 (301) 638-3152; *Yearbook of Labour Statistics.*

St. Martin's Press, Inc., 175 Fifth Avenue, New York, New York 10010 (800) 221-7945; *The Statesman's Year-Book.*

The World Bank, 1818 H Street, NW, Washington, D.C. 20433 (202) 477-1234; *The World Bank Atlas.*

NETHERLANDS ANTILLES - LAND USE

Central Intelligence Agency, Washington, D.C. 20505 (703) 482-1100, www.cia.gov; *The World Factbook.*

Euromonitor International, Inc., 122 South Michigan Avenue, Suite 1200, Chicago, Illinois 60603 (800) 577-EURO; *International Marketing Data and Statistics.*

Food and Agricultural Organization of the United Nations (FAO), Via delle Terme di Caracalla, 00100 Rome, Italy (Telephone Number in U.S. (202) 653-2400); *Production Yearbook.*

NETHERLANDS ANTILLES - LIBRARIES

United Nations Educational, Scientific and Cultural Organization (UNESCO), 7 Place de Fontenoy, F-75700 Paris, France (Telephone Number in U.S. (212) 963-5981); *Statistical Yearbook.*

NETHERLANDS ANTILLES - LIFE EXPECTANCY

Central Intelligence Agency, Washington, D.C. 20505 (703) 482-1100, www.cia.gov; *The World Factbook.*

Euromonitor International, Inc., 122 South Michigan Avenue, Suite 1200, Chicago, Illinois 60603 (800) 577-EURO; *The World Economic Factbook.*

The World Bank, 1818 H Street, NW,

Washington, D.C. 20433 (202) 477-1234; *The World Bank Atlas.*

NETHERLANDS ANTILLES - LITERACY RATE

Euromonitor International, Inc., 122 South Michigan Avenue, Suite 1200, Chicago, Illinois 60603 (800) 577-EURO; *World Marketing Data and Statistics.*

NETHERLANDS ANTILLES - LIVESTOCK AND POULTRY

Europa Publications Limited, 18 Bedford Square, London, WC1B 3JN, England; *The Europa World Year Book.*

Food and Agricultural Organization of the United Nations (FAO), Via delle Terme di Caracalla, 00100 Rome, Italy (Telephone Number in U.S. (202) 653-2400); *Production Yearbook;* and *The State of Food and Agriculture.*

St. Martin's Press, Inc., 175 Fifth Avenue, New York, New York 10010 (800) 221-7945; *The Statesman's Year-Book.*

Statistical Office of the United Nations, Publishing Service, New York, New York 10017 (800) 253-9646; *Statistical Yearbook.*

United Nations Conference on Trade and Development, Central Statistical Service, Palais des Nations, Geneva, Switzerland (Telephone in U.S. (800) 253-9646); *UNCTAD Commodity Yearbook.*

NETHERLANDS ANTILLES - MAIL - PIECES SENT OR RECEIVED

Statistical Office of the United Nations, Publishing Service, New York, New York 10017 (800) 253-9646; *Statistical Yearbook.*

NETHERLANDS ANTILLES - MANUFACTURING

NETHERLANDS ANTILLES - MARRIAGE RATES

Europa Publications Limited, 18 Bedford Square, London, WC1B 3JN, England; *The Europa World Year Book.*

Statistical Office of the United Nations, Publishing Service, New York, New York 10017 (800) 253-9646; *Demographic Yearbook;* and *Statistical Yearbook.*

NETHERLANDS ANTILLES - MEAT PRODUCTION - See - NETHERLANDS ANTILLES - LIVESTOCK AND POULTRY

NETHERLANDS ANTILLES - MERCHANT SHIPPING

Europa Publications Limited, 18 Bedford Square, London, WC1B 3JN, England; *The Europa World Year Book.*

St. Martin's Press, Inc., 175 Fifth Avenue, New York, New York 10010 (800) 221-7945; *The Statesman's Year-Book.*

Statistical Office of the United Nations, Publishing Service, New York, New York 10017 (800) 253-9646; *Statistical Yearbook.*

NETHERLANDS ANTILLES - MILITARY

Central Intelligence Agency, Washington, D.C. 20505 (703) 482-1100, www.cia.gov; *The World Factbook.*

Euromonitor International, Inc., 122 South Michigan Avenue, Suite 1200, Chicago, Illinois 60603 (800) 577-EURO; *World Marketing Data and Statistics.*

International Monetary Fund, 700 Nineteenth Street, NW, Washington, D.C. 20431 (202) 623-7000; *Government Finance Statistics Yearbook.*

NETHERLANDS ANTILLES - MINING AND MINERAL PRODUCTS

Europa Publications Limited, 18 Bedford Square, London, WC1B 3JN, England; *The Europa World Year Book.*

St. Martin's Press, Inc., 175 Fifth Avenue, New York, New York 10010 (800) 221-7945; *The Statesman's Year-Book.*

Statistical Office of the United Nations, Publishing Service, New York, New York 10017 (800) 253-9646; *Statistical Yearbook.*

United Nations Conference on Trade and Development, Central Statistical Service, Palais des Nations, Geneva, Switzerland (Telephone in U.S. (800) 253-9646); *UNCTAD Commodity Yearbook.*

NETHERLANDS ANTILLES - MONEY EXCHANGE RATES - See NETHERLANDS ANTILLES - EXCHANGE RATES

NETHERLANDS ANTILLES - MONEY SUPPLY

Economist Intelligence Unit, 111 West 57th Street, New York, New York 10019 (800) 938-4685; *Netherlands Antilles Country Report.*

Europa Publications Limited, 18 Bedford Square, London, WC1B 3JN, England; *The Europa World Year Book.*

International Monetary Fund, 700 Nineteenth Street, NW, Washington, D.C. 20431 (202) 623-7000; *International Financial Statistics.*

NETHERLANDS ANTILLES - MORTALITY

Central Intelligence Agency, Washington, D.C. 20505 (703) 482-1100, www.cia.gov; *The World Factbook.*

Euromonitor International, Inc., 122 South Michigan Avenue, Suite 1200, Chicago, Illinois 60603 (800) 577-EURO; *International Marketing Data and Statistics;* and *The World Economic Factbook.*

St. Martin's Press, Inc., 175 Fifth Avenue, New York, New York 10010 (800) 221-7945; *The Statesman's Year-Book.*

Statistical Office of the United Nations, Publishing Service, New York, New York 10017 (800) 253-9646; *Demographic Yearbook; World Statistics Pocketbook;* and *Statistical Yearbook.*

The World Bank, 1818 H Street, NW, Washington, D.C. 20433 (202) 477-1234; *The World Bank Atlas.*

NETHERLANDS ANTILLES - MOTOR VEHICLES IN USE

Europa Publications Limited, 18 Bedford Square, London, WC1B 3JN, England; *The Europa World Year Book.*

Statistical Office of the United Nations, Publishing Service, New York, New York 10017 (800) 253-9646; *Statistical Yearbook.*

NETHERLANDS ANTILLES - NATALITY - See NETHERLANDS ANTILLES - BIRTH RATES

NETHERLANDS ANTILLES - NATIONAL ACCOUNTS

Statistical Office of the United Nations, Publishing Service, New York, New York 10017 (800) 253-9646; *National Accounts Statistics;* and *Statistical Yearbook.*

NETHERLANDS ANTILLES - NATIONAL INCOME

Statistical Office of the United Nations, Publishing Service, New York, New York 10017 (800) 253-9646; *National Accounts Statistics;* and *Statistical Yearbook.*

NETHERLANDS ANTILLES - NEWSPAPER PRODUCTION - See NETHERLANDS ANTILLES - FORESTRY AND FOREST PRODUCTS

NETHERLANDS ANTILLES - NEWSPRINT - See NETHERLANDS ANTILLES - FORESTRY AND FOREST PRODUCTS

NETHERLANDS ANTILLES - OCCUPATIONS - See NETHERLANDS ANTILLES - LABOR

NETHERLANDS ANTILLES - PAPER EXPORTS AND IMPORTS - See NETHERLANDS ANTILLES - FORESTRY AND FOREST PRODUCTS

NETHERLANDS ANTILLES - PESTICIDE USE

Food and Agricultural Organization of the United Nations (FAO) Via delle Terme di Caracalla, 00100 Rome, Italy (Telephone Number in U.S. (202) 653-2400); *The State of Food and Agriculture.*

NETHERLANDS ANTILLES - PETROLEUM INDUSTRY

Food and Agricultural Organization of the United Nations (FAO) Via delle Terme di Caracalla, 00100 Rome, Italy (Telephone Number in U.S. (202) 653-2400); *The State of Food and Agriculture.*

St. Martin's Press, Inc., 175 Fifth Avenue, New York, New York 10010 (800) 221-7945; *The Statesman's Year-Book.*

Statistical Office of the United Nations, Publishing Service, New York, New York 10017 (800) 253-9646; *Statistical Yearbook.*

United Nations Conference on Trade and Development, Central Statistical Service, Palais des Nations, Geneva, Switzerland (Telephone in U.S. (800) 253-9646); *UNCTAD Commodity Yearbook.*

NETHERLANDS ANTILLES - PHOSPHATE ROCK PRODUCTION - See NETHERLANDS ANTILLES - MINING AND MINERAL PRODUCTS

NETHERLANDS ANTILLES - PIGS - See NETHERLANDS ANTILLES - LIVESTOCK AND POULTRY

NETHERLANDS ANTILLES - POPULATION

Central Intelligence Agency, Washington, D.C. 20505 (703) 482-1100, www.cia.gov; *The World Factbook.*

The Economist Intelligence Unit, 111 West 57th Street, New York, New York 10019 (800) 938-4685; *Netherlands Antilles Country Report;* and *The World Market Atlas.*

Euromonitor International, Inc., 122 South Michigan Avenue, Suite 1200, Chicago, Illinois 60603 (800) 577-EURO; *International Marketing Data and Statistics;* and *The World Economic Factbook.*

Europa Publications Limited, 18 Bedford Square, London, WC1B 3JN, England; *The Europa World Year Book.*

Food and Agricultural Organization of the United Nations (FAO), Via delle Terme di Caracalla, 00100 Rome, Italy (Telephone Number in U.S. (202) 653-2400); *Production Yearbook.*

International Labour Office, I.L.O. Publications, 1828 L Street, NW, Suite 801, Washington, D.C. 20036 (301) 638-3152; *Yearbook of Labour Statistics.*

St. Martin's Press, Inc., 175 Fifth Avenue, New York, New York 10010 (800) 221-7945; *The Statesman's Year-Book.*

Statistical Office of the United Nations, Publishing Service, New York, New York 10017 (800) 253-9646; *Demographic Yearbook; World Statistics Pocketbook;* and *Statistical Yearbook.*

United Nations Educational, Scientific and Cultural Organization (UNESCO), 7 Place de Fontenoy, F-75700 Paris, France (Telephone Number in U.S. (212) 963-5981); *Statistical Yearbook.*

The World Bank, 1818 H Street, NW, Washington, D.C. 20433 (202) 477-1234; *The World Bank Atlas.*

World Health Organization, Office of Publications, 20 Avenue Appia, CH-1211 Geneva 27, Switzerland (Telephone Number in U.S. (518) 436-9686); *World Health Statistics Annual.*

NETHERLANDS ANTILLES - PRICES

Food and Agricultural Organization of the United Nations (FAO), Via delle Terme di Caracalla, 00100 Rome, Italy (Telephone Number in U.S. (202) 653-2400); *Production Yearbook;* and *The State of Food and Agriculture.*

International Labour Office, I.L.O. Publications, 1828 L Street, NW, Suite 801, Washington, D.C. 20036 (301) 638-3152; *Yearbook of Labour Statistics.*

International Monetary Fund, 700 Nineteenth Street, NW, Washington, D.C. 20431 (202) 623-7000; *International Financial Statistics.*

NETHERLANDS ANTILLES - PRINTING AND WRITING PAPER - See NETHERLANDS ANTILLES - FORESTRY AND FOREST PRODUCTS

NETHERLANDS ANTILLES - PROPERTY TAXES - See NETHERLANDS ANTILLES - TAXATION

NETHERLANDS ANTILLES - RADIO BROADCASTING - See NETHERLANDS ANTILLES - BROADCASTING

NETHERLANDS ANTILLES - RADIO RECEIVERS

St. Martin's Press, Inc., 175 Fifth Avenue, New York, New York 10010 (800) 221-7945; *The Statesman's Year-Book.*

NETHERLANDS ANTILLES - RELIGION

Central Intelligence Agency, Washington, D.C. 20505 (703) 482-1100, www.cia.gov; *The World Factbook.*

St. Martin's Press, Inc., 175 Fifth Avenue, New York, New York 10010 (800) 221-7945; *The Statesman's Year-Book.*

NETHERLANDS ANTILLES - RENT PRICES

International Labour Office, I.L.O. Publications, 1828 L Street, NW, Suite 801, Washington, D.C. 20036 (301) 638-3152; *Yearbook of Labour Statistics.*

NETHERLANDS ANTILLES - RETAIL TRADE

Euromonitor International, Inc., 122 South Michigan Avenue, Suite 1200, Chicago, Illinois 60603 (800) 577-EURO; *World Marketing Data and Statistics.*

NETHERLANDS ANTILLES - ROUNDWOOD PRODUCTION - See NETHERLANDS ANTILLES - FORESTRY AND FOREST PRODUCTS

NETHERLANDS ANTILLES - SALT PRODUCTION - See NETHERLANDS ANTILLES - MINING AND MINERAL PRODUCTS

NETHERLANDS ANTILLES - SAWNWOOD PRODUCTION - See NETHERLANDS ANTILLES - FORESTRY AND FOREST PRODUCTS

NETHERLANDS ANTILLES - SHEEP - See NETHERLANDS ANTILLES - LIVESTOCK AND POULTRY

NETHERLANDS ANTILLES - SOCIAL DATA

Statistical Office of the United Nations, Publishing Service, New York, New York 10017 (800) 253-9646; *World Statistics Pocketbook.*

NETHERLANDS ANTILLES - SOCIAL SECURITY

International Monetary Fund, 700 Nineteenth Street, NW, Washington, D.C. 20431 (202) 623-7000; *Government Finance Statistics Yearbook.*

Statistical Office of the United Nations, Publishing Service, New York, New York 10017 (800) 253-9646; *National Accounts Statistics.*

NETHERLANDS ANTILLES - STAMP TAXES AND DUTIES - See NETHERLANDS ANTILLES - TAXATION

NETHERLANDS ANTILLES - STOCKS - COMMODITY - MARKET PRICE - INDEX

Food and Agricultural Organization of the United Nations (FAO) Via delle Terme di Caracalla, 00100 Rome, Italy (Telephone Number in U.S. (202) 653-2400); *The State of Food and Agriculture.*

NETHERLANDS ANTILLES - TAXATION

International Monetary Fund, 700 Nineteenth Street, NW, Washington, D.C. 20431 (202) 623-7000; *Government Finance Statistics Yearbook.*

NETHERLANDS ANTILLES - TELEGRAPH SERVICE

Statistical Office of the United Nations, Publishing Service, New York, New York 10017 (800) 253-9646; *Statistical Yearbook.*

NETHERLANDS ANTILLES - TELEPHONES IN USE

American Telephone and Telegraph Company, 26 Parsippany Road, Whippany, New Jersey 07981 (800) 222-0300; *The World's Telephones.*

Central Intelligence Agency, Washington, D.C. 20505 (703) 482-1100, www.cia.gov; *The World Factbook.*

Europa Publications Limited, 18 Bedford Square, London, WC1B 3JN, England; *The Europa World Year Book.*

St. Martin's Press, Inc., 175 Fifth Avenue, New York, New York 10010 (800) 221-7945; *The Statesman's Year-Book.*

Statistical Office of the United Nations, Publishing Service, New York, New York 10017 (800) 253-9646; *Statistical Yearbook;* and *World Statistics Pocketbook.*

NETHERLANDS ANTILLES - TELEVISION BROADCASTING - See NETHERLANDS ANTILLES - BROADCASTING

NETHERLANDS ANTILLES - TEXTILE INDUSTRY

United Nations Conference on Trade and Development, Central Statistical Service, Palais des Nations, Geneva, Switzerland (Telephone in U.S. (800) 253-9646); *UNCTAD Commodity Yearbook.*

NETHERLANDS ANTILLES - TOURISM

Euromonitor International, Inc., 122 South Michigan Avenue, Suite 1200, Chicago, Illinois 60603 (800) 577-EURO; *The World Economic Factbook;* and *World Marketing Data and Statistics.*

Europa Publications Limited, 18 Bedford Square, London, WC1B 3JN, England; *The Europa World Year Book.*

St. Martin's Press, Inc., 175 Fifth Avenue, New York, New York 10010 (800) 221-7945; *The Statesman's Year-Book.*

Statistical Office of the United Nations, Publishing Service, New York, New York 10017 (800) 253-9646; *Statistical Yearbook.*

NETHERLANDS ANTILLES - TRACTORS IN

USE

Statistical Office of the United Nations, Publishing Service, New York, New York 10017 (800) 253-9646; *Statistical Yearbook.*

NETHERLANDS ANTILLES - TRADE - See NETHERLANDS ANTILLES - FOREIGN TRADE

NETHERLANDS ANTILLES - TRANSPORTA-TION AND COMMUNICATIONS

Central Intelligence Agency, Washington, D.C. 20505 (703) 482-1100, www.cia.gov; *The World Factbook.*

Euromonitor International, Inc., 122 South Michigan Avenue, Suite 1200, Chicago, Illinois 60603 (800) 577-EURO; *International Marketing Data and Statistics;* and *World Marketing Data and Statistics.*

Europa Publications Limited, 18 Bedford Square, London, WC1B 3JN, England; *The Europa World Year Book.*

St. Martin's Press, Inc., 175 Fifth Avenue, New York, New York 10010 (800) 221-7945; *The Statesman's Year-Book.*

NETHERLANDS ANTILLES - UNEMPLOYMENT

Central Intelligence Agency, Washington, D.C. 20505 (703) 482-1100, www.cia.gov; *The World Factbook.*

International Labour Office, I.L.O. Publications,1828 L Street, NW, Suite 801, Washington, D.C. 20036 (301) 638-3152; *Yearbook of Labour Statistics.*

NETHERLANDS ANTILLES - VITAL STATISTICS

St. Martin's Press, Inc., 175 Fifth Avenue, New York, New York 10010 (800) 221-7945; *The Statesman's Year-Book.*

Statistical Office of the United Nations, Publishing Service, New York, New York 10017 (800) 253-9646; *Statistical Yearbook.*

World Health Organization, Office of Publications, 20 Avenue Appia, CH-1211 Geneva 27, Switzerland (Telephone Number in U.S. (518) 436-9686); *World Health Statistics Annual.*

NETHERLANDS ANTILLES - WAGES

International Labour Office, I.L.O. Publications, 1828 L Street, NW, Suite 801, Washington, D.C. 20036 (301) 638-3152; *Yearbook of Labour Statistics.*

Statistical Office of the United Nations, Publishing Service, New York, New York 10017 (800) 253-9646; *Statistical Yearbook.*

NETHERLANDS ANTILLES - WEATHER - See NETHERLANDS ANTILLES - CLIMATE

NETHERLANDS ANTILLES - WELFARE

International Monetary Fund, 700 Nineteenth Street, NW, Washington, D.C. 20431 (202) 623-7000; *Government Finance Statistics Yearbook.*

NEUROLOGISTS

American Medical Association, 515 North State Street, Chicago, Illinois 60610 (312) 464-5000; *Physician Characteristics and Distribution in the U.S.*

NEVADA - See also STATE DATA (FOR INDIVIDUAL STATES)

Nevada - Primary Statistics Source

Department of Administration, Budget and Planning Division, Capitol Complex, Carson City, Nevada 89710 (702) 687-4065; *Nevada Statistical Abstract.*

Nevada - State Data Center

Nevada State Library and Archives, 100 Stewart Street, Carson City, Nevada 89710, Ms. Joyce M. Cox (775) 684-3326.

Nevada Medicaid Office, 2527 N. Carson Street, Carson City, Nevada 89701, Ms. Diane Nassir (775) 687-5757.

NEW BUSINESS INCORPORATIONS

Dun and Bradstreet Corporation, 299 Park Avenue, Twenty-fourth Floor, New York, New York 10171 (212) 593-6800; *A Decade of Business Starts;* and *Business Failure Record.*

New Caledonia - National Statistical Office

Direction Territoriale de la Statistique et des Etudes Economiques, BP 823, Noumea, New Caledonia.

New Caledonia - Primary Statistics Source

Direction Territoriale de la Statistique et des Etudes Economiques, BP 323, Noumea, New Caledonia, *Annuaire Statistique de la Nouvelle Caledonia et Dependances.*

NEW CALEDONIA - AGRICULTURE

Economist Intelligence Unit, 111 West 57th Street, New York, New York 10019 (800) 938-4685; *New Caledonia Country Report.*

Euromonitor International, Inc., 122 South Michigan Avenue, Suite 1200, Chicago, Illinois 60603 (800) 577-EURO; *World Marketing Data and Statistics*.

Europa Publications Limited, 18 Bedford Square, London, WC1B 3JN, England; *The Europa World Year Book*.

Food and Agricultural Organization of the United Nations (FAO) Via delle Terme di Caracalla, 00100 Rome, Italy (Telephone Number in U.S. (202) 653-2400); *Production Yearbook; The State of Food and Agriculture;* and *Trade Yearbook*.

St. Martin's Press, Inc., 175 Fifth Avenue, New York, New York 10010 (800) 221-7945; *The Statesman's Year-Book*.

Statistical Office of the United Nations, Publishing Service, New York, New York 10017 (800) 253-9646; *Statistical Yearbook*.

United Nations Conference on Trade and Development, Central Statistical Service, Palais des Nations, Geneva, Switzerland (Telephone in U.S. (800) 253-9646); *UNCTAD Commodity Yearbook*.

NEW CALEDONIA - AIRLINE SERVICE

Europa Publications Limited, 18 Bedford Square, London, WC1B 3JN, England; *The Europa World Year Book*.

St. Martin's Press, Inc., 175 Fifth Avenue, New York, New York 10010 (800) 221-7945; *The Statesman's Year-Book*.

NEW CALEDONIA - AIRPORTS

Central Intelligence Agency, Washington, D.C. 20505 (703) 482-1100, www.cia.gov; *The World Factbook*.

NEW CALEDONIA - ANIMAL HEALTH

Food and Agricultural Organization of the United Nations (FAO), Via delle Terme di Caracalla, 00100 Rome, Italy (Telephone Number in U.S. (202) 653-2400); *Animal Health Yearbook*.

NEW CALEDONIA - AREA AND DENSITY OF POPULATION

Central Intelligence Agency, Washington, D.C. 20505 (703) 482-1100, www.cia.gov; *The World Factbook*.

Euromonitor International, Inc., 122 South Michigan Avenue, Suite 1200, Chicago, Illinois 60603 (800) 577-EURO; *The World Economic Factbook*.

Europa Publications Limited, 18 Bedford Square, London, WC1B 3JN, England; *The Europa World Year Book*.

Food and Agricultural Organization of the United Nations (FAO) Via delle Terme di Caracalla, 00100 Rome, Italy (Telephone Number in U.S. (202) 653-2400); *The State of Food and Agriculture*.

St. Martin's Press, Inc., 175 Fifth Avenue, New York, New York 10010 (800) 221-7945; *The Statesman's Year-Book*.

Statistical Office of the United Nations, Publishing Service, New York, New York 10017 (800) 253-9646; *Statistical Yearbook*.

United Nations Educational, Scientific and Cultural Organization (UNESCO), 7 Place de Fontenoy, F-75700 Paris, France (Telephone Number in U.S. (212) 963-5981); *Statistical Yearbook*.

NEW CALEDONIA - BANKING

Euromonitor International, Inc., 122 South Michigan Avenue, Suite 1200, Chicago, Illinois 60603 (800) 577-EURO; *World Marketing Data and Statistics*.

St. Martin's Press, Inc., 175 Fifth Avenue, New York, New York 10010 (800) 221-7945; *The Statesman's Year-Book*.

NEW CALEDONIA - BEER PRODUCTION - See NEW CALEDONIA - BEVERAGES

NEW CALEDONIA - BEVERAGES

Statistical Office of the United Nations, Publishing Service, New York, New York 10017 (800) 253-9646; *Statistical Yearbook*.

NEW CALEDONIA - BIRTH RATES

Central Intelligence Agency, Washington, D.C. 20505 (703) 482-1100, www.cia.gov; *The World Factbook*.

Euromonitor International, Inc., 122 South Michigan Avenue, Suite 1200, Chicago, Illinois 60603 (800) 577-EURO; *International Marketing Data and Statistics;* and *The World Economic Factbook*.

Europa Publications Limited, 18 Bedford Square, London, WC1B 3JN, England; *The Europa World Year Book*.

St. Martin's Press, Inc., 175 Fifth Avenue, New York, New York 10010 (800) 221-7945; *The Statesman's Year-Book*.

Statistical Office of the United Nations, Publishing Service, New York, New York 10017 (800) 253-9646; *Demographic Yearbook;* and *Statistical Yearbook*.

World Health Organization, Office of Publications, 20 Avenue Appia, CH-1211 Geneva 27, Switzerland (Telephone Number in U.S. (518) 436-9686); *World Health Statistics Annual*.

NEW CALEDONIA - BROADCASTING

Billboard Limited, Post Office Box 9027, 1006 AA Amsterdam, The Netherlands (Telephone Number in U.S. (212) 764-7300); *World Radio TV Handbook*.

Central Intelligence Agency, Washington, D.C. 20505 (703) 482-1100, www.cia.gov; *The World Factbook*.

Euromonitor International, Inc., 122 South Michigan Avenue, Suite 1200, Chicago, Illinois 60603 (800) 577-EURO; *World Marketing Data and Statistics*.

St. Martin's Press, Inc., 175 Fifth Avenue, New York, New York 10010 (800) 221-7945; *The Statesman's Year-Book*.

NEW CALEDONIA - BUDGET

Central Intelligence Agency, Washington, D.C. 20505 (703) 482-1100, www.cia.gov; *The World Factbook*.

NEW CALEDONIA - CALORIE SUPPLY

Food and Agricultural Organization of the United Nations (FAO) Via delle Terme di Caracalla, 00100 Rome, Italy (Telephone Number in U.S. (202) 653-2400); *The State of Food and Agriculture*.

NEW CALEDONIA - CATTLE - See NEW CALEDONIA - LIVESTOCK AND POULTRY

NEW CALEDONIA - CEMENT PRODUCTION - See NEW CALEDONIA - MINING AND MINERAL PRODUCTS

NEW CALEDONIA - CLIMATE

St. Martin's Press, Inc., 175 Fifth Avenue, New York, New York 10010 (800) 221-7945; *The Statesman's Year-Book*.

NEW CALEDONIA - CLOTHING EXPORTS AND IMPORTS - See NEW CALEDONIA - TEXTILE INDUSTRY

NEW CALEDONIA - COAL PRODUCTION - See NEW CALEDONIA - MINING AND MINERAL PRODUCTS

NEW CALEDONIA - COBALT PRODUCTION AND CONSUMPTION - See NEW CALEDONIA - MINING AND MINERAL PRODUCTS

NEW CALEDONIA - COMMERCE

St. Martin's Press, Inc., 175 Fifth Avenue, New York, New York 10010 (800) 221-7945; *The Statesman's Year-Book*.

NEW CALEDONIA - CONSTRUCTION INDUSTRY

Statistical Office of the United Nations, Publishing Service, New York, New York

10017 (800) 253-9646; *Statistical Yearbook.*

NEW CALEDONIA - CONSUMER PRICE INDEX

Europa Publications Limited, 18 Bedford Square, London, WC1B 3JN, England; *The Europa World Year Book.*

Statistical Office of the United Nations, Publishing Service, New York, New York 10017 (800) 253-9646; *Statistical Yearbook.*

NEW CALEDONIA - CONSUMER PRICES

Euromonitor International, Inc., 122 South Michigan Avenue, Suite 1200, Chicago, Illinois 60603 (800) 577-EURO; *World Marketing Data and Statistics.*

International Labour Office, I.L.O. Publications, 1828 L Street, NW, Suite 801, Washington, D.C. 20036 (301) 638-3152; *Yearbook of Labour Statistics.*

NEW CALEDONIA - CORN PRODUCTION - See NEW CALEDONIA - CROPS

NEW CALEDONIA - CROPS

Europa Publications Limited, 18 Bedford Square, London, WC1B 3JN, England; *The Europa World Year Book.*

Food and Agricultural Organization of the United Nations (FAO) Via delle Terme di Caracalla, 00100 Rome, Italy (Telephone Number in U.S. (202) 653-2400); *Production Yearbook;* and *The State of Food and Agriculture.*

St. Martin's Press, Inc., 175 Fifth Avenue, New York, New York 10010 (800) 221-7945; *The Statesman's Year-Book.*

Statistical Office of the United Nations, Publishing Service, New York, New York 10017 (800) 253-9646; *Statistical Yearbook.*

United Nations Conference on Trade and Development, Central Statistical Service, Palais des Nations, Geneva, Switzerland (Telephone in U.S. (800) 253-9646); *UNCTAD Commodity Yearbook.*

NEW CALEDONIA - CUSTOMS DUTIES

St. Martin's Press, Inc., 175 Fifth Avenue, New York, New York 10010 (800) 221-7945; *The Statesman's Year-Book.*

NEW CALEDONIA - DAIRY PRODUCTS

Food and Agricultural Organization of the United Nations (FAO) Via delle Terme di Caracalla, 00100 Rome, Italy (Telephone Number in U.S. (202) 653-2400); *The State of Food and Agriculture.*

St. Martin's Press, Inc., 175 Fifth

Avenue, New York, New York 10010 (800) 221-7945; *The Statesman's Year-Book.*

NEW CALEDONIA - DEATH RATES - See NEW CALEDONIA - MORTALITY

NEW CALEDONIA - DEMOGRAPHY

Euromonitor International, Inc., 122 South Michigan Avenue, Suite 1200, Chicago, Illinois 60603 (800) 577-EURO; *International Marketing Data and Statistics; The World Economic Factbook;* and *World Marketing Data and Statistics.*

NEW CALEDONIA - DEVELOPMENT ASSISTANCE

Statistical Office of the United Nations, Publishing Service, New York, New York 10017 (800) 253-9646; *Statistical Yearbook.*

NEW CALEDONIA - DISEASES - See NEW CALEDONIA - HEALTH

NEW CALEDONIA - DIVORCE RATES

Statistical Office of the United Nations, Publishing Service, New York, New York 10017 (800) 253-9646; *Demographic Yearbook;* and *Statistical Yearbook.*

NEW CALEDONIA - ECONOMY

Central Intelligence Agency, Washington, D.C. 20505 (703) 482-1100, www.cia.gov; *The World Factbook.*

Economist Intelligence Unit, 111 West 57th Street, New York, New York 10019 (800) 938-4685; *New Caledonia Country Report.*

Euromonitor International, Inc., 122 South Michigan Avenue, Suite 1200, Chicago, Illinois 60603 (800) 577-EURO; *The World Economic Factbook;* and *World Marketing Data and Statistics.*

Europa Publications Limited, 18 Bedford Square, London, WC1B 3JN, England; *The Europa World Year Book.*

St. Martin's Press, Inc., 175 Fifth Avenue, New York, New York 10010 (800) 221-7945; *The Statesman's Year-Book.*

Statistical Office of the United Nations, Publishing Service, New York, New York 10017 (800) 253-9646; *World Statistics Pocketbook.*

The World Bank, 1818 H Street, NW, Washington, D.C. 20433 (202) 477-1234; *The World Bank Atlas.*

NEW CALEDONIA - EDUCATION

Euromonitor International, Inc., 122 South Michigan Avenue, Suite 1200, Chicago, Illinois 60603 (800) 577-EURO;

International Marketing Data and Statistics; and *World Marketing Data and Statistics.*

Europa Publications Limited, 18 Bedford Square, London, WC1B 3JN, England; *The Europa World Year Book.*

St. Martin's Press, Inc., 175 Fifth Avenue, New York, New York 10010 (800) 221-7945; *The Statesman's Year-Book.*

United Nations Educational, Scientific and Cultural Organization (UNESCO), 7 Place de Fontenoy, F-75700 Paris, France (Telephone Number in U.S. (212) 963-5981); *Statistical Yearbook.*

NEW CALEDONIA - EGG PRODUCTION AND CONSUMPTION - See NEW CALEDONIA - DAIRY PRODUCTS

NEW CALEDONIA - ELECTRICITY

Central Intelligence Agency, Washington, D.C. 20505 (703) 482-1100, www.cia.gov; *The World Factbook.*

St. Martin's Press, Inc., 175 Fifth Avenue, New York, New York 10010 (800) 221-7945; *The Statesman's Year-Book.*

Statistical Office of the United Nations, Publishing Service, New York, New York 10017 (800) 253-9646; *Statistical Yearbook.*

NEW CALEDONIA - EMPLOYMENT

Euromonitor International, Inc., 122 South Michigan Avenue, Suite 1200, Chicago, Illinois 60603 (800) 577-EURO; *International Marketing Data and Statistics.*

International Labour Office, I.L.O. Publications, 1828 L Street, NW, Suite 801, Washington, D.C. 20036 (301) 638-3152; *Yearbook of Labour Statistics.*

NEW CALEDONIA - ENERGY

Euromonitor International, Inc., 122 South Michigan Avenue, Suite 1200, Chicago, Illinois 60603 (800) 577-EURO; *International Marketing Data and Statistics; The World Economic Factbook;* and *World Marketing Data and Statistics.*

Food and Agricultural Organization of the United Nations (FAO) Via delle Terme di Caracalla, 00100 Rome, Italy (Telephone Number in U.S. (202) 653-2400); *The State of Food and Agriculture.*

St. Martin's Press, Inc., 175 Fifth Avenue, New York, New York 10010 (800) 221-7945; *The Statesman's Year-Book.*

Statistical Office of the United Nations, Publishing Service, New York, New York 10017 (800) 253-9646; *Energy Statistics Yearbook; World Statistics Pocketbook;* and *Statistical Yearbook.*

The World Bank, 1818 H Street, NW, Washington, D.C. 20433 (202) 477-1234; *The World Bank Atlas*.

NEW CALEDONIA - ENVIRONMENT

Economist Intelligence Unit, 111 West 57th Street, New York, New York 10019 (800) 938-4685; *New Caledonia Country Report*.

Statistical Office of the United Nations, Publishing Service, New York, New York 10017 (800) 253-9646; *World Statistics Pocketbook*.

NEW CALEDONIA - EXCHANGE RATES

Central Intelligence Agency, Washington, D.C. 20505 (703) 482-1100, www.cia.gov; *The World Factbook*.

Euromonitor International, Inc., 122 South Michigan Avenue, Suite 1200, Chicago, Illinois 60603 (800) 577-EURO; *International Marketing Data and Statistics;* and *The World Economic Factbook*.

Europa Publications Limited, 18 Bedford Square, London, WC1B 3JN, England; *The Europa World Year Book*.

Statistical Office of the United Nations, Publishing Service, New York, New York 10017 (800) 253-9646; *World Statistics Pocketbook*.

Walden Publishing Ltd., Two Market Street, Saffron Walden Essex, CB10 1HZ, England; *The World of Information Asia and Pacific Review*.

NEW CALEDONIA - EXPORTS

Central Intelligence Agency, Washington, D.C. 20505 (703) 482-1100, www.cia.gov; *The World Factbook*.

Economist Intelligence Unit, 111 West 57th Street, New York, New York 10019 (800) 938-4685; *New Caledonia Country Report*.

Euromonitor International, Inc., 122 South Michigan Avenue, Suite 1200, Chicago, Illinois 60603 (800) 577-EURO; *International Marketing Data and Statistics;* and *The World Economic Factbook*.

Europa Publications Limited, 18 Bedford Square, London, WC1B 3JN, England; *The Europa World Year Book*.

Food and Agricultural Organization of the United Nations (FAO) Via delle Terme di Caracalla, 00100 Rome, Italy (Telephone Number in U.S. (202) 653-2400); *The State of Food and Agriculture*.

International Monetary Fund, 700 Nineteenth Street, NW, Washington, D.C.

20431 (202) 623-7000; *Direction of Trade Statistics*.

South Pacific Commission, Post Box D5, Noumea Cedex, New Caledonia; *Statistical Bulletin of the South Pacific: Overseas Trade*.

St. Martin's Press, Inc., 175 Fifth Avenue, New York, New York 10010 (800) 221-7945; *The Statesman's Year-Book*.

Walden Publishing Ltd., Two Market Street, Saffron Walden Essex, CB10 1HZ, England; *The World of Information Asia and Pacific Review*.

NEW CALEDONIA - EXTERNAL TRADE

Euromonitor International, Inc., 122 South Michigan Avenue, Suite 1200, Chicago, Illinois 60603 (800) 577-EURO; *World Marketing Data and Statistics*.

Food and Agricultural Organization of the United Nations (FAO) Via delle Terme di Caracalla, 00100 Rome, Italy (Telephone Number in U.S. (202) 653-2400); *The State of Food and Agriculture;* and *Trade Yearbook*.

Statistical Office of the United Nations, Publishing Service, New York, New York 10017 (800) 253-9646; *Statistical Yearbook*.

NEW CALEDONIA - FARM CROPS - See NEW CALEDONIA - CROPS

NEW CALEDONIA - FERTILITY RATES

Central Intelligence Agency, Washington, D.C. 20505 (703) 482-1100, www.cia.gov; *The World Factbook*.

The World Bank, 1818 H Street, NW, Washington, D.C. 20433 (202) 477-1234; *The World Bank Atlas*.

NEW CALEDONIA - FERTILIZER

Food and Agricultural Organization of the United Nations (FAO), Via delle Terme di Caracalla, 00100 Rome, Italy (Telephone Number in U.S. (202) 653-2400); *Fertilizer Yearbook;* and *The State of Food and Agriculture*.

Statistical Office of the United Nations, Publishing Service, New York, New York 10017 (800) 253-9646; *Statistical Yearbook*.

NEW CALEDONIA - FETAL MORTALITY - See NEW CALEDONIA - MORTALITY

NEW CALEDONIA - FINANCE

Economist Intelligence Unit, 111 West 57th Street, New York, New York 10019 (800) 938-4685; *New Caledonia Country Report*.

Europa Publications Limited, 18 Bedford Square, London, WC1B 3JN, England; *The Europa World Year Book*.

NEW CALEDONIA - FISHERIES

Europa Publications Limited, 18 Bedford Square, London, WC1B 3JN, England; *The Europa World Year Book*.

Food and Agricultural Organization of the United Nations (FAO) Via delle Terme di Caracalla, 00100 Rome, Italy (Telephone Number in U.S. (202) 653-2400); *The State of Food and Agriculture;* and *Yearbook of Fishery Statistics*.

St. Martin's Press, Inc., 175 Fifth Avenue, New York, New York 10010 (800) 221-7945; *The Statesman's Year-Book*.

United Nations Conference on Trade and Development, Central Statistical Service, Palais des Nations, Geneva, Switzerland (Telephone in U.S. (800) 253-9646); *UNCTAD Commodity Yearbook*.

NEW CALEDONIA - FOOD

Food and Agricultural Organization of the United Nations (FAO), Via delle Terme di Caracalla, 00100 Rome, Italy (Telephone Number in U.S. (202) 653-2400); *Production Yearbook;* and *The State of Food and Agriculture*.

South Pacific Commission, Post Box D5, Noumea Cedex, New Caledonia; *Statistical Bulletin of the South Pacific: Retail Price Indexes*.

United Nations Conference on Trade and Development, Central Statistical Service, Palais des Nations, Geneva, Switzerland (Telephone in U.S. (800) 253-9646); *UNCTAD Commodity Yearbook*.

NEW CALEDONIA - FOREIGN DEBT

Walden Publishing Ltd., Two Market Street, Saffron Walden Essex, CB10 1HZ, England; *The World of Information Asia and Pacific Review*.

NEW CALEDONIA - FOREIGN TRADE

Economist Intelligence Unit, 111 West 57th Street, New York, New York 10019 (800) 938-4685; *New Caledonia Country Report*.

Euromonitor International, Inc., 122 South Michigan Avenue, Suite 1200, Chicago, Illinois 60603 (800) 577-EURO; *The World Economic Factbook*.

Europa Publications Limited, 18 Bedford Square, London, WC1B 3JN, England; *The Europa World Year Book*.

Food and Agricultural Organization of

the United Nations (FAO) Via delle Terme di Caracalla, 00100 Rome, Italy (Telephone Number in U.S. (202) 653-2400); *The State of Food and Agriculture.*

South Pacific Commission, Post Box D5, Noumea Cedex, New Caledonia; *Statistical Bulletin of the South Pacific: Overseas Trade.*

St. Martin's Press, Inc., 175 Fifth Avenue, New York, New York 10010 (800) 221-7945; *The Statesman's Year-Book.*

Statistical Office of the United Nations, Publishing Service, New York, New York 10017 (800) 253-9646; *International Trade Statistics Yearbook;* and *Statistical Yearbook.*

United Nations Conference on Trade and Development, Central Statistical Service, Palais des Nations, Geneva, Switzerland (Telephone in U.S. (800) 253-9646); *UNCTAD Commodity Yearbook.*

NEW CALEDONIA - FORESTRY AND FOREST PRODUCTS

Europa Publications Limited, 18 Bedford Square, London, WC1B 3JN, England; *The Europa World Year Book.*

Food and Agricultural Organization of the United Nations (FAO) Via delle Terme di Caracalla, 00100 Rome, Italy (Telephone Number in U.S. (202) 653-2400); *The State of Food and Agriculture;* and *Yearbook of Forest Products.*

St. Martin's Press, Inc., 175 Fifth Avenue, New York, New York 10010 (800) 221-7945; *The Statesman's Year-Book.*

United Nations Conference on Trade and Development, Central Statistical Service, Palais des Nations, Geneva, Switzerland (Telephone in U.S. (800) 253-9646); *UNCTAD Commodity Yearbook.*

NEW CALEDONIA - GENERAL MORTALITY - See NEW CALEDONIA - MORTALITY

NEW CALEDONIA - GOVERNMENT

Central Intelligence Agency, Washington, D.C. 20505 (703) 482-1100, www.cia.gov; *The World Factbook.*

St. Martin's Press, Inc., 175 Fifth Avenue, New York, New York 10010 (800) 221-7945; *The Statesman's Year-Book.*

Statistical Office of the United Nations, Publishing Service, New York, New York 10017 (800) 253-9646; *National Accounts Statistics.*

NEW CALEDONIA - GRAIN PRODUCTION - See NEW CALEDONIA - CROPS

NEW CALEDONIA - GROSS DOMESTIC PRODUCT

Economist Intelligence Unit, 111 West 57th Street, New York, New York 10019 (800) 938-4685; *New Caledonia Country Report.*

Euromonitor International, Inc., 122 South Michigan Avenue, Suite 1200, Chicago, Illinois 60603 (800) 577-EURO; *International Marketing Data and Statistics;* and *The World Economic Factbook.*

Europa Publications Limited, 18 Bedford Square, London, WC1B 3JN, England; *The Europa World Year Book.*

Statistical Office of the United Nations, Publishing Service, New York, New York 10017 (800) 253-9646; *National Accounts Statistics;* and *Statistical Yearbook.*

NEW CALEDONIA - GROSS NATIONAL PRODUCT

Walden Publishing Ltd., Two Market Street, Saffron Walden Essex, CB10 1HZ, England; *The World of Information Asia and Pacific Review.*

The World Bank, 1818 H Street, NW, Washington, D.C. 20433 (202) 477-1234; *The World Bank Atlas.*

NEW CALEDONIA - HEALTH

Euromonitor International, Inc., 122 South Michigan Avenue, Suite 1200, Chicago, Illinois 60603 (800) 577-EURO; *World Marketing Data and Statistics.*

South Pacific Commission, Post Box D5, Noumea Cedex, New Caledonia; *Statistical Bulletin of the South Pacific: Retail Price Indexes.*

St. Martin's Press, Inc., 175 Fifth Avenue, New York, New York 10010 (800) 221-7945; *The Statesman's Year-Book.*

Statistical Office of the United Nations, Publishing Service, New York, New York 10017 (800) 253-9646; *Statistical Yearbook.*

World Health Organization, Office of Publications, 20 Avenue Appia, CH-1211 Geneva 27, Switzerland (Telephone Number in U.S. (518) 436-9686); *World Health Statistics Annual.*

NEW CALEDONIA - HIDE PRODUCTION

Food and Agricultural Organization of the United Nations (FAO), Via delle Terme di Caracalla, 00100 Rome, Italy (Telephone Number in U.S. (202) 653-2400); *Production Yearbook.*

NEW CALEDONIA - HIGHWAYS

Central Intelligence Agency, Washington, D.C. 20505 (703) 482-1100, www.cia.gov; *The World Factbook.*

St. Martin's Press, Inc., 175 Fifth Avenue, New York, New York 10010 (800) 221-7945; *The Statesman's Year-Book.*

NEW CALEDONIA - HORSES - See NEW CALEDONIA - LIVESTOCK AND POULTRY

NEW CALEDONIA - HOURS OF WORK - See NEW CALEDONIA - EMPLOYMENT

NEW CALEDONIA - HOUSING AND HOUSING UNITS

Euromonitor International, Inc., 122 South Michigan Avenue, Suite 1200, Chicago, Illinois 60603 (800) 577-EURO; *World Marketing Data and Statistics.*

South Pacific Commission, Post Box D5, Noumea Cedex, New Caledonia; *Statistical Bulletin of the South Pacific: Retail Price Indexes.*

NEW CALEDONIA - HOUSING EXPENDITURES

South Pacific Commission, Post Box D5, Noumea Cedex, New Caledonia; *Statistical Bulletin of the South Pacific: Retail Price Indexes.*

NEW CALEDONIA - ILLITERATE POPULATION

Central Intelligence Agency, Washington, D.C. 20505 (703) 482-1100, www.cia.gov; *The World Factbook.*

Euromonitor International, Inc., 122 South Michigan Avenue, Suite 1200, Chicago, Illinois 60603 (800) 577-EURO; *The World Economic Factbook.*

United Nations Educational, Scientific and Cultural Organization (UNESCO), 7 Place de Fontenoy, F-75700 Paris, France (Telephone Number in U.S. (212) 963-5981); *Statistical Yearbook.*

NEW CALEDONIA - IMPORTS

Central Intelligence Agency, Washington, D.C. 20505 (703) 482-1100, www.cia.gov; *The World Factbook.*

Economist Intelligence Unit, 111 West 57th Street, New York, New York 10019 (800) 938-4685; *New Caledonia Country Report.*

Euromonitor International, Inc., 122 South Michigan Avenue, Suite 1200, Chicago, Illinois 60603 (800) 577-EURO; *International Marketing Data and Statistics;* and *The World Economic Factbook.*

Europa Publications Limited, 18

Bedford Square, London, WC1B 3JN, England; *The Europa World Year Book.*

Food and Agricultural Organization of the United Nations (FAO) Via delle Terme di Caracalla, 00100 Rome, Italy (Telephone Number in U.S. (202) 653-2400); *The State of Food and Agriculture.*

International Monetary Fund, 700 Nineteenth Street, NW, Washington, D.C. 20431 (202) 623-7000; *Direction of Trade Statistics.*

South Pacific Commission, Post Box D5, Noumea Cedex, New Caledonia; *Statistical Bulletin of the South Pacific: Overseas Trade.*

St. Martin's Press, Inc., 175 Fifth Avenue, New York, New York 10010 (800) 221-7945; *The Statesman's Year-Book.*

Walden Publishing Ltd., Two Market Street, Saffron Walden Essex, CB10 1HZ, England; *The World of Information Asia and Pacific Review.*

NEW CALEDONIA - INDUSTRY

Central Intelligence Agency, Washington, D.C. 20505 (703) 482-1100, www.cia.gov; *The World Factbook.*

Economist Intelligence Unit, 111 West 57th Street, New York, New York 10019 (800) 938-4685; *New Caledonia Country Report.*

Euromonitor International, Inc., 122 South Michigan Avenue, Suite 1200, Chicago, Illinois 60603 (800) 577-EURO; *The World Economic Factbook;* and *World Marketing Data and Statistics.*

Europa Publications Limited, 18 Bedford Square, London, WC1B 3JN, England; *The Europa World Year Book.*

International Labour Office, I.L.O. Publications, 1828 L Street, NW, Suite 801, Washington, D.C. 20036 (301) 638-3152; *Yearbook of Labour Statistics.*

St. Martin's Press, Inc., 175 Fifth Avenue, New York, New York 10010 (800) 221-7945; *The Statesman's Year-Book.*

NEW CALEDONIA - INFANT AND MATERNAL MORTALITY - See NEW CALEDONIA - MORTALITY

NEW CALEDONIA - IRON ORE PRODUCTION AND CONSUMPTION - See NEW CALEDONIA - MINING AND MINERAL PRODUCTS

NEW CALEDONIA - LABOR

Central Intelligence Agency, Washington, D.C. 20505 (703) 482-1100,

www.cia.gov; *The World Factbook.*

Euromonitor International, Inc., 122 South Michigan Avenue, Suite 1200, Chicago, Illinois 60603 (800) 577-EURO; *International Marketing Data and Statistics;* and *World Marketing Data and Statistics.*

Europa Publications Limited, 18 Bedford Square, London, WC1B 3JN, England; *The Europa World Year Book.*

Food and Agricultural Organization of the United Nations (FAO) Via delle Terme di Caracalla, 00100 Rome, Italy (Telephone Number in U.S. (202) 653-2400); *The State of Food and Agriculture.*

International Labour Office, I.L.O. Publications, 1828 L Street, NW, Suite 801, Washington, D.C. 20036 (301) 638-3152; *Yearbook of Labour Statistics.*

St. Martin's Press, Inc., 175 Fifth Avenue, New York, New York 10010 (800) 221-7945; *The Statesman's Year-Book.*

The World Bank, 1818 H Street, NW, Washington, D.C. 20433 (202) 477-1234; *The World Bank Atlas.*

NEW CALEDONIA - LAND USE

Central Intelligence Agency, Washington, D.C. 20505 (703) 482-1100, www.cia.gov; *The World Factbook.*

Euromonitor International, Inc., 122 South Michigan Avenue, Suite 1200, Chicago, Illinois 60603 (800) 577-EURO; *International Marketing Data and Statistics.*

Food and Agricultural Organization of the United Nations (FAO), Via delle Terme di Caracalla, 00100 Rome, Italy (Telephone Number in U.S. (202) 653-2400); *Production Yearbook.*

NEW CALEDONIA - LIBRARIES

United Nations Educational, Scientific and Cultural Organization (UNESCO), 7 Place de Fontenoy, F-75700 Paris, France (Telephone Number in U.S. (212) 963-5981); *Statistical Yearbook.*

NEW CALEDONIA - LIFE EXPECTANCY

Central Intelligence Agency, Washington, D.C. 20505 (703) 482-1100, www.cia.gov; *The World Factbook.*

Euromonitor International, Inc., 122 South Michigan Avenue, Suite 1200, Chicago, Illinois 60603 (800) 577-EURO; *The World Economic Factbook.*

Statistical Office of the United Nations, Publishing Service, New York, New York 10017 (800) 253-9646; *World Statistics Pocketbook.*

The World Bank, 1818 H Street, NW, Washington, D.C. 20433 (202) 477-1234; *The World Bank Atlas.*

NEW CALEDONIA - LITERACY RATE

Euromonitor International, Inc., 122 South Michigan Avenue, Suite 1200, Chicago, Illinois 60603 (800) 577-EURO; *World Marketing Data and Statistics.*

NEW CALEDONIA - LIVESTOCK AND POULTRY

Europa Publications Limited, 18 Bedford Square, London, WC1B 3JN, England; *The Europa World Year Book.*

Food and Agricultural Organization of the United Nations (FAO), Via delle Terme di Caracalla, 00100 Rome, Italy (Telephone Number in U.S. (202) 653-2400); *Production Yearbook;* and *The State of Food and Agriculture.*

St. Martin's Press, Inc., 175 Fifth Avenue, New York, New York 10010 (800) 221-7945; *The Statesman's Year-Book.*

Statistical Office of the United Nations, Publishing Service, New York, New York 10017 (800) 253-9646; *Statistical Yearbook.*

United Nations Conference on Trade and Development, Central Statistical Service, Palais des Nations, Geneva, Switzerland (Telephone in U.S. (800) 253-9646); *UNCTAD Commodity Yearbook.*

NEW CALEDONIA - MAIL - PIECES SENT OR RECEIVED

Statistical Office of the United Nations, Publishing Service, New York, New York 10017 (800) 253-9646; *Statistical Yearbook.*

NEW CALEDONIA - MARRIAGE RATES

Statistical Office of the United Nations, Publishing Service, New York, New York 10017 (800) 253-9646; *Demographic Yearbook;* and *Statistical Yearbook.*

NEW CALEDONIA - MEAT PRODUCTION - See NEW CALEDONIA - LIVESTOCK AND POULTRY

NEW CALEDONIA - MERCHANT SHIPPING

Europa Publications Limited, 18 Bedford Square, London, WC1B 3JN, England; *The Europa World Year Book.*

St. Martin's Press, Inc., 175 Fifth Avenue, New York, New York 10010 (800) 221-7945; *The Statesman's Year-Book.*

Statistical Office of the United Nations, Publishing Service, New York, New York 10017 (800) 253-9646; *Statistical Yearbook.*

NEW CALEDONIA - MILITARY

Central Intelligence Agency, Washington, D.C. 20505 (703) 482-1100, www.cia.gov; *The World Factbook.*

Euromonitor International, Inc., 122 South Michigan Avenue, Suite 1200, Chicago, Illinois 60603 (800) 577-EURO; *World Marketing Data and Statistics.*

NEW CALEDONIA - MINING AND MINERAL PRODUCTS

Commodity Research Bureau, Inc., 30 South Wacker Drive, Chicago, Illinois 60606 (312) 454-1801; *Commodity Year Book.*

Europa Publications Limited, 18 Bedford Square, London, WC1B 3JN, England; *The Europa World Year Book.*

South Pacific Commission, Post Box D5, Noumea Cedex, New Caledonia; *Statistical Bulletin of the South Pacific: Retail Price Indexes.*

St. Martin's Press, Inc., 175 Fifth Avenue, New York, New York 10010 (800) 221-7945; *The Statesman's Year-Book.*

Statistical Office of the United Nations, Publishing Service, New York, New York 10017 (800) 253-9646; *Statistical Yearbook.*

United Nations Conference on Trade and Development, Central Statistical Service, Palais des Nations, Geneva, Switzerland (Telephone in U.S. (800) 253-9646); *UNCTAD Commodity Yearbook.*

NEW CALEDONIA - MONEY SUPPLY

Economist Intelligence Unit, 111 West 57th Street, New York, New York 10019 (800) 938-4685; *New Caledonia Country Report.*

Europa Publications Limited, 18 Bedford Square, London, WC1B 3JN, England; *The Europa World Year Book.*

NEW CALEDONIA - MORTALITY

Central Intelligence Agency, Washington, D.C. 20505 (703) 482-1100, www.cia.gov; *The World Factbook.*

Euromonitor International, Inc., 122 South Michigan Avenue, Suite 1200, Chicago, Illinois 60603 (800) 577-EURO; *International Marketing Data and Statistics;* and *The World Economic Factbook.*

Europa Publications Limited, 18 Bedford Square, London, WC1B 3JN, England; *The Europa World Year Book.*

St. Martin's Press, Inc., 175 Fifth Avenue, New York, New York 10010 (800) 221-7945; *The Statesman's Year-Book.*

Statistical Office of the United Nations, Publishing Service, New York, New York 10017 (800) 253-9646; *Demographic Yearbook; World Statistics Pocketbook;* and *Statistical Yearbook.*

The World Bank, 1818 H Street, NW, Washington, D.C. 20433 (202) 477-1234; *The World Bank Atlas.*

World Health Organization, Office of Publications, 20 Avenue Appia, CH-1211 Geneva 27, Switzerland (Telephone Number in U.S. (518) 436-9686); *World Health Statistics Annual.*

NEW CALEDONIA - MOTION PICTURES

St. Martin's Press, Inc., 175 Fifth Avenue, New York, New York 10010 (800) 221-7945; *The Statesman's Year-Book.*

Statistical Office of the United Nations, Publishing Service, New York, New York 10017 (800) 253-9646; *Statistical Yearbook.*

NEW CALEDONIA - MOTOR VEHICLES IN USE

Europa Publications Limited, 18 Bedford Square, London, WC1B 3JN, England; *The Europa World Year Book.*

Statistical Office of the United Nations, Publishing Service, New York, New York 10017 (800) 253-9646; *Statistical Yearbook.*

NEW CALEDONIA - MUSEUMS

United Nations Educational, Scientific and Cultural Organization (UNESCO), 7 Place de Fontenoy, F-75700 Paris, France (Telephone Number in U.S. (212) 963-5981); *Statistical Yearbook.*

NEW CALEDONIA - NATALITY - See NEW CALEDONIA - BIRTH RATES

NEW CALEDONIA - NATIONAL ACCOUNTS

Statistical Office of the United Nations, Publishing Service, New York, New York 10017 (800) 253-9646; *National Accounts Statistics;* and *Statistical Yearbook.*

NEW CALEDONIA - NATIONAL INCOME

Statistical Office of the United Nations, Publishing Service, New York, New York 10017 (800) 253-9646; *National Accounts Statistics;* and *Statistical Yearbook.*

NEW CALEDONIA - NEWSPAPER PRODUCTION

Statistical Office of the United Nations, Publishing Service, New York, New York 10017 (800) 253-9646; *Statistical Yearbook.*

United Nations Educational, Scientific and Cultural Organization (UNESCO), 7

Place de Fontenoy, F-75700 Paris, France (Telephone Number in U.S. (212) 963-5981); *Statistical Yearbook.*

NEW CALEDONIA - NICKEL AND NICKEL ORE PRODUCTION AND CONSUMPTION - See NEW CALEDONIA - MINING AND MINERAL PRODUCTS

NEW CALEDONIA - PERIODICALS

United Nations Educational, Scientific and Cultural Organization (UNESCO), 7 Place de Fontenoy, F-75700 Paris, France (Telephone Number in U.S. (212) 963-5981); *Statistical Yearbook.*

NEW CALEDONIA - PESTICIDE USE

Food and Agricultural Organization of the United Nations (FAO) Via delle Terme di Caracalla, 00100 Rome, Italy (Telephone Number in U.S. (202) 653-2400); *The State of Food and Agriculture.*

NEW CALEDONIA - PETROLEUM INDUSTRY

Food and Agricultural Organization of the United Nations (FAO) Via delle Terme di Caracalla, 00100 Rome, Italy (Telephone Number in U.S. (202) 653-2400); *The State of Food and Agriculture.*

United Nations Conference on Trade and Development, Central Statistical Service, Palais des Nations, Geneva, Switzerland (Telephone in U.S. (800) 253-9646); *UNCTAD Commodity Yearbook.*

NEW CALEDONIA - PIGS - See NEW CALEDONIA - LIVESTOCK AND POULTRY

NEW CALEDONIA - POPULATION

Central Intelligence Agency, Washington, D.C. 20505 (703) 482-1100, www.cia.gov; *The World Factbook.*

Economist Intelligence Unit, 111 West 57th Street, New York, New York 10019 (800) 938-4685; *New Caledonia Country Report.*

Euromonitor International, Inc., 122 South Michigan Avenue, Suite 1200, Chicago, Illinois 60603 (800) 577-EURO; *International Marketing Data and Statistics;* and *The World Economic Factbook.*

Europa Publications Limited, 18 Bedford Square, London, WC1B 3JN, England; *The Europa World Year Book.*

Food and Agricultural Organization of the United Nations (FAO), Via delle Terme di Caracalla, 00100 Rome, Italy (Telephone Number in U.S. (202) 653-2400); *Production Yearbook.*

International Labour Office,

I.L.O. Publications, 1828 L Street, NW, Suite 801, Washington, D.C. 20036 (301) 638-3152; *Yearbook of Labour Statistics.*

St. Martin's Press, Inc., 175 Fifth Avenue, New York, New York 10010 (800) 221-7945; *The Statesman's Year-Book.*

Statistical Office of the United Nations, Publishing Service, New York, New York 10017 (800) 253-9646; *Demographic Yearbook; World Statistics Pocketbook;* and *Statistical Yearbook.*

United Nations Educational, Scientific and Cultural Organization (UNESCO), 7 Place de Fontenoy, F-75700 Paris, France (Telephone Number in U.S. (212) 963-5981); *Statistical Yearbook.*

Walden Publishing Ltd., Two Market Street, Saffron Walden Essex, CB10 1HZ, England; *The World of Information Asia and Pacific Review.*

The World Bank, 1818 H Street, NW, Washington, D.C. 20433 (202) 477-1234; *The World Bank Atlas.*

World Health Organization, Office of Publications, 20 Avenue Appia, CH-1211 Geneva 27, Switzerland (Telephone Number in U.S. (518) 436-9686); *World Health Statistics Annual.*

NEW CALEDONIA - POST OFFICES

St. Martin's Press, Inc., 175 Fifth Avenue, New York, New York 10010 (800) 221-7945; *The Statesman's Year-Book.*

NEW CALEDONIA - POTATO PRODUCTION - See NEW CALEDONIA - CROPS

NEW CALEDONIA - PRICES

Food and Agricultural Organization of the United Nations (FAO), Via delle Terme di Caracalla, 00100 Rome, Italy (Telephone Number in U.S. (202) 653-2400); *Production Yearbook;* and *The State of Food and Agriculture.*

International Labour Office, I.L.O. Publications, 1828 L Street, NW, Suite 801, Washington, D.C. 20036 (301) 638-3152; *Yearbook of Labour Statistics.*

South Pacific Commission, Post Box D5, Noumea Cedex, New Caledonia; *Statistical Bulletin of the South Pacific: Overseas Trade;* and *Statistical Bulletin of the South Pacific: Retail Price Indexes.*

NEW CALEDONIA - RADIO RECEIVERS

St. Martin's Press, Inc., 175 Fifth Avenue, New York, New York 10010 (800) 221-7945; *The Statesman's Year-Book.*

NEW CALEDONIA - RELIGION

Central Intelligence Agency, Washington, D.C. 20505 (703) 482-1100, www.cia.gov; *The World Factbook.*

St. Martin's Press, Inc., 175 Fifth Avenue, New York, New York 10010 (800) 221-7945; *The Statesman's Year-Book.*

NEW CALEDONIA - RENT PRICES

International Labour Office, I.L.O. Publications, 1828 L Street, NW, Suite 801, Washington, D.C. 20036 (301) 638-3152; *Yearbook of Labour Statistics.*

NEW CALEDONIA - RETAIL TRADE

Euromonitor International, Inc., 122 South Michigan Avenue, Suite 1200, Chicago, Illinois 60603 (800) 577-EURO; *World Marketing Data and Statistics.*

NEW CALEDONIA - ROOT AND TUBER PRODUCTION - See NEW CALEDONIA - CROPS

NEW CALEDONIA - ROUNDWOOD PRODUCTION - See NEW CALEDONIA - FORESTRY AND FOREST PRODUCTS

NEW CALEDONIA - SAWNWOOD PRODUCTION - See NEW CALEDONIA - FORESTRY AND FOREST PRODUCTS

NEW CALEDONIA - SCIENCE AND TECHNOLOGY - EXPENDITURE FOR RESEARCH - See NEW CALEDONIA - SCIENTISTS, TECHNICIANS AND ENGINEERS

NEW CALEDONIA - SCIENTISTS, TECHNICIANS AND ENGINEERS

Statistical Office of the United Nations, Publishing Service, New York, New York 10017 (800) 253-9646; *Statistical Yearbook.*

NEW CALEDONIA - SHEEP - See NEW CALEDONIA - LIVESTOCK AND POULTRY

NEW CALEDONIA - SOCIAL DATA

Statistical Office of the United Nations, Publishing Service, New York, New York 10017 (800) 253-9646; *World Statistics Pocketbook.*

NEW CALEDONIA - SOCIAL SECURITY

Statistical Office of the United Nations, Publishing Service, New York, New York 10017 (800) 253-9646; *National Accounts Statistics.*

NEW CALEDONIA - STOCKS - COMMODITY - MARKET PRICE - INDEX

Food and Agricultural Organization of the United Nations (FAO) Via delle Terme

di Caracalla, 00100 Rome, Italy (Telephone Number in U.S. (202) 653-2400); *The State of Food and Agriculture.*

NEW CALEDONIA - TELEGRAPH SERVICE

Statistical Office of the United Nations, Publishing Service, New York, New York 10017 (800) 253-9646; *Statistical Yearbook.*

NEW CALEDONIA - TELEPHONES IN USE

American Telephone and Telegraph Company, 26 Parsippany Road, Whippany, New Jersey 07981 (800) 222-0300; *The World's Telephones.*

Central Intelligence Agency, Washington, D.C. 20505 (703) 482-1100, www.cia.gov; *The World Factbook.*

St. Martin's Press, Inc., 175 Fifth Avenue, New York, New York 10010 (800) 221-7945; *The Statesman's Year-Book.*

Statistical Office of the United Nations, Publishing Service, New York, New York 10017 (800) 253-9646; *Statistical Yearbook;* and *World Statistics Pocketbook.*

NEW CALEDONIA - TELEVISION RECEIVERS - IN USE

Statistical Office of the United Nations, Publishing Service, New York, New York 10017 (800) 253-9646; *Statistical Yearbook.*

NEW CALEDONIA - TEXTILE INDUSTRY

South Pacific Commission, Post Box D5, Noumea Cedex, New Caledonia; *Statistical Bulletin of the South Pacific: Retail Price Indexes.*

United Nations Conference on Trade and Development, Central Statistical Service, Palais des Nations, Geneva, Switzerland (Telephone in U.S. (800) 253-9646); *UNCTAD Commodity Yearbook.*

NEW CALEDONIA - TOBACCO PRODUCTION

South Pacific Commission, Post Box D5, Noumea Cedex, New Caledonia; *Statistical Bulletin of the South Pacific: Retail Price Indexes.*

NEW CALEDONIA - TOURISM

Euromonitor International, Inc., 122 South Michigan Avenue, Suite 1200, Chicago, Illinois 60603 (800) 577-EURO; *The World Economic Factbook;* and *World Marketing Data and Statistics.*

Europa Publications Limited, 18 Bedford Square, London, WC1B 3JN, England; *The Europa World Year Book.*

South Pacific Commission, Post Box

D5, Noumea Cedex, New Caledonia; *Statistical Bulletin of the South Pacific: Retail Price Indexes.*

St. Martin's Press, Inc., 175 Fifth Avenue, New York, New York 10010 (800) 221-7945; *The Statesman's Year-Book.*

Statistical Office of the United Nations, Publishing Service, New York, New York 10017 (800) 253-9646; *Statistical Yearbook.*

World Tourism Organization, Calle Capitan Haya 42, E-28020 Madrid, Spain; *Yearbook of Tourism Statistics.*

NEW CALEDONIA - TRACTORS IN USE

Statistical Office of the United Nations, Publishing Service, New York, New York 10017 (800) 253-9646; *Statistical Yearbook.*

NEW CALEDONIA - TRADE - See NEW CALEDONIA - FOREIGN TRADE

NEW CALEDONIA - TRANSPORTATION AND COMMUNICATIONS

Central Intelligence Agency, Washington, D.C. 20505 (703) 482-1100, www.cia.gov; *The World Factbook.*

Euromonitor International, Inc., 122 South Michigan Avenue, Suite 1200, Chicago, Illinois 60603 (800) 577-EURO; *International Marketing Data and Statistics;* and *World Marketing Data and Statistics.*

Europa Publications Limited, 18 Bedford Square, London, WC1B 3JN, England; *The Europa World Year Book.*

South Pacific Commission, Post Box D5, Noumea Cedex, New Caledonia; *Statistical Bulletin of the South Pacific: Retail Price Indexes.*

St. Martin's Press, Inc., 175 Fifth Avenue, New York, New York 10010 (800) 221-7945; *The Statesman's Year-Book.*

NEW CALEDONIA - UNEMPLOYMENT

Central Intelligence Agency, Washington, D.C. 20505 (703) 482-1100, www.cia.gov; *The World Factbook.*

International Labour Office, I.L.O. Publications, 1828 L Street, NW, Suite 801, Washington, D.C. 20036 (301) 638-3152; *Yearbook of Labour Statistics.*

Statistical Office of the United Nations, Publishing Service, New York, New York 10017 (800) 253-9646; *Statistical Yearbook.*

NEW CALEDONIA - VITAL STATISTICS

St. Martin's Press, Inc., 175 Fifth Avenue, New York, New York 10010 (800) 221-7945; *The Statesman's Year-Book.*

Statistical Office of the United Nations, Publishing Service, New York, New York 10017 (800) 253-9646; *Statistical Yearbook.*

World Health Organization, Office of Publications, 20 Avenue Appia, CH-1211 Geneva 27, Switzerland (Telephone Number in U.S. (518) 436-9686); *World Health Statistics Annual.*

NEW CALEDONIA - WAGES

International Labour Office, I.L.O. Publications, 1828 L Street, NW, Suite 801, Washington, D.C. 20036 (301) 638-3152; *Yearbook of Labour Statistics.*

Statistical Office of the United Nations, Publishing Service, New York, New York 10017 (800) 253-9646; *Statistical Yearbook.*

NEW GUINEA - See PAPUA NEW GUINEA

NEW HAMPSHIRE - See also STATE DATA (FOR INDIVIDUAL STATES)

New Hampshire - Primary Statistics Source

Office of State Planning, 2 ½ Beacon Street, Concord, New Hampshire 03301 (603) 271-2155; *Population Estimates for New Hampshire Cities and Towns; New Hampshire Population Projections for Cities and Towns;* and *Current Estimates and Trends in New Hampshire's Housing Supply.*

New Hampshire - State Data Centers

Office of State Planning, 2 ½ Beacon Street, Concord, New Hampshire 03301, Mr. Tom Duffy (603) 271-2155.

New Hampshire State Library, 20 Park Street, Concord, New Hampshire 03301-6303, Mr. John McCornick (603) 271-2060.

NEW JERSEY - See also STATE DATA (FOR INDIVIDUAL STATES)

New Jersey - Primary Statistics Source

New Jersey State Data Center, Department of Labor, CN 388, Trenton, New Jersey 08625 (609) 984-2593; *New Jersey Source Book.*

New Jersey - State Data Centers

New Jersey State Data Center, Division of Labor Market and Demographic Research, New Jersey Department of Labor, Post Office Box 388, Trenton, New

Jersey 08625-0388, Mr. David Joye (609) 984-2595.

New Jersey State Library, U.S. Documents Office, Post Office Box 520, 185 West State Street, Trenton, New Jersey 08625-0520, Ms. Beverly Railsback (609) 292-6259.

Princeton University, Data and Statistical Services, 1 Washington Road, Princeton, New Jersey 08544, Ms. Ann S. Gray (609) 258-5316.

Rutgers Regional Report, 33 Livingston Avenue, Suite 300, New Brunswick, New Jersey 08911-1981, Dr. James W. Hughes (732) 932-5475, ext. 756.

NEW MEXICO - See also STATE DATA (FOR INDIVIDUAL STATES)

New Mexico - Primary Statistics Source

University of New Mexico, Bureau of Business and Economic Research, 1920 Lomas, NE, Albuquerque, New Mexico 87131 (505) 277-2216; *County Profiles.*

New Mexico - State Data Centers

New Mexico Economic Development Department, 1100 St. Francis Drive, Post Office Box 20003, Santa Fe, New Mexico 87504-5003, Ms. Beth Davis (505) 827-0264.

Bureau of Business and Economic Research, University of New Mexico, 1920 Lomas NE, Albuquerque, New Mexico 87131, Mr. Kevin Kargacin (505) 277-6626.

Department of Economics, New Mexico State University, Business Complex 143, University Avenue and Solano, Box 30001, Las Cruces, New Mexico 88003, Dr. Kathleen Brook (505) 646-4905.

New Mexico State Library, 1209 Camino Carols Rey, Santa Fe, New Mexico 87505-9860, Ms. Laurie Canepa (505) 476-9717.

NEW PRODUCT INTRODUCTIONS

Marketing Intelligence Service Limited, 6473 D Route 64, Naples, New York 14512 (716) 374-6326; *Product Alert Weekly.*

NEW YORK - See also STATE DATA (FOR INDIVIDUAL STATES)

New York - Primary Statistics Source

Nelson Rockefeller Institute of Government, 411 State Street, Albany, New York 12203 (518) 443-5522; *New York*

State Statistical Yearbook.

New York - State Data Centers

New York State Data Center, Empire State Development, 30 South Pearl Street, Albany, New York 12245, Mr. Robert Scardamalia (518) 292-5300.

Cornell University, CISER Data Archive, 201 Caldwell Hall, Ithaca, New York 14853, Mr. Warren Brown (607) 255-4801.

New York State Library, 6th Floor, Cultural Education Center, Empire State Plaza, Albany, New York 12245, Ms. Mary Redmond (518) 474-3940.

Office of Real Property Services, 16 Sheridan Avenue, Albany, New York 12210, Ms. Rebecca Stegman (518) 484-3453.

NEW YORK STOCK EXCHANGE

Global Financial Data, 784 Fremont Villas, Los Angeles, California 90042 (310) 642-4659; Internet site: http://globalfindata.com.

Securities and Exchange Commission, 450 Fifth Street, NW, Washington, D.C. 20549 (202) 942-4040, www.sec.gov; unpublished data.

NEW YORK STOCK EXCHANGE - STOCK INDICES

Global Financial Data, 784 Fremont Villas, Los Angeles, California 90042 (310) 642-4659; Internet site: http://globalfindata.com.

New Zealand - National Statistical Office

Department of Statistics, Post Office Box 2922, Wellington, New Zealand.

New Zealand - Primary Statistics Sources

Government Bookshop, Mulgrave Street, Wellington, New Zealand; *New Zealand Official Yearbook; Monthly Abstracts of Statistics;* and *New Zealand Pocket Digest of Statistics.*

New Zealand - Databases

Information Network for Official Statistics (INFOS), New Zealand Department of Statistics, Post Office Box 2922, Wellington, New Zealand. Subject coverage: New Zealand national and regional statistical data.

Regional Population Database, New Zealand Department of Statistics, Head Office, Post Office Box 2922, Wellington, New Zealand. Subject coverage: Data for the entire country, local authorities and area units.

NEW ZEALAND - ABORTIONS

Statistical Office of the United Nations, Publishing Service, New York, New York 10017 (800) 253-9646; *Demographic Yearbook.*

NEW ZEALAND - AGRICULTURE

Economist Intelligence Unit, 111 West 57th Street, New York, New York 10019 (800) 938-4685; *New Zealand Country Report.*

Euromonitor International, Inc., 122 South Michigan Avenue, Suite 1200, Chicago, Illinois 60603 (800) 577-EURO; *International Marketing Data and Statistics;* and *World Marketing Data and Statistics.*

Europa Publications Limited, 18 Bedford Square, London, WC1B 3JN, England; *The Europa World Year Book.*

Food and Agricultural Organization of the United Nations (FAO) Via delle Terme di Caracalla, 00100 Rome, Italy (Telephone Number in U.S. (202) 653-2400); *Production Yearbook; The State of Food and Agriculture;* and *Trade Yearbook.*

M.E. Sharpe, 80 Business Park Drive, Armonk, New York 10504 (800) 541-6563; *The Illustrated Book of World Rankings.*

Organisation for Economic Co-operation and Development (OECD), 2 rue Andre-Pascal, 75 Paris 16, France (Telephone Number in U.S. (202) 785-6323); *Economic Accounts for Agriculture; Industrial Structure Statistics;* and *OECD Economic Surveys: New Zealand.*

St. Martin's Press, Inc., 175 Fifth Avenue, New York, New York 10010 (800) 221-7945; *The Statesman's Year-Book.*

Statistical Office of the United Nations, Publishing Service, New York, New York 10017 (800) 253-9646; *Asia-Pacific in Figure; Statistical Yearbook;* and *Statistical Yearbook for Asia and the Pacific.*

United Nations Conference on Trade and Development, Central Statistical Service, Palais des Nations, Geneva, Switzerland (Telephone in U.S. (800) 253-9646); *UNCTAD Commodity Yearbook.*

The World Bank, 1818 H Street, NW, Washington, D.C. 20433 (202) 477-1234; *World Development Indicators.*

NEW ZEALAND - AIRLINE SERVICE

The Economist Intelligence Unit (Asia) Limited, 10th Floor, Luk Kwok Centre, 72 Gloucester Road, Wanchai, Hong Kong (Phone Number in U.S. (800) 938-4685); *Asian Market Atlas.*

Europa Publications Limited, 18 Bedford Square, London, WC1B 3JN, England; *The Europa World Year Book.*

International Civil Aviation Organization, 999 University Street, Montreal, Quebec, Canada H3C 5H7 (514) 954-8219; *Civil Aviation Statistics of the World.*

M.E. Sharpe, 80 Business Park Drive, Armonk, New York 10504 (800) 541-6563; *The Illustrated Book of World Rankings.*

Organisation for Economic Co-operation and Development (OECD), 2 rue Andre-Pascal, 75 Paris 16, France (Telephone Number in U.S. (202) 785-6323); *Tourism Policy and International Tourism in OECD Member Countries.*

St. Martin's Press, Inc., 175 Fifth Avenue, New York, New York 10010 (800) 221-7945; *The Statesman's Year-Book.*

Statistical Office of the United Nations, Publishing Service, New York, New York 10017 (800) 253-9646; *Statistical Yearbook.*

NEW ZEALAND - AIRPORTS

Central Intelligence Agency, Washington, D.C. 20505 (703) 482-1100, www.cia.gov; *The World Factbook.*

NEW ZEALAND - ALUMINUM PRODUCTION AND CONSUMPTION - See NEW ZEALAND - MINING AND MINERAL PRODUCTS

NEW ZEALAND - ANIMAL FEEDINGSTUFFS

Organisation for Economic Co-operation and Development (OECD), 2 rue Andre-Pascal, 75 Paris 16, France (Telephone Number in U.S. (202) 785-6323); *Foreign Trade by Commodities.*

NEW ZEALAND - ANIMAL HEALTH

Food and Agricultural Organization of the United Nations (FAO), Via delle Terme di Caracalla, 00100 Rome, Italy (Telephone Number in U.S. (202) 653-2400); *Animal Health Yearbook.*

NEW ZEALAND - AREA AND DENSITY OF POPULATION

Central Intelligence Agency, Washington, D.C. 20505 (703) 482-1100, www.cia.gov; *The World Factbook.*

Euromonitor International, Inc., 122

South Michigan Avenue, Suite 1200, Chicago, Illinois 60603 (800) 577-EURO; *International Marketing Data and Statistics;* and *The World Economic Factbook.*

Europa Publications Limited, 18 Bedford Square, London, WC1B 3JN, England; *The Europa World Year Book.*

Food and Agricultural Organization of the United Nations (FAO) Via delle Terme di Caracalla, 00100 Rome, Italy (Telephone Number in U.S. (202) 653-2400); *The State of Food and Agriculture.*

M.E. Sharpe, 80 Business Park Drive, Armonk, New York 10504 (800) 541-6563; *The Illustrated Book of World Rankings.*

St. Martin's Press, Inc., 175 Fifth Avenue, New York, New York 10010 (800) 221-7945; *The Statesman's Year-Book.*

Statistical Office of the United Nations, Publishing Service, New York, New York 10017 (800) 253-9646; *Statistical Yearbook.*

United Nations Educational, Scientific and Cultural Organization (UNESCO), 7 Place de Fontenoy, F-75700 Paris, France (Telephone Number in U.S. (212) 963-5981); *Statistical Yearbook.*

The World Bank, 1818 H Street, NW, Washington, D.C. 20433 (202) 477-1234; *World Development Report.*

NEW ZEALAND - ARMS EXPORTS AND IMPORTS - See NEW ZEALAND - MILITARY

NEW ZEALAND - BALANCE OF PAYMENTS

The Economist Intelligence Unit, 111 West 57th Street, New York, New York 10019 (800) 938-4685; *The World Market Atlas.*

Europa Publications Limited, 18 Bedford Square, London, WC1B 3JN, England; *The Europa World Year Book.*

International Monetary Fund, 700 Nineteenth Street, NW, Washington, D.C. 20431 (202) 623-7000; *Balance of Payments Yearbook;* and *International Financial Statistics.*

Organisation for Economic Co-operation and Development (OECD), 2 rue Andre-Pascal, 75 Paris 16, France (Telephone Number in U.S. (202) 785-6323); *Economic Outlook; Geographical Distribution of Financial Flows to Developing Countries; Main Economic Indicators - Historical Statistics;* and *OECD Economic Surveys: New Zealand.*

United Nations Conference on Trade and Development (UNCTAD), New York, New York 10017 (800) 253-9646; *Handbook of International Trade and Development*

Statistics.

The World Bank, 1818 H Street, NW, Washington, D.C. 20433 (202) 477-1234; *World Development Report;* and *World Development Indicators.*

NEW ZEALAND - BANKING

Euromonitor International, Inc., 122 South Michigan Avenue, Suite 1200, Chicago, Illinois 60603 (800) 577-EURO; *World Marketing Data and Statistics.*

Europa Publications Limited, 18 Bedford Square, London, WC1B 3JN, England; *The Europa World Year Book.*

International Monetary Fund, 700 Nineteenth Street, NW, Washington, D.C. 20431 (202) 623-7000; *Government Finance Statistics Yearbook;* and *International Financial Statistics.*

M.E. Sharpe, 80 Business Park Drive, Armonk, New York 10504 (800) 541-6563; *The Illustrated Book of World Rankings.*

Organisation for Economic Co-operation and Development (OECD), 2 rue Andre-Pascal, 75 Paris 16, France (Telephone Number in U.S. (202) 785-6323); *Economic Outlook; Financial Market Trends;* and *OECD Economic Surveys: New Zealand.*

St. Martin's Press, Inc., 175 Fifth Avenue, New York, New York 10010 (800) 221-7945; *The Statesman's Year-Book.*

Statistical Office of the United Nations, Publishing Service, New York, New York 10017 (800) 253-9646; *Statistical Yearbook.*

NEW ZEALAND - BARLEY PRODUCTION - See NEW ZEALAND - CROPS

NEW ZEALAND - BEEF EXPORTS - See NEW ZEALAND - LIVESTOCK AND POULTRY

NEW ZEALAND - BEER PRODUCTION - See NEW ZEALAND - BEVERAGES

NEW ZEALAND - BEVERAGES

M.E. Sharpe, 80 Business Park Drive, Armonk, New York 10504 (800) 541-6563; *The Illustrated Book of World Rankings.*

Statistical Office of the United Nations, Publishing Service, New York, New York 10017 (800) 253-9646; *Statistical Yearbook.*

NEW ZEALAND - BIRTH RATES

Central Intelligence Agency, Washington, D.C. 20505 (703) 482-1100, www.cia.gov; *The World Factbook.*

The Economist Intelligence Unit (Asia) Limited, 10th Floor, Luk Kwok Centre, 72 Gloucester Road, Wanchai, Hong Kong (Phone Number in U.S. (800) 938-4685); *Asian Market Atlas.*

Euromonitor International, Inc., 122 South Michigan Avenue, Suite 1200, Chicago, Illinois 60603 (800) 577-EURO; *International Marketing Data and Statistics;* and *The World Economic Factbook.*

Europa Publications Limited, 18 Bedford Square, London, WC1B 3JN, England; *The Europa World Year Book.*

M.E. Sharpe, 80 Business Park Drive, Armonk, New York 10504 (800) 541-6563; *The Illustrated Book of World Rankings.*

St. Martin's Press, Inc., 175 Fifth Avenue, New York, New York 10010 (800) 221-7945; *The Statesman's Year-Book.*

Statistical Office of the United Nations, Publishing Service, New York, New York 10017 (800) 253-9646; *Asia-Pacific in Figures; Demographic Yearbook;* and *Statistical Yearbook.*

The World Bank, 1818 H Street, NW, Washington, D.C. 20433 (202) 477-1234; *World Development Indicators.*

World Health Organization, Office of Publications, 20 Avenue Appia, CH-1211 Geneva 27, Switzerland (Telephone Number in U.S. (518) 436-9686); *World Health Statistics Annual.*

NEW ZEALAND - BONDS

International Monetary Fund, 700 Nineteenth Street, NW, Washington, D.C. 20431 (202) 623-7000; *Government Finance Statistics Yearbook.*

Organisation for Economic Co-operation and Development (OECD), 2 rue Andre-Pascal, 75 Paris 16, France (Telephone Number in U.S. (202) 785-6323); *Financial Market Trends;* and *Main Economic Indicators - Historical Statistics.*

Statistical Office of the United Nations, Publishing Service, New York, New York 10017 (800) 253-9646; *Statistical Yearbook.*

NEW ZEALAND - BOOK PRODUCTION

Europa Publications Limited, 18 Bedford Square, London, WC1B 3JN, England; *The Europa World Year Book.*

St. Martin's Press, Inc., 175 Fifth Avenue, New York, New York 10010 (800) 221-7945; *The Statesman's Year-Book.*

United Nations Educational, Scientific and Cultural Organization (UNESCO), 7 Place de Fontenoy, F-75700 Paris, France

(Telephone Number in U.S. (212) 963-5981); *Statistical Yearbook.*

NEW ZEALAND - BROADCASTING

Billboard Limited, Post Office Box 9027, 1006 AA Amsterdam, The Netherlands (Telephone Number in U.S. (212) 764-7300); *World Radio TV Handbook.*

Central Intelligence Agency, Washington, D.C. 20505 (703) 482-1100, www.cia.gov; *The World Factbook.*

The Economist Intelligence Unit (Asia) Limited, 10th Floor, Luk Kwok Centre, 72 Gloucester Road, Wanchai, Hong Kong (Phone Number in U.S. (800) 938-4685); *Asian Market Atlas.*

Euromonitor International, Inc., 122 South Michigan Avenue, Suite 1200, Chicago, Illinois 60603 (800) 577-EURO; *World Marketing Data and Statistics.*

M.E. Sharpe, 80 Business Park Drive, Armonk, New York 10504 (800) 541-6563; *The Illustrated Book of World Rankings.*

St. Martin's Press, Inc., 175 Fifth Avenue, New York, New York 10010 (800) 221-7945; *The Statesman's Year-Book.*

NEW ZEALAND - BUDGET

Central Intelligence Agency, Washington, D.C. 20505 (703) 482-1100, www.cia.gov; *The World Factbook.*

NEW ZEALAND - BUTTER - See NEW ZEALAND - DAIRY PRODUCTS

NEW ZEALAND - CABBAGE PRODUCTION - See NEW ZEALAND - CROPS

NEW ZEALAND - CALORIE SUPPLY

Food and Agricultural Organization of the United Nations (FAO) Via delle Terme di Caracalla, 00100 Rome, Italy (Telephone Number in U.S. (202) 653-2400); *The State of Food and Agriculture.*

NEW ZEALAND - CAPITAL INVESTMENT
Organisation for Economic Co-operation and Development (OECD), 2 rue Andre-Pascal, 75 Paris 16, France (Telephone Number in U.S. (202) 785-6323); *Economic Outlook;* and *Financial Market Trends.*

NEW ZEALAND - CAPITAL REVENUE

International Monetary Fund, 700 Nineteenth Street, NW, Washington, D.C. 20431 (202) 623-7000; *Government Finance Statistics Yearbook.*

Organisation for Economic Co-operation and Development (OECD), 2 rue

Andre-Pascal, 75 Paris 16, France (Telephone Number in U.S. (202) 785-6323); *Economic Outlook;* and *Financial Market Trends.*

NEW ZEALAND - CATTLE - See NEW ZEALAND - LIVESTOCK AND POULTRY

NEW ZEALAND - CAULIFLOWER PRODUCTION - See NEW ZEALAND - CROPS

NEW ZEALAND - CEMENT PRODUCTION - See NEW ZEALAND - MINING AND MINERAL PRODUCTS

NEW ZEALAND - CEREAL PRODUCTION - See NEW ZEALAND - CROPS

NEW ZEALAND - CHEESE - See NEW ZEALAND - DAIRY PRODUCTS

NEW ZEALAND - CHEMICAL (ORGANIC) PRODUCTION - See NEW ZEALAND - MINING AND MINERAL PRODUCTS

NEW ZEALAND - CHICKENS - See NEW ZEALAND - LIVESTOCK AND POULTRY

NEW ZEALAND - CIGARETTE PRODUCTION - See NEW ZEALAND -TOBACCO PRODUCTION

NEW ZEALAND - CLIMATE

M.E. Sharpe, 80 Business Park Drive, Armonk, New York 10504 (800) 541-6563; *The Illustrated Book of World Rankings.*

St. Martin's Press, Inc., 175 Fifth Avenue, New York, New York 10010 (800) 221-7945; *The Statesman's Year-Book.*

NEW ZEALAND - CLOTHING EXPORTS AND IMPORTS - See NEW ZEALAND - TEXTILE INDUSTRY

NEW ZEALAND - COAL PRODUCTION - See NEW ZEALAND - MINING AND MINERAL PRODUCTS

NEW ZEALAND - COBALT PRODUCTION AND CONSUMPTION - See NEW ZEALAND - MINING AND MINERAL PRODUCTS

NEW ZEALAND - COFFEE PRODUCTION AND CONSUMPTION - See NEW ZEALAND - CROPS

NEW ZEALAND - COKE, COKE OVEN COKE, AND COKE OVEN ORE PRODUCTION AND CONSUMPTION - See NEW ZEALAND - MINING AND MINERAL PRODUCTS

NEW ZEALAND - COMMERCE

St. Martin's Press, Inc., 175 Fifth Avenue, New York, New York 10010 (800) 221-7945; *The Statesman's Year-Book.*

NEW ZEALAND - COMMUNICATIONS - See NEW ZEALAND - TRANSPORTATION AND COMMUNICATIONS

NEW ZEALAND - CONSTRUCTION INDUSTRY

M.E. Sharpe, 80 Business Park Drive, Armonk, New York 10504 (800) 541-6563; *The Illustrated Book of World Rankings.*

Organisation for Economic Co-operation and Development (OECD), 2 rue Andre-Pascal, 75 Paris 16, France (Telephone Number in U.S. (202) 785-6323); *Industrial Structure Statistics; The Iron and Steel Industry; Main Economic Indicators - Historical Statistics;* and *OECD Economic Surveys: New Zealand.*

St. Martin's Press, Inc., 175 Fifth Avenue, New York, New York 10010 (800) 221-7945; *The Statesman's Year-Book.*

Statistical Office of the United Nations, Publishing Service, New York, New York 10017 (800) 253-9646; *Statistical Yearbook.*

NEW ZEALAND - CONSUMER PRICE INDEX

Europa Publications Limited, 18 Bedford Square, London, WC1B 3JN, England; *The Europa World Year Book.*

Organisation for Economic Co-operation and Development (OECD), 2 rue Andre-Pascal, 75 Paris 16, France (Telephone Number in U.S. (202) 785-6323); *Economic Outlook.*

Statistical Office of the United Nations, Publishing Service, New York, New York 10017 (800) 253-9646; *Statistical Yearbook.*

NEW ZEALAND - CONSUMER PRICES

Euromonitor International, Inc., 122 South Michigan Avenue, Suite 1200, Chicago, Illinois 60603 (800) 577-EURO; *World Marketing Data and Statistics.*

International Labour Office, I.L.O. Publications, 1828 L Street, NW, Suite 801, Washington, D.C. 20036 (301) 638-3152; *Yearbook of Labour Statistics.*

International Monetary Fund, 700 Nineteenth Street, NW, Washington, D.C. 20431 (202) 623-7000; *International Financial Statistics.*

Organisation for Economic Co-operation and Development (OECD), 2 rue Andre-Pascal, 75 Paris 16, France (Telephone Number in U.S. (202) 785-6323); *Economic Outlook;* and *Main Economic Indicators - Historical Statistics.*

NEW ZEALAND - CONSUMPTION

Organisation for Economic Co-

operation and Development (OECD), 2 rue Andre-Pascal, 75 Paris 16, France (Telephone Number in U.S. (202) 785-6323); *The Footwear, Raw Hides and Skins, and Leather Industry in OECD Countries; The Iron and Steel Industry; Meat Balances in OECD Member Countries; The Non-Ferrous Metals Industry; The Pulp and Paper Industry;* and *Textile Industry in OECD Countries.*

The World Bank, 1818 H Street, NW, Washington, D.C. 20433 (202) 477-1234; *World Development Report.*

NEW ZEALAND - COPPER AND COPPER ORE PRODUCTION AND CONSUMPTION - See NEW ZEALAND - MINING AND MINERAL PRODUCTS

NEW ZEALAND - CORN PRODUCTION - See NEW ZEALAND - CROPS

NEW ZEALAND - CORPORATE INCOME TAXES - See NEW ZEALAND - TAXATION

NEW ZEALAND - CORPORATE TAXES - See NEW ZEALAND - TAXATION

NEW ZEALAND - COTTON - See NEW ZEALAND - CROPS

NEW ZEALAND - CRIME

International Criminal Police Organization (INTERPOL), 50 quai Achille Lignon, F-69006 Lyon, France; *International Crime Statistics.*

Yale University Press, Yale Station, New Haven, Connecticut 06520 (800) 987-7323; *Violence and Crime in Cross-National Perspective.*

NEW ZEALAND - CROPS

Europa Publications Limited, 18 Bedford Square, London, WC1B 3JN, England; *The Europa World Year Book.*

Food and Agricultural Organization of the United Nations (FAO), Via delle Terme di Caracalla, 00100 Rome, Italy (Telephone Number in U.S. (202) 653-2400); *Production Yearbook;* and *The State of Food and Agriculture.*

M.E. Sharpe, 80 Business Park Drive, Armonk, New York 10504 (800) 541-6563; *The Illustrated Book of World Rankings.*

Organisation for Economic Co-operation and Development (OECD), 2 rue Andre-Pascal, 75 Paris 16, France (Telephone Number in U.S. (202) 785-6323); *Economic Accounts for Agriculture; Foreign Trade by Commodities;* and *Textile Industry in OECD Countries.*

St. Martin's Press, Inc., 175 Fifth Avenue, New York, New York 10010 (800)

221-7945; *The Statesman's Year-Book.*

Statistical Office of the United Nations, Publishing Service, New York, New York 10017 (800) 253-9646; *Statistical Yearbook.*

United Nations Conference on Trade and Development, Central Statistical Service, Palais des Nations, Geneva, Switzerland (Telephone in U.S. (800) 253-9646); *UNCTAD Commodity Yearbook.*

NEW ZEALAND - CUSTOMS DUTIES

International Monetary Fund, 700 Nineteenth Street, NW, Washington, D.C. 20431 (202) 623-7000; *Government Finance Statistics Yearbook.*

Organisation for Economic Co-operation and Development (OECD), 2 rue Andre-Pascal, 75 Paris 16, France (Telephone Number in U.S. (202) 785-6323); *The Non-Ferrous Metals Industry.*

St. Martin's Press, Inc., 175 Fifth Avenue, New York, New York 10010 (800) 221-7945; *The Statesman's Year-Book.*

NEW ZEALAND - DAIRY PRODUCTS

Commodity Research Bureau, Inc., 30 South Wacker Drive, Chicago, Illinois 60606 (312) 454-1801; *Commodity Year Book.*

Europa Publications Limited, 18 Bedford Square, London, WC1B 3JN, England; *The Europa World Year Book.*

Food and Agricultural Organization of the United Nations (FAO), Via delle Terme di Caracalla, 00100 Rome, Italy (Telephone Number in U.S. (202) 653-2400); *Production Yearbook;* and *The State of Food and Agriculture.*

International Monetary Fund, 700 Nineteenth Street, NW, Washington, D.C. 20431 (202) 623-7000; *International Financial Statistics.*

M.E. Sharpe, 80 Business Park Drive, Armonk, New York 10504 (800) 541-6563; *The Illustrated Book of World Rankings.*

Organisation for Economic Co-operation and Development (OECD), 2 rue Andre-Pascal, 75 Paris 16, France (Telephone Number in U.S. (202) 785-6323); *Economic Accounts for Agriculture;* and *Milk, Milk Products, and Egg Balances in OECD Member Countries.*

St. Martin's Press, Inc., 175 Fifth Avenue, New York, New York 10010 (800) 221-7945; *The Statesman's Year-Book.*

Statistical Office of the United Nations, Publishing Service, New York, New York 10017 (800) 253-9646; *Statistical Yearbook.*

NEW ZEALAND - DEATH RATES - See NEW ZEALAND - MORTALITY

NEW ZEALAND - DEFENSE EXPENDITURES - See NEW ZEALAND - MILITARY

NEW ZEALAND - DEMOGRAPHY

The Economist Intelligence Unit (Asia) Limited, 10th Floor, Luk Kwok Centre, 72 Gloucester Road, Wanchai, Hong Kong (Phone Number in U.S. (800) 938-4685); *Asian Market Atlas.*

Euromonitor International, Inc., 122 South Michigan Avenue, Suite 1200, Chicago, Illinois 60603 (800) 577-EURO; *International Marketing Data and Statistics; The World Economic Factbook;* and *World Marketing Data and Statistics.*

M.E. Sharpe, 80 Business Park Drive, Armonk, New York 10504 (800) 541-6563; *The Illustrated Book of World Rankings.*

Statistical Office of the United Nations, Publishing Service, New York, New York 10017 (800) 253-9646; *Asia-Pacific in Figures;* and *Human Development Report.*

NEW ZEALAND - DEVELOPMENT ASSISTANCE

Organisation for Economic Co-operation and Development (OECD), 2 rue Andre-Pascal, 75 Paris 16, France (Telephone Number in U.S. (202) 785-6323); *Geographical Distribution of Financial Flows to Developing Countries.*

Statistical Office of the United Nations, Publishing Service, New York, New York 10017 (800) 253-9646; *Statistical Yearbook.*

NEW ZEALAND - DIAMOND PRODUCTION - See NEW ZEALAND - MINING AND MINERAL PRODUCTS

NEW ZEALAND - DISCOUNT RATES - See NEW ZEALAND - BANKING

NEW ZEALAND - DISEASES - See NEW ZEALAND - HEALTH

NEW ZEALAND - DIVORCE RATES

M.E. Sharpe, 80 Business Park Drive, Armonk, New York 10504 (800) 541-6563; *The Illustrated Book of World Rankings.*

Statistical Office of the United Nations, Publishing Service, New York, New York 10017 (800) 253-9646; *Demographic Yearbook.*

NEW ZEALAND - DUCKS - See NEW ZEALAND - LIVESTOCK AND POULTRY

NEW ZEALAND - ECONOMY

Central Intelligence Agency,

Washington, D.C. 20505 (703) 482-1100, www.cia.gov; *The World Factbook*.

Economist Intelligence Unit, 111 West 57th Street, New York, New York 10019 (800) 938-4685; *New Zealand Country Report*.

Euromonitor International, Inc., 122 South Michigan Avenue, Suite 1200, Chicago, Illinois 60603 (800) 577-EURO; *International Marketing Data and Statistics; The World Economic Factbook;* and *World Marketing Data and Statistics*.

Europa Publications Limited, 18 Bedford Square, London, WC1B 3JN, England; *The Europa World Year Book*.

M.E. Sharpe, 80 Business Park Drive, Armonk, New York 10504 (800) 541-6563; *The Illustrated Book of World Rankings*.

Organisation for Economic Co-operation and Development (OECD), 2 rue Andre-Pascal, 75 Paris 16, France (Telephone Number in U.S. (202) 785-6323); *Economic Outlook; Geographical Distribution of Financial Flows to Developing Countries; Main Economic Indicators - Historical Statistics; OECD Economic Surveys: New Zealand;* and *OECD Employment Outlook*.

St. Martin's Press, Inc., 175 Fifth Avenue, New York, New York 10010 (800) 221-7945; *The Statesman's Year-Book*.

Statistical Office of the United Nations, Publishing Service, New York, New York 10017 (800) 253-9646; *World Statistics Pocketbook*.

The World Bank, 1818 H Street, NW, Washington, D.C. 20433 (202) 477-1234; *The World Bank Atlas;* and *World Development Report*.

NEW ZEALAND - EDUCATION

The Economist Intelligence Unit, 111 West 57th Street, New York, New York 10019 (800) 938-4685; *The World Market Atlas*.

The Economist Intelligence Unit (Asia) Limited, 10th Floor, Luk Kwok Centre, 72 Gloucester Road, Wanchai, Hong Kong (Phone Number in U.S. (800) 938-4685); *Asian Market Atlas*.

Euromonitor International, Inc., 122 South Michigan Avenue, Suite 1200, Chicago, Illinois 60603 (800) 577-EURO; *International Marketing Data and Statistics;* and *World Marketing Data and Statistics*.

Europa Publications Limited, 18 Bedford Square, London, WC1B 3JN, England; *The Europa World Year Book*.

International Monetary Fund, 700 Nineteenth Street, NW, Washington, D.C. 20431 (202) 623-7000; *Government Finance Statistics Yearbook*.

M.E. Sharpe, 80 Business Park Drive, Armonk, New York 10504 (800) 541-6563; *The Illustrated Book of World Rankings*.

Organisation for Economic Co-operation and Development (OECD), 2 rue Andre-Pascal, 75 Paris 16, France (Telephone Number in U.S. (202) 785-6323); *Education in OECD Countries*.

St. Martin's Press, Inc., 175 Fifth Avenue, New York, New York 10010 (800) 221-7945; *The Statesman's Year-Book*.

Statistical Office of the United Nations, Publishing Service, New York, New York 10017 (800) 253-9646; *Asia-Pacific in Figures; Human Development Report; Statistical Yearbook;* and *Statistical Yearbook for Asia and the Pacific*.

United Nations Educational, Scientific and Cultural Organization (UNESCO), 7 Place de Fontenoy, F-75700 Paris, France (Telephone Number in U.S. (212) 963-5981); *Statistical Yearbook*.

The World Bank, 1818 H Street, NW, Washington, D.C. 20433 (202) 477-1234; *World Development Report;* and *World Development Indicators*.

NEW ZEALAND - EGG PRODUCTION AND CONSUMPTION - See NEW ZEALAND - DAIRY PRODUCTS

NEW ZEALAND - ELECTRICITY

Central Intelligence Agency, Washington, D.C. 20505 (703) 482-1100, www.cia.gov; *The World Factbook*.

M.E. Sharpe, 80 Business Park Drive, Armonk, New York 10504 (800) 541-6563; *The Illustrated Book of World Rankings*.

Organisation for Economic Co-operation and Development (OECD), 2 rue Andre-Pascal, 75 Paris 16, France (Telephone Number in U.S. (202) 785-6323); *Coal Information; Energy Statistics of OECD Countries;* and *Industrial Structure Statistics*.

Penn Well Publishing Company, 1421 South Sheridan Road, Post Office Box 1260, Tulsa, Oklahoma 74101 (800) 752-9764; *International Energy Statistics Sourcebook*.

St. Martin's Press, Inc., 175 Fifth Avenue, New York, New York 10010 (800) 221-7945; *The Statesman's Year-Book*.

Statistical Office of the United Nations, Publishing Service, New York, New York 10017 (800) 253-9646; *Human*

Development Report; and *Statistical Yearbook*.

NEW ZEALAND - EMPLOYMENT

Euromonitor International, Inc., 122 South Michigan Avenue, Suite 1200, Chicago, Illinois 60603 (800) 577-EURO; *International Marketing Data and Statistics*.

International Labour Office, I.L.O. Publications, 1828 L Street, NW, Suite 801, Washington, D.C. 20036 (301) 638-3152; *Yearbook of Labour Statistics*.

M.E. Sharpe, 80 Business Park Drive, Armonk, New York 10504 (800) 541-6563; *The Illustrated Book of World Rankings*.

Organisation for Economic Co-operation and Development (OECD), 2 rue Andre-Pascal, 75 Paris 16, France (Telephone Number in U.S. (202) 785-6323); *The Iron and Steel Industry; OECD Economic Surveys: New Zealand; OECD Employment Outlook;* and *Textile Industry in OECD Countries*.

Statistical Office of the United Nations, Publishing Service, New York, New York 10017 (800) 253-9646; *Asia-Pacific in Figures;* and *Statistical Yearbook*.

NEW ZEALAND - ENERGY

Euromonitor International, Inc., 122 South Michigan Avenue, Suite 1200, Chicago, Illinois 60603 (800) 577-EURO; *International Marketing Data and Statistics; The World Economic Factbook;* and *World Marketing Data and Statistics*.

Food and Agricultural Organization of the United Nations (FAO) Via delle Terme di Caracalla, 00100 Rome, Italy (Telephone Number in U.S. (202) 653-2400); *The State of Food and Agriculture*.

M.E. Sharpe, 80 Business Park Drive, Armonk, New York 10504 (800) 541-6563; *The Illustrated Book of World Rankings*.

Organisation for Economic Co-operation and Development (OECD), 2 rue Andre-Pascal, 75 Paris 16, France (Telephone Number in U.S. (202) 785-6323); *Coal Information; Energy Statistics of OECD Countries; OECD Environmental Data;* and *Oil and Gas Information*.

Penn Well Publishing Company, 1421 South Sheridan Road, Post Office Box 1260, Tulsa, Oklahoma 74101 (800) 752-9764; *International Energy Statistics Sourcebook*.

St. Martin's Press, Inc., 175 Fifth Avenue, New York, New York 10010 (800) 221-7945; *The Statesman's Year-Book*.

Statistical Office of the United Nations, Publishing Service, New York, New York

10017 (800) 253-9646; *Asia-Pacific in Figures; Energy Statistics Yearbook; Human Development Report; Statistical Yearbook; World Statistics Pocketbook;* and *Statistical Yearbook for Asia and the Pacific.*

The World Bank, 1818 H Street, NW, Washington, D.C. 20433 (202) 477-1234; *The World Bank Atlas;* and *World Development Report.*

NEW ZEALAND - ENVIRONMENT

Economist Intelligence Unit, 111 West 57th Street, New York, New York 10019 (800) 938-4685; *New Zealand Country Report.*

Organization for Economic Co-operation and Development (OECD), 2 rue Andre-Pascal, 75 Paris 16, France (Telephone Number in the U.S. (202) 785-6323); *OECD Environmental Data.*

Statistical Office of the United Nations, Publishing Service, New York, New York 10017 (800) 253-9646; *World Statistics Pocketbook.*

NEW ZEALAND - EXCHANGE RATES

Central Intelligence Agency, Washington, D.C. 20505 (703) 482-1100, www.cia.gov; *The World Factbook.*

The Economist Intelligence Unit (Asia) Limited, 10th Floor, Luk Kwok Centre, 72 Gloucester Road, Wanchai, Hong Kong (Phone Number in U.S. (800) 938-4685; *Asian Market Atlas.*

Euromonitor International, Inc., 122 South Michigan Avenue, Suite 1200, Chicago, Illinois 60603 (800) 577-EURO; *International Marketing Data and Statistics;* and *The World Economic Factbook.*

Europa Publications Limited, 18 Bedford Square, London, WC1B 3JN, England; *The Europa World Year Book.*

International Civil Aviation Organization, 999 University Street, Montreal, Quebec, Canada H3C 5H7 (514) 954-8219; *Civil Aviation Statistics of the World.*

International Monetary Fund, 700 Nineteenth Street, NW, Washington, D.C. 20431 (202) 623-7000; *International Financial Statistics.*

Organisation for Economic Co-operation and Development (OECD), 2 rue Andre-Pascal, 75 Paris 16, France (Telephone Number in U.S. (202) 785-6323); *Economic Outlook; Financial Market Trends; Revenue Statistics of OECD Member Countries;* and *Tourism Policy and International Tourism in OECD Member Countries.*

Statistical Office of the United Nations, Publishing Service, New York, New York 10017 (800) 253-9646; *Statistical Yearbook;* and *World Statistics Pocketbook.*

Walden Publishing Ltd., Two Market Street, Saffron Walden Essex, CB10 1HZ, England; *The World of Information Asia and Pacific Review.*

NEW ZEALAND - EXCISE TAXES - See NEW ZEALAND - TAXATION

NEW ZEALAND - EXPORTS

The Economist Intelligence Unit, 111 West 57th Street, New York, New York 10019 (800) 938-4685; *New Zealand Country Report;* and *The World Market Atlas.*

The Economist Intelligence Unit (Asia) Limited, 10th Floor, Luk Kwok Centre, 72 Gloucester Road, Wanchai, Hong Kong (Phone Number in U.S. (800) 938-4685); *Asian Market Atlas.*

Euromonitor International, Inc., 122 South Michigan Avenue, Suite 1200, Chicago, Illinois 60603 (800) 577-EURO; *International Marketing Data and Statistics;* and *The World Economic Factbook.*

Europa Publications Limited, 18 Bedford Square, London, WC1B 3JN, England; *The Europa World Year Book.*

Food and Agricultural Organization of the United Nations (FAO) Via delle Terme di Caracalla, 00100 Rome, Italy (Telephone Number in U.S. (202) 653-2400); *The State of Food and Agriculture.*

International Monetary Fund, 700 Nineteenth Street, NW, Washington, D.C. 20431 (202) 623-7000; *Direction of Trade Statistics;* and *International Financial Statistics.*

Organisation for Economic Co-operation and Development (OECD), 2 rue Andre-Pascal, 75 Paris 16, France (Telephone Number in U.S. (202) 785-6323); *Economic Outlook; The Footwear, Raw Hides and Skins, and Leather Industry in OECD Countries; Foreign Trade by Commodities; Geographical Distribution of Financial Flows to Developing Countries; Industrial Structure Statistics; The Iron and Steel Industry; Milk, Milk Products, and Egg Balances in OECD Member Countries; The Pulp and Paper Industry; OECD Economic Surveys: New Zealand;* and *Review of Fisheries in OECD Member Countries.*

St. Martin's Press, Inc., 175 Fifth Avenue, New York, New York 10010 (800) 221-7945; *The Statesman's Year-Book.*

Statistical Office of the United Nations,

Publishing Service, New York, New York 10017 (800) 253-9646; *Foreign Trade Statistics of Asia and the Pacific.*

United Nations Conference on Trade and Development (UNCTAD), New York, New York 10017 (800) 253-9646; *Handbook of International Trade and Development Statistics.*

Walden Publishing Ltd., Two Market Street, Saffron Walden Essex, CB10 1HZ, England; *The World of Information Asia and Pacific Review.*

The World Bank, 1818 H Street, NW, Washington, D.C. 20433 (202) 477-1234; *World Development Report;* and *World Development Indicators.*

NEW ZEALAND - EXTERNAL FINANCING

Organisation for Economic Co-operation and Development (OECD), 2 rue Andre-Pascal, 75 Paris 16, France (Telephone Number in U.S. (202) 785-6323); *Economic Outlook;* and *Financial Market Trends.*

NEW ZEALAND - EXTERNAL INDEBTEDNESS

Organisation for Economic Co-operation and Development (OECD), 2 rue Andre-Pascal, 75 Paris 16, France (Telephone Number in U.S. (202) 785-6323); *Financial Market Trends;* and *Geographical Distribution of Financial Flows to Developing Countries.*

The World Bank, 1818 H Street, NW, Washington, D.C. 20433 (202) 477-1234; *World Development Report;* and *World Development Indicators.*

NEW ZEALAND - EXTERNAL TRADE

Euromonitor International, Inc., 122 South Michigan Avenue, Suite 1200, Chicago, Illinois 60603 (800) 577-EURO; *World Marketing Data and Statistics.*

Food and Agricultural Organization of the United Nations (FAO) Via delle Terme di Caracalla, 00100 Rome, Italy (Telephone Number in U.S. (202) 653-2400); *The State of Food and Agriculture;* and *Trade Yearbook.*

Statistical Office of the United Nations, Publishing Service, New York, New York 10017 (800) 253-9646; *Asia-Pacific in Figures; Statistical Yearbook;* and *Statistical Yearbook for Asia and the Pacific.*

NEW ZEALAND - FABRIC PRODUCTION - See NEW ZEALAND - TEXTILE INDUSTRY

NEW ZEALAND - FARM CROPS - See NEW ZEALAND - CROPS

NEW ZEALAND - FEMALE WORKING POPULATION - See NEW ZEALAND - EMPLOYMENT

NEW ZEALAND - FERTILITY RATES

The Economist Intelligence Unit (Asia) Limited, 10th Floor, Luk Kwok Centre, 72 Gloucester Road, Wanchai, Hong Kong (Phone Number in U.S. (800) 938-4685); *Asian Market Atlas.*

M.E. Sharpe, 80 Business Park Drive, Armonk, New York 10504 (800) 541-6563; *The Illustrated Book of World Rankings.*

Statistical Office of the United Nations, Publishing Service, New York, New York 10017 (800) 253-9646; *Human Development Report.*

The World Bank, 1818 H Street, NW, Washington, D.C. 20433 (202) 477-1234; *The World Bank Atlas; World Development Report;* and *World Development Indicators.*

NEW ZEALAND - FERTILIZER

Food and Agricultural Organization of the United Nations (FAO) Via delle Terme di Caracalla, 00100 Rome, Italy (Telephone Number in U.S. (202) 653-2400); *The State of Food and Agriculture.*

Organisation for Economic Co-operation and Development (OECD), 2 rue Andre-Pascal, 75 Paris 16, France (Telephone Number in U.S. (202) 785-6323); *Economic Accounts for Agriculture;* and *Foreign Trade by Commodities.*

Statistical Office of the United Nations, Publishing Service, New York, New York 10017 (800) 253-9646; *Statistical Yearbook.*

NEW ZEALAND - FETAL MORTALITY - See NEW ZEALAND - MORTALITY

NEW ZEALAND - FIBRE PRODUCTION - See NEW ZEALAND - TEXTILE INDUSTRY

NEW ZEALAND - FILAMENT PRODUCTION - See NEW ZEALAND - TEXTILE INDUSTRY

NEW ZEALAND - FILMS PRODUCED - LONG - See NEW ZEALAND - MOTION PICTURES

NEW ZEALAND - FINANCE

Economist Intelligence Unit, 111 West 57th Street, New York, New York 10019 (800) 938-4685; *New Zealand Country Report.*

Europa Publications Limited, 18 Bedford Square, London, WC1B 3JN, England; *The Europa World Year Book.*

International Monetary Fund, 700 Nineteenth Street, NW, Washington, D.C.

20431 (202) 623-7000; *Government Finance Statistics Yearbook,* and *International Financial Statistics.*

M.E. Sharpe, 80 Business Park Drive, Armonk, New York 10504 (800) 541-6563; *The Illustrated Book of World Rankings.*

Organisation for Economic Co-operation and Development (OECD), 2 rue Andre-Pascal, 75 Paris 16, France (Telephone Number in U.S. (202) 785-6323); *Economic Outlook; Financial Market Trends; Geographical Distribution of Financial Flows to Developing Countries; Main Economic Indicators - Historical Statistics; OECD Financial Statistics;* and *Revenue Statistics of OECD Member Countries.*

St. Martin's Press, Inc., 175 Fifth Avenue, New York, New York 10010 (800) 221-7945; *The Statesman's Year-Book.*

Statistical Office of the United Nations, Publishing Service, New York, New York 10017 (800) 253-9646; *Statistical Yearbook for Asia and the Pacific.*

NEW ZEALAND - FISHERIES

Europa Publications Limited, 18 Bedford Square, London, WC1B 3JN, England; *The Europa World Year Book.*

Food and Agricultural Organization of the United Nations (FAO) Via delle Terme di Caracalla, 00100 Rome, Italy (Telephone Number in U.S. (202) 653-2400); *The State of Food and Agriculture;* and *Yearbook of Fishery Statistics.*

M.E. Sharpe, 80 Business Park Drive, Armonk, New York 10504 (800) 541-6563; *The Illustrated Book of World Rankings.*

Organisation for Economic Co-operation and Development (OECD), 2 rue Andre-Pascal, 75 Paris 16, France (Telephone Number in U.S. (202) 785-6323); *Foreign Trade by Commodities; Industrial Structure Statistics;* and *Review of Fisheries in OECD Member Countries.*

St. Martin's Press, Inc., 175 Fifth Avenue, New York, New York 10010 (800) 221-7945; *The Statesman's Year-Book.*

Statistical Office of the United Nations, Publishing Service, New York, New York 10017 (800) 253-9646; *Statistical Yearbook.*

United Nations Conference on Trade and Development, Central Statistical Service, Palais des Nations, Geneva, Switzerland (Telephone in U.S. (800) 253-9646); *UNCTAD Commodity Yearbook.*

NEW ZEALAND - FLOUR PRODUCTION

Statistical Office of the United Nations,

Publishing Service, New York, New York 10017 (800) 253-9646; *Statistical Yearbook.*

NEW ZEALAND - FOOD

Euromonitor International, Inc., 122 South Michigan Avenue, Suite 1200, Chicago, Illinois 60603 (800) 577-EURO; *Retail Trade International.*

Food and Agricultural Organization of the United Nations (FAO), Via delle Terme di Caracalla, 00100 Rome, Italy (Telephone Number in U.S. (202) 653-2400); *Production Yearbook;* and *The State of Food and Agriculture.*

Organisation for Economic Co-operation and Development (OECD), 2 rue Andre-Pascal, 75 Paris 16, France (Telephone Number in U.S. (202) 785-6323); *Food Consumption Statistics;* and *Foreign Trade by Commodities.*

Statistical Office of the United Nations, Publishing Service, New York, New York 10017 (800) 253-9646; *Human Development Report;* and *Statistical Yearbook for Asia and the Pacific.*

United Nations Conference on Trade and Development, Central Statistical Service, Palais des Nations, Geneva, Switzerland (Telephone in U.S. (800) 253-9646); *UNCTAD Commodity Yearbook.*

NEW ZEALAND - FOREIGN DEBT

International Monetary Fund, 700 Nineteenth Street, NW, Washington, D.C. 20431 (202) 623-7000; *Government Finance Statistics Yearbook.*

Organisation for Economic Co-operation and Development (OECD), 2 rue Andre-Pascal, 75 Paris 16, France (Telephone Number in U.S. (202) 785-6323); *Economic Outlook.*

St. Martin's Press, Inc., 175 Fifth Avenue, New York, New York 10010 (800) 221-7945; *The Statesman's Year-Book.*

Walden Publishing Ltd., Two Market Street, Saffron Walden Essex, CB10 1HZ, England; The World of Information Asia and Pacific Review.

NEW ZEALAND - FOREIGN INDEBTEDNESS

Organisation for Economic Co-operation and Development (OECD), 2 rue Andre-Pascal, 75 Paris 16, France (Telephone Number in U.S. (202) 785-6323); *Economic Outlook;* and *Financial Market Trends.*

NEW ZEALAND - FOREIGN TRADE

Economist Intelligence Unit, 111 West

57th Street, New York, New York 10019 (800) 938-4685; *New Zealand Country Report.*

The Economist Intelligence Unit (Asia) Limited, 10th Floor, Luk Kwok Centre, 72 Gloucester Road, Wanchai, Hong Kong (Phone Number in U.S. (800) 938-4685); *Asian Market Atlas.*

Euromonitor International, Inc., 122 South Michigan Avenue, Suite 1200, Chicago, Illinois 60603 (800) 577-EURO; *International Marketing Data and Statistics;* and *The World Economic Factbook.*

Europa Publications Limited, 18 Bedford Square, London, WC1B 3JN, England; *The Europa World Year Book.*

Food and Agricultural Organization of the United Nations (FAO) Via delle Terme di Caracalla, 00100 Rome, Italy (Telephone Number in U.S. (202) 653-2400); *The State of Food and Agriculture.*

M.E. Sharpe, 80 Business Park Drive, Armonk, New York 10504 (800) 541-6563; *The Illustrated Book of World Rankings.*

Organisation for Economic Co-operation and Development (OECD), 2 rue Andre-Pascal, 75 Paris 16, France (Telephone Number in U.S. (202) 785-6323); *Economic Outlook; The Footwear, Raw Hides and Skins, and Leather Industry in OECD Countries; Foreign Trade by Commodities; Main Economic Indicators - Historical Statistics; Maritime Transport; Meat Balances in OECD Member Countries;* and *OECD Economic Surveys: New Zealand.*

St. Martin's Press, Inc., 175 Fifth Avenue, New York, New York 10010 (800) 221-7945; *The Statesman's Year-Book.*

Statistical Office of the United Nations, Publishing Service, New York, New York 10017 (800) 253-9646; *International Trade Statistics Yearbook;* and *Statistical Yearbook.*

United Nations Conference on Trade and Development, Central Statistical Service, Palais des Nations, Geneva, Switzerland (Telephone in U.S. (800) 253-9646); *UNCTAD Commodity Yearbook.*

The World Bank, 1818 H Street, NW, Washington, D.C. 20433 (202) 477-1234; *World Development Report;* and *World Development Indicators.*

NEW ZEALAND - FORESTRY AND FOREST PRODUCTS

American Forest and Paper Association, 1111 Nineteenth Street, NW, Suite 800, Washington, D.C. 20036 (202) 463-2700; *Wood Pulp and Fiber Statistics.*

Europa Publications Limited, 18 Bedford Square, London, WC1B 3JN, England; *The Europa World Year Book.*

Food and Agricultural Organization of the United Nations (FAO) Via delle Terme di Caracalla, 00100 Rome, Italy (Telephone Number in U.S. (202) 653-2400); *The State of Food and Agriculture;* and *Yearbook of Forest Products.*

M.E. Sharpe, 80 Business Park Drive, Armonk, New York 10504 (800) 541-6563; *The Illustrated Book of World Rankings.*

Organisation for Economic Co-operation and Development (OECD), 2 rue Andre-Pascal, 75 Paris 16, France (Telephone Number in U.S. (202) 785-6323); *Foreign Trade by Commodities; Industrial Structure Statistics;* and *The Pulp and Paper Industry.*

St. Martin's Press, Inc., 175 Fifth Avenue, New York, New York 10010 (800) 221-7945; *The Statesman's Year-Book.*

Statistical Office of the United Nations, Publishing Service, New York, New York 10017 (800) 253-9646; *Statistical Yearbook.*

United Nations Conference on Trade and Development, Central Statistical Service, Palais des Nations, Geneva, Switzerland (Telephone in U.S. (800) 253-9646); *UNCTAD Commodity Yearbook.*

The World Bank, 1818 H Street, NW, Washington, D.C. 20433 (202) 477-1234; *World Development Report.*

NEW ZEALAND - FRUIT PRODUCTION - See NEW ZEALAND - CROPS

NEW ZEALAND - FURNITURE AND WOOD PRODUCTS - EXPORTS AND IMPORTS

Organisation for Economic Co-operation and Development (OECD), 2 rue Andre-Pascal, 75 Paris 16, France (Telephone Number in U.S. (202) 785-6323); *Foreign Trade by Commodities;* and *Industrial Structure Statistics.*

NEW ZEALAND - GAS PRODUCTION - See NEW ZEALAND - MINING AND MINERAL PRODUCTS

NEW ZEALAND - GENERAL INDUSTRIAL STATISTICS

Statistical Office of the United Nations, Publishing Service, New York, New York 10017 (800) 253-9646; *Industrial Commodity Statistics Yearbook.*

NEW ZEALAND - GENERAL MORTALITY - See NEW ZEALAND - MORTALITY

NEW ZEALAND - GEOGRAPHIC DATA

M.E. Sharpe, 80 Business Park Drive, Armonk, New York 10504 (800) 541-6563; *The Illustrated Book of World Rankings.*

NEW ZEALAND - GOATS - See NEW ZEALAND - LIVESTOCK AND POULTRY

NEW ZEALAND - GOLD HOLDINGS

International Monetary Fund, 700 Nineteenth Street, NW, Washington, D.C. 20431 (202) 623-7000; *International Financial Statistics.*

Statistical Office of the United Nations, Publishing Service, New York, New York 10017 (800) 253-9646; *Statistical Yearbook.*

The World Bank, 1818 H Street, NW, Washington, D.C. 20433 (202) 477-1234; *World Development Indicators.*

NEW ZEALAND - GOLD PRODUCTION AND CONSUMPTION - See NEW ZEALAND - MINING AND MINERAL PRODUCTS

NEW ZEALAND - GOVERNMENT

Central Intelligence Agency, Washington, D.C. 20505 (703) 482-1100, www.cia.gov; *The World Factbook.*

Europa Publications Limited, 18 Bedford Square, London, WC1B 3JN, England; *The Europa World Year Book.*

International Monetary Fund, 700 Nineteenth Street, NW, Washington, D.C. 20431 (202) 623-7000; *Government Finance Statistics Yearbook;* and *International Financial Statistics.*

Organisation for Economic Co-operation and Development (OECD), 2 rue Andre-Pascal, 75 Paris 16, France (Telephone Number in U.S. (202) 785-6323); *Economic Outlook;* and *Revenue Statistics of OECD Member Countries.*

St. Martin's Press, Inc., 175 Fifth Avenue, New York, New York 10010 (800) 221-7945; *The Statesman's Year-Book.*

Statistical Office of the United Nations, Publishing Service, New York, New York 10017 (800) 253-9646; *Asia-Pacific in Figures; National Accounts Statistics;* and *Statistical Yearbook.*

The World Bank, 1818 H Street, NW, Washington, D.C. 20433 (202) 477-1234; *World Development Report;* and *World Development Indicators.*

NEW ZEALAND - GRAIN PRODUCTION - See NEW ZEALAND - CROPS

NEW ZEALAND - GRANTS

International Monetary Fund, 700 Nineteenth Street, NW, Washington, D.C.

20431 (202) 623-7000; *Government Finance Statistics Yearbook.*

Organisation for Economic Co-operation and Development (OECD), 2 rue Andre-Pascal, 75 Paris 16, France (Telephone Number in U.S. (202) 785-6323); *Geographical Distribution of Financial Flows to Developing Countries.*

NEW ZEALAND - GROSS DOMESTIC PRODUCT

The Economist Intelligence Unit, 111 West 57th Street, New York, New York 10019 (800) 938-4685; *New Zealand Country Report;* and *The World Market Atlas.*

The Economist Intelligence Unit (Asia) Limited, 10th Floor, Luk Kwok Centre, 72 Gloucester Road, Wanchai, Hong Kong (Phone Number in U.S. (800) 938-4685); *Asian Market Atlas.*

Euromonitor International, Inc., 122 South Michigan Avenue, Suite 1200, Chicago, Illinois 60603 (800) 577-EURO; *International Marketing Data and Statistics;* and *The World Economic Factbook.*

Europa Publications Limited, 18 Bedford Square, London, WC1B 3JN, England; *The Europa World Year Book.*

M.E. Sharpe, 80 Business Park Drive, Armonk, New York 10504 (800) 541-6563; *The Illustrated Book of World Rankings.*

Organisation for Economic Co-operation and Development (OECD), 2 rue Andre-Pascal, 75 Paris 16, France (Telephone Number in U.S. (202) 785-6323); *Economic Outlook; Geographical Distribution of Financial Flows to Developing Countries;* and *Revenue Statistics of OECD Member Countries.*

Statistical Office of the United Nations, Publishing Service, New York, New York 10017 (800) 253-9646; *Human Development Report; National Accounts Statistics;* and *Statistical Yearbook.*

The World Bank, 1818 H Street, NW, Washington, D.C. 20433 (202) 477-1234; *World Development Report;* and *World Development Indicators.*

NEW ZEALAND - GROSS NATIONAL PRODUCT

Euromonitor International, Inc., 122 South Michigan Avenue, Suite 1200, Chicago, Illinois 60603 (800) 577-EURO; *International Marketing Data and Statistics.*

Europa Publications Limited, 18 Bedford Square, London, WC1B 3JN, England; *The Europa World Year Book.*

Organisation for Economic Co-operation and Development (OECD), 2 rue Andre-Pascal, 75 Paris 16, France (Telephone Number in U.S. (202) 785-6323); *Economic Outlook;* and *Geographical Distribution of Financial Flows to Developing Countries.*

U.S. Arms Control and Disarmament Agency, 320 Twenty-first Street, NW, Washington, D.C. 20451 (202) 647-8677; *World Military Expenditures and Arms Transfers.*

Walden Publishing Ltd., Two Market Street, Saffron Walden Essex, CB10 1HZ, England; *The World of Information Asia and Pacific Review.*

The World Bank, 1818 H Street, NW, Washington, D.C. 20433 (202) 477-1234; *The World Bank Atlas; World Development Report;* and *World Development Indicators.*

NEW ZEALAND - HEALTH

The Economist Intelligence Unit (Asia) Limited, 10th Floor, Luk Kwok Centre, 72 Gloucester Road, Wanchai, Hong Kong (Phone Number in U.S. (800) 938-4685); *Asian Market Atlas.*

Euromonitor International, Inc., 122 South Michigan Avenue, Suite 1200, Chicago, Illinois 60603 (800) 577-EURO; *World Marketing Data and Statistics.*

M.E. Sharpe, 80 Business Park Drive, Armonk, New York 10504 (800) 541-6563; *The Illustrated Book of World Rankings.*

Organisation for Economic Co-operation and Development (OECD), 2 rue Andre-Pascal, 75 Paris 16, France (Telephone Number in U.S. (202) 785-6323); *OECD Health Systems: Facts and Trends.*

St. Martin's Press, Inc., 175 Fifth Avenue, New York, New York 10010 (800) 221-7945; *The Statesman's Year-Book.*

Statistical Office of the United Nations, Publishing Service, New York, New York 10017 (800) 253-9646; *Asia-Pacific in Figures; Human Development Report;* and *Statistical Yearbook.*

United Nations Children's Fund (UNICEF), 3 United Nations Plaza, New York, New York 10017 (800) 253-9646; *State of the World's Children.*

The World Bank, 1818 H Street, NW, Washington, D.C. 20433 (202) 477-1234; *World Development Report.*

World Health Organization, Office of Publications, 20 Avenue Appia, CH-1211 Geneva 27, Switzerland (Telephone Number in U.S. (518) 436-9686); *World*

Health Statistics Annual.

NEW ZEALAND - HEALTH EXPENDITURES

International Monetary Fund, 700 Nineteenth Street, NW, Washington, D.C. 20431 (202) 623-7000; *Government Finance Statistics Yearbook.*

NEW ZEALAND - HIDE PRODUCTION

Food and Agricultural Organization of the United Nations (FAO), Via delle Terme di Caracalla, 00100 Rome, Italy (Telephone Number in U.S. (202) 653-2400); *Production Yearbook.*

Organisation for Economic Co-operation and Development (OECD), 2 rue Andre-Pascal, 75 Paris 16, France (Telephone Number in U.S. (202) 785-6323); *The Footwear, Raw Hides and Skins, and Leather Industry in OECD Countries,* and *Foreign Trade by Commodities.*

NEW ZEALAND - HIGHWAYS

Central Intelligence Agency, Washington, D.C. 20505 (703) 482-1100, www.cia.gov; *The World Factbook.*

The Economist Intelligence Unit (Asia) Limited, 10th Floor, Luk Kwok Centre, 72 Gloucester Road, Wanchai, Hong Kong (Phone Number in U.S. (800) 938-4685); *Asian Market Atlas.*

International Road Federation, 2600 Virginia Avenue, NW, Washington, D.C. 20037 (202) 338-4641; *World Road Statistics.*

St. Martin's Press, Inc., 175 Fifth Avenue, New York, New York 10010 (800) 221-7945; *The Statesman's Year-Book.*

NEW ZEALAND - HOME FINANCE

Organisation for Economic Co-operation and Development (OECD), 2 rue Andre-Pascal, 75 Paris 16, France (Telephone Number in U.S. (202) 785-6323); *Main Economic Indicators - Historical Statistics.*

NEW ZEALAND - HORSES - See NEW ZEALAND - LIVESTOCK AND POULTRY

NEW ZEALAND - HOURS OF WORK - See NEW ZEALAND - EMPLOYMENT

NEW ZEALAND - HOUSING AND HOUSING UNITS

Euromonitor International, Inc., 122 South Michigan Avenue, Suite 1200, Chicago, Illinois 60603 (800) 577-EURO; *World Marketing Data and Statistics.*

M.E. Sharpe, 80 Business Park Drive, Armonk, New York 10504 (800) 541-6563; *The Illustrated Book of World Rankings.*

NEW ZEALAND - HOUSING CONSTRUCTION - See NEW ZEALAND - CONSTRUCTION INDUSTRY

NEW ZEALAND - HOUSING EXPENDITURES

International Monetary Fund, 700 Nineteenth Street, NW, Washington, D.C. 20431 (202) 623-7000; *Government Finance Statistics Yearbook.*

NEW ZEALAND - ILLITERATE POPULATION

Central Intelligence Agency, Washington, D.C. 20505 (703) 482-1100, www.cia.gov; *The World Factbook.*

The Economist Intelligence Unit, 111 West 57th Street, New York, New York 10019 (800) 938-4685; *The World Market Atlas.*

Euromonitor International, Inc., 122 South Michigan Avenue, Suite 1200, Chicago, Illinois 60603 (800) 577-EURO; *The World Economic Factbook.*

Statistical Office of the United Nations, Publishing Service, New York, New York 10017 (800) 253-9646; *Asia-Pacific in Figures;* and *Human Development Report.*

NEW ZEALAND - IMPORTS

Central Intelligence Agency, Washington, D.C. 20505 (703) 482-1100, www.cia.gov; *The World Factbook.*

The Economist Intelligence Unit, 111 West 57th Street, New York, New York 10019 (800) 938-4685; *New Zealand Country Report;* and *The World Market Atlas.*

The Economist Intelligence Unit (Asia) Limited, 10th Floor, Luk Kwok Centre, 72 Gloucester Road, Wanchai, Hong Kong (Phone Number in U.S. (800) 938-4685); *Asian Market Atlas.*

Euromonitor International, Inc., 122 South Michigan Avenue, Suite 1200, Chicago, Illinois 60603 (800) 577-EURO; *International Marketing Data and Statistics;* and *The World Economic Factbook.*

Europa Publications Limited, 18 Bedford Square, London, WC1B 3JN, England; *The Europa World Year Book.*

Food and Agricultural Organization of the United Nations (FAO) Via delle Terme di Caracalla, 00100 Rome, Italy (Telephone Number in U.S. (202) 653-2400); *The State of Food and Agriculture.*

International Monetary Fund, 700 Nineteenth Street, NW, Washington, D.C. 20431 (202) 623-7000; *Direction of Trade Statistics; Government Finance Statistics Yearbook;* and *International Financial Statistics.*

Organisation for Economic Co-operation and Development (OECD), 2 rue Andre-Pascal, 75 Paris 16, France (Telephone Number in U.S. (202) 785-6323); *Economic Outlook; The Footwear, Raw Hides and Skins, and Leather Industry in OECD Countries; Industrial Structure Statistics; The Iron and Steel Industry; Milk, Milk Products, and Egg Balances in OECD Member Countries; The Pulp and Paper Industry; OECD Economic Surveys: New Zealand;* and *Review of Fisheries in OECD Member Countries.*

St. Martin's Press, Inc., 175 Fifth Avenue, New York, New York 10010 (800) 221-7945; *The Statesman's Year-Book.*

Statistical Office of the United Nations, Publishing Service, New York, New York 10017 (800) 253-9646; *Foreign Trade Statistics of Asia and the Pacific.*

United Nations Conference on Trade and Development (UNCTAD), New York, New York 10017 (800) 253-9646; *Handbook of International Trade and Development Statistics.*

Walden Publishing Ltd., Two Market Street, Saffron Walden Essex, CB10 1HZ, England; *The World of Information Asia and Pacific Review.*

The World Bank, 1818 H Street, NW, Washington, D.C. 20433 (202) 477-1234; *World Development Report;* and *World Development Indicators.*

NEW ZEALAND - INCOME TAXES - See NEW ZEALAND - TAXATION

NEW ZEALAND - INDUSTRY

Central Intelligence Agency, Washington, D.C. 20505 (703) 482-1100, www.cia.gov; *The World Factbook.*

Economist Intelligence Unit, 111 West 57th Street, New York, New York 10019 (800) 938-4685; *New Zealand Country Report.*

Euromonitor International, Inc., 122 South Michigan Avenue, Suite 1200, Chicago, Illinois 60603 (800) 577-EURO; *International Marketing Data and Statistics; The World Economic Factbook;* and *World Marketing Data and Statistics.*

Europa Publications Limited, 18 Bedford Square, London, WC1B 3JN, England; *The Europa World Year Book.*

International Labour Office, I.L.O. Publications, 1828 L Street, NW, Suite 801, Washington, D.C. 20036 (301) 638-3152; *Yearbook of Labour Statistics.*

M.E. Sharpe, 80 Business Park Drive, Armonk, New York 10504 (800) 541-6563; *The Illustrated Book of World Rankings.*

Organisation for Economic Co-operation and Development (OECD), 2 rue Andre-Pascal, 75 Paris 16, France (Telephone Number in U.S. (202) 785-6323); *Economic Outlook; Industrial Structure Statistics;* and *OECD Environmental Data.*

St. Martin's Press, Inc., 175 Fifth Avenue, New York, New York 10010 (800) 221-7945; *The Statesman's Year-Book.*

Statistical Office of the United Nations, Publishing Service, New York, New York 10017 (800) 253-9646; *Asia-Pacific in Figures; Statistical Yearbook;* and *Statistical Yearbook for Asia and the Pacific.*

The World Bank, 1818 H Street, NW, Washington, D.C. 20433 (202) 477-1234; *World Development Indicators.*

World Intellectual Property Organization, 34 Chemin des Colombettes, CH-1211 Geneva 20, Switzerland; *Industrial Property Statistics.*

NEW ZEALAND - INFANT AND MATERNAL MORTALITY - See NEW ZEALAND - MORTALITY

NEW ZEALAND - INTEREST RATES

Organisation for Economic Co-operation and Development (OECD), 2 rue Andre-Pascal, 75 Paris 16, France (Telephone Number in U.S. (202) 785-6323); *Economic Outlook; Financial Market Trends;* and *OECD Financial Statistics.*

NEW ZEALAND - INTERNAL TRADE

Organisation for Economic Co-operation and Development (OECD), 2 rue Andre-Pascal, 75 Paris 16, France (Telephone Number in U.S. (202) 785-6323); *Main Economic Indicators - Historical Statistics.*

Statistical Office of the United Nations, Publishing Service, New York, New York 10017 (800) 253-9646; *Statistical Yearbook for Asia and the Pacific.*

NEW ZEALAND - INTERNATIONAL FINANCE

Organisation for Economic Co-operation and Development (OECD), 2 rue Andre-Pascal, 75 Paris 16, France (Telephone Number in U.S. (202) 785-6323); *Economic Outlook;* and *Financial*

Market Trends.

NEW ZEALAND - INTERNATIONAL LIQUIDITY

International Monetary Fund, 700 Nineteenth Street, NW, Washington, D.C. 20431 (202) 623-7000; *International Financial Statistics.*

Organisation for Economic Co-operation and Development (OECD), 2 rue Andre-Pascal, 75 Paris 16, France (Telephone Number in U.S. (202) 785-6323); *Economic Outlook;* and *Financial Market Trends.*

NEW ZEALAND - INTERNATIONAL RESERVES EXCLUDING GOLD

Statistical Office of the United Nations, Publishing Service, New York, New York 10017 (800) 253-9646; *Statistical Yearbook.*

The World Bank, 1818 H Street, NW, Washington, D.C. 20433 (202) 477-1234; *World Development Indicators.*

NEW ZEALAND - INTERNATIONAL STATISTICS

Organisation for Economic Co-operation and Development (OECD), 2 rue Andre-Pascal, 75 Paris 16, France (Telephone Number in U.S. (202) 785-6323); *Financial Market Trends;* and *Tourism Policy and International Tourism in OECD Member Countries.*

NEW ZEALAND - INVESTMENTS

International Monetary Fund, 700 Nineteenth Street, NW, Washington, D.C. 20431 (202) 623-7000; *International Financial Statistics.*

Organisation for Economic Co-operation and Development (OECD), 2 rue Andre-Pascal, 75 Paris 16, France (Telephone Number in U.S. (202) 785-6323); *Economic Outlook; Financial Market Trends; Industrial Structure Statistics; The Iron and Steel Industry;* and *Textile Industry in OECD Countries.*

NEW ZEALAND - IRON ORE PRODUCTION AND CONSUMPTION - See NEW ZEALAND - MINING AND MINERAL PRODUCTS

NEW ZEALAND - IRRIGATION

Euromonitor International, Inc., 122 South Michigan Avenue, Suite 1200, Chicago, Illinois 60603 (800) 577-EURO; *International Marketing Data and Statistics.*

NEW ZEALAND - LABOR

Central Intelligence Agency, Washington, D.C. 20505 (703) 482-1100, www.cia.gov; *The World Factbook.*

The Economist Intelligence Unit (Asia) Limited, 10th Floor, Luk Kwok Centre, 72 Gloucester Road, Wanchai, Hong Kong (Phone Number in U.S. (800) 938-4685); *Asian Market Atlas.*

Euromonitor International, Inc., 122 South Michigan Avenue, Suite 1200, Chicago, Illinois 60603 (800) 577-EURO; *International Marketing Data and Statistics;* and *World Marketing Data and Statistics.*

Europa Publications Limited, 18 Bedford Square, London, WC1B 3JN, England; *The Europa World Year Book.*

Food and Agricultural Organization of the United Nations (FAO) Via delle Terme di Caracalla, 00100 Rome, Italy (Telephone Number in U.S. (202) 653-2400); *The State of Food and Agriculture.*

International Labour Office, I.L.O. Publications, 1828 L Street, NW, Suite 801, Washington, D.C. 20036 (301) 638-3152; *Yearbook of Labour Statistics.*

M.E. Sharpe, 80 Business Park Drive, Armonk, New York 10504 (800) 541-6563; *The Illustrated Book of World Rankings.*

Organisation for Economic Co-operation and Development (OECD), 2 rue Andre-Pascal, 75 Paris 16, France (Telephone Number in U.S. (202) 785-6323); *Economic Outlook; Main Economic Indicators - Historical Statistics; Maritime Transport; OECD Economic Surveys: New Zealand; OECD Employment Outlook;* and *Textile Industry in OECD Countries.*

St. Martin's Press, Inc., 175 Fifth Avenue, New York, New York 10010 (800) 221-7945; *The Statesman's Year-Book.*

Statistical Office of the United Nations, Publishing Service, New York, New York 10017 (800) 253-9646; *Human Development Report.*

The World Bank, 1818 H Street, NW, Washington, D.C. 20433 (202) 477-1234; *The World Bank Atlas; World Development Report;* and *World Development Indicators.*

NEW ZEALAND - LAMB AND MUTTON EXPORTS

International Monetary Fund, 700 Nineteenth Street, NW, Washington, D.C. 20431 (202) 623-7000; *International Financial Statistics.*

NEW ZEALAND - LAND USE

Central Intelligence Agency, Washington, D.C. 20505 (703) 482-1100, www.cia.gov; *The World Factbook.*

Euromonitor International, Inc., 122 South Michigan Avenue, Suite 1200,

Chicago, Illinois 60603 (800) 577-EURO; *International Marketing Data and Statistics.*

Food and Agricultural Organization of the United Nations (FAO), Via delle Terme di Caracalla, 00100 Rome, Italy (Telephone Number in U.S. (202) 653-2400); *Production Yearbook.*

The World Bank, 1818 H Street, NW, Washington, D.C. 20433 (202) 477-1234; *World Development Report.*

NEW ZEALAND - LEAD AND LEAD ORE PRODUCTION AND CONSUMPTION - See NEW ZEALAND - MINING AND MINERAL PRODUCTS

NEW ZEALAND - LEATHER AND FOOTWEAR EXPORTS AND IMPORTS

Organisation for Economic Co-operation and Development (OECD), 2 rue Andre-Pascal, 75 Paris 16, France (Telephone Number in U.S. (202) 785-6323); *The Footwear, Raw Hides and Skins, and Leather Industry in OECD Countries.*

NEW ZEALAND - LIBRARIES

M.E. Sharpe, 80 Business Park Drive, Armonk, New York 10504 (800) 541-6563; *The Illustrated Book of World Rankings.*

United Nations Educational, Scientific and Cultural Organization (UNESCO), 7 Place de Fontenoy, F-75700 Paris, France (Telephone Number in U.S. (212) 963-5981); *Statistical Yearbook.*

NEW ZEALAND - LIFE EXPECTANCY

Central Intelligence Agency, Washington, D.C. 20505 (703) 482-1100, www.cia.gov; *The World Factbook.*

The Economist Intelligence Unit (Asia) Limited, 10th Floor, Luk Kwok Centre, 72 Gloucester Road, Wanchai, Hong Kong (Phone Number in U.S. (800) 938-4685); *Asian Market Atlas.*

Euromonitor International, Inc., 122 South Michigan Avenue, Suite 1200, Chicago, Illinois 60603 (800) 577-EURO; *The World Economic Factbook.*

Organisation for Economic Co-operation and Development (OECD), 2 rue Andre-Pascal, 75 Paris 16, France (Telephone Number in U.S. (202) 785-6323); *Economic Outlook.*

St. Martin's Press, Inc., 175 Fifth Avenue, New York, New York 10010 (800) 221-7945; *The Statesman's Year-Book.*

Statistical Office of the United Nations, Publishing Service, New York, New York 10017 (800) 253-9646; *Asia-Pacific in*

Figures; and *Human Development Report.*

The World Bank, 1818 H Street, NW, Washington, D.C. 20433 (202) 477-1234; *The World Bank Atlas;* and *World Development Report.*

NEW ZEALAND - LIGNITE PRODUCTION - See NEW ZEALAND - MINING AND MINERAL PRODUCTS

NEW ZEALAND - LITERACY RATE

Euromonitor International, Inc., 122 South Michigan Avenue, Suite 1200, Chicago, Illinois 60603 (800) 577-EURO; *World Marketing Data and Statistics.*

NEW ZEALAND - LIVESTOCK AND POULTRY

Commodity Research Bureau, Inc., 30 South Wacker Drive, Chicago, Illinois 60606 (312) 454-1801; *Commodity Year Book.*

Euromonitor International, Inc., 122 South Michigan Avenue, Suite 1200, Chicago, Illinois 60603 (800) 577-EURO; *International Marketing Data and Statistics.*

Europa Publications Limited, 18 Bedford Square, London, WC1B 3JN, England; *The Europa World Year Book.*

Food and Agricultural Organization of the United Nations (FAO), Via delle Terme di Caracalla, 00100 Rome, Italy (Telephone Number in U.S. (202) 653-2400); *Production Yearbook;* and *The State of Food and Agriculture.*

International Monetary Fund, 700 Nineteenth Street, NW, Washington, D.C. 20431 (202) 623-7000; *International Financial Statistics.*

M.E. Sharpe, 80 Business Park Drive, Armonk, New York 10504 (800) 541-6563; *The Illustrated Book of World Rankings.*

Organisation for Economic Co-operation and Development (OECD), 2 rue Andre-Pascal, 75 Paris 16, France (Telephone Number in U.S. (202) 785-6323); *Economic Accounts for Agriculture;* and *Meat Balances in OECD Member Countries.*

St. Martin's Press, Inc., 175 Fifth Avenue, New York, New York 10010 (800) 221-7945; *The Statesman's Year-Book.*

Statistical Office of the United Nations, Publishing Service, New York, New York 10017 (800) 253-9646; *Statistical Yearbook.*

United Nations Conference on Trade and Development, Central Statistical Service, Palais des Nations, Geneva, Switzerland (Telephone in U.S. (800) 253-9646); *UNCTAD Commodity Yearbook.*

NEW ZEALAND - LIVING LEVELS - See NEW ZEALAND - LIFE EXPECTANCY

NEW ZEALAND - MAIL - NUMBER OF PIECES SENT OR RECEIVED

Statistical Office of the United Nations, Publishing Service, New York, New York 10017 (800) 253-9646; *Statistical Yearbook.*

NEW ZEALAND - MANGANESE PRODUCTION AND CONSUMPTION - See NEW ZEALAND - MINING AND MINERAL PRODUCTS

NEW ZEALAND - MANPOWER

Statistical Office of the United Nations, Publishing Service, New York, New York 10017 (800) 253-9646; *Statistical Yearbook for Asia and the Pacific.*

NEW ZEALAND - MANUFACTURING

American Automobile Manufacturers Association, 1401 H Eye Street, NW, Suite 900, Washington, D.C. 20005 (202) 326-5500; *World Motor Vehicle Data.*

M.E. Sharpe, 80 Business Park Drive, Armonk, New York 10504 (800) 541-6563; *The Illustrated Book of World Rankings.*

Organisation for Economic Co-operation and Development (OECD), 2 rue Andre-Pascal, 75 Paris 16, France (Telephone Number in U.S. (202) 785-6323); *Foreign Trade by Commodities; Industrial Structure Statistics;* and *OECD Economic Surveys: New Zealand.*

Statistical Office of the United Nations, Publishing Service, New York, New York 10017 (800) 253-9646; *Statistical Yearbook.*

The World Bank, 1818 H Street, NW, Washington, D.C. 20433 (202) 477-1234; *World Development Indicators.*

NEW ZEALAND - MARRIAGE RATES

Europa Publications Limited, 18 Bedford Square, London, WC1B 3JN, England; *The Europa World Year Book.*

M.E. Sharpe, 80 Business Park Drive, Armonk, New York 10504 (800) 541-6563; *The Illustrated Book of World Rankings.*

Statistical Office of the United Nations, Publishing Service, New York, New York 10017 (800) 253-9646; *Demographic Yearbook.*

NEW ZEALAND - MEAT PRODUCTION - See NEW ZEALAND - LIVESTOCK AND POULTRY

NEW ZEALAND - MERCHANT SHIPPING

Europa Publications Limited, 18

Bedford Square, London, WC1B 3JN, England; *The Europa World Year Book.*

Lloyd's Register of Shipping, 17 Battery Place, New York, New York 10004; *Register of Ships.*

Organisation for Economic Co-operation and Development (OECD), 2 rue Andre-Pascal, 75 Paris 16, France (Telephone Number in U.S. (202) 785-6323); *Maritime Transport.*

St. Martin's Press, Inc., 175 Fifth Avenue, New York, New York 10010 (800) 221-7945; *The Statesman's Year-Book.*

Statistical Office of the United Nations, Publishing Service, New York, New York 10017 (800) 253-9646; *Statistical Yearbook.*

U.S. Department of Transportation, Maritime Administration, 400 Seventh Street, SW, Washington, D.C. 20590 (202) 366-5807, www.marad.dot.gov; *A Statistical Analysis of the World's Merchant Fleets.*

NEW ZEALAND - MILITARY

Central Intelligence Agency, Washington, D.C. 20505 (703) 482-1100, www.cia.gov; *The World Factbook.*

The Economist Intelligence Unit (Asia) Limited, 10th Floor, Luk Kwok Centre, 72 Gloucester Road, Wanchai, Hong Kong (Phone Number in U.S. (800) 938-4685); *Asian Market Atlas.*

Euromonitor International, Inc., 122 South Michigan Avenue, Suite 1200, Chicago, Illinois 60603 (800) 577-EURO; *World Marketing Data and Statistics.*

The International Institute for Strategic Studies, 23 Tavistock Street, London WC2E 7NQ, England; *The Military Balance.*

International Monetary Fund, 700 Nineteenth Street, NW, Washington, D.C. 20431 (202) 623-7000; *Government Finance Statistics Yearbook.*

U.S. Arms Control and Disarmament Agency, 320 Twenty-first Street, NW, Washington, D.C. 20451 (202) 647-8677; *World Military Expenditures and Arms Transfers.*

St. Martin's Press, Inc., 175 Fifth Avenue, New York, New York 10010 (800) 221-7945; *The Statesman's Year-Book.*

Statistical Office of the United Nations, Publishing Service, New York, New York 10017 (800) 253-9646; *Human Development Report.*

U.S. Arms Control and Disarmament Agency, 320 Twenty-first Street, NW,

Washington, D.C. 20451 (202) 647-8677; *World Military Expenditures and Arms Transfers.*

NEW ZEALAND - MILK PRODUCTION - See NEW ZEALAND - DAIRY PRODUCTS

NEW ZEALAND - MINING AND MINERAL PRODUCTS

Europa Publications Limited, 18 Bedford Square, London, WC1B 3JN, England; *The Europa World Year Book.*

M.E. Sharpe, 80 Business Park Drive, Armonk, New York 10504 (800) 541-6563; *The Illustrated Book of World Rankings.*

Organisation for Economic Co-operation and Development (OECD), 2 rue Andre-Pascal, 75 Paris 16, France (Telephone Number in U.S. (202) 785-6323); *Coal Information, Energy Statistics of OECD Countries; Foreign Trade by Commodities; Industrial Structure Statistics; The Iron and Steel Industry; The Non-Ferrous Metals Industry;* and *OECD Economic Surveys: New Zealand.*

Penn Well Publishing Company, 1421 South Sheridan Road, Post Office Box 1260, Tulsa, Oklahoma 74101 (800) 752-9764; *International Energy Statistics Sourcebook.*

St. Martin's Press, Inc., 175 Fifth Avenue, New York, New York 10010 (800) 221-7945; *The Statesman's Year-Book.*

Statistical Office of the United Nations, Publishing Service, New York, New York 10017 (800) 253-9646; *Statistical Yearbook.*

United Nations Conference on Trade and Development, Central Statistical Service, Palais des Nations, Geneva, Switzerland (Telephone in U.S. (800) 253-9646); *UNCTAD Commodity Yearbook.*

NEW ZEALAND - MONEY AND CREDIT

Organisation for Economic Co-operation and Development (OECD), 2 rue Andre-Pascal, 75 Paris 16, France (Telephone Number in U.S. (202) 785-6323); *OECD Economic Surveys: New Zealand.*

NEW ZEALAND - MONEY EXCHANGE RATE - See NEW ZEALAND EXCHANGE RATES

NEW ZEALAND - MONEY RATES - MARKET

Organisation for Economic Co-operation and Development (OECD), 2 rue Andre-Pascal, 75 Paris 16, France (Telephone Number in U.S. (202) 785-6323); *Economic Outlook;* and *Financial Market Trends.*

NEW ZEALAND - MONEY RESERVES

Euromonitor International, Inc., 122 South Michigan Avenue, Suite 1200, Chicago, Illinois 60603 (800) 577-EURO; *International Marketing Data and Statistics.*

Organisation for Economic Co-operation and Development (OECD), 2 rue Andre-Pascal, 75 Paris 16, France (Telephone Number in U.S. (202) 785-6323); *Economic Outlook;* and *Financial Market Trends.*

NEW ZEALAND - MONEY SUPPLY

Economist Intelligence Unit, 111 West 57th Street, New York, New York 10019 (800) 938-4685; *New Zealand Country Report.*

Euromonitor International, Inc., 122 South Michigan Avenue, Suite 1200, Chicago, Illinois 60603 (800) 577-EURO; *International Marketing Data and Statistics.*

Europa Publications Limited, 18 Bedford Square, London, WC1B 3JN, England; *The Europa World Year Book.*

International Monetary Fund, 700 Nineteenth Street, NW, Washington, D.C. 20431 (202) 623-7000; *International Financial Statistics.*

Organisation for Economic Co-operation and Development (OECD), 2 rue Andre-Pascal, 75 Paris 16, France (Telephone Number in U.S. (202) 785-6323); *Economic Outlook.*

Statistical Office of the United Nations, Publishing Service, New York, New York 10017 (800) 253-9646; *Statistical Yearbook.*

The World Bank, 1818 H Street, NW, Washington, D.C. 20433 (202) 477-1234; *World Development Indicators.*

NEW ZEALAND - MORTALITY

Central Intelligence Agency, Washington, D.C. 20505 (703) 482-1100, www.cia.gov; *The World Factbook.*

The Economist Intelligence Unit (Asia) Limited, 10th Floor, Luk Kwok Centre, 72 Gloucester Road, Wanchai, Hong Kong (Phone Number in U.S. (800) 938-4685); *Asian Market Atlas.*

Euromonitor International, Inc., 122 South Michigan Avenue, Suite 1200, Chicago, Illinois 60603 (800) 577-EURO; *International Marketing Data and Statistics;* and *The World Economic Factbook.*

Europa Publications Limited, 18 Bedford Square, London, WC1B 3JN, England; *The Europa World Year Book.*

St. Martin's Press, Inc., 175 Fifth Avenue, New York, New York 10010 (800) 221-7945;

The Statesman's Year-Book.

Statistical Office of the United Nations, Publishing Service, New York, New York 10017 (800) 253-9646; *Asia-Pacific in Figures; Demographic Yearbook; Human Development Report; World Statistics Pocketbook* and *Statistical Yearbook.*

United Nations Children's Fund (UNICEF), 3 United Nations Plaza, New York, New York 10017 (800) 253-9646; *State of the World's Children.*

The World Bank, 1818 H Street, NW, Washington, D.C. 20433 (202) 477-1234; *The World Bank Atlas; World Development Report;* and *World Development Indicators.*

World Health Organization, Office of Publications, 20 Avenue Appia, CH-1211 Geneva 27, Switzerland (Telephone Number in U.S. (518) 436-9686); *World Health Statistics Annual.*

NEW ZEALAND - MOTION PICTURES

St. Martin's Press, Inc., 175 Fifth Avenue, New York, New York 10010 (800) 221-7945; *The Statesman's Year-Book.*

Statistical Office of the United Nations, Publishing Service, New York, New York 10017 (800) 253-9646; *Statistical Yearbook.*

United Nations Educational, Scientific and Cultural Organization (UNESCO), 7 Place de Fontenoy, F-75700 Paris, France (Telephone Number in U.S. (212) 963-5981); *Statistical Yearbook.*

NEW ZEALAND - MOTOR VEHICLE PRODUCTION

American Automobile Manufacturers Association, 1401 H Street, NW, Suite 900, Washington, D.C. 20005 (202) 326-5500; *World Motor Vehicle Data.*

Organisation for Economic Co-operation and Development (OECD), 2 rue Andre-Pascal, 75 Paris 16, France (Telephone Number in U.S. (202) 785-6323); *Foreign Trade by Commodities.*

Statistical Office of the United Nations, Publishing Service, New York, New York 10017 (800) 253-9646; *Statistical Yearbook.*

NEW ZEALAND - MOTOR VEHICLE TAXES - See NEW ZEALAND - TAXATION

NEW ZEALAND - MOTOR VEHICLES IN USE

American Automobile Manufacturers Association, 1401 H Street, NW, Suite 900, Washington, D.C. 20005 (202) 326-5500; *World Motor Vehicle Data.*

Europa Publications Limited, 18 Bedford Square, London, WC1B 3JN,

England; *The Europa World Year Book.*

International Road Federation, 2600 Virginia Avenue, NW, Washington, D.C. 20037 (202) 338-4641; *World Road Statistics.*

Statistical Office of the United Nations, Publishing Service, New York, New York 10017 (800) 253-9646; *Statistical Yearbook.*

NEW ZEALAND - MUSEUMS

M.E. Sharpe, 80 Business Park Drive, Armonk, New York 10504 (800) 541-6563; *The Illustrated Book of World Rankings.*

United Nations Educational, Scientific and Cultural Organization (UNESCO), 7 Place de Fontenoy, F-75700 Paris, France (Telephone Number in U.S. (212) 963-5981); *Statistical Yearbook.*

NEW ZEALAND - MUTTON AND LAMB EXPORTS

International Monetary Fund, 700 Nineteenth Street, NW, Washington, D.C. 20431 (202) 623-7000; *International Financial Statistics.*

NEW ZEALAND - NATALITY - See NEW ZEALAND - BIRTH RATES

NEW ZEALAND - NATIONAL ACCOUNTS

Europa Publications Limited, 18 Bedford Square, London, WC1B 3JN, England; *The Europa World Year Book.*

Organisation for Economic Co-operation and Development (OECD), 2 rue Andre-Pascal, 75 Paris 16, France (Telephone Number in U.S. (202) 785-6323); *Economic Outlook.*

Statistical Office of the United Nations, Publishing Service, New York, New York 10017 (800) 253-9646; *Asia-Pacific in Figures; National Accounts Statistics;* and *Statistical Yearbook.*

NEW ZEALAND - NATIONAL INCOME

M.E. Sharpe, 80 Business Park Drive, Armonk, New York 10504 (800) 541-6563; *The Illustrated Book of World Rankings.*

Organisation for Economic Co-operation and Development (OECD), 2 rue Andre-Pascal, 75 Paris 16, France (Telephone Number in U.S. (202) 785-6323); *Economic Outlook.*

Statistical Office of the United Nations, Publishing Service, New York, New York 10017 (800) 253-9646; *National Accounts Statistics;* and *Statistical Yearbook.*

NEW ZEALAND - NATIONAL PRODUCT

M.E. Sharpe, 80 Business Park Drive, Armonk, New York 10504 (800) 541-6563; *The Illustrated Book of World Rankings.*

Organisation for Economic Co-operation and Development (OECD), 2 rue Andre-Pascal, 75 Paris 16, France (Telephone Number in U.S. (202) 785-6323); *Economic Outlook.*

NEW ZEALAND - NATURAL GAS PRODUCTION - See NEW ZEALAND - MINING AND MINERAL PRODUCTS

NEW ZEALAND - NEWSPAPER PRODUCTION

The Economist Intelligence Unit (Asia) Limited, 10th Floor, Luk Kwok Centre, 72 Gloucester Road, Wanchai, Hong Kong (Phone Number in U.S. (800) 938-4685); *Asian Market Atlas.*

Statistical Office of the United Nations, Publishing Service, New York, New York 10017 (800) 253-9646; *Statistical Yearbook.*

United Nations Educational, Scientific and Cultural Organization (UNESCO), 7 Place de Fontenoy, F-75700 Paris, France (Telephone Number in U.S. (212) 963-5981); *Statistical Yearbook.*

NEW ZEALAND - NEWSPRINT PRODUCTION AND CONSUMPTION - See NEW ZEALAND - FORESTRY AND FOREST PRODUCTS

NEW ZEALAND - NICKEL PRODUCTION AND CONSUMPTION - See NEW ZEALAND - MINING AND MINERAL PRODUCTS

NEW ZEALAND - OIL PRODUCING CROPS - See NEW ZEALAND - CROPS

NEW ZEALAND - PAPER - See NEW ZEALAND - FORESTRY AND FOREST PRODUCTS

NEW ZEALAND - PATENTS, TRADEMARKS AND SERVICE MARKS

Statistical Office of the United Nations, Publishing Service, New York, New York 10017 (800) 253-9646; *Statistical Yearbook.*

World Intellectual Property Organization, 34 Chemin des Colombettes, CH-1211 Geneva 20, Switzerland; *Industrial Property Statistics.*

NEW ZEALAND - PEANUT PRODUCTION - See NEW ZEALAND - CROPS

NEW ZEALAND - PERIODICALS

United Nations Educational, Scientific and Cultural Organization (UNESCO), 7 Place de Fontenoy, F-75700 Paris, France (Telephone Number in U.S. (212) 963-5981); *Statistical Yearbook.*

NEW ZEALAND - PESTICIDE USE

Food and Agricultural Organization of the United Nations (FAO) Via delle Terme di Caracalla, 00100 Rome, Italy (Telephone Number in U.S. (202) 653-2400); *The State of Food and Agriculture.*

NEW ZEALAND - PETROLEUM INDUSTRY

Food and Agricultural Organization of the United Nations (FAO) Via delle Terme di Caracalla, 00100 Rome, Italy (Telephone Number in U.S. (202) 653-2400); *The State of Food and Agriculture.*

M.E. Sharpe, 80 Business Park Drive, Armonk, New York 10504 (800) 541-6563; *The Illustrated Book of World Rankings.*

Organisation for Economic Co-operation and Development (OECD), 2 rue Andre-Pascal, 75 Paris 16, France (Telephone Number in U.S. (202) 785-6323); *Energy Statistics of OECD Countries; Foreign Trade by Commodities;* and *Oil and Gas Information.*

Penn Well Publishing Company, 1421 South Sheridan Road, Post Office Box 1260, Tulsa, Oklahoma 74101 (800) 752-9764; *International Energy Statistics Sourcebook.*

St. Martin's Press, Inc., 175 Fifth Avenue, New York, New York 10010 (800) 221-7945; *The Statesman's Year-Book.*

Statistical Office of the United Nations, Publishing Service, New York, New York 10017 (800) 253-9646; *Statistical Yearbook.*

United Nations Conference on Trade and Development, Central Statistical Service, Palais des Nations, Geneva, Switzerland (Telephone in U.S. (800) 253-9646); *UNCTAD Commodity Yearbook.*

NEW ZEALAND - PIG-IRON AND FERRO-ALLOY PRODUCTION

Organisation for Economic Co-operation and Development (OECD), 2 rue Andre-Pascal, 75 Paris 16, France (Telephone Number in U.S. (202) 785-6323); *The Iron and Steel Industry.*

NEW ZEALAND - PIGS - See NEW ZEALAND - LIVESTOCK AND POULTRY

NEW ZEALAND - PLASTIC AND RESIN PRODUCTION

Organisation for Economic Co-operation and Development (OECD), 2 rue Andre-Pascal, 75 Paris 16, France (Telephone Number in U.S. (202) 785-6323); *Foreign Trade by Commodities.*

NEW ZEALAND - POPULATION

Central Intelligence Agency, Washington, D.C. 20505 (703) 482-1100, www.cia.gov; *The World Factbook.*

The Economist Intelligence Unit, 111 West 57th Street, New York, New York 10019 (800) 938-4685; *New Zealand Country Report;* and *The World Market Atlas.*

The Economist Intelligence Unit (Asia) Limited, 10th Floor, Luk Kwok Centre, 72 Gloucester Road, Wanchai, Hong Kong (Phone Number in U.S. (800) 938-4685); *Asian Market Atlas.*

Euromonitor International, Inc., 122 South Michigan Avenue, Suite 1200, Chicago, Illinois 60603 (800) 577-EURO; *International Marketing Data and Statistics;* and *The World Economic Factbook.*

Europa Publications Limited, 18 Bedford Square, London, WC1B 3JN, England; *The Europa World Year Book.*

Food and Agricultural Organization of the United Nations (FAO), Via delle Terme di Caracalla, 00100 Rome, Italy (Telephone Number in U.S. (202) 653-2400); *Production Yearbook.*

International Labour Office, I.L.O. Publications, 1828 L Street, NW, Suite 801, Washington, D.C. 20036 (301) 638-3152; *Yearbook of Labour Statistics.*

M.E. Sharpe, 80 Business Park Drive, Armonk, New York 10504 (800) 541-6563; *The Illustrated Book of World Rankings.*

St. Martin's Press, Inc., 175 Fifth Avenue, New York, New York 10010 (800) 221-7945; *The Statesman's Year-Book.*

Statistical Office of the United Nations, Publishing Service, New York, New York 10017 (800) 253-9646; *Asia-Pacific in Figures; Demographic Yearbook; Human Development Report; Statistical Yearbook; World Statistics Pocketbook;* and *Statistical Yearbook for Asia and the Pacific.*

United Nations Educational, Scientific and Cultural Organization (UNESCO), 7 Place de Fontenoy, F-75700 Paris, France (Telephone Number in U.S. (212) 963-5981); *Statistical Yearbook.*

U.S. Arms Control and Disarmament Agency, 320 Twenty-first Street, NW, Washington, D.C. 20451 (202) 647-8677; *World Military Expenditures and Arms Transfers.*

Walden Publishing Ltd., Two Market Street, Saffron Walden Essex, CB10 1HZ, England; *The World of Information Asia and Pacific Review.*

The World Bank, 1818 H Street, NW,

Washington, D.C. 20433 (202) 477-1234; *The World Bank Atlas;* and *World Development Report.*

World Health Organization, Office of Publications, 20 Avenue Appia, CH-1211 Geneva 27, Switzerland (Telephone Number in U.S. (518) 436-9686); *World Health Statistics Annual.*

NEW ZEALAND - POST OFFICES

M.E. Sharpe, 80 Business Park Drive, Armonk, New York 10504 (800) 541-6563; *The Illustrated Book of World Rankings.*

St. Martin's Press, Inc., 175 Fifth Avenue, New York, New York 10010 (800) 221-7945; *The Statesman's Year-Book.*

NEW ZEALAND - POTATO PRODUCTION - See NEW ZEALAND - CROPS

NEW ZEALAND - POWER PRODUCTION INDUSTRY

Statistical Office of the United Nations, Publishing Service, New York, New York 10017 (800) 253-9646; *Statistical Yearbook.*

NEW ZEALAND - PRICES

Food and Agricultural Organization of the United Nations (FAO), Via delle Terme di Caracalla, 00100 Rome, Italy (Telephone Number in U.S. (202) 653-2400); *Production Yearbook;* and *The State of Food and Agriculture.*

International Labour Office, I.L.O. Publications, 1828 L Street, NW, Suite 801, Washington, D.C. 20036 (301) 638-3152; *Yearbook of Labour Statistics.*

International Monetary Fund, 700 Nineteenth Street, NW, Washington, D.C. 20431 (202) 623-7000; *International Financial Statistics.*

M.E. Sharpe, 80 Business Park Drive, Armonk, New York 10504 (800) 541-6563; *The Illustrated Book of World Rankings.*

Organisation for Economic Co-operation and Development (OECD), 2 rue Andre-Pascal, 75 Paris 16, France (Telephone Number in U.S. (202) 785-6323); *Economic Accounts for Agriculture; Economic Outlook; The Footwear, Raw Hides and Skins, and Leather Industry in OECD Countries; The Iron and Steel Industry;* and *The Pulp and Paper Industry.*

NEW ZEALAND - PRINTING AND WRITING PAPER PRODUCTION AND CONSUMPTION - See NEW ZEALAND - FORESTRY AND FOREST PRODUCTS

NEW ZEALAND - PRODUCTION

American Automobile Manufacturers Association, 1401 H Street, NW, Suite 900, Washington, D.C. 20005 (202) 326-5500; *World Motor Vehicle Data.*

M.E. Sharpe, 80 Business Park Drive, Armonk, New York 10504 (800) 541-6563; *The Illustrated Book of World Rankings.*

Organisation for Economic Co-operation and Development (OECD), 2 rue Andre-Pascal, 75 Paris 16, France (Telephone Number in U.S. (202) 785-6323); *Economic Outlook; The Footwear, Raw Hides and Skins, and Leather Industry in OECD Countries; Industrial Structure Statistics; The Iron and Steel Industry; Meat Balances in OECD Member Countries; Milk, Milk Products, and Egg Balances in OECD Member Countries; The Non-Ferrous Metals Industry; The Pulp and Paper Industry;* and *Textile Industry in OECD Countries.*

NEW ZEALAND - PRODUCTIVITY

Euromonitor International, Inc., 122 South Michigan Avenue, Suite 1200, Chicago, Illinois 60603 (800) 577-EURO; *International Marketing Data and Statistics.*

Organisation for Economic Co-operation and Development (OECD), 2 rue Andre-Pascal, 75 Paris 16, France (Telephone Number in U.S. (202) 785-6323); *Economic Outlook.*

NEW ZEALAND - PROPERTY TAXES - See NEW ZEALAND - TAXATION

NEW ZEALAND - PUBLIC CONSUMPTION FUND

Organisation for Economic Co-operation and Development (OECD), 2 rue Andre-Pascal, 75 Paris 16, France (Telephone Number in U.S. (202) 785-6323); *Revenue Statistics of OECD Member Countries.*

NEW ZEALAND - PUBLIC EXPENDITURES

Organisation for Economic Co-operation and Development (OECD), 2 rue Andre-Pascal, 75 Paris 16, France (Telephone Number in U.S. (202) 785-6323); *Revenue Statistics of OECD Member Countries.*

NEW ZEALAND - PUBLIC FINANCE - See NEW ZEALAND - FINANCE

NEW ZEALAND - PUBLIC REVENUES

Organisation for Economic Co-operation and Development (OECD), 2 rue Andre-Pascal, 75 Paris 16, France (Telephone Number in U.S. (202) 785-6323); *Revenue Statistics of OECD Member Countries.*

NEW ZEALAND - RADIO
BROADCASTING - See NEW ZEALAND -
BROADCASTING

NEW ZEALAND - RADIO RECEIVER
PRODUCTION

Statistical Office of the United Nations,
Publishing Service, New York, New York
10017 (800) 253-9646; *Statistical Yearbook.*

NEW ZEALAND - RADIO RECEIVERS

St. Martin's Press, Inc., 175 Fifth
Avenue, New York, New York 10010 (800)
221-7945; *The Statesman's Year-Book.*

NEW ZEALAND - RAILWAYS

Europa Publications Limited, 18
Bedford Square, London, WC1B 3JN,
England; *The Europa World Year Book.*

Jane's Information Group, Sentinel
House, 163 Brighton Road, Coulsdon,
Surrey CR5 2NH, England (Telephone
Number in U.S. (703) 683-3700); *Jane's
World Railways.*

St. Martin's Press, Inc., 175 Fifth
Avenue, New York, New York 10010 (800)
221-7945; *The Statesman's Year-Book.*

Statistical Office of the United Nations,
Publishing Service, New York, New York
10017 (800) 253-9646; *Statistical Yearbook.*

NEW ZEALAND - RELIGION

Central Intelligence Agency,
Washington, D.C. 20505 (703) 482-1100,
www.cia.gov; *The World Factbook.*

M.E. Sharpe, 80 Business Park Drive,
Armonk, New York 10504 (800) 541-6563;
The Illustrated Book of World Rankings.

St. Martin's Press, Inc., 175 Fifth
Avenue, New York, New York 10010 (800)
221-7945; *The Statesman's Year-Book.*

NEW ZEALAND - RENT PRICES

International Labour Office,
I.L.O. Publications, 1828 L Street, NW,
Suite 801, Washington, D.C. 20036 (301)
638-3152; *Yearbook of Labour Statistics.*

NEW ZEALAND - RETAIL TRADE

Euromonitor International, Inc., 122
South Michigan Avenue, Suite 1200,
Chicago, Illinois 60603 (800) 577-EURO;
Retail Trade International; and *World
Marketing Data and Statistics.*

Statistical Office of the United Nations,
Publishing Service, New York, New York
10017 (800) 253-9646; *Statistical Yearbook.*

NEW ZEALAND - RICE PRODUCTION - See

NEW ZEALAND - CROPS

NEW ZEALAND - ROOT AND TUBER
PRODUCTION - See NEW ZEALAND -
CROPS

NEW ZEALAND - ROUNDWOOD
PRODUCTION - See NEW ZEALAND -
FORESTRY AND FOREST PRODUCTS

NEW ZEALAND - RUBBER PRODUCTION
AND CONSUMPTION

M.E. Sharpe, 80 Business Park Drive,
Armonk, New York 10504 (800) 541-6563;
The Illustrated Book of World Rankings.

Organisation for Economic Co-
operation and Development (OECD), 2 rue
Andre-Pascal, 75 Paris 16, France
(Telephone Number in U.S. (202) 785-
6323); *Foreign Trade by Commodities.*

NEW ZEALAND - SALT PRODUCTION - See
NEW ZEALAND - MINING AND MINERAL
PRODUCTS

NEW ZEALAND - SAWNWOOD
PRODUCTION - See NEW ZEALAND -
FORESTRY AND FOREST PRODUCTS

NEW ZEALAND - SCIENCE AND
TECHNOLOGY - EXPENDITURE FOR
RESEARCH - See NEW ZEALAND -
SCIENTISTS, TECHNICIANS AND
ENGINEERS

NEW ZEALAND - SCIENTISTS,
TECHNICIANS AND ENGINEERS

Statistical Office of the United Nations,
Publishing Service, New York, New York
10017 (800) 253-9646; *Statistical Yearbook.*

NEW ZEALAND - SENIOR CITIZENS

M.E. Sharpe, 80 Business Park Drive,
Armonk, New York 10504 (800) 541-6563;
The Illustrated Book of World Rankings.

NEW ZEALAND - SERVICE INDUSTRY
EMPLOYMENT - MALE AND FEMALE - See
NEW ZEALAND - EMPLOYMENT

NEW ZEALAND - SHEEP - See NEW
ZEALAND - LIVESTOCK AND POULTRY

NEW ZEALAND - SILVER PRODUCTION
AND CONSUMPTION - See NEW ZEALAND -
MINING AND MINERAL PRODUCTS

NEW ZEALAND - SOCIAL DATA

M.E. Sharpe, 80 Business Park Drive,
Armonk, New York 10504 (800) 541-6563;
The Illustrated Book of World Rankings.

Statistical Office of the United Nations,
Publishing Service, New York, New York
10017 (800) 253-9646; *World Statistics
Pocketbook.*

NEW ZEALAND - SOCIAL SECURITY

International Monetary Fund, 700
Nineteenth Street, NW, Washington, D.C.
20431 (202) 623-7000; *Government
Finance Statistics Yearbook.*

Organisation for Economic Co-
operation and Development (OECD), 2 rue
Andre-Pascal, 75 Paris 16, France
(Telephone Number in U.S. (202) 785-
6323); *Revenue Statistics of OECD Member
Countries.*

St. Martin's Press, Inc., 175 Fifth
Avenue, New York, New York 10010 (800)
221-7945; *The Statesman's Year-Book.*

Statistical Office of the United Nations,
Publishing Service, New York, New York
10017 (800) 253-9646; *National Accounts
Statistics.*

NEW ZEALAND - SOCIOECONOMIC DATA

Organisation for Economic Co-
operation and Development (OECD), 2 rue
Andre-Pascal, 75 Paris 16, France
(Telephone Number in U.S. (202) 785-
6323); *Economic Outlook.*

NEW ZEALAND - STAMP TAXES AND
DUTIES - See NEW ZEALAND - TAXATION

NEW ZEALAND - STATE BUDGET REVENUE
AND EXPENDITURES

Euromonitor International, Inc., 122
South Michigan Avenue, Suite 1200,
Chicago, Illinois 60603 (800) 577-EURO;
International Marketing Data and Statistics.

NEW ZEALAND - STEEL - See NEW
ZEALAND - MINING AND MINERAL
PRODUCTS

NEW ZEALAND - STOCKS -
COMMODITY - MARKET PRICE -
INDEXES

Food and Agricultural Organization of
the United Nations (FAO) Via delle Terme
di Caracalla, 00100 Rome, Italy (Telephone
Number in U.S. (202) 653-2400); *The State
of Food and Agriculture.*

Statistical Office of the United Nations,
Publishing Service, New York, New York
10017 (800) 253-9646; *Statistical Yearbook.*

NEW ZEALAND - SUGAR - See NEW
ZEALAND - CROPS

NEW ZEALAND - TAXATION

Europa Publications Limited, 18
Bedford Square, London, WC1B 3JN,
England; *The Europa World Year Book.*

International Monetary Fund, 700
Nineteenth Street, NW, Washington, D.C.

20431 (202) 623-7000; *Government Finance Statistics Yearbook.*

International Road Federation, 2600 Virginia Avenue, NW., Washington, D.C. 20037 (202) 338-4641; *World Road Statistics.*

Organisation for Economic Co-operation and Development (OECD), 2 rue Andre-Pascal, 75 Paris 16, France (Telephone Number in U.S. (202) 785-6323); *Revenue Statistics of OECD Member Countries.*

St. Martin's Press, Inc., 175 Fifth Avenue, New York, New York 10010 (800) 221-7945; *The Statesman's Year-Book.*

The World Bank, 1818 H Street, NW, Washington, D.C. 20433 (202) 477-1234; *World Development Indicators.*

NEW ZEALAND - TEA CONSUMPTION - See NEW ZEALAND - CROPS

NEW ZEALAND - TELEGRAPH SERVICE

Statistical Office of the United Nations, Publishing Service, New York, New York 10017 (800) 253-9646; *Statistical Yearbook.*

NEW ZEALAND - TELEPHONES IN USE

American Telephone and Telegraph Company, 26 Parsippany Road, Whippany, New Jersey 07981 (800) 222-0300; *The World's Telephones.*

Central Intelligence Agency, Washington, D.C. 20505 (703) 482-1100, www.cia.gov; *The World Factbook.*

The Economist Intelligence Unit (Asia) Limited, 10th Floor, Luk Kwok Centre, 72 Gloucester Road, Wanchai, Hong Kong (Phone Number in U.S. (800) 938-4685); *Asian Market Atlas.*

Europa Publications Limited, 18 Bedford Square, London, WC1B 3JN, England; *The Europa World Year Book.*

St. Martin's Press, Inc., 175 Fifth Avenue, New York, New York 10010 (800) 221-7945; *The Statesman's Year-Book.*

Statistical Office of the United Nations, Publishing Service, New York, New York 10017 (800) 253-9646; *Statistical Yearbook; and World Statistics Pocketbook.*

NEW ZEALAND - TELEVISION BROADCASTING - See NEW ZEALAND - BROADCASTING

NEW ZEALAND - TELEVISION RECEIVER PRODUCTION

Statistical Office of the United Nations, Publishing Service, New York, New York

10017 (800) 253-9646; *Statistical Yearbook.*

NEW ZEALAND - TEXTILE INDUSTRY

American Forest and Paper Association, 1111 Nineteenth Street, NW, Suite 800, Washington, D.C. 20036 (202) 463-2700; *Wood Pulp and Fiber Statistics.*

Commodity Research Bureau, Inc., 30 South Wacker Drive, Chicago, Illinois 60606 (312) 454-1801; *Commodity Year Book.*

Euromonitor International, Inc., 122 South Michigan Avenue, Suite 1200, Chicago, Illinois 60603 (800) 577-EURO; *Retail Trade International.*

International Monetary Fund, 700 Nineteenth Street, NW, Washington, D.C. 20431 (202) 623-7000; *International Financial Statistics.*

M.E. Sharpe, 80 Business Park Drive, Armonk, New York 10504 (800) 541-6563; *The Illustrated Book of World Rankings.*

Organisation for Economic Co-operation and Development (OECD), 2 rue Andre-Pascal, 75 Paris 16, France (Telephone Number in U.S. (202) 785-6323); *Economic Accounts in Agriculture; Foreign Trade by Commodities; Industrial Structure Statistics; and Textile Industry in OECD Countries.*

St. Martin's Press, Inc., 175 Fifth Avenue, New York, New York 10010 (800) 221-7945; *The Statesman's Year-Book.*

Statistical Office of the United Nations, Publishing Service, New York, New York 10017 (800) 253-9646; *Statistical Yearbook.*

United Nations Conference on Trade and Development, Central Statistical Service, Palais des Nations, Geneva, Switzerland (Telephone in U.S. (800) 253-9646); *UNCTAD Commodity Yearbook.*

NEW ZEALAND - THEATRE

United Nations Educational, Scientific and Cultural Organization (UNESCO), 7 Place de Fontenoy, F-75700 Paris, France (Telephone Number in U.S. (212) 963-5981); *Statistical Yearbook.*

NEW ZEALAND - TIN - See NEW ZEALAND - MINING AND MINERAL PRODUCTS

NEW ZEALAND - TIRE (MOTOR VEHICLE) PRODUCTION

Statistical Office of the United Nations, Publishing Service, New York, New York 10017 (800) 253-9646; *Statistical Yearbook.*

NEW ZEALAND - TOBACCO PRODUCTION

M.E. Sharpe, 80 Business Park Drive, Armonk, New York 10504 (800) 541-6563; *The Illustrated Book of World Rankings.*

Organisation for Economic Co-operation and Development (OECD), 2 rue Andre-Pascal, 75 Paris 16, France (Telephone Number in U.S. (202) 785-6323); *Foreign Trade by Commodities; and Industrial Structure Statistics.*

Statistical Office of the United Nations, Publishing Service, New York, New York 10017 (800) 253-9646; *Statistical Yearbook.*

NEW ZEALAND - TOURISM

Euromonitor International, Inc., 122 South Michigan Avenue, Suite 1200, Chicago, Illinois 60603 (800) 577-EURO; *The World Economic Factbook; and World Marketing Data and Statistics.*

Europa Publications Limited, 18 Bedford Square, London, WC1B 3JN, England; *The Europa World Year Book.*

M.E. Sharpe, 80 Business Park Drive, Armonk, New York 10504 (800) 541-6563; *The Illustrated Book of World Rankings.*

Organisation for Economic Co-operation and Development (OECD), 2 rue Andre-Pascal, 75 Paris 16, France (Telephone Number in U.S. (202) 785-6323); *Tourism Policy and International Tourism in OECD Member Countries.*

St. Martin's Press, Inc., 175 Fifth Avenue, New York, New York 10010 (800) 221-7945; *The Statesman's Year-Book.*

Statistical Office of the United Nations, Publishing Service, New York, New York 10017 (800) 253-9646; *Statistical Yearbook.*

World Tourism Organization, Calle Capitan Haya 42, E-28020 Madrid, Spain; *Yearbook of Tourism Statistics.*

NEW ZEALAND - TRACTORS IN USE

Statistical Office of the United Nations, Publishing Service, New York, New York 10017 (800) 253-9646; *Statistical Yearbook.*

NEW ZEALAND - TRADE - See NEW ZEALAND - FOREIGN TRADE

NEW ZEALAND - TRADEMARKS AND SERVICE MARKS - See NEW ZEALAND - PATENTS, TRADEMARKS AND SERVICE MARKS

NEW ZEALAND - TRANSPORTATION AND COMMUNICATIONS

Central Intelligence Agency, Washington, D.C. 20505 (703) 482-1100, www.cia.gov; *The World Factbook.*

The Economist Intelligence Unit (Asia) Limited, 10th Floor, Luk Kwok Centre, 72 Gloucester Road, Wanchai, Hong Kong (Phone Number in U.S. (800) 938-4685); *Asian Market Atlas.*

Euromonitor International, Inc., 122 South Michigan Avenue, Suite 1200, Chicago, Illinois 60603 (800) 577-EURO; *International Marketing Data and Statistics;* and *World Marketing Data and Statistics.*

Europa Publications Limited, 18 Bedford Square, London, WC1B 3JN, England; *The Europa World Year Book.*

M.E. Sharpe, 80 Business Park Drive, Armonk, New York 10504 (800) 541-6563; *The Illustrated Book of World Rankings.*

St. Martin's Press, Inc., 175 Fifth Avenue, New York, New York 10010 (800) 221-7945; *The Statesman's Year-Book.*

Statistical Office of the United Nations, Publishing Service, New York, New York 10017 (800) 253-9646; *Human Development Report;* and *Statistical Yearbook for Asia and the Pacific.*

NEW ZEALAND - TUNGSTEN PRODUCTION AND CONSUMPTION - See NEW ZEALAND - MINING AND MINERAL PRODUCTS

NEW ZEALAND - TURKEYS - See NEW ZEALAND - LIVESTOCK AND POULTRY

NEW ZEALAND - UNEMPLOYMENT

Central Intelligence Agency, Washington, D.C. 20505 (703) 482-1100, www.cia.gov; *The World Factbook.*

Euromonitor International, Inc., 122 South Michigan Avenue, Suite 1200, Chicago, Illinois 60603 (800) 577-EURO; *International Marketing Data and Statistics.*

International Labour Office, I.L.O. Publications, 1828 L Street, NW, Suite 801, Washington, D.C. 20036 (301) 638-3152; *Yearbook of Labour Statistics.*

Organisation for Economic Co-operation and Development (OECD), 2 rue Andre-Pascal, 75 Paris 16, France (Telephone Number in U.S. (202) 785-6323); *Economic Outlook; OECD Economic Surveys: New Zealand;* and *OECD Employment Outlook.*

St. Martin's Press, Inc., 175 Fifth Avenue, New York, New York 10010 (800) 221-7945; *The Statesman's Year-Book.*

Statistical Office of the United Nations, Publishing Service, New York, New York 10017 (800) 253-9646; *Statistical Yearbook.*

NEW ZEALAND - VEAL EXPORTS

International Monetary Fund, 700 Nineteenth Street, NW, Washington, D.C. 20431 (202) 623-7000; *International Financial Statistics.*

NEW ZEALAND - VITAL STATISTICS

Euromonitor International, Inc., 122 South Michigan Avenue, Suite 1200, Chicago, Illinois 60603 (800) 577-EURO; *International Marketing Data and Statistics.*

St. Martin's Press, Inc., 175 Fifth Avenue, New York, New York 10010 (800) 221-7945; *The Statesman's Year-Book.*

World Health Organization, Office of Publications, 20 Avenue Appia, CH-1211 Geneva 27, Switzerland (Telephone Number in U.S. (518) 436-9686); *World Health Statistics Annual.*

NEW ZEALAND - WAGES

International Labour Office, I.L.O. Publications, 1828 L Street, NW, Suite 801, Washington, D.C. 20036 (301) 638-3152; *Yearbook of Labour Statistics.*

Organisation for Economic Co-operation and Development (OECD), 2 rue Andre-Pascal, 75 Paris 16, France (Telephone Number in U.S. (202) 785-6323); *Economic Outlook; Industrial Structure Statistics;* and *Main Economic Indicators - Historical Statistics.*

Statistical Office of the United Nations, Publishing Service, New York, New York 10017 (800) 253-9646; *Statistical Yearbook for Asia and the Pacific;* and *Statistical Yearbook.*

NEW ZEALAND - WALNUT PRODUCTION - See NEW ZEALAND - CROPS

NEW ZEALAND - WATERWAYS IN USE

Organisation for Economic Co-operation and Development (OECD), 2 rue Andre-Pascal, 75 Paris 16, France (Telephone Number in U.S. (202) 785-6323); *Maritime Transport.*

NEW ZEALAND - WEATHER - See NEW ZEALAND - CLIMATE

NEW ZEALAND - WELFARE EXPENDITURES

International Monetary Fund, 700 Nineteenth Street, NW, Washington, D.C. 20431 (202) 623-7000; *Government Finance Statistics Yearbook.*

St. Martin's Press, Inc., 175 Fifth Avenue, New York, New York 10010 (800) 221-7945; *The Statesman's Year-Book.*

NEW ZEALAND - WHEAT PRODUCTION AND PRICES - See NEW ZEALAND - CROPS

NEW ZEALAND - WHOLESALE PRICES

Statistical Office of the United Nations, Publishing Service, New York, New York 10017 (800) 253-9646; *Statistical Yearbook.*

NEW ZEALAND - WHOLESALE TRADE

Statistical Office of the United Nations, Publishing Service, New York, New York 10017 (800) 253-9646; *Statistical Yearbook.*

NEW ZEALAND - WINE PRODUCTION - See NEW ZEALAND - BEVERAGES

NEW ZEALAND - WOOD - See NEW ZEALAND - FORESTRY AND FOREST PRODUCTS

NEW ZEALAND - WOOL - See NEW ZEALAND - TEXTILE INDUSTRY

NEW ZEALAND - YARN PRODUCTION - See NEW ZEALAND - TEXTILE INDUSTRY

NEW ZEALAND - ZINC AND ZINC ORE PRODUCTION AND CONSUMPTION - See NEW ZEALAND - MINING AND MINERAL PRODUCTS

NEWSPAPERS - ADVERTISING EXPENDITURES

McCann-Erickson, Incorporated, 750 Third Avenue, New York, New York 10017 (212) 697-6000; complied for Crain Communications, Incorporated, 740 North Rush Street, Chicago, Illinois 60611 (312) 649-5200; in *Advertising Age.*

Television Bureau of Advertising, Inc., 3 East 54th Street, New York, New York 10022 (212) 486-1111; data compiled by Competitive Media Reporting, 11 West 42nd Street, New York, New York 10036 (212) 789-1400.

NEWSPAPERS - EXPENDITURES - CONSUMER

U.S. Department of Commerce, Bureau of Economic Analysis, Fourteenth Street between Constitution Avenue and E Street, NW, Washington, D.C. 20230 (202) 606-9900, www.bea.doc.gov; *The National Income and Product Accounts of the United States;* and *Survey of Current Business.*

Veronis, Suhler and Associates, 350 Park Avenue, New York, New York 10022 (212) 935-4990; *Communications Industry Forecast Report.*

NEWSPAPERS - FREQUENCY OF PUBLICATION

The Gale Group, 27500 Drake Road, Farmington Hills, Michigan 48331 (800) 877-

4253; *Gale Directory of Publications and Broadcast Media.*

NEWSPAPERS - MANUFACTURING - CAPITAL

U.S. Department of Commerce, Bureau of the Census, Washington, D.C. 20233 (301) 457-4100, www.census.gov; *Census of Manufactures;* and *Annual Survey of Manufactures.*

NEWSPAPERS - MANUFACTURING - EARNINGS

U.S. Department of Commerce, Bureau of the Census, Washington, D.C. 20233 (301) 457-4100, www.census.gov; *Census of Manufactures;* and *Annual Survey of Manufactures.*

U.S. Department of Labor, Bureau of Labor Statistics, Two Massachusetts Avenue, NE, Washington, D.C. 20212 (202) 691-5200, www.stats.bls.gov; *Employment and Earnings;* and Internet site: http://stats.bls.gov/ceshome. htm.

NEWSPAPERS - MANUFACTURING - EMPLOYEES

U.S. Department of Commerce, Bureau of the Census, Washington, D.C. 20233 (301) 457-4100, www.census.gov; *Census of Manufactures;* and *Annual Survey of Manufactures.*

U.S. Department of Labor, Bureau of Labor Statistics, Two Massachusetts Avenue, NE, Washington, D.C. 20212 (202) 691-5200, www.stats.bls.gov; *Employment and Earnings;* and Internet site: http://stats.bls.gov/ceshome. htm.

NEWSPAPERS - MANUFACTURING - ESTABLISHMENTS

U.S. Department of Commerce, Bureau of the Census, Washington, D.C. 20233 (301) 457-4100, www.census.gov; *Census of Manufactures;* and *Annual Survey of Manufactures.*

NEWSPAPERS - MANUFACTURING - FINANCES

U.S. Department of Commerce, Bureau of the Census, Washington, D.C. 20233 (301) 457-4100, www.census.gov; *Census of Manufactures;* and *Annual Survey of Manufactures.*

NEWSPAPERS - MANUFACTURING - INVENTORIES

U.S. Department of Commerce, Bureau of the Census, Washington, D.C. 20233 (301) 457-4100, www.census.gov; *Census of Manufactures;* and *Annual Survey of*

Manufactures.

NEWSPAPERS - MANUFACTURING - PRODUCTIVITY

U.S. Department of Labor, Bureau of Labor Statistics, Two Massachusetts Avenue, NE, Washington, D.C. 20212 (202) 691-5200, www.stats.bls.gov; Internet site: http://stats.bls.gov/iprhome.htm.

NEWSPAPERS - MANUFACTURING - SALES, SHIPMENTS, RECEIPTS

U.S. Department of Commerce, Bureau of the Census, Washington, D.C. 20233 (301) 457-4100, www.census.gov; *Census of Manufactures;* and *Annual Survey of Manufactures.*

NEWSPAPERS - MANUFACTURING - VALUE ADDED

U.S. Department of Commerce, Bureau of the Census, Washington, D.C. 20233 (301) 457-4100, www.census.gov; *Census of Manufactures;* and *Annual Survey of Manufactures.*

NEWSPAPERS - NUMBER AND CIRCULATION

Editor and Publisher Company, 11 West Nineteenth Street, New York, New York 10011 (212) 675-4380; *Editor and Publisher International Year Book.*

NEWSPAPERS - NUMBER AND CIRCULATION - FOREIGN COUNTRIES

United Nations Educational, Scientific, and Cultural Organization (UNESCO), 7 Place de Fontenoy, F-75700 Paris, France (Telephone Number in U.S. (212) 963-5981); *Statistical Yearbook.*

NEWSPAPERS - PUBLIC CONFIDENCE IN MEDIA

Independent Sector, 1200 18th Street, NW, Suite 200, Washington, D.C. 20036 (202) 467-6161; *Giving and Volunteering in the United States.*

NEWSPAPERS - READING

Mediamark Research, Incorporated, 708 Third Avenue, New York, New York 10017 (212) 599-0444; *Multimedia Audiences.*

Veronis, Suhler and Associates, 350 Park Avenue, New York, New York 10022 (212) 935-4990; *Communications Industry Forecast Report.*

NEWSPAPERS - RECEIPTS

Veronis, Suhler and Associates, 350 Park Avenue, New York, New York 10022 (212) 935-4990; *Communications Industry Forecast Report.*

NEWSPRINT

American Forest and Paper Association, 1111 Nineteenth Street, NW, Suite 800, Washington, D.C. 20036 (202) 463-2700; *Monthly Statistical Summary of Paper, Paperboard, and Wood Pulp.*

U.S. Department of Commerce, Bureau of Economic Analysis, Fourteenth Street between Constitution Avenue and E Streets, NW, Washington, D.C. 20230 (202) 606-9900, www.bea.doc.gov; *Survey of Current Business.*

NEWSPRINT - PRODUCER PRICES

U. S. Department of Labor, Bureau of Labor Statistics, Two Massachusetts Avenue, NE, Washington, D.C. 20212 (202) 691-5200, www.stats.bls.gov; *Producer Price Index.*

NEWSPRINT - WORLD PRODUCTION

Statistical Office of the United Nations, Publishing Service, New York, New York 10017 (800) 253-9646; *Monthly Bulletin of Statistics.*

Nicaragua - National Statistical Office

Instituto Nacional de Estadisdicas y Censos, Apartado 4031, Managua, Nicaragua.

Nicaragua - Primary Statistics Source

Instituto Nacional de Estadisticas y Censos, Apartado 4031, Managua, Nicaragua; *Anuario Estadistico de Nicaragua;* and *Boletin de Estadistica.*

NICARAGUA - AGRICULTURE

The Economist Intelligence Unit, 111 West 57th Street, New York, New York 10019 (800) 938-4685; *Nicaragua Country Report;* and *The New Latin America Market Atlas.*

Euromonitor International, Inc., 122 South Michigan Avenue, Suite 1200, Chicago, Illinois 60603 (800) 577-EURO; *International Marketing Data and Statistics;* and *World Marketing Data and Statistics.*

Europa Publications Limited, 18 Bedford Square, London, WC1B 3JN, England; *The Europa World Year Book.*

Food and Agricultural Organization of the United Nations (FAO) Via delle Terme di Caracalla, 00100 Rome, Italy (Telephone Number in U.S. (202) 653-2400); *Production Yearbook; The State of Food and Agriculture;* and *Trade Yearbook.*

Inter-American Development Bank, 1300 New York Avenue, NW, Washington, D.C. 20577 (202) 623-1753; *Economic and Social Progress in Latin America.*

M.E. Sharpe, 80 Business Park Drive, Armonk, New York 10504 (800) 541-6563; *The Illustrated Book of World Rankings.*

St. Martin's Press, Inc., 175 Fifth Avenue, New York, New York 10010 (800) 221-7945; *The Statesman's Year-Book.*

Statistical Office of the United Nations, Publishing Service, New York, New York 10017 (800) 253-9646; *Statistical Yearbook.*

U.C.L.A. Latin American Center Publications, University of California, Los Angeles, California 90024 (310) 825-6634; *Statistical Abstract of Latin America.*

United Nations Conference on Trade and Development, Central Statistical Service, Palais des Nations, Geneva, Switzerland (Telephone in U.S. (800) 253-9646); *UNCTAD Commodity Yearbook.*

The World Bank, 1818 H Street, NW, Washington, D.C. 20433 (202) 477-1234; *World Development Indicators.*

NICARAGUA - AIRLINE SERVICE

The Economist Intelligence Unit, 111 West 57th Street, New York, New York 10019 (800) 938-4685; *The New Latin America Market Atlas.*

Europa Publications Limited, 18 Bedford Square, London, WC1B 3JN, England; *The Europa World Year Book.*

M.E. Sharpe, 80 Business Park Drive, Armonk, New York 10504 (800) 541-6563; *The Illustrated Book of World Rankings.*

St. Martin's Press, Inc., 175 Fifth Avenue, New York, New York 10010 (800) 221-7945; *The Statesman's Year-Book.*

Statistical Office of the United Nations, Publishing Service, New York, New York 10017 (800) 253-9646; *Statistical Yearbook.*

NICARAGUA - AIRPORTS

Central Intelligence Agency, Washington, D.C. 20505 (703) 482-1100, www.cia.gov; *The World Factbook.*

NICARAGUA - ALUMINUM PRODUCTION AND CONSUMPTION - See NICARAGUA - MINING AND MINERAL PRODUCTS

NICARAGUA - ANIMAL HEALTH

Food and Agricultural Organization of the United Nations (FAO), Via delle Terme di Caracalla, 00100 Rome, Italy (Telephone Number in U.S. (202) 653-2400); *Animal Health Yearbook.*

NICARAGUA - AREA AND DENSITY OF POPULATION

Central Intelligence Agency, Washington, D.C. 20505 (703) 482-1100, www.cia.gov; *The World Factbook.*

Euromonitor International, Inc., 122 South Michigan Avenue, Suite 1200, Chicago, Illinois 60603 (800) 577-EURO; *International Marketing Data and Statistics;* and *The World Economic Factbook.*

Europa Publications Limited, 18 Bedford Square, London, WC1B 3JN, England; *The Europa World Year Book.*

Food and Agricultural Organization of the United Nations (FAO) Via delle Terme di Caracalla, 00100 Rome, Italy (Telephone Number in U.S. (202) 653-2400); *The State of Food and Agriculture.*

Inter-American Development Bank, 1300 New York Avenue, NW, Washington, D.C. 20577 (202) 623-1753; *Economic and Social Progress in Latin America.*

M.E. Sharpe, 80 Business Park Drive, Armonk, New York 10504 (800) 541-6563; *The Illustrated Book of World Rankings.*

St. Martin's Press, Inc., 175 Fifth Avenue, New York, New York 10010 (800) 221-7945; *The Statesman's Year-Book.*

Statistical Office of the United Nations, Publishing Service, New York, New York 10017 (800) 253-9646; *Statistical Yearbook.*

United Nations Educational, Scientific and Cultural Organization (UNESCO), 7 Place de Fontenoy, F-75700 Paris, France (Telephone Number in U.S. (212) 963-5981); *Statistical Yearbook.*

The World Bank, 1818 H Street, NW, Washington, D.C. 20433 (202) 477-1234; *World Development Report.*

NICARAGUA - ARMS EXPORTS AND IMPORTS - See NICARAGUA - MILITARY

NICARAGUA - BALANCE OF PAYMENTS

The Economist Intelligence Unit, 111 West 57th Street, New York, New York 10019 (800) 938-4685; *The New Latin America Market Atlas;* and *The World Market Atlas.*

Europa Publications Limited, 18 Bedford Square, London, WC1B 3JN, England; *The Europa World Year Book.*

Inter-American Development Bank, 1300 New York Avenue, NW, Washington,

D.C. 20577 (202) 623-1753; *Economic and Social Progress in Latin America.*

International Monetary Fund, 700 Nineteenth Street, NW, Washington, D.C. 20431 (202) 623-7000; *Balance of Payments Yearbook.*

Statistical Office of the United Nations, Publishing Service, New York, New York 10017 (800) 253-9646; *Economic Survey of Latin America and the Caribbean.*

U.C.L.A. Latin American Center Publications, University of California, Los Angeles, California 90024 (310) 825-6634; *Statistical Abstract of Latin America.*

United Nations Conference on Trade and Development (UNCTAD), New York, New York 10017 (800) 253-9646; *Handbook of International Trade and Development Statistics.*

The World Bank, 1818 H Street, NW, Washington, D.C. 20433 (202) 477-1234; *World Development Report;* and *World Development Indicators.*

NICARAGUA - BANANA PRODUCTION - See NICARAGUA - CROPS

NICARAGUA - BANKING

Euromonitor International, Inc., 122 South Michigan Avenue, Suite 1200, Chicago, Illinois 60603 (800) 577-EURO; *World Marketing Data and Statistics.*

Europa Publications Limited, 18 Bedford Square, London, WC1B 3JN, England; *The Europa World Year Book.*

Inter-American Development Bank, 1300 New York Avenue, NW, Washington, D.C. 20577 (202) 623-1753; *Economic and Social Progress in Latin America.*

International Monetary Fund, 700 Nineteenth Street, NW, Washington, D.C. 20431 (202) 623-7000; *International Financial Statistics.*

M.E. Sharpe, 80 Business Park Drive, Armonk, New York 10504 (800) 541-6563; *The Illustrated Book of World Rankings.*

St. Martin's Press, Inc., 175 Fifth Avenue, New York, New York 10010 (800) 221-7945; *The Statesman's Year-Book.*

Statistical Office of the United Nations, Publishing Service, New York, New York 10017 (800) 253-9646; *Statistical Yearbook.*

NICARAGUA - BARLEY PRODUCTION - See NICARAGUA - CROPS

NICARAGUA - BEER PRODUCTION - See NICARAGUA - BEVERAGES

NICARAGUA - BEVERAGES

M.E. Sharpe, 80 Business Park Drive, Armonk, New York 10504 (800) 541-6563; *The Illustrated Book of World Rankings.*

Statistical Office of the United Nations, Publishing Service, New York, New York 10017 (800) 253-9646; *Statistical Yearbook.*

NICARAGUA - BIRTH RATES

Central Intelligence Agency, Washington, D.C. 20505 (703) 482-1100, www.cia.gov; *The World Factbook.*

Euromonitor International, Inc., 122 South Michigan Avenue, Suite 1200, Chicago, Illinois 60603 (800) 577-EURO; *International Marketing Data and Statistics; and The World Economic Factbook.*

Europa Publications Limited, 18 Bedford Square, London, WC1B 3JN, England; *The Europa World Year Book.*

M.E. Sharpe, 80 Business Park Drive, Armonk, New York 10504 (800) 541-6563; *The Illustrated Book of World Rankings.*

St. Martin's Press, Inc., 175 Fifth Avenue, New York, New York 10010 (800) 221-7945; *The Statesman's Year-Book.*

Statistical Office of the United Nations, Publishing Service, New York, New York 10017 (800) 253-9646; *Demographic Yearbook; and Statistical Yearbook.*

The World Bank, 1818 H Street, NW, Washington, D.C. 20433 (202) 477-1234; *World Development Indicators.*

World Health Organization, Office of Publications, 20 Avenue Appia, CH-1211 Geneva 27, Switzerland (Telephone Number in U.S. (518) 436-9686); *World Health Statistics Annual.*

NICARAGUA - BONDS

Inter-American Development Bank, 1300 New York Avenue, NW, Washington, D.C. 20577 (202) 623-1753; *Economic and Social Progress in Latin America.*

International Monetary Fund, 700 Nineteenth Street, NW, Washington, D.C. 20431 (202) 623-7000; *Government Finance Statistics Yearbook.*

NICARAGUA - BROADCASTING

Billboard Limited, Post Office Box 9027, 1006 AA Amsterdam, The Netherlands (Telephone Number in U.S. (212) 764-7300); *World Radio TV Handbook.*

Central Intelligence Agency, Washington, D.C. 20505 (703) 482-1100, www.cia.gov; *The World Factbook.*

Euromonitor International, Inc., 122 South Michigan Avenue, Suite 1200, Chicago, Illinois 60603 (800) 577-EURO; *World Marketing Data and Statistics.*

M.E. Sharpe, 80 Business Park Drive, Armonk, New York 10504 (800) 541-6563; *The Illustrated Book of World Rankings.*

St. Martin's Press, Inc., 175 Fifth Avenue, New York, New York 10010 (800) 221-7945; *The Statesman's Year-Book.*

NICARAGUA - BUDGET

Central Intelligence Agency, Washington, D.C. 20505 (703) 482-1100, www.cia.gov; *The World Factbook.*

NICARAGUA - BUSINESS

Inter-American Development Bank, 1300 New York Avenue, NW, Washington, D.C. 20577 (202) 623-1753; *Economic and Social Progress in Latin America.*

NICARAGUA - BUSINESS AND PROFESSIONAL LICENSES

International Monetary Fund, 700 Nineteenth Street, NW, Washington, D.C. 20431 (202) 623-7000; *Government Finance Statistics Yearbook.*

NICARAGUA - BUTTER PRODUCTION - See NICARAGUA - DAIRY PRODUCTS

NICARAGUA - CABBAGE PRODUCTION - See NICARAGUA - CROPS

NICARAGUA - CALORIE SUPPLY

Food and Agricultural Organization of the United Nations (FAO) Via delle Terme di Caracalla, 00100 Rome, Italy (Telephone Number in U.S. (202) 653-2400); *The State of Food and Agriculture.*

NICARAGUA - CAPITAL INVESTMENT

Inter-American Development Bank, 1300 New York Avenue, NW, Washington, D.C. 20577 (202) 623-1753; *Economic and Social Progress in Latin America.*

NICARAGUA - CAPITAL REVENUE

Inter-American Development Bank, 1300 New York Avenue, NW, Washington, D.C. 20577 (202) 623-1753; *Economic and Social Progress in Latin America.*

International Monetary Fund, 700 Nineteenth Street, NW, Washington, D.C. 20431 (202) 623-7000; *Government Finance Statistics Yearbook.*

NICARAGUA - CATTLE - See NICARAGUA - LIVESTOCK AND POULTRY

NICARAGUA - CEMENT PRODUCTION - See

NICARAGUA - MINING AND MINERAL PRODUCTS

NICARAGUA - CHEESE PRODUCTION AND CONSUMPTION - See NICARAGUA - DAIRY PRODUCTS

NICARAGUA - CHEMICAL (ORGANIC) PRODUCTION - See NICARAGUA - MINING AND MINERAL PRODUCTS

NICARAGUA - CHICKENS - See NICARAGUA - LIVESTOCK AND POULTRY

NICARAGUA - CIGARETTE PRODUCTION - See NICARAGUA - TOBACCO PRODUCTION

NICARAGUA - CLIMATE

M.E. Sharpe, 80 Business Park Drive, Armonk, New York 10504 (800) 541-6563; *The Illustrated Book of World Rankings.*

St. Martin's Press, Inc., 175 Fifth Avenue, New York, New York 10010 (800) 221-7945; *The Statesman's Year-Book.*

NICARAGUA - COAL PRODUCTION - See NICARAGUA - MINING AND MINERAL PRODUCTS

NICARAGUA - COCOA PRODUCTION

Statistical Office of the United Nations, Publishing Service, New York, New York 10017 (800) 253-9646; *Statistical Yearbook.*

NICARAGUA - COCOA (BEANS) PRODUCTION - See NICARAGUA - CROPS

NICARAGUA - COFFEE - See NICARAGUA - CROPS

NICARAGUA - COMMERCE

St. Martin's Press, Inc., 175 Fifth Avenue, New York, New York 10010 (800) 221-7945; *The Statesman's Year-Book.*

NICARAGUA - COMMUNICATIONS - See NICARAGUA - TRANSPORTATION AND COMMUNICATIONS

NICARAGUA - CONSTRUCTION INDUSTRY

The Economist Intelligence Unit, 111 West 57th Street, New York, New York 10019 (800) 938-4685; *The New Latin America Market Atlas.*

Inter-American Development Bank, 1300 New York Avenue, NW, Washington, D.C. 20577 (202) 623-1753; *Economic and Social Progress in Latin America.*

M.E. Sharpe, 80 Business Park Drive, Armonk, New York 10504 (800) 541-6563; *The Illustrated Book of World Rankings.*

Statistical Office of the United Nations,

Publishing Service, New York, New York 10017 (800) 253-9646; *Statistical Yearbook.*

U.C.L.A. Latin American Center Publications, University of California, Los Angeles, California 90024 (310) 825-6634; *Statistical Abstract of Latin America.*

NICARAGUA - CONSUMER PRICE INDEX

Europa Publications Limited, 18 Bedford Square, London, WC1B 3JN, England; *The Europa World Year Book.*

Statistical Office of the United Nations, Publishing Service, New York, New York 10017 (800) 253-9646; *Statistical Yearbook.*

U.C.L.A. Latin American Center Publications, University of California, Los Angeles, California 90024 (310) 825-6634; *Statistical Abstract of Latin America.*

NICARAGUA - CONSUMER PRICES

The Economist Intelligence Unit, 111 West 57th Street, New York, New York 10019 (800) 938-4685; *The New Latin America Market Atlas.*

Euromonitor International, Inc., 122 South Michigan Avenue, Suite 1200, Chicago, Illinois 60603 (800) 577-EURO; *World Marketing Data and Statistics.*

International Labour Office, I.L.O. Publications, 1828 L Street, NW, Suite 801, Washington, D.C. 20036 (301) 638-3152; *Yearbook of Labour Statistics.*

International Monetary Fund, 700 Nineteenth Street, NW, Washington, D.C. 20431 (202) 623-7000; *International Financial Statistics.*

NICARAGUA - CONSUMPTION

The Economist Intelligence Unit, 111 West 57th Street, New York, New York 10019 (800) 938-4685; *The New Latin America Market Atlas.*

The World Bank, 1818 H Street, NW, Washington, D.C. 20433 (202) 477-1234; *World Development Report.*

NICARAGUA - CONSUMPTION - GOVERNMENT

Inter-American Development Bank, 1300 New York Avenue, NW, Washington, D.C. 20577 (202) 623-1753; *Economic and Social Progress in Latin America.*

NICARAGUA - COOPERATIVES

U.C.L.A. Latin American Center Publications, University of California, Los Angeles, California 90024 (310) 825-6634; *Statistical Abstract of Latin America.*

NICARAGUA - COPPER AND COPPER ORE PRODUCTION AND CONSUMPTION - See NICARAGUA - MINING AND MINERAL PRODUCTS

NICARAGUA - CORN PRODUCTION - See NICARAGUA - CROPS

NICARAGUA - CORPORATE INCOME TAXES - See NICARAGUA - TAXATION

NICARAGUA - CORPORATE TAXES - See NICARAGUA - TAXATION

NICARAGUA - COTTON - See NICARAGUA - CROPS

NICARAGUA - CROPS

The Economist Intelligence Unit, 111 West 57th Street, New York, New York 10019 (800) 938-4685; *The New Latin America Market Atlas.*

Europa Publications Limited, 18 Bedford Square, London, WC1B 3JN, England; *The Europa World Year Book.*

Food and Agricultural Organization of the United Nations (FAO), Via delle Terme di Caracalla, 00100 Rome, Italy (Telephone Number in U.S. (202) 653-2400); *Production Yearbook;* and *The State of Food and Agriculture.*

International Monetary Fund, 700 Nineteenth Street, NW, Washington, D.C. 20431 (202) 623-7000; *International Financial Statistics.*

M.E. Sharpe, 80 Business Park Drive, Armonk, New York 10504 (800) 541-6563; *The Illustrated Book of World Rankings.*

St. Martin's Press, Inc., 175 Fifth Avenue, New York, New York 10010 (800) 221-7945; *The Statesman's Year-Book.*

Statistical Office of the United Nations, Publishing Service, New York, New York 10017 (800) 253-9646; *Statistical Yearbook.*

U.C.L.A. Latin American Center Publications, University of California, Los Angeles, California 90024 (310) 825-6634; *Statistical Abstract of Latin America.*

United Nations Conference on Trade and Development, Central Statistical Service, Palais des Nations, Geneva, Switzerland (Telephone in U.S. (800) 253-9646); *UNCTAD Commodity Yearbook.*

NICARAGUA - CUSTOMS DUTIES

Inter-American Development Bank, 1300 New York Avenue, NW, Washington, D.C. 20577 (202) 623-1753; *Economic and Social Progress in Latin America.*

International Monetary Fund, 700

Nineteenth Street, NW, Washington, D.C. 20431 (202) 623-7000; *Government Finance Statistics Yearbook.*

St. Martin's Press, Inc., 175 Fifth Avenue, New York, New York 10010 (800) 221-7945; *The Statesman's Year-Book.*

NICARAGUA - DAIRY PRODUCTS

Europa Publications Limited, 18 Bedford Square, London, WC1B 3JN, England; *The Europa World Year Book.*

Food and Agricultural Organization of the United Nations (FAO) Via delle Terme di Caracalla, 00100 Rome, Italy (Telephone Number in U.S. (202) 653-2400); *Production Yearbook;* and *The State of Food and Agriculture.*

M.E. Sharpe, 80 Business Park Drive, Armonk, New York 10504 (800) 541-6563; *The Illustrated Book of World Rankings.*

St. Martin's Press, Inc., 175 Fifth Avenue, New York, New York 10010 (800) 221-7945; *The Statesman's Year-Book.*

Statistical Office of the United Nations, Publishing Service, New York, New York 10017 (800) 253-9646; *Statistical Yearbook.*

U.C.L.A. Latin American Center Publications, University of California, Los Angeles, California 90024 (310) 825-6634; *Statistical Abstract of Latin America.*

NICARAGUA - DEATH RATES - See NICARAGUA - MORTALITY

NICARAGUA - DEBT

The Economist Intelligence Unit, 111 West 57th Street, New York, New York 10019 (800) 938-4685; *The New Latin America Market Atlas.*

NICARAGUA - DEFENSE EXPENDITURES - See NICARAGUA - MILITARY

NICARAGUA - DEMOGRAPHY

The Economist Intelligence Unit, 111 West 57th Street, New York, New York 10019 (800) 938-4685; *The World Market Atlas.*

Euromonitor International, Inc., 122 South Michigan Avenue, Suite 1200, Chicago, Illinois 60603 (800) 577-EURO; *International Marketing Data and Statistics; The World Economic Factbook;* and *World Marketing Data and Statistics.*

M.E. Sharpe, 80 Business Park Drive, Armonk, New York 10504 (800) 541-6563; *The Illustrated Book of World Rankings.*

Statistical Office of the United Nations, Publishing Service, New York, New York 10017 (800) 253-9646; *Human Development Report.*

NICARAGUA - DEVELOPMENT ASSISTANCE

Inter-American Development Bank, 1300 New York Avenue, NW, Washington, D.C. 20577 (202) 623-1753; *Economic and Social Progress in Latin America:.*

Statistical Office of the United Nations, Publishing Service, New York, New York 10017 (800) 253-9646; *Statistical Yearbook.*

NICARAGUA - DIAMOND PRODUCTION - See NICARAGUA - MINING AND MINERAL PRODUCTS

NICARAGUA - DISCOUNT RATES - See NICARAGUA - BANKING

NICARAGUA - DISEASE - See NICARAGUA - HEALTH

NICARAGUA - DIVORCE RATES

M.E. Sharpe, 80 Business Park Drive, Armonk, New York 10504 (800) 541-6563; *The Illustrated Book of World Rankings.*

Statistical Office of the United Nations, Publishing Service, New York, New York 10017 (800) 253-9646; *Demographic Yearbook;* and *Statistical Yearbook.*

NICARAGUA - ECONOMY

Central Intelligence Agency, Washington, D.C. 20505 (703) 482-1100, www.cia.gov; *The World Factbook.*

Economist Intelligence Unit, 111 West 57th Street, New York, New York 10019 (800) 938-4685; *Nicaragua Country Report.*

Euromonitor International, Inc., 122 South Michigan Avenue, Suite 1200, Chicago, Illinois 60603 (800) 577-EURO; *International Marketing Data and Statistics; The World Economic Factbook;* and *World Marketing Data and Statistics.*

Europa Publications Limited, 18 Bedford Square, London, WC1B 3JN, England; *The Europa World Year Book.*

Inter-American Development Bank, 1300 New York Avenue, NW, Washington, D.C. 20577 (202) 623-1753; *Economic and Social Progress in Latin America.*

M.E. Sharpe, 80 Business Park Drive, Armonk, New York 10504 (800) 541-6563; *The Illustrated Book of World Rankings.*

St. Martin's Press, Inc., 175 Fifth Avenue, New York, New York 10010 (800) 221-7945; *The Statesman's Year-Book.*

Statistical Office of the United Nations, Publishing Service, New York, New York 10017 (800) 253-9646; *Economic Survey of Latin America and the Caribbean;* and *World Statistics Pocketbook.*

U.C.L.A. Latin American Center Publications, University of California, Los Angeles, California 90024 (310) 825-6634; *Statistical Abstract of Latin America.*

The World Bank, 1818 H Street, NW, Washington, D.C. 20433 (202) 477-1234; *The World Bank Atlas;* and *World Development Report.*

NICARAGUA - EDUCATION

The Economist Intelligence Unit, 111 West 57th Street, New York, New York 10019 (800) 938-4685; *The New Latin America Market Atlas;* and *The World Market Atlas.*

Euromonitor International, Inc., 122 South Michigan Avenue, Suite 1200, Chicago, Illinois 60603 (800) 577-EURO; *International Marketing Data and Statistics;* and *World Marketing Data and Statistics.*

Europa Publications Limited, 18 Bedford Square, London, WC1B 3JN, England; *The Europa World Year Book.*

International Monetary Fund, 700 Nineteenth Street, NW, Washington, D.C. 20431 (202) 623-7000; *Government Finance Statistics Yearbook.*

M.E. Sharpe, 80 Business Park Drive, Armonk, New York 10504 (800) 541-6563; *The Illustrated Book of World Rankings.*

St. Martin's Press, Inc., 175 Fifth Avenue, New York, New York 10010 (800) 221-7945; *The Statesman's Year-Book.*

Statistical Office of the United Nations, Publishing Service, New York, New York 10017 (800) 253-9646; *Human Development Report.*
U.C.L.A. Latin American Center Publications, University of California, Los Angeles, California 90024 (310) 825-6634; *Statistical Abstract of Latin America.*

United Nations Educational, Scientific and Cultural Organization (UNESCO), 7 Place de Fontenoy, F-75700 Paris, France (Telephone Number in U.S. (212) 963-5981); *Statistical Yearbook.*

The World Bank, 1818 H Street, NW, Washington, D.C. 20433 (202) 477-1234; *World Development Report;* and *World Development Indicators.*

NICARAGUA - EGG PRODUCTION AND CONSUMPTION - See NICARAGUA - DAIRY PRODUCTS

NICARAGUA - ELECTRICITY

Central Intelligence Agency, Washington, D.C. 20505 (703) 482-1100, www.cia.gov; *The World Factbook.*

The Economist Intelligence Unit, 111 West 57th Street, New York, New York 10019 (800) 938-4685; *The New Latin America Market Atlas.*

Inter-American Development Bank, 1300 New York Avenue, NW, Washington, D.C. 20577 (202) 623-1753; *Economic and Social Progress in Latin America.*

M.E. Sharpe, 80 Business Park Drive, Armonk, New York 10504 (800) 541-6563; *The Illustrated Book of World Rankings.*

St. Martin's Press, Inc., 175 Fifth Avenue, New York, New York 10010 (800) 221-7945; *The Statesman's Year-Book.*

Statistical Office of the United Nations, Publishing Service, New York, New York 10017 (800) 253-9646; *Human Development Report;* and *Statistical Yearbook.*

NICARAGUA - EMPLOYMENT

Euromonitor International, Inc., 122 South Michigan Avenue, Suite 1200, Chicago, Illinois 60603 (800) 577-EURO; *International Marketing Data and Statistics.*

International Labour Office, I.L.O. Publications, 1828 L Street, NW, Suite 801, Washington, D.C. 20036 (301) 638-3152; *Yearbook of Labour Statistics.*

M.E. Sharpe, 80 Business Park Drive, Armonk, New York 10504 (800) 541-6563; *The Illustrated Book of World Rankings.*

U.C.L.A. Latin American Center Publications, University of California, Los Angeles, California 90024 (310) 825-6634; *Statistical Abstract of Latin America.*

NICARAGUA - ENERGY

The Economist Intelligence Unit, 111 West 57th Street, New York, New York 10019 (800) 938-4685; *The New Latin America Market Atlas.*

Euromonitor International, Inc., 122 South Michigan Avenue, Suite 1200, Chicago, Illinois 60603 (800) 577-EURO; *International Marketing Data and Statistics; The World Economic Factbook;* and *World Marketing Data and Statistics.*

Food and Agricultural Organization of the United Nations (FAO) Via delle Terme di Caracalla, 00100 Rome, Italy (Telephone Number in U.S. (202) 653-2400); *The State of Food and Agriculture.*

M.E. Sharpe, 80 Business Park Drive, Armonk, New York 10504 (800) 541-6563; *The Illustrated Book of World Rankings.*

St. Martin's Press, Inc., 175 Fifth Avenue, New York, New York 10010 (800) 221-7945; *The Statesman's Year-Book.*

Statistical Office of the United Nations, Publishing Service, New York, New York 10017 (800) 253-9646; *Energy Statistics Yearbook; Human Development Report; World Statistics Pocketbook;* and *Statistical Yearbook.*

U.C.L.A. Latin American Center Publications, University of California, Los Angeles, California 90024 (310) 825-6634; *Statistical Abstract of Latin America.*

The World Bank, 1818 H Street, NW, Washington, D.C. 20433 (202) 477-1234; *The World Bank Atlas;* and *World Development Report.*

NICARAGUA - ENVIRONMENT

Economist Intelligence Unit, 111 West 57th Street, New York, New York 10019 (800) 938-4685; *Nicaragua Country Report.*

Statistical Office of the United Nations, Publishing Service, New York, New York 10017 (800) 253-9646; *World Statistics Pocketbook.*

NICARAGUA - EXCHANGE RATES

Central Intelligence Agency, Washington, D.C. 20505 (703) 482-1100, www.cia.gov; *The World Factbook.*

Euromonitor International, Inc., 122 South Michigan Avenue, Suite 1200, Chicago, Illinois 60603 (800) 577-EURO; *International Marketing Data and Statistics;* and *The World Economic Factbook.*

Europa Publications Limited, 18 Bedford Square, London, WC1B 3JN, England; *The Europa World Year Book.*

Inter-American Development Bank, 1300 New York Avenue, NW, Washington, D.C. 20577 (202) 623-1753; *Economic and Social Progress in Latin America.*

International Monetary Fund, 700 Nineteenth Street, NW, Washington, D.C. 20431 (202) 623-7000; *International Financial Statistics.*

Statistical Office of the United Nations, Publishing Service, New York, New York 10017 (800) 253-9646; *Statistical Yearbook;* and *World Statistics Pocketbook.*

U.C.L.A. Latin American Center Publications, University of California, Los Angeles, California 90024 (310) 825-6634; *Statistical Abstract of Latin America.*

NICARAGUA - EXCISE TAXES - See NICARAGUA - TAXATION

NICARAGUA - EXPORTS

Central Intelligence Agency, Washington, D.C. 20505 (703) 482-1100, www.cia.gov; *The World Factbook.*

The Economist Intelligence Unit, 111 West 57th Street, New York, New York 10019 (800) 938-4685; *Nicaragua Country Report; The New Latin America Market Atlas;* and *The World Market Atlas.*

Euromonitor International, Inc., 122 South Michigan Avenue, Suite 1200, Chicago, Illinois 60603 (800) 577-EURO; *International Marketing Data and Statistics;* and *The World Economic Factbook.*

Europa Publications Limited, 18 Bedford Square, London, WC1B 3JN, England; *The Europa World Year Book.*

Food and Agricultural Organization of the United Nations (FAO) Via delle Terme di Caracalla, 00100 Rome, Italy (Telephone Number in U.S. (202) 653-2400); *The State of Food and Agriculture.*

Inter-American Development Bank, 1300 New York Avenue, NW, Washington, D.C. 20577 (202) 623-1753; *Economic and Social Progress in Latin America.*

International Monetary Fund, 700 Nineteenth Street, NW, Washington, D.C. 20431 (202) 623-7000; *Direction of Trade Statistics; Government Finance Statistics Yearbook;* and *International Financial Statistics.*

St. Martin's Press, Inc., 175 Fifth Avenue, New York, New York 10010 (800) 221-7945; *The Statesman's Year-Book*

United Nations Conference on Trade and Development (UNCTAD), New York, New York 10017 (800) 253-9646; *Handbook of International Trade and Development.*

The World Bank, 1818 H Street, NW, Washington, D.C. 20433 (202) 477-1234; *World Development Report;* and *World Development Indicators.*

NICARAGUA - EXTERNAL FINANCING

Inter-American Development Bank, 1300 New York Avenue, NW, Washington, D.C. 20577 (202) 623-1753; *Economic and Social Progress in Latin America.*

NICARAGUA - EXTERNAL INDEBTEDNESS

Inter-American Development Bank, 1300 New York Avenue, NW, Washington, D.C. 20577 (202) 623-1753; *Economic and Social Progress in Latin America.*

The World Bank, 1818 H Street, NW, Washington, D.C. 20433 (202) 477-1234; *World Development Report;* and *World Development Indicators.*

NICARAGUA - EXTERNAL TRADE

Euromonitor International, Inc., 122 South Michigan Avenue, Suite 1200, Chicago, Illinois 60603 (800) 577-EURO; *World Marketing Data and Statistics.*

Food and Agricultural Organization of the United Nations (FAO) Via delle Terme di Caracalla, 00100 Rome, Italy (Telephone Number in U.S. (202) 653-2400); *The State of Food and Agriculture;* and *Trade Yearbook.*

Inter-American Development Bank, 1300 New York Avenue, NW, Washington, D.C. 20577 (202) 623-1753; *Economic and Social Progress in Latin America.*

Statistical Office of the United Nations, Publishing Service, New York, New York 10017 (800) 253-9646; *Statistical Yearbook.*

NICARAGUA - FABRIC PRODUCTION - See NICARAGUA - TEXTILE INDUSTRY

NICARAGUA - FAMILY PLANNING

U.C.L.A. Latin American Center Publications, University of California, Los Angeles, California 90024 (310) 825-6634; *Statistical Abstract of Latin America.*

NICARAGUA - FARM CROPS - See NICARAGUA - CROPS

NICARAGUA - FEMALE WORKING POPULATION - See NICARAGUA - EMPLOYMENT

NICARAGUA - FERTILITY RATES

Central Intelligence Agency, Washington, D.C. 20505 (703) 482-1100, www.cia.gov; *The World Factbook.*

M.E. Sharpe, 80 Business Park Drive, Armonk, New York 10504 (800) 541-6563; *The Illustrated Book of World Rankings.*

Statistical Office of the United Nations, Publishing Service, New York, New York 10017 (800) 253-9646; *Human Development Report.*

The World Bank, 1818 H Street, NW, Washington, D.C. 20433 (202) 477-1234; *The World Bank Atlas; World Development Report;* and *World Development Indicators.*

NICARAGUA - FERTILIZER

The Economist Intelligence Unit, 111 West 57th Street, New York, New York 10019 (800) 938-4685; *The New Latin America Market Atlas.*

Food and Agricultural Organization of the United Nations (FAO), Via delle Terme di Caracalla, 00100 Rome, Italy (Telephone Number in U.S. (202) 653-2400); *Fertilizer Yearbook;* and *The State of Food and Agriculture.*

Statistical Office of the United Nations, Publishing Service, New York, New York 10017 (800) 253-9646; *Statistical Yearbook.*

NICARAGUA - FETAL MORTALITY - See NICARAGUA - MORTALITY

NICARAGUA - FINANCE

Economist Intelligence Unit, 111 West 57th Street, New York, New York 10019 (800) 938-4685; *Nicaragua Country Report.*

Europa Publications Limited, 18 Bedford Square, London, WC1B 3JN, England; *The Europa World Year Book.*

Inter-American Development Bank, 1300 New York Avenue, NW, Washington, D.C. 20577 (202) 623-1753; *Economic and Social Progress in Latin America.*

International Monetary Fund, 700 Nineteenth Street, NW, Washington, D.C. 20431 (202) 623-7000; *Government Finance Statistics Yearbook;* and *International Financial Statistics.*

M.E. Sharpe, 80 Business Park Drive, Armonk, New York 10504 (800) 541-6563; *The Illustrated Book of World Rankings.*

St. Martin's Press, Inc., 175 Fifth Avenue, New York, New York 10010 (800) 221-7945; *The Statesman's Year-Book.*

U.C.L.A. Latin American Center Publications, University of California, Los Angeles, California 90024 (310) 825-6634; *Statistical Abstract of Latin America.*

NICARAGUA - FISHERIES

Europa Publications Limited, 18 Bedford Square, London, WC1B 3JN, England; *The Europa World Year Book.*

Food and Agricultural Organization of the United Nations (FAO) Via delle Terme di Caracalla, 00100 Rome, Italy (Telephone Number in U.S. (202) 653-2400); *The State of Food and Agriculture;* and *Yearbook of Fishery Statistics.*

Inter-American Development Bank, 1300 New York Avenue, NW, Washington, D.C. 20577 (202) 623-1753; *Economic and Social Progress in Latin America.*

M.E. Sharpe, 80 Business Park Drive, Armonk, New York 10504 (800) 541-6563; *The Illustrated Book of World Rankings.*

St. Martin's Press, Inc., 175 Fifth

Avenue, New York, New York 10010 (800) 221-7945; *The Statesman's Year-Book.*

Statistical Office of the United Nations, Publishing Service, New York, New York 10017 (800) 253-9646; *Statistical Yearbook.*

U.C.L.A. Latin American Center Publications, University of California, Los Angeles, California 90024 (310) 825-6634; *Statistical Abstract of Latin America.*

United Nations Conference on Trade and Development, Central Statistical Service, Palais des Nations, Geneva, Switzerland (Telephone in U.S. (800) 253-9646); *UNCTAD Commodity Yearbook.*

NICARAGUA - FLOUR PRODUCTION

Statistical Office of the United Nations, Publishing Service, New York, New York 10017 (800) 253-9646; *Statistical Yearbook.*

NICARAGUA - FOOD

Food and Agricultural Organization of the United Nations (FAO), Via delle Terme di Caracalla, 00100 Rome, Italy (Telephone Number in U.S. (202) 653-2400); *Production Yearbook;* and *The State of Food and Agriculture.*

Statistical Office of the United Nations, Publishing Service, New York, New York 10017 (800) 253-9646; *Human Development Report.*

NICARAGUA - FOREIGN AID

Inter-American Development Bank, 1300 New York Avenue, NW, Washington, D.C. 20577 (202) 623-1753; *Economic and Social Progress in Latin America.*

NICARAGUA - FOREIGN DEBT

The Economist Intelligence Unit, 111 West 57th Street, New York, New York 10019 (800) 938-4685; *The New Latin America Market Atlas.*

Inter-American Development Bank, 1300 New York Avenue, NW, Washington, D.C. 20577 (202) 623-1753; *Economic and Social Progress in Latin America.*

NICARAGUA - FOREIGN INDEBTEDNESS

Inter-American Development Bank, 1300 New York Avenue, NW, Washington, D.C. 20577 (202) 623-1753; *Economic and Social Progress in Latin America.*

Statistical Office of the United Nations, Publishing Service, New York, New York 10017 (800) 253-9646; *Economic Survey of Latin America and the Caribbean.*

NICARAGUA - FOREIGN INVESTMENT

The Economist Intelligence Unit, 111 West 57th Street, New York, New York 10019 (800) 938-4685; *The New Latin America Market Atlas.*

NICARAGUA - FOREIGN TRADE

The Economist Intelligence Unit, 111 West 57th Street, New York, New York 10019 (800) 938-4685; *Nicaragua Country Report;* and *The New Latin America Market Atlas.*

Euromonitor International, Inc., 122 South Michigan Avenue, Suite 1200, Chicago, Illinois 60603 (800) 577-EURO; *International Marketing Data and Statistics;* and *The World Economic Factbook.*

Europa Publications Limited, 18 Bedford Square, London, WC1B 3JN, England; *The Europa World Year Book.*

Food and Agricultural Organization of the United Nations (FAO) Via delle Terme di Caracalla, 00100 Rome, Italy (Telephone Number in U.S. (202) 653-2400); *The State of Food and Agriculture.*

Inter-American Development Bank, 1300 New York Avenue, NW, Washington, D.C. 20577 (202) 623-1753; *Economic and Social Progress in Latin America.*

M.E. Sharpe, 80 Business Park Drive, Armonk, New York 10504 (800) 541-6563; *The Illustrated Book of World Rankings.*

St. Martin's Press, Inc., 175 Fifth Avenue, New York, New York 10010 (800) 221-7945; *The Statesman's Year-Book.*

Statistical Office of the United Nations, Publishing Service, New York, New York 10017 (800) 253-9646; *Economic Survey of Latin America and the Caribbean; International Trade Statistics Yearbook;* and *Statistical Yearbook.*

U.C.L.A. Latin American Center Publications, University of California, Los Angeles, California 90024 (310) 825-6634; *Statistical Abstract of Latin America.*

United Nations Conference on Trade and Development, Central Statistical Service, Palais des Nations, Geneva, Switzerland (Telephone in U.S. (800) 253-9646); *UNCTAD Commodity Yearbook.*

The World Bank, 1818 H Street, NW, Washington, D.C. 20433 (202) 477-1234; *World Development Report;* and *World Development Indicators.*

NICARAGUA - FORESTRY AND FOREST PRODUCTS

The Economist Intelligence Unit, 111 West 57th Street, New York, New York 10019 (800) 938-4685; *The New Latin*

America Market Atlas.

Europa Publications Limited, 18 Bedford Square, London, WC1B 3JN, England; *The Europa World Year Book.*

Food and Agricultural Organization of the United Nations (FAO) Via delle Terme di Caracalla, 00100 Rome, Italy (Telephone Number in U.S. (202) 653-2400); *The State of Food and Agriculture;* and *Yearbook of Forest Products.*

Inter-American Development Bank, 1300 New York Avenue, NW, Washington, D.C. 20577 (202) 623-1753; *Economic and Social Progress in Latin America.*

M.E. Sharpe, 80 Business Park Drive, Armonk, New York 10504 (800) 541-6563; *The Illustrated Book of World Rankings.*

St. Martin's Press, Inc., 175 Fifth Avenue, New York, New York 10010 (800) 221-7945; *The Statesman's Year-Book.*

Statistical Office of the United Nations, Publishing Service, New York, New York 10017 (800) 253-9646; *Statistical Yearbook.*

U.C.L.A. Latin American Center Publications, University of California, Los Angeles, California 90024 (310) 825-6634; *Statistical Abstract of Latin America.*

United Nations Conference on Trade and Development, Central Statistical Service, Palais des Nations, Geneva, Switzerland (Telephone in U.S. (800) 253-9646); *UNCTAD Commodity Yearbook.*

United Nations Educational, Scientific and Cultural Organization (UNESCO), 7 Place de Fontenoy, F-75700 Paris, France (Telephone Number in U.S. (212) 963-5981); *Statistical Yearbook.*

The World Bank, 1818 H Street, NW, Washington, D.C. 20433 (202) 477-1234; *World Development Report.*

NICARAGUA - GAS PRODUCTION - See NICARAGUA - MINING AND MINERAL PRODUCTS

NICARAGUA - GENERAL INDUSTRIAL STATISTICS - See NICARAGUA - INDUSTRY

NICARAGUA - GENERAL MORTALITY - See NICARAGUA - MORTALITY

NICARAGUA - GEOGRAPHIC DATA

M.E. Sharpe, 80 Business Park Drive, Armonk, New York 10504 (800) 541-6563; *The Illustrated Book of World Rankings.*

U.C.L.A. Latin American Center Publications, University of California, Los Angeles, California 90024 (310) 825-6634; *Statistical Abstract of Latin America.*

NICARAGUA - GOATS - See NICARAGUA - LIVESTOCK AND POULTRY

NICARAGUA - GOLD HOLDINGS

International Monetary Fund, 700 Nineteenth Street, NW, Washington, D.C. 20431 (202) 623-7000; *International Financial Statistics.*

Statistical Office of the United Nations, Publishing Service, New York, New York 10017 (800) 253-9646; *Statistical Yearbook.*

The World Bank, 1818 H Street, NW, Washington, D.C. 20433 (202) 477-1234; *World Development Indicators.*

NICARAGUA - GOLD PRODUCTION AND CONSUMPTION - See NICARAGUA - MINING AND MINERAL PRODUCTS

NICARAGUA - GOLD RESERVES

The Economist Intelligence Unit, 111 West 57th Street, New York, New York 10019 (800) 938-4685; *The New Latin America Market Atlas.*

NICARAGUA - GOVERNMENT

Central Intelligence Agency, Washington, D.C. 20505 (703) 482-1100, www.cia.gov; *The World Factbook.*

Europa Publications Limited, 18 Bedford Square, London, WC1B 3JN, England; *The Europa World Year Book.*

Inter-American Development Bank, 1300 New York Avenue, NW, Washington, D.C. 20577 (202) 623-1753; *Economic and Social Progress in Latin America.*

International Monetary Fund, 700 Nineteenth Street, NW, Washington, D.C. 20431 (202) 623-7000; *Government Finance Statistics Yearbook;* and *International Financial Statistics.*

St. Martin's Press, Inc., 175 Fifth Avenue, New York, New York 10010 (800) 221-7945; *The Statesman's Year-Book.*

Statistical Office of the United Nations, Publishing Service, New York, New York 10017 (800) 253-9646; *National Accounts Statistics.*

The World Bank, 1818 H Street, NW, Washington, D.C. 20433 (202) 477-1234; *World Development Report;* and *World Development Indicators.*

NICARAGUA - GRAIN PRODUCTION - See NICARAGUA - CROPS

NICARAGUA - GRANTS

International Monetary Fund, 700 Nineteenth Street, NW, Washington, D.C. 20431 (202) 623-7000; *Government Finance Statistics Yearbook.*

NICARAGUA - GROSS DOMESTIC PRODUCT

The Economist Intelligence Unit, 111 West 57th Street, New York, New York 10019 (800) 938-4685; *Nicaragua Country Report; The New Latin America Market Atlas;* and *The World Market Atlas.*

Euromonitor International, Inc., 122 South Michigan Avenue, Suite 1200, Chicago, Illinois 60603 (800) 577-EURO; *International Marketing Data and Statistics;* and *The World Economic Factbook.*

Europa Publications Limited, 18 Bedford Square, London, WC1B 3JN, England; *The Europa World Year Book.*

Inter-American Development Bank, 1300 New York Avenue, NW, Washington, D.C. 20577 (202) 623-1753; *Economic and Social Progress in Latin America.*

M.E. Sharpe, 80 Business Park Drive, Armonk, New York 10504 (800) 541-6563; *The Illustrated Book of World Rankings.*

Statistical Office of the United Nations, Publishing Service, New York, New York 10017 (800) 253-9646; *Human Development Report; National Accounts Statistics;* and *Statistical Yearbook.*

U.C.L.A. Latin American Center Publications, University of California, Los Angeles, California 90024 (310) 825-6634; *Statistical Abstract of Latin America.*

U.S. Arms Control and Disarmament Agency, 320 Twenty-first Street, NW, Washington, D.C. 20451 (202) 647-8677; *World Military Expenditures and Arms Transfers.*

The World Bank, 1818 H Street, NW, Washington, D.C. 20433 (202) 477-1234; *World Development Report;* and *World Development Indicators.*

NICARAGUA - GROSS NATIONAL PRODUCT

Euromonitor International, Inc., 122 South Michigan Avenue, Suite 1200, Chicago, Illinois 60603 (800) 577-EURO; *International Marketing Data and Statistics.*

Inter-American Development Bank, 1300 New York Avenue, NW, Washington, D.C. 20577 (202) 623-1753; *Economic and Social Progress in Latin America.*

St. Martin's Press, Inc., 175 Fifth Avenue, New York, New York 10010 (800) 221-7945; *The Statesman's Year-Book.*

U.S. Arms Control and Disarmament

Agency, 320 Twenty-first Street, NW, Washington, D.C. 20451 (202) 647-8677; *World Military Expenditures and Arms Transfers.*

The World Bank, 1818 H Street, NW, Washington, D.C. 20433 (202) 477-1234; *The World Bank Atlas; World Development Report;* and *World Development Indicators.*

NICARAGUA - GROUNDNUT PRODUCTION - See NICARAGUA - CROPS

NICARAGUA - HEALTH

The Economist Intelligence Unit, 111 West 57th Street, New York, New York 10019 (800) 938-4685; *The New Latin America Market Atlas.*

Euromonitor International, Inc., 122 South Michigan Avenue, Suite 1200, Chicago, Illinois 60603 (800) 577-EURO; *World Marketing Data and Statistics.*

M.E. Sharpe, 80 Business Park Drive, Armonk, New York 10504 (800) 541-6563; *The Illustrated Book of World Rankings.*

St. Martin's Press, Inc., 175 Fifth Avenue, New York, New York 10010 (800) 221-7945; *The Statesman's Year-Book.*

Statistical Office of the United Nations, Publishing Service, New York, New York 10017 (800) 253-9646; *Human Development Report;* and *Statistical Yearbook.*

U.C.L.A. Latin American Center Publications, University of California, Los Angeles, California 90024 (310) 825-6634; *Statistical Abstract of Latin America.*

United Nations Children's Fund (UNICEF), 3 United Nations Plaza, New York, New York 10017 (800) 253-9646; *State of the World's Children.*

The World Bank, 1818 H Street, NW, Washington, D.C. 20433 (202) 477-1234; *World Development Report.*

World Health Organization, Office of Publications, 20 Avenue Appia, CH-1211 Geneva 27, Switzerland (Telephone Number in U.S. (518) 436-9686); *World Health Statistics Annual.*

NICARAGUA - HEALTH EXPENDITURES

International Monetary Fund, 700 Nineteenth Street, NW, Washington, D.C. 20431 (202) 623-7000; *Government Finance Statistics Yearbook.*

NICARAGUA - HIDE PRODUCTION

Food and Agricultural Organization of the United Nations (FAO), Via delle Terme di Caracalla, 00100 Rome, Italy (Telephone

Number in U.S. (202) 653-2400); *Production Yearbook.*

NICARAGUA - HIGHWAYS

Central Intelligence Agency, Washington, D.C. 20505 (703) 482-1100, www.cia.gov; *The World Factbook.*

The Economist Intelligence Unit, 111 West 57th Street, New York, New York 10019 (800) 938-4685; *The New Latin America Market Atlas.*

International Road Federation, 2600 Virginia Avenue, NW., Washington, D.C. 20037 (202) 338-4641; *World Road Statistics.*

St. Martin's Press, Inc., 175 Fifth Avenue, New York, New York 10010 (800) 221-7945; *The Statesman's Year-Book.*

NICARAGUA - HORSES - See NICARAGUA - LIVESTOCK AND POULTRY

NICARAGUA - HOURS OF WORK - See NICARAGUA - EMPLOYMENT

NICARAGUA - HOUSING AND HOUSING UNITS

Euromonitor International, Inc., 122 South Michigan Avenue, Suite 1200, Chicago, Illinois 60603 (800) 577-EURO; *World Marketing Data and Statistics.*

M.E. Sharpe, 80 Business Park Drive, Armonk, New York 10504 (800) 541-6563; *The Illustrated Book of World Rankings.*

U.C.L.A. Latin American Center Publications, University of California, Los Angeles, California 90024 (310) 825-6634; *Statistical Abstract of Latin America.*

NICARAGUA - HOUSING EXPENDITURES

International Monetary Fund, 700 Nineteenth Street, NW, Washington, D.C. 20431 (202) 623-7000; *Government Finance Statistics Yearbook.*

NICARAGUA - ILLITERACY RATES

The Economist Intelligence Unit, 111 West 57th Street, New York, New York 10019 (800) 938-4685; *The New Latin America Market Atlas.*

Euromonitor International, Inc., 122 South Michigan Avenue, Suite 1200, Chicago, Illinois 60603 (800) 577-EURO; *The World Economic Factbook.*

NICARAGUA - ILLITERATE POPULATION

Central Intelligence Agency, Washington, D.C. 20505 (703) 482-1100, www.cia.gov; *The World Factbook.*

The Economist Intelligence Unit, 111 West 57th Street, New York, New York 10019 (800) 938-4685; *The World Market Atlas.*

St. Martin's Press, Inc., 175 Fifth Avenue, New York, New York 10010 (800) 221-7945; *The Statesman's Year-Book.*

Statistical Office of the United Nations, Publishing Service, New York, New York 10017 (800) 253-9646; *Human Development Report.*

United Nations Educational, Scientific and Cultural Organization (UNESCO), 7 Place de Fontenoy, F-75700 Paris, France (Telephone Number in U.S. (212) 963-5981); *Statistical Yearbook.*

NICARAGUA - IMMIGRATION

U.C.L.A. Latin American Center Publications, University of California, Los Angeles, California 90024 (310) 825-6634; *Statistical Abstract of Latin America.*

NICARAGUA - IMPORTS

Central Intelligence Agency, Washington, D.C. 20505 (703) 482-1100, www.cia.gov; *The World Factbook.*

The Economist Intelligence Unit, 111 West 57th Street, New York, New York 10019 (800) 938-4685; *The New Latin America Market Atlas; Nicaragua Country Report;* and *The World Market Atlas.*

Euromonitor International, Inc., 122 South Michigan Avenue, Suite 1200, Chicago, Illinois 60603 (800) 577-EURO; *International Marketing Data and Statistics;* and *The World Economic Factbook.*

Europa Publications Limited, 18 Bedford Square, London, WC1B 3JN, England; *The Europa World Year Book.*

Food and Agricultural Organization of the United Nations (FAO) Via delle Terme di Caracalla, 00100 Rome, Italy (Telephone Number in U.S. (202) 653-2400); *The State of Food and Agriculture.*

Inter-American Development Bank, 1300 New York Avenue, NW, Washington, D.C. 20577 (202) 623-1753; *Economic and Social Progress in Latin America.*

International Monetary Fund, 700 Nineteenth Street, NW, Washington, D.C. 20431 (202) 623-7000; *Direction of Trade Statistics; Government Finance Statistics Yearbook;* and *International Financial Statistics.*

St. Martin's Press, Inc., 175 Fifth Avenue, New York, New York 10010 (800) 221-7945; *The Statesman's Year-Book*

United Nations Conference on Trade and Development (UNCTAD), New York, New York 10017 (800) 253-9646; *Handbook of International Trade and Development.*

The World Bank, 1818 H Street, NW, Washington, D.C. 20433 (202) 477-1234; *World Development Report;* and *World Development Indicators.*

NICARAGUA - INCOME DISTRIBUTION

U.C.L.A. Latin American Center Publications, University of California, Los Angeles, California 90024 (310) 825-6634; *Statistical Abstract of Latin America.*

NICARAGUA - INCOME TAXES - See NICARAGUA - TAXATION

NICARAGUA - INDUSTRY

Central Intelligence Agency, Washington, D.C. 20505 (703) 482-1100, www.cia.gov; *The World Factbook.*

Economist Intelligence Unit, 111 West 57th Street, New York, New York 10019 (800) 938-4685; *Nicaragua Country Report.*

Euromonitor International, Inc., 122 South Michigan Avenue, Suite 1200, Chicago, Illinois 60603 (800) 577-EURO; *International Marketing Data and Statistics; The World Economic Factbook;* and *World Marketing Data and Statistics.*

Europa Publications Limited, 18 Bedford Square, London, WC1B 3JN, England; *The Europa World Year Book.*

International Labour Office, I.L.O. Publications, 1828 L Street, NW, Suite 801, Washington, D.C. 20036 (301) 638-3152; *Yearbook of Labour Statistics.*

M.E. Sharpe, 80 Business Park Drive, Armonk, New York 10504 (800) 541-6563; *The Illustrated Book of World Rankings.*

St. Martin's Press, Inc., 175 Fifth Avenue, New York, New York 10010 (800) 221-7945; *The Statesman's Year-Book.*

Statistical Office of the United Nations, Publishing Service, New York, New York 10017 (800) 253-9646; *Economic Survey of Latin America and the Caribbean;* and *Industrial Commodity Statistics Yearbook.*

U.C.L.A. Latin American Center Publications, University of California, Los Angeles, California 90024 (310) 825-6634; *Statistical Abstract of Latin America.*

The World Bank, 1818 H Street, NW, Washington, D.C. 20433 (202) 477-1234; *World Development Indicators.*

NICARAGUA - INFANT AND MATERNAL MORTALITY - See NICARAGUA -

MORTALITY

NICARAGUA - INFLATIONARY FACTORS

Statistical Office of the United Nations, Publishing Service, New York, New York 10017 (800) 253-9646; *Economic Survey of Latin America and the Caribbean.*

NICARAGUA - INTEREST RATES

Inter-American Development Bank, 1300 New York Avenue, NW, Washington, D.C. 20577 (202) 623-1753; *Economic and Social Progress in Latin America.*

NICARAGUA - INTERNATIONAL FINANCE

Inter-American Development Bank, 1300 New York Avenue, NW, Washington, D.C. 20577 (202) 623-1753; *Economic and Social Progress in Latin America.*

U.C.L.A. Latin American Center Publications, University of California, Los Angeles, California 90024 (310) 825-6634; *Statistical Abstract of Latin America.*

NICARAGUA - INTERNATIONAL LIQUIDITY

Inter-American Development Bank, 1300 New York Avenue, NW, Washington, D.C. 20577 (202) 623-1753; *Economic and Social Progress in Latin America.*

International Monetary Fund, 700 Nineteenth Street, NW, Washington, D.C. 20431 (202) 623-7000; *International Financial Statistics.*

NICARAGUA - INTERNATIONAL RESERVES EXCLUDING GOLD

Inter-American Development Bank, 1300 New York Avenue, NW, Washington, D.C. 20577 (202) 623-1753; *Economic and Social Progress in Latin America.*

Statistical Office of the United Nations, Publishing Service, New York, New York 10017 (800) 253-9646; *Statistical Yearbook.*

The World Bank, 1818 H Street, NW, Washington, D.C. 20433 (202) 477-1234; *World Development Indicators.*

NICARAGUA - INTERNATIONAL STATISTICS

Inter-American Development Bank, 1300 New York Avenue, NW, Washington, D.C. 20577 (202) 623-1753; *Economic and Social Progress in Latin America.*

U.C.L.A. Latin American Center Publications, University of California, Los Angeles, California 90024 (310) 825-6634; *Statistical Abstract of Latin America.*

NICARAGUA - INVESTMENTS

Inter-American Development Bank, 1300 New York Avenue, NW, Washington, D.C. 20577 (202) 623-1753; *Economic and Social Progress in Latin America.*

NICARAGUA - IRON ORE PRODUCTION AND CONSUMPTION - See NICARAGUA - MINING AND MINERAL PRODUCTS

NICARAGUA - IRRIGATION

Euromonitor International, Inc., 122 South Michigan Avenue, Suite 1200, Chicago, Illinois 60603 (800) 577-EURO; *International Marketing Data and Statistics.*

Inter-American Development Bank, 1300 New York Avenue, NW, Washington, D.C. 20577 (202) 623-1753; *Economic and Social Progress in Latin America.*

NICARAGUA - LABOR

Central Intelligence Agency, Washington, D.C. 20505 (703) 482-1100, www.cia.gov; *The World Factbook.*

The Economist Intelligence Unit, 111 West 57th Street, New York, New York 10019 (800) 938-4685; *The New Latin America Market Atlas.*

Euromonitor International, Inc., 122 South Michigan Avenue, Suite 1200, Chicago, Illinois 60603 (800) 577-EURO; *International Marketing Data and Statistics;* and *World Marketing Data and Statistics.*

Europa Publications Limited, 18 Bedford Square, London, WC1B 3JN, England; *The Europa World Year Book.*

Food and Agricultural Organization of the United Nations (FAO) Via delle Terme di Caracalla, 00100 Rome, Italy (Telephone Number in U.S. (202) 653-2400); *The State of Food and Agriculture.*

International Labour Office, I.L.O. Publications, 1828 L Street, NW, Suite 801, Washington, D.C. 20036 (301) 638-3152; *Yearbook of Labour Statistics.*

M.E. Sharpe, 80 Business Park Drive, Armonk, New York 10504 (800) 541-6563; *The Illustrated Book of World Rankings.*

St. Martin's Press, Inc., 175 Fifth Avenue, New York, New York 10010 (800) 221-7945; *The Statesman's Year-Book.*

Statistical Office of the United Nations, Publishing Service, New York, New York 10017 (800) 253-9646; *Human Development Report.*

The World Bank, 1818 H Street, NW, Washington, D.C. 20433 (202) 477-1234; *The World Bank Atlas; World Development Report;* and *World Development Indicators.*

NICARAGUA - LAND AREA

The Economist Intelligence Unit, 111 West 57th Street, New York, New York 10019 (800) 938-4685; *The New Latin America Market Atlas.*

NICARAGUA - LAND USE

Central Intelligence Agency, Washington, D.C. 20505 (703) 482-1100, www.cia.gov; *The World Factbook.*

Euromonitor International, Inc., 122 South Michigan Avenue, Suite 1200, Chicago, Illinois 60603 (800) 577-EURO; *International Marketing Data and Statistics.*

Food and Agricultural Organization of the United Nations (FAO), Via delle Terme di Caracalla, 00100 Rome, Italy (Telephone Number in U.S. (202) 653-2400); *Production Yearbook.*

Inter-American Development Bank, 1300 New York Avenue, NW, Washington, D.C. 20577 (202) 623-1753; *Economic and Social Progress in Latin America.*

The World Bank, 1818 H Street, NW, Washington, D.C. 20433 (202) 477-1234; *World Development Report.*

NICARAGUA - LIBRARIES

M.E. Sharpe, 80 Business Park Drive, Armonk, New York 10504 (800) 541-6563; *The Illustrated Book of World Rankings.*

United Nations Educational, Scientific and Cultural Organization (UNESCO), 7 Place de Fontenoy, F-75700 Paris, France (Telephone Number in U.S. (212) 963-5981); *Statistical Yearbook.*

NICARAGUA - LIFE EXPECTANCY

Central Intelligence Agency, Washington, D.C. 20505 (703) 482-1100, www.cia.gov; *The World Factbook.*

The Economist Intelligence Unit, 111 West 57th Street, New York, New York 10019 (800) 938-4685; *The New Latin America Market Atlas.*

Euromonitor International, Inc., 122 South Michigan Avenue, Suite 1200, Chicago, Illinois 60603 (800) 577-EURO; *The World Economic Factbook.*

St. Martin's Press, Inc., 175 Fifth Avenue, New York, New York 10010 (800) 221-7945; *The Statesman's Year-Book.*

Statistical Office of the United Nations, Publishing Service, New York, New York 10017 (800) 253-9646; *Human Development Report.*

The World Bank, 1818 H Street, NW,

Washington, D.C. 20433 (202) 477-1234; *The World Bank Atlas;* and *World Development Report.*

NICARAGUA - LITERACY RATE

Euromonitor International, Inc., 122 South Michigan Avenue, Suite 1200, Chicago, Illinois 60603 (800) 577-EURO; *World Marketing Data and Statistics.*

NICARAGUA - LIVESTOCK AND POULTRY

Euromonitor International, Inc., 122 South Michigan Avenue, Suite 1200, Chicago, Illinois 60603 (800) 577-EURO; *International Marketing Data and Statistics.*

Europa Publications Limited, 18 Bedford Square, London, WC1B 3JN, England; *The Europa World Year Book.*

Food and Agricultural Organization of the United Nations (FAO), Via delle Terme di Caracalla, 00100 Rome, Italy (Telephone Number in U.S. (202) 653-2400); *Production Yearbook;* and *The State of Food and Agriculture.*

International Monetary Fund, 700 Nineteenth Street, NW, Washington, D.C. 20431 (202) 623-7000; *International Financial Statistics.*

M.E. Sharpe, 80 Business Park Drive, Armonk, New York 10504 (800) 541-6563; *The Illustrated Book of World Rankings.*

St. Martin's Press, Inc., 175 Fifth Avenue, New York, New York 10010 (800) 221-7945; *The Statesman's Year-Book.*

Statistical Office of the United Nations, Publishing Service, New York, New York 10017 (800) 253-9646; *Statistical Yearbook.*

United Nations Conference on Trade and Development, Central Statistical Service, Palais des Nations, Geneva, Switzerland (Telephone in U.S. (800) 253-9646); *UNCTAD Commodity Yearbook.*

NICARAGUA - LIVING LEVELS - See NICARAGUA - LIFE EXPECTANCY

NICARAGUA - MAIL TRAFFIC

Statistical Office of the United Nations, Publishing Service, New York, New York 10017 (800) 253-9646; *Statistical Yearbook.*

NICARAGUA - MAIN ECONOMIC INDICATORS - See NICARAGUA - ECONOMY

NICARAGUA - MAIN INDICATORS - See NICARAGUA - ECONOMY

NICARAGUA - MANUFACTURING

The Economist Intelligence Unit, 111

West 57th Street, New York, New York 10019 (800) 938-4685; *The New Latin America Market Atlas.*

Inter-American Development Bank, 1300 New York Avenue, NW, Washington, D.C. 20577 (202) 623-1753; *Economic and Social Progress in Latin America.*

M.E. Sharpe, 80 Business Park Drive, Armonk, New York 10504 (800) 541-6563; *The Illustrated Book of World Rankings.*

Statistical Office of the United Nations, Publishing Service, New York, New York 10017 (800) 253-9646; *Statistical Yearbook.*

The World Bank, 1818 H Street, NW, Washington, D.C. 20433 (202) 477-1234; *World Development Indicators.*

NICARAGUA - MARRIAGE RATES

Europa Publications Limited, 18 Bedford Square, London, WC1B 3JN, England; *The Europa World Year Book.*

M.E. Sharpe, 80 Business Park Drive, Armonk, New York 10504 (800) 541-6563; *The Illustrated Book of World Rankings.*

Statistical Office of the United Nations, Publishing Service, New York, New York 10017 (800) 253-9646; *Demographic Yearbook;* and *Statistical Yearbook.*

NICARAGUA - MEAT - See NICARAGUA - LIVESTOCK AND POULTRY

NICARAGUA - MEDICAL PERSONNEL

U.C.L.A. Latin American Center Publications, University of California, Los Angeles, California 90024 (310) 825-6634; *Statistical Abstract of Latin America.*

NICARAGUA - MERCHANT SHIPPING

Europa Publications Limited, 18 Bedford Square, London, WC1B 3JN, England; *The Europa World Year Book.*

St. Martin's Press, Inc., 175 Fifth Avenue, New York, New York 10010 (800) 221-7945; *The Statesman's Year-Book.*

Statistical Office of the United Nations, Publishing Service, New York, New York 10017 (800) 253-9646; *Statistical Yearbook.*

U.S. Department of Transportation, Maritime Administration, 400 Seventh Street, SW, Washington, D.C. 20590 (202) 366-5807, www.marad.dot.gov; *A Statistical Analysis of the World's Merchant Fleets.*

NICARAGUA - MILITARY

Central Intelligence Agency, Washington, D.C. 20505 (703) 482-1100, www.cia.gov; *The World Factbook.*

The Economist Intelligence Unit, 111 West 57th Street, New York, New York 10019 (800) 938-4685; *The New Latin America Market Atlas.*

Euromonitor International, Inc., 122 South Michigan Avenue, Suite 1200, Chicago, Illinois 60603 (800) 577-EURO; *World Marketing Data and Statistics.*

The International Institute for Strategic Studies, 23 Tavistock Street, London WC2E 7NQ, England; *The Military Balance.*

International Monetary Fund, 700 Nineteenth Street, NW, Washington, D.C. 20431 (202) 623-7000; *Government Finance Statistics Yearbook.*

St. Martin's Press, Inc., 175 Fifth Avenue, New York, New York 10010 (800) 221-7945; *The Statesman's Year-Book.*

Statistical Office of the United Nations, Publishing Service, New York, New York 10017 (800) 253-9646; *Human Development Report.*

U.C.L.A. Latin American Center Publications, University of California, Los Angeles, California 90024 (310) 825-6634; *Statistical Abstract of Latin America.*

U.S. Arms Control and Disarmament Agency, 320 Twenty-first Street, NW, Washington, D.C. 20451 (202) 647-8677; *World Military Expenditures and Arms Transfers.*

NICARAGUA - MILK PRODUCTION - See NICARAGUA - DAIRY PRODUCTS

NICARAGUA - MINING AND MINERAL PRODUCTS

Commodity Research Bureau, Inc., 30 South Wacker Drive, Chicago, Illinois 60606 (312) 454-1801; *Commodity Year Book.*

The Economist Intelligence Unit, 111 West 57th Street, New York, New York 10019 (800) 938-4685; *The New Latin America Market Atlas.*

Europa Publications Limited, 18 Bedford Square, London, WC1B 3JN, England; *The Europa World Year Book.*

Inter-American Development Bank, 1300 New York Avenue, NW, Washington, D.C. 20577 (202) 623-1753; *Economic and Social Progress in Latin America.*

M.E. Sharpe, 80 Business Park Drive, Armonk, New York 10504 (800) 541-6563; *The Illustrated Book of World Rankings.*

St. Martin's Press, Inc., 175 Fifth Avenue, New York, New York 10010 (800) 221-7945; *The Statesman's Year-Book.*

Statistical Office of the United Nations, Publishing Service, New York, New York 10017 (800) 253-9646; *Statistical Yearbook.*

U.C.L.A. Latin American Center Publications, University of California, Los Angeles, California 90024 (310) 825-6634; *Statistical Abstract of Latin America.*

United Nations Conference on Trade and Development, Central Statistical Service, Palais des Nations, Geneva, Switzerland (Telephone in U.S. (800) 253-9646); *UNCTAD Commodity Yearbook.*

NICARAGUA - MONEY EXCHANGE RATE - See NICARAGUA - EXCHANGE RATES

NICARAGUA - MONEY RATES - MARKET

Inter-American Development Bank, 1300 New York Avenue, NW, Washington, D.C. 20577 (202) 623-1753; *Economic and Social Progress in Latin America.*

NICARAGUA - MONEY RESERVES

Euromonitor International, Inc., 122 South Michigan Avenue, Suite 1200, Chicago, Illinois 60603 (800) 577-EURO; *International Marketing Data and Statistics.*

Inter-American Development Bank, 1300 New York Avenue, NW, Washington, D.C. 20577 (202) 623-1753; *Economic and Social Progress in Latin America.*

NICARAGUA - MONEY SUPPLY

Economist Intelligence Unit, 111 West 57th Street, New York, New York 10019 (800) 938-4685; *Nicaragua Country Report.*

Euromonitor International, Inc., 122 South Michigan Avenue, Suite 1200, Chicago, Illinois 60603 (800) 577-EURO; *International Marketing Data and Statistics.*

Europa Publications Limited, 18 Bedford Square, London, WC1B 3JN, England; *The Europa World Year Book.*

Inter-American Development Bank, 1300 New York Avenue, NW, Washington, D.C. 20577 (202) 623-1753; *Economic and Social Progress in Latin America.*

International Monetary Fund, 700 Nineteenth Street, NW, Washington, D.C. 20431 (202) 623-7000; *International Financial Statistics.*

Statistical Office of the United Nations, Publishing Service, New York, New York 10017 (800) 253-9646; *Statistical Yearbook.*

U.C.L.A. Latin American Center Publications, University of California, Los Angeles, California 90024 (310) 825-6634; *Statistical Abstract of Latin America.*

The World Bank, 1818 H Street, NW, Washington, D.C. 20433 (202) 477-1234; *World Development Indicators.*

NICARAGUA - MORTALITY

Central Intelligence Agency, Washington, D.C. 20505 (703) 482-1100, www.cia.gov; *The World Factbook.*

The Economist Intelligence Unit, 111 West 57th Street, New York, New York 10019 (800) 938-4685; *The New Latin America Market Atlas.*

Euromonitor International, Inc., 122 South Michigan Avenue, Suite 1200, Chicago, Illinois 60603 (800) 577-EURO; *International Marketing Data and Statistics; and The World Economic Factbook.*

Europa Publications Limited, 18 Bedford Square, London, WC1B 3JN, England; *The Europa World Year Book.*

St. Martin's Press, Inc., 175 Fifth Avenue, New York, New York 10010 (800) 221-7945; *The Statesman's Year-Book.*

Statistical Office of the United Nations, Publishing Service, New York, New York 10017 (800) 253-9646; *Demographic Yearbook; Human Development Report; World Statistics Pocketbook; and Statistical Yearbook.*

United Nations Children's Fund (UNICEF), 3 United Nations Plaza, New York, New York 10017 (800) 253-9646; *State of the World's Children.*

The World Bank, 1818 H Street, NW, Washington, D.C. 20433 (202) 477-1234; *The World Bank Atlas; World Development Report; and World Development Indicators.*

World Health Organization, Office of Publications, 20 Avenue Appia, CH-1211 Geneva 27, Switzerland (Telephone Number in U.S. (518) 436-9686); *World Health Statistics Annual.*

NICARAGUA - MOTOR VEHICLE TAXES - See NICARAGUA - TAXATION

NICARAGUA - MOTOR VEHICLES IN USE

The Economist Intelligence Unit, 111 West 57th Street, New York, New York 10019 (800) 938-4685; *The New Latin America Market Atlas.*

Europa Publications Limited, 18 Bedford Square, London, WC1B 3JN, England; *The Europa World Year Book.*

International Road Federation, 2600 Virginia Avenue, NW., Washington, D.C. 20037 (202) 338-4641; *World Road Statistics.*

Statistical Office of the United Nations, Publishing Service, New York, New York 10017 (800) 253-9646; *Statistical Yearbook*.

NICARAGUA - MULES - See NICARAGUA - LIVESTOCK AND POULTRY

NICARAGUA - MUSEUMS

M.E. Sharpe, 80 Business Park Drive, Armonk, New York 10504 (800) 541-6563; *The Illustrated Book of World Rankings*.

NICARAGUA - NATALITY - See NICARAGUA - BIRTH RATES

NICARAGUA - NATIONAL ACCOUNTS

Europa Publications Limited, 18 Bedford Square, London, WC1B 3JN, England; *The Europa World Year Book*.

Inter-American Development Bank, 1300 New York Avenue, NW, Washington, D.C. 20577 (202) 623-1753; *Economic and Social Progress in Latin America*.

Statistical Office of the United Nations, Publishing Service, New York, New York 10017 (800) 253-9646; *National Accounts Statistics;* and *Statistical Yearbook*.

U.C.L.A. Latin American Center Publications, University of California, Los Angeles, California 90024 (310) 825-6634; *Statistical Abstract of Latin America*.

NICARAGUA - NATIONAL INCOME

Inter-American Development Bank, 1300 New York Avenue, NW, Washington, D.C. 20577 (202) 623-1753; *Economic and Social Progress in Latin America*.

M.E. Sharpe, 80 Business Park Drive, Armonk, New York 10504 (800) 541-6563; *The Illustrated Book of World Rankings*.

Statistical Office of the United Nations, Publishing Service, New York, New York 10017 (800) 253-9646; *National Accounts Statistics;* and *Statistical Yearbook*.

NICARAGUA - NATIONAL PRODUCT

M.E. Sharpe, 80 Business Park Drive, Armonk, New York 10504 (800) 541-6563; *The Illustrated Book of World Rankings*.

Statistical Office of the United Nations, Publishing Service, New York, New York 10017 (800) 253-9646; *Statistical Yearbook*.

NICARAGUA - NATURAL GAS PRODUCTION - See NICARAGUA - MINING AND MINERAL PRODUCTS

NICARAGUA - NEWSPAPER PRODUCTION - See NICARAGUA - FORESTRY AND FOREST PRODUCTS

NICARAGUA - NEWSPRINT - See NICARAGUA - FORESTRY AND FOREST PRODUCTS

NICARAGUA - OCCUPATIONS - See NICARAGUA - LABOR

NICARAGUA - ORANGES PRODUCTION - See NICARAGUA - CROPS

NICARAGUA - PAPER - See NICARAGUA - FORESTRY AND FOREST PRODUCTS

NICARAGUA - PATENTS, TRADEMARKS AND SERVICE MARKS

Statistical Office of the United Nations, Publishing Service, New York, New York 10017 (800) 253-9646; *Statistical Yearbook*.

NICARAGUA - PEANUT PRODUCTION - See NICARAGUA - CROPS

NICARAGUA - PESTICIDE USE

Food and Agricultural Organization of the United Nations (FAO) Via delle Terme di Caracalla, 00100 Rome, Italy (Telephone Number in U.S. (202) 653-2400); *The State of Food and Agriculture*.

NICARAGUA - PETROLEUM INDUSTRY

The Economist Intelligence Unit, 111 West 57th Street, New York, New York 10019 (800) 938-4685; *The New Latin America Market Atlas*.

Food and Agricultural Organization of the United Nations (FAO) Via delle Terme di Caracalla, 00100 Rome, Italy (Telephone Number in U.S. (202) 653-2400); *The State of Food and Agriculture*.

Inter-American Development Bank, 1300 New York Avenue, NW, Washington, D.C. 20577 (202) 623-1753; *Economic and Social Progress in Latin America*.

M.E. Sharpe, 80 Business Park Drive, Armonk, New York 10504 (800) 541-6563; *The Illustrated Book of World Rankings*.

Statistical Office of the United Nations, Publishing Service, New York, New York 10017 (800) 253-9646; *Statistical Yearbook*.

United Nations Conference on Trade and Development, Central Statistical Service, Palais des Nations, Geneva, Switzerland (Telephone in U.S. (800) 253-9646); *UNCTAD Commodity Yearbook*.

NICARAGUA - PIG IRON AND FERRO-ALLOY PRODUCTION - See NICARAGUA - MINING AND MINERAL PRODUCTS

NICARAGUA - PIGS - See NICARAGUA - LIVESTOCK AND POULTRY

NICARAGUA - POLITICAL DATA

U.C.L.A. Latin American Center Publications, University of California, Los Angeles, California 90024 (310) 825-6634; *Statistical Abstract of Latin America*.

NICARAGUA - POPULATION

Central Intelligence Agency, Washington, D.C. 20505 (703) 482-1100, www.cia.gov; *The World Factbook*.

The Economist Intelligence Unit, 111 West 57th Street, New York, New York 10019 (800) 938-4685; *The New Latin America Market Atlas; Nicaragua Country Report;* and *The World Market Atlas*.

Euromonitor International, Inc., 122 South Michigan Avenue, Suite 1200, Chicago, Illinois 60603 (800) 577-EURO; *International Marketing Data and Statistics;* and *The World Economic Factbook*.

Europa Publications Limited, 18 Bedford Square, London, WC1B 3JN, England; *The Europa World Year Book*.

Food and Agricultural Organization of the United Nations (FAO), Via delle Terme di Caracalla, 00100 Rome, Italy (Telephone Number in U.S. (202) 653-2400); *Production Yearbook*.

Inter-American Development Bank, 1300 New York Avenue, NW, Washington, D.C. 20577 (202) 623-1753; *Economic and Social Progress in Latin America*.

International Labour Office, I.L.O. Publications, 1828 L Street, NW, Suite 801, Washington, D.C. 20036 (301) 638-3152; *Yearbook of Labour Statistics*.

M.E. Sharpe, 80 Business Park Drive, Armonk, New York 10504 (800) 541-6563; *The Illustrated Book of World Rankings*.

St. Martin's Press, Inc., 175 Fifth Avenue, New York, New York 10010 (800) 221-7945; *The Statesman's Year-Book*.

Statistical Office of the United Nations, Publishing Service, New York, New York 10017 (800) 253-9646; *Demographic Yearbook; Human Development Report; World Statistics Pocketbook;* and *Statistical Yearbook*.

U.C.L.A. Latin American Center Publications, University of California, Los Angeles, California 90024 (310) 825-6634; *Statistical Abstract of Latin America*.

United Nations Educational, Scientific and Cultural Organization (UNESCO), 7 Place de Fontenoy, F-75700 Paris, France (Telephone Number in U.S. (212) 963-5981); *Statistical Yearbook*.

U.S. Arms Control and Disarmament Agency, 320 Twenty-first Street, NW, Washington, D.C. 20451 (202) 647-8677; *World Military Expenditures and Arms Transfers.*

The World Bank, 1818 H Street, NW, Washington, D.C. 20433 (202) 477-1234; *The World Bank Atlas;* and *World Development Report.*

World Health Organization, Office of Publications, 20 Avenue Appia, CH-1211 Geneva 27, Switzerland (Telephone Number in U.S. (518) 436-9686); *World Health Statistics Annual.*

NICARAGUA - POST OFFICES

M.E. Sharpe, 80 Business Park Drive, Armonk, New York 10504 (800) 541-6563; *The Illustrated Book of World Rankings.*

NICARAGUA - POTATO PRODUCTION - See NICARAGUA - CROPS

NICARAGUA - PRICES

Food and Agricultural Organization of the United Nations (FAO), Via delle Terme di Caracalla, 00100 Rome, Italy (Telephone Number in U.S. (202) 653-2400); *Production Yearbook;* and *The State of Food and Agriculture.*

International Labour Office, I.L.O. Publications, 1828 L Street, NW, Suite 801, Washington, D.C. 20036 (301) 638-3152; *Yearbook of Labour Statistics.*

International Monetary Fund, 700 Nineteenth Street, NW, Washington, D.C. 20431 (202) 623-7000; *International Financial Statistics.*

M.E. Sharpe, 80 Business Park Drive, Armonk, New York 10504 (800) 541-6563; *The Illustrated Book of World Rankings.*

Statistical Office of the United Nations, Publishing Service, New York, New York 10017 (800) 253-9646; *Economic Survey of Latin America and the Caribbean.*

NICARAGUA - PRINTING AND WRITING PAPER - See NICARAGUA - FORESTRY AND FOREST PRODUCTS

NICARAGUA - PRODUCTION

M.E. Sharpe, 80 Business Park Drive, Armonk, New York 10504 (800) 541-6563; *The Illustrated Book of World Rankings.*

NICARAGUA - PRODUCTIVITY

Euromonitor International, Inc., 122 South Michigan Avenue, Suite 1200, Chicago, Illinois 60603 (800) 577-EURO; *International Marketing Data and Statistics.*

NICARAGUA - PROPERTY TAXES - See NICARAGUA - TAXATION

NICARAGUA - PUBLIC CONSUMPTION FUND

Inter-American Development Bank, 1300 New York Avenue, NW, Washington, D.C. 20577 (202) 623-1753; *Economic and Social Progress in Latin America.*

NICARAGUA - PUBLIC EXPENDITURES

Inter-American Development Bank, 1300 New York Avenue, NW, Washington, D.C. 20577 (202) 623-1753; *Economic and Social Progress in Latin America.*

NICARAGUA - PUBLIC FINANCE - See NICARAGUA - FINANCE

NICARAGUA - PUBLIC REVENUES

Inter-American Development Bank, 1300 New York Avenue, NW, Washington, D.C. 20577 (202) 623-1753; *Economic and Social Progress in Latin America.*

NICARAGUA - RADIO BROADCASTING - See NICARAGUA - BROADCASTING

NICARAGUA - RADIO RECEIVER PRODUCTION

Statistical Office of the United Nations, Publishing Service, New York, New York 10017 (800) 253-9646; *Statistical Yearbook.*

NICARAGUA - RADIO RECEIVERS

St. Martin's Press, Inc., 175 Fifth Avenue, New York, New York 10010 (800) 221-7945; *The Statesman's Year-Book.*

NICARAGUA - RAILWAYS

The Economist Intelligence Unit, 111 West 57th Street, New York, New York 10019 (800) 938-4685; *The New Latin America Market Atlas.*

Europa Publications Limited, 18 Bedford Square, London, WC1B 3JN, England; *The Europa World Year Book.*

Jane's Information Group, Sentinel House, 163 Brighton Road, Coulsdon, Surrey CR5 2NH, England (Telephone Number in U.S. (703) 683-3700); *Jane's World Railways.*

St. Martin's Press, Inc., 175 Fifth Avenue, New York, New York 10010 (800) 221-7945; *The Statesman's Year-Book.*

Statistical Office of the United Nations, Publishing Service, New York, New York 10017 (800) 253-9646; *Statistical Yearbook.*

NICARAGUA - RANCHING

U.C.L.A. Latin American Center Publications, University of California, Los Angeles, California 90024 (310) 825-6634; *Statistical Abstract of Latin America.*

NICARAGUA - RELIGION

Central Intelligence Agency, Washington, D.C. 20505 (703) 482-1100, www.cia.gov; *The World Factbook.*

M.E. Sharpe, 80 Business Park Drive, Armonk, New York 10504 (800) 541-6563; *The Illustrated Book of World Rankings.*

St. Martin's Press, Inc., 175 Fifth Avenue, New York, New York 10010 (800) 221-7945; *The Statesman's Year-Book.*

U.C.L.A. Latin American Center Publications, University of California, Los Angeles, California 90024 (310) 825-6634; *Statistical Abstract of Latin America.*

NICARAGUA - RENT PRICES

International Labour Office, I.L.O. Publications, 1828 L Street, NW, Suite 801, Washington, D.C. 20036 (301) 638-3152; *Yearbook of Labour Statistics.*

NICARAGUA - RESERVES EXCLUDING GOLD

The Economist Intelligence Unit, 111 West 57th Street, New York, New York 10019 (800) 938-4685; *The New Latin America Market Atlas.*

NICARAGUA - RETAIL TRADE

Euromonitor International, Inc., 122 South Michigan Avenue, Suite 1200, Chicago, Illinois 60603 (800) 577-EURO; *World Marketing Data and Statistics.*

Inter-American Development Bank, 1300 New York Avenue, NW, Washington, D.C. 20577 (202) 623-1753; *Economic and Social Progress in Latin America.*

NICARAGUA - RICE PRODUCTION - See NICARAGUA - CROPS

NICARAGUA - ROOT AND TUBER PRODUCTION - See NICARAGUA - CROPS

NICARAGUA - ROUNDWOOD PRODUCTION - See NICARAGUA - FORESTRY AND FOREST PRODUCTS

NICARAGUA - RUBBER PRODUCTION AND CONSUMPTION

M.E. Sharpe, 80 Business Park Drive, Armonk, New York 10504 (800) 541-6563; *The Illustrated Book of World Rankings.*

NICARAGUA - SALT PRODUCTION - See NICARAGUA - MINING AND MINERAL PRODUCTS

NICARAGUA - SAWNWOOD
PRODUCTION - See NICARAGUA -
FORESTRY AND FOREST PRODUCTS

NICARAGUA - SCIENCE AND
TECHNOLOGY - See NICARAGUA -
SCIENTISTS, TECHNICIANS AND
ENGINEERS

NICARAGUA - SCIENTISTS, TECHNICIANS
AND ENGINEERS

Statistical Office of the United Nations,
Publishing Service, New York, New York
10017 (800) 253-9646; *Statistical Yearbook.*

U.C.L.A. Latin American Center
Publications, University of California, Los
Angeles, California 90024 (310) 825-6634;
Statistical Abstract of Latin America.

NICARAGUA - SENIOR CITIZENS

M.E. Sharpe, 80 Business Park Drive,
Armonk, New York 10504 (800) 541-6563;
The Illustrated Book of World Rankings.

NICARAGUA - SESAME SEED
PRODUCTION - See NICARAGUA - CROPS

NICARAGUA - SHEEP - See
NICARAGUA - LIVESTOCK AND POULTRY

NICARAGUA - SILVER PRODUCTION AND
CONSUMPTION - See NICARAGUA -
MINING AND MINERAL PRODUCTS

NICARAGUA - SOCIAL DATA

M.E. Sharpe, 80 Business Park Drive,
Armonk, New York 10504 (800) 541-6563;
The Illustrated Book of World Rankings.

Statistical Office of the United Nations,
Publishing Service, New York, New York
10017 (800) 253-9646; *World Statistics
Pocketbook.*

U.C.L.A. Latin American Center
Publications, University of California, Los
Angeles, California 90024 (310) 825-6634;
Statistical Abstract of Latin America.

NICARAGUA - SOCIAL SECURITY

Inter-American Development Bank,
1300 New York Avenue, NW, Washington,
D.C. 20577 (202) 623-1753; *Economic and
Social Progress in Latin America.*

International Monetary Fund, 700
Nineteenth Street, NW, Washington, D.C.
20431 (202) 623-7000; *Government
Finance Statistics Yearbook.*

Statistical Office of the United Nations,
Publishing Service, New York, New York
10017 (800) 253-9646; *National Accounts
Statistics.*

NICARAGUA - SOCIOECONOMIC DATA

Inter-American Development Bank,
1300 New York Avenue, NW, Washington,
D.C. 20577 (202) 623-1753; *Economic and
Social Progress in Latin America.*

U.C.L.A. Latin American Center
Publications, University of California, Los
Angeles, California 90024 (310) 825-6634;
Statistical Abstract of Latin America.

NICARAGUA - SOYBEAN PRODUCTION -
See NICARAGUA - CROPS

NICARAGUA - STAMP TAXES AND DUTIES -
See NICARAGUA - TAXATION

NICARAGUA - STATE BUDGET REVENUE
AND EXPENDITURES

Euromonitor International, Inc., 122
South Michigan Avenue, Suite 1200,
Chicago, Illinois 60603 (800) 577-EURO;
International Marketing Data and Statistics.

Inter-American Development Bank,
1300 New York Avenue, NW, Washington,
D.C. 20577 (202) 623-1753; *Economic and
Social Progress in Latin America.*

NICARAGUA - STEEL - See NICARAGUA -
MINING AND MINERAL PRODUCTS

NICARAGUA - STOCKS - COMMODITY -
MARKET PRICE - INDEX

Food and Agricultural Organization of
the United Nations (FAO) Via delle Terme
di Caracalla, 00100 Rome, Italy (Telephone
Number in U.S. (202) 653-2400); *The State
of Food and Agriculture.*

NICARAGUA - SUGAR PRODUCTION AND
CONSUMPTION - See NICARAGUA -CROPS

NICARAGUA - TAXATION

Europa Publications Limited, 18
Bedford Square, London, WC1B 3JN,
England; *The Europa World Year Book.*

Inter-American Development Bank,
1300 New York Avenue, NW, Washington,
D.C. 20577 (202) 623-1753; *Economic and
Social Progress in Latin America.*

International Monetary Fund, 700
Nineteenth Street, NW, Washington, D.C.
20431 (202) 623-7000; *Government Finance
Statistics Yearbook.*

International Road Federation, 2600
Virginia Avenue, NW., Washington, D.C.
20037 (202) 338-4641; *World Road
Statistics.*

The World Bank, 1818 H Street, NW,
Washington, D.C. 20433 (202) 477-1234;
World Development Indicators.

NICARAGUA - TAX REVENUES - See
NICARAGUA - TAXATION

NICARAGUA - TELEPHONES IN USE

American Telephone and Telegraph
Company, 26 Parsippany Road, Whippany,
New Jersey 07981 (800) 222-0300; *The
World's Telephones.*

Central Intelligence Agency,
Washington, D.C. 20505 (703) 482-1100,
www.cia.gov; *The World Factbook.*

The Economist Intelligence Unit, 111
West 57th Street, New York, New York
10019 (800) 938-4685; *The New Latin
America Market Atlas.*

Europa Publications Limited, 18
Bedford Square, London, WC1B 3JN,
England; *The Europa World Year Book.*

St. Martin's Press, Inc., 175 Fifth
Avenue, New York, New York 10010 (800)
221-7945; *The Statesman's Year-Book.*

Statistical Office of the United Nations,
Publishing Service, New York, New York
10017 (800) 253-9646; *Statistical Yearbook;*
and *World Statistics Pocketbook.*

NICARAGUA - TELEVISION
BROADCASTING - See NICARAGUA -
BROADCASTING

NICARAGUA - TELEVISION RECEIVER
PRODUCTION

Statistical Office of the United Nations,
Publishing Service, New York, New York
10017 (800) 253-9646; *Statistical Yearbook.*

NICARAGUA - TEXTILE INDUSTRY

M.E. Sharpe, 80 Business Park Drive,
Armonk, New York 10504 (800) 541-6563;
The Illustrated Book of World Rankings.

Statistical Office of the United Nations,
Publishing Service, New York, New York
10017 (800) 253-9646; *Statistical Yearbook.*

United Nations Conference on Trade
and Development, Central Statistical
Service, Palais des Nations, Geneva,
Switzerland (Telephone in U.S. (800) 253-
9646); *UNCTAD Commodity Yearbook.*

NICARAGUA - TOBACCO PRODUCTION

M.E. Sharpe, 80 Business Park Drive,
Armonk, New York 10504 (800) 541-6563;
The Illustrated Book of World Rankings.

Statistical Office of the United Nations,
Publishing Service, New York, New York
10017 (800) 253-9646; *Statistical Yearbook.*

U.C.L.A. Latin American Center
Publications, University of California, Los
Angeles, California 90024 (310) 825-6634;
Statistical Abstract of Latin America.

NICARAGUA - TOURISM

The Economist Intelligence Unit, 111 West 57th Street, New York, New York 10019 (800) 938-4685; *The New Latin America Market Atlas.*

Euromonitor International, Inc., 122 South Michigan Avenue, Suite 1200, Chicago, Illinois 60603 (800) 577-EURO; *The World Economic Factbook;* and *World Marketing Data and Statistics.*

Europa Publications Limited, 18 Bedford Square, London, WC1B 3JN, England; *The Europa World Year Book.*

M.E. Sharpe, 80 Business Park Drive, Armonk, New York 10504 (800) 541-6563; *The Illustrated Book of World Rankings.*

St. Martin's Press, Inc., 175 Fifth Avenue, New York, New York 10010 (800) 221-7945; *The Statesman's Year-Book.*

Statistical Office of the United Nations, Publishing Service, New York, New York 10017 (800) 253-9646; *Statistical Yearbook.*

U.C.L.A. Latin American Center Publications, University of California, Los Angeles, California 90024 (310) 825-6634; *Statistical Abstract of Latin America.*

NICARAGUA - TRACTORS IN USE

The Economist Intelligence Unit, 111 West 57th Street, New York, New York 10019 (800) 938-4685; *The New Latin America Market Atlas.*

NICARAGUA - TRADE - See NICARAGUA - FOREIGN TRADE

NICARAGUA - TRADEMARKS AND SERVICE MARKS - See NICARAGUA - PATENTS, TRADEMARKS AND SERVICE MARKS

NICARAGUA - TRANSPORTATION AND COMMUNICATIONS

Central Intelligence Agency, Washington, D.C. 20505 (703) 482-1100, www.cia.gov; *The World Factbook.*

The Economist Intelligence Unit, 111 West 57th Street, New York, New York 10019 (800) 938-4685; *The New Latin America Market Atlas.*

Euromonitor International, Inc., 122 South Michigan Avenue, Suite 1200, Chicago, Illinois 60603 (800) 577-EURO; *International Marketing Data and Statistics;* and *World Marketing Data and Statistics.*

Europa Publications Limited, 18 Bedford Square, London, WC1B 3JN, England; *The Europa World Year Book.*

Inter-American Development Bank, 1300 New York Avenue, NW, Washington, D.C. 20577 (202) 623-1753; *Economic and Social Progress in Latin America.*

M.E. Sharpe, 80 Business Park Drive, Armonk, New York 10504 (800) 541-6563; *The Illustrated Book of World Rankings.*

St. Martin's Press, Inc., 175 Fifth Avenue, New York, New York 10010 (800) 221-7945; *The Statesman's Year-Book.*

Statistical Office of the United Nations, Publishing Service, New York, New York 10017 (800) 253-9646; *Human Development Report.*

U.C.L.A. Latin American Center Publications, University of California, Los Angeles, California 90024 (310) 825-6634; *Statistical Abstract of Latin America.*

NICARAGUA - UNEMPLOYMENT

Central Intelligence Agency, Washington, D.C. 20505 (703) 482-1100, www.cia.gov; *The World Factbook.*

The Economist Intelligence Unit, 111 West 57th Street, New York, New York 10019 (800) 938-4685; *The New Latin America Market Atlas.*

Euromonitor International, Inc., 122 South Michigan Avenue, Suite 1200, Chicago, Illinois 60603 (800) 577-EURO; *International Marketing Data and Statistics.*

International Labour Office, I.L.O. Publications, 1828 L Street, NW, Suite 801, Washington, D.C. 20036 (301) 638-3152; *Yearbook of Labour Statistics.*

St. Martin's Press, Inc., 175 Fifth Avenue, New York, New York 10010 (800) 221-7945; *The Statesman's Year-Book.*

Statistical Office of the United Nations, Publishing Service, New York, New York 10017 (800) 253-9646; *Statistical Yearbook.*

U.C.L.A. Latin American Center Publications, University of California, Los Angeles, California 90024 (310) 825-6634; *Statistical Abstract of Latin America.*

NICARAGUA - UTILITIES

U.C.L.A. Latin American Center Publications, University of California, Los Angeles, California 90024 (310) 825-6634; *Statistical Abstract of Latin America.*

NICARAGUA - VITAL STATISTICS

Euromonitor International, Inc., 122 South Michigan Avenue, Suite 1200, Chicago, Illinois 60603 (800) 577-EURO; *International Marketing Data and Statistics.*

St. Martin's Press, Inc., 175 Fifth Avenue,

New York, New York 10010 (800) 221-7945; *The Statesman's Year-Book.*

Statistical Office of the United Nations, Publishing Service, New York, New York 10017 (800) 253-9646; *Statistical Yearbook.*

World Health Organization, Office of Publications, 20 Avenue Appia, CH-1211 Geneva 27, Switzerland (Telephone Number in U.S. (518) 436-9686); *World Health Statistics Annual.*

NICARAGUA - WAGES

International Labour Office, I.L.O. Publications, 1828 L Street, NW, Suite 801, Washington, D.C. 20036 (301) 638-3152; *Yearbook of Labour Statistics.*

Statistical Office of the United Nations, Publishing Service, New York, New York 10017 (800) 253-9646; *Statistical Yearbook.*

U.C.L.A. Latin American Center Publications, University of California, Los Angeles, California 90024 (310) 825-6634; *Statistical Abstract of Latin America.*

NICARAGUA - WEATHER - See NICARAGUA - CLIMATE

NICARAGUA - WELFARE

Inter-American Development Bank, 1300 New York Avenue, NW, Washington, D.C. 20577 (202) 623-1753; *Economic and Social Progress in Latin America.*

International Monetary Fund, 700 Nineteenth Street, NW, Washington, D.C. 20431 (202) 623-7000; *Government Finance Statistics Yearbook.*

NICARAGUA - WHEAT PRODUCTION AND PRICES - See NICARAGUA - CROPS

NICARAGUA - WHOLESALE PRICES

Inter-American Development Bank, 1300 New York Avenue, NW, Washington, D.C. 20577 (202) 623-1753; *Economic and Social Progress in Latin America.*

NICARAGUA - WHOLESALE TRADE

Inter-American Development Bank, 1300 New York Avenue, NW, Washington, D.C. 20577 (202) 623-1753; *Economic and Social Progress in Latin America.*

NICARAGUA - WINE PRODUCTION - See NICARAGUA - BEVERAGES

NICARAGUA - WOOD PULP PRODUCTION - See NICARAGUA - FORESTRY AND FOREST PRODUCTS

NICARAGUA - WOOL PRODUCTION - See NICARAGUA - TEXTILE INDUSTRY

NICKEL

U.S. Department of Commerce, Bureau of the Census, Washington, D.C. 20233 (301) 457-4100, www.census.gov; *U.S. International Trade in Goods in Services.*

U.S. Department of the Interior, Geological Survey, Office of Minerals Information, 12201 Sunrise Valley Drive, Reston, Virginia 22092 (703) 648-4000, www.usgs.gov; *Annual Reports;* and *Mineral Commodity Summaries.*

NICKEL - CONSUMPTION

U.S. Department of the Interior, Geological Survey, Office of Minerals Information, 12201 Sunrise Valley Drive, Reston, Virginia 22092 (703) 648-4000, www.minerals.usgs.gov; *Mineral Commodity Summaries.*

NICKEL - EMPLOYMENT

U.S. Department of the Interior, Geological Survey, Office of Minerals Information, 12201 Sunrise Valley Drive, Reston, Virginia 22092 (703) 648-4000, www.minerals.usgs.gov; *Mineral Commodity Summaries.*

NICKEL - FOREIGN TRADE

U.S. Department of Commerce, Bureau of the Census, Washington, D.C. 20233 (301) 457-4100, www.census.gov; *U.S. International Trade in Goods and Services.*

U.S. Department of the Interior, Geological Survey, Office of Minerals Information, 12201 Sunrise Valley Drive, Reston, Virginia 22092 (703) 648-4000, www.minerals.usgs.gov; *Mineral Commodity Summaries.*

NICKEL - PRICES

U.S. Department of the Interior, Geological Survey, Office of Minerals Information, 12201 Sunrise Valley Drive, Reston, Virginia 22092 (703) 648-4000, www.minerals.usgs.gov; *Mineral Commodity Summaries.*

NICKEL - PRODUCTION AND VALUE

U.S. Department of the Interior, Geological Survey, Office of Minerals Information, 12201 Sunrise Valley Drive, Reston, Virginia 22092 (703) 648-4000, www.minerals.usgs.gov; *Annual Reports;* and *Mineral Commodity Summaries.*

NICKEL - WORLD PRODUCTION

U.S. Department of the Interior, Geological Survey, Office of Minerals Information, 12201 Sunrise Valley Drive, Reston, Virginia 22092 (703) 648-4000, www.minerals.usgs.gov; *Annual Reports,*

and *Mineral Commodity Summaries.*

Niger - National Statistical Office

Direction de la Statistique, et de la Demographie, Ministere du Plan, BP 467 Niamey, Niger.

Niger - Primary Statistics Sources

Direction de la Statistique, Niamey, Niger; *Annuaire statistique* (Statistical Yearbook); and *Bulletin de statistique* (Statistical bulletin).

NIGER - AGRICULTURE

Economist Intelligence Unit, 111 West 57th Street, New York, New York 10019 (800) 938-4685; *Niger Country Report.*

Euromonitor International, Inc., 122 South Michigan Avenue, Suite 1200, Chicago, Illinois 60603 (800) 577-EURO; *International Marketing Data and Statistics;* and *World Marketing Data and Statistics.*

Europa Publications Limited, 18 Bedford Square, London, WC1B 3JN, England; *The Europa World Year Book.*

Food and Agricultural Organization of the United Nations (FAO) Via delle Terme di Caracalla, 00100 Rome, Italy (Telephone Number in U.S. (202) 653-2400); *Production Yearbook; The State of Food and Agriculture;* and *Trade Yearbook.*

M.E. Sharpe, 80 Business Park Drive, Armonk, New York 10504 (800) 541-6563; *The Illustrated Book of World Rankings.*

St. Martin's Press, Inc., 175 Fifth Avenue, New York, New York 10010 (800) 221-7945; *The Statesman's Year-Book.*

Statistical Office of the United Nations, Publishing Service, New York, New York 10017 (800) 253-9646; *Statistical Yearbook;* and *Survey of Economic and Social Conditions in Africa.*

United Nations Conference on Trade and Development, Central Statistical Service, Palais des Nations, Geneva, Switzerland (Telephone in U.S. (800) 253-9646); *UNCTAD Commodity Yearbook.*

United Nations Economic Commission for Africa, Africa Hall, Post Office Box 3001, Addis Ababa, Ethiopia (Telephone Number in U.S. (800) 253-9646); *African Statistical Yearbook.*

The World Bank, 1818 H Street, NW, Washington, D.C. 20433 (202) 477-1234;

World Development Indicators.

NIGER - AIRLINE SERVICE

Europa Publications Limited, 18 Bedford Square, London, WC1B 3JN, England; *The Europa World Year Book.*

M.E. Sharpe, 80 Business Park Drive, Armonk, New York 10504 (800) 541-6563; *The Illustrated Book of World Rankings.*

St. Martin's Press, Inc., 175 Fifth Avenue, New York, New York 10010 (800) 221-7945; *The Statesman's Year-Book.*

Statistical Office of the United Nations, Publishing Service, New York, New York 10017 (800) 253-9646; *Statistical Yearbook.*

United Nations Economic Commission for Africa, Africa Hall, Post Office Box 3001, Addis Ababa, Ethiopia (Telephone Number in U.S. (800) 253-9646); *African Statistical Yearbook.*

NIGER - AIRPORTS

Central Intelligence Agency, Washington, D.C. 20505 (703) 482-1100, www.cia.gov; *The World Factbook.*

NIGER - ALUMINUM PRODUCTION AND CONSUMPTION - See NIGER - MINING AND MINERAL PRODUCTS

NIGER - ANIMAL HEALTH

Food and Agricultural Organization of the United Nations (FAO), Via delle Terme di Caracalla, 00100 Rome, Italy (Telephone Number in U.S. (202) 653-2400); *Animal Health Yearbook.*

NIGER - AREA AND DENSITY OF POPULATION

African Development Bank, 01 BP 1387, Abidjan 01, Cote d'Ivoire; *Selected Statistics on Regional Member Countries.*

Central Intelligence Agency, Washington, D.C. 20505 (703) 482-1100, www.cia.gov; *The World Factbook.*

Euromonitor International, Inc., 122 South Michigan Avenue, Suite 1200, Chicago, Illinois 60603 (800) 577-EURO; *International Marketing Data and Statistics;* and *The World Economic Factbook.*

Europa Publications Limited, 18 Bedford Square, London, WC1B 3JN, England; *The Europa World Year Book.*

Food and Agricultural Organization of the United Nations (FAO) Via delle Terme di Caracalla, 00100 Rome, Italy (Telephone Number in U.S. (202) 653-2400); *The State of Food and Agriculture.*

M.E. Sharpe, 80 Business Park Drive, Armonk, New York 10504 (800) 541-6563; *The Illustrated Book of World Rankings.*

St. Martin's Press, Inc., 175 Fifth Avenue, New York, New York 10010 (800) 221-7945; *The Statesman's Year-Book.*

Statistical Office of the United Nations, Publishing Service, New York, New York 10017 (800) 253-9646; *Statistical Yearbook* and *Survey of Economic and Social Conditions in Africa.*

United Nations Educational, Scientific and Cultural Organization (UNESCO), 7 Place de Fontenoy, F-75700 Paris, France (Telephone Number in U.S. (212) 963-5981); *Statistical Yearbook.*

The World Bank, 1818 H Street, NW, Washington, D.C. 20433 (202) 477-1234; *World Development Report.*

NIGER - ARMS EXPORTS AND IMPORTS - See **NIGER - MILITARY**

NIGER - BALANCE OF PAYMENTS

African Development Bank, 01 BP 1387, Abidjan 01, Cote d'Ivoire; *Selected Statistics on Regional Member Countries.*

The Economist Intelligence Unit, 111 West 57th Street, New York, New York 10019 (800) 938-4685; *The World Market Atlas.*

Europa Publications Limited, 18 Bedford Square, London, WC1B 3JN, England; *The Europa World Year Book.*

International Monetary Fund, 700 Nineteenth Street, NW, Washington, D.C. 20431 (202) 623-7000; *Balance of Payments Yearbook.*

United Nations Conference on Trade and Development (UNCTAD), New York, New York 10017 (800) 253-9646; *Handbook of International Trade and Development.*

United Nations Economic Commission for Africa, Africa Hall, Post Office Box 3001, Addis Ababa, Ethiopia (Telephone Number in U.S. (800) 253-9646); *African Statistical Yearbook.*

The World Bank, 1818 H Street, NW, Washington, D.C. 20433 (202) 477-1234; *World Development Report;* and *World Development Indicators.*

NIGER - BANKING

Euromonitor International, Inc., 122 South Michigan Avenue, Suite 1200, Chicago, Illinois 60603 (800) 577-EURO; *World Marketing Data and Statistics.*

Europa Publications Limited, 18

Bedford Square, London, WC1B 3JN, England; *The Europa World Year Book.*

International Monetary Fund, 700 Nineteenth Street, NW, Washington, D.C. 20431 (202) 623-7000; *International Financial Statistics.*

M.E. Sharpe, 80 Business Park Drive, Armonk, New York 10504 (800) 541-6563; *The Illustrated Book of World Rankings.*

St. Martin's Press, Inc., 175 Fifth Avenue, New York, New York 10010 (800) 221-7945; *The Statesman's Year-Book.*

Statistical Office of the United Nations, Publishing Service, New York, New York 10017 (800) 253-9646; *Statistical Yearbook.*

United Nations Economic Commission for Africa, Africa Hall, Post Office Box 3001, Addis Ababa, Ethiopia (Telephone Number in U.S. (800) 253-9646); *African Statistical Yearbook.*

NIGER - BARLEY PRODUCTION - See **NIGER - CROPS**

NIGER - BEER PRODUCTION - See **NIGER - BEVERAGES**

NIGER - BEVERAGES

M.E. Sharpe, 80 Business Park Drive, Armonk, New York 10504 (800) 541-6563; *The Illustrated Book of World Rankings.*

Statistical Office of the United Nations, Publishing Service, New York, New York 10017 (800) 253-9646; *Statistical Yearbook.*

NIGER - BIRTH RATES

Central Intelligence Agency, Washington, D.C. 20505 (703) 482-1100, www.cia.gov; *The World Factbook.*

Euromonitor International, Inc., 122 South Michigan Avenue, Suite 1200, Chicago, Illinois 60603 (800) 577-EURO; *International Marketing Data and Statistics;* and *The World Economic Factbook.*

Europa Publications Limited, 18 Bedford Square, London, WC1B 3JN, England; *The Europa World Year Book.*

M.E. Sharpe, 80 Business Park Drive, Armonk, New York 10504 (800) 541-6563; *The Illustrated Book of World Rankings.*

St. Martin's Press, Inc., 175 Fifth Avenue, New York, New York 10010 (800) 221-7945; *The Statesman's Year-Book.*

Statistical Office of the United Nations, Publishing Service, New York, New York 10017 (800) 253-9646; *Demographic Yearbook; Statistical Yearbook;* and *Survey of Economic and Social Conditions in*

Africa.

The World Bank, 1818 H Street, NW, Washington, D.C. 20433 (202) 477-1234; *World Development Indicators.*

NIGER - BOOK PRODUCTION

United Nations Educational, Scientific and Cultural Organization (UNESCO), 7 Place de Fontenoy, F-75700 Paris, France (Telephone Number in U.S. (212) 963-5981); *Statistical Yearbook.*

NIGER - BROADCASTING

Billboard Limited, Post Office Box 9027, 1006 AA Amsterdam, The Netherlands (Telephone Number in U.S. (212) 764-7300); *World Radio TV Handbook.*

Central Intelligence Agency, Washington, D.C. 20505 (703) 482-1100, www.cia.gov; *The World Factbook.*

Euromonitor International, Inc., 122 South Michigan Avenue, Suite 1200, Chicago, Illinois 60603 (800) 577-EURO; *World Marketing Data and Statistics.*

M.E. Sharpe, 80 Business Park Drive, Armonk, New York 10504 (800) 541-6563; *The Illustrated Book of World Rankings.*

St. Martin's Press, Inc., 175 Fifth Avenue, New York, New York 10010 (800) 221-7945; *The Statesman's Year-Book.*

NIGER - BUDGET

Central Intelligence Agency, Washington, D.C. 20505 (703) 482-1100, www.cia.gov; *The World Factbook.*

NIGER - BUSINESS AND PROFESSIONAL LICENSES

International Monetary Fund, 700 Nineteenth Street, NW, Washington, D.C. 20431 (202) 623-7000; *Government Finance Statistics Yearbook.*

NIGER - BUTTER PRODUCTION - See **NIGER - DAIRY PRODUCTS**

NIGER - CALORIE SUPPLY

African Development Bank, 01 BP 1387, Abidjan 01, Cote d'Ivoire; *Selected Statistics on Regional Member Countries.*

Food and Agricultural Organization of the United Nations (FAO) Via delle Terme di Caracalla, 00100 Rome, Italy (Telephone Number in U.S. (202) 653-2400); *The State of Food and Agriculture.*

NIGER - CAPITAL REVENUE

International Monetary Fund, 700 Nineteenth Street, NW, Washington, D.C.

20431 (202) 623-7000; *Government Finance Statistics Yearbook.*

NIGER - CATTLE - See NIGER - LIVESTOCK AND POULTRY

NIGER - CEMENT PRODUCTION - See NIGER - MINING AND MINERAL PRODUCTS

NIGER - CHEESE PRODUCTION AND CONSUMPTION - See NIGER - DAIRY PRODUCTS

NIGER - CHEMICAL (ORGANIC) PRODUCTION - See NIGER - MINING AND MINERAL PRODUCTS

NIGER - CHICKENS - See NIGER - LIVESTOCK AND POULTRY

NIGER - CIGARETTE PRODUCTION - See NIGER - TOBACCO PRODUCTION

NIGER - CLIMATE

M.E. Sharpe, 80 Business Park Drive, Armonk, New York 10504 (800) 541-6563; *The Illustrated Book of World Rankings.*

St. Martin's Press, Inc., 175 Fifth Avenue, New York, New York 10010 (800) 221-7945; *The Statesman's Year-Book.*

NIGER - COAL PRODUCTION - See NIGER - MINING AND MINERAL PRODUCTS

NIGER - COFFEE PRODUCTION AND CONSUMPTION - See NIGER - CROPS

NIGER - COMMERCE

St. Martin's Press, Inc., 175 Fifth Avenue, New York, New York 10010 (800) 221-7945; *The Statesman's Year-Book.*

NIGER - COMMUNICATIONS - See NIGER - TRANSPORTATION AND COMMUNICATIONS

NIGER - CONSTRUCTION INDUSTRY

M.E. Sharpe, 80 Business Park Drive, Armonk, New York 10504 (800) 541-6563; *The Illustrated Book of World Rankings.*

United Nations Economic Commission for Africa, Africa Hall, Post Office Box 3001, Addis Ababa, Ethiopia (Telephone Number in U.S. (800) 253-9646); *African Statistical Yearbook.*

NIGER - CONSUMER PRICE INDEX

African Development Bank, 01 BP 1387, Abidjan 01, Cote d'Ivoire; *Selected Statistics on Regional Member Countries.*

Europa Publications Limited, 18 Bedford Square, London, WC1B 3JN, England; *The Europa World Year Book.*

Statistical Office of the United Nations, Publishing Service, New York, New York 10017 (800) 253-9646; *Statistical Yearbook* and *Survey of Economic and Social Conditions in Africa.*

United Nations Economic Commission for Africa, Africa Hall, Post Office Box 3001, Addis Ababa, Ethiopia (Telephone Number in U.S. (800) 253-9646); *African Statistical Yearbook.*

NIGER - CONSUMER PRICES

Euromonitor International, Inc., 122 South Michigan Avenue, Suite 1200, Chicago, Illinois 60603 (800) 577-EURO; *World Marketing Data and Statistics.*

International Labour Office, I.L.O. Publications, 1828 L Street, NW, Suite 801, Washington, D.C. 20036 (301) 638-3152; *Yearbook of Labour Statistics.*

International Monetary Fund, 700 Nineteenth Street, NW, Washington, D.C. 20431 (202) 623-7000; *International Financial Statistics.*

NIGER - CONSUMPTION

African Development Bank, 01 BP 1387, Abidjan 01, Cote d'Ivoire; *Selected Statistics on Regional Member Countries.*

Statistical Office of the United Nations, Publishing Service, New York 10017 (800) 253-9646; *Survey of Economic and Social Conditions in Africa.*

The World Bank, 1818 H Street, NW, Washington, D.C. 20433 (202) 477-1234; *World Development Report.*

NIGER - COPPER PRODUCTION AND CONSUMPTION - See NIGER - MINING AND MINERAL PRODUCTS

NIGER - CORN PRODUCTION - See NIGER - CROPS

NIGER - CORPORATE TAXES - See NIGER - TAXATION

NIGER - COTTON PRODUCTION - See NIGER - CROPS

NIGER - CROPS

Europa Publications Limited, 18 Bedford Square, London, WC1B 3JN, England; *The Europa World Year Book.*

Food and Agricultural Organization of the United Nations (FAO) Via delle Terme di Caracalla, 00100 Rome, Italy (Telephone Number in U.S. (202) 653-2400); *Production Yearbook;* and *The State of Food and Agriculture.*

M.E. Sharpe, 80 Business Park Drive,

Armonk, New York 10504 (800) 541-6563; *The Illustrated Book of World Rankings.*

St. Martin's Press, Inc., 175 Fifth Avenue, New York, New York 10010 (800) 221-7945; *The Statesman's Year-Book.*

Statistical Office of the United Nations, Publishing Service, New York, New York 10017 (800) 253-9646; *Statistical Yearbook.*

U.C.L.A. Latin American Center Publications, University of California, Los Angeles, California 90024 (310) 825-6634; *Statistical Abstract of Latin America.*

United Nations Conference on Trade and Development, Central Statistical Service, Palais des Nations, Geneva, Switzerland (Telephone in U.S. (800) 253-9646); *UNCTAD Commodity Yearbook.*

United Nations Economic Commission for Africa, Africa Hall, Post Office Box 3001, Addis Ababa, Ethiopia (Telephone Number in U.S. (800) 253-9646); *African Statistical Yearbook.*

NIGER - CUSTOMS DUTIES

International Monetary Fund, 700 Nineteenth Street, NW, Washington, D.C. 20431 (202) 623-7000; *Government Finance Statistics Yearbook.*

St. Martin's Press, Inc., 175 Fifth Avenue, New York, New York 10010 (800) 221-7945; *The Statesman's Year-Book.*

NIGER - DAIRY PRODUCTS

Europa Publications Limited, 18 Bedford Square, London, WC1B 3JN, England; *The Europa World Year Book.*

Food and Agricultural Organization of the United Nations (FAO) Via delle Terme di Caracalla, 00100 Rome, Italy (Telephone Number in U.S. (202) 653-2400); *Production Yearbook;* and *The State of Food and Agriculture.*

M.E. Sharpe, 80 Business Park Drive, Armonk, New York 10504 (800) 541-6563; *The Illustrated Book of World Rankings.*

St. Martin's Press, Inc., 175 Fifth Avenue, New York, New York 10010 (800) 221-7945; *The Statesman's Year-Book.*

Statistical Office of the United Nations, Publishing Service, New York, New York 10017 (800) 253-9646; *Statistical Yearbook.*

NIGER - DEATH RATES - See NIGER - MORTALITY

NIGER - DEFENSE EXPENDITURES - See NIGER - MILITARY

NIGER - DEMOGRAPHY

Euromonitor International, Inc., 122 South Michigan Avenue, Suite 1200, Chicago, Illinois 60603 (800) 577-EURO; *International Marketing Data and Statistics; The World Economic Factbook;* and *World Marketing Data and Statistics.*

M.E. Sharpe, 80 Business Park Drive, Armonk, New York 10504 (800) 541-6563; *The Illustrated Book of World Rankings.*

Statistical Office of the United Nations, Publishing Service, New York 10017 (800) 253-9646; *Human Development Report;* and *Survey of Economic and Social Conditions in Africa.*

NIGER - DEVELOPMENT ASSISTANCE

Statistical Office of the United Nations, Publishing Service, New York, New York 10017 (800) 253-9646; *Statistical Yearbook.*

NIGER - DIAMOND PRODUCTION - See NIGER - MINING AND MINERAL PRODUCTS

NIGER - DISCOUNT RATES - See NIGER - BANKING

NIGER - DISEASES - See NIGER - HEALTH

NIGER - DIVORCE RATES

M.E. Sharpe, 80 Business Park Drive, Armonk, New York 10504 (800) 541-6563; *The Illustrated Book of World Rankings.*

Statistical Office of the United Nations, Publishing Service, New York, New York 10017 (800) 253-9646; *Demographic Yearbook.*

NIGER - ECONOMY

African Development Bank, 01 BP 1387, Abidjan 01, Cote d'Ivoire; *Selected Statistics on Regional Member Countries.*

Central Intelligence Agency, Washington, D.C. 20505 (703) 482-1100, www.cia.gov; *The World Factbook.*

Economist Intelligence Unit, 111 West 57th Street, New York, New York 10019 (800) 938-4685; *Niger Country Report.*

Euromonitor International, Inc., 122 South Michigan Avenue, Suite 1200, Chicago, Illinois 60603 (800) 577-EURO; *International Marketing Data and Statistics; The World Economic Factbook;* and *World Marketing Data and Statistics.*

Europa Publications Limited, 18 Bedford Square, London, WC1B 3JN, England; *The Europa World Year Book.*

M.E. Sharpe, 80 Business Park Drive, Armonk, New York 10504 (800) 541-6563; *The Illustrated Book of World Rankings.*

St. Martin's Press, Inc., 175 Fifth Avenue, New York, New York 10010 (800) 221-7945; *The Statesman's Year-Book.*

Statistical Office of the United Nations, Publishing Service, New York, New York 10017 (800) 253-9646; *Foreign Trade Statistics for Africa;* and *World Statistics Pocketbook.*

The World Bank, 1818 H Street, NW, Washington, D.C. 20433 (202) 477-1234; *The World Bank Atlas;* and *World Development Report.*

NIGER - EDUCATION

African Development Bank, 01 BP 1387, Abidjan 01, Cote d'Ivoire; *Selected Statistics on Regional Member Countries.*

The Economist Intelligence Unit, 111 West 57th Street, New York, New York 10019 (800) 938-4685; *The World Market Atlas.*

Euromonitor International, Inc., 122 South Michigan Avenue, Suite 1200, Chicago, Illinois 60603 (800) 577-EURO; *International Marketing Data and Statistics;* and *World Marketing Data and Statistics.*

Europa Publications Limited, 18 Bedford Square, London, WC1B 3JN, England; *The Europa World Year Book.*

International Monetary Fund, 700 Nineteenth Street, NW, Washington, D.C. 20431 (202) 623-7000; *Government Finance Statistics Yearbook.*

M.E. Sharpe, 80 Business Park Drive, Armonk, New York 10504 (800) 541-6563; *The Illustrated Book of World Rankings.*

St. Martin's Press, Inc., 175 Fifth Avenue, New York, New York 10010 (800) 221-7945; *The Statesman's Year-Book.*

Statistical Office of the United Nations, Publishing Service, New York 10017 (800) 253-9646; *Human Development Report;* and *Survey of Economic and Social Conditions in Africa.*

United Nations Economic Commission for Africa, Africa Hall, Post Office Box 3001, Addis Ababa, Ethiopia (Telephone Number in U.S. (800) 253-9646); *African Statistical Yearbook.*

United Nations Educational, Scientific and Cultural Organization (UNESCO), 7 Place de Fontenoy, F-75700 Paris, France (Telephone Number in U.S. (212) 963-5981); *Statistical Yearbook.*

The World Bank, 1818 H Street, NW, Washington, D.C. 20433 (202) 477-1234; *World Development Report;* and *World Development Indicators.*

NIGER - EGG PRODUCTION AND CONSUMPTION - See NIGER - DAIRY PRODUCTS

NIGER - ELECTRICITY

Central Intelligence Agency, Washington, D.C. 20505 (703) 482-1100, www.cia.gov; *The World Factbook.*

M.E. Sharpe, 80 Business Park Drive, Armonk, New York 10504 (800) 541-6563; *The Illustrated Book of World Rankings.*

St. Martin's Press, Inc., 175 Fifth Avenue, New York, New York 10010 (800) 221-7945; *The Statesman's Year-Book.*

Statistical Office of the United Nations, Publishing Service, New York, New York 10017 (800) 253-9646; *Human Development Report; Statistical Yearbook* and *Survey of Economic and Social Conditions in Africa.*

United Nations Economic Commission for Africa, Africa Hall, Post Office Box 3001, Addis Ababa, Ethiopia (Telephone Number in U.S. (800) 253-9646); *African Statistical Yearbook.*

NIGER - EMPLOYMENT

Euromonitor International, Inc., 122 South Michigan Avenue, Suite 1200, Chicago, Illinois 60603 (800) 577-EURO; *International Marketing Data and Statistics.*

International Labour Office, I.L.O. Publications, 1828 L Street, NW, Suite 801, Washington, D.C. 20036 (301) 638-3152; *Yearbook of Labour Statistics.*

M.E. Sharpe, 80 Business Park Drive, Armonk, New York 10504 (800) 541-6563; *The Illustrated Book of World Rankings.*

Statistical Office of the United Nations, Publishing Service, New York, New York 10017 (800) 253-9646; *Statistical Yearbook;* and *Survey of Economic and Social Conditions in Africa.*

United Nations Economic Commission for Africa, Africa Hall, Post Office Box 3001, Addis Ababa, Ethiopia (Telephone Number in U.S. (800) 253-9646); *African Statistical Yearbook.*

NIGER - ENERGY

Euromonitor International, Inc., 122 South Michigan Avenue, Suite 1200, Chicago, Illinois 60603 (800) 577-EURO; *International Marketing Data and Statistics; The World Economic Factbook;* and *World Marketing Data and Statistics.*

Food and Agricultural Organization of the United Nations (FAO) Via delle Terme di Caracalla, 00100 Rome, Italy (Telephone

Number in U.S. (202) 653-2400); *The State of Food and Agriculture.*

M.E. Sharpe, 80 Business Park Drive, Armonk, New York 10504 (800) 541-6563; *The Illustrated Book of World Rankings.*

St. Martin's Press, Inc., 175 Fifth Avenue, New York, New York 10010 (800) 221-7945; *The Statesman's Year-Book.*

Statistical Office of the United Nations, Publishing Service, New York, New York 10017 (800) 253-9646; *Energy Statistics Yearbook; Human Development Report; Statistical Yearbook; World Statistics Pocketbook;* and *World Energy Supplies.*

United Nations Economic Commission for Africa, Africa Hall, Post Office Box 3001, Addis Ababa, Ethiopia (Telephone Number in U.S. (800) 253-9646); *African Statistical Yearbook.*

The World Bank, 1818 H Street, NW, Washington, D.C. 20433 (202) 477-1234; *The World Bank Atlas;* and *World Development Report.*

NIGER - ENVIRONMENT

Economist Intelligence Unit, 111 West 57th Street, New York, New York 10019 (800) 938-4685; *Niger Country Report.*

Statistical Office of the United Nations, Publishing Service, New York, New York 10017 (800) 253-9646; *World Statistics Pocketbook.*

NIGER - EXCHANGE RATES

African Development Bank, 01 BP 1387, Abidjan 01, Cote d'Ivoire; *Selected Statistics on Regional Member Countries.*

Central Intelligence Agency, Washington, D.C. 20505 (703) 482-1100, www.cia.gov; *The World Factbook.*

Euromonitor International, Inc., 122 South Michigan Avenue, Suite 1200, Chicago, Illinois 60603 (800) 577-EURO; *International Marketing Data and Statistics;* and *The World Economic Factbook.*

Europa Publications Limited, 18 Bedford Square, London, WC1B 3JN, England; *The Europa World Year Book.*

International Monetary Fund, 700 Nineteenth Street, NW, Washington, D.C. 20431 (202) 623-7000; *International Financial Statistics.*

Statistical Office of the United Nations, Publishing Service, New York, New York 10017 (800) 253-9646; *Foreign Trade Statistics for Africa; World Statistics Pocketbook;* and *Statistical Yearbook.*

NIGER - EXCISE TAXES - See NIGER - TAXATION

NIGER - EXPORTS

African Development Bank, 01 BP 1387, Abidjan 01, Cote d'Ivoire; *Selected Statistics on Regional Member Countries.*

Central Intelligence Agency, Washington, D.C. 20505 (703) 482-1100, www.cia.gov; *The World Factbook.*

The Economist Intelligence Unit, 111 West 57th Street, New York, New York 10019 (800) 938-4685; *Niger Country Report;* and *The World Market Atlas.*

Euromonitor International, Inc., 122 South Michigan Avenue, Suite 1200, Chicago, Illinois 60603 (800) 577-EURO; *International Marketing Data and Statistics;* and *The World Economic Factbook.*

Europa Publications Limited, 18 Bedford Square, London, WC1B 3JN, England; *The Europa World Year Book.*

Food and Agricultural Organization of the United Nations (FAO) Via delle Terme di Caracalla, 00100 Rome, Italy (Telephone Number in U.S. (202) 653-2400); *The State of Food and Agriculture.*

International Monetary Fund, 700 Nineteenth Street, NW, Washington, D.C. 20431 (202) 623-7000; *Direction of Trade Statistics;* and *Government Finance Statistics Yearbook.*

St. Martin's Press, Inc., 175 Fifth Avenue, New York, New York 10010 (800) 221-7945; *The Statesman's Year-Book.*

Statistical Office of the United Nations, Publishing Service, New York, New York 10017 (800) 253-9646; *Foreign Trade Statistics for Africa;* and *Survey of Economic and Social Conditions in Africa.*

United Nations Conference on Trade and Development (UNCTAD), New York, New York 10017 (800) 253-9646; *Handbook of International Trade and Development.*

United Nations Economic Commission for Africa, Africa Hall, Post Office Box 3001, Addis Ababa, Ethiopia (Telephone Number in U.S. (800) 253-9646); *African Statistical Yearbook.*

The World Bank, 1818 H Street, NW, Washington, D.C. 20433 (202) 477-1234; *The World Development Report;* and *World Development Indicators.*

NIGER - EXTERNAL INDEBTEDNESS

African Development Bank, 01 BP 1387, Abidjan 01, Cote d'Ivoire; *Selected Statistics on Regional Member Countries.*

Statistical Office of the United Nations, Publishing Service, New York 10017 (800) 253-9646; *Survey of Economic and Social Conditions in Africa.*

The World Bank, 1818 H Street, NW, Washington, D.C. 20433 (202) 477-1234; *World Development Report;* and *World Development Indicators.*

NIGER - EXTERNAL TRADE

African Development Bank, 01 BP 1387, Abidjan 01, Cote d'Ivoire; *Selected Statistics on Regional Member Countries.*

Euromonitor International, Inc., 122 South Michigan Avenue, Suite 1200, Chicago, Illinois 60603 (800) 577-EURO; *World Marketing Data and Statistics.*

Food and Agricultural Organization of the United Nations (FAO) Via delle Terme di Caracalla, 00100 Rome, Italy (Telephone Number in U.S. (202) 653-2400); *The State of Food and Agriculture;* and *Trade Yearbook.*

Statistical Office of the United Nations, Publishing Service, New York, New York 10017 (800) 253-9646; *Statistical Yearbook.*

NIGER - FARM CROPS - See NIGER - CROPS

NIGER - FEMALE WORKING POPULATION - See NIGER - EMPLOYMENT

NIGER - FERTILITY RATES

Central Intelligence Agency, Washington, D.C. 20505 (703) 482-1100, www.cia.gov; *The World Factbook.*

M.E. Sharpe, 80 Business Park Drive, Armonk, New York 10504 (800) 541-6563; *The Illustrated Book of World Rankings.*

Statistical Office of the United Nations, Publishing Service, New York 10017 (800) 253-9646; *Human Development Report;* and *Survey of Economic and Social Conditions in Africa.*

The World Bank, 1818 H Street, NW, Washington, D.C. 20433 (202) 477-1234; *The World Bank Atlas; World Development Report;* and *World Development Indicators.*

NIGER - FERTILIZER

Food and Agricultural Organization of the United Nations (FAO), Via delle Terme di Caracalla, 00100 Rome, Italy (Telephone Number in U.S. (202) 653-2400); *Fertilizer Yearbook;* and *The State of Food and Agriculture.*

Statistical Office of the United Nations, Publishing Service, New York, New York 10017 (800) 253-9646; *Statistical Yearbook.*

NIGER - FETAL MORTALITY - See
NIGER - MORTALITY

NIGER - FINANCE

African Development Bank, 01 BP 1387, Abidjan 01, Cote d'Ivoire; *Selected Statistics on Regional Member Countries.*

Economist Intelligence Unit, 111 West 57th Street, New York, New York 10019 (800) 938-4685; *Niger Country Report.*

Europa Publications Limited, 18 Bedford Square, London, WC1B 3JN, England; *The Europa World Year Book.*

International Monetary Fund, 700 Nineteenth Street, NW, Washington, D.C. 20431 (202) 623-7000; *International Financial Statistics.*

M.E. Sharpe, 80 Business Park Drive, Armonk, New York 10504 (800) 541-6563; *The Illustrated Book of World Rankings.*

St. Martin's Press, Inc., 175 Fifth Avenue, New York, New York 10010 (800) 221-7945; *The Statesman's Year-Book.*

United Nations Economic Commission for Africa, Africa Hall, Post Office Box 3001, Addis Ababa, Ethiopia (Telephone Number in U.S. (800) 253-9646); *African Statistical Yearbook.*

NIGER - FISHERIES

Europa Publications Limited, 18 Bedford Square, London, WC1B 3JN, England; *The Europa World Year Book.*

Food and Agricultural Organization of the United Nations (FAO) Via delle Terme di Caracalla, 00100 Rome, Italy (Telephone Number in U.S. (202) 653-2400); *The State of Food and Agriculture;* and *Yearbook of Fishery Statistics.*

M.E. Sharpe, 80 Business Park Drive, Armonk, New York 10504 (800) 541-6563; *The Illustrated Book of World Rankings.*

St. Martin's Press, Inc., 175 Fifth Avenue, New York, New York 10010 (800) 221-7945; *The Statesman's Year-Book.*

Statistical Office of the United Nations, Publishing Service, New York, New York 10017 (800) 253-9646; *Statistical Yearbook;* and *Survey of Economic and Social Conditions in Africa.*

United Nations Conference on Trade and Development, Central Statistical Service, Palais des Nations, Geneva, Switzerland (Telephone in U.S. (800) 253-9646); *UNCTAD Commodity Yearbook.*

United Nations Economic Commission for Africa, Africa Hall, Post Office Box 3001,

Addis Ababa, Ethiopia (Telephone Number in U.S. (800) 253-9646); *African Statistical Yearbook.*

NIGER - FOOD

African Development Bank, 01 BP 1387, Abidjan 01, Cote d'Ivoire; *Selected Statistics on Regional Member Countries.*

Food and Agricultural Organization of the United Nations (FAO), Via delle Terme di Caracalla, 00100 Rome, Italy (Telephone Number in U.S. (202) 653-2400); *Production Yearbook;* and *The State of Food and Agriculture.*

Statistical Office of the United Nations, Publishing Service, New York, New York 10017 (800) 253-9646; *Human Development Report.*

United Nations Conference on Trade and Development, Central Statistical Service, Palais des Nations, Geneva, Switzerland (Telephone in U.S. (800) 253-9646); *UNCTAD Commodity Yearbook.*

NIGER - FOREIGN DEBT

St. Martin's Press, Inc., 175 Fifth Avenue, New York, New York 10010 (800) 221-7945; *The Statesman's Year-Book.*

NIGER - FOREIGN TRADE

Economist Intelligence Unit, 111 West 57th Street, New York, New York 10019 (800) 938-4685; *Niger Country Report.*

Euromonitor International, Inc., 122 South Michigan Avenue, Suite 1200, Chicago, Illinois 60603 (800) 577-EURO; *International Marketing Data and Statistics;* and *The World Economic Factbook.*

Europa Publications Limited, 18 Bedford Square, London, WC1B 3JN, England; *The Europa World Year Book.*

Food and Agricultural Organization of the United Nations (FAO) Via delle Terme di Caracalla, 00100 Rome, Italy (Telephone Number in U.S. (202) 653-2400); *The State of Food and Agriculture.*

International Monetary Fund, 700 Nineteenth Street, NW, Washington, D.C. 20431 (202) 623-7000; *International Financial Statistics.*

M.E. Sharpe, 80 Business Park Drive, Armonk, New York 10504 (800) 541-6563; *The Illustrated Book of World Rankings.*

St. Martin's Press, Inc., 175 Fifth Avenue, New York, New York 10010 (800) 221-7945; *The Statesman's Year-Book.*

Statistical Office of the United Nations, Publishing Service, New York, New York

10017 (800) 253-9646; *Foreign Trade Statistics for Africa; International Trade Statistics Yearbook;* and *Statistical Yearbook.*

United Nations Conference on Trade and Development, Central Statistical Service, Palais des Nations, Geneva, Switzerland (Telephone in U.S. (800) 253-9646); *UNCTAD Commodity Yearbook.*

United Nations Economic Commission for Africa, Africa Hall, Post Office Box 3001, Addis Ababa, Ethiopia (Telephone Number in U.S. (800) 253-9646); *African Statistical Yearbook.*

The World Bank, 1818 H Street, NW, Washington, D.C. 20433 (202) 477-1234; *World Development Report;* and *World Development Indicators.*

NIGER - FORESTRY AND FOREST PRODUCTS

Europa Publications Limited, 18 Bedford Square, London, WC1B 3JN, England; *The Europa World Year Book.*

Food and Agricultural Organization of the United Nations (FAO) Via delle Terme di Caracalla, 00100 Rome, Italy (Telephone Number in U.S. (202) 653-2400); *The State of Food and Agriculture;* and *Yearbook of Forest Products.*

M.E. Sharpe, 80 Business Park Drive, Armonk, New York 10504 (800) 541-6563; *The Illustrated Book of World Rankings.*

St. Martin's Press, Inc., 175 Fifth Avenue, New York, New York 10010 (800) 221-7945; *The Statesman's Year-Book.*

Statistical Office of the United Nations, Publishing Service, New York, New York 10017 (800) 253-9646; *Statistical Yearbook.*

United Nations Conference on Trade and Development, Central Statistical Service, Palais des Nations, Geneva, Switzerland (Telephone in U.S. (800) 253-9646); *UNCTAD Commodity Yearbook.*

United Nations Economic Commission for Africa, Africa Hall, Post Office Box 3001, Addis Ababa, Ethiopia (Telephone Number in U.S. (800) 253-9646); *African Statistical Yearbook.*

United Nations Educational, Scientific and Cultural Organization (UNESCO), 7 Place de Fontenoy, F-75700 Paris, France (Telephone Number in U.S. (212) 963-5981); *Statistical Yearbook.*

The World Bank, 1818 H Street, NW, Washington, D.C. 20433 (202) 477-1234; *World Development Report.*

NIGER - GAS PRODUCTION - See

NIGER - MINING AND MINERAL PRODUCTS

NIGER - GENERAL MORTALITY - See NIGER - MORTALITY

NIGER - GEOGRAPHIC DATA

M.E. Sharpe, 80 Business Park Drive, Armonk, New York 10504 (800) 541-6563; *The Illustrated Book of World Rankings.*

NIGER - GOATS - See NIGER - LIVESTOCK AND POULTRY

NIGER - GOLD HOLDINGS

International Monetary Fund, 700 Nineteenth Street, NW, Washington, D.C. 20431 (202) 623-7000; *International Financial Statistics.*

Statistical Office of the United Nations, Publishing Service, New York, New York 10017 (800) 253-9646; *Statistical Yearbook.*

The World Bank, 1818 H Street, NW, Washington, D.C. 20433 (202) 477-1234; *World Development Indicators.*

NIGER - GOLD PRODUCTION AND CONSUMPTION - See NIGER - MINING AND MINERAL PRODUCTS

NIGER - GOVERNMENT

Central Intelligence Agency, Washington, D.C. 20505 (703) 482-1100, www.cia.gov; *The World Factbook.*

Europa Publications Limited, 18 Bedford Square, London, WC1B 3JN, England; *The Europa World Year Book.*

International Monetary Fund, 700 Nineteenth Street, NW, Washington, D.C. 20431 (202) 623-7000; *Government Finance Statistics Yearbook;* and *International Financial Statistics.*

St. Martin's Press, Inc., 175 Fifth Avenue, New York, New York 10010 (800) 221-7945; *The Statesman's Year-Book.*

Statistical Office of the United Nations, Publishing Service, New York 10017 (800) 253-9646; *National Accounts Statistics;* and *Survey of Economic and Social Conditions in Africa.*

The World Bank, 1818 H Street, NW, Washington, D.C. 20433 (202) 477-1234; *World Development Report;* and *World Development Indicators.*

NIGER - GRAIN PRODUCTION - See NIGER - CROPS

NIGER - GRANTS

International Monetary Fund, 700

Nineteenth Street, NW, Washington, D.C. 20431 (202) 623-7000; *Government Finance Statistics Yearbook.*

NIGER - GROSS DOMESTIC PRODUCT

African Development Bank, 01 BP 1387, Abidjan 01, Cote d'Ivoire; *Selected Statistics on Regional Member Countries.*

The Economist Intelligence Unit, 111 West 57th Street, New York, New York 10019 (800) 938-4685; *Niger Country Report;* and *The World Market Atlas.*

Euromonitor International, Inc., 122 South Michigan Avenue, Suite 1200, Chicago, Illinois 60603 (800) 577-EURO; *International Marketing Data and Statistics;* and *The World Economic Factbook.*

Europa Publications Limited, 18 Bedford Square, London, WC1B 3JN, England; *The Europa World Year Book.*

M.E. Sharpe, 80 Business Park Drive, Armonk, New York 10504 (800) 541-6563; *The Illustrated Book of World Rankings.*

Statistical Office of the United Nations, Publishing Service, New York, New York 10017 (800) 253-9646; *Human Development Report; National Accounts Statistics; Statistical Yearbook;* and *Survey of Economic and Social Conditions in Africa.*

United Nations Economic Commission for Africa, Africa Hall, Post Office Box 3001, Addis Ababa, Ethiopia (Telephone Number in U.S. (800) 253-9646); *African Statistical Yearbook.*

The World Bank, 1818 H Street, NW, Washington, D.C. 20433 (202) 477-1234; *World Development Report;* and *World Development Indicators.*

NIGER - GROSS NATIONAL PRODUCT

Euromonitor International, Inc., 122 South Michigan Avenue, Suite 1200, Chicago, Illinois 60603 (800) 577-EURO; *International Marketing Data and Statistics.*

St. Martin's Press, Inc., 175 Fifth Avenue, New York, New York 10010 (800) 221-7945; *The Statesman's Year-Book.*

U.S. Arms Control and Disarmament Agency, 320 Twenty-first Street, NW, Washington, D.C. 20451 (202) 647-8677; *World Military Expenditures and Arms Transfers.*

The World Bank, 1818 H Street, NW, Washington, D.C. 20433 (202) 477-1234; *The World Bank Atlas; World Development Report;* and *World Development Indicators.*

NIGER - GROUNDNUT PRODUCTION - See

NIGER - CROPS

NIGER - HEALTH

African Development Bank, 01 BP 1387, Abidjan 01, Cote d'Ivoire; *Selected Statistics on Regional Member Countries.*

Euromonitor International, Inc., 122 South Michigan Avenue, Suite 1200, Chicago, Illinois 60603 (800) 577-EURO; *World Marketing Data and Statistics.*

M.E. Sharpe, 80 Business Park Drive, Armonk, New York 10504 (800) 541-6563; *The Illustrated Book of World Rankings.*

St. Martin's Press, Inc., 175 Fifth Avenue, New York, New York 10010 (800) 221-7945; *The Statesman's Year-Book.*

Statistical Office of the United Nations, Publishing Service, New York, New York 10017 (800) 253-9646; *Human Development Report;* and *Statistical Yearbook.*

United Nations Children's Fund (UNICEF), 3 United Nations Plaza, New York, New York 10017 (800) 253-9646; *State of the World's Children.*

United Nations Economic Commission for Africa, Africa Hall, Post Office Box 3001, Addis Ababa, Ethiopia (Telephone Number in U.S. (800) 253-9646); *African Statistical Yearbook.*

The World Bank, 1818 H Street, NW, Washington, D.C. 20433 (202) 477-1234; *World Development Report.*

World Health Organization, Office of Publications, 20 Avenue Appia, CH-1211 Geneva 27, Switzerland (Telephone Number in U.S. (518) 436-9686); *World Health Statistics Annual.*

NIGER - HEALTH EXPENDITURES

International Monetary Fund, 700 Nineteenth Street, NW, Washington, D.C. 20431 (202) 623-7000; *Government Finance Statistics Yearbook.*

NIGER - HIDE PRODUCTION

Food and Agricultural Organization of the United Nations (FAO), Via delle Terme di Caracalla, 00100 Rome, Italy (Telephone Number in U.S. (202) 653-2400); *Production Yearbook.*

NIGER - HIGHWAYS

Central Intelligence Agency, Washington, D.C. 20505 (703) 482-1100, www.cia.gov; *The World Factbook.*

St. Martin's Press, Inc., 175 Fifth Avenue, New York, New York 10010 (800)

221-7945; *The Statesman's Year-Book.*

Statistical Office of the United Nations, Publishing Service, New York 10017 (800) 253-9646; *Survey of Economic and Social Conditions in Africa.*

United Nations Economic Commission for Africa, Africa Hall, Post Office Box 3001, Addis Ababa, Ethiopia (Telephone Number in U.S. (800) 253-9646); *African Statistical Yearbook.*

NIGER - HORSES - See NIGER - LIVESTOCK AND POULTRY

NIGER - HOURS OF WORK - See NIGER - EMPLOYMENT

NIGER - HOUSING AND HOUSING UNITS

Euromonitor International, Inc., 122 South Michigan Avenue, Suite 1200, Chicago, Illinois 60603 (800) 577-EURO; *World Marketing Data and Statistics.*

NIGER - HOUSING EXPENDITURES

International Monetary Fund, 700 Nineteenth Street, NW, Washington, D.C. 20431 (202) 623-7000; *Government Finance Statistics Yearbook.*

M.E. Sharpe, 80 Business Park Drive, Armonk, New York 10504 (800) 541-6563; *The Illustrated Book of World Rankings.*

NIGER - ILLITERATE POPULATION

Central Intelligence Agency, Washington, D.C. 20505 (703) 482-1100, www.cia.gov; *The World Factbook.*

The Economist Intelligence Unit, 111 West 57th Street, New York, New York 10019 (800) 938-4685; *The World Market Atlas.*

Euromonitor International, Inc., 122 South Michigan Avenue, Suite 1200, Chicago, Illinois 60603 (800) 577-EURO; *The World Economic Factbook.*

St. Martin's Press, Inc., 175 Fifth Avenue, New York, New York 10010 (800) 221-7945; *The Statesman's Year-Book.*

Statistical Office of the United Nations, Publishing Service, New York, New York 10017 (800) 253-9646; *Human Development Report.*

United Nations Educational, Scientific and Cultural Organization (UNESCO), 7 Place de Fontenoy, F-75700 Paris, France (Telephone Number in U.S. (212) 963-5981); *Statistical Yearbook.*

NIGER - IMPORTS

African Development Bank, 01 BP 1387,

Abidjan 01, Cote d'Ivoire; *Selected Statistics on Regional Member Countries.*

Central Intelligence Agency, Washington, D.C. 20505 (703) 482-1100, www.cia.gov; *The World Factbook.*

The Economist Intelligence Unit, 111 West 57th Street, New York, New York 10019 (800) 938-4685; *Niger Country Report;* and *The World Market Atlas.*

Euromonitor International, Inc., 122 South Michigan Avenue, Suite 1200, Chicago, Illinois 60603 (800) 577-EURO; *International Marketing Data and Statistics;* and *The World Economic Factbook.*

Europa Publications Limited, 18 Bedford Square, London, WC1B 3JN, England; *The Europa World Year Book.*

Food and Agricultural Organization of the United Nations (FAO) Via delle Terme di Caracalla, 00100 Rome, Italy (Telephone Number in U.S. (202) 653-2400); *The State of Food and Agriculture.*

International Monetary Fund, 700 Nineteenth Street, NW, Washington, D.C. 20431 (202) 623-7000; *Direction of Trade Statistics;* and *Government Finance Statistics Yearbook.*

St. Martin's Press, Inc., 175 Fifth Avenue, New York, New York 10010 (800) 221-7945; *The Statesman's Year-Book.*

Statistical Office of the United Nations, Publishing Service, New York, New York 10017 (800) 253-9646; *Foreign Trade Statistics for Africa;* and *Survey of Economic and Social Conditions in Africa.*

United Nations Conference on Trade and Development (UNCTAD), New York, New York 10017 (800) 253-9646; *Handbook of International Trade and Development.*

United Nations Economic Commission for Africa, Africa Hall, Post Office Box 3001, Addis Ababa, Ethiopia (Telephone Number in U.S. (800) 253-9646); *African Statistical Yearbook.*

The World Bank, 1818 H Street, NW, Washington, D.C. 20433 (202) 477-1234; *World Development Report;* and *World Development Indicators.*

NIGER - INCOME TAXES - See NIGER - TAXATION

NIGER - INDUSTRY

Central Intelligence Agency, Washington, D.C. 20505 (703) 482-1100, www.cia.gov; *The World Factbook.*

Economist Intelligence Unit, 111 West 57th Street, New York, New York 10019

(800) 938-4685; *Niger Country Report.*

Euromonitor International, Inc., 122 South Michigan Avenue, Suite 1200, Chicago, Illinois 60603 (800) 577-EURO; *International Marketing Data and Statistics; The World Economic Factbook;* and *World Marketing Data and Statistics.*

Europa Publications Limited, 18 Bedford Square, London, WC1B 3JN, England; *The Europa World Year Book.*

International Labour Office, I.L.O. Publications, 1828 L Street, NW, Suite 801, Washington, D.C. 20036 (301) 638-3152; *Yearbook of Labour Statistics.*

M.E. Sharpe, 80 Business Park Drive, Armonk, New York 10504 (800) 541-6563; *The Illustrated Book of World Rankings.*

St. Martin's Press, Inc., 175 Fifth Avenue, New York, New York 10010 (800) 221-7945; *The Statesman's Year-Book.*

Statistical Office of the United Nations, Publishing Service, New York 10017 (800) 253-9646; *Survey of Economic and Social Conditions in Africa.*

United Nations Economic Commission for Africa, Africa Hall, Post Office Box 3001, Addis Ababa, Ethiopia (Telephone Number in U.S. (800) 253-9646); *African Statistical Yearbook.*

The World Bank, 1818 H Street, NW, Washington, D.C. 20433 (202) 477-1234; *World Development Indicators.*

NIGER - INFANT AND MATERNAL MORTALITY - See NIGER - MORTALITY

NIGER - INTERNATIONAL LIQUIDITY

International Monetary Fund, 700 Nineteenth Street, NW, Washington, D.C. 20431 (202) 623-7000; *International Financial Statistics.*

NIGER - INTERNATIONAL RESERVES EXCLUDING GOLD

African Development Bank, 01 BP 1387, Abidjan 01, Cote d'Ivoire; *Selected Statistics on Regional Member Countries.*

Statistical Office of the United Nations, Publishing Service, New York, New York 10017 (800) 253-9646; *Statistical Yearbook.*

The World Bank, 1818 H Street, NW, Washington, D.C. 20433 (202) 477-1234; *World Development Indicators.*

NIGER - IRON ORE PRODUCTION AND CONSUMPTION - See NIGER - MINING AND MINERAL PRODUCTS

NIGER - IRRIGATION

Euromonitor International, Inc., 122 South Michigan Avenue, Suite 1200, Chicago, Illinois 60603 (800) 577-EURO; *International Marketing Data and Statistics.*

NIGER - LABOR

African Development Bank, 01 BP 1387, Abidjan 01, Cote d'Ivoire; *Selected Statistics on Regional Member Countries.*

Central Intelligence Agency, Washington, D.C. 20505 (703) 482-1100, www.cia.gov; *The World Factbook.*

Euromonitor International, Inc., 122 South Michigan Avenue, Suite 1200, Chicago, Illinois 60603 (800) 577-EURO; *International Marketing Data and Statistics; and World Marketing Data and Statistics.*

Europa Publications Limited, 18 Bedford Square, London, WC1B 3JN, England; *The Europa World Year Book.*

Food and Agricultural Organization of the United Nations (FAO) Via delle Terme di Caracalla, 00100 Rome, Italy (Telephone Number in U.S. (202) 653-2400); *The State of Food and Agriculture.*

International Labour Office, I.L.O. Publications, 1828 L Street, NW, Suite 801, Washington, D.C. 20036 (301) 638-3152; *Yearbook of Labour Statistics.*

M.E. Sharpe, 80 Business Park Drive, Armonk, New York 10504 (800) 541-6563; *The Illustrated Book of World Rankings.*

St. Martin's Press, Inc., 175 Fifth Avenue, New York, New York 10010 (800) 221-7945; *The Statesman's Year-Book.*

Statistical Office of the United Nations, Publishing Service, New York, New York 10017 (800) 253-9646; *Human Development Report.*

The World Bank, 1818 H Street, NW, Washington, D.C. 20433 (202) 477-1234; *The World Bank Atlas; World Development Report; and World Development Indicators.*

NIGER - LAND USE

Central Intelligence Agency, Washington, D.C. 20505 (703) 482-1100, www.cia.gov; *The World Factbook.*

Euromonitor International, Inc., 122 South Michigan Avenue, Suite 1200, Chicago, Illinois 60603 (800) 577-EURO; *International Marketing Data and Statistics.*

Food and Agricultural Organization of the United Nations (FAO), Via delle Terme di Caracalla, 00100 Rome, Italy (Telephone Number in U.S. (202) 653-2400); *Production Yearbook.*

The World Bank, 1818 H Street, NW, Washington, D.C. 20433 (202) 477-1234; *World Development Report.*

NIGER - LIBRARIES

M.E. Sharpe, 80 Business Park Drive, Armonk, New York 10504 (800) 541-6563; *The Illustrated Book of World Rankings.*

United Nations Educational, Scientific and Cultural Organization (UNESCO), 7 Place de Fontenoy, F-75700 Paris, France (Telephone Number in U.S. (212) 963-5981); *Statistical Yearbook.*

NIGER - LIFE EXPECTANCY

African Development Bank, 01 BP 1387, Abidjan 01, Cote d'Ivoire; *Selected Statistics on Regional Member Countries.*

Central Intelligence Agency, Washington, D.C. 20505 (703) 482-1100, www.cia.gov; *The World Factbook.*

Euromonitor International, Inc., 122 South Michigan Avenue, Suite 1200, Chicago, Illinois 60603 (800) 577-EURO; *The World Economic Factbook.*

St. Martin's Press, Inc., 175 Fifth Avenue, New York, New York 10010 (800) 221-7945; *The Statesman's Year-Book.*

Statistical Office of the United Nations, Publishing Service, New York, New York 10017 (800) 253-9646; *Human Development Report; and World Statistics Pocketbook.*

The World Bank, 1818 H Street, NW, Washington, D.C. 20433 (202) 477-1234; *The World Bank Atlas; and World Development Report.*

NIGER - LITERACY RATE

Euromonitor International, Inc., 122 South Michigan Avenue, Suite 1200, Chicago, Illinois 60603 (800) 577-EURO; *World Marketing Data and Statistics.*

Statistical Office of the United Nations, Publishing Service, New York, New York 10017 (800) 253-9646; *Survey of Economic and Social Conditions in Africa.*

NIGER - LIVESTOCK AND POULTRY

Euromonitor International, Inc., 122 South Michigan Avenue, Suite 1200, Chicago, Illinois 60603 (800) 577-EURO; *International Marketing Data and Statistics.*

Europa Publications Limited, 18 Bedford Square, London, WC1B 3JN, England; *The Europa World Year Book.*

Food and Agricultural Organization of the United Nations (FAO), Via delle Terme

di Caracalla, 00100 Rome, Italy (Telephone Number in U.S. (202) 653-2400); *Production Yearbook; and The State of Food and Agriculture.*

M.E. Sharpe, 80 Business Park Drive, Armonk, New York 10504 (800) 541-6563; *The Illustrated Book of World Rankings.*

St. Martin's Press, Inc., 175 Fifth Avenue, New York, New York 10010 (800) 221-7945; *The Statesman's Year-Book.*

Statistical Office of the United Nations, Publishing Service, New York, New York 10017 (800) 253-9646; *Statistical Yearbook; and Survey of Economic and Social Conditions in Africa.*

United Nations Conference on Trade and Development, Central Statistical Service, Palais des Nations, Geneva, Switzerland (Telephone in U.S. (800) 253-9646); *UNCTAD Commodity Yearbook.*

United Nations Economic Commission for Africa, Africa Hall, Post Office Box 3001, Addis Ababa, Ethiopia (Telephone Number in U.S. (800) 253-9646); *African Statistical Yearbook.*

NIGER - LIVING LEVELS - See NIGER - LIFE EXPECTANCY

NIGER - MAIL - PIECES SENT OR RECEIVED

Statistical Office of the United Nations, Publishing Service, New York, New York 10017 (800) 253-9646; *Statistical Yearbook.*

NIGER - MANUFACTURING

M.E. Sharpe, 80 Business Park Drive, Armonk, New York 10504 (800) 541-6563; *The Illustrated Book of World Rankings.*

Statistical Office of the United Nations, Publishing Service, New York, New York 10017 (800) 253-9646; *Statistical Yearbook; and Survey of Economic and Social Conditions in Africa.*

United Nations Economic Commission for Africa, Africa Hall, Post Office Box 3001, Addis Ababa, Ethiopia (Telephone Number in U.S. (800) 253-9646); *African Statistical Yearbook.*

The World Bank, 1818 H Street, NW, Washington, D.C. 20433 (202) 477-1234; *World Development Indicators.*

NIGER - MARRIAGE RATES

M.E. Sharpe, 80 Business Park Drive, Armonk, New York 10504 (800) 541-6563; *The Illustrated Book of World Rankings.*

Statistical Office of the United Nations, Publishing Service, New York, New York 10017 (800) 253-9646; *Demographic*

Yearbook.

NIGER - MEAT PRODUCTION - ALL TYPES OF MEAT AND POULTRY

Food and Agricultural Organization of the United Nations (FAO), Via delle Terme di Caracalla, 00100 Rome, Italy (Telephone Number in U.S. (202) 653-2400); *Production Yearbook;* and *The State of Food and Agriculture.*

M.E. Sharpe, 80 Business Park Drive, Armonk, New York 10504 (800) 541-6563; *The Illustrated Book of World Rankings.*

Statistical Office of the United Nations, Publishing Service, New York, New York 10017 (800) 253-9646; *Statistical Yearbook.*

NIGER - MERCHANT SHIPPING

St. Martin's Press, Inc., 175 Fifth Avenue, New York, New York 10010 (800) 221-7945; *The Statesman's Year-Book.*

United Nations Economic Commission for Africa, Africa Hall, Post Office Box 3001, Addis Ababa, Ethiopia (Telephone Number in U.S. (800) 253-9646); *African Statistical Yearbook.*

NIGER - MILITARY

Central Intelligence Agency, Washington, D.C. 20505 (703) 482-1100, www.cia.gov; *The World Factbook.*

Euromonitor International, Inc., 122 South Michigan Avenue, Suite 1200, Chicago, Illinois 60603 (800) 577-EURO; *World Marketing Data and Statistics.*

The International Institute for Strategic Studies, 23 Tavistock Street, London WC2E 7NQ, England; *The Military Balance.*

International Monetary Fund, 700 Nineteenth Street, NW, Washington, D.C. 20431 (202) 623-7000; *Government Finance Statistics Yearbook.*

St. Martin's Press, Inc., 175 Fifth Avenue, New York, New York 10010 (800) 221-7945; *The Statesman's Year-Book.*

Statistical Office of the United Nations, Publishing Service, New York, New York 10017 (800) 253-9646; *Human Development Report.*

U.S. Arms Control and Disarmament Agency, 320 Twenty-first Street, NW, Washington, D.C. 20451 (202) 647-8677; *World Military Expenditures and Arms Transfers.*

NIGER - MILK PRODUCTION - See NIGER - DAIRY PRODUCTS

NIGER - MILLET PRODUCTION - See

NIGER - CROPS

NIGER - MINING AND MINERAL PRODUCTS

Commodity Research Bureau, Inc., 30 South Wacker Drive, Chicago, Illinois 60606 (312) 454-1801; *Commodity Year Book.*

Europa Publications Limited, 18 Bedford Square, London, WC1B 3JN, England; *The Europa World Year Book.*

M.E. Sharpe, 80 Business Park Drive, Armonk, New York 10504 (800) 541-6563; *The Illustrated Book of World Rankings.*

St. Martin's Press, Inc., 175 Fifth Avenue, New York, New York 10010 (800) 221-7945; *The Statesman's Year-Book.*

Statistical Office of the United Nations, Publishing Service, New York, New York 10017 (800) 253-9646; *Statistical Yearbook.*

United Nations Conference on Trade and Development, Central Statistical Service, Palais des Nations, Geneva, Switzerland (Telephone in U.S. (800) 253-9646); *UNCTAD Commodity Yearbook.*

United Nations Economic Commission for Africa, Africa Hall, Post Office Box 3001, Addis Ababa, Ethiopia (Telephone Number in U.S. (800) 253-9646); *African Statistical Yearbook.*

NIGER - MONEY EXCHANGE RATE - See NIGER - EXCHANGE RATES

NIGER - MONEY RESERVES

Euromonitor International, Inc., 122 South Michigan Avenue, Suite 1200, Chicago, Illinois 60603 (800) 577-EURO; *International Marketing Data and Statistics.*

NIGER - MONEY SUPPLY

African Development Bank, 01 BP 1387, Abidjan 01, Cote d'Ivoire; *Selected Statistics on Regional Member Countries.*

Economist Intelligence Unit, 111 West 57th Street, New York, New York 10019 (800) 938-4685; *Niger Country Report.*

Euromonitor International, Inc., 122 South Michigan Avenue, Suite 1200, Chicago, Illinois 60603 (800) 577-EURO; *International Marketing Data and Statistics.*

Europa Publications Limited, 18 Bedford Square, London, WC1B 3JN, England; *The Europa World Year Book.*

International Monetary Fund, 700 Nineteenth Street, NW, Washington, D.C. 20431 (202) 623-7000; *International Financial Statistics.*

Statistical Office of the United Nations, Publishing Service, New York, New York 10017 (800) 253-9646; *Statistical Yearbook.*

The World Bank, 1818 H Street, NW, Washington, D.C. 20433 (202) 477-1234; *World Development Indicators.*

NIGER - MORTALITY

Central Intelligence Agency, Washington, D.C. 20505 (703) 482-1100, www.cia.gov; *The World Factbook.*

Euromonitor International, Inc., 122 South Michigan Avenue, Suite 1200, Chicago, Illinois 60603 (800) 577-EURO; *International Marketing Data and Statistics;* and *The World Economic Factbook.*

Europa Publications Limited, 18 Bedford Square, London, WC1B 3JN, England; *The Europa World Year Book.*

St. Martin's Press, Inc., 175 Fifth Avenue, New York, New York 10010 (800) 221-7945; *The Statesman's Year-Book.*

Statistical Office of the United Nations, Publishing Service, New York, New York 10017 (800) 253-9646; *Demographic Yearbook; Human Development Report; Statistical Yearbook; World Statistics Pocketbook;* and *Survey of Economic and Social Conditions in Africa.*

United Nations Children's Fund (UNICEF), 3 United Nations Plaza, New York, New York 10017 (800) 253-9646; *State of the World's Children.*

The World Bank, 1818 H Street, NW, Washington, D.C. 20433 (202) 477-1234; *The World Bank Atlas; World Development Report;* and *World Development Indicators.*

World Health Organization, Office of Publications, 20 Avenue Appia, CH-1211 Geneva 27, Switzerland (Telephone Number in U.S. (518) 436-9686); *World Health Statistics Annual.*

NIGER - MOTOR VEHICLE TAXES - See NIGER - TAXATION

NIGER - MOTOR VEHICLES IN USE

Europa Publications Limited, 18 Bedford Square, London, WC1B 3JN, England; *The Europa World Year Book.*

Statistical Office of the United Nations, Publishing Service, New York, New York 10017 (800) 253-9646; *Statistical Yearbook;* and *Survey of Economic and Social Conditions in Africa.*

NIGER - MUSEUMS

M.E. Sharpe, 80 Business Park Drive, Armonk, New York 10504 (800) 541-6563;

The Illustrated Book of World Rankings.

United Nations Educational, Scientific and Cultural Organization (UNESCO), 7 Place de Fontenoy, F-75700 Paris, France (Telephone Number in U.S. (212) 963-5981); *Statistical Yearbook.*

NIGER - NATALITY - See NIGER - BIRTH RATES

NIGER - NATIONAL ACCOUNTS

African Development Bank, 01 BP 1387, Abidjan 01, Cote d'Ivoire; *Selected Statistics on Regional Member Countries.*

Europa Publications Limited, 18 Bedford Square, London, WC1B 3JN, England; *The Europa World Year Book.*

International Monetary Fund, 700 Nineteenth Street, NW, Washington, D.C. 20431 (202) 623-7000; *International Financial Statistics.*

Statistical Office of the United Nations, Publishing Service, New York, New York 10017 (800) 253-9646; *Statistical Yearbook.*

United Nations Economic Commission for Africa, Africa Hall, Post Office Box 3001, Addis Ababa, Ethiopia (Telephone Number in U.S. (800) 253-9646); *African Statistical Yearbook.*

NIGER - NATIONAL INCOME

M.E. Sharpe, 80 Business Park Drive, Armonk, New York 10504 (800) 541-6563; *The Illustrated Book of World Rankings.*

Statistical Office of the United Nations, Publishing Service, New York, New York 10017 (800) 253-9646; *National Accounts Statistics;* and *Statistical Yearbook.*

NIGER - NATIONAL PRODUCT

M.E. Sharpe, 80 Business Park Drive, Armonk, New York 10504 (800) 541-6563; *The Illustrated Book of World Rankings.*

NIGER - NATURAL GAS PRODUCTION - See NIGER - MINING AND MINERAL PRODUCTS

NIGER - NEWSPAPER PRODUCTION - See NIGER - FORESTRY AND FOREST PRODUCTS

NIGER - NEWSPRINT - See NIGER - FORESTRY AND FOREST PRODUCTS

NIGER - OCCUPATIONS - See NIGER - LABOR

NIGER - PAPER - See NIGER - FORESTRY AND FOREST PRODUCTS

NIGER - PEANUT PRODUCTION - See

NIGER - CROPS

NIGER - PERIODICALS

United Nations Educational, Scientific and Cultural Organization (UNESCO), 7 Place de Fontenoy, F-75700 Paris, France (Telephone Number in U.S. (212) 963-5981); *Statistical Yearbook.*

NIGER - PESTICIDE USE

Food and Agricultural Organization of the United Nations (FAO) Via delle Terme di Caracalla, 00100 Rome, Italy (Telephone Number in U.S. (202) 653- 400); *The State of Food and Agriculture.*

NIGER - PETROLEUM INDUSTRY

Food and Agricultural Organization of the United Nations (FAO) Via delle Terme di Caracalla, 00100 Rome, Italy (Telephone Number in U.S. (202) 653-2400); *The State of Food and Agriculture.*

M.E. Sharpe, 80 Business Park Drive, Armonk, New York 10504 (800) 541-6563; *The Illustrated Book of World Rankings.*

United Nations Conference on Trade and Development, Central Statistical Service, Palais des Nations, Geneva, Switzerland (Telephone in U.S. (800) 253-9646); *UNCTAD Commodity Yearbook.*

NIGER - PIGS - See NIGER - LIVESTOCK AND POULTRY

NIGER - POPULATION

African Development Bank, 01 BP 1387, Abidjan 01, Cote d'Ivoire; *Selected Statistics on Regional Member Countries.*

Central Intelligence Agency, Washington, D.C. 20505 (703) 482-1100, www.cia.gov; *The World Factbook.*

The Economist Intelligence Unit, 111 West 57th Street, New York, New York 10019 (800) 938-4685; *Niger Country Report;* and *The World Market Atlas.*

Euromonitor International, Inc., 122 South Michigan Avenue, Suite 1200, Chicago, Illinois 60603 (800) 577-EURO; *International Marketing Data and Statistics;* and *The World Economic Factbook.*

Europa Publications Limited, 18 Bedford Square, London, WC1B 3JN, England; *The Europa World Year Book.*

Food and Agricultural Organization of the United Nations (FAO), Via delle Terme di Caracalla, 00100 Rome, Italy (Telephone Number in U.S. (202) 653-2400); *Production Yearbook.*

NIGER - CROPS

International Labour Office, I.L.O. Publications, 1828 L Street, NW, Suite 801, Washington, D.C. 20036 (301) 638-3152; *Yearbook of Labour Statistics.*

M.E. Sharpe, 80 Business Park Drive, Armonk, New York 10504 (800) 541-6563; *The Illustrated Book of World Rankings.*

St. Martin's Press, Inc., 175 Fifth Avenue, New York, New York 10010 (800) 221-7945; *The Statesman's Year-Book.*

Statistical Office of the United Nations, Publishing Service, New York, New York 10017 (800) 253-9646; *Demographic Yearbook; Human Development Report; Statistical Yearbook; World Statistics Pocketbook;* and *Survey of Economic and Social Conditions in Africa.*

United Nations Educational, Scientific and Cultural Organization (UNESCO), 7 Place de Fontenoy, F-75700 Paris, France (Telephone Number in U.S. (212) 963-5981); *Statistical Yearbook.*

U.S. Arms Control and Disarmament Agency, 320 Twenty-first Street, NW, Washington, D.C. 20451 (202) 647-8677; *World Military Expenditures and Arms Transfers.*

The World Bank, 1818 H Street, NW, Washington, D.C. 20433 (202) 477-1234; *The World Bank Atlas;* and *World Development Report.*

World Health Organization, Office of Publications, 20 Avenue Appia, CH-1211 Geneva 27, Switzerland (Telephone Number in U.S. (518) 436-9686); *World Health Statistics Annual.*

NIGER - POST OFFICES

M.E. Sharpe, 80 Business Park Drive, Armonk, New York 10504 (800) 541-6563; *The Illustrated Book of World Rankings.*

St. Martin's Press, Inc., 175 Fifth Avenue, New York, New York 10010 (800) 221-7945; *The Statesman's Year-Book.*

NIGER - POTATO PRODUCTION - See NIGER - CROPS

NIGER - PRICES

Food and Agricultural Organization of the United Nations (FAO), Via delle Terme di Caracalla, 00100 Rome, Italy (Telephone Number in U.S. (202) 653-2400); *Production Yearbook;* and *The State of Food and Agriculture.*

International Labour Office, I.L.O. Publications, 1828 L Street, NW, Suite 801, Washington, D.C. 20036 (301) 638-3152; *Yearbook of Labour Statistics.*

International Monetary Fund, 700 Nineteenth Street, NW, Washington, D.C. 20431 (202) 623-7000; *International Financial Statistics.*

M.E. Sharpe, 80 Business Park Drive, Armonk, New York 10504 (800) 541-6563; *The Illustrated Book of World Rankings.*

United Nations Economic Commission for Africa, Africa Hall, Post Office Box 3001, Addis Ababa, Ethiopia (Telephone Number in U.S. (800) 253-9646); *African Statistical Yearbook.*

NIGER - PRINTING AND WRITING PAPER - See NIGER - FORESTRY AND FOREST PRODUCTS

NIGER - PRODUCTION

M.E. Sharpe, 80 Business Park Drive, Armonk, New York 10504 (800) 541-6563; *The Illustrated Book of World Rankings.*

NIGER - PRODUCTIVITY

Euromonitor International, Inc., 122 South Michigan Avenue, Suite 1200, Chicago, Illinois 60603 (800) 577-EURO; *International Marketing Data and Statistics.*

NIGER - PROPERTY TAXES

International Monetary Fund, 700 Nineteenth Street, NW, Washington, D.C. 20431 (202) 623-7000; *Government Finance Statistics Yearbook.*

NIGER - PUBLIC FINANCE - See NIGER - FINANCE

NIGER - RADIO BROADCASTING - See NIGER - BROADCASTING

NIGER - RADIO RECEIVERS

St. Martin's Press, Inc., 175 Fifth Avenue, New York, New York 10010 (800) 221-7945; *The Statesman's Year-Book.*

NIGER - RAILWAYS

United Nations Economic Commission for Africa, Africa Hall, Post Office Box 3001, Addis Ababa, Ethiopia (Telephone Number in U.S. (800) 253-9646); *African Statistical Yearbook.*

NIGER - RELIGION

Central Intelligence Agency, Washington, D.C. 20505 (703) 482-1100, www.cia.gov; *The World Factbook.*

M.E. Sharpe, 80 Business Park Drive, Armonk, New York 10504 (800) 541-6563; *The Illustrated Book of World Rankings.*

St. Martin's Press, Inc., 175 Fifth Avenue, New York, New York 10010 (800) 221-7945; *The Statesman's Year-Book.*

NIGER - RETAIL TRADE

Euromonitor International, Inc., 122 South Michigan Avenue, Suite 1200, Chicago, Illinois 60603 (800) 577-EURO; *World Marketing Data and Statistics.*

NIGER - RICE PRODUCTION - See NIGER - CROPS

NIGER - ROOT AND TUBER PRODUCTION - See NIGER - CROPS

NIGER - ROUNDWOOD PRODUCTION - See NIGER - FORESTRY AND FOREST PRODUCTS

NIGER - RUBBER PRODUCTION AND CONSUMPTION

M.E. Sharpe, 80 Business Park Drive, Armonk, New York 10504 (800) 541-6563; *The Illustrated Book of World Rankings.*

NIGER - SALT PRODUCTION - See NIGER - MINING AND MINERAL PRODUCTS

NIGER - SAWNWOOD PRODUCTION - See NIGER - FORESTRY AND FOREST PRODUCTS

NIGER - SCIENCE AND TECHNOLOGY - EXPENDITURE FOR RESEARCH - See NIGER - SCIENTISTS, TECHNICIANS AND ENGINEERS

NIGER - SCIENTISTS, TECHNICIANS AND ENGINEERS

Statistical Office of the United Nations, Publishing Service, New York, New York 10017 (800) 253-9646; *Statistical Yearbook.*

NIGER - SENIOR CITIZENS

M.E. Sharpe, 80 Business Park Drive, Armonk, New York 10504 (800) 541-6563; *The Illustrated Book of World Rankings.*

NIGER - SHEEP - See NIGER - LIVESTOCK AND POULTRY

NIGER - SILVER PRODUCTION AND CONSUMPTION - See NIGER - MINING AND MINERAL PRODUCTS

NIGER - SOCIAL DATA

African Development Bank, 01 BP 1387, Abidjan 01, Cote d'Ivoire; *Selected Statistics on Regional Member Countries.*

M.E. Sharpe, 80 Business Park Drive, Armonk, New York 10504 (800) 541-6563; *The Illustrated Book of World Rankings.*

Statistical Office of the United Nations, Publishing Service, New York, New York 10017 (800) 253-9646; *World Statistics Pocketbook.*

NIGER - SOCIAL SECURITY

International Monetary Fund, 700 Nineteenth Street, NW, Washington, D.C. 20431 (202) 623-7000; *Government Finance Statistics Yearbook.*

Statistical Office of the United Nations, Publishing Service, New York, New York 10017 (800) 253-9646; *National Accounts Statistics.*

NIGER - STAMP TAXES AND DUTIES - See NIGER - TAXATION

NIGER - STATE BUDGET REVENUE AND EXPENDITURES

Euromonitor International, Inc., 122 South Michigan Avenue, Suite 1200, Chicago, Illinois 60603 (800) 577-EURO; *International Marketing Data and Statistics.*

NIGER - STEEL PRODUCTION - See NIGER - MINING AND MINERAL PRODUCTS

NIGER - STOCKS - COMMODITY - MARKET PRICE - INDEX

Food and Agricultural Organization of the United Nations (FAO) Via delle Terme di Caracalla, 00100 Rome, Italy (Telephone Number in U.S. (202) 653-2400); *The State of Food and Agriculture.*

NIGER - SUGAR PRODUCTION AND CONSUMPTION - See NIGER - CROPS

NIGER - TAX REVENUES - See NIGER - TAXATION

NIGER - TAXATION

Europa Publications Limited, 18 Bedford Square, London, WC1B 3JN, England; *The Europa World Year Book.*

International Monetary Fund, 700 Nineteenth Street, NW, Washington, D.C. 20431 (202) 623-7000; *Government Finance Statistics Yearbook.*

St. Martin's Press, Inc., 175 Fifth Avenue, New York, New York 10010 (800) 221-7945; *The Statesman's Year-Book.*

The World Bank, 1818 H Street, NW, Washington, D.C. 20433 (202) 477-1234; *World Development Indicators.*

NIGER - TELEGRAPH SERVICE

Statistical Office of the United Nations, Publishing Service, New York, New York 10017 (800) 253-9646; *Statistical Yearbook.*

NIGER - TELEPHONES IN USE

American Telephone and Telegraph

Company, 26 Parsippany Road, Whippany, New Jersey 07981 (800) 222-0300; *The World's Telephones.*

Central Intelligence Agency, Washington, D.C. 20505 (703) 482-1100, www.cia.gov; *The World Factbook.*

Europa Publications Limited, 18 Bedford Square, London, WC1B 3JN, England; *The Europa World Year Book.*

St. Martin's Press, Inc., 175 Fifth Avenue, New York, New York 10010 (800) 221-7945; *The Statesman's Year-Book.*

Statistical Office of the United Nations, Publishing Service, New York, New York 10017 (800) 253-9646; *Statistical Yearbook;* and *World Statistics Pocketbook.*

NIGER - TELEVISION PRODUCTION

M.E. Sharpe, 80 Business Park Drive, Armonk, New York 10504 (800) 541-6563; *The Illustrated Book of World Rankings.*

NIGER - TEXTILE INDUSTRY

M.E. Sharpe, 80 Business Park Drive, Armonk, New York 10504 (800) 541-6563; *The Illustrated Book of World Rankings.*

St. Martin's Press, Inc., 175 Fifth Avenue, New York, New York 10010 (800) 221-7945; *The Statesman's Year-Book.*

United Nations Conference on Trade and Development, Central Statistical Service, Palais des Nations, Geneva, Switzerland (Telephone in U.S. (800) 253-9646); *UNCTAD Commodity Yearbook.*

NIGER - TIN PRODUCTION AND CONSUMPTION - See NIGER - MINING AND MINERAL PRODUCTS

NIGER - TOBACCO PRODUCTION

M.E. Sharpe, 80 Business Park Drive, Armonk, New York 10504 (800) 541-6563; *The Illustrated Book of World Rankings.*

Statistical Office of the United Nations, Publishing Service, New York, New York 10017 (800) 253-9646; *Statistical Yearbook.*

NIGER - TOURISM

Euromonitor International, Inc., 122 South Michigan Avenue, Suite 1200, Chicago, Illinois 60603 (800) 577-EURO; *The World Economic Factbook;* and *World Marketing Data and Statistics.*

Europa Publications Limited, 18 Bedford Square, London, WC1B 3JN, England; *The Europa World Year Book.*

M.E. Sharpe, 80 Business Park Drive, Armonk, New York 10504 (800) 541-6563;

The Illustrated Book of World Rankings.

St. Martin's Press, Inc., 175 Fifth Avenue, New York, New York 10010 (800) 221-7945; *The Statesman's Year-Book.*

United Nations Economic Commission for Africa, Africa Hall, Post Office Box 3001, Addis Ababa, Ethiopia (Telephone Number in U.S. (800) 253-9646); *African Statistical Yearbook.*

World Tourism Organization, Calle Capitan Haya 42, E-28020 Madrid, Spain; *Yearbook of Tourism Statistics.*

NIGER - TRACTORS IN USE

Statistical Office of the United Nations, Publishing Service, New York, New York 10017 (800) 253-9646; *Statistical Yearbook.*

NIGER - TRADE - See NIGER - FOREIGN TRADE

NIGER - TRANSPORTATION AND COMMUNICATIONS

Central Intelligence Agency, Washington, D.C. 20505 (703) 482-1100, www.cia.gov; *The World Factbook.*

Euromonitor International, Inc., 122 South Michigan Avenue, Suite 1200, Chicago, Illinois 60603 (800) 577-EURO; *International Marketing Data and Statistics;* and *World Marketing Data and Statistics.*

Europa Publications Limited, 18 Bedford Square, London, WC1B 3JN, England; *The Europa World Year Book.*

M.E. Sharpe, 80 Business Park Drive, Armonk, New York 10504 (800) 541-6563; *The Illustrated Book of World Rankings.*

St. Martin's Press, Inc., 175 Fifth Avenue, New York, New York 10010 (800) 221-7945; *The Statesman's Year-Book.*

Statistical Office of the United Nations, Publishing Service, New York, New York 10017 (800) 253-9646; *Human Development Report.*

United Nations Economic Commission for Africa, Africa Hall, Post Office Box 3001, Addis Ababa, Ethiopia (Telephone Number in U.S. (800) 253-9646); *African Statistical Yearbook.*

NIGER - UNEMPLOYMENT

Central Intelligence Agency, Washington, D.C. 20505 (703) 482-1100, www.cia.gov; *The World Factbook.*

Euromonitor International, Inc., 122 South Michigan Avenue, Suite 1200, Chicago, Illinois 60603 (800) 577-EURO; *International Marketing Data and Statistics.*

International Labour Office, I.L.O. Publications, 1828 L Street, NW, Suite 801, Washington, D.C. 20036 (301) 638-3152; *Yearbook of Labour Statistics.*

St. Martin's Press, Inc., 175 Fifth Avenue, New York, New York 10010 (800) 221-7945; *The Statesman's Year-Book.*

Statistical Office of the United Nations, Publishing Service, New York, New York 10017 (800) 253-9646; *Statistical Yearbook.*

NIGER - URANIUM PRODUCTION AND CONSUMPTION - See NIGER -MINING AND MINERAL PRODUCTS

NIGER - VITAL STATISTICS

Euromonitor International, Inc., 122 South Michigan Avenue, Suite 1200, Chicago, Illinois 60603 (800) 577-EURO; *International Marketing Data and Statistics.*

St. Martin's Press, Inc., 175 Fifth Avenue, New York, New York 10010 (800) 221-7945; *The Statesman's Year-Book.*

Statistical Office of the United Nations, Publishing Service, New York, New York 10017 (800) 253-9646; *Statistical Yearbook.*

World Health Organization, Office of Publications, 20 Avenue Appia, CH-1211 Geneva 27, Switzerland (Telephone Number in U.S. (518) 436-9686); *World Health Statistics Annual.*

NIGER - WAGES

International Labour Office, I.L.O. Publications, 1828 L Street, NW, Suite 801, Washington, D.C. 20036 (301) 638-3152; *Yearbook of Labour Statistics.*

NIGER - WEATHER - See NIGER - CLIMATE

NIGER - WELFARE

International Monetary Fund, 700 Nineteenth Street, NW, Washington, D.C. 20431 (202) 623-7000; *Government Finance Statistics Yearbook.*

NIGER - WHEAT PRODUCTION AND PRICES - See NIGER - CROPS

NIGER - WINE PRODUCTION - See NIGER - BEVERAGES

NIGER - WOOL PRODUCTION - See NIGER - TEXTILE INDUSTRY

Nigeria - National Statistical Office

Federal Office of Statistics, 36-38 Broad Street, PM Bag 12528, Lagos, Nigeria.

Nigeria - Primary Statistics Sources

Federal Office of Statistics, 36 - 38 Broad Street, PM Bag 12528, Lagos, Nigeria; *Annual Abstract of Statistics;* and *Digest of Statistics,* quarterly.

NIGERIA - AGRICULTURE

Economist Intelligence Unit, 111 West 57th Street, New York, New York 10019 (800) 938-4685; *Nigeria Country Report.*

Euromonitor International, Inc., 122 South Michigan Avenue, Suite 1200, Chicago, Illinois 60603 (800) 577-EURO; *International Marketing Data and Statistics;* and *World Marketing Data and Statistics.*

Europa Publications Limited, 18 Bedford Square, London, WC1B 3JN, England; *The Europa World Year Book.*

Food and Agricultural Organization of the United Nations (FAO) Via delle Terme di Caracalla, 00100 Rome, Italy (Telephone Number in U.S. (202) 653-2400); *Production Yearbook; The State of Food and Agriculture;* and *Trade Yearbook.*

M.E. Sharpe, 80 Business Park Drive, Armonk, New York 10504 (800) 541-6563; *The Illustrated Book of World Rankings.*

St. Martin's Press, Inc., 175 Fifth Avenue, New York, New York 10010 (800) 221-7945; *The Statesman's Year-Book.*

Statistical Office of the United Nations, Publishing Service, New York, New York 10017 (800) 253-9646; *Statistical Yearbook;* and *Survey of Economic and Social Conditions in Africa.*

United Nations Conference on Trade and Development, Central Statistical Service, Palais des Nations, Geneva, Switzerland (Telephone in U.S. (800) 253-9646); *UNCTAD Commodity Yearbook.*

United Nations Economic Commission for Africa, Africa Hall, Post Office Box 3001, Addis Ababa, Ethiopia (Telephone Number in U.S. (800) 253-9646); *African Statistical Yearbook.*

The World Bank, 1818 H Street, NW, Washington, D.C. 20433 (202) 477-1234; *World Development Indicators.*

NIGERIA - AIRLINE SERVICE

Europa Publications Limited, 18 Bedford Square, London, WC1B 3JN, England; *The Europa World Year Book.*

M.E. Sharpe, 80 Business Park Drive, Armonk, New York 10504 (800) 541-6563; *The Illustrated Book of World Rankings.*

St. Martin's Press, Inc., 175 Fifth Avenue, New York, New York 10010 (800) 221-7945; *The Statesman's Year-Book.*

Statistical Office of the United Nations, Publishing Service, New York, New York 10017 (800) 253-9646; *Statistical Yearbook.*

United Nations Economic Commission for Africa, Africa Hall, Post Office Box 3001, Addis Ababa, Ethiopia (Telephone Number in U.S. (800) 253-9646); *African Statistical Yearbook.*

NIGERIA - AIRPORTS

Central Intelligence Agency, Washington, D.C. 20505 (703) 482-1100, www.cia.gov; *The World Factbook.*

NIGERIA - ALUMINUM PRODUCTION AND CONSUMPTION - See NIGERIA - MINING AND MINERAL PRODUCTS

NIGERIA - ANIMAL HEALTH

Food and Agricultural Organization of the United Nations (FAO), Via delle Terme di Caracalla, 00100 Rome, Italy (Telephone Number in U.S. (202) 653-2400); *Animal Health Yearbook.*

NIGERIA - AREA AND DENSITY OF POPULATION

African Development Bank, 01 BP 1387, Abidjan 01, Cote d'Ivoire; *Selected Statistics on Regional Member Countries.*

Central Intelligence Agency, Washington, D.C. 20505 (703) 482-1100, www.cia.gov; *The World Factbook.*

Euromonitor International, Inc., 122 South Michigan Avenue, Suite 1200, Chicago, Illinois 60603 (800) 577-EURO; *International Marketing Data and Statistics;* and *The World Economic Factbook.*

Europa Publications Limited, 18 Bedford Square, London, WC1B 3JN, England; *The Europa World Year Book.*

Food and Agricultural Organization of the United Nations (FAO) Via delle Terme di Caracalla, 00100 Rome, Italy (Telephone Number in U.S. (202) 653-2400); *The State of Food and Agriculture.*

M.E. Sharpe, 80 Business Park Drive, Armonk, New York 10504 (800) 541-6563; *The Illustrated Book of World Rankings.*

St. Martin's Press, Inc., 175 Fifth Avenue, New York, New York 10010 (800) 221-7945; *The Statesman's Year-Book.*

Statistical Office of the United Nations, Publishing Service, New York, New York 10017 (800) 253-9646; *Statistical Yearbook;* and *Survey of Economic and Social Conditions in Africa.*

United Nations Educational, Scientific and Cultural Organization (UNESCO), 7 Place de Fontenoy, F-75700 Paris, France (Telephone Number in U.S. (212) 963-5981); *Statistical Yearbook.*

The World Bank, 1818 H Street, NW, Washington, D.C. 20433 (202) 477-1234; *World Development Report.*

NIGERIA - ARMS EXPORTS AND IMPORTS - See NIGERIA - MILITARY

NIGERIA - BALANCE OF PAYMENTS

African Development Bank, 01 BP 1387, Abidjan 01, Cote d'Ivoire; *Selected Statistics on Regional Member Countries.*

The Economist Intelligence Unit, 111 West 57th Street, New York, New York 10019 (800) 938-4685; *The World Market Atlas.*

Europa Publications Limited, 18 Bedford Square, London, WC1B 3JN, England; *The Europa World Year Book.*

International Monetary Fund, 700 Nineteenth Street, NW, Washington, D.C. 20431 (202) 623-7000; *Balance of Payments Yearbook.*

United Nations Conference on Trade and Development (UNCTAD), New York, New York 10017 (800) 253-9646; *Handbook of International Trade and Development Statistics.*

United Nations Economic Commission for Africa, Africa Hall, Post Office Box 3001, Addis Ababa, Ethiopia (Telephone Number in U.S. (800) 253-9646); *African Statistical Yearbook.*

The World Bank, 1818 H Street, NW, Washington, D.C. 20433 (202) 477-1234; *World Development Report;* and *World Development Indicators.*

NIGERIA - BANKING

Euromonitor International, Inc., 122 South Michigan Avenue, Suite 1200, Chicago, Illinois 60603 (800) 577-EURO; *World Marketing Data and Statistics.*

Europa Publications Limited, 18 Bedford Square, London, WC1B 3JN, England; *The Europa World Year Book.*

International Monetary Fund, 700 Nineteenth Street, NW, Washington, D.C. 20431 (202) 623-7000; *International Financial Statistics.*

M.E. Sharpe, 80 Business Park Drive, Armonk, New York 10504 (800) 541-6563; *The Illustrated Book of World Rankings.*

St. Martin's Press, Inc., 175 Fifth Avenue, New York, New York 10010 (800) 221-7945; *The Statesman's Year-Book.*

Statistical Office of the United Nations, Publishing Service, New York, New York 10017 (800) 253-9646; *Statistical Yearbook.*

United Nations Economic Commission for Africa, Africa Hall, Post Office Box 3001, Addis Ababa, Ethiopia (Telephone Number in U.S. (800) 253-9646); *African Statistical Yearbook.*

NIGERIA - BARLEY PRODUCTION - See NIGERIA - CROPS

NIGERIA - BEER PRODUCTION - See NIGERIA - BEVERAGES

NIGERIA - BEVERAGES

M.E. Sharpe, 80 Business Park Drive, Armonk, New York 10504 (800) 541-6563; *The Illustrated Book of World Rankings.*

Statistical Office of the United Nations, Publishing Service, New York, New York 10017 (800) 253-9646; *Statistical Yearbook.*

NIGERIA - BIRTH RATES

Central Intelligence Agency, Washington, D.C. 20505 (703) 482-1100, www.cia.gov; *The World Factbook.*

Euromonitor International, Inc., 122 South Michigan Avenue, Suite 1200, Chicago, Illinois 60603 (800) 577-EURO; *International Marketing Data and Statistics;* and *The World Economic Factbook.*

Europa Publications Limited, 18 Bedford Square, London, WC1B 3JN, England; *The Europa World Year Book.*

M.E. Sharpe, 80 Business Park Drive, Armonk, New York 10504 (800) 541-6563; *The Illustrated Book of World Rankings.*

Statistical Office of the United Nations, Publishing Service, New York, New York 10017 (800) 253-9646; *Demographic Yearbook; Statistical Yearbook;* and *Survey of Economic and Social Conditions in Africa.*

The World Bank, 1818 H Street, NW, Washington, D.C. 20433 (202) 477-1234; *World Development Indicators.*

NIGERIA - BONDS

International Monetary Fund, 700 Nineteenth Street, NW, Washington, D.C. 20431 (202) 623-7000; *Government Finance Statistics Yearbook.*

NIGERIA - BOOK PRODUCTION

Europa Publications Limited, 18 Bedford Square, London, WC1B 3JN, England; *The Europa World Year Book.*

St. Martin's Press, Inc., 175 Fifth Avenue, New York, New York 10010 (800) 221-7945; *The Statesman's Year-Book.*

United Nations Educational, Scientific and Cultural Organization (UNESCO), 7 Place de Fontenoy, F-75700 Paris, France (Telephone Number in U.S. (212) 963-5981); *Statistical Yearbook.*

NIGERIA - BROADCASTING

Billboard Limited, Post Office Box 9027, 1006 AA Amsterdam, The Netherlands (Telephone Number in U.S. (212) 764-7300); *World Radio TV Handbook.*

Central Intelligence Agency, Washington, D.C. 20505 (703) 482-1100, www.cia.gov; *The World Factbook.*

Euromonitor International, Inc., 122 South Michigan Avenue, Suite 1200, Chicago, Illinois 60603 (800) 577-EURO; *World Marketing Data and Statistics.*

M.E. Sharpe, 80 Business Park Drive, Armonk, New York 10504 (800) 541-6563; *The Illustrated Book of World Rankings.*

St. Martin's Press, Inc., 175 Fifth Avenue, New York, New York 10010 (800) 221-7945; *The Statesman's Year-Book.*

NIGERIA - BUDGET

Central Intelligence Agency, Washington, D.C. 20505 (703) 482-1100, www.cia.gov; *The World Factbook.*

NIGERIA - BUSINESS AND PROFESSIONAL LICENSES

International Monetary Fund, 700 Nineteenth Street, NW, Washington, D.C. 20431 (202) 623-7000; *Government Finance Statistics Yearbook.*

NIGERIA - BUTTER PRODUCTION - See NIGERIA - DAIRY PRODUCTS

NIGERIA - CACAO EXPORTS

International Monetary Fund, 700 Nineteenth Street, NW, Washington, D.C. 20431 (202) 623-7000; *International Financial Statistics.*

NIGERIA - CALORIE SUPPLY

African Development Bank, 01 BP 1387, Abidjan 01, Cote d'Ivoire; *Selected Statistics on Regional Member Countries.*

Food and Agricultural Organization of the United Nations (FAO) Via delle Terme di Caracalla, 00100 Rome, Italy (Telephone Number in U.S. (202) 653-2400); *The State of Food and Agriculture.*

NIGERIA - CAPITAL REVENUE

International Monetary Fund, 700 Nineteenth Street, NW, Washington, D.C. 20431 (202) 623-7000; *Government Finance Statistics Yearbook.*

NIGERIA - CATTLE - See NIGERIA - LIVESTOCK AND POULTRY

NIGERIA - CEMENT PRODUCTION - See NIGERIA - MINING AND MINERAL PRODUCTS

NIGERIA - CHEESE PRODUCTION AND CONSUMPTION - See NIGERIA - DAIRY PRODUCTS

NIGERIA - CHICKENS - See NIGERIA - LIVESTOCK AND POULTRY

NIGERIA - CIGARETTE PRODUCTION - See NIGERIA - TOBACCO PRODUCTION

NIGERIA - CLIMATE

M.E. Sharpe, 80 Business Park Drive, Armonk, New York 10504 (800) 541-6563; *The Illustrated Book of World Rankings.*

St. Martin's Press, Inc., 175 Fifth Avenue, New York, New York 10010 (800) 221-7945; *The Statesman's Year-Book.*

NIGERIA - COAL PRODUCTION - See NIGERIA - MINING AND MINERAL PRODUCTS

NIGERIA - COCOA (BEANS) PRODUCTION - See NIGERIA - CROPS

NIGERIA - COFFEE PRODUCTION AND CONSUMPTION - See NIGERIA - CROPS

NIGERIA - COMMERCE

St. Martin's Press, Inc., 175 Fifth Avenue, New York, New York 10010 (800) 221-7945; *The Statesman's Year-Book.*

NIGERIA - COMMUNICATIONS - See NIGERIA - TRANSPORTATION AND COMMUNICATIONS

NIGERIA - CONSTRUCTION INDUSTRY

M.E. Sharpe, 80 Business Park Drive, Armonk, New York 10504 (800) 541-6563; *The Illustrated Book of World Rankings.*

Statistical Office of the United Nations, Publishing Service, New York, New York 10017 (800) 253-9646; *Statistical Yearbook.*

United Nations Economic Commission for Africa, Africa Hall, Post Office Box 3001, Addis Ababa, Ethiopia (Telephone Number in U.S. (800) 253-9646); *African Statistical Yearbook.*

NIGERIA - CONSUMER PRICE INDEX

African Development Bank, 01 BP 1387, Abidjan 01, Cote d'Ivoire; *Selected Statistics on Regional Member Countries.*

Europa Publications Limited, 18 Bedford Square, London, WC1B 3JN, England; *The Europa World Year Book.*

Statistical Office of the United Nations, Publishing Service, New York, New York 10017 (800) 253-9646; *Statistical Yearbook;* and *Survey of Economic and Social Conditions in Africa.*

United Nations Economic Commission for Africa, Africa Hall, Post Office Box 3001, Addis Ababa, Ethiopia (Telephone Number in U.S. (800) 253-9646); *African Statistical Yearbook.*

NIGERIA - CONSUMER PRICES

Euromonitor International, Inc., 122 South Michigan Avenue, Suite 1200, Chicago, Illinois 60603 (800) 577-EURO; *World Marketing Data and Statistics.*

International Labour Office, I.L.O. Publications, 1828 L Street, NW, Suite 801, Washington, D.C. 20036 (301) 638-3152; *Yearbook of Labour Statistics.*

International Monetary Fund, 700 Nineteenth Street, NW, Washington, D.C. 20431 (202) 623-7000; *International Financial Statistics.*

NIGERIA - CONSUMPTION

African Development Bank, 01 BP 1387, Abidjan 01, Cote d'Ivoire; *Selected Statistics on Regional Member Countries.*

International Rubber Study Group, York House, Eighth Floor, Empire Way, Wembley, London HA9 0PA, England; *Rubber Statistical Bulletin.*

Statistical Office of the United Nations, Publishing Service, New York 10017 (800) 253-9646; *Survey of Economic and Social Conditions in Africa.*

The World Bank, 1818 H Street, NW, Washington, D.C. 20433 (202) 477-1234; *World Development Report.*

NIGERIA - COPPER PRODUCTION AND CONSUMPTION - See NIGERIA - MINING AND MINERAL PRODUCTS

NIGERIA - CORN PRODUCTION - See NIGERIA - CROPS

NIGERIA - CORPORATE TAXES - See NIGERIA - TAXATION

NIGERIA - COTTON - See NIGERIA - CROPS

NIGERIA - CRIME

International Criminal Police Organization (INTERPOL), 50 quai Achille Lignon, F-69006 Lyon, France; *International Crime Statistics.*

Yale University Press, Yale Station, New Haven, Connecticut 06520 (800) 987-7323; *Violence and Crime in Cross-National Perspective.*

NIGERIA - CROPS

Commodity Research Bureau, Inc., 30 South Wacker Drive, Chicago, Illinois 60606 (312) 454-1801; *Commodity Year Book.*

Europa Publications Limited, 18 Bedford Square, London, WC1B 3JN, England; *The Europa World Year Book.*

Food and Agricultural Organization of the United Nations (FAO) Via delle Terme di Caracalla, 00100 Rome, Italy (Telephone Number in U.S. (202) 653-2400); *The State of Food and Agriculture;* and *Production Yearbook.*

M.E. Sharpe, 80 Business Park Drive, Armonk, New York 10504 (800) 541-6563; *The Illustrated Book of World Rankings.*

St. Martin's Press, Inc., 175 Fifth Avenue, New York, New York 10010 (800) 221-7945; *The Statesman's Year-Book.*

Statistical Office of the United Nations, Publishing Service, New York, New York 10017 (800) 253-9646; *Statistical Yearbook.*

United Nations Conference on Trade and Development, Central Statistical Service, Palais des Nations, Geneva, Switzerland (Telephone in U.S. (800) 253-9646); *UNCTAD Commodity Yearbook.*

United Nations Economic Commission for Africa, Africa Hall, Post Office Box 3001, Addis Ababa, Ethiopia (Telephone Number in U.S. (800) 253-9646); *African Statistical Yearbook.*

NIGERIA - CUSTOMS DUTIES

International Monetary Fund, 700 Nineteenth Street, NW, Washington, D.C. 20431 (202) 623-7000; *Government Finance Statistics Yearbook.*

St. Martin's Press, Inc., 175 Fifth Avenue, New York, New York 10010 (800) 221-7945; *The Statesman's Year-Book.*

NIGERIA - DAIRY PRODUCTS

Europa Publications Limited, 18 Bedford Square, London, WC1B 3JN, England; *The Europa World Year Book.*

Food and Agricultural Organization of the United Nations (FAO) Via delle Terme di Caracalla, 00100 Rome, Italy (Telephone Number in U.S. (202) 653-2400); *The State of Food and Agriculture.*

M.E. Sharpe, 80 Business Park Drive, Armonk, New York 10504 (800) 541-6563; *The Illustrated Book of World Rankings.*

St. Martin's Press, Inc., 175 Fifth Avenue, New York, New York 10010 (800) 221-7945; *The Statesman's Year-Book.*

Statistical Office of the United Nations, Publishing Service, New York, New York 10017 (800) 253-9646; *Statistical Yearbook.*

NIGERIA - DEATH RATES - See NIGERIA - MORTALITY

NIGERIA - DEFENSE EXPENDITURES - See NIGERIA - MILITARY

NIGERIA - DEMOGRAPHY

The Economist Intelligence Unit, 111 West 57th Street, New York, New York 10019 (800) 938-4685; *The World Market Atlas.*

Euromonitor International, Inc., 122 South Michigan Avenue, Suite 1200, Chicago, Illinois 60603 (800) 577-EURO; *International Marketing Data and Statistics; The World Economic Factbook;* and *World Marketing Data and Statistics.*

M.E. Sharpe, 80 Business Park Drive, Armonk, New York 10504 (800) 541-6563; *The Illustrated Book of World Rankings.*

Statistical Office of the United Nations, Publishing Service, New York 10017 (800) 253-9646; *Human Development Report;* and *Survey of Economic and Social Conditions in Africa.*

NIGERIA - DEVELOPMENT ASSISTANCE

Statistical Office of the United Nations, Publishing Service, New York, New York 10017 (800) 253-9646; *Statistical Yearbook.*

NIGERIA - DIAMOND PRODUCTION - See NIGERIA - MINING AND MINERAL PRODUCTS

NIGERIA - DISCOUNT RATES - See NIGERIA - BANKING

NIGERIA - DISEASE - See NIGERIA - HEALTH

NIGERIA - DIVORCE RATES

M.E. Sharpe, 80 Business Park Drive, Armonk, New York 10504 (800) 541-6563; *The Illustrated Book of World Rankings.*

Statistical Office of the United Nations, Publishing Service, New York, New York

10017 (800) 253-9646; *Demographic Yearbook.*

NIGERIA - ECONOMY

African Development Bank, 01 BP 1387, Abidjan 01, Cote d'Ivoire; *Selected Statistics on Regional Member Countries.*

Central Intelligence Agency, Washington, D.C. 20505 (703) 482-1100, www.cia.gov; *The World Factbook.*

Economist Intelligence Unit, 111 West 57th Street, New York, New York 10019 (800) 938-4685; *Nigeria Country Report.*

Euromonitor International, Inc., 122 South Michigan Avenue, Suite 1200, Chicago, Illinois 60603 (800) 577-EURO; *International Marketing Data and Statistics; The World Economic Factbook; and World Marketing Data and Statistics.*

Europa Publications Limited, 18 Bedford Square, London, WC1B 3JN, England; *The Europa World Year Book.*

M.E. Sharpe, 80 Business Park Drive, Armonk, New York 10504 (800) 541-6563; *The Illustrated Book of World Rankings.*

St. Martin's Press, Inc., 175 Fifth Avenue, New York, New York 10010 (800) 221-7945; *The Statesman's Year-Book.*

Statistical Office of the United Nations, Publishing Service, New York, New York 10017 (800) 253-9646; *Foreign Trade Statistics for Africa; and World Statistics Pocketbook.*

The World Bank, 1818 H Street, NW, Washington, D.C. 20433 (202) 477-1234; *The World Bank Atlas; and World Development Report.*

NIGERIA - EDUCATION

African Development Bank, 01 BP 1387, Abidjan 01, Cote d'Ivoire; *Selected Statistics on Regional Member Countries.*

The Economist Intelligence Unit, 111 West 57th Street, New York, New York 10019 (800) 938-4685; *The World Market Atlas.*

Euromonitor International, Inc., 122 South Michigan Avenue, Suite 1200, Chicago, Illinois 60603 (800) 577-EURO; *International Marketing Data and Statistics; and World Marketing Data and Statistics.*

Europa Publications Limited, 18 Bedford Square, London, WC1B 3JN, England; *The Europa World Year Book.*

International Monetary Fund, 700 Nineteenth Street, NW, Washington, D.C. 20431 (202) 623-7000; *Government Finance Statistics Yearbook.*

M.E. Sharpe, 80 Business Park Drive, Armonk, New York 10504 (800) 541-6563; *The Illustrated Book of World Rankings.*

St. Martin's Press, Inc., 175 Fifth Avenue, New York, New York 10010 (800) 221-7945; *The Statesman's Year-Book.*

Statistical Office of the United Nations, Publishing Service, New York 10017 (800) 253-9646; *Human Development Report; and Survey of Economic and Social Conditions in Africa.*

United Nations Economic Commission for Africa, Africa Hall, Post Office Box 3001, Addis Ababa, Ethiopia (Telephone Number in U.S. (800) 253-9646); *African Statistical Yearbook.*

United Nations Educational, Scientific and Cultural Organization (UNESCO), 7 Place de Fontenoy, F-75700 Paris, France (Telephone Number in U.S. (212) 963-5981); *Statistical Yearbook.*

The World Bank, 1818 H Street, NW, Washington, D.C. 20433 (202) 477-1234; *World Development Report; and World Development Indicators.*

NIGERIA - EGG PRODUCTION AND CONSUMPTION - See NIGERIA -DAIRY PRODUCTS

NIGERIA - ELECTRICITY

Central Intelligence Agency, Washington, D.C. 20505 (703) 482-1100, www.cia.gov; *The World Factbook.*

M.E. Sharpe, 80 Business Park Drive, Armonk, New York 10504 (800) 541-6563; *The Illustrated Book of World Rankings.*

Penn Well Publishing Company, 1421 South Sheridan Road, Post Office Box 1260, Tulsa, Oklahoma 74101 (800) 752-9764; *International Energy Statistics Sourcebook.*

St. Martin's Press, Inc., 175 Fifth Avenue, New York, New York 10010 (800) 221-7945; *The Statesman's Year-Book.*

Statistical Office of the United Nations, Publishing Service, New York, New York 10017 (800) 253-9646; *Human Development Report; Statistical Yearbook; and Survey of Economic and Social Conditions in Africa.*

United Nations Economic Commission for Africa, Africa Hall, Post Office Box 3001, Addis Ababa, Ethiopia (Telephone Number in U.S. (800) 253-9646); *African Statistical Yearbook.*

NIGERIA - EMPLOYMENT

Euromonitor International, Inc., 122 South Michigan Avenue, Suite 1200, Chicago, Illinois 60603 (800) 577-EURO; *International Marketing Data and Statistics.*

International Labour Office, I.L.O. Publications, 1828 L Street, NW, Suite 801, Washington, D.C. 20036 (301) 638-3152; *Yearbook of Labour Statistics.*

M.E. Sharpe, 80 Business Park Drive, Armonk, New York 10504 (800) 541-6563; *The Illustrated Book of World Rankings.*

Statistical Office of the United Nations, Publishing Service, New York, New York 10017 (800) 253-9646; *Statistical Yearbook; and Survey of Economic and Social Conditions in Africa.*

United Nations Economic Commission for Africa, Africa Hall, Post Office Box 3001, Addis Ababa, Ethiopia (Telephone Number in U.S. (800) 253-9646); *African Statistical Yearbook.*

NIGERIA - ENERGY

Euromonitor International, Inc., 122 South Michigan Avenue, Suite 1200, Chicago, Illinois 60603 (800) 577-EURO; *International Marketing Data and Statistics; The World Economic Factbook; and World Marketing Data and Statistics.*

Food and Agricultural Organization of the United Nations (FAO) Via delle Terme di Caracalla, 00100 Rome, Italy (Telephone Number in U.S. (202) 653-2400); *The State of Food and Agriculture.*

M.E. Sharpe, 80 Business Park Drive, Armonk, New York 10504 (800) 541-6563; *The Illustrated Book of World Rankings.*

Penn Well Publishing Company, 1421 South Sheridan Road, Post Office Box 1260, Tulsa, Oklahoma 74101 (800) 752-9764; *International Energy Statistics Sourcebook.*

St. Martin's Press, Inc., 175 Fifth Avenue, New York, New York 10010 (800) 221-7945; *The Statesman's Year-Book.*

Statistical Office of the United Nations, Publishing Service, New York, New York 10017 (800) 253-9646; *Energy Statistics Yearbook; Human Development Report; World Statistics Pocketbook; and Statistical Yearbook.*

United Nations Economic Commission for Africa, Africa Hall, Post Office Box 3001, Addis Ababa, Ethiopia (Telephone Number in U.S. (800) 253-9646); *African Statistical Yearbook.*

The World Bank, 1818 H Street, NW, Washington, D.C. 20433 (202) 477-1234; *The World Bank Atlas; and World Development Report.*

NIGERIA - ENVIRONMENT

Economist Intelligence Unit, 111 West 57th Street, New York, New York 10019 (800) 938-4685; *Nigeria Country Report.*

Statistical Office of the United Nations, Publishing Service, New York, New York 10017 (800) 253-9646; *World Statistics Pocketbook.*

NIGERIA - EXCHANGE RATES

African Development Bank, 01 BP 1387, Abidjan 01, Cote d'Ivoire; *Selected Statistics on Regional Member Countries.*

Central Intelligence Agency, Washington, D.C. 20505 (703) 482-1100, www.cia.gov; *The World Factbook.*

Euromonitor International, Inc., 122 South Michigan Avenue, Suite 1200, Chicago, Illinois 60603 (800) 577-EURO; *International Marketing Data and Statistics;* and *The World Economic Factbook.*

Europa Publications Limited, 18 Bedford Square, London, WC1B 3JN, England; *The Europa World Year Book.*

International Monetary Fund, 700 Nineteenth Street, NW, Washington, D.C. 20431 (202) 623-7000; *International Financial Statistics.*

Organization of Petroleum Exporting Countries, Obere Donaustrasse 93, 1020 Vienna 2, Austria; *OPEC Annual Statistical Bulletin.*

Statistical Office of the United Nations, Publishing Service, New York, New York 10017 (800) 253-9646; *Foreign Trade Statistics for Africa; World Statistics Pocketbook;* and *Statistical Yearbook.*

NIGERIA - EXCISE TAXES - See NIGERIA - TAXATION

NIGERIA - EXPORT DUTIES

International Monetary Fund, 700 Nineteenth Street, NW, Washington, D.C. 20431 (202) 623-7000; *Government Finance Statistics Yearbook.*

St. Martin's Press, Inc., 175 Fifth Avenue, New York, New York 10010 (800) 221-7945; *The Statesman's Year-Book.*

NIGERIA - EXPORTS

African Development Bank, 01 BP 1387, Abidjan 01, Cote d'Ivoire; *Selected Statistics on Regional Member Countries.*

American Automobile Manufacturers Association, 1401 H Street, NW, Suite 900, Washington, D.C. 20005 (202) 326-5500; *World Motor Vehicle Data.*

Central Intelligence Agency, Washington, D.C. 20505 (703) 482-1100, www.cia.gov; *The World Factbook.*

The Economist Intelligence Unit, 111 West 57th Street, New York, New York 10019 (800) 938-4685; *Nigeria Country Report;* and *The World Market Atlas.*

Euromonitor International, Inc., 122 South Michigan Avenue, Suite 1200, Chicago, Illinois 60603 (800) 577-EURO; *International Marketing Data and Statistics;* and *The World Economic Factbook.*

Europa Publications Limited, 18 Bedford Square, London, WC1B 3JN, England; *The Europa World Year Book.*

Food and Agricultural Organization of the United Nations (FAO) Via delle Terme di Caracalla, 00100 Rome, Italy (Telephone Number in U.S. (202) 653-2400); *The State of Food and Agriculture.*

International Monetary Fund, 700 Nineteenth Street, NW, Washington, D.C. 20431 (202) 623-7000; *Direction of Trade Statistics;* and *International Financial Statistics.*

International Rubber Study Group, York House, Eighth Floor, Empire Way, Wembley, London HA9 0PA, England; *Rubber Statistical Bulletin.*

Organization of Petroleum Exporting Countries, Obere Donaustrasse 93, 1020 Vienna 2, Austria; *OPEC Annual Statistical Bulletin.*

Statistical Office of the United Nations, Publishing Service, New York, New York 10017 (800) 253-9646; *Foreign Trade Statistics for Africa;* and *Survey of Economic and Social Conditions in Africa.*

United Nations Conference on Trade and Development (UNCTAD), New York, New York 10017 (800) 253-9646; *Handbook of International Trade and Development Statistics.*

United Nations Economic Commission for Africa, Africa Hall, Post Office Box 3001, Addis Ababa, Ethiopia (Telephone Number in U.S. (800) 253-9646); *African Statistical Yearbook.*

The World Bank, 1818 H Street, NW, Washington, D.C. 20433 (202) 477-1234; *World Development Report;* and *World Development Indicators.*

NIGERIA - EXTERNAL INDEBTEDNESS

African Development Bank, 01 BP 1387, Abidjan 01, Cote d'Ivoire; *Selected Statistics on Regional Member Countries.*

Statistical Office of the United Nations,

Publishing Service, New York, New York 10017 (800) 253-9646; *Statistical Yearbook;* and *Survey of Economic and Social Conditions in Africa.*

The World Bank, 1818 H Street, NW, Washington, D.C. 20433 (202) 477-1234; *World Development Report;* and *World Development Indicators.*

NIGERIA - EXTERNAL TRADE

African Development Bank, 01 BP 1387, Abidjan 01, Cote d'Ivoire; *Selected Statistics on Regional Member Countries.*

Euromonitor International, Inc., 122 South Michigan Avenue, Suite 1200, Chicago, Illinois 60603 (800) 577-EURO; *World Marketing Data and Statistics.*

Food and Agricultural Organization of the United Nations (FAO) Via delle Terme di Caracalla, 00100 Rome, Italy (Telephone Number in U.S. (202) 653-2400); *The State of Food and Agriculture;* and *Trade Yearbook.*

Statistical Office of the United Nations, Publishing Service, New York, New York 10017 (800) 253-9646; *Statistical Yearbook.*

NIGERIA - FABRIC PRODUCTION - See NIGERIA - TEXTILE INDUSTRY

NIGERIA - FARM CROPS - See NIGERIA - CROPS

NIGERIA - FEMALE WORKING POPULATION - See NIGERIA - EMPLOYMENT

NIGERIA - FERTILITY RATES

Central Intelligence Agency, Washington, D.C. 20505 (703) 482-1100, www.cia.gov; *The World Factbook.*

M.E. Sharpe, 80 Business Park Drive, Armonk, New York 10504 (800) 541-6563; *The Illustrated Book of World Rankings.*

Statistical Office of the United Nations, Publishing Service, New York 10017 (800) 253-9646; *Human Development Report;* and *Survey of Economic and Social Conditions in Africa.*

The World Bank, 1818 H Street, NW, Washington, D.C. 20433 (202) 477-1234; *The World Bank Atlas; World Development Report;* and *World Development Indicators.*

NIGERIA - FERTILIZER

Food and Agricultural Organization of the United Nations (FAO), Via delle Terme di Caracalla, 00100 Rome, Italy (Telephone Number in U.S. (202) 653-2400); *Fertilizer Yearbook;* and *The State of Food and Agriculture.*

Statistical Office of the United Nations, Publishing Service, New York, New York 10017 (800) 253-9646; *Statistical Yearbook.*

NIGERIA - FETAL MORTALITY - See NIGERIA - MORTALITY

NIGERIA - FINANCE

African Development Bank, 01 BP 1387, Abidjan 01, Cote d'Ivoire; *Selected Statistics on Regional Member Countries.*

Economist Intelligence Unit, 111 West 57th Street, New York, New York 10019 (800) 938-4685; *Nigeria Country Report.*

Europa Publications Limited, 18 Bedford Square, London, WC1B 3JN, England; *The Europa World Year Book.*

International Monetary Fund, 700 Nineteenth Street, NW, Washington, D.C. 20431 (202) 623-7000; *Government Finance Statistics Yearbook;* and *International Financial Statistics.*

M.E. Sharpe, 80 Business Park Drive, Armonk, New York 10504 (800) 541-6563; *The Illustrated Book of World Rankings.*

St. Martin's Press, Inc., 175 Fifth Avenue, New York, New York 10010 (800) 221-7945; *The Statesman's Year-Book.*

United Nations Economic Commission for Africa, Africa Hall, Post Office Box 3001, Addis Ababa, Ethiopia (Telephone Number in U.S. (800) 253-9646; *African Statistical Yearbook.*

NIGERIA - FISHERIES

Central Intelligence Agency, Washington, D.C. 20505 (703) 482-1100, www.cia.gov; *The World Factbook.*

Europa Publications Limited, 18 Bedford Square, London, WC1B 3JN, England; *The Europa World Year Book.*

Food and Agricultural Organization of the United Nations (FAO) Via delle Terme di Caracalla, 00100 Rome, Italy (Telephone Number in U.S. (202) 653-2400); *The State of Food and Agriculture;* and *Yearbook of Fishery Statistics.*

M.E. Sharpe, 80 Business Park Drive, Armonk, New York 10504 (800) 541-6563; *The Illustrated Book of World Rankings.*

St. Martin's Press, Inc., 175 Fifth Avenue, New York, New York 10010 (800) 221-7945; *The Statesman's Year-Book.*

Statistical Office of the United Nations, Publishing Service, New York, New York 10017 (800) 253-9646; *Statistical Yearbook;* and *Survey of Economic and Social Conditions in Africa.*

United Nations Conference on Trade and Development, Central Statistical Service, Palais des Nations, Geneva, Switzerland (Telephone in U.S. (800) 253-9646); *UNCTAD Commodity Yearbook.*

United Nations Economic Commission for Africa, Africa Hall, Post Office Box 3001, Addis Ababa, Ethiopia (Telephone Number in U.S. (800) 253-9646); *African Statistical Yearbook.*

NIGERIA - FLOUR PRODUCTION

Statistical Office of the United Nations, Publishing Service, New York, New York 10017 (800) 253-9646; *Statistical Yearbook.*

NIGERIA - FOOD

African Development Bank, 01 BP 1387, Abidjan 01, Cote d'Ivoire; *Selected Statistics on Regional Member Countries.*

Central Intelligence Agency, Washington, D.C. 20505 (703) 482-1100, www.cia.gov; *The World Factbook.*

Food and Agricultural Organization of the United Nations (FAO), Via delle Terme di Caracalla, 00100 Rome, Italy (Telephone Number in U.S. (202) 653-2400); *Production Yearbook;* and *The State of Food and Agriculture.*

Statistical Office of the United Nations, Publishing Service, New York, New York 10017 (800) 253-9646; *Human Development Report.*

United Nations Conference on Trade and Development, Central Statistical Service, Palais des Nations, Geneva, Switzerland (Telephone in U.S. (800) 253-9646); *UNCTAD Commodity Yearbook.*

NIGERIA - FOREIGN DEBT

St. Martin's Press, Inc., 175 Fifth Avenue, New York, New York 10010 (800) 221-7945; *The Statesman's Year-Book.*

NIGERIA - FOREIGN TRADE

Central Intelligence Agency, Washington, D.C. 20505 (703) 482-1100, www.cia.gov; *The World Factbook.*

Economist Intelligence Unit, 111 West 57th Street, New York, New York 10019 (800) 938-4685; *Nigeria Country Report.*

Euromonitor International, Inc., 122 South Michigan Avenue, Suite 1200, Chicago, Illinois 60603 (800) 577-EURO; *International Marketing Data and Statistics;* and *The World Economic Factbook.*

Europa Publications Limited, 18 Bedford Square, London, WC1B 3JN, England; *The Europa World Year Book.*

Food and Agricultural Organization of the United Nations (FAO) Via delle Terme di Caracalla, 00100 Rome, Italy (Telephone Number in U.S. (202) 653-2400); *The State of Food and Agriculture.*

International Monetary Fund, 700 Nineteenth Street, NW, Washington, D.C. 20431 (202) 623-7000; *International Financial Statistics.*

M.E. Sharpe, 80 Business Park Drive, Armonk, New York 10504 (800) 541-6563; *The Illustrated Book of World Rankings.*

St. Martin's Press, Inc., 175 Fifth Avenue, New York, New York 10010 (800) 221-7945; *The Statesman's Year-Book.*

Statistical Office of the United Nations, Publishing Service, New York, New York 10017 (800) 253-9646; *International Trade Statistics Yearbook; Foreign Trade Statistics for Africa;* and *Statistical Yearbook.*

United Nations Conference on Trade and Development, Central Statistical Service, Palais des Nations, Geneva, Switzerland (Telephone in U.S. (800) 253-9646); *UNCTAD Commodity Yearbook.*

United Nations Economic Commission for Africa, Africa Hall, Post Office Box 3001, Addis Ababa, Ethiopia (Telephone Number in U.S. (800) 253-9646); *African Statistical Yearbook.*

The World Bank, 1818 H Street, NW, Washington, D.C. 20433 (202) 477-1234; *World Development Report;* and *World Development Indicators.*

NIGERIA - FORESTRY AND FOREST PRODUCTS

Central Intelligence Agency, Washington, D.C. 20505 (703) 482-1100, www.cia.gov; *The World Factbook.*

Food and Agricultural Organization of the United Nations (FAO) Via delle Terme di Caracalla, 00100 Rome, Italy (Telephone Number in U.S. (202) 653-2400); *The State of Food and Agriculture;* and *Yearbook of Forest Products.*

M.E. Sharpe, 80 Business Park Drive, Armonk, New York 10504 (800) 541-6563; *The Illustrated Book of World Rankings.*

St. Martin's Press, Inc., 175 Fifth Avenue, New York, New York 10010 (800) 221-7945; *The Statesman's Year-Book.*

Statistical Office of the United Nations, Publishing Service, New York, New York 10017 (800) 253-9646; *Statistical Yearbook.*

United Nations Conference on Trade and Development, Central Statistical Service, Palais des Nations, Geneva,

Switzerland (Telephone in U.S. (800) 253-9646); *UNCTAD Commodity Yearbook.*

United Nations Economic Commission for Africa, Africa Hall, Post Office Box 3001, Addis Ababa, Ethiopia (Telephone Number in U.S. (800) 253-9646); *African Statistical Yearbook.*

United Nations Educational, Scientific and Cultural Organization (UNESCO), 7 Place de Fontenoy, F-75700 Paris, France (Telephone Number in U.S. (212) 963-5981); *Statistical Yearbook.*

The World Bank, 1818 H Street, NW, Washington, D.C. 20433 (202) 477-1234; *World Development Report.*

NIGERIA - GAS PRODUCTION - See NIGERIA - MINING AND MINERAL PRODUCTS

NIGERIA - GEOGRAPHIC DATA

M.E. Sharpe, 80 Business Park Drive, Armonk, New York 10504 (800) 541-6563; *The Illustrated Book of World Rankings.*

NIGERIA - GOATS - See NIGERIA - LIVESTOCK AND POULTRY

NIGERIA - GOLD HOLDINGS

International Monetary Fund, 700 Nineteenth Street, NW, Washington, D.C. 20431 (202) 623-7000; *International Financial Statistics.*

Statistical Office of the United Nations, Publishing Service, New York, New York 10017 (800) 253-9646; *Statistical Yearbook.*

The World Bank, 1818 H Street, NW, Washington, D.C. 20433 (202) 477-1234; *World Development Indicators.*

NIGERIA - GOLD PRODUCTION AND CONSUMPTION - See NIGERIA - MINING AND MINERAL PRODUCTS

NIGERIA - GOVERNMENT

Central Intelligence Agency, Washington, D.C. 20505 (703) 482-1100, www.cia.gov; *The World Factbook.*

Europa Publications Limited, 18 Bedford Square, London, WC1B 3JN, England; *The Europa World Year Book.*

International Monetary Fund, 700 Nineteenth Street, NW, Washington, D.C. 20431 (202) 623-7000; *Government Finance Statistics Yearbook.*

St. Martin's Press, Inc., 175 Fifth Avenue, New York, New York 10010 (800) 221-7945; *The Statesman's Year-Book.*

Statistical Office of the United Nations,

Publishing Service, New York, New York 10017 (800) 253-9646; *Statistical Yearbook; National Accounts Statistics;* and *Survey of Economic and Social Conditions in Africa.*

The World Bank, 1818 H Street, NW, Washington, D.C. 20433 (202) 477-1234; *World Development Report;* and *World Development Indicators.*

NIGERIA - GRAIN PRODUCTION - See NIGERIA - CROPS

NIGERIA - GRANTS

International Monetary Fund, 700 Nineteenth Street, NW, Washington, D.C. 20431 (202) 623-7000; *Government Finance Statistics Yearbook.*

NIGERIA - GREEN PEPPER AND CHILIE PRODUCTION - See NIGERIA - CROPS

NIGERIA - GROSS DOMESTIC PRODUCT

African Development Bank, 01 BP 1387, Abidjan 01, Cote d'Ivoire; *Selected Statistics on Regional Member Countries.*

The Economist Intelligence Unit, 111 West 57th Street, New York, New York 10019 (800) 938-4685; *Nigeria Country Report;* and *The World Market Atlas.*

Euromonitor International, Inc., 122 South Michigan Avenue, Suite 1200, Chicago, Illinois 60603 (800) 577-EURO; *International Marketing Data and Statistics;* and *The World Economic Factbook.*

Europa Publications Limited, 18 Bedford Square, London, WC1B 3JN, England; *The Europa World Year Book.*

M.E. Sharpe, 80 Business Park Drive, Armonk, New York 10504 (800) 541-6563; *The Illustrated Book of World Rankings.*

St. Martin's Press, Inc., 175 Fifth Avenue, New York, New York 10010 (800) 221-7945; *The Statesman's Year-Book.*

Statistical Office of the United Nations, Publishing Service, New York, New York 10017 (800) 253-9646; *Human Development Report; National Accounts Statistics; Statistical Yearbook;* and *Survey of Economic and Social Conditions in Africa.*

United Nations Economic Commission for Africa, Africa Hall, Post Office Box 3001, Addis Ababa, Ethiopia (Telephone Number in U.S. (800) 253-9646); *African Statistical Yearbook.*

The World Bank, 1818 H Street, NW, Washington, D.C. 20433 (202) 477-1234; *World Development Report;* and *World Development Indicators.*

NIGERIA - GROSS NATIONAL PRODUCT

Euromonitor International, Inc., 122 South Michigan Avenue, Suite 1200, Chicago, Illinois 60603 (800) 577-EURO; *International Marketing Data and Statistics.*

Europa Publications Limited, 18 Bedford Square, London, WC1B 3JN, England; *The Europa World Year Book.*

Organization of Petroleum Exporting Countries, Obere Donaustrasse 93, 1020 Vienna 2, Austria; *OPEC Annual Statistical Bulletin.*

U.S. Arms Control and Disarmament Agency, 320 Twenty-first Street, NW, Washington, D.C. 20451 (202) 647-8677; *World Military Expenditures and Arms Transfers.*

The World Bank, 1818 H Street, NW, Washington, D.C. 20433 (202) 477-1234; *The World Bank Atlas; World Development Report;* and *World Development Indicators.*

NIGERIA - GROUNDNUTS PRODUCTION - See NIGERIA - CROPS

NIGERIA - HEALTH

African Development Bank, 01 BP 1387, Abidjan 01, Cote d'Ivoire; *Selected Statistics on Regional Member Countries.*

Euromonitor International, Inc., 122 South Michigan Avenue, Suite 1200, Chicago, Illinois 60603 (800) 577-EURO; *World Marketing Data and Statistics.*

M.E. Sharpe, 80 Business Park Drive, Armonk, New York 10504 (800) 541-6563; *The Illustrated Book of World Rankings.*

St. Martin's Press, Inc., 175 Fifth Avenue, New York, New York 10010 (800) 221-7945; *The Statesman's Year-Book.*

Statistical Office of the United Nations, Publishing Service, New York, New York 10017 (800) 253-9646; *Human Development Report;* and *Statistical Yearbook.*

United Nations Children's Fund (UNICEF), 3 United Nations Plaza, New York, New York 10017 (800) 253-9646; *State of the World's Children.*

United Nations Economic Commission for Africa, Africa Hall, Post Office Box 3001, Addis Ababa, Ethiopia (Telephone Number in U.S. (800) 253-9646); *African Statistical Yearbook.*

The World Bank, 1818 H Street, NW, Washington, D.C. 20433 (202) 477-1234; *World Development Report.*

World Health Organization, Office of

Publications, 20 Avenue Appia, CH-1211 Geneva 27, Switzerland (Telephone Number in U.S. (518) 436-9686); *World Health Statistics Annual.*

NIGERIA - HEALTH EXPENDITURES

International Monetary Fund, 700 Nineteenth Street, NW, Washington, D.C. 20431 (202) 623-7000; *Government Finance Statistics Yearbook.*

NIGERIA - HIDE PRODUCTION

Food and Agricultural Organization of the United Nations (FAO), Via delle Terme di Caracalla, 00100 Rome, Italy (Telephone Number in U.S. (202) 653-2400); *Production Yearbook.*

NIGERIA - HIGHWAYS

Central Intelligence Agency, Washington, D.C. 20505 (703) 482-1100, www.cia.gov; *The World Factbook.*

St. Martin's Press, Inc., 175 Fifth Avenue, New York, New York 10010 (800) 221-7945; *The Statesman's Year-Book.*

Statistical Office of the United Nations, Publishing Service, New York 10017 (800) 253-9646; *Survey of Economic and Social Conditions in Africa.*

United Nations Economic Commission for Africa, Africa Hall, Post Office Box 3001, Addis Ababa, Ethiopia (Telephone Number in U.S. (800) 253-9646); *African Statistical Yearbook.*

NIGERIA - HORSES - See NIGERIA - LIVESTOCK AND POULTRY

NIGERIA - HOURS OF WORK - See NIGERIA - EMPLOYMENT

NIGERIA - HOUSING AND HOUSING UNITS

Euromonitor International, Inc., 122 South Michigan Avenue, Suite 1200, Chicago, Illinois 60603 (800) 577-EURO; *World Marketing Data and Statistics.*

M.E. Sharpe, 80 Business Park Drive, Armonk, New York 10504 (800) 541-6563; *The Illustrated Book of World Rankings.*

NIGERIA - HOUSING EXPENDITURES

International Monetary Fund, 700 Nineteenth Street, NW, Washington, D.C. 20431 (202) 623-7000; *Government Finance Statistics Yearbook.*

NIGERIA - ILLITERATE POPULATION

Central Intelligence Agency, Washington, D.C. 20505 (703) 482-1100, www.cia.gov; *The World Factbook.*

The Economist Intelligence Unit, 111 West 57th Street, New York, New York 10019 (800) 938-4685; *The World Market Atlas.*

Euromonitor International, Inc., 122 South Michigan Avenue, Suite 1200, Chicago, Illinois 60603 (800) 577-EURO; *The World Economic Factbook.*

St. Martin's Press, Inc., 175 Fifth Avenue, New York, New York 10010 (800) 221-7945; *The Statesman's Year-Book.*

Statistical Office of the United Nations, Publishing Service, New York, New York 10017 (800) 253-9646; *Human Development Report.*

United Nations Educational, Scientific and Cultural Organization (UNESCO), 7 Place de Fontenoy, F-75700 Paris, France (Telephone Number in U.S. (212) 963-5981); *Statistical Yearbook.*

NIGERIA - IMPORTS

African Development Bank, 01 BP 1387, Abidjan 01, Cote d'Ivoire; *Selected Statistics on Regional Member Countries.*

American Automobile Manufacturers Association, 1401 H Street, NW, Suite 900, Washington, D.C. 20005 (202) 326-5500; *World Motor Vehicle Data.*

Central Intelligence Agency, Washington, D.C. 20505 (703) 482-1100, www.cia.gov; *The World Factbook.*

Economist Intelligence Unit, 111 West 57th Street, New York, New York 10019 (800) 938-4685; *Nigeria Country Report.*

Euromonitor International, Inc., 122 South Michigan Avenue, Suite 1200, Chicago, Illinois 60603 (800) 577-EURO; *International Marketing Data and Statistics;* and *The World Economic Factbook.*

Europa Publications Limited, 18 Bedford Square, London, WC1B 3JN, England; *The Europa World Year Book.*

Food and Agricultural Organization of the United Nations (FAO) Via delle Terme di Caracalla, 00100 Rome, Italy (Telephone Number in U.S. (202) 653-2400); *The State of Food and Agriculture.*

International Monetary Fund, 700 Nineteenth Street, NW, Washington, D.C. 20431 (202) 623-7000; *Direction of Trade Statistics; Government Finance Statistics Yearbook;* and *International Financial Statistics.*

International Rubber Study Group, York House, Eighth Floor, Empire Way, Wembley, London HA9 0PA, England; *Rubber Statistical Bulletin.*

St. Martin's Press, Inc., 175 Fifth Avenue, New York, New York 10010 (800) 221-7945; *The Statesman's Year-Book.*

Statistical Office of the United Nations, Publishing Service, New York, New York 10017 (800) 253-9646; *Foreign Trade Statistics for Africa;* and *Survey of Economic and Social Conditions in Africa.*

United Nations Conference on Trade and Development (UNCTAD), New York, New York 10017 (800) 253-9646; *Handbook of International Trade and Development Statistics.*

United Nations Economic Commission for Africa, Africa Hall, Post Office Box 3001, Addis Ababa, Ethiopia (Telephone Number in U.S. (800) 253-9646); *African Statistical Yearbook.*

The World Bank, 1818 H Street, NW, Washington, D.C. 20433 (202) 477-1234; *World Development Report;* and *World Development Indicators.*

NIGERIA - INCOME TAXES - See NIGERIA - TAXATION

NIGERIA - INDUSTRIAL METALS PRODUCTION - See NIGERIA - MINING AND MINERAL PRODUCTS

NIGERIA - INDUSTRY

Central Intelligence Agency, Washington, D.C. 20505 (703) 482-1100, www.cia.gov; *The World Factbook.*

Economist Intelligence Unit, 111 West 57th Street, New York, New York 10019 (800) 938-4685; *Nigeria Country Report.*

Euromonitor International, Inc., 122 South Michigan Avenue, Suite 1200, Chicago, Illinois 60603 (800) 577-EURO; *International Marketing Data and Statistics; The World Economic Factbook;* and *World Marketing Data and Statistics.*

Europa Publications Limited, 18 Bedford Square, London, WC1B 3JN, England; *The Europa World Year Book.*

International Labour Office, I.L.O. Publications, 1828 L Street, NW, Suite 801, Washington, D.C. 20036 (301) 638-3152; *Yearbook of Labour Statistics.*

M.E. Sharpe, 80 Business Park Drive, Armonk, New York 10504 (800) 541-6563; *The Illustrated Book of World Rankings.*

St. Martin's Press, Inc., 175 Fifth Avenue, New York, New York 10010 (800) 221-7945; *The Statesman's Year-Book.*

Statistical Office of the United Nations, Publishing Service, New York, New York 10017 (800) 253-9646; *Industrial*

Commodity Statistics Yearbook; Statistical Yearbook; and Survey of Economic and Social Conditions in Africa.

United Nations Economic Commission for Africa, Africa Hall, Post Office Box 3001, Addis Ababa, Ethiopia (Telephone Number in U.S. (800) 253-9646); African Statistical Yearbook.

The World Bank, 1818 H Street, NW, Washington, D.C. 20433 (202) 477-1234; World Development Indicators.

NIGERIA - INFANT AND MATERNAL MORTALITY - See NIGERIA - MORTALITY

NIGERIA - INTERNATIONAL LIQUIDITY

International Monetary Fund, 700 Nineteenth Street, NW, Washington, D.C. 20431 (202) 623-7000; International Financial Statistics.

NIGERIA - INTERNATIONAL RESERVES EXCLUDING GOLD

African Development Bank, 01 BP 1387, Abidjan 01, Cote d'Ivoire; Selected Statistics on Regional Member Countries.

Statistical Office of the United Nations, Publishing Service, New York, New York 10017 (800) 253-9646; Statistical Yearbook.

The World Bank, 1818 H Street, NW, Washington, D.C. 20433 (202) 477-1234; World Development Indicators.

NIGERIA - IRON ORE PRODUCTION AND CONSUMPTION - See NIGERIA - MINING AND MINERAL PRODUCTS

NIGERIA - IRRIGATION

Euromonitor International, Inc., 122 South Michigan Avenue, Suite 1200, Chicago, Illinois 60603 (800) 577-EURO; International Marketing Data and Statistics.

NIGERIA - LABOR

African Development Bank, 01 BP 1387, Abidjan 01, Cote d'Ivoire; Selected Statistics on Regional Member Countries.

Central Intelligence Agency, Washington, D.C. 20505 (703) 482-1100, www.cia.gov; The World Factbook.

Euromonitor International, Inc., 122 South Michigan Avenue, Suite 1200, Chicago, Illinois 60603 (800) 577-EURO; International Marketing Data and Statistics; and World Marketing Data and Statistics.

Europa Publications Limited, 18 Bedford Square, London, WC1B 3JN, England; The Europa World Year Book.

Food and Agricultural Organization of

the United Nations (FAO) Via delle Terme di Caracalla, 00100 Rome, Italy (Telephone Number in U.S. (202) 653-2400); The State of Food and Agriculture.

International Labour Office, I.L.O. Publications, 1828 L Street, NW, Suite 801, Washington, D.C. 20036 (301) 638-3152; Yearbook of Labour Statistics.

M.E. Sharpe, 80 Business Park Drive, Armonk, New York 10504 (800) 541-6563; The Illustrated Book of World Rankings.

St. Martin's Press, Inc., 175 Fifth Avenue, New York, New York 10010 (800) 221-7945; The Statesman's Year-Book.

Statistical Office of the United Nations, Publishing Service, New York, New York 10017 (800) 253-9646; Human Development Report.

The World Bank, 1818 H Street, NW, Washington, D.C. 20433 (202) 477-1234; The World Bank Atlas; World Development Report; and World Development Indicators.

NIGERIA - LAND USE

Central Intelligence Agency, Washington, D.C. 20505 (703) 482-1100, www.cia.gov; The World Factbook.

Euromonitor International, Inc., 122 South Michigan Avenue, Suite 1200, Chicago, Illinois 60603 (800) 577-EURO; International Marketing Data and Statistics.

Food and Agricultural Organization of the United Nations (FAO), Via delle Terme di Caracalla, 00100 Rome, Italy (Telephone Number in U.S. (202) 653-2400); Production Yearbook.

The World Bank, 1818 H Street, NW, Washington, D.C. 20433 (202) 477-1234; World Development Report.

NIGERIA - LEAD ORE PRODUCTION AND CONSUMPTION - See NIGERIA - MINING AND MINERAL PRODUCTS

NIGERIA - LIBRARIES

M.E. Sharpe, 80 Business Park Drive, Armonk, New York 10504 (800) 541-6563; The Illustrated Book of World Rankings.

United Nations Educational, Scientific and Cultural Organization (UNESCO), 7 Place de Fontenoy, F-75700 Paris, France (Telephone Number in U.S. (212) 963-5981); Statistical Yearbook.

NIGERIA - LIFE EXPECTANCY

African Development Bank, 01 BP 1387, Abidjan 01, Cote d'Ivoire; Selected Statistics on Regional Member Countries.

Central Intelligence Agency, Washington, D.C. 20505 (703) 482-1100, www.cia.gov; The World Factbook.

Euromonitor International, Inc., 122 South Michigan Avenue, Suite 1200, Chicago, Illinois 60603 (800) 577-EURO; The World Economic Factbook.

St. Martin's Press, Inc., 175 Fifth Avenue, New York, New York 10010 (800) 221-7945; The Statesman's Year-Book.

Statistical Office of the United Nations, Publishing Service, New York, New York 10017 (800) 253-9646; Human Development Report; and World Statistics Pocketbook.

The World Bank, 1818 H Street, NW, Washington, D.C. 20433 (202) 477-1234; The World Bank Atlas; and World Development Report.

NIGERIA - LIGNITE PRODUCTION - See NIGERIA - MINING AND MINERAL PRODUCTS

NIGERIA - LITERACY RATE

Euromonitor International, Inc., 122 South Michigan Avenue, Suite 1200, Chicago, Illinois 60603 (800) 577-EURO; World Marketing Data and Statistics.

Statistical Office of the United Nations, Publishing Service, New York 10017 (800) 253-9646; Survey of Economic and Social Conditions in Africa.

NIGERIA - LIVESTOCK AND POULTRY

Euromonitor International, Inc., 122 South Michigan Avenue, Suite 1200, Chicago, Illinois 60603 (800) 577-EURO; International Marketing Data and Statistics.

Europa Publications Limited, 18 Bedford Square, London, WC1B 3JN, England; The Europa World Year Book.

Food and Agricultural Organization of the United Nations (FAO), Via delle Terme di Caracalla, 00100 Rome, Italy (Telephone Number in U.S. (202) 653-2400); Production Yearbook; and The State of Food and Agriculture.

M.E. Sharpe, 80 Business Park Drive, Armonk, New York 10504 (800) 541-6563; The Illustrated Book of World Rankings.

St. Martin's Press, Inc., 175 Fifth Avenue, New York, New York 10010 (800) 221-7945; The Statesman's Year-Book.

Statistical Office of the United Nations, Publishing Service, New York, New York 10017 (800) 253-9646; Statistical Yearbook; and Survey of Economic and Social Conditions in Africa.

United Nations Conference on Trade and Development, Central Statistical Service, Palais des Nations, Geneva, Switzerland (Telephone in U.S. (800) 253-9646); *UNCTAD Commodity Yearbook.*

United Nations Economic Commission for Africa, Africa Hall, Post Office Box 3001, Addis Ababa, Ethiopia (Telephone Number in U.S. (800) 253-9646); *African Statistical Yearbook.*

NIGERIA - LIVING LEVELS - See NIGERIA - LIFE EXPECTANCY

NIGERIA - MAIL - NUMBER OF PIECES SENT OR RECEIVED

Statistical Office of the United Nations, Publishing Service, New York, New York 10017 (800) 253-9646; *Statistical Yearbook.*

NIGERIA - MANUFACTURING

American Automobile Manufacturers Association, 1401 H Street, NW, Suite 900, Washington, D.C. 20005 (202) 326-5500; *World Motor Vehicle Data.*

M.E. Sharpe, 80 Business Park Drive, Armonk, New York 10504 (800) 541-6563; *The Illustrated Book of World Rankings.*

Statistical Office of the United Nations, Publishing Service, New York, New York 10017 (800) 253-9646; *Statistical Yearbook; and Survey of Economic and Social Conditions in Africa.*

United Nations Economic Commission for Africa, Africa Hall, Post Office Box 3001, Addis Ababa, Ethiopia (Telephone Number in U.S. (800) 253-9646); *African Statistical Yearbook.*

The World Bank, 1818 H Street, NW, Washington, D.C. 20433 (202) 477-1234; *World Development Indicators.*

NIGERIA - MARRIAGE RATES

M.E. Sharpe, 80 Business Park Drive, Armonk, New York 10504 (800) 541-6563; *The Illustrated Book of World Rankings.*

Statistical Office of the United Nations, Publishing Service, New York, New York 10017 (800) 253-9646; *Demographic Yearbook.*

NIGERIA - MEAT PRODUCTION - See NIGERIA - LIVESTOCK AND POULTRY

NIGERIA - MERCHANT SHIPPING

Europa Publications Limited, 18 Bedford Square, London, WC1B 3JN, England; *The Europa World Year Book.*

Lloyd's Register of Shipping, 17 Battery Place, New York, New York 10004 (212) 425-8050; *Register of Ships.*

Organization of Petroleum Exporting Countries, Obere Donaustrasse 93, 1020 Vienna 2, Austria; *OPEC Annual Statistical Bulletin.*

St. Martin's Press, Inc., 175 Fifth Avenue, New York, New York 10010 (800) 221-7945; *The Statesman's Year-Book.*

Statistical Office of the United Nations, Publishing Service, New York, New York 10017 (800) 253-9646; *Statistical Yearbook.*

United Nations Economic Commission for Africa, Africa Hall, Post Office Box 3001, Addis Ababa, Ethiopia (Telephone Number in U.S. (800) 253-9646); *African Statistical Yearbook.*

U.S. Department of Transportation, Maritime Administration, 400 Seventh Street, SW, Washington, D.C. 20590 (202) 366-5807, www.marad.dot.gov; *A Statistical Analysis of the World's Merchant Fleets.*

NIGERIA - MILITARY

Central Intelligence Agency, Washington, D.C. 20505 (703) 482-1100, www.cia.gov; *The World Factbook.*

Euromonitor International, Inc., 122 South Michigan Avenue, Suite 1200, Chicago, Illinois 60603 (800) 577-EURO; *World Marketing Data and Statistics.*

The International Institute for Strategic Studies, 23 Tavistock Street, London WC2E 7NQ, England; *The Military Balance.*

International Monetary Fund, 700 Nineteenth Street, NW, Washington, D.C. 20431 (202) 623-7000; *Government Finance Statistics Yearbook.*

St. Martin's Press, Inc., 175 Fifth Avenue, New York, New York 10010 (800) 221-7945; *The Statesman's Year-Book.*

Statistical Office of the United Nations, Publishing Service, New York, New York 10017 (800) 253-9646; *Human Development Report.*

U.S. Arms Control and Disarmament Agency, 320 Twenty-first Street, NW, Washington, D.C. 20451 (202) 647-8677; *World Military Expenditures and Arms Transfers.*

NIGERIA - MILK PRODUCTION - See NIGERIA - DAIRY PRODUCTS

NIGERIA - MILLET PRODUCTION - See NIGERIA - CROPS

NIGERIA - MINING AND MINERAL PRODUCTS

Europa Publications Limited, 18 Bedford Square, London, WC1B 3JN, England; *The Europa World Year Book.*

M.E. Sharpe, 80 Business Park Drive, Armonk, New York 10504 (800) 541-6563; *The Illustrated Book of World Rankings.*

Organization of Petroleum Exporting Countries, Obere Donaustrasse 93, 1020 Vienna 2, Austria; *OPEC Annual Statistical Bulletin.*

Penn Well Publishing Company, 1421 South Sheridan Road, Post Office Box 1260, Tulsa, Oklahoma 74101 (800) 752-9764; *International Energy Statistics Sourcebook.*

St. Martin's Press, Inc., 175 Fifth Avenue, New York, New York 10010 (800) 221-7945; *The Statesman's Year-Book.*

Statistical Office of the United Nations, Publishing Service, New York, New York 10017 (800) 253-9646; *Statistical Yearbook.*

United Nations Conference on Trade and Development, Central Statistical Service, Palais des Nations, Geneva, Switzerland (Telephone in U.S. (800) 253-9646); *UNCTAD Commodity Yearbook.*

United Nations Economic Commission for Africa, Africa Hall, Post Office Box 3001, Addis Ababa, Ethiopia (Telephone Number in U.S. (800) 253-9646); *African Statistical Yearbook.*

NIGERIA - MONEY EXCHANGE RATE - See NIGERIA - EXCHANGE RATES

NIGERIA - MONEY RESERVES

Euromonitor International, Inc., 122 South Michigan Avenue, Suite 1200, Chicago, Illinois 60603 (800) 577-EURO; *International Marketing Data and Statistics.*

NIGERIA - MONEY SUPPLY

African Development Bank, 01 BP 1387, Abidjan 01, Cote d'Ivoire; *Selected Statistics on Regional Member Countries.*

Economist Intelligence Unit, 111 West 57th Street, New York, New York 10019 (800) 938-4685; *Nigeria Country Report.*

Euromonitor International, Inc., 122 South Michigan Avenue, Suite 1200, Chicago, Illinois 60603 (800) 577-EURO; *International Marketing Data and Statistics.*

Europa Publications Limited, 18 Bedford Square, London, WC1B 3JN, England; *The Europa World Year Book.*

International Monetary Fund, 700 Nineteenth Street, NW, Washington, D.C. 20431 (202) 623-7000; *International Financial Statistics.*

Statistical Office of the United Nations, Publishing Service, New York, New York 10017 (800) 253-9646; *Statistical Yearbook.*

The World Bank, 1818 H Street, NW, Washington, D.C. 20433 (202) 477-1234; *World Development Indicators.*

NIGERIA - MORTALITY

Central Intelligence Agency, Washington, D.C. 20505 (703) 482-1100, www.cia.gov; *The World Factbook.*

Euromonitor International, Inc., 122 South Michigan Avenue, Suite 1200, Chicago, Illinois 60603 (800) 577-EURO; *International Marketing Data and Statistics;* and *The World Economic Factbook.*

Europa Publications Limited, 18 Bedford Square, London, WC1B 3JN, England; *The Europa World Year Book.*

Statistical Office of the United Nations, Publishing Service, New York, New York 10017 (800) 253-9646; *Demographic Yearbook; Human Development Report; Statistical Yearbook; World Statistics Pocketbook;* and *Survey of Economic and Social Conditions in Africa.*

United Nations Children's Fund (UNICEF), 3 United Nations Plaza, New York, New York 10017 (800) 253-9646; *State of the World's Children.*

The World Bank, 1818 H Street, NW, Washington, D.C. 20433 (202) 477-1234; *The World Bank Atlas; World Development Report;* and *World Development Indicators.*

World Health Organization, Office of Publications, 20 Avenue Appia, CH-1211 Geneva 27, Switzerland (Telephone Number in U.S. (518) 436-9686); *World Health Statistics Annual.*

NIGERIA - MOTION PICTURES

St. Martin's Press, Inc., 175 Fifth Avenue, New York, New York 10010 (800) 221-7945; *The Statesman's Year-Book.*

Statistical Office of the United Nations, Publishing Service, New York, New York 10017 (800) 253-9646; *Statistical Yearbook.*

United Nations Educational, Scientific and Cultural Organization (UNESCO), 7 Place de Fontenoy, F-75700 Paris, France (Telephone Number in U.S. (212) 963-5981); *Statistical Yearbook.*

NIGERIA - MOTOR VEHICLES IN USE

American Automobile Manufacturers Association, 1401 H Street, NW, Suite 900, Washington, D.C. 20005 (202) 326-5500; *World Motor Vehicle Data.*

Europa Publications Limited, 18 Bedford Square, London, WC1B 3JN, England; *The Europa World Year Book.*

Statistical Office of the United Nations, Publishing Service, New York, New York 10017 (800) 253-9646; *Statistical Yearbook;* and *Survey of Economic and Social Conditions in Africa.*

NIGERIA - MUSEUMS

M.E. Sharpe, 80 Business Park Drive, Armonk, New York 10504 (800) 541-6563; *The Illustrated Book of World Rankings.*

NIGERIA - NATALITY - See NIGERIA - BIRTH RATES

NIGERIA - NATIONAL ACCOUNTS

African Development Bank, 01 BP 1387, Abidjan 01, Cote d'Ivoire; *Selected Statistics on Regional Member Countries.*

Europa Publications Limited, 18 Bedford Square, London, WC1B 3JN, England; *The Europa World Year Book.*

International Monetary Fund, 700 Nineteenth Street, NW, Washington, D.C. 20431 (202) 623-7000; *International Financial Statistics.*

Statistical Office of the United Nations, Publishing Service, New York, New York 10017 (800) 253-9646; *National Accounts Statistics;* and *Statistical Yearbook.*

United Nations Economic Commission for Africa, Africa Hall, Post Office Box 3001, Addis Ababa, Ethiopia (Telephone Number in U.S. (800) 253-9646); *African Statistical Yearbook.*

NIGERIA - NATIONAL INCOME

M.E. Sharpe, 80 Business Park Drive, Armonk, New York 10504 (800) 541-6563; *The Illustrated Book of World Rankings.*

Statistical Office of the United Nations, Publishing Service, New York, New York 10017 (800) 253-9646; *National Accounts Statistics;* and *Statistical Yearbook.*

NIGERIA - NATIONAL PRODUCT

M.E. Sharpe, 80 Business Park Drive, Armonk, New York 10504 (800) 541-6563; *The Illustrated Book of World Rankings.*

Statistical Office of the United Nations, Publishing Service, New York, New York 10017 (800) 253-9646; *Statistical Yearbook.*

NIGERIA - NATURAL GAS PRODUCTION - See NIGERIA - MINING AND MINERAL PRODUCTS

NIGERIA - NATURAL RUBBER PRODUCTION

International Rubber Study Group, York House, Eighth Floor, Empire Way, Wembley, London HA9 0PA, England; *Rubber Statistical Bulletin.*

Statistical Office of the United Nations, Publishing Service, New York, New York 10017 (800) 253-9646; *Statistical Yearbook.*

NIGERIA - NEWSPAPER PRODUCTION - See NIGERIA - FORESTRY AND FOREST PRODUCTS

NIGERIA - NEWSPRINT - See NIGERIA - FORESTRY AND FOREST PRODUCTS

NIGERIA - PALM OIL AND PALM KERNELS PRODUCTION - See NIGERIA - CROPS

NIGERIA - PAPER - See NIGERIA - FORESTRY AND FOREST PRODUCTS

NIGERIA - PATENTS, TRADEMARKS AND SERVICE MARKS

Statistical Office of the United Nations, Publishing Service, New York, New York 10017 (800) 253-9646; *Statistical Yearbook.*

NIGERIA - PEANUT PRODUCTION - See NIGERIA - CROPS

NIGERIA - PESTICIDE USE

Food and Agricultural Organization of the United Nations (FAO) Via delle Terme di Caracalla, 00100 Rome, Italy (Telephone Number in U.S. (202) 653-2400); *The State of Food and Agriculture.*

NIGERIA - PETROLEUM INDUSTRY

Commodity Research Bureau, Inc., 30 South Wacker Drive, Chicago, Illinois 60606 (312) 454-1801; *Commodity Year Book.*

Food and Agricultural Organization of the United Nations (FAO) Via delle Terme di Caracalla, 00100 Rome, Italy (Telephone Number in U.S. (202) 653-2400); *The State of Food and Agriculture.*

M.E. Sharpe, 80 Business Park Drive, Armonk, New York 10504 (800) 541-6563; *The Illustrated Book of World Rankings.*

Organization of Petroleum Exporting Countries, Obere Donaustrasse 93, 1020 Vienna 2, Austria; *OPEC Annual Statistical Bulletin.*

Penn Well Publishing Company, 1421 South Sheridan Road, Post Office Box 1260, Tulsa, Oklahoma 74101 (800) 752-9764; *International Energy Statistics Sourcebook.*

St. Martin's Press, Inc., 175 Fifth Avenue, New York, New York 10010 (800) 221-7945; *The Statesman's Year-Book.*

Statistical Office of the United Nations, Publishing Service, New York, New York 10017 (800) 253-9646; *Statistical Yearbook.*

United Nations Conference on Trade and Development, Central Statistical Service, Palais des Nations, Geneva, Switzerland (Telephone in U.S. (800) 253-9646); *UNCTAD Commodity Yearbook.*

NIGERIA - PIGS - See NIGERIA - LIVESTOCK AND POULTRY

NIGERIA - PIPELINES FOR OIL AND PETROLEUM PRODUCTS

Organization of Petroleum Exporting Countries, Obere Donaustrasse 93, 1020 Vienna 2, Austria; *OPEC Annual Statistical Bulletin.*

NIGERIA - POPULATION

African Development Bank, 01 BP 1387, Abidjan 01, Cote d'Ivoire; *Selected Statistics on Regional Member Countries.*

Central Intelligence Agency, Washington, D.C. 20505 (703) 482-1100, www.cia.gov; *The World Factbook.*

The Economist Intelligence Unit, 111 West 57th Street, New York, New York 10019 (800) 938-4685; *Nigeria Country Report;* and *The World Market Atlas.*

Euromonitor International, Inc., 122 South Michigan Avenue, Suite 1200, Chicago, Illinois 60603 (800) 577-EURO; *International Marketing Data and Statistics;* and *The World Economic Factbook.*

Europa Publications Limited, 18 Bedford Square, London, WC1B 3JN, England; *The Europa World Year Book.*

Food and Agricultural Organization of the United Nations (FAO), Via delle Terme di Caracalla, 00100 Rome, Italy (Telephone Number in U.S. (202) 653-2400); *Production Yearbook.*

International Labour Office, I.L.O. Publications, 1828 L Street, NW, Suite 801, Washington, D.C. 20036 (301) 638-3152; *Yearbook of Labour Statistics.*

M.E. Sharpe, 80 Business Park Drive, Armonk, New York 10504 (800) 541-6563; *The Illustrated Book of World Rankings.*

St. Martin's Press, Inc., 175 Fifth Avenue, New York, New York 10010 (800) 221-7945; *The Statesman's Year-Book.*

Statistical Office of the United Nations, Publishing Service, New York, New York 10017 (800) 253-9646; *Demographic Yearbook; Human Development Report; Statistical Yearbook; World Statistics Pocketbook;* and *Survey of Economic and Social Conditions in Africa.*

United Nations Educational, Scientific and Cultural Organization (UNESCO), 7 Place de Fontenoy, F-75700 Paris, France (Telephone Number in U.S. (212) 963-5981); *Statistical Yearbook.*

U.S. Arms Control and Disarmament Agency, 320 Twenty-first Street, NW, Washington, D.C. 20451 (202) 647-8677; *World Military Expenditures and Arms Transfers.*

The World Bank, 1818 H Street, NW, Washington, D.C. 20433 (202) 477-1234; *The World Bank Atlas;* and *World Development Report.*

World Health Organization, Office of Publications, 20 Avenue Appia, CH-1211 Geneva 27, Switzerland (Telephone Number in U.S. (518) 436-9686); *World Health Statistics Annual.*

NIGERIA - POST OFFICES

M.E. Sharpe, 80 Business Park Drive, Armonk, New York 10504 (800) 541-6563; *The Illustrated Book of World Rankings.*

St. Martin's Press, Inc., 175 Fifth Avenue, New York, New York 10010 (800) 221-7945; *The Statesman's Year-Book.*

NIGERIA - POTATO PRODUCTION - See NIGERIA - CROPS

NIGERIA - PRICES

Food and Agricultural Organization of the United Nations (FAO), Via delle Terme di Caracalla, 00100 Rome, Italy (Telephone Number in U.S. (202) 653-2400); *Production Yearbook;* and *The State of Food and Agriculture.*

International Labour Office, I.L.O. Publications, 1828 L Street, NW, Suite 801, Washington, D.C. 20036 (301) 638-3152; *Yearbook of Labour Statistics.*

International Monetary Fund, 700 Nineteenth Street, NW, Washington, D.C. 20431 (202) 623-7000; *International Financial Statistics.*

International Rubber Study Group, York House, Eighth Floor, Empire Way, Wembley, London HA9 0PA, England; *Rubber Statistical Bulletin.*

M.E. Sharpe, 80 Business Park Drive, Armonk, New York 10504 (800) 541-6563; *The Illustrated Book of World Rankings.*

United Nations Economic Commission for Africa, Africa Hall, Post Office Box 3001, Addis Ababa, Ethiopia (Telephone Number in U.S. (800) 253-9646); *African Statistical Yearbook.*

NIGERIA - PRINTING AND WRITING PAPER - See NIGERIA - FORESTRY AND FOREST PRODUCTS

NIGERIA - PRODUCTION

American Automobile Manufacturers Association, 1401 H Street, NW, Suite 900, Washington, D.C. 20005 (202) 326-5500; *World Motor Vehicle Data.*

International Rubber Study Group, York House, Eighth Floor, Empire Way, Wembley, London HA9 0PA, England; *Rubber Statistical Bulletin.*

M.E. Sharpe, 80 Business Park Drive, Armonk, New York 10504 (800) 541-6563; *The Illustrated Book of World Rankings.*

NIGERIA - PRODUCTIVITY

Euromonitor International, Inc., 122 South Michigan Avenue, Suite 1200, Chicago, Illinois 60603 (800) 577-EURO; *International Marketing Data and Statistics.*

NIGERIA - PROPERTY TAXES

International Monetary Fund, 700 Nineteenth Street, NW, Washington, D.C. 20431 (202) 623-7000; *Government Finance Statistics Yearbook.*

NIGERIA - RADIO BROADCASTING - See NIGERIA - BROADCASTING

NIGERIA - RADIO RECEIVER PRODUCTION

Statistical Office of the United Nations, Publishing Service, New York, New York 10017 (800) 253-9646; *Statistical Yearbook.*

NIGERIA - RADIO RECEIVERS

St. Martin's Press, Inc., 175 Fifth Avenue, New York, New York 10010 (800) 221-7945; *The Statesman's Year-Book.*

NIGERIA - RAILWAYS

Europa Publications Limited, 18 Bedford Square, London, WC1B 3JN, England; *The Europa World Year Book.*

Jane's Information Group, Sentinel House, 163 Brighton Road, Coulsdon, Surrey CR5 2NH, England (Telephone Number in U.S. (703) 683-3700); *Jane's World Railways.*

St. Martin's Press, Inc., 175 Fifth Avenue, New York, New York 10010 (800) 221-7945; *The Statesman's Year-Book.*

Statistical Office of the United Nations, Publishing Service, New York, New York 10017 (800) 253-9646; *Statistical Yearbook;* and *Survey of Economic and Social Conditions in Africa.*

United Nations Economic Commission for Africa, Africa Hall, Post Office Box 3001, Addis Ababa, Ethiopia (Telephone Number in U.S. (800) 253-9646); *African Statistical Yearbook.*

NIGERIA - RELIGION

Central Intelligence Agency, Washington, D.C. 20505 (703) 482-1100, www.cia.gov; *The World Factbook.*

M.E. Sharpe, 80 Business Park Drive, Armonk, New York 10504 (800) 541-6563; *The Illustrated Book of World Rankings.*

St. Martin's Press, Inc., 175 Fifth Avenue, New York, New York 10010 (800) 221-7945; *The Statesman's Year-Book.*

NIGERIA - RENT PRICES

International Labour Office, I.L.O. Publications, 1828 L Street, NW, Suite 801, Washington, D.C. 20036 (301) 638-3152; *Yearbook of Labour Statistics.*

NIGERIA - RETAIL TRADE

Euromonitor International, Inc., 122 South Michigan Avenue, Suite 1200, Chicago, Illinois 60603 (800) 577-EURO; *World Marketing Data and Statistics.*

NIGERIA - RICE PRODUCTION - See NIGERIA - CROPS

NIGERIA - ROOT AND TUBER PRODUCTION - See NIGERIA - CROPS

NIGERIA - ROUNDWOOD PRODUCTION - See NIGERIA - FORESTRY AND FOREST PRODUCTS

NIGERIA - RUBBER PRODUCTION AND CONSUMPTION

International Rubber Study Group, York House, Eighth Floor, Empire Way, Wembley, London HA9 0PA, England; *Rubber Statistical Bulletin.*

M.E. Sharpe, 80 Business Park Drive, Armonk, New York 10504 (800) 541-6563; *The Illustrated Book of World Rankings.*

Statistical Office of the United Nations, Publishing Service, New York, New York 10017 (800) 253-9646; *Statistical Yearbook.*

NIGERIA - SAWNWOOD PRODUCTION - See NIGERIA - FORESTRY AND FOREST PRODUCTS

NIGERIA - SCIENCE AND TECHNOLOGY - EXPENDITURE FOR RESEARCH - See NIGERIA - SCIENTISTS, TECHNICIANS AND ENGINEERS

NIGERIA - SCIENTISTS, TECHNICIANS AND ENGINEERS

Statistical Office of the United Nations, Publishing Service, New York, New York 10017 (800) 253-9646; *Statistical Yearbook.*

United Nations Educational, Scientific and Cultural Organization (UNESCO), 7 Place de Fontenoy, F-75700 Paris, France (Telephone Number in U.S. (212) 963-5981); *Statistical Yearbook.*

NIGERIA - SENIOR CITIZENS

M.E. Sharpe, 80 Business Park Drive, Armonk, New York 10504 (800) 541-6563; *The Illustrated Book of World Rankings.*

NIGERIA - SESAME SEED PRODUCTION - See NIGERIA - CROPS

NIGERIA - SHEEP - See NIGERIA - LIVESTOCK AND POULTRY

NIGERIA - SILVER PRODUCTION AND CONSUMPTION - See NIGERIA - MINING AND MINERAL PRODUCTS

NIGERIA - SOCIAL DATA

African Development Bank, 01 BP 1387, Abidjan 01, Cote d'Ivoire; *Selected Statistics on Regional Member Countries.*

M.E. Sharpe, 80 Business Park Drive, Armonk, New York 10504 (800) 541-6563; *The Illustrated Book of World Rankings.*

Statistical Office of the United Nations, Publishing Service, New York, New York 10017 (800) 253-9646; *World Statistics Pocketbook.*

NIGERIA - SOCIAL SECURITY

International Monetary Fund, 700 Nineteenth Street, NW, Washington, D.C. 20431 (202) 623-7000; *Government Finance Statistics Yearbook.*

Statistical Office of the United Nations, Publishing Service, New York, New York 10017 (800) 253-9646; *National Accounts Statistics.*

NIGERIA - SOYBEAN PRODUCTION - See NIGERIA - CROPS

NIGERIA - STAMP TAXES AND DUTIES - See NIGERIA - TAXATION

NIGERIA - STATE BUDGET REVENUE AND EXPENDITURES

Euromonitor International, Inc., 122 South Michigan Avenue, Suite 1200, Chicago, Illinois 60603 (800) 577-EURO; *International Marketing Data and Statistics.*

NIGERIA - STEEL - See NIGERIA - MINING AND MINERAL PRODUCTS

NIGERIA - STOCKS - COMMODITY -

MARKET PRICE - INDEX

Food and Agricultural Organization of the United Nations (FAO) Via delle Terme di Caracalla, 00100 Rome, Italy (Telephone Number in U.S. (202) 653-2400); *The State of Food and Agriculture.*

M.E. Sharpe, 80 Business Park Drive, Armonk, New York 10504 (800) 541-6563; *The Illustrated Book of World Rankings.*

NIGERIA - SUGAR PRODUCTION AND CONSUMPTION - See NIGERIA - CROPS

NIGERIA - TAXATION

International Monetary Fund, 700 Nineteenth Street, NW, Washington, D.C. 20431 (202) 623-7000; *Government Finance Statistics Yearbook.*

The World Bank, 1818 H Street, NW, Washington, D.C. 20433 (202) 477-1234; *World Development Indicators.*

NIGERIA - TAX REVENUES - See NIGERIA - TAXATION

NIGERIA - TELEGRAPH SERVICE

Statistical Office of the United Nations, Publishing Service, New York, New York 10017 (800) 253-9646; *Statistical Yearbook.*

NIGERIA - TELEPHONES IN USE

American Telephone and Telegraph Company, 26 Parsippany Road, Whippany, New Jersey 07981 (800) 222-0300; *The World's Telephones.*

Central Intelligence Agency, Washington, D.C. 20505 (703) 482-1100, www.cia.gov; *The World Factbook.*

Europa Publications Limited, 18 Bedford Square, London, WC1B 3JN, England; *The Europa World Year Book.*

St. Martin's Press, Inc., 175 Fifth Avenue, New York, New York 10010 (800) 221-7945; *The Statesman's Year-Book.*

Statistical Office of the United Nations, Publishing Service, New York, New York 10017 (800) 253-9646; *Statistical Yearbook;* and *World Statistics Pocketbook.*

NIGERIA - TELEVISION BROADCASTING - See NIGERIA - BROADCASTING

NIGERIA - TEXTILE INDUSTRY

M.E. Sharpe, 80 Business Park Drive, Armonk, New York 10504 (800) 541-6563; *The Illustrated Book of World Rankings.*

St. Martin's Press, Inc., 175 Fifth Avenue, New York, New York 10010 (800) 221-7945; *The Statesman's Year-Book.*

Statistical Office of the United Nations, Publishing Service, New York, New York 10017 (800) 253-9646; *Statistical Yearbook.*

United Nations Conference on Trade and Development, Central Statistical Service, Palais des Nations, Geneva, Switzerland (Telephone in U.S. (800) 253-9646); *UNCTAD Commodity Yearbook.*

NIGERIA - TIN - See NIGERIA - MINING AND MINERAL PRODUCTS

NIGERIA - TIRE (MOTOR VEHICLE) PRODUCTION

International Rubber Study Group, York House, Eighth Floor, Empire Way, Wembley, London HA9 0PA, England; *Rubber Statistical Bulletin.*

Statistical Office of the United Nations, Publishing Service, New York, New York 10017 (800) 253-9646; *Statistical Yearbook.*

NIGERIA - TOBACCO PRODUCTION

M.E. Sharpe, 80 Business Park Drive, Armonk, New York 10504 (800) 541-6563; *The Illustrated Book of World Rankings.*

Statistical Office of the United Nations, Publishing Service, New York, New York 10017 (800) 253-9646; *Statistical Yearbook.*

NIGERIA - TOURISM

Euromonitor International, Inc., 122 South Michigan Avenue, Suite 1200, Chicago, Illinois 60603 (800) 577-EURO; *The World Economic Factbook;* and *World Marketing Data and Statistics.*

Europa Publications Limited, 18 Bedford Square, London, WC1B 3JN, England; *The Europa World Year Book.*

M.E. Sharpe, 80 Business Park Drive, Armonk, New York 10504 (800) 541-6563; *The Illustrated Book of World Rankings.*

St. Martin's Press, Inc., 175 Fifth Avenue, New York, New York 10010 (800) 221-7945; *The Statesman's Year-Book.*

Statistical Office of the United Nations, Publishing Service, New York, New York 10017 (800) 253-9646; *Statistical Yearbook.*

United Nations Economic Commission for Africa, Africa Hall, Post Office Box 3001, Addis Ababa, Ethiopia (Telephone Number in U.S. (800) 253-9646); *African Statistical Yearbook.*

NIGERIA - TRACTORS IN USE

Statistical Office of the United Nations, Publishing Service, New York, New York 10017 (800) 253-9646; *Statistical Yearbook.*

NIGERIA - TRADE - See NIGERIA - FOREIGN TRADE

NIGERIA - TRADEMARKS AND SERVICE MARKS - See NIGERIA - PATENTS, TRADEMARKS AND SERVICE MARKS

NIGERIA - TRANSPORTATION AND COMMUNICATIONS

Central Intelligence Agency, Washington, D.C. 20505 (703) 482-1100, www.cia.gov; *The World Factbook.*

Euromonitor International, Inc., 122 South Michigan Avenue, Suite 1200, Chicago, Illinois 60603 (800) 577-EURO; *International Marketing Data and Statistics;* and *World Marketing Data and Statistics.*

Europa Publications Limited, 18 Bedford Square, London, WC1B 3JN, England; *The Europa World Year Book.*

M.E. Sharpe, 80 Business Park Drive, Armonk, New York 10504 (800) 541-6563; *The Illustrated Book of World Rankings.*

St. Martin's Press, Inc., 175 Fifth Avenue, New York, New York 10010 (800) 221-7945; *The Statesman's Year-Book.*

Statistical Office of the United Nations, Publishing Service, New York, New York 10017 (800) 253-9646; *Human Development Report.*

United Nations Economic Commission for Africa, Africa Hall, Post Office Box 3001, Addis Ababa, Ethiopia (Telephone Number in U.S. (800) 253-9646); *African Statistical Yearbook.*

NIGERIA - UNEMPLOYMENT

Central Intelligence Agency, Washington, D.C. 20505 (703) 482-1100, www.cia.gov; *The World Factbook.*

Euromonitor International, Inc., 122 South Michigan Avenue, Suite 1200, Chicago, Illinois 60603 (800) 577-EURO; *International Marketing Data and Statistics.*

International Labour Office, I.L.O. Publications, 1828 L Street, NW, Suite 801, Washington, D.C. 20036 (301) 638-3152; *Yearbook of Labour Statistics.*

Statistical Office of the United Nations, Publishing Service, New York, New York 10017 (800) 253-9646; *Statistical Yearbook.*

NIGERIA - VITAL STATISTICS

Euromonitor International, Inc., 122 South Michigan Avenue, Suite 1200, Chicago, Illinois 60603 (800) 577-EURO; *International Marketing Data and Statistics.*

Statistical Office of the United Nations,

Publishing Service, New York, New York 10017 (800) 253-9646; *Statistical Yearbook.*

World Health Organization, Office of Publications, 20 Avenue Appia, CH-1211 Geneva 27, Switzerland (Telephone Number in U.S. (518) 436-9686); *World Health Statistics Annual.*

NIGERIA - WAGES

International Labour Office, I.L.O. Publications, 1828 L Street, NW, Suite 801, Washington, D.C. 20036 (301) 638-3152; *Yearbook of Labour Statistics.*

Statistical Office of the United Nations, Publishing Service, New York, New York 10017 (800) 253-9646; *Statistical Yearbook.*

NIGERIA - WEATHER - See NIGERIA - CLIMATE

NIGERIA - WELFARE

International Monetary Fund, 700 Nineteenth Street, NW, Washington, D.C. 20431 (202) 623-7000; *Government Finance Statistics Yearbook.*

NIGERIA - WHEAT PRODUCTION AND PRICES - See NIGERIA - CROPS

NIGERIA - WINE PRODUCTION - See NIGERIA - BEVERAGES

NIGERIA - WOOD PULP PRODUCTION - See NIGERIA - FORESTRY AND FOREST PRODUCTS

NIGERIA - WOOL PRODUCTION - See NIGERIA - TEXTILE INDUSTRY

NIGERIA - YARN PRODUCTION - See NIGERIA - TEXTILE INDUSTRY

NITROGEN IN AMMONIA - WORLD PRODUCTION

U.S. Department of the Interior, Bureau of the Mines, 810 Seventh Street, NW, Washington, D.C. 20241 (202) 501-9649; *Annual Reports;* and *Mineral Commodity Summaries.*

Niue - National Statistical Office

Government of Niue, Post Office Box 67, Alofi, Niue, South Pacific.

Niue - Primary Statistics Source

Department of Economic Development, Statistics Unit, Post Office Box 42, Niue Island, Niue; *Abstract of Statistics.*

NIUE - AGRICULTURE

Europa Publications Limited, 18 Bedford Square, London, WC1B 3JN, England; *The Europa World Year Book.*

Food and Agricultural Organization of the United Nations (FAO) Via delle Terme di Caracalla, 00100 Rome, Italy (Telephone Number in U.S. (202) 653-2400); *Production Yearbook; The State of Food and Agriculture;* and *Trade Yearbook.*

St. Martin's Press, Inc., 175 Fifth Avenue, New York, New York 10010 (800) 221-7945; *The Statesman's Year-Book.*

Statistical Office of the United Nations, Publishing Service, New York, New York 10017 (800) 253-9646; *Asia-Pacific in Figures; Statistical Yearbook;* and *Statistical Yearbook for Asia and the Pacific.*

United Nations Conference on Trade and Development, Central Statistical Service, Palais des Nations, Geneva, Switzerland (Telephone in U.S. (800) 253-9646); *UNCTAD Commodity Yearbook.*

NIUE - AIRLINE SERVICE

Europa Publications Limited, 18 Bedford Square, London, WC1B 3JN, England; *The Europa World Year Book.*

St. Martin's Press, Inc., 175 Fifth Avenue, New York, New York 10010 (800) 221-7945; *The Statesman's Year-Book.*

NIUE - AIRPORTS

Central Intelligence Agency, Washington, D.C. 20505 (703) 482-1100, www.cia.gov; *The World Factbook.*

NIUE - AREA AND DENSITY OF POPULATION

Central Intelligence Agency, Washington, D.C. 20505 (703) 482-1100, www.cia.gov; *The World Factbook.*

Europa Publications Limited, 18 Bedford Square, London, WC1B 3JN, England; *The Europa World Year Book.*

Food and Agricultural Organization of the United Nations (FAO) Via delle Terme di Caracalla, 00100 Rome, Italy (Telephone Number in U.S. (202) 653-2400); *The State of Food and Agriculture.*

St. Martin's Press, Inc., 175 Fifth Avenue, New York, New York 10010 (800) 221-7945; *The Statesman's Year-Book.*

Statistical Office of the United Nations, Publishing Service, New York, New York 10017 (800) 253-9646; *Statistical Yearbook.*

NIUE - BIRTH RATES

Central Intelligence Agency, Washington, D.C. 20505 (703) 482-1100, www.cia.gov; *The World Factbook.*

Europa Publications Limited, 18 Bedford Square, London, WC1B 3JN, England; *The Europa World Year Book.*

St. Martin's Press, Inc., 175 Fifth Avenue, New York, New York 10010 (800) 221-7945; *The Statesman's Year-Book.*

Statistical Office of the United Nations, Publishing Service, New York, New York 10017 (800) 253-9646; *Asia-Pacific in Figures; Demographic Yearbook;* and *Statistical Yearbook.*

World Health Organization, Office of Publications, 20 Avenue Appia, CH-1211 Geneva 27, Switzerland (Telephone Number in U.S. (518) 436-9686); *World Health Statistics Annual.*

NIUE - BROADCASTING

Billboard Limited, Post Office Box 9027, 1006 AA Amsterdam, The Netherlands (Telephone Number in U.S. (212) 764-7300); *World Radio TV Handbook.*

Central Intelligence Agency, Washington, D.C. 20505 (703) 482-1100, www.cia.gov; *The World Factbook.*

St. Martin's Press, Inc., 175 Fifth Avenue, New York, New York 10010 (800) 221-7945; *The Statesman's Year-Book.*

United Nations Educational, Scientific and Cultural Organization (UNESCO), 7 Place de Fontenoy, F-75700 Paris, France (Telephone Number in U.S. (212) 963-5981); *Statistical Yearbook.*

NIUE - BUDGET

Central Intelligence Agency, Washington, D.C. 20505 (703) 482-1100, www.cia.gov; *The World Factbook.*

NIUE - CALORIE SUPPLY

Food and Agricultural Organization of the United Nations (FAO) Via delle Terme di Caracalla, 00100 Rome, Italy (Telephone Number in U.S. (202) 653-2400); *The State of Food and Agriculture.*

NIUE - CATTLE - See NIUE - LIVESTOCK AND POULTRY

NIUE - CLOTHING EXPORTS AND IMPORTS - See NIUE - TEXTILE INDUSTRY

NIUE - COMMERCE

St. Martin's Press, Inc., 175 Fifth Avenue, New York, New York 10010 (800) 221-7945; *The Statesman's Year-Book.*

NIUE - COMMUNICATIONS - See NIUE - TRANSPORTATION AND COMMUNICATIONS

NIUE - CONSUMER PRICE INDEX

Europa Publications Limited, 18 Bedford Square, London, WC1B 3JN, England; *The Europa World Year Book.*

Statistical Office of the United Nations, Publishing Service, New York, New York 10017 (800) 253-9646; *Statistical Yearbook.*

NIUE - CONSUMER PRICES

International Labour Office, I.L.O. Publications, 1828 L Street, NW, Suite 801, Washington, D.C. 20036 (301) 638-3152; *Yearbook of Labour Statistics.*

NIUE - CONSUMPTION

South Pacific Commission, Post Box D5, Noumea Cedex, New Caledonia; *Statistical Bulletin of the South Pacific: Retail Price Indexes.*

NIUE - CORN PRODUCTION - See NIUE - CROPS

NIUE - CROPS

Europa Publications Limited, 18 Bedford Square, London, WC1B 3JN, England; *The Europa World Year Book.*

Food and Agricultural Organization of the United Nations (FAO) Via delle Terme di Caracalla, 00100 Rome, Italy (Telephone Number in U.S. (202) 653-2400); *Production Yearbook;* and *The State of Food and Agriculture.*

St. Martin's Press, Inc., 175 Fifth Avenue, New York, New York 10010 (800) 221-7945; *The Statesman's Year-Book.*

United Nations Conference on Trade and Development, Central Statistical Service, Palais des Nations, Geneva, Switzerland (Telephone in U.S. (800) 253-9646); *UNCTAD Commodity Yearbook.*

NIUE - DAIRY PRODUCTS

Europa Publications Limited, 18 Bedford Square, London, WC1B 3JN, England; *The Europa World Year Book.*

Food and Agricultural Organization of the United Nations (FAO) Via delle Terme di Caracalla, 00100 Rome, Italy (Telephone Number in U.S. (202) 653-2400); *The State of Food and Agriculture.*

NIUE - DEATH RATES - See NIUE - MORTALITY

NIUE - DEMOGRAPHY

Statistical Office of the United Nations, Publishing Service, New York, New York 10017 (800) 253-9646; *Asia-Pacific in Figures.*

NIUE - DEVELOPMENT ASSISTANCE

Statistical Office of the United Nations, Publishing Service, New York, New York 10017 (800) 253-9646; *Statistical Yearbook.*

NIUE - DIVORCE RATES

Statistical Office of the United Nations, Publishing Service, New York, New York 10017 (800) 253-9646; *Demographic Yearbook;* and *Statistical Yearbook.*

NIUE - ECONOMY

Central Intelligence Agency, Washington, D.C. 20505 (703) 482-1100, www.cia.gov; *The World Factbook.*

NIUE - EDUCATION

Europa Publications Limited, 18 Bedford Square, London, WC1B 3JN, England; *The Europa World Year Book.*

Statistical Office of the United Nations, Publishing Service, New York, New York 10017 (800) 253-9646; *Asia-Pacific in Figures;* and *Statistical Yearbook for Asia and the Pacific.*

United Nations Educational, Scientific and Cultural Organization (UNESCO), 7 Place de Fontenoy, F-75700 Paris, France (Telephone Number in U.S. (212) 963-5981); *Statistical Yearbook.*

NIUE - EGG PRODUCTION AND CONSUMPTION - See NIUE - DAIRY PRODUCTS

NIUE - ELECTRICITY

Central Intelligence Agency, Washington, D.C. 20505 (703) 482-1100, www.cia.gov; *The World Factbook.*

Statistical Office of the United Nations, Publishing Service, New York, New York 10017 (800) 253-9646; *Electric Power in Asia and the Pacific.*

NIUE - EMPLOYMENT

International Labour Office, I.L.O. Publications, 1828 L Street, NW, Suite 801, Washington, D.C. 20036 (301) 638-3152; *Yearbook of Labour Statistics.*

Statistical Office of the United Nations, Publishing Service, New York, New York 10017 (800) 253-9646; *Asia-Pacific in Figures.*

NIUE - ENERGY

Food and Agricultural Organization of the United Nations (FAO) Via delle Terme di Caracalla, 00100 Rome, Italy (Telephone Number in U.S. (202) 653-2400); *The State of Food and Agriculture.*

Statistical Office of the United Nations, Publishing Service, New York, New York 10017 (800) 253-9646; *Asia-Pacific in Figures;* and *Statistical Yearbook for Asia and the Pacific.*

NIUE - EXCHANGE RATES

Central Intelligence Agency, Washington, D.C. 20505 (703) 482-1100, www.cia.gov; *The World Factbook.*

Europa Publications Limited, 18 Bedford Square, London, WC1B 3JN, England; *The Europa World Year Book.*

Walden Publishing Ltd., Two Market Street, Saffron Walden Essex, CB10 1HZ, England; *The World of Information Asia and Pacific Review.*

NIUE - EXPORTS

Central Intelligence Agency, Washington, D.C. 20505 (703) 482-1100, www.cia.gov; *The World Factbook.*

Europa Publications Limited, 18 Bedford Square, London, WC1B 3JN, England; *The Europa World Year Book.*

Food and Agricultural Organization of the United Nations (FAO) Via delle Terme di Caracalla, 00100 Rome, Italy (Telephone Number in U.S. (202) 653-2400); *The State of Food and Agriculture.*

South Pacific Commission, Post Box D5, Noumea Cedex, New Caledonia; *Statistical Bulletin of the South Pacific: Overseas Trade.*

St. Martin's Press, Inc., 175 Fifth Avenue, New York, New York 10010 (800) 221-7945; *The Statesman's Year-Book.*

Walden Publishing Ltd., Two Market Street, Saffron Walden Essex, CB10 1HZ, England; *The World of Information Asia and Pacific Review.*

NIUE - EXTERNAL TRADE

Food and Agricultural Organization of the United Nations (FAO) Via delle Terme di Caracalla, 00100 Rome, Italy (Telephone Number in U.S. (202) 653-2400); *The State of Food and Agriculture;* and *Trade Yearbook.*

Statistical Office of the United Nations, Publishing Service, New York, New York 10017 (800) 253-9646; *Asia-Pacific in Figures;* and *Statistical Yearbook for Asia and the Pacific.*

NIUE - FARM CROPS - See NIUE - CROPS

NIUE - FERTILITY RATES

Central Intelligence Agency, Washington, D.C. 20505 (703) 482-1100, www.cia.gov; *The World Factbook.*

NIUE - FERTILIZER

Food and Agricultural Organization of the United Nations (FAO) Via delle Terme di Caracalla, 00100 Rome, Italy (Telephone Number in U.S. (202) 653-2400); *The State of Food and Agriculture.*

NIUE - FETAL MORTALITY - See NIUE - MORTALITY

NIUE - FINANCE

Europa Publications Limited, 18 Bedford Square, London, WC1B 3JN, England; *The Europa World Year Book.*

Statistical Office of the United Nations, Publishing Service, New York, New York 10017 (800) 253-9646; *Statistical Yearbook for Asia and the Pacific.*

NIUE - FISHERIES

Europa Publications Limited, 18 Bedford Square, London, WC1B 3JN, England; *The Europa World Year Book.*

Food and Agricultural Organization of the United Nations (FAO) Via delle Terme di Caracalla, 00100 Rome, Italy (Telephone Number in U.S. (202) 653-2400); *The State of Food and Agriculture;* and *Yearbook of Fishery Statistics.*

United Nations Conference on Trade and Development, Central Statistical Service, Palais des Nations, Geneva, Switzerland (Telephone in U.S. (800) 253-9646); *UNCTAD Commodity Yearbook.*

NIUE - FOOD

Food and Agricultural Organization of the United Nations (FAO), Via delle Terme di Caracalla, 00100 Rome, Italy (Telephone Number in U.S. (202) 653-2400); *Production Yearbook;* and *The State of Food and Agriculture.*

South Pacific Commission, Post Box D5, Noumea Cedex, New Caledonia; *Statistical Bulletin of the South Pacific: Retail Price Indexes.*

Statistical Office of the United Nations, Publishing Service, New York, New York 10017 (800) 253-9646; *Statistical Yearbook for Asia and the Pacific.*

United Nations Conference on Trade and Development, Central Statistical Service, Palais des Nations, Geneva,

Switzerland (Telephone in U.S. (800) 253-9646); *UNCTAD Commodity Yearbook*.

NIUE - FOREIGN DEBT

Walden Publishing Ltd., Two Market Street, Saffron Walden Essex, CB10 1HZ, England; *The World of Information Asia and Pacific Review*.

NIUE - FOREIGN TRADE

Europa Publications Limited, 18 Bedford Square, London, WC1B 3JN, England; *The Europa World Year Book*.

Food and Agricultural Organization of the United Nations (FAO) Via delle Terme di Caracalla, 00100 Rome, Italy (Telephone Number in U.S. (202) 653-2400); *The State of Food and Agriculture*.

South Pacific Commission, Post Box D5, Noumea Cedex, New Caledonia; *Statistical Bulletin of the South Pacific: Overseas Trade*.

St. Martin's Press, Inc., 175 Fifth Avenue, New York, New York 10010 (800) 221-7945; *The Statesman's Year-Book*.

Statistical Office of the United Nations, Publishing Service, New York, New York 10017 (800) 253-9646; *International Trade Statistics Yearbook*.

United Nations Conference on Trade and Development, Central Statistical Service, Palais des Nations, Geneva, Switzerland (Telephone in U.S. (800) 253-9646); *UNCTAD Commodity Yearbook*.

NIUE - FORESTRY AND FOREST PRODUCTS

Europa Publications Limited, 18 Bedford Square, London, WC1B 3JN, England; *The Europa World Year Book*.

Food and Agricultural Organization of the United Nations (FAO) Via delle Terme di Caracalla, 00100 Rome, Italy (Telephone Number in U.S. (202) 653-2400); *The State of Food and Agriculture*.

Statistical Office of the United Nations, Publishing Service, New York, New York 10017 (800) 253-9646; *Statistical Yearbook*.

United Nations Conference on Trade and Development, Central Statistical Service, Palais des Nations, Geneva, Switzerland (Telephone in U.S. (800) 253-9646); *UNCTAD Commodity Yearbook*.

NIUE - GENERAL MORTALITY - See NIUE - MORTALITY

NIUE - GOVERNMENT

Central Intelligence Agency,

Washington, D.C. 20505 (703) 482-1100, www.cia.gov; *The World Factbook*.

Europa Publications Limited, 18 Bedford Square, London, WC1B 3JN, England; *The Europa World Year Book*.

St. Martin's Press, Inc., 175 Fifth Avenue, New York, New York 10010 (800) 221-7945; *The Statesman's Year-Book*.

Statistical Office of the United Nations, Publishing Service, New York, New York 10017 (800) 253-9646; *Asia-Pacific in Figures*.

NIUE - GRAIN PRODUCTION - See NIUE - CROPS

NIUE - GROSS DOMESTIC PRODUCT

Europa Publications Limited, 18 Bedford Square, London, WC1B 3JN, England; *The Europa World Year Book*.

NIUE - GROSS NATIONAL PRODUCT

Walden Publishing Ltd., Two Market Street, Saffron Walden Essex, CB10 1HZ, England; *The World of Information Asia and Pacific Review*.

NIUE - HEALTH

South Pacific Commission, Post Box D5, Noumea Cedex, New Caledonia; *Statistical Bulletin of the South Pacific: Retail Price Indexes*.

St. Martin's Press, Inc., 175 Fifth Avenue, New York, New York 10010 (800) 221-7945; *The Statesman's Year-Book*.

Statistical Office of the United Nations, Publishing Service, New York, New York 10017 (800) 253-9646; *Asia-Pacific in Figures; and Statistical Yearbook*.

NIUE - HIDE PRODUCTION

Food and Agricultural Organization of the United Nations (FAO), Via delle Terme di Caracalla, 00100 Rome, Italy (Telephone Number in U.S. (202) 653-2400); *Production Yearbook*.

NIUE - HIGHWAYS

Central Intelligence Agency, Washington, D.C. 20505 (703) 482-1100, www.cia.gov; *The World Factbook*.

NIUE - HOURS OF WORK - See NIUE - EMPLOYMENT

NIUE - HOUSING AND HOUSING UNITS

South Pacific Commission, Post Box D5, Noumea Cedex, New Caledonia; *Statistical Bulletin of the South Pacific: Retail Price Indexes*.

NIUE - HOUSING EXPENDITURES

South Pacific Commission, Post Box D5, Noumea Cedex, New Caledonia; *Statistical Bulletin of the South Pacific: Retail Price Indexes*.

NIUE - ILLITERATE POPULATION

Central Intelligence Agency, Washington, D.C. 20505 (703) 482-1100, www.cia.gov; *The World Factbook*.

Statistical Office of the United Nations, Publishing Service, New York, New York 10017 (800) 253-9646; *Asia-Pacific in Figures*.

United Nations Educational, Scientific and Cultural Organization (UNESCO), 7 Place de Fontenoy, F-75700 Paris, France (Telephone Number in U.S. (212) 963-5981); *Statistical Yearbook*.

NIUE - IMPORTS

Central Intelligence Agency, Washington, D.C. 20505 (703) 482-1100, www.cia.gov; *The World Factbook*.

Europa Publications Limited, 18 Bedford Square, London, WC1B 3JN, England; *The Europa World Year Book*.

Food and Agricultural Organization of the United Nations (FAO) Via delle Terme di Caracalla, 00100 Rome, Italy (Telephone Number in U.S. (202) 653-2400); *The State of Food and Agriculture*.

South Pacific Commission, Post Box D5, Noumea Cedex, New Caledonia; *Statistical Bulletin of the South Pacific: Overseas Trade*.

St. Martin's Press, Inc., 175 Fifth Avenue, New York, New York 10010 (800) 221-7945; *The Statesman's Year-Book*.

Walden Publishing Ltd., Two Market Street, Saffron Walden Essex, CB10 1HZ, England; *The World of Information Asia and Pacific Review*.

NIUE - INDUSTRY

Central Intelligence Agency, Washington, D.C. 20505 (703) 482-1100, www.cia.gov; *The World Factbook*.

Europa Publications Limited, 18 Bedford Square, London, WC1B 3JN, England; *The Europa World Year Book*.

International Labour Office, I.L.O. Publications, 1828 L Street, NW, Suite 801, Washington, D.C. 20036 (301) 638-3152; *Yearbook of Labour Statistics*.

Statistical Office of the United Nations, Publishing Service, New York, New York

10017 (800) 253-9646; *Asia-Pacific in Figures;* and *Statistical Yearbook for Asia and the Pacific.*

NIUE - INFANT AND MATERNAL MORTALITY - See NIUE - MORTALITY

NIUE - INTERNAL TRADE

Statistical Office of the United Nations, Publishing Service, New York, New York 10017 (800) 253-9646; *Statistical Yearbook for Asia and the Pacific.*

NIUE - LABOR

Central Intelligence Agency, Washington, D.C. 20505 (703) 482-1100, www.cia.gov; *The World Factbook.*

Food and Agricultural Organization of the United Nations (FAO) Via delle Terme di Caracalla, 00100 Rome, Italy (Telephone Number in U.S. (202) 653-2400); *The State of Food and Agriculture.*

International Labour Office, I.L.O. Publications, 1828 L Street, NW, Suite 801, Washington, D.C. 20036 (301) 638-3152; *Yearbook of Labour Statistics.*

NIUE - LAND USE

Central Intelligence Agency, Washington, D.C. 20505 (703) 482-1100, www.cia.gov; *The World Factbook.*

Food and Agricultural Organization of the United Nations (FAO), Via delle Terme di Caracalla, 00100 Rome, Italy (Telephone Number in U.S. (202) 653-2400); *Production Yearbook.*

NIUE - LIBRARIES

United Nations Educational, Scientific and Cultural Organization (UNESCO), 7 Place de Fontenoy, F-75700 Paris, France (Telephone Number in U.S. (212) 963-5981); *Statistical Yearbook.*

NIUE - LIFE EXPECTANCY

Central Intelligence Agency, Washington, D.C. 20505 (703) 482-1100, www.cia.gov; *The World Factbook.*

Statistical Office of the United Nations, Publishing Service, New York, New York 10017 (800) 253-9646; *Asia-Pacific in Figures.*

NIUE - LIVESTOCK AND POULTRY

Europa Publications Limited, 18 Bedford Square, London, WC1B 3JN, England; *The Europa World Year Book.*

Food and Agricultural Organization of the United Nations (FAO), Via delle Terme di Caracalla, 00100 Rome, Italy (Telephone

Number in U.S. (202) 653-2400); *Production Yearbook;* and *The State of Food and Agriculture.*

St. Martin's Press, Inc., 175 Fifth Avenue, New York, New York 10010 (800) 221-7945; *The Statesman's Year-Book.*

Statistical Office of the United Nations, Publishing Service, New York, New York 10017 (800) 253-9646; *Statistical Yearbook.*

United Nations Conference on Trade and Development, Central Statistical Service, Palais des Nations, Geneva, Switzerland (Telephone in U.S. (800) 253-9646); *UNCTAD Commodity Yearbook.*

NIUE - MANPOWER

Statistical Office of the United Nations, Publishing Service, New York, New York 10017 (800) 253-9646; *Statistical Yearbook for Asia and the Pacific.*

NIUE - MARRIAGE RATES

Europa Publications Limited, 18 Bedford Square, London, WC1B 3JN, England; *The Europa World Year Book.*

Statistical Office of the United Nations, Publishing Service, New York, New York 10017 (800) 253-9646; *Dernographic Yearbook;* and *Statistical Yearbook.*

NIUE - MEAT PRODUCTION - See NIUE - LIVESTOCK AND POULTRY

NIUE - MERCHANT SHIPPING

Europa Publications Limited, 18 Bedford Square, London, WC1B 3JN, England; *The Europa World Year Book.*

NIUE - MILITARY

Central Intelligence Agency, Washington, D.C. 20505 (703) 482-1100, www.cia.gov; *The World Factbook.*

NIUE - MINING AND MINERAL PRODUCTS

United Nations Conference on Trade and Development, Central Statistical Service, Palais des Nations, Geneva, Switzerland (Telephone in U.S. (800) 253-9646); *UNCTAD Commodity Yearbook.*

NIUE - MORTALITY

Central Intelligence Agency, Washington, D.C. 20505 (703) 482-1100, www.cia.gov; *The World Factbook.*

Europa Publications Limited, 18 Bedford Square, London, WC1B 3JN, England; *The Europa World Year Book.*

St. Martin's Press, Inc., 175 Fifth Avenue,

New York, New York 10010 (800) 221-7945; *The Statesman's Year-Book.*

Statistical Office of the United Nations, Publishing Service, New York, New York 10017 (800) 253-9646; *Asia-Pacific in Figures; Demographic Yearbook;* and *Statistical Yearbook.*

World Health Organization, Office of Publications, 20 Avenue Appia, CH-1211 Geneva 27, Switzerland (Telephone Number in U.S. (518) 436-9686); *World Health Statistics Annual.*

NIUE - MOTION PICTURE THEATRES

Statistical Office of the United Nations, Publishing Service, New York, New York 10017 (800) 253-9646; *Statistical Yearbook.*

NIUE - MOTOR VEHICLES IN USE

Europa Publications Limited, 18 Bedford Square, London, WC1B 3JN, England; *The Europa World Year Book.*

NIUE - NATALITY - See NIUE - BIRTH RATES

NIUE - NATIONAL ACCOUNTS

Statistical Office of the United Nations, Publishing Service, New York, New York 10017 (800) 253-9646; *Asia-Pacific in Figures;* and *Statistical Yearbook for Asia and the Pacific.*

NIUE - NEWSPAPER PRODUCTION - See NIUE - FORESTRY AND FOREST PRODUCTS

NIUE - PERIODICALS

United Nations Educational, Scientific and Cultural Organization (UNESCO), 7 Place de Fontenoy, F-75700 Paris, France (Telephone Number in U.S. (212) 963-5981); *Statistical Yearbook.*

NIUE - PESTICIDE USE

Food and Agricultural Organization of the United Nations (FAO) Via delle Terme di Caracalla, 00100 Rome, Italy (Telephone Number in U.S. (202) 653-2400); *The State of Food and Agriculture.*

NIUE - PETROLEUM INDUSTRY

Food and Agricultural Organization of the United Nations (FAO) Via delle Terme di Caracalla, 00100 Rome, Italy (Telephone Number in U.S. (202) 653-2400); *The State of Food and Agriculture.*

United Nations Conference on Trade and Development, Central Statistical Service, Palais des Nations, Geneva, Switzerland (Telephone in U.S. (800) 253-9646); *UNCTAD Commodity Yearbook.*

NIUE - PIGS - See NIUE - LIVESTOCK AND POULTRY

NIUE - POPULATION

Central Intelligence Agency, Washington, D.C. 20505 (703) 482-1100, www.cia.gov; *The World Factbook.*

Europa Publications Limited, 18 Bedford Square, London, WC1B 3JN, England; *The Europa World Year Book.*

Food and Agricultural Organization of the United Nations (FAO), Via delle Terme di Caracalla, 00100 Rome, Italy (Telephone Number in U.S. (202) 653-2400); *Production Yearbook.*

International Labour Office, I.L.O. Publications, 1828 L Street, NW, Suite 801, Washington, D.C. 20036 (301) 638-3152; *Yearbook of Labour Statistics.*

St. Martin's Press, Inc., 175 Fifth Avenue, New York, New York 10010 (800) 221-7945; *The Statesman's Year-Book.*

Statistical Office of the United Nations, Publishing Service, New York, New York 10017 (800) 253-9646; *Asia-Pacific in Figures; Demographic Yearbook;* and *Statistical Yearbook for Asia and the Pacific.*

Walden Publishing Ltd., Two Market Street, Saffron Walden Essex, CB10 1HZ, England; *The World of Information Asia and Pacific Review.*

World Health Organization, Office of Publications, 20 Avenue Appia, CH-1211 Geneva 27, Switzerland (Telephone Number in U.S. (518) 436-9686); *World Health Statistics Annual.*

NIUE - POWER PRODUCTION INDUSTRY

Statistical Office of the United Nations, Publishing Service, New York, New York 10017 (800) 253-9646; *Electric Power in Asia and the Pacific.*

NIUE - PRICES

Food and Agricultural Organization of the United Nations (FAO), Via delle Terme di Caracalla, 00100 Rome, Italy (Telephone Number in U.S. (202) 653-2400); *Production Yearbook.*

International Labour Office, I.L.O. Publications, 1828 L Street, NW, Suite 801, Washington, D.C. 20036 (301) 638-3152; *Yearbook of Labour Statistics.*

South Pacific Commission, Post Box D5, Noumea Cedex, New Caledonia; *Statistical Bulletin of the South Pacific: Overseas Trade;* and *Statistical Bulletin of*

the South Pacific: Retail Price Indexes.

NIUE - RADIO BROADCASTING - See NIUE - BROADCASTING

NIUE - RELIGION

Central Intelligence Agency, Washington, D.C. 20505 (703) 482-1100, www.cia.gov; *The World Factbook.*

St. Martin's Press, Inc., 175 Fifth Avenue, New York, New York 10010 (800) 221-7945; *The Statesman's Year-Book.*

NIUE - ROOT AND TUBER PRODUCTION - NIUE - CROPS

NIUE - SCIENTISTS, TECHNICIANS AND ENGINEERS

Statistical Office of the United Nations, Publishing Service, New York, New York 10017 (800) 253-9646; *Statistical Yearbook.*

NIUE - STOCKS - COMMODITY - MARKET PRICE - INDEX

Food and Agricultural Organization of the United Nations (FAO) Via delle Terme di Caracalla, 00100 Rome, Italy (Telephone Number in U.S. (202) 653-2400); *The State of Food and Agriculture.*

NIUE - TELEPHONES IN USE

American Telephone and Telegraph Company, 26 Parsippany Road, Whippany, New Jersey 07981 (800) 222-0300; *The World's Telephones.*

Central Intelligence Agency, Washington, D.C. 20505 (703) 482-1100, www.cia.gov; *The World Factbook.*

Europa Publications Limited, 18 Bedford Square, London, WC1B 3JN, England; *The Europa World Year Book.*

St. Martin's Press, Inc., 175 Fifth Avenue, New York, New York 10010 (800) 221-7945; *The Statesman's Year-Book.*

NIUE - TEXTILE INDUSTRY

South Pacific Commission, Post Box D5, Noumea Cedex, New Caledonia; *Statistical Bulletin of the South Pacific: Retail Price Indexes.*

United Nations Conference on Trade and Development, Central Statistical Service, Palais des Nations, Geneva, Switzerland (Telephone in U.S. (800) 253-9646); *UNCTAD Commodity Yearbook.*

NIUE - TOBACCO PRODUCTION

South Pacific Commission, Post Box D5, Noumea Cedex, New Caledonia; *Statistical Bulletin of the South Pacific: Retail Price*

Indexes.

NIUE - TOURISM

Europa Publications Limited, 18 Bedford Square, London, WC1B 3JN, England; *The Europa World Year Book.*

St. Martin's Press, Inc., 175 Fifth Avenue, New York, New York 10010 (800) 221-7945; *The Statesman's Year-Book.*

World Tourism Organization, Calle Capitan Haya 42, E-28020 Madrid, Spain; *Yearbook of Tourism Statistics.*

NIUE - TRACTORS IN USE

Statistical Office of the United Nations, Publishing Service, New York, New York 10017 (800) 253-9646; *Statistical Yearbook.*

NIUE - TRADE - See NIUE - FOREIGN TRADE

NIUE - TRANSPORTATION AND COMMUNICATIONS

Central Intelligence Agency, Washington, D.C. 20505 (703) 482-1100, www.cia.gov; *The World Factbook.*

Europa Publications Limited, 18 Bedford Square, London, WC1B 3JN, England; *The Europa World Year Book.*

South Pacific Commission, Post Box D5, Noumea Cedex, New Caledonia; *Statistical Bulletin of the South Pacific: Retail Price Indexes.*

St. Martin's Press, Inc., 175 Fifth Avenue, New York, New York 10010 (800) 221-7945; *The Statesman's Year-Book.*

Statistical Office of the United Nations, Publishing Service, New York, New York 10017 (800) 253-9646; *Statistical Yearbook for Asia and the Pacific.*

NIUE - UNEMPLOYMENT RATE

Central Intelligence Agency, Washington, D.C. 20505 (703) 482-1100, www.cia.gov; *The World Factbook.*

NIUE - UTILITIES

Statistical Office of the United Nations, Publishing Service, New York, New York 10017 (800) 253-9646; *Electric Power in Asia and the Pacific.*

NIUE - VITAL STATISTICS

St. Martin's Press, Inc., 175 Fifth Avenue, New York, New York 10010 (800) 221-7945; *The Statesman's Year-Book.*

Statistical Office of the United Nations, Publishing Service, New York, New York

10017 (800) 253-9646; *Statistical Yearbook.*

World Health Organization, Office of Publications, 20 Avenue Appia, CH-1211 Geneva 27, Switzerland (Telephone Number in U.S. (518) 436-9686); *World Health Statistics Annual.*

NOBEL PRIZE LAUREATES

National Science Foundation, 4201 Wilson Boulevard, Arlington, Virginia 22230 (703) 306-1234, www.nsf.gov; unpublished data.

NONFERROUS METALS AND PRODUCTS - See METALS AND METAL PRODUCTS

NONFINANCIAL CORPORATIONS - See CORPORATIONS

NONPROFIT ASSOCIATIONS

The Gale Group, 27500 Drake Road, Farmington Hills, Michigan 48331 (800) 877-4253; *Encyclopedia of Associations.*

Norfolk Island - Primary Statistics Source

Australian Government Publishing Service, Post Office Box 84, Canberra ACT 26010, Australia; *Annual Report of the Territory of Norfolk Island.*

NORFOLK ISLAND - AGRICULTURE

Food and Agricultural Organization of the United Nations (FAO) Via delle Terme di Caracalla, 00100 Rome, Italy (Telephone Number in U.S. (202) 653-2400); *Production Yearbook; The State of Food and Agriculture;* and *Trade Yearbook.*

Statistical Office of the United Nations, Publishing Service, New York, New York 10017 (800) 253-9646; *Statistical Yearbook.*

NORFOLK ISLAND - AIRPORTS

Central Intelligence Agency, Washington, D.C. 20505 (703) 482-1100, www.cia.gov; *The World Factbook.*

NORFOLK ISLAND - AREA AND DENSITY OF POPULATION

Central Intelligence Agency, Washington, D.C. 20505 (703) 482-1100, www.cia.gov; *The World Factbook.*

Europa Publications Limited, 18 Bedford Square, London, WC1B 3JN, England; *The Europa World Year Book.*

Food and Agricultural Organization of the United Nations (FAO) Via delle Terme di Caracalla, 00100 Rome, Italy (Telephone Number in U.S. (202) 653-2400); *The State of Food and Agriculture.*

Statistical Office of the United Nations, Publishing Service, New York, New York 10017 (800) 253-9646; *Statistical Yearbook.*

NORFOLK ISLAND - BIRTH RATES

Central Intelligence Agency, Washington, D.C. 20505 (703) 482-1100, www.cia.gov; *The World Factbook.*

Europa Publications Limited, 18 Bedford Square, London, WC1B 3JN, England; *The Europa World Year Book.*

Statistical Office of the United Nations, Publishing Service, New York, New York 10017 (800) 253-9646; *Demographic Yearbook;* and *Statistical Yearbook.*

World Health Organization, Office of Publications, 20 Avenue Appia, CH-1211 Geneva 27, Switzerland (Telephone Number in U.S. (518) 436-9686); *World Health Statistics Annual.*

NORFOLK ISLAND - BOOK PRODUCTION

United Nations Educational, Scientific and Cultural Organization (UNESCO), 7 Place de Fontenoy, F-75700 Paris, France (Telephone Number in U.S. (212) 963-5981); *Statistical Yearbook.*

NORFOLK ISLAND - BROADCASTING

Billboard Limited, Post Office Box 9027, 1006 AA Amsterdam, The Netherlands (Telephone Number in U.S. (212) 764-7300); *World Radio TV Handbook.*

Central Intelligence Agency, Washington, D.C. 20505 (703) 482-1100, www.cia.gov; *The World Factbook.*

NORFOLK ISLAND - BUDGET

Central Intelligence Agency, Washington, D.C. 20505 (703) 482-1100, www.cia.gov; *The World Factbook.*

NORFOLK ISLAND - CALORIE SUPPLY

Food and Agricultural Organization of the United Nations (FAO) Via delle Terme di Caracalla, 00100 Rome, Italy (Telephone Number in U.S. (202) 653-2400); *The State of Food and Agriculture.*

NORFOLK ISLAND - CATTLE - See NORFOLK ISLAND - LIVESTOCK AND POULTRY

NORFOLK ISLAND - CORN PRODUCTION - See NORFOLK ISLAND - CROPS

NORFOLK ISLAND - CROPS

Food and Agricultural Organization of the United Nations (FAO) Via delle Terme di Caracalla, 00100 Rome, Italy (Telephone Number in U.S. (202) 653-2400); *The State of Food and Agriculture.*

NORFOLK ISLAND - DAIRY PRODUCTS

Food and Agricultural Organization of the United Nations (FAO) Via delle Terme di Caracalla, 00100 Rome, Italy (Telephone Number in U.S. (202) 653-2400); *The State of Food and Agriculture.*

NORFOLK ISLAND - DEATH RATES - See NORFOLK ISLAND - MORTALITY

NORFOLK ISLAND - DIVORCE RATES

Statistical Office of the United Nations, Publishing Service, New York, New York 10017 (800) 253-9646; *Demographic Yearbook.*

NORFOLK ISLAND - ECONOMY

Central Intelligence Agency, Washington, D.C. 20505 (703) 482-1100, www.cia.gov; *The World Factbook.*

NORFOLK ISLAND - EDUCATION

Europa Publications Limited, 18 Bedford Square, London, WC1B 3JN, England; *The Europa World Year Book.*

St. Martin's Press, Inc., 175 Fifth Avenue, New York, New York 10010 (800) 221-7945; *The Statesman's Year-Book.*

United Nations Educational, Scientific and Cultural Organization (UNESCO), 7 Place de Fontenoy, F-75700 Paris, France (Telephone Number in U.S. (212) 963-5981); *Statistical Yearbook.*

NORFOLK ISLAND - EGG PRODUCTION AND CONSUMPTION - See NORFOLK ISLAND - DAIRY PRODUCTS

NORFOLK ISLAND - ELECTRICITY

Central Intelligence Agency, Washington, D.C. 20505 (703) 482-1100, www.cia.gov; *The World Factbook.*

NORFOLK ISLAND - ENERGY

Food and Agricultural Organization of the United Nations (FAO) Via delle Terme di Caracalla, 00100 Rome, Italy (Telephone Number in U.S. (202) 653-2400); *The State of Food and Agriculture.*

NORFOLK ISLAND - EXCHANGE RATE

Central Intelligence Agency, Washington, D.C. 20505 (703) 482-1100, www.cia.gov; *The World Factbook.*

Europa Publications Limited, 18 Bedford Square, London, WC1B 3JN,

England; *The Europa World Year Book*.

Walden Publishing Ltd., Two Market Street, Saffron Walden Essex, CB10 1HZ, England; *The World of Information Asia and Pacific Review*.

NORFOLK ISLAND - EXPORTS

Central Intelligence Agency, Washington, D.C. 20505 (703) 482-1100, www.cia.gov; *The World Factbook*.

Europa Publications Limited, 18 Bedford Square, London, WC1B 3JN, England; *The Europa World Year Book*.

Food and Agricultural Organization of the United Nations (FAO) Via delle Terme di Caracalla, 00100 Rome, Italy (Telephone Number in U.S. (202) 653-2400); *The State of Food and Agriculture*.

Walden Publishing Ltd., Two Market Street, Saffron Walden Essex, CB10 1HZ, England; *The World of Information Asia and Pacific Review*.

NORFOLK ISLAND - EXTERNAL TRADE

Food and Agricultural Organization of the United Nations (FAO) Via delle Terme di Caracalla, 00100 Rome, Italy (Telephone Number in U.S. (202) 653-2400); *The State of Food and Agriculture;* and *Trade Yearbook*.

NORFOLK ISLAND - FARM CROPS - See NORFOLK ISLAND - CROPS

NORFOLK ISLAND - FERTILITY RATE

Central Intelligence Agency, Washington, D.C. 20505 (703) 482-1100, www.cia.gov; *The World Factbook*.

NORFOLK ISLAND - FERTILIZER

Food and Agricultural Organization of the United Nations (FAO) Via delle Terme di Caracalla, 00100 Rome, Italy (Telephone Number in U.S. (202) 653-2400); *The State of Food and Agriculture*.

NORFOLK ISLAND - FETAL MORTALITY - See NORFOLK ISLAND - MORTALITY

NORFOLK ISLAND - FINANCE

Europa Publications Limited, 18 Bedford Square, London, WC1B 3JN, England; *The Europa World Year Book*.

NORFOLK ISLAND - FISHERIES

Food and Agricultural Organization of the United Nations (FAO) Via delle Terme di Caracalla, 00100 Rome, Italy (Telephone Number in U.S. (202) 653-2400); *The State of Food and Agriculture;* and *Yearbook of Fishery Statistics*.

NORFOLK ISLAND - FOOD

Food and Agricultural Organization of the United Nations (FAO), Via delle Terme di Caracalla, 00100 Rome, Italy (Telephone Number in U.S. (202) 653-2400); *Production Yearbook;* and *The State of Food and Agriculture*.

NORFOLK ISLAND - FOREIGN DEBT

Walden Publishing Ltd., Two Market Street, Saffron Walden Essex, CB10 1HZ, England; *The World of Information Asia and Pacific Review*.

NORFOLK ISLAND - FOREIGN TRADE

Food and Agricultural Organization of the United Nations (FAO) Via delle Terme di Caracalla, 00100 Rome, Italy (Telephone Number in U.S. (202) 653-2400); *The State of Food and Agriculture*.

NORFOLK ISLAND - FORESTRY AND FOREST PRODUCTS

Food and Agricultural Organization of the United Nations (FAO) Via delle Terme di Caracalla, 00100 Rome, Italy (Telephone Number in U.S. (202) 653-2400); *The State of Food and Agriculture*.

Statistical Office of the United Nations, Publishing Service, New York, New York 10017 (800) 253-9646; *Statistical Yearbook*.

NORFOLK ISLAND - GENERAL MORTALITY - See NORFOLK ISLAND - MORTALITY

NORFOLK ISLAND - GOVERNMENT

Central Intelligence Agency, Washington, D.C. 20505 (703) 482-1100, www.cia.gov; *The World Factbook*.

Europa Publications Limited, 18 Bedford Square, London, WC1B 3JN, England; *The Europa World Year Book*.

St. Martin's Press, Inc., 175 Fifth Avenue, New York, New York 10010 (800) 221-7945; *The Statesman's Year-Book*.

NORFOLK ISLAND - GRAIN PRODUCTION - See NORFOLK ISLAND - CROPS

NORFOLK ISLAND - GROSS NATIONAL PRODUCT

Walden Publishing Ltd., Two Market Street, Saffron Walden Essex, CB10 1HZ, England; *The World of Information Asia and Pacific Review*.

NORFOLK ISLAND - HEALTH

St. Martin's Press, Inc., 175 Fifth Avenue, New York, New York 10010 (800) 221-7945; *The Statesman's Year-Book*.

NORFOLK - HIGHWAYS

Central Intelligence Agency, Washington, D.C. 20505 (703) 482-1100, www.cia.gov; *The World Factbook*.

St. Martin's Press, Inc., 175 Fifth Avenue, New York, New York 10010 (800) 221-7945; *The Statesman's Year-Book*.

NORFOLK ISLAND - HOUSING AND HOUSING UNITS

Statistical Office of the United Nations, Publishing Service, New York, New York 10017 (800) 253-9646; *Statistical Yearbook*.

NORFOLK ISLAND - ILLITERATE POPULATION

Central Intelligence Agency, Washington, D.C. 20505 (703) 482-1100, www.cia.gov; *The World Factbook*.

NORFOLK ISLAND - IMPORTS

Central Intelligence Agency, Washington, D.C. 20505 (703) 482-1100, www.cia.gov; *The World Factbook*.

Europa Publications Limited, 18 Bedford Square, London, WC1B 3JN, England; *The Europa World Year Book*.

Food and Agricultural Organization of the United Nations (FAO) Via delle Terme di Caracalla, 00100 Rome, Italy (Telephone Number in U.S. (202) 653-2400); *The State of Food and Agriculture*.

Walden Publishing Ltd., Two Market Street, Saffron Walden Essex, CB10 1HZ, England; *The World of Information Asia and Pacific Review*.

NORFOLK ISLAND - INDUSTRY

Central Intelligence Agency, Washington, D.C. 20505 (703) 482-1100, www.cia.gov; *The World Factbook*.

NORFOLK ISLAND - INFANT AND MATERNAL MORTALITY - See NORFOLK ISLAND - MORTALITY

NORFOLK ISLAND - LABOR

Central Intelligence Agency, Washington, D.C. 20505 (703) 482-1100, www.cia.gov; *The World Factbook*.

Europa Publications Limited, 18 Bedford Square, London, WC1B 3JN, England; *The Europa World Year Book*.

Food and Agricultural Organization of the United Nations (FAO) Via delle Terme di Caracalla, 00100 Rome, Italy (Telephone Number in U.S. (202) 653-2400); *The State of Food and Agriculture*.

NORFOLK ISLAND - LAND USE

Central Intelligence Agency, Washington, D.C. 20505 (703) 482-1100, www.cia.gov; *The World Factbook*.

Food and Agricultural Organization of the United Nations (FAO), Via delle Terme di Caracalla, 00100 Rome, Italy (Telephone Number in U.S. (202) 653-2400); *Production Yearbook*.

NORFOLK ISLAND - LIBRARIES

United Nations Educational, Scientific and Cultural Organization (UNESCO), 7 Place de Fontenoy, F-75700 Paris, France (Telephone Number in U.S. (212) 963-5981); *Statistical Yearbook*.

NORFOLK ISLAND - LIFE EXPECTANCY

Central Intelligence Agency, Washington, D.C. 20505 (703) 482-1100, www.cia.gov; *The World Factbook*.

NORFOLK ISLAND - LIVESTOCK AND POULTRY

Food and Agricultural Organization of the United Nations (FAO), Via delle Terme di Caracalla, 00100 Rome, Italy (Telephone Number in U.S. (202) 653-2400); *Production Yearbook;* and *The State of Food and Agriculture*.

Statistical Office of the United Nations, Publishing Service, New York, New York 10017 (800) 253-9646; *Statistical Yearbook*.

NORFOLK ISLAND - MAIL - NUMBER OF ITEMS SENT OR RECEIVED

Statistical Office of the United Nations, Publishing Service, New York, New York 10017 (800) 253-9646; *Statistical Yearbook*.

NORFOLK ISLAND - MARRIAGE RATES

Statistical Office of the United Nations, Publishing Service, New York, New York 10017 (800) 253-9646; *Demographic Yearbook;* and *Statistical Yearbook*.

NORFOLK ISLAND - MEAT PRODUCTION - See NORFOLK ISLAND - LIVESTOCK AND POULTRY

NORFOLK ISLAND - MILITARY

Central Intelligence Agency, Washington, D.C. 20505 (703) 482-1100, www.cia.gov; *The World Factbook*.

NORFOLK ISLAND - MONUMENTS AND HISTORICAL SITES

United Nations Educational, Scientific and Cultural Organization (UNESCO), 7 Place de Fontenoy, F-75700 Paris, France (Telephone Number in U.S. (212) 963-

5981); *Statistical Yearbook*.

NORFOLK ISLAND - MORTALITY

Central Intelligence Agency, Washington, D.C. 20505 (703) 482-1100, www.cia.gov; *The World Factbook*.

Europa Publications Limited, 18 Bedford Square, London, WC1B 3JN, England; *The Europa World Year Book*.

Statistical Office of the United Nations, Publishing Service, New York, New York 10017 (800) 253-9646; *Demographic Yearbook;* and *Statistical Yearbook*.

World Health Organization, Office of Publications, 20 Avenue Appia, CH-1211 Geneva 27, Switzerland (Telephone Number in U.S. (518) 436-9686); *World Health Statistics Annual*.

NORFOLK ISLAND - MOTION PICTURE THEATRES

Statistical Office of the United Nations, Publishing Service, New York, New York 10017 (800) 253-9646; *Statistical Yearbook*.

NORFOLK ISLAND - MUSEUMS

United Nations Educational, Scientific and Cultural Organization (UNESCO), 7 Place de Fontenoy, F-75700 Paris, France (Telephone Number in U.S. (212) 963-5981); *Statistical Yearbook*.

NORFOLK ISLAND - NATALITY - See NORFOLK ISLAND - BIRTH RATES

NORFOLK ISLAND - NEWSPAPER PRODUCTION - See NORFOLK ISLAND - FORESTRY AND FOREST PRODUCTS

NORFOLK ISLAND - PERIODICALS

United Nations Educational, Scientific and Cultural Organization (UNESCO), 7 Place de Fontenoy, F-75700 Paris, France (Telephone Number in U.S. (212) 963-5981); *Statistical Yearbook*.

NORFOLK ISLAND - PESTICIDE USE

Food and Agricultural Organization of the United Nations (FAO) Via delle Terme di Caracalla, 00100 Rome, Italy (Telephone Number in U.S. (202) 653-2400); *The State of Food and Agriculture*.

NORFOLK ISLAND - PETROLEUM INDUSTRY

Food and Agricultural Organization of the United Nations (FAO) Via delle Terme di Caracalla, 00100 Rome, Italy (Telephone Number in U.S. (202) 653-2400); *The State of Food and Agriculture*.

NORFOLK ISLAND - POPULATION

Central Intelligence Agency, Washington, D.C. 20505 (703) 482-1100, www.cia.gov; *The World Factbook*.

Europa Publications Limited, 18 Bedford Square, London, WC1B 3JN, England; *The Europa World Year Book*.

Food and Agricultural Organization of the United Nations (FAO), Via delle Terme di Caracalla, 00100 Rome, Italy (Telephone Number in U.S. (202) 653-2400); *Production Yearbook*.

St. Martin's Press, Inc., 175 Fifth Avenue, New York, New York 10010 (800) 221-7945; *The Statesman's Year-Book*.

Statistical Office of the United Nations, Publishing Service, New York, New York 10017 (800) 253-9646; *Demographic Yearbook;* and *Statistical Yearbook*.

Walden Publishing Ltd., Two Market Street, Saffron Walden Essex, CB10 1HZ, England; *The World of Information Asia and Pacific Review*.

World Health Organization, Office of Publications, 20 Avenue Appia, CH-1211 Geneva 27, Switzerland (Telephone Number in U.S. (518) 436-9686); *World Health Statistics Annual*.

NORFOLK ISLAND - POST OFFICES

St. Martin's Press, Inc., 175 Fifth Avenue, New York, New York 10010 (800) 221-7945; *The Statesman's Year-Book*.

NORFOLK ISLAND - PRICES

Food and Agricultural Organization of the United Nations (FAO), Via delle Terme di Caracalla, 00100 Rome, Italy (Telephone Number in U.S. (202) 653-2400); *Production Yearbook;* and *The State of Food and Agriculture*.

NORFOLK ISLAND - RADIO RECEIVERS

St. Martin's Press, Inc., 175 Fifth Avenue, New York, New York 10010 (800) 221-7945; *The Statesman's Year-Book*.

NORFOLK ISLAND - RELIGION

Central Intelligence Agency, Washington, D.C. 20505 (703) 482-1100, www.cia.gov; *The World Factbook*.

St. Martin's Press, Inc., 175 Fifth Avenue, New York, New York 10010 (800) 221-7945; *The Statesman's Year-Book*.

NORFOLK ISLAND - SCIENTISTS, TECHNICIANS AND ENGINEERS

Statistical Office of the United Nations, Publishing Service, New York, New York 10017 (800) 253-9646; *Statistical Yearbook*.

NORFOLK ISLAND - STOCKS - COMMODITY - MARKET PRICE - INDEX

Food and Agricultural Organization of the United Nations (FAO) Via delle Terme di Caracalla, 00100 Rome, Italy (Telephone Number in U.S. (202) 653-2400); *The State of Food and Agriculture.*

NORFOLK ISLAND - TAXATION

St. Martin's Press, Inc., 175 Fifth Avenue, New York, New York 10010 (800) 221-7945; *The Statesman's Year-Book.*

NORFOLK ISLAND - TELEPHONES IN USE

American Telephone and Telegraph Company, 26 Parsippany Road, Whippany, New Jersey 07981 (800) 222-0300; *The World's Telephones.*

Central Intelligence Agency, Washington, D.C. 20505 (703) 482-1100, www.cia.gov; *The World Factbook.*

St. Martin's Press, Inc., 175 Fifth Avenue, New York, New York 10010 (800) 221-7945; *The Statesman's Year-Book.*

NORFOLK ISLAND - THEATRE

United Nations Educational, Scientific and Cultural Organization (UNESCO), 7 Place de Fontenoy, F-75700 Paris, France (Telephone Number in U.S. (212) 963-5981); *Statistical Yearbook.*

NORFOLK ISLAND - TOURISM

Europa Publications Limited, 18 Bedford Square, London, WC1B 3JN, England; *The Europa World Year Book.*

St. Martin's Press, Inc., 175 Fifth Avenue, New York, New York 10010 (800) 221-7945; *The Statesman's Year-Book.*

NORFOLK ISLAND - TRACTORS IN USE

Statistical Office of the United Nations, Publishing Service, New York, New York 10017 (800) 253-9646; *Statistical Yearbook.*

NORFOLK ISLAND - TRADE - See NORFOLK ISLAND - FOREIGN TRADE

NORFOLK ISLAND - TRANSPORTATION AND COMMUNICATIONS

Central Intelligence Agency, Washington, D.C. 20505 (703) 482-1100, www.cia.gov; *The World Factbook.*

St. Martin's Press, Inc., 175 Fifth Avenue, New York, New York 10010 (800) 221-7945; *The Statesman's Year-Book.*

NORFOLK ISLAND - UNEMPLOYMENT RATE

Central Intelligence Agency, Washington, D.C. 20505 (703) 482-1100, www.cia.gov; *The World Factbook.*

NORFOLK ISLAND - VITAL STATISTICS

World Health Organization, Office of Publications, 20 Avenue Appia, CH-1211 Geneva 27, Switzerland (Telephone Number in U.S. (518) 436-9686); *World Health Statistics Annual.*

NORTH CAROLINA - See also STATE DATA (FOR INDIVIDUAL STATES)

North Carolina - Primary Statistics Sources

Office of the Governor, Office of State Planning, 116 West Jones Street, Raleigh, North Carolina 27603 (919) 733-4131; *Statistical Abstract of North Carolina Counties.*

North Carolina - State Data Centers

North Carolina Office of State Budget, Planning, and Management, 20321 Mail Service Center, Raleigh, North Carolina 27699-0321, Francine Stephenson (919) 733-3270.

Center for Geographic Information and Analysis, Office of State Budget, Planning and Management, 20322 Mail Service Center, Raleigh, North Carolina 27699-0322, Mr. Justin Flint (919) 715-3820.

Odum Institute for Research in Social Science, University of North Carolina, Manning Hall CB 3355, Chapel Hill, North Carolina 27599-3355, Mr. Ed. Bachmann (919) 962-0512.

State Library of North Carolina, 4641 Mail Service Center, Raleigh, North Carolina 27699-4641, Ms. Cheryl McLean (919) 733-3683.

NORTH DAKOTA - See also STATE DATA (FOR INDIVIDUAL STATES)

North Dakota - Primary Statistics Sources

Bureau of Business and Economic Research, University of North Dakota, Grand Forks, North Dakota 58202 (701) 777-2637; *The Statistical Abstract of North Dakota.*

North Dakota - State Data Centers

North Dakota State Data Center, North

Dakota State University, IACC 424, Fargo, North Dakota 58105, Dr. Richard Rathge (701) 231-8621.

Department of Geography, University of North Dakota, Post Office Box 9020, Grand Forks, North Dakota 58202-9020, Mohammad Hemmasi (701) 777-4246.

North Dakota State Library, Liberty Memorial Building, Capitol Grounds, Bismarck, North Dakota 58505-0800, Ms. Susan Pahlmeyer (701) 328-4622.

Office of Intergovernmental Assistance, State Capitol, 14th Floor, 600 East Boulevard Avenue, Bismarck, North Dakota 58505-0170, Mr. Jim Boyd (701) 328-2094.

NORTHERN IRELAND - See UNITED KINGDOM

Northern Mariana Islands - National Statistical Office

Department of Commerce and Labor, Saipan, M.P. 96950, Commonwealth of the Northern Mariana Islands.

Northern Mariana Islands - State Data Centers

Department of Commerce, Central Statistics Division, Caller Box 10007, Donnie Hill Apts., Saipan, Mariana Islands 96950, Mr. Diego Sasamoto (670) 664-3033.

NORTHERN MARIANA ISLANDS - AGRICULTURE

Europa Publications Limited, 18 Bedford Square, London, WC1B 3JN, England; *The Europa World Year Book.*

Statistical Office of the United Nations, Publishing Service, New York, New York 10017 (800) 253-9646; *Asia-Pacific in Figures.*

NORTHERN MARIANA ISLANDS - AIRLINE SERVICE

St. Martin's Press, Inc., 175 Fifth Avenue, New York, New York 10010 (800) 221-7945; *The Statesman's Year-Book.*

NORTHERN MARIANA ISLANDS - AIRPORTS

Central Intelligence Agency, Washington, D.C. 20505 (703) 482-1100, www.cia.gov; *The World Factbook.*

NORTHERN MARIANA ISLANDS - AREA AND DENSITY OF POPULATION

Central Intelligence Agency, Washington, D.C. 20505 (703) 482-1100,

www.cia.gov; *The World Factbook.*

Europa Publications Limited, 18 Bedford Square, London, WC1B 3JN, England; *The Europa World Year Book.*

St. Martin's Press, Inc., 175 Fifth Avenue, New York, New York 10010 (800) 221-7945; *The Statesman's Year-Book.*

NORTHERN MARIANA ISLANDS - BIRTH RATES

Central Intelligence Agency, Washington, D.C. 20505 (703) 482-1100, www.cia.gov; *The World Factbook.*

Europa Publications Limited, 18 Bedford Square, London, WC1B 3JN, England; *The Europa World Year Book.*

St. Martin's Press, Inc., 175 Fifth Avenue, New York, New York 10010 (800) 221-7945; *The Statesman's Year-Book.*

Statistical Office of the United Nations, Publishing Service, New York, New York 10017 (800) 253-9646; *Asia-Pacific in Figures.*

NORTHERN MARIANA ISLANDS - BROADCASTING

Billboard Limited, Post Office Box 9027, 1006 AA Amsterdam, The Netherlands (Telephone Number in U.S. (212) 764-7300); *World Radio TV Handbook.*

Central Intelligence Agency, Washington, D.C. 20505 (703) 482-1100, www.cia.gov; *The World Factbook.*

St. Martin's Press, Inc., 175 Fifth Avenue, New York, New York 10010 (800) 221-7945; *The Statesman's Year-Book.*

NORTHERN MARIANA ISLANDS - BUDGET

Central Intelligence Agency, Washington, D.C. 20505 (703) 482-1100, www.cia.gov; *The World Factbook.*

NORTHERN MARIANA ISLANDS - COMMERCE

St. Martin's Press, Inc., 175 Fifth Avenue, New York, New York 10010 (800) 221-7945; *The Statesman's Year-Book.*

NORTHERN MARIANA ISLANDS - CONSUMER PRICE INDEX

Europa Publications Limited, 18 Bedford Square, London, WC1B 3JN, England; *The Europa World Year Book.*

NORTHERN MARIANA ISLANDS - DEATH RATES - SEE NORTHERN MARIANA ISLANDS - MORTALITY

NORTHERN MARIANA ISLANDS -

DEMOGRAPHY

Statistical Office of the United Nations, Publishing Service, New York, New York 10017 (800) 253-9646; *Asia-Pacific in Figures.*

NORTHERN MARIANA ISLANDS - ECONOMY

Central Intelligence Agency, Washington, D.C. 20505 (703) 482-1100, www.cia.gov; *The World Factbook.*

Europa Publications Limited, 18 Bedford Square, London, WC1B 3JN, England; *The Europa World Year Book.*

Statistical Office of the United Nations, Publishing Service, New York, New York 10017 (800) 253-9646; *World Statistics Pocketbook.*

The World Bank, 1818 H Street, NW, Washington, D.C. 20433 (202) 477-1234; *The World Bank Atlas.*

NORTHERN MARIANA ISLANDS - EDUCATION

Europa Publications Limited, 18 Bedford Square, London, WC1B 3JN, England; *The Europa World Year Book.*

St. Martin's Press, Inc., 175 Fifth Avenue, New York, New York 10010 (800) 221-7945; *The Statesman's Year-Book.*

Statistical Office of the United Nations, Publishing Service, New York, New York 10017 (800) 253-9646; *Asia-Pacific in Figures.*

NORTHERN MARIANA ISLANDS - ELECTRICITY

Central Intelligence Agency, Washington, D.C. 20505 (703) 482-1100, www.cia.gov; *The World Factbook.*

NORTHERN MARIANA ISLANDS - EMPLOYMENT

Statistical Office of the United Nations, Publishing Service, New York, New York 10017 (800) 253-9646; *Asia-Pacific in Figures.*

NORTHERN MARIANA ISLANDS - ENERGY

Statistical Office of the United Nations, Publishing Service, New York, New York 10017 (800) 253-9646; *Asia-Pacific in Figures;* and *World Statistics Pocketbook.*

The World Bank, 1818 H Street, NW, Washington, D.C. 20433 (202) 477-1234; *The World Bank Atlas.*

NORTHERN MARIANA ISLANDS -

ENVIRONMENT

Statistical Office of the United Nations, Publishing Service, New York, New York 10017 (800) 253-9646; *World Statistics Pocketbook.*

NORTHERN MARIANA ISLANDS - EXCHANGE RATES

Central Intelligence Agency, Washington, D.C. 20505 (703) 482-1100, www.cia.gov; *The World Factbook.*

Europa Publications Limited, 18 Bedford Square, London, WC1B 3JN, England; *The Europa World Year Book.*

Statistical Office of the United Nations, Publishing Service, New York, New York 10017 (800) 253-9646; *World Statistics Pocketbook.*

Walden Publishing Ltd., Two Market Street, Saffron Walden Essex, CB10 1HZ, England; *The World of Information Asia and Pacific Review.*

NORTHERN MARIANA ISLANDS - EXPORTS

Central Intelligence Agency, Washington, D.C. 20505 (703) 482-1100, www.cia.gov; *The World Factbook.*

St. Martin's Press, Inc., 175 Fifth Avenue, New York, New York 10010 (800) 221-7945; *The Statesman's Year-Book.*

Walden Publishing Ltd., Two Market Street, Saffron Walden Essex, CB10 1HZ, England; *The World of Information Asia and Pacific Review.*

NORTHERN MARIANA ISLANDS - EXTERNAL TRADE

Statistical Office of the United Nations, Publishing Service, New York, New York 10017 (800) 253-9646; *Asia-Pacific in Figures.*

NORTHERN MARIANA ISLANDS - FERTILITY RATES

Central Intelligence Agency, Washington, D.C. 20505 (703) 482-1100, www.cia.gov; *The World Factbook.*

The World Bank, 1818 H Street, NW, Washington, D.C. 20433 (202) 477-1234; *The World Bank Atlas.*

NORTHERN MARIANA ISLANDS - FINANCE

Europa Publications Limited, 18 Bedford Square, London, WC1B 3JN, England; *The Europa World Year Book.*

NORTHERN MARIANA ISLANDS - FISHERIES

Europa Publications Limited, 18 Bedford Square, London, WC1B 3JN, England; *The Europa World Year Book.*

NORTHERN MARIANA ISLANDS - GROSS NATIONAL PRODUCT

Walden Publishing Ltd., Two Market Street, Saffron Walden Essex, CB10 1HZ, England; *The World of Information Asia and Pacific Review.*

NORTHERN MARIANA ISLANDS - GOVERNMENT

Central Intelligence Agency, Washington, D.C. 20505 (703) 482-1100, www.cia.gov; *The World Factbook.*

Europa Publications Limited, 18 Bedford Square, London, WC1B 3JN, England; *The Europa World Year Book.*

St. Martin's Press, Inc., 175 Fifth Avenue, New York, New York 10010 (800) 221-7945; *The Statesman's Year-Book.*

Statistical Office of the United Nations, Publishing Service, New York, New York 10017 (800) 253-9646; *Asia-Pacific in Figures.*

NORTHERN MARIANA ISLANDS - GROSS NATIONAL PRODUCT

Europa Publications Limited, 18 Bedford Square, London, WC1B 3JN, England; *The Europa World Year Book.*

The World Bank, 1818 H Street, NW, Washington, D.C. 20433 (202) 477-1234; *The World Bank Atlas.*

NORTHERN MARIANA ISLANDS - HEALTH

St. Martin's Press, Inc., 175 Fifth Avenue, New York, New York 10010 (800) 221-7945; *The Statesman's Year-Book.*

Statistical Office of the United Nations, Publishing Service, New York, New York 10017 (800) 253-9646; *Asia-Pacific in Figures.*

NORTHERN MARIANA ISLANDS - HIGHWAYS

Central Intelligence Agency, Washington, D.C. 20505 (703) 482-1100, www.cia.gov; *The World Factbook.*

St. Martin's Press, Inc., 175 Fifth Avenue, New York, New York 10010 (800) 221-7945; *The Statesman's Year-Book.*

NORTHERN MARIANA ISLANDS - ILLITERATE POPULATION

Central Intelligence Agency, Washington, D.C. 20505 (703) 482-1100, www.cia.gov; *The World Factbook.*

Statistical Office of the United Nations, Publishing Service, New York, New York 10017 (800) 253-9646; *Asia-Pacific in Figures.*

NORTHERN MARIANA ISLANDS - IMPORTS

Central Intelligence Agency, Washington, D.C. 20505 (703) 482-1100, www.cia.gov; *The World Factbook.*

Europa Publications Limited, 18 Bedford Square, London, WC1B 3JN, England; *The Europa World Year Book.*

St. Martin's Press, Inc., 175 Fifth Avenue, New York, New York 10010 (800) 221-7945; *The Statesman's Year-Book.*

Walden Publishing Ltd., Two Market Street, Saffron Walden Essex, CB10 1HZ, England; *The World of Information Asia and Pacific Review.*

NORTHERN MARIANA ISLANDS - INDUSTRY

Central Intelligence Agency, Washington, D.C. 20505 (703) 482-1100, www.cia.gov; *The World Factbook.*

Statistical Office of the United Nations, Publishing Service, New York, New York 10017 (800) 253-9646; *Asia-Pacific in Figures.*

NORTHERN MARIANA ISLANDS - LABOR

Central Intelligence Agency, Washington, D.C. 20505 (703) 482-1100, www.cia.gov; *The World Factbook.*

Europa Publications Limited, 18 Bedford Square, London, WC1B 3JN, England; *The Europa World Year Book.*

St. Martin's Press, Inc., 175 Fifth Avenue, New York, New York 10010 (800) 221-7945; *The Statesman's Year-Book.*

The World Bank, 1818 H Street, NW, Washington, D.C. 20433 (202) 477-1234; *The World Bank Atlas.*

NORTHERN MARIANA ISLANDS - LAND USE

Central Intelligence Agency, Washington, D.C. 20505 (703) 482-1100, www.cia.gov; *The World Factbook.*

NORTHERN MARIANA ISLANDS - LIFE EXPECTANCY

Central Intelligence Agency, Washington, D.C. 20505 (703) 482-1100, www.cia.gov; *The World Factbook.*

Statistical Office of the United Nations, Publishing Service, New York, New York 10017 (800) 253-9646; *Asia-Pacific in Figures;* and *World Statistics Pocketbook.*

The World Bank, 1818 H Street, NW, Washington, D.C. 20433 (202) 477-1234; *The World Bank Atlas.*

NORTHERN MARIANA ISLANDS - MERCHANT SHIPPING

Europa Publications Limited, 18 Bedford Square, London, WC1B 3JN, England; *The Europa World Year Book.*

NORTHERN MARIANA ISLANDS - MILITARY

Central Intelligence Agency, Washington, D.C. 20505 (703) 482-1100, www.cia.gov; *The World Factbook.*

NORTHERN MARIANA ISLANDS - MORTALITY

Central Intelligence Agency, Washington, D.C. 20505 (703) 482-1100, www.cia.gov; *The World Factbook.*

Europa Publications Limited, 18 Bedford Square, London, WC1B 3JN, England; *The Europa World Year Book.*

St. Martin's Press, Inc., 175 Fifth Avenue, New York, New York 10010 (800) 221-7945; *The Statesman's Year-Book.*

Statistical Office of the United Nations, Publishing Service, New York, New York 10017 (800) 253-9646; *Asia-Pacific in Figures;* and *World Statistics Pocketbook.*

The World Bank, 1818 H Street, NW, Washington, D.C. 20433 (202) 477-1234; *The World Bank Atlas.*

NORTHERN MARIANA ISLANDS - NATIONAL ACCOUNTS

Statistical Office of the United Nations, Publishing Service, New York, New York 10017 (800) 253-9646; *Asia-Pacific in Figures.*

NORTHERN MARIANA ISLANDS - POPULATION

Central Intelligence Agency, Washington, D.C. 20505 (703) 482-1100, www.cia.gov; *The World Factbook.*

Europa Publications Limited, 18 Bedford Square, London, WC1B 3JN, England; *The Europa World Year Book.*

St. Martin's Press, Inc., 175 Fifth Avenue, New York, New York 10010 (800) 221-7945; *The Statesman's Year-Book.*

Statistical Office of the United Nations, Publishing Service, New York, New York 10017 (800) 253-9646; *Asia-Pacific in Figures;* and *World Statistics Pocketbook.*

Walden Publishing Ltd., Two Market

Street, Saffron Walden Essex, CB10 1HZ, England; *The World of Information Asia and Pacific Review*.

The World Bank, 1818 H Street, NW, Washington, D.C. 20433 (202) 477-1234; *The World Bank Atlas*.

NORTHERN MARIANA ISLANDS - RADIO RECEIVERS

St. Martin's Press, Inc., 175 Fifth Avenue, New York, New York 10010 (800) 221-7945; *The Statesman's Year-Book*.

NORTHERN MARIANA ISLANDS - RELIGION

Central Intelligence Agency, Washington, D.C. 20505 (703) 482-1100, www.cia.gov; *The World Factbook*.

St. Martin's Press, Inc., 175 Fifth Avenue, New York, New York 10010 (800) 221-7945; *The Statesman's Year-Book*.

NORTHERN MARIANA ISLANDS - SOCIAL DATA

Statistical Office of the United Nations, Publishing Service, New York, New York 10017 (800) 253-9646; *World Statistics Pocketbook*.

NORTHERN MARIANA ISLANDS - TELEPHONES IN USE

Central Intelligence Agency, Washington, D.C. 20505 (703) 482-1100, www.cia.gov; *The World Factbook*.

Europa Publications Limited, 18 Bedford Square, London, WC1B 3JN, England; *The Europa World Year Book*.

Statistical Office of the United Nations, Publishing Service, New York, New York 10017 (800) 253-9646; *World Statistics Pocketbook*.

NORTHERN MARIANA ISLANDS - TOURISM

Europa Publications Limited, 18 Bedford Square, London, WC1B 3JN, England; *The Europa World Year Book*.

St. Martin's Press, Inc., 175 Fifth Avenue, New York, New York 10010 (800) 221-7945; *The Statesman's Year-Book*.

World Tourism Organization, Calle Capitan Haya 42, E-28020 Madrid, Spain; *Yearbook of Tourism Statistics*.

NORTHERN MARIANA ISLANDS - TRANS- PORTATION AND COMMUNICATIONS

Central Intelligence Agency, Washington, D.C. 20505 (703) 482-1100, www.cia.gov; *The World Factbook*.

Europa Publications Limited, 18 Bedford Square, London, WC1B 3JN, England; *The Europa World Year Book*.

St. Martin's Press, Inc., 175 Fifth Avenue, New York, New York 10010 (800) 221-7945; *The Statesman's Year-Book*.

NORTHERN MARIANA ISLANDS - UNEMPLOYMENT

Central Intelligence Agency, Washington, D.C. 20505 (703) 482-1100, www.cia.gov; *The World Factbook*.

St. Martin's Press, Inc., 175 Fifth Avenue, New York, New York 10010 (800) 221-7945; *The Statesman's Year-Book*.

Norway - National Statistical Office

Statistisk Sentralbyra, Skippergate 15, Postboks 8131, DEP N-0033, Oslo 1, Norway.

Norway - Primary Statistics Sources

Statistisk Sentralbyra (Central Bureau of Statistics), Skippergate 15, P.B. 8131, DEP N-0033, Oslo 1, Norway; *Statistisk monedshefte (Monthly Bulletin of Statistics*; *Okonomisk utsyn (Economic Survey)*; and *Statistisk arbok (Statistical Yearbook)*.

Norway - Databases

NSD Kommunedatabase, Hans Holmboesgate 22, N-5007 Bergen, Norway. Subject coverage: Norwegian municipal units: vital statistics and population movement, social conditions and services, population censuses, labour market, education, accounts, and elections.

NSD Statistikk om Hoyere Utdanning, Hams Holmboesgate 22, N-5007 Bergen, Norway. Subject coverage: Public institutions of higher education.

SSB-DATA, Norway Ministry of Finances and Customs, Statistics Norway, Kongensgt 6, Post Office Box 4131 DEP, –0033 Oslo, Norway. Subject coverage: Norwegian statistics.

NORWAY - ABORTIONS

Nordic Council of Ministers, Store Strandstraede 18, DK-1255 Copenhagen K, Denmark and the Nordic Statistical Secretariat, Postboks 2550, DK-2100 Copenhagen 0, Denmark; *The Yearbook of Nordic Statistics*.

Statistical Office of the United Nations, Publishing Service, New York, New York

10017 (800) 253-9646; *Demographic Yearbook;* and *Trends in Europe and North America: The Statistical Yearbook of the Economic Commission for Europe*.

NORWAY - AGRICULTURE

Economist Intelligence Unit, 111 West 57th Street, New York, New York 10019 (800) 938-4685; *Norway Country Report*.

Euromonitor International, Inc., 122 South Michigan Avenue, Suite 1200, Chicago, Illinois 60603 (800) 577-EURO; *World Marketing Data and Statistics*.

Europa Publications Limited, 18 Bedford Square, London, WC1B 3JN, England; *The Europa World Year Book*.

Food and Agricultural Organization of the United Nations (FAO) Via delle Terme di Caracalla, 00100 Rome, Italy (Telephone Number in U.S. (202) 653-2400); *Production Yearbook; The State of Food and Agriculture;* and *Trade Yearbook*.

M.E. Sharpe, 80 Business Park Drive, Armonk, New York 10504 (800) 541-6563; *The Illustrated Book of World Rankings*.

Nordic Council of Ministers, Store Strandstraede 18, DK-1255 Copenhagen K, Denmark and the Nordic Statistical Secretariat, Postboks 2550, DK-2100 Copenhagen 0, Denmark; *The Yearbook of Nordic Statistics*.

Organisation for Economic Co-operation and Development (OECD), 2 rue Andre-Pascal, 75 Paris 16, France (Telephone Number in U.S. (202) 785-6323); *Economic Accounts for Agriculture; Indicators of Industrial Activity; Industrial Structure Statistics;* and *OECD Economic Surveys: Norway*.

St. Martin's Press, Inc., 175 Fifth Avenue, New York, New York 10010 (800) 221-7945; *The Statesman's Year-Book*.

Statistical Office of the United Nations, Publishing Service, New York, New York 10017 (800) 253-9646; *Statistical Yearbook*.

United Nations Conference on Trade and Development, Central Statistical Service, Palais des Nations, Geneva, Switzerland (Telephone in U.S. (800) 253-9646); *UNCTAD Commodity Yearbook*.

The World Bank, 1818 H Street, NW, Washington, D.C. 20433 (202) 477-1234; *World Development Indicators*.

NORWAY - AIRLINE SERVICE

Europa Publications Limited, 18 Bedford Square, London, WC1B 3JN, England; *The Europa World Year Book*.

International Civil Aviation Organization, 1000 Sherbrooke Street, West, Montreal, Quebec, Canada H3A 2R2 (514) 285-8219; *Civil Aviation Statistics of the World.*

M.E. Sharpe, 80 Business Park Drive, Armonk, New York 10504 (800) 541-6563; *The Illustrated Book of World Rankings.*

Nordic Council of Ministers, Store Strandstraede 18, D-K-1255 Copenhagen k, Denmark and the Nordic Statistical Secretariat, Postboks 2550, DK-2100 Copenhagen O, Denmark; *The Yearbook of Nordic Statistics.*

Organisation for Economic Co-operation and Development (OECD), 2 rue Andre-Pascal, 75 Paris 16, France (Telephone Number in U.S. (202) 785-6323); *Tourism Policy and International Tourism in OECD Member Countries.*

St. Martin's Press, Inc., 175 Fifth Avenue, New York, New York 10010 (800) 221-7945; *The Statesman's Year-Book.*

Statistical Office of the United Nations, Publishing Service, New York, New York 10017 (800) 253-9646; *Statistical Yearbook.*

NORWAY - AIRPORTS

Central Intelligence Agency, Washington, D.C. 20505 (703) 482-1100, www.cia.gov; *The World Factbook.*

NORWAY - ALUMINUM EXPORTS

International Monetary Fund, 700 Nineteenth Street, NW, Washington, D.C. 20431 (202) 623-7000; *International Financial Statistics.*

NORWAY - ALUMINUM PRODUCTION AND CONSUMPTION - See NORWAY - MINING AND MINERAL PRODUCTS

NORWAY - ANIMAL FEEDINGSTUFFS

Organisation for Economic Co-operation and Development (OECD), 2 rue Andre-Pascal, 75 Paris 16, France (Telephone Number in U.S. (202) 785-6323); *Foreign Trade by Commodities.*

Statistical Office of the United Nations, Publishing Service, New York, New York 10017 (800) 253-9646; *Statistical Yearbook.*

NORWAY - ANIMAL HEALTH

Food and Agricultural Organization of the United Nations (FAO), Via delle Terme di Caracalla, 00100 Rome, Italy (Telephone Number in U.S. (202) 653-2400); *Animal Health Yearbook.*

NORWAY - ANTIMONY AND ANTIMONY ORE PRODUCTION AND

CONSUMPTION - See NORWAY - MINING AND MINERAL PRODUCTS

NORWAY - AREA AND DENSITY OF POPULATION

Central Intelligence Agency, Washington, D.C. 20505 (703) 482-1100, www.cia.gov; *The World Factbook.*

Euromonitor International, Inc., 122 South Michigan Avenue, Suite 1200, Chicago, Illinois 60603 (800) 577-EURO; *The World Economic Factbook.*

Europa Publications Limited, 18 Bedford Square, London, WC1B 3JN, England; *The Europa World Year Book.*

Food and Agricultural Organization of the United Nations (FAO) Via delle Terme di Caracalla, 00100 Rome, Italy (Telephone Number in U.S. (202) 653-2400); *The State of Food and Agriculture.*

M.E. Sharpe, 80 Business Park Drive, Armonk, New York 10504 (800) 541-6563; *The Illustrated Book of World Rankings.*

Nordic Council of Ministers, Store Strandstraede 18, DK-1255 Copenhagen K, Denmark and the Nordic Statistical Secretariat, Postboks 2550, DK-2100 Copenhagen 0, Denmark; *The Yearbook of Nordic Statistics.*

St. Martin's Press, Inc., 175 Fifth Avenue, New York, New York 10010 (800) 221-7945; *The Statesman's Year-Book.*

Statistical Office of the United Nations, Publishing Service, New York, New York 10017 (800) 253-9646; *Statistical Yearbook;* and *Trends in Europe and North America: The Statistical Yearbook of the Economic Commission for Europe.*

United Nations Educational, Scientific and Cultural Organization (UNESCO), 7 Place de Fontenoy, F-75700 Paris, France (Telephone Number in U.S. (212) 963-5981); *Statistical Yearbook.*

The World Bank, 1818 H Street, NW, Washington, D.C. 20433 (202) 477-1234; *World Development Report.*

NORWAY - ARMS EXPORTS AND IMPORTS - See NORWAY - MILITARY

NORWAY - ARSENIC PRODUCTION AND CONSUMPTION - See NORWAY - MINING AND MINERAL PRODUCTS

NORWAY - BALANCE OF PAYMENTS

The Economist Intelligence Unit, 111 West 57th Street, New York, New York 10019 (800) 938-4685; *The World Market Atlas.*

Europa Publications Limited, 18 Bedford Square, London, WC1B 3JN, England; *The Europa World Year Book.*

International Monetary Fund, 700 Nineteenth Street, NW, Washington, D.C. 20431 (202) 623-7000; *International Financial Statistics.*

Nordic Council of Ministers, Store Strandstraede 18, DK-1255 Copenhagen K, Denmark and the Nordic Statistical Secretariat, Postboks 2550, DK-2100 Copenhagen 0, Denmark; *The Yearbook of Nordic Statistics.*

Organisation for Economic Co-operation and Development (OECD), 2 rue Andre-Pascal, 75 Paris 16, France (Telephone Number in U.S. (202) 785-6323); *Economic Outlook; Geographical Distribution of Financial Flows to Developing Countries; Main Economic Indicators - Historical Statistics;* and *OECD Economic Surveys: Norway.*

United Nations Conference on Trade and Development (UNCTAD), New York, New York 10017 (800) 253-9646; *Handbook of International Trade and Development Statistics.*

The World Bank, 1818 H Street, NW, Washington, D.C. 20433 (202) 477-1234; *World Development Report;* and *World Development Indicators.*

NORWAY - BANKING

Euromonitor International, Inc., 122 South Michigan Avenue, Suite 1200, Chicago, Illinois 60603 (800) 577-EURO; *World Marketing Data and Statistics.*

Europa Publications Limited, 18 Bedford Square, London, WC1B 3JN, England; *The Europa World Year Book.*

International Monetary Fund, 700 Nineteenth Street, NW, Washington, D.C. 20431 (202) 623-7000; *Government Finance Statistics Yearbook;* and *International Financial Statistics.*

M.E. Sharpe, 80 Business Park Drive, Armonk, New York 10504 (800) 541-6563; *The Illustrated Book of World Rankings.*

Nordic Council of Ministers, Store Strandstraede 18, DK-1255 Copenhagen K, Denmark and the Nordic Statistical Secretariat, Postboks 2550, DK-2100 Copenhagen 0, Denmark; *The Yearbook of Nordic Statistics.*

Organisation for Economic Co-operation and Development (OECD), 2 rue Andre-Pascal, 75 Paris 16, France (Telephone Number in U.S. (202) 785-6323); *Economic Outlook; Financial Market Trends;* and *OECD Economic Surveys:*

Norway.

St. Martin's Press, Inc., 175 Fifth Avenue, New York, New York 10010 (800) 221-7945; *The Statesman's Year-Book.*

Statistical Office of the United Nations, Publishing Service, New York, New York 10017 (800) 253-9646; *Statistical Yearbook.*

NORWAY - BARLEY PRODUCTION - See NORWAY - CROPS

NORWAY - BAUXITE PRODUCTION AND CONSUMPTION - See NORWAY - MINING AND MINERAL PRODUCTS

NORWAY - BEER PRODUCTION - See NORWAY - BEVERAGES

NORWAY - BEVERAGES

M.E. Sharpe, 80 Business Park Drive, Armonk, New York 10504 (800) 541-6563; *The Illustrated Book of World Rankings.*

Organisation for Economic Co-operation and Development (OECD), 2 rue Andre-Pascal, 75 Paris 16, France (Telephone Number in U.S. (202) 785-6323); *Indicators of Industrial Activity.*

Statistical Office of the United Nations, Publishing Service, New York, New York 10017 (800) 253-9646; *Statistical Yearbook.*

NORWAY - BIRTH RATES

Central Intelligence Agency, Washington, D.C. 20505 (703) 482-1100, www.cia.gov; *The World Factbook.*

Euromonitor International, Inc., 122 South Michigan Avenue, Suite 1200, Chicago, Illinois 60603 (800) 577-EURO; *The World Economic Factbook.*

Europa Publications Limited, 18 Bedford Square, London, WC1B 3JN, England; *The Europa World Year Book.*

M.E. Sharpe, 80 Business Park Drive, Armonk, New York 10504 (800) 541-6563; *The Illustrated Book of World Rankings.*

Nordic Council of Ministers, Store Strandstraede 18, DK-1255 Copenhagen K, Denmark and the Nordic Statistical Secretariat, Postboks 2550, DK-2100 Copenhagen 0, Denmark; *The Yearbook of Nordic Statistics.*

St. Martin's Press, Inc., 175 Fifth Avenue, New York, New York 10010 (800) 221-7945; *The Statesman's Year-Book.*

Statistical Office of the United Nations, Publishing Service, New York, New York 10017 (800) 253-9646; *Demographic Yearbook;* and *Statistical Yearbook.*

The World Bank, 1818 H Street, NW, Washington, D.C. 20433 (202) 477-1234; *World Development Indicators.*

World Health Organization, Office of Publications, 20 Avenue Appia, CH-1211 Geneva 27, Switzerland (Telephone Number in U.S. (518) 436-9686); *World Health Statistics Annual.*

NORWAY - BISMUTH PRODUCTION AND CONSUMPTION

Organisation for Economic Co-operation and Development (OECD), 2 rue Andre-Pascal, 75 Paris 16, France (Telephone Number in U.S. (202) 785-6323); *Indicators of Industrial Activity.*

NORWAY - BONDS

International Monetary Fund, 700 Nineteenth Street, NW, Washington, D.C. 20431 (202) 623-7000; *Government Finance Statistics Yearbook.*

Organisation for Economic Co-operation and Development (OECD), 2 rue Andre-Pascal, 75 Paris 16, France (Telephone Number in U.S. (202) 785-6323); *Financial Market Trends;* and *Main Economic - Historical Statistics.*

Statistical Office of the United Nations, Publishing Service, New York, New York 10017 (800) 253-9646; *Statistical Yearbook.*

NORWAY - BOOK PRODUCTION

Europa Publications Limited, 18 Bedford Square, London, WC1B 3JN, England; *The Europa World Year Book.*

Nordic Council of Ministers, Store Strandstraede 18, DK-1255 Copenhagen K, Denmark and the Nordic Statistical Secretariat, Postboks 2550, DK-2100 Copenhagen 0, Denmark; *The Yearbook of Nordic Statistics.*

Organisation for Economic Co-operation and Development (OECD), 2 rue Andre-Pascal, 75 Paris 16, France (Telephone Number in U.S. (202) 785-6323); *Indicators of Industrial Activity.*

St. Martin's Press, Inc., 175 Fifth Avenue, New York, New York 10010 (800) 221-7945; *The Statesman's Year-Book.*

Statistical Office of the United Nations, Publishing Service, New York, New York 10017 (800) 253-9646; *Trends in Europe and North America: The Statistical Yearbook of the Economic Commission for Europe.*

United Nations Educational, Scientific and Cultural Organization (UNESCO), 7 Place de Fontenoy, F-75700 Paris, France (Telephone Number in U.S. (212) 963-5981); *Statistical Yearbook.*

NORWAY - BROADCASTING

Billboard Limited, Post Office Box 9027, 1006 AA Amsterdam, The Netherlands (Telephone Number in U.S. (212) 764-7300); *World Radio TV Handbook.*

Central Intelligence Agency, Washington, D.C. 20505 (703) 482-1100, www.cia.gov; *The World Factbook.*

Euromonitor International, Inc., 122 South Michigan Avenue, Suite 1200, Chicago, Illinois 60603 (800) 577-EURO; *World Marketing Data and Statistics.*

Europa Publications Limited, 18 Bedford Square, London, WC1B 3JN, England; *The Europa World Year Book.*

M.E. Sharpe, 80 Business Park Drive, Armonk, New York 10504 (800) 541-6563; *The Illustrated Book of World Rankings.*

Nordic Council of Ministers, Store Strandstraede 18, DK-1255 Copenhagen K, Denmark and the Nordic Statistical Secretariat, Postboks 2550, DK-2100 Copenhagen 0, Denmark; *The Yearbook of Nordic Statistics.*

St. Martin's Press, Inc., 175 Fifth Avenue, New York, New York 10010 (800) 221-7945; *The Statesman's Year-Book.*

Statistical Office of the United Nations, Publishing Service, New York, New York 10017 (800) 253-9646; *Trends in Europe and North America: The Statistical Yearbook of the Economic Commission for Europe.*

United Nations Educational, Scientific and Cultural Organization (UNESCO), 7 Place de Fontenoy, F-75700 Paris, France (Telephone Number in U.S. (212) 963-5981); *Statistical Yearbook.*

NORWAY - BUDGET

Central Intelligence Agency, Washington, D.C. 20505 (703) 482-1100, www.cia.gov; *The World Factbook.*

NORWAY - BUSINESS

Organisation for Economic Co-operation and Development (OECD), 2 rue Andre-Pascal, 75 Paris 16, France (Telephone Number in U.S. (202) 785-6323); *Main Economic Indicators - Historical Statistics.*

NORWAY - BUSINESS AND PROFESSIONAL LICENSES

International Monetary Fund, 700 Nineteenth Street, NW, Washington, D.C. 20431 (202) 623-7000; *Government Finance Statistics Yearbook.*

NORWAY - BUTTER - See NORWAY -

DAIRY PRODUCTS

NORWAY - CABBAGE PRODUCTION - See
NORWAY - CROPS

NORWAY - CADMIUM PRODUCTION AND
CONSUMPTION - See NORWAY - MINING
AND MINERAL PRODUCTS

NORWAY - CALORIE SUPPLY

Food and Agricultural Organization of
the United Nations (FAO) Via delle Terme
di Caracalla, 00100 Rome, Italy (Telephone
Number in U.S. (202) 653-2400); *The State
of Food and Agriculture.*

NORWAY - CAPITAL INVESTMENT

Organisation for Economic Co-
operation and Development (OECD), 2 rue
Andre-Pascal, 75 Paris 16, France
(Telephone Number in U.S. (202) 785-
6323); *Economic Outlook;* and *Financial
Market Trends.*

NORWAY - CAPITAL REVENUE

International Monetary Fund, 700
Nineteenth Street, NW, Washington, D.C.
20431 (202) 623-7000; *Government
Finance Statistics Yearbook.*

Organisation for Economic Co-
operation and Development (OECD), 2 rue
Andre-Pascal, 75 Paris 16, France
(Telephone Number in U.S. (202) 785-
6323); *Economic Outlook;* and *Financial
Market Trends.*

NORWAY - CATTLE - See NORWAY -
LIVESTOCK AND POULTRY

NORWAY - CAULIFLOWER
PRODUCTION - See NORWAY - CROPS

NORWAY - CAUSTIC SODA
PRODUCTION - See NORWAY -
BEVERAGES

NORWAY - CEMENT PRODUCTION - See
NORWAY - MINING AND MINERAL
PRODUCTS

NORWAY - CEREAL PRODUCTION - See
NORWAY - CROPS

NORWAY - CHEESE - See NORWAY -
DAIRY PRODUCTS

NORWAY - CHEMICAL (ORGANIC)
PRODUCTION - See NORWAY - MINING
AND MINERAL PRODUCTS

NORWAY - CHROMITE PRODUCTION
AND CONSUMPTION - See NORWAY -
MINING AND MINERAL PRODUCTS

NORWAY - CHROMIUM ORE PRODUCTION
AND CONSUMPTION - See NORWAY -

MINING AND MINERAL PRODUCTS

NORWAY - CIGARETTE PRODUCTION - See
NORWAY - TOBACCO PRODUCTION

NORWAY - CLIMATE

M.E. Sharpe, 80 Business Park Drive,
Armonk, New York 10504 (800) 541-6563;
The Illustrated Book of World Rankings.

Nordic Council of Ministers, Store
Strandstraede 18, DK-1255 Copenhagen K,
Denmark and the Nordic Statistical
Secretariat, Postboks 2550, DK-2100
Copenhagen 0, Denmark; *The Yearbook of
Nordic Statistics.*

St. Martin's Press, Inc., 175 Fifth Avenue,
New York, New York 10010 (800) 221-7945;
The Statesman's Year-Book.

NORWAY - CLOTHING - See NORWAY -
TEXTILE INDUSTRY

NORWAY - COAL PRODUCTION - See
NORWAY - MINING AND MINERAL
PRODUCTS

NORWAY - COBALT PRODUCTION AND
CONSUMPTION - See NORWAY - MINING
AND MINERAL PRODUCTS

NORWAY - COFFEE PRODUCTION AND
CONSUMPTION - See NORWAY - CROPS

NORWAY - COKE AND COKE OVEN COKE
PRODUCTION AND CONSUMPTION - See
NORWAY - MINING AND MINERAL
PRODUCTS

NORWAY - COKE OVEN ORE PRODUCTION
AND CONSUMPTION - See NORWAY -
MINING AND MINERAL PRODUCTS

NORWAY - COMMERCE

St. Martin's Press, Inc., 175 Fifth Avenue,
New York, New York 10010 (800) 221-7945;
The Statesman's Year-Book.

NORWAY - CONSTRUCTION INDUSTRY

M.E. Sharpe, 80 Business Park Drive,
Armonk, New York 10504 (800) 541-6563;
The Illustrated Book of World Rankings.

Nordic Council of Ministers, Store
Strandstraede 18, DK-1255 Copenhagen K,
Denmark and the Nordic Statistical
Secretariat, Postboks 2550, DK-2100
Copenhagen 0, Denmark; *The Yearbook of
Nordic Statistics.*

Organisation for Economic Co-
operation and Development (OECD), 2 rue
Andre-Pascal, 75 Paris 16, France
(Telephone Number in U.S. (202) 785-
6323); *Industrial Structure Statistics; The
Iron and Steel Industry; Main Economic*

Indicators - Historical Statistics; and *OECD
Economic Surveys: Norway.*

St. Martin's Press, Inc., 175 Fifth
Avenue, New York, New York 10010 (800)
221-7945; *The Statesman's Year-Book.*

Statistical Office of the United Nations,
Publishing Service, New York, New York
10017 (800) 253-9646; *Statistical Yearbook.*

NORWAY - CONSUMER PRICE INDEX

Europa Publications Limited, 18
Bedford Square, London, WC1B 3JN,
England; *The Europa World Year Book.*

Nordic Council of Ministers, Store
Strandstraede 18, DK-1255 Copenhagen K,
Denmark and the Nordic Statistical
Secretariat, Postboks 2550, DK-2100
Copenhagen 0, Denmark; *The Yearbook of
Nordic Statistics.*

Organisation for Economic Co-
operation and Development (OECD), 2 rue
Andre-Pascal, 75 Paris 16, France
(Telephone Number in U.S. (202) 785-
6323); *Economic Outlook.*

Statistical Office of the United Nations,
Publishing Service, New York, New York
10017 (800) 253-9646; *Statistical Yearbook;*
and *Trends in Europe and North America:
The Statistical Yearbook of the Economic
Commission for Europe.*

NORWAY - CONSUMER PRICES

Euromonitor International, Inc., 122
South Michigan Avenue, Suite 1200,
Chicago, Illinois 60603 (800) 577-EURO;
World Marketing Data and Statistics.

International Labour Office,
I.L.O. Publications, 1828 L Street, NW, Suite
801, Washington, D.C. 20036 (301) 638-
3152; *Yearbook of Labour Statistics.*

International Monetary Fund, 700
Nineteenth Street, NW, Washington, D.C.
20431 (202) 623-7000; *International
Financial Statistics.*

Organisation for Economic Co-
operation and Development (OECD), 2 rue
Andre-Pascal, 75 Paris 16, France
(Telephone Number in U.S. (202) 785-
6323); *Economic Outlook.*

NORWAY - CONSUMPTION

International Lead and Zinc Study
Group, Metro House, 58 St. James's Street,
London SW1A 1LD England; *Lead and Zinc
Statistics.*

Nordic Council of Ministers, Store
Strandstraede 18, DK-1255 Copenhagen K,
Denmark and the Nordic Statistical
Secretariat, Postboks 2550, DK-2100

Copenhagen 0, Denmark; *The Yearbook of Nordic Statistics.*

Organisation for Economic Co-operation and Development (OECD), 2 rue Andre-Pascal, 75 Paris 16, France (Telephone Number in U.S. (202) 785-6323); *The Footwear, Raw Hides and Skins, and Leather Industry in OECD Countries; The Iron and Steel Industry; Meat Balances in OECD Member Countries; The Non-Ferrous Metals Industry; The Pulp and Paper Industry;* and *Textile Industry in OECD Countries.*

The World Bank, 1818 H Street, NW, Washington, D.C. 20433 (202) 477-1234; *World Development Report.*

NORWAY - COPPER AND COPPER ORE PRODUCTION AND CONSUMPTION - See NORWAY - MINING AND MINERAL PRODUCTS

NORWAY - CORN PRODUCTION - See NORWAY - CROPS

NORWAY - CORPORATE INCOME TAXES - See NORWAY - TAXATION

NORWAY - CORPORATE TAXES - See NORWAY - TAXATION

NORWAY - COTTON - See NORWAY - CROPS

NORWAY - CRIME

International Criminal Police Organization (INTERPOL), 50 quai achille Lignon, F-69006 Lyon, France; *International Crime Statistics.*

Nordic Council of Ministers, Store Strandstraede 18, DK-1255 Copenhagen K, Denmark and the Nordic Statistical Secretariat, Postboks 2550, DK-2100 Copenhagen 0, Denmark; *The Yearbook of Nordic Statistics.*

Statistical Office of the United Nations, Publishing Service, New York, New York 10017 (800) 253-9646; *Trends in Europe and North America: The Statistical Yearbook of the Economic Commission for Europe.*

Yale University Press, Yale Station, New Haven, Connecticut 06520 (800) 987-7323; *Violence and Crime in Cross-National Perspective.*

NORWAY - CROPS

Europa Publications Limited, 18 Bedford Square, London, WC1B 3JN, England; *The Europa World Year Book.*

Food and Agricultural Organization of the United Nations (FAO), Via delle Terme di Caracalla, 00100 Rome, Italy (Telephone

Number in U.S. (202) 653-2400); *Production Yearbook;* and *The State of Food and Agriculture.*

M.E. Sharpe, 80 Business Park Drive, Armonk, New York 10504 (800) 541-6563; *The Illustrated Book of World Rankings.*

Organisation for Economic Co-operation and Development (OECD), 2 rue Andre-Pascal, 75 Paris 16, France (Telephone Number in U.S. (202) 785-6323); *Economic Accounts for Agriculture; Foreign Trade by Commodities;* and *Textile Industry in OECD Countries.*

St. Martin's Press, Inc., 175 Fifth Avenue, New York, New York 10010 (800) 221-7945; *The Statesman's Year-Book.*

Statistical Office of the United Nations, Publishing Service, New York, New York 10017 (800) 253-9646; *Statistical Yearbook.*

United Nations Conference on Trade and Development, Central Statistical Service, Palais des Nations, Geneva, Switzerland (Telephone in U.S. (800) 253-9646); *UNCTAD Commodity Yearbook.*

NORWAY - CUSTOMS DUTIES

International Monetary Fund, 700 Nineteenth Street, NW, Washington, D.C. 20431 (202) 623-7000; *Government Finance Statistics Yearbook.*

Organisation for Economic Co-operation and Development (OECD), 2 rue Andre-Pascal, 75 Paris 16, France (Telephone Number in U.S. (202) 785-6323); *The Non-Ferrous Metals Industry.*

St. Martin's Press, Inc., 175 Fifth Avenue, New York, New York 10010 (800) 221-7945; *The Statesman's Year-Book.*

NORWAY - DAIRY PRODUCTS

Europa Publications Limited, 18 Bedford Square, London, WC1B 3JN, England; *The Europa World Year Book.*

Food and Agricultural Organization of the United Nations (FAO) Via delle Terme di Caracalla, 00100 Rome, Italy (Telephone Number in U.S. (202) 653-2400); *Production Yearbook;* and *The State of Food and Agriculture.*

M.E. Sharpe, 80 Business Park Drive, Armonk, New York 10504 (800) 541-6563; *The Illustrated Book of World Rankings.*

Nordic Council of Ministers, Store Strandstraede 18, DK-1255 Copenhagen K, Denmark and the Nordic Statistical Secretariat, Postboks 2550, DK-2100 Copenhagen 0, Denmark; *The Yearbook of Nordic Statistics.*

Organisation for Economic Co-operation and Development (OECD), 2 rue Andre-Pascal, 75 Paris 16, France (Telephone Number in U.S. (202) 785-6323); *Economic Accounts for Agriculture;* and *Milk, Milk Products, and Egg Balances in OECD Member Countries.*

St. Martin's Press, Inc., 175 Fifth Avenue, New York, New York 10010 (800) 221-7945; *The Statesman's Year-Book.*

Statistical Office of the United Nations, Publishing Service, New York, New York 10017 (800) 253-9646; *Statistical Yearbook.*

NORWAY - DEATH RATES - See NORWAY - MORTALITY

NORWAY - DEFENSE EXPENDITURES - See NORWAY - MILITARY

NORWAY - DEMOGRAPHY

The Economist Intelligence Unit, 111 West 57th Street, New York, New York 10019 (800) 938-4685; *The World Market Atlas.*

Euromonitor International, Inc., 122 South Michigan Avenue, Suite 1200, Chicago, Illinois 60603 (800) 577-EURO; *The World Economic Factbook;* and *World Marketing Data and Statistics.*

M.E. Sharpe, 80 Business Park Drive, Armonk, New York 10504 (800) 541-6563; *The Illustrated Book of World Rankings.*

Nordic Council of Ministers, Store Strandstraede 18, DK-1255 Copenhagen K, Denmark and the Nordic Statistical Secretariat, Postboks 2550, DK-2100 Copenhagen 0, Denmark; *The Yearbook of Nordic Statistics.*

Statistical Office of the United Nations, Publishing Service, New York, New York 10017 (800) 253-9646; *Human Development Report.*

NORWAY - DEVELOPMENT ASSISTANCE

Organisation for Economic Co-operation and Development (OECD), 2 rue Andre-Pascal, 75 Paris 16, France (Telephone Number in U.S. (202) 785-6323); *Geographical Distribution of Financial Flows to Developing Countries.*

Statistical Office of the United Nations, Publishing Service, New York, New York 10017 (800) 253-9646; *Statistical Yearbook.*

NORWAY - DIAMOND PRODUCTION - See NORWAY - MINING AND MINERAL PRODUCTS

NORWAY - DISCOUNT RATES - See NORWAY - BANKING

NORWAY - DISEASES - See NORWAY - HEALTH

NORWAY - DIVORCE RATES

M.E. Sharpe, 80 Business Park Drive, Armonk, New York 10504 (800) 541-6563; *The Illustrated Book of World Rankings.*

Nordic Council of Ministers, Store Strandstraede 18, DK-1255 Copenhagen K, Denmark and the Nordic Statistical Secretariat, Postboks 2550, DK-2100 Copenhagen 0, Denmark; *The Yearbook of Nordic Statistics.*

Statistical Office of the United Nations, Publishing Service, New York, New York 10017 (800) 253-9646; *Demographic Yearbook; Trends in Europe and North America: The Statistical Yearbook of the Economic Commission for Europe;* and *Statistical Yearbook.*

NORWAY - DUCKS - See NORWAY - LIVESTOCK AND POULTRY

NORWAY - ECONOMY

Central Intelligence Agency, Washington, D.C. 20505 (703) 482-1100, www.cia.gov; *The World Factbook.*

Economist Intelligence Unit, 111 West 57th Street, New York, New York 10019 (800) 938-4685; *Norway Country Report.*

Euromonitor International, Inc., 122 South Michigan Avenue, Suite 1200, Chicago, Illinois 60603 (800) 577-EURO; *The World Economic Factbook;* and *World Marketing Data and Statistics.*

Europa Publications Limited, 18 Bedford Square, London, WC1B 3JN, England; *The Europa World Year Book.*

M.E. Sharpe, 80 Business Park Drive, Armonk, New York 10504 (800) 541-6563; *The Illustrated Book of World Rankings.*

Organisation for Economic Co-operation and Development (OECD), 2 rue Andre-Pascal, 75 Paris 16, France (Telephone Number in U.S. (202) 785-6323); *Economic Outlook; Geographical Distribution of Financial Flows to Developing Countries; Main Economic Indicators - Historical Statistics; OECD Economic Surveys: Norway;* and *OECD Employment Outlook.*

St. Martin's Press, Inc., 175 Fifth Avenue, New York, New York 10010 (800) 221-7945; *The Statesman's Year-Book.*

Statistical Office of the United Nations, Publishing Service, New York, New York 10017 (800) 253-9646; *World Statistics Pocketbook.*

The World Bank, 1818 H Street, NW, Washington, D.C. 20433 (202) 477-1234; *The World Bank Atlas;* and *World Development Report.*

NORWAY - EDUCATION

The Economist Intelligence Unit, 111 West 57th Street, New York, New York 10019 (800) 938-4685; *The World Market Atlas.*

Euromonitor International, Inc., 122 South Michigan Avenue, Suite 1200, Chicago, Illinois 60603 (800) 577-EURO; *World Marketing Data and Statistics.*

Europa Publications Limited, 18 Bedford Square, London, WC1B 3JN, England; *The Europa World Year Book.*

M.E. Sharpe, 80 Business Park Drive, Armonk, New York 10504 (800) 541-6563; *The Illustrated Book of World Rankings.*

International Monetary Fund, 700 Nineteenth Street, NW, Washington, D.C. 20431 (202) 623-7000; *Government Finance Statistics Yearbook.*

Nordic Council of Ministers, Store Strandstraede 18, DK-1255 Copenhagen K, Denmark and the Nordic Statistical Secretariat, Postboks 2550, DK-2100 Copenhagen 0, Denmark; *The Yearbook of Nordic Statistics.*

Organisation for Economic Co-operation and Development (OECD), 2 rue Andre-Pascal, 75 Paris 16, France (Telephone Number in U.S. (202) 785-6323); *Education in OECD.*

St. Martin's Press, Inc., 175 Fifth Avenue, New York, New York 10010 (800) 221-7945; *The Statesman's Year-Book.*

Statistical Office of the United Nations, Publishing Service, New York, New York 10017 (800) 253-9646; *Human Development Report; and Trends in Europe and North America: The Statistical Yearbook of the Economic Commission for Europe;.*

United Nations Educational, Scientific and Cultural Organization (UNESCO), 7 Place de Fontenoy, F-75700 Paris, France (Telephone Number in U.S. (212) 963-5981); *Statistical Yearbook.*

The World Bank, 1818 H Street, NW, Washington, D.C. 20433 (202) 477-1234; *World Development Report;* and *World Development Indicators.*

NORWAY - EGG PRODUCTION AND CONSUMPTION - See NORWAY DAIRY PRODUCTS

NORWAY - ELECTRICITY

Central Intelligence Agency, Washington, D.C. 20505 (703) 482-1100, www.cia.gov; *The World Factbook.*

Commodity Research Bureau, Inc., 30 South Wacker Drive, Chicago, Illinois 60606 (312) 454-1801; *Commodity Year Book.*

M.E. Sharpe, 80 Business Park Drive, Armonk, New York 10504 (800) 541-6563; *The Illustrated Book of World Rankings.*

Nordic Council of Ministers, Store Strandstraede 18, DK-1255 Copenhagen K, Denmark and the Nordic Statistical Secretariat, Postboks 2550, DK-2100 Copenhagen 0, Denmark; *The Yearbook of Nordic Statistics.*

Organisation for Economic Co-operation and Development (OECD), 2 rue Andre-Pascal, 75 Paris 16, France (Telephone Number in U.S. (202) 785-6323); *Coal Information; Energy Statistics of OECD Countries; Indicators of Industrial Activity;* and *Industrial Structure Statistics.*

Penn Well Publishing Company, 1421 South Sheridan Road, Post Office Box 1260, Tulsa, Oklahoma 74101 (800) 752-9764; *International Energy Statistics Sourcebook.*

St. Martin's Press, Inc., 175 Fifth Avenue, New York, New York 10010 (800) 221-7945; *The Statesman's Year-Book.*

Statistical Office of the United Nations, Publishing Service, New York, New York 10017 (800) 253-9646; *Human Development Report; Trends in Europe and North America: The Statistical Yearbook of the Economic Commission for Europe;* and *Statistical Yearbook.*

NORWAY - EMPLOYMENT

International Labour Office, I.L.O. Publications, 1828 L Street, NW, Suite 801, Washington, D.C. 20036 (301) 638-3152; *Yearbook of Labour Statistics.*

M.E. Sharpe, 80 Business Park Drive, Armonk, New York 10504 (800) 541-6563; *The Illustrated Book of World Rankings.*

Nordic Council of Ministers, Store Strandstraede 18, DK-1255 Copenhagen K, Denmark and the Nordic Statistical Secretariat, Postboks 2550, DK-2100 Copenhagen 0, Denmark; *The Yearbook of Nordic Statistics.*

Organisation for Economic Co-operation and Development (OECD), 2 rue Andre-Pascal, 75 Paris 16, France (Telephone Number in U.S. (202) 785-6323); *Economic Outlook; The Iron and Steel Industry; OECD Economic Surveys: Norway; OECD Employment Outlook;* and *Textile Industry in OECD Countries.*

Statistical Office of the United Nations, Publishing Service, New York, New York 10017 (800) 253-9646; *Statistical Yearbook;* and *Trends in Europe and North America: The Statistical Yearbook of the Economic Commission for Europe.*

NORWAY - ENERGY

Euromonitor International, Inc., 122 South Michigan Avenue, Suite 1200, Chicago, Illinois 60603 (800) 577-EURO; *The World Economic Factbook;* and *World Marketing Data and Statistics.*

Food and Agricultural Organization of the United Nations (FAO) Via delle Terme di Caracalla, 00100 Rome, Italy (Telephone Number in U.S. (202) 653-2400); *The State of Food and Agriculture.*

M.E. Sharpe, 80 Business Park Drive, Armonk, New York 10504 (800) 541-6563; *The Illustrated Book of World Rankings.*

Nordic Council of Ministers, Store Strandstraede 18, DK-1255 Copenhagen K, Denmark and the Nordic Statistical Secretariat, Postboks 2550, DK-2100 Copenhagen 0, Denmark; *The Yearbook of Nordic Statistics.*

Organisation for Economic Co-operation and Development (OECD), 2 rue Andre-Pascal, 75 Paris 16, France (Telephone Number in U.S. (202) 785-6323); *Coal Information; Energy Statistics of OECD Countries;* and *Oil and Gas Information.*

Penn Well Publishing Company, 1421 South Sheridan Road, Post Office Box 1260, Tulsa, Oklahoma 74101 (800) 752-9764; *International Energy Statistics Sourcebook.*

St. Martin's Press, Inc., 175 Fifth Avenue, New York, New York 10010 (800) 221-7945; *The Statesman's Year-Book.*

Statistical Office of the United Nations, Publishing Service, New York, New York 10017 (800) 253-9646; *Energy Statistics Yearbook; Human Development Report; OECD Environmental Data; Trends in Europe and North America: The Statistical Yearbook of the Economic Commission for Europe; World Statistics Pocketbook;* and *Statistical Yearbook.*

The World Bank, 1818 H Street, NW, Washington, D.C. 20433 (202) 477-1234; *The World Bank Atlas;* and *World Development Report.*

NORWAY - ENVIRONMENT

Economist Intelligence Unit, 111 West 57th Street, New York, New York 10019 (800) 938-4685; *Norway Country Report.*

Statistical Office of the United Nations,

Publishing Service, New York, New York 10017 (800) 253-9646; *Trends in Europe and North America: The Statistical Yearbook of the Economic Commission for Europe;* and *World Statistics Pocketbook.*

NORWAY - EXCHANGE RATES

Central Intelligence Agency, Washington, D.C. 20505 (703) 482-1100, www.cia.gov; *The World Factbook.*

Euromonitor International, Inc., 122 South Michigan Avenue, Suite 1200, Chicago, Illinois 60603 (800) 577-EURO; *The World Economic Factbook.*

Europa Publications Limited, 18 Bedford Square, London, WC1B 3JN, England; *The Europa World Year Book.*

International Civil Aviation Organization, 1000 Sherbrooke Street, West, Montreal, Quebec, Canada H3A 2R2 (514) 285-8219; *Civil Aviation Statistics of the World.*

International Monetary Fund, 700 Nineteenth Street, NW, Washington, D.C. 20431 (202) 623-7000; *International Financial Statistics.*

Nordic Council of Ministers, Store Strandstraede 18, DK-1255 Copenhagen K, Denmark and the Nordic Statistical Secretariat, Postboks 2550, DK-2100 Copenhagen 0, Denmark; *The Yearbook of Nordic Statistics.*

Organisation for Economic Co-operation and Development (OECD), 2 rue Andre-Pascal, 75 Paris 16, France (Telephone Number in U.S. (202) 785-6323); *Economic Outlook; Financial Market Trends; Revenue Statistics of OECD Member Countries;* and *Tourism Policy and International Tourism in OECD Member Countries.*

Statistical Office of the United Nations, Publishing Service, New York, New York 10017 (800) 253-9646; *Statistical Yearbook; Trends in Europe and North America: The Statistical Yearbook of the Economic Commission for Europe;* and *World Statistics Pocketbook*

NORWAY - EXCISE TAXES - See NORWAY - TAXATION

NORWAY - EXPORTS

Central Intelligence Agency, Washington, D.C. 20505 (703) 482-1100, www.cia.gov; *The World Factbook.*

The Economist Intelligence Unit, 111 West 57th Street, New York, New York 10019 (800) 938-4685; *Norway Country Report;* and *The World Market Atlas.*

Euromonitor International, Inc., 122 South Michigan Avenue, Suite 1200, Chicago, Illinois 60603 (800) 577-EURO; *The World Economic Factbook.*

Europa Publications Limited, 18 Bedford Square, London, WC1B 3JN, England; *The Europa World Year Book.*

Food and Agricultural Organization of the United Nations (FAO) Via delle Terme di Caracalla, 00100 Rome, Italy (Telephone Number in U.S. (202) 653-2400); *The State of Food and Agriculture.*

International Lead and Zinc Study Group, Metro House, 58 St. James's Street, London SW1A 1LD England; *Lead and Zinc Statistics.*

International Monetary Fund, 700 Nineteenth Street, NW, Washington, D.C. 20431 (202) 623-7000; *Direction of Trade Statistics; Government Finance Statistics Yearbook;* and *International Financial Statistics.*

Nordic Council of Ministers, Store Strandstraede 18, DK-1255 Copenhagen K, Denmark and the Nordic Statistical Secretariat, Postboks 2550, DK-2100 Copenhagen 0, Denmark; *The Yearbook of Nordic Statistics.*

Organisation for Economic Co-operation and Development (OECD), 2 rue Andre-Pascal, 75 Paris 16, France (Telephone Number in U.S. (202) 785-6323); *Economic Outlook; The Footwear, Raw Hides and Skins, and Leather Industry in OECD Countries; Foreign Trade by Commodities; Geographical Distribution of Financial Flows to Developing Countries; Industrial Structure Statistics; The Iron and Steel Industry; Milk, Milk Products, and Egg Balances in OECD Member Countries; The Pulp and Paper Industry; OECD Economic Surveys: Norway;* and *Review of Fisheries in OECD Member Countries.*

St. Martin's Press, Inc., 175 Fifth Avenue, New York, New York 10010 (800) 221-7945; *The Statesman's Year-Book.*

Statistical Office of the United Nations, Publishing Service, New York, New York 10017 (800) 253-9646; *Trends in Europe and North America: The Statistical Yearbook of the Economic Commission for Europe.*

United Nations Conference on Trade and Development (UNCTAD), New York, New York 10017 (800) 253-9646; *Handbook of International Trade and Development Statistics.*

The World Bank, 1818 H Street, NW, Washington, D.C. 20433 (202) 477-1234; *World Development Report;* and *World Development Indicators.*

NORWAY - EXTERNAL FINANCING

Organisation for Economic Co-operation and Development (OECD), 2 rue Andre-Pascal, 75 Paris 16, France (Telephone Number in U.S. (202) 785-6323); *Economic Outlook;* and *Financial Market Trends.*

NORWAY - EXTERNAL INDEBTEDNESS

Organisation for Economic Co-operation and Development (OECD), 2 rue Andre-Pascal, 75 Paris 16, France (Telephone Number in U.S. (202) 785-6323); *Financial Market Trends;* and *Geographical Distribution of Financial Flows to Developing Countries.*

The World Bank, 1818 H Street, NW, Washington, D.C. 20433 (202) 477-1234; *World Development Report;* and *World Development Indicators.*

NORWAY - EXTERNAL TRADE

Euromonitor International, Inc., 122 South Michigan Avenue, Suite 1200, Chicago, Illinois 60603 (800) 577-EURO; *World Marketing Data and Statistics.*

Food and Agricultural Organization of the United Nations (FAO) Via delle Terme di Caracalla, 00100 Rome, Italy (Telephone Number in U.S. (202) 653-2400); *The State of Food and Agriculture;* and *Trade Yearbook.*

Nordic Council of Ministers, Store Strandstraede 18, DK-1255 Copenhagen K, Denmark and the Nordic Statistical Secretariat, Postboks 2550, DK-2100 Copenhagen 0, Denmark; *The Yearbook of Nordic Statistics.*

Statistical Office of the United Nations, Publishing Service, New York, New York 10017 (800) 253-9646; *Statistical Yearbook.*

NORWAY - FABRIC PRODUCTION - See NORWAY - TEXTILE INDUSTRY

NORWAY - FARM CROPS - See NORWAY - CROPS

NORWAY - FERTILITY RATES

Central Intelligence Agency, Washington, D.C. 20505 (703) 482-1100, www.cia.gov; *The World Factbook.*

M.E. Sharpe, 80 Business Park Drive, Armonk, New York 10504 (800) 541-6563; *The Illustrated Book of World Rankings.*

Nordic Council of Ministers, Store Strandstraede 18, DK-1255 Copenhagen K, Denmark and the Nordic Statistical Secretariat, Postboks 2550, DK-2100 Copenhagen 0, Denmark; *The Yearbook of Nordic Statistics.*

Statistical Office of the United Nations, Publishing Service, New York, New York 10017 (800) 253-9646; *Human Development Report;* and *Trends in Europe and North America: The Statistical Yearbook of the Economic Commission for Europe.*

The World Bank, 1818 H Street, NW, Washington, D.C. 20433 (202) 477-1234; *The World Bank Atlas; World Development Report;* and *World Development Indicators.*

NORWAY - FERTILIZER

Food and Agricultural Organization of the United Nations (FAO), Via delle Terme di Caracalla, 00100 Rome, Italy (Telephone Number in U.S. (202) 653-2400); *Fertilizer Yearbook;* and *The State of Food and Agriculture.*

Organisation for Economic Co-operation and Development (OECD), 2 rue Andre-Pascal, 75 Paris 16, France (Telephone Number in U.S. (202) 785-6323); *Economic Accounts for Agriculture;* and *Foreign Trade by Commodities.*

Statistical Office of the United Nations, Publishing Service, New York, New York 10017 (800) 253-9646; *Human Development Report;* and *Statistical Yearbook.*

NORWAY - FETAL MORTALITY - See NORWAY - MORTALITY

NORWAY - FILAMENT PRODUCTION - See NORWAY - TEXTILE INDUSTRY

NORWAY - FILMS PRODUCED - LONG - See NORWAY - MOTION PICTURES

NORWAY - FINANCE

Economist Intelligence Unit, 111 West 57th Street, New York, New York 10019 (800) 938-4685; *Norway Country Report.*

Europa Publications Limited, 18 Bedford Square, London, WC1B 3JN, England; *The Europa World Year Book.*

International Monetary Fund, 700 Nineteenth Street, NW, Washington, D.C. 20431 (202) 623-7000; *Government Finance Statistics Yearbook;* and *International Financial Statistics.*

M.E. Sharpe, 80 Business Park Drive, Armonk, New York 10504 (800) 541-6563; *The Illustrated Book of World Rankings.*

Nordic Council of Ministers, Store Strandstraede 18, DK-1255 Copenhagen K, Denmark and the Nordic Statistical Secretariat, Postboks 2550, DK-2100 Copenhagen 0, Denmark; *The Yearbook of Nordic Statistics.*

Organisation for Economic Co-operation and Development (OECD), 2 rue Andre-Pascal, 75 Paris 16, France (Telephone Number in U.S. (202) 785-6323); *Economic Outlook; Financial Market Trends; Geographical Distribution of Financial Flows to Developing Countries; Main Economic Indicators - Historical Statistics; OECD Financial Statistics;* and *Revenue Statistics of OECD Member Countries.*

St. Martin's Press, Inc., 175 Fifth Avenue, New York, New York 10010 (800) 221-7945; *The Statesman's Year-Book.*

NORWAY - FISHERIES

Europa Publications Limited, 18 Bedford Square, London, WC1B 3JN, England; *The Europa World Year Book.*

Food and Agricultural Organization of the United Nations (FAO) Via delle Terme di Caracalla, 00100 Rome, Italy (Telephone Number in U.S. (202) 653-2400); *The State of Food and Agriculture;* and *Yearbook of Fishery Statistics.*

International Monetary Fund, 700 Nineteenth Street, NW, Washington, D.C. 20431 (202) 623-7000; *International Financial Statistics.*

M.E. Sharpe, 80 Business Park Drive, Armonk, New York 10504 (800) 541-6563; *The Illustrated Book of World Rankings.*

Nordic Council of Ministers, Store Strandstraede 18, DK-1255 Copenhagen K, Denmark and the Nordic Statistical Secretariat, Postboks 2550, DK-2100 Copenhagen 0, Denmark; *The Yearbook of Nordic Statistics.*

Organisation for Economic Co-operation and Development (OECD), 2 rue Andre-Pascal, 75 Paris 16, France (Telephone Number in U.S. (202) 785-6323); *Foreign Trade by Commodities; Industrial Structure Statistics;* and *Review of Fisheries in OECD Member Countries.*

St. Martin's Press, Inc., 175 Fifth Avenue, New York, New York 10010 (800) 221-7945; *The Statesman's Year-Book.*

Statistical Office of the United Nations, Publishing Service, New York, New York 10017 (800) 253-9646; *Statistical Yearbook.*

United Nations Conference on Trade and Development, Central Statistical Service, Palais des Nations, Geneva, Switzerland (Telephone in U.S. (800) 253-9646); *UNCTAD Commodity Yearbook.*

NORWAY - FLOUR PRODUCTION

Statistical Office of the United Nations, Publishing Service, New York, New York

10017 (800) 253-9646; *Statistical Yearbook.*

NORWAY - FOOD

Euromonitor International, Inc., 122 South Michigan Avenue, Suite 1200, Chicago, Illinois 60603 (800) 577-EURO; *Retail Trade International.*

Food and Agricultural Organization of the United Nations (FAO) Via delle Terme di Caracalla, 00100 Rome, Italy (Telephone Number in U.S. (202) 653-2400); *The State of Food and Agriculture;* and *Production Yearbook.*

Organisation for Economic Co-operation and Development (OECD), 2 rue Andre-Pascal, 75 Paris 16, France (Telephone Number in U.S. (202) 785-6323); *Food Consumption Statistics;* and *Foreign Trade by Commodities.*

United Nations Conference on Trade and Development, Central Statistical Service, Palais des Nations, Geneva, Switzerland (Telephone in U.S. (800) 253-9646); *UNCTAD Commodity Yearbook.*

NORWAY - FOOTWEAR - PRODUCTION INDEX

Organisation for Economic Co-operation and Development (OECD), 2 rue Andre-Pascal, 75 Paris 16, France (Telephone Number in U.S. (202) 785-6323); *Indicators of Industrial Activity.*

NORWAY - FOREIGN DEBT

International Monetary Fund, 700 Nineteenth Street, NW, Washington, D.C. 20431 (202) 623-7000; *Government Finance Statistics Yearbook.*

Organisation for Economic Co-operation and Development (OECD), 2 rue Andre-Pascal, 75 Paris 16, France (Telephone Number in U.S. (202) 785-6323); *Economic Outlook.*

St. Martin's Press, Inc., 175 Fifth Avenue, New York, New York 10010 (800) 221-7945; *The Statesman's Year-Book.*

NORWAY - FOREIGN INDEBTEDNESS

Organisation for Economic Co-operation and Development (OECD), 2 rue Andre-Pascal, 75 Paris 16, France (Telephone Number in U.S. (202) 785-6323); *Economic Outlook;* and *Financial Market Trends.*

St. Martin's Press, Inc., 175 Fifth Avenue, New York, New York 10010 (800) 221-7945; *The Statesman's Year-Book.*

NORWAY - FOREIGN TRADE

Economist Intelligence Unit, 111 West

57th Street, New York, New York 10019 (800) 938-4685; *Norway Country Report.*

Euromonitor International, Inc., 122 South Michigan Avenue, Suite 1200, Chicago, Illinois 60603 (800) 577-EURO; *The World Economic Factbook.*

Europa Publications Limited, 18 Bedford Square, London, WC1B 3JN, England; *The Europa World Year Book.*

Food and Agricultural Organization of the United Nations (FAO) Via delle Terme di Caracalla, 00100 Rome, Italy (Telephone Number in U.S. (202) 653-2400); *The State of Food and Agriculture.*

International Monetary Fund, 700 Nineteenth Street, NW, Washington, D.C. 20431 (202) 623-7000; *International Financial Statistics.*

M.E. Sharpe, 80 Business Park Drive, Armonk, New York 10504 (800) 541-6563; *The Illustrated Book of World Rankings.*

Organisation for Economic Co-operation and Development (OECD), 2 rue Andre-Pascal, 75 Paris 16, France (Telephone Number in U.S. (202) 785-6323); *Economic Outlook; The Footwear, Raw Hides and Skins, and Leather Industry in OECD Countries; Foreign Trade by Commodities; Main Economic Indicators - Historical Statistics; Maritime Transport; Meat Balances in OECD Member Countries;* and *OECD Economic Surveys: Norway.*

Statistical Office of the United Nations, Publishing Service, New York, New York 10017 (800) 253-9646; *International Trade Statistics Yearbook;* and *Statistical Yearbook.*

United Nations Conference on Trade and Development, Central Statistical Service, Palais des Nations, Geneva, Switzerland (Telephone in U.S. (800) 253-9646); *UNCTAD Commodity Yearbook.*

The World Bank, 1818 H Street, NW, Washington, D.C. 20433 (202) 477-1234; *World Development Report;* and *World Development Indicators.*

World Bureau of Metal Statistics, 27-A High Street, Ware, Herts. SG12 9BA, England; *World Metal Statistics.*

NORWAY - FORESTRY AND FOREST PRODUCTS

Europa Publications Limited, 18 Bedford Square, London, WC1B 3JN, England; *The Europa World Year Book.*

Food and Agricultural Organization of the United Nations (FAO) Via delle Terme di Caracalla, 00100 Rome, Italy (Telephone Number in U.S. (202) 653-2400); *The State*

of Food and Agriculture; and *Yearbook of Forest Products.*

International Monetary Fund, 700 Nineteenth Street, NW, Washington, D.C. 20431 (202) 623-7000; *International Financial Statistics.*

M.E. Sharpe, 80 Business Park Drive, Armonk, New York 10504 (800) 541-6563; *The Illustrated Book of World Rankings.*

Nordic Council of Ministers, Store Strandstraede 18, DK-1255 Copenhagen K, Denmark and the Nordic Statistical Secretariat, Postboks 2550, DK-2100 Copenhagen 0, Denmark; *The Yearbook of Nordic Statistics.*

Organisation for Economic Co-operation and Development (OECD), 2 rue Andre-Pascal, 75 Paris 16, France (Telephone Number in U.S. (202) 785-6323); *Foreign Trade by Commodities; Indicators of Industrial Activity; Industrial Structure Statistics;* and *The Pulp and Paper Industry.*

St. Martin's Press, Inc., 175 Fifth Avenue, New York, New York 10010 (800) 221-7945; *The Statesman's Year-Book.*

Statistical Office of the United Nations, Publishing Service, New York, New York 10017 (800) 253-9646; *Statistical Yearbook;* and *Trends in Europe and North America: The Statistical Yearbook of the Economic Commission for Europe.*

United Nations Conference on Trade and Development, Central Statistical Service, Palais des Nations, Geneva, Switzerland (Telephone in U.S. (800) 253-9646); *UNCTAD Commodity Yearbook.*

United Nations Educational, Scientific and Cultural Organization (UNESCO), 7 Place de Fontenoy, F-75700 Paris, France (Telephone Number in U.S. (212) 963-5981); *Statistical Yearbook.*

The World Bank, 1818 H Street, NW, Washington, D.C. 20433 (202) 477-1234; *World Development Report.*

NORWAY - FRUIT PRODUCTION - See NORWAY - CROPS

NORWAY - FURNITURE AND WOOD PRODUCTS - EXPORTS AND IMPORTS

Organisation for Economic Co-operation and Development (OECD), 2 rue Andre-Pascal, 75 Paris 16, France (Telephone Number in U.S. (202) 785-6323); *Foreign Trade by Commodities;* and *Industrial Structure Statistics.*

NORWAY - GAS - See NORWAY - MINING AND MINERAL PRODUCTS

NORWAY - GENERAL INDUSTRIAL STATISTICS - See NORWAY - INDUSTRY

NORWAY - GENERAL MORTALITY - See NORWAY - MORTALITY

NORWAY - GEOGRAPHIC DATA

M.E. Sharpe, 80 Business Park Drive, Armonk, New York 10504 (800) 541-6563; *The Illustrated Book of World Rankings.*

NORWAY - GLASS AND GLASS PRODUCTS - PRODUCTION INDEX

Organisation for Economic Co-operation and Development (OECD), 2 rue Andre-Pascal, 75 Paris 16, France (Telephone Number in U.S. (202) 785-6323); *Indicators of Industrial Activity.*

NORWAY - GOATS - See NORWAY - LIVESTOCK AND POULTRY

NORWAY - GOLD HOLDINGS

International Monetary Fund, 700 Nineteenth Street, NW, Washington, D.C. 20431 (202) 623-7000; *International Financial Statistics.*

Statistical Office of the United Nations, Publishing Service, New York, New York 10017 (800) 253-9646; *Statistical Yearbook.*

The World Bank, 1818 H Street, NW, Washington, D.C. 20433 (202) 477-1234; *World Development Indicators.*

NORWAY - GOLD PRODUCTION AND CONSUMPTION - See NORWAY - MINING AND MINERAL PRODUCTS

NORWAY - GOVERNMENT

Central Intelligence Agency, Washington, D.C. 20505 (703) 482-1100, www.cia.gov; *The World Factbook.*

Europa Publications Limited, 18 Bedford Square, London, WC1B 3JN, England; *The Europa World Year Book.*

International Monetary Fund, 700 Nineteenth Street, NW, Washington, D.C. 20431 (202) 623-7000; *Government Finance Statistics Yearbook.*

Nordic Council of Ministers, Store Strandstraede 18, DK-1255 Copenhagen K, Denmark and the Nordic Statistical Secretariat, Postboks 2550, DK-2100 Copenhagen 0, Denmark; *The Yearbook of Nordic Statistics.*

Organisation for Economic Co-operation and Development (OECD), 2 rue Andre-Pascal, 75 Paris 16, France (Telephone Number in U.S. (202) 785-6323); *Economic Outlook;* and *Revenue Statistics of OECD Member Countries.*

St. Martin's Press, Inc., 175 Fifth Avenue, New York, New York 10010 (800) 221-7945; *The Statesman's Year-Book.*

Statistical Office of the United Nations, Publishing Service, New York, New York 10017 (800) 253-9646; *National Accounts Statistics;* and *Statistical Yearbook.*

The World Bank, 1818 H Street, NW, Washington, D.C. 20433 (202) 477-1234; *World Development Report;* and *World Development Indicators.*

NORWAY - GRAIN PRODUCTION - See NORWAY - CROPS

NORWAY - GRANTS

International Monetary Fund, 700 Nineteenth Street, NW, Washington, D.C. 20431 (202) 623-7000; *Government Finance Statistics Yearbook.*

Organisation for Economic Co-operation and Development (OECD), 2 rue Andre-Pascal, 75 Paris 16, France (Telephone Number in U.S. (202) 785-6323); *Geographical Distribution of Financial Flows to Developing Countries.*

NORWAY - GROSS DOMESTIC PRODUCT

The Economist Intelligence Unit, 111 West 57th Street, New York, New York 10019 (800) 938-4685; *Norway Country Report;* and *The World Market Atlas.*

Euromonitor International, Inc., 122 South Michigan Avenue, Suite 1200, Chicago, Illinois 60603 (800) 577-EURO; *The World Economic Factbook.*

Europa Publications Limited, 18 Bedford Square, London, WC1B 3JN, England; *The Europa World Year Book.*

M.E. Sharpe, 80 Business Park Drive, Armonk, New York 10504 (800) 541-6563; *The Illustrated Book of World Rankings.*

Nordic Council of Ministers, Store Strandstraede 18, DK-1255 Copenhagen K, Denmark and the Nordic Statistical Secretariat, Postboks 2550, DK-2100 Copenhagen 0, Denmark; *The Yearbook of Nordic Statistics.*

Organisation for Economic Co-operation and Development (OECD), 2 rue Andre-Pascal, 75 Paris 16, France (Telephone Number in U.S. (202) 785-6323); *Economic Outlook; Geographical Distribution of Financial Flows to Developing Countries;* and *Revenue Statistics of OECD Member Countries.*

Statistical Office of the United Nations, Publishing Service, New York, New York 10017 (800) 253-9646; *Human*

Development Report; National Accounts Statistics; Trends in Europe and North America: The Statistical Yearbook of the Economic Commission for Europe; and Statistical Yearbook.

The World Bank, 1818 H Street, NW, Washington, D.C. 20433 (202) 477-1234; *World Development Report;* and *World Development Indicators.*

NORWAY - GROSS NATIONAL PRODUCT

Organisation for Economic Co-operation and Development (OECD), 2 rue Andre-Pascal, 75 Paris 16, France (Telephone Number in U.S. (202) 785-6323); *Economic Outlook;* and *Geographical Distribution of Financial Flows to Developing Countries.*

St. Martin's Press, Inc., 175 Fifth Avenue, New York, New York 10010 (800) 221-7945; *The Statesman's Year-Book.*

U.S. Arms Control and Disarmament Agency, 320 Twenty-first Street, NW, Washington, D.C. 20451 (202) 647-8677; *World Military Expenditures and Arms Transfers.*

The World Bank, 1818 H Street, NW, Washington, D.C. 20433 (202) 477-1234; *The World Bank Atlas; World Development Report;* and *World Development Indicators.*

NORWAY - HEALTH

Euromonitor International, Inc., 122 South Michigan Avenue, Suite 1200, Chicago, Illinois 60603 (800) 577-EURO; *World Marketing Data and Statistics.*

M.E. Sharpe, 80 Business Park Drive, Armonk, New York 10504 (800) 541-6563; *The Illustrated Book of World Rankings.*

Nordic Council of Ministers, Store Strandstraede 18, DK-1255 Copenhagen K, Denmark and the Nordic Statistical Secretariat, Postboks 2550, DK-2100 Copenhagen 0, Denmark; *The Yearbook of Nordic Statistics.*

Organisation for Economic Co-operation and Development (OECD), 2 rue Andre-Pascal, 75 Paris 16, France (Telephone Number in U.S. (202) 785-6323); *OECD Health Systems: Facts and Trends.*

St. Martin's Press, Inc., 175 Fifth Avenue, New York, New York 10010 (800) 221-7945; *The Statesman's Year-Book.*

Statistical Office of the United Nations, Publishing Service, New York, New York 10017 (800) 253-9646; *Human Development Report; Trends in Europe and North America: The Statistical Yearbook of the Economic Commission for Europe;* and

Statistical Yearbook.

United Nations Children's Fund (UNICEF), 3 United Nations Plaza, New York, New York 10017 (800) 253-9646; *State of the World's Children.*

The World Bank, 1818 H Street, NW, Washington, D.C. 20433 (202) 477-1234; *World Development Report.*

World Health Organization, Office of Publications, 20 Avenue Appia, CH-1211 Geneva 27, Switzerland (Telephone Number in U.S. (518) 436-9686); *World Health Statistics Annual.*

NORWAY - HEALTH EXPENDITURES

International Monetary Fund, 700 Nineteenth Street, NW, Washington, D.C. 20431 (202) 623-7000; *Government Finance Statistics Yearbook.*

NORWAY - HIDE PRODUCTION

Food and Agricultural Organization of the United Nations (FAO), Via delle Terme di Caracalla, 00100 Rome, Italy (Telephone Number in U.S. (202) 653-2400); *Production Yearbook.*

Organisation for Economic Co-operation and Development (OECD), 2 rue Andre-Pascal, 75 Paris 16, France (Telephone Number in U.S. (202) 785-6323); *The Footwear, Raw Hides and Skins, and Leather Industry in OECD Countries; Foreign Trade by Commodities;* and *Indicators of Industrial Activity.*

NORWAY - HIGHWAYS

Central Intelligence Agency, Washington, D.C. 20505 (703) 482-1100, www.cia.gov; *The World Factbook.*

International Road Federation, 2600 Virginia Avenue, NW., Washington, D.C. 20037 (202) 338-4641; *World Road Statistics.*

Nordic Council of Ministers, Store Strandstraede 18, DK-1255 Copenhagen K, Denmark and the Nordic Statistical Secretariat, Postboks 2550, DK-2100 Copenhagen 0, Denmark; *The Yearbook of Nordic Statistics.*

St. Martin's Press, Inc., 175 Fifth Avenue, New York, New York 10010 (800) 221-7945; *The Statesman's Year-Book.*

Statistical Office of the United Nations, Publishing Service, New York, New York 10017 (800) 253-9646; *Annual Bulletin of Transport Statistics for Europe;* and *Trends in Europe and North America: The Statistical Yearbook of the Economic Commission for Europe.*

NORWAY - HOME FINANCE

Organisation for Economic Co-operation and Development (OECD), 2 rue Andre-Pascal, 75 Paris 16, France (Telephone Number in U.S. (202) 785-6323); *Main Economic Indicators - Historical Statistics.*

NORWAY - HORSES - See NORWAY - LIVESTOCK AND POULTRY

NORWAY - HOURS OF WORK - See NORWAY - EMPLOYMENT

NORWAY - HOUSING AND HOUSING UNITS

Euromonitor International, Inc., 122 South Michigan Avenue, Suite 1200, Chicago, Illinois 60603 (800) 577-EURO; *World Marketing Data and Statistics.*

M.E. Sharpe, 80 Business Park Drive, Armonk, New York 10504 (800) 541-6563; *The Illustrated Book of World Rankings.*

Nordic Council of Ministers, Store Strandstraede 18, DK-1255 Copenhagen K, Denmark and the Nordic Statistical Secretariat, Postboks 2550, DK-2100 Copenhagen 0, Denmark; *The Yearbook of Nordic Statistics.*

Statistical Office of the United Nations, Publishing Service, New York, New York 10017 (800) 253-9646; *Trends in Europe and North America: The Statistical Yearbook of the Economic Commission for Europe.*

NORWAY - HOUSING CONSTRUCTION - See NORWAY - CONSTRUCTION INDUSTRY

NORWAY - HOUSING EXPENDITURES

International Monetary Fund, 700 Nineteenth Street, NW, Washington, D.C. 20431 (202) 623-7000; *Government Finance Statistics Yearbook.*

NORWAY - HYDROCHLORIC ACID PRODUCTION

Statistical Office of the United Nations, Publishing Service, New York, New York 10017 (800) 253-9646; *Statistical Yearbook.*

NORWAY - ILLITERATE POPULATION

Central Intelligence Agency, Washington, D.C. 20505 (703) 482-1100, www.cia.gov; *The World Factbook.*

The Economist Intelligence Unit, 111 West 57th Street, New York, New York 10019 (800) 938-4685; *The World Market Atlas.*

Euromonitor International, Inc., 122 South Michigan Avenue, Suite 1200, Chicago, Illinois 60603 (800) 577-EURO; *The World Economic Factbook.*

Statistical Office of the United Nations, Publishing Service, New York, New York 10017 (800) 253-9646; *Human Development Report.*

NORWAY - IMPORTS

Central Intelligence Agency, Washington, D.C. 20505 (703) 482-1100, www.cia.gov; *The World Factbook.*

The Economist Intelligence Unit, 111 West 57th Street, New York, New York 10019 (800) 938-4685; *Norway Country Report;* and *The World Market Atlas.*

Euromonitor International, Inc., 122 South Michigan Avenue, Suite 1200, Chicago, Illinois 60603 (800) 577-EURO; *The World Economic Factbook.*

Europa Publications Limited, 18 Bedford Square, London, WC1B 3JN, England; *The Europa World Year Book.*

Food and Agricultural Organization of the United Nations (FAO) Via delle Terme di Caracalla, 00100 Rome, Italy (Telephone Number in U.S. (202) 653-2400); *The State of Food and Agriculture.*

International Lead and Zinc Study Group, Metro House, 58 St. James's Street, London SW1A 1LD England; *Lead and Zinc Statistics.*

International Monetary Fund, 700 Nineteenth Street, NW, Washington, D.C. 20431 (202) 623-7000; *Direction of Trade Statistics; Government Finance Statistics Yearbook;* and *International Financial Statistics.*

Nordic Council of Ministers, Store Strandstraede 18, DK-1255 Copenhagen K, Denmark and the Nordic Statistical Secretariat, Postboks 2550, DK-2100 Copenhagen 0, Denmark; *The Yearbook of Nordic Statistics.*

Organisation for Economic Co-operation and Development (OECD), 2 rue Andre-Pascal, 75 Paris 16, France (Telephone Number in U.S. (202) 785-6323); *Economic Outlook; The Footwear, Raw Hides and Skins, and Leather Industry in OECD Countries; Industrial Structure Statistics; The Iron and Steel Industry; Milk, Milk Products, and Egg Balances in OECD Member Countries; OECD Economic Surveys: Norway; The Pulp and Paper Industry;* and *Review of Fisheries in OECD Member Countries.*

St. Martin's Press, Inc., 175 Fifth Avenue, New York, New York 10010 (800) 221-7945; *The Statesman's Year-Book.*

Statistical Office of the United Nations, Publishing Service, New York, New York

10017 (800) 253-9646; *Trends in Europe and North America: The Statistical Yearbook of the Economic Commission for Europe.*

United Nations Conference on Trade and Development (UNCTAD), New York, New York 10017 (800) 253-9646; *Handbook of International Trade and Development Statistics.*

The World Bank, 1818 H Street, NW, Washington, D.C. 20433 (202) 477-1234; *World Development Report;* and *World Development Indicators.*

NORWAY - INCOME TAXES - See NORWAY - TAXATION

NORWAY - INDUSTRIAL METALS PRODUCTION - See NORWAY - MINING AND MINERAL PRODUCTS

NORWAY - INDUSTRY

Central Intelligence Agency, Washington, D.C. 20505 (703) 482-1100, www.cia.gov; *The World Factbook.*

Economist Intelligence Unit, 111 West 57th Street, New York, New York 10019 (800) 938-4685; *Norway Country Report.*

Euromonitor International, Inc., 122 South Michigan Avenue, Suite 1200, Chicago, Illinois 60603 (800) 577-EURO; *The World Economic Factbook;* and *World Marketing Data and Statistics.*

Europa Publications Limited, 18 Bedford Square, London, WC1B 3JN, England; *The Europa World Year Book.*

International Labour Office, I.L.O. Publications, 1828 L Street, NW, Suite 801, Washington, D.C. 20036 (301) 638-3152; *Yearbook of Labour Statistics.*

M.E. Sharpe, 80 Business Park Drive, Armonk, New York 10504 (800) 541-6563; *The Illustrated Book of World Rankings.*

Nordic Council of Ministers, Store Strandstraede 18, DK-1255 Copenhagen K, Denmark and the Nordic Statistical Secretariat, Postboks 2550, DK-2100 Copenhagen 0, Denmark; *The Yearbook of Nordic Statistics.*

Organisation for Economic Co-operation and Development (OECD), 2 rue Andre-Pascal, 75 Paris 16, France (Telephone Number in U.S. (202) 785-6323); *Economic Outlook; Indicators of Industrial Activity; Industrial Structure Statistics;* and *Main Economic Indicators - Historical Statistics.*

St. Martin's Press, Inc., 175 Fifth Avenue, New York, New York 10010 (800) 221-7945; *The Statesman's Year-Book.*

Statistical Office of the United Nations, Publishing Service, New York, New York 10017 (800) 253-9646; *Industrial Commodity Statistics Yearbook; Trends in Europe and North America: The Statistical Yearbook of the Economic Commission for Europe;* and *Statistical Yearbook.*

The World Bank, 1818 H Street, NW, Washington, D.C. 20433 (202) 477-1234; *World Development Indicators.*

World Intellectual Property Organization, 34 Chemin des Colombettes, CH-1211 Geneva 20, Switzerland; *Industrial Property Statistics.*

NORWAY - INFANT AND MATERNAL MORTALITY - See NORWAY - MORTALITY

NORWAY - INTEREST RATES

Organisation for Economic Co-operation and Development (OECD), 2 rue Andre-Pascal, 75 Paris 16, France (Telephone Number in U.S. (202) 785-6323); *Economic Outlook; Financial Market Trends;* and *OECD Financial Statistics.*

NORWAY - INTERNAL TRADE

Nordic Council of Ministers, Store Strandstraede 18, DK-1255 Copenhagen K, Denmark and the Nordic Statistical Secretariat, Postboks 2550, DK-2100 Copenhagen 0, Denmark; *The Yearbook of Nordic Statistics.*

Organisation for Economic Co-operation and Development (OECD), 2 rue Andre-Pascal, 75 Paris 16, France (Telephone Number in U.S. (202) 785-6323); *Main Economic Indicators - Historical Statistics.*

NORWAY - INTERNATIONAL FINANCE

Organisation for Economic Co-operation and Development (OECD), 2 rue Andre-Pascal, 75 Paris 16, France (Telephone Number in U.S. (202) 785-6323); *Economic Outlook;* and *Financial Market Trends.*

NORWAY - INTERNATIONAL LIQUIDITY

International Monetary Fund, 700 Nineteenth Street, NW, Washington, D.C. 20431 (202) 623-7000; *International Financial Statistics.*

Organisation for Economic Co-operation and Development (OECD), 2 rue Andre-Pascal, 75 Paris 16, France (Telephone Number in U.S. (202) 785-6323); *Economic Outlook;* and *Financial Market Trends.*

NORWAY - INTERNATIONAL RESERVES EXCLUDING GOLD

Statistical Office of the United Nations, Publishing Service, New York, New York 10017 (800) 253-9646; *Statistical Yearbook.*

The World Bank, 1818 H Street, NW, Washington, D.C. 20433 (202) 477-1234; *World Development Indicators.*

NORWAY - INTERNATIONAL STATISTICS

Organisation for Economic Co-operation and Development (OECD), 2 rue Andre-Pascal, 75 Paris 16, France (Telephone Number in U.S. (202) 785-6323); *Financial Market Trends;* and *Tourism Policy and International Tourism in OECD Member Countries.*

NORWAY - INVESTMENTS

International Monetary Fund, 700 Nineteenth Street, NW, Washington, D.C. 20431 (202) 623-7000; *International Financial Statistics.*

Organisation for Economic Co-operation and Development (OECD), 2 rue Andre-Pascal, 75 Paris 16, France (Telephone Number in U.S. (202) 785-6323); *Economic Outlook; Financial Market Trends; Industrial Structure Statistics; The Iron and Steel Industry;* and *Textile Industry in OECD Countries.*

NORWAY - IRON ORE PRODUCTION AND CONSUMPTION - See NORWAY - MINING AND MINERAL PRODUCTS

NORWAY - LABOR

Central Intelligence Agency, Washington, D.C. 20505 (703) 482-1100, www.cia.gov; *The World Factbook.*

Euromonitor International, Inc., 122 South Michigan Avenue, Suite 1200, Chicago, Illinois 60603 (800) 577-EURO; *World Marketing Data and Statistics.*

Europa Publications Limited, 18 Bedford Square, London, WC1B 3JN, England; *The Europa World Year Book.*

Food and Agricultural Organization of the United Nations (FAO) Via delle Terme di Caracalla, 00100 Rome, Italy (Telephone Number in U.S. (202) 653-2400); *The State of Food and Agriculture.*

International Labour Office, I.L.O. Publications, 1828 L Street, NW, Suite 801, Washington, D.C. 20036 (301) 638-3152; *Yearbook of Labour Statistics.*

M.E. Sharpe, 80 Business Park Drive, Armonk, New York 10504 (800) 541-6563; *The Illustrated Book of World Rankings.*

Nordic Council of Ministers, Store

Strandstraede 18, DK-1255 Copenhagen K, Denmark and the Nordic Statistical Secretariat, Postboks 2550, DK-2100 Copenhagen 0, Denmark; *The Yearbook of Nordic Statistics.*

Organisation for Economic Co-operation and Development (OECD), 2 rue Andre-Pascal, 75 Paris 16, France (Telephone Number in U.S. (202) 785-6323); *Economic Outlook; The Iron and Steel Industry; Maritime Transport; OECD Economic Surveys: Norway, OECD Employment Outlook;* and *Textile Industry in OECD Countries.*

St. Martin's Press, Inc., 175 Fifth Avenue, New York, New York 10010 (800) 221-7945; *The Statesman's Year-Book.*

Statistical Office of the United Nations, Publishing Service, New York, New York 10017 (800) 253-9646; *Human Development Report.*

The World Bank, 1818 H Street, NW, Washington, D.C. 20433 (202) 477-1234; *The World Bank Atlas; World Development Report;* and *World Development Indicators.*

NORWAY - LAND USE

Central Intelligence Agency, Washington, D.C. 20505 (703) 482-1100, www.cia.gov; *The World Factbook.*

Food and Agricultural Organization of the United Nations (FAO), Via delle Terme di Caracalla, 00100 Rome, Italy (Telephone Number in U.S. (202) 653-2400); *Production Yearbook.*

The World Bank, 1818 H Street, NW, Washington, D.C. 20433 (202) 477-1234; *World Development Report.*

NORWAY - LEAD - See NORWAY - MINING AND MINERAL PRODUCTS

NORWAY - LEATHER - PRODUCTION INDEX

Organisation for Economic Co-operation and Development (OECD), 2 rue Andre-Pascal, 75 Paris 16, France (Telephone Number in U.S. (202) 785-6323); *Indicators of Industrial Activity.*

NORWAY - LEATHER AND FOOTWEAR - EXPORTS AND IMPORTS

Organisation for Economic Co-operation and Development (OECD), 2 rue Andre-Pascal, 75 Paris 16, France (Telephone Number in U.S. (202) 785-6323); *The Footwear, Raw Hides and Skins, and Leather Industry in OECD Countries.*

NORWAY - LIBRARIES

M.E. Sharpe, 80 Business Park Drive, Armonk, New York 10504 (800) 541-6563; *The Illustrated Book of World Rankings.*

Nordic Council of Ministers, Store Strandstraede 18, DK-1255 Copenhagen K, Denmark and the Nordic Statistical Secretariat, Postboks 2550, DK-2100 Copenhagen 0, Denmark; *The Yearbook of Nordic Statistics.*

Statistical Office of the United Nations, Publishing Service, New York, New York 10017 (800) 253-9646; *Statistical Yearbook;* and *Trends in Europe and North America: The Statistical Yearbook of the Economic Commission for Europe.*

NORWAY - LIFE EXPECTANCY

Central Intelligence Agency, Washington, D.C. 20505 (703) 482-1100, www.cia.gov; *The World Factbook.*

Euromonitor International, Inc., 122 South Michigan Avenue, Suite 1200, Chicago, Illinois 60603 (800) 577-EURO; *The World Economic Factbook.*

Organisation for Economic Co-operation and Development (OECD), 2 rue Andre-Pascal, 75 Paris 16, France (Telephone Number in U.S. (202) 785-6323); *Economic Outlook.*

St. Martin's Press, Inc., 175 Fifth Avenue, New York, New York 10010 (800) 221-7945; *The Statesman's Year-Book.*

Statistical Office of the United Nations, Publishing Service, New York, New York 10017 (800) 253-9646; *Human Development Report; Trends in Europe and North America: The Statistical Yearbook of the Economic Commission for Europe;* and *World Statistics Pocketbook.*

The World Bank, 1818 H Street, NW, Washington, D.C. 20433 (202) 477-1234; *The World Bank Atlas;* and *World Development Report.*

NORWAY - LIGNITE PRODUCTION - See NORWAY - MINING AND MINERAL PRODUCTS

NORWAY - LITERACY RATE

Euromonitor International, Inc., 122 South Michigan Avenue, Suite 1200, Chicago, Illinois 60603 (800) 577-EURO; *World Marketing Data and Statistics.*

NORWAY - LIVESTOCK AND POULTRY

Europa Publications Limited, 18 Bedford Square, London, WC1B 3JN, England; *The Europa World Year Book.*

Food and Agricultural Organization of the United Nations (FAO) Via delle Terme

di Caracalla, 00100 Rome, Italy (Telephone Number in U.S. (202) 653-2400); *Production Yearbook;* and *The State of Food and Agriculture.*

M.E. Sharpe, 80 Business Park Drive, Armonk, New York 10504 (800) 541-6563; *The Illustrated Book of World Rankings.*

Nordic Council of Ministers, Store Strandstraede 18, DK-1255 Copenhagen K, Denmark and the Nordic Statistical Secretariat, Postboks 2550, DK-2100 Copenhagen 0, Denmark; *The Yearbook of Nordic Statistics.*

Organisation for Economic Co-operation and Development (OECD), 2 rue Andre-Pascal, 75 Paris 16, France (Telephone Number in U.S. (202) 785-6323); *Economic Accounts in Agriculture;* and *Meat Balances in OECD Member Countries.*

St. Martin's Press, Inc., 175 Fifth Avenue, New York, New York 10010 (800) 221-7945; *The Statesman's Year-Book.*

Statistical Office of the United Nations, Publishing Service, New York, New York 10017 (800) 253-9646; *Statistical Yearbook.*

United Nations Conference on Trade and Development, Central Statistical Service, Palais des Nations, Geneva, Switzerland (Telephone in U.S. (800) 253-9646); *UNCTAD Commodity Yearbook.*

NORWAY - LIVING LEVELS - See NORWAY - LIFE EXPECTANCY

NORWAY - MACHINERY - PRODUCTION INDEX

Organisation for Economic Co-operation and Development (OECD), 2 rue Andre-Pascal, 75 Paris 16, France (Telephone Number in U.S. (202) 785-6323); *Indicators of Industrial Activity.*

NORWAY - MAGNESIUM PRODUCTION AND CONSUMPTION - See NORWAY - MINING AND MINERAL PRODUCTS

NORWAY - MAIL - NUMBER OF PIECES SENT OR RECEIVED

Nordic Council of Ministers, Store Strandstraede 18, DK-1255 Copenhagen K, Denmark and the Nordic Statistical Secretariat, Postboks 2550, DK-2100 Copenhagen 0, Denmark; *The Yearbook of Nordic Statistics.*

Statistical Office of the United Nations, Publishing Service, New York, New York 10017 (800) 253-9646; *Statistical Yearbook.*

NORWAY - MANGANESE PRODUCTION AND CONSUMPTION - See NORWAY - MINING AND MINERAL PRODUCTS

NORWAY - MANUFACTURING

American Automobile Manufacturers Association, 1401 H Street, NW, Suite 900, Washington, D.C. 20005 (202) 326-5500; *World Motor Vehicle Data.*

M.E. Sharpe, 80 Business Park Drive, Armonk, New York 10504 (800) 541-6563; *The Illustrated Book of World Rankings.*

Nordic Council of Ministers, Store Strandstraede 18, DK-1255 Copenhagen K, Denmark and the Nordic Statistical Secretariat, Postboks 2550, DK-2100 Copenhagen 0, Denmark; *The Yearbook of Nordic Statistics.*

Organisation for Economic Co-operation and Development (OECD), 2 rue Andre-Pascal, 75 Paris 16, France (Telephone Number in U.S. (202) 785-6323); *Foreign Trade by Commodities; Indicators of Industrial Activity; Industrial Structure Statistics;* and *OECD Economic Surveys: Norway.*

Statistical Office of the United Nations, Publishing Service, New York, New York 10017 (800) 253-9646; *Statistical Yearbook.*

The World Bank, 1818 H Street, NW, Washington, D.C. 20433 (202) 477-1234; *World Development Indicators.*

NORWAY - MARRIAGE RATES

Europa Publications Limited, 18 Bedford Square, London, WC1B 3JN, England; *The Europa World Year Book.*

M.E. Sharpe, 80 Business Park Drive, Armonk, New York 10504 (800) 541-6563; *The Illustrated Book of World Rankings.*

Nordic Council of Ministers, Store Strandstraede 18, DK-1255 Copenhagen K, Denmark and the Nordic Statistical Secretariat, Postboks 2550, DK-2100 Copenhagen 0, Denmark; *The Yearbook of Nordic Statistics.*

Statistical Office of the United Nations, Publishing Service, New York, New York 10017 (800) 253-9646; *Demographic Yearbook; Trends in Europe and North America: The Statistical Yearbook of the Economic Commission for Europe;* and *Statistical Yearbook.*

NORWAY - MEAT PRODUCTION - See NORWAY - LIVESTOCK AND POULTRY

NORWAY - MERCHANT SHIPPING

Europa Publications Limited, 18 Bedford Square, London, WC1B 3JN, England; *The Europa World Year Book.*

Lloyd's Register of Shipping, 17 Battery Place, New York, New York 10004 (212) 425-8050; *Register of Ships.*

Nordic Council of Ministers, Store Strandstraede 18, DK-1255 Copenhagen K, Denmark and the Nordic Statistical Secretariat, Postboks 2550, DK-2100 Copenhagen 0, Denmark; *The Yearbook of Nordic Statistics.*

Organisation for Economic Co-operation and Development (OECD), 2 rue Andre-Pascal, 75 Paris 16, France (Telephone Number in U.S. (202) 785-6323); *Maritime Transport.*

St. Martin's Press, Inc., 175 Fifth Avenue, New York, New York 10010 (800) 221-7945; *The Statesman's Year-Book.*

Statistical Office of the United Nations, Publishing Service, New York, New York 10017 (800) 253-9646; *Statistical Yearbook.*

U.S. Department of Transportation, Maritime Administration, 400 Seventh Street, SW, Washington, D.C. 20590 (202) 366-5807, www.marad.dot.gov; *A Statistical Analysis of the World's Merchant Fleets.*

NORWAY - MERCURY PRODUCTION AND CONSUMPTION - See NORWAY - MINING AND MINERAL PRODUCTS

NORWAY - MILITARY

Central Intelligence Agency, Washington, D.C. 20505 (703) 482-1100, www.cia.gov; *The World Factbook.*

Euromonitor International, Inc., 122 South Michigan Avenue, Suite 1200, Chicago, Illinois 60603 (800) 577-EURO; *World Marketing Data and Statistics.*

The International Institute for Strategic Studies, 23 Tavistock Street, London WC2E 7NQ, England; *The Military Balance.*

Nordic Council of Ministers, Store Strandstraede 18, DK-1255 Copenhagen K, Denmark and the Nordic Statistical Secretariat, Postboks 2550, DK-2100 Copenhagen 0, Denmark; *The Yearbook of Nordic Statistics.*

St. Martin's Press, Inc., 175 Fifth Avenue, New York, New York 10010 (800) 221-7945; *The Statesman's Year-Book.*

Statistical Office of the United Nations, Publishing Service, New York, New York 10017 (800) 253-9646; *Human Development Report.*

U.S. Arms Control and Disarmament Agency, 320 Twenty-first Street, NW, Washington, D.C. 20451 (202) 647-8677; *World Military Expenditures and Arms Transfers.*

NORWAY - MILK PRODUCTION - See

NORWAY - DAIRY PRODUCTS

NORWAY - MINING AND MINERAL PRODUCTS

Commodity Research Bureau, Inc., 30 South Wacker Drive, Chicago, Illinois 60606 (312) 454-1801; *Commodity Year Book.*

Europa Publications Limited, 18 Bedford Square, London, WC1B 3JN, England; *The Europa World Year Book.*

International Lead and Zinc Study Group, Metro House, 58 St. James's Street, London SW1A 1LD England; *Lead and Zinc Statistics.*

M.E. Sharpe, 80 Business Park Drive, Armonk, New York 10504 (800) 541-6563; *The Illustrated Book of World Rankings.*

Nordic Council of Ministers, Store Strandstraede 18, DK-1255 Copenhagen K, Denmark and the Nordic Statistical Secretariat, Postboks 2550, DK-2100 Copenhagen 0, Denmark; *The Yearbook of Nordic Statistics.*

Organisation for Economic Co-operation and Development (OECD), 2 rue Andre-Pascal, 75 Paris 16, France (Telephone Number in U.S. (202) 785-6323); *Coal Information; Energy Statistics of OECD Countries; Foreign Trade by Commodities; Indicators of Industrial Activity; Industrial Structure Statistics; The Iron and Steel Industry; The Non-Ferrous Metals Industry;* and *OECD Economic Surveys: Norway.*

Penn Well Publishing Company, 1421 South Sheridan Road, Post Office Box 1260, Tulsa, Oklahoma 74101 (800) 752-9764; *International Energy Statistics Sourcebook.*

St. Martin's Press, Inc., 175 Fifth Avenue, New York, New York 10010 (800) 221-7945; *The Statesman's Year-Book.*

Statistical Office of the United Nations, Publishing Service, New York, New York 10017 (800) 253-9646; *Statistical Yearbook.*

United Nations Conference on Trade and Development, Central Statistical Service, Palais des Nations, Geneva, Switzerland (Telephone in U.S. (800) 253-9646); *UNCTAD Commodity Yearbook.*

World Bureau of Metal Statistics, 27-A High Street, Ware, Herts. SG12 9BA, England; *World Metal Statistics.*

NORWAY - MOLYBDENUM - See NORWAY - MINING AND MINERAL PRODUCTS

NORWAY - MONEY AND CREDIT

Organisation for Economic Co-

operation and Development (OECD), 2 rue Andre-Pascal, 75 Paris 16, France (Telephone Number in U.S. (202) 785-6323); *OECD Economic Surveys: Norway.*

NORWAY - MONEY EXCHANGE RATE - See NORWAY - EXCHANGE RATES

NORWAY - MONEY RATES - MARKET

Organisation for Economic Co-operation and Development (OECD), 2 rue Andre-Pascal, 75 Paris 16, France (Telephone Number in U.S. (202) 785-6323); *Economic Outlook;* and *Financial Market Trends.*

NORWAY - MONEY RESERVES

Organisation for Economic Co-operation and Development (OECD), 2 rue Andre-Pascal, 75 Paris 16, France (Telephone Number in U.S. (202) 785-6323); *Economic Outlook;* and *Financial Market Trends.*

NORWAY - MONEY SUPPLY

Economist Intelligence Unit, 111 West 57th Street, New York, New York 10019 (800) 938-4685; *Norway Country Report.*

Europa Publications Limited, 18 Bedford Square, London, WC1B 3JN, England; *The Europa World Year Book.*

International Monetary Fund, 700 Nineteenth Street, NW, Washington, D.C. 20431 (202) 623-7000; *International Financial Statistics.*

Nordic Council of Ministers, Store Strandstraede 18, DK-1255 Copenhagen K, Denmark and the Nordic Statistical Secretariat, Postboks 2550, DK-2100 Copenhagen 0, Denmark; *The Yearbook of Nordic Statistics.*

Organisation for Economic Co-operation and Development (OECD), 2 rue Andre-Pascal, 75 Paris 16, France (Telephone Number in U.S. (202) 785-6323); *Economic Outlook.*

Statistical Office of the United Nations, Publishing Service, New York, New York 10017 (800) 253-9646; *Statistical Yearbook.*

The World Bank, 1818 H Street, NW, Washington, D.C. 20433 (202) 477-1234; *World Development Indicators.*

NORWAY - MORTALITY

Central Intelligence Agency, Washington, D.C. 20505 (703) 482-1100, www.cia.gov; *The World Factbook.*

Euromonitor International, Inc., 122 South Michigan Avenue, Suite 1200, Chicago, Illinois 60603 (800) 577-EURO;

The World Economic Factbook.

Europa Publications Limited, 18 Bedford Square, London, WC1B 3JN, England; *The Europa World Year Book.*

Nordic Council of Ministers, Store Strandstraede 18, DK-1255 Copenhagen K, Denmark and the Nordic Statistical Secretariat, Postboks 2550, DK-2100 Copenhagen 0, Denmark; *The Yearbook of Nordic Statistics.*

St. Martin's Press, Inc., 175 Fifth Avenue, New York, New York 10010 (800) 221-7945; *The Statesman's Year-Book.*

Statistical Office of the United Nations, Publishing Service, New York, New York 10017 (800) 253-9646; *Demographic Yearbook; Human Development Report; Trends in Europe and North America: The Statistical Yearbook of the Economic Commission for Europe; World Statistics Pocketbook;* and *Statistical Yearbook.*

United Nations Children's Fund (UNICEF), 3 United Nations Plaza, New York, New York 10017 (800) 253-9646; *State of the World's Children.*

The World Bank, 1818 H Street, NW, Washington, D.C. 20433 (202) 477-1234; *The World Bank Atlas; World Development Report;* and *World Development Indicators.*

World Health Organization, Office of Publications, 20 Avenue Appia, CH-1211 Geneva 27, Switzerland (Telephone Number in U.S. (518) 436-9686); *World Health Statistics Annual.*

NORWAY - MOTION PICTURES

St. Martin's Press, Inc., 175 Fifth Avenue, New York, New York 10010 (800) 221-7945; *The Statesman's Year-Book.*

Statistical Office of the United Nations, Publishing Service, New York, New York 10017 (800) 253-9646; *Statistical Yearbook.*

United Nations Educational, Scientific and Cultural Organization (UNESCO), 7 Place de Fontenoy, F-75700 Paris, France (Telephone Number in U.S. (212) 963-5981); *Statistical Yearbook.*

NORWAY - MOTOR VEHICLE PRODUCTION

American Automobile Manufacturers Association, 1401 H Street, NW, Suite 900, Washington, D.C. 20005 (202) 326-5500; *World Motor Vehicle Data.*

Nordic Council of Ministers, Store Strandstraede 18, DK-1255 Copenhagen K, Denmark and the Nordic Statistical Secretariat, Postboks 2550, DK-2100 Copenhagen 0, Denmark; *The Yearbook of*

Nordic Statistics.

Organisation for Economic Co-operation and Development (OECD), 2 rue Andre-Pascal, 75 Paris 16, France (Telephone Number in U.S. (202) 785-6323); *Foreign Trade by Commodities;* and *Indicators of Industrial Activity.*

NORWAY - MOTOR VEHICLE TAXES - See NORWAY - TAXATION

NORWAY - MOTOR VEHICLES IN USE

American Automobile Manufacturers Association, 1401 H Street, NW, Suite 900, Washington, D.C. 20005 (202) 326-5500; *World Motor Vehicle Data.*

Europa Publications Limited, 18 Bedford Square, London, WC1B 3JN, England; *The Europa World Year Book.*

International Road Federation, 2600 Virginia Avenue, NW., Washington, D.C. 20037 (202) 338-4641; *World Road Statistics.*

Statistical Office of the United Nations, Publishing Service, New York, New York 10017 (800) 253-9646; *Statistical Yearbook.*

NORWAY - MUSEUMS

M.E. Sharpe, 80 Business Park Drive, Armonk, New York 10504 (800) 541-6563; *The Illustrated Book of World Rankings.*

Nordic Council of Ministers, Store Strandstraede 18, DK-1255 Copenhagen K, Denmark and the Nordic Statistical Secretariat, Postboks 2550, DK-2100 Copenhagen 0, Denmark; *The Yearbook of Nordic Statistics.*

United Nations Educational, Scientific and Cultural Organization (UNESCO), 7 Place de Fontenoy, F-75700 Paris, France (Telephone Number in U.S. (212) 963-5981); *Statistical Yearbook.*

NORWAY - NATALITY - See NORWAY - BIRTH RATES

NORWAY - NATIONAL ACCOUNTS

Europa Publications Limited, 18 Bedford Square, London, WC1B 3JN, England; *The Europa World Year Book.*

International Monetary Fund, 700 Nineteenth Street, NW, Washington, D.C. 20431 (202) 623-7000; *International Financial Statistics.*

Nordic Council of Ministers, Store Strandstraede 18, DK-1255 Copenhagen K, Denmark and the Nordic Statistical Secretariat, Postboks 2550, DK-2100 Copenhagen 0, Denmark; *The Yearbook of Nordic Statistics.*

Organisation for Economic Co-operation and Development (OECD), 2 rue Andre-Pascal, 75 Paris 16, France (Telephone Number in U.S. (202) 785-6323); *Economic Outlook.*

Statistical Office of the United Nations, Publishing Service, New York, New York 10017 (800) 253-9646; *National Accounts Statistics;* and *Statistical Yearbook.*

NORWAY - NATIONAL INCOME

M.E. Sharpe, 80 Business Park Drive, Armonk, New York 10504 (800) 541-6563; *The Illustrated Book of World Rankings.*

Nordic Council of Ministers, Store Strandstraede 18, DK-1255 Copenhagen K, Denmark and the Nordic Statistical Secretariat, Postboks 2550, DK-2100 Copenhagen 0, Denmark; *The Yearbook of Nordic Statistics.*

Organisation for Economic Co-operation and Development (OECD), 2 rue Andre-Pascal, 75 Paris 16, France (Telephone Number in U.S. (202) 785-6323); *Economic Outlook.*

Statistical Office of the United Nations, Publishing Service, New York, New York 10017 (800) 253-9646; *National Accounts Statistics;* and *Statistical Yearbook.*

NORWAY - NATIONAL PRODUCT

M.E. Sharpe, 80 Business Park Drive, Armonk, New York 10504 (800) 541-6563; *The Illustrated Book of World Rankings.*

Organisation for Economic Co-operation and Development (OECD), 2 rue Andre-Pascal, 75 Paris 16, France (Telephone Number in U.S. (202) 785-6323); *Economic Outlook;* and *Main Economic Indicators - Historical Statistics.*

Statistical Office of the United Nations, Publishing Service, New York, New York 10017 (800) 253-9646; *Statistical Yearbook.*

NORWAY - NATURAL GAS PRODUCTION - See NORWAY - MINING AND MINERAL PRODUCTS

NORWAY - NEWSPAPER PRODUCTION - See NORWAY - FORESTRY AND FOREST PRODUCTS

NORWAY - NEWSPRINT PRODUCTION AND CONSUMPTION - See NORWAY - FORESTRY AND FOREST PRODUCTS

NORWAY - NICKEL - See NORWAY - MINING AND MINERAL PRODUCTS

NORWAY - NITRIC ACID PRODUCTION - See NORWAY - MINING AND MINERAL PRODUCTS

NORWAY - OATS PRODUCTION - See NORWAY - CROPS

NORWAY - OIL PRODUCING CROPS

Organisation for Economic Co-operation and Development (OECD), 2 rue Andre-Pascal, 75 Paris 16, France (Telephone Number in U.S. (202) 785-6323); *Foreign Trade by Commodities.*

NORWAY - PAPER - See NORWAY - FORESTRY AND FOREST PRODUCTS

NORWAY - PATENTS, TRADEMARKS AND SERVICE MARKS

Nordic Council of Ministers, Store Strandstraede 18, DK-1255 Copenhagen K, Denmark and the Nordic Statistical Secretariat, Postboks 2550, DK-2100 Copenhagen 0, Denmark; *The Yearbook of Nordic Statistics.*

Statistical Office of the United Nations, Publishing Service, New York, New York 10017 (800) 253-9646; *Statistical Yearbook.*

World Intellectual Property Organization, 34 Chemin des Colombettes, CH-1211 Geneva 20, Switzerland; *Industrial Property Statistics.*

NORWAY - PEANUT PRODUCTION - See NORWAY - CROPS

NORWAY - PERIODICALS

United Nations Educational, Scientific and Cultural Organization (UNESCO), 7 Place de Fontenoy, F-75700 Paris, France (Telephone Number in U.S. (212) 963-5981); *Statistical Yearbook.*

NORWAY - PESTICIDE USE

Food and Agricultural Organization of the United Nations (FAO) Via delle Terme di Caracalla, 00100 Rome, Italy (Telephone Number in U.S. (202) 653-2400); *The State of Food and Agriculture.*

NORWAY - PETROLEUM INDUSTRY

Food and Agricultural Organization of the United Nations (FAO) Via delle Terme di Caracalla, 00100 Rome, Italy (Telephone Number in U.S. (202) 653-2400); *The State of Food and Agriculture.*

M.E. Sharpe, 80 Business Park Drive, Armonk, New York 10504 (800) 541-6563; *The Illustrated Book of World Rankings.*

Organisation for Economic Co-operation and Development (OECD), 2 rue Andre-Pascal, 75 Paris 16, France (Telephone Number in U.S. (202) 785-6323); *Energy Statistics of OECD Countries, Foreign Trade by Commodities, Indicators of Industrial Activity, Oil and Gas Information.*

Penn Well Publishing Company, 1421 South Sheridan Road, Post Office Box 1260, Tulsa, Oklahoma 74101 (800) 752-9764; *International Energy Statistics Sourcebook.*

St. Martin's Press, Inc., 175 Fifth Avenue, New York, New York 10010 (800) 221-7945; *The Statesman's Year-Book.*

Statistical Office of the United Nations, Publishing Service, New York, New York 10017 (800) 253-9646; *Statistical Yearbook;* and *Trends in Europe and North America: The Statistical Yearbook of the Economic Commission for Europe.*

United Nations Conference on Trade and Development, Central Statistical Service, Palais des Nations, Geneva, Switzerland (Telephone in U.S. (800) 253-9646); *UNCTAD Commodity Yearbook.*

NORWAY - PHOSPHATES PRODUCTION - See NORWAY - MINING AND MINERAL PRODUCTS

NORWAY - PHOSPHATES ROCK PRODUCTION - See NORWAY - MINING AND MINERAL PRODUCTS

NORWAY - PIG-IRON AND FERRO-ALLOY PRODUCTION - See NORWAY - MINING AND MINERAL PRODUCTS

NORWAY - PIGS - See NORWAY - LIVESTOCK AND POULTRY

NORWAY - PIPELINES FOR OIL AND PETROLEUM PRODUCTS

Statistical Office of the United Nations, Publishing Service, New York, New York 10017 (800) 253-9646; *Annual Bulletin of Transport Statistics for Europe.*

NORWAY - PLASTIC AND RESIN PRODUCTION

Organisation for Economic Co-operation and Development (OECD), 2 rue Andre-Pascal, 75 Paris 16, France (Telephone Number in U.S. (202) 785-6323); *Foreign Trade by Commodities.*

Statistical Office of the United Nations, Publishing Service, New York, New York 10017 (800) 253-9646; *Statistical Yearbook.*

NORWAY - PLATINUM PRODUCTION - See NORWAY - MINING AND MINERAL PRODUCTS

NORWAY - POPULATION

Central Intelligence Agency, Washington, D.C. 20505 (703) 482-1100, www.cia.gov; *The World Factbook.*

Economist Intelligence Unit, 111 West

57th Street, New York, New York 10019 (800) 938-4685; *Norway Country Report*.

Euromonitor International, Inc., 122 South Michigan Avenue, Suite 1200, Chicago, Illinois 60603 (800) 577-EURO; *The World Economic Factbook*.

Europa Publications Limited, 18 Bedford Square, London, WC1B 3JN, England; *The Europa World Year Book*.

Food and Agricultural Organization of the United Nations (FAO), Via delle Terme di Caracalla, 00100 Rome, Italy (Telephone Number in U.S. (202) 653-2400); *Production Yearbook*.

International Labour Office, I.L.O. Publications, 1828 L Street, NW, Suite 801, Washington, D.C. 20036 (301) 638-3152; *Yearbook of Labour Statistics*.

M.E. Sharpe, 80 Business Park Drive, Armonk, New York 10504 (800) 541-6563; *The Illustrated Book of World Rankings*.

Nordic Council of Ministers, Store Strandstraede 18, DK-1255 Copenhagen K, Denmark and the Nordic Statistical Secretariat, Postboks 2550, DK-2100 Copenhagen 0, Denmark; *The Yearbook of Nordic Statistics*.

St. Martin's Press, Inc., 175 Fifth Avenue, New York, New York 10010 (800) 221-7945; *The Statesman's Year-Book*.

Statistical Office of the United Nations, Publishing Service, New York, New York 10017 (800) 253-9646; *Demographic Yearbook; Human Development Report; Trends in Europe and North America: The Statistical Yearbook of the Economic Commission for Europe; World Statistics Pocketbook;* and *Statistical Yearbook*.

United Nations Educational, Scientific and Cultural Organization (UNESCO), 7 Place de Fontenoy, F-75700 Paris, France (Telephone Number in U.S. (212) 963-5981); *Statistical Yearbook*.

U.S. Arms Control and Disarmament Agency, 320 Twenty-first Street, NW, Washington, D.C. 20451 (202) 647-8677; *World Military Expenditures and Arms Transfers*.

The World Bank, 1818 H Street, NW, Washington, D.C. 20433 (202) 477-1234; *The World Bank Atlas;* and *World Development Report*.

World Health Organization, Office of Publications, 20 Avenue Appia, CH-1211 Geneva 27, Switzerland (Telephone Number in U.S. (518) 436-9686); *World Health Statistics Annual*.

NORWAY - POST OFFICES

M.E. Sharpe, 80 Business Park Drive, Armonk, New York 10504 (800) 541-6563; *The Illustrated Book of World Rankings*.

St. Martin's Press, Inc., 175 Fifth Avenue, New York, New York 10010 (800) 221-7945; *The Statesman's Year-Book*.

Statistical Office of the United Nations, Publishing Service, New York, New York 10017 (800) 253-9646; *Trends in Europe and North America: The Statistical Yearbook of the Economic Commission for Europe*.

NORWAY - POTATO PRODUCTION - See NORWAY - CROPS

NORWAY - POWER PRODUCTION INDUSTRY

Statistical Office of the United Nations, Publishing Service, New York, New York 10017 (800) 253-9646; *Statistical Yearbook*.

NORWAY - PRICES

Food and Agricultural Organization of the United Nations (FAO), Via delle Terme di Caracalla, 00100 Rome, Italy (Telephone Number in U.S. (202) 653-2400); *Production Yearbook;* and *The State of Food and Agriculture*.

International Labour Office, I.L.O. Publications, 1828 L Street, NW, Suite 801, Washington, D.C. 20036 (301) 638-3152; *Yearbook of Labour Statistics*.

International Lead and Zinc Study Group, Metro House, 58 St. James's Street, London SW1A 1LD England; *Lead and Zinc Statistics*.

International Monetary Fund, 700 Nineteenth Street, NW, Washington, D.C. 20431 (202) 623-7000; *International Financial Statistics*.

M.E. Sharpe, 80 Business Park Drive, Armonk, New York 10504 (800) 541-6563; *The Illustrated Book of World Rankings*.

Nordic Council of Ministers, Store Strandstraede 18, DK-1255 Copenhagen K, Denmark and the Nordic Statistical Secretariat, Postboks 2550, DK-2100 Copenhagen 0, Denmark; *The Yearbook of Nordic Statistics*.

Organisation for Economic Co-operation and Development (OECD), 2 rue Andre-Pascal, 75 Paris 16, France (Telephone Number in U.S. (202) 785-6323); *Economic Outlook; The Footwear, Raw Hides and Skins, and Leather Industry in OECD Countries; Indicators of Industrial Activity; The Iron and Steel Industry; Main Economic Indicators - Historical Statistics;* and *The Pulp and Paper Industry*.

World Bureau of Metal Statistics, 27-A

High Street, Ware, Herts. SG12 9BA, England; *World Metal Statistics*.

NORWAY - PRINTING AND WRITING PAPER PRODUCTION AND CONSUMPTION - See NORWAY - FORESTRY AND FOREST INDUSTRY

NORWAY - PRODUCTION

American Automobile Manufacturers Association, 1401 H Street, NW, Suite 900, Washington, D.C. 20005 (202) 326-5500; *World Motor Vehicle Data*.

International Lead and Zinc Study Group, Metro House, 58 St. James's Street, London SW1A 1LD England; *Lead and Zinc Statistics*.

M.E. Sharpe, 80 Business Park Drive, Armonk, New York 10504 (800) 541-6563; *The Illustrated Book of World Rankings*.

Organisation for Economic Co-operation and Development (OECD), 2 rue Andre-Pascal, 75 Paris 16, France (Telephone Number in U.S. (202) 785-6323); *Economic Outlook; The Footwear, Raw Hides and Skins, and Leather Industry in OECD Countries; Indicators of Industrial Activity; Industrial Structure Statistics; The Iron and Steel Industry; Meat Balances in OECD Member Countries; Milk, Milk Products, and Egg Balances in OECD Member Countries; The Non-Ferrous Metals Industry; The Pulp and Paper Industry;* and *Textile Industry in OECD Countries*.

NORWAY - PRODUCTIVITY

Organisation for Economic Co-operation and Development (OECD), 2 rue Andre-Pascal, 75 Paris 16, France (Telephone Number in U.S. (202) 785-6323); *Economic Outlook*.

NORWAY - PROPERTY TAXES - See NORWAY - TAXATION

NORWAY - PUBLIC CONSUMPTION FUND

Organisation for Economic Co-operation and Development (OECD), 2 rue Andre-Pascal, 75 Paris 16, France (Telephone Number in U.S. (202) 785-6323); *Revenue Statistics of OECD Member Countries*.

NORWAY - PUBLIC EXPENDITURES

Organisation for Economic Co-operation and Development (OECD), 2 rue Andre-Pascal, 75 Paris 16, France (Telephone Number in U.S. (202) 785-6323); *Revenue Statistics of OECD Member Countries*.

NORWAY - PUBLIC FINANCE - See NORWAY - FINANCE

NORWAY - PUBLIC REVENUES

Organisation for Economic Co-operation and Development (OECD), 2 rue Andre-Pascal, 75 Paris 16, France (Telephone Number in U.S. (202) 785-6323); *Revenue Statistics of OECD Member Countries.*

NORWAY - RADIO BROADCASTING - See NORWAY - BROADCASTING

NORWAY - RADIO RECEIVER PRODUCTION

Statistical Office of the United Nations, Publishing Service, New York, New York 10017 (800) 253-9646; *Statistical Yearbook.*

NORWAY - RADIO RECEIVERS

St. Martin's Press, Inc., 175 Fifth Avenue, New York, New York 10010 (800) 221-7945; *The Statesman's Year-Book.*

NORWAY - RAILWAYS

Europa Publications Limited, 18 Bedford Square, London, WC1B 3JN, England; *The Europa World Year Book.*

Jane's Information Group, Sentinel House, 163 Brighton Road, Coulsdon, Surrey CR5 2NH, England (Telephone Number in U.S. (703) 683-3700); *Jane's World Railways.*

Nordic Council of Ministers, Store Strandstraede 18, DK-1255 Copenhagen K, Denmark and the Nordic Statistical Secretariat, Postboks 2550, DK-2100 Copenhagen 0, Denmark; *The Yearbook of Nordic Statistics.*

St. Martin's Press, Inc., 175 Fifth Avenue, New York, New York 10010 (800) 221-7945; *The Statesman's Year-Book.*

Statistical Office of the United Nations, Publishing Service, New York, New York 10017 (800) 253-9646; *Annual Bulletin of Transport Statistics for Europe; Trends in Europe and North America: The Statistical Yearbook of the Economic Commission for Europe;* and *Statistical Yearbook.*

NORWAY - RAPESEED PRODUCTION - See NORWAY - CROPS

NORWAY - RELIGION

Central Intelligence Agency, Washington, D.C. 20505 (703) 482-1100, www.cia.gov; *The World Factbook.*

M.E. Sharpe, 80 Business Park Drive, Armonk, New York 10504 (800) 541-6563; *The Illustrated Book of World Rankings.*

St. Martin's Press, Inc., 175 Fifth Avenue, New York, New York 10010 (800)

221-7945; *The Statesman's Year-Book.*

NORWAY - RENT PRICES

International Labour Office, I.L.O. Publications, 1828 L Street, NW, Suite 801, Washington, D.C. 20036 (301) 638-3152; *Yearbook of Labour Statistics.*

NORWAY - RETAIL TRADE

Euromonitor International, Inc., 122 South Michigan Avenue, Suite 1200, Chicago, Illinois 60603 (800) 577-EURO; *Retail Trade International;* and *World Marketing Data and Statistics.*

Statistical Office of the United Nations, Publishing Service, New York, New York 10017 (800) 253-9646; *Statistical Yearbook.*

NORWAY - RICE PRODUCTION - See NORWAY - CROPS

NORWAY - ROOT AND TUBER PRODUCTION - See NORWAY - CROPS

NORWAY - ROUNDWOOD PRODUCTION - See NORWAY - FORESTRY AND FOREST PRODUCTS

NORWAY - RUBBER PRODUCTION AND CONSUMPTION

M.E. Sharpe, 80 Business Park Drive, Armonk, New York 10504 (800) 541-6563; *The Illustrated Book of World Rankings.*

Organisation for Economic Co-operation and Development (OECD), 2 rue Andre-Pascal, 75 Paris 16, France (Telephone Number in U.S. (202) 785-6323); *Foreign Trade by Commodities.*

NORWAY - SALT PRODUCTION - See NORWAY - MINING AND MINERAL PRODUCTS

NORWAY - SAWNWOOD PRODUCTION - See NORWAY - FORESTRY AND FOREST PRODUCTS

NORWAY - SCIENCE AND TECHNOLOGY - EXPENDITURE FOR RESEARCH - See NORWAY - SCIENTISTS, TECHNICIANS AND ENGINEERS

NORWAY - SCIENTISTS, TECHNICIANS AND ENGINEERS

Statistical Office of the United Nations, Publishing Service, New York, New York 10017 (800) 253-9646; *Statistical Yearbook.*

NORWAY - SENIOR CITIZENS

M.E. Sharpe, 80 Business Park Drive, Armonk, New York 10504 (800) 541-6563; *The Illustrated Book of World Rankings.*

NORWAY - SHEEP - See NORWAY -

LIVESTOCK AND POULTRY

NORWAY - SHIP EXPORTS

International Monetary Fund, 700 Nineteenth Street, NW, Washington, D.C. 20431 (202) 623-7000; *International Financial Statistics.*

NORWAY - SHIPBUILDING - PRODUCTION INDEX

Organisation for Economic Co-operation and Development (OECD), 2 rue Andre-Pascal, 75 Paris 16, France (Telephone Number in U.S. (202) 785-6323); *Indicators of Industrial Activity.*

NORWAY - SILVER PRODUCTION AND CONSUMPTION - See NORWAY - MINING AND MINERAL PRODUCTS

NORWAY - SOCIAL DATA

M.E. Sharpe, 80 Business Park Drive, Armonk, New York 10504 (800) 541-6563; *The Illustrated Book of World Rankings.*

Statistical Office of the United Nations, Publishing Service, New York, New York 10017 (800) 253-9646; *World Statistics Pocketbook.*

NORWAY - SOCIAL SECURITY

Nordic Council of Ministers, Store Strandstraede 18, DK-1255 Copenhagen K, Denmark and the Nordic Statistical Secretariat, Postboks 2550, DK-2100 Copenhagen 0, Denmark; *The Yearbook of Nordic Statistics.*

Organisation for Economic Co-operation and Development (OECD), 2 rue Andre-Pascal, 75 Paris 16, France (Telephone Number in U.S. (202) 785-6323); *Revenue Statistics of OECD Member Countries.*

St. Martin's Press, Inc., 175 Fifth Avenue, New York, New York 10010 (800) 221-7945; *The Statesman's Year-Book.*

Statistical Office of the United Nations, Publishing Service, New York, New York 10017 (800) 253-9646; *National Accounts Statistics.*

NORWAY - SOCIOECONOMIC DATA

Organisation for Economic Co-operation and Development (OECD), 2 rue Andre-Pascal, 75 Paris 16, France (Telephone Number in U.S. (202) 785-6323); *Economic Outlook.*

NORWAY - STEEL - See NORWAY - MINING AND MINERAL PRODUCTS

NORWAY - STOCKS - COMMODITY -

MARKET PRICE - INDEXES

Food and Agricultural Organization of the United Nations (FAO) Via delle Terme di Caracalla, 00100 Rome, Italy (Telephone Number in U.S. (202) 653-2400); *The State of Food and Agriculture.*

International Lead and Zinc Study Group, Metro House, 58 St. James's Street, London SW1A 1LD England; *Lead and Zinc Statistics.*

Statistical Office of the United Nations, Publishing Service, New York, New York 10017 (800) 253-9646; *Statistical Yearbook.*

World Bureau of Metal Statistics, 27-A High Street, Ware, Herts. SG12 9BA, England; *World Metal Statistics.*

NORWAY - SUGAR - See NORWAY - CROPS

NORWAY - SULPHUR PRODUCTION - See NORWAY - MINING AND MINERAL PRODUCTS

NORWAY - TAX REVENUES - See NORWAY - TAXATION

NORWAY - TAXATION

Europa Publications Limited, 18 Bedford Square, London, WC1B 3JN, England; *The Europa World Year Book.*

International Monetary Fund, 700 Nineteenth Street, NW, Washington, D.C. 20431 (202) 623-7000; *Government Finance Statistics Yearbook.*

International Road Federation, 2600 Virginia Avenue, NW., Washington, D.C. 20037 (202) 338-4641; *World Road Statistics.*

Nordic Council of Ministers, Store Strandstraede 18, DK-1255 Copenhagen K, Denmark and the Nordic Statistical Secretariat, Postboks 2550, DK-2100 Copenhagen 0, Denmark; *The Yearbook of Nordic Statistics.*

Organisation for Economic Co-operation and Development (OECD), 2 rue Andre-Pascal, 75 Paris 16, France (Telephone Number in U.S. (202) 785-6323); *Revenue Statistics of OECD Member Countries.*

The World Bank, 1818 H Street, NW, Washington, D.C. 20433 (202) 477-1234; *World Development Indicators.*

NORWAY - TELEGRAPH SERVICE

Nordic Council of Ministers, Store Strandstraede 18, DK-1255 Copenhagen K, Denmark and the Nordic Statistical Secretariat, Postboks 2550, DK-2100 Copenhagen 0, Denmark; *The Yearbook of Nordic Statistics.*

Statistical Office of the United Nations, Publishing Service, New York, New York 10017 (800) 253-9646; *Statistical Yearbook.*

NORWAY - TELEPHONES IN USE

American Telephone and Telegraph Company, 26 Parsippany Road, Whippany, New Jersey 07981 (800) 222-0300; *The World's Telephones.*

Central Intelligence Agency, Washington, D.C. 20505 (703) 482-1100, www.cia.gov; *The World Factbook.*

Europa Publications Limited, 18 Bedford Square, London, WC1B 3JN, England; *The Europa World Year Book.*

Nordic Council of Ministers, Store Strandstraede 18, DK-1255 Copenhagen K, Denmark and the Nordic Statistical Secretariat, Postboks 2550, DK-2100 Copenhagen 0, Denmark; *The Yearbook of Nordic Statistics.*

St. Martin's Press, Inc., 175 Fifth Avenue, New York, New York 10010 (800) 221-7945; *The Statesman's Year-Book.*

Statistical Office of the United Nations, Publishing Service, New York, New York 10017 (800) 253-9646; *Statistical Yearbook; Trends in Europe and North America: The Statistical Yearbook of the Economic Commission for Europe;* and *World Statistics Pocketbook.*

NORWAY - TELEVISION BROADCASTING - See NORWAY - BROADCASTING

NORWAY - TELEVISION RECEIVER PRODUCTION

Statistical Office of the United Nations, Publishing Service, New York, New York 10017 (800) 253-9646; *Statistical Yearbook.*

NORWAY - TEXTILE INDUSTRY

Euromonitor International, Inc., 122 South Michigan Avenue, Suite 1200, Chicago, Illinois 60603 (800) 577-EURO; *Retail Trade International.*

M.E. Sharpe, 80 Business Park Drive, Armonk, New York 10504 (800) 541-6563; *The Illustrated Book of World Rankings.*

Organisation for Economic Co-operation and Development (OECD), 2 rue Andre-Pascal, 75 Paris 16, France (Telephone Number in U.S. (202) 785-6323); *Economic Accounts for Agriculture; Foreign Trade by Commodities; Indicators of Industrial Activity; Industrial Structure Statistics;* and *Textile Industry in OECD Countries.*

St. Martin's Press, Inc., 175 Fifth Avenue, New York, New York 10010 (800) 221-7945; *The Statesman's Year-Book.*

Statistical Office of the United Nations, Publishing Service, New York, New York 10017 (800) 253-9646; *Statistical Yearbook.*

United Nations Conference on Trade and Development, Central Statistical Service, Palais des Nations, Geneva, Switzerland (Telephone in U.S. (800) 253-9646); *UNCTAD Commodity Yearbook.*

NORWAY - THEATRE

United Nations Educational, Scientific and Cultural Organization (UNESCO), 7 Place de Fontenoy, F-75700 Paris, France (Telephone Number in U.S. (212) 963-5981); *Statistical Yearbook.*

NORWAY - TIN - INDUSTRIAL CONSUMPTION - See NORWAY - MINING AND MINERAL PRODUCTS

NORWAY - TIN PRODUCTION AND CONSUMPTION - See NORWAY - MINING AND MINERAL PRODUCTS

NORWAY - TOBACCO PRODUCTION

M.E. Sharpe, 80 Business Park Drive, Armonk, New York 10504 (800) 541-6563; *The Illustrated Book of World Rankings.*

Organisation for Economic Co-operation and Development (OECD), 2 rue Andre-Pascal, 75 Paris 16, France (Telephone Number in U.S. (202) 785-6323); *Foreign Trade by Commodities; Indicators of Industrial Activity;* and *Industrial Structure Statistics.*

Statistical Office of the United Nations, Publishing Service, New York, New York 10017 (800) 253-9646; *Statistical Yearbook.*

NORWAY - TOURISM

Euromonitor International, Inc., 122 South Michigan Avenue, Suite 1200, Chicago, Illinois 60603 (800) 577-EURO; *The World Economic Factbook;* and *World Marketing Data and Statistics.*

Europa Publications Limited, 18 Bedford Square, London, WC1B 3JN, England; *The Europa World Year Book.*

M.E. Sharpe, 80 Business Park Drive, Armonk, New York 10504 (800) 541-6563; *The Illustrated Book of World Rankings.*

Organisation for Economic Co-operation and Development (OECD), 2 rue Andre-Pascal, 75 Paris 16, France (Telephone Number in U.S. (202) 785-6323); *Tourism Policy and International Tourism in OECD Member Countries.*

St. Martin's Press, Inc., 175 Fifth Avenue, New York, New York 10010 (800) 221-7945; *The Statesman's Year-Book.*

Statistical Office of the United Nations, Publishing Service, New York, New York 10017 (800) 253-9646; *Statistical Yearbook; and Trends in Europe and North America: The Statistical Yearbook of the Economic Commission for Europe.*

World Tourism Organization, Calle Capitan Haya 42, E-28020 Madrid, Spain; *Yearbook of Tourism Statistics.*

NORWAY - TRACTORS IN USE

Statistical Office of the United Nations, Publishing Service, New York, New York 10017 (800) 253-9646; *Statistical Yearbook.*

NORWAY - TRADE - See NORWAY - FOREIGN TRADE

NORWAY - TRADEMARKS AND SERVICE MARKS - See NORWAY - PATENTS, TRADEMARKS AND SERVICE MARKS

NORWAY - TRANSPORTATION AND COMMUNICATIONS

Central Intelligence Agency, Washington, D.C. 20505 (703) 482-1100, www.cia.gov; *The World Factbook.*

Euromonitor International, Inc., 122 South Michigan Avenue, Suite 1200, Chicago, Illinois 60603 (800) 577-EURO; *World Marketing Data and Statistics.*

Europa Publications Limited, 18 Bedford Square, London, WC1B 3JN, England; *The Europa World Year Book.*

Nordic Council of Ministers, Store Strandstraede 18, DK-1255 Copenhagen K, Denmark and the Nordic Statistical Secretariat, Postboks 2550, DK-2100 Copenhagen 0, Denmark; *The Yearbook of Nordic Statistics.*

St. Martin's Press, Inc., 175 Fifth Avenue, New York, New York 10010 (800) 221-7945; *The Statesman's Year-Book.*

Statistical Office of the United Nations, Publishing Service, New York, New York 10017 (800) 253-9646; *Human Development Report; and Trends in Europe and North America: The Statistical Yearbook of the Economic Commission for Europe.*

NORWAY - TUNGSTEN PRODUCTION AND CONSUMPTION - See NORWAY - MINING AND MINERAL PRODUCTS

NORWAY - TURKEYS - See NORWAY - LIVESTOCK AND POULTRY

NORWAY - UNEMPLOYMENT

Central Intelligence Agency, Washington, D.C. 20505 (703) 482-1100, www.cia.gov; *The World Factbook.*

International Labour Office, I.L.O. Publications, 1828 L Street, NW, Suite 801, Washington, D.C. 20036 (301) 638-3152; *Yearbook of Labour Statistics.*

Nordic Council of Ministers, Store Strandstraede 18, DK-1255 Copenhagen K, Denmark and the Nordic Statistical Secretariat, Postboks 2550, DK-2100 Copenhagen 0, Denmark; *The Yearbook of Nordic Statistics.*

Organisation for Economic Co-operation and Development (OECD), 2 rue Andre-Pascal, 75 Paris 16, France (Telephone Number in U.S. (202) 785-6323); *Economic Outlook; OECD Economic Surveys: Norway; and OECD Employment Outlook.*

St. Martin's Press, Inc., 175 Fifth Avenue, New York, New York 10010 (800) 221-7945; *The Statesman's Year-Book.*

Statistical Office of the United Nations, Publishing Service, New York, New York 10017 (800) 253-9646; *Statistical Yearbook; and Trends in Europe and North America: The Statistical Yearbook of the Economic Commission for Europe.*

NORWAY - URANIUM PRODUCTION AND CONSUMPTION - See NORWAY - MINING AND MINERAL PRODUCTS

NORWAY - VANADIUM AND VANADIUM ORE PRODUCTION AND CONSUMPTION - See NORWAY - MINING AND MINERAL PRODUCTS

NORWAY - VITAL STATISTICS

Nordic Council of Ministers, Store Strandstraede 18, DK-1255 Copenhagen K, Denmark and the Nordic Statistical Secretariat, Postboks 2550, DK-2100 Copenhagen 0, Denmark; *The Yearbook of Nordic Statistics.*

St. Martin's Press, Inc., 175 Fifth Avenue, New York, New York 10010 (800) 221-7945; *The Statesman's Year-Book.*

Statistical Office of the United Nations, Publishing Service, New York, New York 10017 (800) 253-9646; *Statistical Yearbook.*

World Health Organization, Office of Publications, 20 Avenue Appia, CH-1211 Geneva 27, Switzerland (Telephone Number in U.S. (518) 436-9686); *World Health Statistics Annual.*

NORWAY - WAGES

International Labour Office, I.L.O. Publications, 1828 L Street, NW, Suite 801, Washington, D.C. 20036 (301) 638-3152; *Yearbook of Labour Statistics.*

Nordic Council of Ministers, Store Strandstraede 18, DK-1255 Copenhagen K, Denmark and the Nordic Statistical Secretariat, Postboks 2550, DK-2100 Copenhagen 0, Denmark; *The Yearbook of Nordic Statistics.*

Organisation for Economic Co-operation and Development (OECD), 2 rue Andre-Pascal, 75 Paris 16, France (Telephone Number in U.S. (202) 785-6323); *Economic Outlook; Industrial Structure Statistics; and Main Economic Indicators - Historical Statistics.*

Statistical Office of the United Nations, Publishing Service, New York, New York 10017 (800) 253-9646; *Statistical Yearbook.*

NORWAY - WATERWAYS IN USE

Organisation for Economic Co-operation and Development (OECD), 2 rue Andre-Pascal, 75 Paris 16, France (Telephone Number in U.S. (202) 785-6323); *Maritime Transport.*

NORWAY - WEATHER - See NORWAY - CLIMATE

NORWAY - WELFARE

Nordic Council of Ministers, Store Strandstraede 18, DK-1255 Copenhagen K, Denmark and the Nordic Statistical Secretariat, Postboks 2550, DK-2100 Copenhagen 0, Denmark; *The Yearbook of Nordic Statistics.*

NORWAY - WHALE AND SPERM OIL PRODUCTION

Statistical Office of the United Nations, Publishing Service, New York, New York 10017 (800) 253-9646; *Statistical Yearbook.*

NORWAY - WHALES CAUGHT

Statistical Office of the United Nations, Publishing Service, New York, New York 10017 (800) 253-9646; *Statistical Yearbook.*

NORWAY - WHALING APPARATUS IN OPERATION

Statistical Office of the United Nations, Publishing Service, New York, New York 10017 (800) 253-9646; *Statistical Yearbook.*

NORWAY - WHEAT PRODUCTION AND PRICES - See NORWAY - CROPS

NORWAY - WHOLESALE PRICES - INDEX NUMBERS

Nordic Council of Ministers, Store

Strandstraede 18, DK-1255 Copenhagen K, Denmark and the Nordic Statistical Secretariat, Postboks 2550, DK-2100 Copenhagen 0, Denmark; *The Yearbook of Nordic Statistics.*

Statistical Office of the United Nations, Publishing Service, New York, New York 10017 (800) 253-9646; *Statistical Yearbook.*

NORWAY - WHOLESALE TRADE

Statistical Office of the United Nations, Publishing Service, New York, New York 10017 (800) 253-9646; *Statistical Yearbook.*

NORWAY - WINE PRODUCTION - See NORWAY - BEVERAGES

NORWAY - WOOD AND WOOD PULP - See NORWAY - FORESTRY AND FOREST PRODUCTS

NORWAY - WOOL - See NORWAY - TEXTILE INDUSTRY

NORWAY - YARN PRODUCTION - See NORWAY - TEXTILE INDUSTRY

NORWAY - ZINC - See NORWAY - MINING AND MINERAL PRODUCTS

NUCLEAR POWER

U.S. Department of Energy, Energy Information Administration, 1000 Independence Avenue, SW, Washington, D.C. 20585 (202) 208-0300; *Annual Energy Review; Uranium Industry Annual;* and unpublished data.

NUCLEAR POWER - CAPABILITY

McGraw-Hill, Incorporated, 1221 Avenue of the Americas, New York, New York 10020 (800) 722-4726; *Nucleonics Week.*

U.S. Department of Energy, Energy Information Administration, Washington, D.C. 20585 (202) 208-0300; *Electric Power Annual; Annual Energy Review; Monthly Energy Review;* and unpublished data.

NUCLEAR POWER - COMMERCIAL GENERATION - BY COUNTRY

McGraw-Hill, Incorporated, 1221 Avenue of the Americas, New York, New York 10020 (800) 722-4726; *Nucleonics Week.*

NUCLEAR POWER - CONSUMPTION

U.S. Department of Energy, Energy Information Administration, Washington, D.C. 20585 (202) 208-0300; *Annual Energy Outlook; State Energy Data Report; International Energy Review; International Energy Outlook;* and *Monthly Energy Review.*

NUCLEAR POWER - PRODUCTION

McGraw-Hill Incorporated, 1221 Avenue of the Americas, New York, New York 10020 (800) 722-4726; *Nucleonics Week.*

U.S. Department of Energy, Energy Information Administration, Washington, D.C. 20585 (202) 208-0300; *Annual Energy Review; Monthly Energy Review; Electric Power Monthly; Electric Power Annual; International Energy Annual;* and unpublished data.

NUCLEAR POWER - REACTORS

McGraw-Hill, Incorporated, 1221 Avenue of the Americas, New York, New York 10020 (800) 722-4726; *Nucleonics Week.*

U.S. Department of Energy, Energy Information Administration, Washington, D.C. 20585 (202) 208-0300; *Annual Energy Review;* and *Monthly Energy Review.*

NUCLEAR POWER - STATE DATA

U.S. Department of Energy, Energy Information Administration, Washington, D.C. 20585 (202) 208-0300; *Electric Power Monthly;* and *Electric Power Annual.*

NUCLEAR POWER - WASTE DISCHARGED FUEL

Organization for Economic Cooperation and Development, 2 rue Andre-Pascal, 75 Paris 16, France (Telephone Number in U.S. (202) 785-6323); *Toward Sustainable Development: Environmental Indicators;* and *OECD in Figures.*

U.S. Department of Energy, Energy Information Administration, Washington, D.C. 20585 (202) 208-0300; *Annual Energy Review; Uranium Industry Annual;* and unpublished data.

NURSERY AND GREENHOUSE PRODUCTS

U.S. Department of Agriculture, Economic Research Service, 1800 M Street, NW, Washington, D.C. 20036 (202) 694-5050, www.ers.usda.gov; *Farm Business Economic Report* and unpublished data.

NURSING AND PERSONAL CARE FACILITIES - EARNINGS

U.S. Department of Commerce, Bureau of the Census, Washington, D.C. 20233 (301) 457-4100, www.census.gov; *Census of Service Industries;* and *1997 Economic Census.*

NURSING AND PERSONAL CARE FACILITIES - EMPLOYEES

U.S. Department of Commerce, Bureau of the Census, Washington, D.C. 20233

(301) 457-4100, www.census.gov; *Census of Service Industries;* and *1997 Economic Census.*

U.S. Department of Health and Human Services, National Center for Health Statistics, 3700 East West Highway, Hyattsville, Maryland 20782 (301) 436-8500, www.cdc.gov/nchs; *Advance Data, No. 280.*

U.S. Department of Labor, Bureau of Labor Statistics, Two Massachusetts Avenue, NE, Washington, D.C. 20212 (202) 691-5200, www.stats.bls.gov; *Monthly Labor Review; Employment and Earnings;* Bulletins 2445 and 2481; and Internet site: http://stats.bls.gov/ceshome.htm.

NURSING AND PERSONAL CARE FACILITIES - ESTABLISHMENTS

U.S. Department of Commerce, Bureau of the Census, Washington, D.C. 20233 (301) 457-4100, www.census.gov; *Census of Service Industries;* and *1997 Economic Census.*

U.S. Department of Health and Human Services, Health Care Financing Administration, 200 Independence Avenue, SW, Washington, D.C. 20201 (202) 690-6145, www.hcfa.gov; *Medicare Participating Providers and Suppliers of Health Services;* and unpublished data.

U.S. Department of Health and Human Services, National Center for Health Statistics, 3700 East West Highway, Hyattsville, Maryland 20782 (301) 436-8500, www.cdc.gov/nchs; *Advance Data; No.280.*

NURSING AND PERSONAL CARE FACILITIES - EXPENDITURES

U.S. Department of Health and Human Services, Health Care Financing Administration, 200 Independence Avenue, SW, Washington, D.C. 20201 (202) 690-6145, www.hcfa.gov; *Health Care Financing Review;* and Internet site: http://www.hcfa.gov/ stats/NHE-Proj/tables/t02.htm.

NURSING AND PERSONAL CARE FACILITIES - EXPENDITURES -CONSUMER

U.S. Department of Health and Human Services, Health Care Financing Administration, 200 Independence Avenue, SW, Washington, D.C. 20201 (202) 690-6145, www.hcfa.gov; *Health Care Financing Review.*

NURSING AND PERSONAL CARE FACILITIES - FINANCES

U.S. Department of Commerce, Bureau of the Census, Washington, D.C. 20233 (301) 457-4100, www.census.gov; *Census of Service Industries; Current Business*

Reports; and *Service Annual Survey.*

NURSING AND PERSONAL CARE FACILITIES - RECEIPTS

U.S. Department of Commerce, Bureau of the Census, Washington, D.C. 20233 (301) 457-4100, www.census.gov; *Census of Service Industries; Current Business Reports;* and *Service Annual Survey.*

NURSING AND PERSONAL CARE FACILITIES - RESIDENTS

U.S. Department of Health and Human Services, National Center for Health Statistics, 3700 East West Highway, Hyattsville, Maryland 20782 (301) 436-

8500, www.cdc.gov/nchs; *Advance Data, No. 280 and 289.*

NURSING PERSONNEL

U.S. Department of Health and Human Services, Health Resources and Services Administration, 5600 Fishers Lane, Rockville, Maryland 20857 (301) 443-3376, www.hrsa.gov; unpublished data.

U.S. Department of Justice, Immigration and Nationalization Service, 425 I Street, NW, Washington, D.C. 20536 (202) 305-1613, www.ins.usdoj.gov; *Statistical Yearbook.*

NURSING PERSONNEL - EMPLOYMENT

U.S. Department of Labor, Bureau of Labor Statistics, Two Massachusetts Avenue, NE, Washington, D.C. 20212 (202) 691-5200, www.stats.bls.gov; *Employment and Earnings;* and unpublished data.

NURSING PERSONNEL - EMPLOYMENT - PROJECTIONS

U.S. Department of Labor, Bureau of Labor Statistics, Two Massachusetts Avenue, NE, Washington, D.C. 20212 (202) 691-5200, www.stats.bls.gov; *Monthly Labor Review.*

NURSING PERSONNEL - WORKPLACE VIOLENCE

U.S. Department of Justice, Bureau of Justice Statistics, 810 Seventh Street, NW, 2nd Floor, Washington, D.C. 20531 (800) 732-3277, www.ojp.usdoj.gov/bjs; *Workplace Violence.*

NURSING PROGRAMS - STUDENTS AND GRADUATES

U.S. Department of Health and Human Services, National Center for Health Statistics, 3700 East West Highway, Hyattsville, Maryland 20782 (301) 436-8500, www.cdc.gov/nchs; *Health United States.*

NUTRITION - CONSUMPTION OF MAJOR COMMODITIES

U.S. Department of Agriculture, Economic Research Service, 1800 M Street, NW, Washington, D.C. 20036 (202) 694-

5050, www.ers.usda.gov; *Food Consumption, Prices, and Expenditures;* and *Agricultural Outlook.*

NUTRITION - NUTRIENTS AND NUTRITIONAL INTAKE

U.S. Department of Agriculture, Economic Research Service, 1800 M Street, NW, Washington, D.C. 20036 (202) 694-5050, www.ers.usda.gov; *Food Consumption, Prices and Expenditures.*

NUTRITIONAL DEFICIENCIES - DEATHS

U.S. Department of Health and Human Services, National Center for Health Statistics, 3700 East West Highway, Hyattsville, Maryland 20782 (301) 436-8500, www.cdc.gov/nchs; *Vital Statistics of the U.S.; National Vital Statistical Report;* and unpublished data.

NUTS - CASH RECEIPTS - MARKETING

U.S. Department of Agriculture, Economic Research Service, 1800 M Street, NW, Washington, D.C. 20036 (202) 694-5050, www.ers.usda.gov; *Farm Business Economic Report.*

NUTS - CONSUMPTION

U.S. Department of Agriculture, Economic Research Service, 1800 M Street, NW, Washington, D.C. 20036 (202) 694-5050, www.ers.usda.gov; *Fruit and Tree Nuts Situation and Outlook Yearbook.*

NUTS - FOREIGN TRADE

U.S. Department of Agriculture, Economic Research Service, 1800 M Street, NW, Washington, D.C. 20036 (202) 694-5050, www.ers.usda.gov; *Agricultural Statistics; Foreign Agricultural Trade of the U.S.; Fruit and Tree Nuts Situation and Outlook Yearbook;* and *U.S. Agricultural Trade Update.*

NUTS - PRODUCTION

U.S. Department of Agriculture, Economic Research Service, 1800 M Street, NW, Washington, D.C. 20036 (202) 694-5050, www.ers.usda.gov; *Agricultural Outlook;* and *Fruit and Tree Nuts Situation and Outlook Yearbook.*

O

OBSTETRICIANS - See also PHYSICIANS

American Medical Association, 515 North State Street, Chicago, Illinois 60610 (312) 464-5000; *Physician Characteristics and Distribution in the United States.*

OCCUPATIONAL SAFETY

U.S. Department of Labor, Bureau of Labor Statistics, Two Massachusetts Avenue, NE, Washington, D.C. 20212 (202) 606-5900, www.stats.bls.gov; *Occupational Injuries and Illnesses in the United States By Industry.*

OCCUPATIONS - See also Individual Occupations

OCCUPATIONS - ADULT EDUCATION

U.S. Department of Education, National Center for Education Statistics, 555 New Jersey Avenue, NW, Washington, D.C. 20208-5574 (202) 219-1828, http://hces.ed.gov; *National Household Education Survey;* and *Adult Participation in Work-Related Courses.*

OCCUPATIONS - BLACK POPULATION

U.S. Department of Labor, Bureau of Labor Statistics, Two Massachusetts Avenue, NE, Washington, D.C. 20212 (202) 606-5900, www.stats.bls.gov; *Employment and Earnings;* and unpublished data.

OCCUPATIONS - EARNINGS

U.S. Department of Commerce, Bureau of the Census, Washington, D.C. 20233 (301) 457-4100, www.census.gov; *Current Population Reports.*

U.S. Department of Labor, Bureau of Labor Statistics, Two Massachusetts Avenue, NE, Washington, D.C. 20212 (202) 606-5900, www.stats.bls.gov; *Employment and Earnings;* Bulletin 2307; and unpublished data.

OCCUPATIONS - EMPLOYMENT - BLACK POPULATION

U.S. Department of Labor, Bureau of Labor Statistics, Two Massachusetts Avenue, NE, Washington, D.C. 20212 (202) 606-5900, www.stats.bls.gov; *Employment and Earnings;* and unpublished data.

OCCUPATIONS - EMPLOYMENT - HISPANIC ORIGIN POPULATION

U.S. Department of Labor, Bureau of Labor Statistics, Two Massachusetts Avenue, NE, Washington, D.C. 20212 (202) 606-5900, www.stats.bls.gov; *Employment and Earnings;* and unpublished data.

OCCUPATIONS - EMPLOYMENT - PROJECTIONS

U.S. Department of Labor, Bureau of Labor Statistics, Two Massachusetts Avenue, NE, Washington, D.C. 20212 (202) 606-5900, www.stats.bls.gov; *Monthly Labor Review.*

OCCUPATIONS - EMPLOYMENT - RACE

U.S. Department of Labor, Bureau of Labor Statistics, Two Massachusetts Avenue, NE, Washington, D.C. 20212 (202) 606-5900, www.stats.bls.gov; *Employment and Earnings;* and unpublished data.

OCCUPATIONS - EMPLOYMENT - SEX

U.S. Department of Labor, Bureau of Labor Statistics, Two Massachusetts Avenue, NE, Washington, D.C. 20212 (202) 606-5900, www.stats.bls.gov; *Employment and Earnings;* and unpublished data.

OCCUPATIONS - EMPLOYMENT COST INDEX

U.S. Department of Labor, Bureau of Labor Statistics, Two Massachusetts Avenue, NE, Washington, D.C. 20212 (202) 606-5900, www.stats.bls.gov; *News; Employment Cost Index;* and Internet site: http://stats.bls.gov/ ecthome.htm..

OCCUPATIONS - HISPANIC ORIGIN POPULATION

U.S. Department of Labor, Bureau of Labor Statistics, Two Massachusetts Avenue, NE, Washington, D.C. 20212 (202) 606-5900, www.stats.bls.gov; *Employment and Earnings;* and unpublished data.

OCCUPATIONS - LABOR UNION MEMBERSHIP

U.S. Department of Labor, Bureau of Labor Statistics, Two Massachusetts Avenue, NE, Washington, D.C. 20212 (202) 606-5900, www.stats.bls.gov; *Employment and Earnings.*

OCCUPATIONS - PENSION PLAN - HEALTH PLAN COVERAGE

U.S. Department of Commerce, Bureau of the Census, Washington, D.C. 20233 (301) 457-4100, www.census.gov; unpublished data.

OCCUPATIONS - SEX AND EDUCATIONAL ATTAINMENT

U.S. Department of Labor, Bureau of Labor Statistics, Two Massachusetts Avenue, NE, Washington, D.C. 20212 (202) 606-5900, www.stats.bls.gov; unpublished data.

OCCUPATIONS - WHITE-COLLAR AND BLUE-COLLAR WORKERS

U.S. Department of Labor, Bureau of Labor Statistics, Two Massachusetts Avenue, NE, Washington, D.C. 20212 (202) 606-5900, www.stats.bls.gov; *News; Employment Cost Index;* and Internet site http://stats.bls.gov/ ecthome.htm.

OCEAN PERCH - ATLANTIC

U.S. Department of Commerce, National Oceanic and Atmospheric Administration, National Marine Fisheries Service, 1315 East-West Highway, Silver Spring, Maryland 20910 (301) 713-2239, www.nmfs.noaa.gov; *Fisheries of the United States.*

OFFICE BUILDINGS - See also

COMMERCIAL BUILDINGS

U.S. Department of Commerce, Bureau of the Census, Washington, D.C. 20233 (301) 457-4100, www.census.gov; *Current Construction Reports, Value of Construction.*

U.S. Department of Energy, Energy Information Administration, 1000 Independence Avenue, SW, Washington, D.C. 20585 (202) 586-1185; *Commercial Buildings Energy Consumption Survey;* and Internet site http://www.eia.doe.gov/emeu/cbecs/contents.html.

OFFICE BUILDINGS - CONSTRUCTION

U.S. Department of Commerce, Bureau of the Census, Washington, D.C. 20233 (301) 457-4100, www.census.gov; *Current Construction Reports;* and *Value of Construction.*

OFFICE BUILDINGS - VACANCY RATES

Society of Industrial and Office Realtors, 700 Eleventh Street, NW, Suite 510, Washington, D.C. 20001 (202) 283-1150; *Comparative Statistics of Industrial and Office Real Estate Markets.*

ONCOR International, 3040 Post Oak Boulevard, Houston, Texas 77056 (713) 961-0600; *Year-End Market Data Book.*

OFFICE EQUIPMENT - See COMPUTER AND OFFICE EQUIPMENT

OFFSHORE LEASES

U.S. Department of Energy, Energy Information Administration, 1000 Independence Avenue, SW, Washington, D.C. 20585 (202) 586-1185; *Petroleum Supply Annual.*

OHIO - See also STATE DATA (FOR INDIVIDUAL STATES)

Ohio - Primary Statistics Sources

Department of Development, Ohio Data Users Center (ODUC), Post Office Box 1001, Columbus, Ohio 43266-0101 (614) 466-2115; *Value-added Census Products,* updated continuously.

The Ohio State University, School of Public Policy and Management, 1775 College Road, Columbus, Ohio 43210-1399 (614) 292-8696; *Benchmark Ohio.*

Ohio - State Data Centers

Office of Strategic Research, Ohio Department of Development, Post Office Box 1001, 77 High Street, 27th Floor,

Columbus, Ohio 43266-0101, Mr. Barry Bennett (614) 466-2115.

Buckeye Hills Hocking Valley Regional Development District, Route 1, County Road 9, Box 299D, Marietta, Ohio 45750, Sybil Haney (614) 374-9436.

Cleveland State University, Northern Ohio Data and Information Service/The Urban Center, 1737 Euclid Avenue, Room 45, Cleveland, Ohio 44115-9239, Mr. Mark Salling (216) 687-2209.

Ohio Occupational Information Coordinating Commission, Division of Labor Market Information, Ohio Bureau of Employment Services, 145 S. Front Street, Columbus, Ohio 43215, Mr. Keith Ewald (614) 752-9494.

OSD Data Center, Department of Human and Community Resource Development, 248 Agricultural Administration Building, 2120 Fyffe Road, Columbus, Ohio 43210-1067, Ms. Rosemary Gliem (614) 292-2433.

State Library of Ohio, 65 South Front Street, Columbus, Ohio 43215, Ms. Barbara Kussow (614) 644-6952.

OIL - See PETROLEUM AND PRODUCTS

OIL AND GAS EXTRACTION INDUSTRY - CAPITAL

U.S. Department of Labor, Bureau of Labor Statistics, Two Massachusetts Avenue, NE, Washington, D.C. 20212 (202) 606-5900, www.stats.bls.gov; *Employment and Earnings*; and Bulletin 2370.

Time Warner, 1675 Broadway, Rockefeller Center, New York, New York 10019 (212) 522-1212; *The Fortune Directories.*

OIL AND GAS EXTRACTION INDUSTRY - EARNINGS

U.S. Department of Labor, Bureau of Labor Statistics, Two Massachusetts Avenue, NE, Washington, D.C. 20212 (202) 606-5900, www.stats.bls.gov; *Employment and Earnings;* and Bulletins 2370.

OIL AND GAS EXTRACTION INDUSTRY - EMPLOYEES

U.S. Department of Labor, Bureau of Labor Statistics, Two Massachusetts Avenue, NE, Washington, D.C. 20212 (202) 606-5900, www.stats.bls.gov; *Employment and Earnings;* and Bulletins 2370.

OIL AND GAS EXTRACTION INDUSTRY - ESTABLISHMENTS

U.S. Department of Commerce, Bureau of the Census, Washington, D.C. 20233

(301) 457-4100, www.census.gov; *Census of Mineral Industries.*

U.S. Department of Labor, Bureau of Labor Statistics, Two Massachusetts Avenue, NE, Washington, D.C. 20212 (202) 606-5900, www.stats.bls.gov; *Employment and Earnings;* and Bulletins 2370.

OIL AND GAS EXTRACTION INDUSTRY - FINANCES

U.S. Department of the Treasury, Internal Revenue Service, 1111 Constitution Avenue, NW, Washington, D.C. 20224 (202) 874-0410, www.irs.ustreas.gov; *Statistics of Income Bulletin.*

OIL AND GAS EXTRACTION INDUSTRY - GROSS DOMESTIC PRODUCT

U.S. Department of Commerce, Bureau of Economic Analysis, Fourteenth Street between Constitution Avenue and E Street, NW, Washington, D.C. 20230 (202) 606-9900; *Survey of Current Business.*

OIL AND GAS EXTRACTION INDUSTRY - MERGERS AND ACQUISITIONS

Thomson Financial Securities Data, Two Gateway Center, Newark, New Jersey 07006 (973) 622-3100; *Merger and Corporate Transactions Database.*

OIL AND GAS EXTRACTION INDUSTRY - OCCUPATIONAL SAFETY

U.S. Department of Labor, Bureau of Labor Statistics, Two Massachusetts Avenue, NE, Washington, D.C. 20212 (202) 606-5900, www.stats.bls.gov; *Occupational Injuries and Illnesses in the United States by Industry.*

OIL AND GAS EXTRACTION INDUSTRY - OUTPUT

Board of Governors of the Federal Reserve System, Twentieth Street and Constitution Avenue, NW, Washington, D.C. 20551 (202) 452-3000, www.bog.frb.fed.us; *Federal Reserve Bulletin;* and *Industrial Production and Capacity Utilization.*

OIL AND GAS EXTRACTION INDUSTRY - PARTNERSHIPS

U.S. Department of the Treasury, Internal Revenue Service, 1111 Constitution Avenue, NW, Washington, D.C. 20224 (202) 874-0410, www.irs.ustreas.gov; *Statistics of Income Bulletin.*

OIL AND GAS EXTRACTION INDUSTRY - PATENTS

U.S. Department of Commerce, Patent and Trademark Office, 2011 Crystal Drive, Arlington, Virginia 22202 (703) 305-8341;

Patenting Trends in the United States, State Country Report.

OIL AND GAS EXTRACTION INDUSTRY - PRODUCTION INDEXES

Board of Governors of the Federal Reserve System, Twentieth Street and Constitution Avenue, NW, Washington, D.C. 20551 (202) 452-3000, www.bog.frb.fed.us; *Federal Reserve Bulletin;* and *Industrial Production and Capacity Utilization.*

OIL AND GAS EXTRACTION INDUSTRY - SHIPMENTS, RECEIPTS

U.S. Department of Labor, Bureau of Labor Statistics, Two Massachusetts Avenue, NE, Washington, D.C. 20212 (202) 606-5900, www.stats.bls.gov; *Employment and Earnings*; and Bulletin 2370.

OIL AND GAS EXTRACTION INDUSTRY - VALUE ADDED

U.S. Department of Labor, Bureau of Labor Statistics, Two Massachusetts Avenue, NE, Washington, D.C. 20212 (202) 606-5900, www.stats.bls.gov; *Employment and Earnings*; and Bulletin 2370.

OIL CROPS

Executive Office of the President, Council of Economic Advisers, Old Executive Office Building, Washington, D.C. 20502 (202) 395-5084, www.whitehouse.gov/cea; *Economic Report of the President.*

U.S. Department of Agriculture, Economic Research Service, 1800 M Street, NW, Washington, D.C. 20036 (202) 694-5050, www.ers.usda.gov; *Agricultural Outlook; Foreign Agricultural Trade of the United States; U.S. Agricultural Trade Update;* and *Farm Business Economic Report.*

U.S. Department of Agriculture, National Agricultural Statistics Service, Fourteenth Street and Independence Avenue, SW, Washington, D.C. 20250 (800) 727-9540, www.usda.gov/nass; *Agricultural Prices: Annual Summary.*

OIL SPILLS

Tanker Advisory Center, 10 East End Avenue, New York, New York 10028 (212) 628-7686; *Worldwide Tanker Casualty Returns.*

U.S. Department of Transportation, United States Coast Guard, 2100 Second Street, SW, Washington, D.C. 20593 (202) 267-2229; Internet site: http://www.uscg. mil/nq/g-m/nmc/response/stats/summary. htm.

OILS - ANIMAL (OILS AND FATS)

U.S. Department of Agriculture, Economic Research Service, 1800 M Street, NW, Washington, D.C. 20036 (202) 694-5050, www.ers.usda.gov; *Food Consumption, Prices and Expenditures; Agricultural Statistics; Foreign Agricultural Trade of the U.S.; U.S. Agricultural Trade Update;* and *Agricultural Outlook.*

OILS - ANIMAL AND VEGETABLE - FOREIGN TRADE

U.S. Department of Agriculture, Economic Research Service, 1800 M Street, NW, Washington, D.C. 20036 (202) 694-5050, www.ers.usda.gov; *Agricultural Outlook; Agricultural Statistics; Food Consumption, Prices and Expenditures; U.S. Agricultural Trade Update;* and *Foreign Agricultural Trade of the U.S.*

OILS - VEGETABLE - FOREIGN TRADE

U.S. Department of Agriculture, Economic Research Service, 1800 M Street, NW, Washington, D.C. 20036 (202) 694-5050, www.ers.usda.gov; *Foreign Agricultural Trade of the U.S.; Food Consumption, Prices, and Expenditures;* and *Agricultural Statistics.*

U.S. Department of Agriculture, Foreign Agricultural Service, Fourteenth Street and Independence Avenue, SW, Washington, D.C. 20250 (202) 720-7115, www.fas.usda.gov; *Foreign Agricultural Commodity Circular Series.*

U.S. Department of Commerce, Bureau of the Census, Washington, D.C. 20233 (301) 457-4100, www.census.gov; *U.S. Merchandise Trade;* and *U.S. International Trade in Goods and Services.*

OILS - VEGETABLE - PRODUCTION, CONSUMPTION, AND STOCKS

U.S. Department of Agriculture, Economic Research Service, 1800 M Street, NW, Washington, D.C. 20036 (202) 694-5050, www.ers.usda.gov; *Food Consumption, Prices, and Expenditures;* and *Agricultural Outlook.*

U.S. Department of Agriculture, Foreign Agricultural Service, Fourteenth Street and Independence Avenue, SW, Washington, D.C. 20250 (202) 720-7115, www.fas.usda.gov; *Foreign Agricultural Commodity Circular Series.*

OKLAHOMA - See also STATE DATE (FOR INDIVIDUAL STATES)

Oklahoma - Primary Statistics Source

Center for Economic and Management

Research, University of Oklahoma, 307 West Brooks Street, Room 4, Norman, Oklahoma 73109 (405) 325-2931; *Statistical Abstract of Oklahoma.*

Oklahoma - State Data Centers

Oklahoma State Data Center, Oklahoma Department of Commerce, Post Office Box 26980, Oklahoma City, Oklahoma 73126-0980, Mr. Jeff Wallace (405) 815-5184.

Oklahoma Department of Libraries, 200 N.E. 18th Street, Oklahoma City, Oklahoma 73105-3205, Mr. Steve Beleu (405) 521-2502.

University of Oklahoma, Center for Economic and Management Research, 307 West Brooks, Norman, Oklahoma 73019-0450, Mr. John McCraw (405) 325-2931.

OLD-AGE PENSIONS - See PENSIONS

OLD-AGE, SURVIVORS, DISABILITY, AND HEALTH INSURANCE - See SOCIAL INSURANCE

OLIVES

U.S. Department of Agriculture, National Agricultural Statistics Service, Fourteenth Street and Independence Avenue, SW, Washington, D.C. 20250 (800) 727-9540, www.usda.gov/nass; *Noncitrus Fruits and Nuts.*

Oman - National Statistical Office

Directorate General of National Statistics, Development Council, Post Office Box 881, Muscat, Oman.

Oman - Primary Statistics Source

Directorate General of National Statistics, Development Council, P.O. Box 881, Muscat, Oman; *Statistical Year Book.*

OMAN - AGRICULTURE

Economic Commission for Western Asia, Post Office Box 27, Baghdad, Iraq; *Statistical Abstract of Western Asia.*

Economist Intelligence Unit, 111 West 57th Street, New York, New York 10019 (800) 938-4685; *Oman Country Report.*

Euromonitor International, Inc., 122 South Michigan Avenue, Suite 1200, Chicago, Illinois 60603 (800) 577-EURO; *International Marketing Data and Statistics;* and *World Marketing Data and Statistics.*

Europa Publications Limited, 18 Bedford Square, London, WC1B 3JN, England; *The Europa World Year Book*.

Federal Statistical Office, Gustav - Stresemann - Ring 11, D-6200 Wiesbaden, Germany; *Oman*.

Food and Agricultural Organization of the United Nations (FAO), Via delle Terme di Caracalla, 00100 Rome, Italy (Telephone Number in U.S. (202) 653-2400); *Production Yearbook; The State of Food and Agriculture;* and *Trade Yearbook*.

M.E. Sharpe, 80 Business Park Drive, Armonk, New York 10504 (800) 541-6563; *The Illustrated Book of World Rankings*.

St. Martin's Press, Inc., 175 Fifth Avenue, New York, New York 10010 (800) 221-7945; *The Statesman's Year-Book*.

United Nations Conference on Trade and Development, Central Statistical Service, Palais des Nations, Geneva, Switzerland (Telephone in U.S. (800) 253-9646); *UNCTAD Commodity Yearbook*.

The World Bank, 1818 H Street, NW, Washington, D.C. 20433 (202) 477-1234; *World Development Indicators*.

OMAN - AIRLINE SERVICE

Economic Commission for Western Asia, Post Office Box 27, Baghdad, Iraq; *Statistical Abstract of Western Asia*.

Europa Publications Limited, 18 Bedford Square, London, WC1B 3JN, England; *The Europa World Year Book*.

M.E. Sharpe, 80 Business Park Drive, Armonk, New York 10504 (800) 541-6563; *The Illustrated Book of World Rankings*.

St. Martin's Press, Inc., 175 Fifth Avenue, New York, New York 10010 (800) 221-7945; *The Statesman's Year-Book*.

OMAN - AIRPORTS

Central Intelligence Agency, Washington, D.C. 20505 (703) 482-1100, www.cia.gov; *The World Factbook*.

OMAN - ALUMINUM PRODUCTION AND CONSUMPTION - See OMAN - MINING AND MINERAL PRODUCTS

OMAN - ANIMAL HEALTH

Food and Agricultural Organization of the United Nations (FAO), Via delle Terme di Caracalla, 00100 Rome, Italy (Telephone Number in U.S. (202) 653-2400); *Animal Health Yearbook*.

OMAN - AREA AND DENSITY OF POPULATION

Central Intelligence Agency, Washington, D.C. 20505 (703) 482-1100, www.cia.gov; *The World Factbook*.

Economic Commission for Western Asia, Post Office Box 27, Baghdad, Iraq; *Statistical Abstract of Western Asia*.

Euromonitor International, Inc., 122 South Michigan Avenue, Suite 1200, Chicago, Illinois 60603 (800) 577-EURO; *International Marketing Data and Statistics;* and *The World Economic Factbook*.

Europa Publications Limited, 18 Bedford Square, London, WC1B 3JN, England; *The Europa World Year Book*.

Federal Statistical Office, Gustav - Stresemann - Ring 11, D-6200 Wiesbaden, Germany; *Oman*.

Food and Agricultural Organization of the United Nations (FAO) Via delle Terme di Caracalla, 00100 Rome, Italy (Telephone Number in U.S. (202) 653-2400); *The State of Food and Agriculture*.

M.E. Sharpe, 80 Business Park Drive, Armonk, New York 10504 (800) 541-6563; *The Illustrated Book of World Rankings*.

St. Martin's Press, Inc., 175 Fifth Avenue, New York, New York 10010 (800) 221-7945; *The Statesman's Year-Book*.

Statistical Office of the United Nations, Publishing Service, New York, New York 10017 (800) 253-9646; *Statistical Yearbook*.

The World Bank, 1818 H Street, NW, Washington, D.C. 20433 (202) 477-1234; *World Development Report*.

OMAN - ARMS EXPORTS AND IMPORTS - See OMAN - MILITARY

OMAN - BALANCE OF PAYMENTS

Economic Commission for Western Asia, Post Office Box 27, Baghdad, Iraq; *Statistical Abstract of Western Asia*.

The Economist Intelligence Unit, 111 West 57th Street, New York, New York 10019 (800) 938-4685; *The World Market Atlas*.

Europa Publications Limited, 18 Bedford Square, London, WC1B 3JN, England; *The Europa World Year Book*.

Federal Statistical Office, Gustav - Stresemann - Ring 11, D-6200 Wiesbaden, Germany; *Oman*.

International Monetary Fund, 700 Nineteenth Street, NW, Washington, D.C. 20431 (202) 623-7000; *Balance of Payments Yearbook*.

United Nations Conference on Trade and Development (UNCTAD), New York, New York 10017 (800) 253-9646; *Handbook of International Trade and Development Statistics*.

The World Bank, 1818 H Street, NW, Washington, D.C. 20433 (202) 477-1234; *World Development Report;* and *World Development Indicators*.

OMAN - BALANCE OF TRADE

Economic Commission for Western Asia, Post Office Box 27, Baghdad, Iraq; *Statistical Abstract of Western Asia*.

OMAN - BANKING

Economic Commission for Western Asia, Post Office Box 27, Baghdad, Iraq; *Statistical Abstract of Western Asia*.

Euromonitor International, Inc., 122 South Michigan Avenue, Suite 1200, Chicago, Illinois 60603 (800) 577-EURO; *World Marketing Data and Statistics*.

Europa Publications Limited, 18 Bedford Square, London, WC1B 3JN, England; *The Europa World Year Book*.

International Monetary Fund, 700 Nineteenth Street, NW, Washington, D.C. 20431 (202) 623-7000; *Government Finance Statistics Yearbook;* and *International Financial Statistics*.

M.E. Sharpe, 80 Business Park Drive, Armonk, New York 10504 (800) 541-6563; *The Illustrated Book of World Rankings*.

St. Martin's Press, Inc., 175 Fifth Avenue, New York, New York 10010 (800) 221-7945; *The Statesman's Year-Book*.

OMAN - BARLEY PRODUCTION - See OMAN - CROPS

OMAN - BEER PRODUCTION - See OMAN - BEVERAGES

OMAN - BEVERAGES

M.E. Sharpe, 80 Business Park Drive, Armonk, New York 10504 (800) 541-6563; *The Illustrated Book of World Rankings*.

OMAN - BIRTH RATES

Central Intelligence Agency, Washington, D.C. 20505 (703) 482-1100, www.cia.gov; *The World Factbook*.

Euromonitor International, Inc., 122 South Michigan Avenue, Suite 1200, Chicago, Illinois 60603 (800) 577-EURO; *International Marketing Data and Statistics;* and *The World Economic Factbook*.

Europa Publications Limited, 18

Bedford Square, London, WC1B 3JN, England; *The Europa World Year Book*.

M.E. Sharpe, 80 Business Park Drive, Armonk, New York 10504 (800) 541-6563; *The Illustrated Book of World Rankings*.

Statistical Office of the United Nations, Publishing Service, New York, New York 10017 (800) 253-9646; *Demographic Yearbook*.

The World Bank, 1818 H Street, NW, Washington, D.C. 20433 (202) 477-1234; *World Development Indicators*.

OMAN - BROADCASTING

Billboard Limited, Post Office Box 9027, 1006 AA Amsterdam, The Netherlands (Telephone Number in U.S. (212) 764-7300); *World Radio TV Handbook*.

Central Intelligence Agency, Washington, D.C. 20505 (703) 482-1100, www.cia.gov; *The World Factbook*.

Euromonitor International, Inc., 122 South Michigan Avenue, Suite 1200, Chicago, Illinois 60603 (800) 577-EURO; *World Marketing Data and Statistics*.

M.E. Sharpe, 80 Business Park Drive, Armonk, New York 10504 (800) 541-6563; *The Illustrated Book of World Rankings*.

St. Martin's Press, Inc., 175 Fifth Avenue, New York, New York 10010 (800) 221-7945; *The Statesman's Year-Book*.

OMAN - BUDGET

Central Intelligence Agency, Washington, D.C. 20505 (703) 482-1100, www.cia.gov; *The World Factbook*.

OMAN - BUSINESS AND PROFESSIONAL LICENSES

International Monetary Fund, 700 Nineteenth Street, NW, Washington, D.C. 20431 (202) 623-7000; *Government Finance Statistics Yearbook*.

OMAN - BUTTER PRODUCTION - See OMAN - DAIRY PRODUCTS

OMAN - CALORIE SUPPLY

Food and Agricultural Organization of the United Nations (FAO) Via delle Terme di Caracalla, 00100 Rome, Italy (Telephone Number in U.S. (202) 653-2400); *The State of Food and Agriculture*.

OMAN - CAPITAL REVENUE

International Monetary Fund, 700 Nineteenth Street, NW, Washington, D.C. 20431 (202) 623-7000; *Government Finance Statistics Yearbook*.

OMAN - CATTLE - See OMAN - LIVESTOCK AND POULTRY

OMAN - CEMENT PRODUCTION - See OMAN - MINING AND MINERAL PRODUCTS

OMAN - CHICKENS - See OMAN - LIVESTOCK AND POULTRY

OMAN - CIGARETTE PRODUCTION - See OMAN - TOBACCO PRODUCTION

OMAN - CLIMATE

M.E. Sharpe, 80 Business Park Drive, Armonk, New York 10504 (800) 541-6563; *The Illustrated Book of World Rankings*.

St. Martin's Press, Inc., 175 Fifth Avenue, New York, New York 10010 (800) 221-7945; *The Statesman's Year-Book*.

OMAN - COAL PRODUCTION - See OMAN - MINING AND MINERAL PRODUCTS

OMAN - COFFEE PRODUCTION AND CONSUMPTION - See OMAN - CROPS

OMAN - COMMERCE

St. Martin's Press, Inc., 175 Fifth Avenue, New York, New York 10010 (800) 221-7945; *The Statesman's Year-Book*.

OMAN - COMMUNICATIONS - See OMAN - TRANSPORTATION AND COMMUNICATIONS

OMAN - CONSTRUCTION

M.E. Sharpe, 80 Business Park Drive, Armonk, New York 10504 (800) 541-6563; *The Illustrated Book of World Rankings*.

OMAN - CONSUMER PRICES

Euromonitor International, Inc., 122 South Michigan Avenue, Suite 1200, Chicago, Illinois 60603 (800) 577-EURO; *World Marketing Data and Statistics*.

OMAN - CONSUMPTION

The World Bank, 1818 H Street, NW, Washington, D.C. 20433 (202) 477-1234; *World Development Report*.

OMAN - COPPER PRODUCTION AND CONSUMPTION - See OMAN - MINING AND MINERAL PRODUCTS

OMAN - CORN PRODUCTION - See OMAN - CROPS

OMAN - CORPORATE TAXES - See OMAN - TAXATION

OMAN - COTTON PRODUCTION - See OMAN - CROPS

OMAN - CRIME

International Criminal Police Organization (INTERPOL), 50 quai Achille Lignon, F-69006 Lyon, France; *International Crime Statistics*.

OMAN - CROPS

Europa Publications Limited, 18 Bedford Square, London, WC1B 3JN, England; *The Europa World Year Book*.

Food and Agricultural Organization of the United Nations (FAO) Via delle Terme di Caracalla, 00100 Rome, Italy (Telephone Number in U.S. (202) 653-2400); *The State of Food and Agriculture*.

M.E. Sharpe, 80 Business Park Drive, Armonk, New York 10504 (800) 541-6563; *The Illustrated Book of World Rankings*.

St. Martin's Press, Inc., 175 Fifth Avenue, New York, New York 10010 (800) 221-7945; *The Statesman's Year-Book*.

Statistical Office of the United Nations, Publishing Service, New York, New York 10017 (800) 253-9646; *Statistical Yearbook*.

United Nations Conference on Trade and Development, Central Statistical Service, Palais des Nations, Geneva, Switzerland (Telephone in U.S. (800) 253-9646); *UNCTAD Commodity Yearbook*.

OMAN - CUSTOMS DUTIES

International Monetary Fund, 700 Nineteenth Street, NW, Washington, D.C. 20431 (202) 623-7000; *Government Finance Statistics Yearbook*.

OMAN - DAIRY PRODUCTS

Economic Commission for Western Asia, Post Office Box 27, Baghdad, Iraq; *Statistical Abstract of Western Asia*.

Europa Publications Limited, 18 Bedford Square, London, WC1B 3JN, England; *The Europa World Year Book*.

Food and Agricultural Organization of the United Nations (FAO) Via delle Terme di Caracalla, 00100 Rome, Italy (Telephone Number in U.S. (202) 653-2400); *Production Yearbook;* and *The State of Food and Agriculture*.

M.E. Sharpe, 80 Business Park Drive, Armonk, New York 10504 (800) 541-6563; *The Illustrated Book of World Rankings*.

Statistical Office of the United Nations, Publishing Service, New York, New York 10017 (800) 253-9646; *Statistical Yearbook*.

OMAN - DEATH RATES - See OMAN - MORTALITY

OMAN - DEFENSE EXPENDITURES - See OMAN - MILITARY

OMAN - DEMOGRAPHY

The Economist Intelligence Unit, 111 West 57th Street, New York, New York 10019 (800) 938-4685; *The World Market Atlas.*

Euromonitor International, Inc., 122 South Michigan Avenue, Suite 1200, Chicago, Illinois 60603 (800) 577-EURO; *International Marketing Data and Statistics; The World Economic Factbook;* and *World Marketing Data and Statistics.*

M.E. Sharpe, 80 Business Park Drive, Armonk, New York 10504 (800) 541-6563; *The Illustrated Book of World Rankings.*

Statistical Office of the United Nations, Publishing Service, New York, New York 10017 (800) 253-9646; *Human Development Report.*

OMAN - DEVELOPMENT ASSISTANCE

Statistical Office of the United Nations, Publishing Service, New York, New York 10017 (800) 253-9646; *Statistical Yearbook.*

OMAN - DIAMOND PRODUCTION - See OMAN - MINING AND MINERAL PRODUCTS

OMAN - DISEASES - See OMAN - HEALTH

OMAN - DIVORCE RATES

M.E. Sharpe, 80 Business Park Drive, Armonk, New York 10504 (800) 541-6563; *The Illustrated Book of World Rankings.*

Statistical Office of the United Nations, Publishing Service, New York, New York 10017 (800) 253-9646; *Demographic Yearbook.*

OMAN - ECONOMY

Central Intelligence Agency, Washington, D.C. 20505 (703) 482-1100, www.cia.gov; *The World Factbook.*

Economist Intelligence Unit, 111 West 57th Street, New York, New York 10019 (800) 938-4685; *Oman Country Report.*

Euromonitor International, Inc., 122 South Michigan Avenue, Suite 1200, Chicago, Illinois 60603 (800) 577-EURO; *International Marketing Data and Statistics; The World Economic Factbook;* and *World Marketing Data and Statistics.*

Europa Publications Limited, 18 Bedford Square, London, WC1B 3JN, England; *The Europa World Year Book.*

M.E. Sharpe, 80 Business Park Drive, Armonk, New York 10504 (800) 541-6563;

The Illustrated Book of World Rankings.

St. Martin's Press, Inc., 175 Fifth Avenue, New York, New York 10010 (800) 221-7945; *The Statesman's Year-Book.*

Statistical Office of the United Nations, Publishing Service, New York, New York 10017 (800) 253-9646; *World Statistics Pocketbook.*

The World Bank, 1818 H Street, NW, Washington, D.C. 20433 (202) 477-1234; *The World Bank Atlas;* and *World Development Report.*

OMAN - EDUCATION

Economic Commission for Western Asia, Post Office Box 27, Baghdad, Iraq; *Statistical Abstract of Western Asia.*

The Economist Intelligence Unit, 111 West 57th Street, New York, New York 10019 (800) 938-4685; *The World Market Atlas.*

Euromonitor International, Inc., 122 South Michigan Avenue, Suite 1200, Chicago, Illinois 60603 (800) 577-EURO; *International Marketing Data and Statistics;* and *World Marketing Data and Statistics.*

Europa Publications Limited, 18 Bedford Square, London, WC1B 3JN, England; *The Europa World Year Book.*

Federal Statistical Office, Gustav - Stresemann - Ring 11, D-6200 Wiesbaden, Germany; *Oman.*

International Monetary Fund, 700 Nineteenth Street, NW, Washington, D.C. 20431 (202) 623-7000; *Government Finance Statistics Yearbook.*

M.E. Sharpe, 80 Business Park Drive, Armonk, New York 10504 (800) 541-6563; *The Illustrated Book of World Rankings.*

St. Martin's Press, Inc., 175 Fifth Avenue, New York, New York 10010 (800) 221-7945; *The Statesman's Year-Book.*

Statistical Office of the United Nations, Publishing Service, New York, New York 10017 (800) 253-9646; *Human Development Report.*

United Nations Educational, Scientific and Cultural Organization (UNESCO), 7 Place de Fontenoy, F-75700 Paris, France (Telephone Number in U.S. (212) 963-5981); *Statistical Yearbook.*

The World Bank, 1818 H Street, NW, Washington, D.C. 20433 (202) 477-1234; *World Development Report;* and *World Development Indicators.*

OMAN - EGG PRODUCTION AND

CONSUMPTION - See OMAN - DAIRY PRODUCTS

OMAN - ELECTRICITY

Central Intelligence Agency, Washington, D.C. 20505 (703) 482-1100, www.cia.gov; *The World Factbook.*

M.E. Sharpe, 80 Business Park Drive, Armonk, New York 10504 (800) 541-6563; *The Illustrated Book of World Rankings.*

Penn Well Publishing Company, 1421 South Sheridan Road, Post Office Box 1260, Tulsa, Oklahoma 74101 (800) 752-9764; *International Energy Statistics Sourcebook.*

St. Martin's Press, Inc., 175 Fifth Avenue, New York, New York 10010 (800) 221-7945; *The Statesman's Year-Book.*

Statistical Office of the United Nations, Publishing Service, New York, New York 10017 (800) 253-9646; *Human Development Report;* and *Statistical Yearbook.*

OMAN - EMPLOYMENT

Economic Commission for Western Asia, Post Office Box 27, Baghdad, Iraq; *Statistical Abstract of Western Asia.*

Euromonitor International, Inc., 122 South Michigan Avenue, Suite 1200, Chicago, Illinois 60603 (800) 577-EURO; *International Marketing Data and Statistics.*

Federal Statistical Office, Gustav - Stresemann - Ring 11, D-6200 Wiesbaden, Germany; *Oman.*

M.E. Sharpe, 80 Business Park Drive, Armonk, New York 10504 (800) 541-6563; *The Illustrated Book of World Rankings.*

Statistical Office of the United Nations, Publishing Service, New York, New York 10017 (800) 253-9646; *Bulletin of Industrial Statistics for the Arab Countries.*

OMAN - ENERGY

Economic Commission for Western Asia, Post Office Box 27, Baghdad, Iraq; *Statistical Abstract of Western Asia.*

Euromonitor International, Inc., 122 South Michigan Avenue, Suite 1200, Chicago, Illinois 60603 (800) 577-EURO; *International Marketing Data and Statistics; The World Economic Factbook;* and *World Marketing Data and Statistics.*

Food and Agricultural Organization of the United Nations (FAO) Via delle Terme di Caracalla, 00100 Rome, Italy (Telephone Number in U.S. (202) 653-2400); *The State of Food and Agriculture.*

M.E. Sharpe, 80 Business Park Drive, Armonk, New York 10504 (800) 541-6563; *The Illustrated Book of World Rankings.*

Penn Well Publishing Company, 1421 South Sheridan Road, Post Office Box 1260, Tulsa, Oklahoma 74101 (800) 752-9764; *International Energy Statistics Sourcebook.*

St. Martin's Press, Inc., 175 Fifth Avenue, New York, New York 10010 (800) 221-7945; *The Statesman's Year-Book.*

Statistical Office of the United Nations, Publishing Service, New York, New York 10017 (800) 253-9646; *Energy Statistics Yearbook; Human Development Report; World Statistics Pocketbook;* and *Statistical Yearbook.*

The World Bank, 1818 H Street, NW, Washington, D.C. 20433 (202) 477-1234; *The World Bank Atlas;* and *World Development Report.*

OMAN - ENVIRONMENT

Economist Intelligence Unit, 111 West 57th Street, New York, New York 10019 (800) 938-4685; *Oman Country Report.*

Statistical Office of the United Nations, Publishing Service, New York, New York 10017 (800) 253-9646; *World Statistics Pocketbook.*

OMAN - EXCHANGE RATES

Central Intelligence Agency, Washington, D.C. 20505 (703) 482-1100, www.cia.gov; *The World Factbook.*

Euromonitor International, Inc., 122 South Michigan Avenue, Suite 1200, Chicago, Illinois 60603 (800) 577-EURO; *International Marketing Data and Statistics;* and *The World Economic Factbook.*

Europa Publications Limited, 18 Bedford Square, London, WC1B 3JN, England; *The Europa World Year Book.*

International Monetary Fund, 700 Nineteenth Street, NW, Washington, D.C. 20431 (202) 623-7000; *International Financial Statistics.*

Statistical Office of the United Nations, Publishing Service, New York, New York 10017 (800) 253-9646; *Bulletin of Industrial Statistics for the Arab Countries; World Statistics Pocketbook;* and *Statistical Yearbook.*

OMAN - EXPORTS

Central Intelligence Agency, Washington, D.C. 20505 (703) 482-1100, www.cia.gov; *The World Factbook.*

Economic Commission for Western

Asia, Post Office Box 27, Baghdad, Iraq; *Statistical Abstract of Western Asia.*

The Economist Intelligence Unit, 111 West 57th Street, New York, New York 10019 (800) 938-4685; *Oman Country Report;* and *The World Market Atlas.*

Euromonitor International, Inc., 122 South Michigan Avenue, Suite 1200, Chicago, Illinois 60603 (800) 577-EURO; *International Marketing Data and Statistics;* and *The World Economic Factbook.*

Europa Publications Limited, 18 Bedford Square, London, WC1B 3JN, England; *The Europa World Year Book.*

Food and Agricultural Organization of the United Nations (FAO) Via delle Terme di Caracalla, 00100 Rome, Italy (Telephone Number in U.S. (202) 653-2400); *The State of Food and Agriculture.*

International Monetary Fund, 700 Nineteenth Street, NW, Washington, D.C. 20431 (202) 623-7000; *Direction of Trade Statistics;* and *International Financial Statistics.*

St. Martin's Press, Inc., 175 Fifth Avenue, New York, New York 10010 (800) 221-7945; *The Statesman's Year-Book.*

Statistical Office of the United Nations, Publishing Service, New York, New York 10017 (800) 253-9646; *Bulletin of Industrial Statistics for the Arab Countries.*

United Nations Conference on Trade and Development (UNCTAD), New York, New York 10017 (800) 253-9646; *Handbook of International Trade and Development Statistics.*

The World Bank, 1818 H Street, NW, Washington, D.C. 20433 (202) 477-1234; *World Development Report;* and *World Development Indicators.*

OMAN - EXTERNAL INDEBTEDNESS

The World Bank, 1818 H Street, NW, Washington, D.C. 20433 (202) 477-1234; *World Development Report.*

OMAN - EXTERNAL TRADE

Euromonitor International, Inc., 122 South Michigan Avenue, Suite 1200, Chicago, Illinois 60603 (800) 577-EURO; *World Marketing Data and Statistics.*

Food and Agricultural Organization of the United Nations (FAO) Via delle Terme di Caracalla, 00100 Rome, Italy (Telephone Number in U.S. (202) 653-2400); *The State of Food and Agriculture;* and *Trade Yearbook.*

Statistical Office of the United Nations,

Publishing Service, New York, New York 10017 (800) 253-9646; *Statistical Yearbook.*

OMAN - FARM CROPS - See OMAN - CROPS

OMAN - FEMALE WORKING POPULATION - See OMAN - EMPLOYMENT

OMAN - FERTILITY RATES

Central Intelligence Agency, Washington, D.C. 20505 (703) 482-1100, www.cia.gov; *The World Factbook.*

M.E. Sharpe, 80 Business Park Drive, Armonk, New York 10504 (800) 541-6563; *The Illustrated Book of World Rankings.*

Statistical Office of the United Nations, Publishing Service, New York, New York 10017 (800) 253-9646; *Human Development Report.*

The World Bank, 1818 H Street, NW, Washington, D.C. 20433 (202) 477-1234; *The World Bank Atlas; World Development Report;* and *World Development Indicators.*

OMAN - FERTILIZER

Food and Agricultural Organization of the United Nations (FAO) Via delle Terme di Caracalla, 00100 Rome, Italy (Telephone Number in U.S. (202) 653-2400); *The State of Food and Agriculture.*

Statistical Office of the United Nations, Publishing Service, New York, New York 10017 (800) 253-9646; *Statistical Yearbook.*

OMAN - FETAL MORTALITY - See OMAN - MORTALITY

OMAN - FINANCE

Economic Commission for Western Asia, Post Office Box 27, Baghdad, Iraq; *Statistical Abstract of Western Asia.*

Economist Intelligence Unit, 111 West 57th Street, New York, New York 10019 (800) 938-4685; *Oman Country Report.*

Europa Publications Limited, 18 Bedford Square, London, WC1B 3JN, England; *The Europa World Year Book.*

Federal Statistical Office, Gustav - Stresemann - Ring 11, D-6200 Wiesbaden, Germany; *Oman.*

International Monetary Fund, 700 Nineteenth Street, NW, Washington, D.C. 20431 (202) 623-7000; *Government Finance Statistics Yearbook;* and *International Financial Statistics.*

M.E. Sharpe, 80 Business Park Drive, Armonk, New York 10504 (800) 541-6563; *The Illustrated Book of World Rankings.*

St. Martin's Press, Inc., 175 Fifth Avenue, New York, New York 10010 (800) 221-7945; *The Statesman's Year-Book.*

OMAN - FISHERIES

Economic Commission for Western Asia, Post Office Box 27, Baghdad, Iraq; *Statistical Abstract of Western Asia.*

Europa Publications Limited, 18 Bedford Square, London, WC1B 3JN, England; *The Europa World Year Book.*

Federal Statistical Office, Gustav - Stresemann - Ring 11, D-6200 Wiesbaden, Germany; *Oman.*

Food and Agricultural Organization of the United Nations (FAO) Via delle Terme di Caracalla, 00100 Rome, Italy (Telephone Number in U.S. (202) 653-2400); *The State of Food and Agriculture;* and *Yearbook of Fishery Statistics.*

M.E. Sharpe, 80 Business Park Drive, Armonk, New York 10504 (800) 541-6563; *The Illustrated Book of World Rankings.*

St. Martin's Press, Inc., 175 Fifth Avenue, New York, New York 10010 (800) 221-7945; *The Statesman's Year-Book.*

Statistical Office of the United Nations, Publishing Service, New York, New York 10017 (800) 253-9646; *Statistical Yearbook.*

United Nations Conference on Trade and Development, Central Statistical Service, Palais des Nations, Geneva, Switzerland (Telephone in U.S. (800) 253-9646); *UNCTAD Commodity Yearbook.*

OMAN - FOOD

Food and Agricultural Organization of the United Nations (FAO), Via delle Terme di Caracalla, 00100 Rome, Italy (Telephone Number in U.S. (202) 653-2400); *Production Yearbook;* and *The State of Food and Agriculture.*

Statistical Office of the United Nations, Publishing Service, New York, New York 10017 (800) 253-9646; *Human Development Report.*

United Nations Conference on Trade and Development, Central Statistical Service, Palais des Nations, Geneva, Switzerland (Telephone in U.S. (800) 253-9646); *UNCTAD Commodity Yearbook.*

OMAN - FOREIGN DEBT

International Monetary Fund, 700 Nineteenth Street, NW, Washington, D.C. 20431 (202) 623-7000; *Government Finance Statistics Yearbook.*

OMAN - FOREIGN TRADE

Economic Commission for Western Asia, Post Office Box 27, Baghdad, Iraq; *Statistical Abstract of Western Asia.*

Economist Intelligence Unit, 111 West 57th Street, New York, New York 10019 (800) 938-4685; *Oman Country Report.*

Euromonitor International, Inc., 122 South Michigan Avenue, Suite 1200, Chicago, Illinois 60603 (800) 577-EURO; *International Marketing Data and Statistics;* and *The World Economic Factbook.*

Europa Publications Limited, 18 Bedford Square, London, WC1B 3JN, England; *The Europa World Year Book.*

Federal Statistical Office, Gustav - Stresemann - Ring 11, D-6200 Wiesbaden, Germany; *Oman.*

Food and Agricultural Organization of the United Nations (FAO) Via delle Terme di Caracalla, 00100 Rome, Italy (Telephone Number in U.S. (202) 653-2400); *The State of Food and Agriculture.*

M.E. Sharpe, 80 Business Park Drive, Armonk, New York 10504 (800) 541-6563; *The Illustrated Book of World Rankings.*

St. Martin's Press, Inc., 175 Fifth Avenue, New York, New York 10010 (800) 221-7945; *The Statesman's Year-Book.*

Statistical Office of the United Nations, Publishing Service, New York, New York 10017 (800) 253-9646; *Bulletin of Industrial Statistics for the Arab Countries; International Trade Statistics Yearbook;* and *Statistical Yearbook.*

United Nations Conference on Trade and Development, Central Statistical Service, Palais des Nations, Geneva, Switzerland (Telephone in U.S. (800) 253-9646); *UNCTAD Commodity Yearbook.*

The World Bank, 1818 H Street, NW, Washington, D.C. 20433 (202) 477-1234; *World Development Report;* and *World Development Indicators.*

OMAN - FOREIGN TRADE - INDEX NUMBERS

Economic Commission for Western Asia, Post Office Box 27, Baghdad, Iraq; *Statistical Abstract of Western Asia.*

OMAN - FORESTRY AND FOREST PRODUCTS

Food and Agricultural Organization of the United Nations (FAO) Via delle Terme di Caracalla, 00100 Rome, Italy (Telephone Number in U.S. (202) 653-2400); *The State of Food and Agriculture;* and *Yearbook of Forest Products.*

M.E. Sharpe, 80 Business Park Drive, Armonk, New York 10504 (800) 541-6563; *The Illustrated Book of World Rankings.*

United Nations Conference on Trade and Development, Central Statistical Service, Palais des Nations, Geneva, Switzerland (Telephone in U.S. (800) 253-9646); *UNCTAD Commodity Yearbook.*

The World Bank, 1818 H Street, NW, Washington, D.C. 20433 (202) 477-1234; *World Development Report.*

OMAN - GAS (NATURAL) PRODUCTION - See OMAN - MINING AND MINERAL PRODUCTS

OMAN - GENERAL MORTALITY - See OMAN - MORTALITY

OMAN - GOLD HOLDINGS

International Monetary Fund, 700 Nineteenth Street, NW, Washington, D.C. 20431 (202) 623-7000; *International Financial Statistics.*

Statistical Office of the United Nations, Publishing Service, New York, New York 10017 (800) 253-9646; *Statistical Yearbook.*

The World Bank, 1818 H Street, NW, Washington, D.C. 20433 (202) 477-1234; *World Development Indicators.*

OMAN - GOLD PRODUCTION AND CONSUMPTION - See OMAN - MINING AND MINERAL PRODUCTS

OMAN - GOVERNMENT

Central Intelligence Agency, Washington, D.C. 20505 (703) 482-1100, www.cia.gov; *The World Factbook.*

Economic Commission for Western Asia, Post Office Box 27, Baghdad, Iraq; *Statistical Abstract of Western Asia.*

Europa Publications Limited, 18 Bedford Square, London, WC1B 3JN, England; *The Europa World Year Book.*

International Monetary Fund, 700 Nineteenth Street, NW, Washington, D.C. 20431 (202) 623-7000; *Government Finance Statistics Yearbook.*

St. Martin's Press, Inc., 175 Fifth Avenue, New York, New York 10010 (800) 221-7945; *The Statesman's Year-Book.*

Statistical Office of the United Nations, Publishing Service, New York, New York 10017 (800) 253-9646; *National Accounts Statistics.*

The World Bank, 1818 H Street, NW, Washington, D.C. 20433 (202) 477-1234; *World Development Report;* and *World*

Development Indicators.

OMAN - GRAIN PRODUCTION - See OMAN - CROPS

OMAN - GRANTS

International Monetary Fund, 700 Nineteenth Street, NW, Washington, D.C. 20431 (202) 623-7000; *Government Finance Statistics Yearbook.*

OMAN - GROSS DOMESTIC PRODUCT

Economic Commission for Western Asia, Post Office Box 27, Baghdad, Iraq; *Statistical Abstract of Western Asia.*

The Economist Intelligence Unit, 111 West 57th Street, New York, New York 10019 (800) 938-4685; *Oman Country Report;* and *The World Market Atlas.*

Euromonitor International, Inc., 122 South Michigan Avenue, Suite 1200, Chicago, Illinois 60603 (800) 577-EURO; *International Marketing Data and Statistics;* and *The World Economic Factbook.*

Europa Publications Limited, 18 Bedford Square, London, WC1B 3JN, England; *The Europa World Year Book.*

M.E. Sharpe, 80 Business Park Drive, Armonk, New York 10504 (800) 541-6563; *The Illustrated Book of World Rankings.*

Statistical Office of the United Nations, Publishing Service, New York, New York 10017 (800) 253-9646; *Bulletin of Industrial Statistics for the Arab Countries; Human Development Report; National Accounts Statistics;* and *Statistical Yearbook.*

The World Bank, 1818 H Street, NW, Washington, D.C. 20433 (202) 477-1234; *World Development Report;* and *World Development Indicators.*

OMAN - GROSS NATIONAL PRODUCT

Euromonitor International, Inc., 122 South Michigan Avenue, Suite 1200, Chicago, Illinois 60603 (800) 577-EURO; *International Marketing Data and Statistics.*

St. Martin's Press, Inc., 175 Fifth Avenue, New York, New York 10010 (800) 221-7945; *The Statesman's Year-Book.*

U.S. Arms Control and Disarmament Agency, 320 Twenty-first Street, NW, Washington, D.C. 20451 (202) 647-8677; *World Military Expenditures and Arms Transfers.*

The World Bank, 1818 H Street, NW, Washington, D.C. 20433 (202) 477-1234; *The World Bank Atlas; World Development Report;* and *World Development Indicators.*

OMAN - HEALTH

Economic Commission for Western Asia, Post Office Box 27, Baghdad, Iraq; *Statistical Abstract of Western Asia.*

Euromonitor International, Inc., 122 South Michigan Avenue, Suite 1200, Chicago, Illinois 60603 (800) 577-EURO; *World Marketing Data and Statistics.*

Federal Statistical Office, Gustav - Stresemann - Ring 11, D-6200 Wiesbaden, Germany; *Oman.*

M.E. Sharpe, 80 Business Park Drive, Armonk, New York 10504 (800) 541-6563; *The Illustrated Book of World Rankings.*

St. Martin's Press, Inc., 175 Fifth Avenue, New York, New York 10010 (800) 221-7945; *The Statesman's Year-Book.*

Statistical Office of the United Nations, Publishing Service, New York, New York 10017 (800) 253-9646; *Human Development Report;* and *Statistical Yearbook.*

United Nations Children's Fund (UNICEF), 3 United Nations Plaza, New York, New York 10017 (800) 253-9646; *State of the World's Children.*

The World Bank, 1818 H Street, NW, Washington, D.C. 20433 (202) 477-1234; *World Development Report.*

World Health Organization, Office of Publications, 20 Avenue Appia, CH-1211 Geneva 27, Switzerland (Telephone Number in U.S. (518) 436-9686); *World Health Statistics Annual.*

OMAN - HEALTH EXPENDITURES

International Monetary Fund, 700 Nineteenth Street, NW, Washington, D.C. 20431 (202) 623-7000; *Government Finance Statistics Yearbook.*

OMAN - HIDE PRODUCTION

Food and Agricultural Organization of the United Nations (FAO), Via delle Terme di Caracalla, 00100 Rome, Italy (Telephone Number in U.S. (202) 653-2400); *Production Yearbook.*

OMAN - HIGHWAYS

Central Intelligence Agency, Washington, D.C. 20505 (703) 482-1100, www.cia.gov; *The World Factbook.*

Economic Commission for Western Asia, Post Office Box 27, Baghdad, Iraq; *Statistical Abstract of Western Asia.*

St. Martin's Press, Inc., 175 Fifth Avenue, New York, New York 10010 (800)

221-7945; *The Statesman's Year-Book.*

OMAN - HORSES - See OMAN - LIVESTOCK AND POULTRY

OMAN - HOURS OF WORK - See OMAN - EMPLOYMENT

OMAN - HOUSING AND HOUSING UNITS

Euromonitor International, Inc., 122 South Michigan Avenue, Suite 1200, Chicago, Illinois 60603 (800) 577-EURO; *World Marketing Data and Statistics.*

OMAN - HOUSING EXPENDITURES

International Monetary Fund, 700 Nineteenth Street, NW, Washington, D.C. 20431 (202) 623-7000; *Government Finance Statistics Yearbook.*

M.E. Sharpe, 80 Business Park Drive, Armonk, New York 10504 (800) 541-6563; *The Illustrated Book of World Rankings.*

OMAN - ILLITERATE POPULATION

Central Intelligence Agency, Washington, D.C. 20505 (703) 482-1100, www.cia.gov; *The World Factbook.*

The Economist Intelligence Unit, 111 West 57th Street, New York, New York 10019 (800) 938-4685; *The World Market Atlas.*

Euromonitor International, Inc., 122 South Michigan Avenue, Suite 1200, Chicago, Illinois 60603 (800) 577-EURO; *The World Economic Factbook.*

Statistical Office of the United Nations, Publishing Service, New York, New York 10017 (800) 253-9646; *Human Development Report.*

OMAN - IMPORTS

Central Intelligence Agency, Washington, D.C. 20505 (703) 482-1100, www.cia.gov; *The World Factbook.*

Economic Commission for Western Asia, Post Office Box 27, Baghdad, Iraq; *Statistical Abstract of Western Asia.*

The Economist Intelligence Unit, 111 West 57th Street, New York, New York 10019 (800) 938-4685; *Oman Country Report;* and *The World Market Atlas.*

Euromonitor International, Inc., 122 South Michigan Avenue, Suite 1200, Chicago, Illinois 60603 (800) 577-EURO; *International Marketing Data and Statistics;* and *The World Economic Factbook.*

Europa Publications Limited, 18 Bedford Square, London, WC1B 3JN, England; *The Europa World Year Book.*

Food and Agricultural Organization of the United Nations (FAO) Via delle Terme di Caracalla, 00100 Rome, Italy (Telephone Number in U.S. (202) 653-2400); *The State of Food and Agriculture.*

International Monetary Fund, 700 Nineteenth Street, NW, Washington, D.C. 20431 (202) 623-7000; *Direction of Trade Statistics; Government Finance Statistics Yearbook;* and *International Financial Statistics.*

St. Martin's Press, Inc., 175 Fifth Avenue, New York, New York 10010 (800) 221-7945; *The Statesman's Year-Book.*

Statistical Office of the United Nations, Publishing Service, New York, New York 10017 (800) 253-9646; *Bulletin of Industrial Statistics for the Arab Countries.*

United Nations Conference on Trade and Development (UNCTAD), New York, New York 10017 (800) 253-9646; *Handbook of International Trade and Development Statistics.*

The World Bank, 1818 H Street, NW, Washington, D.C. 20433 (202) 477-1234; *World Development Report;* and *World Development Indicators.*

OMAN - INDUSTRY

Central Intelligence Agency, Washington, D.C. 20505 (703) 482-1100, www.cia.gov; *The World Factbook.*

Economist Intelligence Unit, 111 West 57th Street, New York, New York 10019 (800) 938-4685; *Oman Country Report.*

Euromonitor International, Inc., 122 South Michigan Avenue, Suite 1200, Chicago, Illinois 60603 (800) 577-EURO; *International Marketing Data and Statistics; The World Economic Factbook;* and *World Marketing Data and Statistics.*

Europa Publications Limited, 18 Bedford Square, London, WC1B 3JN, England; *The Europa World Year Book.*

Federal Statistical Office, Gustav - Stresemann - Ring 11, D-6200 Wiesbaden, Germany; *Oman.*

M.E. Sharpe, 80 Business Park Drive, Armonk, New York 10504 (800) 541-6563; *The Illustrated Book of World Rankings.*

St. Martin's Press, Inc., 175 Fifth Avenue, New York, New York 10010 (800) 221-7945; *The Statesman's Year-Book.*

Statistical Office of the United Nations, Publishing Service, New York, New York 10017 (800) 253-9646; *Bulletin of Industrial Statistics for the Arab Countries.*

The World Bank, 1818 H Street, NW, Washington, D.C. 20433 (202) 477-1234; *World Development Indicators.*

OMAN - INFANT AND MATERNAL MORTALITY - See OMAN - MORTALITY

OMAN - INTERNATIONAL LIQUIDITY

International Monetary Fund, 700 Nineteenth Street, NW, Washington, D.C. 20431 (202) 623-7000; *International Financial Statistics.*

OMAN - INTERNATIONAL RESERVES EXCLUDING GOLD

Statistical Office of the United Nations, Publishing Service, New York, New York 10017 (800) 253-9646; *Statistical Yearbook.*

The World Bank, 1818 H Street, NW, Washington, D.C. 20433 (202) 477-1234; *World Development Indicators.*

OMAN - IRON ORE PRODUCTION AND CONSUMPTION - See OMAN - MINING AND MINERAL PRODUCTS

OMAN - IRRIGATION

Euromonitor International, Inc., 122 South Michigan Avenue, Suite 1200, Chicago, Illinois 60603 (800) 577-EURO; *International Marketing Data and Statistics.*

OMAN - LABOR

Central Intelligence Agency, Washington, D.C. 20505 (703) 482-1100, www.cia.gov; *The World Factbook.*

Economic Commission for Western Asia, Post Office Box 27, Baghdad, Iraq; *Statistical Abstract of Western Asia.*

Euromonitor International, Inc., 122 South Michigan Avenue, Suite 1200, Chicago, Illinois 60603 (800) 577-EURO; *International Marketing Data and Statistics;* and *World Marketing Data and Statistics.*

Europa Publications Limited, 18 Bedford Square, London, WC1B 3JN, England; *The Europa World Year Book.*

Food and Agricultural Organization of the United Nations (FAO) Via delle Terme di Caracalla, 00100 Rome, Italy (Telephone Number in U.S. (202) 653-2400); *The State of Food and Agriculture.*

M.E. Sharpe, 80 Business Park Drive, Armonk, New York 10504 (800) 541-6563; *The Illustrated Book of World Rankings.*

St. Martin's Press, Inc., 175 Fifth Avenue, New York, New York 10010 (800) 221-7945; *The Statesman's Year-Book.*

Statistical Office of the United Nations, Publishing Service, New York, New York 10017 (800) 253-9646; *Human Development Report.*

The World Bank, 1818 H Street, NW, Washington, D.C. 20433 (202) 477-1234; *The World Bank Atlas; World Development Report;* and *World Development Indicators.*

OMAN - LAND USE

Central Intelligence Agency, Washington, D.C. 20505 (703) 482-1100, www.cia.gov; *The World Factbook.*

Economic Commission for Western Asia, Post Office Box 27, Baghdad, Iraq; *Statistical Abstract of Western Asia.*

Euromonitor International, Inc., 122 South Michigan Avenue, Suite 1200, Chicago, Illinois 60603 (800) 577-EURO; *International Marketing Data and Statistics.*

Food and Agricultural Organization of the United Nations (FAO), Via delle Terme di Caracalla, 00100 Rome, Italy (Telephone Number in U.S. (202) 653-2400); *Production Yearbook.*

The World Bank, 1818 H Street, NW, Washington, D.C. 20433 (202) 477-1234; *World Development Report.*

OMAN - LIBRARIES

M.E. Sharpe, 80 Business Park Drive, Armonk, New York 10504 (800) 541-6563; *The Illustrated Book of World Rankings.*

OMAN - LIFE EXPECTANCY

Central Intelligence Agency, Washington, D.C. 20505 (703) 482-1100, www.cia.gov; *The World Factbook.*

Euromonitor International, Inc., 122 South Michigan Avenue, Suite 1200, Chicago, Illinois 60603 (800) 577-EURO; *The World Economic Factbook.*

St. Martin's Press, Inc., 175 Fifth Avenue, New York, New York 10010 (800) 221-7945; *The Statesman's Year-Book.*

Statistical Office of the United Nations, Publishing Service, New York, New York 10017 (800) 253-9646; *Human Development Report;* and *World Statistics Pocketbook.*

The World Bank, 1818 H Street, NW, Washington, D.C. 20433 (202) 477-1234; *The World Bank Atlas;* and *World Development Report.*

OMAN - LITERACY RATE

Euromonitor International, Inc., 122

South Michigan Avenue, Suite 1200, Chicago, Illinois 60603 (800) 577-EURO; *World Marketing Data and Statistics.*

OMAN - LIVESTOCK AND POULTRY

Economic Commission for Western Asia, Post Office Box 27, Baghdad, Iraq; *Statistical Abstract of Western Asia.*

Euromonitor International, Inc., 122 South Michigan Avenue, Suite 1200, Chicago, Illinois 60603 (800) 577-EURO; *International Marketing Data and Statistics.*

Europa Publications Limited, 18 Bedford Square, London, WC1B 3JN, England; *The Europa World Year Book.*

Food and Agricultural Organization of the United Nations (FAO), Via delle Terme di Caracalla, 00100 Rome, Italy (Telephone Number in U.S. (202) 653-2400); *Production Yearbook;* and *The State of Food and Agriculture.*

M.E. Sharpe, 80 Business Park Drive, Armonk, New York 10504 (800) 541-6563; *The Illustrated Book of World Rankings.*

Statistical Office of the United Nations, Publishing Service, New York, New York 10017 (800) 253-9646; *Statistical Yearbook.*

United Nations Conference on Trade and Development, Central Statistical Service, Palais des Nations, Geneva, Switzerland (Telephone in U.S. (800) 253-9646); *UNCTAD Commodity Yearbook.*

OMAN - LIVING LEVELS - See OMAN - LIFE EXPECTANCY

OMAN - MANUFACTURING

M.E. Sharpe, 80 Business Park Drive, Armonk, New York 10504 (800) 541-6563; *The Illustrated Book of World Rankings.*

Statistical Office of the United Nations, Publishing Service, New York, New York 10017 (800) 253-9646; *Bulletin of Industrial Statistics for the Arab Countries.*

The World Bank, 1818 H Street, NW, Washington, D.C. 20433 (202) 477-1234; *World Development Indicators.*

OMAN - MARRIAGE RATES

M.E. Sharpe, 80 Business Park Drive, Armonk, New York 10504 (800) 541-6563; *The Illustrated Book of World Rankings.*

Statistical Office of the United Nations, Publishing Service, New York, New York 10017 (800) 253-9646; *Demographic Yearbook.*

OMAN - MEAT PRODUCTION - See OMAN -

LIVESTOCK AND POULTRY

OMAN - MERCHANT SHIPPING

Economic Commission for Western Asia, Post Office Box 27, Baghdad, Iraq; *Statistical Abstract of Western Asia.*

Europa Publications Limited, 18 Bedford Square, London, WC1B 3JN, England; *The Europa World Year Book.*

Lloyd's Register of Shipping, 17 Battery Place, New York, New York 10004 (212) 425-8050; *Register of Ships.*

St. Martin's Press, Inc., 175 Fifth Avenue, New York, New York 10010 (800) 221-7945; *The Statesman's Year-Book.*

Statistical Office of the United Nations, Publishing Service, New York, New York 10017 (800) 253-9646; *Statistical Yearbook.*

OMAN - MILITARY

Central Intelligence Agency, Washington, D.C. 20505 (703) 482-1100, www.cia.gov; *The World Factbook.*

Euromonitor International, Inc., 122 South Michigan Avenue, Suite 1200, Chicago, Illinois 60603 (800) 577-EURO; *World Marketing Data and Statistics.*

The International Institute for Strategic Studies, 23 Tavistock Street, London WC2E 7NQ, England; *The Military Balance.*

International Monetary Fund, 700 Nineteenth Street, NW, Washington, D.C. 20431 (202) 623-7000; *Government Finance Statistics Yearbook.*

St. Martin's Press, Inc., 175 Fifth Avenue, New York, New York 10010 (800) 221-7945; *The Statesman's Year-Book.*

Statistical Office of the United Nations, Publishing Service, New York, New York 10017 (800) 253-9646; *Human Development Report.*

U.S. Arms Control and Disarmament Agency, 320 Twenty-first Street, NW, Washington, D.C. 20451 (202) 647-8677; *World Military Expenditures and Arms Transfers.*

OMAN - MILK PRODUCTION - See OMAN - DAIRY PRODUCTS

OMAN - MINING AND MINERAL PRODUCTS

Economic Commission for Western Asia, Post Office Box 27, Baghdad, Iraq; *Statistical Abstract of Western Asia.*

Europa Publications Limited, 18 Bedford Square, London, WC1B 3JN, England; *The Europa World Year Book.*

M.E. Sharpe, 80 Business Park Drive, Armonk, New York 10504 (800) 541-6563; *The Illustrated Book of World Rankings.*

Penn Well Publishing Company, 1421 South Sheridan Road, Post Office Box 1260, Tulsa, Oklahoma 74101 (800) 752-9764; *International Energy Statistics Sourcebook.*

St. Martin's Press, Inc., 175 Fifth Avenue, New York, New York 10010 (800) 221-7945; *The Statesman's Year-Book.*

Statistical Office of the United Nations, Publishing Service, New York, New York 10017 (800) 253-9646; *Bulletin of Industrial Statistics for the Arab Countries;* and *Statistical Yearbook.*

United Nations Conference on Trade and Development, Central Statistical Service, Palais des Nations, Geneva, Switzerland (Telephone in U.S. (800) 253-9646); *UNCTAD Commodity Yearbook.*

OMAN - MONEY EXCHANGE RATES - See OMAN - EXCHANGE RATES

OMAN - MONEY RESERVES

Euromonitor International, Inc., 122 South Michigan Avenue, Suite 1200, Chicago, Illinois 60603 (800) 577-EURO; *International Marketing Data and Statistics.*

OMAN - MONEY SUPPLY

Economic Commission for Western Asia, Post Office Box 27, Baghdad, Iraq; *Statistical Abstract of Western Asia.*

Economist Intelligence Unit, 111 West 57th Street, New York, New York 10019 (800) 938-4685; *Oman Country Report.*

Euromonitor International, Inc., 122 South Michigan Avenue, Suite 1200, Chicago, Illinois 60603 (800) 577-EURO; *International Marketing Data and Statistics.*

Europa Publications Limited, 18 Bedford Square, London, WC1B 3JN, England; *The Europa World Year Book.*

International Monetary Fund, 700 Nineteenth Street, NW, Washington, D.C. 20431 (202) 623-7000; *International Financial Statistics.*

The World Bank, 1818 H Street, NW, Washington, D.C. 20433 (202) 477-1234; *World Development Indicators.*

OMAN - MORTALITY

Central Intelligence Agency, Washington, D.C. 20505 (703) 482-1100, www.cia.gov; *The World Factbook.*

Euromonitor International, Inc., 122 South Michigan Avenue, Suite 1200, Chicago, Illinois 60603 (800) 577-EURO; *International Marketing Data and Statistics;* and *The World Economic Factbook.*

Europa Publications Limited, 18 Bedford Square, London, WC1B 3JN, England; *The Europa World Year Book.*

M.E. Sharpe, 80 Business Park Drive, Armonk, New York 10504 (800) 541-6563; *The Illustrated Book of World Rankings.*

Statistical Office of the United Nations, Publishing Service, New York, New York 10017 (800) 253-9646; *Demographic Yearbook; Human Development Report;* and *World Statistics Pocketbook.*

United Nations Children's Fund (UNICEF), 3 United Nations Plaza, New York, New York 10017 (800) 253-9646; *State of the World's Children.*

The World Bank, 1818 H Street, NW, Washington, D.C. 20433 (202) 477-1234; *The World Bank Atlas; World Development Report;* and *World Development Indicators.*

World Health Organization, Office of Publications, 20 Avenue Appia, CH-1211 Geneva 27, Switzerland (Telephone Number in U.S. (518) 436-9686); *World Health Statistics Annual.*

OMAN - MOTION PICTURES

Statistical Office of the United Nations, Publishing Service, New York, New York 10017 (800) 253-9646; *Statistical Yearbook.*

OMAN - MOTOR VEHICLE PRODUCTION

American Automobile Manufacturers Association, 1401 H Street, NW, Suite 900, Washington, D.C. 20005 (202) 326-5500; *World Motor Vehicle Data.*

Europa Publications Limited, 18 Bedford Square, London, WC1B 3JN, England; *The Europa World Year Book.*

OMAN - MOTOR VEHICLE TAXES - See OMAN - TAXATION

OMAN - MOTOR VEHICLES

Economic Commission for Western Asia, Post Office Box 27, Baghdad, Iraq; *Statistical Abstract of Western Asia.*

OMAN - MOTOR VEHICLES IN USE

American Automobile Manufacturers Association, 1401 H Street, NW, Suite 900, Washington, D.C. 20005 (202) 326-5500; *World Motor Vehicle Data.*

OMAN - MUSEUMS

M.E. Sharpe, 80 Business Park Drive, Armonk, New York 10504 (800) 541-6563; *The Illustrated Book of World Rankings.*

OMAN - NATALITY - See OMAN - BIRTH RATES

OMAN - NATIONAL ACCOUNTS

Economic Commission for Western Asia, Post Office Box 27, Baghdad, Iraq; *Statistical Abstract of Western Asia.*

Europa Publications Limited, 18 Bedford Square, London, WC1B 3JN, England; *The Europa World Year Book.*

Federal Statistical Office, Gustav - Stresemann - Ring 11, D-6200 Wiesbaden, Germany; *Oman.*

Statistical Office of the United Nations, Publishing Service, New York, New York 10017 (800) 253-9646; *Statistical Yearbook.*

OMAN - NATIONAL INCOME

M.E. Sharpe, 80 Business Park Drive, Armonk, New York 10504 (800) 541-6563; *The Illustrated Book of World Rankings.*

Statistical Office of the United Nations, Publishing Service, New York, New York 10017 (800) 253-9646; *National Accounts Statistics;* and *Statistical Yearbook.*

OMAN - NATIONAL PRODUCT

M.E. Sharpe, 80 Business Park Drive, Armonk, New York 10504 (800) 541-6563; *The Illustrated Book of World Rankings.*

OMAN - NATURAL GAS PRODUCTION - See OMAN - MINING AND MINERAL PRODUCTS

OMAN - PEANUT PRODUCTION - See OMAN - CROPS

OMAN - PESTICIDE USE

Food and Agricultural Organization of the United Nations (FAO) Via delle Terme di Caracalla, 00100 Rome, Italy (Telephone Number in U.S. (202) 653-2400); *The State of Food and Agriculture.*

OMAN - PETROLEUM INDUSTRY

Food and Agricultural Organization of the United Nations (FAO) Via delle Terme di Caracalla, 00100 Rome, Italy (Telephone Number in U.S. (202) 653-2400); *The State of Food and Agriculture.*

M.E. Sharpe, 80 Business Park Drive, Armonk, New York 10504 (800) 541-6563; *The Illustrated Book of World Rankings.*

Penn Well Publishing Company, 1421 South Sheridan Road, Post Office Box 1260, Tulsa, Oklahoma 74101 (800) 752-9764;

M.E. Sharpe, 80 Business Park Drive, Armonk, New York 10504 (800) 541-6563; *The Illustrated Book of World Rankings.*

International Energy Statistics Sourcebook.

St. Martin's Press, Inc., 175 Fifth Avenue, New York, New York 10010 (800) 221-7945; *The Statesman's Year-Book.*

Statistical Office of the United Nations, Publishing Service, New York, New York 10017 (800) 253-9646; *Statistical Yearbook.*

United Nations Conference on Trade and Development, Central Statistical Service, Palais des Nations, Geneva, Switzerland (Telephone in U.S. (800) 253-9646); *UNCTAD Commodity Yearbook.*

OMAN - PIGS - See OMAN - LIVESTOCK AND POULTRY

OMAN - POPULATION

Central Intelligence Agency, Washington, D.C. 20505 (703) 482-1100, www.cia.gov; *The World Factbook.*

Economic Commission for Western Asia, Post Office Box 27, Baghdad, Iraq; *Statistical Abstract of Western Asia.*

The Economist Intelligence Unit, 111 West 57th Street, New York, New York 10019 (800) 938-4685; *Oman Country Report;* and *The World Market Atlas.*

Euromonitor International, Inc., 122 South Michigan Avenue, Suite 1200, Chicago, Illinois 60603 (800) 577-EURO; *International Marketing Data and Statistics;* and *The World Economic Factbook.*

Europa Publications Limited, 18 Bedford Square, London, WC1B 3JN, England; *The Europa World Year Book.*

Federal Statistical Office, Gustav - Stresemann - Ring 11, D-6200 Wiesbaden, Germany; *Oman.*

Food and Agricultural Organization of the United Nations (FAO), Via delle Terme di Caracalla, 00100 Rome, Italy (Telephone Number in U.S. (202) 653-2400); *Production Yearbook.*

M.E. Sharpe, 80 Business Park Drive, Armonk, New York 10504 (800) 541-6563; *The Illustrated Book of World Rankings.*

St. Martin's Press, Inc., 175 Fifth Avenue, New York, New York 10010 (800) 221-7945; *The Statesman's Year-Book.*

Statistical Office of the United Nations, Publishing Service, New York, New York 10017 (800) 253-9646; *Demographic Yearbook; Human Development Report; Statistical Yearbook;* and *World Statistics Pocketbook.*

U.S. Arms Control and Disarmament Agency, 320 Twenty-first Street, NW,

Washington, D.C. 20451 (202) 647-8677; *World Military Expenditures and Arms Transfers.*

The World Bank, 1818 H Street, NW, Washington, D.C. 20433 (202) 477-1234; *The World Bank Atlas;* and *World Development Report.*

World Health Organization, Office of Publications, 20 Avenue Appia, CH-1211 Geneva 27, Switzerland (Telephone Number in U.S. (518) 436-9686); *World Health Statistics Annual.*

OMAN - POST OFFICES

M.E. Sharpe, 80 Business Park Drive, Armonk, New York 10504 (800) 541-6563; *The Illustrated Book of World Rankings.*

St. Martin's Press, Inc., 175 Fifth Avenue, New York, New York 10010 (800) 221-7945; *The Statesman's Year-Book.*

OMAN - POTATO PRODUCTION - See OMAN - CROPS

OMAN - PRICES

Economic Commission for Western Asia, Post Office Box 27, Baghdad, Iraq; *Statistical Abstract of Western Asia.*

Federal Statistical Office, Gustav - Stresemann - Ring 11, D-6200 Wiesbaden, Germany; *Oman.*

Food and Agricultural Organization of the United Nations (FAO), Via delle Terme di Caracalla, 00100 Rome, Italy (Telephone Number in U.S. (202) 653-2400); *Production Yearbook;* and *The State of Food and Agriculture.*

M.E. Sharpe, 80 Business Park Drive, Armonk, New York 10504 (800) 541-6563; *The Illustrated Book of World Rankings.*

OMAN - PRODUCTION

American Automobile Manufacturers Association, 1401 H Street, NW, Suite 900, Washington, D.C. 20005 (202) 326-5500; *World Motor Vehicle Data.*

M.E. Sharpe, 80 Business Park Drive, Armonk, New York 10504 (800) 541-6563; *The Illustrated Book of World Rankings.*

OMAN - PRODUCTIVITY

Euromonitor International, Inc., 122 South Michigan Avenue, Suite 1200, Chicago, Illinois 60603 (800) 577-EURO; *International Marketing Data and Statistics.*

OMAN - PROPERTY TAXES - See OMAN - TAXATION

OMAN - PUBLIC FINANCE - See OMAN - FINANCE

OMAN - RADIO BROADCASTING - See OMAN - BROADCASTING

OMAN - RADIO RECEIVERS

St. Martin's Press, Inc., 175 Fifth Avenue, New York, New York 10010 (800) 221-7945; *The Statesman's Year-Book.*

OMAN - RELIGION

Central Intelligence Agency, Washington, D.C. 20505 (703) 482-1100, www.cia.gov; *The World Factbook.*

M.E. Sharpe, 80 Business Park Drive, Armonk, New York 10504 (800) 541-6563; *The Illustrated Book of World Rankings.*

OMAN - RETAIL TRADE

Euromonitor International, Inc., 122 South Michigan Avenue, Suite 1200, Chicago, Illinois 60603 (800) 577-EURO; *World Marketing Data and Statistics.*

OMAN - RICE PRODUCTION - See OMAN - CROPS

OMAN - ROUNDWOOD PRODUCTION - See OMAN - FORESTRY AND FOREST PRODUCTS

OMAN - RUBBER PRODUCTION AND CONSUMPTION

M.E. Sharpe, 80 Business Park Drive, Armonk, New York 10504 (800) 541-6563; *The Illustrated Book of World Rankings.*

OMAN - SAWNWOOD PRODUCTION - See OMAN - FORESTRY AND FOREST PRODUCTS

OMAN - SENIOR CITIZENS

M.E. Sharpe, 80 Business Park Drive, Armonk, New York 10504 (800) 541-6563; *The Illustrated Book of World Rankings.*

OMAN - SHEEP - See OMAN - LIVESTOCK AND POULTRY

OMAN - SILVER PRODUCTION AND CONSUMPTION - See OMAN - MINING AND MINERAL PRODUCTS

OMAN - SOCIAL DATA

M.E. Sharpe, 80 Business Park Drive, Armonk, New York 10504 (800) 541-6563; *The Illustrated Book of World Rankings.*

Statistical Office of the United Nations, Publishing Service, New York, New York 10017 (800) 253-9646; *World Statistics Pocketbook.*

OMAN - SOCIAL SECURITY

International Monetary Fund, 700 Nineteenth Street, NW, Washington, D.C. 20431 (202) 623-7000; *Government Finance Statistics Yearbook.*

Statistical Office of the United Nations, Publishing Service, New York, New York 10017 (800) 253-9646; *National Accounts Statistics.*

OMAN - STATE BUDGET REVENUE AND EXPENDITURES

Euromonitor International, Inc., 122 South Michigan Avenue, Suite 1200, Chicago, Illinois 60603 (800) 577-EURO; *International Marketing Data and Statistics.*

OMAN - STEEL PRODUCTION - See OMAN - MINING AND MINERAL PRODUCTS

OMAN - STOCKS - COMMODITY - MARKET PRICE - INDEX

Food and Agricultural Organization of the United Nations (FAO) Via delle Terme di Caracalla, 00100 Rome, Italy (Telephone Number in U.S. (202) 653-2400); *The State of Food and Agriculture.*

OMAN - SUGAR PRODUCTION AND CONSUMPTION - See OMAN - CROPS

OMAN - TAX REVENUES - See OMAN - TAXATION

OMAN - TAXATION

Europa Publications Limited, 18 Bedford Square, London, WC1B 3JN, England; *The Europa World Year Book.*

International Monetary Fund, 700 Nineteenth Street, NW, Washington, D.C. 20431 (202) 623-7000; *Government Finance Statistics Yearbook.*

The World Bank, 1818 H Street, NW, Washington, D.C. 20433 (202) 477-1234; *World Development Indicators.*

OMAN - TELEPHONES IN USE

American Telephone and Telegraph Company, 26 Parsippany Road, Whippany, New Jersey 07981 (800) 222-0300; *The World's Telephones.*

Central Intelligence Agency, Washington, D.C. 20505 (703) 482-1100, www.cia.gov; *The World Factbook.*

Europa Publications Limited, 18 Bedford Square, London, WC1B 3JN, England; *The Europa World Year Book.*

St. Martin's Press, Inc., 175 Fifth Avenue, New York, New York 10010 (800)

221-7945; *The Statesman's Year-Book.*

Statistical Office of the United Nations, Publishing Service, New York, New York 10017 (800) 253-9646; *Statistical Yearbook;* and *World Statistics Pocketbook.*

OMAN - TELEVISION BROADCASTING - See OMAN - BROADCASTING

OMAN - TEXTILE INDUSTRY

M.E. Sharpe, 80 Business Park Drive, Armonk, New York 10504 (800) 541-6563; *The Illustrated Book of World Rankings.*

United Nations Conference on Trade and Development, Central Statistical Service, Palais des Nations, Geneva, Switzerland (Telephone in U.S. (800) 253-9646); *UNCTAD Commodity Yearbook.*

OMAN - TOBACCO PRODUCTION

M.E. Sharpe, 80 Business Park Drive, Armonk, New York 10504 (800) 541-6563; *The Illustrated Book of World Rankings.*

Statistical Office of the United Nations, Publishing Service, New York, New York 10017 (800) 253-9646; *Statistical Yearbook.*

OMAN - TOURISM

Economic Commission for Western Asia, Post Office Box 27, Baghdad, Iraq; *Statistical Abstract of Western Asia.*

Euromonitor International, Inc., 122 South Michigan Avenue, Suite 1200, Chicago, Illinois 60603 (800) 577-EURO; *The World Economic Factbook;* and *World Marketing Data and Statistics.*

Federal Statistical Office, Gustav - Stresemann - Ring 11, D-6200 Wiesbaden, Germany; *Oman.*

M.E. Sharpe, 80 Business Park Drive, Armonk, New York 10504 (800) 541-6563; *The Illustrated Book of World Rankings.*

World Tourism Organization, Calle Capitan Haya 42, E-28020 Madrid, Spain; *Yearbook of Tourism Statistics.*

OMAN - TRADE - See OMAN - FOREIGN TRADE

OMAN - TRANSPORTATION AND COMMUNICATIONS

Central Intelligence Agency, Washington, D.C. 20505 (703) 482-1100, www.cia.gov; *The World Factbook.*

Economic Commission for Western Asia, Post Office Box 27, Baghdad, Iraq; *Statistical Abstract of Western Asia.*

Euromonitor International, Inc., 122

South Michigan Avenue, Suite 1200, Chicago, Illinois 60603 (800) 577-EURO; *International Marketing Data and Statistics;* and *World Marketing Data and Statistics.*

Europa Publications Limited, 18 Bedford Square, London, WC1B 3JN, England; *The Europa World Year Book.*

Federal Statistical Office, Gustav - Stresemann - Ring 11, D-6200 Wiesbaden, Germany; *Oman.*

M.E. Sharpe, 80 Business Park Drive, Armonk, New York 10504 (800) 541-6563; *The Illustrated Book of World Rankings.*

St. Martin's Press, Inc., 175 Fifth Avenue, New York, New York 10010 (800) 221-7945; *The Statesman's Year-Book.*

Statistical Office of the United Nations, Publishing Service, New York, New York 10017 (800) 253-9646; *Human Development Report.*

OMAN - UNEMPLOYMENT

Central Intelligence Agency, Washington, D.C. 20505 (703) 482-1100, www.cia.gov; *The World Factbook.*

Euromonitor International, Inc., 122 South Michigan Avenue, Suite 1200, Chicago, Illinois 60603 (800) 577-EURO; *International Marketing Data and Statistics.*

OMAN - VITAL STATISTICS

Euromonitor International, Inc., 122 South Michigan Avenue, Suite 1200, Chicago, Illinois 60603 (800) 577-EURO; *International Marketing Data and Statistics.*

World Health Organization, Office of Publications, 20 Avenue Appia, CH-1211 Geneva 27, Switzerland (Telephone Number in U.S. (518) 436-9686); *World Health Statistics Annual.*

OMAN - WAGES

Federal Statistical Office, Gustav - Stresemann - Ring 11, D-6200 Wiesbaden, Germany; *Oman.*

OMAN - WEATHER - See OMAN - CLIMATE

OMAN - WELFARE

International Monetary Fund, 700 Nineteenth Street, NW, Washington, D.C. 20431 (202) 623-7000; *Government Finance Statistics Yearbook.*

OMAN - WHEAT PRODUCTION AND CONSUMPTION - See OMAN - CROPS

OMAN - WINE PRODUCTION - See OMAN - BEVERAGES

OMAN - WOOL PRODUCTION - See OMAN - TEXTILE INDUSTRY

ONIONS

U.S. Department of Agriculture, Economic Research Service, 1800 M Street, NW, Washington, D.C. 20036 (202) 694-5050, www.ers.usda.gov; *Food Consumption, Prices, and Expenditures; Agricultural Outlook;* and *Farm Business Economic Report.*

U.S. Department of Agriculture, National Agricultural Statistics Service, Fourteenth Street and Independence Avenue, SW, Washington, D.C. 20250 (800) 727-9540, www.usda.gov/nass; *Agricultural Statistics;* and *Vegetables.*

OPERA

Opera America, 777 Fourteenth Street, NW, Suite 520, Washington, D.C. 20005 (202) 347-9262; unpublished data.

OPERATIONS PERFORMED - MEDICAL

U.S. Department of Health and Human Services, National Center for Health Statistics, 3700 East-West Highway, Hyattsville, Maryland 20782 (301) 436-8500, www.cdc.gov.nchs; *Vital and Health Statistics;* and unpublished data.

OPHTHALMOLOGISTS

American Medical Association, 515 North State Street, Chicago, Illinois 60610 (312) 464-5000; *Physician Characteristics and Distribution in the United States.*

OPTOMETRISTS

U.S. Department of Commerce, Bureau of the Census, Washington, D.C. 20233 (301) 457-4100, www.census.gov; *1997 Economic Census.*

U.S. Department of Health and Human Services, Health Care Financing Administration, 200 Independence Avenue, SW, Washington, D.C. 20201 (202) 690-6145, www.hcfa.gov; *Health Care Financing Review.*

OPTOMETRY SCHOOLS - STUDENTS, GRADUATES

U.S. Department of Health and Human Services, National Center for Health Statistics, 3700 East-West Highway, Hyattsville, Maryland 20782 (301) 436-8500, www.cdc.gov/nchs; *Health United States.*

ORANGES

U.S. Department of Agriculture, Economic Research Service, 1800 M Street, NW, Washington, D.C. 20036 (202) 694-5050, www.ers.usda.gov; *Food*

Consumption, Prices and Expenditures; and *Agricultural Outlook.*

U.S. Department of Agriculture, National Agricultural Statistics Service, Fourteenth Street and Independence Avenue, SW, Washington, D.C 20250 (800) 727-9540, www.usda.gov/nass; *Citrus Fruits.*

OREGON - See also STATE DATA (FOR INDIVIDUAL STATES)

Oregon - Primary Statistics Source

Oregon Secretary of State, Room 136, State Capitol, Salem, Oregon 97310; *Oregon Blue Book.*

Oregon - State Data Centers

Center for Population Research and Census, Portland State University, Post Office Box 751, Portland, Oregon 97207-0751, Mr. George Hough (503) 725-5159.

Documents and Microform Department, University of Oregon Library, Eugene, Oregon 97403-1299, Mr. Tom Stave (541) 346-3070.

Office of Economic Analysis, 155 Cottage Street, NE, Salem, Oregon 97310-0310, Kanhaiya L. Vaidya (503) 378-4967.

Oregon State Library, State Library Building, Salem, Oregon 97310, Mr. Craig Smith (503) 378-4277, ext. 238.

ORES, CRUDE - See also Individual Ores

ORES - CRUDE - WORLD PRODUCTION

U.S. Department of the Interior, Geological Survey, Office of Minerals Information, 12201 Sunrise Valley Drive, Reston, Virginia 22092 (703) 648-4000, www.minerals.usgs.gov; *Annual Reports;* and *Mineral Commodity Summaries.*

ORGAN TRANSPLANTS

American Association of Tissue Banks, 1350 Beverly Road, Suite 220-A, McLean, Virginia 22101 (703) 827-9582.

Eye Bank Association of America, 1001 Connecticut Avenue, NW, Suite 601, Washington, D.C. 20036-5504 (202) 775-4999.

United Network for Organ Sharing, 1100 Boulders Parkway, Suite 500, Post Office Box 13770, Richmond, Virginia 23225 (804) 330-8500.

ORPHANS

U.S. Department of Justice, Immigration and Naturalization, 425 I Street, NW, Washington, D.C. 20536 (202) 305-1613, www.ins.usdoj.gov; *Statistical Yearbook.*

OSTEOPATHS - See also PHYSICIANS

American Medical Association, 515 North State Street, Chicago, Illinois 60610 (312) 464-5000; *Physician Characteristics and Distribution in the United States.*

OTOLARYNGOLOGY

American Medical Association, 515 North State Street, Chicago, Illinois 60610 (312) 464-5000; *Physician Characteristics and Distribution in the U.S.*

OUTDOOR RECREATION ACTIVITIES - See also AMUSEMENTS, AND RECREATIONAL SERVICES, RECREATION, and Specific Forms of Recreation

National Sporting Goods Association, 1601 Feehanville Drive, Suite 300, Mount Prospect, Illinois 60056 (847) 296-6742; *Sports Participation in 1998.*

U.S. Department of Agriculture, Forest Service, Post Office Box 96090, Washington, D.C. 20090 (202) 205-8333, www.fs.fed.us; *Annual Report.*

U.S. Department of the Interior, Fish and Wildlife Service, C Street between Eighteenth and Nineteenth Streets, NW, Washington, D.C. 20240 (202) 208-5634, www.fws.gov; *National Survey of Fishing, Hunting, and Wildlife Associated Recreation.*

OUTLAYS - FEDERAL BUDGET

Executive Office of the President, Office of Management and Budget, Executive Office Building, Washington, D.C. 20503 (202) 395-3080, www.whitehouse.gov/omb; *Analytical Perspectives.*

OUTLYING AREAS - AID BY UNITED STATES GOVERNMENT

U.S. Department of Commerce, Bureau of Economic Analysis, Fourteenth Street between Constitution Avenue and E Street, NW, Washington, D.C. 20230 (202) 606-9900; *Economic Census of Outlaying Areas.*

OUTLYING AREAS - AREA

U.S. Department of Commerce, Bureau of the Census, Washington, D.C. 20233 (301) 457-4100, www.census.gov; *Census of Population and Housing;* and *Census of Population.*

OUTLYING AREAS - BANKS AND BANKING

Puerto Rico Planning Board, San Juan Puerto Rico; *Income and Product;* and *Socioeconomic Statistics.*

Federal Deposit Insurance Corporation, 550 Seventeenth Street, NW, Washington, D.C. 20429 (202) 393-8400, www.fdic.gov; *Statistics on Banking.*

OUTLYING AREAS - BIRTHS AND DEATHS

U.S. Department of Health and Human Services, National Center for Health Statistics, 3700 East-West Highway, Hyattsville, Maryland 20782 (301) 436-8500, www.cdc.gov/nchs; *Vital Statistics of the United States.*

OUTLYING AREAS - BUSINESS SUMMARY

U.S. Department of Commerce, Bureau of the Census, Washington, D.C. 20233 (301) 457-4100, www.census.gov; *Economic Census of Outlying Areas;* and *County Business Patterns.*

OUTLYING AREAS - CLIMATE (PUERTO RICO)

U.S. Department of Commerce, National Oceanic and Atmospheric Administration, National Climatic Data Center, 151 Patton Avenue, Asheville, North Carolina 28801 (828) 271-4800, www.ncdc.noaa.gov; *Climatography of the United States;* and *Comparative Climatic Data.*

OUTLYING AREAS - COMMERCE

U.S. Department of Commerce, Bureau of the Census, Washington, D.C. 20233 (301) 457-4100, www.census.gov; *Foreign Commerce and Navigation of the United States; United States Trade with Puerto Rico and United States Possessions;* and *Highlights of U.S. Export and Import Trade.*

OUTLYING AREAS - EARNINGS

U.S. Department of Commerce, Bureau of the Census, Washington, D.C. 20233 (301) 457-4100, www.census.gov; *County Business Patterns;* and *Economic Census of Outlying Areas.*

OUTLYING AREAS - EDUCATION

Puerto Rico Planning Board, San Juan, Puerto Rico; *Socioeconomic Statistics;* and *Income and Product.*

U.S. Department of Education, National Center for Education Statistics, 555 New Jersey Avenue, NW, Washington, D.C. 20208-5574 (202) 219-1828, http://hces.ed.gov; *Digest of Education Statistics.*

OUTLYING AREAS - EDUCATION - ATTAINMENT

U.S. Department of Commerce, Bureau of the Census, Washington, D.C. 20233 (301) 457-4100, www.census.gov; *Census of Population and Housing;* and *Census of Population.*

OUTLYING AREAS - EDUCATION - ENROLLMENT

U.S. Department of Education, National Center for Education Statistics, 555 New Jersey Avenue, NW, Washington, D.C. 20208-5574 (202) 219-1828, http://hces.ed.gov; unpublished data.

OUTLYING AREAS - EMPLOYEES

U.S. Department of Commerce, Bureau of the Census, Washington, D.C. 20233 (301) 457-4100, www.census.gov; *County Business Patterns;* and *Economic Census of Outlying Areas.*

OUTLYING AREAS - ESTABLISHMENTS

U.S. Department of Commerce, Bureau of the Census, Washington, D.C. 20233 (301) 457-4100, www.census.gov; *County Business Patterns;* and *Economic Census of Outlying Areas.*

OUTLYING AREAS - FEDERAL PAYMENT TO INDIVIDUALS

U.S. Department of Commerce, Bureau of the Census, Washington, D.C. 20233 (301) 457-4100, www.census.gov; *Consolidated Federal Funds Report;* and Internet site: http://www.census.gov/govs/www/cffr.htm.

OUTLYING AREAS - FINANCES

Puerto Rico Planning Board, San Juan, Puerto Rico; *Economic Report of the Governor.*

OUTLYING AREAS - FOREIGN INVESTMENT

U.S. Department of Commerce, Bureau of Economic Analysis, Fourteenth Street between Constitution Avenue and E Street, NW, Washington, D.C. 20230 (202) 606-9900, www.bea.doc.gov; *Survey of Current Business;* and *Foreign Direct Investment in the United States, Operations of U.S. Affiliates of Foreign Companies.*

OUTLYING AREAS - FOREIGN TRADE

U.S. Department of Commerce, Bureau of the Census, Washington, D.C. 20233 (301) 457-4100, www.census.gov; *Foreign Commerce and Navigation of the United States; United States Trade with Puerto Rico and United States Possessions;* and *Highlights of U.S. Export and Import Trade.*

OUTLYING AREAS - GEOGRAPHIC DATA

U.S. Department of the Interior, Geological Survey, National Center, 12201 Sunrise Valley Drive, Reston, Virginia 22092 (703) 648-4000, www.usgs.gov; *Elevations and Distances in the United States.*

OUTLYING AREAS - GROSS DOMESTIC PRODUCT

Puerto Rico Planning Board, San Juan, Puerto Rico; *Economic Report of the Governor.*

OUTLYING AREAS - HIGHWAY STATISTICS

U.S. Department of Transportation, Federal Highway Administration, 400 Seventh Street, SW, Washington, D.C. 20590 (202) 366-0660, www.fhwa.dot.gov; *Highway Statistics.*

OUTLYING AREAS - HOSPITAL FACILITIES

American Hospital Association, One North Franklin, Suite 27, Chicago, Illinois 60606 (800) 242-2626; *Hospital Statistics.*

OUTLYING AREAS - INCOME

Puerto Rico Planning Board, San Juan, Puerto Rico; *Income and Product;* and *Socioeconomic Statistics.*

U.S. Department of Commerce, Bureau of the Census, Washington, D.C. 20233 (301) 457-4100, www.census.gov; *Census of the Population and Housing;* and *Census of Population.*

OUTLYING AREAS - LABOR FORCE AND EMPLOYMENT

Puerto Rico Planning Board, San Juan, Puerto Rico; *Income and Product;* and *Socioeconomic Statistics.*

U.S. Department of Commerce, Bureau of the Census, Washington, D.C. 20233 (301) 457-4100, www.census.gov; *Census of Population and Housing;* and *Census of Population.*

OUTLYING AREAS - LANGUAGE SPOKEN

U.S. Department of Commerce, Bureau of the Census, Washington, D.C. 20233 (301) 457-4100, www.census.gov; *U.S. Census of Population and Housing;* and *Census of Population.*

OUTLYING AREAS - MARITAL STATUS

U.S. Department of Commerce, Bureau of the Census, Washington, D.C. 20233 (301) 457-4100, www.census.gov; *Census of Population.*

OUTLYING AREAS - MARRIAGE AND DIVORCE

U.S. Department of Health and Human Services, National Center for Health Statistics 3700 East-West Highway, Hyattsville, Maryland 20782 (301) 436-8500, www.cdc.gov/nchs; *Vital Statistics of the United States.*

OUTLYING AREAS - MOBILITY

U.S. Department of Commerce, Bureau of the Census, Washington, D.C. 20233 (301) 457-4100, www.census.gov; *Census of Population and Housing;* and *Census of Population.*

OUTLYING AREAS - POPULATION AND/OR AREA

Puerto Rico Planning Board, San Juan, Puerto Rico; *Socioeconomic Statistics;* and *Income and Product.*

U.S. Department of Commerce, Bureau of the Census, Washington, D.C. 20233 (301) 457-4100, www.census.gov; *Census of Population and Housing;* International Data Base; and Internet site: http://www.census.gov/population/www.estimates/puerto–rico.htm.

OUTLYING AREAS - PUBLIC AID

Social Security Administration, 6400 Security Boulevard, Baltimore, Maryland 21235 (800) 772-1213, www.ssa.gov; *Annual Statistical Supplement to the Social Security Bulletin;* and *Social Security Bulletin.*

OUTLYING AREAS - PUBLIC LIBRARIES

R.R. Bowker Company, 121 Chanlon Road, New Providence, New Jersey 07974 (908) 464-6800; *The Bowker Annual: Library and Book Trade Almanac;* and *American Library Directory.*

OUTLYING AREAS - SALES, SHIPMENTS, RECEIPTS

U.S. Department of Commerce, Bureau of the Census, Washington, D.C. 20233 (301) 457-4100, www.census.gov; *Census of Agriculture;* and *Economic Census of Outlying Areas.*

OUTLYING AREAS - SOCIAL INSURANCE

Social Security Administration, 6400 Security Boulevard, Baltimore, Maryland 21235 (800) 772-1213, www.ssa.gov; *Social Security Bulletin.*

OUTLYING AREAS - TOURISM

Puerto Rico Planning Board, San Juan, Puerto Rico; *Income and Product;* and *Socioeconomic Statistics.*

OUTLYING AREAS - UNEMPLOYMENT

INSURANCE

U.S. Department of Labor, Employment and Training Administration, 200 Constitution Avenue, NW, Washington, D.C. 20210 (202) 219-6050; *Unemployment Insurance Financial Handbook.*

OUTLYING AREAS - VITAL STATISTICS

U.S. Department of Health and Human Services, National Center for Health Statistics, 3700 East-West Highway, Hyattsville, Maryland 20782 (301) 436-8500, www.cdc.gov/nchs; *Vital Statistics of the United States.*

OUTPATIENT HOSPITAL VISITS

American Hospital Association, One North Franklin, Suite 27, Chicago, Illinois 60606 (800) 242-2626; *Hospital Statistics;* and *Annual Survey of Hospitals.*

U.S. Department of Health and Human Services, National Center for Health Statistics, 3700 East-West Highway, Hyattsville, Maryland 20782 (301) 436-8500, www.cdc.gov/nchs; *Advance Data, No. 204;* and unpublished data.

OVERWEIGHT

U.S. Department of Health and Human Services, National Center for Health Statistics, 3700 East-West Highway, Hyattsville, Maryland 20782 (301) 436-8500, www.cdc.gov/nchs; *Health United States;* and unpublished data.

OYSTERS

U.S. Department of Commerce, National Oceanic and Atmospheric Administration, National Marine Fisheries Service, 1315 East-West Highway, Silver Spring, Maryland 20910 (301) 713-2239, www.nmfs.noaa.gov; *Fisheries of the United States.*

P

PACIFIC ISLANDER POPULATION

U.S. Department of Commerce, Bureau of the Census, Washington, D.C. 20233 (301) 457-4100, www.census.gov; *Current Population Reports;* and Internet site: http://www.census.gov/population/estimates/nation/intfile3-1.txt.

PACIFIC ISLANDER POPULATION - DEGREES CONFERRED

National Science Foundation, Division of Science Resources Studies, 4201 Wilson Boulevard, Arlington, Virginia 22230 (703) 306-1234, www.nsf.gov; *Survey of Earned Doctorates, Selected Data on Science and Engineering Doctorate Awards.*

PACIFIC ISLANDS - See PALAU (REPUBLIC OF)

PAGERS

Electronics Industries Association, 2500 Wilson Boulevard, Arlington, Virginia 22201 (703) 907-7500; *Electronic Market Data Book.*

Pakistan - National Statistical Office

Federal Bureau of Statistics, Ministry of Finance and Economic Affairs, S-SLIC Building Blue Area, F-6/4, Islamabad, Pakistan.

Pakistan - Primary Statistics Sources

Manager of Publications, Government of Pakistan, Block Number 44, Shahrah-e-iraq, Karachi, Pakistan; *Statistical Pocketbook of Pakistan, Statistical Bulletin;* and *Pakistan Statistical Yearbook.*

PAKISTAN - AGRICULTURE

Asian Development Bank, Post Office Box 789, 1099 Manila, Philippines; *Key Indicators of Developing Asian and Pacific Countries.*

Economist Intelligence Unit, 111 West 57th Street, New York, New York 10019 (800) 938-4685; *Pakistan Country Report.*

Euromonitor International, Inc., 122 South Michigan Avenue, Suite 1200, Chicago. Illinois 60603 (800) 577-EURO; *International Marketing Data and Statistics;* and *World Marketing Data and Statistics.*

Europa Publications Limited, 18 Bedford Square, London, WC1B 3JN, England; *The Europa World Year Book.*

Food and Agricultural Organization of the United Nations (FAO) Via delle Terme di Caracalla, 00100 Rome, Italy (Telephone Number in U.S. (202) 653-2400); *Production Yearbook; The State of Food and Agriculture;* and *Trade Yearbook.*

M.E. Sharpe, 80 Business Park Drive, Armonk, New York 10504 (800) 541-6563; *The Illustrated Book of World Rankings.*

St. Martin's Press, Inc., 175 Fifth Avenue, New York, New York 10010 (800) 221-7945; *The Statesman's Year-Book.*

Statistical Office of the United Nations, Publishing Service, New York, New York 10017 (800) 253-9646; *Asia-Pacific in Figures; Statistical Yearbook;* and *Statistical Yearbook for Asia and the Pacific.*

United Nations Conference on Trade and Development, Central Statistical Service, Palais des Nations, Geneva, Switzerland (Telephone in U.S. (800) 253-9646); *UNCTAD Commodity Yearbook.*

The World Bank, 1818 H Street, NW, Washington, D.C. 20433 (202) 477-1234; *World Development Indicators.*

PAKISTAN - AIRLINE SERVICE

The Economist Intelligence Unit (Asia) Limited, 10th Floor, Luk Kwok Centre, 72 Gloucester Road, Wanchai, Hong Kong (Phone Number in U.S. (800) 938-4685); *Asian Market Atlas.*

Europa Publications Limited, 18 Bedford Square, London, WC1B 3JN, England; *The Europa World Year Book.*

International Civil Aviation Organization, 999 University Street, Montreal, Quebec, Canada H3C 5H7 (514) 954-8219; *Civil Aviation Statistics of the World.*

M.E. Sharpe, 80 Business Park Drive, Armonk, New York 10504 (800) 541-6563; *The Illustrated Book of World Rankings.*

St. Martin's Press, Inc., 175 Fifth Avenue, New York, New York 10010 (800) 221-7945; *The Statesman's Year-Book.*

Statistical Office of the United Nations, Publishing Service, New York, New York 10017 (800) 253-9646; *Statistical Yearbook.*

PAKISTAN - AIRPORTS

Central Intelligence Agency, Washington, D.C. 20505 (703) 482-1100, www.cia.gov; *The World Factbook.*

PAKISTAN - ALUMINUM PRODUCTION AND CONSUMPTION - See PAKISTAN - MINING AND MINERAL PRODUCTS

PAKISTAN - ANIMAL HEALTH

Food and Agricultural Organization of the United Nations (FAO), Via delle Terme di Caracalla, 00100 Rome, Italy (Telephone Number in U.S. (202) 653-2400); *Animal Health Yearbook.*

PAKISTAN - AREA AND DENSITY OF POPULATION

Central Intelligence Agency, Washington, D.C. 20505 (703) 482-1100, www.cia.gov; *The World Factbook.*

Euromonitor International, Inc., 122 South Michigan Avenue, Suite 1200, Chicago. Illinois 60603 (800) 577-EURO;

International Marketing Data and Statistics; and *The World Economic Factbook.*

Europa Publications Limited, 18 Bedford Square, London, WC1B 3JN, England; *The Europa World Year Book.*

Food and Agricultural Organization of the United Nations (FAO) Via delle Terme di Caracalla, 00100 Rome, Italy (Telephone Number in U.S. (202) 653-2400); *The State of Food and Agriculture.*

M.E. Sharpe, 80 Business Park Drive, Armonk, New York 10504 (800) 541-6563; *The Illustrated Book of World Rankings.*

St. Martin's Press, Inc., 175 Fifth Avenue, New York, New York 10010 (800) 221-7945; *The Statesman's Year-Book.*

Statistical Office of the United Nations, Publishing Service, New York, New York 10017 (800) 253-9646; *Statistical Yearbook.*

United Nations Educational, Scientific and Cultural Organization (UNESCO), 7 Place de Fontenoy, F-75700 Paris, France (Telephone Number in U.S. (212) 963-5981); *Statistical Yearbook.*

The World Bank, 1818 H Street, NW, Washington, D.C. 20433 (202) 477-1234; *World Development Report.*

PAKISTAN - ARMS EXPORTS AND IMPORTS - See PAKISTAN - MILITARY

PAKISTAN - BALANCE OF PAYMENTS

The Economist Intelligence Unit, 111 West 57th Street, New York, New York 10019 (800) 938-4685; *The World Market Atlas.*

Europa Publications Limited, 18 Bedford Square, London, WC1B 3JN, England; *The Europa World Year Book.*

International Monetary Fund, 700 Nineteenth Street, NW, Washington, D.C. 20431 (202) 623-7000; *Balance of Payments Yearbook;* and *International Financial Statistics.*

United Nations Conference on Trade and Development (UNCTAD), New York, New York 10017 (800) 253-9646; *Handbook of International Trade and Development Statistics.*

The World Bank, 1818 H Street, NW, Washington, D.C. 20433 (202) 477-1234; *World Development Report;* and *World Development Indicators.*

PAKISTAN - BANKING

Asian Development Bank, Post Office Box 789, 1099 Manila, Philippines; *Key Indicators of Developing Asian and Pacific*

Countries.

Euromonitor International, Inc., 122 South Michigan Avenue, Suite 1200, Chicago. Illinois 60603 (800) 577-EURO; *International Marketing Data and Statistics;* and *World Marketing Data and Statistics.*

Europa Publications Limited, 18 Bedford Square, London, WC1B 3JN, England; *The Europa World Year Book.*

International Monetary Fund, 700 Nineteenth Street, NW, Washington, D.C. 20431 (202) 623-7000; *Government Finance Statistics Yearbook;* and *International Financial Statistics.*

M.E. Sharpe, 80 Business Park Drive, Armonk, New York 10504 (800) 541-6563; *The Illustrated Book of World Rankings.*

St. Martin's Press, Inc., 175 Fifth Avenue, New York, New York 10010 (800) 221-7945; *The Statesman's Year-Book.*

Statistical Office of the United Nations, Publishing Service, New York, New York 10017 (800) 253-9646; *Statistical Yearbook.*

PAKISTAN - BARLEY PRODUCTION - See PAKISTAN - CROPS

PAKISTAN - BEER PRODUCTION - See PAKISTAN - BEVERAGES

PAKISTAN - BEVERAGES

M.E. Sharpe, 80 Business Park Drive, Armonk, New York 10504 (800) 541-6563; *The Illustrated Book of World Rankings.*

Statistical Office of the United Nations, Publishing Service, New York, New York 10017 (800) 253-9646; *Statistical Yearbook.*

PAKISTAN - BIRTH RATES

Central Intelligence Agency, Washington, D.C. 20505 (703) 482-1100, www.cia.gov; *The World Factbook.*

The Economist Intelligence Unit (Asia) Limited, 10th Floor, Luk Kwok Centre, 72 Gloucester Road, Wanchai, Hong Kong (Phone Number in U.S. (800) 938-4685); *Asian Market Atlas.*

Euromonitor International, Inc., 122 South Michigan Avenue, Suite 1200, Chicago. Illinois 60603 (800) 577-EURO; *International Marketing Data and Statistics;* and *The World Economic Factbook.*

Europa Publications Limited, 18 Bedford Square, London, WC1B 3JN, England; *The Europa World Year Book.*

M.E. Sharpe, 80 Business Park Drive, Armonk, New York 10504 (800) 541-6563; *The Illustrated Book of World Rankings.*

St. Martin's Press, Inc., 175 Fifth Avenue, New York, New York 10010 (800) 221-7945; *The Statesman's Year-Book.*

Statistical Office of the United Nations, Publishing Service, New York, New York 10017 (800) 253-9646; *Asia-Pacific in Figures; Demographic Yearbook;* and *Statistical Yearbook.*

The World Bank, 1818 H Street, NW, Washington, D.C. 20433 (202) 477-1234; *World Development Indicators.*

PAKISTAN - BONDS

Asian Development Bank, Post Office Box 789, 1099 Manila, Philippines; *Key Indicators of Developing Asian and Pacific Countries.*

International Monetary Fund, 700 Nineteenth Street, NW, Washington, D.C. 20431 (202) 623-7000; *Government Finance Statistics Yearbook.*

Statistical Office of the United Nations, Publishing Service, New York, New York 10017 (800) 253-9646; *Statistical Yearbook.*

PAKISTAN - BOOK PRODUCTION

St. Martin's Press, Inc., 175 Fifth Avenue, New York, New York 10010 (800) 221-7945; *The Statesman's Year-Book.*

United Nations Educational, Scientific and Cultural Organization (UNESCO), 7 Place de Fontenoy, F-75700 Paris, France (Telephone Number in U.S. (212) 963-5981); *Statistical Yearbook.*

PAKISTAN - BROADCASTING

Billboard Limited, Post Office Box 9027, 1006 AA Amsterdam, The Netherlands (Telephone Number in U.S. (212) 764-7300); *World Radio TV Handbook.*

Central Intelligence Agency, Washington, D.C. 20505 (703) 482-1100, www.cia.gov; *The World Factbook.*

The Economist Intelligence Unit (Asia) Limited, 10th Floor, Luk Kwok Centre, 72 Gloucester Road, Wanchai, Hong Kong (Phone Number in U.S. (800) 938-4685); *Asian Market Atlas.*

Euromonitor International, Inc., 122 South Michigan Avenue, Suite 1200, Chicago. Illinois 60603 (800) 577-EURO; *World Marketing Data and Statistics.*

M.E. Sharpe, 80 Business Park Drive, Armonk, New York 10504 (800) 541-6563; *The Illustrated Book of World Rankings.*

St. Martin's Press, Inc., 175 Fifth Avenue, New York, New York 10010 (800) 221-7945; *The Statesman's Year-Book.*

United Nations Educational, Scientific and Cultural Organization (UNESCO), 7 Place de Fontenoy, F-75700 Paris, France (Telephone Number in U.S. (212) 963-5981); *Statistical Yearbook.*

PAKISTAN - BUDGET

Central Intelligence Agency, Washington, D.C. 20505 (703) 482-1100, www.cia.gov; *The World Factbook.*

PAKISTAN - BUTTER PRODUCTION - See PAKISTAN - DAIRY PRODUCTS

PAKISTAN - CALORIE SUPPLY

Asian Development Bank, Post Office Box 789, 1099 Manila, Philippines; *Key Indicators of Developing Asian and Pacific Countries.*

Food and Agricultural Organization of the United Nations (FAO) Via delle Terme di Caracalla, 00100 Rome, Italy (Telephone Number in U.S. (202) 653-2400); *The State of Food and Agriculture.*

PAKISTAN - CAPITAL INVESTMENT

Asian Development Bank, Post Office Box 789, 1099 Manila, Philippines; *Key Indicators of Developing Asian and Pacific Countries.*

PAKISTAN - CAPITAL REVENUE

Asian Development Bank, Post Office Box 789, 1099 Manila, Philippines; *Key Indicators of Developing Asian and Pacific Countries.*

International Monetary Fund, 700 Nineteenth Street, NW, Washington, D.C. 20431 (202) 623-7000; *Government Finance Statistics Yearbook.*

PAKISTAN - CASTOR BEAN PRODUCTION - See PAKISTAN - CROPS

PAKISTAN - CATTLE - See PAKISTAN - LIVESTOCK AND POULTRY

PAKISTAN - CAUSTIC SODA PRODUCTION - See PAKISTAN - BEVERAGES

PAKISTAN - CEMENT PRODUCTION - See PAKISTAN - MINING AND MINERAL PRODUCTS

PAKISTAN - CHEMICAL (ORGANIC) PRODUCTION - See PAKISTAN - MINING AND MINERAL PRODUCTS

PAKISTAN - CHICK PEA PRODUCTION - See PAKISTAN - CROPS

PAKISTAN - CHICKENS - See PAKISTAN - LIVESTOCK AND POULTRY

PAKISTAN - CHROMITE PRODUCTION

AND CONSUMPTION - See PAKISTAN - MINING AND MINERAL PRODUCTS

PAKISTAN - CHROMIUM ORE PRODUCTION AND CONSUMPTION - See PAKISTAN - MINING AND MINERAL PRODUCTS

PAKISTAN - CIGARETTE PRODUCTION - See PAKISTAN - TOBACCO PRODUCTION

PAKISTAN - CLIMATE

M.E. Sharpe, 80 Business Park Drive, Armonk, New York 10504 (800) 541-6563; *The Illustrated Book of World Rankings.*

St. Martin's Press, Inc., 175 Fifth Avenue, New York, New York (800) 221-7945; *The Statesman's Year-Book.*

PAKISTAN - CLOTHING EXPORTS AND IMPORTS - See PAKISTAN - TEXTILE INDUSTRY

PAKISTAN - COAL PRODUCTION - See PAKISTAN - MINING AND MINERAL PRODUCTS

PAKISTAN - COFFEE PRODUCTION AND CONSUMPTION - See PAKISTAN - CROPS

PAKISTAN - COMMERCE

St. Martin's Press, Inc., 175 Fifth Avenue, New York, New York 10010 (800) 221-7945; *The Statesman's Year-Book.*

PAKISTAN - COMMUNICATIONS - See PAKISTAN - TRANSPORTATION AND COMMUNICATIONS

PAKISTAN - CONSTRUCTION INDUSTRY

M.E. Sharpe, 80 Business Park Drive, Armonk, New York 10504 (800) 541-6563; *The Illustrated Book of World Rankings.*

St. Martin's Press, Inc., 175 Fifth Avenue, New York, New York 10010 (800) 221-7945; *The Statesman's Year-Book.*

Statistical Office of the United Nations, Publishing Service, New York, New York 10017 (800) 253-9646; *Statistical Yearbook.*

PAKISTAN - CONSUMER PRICE INDEX

Asian Development Bank, Post Office Box 789, 1099 Manila, Philippines; *Key Indicators of Developing Asian and Pacific Countries.*

Europa Publications Limited, 18 Bedford Square, London, WC1B 3JN, England; *The Europa World Year Book.*

Statistical Office of the United Nations, Publishing Service, New York, New York 10017 (800) 253-9646; *Statistical Yearbook.*

PAKISTAN - CONSUMER PRICES

Euromonitor International, Inc., 122 South Michigan Avenue, Suite 1200, Chicago. Illinois 60603 (800) 577-EURO; *World Marketing Data and Statistics.*

International Labour Office, I.L.O. Publications, 1828 L Street, NW., Suite 801, Washington, D.C. 20036 (301) 638-3152; *Yearbook of Labour Statistics.*

International Monetary Fund, 700 Nineteenth Street, NW, Washington, D.C. 20431 (202) 623-7000; *International Financial Statistics.*

PAKISTAN - CONSUMPTION

The World Bank, 1818 H Street, NW, Washington, D.C. 20433 (202) 477-1234; *World Development Report.*

PAKISTAN - COPPER PRODUCTION AND CONSUMPTION - See PAKISTAN - MINING AND MINERAL PRODUCTS

PAKISTAN - CORN PRODUCTION - See PAKISTAN - CROPS

PAKISTAN - CORPORATE TAXES - See PAKISTAN - TAXATION

PAKISTAN - COTTON - See PAKISTAN - CROPS

PAKISTAN - CRIME

Yale University Press, Yale Station, New Haven, Connecticut 06520 (800) 987-7323; *Violence and Crime in Cross-National Perspective.*

PAKISTAN - CROPS

Asian Development Bank, Post Office Box 789, 1099 Manila, Philippines; *Key Indicators of Developing Asian and Pacific Countries.*

Commodity Research Bureau, Inc., 30 South Wacker Drive, Chicago Illinois 60606 (312) 454-1801; *Commodity Year Book.*

Europa Publications Limited, 18 Bedford Square, London, WC1B 3JN, England; *The Europa World Year Book.*

Food and Agricultural Organization of the United Nations (FAO), Via delle Terme di Caracalla, 00100 Rome, Italy (Telephone Number in U.S. (202) 653-2400); *Production Yearbook;* and *The State of Food and Agriculture.*

International Monetary Fund, 700 Nineteenth Street, NW, Washington, D.C. 20431 (202) 623-7000; *International Financial Statistics.*

M.E. Sharpe, 80 Business Park Drive,

Armonk, New York 10504 (800) 541-6563; *The Illustrated Book of World Rankings*.

St. Martin's Press, Inc., 175 Fifth Avenue, New York, New York 10010 (800) 221-7945; *The Statesman's Year-Book*.

Statistical Office of the United Nations, Publishing Service, New York, New York 10017 (800) 253-9646; *Statistical Yearbook*.

United Nations Conference on Trade and Development, Central Statistical Service, Palais des Nations, Geneva, Switzerland (Telephone in U.S. (800) 253-9646); *UNCTAD Commodity Yearbook*.

PAKISTAN - CUSTOMS DUTIES

St. Martin's Press, Inc., 175 Fifth Avenue, New York, New York 10010 (800) 221-7945; *The Statesman's Year-Book*.

PAKISTAN - DAIRY PRODUCTS

Europa Publications Limited, 18 Bedford Square, London, WC1B 3JN, England; *The Europa World Year Book*.

Food and Agricultural Organization of the United Nations (FAO), Via delle Terme di Caracalla, 00100 Rome, Italy (Telephone Number in U.S. (202) 653-2400); *Production Yearbook;* and *The State of Food and Agriculture*.

M.E. Sharpe, 80 Business Park Drive, Armonk, New York 10504 (800) 541-6563; *The Illustrated Book of World Rankings*.

St. Martin's Press, Inc., 175 Fifth Avenue, New York, New York 10010 (800) 221-7945; *The Statesman's Year-Book*.

Statistical Office of the United Nations, Publishing Service, New York, New York 10017 (800) 253-9646; *Statistical Yearbook*.

PAKISTAN - DEATH RATES - See PAKISTAN - MORTALITY

PAKISTAN - DEFENSE EXPENDITURES - See PAKISTAN - MILITARY

PAKISTAN - DEMOGRAPHY

The Economist Intelligence Unit, 111 West 57th Street, New York, New York 10019 (800) 938-4685; *The World Market Atlas*.

The Economist Intelligence Unit (Asia) Limited, 10th Floor, Luk Kwok Centre, 72 Gloucester Road, Wanchai, Hong Kong (Phone Number in U.S. (800) 938-4685); *Asian Market Atlas*.

Euromonitor International, Inc., 122 South Michigan Avenue, Suite 1200, Chicago. Illinois 60603 (800) 577-EURO; *International Marketing Data and Statistics;*

The World Economic Factbook; and *World Marketing Data and Statistics*.

M.E. Sharpe, 80 Business Park Drive, Armonk, New York 10504 (800) 541-6563; *The Illustrated Book of World Rankings*.

Statistical Office of the United Nations, Publishing Service, New York, New York 10017 (800) 253-9646; *Asia-Pacific in Figures;* and *Human Development Report*.

PAKISTAN - DEVELOPMENT ASSISTANCE

Asian Development Bank, Post Office Box 789, 1099 Manila, Philippines; *Key Indicators of Developing Asian and Pacific Countries*.

Statistical Office of the United Nations, Publishing Service, New York, New York 10017 (800) 253-9646; *Statistical Yearbook*.

PAKISTAN - DIAMOND PRODUCTION - See PAKISTAN - MINING AND MINERAL PRODUCTS

PAKISTAN - DISCOUNT RATES - See PAKISTAN - BANKING

PAKISTAN - DISEASES - See PAKISTAN - HEALTH

PAKISTAN - DIVORCE RATES

M.E. Sharpe, 80 Business Park Drive, Armonk, New York 10504 (800) 541-6563; *The Illustrated Book of World Rankings*.

Statistical Office of the United Nations, Publishing Service, New York, New York 10017 (800) 253-9646; *Demographic Yearbook*.

PAKISTAN - DUCKS - See PAKISTAN - LIVESTOCK AND POULTRY

PAKISTAN - ECONOMY

Asian Development Bank, Post Office Box 789, 1099 Manila, Philippines; *Key Indicators of Developing Asian and Pacific Countries*.

Central Intelligence Agency, Washington, D.C. 20505 (703) 482-1100, www.cia.gov; *The World Factbook*.

Economist Intelligence Unit, 111 West 57th Street, New York, New York 10019 (800) 938-4685; *Pakistan Country Report*.

Euromonitor International, Inc., 122 South Michigan Avenue, Suite 1200, Chicago. Illinois 60603 (800) 577-EURO; *International Marketing Data and Statistics; The World Economic Factbook;* and *World Marketing Data and Statistics*.

Europa Publications Limited, 18

Bedford Square, London, WC1B 3JN, England; *The Europa World Year Book*.

M.E. Sharpe, 80 Business Park Drive, Armonk, New York 10504 (800) 541-6563; *The Illustrated Book of World Rankings*.

St. Martin's Press, Inc., 175 Fifth Avenue, New York, New York 10010 (800) 221-7945; *The Statesman's Year-Book*.

Statistical Office of the United Nations, Publishing Service, New York, New York 10017 (800) 253-9646; *World Statistics Pocketbook*.

The World Bank, 1818 H Street, NW, Washington, D.C. 20433 (202) 477-1234; *The World Bank Atlas;* and *World Development Report*.

PAKISTAN - EDUCATION

The Economist Intelligence Unit, 111 West 57th Street, New York, New York 10019 (800) 938-4685; *The World Market Atlas*.

The Economist Intelligence Unit (Asia) Limited, 10th Floor, Luk Kwok Centre, 72 Gloucester Road, Wanchai, Hong Kong (Phone Number in U.S. (800) 938-4685); *Asian Market Atlas*.

Euromonitor International, Inc., 122 South Michigan Avenue, Suite 1200, Chicago. Illinois 60603 (800) 577-EURO; *International Marketing Data and Statistics;* and *World Marketing Data and Statistics*.

Europa Publications Limited, 18 Bedford Square, London, WC1B 3JN, England; *The Europa World Year Book*.

International Monetary Fund, 700 Nineteenth Street, NW, Washington, D.C. 20431 (202) 623-7000; *Government Finance Statistics Yearbook*.

M.E. Sharpe, 80 Business Park Drive, Armonk, New York 10504 (800) 541-6563; *The Illustrated Book of World Rankings*.

St. Martin's Press, Inc., 175 Fifth Avenue, New York, New York 10010 (800) 221-7945; *The Statesman's Year-Book*.

Statistical Office of the United Nations, Publishing Service, New York, New York 10017 (800) 253-9646; *Asia-Pacific in Figures; Human Development Report;* and *Statistical Yearbook for Asia and the Pacific*.

United Nations Educational, Scientific and Cultural Organization (UNESCO), 7 Place de Fontenoy, F-75700 Paris, France (Telephone Number in U.S. (212) 963-5981); *Statistical Yearbook*.

The World Bank, 1818 H Street, NW,

Washington, D.C. 20433 (202) 477-1234; *World Development Report;* and *World Development Indicators.*

PAKISTAN - EGG PRODUCTION AND CONSUMPTION - See PAKISTAN - DAIRY PRODUCTS

PAKISTAN - ELECTRICITY

Asian Development Bank, Post Office Box 789, 1099 Manila, Philippines; *Key Indicators of Developing Asian and Pacific Countries.*

Central Intelligence Agency, Washington, D.C. 20505 (703) 482-1100, www.cia.gov; *The World Factbook.*

M.E. Sharpe, 80 Business Park Drive, Armonk, New York 10504 (800) 541-6563; *The Illustrated Book of World Rankings.*

Penn Well Publishing Company, 1421 South Sheridan Road, Post Office Box 1260, Tulsa, Oklahoma 74101 (800) 752-9764; *International Energy Statistics Sourcebook.*

St. Martin's Press, Inc., 175 Fifth Avenue, New York, New York 10010 (800) 221-7945; *The Statesman's Year-Book.*

Statistical Office of the United Nations, Publishing Service, New York, New York 10017 (800) 253-9646; *Electric Power in Asia and the Pacific; Human Development Report;* and *Statistical Yearbook.*

PAKISTAN - EMPLOYMENT

Euromonitor International, Inc., 122 South Michigan Avenue, Suite 1200, Chicago. Illinois 60603 (800) 577-EURO; *International Marketing Data and Statistics.*

International Labour Office, I.L.O. Publications, 1828 L Street, NW., Suite 801, Washington, D.C. 20036 (301) 638-3152; *Yearbook of Labour Statistics.*

M.E. Sharpe, 80 Business Park Drive, Armonk, New York 10504 (800) 541-6563; *The Illustrated Book of World Rankings.*

Statistical Office of the United Nations, Publishing Service, New York, New York 10017 (800) 253-9646; *Asia-Pacific in Figures;* and *Statistical Yearbook.*

PAKISTAN - ENERGY

Euromonitor International, Inc., 122 South Michigan Avenue, Suite 1200, Chicago. Illinois 60603 (800) 577-EURO; *International Marketing Data and Statistics; The World Economic Factbook;* and *World Marketing Data and Statistics.*

Food and Agricultural Organization of the United Nations (FAO) Via delle Terme

di Caracalla, 00100 Rome, Italy (Telephone Number in U.S. (202) 653-2400); *The State of Food and Agriculture.*

M.E. Sharpe, 80 Business Park Drive, Armonk, New York 10504 (800) 541-6563; *The Illustrated Book of World Rankings.*

Penn Well Publishing Company, 1421 South Sheridan Road, Post Office Box 1260, Tulsa, Oklahoma 74101 (800) 752-9764; *International Energy Statistics Sourcebook.*

St. Martin's Press, Inc., 175 Fifth Avenue, New York, New York 10010 (800) 221-7945; *The Statesman's Year-Book.*

Statistical Office of the United Nations, Publishing Service, New York, New York 10017 (800) 253-9646; *Asia-Pacific in Figures; Foreign Trade Statistics of Asia and the Pacific; Human Development Report; Statistical Yearbook; Statistical Yearbook for Asia and the Pacific;* and *World Statistics Pocketbook.*

The World Bank, 1818 H Street, NW, Washington, D.C. 20433 (202) 477-1234; *The World Bank Atlas;* and *World Development Report.*

PAKISTAN - ENVIRONMENT

Economist Intelligence Unit, 111 West 57th Street, New York, New York 10019 (800) 938-4685; *Pakistan Country Report.*

Statistical Office of the United Nations, Publishing Service, New York, New York 10017 (800) 253-9646; *World Statistics Pocketbook.*

PAKISTAN - EXCHANGE RATES

Asian Development Bank, Post Office Box 789, 1099 Manila, Philippines; *Key Indicators of Developing Asian and Pacific Countries.*

Central Intelligence Agency, Washington, D.C. 20505 (703) 482-1100, www.cia.gov; *The World Factbook.*

The Economist Intelligence Unit (Asia) Limited, 10th Floor, Luk Kwok Centre, 72 Gloucester Road, Wanchai, Hong Kong (Phone Number in U.S. (800) 938-4685); *Asian Market Atlas.*

Euromonitor International, Inc., 122 South Michigan Avenue, Suite 1200, Chicago. Illinois 60603 (800) 577-EURO; *International Marketing Data and Statistics;* and *The World Economic Factbook.*

Europa Publications Limited, 18 Bedford Square, London, WC1B 3JN, England; *The Europa World Year Book.*

International Civil Aviation Organization, 999 University Street,

Montreal, Quebec, Canada H3C 5H7 (514) 954-8219; *Civil Aviation Statistics of the World.*

International Monetary Fund, 700 Nineteenth Street, NW, Washington, D.C. 20431 (202) 623-7000; *International Financial Statistics.*

Statistical Office of the United Nations, Publishing Service, New York, New York 10017 (800) 253-9646; *Statistical Yearbook;* and *World Statistics Pocketbook.*

Walden Publishing, Ltd., Two Market Street, Saffron Walden Essex, CB10 1HZ, England; *The World of Information Asia and Pacific Review.*

PAKISTAN - EXCISE TAXES - See PAKISTAN - TAXATION

PAKISTAN - EXPORTS

Asian Development Bank, Post Office Box 789, 1099 Manila, Philippines; *Key Indicators of Developing Asian and Pacific Countries.*

Central Intelligence Agency, Washington, D.C. 20505 (703) 482-1100, www.cia.gov; *The World Factbook.*

The Economist Intelligence Unit, 111 West 57th Street, New York, New York 10019 (800) 938-4685; *Pakistan Country Report;* and *The World Market Atlas.*

The Economist Intelligence Unit (Asia) Limited, 10th Floor, Luk Kwok Centre, 72 Gloucester Road, Wanchai, Hong Kong (Phone Number in U.S. (800) 938-4685); *Asian Market Atlas.*

Euromonitor International, Inc., 122 South Michigan Avenue, Suite 1200, Chicago. Illinois 60603 (800) 577-EURO; *International Marketing Data and Statistics;* and *The World Economic Factbook.*

Europa Publications Limited, 18 Bedford Square, London, WC1B 3JN, England; *The Europa World Year Book.*

Food and Agricultural Organization of the United Nations (FAO) Via delle Terme di Caracalla, 00100 Rome, Italy (Telephone Number in U.S. (202) 653-2400); *The State of Food and Agriculture.*

International Monetary Fund, 700 Nineteenth Street, NW, Washington, D.C. 20431 (202) 623-7000; *Direction of Trade Statistics;* and *Government Finance Statistics Yearbook.*

St. Martin's Press, Inc., 175 Fifth Avenue, New York, New York 10010 (800) 221-7945; *The Statesman's Year-Book.*

Statistical Office of the United Nations,

Publishing Service, New York, New York 10017 (800) 253-9646; *Foreign Trade Statistics of Asia and the Pacific.*

United Nations Conference on Trade and Development (UNCTAD), New York, New York 10017 (800) 253-9646; *Handbook of International Trade and Development Statistics.*

Walden Publishing, Ltd., Two Market Street, Saffron Walden Essex, CB10 1HZ, England; *The World of Information Asia and Pacific Review.*

The World Bank, 1818 H Street, NW, Washington, D.C. 20433 (202) 477-1234; *World Development Report;* and *World Development Indicators.*

PAKISTAN - EXTERNAL FINANCING

Asian Development Bank, Post Office Box 789, 1099 Manila, Philippines; *Key Indicators of Developing Asian and Pacific Countries.*

PAKISTAN - EXTERNAL INDEBTEDNESS

Asian Development Bank, Post Office Box 789, 1099 Manila, Philippines; *Key Indicators of Developing Asian and Pacific Countries.*

The World Bank, 1818 H Street, NW, Washington, D.C. 20433 (202) 477-1234; *World Development Report;* and *World Development Indicators.*

PAKISTAN - EXTERNAL TRADE

Asian Development Bank, Post Office Box 789, 1099 Manila, Philippines; *Key Indicators of Developing Asian and Pacific Countries.*

Euromonitor International, Inc., 122 South Michigan Avenue, Suite 1200, Chicago. Illinois 60603 (800) 577-EURO; *World Marketing Data and Statistics.*

Food and Agricultural Organization of the United Nations (FAO) Via delle Terme di Caracalla, 00100 Rome, Italy (Telephone Number in U.S. (202) 653-2400); *The State of Food and Agriculture;* and *Trade Yearbook.*

Statistical Office of the United Nations, Publishing Service, New York, New York 10017 (800) 253-9646; *Asia-Pacific in Figures; Statistical Yearbook;* and *Statistical Yearbook for Asia and the Pacific.*

PAKISTAN - FABRIC PRODUCTION - See PAKISTAN - TEXTILE INDUSTRY

PAKISTAN - FARM CROPS - See PAKISTAN - CROPS

PAKISTAN - FEMALE WORKING

POPULATION - See PAKISTAN - EMPLOYMENT

PAKISTAN - FERTILITY RATES

Central Intelligence Agency, Washington, D.C. 20505 (703) 482-1100, www.cia.gov; *The World Factbook.*

The Economist Intelligence Unit (Asia) Limited, 10th Floor, Luk Kwok Centre, 72 Gloucester Road, Wanchai, Hong Kong (Phone Number in U.S. (800) 938-4685); *Asian Market Atlas.*

M.E. Sharpe, 80 Business Park Drive, Armonk, New York 10504 (800) 541-6563; *The Illustrated Book of World Rankings.*

Statistical Office of the United Nations, Publishing Service, New York, New York 10017 (800) 253-9646; *Human Development Report.*

The World Bank, 1818 H Street, NW, Washington, D.C. 20433 (202) 477-1234; *The World Bank Atlas;* and *World Development Report;* and *World Development Indicators.*

PAKISTAN - FERTILIZER

Food and Agricultural Organization of the United Nations (FAO), Via delle Terme di Caracalla, 00100 Rome, Italy (Telephone Number in U.S. (202) 653-2400); *Fertilizer Yearbook;* and *The State of Food and Agriculture.*

Statistical Office of the United Nations, Publishing Service, New York, New York 10017 (800) 253-9646; *Statistical Yearbook.*

PAKISTAN - FETAL MORTALITY - See PAKISTAN - MORTALITY

PAKISTAN - FIBRE PRODUCTION - See PAKISTAN - TEXTILE INDUSTRY

PAKISTAN - FILAMENT PRODUCTION - See PAKISTAN - TEXTILE INDUSTRY

PAKISTAN - FILMS - See PAKISTAN - MOTION PICTURES

PAKISTAN - FINANCE

Asian Development Bank, Post Office Box 789, 1099 Manila, Philippines; *Key Indicators of Developing Asian and Pacific Countries.*

Economist Intelligence Unit, 111 West 57th Street, New York, New York 10019 (800) 938-4685; *Pakistan Country Report.*

Europa Publications Limited, 18 Bedford Square, London, WC1B 3JN, England; *The Europa World Year Book.*

International Monetary Fund, 700

Nineteenth Street, NW, Washington, D.C. 20431 (202) 623-7000; *Government Finance Statistics Yearbook;* and *International Financial Statistics.*

M.E. Sharpe, 80 Business Park Drive, Armonk, New York 10504 (800) 541-6563; *The Illustrated Book of World Rankings.*

St. Martin's Press, Inc., 175 Fifth Avenue, New York, New York 10010 (800) 221-7945; *The Statesman's Year-Book.*

Statistical Office of the United Nations, Publishing Service, New York, New York 10017 (800) 253-9646; *Statistical Yearbook for Asia and the Pacific.*

PAKISTAN - FISHERIES

Europa Publications Limited, 18 Bedford Square, London, WC1B 3JN, England; *The Europa World Year Book.*

Food and Agricultural Organization of the United Nations (FAO) Via delle Terme di Caracalla, 00100 Rome, Italy (Telephone Number in U.S. (202) 653-2400); *The State of Food and Agriculture;* and *Yearbook of Fishery Statistics.*

M.E. Sharpe, 80 Business Park Drive, Armonk, New York 10504 (800) 541-6563; *The Illustrated Book of World Rankings.*

St. Martin's Press, Inc., 175 Fifth Avenue, New York, New York 10010 (800) 221-7945; *The Statesman's Year-Book.*

Statistical Office of the United Nations, Publishing Service, New York, New York 10017 (800) 253-9646; *Statistical Yearbook.*

United Nations Conference on Trade and Development, Central Statistical Service, Palais des Nations, Geneva, Switzerland (Telephone in U.S. (800) 253-9646); *UNCTAD Commodity Yearbook.*

PAKISTAN - FOOD

Food and Agricultural Organization of the United Nations (FAO) Via delle Terme di Caracalla, 00100 Rome, Italy (Telephone Number in U.S. (202) 653-2400); *Production Yearbook;* and *The State of Food and Agriculture.*

Statistical Office of the United Nations, Publishing Service, New York, New York 10017 (800) 253-9646; *Human Development Report;* and *Statistical Yearbook for Asia and the Pacific.*

United Nations Conference on Trade and Development, Central Statistical Service, Palais des Nations, Geneva, Switzerland (Telephone in U.S. (800) 253-9646); *UNCTAD Commodity Yearbook.*

PAKISTAN - FOREIGN DEBT

International Monetary Fund, 700 Nineteenth Street, NW, Washington, D.C. 20431 (202) 623-7000; *Government Finance Statistics Yearbook.*

St. Martin's Press, Inc., 175 Fifth Avenue, New York, New York 10010 (800) 221-7945; *The Statesman's Year-Book.*

Walden Publishing, Ltd., Two Market Street, Saffron Walden Essex, CB10 1HZ, England; *The World of Information Asia and Pacific Review.*

PAKISTAN - FOREIGN TRADE

Asian Development Bank, Post Office Box 789, 1099 Manila, Philippines; *Key Indicators of Developing Asian and Pacific Countries.*

Economist Intelligence Unit, 111 West 57th Street, New York, New York 10019 (800) 938-4685; *Pakistan Country Report.*

The Economist Intelligence Unit (Asia) Limited, 10th Floor, Luk Kwok Centre, 72 Gloucester Road, Wanchai, Hong Kong (Phone Number in U.S. (800) 938-4685); *Asian Market Atlas.*

Euromonitor International, Inc., 122 South Michigan Avenue, Suite 1200, Chicago. Illinois 60603 (800) 577-EURO; *International Marketing Data and Statistics;* and *The World Economic Factbook.*

Europa Publications Limited, 18 Bedford Square, London, WC1B 3JN, England; *The Europa World Year Book.*

Food and Agricultural Organization of the United Nations (FAO) Via delle Terme di Caracalla, 00100 Rome, Italy (Telephone Number in U.S. (202) 653-2400); *The State of Food and Agriculture.*

International Monetary Fund, 700 Nineteenth Street, NW, Washington, D.C. 20431 (202) 623-7000; *International Financial Statistics.*

M.E. Sharpe, 80 Business Park Drive, Armonk, New York 10504 (800) 541-6563; *The Illustrated Book of World Rankings.*

St. Martin's Press, Inc., 175 Fifth Avenue, New York, New York 10010 (800) 221-7945; *The Statesman's Year-Book.*

Statistical Office of the United Nations, Publishing Service, New York, New York 10017 (800) 253-9646; *International Trade Statistics Yearbook;* and *Statistical Yearbook.*

United Nations Conference on Trade and Development, Central Statistical Service, Palais des Nations, Geneva,

Switzerland (Telephone in U.S. (800) 253-9646); *UNCTAD Commodity Yearbook.*

The World Bank, 1818 H Street, NW, Washington, D.C. 20433 (202) 477-1234; *World Development Report;* and *World Development Indicators.*

PAKISTAN - FORESTRY AND FOREST PRODUCTS

American Forest and Paper Association, 1111 Nineteenth Street, NW, Washington, D.C. 20036 (202) 463-2700; *Wood Pulp and Fiber Statistics.*

The Economist Intelligence Unit (Asia) Limited, 10th Floor, Luk Kwok Centre, 72 Gloucester Road, Wanchai, Hong Kong (Phone Number in U.S. (800) 938-4685); *Asian Market Atlas.*

Europa Publications Limited, 18 Bedford Square, London, WC1B 3JN, England; *The Europa World Year Book.*

Food and Agricultural Organization of the United Nations (FAO) Via delle Terme di Caracalla, 00100 Rome, Italy (Telephone Number in U.S. (202) 653-2400); *The State of Food and Agriculture;* and *Yearbook of Forest Products.*

M.E. Sharpe, 80 Business Park Drive, Armonk, New York 10504 (800) 541-6563; *The Illustrated Book of World Rankings.*

St. Martin's Press, Inc., 175 Fifth Avenue, New York, New York 10010 (800) 221-7945; *The Statesman's Year-Book.*

Statistical Office of the United Nations, Publishing Service, New York, New York 10017 (800) 253-9646; *Statistical Yearbook.*

United Nations Conference on Trade and Development, Central Statistical Service, Palais des Nations, Geneva, Switzerland (Telephone in U.S. (800) 253-9646); *UNCTAD Commodity Yearbook.*

United Nations Educational, Scientific and Cultural Organization (UNESCO), 7 Place de Fontenoy, F-75700 Paris, France (Telephone Number in U.S. (212) 963-5981); *Statistical Yearbook.*

The World Bank, 1818 H Street, NW, Washington, D.C. 20433 (202) 477-1234; *World Development Report.*

PAKISTAN - GARLIC PRODUCTION - See PAKISTAN - CROPS

PAKISTAN - GAS PRODUCTION - See PAKISTAN - MINING AND MINERAL PRODUCTS

PAKISTAN - GENERAL MORTALITY - See PAKISTAN - MORTALITY

PAKISTAN - GEOGRAPHIC DATA

M.E. Sharpe, 80 Business Park Drive, Armonk, New York 10504 (800) 541-6563; *The Illustrated Book of World Rankings.*

PAKISTAN - GOATS - See PAKISTAN - LIVESTOCK AND POULTRY

PAKISTAN - GOLD HOLDINGS

International Monetary Fund, 700 Nineteenth Street, NW, Washington, D.C. 20431 (202) 623-7000; *International Financial Statistics.*

Statistical Office of the United Nations, Publishing Service, New York, New York 10017 (800) 253-9646; *Statistical Yearbook.*

The World Bank, 1818 H Street, NW, Washington, D.C. 20433 (202) 477-1234; *World Development Indicators.*

PAKISTAN - GOLD PRODUCTION AND CONSUMPTION - See PAKISTAN - MINING AND MINERAL PRODUCTS

PAKISTAN - GOVERNMENT

Asian Development Bank, Post Office Box 789, 1099 Manila, Philippines; *Key Indicators of Developing Asian and Pacific Countries.*

Central Intelligence Agency, Washington, D.C. 20505 (703) 482-1100, www.cia.gov; *The World Factbook.*

Europa Publications Limited, 18 Bedford Square, London, WC1B 3JN, England; *The Europa World Year Book.*

International Monetary Fund, 700 Nineteenth Street, NW, Washington, D.C. 20431 (202) 623-7000; *Government Finance Statistics Yearbook;* and *International Financial Statistics.*

St. Martin's Press, Inc., 175 Fifth Avenue, New York, New York 10010 (800) 221-7945; *The Statesman's Year-Book.*

Statistical Office of the United Nations, Publishing Service, New York, New York 10017 (800) 253-9646; *Asia-Pacific in Figures;* and *National Accounts Statistics.*

The World Bank, 1818 H Street, NW, Washington, D.C. 20433 (202) 477-1234; *World Development Report;* and *World Development Indicators.*

PAKISTAN - GRAIN PRODUCTION - See PAKISTAN - CROPS

PAKISTAN - GRANTS

International Monetary Fund, 700 Nineteenth Street, NW, Washington, D.C. 20431 (202) 623-7000; *Government*

Finance Statistics Yearbook.

PAKISTAN - GREEN PEPPER AND CHILIE
PRODUCTION - See PAKISTAN - CROPS

PAKISTAN - GROSS DOMESTIC PRODUCT

Asian Development Bank, Post Office
Box 789, 1099 Manila, Philippines; *Key
Indicators of Developing Asian and Pacific
Countries.*

The Economist Intelligence Unit, 111
West 57th Street, New York, New York
10019 (800) 938-4685; *Pakistan Country
Report;* and *The World Market Atlas.*

The Economist Intelligence Unit (Asia)
Limited, 10th Floor, Luk Kwok Centre, 72
Gloucester Road, Wanchai, Hong Kong
(Phone Number in U.S. (800) 938-4685);
Asian Market Atlas.

Euromonitor International, Inc., 122
South Michigan Avenue, Suite 1200,
Chicago. Illinois 60603 (800) 577-EURO;
International Marketing Data and Statistics;
and *The World Economic Factbook.*

Europa Publications Limited, 18
Bedford Square, London, WC1B 3JN,
England; *The Europa World Year Book.*

M.E. Sharpe, 80 Business Park Drive,
Armonk, New York 10504 (800) 541-6563;
The Illustrated Book of World Rankings.

Statistical Office of the United Nations,
Publishing Service, New York, New York
10017 (800) 253-9646; *Human
Development Report; National Accounts
Statistics;* and *Statistical Yearbook.*

The World Bank, 1818 H Street, NW,
Washington, D.C. 20433 (202) 477-1234;
World Development Report; and *World
Development Indicators.*

PAKISTAN - GROSS NATIONAL PRODUCT

Asian Development Bank, Post Office
Box 789, 1099 Manila, Philippines; *Key
Indicators of Developing Asian and Pacific
Countries.*

Euromonitor International, Inc., 122
South Michigan Avenue, Suite 1200,
Chicago. Illinois 60603 (800) 577-EURO;
*International Marketing Data and
Statistics.*

Europa Publications Limited, 18
Bedford Square, London, WC1B 3JN,
England; *The Europa World Year Book.*

St. Martin's Press, Inc., 175 Fifth
Avenue, New York, New York 10010 (800)
221-7945; *The Statesman's Year-Book.*

U.S. Arms Control and Disarmament
Agency, 320 Twenty-first Street, NW,

Washington, D.C. 20451 (202) 647-8677;
*World Military Expenditures and Arms
Transfers.*

Walden Publishing, Ltd., Two Market
Street, Saffron Walden Essex, CB10 1HZ,
England; *The World of Information Asia
and Pacific Review.*

The World Bank, 1818 H Street, NW,
Washington, D.C. 20433 (202) 477-1234;
*The World Bank Atlas; World Development
Report;* and *World Development Indicators.*

PAKISTAN - GROUNDNUTS
PRODUCTION - See PAKISTAN - CROPS

PAKISTAN - HEALTH

The Economist Intelligence Unit (Asia)
Limited, 10th Floor, Luk Kwok Centre, 72
Gloucester Road, Wanchai, Hong Kong
(Phone Number in U.S. (800) 938-4685);
Asian Market Atlas.

Euromonitor International, Inc., 122
South Michigan Avenue, Suite 1200,
Chicago. Illinois 60603 (800) 577-EURO;
World Marketing Data and Statistics.

M.E. Sharpe, 80 Business Park Drive,
Armonk, New York 10504 (800) 541-6563;
The Illustrated Book of World Rankings.

St. Martin's Press, Inc., 175 Fifth
Avenue, New York, New York 10010 (800)
221-7945; *The Statesman's Year-Book.*

Statistical Office of the United Nations,
Publishing Service, New York, New York
10017 (800) 253-9646; *Asia-Pacific in
Figures; Human Development Report;* and
Statistical Yearbook.

United Nations Children's Fund
(UNICEF), 3 United Nations Plaza, New
York, New York 10017 (800) 253-9646; *State
of the World's Children.*

The World Bank, 1818 H Street, NW,
Washington, D.C. 20433 (202) 477-1234;
World Development Report.

World Health Organization, Office of
Publications, 20 Avenue Appia, CH-1211
Geneva 27, Switzerland (Telephone
Number in U.S. (518) 436-9686); *World
Health Statistics Annual.*

PAKISTAN - HEALTH EXPENDITURES

International Monetary Fund, 700
Nineteenth Street, NW, Washington, D.C.
20431 (202) 623-7000; *Government
Finance Statistics Yearbook.*

PAKISTAN - HEMP FIBRE PRODUCTION -
See PAKISTAN - TEXTILE INDUSTRY

PAKISTAN - HIDE PRODUCTION

Food and Agricultural Organization of
the United Nations (FAO), Via delle Terme
di Caracalla, 00100 Rome, Italy (Telephone
Number in U.S. (202) 653-2400);
Production Yearbook.

PAKISTAN - HIGHWAYS

Central Intelligence Agency,
Washington, D.C. 20505 (703) 482-1100,
www.cia.gov; *The World Factbook.*

The Economist Intelligence Unit (Asia)
Limited, 10th Floor, Luk Kwok Centre, 72
Gloucester Road, Wanchai, Hong Kong
(Phone Number in U.S. (800) 938-4685);
Asian Market Atlas.

International Road Federation, 2600
Virginia Avenue, NW., Washington, D.C.
20037 (202) 338-4641; *World Road
Statistics.*

St. Martin's Press, Inc., 175 Fifth
Avenue, New York, New York 10010 (800)
221-7945; *The Statesman's Year-Book.*

PAKISTAN - HORSES - See PAKISTAN -
LIVESTOCK AND POULTRY

PAKISTAN - HOURS OF WORK - See
PAKISTAN - EMPLOYMENT

PAKISTAN - HOUSING AND HOUSING
UNITS

Euromonitor International, Inc., 122
South Michigan Avenue, Suite 1200,
Chicago. Illinois 60603 (800) 577-EURO;
World Marketing Data and Statistics.

PAKISTAN - HOUSING EXPENDITURES

International Monetary Fund, 700
Nineteenth Street, NW, Washington, D.C.
20431 (202) 623-7000; *Government
Finance Statistics Yearbook.*

M.E. Sharpe, 80 Business Park Drive,
Armonk, New York 10504 (800) 541-6563;
The Illustrated Book of World Rankings.

PAKISTAN - ILLITERATE POPULATION

Central Intelligence Agency,
Washington, D.C. 20505 (703) 482-1100,
www.cia.gov; *The World Factbook.*

The Economist Intelligence Unit, 111
West 57th Street, New York, New York
10019 (800) 938-4685; *The World Market
Atlas.*

Euromonitor International, Inc., 122
South Michigan Avenue, Suite 1200,
Chicago. Illinois 60603 (800) 577-EURO;
The World Economic Factbook.

St. Martin's Press, Inc., 175 Fifth
Avenue, New York, New York 10010 (800)
221-7945; *The Statesman's Year-Book.*

Statistical Office of the United Nations, Publishing Service, New York, New York 10017 (800) 253-9646; *Asia-Pacific in Figures;* and *Human Development Report.*

United Nations Educational, Scientific and Cultural Organization (UNESCO), 7 Place de Fontenoy, F-75700 Paris, France (Telephone Number in U.S. (212) 963-5981); *Statistical Yearbook.*

PAKISTAN - IMPORTS

Asian Development Bank, Post Office Box 789, 1099 Manila, Philippines; *Key Indicators of Developing Asian and Pacific Countries.*

The Economist Intelligence Unit, 111 West 57th Street, New York, New York 10019 (800) 938-4685; *Pakistan Country Report;* and *The World Market Atlas.*

The Economist Intelligence Unit (Asia) Limited, 10th Floor, Luk Kwok Centre, 72 Gloucester Road, Wanchai, Hong Kong (Phone Number in U.S. (800) 938-4685); *Asian Market Atlas.*

Euromonitor International, Inc., 122 South Michigan Avenue, Suite 1200, Chicago. Illinois 60603 (800) 577-EURO; *International Marketing Data and Statistics;* and *The World Economic Factbook.*

Europa Publications Limited, 18 Bedford Square, London, WC1B 3JN, England; *The Europa World Year Book.*

Food and Agricultural Organization of the United Nations (FAO) Via delle Terme di Caracalla, 00100 Rome, Italy (Telephone Number in U.S. (202) 653-2400); *The State of Food and Agriculture.*

International Monetary Fund, 700 Nineteenth Street, NW, Washington, D.C. 20431 (202) 623-7000; *Direction of Trade Statistics; Government Finance Statistics Yearbook;* and *International Financial Statistics.*

St. Martin's Press, Inc., 175 Fifth Avenue, New York, New York 10010 (800) 221-7945; *The Statesman's Year-Book.*

Statistical Office of the United Nations, Publishing Service, New York, New York 10017 (800) 253-9646; *Foreign Trade Statistics of Asia and the Pacific.*

United Nations Conference on Trade and Development (UNCTAD), New York, New York 10017 (800) 253-9646; *Handbook of International Trade and Development Statistics.*

Walden Publishing, Ltd., Two Market Street, Saffron Walden Essex, CB10 1HZ, England; *The World of Information Asia and Pacific Review.*

The World Bank, 1818 H Street, NW, Washington, D.C. 20433 (202) 477-1234; *World Development Report;* and *World Development Indicators.*

PAKISTAN - INCOME TAXES - See PAKISTAN - TAXATION

PAKISTAN - INDUSTRIAL METALS PRODUCTION - See PAKISTAN - MINING AND MINERAL PRODUCTS

PAKISTAN - INDUSTRY

Central Intelligence Agency, Washington, D.C. 20505 (703) 482-1100, www.cia.gov; *The World Factbook.*

Economist Intelligence Unit, 111 West 57th Street, New York, New York 10019 (800) 938-4685; *Pakistan Country Report.*

Euromonitor International, Inc., 122 South Michigan Avenue, Suite 1200, Chicago. Illinois 60603 (800) 577-EURO; *International Marketing Data and Statistics; The World Economic Factbook;* and *World Marketing Data and Statistics.*

Europa Publications Limited, 18 Bedford Square, London, WC1B 3JN, England; *The Europa World Year Book.*

International Labour Office, I.L.O. Publications, 1828 L Street, NW., Suite 801, Washington, D.C. 20036 (301) 638-3152; *Yearbook of Labour Statistics.*

M.E. Sharpe, 80 Business Park Drive, Armonk, New York 10504 (800) 541-6563; *The Illustrated Book of World Rankings.*

St. Martin's Press, Inc., 175 Fifth Avenue, New York, New York 10010 (800) 221-7945; *The Statesman's Year-Book.*

Statistical Office of the United Nations, Publishing Service, New York, New York 10017 (800) 253-9646; *Asia-Pacific in Figures; Statistical Yearbook;* and *Statistical Yearbook for Asia and the Pacific.*

The World Bank, 1818 H Street, NW, Washington, D.C. 20433 (202) 477-1234; *World Development Indicators.*

World Intellectual Property Organization, 34 Chemin des Colombettes, CH-1211 Geneva 20, Switzerland; *Industrial Property Statistics.*

PAKISTAN - INFANT AND MATERNAL MORTALITY - See PAKISTAN - MORTALITY

PAKISTAN - INTERNAL TRADE

Statistical Office of the United Nations, Publishing Service, New York, New York 10017 (800) 253-9646; *Statistical Yearbook for Asia and the Pacific.*

PAKISTAN - INTERNATIONAL LIQUIDITY

International Monetary Fund, 700 Nineteenth Street, NW, Washington, D.C. 20431 (202) 623-7000; *International Financial Statistics.*

PAKISTAN - INTERNATIONAL RESERVES EXCLUDING GOLD

Asian Development Bank, Post Office Box 789, 1099 Manila, Philippines; *Key Indicators of Developing Asian and Pacific Countries.*

Statistical Office of the United Nations, Publishing Service, New York, New York 10017 (800) 253-9646; *Statistical Yearbook.*

The World Bank, 1818 H Street, NW, Washington, D.C. 20433 (202) 477-1234; *World Development Indicators.*

PAKISTAN - INTERNATIONAL STATISTICS

Asian Development Bank, Post Office Box 789, 1099 Manila, Philippines; *Key Indicators of Developing Asian and Pacific Countries.*

PAKISTAN - INVESTMENTS

International Monetary Fund, 700 Nineteenth Street, NW, Washington, D.C. 20431 (202) 623-7000; *International Financial Statistics.*

PAKISTAN - IRON ORE PRODUCTION AND CONSUMPTION - See PAKISTAN - MINING AND MINERAL PRODUCTS

PAKISTAN - IRRIGATION

Euromonitor International, Inc., 122 South Michigan Avenue, Suite 1200, Chicago. Illinois 60603 (800) 577-EURO; *International Marketing Data and Statistics.*

PAKISTAN - JUTE PRODUCTION - See PAKISTAN - CROPS

PAKISTAN - LABOR

Central Intelligence Agency, Washington, D.C. 20505 (703) 482-1100, www.cia.gov; *The World Factbook.*

The Economist Intelligence Unit (Asia) Limited, 10th Floor, Luk Kwok Centre, 72 Gloucester Road, Wanchai, Hong Kong (Phone Number in U.S. (800) 938-4685); *Asian Market Atlas.*

Euromonitor International, Inc., 122 South Michigan Avenue, Suite 1200, Chicago. Illinois 60603 (800) 577-EURO; *International Marketing Data and Statistics;* and *World Marketing Data and Statistics.*

Europa Publications Limited, 18 Bedford Square, London, WC1B 3JN, England; *The Europa World Year Book*.

Food and Agricultural Organization of the United Nations (FAO) Via delle Terme di Caracalla, 00100 Rome, Italy (Telephone Number in U.S. (202) 653-2400); *The State of Food and Agriculture*.

International Labour Office, I.L.O. Publications, 1828 L Street, NW., Suite 801, Washington, D.C. 20036 (301) 638-3152; *Yearbook of Labour Statistics*.

M.E. Sharpe, 80 Business Park Drive, Armonk, New York 10504 (800) 541-6563; *The Illustrated Book of World Rankings*.

St. Martin's Press, Inc., 175 Fifth Avenue, New York, New York 10010 (800) 221-7945; *The Statesman's Year-Book*.

Statistical Office of the United Nations, Publishing Service, New York, New York 10017 (800) 253-9646; *Human Development Report*

The World Bank, 1818 H Street, NW, Washington, D.C. 20433 (202) 477-1234; *The World Bank Atlas; World Development Report;* and *World Development Indicators*.

PAKISTAN - LAND USE

Central Intelligence Agency, Washington, D.C. 20505 (703) 482-1100, www.cia.gov; *The World Factbook*.

Euromonitor International, Inc., 122 South Michigan Avenue, Suite 1200, Chicago. Illinois 60603 (800) 577-EURO; *International Marketing Data and Statistics*.

Food and Agricultural Organization of the United Nations (FAO), Via delle Terme di Caracalla, 00100 Rome, Italy (Telephone Number in U.S. (202) 653-2400); *Production Yearbook*.

The World Bank, 1818 H Street, NW, Washington, D.C. 20433 (202) 477-1234; *World Development Report*.

PAKISTAN - LIBRARIES

M.E. Sharpe, 80 Business Park Drive, Armonk, New York 10504 (800) 541-6563; *The Illustrated Book of World Rankings*.

United Nations Educational, Scientific and Cultural Organization (UNESCO), 7 Place de Fontenoy, F-75700 Paris, France (Telephone Number in U.S. (212) 963-5981); *Statistical Yearbook*.

PAKISTAN - LIFE EXPECTANCY

Central Intelligence Agency, Washington, D.C. 20505 (703) 482-1100,

www.cia.gov; *The World Factbook*.

The Economist Intelligence Unit (Asia) Limited, 10th Floor, Luk Kwok Centre, 72 Gloucester Road, Wanchai, Hong Kong (Phone Number in U.S. (800) 938-4685); *Asian Market Atlas*.

Euromonitor International, Inc., 122 South Michigan Avenue, Suite 1200, Chicago. Illinois 60603 (800) 577-EURO; *The World Economic Factbook*.

St. Martin's Press, Inc., 175 Fifth Avenue, New York, New York 10010 (800) 221-7945; *The Statesman's Year-Book*.

Statistical Office of the United Nations, Publishing Service, New York, New York 10017 (800) 253-9646; *Asia-Pacific in Figures; World Statistics Pocketbook;* and *Human Development Report*.

The World Bank, 1818 H Street, NW, Washington, D.C. 20433 (202) 477-1234; *The World Bank Atlas;* and *World Development Report*.

PAKISTAN - LIGNITE PRODUCTION - See PAKISTAN - MINING AND MINERAL PRODUCTS

PAKISTAN - LITERACY RATE

Euromonitor International, Inc., 122 South Michigan Avenue, Suite 1200, Chicago. Illinois 60603 (800) 577-EURO; *World Marketing Data and Statistics*.

PAKISTAN - LIVESTOCK AND POULTRY

Euromonitor International, Inc., 122 South Michigan Avenue, Suite 1200, Chicago. Illinois 60603 (800) 577-EURO; *International Marketing Data and Statistics*.

Europa Publications Limited, 18 Bedford Square, London, WC1B 3JN, England; *The Europa World Year Book*.

Food and Agricultural Organization of the United Nations (FAO), Via delle Terme di Caracalla, 00100 Rome, Italy (Telephone Number in U.S. (202) 653-2400); *Production Yearbook;* and *The State of Food and Agriculture*.

M.E. Sharpe, 80 Business Park Drive, Armonk, New York 10504 (800) 541-6563; *The Illustrated Book of World Rankings*.

St. Martin's Press, Inc., 175 Fifth Avenue, New York, New York 10010 (800) 221-7945; *The Statesman's Year-Book*.

Statistical Office of the United Nations, Publishing Service, New York, New York 10017 (800) 253-9646; *Statistical Yearbook*.

United Nations Conference on Trade and Development, Central Statistical Service, Palais des Nations, Geneva, Switzerland (Telephone in U.S. (800) 253-9646); *UNCTAD Commodity Yearbook*.

PAKISTAN - LIVING LEVELS - See PAKISTAN - LIFE EXPECTANCY

PAKISTAN - MAIL - NUMBER OF PIECES SENT OR RECEIVED

Statistical Office of the United Nations, Publishing Service, New York, New York 10017 (800) 253-9646; *Statistical Yearbook*.

PAKISTAN - MANGANESE ORE PRODUCTION AND CONSUMPTION - See PAKISTAN - MINING AND MINERAL PRODUCTS

PAKISTAN - MANPOWER

Statistical Office of the United Nations, Publishing Service, New York, New York 10017 (800) 253-9646; *Statistical Yearbook for Asia and the Pacific*.

PAKISTAN - MANUFACTURING

Asian Development Bank, Post Office Box 789, 1099 Manila, Philippines; *Key Indicators of Developing Asian and Pacific Countries*.

M.E. Sharpe, 80 Business Park Drive, Armonk, New York 10504 (800) 541-6563; *The Illustrated Book of World Rankings*.

Statistical Office of the United Nations, Publishing Service, New York, New York 10017 (800) 253-9646; *Statistical Yearbook*.

The World Bank, 1818 H Street, NW, Washington, D.C. 20433 (202) 477-1234; *World Development Indicators*.

PAKISTAN - MARRIAGE RATES

M.E. Sharpe, 80 Business Park Drive, Armonk, New York 10504 (800) 541-6563; *The Illustrated Book of World Rankings*.

Statistical Office of the United Nations, Publishing Service, New York, New York 10017 (800) 253-9646; *Demographic Yearbook*.

PAKISTAN - MEAT PRODUCTION - See PAKISTAN - LIVESTOCK AND POULTRY

PAKISTAN - MERCHANT SHIPPING

Europa Publications Limited, 18 Bedford Square, London, WC1B 3JN, England; *The Europa World Year Book*.

Lloyd's Register of Shipping, 17 Battery Place, New York, New York 10004 (212) 425-8050; *Register of Ships*.

St. Martin's Press, Inc., 175 Fifth Avenue, New York, New York 10010 (800) 221-7945; *The Statesman's Year-Book.*

Statistical Office of the United Nations, Publishing Service, New York, New York 10017 (800) 253-9646; *Statistical Yearbook.*

U.S. Department of Transportation, Maritime Administration, 400 Seventh Street, SW, Washington, D.C. 20590 (202) 366-5807, www.marad.dot.gov; *A Statistical Analysis of the World's Merchant Fleets.*

PAKISTAN - MILITARY

Central Intelligence Agency, Washington, D.C. 20505 (703) 482-1100, www.cia.gov; *The World Factbook.*

The Economist Intelligence Unit (Asia) Limited, 10th Floor, Luk Kwok Centre, 72 Gloucester Road, Wanchai, Hong Kong (Phone Number in U.S. (800) 938-4685); *Asian Market Atlas.*

Euromonitor International, Inc., 122 South Michigan Avenue, Suite 1200, Chicago. Illinois 60603 (800) 577-EURO; *World Marketing Data and Statistics.*

The International Institute for Strategic Studies, 23 Tavistock Street, London WC2E 7NQ, England 44 171 3797676; *The Military Balance.*

International Monetary Fund, 700 Nineteenth Street, NW, Washington, D.C. 20431 (202) 623-7000; *Government Finance Statistics Yearbook.*

St. Martin's Press, Inc., 175 Fifth Avenue, New York, New York 10010 (800) 221-7945; *The Statesman's Year-Book.*

Statistical Office of the United Nations, Publishing Service, New York, New York 10017 (800) 253-9646; *Human Development Report.*

U.S. Arms Control and Disarmament Agency, 320 Twenty-first Street, NW, Washington, D.C. 20451 (202) 647-8677; *World Military Expenditures and Arms Transfers.*

PAKISTAN - MILK PRODUCTION - See PAKISTAN - DAIRY PRODUCTS

PAKISTAN - MILLET PRODUCTION - See PAKISTAN - CROPS

PAKISTAN - MINING AND MINERAL PRODUCTS

Asian Development Bank, Post Office Box 789, 1099 Manila, Philippines; *Key Indicators of Developing Asian and Pacific Countries.*

Commodity Research Bureau, Inc., 30 South Wacker Drive, Chicago Illinois 60606 (312) 454-1801; *Commodity Year Book.*

Europa Publications Limited, 18 Bedford Square, London, WC1B 3JN, England; *The Europa World Year Book.*

M.E. Sharpe, 80 Business Park Drive, Armonk, New York 10504 (800) 541-6563; *The Illustrated Book of World Rankings.*

Penn Well Publishing Company, 1421 South Sheridan Road, Post Office Box 1260, Tulsa, Oklahoma 74101 (800) 752-9764; *International Energy Statistics Sourcebook.*

St. Martin's Press, Inc., 175 Fifth Avenue, New York, New York 10010 (800) 221-7945; *The Statesman's Year-Book.*

Statistical Office of the United Nations, Publishing Service, New York, New York 10017 (800) 253-9646; *Statistical Yearbook.*

United Nations Conference on Trade and Development, Central Statistical Service, Palais des Nations, Geneva, Switzerland (Telephone in U.S. (800) 253-9646); *UNCTAD Commodity Yearbook.*

PAKISTAN - MONEY EXCHANGE RATE - See PAKISTAN - EXCHANGE RATES

PAKISTAN - MONEY MARKET RATES

Statistical Office of the United Nations, Publishing Service, New York, New York 10017 (800) 253-9646; *Statistical Yearbook.*

PAKISTAN - MONEY RESERVES

Euromonitor International, Inc., 122 South Michigan Avenue, Suite 1200, Chicago. Illinois 60603 (800) 577-EURO; *International Marketing Data and Statistics.*

PAKISTAN - MONEY SUPPLY

Asian Development Bank, Post Office Box 789, 1099 Manila, Philippines; *Key Indicators of Developing Asian and Pacific Countries.*

Economist Intelligence Unit, 111 West 57th Street, New York, New York 10019 (800) 938-4685; *Pakistan Country Report.*

Euromonitor International, Inc., 122 South Michigan Avenue, Suite 1200, Chicago. Illinois 60603 (800) 577-EURO; *International Marketing Data and Statistics.*

Europa Publications Limited, 18 Bedford Square, London, WC1B 3JN, England; *The Europa World Year Book.*

International Monetary Fund, 700 Nineteenth Street, NW, Washington, D.C.

20431 (202) 623-7000; *International Financial Statistics.*

Statistical Office of the United Nations, Publishing Service, New York, New York 10017 (800) 253-9646; *Statistical Yearbook.*

The World Bank, 1818 H Street, NW, Washington, D.C. 20433 (202) 477-1234; *World Development Indicators.*

PAKISTAN - MORTALITY

Central Intelligence Agency, Washington, D.C. 20505 (703) 482-1100, www.cia.gov; *The World Factbook.*

The Economist Intelligence Unit (Asia) Limited, 10th Floor, Luk Kwok Centre, 72 Gloucester Road, Wanchai, Hong Kong (Phone Number in U.S. (800) 938-4685); *Asian Market Atlas.*

Euromonitor International, Inc., 122 South Michigan Avenue, Suite 1200, Chicago. Illinois 60603 (800) 577-EURO; *International Marketing Data and Statistics;* and *The World Economic Factbook.*

Europa Publications Limited, 18 Bedford Square, London, WC1B 3JN, England; *The Europa World Year Book.*

St. Martin's Press, Inc., 175 Fifth Avenue, New York, New York 10010 (800) 221-7945; *The Statesman's Year-Book.*

Statistical Office of the United Nations, Publishing Service, New York, New York 10017 (800) 253-9646; *Asia-Pacific in Figures; Demographic Yearbook; Human Development Report; World Statistics Pocketbook;* and *Statistical Yearbook.*

United Nations Children's Fund (UNICEF), 3 United Nations Plaza, New York, New York 10017 (800) 253-9646; *State of the World's Children.*

The World Bank, 1818 H Street, NW, Washington, D.C. 20433 (202) 477-1234; *The World Bank Atlas; World Development Report;* and *World Development Indicators.*

World Health Organization, Office of Publications, 20 Avenue Appia, CH-1211 Geneva 27, Switzerland (Telephone Number in U.S. (518) 436-9686); *World Health Statistics Annual.*

PAKISTAN - MOTION PICTURES

St. Martin's Press, Inc., 175 Fifth Avenue, New York, New York 10010 (800) 221-7945; *The Statesman's Year-Book.*

Statistical Office of the United Nations, Publishing Service, New York, New York 10017 (800) 253-9646; *Statistical Yearbook.*

United Nations Educational, Scientific and Cultural Organization (UNESCO), 7 Place de Fontenoy, F-75700 Paris, France (Telephone Number in U.S. (212) 963-5981); *Statistical Yearbook*.

PAKISTAN - MOTOR VEHICLE TAXES - See PAKISTAN - TAXATION

PAKISTAN - MOTOR VEHICLES IN USE

Europa Publications Limited, 18 Bedford Square, London, WC1B 3JN, England; *The Europa World Year Book*.

International Road Federation, 2600 Virginia Avenue, NW., Washington, D.C. 20037 (202) 338-4641; *World Road Statistics*.

Statistical Office of the United Nations, Publishing Service, New York, New York 10017 (800) 253-9646; *Statistical Yearbook*.

PAKISTAN - MULES - See PAKISTAN - LIVESTOCK AND POULTRY

PAKISTAN - MUSEUMS

M.E. Sharpe, 80 Business Park Drive, Armonk, New York 10504 (800) 541-6563; *The Illustrated Book of World Rankings*.

United Nations Educational, Scientific and Cultural Organization (UNESCO), 7 Place de Fontenoy, F-75700 Paris, France (Telephone Number in U.S. (212) 963-5981); *Statistical Yearbook*.

PAKISTAN - NATALITY - See PAKISTAN - BIRTH RATES

PAKISTAN - NATIONAL ACCOUNTS

Europa Publications Limited, 18 Bedford Square, London, WC1B 3JN, England; *The Europa World Year Book*.

International Monetary Fund, 700 Nineteenth Street, NW, Washington, D.C. 20431 (202) 623-7000; *International Financial Statistics*.

Statistical Office of the United Nations, Publishing Service, New York, New York 10017 (800) 253-9646; *Asia-Pacific in Figures; National Accounts Statistics; Statistical Yearbook;* and *Statistical Yearbook for Asia and the Pacific*.

PAKISTAN - NATIONAL INCOME

M.E. Sharpe, 80 Business Park Drive, Armonk, New York 10504 (800) 541-6563; *The Illustrated Book of World Rankings*.

Statistical Office of the United Nations, Publishing Service, New York, New York 10017 (800) 253-9646; *National Accounts Statistics;* and *Statistical Yearbook*.

PAKISTAN - NATIONAL PRODUCT

M.E. Sharpe, 80 Business Park Drive, Armonk, New York 10504 (800) 541-6563; *The Illustrated Book of World Rankings*.

Statistical Office of the United Nations, Publishing Service, New York, New York 10017 (800) 253-9646; *Statistical Yearbook*.

PAKISTAN - NATURAL GAS - PRODUCTION - See PAKISTAN - MINING AND MINERAL PRODUCTS

PAKISTAN - NEWSPAPER PRODUCTION AND CONSUMPTION - See PAKISTAN - FORESTRY AND FOREST PRODUCTS

PAKISTAN - NEWSPRINT - See PAKISTAN - FORESTRY AND FOREST PRODUCTS

PAKISTAN - OCCUPATIONS - See PAKISTAN - LABOR

PAKISTAN - PAPER - See PAKISTAN - FORESTRY AND FOREST PRODUCTS

PAKISTAN - PATENTS, TRADEMARKS AND SERVICE MARKS

Statistical Office of the United Nations, Publishing Service, New York, New York 10017 (800) 253-9646; *Statistical Yearbook*.

World Intellectual Property Organization, 34 Chemin des Colombettes, CH-1211 Geneva 20, Switzerland; *Industrial Property Statistics*.

PAKISTAN - PEANUT PRODUCTION - See PAKISTAN - CROPS

PAKISTAN - PERIODICALS

United Nations Educational, Scientific and Cultural Organization (UNESCO), 7 Place de Fontenoy, F-75700 Paris, France (Telephone Number in U.S. (212) 963-5981); *Statistical Yearbook*.

PAKISTAN - PESTICIDE USE

Food and Agricultural Organization of the United Nations (FAO) Via delle Terme di Caracalla, 00100 Rome, Italy (Telephone Number in U.S. (202) 653-2400); *The State of Food and Agriculture*.

PAKISTAN - PETROLEUM INDUSTRY

Asian Development Bank, Post Office Box 789, 1099 Manila, Philippines; *Key Indicators of Developing Asian and Pacific Countries*.

Food and Agricultural Organization of the United Nations (FAO) Via delle Terme di Caracalla, 00100 Rome, Italy (Telephone Number in U.S. (202) 653-2400); *The State of Food and Agriculture*.

M.E. Sharpe, 80 Business Park Drive, Armonk, New York 10504 (800) 541-6563; *The Illustrated Book of World Rankings*.

Penn Well Publishing Company, 1421 South Sheridan Road, Post Office Box 1260, Tulsa, Oklahoma 74101 (800) 752-9764; *International Energy Statistics Sourcebook*.

St. Martin's Press, Inc., 175 Fifth Avenue, New York, New York 10010 (800) 221-7945; *The Statesman's Year-Book*.

Statistical Office of the United Nations, Publishing Service, New York, New York 10017 (800) 253-9646; *Statistical Yearbook*.

United Nations Conference on Trade and Development, Central Statistical Service, Palais des Nations, Geneva, Switzerland (Telephone in U.S. (800) 253-9646); *UNCTAD Commodity Yearbook*.

PAKISTAN - PHOSPHATE ROCK PRODUCTION - See PAKISTAN - MINING AND MINERAL PRODUCTS

PAKISTAN - PIGS - See PAKISTAN - LIVESTOCK AND POULTRY

PAKISTAN - POPULATION

Asian Development Bank, Post Office Box 789, 1099 Manila, Philippines; *Key Indicators of Developing Asian and Pacific Countries*.

Central Intelligence Agency, Washington, D.C. 20505 (703) 482-1100, www.cia.gov; *The World Factbook*.

The Economist Intelligence Unit, 111 West 57th Street, New York, New York 10019 (800) 938-4685; *Pakistan Country Report;* and *The World Market Atlas*.

The Economist Intelligence Unit (Asia) Limited, 10th Floor, Luk Kwok Centre, 72 Gloucester Road, Wanchai, Hong Kong (Phone Number in U.S. (800) 938-4685); *Asian Market Atlas*.

Euromonitor International, Inc., 122 South Michigan Avenue, Suite 1200, Chicago. Illinois 60603 (800) 577-EURO; *International Marketing Data and Statistics;* and *The World Economic Factbook*.

Europa Publications Limited, 18 Bedford Square, London, WC1B 3JN, England; *The Europa World Year Book*.

Food and Agricultural Organization of the United Nations (FAO), Via delle Terme di Caracalla, 00100 Rome, Italy (Telephone Number in U.S. (202) 653-2400); *Production Yearbook*.

International Labour Office, I.L.O. Publications, 1828 L Street, NW., Suite 801, Washington, D.C. 20036 (301)

638-3152; *Yearbook of Labour Statistics.*

M.E. Sharpe, 80 Business Park Drive, Armonk, New York 10504 (800) 541-6563; *The Illustrated Book of World Rankings.*

St. Martin's Press, Inc., 175 Fifth Avenue, New York, New York 10010 (800) 221-7945; *The Statesman's Year-Book.*

Statistical Office of the United Nations, Publishing Service, New York, New York 10017 (800) 253-9646; *Asia-Pacific in Figures; Demographic Yearbook; Human Development Report; Statistical Yearbook; World Statistics Pocketbook;* and *Statistical Yearbook for Asia and the Pacific.*

United Nations Educational, Scientific and Cultural Organization (UNESCO), 7 Place de Fontenoy, F-75700 Paris, France (Telephone Number in U.S. (212) 963-5981); *Statistical Yearbook.*

U.S. Arms Control and Disarmament Agency, 320 Twenty-first Street, NW, Washington, D.C. 20451 (202) 647-8677; *World Military Expenditures and Arms Transfers.*

Walden Publishing, Ltd., Two Market Street, Saffron Walden Essex, CB10 1HZ, England; *The World of Information Asia and Pacific Review.*

The World Bank, 1818 H Street, NW, Washington, D.C. 20433 (202) 477-1234; *The World Bank Atlas;* and *World Development Report.*

PAKISTAN - POST OFFICES

M.E. Sharpe, 80 Business Park Drive, Armonk, New York 10504 (800) 541-6563; *The Illustrated Book of World Rankings.*

St. Martin's Press, Inc., 175 Fifth Avenue, New York, New York 10010 (800) 221-7945; *The Statesman's Year-Book.*

PAKISTAN - POTATO PRODUCTION - See PAKISTAN - CROPS

PAKISTAN - POWER PRODUCTION INDUSTRY

Statistical Office of the United Nations, Publishing Service, New York, New York 10017 (800) 253-9646; *Electric Power in Asia and the Pacific.*

PAKISTAN - PRICES

Asian Development Bank, Post Office Box 789, 1099 Manila, Philippines; *Key Indicators of Developing Asian and Pacific Countries.*

Food and Agricultural Organization of the United Nations (FAO), Via delle Terme di Caracalla, 00100 Rome, Italy (Telephone

Number in U.S. (202) 653-2400); *Production Yearbook;* and *The State of Food and Agriculture.*

International Labour Office, I.L.O. Publications, 1828 L Street, NW., Suite 801, Washington, D.C. 20036 (301) 638-3152; *Yearbook of Labour Statistics.*

International Monetary Fund, 700 Nineteenth Street, NW, Washington, D.C. 20431 (202) 623-7000; *International Financial Statistics.*

M.E. Sharpe, 80 Business Park Drive, Armonk, New York 10504 (800) 541-6563; *The Illustrated Book of World Rankings.*

PAKISTAN - PRINTING AND WRITING PAPER - See PAKISTAN - FORESTRY AND FOREST PRODUCTS

PAKISTAN - PRODUCTION

M.E. Sharpe, 80 Business Park Drive, Armonk, New York 10504 (800) 541-6563; *The Illustrated Book of World Rankings.*

PAKISTAN - PRODUCTIVITY

Euromonitor International, Inc., 122 South Michigan Avenue, Suite 1200, Chicago. Illinois 60603 (800) 577-EURO; *International Marketing Data and Statistics.*

PAKISTAN - PROPERTY TAXES - See PAKISTAN - TAXATION

PAKISTAN - PUBLIC FINANCE - See PAKISTAN - FINANCE

PAKISTAN - RADIO BROADCASTING - See PAKISTAN - BROADCASTING

PAKISTAN - RADIO RECEIVERS

St. Martin's Press, Inc., 175 Fifth Avenue, New York, New York 10010 (800) 221-7945; *The Statesman's Year-Book.*

PAKISTAN - RAILWAYS

Europa Publications Limited, 18 Bedford Square, London, WC1B 3JN, England; *The Europa World Year Book.*

Jane's Information Group, Sentinel House, 163 Brighton Road, Coulsdon, Surrey CR5 2NH, England (Telephone Number in U.S. (703) 683-3700); *Jane's World Railways.*

St. Martin's Press, Inc., 175 Fifth Avenue, New York, New York 10010 (800) 221-7945; *The Statesman's Year-Book.*

Statistical Office of the United Nations, Publishing Service, New York, New York 10017 (800) 253-9646; *Statistical Yearbook.*

PAKISTAN - RAPESEED PRODUCTION - See PAKISTAN - CROPS

PAKISTAN - RELIGION

Central Intelligence Agency, Washington, D.C. 20505 (703) 482-1100, www.cia.gov; *The World Factbook.*

M.E. Sharpe, 80 Business Park Drive, Armonk, New York 10504 (800) 541-6563; *The Illustrated Book of World Rankings.*

St. Martin's Press, Inc., 175 Fifth Avenue, New York, New York 10010 (800) 221-7945; *The Statesman's Year-Book.*

PAKISTAN - RENT PRICES

International Labour Office, I.L.O. Publications, 1828 L Street, NW., Suite 801, Washington, D.C. 20036 (301) 638-3152; *Yearbook of Labour Statistics.*

PAKISTAN - RETAIL TRADE

Euromonitor International, Inc., 122 South Michigan Avenue, Suite 1200, Chicago. Illinois 60603 (800) 577-EURO; *World Marketing Data and Statistics.*

PAKISTAN - RICE - See PAKISTAN - CROPS

PAKISTAN - ROOT AND TUBER PRODUCTION - See PAKISTAN - CROPS

PAKISTAN - ROUNDWOOD PRODUCTION - See PAKISTAN - FORESTRY AND FOREST PRODUCTS

PAKISTAN - RUBBER PRODUCTION AND CONSUMPTION

M.E. Sharpe, 80 Business Park Drive, Armonk, New York 10504 (800) 541-6563; *The Illustrated Book of World Rankings.*

PAKISTAN - SALT PRODUCTION - See PAKISTAN - MINING AND MINERAL PRODUCTS

PAKISTAN - SAWNWOOD PRODUCTION - See PAKISTAN - FORESTRY AND FOREST PRODUCTS

PAKISTAN - SCIENCE AND TECHNOLOGY - EXPENDITURE FOR RESEARCH - See PAKISTAN - SCIENTISTS, TECHNICIANS AND ENGINEERS

PAKISTAN - SCIENTISTS, TECHNICIANS AND ENGINEERS

Statistical Office of the United Nations, Publishing Service, New York, New York 10017 (800) 253-9646; *Statistical Yearbook.*

United Nations Educational, Scientific and Cultural Organization (UNESCO), 7 Place de Fontenoy, F-75700 Paris, France (Telephone Number in U.S. (212) 963-

5981); *Statistical Yearbook.*

PAKISTAN - SENIOR CITIZENS

M.E. Sharpe, 80 Business Park Drive, Armonk, New York 10504 (800) 541-6563; *The Illustrated Book of World Rankings.*

PAKISTAN - SESAME SEED PRODUCTION - See PAKISTAN - CROPS

PAKISTAN - SHEEP - See PAKISTAN - LIVESTOCK AND POULTRY

PAKISTAN - SILVER PRODUCTION AND CONSUMPTION - See PAKISTAN - MINING AND MINERAL PRODUCTS

PAKISTAN - SOCIAL DATA

Asian Development Bank, Post Office Box 789, 1099 Manila, Philippines; *Key Indicators of Developing Asian and Pacific Countries.*

M.E. Sharpe, 80 Business Park Drive, Armonk, New York 10504 (800) 541-6563; *The Illustrated Book of World Rankings.*

Statistical Office of the United Nations, Publishing Service, New York, New York 10017 (800) 253-9646; *World Statistics Pocketbook.*

PAKISTAN - SOCIAL SECURITY

International Monetary Fund, 700 Nineteenth Street, NW, Washington, D.C. 20431 (202) 623-7000; *Government Finance Statistics Yearbook.*

Statistical Office of the United Nations, Publishing Service, New York, New York 10017 (800) 253-9646; *National Accounts Statistics.*

PAKISTAN - STATE BUDGET REVENUE AND EXPENDITURES

Euromonitor International, Inc., 122 South Michigan Avenue, Suite 1200, Chicago. Illinois 60603 (800) 577-EURO; *International Marketing Data and Statistics.*

PAKISTAN - STEEL - See PAKISTAN - MINING AND MINERAL PRODUCTS

PAKISTAN - STOCKS - COMMODITY - MARKET PRICE - INDEX

Food and Agricultural Organization of the United Nations (FAO) Via delle Terme di Caracalla, 00100 Rome, Italy (Telephone Number in U.S. (202) 653-2400); *The State of Food and Agriculture.*

PAKISTAN - SUGAR PRODUCTION AND CONSUMPTION - See PAKISTAN - CROPS

PAKISTAN - SULPHURIC ACID

PRODUCTION - See PAKISTAN - MINING AND MINERAL PRODUCTS

PAKISTAN - TAX REVENUES - See PAKISTAN - TAXATION

PAKISTAN - TAXATION

Europa Publications Limited, 18 Bedford Square, London, WC1B 3JN, England; *The Europa World Year Book.*

International Monetary Fund, 700 Nineteenth Street, NW, Washington, D.C. 20431 (202) 623-7000; *Government Finance Statistics Yearbook.*

International Road Federation, 2600 Virginia Avenue, NW., Washington, D.C. 20037 (202) 338-4641; *World Road Statistics.*

The World Bank, 1818 H Street, NW, Washington, D.C. 20433 (202) 477-1234; *World Development Indicators.*

PAKISTAN - TEA PRODUCTION AND CONSUMPTION - See PAKISTAN - CROPS

PAKISTAN - TELEGRAPH SERVICE

Statistical Office of the United Nations, Publishing Service, New York, New York 10017 (800) 253-9646; *Statistical Yearbook.*

PAKISTAN - TELEPHONES IN USE

American Telephone and Telegraph Company, 26 Parsippany Road, Whippany, New Jersey 07981 (800) 222-0300; *The World's Telephones.*

Central Intelligence Agency, Washington, D.C. 20505 (703) 482-1100, www.cia.gov; *The World Factbook.*

The Economist Intelligence Unit (Asia) Limited, 10th Floor, Luk Kwok Centre, 72 Gloucester Road, Wanchai, Hong Kong (Phone Number in U.S. (800) 938-4685); *Asian Market Atlas.*

St. Martin's Press, Inc., 175 Fifth Avenue, New York, New York 10010 (800) 221-7945; *The Statesman's Year-Book.*

Statistical Office of the United Nations, Publishing Service, New York, New York 10017 (800) 253-9646; *Statistical Yearbook;* and *World Statistics Pocketbook.*

PAKISTAN - TELEVISION BROADCASTING - See PAKISTAN - BROADCASTING

PAKISTAN - TEXTILE INDUSTRY

American Forest and Paper Association, 1111 Nineteenth Street, NW, Washington, D.C. 20036 (202) 463-2700; *Wood Pulp and Fiber Statistics.*

Food and Agricultural Organization of the United Nations (FAO), Via delle Terme di Caracalla, 00100 Rome, Italy (Telephone Number in U.S. (202) 653-2400); *Production Yearbook.*

M.E. Sharpe, 80 Business Park Drive, Armonk, New York 10504 (800) 541-6563; *The Illustrated Book of World Rankings.*

St. Martin's Press, Inc., 175 Fifth Avenue, New York, New York 10010 (800) 221-7945; *The Statesman's Year-Book.*

Statistical Office of the United Nations, Publishing Service, New York, New York 10017 (800) 253-9646; *Statistical Yearbook.*

United Nations Conference on Trade and Development, Central Statistical Service, Palais des Nations, Geneva, Switzerland (Telephone in U.S. (800) 253-9646); *UNCTAD Commodity Yearbook.*

PAKISTAN - THEATRE

United Nations Educational, Scientific and Cultural Organization (UNESCO), 7 Place de Fontenoy, F-75700 Paris, France (Telephone Number in U.S. (212) 963-5981); *Statistical Yearbook.*

PAKISTAN - TIN - INDUSTRIAL CONSUMPTION - See PAKISTAN - MINING AND MINERAL PRODUCTS

PAKISTAN - TIRE (MOTOR VEHICLE) PRODUCTION

Statistical Office of the United Nations, Publishing Service, New York, New York 10017 (800) 253-9646; *Statistical Yearbook.*

PAKISTAN - TOBACCO PRODUCTION

Commodity Research Bureau, Inc., 30 South Wacker Drive, Chicago Illinois 60606 (312) 454-1801; *Commodity Year Book.*

M.E. Sharpe, 80 Business Park Drive, Armonk, New York 10504 (800) 541-6563; *The Illustrated Book of World Rankings.*

Statistical Office of the United Nations, Publishing Service, New York, New York 10017 (800) 253-9646; *Statistical Yearbook.*

PAKISTAN - TOURISM

Euromonitor International, Inc., 122 South Michigan Avenue, Suite 1200, Chicago. Illinois 60603 (800) 577-EURO; *The World Economic Factbook;* and *World Marketing Data and Statistics.*

Europa Publications Limited, 18 Bedford Square, London, WC1B 3JN, England; *The Europa World Year Book.*

M.E. Sharpe, 80 Business Park Drive, Armonk, New York 10504 (800) 541-6563;

The Illustrated Book of World Rankings.

St. Martin's Press, Inc., 175 Fifth Avenue, New York, New York 10010 (800) 221-7945; *The Statesman's Year-Book.*

Statistical Office of the United Nations, Publishing Service, New York, New York 10017 (800) 253-9646; *Statistical Yearbook.*

World Tourism Organization, Calle Capitan Haya 42, E-28020 Madrid, Spain; *Yearbook of Tourism Statistics.*

PAKISTAN - TRACTORS IN USE

Statistical Office of the United Nations, Publishing Service, New York, New York 10017 (800) 253-9646; *Statistical Yearbook.*

PAKISTAN - TRADE - See PAKISTAN - FOREIGN TRADE

PAKISTAN - TRADEMARKS AND SERVICE MARKS - See PAKISTAN - PATENTS, TRADEMARKS AND SERVICE MARKS

PAKISTAN - TRANSPORTATION AND COMMUNICATIONS

Central Intelligence Agency, Washington, D.C. 20505 (703) 482-1100, www.cia.gov; *The World Factbook.*

The Economist Intelligence Unit (Asia) Limited, 10th Floor, Luk Kwok Centre, 72 Gloucester Road, Wanchai, Hong Kong (Phone Number in U.S. (800) 938-4685); *Asian Market Atlas.*

Euromonitor International, Inc., 122 South Michigan Avenue, Suite 1200, Chicago. Illinois 60603 (800) 577-EURO; *International Marketing Data and Statistics;* and *World Marketing Data and Statistics.*

Europa Publications Limited, 18 Bedford Square, London, WC1B 3JN, England; *The Europa World Year Book.*

M.E. Sharpe, 80 Business Park Drive, Armonk, New York 10504 (800) 541-6563; *The Illustrated Book of World Rankings.*

St. Martin's Press, Inc., 175 Fifth Avenue, New York, New York 10010 (800) 221-7945; *The Statesman's Year-Book.*

Statistical Office of the United Nations, Publishing Service, New York, New York 10017 (800) 253-9646; *Asia-Pacific in Figures;* and *Statistical Yearbook for Asia and the Pacific.*

PAKISTAN - UNEMPLOYMENT

Central Intelligence Agency, Washington, D.C. 20505 (703) 482-1100, www.cia.gov; *The World Factbook.*

Euromonitor International, Inc., 122

South Michigan Avenue, Suite 1200, Chicago. Illinois 60603 (800) 577-EURO; *International Marketing Data and Statistics.*

International Labour Office, I.L.O. Publications, 1828 L Street, NW., Suite 801, Washington, D.C. 20036 (301) 638-3152; *Yearbook of Labour Statistics.*

St. Martin's Press, Inc., 175 Fifth Avenue, New York, New York 10010 (800) 221-7945; *The Statesman's Year-Book.*

Statistical Office of the United Nations, Publishing Service, New York, New York 10017 (800) 253-9646; *Statistical Yearbook.*

PAKISTAN - UTILITIES

Statistical Office of the United Nations, Publishing Service, New York, New York 10017 (800) 253-9646; *Electric Power in Asia and the Pacific.*

PAKISTAN - VITAL STATISTICS

Euromonitor International, Inc., 122 South Michigan Avenue, Suite 1200, Chicago. Illinois 60603 (800) 577-EURO; *International Marketing Data and Statistics.*

St. Martin's Press, Inc., 175 Fifth Avenue, New York, New York 10010 (800) 221-7945; *The Statesman's Year-Book.*

Statistical Office of the United Nations, Publishing Service, New York, New York 10017 (800) 253-9646; *Statistical Yearbook.*

PAKISTAN - WAGES

International Labour Office, I.L.O. Publications, 1828 L Street, NW., Suite 801, Washington, D.C. 20036 (301) 638-3152; *Yearbook of Labour Statistics.*

Statistical Office of the United Nations, Publishing Service, New York, New York 10017 (800) 253-9646; *Statistical Yearbook.*

PAKISTAN - WAGES AND PRICES

Statistical Office of the United Nations, Publishing Service, New York, New York 10017 (800) 253-9646; *Statistical Yearbook for Asia and the Pacific.*

PAKISTAN - WEATHER - See PAKISTAN - CLIMATE

PAKISTAN - WELFARE

International Monetary Fund, 700 Nineteenth Street, NW, Washington, D.C. 20431 (202) 623-7000; *Government Finance Statistics Yearbook.*

PAKISTAN - WHEAT PRODUCTION AND PRICES - See PAKISTAN - CROPS

PAKISTAN - WHOLESALE PRICES

Asian Development Bank, Post Office Box 789, 1099 Manila, Philippines; *Key Indicators of Developing Asian and Pacific Countries.*

International Monetary Fund, 700 Nineteenth Street, NW, Washington, D.C. 20431 (202) 623-7000; *International Financial Statistics.*

Statistical Office of the United Nations, Publishing Service, New York, New York 10017 (800) 253-9646; *Statistical Yearbook.*

PAKISTAN - WINE PRODUCTION - See PAKISTAN - BEVERAGES

PAKISTAN - WOOD AND WOOD PULP - See FORESTRY AND FOREST PRODUCTS

PAKISTAN - WOOL PRODUCTION AND CONSUMPTION - See PAKISTAN - TEXTILE INDUSTRY

PAKISTAN - YARN PRODUCTION - See PAKISTAN - TEXTILE INDUSTRY

PAKISTANI POPULATION

U.S. Department of Commerce, Bureau of the Census, Washington, D.C. 20233 (301) 457-4100, www.census.gov; *Census of Population;* and *General Population Characteristics.*

Palau (Republic of) - National Statistical Office

Office of Planning and Statistics, Post Office Box 100, Koror, Republic of Palau, Western Caroline Islands 96940.

Superintendent of Documents, U.S. Government Printing Office, Washington, D.C. 20402; *Annual Report to the United Nations on the Administration of the Trust Territory of the Pacific Islands.*

PALAU (REPUBLIC OF) - AGRICULTURE

Economist Intelligence Unit, 111 West 57th Street, New York, New York 10019 (800) 938-4685; *Pacific Islands Country Report.*

Europa Publications Limited, 18 Bedford Square, London, WC1B 3JN, England; *The Europa World Year Book.*

Food and Agricultural Organization of the United Nations (FAO) Via delle Terme di Caracalla, 00100 Rome, Italy (Telephone Number in U.S. (202) 653-2400); *Production Yearbook; The State of Food and Agriculture;* and *Trade Yearbook.*

Statistical Office of the United Nations, Publishing Service, New York, New York

10017 (800) 253-9646; *Asia-Pacific in Figures; Industrial Commodity Statistics Yearbook; Statistical Yearbook;* and *Statistical Yearbook for Asia and the Pacific.*

United Nations Conference on Trade and Development, Central Statistical Service, Palais des Nations, Geneva, Switzerland (Telephone in U.S. (800) 253-9646); *UNCTAD Commodity Yearbook.*

PALAU (REPUBLIC OF) - AIRLINE SERVICE

Statistical Office of the United Nations, Publishing Service, New York, New York 10017 (800) 253-9646; *Statistical Yearbook.*

PALAU (REPUBLIC OF) - AIRPORTS

Central Intelligence Agency, Washington, D.C. 20505 (703) 482-1100, www.cia.gov; *The World Factbook.*

PALAU (REPUBLIC OF) - AREA AND DENSITY OF POPULATION

Central Intelligence Agency, Washington, D.C. 20505 (703) 482-1100, www.cia.gov; *The World Factbook.*

Europa Publications Limited, 18 Bedford Square, London, WC1B 3JN, England; *The Europa World Year Book.*

Food and Agricultural Organization of the United Nations (FAO) Via delle Terme di Caracalla, 00100 Rome, Italy (Telephone Number in U.S. (202) 653-2400); *The State of Food and Agriculture.*

St. Martin's Press, Inc., 175 Fifth Avenue, New York, New York 10010 (800) 221-7945; *The Statesman's Year-Book.*

United Nations Educational, Scientific and Cultural Organization (UNESCO), 7 Place de Fontenoy, F-75700 Paris, France (Telephone Number in U.S. (212) 963-5981); *Statistical Yearbook.*

PALAU (REPUBLIC OF) - BANKING

St. Martin's Press, Inc., 175 Fifth Avenue, New York, New York 10010 (800) 221-7945; *The Statesman's Year-Book.*

PALAU (REPUBLIC OF) - BEVERAGES

Statistical Office of the United Nations, Publishing Service, New York, New York 10017 (800) 253-9646; *Statistical Yearbook.*

PALAU (REPUBLIC OF) - BIRTH RATES

Central Intelligence Agency, Washington, D.C. 20505 (703) 482-1100, www.cia.gov; *The World Factbook.*

Europa Publications Limited, 18 Bedford Square, London, WC1B 3JN,

England; *The Europa World Year Book.*

Statistical Office of the United Nations, Publishing Service, New York, New York 10017 (800) 253-9646; *Asia-Pacific in Figures; Demographic Yearbook;* and *Statistical Yearbook.*

World Health Organization, Office of Publications, 20 Avenue Appia, CH-1211 Geneva 27, Switzerland (Telephone Number in U.S. (518) 436-9686); *World Health Statistics Annual.*

PALAU (REPUBLIC OF) - BOOK PRODUCTION

United Nations Educational, Scientific and Cultural Organization (UNESCO), 7 Place de Fontenoy, F-75700 Paris, France (Telephone Number in U.S. (212) 963-5981); *Statistical Yearbook.*

PALAU (REPUBLIC OF) - BROADCASTING

Billboard Limited, Post Office Box 9027, 1006 AA Amsterdam, The Netherlands (Telephone Number in U.S. (212) 764-7300); *World Radio TV Handbook.*

Central Intelligence Agency, Washington, D.C. 20505 (703) 482-1100, www.cia.gov; *The World Factbook.*

St. Martin's Press, Inc., 175 Fifth Avenue, New York, New York 10010 (800) 221-7945; *The Statesman's Year-Book.*

United Nations Educational, Scientific and Cultural Organization (UNESCO), 7 Place de Fontenoy, F-75700 Paris, France (Telephone Number in U.S. (212) 963-5981); *Statistical Yearbook.*

PALAU (REPUBLIC OF) - BUDGET

Central Intelligence Agency, Washington, D.C. 20505 (703) 482-1100, www.cia.gov; *The World Factbook.*

PALAU (REPUBLIC OF) - CALORIE SUPPLY

Food and Agricultural Organization of the United Nations (FAO) Via delle Terme di Caracalla, 00100 Rome, Italy (Telephone Number in U.S. (202) 653-2400); *The State of Food and Agriculture.*

PALAU (REPUBLIC OF) - CATTLE - See PALAU (REPUBLIC OF) - LIVESTOCK AND POULTRY

PALAU (REPUBLIC OF) - COMMERCE

St. Martin's Press, Inc., 175 Fifth Avenue, New York, New York 10010 (800) 221-7945; *The Statesman's Year-Book.*

PALAU (REPUBLIC OF) - COMMUNICATIONS - See PALAU

(REPUBLIC OF) - TRANSPORTATION AND COMMUNICATIONS

PALAU (REPUBLIC OF) - CONSTRUCTION INDUSTRY

Statistical Office of the United Nations, Publishing Service, New York, New York 10017 (800) 253-9646; *Statistical Yearbook.*

PALAU (REPUBLIC OF) - CONSUMER PRICE INDEX

Statistical Office of the United Nations, Publishing Service, New York, New York 10017 (800) 253-9646; *Statistical Yearbook.*

PALAU (REPUBLIC OF) - CORN PRODUCTION - See PALAU (REPUBLIC OF) - CROPS

PALAU (REPUBLIC OF) - CROPS

Food and Agricultural Organization of the United Nations (FAO) Via delle Terme di Caracalla, 00100 Rome, Italy (Telephone Number in U.S. (202) 653-2400); *Production Yearbook;* and *The State of Food and Agriculture.*

Statistical Office of the United Nations, Publishing Service, New York, New York 10017 (800) 253-9646; *Industrial Commodity Statistics Yearbook;* and *Statistical Yearbook.*

United Nations Conference on Trade and Development, Central Statistical Service, Palais des Nations, Geneva, Switzerland (Telephone in U.S. (800) 253-9646); *UNCTAD Commodity Yearbook.*

PALAU (REPUBLIC OF) - DAIRY PRODUCTS

Food and Agricultural Organization of the United Nations (FAO) Via delle Terme di Caracalla, 00100 Rome, Italy (Telephone Number in U.S. (202) 653-2400); *The State of Food and Agriculture.*

Statistical Office of the United Nations, Publishing Service, New York, New York 10017 (800) 253-9646; *Industrial Commodity Statistics Yearbook;* and *Statistical Yearbook.*

PALAU (REPUBLIC OF) - DEATH RATES - See PALAU (REPUBLIC OF) - MORTALITY

PALAU (REPUBLIC OF) - DEMOGRAPHY

Statistical Office of the United Nations, Publishing Service, New York, New York 10017 (800) 253-9646; *Asia-Pacific in Figures;* and *Demographic Yearbook.*

PALAU (REPUBLIC OF) - DEVELOPMENT ASSISTANCE

Statistical Office of the United Nations, Publishing Service, New York, New York

10017 (800) 253-9646; *Statistical Yearbook.*

PALAU (REPUBLIC OF) - DISEASES - See PALAU (REPUBLIC OF) - HEALTH

PALAU (REPUBLIC OF) - DIVORCE RATES

Statistical Office of the United Nations, Publishing Service, New York, New York 10017 (800) 253-9646; *Demographic Yearbook;* and *Statistical Yearbook.*

PALAU (REPUBLIC OF) - DUCKS - See PALAU (REPUBLIC OF) - LIVESTOCK AND POULTRY

PALAU (REPUBLIC OF) - ECONOMY

Economist Intelligence Unit, 111 West 57th Street, New York, New York 10019 (800) 938-4685; *Pacific Islands Country Report.*

Central Intelligence Agency, Washington, D.C. 20505 (703) 482-1100, www.cia.gov; *The World Factbook.*

Statistical Office of the United Nations, Publishing Service, New York, New York 10017 (800) 253-9646; *World Statistics Pocketbook.*

PALAU (REPUBLIC OF) - EDUCATION

Europa Publications Limited, 18 Bedford Square, London, WC1B 3JN, England; *The Europa World Year Book.*

St. Martin's Press, Inc., 175 Fifth Avenue, New York, New York 10010 (800) 221-7945; *The Statesman's Year-Book.*

Statistical Office of the United Nations, Publishing Service, New York, New York 10017 (800) 253-9646; *Asia-Pacific in Figures;* and *Statistical Yearbook for Asia and the Pacific.*

United Nations Educational, Scientific and Cultural Organization (UNESCO), 7 Place de Fontenoy, F-75700 Paris, France (Telephone Number in U.S. (212) 963-5981); *Statistical Yearbook.*

PALAU (REPUBLIC OF) - EGG PRODUCTION AND CONSUMPTION - See PALAU (REPUBLIC OF) - DAIRY PRODUCTS

PALAU (REPUBLIC OF) - ELECTRICITY

Central Intelligence Agency, Washington, D.C. 20505 (703) 482-1100, www.cia.gov; *The World Factbook.*

Statistical Office of the United Nations, Publishing Service, New York, New York 10017 (800) 253-9646; *Energy Statistics Yearbook;* and *Statistical Yearbook.*

PALAU (REPUBLIC OF) - EMPLOYMENT

Statistical Office of the United Nations, Publishing Service, New York, New York 10017 (800) 253-9646; *Asia-Pacific in Figures;* and *Statistical Yearbook.*

PALAU (REPUBLIC OF) - ENERGY

Food and Agricultural Organization of the United Nations (FAO) Via delle Terme di Caracalla, 00100 Rome, Italy (Telephone Number in U.S. (202) 653-2400); *The State of Food and Agriculture.*

Statistical Office of the United Nations, Publishing Service, New York, New York 10017 (800) 253-9646; *Asia-Pacific in Figures; Energy Statistics Yearbook; Statistical Yearbook; World Statistics Pocketbook;* and *Statistical Yearbook for Asia and the Pacific;*

PALAU (REPUBLIC OF) - ENVIRONMENT

Economist Intelligence Unit, 111 West 57th Street, New York, New York 10019 (800) 938-4685; *Pacific Islands Country Report.*

Statistical Office of the United Nations, Publishing Service, New York, New York 10017 (800) 253-9646; *Statistical Yearbook;* and *World Statistics Pocketbook.*

PALAU (REPUBLIC OF) - EXCHANGE RATES

Central Intelligence Agency, Washington, D.C. 20505 (703) 482-1100, www.cia.gov; *The World Factbook.*

Statistical Office of the United Nations, Publishing Service, New York, New York 10017 (800) 253-9646; *Statistical Yearbook;* and *World Statistics Pocketbook.*

Walden Publishing, Ltd., Two Market Street, Saffron Walden Essex, CB10 1HZ, England; *The World of Information Asia and Pacific Review.*

PALAU (REPUBLIC OF) - EXPORTS

Central Intelligence Agency, Washington, D.C. 20505 (703) 482-1100, www.cia.gov; *The World Factbook.*

Economist Intelligence Unit, 111 West 57th Street, New York, New York 10019 (800) 938-4685; *Pacific Islands Country Report.*

Europa Publications Limited, 18 Bedford Square, London, WC1B 3JN, England; *The Europa World Year Book.*

Food and Agricultural Organization of the United Nations (FAO) Via delle Terme di Caracalla, 00100 Rome, Italy (Telephone Number in U.S. (202) 653-2400); *The State of Food and Agriculture.*

South Pacific Commission, Post Box D5, Noumea Cedex, New Caledonia; *Statistical Bulletin of the South Pacific: Overseas Trade.*

Statistical Office of the United Nations, Publishing Service, New York, New York 10017 (800) 253-9646; *International Trade Statistics Yearbook.*

Walden Publishing, Ltd., Two Market Street, Saffron Walden Essex, CB10 1HZ, England; *The World of Information Asia and Pacific Review.*

PALAU (REPUBLIC OF) - EXTERNAL TRADE

Food and Agricultural Organization of the United Nations (FAO) Via delle Terme di Caracalla, 00100 Rome, Italy (Telephone Number in U.S. (202) 653-2400); *The State of Food and Agriculture;* and *Trade Yearbook.*

Statistical Office of the United Nations, Publishing Service, New York, New York 10017 (800) 253-9646; *Asia-Pacific in Figures; Statistical Yearbook for Asia and the Pacific;* and *Statistical Yearbook.*

PALAU (REPUBLIC OF) - FARM CROPS - See PALAU (REPUBLIC OF) - CROPS

PALAU (REPUBLIC OF) - FERTILITY RATE

Central Intelligence Agency, Washington, D.C. 20505 (703) 482-1100, www.cia.gov; *The World Factbook.*

World Health Organization, Office of Publications, 20 Avenue Appia, CH-1211 Geneva 27, Switzerland (Telephone Number in U.S. (518) 436-9686); *World Health Statistics Annual.*

PALAU (REPUBLIC OF) - FERTILIZER

Food and Agricultural Organization of the United Nations (FAO) Via delle Terme di Caracalla, 00100 Rome, Italy (Telephone Number in U.S. (202) 653-2400); *The State of Food and Agriculture.*

Statistical Office of the United Nations, Publishing Service, New York, New York 10017 (800) 253-9646; *Industrial Commodity Statistics Yearbook;* and *Statistical Yearbook.*

PALAU (REPUBLIC OF) - FETAL MORTALITY - See PALAU (REPUBLIC OF) - MORTALITY

PALAU (REPUBLIC OF) - FINANCE

Economist Intelligence Unit, 111 West 57th Street, New York, New York 10019 (800) 938-4685; *Pacific Islands Country Report.*

Statistical Office of the United Nations, Publishing Service, New York, New York 10017 (800) 253-9646; *Statistical Yearbook for Asia and the Pacific.*

PALAU (REPUBLIC OF) - FISHERIES

Europa Publications Limited, 18 Bedford Square, London, WC1B 3JN, England; *The Europa World Year Book.*

Food and Agricultural Organization of the United Nations (FAO) Via delle Terme di Caracalla, 00100 Rome, Italy (Telephone Number in U.S. (202) 653-2400); *The State of Food and Agriculture; and Trade Yearbook.*

St. Martin's Press, Inc., 175 Fifth Avenue, New York, New York 10010 (800) 221-7945; *The Statesman's Year-Book.*

Statistical Office of the United Nations, Publishing Service, New York, New York 10017 (800) 253-9646; *Industrial Commodity Statistics Yearbook; and Statistical Yearbook.*

United Nations Conference on Trade and Development, Central Statistical Service, Palais des Nations, Geneva, Switzerland (Telephone in U.S. (800) 253-9646); *UNCTAD Commodity Yearbook.*

PALAU (REPUBLIC OF) - FOOD

Food and Agricultural Organization of the United Nations (FAO) Via delle Terme di Caracalla, 00100 Rome, Italy (Telephone Number in U.S. (202) 653-2400); *Production Yearbook; and The State of Food and Agriculture.*

Statistical Office of the United Nations, Publishing Service, New York, New York 10017 (800) 253-9646; *Industrial Commodity Statistics Yearbook; and Statistical Yearbook for Asia and the Pacific.*

United Nations Conference on Trade and Development, Central Statistical Service, Palais des Nations, Geneva, Switzerland (Telephone in U.S. (800) 253-9646); *UNCTAD Commodity Yearbook.*

PALAU (REPUBLIC OF) - FOREIGN DEBT

Walden Publishing, Ltd., Two Market Street, Saffron Walden Essex, CB10 1HZ, England; *The World of Information Asia and Pacific Review.*

PALAU (REPUBLIC OF) - FOREIGN TRADE

Economist Intelligence Unit, 111 West 57th Street, New York, New York 10019 (800) 938-4685; *Pacific Islands Country Report.*

Food and Agricultural Organization of

the United Nations (FAO) Via delle Terme di Caracalla, 00100 Rome, Italy (Telephone Number in U.S. (202) 653-2400); *The State of Food and Agriculture.*

South Pacific Commission, Post Box D5, Noumea Cedex, New Caledonia; *Statistical Bulletin of the South Pacific: Overseas Trade.*

Statistical Office of the United Nations, Publishing Service, New York, New York 10017 (800) 253-9646; *International Trade Statistics Yearbook; and Statistical Yearbook.*

United Nations Conference on Trade and Development, Central Statistical Service, Palais des Nations, Geneva, Switzerland (Telephone in U.S. (800) 253-9646); *UNCTAD Commodity Yearbook.*

PALAU (REPUBLIC OF) - FORESTRY AND FOREST PRODUCTS

Food and Agricultural Organization of the United Nations (FAO) Via delle Terme di Caracalla, 00100 Rome, Italy (Telephone Number in U.S. (202) 653-2400); *The State of Food and Agriculture.*

Statistical Office of the United Nations, Publishing Service, New York, New York 10017 (800) 253-9646; *Industrial Commodity Statistics Yearbook; and Statistical Yearbook.*

United Nations Conference on Trade and Development, Central Statistical Service, Palais des Nations, Geneva, Switzerland (Telephone in U.S. (800) 253-9646); *UNCTAD Commodity Yearbook.*

United Nations Educational, Scientific and Cultural Organization (UNESCO), 7 Place de Fontenoy, F-75700 Paris, France (Telephone Number in U.S. (212) 963-5981); *Statistical Yearbook.*

PALAU (REPUBLIC OF) - GENERAL MORTALITY - See PALAU (REPUBLIC OF) - MORTALITY

PALAU (REPUBLIC OF) - GOVERNMENT

Central Intelligence Agency, Washington, D.C. 20505 (703) 482-1100, www.cia.gov; *The World Factbook.*

St. Martin's Press, Inc., 175 Fifth Avenue, New York, New York 10010 (800) 221-7945; *The Statesman's Year-Book.*

Statistical Office of the United Nations, Publishing Service, New York, New York 10017 (800) 253-9646; *Asia-Pacific in Figures; and Statistical Yearbook.*

PALAU (REPUBLIC OF) - GRAIN PRODUCTION - See PALAU (REPUBLIC OF) - CROPS

PALAU (REPUBLIC OF) - GROSS DOMESTIC PRODUCT

Economist Intelligence Unit, 111 West 57th Street, New York, New York 10019 (800) 938-4685; *Pacific Islands Country Report.*

Statistical Office of the United Nations, Publishing Service, New York, New York 10017 (800) 253-9646; *Statistical Yearbook.*

PALAU (REPUBLIC OF) - GROSS NATIONAL PRODUCT

Walden Publishing, Ltd., Two Market Street, Saffron Walden Essex, CB10 1HZ, England; *The World of Information Asia and Pacific Review.*

PALAU (REPUBLIC OF) - HEALTH

St. Martin's Press, Inc., 175 Fifth Avenue, New York, New York 10010 (800) 221-7945; *The Statesman's Year-Book.*

Statistical Office of the United Nations, Publishing Service, New York, New York 10017 (800) 253-9646; *Asia-Pacific in Figures; and Statistical Yearbook.*

World Health Organization, Office of Publications, 20 Avenue Appia, CH-1211 Geneva 27, Switzerland (Telephone Number in U.S. (518) 436-9686); *World Health Statistics Annual.*

PALAU (REPUBLIC OF) - HIDE PRODUCTION

Food and Agricultural Organization of the United Nations (FAO), Via delle Terme di Caracalla, 00100 Rome, Italy (Telephone Number in U.S. (202) 653-2400); *Production Yearbook.*

PALAU (REPUBLIC OF) - HIGHWAYS

Central Intelligence Agency, Washington, D.C. 20505 (703) 482-1100, www.cia.gov; *The World Factbook.*

St. Martin's Press, Inc., 175 Fifth Avenue, New York, New York 10010 (800) 221-7945; *The Statesman's Year-Book.*

PALAU (REPUBLIC OF) - ILLITERATE POPULATION

Central Intelligence Agency, Washington, D.C. 20505 (703) 482-1100, www.cia.gov; *The World Factbook.*

Statistical Office of the United Nations, Publishing Service, New York, New York 10017 (800) 253-9646; *Asia-Pacific in Figures.*

United Nations Educational, Scientific and Cultural Organization (UNESCO), 7 Place de Fontenoy, F-75700 Paris, France

(Telephone Number in U.S. (212) 963-5981); *Statistical Yearbook.*

PALAU (REPUBLIC OF) - IMPORTS

Central Intelligence Agency, Washington, D.C. 20505 (703) 482-1100, www.cia.gov; *The World Factbook.*

Economist Intelligence Unit, 111 West 57th Street, New York, New York 10019 (800) 938-4685; *Pacific Islands Country Report.*

Europa Publications Limited, 18 Bedford Square, London, WC1B 3JN, England; *The Europa World Year Book.*

Food and Agricultural Organization of the United Nations (FAO) Via delle Terme di Caracalla, 00100 Rome, Italy (Telephone Number in U.S. (202) 653-2400); *The State of Food and Agriculture.*

South Pacific Commission, Post Box D5, Noumea Cedex, New Caledonia; *Statistical Bulletin of the South Pacific: Overseas Trade.*

St. Martin's Press, Inc., 175 Fifth Avenue, New York, New York 10010 (800) 221-7945; *The Statesman's Year-Book.*

Statistical Office of the United Nations, Publishing Service, New York, New York 10017 (800) 253-9646; *International Trade Statistics Yearbook.*

Walden Publishing, Ltd., Two Market Street, Saffron Walden Essex, CB10 1HZ, England; *The World of Information Asia and Pacific Review.*

PALAU (REPUBLIC OF) - INDUSTRY

Central Intelligence Agency, Washington, D.C. 20505 (703) 482-1100, www.cia.gov; *The World Factbook.*

Economist Intelligence Unit, 111 West 57th Street, New York, New York 10019 (800) 938-4685; *Pacific Islands Country Report.*

Statistical Office of the United Nations, Publishing Service, New York, New York 10017 (800) 253-9646; *Asia-Pacific in Figures; Industrial Commodity Statistics Yearbook;* and *Statistical Yearbook for Asia and the Pacific.*

PALAU (REPUBLIC OF) - INFANT AND MATERNAL MORTALITY - See PALAU (REPUBLIC OF) - MORTALITY

PALAU (REPUBLIC OF) - INTERNAL TRADE

Statistical Office of the United Nations, Publishing Service, New York, New York 10017 (800) 253-9646; *Statistical Yearbook for Asia and the Pacific;* and Statistical

Yearbook.

PALAU (REPUBLIC OF) - LABOR

Central Intelligence Agency, Washington, D.C. 20505 (703) 482-1100, www.cia.gov; *The World Factbook.*

Food and Agricultural Organization of the United Nations (FAO) Via delle Terme di Caracalla, 00100 Rome, Italy (Telephone Number in U.S. (202) 653-2400); *The State of Food and Agriculture.*

Statistical Office of the United Nations, Publishing Service, New York, New York 10017 (800) 253-9646; *Statistical Yearbook.*

PALAU (REPUBLIC OF) - LAND USE

Central Intelligence Agency, Washington, D.C. 20505 (703) 482-1100, www.cia.gov; *The World Factbook.*

Food and Agricultural Organization of the United Nations (FAO), Via delle Terme di Caracalla, 00100 Rome, Italy (Telephone Number in U.S. (202) 653-2400); *Production Yearbook.*

PALAU (REPUBLIC OF) - LIBRARIES

United Nations Educational, Scientific and Cultural Organization (UNESCO), 7 Place de Fontenoy, F-75700 Paris, France (Telephone Number in U.S. (212) 963-5981); *Statistical Yearbook.*

PALAU (REPUBLIC OF) - LIFE EXPECTANCY

Central Intelligence Agency, Washington, D.C. 20505 (703) 482-1100, www.cia.gov; *The World Factbook.*

Statistical Office of the United Nations, Publishing Service, New York, New York 10017 (800) 253-9646; *Asia-Pacific in Figures; Demographic Yearbook;* and *World Statistics Pocketbook.*

World Health Organization, Office of Publications, 20 Avenue Appia, CH-1211 Geneva 27, Switzerland (Telephone Number in U.S. (518) 436-9686); *World Health Statistics Annual.*

PALAU (REPUBLIC OF) - LIVESTOCK AND POULTRY

Food and Agricultural Organization of the United Nations (FAO), Via delle Terme di Caracalla, 00100 Rome, Italy (Telephone Number in U.S. (202) 653-2400); *Production Yearbook;* and *The State of Food and Agriculture.*

Statistical Office of the United Nations, Publishing Service, New York, New York 10017 (800) 253-9646; *Industrial Commodity Statistics Yearbook;* and

Statistical Yearbook.

United Nations Conference on Trade and Development, Central Statistical Service, Palais des Nations, Geneva, Switzerland (Telephone in U.S. (800) 253-9646); *UNCTAD Commodity Yearbook.*

PALAU (REPUBLIC OF) - MACHINERY

Statistical Office of the United Nations, Publishing Service, New York, New York 10017 (800) 253-9646; *Industrial Commodity Statistics Yearbook.*

PALAU (REPUBLIC OF) - MAIL - NUMBER OF PIECES SENT OR RECEIVED

Statistical Office of the United Nations, Publishing Service, New York, New York 10017 (800) 253-9646; *Statistical Yearbook.*

PALAU (REPUBLIC OF) - MANPOWER

Statistical Office of the United Nations, Publishing Service, New York, New York 10017 (800) 253-9646; *Statistical Yearbook for Asia and the Pacific.*

PALAU (REPUBLIC OF) - MANUFACTURING

Statistical Office of the United Nations, Publishing Service, New York, New York 10017 (800) 253-9646; *Industrial Commodity Statistics Yearbook;* and *Statistical Yearbook.*

PALAU (REPUBLIC OF) - MARRIAGE RATES

Statistical Office of the United Nations, Publishing Service, New York, New York 10017 (800) 253-9646; *Demographic Yearbook;* and *Statistical Yearbook.*

PALAU (REPUBLIC OF) - MEAT PRODUCTION - See PALAU (REPUBLIC OF) - LIVESTOCK AND POULTRY

PALAU (REPUBLIC OF) - MERCHANT SHIPPING

St. Martin's Press, Inc., 175 Fifth Avenue, New York, New York 10010 (800) 221-7945; *The Statesman's Year-Book.*

Statistical Office of the United Nations, Publishing Service, New York, New York 10017 (800) 253-9646; *Statistical Yearbook.*

PALAU (REPUBLIC OF) - MILITARY

Central Intelligence Agency, Washington, D.C. 20505 (703) 482-1100, www.cia.gov; *The World Factbook.*

PALAU (REPUBLIC OF) - MINING AND MINERAL PRODUCTS

Statistical Office of the United Nations, Publishing Service, New York, New York

10017 (800) 253-9646; *Energy Statistics Yearbook; Industrial Commodity Statistics Yearbook;* and *Statistical Yearbook.*

United Nations Conference on Trade and Development, Central Statistical Service, Palais des Nations, Geneva, Switzerland (Telephone in U.S. (800) 253-9646); *UNCTAD Commodity Yearbook.*

PALAU (REPUBLIC OF) - MONEY SUPPLY

Economist Intelligence Unit, 111 West 57th Street, New York, New York 10019 (800) 938-4685; *Pacific Islands Country Report.*

PALAU (REPUBLIC OF) - MONUMENTS AND HISTORICAL SITES

United Nations Educational, Scientific and Cultural Organization (UNESCO), 7 Place de Fontenoy, F-75700 Paris, France (Telephone Number in U.S. (212) 963-5981); *Statistical Yearbook.*

PALAU (REPUBLIC OF) - MORTALITY

Central Intelligence Agency, Washington, D.C. 20505 (703) 482-1100, www.cia.gov; *The World Factbook.*

Europa Publications Limited, 18 Bedford Square, London, WC1B 3JN, England; *The Europa World Year Book.*

Statistical Office of the United Nations, Publishing Service, New York, New York 10017 (800) 253-9646; *Asia-Pacific in Figures; Demographic Yearbook; Statistical Yearbook;* and *World Statistics Pocketbook.*

World Health Organization, Office of Publications, 20 Avenue Appia, CH-1211 Geneva 27, Switzerland (Telephone Number in U.S. (518) 436-9686); *World Health Statistics Annual.*

PALAU (REPUBLIC OF) - MOTION PICTURES

Statistical Office of the United Nations, Publishing Service, New York, New York 10017 (800) 253-9646; *Statistical Yearbook.*

United Nations Educational, Scientific and Cultural Organization (UNESCO), 7 Place de Fontenoy, F-75700 Paris, France (Telephone Number in U.S. (212) 963-5981); *Statistical Yearbook.*

PALAU (REPUBLIC OF) - MOTOR VEHICLE PRODUCTION

Statistical Office of the United Nations, Publishing Service, New York, New York 10017 (800) 253-9646; *Statistical Yearbook.*

PALAU (REPUBLIC OF) - MUSEUMS

United Nations Educational, Scientific

and Cultural Organization (UNESCO), 7 Place de Fontenoy, F-75700 Paris, France (Telephone Number in U.S. (212) 963-5981); *Statistical Yearbook.*

PALAU (REPUBLIC OF) - NATALITY - See PALAU (REPUBLIC OF) - BIRTH RATES

PALAU (REPUBLIC OF) - NATIONAL ACCOUNTS

Statistical Office of the United Nations, Publishing Service, New York, New York 10017 (800) 253-9646; *Asia-Pacific in Figures; National Accounts Statistics; Statistical Yearbook for Asia and the Pacific;* and *Statistical Yearbook.*

PALAU (REPUBLIC OF) - NATIONAL INCOME

Statistical Office of the United Nations, Publishing Service, New York, New York 10017 (800) 253-9646; *Statistical Yearbook.*

PALAU (REPUBLIC OF) - NATIONAL PRODUCT

Statistical Office of the United Nations, Publishing Service, New York, New York 10017 (800) 253-9646; *Statistical Yearbook.*

PALAU (REPUBLIC OF) - NEWSPAPER PRODUCTION - See PALAU (REPUBLIC OF) - FORESTRY AND FOREST PRODUCTS

PALAU (REPUBLIC OF) - OCCUPATIONS - See PALAU (REPUBLIC OF) - LABOR

PALAU (REPUBLIC OF) - PATENTS, TRADEMARKS AND SERVICE MARKS

Statistical Office of the United Nations, Publishing Service, New York, New York 10017 (800) 253-9646; *Statistical Yearbook.*

PALAU (REPUBLIC OF) - PERIODICALS

United Nations Educational, Scientific and Cultural Organization (UNESCO), 7 Place de Fontenoy, F-75700 Paris, France (Telephone Number in U.S. (212) 963-5981); *Statistical Yearbook.*

PALAU (REPUBLIC OF) - PESTICIDE USE

Food and Agricultural Organization of the United Nations (FAO) Via delle Terme di Caracalla, 00100 Rome, Italy (Telephone Number in U.S. (202) 653-2400); *The State of Food and Agriculture.*

PALAU (REPUBLIC OF) - PETROLEUM INDUSTRY

Food and Agricultural Organization of the United Nations (FAO) Via delle Terme di Caracalla, 00100 Rome, Italy (Telephone Number in U.S. (202) 653-2400); *The State of Food and Agriculture.*

Statistical Office of the United Nations, Publishing Service, New York, New York 10017 (800) 253-9646; *Energy Statistics Yearbook; Industrial Commodity Statistics Yearbook;* and *Statistical Yearbook.*

United Nations Conference on Trade and Development, Central Statistical Service, Palais des Nations, Geneva, Switzerland (Telephone in U.S. (800) 253-9646); *UNCTAD Commodity Yearbook.*

PALAU (REPUBLIC OF) - PIGS - See PALAU (REPUBLIC OF) - LIVESTOCK AND POULTRY

PALAU (REPUBLIC OF) - POPULATION

Central Intelligence Agency, Washington, D.C. 20505 (703) 482-1100, www.cia.gov; *The World Factbook.*

Economist Intelligence Unit, 111 West 57th Street, New York, New York 10019 (800) 938-4685; *Pacific Islands Country Report.*

Europa Publications Limited, 18 Bedford Square, London, WC1B 3JN, England; *The Europa World Year Book.*

Food and Agricultural Organization of the United Nations (FAO), Via delle Terme di Caracalla, 00100 Rome, Italy (Telephone Number in U.S. (202) 653-2400); *Production Yearbook.*

St. Martin's Press, Inc., 175 Fifth Avenue, New York, New York 10010 (800) 221-7945; *The Statesman's Year-Book.*

Statistical Office of the United Nations, Publishing Service, New York, New York 10017 (800) 253-9646; *Asia-Pacific in Figures; Demographic Yearbook; Statistical Yearbook; Statistical Yearbook for Asia and the Pacific;* and *World Statistics Pocketbook.*

United Nations Educational, Scientific and Cultural Organization (UNESCO), 7 Place de Fontenoy, F-75700 Paris, France (Telephone Number in U.S. (212) 963-5981); *Statistical Yearbook.*

Walden Publishing, Ltd., Two Market Street, Saffron Walden Essex, CB10 1HZ, England; *The World of Information Asia and Pacific Review.*

World Health Organization, Office of Publications, 20 Avenue Appia, CH-1211 Geneva 27, Switzerland (Telephone Number in U.S. (518) 436-9686); *World Health Statistics Annual.*

PALAU (REPUBLIC OF) - PRICES

Food and Agricultural Organization of the United Nations (FAO), Via delle Terme di Caracalla, 00100 Rome, Italy (Telephone

Number in U.S. (202) 653-2400); *Production Yearbook;* and *The State of Food and Agriculture.*

South Pacific Commission, Post Box D5, Noumea Cedex, New Caledonia; *Statistical Bulletin of the South Pacific: Overseas Trade.*

PALAU (REPUBLIC OF) - RADIO RECEIVER PRODUCTION

Statistical Office of the United Nations, Publishing Service, New York, New York 10017 (800) 253-9646; *Statistical Yearbook.*

PALAU (REPUBLIC OF) - RADIO RECEIVERS

St. Martin's Press, Inc., 175 Fifth Avenue, New York, New York 10010 (800) 221-7945; *The Statesman's Year-Book.*

PALAU (REPUBLIC OF) - RAILWAYS

Statistical Office of the United Nations, Publishing Service, New York, New York 10017 (800) 253-9646; *Statistical Yearbook.*

PALAU (REPUBLIC OF) - RELIGION

Central Intelligence Agency, Washington, D.C. 20505 (703) 482-1100, www.cia.gov; *The World Factbook.*

St. Martin's Press, Inc., 175 Fifth Avenue, New York, New York 10010 (800) 221-7945; *The Statesman's Year-Book.*

PALAU (REPUBLIC OF) - RETAIL TRADE

Statistical Office of the United Nations, Publishing Service, New York, New York 10017 (800) 253-9646; *Statistical Yearbook.*

PALAU (REPUBLIC OF) - ROOT AND TUBER PRODUCTION - See PALAU (REPUBLIC OF) - CROPS

PALAU (REPUBLIC OF) - RUBBER PRODUCTION AND CONSUMPTION

Statistical Office of the United Nations, Publishing Service, New York, New York 10017 (800) 253-9646; *Statistical Yearbook.*

PALAU (REPUBLIC OF) - SCIENTISTS, TECHNICIANS AND ENGINEERS

Statistical Office of the United Nations, Publishing Service, New York, New York 10017 (800) 253-9646; *Statistical Yearbook.*

PALAU (REPUBLIC OF) - SOCIAL DATA

Statistical Office of the United Nations, Publishing Service, New York, New York 10017 (800) 253-9646; *World Statistics Pocketbook.*

PALAU (REPUBLIC OF) - STOCKS -

COMMODITY - MARKET PRICE - INDEX

Food and Agricultural Organization of the United Nations (FAO) Via delle Terme di Caracalla, 00100 Rome, Italy (Telephone Number in U.S. (202) 653-2400); *The State of Food and Agriculture.*

PALAU (REPUBLIC OF) - TELEPHONES IN USE

Central Intelligence Agency, Washington, D.C. 20505 (703) 482-1100, www.cia.gov; *The World Factbook.*

St. Martin's Press, Inc., 175 Fifth Avenue, New York, New York 10010 (800) 221-7945; *The Statesman's Year-Book.*

Statistical Office of the United Nations, Publishing Service, New York, New York 10017 (800) 253-9646; *Statistical Yearbook;* and *World Statistics Pocketbook.*

PALAU (REPUBLIC OF) - TEXTILE INDUSTRY

Statistical Office of the United Nations, Publishing Service, New York, New York 10017 (800) 253-9646; *Industrial Commodity Statistics Yearbook;* and *Statistical Yearbook.*

United Nations Conference on Trade and Development, Central Statistical Service, Palais des Nations, Geneva, Switzerland (Telephone in U.S. (800) 253-9646); *UNCTAD Commodity Yearbook.*

PALAU (REPUBLIC OF) - THEATRE

United Nations Educational, Scientific and Cultural Organization (UNESCO), 7 Place de Fontenoy, F-75700 Paris, France (Telephone Number in U.S. (212) 963-5981); *Statistical Yearbook.*

PALAU (REPUBLIC OF) - TIRE (MOTOR VEHICLE) PRODUCTION

Statistical Office of the United Nations, Publishing Service, New York, New York 10017 (800) 253-9646; *Statistical Yearbook.*

PALAU (REPUBLIC OF) - TOBACCO PRODUCTION

Statistical Office of the United Nations, Publishing Service, New York, New York 10017 (800) 253-9646; *Statistical Yearbook.*

PALAU (REPUBLIC OF) - TOURISM

Europa Publications Limited, 18 Bedford Square, London, WC1B 3JN, England; *The Europa World Year Book.*

Statistical Office of the United Nations, Publishing Service, New York, New York 10017 (800) 253-9646; *Statistical Yearbook.*

PALAU (REPUBLIC OF) - TRACTORS IN USE

Statistical Office of the United Nations, Publishing Service, New York, New York 10017 (800) 253-9646; *Statistical Yearbook.*

PALAU (REPUBLIC OF) - TRADE - See PALAU (REPUBLIC OF) - FOREIGN TRADE

PALAU (REPUBLIC OF) - TRADEMARKS AND SERVICE MARKS - See PATENTS, TRADEMARKS AND SERVICE MARKS

PALAU (REPUBLIC OF) - TRANSPORTATION AND COMMUNICATIONS

Central Intelligence Agency, Washington, D.C. 20505 (703) 482-1100, www.cia.gov; *The World Factbook.*

Europa Publications Limited, 18 Bedford Square, London, WC1B 3JN, England; *The Europa World Year Book.*

St. Martin's Press, Inc., 175 Fifth Avenue, New York, New York 10010 (800) 221-7945; *The Statesman's Year-Book.*

Statistical Office of the United Nations, Publishing Service, New York, New York 10017 (800) 253-9646; *Statistical Yearbook for Asia and the Pacific.*

PALAU (REPUBLIC OF) - UNEMPLOYMENT

Central Intelligence Agency, Washington, D.C. 20505 (703) 482-1100, www.cia.gov; *The World Factbook.*

Statistical Office of the United Nations, Publishing Service, New York, New York 10017 (800) 253-9646; *Statistical Yearbook.*

PALAU (REPUBLIC OF) - VITAL STATISTICS

Statistical Office of the United Nations, Publishing Service, New York, New York 10017 (800) 253-9646; *Statistical Yearbook.*

World Health Organization, Office of Publications, 20 Avenue Appia, CH-1211 Geneva 27, Switzerland (Telephone Number in U.S. (518) 436-9686); *World Health Statistics Annual.*

PALAU (REPUBLIC OF) - WAGES AND PRICES

Statistical Office of the United Nations, Publishing Service, New York, New York 10017 (800) 253-9646; *Statistical Yearbook for Asia and the Pacific;* and *Statistical Yearbook.*

PALAU (REPUBLIC OF) - WHOLESALE PRICES

Statistical Office of the United Nations,

Publishing Service, New York, New York 10017 (800) 253-9646; *Statistical Yearbook.*

PALAU (REPUBLIC OF) - WHOLESALE TRADE

Statistical Office of the United Nations, Publishing Service, New York, New York 10017 (800) 253-9646; *Statistical Yearbook.*

Panama - National Statistical Office

Direccion de Estadistica y Censo, Apartado 5213, Panama 5, Panama.

Panama - Primary Statistics Source

Direccion de Estadistica y Censo, Apartado 5213, Panama 5, Panama; *Panama en Cifras* (Panama in figures).

PANAMA - ABORTIONS

Statistical Office of the United Nations, Publishing Service, New York, New York 10017 (800) 253-9646; *Demographic Yearbook.*

PANAMA - AGRICULTURE

The Economist Intelligence Unit, 111 West 57th Street, New York, New York 10019 (800) 938-4685; *Panama Country Report;* and *The New Latin America Market Atlas.*

Euromonitor International, Inc., 122 South Michigan Avenue, Suite 1200, Chicago. Illinois 60603 (800) 577-EURO; *International Marketing Data and Statistics;* and *World Marketing Data and Statistics.*

Europa Publications Limited, 18 Bedford Square, London, WC1B 3JN, England; *The Europa World Year Book.*

Food and Agricultural Organization of the United Nations (FAO) Via delle Terme di Caracalla, 00100 Rome, Italy (Telephone Number in U.S. (202) 653-2400); *Production Yearbook;* and *The State of Food and Agriculture,* and *Trade Yearbook.*

Inter-American Development Bank, 1300 New York Avenue, NW, Washington, D.C. 20577 (202) 623-1753; *Economic and Social Progress in Latin America.*

M.E. Sharpe, 80 Business Park Drive, Armonk, New York 10504 (800) 541-6563; *The Illustrated Book of World Rankings.*

St. Martin's Press, Inc., 175 Fifth Avenue, New York, New York 10010 (800) 221-7945; *The Statesman's Year-Book.*

Statistical Office of the United Nations,

Publishing Service, New York, New York 10017 (800) 253-9646; *Statistical Yearbook;* and *Statistical Yearbook for Latin America and the Caribbean.*

U.C.L.A. Latin American Center Publications, University of California, Los Angeles, California 90024 (310) 825-6634; *Statistical Abstract of Latin America.*

United Nations Conference on Trade and Development, Central Statistical Service, Palais des Nations, Geneva, Switzerland (Telephone in U.S. (800) 253-9646); *UNCTAD Commodity Yearbook.*

The World Bank, 1818 H Street, NW, Washington, D.C. 20433 (202) 477-1234; *World Development Indicators.*

PANAMA - AIRLINE SERVICE

The Economist Intelligence Unit, 111 West 57th Street, New York, New York 10019 (800) 938-4685; *The New Latin America Market Atlas.*

Europa Publications Limited, 18 Bedford Square, London, WC1B 3JN, England; *The Europa World Year Book.*

International Civil Aviation Organization, 999 University Street, Montreal, Quebec, Canada H3C 5H7 (514) 954-8219; *Civil Aviation Statistics of the World.*

M.E. Sharpe, 80 Business Park Drive, Armonk, New York 10504 (800) 541-6563; *The Illustrated Book of World Rankings.*

St. Martin's Press, Inc., 175 Fifth Avenue, New York, New York 10010 (800) 221-7945; *The Statesman's Year-Book.*

Statistical Office of the United Nations, Publishing Service, New York, New York 10017 (800) 253-9646; *Statistical Yearbook.*

PANAMA - AIRPORTS

Central Intelligence Agency, Washington, D.C. 20505 (703) 482-1100, www.cia.gov; *The World Factbook.*

PANAMA - ALUMINUM PRODUCTION AND CONSUMPTION - See PANAMA - MINING AND MINERAL PRODUCTS

PANAMA - ANIMAL HEALTH

Food and Agricultural Organization of the United Nations (FAO), Via delle Terme di Caracalla, 00100 Rome, Italy (Telephone Number in U.S. (202) 653-2400); *Animal Health Yearbook.*

PANAMA - AREA AND DENSITY OF POPULATION

Central Intelligence Agency,

Washington, D.C. 20505 (703) 482-1100, www.cia.gov; *The World Factbook.*

Euromonitor International, Inc., 122 South Michigan Avenue, Suite 1200, Chicago. Illinois 60603 (800) 577-EURO; *International Marketing Data and Statistics;* and *The World Economic Factbook.*

Europa Publications Limited, 18 Bedford Square, London, WC1B 3JN, England; *The Europa World Year Book.*

Food and Agricultural Organization of the United Nations (FAO) Via delle Terme di Caracalla, 00100 Rome, Italy (Telephone Number in U.S. (202) 653-2400); *The State of Food and Agriculture.*

Inter-American Development Bank, 1300 New York Avenue, NW, Washington, D.C. 20577 (202) 623-1753; *Economic and Social Progress in Latin America.*

M.E. Sharpe, 80 Business Park Drive, Armonk, New York 10504 (800) 541-6563; *The Illustrated Book of World Rankings.*

St. Martin's Press, Inc., 175 Fifth Avenue, New York, New York 10010 (800) 221-7945; *The Statesman's Year-Book.*

Statistical Office of the United Nations, Publishing Service, New York, New York 10017 (800) 253-9646; *Statistical Yearbook.*

United Nations Educational, Scientific and Cultural Organization (UNESCO), 7 Place de Fontenoy, F-75700 Paris, France (Telephone Number in U.S. (212) 963-5981); *Statistical Yearbook.*

The World Bank, 1818 H Street, NW, Washington, D.C. 20433 (202) 477-1234; *World Development Report.*

PANAMA - ARMS EXPORTS AND IMPORTS - See PANAMA - MILITARY

PANAMA - BALANCE OF PAYMENTS

The Economist Intelligence Unit, 111 West 57th Street, New York, New York 10019 (800) 938-4685; *The New Latin America Market Atlas;* and *The World Market Atlas.*

Europa Publications Limited, 18 Bedford Square, London, WC1B 3JN, England; *The Europa World Year Book.*

Inter-American Development Bank, 1300 New York Avenue, NW, Washington, D.C. 20577 (202) 623-1753; *Economic and Social Progress in Latin America.*

International Monetary Fund, 700 Nineteenth Street, NW, Washington, D.C. 20431 (202) 623-7000; *Balance of Payments Yearbook.*

Organization of American States (OAS), General Secretariat, Washington, D.C. 20006 (202) 458-3533; *Statistical Bulletin of the OAS.*

Statistical Office of the United Nations, Publishing Service, New York, New York 10017 (800) 253-9646; *Economic Survey of Latin America and the Caribbean;* and *Statistical Yearbook for Latin America and the Caribbean.*

U.C.L.A. Latin American Center Publications, University of California, Los Angeles, California 90024 (310) 825-6634; *Statistical Abstract of Latin America.*

United Nations Conference on Trade and Development (UNCTAD), New York, New York 10017 (800) 253-9646; *Handbook of International Trade and Development Statistics.*

The World Bank, 1818 H Street, NW, Washington, D.C. 20433 (202) 477-1234; *World Development Report;* and *World Development Indicators.*

PANAMA - BANANAS - See PANAMA - CROPS

PANAMA - BANKING

Euromonitor International, Inc., 122 South Michigan Avenue, Suite 1200, Chicago. Illinois 60603 (800) 577-EURO; *World Marketing Data and Statistics.*

Europa Publications Limited, 18 Bedford Square, London, WC1B 3JN, England; *The Europa World Year Book.*

Inter-American Development Bank, 1300 New York Avenue, NW, Washington, D.C. 20577 (202) 623-1753; *Economic and Social Progress in Latin America.*

International Monetary Fund, 700 Nineteenth Street, NW, Washington, D.C. 20431 (202) 623-7000; *Government Finance Statistics Yearbook;* and *International Financial Statistics.*

M.E. Sharpe, 80 Business Park Drive, Armonk, New York 10504 (800) 541-6563; *The Illustrated Book of World Rankings.*

St. Martin's Press, Inc., 175 Fifth Avenue, New York, New York 10010 (800) 221-7945; *The Statesman's Year-Book.*

Statistical Office of the United Nations, Publishing Service, New York, New York 10017 (800) 253-9646; *Statistical Yearbook for Latin America and the Caribbean.*

PANAMA - BARLEY PRODUCTION - See PANAMA - CROPS

PANAMA - BEER PRODUCTION - See PANAMA - BEVERAGES

PANAMA - BEVERAGES

M.E. Sharpe, 80 Business Park Drive, Armonk, New York 10504 (800) 541-6563; *The Illustrated Book of World Rankings.*

Statistical Office of the United Nations, Publishing Service, New York, New York 10017 (800) 253-9646; *Statistical Yearbook.*

PANAMA - BIRTH RATES

Central Intelligence Agency, Washington, D.C. 20505 (703) 482-1100, www.cia.gov; *The World Factbook.*

Euromonitor International, Inc., 122 South Michigan Avenue, Suite 1200, Chicago. Illinois 60603 (800) 577-EURO; *International Marketing Data and Statistics;* and *The World Economic Factbook.*

Europa Publications Limited, 18 Bedford Square, London, WC1B 3JN, England; *The Europa World Year Book.*

M.E. Sharpe, 80 Business Park Drive, Armonk, New York 10504 (800) 541-6563; *The Illustrated Book of World Rankings.*

St. Martin's Press, Inc., 175 Fifth Avenue, New York, New York 10010 (800) 221-7945; *The Statesman's Year-Book.*

Statistical Office of the United Nations, Publishing Service, New York, New York 10017 (800) 253-9646; *Demographic Yearbook; Statistical Yearbook;* and *Statistical Yearbook for Latin America and the Caribbean.*

The World Bank, 1818 H Street, NW, Washington, D.C. 20433 (202) 477-1234; *World Development Indicators.*

World Health Organization, Office of Publications, 20 Avenue Appia, CH-1211 Geneva 27, Switzerland (Telephone Number in U.S. (518) 436-9686); *World Health Statistics Annual.*

PANAMA - BONDS

Inter-American Development Bank, 1300 New York Avenue, NW, Washington, D.C. 20577 (202) 623-1753; *Economic and Social Progress in Latin America.*

International Monetary Fund, 700 Nineteenth Street, NW, Washington, D.C. 20431 (202) 623-7000; *Government Finance Statistics Yearbook.*

PANAMA - BOOK PRODUCTION

United Nations Educational, Scientific and Cultural Organization (UNESCO), 7 Place de Fontenoy, F-75700 Paris, France (Telephone Number in U.S. (212) 963-5981); *Statistical Yearbook.*

PANAMA - BROADCASTING

Billboard Limited, Post Office Box 9027, 1006 AA Amsterdam, The Netherlands (Telephone Number in U.S. (212) 764-7300); *World Radio TV Handbook.*

Central Intelligence Agency, Washington, D.C. 20505 (703) 482-1100, www.cia.gov; *The World Factbook.*

Euromonitor International, Inc., 122 South Michigan Avenue, Suite 1200, Chicago. Illinois 60603 (800) 577-EURO; *World Marketing Data and Statistics.*

M.E. Sharpe, 80 Business Park Drive, Armonk, New York 10504 (800) 541-6563; *The Illustrated Book of World Rankings.*

St. Martin's Press, Inc., 175 Fifth Avenue, New York, New York 10010 (800) 221-7945; *The Statesman's Year-Book.*

United Nations Educational, Scientific and Cultural Organization (UNESCO), 7 Place de Fontenoy, F-75700 Paris, France (Telephone Number in U.S. (212) 963-5981); *Statistical Yearbook.*

PANAMA - BUDGET

Central Intelligence Agency, Washington, D.C. 20505 (703) 482-1100, www.cia.gov; *The World Factbook.*

PANAMA - BUSINESS

Inter-American Development Bank, 1300 New York Avenue, NW, Washington, D.C. 20577 (202) 623-1753; *Economic and Social Progress in Latin America.*

PANAMA - BUSINESS AND PROFESSIONAL LICENSES

International Monetary Fund, 700 Nineteenth Street, NW, Washington, D.C. 20431 (202) 623-7000; *Government Finance Statistics Yearbook.*

PANAMA - BUTTER PRODUCTION - See PANAMA - DAIRY PRODUCTS

PANAMA - CALORIE SUPPLY

Food and Agricultural Organization of the United Nations (FAO) Via delle Terme di Caracalla, 00100 Rome, Italy (Telephone Number in U.S. (202) 653-2400); *The State of Food and Agriculture.*

Statistical Office of the United Nations, Publishing Service, New York, New York 10017 (800) 253-9646; *Statistical Yearbook for Latin America and the Caribbean.*

PANAMA - CAPITAL INVESTMENT

Inter-American Development Bank,

1300 New York Avenue, NW, Washington, D.C. 20577 (202) 623-1753; *Economic and Social Progress in Latin America.*

PANAMA - CAPITAL REVENUE

Inter-American Development Bank, 1300 New York Avenue, NW, Washington, D.C. 20577 (202) 623-1753; *Economic and Social Progress in Latin America.*

International Monetary Fund, 700 Nineteenth Street, NW, Washington, D.C. 20431 (202) 623-7000; *Government Finance Statistics Yearbook.*

PANAMA - CATTLE - See PANAMA - LIVESTOCK AND POULTRY

PANAMA - CEMENT PRODUCTION - See PANAMA - MINING AND MINERAL PRODUCTS

PANAMA - CHEESE PRODUCTION AND CONSUMPTION - See PANAMA - DAIRY PRODUCTS

PANAMA - CHEMICAL (ORGANIC) PRODUCTION - See PANAMA - MINING AND MINERAL PRODUCTS

PANAMA - CHICKENS - See PANAMA - LIVESTOCK AND POULTRY

PANAMA - CIGARETTE PRODUCTION - See PANAMA - TOBACCO PRODUCTION

PANAMA - CLIMATE

M.E. Sharpe, 80 Business Park Drive, Armonk, New York 10504 (800) 541-6563; *The Illustrated Book of World Rankings.*

St. Martin's Press, Inc., 175 Fifth Avenue, New York, New York 10010 (800) 221-7945; *The Statesman's Year-Book.*

PANAMA - COAL PRODUCTION - See PANAMA - MINING AND MINERAL PRODUCTS

PANAMA - COCOA (BEANS) PRODUCTION - See PANAMA - CROPS

PANAMA - COFFEE PRODUCTION AND CONSUMPTION - See PANAMA - CROPS

PANAMA - COMMERCE

St. Martin's Press, Inc., 175 Fifth Avenue, New York, New York 10010 (800) 221-7945; *The Statesman's Year-Book.*

PANAMA - COMMUNICATIONS - See PANAMA - TRANSPORTATION AND COMMUNICATIONS

PANAMA - CONSTRUCTION INDUSTRY

The Economist Intelligence Unit, 111 West 57th Street, New York, New York

10019 (800) 938-4685; *The New Latin America Market Atlas.*

Inter-American Development Bank, 1300 New York Avenue, NW, Washington, D.C. 20577 (202) 623-1753; *Economic and Social Progress in Latin America.*

M.E. Sharpe, 80 Business Park Drive, Armonk, New York 10504 (800) 541-6563; *The Illustrated Book of World Rankings.*

Statistical Office of the United Nations, Publishing Service, New York, New York 10017 (800) 253-9646; *Statistical Yearbook.*

U.C.L.A. Latin American Center Publications, University of California, Los Angeles, California 90024 (310) 825-6634; *Statistical Abstract of Latin America.*

PANAMA - CONSUMER PRICE INDEX

Europa Publications Limited, 18 Bedford Square, London, WC1B 3JN, England; *The Europa World Year Book.*

Statistical Office of the United Nations, Publishing Service, New York, New York 10017 (800) 253-9646; *Statistical Yearbook.*

PANAMA - CONSUMER PRICES

The Economist Intelligence Unit, 111 West 57th Street, New York, New York 10019 (800) 938-4685; *The New Latin America Market Atlas.*

Euromonitor International, Inc., 122 South Michigan Avenue, Suite 1200, Chicago. Illinois 60603 (800) 577-EURO; *World Marketing Data and Statistics.*

International Labour Office, I.L.O. Publications, 1828 L Street, NW., Suite 801, Washington, D.C. 20036 (301) 638-3152; *Yearbook of Labour Statistics.*

International Monetary Fund, 700 Nineteenth Street, NW, Washington, D.C. 20431 (202) 623-7000; *International Financial Statistics.*

Organization of American States (OAS), General Secretariat, Washington, D.C. 20006 (202) 458-3533; *Statistical Bulletin of the OAS.*

U.C.L.A. Latin American Center Publications, University of California, Los Angeles, California 90024 (310) 825-6634; *Statistical Abstract of Latin America.*

PANAMA - CONSUMPTION

The Economist Intelligence Unit, 111 West 57th Street, New York, New York 10019 (800) 938-4685; *The New Latin America Market Atlas.*

Inter-American Development Bank,

1300 New York Avenue, NW, Washington, D.C. 20577 (202) 623-1753; *Economic and Social Progress in Latin America.*

Statistical Office of the United Nations, Publishing Service, New York, New York 10017 (800) 253-9646; *Statistical Yearbook for Latin America and the Caribbean.*

The World Bank, 1818 H Street, NW, Washington, D.C. 20433 (202) 477-1234; *World Development Report.*

PANAMA - COOPERATIVES

U.C.L.A. Latin American Center Publications, University of California, Los Angeles, California 90024 (310) 825-6634; *Statistical Abstract of Latin America.*

PANAMA - COPPER PRODUCTION AND CONSUMPTION - See PANAMA - MINING AND MINERAL PRODUCTS

PANAMA - CORN PRODUCTION - See PANAMA - CROPS

PANAMA - CORPORATE INCOME TAXES - See PANAMA - TAXATION

PANAMA - CORPORATE TAXES - See PANAMA - TAXATION

PANAMA - COTTON PRODUCTION - See PANAMA - CROPS

PANAMA - CRIME

Yale University Press, Yale Station, New Haven, Connecticut 06520 (800) 987-7323; *Violence and Crime in Cross-National Perspective.*

PANAMA - CROPS

The Economist Intelligence Unit, 111 West 57th Street, New York, New York 10019 (800) 938-4685; *The New Latin America Market Atlas.*

Europa Publications Limited, 18 Bedford Square, London, WC1B 3JN, England; *The Europa World Year Book.*

Food and Agricultural Organization of the United Nations (FAO) Via delle Terme di Caracalla, 00100 Rome, Italy (Telephone Number in U.S. (202) 653-2400); *Production Yearbook;* and *The State of Food and Agriculture.*

International Monetary Fund, 700 Nineteenth Street, NW, Washington, D.C. 20431 (202) 623-7000; *International Financial Statistics.*

M.E. Sharpe, 80 Business Park Drive, Armonk, New York 10504 (800) 541-6563; *The Illustrated Book of World Rankings.*

Organization of American States (OAS),

General Secretariat, Washington, D.C. 20006 (202) 458-3533; *Statistical Bulletin of the OAS.*

St. Martin's Press, Inc., 175 Fifth Avenue, New York, New York 10010 (800) 221-7945; *The Statesman's Year-Book.*

Statistical Office of the United Nations, Publishing Service, New York, New York 10017 (800) 253-9646; *Statistical Yearbook.*

U.C.L.A. Latin American Center Publications, University of California, Los Angeles, California 90024 (310) 825-6634; *Statistical Abstract of Latin America.*

United Nations Conference on Trade and Development, Central Statistical Service, Palais des Nations, Geneva, Switzerland (Telephone in U.S. (800) 253-9646); *UNCTAD Commodity Yearbook.*

PANAMA - CUSTOMS DUTIES

Inter-American Development Bank, 1300 New York Avenue, NW, Washington, D.C. 20577 (202) 623-1753; *Economic and Social Progress in Latin America.*

International Monetary Fund, 700 Nineteenth Street, NW, Washington, D.C. 20431 (202) 623-7000; *Government Finance Statistics Yearbook.*

St. Martin's Press, Inc., 175 Fifth Avenue, New York, New York 10010 (800) 221-7945; *The Statesman's Year-Book.*

PANAMA - DAIRY PRODUCTS

Europa Publications Limited, 18 Bedford Square, London, WC1B 3JN, England; *The Europa World Year Book.*

Food and Agricultural Organization of the United Nations (FAO) Via delle Terme di Caracalla, 00100 Rome, Italy (Telephone Number in U.S. (202) 653-2400); *Production Yearbook;* and *The State of Food and Agriculture.*

M.E. Sharpe, 80 Business Park Drive, Armonk, New York 10504 (800) 541-6563; *The Illustrated Book of World Rankings.*

St. Martin's Press, Inc., 175 Fifth Avenue, New York, New York 10010 (800) 221-7945; *The Statesman's Year-Book.*

Statistical Office of the United Nations, Publishing Service, New York, New York 10017 (800) 253-9646; *Statistical Yearbook.*

U.C.L.A. Latin American Center Publications, University of California, Los Angeles, California 90024 (310) 825-6634; *Statistical Abstract of Latin America.*

PANAMA - DEATH RATES

Statistical Office of the United Nations, Publishing Service, New York, New York 10017 (800) 253-9646; *Statistical Yearbook;* and *Statistical Yearbook for Latin America and the Caribbean.*

World Health Organization, Office of Publications, 20 Avenue Appia, CH-1211 Geneva 27, Switzerland (Telephone Number in U.S. (518) 436-9686); *World Health Statistics Annual.*

PANAMA - DEBT

The Economist Intelligence Unit, 111 West 57th Street, New York, New York 10019 (800) 938-4685; *The New Latin America Market Atlas.*

PANAMA - DEFENSE - See PANAMA - MILITARY

PANAMA - DEFENSE EXPENDITURES

International Monetary Fund, 700 Nineteenth Street, NW, Washington, D.C. 20431 (202) 623-7000; *Government Finance Statistics Yearbook.*

U.S. Arms Control and Disarmament Agency, 320 Twenty-first Street, NW, Washington, D.C. 20451 (202) 647-8677; *World Military Expenditures and Arms Transfers.*

PANAMA - DEMOGRAPHY

The Economist Intelligence Unit, 111 West 57th Street, New York, New York 10019 (800) 938-4685; *The World Market Atlas.*

Euromonitor International, Inc., 122 South Michigan Avenue, Suite 1200, Chicago. Illinois 60603 (800) 577-EURO; *International Marketing Data and Statistics; The World Economic Factbook;* and *World Marketing Data and Statistics.*

M.E. Sharpe, 80 Business Park Drive, Armonk, New York 10504 (800) 541-6563; *The Illustrated Book of World Rankings.*

Statistical Office of the United Nations, Publishing Service, New York, New York 10017 (800) 253-9646; *Human Development Report.*

PANAMA - DEVELOPMENT ASSISTANCE

Inter-American Development Bank, 1300 New York Avenue, NW, Washington, D.C. 20577 (202) 623-1753; *Economic and Social Progress in Latin America.*

Statistical Office of the United Nations, Publishing Service, New York, New York 10017 (800) 253-9646; *Statistical Yearbook.*

PANAMA - DIAMOND PRODUCTION - See PANAMA - MINING AND MINERAL

PRODUCTS

PANAMA - DISCOUNT RATES - See PANAMA - BANKING

PANAMA - DISEASES - See PANAMA - HEALTH

PANAMA - DIVORCE RATES

M.E. Sharpe, 80 Business Park Drive, Armonk, New York 10504 (800) 541-6563; *The Illustrated Book of World Rankings.*

Statistical Office of the United Nations, Publishing Service, New York, New York 10017 (800) 253-9646; *Demographic Yearbook;* and *Statistical Yearbook.*

PANAMA - DUCKS - See PANAMA - LIVESTOCK AND POULTRY

PANAMA - ECONOMY

Central Intelligence Agency, Washington, D.C. 20505 (703) 482-1100, www.cia.gov; *The World Factbook.*

Economist Intelligence Unit, 111 West 57th Street, New York, New York 10019 (800) 938-4685; *Panama Country Report.*

Euromonitor International, Inc., 122 South Michigan Avenue, Suite 1200, Chicago. Illinois 60603 (800) 577-EURO; *International Marketing Data and Statistics; The World Economic Factbook;* and *World Marketing Data and Statistics.*

Europa Publications Limited, 18 Bedford Square, London, WC1B 3JN, England; *The Europa World Year Book.*

Inter-American Development Bank, 1300 New York Avenue, NW, Washington, D.C. 20577 (202) 623-1753; *Economic and Social Progress in Latin America.*

M.E. Sharpe, 80 Business Park Drive, Armonk, New York 10504 (800) 541-6563; *The Illustrated Book of World Rankings.*

Organization of American States (OAS), General Secretariat, Washington, D.C. 20006 (202) 458-3533; *Statistical Bulletin of the OAS.*

St. Martin's Press, Inc., 175 Fifth Avenue, New York, New York 10010 (800) 221-7945; *The Statesman's Year-Book.*

Statistical Office of the United Nations, Publishing Service, New York, New York 10017 (800) 253-9646; *Economic Survey of Latin America and the Caribbean;* and *World Statistics Pocketbook.*

U.C.L.A. Latin American Center Publications, University of California, Los Angeles, California 90024 (310) 825-6634; *Statistical Abstract of Latin America.*

The World Bank, 1818 H Street, NW, Washington, D.C. 20433 (202) 477-1234; *The World Bank Atlas;* and *World Development Report.*

PANAMA - EDUCATION

The Economist Intelligence Unit, 111 West 57th Street, New York, New York 10019 (800) 938-4685; *The New Latin America Market Atlas;* and *The World Market Atlas.*

Euromonitor International, Inc., 122 South Michigan Avenue, Suite 1200, Chicago. Illinois 60603 (800) 577-EURO; *International Marketing Data and Statistics;* and *World Marketing Data and Statistics.*

Europa Publications Limited, 18 Bedford Square, London, WC1B 3JN, England; *The Europa World Year Book.*

International Monetary Fund, 700 Nineteenth Street, NW, Washington, D.C. 20431 (202) 623-7000; *Government Finance Statistics Yearbook.*

M.E. Sharpe, 80 Business Park Drive, Armonk, New York 10504 (800) 541-6563; *The Illustrated Book of World Rankings.*

St. Martin's Press, Inc., 175 Fifth Avenue, New York, New York 10010 (800) 221-7945; *The Statesman's Year-Book.*

Statistical Office of the United Nations, Publishing Service, New York, New York 10017 (800) 253-9646; *Human Development Report;* and *Statistical Yearbook for Latin America and the Caribbean.*

U.C.L.A. Latin American Center Publications, University of California, Los Angeles, California 90024 (310) 825-6634; *Statistical Abstract of Latin America.*

United Nations Educational, Scientific and Cultural Organization (UNESCO), 7 Place de Fontenoy, F-75700 Paris, France (Telephone Number in U.S. (212) 963-5981); *Statistical Yearbook.*

The World Bank, 1818 H Street, NW, Washington, D.C. 20433 (202) 477-1234; *World Development Report;* and *World Development Indicators.*

PANAMA - EGG PRODUCTION AND CONSUMPTION - See PANAMA - DAIRY PRODUCTS

PANAMA - ELECTRICITY

Central Intelligence Agency, Washington, D.C. 20505 (703) 482-1100, www.cia.gov; *The World Factbook.*

The Economist Intelligence Unit, 111 West 57th Street, New York, New York 10019 (800) 938-4685; *The New Latin America Market Atlas.*

Inter-American Development Bank, 1300 New York Avenue, NW, Washington, D.C. 20577 (202) 623-1753; *Economic and Social Progress in Latin America.*

M.E. Sharpe, 80 Business Park Drive, Armonk, New York 10504 (800) 541-6563; *The Illustrated Book of World Rankings.*

Organization of American States (OAS), General Secretariat, Washington, D.C. 20006 (202) 458-3533; *Statistical Bulletin of the OAS.*

St. Martin's Press, Inc., 175 Fifth Avenue, New York, New York 10010 (800) 221-7945; *The Statesman's Year-Book.*

Statistical Office of the United Nations, Publishing Service, New York, New York 10017 (800) 253-9646; *Human Development Report;* and *Statistical Yearbook.*

PANAMA - EMPLOYMENT

Euromonitor International, Inc., 122 South Michigan Avenue, Suite 1200, Chicago. Illinois 60603 (800) 577-EURO; *International Marketing Data and Statistics.*

International Labour Office, I.L.O. Publications, 1828 L Street, NW., Suite 801, Washington, D.C. 20036 (301) 638-3152; *Yearbook of Labour Statistics.*

M.E. Sharpe, 80 Business Park Drive, Armonk, New York 10504 (800) 541-6563; *The Illustrated Book of World Rankings.*

Statistical Office of the United Nations, Publishing Service, New York, New York 10017 (800) 253-9646; *Statistical Yearbook;* and *Statistical Yearbook for Latin America and the Caribbean.*

U.C.L.A. Latin American Center Publications, University of California, Los Angeles, California 90024 (310) 825-6634; *Statistical Abstract of Latin America.*

PANAMA - ENERGY

The Economist Intelligence Unit, 111 West 57th Street, New York, New York 10019 (800) 938-4685; *The New Latin America Market Atlas.*

Euromonitor International, Inc., 122 South Michigan Avenue, Suite 1200, Chicago. Illinois 60603 (800) 577-EURO; *International Marketing Data and Statistics; The World Economic Factbook;* and *World Marketing Data.*

Food and Agricultural Organization of the United Nations (FAO) Via delle Terme di Caracalla, 00100 Rome, Italy (Telephone

Number in U.S. (202) 653-2400); *The State of Food and Agriculture.*

M.E. Sharpe, 80 Business Park Drive, Armonk, New York 10504 (800) 541-6563; *The Illustrated Book of World Rankings.*

St. Martin's Press, Inc., 175 Fifth Avenue, New York, New York 10010 (800) 221-7945; *The Statesman's Year-Book.*

Statistical Office of the United Nations, Publishing Service, New York, New York 10017 (800) 253-9646; *Energy Statistics Yearbook; Human Development Report; Statistical Yearbook; World Statistics Pocketbook;* and *Statistical Yearbook for Latin America and the Caribbean.*

U.C.L.A. Latin American Center Publications, University of California, Los Angeles, California 90024 (310) 825-6634; *Statistical Abstract of Latin America.*

The World Bank, 1818 H Street, NW, Washington, D.C. 20433 (202) 477-1234; *The World Bank Atlas;* and *World Development Report.*

PANAMA - ENVIRONMENT

Economist Intelligence Unit, 111 West 57th Street, New York, New York 10019 (800) 938-4685; *Panama Country Report.*

Statistical Office of the United Nations, Publishing Service, New York, New York 10017 (800) 253-9646; *World Statistics Pocketbook.*

PANAMA - EXCHANGE RATES

Central Intelligence Agency, Washington, D.C. 20505 (703) 482-1100, www.cia.gov; *The World Factbook.*

Euromonitor International, Inc., 122 South Michigan Avenue, Suite 1200, Chicago. Illinois 60603 (800) 577-EURO; *International Marketing Data and Statistics;* and *The World Economic Factbook.*

Europa Publications Limited, 18 Bedford Square, London, WC1B 3JN, England; *The Europa World Year Book.*

Inter-American Development Bank, 1300 New York Avenue, NW, Washington, D.C. 20577 (202) 623-1753; *Economic and Social Progress in Latin America.*

International Civil Aviation Organization, 999 University Street, Montreal, Quebec, Canada H3C 5H7 (514) 954-8219; *Civil Aviation Statistics of the World.*

International Monetary Fund, 700 Nineteenth Street, NW, Washington, D.C. 20431 (202) 623-7000; *International Financial Statistics.*

Organization of American States (OAS), General Secretariat, Washington, D.C. 20006 (202) 458-3533; *Statistical Bulletin of the OAS.*

Statistical Office of the United Nations, Publishing Service, New York, New York 10017 (800) 253-9646; *Statistical Yearbook;* and *World Statistics Pocketbook.*

U.C.L.A. Latin American Center Publications, University of California, Los Angeles, California 90024 (310) 825-6634; *Statistical Abstract of Latin America.*

PANAMA - EXCHANGE TAXES

International Monetary Fund, 700 Nineteenth Street, NW, Washington, D.C. 20431 (202) 623-7000; *Government Finance Statistics Yearbook.*

PANAMA - EXCISE TAXES - See PANAMA - TAXATION

PANAMA - EXPENDITURES

Organization of American States (OAS), General Secretariat, Washington, D.C. 20006 (202) 458-3533; *Statistical Bulletin of the OAS.*

PANAMA - EXPORTS

Central Intelligence Agency, Washington, D.C. 20505 (703) 482-1100, www.cia.gov; *The World Factbook.*

The Economist Intelligence Unit, 111 West 57th Street, New York, New York 10019 (800) 938-4685; *The New Latin America Market Atlas; Panama Country Report;* and *The World Market Atlas.*

Euromonitor International, Inc., 122 South Michigan Avenue, Suite 1200, Chicago. Illinois 60603 (800) 577-EURO; *International Marketing Data and Statistics;* and *The World Economic Factbook.*

Europa Publications Limited, 18 Bedford Square, London, WC1B 3JN, England; *The Europa World Year Book.*

Food and Agricultural Organization of the United Nations (FAO) Via delle Terme di Caracalla, 00100 Rome, Italy (Telephone Number in U.S. (202) 653-2400); *The State of Food and Agriculture.*

Inter-American Development Bank, 1300 New York Avenue, NW, Washington, D.C. 20577 (202) 623-1753; *Economic and Social Progress in Latin America.*

International Monetary Fund, 700 Nineteenth Street, NW, Washington, D.C. 20431 (202) 623-7000; *Direction of Trade Statistics; Government Finance Statistics Yearbook;* and *International Financial Statistics.*

Organization of American States (OAS), General Secretariat, Washington, D.C. 20006 (202) 458-3533; *Statistical Bulletin of the OAS.*

St. Martin's Press, Inc., 175 Fifth Avenue, New York, New York 10010 (800) 221-7945; *The Statesman's Year-Book.*

Statistical Office of the United Nations, Publishing Service, New York, New York 10017 (800) 253-9646; *Statistical Yearbook for Latin America and the Caribbean.*

United Nations Conference on Trade and Development (UNCTAD), New York, New York 10017 (800) 253-9646; *Handbook of International Trade and Development Statistics.*

The World Bank, 1818 H Street, NW, Washington, D.C. 20433 (202) 477-1234; *World Development Report;* and *World Development Indicators.*

PANAMA - EXTERNAL FINANCING

Inter-American Development Bank, 1300 New York Avenue, NW, Washington, D.C. 20577 (202) 623-1753; *Economic and Social Progress in Latin America.*

Statistical Office of the United Nations, Publishing Service, New York, New York 10017 (800) 253-9646; *Statistical Yearbook for Latin America and the Caribbean.*

PANAMA - EXTERNAL INDEBTEDNESS

Inter-American Development Bank, 1300 New York Avenue, NW, Washington, D.C. 20577 (202) 623-1753; *Economic and Social Progress in Latin America.*

Statistical Office of the United Nations, Publishing Service, New York, New York 10017 (800) 253-9646; *Statistical Yearbook for Latin America and the Caribbean.*

The World Bank, 1818 H Street, NW, Washington, D.C. 20433 (202) 477-1234; *World Development Report;* and *World Development Indicators.*

PANAMA - EXTERNAL TRADE

Euromonitor International, Inc., 122 South Michigan Avenue, Suite 1200, Chicago. Illinois 60603 (800) 577-EURO; *World Marketing Data and Statistics.*

Food and Agricultural Organization of the United Nations (FAO) Via delle Terme di Caracalla, 00100 Rome, Italy (Telephone Number in U.S. (202) 653-2400); *The State of Food and Agriculture;* and *Trade Yearbook.*

Inter-American Development Bank, 1300 New York Avenue, NW, Washington, D.C. 20577 (202) 623-1753; *Economic and*

Social Progress in Latin America.

Statistical Office of the United Nations, Publishing Service, New York, New York 10017 (800) 253-9646; *Statistical Yearbook;* and *Statistical Yearbook for Latin America and the Caribbean.*

PANAMA - FAMILY PLANNING

U.C.L.A. Latin American Center Publications, University of California, Los Angeles, California 90024 (310) 825-6634; *Statistical Abstract of Latin America.*

PANAMA - FARM CROPS - See PANAMA - CROPS

PANAMA - FEMALE WORKING POPULATION - See PANAMA - EMPLOYMENT

PANAMA - FERTILITY RATES

Central Intelligence Agency, Washington, D.C. 20505 (703) 482-1100, www.cia.gov; *The World Factbook.*

M.E. Sharpe, 80 Business Park Drive, Armonk, New York 10504 (800) 541-6563; *The Illustrated Book of World Rankings.*

Statistical Office of the United Nations, Publishing Service, New York, New York 10017 (800) 253-9646; *Human Development Report.*

The World Bank, 1818 H Street, NW, Washington, D.C. 20433 (202) 477-1234; *The World Bank Atlas; World Development Report;* and *World Development Indicators.*

PANAMA - FERTILIZER

The Economist Intelligence Unit, 111 West 57th Street, New York, New York 10019 (800) 938-4685; *The New Latin America Market Atlas.*

Food and Agricultural Organization of the United Nations (FAO), Via delle Terme di Caracalla, 00100 Rome, Italy (Telephone Number in U.S. (202) 653-2400); *Fertilizer Yearbook;* and *The State of Food and Agriculture.*

Statistical Office of the United Nations, Publishing Service, New York, New York 10017 (800) 253-9646; *Statistical Yearbook.*

PANAMA - FETAL MORTALITY - See PANAMA - MORTALITY

PANAMA - FINANCE

Economist Intelligence Unit, 111 West 57th Street, New York, New York 10019 (800) 938-4685; *Panama Country Report.*

Europa Publications Limited, 18 Bedford Square, London, WC1B 3JN,

England; *The Europa World Year Book.*

Inter-American Development Bank, 1300 New York Avenue, NW, Washington, D.C. 20577 (202) 623-1753; *Economic and Social Progress in Latin America.*

International Monetary Fund, 700 Nineteenth Street, NW, Washington, D.C. 20431 (202) 623-7000; *Government Finance Statistics Yearbook;* and *International Financial Statistics.*

M.E. Sharpe, 80 Business Park Drive, Armonk, New York 10504 (800) 541-6563; *The Illustrated Book of World Rankings.*

Organization of American States (OAS), General Secretariat, Washington, D.C. 20006 (202) 458-3533; *Statistical Bulletin of the OAS.*

St. Martin's Press, Inc., 175 Fifth Avenue, New York, New York 10010 (800) 221-7945; *The Statesman's Year-Book.*

U.C.L.A. Latin American Center Publications, University of California, Los Angeles, California 90024 (310) 825-6634; *Statistical Abstract of Latin America.*

PANAMA - FISHERIES

Europa Publications Limited, 18 Bedford Square, London, WC1B 3JN, England; *The Europa World Year Book.*

Food and Agricultural Organization of the United Nations (FAO) Via delle Terme di Caracalla, 00100 Rome, Italy (Telephone Number in U.S. (202) 653-2400); *The State of Food and Agriculture;* and *Yearbook of Fishery Statistics.*

Inter-American Development Bank, 1300 New York Avenue, NW, Washington, D.C. 20577 (202) 623-1753; *Economic and Social Progress in Latin America.*

M.E. Sharpe, 80 Business Park Drive, Armonk, New York 10504 (800) 541-6563; *The Illustrated Book of World Rankings.*

St. Martin's Press, Inc., 175 Fifth Avenue, New York, New York 10010 (800) 221-7945; *The Statesman's Year-Book.*

Statistical Office of the United Nations, Publishing Service, New York, New York 10017 (800) 253-9646; *Statistical Yearbook.*

U.C.L.A. Latin American Center Publications, University of California, Los Angeles, California 90024 (310) 825-6634; *Statistical Abstract of Latin America.*

United Nations Conference on Trade and Development, Central Statistical Service, Palais des Nations, Geneva, Switzerland (Telephone in U.S. (800) 253-

9646); *UNCTAD Commodity Yearbook.*

PANAMA - FLOUR PRODUCTION

Statistical Office of the United Nations, Publishing Service, New York, New York 10017 (800) 253-9646; *Statistical Yearbook.*

PANAMA - FOOD

Food and Agricultural Organization of the United Nations (FAO) Via delle Terme di Caracalla, 00100 Rome, Italy (Telephone Number in U.S. (202) 653-2400); *Production Yearbook;* and *The State of Food and Agriculture.*

Statistical Office of the United Nations, Publishing Service, New York, New York 10017 (800) 253-9646; *Human Development Report.*

United Nations Conference on Trade and Development, Central Statistical Service, Palais des Nations, Geneva, Switzerland (Telephone in U.S. (800) 253-9646); *UNCTAD Commodity Yearbook.*

PANAMA - FOOTWEAR PRODUCTION

Statistical Office of the United Nations, Publishing Service, New York, New York 10017 (800) 253-9646; *Statistical Yearbook.*

PANAMA - FOREIGN AID

Inter-American Development Bank, 1300 New York Avenue, NW, Washington, D.C. 20577 (202) 623-1753; *Economic and Social Progress in Latin America.*

PANAMA - FOREIGN DEBT

The Economist Intelligence Unit, 111 West 57th Street, New York, New York 10019 (800) 938-4685; *The New Latin America Market Atlas.*

Inter-American Development Bank, 1300 New York Avenue, NW, Washington, D.C. 20577 (202) 623-1753; *Economic and Social Progress in Latin America.*

International Monetary Fund, 700 Nineteenth Street, NW, Washington, D.C. 20431 (202) 623-7000; *Government Finance Statistics Yearbook.*

St. Martin's Press, Inc., 175 Fifth Avenue, New York, New York 10010 (800) 221-7945; *The Statesman's Year-Book.*

PANAMA - FOREIGN INDEBTEDNESS

Inter-American Development Bank, 1300 New York Avenue, NW, Washington, D.C. 20577 (202) 623-1753; *Economic and Social Progress in Latin America.*

Statistical Office of the United Nations, Publishing Service, New York, New York

10017 (800) 253-9646; *Economic Survey of Latin America and the Caribbean.*

PANAMA - FOREIGN INVESTMENT

The Economist Intelligence Unit, 111 West 57th Street, New York, New York 10019 (800) 938-4685; *The New Latin America Market Atlas.*

PANAMA - FOREIGN TRADE

The Economist Intelligence Unit, 111 West 57th Street, New York, New York 10019 (800) 938-4685; *Panama Country Report;* and *The New Latin America Market Atlas.*

Euromonitor International, Inc., 122 South Michigan Avenue, Suite 1200, Chicago. Illinois 60603 (800) 577-EURO; *International Marketing Data and Statistics;* and *The World Economic Factbook.*

Europa Publications Limited, 18 Bedford Square, London, WC1B 3JN, England; *The Europa World Year Book.*

Food and Agricultural Organization of the United Nations (FAO) Via delle Terme di Caracalla, 00100 Rome, Italy (Telephone Number in U.S. (202) 653-2400); *The State of Food and Agriculture.*

Inter-American Development Bank, 1300 New York Avenue, NW, Washington, D.C. 20577 (202) 623-1753; *Economic and Social Progress in Latin America.*

International Monetary Fund, 700 Nineteenth Street, NW, Washington, D.C. 20431 (202) 623-7000; *International Financial Statistics.*

M.E. Sharpe, 80 Business Park Drive, Armonk, New York 10504 (800) 541-6563; *The Illustrated Book of World Rankings.*

St. Martin's Press, Inc., 175 Fifth Avenue, New York, New York 10010 (800) 221-7945; *The Statesman's Year-Book.*

Statistical Office of the United Nations, Publishing Service, New York, New York 10017 (800) 253-9646; *Economic Survey of Latin America and the Caribbean; International Trade Statistics Yearbook;* and *Statistical Yearbook.*

U.C.L.A. Latin American Center Publications, University of California, Los Angeles, California 90024 (310) 825-6634; *Statistical Abstract of Latin America.*

United Nations Conference on Trade and Development, Central Statistical Service, Palais des Nations, Geneva, Switzerland (Telephone in U.S. (800) 253-9646); *UNCTAD Commodity Yearbook.*

The World Bank, 1818 H Street, NW,

Washington, D.C. 20433 (202) 477-1234; *World Development Report;* and *World Development Indicators.*

PANAMA - FORESTRY AND FOREST PRODUCTS

The Economist Intelligence Unit, 111 West 57th Street, New York, New York 10019 (800) 938-4685; *The New Latin America Market Atlas.*

Europa Publications Limited, 18 Bedford Square, London, WC1B 3JN, England; *The Europa World Year Book.*

Food and Agricultural Organization of the United Nations (FAO) Via delle Terme di Caracalla, 00100 Rome, Italy (Telephone Number in U.S. (202) 653-2400); *The State of Food and Agriculture;* and *Yearbook of Forest Products.*

Inter-American Development Bank, 1300 New York Avenue, NW, Washington, D.C. 20577 (202) 623-1753; *Economic and Social Progress in Latin America.*

M.E. Sharpe, 80 Business Park Drive, Armonk, New York 10504 (800) 541-6563; *The Illustrated Book of World Rankings.*

St. Martin's Press, Inc., 175 Fifth Avenue, New York, New York 10010 (800) 221-7945; *The Statesman's Year-Book.*

Statistical Office of the United Nations, Publishing Service, New York, New York 10017 (800) 253-9646; *Statistical Yearbook.*

U.C.L.A. Latin American Center Publications, University of California, Los Angeles, California 90024 (310) 825-6634; *Statistical Abstract of Latin America.*

United Nations Conference on Trade and Development, Central Statistical Service, Palais des Nations, Geneva, Switzerland (Telephone in U.S. (800) 253-9646); *UNCTAD Commodity Yearbook.*

United Nations Educational, Scientific and Cultural Organization (UNESCO), 7 Place de Fontenoy, F-75700 Paris, France (Telephone Number in U.S. (212) 963-5981); *Statistical Yearbook.*

The World Bank, 1818 H Street, NW, Washington, D.C. 20433 (202) 477-1234; *World Development Report.*

PANAMA - GAS PRODUCTION - See PANAMA - MINING AND MINERAL PRODUCTS

PANAMA - GENERAL INDUSTRIAL STATISTICS - See PANAMA - INDUSTRY

PANAMA - GENERAL MORTALITY - See PANAMA - MORTALITY

PANAMA - GEOGRAPHIC DATA

M.E. Sharpe, 80 Business Park Drive, Armonk, New York 10504 (800) 541-6563; *The Illustrated Book of World Rankings.*

U.C.L.A. Latin American Center Publications, University of California, Los Angeles, California 90024 (310) 825-6634; *Statistical Abstract of Latin America.*

PANAMA - GOATS - See PANAMA - LIVESTOCK AND POULTRY

PANAMA - GOLD HOLDINGS

International Monetary Fund, 700 Nineteenth Street, NW, Washington, D.C. 20431 (202) 623-7000; *International Financial Statistics.*

Statistical Office of the United Nations, Publishing Service, New York, New York 10017 (800) 253-9646; *Statistical Yearbook.*

The World Bank, 1818 H Street, NW, Washington, D.C. 20433 (202) 477-1234; *World Development Indicators.*

PANAMA - GOLD PRODUCTION AND CONSUMPTION - See PANAMA - MINING AND MINERAL PRODUCTS

PANAMA - GOLD RESERVES

The Economist Intelligence Unit, 111 West 57th Street, New York, New York 10019 (800) 938-4685; *The New Latin America Market Atlas.*

PANAMA - GOVERNMENT

Central Intelligence Agency, Washington, D.C. 20505 (703) 482-1100, www.cia.gov; *The World Factbook.*

Europa Publications Limited, 18 Bedford Square, London, WC1B 3JN, England; *The Europa World Year Book.*

Inter-American Development Bank, 1300 New York Avenue, NW, Washington, D.C. 20577 (202) 623-1753; *Economic and Social Progress in Latin America.*

International Monetary Fund, 700 Nineteenth Street, NW, Washington, D.C. 20431 (202) 623-7000; *Government Finance Statistics Yearbook;* and *International Financial Statistics.*

St. Martin's Press, Inc., 175 Fifth Avenue, New York, New York 10010 (800) 221-7945; *The Statesman's Year-Book.*

Statistical Office of the United Nations, Publishing Service, New York, New York 10017 (800) 253-9646; *National Accounts Statistics;* and *Statistical Yearbook.*

The World Bank, 1818 H Street, NW,

Washington, D.C. 20433 (202) 477-1234; *World Development Report;* and *World Development Indicators.*

PANAMA - GRAIN PRODUCTION - See PANAMA - CROPS

PANAMA - GRANTS

International Monetary Fund, 700 Nineteenth Street, NW, Washington, D.C. 20431 (202) 623-7000; *Government Finance Statistics Yearbook.*

PANAMA - GROSS DOMESTIC PRODUCT

The Economist Intelligence Unit, 111 West 57th Street, New York, New York 10019 (800) 938-4685; *Panama Country Report; The New Latin America Market Atlas;* and *The World Market Atlas.*

Euromonitor International, Inc., 122 South Michigan Avenue, Suite 1200, Chicago. Illinois 60603 (800) 577-EURO; *International Marketing Data and Statistics;* and *The World Economic Factbook.*

Europa Publications Limited, 18 Bedford Square, London, WC1B 3JN, England; *The Europa World Year Book.*

Inter-American Development Bank, 1300 New York Avenue, NW, Washington, D.C. 20577 (202) 623-1753; *Economic and Social Progress in Latin America.*

M.E. Sharpe, 80 Business Park Drive, Armonk, New York 10504 (800) 541-6563; *The Illustrated Book of World Rankings.*

Organization of American States (OAS), General Secretariat, Washington, D.C. 20006 (202) 458-3533; *Statistical Bulletin of the OAS.*

Statistical Office of the United Nations, Publishing Service, New York, New York 10017 (800) 253-9646; *Human Development Report; National Accounts Statistics; Statistical Yearbook;* and *Statistical Yearbook for Latin America and the Caribbean.*

U.C.L.A. Latin American Center Publications, University of California, Los Angeles, California 90024 (310) 825-6634; *Statistical Abstract of Latin America.*

The World Bank, 1818 H Street, NW, Washington, D.C. 20433 (202) 477-1234; *World Development Report;* and *World Development Indicators.*

PANAMA - GROSS NATIONAL PRODUCT

Euromonitor International, Inc., 122 South Michigan Avenue, Suite 1200, Chicago. Illinois 60603 (800) 577-EURO; *International Marketing Data and Statistics.*

Europa Publications Limited, 18 Bedford Square, London, WC1B 3JN, England; *The Europa World Year Book.*

Inter-American Development Bank, 1300 New York Avenue, NW, Washington, D.C. 20577 (202) 623-1753; *Economic and Social Progress in Latin America.*

St. Martin's Press, Inc., 175 Fifth Avenue, New York, New York 10010 (800) 221-7945; *The Statesman's Year-Book.*

U.S. Arms Control and Disarmament Agency, 320 Twenty-first Street, NW, Washington, D.C. 20451 (202) 647-8677; *World Military Expenditures and Arms Transfers.*

The World Bank, 1818 H Street, NW, Washington, D.C. 20433 (202) 477-1234; *The World Bank Atlas; World Development Report;* and *World Development Indicators.*

PANAMA - HEALTH

The Economist Intelligence Unit, 111 West 57th Street, New York, New York 10019 (800) 938-4685; *The New Latin America Market Atlas.*

Euromonitor International, Inc., 122 South Michigan Avenue, Suite 1200, Chicago. Illinois 60603 (800) 577-EURO; *World Marketing Data and Statistics.*

M.E. Sharpe, 80 Business Park Drive, Armonk, New York 10504 (800) 541-6563; *The Illustrated Book of World Rankings.*

St. Martin's Press, Inc., 175 Fifth Avenue, New York, New York 10010 (800) 221-7945; *The Statesman's Year-Book.*

Statistical Office of the United Nations, Publishing Service, New York, New York 10017 (800) 253-9646; *Human Development Report; Statistical Yearbook;* and *Statistical Yearbook for Latin America and the Caribbean.*

U.C.L.A. Latin American Center Publications, University of California, Los Angeles, California 90024 (310) 825-6634; *Statistical Abstract of Latin America.*

United Nations Children's Fund (UNICEF), 3 United Nations Plaza, New York, New York 10017 (800) 253-9646; *State of the World's Children.*

The World Bank, 1818 H Street, NW, Washington, D.C. 20433 (202) 477-1234; *World Development Report.*

World Health Organization, Office of Publications, 20 Avenue Appia, CH-1211 Geneva 27, Switzerland (Telephone Number in U.S. (518) 436-9686); *World Health Statistics Annual.*

PANAMA - HEALTH EXPENDITURES

International Monetary Fund, 700 Nineteenth Street, NW, Washington, D.C. 20431 (202) 623-7000; *Government Finance Statistics Yearbook.*

PANAMA - HIDE PRODUCTION

Food and Agricultural Organization of the United Nations (FAO), Via delle Terme di Caracalla, 00100 Rome, Italy (Telephone Number in U.S. (202) 653-2400); *Production Yearbook.*

PANAMA - HIGHWAYS

Central Intelligence Agency, Washington, D.C. 20505 (703) 482-1100, www.cia.gov; *The World Factbook.*

The Economist Intelligence Unit, 111 West 57th Street, New York, New York 10019 (800) 938-4685; *The New Latin America Market Atlas.*

International Road Federation, 2600 Virginia Avenue, NW., Washington, D.C. 20037 (202) 338-4641; *World Road Statistics.*

St. Martin's Press, Inc., 175 Fifth Avenue, New York, New York 10010 (800) 221-7945; *The Statesman's Year-Book.*

PANAMA - HORSES - See PANAMA - LIVESTOCK AND POULTRY

PANAMA - HOURS OF WORK - See PANAMA - EMPLOYMENT

PANAMA - HOUSING AND HOUSING UNITS

Euromonitor International, Inc., 122 South Michigan Avenue, Suite 1200, Chicago. Illinois 60603 (800) 577-EURO; *World Marketing Data and Statistics.*

M.E. Sharpe, 80 Business Park Drive, Armonk, New York 10504 (800) 541-6563; *The Illustrated Book of World Rankings.*

Statistical Office of the United Nations, Publishing Service, New York, New York 10017 (800) 253-9646; *Statistical Yearbook for Latin America and the Caribbean.*

U.C.L.A. Latin American Center Publications, University of California, Los Angeles, California 90024 (310) 825-6634; *Statistical Abstract of Latin America.*

PANAMA - HOUSING EXPENDITURES

International Monetary Fund, 700 Nineteenth Street, NW, Washington, D.C. 20431 (202) 623-7000; *Government Finance Statistics Yearbook.*

PANAMA - ILLITERACY RATES

The Economist Intelligence Unit, 111 West 57th Street, New York, New York 10019 (800) 938-4685; *The New Latin America Market Atlas.*

PANAMA - ILLITERATE POPULATION

Central Intelligence Agency, Washington, D.C. 20505 (703) 482-1100, www.cia.gov; *The World Factbook.*

The Economist Intelligence Unit, 111 West 57th Street, New York, New York 10019 (800) 938-4685; *The World Market Atlas.*

Euromonitor International, Inc., 122 South Michigan Avenue, Suite 1200, Chicago. Illinois 60603 (800) 577-EURO; *The World Economic Factbook.*

Statistical Office of the United Nations, Publishing Service, New York, New York 10017 (800) 253-9646; *Human Development Report;* and *Statistical Yearbook for Latin America and the Caribbean.*

United Nations Educational, Scientific and Cultural Organization (UNESCO), 7 Place de Fontenoy, F-75700 Paris, France (Telephone Number in U.S. (212) 963-5981); *Statistical Yearbook.*

PANAMA - IMMIGRATION

U.C.L.A. Latin American Center Publications, University of California, Los Angeles, California 90024 (310) 825-6634; *Statistical Abstract of Latin America.*

PANAMA - IMPORTS

Central Intelligence Agency, Washington, D.C. 20505 (703) 482-1100, www.cia.gov; *The World Factbook.*

The Economist Intelligence Unit, 111 West 57th Street, New York, New York 10019 (800) 938-4685; *Panama Country Report; The New Latin America Market Atlas;* and *The World Market Atlas.*

Euromonitor International, Inc., 122 South Michigan Avenue, Suite 1200, Chicago. Illinois 60603 (800) 577-EURO; *International Marketing Data and Statistics;* and *The World Economic Factbook.*

Europa Publications Limited, 18 Bedford Square, London, WC1B 3JN, England; *The Europa World Year Book.*

Food and Agricultural Organization of the United Nations (FAO) Via delle Terme di Caracalla, 00100 Rome, Italy (Telephone Number in U.S. (202) 653-2400); *The State of Food and Agriculture.*

Inter-American Development Bank, 1300 New York Avenue, NW, Washington,

D.C. 20577 (202) 623-1753; *Economic and Social Progress in Latin America.*

International Monetary Fund, 700 Nineteenth Street, NW, Washington, D.C. 20431 (202) 623-7000; *Direction of Trade Statistics; Government Finance Statistics Yearbook;* and *International Financial Statistics.*

Organization of American States (OAS), General Secretariat, Washington, D.C. 20006 (202) 458-3533; *Statistical Bulletin of the OAS.*

St. Martin's Press, Inc., 175 Fifth Avenue, New York, New York 10010 (800) 221-7945; *The Statesman's Year-Book.*

Statistical Office of the United Nations, Publishing Service, New York, New York 10017 (800) 253-9646; *Statistical Yearbook for Latin America and the Caribbean.*

United Nations Conference on Trade and Development (UNCTAD), New York, New York 10017 (800) 253-9646; *Handbook of International Trade and Development Statistics.*

The World Bank, 1818 H Street, NW, Washington, D.C. 20433 (202) 477-1234; *World Development Report;* and *World Development Indicators.*

PANAMA - INCOME DISTRIBUTION

Statistical Office of the United Nations, Publishing Service, New York, New York 10017 (800) 253-9646; *Statistical Yearbook for Latin America and the Caribbean.*

U.C.L.A. Latin American Center Publications, University of California, Los Angeles, California 90024 (310) 825-6634; *Statistical Abstract of Latin America.*

PANAMA - INCOME TAXES - See PANAMA - TAXATION

PANAMA - INDUSTRY

Central Intelligence Agency, Washington, D.C. 20505 (703) 482-1100, www.cia.gov; *The World Factbook.*

Economist Intelligence Unit, 111 West 57th Street, New York, New York 10019 (800) 938-4685; *Panama Country Report.*

Euromonitor International, Inc., 122 South Michigan Avenue, Suite 1200, Chicago. Illinois 60603 (800) 577-EURO; *International Marketing Data and Statistics; The World Economic Factbook;* and *World Marketing Data and Statistics.*

Europa Publications Limited, 18 Bedford Square, London, WC1B 3JN, England; *The Europa World Year Book.*

International Labour Office, I.L.O. Publications, 1828 L Street, NW., Suite 801, Washington, D.C. 20036 (301) 638-3152; *Yearbook of Labour Statistics.*

M.E. Sharpe, 80 Business Park Drive, Armonk, New York 10504 (800) 541-6563; *The Illustrated Book of World Rankings.*

St. Martin's Press, Inc., 175 Fifth Avenue, New York, New York 10010 (800) 221-7945; *The Statesman's Year-Book.*

Statistical Office of the United Nations, Publishing Service, New York, New York 10017 (800) 253-9646; *Economic Survey of Latin America and the Caribbean; Industrial Commodity Statistics Yearbook;* and *Statistical Yearbook.*

U.C.L.A. Latin American Center Publications, University of California, Los Angeles, California 90024 (310) 825-6634; *Statistical Abstract of Latin America.*

The World Bank, 1818 H Street, NW, Washington, D.C. 20433 (202) 477-1234; *World Development Indicators.*

World Intellectual Property Organization, 34 Chemin des Colombettes, CH-1211 Geneva 20, Switzerland; *Industrial Property Statistics.*

PANAMA - INFANT AND MATERNAL MORTALITY - See PANAMA - MORTALITY

PANAMA - INFLATIONARY FACTORS

Statistical Office of the United Nations, Publishing Service, New York, New York 10017 (800) 253-9646; *Economic Survey of Latin America and the Caribbean.*

PANAMA - INTEREST RATES

Inter-American Development. Bank, 1300 New York Avenue, NW, Washington, D.C. 20577 (202) 623-1753; *Economic and Social Progress in Latin America.*

PANAMA - INTERNAL TRADE

Statistical Office of the United Nations, Publishing Service, New York, New York 10017 (800) 253-9646; *Statistical Yearbook.*

PANAMA - INTERNATIONAL FINANCE

Inter-American Development Bank, 1300 New York Avenue, NW, Washington, D.C. 20577 (202) 623-1753; *Economic and Social Progress in Latin America.*

U.C.L.A. Latin American Center Publications, University of California, Los Angeles, California 90024 (310) 825-6634; *Statistical Abstract of Latin America.*

PANAMA - INTERNATIONAL LIQUIDITY

Inter-American Development Bank, 1300 New York Avenue, NW, Washington, D.C. 20577 (202) 623-1753; *Economic and Social Progress in Latin America.*

International Monetary Fund, 700 Nineteenth Street, NW, Washington, D.C. 20431 (202) 623-7000; *International Financial Statistics.*

PANAMA - INTERNATIONAL RESERVES

Organization of American States (OAS), General Secretariat, Washington, D.C. 20006 (202) 458-3533; *Statistical Bulletin of the OAS.*

PANAMA - INTERNATIONAL RESERVES EXCLUDING GOLD

Inter-American Development Bank, 1300 New York Avenue, NW, Washington, D.C. 20577 (202) 623-1753; *Economic and Social Progress in Latin America.*

Statistical Office of the United Nations, Publishing Service, New York, New York 10017 (800) 253-9646; *Statistical Yearbook.*

The World Bank, 1818 H Street, NW, Washington, D.C. 20433 (202) 477-1234; *World Development Indicators.*

PANAMA - INTERNATIONAL STATISTICS

Inter-American Development Bank, 1300 New York Avenue, NW, Washington, D.C. 20577 (202) 623-1753; *Economic and Social Progress in Latin America.*

U.C.L.A. Latin American Center Publications, University of California, Los Angeles, California 90024 (310) 825-6634; *Statistical Abstract of Latin America.*

PANAMA - INVESTMENTS

Inter-American Development Bank, 1300 New York Avenue, NW, Washington, D.C. 20577 (202) 623-1753; *Economic and Social Progress in Latin America.*

International Monetary Fund, 700 Nineteenth Street, NW, Washington, D.C. 20431 (202) 623-7000; *International Financial Statistics.*

Statistical Office of the United Nations, Publishing Service, New York, New York 10017 (800) 253-9646; *Statistical Yearbook for Latin America and the Caribbean.*

PANAMA - IRON ORE PRODUCTION AND CONSUMPTION - See PANAMA - MINING AND MINERAL PRODUCTS

PANAMA - IRRIGATION

Euromonitor International, Inc., 122 South Michigan Avenue, Suite 1200, Chicago. Illinois 60603 (800) 577-EURO;

International Marketing Data and Statistics.

Inter-American Development Bank, 1300 New York Avenue, NW, Washington, D.C. 20577 (202) 623-1753; *Economic and Social Progress in Latin America.*

PANAMA - LABOR

Central Intelligence Agency, Washington, D.C. 20505 (703) 482-1100, www.cia.gov; *The World Factbook.*

The Economist Intelligence Unit, 111 West 57th Street, New York, New York 10019 (800) 938-4685; *The New Latin America Market Atlas.*

Euromonitor International, Inc., 122 South Michigan Avenue, Suite 1200, Chicago. Illinois 60603 (800) 577-EURO; *International Marketing Data and Statistics;* and *World Marketing Data and Statistics.*

Europa Publications Limited, 18 Bedford Square, London, WC1B 3JN, England; *The Europa World Year Book.*

Food and Agricultural Organization of the United Nations (FAO) Via delle Terme di Caracalla, 00100 Rome, Italy (Telephone Number in U.S. (202) 653-2400); *The State of Food and Agriculture.*

International Labour Office, I.L.O. Publications, 1828 L Street, NW., Suite 801, Washington, D.C. 20036 (301) 638-3152; *Yearbook of Labour Statistics.*

M.E. Sharpe, 80 Business Park Drive, Armonk, New York 10504 (800) 541-6563; *The Illustrated Book of World Rankings.*

St. Martin's Press, Inc., 175 Fifth Avenue, New York, New York 10010 (800) 221-7945; *The Statesman's Year-Book.*

Statistical Office of the United Nations, Publishing Service, New York, New York 10017 (800) 253-9646; *Human Development Report.*

The World Bank, 1818 H Street, NW, Washington, D.C. 20433 (202) 477-1234; *The World Bank Atlas; World Development Report;* and *World Development Indicators.*

PANAMA - LAND AREA

The Economist Intelligence Unit, 111 West 57th Street, New York, New York 10019 (800) 938-4685; *The New Latin America Market Atlas.*

PANAMA - LAND USE

Central Intelligence Agency, Washington, D.C. 20505 (703) 482-1100, www.cia.gov; *The World Factbook.*

Euromonitor International, Inc., 122 South Michigan Avenue, Suite 1200, Chicago. Illinois 60603 (800) 577-EURO; *International Marketing Data and Statistics.*

Food and Agricultural Organization of the United Nations (FAO), Via delle Terme di Caracalla, 00100 Rome, Italy (Telephone Number in U.S. (202) 653-2400); *Production Yearbook.*

Inter-American Development Bank, 1300 New York Avenue, NW, Washington, D.C. 20577 (202) 623-1753; *Economic and Social Progress in Latin America.*

The World Bank, 1818 H Street, NW, Washington, D.C. 20433 (202) 477-1234; *World Development Report.*

PANAMA - LIBRARIES

M.E. Sharpe, 80 Business Park Drive, Armonk, New York 10504 (800) 541-6563; *The Illustrated Book of World Rankings.*

United Nations Educational, Scientific and Cultural Organization (UNESCO), 7 Place de Fontenoy, F-75700 Paris, France (Telephone Number in U.S. (212) 963-5981); *Statistical Yearbook.*

PANAMA - LIFE EXPECTANCY

Central Intelligence Agency, Washington, D.C. 20505 (703) 482-1100, www.cia.gov; *The World Factbook.*

The Economist Intelligence Unit, 111 West 57th Street, New York, New York 10019 (800) 938-4685; *The New Latin America Market Atlas.*

Euromonitor International, Inc., 122 South Michigan Avenue, Suite 1200, Chicago. Illinois 60603 (800) 577-EURO; *The World Economic Factbook.*

Statistical Office of the United Nations, Publishing Service, New York, New York 10017 (800) 253-9646; *Human Development Report; Statistical Yearbook for Latin America and the Caribbean;* and *World Statistics Pocketbook.*

The World Bank, 1818 H Street, NW, Washington, D.C. 20433 (202) 477-1234; *The World Bank Atlas;* and *World Development Report.*

PANAMA - LITERACY RATE

Euromonitor International, Inc., 122 South Michigan Avenue, Suite 1200, Chicago. Illinois 60603 (800) 577-EURO; *World Marketing Data and Statistics.*

PANAMA - LIVESTOCK AND POULTRY

Euromonitor International, Inc., 122

South Michigan Avenue, Suite 1200, Chicago. Illinois 60603 (800) 577-EURO; *International Marketing Data and Statistics.*

Europa Publications Limited, 18 Bedford Square, London, WC1B 3JN, England; *The Europa World Year Book.*

Food and Agricultural Organization of the United Nations (FAO), Via delle Terme di Caracalla, 00100 Rome, Italy (Telephone Number in U.S. (202) 653-2400); *Production Yearbook;* and *The State of Food and Agriculture.*

M.E. Sharpe, 80 Business Park Drive, Armonk, New York 10504 (800) 541-6563; *The Illustrated Book of World Rankings.*

St. Martin's Press, Inc., 175 Fifth Avenue, New York, New York 10010 (800) 221-7945; *The Statesman's Year-Book.*

Statistical Office of the United Nations, Publishing Service, New York, New York 10017 (800) 253-9646; *Statistical Yearbook.*

United Nations Conference on Trade and Development, Central Statistical Service, Palais des Nations, Geneva, Switzerland (Telephone in U.S. (800) 253-9646); *UNCTAD Commodity Yearbook.*

PANAMA - LIVING LEVELS - See PANAMA - LIFE EXPECTANCY

PANAMA - MAIL - NUMBER OF ITEMS SENT AND RECEIVED

Statistical Office of the United Nations, Publishing Service, New York, New York 10017 (800) 253-9646; *Statistical Yearbook.*

PANAMA - MAIN ECONOMIC INDICATORS - See PANAMA - ECONOMY

PANAMA - MANUFACTURING

The Economist Intelligence Unit, 111 West 57th Street, New York, New York 10019 (800) 938-4685; *The New Latin America Market Atlas.*

Inter-American Development Bank, 1300 New York Avenue, NW, Washington, D.C. 20577 (202) 623-1753; *Economic and Social Progress in Latin America.*

M.E. Sharpe, 80 Business Park Drive, Armonk, New York 10504 (800) 541-6563; *The Illustrated Book of World Rankings.*

Statistical Office of the United Nations, Publishing Service, New York, New York 10017 (800) 253-9646; *Statistical Yearbook;* and *Statistical Yearbook for Latin America and the Caribbean.*

The World Bank, 1818 H Street, NW,

Washington, D.C. 20433 (202) 477-1234; *World Development Indicators.*

PANAMA - MARRIAGE RATES

Europa Publications Limited, 18 Bedford Square, London, WC1B 3JN, England; *The Europa World Year Book.*

M.E. Sharpe, 80 Business Park Drive, Armonk, New York 10504 (800) 541-6563; *The Illustrated Book of World Rankings.*

Statistical Office of the United Nations, Publishing Service, New York, New York 10017 (800) 253-9646; *Demographic Yearbook;* and *Statistical Yearbook.*

PANAMA - MEAT PRODUCTION - See PANAMA - LIVESTOCK AND POULTRY

PANAMA - MEDICAL PERSONNEL

U.C.L.A. Latin American Center Publications, University of California, Los Angeles, California 90024 (310) 825-6634; *Statistical Abstract of Latin America.*

PANAMA - MERCHANT SHIPPING

Europa Publications Limited, 18 Bedford Square, London, WC1B 3JN, England; *The Europa World Year Book.*

Lloyd's Register of Shipping, 17 Battery Place, New York, New York 10004 (212) 425-8050; *Register of Ships.*

St. Martin's Press, Inc., 175 Fifth Avenue, New York, New York 10010 (800) 221-7945; *The Statesman's Year-Book.*

Statistical Office of the United Nations, Publishing Service, New York, New York 10017 (800) 253-9646; *Statistical Yearbook.*

U.S. Department of Transportation, Maritime Administration,400 Seventh Street, SW, Washington, D.C. 20590 (202) 366-5807, www.marad.dot.gov; *A Statistical Analysis of the World's Merchant Fleets.*

PANAMA - MILITARY

Central Intelligence Agency, Washington, D.C. 20505 (703) 482-1100, www.cia.gov; *The World Factbook.*

The Economist Intelligence Unit, 111 West 57th Street, New York, New York 10019 (800) 938-4685; *The New Latin America Market Atlas.*

Euromonitor International, Inc., 122 South Michigan Avenue, Suite 1200, Chicago. Illinois 60603 (800) 577-EURO; *World Marketing Data and Statistics.*

The International Institute for Strategic Studies, 23 Tavistock Street, London WC2E

7NQ, England 44 171 3797676; *The Military Balance.*

St. Martin's Press, Inc., 175 Fifth Avenue, New York, New York 10010 (800) 221-7945; *The Statesman's Year-Book.*

Statistical Office of the United Nations, Publishing Service, New York, New York 10017 (800) 253-9646; *Human Development Report.*

U.C.L.A. Latin American Center Publications, University of California, Los Angeles, California 90024 (310) 825-6634; *Statistical Abstract of Latin America.*

U.S. Arms Control and Disarmament Agency, 320 Twenty-first Street, NW, Washington, D.C. 20451 (202) 647-8677; *World Military Expenditures and Arms Transfers.*

PANAMA - MILK PRODUCTION - See PANAMA - DAIRY PRODUCTS

PANAMA - MINING AND MINERAL PRODUCTS

The Economist Intelligence Unit, 111 West 57th Street, New York, New York 10019 (800) 938-4685; *The New Latin America Market Atlas.*

Inter-American Development Bank, 1300 New York Avenue, NW, Washington, D.C. 20577 (202) 623-1753; *Economic and Social Progress in Latin America.*

M.E. Sharpe, 80 Business Park Drive, Armonk, New York 10504 (800) 541-6563; *The Illustrated Book of World Rankings.*

St. Martin's Press, Inc., 175 Fifth Avenue, New York, New York 10010 (800) 221-7945; *The Statesman's Year-Book.*

Statistical Office of the United Nations, Publishing Service, New York, New York 10017 (800) 253-9646; *Statistical Yearbook;* and *Statistical Yearbook for Latin America and the Caribbean.*

U.C.L.A. Latin American Center Publications, University of California, Los Angeles, California 90024 (310) 825-6634; *Statistical Abstract of Latin America.*

United Nations Conference on Trade and Development, Central Statistical Service, Palais des Nations, Geneva, Switzerland (Telephone in U.S. (800) 253-9646); *UNCTAD Commodity Yearbook.*

PANAMA - MONEY EXCHANGE RATE - See PANAMA - EXCHANGE RATES

PANAMA - MONEY RESERVES

Euromonitor International, Inc., 122 South Michigan Avenue, Suite 1200,

Chicago. Illinois 60603 (800) 577-EURO; *International Marketing Data and Statistics.*

Inter-American Development Bank, 1300 New York Avenue, NW, Washington, D.C. 20577 (202) 623-1753; *Economic and Social Progress in Latin America.*

PANAMA - MONEY SUPPLY

Economist Intelligence Unit, 111 West 57th Street, New York, New York 10019 (800) 938-4685; *Panama Country Report.*

Euromonitor International, Inc., 122 South Michigan Avenue, Suite 1200, Chicago. Illinois 60603 (800) 577-EURO; *International Marketing Data and Statistics.*

Inter-American Development Bank, 1300 New York Avenue, NW, Washington, D.C. 20577 (202) 623-1753; *Economic and Social Progress in Latin America.*

International Monetary Fund, 700 Nineteenth Street, NW, Washington, D.C. 20431 (202) 623-7000; *International Financial Statistics.*

Statistical Office of the United Nations, Publishing Service, New York, New York 10017 (800) 253-9646; *Statistical Yearbook.*

U.C.L.A. Latin American Center Publications, University of California, Los Angeles, California 90024 (310) 825-6634; *Statistical Abstract of Latin America.*

The World Bank, 1818 H Street, NW, Washington, D.C. 20433 (202) 477-1234; *World Development Indicators.*

PANAMA - MORTALITY

Central Intelligence Agency, Washington, D.C. 20505 (703) 482-1100, www.cia.gov; *The World Factbook.*

The Economist Intelligence Unit, 111 West 57th Street, New York, New York 10019 (800) 938-4685; *The New Latin America Market Atlas.*

Euromonitor International, Inc., 122 South Michigan Avenue, Suite 1200, Chicago. Illinois 60603 (800) 577-EURO; *International Marketing Data and Statistics;* and *The World Economic Factbook.*

Europa Publications Limited, 18 Bedford Square, London, WC1B 3JN, England; *The Europa World Year Book.*

St. Martin's Press, Inc., 175 Fifth Avenue, New York, New York 10010 (800) 221-7945; *The Statesman's Year-Book.*

Statistical Office of the United Nations, Publishing Service, New York, New York

10017 (800) 253-9646; *Demographic Yearbook; Human Development Report; Statistical Yearbook;* and *World Statistics Pocketbook.*

United Nations Children's Fund (UNICEF), 3 United Nations Plaza, New York, New York 10017 (800) 253-9646; *State of the World's Children.*

The World Bank, 1818 H Street, NW, Washington, D.C. 20433 (202) 477-1234; *The World Bank Atlas; World Development Report;* and *World Development Indicators.*

World Health Organization, Office of Publications, 20 Avenue Appia, CH-1211 Geneva 27, Switzerland (Telephone Number in U.S. (518) 436-9686); *World Health Statistics Annual.*

PANAMA - MOTION PICTURES

Statistical Office of the United Nations, Publishing Service, New York, New York 10017 (800) 253-9646; *Statistical Yearbook.*

PANAMA - MOTOR VEHICLE TAXES - See PANAMA - TAXATION

PANAMA - MOTOR VEHICLES IN USE

The Economist Intelligence Unit, 111 West 57th Street, New York, New York 10019 (800) 938-4685; *The New Latin America Market Atlas.*

Europa Publications Limited, 18 Bedford Square, London, WC1B 3JN, England; *The Europa World Year Book.*

International Road Federation, 2600 Virginia Avenue, NW., Washington, D.C. 20037 (202) 338-4641; *World Road Statistics.*

Statistical Office of the United Nations, Publishing Service, New York, New York 10017 (800) 253-9646; *Statistical Yearbook.*

PANAMA - MULES - See PANAMA - LIVESTOCK AND POULTRY

PANAMA - MUSEUMS

M.E. Sharpe, 80 Business Park Drive, Armonk, New York 10504 (800) 541-6563; *The Illustrated Book of World Rankings.*

PANAMA - NATALITY - See PANAMA - BIRTH RATES

PANAMA - NATIONAL ACCOUNTS

Europa Publications Limited, 18 Bedford Square, London, WC1B 3JN, England; *The Europa World Year Book.*

Inter-American Development Bank, 1300 New York Avenue, NW, Washington, D.C. 20577 (202) 623-1753; *Economic and*

Social Progress in Latin America.

Organization of American States (OAS), General Secretariat, Washington, D.C. 20006 (202) 458-3533; *Statistical Bulletin of the OAS.*

Statistical Office of the United Nations, Publishing Service, New York, New York 10017 (800) 253-9646; *National Accounts Statistics;* and *Statistical Yearbook.*

U.C.L.A. Latin American Center Publications, University of California, Los Angeles, California 90024 (310) 825-6634; *Statistical Abstract of Latin America.*

PANAMA - NATIONAL INCOME

Inter-American Development Bank, 1300 New York Avenue, NW, Washington, D.C. 20577 (202) 623-1753; *Economic and Social Progress in Latin America.*

M.E. Sharpe, 80 Business Park Drive, Armonk, New York 10504 (800) 541-6563; *The Illustrated Book of World Rankings.*

Statistical Office of the United Nations, Publishing Service, New York, New York 10017 (800) 253-9646; *National Accounts Statistics; Statistical Yearbook;* and *Statistical Yearbook for Latin America and the Caribbean.*

PANAMA - NATIONAL PRODUCT

M.E. Sharpe, 80 Business Park Drive, Armonk, New York 10504 (800) 541-6563; *The Illustrated Book of World Rankings.*

Statistical Office of the United Nations, Publishing Service, New York, New York 10017 (800) 253-9646; *Statistical Yearbook.*

PANAMA - NATURAL GAS PRODUCTION - See PANAMA - MINING AND MINERAL PRODUCTS

PANAMA - NEWSPAPER PRODUCTION - See PANAMA - FORESTRY AND FOREST PRODUCTS

PANAMA - NEWSPRINT - See PANAMA - FORESTRY AND FOREST PRODUCTS

PANAMA - NUTRITION

Statistical Office of the United Nations, Publishing Service, New York, New York 10017 (800) 253-9646; *Statistical Yearbook for Latin America and the Caribbean.*

PANAMA - OCCUPATIONS - See PANAMA - LABOR FORCE

PANAMA - ORANGES PRODUCTION - See PANAMA - CROPS

PANAMA - PAPER - See PANAMA - FORESTRY AND FOREST PRODUCTS

PANAMA - PATENTS, TRADEMARKS AND SERVICE MARKS

Statistical Office of the United Nations, Publishing Service, New York, New York 10017 (800) 253-9646; *Statistical Yearbook.*

World Intellectual Property Organization, 34 Chemin des Colombettes, CH-1211 Geneva 20, Switzerland; *Industrial Property Statistics.*

PANAMA - PEANUT PRODUCTION - See PANAMA - CROPS

PANAMA - PERIODICALS

Statistical Office of the United Nations, Publishing Service, New York, New York 10017 (800) 253-9646; *Statistical Yearbook.*

PANAMA - PESTICIDE USE

Food and Agricultural Organization of the United Nations (FAO) Via delle Terme di Caracalla, 00100 Rome, Italy (Telephone Number in U.S. (202) 653-2400); *The State of Food and Agriculture.*

PANAMA - PETROLEUM INDUSTRY

The Economist Intelligence Unit, 111 West 57th Street, New York, New York 10019 (800) 938-4685; *The New Latin America Market Atlas.*

Food and Agricultural Organization of the United Nations (FAO) Via delle Terme di Caracalla, 00100 Rome, Italy (Telephone Number in U.S. (202) 653-2400); *The State of Food and Agriculture.*

Inter-American Development Bank, 1300 New York Avenue, NW, Washington, D.C. 20577 (202) 623-1753; *Economic and Social Progress in Latin America.*

M.E. Sharpe, 80 Business Park Drive, Armonk, New York 10504 (800) 541-6563; *The Illustrated Book of World Rankings.*

Organization of American States (OAS), General Secretariat, Washington, D.C. 20006 (202) 458-3533; *Statistical Bulletin of the OAS.*

Statistical Office of the United Nations, Publishing Service, New York, New York 10017 (800) 253-9646; *Statistical Yearbook.*

United Nations Conference on Trade and Development, Central Statistical Service, Palais des Nations, Geneva, Switzerland (Telephone in U.S. (800) 253-9646); *UNCTAD Commodity Yearbook.*

PANAMA - PIG-IRON AND FERRO-ALLOY PRODUCTION - See PANAMA - MINING AND MINERAL PRODUCTS

PANAMA - PIGS - See PANAMA - LIVESTOCK AND POULTRY

PANAMA - POLITICAL DATA

U.C.L.A. Latin American Center Publications, University of California, Los Angeles, California 90024 (310) 825-6634; *Statistical Abstract of Latin America.*

PANAMA - POPULATION

Central Intelligence Agency, Washington, D.C. 20505 (703) 482-1100, www.cia.gov; *The World Factbook.*

The Economist Intelligence Unit, 111 West 57th Street, New York, New York 10019 (800) 938-4685; *Panama Country Report; The New Latin America Market Atlas;* and *The World Market Atlas.*

Euromonitor International, Inc., 122 South Michigan Avenue, Suite 1200, Chicago. Illinois 60603 (800) 577-EURO; *International Marketing Data and Statistics;* and *The World Economic Factbook.*

Europa Publications Limited, 18 Bedford Square, London, WC1B 3JN, England; *The Europa World Year Book.*

Food and Agricultural Organization of the United Nations (FAO), Via delle Terme di Caracalla, 00100 Rome, Italy (Telephone Number in U.S. (202) 653-2400); *Production Yearbook.*

Inter-American Development Bank, 1300 New York Avenue, NW, Washington, D.C. 20577 (202) 623-1753; *Economic and Social Progress in Latin America.*

International Labour Office, I.L.O. Publications, 1828 L Street, NW., Suite 801, Washington, D.C. 20036 (301) 638-3152; *Yearbook of Labour Statistics.*

M.E. Sharpe, 80 Business Park Drive, Armonk, New York 10504 (800) 541-6563; *The Illustrated Book of World Rankings.*

Organization of American States (OAS), General Secretariat, Washington, D.C. 20006 (202) 458-3533; *Statistical Bulletin of the OAS.*

St. Martin's Press, Inc., 175 Fifth Avenue, New York, New York 10010 (800) 221-7945; *The Statesman's Year-Book.*

Statistical Office of the United Nations, Publishing Service, New York, New York 10017 (800) 253-9646; *Demographic Yearbook; Human Development Report; Statistical Yearbook; Statistical Yearbook for Latin America and the Caribbean;* and *World Statistics Pocketbook.*

U.C.L.A. Latin American Center Publications, University of California, Los Angeles, California 90024 (310) 825-6634; *Statistical Abstract of Latin America.*

United Nations Educational, Scientific and Cultural Organization (UNESCO), 7 Place de Fontenoy, F-75700 Paris, France (Telephone Number in U.S. (212) 963-5981); *Statistical Yearbook.*

U.S. Arms Control and Disarmament Agency, 320 Twenty-first Street, NW, Washington, D.C. 20451 (202) 647-8677; *World Military Expenditures and Arms Transfers.*

The World Bank, 1818 H Street, NW, Washington, D.C. 20433 (202) 477-1234; *The World Bank Atlas;* and *World Development Report.*

World Health Organization, Office of Publications, 20 Avenue Appia, CH-1211 Geneva 27, Switzerland (Telephone Number in U.S. (518) 436-9686); *World Health Statistics Annual.*

PANAMA - POST OFFICES

M.E. Sharpe, 80 Business Park Drive, Armonk, New York 10504 (800) 541-6563; *The Illustrated Book of World Rankings.*

PANAMA - POTATO PRODUCTION - See PANAMA - CROPS

PANAMA - POWER PRODUCTION INDUSTRY

Statistical Office of the United Nations, Publishing Service, New York, New York 10017 (800) 253-9646; *Statistical Yearbook.*

PANAMA - PRICES

Food and Agricultural Organization of the United Nations (FAO), Via delle Terme di Caracalla, 00100 Rome, Italy (Telephone Number in U.S. (202) 653-2400); *Production Yearbook;* and *The State of Food and Agriculture.*

International Labour Office, I.L.O. Publications, 1828 L Street, NW., Suite 801, Washington, D.C. 20036 (301) 638-3152; *Yearbook of Labour Statistics.*

International Monetary Fund, 700 Nineteenth Street, NW, Washington, D.C. 20431 (202) 623-7000; *International Financial Statistics.*

M.E. Sharpe, 80 Business Park Drive, Armonk, New York 10504 (800) 541-6563; *The Illustrated Book of World Rankings.*

Statistical Office of the United Nations, Publishing Service, New York, New York 10017 (800) 253-9646; *Economic Survey of Latin America and the Caribbean;* and *Statistical Yearbook for Latin America and the Caribbean.*

PANAMA - PRINTING AND WRITING PAPER - See PANAMA - FORESTRY AND FOREST PRODUCTS

PANAMA - PRODUCTION

M.E. Sharpe, 80 Business Park Drive, Armonk, New York 10504 (800) 541-6563; *The Illustrated Book of World Rankings.*

PANAMA - PRODUCTIVITY

Euromonitor International, Inc., 122 South Michigan Avenue, Suite 1200, Chicago. Illinois 60603 (800) 577-EURO; *International Marketing Data and Statistics.*

PANAMA - PROPERTY TAXES - See PANAMA - TAXATION

PANAMA - PUBLIC CONSUMPTION FUND

Inter-American Development Bank, 1300 New York Avenue, NW, Washington, D.C. 20577 (202) 623-1753; *Economic and Social Progress in Latin America.*

PANAMA - PUBLIC EXPENDITURE

Inter-American Development Bank, 1300 New York Avenue, NW, Washington, D.C. 20577 (202) 623-1753; *Economic and Social Progress in Latin America.*

Organization of American States (OAS), General Secretariat, Washington, D.C. 20006 (202) 458-3533; *Statistical Bulletin of the OAS.*

Statistical Office of the United Nations, Publishing Service, New York, New York 10017 (800) 253-9646; *Statistical Yearbook for Latin America and the Caribbean.*

PANAMA - PUBLIC FINANCE - See PANAMA - FINANCE

PANAMA - PUBLIC REVENUE

Inter-American Development Bank, 1300 New York Avenue, NW, Washington, D.C. 20577 (202) 623-1753; *Economic and Social Progress in Latin America.*

Organization of American States (OAS), General Secretariat, Washington, D.C. 20006 (202) 458-3533; *Statistical Bulletin of the OAS.*

PANAMA - RADIO BROADCASTING - See PANAMA - BROADCASTING

PANAMA - RADIO RECEIVERS

St. Martin's Press, Inc., 175 Fifth Avenue, New York, New York 10010 (800) 221-7945; *The Statesman's Year-Book.*

PANAMA - RAILWAYS

The Economist Intelligence Unit, 111 West 57th Street, New York, New York 10019 (800) 938-4685; *The New Latin America Market Atlas.*

Europa Publications Limited, 18 Bedford Square, London, WC1B 3JN, England; *The Europa World Year Book.*

Jane's Information Group, Sentinel House, 163 Brighton Road, Coulsdon, Surrey CR5 2NH, England (Telephone Number in U.S. (703) 683-3700); *Jane's World Railways.*

St. Martin's Press, Inc., 175 Fifth Avenue, New York, New York 10010 (800) 221-7945; *The Statesman's Year-Book.*

PANAMA - RANCHING

U.C.L.A. Latin American Center Publications, University of California, Los Angeles, California 90024 (310) 825-6634; *Statistical Abstract of Latin America.*

PANAMA - RELIGION

Central Intelligence Agency, Washington, D.C. 20505 (703) 482-1100, www.cia.gov; *The World Factbook.*

M.E. Sharpe, 80 Business Park Drive, Armonk, New York 10504 (800) 541-6563; *The Illustrated Book of World Rankings.*

St. Martin's Press, Inc., 175 Fifth Avenue, New York, New York 10010 (800) 221-7945; *The Statesman's Year-Book.*

U.C.L.A. Latin American Center Publications, University of California, Los Angeles, California 90024 (310) 825-6634; *Statistical Abstract of Latin America.*

PANAMA - RENT PRICES

International Labour Office, I.L.O. Publications, 1828 L Street, NW., Suite 801, Washington, D.C. 20036 (301) 638-3152; *Yearbook of Labour Statistics.*

PANAMA - RESERVES EXCLUDING GOLD

The Economist Intelligence Unit, 111 West 57th Street, New York, New York 10019 (800) 938-4685; *The New Latin America Market Atlas.*

PANAMA - RETAIL TRADE

Euromonitor International, Inc., 122 South Michigan Avenue, Suite 1200, Chicago. Illinois 60603 (800) 577-EURO; *World Marketing Data and Statistics.*

Inter-American Development Bank, 1300 New York Avenue, NW, Washington, D.C. 20577 (202) 623-1753; *Economic and Social Progress in Latin America.*

Statistical Office of the United Nations, Publishing Service, New York, New York 10017 (800) 253-9646; *Statistical Yearbook.*

PANAMA - REVENUES

Organization of American States (OAS), General Secretariat, Washington, D.C. 20006 (202) 458-3533; *Statistical Bulletin of the OAS.*

PANAMA - RICE PRODUCTION - See PANAMA - CROPS

PANAMA - ROOT AND TUBER PRODUCTION - See PANAMA - CROPS

PANAMA - ROUNDWOOD PRODUCTION - See PANAMA - FORESTRY AND FOREST PRODUCTS

PANAMA - RUBBER PRODUCTION AND CONSUMPTION

M.E. Sharpe, 80 Business Park Drive, Armonk, New York 10504 (800) 541-6563; *The Illustrated Book of World Rankings.*

PANAMA - SALT PRODUCTION - See PANAMA - MINING AND MINERAL PRODUCTS

PANAMA - SAWNWOOD PRODUCTION - See PANAMA - FORESTRY AND FOREST PRODUCTS

PANAMA - SCIENCE AND TECHNOLOGY - See PANAMA - SCIENTISTS, TECHNICIANS AND ENGINEERS

PANAMA - SCIENTISTS, TECHNICIANS AND ENGINEERS

Statistical Office of the United Nations, Publishing Service, New York, New York 10017 (800) 253-9646; *Statistical Yearbook.*

U.C.L.A. Latin American Center Publications, University of California, Los Angeles, California 90024 (310) 825-6634; *Statistical Abstract of Latin America.*

PANAMA - SENIOR CITIZENS

M.E. Sharpe, 80 Business Park Drive, Armonk, New York 10504 (800) 541-6563; *The Illustrated Book of World Rankings.*

PANAMA - SHEEP - See PANAMA - LIVESTOCK AND POULTRY

PANAMA - SHRIMP EXPORTS

International Monetary Fund, 700 Nineteenth Street, NW, Washington, D.C. 20431 (202) 623-7000; *International Financial Statistics.*

PANAMA - SILVER PRODUCTION AND CONSUMPTION - See PANAMA - MINING

AND MINERAL PRODUCTS

PANAMA - SOCIAL DATA

M.E. Sharpe, 80 Business Park Drive, Armonk, New York 10504 (800) 541-6563; *The Illustrated Book of World Rankings.*

Statistical Office of the United Nations, Publishing Service, New York, New York 10017 (800) 253-9646; *World Statistics Pocketbook.*

U.C.L.A. Latin American Center Publications, University of California, Los Angeles, California 90024 (310) 825-6634; *Statistical Abstract f Latin America.*

PANAMA - SOCIAL SECURITY

Inter-American Development Bank, 1300 New York Avenue, NW, Washington, D.C. 20577 (202) 623-1753; *Economic and Social Progress in Latin America.*

International Monetary Fund, 700 Nineteenth Street, NW, Washington, D.C. 20431 (202) 623-7000; *Government Finance Statistics Yearbook.*

Statistical Office of the United Nations, Publishing Service, New York, New York 10017 (800) 253-9646; *National Accounts Statistics.*

PANAMA - SOCIOECONOMIC DATA

Inter-American Development Bank, 1300 New York Avenue, NW, Washington, D.C. 20577 (202) 623-1753; *Economic and Social Progress in Latin America.*

U.C.L.A. Latin American Center Publications, University of California, Los Angeles, California 90024 (310) 825-6634; *Statistical Abstract of Latin America.*

PANAMA - SOYBEAN PRODUCTION - See PANAMA - CROPS

PANAMA - STAMP TAXES AND DUTIES -See PANAMA - TAXATION

PANAMA - STATE BUDGET REVENUE AND EXPENDITURES

Euromonitor International, Inc., 122 South Michigan Avenue, Suite 1200, Chicago, Illinois 60603; *International Marketing Data and Statistics.*

Inter-American Development Bank, 1300 New York Avenue, NW, Washington, D.C. 20577 (202) 623-1753; *Economic and Social Progress in Latin America.*

PANAMA - STEEL - See PANAMA - MINING AND MINERAL PRODUCTS

PANAMA - STOCKS - COMMODITY - MARKET PRICE - INDEX

Food and Agricultural Organization of the United Nations (FAO) Via delle Terme di Caracalla, 00100 Rome, Italy (Telephone Number in U.S. (202) 653-2400); *The State of Food and Agriculture.*

PANAMA - SUGAR - See PANAMA - CROPS

PANAMA - TAX REVENUES - See PANAMA - TAXATION

PANAMA - TAXATION

Europa Publications Limited, 18 Bedford Square, London, WC1B 3JN, England; *The Europa World Year Book.*

Inter-American Development Bank, 1300 New York Avenue, NW, Washington, D.C. 20577 (202) 623-1753; *Economic and Social Progress in Latin America.*

International Monetary Fund, 700 Nineteenth Street, NW, Washington, D.C. 20431 (202) 623-7000; *Government Finance Statistics Yearbook.*

International Road Federation, 2600 Virginia Avenue, NW., Washington, D.C. 20037 (202) 338-4641; *World Road Statistics.*

Statistical Office of the United Nations, Publishing Service, New York, New York 10017 (800) 253-9646; *Statistical Yearbook for Latin America and the Caribbean.*

The World Bank, 1818 H Street, NW, Washington, D.C. 20433 (202) 477-1234; *World Development Indicators.*

PANAMA - TELEPHONES IN USE

American Telephone and Telegraph Company, 26 Parsippany Road, Whippany, New Jersey 07981 (800) 222-0300; *The World's Telephones.*

Central Intelligence Agency, Washington, D.C. 20505 (703) 482-1100, www.cia.gov; *The World Factbook.*

The Economist Intelligence Unit, 111 West 57th Street, New York, New York 10019 (800) 938-4685; *The New Latin America Market Atlas.*

Europa Publications Limited, 18 Bedford Square, London, WC1B 3JN, England; *The Europa World Year Book.*

St. Martin's Press, Inc., 175 Fifth Avenue, New York, New York 10010 (800) 221-7945; *The Statesman's Year-Book.*

Statistical Office of the United Nations, Publishing Service, New York, New York 10017 (800) 253-9646; *Statistical Yearbook;* and *World Statistics Pocketbook.*

PANAMA - TELEVISION BROADCAST-

ING - See PANAMA - BROADCASTING

PANAMA - TEXTILE INDUSTRY

M.E. Sharpe, 80 Business Park Drive, Armonk, New York 10504 (800) 541-6563; *The Illustrated Book of World Rankings.*

St. Martin's Press, Inc., 175 Fifth Avenue, New York, New York 10010 (800) 221-7945; *The Statesman's Year-Book.*

Statistical Office of the United Nations, Publishing Service, New York, New York 10017 (800) 253-9646; *Statistical Yearbook.*

United Nations Conference on Trade and Development, Central Statistical Service, Palais des Nations, Geneva, Switzerland (Telephone in U.S. (800) 253-9646); *UNCTAD Commodity Yearbook.*

PANAMA - THEATRE

United Nations Educational, Scientific and Cultural Organization (UNESCO), 7 Place de Fontenoy, F-75700 Paris, France (Telephone Number in U.S. (212) 963-5981); *Statistical Yearbook.*

PANAMA - TIRE (MOTOR VEHICLE) PRODUCTION

Statistical Office of the United Nations, Publishing Service, New York, New York 10017 (800) 253-9646; *Statistical Yearbook.*

PANAMA - TOBACCO PRODUCTION

o M.E. Sharpe, 80 Business Park Drive, Armonk, New York 10504 (800) 541-6563; *The Illustrated Book of World Rankings.*

Statistical Office of the United Nations, Publishing Service, New York, New York 10017 (800) 253-9646; *Statistical Yearbook.*

U.C.L.A. Latin American Center Publications, University of California, Los Angeles, California 90024 (310) 825-6634; *Statistical Abstract f Latin America.*

PANAMA - TOURISM

The Economist Intelligence Unit, 111 West 57th Street, New York, New York 10019 (800) 938-4685; *The New Latin America Market Atlas.*

Euromonitor International, Inc., 122 South Michigan Avenue, Suite 1200, Chicago, Illinois 60603; *The World Economic Factbook;* and *World Marketing Data and Statistics.*

Europa Publications Limited, 18 Bedford Square, London, WC1B 3JN, England; *The Europa World Year Book.*

M.E. Sharpe, 80 Business Park Drive, Armonk, New York 10504 (800) 541-6563;

The Illustrated Book of World Rankings.

Organization of American States (OAS), General Secretariat, Washington, D.C. 20006 (202) 458-3533; *Statistical Bulletin of the OAS.*

St. Martin's Press, Inc., 175 Fifth Avenue, New York, New York 10010 (800) 221-7945; *The Statesman's Year-Book.*

Statistical Office of the United Nations, Publishing Service, New York, New York 10017 (800) 253-9646; *Statistical Yearbook;* and *Statistical Yearbook for Latin America and the Caribbean.*

U.C.L.A. Latin American Center Publications, University of California, Los Angeles, California 90024 (310) 825-6634; *Statistical Abstract of Latin America.*

World Tourism Organization, Calle Capitan Haya 42, E-28020 Madrid, Spain; *Yearbook of Tourism Statistics.*

PANAMA - TRACTORS IN USE

The Economist Intelligence Unit, 111 West 57th Street, New York, New York 10019 (800) 938-4685; *The New Latin America Market Atlas.*

Statistical Office of the United Nations, Publishing Service, New York, New York 10017 (800) 253-9646; *Statistical Yearbook.*

PANAMA - TRADE - See PANAMA - FOREIGN TRADE

PANAMA - TRADEMARKS AND SERVICE MARKS - See PANAMA - PATENTS, TRADEMARKS AND SERVICE MARKS

PANAMA - TRANSPORTATION AND COMMUNICATIONS

Central Intelligence Agency, Washington, D.C. 20505 (703) 482-1100, www.cia.gov; *The World Factbook.*

The Economist Intelligence Unit, 111 West 57th Street, New York, New York 10019 (800) 938-4685; *The New Latin America Market Atlas.*

Euromonitor International, Inc., 122 South Michigan Avenue, Suite 1200, Chicago, Illinois 60603; *International Marketing Data and Statistics;* and *World Marketing Data and Statistics.*

Europa Publications Limited, 18 Bedford Square, London, WC1B 3JN, England; *The Europa World Year Book.*

Inter-American Development Bank, 1300 New York Avenue, NW, Washington, D.C. 20577 (202) 623-1753; *Economic and Social Progress in Latin America.*

M.E. Sharpe, 80 Business Park Drive, Armonk, New York 10504 (800) 541-6563; *The Illustrated Book of World Rankings.*

St. Martin's Press, Inc., 175 Fifth Avenue, New York, New York 10010 (800) 221-7945; *The Statesman's Year-Book.*

Statistical Office of the United Nations, Publishing Service, New York, New York 10017 (800) 253-9646; *Human Development Report;* and *Statistical Yearbook for Latin America and the Caribbean.*

U.C.L.A. Latin American Center Publications, University of California, Los Angeles, California 90024 (310) 825-6634; *Statistical Abstract of Latin America.*

PANAMA - TURKEYS - See PANAMA - LIVESTOCK AND POULTRY

PANAMA - UNEMPLOYMENT

Central Intelligence Agency, Washington, D.C. 20505 (703) 482-1100, www.cia.gov; *The World Factbook.*

The Economist Intelligence Unit, 111 West 57th Street, New York, New York 10019 (800) 938-4685; *The New Latin America Market Atlas.*

Euromonitor International, Inc., 122 South Michigan Avenue, Suite 1200, Chicago, Illinois 60603; *International Marketing Data and Statistics.*

International Labour Office, I.L.O. Publications, 1828 L Street, NW., Suite 801, Washington, D.C. 20036 (301) 638-3152; *Yearbook of Labour Statistics.*

Organization of American States (OAS), General Secretariat, Washington, D.C. 20006 (202) 458-3533; *Statistical Bulletin of the OAS.*

Statistical Office of the United Nations, Publishing Service, New York, New York 10017 (800) 253-9646; *Statistical Yearbook.*

U.C.L.A. Latin American Center Publications, University of California, Los Angeles, California 90024 (310) 825-6634; *Statistical Abstract of Latin America.*

PANAMA - UTILITIES

U.C.L.A. Latin American Center Publications, University of California, Los Angeles, California 90024 (310) 825-6634; *Statistical Abstract of Latin America.*

PANAMA - VITAL STATISTICS

Euromonitor International, Inc., 122 South Michigan Avenue, Suite 1200, Chicago, Illinois 60603; *International*

Marketing Data and Statistics.

St. Martin's Press, Inc., 175 Fifth Avenue, New York, New York 10010 (800) 221-7945; *The Statesman's Year-Book.*

Statistical Office of the United Nations, Publishing Service, New York, New York 10017 (800) 253-9646; *Statistical Yearbook.*

World Health Organization, Office of Publications, 20 Avenue Appia, CH-1211 Geneva 27, Switzerland (Telephone Number in U.S. (518) 436-9686); *World Health Statistics Annual.*

PANAMA - WAGES

International Labour Office, I.L.O. Publications, 1828 L Street, NW., Suite 801, Washington, D.C. 20036 (301) 638-3152; *Yearbook of Labour Statistics.*

Statistical Office of the United Nations, Publishing Service, New York, New York 10017 (800) 253-9646; *Statistical Yearbook.*

U.C.L.A. Latin American Center Publications, University of California, Los Angeles, California 90024 (310) 825-6634; *Statistical Abstract of Latin America.*

PANAMA - WEATHER - See PANAMA - CLIMATE

PANAMA - WELFARE

Inter-American Development Bank, 1300 New York Avenue, NW, Washington, D.C. 20577 (202) 623-1753; *Economic and Social Progress in Latin America.*

International Monetary Fund, 700 Nineteenth Street, NW, Washington, D.C. 20431 (202) 623-7000; *Government Finance Statistics Yearbook.*

PANAMA - WHEAT PRODUCTION AND PRICES - See PANAMA - CROPS

PANAMA - WHOLESALE PRICES

Inter-American Development Bank, 1300 New York Avenue, NW, Washington, D.C. 20577 (202) 623-1753; *Economic and Social Progress in Latin America.*

International Monetary Fund, 700 Nineteenth Street, NW, Washington, D.C. 20431 (202) 623-7000; *International Financial Statistics.*

Organization of American States (OAS), General Secretariat, Washington, D.C. 20006 (202) 458-3533; *Statistical Bulletin of the OAS.*

Statistical Office of the United Nations, Publishing Service, New York, New York 10017 (800) 253-9646; *Statistical Yearbook.*

PANAMA - WHOLESALE TRADE

Inter-American Development Bank, 1300 New York Avenue, NW, Washington, D.C. 20577 (202) 623-1753; *Economic and Social Progress in Latin America.*

Statistical Office of the United Nations, Publishing Service, New York, New York 10017 (800) 253-9646; *Statistical Yearbook.*

PANAMA - WINE PRODUCTION - See PANAMA - BEVERAGES

PANAMA - WOOD PULP PRODUCTION - See PANAMA - FORESTRY AND FOREST PRODUCTS

PANAMA - WOOL PRODUCTION - See PANAMA - TEXTILE INDUSTRY

PAPAYAS

U.S. Department of Agriculture, National Agricultural Statistics Service, Fourteenth Street and Independence Avenue, SW, Washington, D.C. 20250 (800) 727-9540, www.usda.gov/nass; *Noncitrus Fruits and Nuts.*

PAPER AND ALLIED PRODUCTS INDUSTRY - MANUFACTURING - CAPITAL

U.S. Department of Commerce, Bureau of Economic Analysis, Fourteenth Street between Constitution Avenue and E Street, NW, Washington, D.C. 20230 (202) 606-9900, www.bea.doc.gov; *Survey of Current Business.*

PAPER AND ALLIED PRODUCTS INDUSTRY - MANUFACTURING - EARNINGS

U.S. Department of Commerce, Bureau of the Census, Washington, D.C. 20233 (301) 457-4100, www.census.gov; *Census of Manufactures; County Business Patterns; 1997 Economic Census, Core Business Statistics Series;* and *Annual Survey of Manufactures.*

U.S. Department of Labor, Bureau of Labor Statistics, Two Massachusetts Avenue, NE, Washington, D.C. 20212 (202) 691-5200, www.stats.bls.gov; *Employment and Earnings;* and Internet site: http://stats.bls.gov/ ceshome.htm.

PAPER AND ALLIED PRODUCTS INDUSTRY - MANUFACTURING - EMPLOYEES

U.S. Department of Commerce, Bureau of the Census, Washington, D.C. 20233 (301) 457-4100, www.census.gov; *Census of Manufactures; Annual Survey of Manufactures, Final Industry Series; 1997 Economic Census, Core Business Statistics Series;* and *County Business Patterns.*

U.S. Department of Labor, Bureau of

Labor Statistics, Two Massachusetts Avenue, NE, Washington, D.C. 20212 (202) 691-5200, www.stats.bls.gov; *Employment and Earnings;* and Internet site: http://stats.bls.gov/ ceshome.htm.

PAPER AND ALLIED PRODUCTS INDUSTRY - MANUFACTURING - ENERGY CONSUMPTION

U.S. Department of Energy, Energy Information Administration, 1000 Independence Avenue, SW, Washington, D.C. 20585 (202) 586-8800, www.eia.doe.gov; *Manufacturing Energy Consumption.*

PAPER AND ALLIED PRODUCTS INDUSTRY - MANUFACTURING - ESTABLISHMENTS

U.S. Department of Commerce, Bureau of the Census, Washington, D.C. 20233 (301) 457-4100, www.census.gov; *1997 Economic Census, Core Business Statistics Series; Annual Survey of Manufactures; Census of Manufactures, Final Industry Series;* and *County Business Patterns.*

PAPER AND ALLIED PRODUCTS INDUSTRY - MANUFACTURING - FAILURES

Dun and Bradstreet Corporation, 299 Park Avenue, 24th Floor, New York, New York 10171 (212) 593-6800; *Business Failure Record.*

PAPER AND ALLIED PRODUCTS - MANUFACTURING - FOREIGN TRADE

U.S. Department of Commerce, Bureau of the Census, Washington, D.C. 20233 (301) 457-4100, www.census.gov; *U.S. International Trade in Goods and Services.*

PAPER AND ALLIED PRODUCTS INDUSTRY - MANUFACTURING - GROSS DOMESTIC PRODUCT

U.S. Department of Commerce, Bureau of Economic Analysis, Fourteenth Street between Constitution Avenue and E Street, NW, Washington, D.C. 20230 (202) 606-9900, www.bea.doc.gov; *Survey of Current Business.*

PAPER AND ALLIED PRODUCTS INDUSTRY - MANUFACTURING - MERGERS AND ACQUISITIONS

Thomson Financial Securities Data, 2 Gateway Center, Newark, New Jersey 07006 (973) 622-3100; *Merger and Corporate Transactions Database.*

PAPER AND ALLIED PRODUCTS INDUSTRY - MANUFACTURING - OCCUPATIONAL SAFETY

U.S. Department of Labor, Bureau of Labor Statistics, Two Massachusetts Avenue, NE, Washington, D.C. 20212 (202) 691-5200, www.stats.bls.gov; *Occupational Injuries and Illnesses in the United States by Industry.*

PAPER AND ALLIED PRODUCTS INDUSTRY - MANUFACTURING - OUTPUT

American Forest and Paper Association, 1111 Nineteenth Street, NW, Washington, D.C. 20036 (202) 463-2700; *Monthly Statistical Summary of Paper, Paperboard, and Woodpulp.*

PAPER AND ALLIED PRODUCTS INDUSTRY - MANUFACTURING - PRODUCTIVITY

Board of Governors of the Federal Reserve System, Twentieth Street and Constitution Avenue, NW, Washington, D.C. 20551 (202)452-3000, www.bog.frb.fed.us; *Federal Reserve Bulletin;* and *Industrial Production and Capacity Utilization.*

U.S. Department of Labor, Bureau of Labor Statistics, Two Massachusetts Avenue, NE, Washington, D.C. 20212 (202) 691-5200, www.stats.bls.gov; Internet site http://stats.bls.gov/iprhome.htm.

PAPER AND ALLIED PRODUCTS INDUSTRY - MANUFACTURING - RESEARCH AND DEVELOPMENT

National Science Foundation, 4201 Wilson Boulevard, Arlington, Virginia 22230 (703) 306-1234, www.nsf.gov; *Research and Development in Industry.*

PAPER AND ALLIED PRODUCTS INDUSTRY - MANUFACTURING - SALES, SHIPMENTS, RECEIPTS

U.S. Department of Commerce, Bureau of the Census, Washington, D.C. 20233 (301) 457-4100, www.census.gov; *Census of Manufactures; Annual Survey of Manufactures; Exports from Manufacturing Establishments; Current Industrial Reports, Manufactures' Shipments, Inventories and Orders; Census of Manufactures, Final Industry Series;* and *1997 Economic Census, Core Business Statistics Series.*

PAPER AND ALLIED PRODUCTS INDUSTRY - MANUFACTURING - TOXIC CHEMICAL RELEASES

Environmental Protection Agency, 1200 Pennsylvania Avenue, NW, Washington, D.C. 20460 (888) 372-8255, www.epa.gov; *Toxics Release Inventory.*

PAPER AND PAPERBOARD PRODUCTS - FOREIGN TRADE

U.S. Department of Commerce, Bureau of the Census, Washington, D.C. 20233 (301) 457-4100, www.census.gov; *U.S. International Trade in Goods and Services.*

PAPER AND PAPERBOARD PRODUCTS - PRODUCER PRICES

U.S. Department of Agricultural, Forest Service, Post Office Box 96090, Washington, D.C. 20090 (202) 205-8333, www.fs.fed.us; *Timber Demand and Technology Assessment.*

PAPER AND PAPERBOARD PRODUCTS - PRODUCTION

American Forest and Paper Association, 1111 Nineteenth Street, NW, Washington, D.C. 20036 (202) 463-2700; *Monthly Statistical Summary of Paper, Paperboard, and Woodpulp.*

U.S. Department of Commerce, Bureau of Economic Analysis, Fourteenth Street between Constitution Avenue and E Street, NW, Washington, D.C. 20230 (202) 606-9900, www.bea.doc.gov; *Survey of Current Business.*

PAPER AND PAPERBOARD PRODUCTS - RAILROAD CAR LOADINGS

Association of American Railroads, American Railroads Building, 50 F Street, NW, Washington, D.C. 20001 (202) 639-2100; *Freight Commodity Statistics;* and *Weekly Railroad Traffic.*

PAPER AND PAPERBOARD PRODUCTS - RECYCLING

Franklin Associates Limited, 4121 West 83rd Street, Suite 108, Prairie Village, Kansas 66208 (913) 649-2225; *Characterization of Municipal Solid Waste in the United States.*

Papua New Guinea - National Statistical Office

National Statistics Office, Central Government Offices, Post Office Wards Strip, Waigani, Papua New Guinea.

Papua New Guinea - Primary Statistics Sources

National Statistics Office, Central Government Offices, Post Office Wards Strip, Waigani, Papua New Guinea; *Statistical Digest;* and *Abstract of Statistics.*

PAPUA NEW GUINEA - AGRICULTURE

Asian Development Bank, Post Office Box 789, 1099 Manila, Philippines; *Key Indicators of Developing Asian and Pacific Countries.*

Economist Intelligence Unit, 111 West 57th Street, New York, New York 10019 (800) 938-4685; *Papua New Guinea*

Country Report.

Euromonitor International, Inc., 122 South Michigan Avenue, Suite 1200, Chicago, Illinois 60603; *International Marketing Data and Statistics;* and *World Marketing Data and Statistics.*

Europa Publications Limited, 18 Bedford Square, London, WC1B 3JN, England; *The Europa World Year Book.*

Federal Statistical Office, Gustav-Stresemann - Ring 11, D-6200, Wiesbaden, Germany; *Papua-Neuguinea.*

Food and Agricultural Organization of the United Nations (FAO), Via delle Terme di Caracalla, 00100 Rome, Italy (Telephone Number in U.S. (202) 653-2400); *Production Yearbook; The State of Food and Agriculture;* and *Trade Yearbook.*

M.E. Sharpe, 80 Business Park Drive, Armonk, New York 10504 (800) 541-6563; *The Illustrated Book of World Rankings.*

St. Martin's Press, Inc., 175 Fifth Avenue, New York, New York 10010 (800) 221-7945; *The Statesman's Year-Book.*

Statistical Office of the United Nations, Publishing Service, New York, New York 10017 (800) 253-9646; *Asia-Pacific in Figures; Statistical Yearbook;* and *Statistical Yearbook for Asia and the Pacific.*

United Nations Conference on Trade and Development, Central Statistical Service, Palais des Nations, Geneva, Switzerland (Telephone in U.S. (800) 253-9646); *UNCTAD Commodity Yearbook.*

The World Bank, 1818 H Street, NW, Washington, D.C. 20433 (202) 477-1234; *World Development Indicators.*

PAPUA NEW GUINEA - AIRLINE SERVICE

The Economist Intelligence Unit (Asia) Limited, 10th Floor, Luk Kwok Centre, 72 Gloucester Road, Wanchai, Hong Kong (Phone Number in U.S. (800) 938-4685); *Asian Market Atlas.*

Europa Publications Limited, 18 Bedford Square, London, WC1B 3JN, England; *The Europa World Year Book.*

International Civil Aviation Organization, 999 University Street, Montreal, Quebec, Canada H3C 5H7 (514) 954-8219; *Civil Aviation Statistics of the World.*

M.E. Sharpe, 80 Business Park Drive, Armonk, New York 10504 (800) 541-6563; *The Illustrated Book of World Rankings.*

St. Martin's Press, Inc., 175 Fifth Avenue, New York, New York 10010 (800) 221-7945; *The Statesman's Year-Book.*

PAPUA NEW GUINEA - AIRPORTS

Central Intelligence Agency, Washington, D.C. 20505 (703) 482-1100, www.cia.gov; *The World Factbook.*

PAPUA NEW GUINEA - ALUMINUM PRODUCTION AND CONSUMPTION - See PAPUA NEW GUINEA - MINING AND MINERAL PRODUCTS

PAPUA NEW GUINEA - ANTIMONY AND ANTIMONY ORE PRODUCTION AND CONSUMPTION - See PAPUA NEW GUINEA - MINING AND MINERAL PRODUCTS

PAPUA NEW GUINEA - AREA AND DENSITY OF POPULATION

Central Intelligence Agency, Washington, D.C. 20505 (703) 482-1100, www.cia.gov; *The World Factbook.*

Euromonitor International, Inc., 122 South Michigan Avenue, Suite 1200, Chicago, Illinois 60603; *International Marketing Data and Statistics;* and *The World Economic Factbook.*

Europa Publications Limited, 18 Bedford Square, London, WC1B 3JN, England; *The Europa World Year Book.*

Federal Statistical Office, Gustav - Stresemann - Ring 11, D-6200 Wiesbaden, Germany; *Papua-Neuguinea.*

Food and Agricultural Organization of the United Nations (FAO) Via delle Terme di Caracalla, 00100 Rome, Italy (Telephone Number in U.S. (202) 653-2400); *The State of Food and Agriculture.*

M.E. Sharpe, 80 Business Park Drive, Armonk, New York 10504 (800) 541-6563; *The Illustrated Book of World Rankings.*

St. Martin's Press, Inc., 175 Fifth Avenue, New York, New York 10010 (800) 221-7945; *The Statesman's Year-Book.*

Statistical Office of the United Nations, Publishing Service, New York, New York 10017 (800) 253-9646; *Statistical Yearbook.*

United Nations Educational, Scientific and Cultural Organization (UNESCO), 7 Place de Fontenoy, F-75700 Paris, France (Telephone Number in U.S. (212) 963-5981); *Statistical Yearbook.*

The World Bank, 1818 H Street, NW, Washington, D.C. 20433 (202) 477-1234; *World Development Report.*

PAPUA NEW GUINEA - ARMS EXPORTS AND IMPORTS - See PAPUA NEW GUINEA - MILITARY

PAPUA NEW GUINEA - BALANCE OF PAYMENTS

The Economist Intelligence Unit, 111 West 57th Street, New York, New York 10019 (800) 938-4685; *The World Market Atlas.*

Europa Publications Limited, 18 Bedford Square, London, WC1B 3JN, England; *The Europa World Year Book.*

Federal Statistical Office, Gustav - Stresemann - Ring 11, D-6200 Wiesbaden, Germany; *Papua-Neuguinea.*

International Monetary Fund, 700 Nineteenth Street, NW, Washington, D.C. 20431 (202) 623-7000; *Balance of Payments Yearbook.*

United Nations Conference on Trade and Development (UNCTAD), New York, New York 10017 (800) 253-9646; *Handbook of International Trade and Development Statistics.*

The World Bank, 1818 H Street, NW, Washington, D.C. 20433 (202) 477-1234; *World Development Report;* and *World Development Indicators.*

PAPUA NEW GUINEA - BANKING

Asian Development Bank, Post Office Box 789, 1099 Manila, Philippines; *Key Indicators of Developing Asian and Pacific Countries.*

Euromonitor International, Inc., 122 South Michigan Avenue, Suite 1200, Chicago, Illinois 60603 (800) 577-EURO; *World Marketing Data and Statistics.*

Europa Publications Limited, 18 Bedford Square, London, WC1B 3JN, England; *The Europa World Year Book.*

International Monetary Fund, 700 Nineteenth Street, NW, Washington, D.C. 20431 (202) 623-7000; *International Financial Statistics.*

M.E. Sharpe, 80 Business Park Drive, Armonk, New York 10504 (800) 541-6563; *The Illustrated Book of World Rankings.*

St. Martin's Press, Inc., 175 Fifth Avenue, New York, New York 10010 (800) 221-7945; *The Statesman's Year-Book.*

PAPUA NEW GUINEA - BARLEY PRODUCTION - See PAPUA NEW GUINEA - CROPS

PAPUA NEW GUINEA - BAUXITE PRODUCTION AND CONSUMPTION - See PAPUA NEW GUINEA - MINING AND MINERAL PRODUCTS

PAPUA NEW GUINEA - BEER
PRODUCTION - See PAPUA NEW GUINEA -
BEVERAGES

PAPUA NEW GUINEA - BEVERAGES

M.E. Sharpe, 80 Business Park Drive,
Armonk, New York 10504 (800) 541-6563;
The Illustrated Book of World Rankings.

PAPUA NEW GUINEA - BIRTH RATES

Central Intelligence Agency,
Washington, D.C. 20505 (703) 482-1100,
www.cia.gov; *The World Factbook.*

The Economist Intelligence Unit (Asia)
Limited, 10th Floor, Luk Kwok Centre, 72
Gloucester Road, Wanchai, Hong Kong
(Phone Number in U.S. (800) 938-4685);
Asian Market Atlas.

Euromonitor International, Inc., 122
South Michigan Avenue, Suite 1200,
Chicago, Illinois 60603; *International
Marketing Data and Statistics;* and *The
World Economic Factbook.*

Europa Publications Limited, 18
Bedford Square, London, WC1B 3JN,
England; *The Europa World Year Book.*

M.E. Sharpe, 80 Business Park Drive,
Armonk, New York 10504 (800) 541-6563;
The Illustrated Book of World Rankings.

St. Martin's Press, Inc., 175 Fifth
Avenue, New York, New York 10010 (800)
221-7945; *The Statesman's Year-Book.*

Statistical Office of the United Nations,
Publishing Service, New York, New York
10017 (800) 253-9646; *Asia-Pacific in
Figures; Demographic Yearbook;* and
Statistical Yearbook.

The World Bank, 1818 H Street, NW,
Washington, D.C. 20433 (202) 477-1234;
World Development Indicators.

World Health Organization, Office of
Publications, 20 Avenue Appia, CH-1211
Geneva 27, Switzerland (Telephone
Number in U.S. (518) 436-9686); *World
Health Statistics Annual.*

PAPUA NEW GUINEA - BONDS

Asian Development Bank, Post Office
Box 789, 1099 Manila, Philippines; *Key
Indicators of Developing Asian and Pacific
Countries.*

International Monetary Fund, 700
Nineteenth Street, NW, Washington, D.C.
20431 (202) 623-7000; *Government
Finance Statistics Yearbook.*

PAPUA NEW GUINEA - BROADCASTING

Billboard Limited, Post Office Box 9027,

1006 AA Amsterdam, The Netherlands
(Telephone Number in U.S. (212) 764-
7300); *World Radio TV Handbook.*

Central Intelligence Agency,
Washington, D.C. 20505 (703) 482-1100,
www.cia.gov; *The World Factbook.*

The Economist Intelligence Unit (Asia)
Limited, 10th Floor, Luk Kwok Centre, 72
Gloucester Road, Wanchai, Hong Kong
(Phone Number in U.S. (800) 938-4685);
Asian Market Atlas.

Euromonitor International, Inc., 122
South Michigan Avenue, Suite 1200,
Chicago, Illinois 60603 (800) 577-EURO;
World Marketing Data and Statistics.

M.E. Sharpe, 80 Business Park Drive,
Armonk, New York 10504 (800) 541-6563;
The Illustrated Book of World Rankings.

St. Martin's Press, Inc., 175 Fifth
Avenue, New York, New York 10010 (800)
221-7945; *The Statesman's Year-Book.*

United Nations Educational, Scientific
and Cultural Organization (UNESCO), 7
Place de Fontenoy, F-75700 Paris, France
(Telephone Number in U.S. (212) 963-
5981); *Statistical Yearbook.*

PAPUA NEW GUINEA - BUDGET

Central Intelligence Agency,
Washington, D.C. 20505 (703) 482-1100,
www.cia.gov; *The World Factbook.*

PAPUA NEW GUINEA - BUSINESS AND
PROFESSIONAL LICENSES

International Monetary Fund, 700
Nineteenth Street, NW, Washington, D.C.
20431 (202) 623-7000; *Government
Finance Statistics Yearbook.*

PAPUA NEW GUINEA - CACAO EXPORTS

International Monetary Fund, 700
Nineteenth Street, NW, Washington, D.C.
20431 (202) 623-7000; *International
Financial Statistics.*

PAPUA NEW GUINEA - CADMIUM
PRODUCTION AND CONSUMPTION - See
PAPUA NEW GUINEA - MINING AND
MINERAL PRODUCTS

PAPUA NEW GUINEA - CALORIE SUPPLY

Asian Development Bank, Post Office
Box 789, 1099 Manila, Philippines; *Key
Indicators of Developing Asian and Pacific
Countries.*

Food and Agricultural Organization of
the United Nations (FAO) Via delle Terme
di Caracalla, 00100 Rome, Italy (Telephone
Number in U.S. (202) 653-2400); *The State
of Food and Agriculture.*

PAPUA NEW GUINEA - CAPITAL
INVESTMENT

Asian Development Bank, Post Office
Box 789, 1099 Manila, Philippines; *Key
Indicators of Developing Asian and Pacific
Countries.*

PAPUA NEW GUINEA - CAPITAL REVENUE

Asian Development Bank, Post Office
Box 789, 1099 Manila, Philippines; *Key
Indicators of Developing Asian and Pacific
Countries.*

International Monetary Fund, 700
Nineteenth Street, NW, Washington, D.C.
20431 (202) 623-7000; *Government
Finance Statistics Yearbook.*

PAPUA NEW GUINEA - CATTLE - See
PAPUA NEW GUINEA - LIVESTOCK AND
POULTRY

PAPUA NEW GUINEA - CEMENT
PRODUCTION - See PAPUA NEW GUINEA -
MINING AND MINERAL PRODUCTS

PAPUA NEW GUINEA - CHEMICAL
(ORGANIC) PRODUCTION - See PAPUA
NEW GUINEA - MINING AND MINERAL
PRODUCTS

PAPUA NEW GUINEA - CHICKENS - See
PAPUA NEW GUINEA - LIVESTOCK AND
POULTRY

PAPUA NEW GUINEA - CIGARETTE
PRODUCTION - See PAPUA NEW GUINEA -
TOBACCO PRODUCTION

PAPUA NEW GUINEA - CLIMATE

M.E. Sharpe, 80 Business Park Drive,
Armonk, New York 10504 (800) 541-6563;
The Illustrated Book of World Rankings.

St. Martin's Press, Inc., 175 Fifth
Avenue, New York, New York 10010 (800)
221-7945; *The Statesman's Year-Book.*

PAPUA NEW GUINEA - CLOTHING
EXPORTS AND IMPORTS - See PAPUA
NEW GUINEA - TEXTILE INDUSTRY

PAPUA NEW GUINEA - COAL
PRODUCTION - See PAPUA NEW GUINEA -
MINING AND MINERAL PRODUCTS

PAPUA NEW GUINEA - COCOA
PRODUCTION - See PAPUA NEW GUINEA -
CROPS

PAPUA NEW GUINEA - COFFEE - See
PAPUA NEW GUINEA - CROPS

PAPUA NEW GUINEA - COMMERCE

St. Martin's Press, Inc., 175 Fifth
Avenue, New York, New York 10010 (800)
221-7945; *The Statesman's Year-Book.*

PAPUA NEW GUINEA - COMMUNICATIONS - See PAPUA NEW GUINEA - TRANSPORTATION AND COMMUNICATIONS

PAPUA NEW GUINEA - CONSTRUCTION INDUSTRY

M.E. Sharpe, 80 Business Park Drive, Armonk, New York 10504 (800) 541-6563; *The Illustrated Book of World Rankings.*

Statistical Office of the United Nations, Publishing Service, New York, New York 10017 (800) 253-9646; *Statistical Yearbook.*

PAPUA NEW GUINEA - CONSUMER PRICE INDEX

Asian Development Bank, Post Office Box 789, 1099 Manila, Philippines; *Key Indicators of Developing Asian and Pacific Countries.*

Europa Publications Limited, 18 Bedford Square, London, WC1B 3JN, England; *The Europa World Year Book.*

Statistical Office of the United Nations, Publishing Service, New York, New York 10017 (800) 253-9646; *Statistical Yearbook.*

PAPUA NEW GUINEA - CONSUMER PRICES

Euromonitor International, Inc., 122 South Michigan Avenue, Suite 1200, Chicago, Illinois 60603 (800) 577-EURO; *World Marketing Data and Statistics.*

International Labour Office, I.L.O. Publications, 1828 L Street, NW., Suite 801, Washington, D.C. 20036 (301) 638-3152; *Yearbook of Labour Statistics.*

International Monetary Fund, 700 Nineteenth Street, NW, Washington, D.C. 20431 (202) 623-7000; *International Financial Statistics.*

PAPUA NEW GUINEA - CONSUMPTION

South Pacific Commission, Post Box D5, Noumea Cedex, New Caledonia; *Statistical Bulletin of the South Pacific: Retail Price Indexes.*

The World Bank, 1818 H Street, NW, Washington, D.C. 20433 (202) 477-1234; *World Development Report.*

PAPUA NEW GUINEA - COPPER - See PAPUA NEW GUINEA - MINING AND MINERAL PRODUCTS

PAPUA NEW GUINEA - COPRA EXPORTS

International Monetary Fund, 700 Nineteenth Street, NW, Washington, D.C. 20431 (202) 623-7000; *International Financial Statistics.*

PAPUA NEW GUINEA - CORN PRODUCTION - See PAPUA NEW GUINEA - CROPS

PAPUA NEW GUINEA - CORPORATE TAXES - See PAPUA NEW GUINEA - TAXATION

PAPUA NEW GUINEA - COTTON PRODUCTION - See PAPUA NEW GUINEA - CROPS

PAPUA NEW GUINEA - CRIME

International Criminal Police Organization (INTERPOL), 50 quai Achille Lignon, F-69006 Lyon, France; *International Crime Statistics.*

PAPUA NEW GUINEA - CROPS

Asian Development Bank, Post Office Box 789, 1099 Manila, Philippines; *Key Indicators of Developing Asian and Pacific Countries.*

Europa Publications Limited, 18 Bedford Square, London, WC1B 3JN, England; *The Europa World Year Book.*

Food and Agricultural Organization of the United Nations (FAO) Via delle Terme di Caracalla, 00100 Rome, Italy (Telephone Number in U.S. (202) 653-2400); *Production Yearbook;* and *The State of Food and Agriculture.*

International Monetary Fund, 700 Nineteenth Street, NW, Washington, D.C. 20431 (202) 623-7000; *International Financial Statistics.*

M.E. Sharpe, 80 Business Park Drive, Armonk, New York 10504 (800) 541-6563; *The Illustrated Book of World Rankings.*

St. Martin's Press, Inc., 175 Fifth Avenue, New York, New York 10010 (800) 221-7945; *The Statesman's Year-Book.*

Statistical Office of the United Nations, Publishing Service, New York, New York 10017 (800) 253-9646; *Statistical Yearbook.*

United Nations Conference on Trade and Development, Central Statistical Service, Palais des Nations, Geneva, Switzerland (Telephone in U.S. (800) 253-9646); *UNCTAD Commodity Yearbook.*

PAPUA NEW GUINEA - CUSTOMS DUTIES

International Monetary Fund, 700 Nineteenth Street, NW, Washington, D.C. 20431 (202) 623-7000; *Government Finance Statistics Yearbook.*

St. Martin's Press, Inc., 175 Fifth Avenue, New York, New York 10010 (800) 221-7945; *The Statesman's Year-Book.*

PAPUA NEW GUINEA - DAIRY PRODUCTS

Europa Publications Limited, 18 Bedford Square, London, WC1B 3JN, England; *The Europa World Year Book.*

Food and Agricultural Organization of the United Nations (FAO), Via delle Terme di Caracalla, 00100 Rome, Italy (Telephone Number in U.S. (202) 653-2400); *Production Yearbook;* and *The State of Food and Agriculture.*

M.E. Sharpe, 80 Business Park Drive, Armonk, New York 10504 (800) 541-6563; *The Illustrated Book of World Rankings.*

St. Martin's Press, Inc., 175 Fifth Avenue, New York, New York 10010 (800) 221-7945; *The Statesman's Year-Book.*

PAPUA NEW GUINEA - DEATH RATES - See PAPUA NEW GUINEA - MORTALITY

PAPUA NEW GUINEA - DEFENSE EXPENDITURES - See PAPUA NEW GUINEA - MILITARY

PAPUA NEW GUINEA - DEMOGRAPHY

The Economist Intelligence Unit (Asia) Limited, 10th Floor, Luk Kwok Centre, 72 Gloucester Road, Wanchai, Hong Kong (Phone Number in U.S. (800) 938-4685); *Asian Market Atlas.*

Euromonitor International, Inc., 122 South Michigan Avenue, Suite 1200, Chicago, Illinois 60603; *International Marketing Data and Statistics; World Marketing Data and Statistics;* and *The World Economic Factbook.*

Federal Statistical Office, Gustav-Stresemann - Ring 11, D-6200, Wiesbaden, Germany; *Papua-Neuguinea.*

M.E. Sharpe, 80 Business Park Drive, Armonk, New York 10504 (800) 541-6563; *The Illustrated Book of World Rankings.*

Statistical Office of the United Nations, Publishing Service, New York, New York 10017 (800) 253-9646; *Asia-Pacific in Figures;* and *Human Development Report.*

PAPUA NEW GUINEA - DEVELOPMENT ASSISTANCE

Asian Development Bank, Post Office Box 789, 1099 Manila, Philippines; Key Indicators of Developing Asian and Pacific Countries.

Statistical Office of the United Nations, Publishing Service, New York, New York 10017 (800) 253-9646; *Statistical Yearbook.*

PAPUA NEW GUINEA - DIAMOND PRODUCTION - See PAPUA NEW GUINEA - MINING AND MINERAL PRODUCTS

PAPUA NEW GUINEA - DISEASES - See PAPUA NEW GUINEA - HEALTH

PAPUA NEW GUINEA - DIVORCE RATES

M.E. Sharpe, 80 Business Park Drive, Armonk, New York 10504 (800) 541-6563; *The Illustrated Book of World Rankings.*

Statistical Office of the United Nations, Publishing Service, New York, New York 10017 (800) 253-9646; *Demographic Yearbook.*

PAPUA NEW GUINEA - DUCKS - See PAPUA NEW GUINEA - LIVESTOCK AND POULTRY

PAPUA NEW GUINEA - ECONOMY

Asian Development Bank, Post Office Box 789, 1099 Manila, Philippines; *Key Indicators of Developing Asian and Pacific Countries.*

Central Intelligence Agency, Washington, D.C. 20505 (703) 482-1100, www.cia.gov; *The World Factbook.*

Economist Intelligence Unit, 111 West 57th Street, New York, New York 10019 (800) 938-4685; *Papua New Guinea Country Report.*

Euromonitor International, Inc., 122 South Michigan Avenue, Suite 1200, Chicago, Illinois 60603; *International Marketing Data and Statistics; World Marketing Data and Statistics;* and *The World Economic Yearbook.*

Europa Publications Limited, 18 Bedford Square, London, WC1B 3JN, England; *The Europa World Year Book.*

Federal Statistical Office, Gustav-Stresemann - Ring 11, D-6200, Wiesbaden, Germany; *Papua-Neuguinea.*

M.E. Sharpe, 80 Business Park Drive, Armonk, New York 10504 (800) 541-6563; *The Illustrated Book of World Rankings.*

St. Martin's Press, Inc., 175 Fifth Avenue, New York, New York 10010 (800) 221-7945; *The Statesman's Year-Book.*

Statistical Office of the United Nations, Publishing Service, New York, New York 10017 (800) 253-9646; *World Statistics Pocketbook.*

The World Bank, 1818 H Street, NW, Washington, D.C. 20433 (202) 477-1234; *The World Bank Atlas;* and *World Development Report.*

PAPUA NEW GUINEA - EDUCATION

The Economist Intelligence Unit, 111 West 57th Street, New York, New York

10019 (800) 938-4685; *The World Market Atlas.*

The Economist Intelligence Unit (Asia) Limited, 10th Floor, Luk Kwok Centre, 72 Gloucester Road, Wanchai, Hong Kong (Phone Number in U.S. (800) 938-4685); *Asian Market Atlas.*

Euromonitor International, Inc., 122 South Michigan Avenue, Suite 1200, Chicago, Illinois 60603; *International Marketing Data and Statistics;* and *World Marketing Data and Statistics.*

Europa Publications Limited, 18 Bedford Square, London, WC1B 3JN, England; *The Europa World Year Book.*

Federal Statistical Office, Gustav - Stresemann - Ring 11, D-6200 Wiesbaden, Germany; *Papua-Neuguinea.*

International Monetary Fund, 700 Nineteenth Street, NW, Washington, D.C. 20431 (202) 623-7000; *Government Finance Statistics Yearbook.*

M.E. Sharpe, 80 Business Park Drive, Armonk, New York 10504 (800) 541-6563; *The Illustrated Book of World Rankings.*

St. Martin's Press, Inc., 175 Fifth Avenue, New York, New York 10010 (800) 221-7945; *The Statesman's Year-Book.*

Statistical Office of the United Nations, Publishing Service, New York, New York 10017 (800) 253-9646; *Asia-Pacific in Figures; Human Development Report;* and *Statistical Yearbook for Asia and the Pacific.*

United Nations Educational, Scientific and Cultural Organization (UNESCO), 7 Place de Fontenoy, F-75700 Paris, France (Telephone Number in U.S. (212) 963-5981); *Statistical Yearbook.*

The World Bank, 1818 H Street, NW, Washington, D.C. 20433 (202) 477-1234; *World Development Report;* and *World Development Indicators.*

PAPUA NEW GUINEA - EGG PRODUCTION AND CONSUMPTION - See PAPUA NEW GUINEA - DAIRY PRODUCTS

PAPUA NEW GUINEA - ELECTRICITY

Asian Development Bank, Post Office Box 789, 1099 Manila, Philippines; *Key Indicators of Developing Asian and Pacific Countries.*

Central Intelligence Agency, Washington, D.C. 20505 (703) 482-1100, www.cia.gov; *The World Factbook.*

M.E. Sharpe, 80 Business Park Drive,

Armonk, New York 10504 (800) 541-6563; *The Illustrated Book of World Rankings.*

Penn Well Publishing Company, 1421 South Sheridan Road, Post Office Box 1260, Tulsa, Oklahoma 74101 (800) 752-9764; *International Energy Statistics Sourcebook.*

St. Martin's Press, Inc., 175 Fifth Avenue, New York, New York 10010 (800) 221-7945; *The Statesman's Year-Book.*

Statistical Office of the United Nations, Publishing Service, New York, New York 10017 (800) 253-9646; *Human Development Report;* and *Statistical Yearbook.*

PAPUA NEW GUINEA - EMPLOYMENT

Euromonitor International, Inc., 122 South Michigan Avenue, Suite 1200, Chicago, Illinois 60603; *International Marketing Data and Statistics.*

Federal Statistical Office, Gustav - Stresemann - Ring 11, D-6200 Wiesbaden, Germany; *Papua-Neuguinea.*

International Labour Office, I.L.O. Publications, 1828 L Street, NW., Suite 801, Washington, D.C. 20036 (301) 638-3152; *Yearbook of Labour Statistics.*

M.E. Sharpe, 80 Business Park Drive, Armonk, New York 10504 (800) 541-6563; *The Illustrated Book of World Rankings.*

Statistical Office of the United Nations, Publishing Service, New York, New York 10017 (800) 253-9646; *Asia-Pacific in Figures;* and *Statistical Yearbook.*

PAPUA NEW GUINEA - ENERGY

Euromonitor International, Inc., 122 South Michigan Avenue, Suite 1200, Chicago, Illinois 60603; *International Marketing Data and Statistics; World Marketing Data and Statistics;* and *The World Economic Factbook.*

Food and Agricultural Organization of the United Nations (FAO) Via delle Terme di Caracalla, 00100 Rome, Italy (Telephone Number in U.S. (202) 653-2400); *The State of Food and Agriculture.*

M.E. Sharpe, 80 Business Park Drive, Armonk, New York 10504 (800) 541-6563; *The Illustrated Book of World Rankings.*

Penn Well Publishing Company, 1421 South Sheridan Road, Post Office Box 1260, Tulsa, Oklahoma 74101 (800) 752-9764; *International Energy Statistics Sourcebook.*

St. Martin's Press, Inc., 175 Fifth Avenue, New York, New York 10010 (800) 221-7945; *The Statesman's Year-Book.*

Statistical Office of the United Nations, Publishing Service, New York, New York 10017 (800) 253-9646; *Asia-Pacific in Figures; Energy Statistics Yearbook; Human Development Report; Statistical Yearbook; World Statistics Pocketbook;* and *Statistical Yearbook for Asia and the Pacific.*

The World Bank, 1818 H Street, NW, Washington, D.C. 20433 (202) 477-1234; *The World Bank Atlas;* and *World Development Report.*

PAPUA NEW GUINEA - ENVIRONMENT

Economist Intelligence Unit, 111 West 57th Street, New York, New York 10019 (800) 938-4685; *Papua New Guinea Country Report.*

PAPUA NEW GUINEA - EXCHANGE RATES

Asian Development Bank, Post Office Box 789, 1099 Manila, Philippines; *Key Indicators of Developing Asian and Pacific Countries.*

Central Intelligence Agency, Washington, D.C. 20505 (703) 482-1100, www.cia.gov; *The World Factbook.*

The Economist Intelligence Unit (Asia) Limited, 10th Floor, Luk Kwok Centre, 72 Gloucester Road, Wanchai, Hong Kong (Phone Number in U.S. (800) 938-4685); *Asian Market Atlas.*

Euromonitor International, Inc., 122 South Michigan Avenue, Suite 1200, Chicago, Illinois 60603; *International Marketing Data and Statistics;* and *The World Economic Factbook.*

Europa Publications Limited, 18 Bedford Square, London, WC1B 3JN, England; *The Europa World Year Book.*

International Civil Aviation Organization, 999 University Street, Montreal, Quebec, Canada H3C 5H7 (514) 954-8219; *Civil Aviation Statistics of the World.*

International Monetary Fund, 700 Nineteenth Street, NW, Washington, D.C. 20431 (202) 623-7000; *International Financial Statistics.*

Statistical Office of the United Nations, Publishing Service, New York, New York 10017 (800) 253-9646; *Statistical Yearbook;* and *World Statistics Pocketbook.*

Walden Publishing, Ltd., Two Market Street, Saffron Walden Essex, CB10 1HZ, England; *The World of Information Asia and Pacific Review.*

PAPUA NEW GUINEA - EXCISE TAXES - See PAPUA NEW GUINEA -TAXATION

PAPUA NEW GUINEA - EXPORTS

Asian Development Bank, Post Office Box 789, 1099 Manila, Philippines; *Key Indicators of Developing Asian and Pacific Countries.*

Central Intelligence Agency, Washington, D.C. 20505 (703) 482-1100, www.cia.gov; *The World Factbook.*

The Economist Intelligence Unit, 111 West 57th Street, New York, New York 10019 (800) 938-4685; *Papua New Guinea Country Report;* and *The World Market Atlas.*

The Economist Intelligence Unit (Asia) Limited, 10th Floor, Luk Kwok Centre, 72 Gloucester Road, Wanchai, Hong Kong (Phone Number in U.S. (800) 938-4685); *Asian Market Atlas.*

Euromonitor International, Inc., 122 South Michigan Avenue, Suite 1200, Chicago, Illinois 60603; *International Marketing Data and Statistics;* and *The World Economic Factbook.*

Europa Publications Limited, 18 Bedford Square, London, WC1B 3JN, England; *The Europa World Year Book.*

Food and Agricultural Organization of the United Nations (FAO) Via delle Terme di Caracalla, 00100 Rome, Italy (Telephone Number in U.S. (202) 653-2400); *The State of Food and Agriculture.*

International Monetary Fund, 700 Nineteenth Street, NW, Washington, D.C. 20431 (202) 623-7000; *Direction of Trade Statistics; Government Finance Statistics Yearbook;* and *International Financial Statistics.*

South Pacific Commission, Post Box D5, Noumea Cedex, New Caledonia; *Statistical Bulletin of the South Pacific: Overseas Trade.*

St. Martin's Press, Inc., 175 Fifth Avenue, New York, New York 10010 (800) 221-7945; *The Statesman's Year-Book.*

United Nations Conference on Trade and Development (UNCTAD), New York, New York 10017 (800) 253-9646; *Handbook of International Trade and Development Statistics.*

Walden Publishing, Ltd., Two Market Street, Saffron Walden Essex, CB10 1HZ, England; *The World of Information Asia and Pacific Review.*

The World Bank, 1818 H Street, NW, Washington, D.C. 20433 (202) 477-1234; *World Development Report;* and *World Development Indicators.*

PAPUA NEW GUINEA - EXTERNAL FINANCING

Asian Development Bank, Post Office Box 789, 1099 Manila, Philippines; *Key Indicators of Developing Asian and Pacific Countries.*

PAPUA NEW GUINEA - EXTERNAL INDEBTEDNESS

Asian Development Bank, Post Office Box 789, 1099 Manila, Philippines; *Key Indicators of Developing Asian and Pacific Countries.*

The World Bank, 1818 H Street, NW, Washington, D.C. 20433 (202) 477-1234; *World Development Report.*

PAPUA NEW GUINEA - EXTERNAL TRADE

Asian Development Bank, Post Office Box 789, 1099 Manila, Philippines; *Key Indicators of Developing Asian and Pacific Countries.*

Euromonitor International, Inc., 122 South Michigan Avenue, Suite 1200, Chicago, Illinois 60603 (800) 577-EURO; *World Marketing Data and Statistics.*

Food and Agricultural Organization of the United Nations (FAO) Via delle Terme di Caracalla, 00100 Rome, Italy (Telephone Number in U.S. (202) 653-2400); *The State of Food and Agriculture;* and *Trade Yearbook.*

Statistical Office of the United Nations, Publishing Service, New York, New York 10017 (800) 253-9646; *Asia-Pacific in Figures; Statistical Yearbook;* and *Statistical Yearbook for Asia and the Pacific.*

PAPUA NEW GUINEA - FARM CROPS - See PAPUA NEW GUINEA - CROPS

PAPUA NEW GUINEA - FEMALE WORKING POPULATION - See PAPUA NEW GUINEA - EMPLOYMENT

PAPUA NEW GUINEA - FERTILITY RATES

Central Intelligence Agency, Washington, D.C. 20505 (703) 482-1100, www.cia.gov; *The World Factbook.*

The Economist Intelligence Unit (Asia) Limited, 10th Floor, Luk Kwok Centre, 72 Gloucester Road, Wanchai, Hong Kong (Phone Number in U.S. (800) 938-4685); *Asian Market Atlas.*

M.E. Sharpe, 80 Business Park Drive, Armonk, New York 10504 (800) 541-6563; *The Illustrated Book of World Rankings.*

Statistical Office of the United Nations, Publishing Service, New York, New York 10017 (800) 253-9646; *Human*

Development Report.

The World Bank, 1818 H Street, NW, Washington, D.C. 20433 (202) 477-1234; *The World Bank Atlas; World Development Report;* and *World Development Indicators.*

PAPUA NEW GUINEA - FERTILIZER

Food and Agricultural Organization of the United Nations (FAO), Via delle Terme di Caracalla, 00100 Rome, Italy (Telephone Number in U.S. (202) 653-2400); *Fertilizer Yearbook;* and *The State of Food and Agriculture.*

Statistical Office of the United Nations, Publishing Service, New York, New York 10017 (800) 253-9646; *Statistical Yearbook.*

PAPUA NEW GUINEA - FETAL MORTALITY - See PAPUA NEW GUINEA - MORTALITY

PAPUA NEW GUINEA - FINANCE

Asian Development Bank, Post Office Box 789, 1099 Manila, Philippines; *Key Indicators of Developing Asian and Pacific Countries.*

Economist Intelligence Unit, 111 West 57th Street, New York, New York 10019 (800) 938-4685; *Papua New Guinea Country Report.*

Europa Publications Limited, 18 Bedford Square, London, WC1B 3JN, England; *The Europa World Year Book.*

Federal Statistical Office, Gustav - Stresemann - Ring 11, D-6200 Wiesbaden, Germany; *Papua-Neuguinea.*

International Monetary Fund, 700 Nineteenth Street, NW, Washington, D.C. 20431 (202) 623-7000; *Government Finance Statistics Yearbook;* and *International Financial Statistics.*

M.E. Sharpe, 80 Business Park Drive, Armonk, New York 10504 (800) 541-6563; *The Illustrated Book of World Rankings.*

St. Martin's Press, Inc., 175 Fifth Avenue, New York, New York 10010 (800) 221-7945; *The Statesman's Year-Book.*

Statistical Office of the United Nations, Publishing Service, New York, New York 10017 (800) 253-9646; *Statistical Yearbook for Asia and the Pacific.*

PAPUA NEW GUINEA - FISHERIES

Europa Publications Limited, 18 Bedford Square, London, WC1B 3JN, England; *The Europa World Year Book.*

Federal Statistical Office, Gustav - Stresemann - Ring 11, D-6200 Wiesbaden,

Germany; *Papua-Neuguinea.*

Food and Agricultural Organization of the United Nations (FAO) Via delle Terme di Caracalla, 00100 Rome, Italy (Telephone Number in U.S. (202) 653-2400); *The State of Food and Agriculture;* and *Yearbook of Fishery Statistics.*

M.E. Sharpe, 80 Business Park Drive, Armonk, New York 10504 (800) 541-6563; *The Illustrated Book of World Rankings.*

St. Martin's Press, Inc., 175 Fifth Avenue, New York, New York 10010 (800) 221-7945; *The Statesman's Year-Book.*

Statistical Office of the United Nations, Publishing Service, New York, New York 10017 (800) 253-9646; *Statistical Yearbook.*

United Nations Conference on Trade and Development, Central Statistical Service, Palais des Nations, Geneva, Switzerland (Telephone in U.S. (800) 253-9646); *UNCTAD Commodity Yearbook.*

PAPUA NEW GUINEA - FOOD

Food and Agricultural Organization of the United Nations (FAO), Via delle Terme di Caracalla, 00100 Rome, Italy (Telephone Number in U.S. (202) 653-2400); *Production Yearbook;* and *The State of Food and Agriculture.*

South Pacific Commission, Post Box D5, Noumea Cedex, New Caledonia; *Statistical Bulletin of the South Pacific: Retail Price Indexes.*

Statistical Office of the United Nations, Publishing Service, New York, New York 10017 (800) 253-9646; *Human Development Report;* and *Statistical Yearbook for Asia and the Pacific.*

United Nations Conference on Trade and Development, Central Statistical Service, Palais des Nations, Geneva, Switzerland (Telephone in U.S. (800) 253-9646); *UNCTAD Commodity Yearbook.*

PAPUA NEW GUINEA - FOREIGN DEBT

International Monetary Fund, 700 Nineteenth Street, NW, Washington, D.C. 20431 (202) 623-7000; *Government Finance Statistics Yearbook.*

St. Martin's Press, Inc., 175 Fifth Avenue, New York, New York 10010 (800) 221-7945; *The Statesman's Year-Book.*

Walden Publishing, Ltd., Two Market Street, Saffron Walden Essex, CB10 1HZ, England; *The World of Information Asia and Pacific Review.*

PAPUA NEW GUINEA - FOREIGN TRADE

Asian Development Bank, Post Office Box 789, 1099 Manila, Philippines; *Key Indicators of Developing Asian and Pacific Countries.*

Economist Intelligence Unit, 111 West 57th Street, New York, New York 10019 (800) 938-4685; *Papua New Guinea Country Report.*

The Economist Intelligence Unit (Asia) Limited, 10th Floor, Luk Kwok Centre, 72 Gloucester Road, Wanchai, Hong Kong (Phone Number in U.S. (800) 938-4685); *Asian Market Atlas.*

Euromonitor International, Inc., 122 South Michigan Avenue, Suite 1200, Chicago, Illinois 60603; *International Marketing Data and Statistics;* and *The World Economic Factbook.*

Europa Publications Limited, 18 Bedford Square, London, WC1B 3JN, England; *The Europa World Year Book.*

Federal Statistical Office, Gustav - Stresemann - Ring 11, D-6200 Wiesbaden, Germany; *Papua-Neuguinea.*

Food and Agricultural Organization of the United Nations (FAO) Via delle Terme di Caracalla, 00100 Rome, Italy (Telephone Number in U.S. (202) 653-2400); *The State of Food and Agriculture.*

M.E. Sharpe, 80 Business Park Drive, Armonk, New York 10504 (800) 541-6563; *The Illustrated Book of World Rankings.*

South Pacific Commission, Post Box D5, Noumea Cedex, New Caledonia; *Statistical Bulletin of the South Pacific: Overseas Trade.*

St. Martin's Press, Inc., 175 Fifth Avenue, New York, New York 10010 (800) 221-7945; *The Statesman's Year-Book.*

Statistical Office of the United Nations, Publishing Service, New York, New York 10017 (800) 253-9646; *International Trade Statistics Yearbook;* and *Statistical Yearbook.*

United Nations Conference on Trade and Development, Central Statistical Service, Palais des Nations, Geneva, Switzerland (Telephone in U.S. (800) 253-9646); *UNCTAD Commodity Yearbook.*

The World Bank, 1818 H Street, NW, Washington, D.C. 20433 (202) 477-1234; *World Development Report; World Metal Statistics;* and *World Development Indicators.*

PAPUA NEW GUINEA - FORESTRY AND FOREST PRODUCTS

The Economist Intelligence Unit (Asia) Limited, 10th Floor, Luk Kwok Centre, 72 Gloucester Road, Wanchai, Hong Kong (Phone Number in U.S. (800) 938-4685); *Asian Market Atlas.*

Europa Publications Limited, 18 Bedford Square, London, WC1B 3JN, England; *The Europa World Year Book.*

Federal Statistical Office, Gustav - Stresemann - Ring 11, D-6200 Wiesbaden, Germany; *Papua-Neuguinea.*

Food and Agricultural Organization of the United Nations (FAO) Via delle Terme di Caracalla, 00100 Rome, Italy (Telephone Number in U.S. (202) 653-2400); *The State of Food and Agriculture;* and *Yearbook of Forest Products.*

M.E. Sharpe, 80 Business Park Drive, Armonk, New York 10504 (800) 541-6563; *The Illustrated Book of World Rankings.*

St. Martin's Press, Inc., 175 Fifth Avenue, New York, New York 10010 (800) 221-7945; *The Statesman's Year-Book.*

Statistical Office of the United Nations, Publishing Service, New York, New York 10017 (800) 253-9646; *Statistical Yearbook.*

United Nations Conference on Trade and Development, Central Statistical Service, Palais des Nations, Geneva, Switzerland (Telephone in U.S. (800) 253-9646); *UNCTAD Commodity Yearbook.*

United Nations Educational, Scientific and Cultural Organization (UNESCO), 7 Place de Fontenoy, F-75700 Paris, France (Telephone Number in U.S. (212) 963-5981); *Statistical Yearbook.*

The World Bank, 1818 H Street, NW, Washington, D.C. 20433 (202) 477-1234; *World Development Report.*

PAPUA NEW GUINEA - GAS PRODUCTION - See PAPUA NEW GUINEA - MINING AND MINERAL PRODUCTS

PAPUA NEW GUINEA - GENERAL INDUSTRIAL STATISTICS - See PAPUA NEW GUINEA - INDUSTRY

PAPUA NEW GUINEA - GENERAL MORTALITY - See PAPUA NEW GUINEA - MORTALITY

PAPUA NEW GUINEA - GEOGRAPHIC DATA

M.E. Sharpe, 80 Business Park Drive, Armonk, New York 10504 (800) 541-6563; *The Illustrated Book of World Rankings.*

PAPUA NEW GUINEA - GOATS - See PAPUA NEW GUINEA - LIVESTOCK AND POULTRY

PAPUA NEW GUINEA - GOLD HOLDINGS

International Monetary Fund, 700 Nineteenth Street, NW, Washington, D.C. 20431 (202) 623-7000; *International Financial Statistics.*

Statistical Office of the United Nations, Publishing Service, New York, New York 10017 (800) 253-9646; *Statistical Yearbook.*

The World Bank, 1818 H Street, NW, Washington, D.C. 20433 (202) 477-1234; *World Development Indicators.*

PAPUA NEW GUINEA - GOLD PRODUCTION AND CONSUMPTION - See PAPUA NEW GUINEA - MINING AND MINERAL PRODUCTS

PAPUA NEW GUINEA - GOVERNMENT

Asian Development Bank, Post Office Box 789, 1099 Manila, Philippines; *Key Indicators of Developing Asian and Pacific Countries.*

Central Intelligence Agency, Washington, D.C. 20505 (703) 482-1100, www.cia.gov; *The World Factbook.*

Europa Publications Limited, 18 Bedford Square, London, WC1B 3JN, England; *The Europa World Year Book.*

International Monetary Fund, 700 Nineteenth Street, NW, Washington, D.C. 20431 (202) 623-7000; *Government Finance Statistics Yearbook.*

St. Martin's Press, Inc., 175 Fifth Avenue, New York, New York 10010 (800) 221-7945; *The Statesman's Year-Book.*

Statistical Office of the United Nations, Publishing Service, New York, New York 10017 (800) 253-9646; *Asia-Pacific in Figures;* and *National Accounts Statistics.*

The World Bank, 1818 H Street, NW, Washington, D.C. 20433 (202) 477-1234; *World Development Report;* and *World Development Indicators.*

PAPUA NEW GUINEA - GRAIN PRODUCTION - See PAPUA NEW GUINEA - CROPS

PAPUA NEW GUINEA - GRANTS

International Monetary Fund, 700 Nineteenth Street, NW, Washington, D.C. 20431 (202) 623-7000; *Government Finance Statistics Yearbook.*

PAPUA NEW GUINEA - GROSS DOMESTIC PRODUCT

Asian Development Bank, Post Office Box 789, 1099 Manila, Philippines; *Key Indicators of Developing Asian and Pacific Countries.*

The Economist Intelligence Unit, 111 West 57th Street, New York, New York 10019 (800) 938-4685; *Papua New Guinea Country Report;* and *The World Market Atlas.*

The Economist Intelligence Unit (Asia) Limited, 10th Floor, Luk Kwok Centre, 72 Gloucester Road, Wanchai, Hong Kong (Phone Number in U.S. (800) 938-4685); *Asian Market Atlas.*

Euromonitor International, Inc., 122 South Michigan Avenue, Suite 1200, Chicago, Illinois 60603; *International Marketing Data and Statistics;* and *The World Economic Factbook.*

Europa Publications Limited, 18 Bedford Square, London, WC1B 3JN, England; *The Europa World Year Book.*

M.E. Sharpe, 80 Business Park Drive, Armonk, New York 10504 (800) 541-6563; *The Illustrated Book of World Rankings.*

Statistical Office of the United Nations, Publishing Service, New York, New York 10017 (800) 253-9646; *Human Development Report; National Accounts Statistics;* and *Statistical Yearbook.*

Walden Publishing, Ltd., Two Market Street, Saffron Walden Essex, CB10 1HZ, England; *The World of Information Asia and Pacific Review.*

The World Bank, 1818 H Street, NW, Washington, D.C. 20433 (202) 477-1234; *World Development Report;* and *World Development Indicators.*

PAPUA NEW GUINEA - GROSS NATIONAL PRODUCT

Asian Development Bank, Post Office Box 789, 1099 Manila, Philippines; *Key Indicators of Developing Asian and Pacific Countries.*

Euromonitor International, Inc., 122 South Michigan Avenue, Suite 1200, Chicago, Illinois 60603; *International Marketing Data and Statistics.*

St. Martin's Press, Inc., 175 Fifth Avenue, New York, New York 10010 (800) 221-7945; *The Statesman's Year-Book.*

U.S. Arms Control and Disarmament Agency, 320 Twenty-first Street, NW, Washington, D.C. 20451 (202) 647-8677; *World Military Expenditures and Arms Transfers.*

The World Bank, 1818 H Street, NW, Washington, D.C. 20433 (202) 477-1234; *The World Bank Atlas; World Development Report;* and *World Development Indicators.*

PAPUA NEW GUINEA - GROUNDNUT PRODUCTION - See PAPUA NEW GUINEA - CROPS

PAPUA NEW GUINEA - HEALTH

The Economist Intelligence Unit (Asia) Limited, 10th Floor, Luk Kwok Centre, 72 Gloucester Road, Wanchai, Hong Kong (Phone Number in U.S. (800) 938-4685); *Asian Market Atlas.*

Euromonitor International, Inc., 122 South Michigan Avenue, Suite 1200, Chicago, Illinois 60603 (800) 577-EURO; *World Marketing Data and Statistics.*

Federal Statistical Office, Gustav - Stresemann - Ring 11, D-6200 Wiesbaden, Germany; *Papua-Neuguinea.*

M.E. Sharpe, 80 Business Park Drive, Armonk, New York 10504 (800) 541-6563; *The Illustrated Book of World Rankings.*

South Pacific Commission, Post Box D5, Noumea Cedex, New Caledonia; *Statistical Bulletin of the South Pacific: Retail Price Indexes.*

St. Martin's Press, Inc., 175 Fifth Avenue, New York, New York 10010 (800) 221-7945; *The Statesman's Year-Book.*

Statistical Office of the United Nations, Publishing Service, New York, New York 10017 (800) 253-9646; *Asia-Pacific in Figures; Human Development Report;* and *Statistical Yearbook.*

United Nations Children's Fund (UNICEF), 3 United Nations Plaza, New York, New York 10017 (800) 253-9646; *State of the World's Children.*

The World Bank, 1818 H Street, NW, Washington, D.C. 20433 (202) 477-1234; *World Development Report.*

World Health Organization, Office of Publications, 20 Avenue Appia, CH-1211 Geneva 27, Switzerland (Telephone Number in U.S. (518) 436-9686); *World Health Statistics Annual.*

PAPUA NEW GUINEA - HEALTH EXPENDITURES

International Monetary Fund, 700 Nineteenth Street, NW, Washington, D.C. 20431 (202) 623-7000; *Government Finance Statistics Yearbook.*

PAPUA NEW GUINEA - HIDE PRODUCTION

Food and Agricultural Organization of the United Nations (FAO), Via delle Terme di Caracalla, 00100 Rome, Italy (Telephone Number in U.S. (202) 653-2400); *Production Yearbook.*

PAPUA NEW GUINEA - HIGHWAYS

Central Intelligence Agency, Washington, D.C. 20505 (703) 482-1100, www.cia.gov; *The World Factbook.*

The Economist Intelligence Unit (Asia) Limited, 10th Floor, Luk Kwok Centre, 72 Gloucester Road, Wanchai, Hong Kong (Phone Number in U.S. (800) 938-4685); *Asian Market Atlas.*

St. Martin's Press, Inc., 175 Fifth Avenue, New York, New York 10010 (800) 221-7945; *The Statesman's Year-Book.*

PAPUA NEW GUINEA - HORSES - See PAPUA NEW GUINEA - LIVESTOCK AND POULTRY

PAPUA NEW GUINEA - HOURS OF WORK - See PAPUA NEW GUINEA - EMPLOYMENT

PAPUA NEW GUINEA - HOUSING AND HOUSING UNITS

Euromonitor International, Inc., 122 South Michigan Avenue, Suite 1200, Chicago, Illinois 60603 (800) 577-EURO; *World Marketing Data and Statistics.*

M.E. Sharpe, 80 Business Park Drive, Armonk, New York 10504 (800) 541-6563; *The Illustrated Book of World Rankings.*

South Pacific Commission, Post Box D5, Noumea Cedex, New Caledonia; *Statistical Bulletin of the South Pacific: Retail Price Indexes.*

PAPUA NEW GUINEA - HOUSING EXPENDITURES

International Monetary Fund, 700 Nineteenth Street, NW, Washington, D.C. 20431 (202) 623-7000; *Government Finance Statistics Yearbook.*

South Pacific Commission, Post Box D5, Noumea Cedex, New Caledonia; *Statistical Bulletin of the South Pacific: Retail Price Indexes.*

PAPUA NEW GUINEA - ILLITERATE POPULATION

Central Intelligence Agency, Washington, D.C. 20505 (703) 482-1100, www.cia.gov; *The World Factbook.*

The Economist Intelligence Unit, 111 West 57th Street, New York, New York 10019 (800) 938-4685; *The World Market Atlas.*

Euromonitor International, Inc., 122 South Michigan Avenue, Suite 1200, Chicago, Illinois 60603; *The World Economic Factbook.*

Statistical Office of the United Nations,

Publishing Service, New York, New York 10017 (800) 253-9646; *Asia-Pacific in Figures;* and *Human Development Report.*

PAPUA NEW GUINEA - IMPORTS

Asian Development Bank, Post Office Box 789, 1099 Manila, Philippines; *Key Indicators of Developing Asian and Pacific Countries.*

Central Intelligence Agency, Washington, D.C. 20505 (703) 482-1100, www.cia.gov; *The World Factbook.*

The Economist Intelligence Unit, 111 West 57th Street, New York, New York 10019 (800) 938-4685; *Papua Country Report;* and *The World Market Atlas.*

The Economist Intelligence Unit (Asia) Limited, 10th Floor, Luk Kwok Centre, 72 Gloucester Road, Wanchai, Hong Kong (Phone Number in U.S. (800) 938-4685); *Asian Market Atlas.*

Euromonitor International, Inc., 122 South Michigan Avenue, Suite 1200, Chicago, Illinois 60603; *International Marketing Data and Statistics;* and *The World Economic Factbook.*

Europa Publications Limited, 18 Bedford Square, London, WC1B 3JN, England; *The Europa World Year Book.*

Food and Agricultural Organization of the United Nations (FAO) Via delle Terme di Caracalla, 00100 Rome, Italy (Telephone Number in U.S. (202) 653-2400); *The State of Food and Agriculture.*

International Monetary Fund, 700 Nineteenth Street, NW, Washington, D.C. 20431 (202) 623-7000; *Direction of Trade Statistics; Government Finance Statistics Yearbook;* and *International Financial Statistics.*

South Pacific Commission, Post Box D5, Noumea Cedex, New Caledonia; *Statistical Bulletin of the South Pacific: Overseas Trade.*

St. Martin's Press, Inc., 175 Fifth Avenue, New York, New York 10010 (800) 221-7945; *The Statesman's Year-Book.*

United Nations Conference on Trade and Development (UNCTAD), New York, New York 10017 (800) 253-9646; *Handbook of International Trade and Development Statistics.*

Walden Publishing, Ltd., Two Market Street, Saffron Walden Essex, CB10 1HZ, England; *The World of Information Asia and Pacific Review.*

The World Bank, 1818 H Street, NW, Washington, D.C. 20433 (202) 477-1234;

World Development Report; and *World Development Indicators.*

PAPUA NEW GUINEA - INCOME TAXES - See PAPUA NEW GUINEA - TAXATION

PAPUA NEW GUINEA - INDUSTRY

Central Intelligence Agency, Washington, D.C. 20505 (703) 482-1100, www.cia.gov; *The World Factbook.*

Economist Intelligence Unit, 111 West 57th Street, New York, New York 10019 (800) 938-4685; *Papua New Guinea Country Report.*

Euromonitor International, Inc., 122 South Michigan Avenue, Suite 1200, Chicago, Illinois 60603; *Industrial Marketing Data and Statistics; World Marketing Data and Statistics;* and *The World Economic Factbook.*

Europa Publications Limited, 18 Bedford Square, London, WC1B 3JN, England; *The Europa World Year Book.*

Federal Statistical Office, Gustav - Stresemann - Ring 11, D-6200 Wiesbaden, Germany; *Papua-Neuguinea.*

International Labour Office, I.L.O. Publications, 1828 L Street, NW., Suite 801, Washington, D.C. 20036 (301) 638-3152; *Yearbook of Labour Statistics.*

M.E. Sharpe, 80 Business Park Drive, Armonk, New York 10504 (800) 541-6563; *The Illustrated Book of World Rankings.*

St. Martin's Press, Inc., 175 Fifth Avenue, New York, New York 10010 (800) 221-7945; *The Statesman's Year-Book.*

Statistical Office of the United Nations, Publishing Service, New York, New York 10017 (800) 253-9646; *Asia-Pacific in Figures; Industrial Commodities Statistics Yearbook;* and *Statistical Yearbook for Asia and the Pacific.*

The World Bank, 1818 H Street, NW, Washington, D.C. 20433 (202) 477-1234; *World Development Indicators.*

PAPUA NEW GUINEA - INFANT AND MATERNAL MORTALITY - See PAPUA NEW GUINEA - MORTALITY

PAPUA NEW GUINEA - INTERNAL TRADE

Statistical Office of the United Nations, Publishing Service, New York, New York 10017 (800) 253-9646; *Statistical Yearbook Asia and the Pacific.*

PAPUA NEW GUINEA - INTERNATIONAL LIQUIDITY

International Monetary Fund, 700

Nineteenth Street, NW, Washington, D.C. 20431 (202) 623-7000; *International Financial Statistics.*

PAPUA NEW GUINEA - INTERNATIONAL RESERVES EXCLUDING GOLD

Asian Development Bank, Post Office Box 789, 1099 Manila, Philippines; *Key Indicators of Developing Asian and Pacific Countries.*

Statistical Office of the United Nations, Publishing Service, New York, New York 10017 (800) 253-9646; *Statistical Yearbook.*

The World Bank, 1818 H Street, NW, Washington, D.C. 20433 (202) 477-1234; *World Development Indicators.*

PAPUA NEW GUINEA - INTERNATIONAL STATISTICS

Asian Development Bank, Post Office Box 789, 1099 Manila, Philippines; *Key Indicators of Developing Asian and Pacific Countries.*

PAPUA NEW GUINEA - IRON ORE PRODUCTION AND CONSUMPTION - See PAPUA NEW GUINEA - MINING AND MINERAL PRODUCTS

PAPUA NEW GUINEA - IRRIGATION

Euromonitor International, Inc., 122 South Michigan Avenue, Suite 1200, Chicago, Illinois 60603; *International Marketing Data and Statistics.*

PAPUA NEW GUINEA - LABOR

Central Intelligence Agency, Washington, D.C. 20505 (703) 482-1100, www.cia.gov; *The World Factbook.*

The Economist Intelligence Unit (Asia) Limited, 10th Floor, Luk Kwok Centre, 72 Gloucester Road, Wanchai, Hong Kong (Phone Number in U.S. (800) 938-4685); *Asian Market Atlas.*

Euromonitor International, Inc., 122 South Michigan Avenue, Suite 1200, Chicago, Illinois 60603; *International Marketing Data and Statistics;* and *World Marketing Data and Statistics.*

Europa Publications Limited, 18 Bedford Square, London, WC1B 3JN, England; *The Europa World Year Book.*

Food and Agricultural Organization of the United Nations (FAO) Via delle Terme di Caracalla, 00100 Rome, Italy (Telephone Number in U.S. (202) 653-2400); *The State of Food and Agriculture.*

International Labour Office, I.L.O. Publications, 1828 L Street, NW., Suite 801, Washington, D.C. 20036 (301)

638-3152; *Yearbook of Labour Statistics.*

M.E. Sharpe, 80 Business Park Drive, Armonk, New York 10504 (800) 541-6563; *The Illustrated Book of World Rankings.*

St. Martin's Press, Inc., 175 Fifth Avenue, New York, New York 10010 (800) 221-7945; *The Statesman's Year-Book.*

Statistical Office of the United Nations, Publishing Service, New York, New York 10017 (800) 253-9646; *Human Development Report.*

The World Bank, 1818 H Street, NW, Washington, D.C. 20433 (202) 477-1234; *The World Bank Atlas; World Development Report;* and *World Development Indicators.*

PAPUA NEW GUINEA - LAND USE

Central Intelligence Agency, Washington, D.C. 20505 (703) 482-1100, www.cia.gov; *The World Factbook.*

Euromonitor International, Inc., 122 South Michigan Avenue, Suite 1200, Chicago, Illinois 60603; *International Marketing Data and Statistics.*

Food and Agricultural Organization of the United Nations (FAO), Via delle Terme di Caracalla, 00100 Rome, Italy (Telephone Number in U.S. (202) 653-2400); *Production Yearbook.*

The World Bank, 1818 H Street, NW, Washington, D.C. 20433 (202) 477-1234; *World Development Report.*

PAPUA NEW GUINEA - LEAD AND LEAD ORE PRODUCTION AND CONSUMPTION - See PAPUA NEW GUINEA - MINING AND MINERAL PRODUCTS

PAPUA NEW GUINEA - LIBRARIES

M.E. Sharpe, 80 Business Park Drive, Armonk, New York 10504 (800) 541-6563; *The Illustrated Book of World Rankings.*

United Nations Educational, Scientific and Cultural Organization (UNESCO), 7 Place de Fontenoy, F-75700 Paris, France (Telephone Number in U.S. (212) 963-5981); *Statistical Yearbook.*

PAPUA NEW GUINEA - LIFE EXPECTANCY

Central Intelligence Agency, Washington, D.C. 20505 (703) 482-1100, www.cia.gov; *The World Factbook.*

The Economist Intelligence Unit (Asia) Limited, 10th Floor, Luk Kwok Centre, 72 Gloucester Road, Wanchai, Hong Kong (Phone Number in U.S. (800) 938-4685); *Asian Market Atlas.*

Euromonitor International, Inc., 122 South Michigan Avenue, Suite 1200, Chicago, Illinois 60603; *The World Economic Factbook.*

St. Martin's Press, Inc., 175 Fifth Avenue, New York, New York 10010 (800) 221-7945; *The Statesman's Year-Book.*

Statistical Office of the United Nations, Publishing Service, New York, New York 10017 (800) 253-9646; *Asia-Pacific in Figures; Human Development Report;* and *World Statistics Pocketbook.*

The World Bank, 1818 H Street, NW, Washington, D.C. 20433 (202) 477-1234; *The World Bank Atlas;* and *World Development Report.*

PAPUA NEW GUINEA - LITERACY RATE

Euromonitor International, Inc., 122 South Michigan Avenue, Suite 1200, Chicago, Illinois 60603 (800) 577-EURO; *World Marketing Data and Statistics.*

PAPUA NEW GUINEA - LIVESTOCK AND POULTRY

Euromonitor International, Inc., 122 South Michigan Avenue, Suite 1200, Chicago, Illinois 60603; *International Marketing Data and Statistics.*

Europa Publications Limited, 18 Bedford Square, London, WC1B 3JN, England; *The Europa World Year Book.*

Food and Agricultural Organization of the United Nations (FAO), Via delle Terme di Caracalla, 00100 Rome, Italy (Telephone Number in U.S. (202) 653-2400); *Production Yearbook;* and *The State of Food and Agriculture.*

M.E. Sharpe, 80 Business Park Drive, Armonk, New York 10504 (800) 541-6563; *The Illustrated Book of World Rankings.*

St. Martin's Press, Inc., 175 Fifth Avenue, New York, New York 10010 (800) 221-7945; *The Statesman's Year-Book.*

Statistical Office of the United Nations, Publishing Service, New York, New York 10017 (800) 253-9646; *Statistical Yearbook.*

United Nations Conference on Trade and Development, Central Statistical Service, Palais des Nations, Geneva, Switzerland (Telephone in U.S. (800) 253-9646); *UNCTAD Commodity Yearbook.*

PAPUA NEW GUINEA - LIVING LEVELS - See PAPUA NEW GUINEA LIFE EXPECTANCY

PAPUA NEW GUINEA - MANPOWER

Statistical Office of the United Nations, Publishing Service, New York, New York

10017 (800) 253-9646; *Statistical Yearbook for Asia and the Pacific.*

PAPUA NEW GUINEA - MANUFACTURING

Asian Development Bank, Post Office Box 789, 1099 Manila, Philippines; *Key Indicators of Developing Asian and Pacific Countries.*

M.E. Sharpe, 80 Business Park Drive, Armonk, New York 10504 (800) 541-6563; *The Illustrated Book of World Rankings.*

Statistical Office of the United Nations, Publishing Service, New York, New York 10017 (800) 253-9646; *Statistical Yearbook.*

The World Bank, 1818 H Street, NW, Washington, D.C. 20433 (202) 477-1234; *World Development Indicators.*

PAPUA NEW GUINEA - MARRIAGE RATES

M.E. Sharpe, 80 Business Park Drive, Armonk, New York 10504 (800) 541-6563; *The Illustrated Book of World Rankings.*

Statistical Office of the United Nations, Publishing Service, New York, New York 10017 (800) 253-9646; *Demographic Yearbook.*

PAPUA NEW GUINEA - MEAT PRODUCTION - See PAPUA NEW GUINEA - LIVESTOCK AND POULTRY

PAPUA NEW GUINEA - MERCHANT SHIPPING

Europa Publications Limited, 18 Bedford Square, London, WC1B 3JN, England; *The Europa World Year Book.*

Lloyd's Register of Shipping, 17 Battery Place, New York, New York 10004 (212) 425-8050; *Register of Ships.*

St. Martin's Press, Inc., 175 Fifth Avenue, New York, New York 10010 (800) 221-7945; *The Statesman's Year-Book.*

Statistical Office of the United Nations, Publishing Service, New York, New York 10017 (800) 253-9646; *Statistical Yearbook.*

PAPUA NEW GUINEA - MILITARY

Central Intelligence Agency, Washington, D.C. 20505 (703) 482-1100, www.cia.gov; *The World Factbook.*

The Economist Intelligence Unit (Asia) Limited, 10th Floor, Luk Kwok Centre, 72 Gloucester Road, Wanchai, Hong Kong (Phone Number in U.S. (800) 938-4685); *Asian Market Atlas.*

Euromonitor International, Inc., 122 South Michigan Avenue, Suite 1200,

Chicago, Illinois 60603 (800) 577-EURO; *World Marketing Data and Statistics.*

The International Institute for Strategic Studies, 23 Tavistock Street, London WC2E 7NQ, England 44 171 3797676; *The Military Balance.*

International Monetary Fund, 700 Nineteenth Street, NW, Washington, D.C. 20431 (202) 623-7000; *Government Finance Statistics Yearbook.*

St. Martin's Press, Inc., 175 Fifth Avenue, New York, New York 10010 (800) 221-7945; *The Statesman's Year-Book.*

Statistical Office of the United Nations, Publishing Service, New York, New York 10017 (800) 253-9646; *Human Development Report.*

U.S. Arms Control and Disarmament Agency, 320 Twenty-first Street, NW, Washington, D.C. 20451 (202) 647-8677; *World Military Expenditures and Arms Transfers.*

PAPUA NEW GUINEA - MILK PRODUCTION - See PAPUA NEW GUINEA - DAIRY PRODUCTS

PAPUA NEW GUINEA - MINING AND MINERAL PRODUCTS

Asian Development Bank, Post Office Box 789, 1099 Manila, Philippines; *Key Indicators of Developing Asian and Pacific Countries.*

Europa Publications Limited, 18 Bedford Square, London, WC1B 3JN, England; *The Europa World Year Book.*

International Monetary Fund, 700 Nineteenth Street, NW, Washington, D.C. 20431 (202) 623-7000; *International Financial Statistics.*

M.E. Sharpe, 80 Business Park Drive, Armonk, New York 10504 (800) 541-6563; *The Illustrated Book of World Rankings.*

Penn Well Publishing Company, 1421 South Sheridan Road, Post Office Box 1260, Tulsa, Oklahoma 74101 (800) 752-9764; *International Energy Statistics Sourcebook.*

St. Martin's Press, Inc., 175 Fifth Avenue, New York, New York 10010 (800) 221-7945; *The Statesman's Year-Book.*

Statistical Office of the United Nations, Publishing Service, New York, New York 10017 (800) 253-9646; *Statistical Yearbook.*

United Nations Conference on Trade and Development, Central Statistical Service, Palais des Nations, Geneva, Switzerland (Telephone in U.S. (800) 253-9646); *UNCTAD Commodity Yearbook.*

World Bureau of Metal Statistics, 27-A High Street, Ware, Herts. SG12 9BA, England; *World Metal Statistics.*

PAPUA NEW GUINEA - MOLYBDENUM - See PAPUA NEW GUINEA - MINING AND MINERAL PRODUCTS

PAPUA NEW GUINEA - MONEY EXCHANGE RATES - See PAPUA NEW GUINEA - EXCHANGE RATES

PAPUA NEW GUINEA - MONEY RESERVES

Euromonitor International, Inc., 122 South Michigan Avenue, Suite 1200, Chicago, Illinois 60603; *International Marketing Data and Statistics.*

PAPUA NEW GUINEA - MONEY SUPPLY

Asian Development Bank, Post Office Box 789, 1099 Manila, Philippines; *Key Indicators of Developing Asian and Pacific Countries.*

Economist Intelligence Unit, 111 West 57th Street, New York, New York 10019 (800) 938-4685; *Papua New Guinea Country Report.*

Euromonitor International, Inc., 122 South Michigan Avenue, Suite 1200, Chicago, Illinois 60603; *International Marketing Data and Statistics.*

Europa Publications Limited, 18 Bedford Square, London, WC1B 3JN, England; *The Europa World Year Book.*

The World Bank, 1818 H Street, NW, Washington, D.C. 20433 (202) 477-1234; *World Development Indicators.*

PAPUA NEW GUINEA - MORTALITY

Central Intelligence Agency, Washington, D.C. 20505 (703) 482-1100, www.cia.gov; *The World Factbook.*

The Economist Intelligence Unit (Asia) Limited, 10th Floor, Luk Kwok Centre, 72 Gloucester Road, Wanchai, Hong Kong (Phone Number in U.S. (800) 938-4685); *Asian Market Atlas.*

Euromonitor International, Inc., 122 South Michigan Avenue, Suite 1200, Chicago, Illinois 60603; *International Marketing Data and Statistics;* and *The World Economic Factbook.*

Europa Publications Limited, 18 Bedford Square, London, WC1B 3JN, England; *The Europa World Year Book.*

St. Martin's Press, Inc., 175 Fifth Avenue, New York, New York 10010 (800) 221-7945; *The Statesman's Year-Book.*

Statistical Office of the United Nations,

Publishing Service, New York, New York 10017 (800) 253-9646; *Demographic Yearbook; Human Development Report; Statistical Yearbook;* and *World Statistics Pocketbook.*

United Nations Children's Fund (UNICEF), 3 United Nations Plaza, New York, New York 10017 (800) 253-9646; *State of the World's Children.*

The World Bank, 1818 H Street, NW, Washington, D.C. 20433 (202) 477-1234; *The World Bank Atlas; World Development Report;* and *World Development Indicators.*

World Health Organization, Office of Publications, 20 Avenue Appia, CH-1211 Geneva 27, Switzerland (Telephone Number in U.S. (518) 436-9686); *World Health Statistics Annual.*

PAPUA NEW GUINEA - MOTION PICTURES

Statistical Office of the United Nations, Publishing Service, New York, New York 10017 (800) 253-9646; *Statistical Yearbook.*

PAPUA NEW GUINEA - MOTOR VEHICLE TAXES - See PAPUA NEW GUINEA - TAXATION

PAPUA NEW GUINEA - MOTOR VEHICLES IN USE

Europa Publications Limited, 18 Bedford Square, London, WC1B 3JN, England; *The Europa World Year Book.*

Statistical Office of the United Nations, Publishing Service, New York, New York 10017 (800) 253-9646; *Statistical Yearbook.*

PAPUA NEW GUINEA - MUSEUMS

M.E. Sharpe, 80 Business Park Drive, Armonk, New York 10504 (800) 541-6563; *The Illustrated Book of World Rankings.*

United Nations Educational, Scientific and Cultural Organization (UNESCO), 7 Place de Fontenoy, F-75700 Paris, France (Telephone Number in U.S. (212) 963-5981); *Statistical Yearbook.*

PAPUA NEW GUINEA - NATALITY - See PAPUA NEW GUINEA - BIRTH RATES

PAPUA NEW GUINEA - NATIONAL ACCOUNTS

Europa Publications Limited, 18 Bedford Square, London, WC1B 3JN, England; *The Europa World Year Book.*

Federal Statistical Office, Gustav - Stresemann - Ring 11, D-6200 Wiesbaden, Germany; *Papua-Neuguinea.*

Statistical Office of the United Nations, Publishing Service, New York, New York

10017 (800) 253-9646; *Asia-Pacific in Figures; National Accounts Statistics; Statistical Yearbook;* and *Statistical Yearbook for Asia and the Pacific.*

PAPUA NEW GUINEA - NATIONAL INCOME

M.E. Sharpe, 80 Business Park Drive, Armonk, New York 10504 (800) 541-6563; *The Illustrated Book of World Rankings.*

Statistical Office of the United Nations, Publishing Service, New York, New York 10017 (800) 253-9646; *National Accounts Statistics;* and *Statistical Yearbook.*

PAPUA NEW GUINEA - NATIONAL PRODUCT

M.E. Sharpe, 80 Business Park Drive, Armonk, New York 10504 (800) 541-6563; *The Illustrated Book of World Rankings.*

Statistical Office of the United Nations, Publishing Service, New York, New York 10017 (800) 253-9646; *Statistical Yearbook.*

PAPUA NEW GUINEA - NATURAL GAS PRODUCTION - See PAPUA NEW GUINEA - MINING AND MINERAL PRODUCTS

PAPUA NEW GUINEA - NATURAL RUBBER PRODUCTION

Statistical Office of the United Nations, Publishing Service, New York, New York 10017 (800) 253-9646; *Statistical Yearbook.*

PAPUA NEW GUINEA - NEWSPAPER PRODUCTION AND CONSUMPTION - See PAPUA NEW GUINEA - FORESTRY AND FOREST PRODUCTS

PAPUA NEW GUINEA - NEWSPRINT PRODUCTION AND CONSUMPTION - See PAPUA NEW GUINEA - FORESTRY AND FOREST INDUSTRY

PAPUA NEW GUINEA - NICKEL AND NICKEL ORE PRODUCTION AND CONSUMPTION - See PAPUA NEW GUINEA - MINING AND MINERAL PRODUCTS

PAPUA NEW GUINEA - OCCUPATIONS - See PAPUA NEW GUINEA -LABOR

PAPUA NEW GUINEA - PALM KERNELS AND PALM OIL - See PAPUA NEW GUINEA - CROPS

PAPUA NEW GUINEA - PEANUT PRODUCTION - See PAPUA NEW GUINEA - CROPS

PAPUA NEW GUINEA - PERIODICALS

United Nations Educational, Scientific and Cultural Organization (UNESCO), 7 Place de Fontenoy, F-75700 Paris, France (Telephone Number in U.S. (212) 963-

5981); *Statistical Yearbook.*

PAPUA NEW GUINEA - PESTICIDE USE

Food and Agricultural Organization of the United Nations (FAO) Via delle Terme di Caracalla, 00100 Rome, Italy (Telephone Number in U.S. (202) 653-2400); *The State of Food and Agriculture.*

PAPUA NEW GUINEA - PETROLEUM INDUSTRY

Asian Development Bank, Post Office Box 789, 1099 Manila, Philippines; *Key Indicators of Developing Asian and Pacific Countries.*

Food and Agricultural Organization of the United Nations (FAO) Via delle Terme di Caracalla, 00100 Rome, Italy (Telephone Number in U.S. (202) 653-2400); *The State of Food and Agriculture.*

M.E. Sharpe, 80 Business Park Drive, Armonk, New York 10504 (800) 541-6563; *The Illustrated Book of World Rankings.*

Penn Well Publishing Company, 1421 South Sheridan Road, Post Office Box 1260, Tulsa, Oklahoma 74101 (800) 752-9764; *International Energy Statistics Sourcebook.*

St. Martin's Press, Inc., 175 Fifth Avenue, New York, New York 10010 (800) 221-7945; *The Statesman's Year-Book.*

United Nations Conference on Trade and Development, Central Statistical Service, Palais des Nations, Geneva, Switzerland (Telephone in U.S. (800) 253-9646); *UNCTAD Commodity Yearbook.*

PAPUA NEW GUINEA - PIGS - See PAPUA NEW GUINEA - LIVESTOCK AND POULTRY

PAPUA NEW GUINEA - POPULATION

Asian Development Bank, Post Office Box 789, 1099 Manila, Philippines; *Key Indicators of Developing Asian and Pacific Countries.*

Central Intelligence Agency, Washington, D.C. 20505 (703) 482-1100, www.cia.gov; *The World Factbook.*

The Economist Intelligence Unit, 111 West 57th Street, New York, New York 10019 (800) 938-4685; *Papua New Guinea Country Report;* and *The World Market Atlas.*

The Economist Intelligence Unit (Asia) Limited, 10th Floor, Luk Kwok Centre, 72 Gloucester Road, Wanchai, Hong Kong (Phone Number in U.S. (800) 938-4685); *Asian Market Atlas.*

Euromonitor International, Inc., 122 South Michigan Avenue, Suite 1200,

Chicago, Illinois 60603; *International Marketing Data and Statistics;* and *The World Economic Factbook.*

Europa Publications Limited, 18 Bedford Square, London, WC1B 3JN, England; *The Europa World Year Book.*

Federal Statistical Office, Gustav - Stresemann - Ring 11, D-6200 Wiesbaden, Germany; *Papua-Neuguinea.*

Food and Agricultural Organization of the United Nations (FAO), Via delle Terme di Caracalla, 00100 Rome, Italy (Telephone Number in U.S. (202) 653-2400); *Production Yearbook.*

International Labour Office, I.L.O. Publications, 1828 L Street, NW., Suite 801, Washington, D.C. 20036 (301) 638-3152; *Yearbook of Labour Statistics.*

M.E. Sharpe, 80 Business Park Drive, Armonk, New York 10504 (800) 541-6563; *The Illustrated Book of World Rankings.*

St. Martin's Press, Inc., 175 Fifth Avenue, New York, New York 10010 (800) 221-7945; *The Statesman's Year-Book.*

Statistical Office of the United Nations, Publishing Service, New York, New York 10017 (800) 253-9646; *Asia-Pacific in Figures; Demographic Yearbook; Human Development Report; Statistical Yearbook; World Statistics Pocketbook;* and *Statistical Yearbook for Asia and the Pacific.*

United Nations Educational, Scientific and Cultural Organization (UNESCO), 7 Place de Fontenoy, F-75700 Paris, France (Telephone Number in U.S. (212) 963-5981); *Statistical Yearbook.*

U.S. Arms Control and Disarmament Agency, 320 Twenty-first Street, NW, Washington, D.C. 20451 (202) 647-8677; *World Military Expenditures and Arms Transfers.*

Walden Publishing, Ltd., Two Market Street, Saffron Walden Essex, CB10 1HZ, England; *The World of Information Asia and Pacific Review.*

The World Bank, 1818 H Street, NW, Washington, D.C. 20433 (202) 477-1234; *The World Bank Atlas;* and *World Development Report.*

World Health Organization, Office of Publications, 20 Avenue Appia, CH-1211 Geneva 27, Switzerland (Telephone Number in U.S. (518) 436-9686); *World Health Statistics Annual.*

PAPUA NEW GUINEA - POST OFFICES

M.E. Sharpe, 80 Business Park Drive, Armonk, New York 10504 (800) 541-6563;

The Illustrated Book of World Rankings.

PAPUA NEW GUINEA - POTATO PRODUCTION - See PAPUA NEW GUINEA - CROPS

PAPUA NEW GUINEA - PRICES

Asian Development Bank, Post Office Box 789, 1099 Manila, Philippines; *Key Indicators of Developing Asian and Pacific Countries.*

Food and Agricultural Organization of the United Nations (FAO), Via delle Terme di Caracalla, 00100 Rome, Italy (Telephone Number in U.S. (202) 653-2400); *Production Yearbook;* and *The State of Food and Agriculture.*

International Labour Office, I.L.O. Publications, 1828 L Street, NW., Suite 801, Washington, D.C. 20036 (301) 638-3152; *Yearbook of Labour Statistics.*

International Monetary Fund, 700 Nineteenth Street, NW, Washington, D.C. 20431 (202) 623-7000; *International Financial Statistics.*

M.E. Sharpe, 80 Business Park Drive, Armonk, New York 10504 (800) 541-6563; *The Illustrated Book of World Rankings.*

South Pacific Commission, Post Box D5, Noumea Cedex, New Caledonia; *Statistical Bulletin of the South Pacific: Overseas Trade;* and *Statistical Bulletin of the South Pacific: Retail Price Indexes.*

World Bureau of Metal Statistics, 27-A High Street, Ware, Herts. SG12 9BA, England; *World Metal Statistics.*

PAPUA NEW GUINEA - PRODUCTION

M.E. Sharpe, 80 Business Park Drive, Armonk, New York 10504 (800) 541-6563; *The Illustrated Book of World Rankings.*

PAPUA NEW GUINEA - PRODUCTIVITY

Euromonitor International, Inc., 122 South Michigan Avenue, Suite 1200, Chicago, Illinois 60603; *International Marketing Data and Statistics.*

PAPUA NEW GUINEA - PROPERTY TAXES - See PAPUA NEW GUINEA - TAXATION

PAPUA NEW GUINEA - PUBLIC FINANCE - See PAPUA NEW GUINEA - FINANCE

PAPUA NEW GUINEA - RADIO BROADCASTING - See PAPUA NEW GUINEA - BROADCASTING

PAPUA NEW GUINEA - RADIO RECEIVERS

St. Martin's Press, Inc., 175 Fifth Avenue, New York, New York 10010 (800)

221-7945; *The Statesman's Year-Book.*

PAPUA NEW GUINEA - RELIGION

Central Intelligence Agency, Washington, D.C. 20505 (703) 482-1100, www.cia.gov; *The World Factbook.*

M.E. Sharpe, 80 Business Park Drive, Armonk, New York 10504 (800) 541-6563; *The Illustrated Book of World Rankings.*

St. Martin's Press, Inc., 175 Fifth Avenue, New York, New York 10010 (800) 221-7945; *The Statesman's Year-Book.*

PAPUA NEW GUINEA - RENT PRICES

International Labour Office, I.L.O. Publications, 1828 L Street, NW., Suite 801, Washington, D.C. 20036 (301) 638-3152; *Yearbook of Labour Statistics.*

PAPUA NEW GUINEA - RETAIL TRADE

Euromonitor International, Inc., 122 South Michigan Avenue, Suite 1200, Chicago, Illinois 60603 (800) 577-EURO; *World Marketing Data and Statistics.*

Statistical Office of the United Nations, Publishing Service, New York, New York 10017 (800) 253-9646; *Statistical Yearbook.*

PAPUA NEW GUINEA - RICE PRODUCTION - See PAPUA NEW GUINEA - CROPS

PAPUA NEW GUINEA - ROOT AND TUBER PRODUCTION - See PAPUA NEW GUINEA - CROPS

PAPUA NEW GUINEA - ROUNDWOOD PRODUCTION - See PAPUA NEW GUINEA - FORESTRY AND FOREST PRODUCTS

PAPUA NEW GUINEA - RUBBER PRODUCTION AND CONSUMPTION

M.E. Sharpe, 80 Business Park Drive, Armonk, New York 10504 (800) 541-6563; *The Illustrated Book of World Rankings.*

Statistical Office of the United Nations, Publishing Service, New York, New York 10017 (800) 253-9646; *Statistical Yearbook.*

PAPUA NEW GUINEA - SAWNWOOD PRODUCTION - PAPUA NEW GUINEA - FORESTRY AND FOREST PRODUCTS

PAPUA NEW GUINEA - SENIOR CITIZENS

M.E. Sharpe, 80 Business Park Drive, Armonk, New York 10504 (800) 541-6563; *The Illustrated Book of World Rankings.*

PAPUA NEW GUINEA - SHEEP - See PAPUA NEW GUINEA - LIVESTOCK AND POULTRY

PAPUA NEW GUINEA - SILVER

PRODUCTION AND CONSUMPTION - See PAPUA NEW GUINEA - MINING AND MINERAL PRODUCTS

PAPUA NEW GUINEA - SOCIAL DATA

Asian Development Bank, Post Office Box 789, 1099 Manila, Philippines; *Key Indicators of Developing Asian and Pacific Countries.*

M.E. Sharpe, 80 Business Park Drive, Armonk, New York 10504 (800) 541-6563; *The Illustrated Book of World Rankings.*

Statistical Office of the United Nations, Publishing Service, New York, New York 10017 (800) 253-9646; *World Statistics Pocketbook.*

PAPUA NEW GUINEA - SOCIAL SECURITY

International Monetary Fund, 700 Nineteenth Street, NW, Washington, D.C. 20431 (202) 623-7000; *Government Finance Statistics Yearbook.*

Statistical Office of the United Nations, Publishing Service, New York, New York 10017 (800) 253-9646; *National Accounts Statistics.*

PAPUA NEW GUINEA - STAMP TAXES AND DUTIES - See PAPUA NEW GUINEA - TAXATION

PAPUA NEW GUINEA - STATE BUDGET REVENUE AND EXPENDITURES

Euromonitor International, Inc., 122 South Michigan Avenue, Suite 1200, Chicago, Illinois 60603; *International Marketing Data and Statistics.*

PAPUA NEW GUINEA - STEEL PRODUCTION - See PAPUA NEW GUINEA - MINING AND MINERAL PRODUCTS

PAPUA NEW GUINEA - STOCKS - COMMODITY - MARKET PRICE -INDEX

Food and Agricultural Organization of the United Nations (FAO) Via delle Terme di Caracalla, 00100 Rome, Italy (Telephone Number in U.S. (202) 653-2400); *The State of Food and Agriculture.*

World Bureau of Metal Statistics, 27-A High Street, Ware, Herts. SG12 9BA, England; *World Metal Statistics.*

PAPUA NEW GUINEA - SUGAR PRODUCTION AND CONSUMPTION - See PAPUA NEW GUINEA - CROPS

PAPUA NEW GUINEA - TAX REVENUES - See PAPUA NEW GUINEA - TAXATION

PAPUA NEW GUINEA - TAXATION

Europa Publications Limited, 18

Bedford Square, London, WC1B 3JN, England; *The Europa World Year Book.*

International Monetary Fund, 700 Nineteenth Street, NW, Washington, D.C. 20431 (202) 623-7000; *Government Finance Statistics Yearbook.*

St. Martin's Press, Inc., 175 Fifth Avenue, New York, New York 10010 (800) 221-7945; *The Statesman's Year-Book.*

The World Bank, 1818 H Street, NW, Washington, D.C. 20433 (202) 477-1234; *World Development Indicators.*

PAPUA NEW GUINEA - TEA PRODUCTION - See PAPUA NEW GUINEA - CROPS

PAPUA NEW GUINEA - TELEPHONES IN USE

American Telephone and Telegraph Company, 26 Parsippany Road, Whippany, New Jersey 07981 (800) 222-0300; *The World's Telephones.*

Central Intelligence Agency, Washington, D.C. 20505 (703) 482-1100, www.cia.gov; *The World Factbook.*

The Economist Intelligence Unit (Asia) Limited, 10th Floor, Luk Kwok Centre, 72 Gloucester Road, Wanchai, Hong Kong (Phone Number in U.S. (800) 938-4685); *Asian Market Atlas.*

Europa Publications Limited, 18 Bedford Square, London, WC1B 3JN, England; *The Europa World Year Book.*

St. Martin's Press, Inc., 175 Fifth Avenue, New York, New York 10010 (800) 221-7945; *The Statesman's Year-Book.*

Statistical Office of the United Nations, Publishing Service, New York, New York 10017 (800) 253-9646; *Statistical Yearbook;* and *World Statistics Pocketbook.*

PAPUA NEW GUINEA - TELEVISION

The Economist Intelligence Unit (Asia) Limited, 10th Floor, Luk Kwok Centre, 72 Gloucester Road, Wanchai, Hong Kong (Phone Number in U.S. (800) 938-4685); *Asian Market Atlas.*

M.E. Sharpe, 80 Business Park Drive, Armonk, New York 10504 (800) 541-6563; *The Illustrated Book of World Rankings.*

PAPUA NEW GUINEA - TELEVISION BROADCASTING - See PAPUA NEW GUINEA - BROADCASTING

PAPUA NEW GUINEA - TEXTILE INDUSTRY

M.E. Sharpe, 80 Business Park Drive, Armonk, New York 10504 (800) 541-6563; *The Illustrated Book of World Rankings.*

South Pacific Commission, Post Box D5, Noumea Cedex, New Caledonia; *Statistical Bulletin of the South Pacific: Retail Price Indexes.*

United Nations Conference on Trade and Development, Central Statistical Service, Palais des Nations, Geneva, Switzerland (Telephone in U.S. (800) 253-9646); *UNCTAD Commodity Yearbook.*

PAPUA NEW GUINEA - THEATRE

United Nations Educational, Scientific and Cultural Organization (UNESCO), 7 Place de Fontenoy, F-75700 Paris, France (Telephone Number in U.S. (212) 963-5981); *Statistical Yearbook.*

PAPUA NEW GUINEA - TIN - See PAPUA NEW GUINEA - MINING AND MINERAL PRODUCTS

PAPUA NEW GUINEA - TOBACCO PRODUCTION

M.E. Sharpe, 80 Business Park Drive, Armonk, New York 10504 (800) 541-6563; *The Illustrated Book of World Rankings.*

South Pacific Commission, Post Box D5, Noumea Cedex, New Caledonia; *Statistical Bulletin of the South Pacific: Retail Price Indexes.*

PAPUA NEW GUINEA - TOURISM

Euromonitor International, Inc., 122 South Michigan Avenue, Suite 1200, Chicago, Illinois 60603; *The World Economic Factbook;* and *World Marketing Data and Statistics.*

Europa Publications Limited, 18 Bedford Square, London, WC1B 3JN, England; *The Europa World Year Book.*

Federal Statistical Office, Gustav - Stresemann - Ring 11, D-6200 Wiesbaden, Germany; *Papua-Neuguineu.*

M.E. Sharpe, 80 Business Park Drive, Armonk, New York 10504 (800) 541-6563; *The Illustrated Book of World Rankings.*

St. Martin's Press, Inc., 175 Fifth Avenue, New York, New York 10010 (800) 221-7945; *The Statesman's Year-Book.*

Statistical Office of the United Nations, Publishing Service, New York, New York 10017 (800) 253-9646; *Statistical Yearbook.*

World Tourism Organization, Calle Capitan Haya 42, E-28020 Madrid, Spain; *Yearbook of Tourism Statistics.*

PAPUA NEW GUINEA - TRACTORS IN USE

Statistical Office of the United Nations, Publishing Service, New York, New York

10017 (800) 253-9646; *Statistical Yearbook.*

PAPUA NEW GUINEA - TRADE - See PAPUA NEW GUINEA - FOREIGN TRADE

PAPUA NEW GUINEA - TRANSPORTATION AND COMMUNICATIONS

Central Intelligence Agency, Washington, D.C. 20505 (703) 482-1100, www.cia.gov; *The World Factbook.*

The Economist Intelligence Unit (Asia) Limited, 10th Floor, Luk Kwok Centre, 72 Gloucester Road, Wanchai, Hong Kong (Phone Number in U.S. (800) 938-4685); *Asian Market Atlas.*

Euromonitor International, Inc., 122 South Michigan Avenue, Suite 1200, Chicago, Illinois 60603; *International Marketing Data and Statistics;* and *World Marketing Data and Statistics.*

Europa Publications Limited, 18 Bedford Square, London, WC1B 3JN, England; *The Europa World Year Book.*

Federal Statistical Office, Gustav - Stresemann - Ring 11, D-6200 Wiesbaden, Germany; *Papua-Neuguinea.*

M.E. Sharpe, 80 Business Park Drive, Armonk, New York 10504 (800) 541-6563; *The Illustrated Book of World Rankings.*

South Pacific Commission, Post Box D5, Noumea Cedex, New Caledonia; *Statistical Bulletin of the South Pacific: Retail Price Indexes.*

St. Martin's Press, Inc., 175 Fifth Avenue, New York, New York 10010 (800) 221-7945; *The Statesman's Year-Book.*

Statistical Office of the United Nations, Publishing Service, New York, New York 10017 (800) 253-9646; *Human Development Report;* and *Statistical Yearbook for Asia and the Pacific.*

PAPUA NEW GUINEA - UNEMPLOYMENT

Central Intelligence Agency, Washington, D.C. 20505 (703) 482-1100, www.cia.gov; *The World Factbook.*

Euromonitor International, Inc., 122 South Michigan Avenue, Suite 1200, Chicago, Illinois 60603; *International Marketing Data and Statistics.*

International Labour Office, I.L.O. Publications, 1828 L Street, NW., Suite 801, Washington, D.C. 20036 (301) 638-3152; *Yearbook of Labour Statistics.*

PAPUA NEW GUINEA - VITAL STATISTICS

Euromonitor International, Inc., 122 South Michigan Avenue, Suite 1200, Chicago, Illinois 60603; *International Marketing Data and Statistics.*

St. Martin's Press, Inc., 175 Fifth Avenue, New York, New York 10010 (800) 221-7945; *The Statesman's Year-Book.*

Statistical Office of the United Nations, Publishing Service, New York, New York 10017 (800) 253-9646; *Statistical Yearbook.*

World Health Organization, Office of Publications, 20 Avenue Appia, CH-1211 Geneva 27, Switzerland (Telephone Number in U.S. (518) 436-9686); *World Health Statistics Annual.*

PAPUA NEW GUINEA - WAGES

Federal Statistical Office, Gustav - Stresemann - Ring 11, D-6200 Wiesbaden, Germany; *Papua-Neuguinea.*

International Labour Office, I.L.O. Publications, 1828 L Street, NW., Suite 801, Washington, D.C. 20036 (301) 638-3152; *Yearbook of Labour Statistics.*

PAPUA NEW GUINEA - WAGES AND PRICES

Federal Statistical Office, Gustav - Stresemann - Ring 11, D-6200 Wiesbaden, Germany; *Papua-Neuguinea.*

Statistical Office of the United Nations, Publishing Service, New York, New York 10017 (800) 253-9646; *Statistical Yearbook for Asia and the Pacific.*

PAPUA NEW GUINEA - WEATHER - See PAPUA NEW GUINEA - CLIMATE

PAPUA NEW GUINEA - WELFARE

International Monetary Fund, 700 Nineteenth Street, NW, Washington, D.C. 20431 (202) 623-7000; *Government Finance Statistics Yearbook.*

PAPUA NEW GUINEA - WHEAT PRODUCTION AND CONSUMPTION - See PAPUA NEW GUINEA - CROPS

PAPUA NEW GUINEA - WHOLESALE PRICES - INDEX NUMBERS

Asian Development Bank, Post Office Box 789, 1099 Manila, Philippines; *Key Indicators of Developing Asian and Pacific Countries.*

PAPUA NEW GUINEA - WHOLESALE TRADE

Statistical Office of the United Nations, Publishing Service, New York, New York 10017 (800) 253-9646; *Statistical Yearbook.*

PAPUA NEW GUINEA - WINE PRODUCTION - See PAPUA NEW GUINEA - BEVERAGES

PAPUA NEW GUINEA - WOOL PRODUCTION - See PAPUA NEW GUINEA - TEXTILE INDUSTRY

PAPUA NEW GUINEA - ZINC - See PAPUA NEW GUINEA - MINING AND MINERAL PRODUCTS

Paraguay - National Statistical Offices

Departmento de Estudios Economicos del Banco Central del Paraguay, Pablo VI y San Rafael, Barrio Santa Domingo, Asuncion, Paraguay; economic and trade monthly statistics.

Direccion General de Estadistica y Censos, Humaita 473, Asuncion, Paraguay; general statistics.

Paraguay - Primary Statistics Source

Direccion General de Estadistica y Censos, Humaita 473, Asuncion, Paraguay; *Annuario estadistico del Paraguay* (Statistical Yearbook of Paraguay).

PARAGUAY - AGRICULTURE

The Economist Intelligence Unit, 111 West 57th Street, New York, New York 10019 (800) 938-4685; *Paraguay Country Report;* and *The New Latin America Market Atlas.*

Euromonitor International, Inc., 122 South Michigan Avenue, Suite 1200, Chicago, Illinois 60603; *International Marketing Data and Statistics;* and *World Marketing Data and Statistics.*

Europa Publications Limited, 18 Bedford Square, London, WC1B 3JN, England; *The Europa World Year Book.*

Food and Agricultural Organization of the United Nations (FAO), Via delle Terme di Caracalla, 00100 Rome, Italy (Telephone Number in U.S. (202) 653-2400); *Production Yearbook; The State of Food and Agriculture;* and *Trade Yearbook.*

Inter-American Development Bank, 1300 New York Avenue, NW, Washington, D.C. 20577 (202) 623-1753; *Economic and Social Progress in Latin America.*

M.E. Sharpe, 80 Business Park Drive, Armonk, New York 10504 (800) 541-6563; *The Illustrated Book of World Rankings.*

St. Martin's Press, Inc., 175 Fifth Avenue, New York, New York 10010 (800)

221-7945; *The Statesman's Year-Book.*

Statistical Office of the United Nations, Publishing Service, New York, New York 10017 (800) 253-9646; *Statistical Yearbook;* and *Statistical Yearbook for Latin America and the Caribbean.*

U.C.L.A. Latin American Center Publications, University of California, Los Angeles, California 90024 (310) 825-6634; *Statistical Abstract of Latin America.*

United Nations Conference on Trade and Development, Central Statistical Service, Palais des Nations, Geneva, Switzerland (Telephone in U.S. (800) 253-9646); *UNCTAD Commodity Yearbook.*

The World Bank, 1818 H Street, NW, Washington, D.C. 20433 (202) 477-1234; *World Development Indicators.*

PARAGUAY - AIRLINE SERVICE

The Economist Intelligence Unit, 111 West 57th Street, New York, New York 10019 (800) 938-4685; *The New Latin America Market Atlas.*

Europa Publications Limited, 18 Bedford Square, London, WC1B 3JN, England; *The Europa World Year Book.*

M.E. Sharpe, 80 Business Park Drive, Armonk, New York 10504 (800) 541-6563; *The Illustrated Book of World Rankings.*

St. Martin's Press, Inc., 175 Fifth Avenue, New York, New York 10010 (800) 221-7945; *The Statesman's Year-Book.*

PARAGUAY - AIRPORTS

Central Intelligence Agency, Washington, D.C. 20505 (703) 482-1100, www.cia.gov; *The World Factbook.*

PARAGUAY - ALUMINUM PRODUCTION AND CONSUMPTION - See PARAGUAY - MINING AND MINERAL PRODUCTS

PARAGUAY - ANIMAL HEALTH

Food and Agricultural Organization of the United Nations (FAO), Via delle Terme di Caracalla, 00100 Rome, Italy (Telephone Number in U.S. (202) 653-2400); *Animal Health Yearbook.*

PARAGUAY - AREA AND DENSITY OF POPULATION

Central Intelligence Agency, Washington, D.C. 20505 (703) 482-1100, www.cia.gov; *The World Factbook.*

Euromonitor International, Inc., 122 South Michigan Avenue, Suite 1200, Chicago, Illinois 60603; *International Marketing Data and Statistics;* and *The*

World Economic Factbook.

Europa Publications Limited, 18 Bedford Square, London, WC1B 3JN, England; *The Europa World Year Book.*

Food and Agricultural Organization of the United Nations (FAO) Via delle Terme di Caracalla, 00100 Rome, Italy (Telephone Number in U.S. (202) 653-2400); *The State of Food and Agriculture.*

Inter-American Development Bank, 1300 New York Avenue, NW, Washington, D.C. 20577 (202) 623-1753; *Economic and Social Progress in Latin America.*

M.E. Sharpe, 80 Business Park Drive, Armonk, New York 10504 (800) 541-6563; *The Illustrated Book of World Rankings.*

St. Martin's Press, Inc., 175 Fifth Avenue, New York, New York 10010 (800) 221-7945; *The Statesman's Year-Book.*

Statistical Office of the United Nations, Publishing Service, New York, New York 10017 (800) 253-9646; *Statistical Yearbook.*

United Nations Educational, Scientific and Cultural Organization (UNESCO), 7 Place de Fontenoy, F-75700 Paris, France (Telephone Number in U.S. (212) 963-5981); *Statistical Yearbook.*

The World Bank, 1818 H Street, NW, Washington, D.C. 20433 (202) 477-1234; *World Development Report.*

PARAGUAY - ARMS EXPORTS AND IMPORTS - See PARAGUAY - MILITARY

PARAGUAY - BALANCE OF PAYMENTS

The Economist Intelligence Unit, 111 West 57th Street, New York, New York 10019 (800) 938-4685; *The New Latin America Market Atlas;* and *The World Market Atlas.*

Europa Publications Limited, 18 Bedford Square, London, WC1B 3JN, England; *The Europa World Year Book.*

Inter-American Development Bank, 1300 New York Avenue, NW, Washington, D.C. 20577 (202) 623-1753; *Economic and Social Progress in Latin America.*

International Monetary Fund, 700 Nineteenth Street, NW, Washington, D.C. 20431 (202) 623-7000; *Balance of Payments Yearbook;* and *International Financial Statistics.*

Organization of American States (OAS), General Secretariat, Washington, D.C. 20006 (202) 458-3533; *Statistical Bulletin of the OAS.*

Statistical Office of the United Nations,

Publishing Service, New York, New York 10017 (800) 253-9646; *Economic Survey of Latin America and the Caribbean;* and *Statistical Yearbook for Latin America and the Caribbean.*

U.C.L.A. Latin American Center Publications, University of California, Los Angeles, California 90024 (310) 825-6634; *Statistical Abstract of Latin America.*

United Nations Conference on Trade and Development (UNCTAD), New York, New York 10017 (800) 253-9646; *Handbook of International Trade and Development Statistics.*

The World Bank, 1818 H Street, NW, Washington, D.C. 20433 (202) 477-1234; *World Development Report;* and *World Development Indicators.*

PARAGUAY - BANANA PRODUCTION - See PARAGUAY - CROPS

PARAGUAY - BANKING

Euromonitor International, Inc., 122 South Michigan Avenue, Suite 1200, Chicago, Illinois 60603 (800) 577-EURO; *World Marketing Data and Statistics.*

Europa Publications Limited, 18 Bedford Square, London, WC1B 3JN, England; *The Europa World Year Book.*

Inter-American Development Bank, 1300 New York Avenue, NW, Washington, D.C. 20577 (202) 623-1753; *Economic and Social Progress in Latin America.*

International Monetary Fund, 700 Nineteenth Street, NW, Washington, D.C. 20431 (202) 623-7000; *Government Finance Statistics Yearbook;* and *International Financial Statistics.*

M.E. Sharpe, 80 Business Park Drive, Armonk, New York 10504 (800) 541-6563; *The Illustrated Book of World Rankings.*

St. Martin's Press, Inc., 175 Fifth Avenue, New York, New York 10010 (800) 221-7945; *The Statesman's Year-Book.*

Statistical Office of the United Nations, Publishing Service, New York, New York 10017 (800) 253-9646; *Statistical Yearbook for Latin America and the Caribbean.*

PARAGUAY - BARLEY PRODUCTION - See PARAGUAY - CROPS

PARAGUAY - BEER PRODUCTION - See PARAGUAY - BEVERAGES

PARAGUAY - BEVERAGES

M.E. Sharpe, 80 Business Park Drive, Armonk, New York 10504 (800) 541-6563; *The Illustrated Book of World Rankings.*

Statistical Office of the United Nations, Publishing Service, New York, New York 10017 (800) 253-9646; *Statistical Yearbook.*

PARAGUAY - BIRTH RATES

Central Intelligence Agency, Washington, D.C. 20505 (703) 482-1100, www.cia.gov; *The World Factbook.*

Euromonitor International, Inc., 122 South Michigan Avenue, Suite 1200, Chicago, Illinois 60603; *International Marketing Data and Statistics;* and *The World Economic Factbook.*

Europa Publications Limited, 18 Bedford Square, London, WC1B 3JN, England; *The Europa World Year Book.*

M.E. Sharpe, 80 Business Park Drive, Armonk, New York 10504 (800) 541-6563; *The Illustrated Book of World Rankings.*

St. Martin's Press, Inc., 175 Fifth Avenue, New York, New York 10010 (800) 221-7945; *The Statesman's Year-Book.*

Statistical Office of the United Nations, Publishing Service, New York, New York 10017 (800) 253-9646; *Demographic Yearbook; Statistical Yearbook;* and *Statistical Yearbook for Latin America and the Caribbean.*

The World Bank, 1818 H Street, NW, Washington, D.C. 20433 (202) 477-1234; *World Development Indicators.*

World Health Organization, Office of Publications, 20 Avenue Appia, CH-1211 Geneva 27, Switzerland (Telephone Number in U.S. (518) 436-9686); *World Health Statistics Annual.*

PARAGUAY - BONDS

Inter-American Development Bank, 1300 New York Avenue, NW, Washington, D.C. 20577 (202) 623-1753; *Economic and Social Progress in Latin America.*

International Monetary Fund, 700 Nineteenth Street, NW, Washington, D.C. 20431 (202) 623-7000; *Government Finance Statistics Yearbook.*

PARAGUAY - BROADCASTING

Billboard Limited, Post Office Box 9027, 1006 AA Amsterdam, The Netherlands (Telephone Number in U.S. (212) 764-7300); *World Radio TV Handbook.*

Central Intelligence Agency, Washington, D.C. 20505 (703) 482-1100, www.cia.gov; *The World Factbook.*

Euromonitor International, Inc., 122 South Michigan Avenue, Suite 1200, Chicago, Illinois 60603 (800) 577-EURO; *World Marketing Data and Statistics.*

M.E. Sharpe, 80 Business Park Drive, Armonk, New York 10504 (800) 541-6563; *The Illustrated Book of World Rankings.*

St. Martin's Press, Inc., 175 Fifth Avenue, New York, New York 10010 (800) 221-7945; *The Statesman's Year-Book.*

PARAGUAY - BUDGET

Central Intelligence Agency, Washington, D.C. 20505 (703) 482-1100, www.cia.gov; *The World Factbook.*

PARAGUAY - BUSINESS

Inter-American Development Bank, 1300 New York Avenue, NW, Washington, D.C. 20577 (202) 623-1753; *Economic and Social Progress in Latin America.*

PARAGUAY - BUTTER PRODUCTION - See PARAGUAY - DAIRY PRODUCTS

PARAGUAY - CALORIE SUPPLY

Food and Agricultural Organization of the United Nations (FAO) Via delle Terme di Caracalla, 00100 Rome, Italy (Telephone Number in U.S. (202) 653-2400); *The State of Food and Agriculture.*

Statistical Office of the United Nations, Publishing Service, New York, New York 10017 (800) 253-9646; *Statistical Yearbook for Latin America and the Caribbean.*

PARAGUAY - CAPITAL INVESTMENT

Inter-American Development Bank, 1300 New York Avenue, NW, Washington, D.C. 20577 (202) 623-1753; *Economic and Social Progress in Latin America.*

PARAGUAY - CAPITAL REVENUE

Inter-American Development Bank, 1300 New York Avenue, NW, Washington, D.C. 20577 (202) 623-1753; *Economic and Social Progress in Latin America.*

International Monetary Fund, 700 Nineteenth Street, NW, Washington, D.C. 20431 (202) 623-7000; *Government Finance Statistics Yearbook.*

PARAGUAY - CASTOR BEAN PRODUCTION - See PARAGUAY - CROPS

PARAGUAY - CATTLE - See PARAGUAY - LIVESTOCK AND POULTRY

PARAGUAY - CEMENT PRODUCTION - See PARAGUAY - MINING AND MINERAL PRODUCTS

PARAGUAY - CHEESE PRODUCTION AND CONSUMPTION - See PARAGUAY - DAIRY PRODUCTS

PARAGUAY - CHEMICAL (ORGANIC) PRODUCTION - See PARAGUAY - MINING AND MINERAL PRODUCTS

PARAGUAY - CHICKENS - See PARAGUAY - LIVESTOCK AND POULTRY

PARAGUAY - CIGAR PRODUCTION - See PARAGUAY - TOBACCO PRODUCTION

PARAGUAY - CIGARETTE PRODUCTION - See PARAGUAY - TOBACCO PRODUCTION

PARAGUAY - CLIMATE

M.E. Sharpe, 80 Business Park Drive, Armonk, New York 10504 (800) 541-6563; *The Illustrated Book of World Rankings.*

St. Martin's Press, Inc., 175 Fifth Avenue, New York, New York 10010 (800) 221-7945; *The Statesman's Year-Book.*

PARAGUAY - COAL PRODUCTION - See PARAGUAY - MINING AND MINERAL PRODUCTS

PARAGUAY - COCOA (BEANS) PRODUCTION - See PARAGUAY - CROPS

PARAGUAY - COFFEE - See PARAGUAY - CROPS

PARAGUAY - COMMERCE

St. Martin's Press, Inc., 175 Fifth Avenue, New York, New York 10010 (800) 221-7945; *The Statesman's Year-Book.*

PARAGUAY - COMMUNICATIONS - See PARAGUAY - TRANSPORTATION AND COMMUNICATIONS

PARAGUAY - CONSTRUCTION INDUSTRY

The Economist Intelligence Unit, 111 West 57th Street, New York, New York 10019 (800) 938-4685; *The New Latin America Market Atlas.*

Inter-American Development Bank, 1300 New York Avenue, NW, Washington, D.C. 20577 (202) 623-1753; *Economic and Social Progress in Latin America.*

M.E. Sharpe, 80 Business Park Drive, Armonk, New York 10504 (800) 541-6563; *The Illustrated Book of World Rankings.*

Statistical Office of the United Nations, Publishing Service, New York, New York 10017 (800) 253-9646; *Statistical Yearbook.*

U.C.L.A. Latin American Center Publications, University of California, Los Angeles, California 90024 (310) 825-6634; *Statistical Abstract of Latin America.*

PARAGUAY - CONSUMER PRICE INDEX

Europa Publications Limited, 18 Bedford Square, London, WC1B 3JN, England; *The Europa World Year Book.*

Statistical Office of the United Nations, Publishing Service, New York, New York 10017 (800) 253-9646; *Statistical Yearbook.*

U.C.L.A. Latin American Center Publications, University of California, Los Angeles, California 90024 (310) 825-6634; *Statistical Abstract of Latin America.*

PARAGUAY - CONSUMER PRICES

The Economist Intelligence Unit, 111 West 57th Street, New York, New York 10019 (800) 938-4685; *The New Latin America Market Atlas.*

Euromonitor International, Inc., 122 South Michigan Avenue, Suite 1200, Chicago, Illinois 60603 (800) 577-EURO; *World Marketing Data and Statistics.*

International Labour Office, I.L.O. Publications, 1828 L Street, NW., Suite 801, Washington, D.C. 20036 (301) 638-3152; *Yearbook of Labour Statistics.*

International Monetary Fund, 700 Nineteenth Street, NW, Washington, D.C. 20431 (202) 623-7000; *International Financial Statistics.*

Organization of American States (OAS), General Secretariat, Washington, D.C. 20006 (202) 458-3533; *Statistical Bulletin of the OAS.*

PARAGUAY - CONSUMPTION

The Economist Intelligence Unit, 111 West 57th Street, New York, New York 10019 (800) 938-4685; *The New Latin America Market Atlas.*

Inter-American Development Bank, 1300 New York Avenue, NW, Washington, D.C. 20577 (202) 623-1753; *Economic and Social Progress in Latin America.*

Statistical Office of the United Nations, Publishing Service, New York, New York 10017 (800) 253-9646; *Statistical Yearbook for Latin America and the Caribbean.*

The World Bank, 1818 H Street, NW, Washington, D.C. 20433 (202) 477-1234; *World Development Report.*

PARAGUAY - COOPERATIVES

U.C.L.A. Latin American Center Publications, University of California, Los Angeles, California 90024 (310) 825-6634; *Statistical Abstract of Latin America.*

PARAGUAY - COPPER PRODUCTION AND CONSUMPTION - See PARAGUAY - MINING AND MINERAL PRODUCTS

PARAGUAY - CORN PRODUCTION - See PARAGUAY - CROPS

PARAGUAY - CORPORATE INCOME TAXES - See PARAGUAY - TAXATION

PARAGUAY - CORPORATE TAXES - See PARAGUAY - TAXATION

PARAGUAY - COTTON - See PARAGUAY - CROPS

PARAGUAY - CROPS

The Economist Intelligence Unit, 111 West 57th Street, New York, New York 10019 (800) 938-4685; *The New Latin America Market Atlas.*

Europa Publications Limited, 18 Bedford Square, London, WC1B 3JN, England; *The Europa World Year Book.*

Food and Agricultural Organization of the United Nations (FAO), Via delle Terme di Caracalla, 00100 Rome, Italy (Telephone Number in U.S. (202) 653-2400); *Production Yearbook;* and *The State of Food and Agriculture.*

International Monetary Fund, 700 Nineteenth Street, NW, Washington, D.C. 20431 (202) 623-7000; *International Financial Statistics.*

M.E. Sharpe, 80 Business Park Drive, Armonk, New York 10504 (800) 541-6563; *The Illustrated Book of World Rankings.*

Organization of American States (OAS), General Secretariat, Washington, D.C. 20006 (202) 458-3533; *Statistical Bulletin of the OAS.*

St. Martin's Press, Inc., 175 Fifth Avenue, New York, New York 10010 (800) 221-7945; *The Statesman's Year-Book.*

Statistical Office of the United Nations, Publishing Service, New York, New York 10017 (800) 253-9646; *Statistical Yearbook.*

U.C.L.A. Latin American Center Publications, University of California, Los Angeles, California 90024 (310) 825-6634; *Statistical Abstract of Latin America.*

United Nations Conference on Trade and Development, Central Statistical Service, Palais des Nations, Geneva, Switzerland (Telephone in U.S. (800) 253-9646); *UNCTAD Commodity Yearbook.*

PARAGUAY - CUSTOMS DUTIES

Inter-American Development Bank, 1300 New York Avenue, NW, Washington, D.C. 20577 (202) 623-1753; *Economic and Social Progress in Latin America.*

International Monetary Fund, 700

Nineteenth Street, NW, Washington, D.C. 20431 (202) 623-7000; *Government Finance Statistics Yearbook.*

St. Martin's Press, Inc., 175 Fifth Avenue, New York, New York 10010 (800) 221-7945; *The Statesman's Year-Book.*

PARAGUAY - DAIRY PRODUCTS

Europa Publications Limited, 18 Bedford Square, London, WC1B 3JN, England; *The Europa World Year Book.*

Food and Agricultural Organization of the United Nations (FAO), Via delle Terme di Caracalla, 00100 Rome, Italy (Telephone Number in U.S. (202) 653-2400); *Production Yearbook;* and *The State of Food and Agriculture.*

M.E. Sharpe, 80 Business Park Drive, Armonk, New York 10504 (800) 541-6563; *The Illustrated Book of World Rankings.*

St. Martin's Press, Inc., 175 Fifth Avenue, New York, New York 10010 (800) 221-7945; *The Statesman's Year-Book.*

Statistical Office of the United Nations, Publishing Service, New York, New York 10017 (800) 253-9646; *Statistical Yearbook.*

U.C.L.A. Latin American Center Publications, University of California, Los Angeles, California 90024 (310) 825-6634; *Statistical Abstract of Latin America.*

PARAGUAY - DEATH RATES - See PARAGUAY - MORTALITY

PARAGUAY - DEBT

The Economist Intelligence Unit, 111 West 57th Street, New York, New York 10019 (800) 938-4685; *The New Latin America Market Atlas.*

PARAGUAY - DEFENSE EXPENDITURES - See PARAGUAY - MILITARY

PARAGUAY - DEMOGRAPHY

The Economist Intelligence Unit, 111 West 57th Street, New York, New York 10019 (800) 938-4685; *The World Market Atlas.*

Euromonitor International, Inc., 122 South Michigan Avenue, Suite 1200, Chicago, Illinois 60603; *International Marketing Data and Statistics; World Marketing Data and Statistics;* and *The World Economic Factbook.*

M.E. Sharpe, 80 Business Park Drive, Armonk, New York 10504 (800) 541-6563; *The Illustrated Book of World Rankings.*

Statistical Office of the United Nations, Publishing Service, New York, New York

10017 (800) 253-9646; *Human Development Report.*

PARAGUAY - DEVELOPMENT ASSISTANCE

Inter-American Development Bank, 1300 New York Avenue, NW, Washington, D.C. 20577 (202) 623-1753; *Economic and Social Progress in Latin America.*

Statistical Office of the United Nations, Publishing Service, New York, New York 10017 (800) 253-9646; *Statistical Yearbook.*

PARAGUAY - DIAMOND PRODUCTION - See PARAGUAY - MINING AND MINERAL PRODUCTS

PARAGUAY - DISCOUNT RATES - See PARAGUAY - BANKING

PARAGUAY - DISEASES - See PARAGUAY - HEALTH

PARAGUAY - DIVORCE RATES

M.E. Sharpe, 80 Business Park Drive, Armonk, New York 10504 (800) 541-6563; *The Illustrated Book of World Rankings.*

Statistical Office of the United Nations, Publishing Service, New York, New York 10017 (800) 253-9646; *Demographic Yearbook.*

PARAGUAY - DUCKS - See PARAGUAY - LIVESTOCK AND POULTRY

PARAGUAY - ECONOMY

Central Intelligence Agency, Washington, D.C. 20505 (703) 482-1100, www.cia.gov; *The World Factbook.*

Economist Intelligence Unit, 111 West 57th Street, New York, New York 10019 (800) 938-4685; *Paraguay Country Report.*

Euromonitor International, Inc., 122 South Michigan Avenue, Suite 1200, Chicago, Illinois 60603; *International Marketing Data and Statistics; World Marketing Data and Statistics;* and *The World Economy Factbook.*

Europa Publications Limited, 18 Bedford Square, London, WC1B 3JN, England; *The Europa World Year Book.*

Inter-American Development Bank, 1300 New York Avenue, NW, Washington, D.C. 20577 (202) 623-1753; *Economic and Social Progress in Latin America.*

M.E. Sharpe, 80 Business Park Drive, Armonk, New York 10504 (800) 541-6563; *The Illustrated Book of World Rankings.*

Organization of American States (OAS), General Secretariat, Washington, D.C.

20006 (202) 458-3533; *Statistical Bulletin of the OAS.*

St. Martin's Press, Inc., 175 Fifth Avenue, New York, New York 10010 (800) 221-7945; *The Statesman's Year-Book.*

Statistical Office of the United Nations, Publishing Service, New York, New York 10017 (800) 253-9646; *Economic Survey of Latin America and the Caribbean;* and *World Statistics Pocketbook.*

U.C.L.A. Latin American Center Publications, University of California, Los Angeles, California 90024 (310) 825-6634; *Statistical Abstract of Latin America.*

The World Bank, 1818 H Street, NW, Washington, D.C. 20433 (202) 477-1234; *The World Bank Atlas;* and *World Development Report.*

PARAGUAY - EDUCATION

The Economist Intelligence Unit, 111 West 57th Street, New York, New York 10019 (800) 938-4685; *The New Latin America Market Atlas;* and *The World Market Atlas.*

Euromonitor International, Inc., 122 South Michigan Avenue, Suite 1200, Chicago, Illinois 60603; *International Marketing Data and Statistics;* and *World Marketing Data and Statistics.*

Europa Publications Limited, 18 Bedford Square, London, WC1B 3JN, England; *The Europa World Year Book.*

International Monetary Fund, 700 Nineteenth Street, NW, Washington, D.C. 20431 (202) 623-7000; *Government Finance Statistics Yearbook.*

M.E. Sharpe, 80 Business Park Drive, Armonk, New York 10504 (800) 541-6563; *The Illustrated Book of World Rankings.*

St. Martin's Press, Inc., 175 Fifth Avenue, New York, New York 10010 (800) 221-7945; *The Statesman's Year-Book.*

Statistical Office of the United Nations, Publishing Service, New York, New York 10017 (800) 253-9646; *Human Development Report;* and *Statistical Yearbook for Latin America and the Caribbean.*

U.C.L.A. Latin American Center Publications, University of California, Los Angeles, California 90024 (310) 825-6634; *Statistical Abstract of Latin America.*

United Nations Educational, Scientific and Cultural Organization (UNESCO), 7 Place de Fontenoy, F-75700 Paris, France (Telephone Number in U.S. (212) 963-5981); *Statistical Yearbook.*

The World Bank, 1818 H Street, NW, Washington, D.C. 20433 (202) 477-1234; *World Development Report;* and *World Development Indicators.*

PARAGUAY - EGG PRODUCTION AND CONSUMPTION - See PARAGUAY - DAIRY PRODUCTS

PARAGUAY - ELECTRICITY

Central Intelligence Agency, Washington, D.C. 20505 (703) 482-1100, www.cia.gov; *The World Factbook.*

The Economist Intelligence Unit, 111 West 57th Street, New York, New York 10019 (800) 938-4685; *The New Latin America Market Atlas.*

Inter-American Development Bank, 1300 New York Avenue, NW, Washington, D.C. 20577 (202) 623-1753; *Economic and Social Progress in Latin America.*

M.E. Sharpe, 80 Business Park Drive, Armonk, New York 10504 (800) 541-6563; *The Illustrated Book of World Rankings.*

St. Martin's Press, Inc., 175 Fifth Avenue, New York, New York 10010 (800) 221-7945; *The Statesman's Year-Book.*

Statistical Office of the United Nations, Publishing Service, New York, New York 10017 (800) 253-9646; *Human Development Report;* and *Statistical Yearbook.*

PARAGUAY - EMPLOYMENT

Euromonitor International, Inc., 122 South Michigan Avenue, Suite 1200, Chicago, Illinois 60603; *International Marketing Data and Statistics.*

International Labour Office, I.L.O. Publications, 1828 L Street, NW., Suite 801, Washington, D.C. 20036 (301) 638-3152; *Yearbook of Labour Statistics.*

M.E. Sharpe, 80 Business Park Drive, Armonk, New York 10504 (800) 541-6563; *The Illustrated Book of World Rankings.*

Statistical Office of the United Nations, Publishing Service, New York, New York 10017 (800) 253-9646; *Statistical Yearbook for Latin America and the Caribbean.*

U.C.L.A. Latin American Center Publications, University of California, Los Angeles, California 90024 (310) 825-6634; *Statistical Abstract of Latin America.*

PARAGUAY - ENERGY

The Economist Intelligence Unit, 111 West 57th Street, New York, New York 10019 (800) 938-4685; *The New Latin America Market Atlas.*

Euromonitor International, Inc., 122 South Michigan Avenue, Suite 1200, Chicago, Illinois 60603; *International Marketing Data and Statistics; World Marketing Data and Statistics;* and *The World Economic Factbook.*

Food and Agricultural Organization of the United Nations (FAO) Via delle Terme di Caracalla, 00100 Rome, Italy (Telephone Number in U.S. (202) 653-2400); *The State of Food and Agriculture.*

M.E. Sharpe, 80 Business Park Drive, Armonk, New York 10504 (800) 541-6563; *The Illustrated Book of World Rankings.*

St. Martin's Press, Inc., 175 Fifth Avenue, New York, New York 10010 (800) 221-7945; *The Statesman's Year-Book.*

Statistical Office of the United Nations, Publishing Service, New York, New York 10017 (800) 253-9646; *Energy Statistics Yearbook; Human Development Report; Statistical Yearbook; Statistical Yearbook for Latin America and the Caribbean;* and *World Statistics Pocketbook.*

U.C.L.A. Latin American Center Publications, University of California, Los Angeles, California 90024 (310) 825-6634; *Statistical Abstract of Latin America.*

The World Bank, 1818 H Street, NW, Washington, D.C. 20433 (202) 477-1234; *The World Bank Atlas;* and *World Development Report.*

PARAGUAY - ENVIRONMENT

Economist Intelligence Unit, 111 West 57th Street, New York, New York 10019 (800) 938-4685; *Paraguay Country Report.*

Statistical Office of the United Nations, Publishing Service, New York, New York 10017 (800) 253-9646; *World Statistics Pocketbook.*

PARAGUAY - EXCHANGE RATES

Central Intelligence Agency, Washington, D.C. 20505 (703) 482-1100, www.cia.gov; *The World Factbook.*

Euromonitor International, Inc., 122 South Michigan Avenue, Suite 1200, Chicago, Illinois 60603; *International Marketing Data and Statistics;* and *The World Economic Factbook.*

Europa Publications Limited, 18 Bedford Square, London, WC1B 3JN, England; *The Europa World Year Book.*

Inter-American Development Bank, 1300 New York Avenue, NW, Washington, D.C. 20577 (202) 623-1753; *Economic and Social Progress in Latin America.*

International Monetary Fund, 700 Nineteenth Street, NW, Washington, D.C. 20431 (202) 623-7000; *Government Finance Statistics Yearbook;* and *International Financial Statistics.*

Organization of American States (OAS), General Secretariat, Washington, D.C. 20006 (202) 458-3533; *Statistical Bulletin of the OAS.*

Statistical Office of the United Nations, Publishing Service, New York, New York 10017 (800) 253-9646; *Statistical Yearbook;* and *World Statistics Pocketbook.*

U.C.L.A. Latin American Center Publications, University of California, Los Angeles, California 90024 (310) 825-6634; *Statistical Abstract of Latin America.*

PARAGUAY - EXCISE TAXES - See PARAGUAY - TAXATION

PARAGUAY - EXPENDITURES

Organization of American States (OAS), General Secretariat, Washington, D.C. 20006 (202) 458-3533; *Statistical Bulletin of the OAS.*

PARAGUAY - EXPORTS

Central Intelligence Agency, Washington, D.C. 20505 (703) 482-1100, www.cia.gov; *The World Factbook.*

The Economist Intelligence Unit, 111 West 57th Street, New York, New York 10019 (800) 938-4685;*The New Latin America Market Atlas; Paraguay Country Report;* and *The World Market Atlas.*

Euromonitor International, Inc., 122 South Michigan Avenue, Suite 1200, Chicago, Illinois 60603; *International Marketing Data and Statistics;* and *The World Economic Factbook.*

Europa Publications Limited, 18 Bedford Square, London, WC1B 3JN, England; *The Europa World Year Book.*

Food and Agricultural Organization of the United Nations (FAO) Via delle Terme di Caracalla, 00100 Rome, Italy (Telephone Number in U.S. (202) 653-2400); *The State of Food and Agriculture.*

Inter-American Development Bank, 1300 New York Avenue, NW, Washington, D.C. 20577 (202) 623-1753; *Economic and Social Progress in Latin America.*

International Monetary Fund, 700 Nineteenth Street, NW, Washington, D.C. 20431 (202) 623-7000; *Direction of Trade Statistics; Government Finance Statistics Yearbook;* and *International Financial Statistics.*

Organization of American States (OAS), General Secretariat, Washington, D.C. 20006 (202) 458-3533; *Statistical Bulletin of the OAS.*

St. Martin's Press, Inc., 175 Fifth Avenue, New York, New York 10010 (800) 221-7945; *The Statesman's Year-Book.*

Statistical Office of the United Nations, Publishing Service, New York, New York 10017 (800) 253-9646; *Statistical Yearbook for Latin America and the Caribbean.*

United Nations Conference on Trade and Development (UNCTAD), New York, New York 10017 (800) 253-9646; *Handbook of International Trade and Development Statistics.*

The World Bank, 1818 H Street, NW, Washington, D.C. 20433 (202) 477-1234; *World Development Report;* and *World Development Indicators.*

PARAGUAY - EXTERNAL FINANCING

Inter-American Development Bank, 1300 New York Avenue, NW, Washington, D.C. 20577 (202) 623-1753; *Economic and Social Progress in Latin America.*

Statistical Office of the United Nations, Publishing Service, New York, New York 10017 (800) 253-9646; *Statistical Yearbook for Latin America and the Caribbean.*

PARAGUAY - EXTERNAL INDEBTEDNESS

Inter-American Development Bank, 1300 New York Avenue, NW, Washington, D.C. 20577 (202) 623-1753; *Economic and Social Progress in Latin America.*

Statistical Office of the United Nations, Publishing Service, New York, New York 10017 (800) 253-9646; *Statistical Yearbook for Latin America and the Caribbean.*

The World Bank, 1818 H Street, NW, Washington, D.C. 20433 (202) 477-1234; *World Development Report;* and *World Development Indicators.*

PARAGUAY - EXTERNAL TRADE

Euromonitor International, Inc., 122 South Michigan Avenue, Suite 1200, Chicago, Illinois 60603 (800) 577-EURO; *World Marketing Data and Statistics.*

Food and Agricultural Organization of the United Nations (FAO) Via delle Terme di Caracalla, 00100 Rome, Italy (Telephone Number in U.S. (202) 653-2400); *The State of Food and Agriculture;* and *Trade Yearbook.*

Inter-American Development Bank, 1300 New York Avenue, NW, Washington, D.C. 20577 (202) 623-1753; *Economic and Social Progress in Latin America.*

Statistical Office of the United Nations, Publishing Service, New York, New York 10017 (800) 253-9646; *Statistical Yearbook;* and *Statistical Yearbook for Latin America and the Caribbean.*

PARAGUAY - FABRIC PRODUCTION - See PARAGUAY - TEXTILE INDUSTRY

PARAGUAY - FAMILY PLANNING

Food and Agricultural Organization of the United Nations (FAO) Via delle Terme di Caracalla, 00100 Rome, Italy (Telephone Number in U.S. (202) 653-2400); *The State of Food and Agriculture.*

U.C.L.A. Latin American Center Publications, University of California, Los Angeles, California 90024 (310) 825-6634; *Statistical Abstract of Latin America.*

PARAGUAY - FARM CROPS - See PARAGUAY - CROPS

PARAGUAY - FEMALE WORKING POPULATION - See PARAGUAY - EMPLOYMENT

PARAGUAY - FERTILITY RATES

Central Intelligence Agency, Washington, D.C. 20505 (703) 482-1100; www.cia.gov; *The World Factbook.*

M.E. Sharpe, 80 Business Park Drive, Armonk, New York 10504 (800) 541-6563; *The Illustrated Book of World Rankings.*

Statistical Office of the United Nations, Publishing Service, New York, New York 10017 (800) 253-9646; *Human Development Report.*

The World Bank, 1818 H Street, NW, Washington, D.C. 20433 (202) 477-1234; *The World Bank Atlas; World Development Report;* and *World Development Indicators.*

PARAGUAY - FERTILIZER

The Economist Intelligence Unit, 111 West 57th Street, New York, New York 10019 (800) 938-4685; *The New Latin America Market Atlas.*

Food and Agricultural Organization of the United Nations (FAO), Via delle Terme di Caracalla, 00100 Rome, Italy (Telephone Number in U.S. (202) 653-2400); *Fertilizer Yearbook;* and *The State of Food and Agriculture.*

Statistical Office of the United Nations, Publishing Service, New York, New York 10017 (800) 253-9646; *Statistical Yearbook.*

PARAGUAY - FETAL MORTALITY - See PARAGUAY - MORTALITY

PARAGUAY - FINANCE

Economist Intelligence Unit, 111 West 57th Street, New York, New York 10019 (800) 938-4685; *Paraguay Country Report.*

Europa Publications Limited, 18 Bedford Square, London, WC1B 3JN, England; *The Europa World Year Book.*

Inter-American Development Bank, 1300 New York Avenue, NW, Washington, D.C. 20577 (202) 623-1753; *Economic and Social Progress in Latin America;* and *Statistical Bulletin of the OAS.*

International Monetary Fund, 700 Nineteenth Street, NW, Washington, D.C. 20431 (202) 623-7000; *Government Finance Statistics Yearbook;* and *International Financial Statistics.*

M.E. Sharpe, 80 Business Park Drive, Armonk, New York 10504 (800) 541-6563; *The Illustrated Book of World Rankings.*

Organization of American States (OAS), General Secretariat, Washington, D.C. 20006 (202) 458-3533; *Statistical Bulletin of the OAS.*

St. Martin's Press, Inc., 175 Fifth Avenue, New York, New York 10010 (800) 221-7945; *The Statesman's Year-Book.*

U.C.L.A. Latin American Center Publications, University of California, Los Angeles, California 90024 (310) 825-6634; *Statistical Abstract of Latin America.*

PARAGUAY - FISHERIES

Europa Publications Limited, 18 Bedford Square, London, WC1B 3JN, England; *The Europa World Year Book.*

Food and Agricultural Organization of the United Nations (FAO) Via delle Terme di Caracalla, 00100 Rome, Italy (Telephone Number in U.S. (202) 653-2400); *The State of Food and Agriculture;* and *Yearbook of Fishery Statistics.*

Inter-American Development Bank, 1300 New York Avenue, NW, Washington, D.C. 20577 (202) 623-1753; *Economic and Social Progress in Latin America.*

M.E. Sharpe, 80 Business Park Drive, Armonk, New York 10504 (800) 541-6563; *The Illustrated Book of World Rankings.*

Statistical Office of the United Nations, Publishing Service, New York, New York 10017 (800) 253-9646; *Statistical Yearbook.*

U.C.L.A. Latin American Center Publications, University of California, Los Angeles, California 90024 (310) 825-6634; *Statistical Abstract of Latin America.*

United Nations Conference on Trade and Development, Central Statistical Service, Palais des Nations, Geneva, Switzerland (Telephone in U.S. (800) 253-9646); *UNCTAD Commodity Yearbook*.

PARAGUAY - FLOUR PRODUCTION

Statistical Office of the United Nations, Publishing Service, New York, New York 10017 (800) 253-9646; *Statistical Yearbook*.

PARAGUAY - FOOD

Food and Agricultural Organization of the United Nations (FAO), Via delle Terme di Caracalla, 00100 Rome, Italy (Telephone Number in U.S. (202) 653-2400); *Production Yearbook;* and *The State of Food and Agriculture*.

Statistical Office of the United Nations, Publishing Service, New York, New York 10017 (800) 253-9646; *Human Development Report*.

United Nations Conference on Trade and Development, Central Statistical Service, Palais des Nations, Geneva, Switzerland (Telephone in U.S. (800) 253-9646); *UNCTAD Commodity Yearbook*.

PARAGUAY - FOREIGN AID

Inter-American Development Bank, 1300 New York Avenue, NW, Washington, D.C. 20577 (202) 623-1753; *Economic and Social Progress in Latin America*.

PARAGUAY - FOREIGN DEBT

The Economist Intelligence Unit, 111 West 57th Street, New York, New York 10019 (800) 938-4685; *The New Latin America Market Atlas*.

Inter-American Development Bank, 1300 New York Avenue, NW, Washington, D.C. 20577 (202) 623-1753; *Economic and Social Progress in Latin America*.

International Monetary Fund, 700 Nineteenth Street, NW, Washington, D.C. 20431 (202) 623-7000; *Government Finance Statistics Yearbook*.

PARAGUAY - FOREIGN INDEBTEDNESS

Inter-American Development Bank, 1300 New York Avenue, NW, Washington, D.C. 20577 (202) 623-1753; *Economic and Social Progress in Latin America*.

Statistical Office of the United Nations, Publishing Service, New York, New York 10017 (800) 253-9646; *Economic Survey of Latin America and the Caribbean*.

PARAGUAY - FOREIGN INVESTMENT

The Economist Intelligence Unit, 111 West 57th Street, New York, New York 10019 (800) 938-4685; *The New Latin America Market Atlas*.

PARAGUAY - FOREIGN TRADE

The Economist Intelligence Unit, 111 West 57th Street, New York, New York 10019 (800) 938-4685; *The New Latin America Market Atlas;* and *Paraguay Country Report*.

Euromonitor International, Inc., 122 South Michigan Avenue, Suite 1200, Chicago, Illinois 60603; *International Marketing Data and Statistics;* and *The World Economic Factbook*.

Europa Publications Limited, 18 Bedford Square, London, WC1B 3JN, England; *The Europa World Year Book*.

Food and Agricultural Organization of the United Nations (FAO) Via delle Terme di Caracalla, 00100 Rome, Italy (Telephone Number in U.S. (202) 653-2400); *The State of Food and Agriculture*.

Inter-American Development Bank, 1300 New York Avenue, NW, Washington, D.C. 20577 (202) 623-1753; *Economic and Social Progress in Latin America*.

International Monetary Fund, 700 Nineteenth Street, NW, Washington, D.C. 20431 (202) 623-7000; *International Financial Statistics*.

M.E. Sharpe, 80 Business Park Drive, Armonk, New York 10504 (800) 541-6563; *The Illustrated Book of World Rankings*.

St. Martin's Press, Inc., 175 Fifth Avenue, New York, New York 10010 (800) 221-7945; *The Statesman's Year-Book*.

Statistical Office of the United Nations, Publishing Service, New York, New York 10017 (800) 253-9646; *Economic Survey of Latin America and the Caribbean; International Trade Statistics Yearbook;* and *Statistical Yearbook*.

U.C.L.A. Latin American Center Publications, University of California, Los Angeles, California 90024 (310) 825-6634; *Statistical Abstract of Latin America*.

United Nations Conference on Trade and Development, Central Statistical Service, Palais des Nations, Geneva, Switzerland (Telephone in U.S. (800) 253-9646); *UNCTAD Commodity Yearbook*.

The World Bank, 1818 H Street, NW, Washington, D.C. 20433 (202) 477-1234; *World Development Report;* and *World Development Indicators*.

PARAGUAY - FORESTRY AND FOREST PRODUCTS

The Economist Intelligence Unit, 111 West 57th Street, New York, New York 10019 (800) 938-4685; *The New Latin America Market Atlas*.

Europa Publications Limited, 18 Bedford Square, London, WC1B 3JN, England; *The Europa World Year Book*.

Food and Agricultural Organization of the United Nations (FAO) Via delle Terme di Caracalla, 00100 Rome, Italy (Telephone Number in U.S. (202) 653-2400); *The State of Food and Agriculture;* and *Yearbook of Forest Products*.

Inter-American Development Bank, 1300 New York Avenue, NW, Washington, D.C. 20577 (202) 623-1753; *Economic and Social Progress in Latin America*.

International Monetary Fund, 700 Nineteenth Street, NW, Washington, D.C. 20431 (202) 623-7000; *International Financial Statistics*.

M.E. Sharpe, 80 Business Park Drive, Armonk, New York 10504 (800) 541-6563; *The Illustrated Book of World Rankings*.

St. Martin's Press, Inc., 175 Fifth Avenue, New York, New York 10010 (800) 221-7945; *The Statesman's Year-Book*.

Statistical Office of the United Nations, Publishing Service, New York, New York 10017 (800) 253-9646; *Statistical Yearbook*.

U.C.L.A. Latin American Center Publications, University of California, Los Angeles, California 90024 (310) 825-6634; *Statistical Abstract of Latin America*.

United Nations Conference on Trade and Development, Central Statistical Service, Palais des Nations, Geneva, Switzerland (Telephone in U.S. (800) 253-9646); *UNCTAD Commodity Yearbook*.

United Nations Educational, Scientific and Cultural Organization (UNESCO), 7 Place de Fontenoy, F-75700 Paris, France (Telephone Number in U.S. (212) 963-5981); *Statistical Yearbook*.

The World Bank, 1818 H Street, NW, Washington, D.C. 20433 (202) 477-1234; *World Development Report*.

PARAGUAY - GARLIC PRODUCTION - See PARAGUAY - CROPS

PARAGUAY - GAS PRODUCTION - See PARAGUAY - MINING AND MINERAL PRODUCTS

PARAGUAY - GENERAL MORTALITY - See PARAGUAY - MORTALITY

PARAGUAY - GEOGRAPHIC DATA

M.E. Sharpe, 80 Business Park Drive, Armonk, New York 10504 (800) 541-6563; *The Illustrated Book of World Rankings.*

U.C.L.A. Latin American Center Publications, University of California, Los Angeles, California 90024 (310) 825-6634; *Statistical Abstract of Latin America.*

PARAGUAY - GOATS - See PARAGUAY - LIVESTOCK AND POULTRY

PARAGUAY - GOLD HOLDINGS

International Monetary Fund, 700 Nineteenth Street, NW, Washington, D.C. 20431 (202) 623-7000; *International Financial Statistics.*

Statistical Office of the United Nations, Publishing Service, New York, New York 10017 (800) 253-9646; *Statistical Yearbook.*

The World Bank, 1818 H Street, NW, Washington, D.C. 20433 (202) 477-1234; *World Development Indicators.*

PARAGUAY - GOLD PRODUCTION AND CONSUMPTION - See PARAGUAY - MINING AND MINERAL PRODUCTS

PARAGUAY - GOLD RESERVES

The Economist Intelligence Unit, 111 West 57th Street, New York, New York 10019 (800) 938-4685; *The New Latin America Market Atlas.*

PARAGUAY - GOVERNMENT

Central Intelligence Agency, Washington, D.C. 20505 (703) 482-1100, www.cia.gov; *The World Factbook.*

Europa Publications Limited, 18 Bedford Square, London, WC1B 3JN, England; *The Europa World Year Book.*

Inter-American Development Bank, 1300 New York Avenue, NW, Washington, D.C. 20577 (202) 623-1753; *Economic and Social Progress in Latin America.*

International Monetary Fund, 700 Nineteenth Street, NW, Washington, D.C. 20431 (202) 623-7000; *Government Finance Statistics Yearbook;* and *International Financial Statistics.*

St. Martin's Press, Inc., 175 Fifth Avenue, New York, New York 10010 (800) 221-7945; *The Statesman's Year-Book.*

Statistical Office of the United Nations, Publishing Service, New York, New York 10017 (800) 253-9646; *National Accounts Statistics;* and *Statistical Yearbook.*

The World Bank, 1818 H Street, NW, Washington, D.C. 20433 (202) 477-1234; *World Development Report;* and *World*

Development Indicators.

PARAGUAY - GRAIN PRODUCTION - See PARAGUAY - CROPS

PARAGUAY - GRANTS

International Monetary Fund, 700 Nineteenth Street, NW, Washington, D.C. 20431 (202) 623-7000; *Government Finance Statistics Yearbook.*

PARAGUAY - GROSS DOMESTIC PRODUCT

The Economist Intelligence Unit, 111 West 57th Street, New York, New York 10019 (800) 938-4685; *The New Latin America Market Atlas; Paraguay Country Report*; and *The World Market Atlas.*

Euromonitor International, Inc., 122 South Michigan Avenue, Suite 1200, Chicago, Illinois 60603; *International Marketing Data and Statistics;* and *The World Economic Factbook.*

Europa Publications Limited, 18 Bedford Square, London, WC1B 3JN, England; *The Europa World Year Book.*

Inter-American Development Bank, 1300 New York Avenue, NW, Washington, D.C. 20577 (202) 623-1753; *Economic and Social Progress in Latin America.*

M.E. Sharpe, 80 Business Park Drive, Armonk, New York 10504 (800) 541-6563; *The Illustrated Book of World Rankings.*

Organization of American States (OAS), General Secretariat, Washington, D.C. 20006 (202) 458-3533; *Statistical Bulletin of the OAS.*

Statistical Office of the United Nations, Publishing Service, New York, New York 10017 (800) 253-9646; *Human Development Report; National Accounts Statistics; Statistical Yearbook;* and *Statistical Yearbook for Latin America and the Caribbean.*

U.C.L.A. Latin American Center Publications, University of California, Los Angeles, California 90024 (310) 825-6634; *Statistical Abstract of Latin America.*

The World Bank, 1818 H Street, NW, Washington, D.C. 20433 (202) 477-1234; *World Development Report;* and *World Development Indicators.*

PARAGUAY - GROSS NATIONAL PRODUCT

Euromonitor International, Inc., 122 South Michigan Avenue, Suite 1200, Chicago, Illinois 60603; *International Marketing Data and Statistics.*

Europa Publications Limited, 18

Bedford Square, London, WC1B 3JN, England; *The Europa World Year Book.*

Inter-American Development Bank, 1300 New York Avenue, NW, Washington, D.C. 20577 (202) 623-1753; *Economic and Social Progress in Latin America.*

St. Martin's Press, Inc., 175 Fifth Avenue, New York, New York 10010 (800) 221-7945; *The Statesman's Year-Book.*

U.S. Arms Control and Disarmament Agency, 320 Twenty-first Street, NW, Washington, D.C. 20451 (202) 647-8677; *World Military Expenditures and Arms Transfers.*

The World Bank, 1818 H Street, NW, Washington, D.C. 20433 (202) 477-1234; *The World Bank Atlas; World Development Report;* and *World Development Indicators.*

PARAGUAY - GROUNDNUTS PRODUCTION - See PARAGUAY - CROPS

PARAGUAY - HEALTH

The Economist Intelligence Unit, 111 West 57th Street, New York, New York 10019 (800) 938-4685; *The New Latin America Market Atlas.*

Euromonitor International, Inc., 122 South Michigan Avenue, Suite 1200, Chicago, Illinois 60603 (800) 577-EURO; *World Marketing Data and Statistics.*

M.E. Sharpe, 80 Business Park Drive, Armonk, New York 10504 (800) 541-6563; *The Illustrated Book of World Rankings.*

St. Martin's Press, Inc., 175 Fifth Avenue, New York, New York 10010 (800) 221-7945; *The Statesman's Year-Book.*

Statistical Office of the United Nations, Publishing Service, New York, New York 10017 (800) 253-9646; *Human Development Report; Statistical Yearbook for Latin America and the Caribbean;* and *Statistical Yearbook.*

U.C.L.A. Latin American Center Publications, University of California, Los Angeles, California 90024 (310) 825-6634; *Statistical Abstract of Latin America.*

United Nations Children's Fund (UNICEF), 3 United Nations Plaza, New York, New York 10017 (800) 253-9646; *State of the World's Children.*

The World Bank, 1818 H Street, NW, Washington, D.C. 20433 (202) 477-1234; *World Development Report.*

World Health Organization, Office of Publications, 20 Avenue Appia, CH-1211 Geneva 27, Switzerland (Telephone Number in U.S. (518) 436-9686); *World*

Health Statistics Annual.

PARAGUAY - HEALTH EXPENDITURES

International Monetary Fund, 700 Nineteenth Street, NW, Washington, D.C. 20431 (202) 623-7000; *Government Finance Statistics Yearbook.*

PARAGUAY - HIDE PRODUCTION

Food and Agricultural Organization of the United Nations (FAO), Via delle Terme di Caracalla, 00100 Rome, Italy (Telephone Number in U.S. (202) 653-2400); *Production Yearbook.*

PARAGUAY - HIDES EXPORTS

International Monetary Fund, 700 Nineteenth Street, NW, Washington, D.C. 20431 (202) 623-7000; *International Financial Statistics.*

PARAGUAY - HIGHWAYS

Central Intelligence Agency, Washington, D.C. 20505 (703) 482-1100, www.cia.gov; *The World Factbook.*

The Economist Intelligence Unit, 111 West 57th Street, New York, New York 10019 (800) 938-4685; *The New Latin America Market Atlas.*

International Road Federation, 2600 Virginia Avenue, NW.; *World Road Statistics.*

St. Martin's Press, Inc., 175 Fifth Avenue, New York, New York 10010 (800) 221-7945; *The Statesman's Year-Book.*

PARAGUAY - HORSES - See PARAGUAY - LIVESTOCK AND POULTRY

PARAGUAY - HOURS OF WORK - See PARAGUAY - EMPLOYMENT

PARAGUAY - HOUSING AND HOUSING UNITS

Euromonitor International, Inc., 122 South Michigan Avenue, Suite 1200, Chicago, Illinois 60603 (800) 577-EURO; *World Marketing Data and Statistics.*

M.E. Sharpe, 80 Business Park Drive, Armonk, New York 10504 (800) 541-6563; *The Illustrated Book of World Rankings.*

Statistical Office of the United Nations, Publishing Service, New York, New York 10017 (800) 253-9646; *Statistical Yearbook for Latin America and the Caribbean.*

U.C.L.A. Latin American Center Publications, University of California, Los Angeles, California 90024 (310) 825-6634; *Statistical Abstract of Latin America.*

PARAGUAY - HOUSING EXPENDITURES

International Monetary Fund, 700 Nineteenth Street, NW, Washington, D.C. 20431 (202) 623-7000; *Government Finance Statistics Yearbook.*

PARAGUAY - ILLITERATE POPULATION

Central Intelligence Agency, Washington, D.C. 20505 (703) 482-1100, www.cia.gov; *The World Factbook.*

The Economist Intelligence Unit, 111 West 57th Street, New York, New York 10019 (800) 938-4685; *The World Market Atlas.*

Euromonitor International, Inc., 122 South Michigan Avenue, Suite 1200, Chicago, Illinois 60603; *The World Economic Factbook.*

St. Martin's Press, Inc., 175 Fifth Avenue, New York, New York 10010 (800) 221-7945; *The Statesman's Year-Book.*

Statistical Office of the United Nations, Publishing Service, New York, New York 10017 (800) 253-9646; *Human Development Report;* and *Statistical Yearbook for Latin America and the Caribbean.*

United Nations Educational, Scientific and Cultural Organization (UNESCO), 7 Place de Fontenoy, F-75700 Paris, France (Telephone Number in U.S. (212) 963-5981); *Statistical Yearbook.*

PARAGUAY - IMMIGRATION

U.C.L.A. Latin American Center Publications, University of California, Los Angeles, California 90024 (310) 825-6634; *Statistical Abstract of Latin America.*

PARAGUAY - IMPORTS

Central Intelligence Agency, Washington, D.C. 20505 (703) 482-1100, www.cia.gov; *The World Factbook.*

The Economist Intelligence Unit, 111 West 57th Street, New York, New York 10019 (800) 938-4685; *The New Latin America Market Atlas; Paraguay Country Report;* and *The World Market Atlas.*

Euromonitor International, Inc., 122 South Michigan Avenue, Suite 1200, Chicago, Illinois 60603; *International Marketing Data and Statistics;* and *The World Economic Factbook.*

Europa Publications Limited, 18 Bedford Square, London, WC1B 3JN, England; *The Europa World Year Book.*

Food and Agricultural Organization of the United Nations (FAO) Via delle Terme

di Caracalla, 00100 Rome, Italy (Telephone Number in U.S. (202) 653-2400); *The State of Food and Agriculture.*

Inter-American Development Bank, 1300 New York Avenue, NW, Washington, D.C. 20577 (202) 623-1753; *Economic and Social Progress in Latin America.*

International Monetary Fund, 700 Nineteenth Street, NW, Washington, D.C. 20431 (202) 623-7000; *Direction of Trade Statistics;* and *Government Finance Statistics Yearbook.*

Organization of American States (OAS), General Secretariat, Washington, D.C. 20006 (202) 458-3533; *Statistical Bulletin of the OAS.*

St. Martin's Press, Inc., 175 Fifth Avenue, New York, New York 10010 (800) 221-7945; *The Statesman's Year-Book.*

Statistical Office of the United Nations, Publishing Service, New York, New York 10017 (800) 253-9646; *Statistical Yearbook for Latin America and the Caribbean.*

United Nations Conference on Trade and Development (UNCTAD), New York, New York 10017 (800) 253-9646; *Handbook of International Trade and Development Statistics.*

The World Bank, 1818 H Street, NW, Washington, D.C. 20433 (202) 477-1234; *World Development Report;* and *World Development Indicators.*

PARAGUAY - INCOME DISTRIBUTION

Statistical Office of the United Nations, Publishing Service, New York, New York 10017 (800) 253-9646; *Statistical Yearbook for Latin America and the Caribbean.*

U.C.L.A. Latin American Center Publications, University of California, Los Angeles, California 90024 (310) 825-6634; *Statistical Abstract of Latin America.*

PARAGUAY - INCOME TAXES - See PARAGUAY - TAXATION

PARAGUAY - INDUSTRY

Central Intelligence Agency, Washington, D.C. 20505 (703) 482-1100, www.cia.gov; *The World Factbook.*

Economist Intelligence Unit, 111 West 57th Street, New York, New York 10019 (800) 938-4685; *Paraguay Country Report.*

Euromonitor International, Inc., 122 South Michigan Avenue, Suite 1200, Chicago, Illinois 60603; *International Marketing Data and Statistics; World Marketing Data and Statistics;* and *The World Economic Factbook.*

Europa Publications Limited, 18 Bedford Square, London, WC1B 3JN, England; *The Europa World Year Book.*

International Labour Office, I.L.O. Publications, 1828 L Street, NW., Suite 801, Washington, D.C. 20036 (301) 638-3152; *Yearbook of Labour Statistics.*

M.E. Sharpe, 80 Business Park Drive, Armonk, New York 10504 (800) 541-6563; *The Illustrated Book of World Rankings.*

St. Martin's Press, Inc., 175 Fifth Avenue, New York, New York 10010 (800) 221-7945; *The Statesman's Year-Book.*

Statistical Office of the United Nations, Publishing Service, New York, New York 10017 (800) 253-9646; *Economic Survey of Latin America and the Caribbean;* and *Statistical Yearbook.*

U.C.L.A. Latin American Center Publications, University of California, Los Angeles, California 90024 (310) 825-6634; *Statistical Abstract of Latin America.*

The World Bank, 1818 H Street, NW, Washington, D.C. 20433 (202) 477-1234; *World Development Indicators.*

PARAGUAY - INFANT AND MATERNAL MORTALITY - See PARAGUAY - MORTALITY

PARAGUAY - INFLATIONARY FACTORS

Statistical Office of the United Nations, Publishing Service, New York, New York 10017 (800) 253-9646; *Economic Survey of Latin America and the Caribbean.*

PARAGUAY - INTEREST RATES

Inter-American Development Bank, 1300 New York Avenue, NW, Washington, D.C. 20577 (202) 623-1753; *Economic and Social Progress in Latin America.*

PARAGUAY - INTERNATIONAL FINANCE

Inter-American Development Bank, 1300 New York Avenue, NW, Washington, D.C. 20577 (202) 623-1753; *Economic and Social Progress in Latin America.*

U.C.L.A. Latin American Center Publications, University of California, Los Angeles, California 90024 (310) 825-6634; *Statistical Abstract of Latin America.*

PARAGUAY - INTERNATIONAL LIQUIDITY

Inter-American Development Bank, 1300 New York Avenue, NW, Washington, D.C. 20577 (202) 623-1753; *Economic and Social Progress in Latin America.*

International Monetary Fund, 700 Nineteenth Street, NW, Washington, D.C.

20431 (202) 623-7000; *International Financial Statistics.*

PARAGUAY - INTERNATIONAL RESERVES

Organization of American States (OAS), General Secretariat, Washington, D.C. 20006 (202) 458-3533; *Statistical Bulletin of the OAS.*

PARAGUAY - INTERNATIONAL RESERVES EXCLUDING GOLD

Inter-American Development Bank, 1300 New York Avenue, NW, Washington, D.C. 20577 (202) 623-1753; *Economic and Social Progress in Latin America.*

Statistical Office of the United Nations, Publishing Service, New York, New York 10017 (800) 253-9646; *Statistical Yearbook.*

PARAGUAY - INTERNATIONAL STATISTICS

Inter-American Development Bank, 1300 New York Avenue, NW, Washington, D.C. 20577 (202) 623-1753; *Economic and Social Progress in Latin America.*

U.C.L.A. Latin American Center Publications, University of California, Los Angeles, California 90024 (310) 825-6634; *Statistical Abstract of Latin America.*

PARAGUAY - INVESTMENT

Inter-American Development Bank, 1300 New York Avenue, NW, Washington, D.C. 20577 (202) 623-1753; *Economic and Social Progress in Latin America.*

Statistical Office of the United Nations, Publishing Service, New York, New York 10017 (800) 253-9646; *Statistical Yearbook for Latin America and the Caribbean.*

PARAGUAY - IRON ORE PRODUCTION AND CONSUMPTION - See PARAGUAY - MINING AND MINERAL PRODUCTS

PARAGUAY - IRRIGATION

Euromonitor International, Inc., 122 South Michigan Avenue, Suite 1200, Chicago, Illinois 60603; *International Marketing Data and Statistics.*

Inter-American Development Bank, 1300 New York Avenue, NW, Washington, D.C. 20577 (202) 623-1753; *Economic and Social Progress in Latin America.*

PARAGUAY - LABOR

Central Intelligence Agency, Washington, D.C. 20505 (703) 482-1100, www.cia.gov; *The World Factbook.*

The Economist Intelligence Unit, 111

West 57th Street, New York, New York 10019 (800) 938-4685; *The New Latin America Market Atlas.*

Euromonitor International, Inc., 122 South Michigan Avenue, Suite 1200, Chicago, Illinois 60603; *International Marketing Data and Statistics;* and *World Marketing Data and Statistics.*

Europa Publications Limited, 18 Bedford Square, London, WC1B 3JN, England; *The Europa World Year Book.*

Food and Agricultural Organization of the United Nations (FAO) Via delle Terme di Caracalla, 00100 Rome, Italy (Telephone Number in U.S. (202) 653-2400); *The State of Food and Agriculture.*

International Labour Office, I.L.O. Publications, 1828 L Street, NW., Suite 801, Washington, D.C. 20036 (301) 638-3152; *Yearbook of Labour Statistics.*

M.E. Sharpe, 80 Business Park Drive, Armonk, New York 10504 (800) 541-6563; *The Illustrated Book of World Rankings.*

St. Martin's Press, Inc., 175 Fifth Avenue, New York, New York 10010 (800) 221-7945; *The Statesman's Year-Book.*

Statistical Office of the United Nations, Publishing Service, New York, New York 10017 (800) 253-9646; *Human Development Report.*

The World Bank, 1818 H Street, NW, Washington, D.C. 20433 (202) 477-1234; *The World Bank Atlas; World Development Report;* and *World Development Indicators.*

PARAGUAY - LAND AREA

The Economist Intelligence Unit, 111 West 57th Street, New York, New York 10019 (800) 938-4685; *The New Latin America Market Atlas.*

PARAGUAY - LAND USE

Central Intelligence Agency, Washington, D.C. 20505 (703) 482-1100, www.cia.gov; *The World Factbook.*

Euromonitor International, Inc., 122 South Michigan Avenue, Suite 1200, Chicago, Illinois 60603; *International Marketing Data and Statistics.*

Food and Agricultural Organization of the United Nations (FAO), Via delle Terme di Caracalla, 00100 Rome, Italy (Telephone Number in U.S. (202) 653-2400); *Production Yearbook.*

Inter-American Development Bank, 1300 New York Avenue, NW, Washington, D.C. 20577 (202) 623-1753; *Economic and Social Progress in Latin America.*

The World Bank, 1818 H Street, NW, Washington, D.C. 20433 (202) 477-1234; *World Development Report.*

PARAGUAY - LIBRARIES

M.E. Sharpe, 80 Business Park Drive, Armonk, New York 10504 (800) 541-6563; *The Illustrated Book of World Rankings.*

PARAGUAY - LIFE EXPECTANCY

Central Intelligence Agency, Washington, D.C. 20505 (703) 482-1100, www.cia.gov; *The World Factbook.*

The Economist Intelligence Unit, 111 West 57th Street, New York, New York 10019 (800) 938-4685; *The New Latin America Market Atlas.*

Euromonitor International, Inc., 122 South Michigan Avenue, Suite 1200, Chicago, Illinois 60603; *The World Economic Factbook.*

St. Martin's Press, Inc., 175 Fifth Avenue, New York, New York 10010 (800) 221-7945; *The Statesman's Year-Book.*

Statistical Office of the United Nations, Publishing Service, New York, New York 10017 (800) 253-9646; *Human Development Report; Statistical Yearbook for Latin America and the Caribbean;* and *World Statistics Pocketbook.*

The World Bank, 1818 H Street, NW, Washington, D.C. 20433 (202) 477-1234; *The World Bank Atlas;* and *World Development Report.*

PARAGUAY - LITERACY RATE

Euromonitor International, Inc., 122 South Michigan Avenue, Suite 1200, Chicago, Illinois 60603 (800) 577-EURO; *World Marketing Data and Statistics.*

PARAGUAY - LIVESTOCK AND POULTRY

Euromonitor International, Inc., 122 South Michigan Avenue, Suite 1200, Chicago, Illinois 60603; *International Marketing Data and Statistics.*

Europa Publications Limited, 18 Bedford Square, London, WC1B 3JN, England; *The Europa World Year Book.*

Food and Agricultural Organization of the United Nations (FAO), Via delle Terme di Caracalla, 00100 Rome, Italy (Telephone Number in U.S. (202) 653-2400); *Production Yearbook;* and *The State of Food and Agriculture.*

International Monetary Fund, 700 Nineteenth Street, NW, Washington, D.C. 20431 (202) 623-7000; *International Financial Statistics.*

M.E. Sharpe, 80 Business Park Drive, Armonk, New York 10504 (800) 541-6563; *The Illustrated Book of World Rankings.*

Organization of American States (OAS), General Secretariat, Washington, D.C. 20006 (202) 458-3533; *Statistical Bulletin of the OAS.*

St. Martin's Press, Inc., 175 Fifth Avenue, New York, New York 10010 (800) 221-7945; *The Statesman's Year-Book.*

Statistical Office of the United Nations, Publishing Service, New York, New York 10017 (800) 253-9646; *Statistical Yearbook.*

United Nations Conference on Trade and Development, Central Statistical Service, Palais des Nations, Geneva, Switzerland (Telephone in U.S. (800) 253-9646); *UNCTAD Commodity Yearbook.*

PARAGUAY - LIVING LEVELS - See PARAGUAY - LIFE EXPECTANCY

PARAGUAY - MAIN ECONOMIC INDICATORS - See PARAGUAY - ECONOMY

PARAGUAY - MANUFACTURING

The Economist Intelligence Unit, 111 West 57th Street, New York, New York 10019 (800) 938-4685; *The New Latin America Market Atlas.*

Inter-American Development Bank, 1300 New York Avenue, NW, Washington, D.C. 20577 (202) 623-1753; *Economic and Social Progress in Latin America.*

M.E. Sharpe, 80 Business Park Drive, Armonk, New York 10504 (800) 541-6563; *The Illustrated Book of World Rankings.*

Statistical Office of the United Nations, Publishing Service, New York, New York 10017 (800) 253-9646; *Statistical Yearbook for Latin America and the Caribbean.*

The World Bank, 1818 H Street, NW, Washington, D.C. 20433 (202) 477-1234; *World Development Indicators.*

PARAGUAY - MARRIAGE RATES

Europa Publications Limited, 18 Bedford Square, London, WC1B 3JN, England; *The Europa World Year Book.*

M.E. Sharpe, 80 Business Park Drive, Armonk, New York 10504 (800) 541-6563; *The Illustrated Book of World Rankings.*

Statistical Office of the United Nations, Publishing Service, New York, New York 10017 (800) 253-9646; *Demographic Yearbook;* and *Statistical Yearbook.*

PARAGUAY - MEAT PRODUCTION - See PARAGUAY - LIVESTOCK AND POULTRY

PARAGUAY - MEDICAL PERSONNEL

U.C.L.A. Latin American Center Publications, University of California, Los Angeles, California 90024 (310) 825-6634; *Statistical Abstract of Latin America.*

PARAGUAY - MERCHANT SHIPPING

St. Martin's Press, Inc., 175 Fifth Avenue, New York, New York 10010 (800) 221-7945; *The Statesman's Year-Book.*

PARAGUAY - MILITARY

Central Intelligence Agency, Washington, D.C. 20505 (703) 482-1100, www.cia.gov; *The World Factbook.*

The Economist Intelligence Unit, 111 West 57th Street, New York, New York 10019 (800) 938-4685; *The New Latin America Market Atlas.*

Euromonitor International, Inc., 122 South Michigan Avenue, Suite 1200, Chicago, Illinois 60603 (800) 577-EURO; *World Marketing Data and Statistics.*

The International Institute for Strategic Studies, 23 Tavistock Street, London WC2E 7NQ, England 44 171 3797676; *The Military Balance.*

International Monetary Fund, 700 Nineteenth Street, NW, Washington, D.C. 20431 (202) 623-7000; *Government Finance Statistics Yearbook.*

St. Martin's Press, Inc., 175 Fifth Avenue, New York, New York 10010 (800) 221-7945; *The Statesman's Year-Book.*

Statistical Office of the United Nations, Publishing Service, New York, New York 10017 (800) 253-9646; *Human Development Report.*

U.C.L.A. Latin American Center Publications, University of California, Los Angeles, California 90024 (310) 825-6634; *Statistical Abstract of Latin America.*

U.S. Arms Control and Disarmament Agency, 320 Twenty-first Street, NW, Washington, D.C. 20451 (202) 647-8677; *World Military Expenditures and Arms Transfers.*

PARAGUAY - MILK PRODUCTION - ALL TYPES OF MILK

M.E. Sharpe, 80 Business Park Drive, Armonk, New York 10504 (800) 541-6563; *The Illustrated Book of World Rankings.*

Statistical Office of the United Nations, Publishing Service, New York, New York

10017 (800) 253-9646; *Statistical Yearbook.*

PARAGUAY - MINING AND MINERAL PRODUCTS

The Economist Intelligence Unit, 111 West 57th Street, New York, New York 10019 (800) 938-4685; *The New Latin America Market Atlas.*

Inter-American Development Bank, 1300 New York Avenue, NW, Washington, D.C. 20577 (202) 623-1753; *Economic and Social Progress in Latin America.*

M.E. Sharpe, 80 Business Park Drive, Armonk, New York 10504 (800) 541-6563; *The Illustrated Book of World Rankings.*

St. Martin's Press, Inc., 175 Fifth Avenue, New York, New York 10010 (800) 221-7945; *The Statesman's Year-Book.*

Statistical Office of the United Nations, Publishing Service, New York, New York 10017 (800) 253-9646; *Statistical Yearbook;* and *Statistical Yearbook for Latin America and the Caribbean.*

U.C.L.A. Latin American Center Publications, University of California, Los Angeles, California 90024 (310) 825-6634; *Statistical Abstract of Latin America.*

United Nations Conference on Trade and Development, Central Statistical Service, Palais des Nations, Geneva, Switzerland (Telephone in U.S. (800) 253-9646); *UNCTAD Commodity Yearbook.*

PARAGUAY - MONEY EXCHANGE RATES - See PARAGUAY - EXCHANGE RATES

PARAGUAY - MONEY RATES - MARKET

Inter-American Development Bank, 1300 New York Avenue, NW, Washington, D.C. 20577 (202) 623-1753; *Economic and Social Progress in Latin America.*

PARAGUAY - MONEY RESERVES

Euromonitor International, Inc., 122 South Michigan Avenue, Suite 1200, Chicago, Illinois 60603; *International Marketing Data and Statistics.*

Inter-American Development Bank, 1300 New York Avenue, NW, Washington, D.C. 20577 (202) 623-1753; *Economic and Social Progress in Latin America.*

PARAGUAY - MONEY SUPPLY

Economist Intelligence Unit, 111 West 57th Street, New York, New York 10019 (800) 938-4685; *Paraguay Country Report.*

Euromonitor International, Inc., 122 South Michigan Avenue, Suite 1200, Chicago, Illinois 60603; *International*

Marketing Data and Statistics.

Europa Publications Limited, 18 Bedford Square, London, WC1B 3JN, England; *The Europa World Year Book.*

Inter-American Development Bank, 1300 New York Avenue, NW, Washington, D.C. 20577 (202) 623-1753; *Economic and Social Progress in Latin America.*

International Monetary Fund, 700 Nineteenth Street, NW, Washington, D.C. 20431 (202) 623-7000; *International Financial Statistics.*

Statistical Office of the United Nations, Publishing Service, New York, New York 10017 (800) 253-9646; *Statistical Yearbook.*

U.C.L.A. Latin American Center Publications, University of California, Los Angeles, California 90024 (310) 825-6634; *Statistical Abstract of Latin America.*

The World Bank, 1818 H Street, NW, Washington, D.C. 20433 (202) 477-1234; *World Development Indicators.*

PARAGUAY - MORTALITY

Central Intelligence Agency, Washington, D.C. 20505 (703) 482-1100, www.cia.gov; *The World Factbook.*

The Economist Intelligence Unit, 111 West 57th Street, New York, New York 10019 (800) 938-4685; *The New Latin America Market Atlas.*

Euromonitor International, Inc., 122 South Michigan Avenue, Suite 1200, Chicago, Illinois 60603; *International Marketing Data and Statistics;* and *The World Economic Factbook.*

Europa Publications Limited, 18 Bedford Square, London, WC1B 3JN, England; *The Europa World Year Book.*

St. Martin's Press, Inc., 175 Fifth Avenue, New York, New York 10010 (800) 221-7945; *The Statesman's Year-Book.*

Statistical Office of the United Nations, Publishing Service, New York, New York 10017 (800) 253-9646; *Demographic Yearbook; Human Development Report; Statistical Yearbook; Statistical Yearbook for Latin America and the Caribbean;* and *World Statistics Pocketbook.*

United Nations Children's Fund (UNICEF), 3 United Nations Plaza, New York, New York 10017 (800) 253-9646; *State of the World's Children.*

The World Bank, 1818 H Street, NW, Washington, D.C. 20433 (202) 477-1234; *The World Bank Atlas; World Development Report;* and *World Development Indicators.*

World Health Organization, Office of Publications, 20 Avenue Appia, CH-1211 Geneva 27, Switzerland (Telephone Number in U.S. (518) 436-9686); *World Health Statistics Annual.*

PARAGUAY - MOTION PICTURES

St. Martin's Press, Inc., 175 Fifth Avenue, New York, New York 10010 (800) 221-7945; *The Statesman's Year-Book.*

PARAGUAY - MOTOR VEHICLE TAXES - See PARAGUAY - TAXATION

PARAGUAY - MOTOR VEHICLES IN USE

The Economist Intelligence Unit, 111 West 57th Street, New York, New York 10019 (800) 938-4685; *The New Latin America Market Atlas.*

Europa Publications Limited, 18 Bedford Square, London, WC1B 3JN, England; *The Europa World Year Book.*

International Road Federation, 2600 Virginia Avenue, NW.; *World Road Statistics.*

Statistical Office of the United Nations, Publishing Service, New York, New York 10017 (800) 253-9646; *Statistical Yearbook.*

PARAGUAY - MULES - See PARAGUAY - LIVESTOCK AND POULTRY

PARAGUAY - MUSEUMS

M.E. Sharpe, 80 Business Park Drive, Armonk, New York 10504 (800) 541-6563; *The Illustrated Book of World Rankings.*

PARAGUAY - NATALITY - See PARAGUAY - BIRTH RATES

PARAGUAY - NATIONAL ACCOUNTS

Europa Publications Limited, 18 Bedford Square, London, WC1B 3JN, England; *The Europa World Year Book.*

Inter-American Development Bank, 1300 New York Avenue, NW, Washington, D.C. 20577 (202) 623-1753; *Economic and Social Progress in Latin America.*

International Monetary Fund, 700 Nineteenth Street, NW, Washington, D.C. 20431 (202) 623-7000; *International Financial Statistics.*

Organization of American States (OAS), General Secretariat, Washington, D.C. 20006 (202) 458-3533; *Statistical Bulletin of the OAS.*

Statistical Office of the United Nations, Publishing Service, New York, New York 10017 (800) 253-9646; *National Accounts Statistics;* and *Statistical Yearbook.*

U.C.L.A. Latin American Center Publications, University of California, Los Angeles, California 90024 (310) 825-6634; *Statistical Abstract of Latin America.*

PARAGUAY - NATIONAL INCOME

Inter-American Development Bank, 1300 New York Avenue, NW, Washington, D.C. 20577 (202) 623-1753; *Economic and Social Progress in Latin America.*

M.E. Sharpe, 80 Business Park Drive, Armonk, New York 10504 (800) 541-6563; *The Illustrated Book of World Rankings.*

Statistical Office of the United Nations, Publishing Service, New York, New York 10017 (800) 253-9646; *National Accounts Statistics; Statistical Yearbook;* and *Statistical Yearbook for Latin America and the Caribbean.*

PARAGUAY - NATIONAL PRODUCT

M.E. Sharpe, 80 Business Park Drive, Armonk, New York 10504 (800) 541-6563; *The Illustrated Book of World Rankings.*

Statistical Office of the United Nations, Publishing Service, New York, New York 10017 (800) 253-9646; *Statistical Yearbook.*

PARAGUAY - NATURAL GAS PRODUCTION - See PARAGUAY - MINING AND MINERAL PRODUCTS

PARAGUAY - NEWSPAPER PRODUCTION - See PARAGUAY - FORESTRY AND FOREST PRODUCTS

PARAGUAY - NEWSPRINT - See PARAGUAY - FORESTRY AND FOREST PRODUCTS

PARAGUAY - NUTRITION

Statistical Office of the United Nations, Publishing Service, New York, New York 10017 (800) 253-9646; *Statistical Yearbook for Latin America and the Caribbean.*

PARAGUAY - OCCUPATIONS - See PARAGUAY - LABOR

PARAGUAY - ORANGES PRODUCTION - See PARAGUAY - CROPS

PARAGUAY - PALM KERNELS PRODUCTION - See PARAGUAY - CROPS

PARAGUAY - PAPER - See PARAGUAY - FORESTRY AND FOREST PRODUCTS

PARAGUAY - PEANUT PRODUCTION - See PARAGUAY - CROPS

PARAGUAY - PESTICIDE USE

Food and Agricultural Organization of the United Nations (FAO) Via delle Terme di Caracalla, 00100 Rome, Italy (Telephone Number in U.S. (202) 653-2400); *The State of Food and Agriculture.*

PARAGUAY - PETROLEUM INDUSTRY

The Economist Intelligence Unit, 111 West 57th Street, New York, New York 10019 (800) 938-4685; *The New Latin America Market Atlas.*

Food and Agricultural Organization of the United Nations (FAO) Via delle Terme di Caracalla, 00100 Rome, Italy (Telephone Number in U.S. (202) 653-2400); *The State of Food and Agriculture.*

Inter-American Development Bank, 1300 New York Avenue, NW, Washington, D.C. 20577 (202) 623-1753; *Economic and Social Progress in Latin America.*

M.E. Sharpe, 80 Business Park Drive, Armonk, New York 10504 (800) 541-6563; *The Illustrated Book of World Rankings.*

Statistical Office of the United Nations, Publishing Service, New York, New York 10017 (800) 253-9646; *Statistical Yearbook.*

United Nations Conference on Trade and Development, Central Statistical Service, Palais des Nations, Geneva, Switzerland (Telephone in U.S. (800) 253-9646); *UNCTAD Commodity Yearbook.*

PARAGUAY - PIG-IRON AND FERRO-ALLOY PRODUCTION - See PARAGUAY - MINING AND MINERAL PRODUCTS

PARAGUAY - PIGS - See PARAGUAY - LIVESTOCK AND POULTRY

PARAGUAY - POLITICAL DATA

U.C.L.A. Latin American Center Publications, University of California, Los Angeles, California 90024 (310) 825-6634; *Statistical Abstract of Latin America.*

PARAGUAY - POPULATION

Central Intelligence Agency, Washington, D.C. 20505 (703) 482-1100, www.cia.gov; *The World Factbook.*

The Economist Intelligence Unit, 111 West 57th Street, New York, New York 10019 (800) 938-4685; *The New Latin America Market Atlas; Paraguay Country Report;* and *The World Market Atlas.*

Euromonitor International, Inc., 122 South Michigan Avenue, Suite 1200, Chicago, Illinois 60603; *International Marketing Data and Statistics;* and *The World Economic Factbook.*

Europa Publications Limited, 18 Bedford Square, London, WC1B 3JN, England; *The Europa World Year Book.*

Food and Agricultural Organization of the United Nations (FAO), Via delle Terme di Caracalla, 00100 Rome, Italy (Telephone Number in U.S. (202) 653-2400); *Production Yearbook.*

Inter-American Development Bank, 1300 New York Avenue, NW, Washington, D.C. 20577 (202) 623-1753; *Economic and Social Progress in Latin America.*

International Labour Office, I.L.O. Publications, 1828 L Street, NW., Suite 801, Washington, D.C. 20036 (301) 638-3152; *Yearbook of Labour Statistics.*

M.E. Sharpe, 80 Business Park Drive, Armonk, New York 10504 (800) 541-6563; *The Illustrated Book of World Rankings.*

Organization of American States (OAS), General Secretariat, Washington, D.C. 20006 (202) 458-3533; *Statistical Bulletin of the OAS.*

St. Martin's Press, Inc., 175 Fifth Avenue, New York, New York 10010 (800) 221-7945; *The Statesman's Year-Book.*

Statistical Office of the United Nations, Publishing Service, New York, New York 10017 (800) 253-9646; *Demographic Yearbook; Human Development Report; Statistical Yearbook; Statistical Yearbook for Latin America and the Caribbean;* and *World Statistics Pocketbook.*

U.C.L.A. Latin American Center Publications, University of California, Los Angeles, California 90024 (310) 825-6634; *Statistical Abstract of Latin America.*

United Nations Educational, Scientific and Cultural Organization (UNESCO), 7 Place de Fontenoy, F-75700 Paris, France (Telephone Number in U.S. (212) 963-5981); *Statistical Yearbook.*

U.S. Arms Control and Disarmament Agency, 320 Twenty-first Street, NW, Washington, D.C. 20451 (202) 647-8677; *World Military Expenditures and Arms Transfers.*

The World Bank, 1818 H Street, NW, Washington, D.C. 20433 (202) 477-1234; *The World Bank Atlas;* and *World Development Report.*

World Health Organization, Office of Publications, 20 Avenue Appia, CH-1211 Geneva 27, Switzerland (Telephone Number in U.S. (518) 436-9686); *World Health Statistics Annual.*

PARAGUAY - POST OFFICES

M.E. Sharpe, 80 Business Park Drive, Armonk, New York 10504 (800) 541-6563; *The Illustrated Book of World Rankings.*

St. Martin's Press, Inc., 175 Fifth Avenue, New York, New York 10010 (800) 221-7945; *The Statesman's Year-Book.*

PARAGUAY - POTATO PRODUCTION - See PARAGUAY - CROPS

PARAGUAY - PRICES

Food and Agricultural Organization of the United Nations (FAO), Via delle Terme di Caracalla, 00100 Rome, Italy (Telephone Number in U.S. (202) 653-2400); *Production Yearbook;* and *The State of Food and Agriculture.*

International Labour Office, I.L.O. Publications, 1828 L Street, NW., Suite 801, Washington, D.C. 20036 (301) 638-3152; *Yearbook of Labour Statistics.*

International Monetary Fund, 700 Nineteenth Street, NW, Washington, D.C. 20431 (202) 623-7000; *International Financial Statistics.*

M.E. Sharpe, 80 Business Park Drive, Armonk, New York 10504 (800) 541-6563; *The Illustrated Book of World Rankings.*

Statistical Office of the United Nations, Publishing Service, New York, New York 10017 (800) 253-9646; *Economic Survey of Latin America and the Caribbean;* and *Statistical Yearbook for Latin America and the Caribbean.*

PARAGUAY - PRINTING AND WRITING PAPER - See PARAGUAY - FORESTRY AND FOREST PRODUCTS

PARAGUAY - PRODUCTION

M.E. Sharpe, 80 Business Park Drive, Armonk, New York 10504 (800) 541-6563; *The Illustrated Book of World Rankings.*

PARAGUAY - PRODUCTIVITY

Euromonitor International, Inc., 122 South Michigan Avenue, Suite 1200, Chicago, Illinois 60603; *International Marketing Data and Statistics.*

PARAGUAY - PROPERTY TAXES - See PARAGUAY - TAXATION

PARAGUAY - PUBLIC CONSUMPTION FUND

Inter-American Development Bank, 1300 New York Avenue, NW, Washington, D.C. 20577 (202) 623-1753; *Economic and Social Progress in Latin America.*

PARAGUAY - PUBLIC EXPENDITURE

Inter-American Development Bank, 1300 New York Avenue, NW, Washington, D.C. 20577 (202) 623-1753; *Economic and Social Progress in Latin America.*

Organization of American States (OAS), General Secretariat, Washington, D.C. 20006 (202) 458-3533; *Statistical Bulletin of the OAS.*

Statistical Office of the United Nations, Publishing Service, New York, New York 10017 (800) 253-9646; *Statistical Yearbook for Latin America and the Caribbean.*

PARAGUAY - PUBLIC FINANCE - See PARAGUAY - FINANCE

PARAGUAY - PUBLIC REVENUE

Inter-American Development Bank, 1300 New York Avenue, NW, Washington, D.C. 20577 (202) 623-1753; *Economic and Social Progress in Latin America.*

Organization of American States (OAS), General Secretariat, Washington, D.C. 20006 (202) 458-3533; *Statistical Bulletin of the OAS.*

PARAGUAY - RADIO BROADCASTING - See PARAGUAY - BROADCASTING

PARAGUAY - RADIO RECEIVERS

St. Martin's Press, Inc., 175 Fifth Avenue, New York, New York 10010 (800) 221-7945; *The Statesman's Year-Book.*

PARAGUAY - RAILWAYS

The Economist Intelligence Unit, 111 West 57th Street, New York, New York 10019 (800) 938-4685; *The New Latin America Market Atlas.*

Europa Publications Limited, 18 Bedford Square, London, WC1B 3JN, England; *The Europa World Year Book.*

Jane's Information Group, Sentinel House, 163 Brighton Road, Coulsdon, Surrey CR5 2NH, England (Telephone Number in U.S. (703) 683-3700); *Jane's World Railways.*

St. Martin's Press, Inc., 175 Fifth Avenue, New York, New York 10010 (800) 221-7945; *The Statesman's Year-Book.*

Statistical Office of the United Nations, Publishing Service, New York, New York 10017 (800) 253-9646; *Statistical Yearbook.*

PARAGUAY - RANCHING

U.C.L.A. Latin American Center Publications, University of California, Los Angeles, California 90024 (310) 825-6634; *Statistical Abstract of Latin America.*

PARAGUAY - RELIGION

Central Intelligence Agency, Washington, D.C. 20505 (703) 482-1100,

www.cia.gov; *The World Factbook.*

M.E. Sharpe, 80 Business Park Drive, Armonk, New York 10504 (800) 541-6563; *The Illustrated Book of World Rankings.*

St. Martin's Press, Inc., 175 Fifth Avenue, New York, New York 10010 (800) 221-7945; *The Statesman's Year-Book.*

U.C.L.A. Latin American Center Publications, University of California, Los Angeles, California 90024 (310) 825-6634; *Statistical Abstract of Latin America.*

PARAGUAY - RENT PRICES

International Labour Office, I.L.O. Publications, 1828 L Street, NW., Suite 801, Washington, D.C. 20036 (301) 638-3152; *Yearbook of Labour Statistics.*

PARAGUAY - RESERVES EXCLUDING GOLD

The Economist Intelligence Unit, 111 West 57th Street, New York, New York 10019 (800) 938-4685; *The New Latin America Market Atlas.*

PARAGUAY - RETAIL TRADE

Euromonitor International, Inc., 122 South Michigan Avenue, Suite 1200, Chicago, Illinois 60603 (800) 577-EURO; *World Marketing Data and Statistics.*

Inter-American Development Bank, 1300 New York Avenue, NW, Washington, D.C. 20577 (202) 623-1753; *Economic and Social Progress in Latin America.*

PARAGUAY - REVENUE

Organization of American States (OAS), General Secretariat, Washington, D.C. 20006 (202) 458-3533; *Statistical Bulletin of the OAS.*

PARAGUAY - RICE PRODUCTION - See PARAGUAY - CROPS

PARAGUAY - ROOT AND TUBER PRODUCTION - See PARAGUAY - CROPS

PARAGUAY - ROUNDWOOD PRODUCTION - See PARAGUAY - FORESTRY AND FOREST PRODUCTS

PARAGUAY - RUBBER PRODUCTION AND CONSUMPTION

M.E. Sharpe, 80 Business Park Drive, Armonk, New York 10504 (800) 541-6563; *The Illustrated Book of World Rankings.*

PARAGUAY - SAWNWOOD PRODUCTION - See PARAGUAY - FORESTRY AND FOREST PRODUCTS

PARAGUAY - SCIENTISTS, TECHNICIANS AND ENGINEERS

Statistical Office of the United Nations, Publishing Service, New York, New York 10017 (800) 253-9646; *Statistical Yearbook.*

U.C.L.A. Latin American Center Publications, University of California, Los Angeles, California 90024 (310) 825-6634; *Statistical Abstract of Latin America.*

PARAGUAY - SENIOR CITIZENS

M.E. Sharpe, 80 Business Park Drive, Armonk, New York 10504 (800) 541-6563; *The Illustrated Book of World Rankings.*

PARAGUAY - SHEEP - See PARAGUAY - LIVESTOCK AND POULTRY

PARAGUAY - SILVER PRODUCTION AND CONSUMPTION - See PAPUA NEW GUINEA - MINING AND MINERAL PRODUCTS

PARAGUAY - SOCIAL DATA

M.E. Sharpe, 80 Business Park Drive, Armonk, New York 10504 (800) 541-6563; *The Illustrated Book of World Rankings.*

Statistical Office of the United Nations, Publishing Service, New York, New York 10017 (800) 253-9646; *World Statistics Pocketbook.*

U.C.L.A. Latin American Center Publications, University of California, Los Angeles, California 90024 (310) 825-6634; *Statistical Abstract of Latin America.*

PARAGUAY - SOCIAL SECURITY

Inter-American Development Bank, 1300 New York Avenue, NW, Washington, D.C. 20577 (202) 623-1753; *Economic and Social Progress in Latin America.*

International Monetary Fund, 700 Nineteenth Street, NW, Washington, D.C. 20431 (202) 623-7000; *Government Finance Statistics Yearbook.*

Statistical Office of the United Nations, Publishing Service, New York, New York 10017 (800) 253-9646; *National Accounts Statistics.*

PARAGUAY - SOCIOECONOMIC DATA

Inter-American Development Bank, 1300 New York Avenue, NW, Washington, D.C. 20577 (202) 623-1753; *Economic and Social Progress in Latin America.*

U.C.L.A. Latin American Center Publications, University of California, Los Angeles, California 90024 (310) 825-6634; *Statistical Abstract of Latin America.*

PARAGUAY - SOYBEANS - See PARAGUAY - CROPS

PARAGUAY - STAMP TAXES AND DUTIES - See PARAGUAY - TAXATION

PARAGUAY - STATE BUDGET REVENUE AND EXPENDITURES

Euromonitor International, Inc., 122 South Michigan Avenue, Suite 1200, Chicago, Illinois 60603; *International Marketing Data and Statistics.*

Inter-American Development Bank, 1300 New York Avenue, NW, Washington, D.C. 20577 (202) 623-1753; *Economic and Social Progress in Latin America.*

PARAGUAY - STEEL - See PARAGUAY - MINING AND MINERAL PRODUCTS

PARAGUAY - STOCKS - COMMODITY - MARKET PRICE - INDEX

Food and Agricultural Organization of the United Nations (FAO) Via delle Terme di Caracalla, 00100 Rome, Italy (Telephone Number in U.S. (202) 653-2400); *The State of Food and Agriculture.*

PARAGUAY - SUGAR PRODUCTION AND CONSUMPTION - See PARAGUAY - CROPS

PARAGUAY - TAX REVENUE - See PARAGUAY - TAXATION

PARAGUAY - TAXATION

Europa Publications Limited, 18 Bedford Square, London, WC1B 3JN, England; *The Europa World Year Book.*

Inter-American Development Bank, 1300 New York Avenue, NW, Washington, D.C. 20577 (202) 623-1753; *Economic and Social Progress in Latin America.*

International Monetary Fund, 700 Nineteenth Street, NW, Washington, D.C. 20431 (202) 623-7000; *Government Finance Statistics Yearbook.*

International Road Federation, 2600 Virginia Avenue, NW.; *World Road Statistics.*

St. Martin's Press, Inc., 175 Fifth Avenue, New York, New York 10010 (800) 221-7945; *The Statesman's Year-Book.*

Statistical Office of the United Nations, Publishing Service, New York, New York 10017 (800) 253-9646; *Statistical Yearbook for Latin America and the Caribbean.*

The World Bank, 1818 H Street, NW, Washington, D.C. 20433 (202) 477-1234; *World Development Indicators.*

PARAGUAY - TELEGRAPH SERVICE

Statistical Office of the United Nations, Publishing Service, New York, New York

10017 (800) 253-9646; *Statistical Yearbook.*

PARAGUAY - TELEPHONES IN USE

American Telephone and Telegraph Company, 26 Parsippany Road, Whippany, New Jersey 07981 (800) 222-0300; *The World's Telephones.*

Central Intelligence Agency, Washington, D.C. 20505 (703) 482-1100, www.cia.gov; *The World Factbook.*

The Economist Intelligence Unit, 111 West 57th Street, New York, New York 10019 (800) 938-4685; *The New Latin America Market Atlas.*

Europa Publications Limited, 18 Bedford Square, London, WC1B 3JN, England; *The Europa World Year Book.*

St. Martin's Press, Inc., 175 Fifth Avenue, New York, New York 10010 (800) 221-7945; *The Statesman's Year-Book.*

Statistical Office of the United Nations, Publishing Service, New York, New York 10017 (800) 253-9646; *Statistical Yearbook;* and *World Statistics Pocketbook.*

PARAGUAY - TELEVISION BROADCASTING - See PARAGUAY - BROADCASTING

PARAGUAY - TEXTILE INDUSTRY

M.E. Sharpe, 80 Business Park Drive, Armonk, New York 10504 (800) 541-6563; *The Illustrated Book of World Rankings.*

Statistical Office of the United Nations, Publishing Service, New York, New York 10017 (800) 253-9646; *Statistical Yearbook.*

United Nations Conference on Trade and Development, Central Statistical Service, Palais des Nations, Geneva, Switzerland (Telephone in U.S. (800) 253-9646); *UNCTAD Commodity Yearbook.*

PARAGUAY - TIMBER EXPORTS - See PARAGUAY - FORESTRY AND FOREST PRODUCTS

PARAGUAY - TOBACCO EXPORTS

International Monetary Fund, 700 Nineteenth Street, NW, Washington, D.C. 20431 (202) 623-7000; *International Financial Statistics.*

PARAGUAY - TOBACCO PRODUCTION

M.E. Sharpe, 80 Business Park Drive, Armonk, New York 10504 (800) 541-6563; *The Illustrated Book of World Rankings.*

Statistical Office of the United Nations, Publishing Service, New York, New York 10017 (800) 253-9646; *Statistical Yearbook.*

U.C.L.A. Latin American Center Publications, University of California, Los Angeles, California 90024 (310) 825-6634; *Statistical Abstract of Latin America.*

PARAGUAY - TOURISM

The Economist Intelligence Unit, 111 West 57th Street, New York, New York 10019 (800) 938-4685; *The New Latin America Market Atlas.*

Euromonitor International, Inc., 122 South Michigan Avenue, Suite 1200, Chicago, Illinois 60603; *The World Economic Factbook;* and *World Marketing Data and Statistics.*

Europa Publications Limited, 18 Bedford Square, London, WC1B 3JN, England; *The Europa World Year Book.*

M.E. Sharpe, 80 Business Park Drive, Armonk, New York 10504 (800) 541-6563; *The Illustrated Book of World Rankings.*

Organization of American States (OAS), General Secretariat, Washington, D.C. 20006 (202) 458-3533; *Statistical Bulletin of the OAS.*

St. Martin's Press, Inc., 175 Fifth Avenue, New York, New York 10010 (800) 221-7945; *The Statesman's Year-Book.*

Statistical Office of the United Nations, Publishing Service, New York, New York 10017 (800) 253-9646; *Statistical Yearbook;* and *Statistical Yearbook for Latin America and the Caribbean.*

U.C.L.A. Latin American Center Publications, University of California, Los Angeles, California 90024 (310) 825-6634; *Statistical Abstract of Latin America.*

World Tourism Organization, Calle Capitan Haya 42, E-28020 Madrid, Spain; *Yearbook of Tourism Statistics.*

PARAGUAY - TRACTORS IN USE

The Economist Intelligence Unit, 111 West 57th Street, New York, New York 10019 (800) 938-4685; *The New Latin America Market Atlas.*

Statistical Office of the United Nations, Publishing Service, New York, New York 10017 (800) 253-9646; *Statistical Yearbook.*

PARAGUAY - TRADE - See PARAGUAY - FOREIGN TRADE

PARAGUAY - TRANSPORTATION AND COMMUNICATIONS

Central Intelligence Agency, Washington, D.C. 20505 (703) 482-1100, www.cia.gov; *The World Factbook.*

The Economist Intelligence Unit, 111 West 57th Street, New York, New York 10019 (800) 938-4685; *The New Latin America Market Atlas.*

Euromonitor International, Inc., 122 Michigan Avenue, Suite 1200, Chicago, Illinois 60603 (800) 577-EURO; *International Marketing Data and Statistics;* and *World Marketing Data and Statistics.*

Europa Publications Limited, 18 Bedford Square, London, WC1B 3JN, England; *The Europa World Year Book.*

Inter-American Development Bank, 1300 New York Avenue, NW, Washington, D.C. 20577 (202) 623-1753; *Economic and Social Progress in Latin America.*

M.E. Sharpe, 80 Business Park Drive, Armonk, New York 10504 (800) 541-6563; *The Illustrated Book of World Rankings.*

St. Martin's Press, Inc., 175 Fifth Avenue, New York, New York 10010 (800) 221-7945; *The Statesman's Year-Book.*

Statistical Office of the United Nations, Publishing Service, New York, New York 10017 (800) 253-9646; *Human Development Report;* and *Statistical Yearbook for Latin America and the Caribbean.*

U.C.L.A. Latin American Center Publications, University of California, Los Angeles, California 90024 (310) 825-6634; *Statistical Abstract of Latin America.*

PARAGUAY - TRAVEL FARES ABROAD

International Monetary Fund, 700 Nineteenth Street, NW, Washington, D.C. 20431 (202) 623-7000; *Government Finance Statistics Yearbook.*

PARAGUAY - TURKEYS - See PARAGUAY - LIVESTOCK AND POULTRY

PARAGUAY - UNEMPLOYMENT

Central Intelligence Agency, Washington, D.C. 20505 (703) 482-1100, www.cia.gov; *The World Factbook.*

The Economist Intelligence Unit, 111 West 57th Street, New York, New York 10019 (800) 938-4685; *The New Latin America Market Atlas.*

Euromonitor International, Inc., 122 Michigan Avenue, Suite 1200, Chicago, Illinois 60603 (800) 577-EURO; *International Marketing Data and Statistics.*

International Labour Office, I.L.O. Publications, 1828 L Street, NW., Suite 801, Washington, D.C. 20036 (301) 638-3152; *Yearbook of Labour Statistics.*

U.C.L.A. Latin American Center Publications, University of California, Los Angeles, California 90024 (310) 825-6634; *Statistical Abstract of Latin America.*

PARAGUAY - UTILITIES

U.C.L.A. Latin American Center Publications, University of California, Los Angeles, California 90024 (310) 825-6634; *Statistical Abstract of Latin America.*

PARAGUAY - VEGETABLE OIL EXPORTS

International Monetary Fund, 700 Nineteenth Street, NW, Washington, D.C. 20431 (202) 623-7000; *International Financial Statistics.*

PARAGUAY - VITAL STATISTICS

Euromonitor International, Inc., 122 Michigan Avenue, Suite 1200, Chicago, Illinois 60603 (800) 577-EURO; *International Marketing Data and Statistics.*

St. Martin's Press, Inc., 175 Fifth Avenue, New York, New York 10010 (800) 221-7945; *The Statesman's Year-Book.*

Statistical Office of the United Nations, Publishing Service, New York, New York 10017 (800) 253-9646; *Statistical Yearbook.*

World Health Organization, Office of Publications, 20 Avenue Appia, CH-1211 Geneva 27, Switzerland (Telephone Number in U.S. (518) 436-9686); *World Health Statistics Annual.*

PARAGUAY - WAGES

International Labour Office, I.L.O. Publications, 1828 L Street, NW., Suite 801, Washington, D.C. 20036 (301) 638-3152; *Yearbook of Labour Statistics.*

Organization of American States (OAS), General Secretariat, Washington, D.C. 20006 (202) 458-3533; *Statistical Bulletin of the OAS.*

U.C.L.A. Latin American Center Publications, University of California, Los Angeles, California 90024 (310) 825-6634; *Statistical Abstract of Latin America.*

PARAGUAY - WATERMELON PRODUCTION - See PARAGUAY - CROPS

PARAGUAY - WEATHER - See PARAGUAY - CLIMATE

PARAGUAY - WELFARE

Inter-American Development Bank, 1300 New York Avenue, NW, Washington, D.C. 20577 (202) 623-1753; *Economic and Social Progress in Latin America.*

International Monetary Fund, 700 Nineteenth Street, NW, Washington, D.C. 20431 (202) 623-7000; *Government Finance Statistics Yearbook.*

PARAGUAY - WHEAT PRODUCTION AND PRICES - See PARAGUAY - CROPS

PARAGUAY - WHOLESALE PRICES

Inter-American Development Bank, 1300 New York Avenue, NW, Washington, D.C. 20577 (202) 623-1753; *Economic and Social Progress in Latin America.*

International Monetary Fund, 700 Nineteenth Street, NW, Washington, D.C. 20431 (202) 623-7000; *International Financial Statistics.*

Organization of American States (OAS), General Secretariat, Washington, D.C. 20006 (202) 458-3533; *Statistical Bulletin of the OAS.*

PARAGUAY - WHOLESALE TRADE

Inter-American Development Bank, 1300 New York Avenue, NW, Washington, D.C. 20577 (202) 623-1753; *Economic and Social Progress in Latin America.*

PARAGUAY - WINE PRODUCTION - See PARAGUAY - BEVERAGES

PARAGUAY - WOOD PULP PRODUCTION - See PARAGUAY - FORESTRY AND FOREST PRODUCTS

PARAGUAY - WOOL PRODUCTION - See PARAGUAY - TEXTILE INDUSTRY

PARAGUAY - YARN PRODUCTION - See PARAGUAY - TEXTILE INDUSTRY

PARIS CAC-40 STOCK MARKET INDEX

Global Financial Data, 784 Fremont Villas, Los Angeles, California 90042 (310) 642-4659; unpublished data.

PARKS

National Association of State Park Directors, 126 Mill Branch Road, Tallahassee, Florida 32312 (904) 893-4959; *Annual Information Exchange.*

U.S. Department of the Interior, National Park Service, C Street between Eighteenth and Nineteenth Streets, NW, Washington, D.C. 20240 (202) 208-6843, www.nps.gov; *National Park Statistical Abstract;* and unpublished data.

PARKS - FINANCES

National Association of State Park Directors, 126 Mill Branch road, Tallahassee, Florida 32312 (904) 893-4959; *Annual Information Exchange.*

U.S. Department of the Interior, National Park Service, C Street between Eighteenth and Nineteenth Streets, NW, Washington, D.C. 20240 (202) 208-6843, www.nps.gov; *National Park Statistical Abstract;* and unpublished data.

PARKS - GOVERNMENT EMPLOYMENT AND PAYROLLS

U.S. Department of Commerce, Bureau of the Census, Washington, D.C. 20233 (301) 457-4100, www.census.gov; Internet site: http://www.census.gov/pub/govs/www/apes.html.

PARKS - NATIONAL

U.S. Department of the Interior, National Park Service, C Street between Eighteenth and Nineteenth Streets, NW, Washington, D.C. 20240 (202) 208-6843, www.nps.gov; *National Park Statistical Abstract;* and unpublished data.

PARKS - STATE

National Association of State Park Directors, 126 Mill Branch Road, Tallahassee, Florida 32312 (904) 893-4959; *Annual Information Exchange.*

PAROLEES - See also CORRECTIONAL INSTITUTIONS and PRISONS AND PRISONERS

U.S. Department of Justice, Bureau of Justice Statistics, 810 Seventh Street, NW, 2nd Floor, Washington, D.C. 20531 (800) 732-3277, www.ojp.usdoj.gov/bjs; *Correctional Populations in the United States.*

PARTIES, POLITICAL - See POLITICAL PARTIES

PARTNERSHIPS - ESTABLISHMENTS AND FINANCES

U.S. Department of the Treasury, Internal Revenue Service, 1111 Constitution Avenue, NW, Washington, D.C. 20224 (202) 874-0410, www.irs.ustreas.gov; *Statistics of Income; Statistics of Income Bulletin;* and unpublished data.

PASSENGER TRANSIT INDUSTRY - See also PASSENGERS

PASSENGER TRANSIT INDUSTRY - EARNINGS

U.S. Department of Labor, Bureau of Labor Statistics, Two Massachusetts Avenue, NE, Washington, D.C. 20212 (202) 691-5200, www.stats.bls.gov; *Employment and Earnings;* Bulletins 2445 and 2481; and Internet Site: http://stats.bls.gov/ceshome.htm.

PASSENGER TRANSIT INDUSTRY -

EMPLOYEES

U.S. Department of Labor, Bureau of Labor Statistics, Two Massachusetts Avenue, NE, Washington, D.C. 20212 (202) 691-5200, www.stats.bls.gov; *Employment and Earnings;* Bulletins 2445 and 2481; and Internet site: http://stats.bls.gov/ceshome.htm.

PASSENGER TRANSIT INDUSTRY - OCCUPATIONAL SAFETY

U.S. Department of Labor, Bureau of Labor Statistics, Two Massachusetts Avenue, NE, Washington, D.C. 20212 (202) 691-5200, www.stats.bls.gov; *Occupational Injuries and Illnesses in the United States by Industry.*

PASSENGER TRANSIT INDUSTRY - PRODUCTIVITY

U.S. Department of Labor, Bureau of Labor Statistics, Two Massachusetts Avenue, NE, Washington, D.C. 20212 (202) 691-5200, www.stats.bls.gov; Internet site http://stats.bls.gov/iprhome.htm.

PASSENGERS - See also PASSENGER TRANSIT INDUSTRY and Various Transportation Modes

PASSENGERS - ARRIVING FROM OVERSEAS

U.S. Department of Commerce, International Trade Administration, Fourteenth Street between Constitution Avenue and E Street, NW, Washington, D.C. 20230 (202) 482-2185, www.ita.doc.gov; Internet site http://www.tinet.ita.doc.gov.

U.S. Department of Justice, Immigration and Naturalization Service, 425 I Street, NW, Washington, D.C. 20536 (202) 305-1613, www.ins.usdoj.gov; *Statistical Yearbook.*

PASSENGERS - CARRIER OPERATION - SUMMARY

Air Transport Association of America, 1301 Pennsylvania, Suite 1100, Washington, D.C. 20004-7017 (202) 626-4000; *Air Transport;* and *Air Transport, Facts and Figures.*

American Public Transportation Association, 1201 New York Avenue, NW, Suite 400 Washington, D.C. 20005 (202) 898-4000; *Transit Fact Book;* and Internet site: http://www.apta.com/pubs/stats/index.htm.

Association of American Railroads, American Railroads Building, 50 F Street, NW, Washington, D.C. 20001 (202) 639-2100; *Railroad Facts, Statistics of Railroads of Class I;* and *Analysis of Class I Railroads.*

U.S. Department of Transportation, Bureau of Transportation Statistics, 400 Seventh Street, SW, Washington, D.C. 20590 (800) 853-1351, www.bts.gov: *Selected Earnings Data, Class I Motor Carriers of Passengers.*

U.S. Interstate Commerce Commission, Twelfth Street and Constitution Avenue, NW, Washington, D.C. 20433 (202) 275-7119; *Transport Statistics in the United States.*

PASSENGERS - CARRIER OPERATION SUMMARY - AIR

Air Transport Association of America, 1301 Pennsylvania, Suite 1100, Washington, D.C. 20004-7017 (202) 626-4000; *Air Transport;* and *Air Transport, Facts and Figures.*

Regional Airline Association, 2025 M Street, NW, Suite 800, Washington, D.C. 20036 (202) 367-1170; *Annual Report of the Regional Airline Industry.*

PASSENGERS - CARRIER OPERATION SUMMARY - RAIL

Association of American Railroads, American Railroads Building, 50 F Street, NW, Washington, D.C. 20001 (202) 639-2100; *Railroad Facts; Statistics of Railroads of Class I;* and *Analysis of Class I Railroads.*

PASSENGERS - OUTLAYS - BY TYPE OF TRANSPORT

Eno Transportation Foundation, One Farragut Square, South, Suite 500, Washington, D.C. 20006 (202) 879-4700; *Transportation in America.*

PASSENGERS - PASSENGER TRAFFIC - VOLUME

Eno Transportation Foundation, One Farragut Square, South, Suite 500, Washington, D.C. 20006 (202) 879-4700; *Transportation in America.*

PASSENGERS - RAILROADS

Association of American Railroads, American Railroads Building, 50 F Street, NW Washington, D.C. 20001 (202) 639-2100; *Railroad Facts; Statistics of Railroads of Class I;* and *Analysis of Class I Railroads.*

PATENTS AND TRADEMARKS

U.S. Department of Commerce, Patent and Trademark Office, 2011 Crystal Drive, Arlington, Virginia 22202 (703) 305-8341, www.uspto.gov; *Commissioner of Patents and Trademarks Annual Report; Patenting Trends in the United States, State Country Report;* and *Technology Assessment and Forecast Database.*

PATHOLOGISTS

American Medical Association, 515 North State Street, Chicago, Illinois 60610 (312) 464-5000; *Physician Characteristics and Distribution in the United States.*

PEACHES

U.S. Department of Agriculture, Economic Research Service, 1800 M Street, NW, Washington, D.C. 20036 (202) 694-5050, www.ers.usda.gov; *Food Consumption, Prices, and Expenditures;* and *Agricultural Outlook.*

U.S. Department of Agriculture, National Agricultural Statistics Service, Fourteenth Street and Independence Avenue, SW, Washington, D.C. 20250 (800) 727-9540, www.usda.gov/nass; *Noncitrus Fruits and Nuts.*

PEANUT BUTTER

U.S. Department of Labor, Bureau of Labor Statistics, 2 Massachusetts Avenue, NE, Washington, D.C. 20212 (202) 691-5200, www.stats.bls.gov; *CPI Detailed Report.*

PEANUTS

U.S. Department of Agriculture, Economic Research Service, 1800 M Street, NW, Washington, D.C. 20036 (202) 694-5050, www.ers.usda.gov; *Food Consumption, Prices and Expenditures; Farm Business Economic Report;* and *Agricultural Outlook.*

PEARS

U.S. Department of Agriculture, Economic Research Service, 1800 M Street, NW, Washington, D.C. 20036 (202) 694-5050, www.ers.usda.gov; *Food Consumption, Prices, and Expenditures;* and *Farm Business Economic Report.*

U.S. Department of Agriculture, National Agricultural Statistics Service, Fourteenth Street and Independence Avenue, SW, Washington, D.C. 20250 (800) 727-9540, www.usda.gov/nass; *Noncitrus Fruits and Nuts.*

U.S. Department of Labor, Bureau of Labor Statistics, Two Massachusetts Avenue, NE, Washington, D.C. 20212 (202) 691-5200, www.stats.bls.gov; *CPI Detailed Report.*

PEAS

U.S. Department of Agriculture, National Agricultural Statistics Service, Fourteenth Street and Independence Avenue, SW, Washington, D.C. 20250 (800) 727-9540, www.usda.gov/nass; *Vegetables;* and *Agricultural Statistics.*

PEAT

U.S. Department of the Interior, Geological Survey, Office of Minerals Information, 12201 Sunrise Valley Drive, Reston, Virginia 22092 (703) 648-4000, www.minerals.usgs.gov; *Annual Reports;* and *Mineral Commodity Summaries.*

PECANS

U.S. Department of Agriculture, National Agricultural Statistics Service, Fourteenth Street and Independence Avenue, SW, Washington, D.C. 20250 (800) 727-9540, www.usda.gov/nass; *Farm Business Economic Report;* and *Noncitrus Fruit and Nuts.*

PEDIATRICIANS - See also PHYSICIANS

American Medical Association, 515 North State Street, Chicago, Illinois 60610 (312) 464-5000; *Physician Characteristics and Distribution in the United States;* and *Socioeconomic Characteristics of Medical Practice.*

PENNSYLVANIA - See also STATE DATA (FOR INDIVIDUAL STATES)

Pennsylvania - Primary Statistics Source

Pennsylvania State Data Center, Pennsylvania State University at Harrisburg, 777 West Harrisburg Pike, Middletown, Pennsylvania 15057 (717) 948-6336; *Pennsylvania Statistical Abstract.*

Pennsylvania - State Data Centers

Pennsylvania State Data Center, Institute of State and Regional Affairs, Pennsylvania State University at Harrisburg, 777 West Harrisburg Pike, Middletown, Pennsylvania 17057-4898, Diane Shoop (717) 948-6336.

Pennsylvania State Library, Forum Building, Harrisburg, Pennsylvania 17105, Mr. John Gerswindt (717) 787-2327.

State Capitol Office, Pennsylvania State Data Center, B57 Main Capital Building, Harrisburg, Pennsylvania 17120-0001, (717) 772-2710.

PENS, PENCILS, OFFICE AND ART SUPPLIES - MANUFACTURING - EARNINGS

U.S. Department of Commerce, Bureau of the Census, Washington, D.C. 20233 (301) 457-4100, www.census.gov; *Census of Manufactures;* and *Annual Survey of Manufactures.*

U.S. Department of Labor, Bureau of Labor Statistics, Two Massachusetts Avenue, NE, Washington, D.C. 20212 (202) 691-5200, www.stats.bls.gov; *Employment and Earnings*, and Internet site: http://stats.bls.gov/ceshome.htm.

PENS, PENCILS, OFFICE AND ART SUPPLIES - MANUFACTURING - EMPLOYEES

U.S. Department of Commerce, Bureau of the Census, Washington, D.C. 20233 (301) 457-4100, www.census.gov; *Census of Manufactures;* and *Annual Survey of Manufactures.*

U.S. Department of Labor, Bureau of Labor Statistics, Two Massachusetts Avenue, NE, Washington, D.C. 20212 (202) 691-5200, www.stats.bls.gov; *Employment and Earnings;* and Internet site: http://stats.bls/gov/ceshome.htm.

PENS, PENCILS, OFFICE AND ART SUPPLIES - MANUFACTURING - ESTABLISHMENTS

U.S. Department of Commerce, Bureau of the Census, Washington, D.C. 20233 (301) 457-4100, www.census.gov; *Census of Manufactures,* and *Annual Survey of Manufactures.*

PENS, PENCILS, OFFICE AND ART SUPPLIES - MANUFACTURING - SALES, SHIPMENTS, RECEIPTS

U.S. Department of Commerce, Bureau of the Census, Washington, D.C. 20233 (301) 457-4100, www.census.gov; *Census of Manufactures;* and *Annual Survey of Manufactures.*

PENS, PENCILS, OFFICE AND ART SUPPLIES - MANUFACTURING - VALUE ADDED

U.S. Department of Commerce, Bureau of the Census, Washington, D.C. 20233 (301) 457-4100, www.census.gov; *Census of Manufactures;* and *Annual Survey of Manufactures.*

PENSIONS AND RETIREMENT BENEFITS - See also SOCIAL INSURANCE

PENSIONS AND RETIREMENT BENEFITS - EXPENDITURES

Employee Benefit Research Institute, 2121 K Street, NW, Suite 600, Washington, D.C. 20037 (202) 659-0670; *EBRI Databook on Employee Benefits.*

U.S. Department of Labor, Bureau of Labor Statistics, Two Massachusetts Avenue, NE, Washington, D.C. 20212 (202) 691-5200, www.stats.bls.gov; *Consumer Expenditures in 1997.*

PENSION AND RETIREMENT BENEFITS - FAMILIES RECEIVING

U.S. Department of Commerce, Bureau of the Census, Washington, D.C. 20233 (301) 457-4100, www.census.gov; Internet site: http://ferret.bls.gov/macro/031998/faminc/09000.htm.

PENSIONS AND RETIREMENT BENEFITS - FUNDS - FLOW OF FUNDS

Board of Governors of the Federal Reserve System, Twentieth Street and Constitution Avenue, NW, Washington, D.C. 20551 (202) 452-3000, www.bog.frb.fed.us; *Flow of Funds Accounts.*

PENSIONS AND RETIREMENT BENEFITS - GOVERNMENT EMPLOYEES

Employee Benefit Research Institute, 2121 K Street, NW, Suite 600, Washington, D.C. 20037 (202) 659-0670; *EBRI Databook on Employee Benefits.*

Social Security Administration, 6400 Security Boulevard, Baltimore, Maryland 21235 (800) 772-1213, www.ssa.gov; *Social Security Bulletin;* and unpublished data.

U.S. Department of Commerce, Bureau of the Census, Washington, D.C. 20233 (301) 457-4100, www.census.gov; *Finances of Employee - Retirement Systems of State and Local Governments.*

U.S. Office of Personnel Management, 1900 E Street, NW, Washington, D.C. 20415 (202) 606-1800; *Civil Service Retirement and Disability Trust Fund Annual Report.*

PENSIONS AND RETIREMENT BENEFITS - PENSION PLANS

Access Research, Inc., 8 Griffin Road North, Windsor, Connecticut 06095 (860) 688-8821; *Marketplace Update.*

Board of Governors of the Federal Reserve System, 20th Street and Constitution Avenue, NW, Washington, D.C. 20551 (202) 452-3000, www.bog.frb.fed.us, www.bog.frb.fed.us; *Flow of Funds Accounts.*

Employee Benefit Research Institute, 2121 K Street, NW, Suite 600, Washington, D.C. 20037 (202) 659-0670; *EBRI Databook on Employee Benefits.*

Investment Company Institute, 1401 H Street, NW, Washington, D.C. 20005 (202) 326-5800; *Fundamentals, Investment Company Institute Research in Brief; Retirement Assets Held in Mutual Funds by Type of Plan, Mutual Fund Fact Book;* and Internet site: http://www.ici.org/retirement/retirementstatshist.html.

U.S. Department of Commerce, Bureau of the Census, Washington, D.C. 20233 (301) 457-4100, www.census.gov; unpublished data.

U.S. Department of Labor, Bureau of Labor Statistics, Two Massachusetts Avenue, NE, Washington, D.C. 20212 (202) 691-5200, www.stats.bls.gov; *News.*

U.S. Department of Labor, Pension and Welfare Benefits Administration, 200 Constitution Avenue, NW, Washington, D.C. 20210 (202) 219-8921; *Private Pension Plan Bulletin.*

PENSIONS AND RETIREMENT BENEFITS - RAILROAD

Social Security Administration, 6400 Security Boulevard, Baltimore, Maryland 21235 (800) 772-1213, www.ssa.gov; *Social Security Bulletin.*

U.S. Department of Commerce, Bureau of the Census, Washington, D.C. 20233 (301) 457-4100, www.census.gov; Internet site: http://ferret.bls.census.gov/macro/031998/faminc/09000.htm.

PENSIONS AND RETIREMENT BENEFITS - VETERANS

U.S. Department of Commerce, Bureau of the Census, Washington, D.C. 20233 (301) 457-4100, www.census.gov; Internet site: http://ferret.bls.census.gov/macro/031998/faminc/09000.htm.

U.S. Department of Veterans Affairs, Management Sciences Service, 810 Vermont Avenue, NW, Washington, D.C. 20420 (202) 273-5400, www.va.gov; *Annual Report of the Secretary of Veterans Affairs.*

PEPPERS

U.S. Department of Agriculture, Economic Research Service, 1800 M Street, NW, Washington, D.C. 20036 (202) 694-5050, www.ers.usda.gov; *Farm Business Economic Report*; and *Food, Consumption, Prices, and Expenditures.*

U.S. Department of Agriculture, National Agricultural Statistics Service, Fourteenth Street and Independence Avenue, SW, Washington, D.C. 20250 (800) 727-9540, www.usda.gov/nass; *Vegetables;* and *Agricultural Outlook.*

U.S. Department of Labor, Bureau of Labor Statistics, Two Massachusetts Avenue, NE, Washington, D.C. 20212 (202) 691-5200, www.stats.bls.gov; *CPI Detailed Report*; and *Monthly Labor Review.*

PERCH

U.S. Department of Commerce, Bureau of Economic Analysis, Fourteenth Street between Constitution Avenue and E Street, NW, Washington, D.C. 20230 (202) 606-9900, www.bea.doc.gov; *Survey of Current Business*.

U.S. Department of Commerce, National Oceanic and Atmospheric Administration, National Marine Fisheries Service, 1315 East-West Highway, Silver Spring, Maryland 20910 (301) 713-2239, www.nmfs.noaa.gov; *Fisheries of the United States*.

PERFORMING ARTS

American Symphony Orchestra League, 33 West 60th Street, 5th Floor, New York, New York 10023 (212) 262-5161.

League of American Theaters and Producers, Inc., 266 West 47th Street, New York, New York 10036 (212) 764-1122.

Opera America, 1156 15th Street, NW, Suite 810, Washington, D.C. 20005 (202) 293-4466; *Opera America - Profile*.

Theatre Communications Group, 355 Lexington Avenue, New York, New York 10017 (212) 697-5230.

PERIODICALS - See PRINTING AND PUBLISHING INDUSTRIES

PERLITE

U.S. Department of the Interior, Geological Survey, Office of Minerals Information, 12201 Sunrise Valley Drive, Reston, Virginia 22092 (703) 648-4000, www.minerals.usgs.gov; *Annual Reports;* and *Mineral Commodity Summaries*.

PERSONAL CARE PRICE INDEXES

U.S. Department of Labor Bureau of Labor Statistics, Two Massachusetts Avenue, NE, Washington, D.C. 20212 (202) 691-5200, www.stats.bls.gov; *Monthly Labor Review*; and *CPI Detailed Report*.

PERSONAL COMPUTERS - See COMPUTERS

PERSONAL CONSUMPTION EXPENDITURES

U.S. Department of Commerce, Bureau of Economic Analysis, Fourteenth Street between Constitution Avenue and E Street, NW, Washington, D.C. 20230 (202) 606-9900, www.bea.doc.gov; *The National Income and Product Accounts of the United States;* and *Survey of Current Business*.

PERSONAL CONSUMPTION EXPENDITURES - CHAIN-TYPE PRICE INDEX

U.S. Department of Commerce, Bureau of Economic Analysis, Fourteenth Street

between Constitution Avenue and E Street, NW, Washington, D.C. 20230 (202) 606-9900, www.bea.doc.gov; *National Income and Product Accounts of the United States;* and *Survey of Current Business*.

PERSONAL CONSUMPTION EXPENDITURES - FOOD AND BEVERAGES - FOREIGN COUNTRIES

U.S. Department of Agriculture, Economic Research Service, 1800 M Street, NW, Washington, D.C. 20036 (202) 694-5050, www.ers.usda.gov; *Food Consumption, Prices, and Expenditures*.

PERSONAL CONSUMPTION EXPENDITURES - RECREATION

U.S. Department of Commerce, Bureau of Economic Analysis, Fourteenth Street between Constitution Avenue and E Street, NW, Washington, D.C. 20230 (202) 606-9900, www.bea.doc.gov; *The National Income and Product Accounts of the United States;* and *Survey of Current Business*.

PERSONAL HEALTH CARE - EXPENDITURES

U.S. Department of Health and Human Services, Health Care Financing Administration, 200 Independence Avenue, SW, Washington, D.C. 20201 (202) 690-6145, www.hcfa.gov; *Health Care Financing Review*.

PERSONAL HEALTH CARE - PRACTICES

U.S. Department of Health and Human Services, Substance Abuse and Mental Health Services Administration, 5600 Fishers Lane, Rockville, Maryland 20857 (800) 729-6686, www.samhsa.gov; *National Household Survey on Drug Abuse*.

U.S. Department of Health and Human Services, National Center for Health Statistics, 3700 East-West Highway, Hyattsville, Maryland 20782 (301) 436-8500, www.cdc.gov/nchs; *Health, United States*.

PERSONAL INCOME

U.S. Department of Commerce, Bureau of Economic Analysis, Fourteenth Street between Constitution Avenue and E Street, NW, Washington, D.C. 20230 (202) 606-9900, www.bea.doc.gov; *The National Income and Product Accounts of the United States; Survey of Current Business;* and unpublished data.

PERSONAL SAVINGS

Board of Governors of the Federal Reserve System, Twentieth Street and Constitution Avenue, NW, Washington, D.C. 20551 (202) 452-3000, www.bog.frb.fed.us; *Flow of Funds Accounts*.

U.S. Department of Commerce, Bureau of Economic Analysis, Fourteenth Street between Constitution Avenue and E Street, NW, Washington, D.C. 20230 (202) 606-9900, www.bea.doc.gov; *The National Income and Product Accounts of the United States;* and *Survey of Current Business*.

PERSONAL SERVICES INDUSTRY - EARNINGS

U.S. Department of Commerce, Bureau of the Census, Washington, D.C. 20233 (301) 457-4100, www.census.gov; *County Business Patterns; 1997 Economic Census;* and *Census of Service Industries*.

U.S. Department of Labor, Bureau of Labor Statistics, Two Massachusetts Avenue, NE, Washington, D.C. 20212 (202) 691-5200, www.stats.bls.gov; *Employment and Earnings;* Bulletins 2445 and 2481; and Internet site: http://www.stats.bls.gov/ceshome.htm.

PERSONAL SERVICES INDUSTRY - EMPLOYEES

U.S. Department of Commerce, Bureau of the Census, Washington, D.C. 20233 (301) 457-4100, www.census.gov; *County Business Patterns; 1997 Economic Census;* and *Census of Service Industries*.

U.S. Department of Labor, Bureau of Labor Statistics, Two Massachusetts Avenue, NE, Washington, D.C. 20212 (202) 691-5200, www.stats.bls.gov; *Employment and Earnings; Monthly Labor Review*; unpublished data; and Internet site: http://stats.bls.gov/ceshome.htm.

PERSONAL SERVICES INDUSTRY - ESTABLISHMENTS

U.S. Department of Commerce, Bureau of the Census, Washington, D.C. 20233 (301) 457-4100, www.census.gov; *Census of Service Industries; 1997 Economic Census;* and *County Business Patterns*.

PERSONAL SERVICES INDUSTRY - GROSS DOMESTIC PRODUCT

U.S. Department of Commerce, Bureau of Economic Analysis, Fourteenth Street between Constitution Avenue and E Streets, NW, Washington, D.C. 20230 (202) 606-9900, www.bea.doc.gov; *Survey of Current Business*.

PERSONAL SERVICES INDUSTRY - OCCUPATIONAL SAFETY

U.S. Department of Labor, Bureau of Labor Statistics, Two Massachusetts Avenue, NE, Washington, D.C. 20212 (202) 691-5200, www.stats.bls.gov; *Occupational Injuries and Illnesses in the United States by Industry*.

PERSONAL SERVICES INDUSTRY - PRODUCTIVITY

U.S. Department of Labor, Bureau of Labor Statistics, Two Massachusetts Avenue, NE, Washington, D.C. 20212 (202) 691-5200, www.stats.bls.gov; Internet sites http://stats.bls.gov/iprhome.htm.

PERSONAL SERVICES INDUSTRY - RECEIPTS

U.S. Department of Commerce, Bureau of the Census, Washington, D.C. 20233 (301) 457-4100, www.census.gov; *Current Business Reports, Service Annual Survey; Census of Service Industries;* and unpublished data.

PERSONNEL SUPPLY SERVICES INDUSTRY - EARNINGS

U.S. Department of Commerce, Bureau of the Census, Washington, D.C. 20233 (301) 457-4100, www.census.gov; *Census of Service Industries.*

U.S. Department of Labor, Bureau of Labor Statistics, Two Massachusetts Avenue, NE, Washington, D.C. 20212 (202) 691-5200, www.stats.bls.gov; *Employment and Earnings;* and Internet site: http://stats.bls.gov/ceshome.htm.

PERSONNEL SUPPLY SERVICES INDUSTRY - EMPLOYEES

U.S. Department of Commerce, Bureau of the Census, Washington, D.C. 20233 (301) 457-4100, www.census.gov; *Census of Service Industries.*

U.S. Department of Labor, Bureau of Labor Statistics, Two Massachusetts Avenue, NE, Washington, D.C. 20212 (202) 691-5200, www.stats.bls.gov; *Employment and Earnings, Monthly Labor Review;* unpublished data; and Internet site: http://stats.bls.gov/ceshome.htm.

PERSONNEL SUPPLY SERVICES INDUSTRY - ESTABLISHMENTS

U.S. Department of Commerce, Bureau of the Census, Washington, D.C. 20233 (301) 457-4100, www.census.gov; *Census of Service Industries.*

PERSONNEL SUPPLY SERVICES INDUSTRY - RECEIPTS

U.S. Department of Commerce, Bureau of the Census, Washington, D.C. 20233 (301) 457-4100, www.census.gov; *Census of Service Industries; Current Business Reports; Service Annual Survey;* and unpublished data.

PERTUSSIS

U.S. Department of Health and Human Services, Centers for Disease Control and Prevention, 1600 Clifton Road, NE, Atlanta, Georgia 30333 (800) 311-3435, www.cdc.gov; *Summary of Notifiable Diseases, United States;* and *Morbidity and Mortality Weekly Report.*

Peru - National Statistical Office

Instituto Nacional de Estadistica, Avenida 28 de Julio 1056, Lima 1, Peru.

Peru - Primary Statistics Source

Direccion General de Estadistica y Censos, Instituto Nacional de Estadistica, Avenida 28 de Julio 1056, Lima 1, Peru; *Anuario estadistico del Peru (Statistical Yearbook of Peru); Compendio estadistico;* and *Informe estadistico.*

PERU - AGRICULTURE

The Economist Intelligence Unit, 111 West 57th Street, New York, New York 10019 (800) 938-4685; *The New Latin America Market Atlas;* and *Peru Country Report.*

Euromonitor International, Inc., 122 Michigan Avenue, Suite 1200, Chicago, Illinois 60603 (800) 577-EURO; *International Marketing Data and Statistics; World Marketing Data and Statistics;* and *The World Economic Factbook.*

Europa Publications Limited, 18 Bedford Square, London, WC1B 3JN, England; *The Europa World Year Book.*

Food and Agricultural Organization of the United Nations (FAO) Via delle Terme di Caracalla, 00100 Rome, Italy (Telephone Number in U.S. (202) 653-2400); *Production Yearbook;* and *The State of Food and Agriculture;* and *Trade Yearbook.*

Inter-American Development Bank, 1300 New York Avenue, NW, Washington, D.C. 20577 (202) 623-1753; *Economic and Social Progress in Latin America.*

M.E. Sharpe, 80 Business Park Drive, Armonk, New York 10504 (800) 541-6563; *The Illustrated Book of World Rankings.*

St. Martin's Press, Inc., 175 Fifth Avenue, New York, New York 10010 (800) 221-7945; *The Statesman's Year-Book.*

Statistical Office of the United Nations, Publishing Service, New York, New York 10017 (800) 253-9646; *Statistical Yearbook;* and *Statistical Yearbook for Latin America and the Caribbean.*

U.C.L.A. Latin American Center Publications, University of California, Los Angeles, California 90024 (310) 825-6634; *Statistical Abstract of Latin America.*

United Nations Conference on Trade and Development, Central Statistical Service, Palais des Nations, Geneva, Switzerland (Telephone in U.S. (800) 253-9646); *UNCTAD Commodity Yearbook.*

The World Bank, 1818 H Street, NW, Washington, D.C. 20433 (202) 477-1234; *World Development Indicators.*

PERU - AIRLINE SERVICE

The Economist Intelligence Unit, 111 West 57th Street, New York, New York 10019 (800) 938-4685; *The New Latin America Market Atlas.*

Europa Publications Limited, 18 Bedford Square, London, WC1B 3JN, England; *The Europa World Year Book.*

International Civil Aviation Organization, 999 University Street, Montreal, Quebec, Canada H3C 5H7 (514) 954-8219; *Civil Aviation Statistics of the World.*

M.E. Sharpe, 80 Business Park Drive, Armonk, New York 10504 (800) 541-6563; *The Illustrated Book of World Rankings.*

St. Martin's Press, Inc., 175 Fifth Avenue, New York, New York 10010 (800) 221-7945; *The Statesman's Year-Book.*

Statistical Office of the United Nations, Publishing Service, New York, New York 10017 (800) 253-9646; *Statistical Yearbook.*

PERU - AIRPORTS

Central Intelligence Agency, Washington, D.C. 20505 (703) 482-1100, www.cia.gov; *The World Factbook.*

PERU - ALUMINUM PRODUCTION AND CONSUMPTION - See PERU - MINING AND MINERAL PRODUCTS

PERU - ANIMAL FEEDINGSTUFFS OF AQUATIC ANIMAL ORIGIN

Statistical Office of the United Nations, Publishing Service, New York, New York 10017 (800) 253-9646; *Statistical Yearbook.*

PERU - ANIMAL HEALTH

Food and Agricultural Organization of the United Nations (FAO), Via delle Terme di Caracalla, 00100 Rome, Italy (Telephone Number in U.S. (202) 653-2400); *Animal Health Yearbook.*

PERU - ANTIMONY AND ANTIMONY ORE PRODUCTION AND CONSUMPTION - See

PERU - MINING AND MINERAL PRODUCTS

PERU - AREA AND DENSITY OF POPULATION

Central Intelligence Agency, Washington, D.C. 20505 (703) 482-1100, www.cia.gov; *The World Factbook*.

Euromonitor International, Inc., 122 Michigan Avenue, Suite 1200, Chicago, Illinois 60603 (800) 577-EURO; *International Marketing Data and Statistics*.

Europa Publications Limited, 18 Bedford Square, London, WC1B 3JN, England; *The Europa World Year Book*.

Food and Agricultural Organization of the United Nations (FAO) Via delle Terme di Caracalla, 00100 Rome, Italy (Telephone Number in U.S. (202) 653-2400); *The State of Food and Agriculture*.

Inter-American Development Bank, 1300 New York Avenue, NW, Washington, D.C. 20577 (202) 623-1753; *Economic and Social Progress in Latin America*.

M.E. Sharpe, 80 Business Park Drive, Armonk, New York 10504 (800) 541-6563; *The Illustrated Book of World Rankings*.

St. Martin's Press, Inc., 175 Fifth Avenue, New York, New York 10010 (800) 221-7945; *The Statesman's Year-Book*.

Statistical Office of the United Nations, Publishing Service, New York, New York 10017 (800) 253-9646; *Statistical Yearbook*.

United Nations Educational, Scientific and Cultural Organization (UNESCO), 7 Place de Fontenoy, F-75700 Paris, France (Telephone Number in U.S. (212) 963-5981); *Statistical Yearbook*.

The World Bank, 1818 H Street, NW, Washington, D.C. 20433 (202) 477-1234; *World Development Report*.

PERU - ARMS EXPORTS AND IMPORTS - See PERU - MILITARY

PERU - ARSENIC PRODUCTION AND CONSUMPTION - See PERU - MINING AND MINERAL PRODUCTS

PERU - BALANCE OF PAYMENTS

The Economist Intelligence Unit, 111 West 57th Street, New York, New York 10019 (800) 938-4685; *The New Latin America Market Atlas;* and *The World Market Atlas*.

Europa Publications Limited, 18 Bedford Square, London, WC1B 3JN, England; *The Europa World Year Book*.

Inter-American Development Bank, 1300 New York Avenue, NW, Washington, D.C. 20577 (202) 623-1753; *Economic and Social Progress in Latin America*.

International Monetary Fund, 700 Nineteenth Street, NW, Washington, D.C. 20431 (202) 623-7000; *Balance of Payments Yearbook;* and *International Financial Statistics*.

Organization of American States (OAS), General Secretariat, Washington, D.C. 20006 (202) 458-3533; *Statistical Bulletin of the OAS*.

Statistical Office of the United Nations, Publishing Service, New York, New York 10017 (800) 253-9646; *Economic Survey of Latin America and the Caribbean;* and *Statistical Yearbook for Latin America and the Caribbean*.

U.C.L.A. Latin American Center Publications, University of California, Los Angeles, California 90024 (310) 825-6634; *Statistical Abstract of Latin America*.

United Nations Conference on Trade and Development (UNCTAD), New York, New York 10017 (800) 253-9646; *Handbook of International Trade and Development Statistics*.

The World Bank, 1818 H Street, NW, Washington, D.C. 20433 (202) 477-1234; *World Development Report;* and *World Development Indicators*.

PERU - BANANA PRODUCTION - See PERU - CROPS

PERU - BANKING

Euromonitor International, Inc., 122 South Michigan Avenue, Suite 1200, Chicago, Illinois 60603 (800) 577-EURO; *World Marketing Data and Statistics*.

Europa Publications Limited, 18 Bedford Square, London, WC1B 3JN, England; *The Europa World Year Book*.

Inter-American Development Bank, 1300 New York Avenue, NW, Washington, D.C. 20577 (202) 623-1753; *Economic and Social Progress in Latin America*.

International Monetary Fund, 700 Nineteenth Street, NW, Washington, D.C. 20431 (202) 623-7000; *International Financial Statistics*.

M.E. Sharpe, 80 Business Park Drive, Armonk, New York 10504 (800) 541-6563; *The Illustrated Book of World Rankings*.

St. Martin's Press, Inc., 175 Fifth Avenue, New York, New York 10010 (800) 221-7945; *The Statesman's Year-Book*.

Statistical Office of the United Nations, Publishing Service, New York, New York 10017 (800) 253-9646; *Statistical Yearbook;* and *Statistical Yearbook for Latin America and the Caribbean*.

PERU - BARLEY PRODUCTION - See PERU - CROPS

PERU - BAUXITE PRODUCTION AND CONSUMPTION - See PERU - MINING AND MINERAL PRODUCTS

PERU - BEER PRODUCTION - See PERU - BEVERAGES

PERU - BEVERAGES

M.E. Sharpe, 80 Business Park Drive, Armonk, New York 10504 (800) 541-6563; *The Illustrated Book of World Rankings*.

Statistical Office of the United Nations, Publishing Service, New York, New York 10017 (800) 253-9646; *Statistical Yearbook*.

PERU - BIRTH RATES

Central Intelligence Agency, Washington, D.C. 20505 (703) 482-1100, www.cia.gov; *The World Factbook*.

Euromonitor International, Inc., 122 Michigan Avenue, Suite 1200, Chicago, Illinois 60603 (800) 577-EURO; *International Marketing Data and Statistics;* and *The World Economic Factbook*.

Europa Publications Limited, 18 Bedford Square, London, WC1B 3JN, England; *The Europa World Year Book*.

M.E. Sharpe, 80 Business Park Drive, Armonk, New York 10504 (800) 541-6563; *The Illustrated Book of World Rankings*.

St. Martin's Press, Inc., 175 Fifth Avenue, New York, New York 10010 (800) 221-7945; *The Statesman's Year-Book*.

Statistical Office of the United Nations, Publishing Service, New York, New York 10017 (800) 253-9646; *Demographic Yearbook; Statistical Yearbook;* and *Statistical Yearbook for Latin America and the Caribbean*.

The World Bank, 1818 H Street, NW, Washington, D.C. 20433 (202) 477-1234; *World Development Indicators*.

PERU - BISMUTH PRODUCTION AND CONSUMPTION

Commodity Research Bureau, Inc., 30 South Wacker Drive, Chicago Illinois 60606 (312) 454-1801; *Commodity Year Book*.

PERU - BONDS

Inter-American Development Bank, 1300 New York Avenue, NW, Washington, D.C. 20577 (202) 623-1753; *Economic and Social Progress in Latin America.*

PERU - BOOK PRODUCTION

Europa Publications Limited, 18 Bedford Square, London, WC1B 3JN, England; *The Europa World Year Book.*

United Nations Educational, Scientific and Cultural Organization (UNESCO), 7 Place de Fontenoy, F-75700 Paris, France (Telephone Number in U.S. (212) 963-5981); *Statistical Yearbook.*

PERU - BROADCASTING

Billboard Limited, Post Office Box 9027, 1006 AA Amsterdam, The Netherlands (Telephone Number in U.S. (212) 764-7300); *World Radio TV Handbook.*

Central Intelligence Agency, Washington, D.C. 20505 (703) 482-1100, www.cia.gov; *The World Factbook.*

Euromonitor International, Inc., 122 South Michigan Avenue, Suite 1200, Chicago, Illinois 60603 (800) 577-EURO; *World Marketing Data and Statistics.*

M.E. Sharpe, 80 Business Park Drive, Armonk, New York 10504 (800) 541-6563; *The Illustrated Book of World Rankings.*

St. Martin's Press, Inc., 175 Fifth Avenue, New York, New York 10010 (800) 221-7945; *The Statesman's Year-Book.*

United Nations Educational, Scientific and Cultural Organization (UNESCO), 7 Place de Fontenoy, F-75700 Paris, France (Telephone Number in U.S. (212) 963-5981); *Statistical Yearbook.*

PERU - BUDGET

Central Intelligence Agency, Washington, D.C. 20505 (703) 482-1100, www.cia.gov; *The World Factbook.*

PERU - BUSINESS

Inter-American Development Bank, 1300 New York Avenue, NW, Washington, D.C. 20577 (202) 623-1753; *Economic and Social Progress in Latin America.*

PERU - BUTTER PRODUCTION - See PERU - DAIRY PRODUCTS

PERU - CABBAGE PRODUCTION - See PERU - CROPS

PERU - CADMIUM PRODUCTION AND CONSUMPTION - See PERU - MINING AND MINERAL PRODUCTS

PERU - CALORIE SUPPLY

Food and Agricultural Organization of the United Nations (FAO) Via delle Terme di Caracalla, 00100 Rome, Italy (Telephone Number in U.S. (202) 653-2400); *The State of Food and Agriculture.*

Statistical Office of the United Nations, Publishing Service, New York, New York 10017 (800) 253-9646; *Statistical Yearbook for Latin America and the Caribbean.*

PERU - CAPITAL INVESTMENT

Inter-American Development Bank, 1300 New York Avenue, NW, Washington, D.C. 20577 (202) 623-1753; *Economic and Social Progress in Latin America.*

PERU - CAPITAL REVENUE

Inter-American Development Bank, 1300 New York Avenue, NW, Washington, D.C. 20577 (202) 623-1753; *Economic and Social Progress in Latin America.*

International Monetary Fund, 700 Nineteenth Street, NW, Washington, D.C. 20431 (202) 623-7000; *Government Finance Statistics Yearbook.*

PERU - CATTLE - See PERU - LIVESTOCK AND POULTRY

PERU - CAULIFLOWER PRODUCTION - See PERU - CROPS

PERU - CAUSTIC SODA PRODUCTION - See PERU - BEVERAGES

PERU - CEMENT PRODUCTION - See PERU - MINING AND MINERAL PRODUCTS

PERU - CHEESE PRODUCTION AND CONSUMPTION - See PERU - DAIRY PRODUCTS

PERU - CHEMICAL (ORGANIC) PRODUCTION - See PERU - MINING AND MINERAL PRODUCTS

PERU - CHICK PEA PRODUCTION - See PERU - CROPS

PERU - CHICKENS - See PERU - LIVESTOCK AND POULTRY

PERU - CHROMITE PRODUCTION AND CONSUMPTION - See PERU - MINING AND MINERAL PRODUCTS

PERU - CHROMIUM ORE PRODUCTION AND CONSUMPTION - See PERU - MINING AND MINERAL PRODUCTS

PERU - CIGAR AND CIGARETTE PRODUCTION - See PERU - TOBACCO PRODUCTION

PERU - CLIMATE

M.E. Sharpe, 80 Business Park Drive, Armonk, New York 10504 (800) 541-6563; *The Illustrated Book of World Rankings.*

St. Martin's Press, Inc., 175 Fifth Avenue, New York, New York 10010 (800) 221-7945; *The Statesman's Year-Book.*

PERU - COAL PRODUCTION - See PERU - MINING AND MINERAL PRODUCTS

PERU - COBALT PRODUCTION AND CONSUMPTION - See PERU - MINING AND MINERAL PRODUCTS

PERU - COCOA (BEANS) PRODUCTION - See PERU - CROPS

PERU - COFFEE - See PERU - CROPS

PERU - COKE, COKE OVEN ORE, AND COKE OVEN COKE PRODUCTION AND CONSUMPTION - See PERU - MINING AND MINERAL PRODUCTS

PERU - COMMERCE

St. Martin's Press, Inc., 175 Fifth Avenue, New York, New York 10010 (800) 221-7945; *The Statesman's Year-Book.*

PERU - COMMUNICATIONS - See PERU - TRANSPORTATION AND COMMUNICATIONS

PERU - CONSTRUCTION INDUSTRY

The Economist Intelligence Unit, 111 West 57th Street, New York, New York 10019 (800) 938-4685; *The New Latin America Market Atlas.*

Inter-American Development Bank, 1300 New York Avenue, NW, Washington, D.C. 20577 (202) 623-1753; *Economic and Social Progress in Latin America.*

M.E. Sharpe, 80 Business Park Drive, Armonk, New York 10504 (800) 541-6563; *The Illustrated Book of World Rankings.*

St. Martin's Press, Inc., 175 Fifth Avenue, New York, New York 10010 (800) 221-7945; *The Statesman's Year-Book.*

Statistical Office of the United Nations, Publishing Service, New York, New York 10017 (800) 253-9646; *Statistical Yearbook.*

U.C.L.A. Latin American Center Publications, University of California, Los Angeles, California 90024 (310) 825-6634; *Statistical Abstract of Latin America.*

PERU - CONSUMER PRICE INDEX

Europa Publications Limited, 18 Bedford Square, London, WC1B 3JN, England; *The Europa World Year Book.*

Statistical Office of the United Nations,

Publishing Service, New York, New York 10017 (800) 253-9646; *Statistical Yearbook*.

U.C.L.A. Latin American Center Publications, University of California, Los Angeles, California 90024 (310) 825-6634; *Statistical Abstract of Latin America*.

PERU - CONSUMER PRICES

The Economist Intelligence Unit, 111 West 57th Street, New York, New York 10019 (800) 938-4685; *The New Latin America Market Atlas*.

Euromonitor International, Inc., 122 South Michigan Avenue, Suite 1200, Chicago, Illinois 60603 (800) 577-EURO; *World Marketing Data and Statistics*.

International Labour Office, I.L.O. Publications, 1828 L Street, NW., Suite 801, Washington, D.C. 20036 (301) 638-3152; *Yearbook of Labour Statistics*.

International Monetary Fund, 700 Nineteenth Street, NW, Washington, D.C. 20431 (202) 623-7000; *International Financial Statistics*.

Organization of American States (OAS), General Secretariat, Washington, D.C. 20006 (202) 458-3533; *Statistical Bulletin of the OAS*.

PERU - CONSUMPTION

The Economist Intelligence Unit, 111 West 57th Street, New York, New York 10019 (800) 938-4685; *The New Latin America Market Atlas*.

Inter-American Development Bank, 1300 New York Avenue, NW, Washington, D.C. 20577 (202) 623-1753; *Economic and Social Progress in Latin America*.

International Lead and Zinc Study Group, Metro House, 58 St. James's Street, London SW1A 1LD, England; *Lead and Zinc Statistics*.

Statistical Office of the United Nations, Publishing Service, New York, New York 10017 (800) 253-9646; *Statistical Yearbook for Latin America and the Caribbean*.

The World Bank, 1818 H Street, NW, Washington, D.C. 20433 (202) 477-1234; *World Development Report*.

PERU - COOPERATIVES

U.C.L.A. Latin American Center Publications, University of California, Los Angeles, California 90024 (310) 825-6634; *Statistical Abstract of Latin America*.

PERU - COPPER AND COPPER ORE PRODUCTION AND CONSUMPTION - See PERU - MINING AND MINERAL PRODUCTS

PERU - CORN PRODUCTION - See PERU - CROPS

PERU - CORPORATE TAXES - See PERU - TAXATION

PERU - COTTON - See PERU - CROPS

International Monetary Fund, 700 Nineteenth Street, NW, Washington, D.C. 20431 (202) 623-7000; *International Financial Statistics*.

M.E. Sharpe, 80 Business Park Drive, Armonk, New York 10504 (800) 541-6563; *The Illustrated Book of World Rankings*.

Organization of American States (OAS), General Secretariat, Washington, D.C. 20006 (202) 458-3533; *Statistical Bulletin of the OAS*.

Statistical Office of the United Nations, Publishing Service, New York, New York 10017 (800) 253-9646; *Statistical Yearbook*.

U.C.L.A. Latin American Center Publications, University of California, Los Angeles, California 90024 (310) 825-6634; *Statistical Abstract of Latin America*.

PERU - CRIME

International Criminal Police Organization (INTERPOL), 50 quai Achille Lignon, F-69006 Lyon, France; *International Crime Statistics*.

Yale University Press, Yale Station, New Haven, Connecticut 06520 (800) 987-7323; *Violence and Crime in Cross-National Perspective*.

PERU - CROPS

The Economist Intelligence Unit, 111 West 57th Street, New York, New York 10019 (800) 938-4685; *The New Latin America Market Atlas*.

Europa Publications Limited, 18 Bedford Square, London, WC1B 3JN, England; *The Europa World Year Book*.

Food and Agricultural Organization of the United Nations (FAO), Via delle Terme di Caracalla, 00100 Rome, Italy (Telephone Number in U.S. (202) 653-2400); *Production Yearbook;* and *The State of Food and Agriculture*.

International Monetary Fund, 700 Nineteenth Street, NW, Washington, D.C. 20431 (202) 623-7000; *International Financial Statistics*.

M.E. Sharpe, 80 Business Park Drive, Armonk, New York 10504 (800) 541-6563; *The Illustrated Book of World Rankings*.

Organization of American States (OAS),

General Secretariat, Washington, D.C. 20006 (202) 458-3533; *Statistical Bulletin of the OAS*.

St. Martin's Press, Inc., 175 Fifth Avenue, New York, New York 10010 (800) 221-7945; *The Statesman's Year-Book*.

Statistical Office of the United Nations, Publishing Service, New York, New York 10017 (800) 253-9646; *Statistical Yearbook*.

U.C.L.A. Latin American Center Publications, University of California, Los Angeles, California 90024 (310) 825-6634; *Statistical Abstract of Latin America*.

United Nations Conference on Trade and Development, Central Statistical Service, Palais des Nations, Geneva, Switzerland (Telephone in U.S. (800) 253-9646); *UNCTAD Commodity Yearbook*.

PERU - CUSTOMS DUTIES

Inter-American Development Bank, 1300 New York Avenue, NW, Washington, D.C. 20577 (202) 623-1753; *Economic and Social Progress in Latin America*.

International Monetary Fund, 700 Nineteenth Street, NW, Washington, D.C. 20431 (202) 623-7000; *Government Finance Statistics Yearbook*.

St. Martin's Press, Inc., 175 Fifth Avenue, New York, New York 10010 (800) 221-7945; *The Statesman's Year-Book*.

PERU - DAIRY PRODUCTS

Europa Publications Limited, 18 Bedford Square, London, WC1B 3JN, England; *The Europa World Year Book*.

Food and Agricultural Organization of the United Nations (FAO) Via delle Terme di Caracalla, 00100 Rome, Italy (Telephone Number in U.S. (202) 653-2400); *Production Yearbook;* and *The State of Food and Agriculture*.

M.E. Sharpe, 80 Business Park Drive, Armonk, New York 10504 (800) 541-6563; *The Illustrated Book of World Rankings*.

St. Martin's Press, Inc., 175 Fifth Avenue, New York, New York 10010 (800) 221-7945; *The Statesman's Year-Book*.

Statistical Office of the United Nations, Publishing Service, New York, New York 10017 (800) 253-9646; *Statistical Yearbook*.

U.C.L.A. Latin American Center Publications, University of California, Los Angeles, California 90024 (310) 825-6634; *Statistical Abstract of Latin America*.

PERU - DEATH RATES - See PERU -

MORTALITY

PERU - DEBT

The Economist Intelligence Unit, 111 West 57th Street, New York, New York 10019 (800) 938-4685; *The New Latin America Market Atlas.*

PERU - DEFENSE EXPENDITURES - See PERU - MILITARY

PERU - DEMOGRAPHY

The Economist Intelligence Unit, 111 West 57th Street, New York, New York 10019 (800) 938-4685; *The World Market Atlas.*

Euromonitor International, Inc., 122 Michigan Avenue, Suite 1200, Chicago, Illinois 60603 (800) 577-EURO; *International Marketing Data and Statistics; World Marketing Data and Statistics;* and *The World Economic Factbook.*

M.E. Sharpe, 80 Business Park Drive, Armonk, New York 10504 (800) 541-6563; *The Illustrated Book of World Rankings.*

Statistical Office of the United Nations, Publishing Service, New York, New York 10017 (800) 253-9646; *Human Development Report.*

PERU - DEVELOPMENT ASSISTANCE

Inter-American Development Bank, 1300 New York Avenue, NW, Washington, D.C. 20577 (202) 623-1753; *Economic and Social Progress in Latin America.*

Statistical Office of the United Nations, Publishing Service, New York, New York 10017 (800) 253-9646; *Statistical Yearbook.*

PERU - DIAMOND PRODUCTION - See PERU - MINING AND MINERAL PRODUCTS

PERU - DISCOUNT RATES - See PERU - BANKING

PERU - DISEASES - See PERU - HEALTH

PERU - DIVORCE RATES

M.E. Sharpe, 80 Business Park Drive, Armonk, New York 10504 (800) 541-6563; *The Illustrated Book of World Rankings.*

Statistical Office of the United Nations, Publishing Service, New York, New York 10017 (800) 253-9646; *Demographic Yearbook;* and *Statistical Yearbook.*

PERU - ECONOMY

Central Intelligence Agency, Washington, D.C. 20505 (703) 482-1100, www.cia.gov; *The World Factbook.*

Economist Intelligence Unit, 111 West 57th Street, New York, New York 10019 (800) 938-4685; *Peru Country Report.*

Euromonitor International, Inc., 122 Michigan Avenue, Suite 1200, Chicago, Illinois 60603 (800) 577-EURO; *International Marketing Data and Statistics; World Marketing Data and Statistics;* and *The World Economic Factbook.*

Europa Publications Limited, 18 Bedford Square, London, WC1B 3JN, England; *The Europa World Year Book.*

Inter-American Development Bank, 1300 New York Avenue, NW, Washington, D.C. 20577 (202) 623-1753; *Economic and Social Progress in Latin America.*

M.E. Sharpe, 80 Business Park Drive, Armonk, New York 10504 (800) 541-6563; *The Illustrated Book of World Rankings.*

Organization of American States (OAS), General Secretariat, Washington, D.C. 20006 (202) 458-3533; *Statistical Bulletin of the OAS.*

St. Martin's Press, Inc., 175 Fifth Avenue, New York, New York 10010 (800) 221-7945; *The Statesman's Year-Book.*

Statistical Office of the United Nations, Publishing Service, New York, New York 10017 (800) 253-9646; *Economic Survey of Latin America and the Caribbean;* and *World Statistics Pocketbook.*

U.C.L.A. Latin American Center Publications, University of California, Los Angeles, California 90024 (310) 825-6634; *Statistical Abstract of Latin America.*

The World Bank, 1818 H Street, NW, Washington, D.C. 20433 (202) 477-1234; *The World Bank Atlas;* and *World Development Report.*

PERU - EDUCATION

The Economist Intelligence Unit, 111 West 57th Street, New York, New York 10019 (800) 938-4685; *The New Latin America Market Atlas;* and *The World Market Atlas.*

Euromonitor International, Inc., 122 Michigan Avenue, Suite 1200, Chicago, Illinois 60603 (800) 577-EURO; *International Marketing Data and Statistics;* and *World Marketing Data and Statistics.*

Europa Publications Limited, 18 Bedford Square, London, WC1B 3JN, England; *The Europa World Year Book.*

International Monetary Fund, 700 Nineteenth Street, NW, Washington, D.C. 20431 (202) 623-7000; *Government Finance Statistics Yearbook.*

M.E. Sharpe, 80 Business Park Drive, Armonk, New York 10504 (800) 541-6563; *The Illustrated Book of World Rankings.*

St. Martin's Press, Inc., 175 Fifth Avenue, New York, New York 10010 (800) 221-7945; *The Statesman's Year-Book.*

Statistical Office of the United Nations, Publishing Service, New York, New York 10017 (800) 253-9646; *Human Development Report;* and *Statistical Yearbook for Latin America and the Caribbean.*

U.C.L.A. Latin American Center Publications, University of California, Los Angeles, California 90024 (310) 825-6634; *Statistical Abstract of Latin America.*

United Nations Educational, Scientific and Cultural Organization (UNESCO), 7 Place de Fontenoy, F-75700 Paris, France (Telephone Number in U.S. (212) 963-5981); *Statistical Yearbook.*

The World Bank, 1818 H Street, NW, Washington, D.C. 20433 (202) 477-1234; *World Development Report;* and *World Development Indicators.*

PERU - EGG PRODUCTION AND CONSUMPTION - See PERU - DAIRY PRODUCTS

PERU - ELECTRICITY

Central Intelligence Agency, Washington, D.C. 20505 (703) 482-1100, www.cia.gov; *The World Factbook.*

The Economist Intelligence Unit, 111 West 57th Street, New York, New York 10019 (800) 938-4685; *The New Latin America Market Atlas.*

Inter-American Development Bank, 1300 New York Avenue, NW, Washington, D.C. 20577 (202) 623-1753; *Economic and Social Progress in Latin America.*

M.E. Sharpe, 80 Business Park Drive, Armonk, New York 10504 (800) 541-6563; *The Illustrated Book of World Rankings.*

Penn Well Publishing Company, 1421 South Sheridan Road, Post Office Box 1260, Tulsa, Oklahoma 74101 (800) 752-9764; *International Energy Statistics Sourcebook.*

St. Martin's Press, Inc., 175 Fifth Avenue, New York, New York 10010 (800) 221-7945; *The Statesman's Year-Book.*

Statistical Office of the United Nations, Publishing Service, New York, New York 10017 (800) 253-9646; *Human Development Report;* and *Statistical Yearbook.*

PERU - EMPLOYMENT

Euromonitor International, Inc., 122 Michigan Avenue, Suite 1200, Chicago, Illinois 60603 (800) 577-EURO; *International Marketing Data and Statistics;* and *International Marketing Data and Statistics.*

International Labour Office, I.L.O. Publications, 1828 L Street, NW., Suite 801, Washington, D.C. 20036 (301) 638-3152; *Yearbook of Labour Statistics.*

M.E. Sharpe, 80 Business Park Drive, Armonk, New York 10504 (800) 541-6563; *The Illustrated Book of World Rankings.*

Statistical Office of the United Nations, Publishing Service, New York, New York 10017 (800) 253-9646; *Statistical Yearbook;* and *Statistical Yearbook for Latin America and the Caribbean.*

U.C.L.A. Latin American Center Publications, University of California, Los Angeles, California 90024 (310) 825-6634; *Statistical Abstract of Latin America.*

PERU - ENERGY

The Economist Intelligence Unit, 111 West 57th Street, New York, New York 10019 (800) 938-4685; *The New Latin America Market Atlas.*

Euromonitor International, Inc., 122 Michigan Avenue, Suite 1200, Chicago, Illinois 60603 (800) 577-EURO; *International Marketing Data and Statistics; World Marketing Data and Statistics;* and *The World Economic Factbook.*

Food and Agricultural Organization of the United Nations (FAO) Via delle Terme di Caracalla, 00100 Rome, Italy (Telephone Number in U.S. (202) 653-2400); *The State of Food and Agriculture.*

M.E. Sharpe, 80 Business Park Drive, Armonk, New York 10504 (800) 541-6563; *The Illustrated Book of World Rankings.*

Penn Well Publishing Company, 1421 South Sheridan Road, Post Office Box 1260, Tulsa, Oklahoma 74101 (800) 752-9764; *International Energy Statistics Sourcebook.*

St. Martin's Press, Inc., 175 Fifth Avenue, New York, New York 10010 (800) 221-7945; *The Statesman's Year-Book.*

Statistical Office of the United Nations, Publishing Service, New York, New York 10017 (800) 253-9646; *Energy Statistics Yearbook; Human Development Report; Statistical Yearbook; Statistical Yearbook for Latin America and the Caribbean;* and *World Statistics Pocketbook.*

U.C.L.A. Latin American Center Publications, University of California, Los Angeles, California 90024 (310) 825-6634;

Statistical Abstract of Latin America.

The World Bank, 1818 H Street, NW, Washington, D.C. 20433 (202) 477-1234; *The World Bank Atlas;* and *World Development Report.*

PERU - ENVIRONMENT

Economist Intelligence Unit, 111 West 57th Street, New York, New York 10019 (800) 938-4685; *Peru Country Report.*

Statistical Office of the United Nations, Publishing Service, New York, New York 10017 (800) 253-9646; *World Statistics Pocketbook.*

PERU - EXCHANGE RATES

Central Intelligence Agency, Washington, D.C. 20505 (703) 482-1100, www.cia.gov; *The World Factbook.*

Euromonitor International, Inc., 122 Michigan Avenue, Suite 1200, Chicago, Illinois 60603 (800) 577-EURO; *International Marketing Data and Statistics;* and *The World Economic Factbook.*

Europa Publications Limited, 18 Bedford Square, London, WC1B 3JN, England; *The Europa World Year Book.*

Inter-American Development Bank, 1300 New York Avenue, NW, Washington, D.C. 20577 (202) 623-1753; *Economic and Social Progress in Latin America.*

International Civil Aviation Organization, 999 University Street, Montreal, Quebec, Canada H3C 5H7 (514) 954-8219; *Civil Aviation Statistics of the World.*

International Monetary Fund, 700 Nineteenth Street, NW, Washington, D.C. 20431 (202) 623-7000; *International Financial Statistics.*

Organization of American States (OAS), General Secretariat, Washington, D.C. 20006 (202) 458-3533; *Statistical Bulletin of the OAS.*

Statistical Office of the United Nations, Publishing Service, New York, New York 10017 (800) 253-9646; *Statistical Yearbook;* and *World Statistics Pocketbook.*

U.C.L.A. Latin American Center Publications, University of California, Los Angeles, California 90024 (310) 825-6634; *Statistical Abstract of Latin America.*

PERU - EXCISE TAXES - See PERU - TAXATION

PERU - EXPENDITURES

Organization of American States (OAS),

General Secretariat, Washington, D.C. 20006 (202) 458-3533; *Statistical Bulletin of the OAS.*

PERU - EXPORTS

Central Intelligence Agency, Washington, D.C. 20505 (703) 482-1100, www.cia.gov; *The World Factbook.*

The Economist Intelligence Unit, 111 West 57th Street, New York, New York 10019 (800) 938-4685; *The New Latin America Market Atlas; Peru Country Report;* and *The World Market Atlas.*

Euromonitor International, Inc., 122 Michigan Avenue, Suite 1200, Chicago, Illinois 60603 (800) 577-EURO; *International Marketing Data and Statistics;* and *The World Economic Factbook.*

Europa Publications Limited, 18 Bedford Square, London, WC1B 3JN, England; *The Europa World Year Book.*

Food and Agricultural Organization of the United Nations (FAO) Via delle Terme di Caracalla, 00100 Rome, Italy (Telephone Number in U.S. (202) 653-2400); *The State of Food and Agriculture.*

Inter-American Development Bank, 1300 New York Avenue, NW, Washington, D.C. 20577 (202) 623-1753; *Economic and Social Progress in Latin America.*

International Lead and Zinc Study Group, Metro House, 58 St. James's Street, London SW1A 1LD, England; *Lead and Zinc Statistics.*

International Monetary Fund, 700 Nineteenth Street, NW, Washington, D.C. 20431 (202) 623-7000; *Direction of Trade Statistics; Government Finance Statistics Yearbook;* and *International Financial Statistics.*

Organization of American States (OAS), General Secretariat, Washington, D.C. 20006 (202) 458-3533; *Statistical Bulletin of the OAS.*

St. Martin's Press, Inc., 175 Fifth Avenue, New York, New York 10010 (800) 221-7945; *The Statesman's Year-Book.*

Statistical Office of the United Nations, Publishing Service, New York, New York 10017 (800) 253-9646; *Statistical Yearbook for Latin America and the Caribbean.*

United Nations Conference on Trade and Development (UNCTAD), New York, New York 10017 9800) 253-9646; *Handbook of International Trade and Development Statistics.*

The World Bank, 1818 H Street, NW, Washington, D.C. 20433 (202) 477-1234;

World Development Report; and *World Development Indicators.*

PERU - EXTERNAL FINANCING

Inter-American Development Bank, 1300 New York Avenue, NW, Washington, D.C. 20577 (202) 623-1753; *Economic and Social Progress in Latin America.*

Statistical Office of the United Nations, Publishing Service, New York, New York 10017 (800) 253-9646; *Statistical Yearbook for Latin America and the Caribbean.*

PERU - EXTERNAL INDEBTEDNESS

Inter-American Development Bank, 1300 New York Avenue, NW, Washington, D.C. 20577 (202) 623-1753; *Economic and Social Progress in Latin America.*

Statistical Office of the United Nations, Publishing Service, New York, New York 10017 (800) 253-9646; *Statistical Yearbook for Latin America and the Caribbean.*

The World Bank, 1818 H Street, NW, Washington, D.C. 20433 (202) 477-1234; *World Development Report;* and *World Development Indicators.*

PERU - EXTERNAL TRADE

Euromonitor International, Inc., 122 South Michigan Avenue, Suite 1200, Chicago, Illinois 60603 (800) 577-EURO; *World Marketing Data and Statistics.*

Food and Agricultural Organization of the United Nations (FAO) Via delle Terme di Caracalla, 00100 Rome, Italy (Telephone Number in U.S. (202) 653-2400); *The State of Food and Agriculture;* and *Trade Yearbook.*

Inter-American Development Bank, 1300 New York Avenue, NW, Washington, D.C. 20577 (202) 623-1753; *Economic and Social Progress in Latin America.*

Statistical Office of the United Nations, Publishing Service, New York, New York 10017 (800) 253-9646; *Statistical Yearbook;* and *Statistical Yearbook for Latin America and the Caribbean.*

PERU - FABRIC PRODUCTION - See PERU - TEXTILE INDUSTRY

PERU - FAMILY PLANNING

U.C.L.A. Latin American Center Publications, University of California, Los Angeles, California 90024 (310) 825-6634; *Statistical Abstract of Latin America.*

PERU - FARM CROPS - See PERU - CROPS

PERU - FEMALE WORKING POPULATION - See PERU - EMPLOYMENT

PERU - FERTILITY RATES

Central Intelligence Agency, Washington, D.C. 20505 (703) 482-1100, www.cia.gov; *The World Factbook.*

M.E. Sharpe, 80 Business Park Drive, Armonk, New York 10504 (800) 541-6563; *The Illustrated Book of World Rankings.*

Statistical Office of the United Nations, Publishing Service, New York, New York 10017 (800) 253-9646; *Human Development Report.*

The World Bank, 1818 H Street, NW, Washington, D.C. 20433 (202) 477-1234; *The World Bank Atlas; World Development Report;* and *World Development Indicators.*

PERU - FERTILIZER

The Economist Intelligence Unit, 111 West 57th Street, New York, New York 10019 (800) 938-4685; *The New Latin America Market Atlas.*

Food and Agricultural Organization of the United Nations (FAO), Via delle Terme di Caracalla, 00100 Rome, Italy (Telephone Number in U.S. (202) 653-2400); *Fertilizer Yearbook;* and *The State of Food and Agriculture.*

Statistical Office of the United Nations, Publishing Service, New York, New York 10017 (800) 253-9646; *Statistical Yearbook.*

PERU - FETAL MORTALITY - See PERU - MORTALITY

PERU - FIBRE PRODUCTION - See PERU - TEXTILE INDUSTRY

PERU - FILAMENT PRODUCTION - See PERU - TEXTILE INDUSTRY

PERU - FILM - See PERU - MOTION PICTURES

PERU - FINANCE

Economist Intelligence Unit, 111 West 57th Street, New York, New York 10019 (800) 938-4685; *Peru Country Report.*

Europa Publications Limited, 18 Bedford Square, London, WC1B 3JN, England; *The Europa World Year Book.*

Inter-American Development Bank, 1300 New York Avenue, NW, Washington, D.C. 20577 (202) 623-1753; *Economic and Social Progress in Latin America.*

International Monetary Fund, 700 Nineteenth Street, NW, Washington, D.C. 20431 (202) 623-7000; *International Financial Statistics.*

M.E. Sharpe, 80 Business Park Drive,

Armonk, New York 10504 (800) 541-6563; *The Illustrated Book of World Rankings.*

Organization of American States (OAS), General Secretariat, Washington, D.C. 20006 (202) 458-3533; *Statistical Bulletin of the OAS.*

St. Martin's Press, Inc., 175 Fifth Avenue, New York, New York 10010 (800) 221-7945; *The Statesman's Year-Book.*

U.C.L.A. Latin American Center Publications, University of California, Los Angeles, California 90024 (310) 825-6634; *Statistical Abstract of Latin America.*

PERU - FISHERIES

Europa Publications Limited, 18 Bedford Square, London, WC1B 3JN, England; *The Europa World Year Book.*

Food and Agricultural Organization of the United Nations (FAO) Via delle Terme di Caracalla, 00100 Rome, Italy (Telephone Number in U.S. (202) 653-2400); *The State of Food and Agriculture;* and *Yearbook of Fishery Statistics.*

Inter-American Development Bank, 1300 New York Avenue, NW, Washington, D.C. 20577 (202) 623-1753; *Economic and Social Progress in Latin America.*

International Monetary Fund, 700 Nineteenth Street, NW, Washington, D.C. 20431 (202) 623-7000; *International Financial Statistics.*

M.E. Sharpe, 80 Business Park Drive, Armonk, New York 10504 (800) 541-6563; *The Illustrated Book of World Rankings.*

St. Martin's Press, Inc., 175 Fifth Avenue, New York, New York 10010 (800) 221-7945; *The Statesman's Year-Book.*

Statistical Office of the United Nations, Publishing Service, New York, New York 10017 (800) 253-9646; *Statistical Yearbook.*

U.C.L.A. Latin American Center Publications, University of California, Los Angeles, California 90024 (310) 825-6634; *Statistical Abstract of Latin America.*

United Nations Conference on Trade and Development, Central Statistical Service, Palais des Nations, Geneva, Switzerland (Telephone in U.S. (800) 253-9646); *UNCTAD Commodity Yearbook.*

PERU - FLOUR PRODUCTION

Statistical Office of the United Nations, Publishing Service, New York, New York 10017 (800) 253-9646; *Statistical Yearbook.*

PERU - FOOD

Euromonitor International, Inc., 122 South Michigan Avenue, Suite 1200, Chicago, Illinois 60603 (800) 577-EURO; *Retail Trade International.*

Food and Agricultural Organization of the United Nations (FAO) Via delle Terme di Caracalla, 00100 Rome, Italy (Telephone Number in U.S. (202) 653-2400); *Production Yearbook;* and *The State of Food and Agriculture.*

Statistical Office of the United Nations, Publishing Service, New York, New York 10017 (800) 253-9646; *Human Development Report.*

United Nations Conference on Trade and Development, Central Statistical Service, Palais des Nations, Geneva, Switzerland (Telephone in U.S. (800) 253-9646); *UNCTAD Commodity Yearbook.*

PERU - FOREIGN AID

Inter-American Development Bank, 1300 New York Avenue, NW, Washington, D.C. 20577 (202) 623-1753; *Economic and Social Progress in Latin America.*

PERU - FOREIGN DEBT

The Economist Intelligence Unit, 111 West 57th Street, New York, New York 10019 (800) 938-4685; *The New Latin America Market Atlas.*

Inter-American Development Bank, 1300 New York Avenue, NW, Washington, D.C. 20577 (202) 623-1753; *Economic and Social Progress in Latin America.*

St. Martin's Press, Inc., 175 Fifth Avenue, New York, New York 10010 (800) 221-7945; *The Statesman's Year-Book.*

PERU - FOREIGN INDEBTEDNESS

Inter-American Development Bank, 1300 New York Avenue, NW, Washington, D.C. 20577 (202) 623-1753; *Economic and Social Progress in Latin America.*

Statistical Office of the United Nations, Publishing Service, New York, New York 10017 (800) 253-9646; *Economic Survey of Latin America and the Caribbean.*

PERU - FOREIGN INVESTMENT

The Economist Intelligence Unit, 111 West 57th Street, New York, New York 10019 (800) 938-4685; *The New Latin America Market Atlas.*

PERU - FOREIGN TRADE

The Economist Intelligence Unit, 111 West 57th Street, New York, New York 10019 (800) 938-4685; *The New Latin America Market Atlas;* and *Peru Country*

Report.

Euromonitor International, Inc., 122 Michigan Avenue, Suite 1200, Chicago, Illinois 60603 (800) 577-EURO; *International Marketing Data and Statistics;* and *The World Economic Factbook.*

Europa Publications Limited, 18 Bedford Square, London, WC1B 3JN, England; *The Europa World Year Book.*

Food and Agricultural Organization of the United Nations (FAO) Via delle Terme di Caracalla, 00100 Rome, Italy (Telephone Number in U.S. (202) 653-2400); *The State of Food and Agriculture.*

Inter-American Development Bank, 1300 New York Avenue, NW, Washington, D.C. 20577 (202) 623-1753; *Economic and Social Progress in Latin America.*

International Monetary Fund, 700 Nineteenth Street, NW, Washington, D.C. 20431 (202) 623-7000; *International Financial Statistics.*

M.E. Sharpe, 80 Business Park Drive, Armonk, New York 10504 (800) 541-6563; *The Illustrated Book of World Rankings.*

St. Martin's Press, Inc., 175 Fifth Avenue, New York, New York 10010 (800) 221-7945; *The Statesman's Year-Book.*

Statistical Office of the United Nations, Publishing Service, New York, New York 10017 (800) 253-9646; *Economic Survey of Latin America and the Caribbean; International Trade Statistics Yearbook;* and *Statistical Yearbook.*

U.C.L.A. Latin American Center Publications, University of California, Los Angeles, California 90024 (310) 825-6634; *Statistical Abstract of Latin America.*

United Nations Conference on Trade and Development, Central Statistical Service, Palais des Nations, Geneva, Switzerland (Telephone in U.S. (800) 253-9646); *UNCTAD Commodity Yearbook.*

The World Bank, 1818 H Street, NW, Washington, D.C. 20433 (202) 477-1234; *World Development Report;* and *World Development Indicators.*

World Bureau of Metal Statistics, 27-A High Street, Ware, Herts. SG12 9BA, England; *World Metal Statistics.*

PERU - FORESTRY AND FOREST PRODUCTS

American Forest and Paper Association, 1111 Nineteenth Street, NW, Washington, D.C. 20036 (202) 463-2700; *Wood Pulp and Fiber Statistics.*

The Economist Intelligence Unit, 111 West 57th Street, New York, New York 10019 (800) 938-4685; *The New Latin America Market Atlas.*

Europa Publications Limited, 18 Bedford Square, London, WC1B 3JN, England; *The Europa World Year Book.*

Food and Agricultural Organization of the United Nations (FAO) Via delle Terme di Caracalla, 00100 Rome, Italy (Telephone Number in U.S. (202) 653-2400); *The State of Food and Agriculture;* and *Yearbook of Forest Products.*

Inter-American Development Bank, 1300 New York Avenue, NW, Washington, D.C. 20577 (202) 623-1753; *Economic and Social Progress in Latin America.*

M.E. Sharpe, 80 Business Park Drive, Armonk, New York 10504 (800) 541-6563; *The Illustrated Book of World Rankings.*

St. Martin's Press, Inc., 175 Fifth Avenue, New York, New York 10010 (800) 221-7945; *The Statesman's Year-Book.*

Statistical Office of the United Nations, Publishing Service, New York, New York 10017 (800) 253-9646; *Statistical Yearbook.*

U.C.L.A. Latin American Center Publications, University of California, Los Angeles, California 90024 (310) 825-6634; *Statistical Abstract of Latin America.*

United Nations Conference on Trade and Development, Central Statistical Service, Palais des Nations, Geneva, Switzerland (Telephone in U.S. (800) 253-9646); *UNCTAD Commodity Yearbook.*

United Nations Educational, Scientific and Cultural Organization (UNESCO), 7 Place de Fontenoy, F-75700 Paris, France (Telephone Number in U.S. (212) 963-5981); *Statistical Yearbook.*

The World Bank, 1818 H Street, NW, Washington, D.C. 20433 (202) 477-1234; *World Development Report.*

PERU - GARLIC PRODUCTION - See PERU - CROPS

PERU - GAS AND GAS LIQUIDS PRODUCTION - See PERU - MINING AND MINERAL PRODUCTS

PERU - GENERAL INDUSTRIAL STATISTICS - See PERU - INDUSTRY

PERU - GENERAL MORTALITY - See PERU - MORTALITY

PERU - GEOGRAPHIC DATA

M.E. Sharpe, 80 Business Park Drive, Armonk, New York 10504 (800) 541-6563;

The Illustrated Book of World Rankings.

U.C.L.A. Latin American Center Publications, University of California, Los Angeles, California 90024 (310) 825-6634; *Statistical Abstract of Latin America.*

PERU - GOATS - See PERU - LIVESTOCK AND POULTRY

PERU - GOLD HOLDINGS

International Monetary Fund, 700 Nineteenth Street, NW, Washington, D.C. 20431 (202) 623-7000; *International Financial Statistics.*

Statistical Office of the United Nations, Publishing Service, New York, New York 10017 (800) 253-9646; *Statistical Yearbook.*

The World Bank, 1818 H Street, NW, Washington, D.C. 20433 (202) 477-1234; *World Development Indicators.*

PERU - GOLD PRODUCTION AND CONSUMPTION - See PERU - MINING AND MINERAL PRODUCTS

PERU - GOLD RESERVES

The Economist Intelligence Unit, 111 West 57th Street, New York, New York 10019 (800) 938-4685; *The New Latin America Market Atlas.*

PERU - GOVERNMENT

Central Intelligence Agency, Washington, D.C. 20505 (703) 482-1100, www.cia.gov; *The World Factbook.*

Europa Publications Limited, 18 Bedford Square, London, WC1B 3JN, England; *The Europa World Year Book.*

Inter-American Development Bank, 1300 New York Avenue, NW, Washington, D.C. 20577 (202) 623-1753; *Economic and Social Progress in Latin America.*

International Monetary Fund, 700 Nineteenth Street, NW, Washington, D.C. 20431 (202) 623-7000; *Government Finance Statistics Yearbook;* and *International Financial Statistics.*

St. Martin's Press, Inc., 175 Fifth Avenue, New York, New York 10010 (800) 221-7945; *The Statesman's Year-Book.*

Statistical Office of the United Nations, Publishing Service, New York, New York 10017 (800) 253-9646; *National Accounts Statistics;* and *Statistical Yearbook.*

The World Bank, 1818 H Street, NW, Washington, D.C. 20433 (202) 477-1234; *World Development Report;* and *World Development Indicators.*

PERU - GRAIN PRODUCTION - See PERU - CROPS

PERU - GRANTS

International Monetary Fund, 700 Nineteenth Street, NW, Washington, D.C. 20431 (202) 623-7000; *Government Finance Statistics Yearbook.*

PERU - GREEN PEPPER AND CHILIE PRODUCTION - See PERU - CROPS

PERU - GROSS DOMESTIC PRODUCT

The Economist Intelligence Unit, 111 West 57th Street, New York, New York 10019 (800) 938-4685; *The New Latin America Market Atlas; Peru Country Report;* and *The World Market Atlas.*

Euromonitor International, Inc., 122 Michigan Avenue, Suite 1200, Chicago, Illinois 60603 (800) 577-EURO; *International Marketing Data and Statistics;* and *The World Economic Factbook.*

Inter-American Development Bank, 1300 New York Avenue, NW, Washington, D.C. 20577 (202) 623-1753; *Economic and Social Progress in Latin America.*

M.E. Sharpe, 80 Business Park Drive, Armonk, New York 10504 (800) 541-6563; *The Illustrated Book of World Rankings.*

Organization of American States (OAS), General Secretariat, Washington, D.C. 20006 (202) 458-3533; *Statistical Bulletin of the OAS.*

Statistical Office of the United Nations, Publishing Service, New York, New York 10017 (800) 253-9646; *Human Development Report; National Accounts Statistics; Statistical Yearbook;* and *Statistical Yearbook for Latin America and the Caribbean.*

U.C.L.A. Latin American Center Publications, University of California, Los Angeles, California 90024 (310) 825-6634; *Statistical Abstract of Latin America.*

The World Bank, 1818 H Street, NW, Washington, D.C. 20433 (202) 477-1234; *World Development Report;* and *World Development Indicators.*

PERU - GROSS NATIONAL PRODUCT

Euromonitor International, Inc., 122 Michigan Avenue, Suite 1200, Chicago, Illinois 60603 (800) 577-EURO; *International Marketing Data and Statistics.*

Europa Publications Limited, 18 Bedford Square, London, WC1B 3JN, England; *The Europa World Year Book.*

Inter-American Development Bank,

1300 New York Avenue, NW, Washington, D.C. 20577 (202) 623-1753; *Economic and Social Progress in Latin America.*

St. Martin's Press, Inc., 175 Fifth Avenue, New York, New York 10010 (800) 221-7945; *The Statesman's Year-Book.*

U.S. Arms Control and Disarmament Agency, 320 Twenty-first Street, NW, Washington, D.C. 20451 (202) 647-8677; *World Military Expenditures and Arms Transfers.*

The World Bank, 1818 H Street, NW, Washington, D.C. 20433 (202) 477-1234; *The World Bank Atlas; World Development Report;* and *World Development Indicators.*

PERU - GROUNDNUT PRODUCTION - See PERU - CROPS

PERU - HEALTH

The Economist Intelligence Unit, 111 West 57th Street, New York, New York 10019 (800) 938-4685; *The New Latin America Market Atlas.*

Euromonitor International, Inc., 122 South Michigan Avenue, Suite 1200, Chicago, Illinois 60603 (800) 577-EURO; *World Marketing Data and Statistics.*

M.E. Sharpe, 80 Business Park Drive, Armonk, New York 10504 (800) 541-6563; *The Illustrated Book of World Rankings.*

St. Martin's Press, Inc., 175 Fifth Avenue, New York, New York 10010 (800) 221-7945; *The Statesman's Year-Book.*

Statistical Office of the United Nations, Publishing Service, New York, New York 10017 (800) 253-9646; *Human Development Report; Statistical Yearbook;* and *Statistical Yearbook for Latin America and the Caribbean.*

United Nations Children's Fund (UNICEF), 3 United Nations Plaza, New York, New York 10017 (800) 253-9646; *State of the World's Children.*

The World Bank, 1818 H Street, NW, Washington, D.C. 20433 (202) 477-1234; *World Development Report.*

World Health Organization, Office of Publications, 20 Avenue Appia, CH-1211 Geneva 27, Switzerland (Telephone Number in U.S. (518) 436-9686); *World Health Statistics Annual.*

PERU - HEALTH EXPENDITURES

International Monetary Fund, 700 Nineteenth Street, NW, Washington, D.C. 20431 (202) 623-7000; *Government Finance Statistics Yearbook.*

PERU - HIDE PRODUCTION

Food and Agricultural Organization of the United Nations (FAO), Via delle Terme di Caracalla, 00100 Rome, Italy (Telephone Number in U.S. (202) 653-2400); *Production Yearbook.*

PERU - HIGHWAYS

Central Intelligence Agency, Washington, D.C. 20505 (703) 482-1100, www.cia.gov; *The World Factbook.*

The Economist Intelligence Unit, 111 West 57th Street, New York, New York 10019 (800) 938-4685; *The New Latin America Market Atlas.*

International Road Federation, 2600 Virginia Avenue, NW., Washington, D.C. 20037 (202) 338-4641; *World Road Statistics.*

St. Martin's Press, Inc., 175 Fifth Avenue, New York, New York 10010 (800) 221-7945; *The Statesman's Year-Book.*

PERU - HORSES - See PERU - LIVESTOCK AND POULTRY

PERU - HOURS OF WORK - See PERU - EMPLOYMENT

PERU - HOUSING AND HOUSING UNITS

Euromonitor International, Inc., 122 South Michigan Avenue, Suite 1200, Chicago, Illinois 60603 (800) 577-EURO; *World Marketing Data and Statistics.*

M.E. Sharpe, 80 Business Park Drive, Armonk, New York 10504 (800) 541-6563; *The Illustrated Book of World Rankings.*

Statistical Office of the United Nations, Publishing Service, New York, New York 10017 (800) 253-9646; *Statistical Yearbook for Latin America and the Caribbean.*

U.C.L.A. Latin American Center Publications, University of California, Los Angeles, California 90024 (310) 825-6634; *Statistical Abstract of Latin America.*

PERU - ILLITERATE POPULATION

Central Intelligence Agency, Washington, D.C. 20505 (703) 482-1100, www.cia.gov; *The World Factbook.*

The Economist Intelligence Unit, 111 West 57th Street, New York, New York 10019 (800) 938-4685; *The New Latin American Market Atlas;* and *The World Market Atlas.*

Euromonitor International, Inc., 122 Michigan Avenue, Suite 1200, Chicago, Illinois 60603 (800) 577-EURO; *The World Economic Factbook.*

Statistical Office of the United Nations, Publishing Service, New York, New York 10017 (800) 253-9646; *Human Development Report;* and *Statistical Yearbook for Latin America and the Caribbean.*

United Nations Educational, Scientific and Cultural Organization (UNESCO), 7 Place de Fontenoy, F-75700 Paris, France (Telephone Number in U.S. (212) 963-5981); *Statistical Yearbook.*

PERU - IMMIGRATION

U.C.L.A. Latin American Center Publications, University of California, Los Angeles, California 90024 (310) 825-6634; *Statistical Abstract of Latin America.*

PERU - IMPORTS

Central Intelligence Agency, Washington, D.C. 20505 (703) 482-1100, www.cia.gov; *The World Factbook.*

The Economist Intelligence Unit, 111 West 57th Street, New York, New York 10019 (800) 938-4685; *The New Latin America Market Atlas; Peru Country Report;* and *The World Market Atlas.*

Euromonitor International, Inc., 122 Michigan Avenue, Suite 1200, Chicago, Illinois 60603 (800) 577-EURO; *International Marketing Data and Statistics;* and *The World Economic Factbook.*

Europa Publications Limited, 18 Bedford Square, London, WC1B 3JN, England; *The Europa World Year Book.*

Food and Agricultural Organization of the United Nations (FAO) Via delle Terme di Caracalla, 00100 Rome, Italy (Telephone Number in U.S. (202) 653-2400); *The State of Food and Agriculture.*

Inter-American Development Bank, 1300 New York Avenue, NW, Washington, D.C. 20577 (202) 623-1753; *Economic and Social Progress in Latin America.*

International Lead and Zinc Study Group, Metro House, 58 St. James's Street, London SW1A 1LD, England; *Lead and Zinc Statistics.*

International Monetary Fund, 700 Nineteenth Street, NW, Washington, D.C. 20431 (202) 623-7000; *Direction of Trade Statistics; Government Finance Statistics Yearbook;* and *International Financial Statistics.*

Organization of American States (OAS), General Secretariat, Washington, D.C. 20006 (202) 458-3533; *Statistical Bulletin of the OAS.*

St. Martin's Press, Inc., 175 Fifth Avenue, New York, New York 10010 (800) 221-7945; *The Statesman's Year-Book.*

Statistical Office of the United Nations, Publishing Service, New York, New York 10017 (800) 253-9646; *Statistical Yearbook for Latin America and the Caribbean.*

United Nations Conference on Trade and Development (UNCTAD), New York, New York 10017 (800) 253-9646; *Handbook of International Trade and Development Statistics.*

The World Bank, 1818 H Street, NW, Washington, D.C. 20433 (202) 477-1234; *World Development Report;* and *World Development Indicators.*

PERU - INCOME DISTRIBUTION

Statistical Office of the United Nations, Publishing Service, New York, New York 10017 (800) 253-9646; *Statistical Yearbook for Latin America and the Caribbean.*

U.C.L.A. Latin American Center Publications, University of California, Los Angeles, California 90024 (310) 825-6634; *Statistical Abstract of Latin America.*

PERU - INCOME TAXES - See PERU - TAXATION

PERU - INDUSTRIAL METALS PRODUCTION - See PERU - MINING AND MINERAL PRODUCTS

PERU - INDUSTRY

Central Intelligence Agency, Washington, D.C. 20505 (703) 482-1100, www.cia.gov; *The World Factbook.*

Economist Intelligence Unit, 111 West 57th Street, New York, New York 10019 (800) 938-4685; *Peru Country Report.*

Euromonitor International, Inc., 122 Michigan Avenue, Suite 1200, Chicago, Illinois 60603 (800) 577-EURO; *International Marketing Data and Statistics; World Marketing Data and Statistics;* and *The World Economic Factbook.*

Europa Publications Limited, 18 Bedford Square, London, WC1B 3JN, England; *The Europa World Year Book.*

International Labour Office, I.L.O. Publications, 1828 L Street, NW., Suite 801, Washington, D.C. 20036 (301) 638-3152; *Yearbook of Labour Statistics.*

M.E. Sharpe, 80 Business Park Drive, Armonk, New York 10504 (800) 541-6563; *The Illustrated Book of World Rankings.*

St. Martin's Press, Inc., 175 Fifth Avenue, New York, New York 10010 (800) 221-7945; *The Statesman's Year-Book.*

Statistical Office of the United Nations, Publishing Service, New York, New York 10017 (800) 253-9646; *Economic Survey of Latin America and the Caribbean; Industrial Commodity Statistics Yearbook;* and *Statistical Yearbook.*

U.C.L.A. Latin American Center Publications, University of California, Los Angeles, California 90024 (310) 825-6634; *Statistical Abstract of Latin America.*

The World Bank, 1818 H Street, NW, Washington, D.C. 20433 (202) 477-1234; *World Development Indicators.*

World Intellectual Property Organization, 34 Chemin des Colombettes, CH-1211 Geneva 20, Switzerland; *Industrial Property Statistics.*

PERU - INFANT AND MATERNAL MORTALITY - See PERU - MORTALITY

PERU - INFLATIONARY FACTORS

Statistical Office of the United Nations, Publishing Service, New York, New York 10017 (800) 253-9646; *Economic Survey of Latin America and the Caribbean.*

PERU - INTEREST RATES

Inter-American Development Bank, 1300 New York Avenue, NW, Washington, D.C. 20577 (202) 623-1753; *Economic and Social Progress in Latin America.*

Organization of American States (OAS), General Secretariat, Washington, D.C. 20006 (202) 458-3533; *Statistical Bulletin of the OAS.*

PERU - INTERNATIONAL FINANCE

Inter-American Development Bank, 1300 New York Avenue, NW, Washington, D.C. 20577 (202) 623-1753; *Economic and Social Progress in Latin America.*

U.C.L.A. Latin American Center Publications, University of California, Los Angeles, California 90024 (310) 825-6634; *Statistical Abstract of Latin America.*

PERU - INTERNATIONAL LIQUIDITY

Inter-American Development Bank, 1300 New York Avenue, NW, Washington, D.C. 20577 (202) 623-1753; *Economic and Social Progress in Latin America.*

International Monetary Fund, 700 Nineteenth Street, NW, Washington, D.C. 20431 (202) 623-7000; *International Financial Statistics.*

PERU - INTERNATIONAL RESERVES

Inter-American Development Bank, 1300 New York Avenue, NW, Washington, D.C. 20577 (202) 623-1753; *Economic and Social Progress in Latin America.*

Organization of American States (OAS), General Secretariat, Washington, D.C. 20006 (202) 458-3533; *Statistical Bulletin of the OAS.*

Statistical Office of the United Nations, Publishing Service, New York, New York 10017 (800) 253-9646; *Statistical Yearbook.*

PERU - INTERNATIONAL RESERVES EXCLUDING GOLD

The World Bank, 1818 H Street, NW, Washington, D.C. 20433 (202) 477-1234; *World Development Indicators.*

PERU - INTERNATIONAL STATISTICS

Inter-American Development Bank, 1300 New York Avenue, NW, Washington, D.C. 20577 (202) 623-1753; *Economic and Social Progress in Latin America.*

U.C.L.A. Latin American Center Publications, University of California, Los Angeles, California 90024 (310) 825-6634; *Statistical Abstract of Latin America.*

PERU - INVESTMENTS

Inter-American Development Bank, 1300 New York Avenue, NW, Washington, D.C. 20577 (202) 623-1753; *Economic and Social Progress in Latin America.*

International Monetary Fund, 700 Nineteenth Street, NW, Washington, D.C. 20431 (202) 623-7000; *International Financial Statistics.*

Statistical Office of the United Nations, Publishing Service, New York, New York 10017 (800) 253-9646; *Statistical Yearbook for Latin America and the Caribbean.*

PERU - IRON ORE - See PERU - MINING AND MINERAL PRODUCTS

PERU - IRRIGATION

Euromonitor International, Inc., 122 Michigan Avenue, Suite 1200, Chicago, Illinois 60603 (800) 577-EURO; *International Marketing Data and Statistics.*

Inter-American Development Bank, 1300 New York Avenue, NW, Washington, D.C. 20577 (202) 623-1753; *Economic and Social Progress in Latin America.*

PERU - JUTE PRODUCTION - See PERU - CROPS

PERU - LABOR

Central Intelligence Agency, Washington, D.C. 20505 (703) 482-1100, www.cia.gov; *The World Factbook.*

The Economist Intelligence Unit, 111 West 57th Street, New York, New York 10019 (800) 938-4685; *The New Latin America Market Atlas.*

Euromonitor International, Inc., 122 Michigan Avenue, Suite 1200, Chicago, Illinois 60603 (800) 577-EURO; *International Marketing Data and Statistics;* and *World Marketing Data and Statistics.*

Europa Publications Limited, 18 Bedford Square, London, WC1B 3JN, England; *The Europa World Year Book.*

Food and Agricultural Organization of the United Nations (FAO) Via delle Terme di Caracalla, 00100 Rome, Italy (Telephone Number in U.S. (202) 653-2400); *The State of Food and Agriculture.*

International Labour Office, I.L.O. Publications, 1828 L Street, NW., Suite 801, Washington, D.C. 20036 (301) 638-3152; *Yearbook of Labour Statistics.*

M.E. Sharpe, 80 Business Park Drive, Armonk, New York 10504 (800) 541-6563; *The Illustrated Book of World Rankings.*

St. Martin's Press, Inc., 175 Fifth Avenue, New York, New York 10010 (800) 221-7945; *The Statesman's Year-Book.*

Statistical Office of the United Nations, Publishing Service, New York, New York 10017 (800) 253-9646; *Human Development Report.*

The World Bank, 1818 H Street, NW, Washington, D.C. 20433 (202) 477-1234; *The World Bank Atlas; World Development Report;* and *World Development Indicators.*

PERU - LAND AREA

The Economist Intelligence Unit, 111 West 57th Street, New York, New York 10019 (800) 938-4685; *The New Latin America Market Atlas.*

PERU - LAND USE

Central Intelligence Agency, Washington, D.C. 20505 (703) 482-1100, www.cia.gov; *The World Factbook.*

Euromonitor International, Inc., 122 Michigan Avenue, Suite 1200, Chicago, Illinois 60603 (800) 577-EURO; *International Marketing Data and Statistics.*

Food and Agricultural Organization of the United Nations (FAO), Via delle Terme di Caracalla, 00100 Rome, Italy (Telephone

Number in U.S. (202) 653-2400); *Production Yearbook.*

Inter-American Development Bank, 1300 New York Avenue, NW, Washington, D.C. 20577 (202) 623-1753; *Economic and Social Progress in Latin America.*

The World Bank, 1818 H Street, NW, Washington, D.C. 20433 (202) 477-1234; *World Development Report.*

PERU - LEAD AND LEAD ORE PRODUCTION AND CONSUMPTION - See PERU - MINING AND MINERAL PRODUCTS

PERU - LIBRARIES

M.E. Sharpe, 80 Business Park Drive, Armonk, New York 10504 (800) 541-6563; *The Illustrated Book of World Rankings.*

PERU - LIBRARIES - HIGHER EDUCATION

United Nations Educational, Scientific and Cultural Organization (UNESCO), 7 Place de Fontenoy, F-75700 Paris, France (Telephone Number in U.S. (212) 963-5981); *Statistical Yearbook.*

PERU - LIFE EXPECTANCY

Central Intelligence Agency, Washington, D.C. 20505 (703) 482-1100, www.cia.gov; *The World Factbook.*

The Economist Intelligence Unit, 111 West 57th Street, New York, New York 10019 (800) 938-4685; *The New Latin America Market Atlas.*

Euromonitor International, Inc., 122 Michigan Avenue, Suite 1200, Chicago, Illinois 60603 (800) 577-EURO; *The World Economic Factbook.*

St. Martin's Press, Inc., 175 Fifth Avenue, New York, New York 10010 (800) 221-7945; *The Statesman's Year-Book.*

Statistical Office of the United Nations, Publishing Service, New York, New York 10017 (800) 253-9646; *Human Development Report; Statistical Yearbook for Latin America and the Caribbean;* and *World Statistics Pocketbook.*

The World Bank, 1818 H Street, NW, Washington, D.C. 20433 (202) 477-1234; *The World Bank Atlas;* and *World Development Report.*

PERU - LIGNITE PRODUCTION - See PERU - MINING AND MINERAL PRODUCTS

PERU - LITERACY RATE

Euromonitor International, Inc., 122 South Michigan Avenue, Suite 1200, Chicago, Illinois 60603 (800) 577-EURO; *World Marketing Data and Statistics.*

PERU - LIVESTOCK AND POULTRY

Commodity Research Bureau, Inc., 30 South Wacker Drive, Chicago Illinois 60606 (312) 454-1801; *Commodity Year Book.*

Euromonitor International, Inc., 122 Michigan Avenue, Suite 1200, Chicago, Illinois 60603 (800) 577-EURO; *International Marketing Data and Statistics.*

Europa Publications Limited, 18 Bedford Square, London, WC1B 3JN, England; *The Europa World Year Book.*

Food and Agricultural Organization of the United Nations (FAO), Via delle Terme di Caracalla, 00100 Rome, Italy (Telephone Number in U.S. (202) 653-2400); *Production Yearbook;* and *The State of Food and Agriculture.*

M.E. Sharpe, 80 Business Park Drive, Armonk, New York 10504 (800) 541-6563; *The Illustrated Book of World Rankings.*

St. Martin's Press, Inc., 175 Fifth Avenue, New York, New York 10010 (800) 221-7945; *The Statesman's Year-Book.*

Statistical Office of the United Nations, Publishing Service, New York, New York 10017 (800) 253-9646; *Statistical Yearbook.*

United Nations Conference on Trade and Development, Central Statistical Service, Palais des Nations, Geneva, Switzerland (Telephone in U.S. (800) 253-9646); *UNCTAD Commodity Yearbook.*

PERU - LIVING LEVELS - See PERU - LIFE EXPECTANCY

PERU - MAGNESIUM PRODUCTION AND CONSUMPTION - See PERU - MINING AND MINERAL PRODUCTS

PERU - MAIN ECONOMIC INDICATORS - See PERU - ECONOMY

PERU - MANGANESE AND MANGANESE ORE PRODUCTION AND CONSUMPTION - See PERU - MINING AND MINERAL PRODUCTS

PERU - MANUFACTURING

The Economist Intelligence Unit, 111 West 57th Street, New York, New York 10019 (800) 938-4685; *The New Latin America Market Atlas.*

Inter-American Development Bank, 1300 New York Avenue, NW, Washington, D.C. 20577 (202) 623-1753; *Economic and Social Progress in Latin America.*

M.E. Sharpe, 80 Business Park Drive, Armonk, New York 10504 (800) 541-6563; *The Illustrated Book of World Rankings.*

Statistical Office of the United Nations, Publishing Service, New York, New York 10017 (800) 253-9646; *Statistical Yearbook;* and *Statistical Yearbook for Latin America and the Caribbean.*

The World Bank, 1818 H Street, NW, Washington, D.C. 20433 (202) 477-1234; *World Development Indicators.*

PERU - MARGARINE PRODUCTION

Statistical Office of the United Nations, Publishing Service, New York, New York 10017 (800) 253-9646; *Statistical Yearbook.*

PERU - MARRIAGE RATES

M.E. Sharpe, 80 Business Park Drive, Armonk, New York 10504 (800) 541-6563; *The Illustrated Book of World Rankings.*

Statistical Office of the United Nations, Publishing Service, New York, New York 10017 (800) 253-9646; *Demographic Yearbook;* and *Statistical Yearbook.*

PERU - MEAT PRODUCTION - See PERU - LIVESTOCK AND POULTRY

PERU - MEDICAL PERSONNEL

U.C.L.A. Latin American Center Publications, University of California, Los Angeles, California 90024 (310) 825-6634; *Statistical Abstract of Latin America.*

PERU - MERCHANT SHIPPING

Europa Publications Limited, 18 Bedford Square, London, WC1B 3JN, England; *The Europa World Year Book.*

Lloyd's Register of Shipping, 17 Battery Place, New York, New York 10004 (212) 425-8050; *Register of Ships.*

St. Martin's Press, Inc., 175 Fifth Avenue, New York, New York 10010 (800) 221-7945; *The Statesman's Year-Book.*

Statistical Office of the United Nations, Publishing Service, New York, New York 10017 (800) 253-9646; *Statistical Yearbook.*

U.S. Department of Transportation, Maritime Administration, 400 Seventh Street, SW, Washington, D.C. 20590 (202) 366-5807, www.marad.dot.gov; *A Statistical Analysis of the World's Merchant Fleets.*

PERU - MERCURY PRODUCTION AND CONSUMPTION - See PERU - MINING AND MINERAL PRODUCTS

PERU - MILITARY

Central Intelligence Agency, Washington, D.C. 20505 (703) 482-1100, www.cia.gov; *The World Factbook.*

The Economist Intelligence Unit, 111 West 57th Street, New York, New York 10019 (800) 938-4685; *The New Latin America Market Atlas*.

Euromonitor International, Inc., 122 South Michigan Avenue, Suite 1200, Chicago, Illinois 60603 (800) 577-EURO; *World Marketing Data and Statistics*.

The International Institute for Strategic Studies, 23 Tavistock Street, London WC2E 7NQ, England 44 171 3797676; *The Military Balance*.

International Monetary Fund, 700 Nineteenth Street, NW, Washington, D.C. 20431 (202) 623-7000; *Government Finance Statistics Yearbook*.

St. Martin's Press, Inc., 175 Fifth Avenue, New York, New York 10010 (800) 221-7945; *The Statesman's Year-Book*.

Statistical Office of the United Nations, Publishing Service, New York, New York 10017 (800) 253-9646; *Human Development Report*.

U.C.L.A. Latin American Center Publications, University of California, Los Angeles, California 90024 (310) 825-6634; *Statistical Abstract of Latin America*.

U.S. Arms Control and Disarmament Agency, 320 Twenty-first Street, NW, Washington, D.C. 20451 (202) 647-8677; *World Military Expenditures and Arms Transfers*.

PERU - MILK PRODUCTION - See PERU - DAIRY PRODUCTS

PERU - MINING AND MINERAL PRODUCTS

Commodity Research Bureau, Inc., 30 South Wacker Drive, Chicago Illinois 60606 (312) 454-1801; *Commodity Year Book*.

The Economist Intelligence Unit, 111 West 57th Street, New York, New York 10019 (800) 938-4685; *The New Latin America Market Atlas*.

Europa Publications Limited, 18 Bedford Square, London, WC1B 3JN, England; *The Europa World Year Book*.

Inter-American Development Bank, 1300 New York Avenue, NW, Washington, D.C. 20577 (202) 623-1753; *Economic and Social Progress in Latin America*.

International Lead and Zinc Study Group, Metro House, 58 St. James's Street, London SW1A 1LD, England; *Lead and Zinc Statistics*.

International Monetary Fund, 700 Nineteenth Street, NW, Washington, D.C. 20431 (202) 623-7000; *International Financial Statistics*.

M.E. Sharpe, 80 Business Park Drive, Armonk, New York 10504 (800) 541-6563; *The Illustrated Book of World Rankings*.

Organization of American States (OAS), General Secretariat, Washington, D.C. 20006 (202) 458-3533; *Statistical Bulletin of the OAS*.

Penn Well Publishing Company, 1421 South Sheridan Road, Post Office Box 1260, Tulsa, Oklahoma 74101 (800) 752-9764; *International Energy Statistics Sourcebook*.

St. Martin's Press, Inc., 175 Fifth Avenue, New York, New York 10010 (800) 221-7945; *The Statesman's Year-Book*.

Statistical Office of the United Nations, Publishing Service, New York, New York 10017 (800) 253-9646; *Statistical Yearbook;* and *Statistical Yearbook for Latin America and the Caribbean*.

U.C.L.A. Latin American Center Publications, University of California, Los Angeles, California 90024 (310) 825-6634; *Statistical Abstract of Latin America*.

United Nations Conference on Trade and Development, Central Statistical Service, Palais des Nations, Geneva, Switzerland (Telephone in U.S. (800) 253-9646); *UNCTAD Commodity Yearbook*.

World Bureau of Metal Statistics, 27-A High Street, Ware, Herts. SG12 9BA, England; *World Metal Statistics*.

PERU - MOLYBDENUM AND MOLYBDENUM ORE PRODUCTION AND CONSUMPTION - See PERU - MINING AND MINERAL PRODUCTS

PERU - MONEY EXCHANGE RATE - See PERU - EXCHANGE RATES

PERU - MONEY RATES - MARKET

Inter-American Development Bank, 1300 New York Avenue, NW, Washington, D.C. 20577 (202) 623-1753; *Economic and Social Progress in Latin America*.

PERU - MONEY RESERVES

Euromonitor International, Inc., 122 Michigan Avenue, Suite 1200, Chicago, Illinois 60603 (800) 577-EURO; *International Marketing Data and Statistics*.

Inter-American Development Bank, 1300 New York Avenue, NW, Washington, D.C. 20577 (202) 623-1753; *Economic and Social Progress in Latin America*.

PERU - MONEY SUPPLY

Economist Intelligence Unit, 111 West 57th Street, New York, New York 10019 (800) 938-4685; *Peru Country Report*.

Euromonitor International, Inc., 122 Michigan Avenue, Suite 1200, Chicago, Illinois 60603 (800) 577-EURO; *International Marketing Data and Statistics*.

Europa Publications Limited, 18 Bedford Square, London, WC1B 3JN, England; *The Europa World Year Book*.

Inter-American Development Bank, 1300 New York Avenue, NW, Washington, D.C. 20577 (202) 623-1753; *Economic and Social Progress in Latin America*.

International Monetary Fund, 700 Nineteenth Street, NW, Washington, D.C. 20431 (202) 623-7000; *International Financial Statistics*.

Statistical Office of the United Nations, Publishing Service, New York, New York 10017 (800) 253-9646; *Statistical Yearbook*.

U.C.L.A. Latin American Center Publications, University of California, Los Angeles, California 90024 (310) 825-6634; *Statistical Abstract of Latin America*.

The World Bank, 1818 H Street, NW, Washington, D.C. 20433 (202) 477-1234; *World Development Indicators*.

PERU - MONUMENTS AND HISTORICAL SITES

United Nations Educational, Scientific and Cultural Organization (UNESCO), 7 Place de Fontenoy, F-75700 Paris, France (Telephone Number in U.S. (212) 963-5981); *Statistical Yearbook*.

PERU - MORTALITY

Central Intelligence Agency, Washington, D.C. 20505 (703) 482-1100, www.cia.gov; *The World Factbook*.

The Economist Intelligence Unit, 111 West 57th Street, New York, New York 10019 (800) 938-4685; *The New Latin America Market Atlas*.

Euromonitor International, Inc., 122 Michigan Avenue, Suite 1200, Chicago, Illinois 60603 (800) 577-EURO; *International Marketing Data and Statistics;* and *The World Economic Factbook*.

Europa Publications Limited, 18 Bedford Square, London, WC1B 3JN, England; *The Europa World Year Book*.

St. Martin's Press, Inc., 175 Fifth Avenue, New York, New York 10010 (800) 221-7945; *The Statesman's Year-Book*.

Statistical Office of the United Nations,

Publishing Service, New York, New York 10017 (800) 253-9646; *Demographic Yearbook; Human Development Report; Statistical Yearbook; Statistical Yearbook for Latin America and the Caribbean;* and *World Statistics Pocketbook.*

United Nations Children's Fund (UNICEF), 3 United Nations Plaza, New York, New York 10017 (800) 253-9646; *State of the World's Children.*

The World Bank, 1818 H Street, NW, Washington, D.C. 20433 (202) 477-1234; *The World Bank Atlas; World Development Report;* and *World Development Indicators.*

World Health Organization, Office of Publications, 20 Avenue Appia, CH-1211 Geneva 27, Switzerland (Telephone Number in U.S. (518) 436-9686); *World Health Statistics Annual.*

PERU - MOTION PICTURES

Statistical Office of the United Nations, Publishing Service, New York, New York 10017 (800) 253-9646; *Statistical Yearbook.*

United Nations Educational, Scientific and Cultural Organization (UNESCO), 7 Place de Fontenoy, F-75700 Paris, France (Telephone Number in U.S. (212) 963-5981); *Statistical Yearbook.*

PERU - MOTOR VEHICLE PRODUCTION

The Economist Intelligence Unit, 111 West 57th Street, New York, New York 10019 (800) 938-4685; *The New Latin America Market Atlas.*

Europa Publications Limited, 18 Bedford Square, London, WC1B 3JN, England; *The Europa World Year Book.*

Statistical Office of the United Nations, Publishing Service, New York, New York 10017 (800) 253-9646; *Statistical Yearbook.*

PERU - MOTOR VEHICLE TAXES - See PERU - TAXATION

PERU - MOTOR VEHICLES IN USE

International Road Federation, 2600 Virginia Avenue, NW., Washington, D.C. 20037 (202) 338-4641; *World Road Statistics.*

Statistical Office of the United Nations, Publishing Service, New York, New York 10017 (800) 253-9646; *Statistical Yearbook.*

PERU - MULES - See PERU - LIVESTOCK AND POULTRY

PERU - MUSEUMS

M.E. Sharpe, 80 Business Park Drive, Armonk, New York 10504 (800) 541-6563;

The Illustrated Book of World Rankings.

United Nations Educational, Scientific and Cultural Organization (UNESCO), 7 Place de Fontenoy, F-75700 Paris, France (Telephone Number in U.S. (212) 963-5981); *Statistical Yearbook.*

PERU - NATALITY - See PERU - BIRTH RATES

PERU - NATIONAL ACCOUNTS

Europa Publications Limited, 18 Bedford Square, London, WC1B 3JN, England; *The Europa World Year Book.*

Inter-American Development Bank, 1300 New York Avenue, NW, Washington, D.C. 20577 (202) 623-1753; *Economic and Social Progress in Latin America.*

International Monetary Fund, 700 Nineteenth Street, NW, Washington, D.C. 20431 (202) 623-7000; *International Financial Statistics.*

Organization of American States (OAS), General Secretariat, Washington, D.C. 20006 (202) 458-3533; *Statistical Bulletin of the OAS.*

Statistical Office of the United Nations, Publishing Service, New York, New York 10017 (800) 253-9646; *National Accounts Statistics;* and *Statistical Yearbook.*

U.C.L.A. Latin American Center Publications, University of California, Los Angeles, California 90024 (310) 825-6634; *Statistical Abstract of Latin America.*

PERU - NATIONAL INCOME

Inter-American Development Bank, 1300 New York Avenue, NW, Washington, D.C. 20577 (202) 623-1753; *Economic and Social Progress in Latin America.*

M.E. Sharpe, 80 Business Park Drive, Armonk, New York 10504 (800) 541-6563; *The Illustrated Book of World Rankings.*

Statistical Office of the United Nations, Publishing Service, New York, New York 10017 (800) 253-9646; *National Accounts Statistics;* and *Statistical Yearbook.*

PERU - NATIONAL PRODUCT

M.E. Sharpe, 80 Business Park Drive, Armonk, New York 10504 (800) 541-6563; *The Illustrated Book of World Rankings.*

Statistical Office of the United Nations, Publishing Service, New York, New York 10017 (800) 253-9646; *Statistical Yearbook.*

PERU - NATURAL GAS PRODUCTION - See PERU - MINING AND MINERAL PRODUCTS

PERU - NEWSPAPER PRODUCTION - See PERU - FORESTRY AND FOREST PRODUCTS

PERU - NEWSPRINT - See PERU - FORESTRY AND FOREST PRODUCTS

PERU - NICKEL - See PERU - MINING AND MINERAL PRODUCTS

PERU - NITRIC ACID PRODUCTION - See PERU - MINING AND MINERAL PRODUCTS

PERU - NUTRITION

Statistical Office of the United Nations, Publishing Service, New York, New York 10017 (800) 253-9646; *Statistical Yearbook for Latin America and the Caribbean.*

PERU - OATS PRODUCTION - See PERU - CROPS

PERU - OCCUPATIONS - See PERU - LABOR

PERU - ORANGES PRODUCTION - See PERU - CROPS

PERU - PALM KERNELS AND PALM OIL PRODUCTION - See PERU - CROPS

PERU - PAPER - See PERU - FORESTRY AND FOREST PRODUCTS

PERU - PATENTS, TRADEMARKS AND SERVICE MARKS

Statistical Office of the United Nations, Publishing Service, New York, New York 10017 (800) 253-9646; *Statistical Yearbook.*

World Intellectual Property Organization, 34 Chemin des Colombettes, CH-1211 Geneva 20, Switzerland; *Industrial Property Statistics.*

PERU - PEANUT PRODUCTION - See PERU - CROPS

PERU - PERIODICALS

United Nations Educational, Scientific and Cultural Organization (UNESCO), 7 Place de Fontenoy, F-75700 Paris, France (Telephone Number in U.S. (212) 963-5981); *Statistical Yearbook.*

PERU - PESTICIDE USE

Food and Agricultural Organization of the United Nations (FAO) Via delle Terme di Caracalla, 00100 Rome, Italy (Telephone Number in U.S. (202) 653-2400); *The State of Food and Agriculture.*

PERU - PETROLEUM INDUSTRY

The Economist Intelligence Unit, 111 West 57th Street, New York, New York

10019 (800) 938-4685; *The New Latin America Market Atlas.*

Food and Agricultural Organization of the United Nations (FAO) Via delle Terme di Caracalla, 00100 Rome, Italy (Telephone Number in U.S. (202) 653-2400); *The State of Food and Agriculture.*

Inter-American Development Bank, 1300 New York Avenue, NW, Washington, D.C. 20577 (202) 623-1753; *Economic and Social Progress in Latin America.*

M.E. Sharpe, 80 Business Park Drive, Armonk, New York 10504 (800) 541-6563; *The Illustrated Book of World Rankings.*

Penn Well Publishing Company, 1421 South Sheridan Road, Post Office Box 1260, Tulsa, Oklahoma 74101 (800) 752-9764; *International Energy Statistics Sourcebook.*

St. Martin's Press, Inc., 175 Fifth Avenue, New York, New York 10010 (800) 221-7945; *The Statesman's Year-Book.*

Statistical Office of the United Nations, Publishing Service, New York, New York 10017 (800) 253-9646; *Statistical Yearbook.*

United Nations Conference on Trade and Development, Central Statistical Service, Palais des Nations, Geneva, Switzerland (Telephone in U.S. (800) 253-9646); *UNCTAD Commodity Yearbook.*

PERU - PHOSPHATE ROCK PRODUCTION - See PERU - MINING AND MINERAL PRODUCTS

PERU - PIG-IRON AND FERRO-ALLOYS PRODUCTION - See PERU - MINING AND MINERAL PRODUCTS

PERU - PIGS - See PERU - LIVESTOCK AND POULTRY

PERU - PLATINUM PRODUCTION AND CONSUMPTION - See PERU -MINING AND MINERAL PRODUCTS

PERU - POLITICAL DATA

U.C.L.A. Latin American Center Publications, University of California, Los Angeles, California 90024 (310) 825-6634; *Statistical Abstract of Latin America.*

PERU - POPULATION

Central Intelligence Agency, Washington, D.C. 20505 (703) 482-1100, www.cia.gov; *The World Factbook.*

The Economist Intelligence Unit, 111 West 57th Street, New York, New York 10019 (800) 938-4685; *The New Latin America Market Atlas; Peru Country Report;* and *The World Market Atlas.*

Euromonitor International, Inc., 122 Michigan Avenue, Suite 1200, Chicago, Illinois 60603 (800) 577-EURO; *International Marketing Data and Statistics;* and *The World Economic Factbook.*

Europa Publications Limited, 18 Bedford Square, London, WC1B 3JN, England; *The Europa World Year Book.*

Food and Agricultural Organization of the United Nations (FAO), Via delle Terme di Caracalla, 00100 Rome, Italy (Telephone Number in U.S. (202) 653-2400); *Production Yearbook.*

Inter-American Development Bank, 1300 New York Avenue, NW, Washington, D.C. 20577 (202) 623-1753; *Economic and Social Progress in Latin America.*

International Labour Office, I.L.O. Publications, 1828 L Street, NW., Suite 801, Washington, D.C. 20036 (301) 638-3152; *Yearbook of Labour Statistics.*

M.E. Sharpe, 80 Business Park Drive, Armonk, New York 10504 (800) 541-6563; *The Illustrated Book of World Rankings.*

Organization of American States (OAS), General Secretariat, Washington, D.C. 20006 (202) 458-3533; *Statistical Bulletin of the OAS.*

St. Martin's Press, Inc., 175 Fifth Avenue, New York, New York 10010 (800) 221-7945; *The Statesman's Year-Book.*

Statistical Office of the United Nations, Publishing Service, New York, New York 10017 (800) 253-9646; *Demographic Yearbook; Human Development Report; Statistical Yearbook; Statistical Yearbook for Latin America and the Caribbean;* and *World Statistics Pocketbook.*

U.C.L.A. Latin American Center Publications, University of California, Los Angeles, California 90024 (310) 825-6634; *Statistical Abstract of Latin America.*

United Nations Educational, Scientific and Cultural Organization (UNESCO), 7 Place de Fontenoy, F-75700 Paris, France (Telephone Number in U.S. (212) 963-5981); *Statistical Yearbook.*

U.S. Arms Control and Disarmament Agency, 320 Twenty-first Street, NW, Washington, D.C. 20451 (202) 647-8677; *World Military Expenditures and Arms Transfers.*

The World Bank, 1818 H Street, NW, Washington, D.C. 20433 (202) 477-1234; *The World Bank Atlas;* and *World Development Report.*

World Health Organization, Office of Publications, 20 Avenue Appia, CH-1211

Geneva 27, Switzerland (Telephone Number in U.S. (518) 436-9686); *World Health Statistics Annual.*

PERU - POST OFFICES

M.E. Sharpe, 80 Business Park Drive, Armonk, New York 10504 (800) 541-6563; *The Illustrated Book of World Rankings.*

St. Martin's Press, Inc., 175 Fifth Avenue, New York, New York 10010 (800) 221-7945; *The Statesman's Year-Book.*

PERU - POTATO PRODUCTION - See PERU - CROPS

PERU - POWER PRODUCTION INDUSTRY

Statistical Office of the United Nations, Publishing Service, New York, New York 10017 (800) 253-9646; *Statistical Yearbook.*

PERU - PRICES

Food and Agricultural Organization of the United Nations (FAO), Via delle Terme di Caracalla, 00100 Rome, Italy (Telephone Number in U.S. (202) 653-2400); *Production Yearbook;* and *The State of Food and Agriculture.*

International Labour Office, I.L.O. Publications, 1828 L Street, NW., Suite 801, Washington, D.C. 20036 (301) 638-3152; *Yearbook of Labour Statistics.*

International Lead and Zinc Study Group, Metro House, 58 St. James's Street, London SW1A 1LD, England; *Lead and Zinc Statistics.*

International Monetary Fund, 700 Nineteenth Street, NW, Washington, D.C. 20431 (202) 623-7000; *International Financial Statistics.*

M.E. Sharpe, 80 Business Park Drive, Armonk, New York 10504 (800) 541-6563; *The Illustrated Book of World Rankings.*

Statistical Office of the United Nations, Publishing Service, New York, New York 10017 (800) 253-9646; *Economic Survey of Latin America and the Caribbean;* and *Statistical Yearbook for Latin America and the Caribbean.*

World Bureau of Metal Statistics, 27-A High Street, Ware, Herts. SG12 9BA, England; *World Metal Statistics.*

PERU - PRINTING AND WRITING PAPER - See PERU - FORESTRY AND FOREST PRODUCTS

PERU - PRODUCTION

International Lead and Zinc Study Group, Metro House, 58 St. James's Street, London SW1A 1LD, England; *Lead and*

Zinc Statistics.

M.E. Sharpe, 80 Business Park Drive, Armonk, New York 10504 (800) 541-6563; *The Illustrated Book of World Rankings.*

PERU - PRODUCTIVITY

Euromonitor International, Inc., 122 Michigan Avenue, Suite 1200, Chicago, Illinois 60603 (800) 577-EURO; *International Marketing Data and Statistics.*

PERU - PROPERTY TAXES - See PERU - TAXATION

PERU - PUBLIC CONSUMPTION FUND

Inter-American Development Bank, 1300 New York Avenue, NW, Washington, D.C. 20577 (202) 623-1753; *Economic and Social Progress in Latin America.*

PERU - PUBLIC EXPENDITURES

Inter-American Development Bank, 1300 New York Avenue, NW, Washington, D.C. 20577 (202) 623-1753; *Economic and Social Progress in Latin America.*

Organization of American States (OAS), General Secretariat, Washington, D.C. 20006 (202) 458-3533; *Statistical Bulletin of the OAS.*

Statistical Office of the United Nations, Publishing Service, New York, New York 10017 (800) 253-9646; *Statistical Yearbook for Latin America and the Caribbean.*

PERU - PUBLIC FINANCE - See PERU - FINANCE

PERU - PUBLIC REVENUE

Inter-American Development Bank, 1300 New York Avenue, NW, Washington, D.C. 20577 (202) 623-1753; *Economic and Social Progress in Latin America.*

Organization of American States (OAS), General Secretariat, Washington, D.C. 20006 (202) 458-3533; *Statistical Bulletin of the OAS.*

PERU - RADIO BROADCASTING - See PERU - BROADCASTING

PERU - RADIO RECEIVER PRODUCTION

Statistical Office of the United Nations, Publishing Service, New York, New York 10017 (800) 253-9646; *Statistical Yearbook.*

PERU - RADIO RECEIVERS

St. Martin's Press, Inc., 175 Fifth Avenue, New York, New York 10010 (800) 221-7945; *The Statesman's Year-Book.*

PERU - RAILWAYS

The Economist Intelligence Unit, 111 West 57th Street, New York, New York 10019 (800) 938-4685; *The New Latin America Market Atlas.*

Europa Publications Limited, 18 Bedford Square, London, WC1B 3JN, England; *The Europa World Year Book.*

Jane's Information Group, Sentinel House, 163 Brighton Road, Coulsdon, Surrey CR5 2NH, England (Telephone Number in U.S. (703) 683-3700); *Jane's World Railways.*

St. Martin's Press, Inc., 175 Fifth Avenue, New York, New York 10010 (800) 221-7945; *The Statesman's Year-Book.*

Statistical Office of the United Nations, Publishing Service, New York, New York 10017 (800) 253-9646; *Statistical Yearbook.*

PERU - RANCHING

U.C.L.A. Latin American Center Publications, University of California, Los Angeles, California 90024 (310) 825-6634; *Statistical Abstract of Latin America.*

PERU - RELIGION

Central Intelligence Agency, Washington, D.C. 20505 (703) 482-1100, www.cia.gov; *The World Factbook.*

M.E. Sharpe, 80 Business Park Drive, Armonk, New York 10504 (800) 541-6563; *The Illustrated Book of World Rankings.*

St. Martin's Press, Inc., 175 Fifth Avenue, New York, New York 10010 (800) 221-7945; *The Statesman's Year-Book.*

U.C.L.A. Latin American Center Publications, University of California, Los Angeles, California 90024 (310) 825-6634; *Statistical Abstract of Latin America.*

PERU - RENT PRICES

International Labour Office, I.L.O. Publications, 1828 L Street, NW., Suite 801, Washington, D.C. 20036 (301) 638-3152; *Yearbook of Labour Statistics.*

PERU - RESERVES EXCLUDING GOLD

The Economist Intelligence Unit, 111 West 57th Street, New York, New York 10019 (800) 938-4685; *The New Latin America Market Atlas.*

PERU - RETAIL TRADE

Euromonitor International, Inc., 122 South Michigan Avenue, Suite 1200, Chicago, Illinois 60603 (800) 577-EURO; *World Marketing Data and Statistics;* and *Retail Trade International.*

Inter-American Development Bank, 1300 New York Avenue, NW, Washington, D.C. 20577 (202) 623-1753; *Economic and Social Progress in Latin America.*

PERU - REVENUES

Organization of American States (OAS), General Secretariat, Washington, D.C. 20006 (202) 458-3533; *Statistical Bulletin of the OAS.*

PERU - RICE PRODUCTION - See PERU - CROPS

PERU - ROOT AND TUBER PRODUCTION - See PERU - CROPS

PERU - ROUNDWOOD PRODUCTION - See PERU - FORESTRY AND FORESTRY PRODUCTS

PERU - RUBBER PRODUCTION AND CONSUMPTION

M.E. Sharpe, 80 Business Park Drive, Armonk, New York 10504 (800) 541-6563; *The Illustrated Book of World Rankings.*

PERU - SALT PRODUCTION - See PERU - MINING AND MINERAL PRODUCTS

PERU - SAWNWOOD PRODUCTION - See PERU - FORESTRY AND FOREST PRODUCTS

PERU - SCIENTISTS, TECHNICIANS AND ENGINEERS

Statistical Office of the United Nations, Publishing Service, New York, New York 10017 (800) 253-9646; *Statistical Yearbook.*

U.C.L.A. Latin American Center Publications, University of California, Los Angeles, California 90024 (310) 825-6634; *Statistical Abstract of Latin America.*

United Nations Educational, Scientific and Cultural Organization (UNESCO), 7 Place de Fontenoy, F-75700 Paris, France (Telephone Number in U.S. (212) 963-5981); *Statistical Yearbook.*

PERU - SENIOR CITIZENS

M.E. Sharpe, 80 Business Park Drive, Armonk, New York 10504 (800) 541-6563; *The Illustrated Book of World Rankings.*

PERU - SHEEP - See PERU - LIVESTOCK AND POULTRY

PERU - SILVER EXPORTS - See PERU - MINING AND MINERAL PRODUCTS

PERU - SILVER PRODUCTION AND CONSUMPTION - See PERU - MINING AND MINERAL PRODUCTS

PERU - SOCIAL DATA

M.E. Sharpe, 80 Business Park Drive, Armonk, New York 10504 (800) 541-6563; *The Illustrated Book of World Rankings.*

Statistical Office of the United Nations, Publishing Service, New York, New York 10017 (800) 253-9646; *World Statistics Pocketbook.*

U.C.L.A. Latin American Center Publications, University of California, Los Angeles, California 90024 (310) 825-6634; *Statistical Abstract of Latin America.*

PERU - SOCIAL SECURITY

Inter-American Development Bank, 1300 New York Avenue, NW, Washington, D.C. 20577 (202) 623-1753; *Economic and Social Progress in Latin America.*

International Monetary Fund, 700 Nineteenth Street, NW, Washington, D.C. 20431 (202) 623-7000; *Government Finance Statistics Yearbook.*

St. Martin's Press, Inc., 175 Fifth Avenue, New York, New York 10010 (800) 221-7945; *The Statesman's Year-Book.*

Statistical Office of the United Nations, Publishing Service, New York, New York 10017 (800) 253-9646; *National Accounts Statistics.*

PERU - SOCIOECONOMIC DATA

Inter-American Development Bank, 1300 New York Avenue, NW, Washington, D.C. 20577 (202) 623-1753; *Economic and Social Progress in Latin America.*

U.C.L.A. Latin American Center Publications, University of California, Los Angeles, California 90024 (310) 825-6634; *Statistical Abstract of Latin America.*

PERU - SOYBEAN PRODUCTION - See PERU - CROPS

PERU - STAMP TAXES AND DUTIES - See PERU - TAXATION

PERU - STATE BUDGET REVENUE AND EXPENDITURES

Euromonitor International, Inc., 122 Michigan Avenue, Suite 1200, Chicago, Illinois 60603 (800) 577-EURO; *International Marketing Data and Statistics.*

Inter-American Development Bank, 1300 New York Avenue, NW, Washington, D.C. 20577 (202) 623-1753; *Economic and Social Progress in Latin America.*

PERU - STEEL - See PERU - MINING AND MINERAL PRODUCTS

PERU - STOCKS - COMMODITY - MARKET PRICE - INDEXES

Food and Agricultural Organization of the United Nations (FAO) Via delle Terme di Caracalla, 00100 Rome, Italy (Telephone Number in U.S. (202) 653-2400); *The State of Food and Agriculture.*

International Lead and Zinc Study Group, Metro House, 58 St. James's Street, London SW1A 1LD, England; *Lead and Zinc Statistics.*

Statistical Office of the United Nations, Publishing Service, New York, New York 10017 (800) 253-9646; *Statistical Yearbook.*

World Bureau of Metal Statistics, 27-A High Street, Ware, Herts. SG12 9BA, England; *World Metal Statistics.*

PERU - SUGAR PRODUCTION - See PERU - CROPS

PERU - SULPHURIC ACID PRODUCTION - See PERU - MINING AND MINERAL PRODUCTS

PERU - TAXATION

Europa Publications Limited, 18 Bedford Square, London, WC1B 3JN, England; *The Europa World Year Book.*

Inter-American Development Bank, 1300 New York Avenue, NW, Washington, D.C. 20577 (202) 623-1753; *Economic and Social Progress in Latin America.*

International Monetary Fund, 700 Nineteenth Street, NW, Washington, D.C. 20431 (202) 623-7000; *Government Finance Statistics Yearbook.*

International Road Federation, 2600 Virginia Avenue, NW., Washington, D.C. 20037 (202) 338-4641; *World Road Statistics.*

Statistical Office of the United Nations, Publishing Service, New York, New York 10017 (800) 253-9646; *Statistical Yearbook for Latin America and the Caribbean.*

The World Bank, 1818 H Street, NW, Washington, D.C. 20433 (202) 477-1234; *World Development Indicators.*

PERU - TEA PRODUCTION - See PERU - CROPS

PERU - TELEGRAPH SERVICE

Statistical Office of the United Nations, Publishing Service, New York, New York 10017 (800) 253-9646; *Statistical Yearbook.*

PERU - TELEPHONES IN USE

American Telephone and Telegraph

Company, 26 Parsippany Road, Whippany, New Jersey 07981 (800) 222-0300; *The World's Telephones.*

Central Intelligence Agency, Washington, D.C. 20505 (703) 482-1100, www.cia.gov; *The World Factbook.*

The Economist Intelligence Unit, 111 West 57th Street, New York, New York 10019 (800) 938-4685; *The New Latin America Market Atlas.*

Europa Publications Limited, 18 Bedford Square, London, WC1B 3JN, England; *The Europa World Year Book.*

St. Martin's Press, Inc., 175 Fifth Avenue, New York, New York 10010 (800) 221-7945; *The Statesman's Year-Book.*

Statistical Office of the United Nations, Publishing Service, New York, New York 10017 (800) 253-9646; *Statistical Yearbook;* and *World Statistics Pocketbook.*

PERU - TELEVISION BROADCASTING - See PERU - BROADCASTING

PERU - TELEVISION RECEIVER PRODUCTION

Statistical Office of the United Nations, Publishing Service, New York, New York 10017 (800) 253-9646; *Statistical Yearbook.*

PERU - TEXTILE INDUSTRY

American Forest and Paper Association, 1111 Nineteenth Street, NW, Washington, D.C. 20036 (202) 463-2700; *Wood Pulp and Fiber Statistics.*

Euromonitor International, Inc., 122 South Michigan Avenue, Suite 1200, Chicago, Illinois 60603 (800) 577-EURO; *Retail Trade International.*

M.E. Sharpe, 80 Business Park Drive, Armonk, New York 10504 (800) 541-6563; *The Illustrated Book of World Rankings.*

Statistical Office of the United Nations, Publishing Service, New York, New York 10017 (800) 253-9646; *Statistical Yearbook.*

United Nations Conference on Trade and Development, Central Statistical Service, Palais des Nations, Geneva, Switzerland (Telephone in U.S. (800) 253-9646); *UNCTAD Commodity Yearbook.*

PERU - THEATRE

United Nations Educational, Scientific and Cultural Organization (UNESCO), 7 Place de Fontenoy, F-75700 Paris, France (Telephone Number in U.S. (212) 963-5981); *Statistical Yearbook.*

PERU - TIN PRODUCTION AND CONSUMPTION - See PERU - MINING AND MINERAL PRODUCTS

PERU - TIRE (MOTOR VEHICLE) PRODUCTION

Statistical Office of the United Nations, Publishing Service, New York, New York 10017 (800) 253-9646; *Statistical Yearbook.*

PERU - TOBACCO PRODUCTION

M.E. Sharpe, 80 Business Park Drive, Armonk, New York 10504 (800) 541-6563; *The Illustrated Book of World Rankings.*

Statistical Office of the United Nations, Publishing Service, New York, New York 10017 (800) 253-9646; *Statistical Yearbook.*

U.C.L.A. Latin American Center Publications, University of California, Los Angeles, California 90024 (310) 825-6634; *Statistical Abstract of Latin America.*

PERU - TOURISM

The Economist Intelligence Unit, 111 West 57th Street, New York, New York 10019 (800) 938-4685; *The New Latin America Market Atlas.*

Euromonitor International, Inc., 122 Michigan Avenue, Suite 1200, Chicago, Illinois 60603 (800) 577-EURO; *The World Economic Factbook;* and *World Marketing Data and Statistics.*

Europa Publications Limited, 18 Bedford Square, London, WC1B 3JN, England; *The Europa World Year Book.*

M.E. Sharpe, 80 Business Park Drive, Armonk, New York 10504 (800) 541-6563; *The Illustrated Book of World Rankings.*

St. Martin's Press, Inc., 175 Fifth Avenue, New York, New York 10010 (800) 221-7945; *The Statesman's Year-Book.*

Statistical Office of the United Nations, Publishing Service, New York, New York 10017 (800) 253-9646; *Statistical Yearbook;* and *Statistical Yearbook for Latin America and the Caribbean.*

U.C.L.A. Latin American Center Publications, University of California, Los Angeles, California 90024 (310) 825-6634; *Statistical Abstract of Latin America.*

PERU - TRACTORS IN USE

The Economist Intelligence Unit, 111 West 57th Street, New York, New York 10019 (800) 938-4685; *The New Latin America Market Atlas.*

Statistical Office of the United Nations, Publishing Service, New York, New York

10017 (800) 253-9646; *Statistical Yearbook.*

PERU - TRADE - See PERU - FOREIGN TRADE

PERU - TRADEMARKS AND SERVICE MARKS - See PERU - PATENTS, TRADEMARKS AND SERVICE MARKS

PERU - TRANSPORTATION AND COMMUNICATIONS

Central Intelligence Agency, Washington, D.C. 20505 (703) 482-1100, www.cia.gov; *The World Factbook.*

The Economist Intelligence Unit, 111 West 57th Street, New York, New York 10019 (800) 938-4685; *The New Latin America Market Atlas.*

Euromonitor International, Inc., 122 Michigan Avenue, Suite 1200, Chicago, Illinois 60603 (800) 577-EURO; *International Marketing Data and Statistics;* and *World Marketing Data and Statistics.*

Europa Publications Limited, 18 Bedford Square, London, WC1B 3JN, England; *The Europa World Year Book.*

Inter-American Development Bank, 1300 New York Avenue, NW, Washington, D.C. 20577 (202) 623-1753; *Economic and Social Progress in Latin America.*

M.E. Sharpe, 80 Business Park Drive, Armonk, New York 10504 (800) 541-6563; *The Illustrated Book of World Rankings.*

St. Martin's Press, Inc., 175 Fifth Avenue, New York, New York 10010 (800) 221-7945; *The Statesman's Year-Book.*

Statistical Office of the United Nations, Publishing Service, New York, New York 10017 (800) 253-9646; *Human Development Report;* and *Statistical Yearbook for Latin America and the Caribbean.*

U.C.L.A. Latin American Center Publications, University of California, Los Angeles, California 90024 (310) 825-6634; *Statistical Abstract of Latin America.*

PERU - TUNGSTEN PRODUCTION AND CONSUMPTION - See PERU -MINING AND MINERAL PRODUCTS

PERU - UNEMPLOYMENT

Central Intelligence Agency, Washington, D.C. 20505 (703) 482-1100, www.cia.gov; *The World Factbook.*

The Economist Intelligence Unit, 111 West 57th Street, New York, New York 10019 (800) 938-4685; *The New Latin America Market Atlas.*

Euromonitor International, Inc., 122 Michigan Avenue, Suite 1200, Chicago, Illinois 60603 (800) 577-EURO; *International Marketing Data and Statistics.*

International Labour Office, I.L.O. Publications, 1828 L Street, NW., Suite 801, Washington, D.C. 20036 (301) 638-3152; *Yearbook of Labour Statistics.*

Statistical Office of the United Nations, Publishing Service, New York, New York 10017 (800) 253-9646; *Statistical Yearbook.*

U.C.L.A. Latin American Center Publications, University of California, Los Angeles, California 90024 (310) 825-6634; *Statistical Abstract of Latin America.*

PERU - URANIUM PRODUCTION AND CONSUMPTION - See PERU - MINING AND MINERAL PRODUCTS

PERU - UTILITIES

U.C.L.A. Latin American Center Publications, University of California, Los Angeles, California 90024 (310) 825-6634; *Statistical Abstract of Latin America.*

PERU - VANADIUM AND VANADIUM ORE PRODUCTION AND CONSUMPTION - See PERU - MINING AND MINERAL PRODUCTS

PERU - VITAL STATISTICS

Euromonitor International, Inc., 122 Michigan Avenue, Suite 1200, Chicago, Illinois 60603 (800) 577-EURO; *International Marketing Data and Statistics.*

St. Martin's Press, Inc., 175 Fifth Avenue, New York, New York 10010 (800) 221-7945; *The Statesman's Year-Book.*

Statistical Office of the United Nations, Publishing Service, New York, New York 10017 (800) 253-9646; *Statistical Yearbook.*

World Health Organization, Office of Publications, 20 Avenue Appia, CH-1211 Geneva 27, Switzerland (Telephone Number in U.S. (518) 436-9686); *World Health Statistics Annual.*

PERU - WAGES

International Labour Office, I.L.O. Publications, 1828 L Street, NW., Suite 801, Washington, D.C. 20036 (301) 638-3152; *Yearbook of Labour Statistics.*

Statistical Office of the United Nations, Publishing Service, New York, New York 10017 (800) 253-9646; *Statistical Yearbook.*

U.C.L.A. Latin American Center Publications, University of California, Los Angeles, California 90024 (310) 825-6634; *Statistical Abstract of Latin America.*

PERU - WATERMELON PRODUCTION - See
PERU - CROPS

PERU - WEATHER - See PERU - CLIMATE

PERU - WELFARE

Inter-American Development Bank,
1300 New York Avenue, NW, Washington,
D.C. 20577 (202) 623-1753; *Economic and
Social Progress in Latin America.*

International Monetary Fund, 700
Nineteenth Street, NW, Washington, D.C.
20431 (202) 623-7000; *Government
Finance Statistics Yearbook.*

PERU - WHALE AND SPERM OIL
PRODUCTION

Statistical Office of the United Nations,
Publishing Service, New York, New York
10017 (800) 253-9646; *Statistical Yearbook.*

PERU - WHALES CAUGHT

Statistical Office of the United Nations,
Publishing Service, New York, New York
10017 (800) 253-9646; *Statistical Yearbook.*

PERU - WHALING APPARATUS IN
OPERATION

Statistical Office of the United Nations,
Publishing Service, New York, New York
10017 (800) 253-9646; *Statistical Yearbook.*

PERU - WHEAT PRODUCTION AND
PRICES - See PERU - CROPS

PERU - WHOLESALE PRICES

Inter-American Development Bank,
1300 New York Avenue, NW, Washington,
D.C. 20577 (202) 623-1753; *Economic and
Social Progress in Latin America.*

Statistical Office of the United Nations,
Publishing Service, New York, New York
10017 (800) 253-9646; *Statistical Yearbook.*

PERU - WHOLESALE TRADE

Inter-American Development Bank,
1300 New York Avenue, NW, Washington,
D.C. 20577 (202) 623-1753; *Economic and
Social Progress in Latin America.*

PERU - WINE PRODUCTION - See PERU -
BEVERAGES

PERU - WOOD AND WOOD PULP - SEE
PERU - FORESTRY AND FOREST
PRODUCTS

PERU - WOOL PRODUCTION - See PERU -
TEXTILE INDUSTRY

PERU - ZINC - See PERU - MINING AND
MINERAL PRODUCTS

PESTICIDES

U.S. Department of Agriculture,
Economic Research Service, 1800 M Street,
NW, Washington, D.C. 20036 (202) 694-
5050, www.ers.usda.gov; *Farm Business
Economic Report.*

PETS - PET OWNERSHIP

American Veterinary Medical
Association, 1931 North Meacham Road,
Suite 100, Schaumburg, Illinois 60173 (847)
925-8070; *U.S. Pet Ownership and
Demographics Sourcebook.*

PETS - PET PRODUCTS

Television Bureau of Advertising, Inc., 3
East 54th Street, New York, New York 10022
(212) 486-1111; from data compiled by
Competitive Media Reporting, 11 West
42nd Street, New York, New York 10036
(212) 789-1400.

PETROLEUM AND PRODUCTS -
CONSUMPTION

U.S. Department of Energy, Energy
Information Administration, Washington,
D.C. 20585 (202) 586-8800,
www.eia.doe.gov; *Annual Energy Outlook;
Annual Energy Review; Monthly Energy
Review; International Energy Annual;
International Energy Outlook;* and *State
Energy Data Report.*

U.S. Department of the Interior,
Geological Survey, Office of Minerals
Information, 12201 Sunrise Valley Drive,
Reston, Virginia 22092 (703) 648-4000,
www.minerals.usgs.gov; *Mineral
Commodity Summaries.*

PETROLEUM AND PRODUCTS - FOREIGN
TRADE

U.S. Department of Commerce, Bureau
of the Census, Washington, D.C. 20233
(301) 457-4100, www.census.gov; *U.S.
International Trade in Goods and Services.*

U.S. Department of Commerce,
International Trade Administration,
Fourteenth Street between Constitution
Avenue and E Street, NW, Washington,
D.C. 20230 (202) 482-2185,
www.itas.doc.gov; *U.S. Foreign Highlights;*
and Internet site:
http://www.ita.doc.gov/industry/otea/usft
h/aggregate/H198to3.

U.S. Department of Energy, Energy
Information Administration, Washington,
D.C. 20585 (202) 586-8800,
www.eia.doe.gov; *Annual Energy Review;
Monthly Energy Review; Natural Gas
Monthly; Petroleum Supply Annual;
Petroleum Supply Monthly; Annual Energy
Outlook; State Energy Data Report;* and
International Energy Annual.

PETROLEUM AND PRODUCTS - LEASE
REVENUES

U.S. Department of Energy, Energy
Information Administration, Washington,
D.C. 20585 (202) 586-8800,
www.eia.doe.gov; *Petroleum Supply
Annual.*

PETROLEUM AND PRODUCTS - OILSPILLS

U.S. Department of Transportation,
United States Coast Guard, 2100 Second
Street, SW, Washington, D.C. 20593 (202)
267-2229, www.uscg.mil; Internet site:
http://www.uscg.mil/hq/g-
m/nmc/response/stats/summary.htm.

PETROLEUM AND PRODUCTS - PRICES

U.S. Department of Energy, Energy
Information Administration, Washington,
D.C. 20585 (202) 586-8800,
www.eia.doe.gov; *Annual Energy Review;*
and *Monthly Energy Review.*

PETROLEUM AND PRODUCTS -
PRODUCTION

U.S. Department of Energy, Energy
Information Administration, Washington,
D.C. 20585 (202) 586-8800,
www.eia.doe.gov; *Annual Energy Review;
Annual Energy Outlook; Monthly Energy
Review; Petroleum Supply Annual;* and
International Energy Annual.

U.S. Department of the Interior,
Minerals Management Service, 1849 C
Street, NW, Washington, D.C. 20240 (202)
208-3985; *Federal Offshore Statistics.*

PETROLEUM AND PRODUCTS -
PRODUCTION - WORLD

U.S. Department of Energy, Energy
Information Administration, Washington,
D.C. 20585 (202) 586-8800,
www.eia.doe.gov; *Annual Energy Review;
Monthly Energy Review;* and *International
Energy Annual.*

U.S. Department of the Interior,
Geological Survey, Office of Minerals
Information, 12201 Sunrise Valley Drive,
Reston, Virginia 22092 (703) 648-4000,
www.minerals.usgs.gov; *Annual Reports;*
and *Mineral Commodity Summaries.*

PETROLEUM AND PRODUCTS -
RAILROAD - CARLOADINGS OF

Association of American Railroads,
American Railroads Building, 50 F Street,
NW, Washington, D.C. 20001 (202) 639-
2100; *Freight Commodity Statistics;* and
Weekly Railroad Traffic.

PETROLEUM AND PRODUCTS -
REFINERIES

U.S. Department of Energy, Energy Information Administration, Washington, D.C. 20585 (202) 586-8800, www.eia.doe.gov; *Annual Energy Review; U.S. Crude Oil, Natural Gas and Natural Liquids Reserves; and Monthly Energy Review;* and *Petroleum Supply Annual.*

PETROLEUM AND PRODUCTS - RESERVES

U.S. Department of Energy, Energy Information Administration, Washington, D.C. 20585 (202) 586-8800, www.eia.doe.gov; *Annual Energy Review; U.S. Crude Oil, Natural Gas and Natural Liquids Reserves; and Monthly Energy Review;* and *Petroleum Supply Annual.*

PETROLEUM AND PRODUCTS - STOCKS

U.S. Department of Energy, Energy Information Administration, Washington, D.C. 20585 (202) 586-8800, www.eia.doe.gov; *Monthly Energy Review.*

PETROLEUM AND PRODUCTS - STRATEGIC RESERVE

U.S. Department of Energy, Energy Information Administration, Washington, D.C. 20585 (202) 586-8800, www.eia.doe.gov; *Monthly Energy Review.*

PETROLEUM AND PRODUCTS - VALUE

U.S. Department of Energy, Energy Information Administration, Washington, D.C. 20585 (202) 586-8800, www.eia.doe.gov; *Annual Energy Review.*

PETROLEUM AND PRODUCTS - WELLS

U.S. Department of Energy, Energy Information Administration, Washington, D.C. 20585 (202) 586-8800, www.eia.doe.gov; *Petroleum Supply Annual; Annual Energy Review; U.S. Crude Oil, Natural Gas, and Natural Gas Liquids;* and *Monthly Energy Review.*

U.S. Department of Interior, Minerals Management Service, C Street between Eighteenth and Nineteenth Street, NW, Washington, D.C. 20240 (202) 208-3983; *Federal Offshore Statistics.*

PETROLEUM AND PRODUCTS - WELLS - DRILLING COSTS

U.S. Department of Energy, Energy Information Administration, Washington, D.C. 20585 (202) 586-8800, www.eia.doe.gov; *Annual Energy Review; Petroleum Supply Annual; U.S. Crude Oil, Natural Gas; Natural As Liquids Reserves;* and *Monthly Energy Review.*

PETROLEUM AND PRODUCTS - WELLS - LEASES AND PRODUCTION

U.S. Department of the Interior,

Minerals Management Service, C Street between Eighteenth and Nineteenth Streets, NW, Washington, D.C. 20240 (202) 208-3983; *Federal Offshore Statistics.*

PETROLEUM AND REFINING PRODUCTS - MANUFACTURING - CAPITAL

U.S. Department of Commerce, Bureau of Economic Analysis, Fourteenth Street between Constitution Avenue and E Street, NW, Washington, D.C. 20230 (202) 606-9900, www.bea.doc.gov; *Survey of Current Business.*

PETROLEUM AND REFINING PRODUCTS - MANUFACTURING - EARNINGS

U.S. Department of Commerce, Bureau of the Census, Washington, D.C. 20233 (301) 457-4100, www.census.gov; *Annual Survey of Manufactures; Census of Manufactures;* and *1997 Economic Census, Core Business Statistics Series.*

U.S. Department of Labor, Bureau of Labor Statistics, Two Massachusetts Avenue, NE, Washington, D.C. 20212 (202) 691-5200, www.stats.bls.gov; *Employment and Earnings; Employment and Wages;* Bulletins 2445, 2467, and 2483; and Internet site: http://stats.bls.gov/ceshome.htm.

PETROLEUM AND REFINING PRODUCTS - MANUFACTURING - EMPLOYEES

U.S. Department of Commerce, Bureau of the Census, Washington, D.C. 20233 (301) 457-4100, www.census.gov; *Annual Survey of Manufactures; Census of Manufactures; 1997 Economic Census, Core Business Statistics Series;* and *County Business Patterns.*

U.S. Department of Labor, Bureau of Labor Statistics, Two Massachusetts Avenue, NE, Washington, D.C. 20212 (202) 691-5200, www.stats.bls.gov; *Employment and Earnings; Monthly Labor Review;* and Internet site: http://stats.bls.gov/ceshome.htm.

PETROLEUM AND REFINING PRODUCTS - MANUFACTURING - ENERGY CONSUMPTION

U.S. Department of Energy, Energy Information Administration, 1000 Independence Avenue, SW, Washington, D.C. 20585 (202) 586-8800, www.eia.doe.gov; *Manufacturing Energy Consumption.*

PETROLEUM AND REFINING PRODUCTS - MANUFACTURING - ESTABLISHMENTS

U.S. Department of Commerce, Bureau

of the Census, Washington, D.C. 20233 (301) 457-4100, www.census.gov; *County Business Patterns;* and *1997 Economic Census, Core Business Statistics Series.*

PETROLEUM AND REFINING PRODUCTS - MANUFACTURING - FAILURES

The Dun and Bradstreet Corporation, One Diamond Hill Road, Murray Hill, New Jersey 07974 (908) 665-5000; *Business Failure Record.*

PETROLEUM AND REFINING PRODUCTS - MANUFACTURING - FINANCES

Carl H. Pforzheimer and Company, 650 Madison Avenue, New York, New York 10022 (212) 223-6500; *Comparative Oil Company Statements.*

PETROLEUM AND REFINING PRODUCTS - MANUFACTURING - FOREIGN INVESTMENTS IN UNITED STATES

U.S. Department of Commerce, Bureau of Economic Analysis, Fourteenth Street between Constitution Avenue and E Street, NW, Washington, D.C. 20230 (202) 606-9900, www.bea.doc.gov; *Foreign Direct Investment in the United States, Operations of U.S. Affiliates of Foreign Countries;* and *Survey of Current Business.*

PETROLEUM AND REFINING PRODUCTS - MANUFACTURING - MERGERS AND ACQUISITIONS

Thomson Financial Securities Data, Two Gateway Center, Newark, New Jersey 07006 (973) 622-3100; Merger and Corporate Transaction Database.

PETROLEUM AND REFINING PRODUCTS - MANUFACTURING - OCCUPATIONAL SAFETY

U.S. Department of Labor, Bureau of Labor Statistics, Two Massachusetts Avenue, NE, Washington, D.C. 20212 (202) 691-5200, www.stats.bls.gov; *Occupational Injuries and Illnesses in the United States by Industry.*

PETROLEUM AND REFINING PRODUCTS - MANUFACTURING - PRODUCTIVITY

U.S. Department of Labor, Bureau of Labor Statistics, Two Massachusetts Avenue, NE, Washington, D.C. 20212 (202) 691-5200, www.stats.bls.gov; Internet site http://stats.bls.gov/iprhome.htm.

PETROLEUM AND REFINING PRODUCTS - MANUFACTURING - PROFITS

Carl H. Pforzheimer and Company, 650

Madison Avenue, New York, New York 10022 (212) 223-6500; *Comparative Oil Company Statements.*

Executive Office of the President, Council of Economic Advisers, Old Executive Office Building, Washington, D.C. 20502 (202) 395-5084, www.whitehouse.gov/cea; *Economic Report of the President.*

U.S. Department of Commerce, Bureau of Economic Analysis, Fourteenth Street between Constitution Avenue and E Street, NW, Washington, D.C. 20230 (202) 606-9900, www.bea.doc.gov; *Survey of Current Business.*

U.S. Department of Commerce, Bureau of the Census, Washington, D.C. 20233 (301) 457-4100, www.census.gov; *Quarterly Financial Report for Manufacturing, Mining and Trade Corporations.*

PETROLEUM AND REFINING PRODUCTS - MANUFACTURING - RESEARCH AND DEVELOPMENT

National Science Foundation, 4201 Wilson Boulevard, Arlington, Virginia 22230 (703) 306-1234, www.nsf.gov; *Research and Development in Industry.*

PETROLEUM AND REFINING PRODUCTS - MANUFACTURING - SALES - SHIPMENTS

U.S. Department of Commerce, Bureau of the Census, Washington, D.C. 20233 (301) 457-4100, www.census.gov; *Census of Manufactures; Annual Survey of Manufactures; 1997 Economic Census, Core Business Statistics Series*; and *Current Industrial Reports, Manufactures' Shipments, Inventories, and Orders.*

PETROLEUM AND REFINING PRODUCTS - MANUFACTURING - TOXIC CHEMICAL RELEASES

Environmental Protection Agency, 1200 Pennsylvania Avenue, NW, Washington, D.C. 20460 (888) 372-8255, www.epa.gov; *Toxics Release Inventory.*

PETROLEUM AND REFINING PRODUCTS - MANUFACTURING - VALUE ADDED

U.S. Department of Commerce, Bureau of the Census, Washington, D.C. 20233 (301) 457-4100, www.census.gov; *Annual Survey of Manufactures;* and *Census of Manufactures.*

PHARMACEUTICAL PREPS

U.S. Department of Commerce, Bureau of the Census, Washington, D.C. 20233 (301) 457-4100, www.census.gov; *Manufacturing Profiles.*

PHARMACISTS

U.S. Department of Labor, Bureau of Labor Statistics, Two Massachusetts Avenue, NE, Washington, D.C. 20212 (202) 691-5200, www.stats.bls.gov; *Employment and Earnings;* and unpublished data.

PHARMACY SCHOOLS - STUDENTS - GRADUATES

U.S. Department of Health and Human Services, National Center for Health Statistics, 3700 East-West Highway, Hyattsville, Maryland 20782 (301) 436-8500, www.cdc.gov/nchs; *Health United States.*

PHILANTHROPY

American Association of Fund Raising Counsel, 10293 North Meridian Street, Suite 175, Indianapolis, Indiana 46290 (800) 462-2372; *Giving U.S.A.*

The Foundation Center, 79 Fifth Avenue, New York, New York 10003 (212) 620-4230; *Foundation Grants Index;* and *Guide to U.S. Foundations, Their Trustees, Officers, and Donors.*

Independent Sector, 1200 18th Street, NW, Suite 200, Washington, D.C. 20036 (202) 467-6161; *Giving and Volunteering in the United States.*

Philippines - National Statistical Office

National Statistical Coordination Board, Marvin Plaza Building, 2153 Pasong Tamo Street, Makati, Metro Manila, Republic of the Philippines.

Philippines - Primary Statistics Sources

Publications Division, Bureau of the Census and Statistics, Post Office Box 779, Manila, Philippines; *Statistical Pocketbook of the Philippines; Journal of Philippine Statistics; Philippine Statistical Yearbook;* and *Philippine Yearbook.*

PHILIPPINES - AGRICULTURE

Asian Development Bank, Post Office Box 789, 1099 Manila, Philippines; *Key Indicators of Developing Asian and Pacific Countries.*

Economist Intelligence Unit, 111 West 57th Street, New York, New York 10019 (800) 938-4685; *Philippines Country Report.*

Euromonitor International, Inc., 122 Michigan Avenue, Suite 1200, Chicago, Illinois 60603 (800) 577-EURO; *International Marketing Data and Statistics;* and *World Marketing Data and Statistics.*

Europa Publications Limited, 18 Bedford Square, London, WC1B 3JN, England; *The Europa World Year Book.*

Food and Agricultural Organization of the United Nations (FAO), Via delle Terme di Caracalla, 00100 Rome, Italy (Telephone Number in U.S. (202) 653-2400); *Production Yearbook; The State of Food and Agriculture;* and *Trade Yearbook.*

M.E. Sharpe, 80 Business Park Drive, Armonk, New York 10504 (800) 541-6563; *The Illustrated Book of World Rankings.*

St. Martin's Press, Inc., 175 Fifth Avenue, New York, New York 10010 (800) 221-7945; *The Statesman's Year-Book.*

Statistical Office of the United Nations, Publishing Service, New York, New York 10017 (800) 253-9646; *Asia-Pacific in Figures; Statistical Yearbook;* and *Statistical Yearbook for Asia and the Pacific.*

United Nations Conference on Trade and Development, Central Statistical Service, Palais des Nations, Geneva, Switzerland (Telephone in U.S. (800) 253-9646); *UNCTAD Commodity Yearbook.*

The World Bank, 1818 H Street, NW, Washington, D.C. 20433 (202) 477-1234; *World Development Indicators.*

PHILIPPINES - AIRLINE SERVICE

The Economist Intelligence Unit (Asia) Limited, 10th Floor, Luk Kwok Centre, 72 Gloucester Road, Wanchai, Hong Kong (Phone Number in U.S. (800) 938-4685); *Asian Market Atlas.*

Europa Publications Limited, 18 Bedford Square, London, WC1B 3JN, England; *The Europa World Year Book.*

International Civil Aviation Organization, 999 University Street, Montreal, Quebec, Canada H3C 5H7 (514) 954-8219; *Civil Aviation Statistics of the World.*

M.E. Sharpe, 80 Business Park Drive, Armonk, New York 10504 (800) 541-6563; *The Illustrated Book of World Rankings.*

St. Martin's Press, Inc., 175 Fifth Avenue, New York, New York 10010 (800) 221-7945; *The Statesman's Year-Book.*

Statistical Office of the United Nations, Publishing Service, New York, New York 10017 (800) 253-9646; *Statistical Yearbook.*

PHILIPPINES - AIRPORTS

Central Intelligence Agency, Washington, D.C. 20505 (703) 482-1100, www.cia.gov; *The World Factbook.*

PHILIPPINES - ALUMINUM PRODUCTION AND CONSUMPTION - See PHILIPPINES - MINING AND MINERAL PRODUCTS

PHILIPPINES - ANIMAL HEALTH

Food and Agricultural Organization of the United Nations (FAO), Via delle Terme di Caracalla, 00100 Rome, Italy (Telephone Number in U.S. (202) 653-2400); *Animal Health Yearbook.*

PHILIPPINES - ANTIMONY AND ANTIMONY ORE PRODUCTION AND CONSUMPTION - See PHILIPPINES - MINING AND MINERAL PRODUCTS

PHILIPPINES - AREA AND DENSITY OF POPULATION

Central Intelligence Agency, Washington, D.C. 20505 (703) 482-1100, www.cia.gov; *The World Factbook.*

Euromonitor International, Inc., 122 Michigan Avenue, Suite 1200, Chicago, Illinois 60603 (800) 577-EURO; *International Marketing Data and Statistics;* and *The World Economic Factbook.*

Europa Publications Limited, 18 Bedford Square, London, WC1B 3JN, England; *The Europa World Year Book.*

Food and Agricultural Organization of the United Nations (FAO) Via delle Terme di Caracalla, 00100 Rome, Italy (Telephone Number in U.S. (202) 653-2400); *The State of Food and Agriculture.*

M.E. Sharpe, 80 Business Park Drive, Armonk, New York 10504 (800) 541-6563; *The Illustrated Book of World Rankings.*

St. Martin's Press, Inc., 175 Fifth Avenue, New York, New York 10010 (800) 221-7945; *The Statesman's Year-Book.*

Statistical Office of the United Nations, Publishing Service, New York, New York 10017 (800) 253-9646; *Statistical Yearbook.*

United Nations Educational, Scientific and Cultural Organization (UNESCO), 7 Place de Fontenoy, F-75700 Paris, France (Telephone Number in U.S. (212) 963-5981); *Statistical Yearbook.*

The World Bank, 1818 H Street, NW, Washington, D.C. 20433 (202) 477-1234; *World Development Report.*

PHILIPPINES - ARMS EXPORTS AND IMPORTS - See PHILIPPINES - MILITARY

PHILIPPINES - BALANCE OF PAYMENTS

The Economist Intelligence Unit, 111 West 57th Street, New York, New York 10019 (800) 938-4685; *The World Market Atlas.*

Europa Publications Limited, 18 Bedford Square, London, WC1B 3JN, England; *The Europa World Year Book.*

International Monetary Fund, 700 Nineteenth Street, NW, Washington, D.C. 20431 (202) 623-7000; *Balance of Payments Yearbook;* and *International Financial Statistics.*

United Nations Conference on Trade and Development (UNCTAD), New York, New York 10017 (800) 253-9646; *Handbook of International Trade and Development Statistics.*

The World Bank, 1818 H Street, NW, Washington, D.C. 20433 (202) 477-1234; *World Development Report;* and *World Development Indicators.*

PHILIPPINES - BANKING

Asian Development Bank, Post Office Box 789, Manila, 1099 Manila, Philippines; *Key Indicators of Developing Asian and Pacific Countries.*

Euromonitor International, Inc., 122 South Michigan Avenue, Suite 1200, Chicago, Illinois 60603 (800) 577-EURO; *World Marketing Data and Statistics.*

Europa Publications Limited, 18 Bedford Square, London, WC1B 3JN, England; *The Europa World Year Book.*

International Monetary Fund, 700 Nineteenth Street, NW, Washington, D.C. 20431 (202) 623-7000; *International Financial Statistics.*

M.E. Sharpe, 80 Business Park Drive, Armonk, New York 10504 (800) 541-6563; *The Illustrated Book of World Rankings.*

St. Martin's Press, Inc., 175 Fifth Avenue, New York, New York 10010 (800) 221-7945; *The Statesman's Year-Book.*

Statistical Office of the United Nations, Publishing Service, New York, New York 10017 (800) 253-9646; *Statistical Yearbook.*

PHILIPPINES - BARLEY PRODUCTION - See PHILIPPINES - CROPS

PHILIPPINES - BAUXITE PRODUCTION AND CONSUMPTION - See PHILIPPINES - MINING AND MINERAL PRODUCTS

PHILIPPINES - BEER PRODUCTION - See PHILIPPINES - BEVERAGES

PHILIPPINES - BEVERAGES

M.E. Sharpe, 80 Business Park Drive, Armonk, New York 10504 (800) 541-6563; *The Illustrated Book of World Rankings.*

Statistical Office of the United Nations,

Publishing Service, New York, New York 10017 (800) 253-9646; *Statistical Yearbook.*

PHILIPPINES - BIRTH RATES

Central Intelligence Agency, Washington, D.C. 20505 (703) 482-1100, www.cia.gov; *The World Factbook.*

The Economist Intelligence Unit (Asia) Limited, 10th Floor, Luk Kwok Centre, 72 Gloucester Road, Wanchai, Hong Kong (Phone Number in U.S. (800) 938-4685); *Asian Market Atlas.*

Euromonitor International, Inc., 122 Michigan Avenue, Suite 1200, Chicago, Illinois 60603 (800) 577-EURO; *International Marketing Data and Statistics;* and *The World Economic Factbook.*

Europa Publications Limited, 18 Bedford Square, London, WC1B 3JN, England; *The Europa World Year Book.*

M.E. Sharpe, 80 Business Park Drive, Armonk, New York 10504 (800) 541-6563; *The Illustrated Book of World Rankings.*

St. Martin's Press, Inc., 175 Fifth Avenue, New York, New York 10010 (800) 221-7945; *The Statesman's Year-Book.*

Statistical Office of the United Nations, Publishing Service, New York, New York 10017 (800) 253-9646; *Asia-Pacific in Figures; Demographic Yearbook;* and *Statistical Yearbook.*

The World Bank, 1818 H Street, NW, Washington, D.C. 20433 (202) 477-1234; *World Development Indicators.*

World Health Organization, Office of Publications, 20 Avenue Appia, CH-1211 Geneva 27, Switzerland (Telephone Number in U.S. (518) 436-9686); *World Health Statistics Annual.*

PHILIPPINES - BONDS

Asian Development Bank, Post Office Box 789, Manila, 1099 Manila, Philippines; *Key Indicators of Developing Asian and Pacific Countries.*

International Monetary Fund, 700 Nineteenth Street, NW, Washington, D.C. 20431 (202) 623-7000; *Government Finance Statistics Yearbook.*

PHILIPPINES - BOOK PRODUCTION

Europa Publications Limited, 18 Bedford Square, London, WC1B 3JN, England; *The Europa World Year Book.*

St. Martin's Press, Inc., 175 Fifth Avenue, New York, New York 10010 (800) 221-7945; *The Statesman's Year-Book.*

United Nations Educational, Scientific and Cultural Organization (UNESCO), 7 Place de Fontenoy, F-75700 Paris, France (Telephone Number in U.S. (212) 963-5981); *Statistical Yearbook.*

PHILIPPINES - BROADCASTING

Billboard Limited, Post Office Box 9027, 1006 AA Amsterdam, The Netherlands (Telephone Number in U.S. (212) 764-7300); *World Radio TV Handbook.*

Central Intelligence Agency, Washington, D.C. 20505 (703) 482-1100, www.cia.gov; *The World Factbook.*

The Economist Intelligence Unit (Asia) Limited, 10th Floor, Luk Kwok Centre, 72 Gloucester Road, Wanchai, Hong Kong (Phone Number in U.S. (800) 938-4685); *Asian Market Atlas.*

Euromonitor International, Inc., 122 South Michigan Avenue, Suite 1200, Chicago, Illinois 60603 (800) 577-EURO; *World Marketing Data and Statistics.*

M.E. Sharpe, 80 Business Park Drive, Armonk, New York 10504 (800) 541-6563; *The Illustrated Book of World Rankings.*

St. Martin's Press, Inc., 175 Fifth Avenue, New York, New York 10010 (800) 221-7945; *The Statesman's Year-Book.*

PHILIPPINES - BUDGET

Central Intelligence Agency, Washington, D.C. 20505 (703) 482-1100, www.cia.gov; *The World Factbook.*

PHILIPPINES - BUSINESS AND PROFESSIONAL LICENSES

International Monetary Fund, 700 Nineteenth Street, NW, Washington, D.C. 20431 (202) 623-7000; *Government Finance Statistics Yearbook.*

PHILIPPINES - CABBAGE PRODUCTION - See PHILIPPINES - CROPS

PHILIPPINES - CADMIUM PRODUCTION AND CONSUMPTION - See PHILIPPINES - MINING AND MINERAL PRODUCTS

PHILIPPINES - CALORIE SUPPLY

Asian Development Bank, Post Office Box 789, Manila, 1099 Manila, Philippines; *Key Indicators of Developing Asian and Pacific Countries.*

Food and Agricultural Organization of the United Nations (FAO) Via delle Terme di Caracalla, 00100 Rome, Italy (Telephone Number in U.S. (202) 653-2400); *The State of Food and Agriculture.*

PHILIPPINES - CAPITAL INVESTMENT

Asian Development Bank, Post Office Box 789, Manila, 1099 Manila, Philippines; *Key Indicators of Developing Asian and Pacific Countries.*

PHILIPPINES - CAPITAL REVENUE

Asian Development Bank, Post Office Box 789, Manila, 1099 Manila, Philippines; *Key Indicators of Developing Asian and Pacific Countries.*

International Monetary Fund, 700 Nineteenth Street, NW, Washington, D.C. 20431 (202) 623-7000; *Government Finance Statistics Yearbook.*

PHILIPPINES - CASHEW NUT PRODUCTION - See PHILIPPINES - CROPS

PHILIPPINES - CASTOR BEAN PRODUCTION - See PHILIPPINES - CROPS

PHILIPPINES - CATTLE - See PHILIPPINES - LIVESTOCK AND POULTRY

PHILIPPINES - CAUSTIC SODA PRODUCTION - See PHILIPPINES - BEVERAGES

PHILIPPINES - CEMENT PRODUCTION - See PHILIPPINES - MINING AND MINERAL PRODUCTS

PHILIPPINES - CHEMICAL (ORGANIC) PRODUCTION - See PHILIPPINES - MINING AND MINERAL PRODUCTS

PHILIPPINES - CHICKENS - See PHILIPPINES - LIVESTOCK AND POULTRY

PHILIPPINES - CHROMITE PRODUCTION AND CONSUMPTION - See PHILIPPINES - MINING AND MINERAL PRODUCTS

PHILIPPINES - CHROMIUM ORE PRODUCTION AND CONSUMPTION - See PHILIPPINES - MINING AND MINERAL PRODUCTS

PHILIPPINES - CIGAR AND CIGARETTE PRODUCTION - See PHILIPPINES - TOBACCO PRODUCTION

PHILIPPINES - CLIMATE

M.E. Sharpe, 80 Business Park Drive, Armonk, New York 10504 (800) 541-6563; *The Illustrated Book of World Rankings.*

St. Martin's Press, Inc., 175 Fifth Avenue, New York, New York 10010 (800) 221-7945; *The Statesman's Year-Book.*

PHILIPPINES - COAL PRODUCTION - See PHILIPPINES - MINING AND MINERAL PRODUCTS

PHILIPPINES - COBALT PRODUCTION AND CONSUMPTION - See PHILIPPINES - MINING AND MINERAL PRODUCTS

PHILIPPINES - COCOA (BEANS) PRODUCTION - See PHILIPPINES - CROPS

PHILIPPINES - COCONUT PRODUCTS EXPORTS

International Monetary Fund, 700 Nineteenth Street, NW, Washington, D.C. 20431 (202) 623-7000; *International Financial Statistics.*

PHILIPPINES - COFFEE PRODUCTION AND CONSUMPTION - See PHILIPPINES -CROPS

PHILIPPINES - COMMERCE

St. Martin's Press, Inc., 175 Fifth Avenue, New York, New York 10010 (800) 221-7945; *The Statesman's Year-Book.*

PHILIPPINES - COMMUNICATIONS - See PHILIPPINES - TRANSPORTATION AND COMMUNICATIONS

PHILIPPINES - CONSTRUCTION INDUSTRY

M.E. Sharpe, 80 Business Park Drive, Armonk, New York 10504 (800) 541-6563; *The Illustrated Book of World Rankings.*

St. Martin's Press, Inc., 175 Fifth Avenue, New York, New York 10010 (800) 221-7945; *The Statesman's Year-Book.*

Statistical Office of the United Nations, Publishing Service, New York, New York 10017 (800) 253-9646; *Statistical Yearbook.*

PHILIPPINES - CONSUMER PRICE INDEX

Asian Development Bank, Post Office Box 789, Manila, 1099 Manila, Philippines; *Key Indicators of Developing Asian and Pacific Countries.*

Europa Publications Limited, 18 Bedford Square, London, WC1B 3JN, England; *The Europa World Year Book.*

PHILIPPINES - CONSUMER PRICES

Euromonitor International, Inc., 122 South Michigan Avenue, Suite 1200, Chicago, Illinois 60603 (800) 577-EURO; *World Marketing Data and Statistics.*

PHILIPPINES - CONSUMPTION

International Monetary Fund, 700 Nineteenth Street, NW, Washington, D.C. 20431 (202) 623-7000; *International Financial Statistics.*

The World Bank, 1818 H Street, NW, Washington, D.C. 20433 (202) 477-1234; *World Development Report.*

PHILIPPINES - COPPER AND COPPER ORE PRODUCTION AND CONSUMPTION - See PHILIPPINES - MINING AND MINERAL PRODUCTS

PHILIPPINES - CORN PRODUCTION - See PHILIPPINES - CROPS

PHILIPPINES - CORPORATE TAXES - See PHILIPPINES - TAXATION

PHILIPPINES - COTTON - See PHILIPPINES - CROPS

PHILIPPINES - CRIME

International Criminal Police Organization (INTERPOL), 50 quai Achille Lignon, F-69006 Lyon, France; *International Crime Statistics.*

Yale University Press, Yale Station, New Haven, Connecticut 06520 (800) 987-7323; *Violence and Crime in Cross-National Perspective.*

PHILIPPINES - CROPS

Asian Development Bank, Post Office Box 789, Manila, 1099 Manila, Philippines; *Key Indicators of Developing Asian and Pacific Countries.*

Commodity Research Bureau, Inc., 30 South Wacker Drive, Chicago Illinois 60606 (312) 454-1801; *Commodity Year Book.*

Europa Publications Limited, 18 Bedford Square, London, WC1B 3JN, England; *The Europa World Year Book.*

Food and Agricultural Organization of the United Nations (FAO) Via delle Terme di Caracalla, 00100 Rome, Italy (Telephone Number in U.S. (202) 653-2400); *Production Yearbook;* and *The State of Food and Agriculture.*

M.E. Sharpe, 80 Business Park Drive, Armonk, New York 10504 (800) 541-6563; *The Illustrated Book of World Rankings.*

St. Martin's Press, Inc., 175 Fifth Avenue, New York, New York 10010 (800) 221-7945; *The Statesman's Year-Book.*

Statistical Office of the United Nations, Publishing Service, New York, New York 10017 (800) 253-9646; *Statistical Yearbook.*

United Nations Conference on Trade and Development, Central Statistical Service, Palais des Nations, Geneva, Switzerland (Telephone in U.S. (800) 253-9646); *UNCTAD Commodity Yearbook.*

PHILIPPINES - CUSTOMS DUTIES

International Monetary Fund, 700 Nineteenth Street, NW, Washington, D.C. 20431 (202) 623-7000; *Government Finance Statistics Yearbook.*

St. Martin's Press, Inc., 175 Fifth Avenue, New York, New York 10010 (800)

221-7945; *The Statesman's Year-Book.*

PHILIPPINES - DAIRY PRODUCTS

Europa Publications Limited, 18 Bedford Square, London, WC1B 3JN, England; *The Europa World Year Book.*

Food and Agricultural Organization of the United Nations (FAO) Via delle Terme di Caracalla, 00100 Rome, Italy (Telephone Number in U.S. (202) 653-2400); *Production Yearbook;* and *The State of Food and Agriculture.*

M.E. Sharpe, 80 Business Park Drive, Armonk, New York 10504 (800) 541-6563; *The Illustrated Book of World Rankings.*

St. Martin's Press, Inc., 175 Fifth Avenue, New York, New York 10010 (800) 221-7945; *The Statesman's Year-Book.*

PHILIPPINES - DEATH RATES - See PHILIPPINES - MORTALITY

PHILIPPINES - DEFENSE EXPENDITURES - See PHILIPPINES - MILITARY

PHILIPPINES - DEMOGRAPHY

The Economist Intelligence Unit, 111 West 57th Street, New York, New York 10019 (800) 938-4685; *The World Market Atlas.*

The Economist Intelligence Unit (Asia) Limited, 10th Floor, Luk Kwok Centre, 72 Gloucester Road, Wanchai, Hong Kong (Phone Number in U.S. (800) 938-4685); *Asian Market Atlas.*

Euromonitor International, Inc., 122 Michigan Avenue, Suite 1200, Chicago, Illinois 60603 (800) 577-EURO; *International Marketing Data and Statistics; World Marketing Data and Statistics;* and *The World Economic Factbook.*

M.E. Sharpe, 80 Business Park Drive, Armonk, New York 10504 (800) 541-6563; *The Illustrated Book of World Rankings.*

Statistical Office of the United Nations, Publishing Service, New York, New York 10017 (800) 253-9646; *Asia-Pacific in Figures;* and *Human Development Report.*

PHILIPPINES - DEVELOPMENT ASSISTANCE

Asian Development Bank, Post Office Box 789, Manila, 1099 Manila, Philippines; *Key Indicators of Developing Asian and Pacific Countries.*

Statistical Office of the United Nations, Publishing Service, New York, New York 10017 (800) 253-9646; *Statistical Yearbook.*

PHILIPPINES - DIAMOND PRODUCTION - See PHILIPPINES - MINING AND MINERAL PRODUCTS

PHILIPPINES - DISEASES - See PHILIPPINES - HEALTH

PHILIPPINES - DIVORCE RATES

M.E. Sharpe, 80 Business Park Drive, Armonk, New York 10504 (800) 541-6563; *The Illustrated Book of World Rankings.*

Statistical Office of the United Nations, Publishing Service, New York, New York 10017 (800) 253-9646; *Demographic Yearbook.*

PHILIPPINES - DUCKS - See PHILIPPINES - LIVESTOCK AND POULTRY

PHILIPPINES - ECONOMY

Asian Development Bank, Post Office Box 789, Manila, 1099 Manila, Philippines; *Key Indicators of Developing Asian and Pacific Countries.*

Central Intelligence Agency, Washington, D.C. 20505 (703) 482-1100, www.cia.gov; *The World Factbook.*

Economist Intelligence Unit, 111 West 57th Street, New York, New York 10019 (800) 938-4685; *Philippines Country Report.*

Euromonitor International, Inc., 122 Michigan Avenue, Suite 1200, Chicago, Illinois 60603 (800) 577-EURO; *International Marketing Data and Statistics; World Marketing Data and Statistics;* and *The World Economic Factbook.*

Europa Publications Limited, 18 Bedford Square, London, WC1B 3JN, England; *The Europa World Year Book.*

M.E. Sharpe, 80 Business Park Drive, Armonk, New York 10504 (800) 541-6563; *The Illustrated Book of World Rankings.*

St. Martin's Press, Inc., 175 Fifth Avenue, New York, New York 10010 (800) 221-7945; *The Statesman's Year-Book.*

Statistical Office of the United Nations, Publishing Service, New York, New York 10017 (800) 253-9646; *World Statistics Pocketbook.*

The World Bank, 1818 H Street, NW, Washington, D.C. 20433 (202) 477-1234; *The World Bank Atlas;* and *World Development Report.*

PHILIPPINES - EDUCATION

The Economist Intelligence Unit, 111 West 57th Street, New York, New York 10019 (800) 938-4685; *The World Market*

Atlas.

The Economist Intelligence Unit (Asia) Limited, 10th Floor, Luk Kwok Centre, 72 Gloucester Road, Wanchai, Hong Kong (Phone Number in U.S. (800) 938-4685); *Asian Market Atlas.*

Euromonitor International, Inc., 122 Michigan Avenue, Suite 1200, Chicago, Illinois 60603 (800) 577-EURO; *International Marketing Data and Statistics;* and *World Marketing Data and Statistics.*

Europa Publications Limited, 18 Bedford Square, London, WC1B 3JN, England; *The Europa World Year Book.*

International Monetary Fund, 700 Nineteenth Street, NW, Washington, D.C. 20431 (202) 623-7000; *Government Finance Statistics Yearbook.*

M.E. Sharpe, 80 Business Park Drive, Armonk, New York 10504 (800) 541-6563; *The Illustrated Book of World Rankings.*

St. Martin's Press, Inc., 175 Fifth Avenue, New York, New York 10010 (800) 221-7945; *The Statesman's Year-Book.*

Statistical Office of the United Nations, Publishing Service, New York, New York 10017 (800) 253-9646; *Asia-Pacific in Figures; Human Development Report;* and *Statistical Yearbook for Asia and the Pacific.*

United Nations Educational, Scientific and Cultural Organization (UNESCO), 7 Place de Fontenoy, F-75700 Paris, France (Telephone Number in U.S. (212) 963-5981); *Statistical Yearbook.*

The World Bank, 1818 H Street, NW, Washington, D.C. 20433 (202) 477-1234; *World Development Report;* and *World Development Indicators.*

PHILIPPINES - EGG PRODUCTION AND CONSUMPTION - See PHILIPPINES - DAIRY PRODUCTS

PHILIPPINES - EGGPLANT PRODUCTION

Food and Agricultural Organization of the United Nations (FAO), Via delle Terme di Caracalla, 00100 Rome, Italy (Telephone Number in U.S. (202) 653-2400); *Production Yearbook.*

PHILIPPINES - ELECTRICITY

Asian Development Bank, Post Office Box 789, Manila, 1099 Manila, Philippines; *Key Indicators of Developing Asian and Pacific Countries.*

Central Intelligence Agency, Washington, D.C. 20505 (703) 482-1100, www.cia.gov; *The World Factbook.*

M.E. Sharpe, 80 Business Park Drive, Armonk, New York 10504 (800) 541-6563; *The Illustrated Book of World Rankings.*

Penn Well Publishing Company, 1421 South Sheridan Road, Post Office Box 1260, Tulsa, Oklahoma 74101 (800) 752-9764; *International Energy Statistics Sourcebook.*

St. Martin's Press, Inc., 175 Fifth Avenue, New York, New York 10010 (800) 221-7945; *The Statesman's Year-Book.*

Statistical Office of the United Nations, Publishing Service, New York, New York 10017 (800) 253-9646; *Human Development Report;* and *Statistical Yearbook.*

PHILIPPINES - EMPLOYMENT

Euromonitor International, Inc., 122 Michigan Avenue, Suite 1200, Chicago, Illinois 60603 (800) 577-EURO; *International Marketing Data and Statistics.*

International Labour Office, I.L.O. Publications, 1828 L Street, NW., Suite 801, Washington, D.C. 20036 (301) 638-3152; *Yearbook of Labour Statistics.*

M.E. Sharpe, 80 Business Park Drive, Armonk, New York 10504 (800) 541-6563; *The Illustrated Book of World Rankings.*

Statistical Office of the United Nations, Publishing Service, New York, New York 10017 (800) 253-9646; *Asia-Pacific in Figures;* and *Statistical Yearbook.*

PHILIPPINES - ENERGY

Euromonitor International, Inc., 122 Michigan Avenue, Suite 1200, Chicago, Illinois 60603 (800) 577-EURO; *International Marketing Data and Statistics; World Marketing Data and Statistics;* and *The World Economic Factbook.*

Food and Agricultural Organization of the United Nations (FAO) Via delle Terme di Caracalla, 00100 Rome, Italy (Telephone Number in U.S. (202) 653-2400); *The State of Food and Agriculture.*

M.E. Sharpe, 80 Business Park Drive, Armonk, New York 10504 (800) 541-6563; *The Illustrated Book of World Rankings.*

Penn Well Publishing Company, 1421 South Sheridan Road, Post Office Box 1260, Tulsa, Oklahoma 74101 (800) 752-9764; *International Energy Statistics Sourcebook.*

St. Martin's Press, Inc., 175 Fifth Avenue, New York, New York 10010 (800) 221-7945; *The Statesman's Year-Book.*

Statistical Office of the United Nations, Publishing Service, New York, New York 10017 (800) 253-9646; *Asia-Pacific in*

Figures; Energy Statistics Yearbook; Human Development Report; Statistical Yearbook; Statistical Yearbook for Asia and the Pacific; and *World Statistics Pocketbook.*

The World Bank, 1818 H Street, NW, Washington, D.C. 20433 (202) 477-1234; *The World Bank Atlas;* and *World Development Report.*

PHILIPPINES - ENVIRONMENT

Economist Intelligence Unit, 111 West 57th Street, New York, New York 10019 (800) 938-4685; *Philippines Country Report.*

Statistical Office of the United Nations, Publishing Service, New York, New York 10017 (800) 253-9646; *World Statistics Pocketbook.*

PHILIPPINES - EXCHANGE RATES

Asian Development Bank, Post Office Box 789, Manila, 1099 Manila, Philippines; *Key Indicators of Developing Asian and Pacific Countries.*

Central Intelligence Agency, Washington, D.C. 20505 (703) 482-1100, www.cia.gov; *The World Factbook.*

The Economist Intelligence Unit (Asia) Limited, 10th Floor, Luk Kwok Centre, 72 Gloucester Road, Wanchai, Hong Kong (Phone Number in U.S. (800) 938-4685); *Asian Market Atlas.*

Euromonitor International, Inc., 122 Michigan Avenue, Suite 1200, Chicago, Illinois 60603 (800) 577-EURO; *International Marketing Data and Statistics;* and *The World Economic Factbook.*

Europa Publications Limited, 18 Bedford Square, London, WC1B 3JN, England; *The Europa World Year Book.*

International Civil Aviation Organization, 999 University Street, Montreal, Quebec, Canada H3C 5H7 (514) 954-8219; *Civil Aviation Statistics of the World.*

International Monetary Fund, 700 Nineteenth Street, NW, Washington, D.C. 20431 (202) 623-7000; *International Financial Statistics.*

Statistical Office of the United Nations, Publishing Service, New York, New York 10017 (800) 253-9646; *Statistical Yearbook;* and *World Statistics Pocketbook.*

Walden Publishing, Ltd., Two Market Street, Saffron Walden Essex, CB10 1HZ, England; *The World of Information Asia and Pacific Review.*

PHILIPPINES - EXCISE TAXES - See PHILIPPINES - TAXATION

PHILIPPINES - EXPORTS

Asian Development Bank, Post Office Box 789, Manila, 1099 Manila, Philippines; *Key Indicators of Developing Asian and Pacific Countries.*

Central Intelligence Agency, Washington, D.C. 20505 (703) 482-1100, www.cia.gov; *The World Factbook.*

The Economist Intelligence Unit, 111 West 57th Street, New York, New York 10019 (800) 938-4685; *Philippines Country Report;* and *The World Market Atlas.*

The Economist Intelligence Unit (Asia) Limited, 10th Floor, Luk Kwok Centre, 72 Gloucester Road, Wanchai, Hong Kong (Phone Number in U.S. (800) 938-4685); *Asian Market Atlas.*

Euromonitor International, Inc., 122 Michigan Avenue, Suite 1200, Chicago, Illinois 60603 (800) 577-EURO; *International Marketing Data and Statistics;* and *The World Economic Factbook.*

Europa Publications Limited, 18 Bedford Square, London, WC1B 3JN, England; *The Europa World Year Book.*

Food and Agricultural Organization of the United Nations (FAO) Via delle Terme di Caracalla, 00100 Rome, Italy (Telephone Number in U.S. (202) 653-2400); *The State of Food and Agriculture.*

International Monetary Fund, 700 Nineteenth Street, NW, Washington, D.C. 20431 (202) 623-7000; *Direction of Trade Statistics; Government Finance Statistics Yearbook;* and *International Financial Statistics.*

St. Martin's Press, Inc., 175 Fifth Avenue, New York, New York 10010 (800) 221-7945; *The Statesman's Year-Book.*

Statistical Office of the United Nations, Publishing Service, New York, New York 10017 (800) 253-9646; *Foreign Trade Statistics of Asia and the Pacific.*

United Nations Conference on Trade and Development (UNCTAD), New York, New York 10017 (800) 253-9646; *Handbook of International Trade and Development Statistics.*

Walden Publishing, Ltd., Two Market Street, Saffron Walden Essex, CB10 1HZ, England; *The World of Information Asia and Pacific Review.*

The World Bank, 1818 H Street, NW, Washington, D.C. 20433 (202) 477-1234; *World Development Report;* and *World Development Indicators.*

PHILIPPINES - EXTERNAL FINANCING

Asian Development Bank, Post Office Box 789, Manila, 1099 Manila, Philippines; *Key Indicators of Developing Asian and Pacific Countries.*

PHILIPPINES - EXTERNAL INDEBTEDNESS

Asian Development Bank, Post Office Box 789, Manila, 1099 Manila, Philippines; *Key Indicators of Developing Asian and Pacific Countries.*

The World Bank, 1818 H Street, NW, Washington, D.C. 20433 (202) 477-1234; *World Development Report;* and *World Development Indicators.*

PHILIPPINES - EXTERNAL TRADE

Asian Development Bank, Post Office Box 789, Manila, 1099 Manila, Philippines; *Key Indicators of Developing Asian and Pacific Countries.*

Euromonitor International, Inc., 122 South Michigan Avenue, Suite 1200, Chicago, Illinois 60603 (800) 577-EURO; *World Marketing Data and Statistics.*

Food and Agricultural Organization of the United Nations (FAO), Via delle Terme di Caracalla, 00100 Rome, Italy (Telephone Number in U.S. (202) 653-2400); *Production Yearbook; The State of Food and Agriculture;* and *Trade Yearbook.*

Statistical Office of the United Nations, Publishing Service, New York, New York 10017 (800) 253-9646; *Asia-Pacific in Figures; Statistical Yearbook;* and *Statistical Yearbook for Asia and the Pacific.*

PHILIPPINES - FABRIC PRODUCTION - See PHILIPPINES - TEXTILE INDUSTRY

PHILIPPINES - FARM CROPS - See PHILIPPINES - CROPS

PHILIPPINES - FEMALE WORKING POPULATION - See PHILIPPINES - EMPLOYMENT

PHILIPPINES - FERTILITY RATES

Central Intelligence Agency, Washington, D.C. 20505 (703) 482-1100, www.cia.gov; *The World Factbook.*

The Economist Intelligence Unit (Asia) Limited, 10th Floor, Luk Kwok Centre, 72 Gloucester Road, Wanchai, Hong Kong (Phone Number in U.S. (800) 938-4685); *Asian Market Atlas.*

M.E. Sharpe, 80 Business Park Drive, Armonk, New York 10504 (800) 541-6563; *The Illustrated Book of World Rankings.*

Statistical Office of the United Nations, Publishing Service, New York, New York

10017 (800) 253-9646; *Human Development Report.*

The World Bank, 1818 H Street, NW, Washington, D.C. 20433 (202) 477-1234; *The World Bank Atlas; World Development Report;* and *World Development Indicators.*

PHILIPPINES - FERTILIZER

Food and Agricultural Organization of the United Nations (FAO), Via delle Terme di Caracalla, 00100 Rome, Italy (Telephone Number in U.S. (202) 653-2400); *Fertilizer Yearbook;* and *The State of Food and Agriculture.*

Statistical Office of the United Nations, Publishing Service, New York, New York 10017 (800) 253-9646; *Statistical Yearbook.*

PHILIPPINES - FETAL MORTALITY - See PHILIPPINES - MORTALITY

PHILIPPINES - FIBRE PRODUCTION - See PHILIPPINES - TEXTILE INDUSTRY

PHILIPPINES - FILAMENT PRODUCTION - See PHILIPPINES - TEXTILE INDUSTRY

PHILIPPINES - FILM - See PHILIPPINES - MOTION PICTURES

PHILIPPINES - FINANCE

Asian Development Bank, Post Office Box 789, Manila, 1099 Manila, Philippines; *Key Indicators of Developing Asian and Pacific Countries.*

Economist Intelligence Unit, 111 West 57th Street, New York, New York 10019 (800) 938-4685; *Philippines Country Report.*

Europa Publications Limited, 18 Bedford Square, London, WC1B 3JN, England; *The Europa World Year Book.*

International Monetary Fund, 700 Nineteenth Street, NW, Washington, D.C. 20431 (202) 623-7000; *Government Finance Statistics Yearbook.*

M.E. Sharpe, 80 Business Park Drive, Armonk, New York 10504 (800) 541-6563; *The Illustrated Book of World Rankings.*

St. Martin's Press, Inc., 175 Fifth Avenue, New York, New York 10010 (800) 221-7945; *The Statesman's Year-Book.*

Statistical Office of the United Nations, Publishing Service, New York, New York 10017 (800) 253-9646; *Statistical Yearbook for Asia and the Pacific.*

PHILIPPINES - FISHERIES

Europa Publications Limited, 18 Bedford Square, London, WC1B 3JN,

England; *The Europa World Year Book.*

Food and Agricultural Organization of the United Nations (FAO) Via delle Terme di Caracalla, 00100 Rome, Italy (Telephone Number in U.S. (202) 653-2400); *The State of Food and Agriculture;* and *Yearbook of Fishery Statistics.*

M.E. Sharpe, 80 Business Park Drive, Armonk, New York 10504 (800) 541-6563; *The Illustrated Book of World Rankings.*

St. Martin's Press, Inc., 175 Fifth Avenue, New York, New York 10010 (800) 221-7945; *The Statesman's Year-Book.*

Statistical Office of the United Nations, Publishing Service, New York, New York 10017 (800) 253-9646; *Statistical Yearbook.*

United Nations Conference on Trade and Development, Central Statistical Service, Palais des Nations, Geneva, Switzerland (Telephone in U.S. (800) 253-9646); *UNCTAD Commodity Yearbook.*

PHILIPPINES - FLOUR PRODUCTION

Statistical Office of the United Nations, Publishing Service, New York, New York 10017 (800) 253-9646; *Statistical Yearbook.*

PHILIPPINES - FOOD

Euromonitor International, Inc., 122 South Michigan Avenue, Suite 1200, Chicago, Illinois 60603 (800) 577-EURO; *Retail Trade International.*

Food and Agricultural Organization of the United Nations (FAO) Via delle Terme di Caracalla, 00100 Rome, Italy (Telephone Number in U.S. (202) 653-2400); *Production Yearbook;* and *The State of Food and Agriculture.*

Statistical Office of the United Nations, Publishing Service, New York, New York 10017 (800) 253-9646; *Human Development Report;* and *Statistical Yearbook for Asia and the Pacific.*

United Nations Conference on Trade and Development, Central Statistical Service, Palais des Nations, Geneva, Switzerland (Telephone in U.S. (800) 253-9646); *UNCTAD Commodity Yearbook.*

PHILIPPINES - FOREIGN DEBT

International Monetary Fund, 700 Nineteenth Street, NW, Washington, D.C. 20431 (202) 623-7000; *Government Finance Statistics Yearbook.*

St. Martin's Press, Inc., 175 Fifth Avenue, New York, New York 10010 (800) 221-7945; *The Statesman's Year-Book.*

Walden Publishing, Ltd., Two Market

Street, Saffron Walden Essex, CB10 1HZ, England; *The World of Information Asia and Pacific Review.*

PHILIPPINES - FOREIGN TRADE

Asian Development Bank, Post Office Box 789, Manila, 1099 Manila, Philippines; *Key Indicators of Developing Asian and Pacific Countries.*

Economist Intelligence Unit, 111 West 57th Street, New York, New York 10019 (800) 938-4685; *Philippines Country Report.*

The Economist Intelligence Unit (Asia) Limited, 10th Floor, Luk Kwok Centre, 72 Gloucester Road, Wanchai, Hong Kong (Phone Number in U.S. (800) 938-4685); *Asian Market Atlas.*

Euromonitor International, Inc., 122 Michigan Avenue, Suite 1200, Chicago, Illinois 60603 (800) 577-EURO; *International Marketing Data and Statistics;* and *The World Economic Factbook.*

Europa Publications Limited, 18 Bedford Square, London, WC1B 3JN, England; *The Europa World Year Book.*

Food and Agricultural Organization of the United Nations (FAO) Via delle Terme di Caracalla, 00100 Rome, Italy (Telephone Number in U.S. (202) 653-2400); *The State of Food and Agriculture.*

M.E. Sharpe, 80 Business Park Drive, Armonk, New York 10504 (800) 541-6563; *The Illustrated Book of World Rankings.*

St. Martin's Press, Inc., 175 Fifth Avenue, New York, New York 10010 (800) 221-7945; *The Statesman's Year-Book.*

Statistical Office of the United Nations, Publishing Service, New York, New York 10017 (800) 253-9646; *International Trade Statistics Yearbook;* and *Statistical Yearbook.*

United Nations Conference on Trade and Development, Central Statistical Service, Palais des Nations, Geneva, Switzerland (Telephone in U.S. (800) 253-9646); *UNCTAD Commodity Yearbook.*

The World Bank, 1818 H Street, NW, Washington, D.C. 20433 (202) 477-1234; *World Development Report;* and *World Development Indicators.*

World Bureau of Metal Statistics, 27-A High Street, Ware, Herts. SG12 9BA, England; *World Metal Statistics.*

PHILIPPINES - FORESTRY AND FOREST PRODUCTS

The Economist Intelligence Unit (Asia) Limited, 10th Floor, Luk Kwok Centre, 72

Gloucester Road, Wanchai, Hong Kong (Phone Number in U.S. (800) 938-4685); *Asian Market Atlas.*

Europa Publications Limited, 18 Bedford Square, London, WC1B 3JN, England; *The Europa World Year Book.*

Food and Agricultural Organization of the United Nations (FAO) Via delle Terme di Caracalla, 00100 Rome, Italy (Telephone Number in U.S. (202) 653-2400); *The State of Food and Agriculture;* and *Yearbook of Forest Products.*

M.E. Sharpe, 80 Business Park Drive, Armonk, New York 10504 (800) 541-6563; *The Illustrated Book of World Rankings.*

St. Martin's Press, Inc., 175 Fifth Avenue, New York, New York 10010 (800) 221-7945; *The Statesman's Year-Book.*

Statistical Office of the United Nations, Publishing Service, New York, New York 10017 (800) 253-9646; *Statistical Yearbook.*

United Nations Conference on Trade and Development, Central Statistical Service, Palais des Nations, Geneva, Switzerland (Telephone in U.S. (800) 253-9646); *UNCTAD Commodity Yearbook.*

United Nations Educational, Scientific and Cultural Organization (UNESCO), 7 Place de Fontenoy, F-75700 Paris, France (Telephone Number in U.S. (212) 963-5981); *Statistical Yearbook.*

The World Bank, 1818 H Street, NW, Washington, D.C. 20433 (202) 477-1234; *World Development Report.*

PHILIPPINES - GARLIC PRODUCTION - See PHILIPPINES - CROPS

PHILIPPINES - GAS PRODUCTION - See PHILIPPINES - MINING AND MINERAL PRODUCTS

PHILIPPINES - GENERAL INDUSTRIAL STATISTICS - See PHILIPPINES - INDUSTRY

PHILIPPINES - GENERAL MORTALITY - See PHILIPPINES - MORTALITY

PHILIPPINES - GEOGRAPHIC DATA

M.E. Sharpe, 80 Business Park Drive, Armonk, New York 10504 (800) 541-6563; *The Illustrated Book of World Rankings.*

PHILIPPINES - GOATS - See PHILIPPINES - LIVESTOCK AND POULTRY

PHILIPPINES - GOLD HOLDINGS

International Monetary Fund, 700 Nineteenth Street, NW, Washington, D.C. 20431 (202) 623-7000; *International*

Financial Statistics.

Statistical Office of the United Nations, Publishing Service, New York, New York 10017 (800) 253-9646; *Statistical Yearbook.*

The World Bank, 1818 H Street, NW, Washington, D.C. 20433 (202) 477-1234; *World Development Indicators.*

PHILIPPINES - GOLD PRODUCTION AND CONSUMPTION - See PHILIPPINES - MINING AND MINERAL PRODUCTS

PHILIPPINES - GOVERNMENT

Asian Development Bank, Post Office Box 789, Manila, 1099 Manila, Philippines; *Key Indicators of Developing Asian and Pacific Countries.*

Central Intelligence Agency, Washington, D.C. 20505 (703) 482-1100, www.cia.gov; *The World Factbook.*

Europa Publications Limited, 18 Bedford Square, London, WC1B 3JN, England; *The Europa World Year Book.*

International Monetary Fund, 700 Nineteenth Street, NW, Washington, D.C. 20431 (202) 623-7000; *Government Finance Statistics Yearbook;* and *International Financial Statistics.*

St. Martin's Press, Inc., 175 Fifth Avenue, New York, New York 10010 (800) 221-7945; *The Statesman's Year-Book.*

Statistical Office of the United Nations, Publishing Service, New York, New York 10017 (800) 253-9646; *Asia-Pacific in Figures; National Accounts Statistics;* and *Statistical Yearbook.*

The World Bank, 1818 H Street, NW, Washington, D.C. 20433 (202) 477-1234; *World Development Report;* and *World Development Indicators.*

PHILIPPINES - GRAIN PRODUCTION - See PHILIPPINES - CROPS

PHILIPPINES - GRANTS

International Monetary Fund, 700 Nineteenth Street, NW, Washington, D.C. 20431 (202) 623-7000; *Government Finance Statistics Yearbook.*

PHILIPPINES - GROSS DOMESTIC PRODUCT

Asian Development Bank, Post Office Box 789, Manila, 1099 Manila, Philippines; *Key Indicators of Developing Asian and Pacific Countries.*

The Economist Intelligence Unit, 111 West 57th Street, New York, New York 10019 (800) 938-4685; *Philippines Country*

Report; and *The World Market Atlas.*

The Economist Intelligence Unit (Asia) Limited, 10th Floor, Luk Kwok Centre, 72 Gloucester Road, Wanchai, Hong Kong (Phone Number in U.S. (800) 938-4685); *Asian Market Atlas.*

Euromonitor International, Inc., 122 Michigan Avenue, Suite 1200, Chicago, Illinois 60603 (800) 577-EURO; *The World Economic Factbook;* and *International Marketing Data and Statistics.*

Europa Publications Limited, 18 Bedford Square, London, WC1B 3JN, England; *The Europa World Year Book.*

International Monetary Fund, 700 Nineteenth Street, NW, Washington, D.C. 20431 (202) 623-7000; *International Financial Statistics.*

M.E. Sharpe, 80 Business Park Drive, Armonk, New York 10504 (800) 541-6563; *The Illustrated Book of World Rankings.*

Statistical Office of the United Nations, Publishing Service, New York, New York 10017 (800) 253-9646; *Human Development Report; National Accounts Statistics;* and *Statistical Yearbook.*

The World Bank, 1818 H Street, NW, Washington, D.C. 20433 (202) 477-1234; *World Development Report;* and *World Development Indicators.*

PHILIPPINES - GROSS NATIONAL PRODUCT

Asian Development Bank, Post Office Box 789, Manila, 1099 Manila, Philippines; *Key Indicators of Developing Asian and Pacific Countries.*

Euromonitor International, Inc., 122 Michigan Avenue, Suite 1200, Chicago, Illinois 60603 (800) 577-EURO; *International Marketing Data and Statistics.*

Europa Publications Limited, 18 Bedford Square, London, WC1B 3JN, England; *The Europa World Year Book.*

St. Martin's Press, Inc., 175 Fifth Avenue, New York, New York 10010 (800) 221-7945; *The Statesman's Year-Book.*

U.S. Arms Control and Disarmament Agency, 320 Twenty-first Street, NW, Washington, D.C. 20451 (202) 647-8677; *World Military Expenditures and Arms Transfers.*

Walden Publishing, Ltd., Two Market Street, Saffron Walden Essex, CB10 1HZ, England; *The World of Information Asia and Pacific Review.*

The World Bank, 1818 H Street, NW,

Washington, D.C. 20433 (202) 477-1234; *The World Bank Atlas; World Development Report;* and *World Development Indicators.*

PHILIPPINES - GROUNDNUT PRODUCTION - PHILIPPINES - CROPS

PHILIPPINES - HEALTH

The Economist Intelligence Unit (Asia) Limited, 10th Floor, Luk Kwok Centre, 72 Gloucester Road, Wanchai, Hong Kong (Phone Number in U.S. (800) 938-4685); *Asian Market Atlas.*

Euromonitor International, Inc., 122 South Michigan Avenue, Suite 1200, Chicago, Illinois 60603 (800) 577-EURO; *World Marketing Data and Statistics.*

M.E. Sharpe, 80 Business Park Drive, Armonk, New York 10504 (800) 541-6563; *The Illustrated Book of World Rankings.*

St. Martin's Press, Inc., 175 Fifth Avenue, New York, New York 10010 (800) 221-7945; *The Statesman's Year-Book.*

Statistical Office of the United Nations, Publishing Service, New York, New York 10017 (800) 253-9646; *Asia-Pacific in Figures; Human Development Report;* and *Statistical Yearbook.*

United Nations Children's Fund (UNICEF), 3 United Nations Plaza, New York, New York 10017 (800) 253-9646; *State of the World's Children.*

The World Bank, 1818 H Street, NW, Washington, D.C. 20433 (202) 477-1234; *World Development Report.*

World Health Organization, Office of Publications, 20 Avenue Appia, CH-1211 Geneva 27, Switzerland (Telephone Number in U.S. (518) 436-9686); *World Health Statistics Annual.*

PHILIPPINES - HEALTH EXPENDITURES

International Monetary Fund, 700 Nineteenth Street, NW, Washington, D.C. 20431 (202) 623-7000; *Government Finance Statistics Yearbook.*

PHILIPPINES - HIDE PRODUCTION

Food and Agricultural Organization of the United Nations (FAO), Via delle Terme di Caracalla, 00100 Rome, Italy (Telephone Number in U.S. (202) 653-2400); *Production Yearbook.*

PHILIPPINES - HIGHWAYS

Central Intelligence Agency, Washington, D.C. 20505 (703) 482-1100, www.cia.gov; *The World Factbook.*

The Economist Intelligence Unit (Asia)

Limited, 10th Floor, Luk Kwok Centre, 72 Gloucester Road, Wanchai, Hong Kong (Phone Number in U.S. (800) 938-4685); *Asian Market Atlas.*

International Road Federation, 2600 Virginia Avenue, NW., Washington, D.C. 20037 (202) 338-4641; *World Road Statistics.*

St. Martin's Press, Inc., 175 Fifth Avenue, New York, New York 10010 (800) 221-7945; *The Statesman's Year-Book.*

PHILIPPINES - HORSES - See PHILIPPINES - LIVESTOCK AND POULTRY

PHILIPPINES - HOURS OF WORK - See PHILIPPINES - EMPLOYMENT

PHILIPPINES - HOUSING AND HOUSING UNITS

Euromonitor International, Inc., 122 South Michigan Avenue, Suite 1200, Chicago, Illinois 60603 (800) 577-EURO; *World Marketing Data and Statistics.*

M.E. Sharpe, 80 Business Park Drive, Armonk, New York 10504 (800) 541-6563; *The Illustrated Book of World Rankings.*

PHILIPPINES - HOUSING EXPENDITURES

International Monetary Fund, 700 Nineteenth Street, NW, Washington, D.C. 20431 (202) 623-7000; *Government Finance Statistics Yearbook.*

PHILIPPINES - HYDROCHLORIC ACID PRODUCTION

Statistical Office of the United Nations, Publishing Service, New York, New York 10017 (800) 253-9646; *Statistical Yearbook.*

PHILIPPINES - ILLITERATE POPULATION

Central Intelligence Agency, Washington, D.C. 20505 (703) 482-1100, www.cia.gov; *The World Factbook.*

The Economist Intelligence Unit, 111 West 57th Street, New York, New York 10019 (800) 938-4685; *The World Market Atlas.*

Euromonitor International, Inc., 122 Michigan Avenue, Suite 1200, Chicago, Illinois 60603 (800) 577-EURO; *The World Economic Factbook.*

Statistical Office of the United Nations, Publishing Service, New York, New York 10017 (800) 253-9646; *Asia-Pacific in Figures;* and *Human Development Report.*

United Nations Educational, Scientific and Cultural Organization (UNESCO), 7 Place de Fontenoy, F-75700 Paris, France (Telephone Number in U.S. (212) 963-

5981); *Statistical Yearbook.*

PHILIPPINES - IMPORTS

Asian Development Bank, Post Office Box 789, Manila, 1099 Manila, Philippines; *Key Indicators of Developing Asian and Pacific Countries.*

Central Intelligence Agency, Washington, D.C. 20505 (703) 482-1100, www.cia.gov; *The World Factbook.*

The Economist Intelligence Unit, 111 West 57th Street, New York, New York 10019 (800) 938-4685; *Philippines Country Report;* and *The World Market Atlas.*

The Economist Intelligence Unit (Asia) Limited, 10th Floor, Luk Kwok Centre, 72 Gloucester Road, Wanchai, Hong Kong (Phone Number in U.S. (800) 938-4685); *Asian Market Atlas.*

Euromonitor International, Inc., 122 Michigan Avenue, Suite 1200, Chicago, Illinois 60603 (800) 577-EURO; *International Marketing Data and Statistics;* and *The World Economic Factbook.*

Europa Publications Limited, 18 Bedford Square, London, WC1B 3JN, England; *The Europa World Year Book.*

Food and Agricultural Organization of the United Nations (FAO) Via delle Terme di Caracalla, 00100 Rome, Italy (Telephone Number in U.S. (202) 653-2400); *The State of Food and Agriculture.*

International Monetary Fund, 700 Nineteenth Street, NW, Washington, D.C. 20431 (202) 623-7000; *Direction of Trade Statistics; Government Finance Statistics Yearbook;* and *International Financial Statistics.*

St. Martin's Press, Inc., 175 Fifth Avenue, New York, New York 10010 (800) 221-7945; *The Statesman's Year-Book.*

Statistical Office of the United Nations, Publishing Service, New York, New York 10017 (800) 253-9646; *Foreign Trade Statistics of Asia and the Pacific.*

United Nations Conference on Trade and Development (UNCTAD), New York, New York 10017 (800) 253-9646; *Handbook of International Trade and Development Statistics.*

Walden Publishing, Ltd., Two Market Street, Saffron Walden Essex, CB10 1HZ, England; *The World of Information Asia and Pacific Review.*

The World Bank, 1818 H Street, NW, Washington, D.C. 20433 (202) 477-1234; *World Development Report;* and *World Development Indicators.*

PHILIPPINES - INCOME TAXES - See PHILIPPINES - TAXATION

PHILIPPINES - INDUSTRY

Central Intelligence Agency, Washington, D.C. 20505 (703) 482-1100, www.cia.gov; *The World Factbook.*

Economist Intelligence Unit, 111 West 57th Street, New York, New York 10019 (800) 938-4685; *Philippines Country Report.*

Euromonitor International, Inc., 122 Michigan Avenue, Suite 1200, Chicago, Illinois 60603 (800) 577-EURO; *International Marketing Data and Statistics; World Marketing Data and Statistics;* and *The World Economic Factbook.*

Europa Publications Limited, 18 Bedford Square, London, WC1B 3JN, England; *The Europa World Year Book.*

International Labour Office, I.L.O. Publications, 1828 L Street, NW., Suite 801, Washington, D.C. 20036 (301) 638-3152; *Yearbook of Labour Statistics.*

M.E. Sharpe, 80 Business Park Drive, Armonk, New York 10504 (800) 541-6563; *The Illustrated Book of World Rankings.*

St. Martin's Press, Inc., 175 Fifth Avenue, New York, New York 10010 (800) 221-7945; *The Statesman's Year-Book.*

Statistical Office of the United Nations, Publishing Service, New York, New York 10017 (800) 253-9646; *Asia-Pacific in Figures; Statistical Yearbook; Industrial Commodity Statistics Yearbook;* and *Statistical Yearbook for Asia and the Pacific.*

The World Bank, 1818 H Street, NW, Washington, D.C. 20433 (202) 477-1234; *World Development Indicators.*

World Intellectual Property Organization, 34 Chemin des Colombettes, CH-1211 Geneva 20, Switzerland; *Industrial Property Statistics.*

PHILIPPINES - INFANT AND MATERNAL MORTALITY - See PHILIPPINES - MORTALITY

PHILIPPINES - INTERNAL TRADE

Statistical Office of the United Nations, Publishing Service, New York, New York 10017 (800) 253-9646; *Statistical Yearbook for Asia and the Pacific.*

PHILIPPINES - INTERNATIONAL LIQUIDITY

International Monetary Fund, 700 Nineteenth Street, NW, Washington, D.C. 20431 (202) 623-7000; *International Financial Statistics.*

PHILIPPINES - INTERNATIONAL RESERVES EXCLUDING GOLD

Asian Development Bank, Post Office Box 789, Manila, 1099 Manila, Philippines; *Key Indicators of Developing Asian and Pacific Countries.*

Statistical Office of the United Nations, Publishing Service, New York, New York 10017 (800) 253-9646; *Statistical Yearbook.*

The World Bank, 1818 H Street, NW, Washington, D.C. 20433 (202) 477-1234; *World Development Indicators.*

PHILIPPINES - INTERNATIONAL STATISTICS

Asian Development Bank, Post Office Box 789, Manila, 1099 Manila, Philippines; *Key Indicators of Developing Asian and Pacific Countries.*

PHILIPPINES - INVESTMENTS

International Monetary Fund, 700 Nineteenth Street, NW, Washington, D.C. 20431 (202) 623-7000; *International Financial Statistics.*

PHILIPPINES - IRON ORE PRODUCTION AND CONSUMPTION - See PHILIPPINES - MINING AND MINERAL PRODUCTS

PHILIPPINES - IRRIGATION

Euromonitor International, Inc., 122 Michigan Avenue, Suite 1200, Chicago, Illinois 60603 (800) 577-EURO; *International Marketing Data and Statistics.*

PHILIPPINES - LABOR

Central Intelligence Agency, Washington, D.C. 20505 (703) 482-1100, www.cia.gov; *The World Factbook.*

The Economist Intelligence Unit (Asia) Limited, 10th Floor, Luk Kwok Centre, 72 Gloucester Road, Wanchai, Hong Kong (Phone Number in U.S. (800) 938-4685); *Asian Market Atlas.*

Euromonitor International, Inc., 122 Michigan Avenue, Suite 1200, Chicago, Illinois 60603 (800) 577-EURO; *International Marketing Data and Statistics;* and *World Marketing Data and Statistics.*

Europa Publications Limited, 18 Bedford Square, London, WC1B 3JN, England; *The Europa World Year Book.*

Food and Agricultural Organization of the United Nations (FAO) Via delle Terme di Caracalla, 00100 Rome, Italy (Telephone Number in U.S. (202) 653-2400); *The State of Food and Agriculture.*

International Labour Office,

I.L.O. Publications, 1828 L Street, NW., Suite 801, Washington, D.C. 20036 (301) 638-3152; *Yearbook of Labour Statistics.*

M.E. Sharpe, 80 Business Park Drive, Armonk, New York 10504 (800) 541-6563; *The Illustrated Book of World Rankings.*

St. Martin's Press, Inc., 175 Fifth Avenue, New York, New York 10010 (800) 221-7945; *The Statesman's Year-Book.*

Statistical Office of the United Nations, Publishing Service, New York, New York 10017 (800) 253-9646; *Human Development Report.*

The World Bank, 1818 H Street, NW, Washington, D.C. 20433 (202) 477-1234; *The World Bank Atlas; World Development Report;* and *World Development Indicators.*

PHILIPPINES - LAND USE

Central Intelligence Agency, Washington, D.C. 20505 (703) 482-1100, www.cia.gov; *The World Factbook.*

Euromonitor International, Inc., 122 Michigan Avenue, Suite 1200, Chicago, Illinois 60603 (800) 577-EURO; *International Marketing Data and Statistics.*

Food and Agricultural Organization of the United Nations (FAO), Via delle Terme di Caracalla, 00100 Rome, Italy (Telephone Number in U.S. (202) 653-2400); *Production Yearbook.*

The World Bank, 1818 H Street, NW, Washington, D.C. 20433 (202) 477-1234; *World Development Report.*

PHILIPPINES - LEAD AND LEAD ORE PRODUCTION AND CONSUMPTION - See PHILIPPINES - MINING AND MINERAL PRODUCTS

PHILIPPINES - LIBRARIES

M.E. Sharpe, 80 Business Park Drive, Armonk, New York 10504 (800) 541-6563; *The Illustrated Book of World Rankings.*

United Nations Educational, Scientific and Cultural Organization (UNESCO), 7 Place de Fontenoy, F-75700 Paris, France (Telephone Number in U.S. (212) 963-5981); *Statistical Yearbook.*

PHILIPPINES - LIFE EXPECTANCY

Central Intelligence Agency, Washington, D.C. 20505 (703) 482-1100, www.cia.gov; *The World Factbook.*

The Economist Intelligence Unit (Asia) Limited, 10th Floor, Luk Kwok Centre, 72 Gloucester Road, Wanchai, Hong Kong (Phone Number in U.S. (800) 938-4685); *Asian Market Atlas.*

Euromonitor International, Inc., 122 Michigan Avenue, Suite 1200, Chicago, Illinois 60603 (800) 577-EURO; *The World Economic Factbook.*

St. Martin's Press, Inc., 175 Fifth Avenue, New York, New York 10010 (800) 221-7945; *The Statesman's Year-Book.*

Statistical Office of the United Nations, Publishing Service, New York, New York 10017 (800) 253-9646; *Asia-Pacific in Figures; Human Development Report;* and *World Statistics Pocketbook.*

The World Bank, 1818 H Street, NW, Washington, D.C. 20433 (202) 477-1234; *The World Bank Atlas;* and *World Development Report.*

PHILIPPINES - LIGNITE PRODUCTION - See PHILIPPINES - MINING AND MINERAL PRODUCTS

PHILIPPINES - LIVESTOCK AND POULTRY

Commodity Research Bureau, Inc., 30 South Wacker Drive, Chicago Illinois 60606 (312) 454-1801; *Commodity Year Book.*

Euromonitor International, Inc., 122 Michigan Avenue, Suite 1200, Chicago, Illinois 60603 (800) 577-EURO; *International Marketing Data and Statistics.*

Europa Publications Limited, 18 Bedford Square, London, WC1B 3JN, England; *The Europa World Year Book.*

Food and Agricultural Organization of the United Nations (FAO), Via delle Terme di Caracalla, 00100 Rome, Italy (Telephone Number in U.S. (202) 653-2400); *Production Yearbook;* and *The State of Food and Agriculture.*

M.E. Sharpe, 80 Business Park Drive, Armonk, New York 10504 (800) 541-6563; *The Illustrated Book of World Rankings.*

St. Martin's Press, Inc., 175 Fifth Avenue, New York, New York 10010 (800) 221-7945; *The Statesman's Year-Book.*

Statistical Office of the United Nations, Publishing Service, New York, New York 10017 (800) 253-9646; *Statistical Yearbook.*

United Nations Conference on Trade and Development, Central Statistical Service, Palais des Nations, Geneva, Switzerland (Telephone in U.S. (800) 253-9646); *UNCTAD Commodity Yearbook.*

PHILIPPINES - LITERACY RATE

Euromonitor International, Inc., 122 South Michigan Avenue, Suite 1200, Chicago, Illinois 60603 (800) 577-EURO; *World Marketing Data and Statistics.*

PHILIPPINES - LIVING LEVELS - See PHILIPPINES - LIFE EXPECTANCY

PHILIPPINES - MANGANESE ORE PRODUCTION AND CONSUMPTION - See PHILIPPINES - MINING AND MINERAL PRODUCTS

PHILIPPINES - MANPOWER

Statistical Office of the United Nations, Publishing Service, New York, New York 10017 (800) 253-9646; *Statistical Yearbook for Asia and the Pacific.*

PHILIPPINES - MANUFACTURING

M.E. Sharpe, 80 Business Park Drive, Armonk, New York 10504 (800) 541-6563; *The Illustrated Book of World Rankings.*

Statistical Office of the United Nations, Publishing Service, New York, New York 10017 (800) 253-9646; *Statistical Yearbook.*

The World Bank, 1818 H Street, NW, Washington, D.C. 20433 (202) 477-1234; *World Development Indicators.*

PHILIPPINES - MARRIAGE RATES

Europa Publications Limited, 18 Bedford Square, London, WC1B 3JN, England; *The Europa World Year Book.*

M.E. Sharpe, 80 Business Park Drive, Armonk, New York 10504 (800) 541-6563; *The Illustrated Book of World Rankings.*

Statistical Office of the United Nations, Publishing Service, New York, New York 10017 (800) 253-9646; *Demographic Yearbook;* and *Statistical Yearbook.*

PHILIPPINES - MEAT PRODUCTION - See PHILIPPINES - LIVESTOCK AND POULTRY

PHILIPPINES - MERCHANT SHIPPING

Europa Publications Limited, 18 Bedford Square, London, WC1B 3JN, England; *The Europa World Year Book.*

Lloyd's Register of Shipping, 17 Battery Place, New York, New York 10004 (212) 425-8050; *Register of Ships.*

St. Martin's Press, Inc., 175 Fifth Avenue, New York, New York 10010 (800) 221-7945; *The Statesman's Year-Book.*

Statistical Office of the United Nations, Publishing Service, New York, New York 10017 (800) 253-9646; *Statistical Yearbook.*

U.S. Department of Transportation, Maritime Administration, 400 Seventh Street, SW, Washington, D.C. 20590 (202) 366-5807, www.marad.dot.gov; *A Statistical Analysis of the World's Merchant Fleets.*

PHILIPPINES - MERCURY PRODUCTION AND CONSUMPTION - See PHILIPPINES - MINING AND MINERAL PRODUCTS

PHILIPPINES - MILITARY

Central Intelligence Agency, Washington, D.C. 20505 (703) 482-1100, www.cia.gov; *The World Factbook.*

The Economist Intelligence Unit (Asia) Limited, 10th Floor, Luk Kwok Centre, 72 Gloucester Road, Wanchai, Hong Kong (Phone Number in U.S. (800) 938-4685); *Asian Market Atlas.*

Euromonitor International, Inc., 122 South Michigan Avenue, Suite 1200, Chicago, Illinois 60603 (800) 577-EURO; *World Marketing Data and Statistics.*

The International Institute for Strategic Studies, 23 Tavistock Street, London WC2E 7NQ, England 44 171 3797676; *The Military Balance.*

International Monetary Fund, 700 Nineteenth Street, NW, Washington, D.C. 20431 (202) 623-7000; *Government Finance Statistics Yearbook.*

St. Martin's Press, Inc., 175 Fifth Avenue, New York, New York 10010 (800) 221-7945; *The Statesman's Year-Book.*

Statistical Office of the United Nations, Publishing Service, New York, New York 10017 (800) 253-9646; *Human Development Report.*

U.S. Arms Control and Disarmament Agency, 320 Twenty-first Street, NW, Washington, D.C. 20451 (202) 647-8677; *World Military Expenditures and Arms Transfers.*

PHILIPPINES - MILK PRODUCTION - See PHILIPPINES - DAIRY PRODUCTS

PHILIPPINES - MINING AND MINERAL PRODUCTS

Asian Development Bank, Post Office Box 789, Manila, 1099 Manila, Philippines; *Key Indicators of Developing Asian and Pacific Countries.*

Commodity Research Bureau, Inc., 30 South Wacker Drive, Chicago Illinois 60606 (312) 454-1801; *Commodity Year Book.*

Europa Publications Limited, 18 Bedford Square, London, WC1B 3JN, England; *The Europa World Year Book.*

International Monetary Fund, 700 Nineteenth Street, NW, Washington, D.C. 20431 (202) 623-7000; *International Financial Statistics.*

M.E. Sharpe, 80 Business Park Drive, Armonk, New York 10504 (800) 541-6563; *The Illustrated Book of World Rankings.*

Penn Well Publishing Company, 1421 South Sheridan Road, Post Office Box 1260, Tulsa, Oklahoma 74101 (800) 752-9764; *International Energy Statistics Sourcebook.*

St. Martin's Press, Inc., 175 Fifth Avenue, New York, New York 10010 (800) 221-7945; *The Statesman's Year-Book.*

Statistical Office of the United Nations, Publishing Service, New York, New York 10017 (800) 253-9646; *Statistical Yearbook.*

United Nations Conference on Trade and Development, Central Statistical Service, Palais des Nations, Geneva, Switzerland (Telephone in U.S. (800) 253-9646); *UNCTAD Commodity Yearbook.*

World Bureau of Metal Statistics, 27-A High Street, Ware, Herts. SG12 9BA, England; *World Metal Statistics.*

PHILIPPINES - MOLASSES PRODUCTION - See PHILIPPINES - CROPS

PHILIPPINES - MOLYBDENUM AND MOLYBDENUM ORE PRODUCTION AND CONSUMPTION- See PHILIPPINES - MINING AND MINERAL PRODUCTS

PHILIPPINES - MONEY EXCHANGE RATE - See PHILIPPINES - EXCHANGE RATES

PHILIPPINES - MONEY RESERVES

Euromonitor International, Inc., 122 Michigan Avenue, Suite 1200, Chicago, Illinois 60603 (800) 577-EURO; *International Marketing Data and Statistics.*

Europa Publications Limited, 18 Bedford Square, London, WC1B 3JN, England; *The Europa World Year Book.*

PHILIPPINES - MONEY SUPPLY

Asian Development Bank, Post Office Box 789, Manila, 1099 Manila, Philippines; *Key Indicators of Developing Asian and Pacific Countries.*

Economist Intelligence Unit, 111 West 57th Street, New York, New York 10019 (800) 938-4685; *Philippines Country Report.*

Euromonitor International, Inc., 122 Michigan Avenue, Suite 1200, Chicago, Illinois 60603 (800) 577-EURO; *International Marketing Data and Statistics.*

International Monetary Fund, 700 Nineteenth Street, NW, Washington, D.C. 20431 (202) 623-7000; *International*

Financial Statistics.

Statistical Office of the United Nations, Publishing Service, New York, New York 10017 (800) 253-9646; *Statistical Yearbook.*

The World Bank, 1818 H Street, NW, Washington, D.C. 20433 (202) 477-1234; *World Development Indicators.*

PHILIPPINES - MONUMENTS AND HISTORICAL SITES

United Nations Educational, Scientific and Cultural Organization (UNESCO), 7 Place de Fontenoy, F-75700 Paris, France (Telephone Number in U.S. (212) 963-5981); *Statistical Yearbook.*

PHILIPPINES - MORTALITY

Central Intelligence Agency, Washington, D.C. 20505 (703) 482-1100, www.cia.gov; *The World Factbook.*

The Economist Intelligence Unit (Asia) Limited, 10th Floor, Luk Kwok Centre, 72 Gloucester Road, Wanchai, Hong Kong (Phone Number in U.S. (800) 938-4685); *Asian Market Atlas.*

Euromonitor International, Inc., 122 Michigan Avenue, Suite 1200, Chicago, Illinois 60603 (800) 577-EURO; *International Marketing Data and Statistics;* and *The World Economic Factbook.*

Europa Publications Limited, 18 Bedford Square, London, WC1B 3JN, England; *The Europa World Year Book.*

St. Martin's Press, Inc., 175 Fifth Avenue, New York, New York 10010 (800) 221-7945; *The Statesman's Year-Book.*

Statistical Office of the United Nations, Publishing Service, New York, New York 10017 (800) 253-9646; *Asia-Pacific in Figures; Demographic Yearbook; Human Development Report; Statistical Yearbook;* and *World Statistics Pocketbook.*

United Nations Children's Fund (UNICEF), 3 United Nations Plaza, New York, New York 10017 (800) 253-9646; *State of the World's Children.*

The World Bank, 1818 H Street, NW, Washington, D.C. 20433 (202) 477-1234; *The World Bank Atlas; World Development Report;* and *World Development Indicators.*

World Health Organization, Office of Publications, 20 Avenue Appia, CH-1211 Geneva 27, Switzerland (Telephone Number in U.S. (518) 436-9686); *World Health Statistics Annual.*

PHILIPPINES - MOTION PICTURES

Statistical Office of the United Nations,

Publishing Service, New York, New York 10017 (800) 253-9646; *Statistical Yearbook.*

United Nations Educational, Scientific and Cultural Organization (UNESCO), 7 Place de Fontenoy, F-75700 Paris, France (Telephone Number in U.S. (212) 963-5981); *Statistical Yearbook.*

PHILIPPINES - MOTOR VEHICLE PRODUCTION

Statistical Office of the United Nations, Publishing Service, New York, New York 10017 (800) 253-9646; *Statistical Yearbook.*

PHILIPPINES - MOTOR VEHICLE TAXES - See PHILIPPINES - TAXATION

PHILIPPINES - MOTOR VEHICLES IN USE

Europa Publications Limited, 18 Bedford Square, London, WC1B 3JN, England; *The Europa World Year Book.*

International Road Federation, 2600 Virginia Avenue, NW., Washington, D.C. 20037 (202) 338-4641; *World Road Statistics.*

Statistical Office of the United Nations, Publishing Service, New York, New York 10017 (800) 253-9646; *Statistical Yearbook.*

PHILIPPINES - MUSEUMS

M.E. Sharpe, 80 Business Park Drive, Armonk, New York 10504 (800) 541-6563; *The Illustrated Book of World Rankings.*

United Nations Educational, Scientific and Cultural Organization (UNESCO), 7 Place de Fontenoy, F-75700 Paris, France (Telephone Number in U.S. (212) 963-5981); *Statistical Yearbook.*

PHILIPPINES - NATALITY - See PHILIPPINES - BIRTH RATES

PHILIPPINES - NATIONAL ACCOUNTS

Europa Publications Limited, 18 Bedford Square, London, WC1B 3JN, England; *The Europa World Year Book.*

International Monetary Fund, 700 Nineteenth Street, NW, Washington, D.C. 20431 (202) 623-7000; *International Financial Statistics.*

Statistical Office of the United Nations, Publishing Service, New York, New York 10017 (800) 253-9646; *Asia-Pacific in Figures; National Accounts Statistics; Statistical Yearbook;* and *Statistical Yearbook for Asia and the Pacific.*

PHILIPPINES - NATIONAL INCOME

M.E. Sharpe, 80 Business Park Drive, Armonk, New York 10504 (800) 541-6563;

The Illustrated Book of World Rankings.

Statistical Office of the United Nations, Publishing Service, New York, New York 10017 (800) 253-9646; *National Accounts Statistics;* and *Statistical Yearbook.*

PHILIPPINES - NATIONAL PRODUCT

M.E. Sharpe, 80 Business Park Drive, Armonk, New York 10504 (800) 541-6563; *The Illustrated Book of World Rankings.*

Statistical Office of the United Nations, Publishing Service, New York, New York 10017 (800) 253-9646; *Statistical Yearbook.*

PHILIPPINES - NATURAL GAS PRODUCTION - See PHILIPPINES - MINING AND MINERAL PRODUCTS

PHILIPPINES - NATURAL RUBBER PRODUCTION

Statistical Office of the United Nations, Publishing Service, New York, New York 10017 (800) 253-9646; *Statistical Yearbook.*

PHILIPPINES - NEWSPAPER PRODUCTION - See PHILIPPINES - FORESTRY AND FOREST PRODUCTS

PHILIPPINES - NEWSPRINT - See PHILIPPINES - FORESTRY AND FOREST PRODUCTS

PHILIPPINES - NICKEL - See PHILIPPINES - MINING AND MINERAL PRODUCTS

PHILIPPINES - OCCUPATIONS - See PHILIPPINES - LABOR

PHILIPPINES - PALM KERNELS AND PALM OIL PRODUCTION - See PHILIPPINES - CROPS

PHILIPPINES - PAPER - See PHILIPPINES - FORESTRY AND FOREST PRODUCTS

PHILIPPINES - PATENTS, TRADEMARKS AND SERVICE MARKS

Statistical Office of the United Nations, Publishing Service, New York, New York 10017 (800) 253-9646; *Statistical Yearbook.*

World Intellectual Property Organization, 34 Chemin des Colombettes, CH-1211 Geneva 20, Switzerland; *Industrial Property Statistics.*

PHILIPPINES - PEANUT PRODUCTION - See PHILIPPINES - CROPS

PHILIPPINES - PERIODICALS

United Nations Educational, Scientific and Cultural Organization (UNESCO), 7 Place de Fontenoy, F-75700 Paris, France (Telephone Number in U.S. (212) 963-

5981); *Statistical Yearbook.*

PHILIPPINES - PESTICIDE USE

Food and Agricultural Organization of the United Nations (FAO) Via delle Terme di Caracalla, 00100 Rome, Italy (Telephone Number in U.S. (202) 653-2400); *The State of Food and Agriculture.*

PHILIPPINES - PETROLEUM INDUSTRY

Asian Development Bank, Post Office Box 789, Manila, 1099 Manila, Philippines; *Key Indicators of Developing Asian and Pacific Countries.*

Food and Agricultural Organization of the United Nations (FAO) Via delle Terme di Caracalla, 00100 Rome, Italy (Telephone Number in U.S. (202) 653-2400); *The State of Food and Agriculture.*

M.E. Sharpe, 80 Business Park Drive, Armonk, New York 10504 (800) 541-6563; *The Illustrated Book of World Rankings.*

Penn Well Publishing Company, 1421 South Sheridan Road, Post Office Box 1260, Tulsa, Oklahoma 74101 (800) 752-9764; *International Energy Statistics Sourcebook.*

Statistical Office of the United Nations, Publishing Service, New York, New York 10017 (800) 253-9646; *Statistical Yearbook.*

United Nations Conference on Trade and Development, Central Statistical Service, Palais des Nations, Geneva, Switzerland (Telephone in U.S. (800) 253-9646); *UNCTAD Commodity Yearbook.*

PHILIPPINES - PHOSPHATE ROCK PRODUCTION - See PHILIPPINES -MINING AND MINERAL PRODUCTS

PHILIPPINES - PIGS - See PHILIPPINES - LIVESTOCK AND POULTRY

PHILIPPINES - PLASTIC AND RESIN PRODUCTION

Statistical Office of the United Nations, Publishing Service, New York, New York 10017 (800) 253-9646; *Statistical Yearbook.*

PHILIPPINES - PLATINUM PRODUCTION AND CONSUMPTION - See PHILIPPINES - MINING AND MINERAL PRODUCTS

PHILIPPINES - POPULATION

Asian Development Bank, Post Office Box 789, Manila, 1099 Manila, Philippines; *Key Indicators of Developing Asian and Pacific Countries.*

Central Intelligence Agency, Washington, D.C. 20505 (703) 482-1100, www.cia.gov; *The World Factbook.*

The Economist Intelligence Unit, 111 West 57th Street, New York, New York 10019 (800) 938-4685; *Philippines Country Report;* and *The World Market Atlas.*

The Economist Intelligence Unit (Asia) Limited, 10th Floor, Luk Kwok Centre, 72 Gloucester Road, Wanchai, Hong Kong (Phone Number in U.S. (800) 938-4685); *Asian Market Atlas.*

Euromonitor International, Inc., 122 Michigan Avenue, Suite 1200, Chicago, Illinois 60603 (800) 577-EURO; *International Marketing Data and Statistics;* and *The World Economic Factbook.*

Europa Publications Limited, 18 Bedford Square, London, WC1B 3JN, England; *The Europa World Year Book.*

Food and Agricultural Organization of the United Nations (FAO), Via delle Terme di Caracalla, 00100 Rome, Italy (Telephone Number in U.S. (202) 653-2400); *Production Yearbook.*

International Labour Office, I.L.O. Publications, 1828 L Street, NW., Suite 801, Washington, D.C. 20036 (301) 638-3152; *Yearbook of Labour Statistics.*

M.E. Sharpe, 80 Business Park Drive, Armonk, New York 10504 (800) 541-6563; *The Illustrated Book of World Rankings.*

St. Martin's Press, Inc., 175 Fifth Avenue, New York, New York 10010 (800) 221-7945; *The Statesman's Year-Book.*

Statistical Office of the United Nations, Publishing Service, New York, New York 10017 (800) 253-9646; *Asia-Pacific in Figures; Demographic Yearbook; Human Development Report; Statistical Yearbook; Statistical Yearbook for Asia and the Pacific;* and *World Statistics Pocketbook.*

United Nations Educational, Scientific and Cultural Organization (UNESCO), 7 Place de Fontenoy, F-75700 Paris, France (Telephone Number in U.S. (212) 963-5981); *Statistical Yearbook.*

U.S. Arms Control and Disarmament Agency, 320 Twenty-first Street, NW, Washington, D.C. 20451 (202) 647-8677; *World Military Expenditures and Arms Transfers.*

Walden Publishing, Ltd., Two Market Street, Saffron Walden Essex, CB10 1HZ, England; *The World of Information Asia and Pacific Review.*

The World Bank, 1818 H Street, NW, Washington, D.C. 20433 (202) 477-1234; *The World Bank Atlas;* and *World Development Report.*

World Health Organization, Office of

Publications, 20 Avenue Appia, CH-1211 Geneva 27, Switzerland (Telephone Number in U.S. (518) 436-9686); *World Health Statistics Annual.*

PHILIPPINES - POST OFFICES

M.E. Sharpe, 80 Business Park Drive, Armonk, New York 10504 (800) 541-6563; *The Illustrated Book of World Rankings.*

St. Martin's Press, Inc., 175 Fifth Avenue, New York, New York 10010 (800) 221-7945; *The Statesman's Year-Book.*

PHILIPPINES - POTATO PRODUCTION - See PHILIPPINES - CROPS

PHILIPPINES - PRICES

Asian Development Bank, Post Office Box 789, Manila, 1099 Manila, Philippines; *Key Indicators of Developing Asian and Pacific Countries.*

Food and Agricultural Organization of the United Nations (FAO), Via delle Terme di Caracalla, 00100 Rome, Italy (Telephone Number in U.S. (202) 653-2400); *Production Yearbook;* and *The State of Food and Agriculture.*

International Labour Office, I.L.O. Publications, 1828 L Street, NW, Suite 801, Washington, D.C. 20036 (301) 638-3152; *Yearbook of Labour Statistics.*

International Monetary Fund, 700 Nineteenth Street, NW, Washington, D.C. 20431 (202) 623-7000; *International Financial Statistics.*

M.E. Sharpe, 80 Business Park Drive, Armonk, New York 10504 (800) 541-6563; *The Illustrated Book of World Rankings.*

World Bureau of Metal Statistics, 27-A High Street, Ware, Herts. SG12 9BA, England; *World Metal Statistics.*

PHILIPPINES - PRINTING AND WRITING PAPER - See PHILIPPINES - FORESTRY AND FOREST PRODUCTS

PHILIPPINES - PRODUCTION

M.E. Sharpe, 80 Business Park Drive, Armonk, New York 10504 (800) 541-6563; *The Illustrated Book of World Rankings.*

PHILIPPINES - PRODUCTIVITY

Euromonitor International, Inc., 122 South Michigan Avenue, Suite 1200, Chicago, Illinois 60603 (800) 577-EURO; *International Marketing Data and Statistics.*

PHILIPPINES - PROPERTY TAXES - See PHILIPPINES - TAXATION

PHILIPPINES - PUBLIC FINANCE - See

PHILIPPINES - FINANCE

PHILIPPINES - RADIO BROADCASTING -
See PHILIPPINES - BROADCASTING

PHILIPPINES - RADIO RECEIVER
PRODUCTION

Statistical Office of the United Nations,
Publishing Service, New York, New York
10017 (800) 253-9646; *Statistical Yearbook.*

PHILIPPINES - RADIO RECEIVERS

St. Martin's Press, Inc., 175 Fifth
Avenue, New York, New York 10010 (800)
221-7945; *The Statesman's Year-Book.*

PHILIPPINES - RAILWAYS

Europa Publications Limited, 18
Bedford Square, London, WC1B 3JN,
England; *The Europa World Year Book.*

Jane's Information Group, Sentinel
House, 163 Brighton Road, Coulsdon,
Surrey CR5 2NH, England (Telephone
Number in U.S. (703) 683-3700); *Jane's
World Railways.*

St. Martin's Press, Inc., 175 Fifth
Avenue, New York, New York 10010 (800)
221-7945; *The Statesman's Year-Book.*

Statistical Office of the United Nations,
Publishing Service, New York, New York
10017 (800) 253-9646; *Statistical Yearbook.*

PHILIPPINES - RELIGION

Central Intelligence Agency,
Washington, D.C. 20505 (703) 482-1100,
www.cia.gov; *The World Factbook.*

M.E. Sharpe, 80 Business Park Drive,
Armonk, New York 10504 (800) 541-6563;
The Illustrated Book of World Rankings.

St. Martin's Press, Inc., 175 Fifth
Avenue, New York, New York 10010 (800)
221-7945; *The Statesman's Year-Book.*

PHILIPPINES - RENT PRICES

International Labour Office,
I.L.O. Publications, 1828 L Street, NW, Suite
801, Washington, D.C. 20036 (301) 638-
3152; *Yearbook of Labour Statistics.*

PHILIPPINES - RETAIL TRADE

Euromonitor International, Inc., 122
South Michigan Avenue, Suite 1200,
Chicago, Illinois 60603 (800) 577-EURO;
World Marketing Data and Statistics; and
Retail Trade International.

Statistical Office of the United Nations,
Publishing Service, New York, New York
10017 (800) 253-9646; *Statistical Yearbook.*

PHILIPPINES - RICE PRODUCTION - See
PHILIPPINES - CROPS

PHILIPPINES - ROOT AND TUBER
PRODUCTION - See PHILIPPINES - CROPS

PHILIPPINES - ROUNDWOOD
PRODUCTION - See PHILIPPINES -
FORESTRY AND FOREST PRODUCTS

PHILIPPINES - RUBBER PRODUCTION AND
CONSUMPTION

M.E. Sharpe, 80 Business Park Drive,
Armonk, New York 10504 (800) 541-6563;
The Illustrated Book of World Rankings.

Statistical Office of the United Nations,
Publishing Service, New York, New York
10017 (800) 253-9646; *Statistical Yearbook.*

PHILIPPINES - SALT PRODUCTION - See
PHILIPPINES - MINING AND MINERAL
PRODUCTS

PHILIPPINES - SAWNWOOD
PRODUCTION - See PHILIPPINES -
FORESTRY AND FOREST PRODUCTS

PHILIPPINES - SCIENCE AND
TECHNOLOGY - EXPENDITURE FOR
RESEARCH - See PHILIPPINES -
SCIENTISTS, TECHNICIANS AND
ENGINEERS

PHILIPPINES - SCIENTISTS, TECHNICIANS
AND ENGINEERS

Statistical Office of the United Nations,
Publishing Service, New York, New York
10017 (800) 253-9646; *Statistical Yearbook.*

United Nations Educational, Scientific
and Cultural Organization (UNESCO), 7
Place de Fontenoy, F-75700 Paris, France
(Telephone Number in U.S. (212) 963-
5981); *Statistical Yearbook.*

PHILIPPINES - SENIOR CITIZENS

M.E. Sharpe, 80 Business Park Drive,
Armonk, New York 10504 (800) 541-6563;
The Illustrated Book of World Rankings.

PHILIPPINES - SHEEP - See
PHILIPPINES - LIVESTOCK AND POULTRY

PHILIPPINES - SILVER PRODUCTION AND
CONSUMPTION - See PHILIPPINES -
MINING AND MINERAL PRODUCTS

PHILIPPINES - SOCIAL DATA

Asian Development Bank, Post Office
Box 789, Manila, 1099 Manila, Philippines;
*Key Indicators of Developing Asian and
Pacific Countries.*

M.E. Sharpe, 80 Business Park Drive,
Armonk, New York 10504 (800) 541-6563;
The Illustrated Book of World Rankings.

Statistical Office of the United Nations,
Publishing Service, New York, New York
10017 (800) 253-9646; *World Statistics
Pocketbook.*

PHILIPPINES - SOCIAL SECURITY

International Monetary Fund, 700
Nineteenth Street, NW, Washington, D.C.
20431 (202) 623-7000; *Government
Finance Statistics Yearbook.*

St. Martin's Press, Inc., 175 Fifth
Avenue, New York, New York 10010 (800)
221-7945; *The Statesman's Year-Book.*

Statistical Office of the United Nations,
Publishing Service, New York, New York
10017 (800) 253-9646; *National Accounts
Statistics.*

PHILIPPINES - SOYBEAN PRODUCTION -
See PHILIPPINES - CROPS

PHILIPPINES - STAMP TAXES AND DUTIES -
See PHILIPPINES - TAXATION

PHILIPPINES - STATE BUDGET REVENUE
AND EXPENDITURES

Euromonitor International, Inc., 122
South Michigan Avenue, Suite 1200,
Chicago, Illinois 60603 (800) 577-EURO;
International Marketing Data and Statistics.

PHILIPPINES - STEEL - See PHILIPPINES -
MINING AND MINERAL PRODUCTS

PHILIPPINES - STOCKS - COMMODITY -
MARKET PRICE - INDEX

Food and Agricultural Organization of
the United Nations (FAO) Via delle Terme
di Caracalla, 00100 Rome, Italy (Telephone
Number in U.S. (202) 653-2400); *The State
of Food and Agriculture.*

World Bureau of Metal Statistics, 27-A
High Street, Ware, Herts. SG12 9BA,
England; *World Metal Statistics.*

PHILIPPINES - SUGAR PRODUCTION AND
CONSUMPTION - See PHILIPPINES - CROPS

PHILIPPINES - SULPHURIC ACID
PRODUCTION - See PHILIPPINES - MINING
AND MINERAL PRODUCTS

PHILIPPINES - TAXATION

Europa Publications Limited, 18
Bedford Square, London, WC1B 3JN,
England; *The Europa World Year Book.*

International Monetary Fund, 700
Nineteenth Street, NW, Washington, D.C.
20431 (202) 623-7000; *Government
Finance Statistics Yearbook.*

International Road Federation, 2600
Virginia Avenue, NW, Washington, D.C.

20037 (202) 338-4641; *World Road Statistics*.

The World Bank, 1818 H Street, NW, Washington, D.C. 20433 (202) 477-1234; *World Development Indicators*.

PHILIPPINES - TELEPHONES IN USE

American Telephone and Telegraph Company, 26 Parsippany Road, Whippany, New Jersey 07981 (800) 222-0300; *The World's Telephones*.

Central Intelligence Agency, Washington, D.C. 20505 (703) 482-1100, www.cia.gov; *The World Factbook*.

The Economist Intelligence Unit (Asia) Limited, 10th Floor, Luk Kwok Centre, 72 Gloucester Road, Wanchai, Hong Kong (Phone Number in U.S. (800) 938-4685); *Asian Market Atlas*.

Europa Publications Limited, 18 Bedford Square, London, WC1B 3JN, England; *The Europa World Year Book*.

St. Martin's Press, Inc., 175 Fifth Avenue, New York, New York 10010 (800) 221-7945; *The Statesman's Year-Book*.

Statistical Office of the United Nations, Publishing Service, New York, New York 10017 (800) 253-9646; *Statistical Yearbook; and World Statistics Pocketbook*.

PHILIPPINES - TELEVISION BROADCASTING - See PHILIPPINES - BROADCASTING

PHILIPPINES - TELEVISION RECEIVER PRODUCTION

Statistical Office of the United Nations, Publishing Service, New York, New York 10017 (800) 253-9646; *Statistical Yearbook*.

PHILIPPINES - TEXTILE INDUSTRY

American Forest and Paper Association, 1111 Nineteenth Street, NW, Washington, D.C. 20036 (202) 463-2700; *Wood Pulp and Fiber Statistics*.

Euromonitor International, Inc., 122 South Michigan Avenue, Suite 1200, Chicago, Illinois 60603 (800) 577-EURO; *Retail Trade International*.

M.E. Sharpe, 80 Business Park Drive, Armonk, New York 10504 (800) 541-6563; *The Illustrated Book of World Rankings*.

Statistical Office of the United Nations, Publishing Service, New York, New York 10017 (800) 253-9646; *Statistical Yearbook*.

United Nations Conference on Trade and Development, Central Statistical

Service, Palais des Nations, Geneva, Switzerland (Telephone in U.S. (800) 253-9646); *UNCTAD Commodity Yearbook*.

PHILIPPINES - THEATRE

United Nations Educational, Scientific and Cultural Organization (UNESCO), 7 Place de Fontenoy, F-75700 Paris, France (Telephone Number in U.S. (212) 963-5981); *Statistical Yearbook*.

PHILIPPINES - TIN PRODUCTION AND CONSUMPTION - See PHILIPPINES - MINING AND MINERAL PRODUCTS

PHILIPPINES - TIRE (MOTOR VEHICLE) PRODUCTION

Statistical Office of the United Nations, Publishing Service, New York, New York 10017 (800) 253-9646; *Statistical Yearbook*.

PHILIPPINES - TOBACCO PRODUCTION

Commodity Research Bureau, Inc., 30 South Wacker Drive, Chicago Illinois 60606 (312) 454-1801; *Commodity Year Book*.

M.E. Sharpe, 80 Business Park Drive, Armonk, New York 10504 (800) 541-6563; *The Illustrated Book of World Rankings*.

Statistical Office of the United Nations, Publishing Service, New York, New York 10017 (800) 253-9646; *Statistical Yearbook*.

PHILIPPINES - TOURISM

Euromonitor International, Inc., 122 South Michigan Avenue, Suite 1200, Chicago, Illinois 60603 (800) 577-EURO; *The World Economic Factbook;* and *World Marketing Data and Statistics*.

Europa Publications Limited, 18 Bedford Square, London, WC1B 3JN, England; *The Europa World Year Book*.

M.E. Sharpe, 80 Business Park Drive, Armonk, New York 10504 (800) 541-6563; *The Illustrated Book of World Rankings*.

St. Martin's Press, Inc., 175 Fifth Avenue, New York, New York 10010 (800) 221-7945; *The Statesman's Year-Book*.

Statistical Office of the United Nations, Publishing Service, New York, New York 10017 (800) 253-9646; *Statistical Yearbook*.

World Tourism Organization, Calle Capitan Haya 42, E-28020 Madrid, Spain; *Yearbook of Tourism Statistics*.

PHILIPPINES - TRACTORS IN USE

Statistical Office of the United Nations, Publishing Service, New York, New York 10017 (800) 253-9646; *Statistical Yearbook*.

PHILIPPINES - TRADE - See PHILIPPINES - FOREIGN TRADE

PHILIPPINES - TRADEMARKS AND SERVICE MARKS - See PHILIPPINES - PATENTS, TRADEMARKS AND SERVICE MARKS

PHILIPPINES - TRANSPORTATION AND COMMUNICATIONS

Central Intelligence Agency, Washington, D.C. 20505 (703) 482-1100, www.cia.gov; *The World Factbook*.

The Economist Intelligence Unit (Asia) Limited, 10th Floor, Luk Kwok Centre, 72 Gloucester Road, Wanchai, Hong Kong (Phone Number in U.S. (800) 938-4685); *Asian Market Atlas*.

Euromonitor International, Inc., 122 South Michigan Avenue, Suite 1200, Chicago, Illinois 60603 (800) 577-EURO; *International Marketing Data and Statistics;* and *World Marketing Data and Statistics*.

Europa Publications Limited, 18 Bedford Square, London, WC1B 3JN, England; *The Europa World Year Book*.

M.E. Sharpe, 80 Business Park Drive, Armonk, New York 10504 (800) 541-6563; *The Illustrated Book of World Rankings*.

St. Martin's Press, Inc., 175 Fifth Avenue, New York, New York 10010 (800) 221-7945; *The Statesman's Year-Book*.

Statistical Office of the United Nations, Publishing Service, New York, New York 10017 (800) 253-9646; *Human Development Report;* and *Statistical Yearbook for Asia and the Pacific*.

PHILIPPINES - TURKEYS - See PHILIPPINES - LIVESTOCK AND POULTRY

PHILIPPINES - UNEMPLOYMENT

Central Intelligence Agency, Washington, D.C. 20505 (703) 482-1100, www.cia.gov; *The World Factbook*.

Euromonitor International, Inc., 122 South Michigan Avenue, Suite 1200, Chicago, Illinois 60603 (800) 577-EURO; *International Marketing Data and Statistics*.

International Labour Office, I.L.O. Publications, 1828 L Street, NW, Suite 801, Washington, D.C. 20036 (301) 638-3152; *Yearbook of Labour Statistics*.

St. Martin's Press, Inc., 175 Fifth Avenue, New York, New York 10010 (800) 221-7945; *The Statesman's Year-Book*.

Statistical Office of the United Nations, Publishing Service, New York, New York 10017 (800) 253-9646; *Statistical Yearbook*.

PHILIPPINES - URANIUM PRODUCTION AND CONSUMPTION - See PHILIPPINES - MINING AND MINERAL PRODUCTS

PHILIPPINES - VITAL STATISTICS

Euromonitor International, Inc., 122 South Michigan Avenue, Suite 1200, Chicago, Illinois 60603 (800) 577-EURO; *International Marketing Data and Statistics.*

St. Martin's Press, Inc., 175 Fifth Avenue, New York, New York 10010 (800) 221-7945; *The Statesman's Year-Book.*

Statistical Office of the United Nations, Publishing Service, New York, New York 10017 (800) 253-9646; *Statistical Yearbook.*

World Health Organization, Office of Publications, 20 Avenue Appia, CH-1211 Geneva 27, Switzerland (Telephone Number in U.S. (518) 436-9686); *World Health Statistics Annual.*

PHILIPPINES - WAGES

International Labour Office, I.L.O. Publications, 1828 L Street, NW, Suite 801, Washington, D.C. 20036 (301) 638-3152; *Yearbook of Labour Statistics.*

Statistical Office of the United Nations, Publishing Service, New York, New York 10017 (800) 253-9646; *Statistical Yearbook;* and *Statistical Yearbook for Asia and the Pacific.*

PHILIPPINES - WATERMELON PRODUCTION - See PHILIPPINES - CROPS

PHILIPPINES - WEATHER - See PHILIPPINES - CLIMATE

PHILIPPINES - WELFARE

International Monetary Fund, 700 Nineteenth Street, NW, Washington, D.C. 20431 (202) 623-7000; *Government Finance Statistics Yearbook.*

St. Martin's Press, Inc., 175 Fifth Avenue, New York, New York 10010 (800) 221-7945; *The Statesman's Year-Book.*

PHILIPPINES - WHEAT PRODUCTION AND PRICES - See PHILIPPINES - CROPS

PHILIPPINES - WHOLESALE PRICES

Asian Development Bank, Post Office Box 789, 1099 Manila, Philippines; *Key Indicators of Developing Asian and Pacific Countries.*

International Monetary Fund, 700 Nineteenth Street, NW, Washington, D.C. 20431 (202) 623-7000; *International Financial Statistics.*

Statistical Office of the United Nations, Publishing Service, New York, New York 10017 (800) 253-9646; *Statistical Yearbook.*

PHILIPPINES - WHOLESALE TRADE

Statistical Office of the United Nations, Publishing Service, New York, New York 10017 (800) 253-9646; *Statistical Yearbook.*

PHILIPPINES - WINE PRODUCTION - See PHILIPPINES - BEVERAGES

PHILIPPINES - WOOD AND WOOD PULP - See PHILIPPINES - FORESTRY AND FOREST PRODUCTS

PHILIPPINES - WOOL PRODUCTION - See PHILIPPINES - TEXTILE INDUSTRY

PHILIPPINES - YARN PRODUCTION - See PHILIPPINES - TEXTILE INDUSTRY

PHILIPPINES - ZINC AND ZINC ORE PRODUCTION AND CONSUMPTION - See PHILIPPINES - MINING AND MINERAL PRODUCTS

PHONOGRAPH RECORDS AND TAPES

Recording Industry Association of America, 1020 Nineteenth Street, NW, Suite 200, Washington, D.C. 20036 (202) 775-0101; Internet site http://www.riaa.com.

PHOSPHATE ROCK - CONSUMPTION

U.S. Department of the Interior, Geological Survey, Office of Minerals Information, 12201 Sunrise Valley Drive, Reston, Virginia 22092 (703) 648-4000, www.minerals.usgs.gov; *Mineral Commodity Summaries.*

PHOSPHATE ROCK - EMPLOYMENT

U.S. Department of the Interior, Geological Survey, Office of Minerals Information, 12201 Sunrise Valley Drive, Reston, Virginia 22092 (703) 648-4000, www.minerals.usgs.gov; *Mineral Commodity Summaries.*

PHOSPHATE ROCK - FOREIGN TRADE

U.S. Department of the Interior, Geological Survey, Office of Minerals Information, 12201 Sunrise Valley Drive, Reston, Virginia 22092 (703) 648-4000, www.minerals.usgs.gov; *Mineral Commodity Summaries.*

PHOSPHATE ROCK - PRICES

U.S. Department of the Interior, Geological Survey, Office of Minerals Information, 12201 Sunrise Valley Drive, Reston, Virginia 22092 (703) 648-4000, www.minerals.usgs.gov; *Mineral Commodity Summaries.*

PHOSPHATE ROCK - PRODUCTION AND VALUE

U.S. Department of the Interior, Geological Survey, Office of Minerals Information, 12201 Sunrise Valley Drive, Reston, Virginia 22092 (703) 648-4000, www.minerals.usgs.gov; *Annual Reports;* and *Mineral Commodity Summaries.*

PHOSPHATE ROCK - WORLD PRODUCTION

U.S. Department of Energy, Energy Information Administration, 1000 Independence Avenue, SW, Washington, D.C. 20585 (202) 586-5000; *Annual Energy Review; International Energy Annual;* and *Monthly Energy Review.*

U.S. Department of the Interior, Geological Survey, Office of Minerals Information, 12201 Sunrise Valley Drive, Reston, Virginia 22092 (703) 648-4000, www.minerals.usgs.gov; *Mineral Commodity Summaries;* and *Annual Reports.*

PHOTOGRAPHIC EQUIPMENT AND SUPPLIES

U.S. Department of Commerce, Bureau of the Census, Washington, D.C. 20233 (301) 457-4100, www.census.gov; *International Trade in Goods and Services.*

PHYSICAL ACTIVITY

U.S. Department of Health and Human Services, National Center for Chronic Disease Prevention and Health Promotion, Centers for Disease Control and Prevention, 1600 Clifton Road, NE, Atlanta, Georgia 30333 (404) 639-3311, www.cdc.gov/nccdphp; unpublished data.

PHYSICAL SCIENCES - DEGREES CONFERRED

National Science Foundation, Division of Science Resources Studies, 4201 Wilson Boulevard, Arlington, Virginia 22230 (703) 306-1234, www.nsf.gov; *Survey of Earned Doctorates, Selected Data on Science and Engineering Doctorate Awards;* and *National Survey of Recent College Graduates.*

U.S. Department of Commerce, Bureau of the Census, Washington, D.C. 20233 (301) 457-4100, www.census.gov; unpublished data.

U.S. Department of Education, National Center for Education Statistics; 555 New Jersey Avenue, NW, Washington, D.C. 20208-5574 (202) 219-1828, http://nces.ed.gov, *Digest of Education Statistics.*

PHYSICAL SCIENCES - EMPLOYEES

U.S. Department of Labor, Bureau of Labor Statistics, Two Massachusetts Avenue, NE, Washington, D.C. 20212 (202) 691-5200, www.stats.bls.gov; *Monthly Labor Review; Employment and Earnings;* and unpublished data.

PHYSICIANS

American Medical Association, 515 North State Street, Chicago, Illinois 60610 (312) 464-5000; *Physician Characteristics and Distribution in the United States.*

U.S. Department of Health and Human Services, National Center for Health Statistics, 3700 East-West Highway, Hyattsville, Maryland 20782 (301) 436-8500, www.cdc.gov/nchs; *Vital and Health Statistics;* and unpublished data.

U.S. Department of Labor, Bureau of Labor Statistics, 2 Massachusetts Avenue, NE, Washington, D.C. 20212 (202) 691-5200, www.stats.bls.gov; *Employment and Earnings;* and Bulletins 2445 and 2481.

PHYSICIANS - DEGREES CONFERRED

U.S. Department of Education, National Center for Education Statistics; 555 New Jersey Avenue, NW, Washington, D.C. 20208-5574 (202) 219-1828, http://nces.ed.gov; *Digest of Education Statistics.*

PHYSICIANS - EARNINGS

American Medical Association, 515 North State Street, Chicago, Illinois 60610 (312) 464-5000; *Socioeconomic Characteristics of Medical Practice.*

PHYSICIANS - EMPLOYMENT

American Medical Association, 515 North State Street, Chicago, Illinois 60610 (312) 464-5000; *Physician Characteristics and Distribution in the United States.*

U.S. Department of Labor, Bureau of Labor Statistics, Two Massachusetts Avenue, NE, Washington, D.C. 20212 (202) 691-5200, www.stats.bls.gov; *Employment and Earnings;* and unpublished data.

PHYSICIANS - EXPENDITURES FOR

U.S. Department of Health and Human Services, Health Care Financing Administration, 200 Independence Avenue, SW, Washington, D.C. 20201 (202) 690-6145, www.hcfa.gov; *Health Care Financing Review.*

PHYSICIANS - FOREIGN MEDICAL SCHOOL GRADUATES

American Medical Association, 515

North State Street, Chicago, Illinois 60610 (312) 464-5000; *Physician Characteristics and Distribution in the United States.*

PHYSICIANS - MEDICAL SCHOOLS - STUDENTS AND GRADUATES

U.S. Department of Education, National Center for Education Statistics, 555 New Jersey Avenue, NW, Washington, D.C. 20208-5574 (202) 219-1828, http://nces.ed.gov; *Digest of Education Statistics.*

U.S. Department of Health and Human Services, National Center for Health Statistics, 3700 East-West Highway, Hyattsville, Maryland 20782 (301) 436-8500, www.cdc.gov/nchs; *Health, United States.*

PHYSICIANS - OFFICES

U.S. Department of Commerce, Bureau of the Census, Washington, D.C. 20233 (301) 457-4100, www.census.gov; *Census of Service Industries; Current Business Report, Service Annual Survey;* and unpublished data.

PHYSICIANS - PATIENT CARE ACTIVITIES

American Medical Association, 515 North State Street, Chicago, Illinois 60610 (312) 464-5000; *Socioeconomic Characteristics of Medical Practice.*

PHYSICIANS - PRICE INDEX

U.S. Department of Labor, Bureau of Labor Statistics, Two Massachusetts Avenue, NE, Washington, D.C. 20212 (202) 691-5200, www.stats.bls.gov; *CPI Detailed Report.*

PHYSICIANS - SPECIALTY AND PROFESSIONAL ACTIVITY

American Medical Association, 515 North State Street, Chicago, Illinois 60610 (312) 464-5000; *Physician Characteristics and Distribution in the United States.*

PHYSICIANS - STATE DATA

American Medical Association, 515 North State Street, Chicago, Illinois 60610 (312) 464-5000; *Physician Characteristics and Distribution in the United States.*

PHYSICIANS - TYPE OF PRACTICE

American Medical Association, 515 North State Street, Chicago, Illinois 60610 (312) 464-5000; *Physician Characteristics and Distribution in the United States.*

PHYSICIANS - VISITS TO

U.S. Department of Health and Human Services, National Center for Health Statistics, 3700 East-West Highway,

Hyattsville, Maryland 20782 (301) 436-8500, www.cdc.gov/nchs; *Vital and Health Statistics; Health, U.S.; Advance Data, No 304;* and unpublished data.

PHYSICIANS - WORKPLACE VIOLENCE

U.S. Department of Justice, Bureau of Justice Statistics, 810 Seventh Street, NW, 2nd Floor, Washington, D.C. 20531 (800) 732-3277, www.ojp.usdoj.gov/bjs; *Workplace Violence.*

PHYSICS - See also PHYSICAL SCIENCES

PHYSICS - NOBEL PRIZE LAUREATES

National Science Foundation, 4201 Wilson Boulevard, Arlington, Virginia 22230 (703) 306-1234, www.nsf.gov; unpublished data.

PHYSICS - SALARY OFFERS

National Association of Colleges and Employers, 62 Highland Avenue, Bethlehem, Pennsylvania 18017 (800) 544-5272; *Salary Survey, A Study of Beginning Offers.*

PHYSIOLOGY - NOBEL PRIZE LAUREATES

National Science Foundation, 4201 Wilson Boulevard, Arlington, Virginia 22230 (703) 306-1234, www.nsf.gov; unpublished data.

PIG IRON - See IRON

PIGGYBACK - RAILROAD CARLOADS

Association of American Railroads, American Railroads Building, 50 F Street, NW, Washington, D.C. 20001 (202) 639-2100; *Weekly Railroad Traffic.*

PIGS - See HOGS

PILCHARD - See SARDINES

PINEAPPLES

U.S. Department of Agriculture, Economic Research Service, 1800 M Street, NW, Washington, D.C. 20036 (202) 694-5050, www.ers.usda.gov; *Food Consumption, Prices, and Expenditures.*

U.S. Department of Agriculture, National Agricultural Statistics Service, Fourteenth Street and Independence Avenue, SW, Washington, D.C. 20250 (800) 727-9540, www.usda.gov/nass; *Citrus Fruits.*

PIPELINES - EXCEPT NATURAL GAS - CAPITAL

Pennwell Publishing Company, 1421 South Sheridan Road, Tulsa, Oklahoma 74101 (800) 752-9764; *Oil and Gas Journal.*

U.S. Department of Commerce, Bureau of Economic Analysis, Fourteenth Street between Constitution Avenue and E Street, NW, Washington, D.C. 20230 (202) 606-9900, www.bea.doc.gov; *Survey of Current Business.*

PIPELINES - EXCEPT NATURAL GAS - EARNINGS

U.S. Department of Labor, Bureau of Labor Statistics, Two Massachusetts Avenue, NE, Washington, D.C. 20212 (202) 691-5200, www.stats.bls.gov; *Employment and Earnings;* and Internet site: http://stats.bls.gov/ ceshome.htm

PIPELINES - EXCEPT NATURAL GAS - EMPLOYEES

U.S. Department of Labor, Bureau of Labor Statistics, Two Massachusetts Avenue, NE, Washington, D.C. 20212 (202) 691-5200, www.stats.bls.gov; *Employment and Earnings;* and Internet site: http://stats.bls.gov/ ceshome.htm

PIPELINES - EXCEPT NATURAL GAS - FINANCES

Pennwell Publishing Company, 1421 South Sheridan Road, Tulsa, Oklahoma 74101 (800) 752-9764; *Oil and Gas Journal.*

PIPELINES - EXCEPT NATURAL GAS - OCCUPATIONAL SAFETY

U.S. Department of Labor, Bureau of Labor Statistics, Two Massachusetts Avenue, NE, Washington, D.C. 20212 (202) 691-5200, www.stats.bls.gov; *Occupational Injuries and Illnesses in the United States by Industry.*

PIPELINES - EXCEPT NATURAL GAS - OUTPUT

Pennwell Publishing Company, 1421 South Sheridan Road, Tulsa, Oklahoma 74101 (800) 752-9764; *Oil and Gas Journal.*

PIPELINES - EXCEPT NATURAL GAS - PRODUCTIVITY

U.S. Department of Labor, Bureau of Labor Statistics, Two Massachusetts Avenue, NE, Washington, D.C. 20212 (202) 691-5200, www.stats.bls.gov; Internet site http://stats.bls.gov/iprhome.htm.

PISTACHIOS

U.S. Department of Agriculture, National Agricultural Statistics Service, Fourteenth Street and Independence Avenue, SW, Washington, D.C. 20250 (800) 727-9540, www.usda.gov/nass; *Noncitrus Fruits and Nuts.*

PISTOLS - See FIREARMS

PITCAIRN ISLAND - AGRICULTURE

Food and Agricultural Organization of the United Nations (FAO) Via delle Terme di Caracalla, 00100 Rome, Italy (Telephone Number in U.S. (202) 653-2400); *Production Yearbook; The State of Food and Agriculture;* and *Trade Yearbook.*

PITCAIRN ISLAND - AIRPORTS

Central Intelligence Agency, Washington, D.C. 20505 (703) 482-1100, www.cia.gov; *The World Factbook.*

PITCAIRN ISLAND - AREA AND DENSITY OF POPULATION

Central Intelligence Agency, Washington, D.C. 20505 (703) 482-1100, www.cia.gov; *The World Factbook.*

Europa Publications Limited, 18 Bedford Square, London, WC1B 3JN, England; *The Europa World Year Book.*

Food and Agricultural Organization of the United Nations (FAO) Via delle Terme di Caracalla, 00100 Rome, Italy (Telephone Number in U.S. (202) 653-2400); *The State of Food and Agriculture.*

St. Martin's Press, Inc., 175 Fifth Avenue, New York, New York 10010 (800) 221-7945; *The Statesman's Year-Book.*

Statistical Office of the United Nations, Publishing Service, New York, New York 10017 (800) 253-9646; *Statistical Yearbook.*

PITCAIRN ISLAND - BIRTH RATES

Central Intelligence Agency, Washington, D.C. 20505 (703) 482-1100, www.cia.gov; *The World Factbook.*

Statistical Office of the United Nations, Publishing Service, New York, New York 10017 (800) 253-9646; *Demographic Yearbook;* and *Statistical Yearbook.*

PITCAIRN ISLAND - BROADCASTING

Central Intelligence Agency, Washington, D.C. 20505 (703) 482-1100, www.cia.gov; *The World Factbook.*

PITCAIRN ISLAND - BUDGET

Central Intelligence Agency, Washington, D.C. 20505 (703) 482-1100, www.cia.gov; *The World Factbook.*

PITCAIRN ISLAND - CALORIE SUPPLY

Food and Agricultural Organization of the United Nations (FAO) Via delle Terme di Caracalla, 00100 Rome, Italy (Telephone Number in U.S. (202) 653-2400); *The State of Food and Agriculture.*

PITCAIRN ISLAND - CLIMATE

St. Martin's Press, Inc., 175 Fifth Avenue, New York, New York 10010 (800) 221-7945; *The Statesman's Year-Book.*

PITCAIRN ISLAND - CORN PRODUCTION - See PITCAIRN ISLAND - CROPS

PITCAIRN ISLAND - CROPS

Food and Agricultural Organization of the United Nations (FAO) Via delle Terme di Caracalla, 00100 Rome, Italy (Telephone Number in U.S. (202) 653-2400); *The State of Food and Agriculture.*

PITCAIRN ISLAND - DAIRY PRODUCTS

Food and Agricultural Organization of the United Nations (FAO) Via delle Terme di Caracalla, 00100 Rome, Italy (Telephone Number in U.S. (202) 653-2400); *The State of Food and Agriculture.*

PITCAIRN ISLAND - DEATH RATES - See PITCAIRN ISLAND - MORTALITY

PITCAIRN ISLAND - DIVORCE RATES

Statistical Office of the United Nations, Publishing Service, New York, New York 10017 (800) 253-9646; *Demographic Yearbook.*

PITCAIRN ISLAND - ECONOMY

Central Intelligence Agency, Washington, D.C. 20505 (703) 482-1100, www.cia.gov; *The World Factbook.*

PITCAIRN ISLAND - EDUCATION

St. Martin's Press, Inc., 175 Fifth Avenue, New York, New York 10010 (800) 221-7945; *The Statesman's Year-Book.*

PITCAIRN ISLAND - EGG PRODUCTION AND CONSUMPTION - See PITCAIRN ISLAND - DAIRY PRODUCTS

PITCAIRN ISLAND - ELECTRICITY

Central Intelligence Agency, Washington, D.C. 20505 (703) 482-1100, www.cia.gov; *The World Factbook.*

PITCAIRN ISLAND - ENERGY

Food and Agricultural Organization of the United Nations (FAO) Via delle Terme di Caracalla, 00100 Rome, Italy (Telephone Number in U.S. (202) 653-2400); *The State of Food and Agriculture.*

PITCAIRN ISLAND - EXCHANGE RATES

Central Intelligence Agency, Washington, D.C. 20505 (703) 482-1100, www.cia.gov; *The World Factbook.*

Europa Publications Limited, 18 Bedford Square, London, WC1B 3JN, England; *The Europa World Year Book*.

Walden Publishing, Ltd., Two Market Street, Saffron Walden Essex, CB10 1HZ, England; *The World of Information Asia and Pacific Review*.

PITCAIRN ISLAND - EXPORTS

Central Intelligence Agency, Washington, D.C. 20505 (703) 482-1100, www.cia.gov; *The World Factbook*.

Food and Agricultural Organization of the United Nations (FAO) Via delle Terme di Caracalla, 00100 Rome, Italy (Telephone Number in U.S. (202) 653-2400); *The State of Food and Agriculture*.

Walden Publishing, Ltd., Two Market Street, Saffron Walden Essex, CB10 1HZ, England; *The World of Information Asia and Pacific Review*.

PITCAIRN ISLAND - EXTERNAL TRADE

Food and Agricultural Organization of the United Nations (FAO) Via delle Terme di Caracalla, 00100 Rome, Italy (Telephone Number in U.S. (202) 653-2400); *The State of Food and Agriculture; and Trade Yearbook*.

PITCAIRN ISLAND - FARM CROPS - See PITCAIRN ISLAND - CROPS

PITCAIRN ISLAND - FETAL MORTALITY - See PITCAIRN ISLAND - MORTALITY

PITCAIRN ISLAND - FERTILITY RATES

Central Intelligence Agency, Washington, D.C. 20505 (703) 482-1100, www.cia.gov; *The World Factbook*.

PITCAIRN ISLAND - FERTILIZER

Food and Agricultural Organization of the United Nations (FAO) Via delle Terme di Caracalla, 00100 Rome, Italy (Telephone Number in U.S. (202) 653-2400); *The State of Food and Agriculture*.

PITCAIRN ISLAND - FINANCE

Europa Publications Limited, 18 Bedford Square, London, WC1B 3JN, England; *The Europa World Year Book*.

St. Martin's Press, Inc., 175 Fifth Avenue, New York, New York 10010 (800) 221-7945; *The Statesman's Year-Book*.

PITCAIRN ISLAND - FISHERIES

Food and Agricultural Organization of the United Nations (FAO) Via delle Terme di Caracalla, 00100 Rome, Italy (Telephone Number in U.S. (202) 653-2400); *The State*

of Food and Agriculture; and *Yearbook of Fishery Statistics*.

PITCAIRN ISLAND - FOOD

Food and Agricultural Organization of the United Nations (FAO), Via delle Terme di Caracalla, 00100 Rome, Italy (Telephone Number in U.S. (202) 653-2400); *Production Yearbook;* and *The State of Food and Agriculture*.

PITCAIRN ISLAND - FOREIGN DEBT

Walden Publishing, Ltd., Two Market Street, Saffron Walden Essex, CB10 1HZ, England; *The World of Information Asia and Pacific Review*.

PITCAIRN ISLAND - FOREIGN TRADE

St. Martin's Press, Inc., 175 Fifth Avenue, New York, New York 10010 (800) 221-7945; *The Statesman's Year-Book*.

PITCAIRN ISLAND - FORESTRY AND FOREST PRODUCTS

Food and Agricultural Organization of the United Nations (FAO) Via delle Terme di Caracalla, 00100 Rome, Italy (Telephone Number in U.S. (202) 653-2400); *The State of Food and Agriculture*.

PITCAIRN ISLAND - GENERAL MORTALITY - See PITCAIRN ISLAND

PITCAIRN ISLAND - GOVERNMENT

Central Intelligence Agency, Washington, D.C. 20505 (703) 482-1100, www.cia.gov; *The World Factbook*.

Europa Publications Limited, 18 Bedford Square, London, WC1B 3JN, England; *The Europa World Year Book*.

St. Martin's Press, Inc., 175 Fifth Avenue, New York, New York 10010 (800) 221-7945; *The Statesman's Year-Book*.

PITCAIRN ISLAND - GRAIN PRODUCTION - See PITCAIRN ISLAND - CROPS

PITCAIRN ISLAND - GROSS NATIONAL PRODUCT

Walden Publishing, Ltd., Two Market Street, Saffron Walden Essex, CB10 1HZ, England; *The World of Information Asia and Pacific Review*.

PITCAIRN ISLAND - HIGHWAYS

Central Intelligence Agency, Washington, D.C. 20505 (703) 482-1100, www.cia.gov; *The World Factbook*.

St. Martin's Press, Inc., 175 Fifth Avenue, New York, New York 10010 (800) 221-7945; *The Statesman's Year-Book*.

PITCAIRN ISLAND - ILLITERATE POPULATION

Central Intelligence Agency, Washington, D.C. 20505 (703) 482-1100, www.cia.gov; *The World Factbook*.

PITCAIRN ISLAND - IMPORTS

Central Intelligence Agency, Washington, D.C. 20505 (703) 482-1100, www.cia.gov; *The World Factbook*.

Food and Agricultural Organization of the United Nations (FAO) Via delle Terme di Caracalla, 00100 Rome, Italy (Telephone Number in U.S. (202) 653-2400); *The State of Food and Agriculture*.

Walden Publishing, Ltd., Two Market Street, Saffron Walden Essex, CB10 1HZ, England; *The World of Information Asia and Pacific Review*.

PITCAIRN ISLAND - INDUSTRY

Central Intelligence Agency, Washington, D.C. 20505 (703) 482-1100, www.cia.gov; *The World Factbook*.

PITCAIRN ISLAND - INFANT AND MATERNAL MORTALITY - See PITCAIRN ISLAND - MORTALITY

PITCAIRN ISLAND - LABOR

Central Intelligence Agency, Washington, D.C. 20505 (703) 482-1100, www.cia.gov; *The World Factbook*.

Europa Publications Limited, 18 Bedford Square, London, WC1B 3JN, England; *The Europa World Year Book*.

Food and Agricultural Organization of the United Nations (FAO) Via delle Terme di Caracalla, 00100 Rome, Italy (Telephone Number in U.S. (202) 653-2400); *The State of Food and Agriculture*.

PITCAIRN ISLAND - LAND USE

Central Intelligence Agency, Washington, D.C. 20505 (703) 482-1100, www.cia.gov; *The World Factbook*.

Food and Agricultural Organization of the United Nations (FAO), Via delle Terme di Caracalla, 00100 Rome, Italy (Telephone Number in U.S. (202) 653-2400); *Production Yearbook*.

PITCAIRN ISLAND - LIFE EXPECTANCY

Central Intelligence Agency, Washington, D.C. 20505 (703) 482-1100, www.cia.gov; *The World Factbook*.

PITCAIRN ISLAND - LIVESTOCK AND POULTRY

Food and Agricultural Organization of the United Nations (FAO), Via delle Terme di Caracalla, 00100 Rome, Italy (Telephone Number in U.S. (202) 653-2400); *Production Yearbook;* and *The State of Food and Agriculture.*

PITCAIRN ISLAND - MARRIAGE RATES

Statistical Office of the United Nations, Publishing Service, New York, New York 10017 (800) 253-9646; *Demographic Yearbook.*

PITCAIRN ISLAND - MEAT PRODUCTION - See PITCAIRN ISLAND - LIVESTOCK AND POULTRY

PITCAIRN ISLAND - MERCHANT SHIPPING

Europa Publications Limited, 18 Bedford Square, London, WC1B 3JN, England; *The Europa World Year Book.*

PITCAIRN ISLAND - MILITARY

Central Intelligence Agency, Washington, D.C. 20505 (703) 482-1100, www.cia.gov; *The World Factbook.*

PITCAIRN ISLAND - MORTALITY

Central Intelligence Agency, Washington, D.C. 20505 (703) 482-1100, www.cia.gov; *The World Factbook.*

Statistical Office of the United Nations, Publishing Service, New York, New York 10017 (800) 253-9646; *Demographic Yearbook;* and *Statistical Yearbook.*

PITCAIRN ISLAND - MOTOR VEHICLES IN USE

Europa Publications Limited, 18 Bedford Square, London, WC1B 3JN, England; *The Europa World Year Book.*

PITCAIRN ISLAND - NATALITY - See PITCAIRN ISLAND - BIRTH RATES

PITCAIRN ISLAND - NEWSPAPER PRODUCTION - See PITCAIRN ISLAND - FORESTRY AND FOREST PRODUCTS

PITCAIRN ISLAND - OCCUPATIONS - See PITCAIRN ISLAND - LABOR

PITCAIRN ISLAND - PESTICIDE USE

Food and Agricultural Organization of the United Nations (FAO) Via delle Terme di Caracalla, 00100 Rome, Italy (Telephone Number in U.S. (202) 653-2400); *The State of Food and Agriculture.*

PITCAIRN ISLAND - PETROLEUM INDUSTRY

Food and Agricultural Organization of the United Nations (FAO) Via delle Terme di Caracalla, 00100 Rome, Italy (Telephone Number in U.S. (202) 653-2400); *The State of Food and Agriculture.*

PITCAIRN ISLAND - POPULATION

Central Intelligence Agency, Washington, D.C. 20505 (703) 482-1100, www.cia.gov; *The World Factbook.*

Europa Publications Limited, 18 Bedford Square, London, WC1B 3JN, England; *The Europa World Year Book.*

Food and Agricultural Organization of the United Nations (FAO), Via delle Terme di Caracalla, 00100 Rome, Italy (Telephone Number in U.S. (202) 653-2400); *Production Yearbook.*

St. Martin's Press, Inc., 175 Fifth Avenue, New York, New York 10010 (800) 221-7945; *The Statesman's Year-Book.*

Statistical Office of the United Nations, Publishing Service, New York, New York 10017 (800) 253-9646; *Demographic Yearbook;* and *Statistical Yearbook.*

Walden Publishing, Ltd., Two Market Street, Saffron Walden Essex, CB10 1HZ, England; *The World of Information Asia and Pacific Review.*

World Health Organization, Office of Publications, 20 Avenue Appia, CH-1211 Geneva 27, Switzerland (Telephone Number in U.S. (518) 436-9686); *World Health Statistics Annual.*

PITCAIRN ISLAND - PRICES

Food and Agricultural Organization of the United Nations (FAO), Via delle Terme di Caracalla, 00100 Rome, Italy (Telephone Number in U.S. (202) 653-2400); *Production Yearbook;* and *The State of Food and Agriculture.*

PITCAIRN ISLAND - RELIGION

Central Intelligence Agency, Washington, D.C. 20505 (703) 482-1100, www.cia.gov; *The World Factbook.*

PITCAIRN ISLAND - STOCKS - COMMODITY - MARKET PRICE - INDEX

Food and Agricultural Organization of the United Nations (FAO) Via delle Terme di Caracalla, 00100 Rome, Italy (Telephone Number in U.S. (202) 653-2400); *The State of Food and Agriculture.*

PITCAIRN ISLAND - TELEPHONES IN USE

Central Intelligence Agency, Washington, D.C. 20505 (703) 482-1100, www.cia.gov; *The World Factbook.*

PITCAIRN ISLAND - TRADE

Food and Agricultural Organization of the United Nations (FAO) Via delle Terme di Caracalla, 00100 Rome, Italy (Telephone Number in U.S. (202) 653-2400); *The State of Food and Agriculture.*

PITCAIRN ISLAND - TRANSPORTATION AND COMMUNICATIONS

Central Intelligence Agency, Washington, D.C. 20505 (703) 482-1100, www.cia.gov; *The World Factbook.*

Europa Publications Limited, 18 Bedford Square, London, WC1B 3JN, England; *The Europa World Year Book.*

PITCAIRN ISLAND - UNEMPLOYMENT RATE

Central Intelligence Agency, Washington, D.C. 20505 (703) 482-1100, www.cia.gov; *The World Factbook.*

PITCAIRN ISLAND - VITAL STATISTICS

World Health Organization, Office of Publications, 20 Avenue Appia, CH-1211 Geneva 27, Switzerland (Telephone Number in U.S. (518) 436-9686); *World Health Statistics Annual.*

PLAGUE

U.S. Health and Human Services, Center for Disease Control, 1600 Clifton Road, NE, Atlanta, Georgia 30333 (800) 311-3435, www.cdc.gov; *Summary of Notifiable Diseases, U.S. Morbidity and Mortality Weekly Report.*

PLANTS

National Gardening Association, 180 Flynn Avenue, Burlington, Vermont 05401 (802) 863-1308; *National Gardening Survey.*

U.S. Department of Agriculture, Economic Research Service, 1800 M Street, NW, Washington, D.C. 20036 (202) 694-5050, www.ers.usda.gov; unpublished data.

PLASTIC SURGEONS

American Medical Association, 515 North State Street, Chicago, Illinois 60610 (312) 464-5000; *Physician Characteristics and Distribution in the U.S.*

PLASTICS

U.S. Department of Commerce, Bureau of the Census, Washington, D.C. 20233 (301) 457-4100, www.census.gov; *U.S. International Trade in Goods and Services;* and *1997 Economic Census, Core Business Statistics Series.*

PLATINUM-GROUP METALS

U.S. Department of the Interior, Geological Survey, Office of Minerals Information, 12201 Sunrise Valley Drive, Reston, Virginia 22092 (703) 648-4000, www.minerals.usgs.gov; *Mineral Commodity Summaries.*

PLATINUM GROUP METALS - CONSUMPTION

U.S. Department of the Interior, Geological Survey, Office of Minerals Information, 12201 Sunrise Valley Drive, Reston, Virginia 22092 (703) 648-4000, www.minerals.usgs.gov; *Mineral Commodity Summaries.*

PLATINUM GROUP METALS - EMPLOYMENT

U.S. Department of the Interior, Geological Survey, Office of Minerals Information, 12201 Sunrise Valley Drive, Reston, Virginia 22092 (703) 648-4000, www.minerals.usgs.gov; *Mineral Commodity Summaries.*

PLATINUM GROUP METALS - FOREIGN TRADE

U.S. Department of the Interior, Geological Survey, Office of Minerals Information, 12201 Sunrise Valley Drive, Reston, Virginia 22092 (703) 648-4000, www.minerals.usgs.gov; *Mineral Commodity Summaries.*

PLATINUM GROUP METALS - PRICES

U.S. Department of the Interior, Geological Survey, Office of Minerals Information, 12201 Sunrise Valley Drive, Reston, Virginia 22092 (703) 648-4000, www.minerals.usgs.gov; *Mineral Commodity Summaries.*

PLATINUM GROUP METALS - PRODUCTION

U.S. Department of the Interior, Geological Survey, Office of Minerals Information, 12201 Sunrise Valley Drive, Reston, Virginia 22092 (703) 648-4000, www.minerals.usgs.gov; *Mineral Commodity Summaries.*

PLATINUM GROUP METALS - STRATEGIC AND CRITICAL MATERIALS

U.S. Department of Defense, Defense Logistics Agency, 8725 John J. Kingman Road, Fort Belvoir, Virginia 22060 (703) 767-6666; *Statistical Supplement, Stockpile Report to the Congress.*

PLUMBING

U.S. Department of Commerce, Bureau of the Census, Washington, D.C. 20233 (301) 457-4100, www.census.gov; *Current Construction Reports; Census of Construction Industries;* and *Expenditures for Residential Improvements.*

PLUMS AND PRUNES

U.S. Department of Agriculture, Economic Research Service, 1800 M Street, NW, Washington, D.C. 20036 (202) 694-5050, www.ers.usda.gov; *Food Consumption, Prices, and Expenditures;* and *Agricultural Outlook.*

U.S. Department of Agriculture, National Agricultural Statistics Service, Fourteenth Street and Independence Avenue, SW, Washington, D.C. 20250 (800) 727-9540, www.usda.gov/nass; *Noncitrus Fruits and Nuts.*

PLURAL BIRTHS

U.S. Department of Health and Human Services, National Center for Health Statistics, 3700 East-West Highway, Hyattsville, Maryland 20782 (301) 436-8500, www.cdc.gov/nchs; *National Vital Statistics.*

PLYWOOD - CONSUMPTION

U.S. Department of Agriculture, Forest Service, Post Office Box 96090, Washington, D.C. 20090 (202) 205-8333, www.fs.fed.us; *Timber Demand and Technology Assessment.*

PLYWOOD - FOREIGN TRADE

U.S. Department of Agriculture, Forest Service, Post Office Box 96090, Washington, D.C. 20090 (202) 205-8333, www.fs.fed.us; *Timber Demand and Technology Assessment;* and *Agricultural Statistics.*

PLYWOOD - OUTPUT

U.S. Department of Agriculture, Forest Service, Post Office Box 96090, Washington, D.C. 20090 (202) 205-8333, www.fs.fed.us; *Timber Demand and Technology Assessment.*

PLYWOOD - PRODUCER PRICE INDEXES

U.S. Department of Labor, Bureau of Labor Statistics, Two Massachusetts Avenue, NE, Washington, D.C. 20212 (202) 691-5200, www.stats.bls.gov; *Producer Price Indexes.*

PNEUMONIA

U.S. Department of Health and Human Services, National Center for Health Statistics, 3700 East-West Highway, Hyattsville, Maryland 20782 (301) 436-8500, www.cdc.gov/nchs; *Vital Statistics of the United States; National Vital Statistics Report;* and unpublished data.

POISONING - DEATHS FROM

U.S. Department of Health and Human Services, National Center for Health Statistics, 3700 East-West Highway, Hyattsville, Maryland 20782 (301) 436-8500, www.cdc.gov/nchs; *Vital Statistics of the United States; Advance Data, No. 303;* and unpublished data.

Poland - National Statistical Office

Glowny Urzad Statystyczny (Central Statistical Office), Al Niepodleglosci 208, 00-925 Warsaw, Poland.

Poland - Primary Statistics Sources

Glowny Urzad Statystyczny (Central Statistical Office), Al Niepodleglosci 208, 00-925 Warsaw, Poland; *Rocznik statystyczny* (Statistical Yearbook); *Maly rocznik statystyczny* (Concise Statistical Yearbook); *Biuletyn statystyczny* (Statistical Bulletin); and *Concise Statistical Yearbook of Poland.*

POLAND - ABORTIONS

Statistical Office of the United Nations, Publishing Service, New York, New York 10017 (800) 253-9646; *Demographic Yearbook;* and *Trends in Europe and North America: The Statistical Yearbook of the Economic Commission for Europe.*

POLAND - AGRICULTURE

Economist Intelligence Unit, 111 West 57th Street, New York, New York 10019 (800) 938-4685; *Poland Country Report.*

Euromonitor International, Inc., 122 South Michigan Avenue, Suite 1200, Chicago, Illinois 60603 (800) 577-EURO; *World Marketing Data and Statistics.*

Europa Publications Limited, 18 Bedford Square, London, WC1B 3JN, England; *The Europa World Year Book.*

Food and Agricultural Organization of the United Nations (FAO), Via delle Terme di Caracalla, 00100 Rome, Italy (Telephone Number in U.S. (202) 653-2400); *Production Yearbook; The State of Food and Agriculture;* and *Trade Yearbook.*

M.E. Sharpe, 80 Business Park Drive, Armonk, New York 10504 (800) 541-6563; *The Illustrated Book of World Rankings.*

St. Martin's Press, Inc., 175 Fifth Avenue, New York, New York 10010 (800) 221-7945; *The Statesman's Year-Book.*

Statistical Office of the United Nations, Publishing Service, New York, New York 10017 (800) 253-9646; *Statistical Yearbook*.

United Nations Conference on Trade and Development, Central Statistical Service, Palais des Nations, Geneva, Switzerland (Telephone in U.S. (800) 253-9646); *UNCTAD Commodity Yearbook*.

The World Bank, 1818 H Street, NW, Washington, D.C. 20433 (202) 477-1234; *World Development Indicators*.

POLAND - AIRLINE SERVICE

Europa Publications Limited, 18 Bedford Square, London, WC1B 3JN, England; *The Europa World Year Book*.

M.E. Sharpe, 80 Business Park Drive, Armonk, New York 10504 (800) 541-6563; *The Illustrated Book of World Rankings*.

St. Martin's Press, Inc., 175 Fifth Avenue, New York, New York 10010 (800) 221-7945; *The Statesman's Year-Book*.

Statistical Office of the United Nations, Publishing Service, New York, New York 10017 (800) 253-9646; *Statistical Yearbook*.

POLAND - AIRPORTS

Central Intelligence Agency, Washington, D.C. 20505 (703) 482-1100, www.cia.gov; *The World Factbook*.

POLAND - ALUMINUM PRODUCTION AND CONSUMPTION - See POLAND - MINING AND MINERAL PRODUCTS

POLAND - ANIMAL FEEDINGSTUFFS OF AQUATIC ANIMAL ORIGIN

Statistical Office of the United Nations, Publishing Service, New York, New York 10017 (800) 253-9646; *Statistical Yearbook*.

POLAND - AREA AND DENSITY OF POPULATION

Central Intelligence Agency, Washington, D.C. 20505 (703) 482-1100, www.cia.gov; *The World Factbook*.

Euromonitor International, Inc., 122 South Michigan Avenue, Suite 1200, Chicago, Illinois 60603 (800) 577-EURO; *The World Economic Factbook*.

Europa Publications Limited, 18 Bedford Square, London, WC1B 3JN, England; *The Europa World Year Book*.

Food and Agricultural Organization of the United Nations (FAO) Via delle Terme di Caracalla, 00100 Rome, Italy (Telephone Number in U.S. (202) 653-2400); *The State of Food and Agriculture*.

M.E. Sharpe, 80 Business Park Drive, Armonk, New York 10504 (800) 541-6563; *The Illustrated Book of World Rankings*.

St. Martin's Press, Inc., 175 Fifth Avenue, New York, New York 10010 (800) 221-7945; *The Statesman's Year-Book*.

Statistical Office of the United Nations, Publishing Service, New York, New York 10017 (800) 253-9646; *Statistical Yearbook*; and *Trends in Europe and North America: The Statistical Yearbook of the Economic Commission for Europe*.

United Nations Educational, Scientific and Cultural Organization (UNESCO), 7 Place de Fontenoy, F-75700 Paris, France (Telephone Number in U.S. (212) 963-5981); *Statistical Yearbook*.

The World Bank, 1818 H Street, NW, Washington, D.C. 20433 (202) 477-1234; *World Development Report*.

POLAND - ARMS EXPORTS AND IMPORTS - See POLAND - MILITARY

POLAND - BALANCE OF PAYMENTS

The Economist Intelligence Unit, 111 West 57th Street, New York, New York 10019 (800) 938-4685; *The World Market Atlas*.

Europa Publications Limited, 18 Bedford Square, London, WC1B 3JN, England; *The Europa World Year Book*.

United Nations Conference on Trade and Development (UNCAD), New York, New York 10017 (800) 253-9646; *Handbook of International Trade and Development Statistics*.

The World Bank, 1818 H Street, NW, Washington, D.C. 20433 (202) 477-1234; *World Development Report*; and *World Development Indicators*.

POLAND - BANKING

Euromonitor International, Inc., 122 South Michigan Avenue, Suite 1200, Chicago, Illinois 60603 (800) 577-EURO; *World Marketing Data and Statistics*.

Europa Publications Limited, 18 Bedford Square, London, WC1B 3JN, England; *The Europa World Year Book*.

M.E. Sharpe, 80 Business Park Drive, Armonk, New York 10504 (800) 541-6563; *The Illustrated Book of World Rankings*.

St. Martin's Press, Inc., 175 Fifth Avenue, New York, New York 10010 (800) 221-7945; *The Statesman's Year-Book*.

POLAND - BARLEY PRODUCTION

M.E. Sharpe, 80 Business Park Drive, Armonk, New York 10504 (800) 541-6563; *The Illustrated Book of World Rankings*.

Statistical Office of the United Nations, Publishing Service, New York, New York 10017 (800) 253-9646; *Statistical Yearbook*.

POLAND - BEER PRODUCTION - See POLAND - BEVERAGES

POLAND - BEVERAGES

M.E. Sharpe, 80 Business Park Drive, Armonk, New York 10504 (800) 541-6563; *The Illustrated Book of World Rankings*.

Statistical Office of the United Nations, Publishing Service, New York, New York 10017 (800) 253-9646; *Statistical Yearbook*.

POLAND - BIRTH RATES

Central Intelligence Agency, Washington, D.C. 20505 (703) 482-1100, www.cia.gov; *The World Factbook*.

Euromonitor International, Inc., 122 South Michigan Avenue, Suite 1200, Chicago, Illinois 60603 (800) 577-EURO; *The World Economic Factbook*.

Europa Publications Limited, 18 Bedford Square, London, WC1B 3JN, England; *The Europa World Year Book*.

M.E. Sharpe, 80 Business Park Drive, Armonk, New York 10504 (800) 541-6563; *The Illustrated Book of World Rankings*.

St. Martin's Press, Inc., 175 Fifth Avenue, New York, New York 10010 (800) 221-7945; *The Statesman's Year-Book*.

Statistical Office of the United Nations, Publishing Service, New York, New York 10017 (800) 253-9646; *Demographic Yearbook*; and *Statistical Yearbook*.

The World Bank, 1818 H Street, NW, Washington, D.C. 20433 (202) 477-1234; *World Development Indicators*.

World Health Organization, Office of Publications, 20 Avenue Appia, CH-1211 Geneva 27, Switzerland (Telephone Number in U.S. (518) 436-9686); *World Health Statistics Annual*.

POLAND - BOOK PRODUCTION

Euromonitor International, Inc., 122 South Michigan Avenue, Suite 1200, Chicago, Illinois 60603 (800) 577-EURO; *European Marketing Data and Statistics*.

Europa Publications Limited, 18 Bedford Square, London, WC1B 3JN, England; *The Europa World Year Book*.

St. Martin's Press, Inc., 175 Fifth Avenue, New York, New York 10010 (800) 221-7945; *The Statesman's Year-Book*.

Statistical Office of the United Nations, Publishing Service, New York, New York 10017 (800) 253-9646; *Trends in Europe and North America: The Statistical Yearbook of the Economic Commission for Europe*.

United Nations Educational, Scientific and Cultural Organization (UNESCO), 7 Place de Fontenoy, F-75700 Paris, France (Telephone Number in U.S. (212) 963-5981); *Statistical Yearbook*.

POLAND - BROADCASTING

Billboard Limited, Post Office Box 9027, 1006 AA Amsterdam, The Netherlands (Telephone Number in U.S. (212) 764-7300); *World Radio TV Handbook*.

Central Intelligence Agency, Washington, D.C. 20505 (703) 482-1100, www.cia.gov; *The World Factbook*.

Euromonitor International, Inc., 122 South Michigan Avenue, Suite 1200, Chicago, Illinois 60603 (800) 577-EURO; *World Marketing Data and Statistics*.

Europa Publications Limited, 18 Bedford Square, London, WC1B 3JN, England; *The Europa World Year Book*.

M.E. Sharpe, 80 Business Park Drive, Armonk, New York 10504 (800) 541-6563; *The Illustrated Book of World Rankings*.

St. Martin's Press, Inc., 175 Fifth Avenue, New York, New York 10010 (800) 221-7945; *The Statesman's Year-Book*.

Statistical Office of the United Nations, Publishing Service, New York, New York 10017 (800) 253-9646; *Trends in Europe and North America: The Statistical Yearbook of the Economic Commission for Europe*.

United Nations Educational, Scientific and Cultural Organization (UNESCO), 7 Place de Fontenoy, F-75700 Paris, France (Telephone Number in U.S. (212) 963-5981); *Statistical Yearbook*.

POLAND - BUDGET

Central Intelligence Agency, Washington, D.C. 20505 (703) 482-1100, www.cia.gov; *The World Factbook*.

POLAND - BUTTER PRODUCTION - See POLAND - DAIRY PRODUCTS

POLAND - CABBAGE PRODUCTION - See POLAND - CROPS

POLAND - CADMIUM PRODUCTION AND CONSUMPTION - See POLAND - MINING AND MINERAL PRODUCTS

POLAND - CALORIE SUPPLY

Food and Agricultural Organization of the United Nations (FAO) Via delle Terme di Caracalla, 00100 Rome, Italy (Telephone Number in U.S. (202) 653-2400); *The State of Food and Agriculture*.

POLAND - CATTLE - See POLAND - LIVESTOCK AND POULTRY

POLAND - CAULIFLOWER PRODUCTION - See POLAND - CROPS

POLAND - CAUSTIC SODA PRODUCTION - See POLAND - BEVERAGES

POLAND - CEMENT PRODUCTION - See POLAND - MINING AND MINERAL PRODUCTS

POLAND - CEREALS PRODUCTION - See POLAND - CROPS

POLAND - CHEESE PRODUCTION AND CONSUMPTION - See POLAND - DAIRY PRODUCTS

POLAND - CHEMICAL (ORGANIC) PRODUCTION - See POLAND - MINING AND MINERAL PRODUCTS

POLAND - CIGAR AND CIGARETTE PRODUCTION - See POLAND - TOBACCO PRODUCTION

POLAND - CLIMATE

M.E. Sharpe, 80 Business Park Drive, Armonk, New York 10504 (800) 541-6563; *The Illustrated Book of World Rankings*.

St. Martin's Press, Inc., 175 Fifth Avenue, New York, New York 10010 (800) 221-7945; *The Statesman's Year-Book*.

POLAND - COAL PRODUCTION - See POLAND - MINING AND MINERAL PRODUCTS

POLAND - COFFEE PRODUCTION AND CONSUMPTION - See POLAND - CROPS

POLAND - COKE OVEN COKE PRODUCTION AND CONSUMPTION - See POLAND - MINING AND MINERAL PRODUCTS

POLAND - COMMERCE

St. Martin's Press, Inc., 175 Fifth Avenue, New York, New York 10010 (800) 221-7945; *The Statesman's Year-Book*.

POLAND - CONSTRUCTION INDUSTRY

M.E. Sharpe, 80 Business Park Drive, Armonk, New York 10504 (800) 541-6563; *The Illustrated Book of World Rankings*.

St. Martin's Press, Inc., 175 Fifth Avenue, New York, New York 10010 (800) 221-7945; *The Statesman's Year-Book*.

Statistical Office of the United Nations, Publishing Service, New York, New York 10017 (800) 253-9646; *Statistical Yearbook*.

POLAND - CONSUMER PRICE INDEX

Europa Publications Limited, 18 Bedford Square, London, WC1B 3JN, England; *The Europa World Year Book*.

Statistical Office of the United Nations, Publishing Service, New York, New York 10017 (800) 253-9646; *Statistical Yearbook*; and *Trends in Europe and North America: The Statistical Yearbook of the Economic Commission for Europe*.

POLAND - CONSUMER PRICES

Euromonitor International, Inc., 122 South Michigan Avenue, Suite 1200, Chicago, Illinois 60603 (800) 577-EURO; *European Marketing Data and Statistics*; and *World Marketing Data and Statistics*.

International Labour Office, I.L.O. Publications, 1828 L Street, NW, Suite 801, Washington, D.C. 20036 (301) 638-3152; *Yearbook of Labour Statistics*.

POLAND - CONSUMPTION

International Lead and Zinc Study Group, Metro House, 58 St. James's Street, London SW1A 1LD, England; *Lead and Zinc Statistics*.

International Rubber Study Group, York House, Eighth Floor, Empire Way, Wembley, London HA9 0PA, England; *Rubber Statistical Bulletin*.

The World Bank, 1818 H Street, NW, Washington, D.C. 20433 (202) 477-1234; *World Development Report*.

POLAND - COPPER AND COPPER ORE PRODUCTION AND CONSUMPTION - See POLAND - MINING AND MINERAL PRODUCTS

POLAND - CORN PRODUCTION - See POLAND - CROPS

POLAND - CORPORATE TAXES - See POLAND - TAXATION

POLAND - COTTON - See POLAND - CROPS

POLAND - CRIME

Statistical Office of the United Nations, Publishing Service, New York, New York 10017 (800) 253-9646; *Trends in Europe and North America: The Statistical Yearbook of the Economic Commission for Europe*.

Yale University Press, Yale Station, New Haven, Connecticut 06520 (800) 987-7323; *Violence and Crime in Cross-National Perspective.*

POLAND - CROPS

Commodity Research Bureau, Inc., 30 South Wacker Drive, Chicago Illinois 60606 (312) 454-1801; *Commodity Year Book.*

Euromonitor International, Inc., 122 South Michigan Avenue, Suite 1200, Chicago, Illinois 60603 (800) 577-EURO; *European Marketing Data and Statistics.*

Europa Publications Limited, 18 Bedford Square, London, WC1B 3JN, England; *The Europa World Year Book.*

Food and Agricultural Organization of the United Nations (FAO), Via delle Terme di Caracalla, 00100 Rome, Italy (Telephone Number in U.S. (202) 653-2400); *Production Yearbook;* and *The State of Food and Agriculture.*

M.E. Sharpe, 80 Business Park Drive, Armonk, New York 10504 (800) 541-6563; *The Illustrated Book of World Rankings.*

St. Martin's Press, Inc., 175 Fifth Avenue, New York, New York 10010 (800) 221-7945; *The Statesman's Year-Book.*

Statistical Office of the United Nations, Publishing Service, New York, New York 10017 (800) 253-9646; *Statistical Yearbook.*

United Nations Conference on Trade and Development, Central Statistical Service, Palais des Nations, Geneva, Switzerland (Telephone in U.S. (800) 253-9646); *UNCTAD Commodity Yearbook.*

POLAND - CUSTOMS DUTIES

St. Martin's Press, Inc., 175 Fifth Avenue, New York, New York 10010 (800) 221-7945; *The Statesman's Year-Book.*

POLAND - DAIRY PRODUCTS

Commodity Research Bureau, Inc., 30 South Wacker Drive, Chicago Illinois 60606 (312) 454-1801; *Commodity Year Book.*

Europa Publications Limited, 18 Bedford Square, London, WC1B 3JN, England; *The Europa World Year Book.*

Food and Agricultural Organization of the United Nations (FAO) Via delle Terme di Caracalla, 00100 Rome, Italy (Telephone Number in U.S. (202) 653-2400); *Production Yearbook;* and *The State of Food and Agriculture.*

M.E. Sharpe, 80 Business Park Drive, Armonk, New York 10504 (800) 541-6563; *The Illustrated Book of World Rankings.*

St. Martin's Press, Inc., 175 Fifth Avenue, New York, New York 10010 (800) 221-7945; *The Statesman's Year-Book.*

Statistical Office of the United Nations, Publishing Service, New York, New York 10017 (800) 253-9646; *Statistical Yearbook.*

POLAND - DEATH RATES - See POLAND - MORTALITY

POLAND - DEFENSE EXPENDITURES - See POLAND - MILITARY

POLAND - DEMOGRAPHY

The Economist Intelligence Unit, 111 West 57th Street, New York, New York 10019 (800) 938-4685; *The World Market Atlas.*

Euromonitor International, Inc., 122 South Michigan Avenue, Suite 1200, Chicago, Illinois 60603 (800) 577-EURO; *The World Economic Factbook;* and *World Marketing Data and Statistics.*

M.E. Sharpe, 80 Business Park Drive, Armonk, New York 10504 (800) 541-6563; *The Illustrated Book of World Rankings.*

Statistical Office of the United Nations, Publishing Service, New York, New York 10017 (800) 253-9646; *Human Development Report.*

POLAND - DEVELOPMENT ASSISTANCE

Statistical Office of the United Nations, Publishing Service, New York, New York 10017 (800) 253-9646; *Statistical Yearbook.*

POLAND - DIAMOND PRODUCTION - See POLAND - MINING AND MINERAL PRODUCTS

POLAND - DISEASES - See POLAND - HEALTH

POLAND - DIVORCE RATES

M.E. Sharpe, 80 Business Park Drive, Armonk, New York 10504 (800) 541-6563; *The Illustrated Book of World Rankings.*

Statistical Office of the United Nations, Publishing Service, New York, New York 10017 (800) 253-9646; *Demographic Yearbook; Statistical Yearbook;* and *Trends in Europe and North America: The Statistical Yearbook of the Economic Commission for Europe.*

POLAND - DUCKS - See POLAND - LIVESTOCK AND POULTRY

POLAND - ECONOMY

Central Intelligence Agency, Washington, D.C. 20505 (703) 482-1100,

www.cia.gov; *The World Factbook.*

Economist Intelligence Unit, 111 West 57th Street, New York, New York 10019 (800) 938-4685; *Poland Country Report.*

Euromonitor International, Inc., 122 South Michigan Avenue, Suite 1200, Chicago, Illinois 60603 (800) 577-EURO; *European Marketing Data and Statistics; World Marketing Data and Statistics;* and *The World Economic Factbook.*

Europa Publications Limited, 18 Bedford Square, London, WC1B 3JN, England; *The Europa World Year Book.*

M.E. Sharpe, 80 Business Park Drive, Armonk, New York 10504 (800) 541-6563; *The Illustrated Book of World Rankings.*

St. Martin's Press, Inc., 175 Fifth Avenue, New York, New York 10010 (800) 221-7945; *The Statesman's Year-Book.*

Statistical Office of the United Nations, Publishing Service, New York, New York 10017 (800) 253-9646; *World Statistics Pocketbook.*

The World Bank, 1818 H Street, NW, Washington, D.C. 20433 (202) 477-1234; *The World Bank Atlas;* and *World Development Report.*

POLAND - EDUCATION

The Economist Intelligence Unit, 111 West 57th Street, New York, New York 10019 (800) 938-4685; *The World Market Atlas.*

Euromonitor International, Inc., 122 South Michigan Avenue, Suite 1200, Chicago, Illinois 60603 (800) 577-EURO; *European Marketing Data and Statistics;* and *World Marketing Data and Statistics.*

Europa Publications Limited, 18 Bedford Square, London, WC1B 3JN, England; *The Europa World Year Book.*

M.E. Sharpe, 80 Business Park Drive, Armonk, New York 10504 (800) 541-6563; *The Illustrated Book of World Rankings.*

St. Martin's Press, Inc., 175 Fifth Avenue, New York, New York 10010 (800) 221-7945; *The Statesman's Year-Book.*

Statistical Office of the United Nations, Publishing Service, New York, New York 10017 (800) 253-9646; *Human Development Report;* and *Trends in Europe and North America: The Statistical Yearbook of the Economic Commission for Europe.*

United Nations Educational, Scientific and Cultural Organization (UNESCO), 7 Place de Fontenoy, F-75700 Paris, France

(Telephone Number in U.S. (212) 963-5981); *Statistical Yearbook*.

The World Bank, 1818 H Street, NW, Washington, D.C. 20433 (202) 477-1234; *World Development Report;* and *World Development Indicators*.

POLAND - EGG PRODUCTION AND CONSUMPTION - See POLAND - DAIRY PRODUCTS

POLAND - ELECTRICITY

Central Intelligence Agency, Washington, D.C. 20505 (703) 482-1100, www.cia.gov; *The World Factbook*.

Commodity Research Bureau, Inc., 30 South Wacker Drive, Chicago Illinois 60606 (312) 454-1801; *Commodity Year Book*.

M.E. Sharpe, 80 Business Park Drive, Armonk, New York 10504 (800) 541-6563; *The Illustrated Book of World Rankings*.

Penn Well Publishing Company, 1421 South Sheridan Road, Post Office Box 1260, Tulsa, Oklahoma 74101 (800) 752-9764; *International Energy Statistics Sourcebook*.

St. Martin's Press, Inc., 175 Fifth Avenue, New York, New York 10010 (800) 221-7945; *The Statesman's Year-Book*.

Statistical Office of the United Nations, Publishing Service, New York, New York 10017 (800) 253-9646; *Human Development Report; Statistical Yearbook;* and *Trends in Europe and North America: The Statistical Yearbook of the Economic Commission for Europe.*

POLAND - EMPLOYMENT

Euromonitor International, Inc., 122 South Michigan Avenue, Suite 1200, Chicago, Illinois 60603 (800) 577-EURO; *European Marketing Data and Statistics*.

International Labour Office, I.L.O. Publications, 1828 L Street, NW, Suite 801, Washington, D.C. 20036 (301) 638-3152; *Yearbook of Labour Statistics*.

M.E. Sharpe, 80 Business Park Drive, Armonk, New York 10504 (800) 541-6563; *The Illustrated Book of World Rankings*.

Statistical Office of the United Nations, Publishing Service, New York, New York 10017 (800) 253-9646; *Statistical Yearbook;* and *Trends in Europe and North America: The Statistical Yearbook of the Economic Commission for Europe*

POLAND - ENERGY

Euromonitor International, Inc., 122 South Michigan Avenue, Suite 1200, Chicago, Illinois 60603 (800) 577-EURO;

European Marketing Data and Statistics; World Marketing Data and Statistics; and *The World Economic Factbook*.

Food and Agricultural Organization of the United Nations (FAO) Via delle Terme di Caracalla, 00100 Rome, Italy (Telephone Number in U.S. (202) 653-2400); *The State of Food and Agriculture*.

M.E. Sharpe, 80 Business Park Drive, Armonk, New York 10504 (800) 541-6563; *The Illustrated Book of World Rankings*.

Penn Well Publishing Company, 1421 South Sheridan Road, Post Office Box 1260, Tulsa, Oklahoma 74101 (800) 752-9764; *International Energy Statistics Sourcebook*.

St. Martin's Press, Inc., 175 Fifth Avenue, New York, New York 10010 (800) 221-7945; *The Statesman's Year-Book*.

Statistical Office of the United Nations, Publishing Service, New York, New York 10017 (800) 253-9646; *Energy Statistics Yearbook; Human Development Report; Statistical Yearbook; Trends in Europe and North America: The Statistical Yearbook of the Economic Commission for Europe;* and *World Statistics Pocketbook*.

The World Bank, 1818 H Street, NW, Washington, D.C. 20433 (202) 477-1234; *The World Bank Atlas;* and *World Development Report*.

POLAND - ENVIRONMENT

Economist Intelligence Unit, 111 West 57th Street, New York, New York 10019 (800) 938-4685; *Poland Country Report*.

Statistical Office of the United Nations, Publishing Service, New York, New York 10017 (800) 253-9646; *Trends in Europe and North America: The Statistical Yearbook of the Economic Commission for Europe;* and *World Statistics Pocketbook*.

POLAND - EXCHANGE RATES

Central Intelligence Agency, Washington, D.C. 20505 (703) 482-1100, www.cia.gov; *The World Factbook*.

Euromonitor International, Inc., 122 South Michigan Avenue, Suite 1200, Chicago, Illinois 60603 (800) 577-EURO; *The World Economic Factbook*.

Europa Publications Limited, 18 Bedford Square, London, WC1B 3JN, England; *The Europa World Year Book*.

Statistical Office of the United Nations, Publishing Service, New York, New York 10017 (800) 253-9646; *Statistical Yearbook; Trends in Europe and North America: The Statistical Yearbook of the Economic Commission for Europe;* and *World*

Statistics Pocketbook.

POLAND - EXPORTS

Central Intelligence Agency, Washington, D.C. 20505 (703) 482-1100, www.cia.gov; *The World Factbook*.

The Economist Intelligence Unit, 111 West 57th Street, New York, New York 10019 (800) 938-4685; *Poland Country Report;* and *The World Market Atlas*.

Euromonitor International, Inc., 122 South Michigan Avenue, Suite 1200, Chicago, Illinois 60603 (800) 577-EURO; *The World Economic Factbook*.

Europa Publications Limited, 18 Bedford Square, London, WC1B 3JN, England; *The Europa World Year Book*.

Food and Agricultural Organization of the United Nations (FAO) Via delle Terme di Caracalla, 00100 Rome, Italy (Telephone Number in U.S. (202) 653-2400); *The State of Food and Agriculture*.

International Lead and Zinc Study Group, Metro House, 58 St. James's Street, London SW1A 1LD, England; *Lead and Zinc Statistics*.

International Monetary Fund, 700 Nineteenth Street, NW, Washington, D.C. 20431 (202) 623-7000; *Direction of Trade Statistics*.

International Rubber Study Group, York House, Eighth Floor, Empire Way, Wembley, London HA9 0PA, England; *Rubber Statistical Bulletin*.

St. Martin's Press, Inc., 175 Fifth Avenue, New York, New York 10010 (800) 221-7945; *The Statesman's Year-Book*.

Statistical Office of the United Nations, Publishing Service, New York, New York 10017 (800) 253-9646; *Trends in Europe and North America: The Statistical Yearbook of the Economic Commission for Europe*.

United Nations Conference on Trade and Development (UNCAD), New York, New York 10017 (800) 253-9646; *Handbook of International Trade and Development Statistics*.

The World Bank, 1818 H Street, NW, Washington, D.C. 20433 (202) 477-1234; *World Development Report*.

POLAND - EXTERNAL INDEBTEDNESS

The World Bank, 1818 H Street, NW, Washington, D.C. 20433 (202) 477-1234; *World Development Report;* and *World Development Indicators*.

POLAND - EXTERNAL TRADE

Euromonitor International, Inc., 122 South Michigan Avenue, Suite 1200, Chicago, Illinois 60603 (800) 577-EURO; *World Marketing Data and Statistics.*

Food and Agricultural Organization of the United Nations (FAO) Via delle Terme di Caracalla, 00100 Rome, Italy (Telephone Number in U.S. (202) 653-2400); *The State of Food and Agriculture;* and *Trade Yearbook.*

Statistical Office of the United Nations, Publishing Service, New York, New York 10017 (800) 253-9646; *Statistical Yearbook.*

POLAND - FABRIC PRODUCTION - See POLAND - TEXTILE INDUSTRY

POLAND - FARM CROPS

Food and Agricultural Organization of the United Nations (FAO) Via delle Terme di Caracalla, 00100 Rome, Italy (Telephone Number in U.S. (202) 653-2400); *The State of Food and Agriculture.*

M.E. Sharpe, 80 Business Park Drive, Armonk, New York 10504 (800) 541-6563; *The Illustrated Book of World Rankings.*

POLAND - FERTILITY RATES

Central Intelligence Agency, Washington, D.C. 20505 (703) 482-1100, www.cia.gov; *The World Factbook.*

M.E. Sharpe, 80 Business Park Drive, Armonk, New York 10504 (800) 541-6563; *The Illustrated Book of World Rankings.*

Statistical Office of the United Nations, Publishing Service, New York, New York 10017 (800) 253-9646; *Human Development Report;* and *Trends in Europe and North America: The Statistical Yearbook of the Economic Commission for Europe*

The World Bank, 1818 H Street, NW, Washington, D.C. 20433 (202) 477-1234; *The World Bank Atlas; World Development Report;* and *World Development Indicators.*

POLAND - FERTILIZER

Food and Agricultural Organization of the United Nations (FAO), Via delle Terme di Caracalla, 00100 Rome, Italy (Telephone Number in U.S. (202) 653-2400); *Fertilizer Yearbook;* and *The State of Food and Agriculture.*

Statistical Office of the United Nations, Publishing Service, New York, New York 10017 (800) 253-9646; *Statistical Yearbook.*

POLAND - FETAL MORTALITY - See POLAND - MORTALITY

POLAND - FIBRE PRODUCTION - See

POLAND - TEXTILE INDUSTRY

POLAND - FILAMENT PRODUCTION - See POLAND - TEXTILE INDUSTRY

POLAND - FILM - See POLAND - MOTION PICTURES

POLAND - FINANCE

Economist Intelligence Unit, 111 West 57th Street, New York, New York 10019 (800) 938-4685; *Poland Country Report.*

Europa Publications Limited, 18 Bedford Square, London, WC1B 3JN, England; *The Europa World Year Book.*

M.E. Sharpe, 80 Business Park Drive, Armonk, New York 10504 (800) 541-6563; *The Illustrated Book of World Rankings.*

St. Martin's Press, Inc., 175 Fifth Avenue, New York, New York 10010 (800) 221-7945; *The Statesman's Year-Book.*

POLAND - FISHERIES

Euromonitor International, Inc., 122 South Michigan Avenue, Suite 1200, Chicago, Illinois 60603 (800) 577-EURO; *European Marketing Data and Statistics.*

Europa Publications Limited, 18 Bedford Square, London, WC1B 3JN, England; *The Europa World Year Book.*

Food and Agricultural Organization of the United Nations (FAO) Via delle Terme di Caracalla, 00100 Rome, Italy (Telephone Number in U.S. (202) 653-2400); *The State of Food and Agriculture;* and *Yearbook of Fishery Statistics.*

M.E. Sharpe, 80 Business Park Drive, Armonk, New York 10504 (800) 541-6563; *The Illustrated Book of World Rankings.*

St. Martin's Press, Inc., 175 Fifth Avenue, New York, New York 10010 (800) 221-7945; *The Statesman's Year-Book.*

Statistical Office of the United Nations, Publishing Service, New York, New York 10017 (800) 253-9646; *Statistical Yearbook.*

United Nations Conference on Trade and Development, Central Statistical Service, Palais des Nations, Geneva, Switzerland (Telephone in U.S. (800) 253-9646); *UNCTAD Commodity Yearbook.*

POLAND - FLAX AND FLAX FIBRE PRODUCTION - See POLAND - TEXTILE INDUSTRY

POLAND - FLOUR PRODUCTION

Commodity Research Bureau, Inc., 30 South Wacker Drive, Chicago Illinois 60606

(312) 454-1801; *Commodity Year Book.*

Statistical Office of the United Nations, Publishing Service, New York, New York 10017 (800) 253-9646; *Statistical Yearbook.*

POLAND - FOOD

Euromonitor International, Inc., 122 South Michigan Avenue, Suite 1200, Chicago, Illinois 60603 (800) 577-EURO; *Retail Trade International.*

Food and Agricultural Organization of the United Nations (FAO), Via delle Terme di Caracalla, 00100 Rome, Italy (Telephone Number in U.S. (202) 653-2400); *Production Yearbook;* and *The State of Food and Agriculture.*

Statistical Office of the United Nations, Publishing Service, New York, New York 10017 (800) 253-9646; *Human Development Report.*

United Nations Conference on Trade and Development, Central Statistical Service, Palais des Nations, Geneva, Switzerland (Telephone in U.S. (800) 253-9646); *UNCTAD Commodity Yearbook.*

POLAND - FOREIGN DEBT

St. Martin's Press, Inc., 175 Fifth Avenue, New York, New York 10010 (800) 221-7945; *The Statesman's Year-Book.*

POLAND - FOREIGN TRADE

Economist Intelligence Unit, 111 West 57th Street, New York, New York 10019 (800) 938-4685; *Poland Country Report.*

Euromonitor International, Inc., 122 South Michigan Avenue, Suite 1200, Chicago, Illinois 60603 (800) 577-EURO; *The World Economic Factbook.*

Europa Publications Limited, 18 Bedford Square, London, WC1B 3JN, England; *The Europa World Year Book.*

M.E. Sharpe, 80 Business Park Drive, Armonk, New York 10504 (800) 541-6563; *The Illustrated Book of World Rankings.*

St. Martin's Press, Inc., 175 Fifth Avenue, New York, New York 10010 (800) 221-7945; *The Statesman's Year-Book.*

Statistical Office of the United Nations, Publishing Service, New York, New York 10017 (800) 253-9646; *International Trade Statistics Yearbook;* and *Statistical Yearbook.*

United Nations Conference on Trade and Development, Central Statistical Service, Palais des Nations, Geneva, Switzerland (Telephone in U.S. (800) 253-

9646); *UNCTAD Commodity Yearbook.*

The World Bank, 1818 H Street, NW, Washington, D.C. 20433 (202) 477-1234; *World Development Report;* and *World Development Indicators.*

POLAND - FORESTRY AND FOREST PRODUCTS

Euromonitor International, Inc., 122 South Michigan Avenue, Suite 1200, Chicago, Illinois 60603 (800) 577-EURO; *European Marketing Data and Statistics.*

Europa Publications Limited, 18 Bedford Square, London, WC1B 3JN, England; *The Europa World Year Book.*

Food and Agricultural Organization of the United Nations (FAO) Via delle Terme di Caracalla, 00100 Rome, Italy (Telephone Number in U.S. (202) 653-2400); *The State of Food and Agriculture;* and *Yearbook of Forest Products.*

M.E. Sharpe, 80 Business Park Drive, Armonk, New York 10504 (800) 541-6563; *The Illustrated Book of World Rankings.*

St. Martin's Press, Inc., 175 Fifth Avenue, New York, New York 10010 (800) 221-7945; *The Statesman's Year-Book.*

Statistical Office of the United Nations, Publishing Service, New York, New York 10017 (800) 253-9646; *Statistical Yearbook;* and *Trends in Europe and North America: The Statistical Yearbook of the Economic Commission for Europe.*

United Nations Conference on Trade and Development, Central Statistical Service, Palais des Nations, Geneva, Switzerland (Telephone in U.S. (800) 253-9646); *UNCTAD Commodity Yearbook.*

United Nations Educational, Scientific and Cultural Organization (UNESCO), 7 Place de Fontenoy, F-75700 Paris, France (Telephone Number in U.S. (212) 963-5981); *Statistical Yearbook.*

The World Bank, 1818 H Street, NW, Washington, D.C. 20433 (202) 477-1234; *World Development Report.*

POLAND - GAS AND GAS LIQUIDS - See POLAND - MINING AND MINERAL PRODUCTS

POLAND - GENERAL INDUSTRIAL STATISTICS - See POLAND - INDUSTRY

POLAND - GENERAL MORTALITY - See POLAND - MORTALITY

POLAND - GEOGRAPHIC DATA

M.E. Sharpe, 80 Business Park Drive, Armonk, New York 10504 (800) 541-6563;

The Illustrated Book of World Rankings.

POLAND - GOLD HOLDINGS

The World Bank, 1818 H Street, NW, Washington, D.C. 20433 (202) 477-1234; *World Development Indicators.*

POLAND - GOLD PRODUCTION AND CONSUMPTION - See POLAND - MINING AND MINERAL PRODUCTS

POLAND - GOVERNMENT

Central Intelligence Agency, Washington, D.C. 20505 (703) 482-1100, www.cia.gov; *The World Factbook.*

Europa Publications Limited, 18 Bedford Square, London, WC1B 3JN, England; *The Europa World Year Book.*

St. Martin's Press, Inc., 175 Fifth Avenue, New York, New York 10010 (800) 221-7945; *The Statesman's Year-Book.*

Statistical Office of the United Nations, Publishing Service, New York, New York 10017 (800) 253-9646; *National Accounts Statistics;* and *Statistical Yearbook.*

The World Bank, 1818 H Street, NW, Washington, D.C. 20433 (202) 477-1234; *World Development Report;* and *World Development Indicators.*

POLAND - GRAIN PRODUCTION - See POLAND - CROPS

POLAND - GROSS DOMESTIC PRODUCT

The Economist Intelligence Unit, 111 West 57th Street, New York, New York 10019 (800) 938-4685; *Poland Country Report;* and *The World Market Atlas.*

Euromonitor International, Inc., 122 South Michigan Avenue, Suite 1200, Chicago, Illinois 60603 (800) 577-EURO; *The World Economic Factbook.*

Europa Publications Limited, 18 Bedford Square, London, WC1B 3JN, England; *The Europa World Year Book.*

M.E. Sharpe, 80 Business Park Drive, Armonk, New York 10504 (800) 541-6563; *The Illustrated Book of World Rankings.*

Statistical Office of the United Nations, Publishing Service, New York, New York 10017 (800) 253-9646; *Human Development Report; National Accounts Statistics; Statistical Yearbook;* and *Trends in Europe and North America: The Statistical Yearbook of the Economic Commission for Europe.*

The World Bank, 1818 H Street, NW, Washington, D.C. 20433 (202) 477-1234; *World Development Report;* and *World*

Development Indicators.

POLAND - GROSS NATIONAL PRODUCT

St. Martin's Press, Inc., 175 Fifth Avenue, New York, New York 10010 (800) 221-7945; *The Statesman's Year-Book.*

U.S. Arms Control and Disarmament Agency, 320 Twenty-first Street, NW, Washington, D.C. 20451 (202) 647-8677; *World Military Expenditures and Arms Transfers.*

The World Bank, 1818 H Street, NW, Washington, D.C. 20433 (202) 477-1234; *The World Bank Atlas; World Development Report;* and *World Development Indicators.*

POLAND - HEALTH

Euromonitor International, Inc., 122 South Michigan Avenue, Suite 1200, Chicago, Illinois 60603 (800) 577-EURO; *World Marketing Data and Statistics.*

M.E. Sharpe, 80 Business Park Drive, Armonk, New York 10504 (800) 541-6563; *The Illustrated Book of World Rankings.*

St. Martin's Press, Inc., 175 Fifth Avenue, New York, New York 10010 (800) 221-7945; *The Statesman's Year-Book.*

Statistical Office of the United Nations, Publishing Service, New York, New York 10017 (800) 253-9646; *Human Development Report; Statistical Yearbook;* and *Trends in Europe and North America: The Statistical Yearbook of the Economic Commission for Europe.*

United Nations Children's Fund (UNICEF), 3 United Nations Plaza, New York, New York 10017 (800) 253-9646; *State of the World's Children.*

The World Bank, 1818 H Street, NW, Washington, D.C. 20433 (202) 477-1234; *World Development Report.*

World Health Organization, Office of Publications, 20 Avenue Appia, CH-1211 Geneva 27, Switzerland (Telephone Number in U.S. (518) 436-9686); *World Health Statistics Annual.*

POLAND - HEMP FIBRE PRODUCTION - See POLAND - TEXTILE INDUSTRY

POLAND - HIDE PRODUCTION

Food and Agricultural Organization of the United Nations (FAO), Via delle Terme di Caracalla, 00100 Rome, Italy (Telephone Number in U.S. (202) 653-2400); *Production Yearbook.*

POLAND - HIGHWAYS

Central Intelligence Agency,

Washington, D.C. 20505 (703) 482-1100, www.cia.gov; *The World Factbook*.

International Road Federation, 2600 Virginia Avenue, NW, Washington, D.C. 20037 (202) 338-4641; *World Road Statistics*.

St. Martin's Press, Inc., 175 Fifth Avenue, New York, New York 10010 (800) 221-7945; *The Statesman's Year-Book*.

Statistical Office of the United Nations, Publishing Service, New York, New York 10017 (800) 253-9646; *Annual Bulletin of Transport Statistics for Europe;* and *Trends in Europe and North America: The Statistical Yearbook of the Economic Commission for Europe*.

POLAND - HONEY PRODUCTION

Commodity Research Bureau, Inc., 30 South Wacker Drive, Chicago Illinois 60606 (312) 454-1801; *Commodity Year Book*.

POLAND - HOPS PRODUCTION - See POLAND - CROPS

POLAND - HORSES - See POLAND - LIVESTOCK AND POULTRY

POLAND - HOURS OF WORK - See POLAND - EMPLOYMENT

POLAND - HOUSING AND HOUSING UNITS

Euromonitor International, Inc., 122 South Michigan Avenue, Suite 1200, Chicago, Illinois 60603 (800) 577-EURO; *World Marketing Data and Statistics*.

M.E. Sharpe, 80 Business Park Drive, Armonk, New York 10504 (800) 541-6563; *The Illustrated Book of World Rankings*.

Statistical Office of the United Nations, Publishing Service, New York, New York 10017 (800) 253-9646; *Trends in Europe and North America: The Statistical Yearbook of the Economic Commission for Europe*.

POLAND - HYDROCHLORIC ACID PRODUCTION

Statistical Office of the United Nations, Publishing Service, New York, New York 10017 (800) 253-9646; *Statistical Yearbook*.

POLAND - ILLITERATE POPULATION

Central Intelligence Agency, Washington, D.C. 20505 (703) 482-1100, www.cia.gov; *The World Factbook*.

The Economist Intelligence Unit, 111 West 57th Street, New York, New York 10019 (800) 938-4685; *The World Market Atlas*.

Euromonitor International, Inc., 122

South Michigan Avenue, Suite 1200, Chicago, Illinois 60603 (800) 577-EURO; *The World Economic Factbook*.

Statistical Office of the United Nations, Publishing Service, New York, New York 10017 (800) 253-9646; *Human Development Report*.

United Nations Educational, Scientific and Cultural Organization (UNESCO), 7 Place de Fontenoy, F-75700 Paris, France (Telephone Number in U.S. (212) 963-5981); *Statistical Yearbook*.

POLAND - IMPORTS

Central Intelligence Agency, Washington, D.C. 20505 (703) 482-1100, www.cia.gov; *The World Factbook*.

The Economist Intelligence Unit, 111 West 57th Street, New York, New York 10019 (800) 938-4685; *Poland Country Report;* and *The World Market Atlas*.

Euromonitor International, Inc., 122 South Michigan Avenue, Suite 1200, Chicago, Illinois 60603 (800) 577-EURO; *The World Economic Factbook*.

Europa Publications Limited, 18 Bedford Square, London, WC1B 3JN, England; *The Europa World Year Book*.

Food and Agricultural Organization of the United Nations (FAO) Via delle Terme di Caracalla, 00100 Rome, Italy (Telephone Number in U.S. (202) 653-2400); *The State of Food and Agriculture*.

International Lead and Zinc Study Group, Metro House, 58 St. James's Street, London SW1A 1LD, England; *Lead and Zinc Statistics*.

International Monetary Fund, 700 Nineteenth Street, NW, Washington, D.C. 20431 (202) 623-7000; *Direction of Trade Statistics*.

International Rubber Study Group, York House, Eighth Floor, Empire Way, Wembley, London HA9 0PA, England; *Rubber Statistical Bulletin*.

St. Martin's Press, Inc., 175 Fifth Avenue, New York, New York 10010 (800) 221-7945; *The Statesman's Year-Book*.

Statistical Office of the United Nations, Publishing Service, New York, New York 10017 (800) 253-9646; *Trends in Europe and North America: The Statistical Yearbook of the Economic Commission for Europe*.

United Nations Conference on Trade and Development (UNCAD), New York, New York 10017 (800) 253-9646; *Handbook of International Trade and Development Statistics*.

The World Bank, 1818 H Street, NW, Washington, D.C. 20433 (202) 477-1234; *World Development Report;* and *World Development Indicators*.

POLAND - INDUSTRIAL METALS PRODUCTION - See POLAND - MINING AND MINERAL PRODUCTS

POLAND - INDUSTRY

Central Intelligence Agency, Washington, D.C. 20505 (703) 482-1100, www.cia.gov; *The World Factbook*.

Economist Intelligence Unit, 111 West 57th Street, New York, New York 10019 (800) 938-4685; *Poland Country Report*.

Euromonitor International, Inc., 122 South Michigan Avenue, Suite 1200, Chicago, Illinois 60603 (800) 577-EURO; *The World Economic Factbook;* and *World Marketing Data and Statistics*.

Europa Publications Limited, 18 Bedford Square, London, WC1B 3JN, England; *The Europa World Year Book*.

International Labour Office, I.L.O. Publications, 1828 L Street, NW, Suite 801, Washington, D.C. 20036 (301) 638-3152; *Yearbook of Labour Statistics*.

M.E. Sharpe, 80 Business Park Drive, Armonk, New York 10504 (800) 541-6563; *The Illustrated Book of World Rankings*.

St. Martin's Press, Inc., 175 Fifth Avenue, New York, New York 10010 (800) 221-7945; *The Statesman's Year-Book*.

Statistical Office of the United Nations, Publishing Service, New York, New York 10017 (800) 253-9646; *Industrial Commodity Statistics Yearbook; Statistical Yearbook;* and *Trends in Europe and North America: The Statistical Yearbook of the Economic Commission for Europe*

The World Bank, 1818 H Street, NW, Washington, D.C. 20433 (202) 477-1234; *World Development Indicators*.

World Intellectual Property Organization, 34 Chemin des Colombettes, CH-1211 Geneva 20, Switzerland; *Industrial Property Statistics*.

POLAND - INFANT AND MATERNAL MORTALITY - See POLAND - MORTALITY

POLAND - INTERNAL TRADE

Statistical Office of the United Nations, Publishing Service, New York, New York 10017 (800) 253-9646; *Statistical Yearbook*.

POLAND - INTERNATIONAL RESERVES EXCLUDING GOLD

The World Bank, 1818 H Street, NW, Washington, D.C. 20433 (202) 477-1234; *World Development Indicators.*

POLAND - IRON ORE PRODUCTION AND CONSUMPTION - See POLAND - MINING AND MINERAL PRODUCTS

POLAND - LABOR

Central Intelligence Agency, Washington, D.C. 20505 (703) 482-1100, www.cia.gov; *The World Factbook.*

Euromonitor International, Inc., 122 South Michigan Avenue, Suite 1200, Chicago, Illinois 60603 (800) 577-EURO; *World Marketing Data and Statistics.*

Europa Publications Limited, 18 Bedford Square, London, WC1B 3JN, England; *The Europa World Year Book.*

Food and Agricultural Organization of the United Nations (FAO) Via delle Terme di Caracalla, 00100 Rome, Italy (Telephone Number in U.S. (202) 653-2400); *The State of Food and Agriculture.*

International Labour Office, I.L.O. Publications, 1828 L Street, NW, Suite 801, Washington, D.C. 20036 (301) 638-3152; *Yearbook of Labour Statistics.*

M.E. Sharpe, 80 Business Park Drive, Armonk, New York 10504 (800) 541-6563; *The Illustrated Book of World Rankings.*

St. Martin's Press, Inc., 175 Fifth Avenue, New York, New York 10010 (800) 221-7945; *The Statesman's Year-Book.*

Statistical Office of the United Nations, Publishing Service, New York, New York 10017 (800) 253-9646; *Human Development Report.*

The World Bank, 1818 H Street, NW, Washington, D.C. 20433 (202) 477-1234; *The World Bank Atlas; World Development Report;* and *World Development Indicators.*

POLAND - LAND USE

Central Intelligence Agency, Washington, D.C. 20505 (703) 482-1100, www.cia.gov; *The World Factbook.*

Euromonitor International, Inc., 122 South Michigan Avenue, Suite 1200, Chicago, Illinois 60603 (800) 577-EURO; *European Marketing Data and Statistics.*

Food and Agricultural Organization of the United Nations (FAO), Via delle Terme di Caracalla, 00100 Rome, Italy (Telephone Number in U.S. (202) 653-2400); *Production Yearbook.*

The World Bank, 1818 H Street, NW, Washington, D.C. 20433 (202) 477-1234;

World Development Report.

POLAND - LEAD AND LEAD ORE PRODUCTION AND CONSUMPTION - See POLAND - MINING AND MINERAL PRODUCTS

POLAND - LIBRARIES

Euromonitor International, Inc., 122 South Michigan Avenue, Suite 1200, Chicago, Illinois 60603 (800) 577-EURO; *European Marketing Data and Statistics.*

M.E. Sharpe, 80 Business Park Drive, Armonk, New York 10504 (800) 541-6563; *The Illustrated Book of World Rankings.*

Statistical Office of the United Nations, Publishing Service, New York, New York 10017 (800) 253-9646; *Trends in Europe and North America: The Statistical Yearbook of the Economic Commission for Europe.*

United Nations Educational, Scientific and Cultural Organization (UNESCO), 7 Place de Fontenoy, F-75700 Paris, France (Telephone Number in U.S. (212) 963-5981); *Statistical Yearbook.*

POLAND - LIFE EXPECTANCY

Central Intelligence Agency, Washington, D.C. 20505 (703) 482-1100, www.cia.gov; *The World Factbook.*

Euromonitor International, Inc., 122 South Michigan Avenue, Suite 1200, Chicago, Illinois 60603 (800) 577-EURO; *The World Economic Factbook.*

St. Martin's Press, Inc., 175 Fifth Avenue, New York, New York 10010 (800) 221-7945; *The Statesman's Year-Book.*

Statistical Office of the United Nations, Publishing Service, New York, New York 10017 (800) 253-9646; *Human Development Report; Trends in Europe and North America: The Statistical Yearbook of the Economic Commission for Europe;* and *World Statistics Pocketbook.*

The World Bank, 1818 H Street, NW, Washington, D.C. 20433 (202) 477-1234; *The World Bank Atlas;* and *World Development Report.*

POLAND - LIGNITE PRODUCTION - See POLAND - MINING AND MINERAL PRODUCTS

POLAND - LITERACY RATE

Euromonitor International, Inc., 122 South Michigan Avenue, Suite 1200, Chicago, Illinois 60603 (800) 577-EURO; *World Marketing Data and Statistics.*

POLAND - LIVESTOCK AND POULTRY

Commodity Research Bureau, Inc., 30 South Wacker Drive, Chicago Illinois 60606 (312) 454-1801; *Commodity Year Book.*

Euromonitor International, Inc., 122 South Michigan Avenue, Suite 1200, Chicago, Illinois 60603 (800) 577-EURO; *European Marketing Data and Statistics.*

Food and Agricultural Organization of the United Nations (FAO), Via delle Terme di Caracalla, 00100 Rome, Italy (Telephone Number in U.S. (202) 653-2400); *Production Yearbook;* and *The State of Food and Agriculture.*

M.E. Sharpe, 80 Business Park Drive, Armonk, New York 10504 (800) 541-6563; *The Illustrated Book of World Rankings.*

St. Martin's Press, Inc., 175 Fifth Avenue, New York, New York 10010 (800) 221-7945; *The Statesman's Year-Book.*

Statistical Office of the United Nations, Publishing Service, New York, New York 10017 (800) 253-9646; *Statistical Yearbook.*

United Nations Conference on Trade and Development, Central Statistical Service, Palais des Nations, Geneva, Switzerland (Telephone in U.S. (800) 253-9646); *UNCTAD Commodity Yearbook.*

POLAND - LIVING LEVELS - See POLAND - LIFE EXPECTANCY

POLAND - MAGNESIUM PRODUCTION AND CONSUMPTION - See POLAND - MINING AND MINERAL PRODUCTS

POLAND - MAIL - NUMBER OF ITEMS SENT OR RECEIVED

Statistical Office of the United Nations, Publishing Service, New York, New York 10017 (800) 253-9646; *Statistical Yearbook.*

POLAND - MANUFACTURING

M.E. Sharpe, 80 Business Park Drive, Armonk, New York 10504 (800) 541-6563; *The Illustrated Book of World Rankings.*

Statistical Office of the United Nations, Publishing Service, New York, New York 10017 (800) 253-9646; *Statistical Yearbook.*

The World Bank, 1818 H Street, NW, Washington, D.C. 20433 (202) 477-1234; *World Development Indicators.*

POLAND - MARRIAGE RATES

Europa Publications Limited, 18 Bedford Square, London, WC1B 3JN, England; *The Europa World Year Book.*

M.E. Sharpe, 80 Business Park Drive,

Armonk, New York 10504 (800) 541-6563; *The Illustrated Book of World Rankings.*

Statistical Office of the United Nations, Publishing Service, New York, New York 10017 (800) 253-9646; *Demographic Yearbook; Statistical Yearbook; and Trends in Europe and North America: The Statistical Yearbook of the Economic Commission for Europe.*

POLAND - MEAT PRODUCTION - See POLAND - LIVESTOCK AND POULTRY

POLAND - MERCHANT SHIPPING

Europa Publications Limited, 18 Bedford Square, London, WC1B 3JN, England; *The Europa World Year Book.*

Lloyd's Register of Shipping, 17 Battery Place, New York, New York 10004 (212) 425-8050; *Register of Ships.*

St. Martin's Press, Inc., 175 Fifth Avenue, New York, New York 10010 (800) 221-7945; *The Statesman's Year-Book.*

Statistical Office of the United Nations, Publishing Service, New York, New York 10017 (800) 253-9646; *Annual Bulletin of Transport Statistics for Europe; and Statistical Yearbook.*

U.S. Department of Transportation, Maritime Administration, 400 Seventh Street, SW, Washington, D.C. 20590 (202) 366-5807, www.marad.dot.gov; *A Statistical Analysis of the World's Merchant Fleets.*

POLAND - MILITARY

Central Intelligence Agency, Washington, D.C. 20505 (703) 482-1100, www.cia.gov; *The World Factbook.*

Euromonitor International, Inc., 122 South Michigan Avenue, Suite 1200, Chicago, Illinois 60603 (800) 577-EURO; *World Marketing Data and Statistics.*

The International Institute for Strategic Studies, 23 Tavistock Street, London WC2E 7NQ, England 44 171 3797676; *The Military Balance.*

St. Martin's Press, Inc., 175 Fifth Avenue, New York, New York 10010 (800) 221-7945; *The Statesman's Year-Book.*

Statistical Office of the United Nations, Publishing Service, New York, New York 10017 (800) 253-9646; *Human Development Report.*

U.S. Arms Control and Disarmament Agency, 320 Twenty-first Street, NW, Washington, D.C. 20451 (202) 647-8677; *World Military Expenditures and Arms Transfers.*

POLAND - MILK PRODUCTION - See POLAND - DAIRY PRODUCTS

POLAND - MILLET PRODUCTION - See POLAND - CROPS

POLAND - MINING AND MINERAL PRODUCTS

Commodity Research Bureau, Inc., 30 South Wacker Drive, Chicago Illinois 60606 (312) 454-1801; *Commodity Year Book.*

Europa Publications Limited, 18 Bedford Square, London, WC1B 3JN, England; *The Europa World Year Book.*

International Lead and Zinc Study Group, Metro House, 58 St. James's Street, London SW1A 1LD, England; *Lead and Zinc Statistics.*

M.E. Sharpe, 80 Business Park Drive, Armonk, New York 10504 (800) 541-6563; *The Illustrated Book of World Rankings.*

Penn Well Publishing Company, 1421 South Sheridan Road, Post Office Box 1260, Tulsa, Oklahoma 74101 (800) 752-9764; *International Energy Statistics Sourcebook.*

St. Martin's Press, Inc., 175 Fifth Avenue, New York, New York 10010 (800) 221-7945; *The Statesman's Year-Book.*

Statistical Office of the United Nations, Publishing Service, New York, New York 10017 (800) 253-9646; *Statistical Yearbook.*

United Nations Conference on Trade and Development, Central Statistical Service, Palais des Nations, Geneva, Switzerland (Telephone in U.S. (800) 253-9646); *UNCTAD Commodity Yearbook.*

POLAND - MOLASSES PRODUCTION - See POLAND - CROPS

POLAND - MONEY EXCHANGE RATES - See POLAND - EXCHANGE RATES

POLAND - MONEY SUPPLY

Economist Intelligence Unit, 111 West 57th Street, New York, New York 10019 (800) 938-4685; *Poland Country Report.*

Europa Publications Limited, 18 Bedford Square, London, WC1B 3JN, England; *The Europa World Year Book.*

The World Bank, 1818 H Street, NW, Washington, D.C. 20433 (202) 477-1234; *World Development Indicators.*

POLAND - MORTALITY

Central Intelligence Agency, Washington, D.C. 20505 (703) 482-1100, www.cia.gov; *The World Factbook.*

Euromonitor International, Inc., 122 South Michigan Avenue, Suite 1200, Chicago, Illinois 60603, (800) 577-EURO; *The World Economic Factbook.*

St. Martin's Press, Inc., 175 Fifth Avenue, New York, New York 10010 (800) 221-7945; *The Statesman's Year-Book.*

Statistical Office of the United Nations, Publishing Service, New York, New York 10017 (800) 253-9646; *Demographic Yearbook; Human Development Report; Statistical Yearbook; Trends in Europe and North America: The Statistical Yearbook of the Economic Commission for Europe; and World Statistics Pocketbook.*

United Nations Children's Fund (UNICEF), 3 United Nations Plaza, New York, New York 10017 (800) 253-9646; *State of the World's Children.*

The World Bank, 1818 H Street, NW, Washington, D.C. 20433 (202) 477-1234; *The World Bank Atlas; World Development Report; and World Development Indicators.*

World Health Organization, Office of Publications, 20 Avenue Appia, CH-1211 Geneva 27, Switzerland (Telephone Number in U.S. (518) 436-9686); *World Health Statistics Annual.*

POLAND - MOTION PICTURES

St. Martin's Press, Inc., 175 Fifth Avenue, New York, New York 10010 (800) 221-7945; *The Statesman's Year-Book.*

Statistical Office of the United Nations, Publishing Service, New York, New York 10017 (800) 253-9646; *Statistical Yearbook.*

United Nations Educational, Scientific and Cultural Organization (UNESCO), 7 Place de Fontenoy, F-75700 Paris, France (Telephone Number in U.S. (212) 963-5981); *Statistical Yearbook.*

POLAND - MOTOR VEHICLE PRODUCTION AND ASSEMBLY

Statistical Office of the United Nations, Publishing Service, New York, New York 10017 (800) 253-9646; *Statistical Yearbook.*

POLAND - MOTOR VEHICLE TAXES - See POLAND - TAXATION

POLAND - MOTOR VEHICLES IN USE

Europa Publications Limited, 18 Bedford Square, London, WC1B 3JN, England; *The Europa World Year Book.*

International Road Federation, 2600 Virginia Avenue, NW, Washington, D.C. 20037 (202) 338-4641; *World Road Statistics.*

Statistical Office of the United Nations, Publishing Service, New York, New York 10017 (800) 253-9646; *Statistical Yearbook.*

POLAND - MUSEUMS

Euromonitor International, Inc., 122 South Michigan Avenue, Suite 1200, Chicago, Illinois 60603 (800) 577-EURO; *European Marketing Data and Statistics.*

M.E. Sharpe, 80 Business Park Drive, Armonk, New York 10504 (800) 541-6563; *The Illustrated Book of World Rankings.*

United Nations Educational, Scientific and Cultural Organization (UNESCO), 7 Place de Fontenoy, F-75700 Paris, France (Telephone Number in U.S. (212) 963-5981); *Statistical Yearbook.*

POLAND - NATALITY - See POLAND - BIRTH RATES

POLAND - NATIONAL ACCOUNTS

Europa Publications Limited, 18 Bedford Square, London, WC1B 3JN, England; *The Europa World Year Book.*

Statistical Office of the United Nations, Publishing Service, New York, New York 10017 (800) 253-9646; *National Accounts Statistics;* and *Statistical Yearbook.*

POLAND - NATIONAL INCOME

M.E. Sharpe, 80 Business Park Drive, Armonk, New York 10504 (800) 541-6563; *The Illustrated Book of World Rankings.*

Statistical Office of the United Nations, Publishing Service, New York, New York 10017 (800) 253-9646; *National Accounts Statistics;* and *Statistical Yearbook.*

POLAND - NATIONAL PRODUCT

M.E. Sharpe, 80 Business Park Drive, Armonk, New York 10504 (800) 541-6563; *The Illustrated Book of World Rankings.*

Statistical Office of the United Nations, Publishing Service, New York, New York 10017 (800) 253-9646; *Statistical Yearbook.*

POLAND - NATURAL GAS PRODUCTION - See POLAND - MINING AND MINERAL PRODUCTS

POLAND - NATURAL RUBBER PRODUCTION

International Rubber Study Group, York House, Eighth Floor, Empire Way, Wembley, London HA9 0PA, England; *Rubber Statistical Bulletin.*

POLAND - NET MATERIAL PRODUCT

Statistical Office of the United Nations,

Publishing Service, New York, New York 10017 (800) 253-9646; *Statistical Yearbook.*

POLAND - NEWSPAPER PRODUCTION - See POLAND - FORESTRY AND FOREST PRODUCTS

POLAND - NEWSPRINT PRODUCTION AND CONSUMPTION - See POLAND - FORESTRY AND FOREST PRODUCTS

POLAND - NICKEL AND NICKEL ORE PRODUCTION AND CONSUMPTION - See POLAND - MINING AND MINERAL PRODUCTS

POLAND - NITRIC ACID PRODUCTION - See POLAND - MINING AND MINERAL PRODUCTS

POLAND - OATS PRODUCTION - See POLAND - CROPS

POLAND - OCCUPATIONS - See POLAND - LABOR

POLAND - ONION PRODUCTION - See POLAND - CROPS

POLAND - PAPER PRODUCTION - See POLAND - FORESTRY AND FOREST PRODUCTS

POLAND - PATENTS, TRADEMARKS AND SERVICE MARKS

Statistical Office of the United Nations, Publishing Service, New York, New York 10017 (800) 253-9646; *Statistical Yearbook.*

World Intellectual Property Organization, 34 Chemin des Colombettes, CH-1211 Geneva 20, Switzerland; *Industrial Property Statistics.*

POLAND - PEANUT PRODUCTION - See POLAND - CROPS

POLAND - PERIODICALS

United Nations Educational, Scientific and Cultural Organization (UNESCO), 7 Place de Fontenoy, F-75700 Paris, France (Telephone Number in U.S. (212) 963-5981); *Statistical Yearbook.*

POLAND - PESTICIDE USE

Food and Agricultural Organization of the United Nations (FAO) Via delle Terme di Caracalla, 00100 Rome, Italy (Telephone Number in U.S. (202) 653-2400); *The State of Food and Agriculture.*

POLAND - PETROLEUM INDUSTRY

Euromonitor International, Inc., 122 South Michigan Avenue, Suite 1200, Chicago, Illinois 60603 (800) 577-EURO; *European Marketing Data and Statistics.*

Food and Agricultural Organization of the United Nations (FAO) Via delle Terme di Caracalla, 00100 Rome, Italy (Telephone Number in U.S. (202) 653-2400); *The State of Food and Agriculture.*

M.E. Sharpe, 80 Business Park Drive, Armonk, New York 10504 (800) 541-6563; *The Illustrated Book of World Rankings.*

Penn Well Publishing Company, 1421 South Sheridan Road, Post Office Box 1260, Tulsa, Oklahoma 74101 (800) 752-9764; *International Energy Statistics Sourcebook.*

St. Martin's Press, Inc., 175 Fifth Avenue, New York, New York 10010 (800) 221-7945; *The Statesman's Year-Book.*

Statistical Office of the United Nations, Publishing Service, New York, New York 10017 (800) 253-9646; *Statistical Yearbook;* and *Trends in Europe and North America: The Statistical Yearbook of the Economic Commission for Europe.*

United Nations Conference on Trade and Development, Central Statistical Service, Palais des Nations, Geneva, Switzerland (Telephone in U.S. (800) 253-9646); *UNCTAD Commodity Yearbook.*

POLAND - PHOSPHATE ROCK PRODUCTION - See POLAND - MINING AND MINERAL PRODUCTS

POLAND - PIG-IRON AND FERRO-ALLOY PRODUCTION - See POLAND - MINING AND MINERAL PRODUCTS

POLAND - PIGS - See POLAND - LIVESTOCK AND POULTRY

POLAND - PIPELINES FOR OIL AND PETROLEUM PRODUCTS

Statistical Office of the United Nations, Publishing Service, New York, New York 10017 (800) 253-9646; *Annual Bulletin of Transport Statistics for Europe.*

POLAND - PLASTIC AND RESIN PRODUCTION

Commodity Research Bureau, Inc., 30 South Wacker Drive, Chicago Illinois 60606 (312) 454-1801; *Commodity Year Book.*

Statistical Office of the United Nations, Publishing Service, New York, New York 10017 (800) 253-9646; *Statistical Yearbook.*

POLAND - POPULATION

Central Intelligence Agency, Washington, D.C. 20505 (703) 482-1100, www.cia.gov; *The World Factbook.*

The Economist Intelligence Unit, 111

West 57th Street, New York, New York 10019 (800) 938-4685; *Poland Country Report;* and *The World Market Atlas.*

Euromonitor International, Inc., 122 South Michigan Avenue, Suite 1200, Chicago, Illinois 60603 (800) 577-EURO; *European Marketing Data and Statistics;* and *The World Economic Factbook.*

Europa Publications Limited, 18 Bedford Square, London, WC1B 3JN, England; *The Europa World Year Book.*

Food and Agricultural Organization of the United Nations (FAO), Via delle Terme di Caracalla, 00100 Rome, Italy (Telephone Number in U.S. (202) 653-2400); *Production Yearbook.*

International Labour Office, I.L.O. Publications, 1828 L Street, NW, Suite 801, Washington, D.C. 20036 (301) 638-3152; *Yearbook of Labour Statistics.*

M.E. Sharpe, 80 Business Park Drive, Armonk, New York 10504 (800) 541-6563; *The Illustrated Book of World Rankings.*

St. Martin's Press, Inc., 175 Fifth Avenue, New York, New York 10010 (800) 221-7945; *The Statesman's Year-Book.*

Statistical Office of the United Nations, Publishing Service, New York, New York 10017 (800) 253-9646; *Demographic Yearbook; Human Development Report; Statistical Yearbook; Trends in Europe and North America: The Statistical Yearbook of the Economic Commission for Europe;* and *World Statistics Pocketbook.*

United Nations Educational, Scientific and Cultural Organization (UNESCO), 7 Place de Fontenoy, F-75700 Paris, France (Telephone Number in U.S. (212) 963-5981); *Statistical Yearbook.*

U.S. Arms Control and Disarmament Agency, 320 Twenty-first Street, NW, Washington, D.C. 20451 (202) 647-8677; *World Military Expenditures and Arms Transfers.*

The World Bank, 1818 H Street, NW, Washington, D.C. 20433 (202) 477-1234; *The World Bank Atlas;* and *World Development Report.*

World Health Organization, Office of Publications, 20 Avenue Appia, CH-1211 Geneva 27, Switzerland (Telephone Number in U.S. (518) 436-9686); *World Health Statistics Annual.*

POLAND - POST OFFICES

M.E. Sharpe, 80 Business Park Drive, Armonk, New York 10504 (800) 541-6563; *The Illustrated Book of World Rankings.*

St. Martin's Press, Inc., 175 Fifth Avenue, New York, New York 10010 (800) 221-7945; *The Statesman's Year-Book.*

Statistical Office of the United Nations, Publishing Service, New York, New York 10017 (800) 253-9646; *Trends in Europe and North America: The Statistical Yearbook of the Economic Commission for Europe.*

POLAND - POTATO PRODUCTION - See POLAND - CROPS

POLAND - POWER PRODUCTION INDUSTRY

Statistical Office of the United Nations, Publishing Service, New York, New York 10017 (800) 253-9646; *Statistical Yearbook.*

POLAND - PRICES

Food and Agricultural Organization of the United Nations (FAO), Via delle Terme di Caracalla, 00100 Rome, Italy (Telephone Number in U.S. (202) 653-2400); *Production Yearbook;* and *The State of Food and Agriculture.*

International Labour Office, I.L.O. Publications, 1828 L Street, NW, Suite 801, Washington, D.C. 20036 (301) 638-3152; *Yearbook of Labour Statistics.*

International Lead and Zinc Study Group, Metro House, 58 St. James's Street, London SW1A 1LD, England; *Lead and Zinc Statistics.*

International Rubber Study Group, York House, Eighth Floor, Empire Way, Wembley, London HA9 0PA, England; *Rubber Statistical Bulletin.*

M.E. Sharpe, 80 Business Park Drive, Armonk, New York 10504 (800) 541-6563; *The Illustrated Book of World Rankings.*

POLAND - PRODUCTION

International Lead and Zinc Study Group, Metro House, 58 St. James's Street, London SW1A 1LD, England; *Lead and Zinc Statistics.*

International Rubber Study Group, York House, Eighth Floor, Empire Way, Wembley, London HA9 0PA, England; *Rubber Statistical Bulletin.*

M.E. Sharpe, 80 Business Park Drive, Armonk, New York 10504 (800) 541-6563; *The Illustrated Book of World Rankings.*

POLAND - PUBLIC FINANCE - See POLAND - FINANCE

POLAND - RADIO BROADCASTING - See POLAND - BROADCASTING

POLAND - RADIO RECEIVER PRODUCTION

Statistical Office of the United Nations, Publishing Service, New York, New York 10017 (800) 253-9646; *Statistical Yearbook.*

POLAND - RADIO RECEIVERS

St. Martin's Press, Inc., 175 Fifth Avenue, New York, New York 10010 (800) 221-7945; *The Statesman's Year-Book.*

POLAND - RAILWAYS

Euromonitor International, Inc., 122 South Michigan Avenue, Suite 1200, Chicago, Illinois 60603 (800) 577-EURO; *European Marketing Data and Statistics.*

Europa Publications Limited, 18 Bedford Square, London, WC1B 3JN, England; *The Europa World Year Book.*

Jane's Information Group, Sentinel House, 163 Brighton Road, Coulsdon, Surrey CR5 2NH, England (Telephone Number in U.S. (703) 683-3700); *Jane's World Railways.*

St. Martin's Press, Inc., 175 Fifth Avenue, New York, New York 10010 (800) 221-7945; *The Statesman's Year-Book.*

Statistical Office of the United Nations, Publishing Service, New York, New York 10017 (800) 253-9646; *Annual Bulletin of Transport Statistics for Europe; Statistical Yearbook;* and *Trends in Europe and North America: The Statistical Yearbook of the Economic Commission for Europe.*

POLAND - RAPESEED PRODUCTION - See POLAND - CROPS

POLAND - RELIGION

Central Intelligence Agency, Washington, D.C. 20505 (703) 482-1100, www.cia.gov; *The World Factbook.*

M.E. Sharpe, 80 Business Park Drive, Armonk, New York 10504 (800) 541-6563; *The Illustrated Book of World Rankings.*

St. Martin's Press, Inc., 175 Fifth Avenue, New York, New York 10010 (800) 221-7945; *The Statesman's Year-Book.*

POLAND - RETAIL TRADE

Euromonitor International, Inc., 122 South Michigan Avenue, Suite 1200, Chicago, Illinois 60603 (800) 577-EURO; *World Marketing Data and Statistics;* and *Retail Trade International.*

Statistical Office of the United Nations, Publishing Service, New York, New York 10017 (800) 253-9646; *Statistical Yearbook.*

POLAND - RICE PRODUCTION - See POLAND - CROPS

POLAND - ROOT AND TUBER

PRODUCTION - See POLAND - CROPS

POLAND - ROUNDWOOD PRODUCTION -
See POLAND - FORESTRY AND FOREST
PRODUCTS

POLAND - RUBBER PRODUCTION AND
CONSUMPTION

Commodity Research Bureau, Inc., 30
South Wacker Drive, Chicago Illinois 60606
(312) 454-1801; *Commodity Year Book.*

International Rubber Study Group, York
House, Eighth Floor, Empire Way,
Wembley, London HA9 0PA, England;
Rubber Statistical Bulletin.

M.E. Sharpe, 80 Business Park Drive,
Armonk, New York 10504 (800) 541-6563;
The Illustrated Book of World Rankings.

Statistical Office of the United Nations,
Publishing Service, New York, New York
10017 (800) 253-9646; *Statistical Yearbook.*

POLAND - RYE PRODUCTION - See
POLAND - CROPS

POLAND - SALT PRODUCTION - See
POLAND - MINING AND MINERAL
PRODUCTS

POLAND - SAWNWOOD PRODUCTION -
See POLAND - FORESTRY AND FOREST
PRODUCTS

POLAND - SCIENCE AND TECHNOLOGY -
EXPENDITURE FOR RESEARCH - See
POLAND - SCIENTISTS, TECHNICIANS AND
ENGINEERS

POLAND - SCIENTISTS, TECHNICIANS AND
ENGINEERS

Statistical Office of the United Nations,
Publishing Service, New York, New York
10017 (800) 253-9646; *Statistical Yearbook.*

United Nations Educational, Scientific
and Cultural Organization (UNESCO), 7
Place de Fontenoy, F-75700 Paris, France
(Telephone Number in U.S. (212) 963-
5981); *Statistical Yearbook.*

POLAND - SENIOR CITIZENS

M.E. Sharpe, 80 Business Park Drive,
Armonk, New York 10504 (800) 541-6563;
The Illustrated Book of World Rankings.

POLAND - SHEEP - See POLAND -
LIVESTOCK AND POULTRY

POLAND - SILVER PRODUCTION AND
CONSUMPTION - See POLAND - MINING
AND MINERAL PRODUCTS

POLAND - SOCIAL DATA

M.E. Sharpe, 80 Business Park Drive,

Armonk, New York 10504 (800) 541-6563;
The Illustrated Book of World Rankings.

Statistical Office of the United Nations,
Publishing Service, New York, New York
10017 (800) 253-9646; *World Statistics
Pocketbook.*

POLAND - SOCIAL SECURITY

St. Martin's Press, Inc., 175 Fifth
Avenue, New York, New York 10010 (800)
221-7945; *The Statesman's Year-Book.*

Statistical Office of the United Nations,
Publishing Service, New York, New York
10017 (800) 253-9646; *National Accounts
Statistics.*

POLAND - STEEL - See POLAND - MINING
AND MINERAL PRODUCTS

POLAND - STOCKS - COMMODITY -
MARKET PRICE - INDEX

Food and Agricultural Organization of
the United Nations (FAO) Via delle Terme
di Caracalla, 00100 Rome, Italy (Telephone
Number in U.S. (202) 653-2400); *The State
of Food and Agriculture.*

International Lead and Zinc Study
Group, Metro House, 58 St. James's Street,
London SW1A 1LD, England; *Lead and
Zinc Statistics.*

POLAND - SUGAR PRODUCTION AND
CONSUMPTION - See POLAND - CROPS

POLAND - SULPHUR AND SULPHURIC
ACID PRODUCTION - See POLAND -
MINING AND MINERAL PRODUCTS
POLAND - TAXATION

Europa Publications Limited, 18
Bedford Square, London, WC1B 3JN,
England; *The Europa World Year Book.*

International Road Federation, 2600
Virginia Avenue, NW., Washington, D.C.
20037 (202) 338-4641; *World Road
Statistics.*

St. Martin's Press, Inc., 175 Fifth
Avenue, New York, New York 10010 (800)
221-7945; *The Statesman's Year-Book.*

The World Bank, 1818 H Street, NW,
Washington, D.C. 20433 (202) 477-1234;
World Development Indicators.

POLAND - TEA CONSUMPTION - See
POLAND - CROPS

POLAND - TELEGRAPH SERVICE

Statistical Office of the United Nations,
Publishing Service, New York, New York
10017 (800) 253-9646; *Statistical Yearbook.*

POLAND - TELEPHONES IN USE

American Telephone and Telegraph
Company, 26 Parsippany Road, Whippany,
New Jersey 07981 (800) 222-0300; *The
World's Telephones.*

Central Intelligence Agency,
Washington, D.C. 20505 (703) 482-1100,
www.cia.gov; *The World Factbook.*

Europa Publications Limited, 18
Bedford Square, London, WC1B 3JN,
England; *The Europa World Year Book.*

St. Martin's Press, Inc., 175 Fifth
Avenue, New York, New York 10010 (800)
221-7945; *The Statesman's Year-Book.*

Statistical Office of the United Nations,
Publishing Service, New York, New York
10017 (800) 253-9646; *Statistical Yearbook;
Trends in Europe and North America: The
Statistical Yearbook of the Economic
Commission for Europe;* and *World
Statistics Pocketbook.*

POLAND - TELEVISION BROADCASTING -
See POLAND - BROADCASTING

POLAND - TELEVISION RECEIVER
PRODUCTION

Statistical Office of the United Nations,
Publishing Service, New York, New York
10017 (800) 253-9646; *Statistical Yearbook.*

POLAND - TEXTILE INDUSTRY

Euromonitor International, Inc., 122
South Michigan Avenue, Suite 1200,
Chicago, Illinois 60603 (800) 577-EURO;
Retail Trade International.

Food and Agricultural Organization of
the United Nations (FAO), Via delle Terme
di Caracalla, 00100 Rome, Italy (Telephone
Number in U.S. (202) 653-2400);
Production Yearbook.

M.E. Sharpe, 80 Business Park Drive,
Armonk, New York 10504 (800) 541-6563;
The Illustrated Book of World Rankings.

St. Martin's Press, Inc., 175 Fifth
Avenue, New York, New York 10010 (800)
221-7945; *The Statesman's Year-Book.*

Statistical Office of the United Nations,
Publishing Service, New York, New York
10017 (800) 253-9646; *Statistical Yearbook.*

United Nations Conference on Trade
and Development, Central Statistical
Service, Palais des Nations, Geneva,
Switzerland (Telephone in U.S. (800) 253-
9646); *UNCTAD Commodity Yearbook.*

POLAND - THEATRE

United Nations Educational, Scientific
and Cultural Organization (UNESCO), 7
Place de Fontenoy, F-75700 Paris, France

(Telephone Number in U.S. (212) 963-5981); *Statistical Yearbook.*

POLAND - TIMBER - RESOURCE FORESTS - See POLAND - FORESTRY AND FOREST PRODUCTS

POLAND - TIN - INDUSTRIAL CONSUMPTION - See POLAND - MINING AND MINERAL PRODUCTS

POLAND - TIRE (MOTOR VEHICLE) PRODUCTION

International Rubber Study Group, York House, Eighth Floor, Empire Way, Wembley, London HA9 0PA, England; *Rubber Statistical Bulletin.*

Statistical Office of the United Nations, Publishing Service, New York, New York 10017 (800) 253-9646; *Statistical Yearbook.*

POLAND - TOBACCO PRODUCTION

Euromonitor International, Inc., 122 South Michigan Avenue, Suite 1200, Chicago, Illinois 60603 (800) 577-EURO; *European Marketing Data and Statistics.*

M.E. Sharpe, 80 Business Park Drive, Armonk, New York 10504 (800) 541-6563; *The Illustrated Book of World Rankings.*

Statistical Office of the United Nations, Publishing Service, New York, New York 10017 (800) 253-9646; *Statistical Yearbook.*

POLAND - TOURISM

Euromonitor International, Inc., 122 South Michigan Avenue, Suite 1200, Chicago, Illinois 60603 (800) 577-EURO; *European Marketing Data and Statistics; World Marketing Data and Statistics;* and *The World Economic Factbook.*

Europa Publications Limited, 18 Bedford Square, London, WC1B 3JN, England; *The Europa World Year Book.*

M.E. Sharpe, 80 Business Park Drive, Armonk, New York 10504 (800) 541-6563; *The Illustrated Book of World Rankings.*

St. Martin's Press, Inc., 175 Fifth Avenue, New York, New York 10010 (800) 221-7945; *The Statesman's Year-Book.*

Statistical Office of the United Nations, Publishing Service, New York, New York 10017 (800) 253-9646; *Statistical Yearbook;* and *Trends in Europe and North America: The Statistical Yearbook of the Economic Commission for Europe.*

World Tourism Organization, Calle Capitan Haya 42, E-28020 Madrid, Spain; *Yearbook of Tourism Statistics.*

POLAND - TRACTORS IN USE

Statistical Office of the United Nations, Publishing Service, New York, New York 10017 (800) 253-9646; *Statistical Yearbook.*

POLAND - TRADE

Euromonitor International, Inc., 122 South Michigan Avenue, Suite 1200, Chicago, Illinois 60603 (800) 577-EURO; *European Marketing Data and Statistics.*

Food and Agricultural Organization of the United Nations (FAO) Via delle Terme di Caracalla, 00100 Rome, Italy (Telephone Number in U.S. (202) 653-2400); *The State of Food and Agriculture.*

POLAND - TRADEMARKS AND SERVICE MARKS - See POLAND - PATENTS, TRADEMARKS AND SERVICE MARKS

POLAND - TRANSPORTATION AND COMMUNICATIONS

Central Intelligence Agency, Washington, D.C. 20505 (703) 482-1100, www.cia.gov; *The World Factbook.*

Euromonitor International, Inc., 122 South Michigan Avenue, Suite 1200, Chicago, Illinois 60603 (800) 577-EURO; *World Marketing Data and Statistics.*

Europa Publications Limited, 18 Bedford Square, London, WC1B 3JN, England; *The Europa World Year Book.*

M.E. Sharpe, 80 Business Park Drive, Armonk, New York 10504 (800) 541-6563; *The Illustrated Book of World Rankings.*

St. Martin's Press, Inc., 175 Fifth Avenue, New York, New York 10010 (800) 221-7945; *The Statesman's Year-Book.*

Statistical Office of the United Nations, Publishing Service, New York, New York 10017 (800) 253-9646; *Human Development Report;* and *Trends in Europe and North America: The Statistical Yearbook of the Economic Commission for Europe.*

POLAND - TURKEYS - See POLAND - LIVESTOCK AND POULTRY

POLAND - UNEMPLOYMENT

Central Intelligence Agency, Washington, D.C. 20505 (703) 482-1100, www.cia.gov; *The World Factbook.*

Euromonitor International, Inc., 122 South Michigan Avenue, Suite 1200, Chicago, Illinois 60603 (800) 577-EURO; *European Marketing Data and Statistics.*

International Labour Office, I.L.O. Publications, 1828 L Street, NW, Suite 801, Washington, D.C. 20036 (301) 638-3152; *Yearbook of Labour Statistics.*

St. Martin's Press, Inc., 175 Fifth Avenue, New York, New York 10010 (800) 221-7945; *The Statesman's Year-Book.*

Statistical Office of the United Nations, Publishing Service, New York, New York 10017 (800) 253-9646; *Trends in Europe and North America: The Statistical Yearbook of the Economic Commission for Europe.*

POLAND - VITAL STATISTICS

St. Martin's Press, Inc., 175 Fifth Avenue, New York, New York 10010 (800) 221-7945; *The Statesman's Year-Book.*

Statistical Office of the United Nations, Publishing Service, New York, New York 10017 (800) 253-9646; *Statistical Yearbook.*

World Health Organization, Office of Publications, 20 Avenue Appia, CH-1211 Geneva 27, Switzerland (Telephone Number in U.S. (518) 436-9686); *World Health Statistics Annual.*

POLAND - WAGES

Euromonitor International, Inc., 122 South Michigan Avenue, Suite 1200, Chicago, Illinois 60603 (800) 577-EURO; *European Marketing Data and Statistics.*

International Labour Office, I.L.O. Publications, 1828 L Street, NW, Suite 801, Washington, D.C. 20036 (301) 638-3152; *Yearbook of Labour Statistics.*

Statistical Office of the United Nations, Publishing Service, New York, New York 10017 (800) 253-9646; *Statistical Yearbook.*

POLAND - WATERWAYS IN USE

Statistical Office of the United Nations, Publishing Service, New York, New York 10017 (800) 253-9646; *Annual Bulletin of Transport Statistics for Europe.*

POLAND - WEATHER - See POLAND - CLIMATE

POLAND - WHEAT PRODUCTION AND PRICES - See POLAND - CROPS

POLAND - WHOLESALE TRADE

Statistical Office of the United Nations, Publishing Service, New York, New York 10017 (800) 253-9646; *Statistical Yearbook.*

POLAND - WINE PRODUCTION - See POLAND - BEVERAGES

POLAND - WOOD PULP PRODUCTION - See POLAND - FORESTRY AND FOREST PRODUCTS

POLAND - WOOL PRODUCTION - See POLAND - TEXTILE INDUSTRY

POLAND - YARN PRODUCTION - See POLAND - TEXTILE INDUSTRY

POLAND - ZINC AND ZINC ORE PRODUCTION AND CONSUMPTION - See POLAND - MINING AND MINERAL PRODUCTS

POLICE - See LAW ENFORCEMENT and PUBLIC SAFETY

POLIOMYELITIS

U.S. Department of Health and Human Services, Centers for Disease Control, 1600 Clifton Road, NE, Atlanta, Georgia 30333 (800) 311-3435, www.cdc.gov; *Morbidity and Mortality Weekly Report: Summary of Notifiable Diseases, U.S.* ; and unpublished data.

POLITICAL ACTION COMMITTEES

Federal Election Commission, 999 E Street, NW, Washington, D.C. 20463 (800) 424-9530, www.fec.gov; *FEC Reports on Financial Activity, Party and Non-Party Political Committees;* and press releases.

POLITICAL PARTIES - ORGANIZATIONS - CAMPAIGN FINANCES

Federal Election Commission, 999 E Street, NW, Washington, D.C. 20463 (800) 424-9530, www.fec.gov; *FEC Reports on Financial Activity, Final Report, Party and Non-Party Political Committees; FEC Reports on Financial Activity, Final Report, Presidential Pre-Nomination Campaigns;* and *FEC Reports on Financial Activity, Final Report, U.S. Senate and House Campaigns.*

POLITICAL PARTIES - ORGANIZATIONS - CAMPAIGN FINANCES - POLITICAL ACTION COMMITTEES

Federal Election Commission, 999 E Street, NW, Washington, D.C. 20463 (800) 424-9530, www.fec.gov; *FEC Reports on Financial Activity; Party and Non-Party Political Committees, Final Report;* and press releases.

POLITICAL PARTIES - ORGANIZATIONS - CONGRESS - COMPOSITION OF

U.S. Congress, Joint Committee on Printing, North Capitol and H Streets, NW, Washington, D.C. 20401 (202) 512-0000; *Congressional Directory;* and unpublished data.

POLITICAL PARTIES - ORGANIZATIONS - CONGRESSIONAL DISTRICTS

Elections Research Center, 5508 Greystone Street, Chevy Chase, Maryland 20815; *America Votes.*

POLITICAL PARTIES - ORGANIZATIONS - GOVERNORS - BY PARTY AFFILIATION

National Governors' Association, Hall of the States, 444 North Capitol, Washington, D.C. 20001 (202) 624-5300; *Directory of Governors of the American States, Commonwealths, and Territories;* and *Directory of Governors.*

POLITICAL PARTIES - ORGANIZATIONS - PUBLIC CONFIDENCE

Independent Sector, 1200 18th Street, NW, Suite 200, Washington, D.C. 20036 (202) 467-6161; *Giving and Volunteering in the United States.*

POLITICAL PARTIES - ORGANIZATIONS - STATE LEGISLATURES - COMPOSITION OF

Council of State Governments, Post Office Box 11910, Lexington, Kentucky 40578 (859) 244-8000; *State Elective Officials and the Legislatures.*

National Conference of State Legislatures, 1560 Broadway, Suite 700, Suite 2100, Denver, Colorado 80202 (303) 830-2200; unpublished data.

POLITICAL PARTIES - ORGANIZATIONS - VOLUNTEERS

Independent Sector, 1200 18th Street, NW, Suite 200, Washington, D.C. 20036 (202) 467-6161; *Giving and Volunteering in the United States.*

POLITICAL PARTIES - ORGANIZATIONS - VOTER IDENTIFICATION

Congressional Quarterly, Inc., 1414 Twenty-second Street, NW, Washington, D.C. 20037 (202) 887-8500; *America Votes.*

U.S. Department of Commerce, Bureau of the Census, Washington, D.C. 20233 (301) 457-4100, www.census.gov; *Current Population Report.*

POLITICAL PARTIES - ORGANIZATIONS - VOTER REGISTRATION

Center for Political Studies, University of Michigan, Post Office Box 1248, Ann Arbor, Michigan 48106 (313) 764-8363; unpublished data.

POLITICAL PARTIES - ORGANIZATIONS - VOTES

Congressional Quarterly, Inc., 1414 Twenty-second Street, NW, Washington, D.C. 20037 (202) 887-8500; *America Votes;* and *Congressional Quarterly Weekly Report.*

POLITICAL TV ADVERTISING

Television Bureau of Advertising, Inc., 3 East 54th Street, New York, New York 10022 (212) 486-1111; data compiled by

Competitive Media Reporting, 11 West 42nd Street, New York, New York 10036 (212) 789-1400.

POLLOCK

U.S. Department of Commerce, National Oceanic and Atmospheric Administration, National Marine Fisheries Service, 1315 East-West Highway, Silver Spring, Maryland 20910 (301) 427-2239, www.nmfs.noaa.gov; *Fisheries of the United States.*

POLLUTION - AIR

Environmental Protection Agency, 1200 Pennsylvania Avenue, NW, Washington, D.C. 20460 (888) 372-8255, www.epa.gov; *National Air Quality and Emissions Trends Report;* and *National Air Pollutant Emission Trends.*

Organisation for Economic Cooperation and Development, 2 rue Andre-Pascal, 75 Paris 16, France (Telephone Number in U.S. (202) 785-6323); *Toward Sustainable Development: Environmental Indicators;* and *OECD in Figures.*

U.S. Department of Commerce, Bureau of Economic Analysis, Fourteenth Street between Constitution Avenue and E Street, NW, Washington, D.C. 20230 (202) 606-9900, www.bea.doc.gov; *Survey of Current Business.*

U.S. Department of Energy, Energy Information Administration, 1000 Independence Avenue, SW, Washington, D.C. 20585 (202) 586-5000; *International Energy Audit;* and *International Energy Outlook.*

POLLUTION - HAZARDOUS WASTE SITES

Environmental Protection Agency, 1200 Pennsylvania Avenue, NW, Washington, D.C. 20460 (888) 372-8255, www.epa.gov; *Supplementary Materials: National Priorities List, Proposed Rule.*

POLLUTION - INDUSTRY

Environmental Business International, Inc., 4452 Park Boulevard, Suite 306, San Diego, California 92116 (619) 295-7685; *Environmental Business Journal.*

POLLUTION - MOTOR VEHICLE EMISSIONS

Environmental Protection Agency, 1200 Pennsylvania Avenue, NW, Washington, D.C. 20460 (888) 372-8255, www.epa.gov; *National Air Pollutant Emission Trends.*

POLLUTION - OIL SPILLS

Tanker Advisory Center, Inc., 10 East End Avenue, New York, New York 10028 (212) 628-7686; *Worldwide Tanker*

Casualty Returns.

U.S. Department of Transportation, United States Coast Guard, 2100 Second Street, SW, Washington, D.C. 20593 (202) 267-2229, www.uscg.mil; Internet site: http://www.uscg.mil/hq/g-m/nmc/response/stats/summary.htm.

POLLUTION TOXIC RELEASES

Environmental Protection Agency, 1200 Pennsylvania Avenue, NW, Washington, D.C. 20460 (888) 372-8255, www.epa.gov; *Toxics Release Inventory.*

POLLUTION - WASTEWATER TREATMENT

Environmental Protection Agency, 1200 Pennsylvania Avenue, NW, Washington, D.C. 20460 (888) 372-8255, www.epa.gov; *Clean Water Needs Survey Report to Congress.*

POLLUTION - WATER

U.S. Department of the Interior, Geological Survey, National Center, 12201 Sunrise Valley Drive, Reston, Virginia 22092 (703) 648-4000, www.usgs.gov; *Water-Data Report.*

U.S. Department of Transportation, United States Coast Guard, 2100 Second Street, SW, Washington, D.C. 20593 (202) 267-2229, www.uscg.mil; Internet site: http://www.uscg.mil /hq/g-m/nmc/response/stats/summary.htm.

POOR PERSONS - See INCOME and POVERTY

POPULATION - See also VITAL STATISTICS

POPULATION - AGE - AMERICAN INDIAN, ESKIMO, ALEUT POPULATION

U.S. Department of Commerce, Bureau of the Census, Washington, D.C. 20233 (301) 457-4100, www.census.gov; *Current Population Reports; Census of Population, Characteristics of American Indians by Tribe and Language;* and unpublished data.

POPULATION - AGE - ASIAN AND PACIFIC ISLANDER POPULATION

U.S. Department of Commerce, Bureau of the Census, Washington, D.C. 20233 (301) 457-4100, www.census.gov; *Current Population Reports;* and unpublished data.

POPULATION - AGE - BLACK POPULATION

U.S. Department of Commerce, Bureau of the Census, Washington, D.C. 20233 (301) 457-4100, www.census.gov; *Current Population Reports;* and unpublished data.

POPULATION - AGE - DISTRIBUTION

U.S. Department of Commerce, Bureau of the Census, Washington, D.C. 20233 (301) 457-4100, www.census.gov; *Current Population Reports;* and unpublished data.

POPULATION - AGE - HISPANIC POPULATION

U.S. Department of Commerce, Bureau of the Census, Washington, D.C. 20233 (301) 457-4100, www.census.gov; *Current Population Reports;* and unpublished data.

POPULATION - AGE - OUTLYING AREAS

U.S. Department of Commerce, Bureau of the Census, Washington, D.C. 20233 (301) 457-4100, www.census.gov; *Census of Population;* and *Census of Population and Housing.*

POPULATION - AGE - RACE

U.S. Department of Commerce, Bureau of the Census, Washington, D.C. 20233 (301) 457-4100, www.census.gov; *Current Population Reports; Census of Population;* and unpublished data.

POPULATION - AGE - SCHOOL ENROLLMENT

U.S. Department of Commerce, Bureau of the Census, Washington, D.C. 20233 (301) 457-4100, www.census.gov; *Current Population Reports.*

U.S. Department of Education, National Center for Education Statistics, 555 New Jersey Avenue, NW, Washington, D.C. 20208-5574 (202) 219-1828, http://nces.ed.gov; *Digest of Education Statistics;* and *Projections of Educational Statistics.*

POPULATION - AGE - SEX

U.S. Department of Commerce, Bureau of the Census, Washington, D.C. 20233 (301) 457-4100, www.census.gov; *Current Population Reports; Census of Population;* and unpublished data.

POPULATION - AGE - VOTING-AGE POPULATION

U.S. Department of Commerce, Bureau of the Census, Washington, D.C. 20233 (301) 457-4100, www.census.gov; *Current Population Reports;* and unpublished data.

POPULATION - ANCESTRY

U.S. Department of Commerce, Bureau of the Census, Washington, D.C. 20233 (301) 457-4100, www.census.gov; *Census of Population, Supplementary Reports, Detailed Ancestry Groups for States.*

POPULATION - CITIES

U.S. Department of Commerce, Bureau of the Census, Washington, D.C. 20233 (301) 457-4100, www.census.gov; *Census of Population and Housing, Population and Housing Counts; General Population Characteristics; Population of the 100 Largest Cities and Other Urban Places in the U.S.;* unpublished data; and Internet sites: http://www.census.gov/population/estimates/metro-city/scts/SC98TS-DR.txt; http://www.census.gov/population/estimates/metro-city/SC100K96.txt.

POPULATION - CIVILIAN

U.S. Department of Commerce, Bureau of the Census, Washington, D.C. 20233 (301) 457-4100, www.census.gov; *Current Population Reports;* and Internet site: http://www.census.gov/population/estimates/nation/intfile1-1.txt..

POPULATION - COASTAL

U.S. Department of Commerce, Bureau of the Census, Washington, D.C. 20233 (301) 457-4100, www.census.gov; *Census of Population and Housing;* and unpublished data.

POPULATION - COMPONENTS OF CHANGE

U.S. Department of Commerce, Bureau of the Census, Washington, D.C. 20233 (301) 457-4100, www.census.gov; *Current Population Reports;* and Internet sites: http://www.census.gov/population/estimates/state/ST-98-7.txt; http://www.census.gov/population/estimates/state/ST-98-2.txt.; http://www.census.gov/population/estimates/state/STCOM96T1.txt.

POPULATION - DENSITY

U.S. Department of Commerce, Bureau of the Census, Washington, D.C. 20233 (301) 457-4100, www.census.gov; *Census of Population and Housing; Population and Housing Unit Counts;* unpublished data; and Internet site http://www.census.gov/population/estimates/state/ST-98-7.txt.

POPULATION - DENSITY - FOREIGN COUNTRIES

U.S. Department of Commerce, Bureau of the Census, Washington, D.C. 20233 (301) 457-4100, www.census.gov; International Data Base; and Internet site: http://www.census.gov/ipc/www/idbnew.htm.

POPULATION - ELDERLY

U.S. Department of Commerce, Bureau of the Census, Washington, D.C. 20233 (301) 457-4100, www.census.gov; *Current Population Reports;* PPL-47; unpublished data; Internet site: http://www.census.gov/population/estimates/state/5age9890.txt..

POPULATION - ETHNIC ORIGIN

U.S. Department of Commerce, Bureau of the Census, Washington, D.C. 20233 (301) 457-4100, www.census.gov; *Census of Population, Supplementary Reports, Detailed Ancestry Groups for States.*

POPULATION - FERTILITY

U.S. Department of Health and Human Services, National Center for Health Statistics, 3700 East-West Highway, Hyattsville, Maryland 20782 (301) 436-8500, www.cdc.gov/nchs; *Vital Statistics of the United States;* and *National Vital Statistics Report.*

POPULATION - FOREIGN BORN

U.S. Department of Commerce, Bureau of the Census, Washington, D.C. 20233 (301) 457-4100, www.census.gov; *Current Population Reports;* and Population Paper Listing PPL-92.

POPULATION - FOREIGN COUNTRIES

U.S. Department of Commerce, Bureau of the Census, Washington, D.C. 20233 (301) 457-4100, www.census.gov; unpublished data from the International Data Base; and Internet site: http://www.census.gov/ipc/www/idbnew.html.

POPULATION - HISPANIC ORIGIN - See HISPANIC ORIGIN POPULATION

POPULATION - HOUSEHOLDS AND/OR FAMILIES - See HOUSEHOLDS OR FAMILIES

POPULATION - IMMIGRANTS

U.S. Department of Justice, Immigration and Naturalization Service, 425 I Street, NW, Washington, D.C. 20536 (202) 305-1613, www.ins.usdoj.gov; *Statistical Yearbook;* and releases.

POPULATION - LABOR FORCE - See LABOR FORCE - EMPLOYMENT AND EARNINGS

POPULATION - MARITAL STATUS - See MARITAL STATUS OF POPULATION

POPULATION - METROPOLITAN AREAS

U.S. Department of Commerce, Bureau of the Census, Washington, D.C. 20233 (301) 457-4100, www.census.gov; *Census of Population and Housing, Supplementary Reports, Metropolitan Areas as Defined by the Office of Management and Budget; Census of Population and Housing, Population and Housing Unit Counts;*

unpublished data; and Internet sites: http://www.census.gov/population/estimates/metro-city/ma96-05.txt; and http://www.census.gov/population/estimates/metro-city/ma96-07.txt.

POPULATION - METROPOLITAN AREAS - AMERICAN INDIAN, ESKIMO, ALEUT

U.S. Department of Commerce, Bureau of the Census, Washington, D.C. 20233 (301) 457-4100, www.census.gov; unpublished data.

POPULATION - METROPOLITAN AREAS - ASIAN, PACIFIC ISLANDER

U.S. Department of Commerce, Bureau of the Census, Washington, D.C. 20233 (301) 457-4100, www.census.gov; unpublished data.

POPULATION - METROPOLITAN AREAS - BLACK

U.S. Department of Commerce, Bureau of the Census, Washington, D.C. 20233 (301) 457-4100, www.census.gov; unpublished data.

POPULATION - METROPOLITAN AREAS - HISPANIC

U.S. Department of Commerce, Bureau of the Census, Washington, D.C. 20233 (301) 457-4100, www.census.gov; unpublished data.

POPULATION - MIGRATION

U.S. Department of Commerce, Bureau of the Census, Washington, D.C. 20233 (301) 457-4100, www.census.gov; *Current Population Reports;* and Internet sites: http://www.census.gov/population/estimates/state/st-98-2.txt; and http://www.census.gov/population/estimates/state/st-98-7.txt.

POPULATION - MOBILITY

U.S. Department of Commerce, Bureau of the Census, Washington, D.C. 20233 (301) 457-4100, www.census.gov; *Current Population Reports.*

POPULATION - NATIVITY

U.S. Department of Commerce, Bureau of the Census, Washington, D.C. 20233 (301) 457-4100, www.census.gov; *Current Population Reports;* Population Paper Listing PPL-92; and Internet site: http://www.census.gov/population/socdemo/foreign/95/95tab-1.txt; and http://www.census.gov/populaton/socdemo/foreign/97/ppltab1.txt.

POPULATION - OUTLYING AREAS OF UNITED STATES

Puerto Rico Planning Board, San Juan, Puerto Rico, *Socioeconomic Statistics.*

U.S. Department of Commerce, Bureau of the Census, Washington, D.C. 20233 (301) 457-4100, www.census.gov; *Census of Population and Housing;* International Data Base; and Internet site http://www.census.gov/population/estimates/state/st-98-7.txt.

U.S. Department of Health and Human Services, National Center for Health Statistics, 3700 East-West Highway, Hyattsville, Maryland 20782 (301) 436-8500, www.cdc.gov/nchs; *Vital Statistics of the United States.*

POPULATION - PLACE OF BIRTH

U.S. Department of Commerce, Bureau of the Census, Washington, D.C. 20233 (301) 457-4100, www.census.gov; *Census of Population.*

POPULATION - PROJECTIONS

U.S. Department of Commerce, Bureau of the Census, Washington, D.C. 20233 (301) 457-4100, www.census.gov; *Current Population Reports;* Population Paper Listings PL-47; and unpublished data.

POPULATION - RACE

U.S. Department of Commerce, Bureau of the Census, Washington, D.C. 20233 (301) 457-4100, www.census.gov; *Census of Population; Current Population Reports;* unpublished data; and Internet site: http://www.census.gov/population/estimates/nation/intfile3-1.txt.

POPULATION - RACE - STATES

U.S. Department of Commerce, Bureau of the Census, Washington, D.C. 20233 (301) 457-4100, www.census.gov; Population Paper Listings PPL-47;and Internet site: http://www.census.gov/population/estimates/state/srh/srhus98.txt.

POPULATION - RESIDENT

U.S. Department of Commerce, Bureau of the Census, Washington, D.C. 20233 (301) 457-4100, www.census.gov; *Census of Population; Current Population Reports; Census of Population and Housing, Population and Housing Unit Counts;* press releases; unpublished data; and Internet site http://www.census.gov/population/estimates/nation/intfile1-1.txt.

POPULATION - RURAL

U.S. Department of Commerce, Bureau of the Census, Washington, D.C. 20233 (301) 457-4100, www.census.gov; *Census of Population and Housing, Population and Housing Unit Counts.*

POPULATION - SEX

U.S. Department of Commerce, Bureau of the Census, Washington, D.C. 20233 (301) 457-4100, www.census.gov; *Census of Population; Current Population Reports;* Population Paper Listing PPL-92; unpublished data; and Internet site: http://www.census.gov/population/estimates/nation/intfile3-1.txt.

POPULATION - STATES

U.S. Department of Commerce, Bureau of the Census, Washington, D.C. 20233 (301) 457-4100, www.census.gov; *Census of Population; Current Population Reports; Census of Population and Housing, Population and Housing Unit Counts;* unpublished data; and Internet sites http://www.census.gov/population/estimates/state/ST-98-7.txt; and http://www.census.gov/population/estimate-extract/state/srh/srhus98.txt.

POPULATION - STATES - AMERICAN INDIAN, ESKIMO, AND ALEUT POPULATION

U.S. Department of Commerce, Bureau of the Census, Washington, D.C. 20233 (301) 457-4100, www.census.gov; Population Paper Listing PPL-47; and Internet site: http://www.census.gov/population/estimate-extract/state/srh/srhus98.txt.

POPULATION - STATES - ASIAN AND PACIFIC ISLANDER POPULATION

U.S. Department of Commerce, Bureau of the Census, Washington, D.C. 20233 (301) 457-4100, www.census.gov; Population Paper Listing PPL47; and Internet site: http://www.census.gov/population/estimate-extract/state/srh/srhus98.txt.

POPULATION - STATES - BLACK POPULATION

U.S. Department of Commerce, Bureau of the Census, Washington, D.C. 20233 (301) 457-4100, www.census.gov; Population Paper Listing PPL-47; and Internet site: http://www.census.gov/population/estimate-extract/state/srh/srhus98.txt.

POPULATION - STATES - DENSITY

U.S. Department of Commerce, Bureau of the Census, Washington, D.C. 20233 (301) 457-4100, www.census.gov; *Census of Population and Housing, Population and Housing Unit Counts, United States;* and Internet site: http://www.census.gov/population/estimates/state/st-98-3.txt.

POPULATION - STATES - HISPANIC ORIGIN POPULATION

U.S. Department of Commerce, Bureau of the Census, Washington, D.C. 20233 (301) 457-4100, www.census.gov; Population Paper Listing PL-47; and Internet site: http://www.census.gov/population/estimate-extract/state/srh/srhus98.txt.

POPULATION - STATES - RACE

U.S. Department of Commerce, Bureau of the Census, Washington, D.C. 20233 (301) 457-4100, www.census.gov; Population Paper Listing PPL-47; and Internet site: http://www.census.gov/population/estimate-extract/state/srh/srhus98.txt.

POPULATION - STATES - VOTING AGE

Congressional Quarterly, Inc., 1414 Twenty-second Street, NW, Washington, D.C. 20037 (202) 887-8500; *Congressional Quarterly Weekly Report.*

U.S. Department of Commerce, Bureau of the Census, Washington, D.C. 20233 (301) 457-4100, www.census.gov; *Current Population Reports;* and unpublished data.

POPULATION - TOTAL - INCLUDING ARMED FORCES OVERSEAS

U.S. Department of Commerce, Bureau of the Census, Washington, D.C. 20233 (301) 457-4100, www.census.gov; *Current Population Reports;* and Internet site: http://www.census.gov/population/estimates/nation/intfile1-1.txt.

POPULATION - TOWNSHIPS AND SPECIAL DISTRICTS

U.S. Department of Commerce, Bureau of the Census, Washington, D.C. 20233 (301) 457-4100, www.census.gov; *Census of Governments, Government Organization.*

POPULATION - URBAN

U.S. Department of Commerce, Bureau of the Census, Washington, D.C. 20233 (301) 457-4100, www.census.gov; *Census of Population and Housing, Population and Housing Unit Counts;* and Internet site: http://www.census.gov/population/estimates/nation/intfile3-1.txt.

POPULATION - WORLD

U.S. Department of Commerce, Bureau of the Census, Washington, D.C. 20233 (301) 457-4100, www.census.gov; unpublished data from the International Data Base; and Internet sites: http://www.census.gov/ipc/www/worldpop.htm; http://www.census.gov/ipc/www/idbnew.html.

PORK - See also MEAT AND MEAT

PRODUCTS

PORK - CONSUMPTION

U.S. Department of Agriculture, Economic Research Service, 1800 M Street, NW, Washington, D.C. 20036 (202) 694-5050, www.ers.usda.gov; *Food Consumption, Prices, and Expenditures;* and *Agricultural Outlook.*

U.S. Department of Agriculture, Foreign Agricultural Service, Fourteenth Street and Independence Avenue, SW, Washington, D.C. 20250 (202) 720-7115, www.fas.usda.gov; *Livestock and Poultry: World Markets and Trade.*

PORK - FOREIGN TRADE

U.S. Department of Agriculture, Economic Research Service, 1800 M Street, NW, Washington, D.C. 20036 (202) 694-5050, www.ers.usda.gov; *Agricultural Outlook; U.S. Agricultural Trade Update; Foreign Agricultural Trade of the U.S.;* and *Food Consumption, Prices, and Expenditures.*

PORK - PRODUCTION

U.S. Department of Agriculture, Economic Research Service, 1800 M Street, NW, Washington, D.C. 20036 (202) 694-5050, www.ers.usda.gov; *Agricultural Outlook;* and *Food Consumption, Prices, and Expenditures.*

U.S. Department of Agriculture, National Agricultural Statistics Service, Fourteenth Street and Independence Avenue, SW, Washington, D.C. 20250 (800) 727-9540, www.usda.gov/nass; *Meat Animals - Production, Disposition and Income;* and *Agricultural Statistics.*

PORK - SUPPLY

U.S. Department of Agriculture, Economic Research Service, 1800 M Street, NW, Washington, D.C. 20036 (202) 694-5050, www.ers.usda.gov; *Agricultural Outlook;* and *Food Consumption, Prices, and Expenditures.*

PORK CHOPS

U.S. Department of Labor, Bureau of Labor Statistics, 2 Massachusetts Avenue, NE, Washington, D.C. 20212 (202) 691-5200, www.stats.bls.gov; *CPI Detailed Report;* and *Monthly Labor Review.*

PORTLAND CEMENT

U.S. Department of the Interior, Geological Survey, Office of Minerals Information, 12201 Sunrise Valley Drive, Reston, Virginia 22092 (703) 648-4000, www.minerals.usgs.gov; *Annual Reports;* and *Mineral Commodities Summaries.*

Portugal - National Statistical Office

Instituto Nacional de Estatistica, Avenida Antonio Jose de Almeida, 13078 Lisbon 1, Portugal.

Portugal - Primary Statistics Sources

Instituto Nacional de Estatistica (National Statistical Institute), Avenida Antonio Jose de Almeida, 1078 Lisbon 1, Portugal; *Anuario estatistico* (Statistical Yearbook); and *Boletin mensal de estatistica* (Monthly Bulletin of Statistics).

PORTUGAL - ABORTIONS

European Commission Office of Press and Public Affairs, 2100 M Street, NW, Washington, D.C. 20037 (202) 862-9500; *Demographic Statistics.*

Statistical Office of the United Nations, Publishing Service, New York, New York 10017 (800) 253-9646; *Trends in Europe and North America: The Statistical Yearbook of the Economic Commission for Europe.*

PORTUGAL - AGRICULTURE

Economist Intelligence Unit, 111 West 57th Street, New York, New York 10019 (800) 938-4685; *Portugal Country Report.*

Euromonitor International, Inc., 122 South Michigan Avenue, Suite 1200, Chicago, Illinois 60603 (800) 577-EURO; *World Marketing Data and Statistics.*

Europa Publications Limited, 18 Bedford Square, London, WC1B 3JN, England; *The Europa World Year Book.*

European Commission Office of Press and Public Affairs, 2100 M Street, NW, Washington, D.C. 20037 (202) 862-9500; *Agriculture: Statistical Yearbook; Basic Statistics of the Community; Eurostatistics: Data for Short-Term Economic Analysis; Labor Force Sample Survey;* and *Regions: Statistical Yearbook.*

Federal Statistical Office, Gustav - Stresemann - Ring 11, D-6200 Wiesbaden, Germany; *Portugal.*

Food and Agricultural Organization of the United Nations (FAO) Via delle Terme di Caracalla, 00100 Rome, Italy (Telephone Number in U.S. (202) 653-2400); *Production Yearbook; The State of Food and Agriculture;* and *Trade Yearbook.*

M.E. Sharpe, 80 Business Park Drive, Armonk, New York 10504 (800) 541-6563; *The Illustrated Book of World Rankings.*

Organisation for Economic Co-operation and Development (OECD), 2 rue Andre-Pascal, 75 Paris 16, France (Telephone Number in U.S. (202) 785-6323); *Economic Accounts for Agriculture; Indicators of Industrial Activity; Industrial Structure Statistics;* and *OECD Economic Surveys: Portugal.*

St. Martin's Press, Inc., 175 Fifth Avenue, New York, New York 10010 (800) 221-7945; *The Statesman's Year-Book.*

Statistical Office of the United Nations, Publishing Service, New York, New York 10017 (800) 253-9646; *Statistical Yearbook.*

United Nations Conference on Trade and Development, Central Statistical Service, Palais des Nations, Geneva, Switzerland (Telephone in U.S. (800) 253-9646); *UNCTAD Commodity Yearbook.*

The World Bank, 1818 H Street, NW, Washington, D.C. 20433 (202) 477-1234; *World Development Indicators.*

PORTUGAL - AIRLINE SERVICE

Europa Publications Limited, 18 Bedford Square, London, WC1B 3JN, England; *The Europa World Year Book.*

European Commission Office of Press and Public Affairs, 2100 M Street, NW, Washington, D.C. 20037 (202) 862-9500; *Basic Statistics of the Community; Regions: Statistical Yearbook;* and *Transport Annual Statistics.*

International Civil Aviation Organization, 999 University Street, Montreal, Quebec, Canada H3C 5H7 (514) 954-8219; *Civil Aviation Statistics of the World.*

M.E. Sharpe, 80 Business Park Drive, Armonk, New York 10504 (800) 541-6563; *The Illustrated Book of World Rankings.*

Organisation for Economic Co-operation and Development (OECD), 2 rue Andre-Pascal, 75 Paris 16, France (Telephone Number in U.S. (202) 785-6323); *Tourism Policy and International Tourism in OECD Member Countries.*

St. Martin's Press, Inc., 175 Fifth Avenue, New York, New York 10010 (800) 221-7945; *The Statesman's Year-Book.*

Statistical Office of the United Nations, Publishing Service, New York, New York 10017 (800) 253-9646; *Statistical Yearbook.* services.

PORTUGAL - AIRPORTS

Central Intelligence Agency, Washington, D.C. 20505 (703) 482-1100, www.cia.gov; *The World Factbook.*

PORTUGAL - ALMOND PRODUCTION - See PORTUGAL - CROPS

PORTUGAL - ALUMINUM PRODUCTION AND CONSUMPTION - See PORTUGAL - MINING AND MINERAL PRODUCTS

PORTUGAL - ANIMAL FEEDINGSTUFFS OF AQUATIC ANIMAL ORIGIN

Organisation for Economic Co-operation and Development (OECD), 2 rue Andre-Pascal, 75 Paris 16, France (Telephone Number in U.S. (202) 785-6323); *Foreign Trade by Commodities.*

Statistical Office of the United Nations, Publishing Service, New York, New York 10017 (800) 253-9646; *Statistical Yearbook.* animal origin.

PORTUGAL - ANIMAL HEALTH

Food and Agricultural Organization of the United Nations (FAO), Via delle Terme di Caracalla, 00100 Rome, Italy (Telephone Number in U.S. (202) 653-2400); *Animal Health Yearbook.*

PORTUGAL - ANTIMONY AND ANTIMONY ORE PRODUCTION AND CONSUMPTION - See PORTUGAL - MINING AND MINERAL PRODUCTS

PORTUGAL - AREA AND DENSITY OF POPULATION

Central Intelligence Agency, Washington, D.C. 20505 (703) 482-1100, www.cia.gov; *The World Factbook.*

Euromonitor International, Inc., 122 South Michigan Avenue, Suite 1200, Chicago, Illinois 60603 (800) 577-EURO; *The World Economic Factbook.*

Europa Publications Limited, 18 Bedford Square, London, WC1B 3JN, England; *The Europa World Year Book.*

European Commission Office of Press and Public Affairs, 2100 M Street, NW, Washington, D.C. 20037 (202) 862-9500; *Basic Statistics of the Community;* and *Demographic Statistics.*

Federal Statistical Office, Gustav - Stresemann - Ring 11, D-6200 Wiesbaden, Germany; *Portugal.*

Food and Agricultural Organization of the United Nations (FAO) Via delle Terme di Caracalla, 00100 Rome, Italy (Telephone Number in U.S. (202) 653-2400); *The State of Food and Agriculture.*

M.E. Sharpe, 80 Business Park Drive, Armonk, New York 10504 (800) 541-6563; *The Illustrated Book of World Rankings.*

St. Martin's Press, Inc., 175 Fifth

Avenue, New York, New York 10010 (800) 221-7945; *The Statesman's Year-Book.*

Statistical Office of the United Nations, Publishing Service, New York, New York 10017 (800) 253-9646; *Statistical Yearbook; and Trends in Europe and North America: The Statistical Yearbook of the Economic Commission for Europe.*

United Nations Educational, Scientific and Cultural Organization (UNESCO), 7 Place de Fontenoy, F-75700 Paris, France (Telephone Number in U.S. (212) 963-5981); *Statistical Yearbook.*

The World Bank, 1818 H Street, NW, Washington, D.C. 20433 (202) 477-1234; *World Development Report.*

PORTUGAL - ARMS EXPORTS AND IMPORTS - See PORTUGAL - MILITARY

PORTUGAL - ARSENIC PRODUCTION AND CONSUMPTION - See PORTUGAL - MINING AND MINERAL PRODUCTS

PORTUGAL - BALANCE OF PAYMENTS

The Economist Intelligence Unit, 111 West 57th Street, New York, New York 10019 (800) 938-4685; *The World Market Atlas.*

Europa Publications Limited, 18 Bedford Square, London, WC1B 3JN, England; *The Europa World Year Book.*

European Commission Office of Press and Public Affairs, 2100 M Street, NW, Washington, D.C. 20037 (202) 862-9500; *ACP: Basic Statistics; Basic Statistics of the Community; Energy Statistics Yearbook; and Eurostatistics: Data for Short-Term Economic Analysis.*

Federal Statistical Office, Gustav - Stresemann - Ring 11, D-6200 Wiesbaden, Germany; *Portugal.*

International Monetary Fund, 700 Nineteenth Street, NW, Washington, D.C. 20431 (202) 623-7000; *Balance of Payments Yearbook; and International Financial Statistics.*

Organisation for Economic Co-operation and Development (OECD), 2 rue Andre-Pascal, 75 Paris 16, France (Telephone Number in U.S. (202) 785-6323); *Economic Outlook; Geographical Distribution of Financial Flows to Developing Countries; Main Economic Indicators - Historical Statistics; and OECD Economic Surveys: Portugal.*

United Nations Conference on Trade and Development (UNCTAD), New York, New York 10017 (800) 253-9646; *Handbook of International Trade and Development Statistics.*

The World Bank, 1818 H Street, NW, Washington, D.C. 20433 (202) 477-1234; *World Development Report;* and *World Development Indicators.*

PORTUGAL - BANKING

Euromonitor International, Inc., 122 South Michigan Avenue, Suite 1200, Chicago, Illinois 60603 (800) 577-EURO; *World Marketing Data and Statistics.*

Europa Publications Limited, 18 Bedford Square, London, WC1B 3JN, England; *The Europa World Year Book.*

European Commission Office of Press and Public Affairs, 2100 M Street, NW, Washington, D.C. 20037 (202) 862-9500; *ACP: Basic Statistics;* and *Eurostatistics: Data for Short-Term Economic Analysis.*

International Monetary Fund, 700 Nineteenth Street, NW, Washington, D.C. 20431 (202) 623-7000; *International Financial Statistics.*

M.E. Sharpe, 80 Business Park Drive, Armonk, New York 10504 (800) 541-6563; *The Illustrated Book of World Rankings.*

Organisation for Economic Co-operation and Development (OECD), 2 rue Andre-Pascal, 75 Paris 16, France (Telephone Number in U.S. (202) 785-6323); *Economic Outlook; Financial Market Trends;* and *OECD Economic Surveys: Portugal.*

St. Martin's Press, Inc., 175 Fifth Avenue, New York, New York 10010 (800) 221-7945; *The Statesman's Year-Book.*

Statistical Office of the United Nations, Publishing Service, New York, New York 10017 (800) 253-9646; *Statistical Yearbook.*

PORTUGAL - BARLEY PRODUCTION - See PORTUGAL - CROPS

PORTUGAL - BAUXITE PRODUCTION AND CONSUMPTION - See PORTUGAL - MINING AND MINERAL PRODUCTS

PORTUGAL - BEER PRODUCTION - See PORTUGAL - BEVERAGES

PORTUGAL - BEVERAGES

European Commission Office of Press and Public Affairs, 2100 M Street, NW, Washington, D.C. 20037 (202) 862-9500; *Basic Statistics of the Community.*

International Monetary Fund, 700 Nineteenth Street, NW, Washington, D.C. 20431 (202) 623-7000; *International Financial Statistics.*

M.E. Sharpe, 80 Business Park Drive, Armonk, New York 10504 (800) 541-6563;

The Illustrated Book of World Rankings.

Organisation for Economic Co-operation and Development (OECD), 2 rue Andre-Pascal, 75 Paris 16, France (Telephone Number in U.S. (202) 785-6323); *Indicators of Industrial Activity.*

Statistical Office of the United Nations, Publishing Service, New York, New York 10017 (800) 253-9646; *Statistical Yearbook.*

PORTUGAL - BIRTH RATES

Central Intelligence Agency, Washington, D.C. 20505 (703) 482-1100, www.cia.gov; *The World Factbook.*

Euromonitor International, Inc., 122 South Michigan Avenue, Suite 1200, Chicago, Illinois 60603 (800) 577-EURO; *The World Economic Factbook.*

Europa Publications Limited, 18 Bedford Square, London, WC1B 3JN, England; *The Europa World Year Book.*

European Commission Office of Press and Public Affairs, 2100 M Street, NW, Washington, D.C. 20037 (202) 862-9500; *Basic Statistics of the Community;* and *Demographic Statistics.*

M.E. Sharpe, 80 Business Park Drive, Armonk, New York 10504 (800) 541-6563; *The Illustrated Book of World Rankings.*

St. Martin's Press, Inc., 175 Fifth Avenue, New York, New York 10010 (800) 221-7945; *The Statesman's Year-Book.*

Statistical Office of the United Nations, Publishing Service, New York, New York 10017 (800) 253-9646; *Demographic Yearbook;* and *Statistical Yearbook.*

The World Bank, 1818 H Street, NW, Washington, D.C. 20433 (202) 477-1234; *World Development Indicators.*

World Health Organization, Office of Publications, 20 Avenue Appia, CH-1211 Geneva 27, Switzerland (Telephone Number in U.S. (518) 436-9686); *World Health Statistics Annual.*

PORTUGAL - BISMUTH PRODUCTION AND CONSUMPTION

Food and Agricultural Organization of the United Nations (FAO) Via delle Terme di Caracalla, 00100 Rome, Italy (Telephone Number in U.S. (202) 653-2400); *The State of Food and Agriculture.*

PORTUGAL - BONDS

European Commission Office of Press and Public Affairs, 2100 M Street, NW, Washington, D.C. 20037 (202) 862-9500; *Basic Statistics of the Community.*

Organisation for Economic Co-operation and Development (OECD), 2 rue Andre-Pascal, 75 Paris 16, France (Telephone Number in U.S. (202) 785-6323); *Financial Market Trends.*

Statistical Office of the United Nations, Publishing Service, New York, New York 10017 (800) 253-9646; *Statistical Yearbook.*

PORTUGAL - BOOK PRODUCTION

Euromonitor International, Inc., 122 South Michigan Avenue, Suite 1200, Chicago, Illinois 60603 (800) 577-EURO; *European Marketing Data and Statistics.*

Europa Publications Limited, 18 Bedford Square, London, WC1B 3JN, England; *The Europa World Year Book.*

Organisation for Economic Co-operation and Development (OECD), 2 rue Andre-Pascal, 75 Paris 16, France (Telephone Number in U.S. (202) 785-6323); *Indicators of Industrial Activity.*

St. Martin's Press, Inc., 175 Fifth Avenue, New York, New York 10010 (800) 221-7945; *The Statesman's Year-Book.*

Statistical Office of the United Nations, Publishing Service, New York, New York 10017 (800) 253-9646; *Trends in Europe and North America: The Statistical Yearbook of the Economic Commission for Europe.*

PORTUGAL - BROADCASTING

Billboard Limited, Post Office Box 9027, 1006 AA Amsterdam, The Netherlands (Telephone Number in U.S. (212) 764-7300); *World Radio TV Handbook.*

Central Intelligence Agency, Washington, D.C. 20505 (703) 482-1100, www.cia.gov; *The World Factbook.*

Euromonitor International, Inc., 122 South Michigan Avenue, Suite 1200, Chicago, Illinois 60603 (800) 577-EURO; *World Marketing Data and Statistics.*

European Commission Office of Press and Public Affairs, 2100 M Street, NW, Washington, D.C. 20037 (202) 862-9500; *Basic Statistics of the Community.*

M.E. Sharpe, 80 Business Park Drive, Armonk, New York 10504 (800) 541-6563; *The Illustrated Book of World Rankings.*

St. Martin's Press, Inc., 175 Fifth Avenue, New York, New York 10010 (800) 221-7945; *The Statesman's Year-Book.*

Statistical Office of the United Nations, Publishing Service, New York, New York 10017 (800) 253-9646; *Trends in Europe and North America: The Statistical Yearbook of the Economic Commission for Europe.*

United Nations Educational, Scientific and Cultural Organization (UNESCO), 7 Place de Fontenoy, F-75700 Paris, France (Telephone Number in U.S. (212) 963-5981); *Statistical Yearbook.*

PORTUGAL - BUDGET

Central Intelligence Agency, Washington, D.C. 20505 (703) 482-1100, www.cia.gov; *The World Factbook.*

PORTUGAL - BUSINESS

European Commission Office of Press and Public Affairs, 2100 M Street, NW, Washington, D.C. 20037 (202) 862-9500; *Basic Statistics of the Community.*

PORTUGAL - BUSINESS AND PROFESSIONAL LICENSES

International Monetary Fund, 700 Nineteenth Street, NW, Washington, D.C. 20431 (202) 623-7000; *Government Finance Statistics Yearbook.*

PORTUGAL - BUTTER PRODUCTION - See PORTUGAL - DAIRY PRODUCTS

PORTUGAL - CABBAGE PRODUCTION - See PORTUGAL - CROPS

PORTUGAL - CADMIUM PRODUCTION - See PORTUGAL - MINING AND MINERAL PRODUCTS

PORTUGAL - CALORIE SUPPLY

Food and Agricultural Organization of the United Nations (FAO) Via delle Terme di Caracalla, 00100 Rome, Italy (Telephone Number in U.S. (202) 653-2400); *The State of Food and Agriculture.*

PORTUGAL - CAPITAL INVESTMENT

Organisation for Economic Co-operation and Development (OECD), 2 rue Andre-Pascal, 75 Paris 16, France (Telephone Number in U.S. (202) 785-6323); *Economic Outlook;* and *Financial Market Trends.*

PORTUGAL - CAPITAL REVENUE

International Monetary Fund, 700 Nineteenth Street, NW, Washington, D.C. 20431 (202) 623-7000; *Government Finance Statistics Yearbook.*

Organisation for Economic Co-operation and Development (OECD), 2 rue Andre-Pascal, 75 Paris 16, France (Telephone Number in U.S. (202) 785-6323); *Economic Outlook;* and *Financial Market Trends.*

PORTUGAL - CAPITAL STRUCTURE

Organisation for Economic Co-

operation and Development (OECD), 2 rue Andre-Pascal, 75 Paris 16, France (Telephone Number in U.S. (202) 785-6323); *Financial Market Trends.*

PORTUGAL - CATTLE - See PORTUGAL - LIVESTOCK AND POULTRY

PORTUGAL - CAUSTIC SODA PRODUCTION - See PORTUGAL - BEVERAGES

PORTUGAL - CEMENT PRODUCTION - See PORTUGAL - MINING AND MINERAL PRODUCTS

PORTUGAL - CEREALS PRODUCTION - See PORTUGAL - CROPS

PORTUGAL - CHEESE PRODUCTION AND CONSUMPTION - See PORTUGAL - DAIRY PRODUCTS

PORTUGAL - CHEMICAL INDUSTRY

European Commission Office of Press and Public Affairs, 2100 M Street, NW, Washington, D.C. 20037 (202) 862-9500; *Industrial Production: Quarterly.*

PORTUGAL - CHEMICAL (ORGANIC) PRODUCTION - See PORTUGAL - MINING AND MINERAL PRODUCTS

PORTUGAL - CHESTNUT PRODUCTION - See PORTUGAL - CROPS

PORTUGAL - CHICK PEA PRODUCTION - See PORTUGAL - CROPS

PORTUGAL - CHROMITE PRODUCTION AND CONSUMPTION - See PORTUGAL - MINING AND MINERAL PRODUCTS

PORTUGAL - CHROMIUM ORE PRODUCTION AND CONSUMPTION - See PORTUGAL - MINING AND MINERAL PRODUCTS

PORTUGAL - CIGAR AND CIGARETTE PRODUCTION - See PORTUGAL - TOBACCO PRODUCTION

PORTUGAL - CLASS STRUCTURE

European Commission Office of Press and Public Affairs, 2100 M Street, NW, Washington, D.C. 20037 (202) 862-9500; *Basic Statistics of the Community.*

PORTUGAL - CLIMATE

M.E. Sharpe, 80 Business Park Drive, Armonk, New York 10504 (800) 541-6563; *The Illustrated Book of World Rankings.*

St. Martin's Press, Inc., 175 Fifth Avenue, New York, New York 10010 (800) 221-7945; *The Statesman's Year-Book.*

Statistical Office of the United Nations,

Publishing Service, New York, New York 10017 (800) 253-9646; *Statistical Yearbook.*

PORTUGAL - CLOTHING - PRODUCTION INDEX - See PORTUGAL - TEXTILE INDUSTRY

PORTUGAL - CLOTHING EXPORTS AND IMPORTS - See PORTUGAL -TEXTILE INDUSTRY

PORTUGAL - COAL PRODUCTION - See PORTUGAL - MINING AND MINERAL PRODUCTS

PORTUGAL - COBALT PRODUCTION AND CONSUMPTION - See PORTUGAL - MINING AND MINERAL PRODUCTS

PORTUGAL - COFFEE PRODUCTION AND CONSUMPTION - See PORTUGAL - CROPS

PORTUGAL - COKE, COKE OVEN ORE, AND COKE OVEN COKE PRODUCTION AND CONSUMPTION - See PORTUGAL - MINING AND MINERAL PRODUCTS

PORTUGAL - COMMERCE

St. Martin's Press, Inc., 175 Fifth Avenue, New York, New York 10010 (800) 221-7945; *The Statesman's Year-Book.*

PORTUGAL - COMMUNICATIONS - See PORTUGAL - TRANSPORTATION AND COMMUNICATIONS

PORTUGAL - CONSTRUCTION INDUSTRY

European Commission Office of Press and Public Affairs, 2100 M Street, NW, Washington, D.C. 20037 (202) 862-9500; *Basic Statistics of the Community;* and *Labor Force Sample Survey.*

M.E. Sharpe, 80 Business Park Drive, Armonk, New York 10504 (800) 541-6563; *The Illustrated Book of World Rankings.*

Organisation for Economic Co-operation and Development (OECD), 2 rue Andre-Pascal, 75 Paris 16, France (Telephone Number in U.S. (202) 785-6323); *Industrial Structure Statistics; The Iron and Steel Industry; Main Economic Indicators - Historical Statistics;* and *OECD Economic Surveys: Portugal.*

St. Martin's Press, Inc., 175 Fifth Avenue, New York, New York 10010 (800) 221-7945; *The Statesman's Year-Book.*

Statistical Office of the United Nations, Publishing Service, New York, New York 10017 (800) 253-9646; *Statistical Yearbook.*

PORTUGAL - CONSUMER PRICE INDEX

Europa Publications Limited, 18 Bedford Square, London, WC1B 3JN, England; *The Europa World Year Book.*

European Commission Office of Press and Public Affairs, 2100 M Street, NW, Washington, D.C. 20037 (202) 862-9500; *Basic Statistics of the Community;* and *Eurostatistics: Data for Short-Term Economic Analysis.*

Organisation for Economic Co-operation and Development (OECD), 2 rue Andre-Pascal, 75 Paris 16, France (Telephone Number in U.S. (202) 785-6323); *Economic Outlook.*

Statistical Office of the United Nations, Publishing Service, New York, New York 10017 (800) 253-9646; *Statistical Yearbook;* and *Trends in Europe and North America: The Statistical Yearbook of the Economic Commission for Europe.*

PORTUGAL - CONSUMER PRICES

Euromonitor International, Inc., 122 South Michigan Avenue, Suite 1200, Chicago, Illinois 60603 (800) 577-EURO; *European Marketing Data and Statistics;* and *World Marketing Data and Statistics.*

European Commission Office of Press and Public Affairs, 2100 M Street, NW, Washington, D.C. 20037 (202) 862-9500; *Basic Statistics for the Community; Eurostatistics: Data for Short-Term Economic Analysis;* and *Money and Finance.*

International Labour Office, I.L.O. Publications, 1828 L Street, NW, Suite 801, Washington, D.C. 20036 (301) 638-3152; *Yearbook of Labour Statistics.*

International Monetary Fund, 700 Nineteenth Street, NW, Washington, D.C. 20431 (202) 623-7000; *International Financial Statistics.*

Organisation for Economic Co-operation and Development (OECD), 2 rue Andre-Pascal, 75 Paris 16, France (Telephone Number in U.S. (202) 785-6323); *Economic Outlook.*

PORTUGAL - CONSUMPTION

European Commission Office of Press and Public Affairs, 2100 M Street, NW, Washington, D.C. 20037 (202) 862-9500; *Basic Statistics of the Community.*

Organisation for Economic Co-operation and Development (OECD), 2 rue Andre-Pascal, 75 Paris 16, France (Telephone Number in U.S. (202) 785-6323); *The Footwear, Raw Hides and Skins, and Leather Industry in OECD Countries; The Iron and Steel Industry; Meat Balances in OECD Member Countries; The Pulp and Paper Industry;* and *Textile Industry in OECD Countries.*

The World Bank, 1818 H Street, NW,

Washington, D.C. 20433 (202) 477-1234; *World Development Report.*

PORTUGAL - COPPER AND COPPER ORE PRODUCTION AND CONSUMPTION - See PORTUGAL - MINING AND MINERAL PRODUCTS

PORTUGAL - CORK EXPORTS

International Monetary Fund, 700 Nineteenth Street, NW, Washington, D.C. 20431 (202) 623-7000; *International Financial Statistics.*

PORTUGAL - CORN PRODUCTION - See PORTUGAL - CROPS

PORTUGAL - CORPORATE TAXES - See PORTUGAL - TAXATION

PORTUGAL - COTTON - See PORTUGAL - CROPS

PORTUGAL - CRIME

International Criminal Police Organization (INTERPOL), 50 quai Achille Lignon, F-69006 Lyon, France; *International Crime Statistics.*

Statistical Office of the United Nations, Publishing Service, New York, New York 10017 (800) 253-9646; *Trends in Europe and North America: The Statistical Yearbook of the Economic Commission for Europe.*

Yale University Press, Yale Station, New Haven, Connecticut 06520 (800) 987-7323; *Violence and Crime in Cross-National Perspective.*

PORTUGAL - CROPS

Euromonitor International, Inc., 122 South Michigan Avenue, Suite 1200, Chicago, Illinois 60603 (800) 577-EURO; *European Marketing Data and Statistics.*

Europa Publications Limited, 18 Bedford Square, London, WC1B 3JN, England; *The Europa World Year Book.*

European Commission Office of Press and Public Affairs, 2100 M Street, NW, Washington, D.C. 20037 (202) 862-9500; *ACP: Basis Statistics; Agriculture: Statistical Yearbook; Basic Statistics of the Community; Crop Production: Quarterly Statistics; Eurostatistics: Data for Short-Term Economic Analysis;* and *Regions: Statistical Yearbook.*

Food and Agricultural Organization of the United Nations (FAO), Via delle Terme di Caracalla, 00100 Rome, Italy (Telephone Number in U.S. (202) 653-2400); *Production Yearbook;* and *The State of Food and Agriculture.*

M.E. Sharpe, 80 Business Park Drive,

Armonk, New York 10504 (800) 541-6563; *The Illustrated Book of World Rankings.*

Organisation for Economic Co-operation and Development (OECD), 2 rue Andre-Pascal, 75 Paris 16, France (Telephone Number in U.S. (202) 785-6323); *Economic Accounts for Agriculture; Foreign Trade by Commodities; The Non-Ferrous Metals Industry;* and *Textile Industry in OECD Countries.*

St. Martin's Press, Inc., 175 Fifth Avenue, New York, New York 10010 (800) 221-7945; *The Statesman's Year-Book.*

Statistical Office of the United Nations, Publishing Service, New York, New York 10017 (800) 253-9646; *Statistical Yearbook.*

United Nations Conference on Trade and Development, Central Statistical Service, Palais des Nations, Geneva, Switzerland (Telephone in U.S. (800) 253-9646); *UNCTAD Commodity Yearbook.*

PORTUGAL - CUSTOMS DUTIES

European Commission Office of Press and Public Affairs, 2100 M Street, NW, Washington, D.C. 20037 (202) 862-9500; *Basic Statistics of the Community.*

International Monetary Fund, 700 Nineteenth Street, NW, Washington, D.C. 20431 (202) 623-7000; *Government Finance Statistics Yearbook.*

Organisation for Economic Co-operation and Development (OECD), 2 rue Andre-Pascal, 75 Paris 16, France (Telephone Number in U.S. (202) 785-6323); *The Non-Ferrous Metals Industry.*

St. Martin's Press, Inc., 175 Fifth Avenue, New York, New York 10010 (800) 221-7945; *The Statesman's Year-Book.*

PORTUGAL - DAIRY PRODUCTS

Europa Publications Limited, 18 Bedford Square, London, WC1B 3JN, England; *The Europa World Year Book.*

European Commission Office of Press and Public Affairs, 2100 M Street, NW, Washington, D.C. 20037 (202) 862-9500; *Eurostatistics: Data for Short-Term Economic Analysis.*

Food and Agricultural Organization of the United Nations (FAO) Via delle Terme di Caracalla, 00100 Rome, Italy (Telephone Number in U.S. (202) 653-2400); *The State of Food and Agriculture.*

M.E. Sharpe, 80 Business Park Drive, Armonk, New York 10504 (800) 541-6563; *The Illustrated Book of World Rankings.*

Organisation for Economic Co-

operation and Development (OECD), 2 rue Andre-Pascal, 75 Paris 16, France (Telephone Number in U.S. (202) 785-6323); *Economic Accounts for Agriculture;* and *Milk, Milk Products, and Egg Balances in OECD Member Countries.*

St. Martin's Press, Inc., 175 Fifth Avenue, New York, New York 10010 (800) 221-7945; *The Statesman's Year-Book.*

Statistical Office of the United Nations, Publishing Service, New York, New York 10017 (800) 253-9646; *Statistical Yearbook.*

PORTUGAL - DEATH RATES - See PORTUGAL - MORTALITY

PORTUGAL - DEFENSE EXPENDITURES - See PORTUGAL - MILITARY

PORTUGAL - DEMOGRAPHY

The Economist Intelligence Unit, 111 West 57th Street, New York, New York 10019 (800) 938-4685; *The World Market Atlas.*

Euromonitor International, Inc., 122 South Michigan Avenue, Suite 1200, Chicago, Illinois 60603 (800) 577-EURO; *The World Economic Factbook;* and *World Marketing Data and Statistics.*

European Commission Office of Press and Public Affairs, 2100 M Street, NW, Washington, D.C. 20037 (202) 862-9500; *Basic Statistics of the Community, Demographic Statistics; Employment and Unemployment;* and *Regions: Statistical Yearbook.*

M.E. Sharpe, 80 Business Park Drive, Armonk, New York 10504 (800) 541-6563; *The Illustrated Book of World Rankings.*

Statistical Office of the United Nations, Publishing Service, New York, New York 10017 (800) 253-9646; *Human Development Report.*

PORTUGAL - DEVELOPMENT ASSISTANCE

European Commission Office of Press and Public Affairs, 2100 M Street, NW, Washington, D.C. 20037 (202) 862-9500; *ACP: Basic Statistics; Basis Statistics of the Community;* and *Government Financing of Research and Development.*

Organisation for Economic Co-operation and Development (OECD), 2 rue Andre-Pascal, 75 Paris 16, France (Telephone Number in U.S. (202) 785-6323); *Geographical Distribution of Financial Flows to Developing Countries.*

Statistical Office of the United Nations, Publishing Service, New York, New York 10017 (800) 253-9646; *Statistical Yearbook.*

PORTUGAL - DIAMOND PRODUCTION - See PORTUGAL - MINING AND MINERAL PRODUCTS

PORTUGAL - DISCOUNT RATES - See PORTUGAL - BANKING

PORTUGAL - DISEASES - See PORTUGAL - HEALTH

PORTUGAL - DIVORCE RATES

European Commission Office of Press and Public Affairs, 2100 M Street, NW, Washington, D.C. 20037 (202) 862-9500; *Demographic Statistics.*

M.E. Sharpe, 80 Business Park Drive, Armonk, New York 10504 (800) 541-6563; *The Illustrated Book of World Rankings.*

Statistical Office of the United Nations, Publishing Service, New York, New York 10017 (800) 253-9646; *Demographic Yearbook; Statistical Yearbook;* and *Trends in Europe and North America: The Statistical Yearbook of the Economic Commission for Europe.*

PORTUGAL - DOMESTIC PRODUCT

European Commission Office of Press and Public Affairs, 2100 M Street, NW, Washington, D.C. 20037 (202) 862-9500; *Basic Statistics of the Community.*

PORTUGAL - ECONOMY

Central Intelligence Agency, Washington, D.C. 20505 (703) 482-1100, www.cia.gov; *The World Factbook.*

Economist Intelligence Unit, 111 West 57th Street, New York, New York 10019 (800) 938-4685; *Portugal Country Report.*

Euromonitor International, Inc., 122 South Michigan Avenue, Suite 1200, Chicago, Illinois 60603 (800) 577-EURO; *ACP: Basic Statistics; Basic Statistics of the Community; Energy Statistics Yearbook; European Marketing Data and Statistics; Labor Force Sample Survey; The World Economic Factbook;* and *World Marketing Data and Statistics.*

Europa Publications Limited, 18 Bedford Square, London, WC1B 3JN, England; *The Europa World Year Book.*

European Commission Office of Press and Public Affairs, 2100 M Street, NW, Washington, D.C. 20037 (202) 862-9500; *Money and Finance.*

M.E. Sharpe, 80 Business Park Drive, Armonk, New York 10504 (800) 541-6563; *The Illustrated Book of World Rankings.*

Organisation for Economic Co-operation and Development (OECD), 2 rue

Andre-Pascal, 75 Paris 16, France (Telephone Number in U.S. (202) 785-6323); *Economic Outlook, Geographical Distribution of Financial Flows to Developing Countries, Main Economic Indicators, OECD Economic Surveys: Portugal;* and *OECD Employment Outlook.*

St. Martin's Press, Inc., 175 Fifth Avenue, New York, New York 10010 (800) 221-7945; *The Statesman's Year-Book.*

Statistical Office of the United Nations, Publishing Service, New York, New York 10017 (800) 253-9646; *World Statistics Pocketbook.*

The World Bank, 1818 H Street, NW, Washington, D.C. 20433 (202) 477-1234; *World Development Report.*

PORTUGAL - EDUCATION

The Economist Intelligence Unit, 111 West 57th Street, New York, New York 10019 (800) 938-4685; *The World Market Atlas.*

Euromonitor International, Inc., 122 South Michigan Avenue, Suite 1200, Chicago, Illinois 60603 (800) 577-EURO; *European Marketing Data and Statistics;* and *World Marketing Data and Statistics.*

Europa Publications Limited, 18 Bedford Square, London, WC1B 3JN, England; *The Europa World Year Book.*

European Commission Office of Press and Public Affairs, 2100 M Street, NW, Washington, D.C. 20037 (202) 862-9500; *Basic Statistics of the Community;* and *Regions: Statistical Yearbook.*

Federal Statistical Office, Gustav - Stresemann - Ring 11, D-6200 Wiesbaden, Germany; *Portugal.*

International Monetary Fund, 700 Nineteenth Street, NW, Washington, D.C. 20431 (202) 623-7000; *Government Finance Statistics Yearbook.*

M.E. Sharpe, 80 Business Park Drive, Armonk, New York 10504 (800) 541-6563; *The Illustrated Book of World Rankings.*

Organisation for Economic Co-operation and Development (OECD), 2 rue Andre-Pascal, 75 Paris 16, France (Telephone Number in U.S. (202) 785-6323); *Education in OECD.*

St. Martin's Press, Inc., 175 Fifth Avenue, New York, New York 10010 (800) 221-7945; *The Statesman's Year-Book.*

Statistical Office of the United Nations, Publishing Service, New York, New York 10017 (800) 253-9646; *Human Development Report;* and *Trends in Europe*

and *North America: The Statistical Yearbook of the Economic Commission for Europe.*

United Nations Educational, Scientific and Cultural Organization (UNESCO), 7 Place de Fontenoy, F-75700 Paris, France (Telephone Number in U.S. (212) 963-5981); *Statistical Yearbook.*

The World Bank, 1818 H Street, NW, Washington, D.C. 20433 (202) 477-1234; *World Development Report;* and *World Development Indicators.*

PORTUGAL - EGG PRODUCTION AND CONSUMPTION - See PORTUGAL - DAIRY PRODUCTS

PORTUGAL - ELECTRICITY

Central Intelligence Agency, Washington, D.C. 20505 (703) 482-1100, www.cia.gov; *The World Factbook.*

European Commission Office of Press and Public Affairs, 2100 M Street, NW, Washington, D.C. 20037 (202) 862-9500; *Basic Statistics of the Community; Energy: Monthly Statistics; Energy Statistics Yearbook; Eurostatistics: Data for Short-Term Economic Analysis;* and *Regions: Statistical Yearbook.*

M.E. Sharpe, 80 Business Park Drive, Armonk, New York 10504 (800) 541-6563; *The Illustrated Book of World Rankings.*

Organisation for Economic Co-operation and Development (OECD), 2 rue Andre-Pascal, 75 Paris 16, France (Telephone Number in U.S. (202) 785-6323); *Coal Information; Energy Statistics of OECD Countries; Indicators of Industrial Activity;* and *Industrial Structure Statistics.*

St. Martin's Press, Inc., 175 Fifth Avenue, New York, New York 10010 (800) 221-7945; *The Statesman's Year-Book.*

Statistical Office of the United Nations, Publishing Service, New York, New York 10017 (800) 253-9646; *Human Development Report; Statistical Yearbook;* and *Trends in Europe and North America: The Statistical Yearbook of the Economic Commission for Europe.*

PORTUGAL - EMPLOYMENT

Euromonitor International, Inc., 122 South Michigan Avenue, Suite 1200, Chicago, Illinois 60603 (800) 577-EURO; *European Marketing Data and Statistics.*

European Commission Office of Press and Public Affairs, 2100 M Street, NW, Washington, D.C. 20037 (202) 862-9500; *Basic Statistics of the Community; Earnings in Agriculture; Employment and Unemployment; Eurostatistics: Data for*

Short-Term Economic Analysis; and *Iron and Steel: Statistical Yearbook.*

Federal Statistical Office, Gustav - Stresemann - Ring 11, D-6200 Wiesbaden, Germany; *Portugal.*

International Labour Office, I.L.O. Publications, 1828 L Street, NW, Suite 801, Washington, D.C. 20036 (301) 638-3152; *Yearbook of Labour Statistics.*

M.E. Sharpe, 80 Business Park Drive, Armonk, New York 10504 (800) 541-6563; *The Illustrated Book of World Rankings.*

Organisation for Economic Co-operation and Development (OECD), 2 rue Andre-Pascal, 75 Paris 16, France (Telephone Number in U.S. (202) 785-6323); *Economic Outlook; The Iron and Steel Industry; OECD Economic Surveys: Portugal; OECD Employment Outlook;* and *Textile Industry in OECD Countries.*

Statistical Office of the United Nations, Publishing Service, New York, New York 10017 (800) 253-9646; *Statistical Yearbook;* and *Trends in Europe and North America: The Statistical Yearbook of the Economic Commission for Europe.*

PORTUGAL - ENERGY

Euromonitor International, Inc., 122 South Michigan Avenue, Suite 1200, Chicago, Illinois 60603 (800) 577-EURO; *European Marketing Data and Statistics; World Marketing Data and Statistics;* and *The World Economic Factbook.*

European Commission Office of Press and Public Affairs, 2100 M Street, NW, Washington, D.C. 20037 (202) 862-9500; *Basic Statistics of the Community; Energy: Monthly Statistics; Energy Statistics Yearbook; Regions: Statistical Yearbook;* and *Transport Annual Statistics.*

Food and Agricultural Organization of the United Nations (FAO) Via delle Terme di Caracalla, 00100 Rome, Italy (Telephone Number in U.S. (202) 653-2400); *The State of Food and Agriculture.*

M.E. Sharpe, 80 Business Park Drive, Armonk, New York 10504 (800) 541-6563; *The Illustrated Book of World Rankings.*

Organisation for Economic Co-operation and Development (OECD), 2 rue Andre-Pascal, 75 Paris 16, France (Telephone Number in U.S. (202) 785-6323); *Coal Information; Energy Statistics of OECD Countries; OECD Environmental Data;* and *Oil and Gas Information.*

St. Martin's Press, Inc., 175 Fifth Avenue, New York, New York 10010 (800) 221-7945; *The Statesman's Year-Book.*

Statistical Office of the United Nations, Publishing Service, New York, New York 10017 (800) 253-9646; *Energy Statistics Yearbook; Human Development Report; Statistical Yearbook; Trends in Europe and North America: The Statistical Yearbook of the Economic Commission for Europe;* and *World Statistics Pocketbook.*

The World Bank, 1818 H Street, NW, Washington, D.C. 20433 (202) 477-1234; *World Development Report.*

PORTUGAL - ENGINEERING - METAL PRODUCTS

European Commission Office of Press and Public Affairs, 2100 M Street, NW, Washington, D.C. 20037 (202) 862-9500; *Basic Statistics of the Community;* and *Industrial Production: Quarterly.*

PORTUGAL - ENVIRONMENT

Economist Intelligence Unit, 111 West 57th Street, New York, New York 10019 (800) 938-4685; *Portugal Country Report.*

Organisation for Economic Co-operation and Development (OECD), 2 rue Andre-Pascal, 75 Paris 16, France (Telephone Number in U.S. (202) 785-6323); *OECD Environmental Data.*

Statistical Office of the United Nations, Publishing Service, New York, New York 10017 (800) 253-9646; *Trends in Europe and North America: The Statistical Yearbook of the Economic Commission for Europe;* and *World Statistics Pocketbook.*

PORTUGAL - EXCHANGE RATES

Central Intelligence Agency, Washington, D.C. 20505 (703) 482-1100, www.cia.gov; *The World Factbook.*

Euromonitor International, Inc., 122 South Michigan Avenue, Suite 1200, Chicago, Illinois 60603 (800) 577-EURO; *The World Economic Factbook.*

Europa Publications Limited, 18 Bedford Square, London, WC1B 3JN, England; *The Europa World Year Book.*

European Commission Office of Press and Public Affairs, 2100 M Street, NW, Washington, D.C. 20037 (202) 862-9500; *Basic Statistics of the Community; Eurostatistics: Data for Short-Term Economic Analysis;* and *Money and Finance.*

International Civil Aviation Organization, 999 University Street, Montreal, Quebec, Canada H3C 5H7 (514) 954-8219; *Civil Aviation Statistics of the World.*

International Monetary Fund, 700

Nineteenth Street, NW, Washington, D.C. 20431 (202) 623-7000; *International Financial Statistics.*

Organisation for Economic Co-operation and Development (OECD), 2 rue Andre-Pascal, 75 Paris 16, France (Telephone Number in U.S. (202) 785-6323); *Economic Outlook; Financial Market Trends; Revenue Statistics of OECD Member Countries;* and *Tourism Policy and International Tourism in OECD Member Countries.*

Statistical Office of the United Nations, Publishing Service, New York, New York 10017 (800) 253-9646; *Statistical Yearbook; Trends in Europe and North America: The Statistical Yearbook of the Economic Commission for Europe;* and *World Statistics Pocketbook.*

PORTUGAL - EXCISE TAXES - See PORTUGAL - TAXATION

PORTUGAL - EXPORTS

Central Intelligence Agency, Washington, D.C. 20505 (703) 482-1100, www.cia.gov; *The World Factbook.*

The Economist Intelligence Unit, 111 West 57th Street, New York, New York 10019 (800) 938-4685; *Portugal Country Report;* and *The World Market Atlas.*

Euromonitor International, Inc., 122 South Michigan Avenue, Suite 1200, Chicago, Illinois 60603 (800) 577-EURO; *The World Economic Factbook.*

Europa Publications Limited, 18 Bedford Square, London, WC1B 3JN, England; *The Europa World Year Book.*

European Commission Office of Press and Public Affairs, 2100 M Street, NW, Washington, D.C. 20037 (202) 862-9500; *Basic Statistics of the Community; Energy: Monthly Statistics; Energy Statistics Yearbook; Eurostatistics: Data for Short-Term Economic Analysis; External Trade: Statistical Yearbook; External Trade: Monthly Statistics;* and *Fisheries: Yearly Statistics.*

Food and Agricultural Organization of the United Nations (FAO) Via delle Terme di Caracalla, 00100 Rome, Italy (Telephone Number in U.S. (202) 653-2400); *The State of Food and Agriculture.*

International Monetary Fund, 700 Nineteenth Street, NW, Washington, D.C. 20431 (202) 623-7000; *Direction of Trade; Government Finance Statistics Yearbook;* and *International Financial Statistics.*

Organisation for Economic Co-operation and Development (OECD), 2 rue Andre-Pascal, 75 Paris 16, France

(Telephone Number in U.S. (202) 785-6323); *Economic Outlook; The Footwear, Raw Hides and Skins, and Leather Industry in OECD Countries; Foreign Trade by Commodities; Geographical Distribution of Financial Flows to Developing Countries; Industrial Structure Statistics; The Iron and Steel Industry; Milk, Milk Products, and Egg Balances in OECD Member Countries; The Pulp and Paper Industry; OECD Economic Surveys: Portugal;* and *Review of Fisheries in OECD Member Countries.*

St. Martin's Press, Inc., 175 Fifth Avenue, New York, New York 10010 (800) 221-7945; *The Statesman's Year-Book.*

Statistical Office of the United Nations, Publishing Service, New York, New York 10017 (800) 253-9646; *Trends in Europe and North America: The Statistical Yearbook of the Economic Commission for Europe.*

United Nations Conference on Trade and Development (UNCTAD), New York, New York 10017 (800) 253-9646; *Handbook of International Trade and Development Statistics.*

The World Bank, 1818 H Street, NW, Washington, D.C. 20433 (202) 477-1234; *World Development Report;* and *World Development Indicators.*

PORTUGAL - EXTERNAL FINANCING

Organisation for Economic Co-operation and Development (OECD), 2 rue Andre-Pascal, 75 Paris 16, France (Telephone Number in U.S. (202) 785-6323); *Economic Outlook;* and *Financial Market Trends.*

PORTUGAL - EXTERNAL INDEBTEDNESS

Organisation for Economic Co-operation and Development (OECD), 2 rue Andre-Pascal, 75 Paris 16, France (Telephone Number in U.S. (202) 785-6323); *Financial Market Trends;* and *Geographical Distribution of Financial Flows to Developing Countries.*

The World Bank, 1818 H Street, NW, Washington, D.C. 20433 (202) 477-1234; *World Development Report;* and *World Development Indicators.*

PORTUGAL - EXTERNAL TRADE

Euromonitor International, Inc., 122 South Michigan Avenue, Suite 1200, Chicago, Illinois 60603 (800) 577-EURO; *World Marketing Data and Statistics.*

European Commission Office of Press and Public Affairs, 2100 M Street, NW, Washington, D.C. 20037 (202) 862-9500; *ACP: Basic Statistics; Basic Statistics of the Community; Eurostatistics: Data for Short-Term Economic Analysis; External Trade:*

Statistical Yearbook; External Trade: Monthly Statistics; and *Foreign Trade of the People's Republic of China.*

Food and Agricultural Organization of the United Nations (FAO) Via delle Terme di Caracalla, 00100 Rome, Italy (Telephone Number in U.S. (202) 653-2400); *The State of Food and Agriculture;* and *Trade Yearbook.*

Statistical Office of the United Nations, Publishing Service, New York, New York 10017 (800) 253-9646; *Statistical Yearbook.*

PORTUGAL - FABRIC PRODUCTION - See PORTUGAL - TEXTILE INDUSTRY

PORTUGAL - FARM CROPS - See PORTUGAL - CROPS

PORTUGAL - FEMALE WORKING POPULATION - See PORTUGAL - EMPLOYMENT

PORTUGAL - FERTILITY RATES

Central Intelligence Agency, Washington, D.C. 20505 (703) 482-1100, www.cia.gov; *The World Factbook.*

European Commission Office of Press and Public Affairs, 2100 M Street, NW, Washington, D.C. 20037 (202) 862-9500; *Demographic Statistics.*

M.E. Sharpe, 80 Business Park Drive, Armonk, New York 10504 (800) 541-6563; *The Illustrated Book of World Rankings.*

Statistical Office of the United Nations, Publishing Service, New York, New York 10017 (800) 253-9646; *Human Development Report;* and *Trends in Europe and North America: The Statistical Yearbook of the Economic Commission for Europe.*

The World Bank, 1818 H Street, NW, Washington, D.C. 20433 (202) 477-1234; *World Development Report;* and *World Development Indicators.*

PORTUGAL - FERTILIZER

European Commission Office of Press and Public Affairs, 2100 M Street, NW, Washington, D.C. 20037 (202) 862-9500; *Basic Statistics of the Community.*

Food and Agricultural Organization of the United Nations (FAO), Via delle Terme di Caracalla, 00100 Rome, Italy (Telephone Number in U.S. (202) 653-2400); *Fertilizer Yearbook;* and *The State of Food and Agriculture.*

Organisation for Economic Co-operation and Development (OECD), 2 rue Andre-Pascal, 75 Paris 16, France (Telephone Number in U.S. (202) 785-

6323); *Economic Accounts for Agriculture;* and *Foreign Trade by Commodities.*

Statistical Office of the United Nations, Publishing Service, New York, New York 10017 (800) 253-9646; *Statistical Yearbook.*

PORTUGAL - FETAL MORTALITY - See PORTUGAL - MORTALITY

PORTUGAL - FIBRE PRODUCTION - See PORTUGAL - TEXTILE INDUSTRY

PORTUGAL - FILAMENT PRODUCTION - See PORTUGAL - TEXTILE INDUSTRY

PORTUGAL - FILM - See PORTUGAL - MOTION PICTURES

PORTUGAL - FINANCE

Economist Intelligence Unit, 111 West 57th Street, New York, New York 10019 (800) 938-4685; *Portugal Country Report.*

Europa Publications Limited, 18 Bedford Square, London, WC1B 3JN, England; *The Europa World Year Book.*

European Commission Office of Press and Public Affairs, 2100 M Street, NW, Washington, D.C. 20037 (202) 862-9500; *ACP: Basic Statistics; Basic Statistics of the Community; Eurostatistics: Data for Short-Term Economic Analysis;* and *Money and Finance.*

Federal Statistical Office, Gustav - Stresemann - Ring 11, D-6200 Wiesbaden, Germany; *Portugal.*

International Monetary Fund, 700 Nineteenth Street, NW, Washington, D.C. 20431 (202) 623-7000; *International Financial Statistics.*

M.E. Sharpe, 80 Business Park Drive, Armonk, New York 10504 (800) 541-6563; *The Illustrated Book of World Rankings.*

Organisation for Economic Co-operation and Development (OECD), 2 rue Andre-Pascal, 75 Paris 16, France (Telephone Number in U.S. (202) 785-6323); *Economic Outlook; Financial Market Trends; Geographical Distribution of Financial Flows to Developing Countries; Main Economic Indicators - Historical Statistics; OECD Financial Statistics;* and *Revenue Statistics of OECD Member Countries.*

St. Martin's Press, Inc., 175 Fifth Avenue, New York, New York 10010 (800) 221-7945; *The Statesman's Year-Book.*

PORTUGAL - FISHERIES

Euromonitor International, Inc., 122 South Michigan Avenue, Suite 1200, Chicago, Illinois 60603 (800) 577-EURO;

European Marketing Data and Statistics.

Europa Publications Limited, 18 Bedford Square, London, WC1B 3JN, England; *The Europa World Year Book.*

European Commission Office of Press and Public Affairs, 2100 M Street, NW, Washington, D.C. 20037 (202) 862-9500; *Agriculture: Statistical Yearbook;* and *Fisheries: Yearly Statistics.*

Federal Statistical Office, Gustav - Stresemann - Ring 11, D-6200 Wiesbaden, Germany; *Portugal.*

Food and Agricultural Organization of the United Nations (FAO) Via delle Terme di Caracalla, 00100 Rome, Italy (Telephone Number in U.S. (202) 653-2400); *The State of Food and Agriculture;* and *Yearbook of Fishery Statistics.*

M.E. Sharpe, 80 Business Park Drive, Armonk, New York 10504 (800) 541-6563; *The Illustrated Book of World Rankings.*

Organisation for Economic Co-operation and Development (OECD), 2 rue Andre-Pascal, 75 Paris 16, France (Telephone Number in U.S. (202) 785-6323); *Foreign Trade by Commodities; Industrial Structure Statistics;* and *Review of Fisheries in OECD Member Countries.*

St. Martin's Press, Inc., 175 Fifth Avenue, New York, New York 10010 (800) 221-7945; *The Statesman's Year-Book.*

United Nations Conference on Trade and Development, Central Statistical Service, Palais des Nations, Geneva, Switzerland (Telephone in U.S. (800) 253-9646); *UNCTAD Commodity Yearbook.*

PORTUGAL - FLOUR PRODUCTION

European Commission Office of Press and Public Affairs, 2100 M Street, NW, Washington, D.C. 20037 (202) 862-9500; *Basic Statistics of the Community.*

Statistical Office of the United Nations, Publishing Service, New York, New York 10017 (800) 253-9646; *Statistical Yearbook.*

PORTUGAL - FOOD

Euromonitor International, Inc., 122 South Michigan Avenue, Suite 1200, Chicago, Illinois 60603 (800) 577-EURO; *Retail Trade International.*

Food and Agricultural Organization of the United Nations (FAO), Via delle Terme di Caracalla, 00100 Rome, Italy (Telephone Number in U.S. (202) 653-2400); *Production Yearbook;* and *The State of Food and Agriculture.*

Organisation for Economic

Co-operation and Development (OECD), 2 rue Andre-Pascal, 75 Paris 16, France (Telephone Number in U.S. (202) 785-6323); *Food Consumption Statistics;* and *Foreign Trade by Commodities.*

Statistical Office of the United Nations, Publishing Service, New York, New York 10017 (800) 253-9646; *Human Development Report.*

United Nations Conference on Trade and Development, Central Statistical Service, Palais des Nations, Geneva, Switzerland (Telephone in U.S. (800) 253-9646); *UNCTAD Commodity Yearbook.*

PORTUGAL - FOOTWEAR - PRODUCTION INDEX

Organisation for Economic Co-operation and Development (OECD), 2 rue Andre-Pascal, 75 Paris 16, France (Telephone Number in U.S. (202) 785-6323); *Indicators of Industrial Activity.*

PORTUGAL - FOREIGN DEBT

Organisation for Economic Co-operation and Development (OECD), 2 rue Andre-Pascal, 75 Paris 16, France (Telephone Number in U.S. (202) 785-6323); *Economic Outlook.*

St. Martin's Press, Inc., 175 Fifth Avenue, New York, New York 10010 (800) 221-7945; *The Statesman's Year-Book.*

PORTUGAL - FOREIGN INDEBTEDNESS

Organisation for Economic Co-operation and Development (OECD), 2 rue Andre-Pascal, 75 Paris 16, France (Telephone Number in U.S. (202) 785-6323); *Economic Outlook;* and *Financial Market Trends.*

PORTUGAL - FOREIGN OFFICIAL RESERVES

European Commission Office of Press and Public Affairs, 2100 M Street, NW, Washington, D.C. 20037 (202) 862-9500; *Money and Finance.*

PORTUGAL - FOREIGN TRADE

Economist Intelligence Unit, 111 West 57th Street, New York, New York 10019 (800) 938-4685; *Portugal Country Report.*

Euromonitor International, Inc., 122 South Michigan Avenue, Suite 1200, Chicago, Illinois 60603 (800) 577-EURO; *European Marketing Data and Statistics;* and *The World Economic Factbook.*

Europa Publications Limited, 18 Bedford Square, London, WC1B 3JN, England; *The Europa World Year Book.*

European Commission Office of Press and Public Affairs, 2100 M Street, NW, Washington, D.C. 20037 (202) 862-9500; *Basic Statistics of the Community; Energy Statistics Yearbook; Foreign Trade of the People's Republic of China;* and *Iron and Steel: Statistical Yearbook.*

Federal Statistical Office, Gustav - Stresemann - Ring 11, D-6200 Wiesbaden, Germany; *Portugal.*

Food and Agricultural Organization of the United Nations (FAO) Via delle Terme di Caracalla, 00100 Rome, Italy (Telephone Number in U.S. (202) 653-2400); *The State of Food and Agriculture.*

International Monetary Fund, 700 Nineteenth Street, NW, Washington, D.C. 20431 (202) 623-7000; *International Financial Statistics.*

M.E. Sharpe, 80 Business Park Drive, Armonk, New York 10504 (800) 541-6563; *The Illustrated Book of World Rankings.*

Organisation for Economic Co-operation and Development (OECD), 2 rue Andre-Pascal, 75 Paris 16, France (Telephone Number in U.S. (202) 785-6323); *Economic Outlook; The Footwear, Raw Hides and Skins, and Leather Industry in OECD Countries; Foreign Trade by Commodities; Main Economic Indicators - Historical Statistics; Maritime Transport; Meat Balances in OECD Member Countries;* and *OECD Economic Surveys: Portugal.*

St. Martin's Press, Inc., 175 Fifth Avenue, New York, New York 10010 (800) 221-7945; *The Statesman's Year-Book.*

Statistical Office of the United Nations, Publishing Service, New York, New York 10017 (800) 253-9646; *International Trade Statistics Yearbook;* and *Statistical Yearbook.*

United Nations Conference on Trade and Development, Central Statistical Service, Palais des Nations, Geneva, Switzerland (Telephone in U.S. (800) 253-9646); *UNCTAD Commodity Yearbook.*

The World Bank, 1818 H Street, NW, Washington, D.C. 20433 (202) 477-1234; *World Development Report;* and *World Development Indicators.*

PORTUGAL - FORESTRY AND FOREST PRODUCTS

American Forest and Paper Association, 1111 Nineteenth Street, NW, Washington, D.C. 20036 (202) 463-2700; *Wood Pulp and Fiber Statistics.*

Euromonitor International, Inc., 122 South Michigan Avenue, Suite 1200, Chicago, Illinois 60603 (800) 577-EURO;

European Marketing Data and Statistics.

Europa Publications Limited, 18 Bedford Square, London, WC1B 3JN, England; *The Europa World Year Book.*

European Commission Office of Press and Public Affairs, 2100 M Street, NW, Washington, D.C. 20037 (202) 862-9500; *Agriculture: Statistical Yearbook; Basic Statistics of the Community;* and *Industrial Production: Quarterly.*

Federal Statistical Office, Gustav - Stresemann - Ring 11, D-6200 Wiesbaden, Germany; *Portugal.*

Food and Agricultural Organization of the United Nations (FAO) Via delle Terme di Caracalla, 00100 Rome, Italy (Telephone Number in U.S. (202) 653-2400); *The State of Food and Agriculture;* and *Yearbook of Forest Products.*

M.E. Sharpe, 80 Business Park Drive, Armonk, New York 10504 (800) 541-6563; *The Illustrated Book of World Rankings.*

Organisation for Economic Co-operation and Development (OECD), 2 rue Andre-Pascal, 75 Paris 16, France (Telephone Number in U.S. (202) 785-6323); *Foreign Trade by Commodities; Indicators of Industrial Activity;* and *The Pulp and Paper Industry.*

St. Martin's Press, Inc., 175 Fifth Avenue, New York, New York 10010 (800) 221-7945; *The Statesman's Year-Book.*

Statistical Office of the United Nations, Publishing Service, New York, New York 10017 (800) 253-9646; *Statistical Yearbook;* and *Trends in Europe and North America: The Statistical Yearbook of the Economic Commission for Europe.*

United Nations Conference on Trade and Development, Central Statistical Service, Palais des Nations, Geneva, Switzerland (Telephone in U.S. (800) 253-9646); *UNCTAD Commodity Yearbook.*

United Nations Educational, Scientific and Cultural Organization (UNESCO), 7 Place de Fontenoy, F-75700 Paris, France (Telephone Number in U.S. (212) 963-5981); *Statistical Yearbook.*

The World Bank, 1818 H Street, NW, Washington, D.C. 20433 (202) 477-1234; *World Development Report.*

PORTUGAL - FRUIT PRODUCTION - See PORTUGAL - CROPS

PORTUGAL - FURNITURE AND WOOD PRODUCTS - EXPORTS AND IMPORTS

European Commission Office of Press and Public Affairs, 2100 M Street, NW,

Washington, D.C. 20037 (202) 862-9500; *Basic Statistics of the Community.*

Organisation for Economic Co-operation and Development (OECD), 2 rue Andre-Pascal, 75 Paris 16, France (Telephone Number in U.S. (202) 785-6323); *Foreign Trade by Commodities;* and *Industrial Structure Statistics.*

PORTUGAL - GAS AND GAS LIQUIDS PRODUCTION - See PORTUGAL - MINING AND MINERAL PRODUCTS

PORTUGAL - GENERAL INDUSTRIAL STATISTICS - See PORTUGAL - INDUSTRY

PORTUGAL - GENERAL MORTALITY - See PORTUGAL - MORTALITY

PORTUGAL - GEOGRAPHIC DATA

European Commission Office of Press and Public Affairs, 2100 M Street, NW, Washington, D.C. 20037 (202) 862-9500; *Basic Statistics of the Community.*

M.E. Sharpe, 80 Business Park Drive, Armonk, New York 10504 (800) 541-6563; *The Illustrated Book of World Rankings.*

PORTUGAL - GLASS AND GLASS PRODUCTS - PRODUCTION INDEX

Organisation for Economic Co-operation and Development (OECD), 2 rue Andre-Pascal, 75 Paris 16, France (Telephone Number in U.S. (202) 785-6323); *Indicators of Industrial Activity.*

PORTUGAL - GOATS - See PORTUGAL - LIVESTOCK AND POULTRY

PORTUGAL - GOLD HOLDINGS

International Monetary Fund, 700 Nineteenth Street, NW, Washington, D.C. 20431 (202) 623-7000; *International Financial Statistics.*

Statistical Office of the United Nations, Publishing Service, New York, New York 10017 (800) 253-9646; *Statistical Yearbook.*

The World Bank, 1818 H Street, NW, Washington, D.C. 20433 (202) 477-1234; *World Development Indicators.*

PORTUGAL - GOLD PRODUCTION AND CONSUMPTION - See PORTUGAL - MINING AND MINERAL PRODUCTS

PORTUGAL - GOVERNMENT

Central Intelligence Agency, Washington, D.C. 20505 (703) 482-1100, www.cia.gov; *The World Factbook.*

Europa Publications Limited, 18 Bedford Square, London, WC1B 3JN, England; *The Europa World Year Book.*

European Commission Office of Press and Public Affairs, 2100 M Street, NW, Washington, D.C. 20037 (202) 862-9500; *Basic Statistics of the Community.*

St. Martin's Press, Inc., 175 Fifth Avenue, New York, New York 10010 (800) 221-7945; *The Statesman's Year-Book.*

Statistical Office of the United Nations, Publishing Service, New York, New York 10017 (800) 253-9646; *National Accounts Statistics.*

The World Bank, 1818 H Street, NW, Washington, D.C. 20433 (202) 477-1234; *World Development Report.*

PORTUGAL - GOVERNMENT CONSUMPTION

European Commission Office of Press and Public Affairs, 2100 M Street, NW, Washington, D.C. 20037 (202) 862-9500; *Basic Statistics of the Community;* and *Government Financing of Research and Development.*

PORTUGAL - GOVERNMENT EXPENDITURES

International Monetary Fund, 700 Nineteenth Street, NW, Washington, D.C. 20431 (202) 623-7000; *Government Finance Statistics Yearbook.*

Organisation for Economic Co-operation and Development (OECD), 2 rue Andre-Pascal, 75 Paris 16, France (Telephone Number in U.S. (202) 785-6323); *Economic Outlook.*

The World Bank, 1818 H Street, NW, Washington, D.C. 20433 (202) 477-1234; *World Development Indicators.*

PORTUGAL - GOVERNMENT FINANCES

European Commission Office of Press and Public Affairs, 2100 M Street, NW, Washington, D.C. 20037 (202) 862-9500; *Basic Statistics of the Community; Government Financing of Research and Development;* and *Money and Finance.*

Organisation for Economic Co-operation and Development (OECD), 2 rue Andre-Pascal, 75 Paris 16, France (Telephone Number in U.S. (202) 785-6323); *Economic Outlook.*

Statistical Office of the United Nations, Publishing Service, New York, New York 10017 (800) 253-9646; *Statistical Yearbook.*

PORTUGAL - GOVERNMENT REVENUE

European Commission Office of Press and Public Affairs, 2100 M Street, NW, Washington, D.C. 20037 (202) 862-9500; *Basic Statistics of the Community;* and

Government Financing of Research and Development.

International Monetary Fund, 700 Nineteenth Street, NW, Washington, D.C. 20431 (202) 623-7000; *Government Finance Statistics Yearbook.*

Organisation for Economic Co-operation and Development (OECD), 2 rue Andre-Pascal, 75 Paris 16, France (Telephone Number in U.S. (202) 785-6323); *Economic Outlook;* and *Revenue Statistics of OECD Member Countries.*

The World Bank, 1818 H Street, NW, Washington, D.C. 20433 (202) 477-1234; *World Development Indicators.*

PORTUGAL - GRAIN PRODUCTION - See PORTUGAL - CROPS

PORTUGAL - GRANTS

International Monetary Fund, 700 Nineteenth Street, NW, Washington, D.C. 20431 (202) 623-7000; *Government Finance Statistics Yearbook.*

Organisation for Economic Co-operation and Development (OECD), 2 rue Andre-Pascal, 75 Paris 16, France (Telephone Number in U.S. (202) 785-6323); *Geographical Distribution of Financial Flows to Developing Countries.*

PORTUGAL - GROSS DOMESTIC PRODUCT

The Economist Intelligence Unit, 111 West 57th Street, New York, New York 10019 (800) 938-4685; *Portugal Country Report;* and *The World Market Atlas.*

Euromonitor International, Inc., 122 South Michigan Avenue, Suite 1200, Chicago, Illinois 60603 (800) 577-EURO; *The World Economic Factbook.*

Europa Publications Limited, 18 Bedford Square, London, WC1B 3JN, England; *The Europa World Year Book.*

European Commission Office of Press and Public Affairs, 2100 M Street, NW, Washington, D.C. 20037 (202) 862-9500; *Basic Statistics of the Community, Eurostatistics: Data for Short-Term Economic Analysis, Government Financing of Research and Development, Iron and Steel: Statistical Yearbook;* and *Money and Finance.*

M.E. Sharpe, 80 Business Park Drive, Armonk, New York 10504 (800) 541-6563; *The Illustrated Book of World Rankings.*

Organisation for Economic Co-operation and Development (OECD), 2 rue Andre-Pascal, 75 Paris 16, France (Telephone Number in U.S. (202) 785-6323); *Economic Outlook; Geographical*

Distribution of Financial Flows to Developing Countries; and *Revenue Statistics of OECD Member Countries.*

Statistical Office of the United Nations, Publishing Service, New York, New York 10017 (800) 253-9646; *Human Development Report; National Accounts Statistics; Statistical Yearbook;* and *Trends in Europe and North America: The Statistical Yearbook of the Economic Commission for Europe.*

The World Bank, 1818 H Street, NW, Washington, D.C. 20433 (202) 477-1234; *World Development Report;* and *World Development Indicators.*

PORTUGAL - GROSS INDUSTRIAL PRODUCT

European Commission Office of Press and Public Affairs, 2100 M Street, NW, Washington, D.C. 20037 (202) 862-9500; *Government Financing of Research and Development.*

PORTUGAL - GROSS NATIONAL PRODUCT

European Commission Office of Press and Public Affairs, 2100 M Street, NW, Washington, D.C. 20037 (202) 862-9500; *ACP: Basic Statistics;* and *Basic Statistics of the Community.*

Organisation for Economic Co-operation and Development (OECD), 2 rue Andre-Pascal, 75 Paris 16, France (Telephone Number in U.S. (202) 785-6323); *Economic Outlook;* and *Geographical Distribution of Financial Flows to Developing Countries.*

St. Martin's Press, Inc., 175 Fifth Avenue, New York, New York 10010 (800) 221-7945; *The Statesman's Year-Book.*

U.S. Arms Control and Disarmament Agency, 320 Twenty-first Street, NW, Washington, D.C. 20451 (202) 647-8677; *World Military Expenditures and Arms Transfers.*

The World Bank, 1818 H Street, NW, Washington, D.C. 20433 (202) 477-1234; *World Development Report;* and *World Development Indicators.*

PORTUGAL - HAZELNUT PRODUCTION - See PORTUGAL - CROPS

PORTUGAL - HEALTH

Euromonitor International, Inc., 122 South Michigan Avenue, Suite 1200, Chicago, Illinois 60603 (800) 577-EURO; *World Marketing Data and Statistics.*

European Commission Office of Press and Public Affairs, 2100 M Street, NW,

Washington, D.C. 20037 (202) 862-9500; *Basic Statistics of the Community;* and *Regions: Statistical Yearbook.*

Federal Statistical Office, Gustav - Stresemann - Ring 11, D-6200 Wiesbaden, Germany; *Portugal.*

International Monetary Fund, 700 Nineteenth Street, NW, Washington, D.C. 20431 (202) 623-7000; *Government Finance Statistics Yearbook.*

M.E. Sharpe, 80 Business Park Drive, Armonk, New York 10504 (800) 541-6563; *The Illustrated Book of World Rankings.*

Organisation for Economic Co-operation and Development (OECD), 2 rue Andre-Pascal, 75 Paris 16, France (Telephone Number in U.S. (202) 785-6323); *OECD Health Systems: Facts and Trends.*

St. Martin's Press, Inc., 175 Fifth Avenue, New York, New York 10010 (800) 221-7945; *The Statesman's Year-Book.*

Statistical Office of the United Nations, Publishing Service, New York, New York 10017 (800) 253-9646; *Human Development Report; Statistical Yearbook;* and *Trends in Europe and North America: The Statistical Yearbook of the Economic Commission for Europe.*

United Nations Children's Fund (UNICEF), 3 United Nations Plaza, New York, New York 10017 (800) 253-9646; *State of the World's Children.*

The World Bank, 1818 H Street, NW, Washington, D.C. 20433 (202) 477-1234; *World Development Report.*

World Health Organization, Office of Publications, 20 Avenue Appia, CH-1211 Geneva 27, Switzerland (Telephone Number in U.S. (518) 436-9686); *World Health Statistics Annual.*

PORTUGAL - HIDE PRODUCTION

Food and Agricultural Organization of the United Nations (FAO), Via delle Terme di Caracalla, 00100 Rome, Italy (Telephone Number in U.S. (202) 653-2400); *Production Yearbook.*

Organisation for Economic Co-operation and Development (OECD), 2 rue Andre-Pascal, 75 Paris 16, France (Telephone Number in U.S. (202) 785-6323); *The Footwear, Raw Hides and Skins, and Leather Industry in OECD Countries; Foreign Trade by Commodities;* and *Indicators of Industrial Activity.*

PORTUGAL - HIGHWAYS

Central Intelligence Agency,

Washington, D.C. 20505 (703) 482-1100, www.cia.gov; *The World Factbook.*

European Commission Office of Press and Public Affairs, 2100 M Street, NW, Washington, D.C. 20037 (202) 862-9500; *Basic Statistics of the Community;* and *Transport Annual Statistics.*

International Road Federation, 2600 Virginia Avenue, NW., Washington, D.C. 20037 (202) 338-4641; *World Road Statistics.*

St. Martin's Press, Inc., 175 Fifth Avenue, New York, New York 10010 (800) 221-7945; *The Statesman's Year-Book.*

Statistical Office of the United Nations, Publishing Service, New York, New York 10017 (800) 253-9646; *Trends in Europe and North America: The Statistical Yearbook of the Economic Commission for Europe.*

PORTUGAL - HOME FINANCE

Organisation for Economic Co-operation and Development (OECD), 2 rue Andre-Pascal, 75 Paris 16, France (Telephone Number in U.S. (202) 785-6323); *Main Economic Indicators - Historical Statistics.*

PORTUGAL - HORSES - See PORTUGAL - LIVESTOCK AND POULTRY

PORTUGAL - HOURS OF WORK - See PORTUGAL - EMPLOYMENT

PORTUGAL - HOUSING AND HOUSING UNITS

Euromonitor International, Inc., 122 South Michigan Avenue, Suite 1200, Chicago, Illinois 60603 (800) 577-EURO; *World Marketing Data and Statistics.*

European Commission Office of Press and Public Affairs, 2100 M Street, NW, Washington, D.C. 20037 (202) 862-9500; *Basic Statistics of the Community; Labor Force Sample Survey;* and *Regions: Statistical Yearbook.*

M.E. Sharpe, 80 Business Park Drive, Armonk, New York 10504 (800) 541-6563; *The Illustrated Book of World Rankings.*

Statistical Office of the United Nations, Publishing Service, New York, New York 10017 (800) 253-9646; *Trends in Europe and North America: The Statistical Yearbook of the Economic Commission for Europe.*

PORTUGAL - HOUSING CONSTRUCTION - See PORTUGAL - CONSTRUCTION INDUSTRY

PORTUGAL - HOUSING EXPENDITURES

European Commission Office of Press

and Public Affairs, 2100 M Street, NW, Washington, D.C. 20037 (202) 862-9500; *Basic Statistics of the Community.*

International Monetary Fund, 700 Nineteenth Street, NW, Washington, D.C. 20431 (202) 623-7000; *Government Finance Statistics Yearbook.*

PORTUGAL - HYDROCHLORIC ACID PRODUCTION

Statistical Office of the United Nations, Publishing Service, New York, New York 10017 (800) 253-9646; *Statistical Yearbook.*

PORTUGAL - ILLITERATE POPULATION

Central Intelligence Agency, Washington, D.C. 20505 (703) 482-1100, www.cia.gov; *The World Factbook.*

The Economist Intelligence Unit, 111 West 57th Street, New York, New York 10019 (800) 938-4685; *The World Market Atlas.*

Euromonitor International, Inc., 122 South Michigan Avenue, Suite 1200, Chicago, Illinois 60603 (800) 577-EURO; *The World Economic Factbook.*

St. Martin's Press, Inc., 175 Fifth Avenue, New York, New York 10010 (800) 221-7945; *The Statesman's Year-Book.*

Statistical Office of the United Nations, Publishing Service, New York, New York 10017 (800) 253-9646; *Human Development Report.*

PORTUGAL - IMPORTS

Central Intelligence Agency, Washington, D.C. 20505 (703) 482-1100, www.cia.gov; *The World Factbook.*

The Economist Intelligence Unit, 111 West 57th Street, New York, New York 10019 (800) 938-4685; *Portugal Country Report;* and *The World Market Atlas.*

Euromonitor International, Inc., 122 South Michigan Avenue, Suite 1200, Chicago, Illinois 60603 (800) 577-EURO; *The World Economic Factbook.*

Europa Publications Limited, 18 Bedford Square, London, WC1B 3JN, England; *The Europa World Year Book.*

European Commission Office of Press and Public Affairs, 2100 M Street, NW, Washington, D.C. 20037 (202) 862-9500; *Basic Statistics of the Community; Energy: Monthly Statistics; Energy Statistics Yearbook; Eurostatistics: Data for Short-Term Economic Analysis; External Trade: Statistical Yearbook; External Trade: Monthly Statistics;* and *Fisheries: Yearly Statistics.*

Food and Agricultural Organization of the United Nations (FAO) Via delle Terme di Caracalla, 00100 Rome, Italy (Telephone Number in U.S. (202) 653-2400); *The State of Food and Agriculture.*

International Monetary Fund, 700 Nineteenth Street, NW, Washington, D.C. 20431 (202) 623-7000; *Direction of Trade;* and *International Financial Statistics.*

Organisation for Economic Co-operation and Development (OECD), 2 rue Andre-Pascal, 75 Paris 16, France (Telephone Number in U.S. (202) 785-6323); *Economic Outlook, The Footwear, Raw Hides and Skins, and Leather Industry in OECD Countries; Industrial Structure Statistics; The Iron and Steel Industry; Milk, Milk Products, and Egg Balances in OECD Member Countries; The Pulp and Paper Industry; OECD Economic Surveys: Portugal;* and *Review of Fisheries in OECD Member Countries.*

St. Martin's Press, Inc., 175 Fifth Avenue, New York, New York 10010 (800) 221-7945; *The Statesman's Year-Book.*

Statistical Office of the United Nations, Publishing Service, New York, New York 10017 (800) 253-9646; *Trends in Europe and North America: The Statistical Yearbook of the Economic Commission for Europe.*

United Nations Conference on Trade and Development (UNCTAD), New York, New York 10017 (800) 253-9646; *Handbook of International Trade and Development Statistics.*

The World Bank, 1818 H Street, NW, Washington, D.C. 20433 (202) 477-1234; *World Development Report;* and *World Development Indicators.*

PORTUGAL - INCOME TAXES - See PORTUGAL - TAXATION

PORTUGAL - INDUSTRIAL ACID PRODUCTION

Statistical Office of the United Nations, Publishing Service, New York, New York 10017 (800) 253-9646; *Statistical Yearbook.*

PORTUGAL - INDUSTRY

Central Intelligence Agency, Washington, D.C. 20505 (703) 482-1100, www.cia.gov; *The World Factbook.*

Economist Intelligence Unit, 111 West 57th Street, New York, New York 10019 (800) 938-4685; *Portugal Country Report.*

Euromonitor International, Inc., 122 South Michigan Avenue, Suite 1200, Chicago, Illinois 60603 (800) 577-EURO; *The World Economic Factbook;* and *World Marketing Data and Statistics.*

Europa Publications Limited, 18 Bedford Square, London, WC1B 3JN, England; *The Europa World Year Book.*

European Commission Office of Press and Public Affairs, 2100 M Street, NW, Washington, D.C. 20037 (202) 862-9500; *Basic Statistics of the Community; Employment and Unemployment; Eurostatistics: Data for Short-Term Economic Analysis;* and *Labor Force Sample Survey.*

Federal Statistical Office, Gustav - Stresemann - Ring 11, D-6200 Wiesbaden, Germany; *Portugal.*

International Labour Office, I.L.O. Publications, 1828 L Street, NW, Suite 801, Washington, D.C. 20036 (301) 638-3152; *Yearbook of Labour Statistics.*

M.E. Sharpe, 80 Business Park Drive, Armonk, New York 10504 (800) 541-6563; *The Illustrated Book of World Rankings.*

Organisation for Economic Co-operation and Development (OECD), 2 rue Andre-Pascal, 75 Paris 16, France (Telephone Number in U.S. (202) 785-6323); *Economic Outlook; Indicators of Industrial Activity; Industrial Structure Statistics; Main Economic Indicators - Historical Statistics;* and *OECD Environmental Data.*

St. Martin's Press, Inc., 175 Fifth Avenue, New York, New York 10010 (800) 221-7945; *The Statesman's Year-Book.*

Statistical Office of the United Nations, Publishing Service, New York, New York 10017 (800) 253-9646; *Industrial Commodity Statistics Yearbook; Statistical Yearbook;* and *Trends in Europe and North America: The Statistical Yearbook of the Economic Commission for Europe.*

The World Bank, 1818 H Street, NW, Washington, D.C. 20433 (202) 477-1234; *World Development Indicators.*

World Intellectual Property Organization, 34 Chemin des Colombettes, CH-1211 Geneva 20, Switzerland; *Industrial Property Statistics.*

PORTUGAL - INFANT AND MATERNAL MORTALITY - See PORTUGAL - MORTALITY

PORTUGAL - INTEREST RATES

European Commission Office of Press and Public Affairs, 2100 M Street, NW, Washington, D.C. 20037 (202) 862-9500; *Money and Finance.*

Organisation for Economic Co-operation and Development (OECD), 2 rue Andre-Pascal, 75 Paris 16, France

(Telephone Number in U.S. (202) 785-6323); *Economic Outlook; Financial Market Trends;* and *OECD Financial Statistics.*

PORTUGAL - INTERNAL TRADE

European Commission Office of Press and Public Affairs, 2100 M Street, NW, Washington, D.C. 20037 (202) 862-9500; *Basic Statistics of the Community.*

Statistical Office of the United Nations, Publishing Service, New York, New York 10017 (800) 253-9646; *Statistical Yearbook.*

PORTUGAL - INTERNATIONAL FINANCE

European Commission Office of Press and Public Affairs, 2100 M Street, NW, Washington, D.C. 20037 (202) 862-9500; *Basic Statistics of the Community.*

Organisation for Economic Co-operation and Development (OECD), 2 rue Andre-Pascal, 75 Paris 16, France (Telephone Number in U.S. (202) 785-6323); *Economic Outlook;* and *Financial Market Trends.*

PORTUGAL - INTERNATIONAL LIQUIDITY

International Monetary Fund, 700 Nineteenth Street, NW, Washington, D.C. 20431 (202) 623-7000; *International Financial Statistics.*

Organisation for Economic Co-operation and Development (OECD), 2 rue Andre-Pascal, 75 Paris 16, France (Telephone Number in U.S. (202) 785-6323); *Economic Outlook;* and *Financial Market Trends.*

PORTUGAL - INTERNATIONAL RESERVES EXCLUDING GOLD

Statistical Office of the United Nations, Publishing Service, New York, New York 10017 (800) 253-9646; *Statistical Yearbook.*

The World Bank, 1818 H Street, NW, Washington, D.C. 20433 (202) 477-1234; *World Development Indicators.*

PORTUGAL - INTERNATIONAL STATISTICS

Organisation for Economic Co-operation and Development (OECD), 2 rue Andre-Pascal, 75 Paris 16, France (Telephone Number in U.S. (202) 785-6323); *Financial Market Trends;* and *Tourism Policy and International Tourism in OECD Member Countries.*

PORTUGAL - INVESTMENTS

International Monetary Fund, 700

Nineteenth Street, NW, Washington, D.C. 20431 (202) 623-7000; *International Financial Statistics.*

Organisation for Economic Co-operation and Development (OECD), 2 rue Andre-Pascal, 75 Paris 16, France (Telephone Number in U.S. (202) 785-6323); *Economic Outlook; Financial Market Trends; Industrial Structure Statistics; The Iron and Steel Industry;* and *Textile Industry in OECD Countries.*

PORTUGAL - IRON ORE PRODUCTION AND CONSUMPTION - See PORTUGAL - MINING AND MINERAL PRODUCTS

PORTUGAL - LABOR

Central Intelligence Agency, Washington, D.C. 20505 (703) 482-1100, www.cia.gov; *The World Factbook.*

Euromonitor International, Inc., 122 South Michigan Avenue, Suite 1200, Chicago, Illinois 60603 (800) 577-EURO; *World Marketing Data and Statistics.*

Europa Publications Limited, 18 Bedford Square, London, WC1B 3JN, England; *The Europa World Year Book.*

European Commission Office of Press and Public Affairs, 2100 M Street, NW, Washington, D.C. 20037 (202) 862-9500; *Basic Statistics of the Community; Labor Force Sample Survey;* and *Regions: Statistical Yearbook.*

Food and Agricultural Organization of the United Nations (FAO) Via delle Terme di Caracalla, 00100 Rome, Italy (Telephone Number in U.S. (202) 653-2400); *The State of Food and Agriculture.*

International Labour Office, I.L.O. Publications, 1828 L Street, NW, Suite 801, Washington, D.C. 20036 (301) 638-3152; *Yearbook of Labour Statistics.*

M.E. Sharpe, 80 Business Park Drive, Armonk, New York 10504 (800) 541-6563; *The Illustrated Book of World Rankings.*

Organisation for Economic Co-operation and Development (OECD), 2 rue Andre-Pascal, 75 Paris 16, France (Telephone Number in U.S. (202) 785-6323); *Economic Outlook, The Iron and Steel Industry, Maritime Transport, OECD Economic Surveys: Portugal, OECD Employment Outlook;* and *Textile Industry in OECD Countries.*

St. Martin's Press, Inc., 175 Fifth Avenue, New York, New York 10010 (800) 221-7945; *The Statesman's Year-Book.*

Statistical Office of the United Nations, Publishing Service, New York, New York 10017 (800) 253-9646; *Human*

Development Report.

The World Bank, 1818 H Street, NW, Washington, D.C. 20433 (202) 477-1234; *World Development Report;* and *World Development Indicators.*

PORTUGAL - LAND USE

Central Intelligence Agency, Washington, D.C. 20505 (703) 482-1100, www.cia.gov; *The World Factbook.*

Euromonitor International, Inc., 122 South Michigan Avenue, Suite 1200, Chicago, Illinois 60603 (800) 577-EURO; *European Marketing Data and Statistics.*

European Commission Office of Press and Public Affairs, 2100 M Street, NW, Washington, D.C. 20037 (202) 862-9500; *Agriculture: Statistical Yearbook; Basic Statistics of the Community; Crop Production: Quarterly Statistics;* and *Regions: Statistical Yearbook.*

Food and Agricultural Organization of the United Nations (FAO), Via delle Terme di Caracalla, 00100 Rome, Italy (Telephone Number in U.S. (202) 653-2400); *Production Yearbook.*

The World Bank, 1818 H Street, NW, Washington, D.C. 20433 (202) 477-1234; *World Development Report.*

PORTUGAL - LEAD AND LEAD ORE PRODUCTION AND CONSUMPTION - See PORTUGAL - MINING AND MINERAL PRODUCTS

PORTUGAL - LEATHER - PRODUCTION INDEX

Organisation for Economic Co-operation and Development (OECD), 2 rue Andre-Pascal, 75 Paris 16, France (Telephone Number in U.S. (202) 785-6323); *Indicators of Industrial Activity.*

PORTUGAL - LEATHER AND FOOTWEAR EXPORTS AND IMPORTS

European Commission Office of Press and Public Affairs, 2100 M Street, NW, Washington, D.C. 20037 (202) 862-9500; *Basic Statistics of the Community.*

Organisation for Economic Co-operation and Development (OECD), 2 rue Andre-Pascal, 75 Paris 16, France (Telephone Number in U.S. (202) 785-6323); *The Footwear, Raw Hides and Skins, and Leather Industry in OECD Countries.*

PORTUGAL - LIBRARIES

Euromonitor International, Inc., 122 South Michigan Avenue, Suite 1200, Chicago, Illinois 60603 (800) 577-EURO;

European Marketing Data and Statistics.

M.E. Sharpe, 80 Business Park Drive, Armonk, New York 10504 (800) 541-6563; *The Illustrated Book of World Rankings.*

Statistical Office of the United Nations, Publishing Service, New York, New York 10017 (800) 253-9646; *Trends in Europe and North America: The Statistical Yearbook of the Economic Commission for Europe.*

United Nations Educational, Scientific and Cultural Organization (UNESCO), 7 Place de Fontenoy, F-75700 Paris, France (Telephone Number in U.S. (212) 963-5981); *Statistical Yearbook.*

PORTUGAL - LIFE EXPECTANCY

Central Intelligence Agency, Washington, D.C. 20505 (703) 482-1100, www.cia.gov; *The World Factbook.*

Euromonitor International, Inc., 122 South Michigan Avenue, Suite 1200, Chicago, Illinois 60603 (800) 577-EURO; *The World Economic Factbook.*

Organisation for Economic Co-operation and Development (OECD), 2 rue Andre-Pascal, 75 Paris 16, France (Telephone Number in U.S. (202) 785-6323); *Economic Outlook.*

St. Martin's Press, Inc., 175 Fifth Avenue, New York, New York 10010 (800) 221-7945; *The Statesman's Year-Book.*

Statistical Office of the United Nations, Publishing Service, New York, New York 10017 (800) 253-9646; *Human Development Report; Trends in Europe and North America: The Statistical Yearbook of the Economic Commission for Europe;* and *World Statistics Pocketbook.*

The World Bank, 1818 H Street, NW, Washington, D.C. 20433 (202) 477-1234; *World Development Report.*

PORTUGAL - LIGNITE PRODUCTION - See PORTUGAL - MINING AND MINERAL PRODUCTS

PORTUGAL - LITERACY RATE

Euromonitor International, Inc., 122 South Michigan Avenue, Suite 1200, Chicago, Illinois 60603 (800) 577-EURO; *World Marketing Data and Statistics.*

PORTUGAL - LIVESTOCK AND POULTRY

Euromonitor International, Inc., 122 South Michigan Avenue, Suite 1200, Chicago, Illinois 60603 (800) 577-EURO; *European Marketing Data and Statistics.*

Europa Publications Limited, 18 Bedford Square, London, WC1B 3JN,

England; *The Europa World Year Book.*

European Commission Office of Press and Public Affairs, 2100 M Street, NW, Washington, D.C. 20037 (202) 862-9500; *Agriculture: Statistical Yearbook; Basic Statistics of the Community; Eurostatistics: Data for Short-Term Economic Analysis;* and *Regions: Statistical Yearbook.*

Food and Agricultural Organization of the United Nations (FAO), Via delle Terme di Caracalla, 00100 Rome, Italy (Telephone Number in U.S. (202) 653-2400); *Production Yearbook,* and *The State of Food and Agriculture.*

M.E. Sharpe, 80 Business Park Drive, Armonk, New York 10504 (800) 541-6563; *The Illustrated Book of World Rankings.*

Organisation for Economic Co-operation and Development (OECD), 2 rue Andre-Pascal, 75 Paris 16, France (Telephone Number in U.S. (202) 785-6323); *Economic Accounts for Agriculture;* and *Meat Balances in OECD Member Countries.*

St. Martin's Press, Inc., 175 Fifth Avenue, New York, New York 10010 (800) 221-7945; *The Statesman's Year-Book.*

Statistical Office of the United Nations, Publishing Service, New York, New York 10017 (800) 253-9646; *Statistical Yearbook.*

United Nations Conference on Trade and Development, Central Statistical Service, Palais des Nations, Geneva, Switzerland (Telephone in U.S. (800) 253-9646); *UNCTAD Commodity Yearbook.*

PORTUGAL - LIVING LEVELS - See PORTUGAL - LIFE EXPECTANCY

PORTUGAL - MACHINERY - PRODUCTION INDEX

Organisation for Economic Co-operation and Development (OECD), 2 rue Andre-Pascal, 75 Paris 16, France (Telephone Number in U.S. (202) 785-6323); *Indicators of Industrial Activity.*

PORTUGAL - MAGNESIUM PRODUCTION AND CONSUMPTION - See PORTUGAL - MINING AND MINERAL PRODUCTS

PORTUGAL - MAIL - NUMBER OF PIECES SENT OR RECEIVED

European Commission Office of Press and Public Affairs, 2100 M Street, NW, Washington, D.C. 20037 (202) 862-9500; *Transport Annual Statistics.*

Statistical Office of the United Nations, Publishing Service, New York, New York 10017 (800) 253-9646; *Statistical Yearbook.*

PORTUGAL - MAIN ECONOMIC INDICATORS - See PORTUGAL - ECONOMY

PORTUGAL - MANGANESE AND MANGANESE ORE PRODUCTION AND CONSUMPTION - See PORTUGAL - MINING AND MINERAL PRODUCTS

PORTUGAL - MANUFACTURING

European Commission Office of Press and Public Affairs, 2100 M Street, NW, Washington, D.C. 20037 (202) 862-9500; *Basic Statistics of the Community; Eurostatistics: Data for Short-Term Economic Analysis;* and *Industrial Production: Quarterly.*

M.E. Sharpe, 80 Business Park Drive, Armonk, New York 10504 (800) 541-6563; *The Illustrated Book of World Rankings.*

Organisation for Economic Co-operation and Development (OECD), 2 rue Andre-Pascal, 75 Paris 16, France (Telephone Number in U.S. (202) 785-6323); *Foreign Trade by Commodities; Indicators of Industrial Activity; Indicators of Industrial Activity; Industrial Structure Statistics; OECD Economic Surveys: Portugal;* and *Statistical Yearbook.*

Statistical Office of the United Nations, Publishing Service, New York, New York 10017 (800) 253-9646; *Statistical Yearbook.*

The World Bank, 1818 H Street, NW, Washington, D.C. 20433 (202) 477-1234; *World Development Indicators.*

PORTUGAL - MARRIAGE RATES

Europa Publications Limited, 18 Bedford Square, London, WC1B 3JN, England; *The Europa World Year Book.*

European Commission Office of Press and Public Affairs, 2100 M Street, NW, Washington, D.C. 20037 (202) 862-9500; *Basic Statistics of the Community.*

M.E. Sharpe, 80 Business Park Drive, Armonk, New York 10504 (800) 541-6563; *The Illustrated Book of World Rankings.*

Statistical Office of the United Nations, Publishing Service, New York, New York 10017 (800) 253-9646; *Demographic Yearbook; Statistical Yearbook;* and *Trends in Europe and North America: The Statistical Yearbook of the Economic Commission for Europe.*

PORTUGAL - MEAT PRODUCTION - See PORTUGAL - LIVESTOCK AND POULTRY

PORTUGAL - MERCHANT SHIPPING

Europa Publications Limited, 18 Bedford Square, London, WC1B 3JN, England; *The Europa World Year Book.*

European Commission Office of Press and Public Affairs, 2100 M Street, NW, Washington, D.C. 20037 (202) 862-9500; *Basic Statistics of the Community; Fisheries: Yearly Statistics; Regions: Statistical Yearbook;* and *Transport Annual Statistics.*

Lloyd's Register of Shipping, 17 Battery Place, New York, New York 10004 (212) 425-8050; *Register of Ships.*

Organisation for Economic Co-operation and Development (OECD), 2 rue Andre-Pascal, 75 Paris 16, France (Telephone Number in U.S. (202) 785-6323); *Maritime Transport.*

St. Martin's Press, Inc., 175 Fifth Avenue, New York, New York 10010 (800) 221-7945; *The Statesman's Year-Book.*

Statistical Office of the United Nations, Publishing Service, New York, New York 10017 (800) 253-9646; *Statistical Yearbook.*

U.S. Department of Transportation, Maritime Administration, 400 Seventh Street, SW, Washington, D.C. 20590 (202) 366-5807, www.marad.dot.gov; *A Statistical Analysis of the World's Merchant Fleets.*

PORTUGAL - MERCURY PRODUCTION AND CONSUMPTION - See PORTUGAL - MINING AND MINERAL PRODUCTS

PORTUGAL - MILITARY

Central Intelligence Agency, Washington, D.C. 20505 (703) 482-1100, www.cia.gov; *The World Factbook.*

Euromonitor International, Inc., 122 South Michigan Avenue, Suite 1200, Chicago, Illinois 60603 (800) 577-EURO; *World Marketing Data and Statistics.*

European Commission Office of Press and Public Affairs, 2100 M Street, NW, Washington, D.C. 20037 (202) 862-9500; *Government Financing of Research and Development.*

The International Institute for Strategic Studies, 23 Tavistock Street, London WC2E 7NQ, England 44 171 3797676; *The Military Balance.*

International Monetary Fund, 700 Nineteenth Street, NW, Washington, D.C. 20431 (202) 623-7000; *Government Finance Statistics Yearbook.*

St. Martin's Press, Inc., 175 Fifth Avenue, New York, New York 10010 (800) 221-7945; *The Statesman's Year-Book.*

Statistical Office of the United Nations, Publishing Service, New York, New York 10017 (800) 253-9646; *Human Development Report.*

U.S. Arms Control and Disarmament Agency, 320 Twenty-first Street, NW, Washington, D.C. 20451 (202) 647-8677; *World Military Expenditures and Arms Transfers.*

PORTUGAL - MILK PRODUCTION - See PORTUGAL - DAIRY PRODUCTS

PORTUGAL - MILLET PRODUCTION - See PORTUGAL - CROPS

PORTUGAL - MINING AND MINERAL PRODUCTS

Commodity Research Bureau, Inc., 30 South Wacker Drive, Chicago Illinois 60606 (312) 454-1801; *Commodity Year Book.*

Europa Publications Limited, 18 Bedford Square, London, WC1B 3JN, England; *The Europa World Year Book.*

European Commission Office of Press and Public Affairs, 2100 M Street, NW, Washington, D.C. 20037 (202) 862-9500; *ACP: Basic Statistics; Basic Statistics of the Community; Energy: Monthly Statistics; Energy Statistics Yearbook; Eurostatistics: Data for Short-Term Economic Analysis; Industrial Production: Quarterly; Iron and Steel: Statistical Yearbook; Labor Force Sample Survey;* and *Regions: Statistical Yearbook.*

Food and Agricultural Organization of the United Nations (FAO), Via delle Terme di Caracalla, 00100 Rome, Italy (Telephone Number in U.S. (202) 653-2400); *Production Yearbook.*

M.E. Sharpe, 80 Business Park Drive, Armonk, New York 10504 (800) 541-6563; *The Illustrated Book of World Rankings.*

Organisation for Economic Co-operation and Development (OECD), 2 rue Andre-Pascal, 75 Paris 16, France (Telephone Number in U.S. (202) 785-6323); *Coal Information; Energy Statistics of OECD Countries; Foreign Trade by Commodities; Indicators of Industrial Activity; Industrial Structure Statistics; The Iron and Steel Industry; The Non-Ferrous Metals Industry;* and *OECD Economic Surveys: Portugal.*

St. Martin's Press, Inc., 175 Fifth Avenue, New York, New York 10010 (800) 221-7945; *The Statesman's Year-Book.*

Statistical Office of the United Nations, Publishing Service, New York, New York 10017 (800) 253-9646; *Statistical Yearbook.*

United Nations Conference on Trade and Development, Central Statistical Service, Palais des Nations, Geneva, Switzerland (Telephone in U.S. (800) 253-9646); *UNCTAD Commodity Yearbook.*

PORTUGAL - MOLYBDENUM AND MOLYBDENUM ORE PRODUCTION AND CONSUMPTION - See PORTUGAL - MINING AND MINERAL PRODUCTS

PORTUGAL - MONEY AND CREDIT

Organisation for Economic Co-operation and Development (OECD), 2 rue Andre-Pascal, 75 Paris 16, France (Telephone Number in U.S. (202) 785-6323); *OECD Economic Surveys: Portugal.*

PORTUGAL - MONEY EXCHANGE RATE - See PORTUGAL - EXCHANGE RATES

PORTUGAL - MONEY RATES - MARKET

European Commission Office of Press and Public Affairs, 2100 M Street, NW, Washington, D.C. 20037 (202) 862-9500; *Basic Statistics of the Community.*

Organisation for Economic Co-operation and Development (OECD), 2 rue Andre-Pascal, 75 Paris 16, France (Telephone Number in U.S. (202) 785-6323); *Economic Outlook;* and *Financial Market Trends.*

PORTUGAL - MONEY RESERVES

European Commission Office of Press and Public Affairs, 2100 M Street, NW, Washington, D.C. 20037 (202) 862-9500; *Basic Statistics of the Community.*

Organisation for Economic Co-operation and Development (OECD), 2 rue Andre-Pascal, 75 Paris 16, France (Telephone Number in U.S. (202) 785-6323); *Economic Outlook;* and *Financial Market Trends.*

PORTUGAL - MONEY SUPPLY

Economist Intelligence Unit, 111 West 57th Street, New York, New York 10019 (800) 938-4685; *Portugal Country Report.*

Europa Publications Limited, 18 Bedford Square, London, WC1B 3JN, England; *The Europa World Year Book.*

European Commission Office of Press and Public Affairs, 2100 M Street, NW, Washington, D.C. 20037 (202) 862-9500; *Basic Statistics of the Community; Eurostatistics: Data for Short-Term Economic Analysis;* and *Money and Finance.*

International Monetary Fund, 700 Nineteenth Street, NW, Washington, D.C. 20431 (202) 623-7000; *International Financial Statistics.*

Organisation for Economic Co-operation and Development (OECD), 2 rue Andre-Pascal, 75 Paris 16, France

(Telephone Number in U.S. (202) 785-6323); *Economic Outlook.*

Statistical Office of the United Nations, Publishing Service, New York, New York 10017 (800) 253-9646; *Statistical Yearbook.*

The World Bank, 1818 H Street, NW, Washington, D.C. 20433 (202) 477-1234; *World Development Indicators.*

PORTUGAL - MORTALITY

Central Intelligence Agency, Washington, D.C. 20505 (703) 482-1100, www.cia.gov; *The World Factbook.*

Euromonitor International, Inc., 122 South Michigan Avenue, Suite 1200, Chicago, Illinois 60603 (800) 577-EURO; *The World Economic Factbook.*

Europa Publications Limited, 18 Bedford Square, London, WC1B 3JN, England; *The Europa World Year Book.*

European Commission Office of Press and Public Affairs, 2100 M Street, NW, Washington, D.C. 20037 (202) 862-9500; *Basic Statistics of the Community;* and *Demographic Statistics.*

St. Martin's Press, Inc., 175 Fifth Avenue, New York, New York 10010 (800) 221-7945; *The Statesman's Year-Book.*

Statistical Office of the United Nations, Publishing Service, New York, New York 10017 (800) 253-9646; *Demographic Yearbook; Human Development Report; Statistical Yearbook; Trends in Europe and North America: The Statistical Yearbook of the Economic Commission for Europe;* and *World Statistics Pocketbook.*

United Nations Children's Fund (UNICEF), 3 United Nations Plaza, New York, New York 10017 (800) 253-9646; *State of the World's Children.*

The World Bank, 1818 H Street, NW, Washington, D.C. 20433 (202) 477-1234; *World Development Report;* and *World Development Indicators.*

World Health Organization, Office of Publications, 20 Avenue Appia, CH-1211 Geneva 27, Switzerland (Telephone Number in U.S. (518) 436-9686); *World Health Statistics Annual.*

PORTUGAL - MOTION PICTURES

St. Martin's Press, Inc., 175 Fifth Avenue, New York, New York 10010 (800) 221-7945; *The Statesman's Year-Book.*

Statistical Office of the United Nations, Publishing Service, New York, New York 10017 (800) 253-9646; *Statistical Yearbook.*

United Nations Educational, Scientific and Cultural Organization (UNESCO), 7 Place de Fontenoy, F-75700 Paris, France (Telephone Number in U.S. (212) 963-5981); *Statistical Yearbook.*

PORTUGAL - MOTOR VEHICLE PRODUCTION

European Commission Office of Press and Public Affairs, 2100 M Street, NW, Washington, D.C. 20037 (202) 862-9500; *Basic Statistics of the Community;* and *Eurostatistics: Data for Short-Term Economic Analysis.*

Organisation for Economic Co-operation and Development (OECD), 2 rue Andre-Pascal, 75 Paris 16, France (Telephone Number in U.S. (202) 785-6323); *Foreign Trade by Commodities;* and *Indicators of Industrial Activity.*

Statistical Office of the United Nations, Publishing Service, New York, New York 10017 (800) 253-9646; *Statistical Yearbook.*

PORTUGAL - MOTOR VEHICLE TAXES - See PORTUGAL - TAXATION

PORTUGAL - MOTOR VEHICLES IN USE

Europa Publications Limited, 18 Bedford Square, London, WC1B 3JN, England; *The Europa World Year Book.*

European Commission Office of Press and Public Affairs, 2100 M Street, NW, Washington, D.C. 20037 (202) 862-9500; *Basic Statistics of the Community;* and *Transport Annual Statistics.*

International Road Federation, 2600 Virginia Avenue, NW., Washington, D.C. 20037 (202) 338-4641; *World Road Statistics.*

Statistical Office of the United Nations, Publishing Service, New York, New York 10017 (800) 253-9646; *Statistical Yearbook.*

PORTUGAL - MULES - See PORTUGAL - LIVESTOCK AND POULTRY

PORTUGAL - MUSEUMS

Euromonitor International, Inc., 122 South Michigan Avenue, Suite 1200, Chicago, Illinois 60603 (800) 577-EURO; *European Marketing Data and Statistics.*

M.E. Sharpe, 80 Business Park Drive, Armonk, New York 10504 (800) 541-6563; *The Illustrated Book of World Rankings.*

United Nations Educational, Scientific and Cultural Organization (UNESCO), 7 Place de Fontenoy, F-75700 Paris, France (Telephone Number in U.S. (212) 963-5981); *Statistical Yearbook.*

PORTUGAL - NATALITY - See PORTUGAL - BIRTH RATES

PORTUGAL - NATIONAL ACCOUNTS

Europa Publications Limited, 18 Bedford Square, London, WC1B 3JN, England; *The Europa World Year Book.*

European Commission Office of Press and Public Affairs, 2100 M Street, NW, Washington, D.C. 20037 (202) 862-9500; *Basic Statistics of the Community;* and *Eurostatistics: Data for Short-Term Economic Analysis.*

Federal Statistical Office, Gustav - Stresemann - Ring 11, D-6200 Wiesbaden, Germany; *Portugal.*

Organisation for Economic Co-operation and Development (OECD), 2 rue Andre-Pascal, 75 Paris 16, France (Telephone Number in U.S. (202) 785-6323); *Economic Outlook.*

Statistical Office of the United Nations, Publishing Service, New York, New York 10017 (800) 253-9646; *National Accounts Statistics,;* and *Statistical Yearbook.*

PORTUGAL - NATIONAL INCOME

M.E. Sharpe, 80 Business Park Drive, Armonk, New York 10504 (800) 541-6563; *The Illustrated Book of World Rankings.*

Organisation for Economic Co-operation and Development (OECD), 2 rue Andre-Pascal, 75 Paris 16, France (Telephone Number in U.S. (202) 785-6323); *Economic Outlook.*

Statistical Office of the United Nations, Publishing Service, New York, New York 10017 (800) 253-9646; *National Accounts Statistics;* and *Statistical Yearbook.*

PORTUGAL - NATIONAL PRODUCT

European Commission Office of Press and Public Affairs, 2100 M Street, NW, Washington, D.C. 20037 (202) 862-9500; *Basic Statistics of the Community.*

M.E. Sharpe, 80 Business Park Drive, Armonk, New York 10504 (800) 541-6563; *The Illustrated Book of World Rankings.*

Organisation for Economic Co-operation and Development (OECD), 2 rue Andre-Pascal, 75 Paris 16, France (Telephone Number in U.S. (202) 785-6323); *Economic Outlook.*

Statistical Office of the United Nations, Publishing Service, New York, New York 10017 (800) 253-9646; *Statistical Yearbook.*

PORTUGAL - NATURAL GAS PRODUCTION - See PORTUGAL - MINING

AND MINERAL PRODUCTS

PORTUGAL - NEWSPAPER PRODUC-
TION - See PORTUGAL - FORESTRY AND
FOREST PRODUCTS

PORTUGAL - NEWSPRINT PRODUCTION
AND CONSUMPTION - See PORTUGAL -
FORESTRY AND FOREST PRODUCTS

PORTUGAL - NICKEL AND NICKEL ORE
PRODUCTION AND CONSUMPTION - See
PORTUGAL - MINING AND MINERAL
PRODUCTS

PORTUGAL - NITRIC ACID PRODUCTION -
See PORTUGAL - MINING AND MINERAL
PRODUCTS

PORTUGAL - OATS PRODUCTION - See
PORTUGAL - CROPS

PORTUGAL - OIL PRODUCING CROPS

European Commission Office of Press
and Public Affairs, 2100 M Street, NW,
Washington, D.C. 20037 (202) 862-9500;
Basic Statistics of the Community.

Organisation for Economic Co-
operation and Development (OECD), 2 rue
Andre-Pascal, 75 Paris 16, France
(Telephone Number in U.S. (202) 785-
6323); *Foreign Trade by Commodities.*

PORTUGAL - PAPER - See PORTUGAL -
FORESTRY AND FOREST PRODUCTS

PORTUGAL - PATENTS, TRADEMARKS AND
SERVICE MARKS

Statistical Office of the United Nations,
Publishing Service, New York, New York
10017 (800) 253-9646; *Statistical Yearbook.*

World Intellectual Property
Organization, 34 Chemin des Colombettes,
CH-1211 Geneva 20, Switzerland; *Industrial
Property Statistics.*

PORTUGAL - PEANUT PRODUCTION - See
PORTUGAL - CROPS

PORTUGAL - PERIODICALS

United Nations Educational, Scientific
and Cultural Organization (UNESCO), 7
Place de Fontenoy, F-75700 Paris, France
(Telephone Number in U.S. (212) 963-
5981); *Statistical Yearbook.*

PORTUGAL - PESTICIDE USE

Food and Agricultural Organization of
the United Nations (FAO) Via delle Terme
di Caracalla, 00100 Rome, Italy (Telephone
Number in U.S. (202) 653-2400); *The State
of Food and Agriculture.*

PORTUGAL - PETROLEUM INDUSTRY

Euromonitor International, Inc., 122
South Michigan Avenue, Suite 1200,
Chicago, Illinois 60603 (800) 577-EURO;
European Marketing Data and Statistics.

European Commission Office of Press
and Public Affairs, 2100 M Street, NW,
Washington, D.C. 20037 (202) 862-9500;
*ACP: Basic Statistics; Basic Statistics of the
Community;* and *Energy Statistics
Yearbook.*

Food and Agricultural Organization of
the United Nations (FAO) Via delle Terme
di Caracalla, 00100 Rome, Italy (Telephone
Number in U.S. (202) 653-2400); *The State
of Food and Agriculture.*

M.E. Sharpe, 80 Business Park Drive,
Armonk, New York 10504 (800) 541-6563;
The Illustrated Book of World Rankings.

Organisation for Economic Co-
operation and Development (OECD), 2 rue
Andre-Pascal, 75 Paris 16, France
(Telephone Number in U.S. (202) 785-
6323); *Energy Statistics of OECD Countries;
Foreign Trade by Commodities; Indicators
of Industrial Activity;* and *Oil and Gas
Information.*

Statistical Office of the United Nations,
Publishing Service, New York, New York
10017 (800) 253-9646; *Statistical Yearbook;*
and *Trends in Europe and North America:
The Statistical Yearbook of the Economic
Commission for Europe.*

United Nations Conference on Trade
and Development, Central Statistical
Service, Palais des Nations, Geneva,
Switzerland (Telephone in U.S. (800) 253-
9646); *UNCTAD Commodity Yearbook.*

PORTUGAL - PHOSPHATE ROCK
PRODUCTION - See PORTUGAL - MINING
AND MINERAL PRODUCTS

PORTUGAL - PHOSPHATES
PRODUCTION - See PORTUGAL - MINING
AND MINERAL PRODUCTS

PORTUGAL - PIG-IRON AND
FERRO-ALLOY PRODUCTION - See
PORTUGAL - MINING AND MINERAL
PRODUCTS

PORTUGAL - PIGS - See PORTUGAL -
LIVESTOCK AND POULTRY

PORTUGAL - PLASTIC RESIN PRODUCTION

Organisation for Economic Co-
operation and Development (OECD), 2 rue
Andre-Pascal, 75 Paris 16, France
(Telephone Number in U.S. (202) 785-
6323); *Foreign Trade by Commodities.*

Statistical Office of the United Nations,
Publishing Service, New York, New York
10017 (800) 253-9646; *Statistical Yearbook.*

PORTUGAL - PLATINUM PRODUCTION -
See PORTUGAL - MINING AND MINERAL
PRODUCTS

PORTUGAL - POPULATION

Central Intelligence Agency,
Washington, D.C. 20505 (703) 482-1100,
www.cia.gov; *The World Factbook.*

The Economist Intelligence Unit, 111
West 57th Street, New York, New York
10019 (800) 938-4685; *Portugal Country
Report;* and *The World Market Atlas.*

Euromonitor International, Inc., 122
South Michigan Avenue, Suite 1200,
Chicago, Illinois 60603 (800) 577-EURO;
European Marketing Data and Statistics;
and *The World Economic Factbook.*

Europa Publications Limited, 18
Bedford Square, London, WC1B 3JN,
England; *The Europa World Year Book.*

European Commission Office of Press
and Public Affairs, 2100 M Street, NW,
Washington, D.C. 20037 (202) 862-9500;
*ACP: Basic Statistics; Basic Statistics of the
Community; Demographic Statistics;
Employment and Unemployment;
Fisheries: Yearly Statistics; Iron and Steel:
Statistical Yearbook; Labor Force Sample
Survey;* and *Regions: Statistical Yearbook.*

Federal Statistical Office, Gustav -
Stresemann - Ring 11, D-6200 Wiesbaden,
Germany; *Portugal.*

Food and Agricultural Organization of
the United Nations (FAO), Via delle Terme
di Caracalla, 00100 Rome, Italy (Telephone
Number in U.S. (202) 653-2400);
Production Yearbook.

International Labour Office,
I.L.O. Publications, 1828 L Street, NW, Suite
801, Washington, D.C. 20036 (301) 638-
3152; *Yearbook of Labour Statistics.*

M.E. Sharpe, 80 Business Park Drive,
Armonk, New York 10504 (800) 541-6563;
The Illustrated Book of World Rankings.

St. Martin's Press, Inc., 175 Fifth
Avenue, New York, New York 10010 (800)
221-7945; *The Statesman's Year-Book.*

Statistical Office of the United Nations,
Publishing Service, New York, New York
10017 (800) 253-9646; *Demographic
Yearbook; Human Development Report;
Statistical Yearbook; Trends in Europe and
North America: The Statistical Yearbook of
the Economic Commission for Europe;* and
World Statistics Pocketbook.

United Nations Educational, Scientific
and Cultural Organization (UNESCO), 7
Place de Fontenoy, F-75700 Paris, France
(Telephone Number in U.S. (212) 963-

5981); *Statistical Yearbook.*

U.S. Arms Control and Disarmament Agency, 320 Twenty-first Street, NW, Washington, D.C. 20451 (202) 647-8677; *World Military Expenditures and Arms Transfers.*

The World Bank, 1818 H Street, NW, Washington, D.C. 20433 (202) 477-1234; *World Development Report.*

World Health Organization, Office of Publications, 20 Avenue Appia, CH-1211 Geneva 27, Switzerland (Telephone Number in U.S. (518) 436-9686); *World Health Statistics Annual.*

PORTUGAL - POST OFFICES

M.E. Sharpe, 80 Business Park Drive, Armonk, New York 10504 (800) 541-6563; *The Illustrated Book of World Rankings.*

St. Martin's Press, Inc., 175 Fifth Avenue, New York, New York 10010 (800) 221-7945; *The Statesman's Year-Book.*

Statistical Office of the United Nations, Publishing Service, New York, New York 10017 (800) 253-9646; *Trends in Europe and North America: The Statistical Yearbook of the Economic Commission for Europe.*

PORTUGAL - POTATO PRODUCTION - See PORTUGAL - CROPS

PORTUGAL - POWER PRODUCTION INDUSTRY - EMPLOYMENT

European Commission Office of Press and Public Affairs, 2100 M Street, NW, Washington, D.C. 20037 (202) 862-9500; *Basic Statistics of the Community.*

Statistical Office of the United Nations, Publishing Service, New York, New York 10017 (800) 253-9646; *Statistical Yearbook.*

PORTUGAL - PRICES

European Commission Office of Press and Public Affairs, 2100 M Street, NW, Washington, D.C. 20037 (202) 862-9500; *Basic Statistics of the Community, Eurostatistics: Data for Short-Term Economic Analysis.*

Food and Agricultural Organization of the United Nations (FAO), Via delle Terme di Caracalla, 00100 Rome, Italy (Telephone Number in U.S. (202) 653-2400); *Production Yearbook;* and *The State of Food and Agriculture.*

International Labour Office, I.L.O. Publications, 1828 L Street, NW, Suite 801, Washington, D.C. 20036 (301) 638-3152; *Yearbook of Labour Statistics.*

International Monetary Fund, 700

Nineteenth Street, NW, Washington, D.C. 20431 (202) 623-7000; *International Financial Statistics.*

M.E. Sharpe, 80 Business Park Drive, Armonk, New York 10504 (800) 541-6563; *The Illustrated Book of World Rankings.*

Organisation for Economic Co-operation and Development (OECD), 2 rue Andre-Pascal, 75 Paris 16, France (Telephone Number in U.S. (202) 785-6323); *Economic Outlook; The Footwear, Raw Hides and Skins, and Leather Industry in OECD Countries; Indicators of Industrial Activity; The Iron and Steel Industry; Main Economic Indicators - Historical Statistics;* and *The Pulp and Paper Industry.*

PORTUGAL - PRINTING AND WRITING PAPER PRODUCTION - See PORTUGAL - FORESTRY AND FOREST PRODUCTS

PORTUGAL - PRODUCTION

European Commission Office of Press and Public Affairs, 2100 M Street, NW, Washington, D.C. 20037 (202) 862-9500; *Basic Statistics of the Community; Eurostatistics: Data for Short-Term Economic Analysis;* and *Fisheries: Yearly Statistics.*

M.E. Sharpe, 80 Business Park Drive, Armonk, New York 10504 (800) 541-6563; *The Illustrated Book of World Rankings.*

Organisation for Economic Co-operation and Development (OECD), 2 rue Andre-Pascal, 75 Paris 16, France (Telephone Number in U.S. (202) 785-6323); *Economic Outlook; The Footwear, Raw Hides and Skins, and Leather Industry in OECD Countries; Indicators of Industrial Activity; Industrial Structure Statistics; The Iron and Steel Industry; Meat Balances in OECD Member Countries; Milk, Milk Products, and Egg Balances in OECD Member Countries; The Non-Ferrous Metals Industry; The Pulp and Paper Industry;* and *Textile Industry in OECD Countries.*

PORTUGAL - PRODUCTIVITY

European Commission Office of Press and Public Affairs, 2100 M Street, NW, Washington, D.C. 20037 (202) 862-9500; *Basic Statistics of the Community.*

Organisation for Economic Co-operation and Development (OECD), 2 rue Andre-Pascal, 75 Paris 16, France (Telephone Number in U.S. (202) 785-6323); *Economic Outlook.*

PORTUGAL - PROPERTY TAXES - See PORTUGAL - TAXATION

PORTUGAL - PUBLIC CONSUMPTION FUND

European Commission Office of Press and Public Affairs, 2100 M Street, NW, Washington, D.C. 20037 (202) 862-9500; *Basic Statistics of the Community.*

Organisation for Economic Co-operation and Development (OECD), 2 rue Andre-Pascal, 75 Paris 16, France (Telephone Number in U.S. (202) 785-6323); *Revenue Statistics of OECD Member Countries.*

PORTUGAL - PUBLIC EXPENDITURES

European Commission Office of Press and Public Affairs, 2100 M Street, NW, Washington, D.C. 20037 (202) 862-9500; *Basic Statistics of the Community.*

Organisation for Economic Co-operation and Development (OECD), 2 rue Andre-Pascal, 75 Paris 16, France (Telephone Number in U.S. (202) 785-6323); *Revenue Statistics of OECD Member Countries.*

PORTUGAL - PUBLIC FINANCE - See PORTUGAL - FINANCE

PORTUGAL - PUBLIC HEALTH - See PORTUGAL - HEALTH

PORTUGAL - PUBLIC REVENUES

Organisation for Economic Co-operation and Development (OECD), 2 rue Andre-Pascal, 75 Paris 16, France (Telephone Number in U.S. (202) 785-6323); *Revenue Statistics of OECD Member Countries.*

PORTUGAL - RADIO BROADCASTING - See PORTUGAL - BROADCASTING

PORTUGAL - RADIO RECEIVER PRODUCTION

Statistical Office of the United Nations, Publishing Service, New York, New York 10017 (800) 253-9646; *Statistical Yearbook.*

PORTUGAL - RADIO RECEIVERS

St. Martin's Press, Inc., 175 Fifth Avenue, New York, New York 10010 (800) 221-7945; *The Statesman's Year-Book.*

PORTUGAL - RAILWAYS

Euromonitor International, Inc., 122 South Michigan Avenue, Suite 1200, Chicago, Illinois 60603 (800) 577-EURO; *European Marketing Data and Statistics.*

Europa Publications Limited, 18 Bedford Square, London, WC1B 3JN, England; *The Europa World Year Book.*

European Commission Office of Press and Public Affairs, 2100 M Street, NW, Washington, D.C. 20037 (202) 862-9500;

Basic Statistics of the Community; Regions: Statistical Yearbook; and *Transport Annual Statistics.*

Jane's Information Group, Sentinel House, 163 Brighton Road, Coulsdon, Surrey CR5 2NH, England (Telephone Number in U.S. (703) 683-3700); *Jane's World Railways.*

St. Martin's Press, Inc., 175 Fifth Avenue, New York, New York 10010 (800) 221-7945; *The Statesman's Year-Book.*

Statistical Office of the United Nations, Publishing Service, New York, New York 10017 (800) 253-9646; *Statistical Yearbook; Annual Bulletin of Transport Statistics for Europe;* and *Trends in Europe and North America: The Statistical Yearbook of the Economic Commission for Europe.*

PORTUGAL - RANCHING

European Commission Office of Press and Public Affairs, 2100 M Street, NW, Washington, D.C. 20037 (202) 862-9500; *Basic Statistics of the Community.*

PORTUGAL - RELIGION

Central Intelligence Agency, Washington, D.C. 20505 (703) 482-1100, www.cia.gov; *The World Factbook.*

M.E. Sharpe, 80 Business Park Drive, Armonk, New York 10504 (800) 541-6563; *The Illustrated Book of World Rankings.*

St. Martin's Press, Inc., 175 Fifth Avenue, New York, New York 10010 (800) 221-7945; *The Statesman's Year-Book.*

PORTUGAL - RENT PRICES

International Labour Office, I.L.O. Publications, 1828 L Street, NW, Suite 801, Washington, D.C. 20036 (301) 638-3152; *Yearbook of Labour Statistics.*

PORTUGAL - RETAIL TRADE

Euromonitor International, Inc., 122 South Michigan Avenue, Suite 1200, Chicago, Illinois 60603 (800) 577-EURO; *World Marketing Data and Statistics;* and *Retail Trade International.*

European Commission Office of Press and Public Affairs, 2100 M Street, NW, Washington, D.C. 20037 (202) 862-9500; *Basic Statistics of the Community;* and *Eurostatistics: Data for Short-Term Economic Analysis.*

Statistical Office of the United Nations, Publishing Service, New York, New York 10017 (800) 253-9646; *Statistical Yearbook.*

PORTUGAL - RICE PRODUCTION - See PORTUGAL - CROPS

PORTUGAL - ROOT AND TUBER PRODUCTION - See PORTUGAL - CROPS

PORTUGAL - ROUNDWOOD PRODUCTION - See PORTUGAL - FORESTRY AND FOREST PRODUCTS

PORTUGAL - RUBBER PRODUCTION AND CONSUMPTION

European Commission Office of Press and Public Affairs, 2100 M Street, NW, Washington, D.C. 20037 (202) 862-9500; *Basic Statistics of the Community.*

M.E. Sharpe, 80 Business Park Drive, Armonk, New York 10504 (800) 541-6563; *The Illustrated Book of World Rankings.*

Organisation for Economic Co-operation and Development (OECD), 2 rue Andre-Pascal, 75 Paris 16, France (Telephone Number in U.S. (202) 785-6323); *Foreign Trade by Commodities.*

Statistical Office of the United Nations, Publishing Service, New York, New York 10017 (800) 253-9646; *Statistical Yearbook.*

PORTUGAL - SAFFLOWER SEED PRODUCTION - See PORTUGAL - CROPS

PORTUGAL - SALT PRODUCTION - See PORTUGAL - MINING AND MINERAL PRODUCTS

PORTUGAL - SAVINGS ACCOUNT DEPOSITS - See PORTUGAL - BANKING

PORTUGAL - SAWNWOOD PRODUCTION - See PORTUGAL - FORESTRY AND FOREST PRODUCTS

PORTUGAL - SCIENCE AND TECHNOLOGY - EXPENDITURE FOR RESEARCH - See PORTUGAL - SCIENTISTS, TECHNICIANS AND ENGINEERS

PORTUGAL - SCIENTISTS, TECHNICIANS AND ENGINEERS

European Commission Office of Press and Public Affairs, 2100 M Street, NW, Washington, D.C. 20037 (202) 862-9500; *Basic Statistics of the Community.*

Statistical Office of the United Nations, Publishing Service, New York, New York 10017 (800) 253-9646; *Statistical Yearbook.*

United Nations Educational, Scientific and Cultural Organization (UNESCO), 7 Place de Fontenoy, F-75700 Paris, France (Telephone Number in U.S. (212) 963-5981); *Statistical Yearbook.*

PORTUGAL - SENIOR CITIZENS

M.E. Sharpe, 80 Business Park Drive, Armonk, New York 10504 (800) 541-6563;

The Illustrated Book of World Rankings.

PORTUGAL - SERVICES INDUSTRY EMPLOYMENT - MALE AND FEMALE

Organisation for Economic Co-operation and Development (OECD), 2 rue Andre-Pascal, 75 Paris 16, France (Telephone Number in U.S. (202) 785-6323); *OECD Employment Outlook.*

PORTUGAL - SHEEP - See PORTUGAL - LIVESTOCK AND POULTRY

PORTUGAL - SHIPBUILDING - PRODUCTION INDEX

Organisation for Economic Co-operation and Development (OECD), 2 rue Andre-Pascal, 75 Paris 16, France (Telephone Number in U.S. (202) 785-6323); *Indicators of Industrial Activity.*

PORTUGAL - SILVER PRODUCTION AND CONSUMPTION - See PORTUGAL - MINING AND MINERAL PRODUCTS

PORTUGAL - SOCIAL DATA

European Commission Office of Press and Public Affairs, 2100 M Street, NW, Washington, D.C. 20037 (202) 862-9500; *Basic Statistics of the Community.*

M.E. Sharpe, 80 Business Park Drive, Armonk, New York 10504 (800) 541-6563; *The Illustrated Book of World Rankings.*

Statistical Office of the United Nations, Publishing Service, New York, New York 10017 (800) 253-9646; *World Statistics Pocketbook.*

PORTUGAL - SOCIAL SECURITY

European Commission Office of Press and Public Affairs, 2100 M Street, NW, Washington, D.C. 20037 (202) 862-9500; *Basic Statistics of the Community.*

International Monetary Fund, 700 Nineteenth Street, NW, Washington, D.C. 20431 (202) 623-7000; *Government Finance Statistics Yearbook.*

Organisation for Economic Co-operation and Development (OECD), 2 rue Andre-Pascal, 75 Paris 16, France (Telephone Number in U.S. (202) 785-6323); *Revenue statistics of OECD Member Countries.*

St. Martin's Press, Inc., 175 Fifth Avenue, New York, New York 10010 (800) 221-7945; *The Statesman's Year-Book.*

Statistical Office of the United Nations, Publishing Service, New York, New York 10017 (800) 253-9646; *National Accounts Statistics.*

PORTUGAL - SOCIOECONOMIC DATA

European Commission Office of Press and Public Affairs, 2100 M Street, NW, Washington, D.C. 20037 (202) 862-9500; *Basic Statistics of the Community.*

Organisation for Economic Co-operation and Development (OECD), 2 rue Andre-Pascal, 75 Paris 16, France (Telephone Number in U.S. (202) 785-6323); *Economic Outlook.*

PORTUGAL - STAMP TAXES AND DUTIES - See PORTUGAL - TAXATION

PORTUGAL - STEEL - See PORTUGAL - MINING AND MINERAL PRODUCTS

PORTUGAL - STOCKS - COMMODITY - MARKET PRICE - INDEXES

European Commission Office of Press and Public Affairs, 2100 M Street, NW, Washington, D.C. 20037 (202) 862-9500; *Basic Statistics of the Community.*

Statistical Office of the United Nations, Publishing Service, New York, New York 10017 (800) 253-9646; *Statistical Yearbook.*

PORTUGAL - SUGAR - See PORTUGAL - CROPS

PORTUGAL - SULPHUR AND SULPHURIC ACID PRODUCTION - See PORTUGAL - MINING AND MINERAL PRODUCTS

PORTUGAL - TAXATION

Europa Publications Limited, 18 Bedford Square, London, WC1B 3JN, England; *The Europa World Year Book.*

European Commission Office of Press and Public Affairs, 2100 M Street, NW, Washington, D.C. 20037 (202) 862-9500; *Basic Statistics of the Community.*

International Monetary Fund, 700 Nineteenth Street, NW, Washington, D.C. 20431 (202) 623-7000; *Government Finance Statistics Yearbook.*

International Road Federation, 2600 Virginia Avenue, NW., Washington, D.C. 20037 (202) 338-4641; *World Road Statistics.*

Organisation for Economic Co-operation and Development (OECD), 2 rue Andre-Pascal, 75 Paris 16, France (Telephone Number in U.S. (202) 785-6323); *Revenue Statistics of OECD Member Countries.*

The World Bank, 1818 H Street, NW, Washington, D.C. 20433 (202) 477-1234; *World Development Indicators.*

PORTUGAL - TAX REVENUE - See

PORTUGAL - TAXATION

PORTUGAL - TELEGRAPH SERVICE

Statistical Office of the United Nations, Publishing Service, New York, New York 10017 (800) 253-9646; *Statistical Yearbook.*

PORTUGAL - TELEPHONES IN USE

American Telephone and Telegraph Company, 26 Parsippany Road, Whippany, New Jersey 07981 (800) 222-0300; *The World's Telephones.*

Central Intelligence Agency, Washington, D.C. 20505 (703) 482-1100, www.cia.gov; *The World Factbook.*

Europa Publications Limited, 18 Bedford Square, London, WC1B 3JN, England; *The Europa World Year Book.*

European Commission Office of Press and Public Affairs, 2100 M Street, NW, Washington, D.C. 20037 (202) 862-9500; *Basic Statistics of the Community;* and *Transport Annual Statistics.*

St. Martin's Press, Inc., 175 Fifth Avenue, New York, New York 10010 (800) 221-7945; *The Statesman's Year-Book.*

Statistical Office of the United Nations, Publishing Service, New York, New York 10017 (800) 253-9646; *Statistical Yearbook; Trends in Europe and North America: The Statistical Yearbook of the Economic Commission for Europe;* and *World Statistics Pocketbook.*

PORTUGAL - TELEVISION BROADCASTING - See PORTUGAL - BROADCASTING

PORTUGAL - TELEVISION RECEIVER PRODUCTION

European Commission Office of Press and Public Affairs, 2100 M Street, NW, Washington, D.C. 20037 (202) 862-9500; *Basic Statistics of the Community.*

Statistical Office of the United Nations, Publishing Service, New York, New York 10017 (800) 253-9646; *Statistical Yearbook.*

PORTUGAL - TEXTILE INDUSTRY

American Forest and Paper Association, 1111 Nineteenth Street, NW, Washington, D.C. 20036 (202) 463-2700; *Wood Pulp and Fiber Statistics.*

Euromonitor International, Inc., 122 South Michigan Avenue, Suite 1200, Chicago, Illinois 60603 (800) 577-EURO; *Retail Trade International.*

European Commission Office of Press and Public Affairs, 2100 M Street, NW,

Washington, D.C. 20037 (202) 862-9500; *Basic Statistics of the Community; Eurostatistics: Data for Short-Term Economic Analysis;* and *Industrial Production: Quarterly.*

Organisation for Economic Co-operation and Development (OECD), 2 rue Andre-Pascal, 75 Paris 16, France (Telephone Number in U.S. (202) 785-6323); *Economic Accounts for Agriculture; Foreign Trade by Commodities; Indicators of Industrial Activity; Industrial Structure Statistics;* and *Textile Industry in OECD Countries.*

St. Martin's Press, Inc., 175 Fifth Avenue, New York, New York 10010 (800) 221-7945; *The Statesman's Year-Book.*

Statistical Office of the United Nations, Publishing Service, New York, New York 10017 (800) 253-9646; *Statistical Yearbook.*

United Nations Conference on Trade and Development, Central Statistical Service, Palais des Nations, Geneva, Switzerland (Telephone in U.S. (800) 253-9646); *UNCTAD Commodity Yearbook.*

PORTUGAL - THEATRE

United Nations Educational, Scientific and Cultural Organization (UNESCO), 7 Place de Fontenoy, F-75700 Paris, France (Telephone Number in U.S. (212) 963-5981); *Statistical Yearbook.*

PORTUGAL - TIN - See PORTUGAL - MINING AND MINERAL PRODUCTS

PORTUGAL - TIRE (MOTOR VEHICLE) PRODUCTION

Statistical Office of the United Nations, Publishing Service, New York, New York 10017 (800) 253-9646; *Statistical Yearbook.*

PORTUGAL - TOBACCO PRODUCTION

Euromonitor International, Inc., 122 South Michigan Avenue, Suite 1200, Chicago, Illinois 60603 (800) 577-EURO; *European Marketing Data and Statistics.*

European Commission Office of Press and Public Affairs, 2100 M Street, NW, Washington, D.C. 20037 (202) 862-9500; *Basic Statistics of the Community;* and *Industrial Production: Quarterly.*

M.E. Sharpe, 80 Business Park Drive, Armonk, New York 10504 (800) 541-6563; *The Illustrated Book of World Rankings.*

Organisation for Economic Co-operation and Development (OECD), 2 rue Andre-Pascal, 75 Paris 16, France (Telephone Number in U.S. (202) 785-6323); *Foreign Trade by Commodities; Indicators of Industrial Activity;* and

Industrial Structure Statistics.

Statistical Office of the United Nations, Publishing Service, New York, New York 10017 (800) 253-9646; *Statistical Yearbook.*

PORTUGAL - TOURISM

Euromonitor International, Inc., 122 South Michigan Avenue, Suite 1200, Chicago, Illinois 60603 (800) 577-EURO; *European Marketing Data and Statistics;* World *Marketing Data and Statistics;* and *World Economic Factbook.*

Europa Publications Limited, 18 Bedford Square, London, WC1B 3JN, England; *The Europa World Year Book.*

European Commission Office of Press and Public Affairs, 2100 M Street, NW, Washington, D.C. 20037 (202) 862-9500; *Transport Annual Statistics.*

Federal Statistical Office, Gustav - Stresemann - Ring 11, D-6200 Wiesbaden, Germany; *Portugal.*

M.E. Sharpe, 80 Business Park Drive, Armonk, New York 10504 (800) 541-6563; *The Illustrated Book of World Rankings.*

Organisation for Economic Co-operation and Development (OECD), 2 rue Andre-Pascal, 75 Paris 16, France (Telephone Number in U.S. (202) 785-6323); *Tourism Policy and International Tourism in OECD Member Countries.*

St. Martin's Press, Inc., 175 Fifth Avenue, New York, New York 10010 (800) 221-7945; *The Statesman's Year-Book.*

Statistical Office of the United Nations, Publishing Service, New York, New York 10017 (800) 253-9646; *Statistical Yearbook;* and *Trends in Europe and North America: The Statistical Yearbook of the Economic Commission for Europe.*

World Tourism Organization, Calle Capitan Haya 42, E-28020 Madrid, Spain; *Yearbook of Tourism Statistics.*

PORTUGAL - TRACTORS IN USE

European Commission Office of Press and Public Affairs, 2100 M Street, NW, Washington, D.C. 20037 (202) 862-9500; *Transport Annual Statistics.*

Statistical Office of the United Nations, Publishing Service, New York, New York 10017 (800) 253-9646; *Statistical Yearbook.*

PORTUGAL - TRADE - See PORTUGAL - FOREIGN TRADE

PORTUGAL - TRADEMARKS AND SERVICE MARKS - See PORTUGAL - PATENTS, TRADEMARKS AND SERVICE MARKS

PORTUGAL - TRANSPORTATION AND COMMUNICATIONS

Central Intelligence Agency, Washington, D.C. 20505 (703) 482-1100, www.cia.gov; *The World Factbook.*

Euromonitor International, Inc., 122 South Michigan Avenue, Suite 1200, Chicago, Illinois 60603 (800) 577-EURO; *World Marketing Data and Statistics.*

Europa Publications Limited, 18 Bedford Square, London, WC1B 3JN, England; *The Europa World Year Book.*

European Commission Office of Press and Public Affairs, 2100 M Street, NW, Washington, D.C. 20037 (202) 862-9500; *Basic Statistics of the Community; Energy Statistics Yearbook; Regions: Statistical Yearbook;* and *Transport Annual Statistics.*

Federal Statistical Office, Gustav - Stresemann - Ring 11, D-6200 Wiesbaden, Germany; *Portugal.*

M.E. Sharpe, 80 Business Park Drive, Armonk, New York 10504 (800) 541-6563; *The Illustrated Book of World Rankings.*

St. Martin's Press, Inc., 175 Fifth Avenue, New York, New York 10010 (800) 221-7945; *The Statesman's Year-Book.*

Statistical Office of the United Nations, Publishing Service, New York, New York 10017 (800) 253-9646; *Human Development Report;* and *Trends in Europe and North America: The Statistical Yearbook of the Economic Commission for Europe.*

PORTUGAL - TRANSPORTATION EMPLOYMENT - MALE AND FEMALE - See PORTUGAL - EMPLOYMENT

PORTUGAL - TUNGSTEN PRODUCTION AND CONSUMPTION - See PORTUGAL - MINING AND MINERAL PRODUCTS

PORTUGAL - UNEMPLOYMENT

Central Intelligence Agency, Washington, D.C. 20505 (703) 482-1100, www.cia.gov; *The World Factbook.*

Euromonitor International, Inc., 122 South Michigan Avenue, Suite 1200, Chicago, Illinois 60603 (800) 577-EURO; *European Marketing Data and Statistics.*

European Commission Office of Press and Public Affairs, 2100 M Street, NW, Washington, D.C. 20037 (202) 862-9500; *Basic Statistics of the Community; Employment and Unemployment; Eurostatistics: Data for Short-Term Economic Analysis; Labor Force Sample Survey;* and *Regions: Statistical Yearbook.*

International Labour Office, I.L.O. Publications, 1828 L Street, NW, Suite 801, Washington, D.C. 20036 (301) 638-3152; *Yearbook of Labour Statistics.*

Organisation for Economic Co-operation and Development (OECD), 2 rue Andre-Pascal, 75 Paris 16, France (Telephone Number in U.S. (202) 785-6323); *Economic Outlook; OECD Economic Surveys: Portugal; OECD Employment Outlook;* and *Statistical Yearbook.*

St. Martin's Press, Inc., 175 Fifth Avenue, New York, New York 10010 (800) 221-7945; *The Statesman's Year-Book.*

Statistical Office of the United Nations, Publishing Service, New York, New York 10017 (800) 253-9646; *Trends in Europe and North America: The Statistical Yearbook of the Economic Commission for Europe.*

PORTUGAL - URANIUM PRODUCTION AND CONSUMPTION - See PORTUGAL - MINING AND MINERAL PRODUCTS

PORTUGAL - VANADIUM AND VANADIUM ORE PRODUCTION AND CONSUMPTION - See PORTUGAL - MINING AND MINERAL PRODUCTS

PORTUGAL - VITAL STATISTICS

European Commission Office of Press and Public Affairs, 2100 M Street, NW, Washington, D.C. 20037 (202) 862-9500; *Basic Statistics of the Community.*

St. Martin's Press, Inc., 175 Fifth Avenue, New York, New York 10010 (800) 221-7945; *The Statesman's Year-Book.*

Statistical Office of the United Nations, Publishing Service, New York, New York 10017 (800) 253-9646; *Statistical Yearbook.*

World Health Organization, Office of Publications, 20 Avenue Appia, CH-1211 Geneva 27, Switzerland (Telephone Number in U.S. (518) 436-9686); *World Health Statistics Annual.*

PORTUGAL - WAGES

Euromonitor International, Inc., 122 South Michigan Avenue, Suite 1200, Chicago, Illinois 60603 (800) 577-EURO; *European Marketing Data and Statistics.*

European Commission Office of Press and Public Affairs, 2100 M Street, NW, Washington, D.C. 20037 (202) 862-9500; *Basic Statistics of the Community; Earnings in Agriculture;* and *Eurostatistics: Data for Short-Term Economic Analysis.*

Federal Statistical Office, Gustav - Stresemann - Ring 11, D-6200 Wiesbaden, Germany; *Portugal.*

International Labour Office, I.L.O. Publications, 1828 L Street, NW, Suite 801, Washington, D.C. 20036 (301) 638-3152; *Yearbook of Labour Statistics.*

Organisation for Economic Co-operation and Development (OECD), 2 rue Andre-Pascal, 75 Paris 16, France (Telephone Number in U.S. (202) 785-6323); *Economic Outlook;* and *Industrial Structure Statistics.*

Statistical Office of the United Nations, Publishing Service, New York, New York 10017 (800) 253-9646; *Statistical Yearbook.*

PORTUGAL - WALNUT PRODUCTION - See PORTUGAL - CROPS

PORTUGAL - WATERWAYS IN USE

European Commission Office of Press and Public Affairs, 2100 M Street, NW, Washington, D.C. 20037 (202) 862-9500; *Basic Statistics of the Community;* and *Transport Annual Statistics.*

Organisation for Economic Co-operation and Development (OECD), 2 rue Andre-Pascal, 75 Paris 16, France (Telephone Number in U.S. (202) 785-6323); *Maritime Transport.*

Statistical Office of the United Nations, Publishing Service, New York, New York 10017 (800) 253-9646; *Annual Bulletin of Transport Statistics for Europe.*

PORTUGAL - WEATHER - See PORTUGAL - CLIMATE

PORTUGAL - WELFARE

European Commission Office of Press and Public Affairs, 2100 M Street, NW, Washington, D.C. 20037 (202) 862-9500; *Basic Statistics of the Community.*

International Monetary Fund, 700 Nineteenth Street, NW, Washington, D.C. 20431 (202) 623-7000; *Government Finance Statistics Yearbook.*

St. Martin's Press, Inc., 175 Fifth Avenue, New York, New York 10010 (800) 221-7945; *The Statesman's Year-Book.*

PORTUGAL - WHALE AND SPERM OIL PRODUCTION

Statistical Office of the United Nations, Publishing Service, New York, New York 10017 (800) 253-9646; *Statistical Yearbook.*

PORTUGAL - WHALES CAUGHT

Statistical Office of the United Nations, Publishing Service, New York, New York 10017 (800) 253-9646; *Statistical Yearbook.*

PORTUGAL - WHEAT PRODUCTION AND

PRICES - See PORTUGAL - CROPS

PORTUGAL - WHOLESALE PRICES - INDEX NUMBERS

European Commission Office of Press and Public Affairs, 2100 M Street, NW, Washington, D.C. 20037 (202) 862-9500; *Basic Statistics of the Community.*

Statistical Office of the United Nations, Publishing Service, New York, New York 10017 (800) 253-9646; *Statistical Yearbook.*

PORTUGAL - WHOLESALE TRADE

Statistical Office of the United Nations, Publishing Service, New York, New York 10017 (800) 253-9646; *Statistical Yearbook.*

PORTUGAL - WINE - See PORTUGAL - BEVERAGES

PORTUGAL - WOOD - See PORTUGAL - FORESTRY AND FOREST PRODUCTS

PORTUGAL - WOOL - INDUSTRIAL CONSUMPTION - See PORTUGAL - TEXTILE INDUSTRY

PORTUGAL - WOOL PRODUCTION - See PORTUGAL - TEXTILE INDUSTRY

PORTUGAL - YARN PRODUCTION - See PORTUGAL - TEXTILE INDUSTRY

PORTUGAL - ZINC AND ZINC ORE PRODUCTION AND CONSUMPTION - See PORTUGAL - MINING AND MINERAL PRODUCTS

POSTAL RATES

U.S. Postal Service, 475 L'Enfant Plaza West, SW, Washington, D.C. 20260-0010 (202) 268-2000, www.usps.gov; *United States Domestic Postage Rates: Recent History;* and unpublished data.

POSTAL SERVICE

U.S. Postal Service, 475 L'Enfant Plaza West, SW, Washington, D.C. 20260-0010 (202) 268-2000, www.usps.gov; *Annual Report of the Postmaster General and Comprehensive Statement on Postal Operations;* and unpublished data.

POSTAL SERVICE - PRODUCTIVITY

U.S. Department of Labor, Bureau of Labor Statistics, Two Massachusetts Avenue, NE, Washington, D.C. 20212 (202) 691-5200, www.stats.bls.gov; Internet site: http://www.stats.bls.gov/irphome.htm.

POTASH (POTASSIUM SALTS)

U.S. Department of Commerce, Bureau of the Census, Washington, D.C. 20233 (301) 457-4100, www.census.gov; import

and export data.

U.S. Department of the Interior, Geological Survey, Office of Minerals Information, 12201 Sunrise Valley Drive, Reston, Virginia 22092 (703) 648-4000, www.minerals.usgs.gov; *Annual Reports;* and *Mineral Commodity Summaries.*

POTASSIUM - FOREIGN TRADE

U.S. Department of Commerce, Bureau of the Census, Washington, D.C. 20233 (301) 457-4100, www.census.gov; import and export data.

U.S. Department of the Interior, Geological Survey, Office of Minerals Information, 12201 Sunrise Valley Drive, Reston, Virginia 22092 (703) 648-4000, www.minerals.usgs.gov; *Mineral Commodity Summaries.*

POTATOES - ACREAGE

U.S. Department of Agriculture, National Agricultural Statistics Service, Fourteenth Street and Independence Avenue, SW, Washington, D.C. 20250 (800) 727-9540, www.usda.gov/nass; *Agricultural Statistics;* and *Vegetables.*

POTATOES - CONSUMPTION

U.S. Department of Agriculture, Economic Research Service, 1800 M Street, NW, Washington, D.C. 20036 (202) 694-5050, www.ers.usda.gov; *Food Consumption, Prices, and Expenditures; Agricultural Outlook;* and *Vegetables and Specialties Situation and Outlook Yearbook.*

POTATOES - FARM MARKETINGS - SALES

U.S. Department of Agriculture, Economic Research Service, 1800 M Street, NW, Washington, D.C. 20036 (202) 694-5050, www.ers.usda.gov; *Farm Business Economic Report.*

POTATOES - FOREIGN TRADE

U.S. Department of Agriculture, Economic Research Service, 1800 M Street, NW, Washington, D.C. 20036 (202) 694-5050, www.ers.usda.gov; *Vegetables and Specialities and Outlook Yearbook.*

POTATOES - PRICES

U.S. Department of Agriculture, National Agricultural Statistics Service, Fourteenth Street and Independence Avenue, SW, Washington, D.C. 20250 (800) 727-9540, www.usda.gov/nass; *Agricultural Prices: Annual Summary.*

U. S. Department of Labor, Bureau of Labor Statistics, Two Massachusetts Avenue, NE, Washington, D.C. 20212 (202)

691-5200, www.stats.bls.gov; *CPI Detailed Report;* and *Monthly Labor Review.*

POTATOES - PRODUCTION

U.S. Department of Agriculture, National Agricultural Statistics Service, Fourteenth Street and Independence Avenue, SW, Washington, D.C. 20250 ((800) 727-9540, www.usda.gov/nass; *Vegetables; Agricultural Statistics;* and *Vegetables and Specialties Situation and Outlook Yearbook.*

POULTRY - See also EGGS

POULTRY - CONSUMER EXPENDITURES

U.S. Department of Labor, Bureau of Labor Statistics, 2 Massachusetts Avenue, NE, Washington, D.C. 20212 (202) 691-5200, www.stats.bls.gov; *Consumer Expenditures in 1997;* and unpublished data.

POULTRY - CONSUMPTION

U.S. Department of Agriculture, Economic Research Service, 1800 M Street, NW, Washington, D.C. 20036 (202) 694-5050, www.ers.usda.gov; *Food Consumption, Prices, and Expenditures; Agricultural Outlook;* and unpublished data.

U.S. Department of Agriculture, Foreign Agricultural Service, Fourteenth Street and Independence Avenue, SW, Washington, D.C. 20250 (202) 720-7115, www.fas.usda.gov; *Livestock and Poultry World Markets and Trade.*

POULTRY - FARM MARKETINGS, SALES

U.S. Department of Agriculture, Economic Research Service, 1800 M Street, NW, Washington, D.C. 20036 (202) 694-5050, www.ers.usda.gov; *Farm Business Economic Report.*

POULTRY - FOREIGN TRADE

U.S. Department of Agriculture, Economic Research Service, 1800 M Street, NW, Washington, D.C. 20036 (202) 694-5050, www.ers.usda.gov; *Foreign Agricultural Trade of the U.S.;* and *Agricultural Statistics.*

POULTRY - NUMBER ON FARMS

U.S. Department of Agriculture, National Agricultural Statistics Service, Fourteenth Street and Independence Avenue, SW, Washington, D.C. 20250 (800) 727-9540, www.usda.gov/nass; *Poultry - Production and Value; Turkeys;* and *Layers and Egg Production.*

POULTRY - PRICES

U.S. Department of Agriculture, National Agricultural Statistics Service,

Fourteenth Street and Independence Avenue, SW, Washington, D.C. 20250 (800) 727-9540, www.usda.gov/nass; *Layers and Egg Production; Poultry-Production and Value; Turkeys;* and *Agricultural Prices: Annual Summary.*

U.S. Department of Labor, Bureau of Labor Statistics, Two Massachusetts Avenue, NE, Washington, D.C. 20212 (202) 691-5200, www.stats.bls.gov; *CPI Detailed Report.*

POULTRY - PRODUCTION AND SALES

Executive Office of the President, Council of Economic Advisors, Old Executive Office Building, Washington, D.C. 20502 (202) 395-5084, www.whitehouse.gov/cea; *Economic Report of the President.*

U.S. Department of Agriculture, Economic Research Service, 1800 M Street, NW, Washington, D.C. 20036 (202) 694-5050, www.ers.usda.gov; *Agricultural Outlook;* and *Food Consumption, Prices, and Expenditures.*

U.S. Department of Agriculture, National Agricultural Statistics Service, Fourteenth Street and Independence Avenue, SW, Washington, D.C. 20250 (800) 727-9540, www.usda.gov/nass; *Poultry - Production and Value; Turkeys;* and *Layers and Egg Production.*

POULTRY - VALUE

U.S. Department of Agriculture, National Agricultural Statistics Service, Fourteenth Street and Independence Avenue, SW, Washington, D.C. 20250 (800) 727-9540, www.usda.gov/nass; *Poultry - Production and Value; Turkeys;* and *Layers and Egg Production.*

POVERTY - CHILDREN

U.S. Department of Commerce, Bureau of the Census, Washington, D.C. 20233 (301) 457-4100, www.census.gov; *Current Population Reports;* and unpublished data.

POVERTY - FAMILIES

U.S. Department of Commerce, Bureau of the Census, Washington, D.C. 20233 (301) 457-4100, www.census.gov; *Current Population Reports.*

POVERTY - AMERICAN INDIAN, ESKIMO, ALEUT POPULATION

U.S. Department of Commerce, Bureau of the Census, Washington, D.C. 20233 (301) 457-4100, www.census.gov; *Census of Population, Characteristics of American Indians by Tribe and Language.*

POVERTY - FAMILIES - ASIAN AND PACIFIC ISLANDER POPULATION

U.S. Department of Commerce, Bureau of the Census, Washington, D.C. 20233 (301) 457-4100, www.census.gov; *Current Population Reports;* and unpublished data.

POVERTY - FAMILIES - BLACK POPULATION

U.S. Department of Commerce, Bureau of the Census, Washington, D.C. 20233 (301) 457-4100, www.census.gov; *Current Population Reports;* and unpublished data.

POVERTY - FAMILIES - EDUCATIONAL ATTAINMENT

U.S. Department of Commerce, Bureau of the Census, Washington, D.C. 20233 (301) 457-4100, www.census.gov; *Current Population Reports.*

POVERTY - FAMILIES - ELDERLY

U.S. Department of Commerce, Bureau of the Census, Washington, D.C. 20233 (301) 457-4100, www.census.gov; *Current Population Reports.*

POVERTY - FAMILIES - HISPANIC ORIGIN POPULATION

U.S. Department of Commerce, Bureau of the Census, Washington, D.C. 20233 (301) 457-4100, www.census.gov; *Current Population Reports;* and unpublished data.

POVERTY - FAMILIES - LABOR FORCE PARTICIPATION

U.S. Department of Commerce, Bureau of the Census, Washington, D.C. 20233 (301) 457-4100, www.census.gov; *Current Population Reports.*

POVERTY - HOUSING

U.S. Department of Commerce, Bureau of the Census, Washington, D.C. 20233 (301) 457-4100, www.census.gov; *Current Housing Reports;* and *American Housing Survey in the U.S.*

POVERTY - PERSONS - AGE

U.S. Department of Commerce, Bureau of the Census, Washington, D.C. 20233 (301) 457-4100, www.census.gov; *Current Population Reports;* and unpublished data.

POVERTY - PERSONS - AMERICAN INDIAN, ESKIMO, ALEUT POPULATION

U.S. Department of Commerce, Bureau of the Census, Washington, D.C. 20233 (301) 457-4100, www.census.gov; *Census of Population, Characteristics of American Indians by Tribe and Language.*

POVERTY - PERSONS - BLACK POPULATION

U.S. Department of Commerce, Bureau of the Census, Washington, D.C. 20233 (301) 457-4100, www.census.gov; *Current Population Reports;* unpublished data; and Internet site: http://www.census.gov/hhes/income/histinc/index.html.

POVERTY - PERSONS - CHILDREN

U.S. Department of Commerce, Bureau of the Census, Washington, D.C. 20233 (301) 457-4100, www.census.gov; *Current Population Reports;* and unpublished data.

POVERTY - PERSONS - ELDERLY

U.S. Department of Commerce, Bureau of the Census, Washington, D.C. 20233 (301) 457-4100, www.census.gov; *Current Population Reports;* and unpublished data.

POVERTY - PERSONS - HISPANIC ORIGIN POPULATION

U.S. Department of Commerce, Bureau of the Census, Washington, D.C. 20233 (301) 457-4100, www.census.gov; *Current Population Reports; Census of Population;* unpublished data; and Internet site: http://www.census.gov/hhes/income/histinc/index.html.

POVERTY - PERSONS - STATE

U.S. Department of Commerce, Bureau of the Census, Washington, D.C. 20233 (301) 457-4100, www.census.gov; *Current Population Reports.*

POVERTY - THRESHOLD

U.S. Department of Commerce, Bureau of the Census, Washington, D.C. 20233 (301) 457-4100, www.census.gov; *Current Population Reports*; and Internet site: http://www.census.gov/hhes/poverty/histpov/hstpov1.htm.

POWER - See also ELECTRIC LIGHT AND POWER INDUSTRY

POWER - ELECTRIC

Edison Electric Institute, 701 Pennsylvania Avenue, NW, Washington, D.C. 20004 (202) 508-5000; ·*Statistical Yearbook of the Electric Utility Industry.*

U.S. Department of Energy, Energy Information Administration, 1000 Independence Avenue, SW, Washington, D.C. 20585 (202) 586-8800, www.eia.doe.gov; *Electric Power Annual; Electric Power Monthly; Annual Energy Review; Monthly Energy Review;* and unpublished data.

POWER - HYDRO

U.S. Department of Energy, Energy Information Administration, 1000 Independence Avenue, SW, Washington, D.C. 20585 (202) 586-8800, www.eia.doe.gov; *Electric Power Annual; Annual Energy Review; International Energy Annual; International Energy Outlook;* and unpublished data.

POWER - NUCLEAR

McGraw-Hill Inc., 1221 Avenue of the Americas, New York, New York 10020 (800) 722-4726; *Nucleonics Week.*

U.S. Department of Energy, Energy Information Administration, 1000 Independence Avenue, SW, Washington, D.C. 20585 (202) 586-8800, www.eia.doe.gov; *Electric Power Annual; Annual Energy Review; International Energy Annual;* and unpublished data.

POWER - PRICES

U.S. Department of Energy, Energy Information Administration, 1000 Independence Avenue, SW, Washington, D.C. 20585 (202) 586-2363; *Monthly Energy Review; State Energy Price and Expenditure Report;* and *Annual Energy Review.*

POWER - WATER

U.S. Department of Energy, Federal Energy Regulatory Commission, 1000 Independence Avenue, SW, Washington, D.C. 20585 (202) 208-0300; *Hydroelectric Power Resources of the United States, Developed and Undeveloped;* and unpublished data.

U.S. Department of the Interior, Geological Survey, National Center, 12201 Sunrise Valley Drive, Reston, Virginia 22092 (703) 648-4000, www.usgs.gov; *Estimated Use of Water in the U.S.*

POWER PLANTS - See ELECTRIC LIGHT AND POWER INDUSTRY

PRECIPITATION - SELECTED CITIES

U.S. Department of Commerce, National Oceanic and Atmospheric Administration, National Climatic Data Center, 151 Patton Avenue, Asheville, North Carolina 28801 (828) 271-4800, www.ncdc.noaa.gov; *Climatography of the United States; Climates of the World;* and *Comparative Climatic Data.*

PREGNANCIES

U.S. Department of Health and Human Services, National Center for Health Statistics, 3700 East-West Highway, Hyattsville, Maryland 20782 (301) 436-8500, www.cdc.gov/nchs; *National Vital Statistics Report;* and *Fertility Family Planning, and Women's Health: New Data from the 1995 National Survey of Family Growth, Vital and Health Statistics.*

PREGNANCIES - DRINKING DURING

U.S. Department of Health and Human Services, National Center for Health Statistics, 3700 East-West Highway, Hyattsville, Maryland 20782 (301) 436-8500, www.cdc.gov/nchs; *National Vital Statistics Report.*

PREGNANCIES - SMOKING DURING

U.S. Department of Health and Human Services, National Center for Health Statistics, 3700 East-West Highway, Hyattsville, Maryland 20782 (301) 436-8500, www.cdc.gov/nchs; *National Vital Statistics Report.*

PREGNANCIES - TESTING

U.S. Department of Health and Human Services, National Center for Health Statistics, 3700 East-West Highway, Hyattsville, Maryland 20782 (301) 436-8500, www.cdc.gov/nchs; *Fertility Family Planning, and Women's Health: New Data from the 1995 National Survey of Family Growth, Vital and Health Statistics.*

PRENATAL CARE

U.S. Department of Health and Human Services, National Center for Health Statistics, 3700 East-West Highway, Hyattsville, Maryland 20782 (301) 436-8500, www.cdc.gov/nchs; *National Vital Statistics Report; Vital Statistics of the United States;* and unpublished data.

PRESCRIPTION DRUGS - See DRUGS AND MEDICINES

PRESIDENT, UNITED STATES - ELECTIONS FOR

Center for Political Studies, University of Michigan, Post Office Box 1248, Ann Arbor, Michigan 48106 (313) 764-8363; unpublished data.

Congressional Quarterly, Inc., 1414 22nd Street, NW, Washington, D.C. 20037 (202) 887-8500; *America Votes;* and *America at the Polls.*

PRESIDENT, UNITED STATES - ELECTIONS FOR - CAMPAIGN FINANCES

Federal Election Commission, 999 E Street, NW, Washington, D.C. 20463 (800) 424-9530, www.fec.gov; *FEC Reports on Financial Activity; Final Report; Presidential Pre-Nomination Campaigns; FEC Index of Independent Expenditures;* press releases; and unpublished data.

PRICES - See also Individual Commodities

PRICES - BONDS

New York Stock Exchange, 11 Wall Street, New York, New York 10005 (212) 656-3000; *Fact Book.*

PRICES - BOOKS AND PERIODICALS

Library Journal, 249 West 17th Street, New York, New York 10011 (212) 463-6819; *Library Journal.*

R.R. Bowker Company, 121 Chanlon Road, New Providence, New Jersey 07974 (908) 464-6800; *Publishers Weekly;* and *Bowker Annual: Library and Book Trade Almanac.*

PRICES - ELECTRICITY

U.S. Department of Energy, Energy Information Administration, 1000 Independence Avenue, SW, Washington, D.C. 20585 (202) 586-8800, www.eia.doe.gov; *Monthly Energy Review; State Energy Price and Expenditure Report;* and *Annual Energy Review.*

PRICES - ENERGY

U.S. Department of Energy, Energy Information Administration, 1000 Independence Avenue, SW, Washington, D.C. 20585 (202) 586-8800, www.eia.doe.gov; *Household Energy Consumption and Expenditures;* and *Annual Energy Review.*

PRICES - FISH, BY SPECIES

U.S. Department of Commerce, National Oceanic and Atmospheric Administration, National Marine Fisheries Service, 1315 East-West Highway, Silver Spring, Maryland 20910 (301) 427-2239, www.nmfs.noaa.gov; *Fisheries of the United States.*

PRICES - FOOD

U.S. Department of Agriculture, Human Nutrition Information Service, Hyattsville, Maryland 20782 (301) 436-7725; *Agricultural Research Service.*

U.S. Department of Labor, Bureau of Labor Statistics, Two Massachusetts Avenue, NE, Washington, D.C. 20212 (202) 691-5200, www.stats.bls.gov; *Consumer Price Index, Detailed Report;* and *Monthly Labor Review.*

PRICES - FOREIGN COUNTRIES

International Monetary Fund, 700 Nineteenth Street, NW, Washington, D.C. 20431 (202) 623-7000; *International Financial Statistics.*

Organization for Economic Co-operation and Development, Publication and Information Center, 2001 L Street, NW, Washington, D.C. 20036 (202) 785-6323;

Main Economic Indicators.

PRICES - HOUSING

Chicago Title Corporation, 171 North Clark Street, Chicago, Illinois 60601 (312) 630-2000; *Who's Buying Homes in America.*

National Association of Realtors, 430 North Michigan Avenue, Chicago, Illinois 60611-4087 (800) 874-6500; *Real Estate Outlook: Market Trends and Insights..*

U.S. Department of Commerce, Bureau of the Census, Washington, D.C. 20233 (301) 457-4100, www.census.gov; *Current Construction Reports; Characteristics of New Housing; Housing Starts;* and *New One-Family Houses Sold.*

PRICES - INDEXES - AIRLINE COST

Air Transport Association of America, 1301 Pennsylvania Avenue, NW, Washington, D.C. 20004 (202) 626-4000; *Air Transport;* and unpublished data.

PRICES - INDEXES - CONSTRUCTION MATERIALS

U.S. Department of Labor, Bureau of Labor Statistics, Two Massachusetts Avenue, NE, Washington, D.C. 20212 (202) 691-5200, www.stats.bls.gov; *Producer Price Indexes.*

PRICES - INDEXES - CONSUMER PRICE

International Monetary Fund, 700 Nineteenth Street, NW, Washington, D.C. 20431 (202) 623-7000; *International Financial Statistics.*

U.S. Department of Commerce. Bureau of Economic Analysis, Fourteenth Street between Constitution Avenue and E Street, NW, Washington, D.C. 20230 (202) 606-9900, www.bea.doc.gov; *Survey of Current Business.*

U.S. Department of Labor, Bureau of Labor Statistics, Two Massachusetts Avenue, NE, Washington, D.C. 20212 (202) 691-5200, www.stats.bls.gov; *Monthly Labor Review; Consumer Price Index, Detailed Report;* and *Handbook of Labor Statistics.*

PRICES - INDEXES - CONSUMER PRICE - FOREIGN COUNTRIES

International Monetary Fund, 700 Nineteenth Street, NW, Washington, D.C. 20431 (202) 623-7000; *International Financial Statistics.*

PRICES - INDEXES - CONSUMER PRICE - MEDICAL CARE

U.S. Department of Labor, Bureau of Labor Statistics, Two Massachusetts

Avenue, NE, Washington, D.C. 20212 (202) 691-5200, www.stats.bls.gov; *Consumer Price Index Detailed Report.*

PRICES - INDEXES - CONSUMER PRICE - SELECTED METRO AREAS

Association for Applied Community Researchers, Post Office Box 407, Arlington, Virginia 22210 (703) 522-4980; *ACCRA Cost of Living Index.*

PRICES - INDEXES - EXPORTS

U.S. Department of Labor, Bureau of Labor Statistics, Two Massachusetts Avenue, NE, Washington, D.C. 20212 (202) 691-5200, www.stats.bls.gov; *U.S. Import and Export Price Indexes.*

PRICES - INDEXES - HOUSES - ONE-FAMILY

U.S. Department of Commerce, International Trade Administration, Fourteenth Street between Constitution Avenue and E Street, NW, Washington, D.C. 20230 (202) 482-2185, www.ita.doc.gov; *Construction Review.*

PRICES - INDEXES - IMPORTS

Commodity Research Bureau, Inc., 30 South Wacker Drive, Chicago Illinois 60606 (312) 454-1801; *Commodity Research Bureau Commodity Index Report.*

U.S. Department of Labor, Bureau of Labor Statistics, Two Massachusetts Avenue, NE, Washington, D.C. 20212 (202) 691-5200, www.stats.bls.gov; *News;* and *U.S. Import and Export Price Indexes.*

PRICES - INDEXES - PRODUCER PRICES

U.S. Department of Labor, Bureau of Labor Statistics, Two Massachusetts Avenue, NE, Washington, D.C. 20212 (202) 691-5200, www.stats.bls.gov; *Producer Price Indexes.*

PRICES - INDEXES - PRODUCER PRICES - CONSTRUCTION MATERIALS

U.S. Department of Labor, Bureau of Labor Statistics, Two Massachusetts Avenue, NE, Washington, D.C. 20212 (202) 691-5200, www.stats.bls.gov; *Producer Price Indexes.*

PRICES - INDEXES - PRODUCER PRICES - NEWSPRINT

U.S. Department of Commerce, Bureau of Economic Analysis, Fourteenth Street between Constitution Avenue and E Street, NW, Washington, D.C. 20230 (202) 606-9900, www.bea.doc.gov; *Survey of Current Business.*

PRICES - INDEXES - PRODUCER PRICES -

RAILROAD FREIGHT

U.S. Department of Labor, Bureau of Labor Statistics, Two Massachusetts Avenue, NE, Washington, D.C. 20212 (202) 691-5200, www.stats.bls.gov; *Producer Price Indexes.*

PRICES - INDEXES - PRODUCER PRICES - STAGE-OF-PROCESSING

U.S. Department of Labor, Bureau of Labor Statistics, Two Massachusetts Avenue, NE, Washington, D.C. 20212 (202) 691-5200, www.stats.bls.gov; *Producer Price Indexes.*

PRICES - INDEXES - PRODUCER PRICES - TIMBER

U.S. Department of Labor, Bureau of Labor Statistics, Two Massachusetts Avenue, NE, Washington, D.C. 20212 (202) 691-5200, www.stats.bls.gov; *Producer Price Indexes.*

PRICES - INDEXES - PURCHASING POWER OF THE DOLLAR

U.S. Department of Labor, Bureau of Labor Statistics, Two Massachusetts Avenue, NE, Washington, D.C. 20212 (202) 691-5200, www.stats.bls.gov; *Monthly Labor Review*; and *CPI Detailed Report.*

PRICES - INDEXES - RECEIVED BY FARMERS

U.S. Department of Agriculture, National Agricultural Statistic Service, Fourteenth Street and Independence Avenue, SW, Washington, D.C. 20250 (800) 727-9540, www.usda.gov/nass; *Agricultural Prices: Annual Summary.*

PRICES - INDEXES - SCHOOL EXPENDITURES

Research Associates of Washington, 1200 North Nash Street #225, Arlington, Virginia 22209 (703) 243-3399; *Inflation Measures for Schools, Colleges and Libraries.*

PRICES - INDEXES - SPOT MARKET PRICE

Commodity Research Bureau, Inc., 30 South Wacker Drive, Chicago Illinois 60606 (312) 454-1801; *CRB Commodity Index Report.*

PRICES - LUMBER AND STUMPAGE

U.S. Department of Agriculture, Forest Service, Post Office Box 96090, Washington, D.C. 20090 (202) 205-8333, www.fs.fed.us; *Timber Demand and Technology Assessment;* and *Agricultural Statistics.*

PRICES - MINERAL PRODUCTS - See also

Individual Minerals

U.S. Department of the Interior, Geological Survey, Office of Minerals Information, 12201 Sunrise Valley Drive, Reston, Virginia 22092 (703) 648-4000, www.minerals.usgs.gov; *Annual Reports;* and *Mineral Commodity Summaries.*

PRICES - RECEIVED BY FARMERS - CROPS

U.S. Department of Agriculture, National Agricultural Statistics Service, Fourteenth Street and Independence Avenue, SW, Washington, D.C. 20250 (800) 727-9540, www.usda.gov/nass; *Crop Production;* and *Field Crops; Crop Values.*

PRICES - RECEIVED BY FARMERS - INDEXES

U.S. Department of Agriculture, National Agricultural Statistics Service, Fourteenth Street and Independence Avenue, SW, Washington, D.C. 20250 (800) 727-9540, www.usda.gov/nass; *Agricultural Prices: Annual Summary.*

PRICES - RECEIVED BY FARMERS - LIVESTOCK AND PRODUCTS - POULTRY

U.S. Department of Agriculture, National Agricultural Statistics Service, Fourteenth Street and Independence Avenue, SW, Washington, D.C. 20250 (800) 727-9540, www.usda.gov/nass; *Agricultural Statistics; Meat Animals - Production Disposition and Income; Layers and Egg Production; Poultry - Production and Value;* and *Turkeys.*

PRICES - STOCKS

Global Financial Data, 784 Fremont Villas, Los Angeles, California 90042 (310) 642-4659; Internet sites: "U.S. Stock Market Capitalization Indices," http://www.globalfindata.com/tbcap.htm; "Global Financial Data Dow Jones Industrial Average," http://www.globalfindata.com/tbdjia.htm; "GFD Standard and Poor's Sectors," http://www.globalfindata.com/tbspect.htm.

New York Stock Exchange, 11 Wall Street, New York, New York 10005 (212) 656-3000; *Fact Book.*

PRIMARIES - PRESIDENTIAL PREFERENCE

Federal Election Commission, 999 E Street, NW, Washington, D.C. 20463 (800) 424-9530, www.fec.gov; *FEC Reports on Financial Activity, Final Report, Presidential Pre-Nomination Campaigns.*

PRIMARY METAL INDUSTRIES - See METAL INDUSTRIES

PRINTING AND PUBLISHING

INDUSTRIES - BOOK AND PERIODICAL PRICES

R.R. Bowker Company, 121 Chanlon Road, New Providence, New Jersey 07974 (908) 464-6800; *Publishers Weekly,* and *The Bowker Annual: Library and Book Trade Almanac.*

Library Journal, 249 West 17th Street, New York, New York 10011 (212) 463-6819; *Library Journal.*

PRINTING AND PUBLISHING INDUSTRIES - CAPITAL

U.S. Department of Commerce, Bureau of the Census, Washington, D.C. 20233 (301) 457-4100, www.census.gov; *Census of Manufactures, Industry Reports;* and *Annual Survey of Manufactures.*

PRINTING AND PUBLISHING INDUSTRIES - EARNINGS

U.S. Department of Commerce, Bureau of the Census, Washington, D.C. 20233 (301) 457-4100, www.census.gov; *Census of Manufactures;* and *Annual Survey of Manufactures.*

U.S. Department of Commerce, Bureau of the Census, Washington, D.C. 20233 (301) 457-4100, www.census.gov; *1997 Economic Census, Core Business Statistics Series.*

U.S. Department of Labor, Bureau of Labor Statistics, Two Massachusetts Avenue, NE, Washington, D.C. 20212 (202) 691-5200, www.stats.bls.gov; *Employment and Earnings,* and Internet site: http://stats.bls.gov/ ceshome.htm.

PRINTING AND PUBLISHING INDUSTRIES - EMPLOYEES

U.S. Department of Commerce, Bureau of the Census, Washington, D.C. 20233 (301) 457-4100, www.census.gov; *Census of Manufactures, Industry Reports;* and *Annual Survey of Manufactures.*

U.S. Department of Commerce, Bureau of the Census, Washington, D.C. 20233 (301) 457-4100, www.census.gov; *1997 Economic Census, Core Business Statistics Series.*

U.S. Department of Labor, Bureau of Labor Statistics, Two Massachusetts Avenue, NE, Washington, D.C. 20212 (202) 691-5200, www.stats.bls.gov; *Employment and Earnings; Monthly Labor Review;* and Internet site: http://stats.bls.gov/ ceshome.htm.

PRINTING AND PUBLISHING INDUSTRIES - ENERGY CONSUMPTION

U.S. Department of Energy, Energy

Information Administration, 1000 Independence Avenue, SW, Washington, D.C. 20585 (202) 586-8800, www.eia.doe.gov; *Manufacturing Energy Consumption.*

PRINTING AND PUBLISHING INDUSTRIES - ESTABLISHMENTS

U.S. Department of Commerce, Bureau of the Census, Washington, D.C. 20233 (301) 457-4100, www.census.gov; *Census of Manufactures;* and *Annual Survey of Manufactures.*

PRINTING AND PUBLISHING INDUSTRIES - FINANCES

U.S. Department of Commerce, Bureau of the Census, Washington, D.C. 20233 (301) 457-4100, www.census.gov; *Annual Survey of Manufactures;* and *Census of Manufactures.*

PRINTING AND PUBLISHING INDUSTRIES - FOREIGN TRADE

U.S. Department of Commerce, Bureau of the Census, Washington, D.C. 20233 (301) 457-4100, www.census.gov; *U.S. International Trade in Goods and Services.*

PRINTING AND PUBLISHING INDUSTRIES - GROSS DOMESTIC PRODUCT

U.S. Department of Commerce, Bureau of Economic Analysis, Fourteenth Street between Constitution Avenue and E Street, NW, Washington, D.C. 20230 (202) 606-9900, www.bea.doc.gov; *Survey of Current Business.*

PRINTING AND PUBLISHING INDUSTRIES - MERGERS AND ACQUISITIONS

Thomson Financial Securities Data, Two Gateway Center, Newark, New Jersey 07006 (973) 622-3100; Merger and Corporate Transactions Database.

PRINTING AND PUBLISHING INDUSTRIES - OCCUPATIONAL SAFETY

U.S. Department of Labor, Bureau of Labor Statistics, Two Massachusetts Avenue, NE, Washington, D.C. 20212 (202) 691-5200, www.stats.bls.gov; *Occupational Injuries and Illnesses in the United States by Industry.*

PRINTING AND PUBLISHING INDUSTRIES - PRODUCTIVITY

Board of Governors of the Federal Reserve System, Twentieth Street and Constitution Avenue, NW, Washington, D.C. 20551 (202) 452-3000, www.bog.frb.fed.us; *Federal Reserve Bulletin;* and *Industrial Production and Capacity Utilization.*

U.S. Department of Labor, Bureau of Labor Statistics, Two Massachusetts Avenue, NE, Washington, D.C. 20212 (202) 691-5200, www.stats.bls.gov; Internet site: http://stats.bls.gov/iprhome.htm.

PRINTING AND PUBLISHING INDUSTRIES - SALES, SHIPMENTS, RECEIPTS

Forbes, Incorporated, 60 Fifth Avenue, New York, New York 10011 (212) 691-6130; *Forbes Annual Report on American Industry.*

U.S. Department of Commerce, Bureau of the Census, Washington, D.C. 20233 (301) 457-4100, www.census.gov; *Census of Manufactures, Industry Reports;* and *Annual Survey of Manufactures.*

U.S. Department of Commerce, Bureau of the Census, Washington, D.C. 20233 (301) 457-4100, www.census.gov; *1997 Economic Census, Core Business Statistics Series.*

PRINTING AND PUBLISHING INDUSTRIES - TOXIC CHEMICAL RELEASES

Environmental Protection Agency, 1200 Pennsylvania Avenue, NW, Washington, D.C. 20460 (888) 372-8255, www.epa.gov; *Toxics Release Inventory.*

PRINTING AND PUBLISHING INDUSTRIES - VALUE ADDED

U.S. Department of Commerce, Bureau of the Census, Washington, D.C. 20233 (301) 457-4100, www.census.gov; *Census of Manufactures, Industry Reports;* and *Annual Survey of Manufactures.*

PRISONS AND PRISONERS - See also CORRECTIONAL INSTITUTIONS

U.S. Department of Justice, Bureau of Justice Statistics, 810 Seventh Street, NW, 2nd Floor, Washington, D.C. 20531 (800) 732-3277, www.ojp.usdoj.gov/bjs; *Prisoners in State and Federal Institutions on December 31; Correctional Populations in the United States; Capital Punishment; Census of State and Federal Correctional Facilities;* and *Prisoners in 1997.*

PRISONS AND PRISONERS - ALCOHOL/DRUG USE

U.S. Department of Justice, Bureau of Justice Statistics, 810 Seventh Street, NW, 2nd Floor, Washington, D.C. 20531 (800) 732-3277, www.ojp.usdoj.gov/bjs; *Substance Abuse and Treatment, State and Federal Prisoners.*

PRISONS AND PRISONERS - DEATH SENTENCE

U.S. Department of Justice, Bureau of

Justice Statistics, 810 Seventh Street, NW, 2nd Floor, Washington, D.C. 20531 (800) 732-3277, www.ojp.usdoj.gov/bjs; *Capital Punishment;* and *Correctional Populations in the United States.*

PRISONS AND PRISONERS - EXECUTIONS

U.S. Department of Justice, Bureau of Justice Statistics, 810 Seventh Street, NW, 2nd Floor, Washington, D.C. 20531 (800) 732-3277, www.ojp.usdoj.gov/bjs; *Capital Punishment;* and *Correctional Projections in the United States.*

PRISONS AND PRISONERS - INMATE CHARACTERISTICS

U.S. Department of Justice, Bureau of Justice Statistics, 810 Seventh Street, NW, 2nd Floor, Washington, D.C. 20531 (800) 732-3277, www.ojp.usdoj.gov/bjs; *Census of State and Federal Correctional Facilities.*

PRISONS AND PRISONERS - SENTENCE -BY OFFENSE

U.S. Department of Justice, Bureau of Justice Statistics, 810 Seventh Street, NW, 2nd Floor, Washington, D.C. 20531 (800) 732-3277, www.ojp.usdoj.gov/bjs; *Compendium of Federal Justice Statistics.*

PRIVATE HOUSEHOLDS (SERVICES)

U.S. Department of Commerce, Bureau of the Census, Washington, D.C. 20233 (301) 457-4100, www.census.gov; *Survey of Current Business.*

PROBATION

U.S. Department of Justice, Bureau of Justice Statistics, 810 Seventh Street, NW, 2nd Floor, Washington, D.C. 20531 (800) 732-3277, www.ojp.usdoj.gov/bjs, *Correctional Populations in the United States.*

PRODUCER PRICE INDEXES

U.S. Department of Labor, Bureau of Labor Statistics, Two Massachusetts Avenue, NE, Washington, D.C. 20212 (202) 691-5200, www.stats.bls.gov; *Producer Price Indexes.*

PRODUCER PRICE INDEXES - CONSTRUCTION MATERIALS

U.S. Department of Labor, Bureau of Labor Statistics, Two Massachusetts Avenue, NE, Washington, D.C. 20212 (202) 691-5200, www.stats.bls.gov; *Producer Price Indexes.*

PRODUCER PRICE INDEXES - NEWSPRINT

U.S. Department of Labor, Bureau of Labor Statistics, Two Massachusetts

Avenue, NE, Washington, D.C. 20212 (202) 691-5200, www.stats.bls.gov; *Producer Price Indexes.*

PRODUCER PRICE INDEXES - RAILROAD FREIGHT

U.S. Department of Labor, Bureau of Labor Statistics, Two Massachusetts Avenue, NE, Washington, D.C. 20212 (202) 691-5200, www.stats.bls.gov; *Producer Price Indexes.*

PRODUCER PRICE INDEXES - STAGE - OF PROCESSING

U.S. Department of Labor, Bureau of Labor Statistics, Two Massachusetts Avenue, NE, Washington, D.C. 20212 (202) 691-5200, www.stats.bls.gov; *Producer Price Indexes.*

PRODUCER PRICE INDEXES - TIMBER

U.S. Department of Labor, Bureau of Labor Statistics, Two Massachusetts Avenue, NE, Washington, D.C. 20212 (202) 691-5200, www.stats.bls.gov; *Producer Price Indexes.*

PRODUCTIVITY - See also Individual Industries

PRODUCTIVITY - CAPACITY UTILIZATION

Board of Governors of the Federal Reserve System, Twentieth Street and Constitution Avenue, NW, Washington, D.C. 20551 (202) 452-3000, www.bog.frb.fed.us; *Capacity Utilization in Manufacturing, Mining, Utilities, and Industrial Materials.*

PRODUCTIVITY - FARM OUTPUT

Executive Office of the President, Council of Economic Advisors, Old Executive Office Building, Washington, D.C. 20502 (202) 395-5084, www.whitehouse.gov/cea; *Economic Report of the President.*

U.S. Department of Agriculture, Economic Research Service, 1800 M Street, NW, Washington, D.C. 20036 (202) 694-5050, www.ers.usda.gov; *Agricultural Statistics; AREI Updates: Cropland Use; Agricultural Resources and Environmental Indicators; Economic Indicators of the Farm Sector: Production and Efficiency Statistics;* and *Agricultural Outlook.*

PRODUCTIVITY - LABOR

Organisation for Economic Cooperation and Development, Publication and Information Center, 2001 L Street, NW, Washington, D.C. 20036 (202) 785-6323; *Science, Technology, and Industry Outlook.*

U.S. Department of Labor, Bureau of Labor Statistics, Two Massachusetts Avenue, NE, Washington, D.C. 20212 (202) 691-5200, www.stats.bls.gov; *Productivity and Costs; International Comparisons of Manufacturing Productivity and Unit Labor Cost Trends, 1997, revised data;* News Releases; unpublished data; and Internet site http://stats.bls.gov/iprhome.htm.

PRODUCTIVITY - MINING INDUSTRIES

U.S. Department of Energy, Energy Information Administration, 1000 Independence Avenue, SW, Washington, D.C. 20585 (202) 586-8800, www.eia.doe.gov; *Coal Industry; Quarterly Coal Report; Annual Energy Review;* and unpublished data.

PROFESSIONAL SCIENTIFIC AND TECHNICAL SERVICES - EARNINGS

U.S. Department of Commerce, Bureau of the Census, Washington, D.C. 20233 (301) 457-4100, www.census.gov; *1997 Economic Census: Advance Summary Statistics for the U.S. 1997 NAICS Basis.*

PROFESSIONAL SCIENTIFIC AND TECHNICAL SERVICES - EMPLOYEES

U.S. Department of Commerce, Bureau of the Census, Washington, D.C. 20233 (301) 457-4100, www.census.gov; *1997 Economic Census: Advance Summary Statistics for the U.S. 1997 NAICS Basis.*

PROFESSIONAL SCIENTIFIC AND TECHNICAL SERVICES - ESTABLISHMENTS

U.S. Department of Commerce, Bureau of the Census, Washington, D.C. 20233 (301) 457-4100, www.census.gov; *1997 Economic Census: Advance Summary Statistics for the U.S. 1997 NAICS Basis.*

PROFESSIONAL SCIENTIFIC AND TECHNICAL SERVICES - PAYROLL - ANNUAL

U.S. Department of Commerce, Bureau of the Census, Washington, D.C. 20233 (301) 457-4100, www.census.gov; *1997 Economic Census: Advance Summary Statistics for the U.S. 1997 NAICS Basis.*

PROFITS

Federal Deposit Insurance Corporation, 550 17th Street, NW, Washington, D.C. 20429 (202) 393-8400, www.fdic.gov; *Annual Report; Statistics on Banking;* and *FDIC Quarterly Banking Profile.*

U.S. Department of the Treasury, Internal Revenue Service, 1111 Constitution Avenue, NW, Washington, D.C. 20224 (202) 874-0410, www.irs.ustreas.gov; *Statistics of Income, Corporation Income Tax Returns.*

PROFITS - CORPORATIONS

U.S. Department of Commerce, Bureau of Economic Analysis, Fourteenth Street between Constitution Avenue and E Street, NW, Washington, D.C. 20230 (202) 606-9900, www.bea.doc.gov; *The National Income and Product Accounts of the United States;* and *Survey of Current Business.*

U.S. Department of Commerce, Bureau of the Census, Washington, D.C. 20233 (301) 457-4100, www.census.gov; *Quarterly Financial Report for Manufacturing, Mining and Trade Corporations.*

U.S. Department of the Treasury, Internal Revenue Service, 1111 Constitution Avenue, NW, Washington, D.C. 20224 (202) 874-0410, www.irs.ustreas.gov; *Statistics of Income,* various publications.

PROFITS - PARTNERSHIPS AND PROPRIETORSHIPS

U.S. Department of the Treasury, Internal Revenue Service, 1111 Constitution Avenue, NW, Washington, D.C. 20224 (202)874-0410, www.irs.ustreas.gov; *Statistics of Income,* various publications; and *Statistics of Income Bulletin.*

PROJECTIONS - BIRTHS

U.S. Department of Commerce, Bureau of the Census, Washington, D.C. 20233 (301) 457-4100, www.census.gov; *Current Population Reports;* and unpublished data.

PROJECTIONS - COLLEGE ENROLLMENT

U.S. Department of Education, National Center for Education Statistics, 555 New Jersey Avenue, NW, Washington, D.C. 20208-5574 (202) 219-1828, http://nces.ed.gov; *Projections of Education Statistics; Digest of Education Statistics;* and unpublished data.

PROJECTIONS - DEATHS

U.S. Department of Commerce, Bureau of the Census, Washington, D.C. 20233 (301) 457-4100, www.census.gov; *Current Population Reports;* and unpublished data.

PROJECTIONS - DEGREES CONFERRED

U.S. Department of Education, National Center for Education Statistics, 555 New Jersey Avenue, NW, Washington, D.C. 20208-5574 (202) 219-1828, http://nces.ed.gov; *Digest of Education Statistics;* and *Projections of Educational Statistics.*

PROJECTIONS - EMPLOYMENT

U.S. Department of Labor, Bureau of

Labor Statistics, Two Massachusetts Avenue, NE, Washington, D.C. 20212 (202) 691-5200, www.stats.bls.gov; *Monthly Labor Review.*

PROJECTIONS - ENERGY

U.S. Department of Energy, Energy Information Administration, 1000 Independence Avenue, SW, Washington, D.C. 20585 (202) 586-5000; *Annual Energy Outlook.*

PROJECTIONS - HEALTH EXPENDITURES

U.S. Department of Health and Human Services, Health Care Financing Administration, 200 Independence Avenue, SW, Washington, D.C. 20201 (202) 690-6145, www.hcfa.gov; Internet sites: http://www.hcfa.gov/stats/NHE-Proj/tables/t01.htm; http://www.hcfa.gov/stats/NHE-Proj/tables/t02.htm; and http://www.hcfa.gov/stats/NHE-Proj/tables/t02a.htm.

PROJECTIONS - HIGH SCHOOL GRADUATES

U.S. Department of Education, National Center for Education Statistics, 555 New Jersey Avenue, NW, Washington, D.C. 20208-5574 (202) 219-1828, http://nces.ed.gov; *Digest of Education Statistics;* and *Projections of Educational Statistics.*

PROJECTIONS - LABOR FORCE

U.S. Department of Labor, Bureau of Labor Statistics, Two Massachusetts Avenue, NE, Washington, D.C. 20212 (202) 691-5200, www.stats.bls.gov; *Employment and Earnings;* and *Monthly Labor Review.*

PROJECTIONS - LIFE EXPECTANCY

U.S. Department of Commerce, Bureau of the Census, Washington, D.C. 20233 (301) 457-4100, www.census.gov; unpublished data from the International Data Base.

U.S. Department of Health and Human Services, National Center for Health Statistics, 3700 East-West Highway, Hyattsville, Maryland 20782 (301) 436-8500 www.cdc.gov/nchs; *Vital Statistics of the United States;* and *National Vital Statistics.*

PROJECTIONS - POPULATION

U.S. Department of Commerce, Bureau of the Census, Washington, D.C. 20233 (301) 457-4100, www.census.gov; *Current Population Reports;* unpublished data; and Internet site: http://www.census.gov/ipc/www/idbnew.html.

PROJECTIONS - SCHOOL ENROLLMENT

U.S. Department of Education, National Center for Education Statistics, 555 New Jersey Avenue, NW, Washington, D.C. 20208-5574 (202) 219-1828, http://nces.ed.gov; *Projections of Education Statistics; Digest of Education Statistics;* and unpublished data.

PROJECTIONS - TEACHERS

U.S. Department of Education, National Center for Education Statistics, 555 New Jersey Avenue, NW, Washington, D.C. 20208-5574 (202) 219-1828, http://nces.ed.gov; *Digest of Education Statistics;* and *Projections of Education Statistics.*

U.S. Department of Labor, Bureau of Labor Statistics, Two Massachusetts Avenue, NE, Washington, D.C. 20212 (202) 691-5200, www.stats.bls.gov; *Monthly Labor Review.*

PROPERTY AND CASUALTY INSURANCE

Insurance Information Institute, 110 William Street, New York, New York 10038 (212) 669-9200; *The Fact Book, Property/Casualty Insurance Facts.*

PROPERTY TAX

U.S. Department of Commerce, Bureau of the Census, Washington, D.C. 20233 (301) 457-4100, www.census.gov; *Government Finances; State Government Finances;* and Internet sites: http://www.census.gov/ftp/pub/govs/www/index.html; http://www.census.gov/ftp/pub/govs/www.state.html.

PROPERTY TAX - HOUSEHOLDS

U.S. Department of Commerce, Bureau of the Census, Washington, D.C. 20233 (301) 457-4100, www.census.gov; Internet site: http://www.census.gov/hhes/income/histinc/rdi02.html.

PROPERTY TAX - RATES - SELECTED CITIES

Government of the District of Columbia, Department of Finance and Revenue, 441 Fourth Street, NW, Washington, D.C. 20001 (202) 727-6103; *Tax Rates and Tax Burdens in the District of Columbia: A Nationwide Comparison.*

PROPERTY TAX - STATE AND LOCAL GOVERNMENT

U.S. Department of Commerce, Bureau of the Census, Washington, D.C. 20233 (301) 457-4100, www.census.gov; *Governmental Finances and Employment;* and Internet site: http://www.census.gov/

govs/www/estimates.html.

PROPRIETORS' INCOME

U.S. Department of Commerce, Bureau of Economic Analysis, Fourteenth Street between Constitution Avenue and E Street, NW, Washington, D.C. 20230 (202) 606-9900, www.bea.doc.gov; *The National Income and Product Accounts of the United States;* and *Survey of Current Business.*

PROPRIETORSHIPS

U.S. Department of the Treasury, Internal Revenue Service, 1111 Constitution Avenue, NW, Washington, D.C. 20224 (202)874-0410, www.irs.ustreas.gov; *Statistics of Income;* various publications; and *Statistics of Income Bulletin.*

PROSTATECTOMY

U.S. Department of Health and Human Services, National Center for Health Statistics, 3700 East-West Highway, Hyattsville, Maryland 20782 (301) 436-8500, www.cdc.gov/nchs; *Vital and Health Statistics;* and unpublished data.

PROSTITUTION AND COMMERCIALIZED VICE - ARRESTS

U.S. Department of Justice, Federal Bureau of Investigation, 935 Pennsylvania Avenue, NW, Washington, D.C. 20535 (202) 324-3691, www.fbi.gov; *Crime in the United States.*

PROTECTIVE SERVICE WORKERS - See PUBLIC SAFETY

PROTESTANTS - See RELIGION

PRUNES AND PLUMS

U.S. Department of Agriculture, Economic Research Service, 1800 M Street, NW, Washington, D.C. 20036 (202) 694-5050, www.ers.usda.gov; *Food Consumption, Prices, and Expenditures;* and *Agricultural Outlook.*

U.S. Department of Agriculture, National Agricultural Statistics Service, Fourteenth Street and Independence Avenue, SW, Washington, D.C. 20250 (800) 727-9540, www.usda.gov/nass; *Noncitrus Fruits and Nuts.*

PSYCHIATRIC CARE AND INSTITUTIONS - See MENTAL HEALTH

PSYCHOLOGY - DEGREES CONFERRED

National Science Foundation, Division of Science Resource Studies, 4201 Wilson Boulevard, Arlington, Virginia 22230 (703) 306-1234, www.nsf.gov; *Survey of Earned Doctorates, Selected Data on Science and Engineering Doctorate Awards.*

U.S. Department of Commerce, Bureau of the Census, Washington, D.C. 20233 (301) 457-4100, www.census.gov; unpublished data.

U.S. Department of Education, National Center for Education Statistics, 555 New Jersey Avenue, NW, Washington, D.C. 20208-5574 (202) 219-1828, http://nces.ed.gov; *Digest of Education Statistics.*

PSYCHOLOGY - EMPLOYMENT

U.S. Department of Labor, Bureau of Labor Statistics, 2 Massachusetts Avenue, NE, Washington, D.C. 20212 (202) 691-5200, www.stats.bls.gov; *Employment and Earnings;* and unpublished data.

PSYCHOLOGY - RESEARCH - UNITED STATES GOVERNMENT OBLIGATIONS FOR

National Science Foundation, 4201 Wilson Boulevard, Arlington, Virginia 22230 (703) 306-1234, www.nsf.gov; *Federal Funds for Research and Development.*

PSYCHOTHERAPEUTIC DRUGS - NONMEDICAL USE

U.S. Department of Health and Human Services, Substance Abuse and Mental Health Services Administration, 5600 Fishers Lane, Rockville, Maryland 20857 (800) 729-6686, www.samhsa.gov; *National Household Survey on Drug Abuse.*

PUBLIC ADMINISTRATION - See GOVERNMENT

PUBLIC AID ASSISTANCE

U.S. Department of Commerce, Bureau of Economic Analysis, Fourteenth Street between Constitution Avenue and E Street, NW, Washington, D.C. 20230 (202) 606-9900, www.bea.doc.gov; *Survey of Current Business.*

Social Security Administration, 6400 Security Boulevard, Baltimore, Maryland 21235 (800) 772-1213, www.ssa.gov; *Social Security Bulletin; Annual Statistical Supplement to the Social Security Bulletin;* and unpublished data.

PUBLIC AID ASSISTANCE - BENEFITS PAID

Social Security Administration, 6400 Security Boulevard, Baltimore, Maryland 21235 (800) 772-1213, www.ssa.gov; *Social Security Bulletin; Annual Statistical Supplement to the Social Security Bulletin;* and unpublished data.

U.S. Department of Health and Human Services, Health Care Financing Administration, 200 Independence Avenue, SW, Washington, D.C. 20201 (202) 690-6145, www.hcfa.gov; unpublished data.

PUBLIC AID ASSISTANCE - FEDERAL AID TO STATE AND LOCAL GOVERNMENTS

Executive Office of the President, Office of Management and Budget, Executive Office Building, Washington, D.C. 20503 (202) 395-3080, www.whitehouse.gov/omb; *Historical Tables, Budget of the United States.*

U.S. Department of Commerce, Bureau of the Census, Washington, D.C. 20233 (301) 457-4100, www.census.gov; *Federal Expenditures by State for Fiscal Year.*

PUBLIC AID ASSISTANCE - FEDERAL EXPENDITURES

The Congress of the U.S., Congressional Research Service, 10 First Street, SE, Washington, D.C. 20540 (202) 707-5700; *Cash and Non-Cash Benefits for Persons With Limited Income: Eligibility Rules, Recipient and Expenditure Data.*

Social Security Administration, 6400 Security Boulevard, Baltimore, Maryland 21235 (800) 772-1213, www.ssa.gov; *Social Security Bulletin;* and unpublished data.

U.S. Department of Health and Human Services, Health Care Financing Administration, 200 Independence Avenue, SW, Washington, D.C. 20201 (202) 690-6145, www.hcfa.gov; *Health Care Financing Review; Statistical Report on Medical Care: Eligibles, Recipients, and Services;* and unpublished data.

PUBLIC AID ASSISTANCE - HEALTH EXPENDITURES

The Congress of the U.S., Congressional Research Service, 10 First Street, SE, Washington, D.C. 20540 (202) 707-5700; *Cash and Non-cash Benefits for Persons With Limited Income: Eligibility Rules, Recipient and Expenditure Data.*

Social Security Administration, 6400 Security Boulevard, Baltimore, Maryland 21235 (800) 772-1213, www.ssa.gov; *Social Security Bulletin;* and unpublished data.

U.S. Department of Commerce, Bureau of the Census, Washington, D.C. 20233 (301) 457-4100, www.census.gov; *Current Population Reports;* and unpublished data.

U.S. Department of Health and Human Services, Health Care Financing Administration, 200 Independence Avenue, SW, Washington, D.C. 20201 (202) 690-6145, www.hcfa.gov; *Health Care Financing Review; Statistical Report on Medical Care: Eligibles, Recipients and Services;* and unpublished data.

PUBLIC AID ASSISTANCE - RECIPIENTS

The Congress of the U.S., Congressional Research Service, 10 First Street, SE, Washington, D.C. 20540 (202) 707-5700; *Cash and Non-Cash Benefits for Persons With Limited Income: Eligibility Rules, Recipient and Expenditure Data.*

Social Security Administration, 6400 Security Boulevard, Baltimore, Maryland 21235 (800) 772-1213, www.ssa.gov; *Social Security Bulletin; Annual Statistical Supplement to the Social Security Bulletin;* and unpublished data.

U.S. Department of Commerce, Bureau of the Census, Washington, D.C. 20233 (301) 457-4100, www.census.gov; *Current Population Survey, Annual Demographic Survey; Current Population Reports;* unpublished data; and Internet site http://ferret.bls.census.gov/macro/031998/faminc/09000.htm.

U.S. Department of Health and Human Services, Administration for Children and Families, 370 L'Enfant Promenade, SW, Washington, D.C. 20447 (202) 401-9200, www.acf.dhhs.gov; *Quarterly Public Assistance Statistics.*

PUBLIC BROADCASTING STATIONS

Corporation for Public Broadcasting, 901 E Street, NW, Washington, D.C. 20004-2006 (202) 879-9600; *Programming Survey; Public Broadcasting Income, Fiscal Year 1997;* and unpublished data.

PUBLIC DOMAIN - See PUBLIC LANDS

PUBLIC HOUSING

The Congress of the U.S., Congressional Research Service, 10 First Street, SE, Washington, D.C. 20540 (202) 707-5700; *Cash and Non-Cash Benefits for Persons With Limited Income: Eligibility Rules, Recipient and Expenditures Data.*

Social Security Administration, 6400 Security Boulevard, Baltimore, Maryland 21235 (800) 772-1213, www.ssa.gov; *Social Security Bulletin;* and unpublished data.

U.S. Department of Commerce, Bureau of Economic Analysis, Fourteenth Street between Constitution Avenue and E Street, NW, Washington, D.C. 20230 (202) 606-9900, www.bea.doc.gov; *Survey of Current Business.*

U.S. Department of Commerce, Bureau of the Census, Washington, D.C. 20233 (301) 457-4100, www.census.gov; *Current Population Reports; Federal Aid to States for Fiscal Year End;* and Internet site: http://ferret.bls.census.gov/macro/031998/noncash/1001.htm.

PUBLIC LANDS - See also FORESTS

PUBLIC LANDS - AREA

General Services Administration, General Services Building, Eighteenth and F Streets, NW, Washington, D.C. 20405 (202) 708-5082, www.gsa.gov; *Inventory Report on Real Property Owned by the United States Throughout the World.*

PUBLIC LANDS - COST AND USAGE

General Services Administration, General Services Building, Eighteenth and F Streets, NW, Washington, D.C. 20405 (202) 708-5082, www.gsa.gov; *Inventory Report on Real Property Owned by the United States Throughout the World.*

PUBLIC LANDS - FOREST LAND - AREA

U.S. Department of Agriculture, Forest Service, Post Office Box 96090, Washington, D.C. 20090 (202) 205-8333, www.fs.fed.us; *Forest Resources of the U.S.;* and *Land Areas of the National Forest System.*

PUBLIC LANDS - LEASES, PERMITS, AND LICENSES

General Services Administration, General Services Building, Eighteenth and F Streets, NW, Washington, D.C. 20405 (202) 708-5082, www.gsa.gov; *Inventory Report on Real Property Owned by the United States Throughout the World.*

PUBLIC LANDS - NATIONAL PARK SYSTEM

U.S. Department of the Interior, National Park Service, C Street between Eighteenth and Nineteenth Streets, NW, Washington, D.C. 20240 (202) 208-6843, www.nps.gov; *National Park Statistical Abstract;* and unpublished data.

PUBLIC LANDS - OWNERSHIP

General Services Administration, General Services Building, Eighteenth and F Streets, NW, Washington, D.C. 20405 (202) 708-5082, www.gsa.gov; *Inventory Report on Real Property Owned by the United States Throughout the World.*

PUBLIC LANDS - RECREATION

U.S. Department of Agriculture, Forest Service, Post Office Box 96090, Washington, D.C. 20090 (202) 205-8333, www.fs.fed.us; *Annual Report.*

U.S. Department of the Interior, National Park Service, C Street between Eighteenth and Nineteenth Streets, NW, Washington, D.C. 20204 (202) 208-6843, www.nps.gov; *National Park Statistical Abstract;* and unpublished data.

PUBLIC OFFICIALS - PROSECUTIONS

U.S. Department of Justice, 950 Pennsylvania Avenue, NW, Washington, D.C. 20530 (202) 514-2000; *Report to Congress on the Activities and Operations of the Public Integrity Section.*

PUBLIC ROADS - See HIGHWAYS

PUBLIC SAFETY - See also LAW ENFORCEMENT

PUBLIC SAFETY - EMPLOYMENT

U.S. Department of Labor, Bureau of Labor Statistics, Two Massachusetts Avenue, NE, Washington, D.C. 20212 (202) 691-5200, www.stats.bls.gov; *Monthly Labor Review; Employment and Earnings;* and unpublished data.

PUBLIC SAFETY - EMPLOYMENT - CITY GOVERNMENT

U.S. Department of Commerce, Bureau of the Census, Washington, D.C. 20233 (301) 457-4100, www.census.gov; *City Employment;* and unpublished data.

PUBLIC SAFETY - EMPLOYMENT - FIRE PROTECTION

U.S. Department of Commerce, Bureau of the Census, Washington, D.C. 20233 (301) 457-4100, www.census.gov; Internet site: http://www.census.gov/pub/govs/www/apes.html.

PUBLIC SAFETY - EMPLOYMENT - POLICE PROTECTION AND CORRECTION

U.S. Department of Commerce, Bureau of the Census, Washington, D.C. 20233 (301) 457-4100, www.census.gov;Internet site: http://www.census.gov/pub/govs/www/apes.html.

U.S. Department of Justice, Bureau of Justice Statistics, 810 Seventh Street, NW, 2nd Floor, Washington, D.C. 20531 (800) 732-3277, www.ojp.usdoj.gov/bjs; *Census of State and Local Law Enforcement Agencies.*

PUBLIC SAFETY - EXPENDITURES

U.S. Department of Justice, Bureau of Justice Statistics, 810 Seventh Street, NW, 2nd Floor, Washington, D.C. 20531 (800) 732-3277, www.ojp.usdoj.gov/bjs; *Census of State and Local Law Enforcement Agencies.*

PUBLIC SAFETY - EXPENDITURES - CITY GOVERNMENTS

U.S. Department of Commerce, Bureau of the Census, Washington, D.C. 20233 (301) 457-4100, www.census.gov; unpublished data.

PUBLIC SAFETY - EXPENDITURES - LOCAL

GOVERNMENT

U.S. Department of Commerce, Bureau of the Census, Washington, D.C. 20233 (301)457-4100, www.census.gov; *Historical Statistics on Government Finances and Employment;* and Internet site: http://www.census.gov/govs/www/esti96.html.

PUBLIC SAFETY - EXPENDITURES - STATE GOVERNMENT

U.S. Department of Commerce, Bureau of the Census, Washington, D.C. 20233 (301) 457-4100, www.census.gov; *State Government Finances;* and Internet site http://www.census.gov/ftp/pub/govs/www.state.html.

PUBLIC SCHOOLS - See EDUCATION

PUBLIC TRANSPORTATION INDEXES

U.S. Department of Labor, Bureau of Labor Statistics, 2 Massachusetts Avenue, NE, Washington, D.C. 20212 (202) 691-5200, www.stats.bls.gov; *Monthly Labor Review,* and *CPI Detailed Report.*

PUBLISHING INDUSTRY - See PRINTING AND PUBLISHING INDUSTRIES

PUERTO RICAN POPULATION - See also HISPANIC ORIGIN POPULATION

U.S. Department of Commerce, Bureau of the Census, Washington, D.C. 20233 (301) 457-4100, www.census.gov; *Census of Population, General Population Characteristics, U.S.;* and unpublished data.

PUERTO RICAN POPULATION - EDUCATIONAL ATTAINMENT

U.S. Department of Commerce, Bureau of the Census, Washington, D.C. 20233 (301) 457-4100, www.census.gov; *Current Population Reports;* and unpublished data.

PUERTO RICAN POPULATION - LABOR FORCE

U.S. Department of Labor, Bureau of Labor Statistics, Two Massachusetts Avenue, NE, Washington, D.C. 20212 (202) 691-5200, www.stats.bls.gov; *Employment and Earnings;* and Bulletin 2307.

Puerto Rico - National Statistical Office

Planning Board, Commonwealth of Puerto Rico, North Building, Box 41119, San Juan, Puerto Rico 00940.

Puerto Rico - Primary Statistics Source

Puerto Rico Planning Board, North Building, Box 41119, San Juan, Puerto Rico 00940; *Anuario estastistico* (Statistical Yearbook).

Puerto Rico - State Data Centers

Puerto Rico Planning Board, Minillas Government Center, North Building, 14th Floor, De Eiego Avenue Pda 22, Post Office Box 41119, Santurce, Puerto Rico 00940-1119, Lillian Torres Aguirre (787) 728-4430.

Departmeno de Educacion, Apartado 190759, San Juan, Puerto Rico 00919-0759, Jorge Banuchi (787) 751-5372.

Recinto Universitario de Mayaguez, Universidad de Puerto Rico, Apartado 5000, Mayaguez, Puerto Rico 00681-5000, Arlene Martinez Rodriguez (787) 832-4040.

PUERTO RICO - AGRICULTURE

Economist Intelligence Unit, 111 West 57th Street, New York, New York 10019 (800) 938-4685; *Puerto Rico Country Report.*

Euromonitor International, Inc., 122 South Michigan Avenue, Suite 1200, Chicago, Illinois 60603 (800) 577-EURO; *International Marketing Data and Statistics;* and *World Marketing Data and Statistics.*

Europa Publications Limited, 18 Bedford Square, London, WC1B 3JN, England; *The Europa World Year Book.*

Food and Agricultural Organization of the United Nations (FAO), Via delle Terme di Caracalla, 00100 Rome, Italy (Telephone Number in U.S. (202) 653-2400); *Production Yearbook; The State of Food and Agriculture;* and *Trade Yearbook.*

Organisation for Economic Co-operation and Development (OECD), 2 rue Andre-Pascal, 75 Paris 16, France (Telephone Number in U.S. (202) 785-6323); *Indicators of Industrial Activity.*

St. Martin's Press, Inc., 175 Fifth Avenue, New York, New York 10010 (800) 221-7945; *The Statesman's Year-Book.*

Statistical Office of the United Nations, Publishing Service, New York, New York 10017 (800) 253-9646; *Statistical Yearbook.*

PUERTO RICO - AIRLINE SERVICE

Europa Publications Limited, 18 Bedford Square, London, WC1B 3JN, England; *The Europa World Year Book.*

PUERTO RICO - AIRPORTS

Central Intelligence Agency, Washington, D.C. 20505 (703) 482-1100,

www.cia.gov; *The World Factbook.*

PUERTO RICO - AREA AND DENSITY OF POPULATION

Central Intelligence Agency, Washington, D.C. 20505 (703) 482-1100, www.cia.gov; *The World Factbook.*

Euromonitor International, Inc., 122 South Michigan Avenue, Suite 1200, Chicago, Illinois 60603 (800) 577-EURO; *International Marketing Data and Statistics;* and *The World Economic Factbook.*

Europa Publications Limited, 18 Bedford Square, London, WC1B 3JN, England; *The Europa World Year Book.*

Food and Agricultural Organization of the United Nations (FAO) Via delle Terme di Caracalla, 00100 Rome, Italy (Telephone Number in U.S. (202) 653-2400); *The State of Food and Agriculture.*

St. Martin's Press, Inc., 175 Fifth Avenue, New York, New York 10010 (800) 221-7945; *The Statesman's Year-Book.*

Statistical Office of the United Nations, Publishing Service, New York, New York 10017 (800) 253-9646; *Statistical Yearbook.*

United Nations Educational, Scientific and Cultural Organization (UNESCO), 7 Place de Fontenoy, F-75700 Paris, France (Telephone Number in U.S. (212) 963-5981); *Statistical Yearbook.*

PUERTO RICO - BALANCE OF PAYMENTS

Europa Publications Limited, 18 Bedford Square, London, WC1B 3JN, England; *The Europa World Year Book.*

International Monetary Fund, 700 Nineteenth Street, NW, Washington, D.C. 20431 (202) 623-7000; *Balance of Payments Yearbook.*

PUERTO RICO - BANKING

Euromonitor International, Inc., 122 South Michigan Avenue, Suite 1200, Chicago, Illinois 60603 (800) 577-EURO; *World Marketing Data and Statistics.*

St. Martin's Press, Inc., 175 Fifth Avenue, New York, New York 10010 (800) 221-7945; *The Statesman's Year-Book.*

PUERTO RICO - BEER PRODUCTION - See PUERTO RICO - BEVERAGES

PUERTO RICO - BEVERAGES

Statistical Office of the United Nations, Publishing Service, New York, New York 10017 (800) 253-9646; *Statistical Yearbook.*

PUERTO RICO - BIRTH RATES

Central Intelligence Agency, Washington, D.C. 20505 (703) 482-1100, www.cia.gov; *The World Factbook.*

Euromonitor International, Inc., 122 South Michigan Avenue, Suite 1200, Chicago, Illinois 60603 (800) 577-EURO; *International Marketing Data and Statistics;* and *The World Economic Factbook.*

Europa Publications Limited, 18 Bedford Square, London, WC1B 3JN, England; *The Europa World Year Book.*

St. Martin's Press, Inc., 175 Fifth Avenue, New York, New York 10010 (800) 221-7945; *The Statesman's Year-Book.*

Statistical Office of the United Nations, Publishing Service, New York, New York 10017 (800) 253-9646; *Demographic Yearbook;* and *Statistical Yearbook.*

World Health Organization, Office of Publications, 20 Avenue Appia, CH-1211 Geneva 27, Switzerland (Telephone Number in U.S. (518) 436-9686); *World Health Statistics Annual.*

PUERTO RICO - BROADCASTING

Billboard Limited, Post Office Box 9027, 1006 AA Amsterdam, The Netherlands (Telephone Number in U.S. (212) 764-7300); *World Radio TV Handbook.*

Central Intelligence Agency, Washington, D.C. 20505 (703) 482-1100, www.cia.gov; *The World Factbook.*

Euromonitor International, Inc., 122 South Michigan Avenue, Suite 1200, Chicago, Illinois 60603 (800) 577-EURO; *World Marketing Data and Statistics.*
St. Martin's Press, Inc., 175 Fifth Avenue, New York, New York 10010 (800) 221-7945; *The Statesman's Year-Book.*

United Nations Educational, Scientific and Cultural Organization (UNESCO), 7 Place de Fontenoy, F-75700 Paris, France (Telephone Number in U.S. (212) 963-5981); *Statistical Yearbook.*

PUERTO RICO - BUDGET

Central Intelligence Agency, Washington, D.C. 20505 (703) 482-1100, www.cia.gov; *The World Factbook.*

PUERTO RICO - BUTTER PRODUCTION - See PUERTO RICO - DAIRY PRODUCTS

PUERTO RICO - CALORIE SUPPLY

Food and Agricultural Organization of the United Nations (FAO) Via delle Terme di Caracalla, 00100 Rome, Italy (Telephone Number in U.S. (202) 653-2400); *The State of Food and Agriculture.*

PUERTO RICO - CATTLE - See PUERTO RICO - LIVESTOCK AND POULTRY

PUERTO RICO - CEMENT PRODUCTION - See PUERTO RICO - MINING AND MINERAL PRODUCTS

PUERTO RICO - CHEMICAL (ORGANIC) PRODUCTION - See PUERTO RICO - MINING AND MINERAL PRODUCTS

PUERTO RICO - CHICKENS - See PUERTO RICO - LIVESTOCK AND POULTRY

PUERTO RICO - COAL PRODUCTION - See PUERTO RICO - MINING AND MINERAL PRODUCTS

PUERTO RICO - COFFEE PRODUCTION AND CONSUMPTION - See PUERTO RICO - CROPS

PUERTO RICO - COMMERCE

St. Martin's Press, Inc., 175 Fifth Avenue, New York, New York 10010 (800) 221-7945; *The Statesman's Year-Book.*

PUERTO RICO - CONSTRUCTION INDUSTRY

Statistical Office of the United Nations, Publishing Service, New York, New York 10017 (800) 253-9646; *Statistical Yearbook.*

PUERTO RICO - CONSUMER PRICE INDEX

Europa Publications Limited, 18 Bedford Square, London, WC1B 3JN, England; *The Europa World Year Book.*

Statistical Office of the United Nations, Publishing Service, New York, New York 10017 (800) 253-9646; *Statistical Yearbook.*

PUERTO RICO - CONSUMER PRICES

Euromonitor International, Inc., 122 South Michigan Avenue, Suite 1200, Chicago, Illinois 60603 (800) 577-EURO; *World Marketing Data and Statistics.*

International Labour Office, I.L.O. Publications, 1828 L Street, NW, Suite 801, Washington, D.C. 20036 (301) 638-3152; *Yearbook of Labour Statistics.*

PUERTO RICO - CORN PRODUCTION - See PUERTO RICO - CROPS

PUERTO RICO - CORPORATE TAXES - See PUERTO RICO - TAXATION

PUERTO RICO - CRIME

Yale University Press, Yale Station, New Haven, Connecticut 06520 (800) 987-7323; *Violence and Crime in Cross-National Perspective.*

PUERTO RICO - CROPS

Europa Publications Limited, 18 Bedford Square, London, WC1B 3JN, England; *The Europa World Year Book.*

Food and Agricultural Organization of the United Nations (FAO) Via delle Terme di Caracalla, 00100 Rome, Italy (Telephone Number in U.S. (202) 653-2400); *Production Yearbook;* and *The State of Food and Agriculture.*

St. Martin's Press, Inc., 175 Fifth Avenue, New York, New York 10010 (800) 221-7945; *The Statesman's Year-Book.*

Statistical Office of the United Nations, Publishing Service, New York, New York 10017 (800) 253-9646; *Statistical Yearbook.*

PUERTO RICO - CUSTOMS DUTIES

St. Martin's Press, Inc., 175 Fifth Avenue, New York, New York 10010 (800) 221-7945; *The Statesman's Year-Book.*

PUERTO RICO - DAIRY PRODUCTS

Food and Agricultural Organization of the United Nations (FAO) Via delle Terme di Caracalla, 00100 Rome, Italy (Telephone Number in U.S. (202) 653-2400); *The State of Food and Agriculture.*

St. Martin's Press, Inc., 175 Fifth Avenue, New York, New York 10010 (800) 221-7945; *The Statesman's Year-Book.*

Statistical Office of the United Nations, Publishing Service, New York, New York 10017 (800) 253-9646; *Statistical Yearbook.*

PUERTO RICO - DEATH RATES - See PUERTO RICO - MORTALITY

PUERTO RICO - DEMOGRAPHY

Euromonitor International, Inc., 122 South Michigan Avenue, Suite 1200, Chicago, Illinois 60603 (800) 577-EURO; *International Marketing Data and Statistics; World Marketing Data and Statistics;* and *The World Economic Factbook.*

PUERTO RICO - DISEASES - See PUERTO RICO - HEALTH

PUERTO RICO - DIVORCE RATES

Statistical Office of the United Nations, Publishing Service, New York, New York 10017 (800) 253-9646; *Demographic Yearbook;* and *Statistical Yearbook.*

PUERTO RICO - ECONOMY

Central Intelligence Agency, Washington, D.C. 20505 (703) 482-1100, www.cia.gov; *The World Factbook.*

Economist Intelligence Unit, 111 West 57th Street, New York, New York 10019 (800) 938-4685; *Puerto Rico Country Report.*

Euromonitor International, Inc., 122 South Michigan Avenue, Suite 1200, Chicago, Illinois 60603 (800) 577-EURO; *International Marketing Data and Statistics; World Marketing Data and Statistics;* and *The World Economic Factbook.*

Europa Publications Limited, 18 Bedford Square, London, WC1B 3JN, England; *The Europa World Year Book.*

St. Martin's Press, Inc., 175 Fifth Avenue, New York, New York 10010 (800) 221-7945; *The Statesman's Year-Book.*

Statistical Office of the United Nations, Publishing Service, New York, New York 10017 (800) 253-9646; *World Statistics Pocketbook.*

The World Bank, 1818 H Street, NW, Washington, D.C. 20433 (202) 477-1234; *World Development Report.*

PUERTO RICO - EDUCATION

Euromonitor International, Inc., 122 South Michigan Avenue, Suite 1200, Chicago, Illinois 60603 (800) 577-EURO; *International Marketing Data and Statistics;* and *World Marketing Data and Statistics.*

Europa Publications Limited, 18 Bedford Square, London, WC1B 3JN, England; *The Europa World Year Book.*

St. Martin's Press, Inc., 175 Fifth Avenue, New York, New York 10010 (800) 221-7945; *The Statesman's Year-Book*

United Nations Educational, Scientific and Cultural Organization (UNESCO), 7 Place de Fontenoy, F-75700 Paris, France (Telephone Number in U.S. (212) 963-5981); *Statistical Yearbook.*

PUERTO RICO - EGG PRODUCTION AND CONSUMPTION - See PUERTO RICO - DAIRY PRODUCTS

PUERTO RICO - ELECTRICITY

Central Intelligence Agency, Washington, D.C. 20505 (703) 482-1100, www.cia.gov; *The World Factbook.*

St. Martin's Press, Inc., 175 Fifth Avenue, New York, New York 10010 (800) 221-7945; *The Statesman's Year-Book.*

Statistical Office of the United Nations, Publishing Service, New York, New York 10017 (800) 253-9646; *Statistical Yearbook.*

PUERTO RICO - EMPLOYMENT

Euromonitor International, Inc., 122 South Michigan Avenue, Suite 1200,

Chicago, Illinois 60603 (800) 577-EURO; *International Marketing Data and Statistics.*

International Labour Office, I.L.O. Publications, 1828 L Street, NW, Suite 801, Washington, D.C. 20036 (301) 638-3152; *Yearbook of Labour Statistics.*

Statistical Office of the United Nations, Publishing Service, New York, New York 10017 (800) 253-9646; *Statistical Yearbook.*

PUERTO RICO - ENERGY

Euromonitor International, Inc., 122 South Michigan Avenue, Suite 1200, Chicago, Illinois 60603 (800) 577-EURO; *International Marketing Data and Statistics; World Marketing Data and Statistics;* and *The World Economic Factbook.*

Food and Agricultural Organization of the United Nations (FAO) Via delle Terme di Caracalla, 00100 Rome, Italy (Telephone Number in U.S. (202) 653-2400); *The State of Food and Agriculture.*

St. Martin's Press, Inc., 175 Fifth Avenue, New York, New York 10010 (800) 221-7945; *The Statesman's Year-Book.*

Statistical Office of the United Nations, Publishing Service, New York, New York 10017 (800) 253-9646; *Energy Statistics Yearbook; Statistical Yearbook;* and *World Statistics Pocketbook.*

The World Bank, 1818 H Street, NW, Washington, D.C. 20433 (202) 477-1234; *World Development Report.*

PUERTO RICO - ENVIRONMENT

Economist Intelligence Unit, 111 West 57th Street, New York, New York 10019 (800) 938-4685; *Puerto Rico Country Report.*

Statistical Office of the United Nations, Publishing Service, New York, New York 10017 (800) 253-9646; *World Statistics Pocketbook.*

PUERTO RICO - EXCHANGE RATES

Central Intelligence Agency, Washington, D.C. 20505 (703) 482-1100, www.cia.gov; *The World Factbook.*

Euromonitor International, Inc., 122 South Michigan Avenue, Suite 1200, Chicago, Illinois 60603 (800) 577-EURO; *International Marketing Data and Statistics;* and *The World Economic Factbook.*

Europa Publications Limited, 18 Bedford Square, London, WC1B 3JN, England; *The Europa World Year Book.*

Statistical Office of the United Nations, Publishing Service, New York, New York 10017 (800) 253-9646; *World Statistics*

Pocketbook.

PUERTO RICO - EXPORTS

Central Intelligence Agency, Washington, D.C. 20505 (703) 482-1100, www.cia.gov; *The World Factbook.*

Economist Intelligence Unit, 111 West 57th Street, New York, New York 10019 (800) 938-4685; *Puerto Rico Country Report.*

Euromonitor International, Inc., 122 South Michigan Avenue, Suite 1200, Chicago, Illinois 60603 (800) 577-EURO; *International Marketing Data and Statistics;* and *The World Economic Factbook.*

Europa Publications Limited, 18 Bedford Square, London, WC1B 3JN, England; *The Europa World Year Book.*

Food and Agricultural Organization of the United Nations (FAO) Via delle Terme di Caracalla, 00100 Rome, Italy (Telephone Number in U.S. (202) 653-2400); *The State of Food and Agriculture.*

St. Martin's Press, Inc., 175 Fifth Avenue, New York, New York 10010 (800) 221-7945; *The Statesman's Year-Book.*

PUERTO RICO - EXTERNAL TRADE

Euromonitor International, Inc., 122 South Michigan Avenue, Suite 1200, Chicago, Illinois 60603 (800) 577-EURO; *World Marketing Data and Statistics.*

Food and Agricultural Organization of the United Nations (FAO) Via delle Terme di Caracalla, 00100 Rome, Italy (Telephone Number in U.S. (202) 653-2400); *The State of Food and Agriculture;* and *Trade Yearbook.*

PUERTO RICO - FARM CROPS - See PUERTO RICO - CROPS

PUERTO RICO - FEMALE WORKING POPULATION - See PUERTO RICO - EMPLOYMENT

PUERTO RICO - FERTILITY RATE

Central Intelligence Agency, Washington, D.C. 20505 (703) 482-1100, www.cia.gov; *The World Factbook.*

The World Bank, 1818 H Street, NW, Washington, D.C. 20433 (202) 477-1234; *World Development Report.*

PUERTO RICO - FERTILIZER

Food and Agricultural Organization of the United Nations (FAO) Via delle Terme di Caracalla, 00100 Rome, Italy (Telephone Number in U.S. (202) 653-2400); *The State of Food and Agriculture.*

PUERTO RICO - FETAL MORTALITY - See PUERTO RICO - MORTALITY

PUERTO RICO - FINANCE

Economist Intelligence Unit, 111 West 57th Street, New York, New York 10019 (800) 938-4685; *Puerto Rico Country Report.*

Europa Publications Limited, 18 Bedford Square, London, WC1B 3JN, England; *The Europa World Year Book.*

St. Martin's Press, Inc., 175 Fifth Avenue, New York, New York 10010 (800) 221-7945; *The Statesman's Year-Book.*

PUERTO RICO - FISHERIES

Europa Publications Limited, 18 Bedford Square, London, WC1B 3JN, England; *The Europa World Year Book.*

Food and Agricultural Organization of the United Nations (FAO) Via delle Terme di Caracalla, 00100 Rome, Italy (Telephone Number in U.S. (202) 653-2400); *The State of Food and Agriculture;* and *Yearbook of Fishery Statistics.*

Statistical Office of the United Nations, Publishing Service, New York, New York 10017 (800) 253-9646; *Statistical Yearbook.*

PUERTO RICO - FOOD

Food and Agricultural Organization of the United Nations (FAO), Via delle Terme di Caracalla, 00100 Rome, Italy (Telephone Number in U.S. (202) 653-2400); *Production Yearbook;* and *The State of Food and Agriculture.*

PUERTO RICO - FOREIGN TRADE

Economist Intelligence Unit, 111 West 57th Street, New York, New York 10019 (800) 938-4685; *Puerto Rico Country Report.*

Euromonitor International, Inc., 122 South Michigan Avenue, Suite 1200, Chicago, Illinois 60603 (800) 577-EURO; *International Marketing Data and Statistics;* and *The World Economic Factbook.*

Europa Publications Limited, 18 Bedford Square, London, WC1B 3JN, England; *The Europa World Year Book.*

Food and Agricultural Organization of the United Nations (FAO) Via delle Terme di Caracalla, 00100 Rome, Italy (Telephone Number in U.S. (202) 653-2400); *The State of Food and Agriculture.*

St. Martin's Press, Inc., 175 Fifth Avenue, New York, New York 10010 (800) 221-7945; *The Statesman's Year-Book.*

PUERTO RICO - FORESTRY AND FOREST PRODUCTS

Food and Agricultural Organization of the United Nations (FAO) Via delle Terme di Caracalla, 00100 Rome, Italy (Telephone Number in U.S. (202) 653-2400); *The State of Food and Agriculture.*

Statistical Office of the United Nations, Publishing Service, New York, New York 10017 (800) 253-9646; *Statistical Yearbook.*

United Nations Educational, Scientific and Cultural Organization (UNESCO), 7 Place de Fontenoy, F-75700 Paris, France (Telephone Number in U.S. (212) 963-5981); *Statistical Yearbook.*

PUERTO RICO - GENERAL INDUSTRIAL STATISTICS

Statistical Office of the United Nations, Publishing Service, New York, New York 10017 (800) 253-9646; *Industrial Commodity Statistics Yearbook.*

PUERTO RICO - GENERAL MORTALITY - See PUERTO RICO - MORTALITY

PUERTO RICO - GOATS - See PUERTO RICO - LIVESTOCK AND POULTRY

PUERTO RICO - GOVERNMENT

Central Intelligence Agency, Washington, D.C. 20505 (703) 482-1100, www.cia.gov; *The World Factbook.*

Europa Publications Limited, 18 Bedford Square, London, WC1B 3JN, England; *The Europa World Year Book.*

St. Martin's Press, Inc., 175 Fifth Avenue, New York, New York 10010 (800) 221-7945; *The Statesman's Year-Book.*

Statistical Office of the United Nations, Publishing Service, New York, New York 10017 (800) 253-9646; *National Accounts Statistics.*

PUERTO RICO - GRAIN PRODUCTION - See PUERTO RICO - CROPS

PUERTO RICO - GREEN PEPPER AND CHILIE PRODUCTION - See PUERTO RICO - CROPS

PUERTO RICO - GROSS DOMESTIC PRODUCT

Economist Intelligence Unit, 111 West 57th Street, New York, New York 10019 (800) 938-4685; *Puerto Rico Country Report.*

Euromonitor International, Inc., 122 South Michigan Avenue, Suite 1200, Chicago, Illinois 60603 (800) 577-EURO; *International Marketing Data and Statistics;* and *The World Economic Factbook.*

Europa Publications Limited, 18 Bedford Square, London, WC1B 3JN,

England; *The Europa World Year Book.*

Statistical Office of the United Nations, Publishing Service, New York, New York 10017 (800) 253-9646; *Human Development Report;* and *Statistical Yearbook.*

PUERTO RICO - GROSS NATIONAL PRODUCT

Euromonitor International, Inc., 122 South Michigan Avenue, Suite 1200, Chicago, Illinois 60603 (800) 577-EURO; *International Marketing Data and Statistics.*

The World Bank, 1818 H Street, NW, Washington, D.C. 20433 (202) 477-1234; *World Development Report.*

PUERTO RICO - HEALTH

Euromonitor International, Inc., 122 South Michigan Avenue, Suite 1200, Chicago, Illinois 60603 (800) 577-EURO; *World Marketing Data and Statistics.*

Statistical Office of the United Nations, Publishing Service, New York, New York 10017 (800) 253-9646; *Statistical Yearbook.*

World Health Organization, Office of Publications, 20 Avenue Appia, CH-1211 Geneva 27, Switzerland (Telephone Number in U.S. (518) 436-9686); *World Health Statistics Annual.*

PUERTO RICO - HIDE PRODUCTION

Food and Agricultural Organization of the United Nations (FAO), Via delle Terme di Caracalla, 00100 Rome, Italy (Telephone Number in U.S. (202) 653-2400); *Production Yearbook.*

PUERTO RICO - HIGHWAYS

Central Intelligence Agency, Washington, D.C. 20505 (703) 482-1100, www.cia.gov; *The World Factbook.*

St. Martin's Press, Inc., 175 Fifth Avenue, New York, New York 10010 (800) 221-7945; *The Statesman's Year-Book.*

PUERTO RICO - HORSES - See PUERTO RICO - LIVESTOCK AND POULTRY

PUERTO RICO - HOURS OF WORK - See PUERTO RICO - EMPLOYMENT

PUERTO RICO - HOUSING AND HOUSING UNITS

Euromonitor International, Inc., 122 South Michigan Avenue, Suite 1200, Chicago, Illinois 60603 (800) 577-EURO; *World Marketing Data and Statistics.*

PUERTO RICO - ILLITERATE POPULATION

Central Intelligence Agency, Washington, D.C. 20505 (703) 482-1100, www.cia.gov; *The World Factbook.*

Euromonitor International, Inc., 122 South Michigan Avenue, Suite 1200, Chicago, Illinois 60603 (800) 577-EURO; *The World Economic Factbook.*

St. Martin's Press, Inc., 175 Fifth Avenue, New York, New York 10010 (800) 221-7945; *The Statesman's Year-Book.*

United Nations Educational, Scientific and Cultural Organization (UNESCO), 7 Place de Fontenoy, F-75700 Paris, France (Telephone Number in U.S. (212) 963-5981); *Statistical Yearbook.*

PUERTO RICO - IMPORTS

Central Intelligence Agency, Washington, D.C. 20505 (703) 482-1100, www.cia.gov; *The World Factbook.*

Economist Intelligence Unit, 111 West 57th Street, New York, New York 10019 (800) 938-4685; *Puerto Rico Country Report.*

Euromonitor International, Inc., 122 South Michigan Avenue, Suite 1200, Chicago, Illinois 60603 (800) 577-EURO; *International Marketing Data and Statistics;* and *The World Economic Factbook.*

Europa Publications Limited, 18 Bedford Square, London, WC1B 3JN, England; *The Europa World Year Book.*

Food and Agricultural Organization of the United Nations (FAO) Via delle Terme di Caracalla, 00100 Rome, Italy (Telephone Number in U.S. (202) 653-2400); *The State of Food and Agriculture.*

St. Martin's Press, Inc., 175 Fifth Avenue, New York, New York 10010 (800) 221-7945; *The Statesman's Year-Book.*

PUERTO RICO - INDUSTRY

Central Intelligence Agency, Washington, D.C. 20505 (703) 482-1100, www.cia.gov; *The World Factbook.*

Economist Intelligence Unit, 111 West 57th Street, New York, New York 10019 (800) 938-4685; *Puerto Rico Country Report.*

Euromonitor International, Inc., 122 South Michigan Avenue, Suite 1200, Chicago, Illinois 60603 (800) 577-EURO; *International Marketing Data and Statistics; World Marketing Data and Statistics;* and *The World Economic Factbook.*

Europa Publications Limited, 18 Bedford Square, London, WC1B 3JN, England; *The Europa World Year Book.*

International Labour Office,

I.L.O. Publications, 1828 L Street, NW, Suite 801, Washington, D.C. 20036 (301) 638-3152; *Yearbook of Labour Statistics*.

St. Martin's Press, Inc., 175 Fifth Avenue, New York, New York 10010 (800) 221-7945; *The Statesman's Year-Book*

PUERTO RICO - INFANT AND MATERNAL MORTALITY - See PUERTO RICO - MORTALITY

PUERTO RICO - INTERNAL TRADE

Statistical Office of the United Nations, Publishing Service, New York, New York 10017 (800) 253-9646; *Statistical Yearbook*.

PUERTO RICO - IRRIGATION

Euromonitor International, Inc., 122 South Michigan Avenue, Suite 1200, Chicago, Illinois 60603 (800) 577-EURO; *International Marketing Data and Statistics*.

PUERTO RICO - LABOR

Central Intelligence Agency, Washington, D.C. 20505 (703) 482-1100, www.cia.gov; *The World Factbook*.

Euromonitor International, Inc., 122 South Michigan Avenue, Suite 1200, Chicago, Illinois 60603 (800) 577-EURO; *International Marketing Data and Statistics; and World Marketing Data and Statistics*.

Europa Publications Limited, 18 Bedford Square, London, WC1B 3JN, England; *The Europa World Year Book*.

Food and Agricultural Organization of the United Nations (FAO) Via delle Terme di Caracalla, 00100 Rome, Italy (Telephone Number in U.S. (202) 653-2400); *The State of Food and Agriculture*.

International Labour Office, I.L.O. Publications, 1828 L Street, NW, Suite 801, Washington, D.C. 20036 (301) 638-3152; *Yearbook of Labour Statistics*.

St. Martin's Press, Inc., 175 Fifth Avenue, New York, New York 10010 (800) 221-7945; *The Statesman's Year-Book*.

The World Bank, 1818 H Street, NW, Washington, D.C. 20433 (202) 477-1234; *World Development Report*.

PUERTO RICO - LAND USE

Central Intelligence Agency, Washington, D.C. 20505 (703) 482-1100, www.cia.gov; *The World Factbook*.

Euromonitor International, Inc., 122 South Michigan Avenue, Suite 1200, Chicago, Illinois 60603 (800) 577-EURO; *International Marketing Data and Statistics*.

Food and Agricultural Organization of the United Nations (FAO), Via delle Terme di Caracalla, 00100 Rome, Italy (Telephone Number in U.S. (202) 653-2400); *Production Yearbook*.

PUERTO RICO - LIBRARIES

United Nations Educational, Scientific and Cultural Organization (UNESCO), 7 Place de Fontenoy, F-75700 Paris, France (Telephone Number in U.S. (212) 963-5981); *Statistical Yearbook*.

PUERTO RICO - LIFE EXPECTANCY

Central Intelligence Agency, Washington, D.C. 20505 (703) 482-1100, www.cia.gov; *The World Factbook*.

Euromonitor International, Inc., 122 South Michigan Avenue, Suite 1200, Chicago, Illinois 60603 (800) 577-EURO; *The World Economic Factbook*.

Statistical Office of the United Nations, Publishing Service, New York, New York 10017 (800) 253-9646; *World Statistics Pocketbook*.

The World Bank, 1818 H Street, NW, Washington, D.C. 20433 (202) 477-1234; *World Development Report*.

PUERTO RICO - LITERACY RATE

Euromonitor International, Inc., 122 South Michigan Avenue, Suite 1200, Chicago, Illinois 60603 (800) 577-EURO; *World Marketing Data and Statistics*.

PUERTO RICO - LIVESTOCK AND POULTRY

Euromonitor International, Inc., 122 South Michigan Avenue, Suite 1200, Chicago, Illinois 60603 (800) 577-EURO; *European Marketing Data and Statistics; and International Marketing Data and Statistics*.

Europa Publications Limited, 18 Bedford Square, London, WC1B 3JN, England; *The Europa World Year Book*.

Food and Agricultural Organization of the United Nations (FAO), Via delle Terme di Caracalla, 00100 Rome, Italy (Telephone Number in U.S. (202) 653-2400); *Production Yearbook;* and *The State of Food and Agriculture*.

M.E. Sharpe, 80 Business Park Drive, Armonk, New York 10504 (800) 541-6563; *The Illustrated Book of World Rankings*.

Organisation for Economic Co-operation and Development (OECD), 2 rue Andre-Pascal, 75 Paris 16, France (Telephone Number in U.S. (202) 785-6323); *Economic Accounts for Agriculture; and Meat Balances in OECD Member Countries*.

St. Martin's Press, Inc., 175 Fifth Avenue, New York, New York 10010 (800) 221-7945; *The Statesman's Year-Book*.

Statistical Office of the United Nations, Publishing Service, New York, New York 10017 (800) 253-9646; *Statistical Yearbook*.

PUERTO RICO - LIVING LEVELS - See PUERTO RICO - LIFE EXPECTANCY

PUERTO RICO - MANUFACTURING

Statistical Office of the United Nations, Publishing Service, New York, New York 10017 (800) 253-9646; *Statistical Yearbook*.

PUERTO RICO - MARRIAGE RATES

Europa Publications Limited, 18 Bedford Square, London, WC1B 3JN, England; *The Europa World Year Book*.

Statistical Office of the United Nations, Publishing Service, New York, New York 10017 (800) 253-9646; *Demographic Yearbook;* and *Statistical Yearbook*.

PUERTO RICO - MEAT PRODUCTION - See PUERTO RICO - LIVESTOCK AND POULTRY

PUERTO RICO - MERCHANT SHIPPING

Europa Publications Limited, 18 Bedford Square, London, WC1B 3JN, England; *The Europa World Year Book*.

St. Martin's Press, Inc., 175 Fifth Avenue, New York, New York 10010 (800) 221-7945; *The Statesman's Year-Book*.

PUERTO RICO - MILITARY

Central Intelligence Agency, Washington, D.C. 20505 (703) 482-1100, www.cia.gov; *The World Factbook*.

Euromonitor International, Inc., 122 South Michigan Avenue, Suite 1200, Chicago, Illinois 60603 (800) 577-EURO; *World Marketing Data and Statistics*.

PUERTO RICO - MILK PRODUCTION - See PUERTO RICO - DAIRY PRODUCTS

PUERTO RICO - MINING AND MINERAL PRODUCTS

St. Martin's Press, Inc., 175 Fifth Avenue, New York, New York 10010 (800) 221-7945; *The Statesman's Year-Book*.

Statistical Office of the United Nations, Publishing Service, New York, New York 10017 (800) 253-9646; *Statistical Yearbook*.

PUERTO RICO - MONEY EXCHANGE RATES - See PUERTO RICO - EXCHANGE RATES

PUERTO RICO - MONEY RESERVES

Euromonitor International, Inc., 122 South Michigan Avenue, Suite 1200, Chicago, Illinois 60603 (800) 577-EURO; *International Marketing Data and Statistics.*

PUERTO RICO - MONEY SUPPLY

Economist Intelligence Unit, 111 West 57th Street, New York, New York 10019 (800) 938-4685; *Puerto Rico Country Report.*

Euromonitor International, Inc., 122 South Michigan Avenue, Suite 1200, Chicago, Illinois 60603 (800) 577-EURO; *International Marketing Data and Statistics.*

PUERTO RICO - MORTALITY

Central Intelligence Agency, Washington, D.C. 20505 (703) 482-1100, www.cia.gov; *The World Factbook.*

Euromonitor International, Inc., 122 South Michigan Avenue, Suite 1200, Chicago, Illinois 60603 (800) 577-EURO; *International Marketing Data and Statistics;* and *The World Economic Factbook.*

Europa Publications Limited, 18 Bedford Square, London, WC1B 3JN, England; *The Europa World Year Book.*

St. Martin's Press, Inc., 175 Fifth Avenue, New York, New York 10010 (800) 221-7945; *The Statesman's Year-Book.*

Statistical Office of the United Nations, Publishing Service, New York, New York 10017 (800) 253-9646; *Demographic Yearbook; Statistical Yearbook;* and *World Statistics Pocketbook.*

The World Bank, 1818 H Street, NW, Washington, D.C. 20433 (202) 477-1234; *World Development Report.*

World Health Organization, Office of Publications, 20 Avenue Appia, CH-1211 Geneva 27, Switzerland (Telephone Number in U.S. (518) 436-9686); *World Health Statistics Annual.*

PUERTO RICO - MOTION PICTURES

Statistical Office of the United Nations, Publishing Service, New York, New York 10017 (800) 253-9646; *Statistical Yearbook.*

PUERTO RICO - MOTOR VEHICLES IN USE

Europa Publications Limited, 18 Bedford Square, London, WC1B 3JN, England; *The Europa World Year Book.*

Statistical Office of the United Nations, Publishing Service, New York, New York 10017 (800) 253-9646; *Statistical Yearbook.*

PUERTO RICO - MULES - See PUERTO RICO - LIVESTOCK AND POULTRY

PUERTO RICO - MUSEUMS

United Nations Educational, Scientific and Cultural Organization (UNESCO), 7 Place de Fontenoy, F-75700 Paris, France (Telephone Number in U.S. (212) 963-5981); *Statistical Yearbook.*

PUERTO RICO - NATALITY - See PUERTO RICO - BIRTH RATES

PUERTO RICO - NATIONAL ACCOUNTS

Europa Publications Limited, 18 Bedford Square, London, WC1B 3JN, England; *The Europa World Year Book.*

Statistical Office of the United Nations, Publishing Service, New York, New York 10017 (800) 253-9646; *National Accounts Statistics;* and *Statistical Yearbook.*

PUERTO RICO - NATIONAL INCOME

Statistical Office of the United Nations, Publishing Service, New York, New York 10017 (800) 253-9646; *Human Development Report;* and *Statistical Yearbook.*

PUERTO RICO - NATIONAL PRODUCT

Statistical Office of the United Nations, Publishing Service, New York, New York 10017 (800) 253-9646; *Statistical Yearbook.*

PUERTO RICO - NEWSPAPER PRODUCTION - See PUERTO RICO - FORESTRY AND FOREST PRODUCTS

PUERTO RICO - OCCUPATIONS - See PUERTO RICO - LABOR

PUERTO RICO - PESTICIDE USE

Food and Agricultural Organization of the United Nations (FAO) Via delle Terme di Caracalla, 00100 Rome, Italy (Telephone Number in U.S. (202) 653-2400); *The State of Food and Agriculture.*

PUERTO RICO - PETROLEUM INDUSTRY

Food and Agricultural Organization of the United Nations (FAO) Via delle Terme di Caracalla, 00100 Rome, Italy (Telephone Number in U.S. (202) 653-2400); *The State of Food and Agriculture.*

Statistical Office of the United Nations, Publishing Service, New York, New York 10017 (800) 253-9646; *Statistical Yearbook.*

PUERTO RICO - PIGS - See PUERTO RICO - LIVESTOCK AND POULTRY

PUERTO RICO - POPULATION

Central Intelligence Agency, Washington, D.C. 20505 (703) 482-1100, www.cia.gov; *The World Factbook.*

Economist Intelligence Unit, 111 West 57th Street, New York, New York 10019 (800) 938-4685; *Puerto Rico Country Report.*

Euromonitor International, Inc., 122 South Michigan Avenue, Suite 1200, Chicago, Illinois 60603 (800) 577-EURO; *International Marketing Data and Statistics;* and *The World Economic Factbook.*

Europa Publications Limited, 18 Bedford Square, London, WC1B 3JN, England; *The Europa World Year Book.*

Food and Agricultural Organization of the United Nations (FAO), Via delle Terme di Caracalla, 00100 Rome, Italy (Telephone Number in U.S. (202) 653-2400); *Production Yearbook.*

International Labour Office, I.L.O. Publications, 1828 L Street, NW, Suite 801, Washington, D.C. 20036 (301) 638-3152; *Yearbook of Labour Statistics.*

St. Martin's Press, Inc., 175 Fifth Avenue, New York, New York 10010 (800) 221-7945; *The Statesman's Year-Book.*

Statistical Office of the United Nations, Publishing Service, New York, New York 10017 (800) 253-9646; *Demographic Yearbook; Statistical Yearbook;* and *World Statistics Pocketbook.*

United Nations Educational, Scientific and Cultural Organization (UNESCO), 7 Place de Fontenoy, F-75700 Paris, France (Telephone Number in U.S. (212) 963-5981); *Statistical Yearbook.*

The World Bank, 1818 H Street, NW, Washington, D.C. 20433 (202) 477-1234; *World Development Report.*

World Health Organization, Office of Publications, 20 Avenue Appia, CH-1211 Geneva 27, Switzerland (Telephone Number in U.S. (518) 436-9686); *World Health Statistics Annual.*

PUERTO RICO - POST OFFICES

St. Martin's Press, Inc., 175 Fifth Avenue, New York, New York 10010 (800) 221-7945; *The Statesman's Year-Book.*

PUERTO RICO - PRICES

Food and Agricultural Organization of the United Nations (FAO), Via delle Terme di Caracalla, 00100 Rome, Italy (Telephone Number in U.S. (202) 653-2400); *Production Yearbook;* and *The State of Food and Agriculture.*

International Labour Office, I.L.O. Publications, 1828 L Street, NW, Suite

801, Washington, D.C. 20036 (301) 638-3152 ; *Yearbook of Labour Statistics.*

PUERTO RICO - PRODUCTIVITY

Euromonitor International, Inc., 122 South Michigan Avenue, Suite 1200, Chicago, Illinois 60603 (800) 577-EURO; *International Marketing Data and Statistics.*

PUERTO RICO - RADIO BROADCASTING - See PUERTO RICO - BROADCASTING

PUERTO RICO - RADIO RECEIVERS

St. Martin's Press, Inc., 175 Fifth Avenue, New York, New York 10010 (800) 221-7945; *The Statesman's Year-Book.*

PUERTO RICO - RELIGION

Central Intelligence Agency, Washington, D.C. 20505 (703) 482-1100, www.cia.gov; *The World Factbook.*

St. Martin's Press, Inc., 175 Fifth Avenue, New York, New York 10010 (800) 221-7945; *The Statesman's Year-Book.*

PUERTO RICO - RENT PRICES

International Labour Office, I.L.O. Publications, 1828 L Street, NW, Suite 801, Washington, D.C. 20036 (301) 638-3152; *Yearbook of Labour Statistics.*

PUERTO RICO - RETAIL TRADE

Euromonitor International, Inc., 122 South Michigan Avenue, Suite 1200, Chicago, Illinois 60603 (800) 577-EURO; *World Marketing Data and Statistics.*

Statistical Office of the United Nations, Publishing Service, New York, New York 10017 (800) 253-9646; *Statistical Yearbook.*

PUERTO RICO - RICE PRODUCTION - See PUERTO RICO - CROPS

PUERTO RICO - ROOT AND TUBER PRODUCTION - See PUERTO RICO - CROPS

PUERTO RICO - SALT PRODUCTION - See PUERTO RICO - MINING AND MINERAL PRODUCTS

PUERTO RICO - SHEEP - See PUERTO RICO - LIVESTOCK AND POULTRY

PUERTO RICO - SOCIAL DATA

Statistical Office of the United Nations, Publishing Service, New York, New York 10017 (800) 253-9646; *World Statistics Pocketbook.*

PUERTO RICO - SOCIAL SECURITY

Statistical Office of the United Nations,

Publishing Service, New York, New York 10017 (800) 253-9646; *National Accounts Statistics.*

PUERTO RICO - STATE BUDGET REVENUE AND EXPENDITURES

Euromonitor International, Inc., 122 South Michigan Avenue, Suite 1200, Chicago, Illinois 60603 (800) 577-EURO; *International Marketing Data and Statistics.*

PUERTO RICO - STOCKS - COMMODITY - MARKET PRICE - INDEX

Food and Agricultural Organization of the United Nations (FAO) Via delle Terme di Caracalla, 00100 Rome, Italy (Telephone Number in U.S. (202) 653-2400); *The State of Food and Agriculture.*

PUERTO RICO - SUGAR PRODUCTION AND CONSUMPTION - See PUERTO RICO - CROPS

PUERTO RICO - TAXATION

Europa Publications Limited, 18 Bedford Square, London, WC1B 3JN, England; *The Europa World Year Book.*

St. Martin's Press, Inc., 175 Fifth Avenue, New York, New York 10010 (800) 221-7945; *The Statesman's Year-Book.*

PUERTO RICO - TAX REVENUE - See PUERTO RICO - TAXATION

PUERTO RICO - TELEPHONES IN USE

American Telephone and Telegraph Company, 26 Parsippany Road, Whippany, New Jersey 07981 (800) 222-0300; *The World's Telephones.*

Central Intelligence Agency, Washington, D.C. 20505 (703) 482-1100, www.cia.gov; *The World Factbook.*

St. Martin's Press, Inc., 175 Fifth Avenue, New York, New York 10010 (800) 221-7945; *The Statesman's Year-Book.*

Statistical Office of the United Nations, Publishing Service, New York, New York 10017 (800) 253-9646; *Statistical Yearbook;* and *World Statistics Pocketbook.*

PUERTO RICO - TELEVISION BROADCASTING - See PUERTO RICO - BROADCASTING

PUERTO RICO - TOBACCO PRODUCTION

Statistical Office of the United Nations, Publishing Service, New York, New York 10017 (800) 253-9646; *Statistical Yearbook.*

PUERTO RICO - TOURISM

Euromonitor International, Inc., 122

South Michigan Avenue, Suite 1200, Chicago, Illinois 60603 (800) 577-EURO; *The World Economic Factbook;* and *World Marketing Data and Statistics.*

Europa Publications Limited, 18 Bedford Square, London, WC1B 3JN, England; *The Europa World Year Book.*

Statistical Office of the United Nations, Publishing Service, New York, New York 10017 (800) 253-9646; *Statistical Yearbook.*

Times Books, 201 East 50th Street, New York, New York 10022 (800) 726-0600; *The Economist Book of Vital World Statistics.*

World Tourism Organization, Calle Capitan Haya 42, E-28020 Madrid, Spain; *Yearbook of Tourism Statistics.*

PUERTO RICO - TRACTORS IN USE

Statistical Office of the United Nations, Publishing Service, New York, New York 10017 (800) 253-9646; *Statistical Yearbook.*

PUERTO RICO - TRADE - See PUERTO RICO - FOREIGN TRADE

PUERTO RICO - TRANSPORTATION AND COMMUNICATIONS

Central Intelligence Agency, Washington, D.C. 20505 (703) 482-1100, www.cia.gov; *The World Factbook.*

Euromonitor International, Inc., 122 South Michigan Avenue, Suite 1200, Chicago, Illinois 60603 (800) 577-EURO; *International Marketing Data and Statistics;* and *World Marketing Data and Statistics.*

Europa Publications Limited, 18 Bedford Square, London, WC1B 3JN, England; *The Europa World Year Book.*

St. Martin's Press, Inc., 175 Fifth Avenue, New York, New York 10010 (800) 221-7945; *The Statesman's Year-Book.*

PUERTO RICO - UNEMPLOYMENT

Central Intelligence Agency, Washington, D.C. 20505 (703) 482-1100, www.cia.gov; *The World Factbook.*

Euromonitor International, Inc., 122 South Michigan Avenue, Suite 1200, Chicago, Illinois 60603 (800) 577-EURO; *International Marketing Data and Statistics.*

International Labour Office, I.L.O. Publications, 1828 L Street, NW, Suite 801, Washington, D.C. 20036 (301) 638-3152; *Yearbook of Labour Statistics.*

St. Martin's Press, Inc., 175 Fifth Avenue, New York, New York 10010 (800) 221-7945; *The Statesman's Year-Book.*

Statistical Office of the United Nations, Publishing Service, New York, New York 10017 (800) 253-9646; *Statistical Yearbook.*

PUERTO RICO - VITAL STATISTICS

Euromonitor International, Inc., 122 South Michigan Avenue, Suite 1200, Chicago, Illinois 60603 (800) 577-EURO; *International Marketing Data and Statistics.*

St. Martin's Press, Inc., 175 Fifth Avenue, New York, New York 10010 (800) 221-7945; *The Statesman's Year-Book.*

Statistical Office of the United Nations, Publishing Service, New York, New York 10017 (800) 253-9646; *Statistical Yearbook.*

World Health Organization, Office of Publications, 20 Avenue Appia, CH-1211 Geneva 27, Switzerland (Telephone Number in U.S. (518) 436-9686); *World Health Statistics Annual.*

PUERTO RICO - WAGES

International Labour Office, I.L.O. Publications, 1828 L Street, NW, Suite 801, Washington, D.C. 20036 (301) 638-3152; *Yearbook of Labour Statistics.*

Statistical Office of the United Nations, Publishing Service, New York, New York 10017 (800) 253-9646; *Statistical Yearbook.*

PUERTO RICO - WHOLESALE PRICES

Statistical Office of the United Nations, Publishing Service, New York, New York 10017 (800) 253-9646; *Statistical Yearbook.*

PUERTO RICO - WHOLESALE TRADE

Statistical Office of the United Nations, Publishing Service, New York, New York 10017 (800) 253-9646; *Statistical Yearbook.*

PULMONARY DISEASES

U.S. Department of Health and Human Services, Centers for Disease Control, 1600 Clifton Road, NE, Atlanta, Georgia 30333 (800) 311-3435, www.cdc.gov; *Summary of Notifiable Disease, United States, Morbidity and Mortality Weekly Report.*

U.S. Department of Health and Human Services, National Center for Health Statistics, 3700 East-West Highway, Hyattsville, Maryland 20782 (301) 436-8500, www.cdc.gov/nchs; *Vital Statistics of the United States; National Vital Statistics Report;* and unpublished data.

PULPWOOD

U.S. Department of Agriculture, Forest Service, Post Office Box 96090, Washington, D.C. 20090 (202) 205-8333, www.fs.fed.us; *Timber Demand and Technology Assessment;* and *Agricultural Statistics.*

U.S. Department of Commerce, Bureau of the Census, Washington, D.C. 20233 (301) 457-4100, www.census.gov; *Census of Manufactures;* and *Annual Survey of Manufactures.*

PULSES

U.S. Department of Agriculture, Economic Research Service, 1800 M Street, NW, Washington, D.C. 20036 (202) 694-5050, www.ers.usda.gov; *Food Consumption, Prices and Expenditures;* and *Agricultural Outlook.*

PUMICE AND PUMICITE

U.S. Department of the Interior, Geological Survey, Office of Minerals Information, 12201 Sunrise Valley Drive, Reston, Virginia 22092 (703) 648-4000, www.minerals.usgs.gov; *Annual Report;* and *Mineral Commodities Summaries.*

PUMPS AND COMPRESSORS

U.S. Department of Commerce, Bureau of the Census, Washington, D.C. 20233 (301)457-4100, www.census.gov; *Manufacturing Profiles.*

PURCHASING POWER OF THE DOLLAR

U.S. Department of Commerce, Bureau of Economic Analysis, Fourteenth Street between Constitution Avenue and E Street, NW, Washington, D.C. 20230 (202) 606-9900, www.bea.doc.gov; *Survey of Current Business.*

PYRITES

U.S. Department of the Interior, Geological Survey, Office of Minerals Information, 12201 Sunrise Valley Drive, Reston, Virginia 22092 (703) 648-4000, www.minerals.usgs.gov; *Annual Report;* and *Mineral Commodities Summaries.*

Q

Qatar - National Statistical Office

Central Statistical Organisation, Post Office Box 7283, Doha, Qatar.

Qatar - Primary Statistics Source

Central Statistical Organization, Post Office Box 7283, Doha, Qatar; *Annual Statistical Abstract.*

QATAR - AGRICULTURE

Economic Commission for Western Asia, Post Office Box 27, Baghdad, Iraq; *Statistical Abstract of Western Asia.*

Economist Intelligence Unit, 111 West 57th Street, New York, New York 10019 (800) 938-4685; *Qatar Country Report.*

Euromonitor International, Inc., 122 South Michigan Avenue, Suite 1200, Chicago, Illinois 60603 (800) 577-EURO; *World Marketing Data and Statistics.*

Europa Publications Limited, 18 Bedford Square, London, WC1B 3JN, England; *The Europa World Year Book.*

Federal Statistical Office, Gustav - Stresemann - Ring 11, D-6200 Wiesbaden, Germany; *Katar.*

Food and Agricultural Organization of the United Nations (FAO) Via delle Terme di Caracalla, 00100 Rome, Italy (Telephone Number in U.S. (202) 653-2400); *Production Yearbook; The State of Food and Agriculture;* and *Trade Yearbook.*

M.E. Sharpe, 80 Business Park Drive, Armonk, New York 10504 (800) 541-6563; *The Illustrated Book of World Rankings.*

Presidency of the Council of Ministers, Central Statistical Organisation, Doha, Qatar; *Annual Statistical Abstract State of Qatar.*

St. Martin's Press, Inc., 175 Fifth Avenue, New York, New York 10010 (800) 221-7945; *The Statesman's Year-Book.*

United Nations Conference on Trade and Development, Central Statistical Service, Palais des Nations, Geneva, Switzerland (Telephone in U.S. (800) 253-9646); UNCTAD Commodity Yearbook.

QATAR - AIRLINE SERVICE

Economic Commission for Western Asia, Post Office Box 27, Baghdad, Iraq; *Statistical Abstract of Western Asia.*

Europa Publications Limited, 18 Bedford Square, London, WC1B 3JN, England; *The Europa World Year Book.*

M.E. Sharpe, 80 Business Park Drive, Armonk, New York 10504 (800) 541-6563; *The Illustrated Book of World Rankings.*

St. Martin's Press, Inc., 175 Fifth Avenue, New York, New York 10010 (800) 221-7945; *The Statesman's Year-Book.*

QATAR - AIRPORTS

Central Intelligence Agency, Washington, D.C. 20505 (703) 482-1100, www.cia.gov; *The World Factbook.*

QATAR - ALUMINUM PRODUCTION AND CONSUMPTION - See QATAR - MINING AND MINERAL PRODUCTS

QATAR - ANIMAL HEALTH

Food and Agricultural Organization of the United Nations (FAO), Via delle Terme di Caracalla, 00100 Rome, Italy (Telephone Number in U.S. (202) 653-2400); *Animal Health Yearbook.*

QATAR - AREA AND DENSITY OF POPULATION

Central Intelligence Agency, Washington, D.C. 20505 (703) 482-1100, www.cia.gov; *The World Factbook.*

Economic Commission for Western Asia, Post Office Box 27, Baghdad, Iraq; *Statistical Abstract of Western Asia.*

Euromonitor International, Inc., 122 South Michigan Avenue, Suite 1200, Chicago, Illinois 60603 (800) 577-EURO; *The World Economic Factbook.*

Europa Publications Limited, 18 Bedford Square, London, WC1B 3JN, England; *The Europa World Year Book.*

Federal Statistical Office, Gustav - Stresemann - Ring 11, D-6200 Wiesbaden, Germany; *Katar.*

Food and Agricultural Organization of the United Nations (FAO) Via delle Terme di Caracalla, 00100 Rome, Italy (Telephone Number in U.S. (202) 653-2400); *The State of Food and Agriculture.*

M.E. Sharpe, 80 Business Park Drive, Armonk, New York 10504 (800) 541-6563; *The Illustrated Book of World Rankings.*

St. Martin's Press, Inc., 175 Fifth Avenue, New York, New York 10010 (800) 221-7945; *The Statesman's Year-Book.*

Statistical Office of the United Nations, Publishing Service, New York, New York 10017 (800) 253-9646; *Statistical Yearbook.*

United Nations Educational, Scientific and Cultural Organization (UNESCO), 7 Place de Fontenoy, F-75700 Paris, France (Telephone Number in U.S. (212) 963-5981); *Statistical Yearbook.*

QATAR - ARMS EXPORTS AND IMPORTS - See QATAR - MILITARY

QATAR - BALANCE OF PAYMENTS

Economic Commission for Western Asia, Post Office Box 27, Baghdad, Iraq; *Statistical Abstract of Western Asia.*

The Economist Intelligence Unit, 111 West 57th Street, New York, New York 10019 (800) 938-4685; *The World Market Atlas.*

Europa Publications Limited, 18 Bedford Square, London, WC1B 3JN, England; *The Europa World Year Book.*

Federal Statistical Office, Gustav - Stresemann - Ring 11, D-6200 Wiesbaden, Germany; *Katar.*

QATAR - BALANCE OF TRADE

Economic Commission for Western Asia, Post Office Box 27, Baghdad, Iraq; *Statistical Abstract of Western Asia.*

QATAR - BANKING

Economic Commission for Western Asia, Post Office Box 27, Baghdad, Iraq; *Statistical Abstract of Western Asia.*

Euromonitor International, Inc., 122 South Michigan Avenue, Suite 1200, Chicago, Illinois 60603 (800) 577-EURO; *World Marketing Data and Statistics.*

Europa Publications Limited, 18 Bedford Square, London, WC1B 3JN, England; *The Europa World Year Book.*

International Monetary Fund, 700 Nineteenth Street, NW, Washington, D.C. 20431 (202) 623-7000; *International Financial Statistics.*

M.E. Sharpe, 80 Business Park Drive, Armonk, New York 10504 (800) 541-6563; *The Illustrated Book of World Rankings.*

Presidency of the Council of Ministers, Central Statistical Organisation, Doha, Qatar; *Annual Statistical Abstract State of Qatar.*

St. Martin's Press, Inc., 175 Fifth Avenue, New York, New York 10010 (800) 221-7945; *The Statesman's Year-Book.*

QATAR - BARLEY PRODUCTION - See QATAR - CROPS

QATAR - BEER PRODUCTION - See QATAR - BEVERAGES

QATAR - BEVERAGES

M.E. Sharpe, 80 Business Park Drive, Armonk, New York 10504 (800) 541-6563; *The Illustrated Book of World Rankings.*

QATAR - BIRTH RATES

Central Intelligence Agency, Washington, D.C. 20505 (703) 482-1100, www.cia.gov; *The World Factbook.*

Euromonitor International, Inc., 122 South Michigan Avenue, Suite 1200, Chicago, Illinois 60603 (800) 577-EURO; *International Marketing Data and Statistics;* and *The World Economic Factbook.*

Europa Publications Limited, 18

Bedford Square, London, WC1B 3JN, England; *The Europa World Year Book.*

M.E. Sharpe, 80 Business Park Drive, Armonk, New York 10504 (800) 541-6563; *The Illustrated Book of World Rankings.*

St. Martin's Press, Inc., 175 Fifth Avenue, New York, New York 10010 (800) 221-7945; *The Statesman's Year-Book.*

Statistical Office of the United Nations, Publishing Service, New York, New York 10017 (800) 253-9646; *Demographic Yearbook.*

QATAR - BOOK PRODUCTION

Europa Publications Limited, 18 Bedford Square, London, WC1B 3JN, England; *The Europa World Year Book.*

United Nations Educational, Scientific and Cultural Organization (UNESCO), 7 Place de Fontenoy, F-75700 Paris, France (Telephone Number in U.S. (212) 963-5981); *Statistical Yearbook.*

QATAR - BROADCASTING

Billboard Limited, Post Office Box 9027, 1006 AA Amsterdam, The Netherlands (Telephone Number in U.S. (212) 764-7300); *World Radio TV Handbook.*

Central Intelligence Agency, Washington, D.C. 20505 (703) 482-1100, www.cia.gov; *The World Factbook.*

Euromonitor International, Inc., 122 South Michigan Avenue, Suite 1200, Chicago, Illinois 60603 (800) 577-EURO; *World Marketing Data and Statistics.*

M.E. Sharpe, 80 Business Park Drive, Armonk, New York 10504 (800) 541-6563; *The Illustrated Book of World Rankings.*

St. Martin's Press, Inc., 175 Fifth Avenue, New York, New York 10010 (800) 221-7945; *The Statesman's Year-Book.*

United Nations Educational, Scientific and Cultural Organization (UNESCO), 7 Place de Fontenoy, F-75700 Paris, France (Telephone Number in U.S. (212) 963-5981); *Statistical Yearbook.*

QATAR - BUDGET

Central Intelligence Agency, Washington, D.C. 20505 (703) 482-1100, www.cia.gov; *The World Factbook.*

QATAR - CALORIE SUPPLY

Food and Agricultural Organization of the United Nations (FAO) Via delle Terme di Caracalla, 00100 Rome, Italy (Telephone Number in U.S. (202) 653-2400); *The State of Food and Agriculture.*

QATAR - CATTLE - See QATAR - LIVESTOCK AND POULTRY

QATAR - CEMENT PRODUCTION - See QATAR - MINING AND MINERAL PRODUCTS

QATAR - CHEMICAL (ORGANIC) PRODUCTION - See QATAR - MINING AND MINERAL PRODUCTS

QATAR - CIGARETTE PRODUCTION - See QATAR - TOBACCO PRODUCTION

QATAR - CLIMATE

M.E. Sharpe, 80 Business Park Drive, Armonk, New York 10504 (800) 541-6563; *The Illustrated Book of World Rankings.*

St. Martin's Press, Inc., 175 Fifth Avenue, New York, New York 10010 (800) 221-7945; *The Statesman's Year-Book.*

QATAR - COAL PRODUCTION - See QATAR - MINING AND MINERAL PRODUCTS

QATAR - COFFEE PRODUCTION AND CONSUMPTION - See QATAR CROPS

QATAR - COMMERCE

St. Martin's Press, Inc., 175 Fifth Avenue, New York, New York 10010 (800) 221-7945; *The Statesman's Year-Book.*

QATAR - COMMUNICATIONS - See QATAR - TRANSPORTATION AND COMMUNICATIONS

QATAR - CONSTRUCTION

M.E. Sharpe, 80 Business Park Drive, Armonk, New York 10504 (800) 541-6563; *The Illustrated Book of World Rankings.*

QATAR - CONSUMER PRICES

Euromonitor International, Inc., 122 South Michigan Avenue, Suite 1200, Chicago, Illinois 60603 (800) 577-EURO; *World Marketing Data and Statistics.*

Europa Publications Limited, 18 Bedford Square, London, WC1B 3JN, England; *The Europa World Year Book.*

QATAR - COPPER PRODUCTION AND CONSUMPTION - See QATAR - MINING AND MINERAL PRODUCTS

QATAR - CORN PRODUCTION - See QATAR - CROPS

QATAR - COTTON PRODUCTION - See QATAR - CROPS

QATAR - CRIME

International Criminal Police

Organization (INTERPOL), 50 quai Achille Lignon, F-69006 Lyon, France; *International Crime Statistics.*

Yale University Press, Yale Station, New Haven, Connecticut 06520 (203) 432-0940; *Violence and Crime in Cross-National Perspective.*

QATAR - CROPS

Europa Publications Limited, 18 Bedford Square, London, WC1B 3JN, England; *The Europa World Year Book.*

Food and Agricultural Organization of the United Nations (FAO) Via delle Terme di Caracalla, 00100 Rome, Italy (Telephone Number in U.S. (202) 653-2400); *The State of Food and Agriculture.*

M.E. Sharpe, 80 Business Park Drive, Armonk, New York 10504 (800) 541-6563; *The Illustrated Book of World Rankings.*

St. Martin's Press, Inc., 175 Fifth Avenue, New York, New York 10010 (800) 221-7945; *The Statesman's Year-Book.*

United Nations Conference on Trade and Development, Central Statistical Service, Palais des Nations, Geneva, Switzerland (Telephone in U.S. (800) 253-9646); *UNCTAD Commodity Yearbook.*

QATAR - CUSTOMS DUTIES

St. Martin's Press, Inc., 175 Fifth Avenue, New York, New York 10010 (800) 221-7945; *The Statesman's Year-Book.*

QATAR - DAIRY PRODUCTS

Economic Commission for Western Asia, Post Office Box 27, Baghdad, Iraq; *Statistical Abstract of Western Asia.*

Food and Agricultural Organization of the United Nations (FAO) Via delle Terme di Caracalla, 00100 Rome, Italy (Telephone Number in U.S. (202) 653-2400); *Production Yearbook;* and *The State of Food and Agriculture.*

M.E. Sharpe, 80 Business Park Drive, Armonk, New York 10504 (800) 541-6563; *The Illustrated Book of World Rankings.*

St. Martin's Press, Inc., 175 Fifth Avenue, New York, New York 10010 (800) 221-7945; *The Statesman's Year-Book.*

QATAR - DEATH RATES - See QATAR - MORTALITY

QATAR - DEFENSE EXPENDITURES - See QATAR - MILITARY

QATAR - DEMOGRAPHY

Euromonitor International, Inc., 122

South Michigan Avenue, Suite 1200, Chicago, Illinois 60603 (800) 577-EURO; *International Marketing Data and Statistics; World Marketing Data and Statistics;* and *The World Economic Factbook.*

Federal Statistical Office, Gustav-Stresemann - Ring 11, D-6200, Wiesbaden, Germany; *Katar.*

M.E. Sharpe, 80 Business Park Drive, Armonk, New York 10504 (800) 541-6563; *The Illustrated Book of World Rankings.*

Statistical Office of the United Nations, Publishing Service, New York, New York 10017 (800) 253-9646; *Human Development Report.*

QATAR - DEVELOPMENT ASSISTANCE

Statistical Office of the United Nations, Publishing Service, New York, New York 10017 (800) 253-9646; *Statistical Yearbook.*

QATAR - DIAMOND PRODUCTION - See QATAR - MINING AND MINERAL PRODUCTS

QATAR - DIVORCE RATES

M.E. Sharpe, 80 Business Park Drive, Armonk, New York 10504 (800) 541-6563; *The Illustrated Book of World Rankings.*

Statistical Office of the United Nations, Publishing Service, New York, New York 10017 (800) 253-9646; *Demographic Yearbook.*

QATAR - ECONOMY

Central Intelligence Agency, Washington, D.C. 20505 (703) 482-1100, www.cia.gov; *The World Factbook.*

Economist Intelligence Unit, 111 West 57th Street, New York, New York 10019 (800) 938-4685; *Qatar Country Report.*

Euromonitor International, Inc., 122 South Michigan Avenue, Suite 1200, Chicago, Illinois 60603 (800) 577-EURO; *The World Economic Factbook;* and *World Marketing Data and Statistics.*

Europa Publications Limited, 18 Bedford Square, London, WC1B 3JN, England; *The Europa World Year Book.*

Federal Statistical Office, Gustav-Stresemann - Ring 11, D-6200, Wiesbaden, Germany; *Katar.*

M.E. Sharpe, 80 Business Park Drive, Armonk, New York 10504 (800) 541-6563; *The Illustrated Book of World Rankings.*

St. Martin's Press, Inc., 175 Fifth Avenue, New York, New York 10010 (800) 221-7945; *The Statesman's Year-Book.*

Statistical Office of the United Nations, Publishing Service, New York, New York 10017 (800) 253-9646; *World Statistics Pocketbook.*

The World Bank, 1818 H Street, NW, Washington, D.C. 20433 (800) 645-7247; *World Development Report.*

QATAR - EDUCATION

Economic Commission for Western Asia, Post Office Box 27, Baghdad, Iraq; *Statistical Abstract of Western Asia.*

The Economist Intelligence Unit, 111 West 57th Street, New York, New York 10019 (800) 938-4685; *The World Market Atlas.*

Euromonitor International, Inc., 122 South Michigan Avenue, Suite 1200, Chicago, Illinois 60603 (800) 577-EURO; *International Marketing Data and Statistics;* and *World Marketing Data and Statistics.*

Europa Publications Limited, 18 Bedford Square, London, WC1B 3JN, England; *The Europa World Year Book.*

Federal Statistical Office, Gustav - Stresemann - Ring 11, D-6200 Wiesbaden, Germany; *Katar.*

M.E. Sharpe, 80 Business Park Drive, Armonk, New York 10504 (800) 541-6563; *The Illustrated Book of World Rankings.*

Presidency of the Council of Ministers, Central Statistical Organisation, Doha, Qatar; *Annual Statistical Abstract State of Qatar.*

St. Martin's Press, Inc., 175 Fifth Avenue, New York, New York 10010 (800) 221-7945; *The Statesman's Year-Book.*

Statistical Office of the United Nations, Publishing Service, New York, New York 10017 (800) 253-9646; *Human Development Report.*

United Nations Educational, Scientific and Cultural Organization (UNESCO), 7 Place de Fontenoy, F-75700 Paris, France (Telephone Number in U.S. (212) 963-5981); *Statistical Yearbook.*

QATAR - EGG PRODUCTION AND CONSUMPTION - See QATAR - DAIRY PRODUCTS

QATAR - ELECTRICITY

Central Intelligence Agency, Washington, D.C. 20505 (703) 482-1100, www.cia.gov; *The World Factbook.*

M.E. Sharpe, 80 Business Park Drive, Armonk, New York 10504 (800) 541-6563; *The Illustrated Book of World Rankings.*

Penn Well Publishing Company, 1421 South Sheridan Road, Post Office Box 1260, Tulsa, Oklahoma 74101 (800) 752-9764; *International Energy Statistics Sourcebook.*

Presidency of the Council of Ministers, Central Statistical Organisation, Doha, Qatar; *Annual Statistical Abstract State of Qatar.*

St. Martin's Press, Inc., 175 Fifth Avenue, New York, New York 10010 (800) 221-7945; *The Statesman's Year-Book.*

Statistical Office of the United Nations, Publishing Service, New York, New York 10017 (800) 253-9646; *Human Development Report;* and *Statistical Yearbook.*

QATAR - EMPLOYMENT

Economic Commission for Western Asia, Post Office Box 27, Baghdad, Iraq; *Statistical Abstract of Western Asia.*

Euromonitor International, Inc., 122 South Michigan Avenue, Suite 1200, Chicago, Illinois 60603 (800) 577-EURO; *International Marketing Data and Statistics.*

Federal Statistical Office, Gustav - Stresemann - Ring 11, D-6200 Wiesbaden, Germany; *Katar.*

International Labour Office, I.L.O. Publications, 1828 L Street, NW., Suite 801, Washington, D.C. 20036 (301) 638-3152; *Yearbook of Labour Statistics.*

M.E. Sharpe, 80 Business Park Drive, Armonk, New York 10504 (800) 541-6563; *The Illustrated Book of World Rankings.*

Statistical Office of the United Nations, Publishing Service, New York, New York 10017 (800) 253-9646; *Bulletin of Industrial Statistics for the Arab Countries.*

QATAR - ENERGY

Economic Commission for Western Asia, Post Office Box 27, Baghdad, Iraq; *Statistical Abstract of Western Asia.*

Euromonitor International, Inc., 122 South Michigan Avenue, Suite 1200, Chicago, Illinois 60603 (800) 577-EURO; *International Marketing Data and Statistics; World Marketing Data and Statistics;* and *The World Economic Factbook.*

Food and Agricultural Organization of the United Nations (FAO) Via delle Terme di Caracalla, 00100 Rome, Italy (Telephone Number in U.S. (202) 653-2400); *The State of Food and Agriculture.*

M.E. Sharpe, 80 Business Park Drive, Armonk, New York 10504 (800) 541-6563; *The Illustrated Book of World Rankings.*

Penn Well Publishing Company, 1421 South Sheridan Road, Post Office Box 1260, Tulsa, Oklahoma 74101 (800) 752-9764; *International Energy Statistics Sourcebook.*

St. Martin's Press, Inc., 175 Fifth Avenue, New York, New York 10010 (800) 221-7945; *The Statesman's Year-Book.*

Statistical Office of the United Nations, Publishing Service, New York, New York 10017 (800) 253-9646; *Energy Statistics Yearbook; Human Development Report; Statistical Yearbook;* and *World Statistics Pocketbook.*

The World Bank, 1818 H Street, NW, Washington, D.C. 20433 (800) 645-7247; *World Development Report.*

QATAR - ENVIRONMENT

Economist Intelligence Unit, 111 West 57th Street, New York, New York 10019 (800) 938-4685; *Qatar Country Report.*

Statistical Office of the United Nations, Publishing Service, New York, New York 10017 (800) 253-9646; *World Statistics Pocketbook.*

QATAR - EXCHANGE RATES

Central Intelligence Agency, Washington, D.C. 20505 (703) 482-1100, www.cia.gov; *The World Factbook.*

Euromonitor International, Inc., 122 South Michigan Avenue, Suite 1200, Chicago, Illinois 60603 (800) 577-EURO; *International Marketing Data and Statistics;* and *The World Economic Factbook.*

Europa Publications Limited, 18 Bedford Square, London, WC1B 3JN, England; *The Europa World Year Book.*

International Monetary Fund, 700 Nineteenth Street, NW, Washington, D.C. 20431 (202) 623-7000; *International Financial Statistics.*

Organization of Petroleum Exporting Countries, Obere Donaustrasse 93, 1020 Vienna 2, Austria; *OPEC Annual Statistical Bulletin.*

Statistical Office of the United Nations, Publishing Service, New York, New York 10017 (800) 253-9646; *Bulletin of Industrial Statistics for the Arab Countries; Statistical Yearbook;* and *World Statistics Pocketbook.*

QATAR - EXPORTS

Central Intelligence Agency, Washington, D.C. 20505 (703) 482-1100, www.cia.gov; *The World Factbook.*

Economic Commission for Western Asia, Post Office Box 27, Baghdad, Iraq;

Statistical Abstract of Western Asia.

The Economist Intelligence Unit, 111 West 57th Street, New York, New York 10019 (800) 938-4685; *Qatar Country Report;* and *The World Market Atlas.*

Euromonitor International, Inc., 122 South Michigan Avenue, Suite 1200, Chicago, Illinois 60603 (800) 577-EURO; *International Marketing Data and Statistics;* and *The World Economic Factbook.*

Europa Publications Limited, 18 Bedford Square, London, WC1B 3JN, England; *The Europa World Year Book.*

Food and Agricultural Organization of the United Nations (FAO) Via delle Terme di Caracalla, 00100 Rome, Italy (Telephone Number in U.S. (202) 653-2400); *The State of Food and Agriculture.*

International Monetary Fund, 700 Nineteenth Street, NW, Washington, D.C. 20431 (202) 623-7000; *Direction of Trade Statistics,;* and *International Financial Statistics.*

Organization of Petroleum Exporting Countries, Obere Donaustrasse 93, 1020 Vienna 2, Austria; *OPEC Annual Statistical Bulletin.*

St. Martin's Press, Inc., 175 Fifth Avenue, New York, New York 10010 (800) 221-7945; *The Statesman's Year-Book.*

Statistical Office of the United Nations, Publishing Service, New York, New York 10017 (800) 253-9646; *Bulletin of Industrial Statistics for the Arab Countries.*

QATAR - EXTERNAL TRADE

Euromonitor International, Inc., 122 South Michigan Avenue, Suite 1200, Chicago, Illinois 60603 (800) 577-EURO; *World Marketing Data and Statistics.*

Food and Agricultural Organization of the United Nations (FAO) Via delle Terme di Caracalla, 00100 Rome, Italy (Telephone Number in U.S. (202) 653-2400); *The State of Food and Agriculture;* and *Trade Yearbook.*

QATAR - FARM CROPS - See QATAR - CROPS

QATAR - FERTILITY RATE

Central Intelligence Agency, Washington, D.C. 20505 (703) 482-1100, www.cia.gov; *The World Factbook.*

M.E. Sharpe, 80 Business Park Drive, Armonk, New York 10504 (800) 541-6563; *The Illustrated Book of World Rankings.*

Statistical Office of the United Nations,

Publishing Service, New York, New York 10017 (800) 253-9646; *Human Development Report.*

The World Bank, 1818 H Street, NW, Washington, D.C. 20433 (800) 645-7247; *World Development Report.*

QATAR - FERTILIZER

Food and Agricultural Organization of the United Nations (FAO), Via delle Terme di Caracalla, 00100 Rome, Italy (Telephone Number in U.S. (202) 653-2400); *Fertilizer Yearbook;* and *The State of Food and Agriculture.*

Statistical Office of the United Nations, Publishing Service, New York, New York 10017 (800) 253-9646; *Statistical Yearbook.*

QATAR - FETAL MORTALITY - See QATAR - MORTALITY

QATAR - FILM - See QATAR - MOTION PICTURES

QATAR - FINANCE

Economic Commission for Western Asia, Post Office Box 27, Baghdad, Iraq; *Statistical Abstract of Western Asia.*

Economist Intelligence Unit, 111 West 57th Street, New York, New York 10019 (800) 938-4685; *Qatar Country Report.*

Europa Publications Limited, 18 Bedford Square, London, WC1B 3JN, England; *The Europa World Year Book.*

Federal Statistical Office, Gustav - Stresemann - Ring 11, D-6200 Wiesbaden, Germany; *Katar.*

International Monetary Fund, 700 Nineteenth Street, NW, Washington, D.C. 20431 (202) 623-7000; *International Financial Statistics.*

M.E. Sharpe, 80 Business Park Drive, Armonk, New York 10504 (800) 541-6563; *The Illustrated Book of World Rankings.*

St. Martin's Press, Inc., 175 Fifth Avenue, New York, New York 10010 (800) 221-7945; *The Statesman's Year-Book.*

QATAR - FISHERIES

Economic Commission for Western Asia, Post Office Box 27, Baghdad, Iraq; *Statistical Abstract of Western Asia.*

Europa Publications Limited, 18 Bedford Square, London, WC1B 3JN, England; *The Europa World Year Book.*

Federal Statistical Office, Gustav - Stresemann - Ring 11, D-6200 Wiesbaden, Germany; *Katar.*

Food and Agricultural Organization of the United Nations (FAO) Via delle Terme di Caracalla, 00100 Rome, Italy (Telephone Number in U.S. (202) 653-2400); *The State of Food and Agriculture;* and *Yearbook of Fishery Statistics.*

M.E. Sharpe, 80 Business Park Drive, Armonk, New York 10504 (800) 541-6563; *The Illustrated Book of World Rankings.*

St. Martin's Press, Inc., 175 Fifth Avenue, New York, New York 10010 (800) 221-7945; *The Statesman's Year-Book.*

Statistical Office of the United Nations, Publishing Service, New York, New York 10017 (800) 253-9646; *Statistical Yearbook.*

United Nations Conference on Trade and Development, Central Statistical Service, Palais des Nations, Geneva, Switzerland (Telephone in U.S. (800) 253-9646); *UNCTAD Commodity Yearbook.*

QATAR - FOOD

Food and Agricultural Organization of the United Nations (FAO), Via delle Terme di Caracalla, 00100 Rome, Italy (Telephone Number in U.S. (202) 653-2400); *Production Yearbook;* and *The State of Food and Agriculture.*

Statistical Office of the United Nations, Publishing Service, New York, New York 10017 (800) 253-9646; *Human Development Report.*

United Nations Conference on Trade and Development, Central Statistical Service, Palais des Nations, Geneva, Switzerland (Telephone in U.S. (800) 253-9646); *UNCTAD Commodity Yearbook.*

QATAR - FOREIGN TRADE

Economic Commission for Western Asia, Post Office Box 27, Baghdad, Iraq; *Statistical Abstract of Western Asia.*

Economist Intelligence Unit, 111 West 57th Street, New York, New York 10019 (800) 938-4685; *Qatar Country Report.*

Euromonitor International, Inc., 122 South Michigan Avenue, Suite 1200, Chicago, Illinois 60603 (800) 577-EURO; *The World Economic Factbook.*

Europa Publications Limited, 18 Bedford Square, London, WC1B 3JN, England; *The Europa World Year Book.*

Federal Statistical Office, Gustav - Stresemann - Ring 11, D-6200 Wiesbaden, Germany; *Katar.*

Food and Agricultural Organization of the United Nations (FAO) Via delle Terme di Caracalla, 00100 Rome, Italy (Telephone

Number in U.S. (202) 653-2400); *The State of Food and Agriculture.*

M.E. Sharpe, 80 Business Park Drive, Armonk, New York 10504 (800) 541-6563; *The Illustrated Book of World Rankings.*

Presidency of the Council of Ministers, Central Statistical Organisation, Doha, Qatar; *Annual Statistical Abstract State of Qatar.*

St. Martin's Press, Inc., 175 Fifth Avenue, New York, New York 10010 (800) 221-7945; *The Statesman's Year-Book.*

Statistical Office of the United Nations, Publishing Service, New York, New York 10017 (800) 253-9646; *Bulletin of Industrial Statistics for the Arab Countries; International Trade Statistics Yearbook;* and *Statistical Yearbook.*

United Nations Conference on Trade and Development, Central Statistical Service, Palais des Nations, Geneva, Switzerland (Telephone in U.S. (800) 253-9646); *UNCTAD Commodity Yearbook.*

QATAR - FORESTRY AND FOREST PRODUCTS

Federal Statistical Office, Gustav - Stresemann - Ring 11, D-6200 Wiesbaden, Germany; *Katar.*

Food and Agricultural Organization of the United Nations (FAO) Via delle Terme di Caracalla, 00100 Rome, Italy (Telephone Number in U.S. (202) 653-2400); *The State of Food and Agriculture;* and *Yearbook of Forest Products.*

M.E. Sharpe, 80 Business Park Drive, Armonk, New York 10504 (800) 541-6563; *The Illustrated Book of World Rankings.*

United Nations Conference on Trade and Development, Central Statistical Service, Palais des Nations, Geneva, Switzerland (Telephone in U.S. (800) 253-9646); *UNCTAD Commodity Yearbook.*

United Nations Educational, Scientific and Cultural Organization (UNESCO), 7 Place de Fontenoy, F-75700 Paris, France (Telephone Number in U.S. (212) 963-5981); *Statistical Yearbook.*

QATAR - GAS PRODUCTION - See QATAR - MINING AND MINERAL PRODUCTS

QATAR - GENERAL MORTALITY - See QATAR - MORTALITY

QATAR - GEOGRAPHIC DATA

M.E. Sharpe, 80 Business Park Drive, Armonk, New York 10504 (800) 541-6563; *The Illustrated Book of World Rankings.*

QATAR - GOLD HOLDINGS

International Monetary Fund, 700 Nineteenth Street, NW, Washington, D.C. 20431 (202) 623-7000; *International Financial Statistics.*

Statistical Office of the United Nations, Publishing Service, New York, New York 10017 (800) 253-9646; *Statistical Yearbook.*

QATAR - GOLD PRODUCTION AND CONSUMPTION - See QATAR - MINING AND MINERAL PRODUCTS

QATAR - GOVERNMENT

Central Intelligence Agency, Washington, D.C. 20505 (703) 482-1100, www.cia.gov; *The World Factbook.*

Economic Commission for Western Asia, Post Office Box 27, Baghdad, Iraq; *Statistical Abstract of Western Asia.*

Europa Publications Limited, 18 Bedford Square, London, WC1B 3JN, England; *The Europa World Year Book.*

St. Martin's Press, Inc., 175 Fifth Avenue, New York, New York 10010 (800) 221-7945; *The Statesman's Year-Book.*

Statistical Office of the United Nations, Publishing Service, New York, New York 10017 (800) 253-9646; *National Accounts Statistics.*

QATAR - GRAIN PRODUCTION - See QATAR - CROPS

QATAR - GROSS DOMESTIC PRODUCT

Economic Commission for Western Asia, Post Office Box 27, Baghdad, Iraq; *Statistical Abstract of Western Asia.*

The Economist Intelligence Unit, 111 West 57th Street, New York, New York 10019 (800) 938-4685; *Qatar Country Report;* and *The World Market Atlas.*

Euromonitor International, Inc., 122 South Michigan Avenue, Suite 1200, Chicago, Illinois 60603 (800) 577-EURO; *International Marketing Data and Statistics;* and *The World Economic Factbook.*

Europa Publications Limited, 18 Bedford Square, London, WC1B 3JN, England; *The Europa World Year Book.*

M.E. Sharpe, 80 Business Park Drive, Armonk, New York 10504 (800) 541-6563; *The Illustrated Book of World Rankings.*

Statistical Office of the United Nations, Publishing Service, New York, New York 10017 (800) 253-9646; *Bulletin of Industrial Statistics for the Arab Countries; Human Development Report;* and *National*

Accounts Statistics.

QATAR - GROSS NATIONAL PRODUCT

Organization of Petroleum Exporting Countries, Obere Donaustrasse 93, 1020 Vienna 2, Austria; *OPEC Annual Statistical Bulletin.*

St. Martin's Press, Inc., 175 Fifth Avenue, New York, New York 10010 (800) 221-7945; *The Statesman's Year-Book.*

U.S. Arms Control and Disarmament Agency, 320 Twenty-first Street, NW, Washington, D.C. 20451 (202) 647-8677; *World Military Expenditures and Arms Transfers.*

The World Bank, 1818 H Street, NW, Washington, D.C. 20433 (800) 645-7247; *World Development Report.*

QATAR - HEALTH

Economic Commission for Western Asia, Post Office Box 27, Baghdad, Iraq; *Statistical Abstract of Western Asia.*

Euromonitor International, Inc., 122 South Michigan Avenue, Suite 1200, Chicago, Illinois 60603 (800) 577-EURO; *World Marketing Data and Statistics.*

Federal Statistical Office, Gustav - Stresemann - Ring 11, D-6200 Wiesbaden, Germany; *Katar.*

M.E. Sharpe, 80 Business Park Drive, Armonk, New York 10504 (800) 541-6563; *The Illustrated Book of World Rankings.*

Presidency of the Council of Ministers, Central Statistical Organisation, Doha, Qatar; *Annual Statistical Abstract State of Qatar.*

St. Martin's Press, Inc., 175 Fifth Avenue, New York, New York 10010 (800) 221-7945; *The Statesman's Year-Book.*

Statistical Office of the United Nations, Publishing Service, New York, New York 10017 (800) 253-9646; *Human Development Report;* and *Statistical Yearbook.*

World Health Organization, Office of Publications, Avenue Appia, CH-1211 Geneva 27, Switzerland (Telephone Number in U.S. (518) 436-9686); *World Health Statistics Annual.*

QATAR - HIDE PRODUCTION

Food and Agricultural Organization of the United Nations (FAO), Via delle Terme di Caracalla, 00100 Rome, Italy (Telephone Number in U.S. (202) 653-2400); *Production Yearbook.*

QATAR - HIGHWAYS

Central Intelligence Agency, Washington, D.C. 20505 (703) 482-1100, www.cia.gov; *The World Factbook.*

Economic Commission for Western Asia, Post Office Box 27, Baghdad, Iraq; *Statistical Abstract of Western Asia.*

St. Martin's Press, Inc., 175 Fifth Avenue, New York, New York 10010 (800) 221-7945; *The Statesman's Year-Book.*

QATAR - HORSES - See QATAR - LIVESTOCK AND POULTRY

QATAR - HOURS OF WORK - See QATAR - EMPLOYMENT

QATAR - HOUSING AND HOUSING UNITS

Euromonitor International, Inc., 122 South Michigan Avenue, Suite 1200, Chicago, Illinois 60603 (800) 577-EURO; *World Marketing Data and Statistics.*

M.E. Sharpe, 80 Business Park Drive, Armonk, New York 10504 (800) 541-6563; *The Illustrated Book of World Rankings.*

QATAR - ILLITERATE POPULATION

Central Intelligence Agency, Washington, D.C. 20505 (703) 482-1100, www.cia.gov; *The World Factbook.*

The Economist Intelligence Unit, 111 West 57th Street, New York, New York 10019 (800) 938-4685; *The World Market Atlas.*

Euromonitor International, Inc., 122 South Michigan Avenue, Suite 1200, Chicago, Illinois 60603 (800) 577-EURO; *The World Economic Factbook.*

Statistical Office of the United Nations, Publishing Service, New York, New York 10017 (800) 253-9646; *Human Development Report.*

QATAR - IMPORTS

Central Intelligence Agency, Washington, D.C. 20505 (703) 482-1100, www.cia.gov; *The World Factbook.*

Economic Commission for Western Asia, Post Office Box 27, Baghdad, Iraq; *Statistical Abstract of Western Asia.*

The Economist Intelligence Unit, 111 West 57th Street, New York, New York 10019 (800) 938-4685; *Qatar Country Report;* and *The World Market Atlas.*

Euromonitor International, Inc., 122 South Michigan Avenue, Suite 1200, Chicago, Illinois 60603 (800) 577-EURO; *International Marketing Data and Statistics;*

and *The World Economic Factbook.*

Europa Publications Limited, 18 Bedford Square, London, WC1B 3JN, England; *The Europa World Year Book.*

Food and Agricultural Organization of the United Nations (FAO) Via delle Terme di Caracalla, 00100 Rome, Italy (Telephone Number in U.S. (202) 653-2400); *The State of Food and Agriculture.*

International Monetary Fund, 700 Nineteenth Street, NW, Washington, D.C. 20431 (202) 623-7000; *Direction of Trade Statistics;* and *International Financial Statistics.*

St. Martin's Press, Inc., 175 Fifth Avenue, New York, New York 10010 (800) 221-7945; *The Statesman's Year-Book.*

Statistical Office of the United Nations, Publishing Service, New York, New York 10017 (800) 253-9646; *Bulletin of Industrial Statistics for the Arab Countries.*

QATAR - INDUSTRY

Central Intelligence Agency, Washington, D.C. 20505 (703) 482-1100, www.cia.gov; *The World Factbook.*

Economist Intelligence Unit, 111 West 57th Street, New York, New York 10019 (800) 938-4685; *Qatar Country Report.*

Euromonitor International, Inc., 122 South Michigan Avenue, Suite 1200, Chicago, Illinois 60603 (800) 577-EURO; *The World Economic Factbook;* and *World Marketing Data and Statistics.*

Europa Publications Limited, 18 Bedford Square, London, WC1B 3JN, England; *The Europa World Year Book.*

Federal Statistical Office, Gustav - Stresemann - Ring 11, D-6200 Wiesbaden, Germany; *Katar.*

M.E. Sharpe, 80 Business Park Drive, Armonk, New York 10504 (800) 541-6563; *The Illustrated Book of World Rankings.*

Presidency of the Council of Ministers, Central Statistical Organisation, Doha, Qatar; *Annual Statistical Abstract State of Qatar.*

St. Martin's Press, Inc., 175 Fifth Avenue, New York, New York 10010 (800) 221-7945; *The Statesman's Year-Book.*

Statistical Office of the United Nations, Publishing Service, New York, New York 10017 (800) 253-9646; *Bulletin of Industrial Statistics for the Arab Countries.*

QATAR - INFANT AND MATERNAL MORTALITY - See QATAR - MORTALITY

QATAR - INTERNATIONAL LIQUIDITY

International Monetary Fund, 700 Nineteenth Street, NW, Washington, D.C. 20431 (202) 623-7000; *International Financial Statistics.*

QATAR - INTERNATIONAL RESERVES EXCLUDING GOLD

Statistical Office of the United Nations, Publishing Service, New York, New York 10017 (800) 253-9646; *Statistical Yearbook.*

QATAR - IRON ORE PRODUCTION AND CONSUMPTION - See QATAR - MINING AND MINERAL PRODUCTS

QATAR - LABOR

Central Intelligence Agency, Washington, D.C. 20505 (703) 482-1100, www.cia.gov; *The World Factbook.*

Economic Commission for Western Asia, Post Office Box 27, Baghdad, Iraq; *Statistical Abstract of Western Asia.*

Euromonitor International, Inc., 122 South Michigan Avenue, Suite 1200, Chicago, Illinois 60603 (800) 577-EURO; *International Marketing Data and Statistics;* and *World Marketing Data and Statistics.*

Europa Publications Limited, 18 Bedford Square, London, WC1B 3JN, England; *The Europa World Year Book.*

Food and Agricultural Organization of the United Nations (FAO) Via delle Terme di Caracalla, 00100 Rome, Italy (Telephone Number in U.S. (202) 653-2400); *The State of Food and Agriculture.*

M.E. Sharpe, 80 Business Park Drive, Armonk, New York 10504 (800) 541-6563; *The Illustrated Book of World Rankings.*

St. Martin's Press, Inc., 175 Fifth Avenue, New York, New York 10010 (800) 221-7945; *The Statesman's Year-Book.*

Statistical Office of the United Nations, Publishing Service, New York, New York 10017 (800) 253-9646; *Human Development Report.*

The World Bank, 1818 H Street, NW, Washington, D.C. 20433 (800) 645-7247; *World Development Report.*

QATAR - LAND USE

Central Intelligence Agency, Washington, D.C. 20505 (703) 482-1100, www.cia.gov; *The World Factbook.*

Economic Commission for Western Asia, Post Office Box 27, Baghdad, Iraq; *Statistical Abstract of Western Asia.*

Euromonitor International, Inc., 122 South Michigan Avenue, Suite 1200, Chicago, Illinois 60603 (800) 577-EURO; *International Marketing Data and Statistics.*

Food and Agricultural Organization of the United Nations (FAO), Via delle Terme di Caracalla, 00100 Rome, Italy (Telephone Number in U.S. (202) 653-2400); *Production Yearbook.*

QATAR - LIBRARIES

M.E. Sharpe, 80 Business Park Drive, Armonk, New York 10504 (800) 541-6563; *The Illustrated Book of World Rankings.*

United Nations Educational, Scientific and Cultural Organization (UNESCO), 7 Place de Fontenoy, F-75700 Paris, France (Telephone Number in U.S. (212) 963-5981); *Statistical Yearbook.*

QATAR - LIFE EXPECTANCY

Central Intelligence Agency, Washington, D.C. 20505 (703) 482-1100, www.cia.gov; *The World Factbook.*

Euromonitor International, Inc., 122 South Michigan Avenue, Suite 1200, Chicago, Illinois 60603 (800) 577-EURO; *The World Economic Factbook.*

St. Martin's Press, Inc., 175 Fifth Avenue, New York, New York 10010 (800) 221-7945; *The Statesman's Year-Book.*

Statistical Office of the United Nations, Publishing Service, New York, New York 10017 (800) 253-9646; *Human Development Report;* and *World Statistics Pocketbook.*

The World Bank, 1818 H Street, NW, Washington, D.C. 20433 (800) 645-7247; *World Development Report.*

QATAR - LITERACY RATE

Euromonitor International, Inc., 122 South Michigan Avenue, Suite 1200, Chicago, Illinois 60603 (800) 577-EURO; *World Marketing Data and Statistics.*

QATAR - LIVESTOCK AND POULTRY

Economic Commission for Western Asia, Post Office Box 27, Baghdad, Iraq; *Statistical Abstract of Western Asia.*

Europa Publications Limited, 18 Bedford Square, London, WC1B 3JN, England; *The Europa World Year Book.*

Food and Agricultural Organization of the United Nations (FAO), Via delle Terme di Caracalla, 00100 Rome, Italy (Telephone Number in U.S. (202) 653-2400); *Production Yearbook;* and *The State of Food and Agriculture.*

M.E. Sharpe, 80 Business Park Drive, Armonk, New York 10504 (800) 541-6563; *The Illustrated Book of World Rankings.*

St. Martin's Press, Inc., 175 Fifth Avenue, New York, New York 10010 (800) 221-7945; *The Statesman's Year-Book.*

Statistical Office of the United Nations, Publishing Service, New York, New York 10017 (800) 253-9646; *Statistical Yearbook.*

United Nations Conference on Trade and Development, Central Statistical Service, Palais des Nations, Geneva, Switzerland (Telephone in U.S. (800) 253-9646); *UNCTAD Commodity Yearbook.*

QATAR - LIVING LEVELS - See QATAR - LIFE EXPECTANCY

QATAR - MANPOWER

Presidency of the Council of Ministers, Central Statistical Organisation, Doha, Qatar; *Annual Statistical Abstract State of Qatar.*

QATAR - MANUFACTURING

M.E. Sharpe, 80 Business Park Drive, Armonk, New York 10504 (800) 541-6563; *The Illustrated Book of World Rankings.*

Statistical Office of the United Nations, Publishing Service, New York, New York 10017 (800) 253-9646; *Bulletin of Industrial Statistics for the Arab Countries.*

QATAR - MARRIAGE RATES

Europa Publications Limited, 18 Bedford Square, London, WC1B 3JN, England; *The Europa World Year Book.*

M.E. Sharpe, 80 Business Park Drive, Armonk, New York 10504 (800) 541-6563; *The Illustrated Book of World Rankings.*

Statistical Office of the United Nations, Publishing Service, New York, New York 10017 (800) 253-9646; *Demographic Yearbook.*

QATAR - MEAT PRODUCTION - See QATAR - LIVESTOCK AND POULTRY

QATAR - MERCHANT SHIPPING

Economic Commission for Western Asia, Post Office Box 27, Baghdad, Iraq; *Statistical Abstract of Western Asia.*

Europa Publications Limited, 18 Bedford Square, London, WC1B 3JN, England; *The Europa World Year Book.*

Organization of Petroleum Exporting Countries, Obere Donaustrasse 93, 1020 Vienna 2, Austria; *OPEC Annual Statistical Bulletin.*

St. Martin's Press, Inc., 175 Fifth Avenue, New York, New York 10010 (800) 221-7945; *The Statesman's Year-Book.*

Statistical Office of the United Nations, Publishing Service, New York, New York 10017 (800) 253-9646; *Statistical Yearbook.*

QATAR - MILITARY

Central Intelligence Agency, Washington, D.C. 20505 (703) 482-1100, www.cia.gov; *The World Factbook.*

Euromonitor International, Inc., 122 South Michigan Avenue, Suite 1200, Chicago, Illinois 60603 (800) 577-EURO; *World Marketing Data and Statistics.*

The International Institute for Strategic Studies, 23 Tavistock Street, London WC2E 7NQ, England; *The Military Balance.*

St. Martin's Press, Inc., 175 Fifth Avenue, New York, New York 10010 (800) 221-7945; *The Statesman's Year-Book.*

Statistical Office of the United Nations, Publishing Service, New York, New York 10017 (800) 253-9646; *Human Development Report.*

U.S. Arms Control and Disarmament Agency, 320 Twenty-first Street, NW, Washington, D.C. 20451 (202) 647-8677; *World Military Expenditures and Arms Transfers.*

QATAR - MILK PRODUCTION - See QATAR - DAIRY PRODUCTS

QATAR - MINING AND MINERAL PRODUCTS

Economic Commission for Western Asia, Post Office Box 27, Baghdad, Iraq; *Statistical Abstract of Western Asia.*

Europa Publications Limited, 18 Bedford Square, London, WC1B 3JN, England; *The Europa World Year Book.*

M.E. Sharpe, 80 Business Park Drive, Armonk, New York 10504 (800) 541-6563; *The Illustrated Book of World Rankings.*

Organization of Petroleum Exporting Countries, Obere Donaustrasse 93, 1020 Vienna 2, Austria; *OPEC Annual Statistical Bulletin.*

Penn Well Publishing Company, 1421 South Sheridan Road, Post Office Box 1260, Tulsa, Oklahoma 74101 (800) 752-9764; *International Energy Statistics Sourcebook.*

Statistical Office of the United Nations, Publishing Service, New York, New York 10017 (800) 253-9646; *Bulletin of Industrial Statistics for the Arab Countries;* and *Statistical Yearbook.*

United Nations Conference on Trade and Development, Central Statistical Service, Palais des Nations, Geneva, Switzerland (Telephone in U.S. (800) 253-9646); *UNCTAD Commodity Yearbook.*

QATAR - MONEY EXCHANGE RATES - See QATAR - EXCHANGE RATES

QATAR - MONEY SUPPLY

Economist Intelligence Unit, 111 West 57th Street, New York, New York 10019 (800) 938-4685; *Qatar Country Report.*

Europa Publications Limited, 18 Bedford Square, London, WC1B 3JN, England; *The Europa World Year Book.*

Federal Statistical Office, Gustav-Stresemann - Ring 11, D-6200, Wiesbaden, Germany; *Katar.*

International Monetary Fund, 700 Nineteenth Street, NW, Washington, D.C. 20431 (202) 623-7000; *International Financial Statistics.*

Statistical Office of the United Nations, Publishing Service, New York, New York 10017 (800) 253-9646; *Statistical Yearbook.*

QATAR - MORTALITY

Central Intelligence Agency, Washington, D.C. 20505 (703) 482-1100, www.cia.gov; *The World Factbook.*

Euromonitor International, Inc., 122 South Michigan Avenue, Suite 1200, Chicago, Illinois 60603 (800) 577-EURO; *International Marketing Data and Statistics;* and *The World Economic Factbook.*

Europa Publications Limited, 18 Bedford Square, London, WC1B 3JN, England; *The Europa World Year Book.*

St. Martin's Press, Inc., 175 Fifth Avenue, New York, New York 10010 (800) 221-7945; *The Statesman's Year-Book.*

Statistical Office of the United Nations, Publishing Service, New York, New York 10017 (800) 253-9646; *Demographic Yearbook; Human Development Report;* and *World Statistics Pocketbook.*

The World Bank, 1818 H Street, NW, Washington, D.C. 20433 (800) 645-7247; *World Development Report.*

World Health Organization, Office of Publications, Avenue Appia, CH-1211 Geneva 27, Switzerland (Telephone Number in U.S. (518) 436-9686); *World Health Statistics Annual.*

QATAR - MOTION PICTURES

St. Martin's Press, Inc., 175 Fifth

Avenue, New York, New York 10010 (800) 221-7945; *The Statesman's Year-Book.*

United Nations Educational, Scientific and Cultural Organization (UNESCO), 7 Place de Fontenoy, F-75700 Paris, France (Telephone Number in U.S. (212) 963-5981); *Statistical Yearbook.*

QATAR - MOTOR VEHICLES

Economic Commission for Western Asia, Post Office Box 27, Baghdad, Iraq; *Statistical Abstract of Western Asia.*

QATAR - MOTOR VEHICLES IN USE

Europa Publications Limited, 18 Bedford Square, London, WC1B 3JN, England; *The Europa World Year Book.*

QATAR - MUSEUMS

M.E. Sharpe, 80 Business Park Drive, Armonk, New York 10504 (800) 541-6563; *The Illustrated Book of World Rankings.*

United Nations Educational, Scientific and Cultural Organization (UNESCO), 7 Place de Fontenoy, F-75700 Paris, France (Telephone Number in U.S. (212) 963-5981); *Statistical Yearbook.*

QATAR - NATALITY - See QATAR - BIRTH RATES

QATAR - NATIONAL ACCOUNTS

Economic Commission for Western Asia, Post Office Box 27, Baghdad, Iraq; *Statistical Abstract of Western Asia.*

Federal Statistical Office, Gustav - Stresemann - Ring 11, D-6200 Wiesbaden, Germany; *Katar.*

QATAR - NATIONAL INCOME

M.E. Sharpe, 80 Business Park Drive, Armonk, New York 10504 (800) 541-6563; *The Illustrated Book of World Rankings.*

Presidency of the Council of Ministers, Central Statistical Organisation, Doha, Qatar; *Annual Statistical Abstract State of Qatar.*

Statistical Office of the United Nations, Publishing Service, New York, New York 10017 (800) 253-9646; *National Accounts Statistics;* and *Statistical Yearbook.*

QATAR - NATURAL GAS PRODUCTION - See QATAR - MINING AND MINERAL PRODUCTS

QATAR - NEWSPAPER PRODUCTION - See QATAR - FORESTRY AND FOREST PRODUCTS

QATAR - OCCUPATIONS - See QATAR -

LABOR

QATAR - PAPER - See QATAR - FORESTRY AND FOREST PRODUCTS

QATAR - PEANUT PRODUCTION - See QATAR - CROPS

QATAR - PERIODICALS

United Nations Educational, Scientific and Cultural Organization (UNESCO), 7 Place de Fontenoy, F-75700 Paris, France (Telephone Number in U.S. (212) 963-5981); *Statistical Yearbook.*

QATAR - PESTICIDE USE

Food and Agricultural Organization of the United Nations (FAO) Via delle Terme di Caracalla, 00100 Rome, Italy (Telephone Number in U.S. (202) 653-2400); *The State of Food and Agriculture.*

QATAR - PETROLEUM INDUSTRY

Food and Agricultural Organization of the United Nations (FAO) Via delle Terme di Caracalla, 00100 Rome, Italy (Telephone Number in U.S. (202) 653-2400); *The State of Food and Agriculture.*

M.E. Sharpe, 80 Business Park Drive, Armonk, New York 10504 (800) 541-6563; *The Illustrated Book of World Rankings.*

Organization of Petroleum Exporting Countries, Obere Donaustrasse 93, 1020 Vienna 2, Austria; *OPEC Annual Statistical Bulletin.*

Penn Well Publishing Company, 1421 South Sheridan Road, Post Office Box 1260, Tulsa, Oklahoma 74101 (800) 752-9764; *International Energy Statistics Sourcebook.*

Presidency of the Council of Ministers, Central Statistical Organisation, Doha, Qatar; *Annual Statistical Abstract State of Qatar.*

St. Martin's Press, Inc., 175 Fifth Avenue, New York, New York 10010 (800) 221-7945; *The Statesman's Year-Book.*

Statistical Office of the United Nations, Publishing Service, New York, New York 10017 (800) 253-9646; *Statistical Yearbook.*

United Nations Conference on Trade and Development, Central Statistical Service, Palais des Nations, Geneva, Switzerland (Telephone in U.S. (800) 253-9646); *UNCTAD Commodity Yearbook.*

QATAR - PIGS - See QATAR - LIVESTOCK AND POULTRY

QATAR - PIPELINES FOR OIL AND PETROLEUM PRODUCTS

Organization of Petroleum Exporting Countries, Obere Donaustrasse 93, 1020 Vienna 2, Austria; *OPEC Annual Statistical Bulletin.*

QATAR - POPULATION

Central Intelligence Agency, Washington, D.C. 20505 (703) 482-1100, www.cia.gov; *The World Factbook.*

Economic Commission for Western Asia, Post Office Box 27, Baghdad, Iraq; *Statistical Abstract of Western Asia.*

The Economist Intelligence Unit, 111 West 57th Street, New York, New York 10019 (800) 938-4685; *Qatar Country Report;* and *The World Market Atlas.*

Euromonitor International, Inc., 122 South Michigan Avenue, Suite 1200, Chicago, Illinois 60603 (800) 577-EURO; *International Marketing Data and Statistics;* and *The World Economic Factbook.*

Europa Publications Limited, 18 Bedford Square, London, WC1B 3JN, England; *The Europa World Year Book.*

Federal Statistical Office, Gustav - Stresemann - Ring 11, D-6200 Wiesbaden, Germany; *Katar.*

Food and Agricultural Organization of the United Nations (FAO), Via delle Terme di Caracalla, 00100 Rome, Italy (Telephone Number in U.S. (202) 653-2400); *Production Yearbook.*

M.E. Sharpe, 80 Business Park Drive, Armonk, New York 10504 (800) 541-6563; *The Illustrated Book of World Rankings.*

Presidency of the Council of Ministers, Central Statistical Organisation, Doha, Qatar; *Annual Statistical Abstract State of Qatar.*

St. Martin's Press, Inc., 175 Fifth Avenue, New York, New York 10010 (800) 221-7945; *The Statesman's Year-Book.*

Statistical Office of the United Nations, Publishing Service, New York, New York 10017 (800) 253-9646; *Demographic Yearbook; Human Development Report; Statistical Yearbook;* and *World Statistics Pocketbook.*

United Nations Educational, Scientific and Cultural Organization (UNESCO), 7 Place de Fontenoy, F-75700 Paris, France (Telephone Number in U.S. (212) 963-5981); *Statistical Yearbook.*

U.S. Arms Control and Disarmament Agency, 320 Twenty-first Street, NW, Washington, D.C. 20451 (202) 647-8677; *World Military Expenditures and Arms Transfers.*

The World Bank, 1818 H Street, NW, Washington, D.C. 20433 (800) 645-7247; *World Development Report.*

World Health Organization, Office of Publications, Avenue Appia, CH-1211 Geneva 27, Switzerland (Telephone Number in U.S. (518) 436-9686); *World Health Statistics Annual.*

QATAR - POST OFFICES

M.E. Sharpe, 80 Business Park Drive, Armonk, New York 10504 (800) 541-6563; *The Illustrated Book of World Rankings.*

St. Martin's Press, Inc., 175 Fifth Avenue, New York, New York 10010 (800) 221-7945; *The Statesman's Year-Book.*

QATAR - POTATO PRODUCTION - See QATAR - CROPS

QATAR - PRICES

Economic Commission for Western Asia, Post Office Box 27, Baghdad, Iraq; *Statistical Abstract of Western Asia.*

Federal Statistical Office, Gustav - Stresemann - Ring 11, D-6200 Wiesbaden, Germany; *Katar.*

Food and Agricultural Organization of the United Nations (FAO) Via delle Terme di Caracalla, 00100 Rome, Italy (Telephone Number in U.S. (202) 653-2400); *The State of Food and Agriculture.*

M.E. Sharpe, 80 Business Park Drive, Armonk, New York 10504 (800) 541-6563; *The Illustrated Book of World Rankings.*

Presidency of the Council of Ministers, Central Statistical Organisation, Doha, Qatar; *Annual Statistical Abstract State of Qatar.*

QATAR - PRODUCTION

M.E. Sharpe, 80 Business Park Drive, Armonk, New York 10504 (800) 541-6563; *The Illustrated Book of World Rankings.*

QATAR - PUBLIC FINANCE - See QATAR - FINANCE

QATAR - RADIO BROADCASTING - See QATAR - BROADCASTING

QATAR - RADIO RECEIVERS

St. Martin's Press, Inc., 175 Fifth Avenue, New York, New York 10010 (800) 221-7945; *The Statesman's Year-Book.*

QATAR - RELIGION

Central Intelligence Agency, Washington, D.C. 20505 (703) 482-1100, www.cia.gov; *The World Factbook.*

M.E. Sharpe, 80 Business Park Drive, Armonk, New York 10504 (800) 541-6563; *The Illustrated Book of World Rankings.*

St. Martin's Press, Inc., 175 Fifth Avenue, New York, New York 10010 (800) 221-7945; *The Statesman's Year-Book.*

QATAR - RETAIL TRADE

Euromonitor International, Inc., 122 South Michigan Avenue, Suite 1200, Chicago, Illinois 60603 (800) 577-EURO; *World Marketing Data and Statistics.*

QATAR - RICE PRODUCTION - See QATAR - CROPS

QATAR - RUBBER PRODUCTION AND CONSUMPTION

M.E. Sharpe, 80 Business Park Drive, Armonk, New York 10504 (800) 541-6563; *The Illustrated Book of World Rankings.*

QATAR - SCIENTISTS, TECHNICIANS AND ENGINEERS

Statistical Office of the United Nations, Publishing Service, New York, New York 10017 (800) 253-9646; *Statistical Yearbook.*

QATAR - SENIOR CITIZENS

M.E. Sharpe, 80 Business Park Drive, Armonk, New York 10504 (800) 541-6563; *The Illustrated Book of World Rankings.*

QATAR - SHEEP - See QATAR - LIVESTOCK AND POULTRY

QATAR - SILVER PRODUCTION AND CONSUMPTION - See QATAR -MINING AND MINERAL PRODUCTS

QATAR - SOCIAL DATA

M.E. Sharpe, 80 Business Park Drive, Armonk, New York 10504 (800) 541-6563; *The Illustrated Book of World Rankings.*

Statistical Office of the United Nations, Publishing Service, New York, New York 10017 (800) 253-9646; *World Statistics Pocketbook.*

QATAR - SOCIAL SECURITY

Statistical Office of the United Nations, Publishing Service, New York, New York 10017 (800) 253-9646; *National Accounts Statistics.*

QATAR - STEEL PRODUCTION - See QATAR - MINING AND MINERAL PRODUCTS

QATAR - STOCKS - COMMODITY - MARKET PRICE - INDEX

Food and Agricultural Organization of

the United Nations (FAO) Via delle Terme di Caracalla, 00100 Rome, Italy (Telephone Number in U.S. (202) 653-2400); *The State of Food and Agriculture.*

QATAR - SUGAR PRODUCTION AND CONSUMPTION - See QATAR - CROPS

QATAR - TELEPHONES IN USE

American Telephone and Telegraph Company, 26 Parsippany Road, Whippany, New Jersey 07981 (800) 338-4038; *The World's Telephones.*

Central Intelligence Agency, Washington, D.C. 20505 (703) 482-1100, www.cia.gov; *The World Factbook.*

Europa Publications Limited, 18 Bedford Square, London, WC1B 3JN, England; *The Europa World Year Book.*

St. Martin's Press, Inc., 175 Fifth Avenue, New York, New York 10010 (800) 221-7945; *The Statesman's Year-Book.*

Statistical Office of the United Nations, Publishing Service, New York, New York 10017 (800) 253-9646; *Statistical Yearbook;* and *World Statistics Pocketbook.*

QATAR - TELEVISION BROADCASTING - See QATAR -BROADCASTING

QATAR - TEXTILE INDUSTRY

M.E. Sharpe, 80 Business Park Drive, Armonk, New York 10504 (800) 541-6563; *The Illustrated Book of World Rankings.*

United Nations Conference on Trade and Development, Central Statistical Service, Palais des Nations, Geneva, Switzerland (Telephone in U.S. (800) 253-9646); *UNCTAD Commodity Yearbook.*

QATAR - THEATRE

United Nations Educational, Scientific and Cultural Organization (UNESCO), 7 Place de Fontenoy, F-75700 Paris, France (Telephone Number in U.S. (212) 963-5981); *Statistical Yearbook.*

QATAR - TOBACCO PRODUCTION

M.E. Sharpe, 80 Business Park Drive, Armonk, New York 10504 (800) 541-6563; *The Illustrated Book of World Rankings.*

QATAR - TOURISM

Economic Commission for Western Asia, Post Office Box 27, Baghdad, Iraq; *Statistical Abstract of Western Asia.*

Euromonitor International, Inc., 122 South Michigan Avenue, Suite 1200, Chicago, Illinois 60603 (800) 577-EURO; *The World Economic Factbook;* and *World*

Marketing Data and Statistics.

Europa Publications Limited, 18 Bedford Square, London, WC1B 3JN, England; *The Europa World Year Book.*

Federal Statistical Office, Gustav - Stresemann - Ring 11, D-6200 Wiesbaden, Germany; *Katar.*

M.E. Sharpe, 80 Business Park Drive, Armonk, New York 10504 (800) 541-6563; *The Illustrated Book of World Rankings.*

Presidency of the Council of Ministers, Central Statistical Organisation, Doha, Qatar; *Annual Statistical Abstract State of Qatar.*

St. Martin's Press, Inc., 175 Fifth Avenue, New York, New York 10010 (800) 221-7945; *The Statesman's Year-Book.*

QATAR - TRADE - See QATAR - FOREIGN TRADE

QATAR - TRANSPORTATION AND COMMUNICATIONS

Central Intelligence Agency, Washington, D.C. 20505 (703) 482-1100, www.cia.gov; *The World Factbook.*

Economic Commission for Western Asia, Post Office Box 27, Baghdad, Iraq; *Statistical Abstract of Western Asia.*

Euromonitor International, Inc., 122 South Michigan Avenue, Suite 1200, Chicago, Illinois 60603 (800) 577-EURO; *International Marketing Data and Statistics;* and *World Marketing Data and Statistics.*

Europa Publications Limited, 18 Bedford Square, London, WC1B 3JN, England; *The Europa World Year Book.*

Federal Statistical Office, Gustav - Stresemann - Ring 11, D-6200 Wiesbaden, Germany; *Katar.*

M.E. Sharpe, 80 Business Park Drive, Armonk, New York 10504 (800) 541-6563; *The Illustrated Book of World Rankings.*

Presidency of the Council of Ministers, Central Statistical Organisation, Doha, Qatar; *Annual Statistical Abstract State of Qatar.*

St. Martin's Press, Inc., 175 Fifth Avenue, New York, New York 10010 (800) 221-7945; *The Statesman's Year-Book.*

Statistical Office of the United Nations, Publishing Service, New York, New York 10017 (800) 253-9646; *Human Development Report.*

QATAR - UNEMPLOYMENT RATE

Central Intelligence Agency, Washington, D.C. 20505 (703) 482-1100, www.cia.gov; *The World Factbook.*

QATAR - VITAL STATISTICS

Presidency of the Council of Ministers, Central Statistical Organisation, Doha,

Qatar; *Annual Statistical Abstract State of Qatar.*

St. Martin's Press, Inc., 175 Fifth Avenue, New York, New York 10010 (800) 221-7945; *The Statesman's Year-Book.*

World Health Organization, Office of Publications, Avenue Appia, CH-1211 Geneva 27, Switzerland (Telephone Number in U.S. (518) 436-9686); *World Health Statistics Annual.*

QATAR - WAGES

Federal Statistical Office, Gustav - Stresemann - Ring 11, D-6200 Wiesbaden, Germany; *Katar.*

QATAR - WEATHER - See QATAR - CLIMATE

QATAR - WHEAT PRODUCTION AND PRICES - See QATAR - CROPS

QATAR - WINE PRODUCTION - See QATAR - BEVERAGES

QATAR - WOOL PRODUCTION - See QATAR - TEXTILE INDUSTRY

QUARRIES - See MINING INDUSTRY

QUICKSILVER (MERCURY)

U.S. Department of the Interior, Geological Survey, Office of Minerals Information, 12201 Sunrise Valley Drive, Reston, Virginia 22092 (703) 648-4000, www,minerals.usgs.gov; *Annual Reports;* and *Mineral Commodities Summaries.*

R

RABIES

U.S. Department of Health and Human Services, Centers for Disease Control, 1600 Clifton Road, NE, Atlanta, Georgia 30333 (800) 311-3435, www.cdc.gov; *Summary of Notifiable Diseases, United States Morbidity and Mortality Weekly Report.*

RACETRACK OPERATIONS

Association of Racing Commissioners International, Incorporated, Two Paragon Centre, 2343 Alexandria Drive, Suite 200, Lexington, Kentucky 40504 (606) 224-7070.

RACQUETBALL

National Sporting Goods Association, 1601 Feehanville Drive, Suite 300, Mount Prospect, Illinois 60056 (847) 296-6742; *Sports Participation in 1998.*

RADIOLOGISTS

American Medical Association, 515 North State Street, Chicago, Illinois 60610 (312) 464-5000; *Physician Characteristics and Distribution in the United States.*

RADIO BROADCASTING STATIONS - ADVERTISING EXPENDITURES

McCann-Erickson, Incorporated, 750 Third Avenue, New York, New York 10017 (212) 697-6000; compiled for Crain Communications, Incorporated, 740 North Rush Street, Chicago, Illinois 60611 (312) 649-5200; *Advertising Age.*

RADIO BROADCASTING STATIONS - EARNINGS

U.S. Department of Commerce, Economics and Statistics Administration, Fourteenth Street and Constitution Avenue, NW, Room 4858, Washington, D.C. 20230 (800) 782-8872, www.esa.doc.gov; *The Emerging Digital EconomyI.*

U.S. Department of Labor, Bureau of Labor Statistics, Two Massachusetts Avenue, NE, Washington, D.C. 20212 (202) 691-5200, www.stats.bls.gov; *Employment and Earnings;* and Internet site: http://stats.bls.gov/ ceshome.htm.

RADIO BROADCASTING STATIONS - EMPLOYEES

U.S. Department of Commerce, Economics and Statistics Administration, Fourteenth Street and Constitution Avenue, NW, Room 4858, Washington, D.C. 20230 (800) 782-8872, www.esa.doc.gov; *The Emerging Digital Economy II.*

U.S. Department of Labor, Bureau of Labor Statistics, Two Massachusetts Avenue, NE, Washington, D.C. 20212 (202) 691-5200, www.stats.bls.gov; *Employment and Earnings;* and Internet site: http://stats.bls.gov/ceshome. htm.

RADIO BROADCASTING STATIONS - FINANCES

U.S. Department of Commerce, Bureau of the Census, Washington, D.C. 20233 (301) 457-4100, www.census.gov; *Annual Survey of Communication Services.*

Veronis, Suhler and Associates, 350 Park Avenue, New York, New York 10022 (212) 935-4990; *Communications Industry Forecast Report.*

RADIO BROADCASTING STATIONS - GROSS DOMESTIC PRODUCTS

U.S. Department of Commerce, Economics and Statistics Administration, Fourteenth Street and Constitution Avenue, NW, Room 4858, Washington, D.C. 20230 (800) 782-8872, www.esa.doc.gov; *The Emerging Digital Economy.*

RADIO BROADCASTING STATIONS - MERGERS AND ACQUISITIONS

Thomson Financial Securities Data, 2 Gateway Center, Newark, New Jersey 07006 (973) 622-3100; Merger and Corporate Transactions Database.

RADIO BROADCASTING STATIONS - STATIONS

Federal Communications Commission, 445 Twelfth Street, SW, Washington, D.C. 20554 (888) 225-5322, www.fcc.gov; various reports.

Radio Advertising Bureau, 261 Madison Avenue, 23rd Floor, New York, New York 10016 (212) 681-7200; *Radio Marketing Guide and Fact Book for Advertisers.*

RADIOS - AUDIENCE CHARACTERISTICS

Mediamark Research, Incorporated, 708 Third Avenue, New York, New York 10017 (212) 599-0444; *Multimedia Audiences.*

Veronis, Suhler and Associates, 350 Park Avenue, New York, New York 10022 (212) 935-4990; *Communications Industry Forecast Report.*

RADIOS - HOUSEHOLDS WITH

Radio Advertising Bureau, 261 Madison Avenue, 23rd Floor, New York, New York 10016 (212) 681-7200; *Radio Marketing Guide and Fact Book for Advertisers.*

United Nations Educational, Scientific and Cultural Organization, (UNESCO). 7 Place de Fontenoy, F-75700 Paris, France (Telephone Number in U.S. (212) 963-5981); *Statistical Yearbook.*

RADIOS - LISTENING

Veronis, Suhler & Associates, 350 Park Avenue, New York, New York 10022 (212) 935-4990; *Communications Industry Report.*

RAILROAD EMPLOYEES RETIREMENT FUNDS

Executive Office of the President, Office of Management and Budget, Executive Office Building, Washington, D.C. 20503 (202) 395-3080, www.whitehouse.gov omb; *Analytical Perspectives.*

Social Security Administration, 6400 Security Boulevard, Baltimore, Maryland 21235 (800) 772-1213, www.ssa.gov; *Social Security Bulletin;* and unpublished data.

RAILROAD RETIREMENT BOARD

Social Security Administration, 6400 Security Boulevard, Baltimore, Maryland 21235 (800) 772-1213, www.ssa.gov; *Social Security Bulletin;* and unpublished data.

RAILROADS - AMTRAK

Association of American Railroads, American Railroads Building, 50 F Street, NW, Washington, D.C. 20001 (202) 639-2100; *Railroad Facts, Statistics of Railroads of Class I;* and *Analysis of Class I Railroads.*

RAILROADS - CAR LOADINGS - BY COMMODITY

Association of American Railroads, American Railroads Building, 50 F Street, NW, Washington, D.C. 20001 (202) 639-2100; *Freight Commodity Statistics;* and *Weekly Railroad Traffic.*

RAILROADS - CONSTRUCTION VALUE

U.S. Department of Commerce, Bureau of the Census, Washington, D.C. 20233 (301) 457-4100, www.census.gov; *Current Construction Reports;* and *Value of Construction.*

RAILROADS - EARNINGS

Association of American Railroads, American Railroads Building, 50 F Street, NW, Washington, D.C. 20001 (202) 639-2222; *Railroad Facts, Statistics of Railroads of Class I;* and *Analysis of Class I Railroads.*

U.S. Department of Labor, Bureau of Labor Statistics, Two Massachusetts Avenue, NE, Washington, D.C. 20212 (202) 691-5200, www.stats.bls.gov; *Employment and Earnings;* Bulletins 2445 and 2481; and Internet site: http://stats.bls.gov/ceshome.htm.

RAILROADS - EMPLOYEES

Association of American Railroads, American Railroads Building, 50 F Street, NW, Washington, D.C. 20001 (202) 639-2100; *Railroad Facts, Statistics of Railroads of Class I;* and *Analysis of Class I Railroads.*

U.S. Department of Labor, Bureau of Labor Statistics, Two Massachusetts Avenue, NE, Washington, D.C. 20212 (202) 691-5200, www.stats.bls.gov; *Employment and Earnings;* Bulletins 2445 and 2481; and Internet site: http://stats.bls.gov/ceshome.htm

RAILROADS - EQUIPMENT IN SERVICE

Association of American Railroads, American Railroads Building, 50 F Street, NW, Washington, D.C. 20001 (202) 639-2100; *Analysis of Class I Railroads;* and *Railroad Facts, Statistics of Railroads of Class I.*

RAILROADS - FINANCES

Association of American Railroads, American Railroads Building, 50 F Street, NW, Washington, D.C. 20001 (202) 639-2100; *Analysis of Class I Railroads;* and *Railroad Facts, Statistics of Railroads of Class I.*

Board of Governors of the Federal Reserve System, Twentieth Street and Constitution Avenue, NW, Washington, D.C. 20551 (202) 452-3000, www.bog.frb.fed.us; *Federal Reserve Bulletin.*

U.S. Department of Commerce, Bureau of Economic Analysis, Fourteenth Street between Constitution Avenue and E Street, NW, Washington, D.C. 20230 (202) 606-9900, www.bea.doc.gov; *Survey of Current Business;* and *Current Business Reports, Service Annual Survey.*

RAILROADS - FREIGHT PRICE INDEXES

U.S. Department of Labor, Bureau of Labor Statistics, Two Massachusetts Avenue, NE, Washington, D.C. 20212 (202) 691-5200, www.stats.bls.gov; *Producer Price Indexes.*

RAILROADS - FREIGHT TRAFFIC

Association of American Railroads, American Railroads Building, 50 F Street, NW, Washington, D.C. 20001 (202) 639-2100; *Railroad Facts, Statistics of Railroads of Class I; Analysis of Class I Railroads; Freight Commodity Statistics;* and *Weekly Railroad Traffic.*

Eno Transportation Foundation, One Farragut Square, South, Suite 500, Washington, D.C. 20006 (202) 879-4700; *Transportation in America.*

RAILROADS - MILEAGE OWNED AND OPERATED

Association of American Railroads, American Railroads Building, 50 F Street, NW, Washington, D.C. 20001 (202) 639-2100; *Railroad Facts, Statistics of Railroads of Class I;* and *Analysis of Class I Railroads.*

RAILROADS - OCCUPATIONAL SAFETY

Association of American Railroads, American Railroads Building, 50 F Street, NW, Washington, D.C. 20001 (202) 639-2100; *Railroad Facts, Statistics of Railroads of Class I;* and *Analysis of Class I Railroads*

U.S. Department of Transportation

U.S. Department of Transportation, Bureau of Transportation Statistics, 400 Seventh Street, SW, Washington, D.C. 20590 (800) 853-1351, www.bts.gov; *National Transportation Statistics.*

RAILROADS - PASSENGER TRAFFIC AND REVENUE

Association of American Railroads, American Railroads Building, 50 F Street, NW, Washington, D.C. 20001 (202) 639-2100; *Railroad Facts, Statistics of Railroads of Class I;* and *Analysis of Class I Railroads.*

Eno Transportation Foundation, One Farragut Square, South, Suite 500, Washington, D.C. 20006 (202) 879-4700; *Transportation in America.*

RAILROADS - PIGGYBACK

Association of American Railroads, American Railroads Building, 50 F Street, NW, Washington, D.C. 20001 (202) 639-2100; *Freight Commodity Statistics;* and *Weekly Railroad Traffic.*

RAILROADS - PRODUCTIVITY

Association of American Railroads, American Railroads Building, 50 F Street, NW, Washington, D.C. 20001 (202) 639-2100; *Railroad Facts, Statistics of Railroads of Class I;* and *Analysis of Class I Railroads.*

RAILROADS - RECEIPTS

United States Travel Data Center, 1100 New York Avenue, NW, Suite 450, Washington, D.C. 20005 (202) 408-8422; *Impact of Travel on State Economies.*

RAINFALL - SELECTED CITIES

U.S. Department of Commerce, National Oceanic and Atmospheric Administration, National Climatic Data Center, 151 Patton Avenue, Asheville, North Carolina 28801 (828) 271-4800, www.ncdc.noaa.gov; *Climatography of the United States; Comparative Climatic Data;* and *Climates of the World.*

RANKINGS - AIRPORT TRAFFIC

U.S. Department of Transportation, Bureau of Transportation Statistics, 400 Seventh Street, SW, Washington, D.C. 20590 (800) 853-1351, www.bts.gov; *Airport Activity Statistics of Certificates Route Air Carriers, Calendar Year 1997*; and *Federal Aviation Administration, Airport Activity Statistics.*

RANKINGS - CITIES - POPULATION

U.S. Department of Commerce, Bureau of the Census, Washington, D.C. 20233 (301) 457-4100, www.census.gov; *Census of Population; Census of Population and*

Housing, Population and Housing Unit Counts; Current Population Reports; General Population Characteristics; unpublished data; and Internet site http://www.census.gov/population/estimates/metro-city/scts/sc98ts-dr.txt.

RANKINGS - CITIES - RESIDENTIAL PROPERTY TAX

Government of the District of Columbia, Department of Finance and Revenue, 441 Fourth Street, NW, Washington, D.C. 20001 (202) 727-6103; *Tax Rates and Tax Burdens in the District of Columbia: A Nationwide Comparison.*

RANKINGS - COUNTRIES - CONSUMPTION OF BEEF, PORK, POULTRY

U.S. Department of Agriculture, Foreign Agricultural Service, Fourteenth Street and Independence Avenue, SW, Washington, D.C. 20250 (202) 720-7115, www.fas.usda.gov; *Livestock and Poultry: World Markets and Trade.*

RANKINGS - COUNTRIES - EXPORTS AND IMPORTS OF WHEAT, RICE AND CORN

U.S. Department of Agriculture, Economic Research Service, 1800 M Street, NW, Washington, D.C. 20036 (202) 694-5050, www.ers.usda.gov; unpublished data from the PS&D Database.

RANKINGS - COUNTRIES - POPULATION

U.S. Department of Commerce, Bureau of the Census, Washington, D.C. 20233 (301) 457-4100, www.census.gov; International Data Base; and Internet site: http://www.census.gov/ipc/www/idbnew.html.

RANKINGS - EXPORTS

U.S. Department of Commerce, Bureau of the Census, Washington, D.C. 20233 (301) 457-4100, www.census.gov; *U.S. Merchandise Trade.*

RANKINGS - FEDERAL RESEARCH AND DEVELOPMENT OBLIGATIONS TO HIGHER EDUCATION

National Science Foundation, 4201 Wilson Boulevard, Arlington, Virginia 22230 (703) 306-1234, www.nsf.gov; *Federal S & E Support to Universities and Colleges and Selected Non-Profit Institutions.*

RANKING - HAZARDOUS WASTE SITES

Environmental Protection Agency, 1200 Pennsylvania Avenue, NW, Washington, D.C. 20460 (888) 372-8255, www.epa.gov; *Toxics Release Inventory.*

RANKINGS - SPORTS PARTICIPATION

National Sporting Goods Association, 1601 Feehanville Drive, Suite 300, Mount Prospect, Illinois 60056 (847) 296-6742; *Sports Participation in 1998.*

RANKINGS - STATE - DOMESTIC TRAVEL EXPENDITURES

United States Travel Data Center, 1100 New York Avenue, NW, Suite 450, Washington, D.C. 20005 (202) 408-8422; *Impact of Travel on State Economies.*

RANKINGS - STATE - FARM MARKETINGS

U.S. Department of Agriculture, Economic Research Service, 1800 M Street, NW, Washington, D.C. 20036 (202) 694-5050, www.ers.usda.gov; *Farm Business Economic Report.*

RANKINGS - STATE - FOREIGN TRADE

U.S. Department of Commerce, Bureau of the Census, Washington, D.C. 20233 (301) 457-4100, www.census.gov; *U.S. Merchandise Trade: Selected Highlights; U.S. Export History;* and *U.S. Import History.*

RANKINGS - STATE - GOVERNMENT FINANCES

U.S. Department of Commerce, Bureau of the Census, Washington, D.C. 20233 (301) 457-4100, www.census.gov; Internet site: http://www.census.gov/govs/www/index.html.

RANKINGS - STATE - PERSONAL INCOME PER CAPITA

U.S. Department of Commerce, Bureau of Economic Analysis, Fourteenth Street between Constitution Avenue and E Street, NW, Washington, D.C. 20230 (202) 606-9900, www.bea.doc.gov; *Survey of Current Business;* and unpublished data.

RANKINGS - STATE - PERSONAL INCOME PER CAPITA - DISPOSABLE

U.S. Department of Commerce, Bureau of Economic Analysis, Fourteenth Street between Constitution Avenue and E Street, NW, Washington, D.C. 20230 (202) 606-9900, www.bea.doc.gov; *Survey of Current Business;* and unpublished data.

RANKINGS - STATE - POPULATION

U.S. Department of Commerce, Bureau of the Census, Washington, D.C. 20233 (301) 457-4100, www.census.gov; *Census of Population and Housing, Population and Housing Unit Counts;* and Internet site http://www.census.gov/population/estimates/state/st-98-3.txt.

RANKINGS - STATE - PUBLIC ELEMENTARY/SECONDARY SCHOOL FINANCES

National Education Association, 1201 Sixteenth Street, NW, Washington, D.C. 20036 (202) 833-4000; Estimates of School Statistics database.

RAPE - FORCIBLE

U.S. Department of Justice, Bureau of Justice Statistics, 810 Seventh Street, NW, 2nd Floor, Washington, D.C. 20531 (800) 732-3277, www.ojp.usdoj.gov/bjs; *Criminal Victimization.*

U.S. Department of Justice, Federal Bureau of Investigation, 935 Pennsylvania Avenue, NW, Washington, D.C. 20535 (202) 324-3691, www.fbi.gov; *Crime in the United States;* and *Population-at-Risk Rates and Selected Crime Indicators.*

RAPESEED

U.S. Department of Agriculture, Economic Research Service, 1800 M Street, NW, Washington, D.C. 20036 (202) 694-5050, www.ers.usda.gov; *Agricultural Outlook.*

RARE - EARTH MINERALS

U.S. Department of the Interior, Geological Survey, Office of Minerals Information, 12201 Sunrise Valley Drive, Reston, Virginia 22092 (703) 648-4000, www.minerals.usgs.gov; *Mineral Commodity Summaries.*

RAW MATERIALS - See CRUDE MATERIALS

READING - See also BOOKS and LIBRARIES

U.S. Department of Labor, Bureau of Labor Statistics, Two Massachusetts Avenue, NE, Washington, D.C. 20212 (202) 691-5200, www.stats.bls.gov; *Consumer Expenditure Survey; Consumer Expenditures;* and unpublished data.

National Endowment for the Arts, 1100 Pennsylvania Avenue, NW, Washington, D.C. 20506 (202) 682-5400, www.arts.gov; *Survey of Public Participation in the Arts.*

READING - CONSUMER PRICE INDEXES

U.S. Department of Labor, Bureau of Labor Statistics, Two Massachusetts Avenue, NE, Washington, D.C. 20212 (202) 691-5200, www.stats.bls.gov; *Monthly Labor Review*; and *CPI Detailed Report.*

REAL ESTATE INDUSTRY - EARNINGS

U.S. Department of Commerce, Bureau of the Census, Washington, D.C. 20233 (301) 457-4100, www.census.gov; *County Business Patterns;* and *1997 Economic Census, Core Business Statistics Series, Advanced.*

U.S. Department of Labor, Bureau of

Labor Statistics, Two Massachusetts Avenue, NE, Washington, D.C. 20212 (202) 691-5200, www.stats.bls.gov; *Employment and Earnings;* and Internet site: http://stats.bls.gov/ceshome. htm.

REAL ESTATE INDUSTRY - EMPLOYEES

U.S. Department of Commerce, Bureau of the Census, Washington, D.C. 20233 (301) 457-4100, www.census.gov; *County Business Patterns;* and *1997 Economic Census, Core Business Statistics Series, Advanced.*

U.S. Department of Labor, Bureau of Labor Statistics, Two Massachusetts Avenue, NE, Washington, D.C. 20212 (202) 691-5200, www.stats.bls.gov; *Employment and Earnings;* and Internet site: http://stats.bls.gov/ceshome. htm.

REAL ESTATE INDUSTRY - ESTABLISHMENTS

U.S. Department of Commerce, Bureau of the Census, Washington, D.C. 20233 (301) 457-4100, www.census.gov; *County Business Patterns;* and *1997 Economic Census, Core Business Statistics Series, Advanced.*

REAL ESTATE INDUSTRY - GROSS DOMESTIC PRODUCT

U.S. Department of Commerce, Bureau of Economic Analysis, Fourteenth Street between Constitution Avenue and E Street, NW, Washington, D.C. 20230 (202) 606-9900, www.bea.doc.gov; *Survey of Current Business.*

REAL ESTATE INDUSTRY - MERGERS AND ACQUISITIONS

Thomson Financial Securities Data, Two Gateway Center, Newark, New Jersey 07006 (973) 622-3100; *Merger and Corporate Transactions Database.*

REAL ESTATE INDUSTRY - RECEIPTS

U.S. Department of Commerce, Bureau of the Census, Washington, D.C. 20233 (301) 457-4100, www.census.gov; *Current Business Reports;* and *1997 Economic Census, Core Business Statistics Series, Advanced.*

RECEIPTS - See also Individual Industries and TAX RECEIPTS

U.S. Department of Commerce, Bureau of the Census, Washington, D.C. 20233 (301) 457-4100, www.census.gov; *Census of Construction Industries; Current Business Reports; Service Annual Survey; Census of Service Industries; 1997 Economic Census, Core Business Statistics*

Series, Advanced Report; and unpublished data.

RECEIPTS - CORPORATIONS - PARTNERSHIPS AND PROPRIETORSHIPS

U.S. Department of the Treasury, Internal Revenue Service, 1111 Constitution Avenue, NW, Washington, D.C. 20224 (202) 874-0410, www.irs.ustreas.gov; *Statistics of Income, Corporation Income Tax Returns; Statistics of Income, Partnership Returns; Statistics of Income,* various publications; *Statistics of Income Bulletin;* and unpublished data.

RECEIPTS - INTERNATIONAL TRANSPORTATION

U.S. Department of Commerce, Bureau of Economic Analysis, Fourteenth Street between Constitution Avenue and E Street, NW, Washington, D.C. 20230 (202) 606-9900, www.bea.doc.gov; *Survey of Current Business;* and unpublished data.

RECEIPTS - REVENUE - LOCAL GOVERNMENTS

U.S. Department of Commerce, Bureau of the Census, Washington, D.C. 20233 (301) 457-4100, www.census.gov; Internet site: http://www.census.gov/govs/www/index.html.; and unpublished data.

RECEIPTS - REVENUE - LOCAL GOVERNMENTS - CITY GOVERNMENTS

U.S. Department of Commerce, Bureau of the Census, Washington, D.C. 20233 (301) 457-4100, www.census.gov; unpublished data.

RECEIPTS - REVENUE - COUNTY GOVERNMENT

U.S. Department of Commerce, Bureau of the Census, Washington, D.C. 20233 (301) 457-4100, www.census.gov; unpublished data.

RECEIPTS - REVENUE - STATE AND LOCAL GOVERNMENTS COMBINED

U.S. Department of Commerce, Bureau of Economic Analysis, Fourteenth Street between Constitution Avenue and E Street, NW, Washington, D.C. 20230 (202) 606-9900, www.bea.doc.gov; *The National Income and Product Accounts of the United States;* and *Survey of Current Business.*

U.S. Department of Commerce, Bureau of the Census, Washington, D.C. 20233 (301) 457-4100, www.census.gov; *Government Finances;* and Internet sites: http://www.census.gov/govs/www/index.html; http://www.census.gov/govs/www/esti96.

html; and http://www. census.gov/govs/www/estimate.html.

RECEIPTS - REVENUE - STATE GOVERNMENTS

National Association of State Budget Officers, Hall of the States, 444 North Capitol Street, NW, Suite 642, Washington, D.C. 20001 (202) 624-5382; *1998 State Expenditure Report;* and *State General Fund from National Governors' Association and NASBO, Fiscal Survey of the States.*

U.S. Department of Commerce, Bureau of the Census, Washington, D.C. 20233 (301) 457-4100, www.census.gov; *State Government Finances;* and Internet sites http://www.census.gov/www/index.html; and http://www.census.gov/govs/www/state.htm.

RECEIPTS - REVENUE - STATE GOVERNMENTS - TAX COLLECTIONS

U.S. Department of Commerce, Bureau of the Census, Washington, D.C. 20233 (301) 457-4100, www.census.gov; Internet site: http://www.census.gov/govs/www/index.html.

RECEIPTS - TRUST FUNDS

Executive Office of the President, Office of Management and Budget, Executive Office Building, Washington, D.C. 20503 (202) 395-3080, www.whitehouse.gov/omb; *Analytical Perspectives.*

RECEIPTS - UNITED STATES GOVERNMENT

Executive Office of the President, Office of Management and Budget, Executive Office Building, Washington, D.C. 20503 (202) 395-3080, www.whitehouse.gov/omb; *Historical Tables.*

U.S. Department of Commerce, Bureau of the Census, Washington, D.C. 20233 (301) 457-4100, www.census.gov; *Government Finances;* and Internet site http://www.census.gov/pub/govs/www/index.html.

U.S. Department of the Treasury, Bureau of Alcohol, Tobacco and Firearms, 650 Massachusetts Avenue, NW, Washington, D.C. 20226 (202) 927-8500, www.atf.treas.gov; *Alcohol and Tobacco Tax Collections.*

RECEIPTS - UNITED STATES GOVERNMENT - FROM NATIONAL FORESTS

U.S. Department of Agriculture, Forest Service, Post Office Box 96090, Washington, D.C. 20090 (202) 205-8333, www.fs.fed.us; *Agricultural Statistics;* and *Timber Demand and Technology Assessment.*

RECREATION - See also AMUSEMENT AND RECREATIONAL SERVICES, TOYS AND SPORTS

RECREATION - ACTIVITIES

American League of Professional Baseball Clubs, 350 Park Avenue, New York, New York 10022 (212) 339-7600; *National League Green Book.*

Boy Scouts of America, 1325 Walnut Hill Lane, P.O. Box 152079, Irving, Texas 75015 (214) 580-2000; *Annual Report.*

Girls Scouts of the United States of America, 420 Fifth Avenue and 51st Street, New York, New York 10018-2702 (212) 852-8000; *Annual Report.*

National Association of State Park Directors, 126 Mill Branch Road, Tallahassee, Florida 32312 (904) 893-4959; *Annual Information Exchange.*

National Endowment for the Arts, 1100 Pennsylvania Avenue, NW, Washington, D.C. 20506 (202) 682-5400, www.arts.gov; *Survey of Public Arts Participation.*

The National Gardening Association, 1100 Dorset Street, South, Burlington, Vermont 05403 (802) 863-5215; *National Gardening Survey.*

National League of Professional Baseball Clubs, 245 Park Avenue, 28th Floor, New York, New York 10167 (212) 339-7700; *American League Red book.*

National Sporting Goods Association, 1601 Feehanville Drive, Suite 300, Mount Prospect, Illinois 60056 (847) 296-6742; *Sports Participation in 1998.*

U.S. Department of Agriculture, Forest Service, Post Office Box 96090, Washington, D.C. 20090 (202) 205-8333, www.fs.fed.us; *Annual Report*; and unpublished data.

U.S. Department of Health and Human Services, National Center for Chronic Disease Prevention and Health Promotion, Centers for Disease Control and Prevention, 1600 Clifton Road, NE, Atlanta, Georgia 30333 (404) 639-3311, www.cdc.gov/nccdphp; unpublished data.

U.S. Department of the Interior, National Park Service, C Street between Eighteenth and Nineteenth Streets, NW, Washington, D.C. 20240 (202) 208-6843, www.nps.gov; *National Park Statistical Abstract;* and unpublished data.

Veronis, Suhler and Associates, 350 Park Avenue, New York, New York 10022 (213) 935-4990; *Communications Industry Report.*

RECREATION - BUILDING CONSTRUCTION - VALUE

F.W. Dodge Division, McGraw-Hill Information Systems Company, 148 Princeton-Hightstown Road, Hightstown, New Jersey 08520-1450 (800) 393-6343; *Dodge Construction Potentials.*

RECREATION - CONSUMER EXPENDITURES

Book Industry Study Group, 160 Fifth Avenue, New York, New York 10010 (212) 929-1393; *Book Industry Trends.*

National Sporting Goods Association, 1601 Feehanville Drive, Suite 300, Mount Prospect, Illinois 60056 (847) 296-6742; *The Sporting Goods Market in 1999.*

U.S. Department of Commerce, Bureau of Economic Analysis, Fourteenth Street between Constitution Avenue and E Street, NW, Washington, D.C. 20230 (202) 606-9900, www.bea.doc.gov; *The National Income and Product Accounts of the United States;* and *Survey of Current Business.*

U.S. Department of Labor, Bureau of Labor Statistics, Two Massachusetts Avenue, NE, Washington, D.C. 20212 (202) 691-5200, www.stats.bls.gov; *Consumer Expenditure Survey.*

Veronis, Suhler and Associates, 350 Park Avenue, New York, New York 10022 (212) 935-4990; *Communications Industry Forecast Report.*

RECREATION - CONSUMER PRICE INDEXES

U.S. Department of Labor, Bureau of Labor Statistics, Two Massachusetts Avenue, NE, Washington, D.C. 20212 (202) 691-5200, www.stats.bls.gov; *Monthly Labor Review;* and *Consumer Price Indexes, Detailed Report.*

RECREATION - EMPLOYMENT AND EXPENDITURES - GOVERNMENT

Executive Office of the President, U.S. Office of Management and Budget, Executive Office Building, Washington, D.C. 20503 (202)395-3080, www.whitehouse.gov/omb ; *Historical Tables.*

RECREATION - EMPLOYMENT AND EXPENDITURES - GOVERNMENT - CITY GOVERNMENTS

U.S. Department of Commerce, Bureau of the Census, Washington, D.C. 20233 (301) 457-4100, www.census.gov; Internet site: http://www.census.gov/pub/govs/www/apes.html.

RECREATION - EMPLOYMENT AND EXPENDITURES - GOVERNMENT - COUNTY GOVERNMENT

U.S. Department of Commerce, Bureau of the Census, Washington, D.C. 20233 (301) 457-4100, www.census.gov; unpublished data.

RECREATION - PARKS - GOVERNMENT EXPENDITURES

U.S. Department of Commerce, Bureau of the Census, Washington, D.C. 20233 (301) 457-4100, www.census.gov; *Government Finances; Historical Statistics on Governmental Finances and Employment;* and Internet site: http://www.census.gov/govs/www/index.html.

RECREATION - PARKS - NATIONAL

U.S. Department of the Interior, National Park Service, C Street between Eighteenth and Nineteenth Streets, NW, Washington, D.C. 20240 (202) 208-6843, www.nps.gov; *National Park Statistical Abstract;* and unpublished data.

RECREATION - PARKS - VISITS

National Association of State Park Directors, 126 Mill Branch Road, Tallahassee, Florida 32312 (904) 893-4959; *Annual Information Exchange.*

U.S. Department of the Interior, National Park Service, C Street between Eighteenth and Nineteenth Streets, NW, Washington, D.C. 20240 (202) 208-6843, www.nps.gov; *National Park Statistical Abstract;* and unpublished data.

RECREATION - PERFORMING ARTS

American Symphony Orchestra League, 33 West 60th Street, 5th Floor, New York, New York 10023 (212) 262-5161.

League of American Theaters and Producers, Inc., 226 West 47th Street, New York, New York 10036 (212) 764-1122.

Opera America, 777 Fourteenth Street, NW, Washington, D.C. 20005 (202) 347-9262.

Theatre Communications Group, 355 Lexington Avenue, New York, New York 10017 (212) 697-5230.

RECREATION - SPECTATOR SPORTS

American League of Professional Baseball Clubs 350 Park Avenue, New York, New York 10022 (212) 339-7600; *American League Red Book.*

Association of Racing Commissioners International, Inc., Two Paragon Centre, 2343 Alexandria Drive, Suite 200, Lexington, Kentucky 40504 (606) 224-7070.

National Basketball Association, 645

Fifth Avenue, Tenth Floor, New York, New York 10022 (212) 826-7000.

National Collegiate Athletic Association, 700 West Washington Street, Indianapolis, Indiana 46206 (317) 917-6222.

National Football League, 2021 L Street, NW, 6th Floor, Washington, D.C. 20036 (202) 463-2200.

National Football League Players Association, 2021 L Street, NW, Washington, D.C. 20036 (202) 463-2200.

National Hockey League, 1251 Avenue of the Americas, New York, New York 10020 (212) 730-1413.

National League of Professional Baseball Clubs, 350 Park Avenue, 18th Floor, New York, New York 10022 (212) 339-7700; *National League Green Book.*

Professional Rodeo Cowboys Association, 101 Prorodeo Drive, Colorado Springs, Colorado 80910 (719) 593-8840.

RECREATION - TRAVEL

U.S. Department of Commerce, International Trade Administration, Fourteenth Street between Constitution Avenue and E Street, NW, Washington, D.C. 20230 (202) 482-3809; Internet site http://www.tinet.ita.doc.gov/

Travel Industry Association of America, 1100 New York Avenue, NW, Suite 450, Washington, D.C. 20005 (202) 408-1832; *Impact of Travel on State Economies;* and *National Travel Survey.*

RECREATION - VOLUNTEERS

Independent Sector, 1200 18th Street, NW, Suite 200, Washington, D.C. 20036 (202) 467-6161; *Giving and Volunteering in the United States.*

RECREATIONAL VEHICLES

American Automobile Manufacturers Association, 1401 H Street, NW, Suite 900, Washington, D.C. 20005 (202) 326-5500; *Motor Vehicle Facts and Figures.*

National Sporting Goods Association, 1601 Feehanville Drive, Suite 300, Mount Prospect, Illinois 60056 (847) 296-6742; *The Sporting Goods Market in 1999.*

Recreation Vehicle Industry Association, Post Office Box 2999, 1896 Preston White Drive, Reston, Virginia 22090 (703) 620-6003; *RVIA Industry Profile.*

RECYCLING WASTE

Environmental Protection Agency, 1200

Pennsylvania Avenue, NW, Washington, D.C. 20460 (888) 372-8255, www.epa.gov; *Toxics Release Inventory.*

Franklin Associates Limited, 4121 West Eighty-third Street, Suite 108, Prairie Village, Kansas 66208 (913) 649-2225; *Characterization of Municipal Solid Waste in the United States.*

REFRACTORIES

U.S. Department of Commerce, Bureau of the Census, Washington, D.C. 20233 (301) 457-4100, www.census.gov; *Current Industrial Reports;* and *Manufacturing Profiles.*

REFRIGERATORS AND REFRIGERATION EQUIPMENT

U.S. Department of Commerce, Bureau of the Census, Washington, D.C. 20233 (301) 457-4100, www.census.gov; *Manufacturing Profiles.*

REFUGEES

U.S. Department of Justice, Immigration and Naturalization Service, 425 I Street, NW, Washington, D.C. 20536 (202) 305-1613, www.ins.usdoj.gov; *Statistical Yearbook;* and releases.

REFUSE COLLECTION

Franklin Associates Limited, 4121 West Eighty-third Street, Suite 108, Prairie Village, Kansas 66208 (913) 649-2225; *Characteristics of Municipal Solid Waste in the United States.*

U.S. Department of Labor, Bureau of Labor Statistics, Two Massachusetts Avenue, NE, Washington, D.C. 20212 (202) 691-5200, www.stats.bls.gov; *Monthly Labor Review*; and *CPI Detailed Report.*

RELIGION

American Jewish Committee, c/o Institute of Human Relations, 165 East 56th Street, New York, New York 10022 (212) 751-4000; *American Jewish Year Book.*

Encyclopedia Britannica, Incorporated, 310 South Michigan Avenue, Chicago, Illinois 60604 (312) 347-7000; *Britannica Book of the Year.*

Glenmary Research Center, 1312 Fifth Avenue, North, Nashville, Tennessee 37208 (615) 256-1905; *Churches and Church Membership in the United States.*

National Council of the Churches of Christ in the USA, 475 Riverside Drive, New York, New York 10115 (212) 870-2227; *Yearbook of American and Canadian Churches.*

Princeton Religion Research Center, 47 Hulfish Street, Princeton, New Jersey 08542 (609) 921-8112; *Religion in America,* based on surveys conducted by The Gallup Organization, Inc., 47 Hulfish Street, Princeton, New Jersey 08542 (609) 924-9600.

RELIGION - BUDDHISTS

Encyclopedia Britannica, Incorporated, 310 South Michigan Avenue, Chicago, Illinois 60604 (312) 347-7000; *Britannica Book of the Year.*

National Council of the Churches of Christ in the USA, 475 Riverside Drive, New York, New York 10115 (212) 870-2227; *Yearbook of American and Canadian Churches.*

RELIGION - CATHOLICS

Encyclopedia Britannica, Incorporated, 310 South Michigan Avenue, Chicago, Illinois 60604 (312) 347-7000; *Britannica Book of the Year.*

National Council of the Churches of Christ in the USA, 475 Riverside Drive, New York, New York 10115 (212) 870-2227; *Yearbook of American and Canadian Churches.*

Princeton Religion Research Center, 47 Hulfish Street, Princeton, New Jersey 08542 (609) 921-8112; *Religion in America,* based on surveys conducted by The Gallup Organization, Inc., 47 Hulfish Street, Princeton, New Jersey 08542 (609) 924-9600.

RELIGION - CHARITABLE CONTRIBUTIONS

Independent Sector, 1200 18th Street, NW, Suite 200, Washington, D.C. 20036 (202) 467-6161; *Giving and Volunteering in the United States.*

RELIGION - CHURCH - SYNAGOGUE ATTENDANCE

Princeton Religion Research Center, 47 Hulfish Street, Princeton, New Jersey 08542 (609) 921-8112; *Religion in America,* based on surveys conducted by The Gallup Organization, Inc., 47 Hulfish Street, Princeton, New Jersey 08542 (609) 924-9600.

RELIGION - HINDUS

National Council of the Churches of Christ in the USA, 475 Riverside Drive, New York, New York 10115 (212) 870-2227; *Yearbook of American and Canadian Churches.*

Encyclopedia Britannica, Incorporated, 310 South Michigan Avenue, Chicago,

Illinois 60604 (312) 347-7000; *Britannica Book of the Year.*

RELIGION - JEWS

American Jewish Committee, c/o Institute of Human Relations, 165 East Fifty-sixth Street, New York, New York 10022 (212) 751-4000; and the Jewish Publication Society, 1930 Chestnut Street, Philadelphia, Pennsylvania 19103 (215) 564-5925; *American Jewish Yearbook.*

Encyclopedia Britannica, Incorporated, 310 South Michigan Avenue, Chicago, Illinois 60604 (312) 347-7000; *Britannica Book of the Year.*

National Council of the Churches of Christ in the USA, 475 Riverside Drive, New York, New York 10115 (212) 870-2227; *Yearbook of American and Canadian Churches.*

Princeton Religion Research Center, 47 Hulfish Street, Princeton, New Jersey 08542 (609) 921-8112; *Religion in America* based on surveys conducted by the Gallup Organization, Inc., 47 Hulfish Street, Princeton, New Jersey 08542 (609) 924-9600.

RELIGION - MUSLIM/ISLAMIC

Encyclopedia Britannica, Incorporated, 310 South Michigan Avenue, Chicago, Illinois 60604 (312) 347-7000; *Britannica Book of the Year.*

National Council of the Churches of Christ in the USA, 475 Riverside Drive, New York, New York 10115 (212) 870-2227; *Yearbook of American and Canadian Churches.*

RELIGION - PHILANTHROPY

American Association of Fund Raising Counsel, 10293 North Meridian Street, Suite 175, Indianapolis, Indiana 46290 (800) 462-2372; *Giving USA.*

The Foundation Center, 79 Fifth Avenue, New York, New York 10003 (212) 620-4230; *Foundation Grants Index.*

Independent Sector, 1200 18th Street, NW, Suite 200, Washington, D.C. 20036 (202) 467-6161; *Giving and Volunteering in the United States.*

RELIGION - PROTESTANTS

Encyclopedia Britannica, Incorporated, 310 South Michigan Avenue, Chicago, Illinois 60604 (312) 347-7000; *Britannica Book of the Year.*

National Council of the Churches of Christ in the USA, 475 Riverside Drive, New York, New York 10115 (212) 870-2227;

Yearbook of American and Canadian Churches.

Princeton Religion Research Center, 47 Hulfish Street, Princeton, New Jersey 08542 (609) 921-8112; *Religions in America,* based on surveys conducted by The Gallup Organization, Inc., 47 Hulfish Street, Princeton, New Jersey 08542 (609) 924-9600.

RELIGIOUS ORGANIZATIONS

Encyclopedia Britannica, Incorporated, 310 South Michigan Avenue, Chicago, Illinois 60604 (312) 347-7000; *Britannica Book of the Year.*

The Gale Group, 27500 Drake Road, Farmington Hills, Michigan 48331-3535 (800) 877-4253; *Encyclopedia of Associations.*

U.S. Department of Commerce, Bureau of the Census, Washington, D.C. 20233 (301) 457-4100, www.census.gov; *1997 Economic Census.*

RELIGIOUS ORGANIZATIONS - PUBLIC CONFIDENCE

Independent Sector, 1200 18th Street, NW, Suite 200, Washington, D.C. 20036 (202) 467-6161; *Giving and Volunteering in the U.S.*

RELIGIOUS ORGANIZATIONS - VOLUNTEERS

Independent Sector, 1200 18th Street, NW, Suite 200, Washington, D.C. 20036 (202) 467-6161; *Giving and Volunteering in the U.S.*

RELIGIOUS PREFERENCE

Princeton Religion Research Center, 47 Hulfish Street, Princeton, New Jersey 08542 (609) 921-8112; *Religions in America,* based on surveys conducted by The Gallup Organization, Inc., 47 Hulfish Street, Princeton, New Jersey 08542 (609) 924-9600.

REMARRIAGES

U.S. Department of Health and Human Services, National Center for Health Statistics, 3700 East-West Highway, Hyattsville, Maryland 20782 (301) 436-8500, www.cdc.gov/nchs; *Advance Data from Vital and Health Statistics.*

RENTS

U.S. Department of Labor, Bureau of Labor Statistics, Two Massachusetts Avenue, NE, Washington, D.C. 20212 (202) 691-5200, www.stats.bls.gov; *Monthly Labor Review;* and *Consumer Price Indexes, Detailed Report.*

REPAIR SERVICES - See AUTOMOTIVE REPAIR, SERVICES AND PARKING

REPRESENTATIVES, UNITED STATES - See CONGRESS, UNITED STATES

RESEARCH AND DEVELOPMENT - EMPLOYMENT

National Science Foundation, 4201 Wilson Boulevard, Arlington, Virginia 22230 (703) 306-1234, www.nsf.gov; *Research and Development in Industry.*

RESEARCH AND DEVELOPMENT - EXPENDITURES - BY COUNTRY

National Science Foundation, 4201 Wilson Boulevard, Arlington, Virginia 22230 (703) 306-1234, www.nsf.gov; *National Patterns of Research and Development Resources.*

RESEARCH AND DEVELOPMENT - EXPENDITURES - COLLEGES AND UNIVERSITIES

National Science Foundation, 4201 Wilson Boulevard, Arlington, Virginia 22230 (703) 306-1234, www.nsf.gov; *Survey of Scientific and Engineering Expenditures of Universities and Colleges;* and *National Patterns of Research and Development Resources.*

RESEARCH AND DEVELOPMENT - EXPENDITURES - FEDERAL

National Science Foundation, 4201 Wilson Boulevard, Arlington, Virginia 22230 (703) 306-1234, www.nsf.gov; *National Patterns of Research and Development Resources; Federal Funds for Research and Development; Federal Research and Development Funding by Budget Function;* and *Survey of Federal Support to Universities, Colleges, and Nonprofit Institutions.*

RESEARCH AND DEVELOPMENT - EXPENDITURES - INDUSTRY

National Science Foundation, 4201 Wilson Boulevard, Arlington, Virginia 22230 (703) 306-1234, www.nsf.gov; *National Patterns of Research and Development Resources;* and *Research and Development in Industry.*

RESEARCH AND DEVELOPMENT - EXPENDITURES - NATIONAL DEFENSE

Executive Office of the President, Office of Management and Budget, Executive Office Building, Washington, D.C. 20503 (202) 395-3080, www.whitehouse.gov/omb; *Historical Tables.*

National Science Foundation, 4201 Wilson Boulevard, Arlington, Virginia 22230 (703) 306-1234, www.nsf.gov; *National*

Patterns of Research and Development Resources.

RESEARCH AND DEVELOPMENT - STATES - BY SECTOR

National Science Foundation, 4201 Wilson Boulevard, Arlington, Virginia 22230 (703) 306-1234, www.nsf.gov; *National Patterns of Research and Development Resources.*

RESEARCH AND TESTING SERVICES - EARNINGS

U.S. Department of Commerce, Bureau of the Census, Washington, D.C. 20233 (301) 457-4100, www.census.gov; *Census of Service Industries.*

RESEARCH AND TESTING SERVICES - EMPLOYEES

U.S. Department of Commerce, Bureau of the Census, Washington, D.C. 20233 (301) 457-4100, www.census.gov; *Census of Service Industries.*

RESEARCH AND TESTING SERVICES - ESTABLISHMENTS

U.S. Department of Commerce, Bureau of the Census, Washington, D.C. 20233 (301) 457-4100, www.census.gov; *Census of Service Industries.*

RESEARCH AND TESTING SERVICES - FINANCES

U.S. Department of Commerce, Bureau of the Census, Washington, D.C. 20233 (301) 457-4100, www.census.gov; *Census of Service Industries;* and *Current Business Reports, Service Annual Survey.*

RESEARCH AND TESTING SERVICES - REVENUES

U.S. Department of Commerce, Bureau of the Census, Washington, D.C. 20233 (301) 457-4100, www.census.gov; *Census of Service Industries.*

RESERVATIONS - AMERICAN INDIAN

U.S. Department of Commerce, Bureau of the Census, Washington, D.C. 20233 (301) 457-4100, www.census.gov; *Census of Population, General Population Characteristics, American Indian and Alaska Native Areas.*

RESIDENTIAL BUILDINGS - See CONSTRUCTION INDUSTRY and HOUSING AND HOUSING UNITS

RESIDENTIAL CAPITAL

U.S. Department of Commerce, Bureau of Economic Analysis, Fourteenth Street between Constitution Avenue and E Street, NW, Washington, D.C. 20230 (202) 606-9900, www.bea.doc.gov; *Survey of Current Business.*

RESTAURANTS - See EATING AND DRINKING PLACES

RETAIL TRADE - CAPITAL EXPENDITURES

U.S. Department of Commerce, Bureau of Economic Analysis, Fourteenth Street between Constitution Avenue and E Street, NW, Washington, D.C. 20230 (202) 606-9900, www.bea.doc.gov; *National Income and Product Accounts;* and *Survey of Current Business.*

RETAIL TRADE - EARNINGS

U.S. Department of Commerce, Bureau of Economic Analysis, Fourteenth Street between Constitution Avenue and E Street, NW, Washington, D.C. 20230 (202) 606-9900, www.bea.doc.gov; *National Income and Products Accounts of the United States;* and *Survey of Current Business.*

U.S. Department of Commerce, Bureau of the Census, Washington, D.C. 20233 (301) 457-4100, www.census.gov; *Economic Census of Outlying Areas; Census of Retail Trade; 1997 Economic Census: Advanced Summary Statistics for the U.S. 1997 NAICS Basis;* and *County Business Patterns.*

U.S. Department of Labor, Bureau of Labor Statistics, Two Massachusetts Avenue, NE, Washington, D.C. 20212 (202) 691-5200, www.stats.bls.gov; *Employment and Earnings;* Bulletins 2445 and 2481; and Internet site: http://stats.bls.gov/ceshome.htm.

RETAIL TRADE - EMPLOYEE TRAINING

U.S. Department of Labor, Bureau of Labor Statistics, Two Massachusetts Avenue, NE, Washington, D.C. 20212 (202) 691-5200, www.stats.bls.gov; *Monthly Labor Review.*

RETAIL TRADE - EMPLOYEES

U.S. Department of Commerce, Bureau of the Census, Washington, D.C. 20233 (301) 457-4100, www.census.gov; *1997 Economic Census: Advance Summary Statistics for the U.S. 1997 NAICS Basis; Census of Retail Trade; County Business Patterns;* and *Economic Census of Outlying Areas.*

U.S. Department of Labor, Bureau of Labor Statistics, Two Massachusetts Avenue, NE, Washington, D.C. 20212 (202) 691-5200, www.stats.bls.gov; *Employment and Earnings; Monthly Labor Review; News, USDL-98-93;* unpublished data; and Internet site: http://stats.bls.gov/ceshome.htm.

RETAIL TRADE - ESTABLISHMENTS

U.S. Department of Commerce, Bureau of the Census, Washington, D.C. 20233 (301) 457-4100, www.census.gov; *Census of Retail Trade; Economic Census of Outlying Areas;* and *County Business Patterns.*

RETAIL TRADE - FINANCES

Board of Governors of the Federal Reserve System, 20th Street and Constitution Avenue, NW, Washington, D.C. 20551 (202) 452-3000, www.bog.frb.fed.us; *Federal Reserve Bulletin;* and *Annual Statistical Digest.*

Puerto Rico Planning Board, North Building, Box 41119, Santurce, Puerto Rico 00940; *Economic Report of the Governor.*

U.S. Department of the Treasury, Internal Revenue Service, 1111 Constitution Avenue, NW, Washington, D.C. 20224 (202) 874-0410, www.irs.ustreas.gov; *Statistics of Income; Statistics of Income Bulletin;* and various publications.

RETAIL TRADE - FOREIGN INVESTMENTS IN THE UNITED STATES

U.S. Department of Commerce, Bureau of Economic Analysis, Fourteenth Street between Constitution Avenue and E Street, NW, Washington, D.C. 20230 (202) 606-9900, www.bea.doc.gov; *Survey of Current Business; Foreign Direct Investment in the United States, Operations of U.S. Affiliates of Foreign Companies;* and unpublished data.

RETAIL TRADE - GROSS DOMESTIC PRODUCT

Puerto Rico Planning Board, North Building, Box 41119, Santurce, Puerto Rico 00940; *Economic Report of the Governor.*

U.S. Department of Commerce, Bureau of Economic Analysis, Fourteenth Street between Constitution Avenue and E Street, NW, Washington, D.C. 20230 (202) 606-9900, www.bea.doc.gov; *Survey of Current Business.*

RETAIL TRADE - HEALTH INSURANCE COVERAGE - EMPLOYEES

U.S. Department of Health and Human Services, National Center for Health Statistics, 3700 East-West Highway, Hyattsville, Maryland 20782 (301) 436-8500, www.cdc.gov/nchs; *Employer-Sponsored Health Insurance, State and National Estimates.*

RETAIL TRADE - INVENTORIES

Executive Office of the President, Council of Economic Advisers, Old

Executive Office Building, Washington, D.C. 20502 (202) 395-5084,www.whitehouse. gov/cea; *Economic Report of the President.*

U.S. Department of Commerce, Bureau of Economic Analysis, Fourteenth Street between Constitution Avenue and E Street, NW, Washington, D.C. 20230 (202) 606-9900, www.bea.doc.gov; *The National Income and Product Accounts of the United States; Survey of Current Business;* and unpublished data.

U.S. Department of Commerce, Bureau of the Census, Washington, D.C. 20233 (301) 457-4100, www.census.gov; *Current Business Reports, Annual Benchmark Report for Retail Trade;* and unpublished data.

RETAIL TRADE - MERGERS AND ACQUISITIONS

Thomson Financial Securities Data, 2 Gateway Center, Newark, New Jersey 07006 (973) 622-3100; *Merger and Corporate Transactions Database.*

RETAIL TRADE - OCCUPATIONAL SAFETY

U.S. Department of Labor, Bureau of Labor Statistics, Two Massachusetts Avenue, NE, Washington, D.C. 20212 (202) 691-5200, www.stats.bls.gov; *Occupational Injuries and Illnesses in the United States by Industry.*

RETAIL TRADE - RECEIPTS

U.S. Department of Commerce, Bureau of the Census, Washington, D.C. 20233 (301) 457-4100, www.census.gov; *1997 Economic Census: Advance Summary Statistics for the U.S. 1997 NAICS Basis;* and *Statistics of U.S. Business.*

RETAIL TRADE - SALES

U.S. Department of Agriculture, Economic Research Service, 1800 M Street, NW, Washington, D.C. 20036 (202) 694-5050, www.ers.usda.gov; *Food Marketing Review.*

U.S. Department of Commerce, Bureau of the Census, Washington, D.C. 20233 (301) 457-4100, www.census.gov; *Census of Retail Trade; Current Business Reports, Annual Benchmark Report for Retail Trade; Merchandise Line Sales; Economic Census of Outlying Areas; 1997 Economic Census;* and *unpublished data.*

RETIREMENT SYSTEM - BENEFITS PAID

Employment Benefit Research Institute, 2121 K Street, NW, Suite 600, Washington, D.C. 20037 (202) 659-0670; *EBRI Databook on Employee Benefits.*

Social Security Administration, 6400

Security Boulevard, Baltimore, Maryland 21235 (800) 772-1213, www.ssa.gov; *Social Security Bulletin;* and unpublished data.

RETIREMENT SYSTEM - CIVIL SERVICE

Board of Governors of the Federal Reserve System, Twentieth Street and Constitution Avenue, NW, Washington, D.C. 20551 (202) 452-3000, www.bog.frb.fed.us; *Flow of Funds Accounts.*

Employment Benefit Research Institute, 2121 K Street, NW, Suite 600, Washington, D.C. 20037 (202) 659-0670; *EBRI Databook on Employee Benefits.*

U.S. Office of Personnel Management, 1900 E Street, NW, Washington, D.C. 20415 (202) 606-1800; *Civil Service Retirement and Disability Trust Fund Annual Report.*

RETIREMENT SYSTEM - FEDERAL - OTHER THAN CIVIL SERVICE

Board of Governors of the Federal Reserve System, Twentieth Street and Constitution Avenue, NW, Washington, D.C. 20551 (202) 452-3000, www.bog.frb.fed.us; *Flow of Funds Accounts.*

Employment Benefit Research Institute, 2121 K Street, NW, Suite 600, Washington, D.C. 20037 (202) 659-0670; *EBRI Databook on Employee Benefits.*

RETIREMENT SYSTEM - OLD AGE, SURVIVORS, DISABILITY, AND HEALTH INSURANCE - See SOCIAL INSURANCE

RETIREMENT SYSTEM - PENSION PLANS

Access Research Inc., 8 Griffen Road North, Windsor, Connecticut 06095 (860) 688-8821; *Marketplace Update.*

Board of Governors of the Federal Reserve System, Twentieth Street and Constitution Avenue, NW, Washington, D.C. 20551 (202) 452-3000, www.bog.frb.fed.us; *Flow of Funds Accounts.*

Employment Benefit Research Institute, 2121 K Street, NW, Suite 600, Washington, D.C. 20037 (202) 659-0670; *EBRI Databook on Employee Benefits.*

U.S. Department of Labor, Pension and Welfare Benefits Administration, 200 Constitution Avenue, NW, Washington, D.C. 20210 (202) 219-8921; *Private Pension Plan Bulletin.*

RETIREMENT SYSTEM - PUBLIC EMPLOYEES

Employment Benefit Research Institute, 2121 K Street, NW, Suite 600, Washington,

D.C. 20037 (202) 659-0670; *EBRI Databook on Employee Benefits.*

RETIREMENT SYSTEM - RAILROAD

Board of Governors of the Federal Reserve System, Twentieth Street and Constitution Avenue, NW, Washington, D.C. 20551 (202) 452-3000, www.bog.frb.fed.us; *Flow of Funds Accounts.*

Executive Office of the President, Office of Management and Budget, Executive Office Building, Washington, D.C. 20503 (202) 395-3080, www.whitehouse.gov omb; *Analytical Perspectives.*

Social Security Administration,6400 Security Boulevard, Baltimore, Maryland 21235 (800) 772-1213, www.ssa.gov; *Social Security Bulletin*; and unpublished data.

RETIREMENT SYSTEM - SOCIAL SECURITY TRUST FUNDS

Social Security Administration, 6400 Security Boulevard, Baltimore, Maryland 21235 (800) 772-1213, www.ssa.gov; *Annual Report of Board of Trustees, OASI, DI, HI, and SMI Trust Funds;* and *Social Security Bulletin.*

RETIREMENT SYSTEM - STATE AND LOCAL GOVERNMENT

Board of Governors of the Federal Reserve System, Twentieth Street and Constitution Avenue, NW, Washington, D.C. 20551 (202) 452-3000, www.bog.frb.fed.us; *Flow of Funds Accounts.*

Social Security Administration, 6400 Security Boulevard, Baltimore, Maryland 21235 (800) 772-1213, www.ssa.gov; *Social Security Bulletin;* and unpublished data.

U.S. Department of Commerce, Bureau of the Census, Washington, D.C. 20233 (301) 457-4100, www.census.gov; *Governmental Finances;* and Internet sites: http://www.census.gov/govs/estimate.html; and http://www.census.gov/ftp/pub/govs/www/apes/97.html.

RETIREMENT SYSTEM - TRUST FUNDS

Executive Office of the President, Office of Management and Budget, Executive Office Building, Washington, D.C. 20503 (202) 395-3080, www.whitehouse.gov/omb; *Analytical Perspectives.*

Reunion - Primary Statistics Sources

Institut National de la Statistique et des Etudes Economiques (France), 4 rue de l'Ecole, Sainte, Clothilde, Reunion 97490; *Tableau Economique de La Reunion.*

REUNION - ABORTIONS

Statistical Office of the United Nations, Publishing Service, New York, New York 10017 (800) 253-9646; *Demographic Yearbook.*

REUNION - AGRICULTURE

Euromonitor International, Inc., 122 South Michigan Avenue, Suite 1200, Chicago, Illinois 60603 (800) 577-EURO; *World Marketing Data and Statistics.*

Europa Publications Limited, 18 Bedford Square, London, WC1B 3JN, England; *The Europa World Year Book.*

Food and Agricultural Organization of the United Nations (FAO) Via delle Terme di Caracalla, 00100 Rome, Italy (Telephone Number in U.S. (202) 653-2400); *Production Yearbook; The State of Food and Agriculture;* and *Trade Yearbook.*

St. Martin's Press, Inc., 175 Fifth Avenue, New York, New York 10010 (800) 221-7945; *The Statesman's Year-Book.*

United Nations Conference on Trade and Development, Central Statistical Service, Palais des Nations, Geneva, Switzerland (Telephone in U.S. (800) 253-9646); *UNCTAD Commodity Yearbook.*

REUNION - AIRLINE SERVICE

Europa Publications Limited, 18 Bedford Square, London, WC1B 3JN, England; *The Europa World Year Book.*

St. Martin's Press, Inc., 175 Fifth Avenue, New York, New York 10010 (800) 221-7945; *The Statesman's Year-Book.*

REUNION - AIRPORTS

Central Intelligence Agency, Washington, D.C. 20505 (703) 482-1100, www.cia.gov; *The World Factbook.*

REUNION - ANIMAL HEALTH

Food and Agricultural Organization of the United Nations (FAO), Via delle Terme di Caracalla, 00100, Rome, Italy (Telephone Number in U.S. (202) 653-2400); *Animal Health Yearbook.*

REUNION - AREA AND DENSITY OF POPULATION

Central Intelligence Agency, Washington, D.C. 20505 (703) 482-1100, www.cia.gov; *The World Factbook.*

Euromonitor International, Inc., 122 South Michigan Avenue, Suite 1200,

Chicago, Illinois 60603 (800) 577-EURO; *The World Economic Factbook.*

Europa Publications Limited, 18 Bedford Square, London, WC1B 3JN, England; *The Europa World Year Book.*

Food and Agricultural Organization of the United Nations (FAO) Via delle Terme di Caracalla, 00100 Rome, Italy (Telephone Number in U.S. (202) 653-2400); *The State of Food and Agriculture.*

St. Martin's Press, Inc., 175 Fifth Avenue, New York, New York 10010 (800) 221-7945; *The Statesman's Year-Book.*

Statistical Office of the United Nations, Publishing Service, New York, New York 10017 (800) 253-9646; *Statistical Yearbook.*

United Nations Educational, Scientific and Cultural Organization (UNESCO), 7 Place de Fontenoy, F-75700 Paris, France (Telephone Number in U.S. (212) 963-5981); *Statistical Yearbook.*

REUNION - BANKING

Euromonitor International, Inc., 122 South Michigan Avenue, Suite 1200, Chicago, Illinois 60603 (800) 577-EURO; *World Marketing Data and Statistics.*

St. Martin's Press, Inc., 175 Fifth Avenue, New York, New York 10010 (800) 221-7945; *The Statesman's Year-Book.*

REUNION - BIRTH RATES

Central Intelligence Agency, Washington, D.C. 20505 (703) 482-1100, www.cia.gov; *The World Factbook.*

Euromonitor International, Inc., 122 South Michigan Avenue, Suite 1200, Chicago, Illinois 60603 (800) 577-EURO; *International Marketing Data and Statistics;* and *The World Economic Factbook.*

Europa Publications Limited, 18 Bedford Square, London, WC1B 3JN, England; *The Europa World Year Book.*

St. Martin's Press, Inc., 175 Fifth Avenue, New York, New York 10010 (800) 221-7945; *The Statesman's Year-Book.*

Statistical Office of the United Nations, Publishing Service, New York, New York 10017 (800) 253-9646; *Demographic Yearbook;* and *Statistical Yearbook.*

World Health Organization, Office of Publications, 20 Avenue Appia, CH-1211 Geneva 27, Switzerland (Telephone Number in U.S. (518) 436-9686); *World Health Statistics Annual.*

REUNION - BOOK PRODUCTION

Europa Publications Limited, 18 Bedford Square, London, WC1B 3JN, England; *The Europa World Year Book.*

United Nations Educational, Scientific and Cultural Organization (UNESCO), 7 Place de Fontenoy, F-75700 Paris, France (Telephone Number in U.S. (212) 963-5981); *Statistical Yearbook.*

REUNION - BROADCASTING

Billboard Limited, P.O. Box 9027, 1006 AA Amsterdam, The Netherlands (Telephone Number in U.S. (212) 764-7300); *World Radio TV Handbook.*

Central Intelligence Agency, Washington, D.C. 20505 (703) 482-1100, www.cia.gov; *The World Factbook.*

Euromonitor International, Inc., 122 South Michigan Avenue, Suite 1200, Chicago, Illinois 60603 (800) 577-EURO; *World Marketing Data and Statistics.*

St. Martin's Press, Inc., 175 Fifth Avenue, New York, New York 10010 (800) 221-7945; *The Statesman's Year-Book.*

REUNION - BUDGET

Central Intelligence Agency, Washington, D.C. 20505 (703) 482-1100, www.cia.gov; *The World Factbook.*

REUNION - CALORIE SUPPLY

Food and Agricultural Organization of the United Nations (FAO) Via delle Terme di Caracalla, 00100 Rome, Italy (Telephone Number in U.S. (202) 653-2400); *The State of Food and Agriculture.*

REUNION - CATTLE - See REUNION - LIVESTOCK AND POULTRY

REUNION - CHEMICAL (ORGANIC) PRODUCTION - See REUNION - MINING AND MINERAL PRODUCTS

REUNION - CLIMATE

St. Martin's Press, Inc., 175 Fifth Avenue, New York, New York 10010 (800) 221-7945; *The Statesman's Year-Book.*

REUNION - COAL PRODUCTION - See REUNION - MINING AND MINERAL PRODUCTS

REUNION - COMMERCE

St. Martin's Press, Inc., 175 Fifth Avenue, New York, New York 10010 (800) 221-7945; *The Statesman's Year-Book.*

REUNION - COMMUNICATIONS - See REUNION - TRANSPORTATION AND COMMUNICATIONS

REUNION - CONSTRUCTION INDUSTRY

United Nations Economic Commission for Africa, Africa Hall, P.O. Box 3001, Addis Ababa, Ethiopia (Telephone Number in U.S. (800) 253-9646); *African Statistical Yearbook.*

REUNION - CONSUMER PRICE INDEX

Europa Publications Limited, 18 Bedford Square, London, WC1B 3JN, England; *The Europa World Year Book.*

Statistical Office of the United Nations, Publishing Service, New York, New York 10017 (800) 253-9646; *Statistical Yearbook.*

REUNION - CONSUMER PRICES

Euromonitor International, Inc., 122 South Michigan Avenue, Suite 1200, Chicago, Illinois 60603 (800) 577-EURO; *World Marketing Data and Statistics.*

International Labour Office, I.L.O. Publications, 1828 L Street, NW, Suite 801, Washington, D.C. 20036 (301) 638-3152; *Yearbook of Labour Statistics.*

REUNION - CORN PRODUCTION - See REUNION - CROPS

REUNION - CROPS

Europa Publications Limited, 18 Bedford Square, London, WC1B 3JN, England; *The Europa World Year Book.*

Food and Agricultural Organization of the United Nations (FAO) Via delle Terme di Caracalla, 00100 Rome, Italy (Telephone Number in U.S. (202) 653-2400); *Production Yearbook;* and *The State of Food and Agriculture.*

St. Martin's Press, Inc., 175 Fifth Avenue, New York, New York 10010 (800) 221-7945; *The Statesman's Year-Book.*

Statistical Office of the United Nations, Publishing Service, New York, New York 10017 (800) 253-9646; *Statistical Yearbook.*

United Nations Conference on Trade and Development, Central Statistical Service, Palais des Nations, Geneva, Switzerland (Telephone in U.S. (800) 253-9646); *UNCTAD Commodity Yearbook.*

REUNION - DAIRY PRODUCTS

Food and Agricultural Organization of the United Nations (FAO) Via delle Terme di Caracalla, 00100 Rome, Italy (Telephone Number in U.S. (202) 653-2400); *The State of Food and Agriculture.*

St. Martin's Press, Inc., 175 Fifth Avenue, New York, New York 10010 (800) 221-7945; *The Statesman's Year-Book.*

Statistical Office of the United Nations, Publishing Service, New York, New York 10017 (800) 253-9646; *Statistical Yearbook.*

REUNION - DEATH RATES - See REUNION - MORTALITY

REUNION - DEMOGRAPHY

Euromonitor International, Inc., 122 South Michigan Avenue, Suite 1200, Chicago, Illinois 60603 (800) 577-EURO; *International Marketing Data and Statistics; World Marketing Data and Statistics;* and *The World Economic Factbook.*

REUNION - DEVELOPMENT ASSISTANCE

Statistical Office of the United Nations, Publishing Service, New York, New York 10017 (800) 253-9646; *Statistical Yearbook.*

REUNION - DISEASE - See REUNION - HEALTH

REUNION - DIVORCE RATES

Statistical Office of the United Nations, Publishing Service, New York, New York 10017 (800) 253-9646; *Demographic Yearbook;* and *Statistical Yearbook.*

REUNION - ECONOMY

Central Intelligence Agency, Washington, D.C. 20505 (703) 482-1100, www.cia.gov; *The World Factbook.*

Euromonitor International, Inc., 122 South Michigan Avenue, Suite 1200, Chicago, Illinois 60603 (800) 577-EURO; *The World Economic Factbook;* and *World Marketing Data and Statistics.*

St. Martin's Press, Inc., 175 Fifth Avenue, New York, New York 10010 (800) 221-7945; *The Statesman's Year-Book.*

Statistical Office of the United Nations, Publishing Service, New York, New York 10017 (800) 253-9646; *World Statistics Pocketbook.*

The World Bank, 1818 H Street, NW, Washington, D.C. 20433 (202) 477-1234; *World Development Report.*

REUNION - EDUCATION

Euromonitor International, Inc., 122 South Michigan Avenue, Suite 1200, Chicago, Illinois 60603 (800) 577-EURO; *International Marketing Data and Statistics;* and *World Marketing Data and Statistics.*

Europa Publications Limited, 18 Bedford Square, London, WC1B 3JN, England; *The Europa World Year Book.*

St. Martin's Press, Inc., 175 Fifth Avenue, New York, New York 10010 (800)

221-7945; *The Statesman's Year-Book.*

United Nations Educational, Scientific and Cultural Organization (UNESCO), 7 Place de Fontenoy, F-75700 Paris, France (Telephone Number in U.S. (212) 963-5981); *Statistical Yearbook.*

REUNION - EGG PRODUCTION AND CONSUMPTION - See REUNION - DAIRY PRODUCTS

REUNION - ELECTRICITY

Central Intelligence Agency, Washington, D.C. 20505 (703) 482-1100, www.cia.gov; *The World Factbook.*

St. Martin's Press, Inc., 175 Fifth Avenue, New York, New York 10010 (800) 221-7945; *The Statesman's Year-Book.*

Statistical Office of the United Nations, Publishing Service, New York, New York 10017 (800) 253-9646; *Statistical Yearbook.*

United Nations Economic Commission for Africa, Africa Hall, P.O. Box 3001, Addis Ababa, Ethiopia (Telephone Number in U.S. (800) 253-9646); *African Statistical Yearbook.*

REUNION - EMPLOYMENT

Euromonitor International, Inc., 122 South Michigan Avenue, Suite 1200, Chicago, Illinois 60603 (800) 577-EURO; *International Marketing Data and Statistics.*

International Labour Office, I.L.O. Publications, 1828 L Street, NW, Suite 801, Washington, D.C. 20036 (301) 638-3152; *Yearbook of Labour Statistics.*

United Nations Economic Commission for Africa, Africa Hall, P.O. Box 3001, Addis Ababa, Ethiopia (Telephone Number in U.S. (800) 253-9646); *African Statistical Yearbook.*

REUNION - ENERGY

Euromonitor International, Inc., 122 South Michigan Avenue, Suite 1200, Chicago, Illinois 60603 (800) 577-EURO; *International Marketing Data and Statistics; World Marketing Data and Statistics;* and *The World Economic Factbook.*

Food and Agricultural Organization of the United Nations (FAO) Via delle Terme di Caracalla, 00100 Rome, Italy (Telephone Number in U.S. (202) 653-2400); *The State of Food and Agriculture.*

St. Martin's Press, Inc., 175 Fifth Avenue, New York, New York 10010 (800) 221-7945; *The Statesman's Year-Book.*

Statistical Office of the United Nations, Publishing Service, New York, New York

10017 (800) 253-9646; *Energy Statistics Yearbook; Statistical Yearbook;* and *World Statistics Pocketbook.*

United Nations Economic Commission for Africa, Africa Hall, P.O. Box 3001, Addis Ababa, Ethiopia (Telephone Number in U.S. (800) 253-9646); *African Statistical Yearbook.*

The World Bank, 1818 H Street, NW, Washington, D.C. 20433 (202) 477-1234; *World Development Report.*

REUNION - ENVIRONMENT

Statistical Office of the United Nations, Publishing Service, New York, New York 10017 (800) 253-9646; *World Statistics Pocketbook.*

REUNION - EXCHANGE RATES

Central Intelligence Agency, Washington, D.C. 20505 (703) 482-1100, www.cia.gov; *The World Factbook.*

Euromonitor International, Inc., 122 South Michigan Avenue, Suite 1200, Chicago, Illinois 60603 (800) 577-EURO; *International Marketing Data and Statistics;* and *The World Economic Factbook.*

Europa Publications Limited, 18 Bedford Square, London, WC1B 3JN, England; *The Europa World Year Book.*

Statistical Office of the United Nations, Publishing Service, New York, New York 10017 (800) 253-9646; *World Statistics Pocketbook.*

REUNION - EXPORTS

Central Intelligence Agency, Washington, D.C. 20505 (703) 482-1100, www.cia.gov; *The World Factbook.*

Euromonitor International, Inc., 122 South Michigan Avenue, Suite 1200, Chicago, Illinois 60603 (800) 577-EURO; *International Marketing Data and Statistics;* and *The World Economic Factbook.*

Europa Publications Limited, 18 Bedford Square, London, WC1B 3JN, England; *The Europa World Year Book.*

Food and Agricultural Organization of the United Nations (FAO) Via delle Terme di Caracalla, 00100 Rome, Italy (Telephone Number in U.S. (202) 653-2400); *The State of Food and Agriculture.*

International Monetary Fund, 700 Nineteenth Street, NW, Washington, D.C. 20431 (202) 623-7000; *Direction of Trade Statistics.*

St. Martin's Press, Inc., 175 Fifth Avenue, New York, New York 10010 (800)

221-7945; *The Statesman's Year-Book.*

United Nations Economic Commission for Africa, Africa Hall, P.O. Box 3001, Addis Ababa, Ethiopia (Telephone Number in U.S. (800) 253-9646); *African Statistical Yearbook.*

REUNION - EXTERNAL TRADE

Euromonitor International, Inc., 122 South Michigan Avenue, Suite 1200, Chicago, Illinois 60603 (800) 577-EURO; *World Marketing Data and Statistics.*

Food and Agricultural Organization of the United Nations (FAO) Via delle Terme di Caracalla, 00100 Rome, Italy (Telephone Number in U.S. (202) 653-2400); *The State of Food and Agriculture;* and *Trade Yearbook.*

Statistical Office of the United Nations, Publishing Service, New York, New York 10017 (800) 253-9646; *Statistical Yearbook.*

REUNION - FARM CROPS - See
REUNION - CROPS

REUNION - FERTILITY RATES

Central Intelligence Agency, Washington, D.C. 20505 (703) 482-1100, www.cia.gov; *The World Factbook.*

The World Bank, 1818 H Street, NW, Washington, D.C. 20433 (202) 477-1234; *World Development Report.*

REUNION - FERTILIZER

Food and Agricultural Organization of the United Nations (FAO), Via delle Terme di Caracalla, 00100, Rome, Italy (Telephone Number in U.S. (202) 653-2400); *Fertilizer Yearbook;* and *The State of Food and Agriculture.*

Statistical Office of the United Nations, Publishing Service, New York, New York 10017 (800) 253-9646; *Statistical Yearbook.*

REUNION - FETAL MORTALITY - See
REUNION - MORTALITY

REUNION - FINANCE

Europa Publications Limited, 18 Bedford Square, London, WC1B 3JN, England; *The Europa World Year Book.*

REUNION - FISHERIES

Europa Publications Limited, 18 Bedford Square, London, WC1B 3JN, England; *The Europa World Year Book.*

Food and Agricultural Organization of the United Nations (FAO) Via delle Terme di Caracalla, 00100 Rome, Italy (Telephone

Number in U.S. (202) 653-2400); *The State of Food and Agriculture;* and *Yearbook of Fishery Statistics.*

St. Martin's Press, Inc., 175 Fifth Avenue, New York, New York 10010 (800) 221-7945; *The Statesman's Year-Book.*

Statistical Office of the United Nations, Publishing Service, New York, New York 10017 (800) 253-9646; *Statistical Yearbook.*

United Nations Conference on Trade and Development, Central Statistical Service, Palais des Nations, Geneva, Switzerland (Telephone in U.S. (800) 253-9646); *UNCTAD Commodity Yearbook.*

REUNION - FINANCE

St. Martin's Press, Inc., 175 Fifth Avenue, New York, New York 10010 (800) 221-7945; *The Statesman's Year-Book.*

REUNION - FOOD

Food and Agricultural Organization of the United Nations (FAO) Via delle Terme di Caracalla, 00100 Rome, Italy (Telephone Number in U.S. (202) 653-2400); *Production Yearbook;* and *The State of Food and Agriculture.*

REUNION - FOREIGN TRADE

Euromonitor International, Inc., 122 South Michigan Avenue, Suite 1200, Chicago, Illinois 60603 (800) 577-EURO; *The World Economic Factbook.*

Europa Publications Limited, 18 Bedford Square, London, WC1B 3JN, England; *The Europa World Year Book.*

Food and Agricultural Organization of the United Nations (FAO) Via delle Terme di Caracalla, 00100 Rome, Italy (Telephone Number in U.S. (202) 653-2400); *The State of Food and Agriculture.*

St. Martin's Press, Inc., 175 Fifth Avenue, New York, New York 10010 (800) 221-7945; *The Statesman's Year-Book.*

Statistical Office of the United Nations, Publishing Service, New York, New York 10017 (800) 253-9646; *International Trade Statistics;* and *Statistical Yearbook.*

United Nations Conference on Trade and Development, Central Statistical Service, Palais des Nations, Geneva, Switzerland (Telephone in U.S. (800) 253-9646); *UNCTAD Commodity Yearbook.*

United Nations Economic Commission for Africa, Africa Hall, P.O. Box 3001, Addis Ababa, Ethiopia (Telephone Number in U.S. (800) 253-9646); *African Statistical Yearbook.*

REUNION - FORESTRY AND FOREST PRODUCTS

Europa Publications Limited, 18 Bedford Square, London, WC1B 3JN, England; *The Europa World Year Book.*

Food and Agricultural Organization of the United Nations (FAO) Via delle Terme di Caracalla, 00100 Rome, Italy (Telephone Number in U.S. (202) 653-2400); *The State of Food and Agriculture;* and *Yearbook of Forest Products.*

St. Martin's Press, Inc., 175 Fifth Avenue, New York, New York 10010 (800) 221-7945; *The Statesman's Year-Book.*

Statistical Office of the United Nations, Publishing Service, New York, New York 10017 (800) 253-9646; *Statistical Yearbook.*

United Nations Conference on Trade and Development, Central Statistical Service, Palais des Nations, Geneva, Switzerland (Telephone in U.S. (800) 253-9646); *UNCTAD Commodity Yearbook.*

United Nations Educational, Scientific and Cultural Organization (UNESCO), 7 Place de Fontenoy, F-75700 Paris, France (Telephone Number in U.S. (212) 963-5981); *Statistical Yearbook.*

REUNION - GENERAL MORTALITY - See REUNION - MORTALITY

REUNION - GOVERNMENT

Central Intelligence Agency, Washington, D.C. 20505 (703) 482-1100, www.cia.gov; *The World Factbook.*

Europa Publications Limited, 18 Bedford Square, London, WC1B 3JN, England; *The Europa World Year Book.*

St. Martin's Press, Inc., 175 Fifth Avenue, New York, New York 10010 (800) 221-7945; *The Statesman's Year-Book.*

Statistical Office of the United Nations, Publishing Service, New York, New York 10017 (800) 253-9646; *National Accounts Statistics.*

REUNION - GRAIN PRODUCTION - See REUNION - CROPS

REUNION - GROSS DOMESTIC PRODUCT

Euromonitor International, Inc., 122 South Michigan Avenue, Suite 1200, Chicago, Illinois 60603 (800) 577-EURO; *International Marketing Data and Statistics;* and *The World Economic Factbook.*

Europa Publications Limited, 18 Bedford Square, London, WC1B 3JN, England; *The Europa World Year Book.*

Statistical Office of the United Nations, Publishing Service, New York, New York 10017 (800) 253-9646; *National Accounts Statistics;* and *Statistical Yearbook.*

United Nations Economic Commission for Africa, Africa Hall, P.O. Box 3001, Addis Ababa, Ethiopia (Telephone Number in U.S. (800) 253-9646); *African Statistical Yearbook.*

REUNION - GROSS NATIONAL PRODUCT

The World Bank, 1818 H Street, NW, Washington, D.C. 20433 (202) 477-1234; *World Development Report.*

REUNION - GROUNDNUT PRODUCTION - See REUNION - CROPS

REUNION - HEALTH

Euromonitor International, Inc., 122 South Michigan Avenue, Suite 1200, Chicago, Illinois 60603 (800) 577-EURO; *World Marketing Data and Statistics.*

St. Martin's Press, Inc., 175 Fifth Avenue, New York, New York 10010 (800) 221-7945; *The Statesman's Year-Book.*

Statistical Office of the United Nations, Publishing Service, New York, New York 10017 (800) 253-9646; *Statistical Yearbook.*

World Health Organization, Office of Publications, 20 Avenue Appia, CH-1211 Geneva 27, Switzerland (Telephone Number in U.S. (518) 436-9686); *World Health Statistics Annual.*

REUNION - HIDE PRODUCTION

Food and Agricultural Organization of the United Nations (FAO), Via delle Terme di Caracalla, 00100, Rome, Italy (Telephone Number in U.S. (202) 653-2400); *Production Yearbook.*

REUNION - HIGHWAYS

Central Intelligence Agency, Washington, D.C. 20505 (703) 482-1100, www.cia.gov; *The World Factbook.*

St. Martin's Press, Inc., 175 Fifth Avenue, New York, New York 10010 (800) 221-7945; *The Statesman's Year-Book.*

REUNION - HOURS OF WORK - See REUNION - EMPLOYMENT

REUNION - HOUSING AND HOUSING UNITS

Euromonitor International, Inc., 122 South Michigan Avenue, Suite 1200, Chicago, Illinois 60603 (800) 577-EURO; *World Marketing Data and Statistics.*

REUNION - ILLITERATE POPULATION

Central Intelligence Agency, Washington, D.C. 20505 (703) 482-1100, www.cia.gov; *The World Factbook.*

Euromonitor International, Inc., 122 South Michigan Avenue, Suite 1200, Chicago, Illinois 60603 (800) 577-EURO; *The World Economic Factbook.*

United Nations Educational, Scientific and Cultural Organization (UNESCO), 7 Place de Fontenoy, F-75700 Paris, France (Telephone Number in U.S. (212) 963-5981); *Statistical Yearbook.*

REUNION - IMPORTS

Central Intelligence Agency, Washington, D.C. 20505 (703) 482-1100, www.cia.gov; *The World Factbook.*

Euromonitor International, Inc., 122 South Michigan Avenue, Suite 1200, Chicago, Illinois 60603 (800) 577-EURO; *International Marketing Data and Statistics;* and *The World Economic Factbook.*

Europa Publications Limited, 18 Bedford Square, London, WC1B 3JN, England; *The Europa World Year Book.*

Food and Agricultural Organization of the United Nations (FAO) Via delle Terme di Caracalla, 00100 Rome, Italy (Telephone Number in U.S. (202) 653-2400); *The State of Food and Agriculture.*

International Labour Office, I.L.O. Publications, 1828 L Street, NW, Suite 801, Washington, D.C. 20036 (301) 638-3152; *Direction of Trade.*

St. Martin's Press, Inc., 175 Fifth Avenue, New York, New York 10010 (800) 221-7945; *The Statesman's Year-Book.*

United Nations Economic Commission for Africa, Africa Hall, P.O. Box 3001, Addis Ababa, Ethiopia (Telephone Number in U.S. (800) 253-9646); *African Statistical Yearbook.*

REUNION - INDUSTRY

Central Intelligence Agency, Washington, D.C. 20505 (703) 482-1100, www.cia.gov; *The World Factbook.*

Euromonitor International, Inc., 122 South Michigan Avenue, Suite 1200, Chicago, Illinois 60603 (800) 577-EURO; *The World Economic Factbook;* and *World Marketing Data and Statistics.*

International Labour Office, I.L.O. Publications, 1828 L Street, NW, Suite 801, Washington, D.C. 20036 (301) 638-3152; *Yearbook of Labour Statistics.*

St. Martin's Press, Inc., 175 Fifth Avenue, New York, New York 10010 (800) 221-7945; *The Statesman's Year-Book.*

United Nations Economic Commission for Africa, Africa Hall, P.O. Box 3001, Addis Ababa, Ethiopia (Telephone Number in U.S. (800) 253-9646); *African Statistical Yearbook.*

REUNION - INFANT AND MATERNAL MORTALITY - See REUNION - MORTALITY

REUNION - LABOR

Central Intelligence Agency, Washington, D.C. 20505 (703) 482-1100, www.cia.gov; *The World Factbook.*

Euromonitor International, Inc., 122 South Michigan Avenue, Suite 1200, Chicago, Illinois 60603 (800) 577-EURO; *International Marketing Data and Statistics;* and *World Marketing Data and Statistics.*

Europa Publications Limited, 18 Bedford Square, London, WC1B 3JN, England; *The Europa World Year Book.*

Food and Agricultural Organization of the United Nations (FAO) Via delle Terme di Caracalla, 00100 Rome, Italy (Telephone Number in U.S. (202) 653-2400); *The State of Food and Agriculture.*

International Labour Office, I.L.O. Publications, 1828 L Street, NW, Suite 801, Washington, D.C. 20036 (301) 638-3152; *Yearbook of Labour Statistics.*

St. Martin's Press, Inc., 175 Fifth Avenue, New York, New York 10010 (800) 221-7945; *The Statesman's Year-Book.*

The World Bank, 1818 H Street, NW, Washington, D.C. 20433 (202) 477-1234; *World Development Report.*

REUNION - LAND USE

Central Intelligence Agency, Washington, D.C. 20505 (703) 482-1100, www.cia.gov; *The World Factbook.*

Euromonitor International, Inc., 122 South Michigan Avenue, Suite 1200, Chicago, Illinois 60603 (800) 577-EURO; *International Marketing Data and Statistics.*

Food and Agricultural Organization of the United Nations (FAO), Via delle Terme di Caracalla, 00100, Rome, Italy (Telephone Number in U.S. (202) 653-2400); *Production Yearbook.*

REUNION - LIBRARIES

United Nations Educational, Scientific and Cultural Organization (UNESCO), 7 Place de Fontenoy, F-75700 Paris, France (Telephone Number in U.S. (212) 963-

5981); *Statistical Yearbook.*

REUNION - LIFE EXPECTANCY

Central Intelligence Agency, Washington, D.C. 20505 (703) 482-1100, www.cia.gov; *The World Factbook.*

Euromonitor International, Inc., 122 South Michigan Avenue, Suite 1200, Chicago, Illinois 60603 (800) 577-EURO; *The World Economic Factbook.*

Statistical Office of the United Nations, Publishing Service, New York, New York 10017 (800) 253-9646; *World Statistics Pocketbook.*

The World Bank, 1818 H Street, NW, Washington, D.C. 20433 (202) 477-1234; *World Development Report.*

REUNION - LITERACY RATE

Euromonitor International, Inc., 122 South Michigan Avenue, Suite 1200, Chicago, Illinois 60603 (800) 577-EURO; *World Marketing Data and Statistics.*

REUNION - LIVESTOCK AND POULTRY

Europa Publications Limited, 18 Bedford Square, London, WC1B 3JN, England; *The Europa World Year Book.*

Food and Agricultural Organization of the United Nations (FAO), Via delle Terme di Caracalla, 00100, Rome, Italy (Telephone Number in U.S. (202) 653-2400); *Production Yearbook;* and *The State of Food and Agriculture.*

St. Martin's Press, Inc., 175 Fifth Avenue, New York, New York 10010 (800) 221-7945; *The Statesman's Year-Book.*

Statistical Office of the United Nations, Publishing Service, New York, New York 10017 (800) 253-9646; *Statistical Yearbook.*

United Nations Conference on Trade and Development, Central Statistical Service, Palais des Nations, Geneva, Switzerland (Telephone in U.S. (800) 253-9646); *UNCTAD Commodity Yearbook.*

REUNION - MANUFACTURING

Statistical Office of the United Nations, Publishing Service, New York, New York 10017 (800) 253-9646; *Statistical Yearbook.*

United Nations Economic Commission for Africa, Africa Hall, P.O. Box 3001, Addis Ababa, Ethiopia (Telephone Number in U.S. (800) 253-9646); *African Statistical Yearbook.*

REUNION - MARRIAGE RATES

Statistical Office of the United Nations,

Publishing Service, New York, New York 10017 (800) 253-9646; *Demographic Yearbook;* and *Statistical Yearbook.*

REUNION - MEAT PRODUCTION - See REUNION - LIVESTOCK AND POULTRY

REUNION - MERCHANT SHIPPING

Europa Publications Limited, 18 Bedford Square, London, WC1B 3JN, England; *The Europa World Year Book.*

St. Martin's Press, Inc., 175 Fifth Avenue, New York, New York 10010 (800) 221-7945; *The Statesman's Year-Book.*

Statistical Office of the United Nations, Publishing Service, New York, New York 10017 (800) 253-9646; *Statistical Yearbook.*

REUNION - MILITARY

Central Intelligence Agency, Washington, D.C. 20505 (703) 482-1100, www.cia.gov; *The World Factbook.*

Euromonitor International, Inc., 122 South Michigan Avenue, Suite 1200, Chicago, Illinois 60603 (800) 577-EURO; *World Marketing Data and Statistics.*

REUNION - MINING AND MINERAL PRODUCTS

United Nations Conference on Trade and Development, Central Statistical Service, Palais des Nations, Geneva, Switzerland (Telephone in U.S. (800) 253-9646); *UNCTAD Commodity Yearbook.*

United Nations Economic Commission for Africa, Africa Hall, P.O. Box 3001, Addis Ababa, Ethiopia (Telephone Number in U.S. (800) 253-9646); *African Statistical Yearbook.*

REUNION - MORTALITY

Central Intelligence Agency, Washington, D.C. 20505 (703) 482-1100, www.cia.gov; *The World Factbook.*

Euromonitor International, Inc., 122 South Michigan Avenue, Suite 1200, Chicago, Illinois 60603 (800) 577-EURO; *International Marketing Data and Statistics;* and *The World Economic Factbook.*

Europa Publications Limited, 18 Bedford Square, London, WC1B 3JN, England; *The Europa World Year Book.*

St. Martin's Press, Inc., 175 Fifth Avenue, New York, New York 10010 (800) 221-7945; *The Statesman's Year-Book.*

Statistical Office of the United Nations, Publishing Service, New York, New York 10017 (800) 253-9646; *Demographic Yearbook; Statistical Yearbook;* and *World Statistics Pocketbook.*

The World Bank, 1818 H Street, NW, Washington, D.C. 20433 (202) 477-1234; *World Development Report.*

World Health Organization, Office of Publications, 20 Avenue Appia, CH-1211 Geneva 27, Switzerland (Telephone Number in U.S. (518) 436-9686); *World Health Statistics Annual.*

REUNION - MOTION PICTURES

St. Martin's Press, Inc., 175 Fifth Avenue, New York, New York 10010 (800) 221-7945; *The Statesman's Year-Book.*

Statistical Office of the United Nations, Publishing Service, New York, New York 10017 (800) 253-9646; *Statistical Yearbook.*

REUNION - MOTOR VEHICLES IN USE

Europa Publications Limited, 18 Bedford Square, London, WC1B 3JN, England; *The Europa World Year Book.*

Statistical Office of the United Nations, Publishing Service, New York, New York 10017 (800) 253-9646; *Statistical Yearbook.*

REUNION - MULES - See REUNION - LIVESTOCK AND POULTRY

REUNION - MUSEUMS

United Nations Educational, Scientific and Cultural Organization (UNESCO), 7 Place de Fontenoy, F-75700 Paris, France (Telephone Number in U.S. (212) 963-5981); *Statistical Yearbook.*

REUNION - NATALITY - See REUNION - BIRTH RATE

REUNION - NATIONAL ACCOUNTS

Statistical Office of the United Nations, Publishing Service, New York, New York 10017 (800) 253-9646; *National Accounts Statistics;* and *Statistical Yearbook.*

United Nations Economic Commission for Africa, Africa Hall, P.O. Box 3001, Addis Ababa, Ethiopia (Telephone Number in U.S. (800) 253-9646); *African Statistical Yearbook.*

REUNION - NATIONAL INCOME

Statistical Office of the United Nations, Publishing Service, New York, New York 10017 (800) 253-9646; *National Accounts Statistics;* and *Statistical Yearbook.*

REUNION - NEWSPAPER PRODUCTION - See REUNION - FORESTRY AND FOREST PRODUCTS

REUNION - NEWSPRINT - See REUNION - FORESTRY AND FOREST PRODUCTS

REUNION - OCCUPATIONS - See REUNION - LABOR

REUNION - PAPER - See REUNION - FORESTRY AND FOREST PRODUCTS

REUNION - PERIODICALS

United Nations Educational, Scientific and Cultural Organization (UNESCO), 7 Place de Fontenoy, F-75700 Paris, France (Telephone Number in U.S. (212) 963-5981); *Statistical Yearbook.*

REUNION - PESTICIDE USE

Food and Agricultural Organization of the United Nations (FAO) Via delle Terme di Caracalla, 00100 Rome, Italy (Telephone Number in U.S. (202) 653-2400); *The State of Food and Agriculture.*

REUNION - PETROLEUM INDUSTRY

Food and Agricultural Organization of the United Nations (FAO) Via delle Terme di Caracalla, 00100 Rome, Italy (Telephone Number in U.S. (202) 653-2400); *The State of Food and Agriculture.*

United Nations Conference on Trade and Development, Central Statistical Service, Palais des Nations, Geneva, Switzerland (Telephone in U.S. (800) 253-9646); *UNCTAD Commodity Yearbook.*

REUNION - PIGS - See REUNION - LIVESTOCK AND POULTRY

REUNION - POPULATION

Central Intelligence Agency, Washington, D.C. 20505 (703) 482-1100, www.cia.gov; *The World Factbook.*

Euromonitor International, Inc., 122 South Michigan Avenue, Suite 1200, Chicago, Illinois 60603 (800) 577-EURO; *International Marketing Data and Statistics;* and *The World Economic Factbook.*

Europa Publications Limited, 18 Bedford Square, London, WC1B 3JN, England; *The Europa World Year Book.*

Food and Agricultural Organization of the United Nations (FAO), Via delle Terme di Caracalla, 00100, Rome, Italy (Telephone Number in U.S. (202) 653-2400); *Production Yearbook.*

International Labour Office, I.L.O. Publications, 1828 L Street, NW, Suite 801, Washington, D.C. 20036 (301) 638-3152; *Yearbook of Labour Statistics.*

St. Martin's Press, Inc., 175 Fifth Avenue, New York, New York 10010 (800) 221-7945; *The Statesman's Year-Book.*

Statistical Office of the United Nations,

Publishing Service, New York, New York 10017 (800) 253-9646; *Demographic Yearbook; Statistical Yearbook;* and *World Statistics Pocketbook.*

United Nations Educational, Scientific and Cultural Organization (UNESCO), 7 Place de Fontenoy, F-75700 Paris, France (Telephone Number in U.S. (212) 963-5981); *Statistical Yearbook.*

The World Bank, 1818 H Street, NW, Washington, D.C. 20433 (202) 477-1234; *World Development Report.*

World Health Organization, Office of Publications, 20 Avenue Appia, CH-1211 Geneva 27, Switzerland (Telephone Number in U.S. (518) 436-9686); *World Health Statistics Annual.*

REUNION - POST OFFICES

St. Martin's Press, Inc., 175 Fifth Avenue, New York, New York 10010 (800) 221-7945; *The Statesman's Year-Book.*

REUNION - POTATO PRODUCTION - See REUNION - CROPS

REUNION - PRICES

Food and Agricultural Organization of the United Nations (FAO), Via delle Terme di Caracalla, 00100, Rome, Italy (Telephone Number in U.S. (202) 653-2400); *Production Yearbook;* and *The State of Food and Agriculture.*

International Labour Office, I.L.O. Publications, 1828 L Street, NW, Suite 801, Washington, D.C. 20036 (301) 638-3152; *Yearbook of Labour Statistics.*

REUNION - PRINTING AND WRITING PAPER - See REUNION - FORESTRY AND FOREST PRODUCTS

REUNION - RADIO RECEIVERS

St. Martin's Press, Inc., 175 Fifth Avenue, New York, New York 10010 (800) 221-7945; *The Statesman's Year-Book.*

REUNION - RELIGION

Central Intelligence Agency, Washington, D.C. 20505 (703) 482-1100, www.cia.gov; *The World Factbook.*

St. Martin's Press, Inc., 175 Fifth Avenue, New York, New York 10010 (800) 221-7945; *The Statesman's Year-Book.*

REUNION - RENT PRICES

International Labour Office, I.L.O. Publications, 1828 L Street, NW, Washington, D.C. 20036 (301) 638-3152; *Yearbook of Labour Statistics.*

REUNION - RETAIL TRADE

Euromonitor International, Inc., 122 South Michigan Avenue, Suite 1200, Chicago, Illinois 60603 (800) 577-EURO; *World Marketing Data and Statistics.*

REUNION - ROOT AND TUBER PRODUCTION - See REUNION - CROPS

REUNION - ROUNDWOOD PRODUCTION - See REUNION - FORESTRY AND FOREST PRODUCTS

REUNION - SAWNWOOD PRODUCTION - See REUNION - FORESTRY AND FOREST PRODUCTS

REUNION - SHEEP - See REUNION - LIVESTOCK AND POULTRY

REUNION - SOCIAL DATA

Statistical Office of the United Nations, Publishing Service, New York, New York 10017 (800) 253-9646; *World Statistics Pocketbook.*

REUNION - SOCIAL SECURITY

Statistical Office of the United Nations, Publishing Service, New York, New York 10017 (800) 253-9646; *National Accounts Statistics.*

REUNION - STOCKS - COMMODITY - MARKET PRICE - INDEX

Food and Agricultural Organization of the United Nations (FAO) Via delle Terme di Caracalla, 00100 Rome, Italy (Telephone Number in U.S. (202) 653-2400); *The State of Food and Agriculture.*

REUNION - SUGAR - See REUNION - CROPS

REUNION - TELEPHONES IN USE

American Telephone and Telegraph Company, 26 Parsippany Road, Whippany, New Jersey 07981 (800) 222-0300; *The World's Telephones.*

Central Intelligence Agency, Washington, D.C. 20505 (703) 482-1100, www.cia.gov; *The World Factbook.*

Europa Publications Limited, 18 Bedford Square, London, WC1B 3JN, England; *The Europa World Year Book.*

St. Martin's Press, Inc., 175 Fifth Avenue, New York, New York 10010 (800) 221-7945; *The Statesman's Year-Book.*

Statistical Office of the United Nations, Publishing Service, New York, New York 10017 (800) 253-9646; *Statistical Yearbook;* and *World Statistics Pocketbook.*

REUNION - TEXTILE INDUSTRY

St. Martin's Press, Inc., 175 Fifth Avenue, New York, New York 10010 (800) 221-7945; *The Statesman's Year-Book.*

United Nations Conference on Trade and Development, Central Statistical Service, Palais des Nations, Geneva, Switzerland (Telephone in U.S. (800) 253-9646); *UNCTAD Commodity Yearbook.*

REUNION - TOURISM

Euromonitor International, Inc., 122 South Michigan Avenue, Suite 1200, Chicago, Illinois 60603 (800) 577-EURO; *The World Economic Factbook;* and *World Marketing Data and Statistics.*

Europa Publications Limited, 18 Bedford Square, London, WC1B 3JN, England; *The Europa World Year Book.*

St. Martin's Press, Inc., 175 Fifth Avenue, New York, New York 10010 (800) 221-7945; *The Statesman's Year-Book.*

REUNION - TRADE - See REUNION - FOREIGN TRADE

REUNION - TRANSPORTATION AND COMMUNICATIONS

Central Intelligence Agency, Washington, D.C. 20505 (703) 482-1100, www.cia.gov; *The World Factbook.*

Euromonitor International, Inc., 122 South Michigan Avenue, Suite 1200, Chicago, Illinois 60603 (800) 577-EURO; *International Marketing Data and Statistics;* and *World Marketing Data and Statistics.*

Europa Publications Limited, 18 Bedford Square, London, WC1B 3JN, England; *The Europa World Year Book.*

St. Martin's Press, Inc., 175 Fifth Avenue, New York, New York 10010 (800) 221-7945; *The Statesman's Year-Book.*

REUNION - UNEMPLOYMENT

Central Intelligence Agency, Washington, D.C. 20505 (703) 482-1100, www.cia.gov; *The World Factbook.*

International Labour Office, I.L.O. Publications, 1828 L Street, NW, Suite 801, Washington, D.C. 20036 (301) 638-3152; *Yearbook of Labour Statistics.*

St. Martin's Press, Inc., 175 Fifth Avenue, New York, New York 10010 (800) 221-7945; *The Statesman's Year-Book.*

REUNION - VITAL STATISTICS

St. Martin's Press, Inc., 175 Fifth Avenue, New York, New York 10010 (800) 221-7945; *The Statesman's Year-Book.*

Statistical Office of the United Nations, Publishing Service, New York, New York 10017 (800) 253-9646; *Statistical Yearbook.*

World Health Organization, Office of Publications, 20 Avenue Appia, CH-1211 Geneva 27, Switzerland (Telephone Number in U.S. (518) 436-9686); *World Health Statistics Annual.*

REUNION - WAGES

International Labour Office, I.L.O. Publications, 1828 L Street, NW, Suite 801, Washington, D.C. 20036 (301) 638-3152; *Yearbook of Labour Statistics.*

REVOLVERS - See FIREARMS

RHEUMATIC FEVER

U.S. Department of Health and Human Services, Centers for Disease Control, 1600 Clifton Road, NE, Atlanta, Georgia 30333 (800) 311-3435, www.cdc.gov; *Summary of Notifiable Diseases, United States, Morbidity and Mortality Weekly Report.*

RHODE ISLAND - See also STATE DATA (FOR INDIVIDUAL STATES)

Rhode Island - Primary Statistics Source

Department of Economic Development, 7 Jackson Walkway, Providence, Rhode Island 02903 (401) 277-2601; *Rhode Island Census of Population and Housing Summary; The Rhode Island Economy;* and *Monthly Economic Trends.*

Rhode Island - State Data Centers

Rhode Island Department of Administration, Statewide Planning Program, One Capitol Hill, Providence, Rhode Island 02908-5872, Mr. Mark G. Brown, Chair (401) 222-6183.

Brown University, Population Studies and Training Center, Post Office Box 1916, Providence, Rhode Island 02912, Anneliese Greenier, Data Archivist (401) 863-2278.

House Fiscal Advisory Office, State House, Room 306, Providence, Rhode Island 02903, Dr. Robert Sieczkiewicz (401) 222-2738.

Rhode Island Department of Education, 225 Westminster Street, Providence, Rhode Island 02903, James Karon, Coordinator, State Assessment Program (401) 222-4600, ext. 2105.

Rhode Island Department of Health,

Office of Health Statistics, 3 Capitol Hill, Providence, Rhode Island 02908-5097, Jay Buechner, Chief, Health Statistics (401) 222-2550.

Rhode Island Development Corporation, 1 West Exchange Street, Providence, Rhode Island 02903, Vincent Harrington (401) 222-2601.

RICE - ACREAGE

U.S. Department of Agriculture, National Agricultural Statistics Service, Fourteenth Street and Independence Avenue, SW, Washington, D.C. 20250 (800) 727-9540; *Agricultural Statistics; Crop Production; Field Crops; Crop Values;* and *Agricultural Outlook.*

RICE - CONSUMPTION

U.S. Department of Agriculture, Economic Research Service, 1800 M Street, NW, Washington, D.C. 20036 (202) 694-5050, www.ers.usda.gov; *Food Consumption, Prices and Expenditures;* and *Agricultural Outlook.*

RICE - FARM MARKETINGS - SALES

U.S. Department of Agriculture, Economic Research Service, 1800 M Street, NW, Washington, D.C. 20036 (202) 694-5050, www.ers.usda.gov; *Farm Business Economic Report.*

RICE - FOREIGN TRADE

U.S. Department of Agriculture, Economic Research Service, 1800 M Street, NW, Washington, D.C. 20036 (202) 694-5050, www.ers.usda.gov; *Agricultural Statistics; Foreign Agricultural Trade of the United States; Food Consumption, Prices, and Expenditures; U.S. Agricultural Trade Update;* and *Agricultural Outlook.*

U.S. Department of Agriculture, Foreign Agricultural Service, Fourteenth Street and Independence Avenue, SW, Washington, D.C. 20250 (202) 720-7115, www.fas.usda.gov; *Foreign Agricultural Commodity Circular Series.*

U.S. Department of Commerce, Bureau of the Census, Washington, D.C. 20233 (301) 457-4100, www.census.gov; *U.S. International Trade in Goods and Services.*

RICE - PRICES

U.S. Department of Agriculture, National Agricultural Statistics Service, Fourteenth Street and Independence Avenue, SW, Washington, D.C. 20250 (800) 727-9540, www.usda.gov/nass; *Agricultural Statistics; Crop Production; Crop Values;* and *Agricultural Outlook.*

RICE - PRODUCTION

U.S. Department of Agriculture, Foreign Agricultural Service, Fourteenth Street and Independence Avenue, SW, Washington, D.C. 20250 (202) 720-7115, www.fas.usda.gov; *Foreign Agricultural Commodity Circular Series.*

U.S. Department of Agriculture, National Agricultural Statistics Service, Fourteenth Street and Independence Avenue, SW, Washington, D.C. 20250 (800) 727-9540; *Agricultural Statistics; Crop Production; Crop Values;* and *Agricultural Outlook.*

RICE - PRODUCTION - WORLD

U.S. Department of Agriculture, Economic Research Service, 1800 M Street, NW, Washington, D.C. 20036 (202) 694-5050, www.ers.usda.gov; *Agricultural Outlook.*

U.S. Department of Agriculture, Foreign Agricultural Service, Fourteenth Street and Independence Avenue, SW, Washington, D.C. 20250 (202) 720-7115, www.fas.usda.gov; *Foreign Agricultural Commodity Circular Series;* and *World Agriculture - Trends and Indicators.*

RICE - SUPPLY AND DISAPPEARANCE

U.S. Department of Agriculture, Economic Research Service, 1800 M Street, NW, Washington, D.C. 20036 (202) 694-5050, www.ers.usda.gov; *Agricultural Supply and Demand Estimates; Agricultural Outlook;* and *Agricultural Statistics.*

RIFLE

National Collegiate Athletic Association, 700 West Washington Street, Indianapolis, Indiana 46206 (317) 917-6222; *1997-98 Participation Study.*

RIVERS, CANALS, HARBORS, ETC. - COMMERCE - DOMESTIC AND FOREIGN

U.S. Department of the Army, Corps of Engineers, The Pentagon, Washington, D.C. 20310 (202) 545-6700; *Waterborne Commerce of the United States.*

RIVERS, CANALS, HARBORS, ETC. - DRAINAGE AREA AND FLOW

U.S. Department of the Interior, Geological Survey, National Center, 12201 Sunrise Valley Drive, Reston, Virginia 22092 (703) 648-4000, www.usgs.gov; *Largest Rivers in the United States.*

RIVERS, CANALS, HARBORS, ETC. - FEDERAL EXPENDITURES FOR

U.S. Department of the Army, Corps of Engineers, The Pentagon, Washington, D.C. 20310 (202) 545-6700; *Report of Civil Works Expenditures by State and Fiscal Year.*

RIVERS, CANALS, HARBORS, ETC. - LENGTH OF PRINCIPAL RIVERS

U.S. Department of the Interior, Geological Survey, National Center, 12201 Sunrise Valley Drive, Reston, Virginia 22092 (703) 648-4000, www.usgs.gov; *Largest Rivers in the United States.*

RIVERS, CANALS, HARBORS, ETC. - WATER QUALITY

U.S. Department of the Interior, Geological Survey, National Center, 12201 Sunrise Valley Drive, Reston, Virginia 22092 (703) 648-4000, www.usgs.gov; *Water - Data Report;* and unpublished data.

ROADS, PUBLIC - See HIGHWAYS

ROADWAY CONGESTION

Texas Transportation Institute, Texas A&M University, Riverside Campus, Building 7751, Safety Division, College Station, Texas 77843 (409) 845-8408; *Roadway Congestion in Major Urban Areas.*

ROBBERY

U.S. Department of Justice, Bureau of Justice Statistics, 810 Seventh Street, NW, 2nd Floor, Washington, D.C. 20531 (800) 732-3277, www.ojp.usdoj.gov/bjs; *Criminal Victimization.*

U.S. Department of Justice, Federal Bureau of Investigation, 935 Pennsylvania Avenue, NW, Washington, D.C. 20535 (202) 324-3691, www.fbi.gov; *Crime in the United States;* and *Population-at-Risk Rates and Selected Crime Indicators.*

ROCKFISH

U.S. Department of Commerce, National Oceanic and Atmospheric Administration, National Marine Fisheries Service, 1315 East-West Highway, Silver Spring, Maryland 20910 (301) 427-2239, www.nmfs.noaa.gov; *Fisheries of the United States.*

RODEOS

Professional Rodeo Cowboys Association, 101 Prorodeo Drive, Colorado Springs, Colorado 80910 (719) 593-8840; *Official Professional Rodeo Media Guide.*

ROLLER SKATING

National Sporting Goods Association, 1601 Feehanville Drive, Suite 300, Mount Prospect, Illinois 60056 (847) 296-6742; *Sports Participation in 1998.*

Romania - National

Statistical Office

Directia Centrala de Statistica, Str. Stavropoleos Number 6, Bucharest, Romania.

Romania - Primary Statistics Source

Comisia Nationala Pentru Statistica, Bucharest, Romania; *Anuarul Statistic Al Romaniei.*

ROMANIA - ABORTIONS

Statistical Office of the United Nations, Publishing Service, New York, New York 10017 (800) 253-9646; *Trends in Europe and North America: The Statistical Yearbook of the Economic Commission for Europe.*

ROMANIA - AGRICULTURE

Economist Intelligence Unit, 111 West 57th Street, New York, New York 10019 (800) 938-4685; *Romania Country Report.*

Euromonitor International, Inc., 122 South Michigan Avenue, Suite 1200, Chicago, Illinois 60603 (800) 577-EURO; *World Marketing Data and Statistics.*

Europa Publications Limited, 18 Bedford Square, London, WC1B 3JN, England; *The Europa World Year Book.*

Food and Agricultural Organization of the United Nations (FAO) Via delle Terme di Caracalla, 00100 Rome, Italy (Telephone Number in U.S. (202) 653-2400); *Production Yearbook; The State of Food and Agriculture;* and *Trade Yearbook.*

M.E. Sharpe, 80 Business Park Drive, Armonk, New York 10504 (800) 541-6563; *The Illustrated Book of World Rankings.*

St. Martin's Press, Inc., 175 Fifth Avenue, New York, New York 10010 (800) 221-7945; *The Statesman's Year-Book.*

Statistical Office of the United Nations, Publishing Service, New York, New York 10017 (800) 253-9646; *Statistical Yearbook.*

United Nations Conference on Trade and Development, Central Statistical Service, Palais des Nations, Geneva, Switzerland (Telephone in U.S. (800) 253-9646); *UNCTAD Commodity Yearbook.*

ROMANIA - AIRLINE SERVICE

Europa Publications Limited, 18 Bedford Square, London, WC1B 3JN, England; *The Europa World Year Book.*

M.E. Sharpe, 80 Business Park Drive, Armonk, New York 10504 (800) 541-6563; *The Illustrated Book of World Rankings.*

St. Martin's Press, Inc., 175 Fifth Avenue, New York, New York 10010 (800) 221-7945; *The Statesman's Year-Book.*

Statistical Office of the United Nations, Publishing Service, New York, New York 10017 (800) 253-9646; *Statistical Yearbook.*

ROMANIA - AIRPORTS

Central Intelligence Agency, Washington, D.C. 20505 (703) 482-1100, www.cia.gov; *The World Factbook.*

ROMANIA - ALUMINUM PRODUCTION AND CONSUMPTION - See ROMANIA - MINING AND MINERAL PRODUCTS

ROMANIA - ANIMAL HEALTH

Food and Agricultural Organization of the United Nations (FAO), Via delle Terme di Caracalla, 00100, Rome, Italy (Telephone Number in U.S. (202) 653-2400); *Animal Health Yearbook.*

ROMANIA - AREA AND DENSITY OF POPULATION

Central Intelligence Agency, Washington, D.C. 20505 (703) 482-1100, www.cia.gov; *The World Factbook.*

Euromonitor International, Inc., 122 South Michigan Avenue, Suite 1200, Chicago, Illinois 60603 (800) 577-EURO; *The World Economic Factbook.*

Europa Publications Limited, 18 Bedford Square, London, WC1B 3JN, England; *The Europa World Year Book.*

Food and Agricultural Organization of the United Nations (FAO) Via delle Terme di Caracalla, 00100 Rome, Italy (Telephone Number in U.S. (202) 653-2400); *The State of Food and Agriculture.*

M.E. Sharpe, 80 Business Park Drive, Armonk, New York 10504 (800) 541-6563; *The Illustrated Book of World Rankings.*

St. Martin's Press, Inc., 175 Fifth Avenue, New York, New York 10010 (800) 221-7945; *The Statesman's Year-Book.*

Statistical Office of the United Nations, Publishing Service, New York, New York 10017 (800) 253-9646; *Statistical Yearbook;* and *Trends in Europe and North America: The Statistical Yearbook of the Economic Commission for Europe..*

United Nations Educational, Scientific and Cultural Organization (UNESCO), 7 Place de Fontenoy, F-75700 Paris, France (Telephone Number in U.S. (212) 963-5981); *Statistical Yearbook.*

The World Bank, 1818 H Street, NW, Washington, D.C. 20433 (202) 477-1234; *World Development Report.*

ROMANIA - ARMS EXPORTS AND IMPORTS - See ROMANIA - MILITARY

ROMANIA - BALANCE OF PAYMENTS

The Economist Intelligence Unit, 111 West 57th Street, New York, New York 10019 (800) 938-4685; *The World Market Atlas.*

Europa Publications Limited, 18 Bedford Square, London, WC1B 3JN, England; *The Europa World Year Book.*

International Monetary Fund, 700 Nineteenth Street, NW, Washington, D.C. 20431 (202) 623-7000; *Balance of Payments Yearbook.*

United Nations Conference on Trade and Development (UNCTAD), New York, New York 10017 (800) 253-9646; *Handbook of International Trade and Development Statistics.*

The World Bank, 1818 H Street, NW, Washington, D.C. 20433 (202) 477-1234; *World Development Report.*

ROMANIA - BANKING

Euromonitor International, Inc., 122 South Michigan Avenue, Suite 1200, Chicago, Illinois 60603 (800) 577-EURO; *World Marketing Data and Statistics.*

Europa Publications Limited, 18 Bedford Square, London, WC1B 3JN, England; *The Europa World Year Book.*

International Monetary Fund, 700 Nineteenth Street, NW, Washington, D.C. 20431 (202) 623-7000; *International Financial Statistics.*

M.E. Sharpe, 80 Business Park Drive, Armonk, New York 10504 (800) 541-6563; *The Illustrated Book of World Rankings.*

St. Martin's Press, Inc., 175 Fifth Avenue, New York, New York 10010 (800) 221-7945; *The Statesman's Year-Book.*

ROMANIA - BARLEY PRODUCTION - See ROMANIA - CROPS

ROMANIA - BAUXITE PRODUCTION AND CONSUMPTION - See ROMANIA - MINING AND MINERAL PRODUCTS

ROMANIA - BEER PRODUCTION - See ROMANIA - BEVERAGES

ROMANIA - BEVERAGES

M.E. Sharpe, 80 Business Park Drive, Armonk, New York 10504 (800) 541-6563;

The Illustrated Book of World Rankings.

Statistical Office of the United Nations, Publishing Service, New York, New York 10017 (800) 253-9646; *Statistical Yearbook.*

ROMANIA - BIRTH RATES

Central Intelligence Agency, Washington, D.C. 20505 (703) 482-1100, www.cia.gov; *The World Factbook.*

Euromonitor International, Inc., 122 South Michigan Avenue, Suite 1200, Chicago, Illinois 60603 (800) 577-EURO; *The World Economic Factbook.*

Europa Publications Limited, 18 Bedford Square, London, WC1B 3JN, England; *The Europa World Year Book.*

M.E. Sharpe, 80 Business Park Drive, Armonk, New York 10504 (800) 541-6563; *The Illustrated Book of World Rankings.*

St. Martin's Press, Inc., 175 Fifth Avenue, New York, New York 10010 (800) 221-7945; *The Statesman's Year-Book.*

Statistical Office of the United Nations, Publishing Service, New York, New York 10017 (800) 253-9646; *Demographic Yearbook;* and *Statistical Yearbook.*

World Health Organization, Office of Publications, 20 Avenue Appia, CH-1211 Geneva 27, Switzerland (Telephone Number in U.S. (518) 436-9686); *World Health Statistics Annual.*

ROMANIA - BISMUTH PRODUCTION AND CONSUMPTION - See ROMANIA - MINING AND MINERAL PRODUCTS

ROMANIA - BOOK PRODUCTION

Euromonitor International, Inc., 122 South Michigan Avenue, Suite 1200, Chicago, Illinois 60603 (800) 577-EURO; *European Marketing Data and Statistics.*

Europa Publications Limited, 18 Bedford Square, London, WC1B 3JN, England; *The Europa World Year Book.*

St. Martin's Press, Inc., 175 Fifth Avenue, New York, New York 10010 (800) 221-7945; *The Statesman's Year-Book.*

Statistical Office of the United Nations, Publishing Service, New York, New York 10017 (800) 253-9646; *Trends in Europe and North America: The Statistical Yearbook of the Economic Commission for Europe.*

United Nations Educational, Scientific and Cultural Organization (UNESCO), 7 Place de Fontenoy, F-75700 Paris, France (Telephone Number in U.S. (212) 963-5981); *Statistical Yearbook.*

ROMANIA - BROADCASTING

Billboard Limited, P.O. Box 9027, 1006 AA Amsterdam, The Netherlands (Telephone Number in U.S. (212) 764-7300); *World Radio TV Handbook.*

Central Intelligence Agency, Washington, D.C. 20505 (703) 482-1100, www.cia.gov; *The World Factbook.*

Euromonitor International, Inc., 122 South Michigan Avenue, Suite 1200, Chicago, Illinois 60603 (800) 577-EURO; *World Marketing Data and Statistics.*

Europa Publications Limited, 18 Bedford Square, London, WC1B 3JN, England; *The Europa World Year Book.*

M.E. Sharpe, 80 Business Park Drive, Armonk, New York 10504 (800) 541-6563; *The Illustrated Book of World Rankings.*

St. Martin's Press, Inc., 175 Fifth Avenue, New York, New York 10010 (800) 221-7945; *The Statesman's Year-Book.*

Statistical Office of the United Nations, Publishing Service, New York, New York 10017 (800) 253-9646; *Trends in Europe and North America: The Statistical Yearbook of the Economic Commission for Europe.*

ROMANIA - BUDGET

Central Intelligence Agency, Washington, D.C. 20505 (703) 482-1100, www.cia.gov; *The World Factbook.*

ROMANIA - BUTTER PRODUCTION - See ROMANIA - DAIRY PRODUCTS

ROMANIA - CABBAGE PRODUCTION - See ROMANIA - CROPS

ROMANIA - CALORIE SUPPLY

Food and Agricultural Organization of the United Nations (FAO) Via delle Terme di Caracalla, 00100 Rome, Italy (Telephone Number in U.S. (202) 653-2400); *The State of Food and Agriculture.*

ROMANIA - CAPITAL REVENUE

International Monetary Fund, 700 Nineteenth Street, NW, Washington, D.C. 20431 (202) 623-7000; *Government Finance Statistics Yearbook.*

ROMANIA - CASTOR BEAN PRODUCTION - See ROMANIA - CROPS

ROMANIA - CATTLE - See ROMANIA - LIVESTOCK AND POULTRY

ROMANIA - CAUSTIC SODA PRODUCTION - See ROMANIA - BEVERAGES

ROMANIA - CEMENT PRODUCTION - See

ROMANIA - MINING AND MINERAL PRODUCTS

ROMANIA - CEREALS PRODUCTION - See ROMANIA - CROPS

ROMANIA - CHEESE PRODUCTION AND CONSUMPTION - See ROMANIA - DAIRY PRODUCTS

ROMANIA - CHEMICAL (ORGANIC) PRODUCTION - See ROMANIA - MINING AND MINERAL PRODUCTS

ROMANIA - CIGARETTE PRODUCTION - See ROMANIA - TOBACCO PRODUCTION

ROMANIA - CLIMATE

M.E. Sharpe, 80 Business Park Drive, Armonk, New York 10504 (800) 541-6563; *The Illustrated Book of World Rankings.*

St. Martin's Press, Inc., 175 Fifth Avenue, New York, New York 10010 (800) 221-7945; *The Statesman's Year-Book.*

ROMANIA - COAL PRODUCTION - See ROMANIA - MINING AND MINERAL PRODUCTS

ROMANIA - COFFEE PRODUCTION AND CONSUMPTION - See ROMANIA - CROPS

ROMANIA - COKE OVEN COKE PRODUCTION AND CONSUMPTION - See ROMANIA - MINING AND MINERAL PRODUCTS

ROMANIA - COMMERCE

St. Martin's Press, Inc., 175 Fifth Avenue, New York, New York 10010 (800) 221-7945; *The Statesman's Year-Book.*

ROMANIA - COMMUNICATIONS - See ROMANIA - TRANSPORTATION AND COMMUNICATIONS

ROMANIA - CONSTRUCTION INDUSTRY

M.E. Sharpe, 80 Business Park Drive, Armonk, New York 10504 (800) 541-6563; *The Illustrated Book of World Rankings.*

St. Martin's Press, Inc., 175 Fifth Avenue, New York, New York 10010 (800) 221-7945; *The Statesman's Year-Book.*

Statistical Office of the United Nations, Publishing Service, New York, New York 10017 (800) 253-9646; *Statistical Yearbook.*

ROMANIA - CONSUMER PRICE INDEX

Statistical Office of the United Nations, Publishing Service, New York, New York 10017 (800) 253-9646; *Statistical Yearbook;* and *Trends in Europe and North America: The Statistical Yearbook of the Economic Commission for Europe.*

ROMANIA - CONSUMER PRICES

Euromonitor International, Inc., 122 South Michigan Avenue, Suite 1200, Chicago, Illinois 60603 (800) 577-EURO; *European Marketing Data and Statistics; and World Marketing Data and Statistics.*

International Labour Office, I.L.O. Publications, 1828 L Street, NW, Suite 801, Washington, D.C. 20036 (301) 638-3152; *Yearbook of Labour Statistics.*

International Monetary Fund, 700 Nineteenth Street, NW, Washington, D.C. 20431 (202) 623-7000; *International Financial Statistics.*

ROMANIA - CONSUMPTION

The World Bank, 1818 H Street, NW, Washington, D.C. 20433 (202) 477-1234; *World Development Report.*

ROMANIA - COPPER PRODUCTION AND CONSUMPTION - See ROMANIA - MINING AND MINERAL PRODUCTS

ROMANIA - CORN PRODUCTION - See ROMANIA - CROPS

ROMANIA - CORPORATE TAXES - See ROMANIA - TAXATION

ROMANIA - COTTON - See ROMANIA - CROPS

ROMANIA - CRIME

Statistical Office of the United Nations, Publishing Service, New York, New York 10017 (800) 253-9646; *Foreign Trade Statistics for Africa; and Trends in Europe and North America: The Statistical Yearbook of the Economic Commission for Europe.*

Yale University Press, Yale Station, New Haven, Connecticut 06520 (800) 987-7323; *Violence and Crime in Cross-National Perspective.*

ROMANIA - CROPS

Commodity Research Bureau, Inc., 30 South Wacker Drive, Chicago Illinois 60606 (312) 454-1801; *Commodity Year Book.*

Euromonitor International, Inc., 122 South Michigan Avenue, Suite 1200, Chicago, Illinois 60603 (800) 577-EURO; *European Marketing Data and Statistics.*

Europa Publications Limited, 18 Bedford Square, London, WC1B 3JN, England; *The Europa World Year Book.*

Food and Agricultural Organization of the United Nations (FAO) Via delle Terme di Caracalla, 00100 Rome, Italy (Telephone Number in U.S. (202) 653-2400);

Production Yearbook; and *The State of Food and Agriculture.*

M.E. Sharpe, 80 Business Park Drive, Armonk, New York 10504 (800) 541-6563; *The Illustrated Book of World Rankings.*

St. Martin's Press, Inc., 175 Fifth Avenue, New York, New York 10010 (800) 221-7945; *The Statesman's Year-Book.*

Statistical Office of the United Nations, Publishing Service, New York, New York 10017 (800) 253-9646; *Statistical Yearbook.*

United Nations Conference on Trade and Development, Central Statistical Service, Palais des Nations, Geneva, Switzerland (Telephone in U.S. (800) 253-9646); *UNCTAD Commodity Yearbook.*

ROMANIA - CUSTOMS DUTIES

St. Martin's Press, Inc., 175 Fifth Avenue, New York, New York 10010 (800) 221-7945; *The Statesman's Year-Book.*

ROMANIA - DAIRY PRODUCTS

Europa Publications Limited, 18 Bedford Square, London, WC1B 3JN, England; *The Europa World Year Book.*

Food and Agricultural Organization of the United Nations (FAO), Via delle Terme di Caracalla, 00100 Rome, Italy (Telephone Number in U.S. (202) 653-2400); *Production Yearbook;* and *The State of Food and Agriculture.*

M.E. Sharpe, 80 Business Park Drive, Armonk, New York 10504 (800) 541-6563; *The Illustrated Book of World Rankings.*

St. Martin's Press, Inc., 175 Fifth Avenue, New York, New York 10010 (800) 221-7945; *The Statesman's Year-Book.*

Statistical Office of the United Nations, Publishing Service, New York, New York 10017 (800) 253-9646; *Statistical Yearbook.*

ROMANIA - DEATH RATES - See ROMANIA - MORTALITY

ROMANIA - DEFENSE EXPENDITURES - See ROMANIA - MILITARY

ROMANIA - DEMOGRAPHY

The Economist Intelligence Unit, 111 West 57th Street, New York, New York 10019 (800) 938-4685; *The World Market Atlas.*

Euromonitor International, Inc., 122 South Michigan Avenue, Suite 1200, Chicago, Illinois 60603 (800) 577-EURO; *The World Economic Factbook;* and *World Marketing Data and Statistics.*

M.E. Sharpe, 80 Business Park Drive, Armonk, New York 10504 (800) 541-6563; *The Illustrated Book of World Rankings.*

Statistical Office of the United Nations, Publishing Service, New York, New York 10017 (800) 253-9646; *Human Development Report.*

ROMANIA - DEVELOPMENT ASSISTANCE

Statistical Office of the United Nations, Publishing Service, New York, New York 10017 (800) 253-9646; *Statistical Yearbook.*

ROMANIA - DIAMOND PRODUCTION - See ROMANIA - MINING AND MINERAL PRODUCTS

ROMANIA - DISEASE - See ROMANIA - HEALTH

ROMANIA - DIVORCE RATES

M.E. Sharpe, 80 Business Park Drive, Armonk, New York 10504 (800) 541-6563; *The Illustrated Book of World Rankings.*

Statistical Office of the United Nations, Publishing Service, New York, New York 10017 (800) 253-9646; *Demographic Yearbook; Statistical Yearbook;* and *Trends in Europe and North America: The Statistical Yearbook of the Economic Commission for Europe.*

ROMANIA - ECONOMY

Central Intelligence Agency, Washington, D.C. 20505 (703) 482-1100, www.cia.gov; *The World Factbook.*

Economist Intelligence Unit, 111 West 57th Street, New York, New York 10019 (800) 938-4685; *Romania Country Report.*

Euromonitor International, Inc., 122 South Michigan Avenue, Suite 1200, Chicago, Illinois 60603 (800) 577-EURO; *European Marketing Data and Statistics; World Marketing Data and Statistics;* and *The World Economic Factbook.*

Europa Publications Limited, 18 Bedford Square, London, WC1B 3JN, England; *The Europa World Year Book.*

M.E. Sharpe, 80 Business Park Drive, Armonk, New York 10504 (800) 541-6563; *The Illustrated Book of World Rankings.*

St. Martin's Press, Inc., 175 Fifth Avenue, New York, New York 10010 (800) 221-7945; *The Statesman's Year-Book.*

Statistical Office of the United Nations, Publishing Service, New York, New York 10017 (800) 253-9646; *World Statistics Pocketbook.*

The World Bank, 1818 H Street, NW, Washington, D.C. 20433 (202) 477-1234; *World Development Report.*

ROMANIA - EDUCATION

The Economist Intelligence Unit, 111 West 57th Street, New York, New York 10019 (800) 938-4685; *The World Market Atlas.*

Euromonitor International, Inc., 122 South Michigan Avenue, Suite 1200, Chicago, Illinois 60603 (800) 577-EURO; *European Marketing Data and Statistics;* and *World Marketing Data and Statistics.*

Europa Publications Limited, 18 Bedford Square, London, WC1B 3JN, England; *The Europa World Year Book.*

M.E. Sharpe, 80 Business Park Drive, Armonk, New York 10504 (800) 541-6563; *The Illustrated Book of World Rankings.*

International Monetary Fund, 700 Nineteenth Street, NW, Washington, D.C. 20431 (202) 623-7000; *Government Finance Statistics Yearbook.*

St. Martin's Press, Inc., 175 Fifth Avenue, New York, New York 10010 (800) 221-7945; *The Statesman's Year-Book.*

Statistical Office of the United Nations, Publishing Service, New York, New York 10017 (800) 253-9646; *Human Development Report;* and *Trends in Europe and North America: The Statistical Yearbook of the Economic Commission for Europe.*

United Nations Educational, Scientific and Cultural Organization (UNESCO), 7 Place de Fontenoy, F-75700 Paris, France (Telephone Number in U.S. (212) 963-5981); *Statistical Yearbook.*

The World Bank, 1818 H Street, NW, Washington, D.C. 20433 (202) 477-1234; *World Development Report.*

ROMANIA - EGG PRODUCTION AND CONSUMPTION - See ROMANIA - DAIRY PRODUCTS

ROMANIA - ELECTRICITY

Central Intelligence Agency, Washington, D.C. 20505 (703) 482-1100, www.cia.gov; *The World Factbook.*

M.E. Sharpe, 80 Business Park Drive, Armonk, New York 10504 (800) 541-6563; *The Illustrated Book of World Rankings.*

Penn Well Publishing Company, 1421 South Sheridan Road, P.O. Box 1260, Tulsa, Oklahoma 74101 (800) 752-9764; *International Energy Statistics Sourcebook.*

St. Martin's Press, Inc., 175 Fifth Avenue, New York, New York 10010 (800) 221-7945; *The Statesman's Year-Book.*

Statistical Office of the United Nations, Publishing Service, New York, New York 10017 (800) 253-9646; *Human Development Report; Statistical Yearbook;* and *Trends in Europe and North America: The Statistical Yearbook of the Economic Commission for Europe.*

ROMANIA - EMPLOYMENT

Euromonitor International, Inc., 122 South Michigan Avenue, Suite 1200, Chicago, Illinois 60603 (800) 577-EURO; *European Marketing Data and Statistics.*

International Labour Office, I.L.O. Publications, 1828 L Street, NW, Suite 801, Washington, D.C. 20036 (301) 638-3152; *Yearbook of Labour Statistics.*

M.E. Sharpe, 80 Business Park Drive, Armonk, New York 10504 (800) 541-6563; *The Illustrated Book of World Rankings.*

Statistical Office of the United Nations, Publishing Service, New York, New York 10017 (800) 253-9646; *Statistical Yearbook;* and *Trends in Europe and North America: The Statistical Yearbook of the Economic Commission for Europe.*

ROMANIA - ENERGY

Euromonitor International, Inc., 122 South Michigan Avenue, Suite 1200, Chicago, Illinois 60603 (800) 577-EURO; *European Marketing Data and Statistics; World Marketing Data and Statistics;* and *The World Economic Factbook.*

Food and Agricultural Organization of the United Nations (FAO) Via delle Terme di Caracalla, 00100 Rome, Italy (Telephone Number in U.S. (202) 653-2400); *The State of Food and Agriculture.*

M.E. Sharpe, 80 Business Park Drive, Armonk, New York 10504 (800) 541-6563; *The Illustrated Book of World Rankings.*

Penn Well Publishing Company, 1421 South Sheridan Road, P.O. Box 1260, Tulsa, Oklahoma 74101 (800) 752-9764; *International Energy Statistics Sourcebook.*

St. Martin's Press, Inc., 175 Fifth Avenue, New York, New York 10010 (800) 221-7945; *The Statesman's Year-Book.*

Statistical Office of the United Nations, Publishing Service, New York, New York 10017 (800) 253-9646; *Energy Statistics Yearbook; Human Development Report; Statistical Yearbook; Trends in Europe and North America: The Statistical Yearbook of the Economic Commission for Europe;* and *World Statistics Pocketbook.*

The World Bank, 1818 H Street, NW, Washington, D.C. 20433 (202) 477-1234; *World Development Report.*

ROMANIA - ENVIRONMENT

Economist Intelligence Unit, 111 West 57th Street, New York, New York 10019 (800) 938-4685; *Romania Country Report.*

Statistical Office of the United Nations, Publishing Service, New York, New York 10017 (800) 253-9646; *Trends in Europe and North America: The Statistical Yearbook of the Economic Commission for Europe;* and *World Statistics Pocketbook.*

ROMANIA - EXCHANGE RATES

Central Intelligence Agency, Washington, D.C. 20505 (703) 482-1100, www.cia.gov; *The World Factbook.*

Euromonitor International, Inc., 122 South Michigan Avenue, Suite 1200, Chicago, Illinois 60603 (800) 577-EURO; *The World Economic Factbook.*

Europa Publications Limited, 18 Bedford Square, London, WC1B 3JN, England; *The Europa World Year Book.*

International Monetary Fund, 700 Nineteenth Street, NW, Washington, D.C. 20431 (202) 623-7000; *International Financial Statistics.*

Statistical Office of the United Nations, Publishing Service, New York, New York 10017 (800) 253-9646; *Statistical Yearbook; Trends in Europe and North America: The Statistical Yearbook of the Economic Commission for Europe;* and *World Statistics Pocketbook.*

ROMANIA - EXPORTS

Central Intelligence Agency, Washington, D.C. 20505 (703) 482-1100, www.cia.gov; *The World Factbook.*

The Economist Intelligence Unit, 111 West 57th Street, New York, New York 10019 (800) 938-4685; *Romania Country Report;* and *The World Market Atlas.*

Euromonitor International, Inc., 122 South Michigan Avenue, Suite 1200, Chicago, Illinois 60603 (800) 577-EURO; *The World Economic Factbook.*

Europa Publications Limited, 18 Bedford Square, London, WC1B 3JN, England; *The Europa World Year Book.*

Food and Agricultural Organization of the United Nations (FAO) Via delle Terme di Caracalla, 00100 Rome, Italy (Telephone Number in U.S. (202) 653-2400); *The State of Food and Agriculture.*

International Monetary Fund, 700 Nineteenth Street, NW, Washington, D.C. 20431 (202) 623-7000; *Direction of Trade Statistics.*

St. Martin's Press, Inc., 175 Fifth Avenue, New York, New York 10010 (800) 221-7945; *The Statesman's Year-Book.*

Statistical Office of the United Nations, Publishing Service, New York, New York 10017 (800) 253-9646; *Trends in Europe and North America: The Statistical Yearbook of the Economic Commission for Europe.*

United Nations Conference on Trade and Development (UNCTAD), New York, New York 10017 (800) 253-9646; *Handbook of International Trade and Development Statistics.*

The World Bank, 1818 H Street, NW, Washington, D.C. 20433 (202) 477-1234; *World Development Report.*

ROMANIA - INTERNAL INDEBTEDNESS

The World Bank, 1818 H Street, NW, Washington, D.C. 20433 (202) 477-1234; *World Development Report.*

ROMANIA - EXTERNAL TRADE

Euromonitor International, Inc., 122 South Michigan Avenue, Suite 1200, Chicago, Illinois 60603 (800) 577-EURO; *World Marketing Data and Statistics.*

Food and Agricultural Organization of the United Nations (FAO) Via delle Terme di Caracalla, 00100 Rome, Italy (Telephone Number in U.S. (202) 653-2400); *The State of Food and Agriculture;* and *Trade Yearbook.*

Statistical Office of the United Nations, Publishing Service, New York, New York 10017 (800) 253-9646; *Statistical Yearbook.*

ROMANIA - FABRIC PRODUCTION - See ROMANIA - TEXTILE INDUSTRY

ROMANIA - FARM CROPS - See ROMANIA - CROPS

ROMANIA - FERTILITY RATES

Central Intelligence Agency, Washington, D.C. 20505 (703) 482-1100, www.cia.gov; *The World Factbook.*

M.E. Sharpe, 80 Business Park Drive, Armonk, New York 10504 (800) 541-6563; *The Illustrated Book of World Rankings.*

Statistical Office of the United Nations, Publishing Service, New York, New York 10017 (800) 253-9646; *Human Development Report;* and *Trends in Europe and North America: The Statistical Yearbook of the Economic Commission for*

Europe.

The World Bank, 1818 H Street, NW, Washington, D.C. 20433 (202) 477-1234; *World Development Report.*

ROMANIA - FERTILIZER

Food and Agricultural Organization of the United Nations (FAO) Via delle Terme di Caracalla, 00100 Rome, Italy (Telephone Number in U.S. (202) 653-2400); *The State of Food and Agriculture.*

Statistical Office of the United Nations, Publishing Service, New York, New York 10017 (800) 253-9646; *Statistical Yearbook.*

ROMANIA - FETAL MORTALITY - See ROMANIA - MORTALITY

ROMANIA - FIBRE PRODUCTION - See ROMANIA - TEXTILE INDUSTRY

ROMANIA - FILAMENT PRODUCTION - See ROMANIA - TEXTILE INDUSTRY

ROMANIA - FILM - See ROMANIA - MOTION PICTURES

ROMANIA - FINANCE

Economist Intelligence Unit, 111 West 57th Street, New York, New York 10019 (800) 938-4685; *Romania Country Report.*

Europa Publications Limited, 18 Bedford Square, London, WC1B 3JN, England; *The Europa World Year Book.*

International Monetary Fund, 700 Nineteenth Street, NW, Washington, D.C. 20431 (202) 623-7000; *International Financial Statistics.*

M.E. Sharpe, 80 Business Park Drive, Armonk, New York 10504 (800) 541-6563; *The Illustrated Book of World Rankings.*

St. Martin's Press, Inc., 175 Fifth Avenue, New York, New York 10010 (800) 221-7945; *The Statesman's Year-Book.*

ROMANIA - FISHERIES

Euromonitor International, Inc., 122 South Michigan Avenue, Suite 1200, Chicago, Illinois 60603 (800) 577-EURO; *European Marketing Data and Statistics.*

Europa Publications Limited, 18 Bedford Square, London, WC1B 3JN, England; *The Europa World Year Book.*

Food and Agricultural Organization of the United Nations (FAO) Via delle Terme di Caracalla, 00100 Rome, Italy (Telephone Number in U.S. (202) 653-2400); *The State of Food and Agriculture;* and *Yearbook of Fishery Statistics.*

M.E. Sharpe, 80 Business Park Drive, Armonk, New York 10504 (800) 541-6563; *The Illustrated Book of World Rankings.*

Statistical Office of the United Nations, Publishing Service, New York, New York 10017 (800) 253-9646; *Statistical Yearbook.*

United Nations Conference on Trade and Development, Central Statistical Service, Palais des Nations, Geneva, Switzerland (Telephone in U.S. (800) 253-9646); *UNCTAD Commodity Yearbook.*

ROMANIA - FLAX PRODUCTION - See ROMANIA - TEXTILE INDUSTRY

ROMANIA - FLOUR PRODUCTION

Statistical Office of the United Nations, Publishing Service, New York, New York 10017 (800) 253-9646; *Statistical Yearbook.*

ROMANIA - FOOD

Euromonitor International, Inc., 122 South Michigan Avenue, Suite 1200, Chicago, Illinois 60603 (800) 577-EURO; *Retail Trade International.*

Food and Agricultural Organization of the United Nations (FAO) Via delle Terme di Caracalla, 00100 Rome, Italy (Telephone Number in U.S. (202) 653-2400); *Production Yearbook;* and *The State of Food and Agriculture.*

Statistical Office of the United Nations, Publishing Service, New York, New York 10017 (800) 253-9646; *Human Development Report.*

United Nations Conference on Trade and Development, Central Statistical Service, Palais des Nations, Geneva, Switzerland (Telephone in U.S. (800) 253-9646); *UNCTAD Commodity Yearbook.*

ROMANIA - FOREIGN DEBT

St. Martin's Press, Inc., 175 Fifth Avenue, New York, New York 10010 (800) 221-7945; *The Statesman's Year-Book.*

ROMANIA - FOREIGN TRADE

Economist Intelligence Unit, 111 West 57th Street, New York, New York 10019 (800) 938-4685; *Romania Country Report.*

Euromonitor International, Inc., 122 South Michigan Avenue, Suite 1200, Chicago, Illinois 60603 (800) 577-EURO; *The World Economic Factbook.*

Europa Publications Limited, 18 Bedford Square, London, WC1B 3JN, England; *The Europa World Year Book.*

M.E. Sharpe, 80 Business Park Drive, Armonk, New York 10504 (800) 541-6563;

The Illustrated Book of World Rankings.

St. Martin's Press, Inc., 175 Fifth Avenue, New York, New York 10010 (800) 221-7945; *The Statesman's Year-Book.*

Statistical Office of the United Nations, Publishing Service, New York, New York 10017 (800) 253-9646; *International Trade Statistics Yearbook;* and *Statistical Yearbook.*

United Nations Conference on Trade and Development, Central Statistical Service, Palais des Nations, Geneva, Switzerland (Telephone in U.S. (800) 253-9646); *UNCTAD Commodity Yearbook.*

The World Bank, 1818 H Street, NW, Washington, D.C. 20433 (202) 477-1234; *World Development Report.*

ROMANIA - FORESTRY AND FOREST PRODUCTS

Euromonitor International, Inc., 122 South Michigan Avenue, Suite 1200, Chicago, Illinois 60603 (800) 577-EURO; *European Marketing Data and Statistics.*

Europa Publications Limited, 18 Bedford Square, London, WC1B 3JN, England; *The Europa World Year Book.*

Food and Agricultural Organization of the United Nations (FAO) Via delle Terme di Caracalla, 00100 Rome, Italy (Telephone Number in U.S. (202) 653-2400); *The State of Food and Agriculture;* and *Yearbook of Forest Products.*

M.E. Sharpe, 80 Business Park Drive, Armonk, New York 10504 (800) 541-6563; *The Illustrated Book of World Rankings.*

St. Martin's Press, Inc., 175 Fifth Avenue, New York, New York 10010 (800) 221-7945; *The Statesman's Year-Book.*

Statistical Office of the United Nations, Publishing Service, New York, New York 10017 (800) 253-9646; *Statistical Yearbook;* and *Trends in Europe and North America: The Statistical Yearbook of the Economic Commission for Europe.*

United Nations Conference on Trade and Development, Central Statistical Service, Palais des Nations, Geneva, Switzerland (Telephone in U.S. (800) 253-9646); *UNCTAD Commodity Yearbook.*

United Nations Educational, Scientific and Cultural Organization (UNESCO), 7 Place de Fontenoy, F-75700 Paris, France (Telephone Number in U.S. (212) 963-5981); *Statistical Yearbook.*

The World Bank, 1818 H Street, NW, Washington, D.C. 20433 (202) 477-1234; *World Development Report.*

ROMANIA - GARLIC PRODUCTION - See ROMANIA - CROPS

ROMANIA - GAS LIQUIDS (NATURAL) PRODUCTION - See ROMANIA - MINING AND MINERAL PRODUCTS

ROMANIA - GAS PRODUCTION - See ROMANIA - MINING AND MINERAL PRODUCTS

ROMANIA - GENERAL MORTALITY - See ROMANIA - MORTALITY

ROMANIA - GEOGRAPHIC DATA

M.E. Sharpe, 80 Business Park Drive, Armonk, New York 10504 (800) 541-6563; *The Illustrated Book of World Rankings.*

ROMANIA - GOLD HOLDINGS

International Monetary Fund, 700 Nineteenth Street, NW, Washington, D.C. 20431 (202) 623-7000; *International Financial Statistics.*

ROMANIA - GOLD PRODUCTION AND CONSUMPTION - See ROMANIA - MINING AND MINERAL PRODUCTS

ROMANIA - GOVERNMENT

Central Intelligence Agency, Washington, D.C. 20505 (703) 482-1100, www.cia.gov; *The World Factbook.*

Europa Publications Limited, 18 Bedford Square, London, WC1B 3JN, England; *The Europa World Year Book.*

International Monetary Fund, 700 Nineteenth Street, NW, Washington, D.C. 20431 (202) 623-7000; *Government Finance Statistics Yearbook;* and *International Financial Statistics.*

St. Martin's Press, Inc., 175 Fifth Avenue, New York, New York 10010 (800) 221-7945; *The Statesman's Year-Book.*

Statistical Office of the United Nations, Publishing Service, New York, New York 10017 (800) 253-9646; *National Accounts Statistics;* and *Statistical Yearbook.*

The World Bank, 1818 H Street, NW, Washington, D.C. 20433 (202) 477-1234; *World Development Report.*

ROMANIA - GRAIN PRODUCTION - See ROMANIA - CROPS

ROMANIA - GRANTS

International Monetary Fund, 700 Nineteenth Street, NW, Washington, D.C. 20431 (202) 623-7000; *Government Finance Statistics Yearbook.*

ROMANIA - GREEN PEPPER AND CHILIE

PRODUCTION - See ROMANIA - CROPS

ROMANIA - GROSS DOMESTIC PRODUCT

The Economist Intelligence Unit, 111 West 57th Street, New York, New York 10019 (800) 938-4685; *Romania Country Report;* and *The World Market Atlas.*

Euromonitor International, Inc., 122 South Michigan Avenue, Suite 1200, Chicago, Illinois 60603 (800) 577-EURO; *The World Economic Factbook.*

M.E. Sharpe, 80 Business Park Drive, Armonk, New York 10504 (800) 541-6563; *The Illustrated Book of World Rankings.*

Statistical Office of the United Nations, Publishing Service, New York, New York 10017 (800) 253-9646; *Human Development Report; National Accounts Statistics; Statistical Yearbook;* and *Trends in Europe and North America: The Statistical Yearbook of the Economic Commission for Europe.*

The World Bank, 1818 H Street, NW, Washington, D.C. 20433 (202) 477-1234; *World Development Report.*

ROMANIA - GROSS NATIONAL PRODUCT

St. Martin's Press, Inc., 175 Fifth Avenue, New York, New York 10010 (800) 221-7945; *The Statesman's Year-Book.*

U.S. Arms Control and Disarmament Agency, 320 Twenty-first Street, NW, Washington, D.C. 20451 (202) 647-8677; *World Military Expenditures and Arms Transfers.*

The World Bank, 1818 H Street, NW, Washington, D.C. 20433 (202) 477-1234; *World Development Report.*

ROMANIA - HEALTH

Euromonitor International, Inc., 122 South Michigan Avenue, Suite 1200, Chicago, Illinois 60603 (800) 577-EURO; *World Marketing Data and Statistics.*

M.E. Sharpe, 80 Business Park Drive, Armonk, New York 10504 (800) 541-6563; *The Illustrated Book of World Rankings.*

St. Martin's Press, Inc., 175 Fifth Avenue, New York, New York 10010 (800) 221-7945; *The Statesman's Year-Book.*

Statistical Office of the United Nations, Publishing Service, New York, New York 10017 (800) 253-9646; *Human Development Report; Statistical Yearbook;* and *Trends in Europe and North America: The Statistical Yearbook of the Economic Commission for Europe.*

United Nations Children's Fund (UNICEF), 3 United Nations Plaza, New York, New York 10017 (800) 253-9646; *State of the World's Children.*

The World Bank, 1818 H Street, NW, Washington, D.C. 20433 (202) 477-1234; *World Development Report.*

World Health Organization, Office of Publications, 20 Avenue Appia, CH-1211 Geneva 27, Switzerland (Telephone Number in U.S. (518) 436-9686); *World Health Statistics Annual.*

ROMANIA - HEALTH EXPENDITURES

International Monetary Fund, 700 Nineteenth Street, NW, Washington, D.C. 20431 (202) 623-7000; *Government Finance Statistics Yearbook.*

ROMANIA - HEMP FIBRE PRODUCTION - See ROMANIA - TEXTILE INDUSTRY

ROMANIA - HIDE PRODUCTION

Food and Agricultural Organization of the United Nations (FAO), Via delle Terme di Caracalla, 00100 Rome, Italy (Telephone Number in U.S. (202) 653-2400); *Production Yearbook.*

ROMANIA - HIGHWAYS

Central Intelligence Agency, Washington, D.C. 20505 (703) 482-1100, www.cia.gov; *The World Factbook.*

International Road Federation, 2600 Virginia Avenue, NW, Washington, D.C. 20037 (202) 338-4641; *World Road Statistics.*

St. Martin's Press, Inc., 175 Fifth Avenue, New York, New York 10010 (800) 221-7945; *The Statesman's Year-Book.*

Statistical Office of the United Nations, Publishing Service, New York, New York 10017 (800) 253-9646; *Annual Bulletin of Transport Statistics for Europe;* and *Trends in Europe and North America: The Statistical Yearbook of the Economic Commission for Europe.*

ROMANIA - HOPS PRODUCTION - See ROMANIA - CROPS

ROMANIA - HORSES - See ROMANIA - LIVESTOCK AND POULTRY

ROMANIA - HOURS OF WORK - See ROMANIA - EMPLOYMENT

ROMANIA - HOUSING AND HOUSING UNITS

Euromonitor International, Inc., 122 South Michigan Avenue, Suite 1200, Chicago, Illinois 60603 (800) 577-EURO; *World Marketing Data and Statistics.*

M.E. Sharpe, 80 Business Park Drive, Armonk, New York 10504 (800) 541-6563; *The Illustrated Book of World Rankings.*

Statistical Office of the United Nations, Publishing Service, New York, New York 10017 (800) 253-9646; *Trends in Europe and North America: The Statistical Yearbook of the Economic Commission for Europe.*

ROMANIA - HYDROCHLORIC ACID PRODUCTION

Statistical Office of the United Nations, Publishing Service, New York, New York 10017 (800) 253-9646; *Statistical Yearbook.*

ROMANIA - ILLITERATE POPULATION

Central Intelligence Agency, Washington, D.C. 20505 (703) 482-1100, www.cia.gov; *The World Factbook.*

The Economist Intelligence Unit, 111 West 57th Street, New York, New York 10019 (800) 938-4685; *The World Market Atlas.*

Euromonitor International, Inc., 122 South Michigan Avenue, Suite 1200, Chicago, Illinois 60603 (800) 577-EURO; *The World Economic Factbook.*

Statistical Office of the United Nations, Publishing Service, New York, New York 10017 (800) 253-9646; *Human Development Report.*

United Nations Educational, Scientific and Cultural Organization (UNESCO), 7 Place de Fontenoy, F-75700 Paris, France (Telephone Number in U.S. (212) 963-5981); *Statistical Yearbook.*

ROMANIA - IMPORTS

Central Intelligence Agency, Washington, D.C. 20505 (703) 482-1100, www.cia.gov; *The World Factbook.*

The Economist Intelligence Unit, 111 West 57th Street, New York, New York 10019 (800) 938-4685; *Romania Country Report;* and *The World Market Atlas.*

Euromonitor International, Inc., 122 South Michigan Avenue, Suite 1200, Chicago, Illinois 60603 (800) 577-EURO; *The World Economic Factbook.*

Europa Publications Limited, 18 Bedford Square, London, WC1B 3JN, England; *The Europa World Year Book.*

Food and Agricultural Organization of the United Nations (FAO) Via delle Terme di Caracalla, 00100 Rome, Italy (Telephone Number in U.S. (202) 653-2400); *The State of Food and Agriculture.*

International Monetary Fund, 700 Nineteenth Street, NW, Washington, D.C. 20431 (202) 623-7000; *Direction of Trade Statistics.*

St. Martin's Press, Inc., 175 Fifth Avenue, New York, New York 10010 (800) 221-7945; *The Statesman's Year-Book.*

Statistical Office of the United Nations, Publishing Service, New York, New York 10017 (800) 253-9646; *Trends in Europe and North America: The Statistical Yearbook of the Economic Commission for Europe.*

United Nations Conference on Trade and Development (UNCTAD), New York, New York 10017 (800) 253-9646; *Handbook of International Trade and Development Statistics.*

The World Bank, 1818 H Street, NW, Washington, D.C. 20433 (202) 477-1234; *World Development Report.*

ROMANIA - INCOME TAXES - See ROMANIA - TAXATION

ROMANIA - INDUSTRIAL METALS PRODUCTION - See ROMANIA - MINING AND MINERAL PRODUCTS

ROMANIA - INDUSTRY

Central Intelligence Agency, Washington, D.C. 20505 (703) 482-1100, www.cia.gov; *The World Factbook.*

Economist Intelligence Unit, 111 West 57th Street, New York, New York 10019 (800) 938-4685; *Romania Country Report.*

Euromonitor International, Inc., 122 South Michigan Avenue, Suite 1200, Chicago, Illinois 60603 (800) 577-EURO; *The World Economic Factbook;* and *World Marketing Data and Statistics.*

Europa Publications Limited, 18 Bedford Square, London, WC1B 3JN, England; *The Europa World Year Book.*

International Labour Office, I.L.O. Publications, 1828 L Street, NW, Suite 801, Washington, D.C. 20036 (301) 638-3152; *Yearbook of Labour Statistics.*

M.E. Sharpe, 80 Business Park Drive, Armonk, New York 10504 (800) 541-6563; *The Illustrated Book of World Rankings.*

St. Martin's Press, Inc., 175 Fifth Avenue, New York, New York 10010 (800) 221-7945; *The Statesman's Year-Book.*

Statistical Office of the United Nations, Publishing Service, New York, New York 10017 (800) 253-9646; *Industrial Commodity Statistics Yearbook; Statistical Yearbook;* and *Trends in Europe and North America: The Statistical Yearbook of the*

Economic Commission for Europe.

World Intellectual Property Organization, 34 Chemin des Colombettes, CH-1211 Geneva 20. Switzerland; *Industrial Property Statistics.*

ROMANIA - INFANT AND MATERNAL MORTALITY - See ROMANIA - MORTALITY

ROMANIA - INTERNATIONAL LIQUIDITY

International Monetary Fund, 700 Nineteenth Street, NW, Washington, D.C. 20431 (202) 623-7000; *International Financial Statistics.*

ROMANIA - INTERNATIONAL RESERVES EXCLUDING GOLD

Statistical Office of the United Nations, Publishing Service, New York, New York 10017 (800) 253-9646; *Statistical Yearbook.*

ROMANIA - IRON ORE PRODUCTION AND CONSUMPTION - See ROMANIA - MINING AND MINERAL PRODUCTS

ROMANIA - LABOR

Central Intelligence Agency, Washington, D.C. 20505 (703) 482-1100, www.cia.gov; *The World Factbook.*

Euromonitor International, Inc., 122 South Michigan Avenue, Suite 1200, Chicago, Illinois 60603 (800) 577-EURO; *World Marketing Data and Statistics.*

Europa Publications Limited, 18 Bedford Square, London, WC1B 3JN, England; *The Europa World Year Book.*

Food and Agricultural Organization of the United Nations (FAO) Via delle Terme di Caracalla, 00100 Rome, Italy (Telephone Number in U.S. (202) 653-2400); *The State of Food and Agriculture.*

International Labour Office, I.L.O. Publications, 1828 L Street, NW, Suite 801, Washington, D.C. 20036 (301) 638-3152; *Yearbook of Labour Statistics.*

M.E. Sharpe, 80 Business Park Drive, Armonk, New York 10504 (800) 541-6563; *The Illustrated Book of World Rankings.*

St. Martin's Press, Inc., 175 Fifth Avenue, New York, New York 10010 (800) 221-7945; *The Statesman's Year-Book.*

Statistical Office of the United Nations, Publishing Service, New York, New York 10017 (800) 253-9646; *Human Development Report.*

The World Bank, 1818 H Street, NW, Washington, D.C. 20433 (202) 477-1234; *World Development Report.*

ROMANIA - LAND USE

Central Intelligence Agency, Washington, D.C. 20505 (703) 482-1100, www.cia.gov; *The World Factbook.*

Euromonitor International, Inc., 122 South Michigan Avenue, Suite 1200, Chicago, Illinois 60603 (800) 577-EURO; *European Marketing Data and Statistics.*

Food and Agricultural Organization of the United Nations (FAO), Via delle Terme di Caracalla, 00100 Rome, Italy (Telephone Number in U.S. (202) 653-2400); *Production Yearbook.*

The World Bank, 1818 H Street, NW, Washington, D.C. 20433 (202) 477-1234; *World Development Report.*

ROMANIA - LEAD AND LEAD ORE PRODUCTION AND CONSUMPTION - See ROMANIA - MINING AND MINERAL PRODUCTS

ROMANIA - LIBRARIES

Euromonitor International, Inc., 122 South Michigan Avenue, Suite 1200, Chicago, Illinois 60603 (800) 577-EURO; *European Marketing Data and Statistics.*

M.E. Sharpe, 80 Business Park Drive, Armonk, New York 10504 (800) 541-6563; *The Illustrated Book of World Rankings.*

Statistical Office of the United Nations, Publishing Service, New York, New York 10017 (800) 253-9646; *Statistical Yearbook;* and *Trends in Europe and North America: The Statistical Yearbook of the Economic Commission for Europe.*

United Nations Educational, Scientific and Cultural Organization (UNESCO), 7 Place de Fontenoy, F-75700 Paris, France (Telephone Number in U.S. (212) 963-5981); *Statistical Yearbook.*

ROMANIA - LIFE EXPECTANCY

Central Intelligence Agency, Washington, D.C. 20505 (703) 482-1100, www.cia.gov; *The World Factbook.*

Euromonitor International, Inc., 122 South Michigan Avenue, Suite 1200, Chicago, Illinois 60603 (800) 577-EURO; *The World Economic Factbook.*

St. Martin's Press, Inc., 175 Fifth Avenue, New York, New York 10010 (800) 221-7945; *The Statesman's Year-Book.*

Statistical Office of the United Nations, Publishing Service, New York, New York 10017 (800) 253-9646; *Human Development Report; Trends in Europe and North America: The Statistical Yearbook of the Economic Commission for Europe;* and

World Statistics Pocketbook.

The World Bank, 1818 H Street, NW, Washington, D.C. 20433 (202) 477-1234; *World Development Report.*

ROMANIA - LIGNITE PRODUCTION - See ROMANIA - MINING AND MINERAL PRODUCTS

ROMANIA - LITERACY RATE

Euromonitor International, Inc., 122 South Michigan Avenue, Suite 1200, Chicago, Illinois 60603 (800) 577-EURO; *World Marketing Data and Statistics.*

ROMANIA - LIVESTOCK AND POULTRY

Euromonitor International, Inc., 122 South Michigan Avenue, Suite 1200, Chicago, Illinois 60603 (800) 577-EURO; *European Marketing Data and Statistics.*

Europa Publications Limited, 18 Bedford Square, London, WC1B 3JN, England; *The Europa World Year Book.*

Food and Agricultural Organization of the United Nations (FAO), Via delle Terme di Caracalla, 00100 Rome, Italy (Telephone Number in U.S. (202) 653-2400); *Production Yearbook;* and *The State of Food and Agriculture.*

M.E. Sharpe, 80 Business Park Drive, Armonk, New York 10504 (800) 541-6563; *The Illustrated Book of World Rankings.*

St. Martin's Press, Inc., 175 Fifth Avenue, New York, New York 10010 (800) 221-7945; *The Statesman's Year-Book.*

Statistical Office of the United Nations, Publishing Service, New York, New York 10017 (800) 253-9646; *Statistical Yearbook.*

United Nations Conference on Trade and Development, Central Statistical Service, Palais des Nations, Geneva, Switzerland (Telephone in U.S. (800) 253-9646); *UNCTAD Commodity Yearbook.*

ROMANIA - LIVING LEVELS - See ROMANIA - LIFE EXPECTANCY
ROMANIA - MAIL - NUMBER OF PIECES SENT OR RECEIVED

Statistical Office of the United Nations, Publishing Service, New York, New York 10017 (800) 253-9646; *Statistical Yearbook.*

ROMANIA - MANGANESE ORE PRODUCTION AND CONSUMPTION - See ROMANIA - MINING AND MINERAL PRODUCTS

ROMANIA - MANUFACTURING

M.E. Sharpe, 80 Business Park Drive,

Armonk, New York 10504 (800) 541-6563; *The Illustrated Book of World Rankings.*

Statistical Office of the United Nations, Publishing Service, New York, New York 10017 (800) 253-9646; *Statistical Yearbook.*

ROMANIA - MARRIAGE RATES

Europa Publications Limited, 18 Bedford Square, London, WC1B 3JN, England; *The Europa World Year Book.*

M.E. Sharpe, 80 Business Park Drive, Armonk, New York 10504 (800) 541-6563; *The Illustrated Book of World Rankings.*

Statistical Office of the United Nations, Publishing Service, New York, New York 10017 (800) 253-9646; *Demographic Yearbook; Statistical Yearbook;* and *Trends in Europe and North America: The Statistical Yearbook of the Economic Commission for Europe.*

ROMANIA - MEAT PRODUCTION - See ROMANIA - LIVESTOCK AND POULTRY

ROMANIA - MERCHANT SHIPPING

Europa Publications Limited, 18 Bedford Square, London, WC1B 3JN, England; *The Europa World Year Book.*

Lloyd's Register of Shipping, 17 Battery Place, New York, New York 10004 (212) 425-8050; *Register of Ships.*

St. Martin's Press, Inc., 175 Fifth Avenue, New York, New York 10010 (800) 221-7945; *The Statesman's Year-Book.*

Statistical Office of the United Nations, Publishing Service, New York, New York 10017 (800) 253-9646; *Annual Bulletin of Transport Statistics for Europe;* and *Statistical Yearbook.*

U.S. Department of Transportation, Maritime Administration, 400 Seventh Street, SW, Washington, D.C. 20590 (202) 366-5807, www.marad.dot.gov; *A Statistical Analysis of the World's Merchant Fleets.*

ROMANIA - MILITARY

Central Intelligence Agency, Washington, D.C. 20505 (703) 482-1100, www.cia.gov; *The World Factbook.*

Euromonitor International, Inc., 122 South Michigan Avenue, Suite 1200, Chicago, Illinois 60603 (800) 577-EURO; *World Marketing Data and Statistics.*

The International Institute for Strategic Studies, 23 Tavistock Street, London WC2E 7NQ, England; *The Military Balance.*

International Monetary Fund, 700

Nineteenth Street, NW, Washington, D.C. 20431 (202) 623-7000; *Government Finance Statistics Yearbook.*

St. Martin's Press, Inc., 175 Fifth Avenue, New York, New York 10010 (800) 221-7945; *The Statesman's Year-Book.*

Statistical Office of the United Nations, Publishing Service, New York, New York 10017 (800) 253-9646; *Human Development Report.*

U.S. Arms Control and Disarmament Agency, 320 Twenty-first Street, NW, Washington, D.C. 20451 (202) 647-8677; *World Military Expenditures and Arms Transfers.*

ROMANIA - MILK - See ROMANIA - DAIRY PRODUCTS

ROMANIA - MINING AND MINERAL PRODUCTS

Commodity Research Bureau, Inc., 30 South Wacker Drive, Chicago Illinois 60606 (312) 454-1801; *Commodity Year Book.*

Europa Publications Limited, 18 Bedford Square, London, WC1B 3JN, England; *The Europa World Year Book.*

M.E. Sharpe, 80 Business Park Drive, Armonk, New York 10504 (800) 541-6563; *The Illustrated Book of World Rankings.*

Penn Well Publishing Company, 1421 South Sheridan Road, P.O. Box 1260, Tulsa, Oklahoma 74101 (800) 752-9764; *International Energy Statistics Sourcebook.*

St. Martin's Press, Inc., 175 Fifth Avenue, New York, New York 10010 (800) 221-7945; *The Statesman's Year-Book.*

Statistical Office of the United Nations, Publishing Service, New York, New York 10017 (800) 253-9646; *Statistical Yearbook.*

United Nations Conference on Trade and Development, Central Statistical Service, Palais des Nations, Geneva, Switzerland (Telephone in U.S. (800) 253-9646); *UNCTAD Commodity Yearbook.*

ROMANIA - MONEY EXCHANGE RATES - See ROMANIA - EXCHANGE RATES

ROMANIA - MONEY SUPPLY

Economist Intelligence Unit, 111 West 57th Street, New York, New York 10019 (800) 938-4685; *Romania Country Report.*

Europa Publications Limited, 18 Bedford Square, London, WC1B 3JN, England; *The Europa World Year Book.*

International Monetary Fund, 700 Nineteenth Street, NW, Washington, D.C.

20431 (202) 623-7000; *International Financial Statistics.*

ROMANIA - MORTALITY

Central Intelligence Agency, Washington, D.C. 20505 (703) 482-1100, www.cia.gov; *The World Factbook.*

Euromonitor International, Inc., 122 South Michigan Avenue, Suite 1200, Chicago, Illinois 60603 (800) 577-EURO; *The World Economic Factbook.*

Europa Publications Limited, 18 Bedford Square, London, WC1B 3JN, England; *The Europa World Year Book.*

St. Martin's Press, Inc., 175 Fifth Avenue, New York, New York 10010 (800) 221-7945; *The Statesman's Year-Book.*

Statistical Office of the United Nations, Publishing Service, New York, New York 10017 (800) 253-9646; *Demographic Yearbook; Human Development Report; Statistical Yearbook; Trends in Europe and North America: The Statistical Yearbook of the Economic Commission for Europe;* and *World Statistics Pocketbook.*

United Nations Children's Fund (UNICEF), 3 United Nations Plaza, New York, New York 10017 (800) 253-9646; *State of the World's Children.*

The World Bank, 1818 H Street, NW, Washington, D.C. 20433 (202) 477-1234; *World Development Report.*

World Health Organization, Office of Publications, 20 Avenue Appia, CH-1211 Geneva 27, Switzerland (Telephone Number in U.S. (518) 436-9686); *World Health Statistics Annual.*

ROMANIA - MOTION PICTURES

St. Martin's Press, Inc., 175 Fifth Avenue, New York, New York 10010 (800) 221-7945; *The Statesman's Year-Book.*

Statistical Office of the United Nations, Publishing Service, New York, New York 10017 (800) 253-9646; *Statistical Yearbook.*

United Nations Educational, Scientific and Cultural Organization (UNESCO), 7 Place de Fontenoy, F-75700 Paris, France (Telephone Number in U.S. (212) 963-5981); *Statistical Yearbook.*

ROMANIA - MOTOR VEHICLE PRODUCTION AND ASSEMBLY

Statistical Office of the United Nations, Publishing Service, New York, New York 10017 (800) 253-9646; *Statistical Yearbook.*

ROMANIA - MOTOR VEHICLES IN USE

International Road Federation, 2600 Virginia Avenue, NW, Washington, D.C. 20037 (202) 338-4641; *World Road Statistics.*

Statistical Office of the United Nations, Publishing Service, New York, New York 10017 (800) 253-9646; *Statistical Yearbook.*

ROMANIA - MUSEUMS

Euromonitor International, Inc., 122 South Michigan Avenue, Suite 1200, Chicago, Illinois 60603 (800) 577-EURO; *European Marketing Data and Statistics.*

M.E. Sharpe, 80 Business Park Drive, Armonk, New York 10504 (800) 541-6563; *The Illustrated Book of World Rankings.*

United Nations Educational, Scientific and Cultural Organization (UNESCO), 7 Place de Fontenoy, F-75700 Paris, France (Telephone Number in U.S. (212) 963-5981); *Statistical Yearbook.*

ROMANIA - NATALITY - See ROMANIA - BIRTH RATE

ROMANIA - NATIONAL ACCOUNTS

Statistical Office of the United Nations, Publishing Service, New York, New York 10017 (800) 253-9646; *National Accounts Statistics;* and *Statistical Yearbook.*

ROMANIA - NATIONAL INCOME

M.E. Sharpe, 80 Business Park Drive, Armonk, New York 10504 (800) 541-6563; *The Illustrated Book of World Rankings.*

Statistical Office of the United Nations, Publishing Service, New York, New York 10017 (800) 253-9646; *National Accounts Statistics;* and *Statistical Yearbook.*

ROMANIA - NATIONAL PRODUCT

M.E. Sharpe, 80 Business Park Drive, Armonk, New York 10504 (800) 541-6563; *The Illustrated Book of World Rankings.*

Statistical Office of the United Nations, Publishing Service, New York, New York 10017 (800) 253-9646; *Statistical Yearbook.*

ROMANIA - NATURAL GAS PRODUCTION - See ROMANIA - MINING AND MINERAL PRODUCTS

ROMANIA - NET MATERIAL PRODUCT

Statistical Office of the United Nations, Publishing Service, New York, New York 10017 (800) 253-9646; *Statistical Yearbook.*

ROMANIA - NEWSPAPER PRODUCTION - See ROMANIA - FORESTRY AND FOREST PRODUCTS

ROMANIA - NEWSPRINT PRODUCTION AND CONSUMPTION - See ROMANIA - FORESTRY AND FOREST PRODUCTS

ROMANIA - NITRIC ACID PRODUCTION - See ROMANIA - MINING AND MINERAL PRODUCTS

ROMANIA - OATS PRODUCTION - See ROMANIA - CROPS

ROMANIA - OCCUPATIONS - See ROMANIA - LABOR

ROMANIA - ONION PRODUCTION - See ROMANIA - CROPS

ROMANIA - PAPER PRODUCTION - See ROMANIA - FORESTRY AND FOREST PRODUCTS

ROMANIA - PATENTS, TRADEMARKS AND SERVICE MARKS

Statistical Office of the United Nations, Publishing Service, New York, New York 10017 (800) 253-9646; *Statistical Yearbook.*

World Intellectual Property Organization, 34 Chemin des Colombettes, CH-1211 Geneva 20. Switzerland; *Industrial Property Statistics.*

ROMANIA - PEANUT PRODUCTION - See ROMANIA - CROPS

ROMANIA - PERIODICALS

United Nations Educational, Scientific and Cultural Organization (UNESCO), 7 Place de Fontenoy, F-75700 Paris, France (Telephone Number in U.S. (212) 963-5981); *Statistical Yearbook.*

ROMANIA - PESTICIDE USE

Food and Agricultural Organization of the United Nations (FAO) Via delle Terme di Caracalla, 00100 Rome, Italy (Telephone Number in U.S. (202) 653-2400); *The State of Food and Agriculture.*

ROMANIA - PETROLEUM INDUSTRY

Commodity Research Bureau, Inc., 30 South Wacker Drive, Chicago Illinois 60606 (312) 454-1801; *Commodity Year Book.*

Euromonitor International, Inc., 122 South Michigan Avenue, Suite 1200, Chicago, Illinois 60603 (800) 577-EURO; *European Marketing Data and Statistics.*

Food and Agricultural Organization of the United Nations (FAO) Via delle Terme di Caracalla, 00100 Rome, Italy (Telephone Number in U.S. (202) 653-2400); *The State of Food and Agriculture.*

M.E. Sharpe, 80 Business Park Drive, Armonk, New York 10504 (800) 541-6563;

The Illustrated Book of World Rankings.

Penn Well Publishing Company, 1421 South Sheridan Road, P.O. Box 1260, Tulsa, Oklahoma 74101 (800) 752-9764; *International Energy Statistics Sourcebook.*

St. Martin's Press, Inc., 175 Fifth Avenue, New York, New York 10010 (800) 221-7945; *The Statesman's Year-Book.*

Statistical Office of the United Nations, Publishing Service, New York, New York 10017 (800) 253-9646; *Statistical Yearbook;* and *Trends in Europe and North America: The Statistical Yearbook of the Economic Commission for Europe.*

United Nations Conference on Trade and Development, Central Statistical Service, Palais des Nations, Geneva, Switzerland (Telephone in U.S. (800) 253-9646); *UNCTAD Commodity Yearbook.*

ROMANIA - PIG-IRON AND FERRO-ALLOYS PRODUCTION - See ROMANIA - MINING AND MINERAL PRODUCTS

ROMANIA - PIGS - See ROMANIA - LIVESTOCK AND POULTRY

ROMANIA - PIPELINES FOR OIL AND PETROLEUM PRODUCTS

Statistical Office of the United Nations, Publishing Service, New York, New York 10017 (800) 253-9646; *Annual Bulletin of Transport Statistics for Europe.*

ROMANIA - PLASTIC AND RESIN PRODUCTION

Statistical Office of the United Nations, Publishing Service, New York, New York 10017 (800) 253-9646; *Statistical Yearbook.*

ROMANIA - POPULATION

Central Intelligence Agency, Washington, D.C. 20505 (703) 482-1100, www.cia.gov; *The World Factbook.*

The Economist Intelligence Unit, 111 West 57th Street, New York, New York 10019 (800) 938-4685; *Romania Country Report;* and *The World Market Atlas.*

Euromonitor International, Inc., 122 South Michigan Avenue, Suite 1200, Chicago, Illinois 60603 (800) 577-EURO; *European Marketing Data and Statistics;* and *The World Economic Factbook.*

Europa Publications Limited, 18 Bedford Square, London, WC1B 3JN, England; *The Europa World Year Book.*

Food and Agricultural Organization of the United Nations (FAO), Via delle Terme di Caracalla, 00100 Rome, Italy (Telephone Number in U.S. (202) 653-2400);

Production Yearbook.

International Labour Office, I.L.O. Publications, 1828 L Street, NW., Suite 801, Washington, D.C. 20036 (301) 638-3152; *Yearbook of Labour Statistics.*

M.E. Sharpe, 80 Business Park Drive, Armonk, New York 10504 (800) 541-6563; *The Illustrated Book of World Rankings.*

St. Martin's Press, Inc., 175 Fifth Avenue, New York, New York 10010 (800) 221-7945; *The Statesman's Year-Book.*

Statistical Office of the United Nations, Publishing Service, New York, New York 10017 (800) 253-9646; *Demographic Yearbook; Human Development Report; Statistical Yearbook; Trends in Europe and North America: The Statistical Yearbook of the Economic Commission for Europe;* and *World Statistics Pocketbook.*

United Nations Educational, Scientific and Cultural Organization (UNESCO), 7 Place de Fontenoy, F-75700 Paris, France (Telephone Number in U.S. (212) 963-5981); *Statistical Yearbook.*

U.S. Arms Control and Disarmament Agency, 320 Twenty-first Street, NW, Washington, D.C. 20451 (202) 647-8677; *World Military Expenditures and Arms Transfers.*

The World Bank, 1818 H Street, NW, Washington, D.C. 20433 (202) 477-1234; *The World Bank Atlas;* and *World Development Report.*

World Health Organization, Office of Publications, 20 Avenue Appia, CH-1211 Geneva 27, Switzerland (Telephone Number in U.S. (518) 436-9686); *World Health Statistics Annual.*

ROMANIA - POST OFFICES

M.E. Sharpe, 80 Business Park Drive, Armonk, New York 10504 (800) 541-6563; *The Illustrated Book of World Rankings.*

St. Martin's Press, Inc., 175 Fifth Avenue, New York, New York 10010 (800) 221-7945; *The Statesman's Year-Book.*

Statistical Office of the United Nations, Publishing Service, New York, New York 10017 (800) 253-9646; *Trends in Europe and North America: The Statistical Yearbook of the Economic Commission for Europe.*

ROMANIA - POTATO PRODUCTION - See ROMANIA - CROPS

ROMANIA - POWER PRODUCTION INDUSTRY

Statistical Office of the United Nations, Publishing Service, New York, New York

10017 (800) 253-9646; *Statistical Yearbook.*

ROMANIA - PRICES

Food and Agricultural Organization of the United Nations (FAO), Via delle Terme di Caracalla, 00100 Rome, Italy (Telephone Number in U.S. (202) 653-2400); *Production Yearbook;* and *The State of Food and Agriculture.*

International Labour Office, I.L.O. Publications, 1828 L Street, NW., Suite 801, Washington, D.C. 20036 (301) 638-3152; *Yearbook of Labour Statistics.*

International Monetary Fund, 700 Nineteenth Street, NW, Washington, D.C. 20431 (202) 623-7000; *International Financial Statistics.*

M.E. Sharpe, 80 Business Park Drive, Armonk, New York 10504 (800) 541-6563; *The Illustrated Book of World Rankings.*

ROMANIA - PRODUCTION

M.E. Sharpe, 80 Business Park Drive, Armonk, New York 10504 (800) 541-6563; *The Illustrated Book of World Rankings.*

ROMANIA - PROPERTY TAXES - See ROMANIA - TAXATION

ROMANIA - PUBLIC FINANCE - See ROMANIA - FINANCE

ROMANIA - RADIO BROADCASTING - See ROMANIA - BROADCASTING

ROMANIA - RADIO RECEIVER PRODUCTION

Statistical Office of the United Nations, Publishing Service, New York, New York 10017 (800) 253-9646; *Statistical Yearbook.*

ROMANIA - RADIO RECEIVERS

St. Martin's Press, Inc., 175 Fifth Avenue, New York, New York 10010 (800) 221-7945; *The Statesman's Year-Book.*

ROMANIA - RAILWAYS

Euromonitor International, Inc., 122 South Michigan Avenue, Suite 1200, Chicago, Illinois 60603 (800) 577-EURO; *European Marketing Data and Statistics.*

Europa Publications Limited, 18 Bedford Square, London, WC1B 3JN, England; *The Europa World Year Book.*

Jane's Information Group, Sentinel House, 163 Brighton Road, Coulsdon, Surrey CR5 2NH, England (Telephone Number in U.S. (703) 683-3700); *Jane's World Railways.*

St. Martin's Press, Inc., 175 Fifth

Avenue, New York, New York 10010 (800) 221-7945; *The Statesman's Year-Book.*

Statistical Office of the United Nations, Publishing Service, New York, New York 10017 (800) 253-9646; *Annual Bulletin of Transport Statistics for Europe; Statistical Yearbook;* and *Trends in Europe and North America: The Statistical Yearbook of the Economic Commission for Europe.*

ROMANIA - RAPESEED PRODUCTION - See ROMANIA - CROPS

ROMANIA - RELIGION

Central Intelligence Agency, Washington, D.C. 20505 (703) 482-1100, www.cia.gov; *The World Factbook.*

M.E. Sharpe, 80 Business Park Drive, Armonk, New York 10504 (800) 541-6563; *The Illustrated Book of World Rankings.*

St. Martin's Press, Inc., 175 Fifth Avenue, New York, New York 10010 (800) 221-7945; *The Statesman's Year-Book.*

ROMANIA - RENT PRICES

International Labour Office, I.L.O. Publications, 1828 L Street, NW., Suite 801, Washington, D.C. 20036 (301) 638-3152; *Yearbook of Labour Statistics.*

ROMANIA - RETAIL TRADE

Euromonitor International, Inc., 122 South Michigan Avenue, Suite 1200, Chicago, Illinois 60603 (800) 577-EURO; *Retail Trade International;* and *World Marketing Data and Statistics.*

Statistical Office of the United Nations, Publishing Service, New York, New York 10017 (800) 253-9646; *Statistical Yearbook.*

ROMANIA - RICE PRODUCTION - See ROMANIA - CROPS

ROMANIA - ROOT AND TUBER PRODUCTION - See ROMANIA - CROPS

ROMANIA - ROUNDWOOD PRODUCTION - See ROMANIA - FORESTRY AND FOREST PRODUCTS

ROMANIA - RUBBER PRODUCTION AND CONSUMPTION

M.E. Sharpe, 80 Business Park Drive, Armonk, New York 10504 (800) 541-6563; *The Illustrated Book of World Rankings.*

Statistical Office of the United Nations, Publishing Service, New York, New York 10017 (800) 253-9646; *Statistical Yearbook.*

ROMANIA - SALT PRODUCTION - See ROMANIA - MINING AND MINERAL PRODUCTS

ROMANIA - SAWNWOOD PRODUCTION - See ROMANIA - FORESTRY AND FOREST PRODUCTS

ROMANIA - SCIENCE AND TECHNOLOGY - EXPENDITURE FOR RESEARCH - See ROMANIA - SCIENTISTS, TECHNICIANS AND ENGINEERS

ROMANIA - SCIENTISTS, TECHNICIANS AND ENGINEERS

Statistical Office of the United Nations, Publishing Service, New York, New York 10017 (800) 253-9646; *Statistical Yearbook*.

United Nations Educational, Scientific and Cultural Organization (UNESCO), 7 Place de Fontenoy, F-75700 Paris, France (Telephone Number in U.S. (212) 963-5981); *Statistical Yearbook*.

ROMANIA - SENIOR CITIZENS

M.E. Sharpe, 80 Business Park Drive, Armonk, New York 10504 (800) 541-6563; *The Illustrated Book of World Rankings*.

ROMANIA - SHEEP - See ROMANIA - LIVESTOCK AND POULTRY

ROMANIA - SILVER PRODUCTION AND CONSUMPTION - See ROMANIA - MINING AND MINERAL PRODUCTS

ROMANIA - SOCIAL DATA

M.E. Sharpe, 80 Business Park Drive, Armonk, New York 10504 (800) 541-6563; *The Illustrated Book of World Rankings*.

Statistical Office of the United Nations, Publishing Service, New York, New York 10017 (800) 253-9646; *World Statistics Pocketbook*.

ROMANIA - SOCIAL SECURITY

International Monetary Fund, 700 Nineteenth Street, NW, Washington, D.C. 20431 (202) 623-7000; *Government Finance Statistics Yearbook*.

St. Martin's Press, Inc., 175 Fifth Avenue, New York, New York 10010 (800) 221-7945; *The Statesman's Year-Book*.

Statistical Office of the United Nations, Publishing Service, New York, New York 10017 (800) 253-9646; *National Accounts Statistics*.

ROMANIA - SOYBEAN PRODUCTION - See ROMANIA - CROPS

ROMANIA - STEEL - See ROMANIA - MINING AND MINERAL PRODUCTS

ROMANIA - STOCKS - COMMODITY - MARKET PRICE - INDEX

Food and Agricultural Organization of the United Nations (FAO) Via delle Terme di Caracalla, 00100 Rome, Italy (Telephone Number in U.S. (202) 653-2400); *The State of Food and Agriculture*.

ROMANIA - SUGAR PRODUCTION AND CONSUMPTION - See ROMANIA - CROPS

ROMANIA - SULPHURIC ACID PRODUCTION - See ROMANIA - MINING AND MINERAL PRODUCTS

ROMANIA - TAXATION

Europa Publications Limited, 18 Bedford Square, London, WC1B 3JN, England; *The Europa World Year Book*.

International Monetary Fund, 700 Nineteenth Street, NW, Washington, D.C. 20431 (202) 623-7000; *Government Finance Statistics Yearbook*.

International Road Federation, 2600 Virginia Avenue, NW, Washington, D.C. 20037 (202) 338-4641; *World Road Statistics*.

St. Martin's Press, Inc., 175 Fifth Avenue, New York, New York 10010 (800) 221-7945; *The Statesman's Year-Book*.

ROMANIA - TELEPHONES IN USE

American Telephone and Telegraph Company, 26 Parsippany Road, Whippany, New Jersey 07981 (800) 222-0300; *The World's Telephones*.

Central Intelligence Agency, Washington, D.C. 20505 (703) 482-1100, www.cia.gov; *The World Factbook*.

Europa Publications Limited, 18 Bedford Square, London, WC1B 3JN, England; *The Europa World Year Book*.

St. Martin's Press, Inc., 175 Fifth Avenue, New York, New York 10010 (800) 221-7945; *The Statesman's Year-Book*.

Statistical Office of the United Nations, Publishing Service, New York, New York 10017 (800) 253-9646; *Statistical Yearbook; Trends in Europe and North America: The Statistical Yearbook of the Economic Commission for Europe;* and *World Statistics Pocketbook*.

ROMANIA - TELEVISION BROADCASTING - See ROMANIA - BROADCASTING

ROMANIA - TELEVISION RECEIVER PRODUCTION

Statistical Office of the United Nations, Publishing Service, New York, New York 10017 (800) 253-9646; *Statistical Yearbook*.

ROMANIA - TEXTILE INDUSTRY

Euromonitor International, Inc., 122 South Michigan Avenue, Suite 1200, Chicago, Illinois 60603 (800) 577-EURO; *Retail Trade International*.

Food and Agricultural Organization of the United Nations (FAO), Via delle Terme di Caracalla, 00100 Rome, Italy (Telephone Number in U.S. (202) 653-2400); *Production Yearbook*.

M.E. Sharpe, 80 Business Park Drive, Armonk, New York 10504 (800) 541-6563; *The Illustrated Book of World Rankings*.

Statistical Office of the United Nations, Publishing Service, New York, New York 10017 (800) 253-9646; *Statistical Yearbook*.

United Nations Conference on Trade and Development, Central Statistical Service, Palais des Nations, Geneva, Switzerland (Telephone in U.S. (800) 253-9646); *UNCTAD Commodity Yearbook*.

ROMANIA - THEATRE

United Nations Educational, Scientific and Cultural Organization (UNESCO), 7 Place de Fontenoy, F-75700 Paris, France (Telephone Number in U.S. (212) 963-5981); *Statistical Yearbook*.

ROMANIA - TIMBER - RESOURCE FORESTS - See ROMANIA - FORESTRY AND FOREST PRODUCTS

ROMANIA - TIN - INDUSTRIAL CONSUMPTION - See ROMANIA - MINING AND MINERAL PRODUCTS

ROMANIA - TIRE (MOTOR VEHICLE) PRODUCTION

Statistical Office of the United Nations, Publishing Service, New York, New York 10017 (800) 253-9646; *Statistical Yearbook*.

ROMANIA - TOBACCO PRODUCTION

Euromonitor International, Inc., 122 South Michigan Avenue, Suite 1200, Chicago, Illinois 60603 (800) 577-EURO; *European Marketing Data and Statistics*.

M.E. Sharpe, 80 Business Park Drive, Armonk, New York 10504 (800) 541-6563; *The Illustrated Book of World Rankings*.

Statistical Office of the United Nations, Publishing Service, New York, New York 10017 (800) 253-9646; *Statistical Yearbook*.

ROMANIA - TOURISM

Euromonitor International, Inc., 122 South Michigan Avenue, Suite 1200, Chicago, Illinois 60603 (800) 577-EURO; *European Marketing Data and Statistics;*

World Marketing Data and Statistics; and *The World Economic Factbook.*

Europa Publications Limited, 18 Bedford Square, London, WC1B 3JN, England; *The Europa World Year Book.*

M.E. Sharpe, 80 Business Park Drive, Armonk, New York 10504 (800) 541-6563; *The Illustrated Book of World Rankings.*

St. Martin's Press, Inc., 175 Fifth Avenue, New York, New York 10010 (800) 221-7945; *The Statesman's Year-Book.*

Statistical Office of the United Nations, Publishing Service, New York, New York 10017 (800) 253-9646; *Statistical Yearbook;* and *Trends in Europe and North America: The Statistical Yearbook of the Economic Commission for Europe.*

World Tourism Organization, Calle Capitan Haya 42, E-28020 Madrid, Spain; *Yearbook of Tourism Statistics.*

ROMANIA - TRACTORS IN USE

Statistical Office of the United Nations, Publishing Service, New York, New York 10017 (800) 253-9646; *Statistical Yearbook.*

ROMANIA - TRADE

Euromonitor International, Inc., 122 South Michigan Avenue, Suite 1200, Chicago, Illinois 60603 (800) 577-EURO; *European Marketing Data and Statistics.*

Food and Agricultural Organization of the United Nations (FAO) Via delle Terme di Caracalla, 00100 Rome, Italy (Telephone Number in U.S. (202) 653-2400); *The State of Food and Agriculture.*

Statistical Office of the United Nations, Publishing Service, New York, New York 10017 (800) 253-9646; *Statistical Yearbook.*

ROMANIA - TRADEMARKS AND SERVICE MARKS - See ROMANIA - PATENTS, TRADEMARKS AND SERVICE MARKS

ROMANIA - TRANSPORTATION AND COMMUNICATIONS

Central Intelligence Agency, Washington, D.C. 20505 (703) 482-1100, www.cia.gov; *The World Factbook.*

Euromonitor International, Inc., 122 South Michigan Avenue, Suite 1200, Chicago, Illinois 60603 (800) 577-EURO; *World Marketing Data and Statistics.*

Europa Publications Limited, 18 Bedford Square, London, WC1B 3JN, England; *The Europa World Year Book.*

M.E. Sharpe, 80 Business Park Drive, Armonk, New York 10504 (800) 541-6563;

The Illustrated Book of World Rankings.

St. Martin's Press, Inc., 175 Fifth Avenue, New York, New York 10010 (800) 221-7945; *The Statesman's Year-Book.*

Statistical Office of the United Nations, Publishing Service, New York, New York 10017 (800) 253-9646; *Human Development Report;* and *Trends in Europe and North America: The Statistical Yearbook of the Economic Commission for Europe.*

ROMANIA - UNEMPLOYMENT

Central Intelligence Agency, Washington, D.C. 20505 (703) 482-1100, www.cia.gov; *The World Factbook.*

Euromonitor International, Inc., 122 South Michigan Avenue, Suite 1200, Chicago, Illinois 60603 (800) 577-EURO; *European Marketing Data and Statistics.*

International Labour Office, I.L.O. Publications, 1828 L Street, NW., Suite 801, Washington, D.C. 20036 (301) 638-3152; *Yearbook of Labour Statistics.*

St. Martin's Press, Inc., 175 Fifth Avenue, New York, New York 10010 (800) 221-7945; *The Statesman's Year-Book.*

Statistical Office of the United Nations, Publishing Service, New York, New York 10017 (800) 253-9646; *Trends in Europe and North America: The Statistical Yearbook of the Economic Commission for Europe.*

ROMANIA - VITAL STATISTICS

St. Martin's Press, Inc., 175 Fifth Avenue, New York, New York 10010 (800) 221-7945; *The Statesman's Year-Book.*

Statistical Office of the United Nations, Publishing Service, New York, New York 10017 (800) 253-9646; *Statistical Yearbook.*

ROMANIA - WAGES

Euromonitor International, Inc., 122 South Michigan Avenue, Suite 1200, Chicago, Illinois 60603 (800) 577-EURO; *European Marketing Data and Statistics.*

International Labour Office, I.L.O. Publications, 1828 L Street, NW., Suite 801, Washington, D.C. 20036 (301) 638-3152; *Yearbook of Labour Statistics.*

Statistical Office of the United Nations, Publishing Service, New York, New York 10017 (800) 253-9646; *Statistical Yearbook.*

ROMANIA - WALNUT PRODUCTION - See ROMANIA - CROPS

ROMANIA - WATERWAYS IN USE

Statistical Office of the United Nations, Publishing Service, New York, New York 10017 (800) 253-9646; *Annual Bulletin of Transport Statistics for Europe.*

ROMANIA - WEATHER - See ROMANIA - CLIMATE

ROMANIA - WELFARE

International Monetary Fund, 700 Nineteenth Street, NW, Washington, D.C. 20431 (202) 623-7000; *Government Finance Statistics Yearbook.*

St. Martin's Press, Inc., 175 Fifth Avenue, New York, New York 10010 (800) 221-7945; *The Statesman's Year-Book.*

ROMANIA - WHEAT PRODUCTION AND CONSUMPTION - See ROMANIA - CROPS

ROMANIA - WINE PRODUCTION - See ROMANIA - BEVERAGES

ROMANIA - WOOD PULP PRODUCTION - See ROMANIA - FORESTRY AND FOREST PRODUCTS

ROMANIA - WOOL PRODUCTION - See ROMANIA - TEXTILE INDUSTRY

ROMANIA - YARN PRODUCTION - See ROMANIA - TEXTILE INDUSTRY

ROWING

National Collegiate Athletic Association, 700 West Washington Street, Indianapolis, Indiana 46206 (317) 917-6222; *1997-98 Participation Study.*

RUBBER - CRUDE NATURAL

U.S. Department of Agriculture, Economic Research, 1800 M Street, NW, Washington, D.C. 20036 (202) 694-5050, www.ers.usda.gov; *Foreign Agricultural Trade of the United States;* and *U.S. Agricultural Trade Update.*

RUBBER AND MISCELLANEOUS PLASTICS - MANUFACTURING -CAPITAL

U.S. Department of Commerce, Bureau of Economic Analysis, Fourteenth Street between Constitution Avenue and E Street, NW, Washington, D.C. 20230 (202) 606-9900, www.bea.doc.gov; *Survey of Current Business.*

U.S. Department of Commerce, Bureau of the Census, Washington, D.C. 20233 (301) 457-4100, www.census.gov; *Census of Manufactures;* and *Annual Survey of Manufactures.*

RUBBER AND MISCELLANEOUS PLASTICS - MANUFACTURING -EARNINGS

U.S. Department of Commerce, Bureau

of the Census, Washington, D.C. 20233 (301) 457-4100, www.census.gov; *Census of Manufactures; Annual Survey of Manufactures;* and *County Business Patterns.*

U.S. Department of Labor, Bureau of Labor Statistics, Two Massachusetts Avenue, NE, Washington, D.C. 20212 (202) 691-5200, www.stats.bls.gov; *Employment and Earnings;* and Internet site: http://stats.bls.gov/ ceshome.htm.

RUBBER AND MISCELLANEOUS PLASTICS - MANUFACTURING - EMPLOYEES

U.S. Department of Commerce, Bureau of the Census, Washington, D.C. 20233 (301) 457-4100, www.census.gov; *Census of Manufactures; Annual Survey of Manufactures;* and *County Business Patterns.*

U.S. Department of Labor, Bureau of Labor Statistics, Two Massachusetts Avenue, NE, Washington, D.C. 20212 (202) 691-5200, www.stats.bls.gov; *Employment and Earnings; Monthly Labor Review;* and Internet site: http://www.stats.bls.gov/ceshome.htm.

RUBBER AND MISCELLANEOUS PLASTICS - ENERGY CONSUMPTION

U.S. Department of Energy, Energy Information Administration, 1000 Independence Avenue, SW, Washington, D.C. 20585 (202) 586-8800, www.eia.doc.gov; *Manufacturing Energy Consumption.*

RUBBER AND MISCELLANEOUS PLASTICS - MANUFACTURING - ESTABLISHMENTS

U.S. Department of Commerce, Bureau of the Census, Washington, D.C. 20233 (301) 457-4100, www.census.gov; *County Business Patterns.*

RUBBER AND MISCELLANEOUS PLASTICS - MANUFACTURING -FOREIGN TRADE

U.S. Department of Commerce, Bureau of the Census, Washington, D.C. 20233 (301) 457-4100, www.census.gov; *U.S. International Trade in Goods and Services.*

RUBBER AND MISCELLANEOUS PLASTICS - MANUFACTURING - GROSS DOMESTIC PRODUCT

U.S. Department of Commerce, Bureau of Economic Analysis, Fourteenth Street between Constitution Avenue and E Street, NW, Washington, D.C. 20230 (202) 606-9900, www.bea.doc.gov; *Survey of Current Business.*

RUBBER AND MISCELLANEOUS PLASTICS - MANUFACTURING - INVENTORIES

U.S. Department of Commerce, Bureau of the Census, Washington, D.C. 20233 (301) 457-4100, www.census.gov; *Current Industrial Reports, Manufactures' Shipments, Inventories, and Orders.*

RUBBER AND MISCELLANEOUS PLASTICS - MANUFACTURING -MERGERS AND ACQUISITIONS

Thomson Financial Securities Data, 2 Gateway Center, Newark, New Jersey 07006 (973) 622-3100; *Merger and Corporate Transactions Database.*

RUBBER AND MISCELLANEOUS PLASTICS - MANUFACTURING - OCCUPATIONAL SAFETY

U.S. Department of Labor, Bureau of Labor Statistics, Two Massachusetts Avenue, NE, Washington, D.C. 20212 (202) 691-5200, www.stats.bls.gov; *Occupational Injuries and Illnesses in the United States by Industry.*

RUBBER AND MISCELLANEOUS PLASTICS - MANUFACTURING -PATENTS

U.S. Department of Commerce, Patent and Trademark Office, 2011 Crystal Drive, Arlington, Virginia 22202 (703) 305-8341, www.uspto.gov; *Patenting Trends in the United States, State Country Report.*

RUBBER AND MISCELLANEOUS PLASTICS - MANUFACTURING - PRODUCTIVITY

U.S. Department of Labor, Bureau of Labor Statistics, Two Massachusetts Avenue, NE, Washington, D.C. 20212 (202) 691-5200, www.stats.bls.gov; Internet site http://stats.bls.gov/iprhome.htm.

RUBBER AND MISCELLANEOUS PLASTICS - MANUFACTURING -PROFITS

Time Warner, Time and Life Building, Rockefeller Center, New York, New York 10019 (212) 522-1212; *The Fortune Directories.*

RUBBER AND MISCELLANEOUS PLASTICS - MANUFACTURING - SALES, SHIPMENTS, RECEIPTS

Time Warner, Time and Life Building, Rockefeller Center, New York, New York 10019 (212) 522-1212; *The Fortune Directories.*

U.S. Department of Commerce, Bureau of the Census, Washington, D.C. 20233 (301) 457-4100, www.census.gov; *Manufactures' Shipments, Inventories, and Orders; Census of Manufactures; Annual Survey of Manufactures;* and *Current Industrial Reports.*

RUBBER AND MISCELLANEOUS - MANUFACTURING - TOXIC CHEMICAL RELEASES

Environmental Protection Agency, 1200 Pennsylvania Avenue, NW, Washington, D.C. 20460 (888) 372-8255, www.epa.gov; *Toxics Release Inventory.*

RUBBER AND MISCELLANEOUS PLASTICS - MANUFACTURING - VALUE ADDED

U.S. Department of Commerce, Bureau of the Census, Washington, D.C. 20233 (301) 457-4100, www.census.gov; *Census of Manufactures;* and *Annual Survey of Manufactures.*

RUBBER PRODUCTS

U.S. Department of Commerce, Bureau of the Census, Washington, D.C. 20233 (301) 457-4100, www.census.gov; *U.S. International Trade in Goods and Services.*

RUBELLA

U.S. Department of Health and Human Services, Centers for Disease Control, 1600 Clifton Road, NE, Atlanta, Georgia 30333 (800) 311-3435, www.cdc.gov; *Summary of Notifiable Diseases, United States;* and *Morbidity and Mortality Weekly Report..*

RUGS

Fiber Economics Bureau, 101 Eisenhower Parkway, Roseland, New Jersey 07068 (201) 228-1107; *Textile Organon.*

National Safety Council, 1121 Spring Lake Drive, Chicago, Illinois 60143-3201 (630) 285-1121; *Accident Facts.*

U.S. Department of Commerce, Bureau of the Census, Washington, D.C. 20233 (301) 457-4100, www.census.gov; *Current Industrial Reports; Annual Survey of Manufactures; Census of Manufactures;* and *Manufacturing Profiles.*

U. S. Department of Labor, Bureau of Labor Statistics, Two Massachusetts Avenue, NE, Washington, D.C. 20212 (202) 691-5200, www.stats.bls.gov; *Employment and Earnings;* Bulletins 2445 and 2481; and Internet site: http://stats.bls.gov/ceshome.htm.

RUNNING AND JOGGING

National Sporting Goods Association, 1601 Feehanville Drive, Suite 300, Mount Prospect, Illinois 60056 (847) 296-6742; *Sports Participation in 1998.*

RURAL POPULATION - See POPULATION

Russia - Primary Statistics Source

Gosudarstvennyi Komitet Rossiiskoi Federatsii Po Statistike, Moscow, Russia; *Narodnoe Khoziaistvo Rossiiskoi Federatsii: Statisticheskii Ezhegodnik.*

RUSSIA - ABORTIONS

Statistical Office of the United Nations, Publishing Service, New York, New York 10017 (800) 253-9646; *Trends in Europe and North America: The Statistical Yearbook of the Economic Commission for Europe.*

RUSSIA - AGRICULTURE

Academic International Press, Box 1111, Gulf Breeze, Florida 32562; *Russia and Eurasia Facts and Figures Annual.*

Business International Moscow, 23 Profsoyuznaya Ulitsa, 117859, Moscow (Telephone Number in U.S. (800) 938-4685); *The CIS Market Atlas.*

Economist Intelligence Unit, 111 West 57th Street, New York, New York 10019 (800) 938-4685; *Russia Country Report.*

Euromonitor International, Inc., 122 South Michigan Avenue, Suite 1200, Chicago, Illinois 60603 (800) 577-EURO; *World Marketing Data and Statistics.*

Europa Publications Limited, 18 Bedford Square, London, WC1B 3JN, England; *The Europa World Year Book.*

Federal Statistical Office, Gustav-Stresemann - Ring 11, D-6200, Wiesbaden, Germany; *Russische Federation.*

Food and Agriculture Organization of the United Nations (FAO), via delle Terme di Caracalla, 00100, Rome, Italy (Telephone Number in the U.S. (202) 653-2400); *Production Yearbook; The State of Food and Agriculture;* and *Trade Yearbook.*

St. Martin's Press, Inc., 175 Fifth Avenue, New York, New York 10010 (800) 221-7945; *The Statesman's Year-Book.*

Statistical Office of the United Nations, Publishing Service, New York, New York 10017 (800) 253-9646; *Industrial Commodity Statistics Yearbook;* and *Statistical Yearbook.*

The World Bank, 1818 H Street, NW, Washington, D.C. 20433 (202) 477-1234; *Statistical Handbook: States of the Former USSR;* and *World Development Indicators.*

RUSSIA - AIRLINE SERVICE

Business International Moscow, 23 Profsoyuznaya Ulitsa, 117859, Moscow (Telephone Number in U.S. (800) 938-4685); *The CIS Market Atlas.*

International Civil Aviation Organization, 999 University Street, Montreal, Quebec, Canada H3C 5H7 (514) 954-8219; *Civil Aviation Statistics of the World.*

Statistical Office of the United Nations, Publishing Service, New York, New York 10017 (800) 253-9646; *Statistical Yearbook.*

RUSSIA - AIRPORTS

Central Intelligence Agency, Washington, D.C. 20505 (703) 482-1100, www.cia.gov; *The World Factbook.*

RUSSIA - ANIMAL HEALTH

Food and Agriculture Organization of the United Nations (FAO), via delle Terme di Caracalla, 00100, Rome, Italy (Telephone Number in the U.S. (202) 653-2400); *Animal Health Yearbook.*

RUSSIA - AREA AND DENSITY OF POPULATION

Academic International Press, Box 1111, Gulf Breeze, Florida 32562; *Russia and Eurasia Facts and Figures Annual.*

Central Intelligence Agency, Washington, D.C. 20505 (703) 482-1100, www.cia.gov; *The World Factbook.*

Business International Moscow, 23 Profsoyuznaya Ulitsa, 117859, Moscow (Telephone Number in U.S. (800) 938-4685); *The CIS Market Atlas.*

Euromonitor International, Inc., 122 South Michigan Avenue, Suite 1200, Chicago, Illinois 60603 (800) 577-EURO; *The World Economic Factbook.*

Europa Publications Limited, 18 Bedford Square, London, WC1B 3JN, England; *The Europa World Year Book.*

Federal Statistical Office, Gustav-Stresemann - Ring 11, D-6200, Wiesbaden, Germany; *Russische Federation.*

St. Martin's Press, Inc., 175 Fifth Avenue, New York, New York 10010 (800) 221-7945; *The Statesman's Year-Book.*

Statistical Office of the United Nations, Publishing Service, New York, New York 10017 (800) 253-9646; *Statistical Yearbook;* and *Trends in Europe and North America: The Statistical Yearbook of the Economic Commission for Europe.*

United Nations Educational, Scientific and Cultural Organization (UNESCO), 7 Place de Fontenoy, F-75700 Paris, France (Telephone Number in U.S. (212) 963-5981); *Statistical Yearbook.*

The World Bank, 1818 H Street, NW, Washington, D.C. 20433 (202) 477-1234; *World Development Report.*

RUSSIA - BALANCE OF PAYMENTS

Europa Publications Limited, 18 Bedford Square, London, WC1B 3JN, England; *The Europa World Year Book.*

Federal Statistical Office, Gustav-Stresemann - Ring 11, D-6200, Wiesbaden, Germany; *Russische Federation.*

United Nations Conference on Trade and Development (UNCTAD), New York, New York 10017 (800) 253-9646; *Handbook of International Trade and Development Statistics.*

The World Bank, 1818 H Street, NW, Washington, D.C. 20433 (202) 477-1234; *World Development Report;* and *World Development Indicators.*

RUSSIA - BANKING

Business International Moscow, 23 Profsoyuznaya Ulitsa, 117859, Moscow (Telephone Number in U.S. (800) 938-4685); *The CIS Market Atlas.*

Euromonitor International, Inc., 122 South Michigan Avenue, Suite 1200, Chicago, Illinois 60603 (800) 577-EURO; *World Marketing Data and Statistics.*

St. Martin's Press, Inc., 175 Fifth Avenue, New York, New York 10010 (800) 221-7945; *The Statesman's Year-Book.*

RUSSIA - BEVERAGES

Statistical Office of the United Nations, Publishing Service, New York, New York 10017 (800) 253-9646; *Statistical Yearbook.*

RUSSIA - BIRTH RATES

Academic International Press, Box 1111, Gulf Breeze, Florida 32562; *Russia and Eurasia Facts and Figures Annual.*

Business International Moscow, 23 Profsoyuznaya Ulitsa, 117859, Moscow (Telephone Number in U.S. (800) 938-4685); *The CIS Market Atlas.*

Central Intelligence Agency, Washington, D.C. 20505 (703) 482-1100, www.cia.gov; *The World Factbook.*

Euromonitor International, Inc., 122 South Michigan Avenue, Suite 1200, Chicago, Illinois 60603 (800) 577-EURO; *The World Economic Factbook.*

Europa Publications Limited, 18 Bedford Square, London, WC1B 3JN, England; *The Europa World Year Book*.

Statistical Office of the United Nations, Publishing Service, New York, New York 10017 (800) 253-9646; *Statistical Yearbook*.

World Health Organization, Office of Publications, 20 Avenue Appia, CH-1211 Geneva 27, Switzerland (Telephone Number in U.S. (518) 436-9686); *World Health Statistics Annual*.

RUSSIA - BOOK PRODUCTION

Europa Publications Limited, 18 Bedford Square, London, WC1B 3JN, England; *The Europa World Year Book*.

Statistical Office of the United Nations, Publishing Service, New York, New York 10017 (800) 253-9646; *Trends in Europe and North America: The Statistical Yearbook of the Economic Commission for Europe*.

United Nations Educational, Scientific and Cultural Organization (UNESCO), 7 Place de Fontenoy, F-75700 Paris, France (Telephone Number in U.S. (212) 963-5981); *Statistical Yearbook*.

RUSSIA - BROADCASTING

Central Intelligence Agency, Washington, D.C. 20505 (703) 482-1100, www.cia.gov; *The World Factbook*.

Euromonitor International, Inc., 122 South Michigan Avenue, Suite 1200, Chicago, Illinois 60603 (800) 577-EURO; *World Marketing Data and Statistics*.

St. Martin's Press, Inc., 175 Fifth Avenue, New York, New York 10010 (800) 221-7945; *The Statesman's Year-Book*.

Statistical Office of the United Nations, Publishing Service, New York, New York 10017 (800) 253-9646; *Trends in Europe and North America: The Statistical Yearbook of the Economic Commission for Europe*.

United Nations Educational, Scientific and Cultural Organization (UNESCO), 7 Place de Fontenoy, F-75700 Paris, France (Telephone Number in U.S. (212) 963-5981); *Statistical Yearbook*.

RUSSIA - BUDGET

Business International Moscow, 23 Profsoyuznaya Ulitsa, 117859, Moscow (Telephone Number in U.S. (800) 938-4685); *The CIS Market Atlas*.

Central Intelligence Agency, Washington, D.C. 20505 (703) 482-1100, www.cia.gov; *The World Factbook*.

RUSSIA - CAPITAL INVESTMENT

The World Bank, 1818 H Street, NW, Washington, D.C. 20433 (202) 477-1234; *Statistical Handbook: States of the Former USSR*.

RUSSIA - CATTLE - See RUSSIA - LIVESTOCK AND POULTRY

RUSSIA - CHEMICALS

Business International Moscow, 23 Profsoyuznaya Ulitsa, 117859, Moscow (Telephone Number in U.S. (800) 938-4685); *The CIS Market Atlas*.

RUSSIA - COAL PRODUCTION AND CONSUMPTION - See RUSSIA - MINING AND MINERAL PRODUCTS

RUSSIA - COMMERCE

St. Martin's Press, Inc., 175 Fifth Avenue, New York, New York 10010 (800) 221-7945; *The Statesman's Year-Book*.

RUSSIA - COMMUNICATIONS - See RUSSIA - TRANSPORTATION AND COMMUNICATIONS

RUSSIA - CONSTRUCTION INDUSTRY

Academic International Press, Box 1111, Gulf Breeze, Florida 32562; *Russia and Eurasia Facts and Figures Annual*.

Business International Moscow, 23 Profsoyuznaya Ulitsa, 117859, Moscow (Telephone Number in U.S. (800) 938-4685); *The CIS Market Atlas*.

Statistical Office of the United Nations, Publishing Service, New York, New York 10017 (800) 253-9646; *Statistical Yearbook*.

RUSSIA - CONSUMER PRICE INDEX

Europa Publications Limited, 18 Bedford Square, London, WC1B 3JN, England; *The Europa World Year Book*.

Statistical Office of the United Nations, Publishing Service, New York, New York 10017 (800) 253-9646; *Statistical Yearbook*; and *Trends in Europe and North America: The Statistical Yearbook of the Economic Commission for Europe*.

RUSSIA - CONSUMER PRICES

Business International Moscow, 23 Profsoyuznaya Ulitsa, 117859, Moscow (Telephone Number in U.S. (800) 938-4685); *The CIS Market Atlas*.

Euromonitor International, Inc., 122 South Michigan Avenue, Suite 1200, Chicago, Illinois 60603 (800) 577-EURO; *World Marketing Data and Statistics*.

RUSSIA - CONSUMPTION

Business International Moscow, 23 Profsoyuznaya Ulitsa, 117859, Moscow (Telephone Number in U.S. (800) 938-4685); *The CIS Market Atlas*.

The World Bank, 1818 H Street, NW, Washington, D.C. 20433 (202) 477-1234; *World Development Report;* and *Statistical Handbook: States of the Former USSR*.

RUSSIA - COTTON PRODUCTION AND CONSUMPTION - See RUSSIA - CROPS

RUSSIA - CRIME

Academic International Press, Box 1111, Gulf Breeze, Florida 32562; *Russia and Eurasia Facts and Figures Annual*.

Statistical Office of the United Nations, Publishing Service, New York, New York 10017 (800) 253-9646; *Trends in Europe and North America: The Statistical Yearbook of the Economic Commission for Europe*.

RUSSIA - CROPS

Academic International Press, Box 1111, Gulf Breeze, Florida 32562; *Russia and Eurasia Facts and Figures Annual*.

Business International Moscow, 23 Profsoyuznaya Ulitsa, 117859, Moscow (Telephone Number in U.S. (800) 938-4685); *The CIS Market Atlas*.

Europa Publications Limited, 18 Bedford Square, London, WC1B 3JN, England; *The Europa World Year Book*.

Food and Agriculture Organization of the United Nations (FAO), via delle Terme di Caracalla, 00100, Rome, Italy (Telephone Number in the U.S. (202) 653-2400); *Production Yearbook; The State of Food and Agriculture;* and *Trade Yearbook*.

Statistical Office of the United Nations, Publishing Service, New York, New York 10017 (800) 253-9646; *Industrial Commodity Statistics Yearbook;* and *Statistical Yearbook*.

St. Martin's Press, Inc., 175 Fifth Avenue, New York, New York 10010 (800) 221-7945; *The Statesman's Year-Book*.

The World Bank, 1818 H Street, NW, Washington, D.C. 20433 (202) 477-1234; *Statistical Handbook: States of the Former USSR*.

RUSSIA - DAIRY PRODUCTS

Europa Publications Limited, 18 Bedford Square, London, WC1B 3JN, England; *The Europa World Year Book*.

Food and Agriculture Organization of the United Nations (FAO), via delle Terme di Caracalla, 00100, Rome, Italy (Telephone

Number in the U.S. (202) 653-2400); *Production Yearbook; The State of Food and Agriculture;* and *Trade Yearbook.*

St. Martin's Press, Inc., 175 Fifth Avenue, New York, New York 10010 (800) 221-7945; *The Statesman's Year-Book.*

Statistical Office of the United Nations, Publishing Service, New York, New York 10017 (800) 253-9646; *Industrial Commodity Statistics Yearbook;* and *Statistical Yearbook.*

RUSSIA - DEATH RATES - See RUSSIA - MORTALITY

RUSSIA - DEMOGRAPHY

Business International Moscow, 23 Profsoyuznaya Ulitsa, 117859, Moscow (Telephone Number in U.S. (800) 938-4685); *The CIS Market Atlas.*

Euromonitor International, Inc., 122 South Michigan Avenue, Suite 1200, Chicago, Illinois 60603 (800) 577-EURO; *The World Economic Factbook;* and *World Marketing Data and Statistics.*

Federal Statistical Office, Gustav-Stresemann - Ring 11, D-6200, Wiesbaden, Germany; *Russische Federation.*

Statistical Office of the United Nations, Publishing Service, New York, New York 10017 (800) 253-9646; *Demographic Yearbook;* and *Human Development Report.*

The World Bank, 1818 H Street, NW, Washington, D.C. 20433 (202) 477-1234; *Statistical Handbook: States of the Former USSR.*

RUSSIA - DISEASES - See RUSSIA - HEALTH

RUSSIA - DIVORCE RATES

Academic International Press, Box 1111, Gulf Breeze, Florida 32562; *Russia and Eurasia Facts and Figures Annual.*

Statistical Office of the United Nations, Publishing Service, New York, New York 10017 (800) 253-9646; *Demographic Yearbook; Statistical Yearbook;* and *Trends in Europe and North America: The Statistical Yearbook of the Economic Commission for Europe.*

RUSSIA - DOMESTIC INVESTMENT

Business International Moscow, 23 Profsoyuznaya Ulitsa, 117859, Moscow (Telephone Number in U.S. (800) 938-4685); *The CIS Market Atlas.*

RUSSIA - ECONOMY

Academic International Press, Box

1111, Gulf Breeze, Florida 32562; *Russia and Eurasia Facts and Figures Annual.*

Business International Moscow, 23 Profsoyuznaya Ulitsa, 117859, Moscow (Telephone Number in U.S. (800) 938-4685); *The CIS Market Atlas.*

Central Intelligence Agency, Washington, D.C. 20505 (703) 482-1100, www.cia.gov; *The World Factbook.*

Economist Intelligence Unit, 111 West 57th Street, New York, New York 10019 (800) 938-4685; *Russia Country Report.*

Euromonitor International, Inc., 122 South Michigan Avenue, Suite 1200, Chicago, Illinois 60603 (800) 577-EURO; *The World Economic Factbook;* and *World Marketing Data and Statistics.*

Europa Publications Limited, 18 Bedford Square, London, WC1B 3JN, England; *The Europa World Year Book.*

Federal Statistical Office, Gustav-Stresemann - Ring 11, D-6200, Wiesbaden, Germany; *Russische Federation.*

St. Martin's Press, Inc., 175 Fifth Avenue, New York, New York 10010 (800) 221-7945; *The Statesman's Year-Book.*

Statistical Office of the United Nations, Publishing Service, New York, New York 10017 (800) 253-9646; *World Statistics Pocketbook.*

The World Bank, 1818 H Street, NW, Washington, D.C. 20433 (202) 477-1234; *The World Bank Atlas;* and *World Development Report.*

RUSSIA - EDUCATION

Academic International Press, Box 1111, Gulf Breeze, Florida 32562; *Russia and Eurasia Facts and Figures Annual.*

Business International Moscow, 23 Profsoyuznaya Ulitsa, 117859, Moscow (Telephone Number in U.S. (800) 938-4685); *The CIS Market Atlas.*

Euromonitor International, Inc., 122 South Michigan Avenue, Suite 1200, Chicago, Illinois 60603 (800) 577-EURO; *World Marketing Data and Statistics.*

Europa Publications Limited, 18 Bedford Square, London, WC1B 3JN, England; *The Europa World Year Book.*

Federal Statistical Office, Gustav-Stresemann - Ring 11, D-6200, Wiesbaden, Germany; *Russische Federation.*

St. Martin's Press, Inc., 175 Fifth Avenue, New York, New York 10010 (800) 221-7945; *The Statesman's Year-Book.*

Statistical Office of the United Nations, Publishing Service, New York, New York 10017 (800) 253-9646; *Human Development Report;* and *Trends in Europe and North America: The Statistical Yearbook of the Economic Commission for Europe.*

United Nations Educational, Scientific and Cultural Organization (UNESCO), 7 Place de Fontenoy, F-75700 Paris, France (Telephone Number in U.S. (212) 963-5981); *Statistical Yearbook.*

The World Bank, 1818 H Street, NW, Washington, D.C. 20433 (202) 477-1234; *World Development Report.*

RUSSIA - ELECTRICITY

Academic International Press, Box 1111, Gulf Breeze, Florida 32562; *Russia and Eurasia Facts and Figures Annual.*

Business International Moscow, 23 Profsoyuznaya Ulitsa, 117859, Moscow (Telephone Number in U.S. (800) 938-4685); *The CIS Market Atlas.*

Central Intelligence Agency, Washington, D.C. 20505 (703) 482-1100, www.cia.gov; *The World Factbook.*

St. Martin's Press, Inc., 175 Fifth Avenue, New York, New York 10010 (800) 221-7945; *The Statesman's Year-Book.*

Statistical Office of the United Nations, Publishing Service, New York, New York 10017 (800) 253-9646; *Human Development Report; Statistical Yearbook;* and *Trends in Europe and North America: The Statistical Yearbook of the Economic Commission for Europe.*

The World Bank, 1818 H Street, NW, Washington, D.C. 20433 (202) 477-1234; *Statistical Handbook: States of the Former USSR.*

RUSSIA - EMPLOYMENT

Federal Statistical Office, Gustav-Stresemann - Ring 11, D-6200, Wiesbaden, Germany; *Russische Federation.*

Statistical Office of the United Nations, Publishing Service, New York, New York 10017 (800) 253-9646; *Statistical Yearbook;* and *Trends in Europe and North America: The Statistical Yearbook of the Economic Commission for Europe.*

The World Bank, 1818 H Street, NW, Washington, D.C. 20433 (202) 477-1234; *Statistical Handbook: States of the Former USSR.*

RUSSIA - ENERGY

Academic International Press, Box

1111, Gulf Breeze, Florida 32562; *Russia and Eurasia Facts and Figures Annual.*

Business International Moscow, 23 Profsoyuznaya Ulitsa, 117859, Moscow (Telephone Number in U.S. (800) 938-4685); *The CIS Market Atlas.*

Euromonitor International, Inc., 122 South Michigan Avenue, Suite 1200, Chicago, Illinois 60603 (800) 577-EURO; *The World Economic Factbook;* and *World Marketing Data and Statistics.*

St. Martin's Press, Inc., 175 Fifth Avenue, New York, New York 10010 (800) 221-7945; *The Statesman's Year-Book.*

Statistical Office of the United Nations, Publishing Service, New York, New York 10017 (800) 253-9646; *Energy Statistics Yearbook; Human Development Report; Statistical Yearbook; Trends in Europe and North America: The Statistical Yearbook of the Economic Commission for Europe;* and *World Statistics Pocketbook.*

The World Bank, 1818 H Street, NW, Washington, D.C. 20433 (202) 477-1234; *Statistical Handbook: States of the Former USSR; The World Bank Atlas;* and *World Development Report.*

RUSSIA - ENVIRONMENT

Business International Moscow, 23 Profsoyuznaya Ulitsa, 117859, Moscow (Telephone Number in U.S. (800) 938-4685); *The CIS Market Atlas.*

Economist Intelligence Unit, 111 West 57th Street, New York, New York 10019 (800) 938-4685; *Russia Country Report.*

Statistical Office of the United Nations, Publishing Service, New York, New York 10017 (800) 253-9646; *Statistical Yearbook; Trends in Europe and North America: The Statistical Yearbook of the Economic Commission for Europe;* and *World Statistics Pocketbook.*

RUSSIA - EXCHANGE RATES

Central Intelligence Agency, Washington, D.C. 20505 (703) 482-1100, www.cia.gov; *The World Factbook.*

Euromonitor International, Inc., 122 South Michigan Avenue, Suite 1200, Chicago, Illinois 60603 (800) 577-EURO; *The World Economic Factbook.*

Europa Publications Limited, 18 Bedford Square, London, WC1B 3JN, England; *The Europa World Year Book.*

Statistical Office of the United Nations, Publishing Service, New York, New York 10017 (800) 253-9646; *Statistical Yearbook; Trends in Europe and North America: The*

Statistical Yearbook of the Economic Commission for Europe; and *World Statistics Pocketbook.*

RUSSIA - EXPORTS

Academic International Press, Box 1111, Gulf Breeze, Florida 32562; *Russia and Eurasia Facts and Figures Annual.*

Business International Moscow, 23 Profsoyuznaya Ulitsa, 117859, Moscow (Telephone Number in U.S. (800) 938-4685); *The CIS Market Atlas.*

Central Intelligence Agency, Washington, D.C. 20505 (703) 482-1100, www.cia.gov; *The World Factbook.*

Economist Intelligence Unit, 111 West 57th Street, New York, New York 10019 (800) 938-4685; *Russia Country Report.*

Euromonitor International, Inc., 122 South Michigan Avenue, Suite 1200, Chicago, Illinois 60603 (800) 577-EURO; *The World Economic Factbook.*

Europa Publications Limited, 18 Bedford Square, London, WC1B 3JN, England; *The Europa World Year Book.*

International Monetary Fund, 700 Nineteenth Street, NW, Washington, D.C. 20431 (202) 623-7000; *Direction of Trade Statistics.*

St. Martin's Press, Inc., 175 Fifth Avenue, New York, New York 10010 (800) 221-7945; *The Statesman's Year-Book.*

Statistical Office of the United Nations, Publishing Service, New York, New York 10017 (800) 253-9646; *International Trade Statistics Yearbook;* and *Trends in Europe and North America: The Statistical Yearbook of the Economic Commission for Europe.*

United Nations Conference on Trade and Development (UNCTAD), New York, New York 10017 (800) 253-9646; *Handbook of International Trade and Development Statistics.*

The World Bank, 1818 H Street, NW, Washington, D.C. 20433 (202) 477-1234; *Statistical Handbook: States of the Former USSR; World Development Report;* and *World Development Indicators.*

RUSSIA - EXTERNAL INDEBTEDNESS

The World Bank, 1818 H Street, NW, Washington, D.C. 20433 (202) 477-1234; *World Development Report;* and *World Development Indicators.*

RUSSIA - EXTERNAL TRADE

Academic International Press, Box

1111, Gulf Breeze, Florida 32562; *Russia and Eurasia Facts and Figures Annual.*

Euromonitor International, Inc., 122 South Michigan Avenue, Suite 1200, Chicago, Illinois 60603 (800) 577-EURO; *World Marketing Data and Statistics.*

Food and Agriculture Organization of the United Nations (FAO), via delle Terme di Caracalla, 00100, Rome, Italy (Telephone Number in the U.S. (202) 653-2400); *Trade Yearbook.*

Statistical Office of the United Nations, Publishing Service, New York, New York 10017 (800) 253-9646; *Statistical Yearbook.*

The World Bank, 1818 H Street, NW, Washington, D.C. 20433 (202) 477-1234; *Statistical Handbook: States of the Former USSR.*

RUSSIA - FABRIC PRODUCTION AND CONSUMPTION - See RUSSIA - TEXTILE INDUSTRY

RUSSIA - FERTILITY RATES

Central Intelligence Agency, Washington, D.C. 20505 (703) 482-1100, www.cia.gov; *The World Factbook.*

Statistical Office of the United Nations, Publishing Service, New York, New York 10017 (800) 253-9646; *Human Development Report;* and *Trends in Europe and North America: The Statistical Yearbook of the Economic Commission for Europe.*

The World Bank, 1818 H Street, NW, Washington, D.C. 20433 (202) 477-1234; *Statistical Handbook: States of the Former USSR; The World Bank Atlas; World Development Report;* and *World Development Indicators.*

World Health Organization, Office of Publications, 20 Avenue Appia, CH-1211 Geneva 27, Switzerland (Telephone Number in U.S. (518) 436-9686); *World Health Statistics Annual.*

RUSSIA - FERTILIZER

Food and Agriculture Organization of the United Nations (FAO), via delle Terme di Caracalla, 00100, Rome, Italy (Telephone Number in the U.S. (202) 653-2400); *Fertilizer Yearbook.*

Statistical Office of the United Nations, Publishing Service, New York, New York 10017 (800) 253-9646; *Industrial Commodity Statistics Yearbook;* and *Statistical Yearbook.*

RUSSIA - FINANCE

Economist Intelligence Unit, 111 West 57th Street, New York, New York 10019 (800) 938-4685; *Russia Country Report*.

Europa Publications Limited, 18 Bedford Square, London, WC1B 3JN, England; *The Europa World Year Book*.

Federal Statistical Office, Gustav-Stresemann - Ring 11, D-6200, Wiesbaden, Germany; *Russische Federation*.

St. Martin's Press, Inc., 175 Fifth Avenue, New York, New York 10010 (800) 221-7945; *The Statesman's Year-Book*.

The World Bank, 1818 H Street, NW, Washington, D.C. 20433 (202) 477-1234; *Statistical Handbook: States of the Former USSR*.

RUSSIA - FISHERIES

Federal Statistical Office, Gustav-Stresemann - Ring 11, D-6200, Wiesbaden, Germany; *Russische Federation*.

Food and Agriculture Organization of the United Nations (FAO), via delle Terme di Caracalla, 00100, Rome, Italy (Telephone Number in the U.S. (202) 653-2400); *The State of Food and Agriculture;* and *Yearbook of Fishery Statistics*.

Statistical Office of the United Nations, Publishing Service, New York, New York 10017 (800) 253-9646; *Industrial Commodity Statistics Yearbook;* and *Statistical Yearbook*.

RUSSIA - FOOD

Euromonitor International, Inc., 122 South Michigan Avenue, Suite 1200, Chicago, Illinois 60603 (800) 577-EURO; *Retail Trade International*.

Food and Agriculture Organization of the United Nations (FAO), via delle Terme di Caracalla, 00100, Rome, Italy (Telephone Number in the U.S. (202) 653-2400); *Production Yearbook; The State of Food and Agriculture;* and *Trade Yearbook*.

Statistical Office of the United Nations, Publishing Service, New York, New York 10017 (800) 253-9646; *Human Development Report;* and *Industrial Commodity Statistics Yearbook*.

RUSSIA - FOOTWEAR PRODUCTION AND CONSUMPTION - See RUSSIA - TEXTILE INDUSTRY

RUSSIA - FOREIGN INVESTMENT

Business International Moscow, 23 Profsoyuznaya Ulitsa, 117859, Moscow (Telephone Number in U.S. (800) 938-4685); *The CIS Market Atlas*.

RUSSIA - FOREIGN TRADE

Business International Moscow, 23 Profsoyuznaya Ulitsa, 117859, Moscow (Telephone Number in U.S. (800) 938-4685); *The CIS Market Atlas*.

Economist Intelligence Unit, 111 West 57th Street, New York, New York 10019 (800) 938-4685; *Russia Country Report*.

Euromonitor International, Inc., 122 South Michigan Avenue, Suite 1200, Chicago, Illinois 60603 (800) 577-EURO; *The World Economic Factbook*.

Europa Publications Limited, 18 Bedford Square, London, WC1B 3JN, England; *The Europa World Year Book*.

Federal Statistical Office, Gustav-Stresemann - Ring 11, D-6200, Wiesbaden, Germany; *Russische Federation*.

Food and Agriculture Organization of the United Nations (FAO), via delle Terme di Caracalla, 00100, Rome, Italy (Telephone Number in the U.S. (202) 653-2400); *Trade Yearbook*.

International Monetary Fund, 700 Nineteenth Street, NW, Washington, D.C. 20431 (202) 623-7000; *Direction of Trade Statistics*.

St. Martin's Press, Inc., 175 Fifth Avenue, New York, New York 10010 (800) 221-7945; *The Statesman's Year-Book*.

Statistical Office of the United Nations, Publishing Service, New York, New York 10017 (800) 253-9646; *International Trade Statistics Yearbook;* and *Statistical Yearbook*.

The World Bank, 1818 H Street, NW, Washington, D.C. 20433 (202) 477-1234; *Statistical Handbook: States of the Former USSR; World Development Report;* and *World Development Indicators*.

RUSSIA - FORESTRY AND FOREST PRODUCTS

Academic International Press, Box 1111, Gulf Breeze, Florida 32562; *Russia and Eurasia Facts and Figures Annual*.

Business International Moscow, 23 Profsoyuznaya Ulitsa, 117859, Moscow (Telephone Number in U.S. (800) 938-4685); *The CIS Market Atlas*.

Federal Statistical Office, Gustav-Stresemann - Ring 11, D-6200, Wiesbaden, Germany; *Russische Federation*.

Food and Agriculture Organization of the United Nations (FAO), via delle Terme di Caracalla, 00100, Rome, Italy (Telephone

Number in the U.S. (202) 653-2400); *The State of Food and Agriculture;* and *Yearbook of Forest Products*.

St. Martin's Press, Inc., 175 Fifth Avenue, New York, New York 10010 (800) 221-7945; *The Statesman's Year-Book*.

Statistical Office of the United Nations, Publishing Service, New York, New York 10017 (800) 253-9646; *Industrial Commodity Statistics Yearbook; Statistical Yearbook;* and *Trends in Europe and North America: The Statistical Yearbook of the Economic Commission for Europe*.

United Nations Educational, Scientific and Cultural Organization (UNESCO), 7 Place de Fontenoy, F-75700 Paris, France (Telephone Number in U.S. (212) 963-5981); *Statistical Yearbook*.

The World Bank, 1818 H Street, NW, Washington, D.C. 20433 (202) 477-1234; *World Development Report*.

RUSSIA - GOATS - See RUSSIA - LIVESTOCK AND POULTRY

RUSSIA - GOVERNMENT

Academic International Press, Box 1111, Gulf Breeze, Florida 32562; *Russia and Eurasia Facts and Figures Annual*.

Central Intelligence Agency, Washington, D.C. 20505 (703) 482-1100, www.cia.gov; *The World Factbook*.

Europa Publications Limited, 18 Bedford Square, London, WC1B 3JN, England; *The Europa World Year Book*.

St. Martin's Press, Inc., 175 Fifth Avenue, New York, New York 10010 (800) 221-7945; *The Statesman's Year-Book*.

Statistical Office of the United Nations, Publishing Service, New York, New York 10017 (800) 253-9646; *National Accounts Statistics;* and *Statistical Yearbook*.

The World Bank, 1818 H Street, NW, Washington, D.C. 20433 (202) 477-1234; *Statistical Handbook: States of the Former USSR;* and *World Development Report*.

RUSSIA - GROSS DOMESTIC PRODUCT

Academic International Press, Box 1111, Gulf Breeze, Florida 32562; *Russia and Eurasia Facts and Figures Annual*.

Economist Intelligence Unit, 111 West 57th Street, New York, New York 10019 (800) 938-4685; *Russia Country Report*.

Euromonitor International, Inc., 122 South Michigan Avenue, Suite 1200, Chicago, Illinois 60603 (800) 577-EURO;

The World Economic Factbook.

Statistical Office of the United Nations, Publishing Service, New York, New York 10017 (800) 253-9646; *Human Development Report; National Accounts Statistics; Statistical Yearbook; and Trends in Europe and North America: The Statistical Yearbook of the Economic Commission for Europe.*

The World Bank, 1818 H Street, NW, Washington, D.C. 20433 (202) 477-1234; *Statistical Handbook: States of the Former USSR; World Development Report; and World Development Indicators.*

RUSSIA - GROSS NATIONAL PRODUCT

St. Martin's Press, Inc., 175 Fifth Avenue, New York, New York 10010 (800) 221-7945; *The Statesman's Year-Book.*

The World Bank, 1818 H Street, NW, Washington, D.C. 20433 (202) 477-1234; *The World Bank Atlas; World Development Report; and World Development Indicators.*

RUSSIA - HEALTH

Academic International Press, Box 1111, Gulf Breeze, Florida 32562; *Russia and Eurasia Facts and Figures Annual.*

Business International Moscow, 23 Profsoyuznaya Ulitsa, 117859, Moscow (Telephone Number in U.S. (800) 938-4685); *The CIS Market Atlas.*

Euromonitor International, Inc., 122 South Michigan Avenue, Suite 1200, Chicago, Illinois 60603 (800) 577-EURO; *World Marketing Data and Statistics.*

Federal Statistical Office, Gustav-Stresemann - Ring 11, D-6200, Wiesbaden, Germany; *Russische Federation.*

St. Martin's Press, Inc., 175 Fifth Avenue, New York, New York 10010 (800) 221-7945; *The Statesman's Year-Book.*

Statistical Office of the United Nations, Publishing Service, New York, New York 10017 (800) 253-9646; *Human Development Report; Statistical Yearbook; and Trends in Europe and North America: The Statistical Yearbook of the Economic Commission for Europe.*

United Nations Children's Fund (UNICEF), 3 United Nations Plaza, New York, New York 10017 (800) 253-9646; *State of the World's Children.*

The World Bank, 1818 H Street, NW, Washington, D.C. 20433 (202) 477-1234; *World Development Report.*

World Health Organization, Office of Publications, 20 Avenue Appia, CH-1211

Geneva 27, Switzerland (Telephone Number in U.S. (518) 436-9686); *World Health Statistics Annual.*

RUSSIA - HIGHWAYS

Academic International Press, Box 1111, Gulf Breeze, Florida 32562; *Russia and Eurasia Facts and Figures Annual.*

Business International Moscow, 23 Profsoyuznaya Ulitsa, 117859, Moscow (Telephone Number in U.S. (800) 938-4685); *The CIS Market Atlas.*

Central Intelligence Agency, Washington, D.C. 20505 (703) 482-1100, www.cia.gov; *The World Factbook.*

St. Martin's Press, Inc., 175 Fifth Avenue, New York, New York 10010 (800) 221-7945; *The Statesman's Year-Book.*

Statistical Office of the United Nations, Publishing Service, New York, New York 10017 (800) 253-9646; *Annual Bulletin of Transport Statistics for Europe; and Trends in Europe and North America: The Statistical Yearbook of the Economic Commission for Europe.*

World Health Organization, Office of Publications, 20 Avenue Appia, CH-1211 Geneva 27, Switzerland (Telephone Number in U.S. (518) 436-9686); *World Health Statistics Annual.*

RUSSIA - HOUSING AND HOUSING UNITS

Business International Moscow, 23 Profsoyuznaya Ulitsa, 117859, Moscow (Telephone Number in U.S. (800) 938-4685); *The CIS Market Atlas.*

Euromonitor International, Inc., 122 South Michigan Avenue, Suite 1200, Chicago, Illinois 60603 (800) 577-EURO; *World Marketing Data and Statistics.*

Statistical Office of the United Nations, Publishing Service, New York, New York 10017 (800) 253-9646; *Trends in Europe and North America: The Statistical Yearbook of the Economic Commission for Europe.*

RUSSIA - ILLITERATE POPULATION

Central Intelligence Agency, Washington, D.C. 20505 (703) 482-1100, www.cia.gov; *The World Factbook.*

Euromonitor International, Inc., 122 South Michigan Avenue, Suite 1200, Chicago, Illinois 60603 (800) 577-EURO; *The World Economic Factbook.*

Statistical Office of the United Nations, Publishing Service, New York, New York 10017 (800) 253-9646; *Human Development Report.*

United Nations Educational, Scientific and Cultural Organization (UNESCO), 7 Place de Fontenoy, F-75700 Paris, France (Telephone Number in U.S. (212) 963-5981); *Statistical Yearbook.*

RUSSIA - IMPORTS

Academic International Press, Box 1111, Gulf Breeze, Florida 32562; *Russia and Eurasia Facts and Figures Annual.*

Business International Moscow, 23 Profsoyuznaya Ulitsa, 117859, Moscow (Telephone Number in U.S. (800) 938-4685); *The CIS Market Atlas.*

Central Intelligence Agency, Washington, D.C. 20505 (703) 482-1100, www.cia.gov; *The World Factbook.*

Economist Intelligence Unit, 111 West 57th Street, New York, New York 10019 (800) 938-4685; *Russia Country Report.*

Euromonitor International, Inc., 122 South Michigan Avenue, Suite 1200, Chicago, Illinois 60603 (800) 577-EURO; *The World Economic Factbook.*

Europa Publications Limited, 18 Bedford Square, London, WC1B 3JN, England; *The Europa World Year Book.*

International Monetary Fund, 700 Nineteenth Street, NW, Washington, D.C. 20431 (202) 623-7000; *Direction of Trade Statistics.*

St. Martin's Press, Inc., 175 Fifth Avenue, New York, New York 10010 (800) 221-7945; *The Statesman's Year-Book.*

Statistical Office of the United Nations, Publishing Service, New York, New York 10017 (800) 253-9646; *International Trade Statistics Yearbook; and Trends in Europe and North America: The Statistical Yearbook of the Economic Commission for Europe.*

United Nations Conference on Trade and Development (UNCTAD), New York, New York 10017 (800) 253-9646; *Handbook of International Trade and Development Statistics.*

The World Bank, 1818 H Street, NW, Washington, D.C. 20433 (202) 477-1234; *Statistical Handbook: States of the Former USSR; World Development Report; and World Development Indicators.*

RUSSIA - INDUSTRY

Academic International Press, Box 1111, Gulf Breeze, Florida 32562; *Russia and Eurasia Facts and Figures Annual.*

Business International Moscow, 23 Profsoyuznaya Ulitsa, 117859, Moscow

(Telephone Number in U.S. (800) 938-4685); *The CIS Market Atlas.*

Central Intelligence Agency, Washington, D.C. 20505 (703) 482-1100, www.cia.gov; *The World Factbook.*

Economist Intelligence Unit, 111 West 57th Street, New York, New York 10019 (800) 938-4685; *Russia Country Report.*

Euromonitor International, Inc., 122 South Michigan Avenue, Suite 1200, Chicago, Illinois 60603 (800) 577-EURO; *The World Economic Factbook;* and *World Marketing Data and Statistics.*

Europa Publications Limited, 18 Bedford Square, London, WC1B 3JN, England; *The Europa World Year Book.*

Federal Statistical Office, Gustav-Stresemann - Ring 11, D-6200, Wiesbaden, Germany; *Russische Federation.*

St. Martin's Press, Inc., 175 Fifth Avenue, New York, New York 10010 (800) 221-7945; *The Statesman's Year-Book.*

Statistical Office of the United Nations, Publishing Service, New York, New York 10017 (800) 253-9646; *Industrial Commodity Statistics Yearbook; Statistical Yearbook;* and *Trends in Europe and North America: The Statistical Yearbook of the Economic Commission for Europe.*

The World Bank, 1818 H Street, NW, Washington, D.C. 20433 (202) 477-1234; *Statistical Handbook: States of the Former USSR;* and *World Development Indicators.*

RUSSIA - INFANT MORTALITY - See RUSSIA - MORTALITY

RUSSIA - INTERNAL TRADE

Statistical Office of the United Nations, Publishing Service, New York, New York 10017 (800) 253-9646; *Statistical Yearbook.*

RUSSIA - LABOR

Academic International Press, Box 1111, Gulf Breeze, Florida 32562; *Russia and Eurasia Facts and Figures Annual.*

Business International Moscow, 23 Profsoyuznaya Ulitsa, 117859, Moscow (Telephone Number in U.S. (800) 938-4685); *The CIS Market Atlas.*

Central Intelligence Agency, Washington, D.C. 20505 (703) 482-1100, www.cia.gov; *The World Factbook.*

Euromonitor International, Inc., 122 South Michigan Avenue, Suite 1200, Chicago, Illinois 60603 (800) 577-EURO; *World Marketing Data and Statistics.*

Europa Publications Limited, 18 Bedford Square, London, WC1B 3JN, England; *The Europa World Year Book.*

St. Martin's Press, Inc., 175 Fifth Avenue, New York, New York 10010 (800) 221-7945; *The Statesman's Year-Book.*

Statistical Office of the United Nations, Publishing Service, New York, New York 10017 (800) 253-9646; *Human Development Report;* and *Statistical Yearbook.*

The World Bank, 1818 H Street, NW, Washington, D.C. 20433 (202) 477-1234; *Statistical Handbook: States of the Former USSR; The World Bank Atlas; World Development Report;* and *World Development Indicators.*

RUSSIA - LAND USE

Central Intelligence Agency, Washington, D.C. 20505 (703) 482-1100, www.cia.gov; *The World Factbook.*

Food and Agriculture Organization of the United Nations (FAO), via delle Terme di Caracalla, 00100, Rome, Italy (Telephone Number in the U.S. (202) 653-2400); *Production Yearbook.*

The World Bank, 1818 H Street, NW, Washington, D.C. 20433 (202) 477-1234; *World Development Report.*

RUSSIA - LIBRARIES

Statistical Office of the United Nations, Publishing Service, New York, New York 10017 (800) 253-9646; *Trends in Europe and North America: The Statistical Yearbook of the Economic Commission for Europe.*

United Nations Educational, Scientific and Cultural Organization (UNESCO), 7 Place de Fontenoy, F-75700 Paris, France (Telephone Number in U.S. (212) 963-5981); *Statistical Yearbook.*

RUSSIA - LIFE EXPECTANCY

Academic International Press, Box 1111, Gulf Breeze, Florida 32562; *Russia and Eurasia Facts and Figures Annual.*

Business International Moscow, 23 Profsoyuznaya Ulitsa, 117859, Moscow (Telephone Number in U.S. (800) 938-4685); *The CIS Market Atlas.*

Central Intelligence Agency, Washington, D.C. 20505 (703) 482-1100, www.cia.gov; *The World Factbook.*

Euromonitor International, Inc., 122 South Michigan Avenue, Suite 1200, Chicago, Illinois 60603 (800) 577-EURO; *The World Economic Factbook.*

Statistical Office of the United Nations, Publishing Service, New York, New York 10017 (800) 253-9646; *Demographic Yearbook; Human Development Report; Trends in Europe and North America: The Statistical Yearbook of the Economic Commission for Europe;* and *World Statistics Pocketbook.*

The World Bank, 1818 H Street, NW, Washington, D.C. 20433 (202) 477-1234; *The World Bank Atlas; World Development Report;* and *World Development Indicators.*

World Health Organization, Office of Publications, 20 Avenue Appia, CH-1211 Geneva 27, Switzerland (Telephone Number in U.S. (518) 436-9686); *World Health Statistics Annual.*

RUSSIA - LIVESTOCK AND POULTRY

Academic International Press, Box 1111, Gulf Breeze, Florida 32562; *Russia and Eurasia Facts and Figures Annual.*

Business International Moscow, 23 Profsoyuznaya Ulitsa, 117859, Moscow (Telephone Number in U.S. (800) 938-4685); *The CIS Market Atlas.*

Europa Publications Limited, 18 Bedford Square, London, WC1B 3JN, England; *The Europa World Year Book.*

Food and Agriculture Organization of the United Nations (FAO), via delle Terme di Caracalla, 00100, Rome, Italy (Telephone Number in the U.S. (202) 653-2400); *Production Yearbook; The State of Food and Agriculture;* and *Trade Yearbook.*

St. Martin's Press, Inc., 175 Fifth Avenue, New York, New York 10010 (800) 221-7945; *The Statesman's Year-Book.*

Statistical Office of the United Nations, Publishing Service, New York, New York 10017 (800) 253-9646; *Industrial Commodity Statistics Yearbook;* and *Statistical Yearbook.*

RUSSIA - MACHINERY

Statistical Office of the United Nations, Publishing Service, New York, New York 10017 (800) 253-9646; *Industrial Commodity Statistics Yearbook.*

RUSSIA - MAIL - NUMBER OF PIECES SENT OR RECEIVED

Statistical Office of the United Nations, Publishing Service, New York, New York 10017 (800) 253-9646; *Statistical Yearbook.*

RUSSIA - MANUFACTURING

Statistical Office of the United Nations, Publishing Service, New York, New York 10017 (800) 253-9646; *Industrial*

Commodity Statistics Yearbook; and *Statistical Yearbook.*

The World Bank, 1818 H Street, NW, Washington, D.C. 20433 (202) 477-1234; *World Development Indicators.*

RUSSIA - MARRIAGE RATES

Academic International Press, Box 1111, Gulf Breeze, Florida 32562; *Russia and Eurasia Facts and Figures Annual.*

Europa Publications Limited, 18 Bedford Square, London, WC1B 3JN, England; *The Europa World Year Book.*

Statistical Office of the United Nations, Publishing Service, New York, New York 10017 (800) 253-9646; *Demographic Yearbook; Statistical Yearbook;* and *Trends in Europe and North America: The Statistical Yearbook of the Economic Commission for Europe.*

RUSSIA - MEAT PRODUCTION - See RUSSIA - LIVESTOCK AND POULTRY

RUSSIA - MERCHANT SHIPPING

St. Martin's Press, Inc., 175 Fifth Avenue, New York, New York 10010 (800) 221-7945; *The Statesman's Year-Book.*

Statistical Office of the United Nations, Publishing Service, New York, New York 10017 (800) 253-9646; *Annual Bulletin of Transport Statistics for Europe;* and *Statistical Yearbook.*

RUSSIA - MILITARY

Academic International Press, Box 1111, Gulf Breeze, Florida 32562; *Russia and Eurasia Facts and Figures Annual.*

Central Intelligence Agency, Washington, D.C. 20505 (703) 482-1100, www.cia.gov; *The World Factbook.*

The International Institute for Strategic Studies, 23 Tavistock Street, London WC2E 7NQ, England; *The Military Balance.*

St. Martin's Press, Inc., 175 Fifth Avenue, New York, New York 10010 (800) 221-7945; *The Statesman's Year-Book.*

Statistical Office of the United Nations, Publishing Service, New York, New York 10017 (800) 253-9646; *Human Development Report.*

RUSSIA - MINING AND MINERAL PRODUCTS

Academic International Press, Box 1111, Gulf Breeze, Florida 32562; *Russia and Eurasia Facts and Figures Annual.*

Business International Moscow, 23

Profsoyuznaya Ulitsa, 117859, Moscow (Telephone Number in U.S. (800) 938-4685); *The CIS Market Atlas.*

Europa Publications Limited, 18 Bedford Square, London, WC1B 3JN, England; *The Europa World Year Book.*

St. Martin's Press, Inc., 175 Fifth Avenue, New York, New York 10010 (800) 221-7945; *The Statesman's Year-Book.*

Statistical Office of the United Nations, Publishing Service, New York, New York 10017 (800) 253-9646; *Energy Statistics Yearbook; Industrial Commodity Statistics Yearbook;* and *Statistical Yearbook.*

RUSSIA - MONEY SUPPLY

Economist Intelligence Unit, 111 West 57th Street, New York, New York 10019 (800) 938-4685; *Russia Country Report.*

Europa Publications Limited, 18 Bedford Square, London, WC1B 3JN, England; *The Europa World Year Book.*

Federal Statistical Office, Gustav-Stresemann - Ring 11, D-6200, Wiesbaden, Germany; *Russische Federation.*

RUSSIA - MONUMENTS AND HISTORICAL SITES

United Nations Educational, Scientific and Cultural Organization (UNESCO), 7 Place de Fontenoy, F-75700 Paris, France (Telephone Number in U.S. (212) 963-5981); *Statistical Yearbook.*

RUSSIA - MORTALITY

Academic International Press, Box 1111, Gulf Breeze, Florida 32562; *Russia and Eurasia Facts and Figures Annual.*

Business International Moscow, 23 Profsoyuznaya Ulitsa, 117859, Moscow (Telephone Number in U.S. (800) 938-4685); *The CIS Market Atlas.*

Central Intelligence Agency, Washington, D.C. 20505 (703) 482-1100, www.cia.gov; *The World Factbook.*

Euromonitor International, Inc., 122 South Michigan Avenue, Suite 1200, Chicago, Illinois 60603 (800) 577-EURO; *The World Economic Factbook.*

Europa Publications Limited, 18 Bedford Square, London, WC1B 3JN, England; *The Europa World Year Book.*

Statistical Office of the United Nations, Publishing Service, New York, New York 10017 (800) 253-9646; *Demographic Yearbook; Human Development Report; Statistical Yearbook; Trends in Europe and North America: The Statistical Yearbook of*

the Economic Commission for Europe; and *World Statistics Pocketbook.*

United Nations Children's Fund (UNICEF), 3 United Nations Plaza, New York, New York 10017 (800) 253-9646; *State of the World's Children.*

The World Bank, 1818 H Street, NW, Washington, D.C. 20433 (202) 477-1234; *The World Bank Atlas; World Development Report;* and *World Development Indicators.*

World Health Organization, Office of Publications, 20 Avenue Appia, CH-1211 Geneva 27, Switzerland (Telephone Number in U.S. (518) 436-9686); *World Health Statistics Annual.*

RUSSIA - MOTION PICTURES

Statistical Office of the United Nations, Publishing Service, New York, New York 10017 (800) 253-9646; *Statistical Yearbook.*

United Nations Educational, Scientific and Cultural Organization (UNESCO), 7 Place de Fontenoy, F-75700 Paris, France (Telephone Number in U.S. (212) 963-5981); *Statistical Yearbook.*

RUSSIA - MOTOR VEHICLE PRODUCTION

Statistical Office of the United Nations, Publishing Service, New York, New York 10017 (800) 253-9646; *Statistical Yearbook.*

RUSSIA - MOTOR VEHICLES

Business International Moscow, 23 Profsoyuznaya Ulitsa, 117859, Moscow (Telephone Number in U.S. (800) 938-4685); *The CIS Market Atlas.*

RUSSIA - MUSEUMS

United Nations Educational, Scientific and Cultural Organization (UNESCO), 7 Place de Fontenoy, F-75700 Paris, France (Telephone Number in U.S. (212) 963-5981); *Statistical Yearbook.*

RUSSIA - NATIONAL ACCOUNTS

Europa Publications Limited, 18 Bedford Square, London, WC1B 3JN, England; *The Europa World Year Book.*

Federal Statistical Office, Gustav-Stresemann - Ring 11, D-6200, Wiesbaden, Germany; *Russische Federation.*

Statistical Office of the United Nations, Publishing Service, New York, New York 10017 (800) 253-9646; *National Accounts Statistics;* and *Statistical Yearbook.*

The World Bank, 1818 H Street, NW, Washington, D.C. 20433 (202) 477-1234; *Statistical Handbook: States of the Former*

USSR.

RUSSIA - NATIONAL INCOME

Business International Moscow, 23 Profsoyuznaya Ulitsa, 117859, Moscow (Telephone Number in U.S. (800) 938-4685); *The CIS Market Atlas.*

Statistical Office of the United Nations, Publishing Service, New York, New York 10017 (800) 253-9646; *National Accounts Statistics;* and *Statistical Yearbook.*

RUSSIA - NATIONAL PRODUCT

Statistical Office of the United Nations, Publishing Service, New York, New York 10017 (800) 253-9646; *Statistical Yearbook.*

RUSSIA - PATENTS, TRADEMARKS AND SERVICE MARKS

Statistical Office of the United Nations, Publishing Service, New York, New York 10017 (800) 253-9646; *Statistical Yearbook.*

RUSSIA - PERIODICALS

United Nations Educational, Scientific and Cultural Organization (UNESCO), 7 Place de Fontenoy, F-75700 Paris, France (Telephone Number in U.S. (212) 963-5981); *Statistical Yearbook.*

RUSSIA - PETROLEUM INDUSTRY

Food and Agriculture Organization of the United Nations (FAO), via delle Terme di Caracalla, 00100, Rome, Italy (Telephone Number in the U.S. (202) 653-2400); *The State of Food and Agriculture;*

St. Martin's Press, Inc., 175 Fifth Avenue, New York, New York 10010 (800) 221-7945; *The Statesman's Year-Book.*

Statistical Office of the United Nations, Publishing Service, New York, New York 10017 (800) 253-9646; *Energy Statistics Yearbook; Industrial Commodity Statistics Yearbook; Statistical Yearbook;* and *Trends in Europe and North America: The Statistical Yearbook of the Economic Commission for Europe.*

RUSSIA - PIGS - See RUSSIA - LIVESTOCK AND POULTRY

RUSSIA - POPULATION

Academic International Press, Box 1111, Gulf Breeze, Florida 32562; *Russia and Eurasia Facts and Figures Annual.*

Business International Moscow, 23 Profsoyuznaya Ulitsa, 117859, Moscow (Telephone Number in U.S. (800) 938-4685); *The CIS Market Atlas.*

Central Intelligence Agency,

Washington, D.C. 20505 (703) 482-1100, www.cia.gov; *The World Factbook.*

Economist Intelligence Unit, 111 West 57th Street, New York, New York 10019 (800) 938-4685; *Russia Country Report.*

Euromonitor International, Inc., 122 South Michigan Avenue, Suite 1200, Chicago, Illinois 60603 (800) 577-EURO; *The World Economic Factbook.*

Europa Publications Limited, 18 Bedford Square, London, WC1B 3JN, England; *The Europa World Year Book.*

Federal Statistical Office, Gustav-Stresemann - Ring 11, D-6200, Wiesbaden, Germany; *Russische Federation.*

Food and Agriculture Organization of the United Nations (FAO), via delle Terme di Caracalla, 00100, Rome, Italy (Telephone Number in the U.S. (202) 653-2400); *Production Yearbook.*

St. Martin's Press, Inc., 175 Fifth Avenue, New York, New York 10010 (800) 221-7945; *The Statesman's Year-Book.*

Statistical Office of the United Nations, Publishing Service, New York, New York 10017 (800) 253-9646; *Demographic Yearbook; Human Development Report; Statistical Yearbook; Trends in Europe and North America: The Statistical Yearbook of the Economic Commission for Europe;* and *World Statistics Pocketbook.*

United Nations Educational, Scientific and Cultural Organization (UNESCO), 7 Place de Fontenoy, F-75700 Paris, France (Telephone Number in U.S. (212) 963-5981); *Statistical Yearbook.*

The World Bank, 1818 H Street, NW, Washington, D.C. 20433 (202) 477-1234; *Statistical Handbook: States of the Former USSR; The World Bank Atlas; World Development Report;* and *World Development Indicators.*

World Health Organization, Office of Publications, 20 Avenue Appia, CH-1211 Geneva 27, Switzerland (Telephone Number in U.S. (518) 436-9686); *World Health Statistics Annual.*

RUSSIA - POST OFFICES

St. Martin's Press, Inc., 175 Fifth Avenue, New York, New York 10010 (800) 221-7945; *The Statesman's Year-Book.*

Statistical Office of the United Nations, Publishing Service, New York, New York 10017 (800) 253-9646; *Trends in Europe and North America: The Statistical Yearbook of the Economic Commission for Europe.*

RUSSIA - POULTRY - See RUSSIA -

LIVESTOCK AND POULTRY

RUSSIA - PRICES

Federal Statistical Office, Gustav-Stresemann - Ring 11, D-6200, Wiesbaden, Germany; *Russische Federation.*

Food and Agriculture Organization of the United Nations (FAO), via delle Terme di Caracalla, 00100, Rome, Italy (Telephone Number in the U.S. (202) 653-2400); *Production Yearbook.*

The World Bank, 1818 H Street, NW, Washington, D.C. 20433 (202) 477-1234; *Statistical Handbook: States of the Former USSR.*

RUSSIA - PRODUCTION

The World Bank, 1818 H Street, NW, Washington, D.C. 20433 (202) 477-1234; *Statistical Handbook: States of the Former USSR.*

RUSSIA - PUBLIC FINANCE - See RUSSIA - FINANCE

RUSSIA - RADIO RECEIVER PRODUCTION

Statistical Office of the United Nations, Publishing Service, New York, New York 10017 (800) 253-9646; *Statistical Yearbook.*

RUSSIA - RADIO RECEIVERS

St. Martin's Press, Inc., 175 Fifth Avenue, New York, New York 10010 (800) 221-7945; *The Statesman's Year-Book.*

RUSSIA - RAILWAYS

Academic International Press, Box 1111, Gulf Breeze, Florida 32562; *Russia and Eurasia Facts and Figures Annual.*

Business International Moscow, 23 Profsoyuznaya Ulitsa, 117859, Moscow (Telephone Number in U.S. (800) 938-4685); *The CIS Market Atlas.*

St. Martin's Press, Inc., 175 Fifth Avenue, New York, New York 10010 (800) 221-7945; *The Statesman's Year-Book.*

Statistical Office of the United Nations, Publishing Service, New York, New York 10017 (800) 253-9646; *Annual Bulletin of Transport Statistics for Europe; Statistical Yearbook;* and *Trends in Europe and North America: The Statistical Yearbook of the Economic Commission for Europe.*

RUSSIA - RELIGION

Academic International Press, Box 1111, Gulf Breeze, Florida 32562; *Russia and Eurasia Facts and Figures Annual.*

Central Intelligence Agency, Washington, D.C. 20505 (703) 482-1100, www.cia.gov; *The World Factbook*.

St. Martin's Press, Inc., 175 Fifth Avenue, New York, New York 10010 (800) 221-7945; *The Statesman's Year-Book*.

RUSSIA - RETAIL TRADE

Business International Moscow, 23 Profsoyuznaya Ulitsa, 117859, Moscow (Telephone Number in U.S. (800) 938-4685); *The CIS Market Atlas*.

Euromonitor International, Inc., 122 South Michigan Avenue, Suite 1200, Chicago, Illinois 60603 (800) 577-EURO; *Retail Trade International*; and *World Marketing Data and Statistics*.

Statistical Office of the United Nations, Publishing Service, New York, New York 10017 (800) 253-9646; *Statistical Yearbook*.

RUSSIA - ROADS - See RUSSIA - HIGHWAYS

RUSSIA - ROUNDWOOD PRODUCTION AND CONSUMPTION - See RUSSIA - FORESTRY AND FOREST PRODUCTS

RUSSIA - RUBBER PRODUCTION AND CONSUMPTION

Statistical Office of the United Nations, Publishing Service, New York, New York 10017 (800) 253-9646; *Statistical Yearbook*.

RUSSIA - SCIENTISTS, TECHNICIANS AND ENGINEERS

Statistical Office of the United Nations, Publishing Service, New York, New York 10017 (800) 253-9646; *Statistical Yearbook*.

RUSSIA - SHEEP - See RUSSIA - LIVESTOCK AND POULTRY

RUSSIA - SOCIAL DATA

Statistical Office of the United Nations, Publishing Service, New York, New York 10017 (800) 253-9646; *World Statistics Pocketbook*.

RUSSIA - SOCIAL SECURITY

St. Martin's Press, Inc., 175 Fifth Avenue, New York, New York 10010 (800) 221-7945; *The Statesman's Year-Book*.

Statistical Office of the United Nations, Publishing Service, New York, New York 10017 (800) 253-9646; *National Accounts Statistics*.

RUSSIA - STEEL PRODUCTION AND CONSUMPTION - See RUSSIA - MINING AND MINERAL PRODUCTS

RUSSIA - TAXATION

St. Martin's Press, Inc., 175 Fifth Avenue, New York, New York 10010 (800) 221-7945; *The Statesman's Year-Book*.

RUSSIA - TELEPHONES IN USE

Academic International Press, Box 1111, Gulf Breeze, Florida 32562; *Russia and Eurasia Facts and Figures Annual*.

Central Intelligence Agency, Washington, D.C. 20505 (703) 482-1100, www.cia.gov; *The World Factbook*.

St. Martin's Press, Inc., 175 Fifth Avenue, New York, New York 10010 (800) 221-7945; *The Statesman's Year-Book*.

Statistical Office of the United Nations, Publishing Service, New York, New York 10017 (800) 253-9646; *Statistical Yearbook; Trends in Europe and North America: The Statistical Yearbook of the Economic Commission for Europe;* and *World Statistics Pocketbook*.

RUSSIA - TEXTILE INDUSTRY

Business International Moscow, 23 Profsoyuznaya Ulitsa, 117859, Moscow (Telephone Number in U.S. (800) 938-4685); *The CIS Market Atlas*.

Euromonitor International, Inc., 122 South Michigan Avenue, Suite 1200, Chicago, Illinois 60603 (800) 577-EURO; *Retail Trade International*.

Statistical Office of the United Nations, Publishing Service, New York, New York 10017 (800) 253-9646; *Industrial Commodity Statistics Yearbook;* and *Statistical Yearbook*.

RUSSIA - THEATRE

United Nations Educational, Scientific and Cultural Organization (UNESCO), 7 Place de Fontenoy, F-75700 Paris, France (Telephone Number in U.S. (212) 963-5981); *Statistical Yearbook*.

RUSSIA - TIRE (MOTOR VEHICLE) PRODUCTION

Statistical Office of the United Nations, Publishing Service, New York, New York 10017 (800) 253-9646; *Statistical Yearbook*.

RUSSIA - TOBACCO PRODUCTION

Statistical Office of the United Nations, Publishing Service, New York, New York 10017 (800) 253-9646; *Statistical Yearbook*.

RUSSIA - TOURISM

Business International Moscow, 23 Profsoyuznaya Ulitsa, 117859, Moscow (Telephone Number in U.S. (800) 938-4685); *The CIS Market Atlas*.

Euromonitor International, Inc., 122 South Michigan Avenue, Suite 1200, Chicago, Illinois 60603 (800) 577-EURO; *The World Economic Factbook;* and *World Marketing Data and Statistics*.

Federal Statistical Office, Gustav-Stresemann - Ring 11, D-6200, Wiesbaden, Germany; *Russische Federation*.

Statistical Office of the United Nations, Publishing Service, New York, New York 10017 (800) 253-9646; *Statistical Yearbook;* and *Trends in Europe and North America: The Statistical Yearbook of the Economic Commission for Europe*.

RUSSIA - TRADEMARKS AND SERVICE MARKS - See RUSSIA - PATENTS, TRADEMARKS AND SERVICE MARKS

RUSSIA - TRANSPORTATION AND COMMUNICATIONS

Academic International Press, Box 1111, Gulf Breeze, Florida 32562; *Russia and Eurasia Facts and Figures Annual*.

Business International Moscow, 23 Profsoyuznaya Ulitsa, 117859, Moscow (Telephone Number in U.S. (800) 938-4685); *The CIS Market Atlas*.

Central Intelligence Agency, Washington, D.C. 20505 (703) 482-1100, www.cia.gov; *The World Factbook*.

Euromonitor International, Inc., 122 South Michigan Avenue, Suite 1200, Chicago, Illinois 60603 (800) 577-EURO; *World Marketing Data and Statistics*.

Europa Publications Limited, 18 Bedford Square, London, WC1B 3JN, England; *The Europa World Year Book*.

Federal Statistical Office, Gustav-Stresemann - Ring 11, D-6200, Wiesbaden, Germany; *Russische Federation*.

St. Martin's Press, Inc., 175 Fifth Avenue, New York, New York 10010 (800) 221-7945; *The Statesman's Year-Book*.

Statistical Office of the United Nations, Publishing Service, New York, New York 10017 (800) 253-9646; *Annual Bulletin of Transport Statistics for Europe; Human Development Report;* and *Trends in Europe and North America: The Statistical Yearbook of the Economic Commission for Europe*.

RUSSIA - UNEMPLOYMENT

Central Intelligence Agency, Washington, D.C. 20505 (703) 482-1100, www.cia.gov; *The World Factbook*.

St. Martin's Press, Inc., 175 Fifth Avenue, New York, New York 10010 (800)

221-7945; *The Statesman's Year-Book.*

Statistical Office of the United Nations, Publishing Service, New York, New York 10017 (800) 253-9646; *Statistical Yearbook;* and *Trends in Europe and North America: The Statistical Yearbook of the Economic Commission for Europe.*

RUSSIA - VITAL STATISTICS

Statistical Office of the United Nations, Publishing Service, New York, New York 10017 (800) 253-9646; *Statistical Yearbook.*

World Health Organization, Office of Publications, 20 Avenue Appia, CH-1211 Geneva 27, Switzerland (Telephone Number in U.S. (518) 436-9686); *World Health Statistics Annual.*

RUSSIA - WAGES

Business International Moscow, 23 Profsoyuznaya Ulitsa, 117859, Moscow (Telephone Number in U.S. (800) 938-4685); *The CIS Market Atlas.*

Federal Statistical Office, Gustav-Stresemann - Ring 11, D-6200, Wiesbaden, Germany; *Russische Federation.*

Statistical Office of the United Nations, Publishing Service, New York, New York 10017 (800) 253-9646; *Statistical Yearbook.*

The World Bank, 1818 H Street, NW, Washington, D.C. 20433 (202) 477-1234; *Statistical Handbook: States of the Former USSR.*

RUSSIA - WELFARE

Academic International Press, Box 1111, Gulf Breeze, Florida 32562; *Russia and Eurasia Facts and Figures Annual.*

St. Martin's Press, Inc., 175 Fifth Avenue, New York, New York 10010 (800) 221-7945; *The Statesman's Year-Book.*

RUSSIA - WHOLESALE PRICES

Academic International Press, Box 1111, Gulf Breeze, Florida 32562; *Russia and Eurasia Facts and Figures Annual.*

Statistical Office of the United Nations, Publishing Service, New York, New York 10017 (800) 253-9646; *Statistical Yearbook.*

RUSSIA - WHOLESALE TRADE

Statistical Office of the United Nations, Publishing Service, New York, New York 10017 (800) 253-9646; *Statistical Yearbook.*

RUSSIA - WOOL PRODUCTION AND CONSUMPTION - See RUSSIA - TEXTILE INDUSTRY

Rwanda - National Statistical Office

Direction Generale de la Statistiques, Ministere du Plan, BP 46, Kigali, Rwanda.

Rwanda - Primary Statistics Source

Direction Generale de la Statistiques, BP 46, Kigali, Rwanda; *Bulletin de Statistique* (Statistical Bulletin).

RWANDA - AGRICULTURE

Economist Intelligence Unit, 111 West 57th Street, New York, New York 10019 (800) 938-4685; *Rwanda Country Report.*

Euromonitor International, Inc., 122 South Michigan Avenue, Suite 1200, Chicago, Illinois 60603 (800) 577-EURO; *International Marketing Data and Statistics;* and *World Marketing Data and Statistics.*

Europa Publications Limited, 18 Bedford Square, London, WC1B 3JN, England; *The Europa World Year Book.*

Food and Agricultural Organization of the United Nations (FAO) Via delle Terme di Caracalla, 00100 Rome, Italy (Telephone Number in U.S. (202) 653-2400); *Production Yearbook; The State of Food and Agriculture;* and *Trade Yearbook.*

M.E. Sharpe, 80 Business Park Drive, Armonk, New York 10504 (800) 541-6563; *The Illustrated Book of World Rankings.*

St. Martin's Press, Inc., 175 Fifth Avenue, New York, New York 10010 (800) 221-7945; *The Statesman's Year-Book.*

Statistical Office of the United Nations, Publishing Service, New York, New York 10017 (800) 253-9646; *Statistical Yearbook;* and *Survey of Economic and Social Conditions in Africa.*

United Nations Conference on Trade and Development, Central Statistical Service, Palais des Nations, Geneva, Switzerland (Telephone in U.S. (800) 253-9646); *UNCTAD Commodity Yearbook.*

United Nations Economic Commission for Africa, Africa Hall, P.O. Box 3001, Addis Ababa, Ethiopia (Telephone Number in U.S. (800) 253-9646); *African Statistical Yearbook.*

The World Bank, 1818 H Street, NW, Washington, D.C. 20433 (202) 477-1234; *World Development Indicators.*

RWANDA - AIRLINE SERVICE

Europa Publications Limited, 18 Bedford Square, London, WC1B 3JN, England; *The Europa World Year Book.*

M.E. Sharpe, 80 Business Park Drive, Armonk, New York 10504 (800) 541-6563; *The Illustrated Book of World Rankings.*

St. Martin's Press, Inc., 175 Fifth Avenue, New York, New York 10010 (800) 221-7945; *The Statesman's Year-Book.*

United Nations Economic Commission for Africa, Africa Hall, P.O. Box 3001, Addis Ababa, Ethiopia (Telephone Number in U.S. (800) 253-9646); *African Statistical Yearbook.*

RWANDA - AIRPORTS

Central Intelligence Agency, Washington, D.C. 20505 (703) 482-1100, www.cia.gov; *The World Factbook.*

RWANDA - ALUMINUM PRODUCTION AND CONSUMPTION - See RWANDA - MINING AND MINERAL PRODUCTS

RWANDA - ANIMAL HEALTH

Food and Agricultural Organization of the United Nations (FAO), Via delle Terme di Caracalla, 00100, Rome, Italy (Telephone Number in U.S. (202) 653-2400); *Animal Health Yearbook.*

RWANDA - AREA AND DENSITY OF POPULATION

African Development Bank, 01 BP 1387, Abidjan 01, Cote d'Ivoire; *Selected Statistics on Regional Member Countries.*

Central Intelligence Agency, Washington, D.C. 20505 (703) 482-1100, www.cia.gov; *The World Factbook.*

Euromonitor International, Inc., 122 South Michigan Avenue, Suite 1200, Chicago, Illinois 60603 (800) 577-EURO; *International Marketing Data and Statistics;* and *The World Economic Factbook.*

Europa Publications Limited, 18 Bedford Square, London, WC1B 3JN, England; *The Europa World Year Book.*

Food and Agricultural Organization of the United Nations (FAO) Via delle Terme di Caracalla, 00100 Rome, Italy (Telephone Number in U.S. (202) 653-2400); *The State of Food and Agriculture.*

M.E. Sharpe, 80 Business Park Drive, Armonk, New York 10504 (800) 541-6563; *The Illustrated Book of World Rankings.*

St. Martin's Press, Inc., 175 Fifth Avenue, New York, New York 10010 (800) 221-7945; *The Statesman's Year-Book.*

Statistical Office of the United Nations, Publishing Service, New York, New York 10017 (800) 253-9646; *Statistical Yearbook;* and *Survey of Economic and Social Conditions in Africa.*

United Nations Educational, Scientific and Cultural Organization (UNESCO), 7 Place de Fontenoy, F-75700 Paris, France (Telephone Number in U.S. (212) 963-5981); *Statistical Yearbook.*

The World Bank, 1818 H Street, NW, Washington, D.C. 20433 (202) 477-1234; *World Development Report.*

RWANDA - ARMS EXPORTS AND IMPORTS - See RWANDA - DEFENSE

RWANDA - BALANCE OF PAYMENTS

African Development Bank, 01 BP 1387, Abidjan 01, Cote d'Ivoire; *Selected Statistics on Regional Member Countries.*

The Economist Intelligence Unit, 111 West 57th Street, New York, New York 10019 (800) 938-4685; *The World Market Atlas.*

Europa Publications Limited, 18 Bedford Square, London, WC1B 3JN, England; *The Europa World Year Book.*

International Monetary Fund, 700 Nineteenth Street, NW, Washington, D.C. 20431 (202) 623-7000; *Balance of Payments Yearbook;* and *International Financial Statistics.*

United Nations Conference on Trade and Development (UNCTAD), New York, New York 10017 (800) 253-9646; *Handbook of International Trade and Development Statistics.*

United Nations Economic Commission for Africa, Africa Hall, P.O. Box 3001, Addis Ababa, Ethiopia (Telephone Number in U.S. (800) 253-9646); *African Statistical Yearbook.*

The World Bank, 1818 H Street, NW, Washington, D.C. 20433 (202) 477-1234; *World Development Report;* and *World Development Indicators.*

RWANDA - BANKING

Euromonitor International, Inc., 122 South Michigan Avenue, Suite 1200, Chicago, Illinois 60603 (800) 577-EURO; *World Marketing Data and Statistics.*

Europa Publications Limited, 18 Bedford Square, London, WC1B 3JN, England; *The Europa World Year Book.*

International Monetary Fund, 700 Nineteenth Street, NW, Washington, D.C. 20431 (202) 623-7000; *International*

Financial Statistics.

M.E. Sharpe, 80 Business Park Drive, Armonk, New York 10504 (800) 541-6563; *The Illustrated Book of World Rankings.*

St. Martin's Press, Inc., 175 Fifth Avenue, New York, New York 10010 (800) 221-7945; *The Statesman's Year-Book.*

Statistical Office of the United Nations, Publishing Service, New York, New York 10017 (800) 253-9646; *Statistical Yearbook.*

United Nations Economic Commission for Africa, Africa Hall, P.O. Box 3001, Addis Ababa, Ethiopia (Telephone Number in U.S. (800) 253-9646); *African Statistical Yearbook.*

RWANDA - BARLEY PRODUCTION - See RWANDA - CROPS

RWANDA - BEER PRODUCTION - See RWANDA - BEVERAGES

RWANDA - BEVERAGES

M.E. Sharpe, 80 Business Park Drive, Armonk, New York 10504 (800) 541-6563; *The Illustrated Book of World Rankings.*

Statistical Office of the United Nations, Publishing Service, New York, New York 10017 (800) 253-9646; *Statistical Yearbook.*

RWANDA - BIRTH RATES

Central Intelligence Agency, Washington, D.C. 20505 (703) 482-1100, www.cia.gov; *The World Factbook.*

Euromonitor International, Inc., 122 South Michigan Avenue, Suite 1200, Chicago, Illinois 60603 (800) 577-EURO; *International Marketing Data and Statistics;* and *The World Economic Factbook.*

Europa Publications Limited, 18 Bedford Square, London, WC1B 3JN, England; *The Europa World Year Book.*

M.E. Sharpe, 80 Business Park Drive, Armonk, New York 10504 (800) 541-6563; *The Illustrated Book of World Rankings.*

Statistical Office of the United Nations, Publishing Service, New York, New York 10017 (800) 253-9646; *Demographic Yearbook; Statistical Yearbook;* and *Survey of Economic and Social Conditions in Africa.*

The World Bank, 1818 H Street, NW, Washington, D.C. 20433 (202) 477-1234; *World Development Indicators.*

World Health Organization, Office of Publications, 20 Avenue Appia, CH-1211 Geneva 27, Switzerland (Telephone Number in U.S. (518) 436-9686); *World*

Health Statistics Annual.

RWANDA - BONDS

International Monetary Fund, 700 Nineteenth Street, NW, Washington, D.C. 20431 (202) 623-7000; *Government Finance Statistics Yearbook.*

RWANDA - BROADCASTING

Billboard Limited, P.O. Box 9027, 1006 AA Amsterdam, The Netherlands (Telephone Number in U.S. (212) 764-7300); *World Radio TV Handbook.*

Central Intelligence Agency, Washington, D.C. 20505 (703) 482-1100, www.cia.gov; *The World Factbook.*

Euromonitor International, Inc., 122 South Michigan Avenue, Suite 1200, Chicago, Illinois 60603 (800) 577-EURO; *World Marketing Data and Statistics.*

M.E. Sharpe, 80 Business Park Drive, Armonk, New York 10504 (800) 541-6563; *The Illustrated Book of World Rankings.*

St. Martin's Press, Inc., 175 Fifth Avenue, New York, New York 10010 (800) 221-7945; *The Statesman's Year-Book.*

RWANDA - BUDGET

Central Intelligence Agency, Washington, D.C. 20505 (703) 482-1100, www.cia.gov; *The World Factbook.*

RWANDA - BUSINESS AND PROFESSIONAL LICENSES

International Monetary Fund, 700 Nineteenth Street, NW, Washington, D.C. 20431 (202) 623-7000; *Government Finance Statistics Yearbook.*

RWANDA - CALORIE SUPPLY

African Development Bank, 01 BP 1387, Abidjan 01, Cote d'Ivoire; *Selected Statistics on Regional Member Countries.*

Food and Agricultural Organization of the United Nations (FAO) Via delle Terme di Caracalla, 00100 Rome, Italy (Telephone Number in U.S. (202) 653-2400); *The State of Food and Agriculture.*

RWANDA - CAPITAL REVENUE

International Monetary Fund, 700 Nineteenth Street, NW, Washington, D.C. 20431 (202) 623-7000; *Government Finance Statistics Yearbook.*

RWANDA - CATTLE - See RWANDA - LIVESTOCK AND POULTRY

RWANDA - CEMENT PRODUCTION - See RWANDA - MINING AND MINERAL

PRODUCTS

RWANDA - CHEMICAL (ORGANIC) PRODUCTION - See RWANDA - MINING AND MINERAL PRODUCTS

RWANDA - CHICKENS - See RWANDA - LIVESTOCK AND POULTRY

RWANDA - CIGARETTE PRODUCTION - See RWANDA - TOBACCO PRODUCTION

RWANDA - CLIMATE

M.E. Sharpe, 80 Business Park Drive, Armonk, New York 10504 (800) 541-6563; *The Illustrated Book of World Rankings.*

St. Martin's Press, Inc., 175 Fifth Avenue, New York, New York 10010 (800) 221-7945; *The Statesman's Year-Book.*

RWANDA - COAL PRODUCTION - See RWANDA - MINING AND MINERAL PRODUCTS

RWANDA - COFFEE - See RWANDA - CROPS

RWANDA - COMMERCE

St. Martin's Press, Inc., 175 Fifth Avenue, New York, New York 10010 (800) 221-7945; *The Statesman's Year-Book.*

RWANDA - COMMUNICATIONS - See RWANDA - TRANSPORTATION AND COMMUNICATIONS

RWANDA - CONSTRUCTION INDUSTRY

M.E. Sharpe, 80 Business Park Drive, Armonk, New York 10504 (800) 541-6563; *The Illustrated Book of World Rankings.*

St. Martin's Press, Inc., 175 Fifth Avenue, New York, New York 10010 (800) 221-7945; *The Statesman's Year-Book.*

Statistical Office of the United Nations, Publishing Service, New York, New York 10017 (800) 253-9646; *Statistical Yearbook.*

United Nations Economic Commission for Africa, Africa Hall, P.O. Box 3001, Addis Ababa, Ethiopia (Telephone Number in U.S. (800) 253-9646); *African Statistical Yearbook.*

RWANDA - CONSUMER PRICE INDEX

African Development Bank, 01 BP 1387, Abidjan 01, Cote d'Ivoire; *Selected Statistics on Regional Member Countries.*

Europa Publications Limited, 18 Bedford Square, London, WC1B 3JN, England; *The Europa World Year Book.*

Statistical Office of the United Nations,

Publishing Service, New York, New York 10017 (800) 253-9646; *Statistical Yearbook;* and *Survey of Economic and Social Conditions in Africa.*

United Nations Economic Commission for Africa, Africa Hall, P.O. Box 3001, Addis Ababa, Ethiopia (Telephone Number in U.S. (800) 253-9646); *African Statistical Yearbook.*

RWANDA - CONSUMER PRICES

Euromonitor International, Inc., 122 South Michigan Avenue, Suite 1200, Chicago, Illinois 60603 (800) 577-EURO; *World Marketing Data and Statistics.*

International Labour Office, I.L.O. Publications, 1828 L Street, NW., Suite 801, Washington, D.C. 20036 (301) 638-3152; *Yearbook of Labour Statistics.*

International Monetary Fund, 700 Nineteenth Street, NW, Washington, D.C. 20431 (202) 623-7000; *International Financial Statistics.*

RWANDA - CONSUMPTION

African Development Bank, 01 BP 1387, Abidjan 01, Cote d'Ivoire; *Selected Statistics on Regional Member Countries.*

Statistical Office of the United Nations, Publishing Service, New York 10017 (800) 253-9646; *Survey of Economic and Social Conditions in Africa.*

The World Bank, 1818 H Street, NW, Washington, D.C. 20433 (202) 477-1234; *World Development Report.*

RWANDA - COPPER PRODUCTION AND CONSUMPTION - See RWANDA - MINING AND MINERAL PRODUCTS

RWANDA - CORN PRODUCTION - See RWANDA - CROPS

RWANDA - CORPORATE TAXES - See RWANDA - TAXATION

RWANDA - COTTON PRODUCTION - See RWANDA - CROPS

RWANDA - CRIME

International Criminal Police Organization (INTERPOL), 50 quai Achille Lignon, F-69006 Lyon, France; *International Crime Statistics.*

RWANDA - CROPS

Europa Publications Limited, 18 Bedford Square, London, WC1B 3JN, England; *The Europa World Year Book.*

Food and Agricultural Organization of

the United Nations (FAO) Via delle Terme di Caracalla, 00100 Rome, Italy (Telephone Number in U.S. (202) 653-2400); *Production Yearbook;* and *The State of Food and Agriculture.*

International Monetary Fund, 700 Nineteenth Street, NW, Washington, D.C. 20431 (202) 623-7000; *International Financial Statistics.*

M.E. Sharpe, 80 Business Park Drive, Armonk, New York 10504 (800) 541-6563; *The Illustrated Book of World Rankings.*

St. Martin's Press, Inc., 175 Fifth Avenue, New York, New York 10010 (800) 221-7945; *The Statesman's Year-Book.*

Statistical Office of the United Nations, Publishing Service, New York, New York 10017 (800) 253-9646; *Statistical Yearbook.*

United Nations Conference on Trade and Development, Central Statistical Service, Palais des Nations, Geneva, Switzerland (Telephone in U.S. (800) 253-9646); *UNCTAD Commodity Yearbook.*

United Nations Economic Commission for Africa, Africa Hall, P.O. Box 3001, Addis Ababa, Ethiopia (Telephone Number in U.S. (800) 253-9646); *African Statistical Yearbook.*

RWANDA - CUSTOMS DUTIES

International Monetary Fund, 700 Nineteenth Street, NW, Washington, D.C. 20431 (202) 623-7000; *Government Finance Statistics Yearbook.*

St. Martin's Press, Inc., 175 Fifth Avenue, New York, New York 10010 (800) 221-7945; *The Statesman's Year-Book.*

RWANDA - DAIRY PRODUCTS

Europa Publications Limited, 18 Bedford Square, London, WC1B 3JN, England; *The Europa World Year Book.*

Food and Agricultural Organization of the United Nations (FAO) Via delle Terme di Caracalla, 00100 Rome, Italy (Telephone Number in U.S. (202) 653-2400); *The State of Food and Agriculture.*

M.E. Sharpe, 80 Business Park Drive, Armonk, New York 10504 (800) 541-6563; *The Illustrated Book of World Rankings.*

St. Martin's Press, Inc., 175 Fifth Avenue, New York, New York 10010 (800) 221-7945; *The Statesman's Year-Book.*

RWANDA - DEATH RATES - See RWANDA - MORTALITY

RWANDA - DEFENSE EXPENDITURES

International Monetary Fund, 700 Nineteenth Street, NW, Washington, D.C. 20431 (202) 623-7000; *Government Finance Statistics Yearbook.*

U.S. Arms Control and Disarmament Agency, 320 Twenty-first Street, NW, Washington, D.C. 20451 (202) 647-8677; *World Military Expenditures and Arms Transfers.*

RWANDA - DEMOGRAPHY

The Economist Intelligence Unit, 111 West 57th Street, New York, New York 10019 (800) 938-4685; *The World Market Atlas.*

Euromonitor International, Inc., 122 South Michigan Avenue, Suite 1200, Chicago, Illinois 60603 (800) 577-EURO; *International Marketing Data and Statistics; World Marketing Data and Statistics;* and *The World Economic Factbook.*

M.E. Sharpe, 80 Business Park Drive, Armonk, New York 10504 (800) 541-6563; *The Illustrated Book of World Rankings.*

Statistical Office of the United Nations, Publishing Service, New York 10017 (800) 253-9646; *Human Development Report;* and *Survey of Economic and Social Conditions in Africa.*

RWANDA - DEVELOPMENT ASSISTANCE

Statistical Office of the United Nations, Publishing Service, New York, New York 10017 (800) 253-9646; *Statistical Yearbook.*

RWANDA - DIAMOND PRODUCTION - See RWANDA - MINING AND MINERAL PRODUCTS

RWANDA - DISCOUNT RATES - See RWANDA - BANKING

RWANDA - DISEASE - See RWANDA - HEALTH

RWANDA - DIVORCE RATES

M.E. Sharpe, 80 Business Park Drive, Armonk, New York 10504 (800) 541-6563; *The Illustrated Book of World Rankings.*

Statistical Office of the United Nations, Publishing Service, New York, New York 10017 (800) 253-9646; *Demographic Yearbook;* and *Statistical Yearbook.*

RWANDA - ECONOMY

African Development Bank, 01 BP 1387, Abidjan 01, Cote d'Ivoire; *Selected Statistics on Regional Member Countries.*

Central Intelligence Agency, Washington, D.C. 20505 (703) 482-1100, www.cia.gov; *The World Factbook.*

Economist Intelligence Unit, 111 West 57th Street, New York, New York 10019 (800) 938-4685; *Rwanda Country Report.*

Euromonitor International, Inc., 122 South Michigan Avenue, Suite 1200, Chicago, Illinois 60603 (800) 577-EURO; *International Marketing Data and Statistics; World Marketing Data and Statistics;* and *The World Economic Factbook.*

Europa Publications Limited, 18 Bedford Square, London, WC1B 3JN, England; *The Europa World Year Book.*

M.E. Sharpe, 80 Business Park Drive, Armonk, New York 10504 (800) 541-6563; *The Illustrated Book of World Rankings.*

St. Martin's Press, Inc., 175 Fifth Avenue, New York, New York 10010 (800) 221-7945; *The Statesman's Year-Book.*

Statistical Office of the United Nations, Publishing Service, New York, New York 10017 (800) 253-9646; *Foreign Trade Statistics for Africa;* and *World Statistics Pocketbook.*

The World Bank, 1818 H Street, NW, Washington, D.C. 20433 (202) 477-1234; *The World Bank Atlas;* and *World Development Report.*

RWANDA - EDUCATION

African Development Bank, 01 BP 1387, Abidjan 01, Cote d'Ivoire; *Selected Statistics on Regional Member Countries.*

The Economist Intelligence Unit, 111 West 57th Street, New York, New York 10019 (800) 938-4685; *The World Market Atlas.*

Euromonitor International, Inc., 122 South Michigan Avenue, Suite 1200, Chicago, Illinois 60603 (800) 577-EURO; *International Marketing Data and Statistics;* and *World Marketing Data and Statistics.*

Europa Publications Limited, 18 Bedford Square, London, WC1B 3JN, England; *The Europa World Year Book.*

International Monetary Fund, 700 Nineteenth Street, NW, Washington, D.C. 20431 (202) 623-7000; *Government Finance Statistics Yearbook.*

M.E. Sharpe, 80 Business Park Drive, Armonk, New York 10504 (800) 541-6563; *The Illustrated Book of World Rankings.*

St. Martin's Press, Inc., 175 Fifth Avenue, New York, New York 10010 (800) 221-7945; *The Statesman's Year-Book.*

Statistical Office of the United Nations, Publishing Service, New York 10017 (800) 253-9646; *Human Development Report;*

and *Survey of Economic and Social Conditions in Africa.*

United Nations Economic Commission for Africa, Africa Hall, P.O. Box 3001, Addis Ababa, Ethiopia (Telephone Number in U.S. (800) 253-9646); *African Statistical Yearbook.*

United Nations Educational, Scientific and Cultural Organization (UNESCO), 7 Place de Fontenoy, F-75700 Paris, France (Telephone Number in U.S. (212) 963-5981); *Statistical Yearbook.*

The World Bank, 1818 H Street, NW, Washington, D.C. 20433 (202) 477-1234; *World Development Report;* and *World Development Indicators.*

RWANDA - EGG PRODUCTION AND CONSUMPTION - See RWANDA - DAIRY PRODUCTS

RWANDA - ELECTRICITY

Central Intelligence Agency, Washington, D.C. 20505 (703) 482-1100, www.cia.gov; *The World Factbook.*

M.E. Sharpe, 80 Business Park Drive, Armonk, New York 10504 (800) 541-6563; *The Illustrated Book of World Rankings.*

St. Martin's Press, Inc., 175 Fifth Avenue, New York, New York 10010 (800) 221-7945; *The Statesman's Year-Book.*

Statistical Office of the United Nations, Publishing Service, New York, New York 10017 (800) 253-9646; *Statistical Yearbook; Human Development Report;* and *Survey of Economic and Social Conditions in Africa.*

United Nations Economic Commission for Africa, Africa Hall, P.O. Box 3001, Addis Ababa, Ethiopia (Telephone Number in U.S. (800) 253-9646); *African Statistical Yearbook.*

RWANDA - EMPLOYMENT

Euromonitor International, Inc., 122 South Michigan Avenue, Suite 1200, Chicago, Illinois 60603 (800) 577-EURO; *International Marketing Data and Statistics.*

International Labour Office, I.L.O. Publications, 1828 L Street, NW., Suite 801, Washington, D.C. 20036 (301) 638-3152; *Yearbook of Labour Statistics.*

M.E. Sharpe, 80 Business Park Drive, Armonk, New York 10504 (800) 541-6563; *The Illustrated Book of World Rankings.*

Statistical Office of the United Nations, Publishing Service, New York, New York 10017 (800) 253-9646; *Statistical Yearbook;* and *Survey of Economic and Social*

Conditions in Africa.

United Nations Economic Commission for Africa, Africa Hall, P.O. Box 3001, Addis Ababa, Ethiopia (Telephone Number in U.S. (800) 253-9646); *African Statistical Yearbook.*

RWANDA - ENERGY

Euromonitor International, Inc., 122 South Michigan Avenue, Suite 1200, Chicago, Illinois 60603 (800) 577-EURO; *International Marketing Data and Statistics; World Marketing Data and Statistics;* and *The World Economic Factbook.*

Food and Agricultural Organization of the United Nations (FAO) Via delle Terme di Caracalla, 00100 Rome, Italy (Telephone Number in U.S. (202) 653-2400); *The State of Food and Agriculture.*

M.E. Sharpe, 80 Business Park Drive, Armonk, New York 10504 (800) 541-6563; *The Illustrated Book of World Rankings.*

St. Martin's Press, Inc., 175 Fifth Avenue, New York, New York 10010 (800) 221-7945; *The Statesman's Year-Book.*

Statistical Office of the United Nations, Publishing Service, New York, New York 10017 (800) 253-9646; *Energy Statistics Yearbook; Human Development Report; Statistical Yearbook;* and *World Statistics Pocketbook.*

United Nations Economic Commission for Africa, Africa Hall, P.O. Box 3001, Addis Ababa, Ethiopia (Telephone Number in U.S. (800) 253-9646); *African Statistical Yearbook.*

The World Bank, 1818 H Street, NW, Washington, D.C. 20433 (202) 477-1234; *The World Bank Atlas;* and *World Development Report.*

RWANDA - ENVIRONMENT

Economist Intelligence Unit, 111 West 57th Street, New York, New York 10019 (800) 938-4685; *Rwanda Country Report.*

Statistical Office of the United Nations, Publishing Service, New York, New York 10017 (800) 253-9646; *World Statistics Pocketbook.*

RWANDA - EXCHANGE RATES

African Development Bank, 01 BP 1387, Abidjan 01, Cote d'Ivoire; *Selected Statistics on Regional Member Countries.*

Central Intelligence Agency, Washington, D.C. 20505 (703) 482-1100, www.cia.gov; *The World Factbook.*

Euromonitor International, Inc., 122

South Michigan Avenue, Suite 1200, Chicago, Illinois 60603 (800) 577-EURO; *International Marketing Data and Statistics;* and *The World Economic Factbook.*

Europa Publications Limited, 18 Bedford Square, London, WC1B 3JN, England; *The Europa World Year Book.*

International Monetary Fund, 700 Nineteenth Street, NW, Washington, D.C. 20431 (202) 623-7000; *International Financial Statistics.*

Statistical Office of the United Nations, Publishing Service, New York, New York 10017 (800) 253-9646; *Foreign Trade Statistics for Africa; Statistical Yearbook;* and *World Statistics Pocketbook.*

RWANDA - EXCISE TAXES - See RWANDA - TAXATION

RWANDA - EXPORTS

African Development Bank, 01 BP 1387, Abidjan 01, Cote d'Ivoire; *Selected Statistics on Regional Member Countries.*

Central Intelligence Agency, Washington, D.C. 20505 (703) 482-1100, www.cia.gov; *The World Factbook.*

The Economist Intelligence Unit, 111 West 57th Street, New York, New York 10019 (800) 938-4685; *Rwanda Country Report;* and *The World Market Atlas.*

Euromonitor International, Inc., 122 South Michigan Avenue, Suite 1200, Chicago, Illinois 60603 (800) 577-EURO; *International Marketing Data and Statistics;* and *The World Economic Factbook.*

Europa Publications Limited, 18 Bedford Square, London, WC1B 3JN, England; *The Europa World Year Book.*

Food and Agricultural Organization of the United Nations (FAO) Via delle Terme di Caracalla, 00100 Rome, Italy (Telephone Number in U.S. (202) 653-2400); *The State of Food and Agriculture.*

International Monetary Fund, 700 Nineteenth Street, NW, Washington, D.C. 20431 (202) 623-7000; *Direction of Trade Statistics; Government Finance Statistics Yearbook;* and *International Financial Statistics.*

St. Martin's Press, Inc., 175 Fifth Avenue, New York, New York 10010 (800) 221-7945; *The Statesman's Year-Book.*

Statistical Office of the United Nations, Publishing Service, New York, New York 10017 (800) 253-9646; *Foreign Trade Statistics for Africa;* and *Survey of Economic and Social Conditions in Africa.*

United Nations Conference on Trade and Development (UNCTAD), New York, New York 10017 (800) 253-9646; *Handbook of International Trade and Development Statistics.*

United Nations Economic Commission for Africa, Africa Hall, P.O. Box 3001, Addis Ababa, Ethiopia (Telephone Number in U.S. (800) 253-9646); *African Statistical Yearbook.*

The World Bank, 1818 H Street, NW, Washington, D.C. 20433 (202) 477-1234; *World Development Report;* and *World Development Indicators.*

RWANDA - EXTERNAL INDEBTEDNESS

African Development Bank, 01 BP 1387, Abidjan 01, Cote d'Ivoire; *Selected Statistics on Regional Member Countries.*

Statistical Office of the United Nations, Publishing Service, New York 10017 (800) 253-9646; *Survey of Economic and Social Conditions in Africa.*

The World Bank, 1818 H Street, NW, Washington, D.C. 20433 (202) 477-1234; *World Development Report;* and *World Development Indicators.*

RWANDA - EXTERNAL TRADE

African Development Bank, 01 BP 1387, Abidjan 01, Cote d'Ivoire; *Selected Statistics on Regional Member Countries.*

Euromonitor International, Inc., 122 South Michigan Avenue, Suite 1200, Chicago, Illinois 60603 (800) 577-EURO; *World Marketing Data and Statistics.*

Food and Agricultural Organization of the United Nations (FAO) Via delle Terme di Caracalla, 00100 Rome, Italy (Telephone Number in U.S. (202) 653-2400); *The State of Food and Agriculture;* and *Trade Yearbook.*

Statistical Office of the United Nations, Publishing Service, New York, New York 10017 (800) 253-9646; *Statistical Yearbook.*

RWANDA - FARM CROPS - See RWANDA - CROPS

RWANDA - FEMALE WORKING POPULATION - See RWANDA - EMPLOYMENT

RWANDA - FERTILITY RATES

Central Intelligence Agency, Washington, D.C. 20505 (703) 482-1100, www.cia.gov; *The World Factbook.*

M.E. Sharpe, 80 Business Park Drive, Armonk, New York 10504 (800) 541-6563; *The Illustrated Book of World Rankings.*

Statistical Office of the United Nations, Publishing Service, New York 10017 (800) 253-9646; *Human Development Report;* and *Survey of Economic and Social Conditions in Africa.*

The World Bank, 1818 H Street, NW, Washington, D.C. 20433 (202) 477-1234; *The World Bank Atlas; World Development Report;* and *World Development Indicators.*

RWANDA - FERTILIZER

Food and Agricultural Organization of the United Nations (FAO), Via delle Terme di Caracalla, 00100, Rome, Italy (Telephone Number in U.S. (202) 653-2400); *Fertilizer Yearbook;* and *The State of Food and Agriculture.*

Statistical Office of the United Nations, Publishing Service, New York, New York 10017 (800) 253-9646; *Statistical Yearbook.*

RWANDA - FETAL MORTALITY - See RWANDA - MORTALITY

RWANDA - FINANCE

African Development Bank, 01 BP 1387, Abidjan 01, Cote d'Ivoire; *Selected Statistics on Regional Member Countries.*

Economist Intelligence Unit, 111 West 57th Street, New York, New York 10019 (800) 938-4685; *Rwanda Country Report.*

Europa Publications Limited, 18 Bedford Square, London, WC1B 3JN, England; *The Europa World Year Book.*

International Monetary Fund, 700 Nineteenth Street, NW, Washington, D.C. 20431 (202) 623-7000; *Government Finance Statistics Yearbook;* and *International Financial Statistics.*

M.E. Sharpe, 80 Business Park Drive, Armonk, New York 10504 (800) 541-6563; *The Illustrated Book of World Rankings.*

St. Martin's Press, Inc., 175 Fifth Avenue, New York, New York 10010 (800) 221-7945; *The Statesman's Year-Book.*

United Nations Economic Commission for Africa, Africa Hall, P.O. Box 3001, Addis Ababa, Ethiopia (Telephone Number in U.S. (800) 253-9646); *African Statistical Yearbook.*

RWANDA - FISHERIES

Europa Publications Limited, 18 Bedford Square, London, WC1B 3JN, England; *The Europa World Year Book.*

Food and Agricultural Organization of the United Nations (FAO) Via delle Terme di Caracalla, 00100 Rome, Italy (Telephone Number in U.S. (202) 653-2400); *The State of Food and Agriculture;* and *Yearbook of Fishery Statistics.*

M.E. Sharpe, 80 Business Park Drive, Armonk, New York 10504 (800) 541-6563; *The Illustrated Book of World Rankings.*

Statistical Office of the United Nations, Publishing Service, New York, New York 10017 (800) 253-9646; *Statistical Yearbook;* and *Survey of Economic and Social Conditions in Africa.*

United Nations Conference on Trade and Development, Central Statistical Service, Palais des Nations, Geneva, Switzerland (Telephone in U.S. (800) 253-9646); *UNCTAD Commodity Yearbook.*

United Nations Economic Commission for Africa, Africa Hall, P.O. Box 3001, Addis Ababa, Ethiopia (Telephone Number in U.S. (800) 253-9646); *African Statistical Yearbook.*

RWANDA - FOOD

African Development Bank, 01 BP 1387, Abidjan 01, Cote d'Ivoire; *Selected Statistics on Regional Member Countries.*

Food and Agricultural Organization of the United Nations (FAO) Via delle Terme di Caracalla, 00100 Rome, Italy (Telephone Number in U.S. (202) 653-2400); *Production Yearbook;* and *The State of Food and Agriculture.*

Statistical Office of the United Nations, Publishing Service, New York, New York 10017 (800) 253-9646; *Human Development Report.*

RWANDA - FOREIGN DEBT

International Monetary Fund, 700 Nineteenth Street, NW, Washington, D.C. 20431 (202) 623-7000; *Government Finance Statistics Yearbook.*

United Nations Conference on Trade and Development, Central Statistical Service, Palais des Nations, Geneva, Switzerland (Telephone in U.S. (800) 253-9646); *UNCTAD Commodity Yearbook.*

RWANDA - FOREIGN TRADE

Economist Intelligence Unit, 111 West 57th Street, New York, New York 10019 (800) 938-4685; *Rwanda Country Report.*

Euromonitor International, Inc., 122 South Michigan Avenue, Suite 1200, Chicago, Illinois 60603 (800) 577-EURO; *International Marketing Data and Statistics;* and *The World Economic Factbook.*

Europa Publications Limited, 18 Bedford Square, London, WC1B 3JN, England; *The Europa World Year Book.*

Food and Agricultural Organization of the United Nations (FAO) Via delle Terme di Caracalla, 00100 Rome, Italy (Telephone Number in U.S. (202) 653-2400); *The State of Food and Agriculture.*

International Monetary Fund, 700 Nineteenth Street, NW, Washington, D.C. 20431 (202) 623-7000; *International Financial Statistics.*

M.E. Sharpe, 80 Business Park Drive, Armonk, New York 10504 (800) 541-6563; *The Illustrated Book of World Rankings.*

St. Martin's Press, Inc., 175 Fifth Avenue, New York, New York 10010 (800) 221-7945; *The Statesman's Year-Book.*

Statistical Office of the United Nations, Publishing Service, New York, New York 10017 (800) 253-9646; *Foreign Trade Statistics for Africa; International Trade Statistics Yearbook;* and *Statistical Yearbook.*

United Nations Conference on Trade and Development, Central Statistical Service, Palais des Nations, Geneva, Switzerland (Telephone in U.S. (800) 253-9646); *UNCTAD Commodity Yearbook.*

United Nations Economic Commission for Africa, Africa Hall, P.O. Box 3001, Addis Ababa, Ethiopia (Telephone Number in U.S. (800) 253-9646); *African Statistical Yearbook.*

The World Bank, 1818 H Street, NW, Washington, D.C. 20433 (202) 477-1234; *World Development Report;* and *World Development Indicators.*

RWANDA - FORESTRY AND FOREST PRODUCTS

Europa Publications Limited, 18 Bedford Square, London, WC1B 3JN, England; *The Europa World Year Book.*

Food and Agricultural Organization of the United Nations (FAO) Via delle Terme di Caracalla, 00100 Rome, Italy (Telephone Number in U.S. (202) 653-2400); *The State of Food and Agriculture;* and *Yearbook of Forest Products.*

M.E. Sharpe, 80 Business Park Drive, Armonk, New York 10504 (800) 541-6563; *The Illustrated Book of World Rankings.*

Statistical Office of the United Nations, Publishing Service, New York, New York 10017 (800) 253-9646; *Statistical Yearbook.*

United Nations Conference on Trade and Development, Central Statistical Service, Palais des Nations, Geneva, Switzerland (Telephone in U.S. (800) 253-9646); *UNCTAD Commodity Yearbook.*

United Nations Economic Commission for Africa, Africa Hall, P.O. Box 3001, Addis Ababa, Ethiopia (Telephone Number in U.S. (800) 253-9646); *African Statistical Yearbook.*

The World Bank, 1818 H Street, NW, Washington, D.C. 20433 (202) 477-1234; *World Development Report.*

RWANDA - GAS (NATURAL) PRODUCTION - See RWANDA - MINING AND MINERAL PRODUCTS

RWANDA - GENERAL INDUSTRIAL STATISTICS - See RWANDA - INDUSTRY

RWANDA - GENERAL MORTALITY - See RWANDA - MORTALITY

RWANDA - GEOGRAPHIC DATA

M.E. Sharpe, 80 Business Park Drive, Armonk, New York 10504 (800) 541-6563; *The Illustrated Book of World Rankings.*

RWANDA - GOATS - See RWANDA - LIVESTOCK AND POULTRY

RWANDA - GOLD HOLDINGS

International Monetary Fund, 700 Nineteenth Street, NW, Washington, D.C. 20431 (202) 623-7000; *International Financial Statistics.*

Statistical Office of the United Nations, Publishing Service, New York, New York 10017 (800) 253-9646; *Statistical Yearbook.*

The World Bank, 1818 H Street, NW, Washington, D.C. 20433 (202) 477-1234; *World Development Indicators.*

RWANDA - GOLD PRODUCTION AND CONSUMPTION - See RWANDA - MINING AND MINERAL PRODUCTS

RWANDA - GOVERNMENT

Central Intelligence Agency, Washington, D.C. 20505 (703) 482-1100, www.cia.gov; *The World Factbook.*

Europa Publications Limited, 18 Bedford Square, London, WC1B 3JN, England; *The Europa World Year Book.*

International Monetary Fund, 700 Nineteenth Street, NW, Washington, D.C. 20431 (202) 623-7000; *Government Finance Statistics Yearbook;* and *International Financial Statistics.*

St. Martin's Press, Inc., 175 Fifth Avenue, New York, New York 10010 (800) 221-7945; *The Statesman's Year-Book.*

Statistical Office of the United Nations, Publishing Service, New York 10017 (800) 253-9646; *National Accounts Statistics;* and

Survey of Economic and Social Conditions in Africa.

The World Bank, 1818 H Street, NW, Washington, D.C. 20433 (202) 477-1234; *World Development Report;* and *World Development Indicators.*

RWANDA - GRAIN PRODUCTION - See RWANDA - CROPS

RWANDA - GRANTS

International Monetary Fund, 700 Nineteenth Street, NW, Washington, D.C. 20431 (202) 623-7000; *Government Finance Statistics Yearbook.*

RWANDA - GROSS DOMESTIC PRODUCT

African Development Bank, 01 BP 1387, Abidjan 01, Cote d'Ivoire; *Selected Statistics on Regional Member Countries.*

The Economist Intelligence Unit, 111 West 57th Street, New York, New York 10019 (800) 938-4685; *Rwanda Country Report;* and *The World Market Atlas.*

Euromonitor International, Inc., 122 South Michigan Avenue, Suite 1200, Chicago, Illinois 60603 (800) 577-EURO; *International Marketing Data and Statistics;* and *The World Economic Factbook.*

Europa Publications Limited, 18 Bedford Square, London, WC1B 3JN, England; *The Europa World Year Book.*

M.E. Sharpe, 80 Business Park Drive, Armonk, New York 10504 (800) 541-6563; *The Illustrated Book of World Rankings.*

Statistical Office of the United Nations, Publishing Service, New York, New York 10017 (800) 253-9646; *Human Development Report; National Accounts Statistics; Statistical Yearbook;* and *Survey of Economic and Social Conditions in Africa.*

United Nations Economic Commission for Africa, Africa Hall, P.O. Box 3001, Ababa, Ethiopia (Telephone Number in U.S. (800) 253-9646); *African Statistical Yearbook.*

The World Bank, 1818 H Street, NW, Washington, D.C. 20433 (202) 477-1234; *World Development Report;* and *World Development Indicators.*

RWANDA - GROSS NATIONAL PRODUCT

Euromonitor International, Inc., 122 South Michigan Avenue, Suite 1200, Chicago, Illinois 60603 (800) 577-EURO; *International Marketing Data and Statistics.*

Europa Publications Limited, 18 Bedford Square, London, WC1B 3JN,

England; *The Europa World Year Book.*

St. Martin's Press, Inc., 175 Fifth Avenue, New York, New York 10010 (800) 221-7945; *The Statesman's Year-Book.*

U.S. Arms Control and Disarmament Agency, 320 Twenty-first Street, NW, Washington, D.C. 20451 (202) 647-8677; *World Military Expenditures and Arms Transfers.*

The World Bank, 1818 H Street, NW, Washington, D.C. 20433 (202) 477-1234; *The World Bank Atlas; World Development Report;* and *World Development Indicators.*

RWANDA - GROUNDNUTS PRODUCTION - See RWANDA - CROPS

RWANDA - HEALTH

African Development Bank, 01 BP 1387, Abidjan 01, Cote d'Ivoire; *Selected Statistics on Regional Member Countries.*

Euromonitor International, Inc., 122 South Michigan Avenue, Suite 1200, Chicago, Illinois 60603 (800) 577-EURO; *World Marketing Data and Statistics.*

M.E. Sharpe, 80 Business Park Drive, Armonk, New York 10504 (800) 541-6563; *The Illustrated Book of World Rankings.*

St. Martin's Press, Inc., 175 Fifth Avenue, New York, New York 10010 (800) 221-7945; *The Statesman's Year-Book.*

Statistical Office of the United Nations, Publishing Service, New York, New York 10017 (800) 253-9646; *Human Development Report;* and *Statistical Yearbook.*

United Nations Children's Fund (UNICEF), 3 United Nations Plaza, New York, New York 10017 (800) 253-9646; *State of the World's Children.*

United Nations Economic Commission for Africa, Africa Hall, P.O. Box 3001, Addis Ababa, Ethiopia (Telephone Number in U.S. (800) 253-9646); *African Statistical Yearbook.*

The World Bank, 1818 H Street, NW, Washington, D.C. 20433 (202) 477-1234; *World Development Report.*

World Health Organization, Office of Publications, 20 Avenue Appia, CH-1211 Geneva 27, Switzerland (Telephone Number in U.S. (518) 436-9686); *World Health Statistics Annual.*

RWANDA - HEALTH EXPENDITURES

International Monetary Fund, 700 Nineteenth Street, NW, Washington, D.C. 20431 (202) 623-7000; *Government*

Finance Statistics Yearbook.

RWANDA - HIDE PRODUCTION

Food and Agricultural Organization of the United Nations (FAO), Via delle Terme di Caracalla, 00100 Rome, Italy (Telephone Number in U.S. (202) 653-2400); *Production Yearbook.*

RWANDA - HIGHWAYS

Central Intelligence Agency, Washington, D.C. 20505 (703) 482-1100, www.cia.gov; *The World Factbook.*

International Road Federation, 2600 Virginia Avenue, NW, Washington, D.C. 20037 (202) 338-4641; *World Road Statistics.*

St. Martin's Press, Inc., 175 Fifth Avenue, New York, New York 10010 (800) 221-7945; *The Statesman's Year-Book.*

Statistical Office of the United Nations, Publishing Service, New York 10017 (800) 253-9646; *Survey of Economic and Social Conditions in Africa.*

United Nations Economic Commission for Africa, Africa Hall, P.O. Box 3001, Addis Ababa, Ethiopia (Telephone Number in U.S. (800) 253-9646); *African Statistical Yearbook.*

RWANDA - HORSES - See RWANDA - LIVESTOCK AND POULTRY

RWANDA - HOURS OF WORK - See RWANDA - EMPLOYMENT

RWANDA - HOUSING AND HOUSING UNITS

Euromonitor International, Inc., 122 South Michigan Avenue, Suite 1200, Chicago, Illinois 60603 (800) 577-EURO; *World Marketing Data and Statistics.*

M.E. Sharpe, 80 Business Park Drive, Armonk, New York 10504 (800) 541-6563; *The Illustrated Book of World Rankings.*

RWANDA - HOUSING EXPENDITURES

International Monetary Fund, 700 Nineteenth Street, NW, Washington, D.C. 20431 (202) 623-7000; *Government Finance Statistics Yearbook.*

RWANDA - ILLITERATE POPULATION

Central Intelligence Agency, Washington, D.C. 20505 (703) 482-1100, www.cia.gov; *The World Factbook.*

The Economist Intelligence Unit, 111 West 57th Street, New York, New York 10019 (800) 938-4685; *The World Market Atlas.*

Euromonitor International, Inc., 122 South Michigan Avenue, Suite 1200, Chicago, Illinois 60603 (800) 577-EURO; *The World Economic Factbook.*

Statistical Office of the United Nations, Publishing Service, New York, New York 10017 (800) 253-9646; *Human Development Report.*

United Nations Educational, Scientific and Cultural Organization (UNESCO), 7 Place de Fontenoy, F-75700 Paris, France (Telephone Number in U.S. (212) 963-5981); *Statistical Yearbook.*

RWANDA - IMPORTS

African Development Bank, 01 BP 1387, Abidjan 01, Cote d'Ivoire; *Selected Statistics on Regional Member Countries.*

Central Intelligence Agency, Washington, D.C. 20505 (703) 482-1100, www.cia.gov; *The World Factbook.*

The Economist Intelligence Unit, 111 West 57th Street, New York, New York 10019 (800) 938-4685; *Rwanda Country Report;* and *The World Market Atlas.*

Euromonitor International, Inc., 122 South Michigan Avenue, Suite 1200, Chicago, Illinois 60603 (800) 577-EURO; *International Marketing Data and Statistics;* and *The World Economic Factbook.*

Europa Publications Limited, 18 Bedford Square, London, WC1B 3JN, England; *The Europa World Year Book.*

Food and Agricultural Organization of the United Nations (FAO) Via delle Terme di Caracalla, 00100 Rome, Italy (Telephone Number in U.S. (202) 653-2400); *The State of Food and Agriculture.*

International Monetary Fund, 700 Nineteenth Street, NW, Washington, D.C. 20431 (202) 623-7000; *Direction of Trade Statistics; Government Finance Statistics Yearbook;* and *International Financial Statistics.*

St. Martin's Press, Inc., 175 Fifth Avenue, New York, New York 10010 (800) 221-7945; *The Statesman's Year-Book.*

Statistical Office of the United Nations, Publishing Service, New York, New York 10017 (800) 253-9646; *Foreign Trade Statistics for Africa;* and *Survey of Economic and Social Conditions in Africa.*

United Nations Conference on Trade and Development (UNCTAD), New York, New York 10017 (800) 253-9646; *Handbook of International Trade and Development Statistics.*

United Nations Economic Commission

for Africa, Africa Hall, P.O. Box 3001, Addis Ababa, Ethiopia (Telephone Number in U.S. (800) 253-9646); *African Statistical Yearbook.*

The World Bank, 1818 H Street, NW, Washington, D.C. 20433 (202) 477-1234; *World Development Report;* and *World Development Indicators.*

RWANDA - INCOME TAXES - See RWANDA - TAXATION

RWANDA - INDUSTRY

Central Intelligence Agency, Washington, D.C. 20505 (703) 482-1100, www.cia.gov; *The World Factbook.*

Economist Intelligence Unit, 111 West 57th Street, New York, New York 10019 (800) 938-4685; *Rwanda Country Report.*

Euromonitor International, Inc., 122 South Michigan Avenue, Suite 1200, Chicago, Illinois 60603 (800) 577-EURO; *International Marketing Data and Statistics; World Marketing Data and Statistics;* and *The World Economic Factbook.*

Europa Publications Limited, 18 Bedford Square, London, WC1B 3JN, England; *The Europa World Year Book.*

International Labour Office, I.L.O. Publications, 1828 L Street, NW., Suite 801, Washington, D.C. 20036 (301) 638-3152; *Yearbook of Labour Statistics.*

M.E. Sharpe, 80 Business Park Drive, Armonk, New York 10504 (800) 541-6563; *The Illustrated Book of World Rankings.*

St. Martin's Press, Inc., 175 Fifth Avenue, New York, New York 10010 (800) 221-7945; *The Statesman's Year-Book.*

Statistical Office of the United Nations, Publishing Service, New York, New York 10017 (800) 253-9646; *Industrial Commodity Statistics Yearbook;* and *Survey of Economic and Social Conditions in Africa.*

United Nations Economic Commission for Africa, Africa Hall, P.O. Box 3001, Addis Ababa, Ethiopia (Telephone Number in U.S. (800) 253-9646); *African Statistical Yearbook.*

The World Bank, 1818 H Street, NW, Washington, D.C. 20433 (202) 477-1234; *World Development Indicators.*

World Intellectual Property Organization, 34 Chemin des Colombettes, CH-1211 Geneva 20. Switzerland; *Industrial Property Statistics.*

RWANDA - INFANT AND MATERNAL MORTALITY - See RWANDA - MORTALITY

RWANDA - INTERNATIONAL RESERVES EXCLUDING GOLD

African Development Bank, 01 BP 1387, Abidjan 01, Cote d'Ivoire; *Selected Statistics on Regional Member Countries.*

Statistical Office of the United Nations, Publishing Service, New York, New York 10017 (800) 253-9646; *Statistical Yearbook.*

The World Bank, 1818 H Street, NW, Washington, D.C. 20433 (202) 477-1234; *World Development Indicators.*

RWANDA - INVESTMENTS

International Monetary Fund, 700 Nineteenth Street, NW, Washington, D.C. 20431 (202) 623-7000; *International Financial Statistics.*

RWANDA - IRON ORE PRODUCTION AND CONSUMPTION - See RWANDA - MINING AND MINERAL PRODUCTS

RWANDA - IRRIGATION

Euromonitor International, Inc., 122 South Michigan Avenue, Suite 1200, Chicago, Illinois 60603 (800) 577-EURO; *International Marketing Data and Statistics.*

RWANDA - LABOR

African Development Bank, 01 BP 1387, Abidjan 01, Cote d'Ivoire; *Selected Statistics on Regional Member Countries.*

Central Intelligence Agency, Washington, D.C. 20505 (703) 482-1100, www.cia.gov; *The World Factbook.*

Euromonitor International, Inc., 122 South Michigan Avenue, Suite 1200, Chicago, Illinois 60603 (800) 577-EURO; *International Marketing Data and Statistics;* and *World Marketing Data and Statistics*

Europa Publications Limited, 18 Bedford Square, London, WC1B 3JN, England; *The Europa World Year Book.*

Food and Agricultural Organization of the United Nations (FAO) Via delle Terme di Caracalla, 00100 Rome, Italy (Telephone Number in U.S. (202) 653-2400); *The State of Food and Agriculture.*

International Labour Office, I.L.O. Publications, 1828 L Street, NW., Suite 801, Washington, D.C. 20036 (301) 638-3152; *Yearbook of Labour Statistics.*

M.E. Sharpe, 80 Business Park Drive, Armonk, New York 10504 (800) 541-6563; *The Illustrated Book of World Rankings.*

St. Martin's Press, Inc., 175 Fifth Avenue, New York, New York 10010 (800) 221-7945; *The Statesman's Year-Book.*

Statistical Office of the United Nations, Publishing Service, New York, New York 10017 (800) 253-9646; *Human Development Report.*

The World Bank, 1818 H Street, NW, Washington, D.C. 20433 (202) 477-1234; *The World Bank Atlas; World Development Report;* and *World Development Indicators.*

RWANDA - LAND USE

Central Intelligence Agency, Washington, D.C. 20505 (703) 482-1100, www.cia.gov; *The World Factbook.*

Euromonitor International, Inc., 122 South Michigan Avenue, Suite 1200, Chicago, Illinois 60603 (800) 577-EURO; *International Marketing Data and Statistics.*

Food and Agricultural Organization of the United Nations (FAO), Via delle Terme di Caracalla, 00100 Rome, Italy (Telephone Number in U.S. (202) 653-2400); *Production Yearbook.*

The World Bank, 1818 H Street, NW, Washington, D.C. 20433 (202) 477-1234; *World Development Report.*

RWANDA - LIBRARIES

M.E. Sharpe, 80 Business Park Drive, Armonk, New York 10504 (800) 541-6563; *The Illustrated Book of World Rankings.*

United Nations Educational, Scientific and Cultural Organization (UNESCO), 7 Place de Fontenoy, F-75700 Paris, France (Telephone Number in U.S. (212) 963-5981); *Statistical Yearbook.*

RWANDA - LIFE EXPECTANCY

African Development Bank, 01 BP 1387, Abidjan 01, Cote d'Ivoire; *Selected Statistics on Regional Member Countries.*

Central Intelligence Agency, Washington, D.C. 20505 (703) 482-1100, www.cia.gov; *The World Factbook.*

Euromonitor International, Inc., 122 South Michigan Avenue, Suite 1200, Chicago, Illinois 60603 (800) 577-EURO; *The World Economic Factbook.*

Statistical Office of the United Nations, Publishing Service, New York, New York 10017 (800) 253-9646; *Human Development Report;* and *World Statistics Pocketbook.*

The World Bank, 1818 H Street, NW, Washington, D.C. 20433 (202) 477-1234; *The World Bank Atlas;* and *World Development Report.*

RWANDA - LITERACY RATE

Euromonitor International, Inc., 122 South Michigan Avenue, Suite 1200, Chicago, Illinois 60603 (800) 577-EURO; *World Marketing Data and Statistics.*

Statistical Office of the United Nations, Publishing Service, New York 10017 (800) 253-9646; *Survey of Economic and Social Conditions in Africa.*

RWANDA - LIVESTOCK AND POULTRY

Euromonitor International, Inc., 122 South Michigan Avenue, Suite 1200, Chicago, Illinois 60603 (800) 577-EURO; *International Marketing Data and Statistics.*

Europa Publications Limited, 18 Bedford Square, London, WC1B 3JN, England; *The Europa World Year Book.*

Food and Agricultural Organization of the United Nations (FAO), Via delle Terme di Caracalla, 00100 Rome, Italy (Telephone Number in U.S. (202) 653-2400); *Production Yearbook;* and *The State of Food and Agriculture.*

M.E. Sharpe, 80 Business Park Drive, Armonk, New York 10504 (800) 541-6563; *The Illustrated Book of World Rankings.*

St. Martin's Press, Inc., 175 Fifth Avenue, New York, New York 10010 (800) 221-7945; *The Statesman's Year-Book.*

Statistical Office of the United Nations, Publishing Service, New York, New York 10017 (800) 253-9646; *Statistical Yearbook;* and *Survey of Economic and Social Conditions in Africa.*

United Nations Conference on Trade and Development, Central Statistical Service, Palais des Nations, Geneva, Switzerland (Telephone in U.S. (800) 253-9646); *UNCTAD Commodity Yearbook.*

United Nations Economic Commission for Africa, Africa Hall, P.O. Box 3001, Addis Ababa, Ethiopia (Telephone Number in U.S. (800) 253-9646); *African Statistical Yearbook.*

RWANDA - LIVING LEVELS - See RWANDA - LIFE EXPECTANCY

RWANDA - MAIL - NUMBER OF PIECES SENT OR RECEIVED

Statistical Office of the United Nations, Publishing Service, New York, New York 10017 (800) 253-9646; *Statistical Yearbook.*

RWANDA - MANUFACTURING

M.E. Sharpe, 80 Business Park Drive, Armonk, New York 10504 (800) 541-6563; *The Illustrated Book of World Rankings.*

Statistical Office of the United Nations,

Publishing Service, New York, New York 10017 (800) 253-9646; *Statistical Yearbook;* and *Survey of Economic and Social Conditions in Africa.*

United Nations Economic Commission for Africa, Africa Hall, P.O. Box 3001, Addis Ababa, Ethiopia (Telephone Number in U.S. (800) 253-9646); *African Statistical Yearbook.*

The World Bank, 1818 H Street, NW, Washington, D.C. 20433 (202) 477-1234; *World Development Indicators.*

RWANDA - MARRIAGE RATES

M.E. Sharpe, 80 Business Park Drive, Armonk, New York 10504 (800) 541-6563; *The Illustrated Book of World Rankings.*

Statistical Office of the United Nations, Publishing Service, New York, New York 10017 (800) 253-9646; *Demographic Yearbook;* and *Statistical Yearbook.*

RWANDA - MEAT PRODUCTION - See RWANDA - LIVESTOCK AND POULTRY

RWANDA - MERCHANT SHIPPING

United Nations Economic Commission for Africa, Africa Hall, P.O. Box 3001, Addis Ababa, Ethiopia (Telephone Number in U.S. (800) 253-9646); *African Statistical Yearbook.*

RWANDA - MILITARY

Central Intelligence Agency, Washington, D.C. 20505 (703) 482-1100, www.cia.gov; *The World Factbook.*

Euromonitor International, Inc., 122 South Michigan Avenue, Suite 1200, Chicago, Illinois 60603 (800) 577-EURO; *World Marketing Data and Statistics.*

The International Institute for Strategic Studies, 23 Tavistock Street, London WC2E 7NQ, England; *The Military Balance.*

St. Martin's Press, Inc., 175 Fifth Avenue, New York, New York 10010 (800) 221-7945; *The Statesman's Year-Book.*

Statistical Office of the United Nations, Publishing Service, New York, New York 10017 (800) 253-9646; *Human Development Report.*

U.S. Arms Control and Disarmament Agency, 320 Twenty-first Street, NW, Washington, D.C. 20451 (202) 647-8677; *World Military Expenditures and Arms Transfers.*

RWANDA - MILK PRODUCTION - See RWANDA - DAIRY PRODUCTS

RWANDA - MILLET PRODUCTION

Food and Agricultural Organization of the United Nations (FAO), Via delle Terme di Caracalla, 00100 Rome, Italy (Telephone Number in U.S. (202) 653-2400); *Production Yearbook.*

RWANDA - MINING AND MINERAL PRODUCTS

Europa Publications Limited, 18 Bedford Square, London, WC1B 3JN, England; *The Europa World Year Book.*

M.E. Sharpe, 80 Business Park Drive, Armonk, New York 10504 (800) 541-6563; *The Illustrated Book of World Rankings.*

St. Martin's Press, Inc., 175 Fifth Avenue, New York, New York 10010 (800) 221-7945; *The Statesman's Year-Book.*

Statistical Office of the United Nations, Publishing Service, New York, New York 10017 (800) 253-9646; *Statistical Yearbook.*

United Nations Conference on Trade and Development, Central Statistical Service, Palais des Nations, Geneva, Switzerland (Telephone in U.S. (800) 253-9646); *UNCTAD Commodity Yearbook.*

United Nations Economic Commission for Africa, Africa Hall, P.O. Box 3001, Addis Ababa, Ethiopia (Telephone Number in U.S. (800) 253-9646); *African Statistical Yearbook.*

RWANDA - MONEY EXCHANGE RATE - See RWANDA - EXCHANGE RATES

RWANDA - MONEY RESERVES

Euromonitor International, Inc., 122 South Michigan Avenue, Suite 1200, Chicago, Illinois 60603 (800) 577-EURO; *International Marketing Data and Statistics.*

RWANDA - MONEY SUPPLY

African Development Bank, 01 BP 1387, Abidjan 01, Cote d'Ivoire; *Selected Statistics on Regional Member Countries.*

Economist Intelligence Unit, 111 West 57th Street, New York, New York 10019 (800) 938-4685; *Rwanda Country Report.*

Euromonitor International, Inc., 122 South Michigan Avenue, Suite 1200, Chicago, Illinois 60603 (800) 577-EURO; *International Marketing Data and Statistics.*

Europa Publications Limited, 18 Bedford Square, London, WC1B 3JN, England; *The Europa World Year Book.*

International Monetary Fund, 700 Nineteenth Street, NW, Washington, D.C. 20431 (202) 623-7000; *International Financial Statistics.*

Statistical Office of the United Nations, Publishing Service, New York, New York 10017 (800) 253-9646; *Statistical Yearbook.*

The World Bank, 1818 H Street, NW, Washington, D.C. 20433 (202) 477-1234; *World Development Indicators.*

RWANDA - MORTALITY

Central Intelligence Agency, Washington, D.C. 20505 (703) 482-1100, www.cia.gov; *The World Factbook.*

Euromonitor International, Inc., 122 South Michigan Avenue, Suite 1200, Chicago, Illinois 60603 (800) 577-EURO; *International Marketing Data and Statistics;* and *The World Economic Factbook.*

Europa Publications Limited, 18 Bedford Square, London, WC1B 3JN, England; *The Europa World Year Book.*

Statistical Office of the United Nations, Publishing Service, New York, New York 10017 (800) 253-9646; *Demographic Yearbook; Human Development Report; Statistical Yearbook; Survey of Economic and Social Conditions in Africa;* and *World Statistics Pocketbook.*

United Nations Children's Fund (UNICEF), 3 United Nations Plaza, New York, New York 10017 (800) 253-9646; *State of the World's Children.*

The World Bank, 1818 H Street, NW, Washington, D.C. 20433 (202) 477-1234; *The World Bank Atlas; World Development Report;* and *World Development Indicators.*

World Health Organization, Office of Publications, 20 Avenue Appia, CH-1211 Geneva 27, Switzerland (Telephone Number in U.S. (518) 436-9686); *World Health Statistics Annual.*

RWANDA - MOTION PICTURES

Statistical Office of the United Nations, Publishing Service, New York, New York 10017 (800) 253-9646; *Statistical Yearbook.*

RWANDA - MOTOR VEHICLES IN USE

Europa Publications Limited, 18 Bedford Square, London, WC1B 3JN, England; *The Europa World Year Book.*

International Road Federation, 2600 Virginia Avenue, NW, Washington, D.C. 20037 (202) 338-4641; *World Road Statistics.*

Statistical Office of the United Nations, Publishing Service, New York, New York 10017 (800) 253-9646; *Statistical Yearbook;* and *Survey of Economic and Social Conditions in Africa.*

RWANDA - MUSEUMS

M.E. Sharpe, 80 Business Park Drive, Armonk, New York 10504 (800) 541-6563; *The Illustrated Book of World Rankings.*

United Nations Educational, Scientific and Cultural Organization (UNESCO), 7 Place de Fontenoy, F-75700 Paris, France (Telephone Number in U.S. (212) 963-5981); *Statistical Yearbook.*

RWANDA - NATALITY - See RWANDA - BIRTH RATE

RWANDA - NATIONAL ACCOUNTS

African Development Bank, 01 BP 1387, Abidjan 01, Cote d'Ivoire; *Selected Statistics on Regional Member Countries.*

Europa Publications Limited, 18 Bedford Square, London, WC1B 3JN, England; *The Europa World Year Book.*

Statistical Office of the United Nations, Publishing Service, New York, New York 10017 (800) 253-9646; *National Accounts Statistics;* and *Statistical Yearbook.*

United Nations Economic Commission for Africa, Africa Hall, P.O. Box 3001, Addis Ababa, Ethiopia (Telephone Number in U.S. (800) 253-9646); *African Statistical Yearbook.*

RWANDA - NATIONAL INCOME

M.E. Sharpe, 80 Business Park Drive, Armonk, New York 10504 (800) 541-6563; *The Illustrated Book of World Rankings.*

Statistical Office of the United Nations, Publishing Service, New York, New York 10017 (800) 253-9646; *National Accounts Statistics;* and *Statistical Yearbook.*

RWANDA - NATIONAL PRODUCT

M.E. Sharpe, 80 Business Park Drive, Armonk, New York 10504 (800) 541-6563; *The Illustrated Book of World Rankings.*

Statistical Office of the United Nations, Publishing Service, New York, New York 10017 (800) 253-9646; *Statistical Yearbook.*

RWANDA - NATURAL GAS PRODUCTION - See RWANDA - MINING AND MINERAL PRODUCTS

RWANDA - NEWSPAPER PRODUCTION - See RWANDA - FORESTRY AND FOREST PRODUCTS

RWANDA - OCCUPATIONS - See RWANDA - LABOR

RWANDA - PATENTS, TRADEMARKS AND SERVICE MARKS

Statistical Office of the United Nations, Publishing Service, New York, New York 10017 (800) 253-9646; *Statistical Yearbook.*

World Intellectual Property Organization, 34 Chemin des Colombettes, CH-1211 Geneva 20. Switzerland; *Industrial Property Statistics.*

RWANDA - PERIODICALS

United Nations Educational, Scientific and Cultural Organization (UNESCO), 7 Place de Fontenoy, F-75700 Paris, France (Telephone Number in U.S. (212) 963-5981); *Statistical Yearbook.*

RWANDA - PEANUT PRODUCTION - See RWANDA - CROPS

RWANDA - PESTICIDE USE

Food and Agricultural Organization of the United Nations (FAO) Via delle Terme di Caracalla, 00100 Rome, Italy (Telephone Number in U.S. (202) 653-2400); *The State of Food and Agriculture.*

RWANDA - PETROLEUM INDUSTRY

Food and Agricultural Organization of the United Nations (FAO) Via delle Terme di Caracalla, 00100 Rome, Italy (Telephone Number in U.S. (202) 653-2400); *The State of Food and Agriculture.*

M.E. Sharpe, 80 Business Park Drive, Armonk, New York 10504 (800) 541-6563; *The Illustrated Book of World Rankings.*

United Nations Conference on Trade and Development, Central Statistical Service, Palais des Nations, Geneva, Switzerland (Telephone in U.S. (800) 253-9646); *UNCTAD Commodity Yearbook.*

RWANDA - PIGS - See RWANDA - LIVESTOCK AND POULTRY

RWANDA - POPULATION

African Development Bank, 01 BP 1387, Abidjan 01, Cote d'Ivoire; *Selected Statistics on Regional Member Countries.*

Central Intelligence Agency, Washington, D.C. 20505 (703) 482-1100, www.cia.gov; *The World Factbook.*

The Economist Intelligence Unit, 111 West 57th Street, New York, New York 10019 (800) 938-4685; *Rwanda Country Report;* and *The World Market Atlas.*

Euromonitor International, Inc., 122 South Michigan Avenue, Suite 1200, Chicago, Illinois 60603 (800) 577-EURO; *International Marketing Data and Statistics;* and *The World Economic Factbook.*

Europa Publications Limited, 18

Bedford Square, London, WC1B 3JN, England; *The Europa World Year Book.*

Food and Agricultural Organization of the United Nations (FAO), Via delle Terme di Caracalla, 00100 Rome, Italy (Telephone Number in U.S. (202) 653-2400); *Production Yearbook.*

International Labour Office, I.L.O. Publications, 1828 L Street, NW., Suite 801, Washington, D.C. 20036 (301) 638-3152; *Yearbook of Labour Statistics.*

M.E. Sharpe, 80 Business Park Drive, Armonk, New York 10504 (800) 541-6563; *The Illustrated Book of World Rankings.*

St. Martin's Press, Inc., 175 Fifth Avenue, New York, New York 10010 (800) 221-7945; *The Statesman's Year-Book.*

Statistical Office of the United Nations, Publishing Service, New York, New York 10017 (800) 253-9646; *Demographic Yearbook; Human Development Report; Statistical Yearbook; Survey of Economic and Social Conditions in Africa;* and *World Statistics Pocketbook.*

United Nations Educational, Scientific and Cultural Organization (UNESCO), 7 Place de Fontenoy, F-75700 Paris, France (Telephone Number in U.S. (212) 963-5981); *Statistical Yearbook.*

U.S. Arms Control and Disarmament Agency, 320 Twenty-first Street, NW, Washington, D.C. 20451 (202) 647-8677; *World Military Expenditures and Arms Transfers.*

The World Bank, 1818 H Street, NW, Washington, D.C. 20433 (202) 477-1234; *The World Bank Atlas;* and *World Development Report.*

World Health Organization, Office of Publications, 20 Avenue Appia, CH-1211 Geneva 27, Switzerland (Telephone Number in U.S. (518) 436-9686); *World Health Statistics Annual.*

RWANDA - POST OFFICES

M.E. Sharpe, 80 Business Park Drive, Armonk, New York 10504 (800) 541-6563; *The Illustrated Book of World Rankings.*

RWANDA - POTATO PRODUCTION - See RWANDA - CROPS

RWANDA - PRICES

Food and Agricultural Organization of the United Nations (FAO), Via delle Terme di Caracalla, 00100 Rome, Italy (Telephone Number in U.S. (202) 653-2400); *Production Yearbook;* and *The State of Food and Agriculture.*

International Labour Office, I.L.O. Publications, 1828 L Street, NW., Suite 801, Washington, D.C. 20036 (301) 638-3152; *Yearbook of Labour Statistics.*

International Monetary Fund, 700 Nineteenth Street, NW, Washington, D.C. 20431 (202) 623-7000; *International Financial Statistics.*

M.E. Sharpe, 80 Business Park Drive, Armonk, New York 10504 (800) 541-6563; *The Illustrated Book of World Rankings.*

United Nations Economic Commission for Africa, Africa Hall, P.O. Box 3001, Addis Ababa, Ethiopia (Telephone Number in U.S. (800) 253-9646); *African Statistical Yearbook.*

RWANDA - PRODUCTION

M.E. Sharpe, 80 Business Park Drive, Armonk, New York 10504 (800) 541-6563; *The Illustrated Book of World Rankings.*

RWANDA - PRODUCTIVITY

Euromonitor International, Inc., 122 South Michigan Avenue, Suite 1200, Chicago, Illinois 60603 (800) 577-EURO; *International Marketing Data and Statistics.*

RWANDA - PROPERTY TAXES - See RWANDA - TAXATION

RWANDA - PUBLIC FINANCE - See RWANDA - FINANCE

RWANDA - RADIO BROADCASTING - See RWANDA - BROADCASTING

RWANDA - RADIO RECEIVER PRODUCTION

Statistical Office of the United Nations, Publishing Service, New York, New York 10017 (800) 253-9646; *Statistical Yearbook.*

RWANDA - RADIO RECEIVERS

St. Martin's Press, Inc., 175 Fifth Avenue, New York, New York 10010 (800) 221-7945; *The Statesman's Year-Book.*

RWANDA - RAILWAYS

United Nations Economic Commission for Africa, Africa Hall, P.O. Box 3001, Addis Ababa, Ethiopia (Telephone Number in U.S. (800) 253-9646); *African Statistical Yearbook.*

RWANDA - RELIGION

Central Intelligence Agency, Washington, D.C. 20505 (703) 482-1100, www.cia.gov; *The World Factbook.*

M.E. Sharpe, 80 Business Park Drive, Armonk, New York 10504 (800) 541-6563;

The Illustrated Book of World Rankings.

St. Martin's Press, Inc., 175 Fifth Avenue, New York, New York 10010 (800) 221-7945; *The Statesman's Year-Book.*

RWANDA - RETAIL TRADE

Euromonitor International, Inc., 122 South Michigan Avenue, Suite 1200, Chicago, Illinois 60603 (800) 577-EURO; *World Marketing Data and Statistics.*

RWANDA - RICE PRODUCTION - See RWANDA - CROPS

RWANDA - ROOT AND TUBER PRODUCTION - See RWANDA - CROPS

RWANDA - ROUNDWOOD PRODUCTION - See RWANDA - FORESTRY AND FOREST PRODUCTS

RWANDA - RUBBER PRODUCTION AND CONSUMPTION

M.E. Sharpe, 80 Business Park Drive, Armonk, New York 10504 (800) 541-6563; *The Illustrated Book of World Rankings.*

RWANDA - SAWNWOOD PRODUCTION - See RWANDA - FORESTRY AND FOREST PRODUCTS

RWANDA - SCIENTISTS, TECHNICIANS AND ENGINEERS

Statistical Office of the United Nations, Publishing Service, New York, New York 10017 (800) 253-9646; *Statistical Yearbook.*

United Nations Educational, Scientific and Cultural Organization (UNESCO), 7 Place de Fontenoy, F-75700 Paris, France (Telephone Number in U.S. (212) 963-5981); *Statistical Yearbook.*

RWANDA - SENIOR CITIZENS

M.E. Sharpe, 80 Business Park Drive, Armonk, New York 10504 (800) 541-6563; *The Illustrated Book of World Rankings.*

RWANDA - SHEEP - See RWANDA - LIVESTOCK AND POULTRY

RWANDA - SILVER PRODUCTION AND CONSUMPTION - See RWANDA - MINING AND MINERAL PRODUCTS

RWANDA - SOCIAL DATA

African Development Bank, 01 BP 1387, Abidjan 01, Cote d'Ivoire; *Selected Statistics on Regional Member Countries.*

M.E. Sharpe, 80 Business Park Drive, Armonk, New York 10504 (800) 541-6563; *The Illustrated Book of World Rankings.*

Statistical Office of the United Nations, Publishing Service, New York, New York 10017 (800) 253-9646; *World Statistics Pocketbook.*

RWANDA - SOCIAL SECURITY

International Monetary Fund, 700 Nineteenth Street, NW, Washington, D.C. 20431 (202) 623-7000; *Government Finance Statistics Yearbook.*

Statistical Office of the United Nations, Publishing Service, New York, New York 10017 (800) 253-9646; *National Accounts Statistics.*

RWANDA - SOYBEAN PRODUCTION - See RWANDA - CROPS

RWANDA - STATE BUDGET REVENUE AND EXPENDITURES

Euromonitor International, Inc., 122 South Michigan Avenue, Suite 1200, Chicago, Illinois 60603 (800) 577-EURO; *International Marketing Data and Statistics.*

RWANDA - STEEL - See RWANDA - MINING AND MINERAL PRODUCTS

RWANDA - STOCKS - COMMODITY - MARKET PRICE - INDEX

Food and Agricultural Organization of the United Nations (FAO) Via delle Terme di Caracalla, 00100 Rome, Italy (Telephone Number in U.S. (202) 653-2400); *The State of Food and Agriculture.*

RWANDA - SUGAR PRODUCTION AND CONSUMPTION - See RWANDA - CROPS

RWANDA - TAXATION

Europa Publications Limited, 18 Bedford Square, London, WC1B 3JN, England; *The Europa World Year Book.*

International Monetary Fund, 700 Nineteenth Street, NW, Washington, D.C. 20431 (202) 623-7000; *Government Finance Statistics Yearbook.*

International Road Federation, 2600 Virginia Avenue, NW, Washington, D.C. 20037 (202) 338-4641; *World Road Statistics.*

The World Bank, 1818 H Street, NW, Washington, D.C. 20433 (202) 477-1234; *World Development Indicators.*

RWANDA - TEA EXPORTS - See RWANDA - CROPS

RWANDA - TELEPHONES IN USE

American Telephone and Telegraph Company, 26 Parsippany Road, Whippany,

New Jersey 07981 (800) 222-0300; *The World's Telephones.*

Central Intelligence Agency, Washington, D.C. 20505 (703) 482-1100, www.cia.gov; *The World Factbook.*

Europa Publications Limited, 18 Bedford Square, London, WC1B 3JN, England; *The Europa World Year Book.*

St. Martin's Press, Inc., 175 Fifth Avenue, New York, New York 10010 (800) 221-7945; *The Statesman's Year-Book.*

Statistical Office of the United Nations, Publishing Service, New York, New York 10017 (800) 253-9646; *Statistical Yearbook; and World Statistics Pocketbook.*

RWANDA - TELEVISION BROADCASTING - See RWANDA - BROADCASTING

RWANDA - TEXTILE INDUSTRY

M.E. Sharpe, 80 Business Park Drive, Armonk, New York 10504 (800) 541-6563; *The Illustrated Book of World Rankings.*

United Nations Conference on Trade and Development, Central Statistical Service, Palais des Nations, Geneva, Switzerland (Telephone in U.S. (800) 253-9646); *UNCTAD Commodity Yearbook.*

RWANDA - TIN PRODUCTION - See RWANDA - MINING AND MINERAL PRODUCTS

RWANDA - TOBACCO PRODUCTION

M.E. Sharpe, 80 Business Park Drive, Armonk, New York 10504 (800) 541-6563; *The Illustrated Book of World Rankings.*

Statistical Office of the United Nations, Publishing Service, New York, New York 10017 (800) 253-9646; *Statistical Yearbook.*

RWANDA - TOURISM

Euromonitor International, Inc., 122 South Michigan Avenue, Suite 1200, Chicago, Illinois 60603 (800) 577-EURO; *The World Economic Factbook; and World Marketing Data and Statistics.*

Europa Publications Limited, 18 Bedford Square, London, WC1B 3JN, England; *The Europa World Year Book.*

M.E. Sharpe, 80 Business Park Drive, Armonk, New York 10504 (800) 541-6563; *The Illustrated Book of World Rankings.*

St. Martin's Press, Inc., 175 Fifth Avenue, New York, New York 10010 (800) 221-7945; *The Statesman's Year-Book.*

United Nations Economic Commission for Africa, Africa Hall, P.O. Box 3001, Addis Ababa, Ethiopia (Telephone Number in U.S. (800) 253-9646); *African Statistical Yearbook.*

RWANDA - TRACTORS IN USE

Statistical Office of the United Nations, Publishing Service, New York, New York 10017 (800) 253-9646; *Statistical Yearbook.*

RWANDA - TRADE - See RWANDA - FOREIGN TRADE

RWANDA - TRADEMARKS AND SERVICE MARKS - See PATENTS, TRADEMARKS AND SERVICE MARKS

RWANDA - TRANSPORTATION AND COMMUNICATIONS

Central Intelligence Agency, Washington, D.C. 20505 (703) 482-1100, www.cia.gov; *The World Factbook.*

Euromonitor International, Inc., 122 South Michigan Avenue, Suite 1200, Chicago, Illinois 60603 (800) 577-EURO; *International Marketing Data and Statistics; and World Marketing Data and Statistics.*

Europa Publications Limited, 18 Bedford Square, London, WC1B 3JN, England; *The Europa World Year Book.*

M.E. Sharpe, 80 Business Park Drive, Armonk, New York 10504 (800) 541-6563; *The Illustrated Book of World Rankings.*

St. Martin's Press, Inc., 175 Fifth Avenue, New York, New York 10010 (800) 221-7945; *The Statesman's Year-Book.*

Statistical Office of the United Nations, Publishing Service, New York, New York 10017 (800) 253-9646; *Human Development Report.*

United Nations Economic Commission for Africa, Africa Hall, P.O. Box 3001, Addis Ababa, Ethiopia (Telephone Number in U.S. (800) 253-9646); *African Statistical Yearbook.*

RWANDA - TUNGSTEN PRODUCTION AND CONSUMPTION - See RWANDA - MINING AND MINERAL PRODUCTS

RWANDA - UNEMPLOYMENT

Central Intelligence Agency, Washington, D.C. 20505 (703) 482-1100, www.cia.gov; *The World Factbook.*

Euromonitor International, Inc., 122 South Michigan Avenue, Suite 1200, Chicago, Illinois 60603 (800) 577-EURO; *International Marketing Data and Statistics.*

International Labour Office, I.L.O. Publications, 1828 L Street, NW., Suite 801, Washington, D.C. 20036 (301) 638-3152; *Yearbook of Labour Statistics.*

RWANDA - VITAL STATISTICS

Euromonitor International, Inc., 122 South Michigan Avenue, Suite 1200, Chicago, Illinois 60603 (800) 577-EURO; *International Marketing Data and Statistics.*

Statistical Office of the United Nations, Publishing Service, New York, New York 10017 (800) 253-9646; *Statistical Yearbook.*

World Health Organization, Office of Publications, 20 Avenue Appia, CH-1211 Geneva 27, Switzerland (Telephone

Number in U.S. (518) 436-9686); *World Health Statistics Annual.*

RWANDA - WAGES

International Labour Office, I.L.O. Publications, 1828 L Street, NW., Suite 801, Washington, D.C. 20036 (301) 638-3152; *Yearbook of Labour Statistics.*

RWANDA - WEATHER - See RWANDA - CLIMATE

RWANDA - WELFARE

International Monetary Fund, 700 Nineteenth Street, NW, Washington, D.C. 20431 (202) 623-7000; *Government Finance Statistics Yearbook.*

RWANDA - WHEAT PRODUCTION AND PRICES - See RWANDA - CROPS

RWANDA - WINE PRODUCTION - See RWANDA - BEVERAGES

RWANDA - WOOL PRODUCTION - See RWANDA - TEXTILE INDUSTRY

S

SABLEFISH

U.S. Department of Commerce, National Oceanic and Atmospheric Administration, National Marine Fisheries Service, 1315 East-West Highway, Silver Spring, Maryland 20910 (301) 427-2239, www.nmfs.noaa.gov; *Fisheries of the United States.*

SAFFLOWER

U.S. Department of Agriculture, Economic Research Service, 1800 M Street, NW, Washington, D.C. 20036 (202) 694-5050, www.ers.usda.gov; *Farm Business Economic Report.*

SAILING

National Sporting Goods Association, 1601 Feehanville Drive, Suite 300, Mount Prospect, Illinois 66056 (847) 296-6742; Sports Participation in 1998.

Saint Helena - National Statistical Office

Information Officer, Broadway House, Saint Helena.

Saint Helena - Primary Statistics Source

HM Stationery Office, Post Office Box 569, London SE1, England: *Saint Helena: Report for the Years...*

SAINT HELENA - AGRICULTURE

Europa Publications Limited, 18 Bedford Square, London, WC1B 3JN, England; *The Europa World Year Book.*

Food and Agricultural Organization of the United Nations (FAO) Via delle Terme di Caracalla, 00100 Rome, Italy (Telephone Number in U.S. (202) 653-2400); *Production Yearbook; The State of Food and Agriculture;* and *Trade Yearbook.*

United Nations Conference on Trade and Development, Central Statistical Service, Palais des Nations, Geneva, Switzerland (Telephone in U.S. (800) 253-9646); *UNCTAD Commodity Yearbook.*

SAINT HELENA - AIRPORTS

Central Intelligence Agency, Washington, D.C. 20505 (703) 482-1100, www.cia.gov; *The World Factbook.*

SAINT HELENA - AREA AND DENSITY OF POPULATION

Central Intelligence Agency, Washington, D.C. 20505 (703) 482-1100, www.cia.gov; *The World Factbook.*

Europa Publications Limited, 18 Bedford Square, London, WC1B 3JN, England; *The Europa World Year Book.*

Food and Agricultural Organization of the United Nations (FAO) Via delle Terme di Caracalla, 00100 Rome, Italy (Telephone Number in U.S. (202) 653-2400); *The State of Food and Agriculture.*

St. Martin's Press, Inc., 175 Fifth Avenue, New York, New York 10010 (800) 221-7945; *The Statesman's Year-Book.*

Statistical Office of the United Nations, Publishing Service, New York, New York 10017 (800) 253-9646; *Statistical Yearbook.*

United Nations Educational, Scientific and Cultural Organization (UNESCO), 7 Place de Fontenoy, F-75700 Paris, France (Telephone Number in U.S. (212) 963-5981); *Statistical Yearbook.*

SAINT HELENA - BANKING

St. Martin's Press, Inc., 175 Fifth Avenue, New York, New York 10010 (800) 221-7945; *The Statesman's Year-Book.*

SAINT HELENA - BIRTH RATES

Central Intelligence Agency,

Washington, D.C. 20505 (703) 482-1100, www.cia.gov; *The World Factbook.*

Europa Publications Limited, 18 Bedford Square, London, WC1B 3JN, England; *The Europa World Year Book.*

St. Martin's Press, Inc., 175 Fifth Avenue, New York, New York 10010 (800) 221-7945; *The Statesman's Year-Book.*

Statistical Office of the United Nations, Publishing Service, New York, New York 10017 (800) 253-9646; *Demographic Yearbook;* and *Statistical Yearbook.*

World Health Organization, Office of Publications, 20 Avenue Appia, CH-1211 Geneva 27, Switzerland (Telephone Number in U.S. (518) 436-9686); *World Health Statistics Annual.*

SAINT HELENA - BROADCASTING

Billboard Limited, P.O. Box 9027, 1006 AA Amsterdam, The Netherlands (Telephone Number in U.S. (212) 764-7300); *World Radio TV Handbook.*

Central Intelligence Agency, Washington, D.C. 20505 (703) 482-1100, www.cia.gov; *The World Factbook.*

St. Martin's Press, Inc., 175 Fifth Avenue, New York, New York 10010 (800) 221-7945; *The Statesman's Year-Book.*

SAINT HELENA - BUDGET

Central Intelligence Agency, Washington, D.C. 20505 (703) 482-1100, www.cia.gov; *The World Factbook.*

SAINT HELENA - CALORIE SUPPLY

Food and Agricultural Organization of the United Nations (FAO) Via delle Terme di Caracalla, 00100 Rome, Italy (Telephone Number in U.S. (202) 653-2400); *The State of Food and Agriculture.*

SAINT HELENA - CATTLE - See SAINT HELENA - LIVESTOCK AND POULTRY

SAINT HELENA - CLIMATE

St. Martin's Press, Inc., 175 Fifth Avenue, New York, New York 10010 (800) 221-7945; *The Statesman's Year-Book.*

SAINT HELENA - COMMERCE

St. Martin's Press, Inc., 175 Fifth Avenue, New York, New York 10010 (800) 221-7945; *The Statesman's Year-Book.*

SAINT HELENA - COMMUNICATIONS - See SAINT HELENA - TRANSPORTATION AND COMMUNICATIONS

SAINT HELENA - CONSUMER PRICE INDEX

Europa Publications Limited, 18 Bedford Square, London, WC1B 3JN, England; *The Europa World Year Book.*

SAINT HELENA - CORN PRODUCTION - See SAINT HELENA - CROPS

SAINT HELENA - CROPS

Food and Agricultural Organization of the United Nations (FAO) Via delle Terme di Caracalla, 00100 Rome, Italy (Telephone Number in U.S. (202) 653-2400); *The State of Food and Agriculture.*

United Nations Conference on Trade and Development, Central Statistical Service, Palais des Nations, Geneva, Switzerland (Telephone in U.S. (800) 253-9646); *UNCTAD Commodity Yearbook.*

SAINT HELENA - DAIRY PRODUCTS

Food and Agricultural Organization of the United Nations (FAO) Via delle Terme di Caracalla, 00100 Rome, Italy (Telephone Number in U.S. (202) 653-2400); *The State of Food and Agriculture.*

SAINT HELENA - DEATH RATES - See SAINT HELENA - MORTALITY

SAINT HELENA - DEVELOPMENT ASSISTANCE

Statistical Office of the United Nations, Publishing Service, New York, New York 10017 (800) 253-9646; *Statistical Yearbook.*

SAINT HELENA - DIVORCE RATES

Statistical Office of the United Nations, Publishing Service, New York, New York 10017 (800) 253-9646; *Demographic Yearbook;* and *Statistical Yearbook.*

SAINT HELENA - ECONOMY

Central Intelligence Agency, Washington, D.C. 20505 (703) 482-1100, www.cia.gov; *The World Factbook.*

St. Martin's Press, Inc., 175 Fifth Avenue, New York, New York 10010 (800) 221-7945; *The Statesman's Year-Book.*

SAINT HELENA - EDUCATION

Europa Publications Limited, 18 Bedford Square, London, WC1B 3JN, England; *The Europa World Year Book.*

St. Martin's Press, Inc., 175 Fifth Avenue, New York, New York 10010 (800) 221-7945; *The Statesman's Year-Book.*

United Nations Educational, Scientific and Cultural Organization (UNESCO), 7 Place de Fontenoy, F-75700 Paris, France (Telephone Number in U.S. (212) 963-5981); *Statistical Yearbook.*

SAINT HELENA - EGG PRODUCTION AND CONSUMPTION - See SAINT HELENA - DAIRY PRODUCTS

SAINT HELENA - ELECTRICITY

Central Intelligence Agency, Washington, D.C. 20505 (703) 482-1100, www.cia.gov; *The World Factbook.*

SAINT HELENA - EMPLOYMENT

International Labour Office, I.L.O. Publications, 1828 L Street, NW, Suite 801, Washington, D.C. 20036 (301) 638-3152; *Yearbook of Labour Statistics.*

SAINT HELENA - ENERGY

Food and Agricultural Organization of the United Nations (FAO) Via delle Terme di Caracalla, 00100 Rome, Italy (Telephone Number in U.S. (202) 653-2400); *The State of Food and Agriculture.*

Statistical Office of the United Nations, Publishing Service, New York, New York 10017 (800) 253-9646; *Energy Statistics Yearbook.*

SAINT HELENA - EXCHANGE RATES

Central Intelligence Agency, Washington, D.C. 20505 (703) 482-1100, www.cia.gov; *The World Factbook.*

Europa Publications Limited, 18 Bedford Square, London, WC1B 3JN, England; *The Europa World Year Book.*

SAINT HELENA - EXPORTS

Central Intelligence Agency, Washington, D.C. 20505 (703) 482-1100, www.cia.gov; *The World Factbook.*

Europa Publications Limited, 18 Bedford Square, London, WC1B 3JN, England; *The Europa World Year Book.*

Food and Agricultural Organization of the United Nations (FAO) Via delle Terme

di Caracalla, 00100 Rome, Italy (Telephone Number in U.S. (202) 653-2400); *The State of Food and Agriculture.*

International Monetary Fund, 700 Nineteenth Street, NW, Washington, D.C. 20431 (202) 623-7000; *Direction of Trade Statistics.*

St. Martin's Press, Inc., 175 Fifth Avenue, New York, New York 10010 (800) 221-7945; *The Statesman's Year-Book.*

SAINT HELENA - EXTERNAL TRADE

Food and Agricultural Organization of the United Nations (FAO) Via delle Terme di Caracalla, 00100 Rome, Italy (Telephone Number in U.S. (202) 653-2400); *The State of Food and Agriculture;* and *Trade Yearbook.*

SAINT HELENA - FARM CROPS - See SAINT HELENA - CROPS

SAINT HELENA - FERTILITY RATES

Central Intelligence Agency, Washington, D.C. 20505 (703) 482-1100, www.cia.gov; *The World Factbook.*

SAINT HELENA - FERTILIZER

Food and Agricultural Organization of the United Nations (FAO) Via delle Terme di Caracalla, 00100 Rome, Italy (Telephone Number in U.S. (202) 653-2400); *The State of Food and Agriculture.*

SAINT HELENA - FETAL MORTALITY - See SAINT HELENA - MORTALITY

SAINT HELENA - FINANCE

Europa Publications Limited, 18 Bedford Square, London, WC1B 3JN, England; *The Europa World Year Book.*

SAINT HELENA - FISHERIES

Europa Publications Limited, 18 Bedford Square, London, WC1B 3JN, England; *The Europa World Year Book.*

Food and Agricultural Organization of the United Nations (FAO) Via delle Terme di Caracalla, 00100 Rome, Italy (Telephone Number in U.S. (202) 653-2400); *The State of Food and Agriculture;* and *Yearbook of Fishery Statistics.*

United Nations Conference on Trade and Development, Central Statistical Service, Palais des Nations, Geneva, Switzerland (Telephone in U.S. (800) 253-9646); *UNCTAD Commodity Yearbook.*

SAINT HELENA - FOOD

Food and Agricultural Organization of the United Nations (FAO), Via delle Terme

di Caracalla, 00100 Rome, Italy (Telephone Number in U.S. (202) 653-2400); *Production Yearbook;* and *The State of Food and Agriculture.*

United Nations Conference on Trade and Development, Central Statistical Service, Palais des Nations, Geneva, Switzerland (Telephone in U.S. (800) 253-9646); *UNCTAD Commodity Yearbook.*

SAINT HELENA - FOREIGN TRADE

Europa Publications Limited, 18 Bedford Square, London, WC1B 3JN, England; *The Europa World Year Book.*

Food and Agricultural Organization of the United Nations (FAO) Via delle Terme di Caracalla, 00100 Rome, Italy (Telephone Number in U.S. (202) 653-2400); *The State of Food and Agriculture.*

United Nations Conference on Trade and Development, Central Statistical Service, Palais des Nations, Geneva, Switzerland (Telephone in U.S. (800) 253-9646); *UNCTAD Commodity Yearbook.*

SAINT HELENA - FORESTRY AND FOREST PRODUCTS

Food and Agricultural Organization of the United Nations (FAO) Via delle Terme di Caracalla, 00100 Rome, Italy (Telephone Number in U.S. (202) 653-2400); *The State of Food and Agriculture.*

United Nations Conference on Trade and Development, Central Statistical Service, Palais des Nations, Geneva, Switzerland (Telephone in U.S. (800) 253-9646); *UNCTAD Commodity Yearbook.*

SAINT HELENA - GENERAL MORTALITY - See SAINT HELENA - MORTALITY

SAINT HELENA - GOVERNMENT

Central Intelligence Agency, Washington, D.C. 20505 (703) 482-1100, www.cia.gov; *The World Factbook.*

Europa Publications Limited, 18 Bedford Square, London, WC1B 3JN, England; *The Europa World Year Book.*

St. Martin's Press, Inc., 175 Fifth Avenue, New York, New York 10010 (800) 221-7945; *The Statesman's Year-Book.*

SAINT HELENA - GRAIN PRODUCTION - See SAINT HELENA - CROPS

SAINT HELENA - GROUNDNUT PRODUCTION - See SAINT HELENA - CROPS

SAINT HELENA - HEALTH

St. Martin's Press, Inc., 175 Fifth

Avenue, New York, New York 10010 (800) 221-7945; *The Statesman's Year-Book.*

Statistical Office of the United Nations, Publishing Service, New York, New York 10017 (800) 253-9646; *Statistical Yearbook.*

SAINT HELENA - HIGHWAYS

Central Intelligence Agency, Washington, D.C. 20505 (703) 482-1100, www.cia.gov; *The World Factbook.*

SAINT HELENA - HOURS OF WORK - See SAINT HELENA - EMPLOYMENT

SAINT HELENA - ILLITERATE POPULATION

Central Intelligence Agency, Washington, D.C. 20505 (703) 482-1100, www.cia.gov; *The World Factbook.*

United Nations Educational, Scientific and Cultural Organization (UNESCO), 7 Place de Fontenoy, F-75700 Paris, France (Telephone Number in U.S. (212) 963-5981); *Statistical Yearbook.*

SAINT HELENA - IMPORTS

Central Intelligence Agency, Washington, D.C. 20505 (703) 482-1100, www.cia.gov; *The World Factbook.*

Europa Publications Limited, 18 Bedford Square, London, WC1B 3JN, England; *The Europa World Year Book.*

Food and Agricultural Organization of the United Nations (FAO) Via delle Terme di Caracalla, 00100 Rome, Italy (Telephone Number in U.S. (202) 653-2400); *The State of Food and Agriculture.*

International Monetary Fund, 700 Nineteenth Street, NW, Washington, D.C. 20431 (202) 623-7000; *Direction of Trade Statistics.*

St. Martin's Press, Inc., 175 Fifth Avenue, New York, New York 10010 (800) 221-7945; *The Statesman's Year-Book.*

SAINT HELENA - INDUSTRY

Central Intelligence Agency, Washington, D.C. 20505 (703) 482-1100, www.cia.gov; *The World Factbook.*

St. Martin's Press, Inc., 175 Fifth Avenue, New York, New York 10010 (800) 221-7945; *The Statesman's Year-Book.*

SAINT HELENA - INFANT AND MATERNAL MORTALITY - See SAINT HELENA - MORTALITY

SAINT HELENA - LABOR

Central Intelligence Agency, Washington, D.C. 20505 (703) 482-1100,

www.cia.gov; *The World Factbook.*

Europa Publications Limited, 18 Bedford Square, London, WC1B 3JN, England; *The Europa World Year Book.*

Food and Agricultural Organization of the United Nations (FAO) Via delle Terme di Caracalla, 00100 Rome, Italy (Telephone Number in U.S. (202) 653-2400); *The State of Food and Agriculture.*

St. Martin's Press, Inc., 175 Fifth Avenue, New York, New York 10010 (800) 221-7945; *The Statesman's Year-Book.*

SAINT HELENA - LAND USE

Central Intelligence Agency, Washington, D.C. 20505 (703) 482-1100, www.cia.gov; *The World Factbook.*

Food and Agricultural Organization of the United Nations (FAO), Via delle Terme di Caracalla, 00100 Rome, Italy (Telephone Number in U.S. (202) 653-2400); *Production Yearbook.*

SAINT HELENA - LIBRARIES

United Nations Educational, Scientific and Cultural Organization (UNESCO), 7 Place de Fontenoy, F-75700 Paris, France (Telephone Number in U.S. (212) 963-5981); *Statistical Yearbook.*

SAINT HELENA - LIFE EXPECTANCY

Central Intelligence Agency, Washington, D.C. 20505 (703) 482-1100, www.cia.gov; *The World Factbook.*

SAINT HELENA - LIVESTOCK AND POULTRY

Europa Publications Limited, 18 Bedford Square, London, WC1B 3JN, England; *The Europa World Year Book.*

Food and Agricultural Organization of the United Nations (FAO), Via delle Terme di Caracalla, 00100 Rome, Italy (Telephone Number in U.S. (202) 653-2400); *Production Yearbook;* and *The State of Food and Agriculture.*

Statistical Office of the United Nations, Publishing Service, New York, New York 10017 (800) 253-9646; *Statistical Yearbook.*

United Nations Conference on Trade and Development, Central Statistical Service, Palais des Nations, Geneva, Switzerland (Telephone in U.S. (800) 253-9646); *UNCTAD Commodity Yearbook.*

SAINT HELENA - MAIL - NUMBER OF ITEMS SENT AND RECEIVED

Statistical Office of the United Nations, Publishing Service, New York, New York

10017 (800) 253-9646; *Statistical Yearbook.*

SAINT HELENA - MARRIAGE RATES

Statistical Office of the United Nations, Publishing Service, New York, New York 10017 (800) 253-9646; *Demographic Yearbook;* and *Statistical Yearbook.*

SAINT HELENA - MEAT PRODUCTION - See SAINT HELENA - LIVESTOCK AND POULTRY

SAINT HELENA - MERCHANT SHIPPING

Europa Publications Limited, 18 Bedford Square, London, WC1B 3JN, England; *The Europa World Year Book.*

St. Martin's Press, Inc., 175 Fifth Avenue, New York, New York 10010 (800) 221-7945; *The Statesman's Year-Book.*

Statistical Office of the United Nations, Publishing Service, New York, New York 10017 (800) 253-9646; *Statistical Yearbook.*

SAINT HELENA - MILITARY

Central Intelligence Agency, Washington, D.C. 20505 (703) 482-1100, www.cia.gov; *The World Factbook.*

SAINT HELENA - MINING AND MINERAL PRODUCTS

United Nations Conference on Trade and Development, Central Statistical Service, Palais des Nations, Geneva, Switzerland (Telephone in U.S. (800) 253-9646); *UNCTAD Commodity Yearbook.*

SAINT HELENA - MORTALITY

Central Intelligence Agency, Washington, D.C. 20505 (703) 482-1100, www.cia.gov; *The World Factbook.*

Europa Publications Limited, 18 Bedford Square, London, WC1B 3JN, England; *The Europa World Year Book.*

St. Martin's Press, Inc., 175 Fifth Avenue, New York, New York 10010 (800) 221-7945; *The Statesman's Year-Book.*

Statistical Office of the United Nations, Publishing Service, New York, New York 10017 (800) 253-9646; *Demographic Yearbook;* and *Statistical Yearbook.*

World Health Organization, Office of Publications, 20 Avenue Appia, CH-1211 Geneva 27, Switzerland (Telephone Number in U.S. (518) 436-9686); *World Health Statistics Annual.*

SAINT HELENA - MOTION PICTURES

Statistical Office of the United Nations, Publishing Service, New York, New York

10017 (800) 253-9646; *Statistical Yearbook.*

SAINT HELENA - MOTOR VEHICLES IN USE

Europa Publications Limited, 18 Bedford Square, London, WC1B 3JN, England; *The Europa World Year Book.*

SAINT HELENA - MUSEUMS

United Nations Educational, Scientific and Cultural Organization (UNESCO), 7 Place de Fontenoy, F-75700 Paris, France (Telephone Number in U.S. (212) 963-5981); *Statistical Yearbook.*

SAINT HELENA - NATALITY - See SAINT HELENA - BIRTH RATE

SAINT HELENA - NEWSPAPER PRODUCTION - See SAINT HELENA - FORESTRY AND FOREST PRODUCTS

SAINT HELENA - OCCUPATIONS - See SAINT HELENA - LABOR

SAINT HELENA - PERIODICALS

United Nations Educational, Scientific and Cultural Organization (UNESCO), 7 Place de Fontenoy, F-75700 Paris, France (Telephone Number in U.S. (212) 963-5981); *Statistical Yearbook.*

SAINT HELENA - PESTICIDE USE

Food and Agricultural Organization of the United Nations (FAO) Via delle Terme di Caracalla, 00100 Rome, Italy (Telephone Number in U.S. (202) 653-2400); *The State of Food and Agriculture.*

SAINT HELENA - PETROLEUM INDUSTRY

Food and Agricultural Organization of the United Nations (FAO) Via delle Terme di Caracalla, 00100 Rome, Italy (Telephone Number in U.S. (202) 653-2400); *The State of Food and Agriculture.*

United Nations Conference on Trade and Development, Central Statistical Service, Palais des Nations, Geneva, Switzerland (Telephone in U.S. (800) 253-9646); *UNCTAD Commodity Yearbook.*

SAINT HELENA - PIGS - See SAINT HELENA - LIVESTOCK AND POULTRY

SAINT HELENA - POPULATION

Central Intelligence Agency, Washington, D.C. 20505 (703) 482-1100, www.cia.gov; *The World Factbook.*

Europa Publications Limited, 18 Bedford Square, London, WC1B 3JN, England; *The Europa World Year Book.*

Food and Agricultural Organization of

the United Nations (FAO), Via delle Terme di Caracalla, 00100 Rome, Italy (Telephone Number in U.S. (202) 653-2400); *Production Yearbook.*

St. Martin's Press, Inc., 175 Fifth Avenue, New York, New York 10010 (800) 221-7945; *The Statesman's Year-Book.*

Statistical Office of the United Nations, Publishing Service, New York, New York 10017 (800) 253-9646; *Demographic Yearbook;* and *Statistical Yearbook.*

United Nations Educational, Scientific and Cultural Organization (UNESCO), 7 Place de Fontenoy, F-75700 Paris, France (Telephone Number in U.S. (212) 963-5981); *Statistical Yearbook.*

World Health Organization, Office of Publications, 20 Avenue Appia, CH-1211 Geneva 27, Switzerland (Telephone Number in U.S. (518) 436-9686); *World Health Statistics Annual.*

SAINT HELENA - PRICES

Food and Agricultural Organization of the United Nations (FAO), Via delle Terme di Caracalla, 00100 Rome, Italy (Telephone Number in U.S. (202) 653-2400); *Production Yearbook;* and *The State of Food and Agriculture.*

SAINT HELENA - RADIO RECEIVERS

St. Martin's Press, Inc., 175 Fifth Avenue, New York, New York 10010 (800) 221-7945; *The Statesman's Year-Book.*

SAINT HELENA - RELIGION

Central Intelligence Agency, Washington, D.C. 20505 (703) 482-1100, www.cia.gov; *The World Factbook.*

St. Martin's Press, Inc., 175 Fifth Avenue, New York, New York 10010 (800) 221-7945; *The Statesman's Year-Book.*

SAINT HELENA - SHEEP - See SAINT HELENA - LIVESTOCK AND POULTRY

SAINT HELENA - STOCKS - COMMODITY - MARKET PRICE - INDEX

Food and Agricultural Organization of the United Nations (FAO) Via delle Terme di Caracalla, 00100 Rome, Italy (Telephone Number in U.S. (202) 653-2400); *The State of Food and Agriculture.*

SAINT HELENA - TELEPHONES IN USE

Central Intelligence Agency, Washington, D.C. 20505 (703) 482-1100, www.cia.gov; *The World Factbook.*

St. Martin's Press, Inc., 175 Fifth Avenue, New York, New York 10010 (800)

221-7945; *The Statesman's Year-Book.*

SAINT HELENA - TEXTILE INDUSTRY

United Nations Conference on Trade and Development, Central Statistical Service, Palais des Nations, Geneva, Switzerland (Telephone in U.S. (800) 253-9646); *UNCTAD Commodity Yearbook.*

SAINT HELENA - TRADE - See SAINT HELENA - FOREIGN TRADE

SAINT HELENA - TRANSPORTATION AND COMMUNICATIONS

Central Intelligence Agency, Washington, D.C. 20505 (703) 482-1100, www.cia.gov; *The World Factbook.*

Europa Publications Limited, 18 Bedford Square, London, WC1B 3JN, England; *The Europa World Year Book.*

St. Martin's Press, Inc., 175 Fifth Avenue, New York, New York 10010 (800) 221-7945; *The Statesman's Year-Book.*

SAINT HELENA - UNEMPLOYMENT RATE

Central Intelligence Agency, Washington, D.C. 20505 (703) 482-1100, www.cia.gov; *The World Factbook.*

SAINT HELENA - VITAL STATISTICS

St. Martin's Press, Inc., 175 Fifth Avenue, New York, New York 10010 (800) 221-7945; *The Statesman's Year-Book.*

Statistical Office of the United Nations, Publishing Service, New York, New York 10017 (800) 253-9646; *Statistical Yearbook.*

World Health Organization, Office of Publications, 20 Avenue Appia, CH-1211 Geneva 27, Switzerland (Telephone Number in U.S. (518) 436-9686); *World Health Statistics Annual.*

SAINT HELENA - WEATHER - See SAINT HELENA - CLIMATE

Saint Kitts and Nevis - National Statistical Office

Statistics Division, Planning Unit, Ministry of Finance, Church Street, Post Office Box 186, Basseterre, Saint Kitts and Nevis.

Saint Kitts and Nevis - Primary Statistics Source

HM Stationery Office, Post Office Box 569, London SE1 9NH, England; *Saint Kitts and Nevis: Report.*

SAINT KITTS AND NEVIS - AGRICULTURE

Euromonitor International, Inc., 122 South Michigan Avenue, Suite 1200, Chicago, Illinois 60603 (800) 577-EURO; *World Marketing Data and Statistics.*

Europa Publications Limited, 18 Bedford Square, London, WC1B 3JN, England; *The Europa World Year Book.*

Federal Statistical Office, Gustav-Stresemann - Ring 11, D-6200, Wiesbaden, Germany; *Saint Kitts and Nevis.*

Food and Agricultural Organization of the United Nations (FAO) Via delle Terme di Caracalla, 00100 Rome, Italy (Telephone Number in U.S. (202) 653-2400); *Production Yearbook; The State of Food and Agriculture;* and *Trade Yearbook.*

St. Martin's Press, Inc., 175 Fifth Avenue, New York, New York 10010 (800) 221-7945; *The Statesman's Year-Book.*

Statistical Office of the United Nations, Publishing Service, New York, New York 10017 (800) 253-9646; *Statistical Yearbook.*

United Nations Conference on Trade and Development, Central Statistical Service, Palais des Nations, Geneva, Switzerland (Telephone in U.S. (800) 253-9646); *UNCTAD Commodity Yearbook.*

The World Bank, 1818 H Street, NW, Washington, D.C. 20433 (202) 477-1234; *World Development Indicators.*

SAINT KITTS AND NEVIS - AIRLINE SERVICE

Europa Publications Limited, 18 Bedford Square, London, WC1B 3JN, England; *The Europa World Year Book.*

St. Martin's Press, Inc., 175 Fifth Avenue, New York, New York 10010 (800) 221-7945; *The Statesman's Year-Book.*

SAINT KITTS AND NEVIS - AIRPORTS

Central Intelligence Agency, Washington, D.C. 20505 (703) 482-1100, www.cia.gov; *The World Factbook.*

SAINT KITTS AND NEVIS - AREA AND DENSITY OF POPULATION

Central Intelligence Agency, Washington, D.C. 20505 (703) 482-1100, www.cia.gov; *The World Factbook.*

Euromonitor International, Inc., 122 South Michigan Avenue, Suite 1200, Chicago, Illinois 60603 (800) 577-EURO; *The World Economic Factbook.*

Europa Publications Limited, 18 Bedford Square, London, WC1B 3JN,

England; *The Europa World Year Book.*

Federal Statistical Office, Gustav-Stresemann - Ring 11, D-6200, Wiesbaden, Germany; *Saint Kitts and Nevis.*

Food and Agricultural Organization of the United Nations (FAO) Via delle Terme di Caracalla, 00100 Rome, Italy (Telephone Number in U.S. (202) 653-2400); *The State of Food and Agriculture.*

St. Martin's Press, Inc., 175 Fifth Avenue, New York, New York 10010 (800) 221-7945; *The Statesman's Year-Book.*

Statistical Office of the United Nations, Publishing Service, New York, New York 10017 (800) 253-9646; *Statistical Yearbook.*

United Nations Educational, Scientific and Cultural Organization (UNESCO), 7 Place de Fontenoy, F-75700 Paris, France (Telephone Number in U.S. (212) 963-5981); *Statistical Yearbook.*

SAINT KITTS AND NEVIS - BALANCE OF PAYMENTS

Europa Publications Limited, 18 Bedford Square, London, WC1B 3JN, England; *The Europa World Year Book.*

Federal Statistical Office, Gustav-Stresemann - Ring 11, D-6200, Wiesbaden, Germany; *Saint Kitts and Nevis.*

United Nations Conference on Trade and Development (UNCTAD), New York, New York 10017 (800) 253-9646; *Handbook of International Trade and Development Statistics.*

The World Bank, 1818 H Street, NW, Washington, D.C. 20433 (202) 477-1234; *World Development Indicators.*

SAINT KITTS AND NEVIS - BANKING

Euromonitor International, Inc., 122 South Michigan Avenue, Suite 1200, Chicago, Illinois 60603 (800) 577-EURO; *World Marketing Data and Statistics.*

Europa Publications Limited, 18 Bedford Square, London, WC1B 3JN, England; *The Europa World Year Book.*

St. Martin's Press, Inc., 175 Fifth Avenue, New York, New York 10010 (800) 221-7945; *The Statesman's Year-Book.*

SAINT KITTS AND NEVIS - BIRTH RATES

Central Intelligence Agency, Washington, D.C. 20505 (703) 482-1100, www.cia.gov; *The World Factbook.*

Euromonitor International, Inc., 122 South Michigan Avenue, Suite 1200, Chicago, Illinois 60603 (800) 577-EURO;

The World Economic Factbook.

Europa Publications Limited, 18 Bedford Square, London, WC1B 3JN, England; *The Europa World Year Book.*

St. Martin's Press, Inc., 175 Fifth Avenue, New York, New York 10010 (800) 221-7945; *The Statesman's Year-Book.*

Statistical Office of the United Nations, Publishing Service, New York, New York 10017 (800) 253-9646; *Demographic Yearbook;* and *Statistical Yearbook.*

The World Bank, 1818 H Street, NW, Washington, D.C. 20433 (202) 477-1234; *World Development Indicators.*

World Health Organization, Office of Publications, 20 Avenue Appia, CH-1211 Geneva 27, Switzerland (Telephone Number in U.S. (518) 436-9686); *World Health Statistics Annual.*

SAINT KITTS AND NEVIS - BOOK PRODUCTION

United Nations Educational, Scientific and Cultural Organization (UNESCO), 7 Place de Fontenoy, F-75700 Paris, France (Telephone Number in U.S. (212) 963-5981); *Statistical Yearbook.*

SAINT KITTS AND NEVIS - BROADCASTING

Billboard Limited, P.O. Box 9027, 1006 AA Amsterdam, The Netherlands (Telephone Number in U.S. (212) 764-7300); *World Radio TV Handbook.*

Central Intelligence Agency, Washington, D.C. 20505 (703) 482-1100, www.cia.gov; *The World Factbook.*

Euromonitor International, Inc., 122 South Michigan Avenue, Suite 1200, Chicago, Illinois 60603 (800) 577-EURO; *World Marketing Data and Statistics.*

St. Martin's Press, Inc., 175 Fifth Avenue, New York, New York 10010 (800) 221-7945; *The Statesman's Year-Book.*

SAINT KITTS AND NEVIS - BUDGET

Central Intelligence Agency, Washington, D.C. 20505 (703) 482-1100, www.cia.gov; *The World Factbook.*

SAINT KITTS AND NEVIS - CALORIE SUPPLY

Food and Agricultural Organization of the United Nations (FAO) Via delle Terme di Caracalla, 00100 Rome, Italy (Telephone Number in U.S. (202) 653-2400); *The State of Food and Agriculture.*

SAINT KITTS AND NEVIS - CATTLE - See SAINT KITTS AND NEVIS - LIVESTOCK AND POULTRY

SAINT KITTS AND NEVIS - CLIMATE

St. Martin's Press, Inc., 175 Fifth Avenue, New York, New York 10010 (800) 221-7945; *The Statesman's Year-Book.*

SAINT KITTS AND NEVIS - COMMERCE

St. Martin's Press, Inc., 175 Fifth Avenue, New York, New York 10010 (800) 221-7945; *The Statesman's Year-Book.*

SAINT KITTS AND NEVIS - COMMUNICATIONS - See SAINT KITTS AND NEVIS - TRANSPORTATION AND COMMUNICATIONS

SAINT KITTS AND NEVIS - CONSUMER PRICE INDEX

Europa Publications Limited, 18 Bedford Square, London, WC1B 3JN, England; *The Europa World Year Book.*

Statistical Office of the United Nations, Publishing Service, New York, New York 10017 (800) 253-9646; *Statistical Yearbook.*

SAINT KITTS AND NEVIS - CONSUMER PRICES

Euromonitor International, Inc., 122 South Michigan Avenue, Suite 1200, Chicago, Illinois 60603 (800) 577-EURO; *World Marketing Data and Statistics.*

International Labour Office, I.L.O. Publications, 1828 L Street, NW, Suite 801, Washington, D.C. 20036 (301) 638-3152; *Yearbook of Labour Statistics.*

SAINT KITTS AND NEVIS - CORN PRODUCTION - See SAINT KITTS AND NEVIS - CROPS

SAINT KITTS AND NEVIS - CORPORATE TAXES - See SAINT KITTS AND NEVIS - TAXATION

SAINT KITTS AND NEVIS - CROPS

Europa Publications Limited, 18 Bedford Square, London, WC1B 3JN, England; *The Europa World Year Book.*

Food and Agricultural Organization of the United Nations (FAO) Via delle Terme di Caracalla, 00100 Rome, Italy (Telephone Number in U.S. (202) 653-2400); *The State of Food and Agriculture.*

St. Martin's Press, Inc., 175 Fifth Avenue, New York, New York 10010 (800) 221-7945; *The Statesman's Year-Book.*

Statistical Office of the United Nations, Publishing Service, New York, New York 10017 (800) 253-9646; *Statistical Yearbook.*

United Nations Conference on Trade and Development, Central Statistical Service, Palais des Nations, Geneva, Switzerland (Telephone in U.S. (800) 253-9646); *UNCTAD Commodity Yearbook.*

SAINT KITTS AND NEVIS - CUSTOMS DUTIES

St. Martin's Press, Inc., 175 Fifth Avenue, New York, New York 10010 (800) 221-7945; *The Statesman's Year-Book.*

SAINT KITTS AND NEVIS - DAIRY PRODUCTS

Food and Agricultural Organization of the United Nations (FAO) Via delle Terme di Caracalla, 00100 Rome, Italy (Telephone Number in U.S. (202) 653-2400); *The State of Food and Agriculture.*

St. Martin's Press, Inc., 175 Fifth Avenue, New York, New York 10010 (800) 221-7945; *The Statesman's Year-Book.*

SAINT KITTS AND NEVIS - DEATH RATES - See SAINT KITTS AND NEVIS - MORTALITY

SAINT KITTS AND NEVIS - DEMOGRAPHY

Euromonitor International, Inc., 122 South Michigan Avenue, Suite 1200, Chicago, Illinois 60603 (800) 577-EURO; *The World Economic Factbook;* and *World Marketing Data and Statistics.*

Federal Statistical Office, Gustav-Stresemann - Ring 11, D-6200, Wiesbaden, Germany; *Saint Kitts and Nevis.*

Statistical Office of the United Nations, Publishing Service, New York, New York 10017 (800) 253-9646; *Human Development Report.*

SAINT KITTS AND NEVIS - DISEASES - See SAINT KITTS AND NEVIS - HEALTH

SAINT KITTS AND NEVIS - DIVORCE RATES

Statistical Office of the United Nations, Publishing Service, New York, New York 10017 (800) 253-9646; *Demographic Yearbook;* and *Statistical Yearbook.*

SAINT KITTS AND NEVIS - ECONOMY

Central Intelligence Agency, Washington, D.C. 20505 (703) 482-1100, www.cia.gov; *The World Factbook.*

Euromonitor International, Inc., 122 South Michigan Avenue, Suite 1200, Chicago, Illinois 60603 (800) 577-EURO; *The World Economic Factbook;* and *World Marketing Data and Statistics.*

Europa Publications Limited, 18 Bedford Square, London, WC1B 3JN, England; *The Europa World Year Book.*

Federal Statistical Office, Gustav-Stresemann - Ring 11, D-6200, Wiesbaden, Germany; *Saint Kitts and Nevis.*

St. Martin's Press, Inc., 175 Fifth Avenue, New York, New York 10010 (800) 221-7945; *The Statesman's Year-Book.*

Statistical Office of the United Nations, Publishing Service, New York, New York 10017 (800) 253-9646; *World Statistics Pocketbook.*

The World Bank, 1818 H Street, NW, Washington, D.C. 20433 (202) 477-1234; *The World Bank Atlas.*

SAINT KITTS AND NEVIS - EDUCATION

Euromonitor International, Inc., 122 South Michigan Avenue, Suite 1200, Chicago, Illinois 60603 (800) 577-EURO; *World Marketing Data and Statistics.*

Federal Statistical Office, Gustav-Stresemann - Ring 11, D-6200, Wiesbaden, Germany; *Saint Kitts and Nevis.*

St. Martin's Press, Inc., 175 Fifth Avenue, New York, New York 10010 (800) 221-7945; *The Statesman's Year-Book.*

Statistical Office of the United Nations, Publishing Service, New York, New York 10017 (800) 253-9646; *Human Development Report.*

United Nations Educational, Scientific and Cultural Organization (UNESCO), 7 Place de Fontenoy, F-75700 Paris, France (Telephone Number in U.S. (212) 963-5981); *Statistical Yearbook.*

The World Bank, 1818 H Street, NW, Washington, D.C. 20433 (202) 477-1234; *World Development Indicators.*

SAINT KITTS AND NEVIS - EGG PRODUCTION - See SAINT KITTS AND NEVIS - DAIRY PRODUCTS

SAINT KITTS AND NEVIS - ELECTRICITY

Central Intelligence Agency, Washington, D.C. 20505 (703) 482-1100, www.cia.gov; *The World Factbook.*

St. Martin's Press, Inc., 175 Fifth Avenue, New York, New York 10010 (800) 221-7945; *The Statesman's Year-Book.*

Statistical Office of the United Nations, Publishing Service, New York, New York 10017 (800) 253-9646; *Human Development Report;* and *Statistical Yearbook.*

SAINT KITTS AND NEVIS - EMPLOYMENT

Federal Statistical Office, Gustav-

Stresemann - Ring 11, D-6200, Wiesbaden, Germany; *Saint Kitts and Nevis.*

International Labour Office, I.L.O. Publications, 1828 L Street, NW, Suite 801, Washington, D.C. 20036 (301) 638-3152; *Yearbook of Labour Statistics.*

SAINT KITTS AND NEVIS - ENERGY

Euromonitor International, Inc., 122 South Michigan Avenue, Suite 1200, Chicago, Illinois 60603 (800) 577-EURO; *The World Economic Factbook;* and *World Marketing Data and Statistics.*

Food and Agricultural Organization of the United Nations (FAO) Via delle Terme di Caracalla, 00100 Rome, Italy (Telephone Number in U.S. (202) 653-2400); *The State of Food and Agriculture.*

St. Martin's Press, Inc., 175 Fifth Avenue, New York, New York 10010 (800) 221-7945; *The Statesman's Year-Book.*

Statistical Office of the United Nations, Publishing Service, New York, New York 10017 (800) 253-9646; *Human Development Report; Statistical Yearbook;* and *World Statistics Pocketbook.*

The World Bank, 1818 H Street, NW, Washington, D.C. 20433 (202) 477-1234; *The World Bank Atlas.*

SAINT KITTS AND NEVIS - ENVIRONMENT

Statistical Office of the United Nations, Publishing Service, New York, New York 10017 (800) 253-9646; *World Statistics Pocketbook.*

SAINT KITTS AND NEVIS - EXCHANGE RATES

Central Intelligence Agency, Washington, D.C. 20505 (703) 482-1100, www.cia.gov; *The World Factbook.*

Euromonitor International, Inc., 122 South Michigan Avenue, Suite 1200, Chicago, Illinois 60603 (800) 577-EURO; *The World Economic Factbook.*

Europa Publications Limited, 18 Bedford Square, London, WC1B 3JN, England; *The Europa World Year Book.*

Statistical Office of the United Nations, Publishing Service, New York, New York 10017 (800) 253-9646; *World Statistics Pocketbook.*

SAINT KITTS AND NEVIS - EXPORTS

Euromonitor International, Inc., 122 South Michigan Avenue, Suite 1200, Chicago, Illinois 60603 (800) 577-EURO; *The World Economic Factbook.*

Europa Publications Limited, 18 Bedford Square, London, WC1B 3JN, England; *The Europa World Year Book.*

Food and Agricultural Organization of the United Nations (FAO) Via delle Terme di Caracalla, 00100 Rome, Italy (Telephone Number in U.S. (202) 653-2400); *The State of Food and Agriculture.*

International Monetary Fund, 700 Nineteenth Street, NW, Washington, D.C. 20431 (202) 623-7000; *Direction of Trade Statistics.*

St. Martin's Press, Inc., 175 Fifth Avenue, New York, New York 10010 (800) 221-7945; *The Statesman's Year-Book.*

United Nations Conference on Trade and Development (UNCTAD), New York, New York 10017 (800) 253-9646; *Handbook of International Trade and Development Statistics.*

The World Bank, 1818 H Street, NW, Washington, D.C. 20433 (202) 477-1234; *World Development Indicators.*

SAINT KITTS AND NEVIS - EXTERNAL INDEBTEDNESS

The World Bank, 1818 H Street, NW, Washington, D.C. 20433 (202) 477-1234; *World Development Indicators.*

SAINT KITTS AND NEVIS - EXTERNAL TRADE

Euromonitor International, Inc., 122 South Michigan Avenue, Suite 1200, Chicago, Illinois 60603 (800) 577-EURO; *World Marketing Data and Statistics.*

Food and Agricultural Organization of the United Nations (FAO) Via delle Terme di Caracalla, 00100 Rome, Italy (Telephone Number in U.S. (202) 653-2400); *The State of Food and Agriculture;* and *Trade Yearbook.*

SAINT KITTS AND NEVIS - FARM CROPS - See SAINT KITTS AND NEVIS - CROPS

SAINT KITTS AND NEVIS - FERTILITY RATES

Central Intelligence Agency, Washington, D.C. 20505 (703) 482-1100, www.cia.gov; *The World Factbook.*

Statistical Office of the United Nations, Publishing Service, New York, New York 10017 (800) 253-9646; *Human Development Report.*

The World Bank, 1818 H Street, NW, Washington, D.C. 20433 (202) 477-1234; *The World Bank Atlas;* and *World Development Indicators.*

SAINT KITTS AND NEVIS - FERTILIZER

Food and Agricultural Organization of the United Nations (FAO) Via delle Terme di Caracalla, 00100 Rome, Italy (Telephone Number in U.S. (202) 653-2400); *The State of Food and Agriculture.*

Statistical Office of the United Nations, Publishing Service, New York, New York 10017 (800) 253-9646; *Statistical Yearbook.*

SAINT KITTS AND NEVIS - FETAL MORTALITY - See SAINT KITTS AND NEVIS - MORTALITY

SAINT KITTS AND NEVIS - FINANCE

Europa Publications Limited, 18 Bedford Square, London, WC1B 3JN, England; *The Europa World Year Book.*

Federal Statistical Office, Gustav-Stresemann - Ring 11, D-6200, Wiesbaden, Germany; *Saint Kitts and Nevis.*

St. Martin's Press, Inc., 175 Fifth Avenue, New York, New York 10010 (800) 221-7945; *The Statesman's Year-Book.*

SAINT KITTS AND NEVIS - FISHERIES

Europa Publications Limited, 18 Bedford Square, London, WC1B 3JN, England; *The Europa World Year Book.*

Federal Statistical Office, Gustav-Stresemann - Ring 11, D-6200, Wiesbaden, Germany; *Saint Kitts and Nevis.*

Food and Agricultural Organization of the United Nations (FAO) Via delle Terme di Caracalla, 00100 Rome, Italy (Telephone Number in U.S. (202) 653-2400); *The State of Food and Agriculture; and Yearbook of Fishery Statistics.*

St. Martin's Press, Inc., 175 Fifth Avenue, New York, New York 10010 (800) 221-7945; *The Statesman's Year-Book.*

United Nations Conference on Trade and Development, Central Statistical Service, Palais des Nations, Geneva, Switzerland (Telephone in U.S. (800) 253-9646); *UNCTAD Commodity Yearbook.*

SAINT KITTS AND NEVIS - FOOD

Food and Agricultural Organization of the United Nations (FAO) Via delle Terme di Caracalla, 00100 Rome, Italy (Telephone Number in U.S. (202) 653-2400); *The State of Food and Agriculture.*

Statistical Office of the United Nations, Publishing Service, New York, New York 10017 (800) 253-9646; *Human Development Report.*

SAINT KITTS AND NEVIS - FOREIGN TRADE

Euromonitor International, Inc., 122 South Michigan Avenue, Suite 1200, Chicago, Illinois 60603 (800) 577-EURO; *The World Economic Factbook.*

Europa Publications Limited, 18 Bedford Square, London, WC1B 3JN, England; *The Europa World Year Book.*

Federal Statistical Office, Gustav-Stresemann - Ring 11, D-6200, Wiesbaden, Germany; *Saint Kitts and Nevis.*

Food and Agricultural Organization of the United Nations (FAO) Via delle Terme di Caracalla, 00100 Rome, Italy (Telephone Number in U.S. (202) 653-2400); *The State of Food and Agriculture.*

St. Martin's Press, Inc., 175 Fifth Avenue, New York, New York 10010 (800) 221-7945; *The Statesman's Year-Book.*

Statistical Office of the United Nations, Publishing Service, New York, New York 10017 (800) 253-9646; *Statistical Yearbook.*

United Nations Conference on Trade and Development, Central Statistical Service, Palais des Nations, Geneva, Switzerland (Telephone in U.S. (800) 253-9646); *UNCTAD Commodity Yearbook.*

The World Bank, 1818 H Street, NW, Washington, D.C. 20433 (202) 477-1234; *World Development Indicators.*

SAINT KITTS AND NEVIS - FORESTRY AND FOREST PRODUCTS

Federal Statistical Office, Gustav-Stresemann - Ring 11, D-6200, Wiesbaden, Germany; *Saint Kitts and Nevis.*

Food and Agricultural Organization of the United Nations (FAO) Via delle Terme di Caracalla, 00100 Rome, Italy (Telephone Number in U.S. (202) 653-2400); *The State of Food and Agriculture.*

Statistical Office of the United Nations, Publishing Service, New York, New York 10017 (800) 253-9646; *Statistical Yearbook.*

United Nations Conference on Trade and Development, Central Statistical Service, Palais des Nations, Geneva, Switzerland (Telephone in U.S. (800) 253-9646); *UNCTAD Commodity Yearbook.*

United Nations Educational, Scientific and Cultural Organization (UNESCO), 7 Place de Fontenoy, F-75700 Paris, France (Telephone Number in U.S. (212) 963-5981); *Statistical Yearbook.*

SAINT KITTS AND NEVIS - GENERAL MORTALITY - See SAINT KITTS AND NEVIS - MORTALITY

SAINT KITTS AND NEVIS - GOLD HOLDINGS

The World Bank, 1818 H Street, NW, Washington, D.C. 20433 (202) 477-1234; *World Development Indicators.*

SAINT KITTS AND NEVIS - GOVERNMENT

Central Intelligence Agency, Washington, D.C. 20505 (703) 482-1100, www.cia.gov; *The World Factbook.*

Europa Publications Limited, 18 Bedford Square, London, WC1B 3JN, England; *The Europa World Year Book.*

St. Martin's Press, Inc., 175 Fifth Avenue, New York, New York 10010 (800) 221-7945; *The Statesman's Year-Book.*

Statistical Office of the United Nations, Publishing Service, New York, New York 10017 (800) 253-9646; *National Accounts Statistics.*

The World Bank, 1818 H Street, NW, Washington, D.C. 20433 (202) 477-1234; *World Development Indicators.*

SAINT KITTS AND NEVIS - GRAIN PRODUCTION - See SAINT KITTS AND NEVIS - CROPS

SAINT KITTS AND NEVIS - GROSS DOMESTIC PRODUCT

Euromonitor International, Inc., 122 South Michigan Avenue, Suite 1200, Chicago, Illinois 60603 (800) 577-EURO; *The World Economic Factbook.*

Statistical Office of the United Nations, Publishing Service, New York, New York 10017 (800) 253-9646; *Human Development Report; National Accounts Statistics; and Statistical Yearbook.*

The World Bank, 1818 H Street, NW, Washington, D.C. 20433 (202) 477-1234; *The World Bank Atlas; and World Development Indicators.*

SAINT KITTS AND NEVIS - GROSS NATIONAL PRODUCT

The World Bank, 1818 H Street, NW, Washington, D.C. 20433 (202) 477-1234; *World Development Indicators.*

SAINT KITTS AND NEVIS - GROUNDNUT PRODUCTION - See SAINT KITTS AND NEVIS - CROPS

SAINT KITTS AND NEVIS - HEALTH

Euromonitor International, Inc., 122 South Michigan Avenue, Suite 1200, Chicago, Illinois 60603 (800) 577-EURO; *World Marketing Data and Statistics.*

Federal Statistical Office, Gustav-Stresemann - Ring 11, D-6200, Wiesbaden, Germany; *Saint Kitts and Nevis.*

St. Martin's Press, Inc., 175 Fifth Avenue, New York, New York 10010 (800) 221-7945; *The Statesman's Year-Book.*

Statistical Office of the United Nations, Publishing Service, New York, New York 10017 (800) 253-9646; *Human Development Report;* and *Statistical Yearbook.*

World Health Organization, Office of Publications, 20 Avenue Appia, CH-1211 Geneva 27, Switzerland (Telephone Number in U.S. (518) 436-9686); *World Health Statistics Annual.*

SAINT KITTS AND NEVIS - HIGHWAYS

Central Intelligence Agency, Washington, D.C. 20505 (703) 482-1100, www.cia.gov; *The World Factbook.*

St. Martin's Press, Inc., 175 Fifth Avenue, New York, New York 10010 (800) 221-7945; *The Statesman's Year-Book.*

SAINT KITTS AND NEVIS - HOURS OF WORK - See SAINT KITTS AND NEVIS - EMPLOYMENT

SAINT KITTS AND NEVIS - HOUSING AND HOUSING UNITS

Euromonitor International, Inc., 122 South Michigan Avenue, Suite 1200, Chicago, Illinois 60603 (800) 577-EURO; *World Marketing Data and Statistics.*

SAINT KITTS AND NEVIS - ILLITERATE POPULATION

Central Intelligence Agency, Washington, D.C. 20505 (703) 482-1100, www.cia.gov; *The World Factbook.*

Euromonitor International, Inc., 122 South Michigan Avenue, Suite 1200, Chicago, Illinois 60603 (800) 577-EURO; *The World Economic Factbook.*

Statistical Office of the United Nations, Publishing Service, New York, New York 10017 (800) 253-9646; *Human Development Report.*

United Nations Educational, Scientific and Cultural Organization (UNESCO), 7 Place de Fontenoy, F-75700 Paris, France (Telephone Number in U.S. (212) 963-5981); *Statistical Yearbook.*

SAINT KITTS AND NEVIS - IMPORTS

Central Intelligence Agency, Washington, D.C. 20505 (703) 482-1100, www.cia.gov; *The World Factbook.*

Euromonitor International, Inc., 122 South Michigan Avenue, Suite 1200, Chicago, Illinois 60603 (800) 577-EURO; *The World Economic Factbook.*

Europa Publications Limited, 18 Bedford Square, London, WC1B 3JN, England; *The Europa World Year Book.*

Food and Agricultural Organization of the United Nations (FAO) Via delle Terme di Caracalla, 00100 Rome, Italy (Telephone Number in U.S. (202) 653-2400); *The State of Food and Agriculture.*

International Monetary Fund, 700 Nineteenth Street, NW, Washington, D.C. 20431 (202) 623-7000; *Direction of Trade Statistics.*

St. Martin's Press, Inc., 175 Fifth Avenue, New York, New York 10010 (800) 221-7945; *The Statesman's Year-Book.*

United Nations Conference on Trade and Development (UNCTAD), New York, New York 10017 (800) 253-9646; *Handbook of International Trade and Development Statistics.*

The World Bank, 1818 H Street, NW, Washington, D.C. 20433 (202) 477-1234; *World Development Indicators.*

SAINT KITTS AND NEVIS - INDUSTRY

Central Intelligence Agency, Washington, D.C. 20505 (703) 482-1100, www.cia.gov; *The World Factbook.*

Euromonitor International, Inc., 122 South Michigan Avenue, Suite 1200, Chicago, Illinois 60603 (800) 577-EURO; *The World Economic Factbook;* and *World Marketing Data and Statistics.*

Europa Publications Limited, 18 Bedford Square, London, WC1B 3JN, England; *The Europa World Year Book.*

Federal Statistical Office, Gustav-Stresemann - Ring 11, D-6200, Wiesbaden, Germany; *Saint Kitts and Nevis.*

International Labour Office, I.L.O. Publications, 1828 L Street, NW, Suite 801, Washington, D.C. 20036 (301) 638-3152; *Yearbook of Labour Statistics.*

St. Martin's Press, Inc., 175 Fifth Avenue, New York, New York 10010 (800) 221-7945; *The Statesman's Year-Book.*

The World Bank, 1818 H Street, NW, Washington, D.C. 20433 (202) 477-1234; *World Development Indicators.*

SAINT KITTS AND NEVIS - INFANT AND MATERNAL MORTALITY - See SAINT KITTS AND NEVIS - MORTALITY

SAINT KITTS AND NEVIS - INTERNATIONAL RESERVES EXCLUDING GOLD

The World Bank, 1818 H Street, NW, Washington, D.C. 20433 (202) 477-1234; *World Development Indicators.*

SAINT KITTS AND NEVIS - LABOR

Central Intelligence Agency, Washington, D.C. 20505 (703) 482-1100, www.cia.gov; *The World Factbook.*

Euromonitor International, Inc., 122 South Michigan Avenue, Suite 1200, Chicago, Illinois 60603 (800) 577-EURO; *World Marketing Data and Statistics.*

Europa Publications Limited, 18 Bedford Square, London, WC1B 3JN, England; *The Europa World Year Book.*

Food and Agricultural Organization of the United Nations (FAO) Via delle Terme di Caracalla, 00100 Rome, Italy (Telephone Number in U.S. (202) 653-2400); *The State of Food and Agriculture.*

International Labour Office, I.L.O. Publications, 1828 L Street, NW, Suite 801, Washington, D.C. 20036 (301) 638-3152; *Yearbook of Labour Statistics.*

St. Martin's Press, Inc., 175 Fifth Avenue, New York, New York 10010 (800) 221-7945; *The Statesman's Year-Book.*

Statistical Office of the United Nations, Publishing Service, New York, New York 10017 (800) 253-9646; *Human Development Report.*

The World Bank, 1818 H Street, NW, Washington, D.C. 20433 (202) 477-1234; *The World Bank Atlas;* and *World Development Indicators.*

SAINT KITTS AND NEVIS - LAND USE

Central Intelligence Agency, Washington, D.C. 20505 (703) 482-1100, www.cia.gov; *The World Factbook.*

Food and Agricultural Organization of the United Nations (FAO), Via delle Terme di Caracalla, 00100 Rome, Italy (Telephone Number in U.S. (202) 653-2400); *Production Yearbook.*

SAINT KITTS AND NEVIS - LIFE EXPECTANCY

Central Intelligence Agency, Washington, D.C. 20505 (703) 482-1100, www.cia.gov; *The World Factbook.*

Euromonitor International, Inc., 122 South Michigan Avenue, Suite 1200, Chicago, Illinois 60603 (800) 577-EURO; *The World Economic Factbook.*

Statistical Office of the United Nations, Publishing Service, New York, New York 10017 (800) 253-9646; *Human Development Report;* and *World Statistics Pocketbook.*

The World Bank, 1818 H Street, NW, Washington, D.C. 20433 (202) 477-1234; *The World Bank Atlas.*

SAINT KITTS AND NEVIS - LITERACY RATE

Euromonitor International, Inc., 122 South Michigan Avenue, Suite 1200, Chicago, Illinois 60603 (800) 577-EURO; *World Marketing Data and Statistics.*

SAINT KITTS AND NEVIS - LIVESTOCK AND POULTRY

Europa Publications Limited, 18 Bedford Square, London, WC1B 3JN, England; *The Europa World Year Book.*

Food and Agricultural Organization of the United Nations (FAO), Via delle Terme di Caracalla, 00100 Rome, Italy (Telephone Number in U.S. (202) 653-2400); *Production Yearbook;* and *The State of Food and Agriculture.*

St. Martin's Press, Inc., 175 Fifth Avenue, New York, New York 10010 (800) 221-7945; *The Statesman's Year-Book.*

Statistical Office of the United Nations, Publishing Service, New York, New York 10017 (800) 253-9646; *Statistical Yearbook.*

United Nations Conference on Trade and Development, Central Statistical Service, Palais des Nations, Geneva, Switzerland (Telephone in U.S. (800) 253-9646); *UNCTAD Commodity Yearbook.*

SAINT KITTS AND NEVIS - MAIL - NUMBER OF ITEMS SENT AND RECEIVED

Statistical Office of the United Nations, Publishing Service, New York, New York 10017 (800) 253-9646; *Statistical Yearbook.*

SAINT KITTS AND NEVIS - MANUFACTURING

The World Bank, 1818 H Street, NW, Washington, D.C. 20433 (202) 477-1234; *World Development Indicators.*

SAINT KITTS AND NEVIS - MARRIAGE RATES

Statistical Office of the United Nations, Publishing Service, New York, New York 10017 (800) 253-9646; *Demographic Yearbook;* and *Statistical Yearbook.*

SAINT KITTS AND NEVIS - MEAT PRODUCTION - See SAINT KITTS AND NEVIS - LIVESTOCK AND POULTRY

SAINT KITTS AND NEVIS - MERCHANT SHIPPING

Europa Publications Limited, 18 Bedford Square, London, WC1B 3JN, England; *The Europa World Year Book.*

St. Martin's Press, Inc., 175 Fifth Avenue, New York, New York 10010 (800) 221-7945; *The Statesman's Year-Book.*

Statistical Office of the United Nations, Publishing Service, New York, New York 10017 (800) 253-9646; *Statistical Yearbook.*

SAINT KITTS AND NEVIS - MILITARY

Central Intelligence Agency, Washington, D.C. 20505 (703) 482-1100, www.cia.gov; *The World Factbook.*

Euromonitor International, Inc., 122 South Michigan Avenue, Suite 1200, Chicago, Illinois 60603 (800) 577-EURO; *World Marketing Data and Statistics.*

Statistical Office of the United Nations, Publishing Service, New York, New York 10017 (800) 253-9646; *Human Development Report.*

SAINT KITTS AND NEVIS - MINING AND MINERAL PRODUCTS

United Nations Conference on Trade and Development, Central Statistical Service, Palais des Nations, Geneva, Switzerland (Telephone in U.S. (800) 253-9646); *UNCTAD Commodity Yearbook.*

SAINT KITTS AND NEVIS - MONEY SUPPLY

Europa Publications Limited, 18 Bedford Square, London, WC1B 3JN, England; *The Europa World Year Book.*

Federal Statistical Office, Gustav-Stresemann - Ring 11, D-6200, Wiesbaden, Germany; *Saint Kitts and Nevis.*

The World Bank, 1818 H Street, NW, Washington, D.C. 20433 (202) 477-1234; *World Development Indicators.*

SAINT KITTS AND NEVIS - MORTALITY

Central Intelligence Agency, Washington, D.C. 20505 (703) 482-1100, www.cia.gov; *The World Factbook.*

Euromonitor International, Inc., 122 South Michigan Avenue, Suite 1200, Chicago, Illinois 60603 (800) 577-EURO; *The World Economic Factbook.*

St. Martin's Press, Inc., 175 Fifth Avenue, New York, New York 10010 (800) 221-7945; *The Statesman's Year-Book.*

Statistical Office of the United Nations, Publishing Service, New York, New York

10017 (800) 253-9646; *Demographic Yearbook; Human Development Report; Statistical Yearbook;* and *World Statistics Pocketbook.*

The World Bank, 1818 H Street, NW, Washington, D.C. 20433 (202) 477-1234; *The World Bank Atlas;* and *World Development Indicators.*

World Health Organization, Office of Publications, 20 Avenue Appia, CH-1211 Geneva 27, Switzerland (Telephone Number in U.S. (518) 436-9686); *World Health Statistics Annual.*

SAINT KITTS AND NEVIS - MOTOR VEHICLES IN USE

Europa Publications Limited, 18 Bedford Square, London, WC1B 3JN, England; *The Europa World Year Book.*

Statistical Office of the United Nations, Publishing Service, New York, New York 10017 (800) 253-9646; *Statistical Yearbook.*

SAINT KITTS AND NEVIS - NATALITY - See SAINT KITTS AND NEVIS - BIRTH RATE

SAINT KITTS AND NEVIS - NATIONAL ACCOUNTS

Europa Publications Limited, 18 Bedford Square, London, WC1B 3JN, England; *The Europa World Year Book.*

Federal Statistical Office, Gustav-Stresemann - Ring 11, D-6200, Wiesbaden, Germany; *Saint Kitts and Nevis.*

Statistical Office of the United Nations, Publishing Service, New York, New York 10017 (800) 253-9646; *Statistical Yearbook.*

SAINT KITTS AND NEVIS - NATIONAL INCOME

Statistical Office of the United Nations, Publishing Service, New York, New York 10017 (800) 253-9646; *National Accounts Statistics;* and *Statistical Yearbook.*

SAINT KITTS AND NEVIS - NEWSPAPER PRODUCTION - See SAINT KITTS AND NEVIS - FORESTRY AND FOREST PRODUCTS

SAINT KITTS AND NEVIS - OCCUPATIONS - See SAINT KITTS AND NEVIS - LABOR

SAINT KITTS AND NEVIS - PESTICIDE USE

Food and Agricultural Organization of the United Nations (FAO) Via delle Terme di Caracalla, 00100 Rome, Italy (Telephone Number in U.S. (202) 653-2400); *The State of Food and Agriculture.*

SAINT KITTS AND NEVIS - PETROLEUM INDUSTRY

Food and Agricultural Organization of the United Nations (FAO) Via delle Terme di Caracalla, 00100 Rome, Italy (Telephone Number in U.S. (202) 653-2400); *The State of Food and Agriculture.*

United Nations Conference on Trade and Development, Central Statistical Service, Palais des Nations, Geneva, Switzerland (Telephone in U.S. (800) 253-9646); *UNCTAD Commodity Yearbook.*

SAINT KITTS AND NEVIS - PIGS - See SAINT KITTS AND NEVIS - LIVESTOCK AND POULTRY

SAINT KITTS AND NEVIS - POPULATION

Central Intelligence Agency, Washington, D.C. 20505 (703) 482-1100, www.cia.gov; *The World Factbook.*

Euromonitor International, Inc., 122 South Michigan Avenue, Suite 1200, Chicago, Illinois 60603 (800) 577-EURO; *The World Economic Factbook.*

Europa Publications Limited, 18 Bedford Square, London, WC1B 3JN, England; *The Europa World Year Book.*

Federal Statistical Office, Gustav-Stresemann - Ring 11, D-6200, Wiesbaden, Germany; *Saint Kitts and Nevis.*

Food and Agricultural Organization of the United Nations (FAO), Via delle Terme di Caracalla, 00100 Rome, Italy (Telephone Number in U.S. (202) 653-2400); *Production Yearbook.*

International Labour Office, I.L.O. Publications, 1828 L Street, NW, Suite 801, Washington, D.C. 20036 (301) 638-3152; *Yearbook of Labour Statistics.*

St. Martin's Press, Inc., 175 Fifth Avenue, New York, New York 10010 (800) 221-7945; *The Statesman's Year-Book.*

Statistical Office of the United Nations, Publishing Service, New York, New York 10017 (800) 253-9646; *Demographic Yearbook; Human Development Report; Statistical Yearbook;* and *World Statistics Pocketbook.*

United Nations Educational, Scientific and Cultural Organization (UNESCO), 7 Place de Fontenoy, F-75700 Paris, France (Telephone Number in U.S. (212) 963-5981); *Statistical Yearbook.*

The World Bank, 1818 H Street, NW, Washington, D.C. 20433 (202) 477-1234; *The World Bank Atlas.*

World Health Organization, Office of Publications, 20 Avenue Appia, CH-1211 Geneva 27, Switzerland (Telephone Number in U.S. (518) 436-9686); *World*

Health Statistics Annual.

SAINT KITTS AND NEVIS - POST OFFICES

St. Martin's Press, Inc., 175 Fifth Avenue, New York, New York 10010 (800) 221-7945; *The Statesman's Year-Book.*

SAINT KITTS AND NEVIS - PRICES

Federal Statistical Office, Gustav-Stresemann - Ring 11, D-6200, Wiesbaden, Germany; *Saint Kitts and Nevis.*

Food and Agricultural Organization of the United Nations (FAO), Via delle Terme di Caracalla, 00100 Rome, Italy (Telephone Number in U.S. (202) 653-2400); *Production Yearbook;* and *The State of Food and Agriculture.*

International Labour Office, I.L.O. Publications, 1828 L Street, NW, Suite 801, Washington, D.C. 20036 (301) 638-3152; *Yearbook of Labour Statistics.*

SAINT KITTS AND NEVIS - RADIO RECEIVERS

St. Martin's Press, Inc., 175 Fifth Avenue, New York, New York 10010 (800) 221-7945; *The Statesman's Year-Book.*

SAINT KITTS AND NEVIS - RAILWAYS

St. Martin's Press, Inc., 175 Fifth Avenue, New York, New York 10010 (800) 221-7945; *The Statesman's Year-Book.*

SAINT KITTS AND NEVIS - RELIGION

Central Intelligence Agency, Washington, D.C. 20505 (703) 482-1100, www.cia.gov; *The World Factbook.*

St. Martin's Press, Inc., 175 Fifth Avenue, New York, New York 10010 (800) 221-7945; *The Statesman's Year-Book.*

SAINT KITTS AND NEVIS - RETAIL TRADE

Euromonitor International, Inc., 122 South Michigan Avenue, Suite 1200, Chicago, Illinois 60603 (800) 577-EURO; *World Marketing Data and Statistics.*

SAINT KITTS AND NEVIS - SHEEP - See SAINT KITTS AND NEVIS - LIVESTOCK AND POULTRY

SAINT KITTS AND NEVIS - SOCIAL DATA

Statistical Office of the United Nations, Publishing Service, New York, New York 10017 (800) 253-9646; *World Statistics Pocketbook.*

SAINT KITTS AND NEVIS - SOCIAL SECURITY

Statistical Office of the United Nations,

Publishing Service, New York, New York 10017 (800) 253-9646; *National Accounts Statistics.*

SAINT KITTS AND NEVIS - STOCKS - COMMODITY - MARKET PRICE - INDEX

Food and Agricultural Organization of the United Nations (FAO) Via delle Terme di Caracalla, 00100 Rome, Italy (Telephone Number in U.S. (202) 653-2400); *The State of Food and Agriculture.*

SAINT KITTS AND NEVIS - SUGAR - See SAINT KITTS AND NEVIS - CROPS

SAINT KITTS AND NEVIS - TAXATION

Europa Publications Limited, 18 Bedford Square, London, WC1B 3JN, England; *The Europa World Year Book.*

The World Bank, 1818 H Street, NW, Washington, D.C. 20433 (202) 477-1234; *World Development Indicators.*

SAINT KITTS AND NEVIS - TELEPHONES IN USE

American Telephone and Telegraph Company, 26 Parsippany Road, Whippany, New Jersey 07981 (800) 222-0300; *The World's Telephones.*

Central Intelligence Agency, Washington, D.C. 20505 (703) 482-1100, www.cia.gov; *The World Factbook.*

Europa Publications Limited, 18 Bedford Square, London, WC1B 3JN, England; *The Europa World Year Book.*

St. Martin's Press, Inc., 175 Fifth Avenue, New York, New York 10010 (800) 221-7945; *The Statesman's Year-Book.*

Statistical Office of the United Nations, Publishing Service, New York, New York 10017 (800) 253-9646; *Statistical Yearbook;* and *World Statistics Pocketbook.*

SAINT KITTS AND NEVIS - TEXTILE INDUSTRY

United Nations Conference on Trade and Development, Central Statistical Service, Palais des Nations, Geneva, Switzerland (Telephone in U.S. (800) 253-9646); *UNCTAD Commodity Yearbook.*

SAINT KITTS AND NEVIS - TOURISM

Euromonitor International, Inc., 122 South Michigan Avenue, Suite 1200, Chicago, Illinois 60603 (800) 577-EURO; *The World Economic Factbook;* and *World Marketing Data and Statistics.*

Europa Publications Limited, 18 Bedford Square, London, WC1B 3JN, England; *The Europa World Year Book.*

Federal Statistical Office, Gustav-Stresemann - Ring 11, D-6200, Wiesbaden, Germany; *Saint Kitts and Nevis*.

St. Martin's Press, Inc., 175 Fifth Avenue, New York, New York 10010 (800) 221-7945; *The Statesman's Year-Book*.

World Tourism Organization, Calle Capitan Haya 42, E-28020 Madrid, Spain; *Yearbook of Tourism Statistics*.

SAINT KITTS AND NEVIS - TRACTORS IN USE

Statistical Office of the United Nations, Publishing Service, New York, New York 10017 (800) 253-9646; *Statistical Yearbook*.

SAINT KITTS AND NEVIS - TRADE - See SAINT KITTS AND NEVIS - FOREIGN TRADE

SAINT KITTS AND NEVIS - TRANSPORTATION AND COMMUNICATIONS

Central Intelligence Agency, Washington, D.C. 20505 (703) 482-1100, www.cia.gov; *The World Factbook*.

Euromonitor International, Inc., 122 South Michigan Avenue, Suite 1200, Chicago, Illinois 60603 (800) 577-EURO; *World Marketing Data and Statistics*.
Europa Publications Limited, 18 Bedford Square, London, WC1B 3JN, England; *The Europa World Year Book*.

Federal Statistical Office, Gustav-Stresemann - Ring 11, D-6200, Wiesbaden, Germany; *Saint Kitts and Nevis*.

St. Martin's Press, Inc., 175 Fifth Avenue, New York, New York 10010 (800) 221-7945; *The Statesman's Year-Book*.

Statistical Office of the United Nations, Publishing Service, New York, New York 10017 (800) 253-9646; *Human Development Report*.

SAINT KITTS AND NEVIS - UNEMPLOYMENT

Central Intelligence Agency, Washington, D.C. 20505 (703) 482-1100, www.cia.gov; *The World Factbook*.

International Labour Office, I.L.O. Publications, 1828 L Street, NW, Suite 801, Washington, D.C. 20036 (301) 638-3152; *Yearbook of Labour Statistics*.

SAINT KITTS AND NEVIS - VITAL STATISTICS

St. Martin's Press, Inc., 175 Fifth Avenue, New York, New York 10010 (800) 221-7945; *The Statesman's Year-Book*.

Statistical Office of the United Nations,

Publishing Service, New York, New York 10017 (800) 253-9646; *Statistical Yearbook*.

World Health Organization, Office of Publications, 20 Avenue Appia, CH-1211 Geneva 27, Switzerland (Telephone Number in U.S. (518) 436-9686); *World Health Statistics Annual*.

SAINT KITTS AND NEVIS - WAGES

Federal Statistical Office, Gustav-Stresemann - Ring 11, D-6200, Wiesbaden, Germany; *Saint Kitts and Nevis*.

International Labour Office, I.L.O. Publications, 1828 L Street, NW, Suite 801, Washington, D.C. 20036 (301) 638-3152; *Yearbook of Labour Statistics*.

SAINT KITTS AND NEVIS - WEATHER - See SAINT KITTS AND NEVIS - CLIMATE

Saint Lucia - National Statistical Office

Statistical Department, Ministry of Trade, Industry, and Tourism, Post Office Building, Castries, Saint Lucia.

Saint Lucia - Primary Statistics Source

Development, Planning and Statistics Division, Premier's Office, Post Office Building, Castries, Saint Lucia; *Annual Statistical Digest*.

SAINT LUCIA - AGRICULTURE

Euromonitor International, Inc., 122 South Michigan Avenue, Suite 1200, Chicago, Illinois 60603 (800) 577-EURO; *World Marketing Data and Statistics*.

Europa Publications Limited, 18 Bedford Square, London, WC1B 3JN, England; *The Europa World Year Book*.

Federal Statistical Office, Gustav-Stresemann - Ring 11, D-6200, Wiesbaden, Germany; *Saint Lucia*.

Food and Agricultural Organization of the United Nations (FAO) Via delle Terme di Caracalla, 00100 Rome, Italy (Telephone Number in U.S. (202) 653-2400); *Production Yearbook; The State of Food and Agriculture;* and *Trade Yearbook*.

St. Martin's Press, Inc., 175 Fifth Avenue, New York, New York 10010 (800) 221-7945; *The Statesman's Year-Book*.

Statistical Office of the United Nations, Publishing Service, New York, New York 10017 (800) 253-9646; *Statistical Yearbook*.

United Nations Conference on Trade

and Development, Central Statistical Service, Palais des Nations, Geneva, Switzerland (Telephone in U.S. (800) 253-9646); *UNCTAD Commodity Yearbook*.

The World Bank, 1818 H Street, NW, Washington, D.C. 20433 (202) 477-1234; *World Development Indicators*.

SAINT LUCIA - AIRLINE SERVICE

Europa Publications Limited, 18 Bedford Square, London, WC1B 3JN, England; *The Europa World Year Book*.

St. Martin's Press, Inc., 175 Fifth Avenue, New York, New York 10010 (800) 221-7945; *The Statesman's Year-Book*.

SAINT LUCIA - AIRPORTS

Central Intelligence Agency, Washington, D.C. 20505 (703) 482-1100, www.cia.gov; *The World Factbook*.

SAINT LUCIA - ANIMAL HEALTH

Food and Agricultural Organization of the United Nations (FAO), Via delle Terme di Caracalla, 00100, Rome, Italy (Telephone Number in U.S. (202) 653-2400); *Animal Health Yearbook*.

SAINT LUCIA - AREA AND DENSITY OF POPULATION

Central Intelligence Agency, Washington, D.C. 20505 (703) 482-1100, www.cia.gov; *The World Factbook*.

Euromonitor International, Inc., 122 South Michigan Avenue, Suite 1200, Chicago, Illinois 60603 (800) 577-EURO; *The World Economic Factbook*.

Europa Publications Limited, 18 Bedford Square, London, WC1B 3JN, England; *The Europa World Year Book*.

Federal Statistical Office, Gustav-Stresemann - Ring 11, D-6200, Wiesbaden, Germany; *Saint Lucia*.

Food and Agricultural Organization of the United Nations (FAO) Via delle Terme di Caracalla, 00100 Rome, Italy (Telephone Number in U.S. (202) 653-2400); *The State of Food and Agriculture*.

St. Martin's Press, Inc., 175 Fifth Avenue, New York, New York 10010 (800) 221-7945; *The Statesman's Year-Book*.

Statistical Office of the United Nations, Publishing Service, New York, New York 10017 (800) 253-9646; *Statistical Yearbook*.

United Nations Educational, Scientific and Cultural Organization (UNESCO), 7 Place de Fontenoy, F-75700 Paris, France (Telephone Number in U.S. (212) 963-

5981); *Statistical Yearbook.*

SAINT LUCIA - BALANCE OF PAYMENTS

Europa Publications Limited, 18 Bedford Square, London, WC1B 3JN, England; *The Europa World Year Book.*

Federal Statistical Office, Gustav-Stresemann - Ring 11, D-6200, Wiesbaden, Germany; *Saint Lucia.*

United Nations Conference on Trade and Development (UNCTAD), New York, New York 10017 (800) 253-9646; *Handbook of International Trade and Development Statistics.*

The World Bank, 1818 H Street, NW, Washington, D.C. 20433 (202) 477-1234; *World Development Indicators.*

SAINT LUCIA - BANKING

Euromonitor International, Inc., 122 South Michigan Avenue, Suite 1200, Chicago, Illinois 60603 (800) 577-EURO; *World Marketing Data and Statistics.*

Europa Publications Limited, 18 Bedford Square, London, WC1B 3JN, England; *The Europa World Year Book.*

St. Martin's Press, Inc., 175 Fifth Avenue, New York, New York 10010 (800) 221-7945; *The Statesman's Year-Book.*

SAINT LUCIA - BIRTH RATES

Central Intelligence Agency, Washington, D.C. 20505 (703) 482-1100, www.cia.gov; *The World Factbook.*

Euromonitor International, Inc., 122 South Michigan Avenue, Suite 1200, Chicago, Illinois 60603 (800) 577-EURO; *The World Economic Factbook.*

Europa Publications Limited, 18 Bedford Square, London, WC1B 3JN, England; *The Europa World Year Book.*

Statistical Office of the United Nations, Publishing Service, New York, New York 10017 (800) 253-9646; *Demographic Yearbook;* and *Statistical Yearbook.*

The World Bank, 1818 H Street, NW, Washington, D.C. 20433 (202) 477-1234; *World Development Indicators.*

World Health Organization, Office of Publications, 20 Avenue Appia, CH-1211 Geneva 27, Switzerland (Telephone Number in U.S. (518) 436-9686); *World Health Statistics Annual.*

SAINT LUCIA - BROADCASTING

Billboard Limited, P.O. Box 9027, 1006 AA Amsterdam, The Netherlands

(Telephone Number in U.S. (212) 764-7300); *World Radio TV Handbook.*

Central Intelligence Agency, Washington, D.C. 20505 (703) 482-1100, www.cia.gov; *The World Factbook.*

Euromonitor International, Inc., 122 South Michigan Avenue, Suite 1200, Chicago, Illinois 60603 (800) 577-EURO; *World Marketing Data and Statistics.*

St. Martin's Press, Inc., 175 Fifth Avenue, New York, New York 10010 (800) 221-7945; *The Statesman's Year-Book.*

SAINT LUCIA - BUDGET

Central Intelligence Agency, Washington, D.C. 20505 (703) 482-1100, www.cia.gov; *The World Factbook.*

SAINT LUCIA - CALORIE SUPPLY

Food and Agricultural Organization of the United Nations (FAO) Via delle Terme di Caracalla, 00100 Rome, Italy (Telephone Number in U.S. (202) 653-2400); *The State of Food and Agriculture.*

SAINT LUCIA - CATTLE - See SAINT LUCIA - LIVESTOCK AND POULTRY

SAINT LUCIA - CLIMATE

St. Martin's Press, Inc., 175 Fifth Avenue, New York, New York 10010 (800) 221-7945; *The Statesman's Year-Book.*

SAINT LUCIA - COCOA PRODUCTION - See SAINT LUCIA - CROPS

SAINT LUCIA - COMMERCE

St. Martin's Press, Inc., 175 Fifth Avenue, New York, New York 10010 (800) 221-7945; *The Statesman's Year-Book.*

SAINT LUCIA - COMMUNICATIONS - See SAINT LUCIA - TRANSPORTATION AND COMMUNICATIONS

SAINT LUCIA - CONSUMER PRICE INDEX

Europa Publications Limited, 18 Bedford Square, London, WC1B 3JN, England; *The Europa World Year Book.*

Statistical Office of the United Nations, Publishing Service, New York, New York 10017 (800) 253-9646; *Statistical Yearbook.*

SAINT LUCIA - CONSUMER PRICES

Euromonitor International, Inc., 122 South Michigan Avenue, Suite 1200, Chicago, Illinois 60603 (800) 577-EURO; *World Marketing Data and Statistics.*

International Labour Office, I.L.O. Publications, 1828 L Street, NW, Suite

801, Washington, D.C. 20036 (301) 638-3152; *Yearbook of Labour Statistics.*

SAINT LUCIA - CORN PRODUCTION - See SAINT LUCIA - CROPS

SAINT LUCIA - CORPORATE TAXES - See SAINT LUCIA - TAXATION

SAINT LUCIA - CROPS

Europa Publications Limited, 18 Bedford Square, London, WC1B 3JN, England; *The Europa World Year Book.*

Food and Agricultural Organization of the United Nations (FAO) Via delle Terme di Caracalla, 00100 Rome, Italy (Telephone Number in U.S. (202) 653-2400); *The State of Food and Agriculture.*

St. Martin's Press, Inc., 175 Fifth Avenue, New York, New York 10010 (800) 221-7945; *The Statesman's Year-Book.*

Statistical Office of the United Nations, Publishing Service, New York, New York 10017 (800) 253-9646; *Statistical Yearbook.*

United Nations Conference on Trade and Development, Central Statistical Service, Palais des Nations, Geneva, Switzerland (Telephone in U.S. (800) 253-9646); *UNCTAD Commodity Yearbook.*

SAINT LUCIA - DAIRY PRODUCTS

Europa Publications Limited, 18 Bedford Square, London, WC1B 3JN, England; *The Europa World Year Book.*

Food and Agricultural Organization of the United Nations (FAO) Via delle Terme di Caracalla, 00100 Rome, Italy (Telephone Number in U.S. (202) 653-2400); *The State of Food and Agriculture.*

SAINT LUCIA - DEATH RATES - See SAINT LUCIA - MORTALITY

SAINT LUCIA - DEMOGRAPHY

Euromonitor International, Inc., 122 South Michigan Avenue, Suite 1200, Chicago, Illinois 60603 (800) 577-EURO; *The World Economic Factbook;* and *World Marketing Data and Statistics.*

Federal Statistical Office, Gustav-Stresemann - Ring 11, D-6200, Wiesbaden, Germany; *Saint Lucia.*

Statistical Office of the United Nations, Publishing Service, New York, New York 10017 (800) 253-9646; *Human Development Report.*

SAINT LUCIA - DISEASES - See SAINT LUCIA - HEALTH

SAINT LUCIA - DIVORCE RATES

Statistical Office of the United Nations, Publishing Service, New York, New York 10017 (800) 253-9646; *Demographic Yearbook.*

SAINT LUCIA - ECONOMY

Central Intelligence Agency, Washington, D.C. 20505 (703) 482-1100, www.cia.gov; *The World Factbook.*

Euromonitor International, Inc., 122 South Michigan Avenue, Suite 1200, Chicago, Illinois 60603 (800) 577-EURO; *The World Economic Factbook;* and *World Marketing Data and Statistics.*

Europa Publications Limited, 18 Bedford Square, London, WC1B 3JN, England; *The Europa World Year Book.*

Federal Statistical Office, Gustav-Stresemann - Ring 11, D-6200, Wiesbaden, Germany; *Saint Lucia.*

St. Martin's Press, Inc., 175 Fifth Avenue, New York, New York 10010 (800) 221-7945; *The Statesman's Year-Book.*

Statistical Office of the United Nations, Publishing Service, New York, New York 10017 (800) 253-9646; *World Statistics Pocketbook.*

The World Bank, 1818 H Street, NW, Washington, D.C. 20433 (202) 477-1234; *The World Bank Atlas.*

SAINT LUCIA - EDUCATION

Euromonitor International, Inc., 122 South Michigan Avenue, Suite 1200, Chicago, Illinois 60603 (800) 577-EURO; *World Marketing Data and Statistics.*

Europa Publications Limited, 18 Bedford Square, London, WC1B 3JN, England; *The Europa World Year Book.*

Federal Statistical Office, Gustav-Stresemann - Ring 11, D-6200, Wiesbaden, Germany; *Saint Lucia.*

St. Martin's Press, Inc., 175 Fifth Avenue, New York, New York 10010 (800) 221-7945; *The Statesman's Year-Book.*

Statistical Office of the United Nations, Publishing Service, New York, New York 10017 (800) 253-9646; *Human Development Report.*

United Nations Educational, Scientific and Cultural Organization (UNESCO), 7 Place de Fontenoy, F-75700 Paris, France (Telephone Number in U.S. (212) 963-5981); *Statistical Yearbook.*

The World Bank, 1818 H Street, NW, Washington, D.C. 20433 (202) 477-1234; *World Development Indicators.*

SAINT LUCIA - EGG PRODUCTION - See SAINT LUCIA - DAIRY PRODUCTS

SAINT LUCIA - ELECTRICITY

Central Intelligence Agency, Washington, D.C. 20505 (703) 482-1100, www.cia.gov; *The World Factbook.*

Statistical Office of the United Nations, Publishing Service, New York, New York 10017 (800) 253-9646; *Human Development Report;* and *Statistical Yearbook.*

SAINT LUCIA - EMPLOYMENT

Federal Statistical Office, Gustav-Stresemann - Ring 11, D-6200, Wiesbaden, Germany; *Saint Lucia.*

International Labour Office, I.L.O. Publications, 1828 L Street, NW, Suite 801, Washington, D.C. 20036 (301) 638-3152; *Yearbook of Labour Statistics.*

SAINT LUCIA - ENERGY

Euromonitor International, Inc., 122 South Michigan Avenue, Suite 1200, Chicago, Illinois 60603 (800) 577-EURO; *The World Economic Factbook;* and *World Marketing Data and Statistics.*

Food and Agricultural Organization of the United Nations (FAO) Via delle Terme di Caracalla, 00100 Rome, Italy (Telephone Number in U.S. (202) 653-2400); *The State of Food and Agriculture.*

Statistical Office of the United Nations, Publishing Service, New York, New York 10017 (800) 253-9646; *Energy Statistics Yearbook; Human Development Report; Statistical Yearbook;* and *World Statistics Pocketbook*

The World Bank, 1818 H Street, NW, Washington, D.C. 20433 (202) 477-1234; *The World Bank Atlas.*

SAINT LUCIA - ENVIRONMENT

Statistical Office of the United Nations, Publishing Service, New York, New York 10017 (800) 253-9646; *World Statistics Pocketbook.*

SAINT LUCIA - EXCHANGE RATES

Central Intelligence Agency, Washington, D.C. 20505 (703) 482-1100, www.cia.gov; *The World Factbook.*

Euromonitor International, Inc., 122 South Michigan Avenue, Suite 1200, Chicago, Illinois 60603 (800) 577-EURO; *The World Economic Factbook.*

Europa Publications Limited, 18 Bedford Square, London, WC1B 3JN,

England; *The Europa World Year Book.*

Statistical Office of the United Nations, Publishing Service, New York, New York 10017 (800) 253-9646; *World Statistics Pocketbook.*

SAINT LUCIA - EXPORTS

Central Intelligence Agency, Washington, D.C. 20505 (703) 482-1100, www.cia.gov; *The World Factbook.*

Euromonitor International, Inc., 122 South Michigan Avenue, Suite 1200, Chicago, Illinois 60603 (800) 577-EURO; *The World Economic Factbook.*

Europa Publications Limited, 18 Bedford Square, London, WC1B 3JN, England; *The Europa World Year Book.*

Food and Agricultural Organization of the United Nations (FAO) Via delle Terme di Caracalla, 00100 Rome, Italy (Telephone Number in U.S. (202) 653-2400); *The State of Food and Agriculture.*

St. Martin's Press, Inc., 175 Fifth Avenue, New York, New York 10010 (800) 221-7945; *The Statesman's Year-Book.*

United Nations Conference on Trade and Development (UNCTAD), New York, New York 10017 (800) 253-9646; *Handbook of International Trade and Development Statistics.*

The World Bank, 1818 H Street, NW, Washington, D.C. 20433 (202) 477-1234; *World Development Indicators.*

SAINT LUCIA - EXTERNAL INDEBTEDNESS

The World Bank, 1818 H Street, NW, Washington, D.C. 20433 (202) 477-1234; *World Development Indicators.*

SAINT LUCIA - EXTERNAL TRADE

Euromonitor International, Inc., 122 South Michigan Avenue, Suite 1200, Chicago, Illinois 60603 (800) 577-EURO; *World Marketing Data and Statistics.*

Food and Agricultural Organization of the United Nations (FAO) Via delle Terme di Caracalla, 00100 Rome, Italy (Telephone Number in U.S. (202) 653-2400); *The State of Food and Agriculture;* and *Trade Yearbook.*

Statistical Office of the United Nations, Publishing Service, New York, New York 10017 (800) 253-9646; *Statistical Yearbook.*

SAINT LUCIA - FARM CROPS - See SAINT LUCIA - CROPS

SAINT LUCIA - FERTILITY RATES

Central Intelligence Agency, Washington, D.C. 20505 (703) 482-1100, www.cia.gov; *The World Factbook.*

Statistical Office of the United Nations, Publishing Service, New York, New York 10017 (800) 253-9646; *Human Development Report.*

The World Bank, 1818 H Street, NW, Washington, D.C. 20433 (202) 477-1234; *The World Bank Atlas;* and *World Development Indicators.*

SAINT LUCIA - FERTILIZER

Food and Agricultural Organization of the United Nations (FAO) Via delle Terme di Caracalla, 00100 Rome, Italy (Telephone Number in U.S. (202) 653-2400); *The State of Food and Agriculture.*

Statistical Office of the United Nations, Publishing Service, New York, New York 10017 (800) 253-9646; *Statistical Yearbook.*

SAINT LUCIA - FETAL MORTALITY - See SAINT LUCIA - MORTALITY

SAINT LUCIA - FINANCE

Europa Publications Limited, 18 Bedford Square, London, WC1B 3JN, England; *The Europa World Year Book.*

Federal Statistical Office, Gustav-Stresemann - Ring 11, D-6200, Wiesbaden, Germany; *Saint Lucia.*

St. Martin's Press, Inc., 175 Fifth Avenue, New York, New York 10010 (800) 221-7945; *The Statesman's Year-Book.*

SAINT LUCIA - FISHERIES

Europa Publications Limited, 18 Bedford Square, London, WC1B 3JN, England; *The Europa World Year Book.*

Federal Statistical Office, Gustav-Stresemann - Ring 11, D-6200, Wiesbaden, Germany; *Saint Lucia.*

Food and Agricultural Organization of the United Nations (FAO) Via delle Terme di Caracalla, 00100 Rome, Italy (Telephone Number in U.S. (202) 653-2400); *The State of Food and Agriculture;* and *Yearbook of Fishery Statistics.*

Statistical Office of the United Nations, Publishing Service, New York, New York 10017 (800) 253-9646; *Statistical Yearbook.*

United Nations Conference on Trade and Development, Central Statistical Service, Palais des Nations, Geneva, Switzerland (Telephone in U.S. (800) 253-9646); *UNCTAD Commodity Yearbook.*

SAINT LUCIA - FOOD

Food and Agricultural Organization of the United Nations (FAO), Via delle Terme di Caracalla, 00100 Rome, Italy (Telephone Number in U.S. (202) 653-2400); *Production Yearbook;* and *The State of Food and Agriculture.*

Statistical Office of the United Nations, Publishing Service, New York, New York 10017 (800) 253-9646; *Human Development Report.*

United Nations Conference on Trade and Development, Central Statistical Service, Palais des Nations, Geneva, Switzerland (Telephone in U.S. (800) 253-9646); *UNCTAD Commodity Yearbook.*

SAINT LUCIA - FOREIGN TRADE

Euromonitor International, Inc., 122 South Michigan Avenue, Suite 1200, Chicago, Illinois 60603 (800) 577-EURO; *The World Economic Factbook.*

Europa Publications Limited, 18 Bedford Square, London, WC1B 3JN, England; *The Europa World Year Book.*

Federal Statistical Office, Gustav-Stresemann - Ring 11, D-6200, Wiesbaden, Germany; *Saint Lucia.*

Food and Agricultural Organization of the United Nations (FAO) Via delle Terme di Caracalla, 00100 Rome, Italy (Telephone Number in U.S. (202) 653-2400); *The State of Food and Agriculture.*

St. Martin's Press, Inc., 175 Fifth Avenue, New York, New York 10010 (800) 221-7945; *The Statesman's Year-Book.*

Statistical Office of the United Nations, Publishing Service, New York, New York 10017 (800) 253-9646; *International Trade Statistics Yearbook;* and *Statistical Yearbook.*

United Nations Conference on Trade and Development, Central Statistical Service, Palais des Nations, Geneva, Switzerland (Telephone in U.S. (800) 253-9646); *UNCTAD Commodity Yearbook.*

The World Bank, 1818 H Street, NW, Washington, D.C. 20433 (202) 477-1234; *World Development Indicators.*

SAINT LUCIA - FORESTRY AND FOREST PRODUCTS

Federal Statistical Office, Gustav-Stresemann - Ring 11, D-6200, Wiesbaden, Germany; *Saint Lucia.*

Food and Agricultural Organization of the United Nations (FAO) Via delle Terme di Caracalla, 00100 Rome, Italy (Telephone Number in U.S. (202) 653-2400); *The State of Food and Agriculture.*

Statistical Office of the United Nations, Publishing Service, New York, New York 10017 (800) 253-9646; *Statistical Yearbook.*

United Nations Conference on Trade and Development, Central Statistical Service, Palais des Nations, Geneva, Switzerland (Telephone in U.S. (800) 253-9646); *UNCTAD Commodity Yearbook.*

United Nations Educational, Scientific and Cultural Organization (UNESCO), 7 Place de Fontenoy, F-75700 Paris, France (Telephone Number in U.S. (212) 963-5981); *Statistical Yearbook.*

SAINT LUCIA - GENERAL MORTALITY - See SAINT LUCIA - MORTALITY

SAINT LUCIA - GOLD HOLDINGS

The World Bank, 1818 H Street, NW, Washington, D.C. 20433 (202) 477-1234; *World Development Indicators.*

SAINT LUCIA - GOVERNMENT

Central Intelligence Agency, Washington, D.C. 20505 (703) 482-1100, www.cia.gov; *The World Factbook.*

Europa Publications Limited, 18 Bedford Square, London, WC1B 3JN, England; *The Europa World Year Book.*

St. Martin's Press, Inc., 175 Fifth Avenue, New York, New York 10010 (800) 221-7945; *The Statesman's Year-Book.*

Statistical Office of the United Nations, Publishing Service, New York, New York 10017 (800) 253-9646; *National Accounts Statistics.*

The World Bank, 1818 H Street, NW, Washington, D.C. 20433 (202) 477-1234; *World Development Indicators.*

SAINT LUCIA - GRAIN PRODUCTION - See SAINT LUCIA - CROPS

SAINT LUCIA - GROSS DOMESTIC PRODUCT

Euromonitor International, Inc., 122 South Michigan Avenue, Suite 1200, Chicago, Illinois 60603 (800) 577-EURO; *The World Economic Factbook.*

Europa Publications Limited, 18 Bedford Square, London, WC1B 3JN, England; *The Europa World Year Book.*

Statistical Office of the United Nations, Publishing Service, New York, New York 10017 (800) 253-9646; *Human Development Report; National Accounts Statistics;* and *Statistical Yearbook.*

The World Bank, 1818 H Street, NW, Washington, D.C. 20433 (202) 477-1234;

World Development Indicators.

SAINT LUCIA - GROSS NATIONAL PRODUCT

St. Martin's Press, Inc., 175 Fifth Avenue, New York, New York 10010 (800) 221-7945; *The Statesman's Year-Book.*

The World Bank, 1818 H Street, NW, Washington, D.C. 20433 (202) 477-1234; *The World Bank Atlas; and World Development Indicators.*

SAINT LUCIA - HEALTH

Euromonitor International, Inc., 122 South Michigan Avenue, Suite 1200, Chicago, Illinois 60603 (800) 577-EURO; *World Marketing Data and Statistics.*

Federal Statistical Office, Gustav-Stresemann - Ring 11, D-6200, Wiesbaden, Germany; *Saint Lucia.*

St. Martin's Press, Inc., 175 Fifth Avenue, New York, New York 10010 (800) 221-7945; *The Statesman's Year-Book.*

Statistical Office of the United Nations, Publishing Service, New York, New York 10017 (800) 253-9646; *Human Development Report; and Statistical Yearbook.*

World Health Organization, Office of Publications, 20 Avenue Appia, CH-1211 Geneva 27, Switzerland (Telephone Number in U.S. (518) 436-9686); *World Health Statistics Annual.*

SAINT LUCIA - HIGHWAYS

Central Intelligence Agency, Washington, D.C. 20505 (703) 482-1100, www.cia.gov; *The World Factbook.*

St. Martin's Press, Inc., 175 Fifth Avenue, New York, New York 10010 (800) 221-7945; *The Statesman's Year-Book.*

SAINT LUCIA - HORSES - See SAINT LUCIA - LIVESTOCK AND POULTRY

SAINT LUCIA - HOURS OF WORK - See SAINT LUCIA - EMPLOYMENT

SAINT LUCIA - HOUSING AND HOUSING UNITS

Euromonitor International, Inc., 122 South Michigan Avenue, Suite 1200, Chicago, Illinois 60603 (800) 577-EURO; *World Marketing Data and Statistics.*

SAINT LUCIA - ILLITERATE POPULATION

Central Intelligence Agency, Washington, D.C. 20505 (703) 482-1100, www.cia.gov; *The World Factbook.*

Euromonitor International, Inc., 122 South Michigan Avenue, Suite 1200, Chicago, Illinois 60603 (800) 577-EURO; *The World Economic Factbook.*

Statistical Office of the United Nations, Publishing Service, New York, New York 10017 (800) 253-9646; *Human Development Report.*

United Nations Educational, Scientific and Cultural Organization (UNESCO), 7 Place de Fontenoy, F-75700 Paris, France (Telephone Number in U.S. (212) 963-5981); *Statistical Yearbook.*

SAINT LUCIA - IMPORTS

Central Intelligence Agency, Washington, D.C. 20505 (703) 482-1100, www.cia.gov; *The World Factbook.*

Euromonitor International, Inc., 122 South Michigan Avenue, Suite 1200, Chicago, Illinois 60603 (800) 577-EURO; *The World Economic Factbook.*

Europa Publications Limited, 18 Bedford Square, London, WC1B 3JN, England; *The Europa World Year Book.*

Food and Agricultural Organization of the United Nations (FAO) Via delle Terme di Caracalla, 00100 Rome, Italy (Telephone Number in U.S. (202) 653-2400); *The State of Food and Agriculture.*

St. Martin's Press, Inc., 175 Fifth Avenue, New York, New York 10010 (800) 221-7945; *The Statesman's Year-Book.*

United Nations Conference on Trade and Development (UNCTAD), New York, New York 10017 (800) 253-9646; *Handbook of International Trade and Development Statistics.*

The World Bank, 1818 H Street, NW, Washington, D.C. 20433 (202) 477-1234; *World Development Indicators.*

SAINT LUCIA - INDUSTRY

Central Intelligence Agency, Washington, D.C. 20505 (703) 482-1100, www.cia.gov; *The World Factbook.*

Euromonitor International, Inc., 122 South Michigan Avenue, Suite 1200, Chicago, Illinois 60603 (800) 577-EURO; *The World Economic Factbook; and World Marketing Data and Statistics.*

Europa Publications Limited, 18 Bedford Square, London, WC1B 3JN, England; *The Europa World Year Book.*

Federal Statistical Office, Gustav-Stresemann - Ring 11, D-6200, Wiesbaden, Germany; *Saint Lucia.*

International Labour Office, I.L.O. Publications, 1828 L Street, NW, Suite 801, Washington, D.C. 20036 (301) 638-3152; *Yearbook of Labour Statistics.*

The World Bank, 1818 H Street, NW, Washington, D.C. 20433 (202) 477-1234; *World Development Indicators.*

SAINT LUCIA - INFANT AND MATERNAL MORTALITY - See SAINT LUCIA - MORTALITY

SAINT LUCIA - INTERNATIONAL RESERVES EXCLUDING GOLD

The World Bank, 1818 H Street, NW, Washington, D.C. 20433 (202) 477-1234; *World Development Indicators.*

SAINT LUCIA - LABOR

Central Intelligence Agency, Washington, D.C. 20505 (703) 482-1100, www.cia.gov; *The World Factbook.*

Euromonitor International, Inc., 122 South Michigan Avenue, Suite 1200, Chicago, Illinois 60603 (800) 577-EURO; *World Marketing Data and Statistics.*

Europa Publications Limited, 18 Bedford Square, London, WC1B 3JN, England; *The Europa World Year Book.*

Food and Agricultural Organization of the United Nations (FAO) Via delle Terme di Caracalla, 00100 Rome, Italy (Telephone Number in U.S. (202) 653-2400); *The State of Food and Agriculture.*

International Labour Office, I.L.O. Publications, 1828 L Street, NW, Suite 801, Washington, D.C. 20036 (301) 638-3152; *Yearbook of Labour Statistics.*

St. Martin's Press, Inc., 175 Fifth Avenue, New York, New York 10010 (800) 221-7945; *The Statesman's Year-Book.*

Statistical Office of the United Nations, Publishing Service, New York, New York 10017 (800) 253-9646; *Human Development Report.*

The World Bank, 1818 H Street, NW, Washington, D.C. 20433 (202) 477-1234; *The World Bank Atlas; and World Development Indicators.*

SAINT LUCIA - LAND USE

Central Intelligence Agency, Washington, D.C. 20505 (703) 482-1100, www.cia.gov; *The World Factbook.*

Food and Agricultural Organization of the United Nations (FAO), Via delle Terme di Caracalla, 00100 Rome, Italy (Telephone Number in U.S. (202) 653-2400); *Production Yearbook.*

SAINT LUCIA - LIBRARIES

United Nations Educational, Scientific and Cultural Organization (UNESCO), 7 Place de Fontenoy, F-75700 Paris, France (Telephone Number in U.S. (212) 963-5981); *Statistical Yearbook.*

SAINT LUCIA - LIFE EXPECTANCY

Central Intelligence Agency, Washington, D.C. 20505 (703) 482-1100, www.cia.gov; *The World Factbook.*

Euromonitor International, Inc., 122 South Michigan Avenue, Suite 1200, Chicago, Illinois 60603 (800) 577-EURO; *The World Economic Factbook.*

St. Martin's Press, Inc., 175 Fifth Avenue, New York, New York 10010 (800) 221-7945; *The Statesman's Year-Book.*

Statistical Office of the United Nations, Publishing Service, New York, New York 10017 (800) 253-9646; *Human Development Report;* and *World Statistics Pocketbook.*

The World Bank, 1818 H Street, NW, Washington, D.C. 20433 (202) 477-1234; *The World Bank Atlas.*

SAINT LUCIA - LITERACY RATE

Euromonitor International, Inc., 122 South Michigan Avenue, Suite 1200, Chicago, Illinois 60603 (800) 577-EURO; *World Marketing Data and Statistics.*

SAINT LUCIA - LIVESTOCK AND POULTRY

Europa Publications Limited, 18 Bedford Square, London, WC1B 3JN, England; *The Europa World Year Book.*

Food and Agricultural Organization of the United Nations (FAO), Via delle Terme di Caracalla, 00100 Rome, Italy (Telephone Number in U.S. (202) 653-2400); *Production Yearbook;* and *The State of Food and Agriculture.*

St. Martin's Press, Inc., 175 Fifth Avenue, New York, New York 10010 (800) 221-7945; *The Statesman's Year-Book.*

Statistical Office of the United Nations, Publishing Service, New York, New York 10017 (800) 253-9646; *Statistical Yearbook.*

United Nations Conference on Trade and Development, Central Statistical Service, Palais des Nations, Geneva, Switzerland (Telephone in U.S. (800) 253-9646); *UNCTAD Commodity Yearbook.*

SAINT LUCIA - LIVING LEVELS - See SAINT LUCIA - LIFE EXPECTANCY

SAINT LUCIA - MAIL TRAFFIC - NUMBER

OF ITEMS SENT AND RECEIVED

Statistical Office of the United Nations, Publishing Service, New York, New York 10017 (800) 253-9646; *Statistical Yearbook.*

SAINT LUCIA - MANUFACTURING

The World Bank, 1818 H Street, NW, Washington, D.C. 20433 (202) 477-1234; *World Development Indicators.*

SAINT LUCIA - MARRIAGE RATES

Statistical Office of the United Nations, Publishing Service, New York, New York 10017 (800) 253-9646; *Demographic Yearbook;* and *Statistical Yearbook.*

SAINT LUCIA - MEAT PRODUCTION - See SAINT LUCIA - LIVESTOCK AND POULTRY

SAINT LUCIA - MERCHANT SHIPPING

Europa Publications Limited, 18 Bedford Square, London, WC1B 3JN, England; *The Europa World Year Book.*

St. Martin's Press, Inc., 175 Fifth Avenue, New York, New York 10010 (800) 221-7945; *The Statesman's Year-Book.*

Statistical Office of the United Nations, Publishing Service, New York, New York 10017 (800) 253-9646; *Statistical Yearbook.*

SAINT LUCIA - MILITARY

Central Intelligence Agency, Washington, D.C. 20505 (703) 482-1100, www.cia.gov; *The World Factbook.*

Euromonitor International, Inc., 122 South Michigan Avenue, Suite 1200, Chicago, Illinois 60603 (800) 577-EURO; *World Marketing Data and Statistics.*

Statistical Office of the United Nations, Publishing Service, New York, New York 10017 (800) 253-9646; *Human Development Report.*

SAINT LUCIA - MINING AND MINERAL PRODUCTS

United Nations Conference on Trade and Development, Central Statistical Service, Palais des Nations, Geneva, Switzerland (Telephone in U.S. (800) 253-9646); *UNCTAD Commodity Yearbook.*

SAINT LUCIA - MONEY SUPPLY

Europa Publications Limited, 18 Bedford Square, London, WC1B 3JN, England; *The Europa World Year Book.*

Federal Statistical Office, Gustav-Stresemann - Ring 11, D-6200, Wiesbaden, Germany; *Saint Lucia.*

The World Bank, 1818 H Street, NW, Washington, D.C. 20433 (202) 477-1234; *World Development Indicators.*

SAINT LUCIA - MORTALITY

Central Intelligence Agency, Washington, D.C. 20505 (703) 482-1100, www.cia.gov; *The World Factbook.*

Euromonitor International, Inc., 122 South Michigan Avenue, Suite 1200, Chicago, Illinois 60603 (800) 577-EURO; *The World Economic Factbook.*

Statistical Office of the United Nations, Publishing Service, New York, New York 10017 (800) 253-9646; *Demographic Yearbook; Human Development Report; Statistical Yearbook;* and *World Statistics Pocketbook.*

The World Bank, 1818 H Street, NW, Washington, D.C. 20433 (202) 477-1234; *The World Bank Atlas;* and *World Development Indicators.*

World Health Organization, Office of Publications, 20 Avenue Appia, CH-1211 Geneva 27, Switzerland (Telephone Number in U.S. (518) 436-9686); *World Health Statistics Annual.*

SAINT LUCIA - MOTION PICTURES

St. Martin's Press, Inc., 175 Fifth Avenue, New York, New York 10010 (800) 221-7945; *The Statesman's Year-Book.*

SAINT LUCIA - MOTOR VEHICLES - IN USE

Europa Publications Limited, 18 Bedford Square, London, WC1B 3JN, England; *The Europa World Year Book.*

Statistical Office of the United Nations, Publishing Service, New York, New York 10017 (800) 253-9646; *Statistical Yearbook.*

SAINT LUCIA - MULES - See SAINT LUCIA - LIVESTOCK AND POULTRY

SAINT LUCIA - MUSEUMS

United Nations Educational, Scientific and Cultural Organization (UNESCO), 7 Place de Fontenoy, F-75700 Paris, France (Telephone Number in U.S. (212) 963-5981); *Statistical Yearbook.*

SAINT LUCIA - NATALITY - See SAINT LUCIA - BIRTH RATE

SAINT LUCIA - NATIONAL ACCOUNTS

Europa Publications Limited, 18 Bedford Square, London, WC1B 3JN, England; *The Europa World Year Book.*

Federal Statistical Office, Gustav-Stresemann - Ring 11, D-6200, Wiesbaden,

Germany; *Saint Lucia.*

Statistical Office of the United Nations, Publishing Service, New York, New York 10017 (800) 253-9646; *National Accounts Statistics;* and *Statistical Yearbook.*

SAINT LUCIA - NATIONAL INCOME

Statistical Office of the United Nations, Publishing Service, New York, New York 10017 (800) 253-9646; *National Accounts Statistics;* and *Statistical Yearbook.*

SAINT LUCIA - NEWSPAPER PRODUCTION - See SAINT LUCIA - FORESTRY AND FOREST PRODUCTS

SAINT LUCIA - OCCUPATIONS - See SAINT LUCIA - LABOR

SAINT LUCIA - PESTICIDE USE

Food and Agricultural Organization of the United Nations (FAO) Via delle Terme di Caracalla, 00100 Rome, Italy (Telephone Number in U.S. (202) 653-2400); *The State of Food and Agriculture.*

SAINT LUCIA - PETROLEUM INDUSTRY

Food and Agricultural Organization of the United Nations (FAO) Via delle Terme di Caracalla, 00100 Rome, Italy (Telephone Number in U.S. (202) 653-2400); *The State of Food and Agriculture.*

United Nations Conference on Trade and Development, Central Statistical Service, Palais des Nations, Geneva, Switzerland (Telephone in U.S. (800) 253-9646); *UNCTAD Commodity Yearbook.*

SAINT LUCIA - PIGS - See SAINT LUCIA - LIVESTOCK AND POULTRY

SAINT LUCIA - POPULATION

Central Intelligence Agency, Washington, D.C. 20505 (703) 482-1100, www.cia.gov; *The World Factbook.*

Euromonitor International, Inc., 122 South Michigan Avenue, Suite 1200, Chicago, Illinois 60603 (800) 577-EURO; *The World Economic Factbook.*

Europa Publications Limited, 18 Bedford Square, London, WC1B 3JN, England; *The Europa World Year Book.*

Federal Statistical Office, Gustav-Stresemann - Ring 11, D-6200, Wiesbaden, Germany; *Saint Lucia.*

Food and Agricultural Organization of the United Nations (FAO), Via delle Terme di Caracalla, 00100 Rome, Italy (Telephone Number in U.S. (202) 653-2400); *Production Yearbook.*

International Labour Office, I.L.O. Publications, 1828 L Street, NW, Suite 801, Washington, D.C. 20036 (301) 638-3152; *Yearbook of Labour Statistics.*

St. Martin's Press, Inc., 175 Fifth Avenue, New York, New York 10010 (800) 221-7945; *The Statesman's Year-Book.*

Statistical Office of the United Nations, Publishing Service, New York, New York 10017 (800) 253-9646; *Demographic Yearbook; Human Development Report; Statistical Yearbook;* and *World Statistics Pocketbook.*

United Nations Educational, Scientific and Cultural Organization (UNESCO), 7 Place de Fontenoy, F-75700 Paris, France (Telephone Number in U.S. (212) 963-5981); *Statistical Yearbook.*

The World Bank, 1818 H Street, NW, Washington, D.C. 20433 (202) 477-1234; *The World Bank Atlas.*

World Health Organization, Office of Publications, 20 Avenue Appia, CH-1211 Geneva 27, Switzerland (Telephone Number in U.S. (518) 436-9686); *World Health Statistics Annual.*

SAINT LUCIA - PRICES

Federal Statistical Office, Gustav-Stresemann - Ring 11, D-6200, Wiesbaden, Germany; *Saint Lucia.*

Food and Agricultural Organization of the United Nations (FAO), Via delle Terme di Caracalla, 00100 Rome, Italy (Telephone Number in U.S. (202) 653-2400); *Production Yearbook;* and *The State of Food and Agriculture.*

International Labour Office, I.L.O. Publications, 1828 L Street, NW, Suite 801, Washington, D.C. 20036 (301) 638-3152; *Yearbook of Labour Statistics.*

SAINT LUCIA - RADIO RECEIVERS

St. Martin's Press, Inc., 175 Fifth Avenue, New York, New York 10010 (800) 221-7945; *The Statesman's Year-Book.*

SAINT LUCIA - RELIGION

Central Intelligence Agency, Washington, D.C. 20505 (703) 482-1100, www.cia.gov; *The World Factbook.*

St. Martin's Press, Inc., 175 Fifth Avenue, New York, New York 10010 (800) 221-7945; *The Statesman's Year-Book.*

SAINT LUCIA - RENT PRICES

International Labour Office, I.L.O. Publications, 1828 L Street, NW, Suite

801, Washington, D.C. 20036 (301) 638-3152; *Yearbook of Labour Statistics.*

SAINT LUCIA - RETAIL TRADE

Euromonitor International, Inc., 122 South Michigan Avenue, Suite 1200, Chicago, Illinois 60603 (800) 577-EURO; *World Marketing Data and Statistics.*

SAINT LUCIA - SHEEP - See SAINT LUCIA - LIVESTOCK AND POULTRY

SAINT LUCIA - SOCIAL SECURITY

Statistical Office of the United Nations, Publishing Service, New York, New York 10017 (800) 253-9646; *National Accounts Statistics;* and *World Statistical Pocketbook.*

SAINT LUCIA - STOCKS - COMMODITY - MARKET PRICE - INDEX

Food and Agricultural Organization of the United Nations (FAO) Via delle Terme di Caracalla, 00100 Rome, Italy (Telephone Number in U.S. (202) 653-2400); *The State of Food and Agriculture.*

SAINT LUCIA - TAXATION

Europa Publications Limited, 18 Bedford Square, London, WC1B 3JN, England; *The Europa World Year Book.*

The World Bank, 1818 H Street, NW, Washington, D.C. 20433 (202) 477-1234; *World Development Indicators.*

SAINT LUCIA - TELEPHONES IN USE

American Telephone and Telegraph Company, 26 Parsippany Road, Whippany, New Jersey 07981 (800) 222-0300; *The World's Telephones.*

Central Intelligence Agency, Washington, D.C. 20505 (703) 482-1100, www.cia.gov; *The World Factbook.*

Europa Publications Limited, 18 Bedford Square, London, WC1B 3JN, England; *The Europa World Year Book.*

St. Martin's Press, Inc., 175 Fifth Avenue, New York, New York 10010 (800) 221-7945; *The Statesman's Year-Book.*

Statistical Office of the United Nations, Publishing Service, New York, New York 10017 (800) 253-9646; *Statistical Yearbook;* and *World Statistics Pocketbook.*

SAINT LUCIA - TEXTILE INDUSTRY

St. Martin's Press, Inc., 175 Fifth Avenue, New York, New York 10010 (800) 221-7945; *The Statesman's Year-Book.*

United Nations Conference on Trade and Development, Central Statistical

Service, Palais des Nations, Geneva, Switzerland (Telephone in U.S. (800) 253-9646); *UNCTAD Commodity Yearbook*.

SAINT LUCIA - TOURISM

Euromonitor International, Inc., 122 South Michigan Avenue, Suite 1200, Chicago, Illinois 60603 (800) 577-EURO; *The World Economic Factbook;* and *World Marketing Data and Statistics.*

Europa Publications Limited, 18 Bedford Square, London, WC1B 3JN, England; *The Europa World Year Book.*

Federal Statistical Office, Gustav-Stresemann - Ring 11, D-6200, Wiesbaden, Germany; *Saint Lucia.*

St. Martin's Press, Inc., 175 Fifth Avenue, New York, New York 10010 (800) 221-7945; *The Statesman's Year-Book.*

World Tourism Organization, Calle Capitan Haya 42, E-28020 Madrid, Spain; *Yearbook of Tourism Statistics.*

SAINT LUCIA - TRACTORS IN USE

Statistical Office of the United Nations, Publishing Service, New York, New York 10017 (800) 253-9646; *Statistical Yearbook.*

SAINT LUCIA - TRADE - See SAINT LUCIA - FOREIGN TRADE

SAINT LUCIA - TRANSPORTATION AND COMMUNICATIONS

Central Intelligence Agency, Washington, D.C. 20505 (703) 482-1100, www.cia.gov; *The World Factbook.*

Euromonitor International, Inc., 122 South Michigan Avenue, Suite 1200, Chicago, Illinois 60603 (800) 577-EURO; *World Marketing Data and Statistics.*

Europa Publications Limited, 18 Bedford Square, London, WC1B 3JN, England; *The Europa World Year Book.*

Federal Statistical Office, Gustav-Stresemann - Ring 11, D-6200, Wiesbaden, Germany; *Saint Lucia.*

St. Martin's Press, Inc., 175 Fifth Avenue, New York, New York 10010 (800) 221-7945; *The Statesman's Year-Book.*

Statistical Office of the United Nations, Publishing Service, New York, New York 10017 (800) 253-9646; *Human Development Report.*

SAINT LUCIA - UNEMPLOYMENT

Central Intelligence Agency, Washington, D.C. 20505 (703) 482-1100, www.cia.gov; *The World Factbook.*

International Labour Office, I.L.O. Publications, 1828 L Street, NW, Suite 801, Washington, D.C. 20036 (301) 638-3152; *Yearbook of Labour Statistics.*

SAINT LUCIA - VITAL STATISTICS

Statistical Office of the United Nations, Publishing Service, New York, New York 10017 (800) 253-9646; *Statistical Yearbook.*

World Health Organization, Office of Publications, 20 Avenue Appia, CH-1211 Geneva 27, Switzerland (Telephone Number in U.S. (518) 436-9686); *World Health Statistics Annual.*

SAINT LUCIA - WAGES

Federal Statistical Office, Gustav-Stresemann - Ring 11, D-6200, Wiesbaden, Germany; *Saint Lucia.*

International Labour Office, I.L.O. Publications, 1828 L Street, NW, Suite 801, Washington, D.C. 20036 (301) 638-3152; *Yearbook of Labour Statistics.*

SAINT LUCIA - WEATHER - See SAINT LUCIA - CLIMATE

Saint Pierre and Miquelon - Primary Statistics Sources

Institut National de la Statistique et des Etudes Economiques (INSEE), 18 boulevard Adolphe Pinard, 75675 Paris Cedex 14, France; *Annuaire Statistique des territories d'outre-mer* (Statistical yearbook of overseas territories).

SAINT PIERRE AND MIQUELON - AGRICULTURE

Food and Agricultural Organization of the United Nations (FAO) Via delle Terme di Caracalla, 00100 Rome, Italy (Telephone Number in U.S. (202) 653-2400); *Production Yearbook; The State of Food and Agriculture;* and *Trade Yearbook.*

St. Martin's Press, Inc., 175 Fifth Avenue, New York, New York 10010 (800) 221-7945; *The Statesman's Year-Book.*

United Nations Conference on Trade and Development, Central Statistical Service, Palais des Nations, Geneva, Switzerland (Telephone in U.S. (800) 253-9646); *UNCTAD Commodity Yearbook.*

SAINT PIERRE AND MIQUELON - AIRLINE SERVICE

Europa Publications Limited, 18 Bedford Square, London, WC1B 3JN, England; *The Europa World Year Book.*

St. Martin's Press, Inc., 175 Fifth Avenue, New York, New York 10010 (800) 221-7945; *The Statesman's Year-Book.*

SAINT PIERRE AND MIQUELON - AIRPORTS

Central Intelligence Agency, Washington, D.C. 20505 (703) 482-1100, www.cia.gov; *The World Factbook.*

SAINT PIERRE AND MIQUELON - AREA AND DENSITY OF POPULATION

Central Intelligence Agency, Washington, D.C. 20505 (703) 482-1100, www.cia.gov; *The World Factbook.*

Europa Publications Limited, 18 Bedford Square, London, WC1B 3JN, England; *The Europa World Year Book.*

Food and Agricultural Organization of the United Nations (FAO) Via delle Terme di Caracalla, 00100 Rome, Italy (Telephone Number in U.S. (202) 653-2400); *The State of Food and Agriculture.*

St. Martin's Press, Inc., 175 Fifth Avenue, New York, New York 10010 (800) 221-7945; *The Statesman's Year-Book.*

Statistical Office of the United Nations, Publishing Service, New York, New York 10017 (800) 253-9646; *Statistical Yearbook.*

United Nations Educational, Scientific and Cultural Organization (UNESCO), 7 Place de Fontenoy, F-75700 Paris, France (Telephone Number in U.S. (212) 963-5981); *Statistical Yearbook.*

SAINT PIERRE AND MIQUELON - BANKING

St. Martin's Press, Inc., 175 Fifth Avenue, New York, New York 10010 (800) 221-7945; *The Statesman's Year-Book.*

SAINT PIERRE AND MIQUELON - BIRTH RATES

Central Intelligence Agency, Washington, D.C. 20505 (703) 482-1100, www.cia.gov; *The World Factbook.*

Europa Publications Limited, 18 Bedford Square, London, WC1B 3JN, England; *The Europa World Year Book.*

St. Martin's Press, Inc., 175 Fifth Avenue, New York, New York 10010 (800) 221-7945; *The Statesman's Year-Book.*

Statistical Office of the United Nations, Publishing Service, New York, New York 10017 (800) 253-9646; *Demographic Yearbook;* and *Statistical Yearbook.*

World Health Organization, Office of Publications, 20 Avenue Appia, CH-1211 Geneva 27, Switzerland (Telephone Number in U.S. (518) 436-9686); *World*

Health Statistics Annual.

SAINT PIERRE AND MIQUELON - BROADCASTING

Billboard Limited, P.O. Box 9027, 1006 AA Amsterdam, The Netherlands (Telephone Number in U.S. (212) 764-7300); *World Radio TV Handbook.*

Central Intelligence Agency, Washington, D.C. 20505 (703) 482-1100, www.cia.gov; *The World Factbook.*

St. Martin's Press, Inc., 175 Fifth Avenue, New York, New York 10010 (800) 221-7945; *The Statesman's Year-Book.*

United Nations Educational, Scientific and Cultural Organization (UNESCO), 7 Place de Fontenoy, F-75700 Paris, France (Telephone Number in U.S. (212) 963-5981); *Statistical Yearbook.*

SAINT PIERRE AND MIQUELON - BUDGET

Central Intelligence Agency, Washington, D.C. 20505 (703) 482-1100, www.cia.gov; *The World Factbook.*

SAINT PIERRE AND MIQUELON - CALORIE SUPPLY

Food and Agricultural Organization of the United Nations (FAO) Via delle Terme di Caracalla, 00100 Rome, Italy (Telephone Number in U.S. (202) 653-2400); *The State of Food and Agriculture.*

SAINT PIERRE AND MIQUELON - COMMERCE

St. Martin's Press, Inc., 175 Fifth Avenue, New York, New York 10010 (800) 221-7945; *The Statesman's Year-Book.*

SAINT PIERRE AND MIQUELON - COMMUNICATIONS - See SAINT PIERRE AND MIQUELON - TRANSPORTATION AND COMMUNICATIONS

SAINT PIERRE AND MIQUELON - CONSUMER PRICE INDEX

Europa Publications Limited, 18 Bedford Square, London, WC1B 3JN, England; *The Europa World Year Book.*

SAINT PIERRE AND MIQUELON - CONSUMER PRICES

International Labour Office, I.L.O. Publications, 1828 L Street, NW, Suite 801, Washington, D.C. 20036 (301) 638-3152; *Yearbook of Labour Statistics.*

SAINT PIERRE AND MIQUELON - CORN PRODUCTION - SAINT PIERRE AND MIQUELON - CROPS

SAINT PIERRE AND MIQUELON - CROPS

Food and Agricultural Organization of the United Nations (FAO) Via delle Terme di Caracalla, 00100 Rome, Italy (Telephone Number in U.S. (202) 653-2400); *The State of Food and Agriculture.*

St. Martin's Press, Inc., 175 Fifth Avenue, New York, New York 10010 (800) 221-7945; *The Statesman's Year-Book.*

United Nations Conference on Trade and Development, Central Statistical Service, Palais des Nations, Geneva, Switzerland (Telephone in U.S. (800) 253-9646); *UNCTAD Commodity Yearbook.*

SAINT PIERRE AND MIQUELON - DAIRY PRODUCTS

Food and Agricultural Organization of the United Nations (FAO) Via delle Terme di Caracalla, 00100 Rome, Italy (Telephone Number in U.S. (202) 653-2400); *The State of Food and Agriculture.*

SAINT PIERRE AND MIQUELON - DEATH RATES - See SAINT PIERRE AND MIQUELON - MORTALITY

SAINT PIERRE AND MIQUELON - DEVELOPMENT ASSISTANCE

Statistical Office of the United Nations, Publishing Service, New York, New York 10017 (800) 253-9646; *Statistical Yearbook.*

SAINT PIERRE AND MIQUELON - DIVORCE RATES

Statistical Office of the United Nations, Publishing Service, New York, New York 10017 (800) 253-9646; *Demographic Yearbook;* and *Statistical Yearbook.*

SAINT PIERRE AND MIQUELON - ECONOMY

Central Intelligence Agency, Washington, D.C. 20505 (703) 482-1100, www.cia.gov; *The World Factbook.*

Europa Publications Limited, 18 Bedford Square, London, WC1B 3JN, England; *The Europa World Year Book.*

St. Martin's Press, Inc., 175 Fifth Avenue, New York, New York 10010 (800) 221-7945; *The Statesman's Year-Book.*

SAINT PIERRE AND MIQUELON - EDUCATION

Europa Publications Limited, 18 Bedford Square, London, WC1B 3JN, England; *The Europa World Year Book.*

St. Martin's Press, Inc., 175 Fifth Avenue, New York, New York 10010 (800) 221-7945; *The Statesman's Year-Book.*

SAINT PIERRE AND MIQUELON - EGG

PRODUCTION AND CONSUMPTION - See SAINT PIERRE AND MIQUELON - DAIRY PRODUCTS

SAINT PIERRE AND MIQUELON - ELECTRICITY

Central Intelligence Agency, Washington, D.C. 20505 (703) 482-1100, www.cia.gov; *The World Factbook.*

St. Martin's Press, Inc., 175 Fifth Avenue, New York, New York 10010 (800) 221-7945; *The Statesman's Year-Book.*

SAINT PIERRE AND MIQUELON - EMPLOYMENT

International Labour Office, I.L.O. Publications, 1828 L Street, NW, Suite 801, Washington, D.C. 20036 (301) 638-3152; *Yearbook of Labour Statistics.*

SAINT PIERRE AND MIQUELON - ENERGY

Food and Agricultural Organization of the United Nations (FAO) Via delle Terme di Caracalla, 00100 Rome, Italy (Telephone Number in U.S. (202) 653-2400); *The State of Food and Agriculture.*

St. Martin's Press, Inc., 175 Fifth Avenue, New York, New York 10010 (800) 221-7945; *The Statesman's Year-Book.*

Statistical Office of the United Nations, Publishing Service, New York, New York 10017 (800) 253-9646; *Energy Statistics Yearbook;* and *Statistical Yearbook.*

SAINT PIERRE AND MIQUELON - EXCHANGE RATES

Central Intelligence Agency, Washington, D.C. 20505 (703) 482-1100, www.cia.gov; *The World Factbook.*

Europa Publications Limited, 18 Bedford Square, London, WC1B 3JN, England; *The Europa World Year Book.*

SAINT PIERRE AND MIQUELON - EXPORTS

Central Intelligence Agency, Washington, D.C. 20505 (703) 482-1100, www.cia.gov; *The World Factbook.*

Europa Publications Limited, 18 Bedford Square, London, WC1B 3JN, England; *The Europa World Year Book.*

Food and Agricultural Organization of the United Nations (FAO) Via delle Terme di Caracalla, 00100 Rome, Italy (Telephone Number in U.S. (202) 653-2400); *The State of Food and Agriculture.*

International Monetary Fund, 700 Nineteenth Street, NW, Washington, D.C. 20431 (202) 623-7000; *Direction of Trade*

Statistics.

St. Martin's Press, Inc., 175 Fifth Avenue, New York, New York 10010 (800) 221-7945; *The Statesman's Year-Book.*

SAINT PIERRE AND MIQUELON - EXTERNAL TRADE

Food and Agricultural Organization of the United Nations (FAO) Via delle Terme di Caracalla, 00100 Rome, Italy (Telephone Number in U.S. (202) 653-2400); *The State of Food and Agriculture;* and *Trade Yearbook.*

Statistical Office of the United Nations, Publishing Service, New York, New York 10017 (800) 253-9646; *Statistical Yearbook.*

SAINT PIERRE AND MIQUELON - FARM CROPS - See SAINT PIERRE AND MIQUELON

SAINT PIERRE AND MIQUELON - FERTILITY RATES

Central Intelligence Agency, Washington, D.C. 20505 (703) 482-1100, www.cia.gov; *The World Factbook.*

SAINT PIERRE AND MIQUELON - FERTILIZER

Food and Agricultural Organization of the United Nations (FAO) Via delle Terme di Caracalla, 00100 Rome, Italy (Telephone Number in U.S. (202) 653-2400); *The State of Food and Agriculture.*

SAINT PIERRE AND MIQUELON - FETAL MORTALITY - See SAINT PIERRE AND MIQUELON - MORTALITY

SAINT PIERRE AND MIQUELON - FINANCE

Europa Publications Limited, 18 Bedford Square, London, WC1B 3JN, England; *The Europa World Year Book.*

SAINT PIERRE AND MIQUELON - FISHERIES

Europa Publications Limited, 18 Bedford Square, London, WC1B 3JN, England; *The Europa World Year Book.*

Food and Agricultural Organization of the United Nations (FAO) Via delle Terme di Caracalla, 00100 Rome, Italy (Telephone Number in U.S. (202) 653-2400); *The State of Food and Agriculture;* and *Yearbook of Fishery Statistics.*

St. Martin's Press, Inc., 175 Fifth Avenue, New York, New York 10010 (800) 221-7945; *The Statesman's Year-Book.*

Statistical Office of the United Nations, Publishing Service, New York, New York 10017 (800) 253-9646; *Statistical Yearbook.*

United Nations Conference on Trade and Development, Central Statistical Service, Palais des Nations, Geneva, Switzerland (Telephone in U.S. (800) 253-9646); *UNCTAD Commodity Yearbook.*

SAINT PIERRE AND MIQUELON - FOOD

Food and Agricultural Organization of the United Nations (FAO), Via delle Terme di Caracalla, 00100 Rome, Italy (Telephone Number in U.S. (202) 653-2400); *Production Yearbook;* and *The State of Food and Agriculture.*

United Nations Conference on Trade and Development, Central Statistical Service, Palais des Nations, Geneva, Switzerland (Telephone in U.S. (800) 253-9646); *UNCTAD Commodity Yearbook.*

SAINT PIERRE AND MIQUELON - FOREIGN TRADE

Europa Publications Limited, 18 Bedford Square, London, WC1B 3JN, England; *The Europa World Year Book.*

Food and Agricultural Organization of the United Nations (FAO) Via delle Terme di Caracalla, 00100 Rome, Italy (Telephone Number in U.S. (202) 653-2400); *The State of Food and Agriculture.*

St. Martin's Press, Inc., 175 Fifth Avenue, New York, New York 10010 (800) 221-7945; *The Statesman's Year-Book.*

Statistical Office of the United Nations, Publishing Service, New York, New York 10017 (800) 253-9646; *International Trade Statistics Yearbook.*

United Nations Conference on Trade and Development, Central Statistical Service, Palais des Nations, Geneva, Switzerland (Telephone in U.S. (800) 253-9646); *UNCTAD Commodity Yearbook.*

SAINT PIERRE AND MIQUELON - FORESTRY AND FOREST PRODUCTS

Food and Agricultural Organization of the United Nations (FAO) Via delle Terme di Caracalla, 00100 Rome, Italy (Telephone Number in U.S. (202) 653-2400); *The State of Food and Agriculture.*

United Nations Conference on Trade and Development, Central Statistical Service, Palais des Nations, Geneva, Switzerland (Telephone in U.S. (800) 253-9646); *UNCTAD Commodity Yearbook.*

SAINT PIERRE AND MIQUELON - GENERAL MORTALITY - See SAINT PIERRE AND MIQUELON - MORTALITY

SAINT PIERRE AND MIQUELON - GOVERNMENT

Central Intelligence Agency, Washington, D.C. 20505 (703) 482-1100, www.cia.gov; *The World Factbook.*

Europa Publications Limited, 18 Bedford Square, London, WC1B 3JN, England; *The Europa World Year Book.*

St. Martin's Press, Inc., 175 Fifth Avenue, New York, New York 10010 (800) 221-7945; *The Statesman's Year-Book.*

SAINT PIERRE AND MIQUELON - GRAIN PRODUCTION - See SAINT HELENA - CROPS

SAINT PIERRE AND MIQUELON - HEALTH

St. Martin's Press, Inc., 175 Fifth Avenue, New York, New York 10010 (800) 221-7945; *The Statesman's Year-Book.*

Statistical Office of the United Nations, Publishing Service, New York, New York 10017 (800) 253-9646; *Statistical Yearbook.*

SAINT PIERRE AND MIQUELON - HIGHWAYS

Central Intelligence Agency, Washington, D.C. 20505 (703) 482-1100, www.cia.gov; *The World Factbook.*

St. Martin's Press, Inc., 175 Fifth Avenue, New York, New York 10010 (800) 221-7945; *The Statesman's Year-Book.*

SAINT PIERRE AND MIQUELON - HOURS OF WORK - See SAINT PIERRE AND MIQUELON - EMPLOYMENT

SAINT PIERRE AND MIQUELON - ILLITERATE POPULATION

Central Intelligence Agency, Washington, D.C. 20505 (703) 482-1100, www.cia.gov; *The World Factbook.*

United Nations Educational, Scientific and Cultural Organization (UNESCO), 7 Place de Fontenoy, F-75700 Paris, France (Telephone Number in U.S. (212) 963-5981); *Statistical Yearbook.*

SAINT PIERRE AND MIQUELON - IMPORTS

Central Intelligence Agency, Washington, D.C. 20505 (703) 482-1100, www.cia.gov; *The World Factbook.*

Europa Publications Limited, 18 Bedford Square, London, WC1B 3JN, England; *The Europa World Year Book.*

Food and Agricultural Organization of the United Nations (FAO) Via delle Terme di Caracalla, 00100 Rome, Italy (Telephone Number in U.S. (202) 653-2400); *The State of Food and Agriculture.*

International Monetary Fund, 700

Nineteenth Street, NW, Washington, D.C. 20431 (202) 623-7000; *Direction of Trade Statistics.*

St. Martin's Press, Inc., 175 Fifth Avenue, New York, New York 10010 (800) 221-7945; *The Statesman's Year-Book.*

SAINT PIERRE AND MIQUELON - INDUSTRY

Central Intelligence Agency, Washington, D.C. 20505 (703) 482-1100, www.cia.gov; *The World Factbook.*

Europa Publications Limited, 18 Bedford Square, London, WC1B 3JN, England; *The Europa World Year Book.*

International Labour Office, I.L.O. Publications, 1828 L Street, NW, Suite 801, Washington, D.C. 20036 (301) 638-3152; *Yearbook of Labour Statistics.*

St. Martin's Press, Inc., 175 Fifth Avenue, New York, New York 10010 (800) 221-7945; *The Statesman's Year-Book.*

SAINT PIERRE AND MIQUELON - INFANT AND MATERNAL MORTALITY - See SAINT PIERRE AND MIQUELON - MORTALITY

SAINT PIERRE AND MIQUELON - LABOR

Central Intelligence Agency, Washington, D.C. 20505 (703) 482-1100, www.cia.gov; *The World Factbook.*

Europa Publications Limited, 18 Bedford Square, London, WC1B 3JN, England; *The Europa World Year Book.*

Food and Agricultural Organization of the United Nations (FAO) Via delle Terme di Caracalla, 00100 Rome, Italy (Telephone Number in U.S. (202) 653-2400); *The State of Food and Agriculture.*

International Labour Office, I.L.O. Publications, 1828 L Street, NW, Suite 801, Washington, D.C. 20036 (301) 638-3152; *Yearbook of Labour Statistics.*

St. Martin's Press, Inc., 175 Fifth Avenue, New York, New York 10010 (800) 221-7945; *The Statesman's Year-Book.*

SAINT PIERRE AND MIQUELON - LAND USE

Central Intelligence Agency, Washington, D.C. 20505 (703) 482-1100, www.cia.gov; *The World Factbook.*

Food and Agricultural Organization of the United Nations (FAO), Via delle Terme di Caracalla, 00100 Rome, Italy (Telephone Number in U.S. (202) 653-2400); *Production Yearbook.*

SAINT PIERRE AND MIQUELON - LIBRARIES

United Nations Educational, Scientific and Cultural Organization (UNESCO), 7 Place de Fontenoy, F-75700 Paris, France (Telephone Number in U.S. (212) 963-5981); *Statistical Yearbook.*

SAINT PIERRE AND MIQUELON - LIFE EXPECTANCY

Central Intelligence Agency, Washington, D.C. 20505 (703) 482-1100, www.cia.gov; *The World Factbook.*

SAINT PIERRE AND MIQUELON - LIVESTOCK AND POULTRY

Food and Agricultural Organization of the United Nations (FAO), Via delle Terme di Caracalla, 00100 Rome, Italy (Telephone Number in U.S. (202) 653-2400); *Production Yearbook;* and *The State of Food and Agriculture.*

St. Martin's Press, Inc., 175 Fifth Avenue, New York, New York 10010 (800) 221-7945; *The Statesman's Year-Book.*

United Nations Conference on Trade and Development, Central Statistical Service, Palais des Nations, Geneva, Switzerland (Telephone in U.S. (800) 253-9646); *UNCTAD Commodity Yearbook.*

SAINT PIERRE AND MIQUELON - MAIL - NUMBER OF ITEMS SENT AND RECEIVED

Statistical Office of the United Nations, Publishing Service, New York, New York 10017 (800) 253-9646; *Statistical Yearbook.*

SAINT PIERRE AND MIQUELON - MARRIAGE RATES

Statistical Office of the United Nations, Publishing Service, New York, New York 10017 (800) 253-9646; *Demographic Yearbook;* and *Statistical Yearbook.*

SAINT PIERRE AND MIQUELON - MEAT PRODUCTION - See SAINT PIERRE AND MIQUELON - LIVESTOCK AND POULTRY

SAINT PIERRE AND MIQUELON - MERCHANT SHIPPING

Europa Publications Limited, 18 Bedford Square, London, WC1B 3JN, England; *The Europa World Year Book.*

St. Martin's Press, Inc., 175 Fifth Avenue, New York, New York 10010 (800) 221-7945; *The Statesman's Year-Book.*

Statistical Office of the United Nations, Publishing Service, New York, New York 10017 (800) 253-9646; *Statistical Yearbook.*

SAINT PIERRE AND MIQUELON - MILITARY

Central Intelligence Agency,

Washington, D.C. 20505 (703) 482-1100, www.cia.gov; *The World Factbook.*

SAINT PIERRE AND MIQUELON - MINING AND MINERAL PRODUCTS

United Nations Conference on Trade and Development, Central Statistical Service, Palais des Nations, Geneva, Switzerland (Telephone in U.S. (800) 253-9646); *UNCTAD Commodity Yearbook.*

SAINT PIERRE AND MIQUELON - MONEY SUPPLY

Europa Publications Limited, 18 Bedford Square, London, WC1B 3JN, England; *The Europa World Year Book.*

SAINT PIERRE AND MIQUELON - MORTALITY

St. Martin's Press, Inc., 175 Fifth Avenue, New York, New York 10010 (800) 221-7945; *The Statesman's Year-Book.*

Statistical Office of the United Nations, Publishing Service, New York, New York 10017 (800) 253-9646; *Demographic Yearbook;* and *Statistical Yearbook.*

World Health Organization, Office of Publications, 20 Avenue Appia, CH-1211 Geneva 27, Switzerland (Telephone Number in U.S. (518) 436-9686); *World Health Statistics Annual.*

SAINT PIERRE AND MIQUELON - MOTION PICTURES

Statistical Office of the United Nations, Publishing Service, New York, New York 10017 (800) 253-9646; *Statistical Yearbook.*

SAINT PIERRE AND MIQUELON - MOTOR VEHICLES IN USE

Europa Publications Limited, 18 Bedford Square, London, WC1B 3JN, England; *The Europa World Year Book.*

SAINT PIERRE AND MIQUELON - MUSEUMS

United Nations Educational, Scientific and Cultural Organization (UNESCO), 7 Place de Fontenoy, F-75700 Paris, France (Telephone Number in U.S. (212) 963-5981); *Statistical Yearbook.*

SAINT PIERRE AND MIQUELON - NATALITY - See SAINT PIERRE AND MIQUELON - BIRTH RATE

SAINT PIERRE AND MIQUELON - NEWSPAPER PRODUCTION - See SAINT PIERRE AND MIQUELON - FORESTRY AND FOREST PRODUCTS

SAINT PIERRE AND MIQUELON - OCCUPATIONS - See SAINT PIERRE AND MIQUELON - LABOR

SAINT PIERRE AND MIQUELON - PESTICIDE USE

Food and Agricultural Organization of the United Nations (FAO) Via delle Terme di Caracalla, 00100 Rome, Italy (Telephone Number in U.S. (202) 653-2400); *The State of Food and Agriculture.*

SAINT PIERRE AND MIQUELON - PETROLEUM INDUSTRY

Food and Agricultural Organization of the United Nations (FAO) Via delle Terme di Caracalla, 00100 Rome, Italy (Telephone Number in U.S. (202) 653-2400); *The State of Food and Agriculture.*

United Nations Conference on Trade and Development, Central Statistical Service, Palais des Nations, Geneva, Switzerland (Telephone in U.S. (800) 253-9646); *UNCTAD Commodity Yearbook.*

SAINT PIERRE AND MIQUELON - POPULATION

Central Intelligence Agency, Washington, D.C. 20505 (703) 482-1100, www.cia.gov; *The World Factbook.*

Europa Publications Limited, 18 Bedford Square, London, WC1B 3JN, England; *The Europa World Year Book.*

Food and Agricultural Organization of the United Nations (FAO), Via delle Terme di Caracalla, 00100 Rome, Italy (Telephone Number in U.S. (202) 653-2400); *Production Yearbook.*

International Labour Office, I.L.O. Publications, 1828 L Street, NW, Suite 801, Washington, D.C. 20036 (301) 638-3152; *Yearbook of Labour Statistics.*

St. Martin's Press, Inc., 175 Fifth Avenue, New York, New York 10010 (800) 221-7945; *The Statesman's Year-Book.*

Statistical Office of the United Nations, Publishing Service, New York, New York 10017 (800) 253-9646; *Demographic Yearbook;* and *Statistical Yearbook.*

United Nations Educational, Scientific and Cultural Organization (UNESCO), 7 Place de Fontenoy, F-75700 Paris, France (Telephone Number in U.S. (212) 963-5981); *Statistical Yearbook.*

World Health Organization, Office of Publications, 20 Avenue Appia, CH-1211 Geneva 27, Switzerland (Telephone Number in U.S. (518) 436-9686); *World Health Statistics Annual.*

SAINT PIERRE AND MIQUELON - PRICES

Food and Agricultural Organization of the United Nations (FAO), Via delle Terme

di Caracalla, 00100 Rome, Italy (Telephone Number in U.S. (202) 653-2400); *Production Yearbook;* and *The State of Food and Agriculture.*

International Labour Office, I.L.O. Publications, 1828 L Street, NW, Suite 801, Washington, D.C. 20036 (301) 638-3152; *Yearbook of Labour Statistics.*

SAINT PIERRE AND MIQUELON - RADIO BROADCASTING - See SAINT PIERRE AND MIQUELON - BROADCASTING

SAINT PIERRE AND MIQUELON - RADIO RECEIVERS

St. Martin's Press, Inc., 175 Fifth Avenue, New York, New York 10010 (800) 221-7945; *The Statesman's Year-Book.*

SAINT PIERRE AND MIQUELON - RELIGION

Central Intelligence Agency, Washington, D.C. 20505 (703) 482-1100, www.cia.gov; *The World Factbook.*

St. Martin's Press, Inc., 175 Fifth Avenue, New York, New York 10010 (800) 221-7945; *The Statesman's Year-Book.*

SAINT PIERRE AND MIQUELON - RENT PRICES

International Labour Office, I.L.O. Publications, 1828 L Street, NW, Suite 801, Washington, D.C. 20036 (301) 638-3152; *Yearbook of Labour Statistics.*

SAINT PIERRE AND MIQUELON - SCIENCE AND TECHNOLOGY - EXPENDITURE FOR RESEARCH - See SAINT PIERRE AND MIQUELON - SCIENTISTS, TECHNICIANS AND ENGINEERS

SAINT PIERRE AND MIQUELON - SCIENTISTS, TECHNICIANS AND ENGINEERS

Statistical Office of the United Nations, Publishing Service, New York, New York 10017 (800) 253-9646; *Statistical Yearbook.*

SAINT PIERRE AND MIQUELON - STOCKS - COMMODITY - MARKET PRICE - INDEX

Food and Agricultural Organization of the United Nations (FAO) Via delle Terme di Caracalla, 00100 Rome, Italy (Telephone Number in U.S. (202) 653-2400); *The State of Food and Agriculture.*

SAINT PIERRE AND MIQUELON - TELEPHONES IN USE

American Telephone and Telegraph Company, 26 Parsippany Road, Whippany, New Jersey 07981 (800) 222-0300; *The World's Telephones.*

Central Intelligence Agency,

Washington, D.C. 20505 (703) 482-1100, www.cia.gov; *The World Factbook.*

St. Martin's Press, Inc., 175 Fifth Avenue, New York, New York 10010 (800) 221-7945; *The Statesman's Year-Book.*

SAINT PIERRE AND MIQUELON - TELEVISION BROADCASTING - See SAINT PIERRE AND MIQUELON - BROADCASTING

SAINT PIERRE AND MIQUELON - TEXTILE INDUSTRY

United Nations Conference on Trade and Development, Central Statistical Service, Palais des Nations, Geneva, Switzerland (Telephone in U.S. (800) 253-9646); *UNCTAD Commodity Yearbook.*

SAINT PIERRE AND MIQUELON - TOURISM

Europa Publications Limited, 18 Bedford Square, London, WC1B 3JN, England; *The Europa World Year Book.*

St. Martin's Press, Inc., 175 Fifth Avenue, New York, New York 10010 (800) 221-7945; *The Statesman's Year-Book.*

SAINT PIERRE AND MIQUELON - TRADE - See SAINT PIERRE AND MIQUELON - FOREIGN TRADE

SAINT PIERRE AND MIQUELON - TRANSPORTATION AND COMMUNICATIONS

Central Intelligence Agency, Washington, D.C. 20505 (703) 482-1100, www.cia.gov; *The World Factbook.*

Europa Publications Limited, 18 Bedford Square, London, WC1B 3JN, England; *The Europa World Year Book.*

St. Martin's Press, Inc., 175 Fifth Avenue, New York, New York 10010 (800) 221-7945; *The Statesman's Year-Book.*

SAINT PIERRE AND MIQUELON - UNEMPLOYMENT

Central Intelligence Agency, Washington, D.C. 20505 (703) 482-1100, www.cia.gov; *The World Factbook.*

International Labour Office, I.L.O. Publications, 1828 L Street, NW, Suite 801, Washington, D.C. 20036 (301) 638-3152; *Yearbook of Labour Statistics.*

SAINT PIERRE AND MIQUELON - VITAL STATISTICS

St. Martin's Press, Inc., 175 Fifth Avenue, New York, New York 10010 (800) 221-7945; *The Statesman's Year-Book.*

Statistical Office of the United Nations, Publishing Service, New York, New York

10017 (800) 253-9646; *Statistical Yearbook.*

World Health Organization, Office of Publications, 20 Avenue Appia, CH-1211 Geneva 27, Switzerland (Telephone Number in U.S. (518) 436-9686); *World Health Statistics Annual.*

SAINT PIERRE AND MIQUELON - WAGES

International Labour Office, I.L.O. Publications, 1828 L Street, NW, Suite 801, Washington, D.C. 20036 (301) 638-3152; *Yearbook of Labour Statistics.*

Saint Vincent and The Grenadines - National Statistical Office

Statistical Office, Ministry of Finance, Kingstown, Saint Vincent and The Grenadines.

Saint Vincent and The Grenadines - Primary Statistics Source

Statistical Office, Ministry of Finance, Kingstown, Saint Vincent and The Grenadines; *Digest of Statistics.*

SAINT VINCENT AND THE GRENADINES - AGRICULTURE

Euromonitor International, Inc., 122 South Michigan Avenue, Suite 1200, Chicago, Illinois 60603 (800) 577-EURO; *World Marketing Data and Statistics.*

Europa Publications Limited, 18 Bedford Square, London, WC1B 3JN, England; *The Europa World Year Book.*

Federal Statistical Office, Gustav-Stresemann - Ring 11, D-6200, Wiesbaden, Germany; *Saint Vincent and die Grenadinen.*

Food and Agricultural Organization of the United Nations (FAO) Via delle Terme di Caracalla, 00100 Rome, Italy (Telephone Number in U.S. (202) 653-2400); *Production Yearbook; The State of Food and Agriculture;* and *Trade Yearbook.*

St. Martin's Press, Inc., 175 Fifth Avenue, New York, New York 10010 (800) 221-7945; *The Statesman's Year-Book.*

Statistical Office of the United Nations, Publishing Service, New York, New York 10017 (800) 253-9646; *Statistical Yearbook.*

United Nations Conference on Trade and Development, Central Statistical Service, Palais des Nations, Geneva, Switzerland (Telephone in U.S. (800) 253-

9646); *UNCTAD Commodity Yearbook.*

The World Bank, 1818 H Street, NW, Washington, D.C. 20433 (202) 477-1234; *World Development Indicators.*

SAINT VINCENT AND THE GRENADINES - AIRLINE SERVICE

Europa Publications Limited, 18 Bedford Square, London, WC1B 3JN, England; *The Europa World Year Book.*

St. Martin's Press, Inc., 175 Fifth Avenue, New York, New York 10010 (800) 221-7945; *The Statesman's Year-Book.*

SAINT VINCENT AND THE GRENADINES - AIRPORTS

Central Intelligence Agency, Washington, D.C. 20505 (703) 482-1100, www.cia.gov; *The World Factbook.*

SAINT VINCENT AND THE GRENADINES - ANIMAL HEALTH

Food and Agricultural Organization of the United Nations (FAO), Via delle Terme di Caracalla, 00100, Rome, Italy (Telephone Number in U.S. (202) 653-2400); *Animal Health Yearbook.*

SAINT VINCENT AND THE GRENADINES - AREA AND DENSITY OF POPULATION

Central Intelligence Agency, Washington, D.C. 20505 (703) 482-1100, www.cia.gov; *The World Factbook.*

Euromonitor International, Inc., 122 South Michigan Avenue, Suite 1200, Chicago, Illinois 60603 (800) 577-EURO; *The World Economic Factbook.*

Europa Publications Limited, 18 Bedford Square, London, WC1B 3JN, England; *The Europa World Year Book.*

Federal Statistical Office, Gustav-Stresemann - Ring 11, D-6200, Wiesbaden, Germany; *Saint Vincent and die Grenadinen.*

Food and Agricultural Organization of the United Nations (FAO) Via delle Terme di Caracalla, 00100 Rome, Italy (Telephone Number in U.S. (202) 653-2400); *The State of Food and Agriculture.*

St. Martin's Press, Inc., 175 Fifth Avenue, New York, New York 10010 (800) 221-7945; *The Statesman's Year-Book.*

Statistical Office of the United Nations, Publishing Service, New York, New York 10017 (800) 253-9646; *Statistical Yearbook.*

United Nations Educational, Scientific and Cultural Organization (UNESCO), 7

Place de Fontenoy, F-75700 Paris, France (Telephone Number in U.S. (212) 963-5981); *Statistical Yearbook.*

SAINT VINCENT AND THE GRENADINES - BALANCE OF PAYMENTS

Europa Publications Limited, 18 Bedford Square, London, WC1B 3JN, England; *The Europa World Year Book.*

Federal Statistical Office, Gustav-Stresemann - Ring 11, D-6200, Wiesbaden, Germany; *Saint Vincent and die Grenadinen.*

United Nations Conference on Trade and Development (UNCTAD), New York, New York 10017 (800) 253-9646; *Handbook of International Trade and Development Statistics.*

The World Bank, 1818 H Street, NW, Washington, D.C. 20433 (202) 477-1234; *World Development Indicators.*

SAINT VINCENT AND THE GRENADINES - BANKING

Euromonitor International, Inc., 122 South Michigan Avenue, Suite 1200, Chicago, Illinois 60603 (800) 577-EURO; *World Marketing Data and Statistics.*

Europa Publications Limited, 18 Bedford Square, London, WC1B 3JN, England; *The Europa World Year Book.*

St. Martin's Press, Inc., 175 Fifth Avenue, New York, New York 10010 (800) 221-7945; *The Statesman's Year-Book.*

SAINT VINCENT AND THE GRENADINES - BIRTH RATES

Central Intelligence Agency, Washington, D.C. 20505 (703) 482-1100, www.cia.gov; *The World Factbook.*

Euromonitor International, Inc., 122 South Michigan Avenue, Suite 1200, Chicago, Illinois 60603 (800) 577-EURO; *The World Economic Factbook.*

Europa Publications Limited, 18 Bedford Square, London, WC1B 3JN, England; *The Europa World Year Book.*

St. Martin's Press, Inc., 175 Fifth Avenue, New York, New York 10010 (800) 221-7945; *The Statesman's Year-Book.*

Statistical Office of the United Nations, Publishing Service, New York, New York 10017 (800) 253-9646; *Demographic Yearbook;* and *Statistical Yearbook.*

The World Bank, 1818 H Street, NW, Washington, D.C. 20433 (202) 477-1234; *World Development Indicators.*

World Health Organization, Office of Publications, 20 Avenue Appia, CH-1211 Geneva 27, Switzerland (Telephone Number in U.S. (518) 436-9686); *World Health Statistics Annual.*

SAINT VINCENT AND THE GRENADINES - BROADCASTING

Billboard Limited, P.O. Box 9027, 1006 AA Amsterdam, The Netherlands (Telephone Number in U.S. (212) 764-7300); *World Radio TV Handbook.*

Central Intelligence Agency, Washington, D.C. 20505 (703) 482-1100, www.cia.gov; *The World Factbook.*

Euromonitor International, Inc., 122 South Michigan Avenue, Suite 1200, Chicago, Illinois 60603 (800) 577-EURO; *World Marketing Data and Statistics.*

St. Martin's Press, Inc., 175 Fifth Avenue, New York, New York 10010 (800) 221-7945; *The Statesman's Year-Book.*

SAINT VINCENT AND THE GRENADINES - BUDGET

Central Intelligence Agency, Washington, D.C. 20505 (703) 482-1100, www.cia.gov; *The World Factbook.*

SAINT VINCENT AND THE GRENADINES - CALORIE SUPPLY

Food and Agricultural Organization of the United Nations (FAO) Via delle Terme di Caracalla, 00100 Rome, Italy (Telephone Number in U.S. (202) 653-2400); *The State of Food and Agriculture.*

SAINT VINCENT AND THE GRENADINES - CATTLE - See SAINT VINCENT AND THE GRENADINES - LIVESTOCK AND POULTRY

SAINT VINCENT AND THE GRENADINES - CLIMATE

St. Martin's Press, Inc., 175 Fifth Avenue, New York, New York 10010 (800) 221-7945; *The Statesman's Year-Book.*

SAINT VINCENT AND THE GRENADINES - COCOA PRODUCTION - See SAINT VINCENT AND THE GRENADINES - CROPS

SAINT VINCENT AND THE GRENADINES - COMMERCE

St. Martin's Press, Inc., 175 Fifth Avenue, New York, New York 10010 (800) 221-7945; *The Statesman's Year-Book.*

SAINT VINCENT AND THE GRENADINES - COMMUNICATIONS - See SAINT VINCENT AND THE GRENADINES - TRANSPORTATION AND COMMUNICATIONS

SAINT VINCENT AND THE GRENADINES - CONSUMER PRICE INDEX

Europa Publications Limited, 18 Bedford Square, London, WC1B 3JN, England; *The Europa World Year Book.*

SAINT VINCENT AND THE GRENADINES - CONSUMER PRICES

Euromonitor International, Inc., 122 South Michigan Avenue, Suite 1200, Chicago, Illinois 60603 (800) 577-EURO; *World Marketing Data and Statistics.*

International Labour Office, I.L.O. Publications, 1828 L Street, NW, Suite 801, Washington, D.C. 20036 (301) 638-3152; *Yearbook of Labour Statistics.*

SAINT VINCENT AND THE GRENADINES - CORN PRODUCTION - See SAINT VINCENT AND THE GRENADINES - CROPS

SAINT VINCENT AND THE GRENADINES - CORPORATE TAXES - See SAINT VINCENT AND THE GRENADINES - TAXATION

SAINT VINCENT AND THE GRENADINES - CROPS

Europa Publications Limited, 18 Bedford Square, London, WC1B 3JN, England; *The Europa World Year Book.*

Food and Agricultural Organization of the United Nations (FAO) Via delle Terme di Caracalla, 00100 Rome, Italy (Telephone Number in U.S. (202) 653-2400); *The State of Food and Agriculture.*

St. Martin's Press, Inc., 175 Fifth Avenue, New York, New York 10010 (800) 221-7945; *The Statesman's Year-Book.*

Statistical Office of the United Nations, Publishing Service, New York, New York 10017 (800) 253-9646; *Statistical Yearbook.*

United Nations Conference on Trade and Development, Central Statistical Service, Palais des Nations, Geneva, Switzerland (Telephone in U.S. (800) 253-9646); *UNCTAD Commodity Yearbook.*

SAINT VINCENT AND THE GRENADINES - CUSTOMS DUTIES

St. Martin's Press, Inc., 175 Fifth Avenue, New York, New York 10010 (800) 221-7945; *The Statesman's Year-Book.*

SAINT VINCENT AND THE GRENADINES - DAIRY PRODUCTS

Europa Publications Limited, 18 Bedford Square, London, WC1B 3JN, England; *The Europa World Year Book.*

Food and Agricultural Organization of the United Nations (FAO) Via delle Terme di Caracalla, 00100 Rome, Italy (Telephone Number in U.S. (202) 653-2400); *The State of Food and Agriculture.*

St. Martin's Press, Inc., 175 Fifth Avenue, New York, New York 10010 (800) 221-7945; *The Statesman's Year-Book.*

SAINT VINCENT AND THE GRENADINES - DEATH RATES - See SAINT VINCENT AND THE GRENADINES - MORTALITY

SAINT VINCENT AND THE GRENADINES - DEMOGRAPHY

Euromonitor International, Inc., 122 South Michigan Avenue, Suite 1200, Chicago, Illinois 60603 (800) 577-EURO; *The World Economic Factbook;* and *World Marketing Data and Statistics.*

Federal Statistical Office, Gustav-Stresemann - Ring 11, D-6200, Wiesbaden, Germany; *Saint Vincent and die Grenadinen.*

Statistical Office of the United Nations, Publishing Service, New York, New York 10017 (800) 253-9646; *Human Development Report.*

SAINT VINCENT AND THE GRENADINES - DISEASES - See SAINT VINCENT AND THE GRENADINES - HEALTH

SAINT VINCENT AND THE GRENADINES - DIVORCE RATES

Statistical Office of the United Nations, Publishing Service, New York, New York 10017 (800) 253-9646; *Demographic Yearbook;* and *Statistical Yearbook.*

SAINT VINCENT AND THE GRENADINES - ECONOMY

Euromonitor International, Inc., 122 South Michigan Avenue, Suite 1200, Chicago, Illinois 60603 (800) 577-EURO; *The World Economic Factbook;* and *World Marketing Data and Statistics.*

Europa Publications Limited, 18 Bedford Square, London, WC1B 3JN, England; *The Europa World Year Book.*

Federal Statistical Office, Gustav-Stresemann - Ring 11, D-6200, Wiesbaden, Germany; *Saint Vincent and die Grenadinen.*

St. Martin's Press, Inc., 175 Fifth Avenue, New York, New York 10010 (800) 221-7945; *The Statesman's Year-Book.*

Statistical Office of the United Nations, Publishing Service, New York, New York 10017 (800) 253-9646; *World Statistics*

Pocketbook.

The World Bank, 1818 H Street, NW, Washington, D.C. 20433 (202) 477-1234; *The World Bank Atlas.*

SAINT VINCENT AND THE
GRENADINES - EDUCATION

Euromonitor International, Inc., 122 South Michigan Avenue, Suite 1200, Chicago, Illinois 60603 (800) 577-EURO; *World Marketing Data and Statistics.*

Europa Publications Limited, 18 Bedford Square, London, WC1B 3JN, England; *The Europa World Year Book.*

Federal Statistical Office, Gustav-Stresemann - Ring 11, D-6200, Wiesbaden, Germany; *Saint Vincent and die Grenadinen.*

St. Martin's Press, Inc., 175 Fifth Avenue, New York, New York 10010 (800) 221-7945; *The Statesman's Year-Book.*

Statistical Office of the United Nations, Publishing Service, New York, New York 10017 (800) 253-9646; *Human Development Report.*

United Nations Educational, Scientific and Cultural Organization (UNESCO), 7 Place de Fontenoy, F-75700 Paris, France (Telephone Number in U.S. (212) 963-5981); *Statistical Yearbook.*

The World Bank, 1818 H Street, NW, Washington, D.C. 20433 (202) 477-1234; *World Development Indicators.*

SAINT VINCENT AND THE
GRENADINES - EGG PRODUCTION AND
CONSUMPTION - See SAINT VINCENT AND
THE GRENADINES - DAIRY PRODUCTS

SAINT VINCENT AND THE
GRENADINES - ELECTRICITY

Central Intelligence Agency, Washington, D.C. 20505 (703) 482-1100, www.cia.gov; *The World Factbook.*

St. Martin's Press, Inc., 175 Fifth Avenue, New York, New York 10010 (800) 221-7945; *The Statesman's Year-Book.*

Statistical Office of the United Nations, Publishing Service, New York, New York 10017 (800) 253-9646; *Human Development Report.*

SAINT VINCENT AND THE
GRENADINES - EMPLOYMENT

Federal Statistical Office, Gustav-Stresemann - Ring 11, D-6200, Wiesbaden, Germany; *Saint Vincent and die Grenadinen.*

International Labour Office, I.L.O. Publications, 1828 L Street, NW, Suite 801, Washington, D.C. 20036 (301) 638-3152; *Yearbook of Labour Statistics.*

SAINT VINCENT AND THE
GRENADINES - ENERGY

Euromonitor International, Inc., 122 South Michigan Avenue, Suite 1200, Chicago, Illinois 60603 (800) 577-EURO; *The World Economic Factbook;* and *World Marketing Data and Statistics.*

Food and Agricultural Organization of the United Nations (FAO) Via delle Terme di Caracalla, 00100 Rome, Italy (Telephone Number in U.S. (202) 653-2400); *The State of Food and Agriculture.*

St. Martin's Press, Inc., 175 Fifth Avenue, New York, New York 10010 (800) 221-7945; *The Statesman's Year-Book.*

Statistical Office of the United Nations, Publishing Service, New York, New York 10017 (800) 253-9646; *Energy Statistics Yearbook;* and *Statistical Yearbook.*

Statistical Office of the United Nations, Publishing Service, New York, New York 10017 (800) 253-9646; *Human Development Report;* and *World Statistics Pocketbook.*

The World Bank, 1818 H Street, NW, Washington, D.C. 20433 (202) 477-1234; *The World Bank Atlas.*

SAINT VINCENT AND THE
GRENADINES - ENVIRONMENT

Statistical Office of the United Nations, Publishing Service, New York, New York 10017 (800) 253-9646; *World Statistics Pocketbook.*

SAINT VINCENT AND THE
GRENADINES - EXCHANGE RATES

Central Intelligence Agency, Washington, D.C. 20505 (703) 482-1100, www.cia.gov; *The World Factbook.*

Euromonitor International, Inc., 122 South Michigan Avenue, Suite 1200, Chicago, Illinois 60603 (800) 577-EURO; *The World Economic Factbook.*

Europa Publications Limited, 18 Bedford Square, London, WC1B 3JN, England; *The Europa World Year Book.*

Statistical Office of the United Nations, Publishing Service, New York, New York 10017 (800) 253-9646; *World Statistics Pocketbook.*

SAINT VINCENT AND THE
GRENADINES - EXPORTS

Central Intelligence Agency, Washington, D.C. 20505 (703) 482-1100, www.cia.gov; *The World Factbook.*

Euromonitor International, Inc., 122 South Michigan Avenue, Suite 1200, Chicago, Illinois 60603 (800) 577-EURO; *The World Economic Factbook.*

Europa Publications Limited, 18 Bedford Square, London, WC1B 3JN, England; *The Europa World Year Book.*

Food and Agricultural Organization of the United Nations (FAO) Via delle Terme di Caracalla, 00100 Rome, Italy (Telephone Number in U.S. (202) 653-2400); *The State of Food and Agriculture.*

St. Martin's Press, Inc., 175 Fifth Avenue, New York, New York 10010 (800) 221-7945; *The Statesman's Year-Book.*

United Nations Conference on Trade and Development (UNCTAD), New York, New York 10017 (800) 253-9646; *Handbook of International Trade and Development Statistics.*

The World Bank, 1818 H Street, NW, Washington, D.C. 20433 (202) 477-1234; *World Development Indicators.*

SAINT VINCENT AND THE
GRENADINES - EXTERNAL INDEBTEDNESS

The World Bank, 1818 H Street, NW, Washington, D.C. 20433 (202) 477-1234; *World Development Indicators.*

SAINT VINCENT AND THE
GRENADINES - EXTERNAL TRADE

Euromonitor International, Inc., 122 South Michigan Avenue, Suite 1200, Chicago, Illinois 60603 (800) 577-EURO; *World Marketing Data and Statistics.*

Food and Agricultural Organization of the United Nations (FAO) Via delle Terme di Caracalla, 00100 Rome, Italy (Telephone Number in U.S. (202) 653-2400); *The State of Food and Agriculture;* and *Trade Yearbook.*

Statistical Office of the United Nations, Publishing Service, New York, New York 10017 (800) 253-9646; *Statistical Yearbook.*

SAINT VINCENT AND THE
GRENADINES - FARM CROPS - See SAINT
VINCENT AND THE GRENADINES - CROPS

SAINT VINCENT AND THE
GRENADINES - FERTILITY RATES

Central Intelligence Agency, Washington, D.C. 20505 (703) 482-1100, www.cia.gov; *The World Factbook.*

Statistical Office of the United Nations, Publishing Service, New York, New York 10017 (800) 253-9646; *Human Development Report.*

The World Bank, 1818 H Street, NW, Washington, D.C. 20433 (202) 477-1234; *The World Bank Atlas; and World Development Indicators.*

SAINT VINCENT AND THE GRENADINES - FERTILIZER

Food and Agricultural Organization of the United Nations (FAO) Via delle Terme di Caracalla, 00100 Rome, Italy (Telephone Number in U.S. (202) 653-2400); *The State of Food and Agriculture.*

Statistical Office of the United Nations, Publishing Service, New York, New York 10017 (800) 253-9646; *Statistical Yearbook.*

SAINT VINCENT AND THE GRENADINES - FETAL MORTALITY - See SAINT VINCENT AND THE GRENADINES - MORTALITY

SAINT VINCENT AND THE GRENADINES - FINANCE

Europa Publications Limited, 18 Bedford Square, London, WC1B 3JN, England; *The Europa World Year Book.*

Federal Statistical Office, Gustav-Stresemann - Ring 11, D-6200, Wiesbaden, Germany; *Saint Vincent and die Grenadinen.*

St. Martin's Press, Inc., 175 Fifth Avenue, New York, New York 10010 (800) 221-7945; *The Statesman's Year-Book.*

SAINT VINCENT AND THE GRENADINES - FISHERIES

Europa Publications Limited, 18 Bedford Square, London, WC1B 3JN, England; *The Europa World Year Book.*

Federal Statistical Office, Gustav-Stresemann - Ring 11, D-6200, Wiesbaden, Germany; *Saint Vincent and die Grenadinen.*

Food and Agricultural Organization of the United Nations (FAO) Via delle Terme di Caracalla, 00100 Rome, Italy (Telephone Number in U.S. (202) 653-2400); *The State of Food and Agriculture; and Yearbook of Fishery Statistics.*

United Nations Conference on Trade and Development, Central Statistical Service, Palais des Nations, Geneva, Switzerland (Telephone in U.S. (800) 253-9646); *UNCTAD Commodity Yearbook.*

SAINT VINCENT AND THE GRENADINES - FOOD

Food and Agricultural Organization of the United Nations (FAO), Via delle Terme di Caracalla, 00100 Rome, Italy (Telephone Number in U.S. (202) 653-2400); *Production Yearbook;* and *The State of Food and Agriculture.*

Statistical Office of the United Nations, Publishing Service, New York, New York 10017 (800) 253-9646; *Human Development Report.*

United Nations Conference on Trade and Development, Central Statistical Service, Palais des Nations, Geneva, Switzerland (Telephone in U.S. (800) 253-9646); *UNCTAD Commodity Yearbook.*

SAINT VINCENT AND THE GRENADINES - FOREIGN TRADE

Euromonitor International, Inc., 122 South Michigan Avenue, Suite 1200, Chicago, Illinois 60603 (800) 577-EURO; *The World Economic Factbook.*

Europa Publications Limited, 18 Bedford Square, London, WC1B 3JN, England; *The Europa World Year Book.*

Federal Statistical Office, Gustav-Stresemann - Ring 11, D-6200, Wiesbaden, Germany; *Saint Vincent and die Grenadinen.*

Food and Agricultural Organization of the United Nations (FAO) Via delle Terme di Caracalla, 00100 Rome, Italy (Telephone Number in U.S. (202) 653-2400); *The State of Food and Agriculture.*

St. Martin's Press, Inc., 175 Fifth Avenue, New York, New York 10010 (800) 221-7945; *The Statesman's Year-Book.*

Statistical Office of the United Nations, Publishing Service, New York, New York 10017 (800) 253-9646; *International Trade Statistics Yearbook;* and *Statistical Yearbook.*

United Nations Conference on Trade and Development, Central Statistical Service, Palais des Nations, Geneva, Switzerland (Telephone in U.S. (800) 253-9646); *UNCTAD Commodity Yearbook.*

The World Bank, 1818 H Street, NW, Washington, D.C. 20433 (202) 477-1234; *World Development Indicators.*

SAINT VINCENT AND THE GRENADINES - FORESTRY AND FOREST PRODUCTS

Federal Statistical Office, Gustav-Stresemann - Ring 11, D-6200, Wiesbaden, Germany; *Saint Vincent and die Grenadinen.*

Food and Agricultural Organization of

the United Nations (FAO) Via delle Terme di Caracalla, 00100 Rome, Italy (Telephone Number in U.S. (202) 653-2400); *The State of Food and Agriculture.*

Statistical Office of the United Nations, Publishing Service, New York, New York 10017 (800) 253-9646; *Statistical Yearbook.*

United Nations Conference on Trade and Development, Central Statistical Service, Palais des Nations, Geneva, Switzerland (Telephone in U.S. (800) 253-9646); *UNCTAD Commodity Yearbook.*

SAINT VINCENT AND THE GRENADINES - GENERAL MORTALITY - See SAINT VINCENT AND THE GRENADINES - MORTALITY

SAINT VINCENT AND THE GRENADINES - GOLD HOLDINGS

The World Bank, 1818 H Street, NW, Washington, D.C. 20433 (202) 477-1234; *World Development Indicators.*

SAINT VINCENT AND THE GRENADINES - GOVERNMENT

Central Intelligence Agency, Washington, D.C. 20505 (703) 482-1100, www.cia.gov; *The World Factbook.*

Europa Publications Limited, 18 Bedford Square, London, WC1B 3JN, England; *The Europa World Year Book.*

St. Martin's Press, Inc., 175 Fifth Avenue, New York, New York 10010 (800) 221-7945; *The Statesman's Year-Book.*

Statistical Office of the United Nations, Publishing Service, New York, New York 10017 (800) 253-9646; *National Accounts Statistics.*

The World Bank, 1818 H Street, NW, Washington, D.C. 20433 (202) 477-1234; *World Development Indicators.*

SAINT VINCENT AND THE GRENADINES - GRAIN PRODUCTION - See SAINT VINCENT AND THE GRENADINES - CROPS

SAINT VINCENT AND THE GRENADINES - GROSS DOMESTIC PRODUCT

Euromonitor International, Inc., 122 South Michigan Avenue, Suite 1200, Chicago, Illinois 60603 (800) 577-EURO; *The World Economic Factbook.*

Europa Publications Limited, 18 Bedford Square, London, WC1B 3JN, England; *The Europa World Year Book.*

Statistical Office of the United Nations, Publishing Service, New York, New York

10017 (800) 253-9646; *Human Development Report; National Accounts Statistics;* and *Statistical Yearbook.*

The World Bank, 1818 H Street, NW, Washington, D.C. 20433 (202) 477-1234; *World Development Indicators.*

SAINT VINCENT AND THE GRENADINES - GROSS NATIONAL PRODUCT

St. Martin's Press, Inc., 175 Fifth Avenue, New York, New York 10010 (800) 221-7945; *The Statesman's Year-Book.*

The World Bank, 1818 H Street, NW, Washington, D.C. 20433 (202) 477-1234; *The World Bank Atlas;* and *World Development Indicators.*

SAINT VINCENT AND THE GRENADINES - GROUNDNUT PRODUCTION - See SAINT VINCENT AND THE GRENADINES - CROPS

SAINT VINCENT AND THE GRENADINES - HEALTH

Euromonitor International, Inc., 122 South Michigan Avenue, Suite 1200, Chicago, Illinois 60603 (800) 577-EURO; *World Marketing Data and Statistics.*

Federal Statistical Office, Gustav-Stresemann - Ring 11, D-6200, Wiesbaden, Germany; *Saint Vincent and die Grenadinen.*

St. Martin's Press, Inc., 175 Fifth Avenue, New York, New York 10010 (800) 221-7945; *The Statesman's Year-Book.*

Statistical Office of the United Nations, Publishing Service, New York, New York 10017 (800) 253-9646; *Human Development Report;* and *Statistical Yearbook.*

World Health Organization, Office of Publications, 20 Avenue Appia, CH-1211 Geneva 27, Switzerland (Telephone Number in U.S. (518) 436-9686); *World Health Statistics Annual.*

SAINT VINCENT AND THE GRENADINES - HIGHWAYS

Central Intelligence Agency, Washington, D.C. 20505 (703) 482-1100, www.cia.gov; *The World Factbook.*

St. Martin's Press, Inc., 175 Fifth Avenue, New York, New York 10010 (800) 221-7945; *The Statesman's Year-Book.*

SAINT VINCENT AND THE GRENADINES - HOURS OF WORK - See SAINT VINCENT AND THE GRENADINES - EMPLOYMENT

SAINT VINCENT AND THE GRENADINES - HOUSING AND HOUSING UNITS

Euromonitor International, Inc., 122 South Michigan Avenue, Suite 1200, Chicago, Illinois 60603 (800) 577-EURO; *World Marketing Data and Statistics.*

SAINT VINCENT AND THE GRENADINES - ILLITERATE POPULATION

Central Intelligence Agency, Washington, D.C. 20505 (703) 482-1100, www.cia.gov; *The World Factbook.*

Euromonitor International, Inc., 122 South Michigan Avenue, Suite 1200, Chicago, Illinois 60603 (800) 577-EURO; *The World Economic Factbook.*

Statistical Office of the United Nations, Publishing Service, New York, New York 10017 (800) 253-9646; *Human Development Report.*

United Nations Educational, Scientific and Cultural Organization (UNESCO), 7 Place de Fontenoy, F-75700 Paris, France (Telephone Number in U.S. (212) 963-5981); *Statistical Yearbook.*

SAINT VINCENT AND THE GRENADINES - IMPORTS

Central Intelligence Agency, Washington, D.C. 20505 (703) 482-1100, www.cia.gov; *The World Factbook.*

Euromonitor International, Inc., 122 South Michigan Avenue, Suite 1200, Chicago, Illinois 60603 (800) 577-EURO; *The World Economic Factbook.*

Europa Publications Limited, 18 Bedford Square, London, WC1B 3JN, England; *The Europa World Year Book.*

Food and Agricultural Organization of the United Nations (FAO) Via delle Terme di Caracalla, 00100 Rome, Italy (Telephone Number in U.S. (202) 653-2400); *The State of Food and Agriculture.*

St. Martin's Press, Inc., 175 Fifth Avenue, New York, New York 10010 (800) 221-7945; *The Statesman's Year-Book.*

United Nations Conference on Trade and Development (UNCTAD), New York, New York 10017 (800) 253-9646; *Handbook of International Trade and Development Statistics.*

The World Bank, 1818 H Street, NW, Washington, D.C. 20433 (202) 477-1234; *World Development Indicators.*

SAINT VINCENT AND THE GRENADINES - INDUSTRY

Central Intelligence Agency,

Washington, D.C. 20505 (703) 482-1100, www.cia.gov; *The World Factbook.*

Euromonitor International, Inc., 122 South Michigan Avenue, Suite 1200, Chicago, Illinois 60603 (800) 577-EURO; *The World Economic Factbook;* and *World Marketing Data and Statistics.*

Europa Publications Limited, 18 Bedford Square, London, WC1B 3JN, England; *The Europa World Year Book.*

Federal Statistical Office, Gustav-Stresemann - Ring 11, D-6200, Wiesbaden, Germany; *Saint Vincent and die Grenadinen.*

International Labour Office, I.L.O. Publications, 1828 L Street, NW, Suite 801, Washington, D.C. 20036 (301) 638-3152; *Yearbook of Labour Statistics.*

St. Martin's Press, Inc., 175 Fifth Avenue, New York, New York 10010 (800) 221-7945; *The Statesman's Year-Book.*

The World Bank, 1818 H Street, NW, Washington, D.C. 20433 (202) 477-1234; *World Development Indicators.*

SAINT VINCENT AND THE GRENADINES - INFANT AND MATERNAL MORTALITY - See SAINT VINCENT AND THE GRENADINES - MORTALITY

SAINT VINCENT AND THE GRENADINES - INTERNATIONAL RESERVES EXCLUDING GOLD

The World Bank, 1818 H Street, NW, Washington, D.C. 20433 (202) 477-1234; *World Development Indicators.*

SAINT VINCENT AND THE GRENADINES - LABOR

Central Intelligence Agency, Washington, D.C. 20505 (703) 482-1100, www.cia.gov; *The World Factbook.*

Euromonitor International, Inc., 122 South Michigan Avenue, Suite 1200, Chicago, Illinois 60603 (800) 577-EURO; *World Marketing Data and Statistics.*

Europa Publications Limited, 18 Bedford Square, London, WC1B 3JN, England; *The Europa World Year Book.*

Food and Agricultural Organization of the United Nations (FAO) Via delle Terme di Caracalla, 00100 Rome, Italy (Telephone Number in U.S. (202) 653-2400); *The State of Food and Agriculture.*

International Labour Office, I.L.O. Publications, 1828 L Street, NW, Suite 801, Washington, D.C. 20036 (301) 638-3152; *Yearbook of Labour Statistics.*

St. Martin's Press, Inc., 175 Fifth Avenue, New York, New York 10010 (800) 221-7945; *The Statesman's Year-Book.*

Statistical Office of the United Nations, Publishing Service, New York, New York 10017 (800) 253-9646; *Human Development Report.*

The World Bank, 1818 H Street, NW, Washington, D.C. 20433 (202) 477-1234; *The World Bank Atlas;* and *World Development Indicators.*

SAINT VINCENT AND THE GRENADINES - LAND USE

Central Intelligence Agency, Washington, D.C. 20505 (703) 482-1100, www.cia.gov; *The World Factbook.*

Food and Agricultural Organization of the United Nations (FAO), Via delle Terme di Caracalla, 00100 Rome, Italy (Telephone Number in U.S. (202) 653-2400); *Production Yearbook.*

SAINT VINCENT AND THE GRENADINES - LIBRARIES

United Nations Educational, Scientific and Cultural Organization (UNESCO), 7 Place de Fontenoy, F-75700 Paris, France (Telephone Number in U.S. (212) 963-5981); *Statistical Yearbook.*

SAINT VINCENT AND THE GRENADINES - LIFE EXPECTANCY

Central Intelligence Agency, Washington, D.C. 20505 (703) 482-1100, www.cia.gov; *The World Factbook.*

Euromonitor International, Inc., 122 South Michigan Avenue, Suite 1200, Chicago, Illinois 60603 (800) 577-EURO; *The World Economic Factbook.*

Statistical Office of the United Nations, Publishing Service, New York, New York 10017 (800) 253-9646; *Human Development Report;* and *World Statistics Pocketbook.*

The World Bank, 1818 H Street, NW, Washington, D.C. 20433 (202) 477-1234; *The World Bank Atlas.*

SAINT VINCENT AND THE GRENADINES - LITERACY RATE

Euromonitor International, Inc., 122 South Michigan Avenue, Suite 1200, Chicago, Illinois 60603 (800) 577-EURO; *World Marketing Data and Statistics.*

SAINT VINCENT AND THE GRENADINES - LIVESTOCK AND POULTRY

Europa Publications Limited, 18 Bedford Square, London, WC1B 3JN,

England; *The Europa World Year Book.*

Food and Agricultural Organization of the United Nations (FAO), Via delle Terme di Caracalla, 00100 Rome, Italy (Telephone Number in U.S. (202) 653-2400); *Production Yearbook;* and *The State of Food and Agriculture.*

St. Martin's Press, Inc., 175 Fifth Avenue, New York, New York 10010 (800) 221-7945; *The Statesman's Year-Book.*

Statistical Office of the United Nations, Publishing Service, New York, New York 10017 (800) 253-9646; *Statistical Yearbook.*

United Nations Conference on Trade and Development, Central Statistical Service, Palais des Nations, Geneva, Switzerland (Telephone in U.S. (800) 253-9646); *UNCTAD Commodity Yearbook.*

SAINT VINCENT AND THE GRENADINES - MANUFACTURING

The World Bank, 1818 H Street, NW, Washington, D.C. 20433 (202) 477-1234; *World Development Indicators.*

SAINT VINCENT AND THE GRENADINES - MARRIAGE RATES

Statistical Office of the United Nations, Publishing Service, New York, New York 10017 (800) 253-9646; *Demographic Yearbook;* and *Statistical Yearbook.*

SAINT VINCENT AND THE GRENADINES - MEAT PRODUCTION - See SAINT VINCENT AND THE GRENADINES - LIVESTOCK AND POULTRY

SAINT VINCENT AND THE GRENADINES - MERCHANT SHIPPING

Europa Publications Limited, 18 Bedford Square, London, WC1B 3JN, England; *The Europa World Year Book.*

St. Martin's Press, Inc., 175 Fifth Avenue, New York, New York 10010 (800) 221-7945; *The Statesman's Year-Book.*

Statistical Office of the United Nations, Publishing Service, New York, New York 10017 (800) 253-9646; *Statistical Yearbook.*

SAINT VINCENT AND THE GRENADINES - MILITARY

Central Intelligence Agency, Washington, D.C. 20505 (703) 482-1100, www.cia.gov; *The World Factbook.*

Euromonitor International, Inc., 122 South Michigan Avenue, Suite 1200, Chicago, Illinois 60603 (800) 577-EURO; *World Marketing Data and Statistics.*

Statistical Office of the United Nations,

Publishing Service, New York, New York 10017 (800) 253-9646; *Human Development Report.*

SAINT VINCENT AND THE GRENADINES - MINING AND MINERAL PRODUCTS

United Nations Conference on Trade and Development, Central Statistical Service, Palais des Nations, Geneva, Switzerland (Telephone in U.S. (800) 253-9646); *UNCTAD Commodity Yearbook.*

SAINT VINCENT AND THE GRENADINES - MONEY SUPPLY

Europa Publications Limited, 18 Bedford Square, London, WC1B 3JN, England; *The Europa World Year Book.*

Federal Statistical Office, Gustav-Stresemann - Ring 11, D-6200, Wiesbaden, Germany; *Saint Vincent and die Grenadinen.*

The World Bank, 1818 H Street, NW, Washington, D.C. 20433 (202) 477-1234; *World Development Indicators.*

SAINT VINCENT AND THE GRENADINES - MORTALITY

Central Intelligence Agency, Washington, D.C. 20505 (703) 482-1100, www.cia.gov; *The World Factbook.*

Euromonitor International, Inc., 122 South Michigan Avenue, Suite 1200, Chicago, Illinois 60603 (800) 577-EURO; *The World Economic Factbook.*

St. Martin's Press, Inc., 175 Fifth Avenue, New York, New York 10010 (800) 221-7945; *The Statesman's Year-Book.*

Statistical Office of the United Nations, Publishing Service, New York, New York 10017 (800) 253-9646; *Demographic Yearbook; Human Development Report; Statistical Yearbook;* and *World Statistics Pocketbook.*

The World Bank, 1818 H Street, NW, Washington, D.C. 20433 (202) 477-1234; *The World Bank Atlas;* and *World Development Indicators.*

World Health Organization, Office of Publications, 20 Avenue Appia, CH-1211 Geneva 27, Switzerland (Telephone Number in U.S. (518) 436-9686); *World Health Statistics Annual.*

SAINT VINCENT AND THE GRENADINES - MOTION PICTURES

St. Martin's Press, Inc., 175 Fifth Avenue, New York, New York 10010 (800) 221-7945; *The Statesman's Year-Book.*

Statistical Office of the United Nations, Publishing Service, New York, New York 10017 (800) 253-9646; *Statistical Yearbook.*

SAINT VINCENT AND THE GRENADINES - MOTOR VEHICLES IN USE

Europa Publications Limited, 18 Bedford Square, London, WC1B 3JN, England; *The Europa World Year Book.*

Statistical Office of the United Nations, Publishing Service, New York, New York 10017 (800) 253-9646; *Statistical Yearbook.*

SAINT VINCENT AND THE GRENADINES - NATALITY - See SAINT VINCENT AND THE GRENADINES - BIRTH RATE

SAINT VINCENT AND THE GRENADINES - NATIONAL ACCOUNTS

Federal Statistical Office, Gustav-Stresemann - Ring 11, D-6200, Wiesbaden, Germany; *Saint Vincent and die Grenadinen.*

Statistical Office of the United Nations, Publishing Service, New York, New York 10017 (800) 253-9646; *National Accounts Statistics;* and *Statistical Yearbook.*

SAINT VINCENT AND THE GRENADINES - NATIONAL INCOME

Statistical Office of the United Nations, Publishing Service, New York, New York 10017 (800) 253-9646; *National Accounts Statistics;* and *Statistical Yearbook.*

SAINT VINCENT AND THE GRENADINES - NEWSPAPER PRODUCTION - See SAINT VINCENT AND THE GRENADINES - FORESTRY AND FOREST PRODUCTS

SAINT VINCENT AND THE GRENADINES - OCCUPATIONS - See SAINT VINCENT AND THE GRENADINES - LABOR

SAINT VINCENT AND THE GRENADINES - PESTICIDE USE

Food and Agricultural Organization of the United Nations (FAO) Via delle Terme di Caracalla, 00100 Rome, Italy (Telephone Number in U.S. (202) 653-2400); *The State of Food and Agriculture.*

SAINT VINCENT AND THE GRENADINES - PETROLEUM INDUSTRY

Food and Agricultural Organization of the United Nations (FAO) Via delle Terme di Caracalla, 00100 Rome, Italy (Telephone Number in U.S. (202) 653-2400); *The State of Food and Agriculture.*

United Nations Conference on Trade and Development, Central Statistical Service, Palais des Nations, Geneva, Switzerland (Telephone in U.S. (800) 253-

9646); *UNCTAD Commodity Yearbook.*

SAINT VINCENT AND THE GRENADINES - PIGS - See SAINT VINCENT AND THE GRENADINES - LIVESTOCK AND POULTRY

SAINT VINCENT AND THE GRENADINES - POPULATION

Central Intelligence Agency, Washington, D.C. 20505 (703) 482-1100, www.cia.gov; *The World Factbook.*

Euromonitor International, Inc., 122 South Michigan Avenue, Suite 1200, Chicago, Illinois 60603 (800) 577-EURO; *The World Economic Factbook.*

Europa Publications Limited, 18 Bedford Square, London, WC1B 3JN, England; *The Europa World Year Book.*

Federal Statistical Office, Gustav-Stresemann - Ring 11, D-6200, Wiesbaden, Germany; *Saint Vincent and die Grenadinen.*

Food and Agricultural Organization of the United Nations (FAO), Via delle Terme di Caracalla, 00100 Rome, Italy (Telephone Number in U.S. (202) 653-2400); *Production Yearbook.*

International Labour Office, I.L.O. Publications, 1828 L Street, NW, Suite 801, Washington, D.C. 20036 (301) 638-3152; *Yearbook of Labour Statistics.*

St. Martin's Press, Inc., 175 Fifth Avenue, New York, New York 10010 (800) 221-7945; *The Statesman's Year-Book.*

Statistical Office of the United Nations, Publishing Service, New York, New York 10017 (800) 253-9646; *Demographic Yearbook; Human Development Report; Statistical Yearbook;* and *World Statistics Pocketbook.*

United Nations Educational, Scientific and Cultural Organization (UNESCO), 7 Place de Fontenoy, F-75700 Paris, France (Telephone Number in U.S. (212) 963-5981); *Statistical Yearbook.*

The World Bank, 1818 H Street, NW, Washington, D.C. 20433 (202) 477-1234; *The World Bank Atlas.*

World Health Organization, Office of Publications, 20 Avenue Appia, CH-1211 Geneva 27, Switzerland (Telephone Number in U.S. (518) 436-9686); *World Health Statistics Annual.*

SAINT VINCENT AND THE GRENADINES - POST OFFICES

St. Martin's Press, Inc., 175 Fifth Avenue, New York, New York 10010 (800)

221-7945; *The Statesman's Year-Book.*

SAINT VINCENT AND THE GRENADINES - PRICES

Federal Statistical Office, Gustav-Stresemann - Ring 11, D-6200, Wiesbaden, Germany; *Saint Vincent and die Grenadinen.*

Food and Agricultural Organization of the United Nations (FAO), Via delle Terme di Caracalla, 00100 Rome, Italy (Telephone Number in U.S. (202) 653-2400); *Production Yearbook;* and *The State of Food and Agriculture.*

International Labour Office, I.L.O. Publications, 1828 L Street, NW, Suite 801, Washington, D.C. 20036 (301) 638-3152; *Yearbook of Labour Statistics.*

SAINT VINCENT AND THE GRENADINES - RADIO RECEIVERS

St. Martin's Press, Inc., 175 Fifth Avenue, New York, New York 10010 (800) 221-7945; *The Statesman's Year-Book.*

SAINT VINCENT AND THE GRENADINES - RELIGION

Central Intelligence Agency, Washington, D.C. 20505 (703) 482-1100, www.cia.gov; *The World Factbook.*

St. Martin's Press, Inc., 175 Fifth Avenue, New York, New York 10010 (800) 221-7945; *The Statesman's Year-Book.*

SAINT VINCENT AND THE GRENADINES - RETAIL TRADE

Euromonitor International, Inc., 122 South Michigan Avenue, Suite 1200, Chicago, Illinois 60603 (800) 577-EURO; *World Marketing Data and Statistics.*

SAINT VINCENT AND THE GRENADINES - SHEEP - See SAINT VINCENT AND THE GRENADINES - LIVESTOCK AND POULTRY

SAINT VINCENT AND THE GRENADINES - SOCIAL SECURITY

Statistical Office of the United Nations, Publishing Service, New York, New York 10017 (800) 253-9646; *National Accounts Statistics;* and *World Statistics Pocketbook.*

SAINT VINCENT AND THE GRENADINES - STOCKS - COMMODITY -MARKET PRICE - INDEX

Food and Agricultural Organization of the United Nations (FAO) Via delle Terme di Caracalla, 00100 Rome, Italy (Telephone Number in U.S. (202) 653-2400); *The State of Food and Agriculture.*

SAINT VINCENT AND THE GRENADINES - TAXATION

Europa Publications Limited, 18 Bedford Square, London, WC1B 3JN, England; *The Europa World Year Book.*

The World Bank, 1818 H Street, NW, Washington, D.C. 20433 (202) 477-1234; *World Development Indicators.*

SAINT VINCENT AND THE GRENADINES - TELEPHONES IN USE

American Telephone and Telegraph Company, 26 Parsippany Road, Whippany, New Jersey 07981 (800) 222-0300; *The World's Telephones.*

Central Intelligence Agency, Washington, D.C. 20505 (703) 482-1100, www.cia.gov; *The World Factbook.*

Europa Publications Limited, 18 Bedford Square, London, WC1B 3JN, England; *The Europa World Year Book.*

St. Martin's Press, Inc., 175 Fifth Avenue, New York, New York 10010 (800) 221-7945; *The Statesman's Year-Book.*

Statistical Office of the United Nations, Publishing Service, New York, New York 10017 (800) 253-9646; *Statistical Yearbook;* and *World Statistics Pocketbook.*

SAINT VINCENT AND THE GRENADINES - TEXTILE INDUSTRY

St. Martin's Press, Inc., 175 Fifth Avenue, New York, New York 10010 (800) 221-7945; *The Statesman's Year-Book.*

United Nations Conference on Trade and Development, Central Statistical Service, Palais des Nations, Geneva, Switzerland (Telephone in U.S. (800) 253-9646); *UNCTAD Commodity Yearbook.*

SAINT VINCENT AND THE GRENADINES - TOURISM

Euromonitor International, Inc., 122 South Michigan Avenue, Suite 1200, Chicago, Illinois 60603 (800) 577-EURO; *The World Economic Factbook;* and *World Marketing Data and Statistics.*

Europa Publications Limited, 18 Bedford Square, London, WC1B 3JN, England; *The Europa World Year Book.*

Federal Statistical Office, Gustav-Stresemann - Ring 11, D-6200, Wiesbaden, Germany; *Saint Vincent and die Grenadinen.*

St. Martin's Press, Inc., 175 Fifth Avenue, New York, New York 10010 (800) 221-7945; *The Statesman's Year-Book.*

World Tourism Organization, Calle Capitan Haya 42, E-28020 Madrid, Spain; *Yearbook of Tourism Statistics.*

SAINT VINCENT AND THE GRENADINES - TRACTORS IN USE

Statistical Office of the United Nations, Publishing Service, New York, New York 10017 (800) 253-9646; *Statistical Yearbook.*

SAINT VINCENT AND THE GRENADINES - TRADE - See SAINT VINCENT AND THE GRENADINES - FOREIGN TRADE

SAINT VINCENT AND THE GRENADINES - TRANSPORTATION AND COMMUNICATIONS

Central Intelligence Agency, Washington, D.C. 20505 (703) 482-1100, www.cia.gov; *The World Factbook.*

Euromonitor International, Inc., 122 South Michigan Avenue, Suite 1200, Chicago, Illinois 60603 (800) 577-EURO; *World Marketing Data and Statistics.*

Europa Publications Limited, 18 Bedford Square, London, WC1B 3JN, England; *The Europa World Year Book.*

Federal Statistical Office, Gustav-Stresemann - Ring 11, D-6200, Wiesbaden, Germany; *Saint Vincent and die Grenadinen.*

St. Martin's Press, Inc., 175 Fifth Avenue, New York, New York 10010 (800) 221-7945; *The Statesman's Year-Book.*

Statistical Office of the United Nations, Publishing Service, New York, New York 10017 (800) 253-9646; *Human Development Report.*

SAINT VINCENT AND THE GRENADINES - UNEMPLOYMENT

Central Intelligence Agency, Washington, D.C. 20505 (703) 482-1100, www.cia.gov; *The World Factbook.*

International Labour Office, I.L.O. Publications, 1828 L Street, NW, Suite 801, Washington, D.C. 20036 (301) 638-3152; *Yearbook of Labour Statistics.*

SAINT VINCENT AND THE GRENADINES - VITAL STATISTICS

St. Martin's Press, Inc., 175 Fifth Avenue, New York, New York 10010 (800) 221-7945; *The Statesman's Year-Book.*

Statistical Office of the United Nations, Publishing Service, New York, New York 10017 (800) 253-9646; *Statistical Yearbook.*

World Health Organization, Office of Publications, 20 Avenue Appia, CH-1211

Geneva 27, Switzerland (Telephone Number in U.S. (518) 436-9686); *World Health Statistics Annual.*

SAINT VINCENT AND THE GRENADINES - WAGES

Federal Statistical Office, Gustav-Stresemann - Ring 11, D-6200, Wiesbaden, Germany; *Saint Vincent and die Grenadinen.*

International Labour Office, I.L.O. Publications, 1828 L Street, NW, Suite 801, Washington, D.C. 20036 (301) 638-3152; *Yearbook of Labour Statistics.*

SAINT VINCENT AND THE GRENADINES - WEATHER - See SAINT VINCENT AND THE GRENADINES - CLIMATE

SALAD AND COOKING OILS - CONSUMPTION

U.S. Department of Agriculture, Economic Research Service, 1800 M Street, NW, Washington, D.C. 20036 (202) 694-5050, www.ers.usda.gov; *Food Consumption, Prices, and Expenditures;* and *Agricultural Outlook.*

SALARIES AND WAGES - See EARNINGS

SALES - See Individual Commodities and Industries

SALES WORKERS

U.S. Department of Labor, Bureau of Labor Statistics, Two Massachusetts Avenue, NE, Washington, D.C. 20212 (202) 691-5200, www.stats.bls.gov; *Employment and Earnings;* and unpublished data.

SALMON

U.S. Department of Commerce, National Oceanic and Atmospheric Administration, National Marine Fisheries Service, 1315 East-West Highway, Silver Spring, Maryland 20910 (301) 427-2239, www.nmfs.noaa.gov; *Fisheries of the United States.*

SALMON - CANNED

U.S. Department of Commerce, National Oceanic and Atmospheric Administration, National Marine Fisheries Service, 1315 East-West Highway, Silver Spring, Maryland 20910 (301) 427-2239, www.nmfs.noaa.gov; *Fisheries of the United States.*

SALMONELLOSIS

U.S. Department of Health and Human Services, Centers for Disease Control, 1600 Clifton Road, NE, Atlanta, Georgia 30333 (800) 311-3435, www.cdc.gov; *Summary of Notifiable Diseases, United States,*

Morbidity and Mortality Weekly Report.

SALT - PRODUCTION AND VALUE

U.S. Department of the Interior, Geological Survey, Office of Minerals Information, 12201 Sunrise Valley Drive, Reston, Virginia 22092 (703) 648-4000, www.minerals.usgs.gov; *Annual Reports; and Mineral Commodities Summaries.*

SAMOA - See AMERICAN SAMOA OR WESTERN SAMOA

SAMOAN POPULATION

U.S. Department of Commerce, Bureau of the Census, Washington, D.C. 20233 (301) 457-4100, www.census.gov; *Census of Population;* and *General Population Characteristics, United States.*

San Marino - National Statistical Office

Ufficio Statale di Statistica, Via Antonio Onofri 87, Repubblica de San Marino.

San Marino - Primary Statistics Sources

Servicio Statale di Statistica, Via G Carducci 145, Repubblica de San Marino; *Sintesi Statistica Socio-economica* (Socio-economic statistical analysis); *Bollettino di statistica* (Statistical bulletin); and *Annuario Statistico* (Statistical Yearbook).

SAN MARINO - ABORTIONS

Statistical Office of the United Nations, Publishing Service, New York, New York 10017 (800) 253-9646; *Trends in Europe and North America: The Statistical Yearbook of the Economic Commission for Europe.*

SAN MARINO - AGRICULTURE

Food and Agricultural Organization of the United Nations (FAO) Via delle Terme di Caracalla, 00100 Rome, Italy (Telephone Number in U.S. (202) 653-2400); *Production Yearbook; The State of Food and Agriculture;* and *Trade Yearbook.*

Statistical Office of the United Nations, Publishing Service, New York, New York 10017 (800) 253-9646; *Industrial Commodity Statistics Yearbook;* and *Statistical Yearbook.*

SAN MARINO - AIRLINE SERVICE

Statistical Office of the United Nations, Publishing Service, New York, New York 10017 (800) 253-9646; *Statistical Yearbook.*

SAN MARINO - AIRPORTS

Central Intelligence Agency, Washington, D.C. 20505 (703) 482-1100, www.cia.gov; *The World Factbook.*

SAN MARINO - ANIMAL HEALTH

Food and Agricultural Organization of the United Nations (FAO) Via delle Terme di Caracalla, 00100 Rome, Italy (Telephone Number in U.S. (202) 653-2400); *Animal Health Yearbook.*

SAN MARINO - AREA AND DENSITY OF POPULATION

Central Intelligence Agency, Washington, D.C. 20505 (703) 482-1100, www.cia.gov; *The World Factbook.*

Europa Publications Limited, 18 Bedford Square, London, WC1B 3JN, England; *The Europa World Year Book.*

Food and Agricultural Organization of the United Nations (FAO) Via delle Terme di Caracalla, 00100 Rome, Italy (Telephone Number in U.S. (202) 653-2400); *The State of Food and Agriculture.*

St. Martin's Press, Inc., 175 Fifth Avenue, New York, New York 10010 (800) 221-7945; *The Statesman's Year-Book.*

Statistical Office of the United Nations, Publishing Service, New York, New York 10017 (800) 253-9646; *Statistical Yearbook;* and *Trends in Europe and North America: The Statistical Yearbook of the Economic Commission for Europe.*

United Nations Educational, Scientific and Cultural Organization (UNESCO), 7 Place de Fontenoy, F-75700 Paris, France (Telephone Number in U.S. (212) 963-5981); *Statistical Yearbook.*

SAN MARINO - BEVERAGES

Statistical Office of the United Nations, Publishing Service, New York, New York 10017 (800) 253-9646; *Statistical Yearbook.*

SAN MARINO - BIRTH RATES

Central Intelligence Agency, Washington, D.C. 20505 (703) 482-1100, www.cia.gov; *The World Factbook.*

Europa Publications Limited, 18 Bedford Square, London, WC1B 3JN, England; *The Europa World Year Book.*

Statistical Office of the United Nations, Publishing Service, New York, New York 10017 (800) 253-9646; *Demographic Yearbook;* and *Statistical Yearbook.*

World Health Organization, Office of Publications, 20 Avenue Appia, CH-1211 Geneva 27, Switzerland (Telephone Number in U.S. (518) 436-9686); *World Health Statistics Annual.*

SAN MARINO - BOOK PRODUCTION

Statistical Office of the United Nations, Publishing Service, New York, New York 10017 (800) 253-9646; *Trends in Europe and North America: The Statistical Yearbook of the Economic Commission for Europe.*

United Nations Educational, Scientific and Cultural Organization (UNESCO), 7 Place de Fontenoy, F-75700 Paris, France (Telephone Number in U.S. (212) 963-5981); *Statistical Yearbook.*

SAN MARINO - BROADCASTING

Billboard Limited, P.O. Box 9027, 1006 AA Amsterdam, The Netherlands (Telephone Number in U.S. (212) 764-7300); *World Radio TV Handbook.*

Central Intelligence Agency, Washington, D.C. 20505 (703) 482-1100, www.cia.gov; *The World Factbook.*

St. Martin's Press, Inc., 175 Fifth Avenue, New York, New York 10010 (800) 221-7945; *The Statesman's Year-Book.*

Statistical Office of the United Nations, Publishing Service, New York, New York 10017 (800) 253-9646; *Trends in Europe and North America: The Statistical Yearbook of the Economic Commission for Europe.*

United Nations Educational, Scientific and Cultural Organization (UNESCO), 7 Place de Fontenoy, F-75700 Paris, France (Telephone Number in U.S. (212) 963-5981); *Statistical Yearbook.*

SAN MARINO - BUDGET

Central Intelligence Agency, Washington, D.C. 20505 (703) 482-1100, www.cia.gov; *The World Factbook.*

SAN MARINO - CALORIE SUPPLY

Food and Agricultural Organization of the United Nations (FAO) Via delle Terme di Caracalla, 00100 Rome, Italy (Telephone Number in U.S. (202) 653-2400); *The State of Food and Agriculture.*

SAN MARINO - CHEMICAL (ORGANIC) PRODUCTION - See SAN MARINO - MINING AND MINERAL PRODUCTS

SAN MARINO - COMMUNICATIONS - See SAN MARINO - TRANSPORTATION AND COMMUNICATIONS

SAN MARINO - CONSTRUCTION INDUSTRY

Statistical Office of the United Nations, Publishing Service, New York, New York 10017 (800) 253-9646; *Statistical Yearbook.*

SAN MARINO - CONSUMER PRICE INDEX

Europa Publications Limited, 18 Bedford Square, London, WC1B 3JN, England; *The Europa World Year Book.*

Statistical Office of the United Nations, Publishing Service, New York, New York 10017 (800) 253-9646; *Statistical Yearbook;* and *Trends in Europe and North America: The Statistical Yearbook of the Economic Commission for Europe.*

SAN MARINO - CORN PRODUCTION - See SAN MARINO - CROPS

SAN MARINO - CRIME

Statistical Office of the United Nations, Publishing Service, New York, New York 10017 (800) 253-9646; *Trends in Europe and North America: The Statistical Yearbook of the Economic Commission for Europe.*

SAN MARINO - CROPS

Food and Agricultural Organization of the United Nations (FAO) Via delle Terme di Caracalla, 00100 Rome, Italy (Telephone Number in U.S. (202) 653-2400); *Production Yearbook; The State of Food and Agriculture;* and *Trade Yearbook.*

Statistical Office of the United Nations, Publishing Service, New York, New York 10017 (800) 253-9646; *Industrial Commodity Statistics Yearbook;* and *Statistical Yearbook.*

SAN MARINO - DAIRY PRODUCTS

Food and Agricultural Organization of the United Nations (FAO) Via delle Terme di Caracalla, 00100 Rome, Italy (Telephone Number in U.S. (202) 653-2400); *Production Yearbook; The State of Food and Agriculture;* and *Trade Yearbook.*

Statistical Office of the United Nations, Publishing Service, New York, New York 10017 (800) 253-9646; *Industrial Commodity Statistics Yearbook;* and *Statistical Yearbook.*

SAN MARINO - DEATH RATES - See SAN MARINO - MORTALITY

SAN MARINO - DEMOGRAPHY

Statistical Office of the United Nations, Publishing Service, New York, New York 10017 (800) 253-9646; *Demographic Yearbook.*

SAN MARINO - DISEASES - See SAN MARINO - HEALTH

SAN MARINO - DIVORCE RATES

Statistical Office of the United Nations, Publishing Service, New York, New York 10017 (800) 253-9646; *Demographic Yearbook; Statistical Yearbook;* and *Trends in Europe and North America: The Statistical Yearbook of the Economic Commission for Europe.*

SAN MARINO - ECONOMY

Central Intelligence Agency, Washington, D.C. 20505 (703) 482-1100, www.cia.gov; *The World Factbook.*

Europa Publications Limited, 18 Bedford Square, London, WC1B 3JN, England; *The Europa World Year Book.*

St. Martin's Press, Inc., 175 Fifth Avenue, New York, New York 10010 (800) 221-7945; *The Statesman's Year-Book.*

Statistical Office of the United Nations, Publishing Service, New York, New York 10017 (800) 253-9646; *World Statistics Pocketbook.*

The World Bank, 1818 H Street, NW, Washington, D.C. 20433 (202) 477-1234; *The World Bank Atlas.*

SAN MARINO - EDUCATION

Europa Publications Limited, 18 Bedford Square, London, WC1B 3JN, England; *The Europa World Year Book.*

St. Martin's Press, Inc., 175 Fifth Avenue, New York, New York 10010 (800) 221-7945; *The Statesman's Year-Book.*

Statistical Office of the United Nations, Publishing Service, New York, New York 10017 (800) 253-9646; *Trends in Europe and North America: The Statistical Yearbook of the Economic Commission for Europe.*

United Nations Educational, Scientific and Cultural Organization (UNESCO), 7 Place de Fontenoy, F-75700 Paris, France (Telephone Number in U.S. (212) 963-5981); *Statistical Yearbook.*

SAN MARINO - EGG PRODUCTION AND CONSUMPTION - See SAN MARINO - DAIRY PRODUCTS

SAN MARINO - ELECTRICITY

Central Intelligence Agency, Washington, D.C. 20505 (703) 482-1100, www.cia.gov; *The World Factbook.*

Statistical Office of the United Nations, Publishing Service, New York, New York 10017 (800) 253-9646; *Energy Statistics Yearbook; Statistical Yearbook;* and *Trends in Europe and North America: The Statistical Yearbook of the Economic Commission for Europe.*

SAN MARINO - EMPLOYMENT

Statistical Office of the United Nations, Publishing Service, New York, New York 10017 (800) 253-9646; *Statistical Yearbook;* and *Trends in Europe and North America: The Statistical Yearbook of the Economic Commission for Europe.*

SAN MARINO - ENERGY

Food and Agricultural Organization of the United Nations (FAO) Via delle Terme di Caracalla, 00100 Rome, Italy (Telephone Number in U.S. (202) 653-2400); *The State of Food and Agriculture.*

Statistical Office of the United Nations, Publishing Service, New York, New York 10017 (800) 253-9646; *Energy Statistics Yearbook; Statistical Yearbook; Trends in Europe and North America: The Statistical Yearbook of the Economic Commission for Europe;* and *World Statistics Pocketbook.*

The World Bank, 1818 H Street, NW, Washington, D.C. 20433 (202) 477-1234; *The World Bank Atlas.*

SAN MARINO - ENVIRONMENT

Statistical Office of the United Nations, Publishing Service, New York, New York 10017 (800) 253-9646; *Statistical Yearbook; Trends in Europe and North America: The Statistical Yearbook of the Economic Commission for Europe;* and *World Statistics Pocketbook.*

SAN MARINO - EXCHANGE RATES

Central Intelligence Agency, Washington, D.C. 20505 (703) 482-1100, www.cia.gov; *The World Factbook.*

Europa Publications Limited, 18 Bedford Square, London, WC1B 3JN, England; *The Europa World Year Book.*

Statistical Office of the United Nations, Publishing Service, New York, New York 10017 (800) 253-9646; *Statistical Yearbook; Trends in Europe and North America: The Statistical Yearbook of the Economic Commission for Europe;* and *World Statistics Pocketbook.*

SAN MARINO - EXPORTS

Central Intelligence Agency, Washington, D.C. 20505 (703) 482-1100, www.cia.gov; *The World Factbook.*

Food and Agricultural Organization of the United Nations (FAO) Via delle Terme di Caracalla, 00100 Rome, Italy (Telephone Number in U.S. (202) 653-2400); *The State of Food and Agriculture.*

Statistical Office of the United Nations, Publishing Service, New York, New York 10017 (800) 253-9646; *International Trade Statistics Yearbook;* and *Trends in Europe and North America: The Statistical Yearbook of the Economic Commission for Europe.*

SAN MARINO - EXTERNAL TRADE

Food and Agricultural Organization of the United Nations (FAO) Via delle Terme di Caracalla, 00100 Rome, Italy (Telephone Number in U.S. (202) 653-2400); *The State of Food and Agriculture;* and *Trade Yearbook.*

Statistical Office of the United Nations, Publishing Service, New York, New York 10017 (800) 253-9646; *Statistical Yearbook.*

SAN MARINO - FARM CROPS - See SAN MARINO - CROPS

SAN MARINO - FERTILITY RATE

Central Intelligence Agency, Washington, D.C. 20505 (703) 482-1100, www.cia.gov; *The World Factbook.*

Statistical Office of the United Nations, Publishing Service, New York, New York 10017 (800) 253-9646; *Trends in Europe and North America: The Statistical Yearbook of the Economic Commission for Europe.*

The World Bank, 1818 H Street, NW, Washington, D.C. 20433 (202) 477-1234; *The World Bank Atlas.*

World Health Organization, Office of Publications, 20 Avenue Appia, CH-1211 Geneva 27, Switzerland (Telephone Number in U.S. (518) 436-9686); *World Health Statistics Annual.*

SAN MARINO - FERTILIZER

Food and Agricultural Organization of the United Nations (FAO) Via delle Terme di Caracalla, 00100 Rome, Italy (Telephone Number in U.S. (202) 653-2400); *Fertilizer Yearbook.*

Statistical Office of the United Nations, Publishing Service, New York, New York 10017 (800) 253-9646; *Industrial Commodity Statistics Yearbook;* and *Statistical Yearbook.*

SAN MARINO - FETAL MORTALITY - See SAN MARINO - MORTALITY

SAN MARINO - FINANCE

Europa Publications Limited, 18 Bedford Square, London, WC1B 3JN, England; *The Europa World Year Book.*

SAN MARINO - FISHERIES

Food and Agricultural Organization of the United Nations (FAO) Via delle Terme di Caracalla, 00100 Rome, Italy (Telephone Number in U.S. (202) 653-2400); *The State of Food and Agriculture;* and *Yearbook of Fishery Statistics.*

Statistical Office of the United Nations, Publishing Service, New York, New York 10017 (800) 253-9646; *Industrial Commodity Statistics Yearbook;* and *Statistical Yearbook.*

SAN MARINO - FOOD

Food and Agricultural Organization of the United Nations (FAO) Via delle Terme di Caracalla, 00100 Rome, Italy (Telephone Number in U.S. (202) 653-2400); *Production Yearbook; The State of Food and Agriculture;* and *Trade Yearbook.*

Statistical Office of the United Nations, Publishing Service, New York, New York 10017 (800) 253-9646; *Industrial Commodity Statistics Yearbook.*

SAN MARINO - FOREIGN TRADE

Food and Agricultural Organization of the United Nations (FAO) Via delle Terme di Caracalla, 00100 Rome, Italy (Telephone Number in U.S. (202) 653-2400); *The State of Food and Agriculture;* and *Trade Yearbook.*

Statistical Office of the United Nations, Publishing Service, New York, New York 10017 (800) 253-9646; *International Trade Statistics Yearbook;* and *Statistical Yearbook.*

SAN MARINO - FORESTRY AND FOREST PRODUCTS

Food and Agricultural Organization of the United Nations (FAO) Via delle Terme di Caracalla, 00100 Rome, Italy (Telephone Number in U.S. (202) 653-2400); *Yearbook of Forest Products.*

Statistical Office of the United Nations, Publishing Service, New York, New York 10017 (800) 253-9646; *Industrial Commodity Statistics Yearbook; Statistical Yearbook;* and *Trends in Europe and North America: The Statistical Yearbook of the Economic Commission for Europe.*

United Nations Educational, Scientific and Cultural Organization (UNESCO), 7 Place de Fontenoy, F-75700 Paris, France (Telephone Number in U.S. (212) 963-5981); *Statistical Yearbook.*

SAN MARINO - GENERAL MORTALITY - See SAN MARINO - MORTALITY

SAN MARINO - GOVERNMENT

Central Intelligence Agency, Washington, D.C. 20505 (703) 482-1100, www.cia.gov; *The World Factbook.*

Europa Publications Limited, 18

Bedford Square, London, WC1B 3JN, England; *The Europa World Year Book.*

St. Martin's Press, Inc., 175 Fifth Avenue, New York, New York 10010 (800) 221-7945; *The Statesman's Year-Book.*

Statistical Office of the United Nations, Publishing Service, New York, New York 10017 (800) 253-9646; *Statistical Yearbook.*

SAN MARINO - GRAIN PRODUCTION - See SAN MARINO - CROPS

SAN MARINO - GROSS DOMESTIC PRODUCT

Statistical Office of the United Nations, Publishing Service, New York, New York 10017 (800) 253-9646; *National Accounts Statistics; Statistical Yearbook;* and *Trends in Europe and North America: The Statistical Yearbook of the Economic Commission for Europe.*

SAN MARINO - GROSS NATIONAL PRODUCT

Statistical Office of the United Nations, Publishing Service, New York, New York 10017 (800) 253-9646; *The World Bank Atlas.*

SAN MARINO - HEALTH

St. Martin's Press, Inc., 175 Fifth Avenue, New York, New York 10010 (800) 221-7945; *The Statesman's Year-Book.*

Statistical Office of the United Nations, Publishing Service, New York, New York 10017 (800) 253-9646; *Statistical Yearbook;* and *Trends in Europe and North America: The Statistical Yearbook of the Economic Commission for Europe.*

World Health Organization, Office of Publications, 20 Avenue Appia, CH-1211 Geneva 27, Switzerland (Telephone Number in U.S. (518) 436-9686); *World Health Statistics Annual.*

SAN MARINO - HIGHWAYS

Central Intelligence Agency, Washington, D.C. 20505 (703) 482-1100, www.cia.gov; *The World Factbook.*

St. Martin's Press, Inc., 175 Fifth Avenue, New York, New York 10010 (800) 221-7945; *The Statesman's Year-Book.*

Statistical Office of the United Nations, Publishing Service, New York, New York 10017 (800) 253-9646; *Trends in Europe and North America: The Statistical Yearbook of the Economic Commission for Europe.*

SAN MARINO - HOUSING AND HOUSING UNITS

Statistical Office of the United Nations, Publishing Service, New York, New York 10017 (800) 253-9646; *Statistical Yearbook;* and *Trends in Europe and North America: The Statistical Yearbook of the Economic Commission for Europe.*

SAN MARINO - ILLITERATE POPULATION

Central Intelligence Agency, Washington, D.C. 20505 (703) 482-1100, www.cia.gov; *The World Factbook.*

United Nations Educational, Scientific and Cultural Organization (UNESCO), 7 Place de Fontenoy, F-75700 Paris, France (Telephone Number in U.S. (212) 963-5981); *Statistical Yearbook.*

SAN MARINO - IMPORTS

Central Intelligence Agency, Washington, D.C. 20505 (703) 482-1100, www.cia.gov; *The World Factbook.*

Food and Agricultural Organization of the United Nations (FAO) Via delle Terme di Caracalla, 00100 Rome, Italy (Telephone Number in U.S. (202) 653-2400); *The State of Food and Agriculture.*

Statistical Office of the United Nations, Publishing Service, New York, New York 10017 (800) 253-9646; *International Trade Statistics Yearbook;* and *Trends in Europe and North America: The Statistical Yearbook of the Economic Commission for Europe.*

SAN MARINO - INDUSTRY

Central Intelligence Agency, Washington, D.C. 20505 (703) 482-1100, www.cia.gov; *The World Factbook.*

Europa Publications Limited, 18 Bedford Square, London, WC1B 3JN, England; *The Europa World Year Book.*

Statistical Office of the United Nations, Publishing Service, New York, New York 10017 (800) 253-9646; *Industrial Commodity Statistics Yearbook; Statistical Yearbook;* and *Trends in Europe and North America: The Statistical Yearbook of the Economic Commission for Europe.*

SAN MARINO - INFANT AND MATERNAL MORTALITY - See SAN MARINO - MORTALITY

SAN MARINO - INTERNAL TRADE

Statistical Office of the United Nations, Publishing Service, New York, New York 10017 (800) 253-9646; *Statistical Yearbook.*

SAN MARINO - LABOR

Central Intelligence Agency,

Washington, D.C. 20505 (703) 482-1100, www.cia.gov; *The World Factbook.*

Europa Publications Limited, 18 Bedford Square, London, WC1B 3JN, England; *The Europa World Year Book.*

Food and Agricultural Organization of the United Nations (FAO) Via delle Terme di Caracalla, 00100 Rome, Italy (Telephone Number in U.S. (202) 653-2400); *The State of Food and Agriculture.*

Statistical Office of the United Nations, Publishing Service, New York, New York 10017 (800) 253-9646; *Statistical Yearbook.*

The World Bank, 1818 H Street, NW, Washington, D.C. 20433 (202) 477-1234; *The World Bank Atlas.*

SAN MARINO - LAND USE

Central Intelligence Agency, Washington, D.C. 20505 (703) 482-1100, www.cia.gov; *The World Factbook.*

Food and Agricultural Organization of the United Nations (FAO), Via delle Terme di Caracalla, 00100 Rome, Italy (Telephone Number in U.S. (202) 653-2400); *Production Yearbook.*

SAN MARINO - LIBRARIES

Statistical Office of the United Nations, Publishing Service, New York, New York 10017 (800) 253-9646; *Trends in Europe and North America: The Statistical Yearbook of the Economic Commission for Europe.*

United Nations Educational, Scientific and Cultural Organization (UNESCO), 7 Place de Fontenoy, F-75700 Paris, France (Telephone Number in U.S. (212) 963-5981); *Statistical Yearbook.*

SAN MARINO - LIFE EXPECTANCY

Central Intelligence Agency, Washington, D.C. 20505 (703) 482-1100, www.cia.gov; *The World Factbook.*

Statistical Office of the United Nations, Publishing Service, New York, New York 10017 (800) 253-9646; *Demographic Yearbook; Trends in Europe and North America: The Statistical Yearbook of the Economic Commission for Europe;* and *World Statistics Pocketbook.*

The World Bank, 1818 H Street, NW, Washington, D.C. 20433 (202) 477-1234; *World Development Report.*

World Health Organization, Office of Publications, 20 Avenue Appia, CH-1211 Geneva 27, Switzerland (Telephone Number in U.S. (518) 436-9686); *World Health Statistics Annual.*

SAN MARINO - LIVESTOCK AND POULTRY

Food and Agricultural Organization of the United Nations (FAO), Via delle Terme di Caracalla, 00100 Rome, Italy (Telephone Number in U.S. (202) 653-2400); *Production Yearbook; The State of Food and Agriculture;* and *Trade Yearbook.*

Statistical Office of the United Nations, Publishing Service, New York, New York 10017 (800) 253-9646; *Industrial Commodity Statistics Yearbook;* and *Statistical Yearbook.*

SAN MARINO - LIVING LEVELS - See SAN MARINO - LIFE EXPECTANCY

SAN MARINO - MACHINERY

Statistical Office of the United Nations, Publishing Service, New York, New York 10017 (800) 253-9646; *Industrial Commodity Statistics Yearbook.*

SAN MARINO - MAIL - PIECES SENT OR RECEIVED

Statistical Office of the United Nations, Publishing Service, New York, New York 10017 (800) 253-9646; *Statistical Yearbook.*

SAN MARINO - MANUFACTURING

Statistical Office of the United Nations, Publishing Service, New York, New York 10017 (800) 253-9646; *Industrial Commodity Statistics Yearbook;* and *Statistical Yearbook.*

SAN MARINO - MARRIAGE RATES

Statistical Office of the United Nations, Publishing Service, New York, New York 10017 (800) 253-9646; *Demographic Yearbook; Statistical Yearbook;* and *Trends in Europe and North America: The Statistical Yearbook of the Economic Commission for Europe.*

SAN MARINO - MEAT PRODUCTION - See SAN MARINO - LIVESTOCK AND POULTRY

SAN MARINO - MERCHANT SHIPPING

Statistical Office of the United Nations, Publishing Service, New York, New York 10017 (800) 253-9646; *Statistical Yearbook.*

SAN MARINO - MILITARY

Central Intelligence Agency, Washington, D.C. 20505 (703) 482-1100, www.cia.gov; *The World Factbook.*

St. Martin's Press, Inc., 175 Fifth Avenue, New York, New York 10010 (800) 221-7945; *The Statesman's Year-Book.*

SAN MARINO - MINING AND MINERAL PRODUCTS

Statistical Office of the United Nations, Publishing Service, New York, New York 10017 (800) 253-9646; *Energy Statistics Yearbook; Industrial Commodity Statistics Yearbook;* and *Statistical Yearbook.*

SAN MARINO - MONUMENTS AND HISTORICAL SITES

United Nations Educational, Scientific and Cultural Organization (UNESCO), 7 Place de Fontenoy, F-75700 Paris, France (Telephone Number in U.S. (212) 963-5981); *Statistical Yearbook.*

SAN MARINO - MORTALITY

Central Intelligence Agency, Washington, D.C. 20505 (703) 482-1100, www.cia.gov; *The World Factbook.*

Europa Publications Limited, 18 Bedford Square, London, WC1B 3JN, England; *The Europa World Year Book.*

Statistical Office of the United Nations, Publishing Service, New York, New York 10017 (800) 253-9646; *Demographic Yearbook; Statistical Yearbook; Trends in Europe and North America: The Statistical Yearbook of the Economic Commission for Europe;* and *World Statistics Pocketbook.*

The World Bank, 1818 H Street, NW, Washington, D.C. 20433 (202) 477-1234; *The World Bank Atlas.*

World Health Organization, Office of Publications, 20 Avenue Appia, CH-1211 Geneva 27, Switzerland (Telephone Number in U.S. (518) 436-9686); *World Health Statistics Annual.*

SAN MARINO - MOTION PICTURES

St. Martin's Press, Inc., 175 Fifth Avenue, New York, New York 10010 (800) 221-7945; *The Statesman's Year-Book.*

Statistical Office of the United Nations, Publishing Service, New York, New York 10017 (800) 253-9646; *Statistical Yearbook.*

United Nations Educational, Scientific and Cultural Organization (UNESCO), 7 Place de Fontenoy, F-75700 Paris, France (Telephone Number in U.S. (212) 963-5981); *Statistical Yearbook.*

SAN MARINO - MOTOR VEHICLE PRODUCTION

Statistical Office of the United Nations, Publishing Service, New York, New York 10017 (800) 253-9646; *Statistical Yearbook.*

SAN MARINO - MUSEUMS

United Nations Educational, Scientific and Cultural Organization (UNESCO), 7 Place de Fontenoy, F-75700 Paris, France

(Telephone Number in U.S. (212) 963-5981); *Statistical Yearbook.*

SAN MARINO - NATALITY - See SAN MARINO - BIRTH RATE

SAN MARINO - NATIONAL ACCOUNTS

Statistical Office of the United Nations, Publishing Service, New York, New York 10017 (800) 253-9646; *National Accounts Statistics;* and *Statistical Yearbook.*

SAN MARINO - NATIONAL INCOME

Statistical Office of the United Nations, Publishing Service, New York, New York 10017 (800) 253-9646; *Statistical Yearbook.*

SAN MARINO - NATIONAL PRODUCT

Statistical Office of the United Nations, Publishing Service, New York, New York 10017 (800) 253-9646; *Statistical Yearbook.*

SAN MARINO - NEWSPAPER PRODUCTION - See SAN MARINO - FORESTRY AND FOREST PRODUCTS

SAN MARINO - OCCUPATIONS - See SAN MARINO - LABOR

SAN MARINO - PATENTS, TRADEMARKS AND SERVICE MARKS

Statistical Office of the United Nations, Publishing Service, New York, New York 10017 (800) 253-9646; *Statistical Yearbook.*

SAN MARINO - PERIODICALS

United Nations Educational, Scientific and Cultural Organization (UNESCO), 7 Place de Fontenoy, F-75700 Paris, France (Telephone Number in U.S. (212) 963-5981); *Statistical Yearbook.*

SAN MARINO - PESTICIDE USE

Food and Agricultural Organization of the United Nations (FAO) Via delle Terme di Caracalla, 00100 Rome, Italy (Telephone Number in U.S. (202) 653-2400); *The State of Food and Agriculture.*

SAN MARINO - PETROLEUM INDUSTRY

Food and Agricultural Organization of the United Nations (FAO) Via delle Terme di Caracalla, 00100 Rome, Italy (Telephone Number in U.S. (202) 653-2400); *The State of Food and Agriculture.*

Statistical Office of the United Nations, Publishing Service, New York, New York 10017 (800) 253-9646; *Energy Statistics Yearbook; Industrial Commodity Statistics Yearbook; Statistical Yearbook;* and *Trends in Europe and North America: The Statistical Yearbook of the Economic*

Commission for Europe.

SAN MARINO - POPULATION

Central Intelligence Agency, Washington, D.C. 20505 (703) 482-1100, www.cia.gov; *The World Factbook.*

Europa Publications Limited, 18 Bedford Square, London, WC1B 3JN, England; *The Europa World Year Book.*

Food and Agricultural Organization of the United Nations (FAO), Via delle Terme di Caracalla, 00100 Rome, Italy (Telephone Number in U.S. (202) 653-2400); *Production Yearbook.*

St. Martin's Press, Inc., 175 Fifth Avenue, New York, New York 10010 (800) 221-7945; *The Statesman's Year-Book.*

Statistical Office of the United Nations, Publishing Service, New York, New York 10017 (800) 253-9646; *Demographic Yearbook; Statistical Yearbook; Trends in Europe and North America: The Statistical Yearbook of the Economic Commission for Europe;* and *World Statistics Pocketbook.*

United Nations Educational, Scientific and Cultural Organization (UNESCO), 7 Place de Fontenoy, F-75700 Paris, France (Telephone Number in U.S. (212) 963-5981); *Statistical Yearbook.*

World Health Organization, Office of Publications, 20 Avenue Appia, CH-1211 Geneva 27, Switzerland (Telephone Number in U.S. (518) 436-9686); *World Health Statistics Annual.*

SAN MARINO - POST OFFICES

St. Martin's Press, Inc., 175 Fifth Avenue, New York, New York 10010 (800) 221-7945; *The Statesman's Year-Book.*

Statistical Office of the United Nations, Publishing Service, New York, New York 10017 (800) 253-9646; *Trends in Europe and North America: The Statistical Yearbook of the Economic Commission for Europe.*

SAN MARINO - PRICES

Food and Agricultural Organization of the United Nations (FAO), Via delle Terme di Caracalla, 00100 Rome, Italy (Telephone Number in U.S. (202) 653-2400); *Production Yearbook;* and *The State of Food and Agriculture.*

SAN MARINO - RADIO RECEIVER PRODUCTION

Statistical Office of the United Nations, Publishing Service, New York, New York 10017 (800) 253-9646; *Statistical Yearbook.*

SAN MARINO - RADIO RECEIVERS

St. Martin's Press, Inc., 175 Fifth Avenue, New York, New York 10010 (800) 221-7945; *The Statesman's Year-Book.*

SAN MARINO - RAILWAYS

Statistical Office of the United Nations, Publishing Service, New York, New York 10017 (800) 253-9646; *Statistical Yearbook;* and *Trends in Europe and North America: The Statistical Yearbook of the Economic Commission for Europe.*

SAN MARINO - RELIGION

Central Intelligence Agency, Washington, D.C. 20505 (703) 482-1100, www.cia.gov; *The World Factbook.*

St. Martin's Press, Inc., 175 Fifth Avenue, New York, New York 10010 (800) 221-7945; *The Statesman's Year-Book.*

SAN MARINO - RETAIL TRADE

Statistical Office of the United Nations, Publishing Service, New York, New York 10017 (800) 253-9646; *Statistical Yearbook.*

SAN MARINO - RUBBER PRODUCTION AND CONSUMPTION

Statistical Office of the United Nations, Publishing Service, New York, New York 10017 (800) 253-9646; *Statistical Yearbook.*

SAN MARINO - SCIENTISTS, TECHNICIANS AND ENGINEERS

Statistical Office of the United Nations, Publishing Service, New York, New York 10017 (800) 253-9646; *Statistical Yearbook.*

SAN MARINO - SOCIAL DATA

Statistical Office of the United Nations, Publishing Service, New York, New York 10017 (800) 253-9646; *World Statistics Pocketbook.*

SAN MARINO - STOCKS - COMMODITY - MARKET PRICE - INDEX

Food and Agricultural Organization of the United Nations (FAO) Via delle Terme di Caracalla, 00100 Rome, Italy (Telephone Number in U.S. (202) 653-2400); *The State of Food and Agriculture.*

SAN MARINO - TELEPHONES IN USE

American Telephone and Telegraph Company, 26 Parsippany Road, Whippany, New Jersey 07981 (800) 222-0300; *The World's Telephones.*

Central Intelligence Agency, Washington, D.C. 20505 (703) 482-1100, www.cia.gov; *The World Factbook.*

Europa Publications Limited, 18

Bedford Square, London, WC1B 3JN, England; *The Europa World Year Book.*

St. Martin's Press, Inc., 175 Fifth Avenue, New York, New York 10010 (800) 221-7945; *The Statesman's Year-Book.*

Statistical Office of the United Nations, Publishing Service, New York, New York 10017 (800) 253-9646; *Statistical Yearbook; Trends in Europe and North America: The Statistical Yearbook of the Economic Commission for Europe;* and *World Statistics Pocketbook.*

SAN MARINO - TEXTILE INDUSTRY

St. Martin's Press, Inc., 175 Fifth Avenue, New York, New York 10010 (800) 221-7945; *The Statesman's Year-Book.*

Statistical Office of the United Nations, Publishing Service, New York, New York 10017 (800) 253-9646; *Industrial Commodity Statistics Yearbook;* and *Statistical Yearbook.*

SAN MARINO - THEATRE

United Nations Educational, Scientific and Cultural Organization (UNESCO), 7 Place de Fontenoy, F-75700 Paris, France (Telephone Number in U.S. (212) 963-5981); *Statistical Yearbook.*

SAN MARINO - TIRE (MOTOR VEHICLE) PRODUCTION

Statistical Office of the United Nations, Publishing Service, New York, New York 10017 (800) 253-9646; *Statistical Yearbook.*

SAN MARINO - TOBACCO PRODUCTION

Statistical Office of the United Nations, Publishing Service, New York, New York 10017 (800) 253-9646; *Statistical Yearbook.*

SAN MARINO - TOURISM

Europa Publications Limited, 18 Bedford Square, London, WC1B 3JN, England; *The Europa World Year Book.*

St. Martin's Press, Inc., 175 Fifth Avenue, New York, New York 10010 (800) 221-7945; *The Statesman's Year-Book.*

Statistical Office of the United Nations, Publishing Service, New York, New York 10017 (800) 253-9646; *Statistical Yearbook;* and *Trends in Europe and North America: The Statistical Yearbook of the Economic Commission for Europe.*

SAN MARINO - TRADE - See SAN MARINO - FOREIGN TRADE

SAN MARINO - TRADEMARKS AND SERVICE MARKS - See SAN MARINO - PATENTS, TRADEMARKS AND SERVICE

MARKS

SAN MARINO - TRANSPORTATION AND COMMUNICATIONS

Central Intelligence Agency, Washington, D.C. 20505 (703) 482-1100, www.cia.gov; *The World Factbook.*

St. Martin's Press, Inc., 175 Fifth Avenue, New York, New York 10010 (800) 221-7945; *The Statesman's Year-Book.*

Statistical Office of the United Nations, Publishing Service, New York, New York 10017 (800) 253-9646; *Trends in Europe and North America: The Statistical Yearbook of the Economic Commission for Europe.*

SAN MARINO - UNEMPLOYMENT

Central Intelligence Agency, Washington, D.C. 20505 (703) 482-1100, www.cia.gov; *The World Factbook.*

Statistical Office of the United Nations, Publishing Service, New York, New York 10017 (800) 253-9646; *Statistical Yearbook;* and *Trends in Europe and North America: The Statistical Yearbook of the Economic Commission for Europe.*

SAN MARINO - VITAL STATISTICS

Statistical Office of the United Nations, Publishing Service, New York, New York 10017 (800) 253-9646; *Statistical Yearbook.*

World Health Organization, Office of Publications, 20 Avenue Appia, CH-1211 Geneva 27, Switzerland (Telephone Number in U.S. (518) 436-9686); *World Health Statistics Annual.*

SAN MARINO - WAGES

Statistical Office of the United Nations, Publishing Service, New York, New York 10017 (800) 253-9646; *Statistical Yearbook.*

SAN MARINO - WHOLESALE PRICES

Statistical Office of the United Nations, Publishing Service, New York, New York 10017 (800) 253-9646; *Statistical Yearbook.*

SAN MARINO - WHOLESALE TRADE

Statistical Office of the United Nations, Publishing Service, New York, New York 10017 (800) 253-9646; *Statistical Yearbook.*

SAND AND GRAVEL INDUSTRY - See also MINING INDUSTRY

SAND AND GRAVEL INDUSTRY

U.S. Department of the Interior, Geological Survey, Office of Minerals Information, 12201 Sunrise Valley Drive, Reston, Virginia 22092 (703) 648-4000, www.minerals.usgs.gov; *Annual Reports; Census of Mineral Industries;* and *Mineral Commodity Summaries.*

SANITATION - See HEALTH AND SEWAGE TREATMENT

Sao Tome and Principe - National Statistical Office

Direccado de Estatistica, CP 256, Sao Tome, Sao Tome e Principe.

Sao Tome and Principe - Primary Statistics Source

Direccao de Economia e Estatistica, Sao Tome, Sao Tome e Principe; *Exposicao: Informacao Estatistica.*

SAO TOME AND PRINCIPE - AGRICULTURE

Economist Intelligence Unit, 111 West 57th Street, New York, New York 10019 (800) 938-4685; *Sao Tome and Principe Country Report.*

Euromonitor International, Inc., 122 South Michigan Avenue, Suite 1200, Chicago, Illinois 60603 (800) 577-EURO; *World Marketing Data and Statistics.*

Europa Publications Limited, 18 Bedford Square, London, WC1B 3JN, England; *The Europa World Year Book.*

Food and Agricultural Organization of the United Nations (FAO) Via delle Terme di Caracalla, 00100 Rome, Italy (Telephone Number in U.S. (202) 653-2400); *Production Yearbook; The State of Food and Agriculture;* and *Trade Yearbook.*

St. Martin's Press, Inc., 175 Fifth Avenue, New York, New York 10010 (800) 221-7945; *The Statesman's Year-Book.*

Statistical Office of the United Nations, Publishing Service, New York, New York 10017 (800) 253-9646; *Statistical Yearbook;* and *Survey of Economic and Social Conditions in Africa.*

United Nations Conference on Trade and Development, Central Statistical Service, Palais des Nations, Geneva, Switzerland (Telephone in U.S. (800) 253-9646); *UNCTAD Commodity Yearbook.*

United Nations Economic Commission for Africa, Africa Hall, P.O. Box 3001, Addis Ababa, Ethiopia (Telephone Number in U.S. (800) 253-9646); *African Statistical Yearbook.*

SAO TOME AND PRINCIPE - AIRLINE SERVICE

Europa Publications Limited, 18

Bedford Square, London, WC1B 3JN, England; *The Europa World Year Book.*

St. Martin's Press, Inc., 175 Fifth Avenue, New York, New York 10010 (800) 221-7945; *The Statesman's Year-Book.*

United Nations Economic Commission for Africa, Africa Hall, P.O. Box 3001, Addis Ababa, Ethiopia (Telephone Number in U.S. (800) 253-9646); *African Statistical Yearbook.*

SAO TOME AND PRINCIPE - AIRPORTS

Central Intelligence Agency, Washington, D.C. 20505 (703) 482-1100, www.cia.gov; *The World Factbook.*

SAO TOME AND PRINCIPE - AREA AND DENSITY OF POPULATION

African Development Bank, 01 BP 1387, Abidjan 01, Cote D'Ivoire; *Selected Statistics on Regional Member Countries.*

Central Intelligence Agency, Washington, D.C. 20505 (703) 482-1100, www.cia.gov; *The World Factbook.*

Europa Publications Limited, 18 Bedford Square, London, WC1B 3JN, England; *The Europa World Year Book.*

Food and Agricultural Organization of the United Nations (FAO) Via delle Terme di Caracalla, 00100 Rome, Italy (Telephone Number in U.S. (202) 653-2400); *The State of Food and Agriculture.*

St. Martin's Press, Inc., 175 Fifth Avenue, New York, New York 10010 (800) 221-7945; *The Statesman's Year-Book.*

Statistical Office of the United Nations, Publishing Service, New York, New York 10017 (800) 253-9646; *Statistical Yearbook;* and *Survey of Economic and Social Conditions in Africa.*

United Nations Educational, Scientific and Cultural Organization (UNESCO), 7 Place de Fontenoy, F-75700 Paris, France (Telephone Number in U.S. (212) 963-5981); *Statistical Yearbook.*

SAO TOME AND PRINCIPE - ARMS EXPORTS AND IMPORTS - See SAO TOME AND PRINCIPE - MILITARY

SAO TOME AND PRINCIPE - BALANCE OF PAYMENTS

African Development Bank, 01 BP 1387, Abidjan 01, Cote D'Ivoire; *Selected Statistics on Regional Member Countries.*

The Economist Intelligence Unit, 111 West 57th Street, New York, New York 10019 (800) 938-4685; *The World Market Atlas.*

Europa Publications Limited, 18 Bedford Square, London, WC1B 3JN, England; *The Europa World Year Book.*

United Nations Conference on Trade and Development (UNCTAD), New York, New York 10017 (800) 253-9646; *Handbook of International Trade and Development Statistics.*

United Nations Economic Commission for Africa, Africa Hall, P.O. Box 3001, Addis Ababa, Ethiopia (Telephone Number in U.S. (800) 253-9646); *African Statistical Yearbook.*

SAO TOME AND PRINCIPE - BANKING

Euromonitor International, Inc., 122 South Michigan Avenue, Suite 1200, Chicago, Illinois 60603 (800) 577-EURO; *World Marketing Data and Statistics.*

St. Martin's Press, Inc., 175 Fifth Avenue, New York, New York 10010 (800) 221-7945; *The Statesman's Year-Book.*

United Nations Economic Commission for Africa, Africa Hall, P.O. Box 3001, Addis Ababa, Ethiopia (Telephone Number in U.S. (800) 253-9646); *African Statistical Yearbook.*

SAO TOME AND PRINCIPE - BIRTH RATES

Central Intelligence Agency, Washington, D.C. 20505 (703) 482-1100, www.cia.gov; *The World Factbook.*

Euromonitor International, Inc., 122 South Michigan Avenue, Suite 1200, Chicago, Illinois 60603 (800) 577-EURO; *International Marketing Data and Statistics.*

Europa Publications Limited, 18 Bedford Square, London, WC1B 3JN, England; *The Europa World Year Book.*

St. Martin's Press, Inc., 175 Fifth Avenue, New York, New York 10010 (800) 221-7945; *The Statesman's Year-Book.*

Statistical Office of the United Nations, Publishing Service, New York, New York 10017 (800) 253-9646; *Demographic Yearbook; Statistical Yearbook;* and *Survey of Economic and Social Conditions in Africa.*

World Health Organization, Office of Publications, 20 Avenue Appia, CH-1211 Geneva 27, Switzerland (Telephone Number in U.S. (518) 436-9686); *World Health Statistics Annual.*

SAO TOME AND PRINCIPE - BROADCASTING

Billboard Limited, P.O. Box 9027, 1006 AA Amsterdam, The Netherlands (Telephone Number in U.S. (212) 764-

7300); *World Radio TV Handbook.*

Central Intelligence Agency, Washington, D.C. 20505 (703) 482-1100, www.cia.gov; *The World Factbook.*

Euromonitor International, Inc., 122 South Michigan Avenue, Suite 1200, Chicago, Illinois 60603 (800) 577-EURO; *World Marketing Data and Statistics.*

St. Martin's Press, Inc., 175 Fifth Avenue, New York, New York 10010 (800) 221-7945; *The Statesman's Year-Book.*

SAO TOME AND PRINCIPE - BUDGET

Central Intelligence Agency, Washington, D.C. 20505 (703) 482-1100, www.cia.gov; *The World Factbook.*

SAO TOME AND PRINCIPE - CALORIE SUPPLY

African Development Bank, 01 BP 1387, Abidjan 01, Cote D'Ivoire; *Selected Statistics on Regional Member Countries.*

Food and Agricultural Organization of the United Nations (FAO) Via delle Terme di Caracalla, 00100 Rome, Italy (Telephone Number in U.S. (202) 653-2400); *The State of Food and Agriculture.*

SAO TOME AND PRINCIPE - CATTLE - See SAO TOME AND PRINCIPE - LIVESTOCK AND POULTRY

SAO TOME AND PRINCIPE - CHEMICAL (ORGANIC) PRODUCTION - SEE SAO TOME AND PRINCIPE - MINING AND MINERAL PRODUCTS

SAO TOME AND PRINCIPE - CHICKENS - See SAO TOME AND PRINCIPE - LIVESTOCK AND POULTRY

SAO TOME AND PRINCIPE - CLIMATE

St. Martin's Press, Inc., 175 Fifth Avenue, New York, New York 10010 (800) 221-7945; *The Statesman's Year-Book.*

SAO TOME AND PRINCIPE - COAL PRODUCTION - See SAO TOME AND PRINCIPE - MINING AND MINERAL PRODUCTS

SAO TOME AND PRINCIPE - COCOA PRODUCTION - See SAO TOME AND PRINCIPE - CROPS

SAO TOME AND PRINCIPE - COMMERCE

St. Martin's Press, Inc., 175 Fifth Avenue, New York, New York 10010 (800) 221-7945; *The Statesman's Year-Book.*

SAO TOME AND PRINCIPE - COMMUNICATIONS - See SAO TOME AND PRINCIPE - TRANSPORTATION AND

COMMUNICATIONS

SAO TOME AND PRINCIPE - CONSTRUCTION INDUSTRY

United Nations Economic Commission for Africa, Africa Hall, P.O. Box 3001, Addis Ababa, Ethiopia (Telephone Number in U.S. (800) 253-9646); *African Statistical Yearbook.*

SAO TOME AND PRINCIPE - CONSUMER PRICE INDEX

African Development Bank, 01 BP 1387, Abidjan 01, Cote D'Ivoire; *Selected Statistics on Regional Member Countries.*

Europa Publications Limited, 18 Bedford Square, London, WC1B 3JN, England; *The Europa World Year Book.*

Statistical Office of the United Nations, Publishing Service, New York, New York 10017 (800) 253-9646; *Survey of Economic and Social Conditions in Africa.*

SAO TOME AND PRINCIPE - CONSUMER PRICES

Euromonitor International, Inc., 122 South Michigan Avenue, Suite 1200, Chicago, Illinois 60603 (800) 577-EURO; *World Marketing Data and Statistics.*

SAO TOME AND PRINCIPE - CONSUMPTION

African Development Bank, 01 BP 1387, Abidjan 01, Cote D'Ivoire; *Selected Statistics on Regional Member Countries.*

Statistical Office of the United Nations, Publishing Service, New York, New York 10017 (800) 253-9646; *Survey of Economic and Social Conditions in Africa.*

SAO TOME AND PRINCIPE - CORN PRODUCTION - See SAO TOME AND PRINCIPE - CROPS

SAO TOME AND PRINCIPE - CORPORATE TAXES - See SAO TOME AND PRINCIPE - TAXATION

SAO TOME AND PRINCIPE - CROPS

Commodity Research Bureau, Inc., 30 South Wacker Drive, Chicago Illinois 60606 (312) 454-1801; *Commodity Year Book.*

Europa Publications Limited, 18 Bedford Square, London, WC1B 3JN, England; *The Europa World Year Book.*

Food and Agricultural Organization of the United Nations (FAO) Via delle Terme di Caracalla, 00100 Rome, Italy (Telephone Number in U.S. (202) 653-2400); *The State of Food and Agriculture.*

St. Martin's Press, Inc., 175 Fifth Avenue, New York, New York 10010 (800) 221-7945; *The Statesman's Year-Book.*

Statistical Office of the United Nations, Publishing Service, New York, New York 10017 (800) 253-9646; *Statistical Yearbook.*

United Nations Conference on Trade and Development, Central Statistical Service, Palais des Nations, Geneva, Switzerland (Telephone in U.S. (800) 253-9646); *UNCTAD Commodity Yearbook.*

United Nations Economic Commission for Africa, Africa Hall, P.O. Box 3001, Addis Ababa, Ethiopia (Telephone Number in U.S. (800) 253-9646); *African Statistical Yearbook.*

SAO TOME AND PRINCIPE - CUSTOMS DUTIES

St. Martin's Press, Inc., 175 Fifth Avenue, New York, New York 10010 (800) 221-7945; *The Statesman's Year-Book.*

SAO TOME AND PRINCIPE - DAIRY PRODUCTS

Food and Agricultural Organization of the United Nations (FAO) Via delle Terme di Caracalla, 00100 Rome, Italy (Telephone Number in U.S. (202) 653-2400); *The State of Food and Agriculture.*

SAO TOME AND PRINCIPE - DEATH RATES - See SAO TOME AND PRINCIPE - MORTALITY

SAO TOME AND PRINCIPE - DEMOGRAPHY

The Economist Intelligence Unit, 111 West 57th Street, New York, New York 10019 (800) 938-4685; *The World Market Atlas.*

Euromonitor International, Inc., 122 South Michigan Avenue, Suite 1200, Chicago, Illinois 60603 (800) 577-EURO; *International Marketing Data and Statistics; and World Marketing Data and Statistics.*

Statistical Office of the United Nations, Publishing Service, New York, New York 10017 (800) 253-9646; *Human Development Report;* and *Survey of Economic and Social Conditions in Africa.*

SAO TOME AND PRINCIPE - DEVELOPMENT ASSISTANCE

Statistical Office of the United Nations, Publishing Service, New York, New York 10017 (800) 253-9646; *Statistical Yearbook.*

SAO TOME AND PRINCIPE - DISEASES - See SAO TOME AND PRINCIPE - HEALTH

SAO TOME AND PRINCIPE - DIVORCE RATES

Statistical Office of the United Nations, Publishing Service, New York, New York 10017 (800) 253-9646; *Demographic Yearbook.*

SAO TOME AND PRINCIPE - ECONOMY

African Development Bank, 01 BP 1387, Abidjan 01, Cote D'Ivoire; *Selected Statistics on Regional Member Countries.*

Central Intelligence Agency, Washington, D.C. 20505 (703) 482-1100, www.cia.gov; *The World Factbook.*

Economist Intelligence Unit, 111 West 57th Street, New York, New York 10019 (800) 938-4685; *Sao Tome and Principe Country Report.*

Euromonitor International, Inc., 122 South Michigan Avenue, Suite 1200, Chicago, Illinois 60603 (800) 577-EURO; *World Marketing Data and Statistics.*

St. Martin's Press, Inc., 175 Fifth Avenue, New York, New York 10010 (800) 221-7945; *The Statesman's Year-Book.*

Statistical Office of the United Nations, Publishing Service, New York, New York 10017 (800) 253-9646; *Foreign Trade Statistics for Africa;* and *World Statistics Pocketbook.*

The World Bank, 1818 H Street, NW, Washington, D.C. 20433 (202) 477-1234; *The World Bank Atlas.*

SAO TOME AND PRINCIPE - EDUCATION

African Development Bank, 01 BP 1387, Abidjan 01, Cote D'Ivoire; *Selected Statistics on Regional Member Countries.*

The Economist Intelligence Unit, 111 West 57th Street, New York, New York 10019 (800) 938-4685; *The World Market Atlas.*

Euromonitor International, Inc., 122 South Michigan Avenue, Suite 1200, Chicago, Illinois 60603 (800) 577-EURO; *International Marketing Data and Statistics;* and *World Marketing Data and Statistics.*

Europa Publications Limited, 18 Bedford Square, London, WC1B 3JN, England; *The Europa World Year Book.*

St. Martin's Press, Inc., 175 Fifth Avenue, New York, New York 10010 (800) 221-7945; *The Statesman's Year-Book.*

Statistical Office of the United Nations, Publishing Service, New York, New York 10017 (800) 253-9646; *Human Development Report;* and *Survey of Economic and Social Conditions in Africa.*

United Nations Economic Commission for Africa, Africa Hall, P.O. Box 3001, Addis Ababa, Ethiopia (Telephone Number in U.S. (800) 253-9646); *African Statistical Yearbook.*

United Nations Educational, Scientific and Cultural Organization (UNESCO), 7 Place de Fontenoy, F-75700 Paris, France (Telephone Number in U.S. (212) 963-5981); *Statistical Yearbook.*

SAO TOME AND PRINCIPE - EGG PRODUCTION AND CONSUMPTION - See SAO TOME AND PRINCIPE - DAIRY PRODUCTS

SAO TOME AND PRINCIPE - ELECTRICITY

Central Intelligence Agency, Washington, D.C. 20505 (703) 482-1100, www.cia.gov; *The World Factbook.*

St. Martin's Press, Inc., 175 Fifth Avenue, New York, New York 10010 (800) 221-7945; *The Statesman's Year-Book.*

Statistical Office of the United Nations, Publishing Service, New York, New York 10017 (800) 253-9646; *Human Development Report;* and *Survey of Economic and Social Conditions in Africa.*

United Nations Economic Commission for Africa, Africa Hall, P.O. Box 3001, Addis Ababa, Ethiopia (Telephone Number in U.S. (800) 253-9646); *African Statistical Yearbook.*

SAO TOME AND PRINCIPE - EMPLOYMENT

Euromonitor International, Inc., 122 South Michigan Avenue, Suite 1200, Chicago, Illinois 60603 (800) 577-EURO; *International Marketing Data and Statistics.*

Statistical Office of the United Nations, Publishing Service, New York, New York 10017 (800) 253-9646; *Survey of Economic and Social Conditions in Africa.*

United Nations Economic Commission for Africa, Africa Hall, P.O. Box 3001, Addis Ababa, Ethiopia (Telephone Number in U.S. (800) 253-9646); *African Statistical Yearbook.*

SAO TOME AND PRINCIPE - ENERGY

Euromonitor International, Inc., 122 South Michigan Avenue, Suite 1200, Chicago, Illinois 60603 (800) 577-EURO; *International Marketing Data and Statistics;* and *World Marketing Data and Statistics.*

Food and Agricultural Organization of the United Nations (FAO) Via delle Terme di Caracalla, 00100 Rome, Italy (Telephone

Number in U.S. (202) 653-2400); *The State of Food and Agriculture.*

St. Martin's Press, Inc., 175 Fifth Avenue, New York, New York 10010 (800) 221-7945; *The Statesman's Year-Book.*

Statistical Office of the United Nations, Publishing Service, New York, New York 10017 (800) 253-9646; *Energy Statistics Yearbook; Human Development Report; Statistical Yearbook;* and *World Statistics Pocketbook.*

United Nations Economic Commission for Africa, Africa Hall, P.O. Box 3001, Addis Ababa, Ethiopia (Telephone Number in U.S. (800) 253-9646); *African Statistical Yearbook.*

The World Bank, 1818 H Street, NW, Washington, D.C. 20433 (202) 477-1234; *The World Bank Atlas.*

SAO TOME AND PRINCIPE - ENVIRONMENT

Economist Intelligence Unit, 111 West 57th Street, New York, New York 10019 (800) 938-4685; *Sao Tome and Principe Country Report.*

Statistical Office of the United Nations, Publishing Service, New York, New York 10017 (800) 253-9646; *World Statistics Pocketbook.*

SAO TOME AND PRINCIPE - EXCHANGE RATES

African Development Bank, 01 BP 1387, Abidjan 01, Cote D'Ivoire; *Selected Statistics on Regional Member Countries.*

Central Intelligence Agency, Washington, D.C. 20505 (703) 482-1100, www.cia.gov; *The World Factbook.*

Euromonitor International, Inc., 122 South Michigan Avenue, Suite 1200, Chicago, Illinois 60603 (800) 577-EURO; *International Marketing Data and Statistics.*

Europa Publications Limited, 18 Bedford Square, London, WC1B 3JN, England; *The Europa World Year Book.*

Statistical Office of the United Nations, Publishing Service, New York, New York 10017 (800) 253-9646; *Foreign Trade Statistics for Africa; Statistical Yearbook;* and *World Statistics Pocketbook.*

SAO TOME AND PRINCIPE - EXPORTS

African Development Bank, 01 BP 1387, Abidjan 01, Cote D'Ivoire; *Selected Statistics on Regional Member Countries.*

Central Intelligence Agency, Washington, D.C. 20505 (703) 482-1100,

www.cia.gov; *The World Factbook*.

The Economist Intelligence Unit, 111 West 57th Street, New York, New York 10019 (800) 938-4685; *Sao Tome and Principe Country Report;* and *The World Market Atlas.*

Euromonitor International, Inc., 122 South Michigan Avenue, Suite 1200, Chicago, Illinois 60603 (800) 577-EURO; *International Marketing Data and Statistics.*

Europa Publications Limited, 18 Bedford Square, London, WC1B 3JN, England; *The Europa World Year Book.*

Food and Agricultural Organization of the United Nations (FAO) Via delle Terme di Caracalla, 00100 Rome, Italy (Telephone Number in U.S. (202) 653-2400); *The State of Food and Agriculture.*

International Monetary Fund, 700 Nineteenth Street, NW, Washington, D.C. 20431 (202) 623-7000; *Direction of Trade Statistics.*

St. Martin's Press, Inc., 175 Fifth Avenue, New York, New York 10010 (800) 221-7945; *The Statesman's Year-Book.*

Statistical Office of the United Nations, Publishing Service, New York, New York 10017 (800) 253-9646; *Foreign Trade Statistics for Africa;* and *Survey of Economic and Social Conditions in Africa.*

United Nations Conference on Trade and Development (UNCTAD), New York, New York 10017 (800) 253-9646; *Handbook of International Trade and Development Statistics.*

United Nations Economic Commission for Africa, Africa Hall, P.O. Box 3001, Addis Ababa, Ethiopia (Telephone Number in U.S. (800) 253-9646); *African Statistical Yearbook.*

SAO TOME AND PRINCIPE - EXTERNAL INDEBTEDNESS

African Development Bank, 01 BP 1387, Abidjan 01, Cote D'Ivoire; *Selected Statistics on Regional Member Countries.*

Statistical Office of the United Nations, Publishing Service, New York, New York 10017 (800) 253-9646; *Survey of Economic and Social Conditions in Africa.*

SAO TOME AND PRINCIPE - EXTERNAL TRADE

African Development Bank, 01 BP 1387, Abidjan 01, Cote D'Ivoire; *Selected Statistics on Regional Member Countries.*

Euromonitor International, Inc., 122

South Michigan Avenue, Suite 1200, Chicago, Illinois 60603 (800) 577-EURO; *World Marketing Data and Statistics.*

Food and Agricultural Organization of the United Nations (FAO) Via delle Terme di Caracalla, 00100 Rome, Italy (Telephone Number in U.S. (202) 653-2400); *The State of Food and Agriculture;* and *Trade Yearbook.*

Statistical Office of the United Nations, Publishing Service, New York, New York 10017 (800) 253-9646; *Statistical Yearbook.*

SAO TOME AND PRINCIPE - FARM CROPS - See SAO TOME AND PRINCIPE -CROPS

SAO TOME AND PRINCIPE - FERTILITY RATES

Central Intelligence Agency, Washington, D.C. 20505 (703) 482-1100, www.cia.gov; *The World Factbook.*

Statistical Office of the United Nations, Publishing Service, New York, New York 10017 (800) 253-9646; *Human Development Report;* and *Survey of Economic and Social Conditions in Africa.*

The World Bank, 1818 H Street, NW, Washington, D.C. 20433 (202) 477-1234; *The World Bank Atlas.*

SAO TOME AND PRINCIPE - FERTILIZER

Food and Agricultural Organization of the United Nations (FAO) Via delle Terme di Caracalla, 00100 Rome, Italy (Telephone Number in U.S. (202) 653-2400); *The State of Food and Agriculture.*

SAO TOME AND PRINCIPE - FETAL MORTALITY - See SAO TOME AND PRINCIPE - MORTALITY

SAO TOME AND PRINCIPE - FINANCE

Economist Intelligence Unit, 111 West 57th Street, New York, New York 10019 (800) 938-4685; *Sao Tome and Principe Country Report.*

Europa Publications Limited, 18 Bedford Square, London, WC1B 3JN, England; *The Europa World Year Book.*

St. Martin's Press, Inc., 175 Fifth Avenue, New York, New York 10010 (800) 221-7945; *The Statesman's Year-Book.*

United Nations Economic Commission for Africa, Africa Hall, P.O. Box 3001, Addis Ababa, Ethiopia (Telephone Number in U.S. (800) 253-9646); *African Statistical Yearbook.*

SAO TOME AND PRINCIPE - FINANCIAL CHARACTERISTICS

African Development Bank, 01 BP 1387, Abidjan 01, Cote D'Ivoire; *Selected Statistics on Regional Member Countries.*

SAO TOME AND PRINCIPE - FISHERIES

Europa Publications Limited, 18 Bedford Square, London, WC1B 3JN, England; *The Europa World Year Book.*

Food and Agricultural Organization of the United Nations (FAO) Via delle Terme di Caracalla, 00100 Rome, Italy (Telephone Number in U.S. (202) 653-2400); *The State of Food and Agriculture;* and *Yearbook of Fishery Statistics.*

St. Martin's Press, Inc., 175 Fifth Avenue, New York, New York 10010 (800) 221-7945; *The Statesman's Year-Book.*

Statistical Office of the United Nations, Publishing Service, New York, New York 10017 (800) 253-9646; *Survey of Economic and Social Conditions in Africa.*

United Nations Conference on Trade and Development, Central Statistical Service, Palais des Nations, Geneva, Switzerland (Telephone in U.S. (800) 253-9646); *UNCTAD Commodity Yearbook.*

United Nations Economic Commission for Africa, Africa Hall, P.O. Box 3001, Addis Ababa, Ethiopia (Telephone Number in U.S. (800) 253-9646); *African Statistical Yearbook.*

SAO TOME AND PRINCIPE - FOOD

African Development Bank, 01 BP 1387, Abidjan 01, Cote D'Ivoire; *Selected Statistics on Regional Member Countries.*

Food and Agricultural Organization of the United Nations (FAO) Via delle Terme di Caracalla, 00100 Rome, Italy (Telephone Number in U.S. (202) 653-2400); *Production Yearbook;* and *The State of Food and Agriculture.*

Statistical Office of the United Nations, Publishing Service, New York, New York 10017 (800) 253-9646; *Human Development Report.*

United Nations Conference on Trade and Development, Central Statistical Service, Palais des Nations, Geneva, Switzerland (Telephone in U.S. (800) 253-9646); *UNCTAD Commodity Yearbook.*

SAO TOME AND PRINCIPE - FOREIGN TRADE

Economist Intelligence Unit, 111 West 57th Street, New York, New York 10019 (800) 938-4685; *Sao Tome and Principe Country Report.*

Europa Publications Limited, 18

Bedford Square, London, WC1B 3JN, England; *The Europa World Year Book.*

Food and Agricultural Organization of the United Nations (FAO) Via delle Terme di Caracalla, 00100 Rome, Italy (Telephone Number in U.S. (202) 653-2400); *The State of Food and Agriculture.*

St. Martin's Press, Inc., 175 Fifth Avenue, New York, New York 10010 (800) 221-7945; *The Statesman's Year-Book.*

Statistical Office of the United Nations, Publishing Service, New York, New York 10017 (800) 253-9646; *Foreign Trade Statistics for Africa;* and *Statistical Yearbook.*

United Nations Conference on Trade and Development, Central Statistical Service, Palais des Nations, Geneva, Switzerland (Telephone in U.S. (800) 253-9646); *UNCTAD Commodity Yearbook.*

United Nations Economic Commission for Africa, Africa Hall, P.O. Box 3001, Addis Ababa, Ethiopia (Telephone Number in U.S. (800) 253-9646); *African Statistical Yearbook.*

SAO TOME AND PRINCIPE - FORESTRY AND FOREST PRODUCTS

Europa Publications Limited, 18 Bedford Square, London, WC1B 3JN, England; *The Europa World Year Book.*

Food and Agricultural Organization of the United Nations (FAO) Via delle Terme di Caracalla, 00100 Rome, Italy (Telephone Number in U.S. (202) 653-2400); *The State of Food and Agriculture;* and *Yearbook of Forest Products.*

St. Martin's Press, Inc., 175 Fifth Avenue, New York, New York 10010 (800) 221-7945; *The Statesman's Year-Book.*

United Nations Conference on Trade and Development, Central Statistical Service, Palais des Nations, Geneva, Switzerland (Telephone in U.S. (800) 253-9646); *UNCTAD Commodity Yearbook.*

United Nations Economic Commission for Africa, Africa Hall, P.O. Box 3001, Addis Ababa, Ethiopia (Telephone Number in U.S. (800) 253-9646); *African Statistical Yearbook.*

SAO TOME AND PRINCIPE - GENERAL MORTALITY - See SAO TOME AND PRINCIPE - MORTALITY

SAO TOME AND PRINCIPE - GOATS - See SAO TOME AND PRINCIPE - LIVESTOCK AND POULTRY

SAO TOME AND PRINCIPE - GOVERNMENT

Central Intelligence Agency, Washington, D.C. 20505 (703) 482-1100, www.cia.gov; *The World Factbook.*

Europa Publications Limited, 18 Bedford Square, London, WC1B 3JN, England; *The Europa World Year Book.*

St. Martin's Press, Inc., 175 Fifth Avenue, New York, New York 10010 (800) 221-7945; *The Statesman's Year-Book.*

Statistical Office of the United Nations, Publishing Service, New York, New York 10017 (800) 253-9646; *National Accounts Statistics;* and *Survey of Economic and Social Conditions in Africa.*

SAO TOME AND PRINCIPE - GRAIN PRODUCTION - See SAO TOME AND PRINCIPE - CROPS

SAO TOME AND PRINCIPE - GROSS DOMESTIC PRODUCT

African Development Bank, 01 BP 1387, Abidjan 01, Cote D'Ivoire; *Selected Statistics on Regional Member Countries.*

The Economist Intelligence Unit, 111 West 57th Street, New York, New York 10019 (800) 938-4685; *Sao Tome and Principe Country Report;* and *The World Market Atlas.*

Euromonitor International, Inc., 122 South Michigan Avenue, Suite 1200, Chicago, Illinois 60603 (800) 577-EURO; *International Marketing Data and Statistics.*

Europa Publications Limited, 18 Bedford Square, London, WC1B 3JN, England; *The Europa World Year Book.*

Statistical Office of the United Nations, Publishing Service, New York, New York 10017 (800) 253-9646; *Human Development Report; National Accounts Statistics; Statistical Yearbook;* and *Survey of Economic and Social Conditions in Africa.*

United Nations Economic Commission for Africa, Africa Hall, P.O. Box 3001, Addis Ababa, Ethiopia (Telephone Number in U.S. (800) 253-9646); *African Statistical Yearbook.*

SAO TOME AND PRINCIPE - GROSS NATIONAL PRODUCT

St. Martin's Press, Inc., 175 Fifth Avenue, New York, New York 10010 (800) 221-7945; *The Statesman's Year-Book.*

U.S. Arms Control and Disarmament Agency, 320 Twenty-first Street, NW, Washington, D.C. 20451 (202) 647-8677; *World Military Expenditures and Arms Transfers.*

The World Bank, 1818 H Street, NW, Washington, D.C. 20433 (202) 477-1234; *The World Bank Atlas.*

SAO TOME AND PRINCIPE - HEALTH

African Development Bank, 01 BP 1387, Abidjan 01, Cote D'Ivoire; *Selected Statistics on Regional Member Countries.*

Euromonitor International, Inc., 122 South Michigan Avenue, Suite 1200, Chicago, Illinois 60603 (800) 577-EURO; *World Marketing Data and Statistics.*

St. Martin's Press, Inc., 175 Fifth Avenue, New York, New York 10010 (800) 221-7945; *The Statesman's Year-Book.*

Statistical Office of the United Nations, Publishing Service, New York, New York 10017 (800) 253-9646; *Human Development Report;* and *Statistical Yearbook.*

United Nations Economic Commission for Africa, Africa Hall, P.O. Box 3001, Addis Ababa, Ethiopia (Telephone Number in U.S. (800) 253-9646); *African Statistical Yearbook.*

World Health Organization, Office of Publications, 20 Avenue Appia, CH-1211 Geneva 27, Switzerland (Telephone Number in U.S. (518) 436-9686); *World Health Statistics Annual.*

SAO TOME AND PRINCIPE - HIGHWAYS

Central Intelligence Agency, Washington, D.C. 20505 (703) 482-1100, www.cia.gov; *The World Factbook.*

St. Martin's Press, Inc., 175 Fifth Avenue, New York, New York 10010 (800) 221-7945; *The Statesman's Year-Book.*

Statistical Office of the United Nations, Publishing Service, New York, New York 10017 (800) 253-9646; *Survey of Economic and Social Conditions in Africa.*

United Nations Economic Commission for Africa, Africa Hall, P.O. Box 3001, Addis Ababa, Ethiopia (Telephone Number in U.S. (800) 253-9646); *African Statistical Yearbook.*

SAO TOME AND PRINCIPE - HOUSING AND HOUSING UNITS

Euromonitor International, Inc., 122 South Michigan Avenue, Suite 1200, Chicago, Illinois 60603 (800) 577-EURO; *World Marketing Data and Statistics.*

SAO TOME AND PRINCIPE - ILLITERATE POPULATION

Central Intelligence Agency, Washington, D.C. 20505 (703) 482-1100,

www.cia.gov; *The World Factbook.*

The Economist Intelligence Unit, 111 West 57th Street, New York, New York 10019 (800) 938-4685; *The World Market Atlas.*

Statistical Office of the United Nations, Publishing Service, New York, New York 10017 (800) 253-9646; *Human Development Report.*

SAO TOME AND PRINCIPE - IMPORTS

African Development Bank, 01 BP 1387, Abidjan 01, Cote D'Ivoire; *Selected Statistics on Regional Member Countries.*

Central Intelligence Agency, Washington, D.C. 20505 (703) 482-1100, www.cia.gov; *The World Factbook.*

The Economist Intelligence Unit, 111 West 57th Street, New York, New York 10019 (800) 938-4685; *Sao Tome and Principe Country Report;* and *The World Market Atlas.*

Euromonitor International, Inc., 122 South Michigan Avenue, Suite 1200, Chicago, Illinois 60603 (800) 577-EURO; *International Marketing Data and Statistics.*

Europa Publications Limited, 18 Bedford Square, London, WC1B 3JN, England; *The Europa World Year Book.*

Food and Agricultural Organization of the United Nations (FAO) Via delle Terme di Caracalla, 00100 Rome, Italy (Telephone Number in U.S. (202) 653-2400); *The State of Food and Agriculture.*

International Monetary Fund, 700 Nineteenth Street, NW, Washington, D.C. 20431 (202) 623-7000; *Direction of Trade Statistics.*

St. Martin's Press, Inc., 175 Fifth Avenue, New York, New York 10010 (800) 221-7945; *The Statesman's Year-Book.*

Statistical Office of the United Nations, Publishing Service, New York, New York 10017 (800) 253-9646; *Foreign Trade Statistics for Africa;* and *Survey of Economic and Social Conditions in Africa.*

United Nations Conference on Trade and Development (UNCTAD), New York, New York 10017 (800) 253-9646; *Handbook of International Trade and Development Statistics.*

United Nations Economic Commission for Africa, Africa Hall, P.O. Box 3001, Addis Ababa, Ethiopia (Telephone Number in U.S. (800) 253-9646); *African Statistical Yearbook.*

SAO TOME AND PRINCIPE - INDUSTRY

Central Intelligence Agency, Washington, D.C. 20505 (703) 482-1100, www.cia.gov; *The World Factbook.*

Economist Intelligence Unit, 111 West 57th Street, New York, New York 10019 (800) 938-4685; *Sao Tome and Principe Country Report.*

Euromonitor International, Inc., 122 South Michigan Avenue, Suite 1200, Chicago, Illinois 60603 (800) 577-EURO; *World Marketing Data and Statistics.*

Europa Publications Limited, 18 Bedford Square, London, WC1B 3JN, England; *The Europa World Year Book.*

Statistical Office of the United Nations, Publishing Service, New York, New York 10017 (800) 253-9646; *Survey of Economic and Social Conditions in Africa.*

United Nations Economic Commission for Africa, Africa Hall, P.O. Box 3001, Addis Ababa, Ethiopia (Telephone Number in U.S. (800) 253-9646); *African Statistical Yearbook.*

SAO TOME AND PRINCIPE - INFANT AND MATERNAL MORTALITY - See SAO TOME AND PRINCIPE - MORTALITY

SAO TOME AND PRINCIPE - INTERNATIONAL RESERVES EXCLUDING GOLD

African Development Bank, 01 BP 1387, Abidjan 01, Cote D'Ivoire; *Selected Statistics on Regional Member Countries.*

SAO TOME AND PRINCIPE - LABOR

African Development Bank, 01 BP 1387, Abidjan 01, Cote D'Ivoire; *Selected Statistics on Regional Member Countries.*

Central Intelligence Agency, Washington, D.C. 20505 (703) 482-1100, www.cia.gov; *The World Factbook.*

Euromonitor International, Inc., 122 South Michigan Avenue, Suite 1200, Chicago, Illinois 60603 (800) 577-EURO; *International Marketing Data and Statistics;* and *World Marketing Data and Statistics.*

Europa Publications Limited, 18 Bedford Square, London, WC1B 3JN, England; *The Europa World Year Book.*

Food and Agricultural Organization of the United Nations (FAO) Via delle Terme di Caracalla, 00100 Rome, Italy (Telephone Number in U.S. (202) 653-2400); *The State of Food and Agriculture.*

Statistical Office of the United Nations, Publishing Service, New York, New York 10017 (800) 253-9646; *Human Development Report.*

The World Bank, 1818 H Street, NW, Washington, D.C. 20433 (202) 477-1234; *The World Bank Atlas.*

SAO TOME AND PRINCIPE - LAND USE

Central Intelligence Agency, Washington, D.C. 20505 (703) 482-1100, www.cia.gov; *The World Factbook.*

Euromonitor International, Inc., 122 South Michigan Avenue, Suite 1200, Chicago, Illinois 60603 (800) 577-EURO; *International Marketing Data and Statistics.*

Food and Agricultural Organization of the United Nations (FAO), Via delle Terme di Caracalla, 00100 Rome, Italy (Telephone Number in U.S. (202) 653-2400); *Production Yearbook.*

SAO TOME AND PRINCIPE - LIBRARIES

United Nations Educational, Scientific and Cultural Organization (UNESCO), 7 Place de Fontenoy, F-75700 Paris, France (Telephone Number in U.S. (212) 963-5981); *Statistical Yearbook.*

SAO TOME AND PRINCIPE - LIFE EXPECTANCY

African Development Bank, 01 BP 1387, Abidjan 01, Cote D'Ivoire; *Selected Statistics on Regional Member Countries.*

Central Intelligence Agency, Washington, D.C. 20505 (703) 482-1100, www.cia.gov; *The World Factbook.*

St. Martin's Press, Inc., 175 Fifth Avenue, New York, New York 10010 (800) 221-7945; *The Statesman's Year-Book.*

Statistical Office of the United Nations, Publishing Service, New York, New York 10017 (800) 253-9646; *Human Development Report;* and *World Statistics Pocketbook.*

The World Bank, 1818 H Street, NW, Washington, D.C. 20433 (202) 477-1234; *The World Bank Atlas.*

SAO TOME AND PRINCIPE - LITERACY RATE

Euromonitor International, Inc., 122 South Michigan Avenue, Suite 1200, Chicago, Illinois 60603 (800) 577-EURO; *World Marketing Data and Statistics.*

Statistical Office of the United Nations, Publishing Service, New York, New York 10017 (800) 253-9646; *Survey of Economic and Social Conditions in Africa.*

SAO TOME AND PRINCIPE - LIVESTOCK AND POULTRY

Europa Publications Limited, 18

Bedford Square, London, WC1B 3JN, England; *The Europa World Year Book.*

Food and Agricultural Organization of the United Nations (FAO), Via delle Terme di Caracalla, 00100 Rome, Italy (Telephone Number in U.S. (202) 653-2400); *Production Yearbook;* and *The State of Food and Agriculture.*

St. Martin's Press, Inc., 175 Fifth Avenue, New York, New York 10010 (800) 221-7945; *The Statesman's Year-Book.*

Statistical Office of the United Nations, Publishing Service, New York, New York 10017 (800) 253-9646; *Statistical Yearbook;* and *Survey of Economic and Social Conditions in Africa.*

United Nations Conference on Trade and Development, Central Statistical Service, Palais des Nations, Geneva, Switzerland (Telephone in U.S. (800) 253-9646); *UNCTAD Commodity Yearbook.*

United Nations Economic Commission for Africa, Africa Hall, P.O. Box 3001, Addis Ababa, Ethiopia (Telephone Number in U.S. (800) 253-9646); *African Statistical Yearbook.*

SAO TOME AND PRINCIPE - LIVING LEVELS - See SAO TOME AND PRINCIPE - LIFE EXPECTANCY

SAO TOME AND PRINCIPE - MAIL TRAFFIC - NUMBER OF ITEMS SENT AND RECEIVED

Statistical Office of the United Nations, Publishing Service, New York, New York 10017 (800) 253-9646; *Statistical Yearbook.*

SAO TOME AND PRINCIPE - MANUFACTURING

Statistical Office of the United Nations, Publishing Service, New York, New York 10017 (800) 253-9646; *Survey of Economic and Social Conditions in Africa.*

United Nations Economic Commission for Africa, Africa Hall, P.O. Box 3001, Addis Ababa, Ethiopia (Telephone Number in U.S. (800) 253-9646); *African Statistical Yearbook.*

SAO TOME AND PRINCIPE - MARRIAGE RATES

Statistical Office of the United Nations, Publishing Service, New York, New York 10017 (800) 253-9646; *Statistical Yearbook.*

SAO TOME AND PRINCIPE - MEAT PRODUCTION - See SAO TOME AND PRINCIPE - LIVESTOCK AND POULTRY

SAO TOME AND PRINCIPE - MERCHANT SHIPPING

Europa Publications Limited, 18 Bedford Square, London, WC1B 3JN, England; *The Europa World Year Book.*

Statistical Office of the United Nations, Publishing Service, New York, New York 10017 (800) 253-9646; *Statistical Yearbook.*

United Nations Economic Commission for Africa, Africa Hall, P.O. Box 3001, Addis Ababa, Ethiopia (Telephone Number in U.S. (800) 253-9646); *African Statistical Yearbook.*

SAO TOME AND PRINCIPE - MILITARY

Central Intelligence Agency, Washington, D.C. 20505 (703) 482-1100, www.cia.gov; *The World Factbook.*

Euromonitor International, Inc., 122 South Michigan Avenue, Suite 1200, Chicago, Illinois 60603 (800) 577-EURO; *World Marketing Data and Statistics.*

Statistical Office of the United Nations, Publishing Service, New York, New York 10017 (800) 253-9646; *Human Development Report.*

U.S. Arms Control and Disarmament Agency, 320 Twenty-first Street, NW, Washington, D.C. 20451 (202) 647-8677; *World Military Expenditures and Arms Transfers.*

SAO TOME AND PRINCIPE - MINING AND MINERAL PRODUCTS

United Nations Conference on Trade and Development, Central Statistical Service, Palais des Nations, Geneva, Switzerland (Telephone in U.S. (800) 253-9646); *UNCTAD Commodity Yearbook.*

United Nations Economic Commission for Africa, Africa Hall, P.O. Box 3001, Addis Ababa, Ethiopia (Telephone Number in U.S. (800) 253-9646); *African Statistical Yearbook.*

SAO TOME AND PRINCIPE - MONEY EXCHANGE RATES - See SAO TOME AND PRINCIPE - EXCHANGE RATES

SAO TOME AND PRINCIPE - MONEY SUPPLY

African Development Bank, 01 BP 1387, Abidjan 01, Cote D'Ivoire; *Selected Statistics on Regional Member Countries.*

Economist Intelligence Unit, 111 West 57th Street, New York, New York 10019 (800) 938-4685; *Sao Tome and Principe Country Report.*

SAO TOME AND PRINCIPE - MORTALITY

Central Intelligence Agency, Washington, D.C. 20505 (703) 482-1100,

www.cia.gov; *The World Factbook.*

Euromonitor International, Inc., 122 South Michigan Avenue, Suite 1200, Chicago, Illinois 60603 (800) 577-EURO; *International Marketing Data and Statistics.*

St. Martin's Press, Inc., 175 Fifth Avenue, New York, New York 10010 (800) 221-7945; *The Statesman's Year-Book.*

Statistical Office of the United Nations, Publishing Service, New York, New York 10017 (800) 253-9646; *Human Development Report; Statistical Yearbook; Survey of Economic and Social Conditions in Africa;* and *World Statistics Pocketbook.*

The World Bank, 1818 H Street, NW, Washington, D.C. 20433 (202) 477-1234; *The World Bank Atlas.*

World Health Organization, Office of Publications, 20 Avenue Appia, CH-1211 Geneva 27, Switzerland (Telephone Number in U.S. (518) 436-9686); *World Health Statistics Annual.*

SAO TOME AND PRINCIPE - MOTION PICTURES

Statistical Office of the United Nations, Publishing Service, New York, New York 10017 (800) 253-9646; *Statistical Yearbook.*

SAO TOME AND PRINCIPE - MOTOR VEHICLES IN USE

Europa Publications Limited, 18 Bedford Square, London, WC1B 3JN, England; *The Europa World Year Book.*

Statistical Office of the United Nations, Publishing Service, New York, New York 10017 (800) 253-9646; *Statistical Yearbook;* and *Survey of Economic and Social Conditions in Africa.*

SAO TOME AND PRINCIPE - NATALITY -See SAO TOME AND PRINCIPE - BIRTH RATE

SAO TOME AND PRINCIPE - NATIONAL ACCOUNTS

African Development Bank, 01 BP 1387, Abidjan 01, Cote D'Ivoire; *Selected Statistics on Regional Member Countries.*

United Nations Economic Commission for Africa, Africa Hall, P.O. Box 3001, Addis Ababa, Ethiopia (Telephone Number in U.S. (800) 253-9646); *African Statistical Yearbook.*

SAO TOME AND PRINCIPE - NATIONAL INCOME

Statistical Office of the United Nations, Publishing Service, New York, New York 10017 (800) 253-9646; *National Accounts Statistics.*

SAO TOME AND PRINCIPE - NEWSPAPER PRODUCTION - See SAO TOME AND PRINCIPE - FORESTRY AND FOREST PRODUCTS

SAO TOME AND PRINCIPE - OCCUPATIONS - See SAO TOME AND PRINCIPE - LABOR

SAO TOME AND PRINCIPE - PALM KERNELS AND PALM OIL

Statistical Office of the United Nations, Publishing Service, New York, New York 10017 (800) 253-9646; *Statistical Yearbook.*

SAO TOME AND PRINCIPE - PESTICIDE USE

Food and Agricultural Organization of the United Nations (FAO) Via delle Terme di Caracalla, 00100 Rome, Italy (Telephone Number in U.S. (202) 653-2400); *The State of Food and Agriculture.*

SAO TOME AND PRINCIPE - PETROLEUM INDUSTRY

Food and Agricultural Organization of the United Nations (FAO) Via delle Terme di Caracalla, 00100 Rome, Italy (Telephone Number in U.S. (202) 653-2400); *The State of Food and Agriculture.*

United Nations Conference on Trade and Development, Central Statistical Service, Palais des Nations, Geneva, Switzerland (Telephone in U.S. (800) 253-9646); *UNCTAD Commodity Yearbook.*

SAO TOME AND PRINCIPE - PIGS - See SAO TOME AND PRINCIPE - LIVESTOCK AND POULTRY

SAO TOME AND PRINCIPE - POPULATION

African Development Bank, 01 BP 1387, Abidjan 01, Cote D'Ivoire; *Selected Statistics on Regional Member Countries.*

Central Intelligence Agency, Washington, D.C. 20505 (703) 482-1100, www.cia.gov; *The World Factbook.*

The Economist Intelligence Unit, 111 West 57th Street, New York, New York 10019 (800) 938-4685; *Sao Tome and Principe Country Report;* and *The World Market Atlas.*

Euromonitor International, Inc., 122 South Michigan Avenue, Suite 1200, Chicago, Illinois 60603 (800) 577-EURO; *International Marketing Data and Statistics.*

Europa Publications Limited, 18 Bedford Square, London, WC1B 3JN, England; *The Europa World Year Book.*

Food and Agricultural Organization of the United Nations (FAO), Via delle Terme di Caracalla, 00100 Rome, Italy (Telephone

Number in U.S. (202) 653-2400); *Production Yearbook.*

St. Martin's Press, Inc., 175 Fifth Avenue, New York, New York 10010 (800) 221-7945; *The Statesman's Year-Book.*

Statistical Office of the United Nations, Publishing Service, New York, New York 10017 (800) 253-9646; *Human Development Report; Statistical Yearbook; Survey of Economic and Social Conditions in Africa;* and *World Statistics Pocketbook.*

United Nations Educational, Scientific and Cultural Organization (UNESCO), 7 Place de Fontenoy, F-75700 Paris, France; *Statistical Yearbook.*

U.S. Arms Control and Disarmament Agency, 320 Twenty-first Street, NW, Washington, D.C. 20451 (202) 647-8677; *World Military Expenditures and Arms Transfers.*

The World Bank, 1818 H Street, NW, Washington, D.C. 20433 (202) 477-1234; *The World Bank Atlas.*

World Health Organization, Office of Publications, 20 Avenue Appia, CH-1211 Geneva 27, Switzerland (Telephone Number in U.S. (518) 436-9686); *World Health Statistics Annual.*

SAO TOME AND PRINCIPE - PRICES

Food and Agricultural Organization of the United Nations (FAO), Via delle Terme di Caracalla, 00100 Rome, Italy (Telephone Number in U.S. (202) 653-2400); *Production Yearbook;* and *The State of Food and Agriculture.*

SAO TOME AND PRINCIPE - RADIO RECEIVERS

St. Martin's Press, Inc., 175 Fifth Avenue, New York, New York 10010 (800) 221-7945; *The Statesman's Year-Book.*

SAO TOME AND PRINCIPE - RAILWAYS

United Nations Economic Commission for Africa, Africa Hall, P.O. Box 3001, Addis Ababa, Ethiopia (Telephone Number in U.S. (800) 253-9646); *African Statistical Yearbook.*

SAO TOME AND PRINCIPE - RELIGION

Central Intelligence Agency, Washington, D.C. 20505 (703) 482-1100, www.cia.gov; *The World Factbook.*

St. Martin's Press, Inc., 175 Fifth Avenue, New York, New York 10010 (800) 221-7945; *The Statesman's Year-Book.*

SAO TOME AND PRINCIPE - RETAIL TRADE

Euromonitor International, Inc., 122 South Michigan Avenue, Suite 1200, Chicago, Illinois 60603 (800) 577-EURO; *World Marketing Data and Statistics.*

SAO TOME AND PRINCIPE - ROUNDWOOD PRODUCTION - See SAO TOME AND PRINCIPE - FORESTRY AND FOREST PRODUCTS

SAO TOME AND PRINCIPE - SAWNWOOD PRODUCTION - See SAO TOME AND PRINCIPE - FORESTRY AND FOREST PRODUCTS

SAO TOME AND PRINCIPE - SHEEP - See SAO TOME AND PRINCIPE - LIVESTOCK AND POULTRY

SAO TOME AND PRINCIPE - SOCIAL DATA

African Development Bank, 01 BP 1387, Abidjan 01, Cote D'Ivoire; *Selected Statistics on Regional Member Countries.*

Statistical Office of the United Nations, Publishing Service, New York, New York 10017 (800) 253-9646; *World Statistics Pocketbook.*

SAO TOME AND PRINCIPE - SOCIAL SECURITY

Statistical Office of the United Nations, Publishing Service, New York, New York 10017 (800) 253-9646; *National Accounts Statistics.*

SAO TOME AND PRINCIPE - STOCKS - COMMODITY - MARKET PRICE - INDEX

Food and Agricultural Organization of the United Nations (FAO) Via delle Terme di Caracalla, 00100 Rome, Italy (Telephone Number in U.S. (202) 653-2400); *The State of Food and Agriculture.*

SAO TOME AND PRINCIPE - TELEPHONES IN USE

American Telephone and Telegraph Company, 26 Parsippany Road, Whippany, New Jersey 07981 (800) 222-0300; *The World's Telephones.*

Central Intelligence Agency, Washington, D.C. 20505 (703) 482-1100, www.cia.gov; *The World Factbook.*

Europa Publications Limited, 18 Bedford Square, London, WC1B 3JN, England; *The Europa World Year Book.*

St. Martin's Press, Inc., 175 Fifth Avenue, New York, New York 10010 (800) 221-7945; *The Statesman's Year-Book.*

Statistical Office of the United Nations, Publishing Service, New York, New York 10017 (800) 253-9646; *World Statistics Pocketbook.*

SAO TOME AND PRINCIPE - TEXTILE INDUSTRY

United Nations Conference on Trade and Development, Central Statistical Service, Palais des Nations, Geneva, Switzerland (Telephone in U.S. (800) 253-9646); *UNCTAD Commodity Yearbook.*

SAO TOME AND PRINCIPE - TOURISM

Euromonitor International, Inc., 122 South Michigan Avenue, Suite 1200, Chicago, Illinois 60603 (800) 577-EURO; *World Marketing Data and Statistics.*

United Nations Economic Commission for Africa, Africa Hall, P.O. Box 3001, Addis Ababa, Ethiopia (Telephone Number in U.S. (800) 253-9646); *African Statistical Yearbook.*

World Tourism Organization, Calle Capitan Haya 42, E-28020 Madrid, Spain; *Yearbook of Tourism Statistics.*

SAO TOME AND PRINCIPE - TRACTORS IN USE

Statistical Office of the United Nations, Publishing Service, New York, New York 10017 (800) 253-9646; *Statistical Yearbook.*

SAO TOME AND PRINCIPE - TRADE - See SAO TOME AND PRINCIPE - FOREIGN TRADE

SAO TOME AND PRINCIPE - TRANSPORTATION AND COMMUNICATIONS

Central Intelligence Agency, Washington, D.C. 20505 (703) 482-1100, www.cia.gov; *The World Factbook.*

Euromonitor International, Inc., 122 South Michigan Avenue, Suite 1200, Chicago, Illinois 60603 (800) 577-EURO; *International Marketing Data and Statistics;* and *World Marketing Data and Statistics.*

Europa Publications Limited, 18 Bedford Square, London, WC1B 3JN, England; *The Europa World Year Book.*

St. Martin's Press, Inc., 175 Fifth Avenue, New York, New York 10010 (800) 221-7945; *The Statesman's Year-Book.*

Statistical Office of the United Nations, Publishing Service, New York, New York 10017 (800) 253-9646; *Human Development Report.*

United Nations Economic Commission for Africa, Africa Hall, P.O. Box 3001, Addis Ababa, Ethiopia (Telephone Number in U.S. (800) 253-9646); *African Statistical Yearbook.*

SAO TOME AND PRINCIPE - UNEMPLOYMENT RATE

Central Intelligence Agency, Washington, D.C. 20505 (703) 482-1100, www.cia.gov; *The World Factbook.*

SAO TOME AND PRINCIPE - VITAL STATISTICS

St. Martin's Press, Inc., 175 Fifth Avenue, New York, New York 10010 (800) 221-7945; *The Statesman's Year-Book.*

Statistical Office of the United Nations, Publishing Service, New York, New York 10017 (800) 253-9646; *Statistical Yearbook.*

World Health Organization, Office of Publications, 20 Avenue Appia, CH-1211 Geneva 27, Switzerland (Telephone Number in U.S. (518) 436-9686); *World Health Statistics Annual.*

SAO TOME AND PRINCIPE - WEATHER - See SAO TOME AND PRINCIPE - CLIMATE

SARDINES

U.S. Department of Commerce, National Oceanic and Atmospheric Administration, National Marine Fisheries Service, 1315 East-West Highway, Silver Spring, Maryland 20910 (301) 427-2239, www.nmfs.noaa.gov; *Fisheries of the United States.*

Saudi Arabia - National Statistical Office

Central Department of Statistics, Ministry of Finance and National Economy, Post Office Box 3735, Riyadh, Saudi Arabia.

Saudi Arabia - Primary Statistics Source

Central Department of Statistics, Ministry of Finance and National Economy, Riyadh, Saudi Arabia; *Statistical Yearbook.*

SAUDI ARABIA - AGRICULTURE

Economic Commission for Western Asia, Post Office Box 27, Baghdad, Iraq; *Statistical Abstract of Western Asia.*

Economist Intelligence Unit, 111 West 57th Street, New York, New York 10019 (800) 938-4685; *Saudi Arabia Country Report.*

Euromonitor International, Inc., 122 South Michigan Avenue, Suite 1200, Chicago, Illinois 60603 (800) 577-EURO; *International Marketing Data and Statistics;* and *World Marketing Data and Statistics.*

Europa Publications Limited, 18 Bedford Square, London, WC1B 3JN, England; *The Europa World Year Book.*

Federal Statistical Office, Gustav-Stresemann-Ring 11, D-6200 Wiesbaden, Germany; *Saudi-Arabien.*

Food and Agricultural Organization of the United Nations (FAO) Via delle Terme di Caracalla, 00100 Rome, Italy (Telephone Number in U.S. (202) 653-2400); *Production Yearbook; The State of Food and Agriculture;* and *Trade Yearbook.*

M.E. Sharpe, 80 Business Park Drive, Armonk, New York 10504 (800) 541-6563; *The Illustrated Book of World Rankings.*

St. Martin's Press, Inc., 175 Fifth Avenue, New York, New York 10010 (800) 221-7945; *The Statesman's Year-Book.*

Statistical Office of the United Nations, Publishing Service, New York, New York 10017 (800) 253-9646; *Statistical Yearbook.*

United Nations Conference on Trade and Development, Central Statistical Service, Palais des Nations, Geneva, Switzerland (Telephone in U.S. (800) 253-9646); *UNCTAD Commodity Yearbook.*

The World Bank, 1818 H Street, NW, Washington, D.C. 20433 (202) 477-1234; *World Development Indicators.*

SAUDI ARABIA - AIRLINE SERVICE

Economic Commission for Western Asia, Post Office Box 27, Baghdad, Iraq; *Statistical Abstract of Western Asia.*

Europa Publications Limited, 18 Bedford Square, London, WC1B 3JN, England; *The Europa World Year Book.*

International Civil Aviation Organization, 999 University Street, Montreal, Quebec, Canada H3C 5H7 (514) 954-8219; *Civil Aviation Statistics of the World.*

M.E. Sharpe, 80 Business Park Drive, Armonk, New York 10504 (800) 541-6563; *The Illustrated Book of World Rankings.*

St. Martin's Press, Inc., 175 Fifth Avenue, New York, New York 10010 (800) 221-7945; *The Statesman's Year-Book.*

Statistical Office of the United Nations, Publishing Service, New York, New York 10017 (800) 253-9646; *Statistical Yearbook.*

SAUDI ARABIA - AIRPORTS

Central Intelligence Agency, Washington, D.C. 20505 (703) 482-1100, www.cia.gov; *The World Factbook.*

SAUDI ARABIA - ALUMINUM PRODUCTION AND CONSUMPTION - See SAUDI ARABIA - MINING AND MINERAL PRODUCTS

SAUDI ARABIA - ANIMAL HEALTH

Food and Agricultural Organization of the United Nations (FAO), Via delle Terme di Caracalla, 00100, Rome, Italy (Telephone Number in U.S. (202) 653-2400); *Animal Health Yearbook*.

SAUDI ARABIA - AREA AND DENSITY OF POPULATION

Central Intelligence Agency, Washington, D.C. 20505 (703) 482-1100, www.cia.gov; *The World Factbook*.

Economic Commission for Western Asia, Post Office Box 27, Baghdad, Iraq; *Statistical Abstract of Western Asia*.

Euromonitor International, Inc., 122 South Michigan Avenue, Suite 1200, Chicago, Illinois 60603 (800) 577-EURO; *International Marketing Data and Statistics*; and *The World Economic Factbook*.

Europa Publications Limited, 18 Bedford Square, London, WC1B 3JN, England; *The Europa World Year Book*.

Federal Statistical Office, Gustav-Stresemann-Ring 11, D-6200 Wiesbaden, Germany; *Saudi-Arabien*.

Food and Agricultural Organization of the United Nations (FAO) Via delle Terme di Caracalla, 00100 Rome, Italy (Telephone Number in U.S. (202) 653-2400); *The State of Food and Agriculture*.

M.E. Sharpe, 80 Business Park Drive, Armonk, New York 10504 (800) 541-6563; *The Illustrated Book of World Rankings*.

St. Martin's Press, Inc., 175 Fifth Avenue, New York, New York 10010 (800) 221-7945; *The Statesman's Year-Book*.

Statistical Office of the United Nations, Publishing Service, New York, New York 10017 (800) 253-9646; *Statistical Yearbook*.

The World Bank, 1818 H Street, NW, Washington, D.C. 20433 (202) 477-1234; *World Development Report*.

SAUDI ARABIA - ARMS EXPORTS AND IMPORTS - See SAUDI ARABIA - MILITARY

SAUDI ARABIA - BALANCE OF PAYMENTS

Economic Commission for Western Asia, Post Office Box 27, Baghdad, Iraq; *Statistical Abstract of Western Asia*.

The Economist Intelligence Unit, 111 West 57th Street, New York, New York 10019 (800) 938-4685; *The World Market Atlas*.

Europa Publications Limited, 18 Bedford Square, London, WC1B 3JN,

England; *The Europa World Year Book*.

Federal Statistical Office, Gustav-Stresemann-Ring 11, D-6200 Wiesbaden, Germany; *Saudi-Arabien*.

International Monetary Fund, 700 Nineteenth Street, NW, Washington, D.C. 20431 (202) 623-700; *Balance of Payments Yearbook*.

Statistical Office of the United Nations, Publishing Service, New York, New York 10017 (800) 253-9646; *Statistical Yearbook*.

United Nations Conference on Trade and Development (UNCTAD), New York, New York 10017 (800) 253-9646; *Handbook of International Trade and Development Statistics*.

The World Bank, 1818 H Street, NW, Washington, D.C. 20433 (202) 477-1234; *World Development Report;* and *World Development Indicators*.

SAUDI ARABIA - BALANCE OF TRADE

Economic Commission for Western Asia, Post Office Box 27, Baghdad, Iraq; *Statistical Abstract of Western Asia*.

SAUDI ARABIA - BANKING

Economic Commission for Western Asia, Post Office Box 27, Baghdad, Iraq; *Statistical Abstract of Western Asia*.

Euromonitor International, Inc., 122 South Michigan Avenue, Suite 1200, Chicago, Illinois 60603 (800) 577-EURO; *World Marketing Data and Statistics*.

Europa Publications Limited, 18 Bedford Square, London, WC1B 3JN, England; *The Europa World Year Book*.

International Monetary Fund, 700 Nineteenth Street, NW, Washington, D.C. 20431 (202) 623-7000; *International Financial Statistics*.

M.E. Sharpe, 80 Business Park Drive, Armonk, New York 10504 (800) 541-6563; *The Illustrated Book of World Rankings*.

St. Martin's Press, Inc., 175 Fifth Avenue, New York, New York 10010 (800) 221-7945; *The Statesman's Year-Book*.

SAUDI ARABIA - BARLEY PRODUCTION - See SAUDI ARABIA - CROPS

SAUDI ARABIA - BEER PRODUCTION - See SAUDI ARABIA - BEVERAGES

SAUDI ARABIA - BEVERAGES

M.E. Sharpe, 80 Business Park Drive, Armonk, New York 10504 (800) 541-6563; *The Illustrated Book of World Rankings*.

SAUDI ARABIA - BIRTH RATES

Central Intelligence Agency, Washington, D.C. 20505 (703) 482-1100, www.cia.gov; *The World Factbook*.

Euromonitor International, Inc., 122 South Michigan Avenue, Suite 1200, Chicago, Illinois 60603 (800) 577-EURO; *International Marketing Data and Statistics;* and *The World Economic Factbook*.

Europa Publications Limited, 18 Bedford Square, London, WC1B 3JN, England; *The Europa World Year Book*.

M.E. Sharpe, 80 Business Park Drive, Armonk, New York 10504 (800) 541-6563; *The Illustrated Book of World Rankings*.

St. Martin's Press, Inc., 175 Fifth Avenue, New York, New York 10010 (800) 221-7945; *The Statesman's Year-Book*.

Statistical Office of the United Nations, Publishing Service, New York, New York 10017 (800) 253-9646; *Demographic Yearbook;* and *Statistical Yearbook*.

The World Bank, 1818 H Street, NW, Washington, D.C. 20433 (202) 477-1234; *World Development Indicators*.

SAUDI ARABIA - BROADCASTING

Billboard Limited, P.O. Box 9027, 1006 AA Amsterdam, The Netherlands (Telephone Number in U.S. (212) 764-7300); *World Radio TV Handbook*.

Central Intelligence Agency, Washington, D.C. 20505 (703) 482-1100, www.cia.gov; *The World Factbook*.

Euromonitor International, Inc., 122 South Michigan Avenue, Suite 1200, Chicago, Illinois 60603 (800) 577-EURO; *World Marketing Data and Statistics*.

M.E. Sharpe, 80 Business Park Drive, Armonk, New York 10504 (800) 541-6563; *The Illustrated Book of World Rankings*.

St. Martin's Press, Inc., 175 Fifth Avenue, New York, New York 10010 (800) 221-7945; *The Statesman's Year-Book*.

United Nations Educational, Scientific and Cultural Organization (UNESCO), 7 Place de Fontenoy, F-75700 Paris, France (Telephone Number in U.S. (212) 963-5981); *Statistical Yearbook*.

SAUDI ARABIA - BUDGET

Central Intelligence Agency, Washington, D.C. 20505 (703) 482-1100, www.cia.gov; *The World Factbook*.

SAUDI ARABIA - BUTTER PRODUCTION - See SAUDI ARABIA -

DAIRY PRODUCTS

SAUDI ARABIA - CALORIE SUPPLY

Food and Agricultural Organization of the United Nations (FAO) Via delle Terme di Caracalla, 00100 Rome, Italy (Telephone Number in U.S. (202) 653-2400); *The State of Food and Agriculture.*

SAUDI ARABIA - CATTLE - See SAUDI ARABIA - LIVESTOCK AND POULTRY

SAUDI ARABIA - CEMENT PRODUCTION - See SAUDI ARABIA - MINING AND MINERAL PRODUCTS

SAUDI ARABIA - CHEMICAL (ORGANIC) PRODUCTION - See SAUDI ARABIA - MINING AND MINERAL PRODUCTS

SAUDI ARABIA - CHICKENS - See SAUDI ARABIA - LIVESTOCK AND POULTRY

SAUDI ARABIA - CIGARETTE PRODUCTION - See SAUDI ARABIA - TOBACCO PRODUCTION

SAUDI ARABIA - CLIMATE

M.E. Sharpe, 80 Business Park Drive, Armonk, New York 10504 (800) 541-6563; *The Illustrated Book of World Rankings.*

St. Martin's Press, Inc., 175 Fifth Avenue, New York, New York 10010 (800) 221-7945; *The Statesman's Year-Book.*

SAUDI ARABIA - COAL PRODUCTION - See SAUDI ARABIA - MINING AND MINERAL PRODUCTS

SAUDI ARABIA - COFFEE - See SAUDI ARABIA - CROPS

SAUDI ARABIA - COMMERCE

St. Martin's Press, Inc., 175 Fifth Avenue, New York, New York 10010 (800) 221-7945; *The Statesman's Year-Book.*

SAUDI ARABIA - COMMUNICATIONS - See SAUDI ARABIA - TRANSPORTATION AND COMMUNICATIONS

SAUDI ARABIA - CONSTRUCTION INDUSTRY

M.E. Sharpe, 80 Business Park Drive, Armonk, New York 10504 (800) 541-6563; *The Illustrated Book of World Rankings.*

Statistical Office of the United Nations, Publishing Service, New York, New York 10017 (800) 253-9646; *Statistical Yearbook.*

SAUDI ARABIA - CONSUMER PRICE INDEX

Europa Publications Limited, 18 Bedford Square, London, WC1B 3JN, England; *The Europa World Year Book.*

SAUDI ARABIA - CONSUMER PRICES

Euromonitor International, Inc., 122 South Michigan Avenue, Suite 1200, Chicago, Illinois 60603 (800) 577-EURO; *World Marketing Data and Statistics.*

International Labour Office, I.L.O. Publications, 1828 L Street, NW, Suite 801, Washington, D.C. 20036 (301) 638-3152; *Yearbook of Labour Statistics.*

International Monetary Fund, 700 Nineteenth Street, NW, Washington, D.C. 20431 (202) 623-7000; *International Financial Statistics.*

SAUDI ARABIA - CONSUMPTION

The World Bank, 1818 H Street, NW, Washington, D.C. 20433 (202) 477-1234; *World Development Report.*

SAUDI ARABIA - COPPER PRODUCTION AND CONSUMPTION - See SAUDI ARABIA - MINING AND MINERAL PRODUCTS

SAUDI ARABIA - CORN PRODUCTION - See SAUDI ARABIA - CROPS

SAUDI ARABIA - CORPORATE TAXES - See SAUDI ARABIA - TAXATION

SAUDI ARABIA - COTTON PRODUCTION - See SAUDI ARABIA - CROPS

SAUDI ARABIA - CROPS

Europa Publications Limited, 18 Bedford Square, London, WC1B 3JN, England; *The Europa World Year Book.*

Food and Agricultural Organization of the United Nations (FAO) Via delle Terme di Caracalla, 00100 Rome, Italy (Telephone Number in U.S. (202) 653-2400); *The State of Food and Agriculture.*

M.E. Sharpe, 80 Business Park Drive, Armonk, New York 10504 (800) 541-6563; *The Illustrated Book of World Rankings.*

St. Martin's Press, Inc., 175 Fifth Avenue, New York, New York 10010 (800) 221-7945; *The Statesman's Year-Book.*

Statistical Office of the United Nations, Publishing Service, New York, New York 10017 (800) 253-9646; *Statistical Yearbook.*

United Nations Conference on Trade and Development, Central Statistical Service, Palais des Nations, Geneva, Switzerland (Telephone in U.S. (800) 253-9646); *UNCTAD Commodity Yearbook.*

SAUDI ARABIA - CUSTOMS DUTIES

St. Martin's Press, Inc., 175 Fifth Avenue, New York, New York 10010 (800) 221-7945; *The Statesman's Year-Book.*

SAUDI ARABIA - DAIRY PRODUCTS

Economic Commission for Western Asia, Post Office Box 27, Baghdad, Iraq; *Statistical Abstract of Western Asia.*

Europa Publications Limited, 18 Bedford Square, London, WC1B 3JN, England; *The Europa World Year Book.*

Food and Agricultural Organization of the United Nations (FAO) Via delle Terme di Caracalla, 00100 Rome, Italy (Telephone Number in U.S. (202) 653-2400); *The State of Food and Agriculture.*

M.E. Sharpe, 80 Business Park Drive, Armonk, New York 10504 (800) 541-6563; *The Illustrated Book of World Rankings.*

St. Martin's Press, Inc., 175 Fifth Avenue, New York, New York 10010 (800) 221-7945; *The Statesman's Year-Book.*

SAUDI ARABIA - DEATH RATES - See SAUDI ARABIA - MORTALITY

SAUDI ARABIA - DEFENSE EXPENDITURES - See SAUDI ARABIA - MILITARY

SAUDI ARABIA - DEMOGRAPHY

The Economist Intelligence Unit, 111 West 57th Street, New York, New York 10019 (800) 938-4685; *The World Market Atlas.*

Euromonitor International, Inc., 122 South Michigan Avenue, Suite 1200, Chicago, Illinois 60603 (800) 577-EURO; *International Marketing Data and Statistics; World Marketing Data and Statistics;* and *The World Economic Factbook.*

Federal Statistical Office, Gustav-Stresemann - Ring 11, D-6200, Wiesbaden, Germany; *Saudi-Arabien.*

M.E. Sharpe, 80 Business Park Drive, Armonk, New York 10504 (800) 541-6563; *The Illustrated Book of World Rankings.*

Statistical Office of the United Nations, Publishing Service, New York, New York 10017 (800) 253-9646; *Human Development Report.*

SAUDI ARABIA - DEVELOPMENT ASSISTANCE

Statistical Office of the United Nations, Publishing Service, New York, New York 10017 (800) 253-9646; *Statistical Yearbook.*

SAUDI ARABIA - DIAMOND PRODUCTION - See SAUDI ARABIA - MINING AND MINERAL PRODUCTS

SAUDI ARABIA - DISEASES - See SAUDI

ARABIA - HEALTH

SAUDI ARABIA - DIVORCE RATES

M.E. Sharpe, 80 Business Park Drive, Armonk, New York 10504 (800) 541-6563; *The Illustrated Book of World Rankings.*

Statistical Office of the United Nations, Publishing Service, New York, New York 10017 (800) 253-9646; *Demographic Yearbook.*

SAUDI ARABIA - ECONOMY

Central Intelligence Agency, Washington, D.C. 20505 (703) 482-1100, www.cia.gov; *The World Factbook.*

Economist Intelligence Unit, 111 West 57th Street, New York, New York 10019 (800) 938-4685; *Saudi Arabia Country Report.*

Euromonitor International, Inc., 122 South Michigan Avenue, Suite 1200, Chicago, Illinois 60603 (800) 577-EURO; *International Marketing Data and Statistics; World Marketing Data and Statistics;* and *The World Economic Factbook.*

Europa Publications Limited, 18 Bedford Square, London, WC1B 3JN, England; *The Europa World Year Book.*

Federal Statistical Office, Gustav-Stresemann - Ring 11, D-6200, Wiesbaden, Germany; *Saudi-Arabien.*

M.E. Sharpe, 80 Business Park Drive, Armonk, New York 10504 (800) 541-6563; *The Illustrated Book of World Rankings.*

St. Martin's Press, Inc., 175 Fifth Avenue, New York, New York 10010 (800) 221-7945; *The Statesman's Year-Book.*

Statistical Office of the United Nations, Publishing Service, New York, New York 10017 (800) 253-9646; *World Statistics Pocketbook.*

The World Bank, 1818 H Street, NW, Washington, D.C. 20433 (202) 477-1234; *The World Bank Atlas;* and *World Development Report.*

SAUDI ARABIA - EDUCATION

Economic Commission for Western Asia, Post Office Box 27, Baghdad, Iraq; *Statistical Abstract of Western Asia.*

The Economist Intelligence Unit, 111 West 57th Street, New York, New York 10019 (800) 938-4685; *The World Market Atlas.*

Euromonitor International, Inc., 122 South Michigan Avenue, Suite 1200, Chicago, Illinois 60603 (800) 577-EURO;

International Marketing Data and Statistics; and *World Marketing Data and Statistics.*

Europa Publications Limited, 18 Bedford Square, London, WC1B 3JN, England; *The Europa World Year Book.*

Federal Statistical Office, Gustav-Stresemann-Ring 11, D-6200 Wiesbaden, Germany; *Saudi Arabia.*

M.E. Sharpe, 80 Business Park Drive, Armonk, New York 10504 (800) 541-6563; *The Illustrated Book of World Rankings.*

St. Martin's Press, Inc., 175 Fifth Avenue, New York, New York 10010 (800) 221-7945; *The Statesman's Year-Book.*

Statistical Office of the United Nations, Publishing Service, New York, New York 10017 (800) 253-9646; *Human Development Report.*

United Nations Educational, Scientific and Cultural Organization (UNESCO), 7 Place de Fontenoy, F-75700 Paris, France (Telephone Number in U.S. (212) 963-5981); *Statistical Yearbook.*

The World Bank, 1818 H Street, NW, Washington, D.C. 20433 (202) 477-1234; *World Development Report;* and *World Development Indicators.*

SAUDI ARABIA - EGG PRODUCTION AND CONSUMPTION - See SAUDI ARABIA - DAIRY PRODUCTS

SAUDI ARABIA - ELECTRICITY

Central Intelligence Agency, Washington, D.C. 20505 (703) 482-1100, www.cia.gov; *The World Factbook.*

Federal Statistical Office, Gustav-Stresemann - Ring 11, D-6200, Wiesbaden, Germany; *Saudi-Arabien.*

M.E. Sharpe, 80 Business Park Drive, Armonk, New York 10504 (800) 541-6563; *The Illustrated Book of World Rankings.*

Penn Well Publishing Company, 1421 South Sheridan Road, P.O. Box 1260, Tulsa, Oklahoma 74101 (800) 752-9764; *International Energy Statistics Sourcebook.*

St. Martin's Press, Inc., 175 Fifth Avenue, New York, New York 10010 (800) 221-7945; *The Statesman's Year-Book.*

Statistical Office of the United Nations, Publishing Service, New York, New York 10017 (800) 253-9646; *Human Development Report;* and *Statistical Yearbook.*

SAUDI ARABIA - EMPLOYMENT

Economic Commission for Western

Asia, Post Office Box 27, Baghdad, Iraq; *Statistical Abstract of Western Asia.*

Euromonitor International, Inc., 122 South Michigan Avenue, Suite 1200, Chicago, Illinois 60603 (800) 577-EURO; *International Marketing Data and Statistics.*

Federal Statistical Office, Gustav-Stresemann-Ring 11, D-6200 Wiesbaden, Germany; *Saudi-Arabien.*

International Labour Office, I.L.O. Publications, 1828 L Street, NW, Suite 801, Washington, D.C. 20036 (301) 638-3152; *Yearbook of Labour Statistics.*

M.E. Sharpe, 80 Business Park Drive, Armonk, New York 10504 (800) 541-6563; *The Illustrated Book of World Rankings.*

Statistical Office of the United Nations, Publishing Service, New York, New York 10017 (800) 253-9646; *Bulletin of Industrial Statistics for the Arab Countries.*

SAUDI ARABIA - ENERGY

Economic Commission for Western Asia, Post Office Box 27, Baghdad, Iraq; *Statistical Abstract of Western Asia.*

Euromonitor International, Inc., 122 South Michigan Avenue, Suite 1200, Chicago, Illinois 60603 (800) 577-EURO; *International Marketing Data and Statistics; World Marketing Data and Statistics;* and *The World Economic Factbook.*

Food and Agricultural Organization of the United Nations (FAO) Via delle Terme di Caracalla, 00100 Rome, Italy (Telephone Number in U.S. (202) 653-2400); *The State of Food and Agriculture.*

M.E. Sharpe, 80 Business Park Drive, Armonk, New York 10504 (800) 541-6563; *The Illustrated Book of World Rankings.*

Penn Well Publishing Company, 1421 South Sheridan Road, P.O. Box 1260, Tulsa, Oklahoma 74101 (800) 752-9764; *International Energy Statistics Sourcebook.*

St. Martin's Press, Inc., 175 Fifth Avenue, New York, New York 10010 (800) 221-7945; *The Statesman's Year-Book.*

Statistical Office of the United Nations, Publishing Service, New York, New York 10017 (800) 253-9646; *Energy Statistics Yearbook; Human Development Report; Statistical Yearbook;* and *World Statistics Pocketbook.*

The World Bank, 1818 H Street, NW, Washington, D.C. 20433 (202) 477-1234; *The World Bank Atlas;* and *World Development Report.*

SAUDI ARABIA - ENVIRONMENT

Economist Intelligence Unit, 111 West 57th Street, New York, New York 10019 (800) 938-4685; *Saudi Arabia Country Report.*

Statistical Office of the United Nations, Publishing Service, New York, New York 10017 (800) 253-9646; *World Statistics Pocketbook.*

SAUDI ARABIA - EXCHANGE RATES

Central Intelligence Agency, Washington, D.C. 20505 (703) 482-1100, www.cia.gov; *The World Factbook.*

Euromonitor International, Inc., 122 South Michigan Avenue, Suite 1200, Chicago, Illinois 60603 (800) 577-EURO; *International Marketing Data and Statistics;* and *The World Economic Factbook.*

Europa Publications Limited, 18 Bedford Square, London, WC1B 3JN, England; *The Europa World Year Book.*

International Civil Aviation Organization, 999 University Street, Montreal, Quebec, Canada H3C 5H7 (514) 954-8219; *Civil Aviation Statistics of the World.*

International Monetary Fund, 700 Nineteenth Street, NW, Washington, D.C. 20431 (202) 623-7000; *International Financial Statistics.*

Organization of Petroleum Exporting Countries, Obere Donaustrasse 93, 1020 Vienna 2, Austria; *OPEC Annual Statistical Bulletin.*

Statistical Office of the United Nations, Publishing Service, New York, New York 10017 (800) 253-9646; *Bulletin of Industrial Statistics for the Arab Countries; Statistical Yearbook;* and *World Statistics Pocketbook.*

SAUDI ARABIA - EXPORTS

Central Intelligence Agency, Washington, D.C. 20505 (703) 482-1100, www.cia.gov; *The World Factbook.*

Economic Commission for Western Asia, Post Office Box 27, Baghdad, Iraq; *Statistical Abstract of Western Asia.*

The Economist Intelligence Unit, 111 West 57th Street, New York, New York 10019 (800) 938-4685; *Saudi Arabia Country Report;* and *The World Market Atlas.*

Euromonitor International, Inc., 122 South Michigan Avenue, Suite 1200, Chicago, Illinois 60603 (800) 577-EURO; *International Marketing Data and Statistics;* and *The World Economic Factbook.*

Europa Publications Limited, 18 Bedford Square, London, WC1B 3JN,

England; *The Europa World Year Book.*

Food and Agricultural Organization of the United Nations (FAO) Via delle Terme di Caracalla, 00100 Rome, Italy (Telephone Number in U.S. (202) 653-2400); *The State of Food and Agriculture.*

International Monetary Fund, 700 Nineteenth Street, NW, Washington, D.C. 20431 (202) 623-7000; *Direction of Trade Statistics;* and *International Financial Statistics.*

Organization of Petroleum Exporting Countries, Obere Donaustrasse 93, 1020 Vienna 2, Austria; *OPEC Annual Statistical Bulletin.*

St. Martin's Press, Inc., 175 Fifth Avenue, New York, New York 10010 (800) 221-7945; *The Statesman's Year-Book.*

Statistical Office of the United Nations, Publishing Service, New York, New York 10017 (800) 253-9646; *Bulletin of Industrial Statistics for the Arab Countries.*

United Nations Conference on Trade and Development (UNCTAD), New York, New York 10017 (800) 253-9646; *Handbook of International Trade and Development Statistics.*

The World Bank, 1818 H Street, NW, Washington, D.C. 20433 (202) 477-1234; *World Development Report;* and *World Development Indicators.*

SAUDI ARABIA - EXTERNAL INDEBTEDNESS

The World Bank, 1818 H Street, NW, Washington, D.C. 20433 (202) 477-1234; *World Development Report;* and *World Development Indicators.*

SAUDI ARABIA - EXTERNAL TRADE

Euromonitor International, Inc., 122 South Michigan Avenue, Suite 1200, Chicago, Illinois 60603 (800) 577-EURO; *World Marketing Data and Statistics.*

Food and Agricultural Organization of the United Nations (FAO), Via delle Terme di Caracalla, 00100, Rome, Italy (Telephone Number in U.S. (202) 653-2400); *Trade Yearbook;* and *The State of Food and Agriculture.*

Statistical Office of the United Nations, Publishing Service, New York, New York 10017 (800) 253-9646; *Statistical Yearbook.*

SAUDI ARABIA - FARM CROPS - See SAUDI ARABIA - CROPS

SAUDI ARABIA - FEMALE WORKING POPULATION - See SAUDI ARABIA - EMPLOYMENT

SAUDI ARABIA - FERTILITY RATES

Central Intelligence Agency, Washington, D.C. 20505 (703) 482-1100, www.cia.gov; *The World Factbook.*

M.E. Sharpe, 80 Business Park Drive, Armonk, New York 10504 (800) 541-6563; *The Illustrated Book of World Rankings.*

Statistical Office of the United Nations, Publishing Service, New York, New York 10017 (800) 253-9646; *Human Development Report.*

The World Bank, 1818 H Street, NW, Washington, D.C. 20433 (202) 477-1234; *The World Bank Atlas; World Development Report;* and *World Development Indicators.*

SAUDI ARABIA - FERTILIZER PRICES

Food and Agricultural Organization of the United Nations (FAO) Via delle Terme di Caracalla, 00100 Rome, Italy (Telephone Number in U.S. (202) 653-2400); *The State of Food and Agriculture.*

SAUDI ARABIA - FERTILIZER PRODUCTION AND CONSUMPTION

Food and Agricultural Organization of the United Nations (FAO) Via delle Terme di Caracalla, 00100 Rome, Italy (Telephone Number in U.S. (202) 653-2400); *The State of Food and Agriculture.*

Statistical Office of the United Nations, Publishing Service, New York, New York 10017 (800) 253-9646; *Statistical Yearbook.*

SAUDI ARABIA - FETAL MORTALITY - See SAUDI - ARABIA - MORTALITY

SAUDI ARABIA - FINANCE

Economic Commission for Western Asia, Post Office Box 27, Baghdad, Iraq; *Statistical Abstract of Western Asia.*

Economist Intelligence Unit, 111 West 57th Street, New York, New York 10019 (800) 938-4685; *Saudi Arabia Country Report.*

Europa Publications Limited, 18 Bedford Square, London, WC1B 3JN, England; *The Europa World Year Book.*

Federal Statistical Office, Gustav-Stresemann-Ring 11, D-6200 Wiesbaden, Germany; *Saudi-Arabien.*

International Monetary Fund, 700 Nineteenth Street, NW, Washington, D.C. 20431 (202) 623-7000; *International Financial Statistics.*

M.E. Sharpe, 80 Business Park Drive, Armonk, New York 10504 (800) 541-6563; *The Illustrated Book of World Rankings.*

St. Martin's Press, Inc., 175 Fifth Avenue, New York, New York 10010 (800) 221-7945; *The Statesman's Year-Book.*

SAUDI ARABIA - FISHERIES

Economic Commission for Western Asia, Post Office Box 27, Baghdad, Iraq; *Statistical Abstract of Western Asia.*

Europa Publications Limited, 18 Bedford Square, London, WC1B 3JN, England; *The Europa World Year Book.*

Federal Statistical Office, Gustav-Stresemann - Ring 11, D-6200, Wiesbaden, Germany; *Saudi-Arabien.*

Food and Agricultural Organization of the United Nations (FAO) Via delle Terme di Caracalla, 00100 Rome, Italy (Telephone Number in U.S. (202) 653-2400); *The State of Food and Agriculture;* and *Yearbook of Fishery Statistics.*

M.E. Sharpe, 80 Business Park Drive, Armonk, New York 10504 (800) 541-6563; *The Illustrated Book of World Rankings.*

St. Martin's Press, Inc., 175 Fifth Avenue, New York, New York 10010 (800) 221-7945; *The Statesman's Year-Book.*

Statistical Office of the United Nations, Publishing Service, New York, New York 10017 (800) 253-9646; *Statistical Yearbook.*

United Nations Conference on Trade and Development, Central Statistical Service, Palais des Nations, Geneva, Switzerland (Telephone in U.S. (800) 253-9646); *UNCTAD Commodity Yearbook.*

SAUDI ARABIA - FOOD

Food and Agricultural Organization of the United Nations (FAO) Via delle Terme di Caracalla, 00100 Rome, Italy (Telephone Number in U.S. (202) 653-2400); *Production Yearbook;* and *The State of Food and Agriculture.*

Statistical Office of the United Nations, Publishing Service, New York, New York 10017 (800) 253-9646; *Human Development Report.*

United Nations Conference on Trade and Development, Central Statistical Service, Palais des Nations, Geneva, Switzerland (Telephone in U.S. (800) 253-9646); *UNCTAD Commodity Yearbook.*

SAUDI ARABIA - FOREIGN TRADE

Economic Commission for Western Asia, Post Office Box 27, Baghdad, Iraq; *Statistical Abstract of Western Asia.*

Economist Intelligence Unit, 111 West 57th Street, New York, New York 10019

(800) 938-4685; *Saudi Arabia Country Report.*

Euromonitor International, Inc., 122 South Michigan Avenue, Suite 1200, Chicago, Illinois 60603 (800) 577-EURO; *International Marketing Data and Statistics;* and *The World Economic Factbook.*

Europa Publications Limited, 18 Bedford Square, London, WC1B 3JN, England; *The Europa World Year Book.*

Federal Statistical Office, Gustav-Stresemann-Ring 11, D-6200 Wiesbaden, Germany; *Saudi-Arabien.*

Food and Agricultural Organization of the United Nations (FAO) Via delle Terme di Caracalla, 00100 Rome, Italy (Telephone Number in U.S. (202) 653-2400); *The State of Food and Agriculture.*

International Monetary Fund, 700 Nineteenth Street, NW, Washington, D.C. 20431 (202) 623-7000; *International Financial Statistics.*

M.E. Sharpe, 80 Business Park Drive, Armonk, New York 10504 (800) 541-6563; *The Illustrated Book of World Rankings.*

St. Martin's Press, Inc., 175 Fifth Avenue, New York, New York 10010 (800) 221-7945; *The Statesman's Year-Book.*

Statistical Office of the United Nations, Publishing Service, New York, New York 10017 (800) 253-9646; *Bulletin of Industrial Statistics for the Arab Countries; International Trade Statistics Yearbook;* and *Statistical Yearbook..*

United Nations Conference on Trade and Development, Central Statistical Service, Palais des Nations, Geneva, Switzerland (Telephone in U.S. (800) 253-9646); *UNCTAD Commodity Yearbook.*

The World Bank, 1818 H Street, NW, Washington, D.C. 20433 (202) 477-1234; *World Development Report;* and *World Development Indicators.*

SAUDI ARABIA - FORESTRY AND FOREST PRODUCTS

Federal Statistical Office, Gustav-Stresemann-Ring 11, D-6200 Wiesbaden, Germany; *Saudi-Arabien.*

Food and Agricultural Organization of the United Nations (FAO) Via delle Terme di Caracalla, 00100 Rome, Italy (Telephone Number in U.S. (202) 653-2400); *The State of Food and Agriculture;* and *Yearbook of Forest Products.*

M.E. Sharpe, 80 Business Park Drive, Armonk, New York 10504 (800) 541-6563; *The Illustrated Book of World Rankings.*

Statistical Office of the United Nations, Publishing Service, New York, New York 10017 (800) 253-9646; *Statistical Yearbook.*

United Nations Conference on Trade and Development, Central Statistical Service, Palais des Nations, Geneva, Switzerland (Telephone in U.S. (800) 253-9646); *UNCTAD Commodity Yearbook.*

United Nations Educational, Scientific and Cultural Organization (UNESCO), 7 Place de Fontenoy, F-75700 Paris, France (Telephone Number in U.S. (212) 963-5981); *Statistical Yearbook.*

The World Bank, 1818 H Street, NW, Washington, D.C. 20433 (202) 477-1234; *World Development Report.*

SAUDI ARABIA - GAS LIQUIDS PRODUCTION - See SAUDI ARABIA - MINING AND MINERAL PRODUCTS

SAUDI ARABIA - GAS PRODUCTION - See SAUDI ARABIA - MINING AND MINERAL PRODUCTS

SAUDI ARABIA - GENERAL MORTALITY - See SAUDI ARABIA - MORTALITY

SAUDI ARABIA - GEOGRAPHIC DATA

M.E. Sharpe, 80 Business Park Drive, Armonk, New York 10504 (800) 541-6563; *The Illustrated Book of World Rankings.*

SAUDI ARABIA - GOATS - See SAUDI ARABIA - LIVESTOCK AND POULTRY

SAUDI ARABIA - GOLD HOLDINGS

International Monetary Fund, 700 Nineteenth Street, NW, Washington, D.C. 20431 (202) 623-7000; *International Financial Statistics.*

Statistical Office of the United Nations, Publishing Service, New York, New York 10017 (800) 253-9646; *Statistical Yearbook.*

The World Bank, 1818 H Street, NW, Washington, D.C. 20433 (202) 477-1234; *World Development Indicators.*

SAUDI ARABIA - GOLD PRODUCTION AND CONSUMPTION - See SAUDI ARABIA - MINING AND MINERAL PRODUCTS

SAUDI ARABIA - GOVERNMENT

Central Intelligence Agency, Washington, D.C. 20505 (703) 482-1100, www.cia.gov; *The World Factbook.*

Economic Commission for Western Asia, Post Office Box 27, Baghdad, Iraq; *Statistical Abstract of Western Asia.*

Europa Publications Limited, 18 Bedford Square, London, WC1B 3JN,

England; *The Europa World Year Book.*

St. Martin's Press, Inc., 175 Fifth Avenue, New York, New York 10010 (800) 221-7945; *The Statesman's Year-Book.*

Statistical Office of the United Nations, Publishing Service, New York, New York 10017 (800) 253-9646; *National Accounts Statistics.*

The World Bank, 1818 H Street, NW, Washington, D.C. 20433 (202) 477-1234; *World Development Report;* and *World Development Indicators.*

SAUDI ARABIA - GRAIN PRODUCTION - See SAUDI ARABIA - CROPS

SAUDI ARABIA - GROSS DOMESTIC PRODUCT

Economic Commission for Western Asia, Post Office Box 27, Baghdad, Iraq; *Statistical Abstract of Western Asia.*

The Economist Intelligence Unit, 111 West 57th Street, New York, New York 10019 (800) 938-4685; *Saudi Arabia Country Report;* and *The World Market Atlas.*

Euromonitor International, Inc., 122 South Michigan Avenue, Suite 1200, Chicago, Illinois 60603 (800) 577-EURO; *International Marketing Data and Statistics;* and *The World Economic Factbook.*

Europa Publications Limited, 18 Bedford Square, London, WC1B 3JN, England; *The Europa World Year Book.*

M.E. Sharpe, 80 Business Park Drive, Armonk, New York 10504 (800) 541-6563; *The Illustrated Book of World Rankings.*

Statistical Office of the United Nations, Publishing Service, New York, New York 10017 (800) 253-9646; *Bulletin of Industrial Statistics for the Arab Countries; Human Development Report; National Accounts Statistics;* and *Statistical Yearbook.*

The World Bank, 1818 H Street, NW, Washington, D.C. 20433 (202) 477-1234; *World Development Report;* and *World Development Indicators.*

SAUDI ARABIA - GROSS NATIONAL PRODUCT

Euromonitor International, Inc., 122 South Michigan Avenue, Suite 1200, Chicago, Illinois 60603 (800) 577-EURO; *International Marketing Data and Statistics.*

Organization of Petroleum Exporting Countries, Obere Donaustrasse 93, 1020 Vienna 2, Austria; *OPEC Annual Statistical Bulletin.*

St. Martin's Press, Inc., 175 Fifth

Avenue, New York, New York 10010 (800) 221-7945; *The Statesman's Year-Book.*

U.S. Arms Control and Disarmament Agency, 320 Twenty-first Street, NW, Washington, D.C. 20451 (202) 647-8677; *World Military Expenditures and Arms Transfers.*

The World Bank, 1818 H Street, NW, Washington, D.C. 20433 (202) 477-1234; *The World Bank Atlas; World Development Report;* and *World Development Indicators.*

SAUDI ARABIA - HEALTH

Economic Commission for Western Asia, Post Office Box 27, Baghdad, Iraq; *Statistical Abstract of Western Asia.*

Euromonitor International, Inc., 122 South Michigan Avenue, Suite 1200, Chicago, Illinois 60603 (800) 577-EURO; *World Marketing Data and Statistics.*

Federal Statistical Office, Gustav-Stresemann-Ring 11, D-6200 Wiesbaden, Germany; *Saudi-Arabien.*

M.E. Sharpe, 80 Business Park Drive, Armonk, New York 10504 (800) 541-6563; *The Illustrated Book of World Rankings.*

St. Martin's Press, Inc., 175 Fifth Avenue, New York, New York 10010 (800) 221-7945; *The Statesman's Year-Book.*

Statistical Office of the United Nations, Publishing Service, New York, New York 10017 (800) 253-9646; *Human Development Report;* and *Statistical Yearbook.*

United Nations Children's Fund (UNICEF), 3 United Nations Plaza, New York, New York 10017 (800) 253-9646; *State of the World's Children.*

The World Bank, 1818 H Street, NW, Washington, D.C. 20433 (202) 477-1234; *World Development Report.*

World Health Organization, Office of Publications, 20 Avenue Appia, CH-1211 Geneva 27, Switzerland (Telephone Number in U.S. (518) 436-9686); *World Health Statistics Annual.*

SAUDI ARABIA - HIGHWAYS

Central Intelligence Agency, Washington, D.C. 20505 (703) 482-1100, www.cia.gov; *The World Factbook.*

Economic Commission for Western Asia, Post Office Box 27, Baghdad, Iraq; *Statistical Abstract of Western Asia.*

International Road Federation, 2600 Virginia Avenue, NW, Washington, D.C. 20037 (202) 338-4641; *World Road*

Statistics.

St. Martin's Press, Inc., 175 Fifth Avenue, New York, New York 10010 (800) 221-7945; *The Statesman's Year-Book.*

SAUDI ARABIA - HORSES - See SAUDI ARABIA - LIVESTOCK AND POULTRY

SAUDI ARABIA - HOURS OF WORK - See SAUDI ARABIA - EMPLOYMENT

SAUDI ARABIA - HOUSING AND HOUSING UNITS

Euromonitor International, Inc., 122 South Michigan Avenue, Suite 1200, Chicago, Illinois 60603 (800) 577-EURO; *World Marketing Data and Statistics.*

M.E. Sharpe, 80 Business Park Drive, Armonk, New York 10504 (800) 541-6563; *The Illustrated Book of World Rankings.*

SAUDI ARABIA - ILLITERATE POPULATION

Central Intelligence Agency, Washington, D.C. 20505 (703) 482-1100, www.cia.gov; *The World Factbook.*

The Economist Intelligence Unit, 111 West 57th Street, New York, New York 10019 (800) 938-4685; *The World Market Atlas.*

Euromonitor International, Inc., 122 South Michigan Avenue, Suite 1200, Chicago, Illinois 60603 (800) 577-EURO; *The World Economic Factbook.*

St. Martin's Press, Inc., 175 Fifth Avenue, New York, New York 10010 (800) 221-7945; *The Statesman's Year-Book.*

Statistical Office of the United Nations, Publishing Service, New York, New York 10017 (800) 253-9646; *Human Development Report.*

United Nations Educational, Scientific and Cultural Organization (UNESCO), 7 Place de Fontenoy, F-75700 Paris, France (Telephone Number in U.S. (212) 963-5981); *Statistical Yearbook.*

SAUDI ARABIA - IMPORTS

Central Intelligence Agency, Washington, D.C. 20505 (703) 482-1100, www.cia.gov; *The World Factbook.*

Economic Commission for Western Asia, Post Office Box 27, Baghdad, Iraq; *Statistical Abstract of Western Asia.*

The Economist Intelligence Unit, 111 West 57th Street, New York, New York 10019 (800) 938-4685; *Saudi Arabia Country Report;* and *The World Market Atlas.*

Euromonitor International, Inc., 122

South Michigan Avenue, Suite 1200, Chicago, Illinois 60603 (800) 577-EURO; *International Marketing Data and Statistics;* and *The World Economic Factbook.*

Europa Publications Limited, 18 Bedford Square, London, WC1B 3JN, England; *The Europa World Year Book.*

Food and Agricultural Organization of the United Nations (FAO) Via delle Terme di Caracalla, 00100 Rome, Italy (Telephone Number in U.S. (202) 653-2400); *The State of Food and Agriculture.*

International Monetary Fund, 700 Nineteenth Street, NW, Washington, D.C. 20431 (202) 623-7000; *Direction of Trade Statistics;* and *International Financial Statistics.*

St. Martin's Press, Inc., 175 Fifth Avenue, New York, New York 10010 (800) 221-7945; *The Statesman's Year-Book.*

Statistical Office of the United Nations, Publishing Service, New York, New York 10017 (800) 253-9646; *Bulletin of Industrial Statistics for the Arab Countries.*

United Nations Conference on Trade and Development (UNCTAD), New York, New York 10017 (800) 253-9646; *Handbook of International Trade and Development Statistics.*

The World Bank, 1818 H Street, NW, Washington, D.C. 20433 (202) 477-1234; *World Development Report;* and *World Development Indicators.*

SAUDI ARABIA - INDUSTRY

Central Intelligence Agency, Washington, D.C. 20505 (703) 482-1100, www.cia.gov; *The World Factbook.*

Economist Intelligence Unit, 111 West 57th Street, New York, New York 10019 (800) 938-4685; *Saudi Arabia Country Report.*

Euromonitor International, Inc., 122 South Michigan Avenue, Suite 1200, Chicago, Illinois 60603 (800) 577-EURO; *The World Economic Factbook;* and *World Marketing Data and Statistics.*

Europa Publications Limited, 18 Bedford Square, London, WC1B 3JN, England; *The Europa World Year Book.*

Federal Statistical Office, Gustav-Stresemann-Ring 11, D-6200 Wiesbaden, Germany; *Saudi-Arabien.*

International Labour Office, I.L.O. Publications, 1828 L Street, NW, Suite 801, Washington, D.C. 20036 (301) 638-3152; *Yearbook of Labour Statistics.*

M.E. Sharpe, 80 Business Park Drive, Armonk, New York 10504 (800) 541-6563; *The Illustrated Book of World Rankings.*

St. Martin's Press, Inc., 175 Fifth Avenue, New York, New York 10010 (800) 221-7945; *The Statesman's Year-Book.*

Statistical Office of the United Nations, Publishing Service, New York, New York 10017 (800) 253-9646; *Bulletin of Industrial Statistics for the Arab Countries.*

The World Bank, 1818 H Street, NW, Washington, D.C. 20433 (202) 477-1234; *World Development Indicators.*

SAUDI ARABIA - INFANT AND MATERNAL MORTALITY - See SAUDI ARABIA - MORTALITY

SAUDI ARABIA - INTERNAL TRADE

Statistical Office of the United Nations, Publishing Service, New York, New York 10017 (800) 253-9646; *Statistical Yearbook.*

SAUDI ARABIA - INTERNATIONAL LIQUIDITY

International Monetary Fund, 700 Nineteenth Street, NW, Washington, D.C. 20431 (202) 623-7000; *International Financial Statistics.*

SAUDI ARABIA - INTERNATIONAL RESERVES EXCLUDING GOLD

Statistical Office of the United Nations, Publishing Service, New York, New York 10017 (800) 253-9646; *Statistical Yearbook.*

The World Bank, 1818 H Street, NW, Washington, D.C. 20433 (202) 477-1234; *World Development Indicators.*

SAUDI ARABIA - IRON ORE PRODUCTION AND CONSUMPTION - See SAUDI ARABIA - MINING AND MINERAL PRODUCTS

SAUDI ARABIA - IRRIGATION

Euromonitor International, Inc., 122 South Michigan Avenue, Suite 1200, Chicago, Illinois 60603 (800) 577-EURO; *International Marketing Data and Statistics.*

SAUDI ARABIA - LABOR

Central Intelligence Agency, Washington, D.C. 20505 (703) 482-1100, www.cia.gov; *The World Factbook.*

Economic Commission for Western Asia, Post Office Box 27, Baghdad, Iraq; *Statistical Abstract of Western Asia.*

Euromonitor International, Inc., 122 South Michigan Avenue, Suite 1200, Chicago, Illinois 60603 (800) 577-EURO; *International Marketing Data and Statistics;*

and *World Marketing Data and Statistics.*

Food and Agricultural Organization of the United Nations (FAO) Via delle Terme di Caracalla, 00100 Rome, Italy (Telephone Number in U.S. (202) 653-2400); *The State of Food and Agriculture.*

International Labour Office, I.L.O. Publications, 1828 L Street, NW, Suite 801, Washington, D.C. 20036 (301) 638-3152; *Yearbook of Labour Statistics.*

M.E. Sharpe, 80 Business Park Drive, Armonk, New York 10504 (800) 541-6563; *The Illustrated Book of World Rankings.*

St. Martin's Press, Inc., 175 Fifth Avenue, New York, New York 10010 (800) 221-7945; *The Statesman's Year-Book.*

Statistical Office of the United Nations, Publishing Service, New York, New York 10017 (800) 253-9646; *Human Development Report.*

The World Bank, 1818 H Street, NW, Washington, D.C. 20433 (202) 477-1234; *The World Bank Atlas; World Development Report;* and *World Development Indicators.*

SAUDI ARABIA - LAND USE

Central Intelligence Agency, Washington, D.C. 20505 (703) 482-1100, www.cia.gov; *The World Factbook.*

Economic Commission for Western Asia, Post Office Box 27, Baghdad, Iraq; *Statistical Abstract of Western Asia.*

Euromonitor International, Inc., 122 South Michigan Avenue, Suite 1200, Chicago, Illinois 60603 (800) 577-EURO; *International Marketing Data and Statistics.*

Food and Agricultural Organization of the United Nations (FAO), Via delle Terme di Caracalla, 00100 Rome, Italy (Telephone Number in U.S. (202) 653-2400); *Production Yearbook.*

The World Bank, 1818 H Street, NW, Washington, D.C. 20433 (202) 477-1234; *World Development Report.*

SAUDI ARABIA - LIBRARIES

M.E. Sharpe, 80 Business Park Drive, Armonk, New York 10504 (800) 541-6563; *The Illustrated Book of World Rankings.*

United Nations Educational, Scientific and Cultural Organization (UNESCO), 7 Place de Fontenoy, F-75700 Paris, France (Telephone Number in U.S. (212) 963-5981); *Statistical Yearbook.*

SAUDI ARABIA - LIFE EXPECTANCY

Central Intelligence Agency,

Washington, D.C. 20505 (703) 482-1100, www.cia.gov; *The World Factbook*.

Euromonitor International, Inc., 122 South Michigan Avenue, Suite 1200, Chicago, Illinois 60603 (800) 577-EURO; *The World Economic Factbook*.

St. Martin's Press, Inc., 175 Fifth Avenue, New York, New York 10010 (800) 221-7945; *The Statesman's Year-Book*.

Statistical Office of the United Nations, Publishing Service, New York, New York 10017 (800) 253-9646; *Human Development Report;* and *World Statistics Pocketbook*.

The World Bank, 1818 H Street, NW, Washington, D.C. 20433 (202) 477-1234; *The World Bank Atlas;* and *World Development Report*.

SAUDI ARABIA - LITERACY RATE

Euromonitor International, Inc., 122 South Michigan Avenue, Suite 1200, Chicago, Illinois 60603 (800) 577-EURO; *World Marketing Data and Statistics*.

SAUDI ARABIA - LIVESTOCK AND POULTRY

Economic Commission for Western Asia, Post Office Box 27, Baghdad, Iraq; *Statistical Abstract of Western Asia*.

Euromonitor International, Inc., 122 South Michigan Avenue, Suite 1200, Chicago, Illinois 60603 (800) 577-EURO; *International Marketing Data and Statistics*.

Europa Publications Limited, 18 Bedford Square, London, WC1B 3JN, England; *The Europa World Year Book*.

Food and Agricultural Organization of the United Nations (FAO), Via delle Terme di Caracalla, 00100 Rome, Italy (Telephone Number in U.S. (202) 653-2400); *Production Yearbook;* and *The State of Food and Agriculture*.

M.E. Sharpe, 80 Business Park Drive, Armonk, New York 10504 (800) 541-6563; *The Illustrated Book of World Rankings*.

St. Martin's Press, Inc., 175 Fifth Avenue, New York, New York 10010 (800) 221-7945; *The Statesman's Year-Book*.

Statistical Office of the United Nations, Publishing Service, New York, New York 10017 (800) 253-9646; *Statistical Yearbook*.

United Nations Conference on Trade and Development, Central Statistical Service, Palais des Nations, Geneva, Switzerland (Telephone in U.S. (800) 253-9646); *UNCTAD Commodity Yearbook*.

SAUDI ARABIA - LIVING LEVELS - See SAUDI ARABIA - LIFE EXPECTANCY

SAUDI ARABIA - MAIL - NUMBER OF PIECES SENT OR RECEIVED

Statistical Office of the United Nations, Publishing Service, New York, New York 10017 (800) 253-9646; *Statistical Yearbook*.

SAUDI ARABIA - MANUFACTURING

M.E. Sharpe, 80 Business Park Drive, Armonk, New York 10504 (800) 541-6563; *The Illustrated Book of World Rankings*.

Statistical Office of the United Nations, Publishing Service, New York, New York 10017 (800) 253-9646; *Bulletin of Industrial Statistics for the Arab Countries*.

The World Bank, 1818 H Street, NW, Washington, D.C. 20433 (202) 477-1234; *World Development Indicators*.

SAUDI ARABIA - MARRIAGE RATES

M.E. Sharpe, 80 Business Park Drive, Armonk, New York 10504 (800) 541-6563; *The Illustrated Book of World Rankings*.

Statistical Office of the United Nations, Publishing Service, New York, New York 10017 (800) 253-9646; *Demographic Yearbook*.

World Health Organization, Office of Publications, 20 Avenue Appia, CH-1211 Geneva 27, Switzerland (Telephone Number in U.S. (518) 436-9686); *World Health Statistics Annual*.

SAUDI ARABIA - MEAT PRODUCTION - See SAUDI ARABIA - LIVESTOCK AND POULTRY

SAUDI ARABIA - MERCHANT SHIPPING

Economic Commission for Western Asia, Post Office Box 27, Baghdad, Iraq; *Statistical Abstract of Western Asia*.

Europa Publications Limited, 18 Bedford Square, London, WC1B 3JN, England; *The Europa World Year Book*.

Lloyd's Register of Shipping, 17 Battery Place, New York, New York 10004 (212) 425-8050; *Register of Ships*.

Organization of Petroleum Exporting Countries, Obere Donaustrasse 93, 1020 Vienna 2, Austria; *OPEC Annual Statistical Bulletin*.

St. Martin's Press, Inc., 175 Fifth Avenue, New York, New York 10010 (800) 221-7945; *The Statesman's Year-Book*.

Statistical Office of the United Nations, Publishing Service, New York, New York

10017 (800) 253-9646; *Statistical Yearbook*.

U.S. Department of Transportation, Maritime Administration, 400 Seventh Street, SW, Washington, D.C. 20590 (202) 366-5807, www.marad.dot.gov; *A Statistical Analysis of the World's Merchant Fleets*.

SAUDI ARABIA - MILITARY

Central Intelligence Agency, Washington, D.C. 20505 (703) 482-1100, www.cia.gov; *The World Factbook*.

Euromonitor International, Inc., 122 South Michigan Avenue, Suite 1200, Chicago, Illinois 60603 (800) 577-EURO; *World Marketing Data and Statistics*.

The International Institute for Strategic Studies, 23 Tavistock Street, London WC2E 7NQ, England 44 171 3797676; *The Military Balance*.

St. Martin's Press, Inc., 175 Fifth Avenue, New York, New York 10010 (800) 221-7945; *The Statesman's Year-Book*.

Statistical Office of the United Nations, Publishing Service, New York, New York 10017 (800) 253-9646; *Human Development Report*.

U.S. Arms Control and Disarmament Agency, 320 Twenty-first Street, NW, Washington, D.C. 20451 (202) 647-8677; *World Military Expenditures and Arms Transfers*.

SAUDI ARABIA - MILK PRODUCTION - See SAUDI ARABIA - DAIRY PRODUCTS

SAUDI ARABIA - MINING AND MINERAL PRODUCTS

Economic Commission for Western Asia, Post Office Box 27, Baghdad, Iraq; *Statistical Abstract of Western Asia*.

Europa Publications Limited, 18 Bedford Square, London, WC1B 3JN, England; *The Europa World Year Book*.

M.E. Sharpe, 80 Business Park Drive, Armonk, New York 10504 (800) 541-6563; *The Illustrated Book of World Rankings*.

Organization of Petroleum Exporting Countries, Obere Donaustrasse 93, 1020 Vienna 2, Austria; *OPEC Annual Statistical Bulletin*.

Penn Well Publishing Company, 1421 South Sheridan Road, P.O. Box 1260, Tulsa, Oklahoma 74101 (800) 752-9764; *International Energy Statistics Sourcebook*.

St. Martin's Press, Inc., 175 Fifth Avenue, New York, New York 10010 (800) 221-7945; *The Statesman's Year-Book*.

Statistical Office of the United Nations, Publishing Service, New York, New York 10017 (800) 253-9646; *Bulletin of Industrial Statistics for the Arab Countries;* and *Statistical Yearbook.*

United Nations Conference on Trade and Development, Central Statistical Service, Palais des Nations, Geneva, Switzerland (Telephone in U.S. (800) 253-9646); *UNCTAD Commodity Yearbook.*

SAUDI ARABIA - MONEY EXCHANGE RATES - See SAUDI ARABIA - EXCHANGE RATES

SAUDI ARABIA - MONEY RESERVES

Euromonitor International, Inc., 122 South Michigan Avenue, Suite 1200, Chicago, Illinois 60603 (800) 577-EURO; *International Marketing Data and Statistics.*

SAUDI ARABIA - MONEY SUPPLY

Economic Commission for Western Asia, Post Office Box 27, Baghdad, Iraq; *Statistical Abstract of Western Asia.*

Economist Intelligence Unit, 111 West 57th Street, New York, New York 10019 (800) 938-4685; *Saudi Arabia Country Report.*

Euromonitor International, Inc., 122 South Michigan Avenue, Suite 1200, Chicago, Illinois 60603 (800) 577-EURO; *International Marketing Data and Statistics.*

Europa Publications Limited, 18 Bedford Square, London, WC1B 3JN, England; *The Europa World Year Book.*

Federal Statistical Office, Gustav-Stresemann - Ring 11, D-6200, Wiesbaden, Germany; *Saudi-Arabien.*

International Monetary Fund, 700 Nineteenth Street, NW, Washington, D.C. 20431 (202) 623-7000; *International Financial Statistics.*

Statistical Office of the United Nations, Publishing Service, New York, New York 10017 (800) 253-9646; *Statistical Yearbook.*

The World Bank, 1818 H Street, NW, Washington, D.C. 20433 (202) 477-1234; *World Development Indicators.*

SAUDI ARABIA - MORTALITY

Central Intelligence Agency, Washington, D.C. 20505 (703) 482-1100, www.cia.gov; *The World Factbook.*

Euromonitor International, Inc., 122 South Michigan Avenue, Suite 1200, Chicago, Illinois 60603 (800) 577-EURO; *International Marketing Data and Statistics;* and *The World Economic Factbook.*

Europa Publications Limited, 18 Bedford Square, London, WC1B 3JN, England; *The Europa World Year Book.*

St. Martin's Press, Inc., 175 Fifth Avenue, New York, New York 10010 (800) 221-7945; *The Statesman's Year-Book.*

Statistical Office of the United Nations, Publishing Service, New York, New York 10017 (800) 253-9646; *Demographic Yearbook; Human Development Report; Statistical Yearbook;* and *World Statistics Pocketbook.*

United Nations Children's Fund (UNICEF), 3 United Nations Plaza, New York, New York 10017 (800) 253-9646; *State of the World's Children.*

The World Bank, 1818 H Street, NW, Washington, D.C. 20433 (202) 477-1234; *The World Bank Atlas; World Development Report;* and *World Development Indicators.*

World Health Organization, Office of Publications, 20 Avenue Appia, CH-1211 Geneva 27, Switzerland (Telephone Number in U.S. (518) 436-9686); *World Health Statistics Annual.*

SAUDI ARABIA - MOTOR VEHICLE TAXES - See SAUDI ARABIA - TAXATION

SAUDI ARABIA - MOTOR VEHICLES

Economic Commission for Western Asia, Post Office Box 27, Baghdad, Iraq; *Statistical Abstract of Western Asia.*

SAUDI ARABIA - MOTOR VEHICLES IN USE

International Road Federation, 2600 Virginia Avenue, NW, Washington, D.C. 20037 (202) 338-4641; *World Road Statistics.*

Statistical Office of the United Nations, Publishing Service, New York, New York 10017 (800) 253-9646; *Statistical Yearbook.*

SAUDI ARABIA - MULES - See SAUDI ARABIA - LIVESTOCK AND POULTRY

SAUDI ARABIA - MUSEUMS

M.E. Sharpe, 80 Business Park Drive, Armonk, New York 10504 (800) 541-6563; *The Illustrated Book of World Rankings.*

United Nations Educational, Scientific and Cultural Organization (UNESCO), 7 Place de Fontenoy, F-75700 Paris, France (Telephone Number in U.S. (212) 963-5981); *Statistical Yearbook.*

SAUDI ARABIA - NATALITY - See SAUDI ARABIA - BIRTH RATE

SAUDI ARABIA - NATIONAL ACCOUNTS

Economic Commission for Western Asia, Post Office Box 27, Baghdad, Iraq; *Statistical Abstract of Western Asia.*

Europa Publications Limited, 18 Bedford Square, London, WC1B 3JN, England; *The Europa World Year Book.*

Federal Statistical Office, Gustav-Stresemann-Ring 11, D-6200 Wiesbaden, Germany; *Saudi-Arabien.*

International Monetary Fund, 700 Nineteenth Street, NW, Washington, D.C. 20431 (202) 623-7000; *International Financial Statistics.*

Statistical Office of the United Nations, Publishing Service, New York, New York 10017 (800) 253-9646; *National Accounts Statistics;* and *Statistical Yearbook.*

SAUDI ARABIA - NATIONAL INCOME

M.E. Sharpe, 80 Business Park Drive, Armonk, New York 10504 (800) 541-6563; *The Illustrated Book of World Rankings.*

Statistical Office of the United Nations, Publishing Service, New York, New York 10017 (800) 253-9646; *National Accounts Statistics;* and *Statistical Yearbook.*

SAUDI ARABIA - NATIONAL PRODUCT

M.E. Sharpe, 80 Business Park Drive, Armonk, New York 10504 (800) 541-6563; *The Illustrated Book of World Rankings.*

Statistical Office of the United Nations, Publishing Service, New York, New York 10017 (800) 253-9646; *Statistical Yearbook.*

SAUDI ARABIA - NATURAL GAS PRODUCTION - See SAUDI ARABIA - MINING AND MINERAL PRODUCTS

SAUDI ARABIA - NEWSPAPER PRODUCTION - See SAUDI ARABIA - FORESTRY AND FOREST PRODUCTS

SAUDI ARABIA - NEWSPRINT - See SAUDI ARABIA - FORESTRY AND FOREST PRODUCTS

SAUDI ARABIA - OCCUPATIONS - See SAUDI ARABIA - LABOR

SAUDI ARABIA - PAPER - See SAUDI ARABIA - FORESTRY AND FOREST PRODUCTS

SAUDI ARABIA - PEANUT PRODUCTION - See SAUDI ARABIA - CROPS

SAUDI ARABIA - PERIODICALS

United Nations Educational, Scientific and Cultural Organization (UNESCO), 7 Place de Fontenoy, F-75700 Paris, France (Telephone Number in U.S. (212) 963-

5981); *Statistical Yearbook*.

SAUDI ARABIA - PESTICIDE USE

Food and Agricultural Organization of the United Nations (FAO) Via delle Terme di Caracalla, 00100 Rome, Italy (Telephone Number in U.S. (202) 653-2400); *The State of Food and Agriculture*.

SAUDI ARABIA - PETROLEUM INDUSTRY

Commodity Research Bureau, Inc., 30 South Wacker Drive, Chicago Illinois 60606 (312) 454-1801; *Commodity Year Book*.

Food and Agricultural Organization of the United Nations (FAO) Via delle Terme di Caracalla, 00100 Rome, Italy (Telephone Number in U.S. (202) 653-2400); *The State of Food and Agriculture*.

International Monetary Fund, 700 Nineteenth Street, NW, Washington, D.C. 20431 (202) 623-7000; *International Financial Statistics*.

M.E. Sharpe, 80 Business Park Drive, Armonk, New York 10504 (800) 541-6563; *The Illustrated Book of World Rankings*.

Organization of Petroleum Exporting Countries, Obere Donaustrasse 93, 1020 Vienna 2, Austria; *OPEC Annual Statistical Bulletin*.

Penn Well Publishing Company, 1421 South Sheridan Road, P.O. Box 1260, Tulsa, Oklahoma 74101 (800) 752-9764; *International Energy Statistics Sourcebook*.

St. Martin's Press, Inc., 175 Fifth Avenue, New York, New York 10010 (800) 221-7945; *The Statesman's Year-Book*.

Statistical Office of the United Nations, Publishing Service, New York, New York 10017 (800) 253-9646; *Statistical Yearbook*.

United Nations Conference on Trade and Development, Central Statistical Service, Palais des Nations, Geneva, Switzerland (Telephone in U.S. (800) 253-9646); *UNCTAD Commodity Yearbook*.

SAUDI ARABIA - PIGS - See SAUDI ARABIA - LIVESTOCK AND POULTRY

SAUDI ARABIA - PIPELINES FOR OIL AND PETROLEUM PRODUCTS

Organization of Petroleum Exporting Countries, Obere Donaustrasse 93, 1020 Vienna 2, Austria; *OPEC Annual Statistical Bulletin*.

SAUDI ARABIA - POPULATION

Central Intelligence Agency, Washington, D.C. 20505 (703) 482-1100, www.cia.gov; *The World Factbook*.

Economic Commission for Western Asia, Post Office Box 27, Baghdad, Iraq; *Statistical Abstract of Western Asia*.

The Economist Intelligence Unit, 111 West 57th Street, New York, New York 10019 (800) 938-4685; *Saudi Arabia Country Report;* and *The World Market Atlas*.

Euromonitor International, Inc., 122 South Michigan Avenue, Suite 1200, Chicago, Illinois 60603 (800) 577-EURO; *International Marketing Data and Statistics;* and *The World Economic Factbook*.

Europa Publications Limited, 18 Bedford Square, London, WC1B 3JN, England; *The Europa World Year Book*.

Federal Statistical Office, Gustav-Stresemann-Ring 11, D-6200 Wiesbaden, Germany; *Saudi-Arabien*.

Food and Agricultural Organization of the United Nations (FAO), Via delle Terme di Caracalla, 00100 Rome, Italy (Telephone Number in U.S. (202) 653-2400); *Production Yearbook*.

International Labour Office, I.L.O. Publications, 1828 L Street, NW, Suite 801, Washington, D.C. 20036 (301) 638-3152; *Yearbook of Labour Statistics*.

M.E. Sharpe, 80 Business Park Drive, Armonk, New York 10504 (800) 541-6563; *The Illustrated Book of World Rankings*.

St. Martin's Press, Inc., 175 Fifth Avenue, New York, New York 10010 (800) 221-7945; *The Statesman's Year-Book*.

Statistical Office of the United Nations, Publishing Service, New York, New York 10017 (800) 253-9646; *Human Development Report; Statistical Yearbook;* and *World Statistics Pocketbook*.

United Nations Educational, Scientific and Cultural Organization (UNESCO), 7 Place de Fontenoy, F-75700 Paris, France (Telephone Number in U.S. (212) 963-5981); *Statistical Yearbook*.

U.S. Arms Control and Disarmament Agency, 320 Twenty-first Street, NW, Washington, D.C. 20451 (202) 647-8677; *World Military Expenditures and Arms Transfers*.

The World Bank, 1818 H Street, NW, Washington, D.C. 20433 (202) 477-1234; *The World Bank Atlas;* and *World Development Report*.

World Health Organization, Office of Publications, 20 Avenue Appia, CH-1211 Geneva 27, Switzerland (Telephone Number in U.S. (518) 436-9686); *World Health Statistics Annual*.

SAUDI ARABIA - POST OFFICES

M.E. Sharpe, 80 Business Park Drive, Armonk, New York 10504 (800) 541-6563; *The Illustrated Book of World Rankings*.

St. Martin's Press, Inc., 175 Fifth Avenue, New York, New York 10010 (800) 221-7945; *The Statesman's Year-Book*.

SAUDI ARABIA - POTATO PRODUCTION - See SAUDI ARABIA - CROPS

SAUDI ARABIA - PRICES

Economic Commission for Western Asia, Post Office Box 27, Baghdad, Iraq; *Statistical Abstract of Western Asia*.

Federal Statistical Office, Gustav-Stresemann-Ring 11, D-6200 Wiesbaden, Germany; *Saudi-Arabien*.

Food and Agricultural Organization of the United Nations (FAO), Via delle Terme di Caracalla, 00100 Rome, Italy (Telephone Number in U.S. (202) 653-2400); *Production Yearbook;* and *The State of Food and Agriculture*.

International Monetary Fund, 700 Nineteenth Street, NW, Washington, D.C. 20431 (202) 623-7000; *International Financial Statistics*.

M.E. Sharpe, 80 Business Park Drive, Armonk, New York 10504 (800) 541-6563; *The Illustrated Book of World Rankings*.

SAUDI ARABIA - PRINTING AND WRITING PAPER - See SAUDI ARABIA - FORESTRY AND FOREST PRODUCTS

SAUDI ARABIA - PRODUCTION

M.E. Sharpe, 80 Business Park Drive, Armonk, New York 10504 (800) 541-6563; *The Illustrated Book of World Rankings*.

SAUDI ARABIA - PRODUCTIVITY

Euromonitor International, Inc., 122 South Michigan Avenue, Suite 1200, Chicago, Illinois 60603 (800) 577-EURO; *International Marketing Data and Statistics*.

SAUDI ARABIA - PUBLIC FINANCE - See SAUDI ARABIA - FINANCE

SAUDI ARABIA - RADIO BROADCASTING - See SAUDI ARABIA - BROADCASTING

SAUDI ARABIA - RADIO RECEIVERS

St. Martin's Press, Inc., 175 Fifth Avenue, New York, New York 10010 (800) 221-7945; *The Statesman's Year-Book*.

SAUDI ARABIA - RAILWAYS

Europa Publications Limited, 18

Bedford Square, London, WC1B 3JN, England; *The Europa World Year Book.*

Jane's Information Group, Sentinel House, 163 Brighton Road, Coulsdon, Surrey CR5 2NH, England (Telephone Number in U.S. (703) 683-3700); *Jane's World Railways.*

St. Martin's Press, Inc., 175 Fifth Avenue, New York, New York 10010 (800) 221-7945; *The Statesman's Year-Book.*

Statistical Office of the United Nations, Publishing Service, New York, New York 10017 (800) 253-9646; *Statistical Yearbook.*

SAUDI ARABIA - RELIGION

Central Intelligence Agency, Washington, D.C. 20505 (703) 482-1100, www.cia.gov; *The World Factbook.*

M.E. Sharpe, 80 Business Park Drive, Armonk, New York 10504 (800) 541-6563; *The Illustrated Book of World Rankings.*

St. Martin's Press, Inc., 175 Fifth Avenue, New York, New York 10010 (800) 221-7945; *The Statesman's Year-Book.*

SAUDI ARABIA - RETAIL TRADE

Euromonitor International, Inc., 122 South Michigan Avenue, Suite 1200, Chicago, Illinois 60603 (800) 577-EURO; *World Marketing Data and Statistics.*

Statistical Office of the United Nations, Publishing Service, New York, New York 10017 (800) 253-9646; *Statistical Yearbook.*

SAUDI ARABIA - RICE PRODUCTION - See SAUDI ARABIA - CROPS

SAUDI ARABIA - ROUNDWOOD PRODUCTION - See SAUDI ARABIA - FORESTRY AND FOREST PRODUCTS

SAUDI ARABIA - RUBBER PRODUCTION AND CONSUMPTION

M.E. Sharpe, 80 Business Park Drive, Armonk, New York 10504 (800) 541-6563; *The Illustrated Book of World Rankings.*

SAUDI ARABIA - SAWNWOOD PRODUCTION - See SAUDI ARABIA - FORESTRY AND FOREST PRODUCTS

SAUDI ARABIA - SCIENTISTS, TECHNICIANS AND ENGINEERS

Statistical Office of the United Nations, Publishing Service, New York, New York 10017 (800) 253-9646; *Statistical Yearbook.*

SAUDI ARABIA - SENIOR CITIZENS

M.E. Sharpe, 80 Business Park Drive, Armonk, New York 10504 (800) 541-6563;

The Illustrated Book of World Rankings.

SAUDI ARABIA - SHEEP - See SAUDI ARABIA - LIVESTOCK AND POULTRY

SAUDI ARABIA - SILVER PRODUCTION AND CONSUMPTION - See SAUDI ARABIA - MINING AND MINERAL PRODUCTS

SAUDI ARABIA - SOCIAL DATA

M.E. Sharpe, 80 Business Park Drive, Armonk, New York 10504 (800) 541-6563; *The Illustrated Book of World Rankings.*

Statistical Office of the United Nations, Publishing Service, New York, New York 10017 (800) 253-9646; *World Statistics Pocketbook.*

SAUDI ARABIA - SOCIAL SECURITY

Statistical Office of the United Nations, Publishing Service, New York, New York 10017 (800) 253-9646; *National Accounts Statistics.*

SAUDI ARABIA - STATE BUDGET REVENUE AND EXPENDITURES

Euromonitor International, Inc., 122 South Michigan Avenue, Suite 1200, Chicago, Illinois 60603 (800) 577-EURO; *International Marketing Data and Statistics.*

SAUDI ARABIA - STEEL - See SAUDI ARABIA - MINING AND MINERAL PRODUCTS

SAUDI ARABIA - STOCKS - COMMODITY - MARKET PRICE - INDEX

Food and Agricultural Organization of the United Nations (FAO) Via delle Terme di Caracalla, 00100 Rome, Italy (Telephone Number in U.S. (202) 653-2400); *The State of Food and Agriculture.*

SAUDI ARABIA - SUGAR - See SAUDI ARABIA - CROPS

SAUDI ARABIA - TAXATION

International Road Federation, 2600 Virginia Avenue, NW, Washington, D.C. 20037 (202) 338-4641; *World Road Statistics.*

The World Bank, 1818 H Street, NW, Washington, D.C. 20433 (202) 477-1234; *World Development Indicators.*

SAUDI ARABIA - TELEPHONES IN USE

American Telephone and Telegraph Company, 26 Parsippany Road, Whippany, New Jersey 07981 (800) 222-0300; *The World's Telephones.*

Central Intelligence Agency,

Washington, D.C. 20505 (703) 482-1100, www.cia.gov; *The World Factbook.*

Europa Publications Limited, 18 Bedford Square, London, WC1B 3JN, England; *The Europa World Year Book.*

St. Martin's Press, Inc., 175 Fifth Avenue, New York, New York 10010 (800) 221-7945; *The Statesman's Year-Book.*

Statistical Office of the United Nations, Publishing Service, New York, New York 10017 (800) 253-9646; *Statistical Yearbook;* and *World Statistics Pocketbook.*

SAUDI ARABIA - TELEVISION BROADCASTING - See SAUDI ARABIA - BROADCASTING

SAUDI ARABIA - TEXTILE INDUSTRY

M.E. Sharpe, 80 Business Park Drive, Armonk, New York 10504 (800) 541-6563; *The Illustrated Book of World Rankings.*

United Nations Conference on Trade and Development, Central Statistical Service, Palais des Nations, Geneva, Switzerland (Telephone in U.S. (800) 253-9646); *UNCTAD Commodity Yearbook.*

SAUDI ARABIA - THEATRE

United Nations Educational, Scientific and Cultural Organization (UNESCO), 7 Place de Fontenoy, F-75700 Paris, France (Telephone Number in U.S. (212) 963-5981); *Statistical Yearbook.*

SAUDI ARABIA - TOBACCO PRODUCTION

M.E. Sharpe, 80 Business Park Drive, Armonk, New York 10504 (800) 541-6563; *The Illustrated Book of World Rankings.*

SAUDI ARABIA - TOURISM

Economic Commission for Western Asia, Post Office Box 27, Baghdad, Iraq; *Statistical Abstract of Western Asia.*

Euromonitor International, Inc., 122 South Michigan Avenue, Suite 1200, Chicago, Illinois 60603 (800) 577-EURO; *The World Economic Factbook;* and *World Marketing Data and Statistics.*

Europa Publications Limited, 18 Bedford Square, London, WC1B 3JN, England; *The Europa World Year Book.*

Federal Statistical Office, Gustav-Stresemann-Ring 11, D-6200 Wiesbaden, Germany; *Saudi-Arabien.*

M.E. Sharpe, 80 Business Park Drive, Armonk, New York 10504 (800) 541-6563; *The Illustrated Book of World Rankings.*

St. Martin's Press, Inc., 175 Fifth Avenue, New York, New York 10010 (800) 221-7945; *The Statesman's Year-Book.*

Statistical Office of the United Nations, Publishing Service, New York, New York 10017 (800) 253-9646; *Statistical Yearbook.*

World Tourism Organization, Calle Capitan Haya 42, E-28020 Madrid, Spain; *Yearbook of Tourism Statistics.*

SAUDI ARABIA - TRACTORS IN USE

Statistical Office of the United Nations, Publishing Service, New York, New York 10017 (800) 253-9646; *Statistical Yearbook.*

SAUDI ARABIA - TRADE - See SAUDI ARABIA - FOREIGN TRADE

SAUDI ARABIA - TRANSPORTATION AND COMMUNICATIONS

Central Intelligence Agency, Washington, D.C. 20505 (703) 482-1100, www.cia.gov; *The World Factbook.*

Economic Commission for Western Asia, Post Office Box 27, Baghdad, Iraq; *Statistical Abstract of Western Asia.*

Euromonitor International, Inc., 122 South Michigan Avenue, Suite 1200, Chicago, Illinois 60603 (800) 577-EURO; *International Marketing Data and Statistics;* and *World Marketing Data and Statistics.*

Europa Publications Limited, 18 Bedford Square, London, WC1B 3JN, England; *The Europa World Year Book.*

Federal Statistical Office, Gustav-Stresemann-Ring 11, D-6200 Wiesbaden, Germany; *Saudi-Arabien.*

M.E. Sharpe, 80 Business Park Drive, Armonk, New York 10504 (800) 541-6563; *The Illustrated Book of World Rankings.*

St. Martin's Press, Inc., 175 Fifth Avenue, New York, New York 10010 (800) 221-7945; *The Statesman's Year-Book.*

Statistical Office of the United Nations, Publishing Service, New York, New York 10017 (800) 253-9646; *Human Development Report.*

SAUDI ARABIA - UNEMPLOYMENT

Central Intelligence Agency, Washington, D.C. 20505 (703) 482-1100, www.cia.gov; *The World Factbook.*

Euromonitor International, Inc., 122 South Michigan Avenue, Suite 1200, Chicago, Illinois 60603 (800) 577-EURO; *International Marketing Data and Statistics.*

International Labour Office,

I.L.O. Publications, 1828 L Street, NW, Suite 801, Washington, D.C. 20036 (301) 638-3152; *Yearbook of Labour Statistics.*

SAUDI ARABIA - VITAL STATISTICS

Euromonitor International, Inc., 122 South Michigan Avenue, Suite 1200, Chicago, Illinois 60603 (800) 577-EURO; *International Marketing Data and Statistics.*

St. Martin's Press, Inc., 175 Fifth Avenue, New York, New York 10010 (800) 221-7945; *The Statesman's Year-Book.*

Statistical Office of the United Nations, Publishing Service, New York, New York 10017 (800) 253-9646; *Statistical Yearbook.*

World Health Organization, Office of Publications, 20 Avenue Appia, CH-1211 Geneva 27, Switzerland (Telephone Number in U.S. (518) 436-9686); *World Health Statistics Annual.*

SAUDI ARABIA - WAGES

Federal Statistical Office, Gustav-Stresemann-Ring 11, D-6200 Wiesbaden, Germany; *Saudi-Arabien.*

International Labour Office, I.L.O. Publications, 1828 L Street, NW, Suite 801, Washington, D.C. 20036 (301) 638-3152; *Yearbook of Labour Statistics.*

SAUDI ARABIA - WEATHER - See SAUDI ARABIA - CLIMATE

SAUDI ARABIA - WELFARE

St. Martin's Press, Inc., 175 Fifth Avenue, New York, New York 10010 (800) 221-7945; *The Statesman's Year-Book.*

SAUDI ARABIA - WHEAT - See SAUDI ARABIA - CROPS

SAUDI ARABIA - WHOLESALE TRADE

Statistical Office of the United Nations, Publishing Service, New York, New York 10017 (800) 253-9646; *Statistical Yearbook.*

SAUDI ARABIA - WINE PRODUCTION - See SAUDI ARABIA - BEVERAGES

SAUDI ARABIA - WOOD PULP PRODUCTION - See SAUDI ARABIA - FORESTRY AND FOREST PRODUCTS

SAUDI ARABIA - WOOL PRODUCTION - See SAUDI ARABIA - TEXTILE INDUSTRY

SAUSAGES

U.S. Department of Labor, Bureau of Labor Statistics, 2 Massachusetts Avenue, NE, Washington, D.C. 20212 (202) 691-5200, www.stats.bls.gov; *CPI Detailed Report;* and *Monthly Labor Review.*

SAVINGS - CREDIT UNIONS

National Credit Union Administration, 1775 Duke Street, Alexandria, Virginia 22314-3428 (703) 518-6300; *Annual Report of the National Credit Union Administration;* and unpublished data.

SAVINGS - DEPOSIT BANK

Board of Governors of the Federal Reserve System, Twentieth Street and Constitution Avenue, NW, Washington, D.C. 20551 (202) 452-3000, www.bog.frb.fed.us; *Flow of Fund Accounts.*

SAVINGS - GROSS SAVINGS - SOURCES AND USES

U.S. Department of Commerce, Bureau of Economic Analysis, Fourteenth Street between Constitution Avenue and E Street, NW, Washington, D.C. 20230 (202) 606-9900, www.bea.doc.gov; *The National Income and Product Accounts of the United States;* and *Survey of Current Business.*

SAVINGS - PERSONAL

U.S. Department of Commerce, Bureau of Economic Analysis, Fourteenth Street between Constitution Avenue and E Street, NW, Washington, D.C. 20230 (202) 606-9900, www.bea.doc.gov; *The National Income and Product Accounts of the United States;* and *Survey of Current Business.*

SAVINGS BANKS - See SAVINGS INSTITUTIONS

SAVINGS BONDS

Board of Governors of the Federal Reserve System, Twentieth Street and Constitution Avenue, NW, Washington, D.C. 20551 (202) 452-3000, www.bog.frb.fed.us; *Federal Reserve Bulletin;* and unpublished data.

U.S. Department of the Treasury, Fifteenth Street and Pennsylvania Avenue, NW, Washington, D.C. 20220 (202) 622-2000; *Treasury Bulletin.*

SAVINGS INSTITUTIONS - EARNINGS

U.S. Department of Commerce, Bureau of the Census, Washington, D.C. 20233 (301) 457-4100, www.census.gov; *County Business Patterns.*

SAVINGS INSTITUTIONS - EMPLOYEES

U.S. Department of Commerce, Bureau of the Census, Washington, D.C. 20233 (301) 457-4100, www.census.gov; *County Business Patterns.*

SAVINGS INSTITUTIONS - ESTABLISHMENTS

Federal Deposit Insurance Corporation, 550 Seventeenth Street, NW, Washington, D.C. 20429 (202) 393-8400, www.fdic.gov; *Statistics on Banking;* and *FDIC Quarterly Banking Profile.*

U.S. Department of Commerce, Bureau of the Census, Washington, D.C. 20233 (301) 457-4100, www.census.gov; *County Business Patterns.*

SAVINGS INSTITUTIONS - FAMILY DEBT

Board of Governors of the Federal Reserve System, 20th Street and Constitution Avenue, NW, Washington, D.C. 20551 (202) 452-3000, www.bog.frb.fed.us; *Federal Reserve Bulletin.*

SAVINGS INSTITUTIONS - FINANCES

Board of Governors of the Federal Reserve System, Twentieth Street and Constitution Avenue, NW, Washington, D.C. 20551 (202) 452-3000, www.bog.frb.fed.us; *Flow of Funds Accounts; Federal Reserve Bulletin;* and *Money Stock, Liquid Assets, and Debt Measures, Federal Reserve Statistical Release H.6.*

Federal Deposit Insurance Corporation, 550 Seventeenth Street, NW, Washington, D.C. 20429 (202) 393-8400, www.fdic.gov; *Statistics on Banking;* and *FDIC Quarterly Banking Profile.*

U.S. Department of Housing and Urban Development, 451 Seventh Street, SW, Washington, D.C. 20410 (202) 708-1422; monthly and quarterly press releases based on the Survey of Mortgage Lending Activity.

SAVINGS INSTITUTIONS - INDIVIDUAL RETIREMENT ACCOUNTS

Investment Company Institute, 1600 M Street, NW, Suite 600, Washington, D.C. 20036 (202) 293-7700; *Mutual Fund Fact Book.*

SAVINGS INSTITUTIONS - MERGERS AND ACQUISITIONS

Thomson Financial Securities Data, 2 Gateway Center, Newark, New Jersey 07006 (973) 622-3100; *Merger and Corporate Transactions Database.*

SAWLOGS

U.S. Department of Agriculture, Forest Service, Post Office Box 96090, Washington, D.C. 20090 (202) 205-8333, www.fs.fed.us; *Timber Demand and Technology Assessment.*

U.S. Department of Labor, Bureau of Labor Statistics, Two Massachusetts Avenue, NE, Washington, D.C. 20212 (202)

691-5200, www.stats.bls.gov; *Producer Price Indexes.*

SAWTIMBER

U.S. Department of Agriculture, Forest Service, Post Office Box 96090, Washington, D.C. 20090 (202) 205-8333, www.fs.fed.us; *Forest Resources of the United States.*

SCALLOPS

U.S. Department of Commerce, National Oceanic and Atmospheric Administration, National Marine Fisheries Service, 1315 East-West Highway, Silver Spring, Maryland 20910 (301) 427-2239, www.nmfs.noaa.gov; *Fisheries of the United States.*

SCHOLASTIC APTITUDE TEST (SAT)

College Entrance Examination Board, 45 Columbus Avenue, New York, New York 10017 (212) 713-8000; *National College-Bound Senior.*

SCHOOLS - See also EDUCATION

SCHOOLS - ACTIVITIES FOR PARENTS

U.S. Department of Education, National Center for Education Statistics, 555 New Jersey Avenue, NW, Washington, D.C. 20208-5574 (202) 219-1828, http://nces.ed.gov; *Fathers' Involvement in Their Children's School; Parent Involvement in Children's Education: Efforts by Public Elementary Schools;* and *Fast Response Survey System.*

SCHOOLS - BOARDS - ELECTED OFFICIALS

Joint Center for Political and Economic Studies, 1090 Vermont Avenue, Suite 1100, NW, Washington, D.C. 20005 (202) 789-3500; *Black Elected Officials: A National Roster.*

National Association of Latino Elected and Appointed Officials, NALEO Education Fund, 5800 South Eastern Avenue, Suite 365, Los Angeles, California 90040 (213) 262-8503; *National Roster of Hispanic Elected Officials.*

U.S. Department of Commerce, Bureau of the Census, Washington, D.C. 20233 (301) 457-4100, www.census.gov; *Census of Governments, Popularly Elected Officials.*

SCHOOLS - CRIMES

U.S. Department of Education, National Center for Education Statistics, 555 New Jersey Avenue, NW, Washington, D.C. 20208-5574 (202) 219-1828, http://nces.ed.gov; *Indicators of School Crime and Safety.*

SCHOOLS - DISTRICTS

National Education Association, 1201 Sixteenth Street, NW, Washington, D.C. 20036 (202) 833-4000; *Estimates of School Statistics Database.*

U.S. Department of Commerce, Bureau of the Census, Washington, D.C. 20233 (301) 457-4100, www.census.gov; *Census of Governments, Government Organization.*

SCHOOLS - INTERNET ACCESS

U.S. Department of Education, National Center for Education Statistics, 555 New Jersey Avenue, NW, Washington, D.C. 20208-5574 (202) 219-1828, http://nces.ed.gov; *Internet Access in Public Schools and Classrooms.*

SCHOOLS - LUNCH PROGRAMS

The Congress of the U.S., Congressional Research Service, 10 First Street, SE, Washington, D.C. 20540 (202) 707-5700; *Cash and Non-Cash Benefits for Persons with Limited Income: Eligibility Rules, Recipient and Expenditure Data.*

U.S. Department of Agriculture, Food and Nutrition Services, 3101 Park Center Drive, Alexandria, Virginia 22302 (703) 305-2286, www.fns.usda.gov/fns; *Annual Historical Review of FNS Programs;* and unpublished data.

U.S. Department of Commerce, Bureau of the Census, Washington, D.C. 20233 (301) 457-4100, www.census.gov; *Current Population Reports;* and unpublished data.

SCHOOLS - NUMBER

U.S. Department of Education, National Center for Education 555 New Jersey Avenue, NW, Washington, D.C. 20208-5574 (202) 219-1828, http://nces.ed.gov; *Digest of Education Statistics; Projections of Education Statistics;* and unpublished data.

SCIENTIFIC, ENGINEERING, AND TECHNICAL ASSOCIATIONS

The Gale Group, 27500 Drake Road, Farmington Hills, Michigan 48331 (800) 877-4253; *Encyclopedia of Associations.*

SCIENTIFIC INSTRUMENTS - See INSTRUMENTS

SCIENTIFIC RESEARCH - See RESEARCH AND DEVELOPMENT

SCIENTISTS AND ENGINEERS - See also Individual Fields

SCIENTISTS AND ENGINEERS - DEGREES CONFERRED

National Science Foundation, 4201 Wilson Boulevard, Arlington, Virginia 22230 (703) 306-1234, wwwnsf.gov; *Survey of Earned Doctorates, Selected Data on Science and Engineering Doctorate Awards.*

U.S. Department of Education, National Center for Education Statistics, 555 New Jersey Avenue, NW, Washington, D.C. 20208-5574 (202) 219-1828, http://nces.ed.gov; *Digest of Education Statistics.*

SCIENTISTS AND ENGINEERS - EMPLOYMENT

National Science Foundation, 4201 Wilson Boulevard, Arlington, Virginia 22230 (703) 306-1234, www.nsf.gov; *Research and Development in Industry; Survey of Federal S&E Support to Universities, Colleges, and Nonprofit Institutions;* and *Federal Funds for Research Land Development.*

U.S. Department of Labor, Bureau of Labor Statistics, Two Massachusetts Avenue, NE, Washington, D.C. 20212 (202) 691-5200, www.stats.bls.gov; *Employment and Earnings; Monthly Labor Review;* and unpublished data.

SCIENTISTS AND ENGINEERS - EMPLOYMENT - BY INDUSTRIAL SECTOR

U.S. Department of Labor, Bureau of Labor Statistics, Two Massachusetts Avenue, NE, Washington, D.C. 20212 (202) 691-5200, www.stats.bls.gov; *Monthly Labor Review;* and unpublished data.

SCOUTS - MEMBERSHIP AND UNITS

Boy Scouts of America, 1325 West Walnut Hill Lane, Post Office Box 152079, Irving, Texas 75015 (972) 580-2000; *Annual Report.*

Girl Scouts of the United States of America, 420 Fifth Avenue, New York, New York 10018 (212) 852-8000; *Annual Report.*

SCRAP METAL - See Individual Commodities

SCUBA DIVING

National Sporting Goods Association, 1601 Feehanville Drive, Suite 300, Mount Prospect, Illinois 66056 (847) 296-6742; *Sports Participation in 1998.*

SCUP - CATCH

U.S. Department of Commerce, National Oceanic and Atmospheric Administration, National Marine Fisheries Service, 1315 East-West Highway, Silver Spring, Maryland 20910 (301) 427-2239, www.nmfs.noaa.gov; *Fisheries of the United States.*

SEA BASS

U.S. Department of Commerce, National Oceanic and Atmospheric Administration, National Marine Fisheries Service, 1315 East-West Highway, Silver Spring, Maryland 20910 (301) 427-2239, www.nmfs.noaa.gov; *Fisheries of the United States.*

SEA TROUT

U.S. Department of Commerce, National Oceanic and Atmospheric Administration, National Marine Fisheries Service, 1315 East-West Highway, Silver Spring, Maryland 20910 (301) 427-2239, www.nmfs.noaa.gov; *Fisheries of the United States.*

SEAFOODS

U.S. Department of Commerce, National Oceanic and Atmospheric Administration, National Marine Fisheries Service, 1315 East-West Highway, Silver Spring, Maryland 20910 (301) 427-2239, www.nmfs.noaa.gov; *Fisheries of the United States.*

SECURITIES - FOREIGN HOLDINGS

International Finance Corporation, 1850 Eye Street, NW, Washington, D.C. 20433 (202) 477-1234; *Emerging Stock Markets Factbook.*

U.S. Department of Commerce, Bureau of Economic Analysis, Fourteenth Street between Constitution Avenue and E Street, NW, Washington, D.C. 20230 (202) 606-9900, www.bea.doc.gov; *Survey of Current Business.*

SECURITIES - FOREIGN PURCHASES AND SALES

Dow Jones and Company Inc., 200 Liberty Street, New York, New York 10006 (212) 597-5600; *Wall Street Journal.*

International Finance Corporation, 1818 H Street, NW, Washington, D.C. 20006 (202) 477-1234; *Emerging Stock Markets Factbook.*

Morgan Stanley Capital International, 1585 Broadway, New York, New York 10036 (212) 761-4000; unpublished data.

U.S. Department of the Treasury, Fifteenth Street and Pennsylvania Avenue, NW, Washington, D.C. 20220 (202) 622-2000; *Treasury Bulletin.*

SECURITIES - GOVERNMENT

Board of Governors of the Federal Reserve System, Twentieth Street and Constitution Avenue, NW, Washington, D.C. 20551 (202) 452-3000,

www.bog.frb.fed.us; *Federal Reserve Bulletin;* and *Banking and Monetary Statistics.*

Thomson Financial Securities Data, Two Gateway Center, Newark, New Jersey 07006 (973) 622-3100; Municipal New Issues Database.

SECURITIES - HELD BY GOVERNMENT CORPORATIONS AND CREDIT AGENCIES

Board of Governors of the Federal Reserve System, Twentieth Street and Constitution Avenue, NW, Washington, D.C. 20551 (202) 452-3000, www.bog.frb.fed.us; *Flow of Funds Accounts.*

SECURITIES - HELD BY LIFE INSURANCE

American Council of Life Insurance, 1001 Pennsylvania Avenue, NW, Washington, D.C. 20004-2599 (202) 624-2000; *Life Insurance Fact Book.*

SECURITIES - HOLDINGS OF BANKS

Board of Governors of the Federal Reserve System, Twentieth Street and Constitution Avenue, NW, Washington, D.C. 20551 (202) 452-3000, www.bog.frb.fed.us; *Flow of Funds Accounts.*

Federal Deposit Insurance Corporation, 500 Seventeenth Street, NW, Washington, D.C. 20429 (202) 393-8400, www.fdic.gov; *Annual Report; The FDIC Quarterly Banking Profile;* and *Statistics on Banking.*

SECURITIES - HOLDINGS OF INDIVIDUALS AND BUSINESSES

Board of Governors of the Federal Reserve System, Twentieth Street and Constitution Avenue, NW, Washington, D.C. 20551 (202) 452-3000, www.bog.frb.fed.us; *Flow of Funds Accounts.*

SECURITIES - NEW ISSUES

Board of Governors of the Federal Reserve System, Twentieth Street and Constitution Avenue, NW, Washington, D.C. 20551 (202) 452-3000, www.bog.frb.fed.us; *Federal Reserve Bulletin;* and *Annual Statistical Digest.*

SECURITIES - PRICES, INDEXES, YIELDS, AND ISSUES

Board of Governors of the Federal Reserve System, Twentieth Street and Constitution Avenue, NW, Washington, D.C. 20551 (202) 452-3000, www.bog.frb.fed.us; *Federal Reserve Bulletin;* and *Banking and Monetary Statistics.*

Dow Jones and Company, Inc., 200 Liberty Street, New York, New York 10006 (212) 597-5600; *Wall Street Journal.*

Morgan Stanley Capital International, 1585 Broadway, New York, New York 10036 (212) 761-4000; unpublished data.

National Association of Securities Dealers, 1735 K Street, NW, Washington, D.C. 20006 (202) 728-8000; *Fact Book.*

New York Stock Exchange, 11 Wall Street, New York, New York 10005 (212) 656-3000; *Fact Book.*

SECURITIES - SALES - STOCKS AND BONDS

Dow Jones and Company, Inc., 200 Liberty Street, New York, New York 10006 (212) 597-5600; *Wall Street Journal.*

International Finance Corporation, 1818 H Street, NW, Washington, D.C. 20006 (202) 477-1234; *Emerging Stock Markets Factbook.*

Morgan Stanley Capital International, 1585 Broadway, New York, New York 10036 (212) 761-4000; unpublished data.

National Association of Security Dealers, 1735 K Street, NW, Washington, D.C. 20006 (202) 728-8000; *Fact Book.*

U.S. Department of the Treasury, Fifteenth Street and Pennsylvania Avenue, NW, Washington, D.C. 20220 (202) 622-2000; *Treasury Bulletin.*

SECURITIES - SAVINGS OF INDIVIDUALS

Board of Governors of the Federal Reserve System, Twentieth Street and Constitution Avenue, NW, Washington, D.C. 20551 (202) 452-3000, www.bog.frb.fed.us; *Flow of Funds Accounts.*

U.S. Department of Commerce, Bureau of Economic Analysis, Fourteenth Street between Constitution Avenue and E Street, NW, Washington, D.C. 20230 (202) 606-9900, www.bea.doc.gov; *The National Income and Product Accounts of the United States;* and *Survey of Current Business.*

SECURITIES - STATE AND LOCAL GOVERNMENT

Board of Governors of the Federal Reserve System, Twentieth Street and Constitution Avenue, NW, Washington, D.C. 20551 (202) 452-3000, www.bog.frb.fed.us; *Annual Statistical Digest;* and *Federal Reserve Bulletin.*

SECURITY AND COMMODITY BROKERS - EARNINGS

U.S. Department of Commerce, Bureau

of the Census, Washington, D.C. 20233 (301) 457-4100, www.census.gov; *1997 Economic Census, Core Business Statistics Series, Advance;* and *County Business Patterns.*

U.S. Department of Labor, Bureau of Labor Statistics, Two Massachusetts Avenue, NE, Washington, D.C. 20212 (202) 691-5200, www.stats.bls.gov; *Employment and Earnings;* and Internet site: http://stats.bls.gov/ ceshome.htm.

SECURITY AND COMMODITY BROKERS - EMPLOYEES

U.S. Department of Commerce, Bureau of the Census, Washington, D.C. 20233 (301) 457-4100, www.census.gov; *1997 Economic Census, Core Business Statistics Series, Advance;* and *County Business Patterns.*

U.S. Department of Labor, Bureau of Labor Statistics, Two Massachusetts Avenue, NE, Washington, D.C. 20212 (202) 691-5200, www.stats.bls.gov; *Employment and Earnings;* and Internet site: http://stats.bls.gov/ ceshome.htm.

SECURITY AND COMMODITY BROKERS - ESTABLISHMENTS

U.S. Department of Commerce, Bureau of the Census, Washington, D.C. 20233 (301) 457-4100, www.census.gov; *1997 Economic Census, Core Business Statistics Series, Advance;* and *County Business Patterns.*

SECURITY AND COMMODITY BROKERS - FINANCES

Board of Governors of the Federal Reserve System, Twentieth Street and Constitution Avenue, NW, Washington, D.C. 20551 (202) 452-3000, www.bog.frb.fed.us, www.bog.frb.fed.us; *Flow of Funds Accounts.*

Securities and Exchange Commission, 450 Fifth Street, NW, Washington, D.C. 20549 (202) 942-4040, www.sec.gov; *Annual Report.*

SECURITY AND COMMODITY BROKERS - GROSS DOMESTIC PRODUCT

U.S. Department of Commerce, Bureau of Economic Analysis, Fourteenth Street between Constitution Avenue and E Street, NW, Washington, D.C. 20230 (202) 606-9900, www.bea.doc.gov; *Survey of Current Business.*

SECURITY AND COMMODITY BROKERS - OCCUPATIONAL SAFETY

U.S. Department of Labor, Bureau of Labor Statistics, Two Massachusetts Avenue, NE, Washington, D.C. 20212 (202)

691-5200, www.stats.bls.gov; *Occupational Injuries and Illnesses in the United States by Industry.*

SECURITY AND COMMODITY BROKERS - MERGERS AND ACQUISITIONS

Thomson Financial Securities Data, Two Gateway Center, Newark, New Jersey 07006 (973) 622-3100; *Merger and Corporate Transactions Database.*

SECURITY AND COMMODITY BROKERS - PROFITS

Securities and Exchange Commission, 450 Fifth Street, NW, Washington, D.C. 20549 (202) 942-4040, www.sec.gov; *Annual Report.*

SEDATIVES - PERSONS USING

U.S. Department of Health and Human Services, Substance Abuse and Mental Health Services Administration, 5600 Fishers Lane, Rockville, Maryland 20857 (800) 729-6686, www.samhsa.gov; *National Household Survey on Drug Abuse.*

SEEDS

Executive Office of the President, Council of Economic Advisers, Old Executive Office Building, Washington, D.C. 20502 (202) 395-5084, www.whitehouse. gov/cea; *Economic Report of the President.*

U.S. Department of Agriculture, Economic Research Service, 1800 M Street, NW, Washington, D.C. 20036 (202) 694-5050, www.ers.usda.gov; *Agricultural Outlook.*

SELENIUM

U.S. Department of the Interior, Geological Survey, Office of Minerals Information, 12201 Sunrise Valley Drive, Reston, Virginia 22092 (703) 648-4000, www.minerals.usgs.gov; *Minerals Commodity Summaries.*

SEMICONDUCTORS AND RELATED DEVISES - MANUFACTURING - See also ELECTRONIC COMPONENTS

U.S. Department of Commerce, Bureau of the Census, Washington, D.C. 20233 (301) 457-4100, www.census.gov; *Manufacturing Profiles;* and Internet site: http://www.census.gov/ industry/ma36q97.txt.

SENATORS, UNITED STATES

Congressional Quarterly, Inc., 1414 22nd Street, NW, Washington, D.C. 20037 (202) 887-8500; *America Votes.*

U.S. Congress, Joint Committee on Printing, North Capitol and H Streets, NW,

Washington, D.C. 20401 (202) 512-0000; *Congressional Directory*.

Senegal - National Statistical Office

Direction de la Statistique, Ministere de l'Economie et des Finances, BP 116, Dakar, Senegal.

Senegal - Primary Statistics Sources

Direction de la Prevision et de la Statistique, BP 116, Dakar, Senegal; *Situation economique du Senegal* (Economic Situation in Senegal); and *Bulletin statistique et economique mensuel* (Monthly Economic and Statistical Bulletin).

SENEGAL - AGRICULTURE

Economist Intelligence Unit, 111 West 57th Street, New York, New York 10019 (800) 938-4685; *Senegal Country Report*.

Euromonitor International, Inc., 122 South Michigan Avenue, Suite 1200, Chicago, Illinois 60603 (800) 577-EURO; *International Marketing Data and Statistics;* and *World Marketing Data and Statistics*.

Europa Publications Limited, 18 Bedford Square, London, WC1B 3JN, England; *The Europa World Year Book*.

Food and Agricultural Organization of the United Nations (FAO) Via delle Terme di Caracalla, 00100 Rome, Italy (Telephone Number in U.S. (202) 653-2400); *Production Yearbook; The State of Food and Agriculture;* and *Trade Yearbook*.

M.E. Sharpe, 80 Business Park Drive, Armonk, New York 10504 (800) 541-6563; *The Illustrated Book of World Rankings*.

St. Martin's Press, Inc., 175 Fifth Avenue, New York, New York 10010 (800) 221-7945; *The Statesman's Year-Book*.

Statistical Office of the United Nations, Publishing Service, New York, New York 10017 (800) 253-9646; *Statistical Yearbook;* and *Survey of Economic and Social Conditions in Africa*.

United Nations Conference on Trade and Development, Central Statistical Service, Palais des Nations, Geneva, Switzerland (Telephone in U.S. (800) 253-9646); *UNCTAD Commodity Yearbook*.

United Nations Economic Commission for Africa, Africa Hall, P.O. Box 3001, Addis Ababa, Ethiopia (Telephone Number in U.S. (800) 253-9646); *African Statistical Yearbook*.

The World Bank, 1818 H Street, NW, Washington, D.C. 20433 (202) 477-1234; *World Development Indicators*.

SENEGAL - AIRLINE SERVICE

Europa Publications Limited, 18 Bedford Square, London, WC1B 3JN, England; *The Europa World Year Book*.

M.E. Sharpe, 80 Business Park Drive, Armonk, New York 10504 (800) 541-6563; *The Illustrated Book of World Rankings*.

St. Martin's Press, Inc., 175 Fifth Avenue, New York, New York 10010 (800) 221-7945; *The Statesman's Year-Book*.

Statistical Office of the United Nations, Publishing Service, New York, New York 10017 (800) 253-9646; *Statistical Yearbook*.

United Nations Economic Commission for Africa, Africa Hall, P.O. Box 3001, Addis Ababa, Ethiopia (Telephone Number in U.S. (800) 253-9646); *African Statistical Yearbook*.

SENEGAL - AIRPORTS

Central Intelligence Agency, Washington, D.C. 20505 (703) 482-1100, www.cia.gov; *The World Factbook*.

SENEGAL - ALUMINUM PRODUCTION AND CONSUMPTION - See SENEGAL - MINING AND MINERAL PRODUCTS

SENEGAL - ANIMAL HEALTH

Food and Agricultural Organization of the United Nations (FAO), Via delle Terme di Caracalla, 00100, Rome, Italy (Telephone Number in U.S. (202) 653-2400); *Animal Health Yearbook*.

SENEGAL - AREA AND DENSITY OF POPULATION

African Development Bank, 01 BP 1387, Abidjan 01, Cote D'Ivoire; *Selected Statistics on Regional Member Countries*.

Central Intelligence Agency, Washington, D.C. 20505 (703) 482-1100, www.cia.gov; *The World Factbook*.

Euromonitor International, Inc., 122 South Michigan Avenue, Suite 1200, Chicago, Illinois 60603 (800) 577-EURO; *International Marketing Data and Statistics;* and *The World Economic Factbook*.

Europa Publications Limited, 18 Bedford Square, London, WC1B 3JN, England; *The Europa World Year Book*.

Food and Agricultural Organization of the United Nations (FAO) Via delle Terme di Caracalla, 00100 Rome, Italy (Telephone Number in U.S. (202) 653-2400); *The State*

of Food and Agriculture.

M.E. Sharpe, 80 Business Park Drive, Armonk, New York 10504 (800) 541-6563; *The Illustrated Book of World Rankings*.

St. Martin's Press, Inc., 175 Fifth Avenue, New York, New York 10010 (800) 221-7945; *The Statesman's Year-Book*.

Statistical Office of the United Nations, Publishing Service, New York, New York 10017 (800) 253-9646; *Statistical Yearbook;* and *Survey of Economic and Social Conditions in Africa*.

United Nations Educational, Scientific and Cultural Organization (UNESCO), 7 Place de Fontenoy, F-75700 Paris, France (Telephone Number in U.S. (212) 963-5981); *Statistical Yearbook*.

The World Bank, 1818 H Street, NW, Washington, D.C. 20433 (202) 477-1234; *World Development Report*.

SENEGAL - ARMS EXPORTS AND IMPORTS - See SENEGAL - MILITARY

SENEGAL - BALANCE OF PAYMENTS

African Development Bank, 01 BP 1387, Abidjan 01, Cote D'Ivoire; *Selected Statistics on Regional Member Countries*.

The Economist Intelligence Unit, 111 West 57th Street, New York, New York 10019 (800) 938-4685; *The World Market Atlas*.

Europa Publications Limited, 18 Bedford Square, London, WC1B 3JN, England; *The Europa World Year Book*.

International Monetary Fund, 700 Nineteenth Street, NW, Washington, D.C. 20431 (202) 623-7000; *Balance of Payments Yearbook*.

United Nations Conference on Trade and Development (UNCTAD), New York, New York 10017 (800) 253-9646; *Handbook of International Trade and Development Statistics*.

United Nations Economic Commission for Africa, Africa Hall, P.O. Box 3001, Addis Ababa, Ethiopia (Telephone Number in U.S. (800) 253-9646); *African Statistical Yearbook*.

The World Bank, 1818 H Street, NW, Washington, D.C. 20433 (202) 477-1234; *World Development Report;* and *World Development Indicators*.

SENEGAL - BANKING

Euromonitor International, Inc., 122 South Michigan Avenue, Suite 1200, Chicago, Illinois 60603 (800) 577-EURO;

World Marketing Data and Statistics.

Europa Publications Limited, 18 Bedford Square, London, WC1B 3JN, England; *The Europa World Year Book.*

International Monetary Fund, 700 Nineteenth Street, NW, Washington, D.C. 20431 (202) 623-7000; *International Financial Statistics.*

M.E. Sharpe, 80 Business Park Drive, Armonk, New York 10504 (800) 541-6563; *The Illustrated Book of World Rankings.*

St. Martin's Press, Inc., 175 Fifth Avenue, New York, New York 10010 (800) 221-7945; *The Statesman's Year-Book.*

Statistical Office of the United Nations, Publishing Service, New York, New York 10017 (800) 253-9646; *Statistical Yearbook.*

United Nations Economic Commission for Africa, Africa Hall, P.O. Box 3001, Addis Ababa, Ethiopia (Telephone Number in U.S. (800) 253-9646); *African Statistical Yearbook.*

SENEGAL - BARLEY PRODUCTION - See SENEGAL - CROPS

SENEGAL - BEER PRODUCTION - See SENEGAL - BEVERAGES

SENEGAL - BEVERAGES

M.E. Sharpe, 80 Business Park Drive, Armonk, New York 10504 (800) 541-6563; *The Illustrated Book of World Rankings.*

Statistical Office of the United Nations, Publishing Service, New York, New York 10017 (800) 253-9646; *Statistical Yearbook.*

SENEGAL - BIRTH RATES

Central Intelligence Agency, Washington, D.C. 20505 (703) 482-1100, www.cia.gov; *The World Factbook.*

Euromonitor International, Inc., 122 South Michigan Avenue, Suite 1200, Chicago, Illinois 60603 (800) 577-EURO; *International Marketing Data and Statistics;* and *The World Economic Factbook.*

Europa Publications Limited, 18 Bedford Square, London, WC1B 3JN, England; *The Europa World Year Book.*

M.E. Sharpe, 80 Business Park Drive, Armonk, New York 10504 (800) 541-6563; *The Illustrated Book of World Rankings.*

St. Martin's Press, Inc., 175 Fifth Avenue, New York, New York 10010 (800) 221-7945; *The Statesman's Year-Book.*

Statistical Office of the United Nations, Publishing Service, New York, New York

10017 (800) 253-9646; *Demographic Yearbook; Statistical Yearbook;* and *Survey of Economic and Social Conditions in Africa.*

The World Bank, 1818 H Street, NW, Washington, D.C. 20433 (202) 477-1234; *World Development Indicators.*

SENEGAL - BOOK PRODUCTION

Europa Publications Limited, 18 Bedford Square, London, WC1B 3JN, England; *The Europa World Year Book.*

United Nations Educational, Scientific and Cultural Organization (UNESCO), 7 Place de Fontenoy, F-75700 Paris, France (Telephone Number in U.S. (212) 963-5981); *Statistical Yearbook.*

SENEGAL - BROADCASTING

Billboard Limited, P.O. Box 9027, 1006 AA Amsterdam, The Netherlands (Telephone Number in U.S. (212) 764-7300); *World Radio TV Handbook.*

Central Intelligence Agency, Washington, D.C. 20505 (703) 482-1100, www.cia.gov; *The World Factbook.*

Euromonitor International, Inc., 122 South Michigan Avenue, Suite 1200, Chicago, Illinois 60603 (800) 577-EURO; *World Marketing Data and Statistics.*

M.E. Sharpe, 80 Business Park Drive, Armonk, New York 10504 (800) 541-6563; *The Illustrated Book of World Rankings.*

St. Martin's Press, Inc., 175 Fifth Avenue, New York, New York 10010 (800) 221-7945; *The Statesman's Year-Book.*

SENEGAL - BUDGET

Central Intelligence Agency, Washington, D.C. 20505 (703) 482-1100, www.cia.gov; *The World Factbook.*

SENEGAL - BUSINESS AND PROFESSIONAL LICENSES

International Monetary Fund, 700 Nineteenth Street, NW, Washington, D.C. 20431 (202) 623-7000; *Government Finance Statistics Yearbook.*

SENEGAL - CALORIE SUPPLY

African Development Bank, 01 BP 1387, Abidjan 01, Cote D'Ivoire; *Selected Statistics on Regional Member Countries.*

Food and Agricultural Organization of the United Nations (FAO) Via delle Terme di Caracalla, 00100 Rome, Italy (Telephone Number in U.S. (202) 653-2400); *The State of Food and Agriculture.*

SENEGAL - CAPITAL REVENUE

International Monetary Fund, 700 Nineteenth Street, NW, Washington, D.C. 20431 (202) 623-7000; *Government Finance Statistics Yearbook.*

SENEGAL - CATTLE - See SENEGAL - LIVESTOCK AND POULTRY

SENEGAL - CEMENT PRODUCTION - See SENEGAL - MINING AND MINERAL PRODUCTS

SENEGAL - CHEMICAL (ORGANIC) PRODUCTION - See SENEGAL - MINING AND MINERAL PRODUCTS

SENEGAL - CHICKENS - See SENEGAL - LIVESTOCK AND POULTRY

SENEGAL - CIGARETTE PRODUCTION - See SENEGAL - TOBACCO PRODUCTION

SENEGAL - CLIMATE

M.E. Sharpe, 80 Business Park Drive, Armonk, New York 10504 (800) 541-6563; *The Illustrated Book of World Rankings.*

St. Martin's Press, Inc., 175 Fifth Avenue, New York, New York 10010 (800) 221-7945; *The Statesman's Year-Book.*

SENEGAL - COAL PRODUCTION - See SENEGAL - MINING AND MINERAL PRODUCTS

SENEGAL - COFFEE - See SENEGAL - CROPS

SENEGAL - COMMERCE

St. Martin's Press, Inc., 175 Fifth Avenue, New York, New York 10010 (800) 221-7945; *The Statesman's Year-Book.*

SENEGAL - COMMUNICATIONS - See SENEGAL - TRANSPORTATION AND COMMUNICATIONS

SENEGAL - CONSTRUCTION INDUSTRY

M.E. Sharpe, 80 Business Park Drive, Armonk, New York 10504 (800) 541-6563; *The Illustrated Book of World Rankings.*

Statistical Office of the United Nations, Publishing Service, New York, New York 10017 (800) 253-9646; *Statistical Yearbook.*

United Nations Economic Commission for Africa, Africa Hall, P.O. Box 3001, Addis Ababa, Ethiopia (Telephone Number in U.S. (800) 253-9646); *African Statistical Yearbook.*

SENEGAL - CONSUMER PRICE INDEX

African Development Bank, 01 BP 1387, Abidjan 01, Cote D'Ivoire; *Selected*

Statistics on Regional Member Countries.

Europa Publications Limited, 18 Bedford Square, London, WC1B 3JN, England; *The Europa World Year Book.*

Statistical Office of the United Nations, Publishing Service, New York, New York 10017 (800) 253-9646; *Statistical Yearbook;* and *Survey of Economic and Social Conditions in Africa.*

United Nations Economic Commission for Africa, Africa Hall, P.O. Box 3001, Addis Ababa, Ethiopia (Telephone Number in U.S. (800) 253-9646); *African Statistical Yearbook.*

SENEGAL - CONSUMER PRICES

Euromonitor International, Inc., 122 South Michigan Avenue, Suite 1200, Chicago, Illinois 60603 (800) 577-EURO; *World Marketing Data and Statistics.*

International Labour Office, I.L.O. Publications, 1828 L Street, NW, Suite 801, Washington, D.C. 20036 (301) 638-3152; *Yearbook of Labour Statistics.*

International Monetary Fund, 700 Nineteenth Street, NW, Washington, D.C. 20431 (202) 623-7000; *International Financial Statistics.*

SENEGAL - CONSUMPTION

African Development Bank, 01 BP 1387, Abidjan 01, Cote D'Ivoire; *Selected Statistics on Regional Member Countries.*

Statistical Office of the United Nations, Publishing Service, New York, New York 10017 (800) 253-9646; *Survey of Economic and Social Conditions in Africa.*

The World Bank, 1818 H Street, NW, Washington, D.C. 20433 (202) 477-1234; *World Development Report.*

SENEGAL - COPPER PRODUCTION AND CONSUMPTION - See SENEGAL - MINING AND MINERAL PRODUCTS

SENEGAL - CORN PRODUCTION - See SENEGAL - CROPS

SENEGAL - CORPORATE TAXES - See SENEGAL - TAXATION

SENEGAL - COTTON - See SENEGAL - CROPS

SENEGAL - CRIME

Yale University Press, Yale Station, New Haven, Connecticut 06520 (800) 987-7323; *Violence and Crime in Cross-National Perspective.*

SENEGAL - CROPS

Commodity Research Bureau, Inc., 30 South Wacker Drive, Chicago Illinois 60606 (312) 454-1801; *Commodity Year Book.*

Europa Publications Limited, 18 Bedford Square, London, WC1B 3JN, England; *The Europa World Year Book.*

Food and Agricultural Organization of the United Nations (FAO) Via delle Terme di Caracalla, 00100 Rome, Italy (Telephone Number in U.S. (202) 653-2400); *The State of Food and Agriculture.*

M.E. Sharpe, 80 Business Park Drive, Armonk, New York 10504 (800) 541-6563; *The Illustrated Book of World Rankings.*

St. Martin's Press, Inc., 175 Fifth Avenue, New York, New York 10010 (800) 221-7945; *The Statesman's Year-Book.*

Statistical Office of the United Nations, Publishing Service, New York, New York 10017 (800) 253-9646; *Statistical Yearbook.*

United Nations Conference on Trade and Development, Central Statistical Service, Palais des Nations, Geneva, Switzerland (Telephone in U.S. (800) 253-9646); *UNCTAD Commodity Yearbook.*

United Nations Economic Commission for Africa, Africa Hall, P.O. Box 3001, Addis Ababa, Ethiopia (Telephone Number in U.S. (800) 253-9646); *African Statistical Yearbook.*

SENEGAL - CUSTOMS DUTIES

International Monetary Fund, 700 Nineteenth Street, NW, Washington, D.C. 20431 (202) 623-7000; *Government Finance Statistics Yearbook.*

St. Martin's Press, Inc., 175 Fifth Avenue, New York, New York 10010 (800) 221-7945; *The Statesman's Year-Book.*

SENEGAL - DAIRY PRODUCTS

Europa Publications Limited, 18 Bedford Square, London, WC1B 3JN, England; *The Europa World Year Book.*

Food and Agricultural Organization of the United Nations (FAO) Via delle Terme di Caracalla, 00100 Rome, Italy (Telephone Number in U.S. (202) 653-2400); *The State of Food and Agriculture.*

M.E. Sharpe, 80 Business Park Drive, Armonk, New York 10504 (800) 541-6563; *The Illustrated Book of World Rankings.*

St. Martin's Press, Inc., 175 Fifth Avenue, New York, New York 10010 (800) 221-7945; *The Statesman's Year-Book.*

Statistical Office of the United Nations, Publishing Service, New York, New York

10017 (800) 253-9646; *Statistical Yearbook.*

SENEGAL - DEATH RATES - See SENEGAL - MORTALITY

SENEGAL - DEFENSE EXPENDITURES

International Monetary Fund, 700 Nineteenth Street, NW, Washington, D.C. 20431 (202) 623-7000; *Government Finance Statistics Yearbook.*

U.S. Arms Control and Disarmament Agency, 320 Twenty-first Street, NW, Washington, D.C. 20451 (202) 647-8677; *World Military Expenditures and Arms Transfers.*

SENEGAL - DEMOGRAPHY

The Economist Intelligence Unit, 111 West 57th Street, New York, New York 10019 (800) 938-4685; *The World Market Atlas.*

Euromonitor International, Inc., 122 South Michigan Avenue, Suite 1200, Chicago, Illinois 60603 (800) 577-EURO; *International Marketing Data and Statistics; World Marketing Data and Statistics;* and *The World Economic Factbook.*

M.E. Sharpe, 80 Business Park Drive, Armonk, New York 10504 (800) 541-6563; *The Illustrated Book of World Rankings.*

Statistical Office of the United Nations, Publishing Service, New York, New York 10017 (800) 253-9646; *Human Development Report;* and *Survey of Economic and Social Conditions in Africa.*

SENEGAL - DEVELOPMENT ASSISTANCE

Statistical Office of the United Nations, Publishing Service, New York, New York 10017 (800) 253-9646; *Statistical Yearbook.*

SENEGAL - DIAMOND PRODUCTION - See SENEGAL - MINING AND MINERAL PRODUCTS

SENEGAL - DISCOUNT RATES - See SENEGAL - BANKING

SENEGAL - DISEASES - See SENEGAL HEALTH

SENEGAL - DIVORCE RATES

M.E. Sharpe, 80 Business Park Drive, Armonk, New York 10504 (800) 541-6563; *The Illustrated Book of World Rankings.*

Statistical Office of the United Nations, Publishing Service, New York, New York 10017 (800) 253-9646; *Demographic Yearbook.*

SENEGAL - ECONOMY

African Development Bank, 01 BP 1387, Abidjan 01, Cote D'Ivoire; *Selected Statistics on Regional Member Countries.*

Central Intelligence Agency, Washington, D.C. 20505 (703) 482-1100, www.cia.gov; *The World Factbook.*

Economist Intelligence Unit, 111 West 57th Street, New York, New York 10019 (800) 938-4685; *Senegal Country Report.*

Euromonitor International, Inc., 122 South Michigan Avenue, Suite 1200, Chicago, Illinois 60603 (800) 577-EURO; *International Marketing Data and Statistics; World Marketing Data and Statistics;* and *The World Economic Factbook.*

Europa Publications Limited, 18 Bedford Square, London, WC1B 3JN, England; *The Europa World Year Book.*

M.E. Sharpe, 80 Business Park Drive, Armonk, New York 10504 (800) 541-6563; *The Illustrated Book of World Rankings.*

St. Martin's Press, Inc., 175 Fifth Avenue, New York, New York 10010 (800) 221-7945; *The Statesman's Year-Book.*

Statistical Office of the United Nations, Publishing Service, New York, New York 10017 (800) 253-9646; *Foreign Trade Statistics for Africa;* and *World Statistics Pocketbook.*

The World Bank, 1818 H Street, NW, Washington, D.C. 20433 (202) 477-1234; *The World Bank Atlas;* and *World Development Report.*

SENEGAL - EDUCATION

African Development Bank, 01 BP 1387, Abidjan 01, Cote D'Ivoire; *Selected Statistics on Regional Member Countries.*

The Economist Intelligence Unit, 111 West 57th Street, New York, New York 10019 (800) 938-4685; *The World Market Atlas.*

Euromonitor International, Inc., 122 South Michigan Avenue, Suite 1200, Chicago, Illinois 60603 (800) 577-EURO; *International Marketing Data and Statistics;* and *World Marketing Data and Statistics.*

Europa Publications Limited, 18 Bedford Square, London, WC1B 3JN, England; *The Europa World Year Book.*

International Monetary Fund, 700 Nineteenth Street, NW, Washington, D.C. 20431 (202) 623-7000; *Government Finance Statistics Yearbook.*

M.E. Sharpe, 80 Business Park Drive, Armonk, New York 10504 (800) 541-6563; *The Illustrated Book of World Rankings.*

St. Martin's Press, Inc., 175 Fifth Avenue, New York, New York 10010 (800) 221-7945; *The Statesman's Year-Book.*

Statistical Office of the United Nations, Publishing Service, New York, New York 10017 (800) 253-9646; *Human Development Report;* and *Survey of Economic and Social Conditions in Africa.*

United Nations Economic Commission for Africa, Africa Hall, P.O. Box 3001, Addis Ababa, Ethiopia (Telephone Number in U.S. (800) 253-9646); *African Statistical Yearbook.*

United Nations Educational, Scientific and Cultural Organization (UNESCO), 7 Place de Fontenoy, F-75700 Paris, France (Telephone Number in U.S. (212) 963-5981); *Statistical Yearbook.*

The World Bank, 1818 H Street, NW, Washington, D.C. 20433 (202) 477-1234; *World Development Report;* and *World Development Indicators.*

SENEGAL - EGG PRODUCTION AND CONSUMPTION - See SENEGAL - DAIRY PRODUCTS

SENEGAL - ELECTRICITY

Central Intelligence Agency, Washington, D.C. 20505 (703) 482-1100, www.cia.gov; *The World Factbook.*

M.E. Sharpe, 80 Business Park Drive, Armonk, New York 10504 (800) 541-6563; *The Illustrated Book of World Rankings.*

St. Martin's Press, Inc., 175 Fifth Avenue, New York, New York 10010 (800) 221-7945; *The Statesman's Year-Book.*

Statistical Office of the United Nations, Publishing Service, New York, New York 10017 (800) 253-9646; *Human Development Report; Statistical Yearbook;* and *Survey of Economic and Social Conditions in Africa.*

United Nations Economic Commission for Africa, Africa Hall, P.O. Box 3001, Addis Ababa, Ethiopia (Telephone Number in U.S. (800) 253-9646); *African Statistical Yearbook.*

SENEGAL - EMPLOYMENT

Euromonitor International, Inc., 122 South Michigan Avenue, Suite 1200, Chicago, Illinois 60603 (800) 577-EURO; *International Marketing Data and Statistics.*

International Labour Office, I.L.O. Publications, 1828 L Street, NW, Suite 801, Washington, D.C. 20036 (301) 638-3152; *Yearbook of Labour Statistics.*

M.E. Sharpe, 80 Business Park Drive,

Armonk, New York 10504 (800) 541-6563; *The Illustrated Book of World Rankings.*

Statistical Office of the United Nations, Publishing Service, New York, New York 10017 (800) 253-9646; *Survey of Economic and Social Conditions in Africa.*

United Nations Economic Commission for Africa, Africa Hall, P.O. Box 3001, Addis Ababa, Ethiopia (Telephone Number in U.S. (800) 253-9646); *African Statistical Yearbook.*

SENEGAL - ENERGY

Euromonitor International, Inc., 122 South Michigan Avenue, Suite 1200, Chicago, Illinois 60603 (800) 577-EURO; *International Marketing Data and Statistics; World Marketing Data and Statistics;* and *The World Economic Factbook.*

Food and Agricultural Organization of the United Nations (FAO) Via delle Terme di Caracalla, 00100 Rome, Italy (Telephone Number in U.S. (202) 653-2400); *The State of Food and Agriculture.*

M.E. Sharpe, 80 Business Park Drive, Armonk, New York 10504 (800) 541-6563; *The Illustrated Book of World Rankings.*

St. Martin's Press, Inc., 175 Fifth Avenue, New York, New York 10010 (800) 221-7945; *The Statesman's Year-Book.*

Statistical Office of the United Nations, Publishing Service, New York, New York 10017 (800) 253-9646; *Energy Statistics Yearbook; Human Development Report; Statistical Yearbook;* and *World Statistics Pocketbook.*

United Nations Economic Commission for Africa, Africa Hall, P.O. Box 3001, Addis Ababa, Ethiopia (Telephone Number in U.S. (800) 253-9646); *African Statistical Yearbook.*

The World Bank, 1818 H Street, NW, Washington, D.C. 20433 (202) 477-1234; *The World Bank Atlas;* and *World Development Report.*

SENEGAL - ENVIRONMENT

Economist Intelligence Unit, 111 West 57th Street, New York, New York 10019 (800) 938-4685; *Senegal Country Report.*

Statistical Office of the United Nations, Publishing Service, New York, New York 10017 (800) 253-9646; *World Statistics Pocketbook.*

SENEGAL - EXCHANGE RATES

African Development Bank, 01 BP 1387, Abidjan 01, Cote D'Ivoire; *Selected Statistics on Regional Member Countries.*

Central Intelligence Agency, Washington, D.C. 20505 (703) 482-1100, www.cia.gov; *The World Factbook*.

Euromonitor International, Inc., 122 South Michigan Avenue, Suite 1200, Chicago, Illinois 60603 (800) 577-EURO; *International Marketing Data and Statistics;* and *The World Economic Factbook*.

Europa Publications Limited, 18 Bedford Square, London, WC1B 3JN, England; *The Europa World Year Book*.

International Monetary Fund, 700 Nineteenth Street, NW, Washington, D.C. 20431 (202) 623-7000; *International Financial Statistics*.

Statistical Office of the United Nations, Publishing Service, New York, New York 10017 (800) 253-9646; *Foreign Trade Statistics for Africa; Statistical Yearbook;* and *World Statistics Pocketbook*.

SENEGAL - EXCISE TAXES - See SENEGAL - TAXATION

SENEGAL - EXPORTS

African Development Bank, 01 BP 1387, Abidjan 01, Cote D'Ivoire; *Selected Statistics on Regional Member Countries*.

Central Intelligence Agency, Washington, D.C. 20505 (703) 482-1100, www.cia.gov; *The World Factbook*.

The Economist Intelligence Unit, 111 West 57th Street, New York, New York 10019 (800) 938-4685; *Senegal Country Report;* and *The World Market Atlas*.

Euromonitor International, Inc., 122 South Michigan Avenue, Suite 1200, Chicago, Illinois 60603 (800) 577-EURO; *International Marketing Data and Statistics;* and *The World Economic Factbook*.

Europa Publications Limited, 18 Bedford Square, London, WC1B 3JN, England; *The Europa World Year Book*.

Food and Agricultural Organization of the United Nations (FAO) Via delle Terme di Caracalla, 00100 Rome, Italy (Telephone Number in U.S. (202) 653-2400); *The State of Food and Agriculture*.

International Monetary Fund, 700 Nineteenth Street, NW, Washington, D.C. 20431 (202) 623-7000; *Direction of Trade Statistics; Government Finance Statistics Yearbook;* and *International Financial Statistics*.

St. Martin's Press, Inc., 175 Fifth Avenue, New York, New York 10010 (800) 221-7945; *The Statesman's Year-Book*.

Statistical Office of the United Nations,

Publishing Service, New York, New York 10017 (800) 253-9646; *Foreign Trade Statistics for Africa;* and *Survey of Economic and Social Conditions in Africa*.

United Nations Conference on Trade and Development (UNCTAD), New York, New York 10017 (800) 253-9646; *Handbook of International Trade and Development Statistics*.

United Nations Economic Commission for Africa, Africa Hall, P.O. Box 3001, Addis Ababa, Ethiopia (Telephone Number in U.S. (800) 253-9646); *African Statistical Yearbook*.

The World Bank, 1818 H Street, NW, Washington, D.C. 20433 (202) 477-1234; *World Development Report;* and *World Development Indicators*.

SENEGAL - EXTERNAL INDEBTEDNESS

African Development Bank, 01 BP 1387, Abidjan 01, Cote D'Ivoire; *Selected Statistics on Regional Member Countries*.

Statistical Office of the United Nations, Publishing Service, New York, New York 10017 (800) 253-9646; *Survey of Economic and Social Conditions in Africa*.

The World Bank, 1818 H Street, NW, Washington, D.C. 20433 (202) 477-1234; *World Development Report;* and *World Development Indicators*.

SENEGAL - EXTERNAL TRADE

African Development Bank, 01 BP 1387, Abidjan 01, Cote D'Ivoire; *Selected Statistics on Regional Member Countries*.

Euromonitor International, Inc., 122 South Michigan Avenue, Suite 1200, Chicago, Illinois 60603 (800) 577-EURO; *World Marketing Data and Statistics*.

Food and Agricultural Organization of the United Nations (FAO) Via delle Terme di Caracalla, 00100 Rome, Italy (Telephone Number in U.S. (202) 653-2400); *The State of Food and Agriculture;* and *Trade Yearbook*.

Statistical Office of the United Nations, Publishing Service, New York, New York 10017 (800) 253-9646; *Statistical Yearbook*.

SENEGAL - FABRIC PRODUCTION - See SENEGAL - TEXTILE INDUSTRY

SENEGAL - FARM CROPS - See SENEGAL - CROPS

SENEGAL - FEMALE WORKING POPULATION - See SENEGAL - EMPLOYMENT

SENEGAL - FERTILITY RATES

Central Intelligence Agency, Washington, D.C. 20505 (703) 482-1100, www.cia.gov; *The World Factbook*.

M.E. Sharpe, 80 Business Park Drive, Armonk, New York 10504 (800) 541-6563; *The Illustrated Book of World Rankings*.

Statistical Office of the United Nations, Publishing Service, New York, New York 10017 (800) 253-9646; *Human Development Report;* and *Survey of Economic and Social Conditions in Africa*.

The World Bank, 1818 H Street, NW, Washington, D.C. 20433 (202) 477-1234; *The World Bank Atlas; World Development Report;* and *World Development Indicators*.

SENEGAL - FERTILIZER

Food and Agricultural Organization of the United Nations (FAO) Via delle Terme di Caracalla, 00100 Rome, Italy (Telephone Number in U.S. (202) 653-2400); *The State of Food and Agriculture;* and *Fertilizer Yearbook*.

Statistical Office of the United Nations, Publishing Service, New York, New York 10017 (800) 253-9646; *Statistical Yearbook*.

SENEGAL - FETAL MORTALITY - See SENEGAL - MORTALITY

SENEGAL - FINANCE

African Development Bank, 01 BP 1387, Abidjan 01, Cote D'Ivoire; *Selected Statistics on Regional Member Countries*.

Economist Intelligence Unit, 111 West 57th Street, New York, New York 10019 (800) 938-4685; *Senegal Country Report*.

Europa Publications Limited, 18 Bedford Square, London, WC1B 3JN, England; *The Europa World Year Book*.

International Monetary Fund, 700 Nineteenth Street, NW, Washington, D.C. 20431 (202) 623-7000; *International Financial Statistics*.

M.E. Sharpe, 80 Business Park Drive, Armonk, New York 10504 (800) 541-6563; *The Illustrated Book of World Rankings*.

St. Martin's Press, Inc., 175 Fifth Avenue, New York, New York 10010 (800) 221-7945; *The Statesman's Year-Book*.

United Nations Economic Commission for Africa, Africa Hall, P.O. Box 3001, Addis Ababa, Ethiopia (Telephone Number in U.S. (800) 253-9646); *African Statistical Yearbook*.

SENEGAL - FISHERIES

Europa Publications Limited, 18 Bedford Square, London, WC1B 3JN, England; *The Europa World Year Book.*

Food and Agricultural Organization of the United Nations (FAO) Via delle Terme di Caracalla, 00100 Rome, Italy (Telephone Number in U.S. (202) 653-2400); *The State of Food and Agriculture; and Yearbook of Fishery Statistics.*

International Monetary Fund, 700 Nineteenth Street, NW, Washington, D.C. 20431 (202) 623-7000; *International Financial Statistics.*

M.E. Sharpe, 80 Business Park Drive, Armonk, New York 10504 (800) 541-6563; *The Illustrated Book of World Rankings.*

St. Martin's Press, Inc., 175 Fifth Avenue, New York, New York 10010 (800) 221-7945; *The Statesman's Year-Book.*

Statistical Office of the United Nations, Publishing Service, New York, New York 10017 (800) 253-9646; *Statistical Yearbook; and Survey of Economic and Social Conditions in Africa.*

United Nations Economic Commission for Africa, Africa Hall, P.O. Box 3001, Addis Ababa, Ethiopia (Telephone Number in U.S. (800) 253-9646); *African Statistical Yearbook.*

SENEGAL - FLOUR PRODUCTION

Statistical Office of the United Nations, Publishing Service, New York, New York 10017 (800) 253-9646; *Statistical Yearbook.*

SENEGAL - FOOD

African Development Bank, 01 BP 1387, Abidjan 01, Cote D'Ivoire; *Selected Statistics on Regional Member Countries.*

Food and Agricultural Organization of the United Nations (FAO) Via delle Terme di Caracalla, 00100 Rome, Italy (Telephone Number in U.S. (202) 653-2400); *Production Yearbook; and The State of Food and Agriculture.*

Statistical Office of the United Nations, Publishing Service, New York, New York 10017 (800) 253-9646; *Human Development Report.*

SENEGAL - FOREIGN DEBT

St. Martin's Press, Inc., 175 Fifth Avenue, New York, New York 10010 (800) 221-7945; *The Statesman's Year-Book.*

SENEGAL - FOREIGN TRADE

Economist Intelligence Unit, 111 West 57th Street, New York, New York 10019 (800) 938-4685; *Senegal Country Report.*

Euromonitor International, Inc., 122 South Michigan Avenue, Suite 1200, Chicago, Illinois 60603 (800) 577-EURO; *International Marketing Data and Statistics; and The World Economic Factbook.*

Europa Publications Limited, 18 Bedford Square, London, WC1B 3JN, England; *The Europa World Year Book.*

Food and Agricultural Organization of the United Nations (FAO) Via delle Terme di Caracalla, 00100 Rome, Italy (Telephone Number in U.S. (202) 653-2400); *The State of Food and Agriculture.*

International Monetary Fund, 700 Nineteenth Street, NW, Washington, D.C. 20431 (202) 623-7000; *International Financial Statistics.*

M.E. Sharpe, 80 Business Park Drive, Armonk, New York 10504 (800) 541-6563; *The Illustrated Book of World Rankings.*

St. Martin's Press, Inc., 175 Fifth Avenue, New York, New York 10010 (800) 221-7945; *The Statesman's Year-Book.*

Statistical Office of the United Nations, Publishing Service, New York, New York 10017 (800) 253-9646; *Foreign Trade Statistics for Africa; International Trade Statistics Yearbook; and Statistical Yearbook.*

United Nations Economic Commission for Africa, Africa Hall, P.O. Box 3001, Addis Ababa, Ethiopia (Telephone Number in U.S. (800) 253-9646); *African Statistical Yearbook.*

The World Bank, 1818 H Street, NW, Washington, D.C. 20433 (202) 477-1234; *World Development Report; and World Development Indicators.*

SENEGAL - FORESTRY AND FOREST PRODUCTS

Europa Publications Limited, 18 Bedford Square, London, WC1B 3JN, England; *The Europa World Year Book.*

Food and Agricultural Organization of the United Nations (FAO) Via delle Terme di Caracalla, 00100 Rome, Italy (Telephone Number in U.S. (202) 653-2400); *The State of Food and Agriculture; and Yearbook of Forest Products.*

M.E. Sharpe, 80 Business Park Drive, Armonk, New York 10504 (800) 541-6563; *The Illustrated Book of World Rankings.*

St. Martin's Press, Inc., 175 Fifth Avenue, New York, New York 10010 (800) 221-7945; *The Statesman's Year-Book.*

Statistical Office of the United Nations, Publishing Service, New York, New York

10017 (800) 253-9646; *Statistical Yearbook.*

United Nations Conference on Trade and Development, Central Statistical Service, Palais des Nations, Geneva, Switzerland (Telephone in U.S. (800) 253-9646); *UNCTAD Commodity Yearbook.*

United Nations Economic Commission for Africa, Africa Hall, P.O. Box 3001, Addis Ababa, Ethiopia (Telephone Number in U.S. (800) 253-9646); *African Statistical Yearbook.*

United Nations Educational, Scientific and Cultural Organization (UNESCO), 7 Place de Fontenoy, F-75700 Paris, France (Telephone Number in U.S. (212) 963-5981); *Statistical Yearbook.*

The World Bank, 1818 H Street, NW, Washington, D.C. 20433 (202) 477-1234; *World Development Report.*

SENEGAL - GAS PRODUCTION - See SENEGAL - MINING AND MINERAL PRODUCTS

SENEGAL - GENERAL INDUSTRIAL STATISTICS - See SENEGAL - INDUSTRY

SENEGAL - GENERAL MORTALITY - See SENEGAL - MORTALITY

SENEGAL - GEOGRAPHIC DATA

M.E. Sharpe, 80 Business Park Drive, Armonk, New York 10504 (800) 541-6563; *The Illustrated Book of World Rankings.*

SENEGAL - GOATS - See SENEGAL - LIVESTOCK AND POULTRY

SENEGAL - GOLD HOLDINGS

International Monetary Fund, 700 Nineteenth Street, NW, Washington, D.C. 20431 (202) 623-7000; *International Financial Statistics.*

Statistical Office of the United Nations, Publishing Service, New York, New York 10017 (800) 253-9646; *Statistical Yearbook.*

The World Bank, 1818 H Street, NW, Washington, D.C. 20433 (202) 477-1234; *World Development Indicators.*

SENEGAL - GOLD PRODUCTION AND CONSUMPTION - See SENEGAL - MINING AND MINERAL PRODUCTS

SENEGAL - GOVERNMENT

Central Intelligence Agency, Washington, D.C. 20505 (703) 482-1100, www.cia.gov; *The World Factbook.*

Europa Publications Limited, 18 Bedford Square, London, WC1B 3JN,

England; *The Europa World Year Book.*

International Monetary Fund, 700 Nineteenth Street, NW, Washington, D.C. 20431 (202) 623-7000; *Government Finance Statistics Yearbook;* and *International Financial Statistics.*

St. Martin's Press, Inc., 175 Fifth Avenue, New York, New York 10010 (800) 221-7945; *The Statesman's Year-Book.*

Statistical Office of the United Nations, Publishing Service, New York, New York 10017 (800) 253-9646; *National Accounts Statistics;* and *Survey of Economic and Social Conditions in Africa.*

The World Bank, 1818 H Street, NW, Washington, D.C. 20433 (202) 477-1234; *World Development Report;* and *World Development Indicators.*

SENEGAL - GRAIN PRODUCTION - See SENEGAL - CROPS

SENEGAL - GRANTS

International Monetary Fund, 700 Nineteenth Street, NW, Washington, D.C. 20431 (202) 623-7000; *Government Finance Statistics Yearbook.*

SENEGAL - GROSS DOMESTIC PRODUCT

African Development Bank, 01 BP 1387, Abidjan 01, Cote D'Ivoire; *Selected Statistics on Regional Member Countries.*

The Economist Intelligence Unit, 111 West 57th Street, New York, New York 10019 (800) 938-4685; *Senegal Country Report;* and *The World Market Atlas.*

Euromonitor International, Inc., 122 South Michigan Avenue, Suite 1200, Chicago, Illinois 60603 (800) 577-EURO; *International Marketing Data and Statistics;* and *The World Economic Factbook.*

Europa Publications Limited, 18 Bedford Square, London, WC1B 3JN, England; *The Europa World Year Book.*

M.E. Sharpe, 80 Business Park Drive, Armonk, New York 10504 (800) 541-6563; *The Illustrated Book of World Rankings.*

Statistical Office of the United Nations, Publishing Service, New York, New York 10017 (800) 253-9646; *Human Development Report; National Accounts Statistics; Statistical Yearbook;* and *Survey of Economic and Social Conditions in Africa.*

United Nations Economic Commission for Africa, Africa Hall, P.O. Box 3001, Addis Ababa, Ethiopia (Telephone Number in U.S. (800) 253-9646); *African Statistical Yearbook.*

The World Bank, 1818 H Street, NW, Washington, D.C. 20433 (202) 477-1234; *World Development Report;* and *World Development Indicators.*

SENEGAL - GROSS NATIONAL PRODUCT

Euromonitor International, Inc., 122 South Michigan Avenue, Suite 1200, Chicago, Illinois 60603 (800) 577-EURO; *International Marketing Data and Statistics.*

St. Martin's Press, Inc., 175 Fifth Avenue, New York, New York 10010 (800) 221-7945; *The Statesman's Year-Book.*

U.S. Arms Control and Disarmament Agency, 320 Twenty-first Street, NW, Washington, D.C. 20451 (202) 647-8677; *World Military Expenditures and Arms Transfers.*

The World Bank, 1818 H Street, NW, Washington, D.C. 20433 (202) 477-1234; *The World Bank Atlas; World Development Report;* and *World Development Indicators.*

SENEGAL - GROUNDNUTS - See SENEGAL - CROPS

SENEGAL - HEALTH

Euromonitor International, Inc., 122 South Michigan Avenue, Suite 1200, Chicago, Illinois 60603 (800) 577-EURO; *World Marketing Data and Statistics.*

M.E. Sharpe, 80 Business Park Drive, Armonk, New York 10504 (800) 541-6563; *The Illustrated Book of World Rankings.*

St. Martin's Press, Inc., 175 Fifth Avenue, New York, New York 10010 (800) 221-7945; *The Statesman's Year-Book.*

Statistical Office of the United Nations, Publishing Service, New York, New York 10017 (800) 253-9646; *Human Development Report;* and *Statistical Yearbook.*
United Nations Children's Fund (UNICEF), 3 United Nations Plaza, New York, New York 10017 (800) 253-9646; *State of the World's Children.*

United Nations Economic Commission for Africa, Africa Hall, P.O. Box 3001, Addis Ababa, Ethiopia (Telephone Number in U.S. (800) 253-9646); *African Statistical Yearbook.*

The World Bank, 1818 H Street, NW, Washington, D.C. 20433 (202) 477-1234; *World Development Report.*

World Health Organization, Office of Publications, 20 Avenue Appia, CH-1211 Geneva 27, Switzerland (Telephone Number in U.S. (518) 436-9686); *World Health Statistics Annual.*

SENEGAL - HEALTH EXPENDITURES

International Monetary Fund, 700 Nineteenth Street, NW, Washington, D.C. 20431 (202) 623-7000; *Government Finance Statistics Yearbook.*

United Nations Economic Commission for Africa, Africa Hall, P.O. Box 3001, Addis Ababa, Ethiopia (Telephone Number in U.S. (800) 253-9646); *African Statistical Yearbook.*

SENEGAL - HIGHWAYS

Central Intelligence Agency, Washington, D.C. 20505 (703) 482-1100, www.cia.gov; *The World Factbook.*

International Road Federation, 2600 Virginia Avenue, NW, Washington, D.C. 20037 (202) 338-4641; *World Road Statistics.*

St. Martin's Press, Inc., 175 Fifth Avenue, New York, New York 10010 (800) 221-7945; *The Statesman's Year-Book.*

Statistical Office of the United Nations, Publishing Service, New York, New York 10017 (800) 253-9646; *Survey of Economic and Social Conditions in Africa.*

United Nations Economic Commission for Africa, Africa Hall, P.O. Box 3001, Addis Ababa, Ethiopia (Telephone Number in U.S. (800) 253-9646); *African Statistical Yearbook.*

SENEGAL - HORSES - See SENEGAL - LIVESTOCK AND POULTRY

SENEGAL - HOURS OF WORK - See SENEGAL - EMPLOYMENT

SENEGAL - HOUSING AND HOUSING UNITS

Euromonitor International, Inc., 122 South Michigan Avenue, Suite 1200, Chicago, Illinois 60603 (800) 577-EURO; *World Marketing Data and Statistics.*

SENEGAL - HOUSING EXPENDITURES

International Monetary Fund, 700 Nineteenth Street, NW, Washington, D.C. 20431 (202) 623-7000; *Government Finance Statistics Yearbook.*

M.E. Sharpe, 80 Business Park Drive, Armonk, New York 10504 (800) 541-6563; *The Illustrated Book of World Rankings.*

SENEGAL - ILLITERATE POPULATION

Central Intelligence Agency, Washington, D.C. 20505 (703) 482-1100, www.cia.gov; *The World Factbook.*

The Economist Intelligence Unit, 111

West 57th Street, New York, New York 10019 (800) 938-4685; *The World Market Atlas.*

Euromonitor International, Inc., 122 South Michigan Avenue, Suite 1200, Chicago, Illinois 60603 (800) 577-EURO; *The World Economic Factbook.*

St. Martin's Press, Inc., 175 Fifth Avenue, New York, New York 10010 (800) 221-7945; *The Statesman's Year-Book.*

Statistical Office of the United Nations, Publishing Service, New York, New York 10017 (800) 253-9646; *Human Development Report.*

United Nations Educational, Scientific and Cultural Organization (UNESCO), 7 Place de Fontenoy, F-75700 Paris, France (Telephone Number in U.S. (212) 963-5981); *Statistical Yearbook.*

SENEGAL - IMPORTS

African Development Bank, 01 BP 1387, Abidjan 01, Cote D'Ivoire; *Selected Statistics on Regional Member Countries.*

Central Intelligence Agency, Washington, D.C. 20505 (703) 482-1100, www.cia.gov; *The World Factbook.*

The Economist Intelligence Unit, 111 West 57th Street, New York, New York 10019 (800) 938-4685; *Senegal Country Report;* and *The World Market Atlas.*

Euromonitor International, Inc., 122 South Michigan Avenue, Suite 1200, Chicago, Illinois 60603 (800) 577-EURO; *International Marketing Data and Statistics;* and *The World Economic Factbook.*

Europa Publications Limited, 18 Bedford Square, London, WC1B 3JN, England; *The Europa World Year Book.*

Food and Agricultural Organization of the United Nations (FAO) Via delle Terme di Caracalla, 00100 Rome, Italy (Telephone Number in U.S. (202) 653-2400); *The State of Food and Agriculture.*

International Monetary Fund, 700 Nineteenth Street, NW, Washington, D.C. 20431 (202) 623-7000; *Direction of Trade Statistics; Government Finance Statistics Yearbook;* and *International Financial Statistics.*

St. Martin's Press, Inc., 175 Fifth Avenue, New York, New York 10010 (800) 221-7945; *The Statesman's Year-Book.*

Statistical Office of the United Nations, Publishing Service, New York, New York 10017 (800) 253-9646; *Foreign Trade Statistics for Africa;* and *Survey of Economic and Social Conditions in Africa.*

United Nations Conference on Trade and Development (UNCTAD), New York, New York 10017 (800) 253-9646; *Handbook of International Trade and Development Statistics.*

United Nations Economic Commission for Africa, Africa Hall, P.O. Box 3001, Addis Ababa, Ethiopia (Telephone Number in U.S. (800) 253-9646); *African Statistical Yearbook.*

The World Bank, 1818 H Street, NW, Washington, D.C. 20433 (202) 477-1234; *World Development Report;* and *World Development Indicators.*

SENEGAL - INCOME TAXES - See SENEGAL - TAXATION

SENEGAL - INDUSTRY

Central Intelligence Agency, Washington, D.C. 20505 (703) 482-1100, www.cia.gov; *The World Factbook.*

Economist Intelligence Unit, 111 West 57th Street, New York, New York 10019 (800) 938-4685; *Senegal Country Report.*

Euromonitor International, Inc., 122 South Michigan Avenue, Suite 1200, Chicago, Illinois 60603 (800) 577-EURO; *International Marketing Data and Statistics; World Marketing Data and Statistics;* and *The World Economic Factbook.*

Europa Publications Limited, 18 Bedford Square, London, WC1B 3JN, England; *The Europa World Year Book.*

International Labour Office, I.L.O. Publications, 1828 L Street, NW, Suite 801, Washington, D.C. 20036 (301) 638-3152; *Yearbook of Labour Statistics.*

M.E. Sharpe, 80 Business Park Drive, Armonk, New York 10504 (800) 541-6563; *The Illustrated Book of World Rankings.*

St. Martin's Press, Inc., 175 Fifth Avenue, New York, New York 10010 (800) 221-7945; *The Statesman's Year-Book.*

Statistical Office of the United Nations, Publishing Service, New York, New York 10017 (800) 253-9646; *Industrial Commodity Statistics Yearbook;* and *Survey of Economic and Social Conditions in Africa.*

International Labour Office, I.L.O. Publications, 1828 L Street, NW, Suite 801, Washington, D.C. 20036 (301) 638-3152; *Yearbook of Labour Statistics.*

M.E. Sharpe, 80 Business Park Drive, Armonk, New York 10504 (800) 541-6563; *The Illustrated Book of World Rankings.*

St. Martin's Press, Inc., 175 Fifth

Avenue, New York, New York 10010 (800) 221-7945; *The Statesman's Year-Book.*

Statistical Office of the United Nations, Publishing Service, New York, New York 10017 (800) 253-9646; *Human Development Report.*

The World Bank, 1818 H Street, NW, Washington, D.C. 20433 (202) 477-1234; *The World Bank Atlas; World Development Report;* and *World Development Indicators.*

SENEGAL - LABOR

Euromonitor International, Inc., 122 South Michigan Avenue, Suite 1200, Chicago, Illinois 60603 (800) 577-EURO; *World Marketing Data and Statistics.*

SENEGAL - LAND USE

Central Intelligence Agency, Washington, D.C. 20505 (703) 482-1100, www.cia.gov; *The World Factbook.*

Euromonitor International, Inc., 122 South Michigan Avenue, Suite 1200, Chicago, Illinois 60603 (800) 577-EURO; *International Marketing Data and Statistics.*

Food and Agricultural Organization of the United Nations (FAO), Via delle Terme di Caracalla, 00100 Rome, Italy (Telephone Number in U.S. (202) 653-2400); *Production Yearbook.*

The World Bank, 1818 H Street, NW, Washington, D.C. 20433 (202) 477-1234; *World Development Report.*

SENEGAL - LIBRARIES

M.E. Sharpe, 80 Business Park Drive, Armonk, New York 10504 (800) 541-6563; *The Illustrated Book of World Rankings.*

United Nations Educational, Scientific and Cultural Organization (UNESCO), 7 Place de Fontenoy, F-75700 Paris, France (Telephone Number in U.S. (212) 963-5981); *Statistical Yearbook.*

SENEGAL - LIFE EXPECTANCY

African Development Bank, 01 BP 1387, Abidjan 01, Cote D'Ivoire; *Selected Statistics on Regional Member Countries.*

Central Intelligence Agency, Washington, D.C. 20505 (703) 482-1100, www.cia.gov; *The World Factbook.*

Euromonitor International, Inc., 122 South Michigan Avenue, Suite 1200, Chicago, Illinois 60603 (800) 577-EURO; *The World Economic Factbook.*

Statistical Office of the United Nations, Publishing Service, New York, New York 10017 (800) 253-9646; *Human*

Development Report; and *World Statistics Pocketbook.*

The World Bank, 1818 H Street, NW, Washington, D.C. 20433 (202) 477-1234; *The World Bank Atlas;* and *World Development Report.*

SENEGAL - LITERACY RATE

Euromonitor International, Inc., 122 South Michigan Avenue, Suite 1200, Chicago, Illinois 60603 (800) 577-EURO; *World Marketing Data and Statistics.*

Statistical Office of the United Nations, Publishing Service, New York, New York 10017 (800) 253-9646; *Survey of Economic and Social Conditions in Africa.*

SENEGAL - LIVESTOCK AND POULTRY

Euromonitor International, Inc., 122 South Michigan Avenue, Suite 1200, Chicago, Illinois 60603 (800) 577-EURO; *International Marketing Data and Statistics.*

Europa Publications Limited, 18 Bedford Square, London, WC1B 3JN, England; *The Europa World Year Book.*

Food and Agricultural Organization of the United Nations (FAO), Via delle Terme di Caracalla, 00100 Rome, Italy (Telephone Number in U.S. (202) 653-2400); *Production Yearbook,* and *The State of Food and Agriculture.*

M.E. Sharpe, 80 Business Park Drive, Armonk, New York 10504 (800) 541-6563; *The Illustrated Book of World Rankings.*

St. Martin's Press, Inc., 175 Fifth Avenue, New York, New York 10010 (800) 221-7945; *The Statesman's Year-Book.*

Statistical Office of the United Nations, Publishing Service, New York, New York 10017 (800) 253-9646; *Statistical Yearbook;* and *Survey of Economic and Social Conditions in Africa.*

United Nations Conference on Trade and Development, Central Statistical Service, Palais des Nations, Geneva, Switzerland (Telephone in U.S. (800) 253-9646); *UNCTAD Commodity Yearbook.*

United Nations Economic Commission for Africa, Africa Hall, P.O. Box 3001, Addis Ababa, Ethiopia (Telephone Number in U.S. (800) 253-9646); *African Statistical Yearbook.*

SENEGAL - LIVING LEVELS - See SENEGAL - LIFE EXPECTANCY

SENEGAL - MAIL TRAFFIC - NUMBER OF ITEMS SENT AND RECEIVED

Statistical Office of the United Nations,

Publishing Service, New York, New York 10017 (800) 253-9646; *Statistical Yearbook.*

SENEGAL - MANUFACTURING

M.E. Sharpe, 80 Business Park Drive, Armonk, New York 10504 (800) 541-6563; *The Illustrated Book of World Rankings.*

Statistical Office of the United Nations, Publishing Service, New York, New York 10017 (800) 253-9646; *Statistical Yearbook;* and *Survey of Economic and Social Conditions in Africa.*

United Nations Economic Commission for Africa, Africa Hall, P.O. Box 3001, Addis Ababa, Ethiopia (Telephone Number in U.S. (800) 253-9646); *African Statistical Yearbook.*

The World Bank, 1818 H Street, NW, Washington, D.C. 20433 (202) 477-1234; *World Development Indicators.*

SENEGAL - MARRIAGE RATES

Europa Publications Limited, 18 Bedford Square, London, WC1B 3JN, England; *The Europa World Year Book.*

M.E. Sharpe, 80 Business Park Drive, Armonk, New York 10504 (800) 541-6563; *The Illustrated Book of World Rankings.*

Statistical Office of the United Nations, Publishing Service, New York, New York 10017 (800) 253-9646; *Demographic Yearbook.*

SENEGAL - MEAT PRODUCTION - See SENEGAL - LIVESTOCK AND POULTRY

SENEGAL - MERCHANT SHIPPING

Europa Publications Limited, 18 Bedford Square, London, WC1B 3JN, England; *The Europa World Year Book.*

St. Martin's Press, Inc., 175 Fifth Avenue, New York, New York 10010 (800) 221-7945; *The Statesman's Year-Book.*

Statistical Office of the United Nations, Publishing Service, New York, New York 10017 (800) 253-9646; *Statistical Yearbook.*

United Nations Economic Commission for Africa, Africa Hall, P.O. Box 3001, Addis Ababa, Ethiopia (Telephone Number in U.S. (800) 253-9646); *African Statistical Yearbook.*

U.S. Department of Transportation, Maritime Administration, 400 Seventh Street, SW, Washington, D.C. 20590 (202) 366-5807, www.marad.dot.gov; *A Statistical Analysis of the World's Merchant Fleets.*

SENEGAL - MILITARY

Central Intelligence Agency, Washington, D.C. 20505 (703) 482-1100, www.cia.gov; *The World Factbook.*

Euromonitor International, Inc., 122 South Michigan Avenue, Suite 1200, Chicago, Illinois 60603 (800) 577-EURO; *World Marketing Data and Statistics.*

The International Institute for Strategic Studies, 23 Tavistock Street, London WC2E 7NQ, England 44 171 3797676; *The Military Balance.*

St. Martin's Press, Inc., 175 Fifth Avenue, New York, New York 10010 (800) 221-7945; *The Statesman's Year-Book.*

Statistical Office of the United Nations, Publishing Service, New York, New York 10017 (800) 253-9646; *Human Development Report.*

U.S. Arms Control and Disarmament Agency, 320 Twenty-first Street, NW, Washington, D.C. 20451 (202) 647-8677; *World Military Expenditures and Arms Transfers.*

SENEGAL - MILK PRODUCTION - See SENEGAL - DAIRY PRODUCTS

SENEGAL - MINING AND MINERAL PRODUCTS

Europa Publications Limited, 18 Bedford Square, London, WC1B 3JN, England; *The Europa World Year Book.*

M.E. Sharpe, 80 Business Park Drive, Armonk, New York 10504 (800) 541-6563; *The Illustrated Book of World Rankings.*

St. Martin's Press, Inc., 175 Fifth Avenue, New York, New York 10010 (800) 221-7945; *The Statesman's Year-Book.*

Statistical Office of the United Nations, Publishing Service, New York, New York 10017 (800) 253-9646; *Statistical Yearbook.*

United Nations Conference on Trade and Development, Central Statistical Service, Palais des Nations, Geneva, Switzerland (Telephone in U.S. (800) 253-9646); *UNCTAD Commodity Yearbook.*

United Nations Economic Commission for Africa, Africa Hall, P.O. Box 3001, Addis Ababa, Ethiopia (Telephone Number in U.S. (800) 253-9646); *African Statistical Yearbook.*

SENEGAL - MONEY EXCHANGE RATES - See SENEGAL - EXCHANGE RATES

SENEGAL - MONEY RESERVES

Euromonitor International, Inc., 122 South Michigan Avenue, Suite 1200, Chicago, Illinois 60603 (800) 577-EURO;

International Marketing Data and Statistics.

SENEGAL - MONEY SUPPLY

African Development Bank, 01 BP 1387, Abidjan 01, Cote D'Ivoire; *Selected Statistics on Regional Member Countries.*

Economist Intelligence Unit, 111 West 57th Street, New York, New York 10019 (800) 938-4685; *Senegal Country Report.*

Euromonitor International, Inc., 122 South Michigan Avenue, Suite 1200, Chicago, Illinois 60603 (800) 577-EURO; *International Marketing Data and Statistics.*

Europa Publications Limited, 18 Bedford Square, London, WC1B 3JN, England; *The Europa World Year Book.*

International Monetary Fund, 700 Nineteenth Street, NW, Washington, D.C. 20431 (202) 623-7000; *International Financial Statistics.*

Statistical Office of the United Nations, Publishing Service, New York, New York 10017 (800) 253-9646; *Statistical Yearbook.*

The World Bank, 1818 H Street, NW, Washington, D.C. 20433 (202) 477-1234; *World Development Indicators.*

SENEGAL - MONUMENTS AND HISTORICAL SITES

United Nations Educational, Scientific and Cultural Organization (UNESCO), 7 Place de Fontenoy, F-75700 Paris, France (Telephone Number in U.S. (212) 963-5981); *Statistical Yearbook.*

SENEGAL - MORTALITY

Central Intelligence Agency, Washington, D.C. 20505 (703) 482-1100, www.cia.gov; *The World Factbook.*

Euromonitor International, Inc., 122 South Michigan Avenue, Suite 1200, Chicago, Illinois 60603 (800) 577-EURO; *International Marketing Data and Statistics;* and *The World Economic Factbook.*

St. Martin's Press, Inc., 175 Fifth Avenue, New York, New York 10010 (800) 221-7945; *The Statesman's Year-Book.*

Statistical Office of the United Nations, Publishing Service, New York, New York 10017 (800) 253-9646; *Demographic Yearbook; Human Development Report; Statistical Yearbook; Survey of Economic and Social Conditions in Africa;* and *World Statistics Pocketbook.*

United Nations Children's Fund (UNICEF), 3 United Nations Plaza, New York, New York 10017 (800) 253-9646; *State of the World's Children.*

The World Bank, 1818 H Street, NW, Washington, D.C. 20433 (202) 477-1234; *The World Bank Atlas; World Development Report;* and *World Development Indicators.*

World Health Organization, Office of Publications, 20 Avenue Appia, CH-1211 Geneva 27, Switzerland (Telephone Number in U.S. (518) 436-9686); *World Health Statistics Annual.*

SENEGAL - MOTION PICTURES

Statistical Office of the United Nations, Publishing Service, New York, New York 10017 (800) 253-9646; *Statistical Yearbook.*

SENEGAL - MOTOR VEHICLE TAXES - See SENEGAL - TAXATION

SENEGAL - MOTOR VEHICLES IN USE

Europa Publications Limited, 18 Bedford Square, London, WC1B 3JN, England; *The Europa World Year Book.*

International Road Federation, 2600 Virginia Avenue, NW, Washington, D.C. 20037 (202) 338-4641; *World Road Statistics.*

Statistical Office of the United Nations, Publishing Service, New York, New York 10017 (800) 253-9646; *Statistical Yearbook;* and *Survey of Economic and Social Conditions in Africa.*

SENEGAL - MUSEUMS

M.E. Sharpe, 80 Business Park Drive, Armonk, New York 10504 (800) 541-6563; *The Illustrated Book of World Rankings.*

United Nations Educational, Scientific and Cultural Organization (UNESCO), 7 Place de Fontenoy, F-75700 Paris, France (Telephone Number in U.S. (212) 963-5981); *Statistical Yearbook.*

SENEGAL - NATALITY - See SENEGAL - BIRTH RATE

SENEGAL - NATIONAL ACCOUNTS

African Development Bank, 01 BP 1387, Abidjan 01, Cote D'Ivoire; *Selected Statistics on Regional Member Countries.*

Europa Publications Limited, 18 Bedford Square, London, WC1B 3JN, England; *The Europa World Year Book.*

International Monetary Fund, 700 Nineteenth Street, NW, Washington, D.C. 20431 (202) 623-7000; *International Financial Statistics.*

Statistical Office of the United Nations, Publishing Service, New York, New York 10017 (800) 253-9646; *National Accounts Statistics,;* and *Statistical Yearbook.*

United Nations Economic Commission for Africa, Africa Hall, P.O. Box 3001, Addis Ababa, Ethiopia (Telephone Number in U.S. (800) 253-9646); *African Statistical Yearbook.*

SENEGAL - NATIONAL INCOME

M.E. Sharpe, 80 Business Park Drive, Armonk, New York 10504 (800) 541-6563; *The Illustrated Book of World Rankings.*

Statistical Office of the United Nations, Publishing Service, New York, New York 10017 (800) 253-9646; *National Accounts Statistics;* and *Statistical Yearbook.*

SENEGAL - NATIONAL PRODUCT

M.E. Sharpe, 80 Business Park Drive, Armonk, New York 10504 (800) 541-6563; *The Illustrated Book of World Rankings.*

SENEGAL - NATURAL GAS PRODUCTION - See SENEGAL - MINING AND MINERAL PRODUCTS

SENEGAL - NEWSPAPER PRODUCTION - See SENEGAL - FORESTRY AND FOREST PRODUCTS

SENEGAL - NEWSPRINT - See SENEGAL - FORESTRY AND FOREST PRODUCTS

SENEGAL - OCCUPATIONS - See SENEGAL - LABOR

SENEGAL - PALM KERNEL PRODUCTION - See SENEGAL - CROPS

SENEGAL - PAPER - See SENEGAL - FORESTRY AND FOREST PRODUCTS

SENEGAL - PEANUT PRODUCTION - See SENEGAL - CROPS

SENEGAL - PESTICIDE USE

Food and Agricultural Organization of the United Nations (FAO) Via delle Terme di Caracalla, 00100 Rome, Italy (Telephone Number in U.S. (202) 653-2400); *The State of Food and Agriculture.*

SENEGAL - PETROLEUM INDUSTRY

Food and Agricultural Organization of the United Nations (FAO) Via delle Terme di Caracalla, 00100 Rome, Italy (Telephone Number in U.S. (202) 653-2400); *The State of Food and Agriculture.*

International Monetary Fund, 700 Nineteenth Street, NW, Washington, D.C. 20431 (202) 623-7000; *International Financial Statistics.*

M.E. Sharpe, 80 Business Park Drive, Armonk, New York 10504 (800) 541-6563; *The Illustrated Book of World Rankings.*

Statistical Office of the United Nations, Publishing Service, New York, New York 10017 (800) 253-9646; *Statistical Yearbook.*

United Nations Conference on Trade and Development, Central Statistical Service, Palais des Nations, Geneva, Switzerland (Telephone in U.S. (800) 253-9646); *UNCTAD Commodity Yearbook.*

SENEGAL - PHOSPHATE EXPORTS

International Monetary Fund, 700 Nineteenth Street, NW, Washington, D.C. 20431 (202) 623-7000; *International Financial Statistics.*

SENEGAL - PHOSPHATE ROCK PRODUCTION - See SENEGAL - MINING AND MINERAL PRODUCTS

SENEGAL - PIGS - See SENEGAL - LIVESTOCK AND POULTRY

SENEGAL - POPULATION

African Development Bank, 01 BP 1387, Abidjan 01, Cote D'Ivoire; *Selected Statistics on Regional Member Countries.*

Central Intelligence Agency, Washington, D.C. 20505 (703) 482-1100, www.cia.gov; *The World Factbook.*

The Economist Intelligence Unit, 111 West 57th Street, New York, New York 10019 (800) 938-4685; *Senegal Country Report;* and *The World Market Atlas.*

Euromonitor International, Inc., 122 South Michigan Avenue, Suite 1200, Chicago, Illinois 60603 (800) 577-EURO; *International Marketing Data and Statistics;* and *The World Economic Factbook.*

Europa Publications Limited, 18 Bedford Square, London, WC1B 3JN, England; *The Europa World Year Book.*

Food and Agricultural Organization of the United Nations (FAO), Via delle Terme di Caracalla, 00100 Rome, Italy (Telephone Number in U.S. (202) 653-2400); *Production Yearbook.*

International Labour Office, I.L.O. Publications, 1828 L Street, NW, Suite 801, Washington, D.C. 20036 (301) 638-3152; *Yearbook of Labour Statistics.*

M.E. Sharpe, 80 Business Park Drive, Armonk, New York 10504 (800) 541-6563; *The Illustrated Book of World Rankings.*

St. Martin's Press, Inc., 175 Fifth Avenue, New York, New York 10010 (800) 221-7945; *The Statesman's Year-Book.*

Statistical Office of the United Nations, Publishing Service, New York, New York 10017 (800) 253-9646; *Demographic*

Yearbook; Human Development Report; Statistical Yearbook; Survey of Economic and Social Conditions in Africa; and *World Statistics Pocketbook.*

United Nations Educational, Scientific and Cultural Organization (UNESCO), 7 Place de Fontenoy, F-75700 Paris, France (Telephone Number in U.S. (212) 963-5981); *Statistical Yearbook.*

U.S. Arms Control and Disarmament Agency, 320 Twenty-first Street, NW, Washington, D.C. 20451 (202) 647-8677; *World Military Expenditures and Arms Transfers.*

The World Bank, 1818 H Street, NW, Washington, D.C. 20433 (202) 477-1234; *The World Bank Atlas;* and *World Development Report.*

World Health Organization, Office of Publications, 20 Avenue Appia, CH-1211 Geneva 27, Switzerland (Telephone Number in U.S. (518) 436-9686); *World Health Statistics Annual.*

SENEGAL - POST OFFICES

M.E. Sharpe, 80 Business Park Drive, Armonk, New York 10504 (800) 541-6563; *The Illustrated Book of World Rankings.*

St. Martin's Press, Inc., 175 Fifth Avenue, New York, New York 10010 (800) 221-7945; *The Statesman's Year-Book.*

SENEGAL - POTATO PRODUCTION - See SENEGAL - CROPS

SENEGAL - PRICES

Food and Agricultural Organization of the United Nations (FAO), Via delle Terme di Caracalla, 00100 Rome, Italy (Telephone Number in U.S. (202) 653-2400); *Production Yearbook;* and *The State of Food and Agriculture.*

International Labour Office, I.L.O. Publications, 1828 L Street, NW, Suite 801, Washington, D.C. 20036 (301) 638-3152; *Yearbook of Labour Statistics.*

International Monetary Fund, 700 Nineteenth Street, NW, Washington, D.C. 20431 (202) 623-7000; *International Financial Statistics.*

M.E. Sharpe, 80 Business Park Drive, Armonk, New York 10504 (800) 541-6563; *The Illustrated Book of World Rankings.*

United Nations Economic Commission for Africa, Africa Hall, P.O. Box 3001, Addis Ababa, Ethiopia (Telephone Number in U.S. (800) 253-9646); *African Statistical Yearbook.*

SENEGAL - PRINTING AND WRITING

PAPER - See SENEGAL - FORESTRY AND FOREST PRODUCTS

SENEGAL - PRODUCTION

M.E. Sharpe, 80 Business Park Drive, Armonk, New York 10504 (800) 541-6563; *The Illustrated Book of World Rankings.*

SENEGAL - PRODUCTIVITY

Euromonitor International, Inc., 122 South Michigan Avenue, Suite 1200, Chicago, Illinois 60603 (800) 577-EURO; *International Marketing Data and Statistics.*

SENEGAL - PROPERTY TAXES - See SENEGAL - TAXATION

SENEGAL - PUBLIC FINANCE

M.E. Sharpe, 80 Business Park Drive, Armonk, New York 10504 (800) 541-6563; *The Illustrated Book of World Rankings.*

SENEGAL - RADIO BROADCASTING - See SENEGAL - BROADCASTING

SENEGAL - RADIO RECEIVERS

St. Martin's Press, Inc., 175 Fifth Avenue, New York, New York 10010 (800) 221-7945; *The Statesman's Year-Book.*

SENEGAL - RAILWAYS

Europa Publications Limited, 18 Bedford Square, London, WC1B 3JN, England; *The Europa World Year Book.*

St. Martin's Press, Inc., 175 Fifth Avenue, New York, New York 10010 (800) 221-7945; *The Statesman's Year-Book.*

Statistical Office of the United Nations, Publishing Service, New York, New York 10017 (800) 253-9646; *Statistical Yearbook;* and *Survey of Economic and Social Conditions in Africa.*

United Nations Economic Commission for Africa, Africa Hall, P.O. Box 3001, Addis Ababa, Ethiopia (Telephone Number in U.S. (800) 253-9646); *African Statistical Yearbook.*

SENEGAL - RELIGION

Central Intelligence Agency, Washington, D.C. 20505 (703) 482-1100, www.cia.gov; *The World Factbook.*

M.E. Sharpe, 80 Business Park Drive, Armonk, New York 10504 (800) 541-6563; *The Illustrated Book of World Rankings.*

St. Martin's Press, Inc., 175 Fifth Avenue, New York, New York 10010 (800) 221-7945; *The Statesman's Year-Book.*

SENEGAL - RENT PRICES

International Labour Office, I.L.O. Publications, 1828 L Street, NW, Suite 801, Washington, D.C. 20036 (301) 638-3152; *Yearbook of Labour Statistics.*

SENEGAL - RETAIL TRADE

Euromonitor International, Inc., 122 South Michigan Avenue, Suite 1200, Chicago, Illinois 60603 (800) 577-EURO; *World Marketing Data and Statistics.*

SENEGAL - RICE PRODUCTION - See SENEGAL - CROPS

SENEGAL - ROUNDWOOD PRODUCTION - See SENEGAL - FORESTRY AND FOREST PRODUCTS

SENEGAL - RUBBER PRODUCTION AND CONSUMPTION

M.E. Sharpe, 80 Business Park Drive, Armonk, New York 10504 (800) 541-6563; *The Illustrated Book of World Rankings.*

SENEGAL - SALT PRODUCTION - See SENEGAL - MINING AND MINERAL PRODUCTS

SENEGAL - SAWNWOOD PRODUCTION - See SENEGAL - FORESTRY AND FOREST PRODUCTS

SENEGAL - SCIENCE AND TECHNOLOGY - EXPENDITURE FOR RESEARCH - See SENEGAL - SCIENTISTS, TECHNICIANS AND ENGINEERS

SENEGAL - SCIENTISTS, TECHNICIANS AND ENGINEERS

Statistical Office of the United Nations, Publishing Service, New York, New York 10017 (800) 253-9646; *Statistical Yearbook.*

SENEGAL - SENIOR CITIZENS

M.E. Sharpe, 80 Business Park Drive, Armonk, New York 10504 (800) 541-6563; *The Illustrated Book of World Rankings.*

SENEGAL - SHEEP

Euromonitor International, Inc., 122 South Michigan Avenue, Suite 1200, Chicago, Illinois 60603 (800) 577-EURO; *International Marketing Data and Statistics.*

M.E. Sharpe, 80 Business Park Drive, Armonk, New York 10504 (800) 541-6563; *The Illustrated Book of World Rankings.*

Statistical Office of the United Nations, Publishing Service, New York, New York 10017 (800) 253-9646; *Statistical Yearbook;* and *Survey of Economic and Social Conditions in Africa.*

SENEGAL - SHELLFISH EXPORTS

International Monetary Fund, 700 Nineteenth Street, NW, Washington, D.C. 20431 (202) 623-7000; *International Financial Statistics.*

SENEGAL - SILVER PRODUCTION AND CONSUMPTION - See SENEGAL - MINING AND MINERAL PRODUCTS

SENEGAL - SOCIAL DATA

African Development Bank, 01 BP 1387, Abidjan 01, Cote D'Ivoire; *Selected Statistics on Regional Member Countries.*

M.E. Sharpe, 80 Business Park Drive, Armonk, New York 10504 (800) 541-6563; *The Illustrated Book of World Rankings.*

Statistical Office of the United Nations, Publishing Service, New York, New York 10017 (800) 253-9646; *World Statistics Pocketbook.*

SENEGAL - SOCIAL SECURITY

International Monetary Fund, 700 Nineteenth Street, NW, Washington, D.C. 20431 (202) 623-7000; *Government Finance Statistics Yearbook.*

Statistical Office of the United Nations, Publishing Service, New York, New York 10017 (800) 253-9646; *National Accounts Statistics.*

SENEGAL - STAMP TAXES AND DUTIES - See SENEGAL - TAXATION

SENEGAL - STATE BUDGET REVENUE AND EXPENDITURES

Euromonitor International, Inc., 122 South Michigan Avenue, Suite 1200, Chicago, Illinois 60603 (800) 577-EURO; *International Marketing Data and Statistics.*

SENEGAL - STEEL - See SENEGAL - MINING AND MINERAL PRODUCTS

SENEGAL - STOCKS - COMMODITY - MARKET PRICE - INDEX

Food and Agricultural Organization of the United Nations (FAO) Via delle Terme di Caracalla, 00100 Rome, Italy (Telephone Number in U.S. (202) 653-2400); *The State of Food and Agriculture.*

SENEGAL - SUGAR - See SENEGAL - CROPS

SENEGAL - TAXATION

Europa Publications Limited, 18 Bedford Square, London, WC1B 3JN, England; *The Europa World Year Book.*

International Monetary Fund, 700 Nineteenth Street, NW, Washington, D.C. 20431 (202) 623-7000; *Government Finance Statistics Yearbook.*

International Road Federation, 2600 Virginia Avenue, NW, Washington, D.C. 20037 (202) 338-4641; *World Road Statistics.*

The World Bank, 1818 H Street, NW, Washington, D.C. 20433 (202) 477-1234; *World Development Indicators.*

SENEGAL - TELEPHONES IN USE

American Telephone and Telegraph Company, 26 Parsippany Road, Whippany, New Jersey 07981 (800) 222-0300; *The World's Telephones.*

Central Intelligence Agency, Washington, D.C. 20505 (703) 482-1100, www.cia.gov; *The World Factbook.*

Europa Publications Limited, 18 Bedford Square, London, WC1B 3JN, England; *The Europa World Year Book.*

St. Martin's Press, Inc., 175 Fifth Avenue, New York, New York 10010 (800) 221-7945; *The Statesman's Year-Book.*

Statistical Office of the United Nations, Publishing Service, New York, New York 10017 (800) 253-9646; *Statistical Yearbook;* and *World Statistics Pocketbook.*

SENEGAL - TELEVISION BROADCASTING - See SENEGAL - BROADCASTING

SENEGAL - TEXTILE INDUSTRY

M.E. Sharpe, 80 Business Park Drive, Armonk, New York 10504 (800) 541-6563; *The Illustrated Book of World Rankings.*

Statistical Office of the United Nations, Publishing Service, New York, New York 10017 (800) 253-9646; *Statistical Yearbook.*

United Nations Conference on Trade and Development, Central Statistical Service, Palais des Nations, Geneva, Switzerland (Telephone in U.S. (800) 253-9646); *UNCTAD Commodity Yearbook.*

SENEGAL - TOBACCO PRODUCTION

M.E. Sharpe, 80 Business Park Drive, Armonk, New York 10504 (800) 541-6563; *The Illustrated Book of World Rankings.*

Statistical Office of the United Nations, Publishing Service, New York, New York 10017 (800) 253-9646; *Statistical Yearbook.*

SENEGAL - TOURISM

Euromonitor International, Inc., 122 South Michigan Avenue, Suite 1200, Chicago, Illinois 60603 (800) 577-EURO; *The World Economic Factbook;* and *World Marketing Data and Statistics.*

Europa Publications Limited, 18

Bedford Square, London, WC1B 3JN, England; *The Europa World Year Book.*

M.E. Sharpe, 80 Business Park Drive, Armonk, New York 10504 (800) 541-6563; *The Illustrated Book of World Rankings.*

St. Martin's Press, Inc., 175 Fifth Avenue, New York, New York 10010 (800) 221-7945; *The Statesman's Year-Book.*

Statistical Office of the United Nations, Publishing Service, New York, New York 10017 (800) 253-9646; *Statistical Yearbook.*

United Nations Economic Commission for Africa, Africa Hall, P.O. Box 3001, Addis Ababa, Ethiopia (Telephone Number in U.S. (800) 253-9646); *African Statistical Yearbook.*

World Tourism Organization, Calle Capitan Haya 42, E-28020 Madrid, Spain; *Yearbook of Tourism Statistics.*

SENEGAL - TRACTORS IN USE

Statistical Office of the United Nations, Publishing Service, New York, New York 10017 (800) 253-9646; *Statistical Yearbook.*

SENEGAL - TRADE - See SENEGAL - FOREIGN TRADE

SENEGAL - TRANSPORTATION AND COMMUNICATIONS

Central Intelligence Agency, Washington, D.C. 20505 (703) 482-1100, www.cia.gov; *The World Factbook.*

Euromonitor International, Inc., 122 South Michigan Avenue, Suite 1200, Chicago, Illinois 60603 (800) 577-EURO; *International Marketing Data and Statistics; and World Marketing Data and Statistics.*

Europa Publications Limited, 18 Bedford Square, London, WC1B 3JN, England; *The Europa World Year Book.*

M.E. Sharpe, 80 Business Park Drive, Armonk, New York 10504 (800) 541-6563; *The Illustrated Book of World Rankings.*

St. Martin's Press, Inc., 175 Fifth Avenue, New York, New York 10010 (800) 221-7945; *The Statesman's Year-Book.*

Statistical Office of the United Nations, Publishing Service, New York, New York 10017 (800) 253-9646; *Human Development Report.*

United Nations Economic Commission for Africa, Africa Hall, P.O. Box 3001, Addis Ababa, Ethiopia (Telephone Number in U.S. (800) 253-9646); *African Statistical Yearbook.*

SENEGAL - UNEMPLOYMENT

Central Intelligence Agency, Washington, D.C. 20505 (703) 482-1100, www.cia.gov; *The World Factbook.*

Euromonitor International, Inc., 122 South Michigan Avenue, Suite 1200, Chicago, Illinois 60603 (800) 577-EURO; *International Marketing Data and Statistics.*

International Labour Office, I.L.O. Publications, 1828 L Street, NW, Suite 801, Washington, D.C. 20036 (301) 638-3152; *Yearbook of Labour Statistics.*

St. Martin's Press, Inc., 175 Fifth Avenue, New York, New York 10010 (800) 221-7945; *The Statesman's Year-Book.*

Statistical Office of the United Nations, Publishing Service, New York, New York 10017 (800) 253-9646; *Statistical Yearbook.*

SENEGAL - VITAL STATISTICS

Euromonitor International, Inc., 122 South Michigan Avenue, Suite 1200, Chicago, Illinois 60603 (800) 577-EURO; *International Marketing Data and Statistics.*

St. Martin's Press, Inc., 175 Fifth Avenue, New York, New York 10010 (800) 221-7945; *The Statesman's Year-Book.*

Statistical Office of the United Nations, Publishing Service, New York, New York 10017 (800) 253-9646; *Statistical Yearbook.*

World Health Organization, Office of Publications, 20 Avenue Appia, CH-1211 Geneva 27, Switzerland (Telephone Number in U.S. (518) 436-9686); *World Health Statistics Annual.*

SENEGAL - WAGES

International Labour Office, I.L.O. Publications, 1828 L Street, NW, Suite 801, Washington, D.C. 20036 (301) 638-3152; *Yearbook of Labour Statistics.*

SENEGAL - WEATHER - See SENEGAL - CLIMATE

SENEGAL - WELFARE

International Monetary Fund, 700 Nineteenth Street, NW, Washington, D.C. 20431 (202) 623-7000; *Government Finance Statistics Yearbook.*

SENEGAL - WHEAT - See SENEGAL - CROPS

SENEGAL - WHOLESALE PRICES

Statistical Office of the United Nations, Publishing Service, New York, New York 10017 (800) 253-9646; *Statistical Yearbook.*

SENEGAL - WINE PRODUCTION - See SENEGAL - BEVERAGES

SENEGAL - WOOL PRODUCTION - See SENEGAL - TEXTILE INDUSTRY

SENEGAL - YARN PRODUCTION - See SENEGAL - TEXTILE INDUSTRY

SEPTICEMIA

U.S. Department of Health and Human Services, National Center for Health Statistics, 3700 East-West Highway, Hyattsville, Maryland 20782 (301) 436-8500, www.cdc.gov/nchs; *Vital Statistics of the United States; National Vital Statistics Report;* and unpublished data.

SERBIA - See YUGOSLAVIA

SERVICE INDUSTRIES - CAPITAL

U.S. Department of Commerce, Bureau of Economic Analysis, Fourteenth Street between Constitution Avenue and E Street, NW, Washington, D.C. 20230 (202) 606-9900, www.bea.doc.gov; *Survey of Current Business.*

SERVICE INDUSTRIES - EARNINGS

U.S. Department of Commerce, Bureau of Economic Analysis, Fourteenth Street between Constitution Avenue and E Street, NW, Washington, D.C. 20230 (202) 606-9900, www.bea.doc.gov; *Survey of Current Business;* and *The National Income and Product Accounts of the United States.*

U.S. Department of Commerce, Bureau of the Census, Washington, D.C. 20233 (301) 457-4100, www.census.gov; *1997 Economic Census: Advance Summary for the United States 1997 NAICS Basis; Census of Service Industries; County Business Patterns;* and *Economic Census of Outlying Areas.*

U.S. Department of Labor, Bureau of Labor Statistics, Two Massachusetts Avenue, NE, Washington, D.C. 20212 (202) 691-5200, www.stats.bls.gov; *Employment and Earnings;* and Internet site: http://stats.bls.gov/ ceshome.htm.

SERVICE INDUSTRIES - EMPLOYEE TRAINING

U.S. Department of Labor, Bureau of Labor Statistics, Two Massachusetts Avenue, NE, Washington, D.C. 20212 (202) 691-5200, www.stats.bls.gov; *Monthly Labor Review.*

SERVICE INDUSTRIES - EMPLOYEES

U.S. Department of Commerce, Bureau of Economic Analysis, Fourteenth Street between Constitution Avenue and E Street, NW, Washington, D.C. 20230 (202) 606-9900, www.bea.doc.gov; *The National Income and Product Accounts of the United States;* and *Survey of Current Business.*

U.S. Department of Commerce, Bureau of the Census, Washington, D.C. 20233 (301) 457-4100, www.census.gov; *1997 Economic Census: Advance Summary Statistics for the United States 1997 NAICS Basis; Statistics of U.S. Businesses; Census of Service Industries; County Business Patterns;* and *Economic Census of Outlying Areas.*

U.S. Department of Labor, Bureau of Labor Statistics, Two Massachusetts Avenue, NE, Washington, D.C. 20212 (202) 691-5200, www.stats.bls.gov; *News, USDL 98-93; Employment and Earnings; Monthly Labor Review;* Bulletins 2445 and 2481; unpublished data; and Internet site: http://stats.bls.gov/ ceshome.htm.

SERVICE INDUSTRIES - ESTABLISHMENTS

U.S. Department of Commerce, Bureau of the Census, Washington, D.C. 20233 (301) 457-4100, www.census.gov; *Census of Service Industries; County Business Patterns;* and *Economic Census of Outlying Areas.*

U.S. Department of the Treasury, Internal Revenue Service, 1111 Constitution Avenue, NW, Washington, D.C. 20224 (202) 874-0410, www.irs.ustreas.gov; *Statistics of Income Bulletin; Statistics of Income;* various publications and unpublished data.

SERVICE INDUSTRIES - FAILURES

Dun and Bradstreet Corporation, 299 Park Avenue, 24th Floor, New York, New York 10171 (212) 593-6800; *Business Failure Record.*

SERVICE INDUSTRIES - FINANCES

U.S. Department of Commerce, Bureau of the Census, Washington, D.C. 20233 (301) 457-4100, www.census.gov; *Census of Service Industries.*

U.S. Department of the Treasury, Internal Revenue Service, 1111 Constitution Avenue, NW, Washington, D.C. 20224 (202) 874-0410, www.irs.ustreas.gov; *Statistics of Income, Corporation Income Tax Returns; Statistics of Income Bulletin; Statistics of Income;* various publications and unpublished data.

SERVICE INDUSTRIES - FOREIGN TRADE

U.S. Department of Commerce, Bureau of Economic Analysis, Fourteenth Street between Constitution Avenue and E Street, NW, Washington, D.C. 20230 (202) 606-9900, www.bea.doc.gov; *Survey of Current Business.*

U.S. Department of Commerce, Bureau of the Census, Washington, D.C. 20233

(301) 457-4100, www.census.gov; *U.S. International Trade in Goods and Services.*

SERVICE INDUSTRIES - GROSS DOMESTIC PRODUCT

U.S. Department of Commerce, Bureau of Economic Analysis, Fourteenth Street between Constitution Avenue and E Street, NW, Washington, D.C. 20230 (202) 606-9900, www.bea.doc.gov; *Survey of Current Business.*

SERVICE INDUSTRIES - HEALTH INSURANCE COVERAGE - EMPLOYEES

U.S. Department of Health and Human Services, National Center for Health Statistics,3700 East-West Highway, Hyattsville, Maryland 20782 (301) 436-8500, www.cdc.gov/nchs; *Employer-Sponsored Health Insurance, State and National Estimates.*

SERVICE INDUSTRIES - MULTINATIONAL COMPANIES

U.S. Department of Commerce, Bureau of Economic Analysis, Fourteenth Street between Constitution Avenue and E Street, NW, Washington, D.C. 20230 (202) 606-9900, www.bea.doc.gov; *Survey of Current Business.*

SERVICE INDUSTRIES - OCCUPATIONAL SAFETY

National Safety Council, 1121 Spring Lake Drive, Itasca, Illinois 60143-3201 (630) 285-1121; *Accident Facts.*

U.S. Department of Labor, Bureau of Labor Statistics, Two Massachusetts Avenue, NE, Washington, D.C. 20212 (202) 691-5200, www.stats.bls.gov; *Occupational Injuries and Illnesses in the United States by Industry.*

SERVICE INDUSTRIES - PRODUCTIVITY

U.S. Department of Labor, Bureau of Labor Statistics, Two Massachusetts Avenue, NE, Washington, D.C. 20212 (202) 691-5200, www.stats.bls.gov; Internet site http://stats.bls.gov/iprhome.htm.

SERVICE INDUSTRIES - PROFITS

U.S. Department of Commerce, Bureau of Economic Analysis, Fourteenth Street between Constitution Avenue and E Street, NW, Washington, D.C. 20230 (202) 606-9900, www.bea.doc.gov; *The National Income and Product Accounts of the United States;* and *Survey of Current Business.*

U.S. Department of the Treasury, Internal Revenue Service, 1111 Constitution Avenue, NW, Washington, D.C. 20224 (202) 874-0410, www.irs.ustreas.gov; *Statistics of Income,* various publications.

SERVICE INDUSTRIES - SALES OR RECEIPTS

Time Warner, Time and Life Building, Rockefeller Center, New York, New York 10019 (212) 522-1212; *The Fortune Directories.*

U.S. Department of Commerce, Bureau of the Census, Washington, D.C. 20233 (301) 457-4100, www.census.gov; *1997 Economic Census: Advance Summary Statistics for the U.S. 1997 NAICS Basis; Statistics of U.S. Businesses; Census of Service Industries; Current Business Reports; Service Annual Survey; Economic Census of Outlying Areas;* and unpublished data.

U.S. Department of the Treasury, Internal Revenue Service, 1111 Constitution Avenue, NW, Washington, D.C. 20224 (202) 874-0410, www.irs.ustreas.gov; *Statistics of Income; Statistics of Income Bulletin;* and unpublished data.

SERVICE OCCUPATIONS - BENEFITS

U.S. Department of Commerce, Bureau of the Census, Washington, D.C. 20233 (301) 457-4100, www.census.gov; unpublished data.

SERVICE OCCUPATIONS - EARNINGS

U.S. Department of Commerce, Bureau of the Census, Washington, D.C. 20233 (301) 457-4100, www.census.gov; *Current Population Report.*

U.S. Department of Labor, Bureau of Labor Statistics, Two Massachusetts Avenue, NE, Washington, D.C. 20212 (202) 691-5200, www.stats.bls.gov; *Employment and Earnings;* Bulletin 2307; and unpublished data.

SERVICE OCCUPATIONS - EMPLOYMENT

U.S. Department of Labor, Bureau of Labor Statistics, Two Massachusetts Avenue, NE, Washington, D.C. 20212 (202) 691-5200, www.stats.bls.gov; *Employment and Earnings; Monthly Labor Review;* and unpublished data.

SERVICE OCCUPATIONS - EMPLOYMENT - BY SEX AND EDUCATIONAL ATTAINMENT

U.S. Department of Labor, Bureau of Labor Statistics, Two Massachusetts Avenue, NE, Washington, D.C. 20212 (202) 691-5200, www.stats.bls.gov; unpublished data.

SERVICE OCCUPATIONS - EMPLOYMENT - PROJECTIONS

U.S. Department of Labor, Bureau of Labor Statistics, Two Massachusetts Avenue, NE, Washington, D.C. 20212 (202)

691-5200, www.stats.bls.gov; *Monthly Labor Review.*

SERVICE OCCUPATIONS - UNEMPLOYMENT

U.S. Department of Labor, Bureau of Labor Statistics, Two Massachusetts Avenue, NE, Washington, D.C. 20212 (202) 691-5200, www.stats.bls.gov; *Employment and Earnings.*

SERVICE OCCUPATIONS - UNION MEMBERSHIP

U.S. Department of Labor, Bureau of Labor Statistics, Two Massachusetts Avenue, NE, Washington, D.C. 20212 (202) 691-5200, www.stats.bls.gov; *Employment and Earnings.*

SERVICE STATIONS - See GASOLINE SERVICE STATIONS

SERVICE WORKERS- See SERVICE INDUSTRIES and SERVICE OCCUPATIONS

SEWAGE TREATMENT SYSTEMS

Environmental Protection Agency, Office of Wastewater Management, 1200 Pennsylvania Avenue, NW, Washington, D.C. 20460 (202) 372-8255, www.epa.gov; *1996 Clean Water Needs Survey Report to Congress.*

U.S. Department of Commerce, Bureau of the Census, Washington, D.C. 20233 (301) 457-4100, www.census.gov; *Federal Expenditures by State for Fiscal Year.*

SEWAGE TREATMENT SYSTEMS - CONSTRUCTION

U.S. Department of Commerce, Bureau of the Census, Washington, D.C. 20233 (301) 457-4100, www.census.gov; *Current Construction Reports;* and *Value for New Construction.*

SEWAGE TREATMENT SYSTEMS - EMPLOYMENT

U.S. Department of Commerce, Bureau of the Census, Washington, D.C. 20233 (301) 457-4100, www.census.gov; Internet site: http://www.census.gov/pub/govs/www/apes.html.

SEWAGE TREATMENT SYSTEMS - EXPENDITURES

U.S. Department of Commerce, Bureau of the Census, Washington, D.C. 20233 (301) 457-4100, www.census.gov; *Historical Statistics on Governmental Finances and Employment;* and Internet site: http://www.census.gov/govs/www/estimate.html.

SEWAGE TREATMENT SYSTEMS -

RESIDENCES

U.S. Department of Commerce, Bureau of the Census, Washington, D.C. 20233 (301) 457-4100, www.census.gov; *Current Housing Reports;* and *American Housing Survey in the U.S.*

SEXUAL PARTNERS

U.S. Department of Health and Human Services, National Center for Health Statistics, 3700 East-West Highway, Hyattsville, Maryland 20782 (301) 436-8500, www.cdc.gov/nchs; *Fertility, Family Planning, and Women's Health: New Data From the 1995 National Survey of Family Growth, Vital and Health Statistics Series.*

Seychelles - National Statistical Office

Chief Statistician, Post Office Box 206, Victoria, Mahe, Seychelles.

Seychelles - Primary Statistics Source

Central Statistical Office, Post Office Box 206, Victoria, Mahe, Seychelles; *Statistical Abstract.*

SEYCHELLES - AGRICULTURE

Economist Intelligence Unit, 111 West 57th Street, New York, New York 10019 (800) 938-4685; *Seychelles Country Report.*

Euromonitor International, Inc., 122 South Michigan Avenue, Suite 1200, Chicago, Illinois 60603 (800) 577-EURO; *World Marketing Data and Statistics.*

Europa Publications Limited, 18 Bedford Square, London, WC1B 3JN, England; *The Europa World Year Book.*

Federal Statistical Office, Gustav-Stresemann - Ring 11, D-6200, Wiesbaden, Germany; *Seychellen.*

Food and Agricultural Organization of the United Nations (FAO) Via delle Terme di Caracalla, 00100 Rome, Italy (Telephone Number in U.S. (202) 653-2400); *Production Yearbook; The State of Food and Agriculture;* and *Trade Yearbook.*

St. Martin's Press, Inc., 175 Fifth Avenue, New York, New York 10010 (800) 221-7945; *The Statesman's Year-Book.*

Statistical Office of the United Nations, Publishing Service, New York, New York 10017 (800) 253-9646; *Statistical Yearbook;* and *Survey of Economic and Social Conditions in Africa.*

United Nations Conference on Trade

and Development, Central Statistical Service, Palais des Nations, Geneva, Switzerland (Telephone in U.S. (800) 253-9646); *UNCTAD Commodity Yearbook.*

United Nations Economic Commission for Africa, Africa Hall, P.O. Box 3001, Addis Ababa, Ethiopia (Telephone Number in U.S. (800) 253-9646); *African Statistical Yearbook.*

The World Bank, 1818 H Street, NW, Washington, D.C. 20433 (202) 477-1234; *World Development Indicators.*

SEYCHELLES - AIRLINE SERVICE

Europa Publications Limited, 18 Bedford Square, London, WC1B 3JN, England; *The Europa World Year Book.*

St. Martin's Press, Inc., 175 Fifth Avenue, New York, New York 10010 (800) 221-7945; *The Statesman's Year-Book.*

United Nations Economic Commission for Africa, Africa Hall, P.O. Box 3001, Addis Ababa, Ethiopia (Telephone Number in U.S. (800) 253-9646); *African Statistical Yearbook.*

SEYCHELLES - AIRPORT

Central Intelligence Agency, Washington, D.C. 20505 (703) 482-1100, www.cia.gov; *The World Factbook.*

SEYCHELLES - ANIMAL HEALTH

Food and Agricultural Organization of the United Nations (FAO), Via delle Terme di Caracalla, 00100, Rome, Italy (Telephone Number in U.S. (202) 653-2400); *Animal Health Yearbook.*

SEYCHELLES - AREA AND DENSITY OF POPULATION

African Development Bank, 01 BP 1387, Abidjan 01, Cote D'Ivoire; *Selected Statistics on Regional Member Countries.*

Central Intelligence Agency, Washington, D.C. 20505 (703) 482-1100, www.cia.gov; *The World Factbook.*

Euromonitor International, Inc., 122 South Michigan Avenue, Suite 1200, Chicago, Illinois 60603 (800) 577-EURO; *The World Economic Factbook.*

Europa Publications Limited, 18 Bedford Square, London, WC1B 3JN, England; *The Europa World Year Book.*

Federal Statistical Office, Gustav-Stresemann - Ring 11, D-6200, Wiesbaden, Germany; *Seychellen.*

Food and Agricultural Organization of the United Nations (FAO) Via delle Terme

di Caracalla, 00100 Rome, Italy (Telephone Number in U.S. (202) 653-2400); *The State of Food and Agriculture.*

St. Martin's Press, Inc., 175 Fifth Avenue, New York, New York 10010 (800) 221-7945; *The Statesman's Year-Book.*

Statistical Office of the United Nations, Publishing Service, New York, New York 10017 (800) 253-9646; *Statistical Yearbook;* and *Survey of Economic and Social Conditions in Africa.*

United Nations Educational, Scientific and Cultural Organization (UNESCO), 7 Place de Fontenoy, F-75700 Paris, France (Telephone Number in U.S. (212) 963-5981); *Statistical Yearbook.*

SEYCHELLES - BALANCE OF PAYMENTS

African Development Bank, 01 BP 1387, Abidjan 01, Cote D'Ivoire; *Selected Statistics on Regional Member Countries.*

The Economist Intelligence Unit, 111 West 57th Street, New York, New York 10019 (800) 938-4685; *The World Market Atlas.*

Europa Publications Limited, 18 Bedford Square, London, WC1B 3JN, England; *The Europa World Year Book.*

Federal Statistical Office, Gustav-Stresemann - Ring 11, D-6200, Wiesbaden, Germany; *Seychellen.*

International Monetary Fund, 700 Nineteenth Street, NW, Washington, D.C. 20431 (202) 623-7000; *Balance of Payments Yearbook;* and *International Financial Statistics.*

United Nations Conference on Trade and Development (UNCTAD), New York, New York 10017 (800) 253-9646; *Handbook of International Trade and Development Statistics.*

United Nations Economic Commission for Africa, Africa Hall, P.O. Box 3001, Addis Ababa, Ethiopia (Telephone Number in U.S. (800) 253-9646); *African Statistical Yearbook.*

The World Bank, 1818 H Street, NW, Washington, D.C. 20433 (202) 477-1234; *World Development Indicators.*

SEYCHELLES - BANKING

Euromonitor International, Inc., 122 South Michigan Avenue, Suite 1200, Chicago, Illinois 60603 (800) 577-EURO; *World Marketing Data and Statistics.*

Europa Publications Limited, 18 Bedford Square, London, WC1B 3JN, England; *The Europa World Year Book.*

International Monetary Fund, 700 Nineteenth Street, NW, Washington, D.C. 20431 (202) 623-7000; *Government Finance Statistics Yearbook;* and *International Financial Statistics.*

St. Martin's Press, Inc., 175 Fifth Avenue, New York, New York 10010 (800) 221-7945; *The Statesman's Year-Book.*

SEYCHELLES - BEER PRODUCTION - See SEYCHELLES - BEVERAGES

SEYCHELLES - BEVERAGES

Statistical Office of the United Nations, Publishing Service, New York, New York 10017 (800) 253-9646; *Statistical Yearbook.*

United Nations Economic Commission for Africa, Africa Hall, P.O. Box 3001, Addis Ababa, Ethiopia (Telephone Number in U.S. (800) 253-9646); *African Statistical Yearbook.*

SEYCHELLES - BIRTH RATES

Central Intelligence Agency, Washington, D.C. 20505 (703) 482-1100, www.cia.gov; *The World Factbook.*

Euromonitor International, Inc., 122 South Michigan Avenue, Suite 1200, Chicago, Illinois 60603 (800) 577-EURO; *International Marketing Data and Statistics;* and *The World Economic Factbook.*

Europa Publications Limited, 18 Bedford Square, London, WC1B 3JN, England; *The Europa World Year Book.*

St. Martin's Press, Inc., 175 Fifth Avenue, New York, New York 10010 (800) 221-7945; *The Statesman's Year-Book.*

Statistical Office of the United Nations, Publishing Service, New York, New York 10017 (800) 253-9646; *Demographic Yearbook; Statistical Yearbook;* and *Survey of Economic and Social Conditions in Africa.*

The World Bank, 1818 H Street, NW, Washington, D.C. 20433 (202) 477-1234; *World Development Indicators.*

World Health Organization, Office of Publications, 20 Avenue Appia, CH-1211 Geneva 27, Switzerland (Telephone Number in U.S. (518) 436-9686); *World Health Statistics Annual.*

SEYCHELLES - BONDS

International Monetary Fund, 700 Nineteenth Street, NW, Washington, D.C. 20431 (202) 623-7000; *Government Finance Statistics Yearbook.*

SEYCHELLES - BOOK PRODUCTION

Europa Publications Limited, 18 Bedford Square, London, WC1B 3JN, England; *The Europa World Year Book.*

United Nations Educational, Scientific and Cultural Organization (UNESCO), 7 Place de Fontenoy, F-75700 Paris, France (Telephone Number in U.S. (212) 963-5981); *Statistical Yearbook.*

SEYCHELLES - BROADCASTING

Billboard Limited, P.O. Box 9027, 1006 AA Amsterdam, The Netherlands (Telephone Number in U.S. (212) 764-7300); *World Radio TV Handbook.*

Central Intelligence Agency, Washington, D.C. 20505 (703) 482-1100, www.cia.gov; *The World Factbook.*

Euromonitor International, Inc., 122 South Michigan Avenue, Suite 1200, Chicago, Illinois 60603 (800) 577-EURO; *World Marketing Data and Statistics.*

St. Martin's Press, Inc., 175 Fifth Avenue, New York, New York 10010 (800) 221-7945; *The Statesman's Year-Book.*

United Nations Educational, Scientific and Cultural Organization (UNESCO), 7 Place de Fontenoy, F-75700 Paris, France (Telephone Number in U.S. (212) 963-5981); *Statistical Yearbook.*

SEYCHELLES - BUDGET

Central Intelligence Agency, Washington, D.C. 20505 (703) 482-1100, www.cia.gov; *The World Factbook.*

SEYCHELLES - BUSINESS AND PROFESSIONAL LICENSES

International Monetary Fund, 700 Nineteenth Street, NW, Washington, D.C. 20431 (202) 623-7000; *Government Finance Statistics Yearbook.*

SEYCHELLES - CALORIE SUPPLY

African Development Bank, 01 BP 1387, Abidjan 01, Cote D'Ivoire; *Selected Statistics on Regional Member Countries.*

Food and Agricultural Organization of the United Nations (FAO) Via delle Terme di Caracalla, 00100 Rome, Italy (Telephone Number in U.S. (202) 653-2400); *The State of Food and Agriculture.*

SEYCHELLES - CAPITAL REVENUE

International Monetary Fund, 700 Nineteenth Street, NW, Washington, D.C. 20431 (202) 623-7000; *Government Finance Statistics Yearbook.*

SEYCHELLES - CATTLE - See SEYCHELLES - LIVESTOCK AND POULTRY

SEYCHELLES - CHEMICAL (ORGANIC) PRODUCTION - See SEYCHELLES - MINING AND MINERAL PRODUCTS

SEYCHELLES - CIGARETTE PRODUCTION - See SEYCHELLES - TOBACCO PRODUCTION

SEYCHELLES - CLIMATE

St. Martin's Press, Inc., 175 Fifth Avenue, New York, New York 10010 (800) 221-7945; *The Statesman's Year-Book.*

SEYCHELLES - COAL PRODUCTION - See SEYCHELLES - MINING AND MINERAL PRODUCTS

SEYCHELLES - COMMERCE

St. Martin's Press, Inc., 175 Fifth Avenue, New York, New York 10010 (800) 221-7945; *The Statesman's Year-Book.*

SEYCHELLES - COMMUNICATIONS - See SEYCHELLES - TRANSPORTATION AND COMMUNICATIONS

SEYCHELLES - CONSTRUCTION INDUSTRY

Statistical Office of the United Nations, Publishing Service, New York, New York 10017 (800) 253-9646; *Statistical Yearbook.*

United Nations Economic Commission for Africa, Africa Hall, P.O. Box 3001, Addis Ababa, Ethiopia (Telephone Number in U.S. (800) 253-9646); *African Statistical Yearbook.*

SEYCHELLES - CONSUMER PRICE INDEX

African Development Bank, 01 BP 1387, Abidjan 01, Cote D'Ivoire; *Selected Statistics on Regional Member Countries.*

Europa Publications Limited, 18 Bedford Square, London, WC1B 3JN, England; *The Europa World Year Book.*

Statistical Office of the United Nations, Publishing Service, New York, New York 10017 (800) 253-9646; *Statistical Yearbook;* and *Survey of Economic and Social Conditions in Africa.*

United Nations Economic Commission for Africa, Africa Hall, P.O. Box 3001, Addis Ababa, Ethiopia (Telephone Number in U.S. (800) 253-9646); *African Statistical Yearbook.*

SEYCHELLES - CONSUMER PRICES

Euromonitor International, Inc., 122 South Michigan Avenue, Suite 1200, Chicago, Illinois 60603 (800) 577-EURO; *World Marketing Data and Statistics.*

International Labour Office, I.L.O. Publications, 1828 L Street, NW, Suite

801, Washington, D.C. 20036 (301) 638-3152; *Yearbook of Labour Statistics.*

International Monetary Fund, 700 Nineteenth Street, NW, Washington, D.C. 20431 (202) 623-7000; *International Financial Statistics.*

SEYCHELLES - CONSUMPTION

African Development Bank, 01 BP 1387, Abidjan 01, Cote D'Ivoire; *Selected Statistics on Regional Member Countries.*

Statistical Office of the United Nations, Publishing Service, New York, New York 10017 (800) 253-9646; *Survey of Economic and Social Conditions in Africa.*

SEYCHELLES - COPRA EXPORTS

International Monetary Fund, 700 Nineteenth Street, NW, Washington, D.C. 20431 (202) 623-7000; *International Financial Statistics.*

SEYCHELLES - CORN PRODUCTION - See SEYCHELLES - CROPS

SEYCHELLES - CORPORATE TAXES - See SEYCHELLES - TAXATION

SEYCHELLES - CRIME

International Criminal Police Organization (INTERPOL), 50 quai Achille Lignon, F-69006 Lyon, France; *International Crime Statistics.*

SEYCHELLES - CROPS

Europa Publications Limited, 18 Bedford Square, London, WC1B 3JN, England; *The Europa World Year Book.*

Food and Agricultural Organization of the United Nations (FAO) Via delle Terme di Caracalla, 00100 Rome, Italy (Telephone Number in U.S. (202) 653-2400); *The State of Food and Agriculture.*

St. Martin's Press, Inc., 175 Fifth Avenue, New York, New York 10010 (800) 221-7945; *The Statesman's Year-Book.*

United Nations Conference on Trade and Development, Central Statistical Service, Palais des Nations, Geneva, Switzerland (Telephone in U.S. (800) 253-9646); *UNCTAD Commodity Yearbook.*

United Nations Economic Commission for Africa, Africa Hall, P.O. Box 3001, Addis Ababa, Ethiopia (Telephone Number in U.S. (800) 253-9646); *African Statistical Yearbook.*

SEYCHELLES - CUSTOMS DUTIES

International Monetary Fund, 700 Nineteenth Street, NW, Washington, D.C.

20431 (202) 623-7000; *Government Finance Statistics Yearbook.*

SEYCHELLES - DAIRY PRODUCTS

Food and Agricultural Organization of the United Nations (FAO) Via delle Terme di Caracalla, 00100 Rome, Italy (Telephone Number in U.S. (202) 653-2400); *The State of Food and Agriculture.*

St. Martin's Press, Inc., 175 Fifth Avenue, New York, New York 10010 (800) 221-7945; *The Statesman's Year-Book.*

SEYCHELLES - DEATH RATES - See SEYCHELLES - MORTALITY

SEYCHELLES - DEFENSE EXPENDITURES - See SEYCHELLES - MILITARY

SEYCHELLES - DEMOGRAPHY

The Economist Intelligence Unit, 111 West 57th Street, New York, New York 10019 (800) 938-4685; *The World Market Atlas.*

Euromonitor International, Inc., 122 South Michigan Avenue, Suite 1200, Chicago, Illinois 60603 (800) 577-EURO; *International Marketing Data and Statistics; World Marketing Data and Statistics;* and *The World Economic Factbook.*

Federal Statistical Office, Gustav-Stresemann - Ring 11, D-6200, Wiesbaden, Germany; *Seychellen.*

Statistical Office of the United Nations, Publishing Service, New York, New York 10017 (800) 253-9646; *Human Development Report;* and *Survey of Economic and Social Conditions in Africa.*

SEYCHELLES - DEVELOPMENT ASSISTANCE

Statistical Office of the United Nations, Publishing Service, New York, New York 10017 (800) 253-9646; *Statistical Yearbook.*

SEYCHELLES - DISEASES - See SEYCHELLES - HEALTH

SEYCHELLES - DIVORCE RATES

Statistical Office of the United Nations, Publishing Service, New York, New York 10017 (800) 253-9646; *Demographic Yearbook;* and *Statistical Yearbook.*

SEYCHELLES - ECONOMY

African Development Bank, 01 BP 1387, Abidjan 01, Cote D'Ivoire; *Selected Statistics on Regional Member Countries.*

Central Intelligence Agency, Washington, D.C. 20505 (703) 482-1100, www.cia.gov; *The World Factbook.*

Economist Intelligence Unit, 111 West 57th Street, New York, New York 10019 (800) 938-4685; *Seychelles Country Report.*

Euromonitor International, Inc., 122 South Michigan Avenue, Suite 1200, Chicago, Illinois 60603 (800) 577-EURO; *The World Economic Factbook; and World Marketing Data and Statistics.*

Europa Publications Limited, 18 Bedford Square, London, WC1B 3JN, England; *The Europa World Year Book.*

Federal Statistical Office, Gustav-Stresemann - Ring 11, D-6200, Wiesbaden, Germany; *Seychellen.*

St. Martin's Press, Inc., 175 Fifth Avenue, New York, New York 10010 (800) 221-7945; *The Statesman's Year-Book.*

Statistical Office of the United Nations, Publishing Service, New York, New York 10017 (800) 253-9646; *Foreign Trade Statistics for Africa; and World Statistics Pocketbook.*

The World Bank, 1818 H Street, NW, Washington, D.C. 20433 (202) 477-1234; *The World Bank Atlas.*

SEYCHELLES - EDUCATION

African Development Bank, 01 BP 1387, Abidjan 01, Cote D'Ivoire; *Selected Statistics on Regional Member Countries.*

The Economist Intelligence Unit, 111 West 57th Street, New York, New York 10019 (800) 938-4685; *The World Market Atlas.*

Euromonitor International, Inc., 122 South Michigan Avenue, Suite 1200, Chicago, Illinois 60603 (800) 577-EURO; *International Marketing Data and Statistics; and World Marketing Data and Statistics.*

Europa Publications Limited, 18 Bedford Square, London, WC1B 3JN, England; *The Europa World Year Book.*

Federal Statistical Office, Gustav-Stresemann - Ring 11, D-6200, Wiesbaden, Germany; *Seychellen.*

International Monetary Fund, 700 Nineteenth Street, NW, Washington, D.C. 20431 (202) 623-7000; *Government Finance Statistics Yearbook.*

St. Martin's Press, Inc., 175 Fifth Avenue, New York, New York 10010 (800) 221-7945; *The Statesman's Year-Book.*

Statistical Office of the United Nations, Publishing Service, New York, New York 10017 (800) 253-9646; *Human Development Report; and Survey of Economic and Social Conditions in Africa.*

United Nations Economic Commission for Africa, Africa Hall, P.O. Box 3001, Addis Ababa, Ethiopia (Telephone Number in U.S. (800) 253-9646); *African Statistical Yearbook.*

United Nations Educational, Scientific and Cultural Organization (UNESCO), 7 Place de Fontenoy, F-75700 Paris, France (Telephone Number in U.S. (212) 963-5981); *Statistical Yearbook.*

The World Bank, 1818 H Street, NW, Washington, D.C. 20433 (202) 477-1234; *World Development Indicators.*

SEYCHELLES - EGG PRODUCTION AND CONSUMPTION - See SEYCHELLES - DAIRY PRODUCTS

SEYCHELLES - ELECTRICITY

Central Intelligence Agency, Washington, D.C. 20505 (703) 482-1100, www.cia.gov; *The World Factbook.*

St. Martin's Press, Inc., 175 Fifth Avenue, New York, New York 10010 (800) 221-7945; *The Statesman's Year-Book.*

Statistical Office of the United Nations, Publishing Service, New York, New York 10017 (800) 253-9646; *Human Development Report; Statistical Yearbook; and Survey of Economic and Social Conditions in Africa.*

United Nations Economic Commission for Africa, Africa Hall, P.O. Box 3001, Addis Ababa, Ethiopia (Telephone Number in U.S. (800) 253-9646); *African Statistical Yearbook.*

SEYCHELLES - EMPLOYMENT

Euromonitor International, Inc., 122 South Michigan Avenue, Suite 1200, Chicago, Illinois 60603 (800) 577-EURO; *International Marketing Data and Statistics.*

Federal Statistical Office, Gustav-Stresemann - Ring 11, D-6200, Wiesbaden, Germany; *Seychellen.*

International Labour Office, I.L.O. Publications, 1828 L Street, NW, Suite 801, Washington, D.C. 20036 (301) 638-3152; *Yearbook of Labour Statistics.*

Statistical Office of the United Nations, Publishing Service, New York, New York 10017 (800) 253-9646; *Statistical Yearbook; and Survey of Economic and Social Conditions in Africa.*

SEYCHELLES - ENERGY

Euromonitor International, Inc., 122 South Michigan Avenue, Suite 1200, Chicago, Illinois 60603 (800) 577-EURO; *International Marketing Data and Statistics;*

World Marketing Data and Statistics; and The World Economic Factbook.

Food and Agricultural Organization of the United Nations (FAO) Via delle Terme di Caracalla, 00100 Rome, Italy (Telephone Number in U.S. (202) 653-2400); *The State of Food and Agriculture.*

St. Martin's Press, Inc., 175 Fifth Avenue, New York, New York 10010 (800) 221-7945; *The Statesman's Year-Book.*

Statistical Office of the United Nations, Publishing Service, New York, New York 10017 (800) 253-9646; *Energy Statistics Yearbook; Human Development Report; Statistical Yearbook; and World Statistics Pocketbook.*

United Nations Economic Commission for Africa, Africa Hall, P.O. Box 3001, Addis Ababa, Ethiopia (Telephone Number in U.S. (800) 253-9646); *African Statistical Yearbook.*

The World Bank, 1818 H Street, NW, Washington, D.C. 20433 (202) 477-1234; *The World Bank Atlas.*

SEYCHELLES - ENVIRONMENT

Economist Intelligence Unit, 111 West 57th Street, New York, New York 10019 (800) 938-4685; *Seychelles Country Report.*

Statistical Office of the United Nations, Publishing Service, New York, New York 10017 (800) 253-9646; *World Statistics Pocketbook.*

SEYCHELLES - EXCHANGE RATES

African Development Bank, 01 BP 1387, Abidjan 01, Cote D'Ivoire; *Selected Statistics on Regional Member Countries.*

Central Intelligence Agency, Washington, D.C. 20505 (703) 482-1100, www.cia.gov; *The World Factbook.*

Euromonitor International, Inc., 122 South Michigan Avenue, Suite 1200, Chicago, Illinois 60603 (800) 577-EURO; *International Marketing Data and Statistics; and The World Economic Factbook.*

Europa Publications Limited, 18 Bedford Square, London, WC1B 3JN, England; *The Europa World Year Book.*

International Monetary Fund, 700 Nineteenth Street, NW, Washington, D.C. 20431 (202) 623-7000; *International Financial Statistics.*

Statistical Office of the United Nations, Publishing Service, New York, New York 10017 (800) 253-9646; *Foreign Trade Statistics for Africa; Statistical Yearbook; and World Statistics Pocketbook.*

SEYCHELLES - EXCISE TAXES - See
SEYCHELLES - TAXATION

SEYCHELLES - EXPORTS

African Development Bank, 01 BP 1387,
Abidjan 01, Cote D'Ivoire; *Selected
Statistics on Regional Member Countries.*

Central Intelligence Agency,
Washington, D.C. 20505 (703) 482-1100,
www.cia.gov; *The World Factbook.*

The Economist Intelligence Unit, 111
West 57th Street, New York, New York
10019 (800) 938-4685; *Seychelles Country
Report;* and *The World Market Atlas.*

Euromonitor International, Inc., 122
South Michigan Avenue, Suite 1200,
Chicago, Illinois 60603 (800) 577-EURO;
International Marketing Data and Statistics;
and *The World Economic Factbook.*

Europa Publications Limited, 18
Bedford Square, London, WC1B 3JN,
England; *The Europa World Year Book.*

Food and Agricultural Organization of
the United Nations (FAO) Via delle Terme
di Caracalla, 00100 Rome, Italy (Telephone
Number in U.S. (202) 653-2400); *The State
of Food and Agriculture.*

International Monetary Fund, 700
Nineteenth Street, NW, Washington, D.C.
20431 (202) 623-7000; *Direction of Trade
Statistics; Government Finance Statistics
Yearbook;* and *International Financial
Statistics.*

St. Martin's Press, Inc., 175 Fifth
Avenue, New York, New York 10010 (800)
221-7945; *The Statesman's Year-Book.*

Statistical Office of the United Nations,
Publishing Service, New York, New York
10017 (800) 253-9646; *Foreign Trade
Statistics for Africa;* and *Survey of Economic
and Social Conditions in Africa.*

United Nations Conference on Trade
and Development (UNCTAD), New York,
New York 10017 (800) 253-9646; *Handbook
of International Trade and Development
Statistics.*

United Nations Economic Commission
for Africa, Africa Hall, P.O. Box 3001, Addis
Ababa, Ethiopia (Telephone Number in
U.S. (800) 253-9646); *African Statistical
Yearbook.*

The World Bank, 1818 H Street, NW,
Washington, D.C. 20433 (202) 477-1234;
World Development Indicators.

SEYCHELLES - EXTERNAL
INDEBTEDNESS

African Development Bank, 01 BP 1387,

Abidjan 01, Cote D'Ivoire; *Selected
Statistics on Regional Member Countries.*

Statistical Office of the United Nations,
Publishing Service, New York, New York
10017 (800) 253-9646; *Survey of Economic
and Social Conditions in Africa.*

The World Bank, 1818 H Street, NW,
Washington, D.C. 20433 (202) 477-1234;
World Development Indicators.

SEYCHELLES - EXTERNAL TRADE

African Development Bank, 01 BP 1387,
Abidjan 01, Cote D'Ivoire; *Selected
Statistics on Regional Member Countries.*

Euromonitor International, Inc., 122
South Michigan Avenue, Suite 1200,
Chicago, Illinois 60603 (800) 577-EURO;
World Marketing Data and Statistics.

Food and Agricultural Organization of
the United Nations (FAO) Via delle Terme
di Caracalla, 00100 Rome, Italy (Telephone
Number in U.S. (202) 653-2400); *The State
of Food and Agriculture;* and *Trade
Yearbook.*

SEYCHELLES - FARM CROPS - See
SEYCHELLES - CROPS

SEYCHELLES - FERTILITY RATES

Central Intelligence Agency,
Washington, D.C. 20505 (703) 482-1100,
www.cia.gov; *The World Factbook.*

Statistical Office of the United Nations,
Publishing Service, New York, New York
10017 (800) 253-9646; *Human
Development Report;* and *Survey of
Economic and Social Conditions in Africa.*

The World Bank, 1818 H Street, NW,
Washington, D.C. 20433 (202) 477-1234;
The World Bank Atlas; and *World
Development Indicators.*

SEYCHELLES - FERTILIZER

Food and Agricultural Organization of
the United Nations (FAO) Via delle Terme
di Caracalla, 00100 Rome, Italy (Telephone
Number in U.S. (202) 653-2400); *The State
of Food and Agriculture.*

SEYCHELLES - FETAL MORTALITY - See
SEYCHELLES - MORTALITY

SEYCHELLES - FINANCE

African Development Bank, 01 BP 1387,
Abidjan 01, Cote D'Ivoire; *Selected
Statistics on Regional Member Countries.*

Economist Intelligence Unit, 111 West
57th Street, New York, New York 10019
(800) 938-4685; *Seychelles Country Report.*

Europa Publications Limited, 18
Bedford Square, London, WC1B 3JN,
England; *The Europa World Year Book.*

Federal Statistical Office, Gustav-
Stresemann - Ring 11, D-6200, Wiesbaden,
Germany; *Seychellen.*

International Monetary Fund, 700
Nineteenth Street, NW, Washington, D.C.
20431 (202) 623-7000; *Government
Finance Statistics Yearbook.*

St. Martin's Press, Inc., 175 Fifth
Avenue, New York, New York 10010 (800)
221-7945; *The Statesman's Year-Book.*

United Nations Economic Commission
for Africa, Africa Hall, P.O. Box 3001, Addis
Ababa, Ethiopia (Telephone Number in
U.S. (800) 253-9646); *African Statistical
Yearbook.*

SEYCHELLES - FISHERIES

Europa Publications Limited, 18
Bedford Square, London, WC1B 3JN,
England; *The Europa World Year Book.*

Federal Statistical Office, Gustav-
Stresemann - Ring 11, D-6200, Wiesbaden,
Germany; *Seychellen.*

Food and Agricultural Organization of
the United Nations (FAO) Via delle Terme
di Caracalla, 00100 Rome, Italy (Telephone
Number in U.S. (202) 653-2400); *The State
of Food and Agriculture;* and *Yearbook of
Fishery Statistics.*

St. Martin's Press, Inc., 175 Fifth
Avenue, New York, New York 10010 (800)
221-7945; *The Statesman's Year-Book.*

Statistical Office of the United Nations,
Publishing Service, New York, New York
10017 (800) 253-9646; *Statistical Yearbook;*
and *Survey of Economic and Social
Conditions in Africa.*

United Nations Conference on Trade
and Development, Central Statistical
Service, Palais des Nations, Geneva,
Switzerland (Telephone in U.S. (800) 253-
9646); *UNCTAD Commodity Yearbook.*

United Nations Economic Commission
for Africa, Africa Hall, P.O. Box 3001, Addis
Ababa, Ethiopia (Telephone Number in
U.S. (800) 253-9646); *African Statistical
Yearbook.*

SEYCHELLES - FOOD

African Development Bank, 01 BP 1387,
Abidjan 01, Cote D'Ivoire; *Selected
Statistics on Regional Member Countries.*

Food and Agricultural Organization of
the United Nations (FAO) Via delle Terme

di Caracalla, 00100 Rome, Italy (Telephone Number in U.S. (202) 653-2400); *Production Yearbook;* and *The State of Food and Agriculture.*

Statistical Office of the United Nations, Publishing Service, New York, New York 10017 (800) 253-9646; *Human Development Report.*

United Nations Conference on Trade and Development, Central Statistical Service, Palais des Nations, Geneva, Switzerland (Telephone in U.S. (800) 253-9646); *UNCTAD Commodity Yearbook.*

SEYCHELLES - FOREIGN DEBT

International Monetary Fund, 700 Nineteenth Street, NW, Washington, D.C. 20431 (202) 623-7000; *Government Finance Statistics Yearbook.*

SEYCHELLES - FOREIGN TRADE

Economist Intelligence Unit, 111 West 57th Street, New York, New York 10019 (800) 938-4685; *Seychelles Country Report.*

Euromonitor International, Inc., 122 South Michigan Avenue, Suite 1200, Chicago, Illinois 60603 (800) 577-EURO; *The World Economic Factbook.*

Europa Publications Limited, 18 Bedford Square, London, WC1B 3JN, England; *The Europa World Year Book.*

Federal Statistical Office, Gustav-Stresemann - Ring 11, D-6200, Wiesbaden, Germany; *Seychellen.*

Food and Agricultural Organization of the United Nations (FAO) Via delle Terme di Caracalla, 00100 Rome, Italy (Telephone Number in U.S. (202) 653-2400); *The State of Food and Agriculture.*

St. Martin's Press, Inc., 175 Fifth Avenue, New York, New York 10010 (800) 221-7945; *The Statesman's Year-Book.*

Statistical Office of the United Nations, Publishing Service, New York, New York 10017 (800) 253-9646; *Foreign Trade Statistics for Africa; International Trade Statistics Yearbook;* and *Statistical Yearbook.*

United Nations Conference on Trade and Development, Central Statistical Service, Palais des Nations, Geneva, Switzerland (Telephone in U.S. (800) 253-9646); *UNCTAD Commodity Yearbook.*

United Nations Economic Commission for Africa, Africa Hall, P.O. Box 3001, Addis Ababa, Ethiopia (Telephone Number in U.S. (800) 253-9646); *African Statistical Yearbook.*

The World Bank, 1818 H Street, NW, Washington, D.C. 20433 (202) 477-1234; *World Development Indicators.*

SEYCHELLES - FORESTRY AND FOREST PRODUCTS

Federal Statistical Office, Gustav-Stresemann - Ring 11, D-6200, Wiesbaden, Germany; *Seychellen.*

Food and Agricultural Organization of the United Nations (FAO) Via delle Terme di Caracalla, 00100 Rome, Italy (Telephone Number in U.S. (202) 653-2400); *The State of Food and Agriculture.*

Statistical Office of the United Nations, Publishing Service, New York, New York 10017 (800) 253-9646; *Statistical Yearbook.*

United Nations Conference on Trade and Development, Central Statistical Service, Palais des Nations, Geneva, Switzerland (Telephone in U.S. (800) 253-9646); *UNCTAD Commodity Yearbook.*

United Nations Economic Commission for Africa, Africa Hall, P.O. Box 3001, Addis Ababa, Ethiopia (Telephone Number in U.S. (800) 253-9646); *African Statistical Yearbook.*

United Nations Educational, Scientific and Cultural Organization (UNESCO), 7 Place de Fontenoy, F-75700 Paris, France (Telephone Number in U.S. (212) 963-5981); *Statistical Yearbook.*

SEYCHELLES - GENERAL INDUSTRIAL STATISTICS - See SEYCHELLES - INDUSTRY

SEYCHELLES - GENERAL MORTALITY - See SEYCHELLES - MORTALITY

SEYCHELLES - GOATS - See SEYCHELLES - LIVESTOCK AND POULTRY

SEYCHELLES - GOLD HOLDINGS

The World Bank, 1818 H Street, NW, Washington, D.C. 20433 (202) 477-1234; *World Development Indicators.*

SEYCHELLES - GOVERNMENT

Central Intelligence Agency, Washington, D.C. 20505 (703) 482-1100, www.cia.gov; *The World Factbook.*

Europa Publications Limited, 18 Bedford Square, London, WC1B 3JN, England; *The Europa World Year Book.*

International Monetary Fund, 700 Nineteenth Street, NW, Washington, D.C. 20431 (202) 623-7000; *Government Finance Statistics Yearbook.*

St. Martin's Press, Inc., 175 Fifth Avenue, New York, New York 10010 (800)

221-7945; *The Statesman's Year-Book.*

Statistical Office of the United Nations, Publishing Service, New York, New York 10017 (800) 253-9646; *National Accounts Statistics;* and *Survey of Economic and Social Conditions in Africa.*

The World Bank, 1818 H Street, NW, Washington, D.C. 20433 (202) 477-1234; *World Development Indicators.*

SEYCHELLES - GRAIN PRODUCTION - See SEYCHELLES - CROPS

SEYCHELLES - GRANTS

International Monetary Fund, 700 Nineteenth Street, NW, Washington, D.C. 20431 (202) 623-7000; *Government Finance Statistics Yearbook.*

SEYCHELLES - GROSS DOMESTIC PRODUCT

African Development Bank, 01 BP 1387, Abidjan 01, Cote D'Ivoire; *Selected Statistics on Regional Member Countries.*

The Economist Intelligence Unit, 111 West 57th Street, New York, New York 10019 (800) 938-4685; *Seychelles Country Report;* and *The World Market Atlas.*

Euromonitor International, Inc., 122 South Michigan Avenue, Suite 1200, Chicago, Illinois 60603 (800) 577-EURO; *International Marketing Data and Statistics;* and *The World Economic Factbook.*

Europa Publications Limited, 18 Bedford Square, London, WC1B 3JN, England; *The Europa World Year Book.*

Statistical Office of the United Nations, Publishing Service, New York, New York 10017 (800) 253-9646; *Human Development Report; National Accounts Statistics; Statistical Yearbook;* and *Survey of Economic and Social Conditions in Africa.*

United Nations Economic Commission for Africa, Africa Hall, P.O. Box 3001, Addis Ababa, Ethiopia (Telephone Number in U.S. (800) 253-9646); *African Statistical Yearbook.*

The World Bank, 1818 H Street, NW, Washington, D.C. 20433 (202) 477-1234; *World Development Indicators.*

SEYCHELLES - GROSS NATIONAL PRODUCT

St. Martin's Press, Inc., 175 Fifth Avenue, New York, New York 10010 (800) 221-7945; *The Statesman's Year-Book.*

The World Bank, 1818 H Street, NW,

Washington, D.C. 20433 (202) 477-1234; *The World Bank Atlas;* and *World Development Indicators.*

SEYCHELLES - HEALTH

African Development Bank, 01 BP 1387, Abidjan 01, Cote D'Ivoire; *Selected Statistics on Regional Member Countries.*

Euromonitor International, Inc., 122 South Michigan Avenue, Suite 1200, Chicago, Illinois 60603 (800) 577-EURO; *World Marketing Data and Statistics.*

Federal Statistical Office, Gustav-Stresemann - Ring 11, D-6200, Wiesbaden, Germany; *Seychellen.*

St. Martin's Press, Inc., 175 Fifth Avenue, New York, New York 10010 (800) 221-7945; *The Statesman's Year-Book.*

Statistical Office of the United Nations, Publishing Service, New York, New York 10017 (800) 253-9646; *Human Development Report;* and *Statistical Yearbook.*

United Nations Economic Commission for Africa, Africa Hall, P.O. Box 3001, Addis Ababa, Ethiopia (Telephone Number in U.S. (800) 253-9646); *African Statistical Yearbook.*

World Health Organization, Office of Publications, 20 Avenue Appia, CH-1211 Geneva 27, Switzerland (Telephone Number in U.S. (518) 436-9686); *World Health Statistics Annual.*

SEYCHELLES - HEALTH EXPENDITURES

International Monetary Fund, 700 Nineteenth Street, NW, Washington, D.C. 20431 (202) 623-7000; *Government Finance Statistics Yearbook.*

SEYCHELLES - HIGHWAYS

Central Intelligence Agency, Washington, D.C. 20505 (703) 482-1100, www.cia.gov; *The World Factbook.*

St. Martin's Press, Inc., 175 Fifth Avenue, New York, New York 10010 (800) 221-7945; *The Statesman's Year-Book.*

Statistical Office of the United Nations, Publishing Service, New York, New York 10017 (800) 253-9646; *Survey of Economic and Social Conditions in Africa.*

United Nations Economic Commission for Africa, Africa Hall, P.O. Box 3001, Addis Ababa, Ethiopia (Telephone Number in U.S. (800) 253-9646); *African Statistical Yearbook.*

SEYCHELLES - HOURS OF WORK - See SEYCHELLES - EMPLOYMENT

SEYCHELLES - HOUSING AND HOUSING UNITS

Euromonitor International, Inc., 122 South Michigan Avenue, Suite 1200, Chicago, Illinois 60603 (800) 577-EURO; *World Marketing Data and Statistics.*

SEYCHELLES - HOUSING EXPENDITURES

International Monetary Fund, 700 Nineteenth Street, NW, Washington, D.C. 20431 (202) 623-7000; *Government Finance Statistics Yearbook.*

SEYCHELLES - ILLITERATE POPULATION

Central Intelligence Agency, Washington, D.C. 20505 (703) 482-1100, www.cia.gov; *The World Factbook.*

The Economist Intelligence Unit, 111 West 57th Street, New York, New York 10019 (800) 938-4685; *The World Market Atlas.*

Euromonitor International, Inc., 122 South Michigan Avenue, Suite 1200, Chicago, Illinois 60603 (800) 577-EURO; *The World Economic Factbook.*

St. Martin's Press, Inc., 175 Fifth Avenue, New York, New York 10010 (800) 221-7945; *The Statesman's Year-Book.*

Statistical Office of the United Nations, Publishing Service, New York, New York 10017 (800) 253-9646; *Human Development Report.*

United Nations Educational, Scientific and Cultural Organization (UNESCO), 7 Place de Fontenoy, F-75700 Paris, France (Telephone Number in U.S. (212) 963-5981); *Statistical Yearbook.*

SEYCHELLES - IMPORTS

African Development Bank, 01 BP 1387, Abidjan 01, Cote D'Ivoire; *Selected Statistics on Regional Member Countries.*

Central Intelligence Agency, Washington, D.C. 20505 (703) 482-1100, www.cia.gov; *The World Factbook.*

The Economist Intelligence Unit, 111 West 57th Street, New York, New York 10019 (800) 938-4685; *Seychelles Country Report;* and *The World Market Atlas.*

Euromonitor International, Inc., 122 South Michigan Avenue, Suite 1200, Chicago, Illinois 60603 (800) 577-EURO; *International Marketing Data and Statistics;* and *The World Economic Factbook.*

Europa Publications Limited, 18 Bedford Square, London, WC1B 3JN, England; *The Europa World Year Book.*

Food and Agricultural Organization of the United Nations (FAO) Via delle Terme di Caracalla, 00100 Rome, Italy (Telephone Number in U.S. (202) 653-2400); *The State of Food and Agriculture.*

International Monetary Fund, 700 Nineteenth Street, NW, Washington, D.C. 20431 (202) 623-7000; *Direction of Trade Statistics; Government Finance Statistics Yearbook;* and *International Financial Statistics.*

St. Martin's Press, Inc., 175 Fifth Avenue, New York, New York 10010 (800) 221-7945; *The Statesman's Year-Book.*

Statistical Office of the United Nations, Publishing Service, New York, New York 10017 (800) 253-9646; *Foreign Trade Statistics for Africa;* and *Survey of Economic and Social Conditions in Africa.*

United Nations Conference on Trade and Development (UNCTAD), New York, New York 10017 (800) 253-9646; *Handbook of International Trade and Development Statistics.*

United Nations Economic Commission for Africa, Africa Hall, P.O. Box 3001, Addis Ababa, Ethiopia (Telephone Number in U.S. (800) 253-9646); *African Statistical Yearbook.*

The World Bank, 1818 H Street, NW, Washington, D.C. 20433 (202) 477-1234; *World Development Indicators.*

SEYCHELLES - INCOME TAXES - See SEYCHELLES - TAXATION

SEYCHELLES - INDUSTRY

Central Intelligence Agency, Washington, D.C. 20505 (703) 482-1100, www.cia.gov; *The World Factbook.*

Economist Intelligence Unit, 111 West 57th Street, New York, New York 10019 (800) 938-4685; *Seychelles Country Report.*

Euromonitor International, Inc., 122 South Michigan Avenue, Suite 1200, Chicago, Illinois 60603 (800) 577-EURO; *The World Economic Factbook;* and *World Marketing Data and Statistics.*

Europa Publications Limited, 18 Bedford Square, London, WC1B 3JN, England; *The Europa World Year Book.*

Federal Statistical Office, Gustav-Stresemann - Ring 11, D-6200, Wiesbaden, Germany; *Seychellen.*

International Labour Office, I.L.O. Publications, 1828 L Street, NW, Suite 801, Washington, D.C. 20036 (301) 638-3152; *Yearbook of Labour Statistics.*

St. Martin's Press, Inc., 175 Fifth Avenue, New York, New York 10010 (800) 221-7945; *The Statesman's Year-Book.*

Statistical Office of the United Nations, Publishing Service, New York, New York 10017 (800) 253-9646; *Industrial Commodity Statistics Yearbook;* and *Survey of Economic and Social Conditions in Africa.*

United Nations Economic Commission for Africa, Africa Hall, P.O. Box 3001, Addis Ababa, Ethiopia (Telephone Number in U.S. (800) 253-9646); *African Statistical Yearbook.*

The World Bank, 1818 H Street, NW, Washington, D.C. 20433 (202) 477-1234; *World Development Indicators.*

SEYCHELLES - INFANT AND MATERNAL MORTALITY - See SEYCHELLES - MORTALITY

SEYCHELLES - INTERNATIONAL LIQUIDITY

International Monetary Fund, 700 Nineteenth Street, NW, Washington, D.C. 20431 (202) 623-7000; *International Financial Statistics.*

SEYCHELLES - INTERNATIONAL RESERVES EXCLUDING GOLD

Statistical Office of the United Nations, Publishing Service, New York, New York 10017 (800) 253-9646; *Statistical Yearbook;* and *Survey of Economic and Social Conditions in Africa.*

The World Bank, 1818 H Street, NW, Washington, D.C. 20433 (202) 477-1234; *World Development Indicators.*

SEYCHELLES - INVESTMENTS

International Monetary Fund, 700 Nineteenth Street, NW, Washington, D.C. 20431 (202) 623-7000; *International Financial Statistics.*

SEYCHELLES - LABOR

African Development Bank, 01 BP 1387, Abidjan 01, Cote D'Ivoire; *Selected Statistics on Regional Member Countries.*

Central Intelligence Agency, Washington, D.C. 20505 (703) 482-1100, www.cia.gov; *The World Factbook.*

Euromonitor International, Inc., 122 South Michigan Avenue, Suite 1200, Chicago, Illinois 60603 (800) 577-EURO; *International Marketing Data and Statistics;* and *World Marketing Data and Statistics.*

Europa Publications Limited, 18 Bedford Square, London, WC1B 3JN, England; *The Europa World Year Book.*

Food and Agricultural Organization of the United Nations (FAO) Via delle Terme di Caracalla, 00100 Rome, Italy (Telephone Number in U.S. (202) 653-2400); *The State of Food and Agriculture.*

International Labour Office, I.L.O. Publications, 1828 L Street, NW, Suite 801, Washington, D.C. 20036 (301) 638-3152; *Yearbook of Labour Statistics.*

St. Martin's Press, Inc., 175 Fifth Avenue, New York, New York 10010 (800) 221-7945; *The Statesman's Year-Book.*

Statistical Office of the United Nations, Publishing Service, New York, New York 10017 (800) 253-9646; *Human Development Report.*

The World Bank, 1818 H Street, NW, Washington, D.C. 20433 (202) 477-1234; *The World Bank Atlas;* and *World Development Indicators.*

SEYCHELLES - LAND USE

Central Intelligence Agency, Washington, D.C. 20505 (703) 482-1100, www.cia.gov; *The World Factbook.*

Euromonitor International, Inc., 122 South Michigan Avenue, Suite 1200, Chicago, Illinois 60603 (800) 577-EURO; *International Marketing Data and Statistics.*

Food and Agricultural Organization of the United Nations (FAO), Via delle Terme di Caracalla, 00100 Rome, Italy (Telephone Number in U.S. (202) 653-2400); *Production Yearbook.*

SEYCHELLES - LIBRARIES

United Nations Educational, Scientific and Cultural Organization (UNESCO), 7 Place de Fontenoy, F-75700 Paris, France (Telephone Number in U.S. (212) 963-5981); *Statistical Yearbook.*

SEYCHELLES - LIFE EXPECTANCY

African Development Bank, 01 BP 1387, Abidjan 01, Cote D'Ivoire; *Selected Statistics on Regional Member Countries.*

Central Intelligence Agency, Washington, D.C. 20505 (703) 482-1100, www.cia.gov; *The World Factbook.*

Euromonitor International, Inc., 122 South Michigan Avenue, Suite 1200, Chicago, Illinois 60603 (800) 577-EURO; *The World Economic Factbook.*

St. Martin's Press, Inc., 175 Fifth Avenue, New York, New York 10010 (800) 221-7945; *The Statesman's Year-Book.*

Statistical Office of the United Nations, Publishing Service, New York, New York

10017 (800) 253-9646; *Human Development Report;* and *World Statistics Pocketbook.*

The World Bank, 1818 H Street, NW, Washington, D.C. 20433 (202) 477-1234; *The World Bank Atlas.*

SEYCHELLES - LITERACY RATE

Euromonitor International, Inc., 122 South Michigan Avenue, Suite 1200, Chicago, Illinois 60603 (800) 577-EURO; *World Marketing Data and Statistics.*

Statistical Office of the United Nations, Publishing Service, New York, New York 10017 (800) 253-9646; *Survey of Economic and Social Conditions in Africa.*

SEYCHELLES - LIVESTOCK AND POULTRY

Europa Publications Limited, 18 Bedford Square, London, WC1B 3JN, England; *The Europa World Year Book.*

Food and Agricultural Organization of the United Nations (FAO), Via delle Terme di Caracalla, 00100 Rome, Italy (Telephone Number in U.S. (202) 653-2400); *Production Yearbook;* and *The State of Food and Agriculture.*

St. Martin's Press, Inc., 175 Fifth Avenue, New York, New York 10010 (800) 221-7945; *The Statesman's Year-Book.*

Statistical Office of the United Nations, Publishing Service, New York, New York 10017 (800) 253-9646; *Statistical Yearbook;* and *Survey of Economic and Social Conditions in Africa.*

United Nations Conference on Trade and Development, Central Statistical Service, Palais des Nations, Geneva, Switzerland (Telephone in U.S. (800) 253-9646); *UNCTAD Commodity Yearbook.*

United Nations Economic Commission for Africa, Africa Hall, P.O. Box 3001, Addis Ababa, Ethiopia (Telephone Number in U.S. (800) 253-9646); *African Statistical Yearbook.*

SEYCHELLES - LIVING LEVELS - See SEYCHELLES - LIFE EXPECTANCY

SEYCHELLES - MAIL - NUMBER OF ITEMS SENT AND RECEIVED

Statistical Office of the United Nations, Publishing Service, New York, New York 10017 (800) 253-9646; *Statistical Yearbook.*

SEYCHELLES - MANUFACTURING

Statistical Office of the United Nations, Publishing Service, New York, New York 10017 (800) 253-9646; *Survey of Economic and Social Conditions in Africa.*

United Nations Economic Commission for Africa, Africa Hall, P.O. Box 3001, Addis Ababa, Ethiopia (Telephone Number in U.S. (800) 253-9646); *African Statistical Yearbook*.

The World Bank, 1818 H Street, NW, Washington, D.C. 20433 (202) 477-1234; *World Development Indicators*.

SEYCHELLES - MARRIAGE RATES

Statistical Office of the United Nations, Publishing Service, New York, New York 10017 (800) 253-9646; *Demographic Yearbook,;* and *Statistical Yearbook*.

SEYCHELLES - MEAT PRODUCTION - See SEYCHELLES - LIVESTOCK AND POULTRY

SEYCHELLES - MERCHANT SHIPPING

Europa Publications Limited, 18 Bedford Square, London, WC1B 3JN, England; *The Europa World Year Book*.

St. Martin's Press, Inc., 175 Fifth Avenue, New York, New York 10010 (800) 221-7945; *The Statesman's Year-Book*.

Statistical Office of the United Nations, Publishing Service, New York, New York 10017 (800) 253-9646; *Statistical Yearbook*.

United Nations Economic Commission for Africa, Africa Hall, P.O. Box 3001, Addis Ababa, Ethiopia (Telephone Number in U.S. (800) 253-9646); *African Statistical Yearbook*.

U.S. Department of Transportation, Maritime Administration, 400 Seventh Street, SW, Washington, D.C. 20590 (202) 366-5807, www.marad.dot.gov; *A Statistical Analysis of the World's Merchant Fleets*.

SEYCHELLES - MILITARY

Central Intelligence Agency, Washington, D.C. 20505 (703) 482-1100, www.cia.gov; *The World Factbook*.

Euromonitor International, Inc., 122 South Michigan Avenue, Suite 1200, Chicago, Illinois 60603 (800) 577-EURO; *World Marketing Data and Statistics*.

The International Institute for Strategic Studies, 23 Tavistock Street, London WC2E 7NQ, England 44 171 3797676; *The Military Balance*.

International Monetary Fund, 700 Nineteenth Street, NW, Washington, D.C. 20431 (202) 623-7000; *Government Finance Statistics Yearbook*.

St. Martin's Press, Inc., 175 Fifth Avenue, New York, New York 10010 (800) 221-7945; *The Statesman's Year-Book*.

Statistical Office of the United Nations, Publishing Service, New York, New York 10017 (800) 253-9646; *Human Development Report*.

SEYCHELLES - MINING AND MINERAL PRODUCTS

Europa Publications Limited, 18 Bedford Square, London, WC1B 3JN, England; *The Europa World Year Book*.

United Nations Conference on Trade and Development, Central Statistical Service, Palais des Nations, Geneva, Switzerland (Telephone in U.S. (800) 253-9646); *UNCTAD Commodity Yearbook*.

United Nations Economic Commission for Africa, Africa Hall, P.O. Box 3001, Addis Ababa, Ethiopia (Telephone Number in U.S. (800) 253-9646); *African Statistical Yearbook*.

SEYCHELLES - MONEY EXCHANGE RATES - See SEYCHELLES - EXCHANGE RATES

SEYCHELLES - MONEY SUPPLY

African Development Bank, 01 BP 1387, Abidjan 01, Cote D'Ivoire; *Selected Statistics on Regional Member Countries*.

Economist Intelligence Unit, 111 West 57th Street, New York, New York 10019 (800) 938-4685; *Seychelles Country Report*.

Europa Publications Limited, 18 Bedford Square, London, WC1B 3JN, England; *The Europa World Year Book*.

Federal Statistical Office, Gustav-Stresemann - Ring 11, D-6200, Wiesbaden, Germany; *Seychellen*.

The World Bank, 1818 H Street, NW, Washington, D.C. 20433 (202) 477-1234; *World Development Indicators*.

SEYCHELLES - MORTALITY

Central Intelligence Agency, Washington, D.C. 20505 (703) 482-1100, www.cia.gov; *The World Factbook*.

Euromonitor International, Inc., 122 South Michigan Avenue, Suite 1200, Chicago, Illinois 60603 (800) 577-EURO; *International Marketing Data and Statistics;* and *The World Economic Factbook*.

Europa Publications Limited, 18 Bedford Square, London, WC1B 3JN, England; *The Europa World Year Book*.

St. Martin's Press, Inc., 175 Fifth Avenue, New York, New York 10010 (800) 221-7945; *The Statesman's Year-Book*.

Statistical Office of the United Nations, Publishing Service, New York, New York

10017 (800) 253-9646; *Demographic Yearbook; Human Development Report; Statistical Yearbook; Survey of Economic and Social Conditions in Africa;* and *World Statistics Pocketbook*.

The World Bank, 1818 H Street, NW, Washington, D.C. 20433 (202) 477-1234; *The World Bank Atlas;* and *World Development Indicators*.

World Health Organization, Office of Publications, 20 Avenue Appia, CH-1211 Geneva 27, Switzerland (Telephone Number in U.S. (518) 436-9686); *World Health Statistics Annual*.

SEYCHELLES - MOTION PICTURES

St. Martin's Press, Inc., 175 Fifth Avenue, New York, New York 10010 (800) 221-7945; *The Statesman's Year-Book*.

Statistical Office of the United Nations, Publishing Service, New York, New York 10017 (800) 253-9646; *Statistical Yearbook*.

SEYCHELLES - MOTOR VEHICLES IN USE

Europa Publications Limited, 18 Bedford Square, London, WC1B 3JN, England; *The Europa World Year Book*.

Statistical Office of the United Nations, Publishing Service, New York, New York 10017 (800) 253-9646; *Statistical Yearbook;* and *Survey of Economic and Social Conditions in Africa*.

SEYCHELLES - MUSEUMS

United Nations Educational, Scientific and Cultural Organization (UNESCO), 7 Place de Fontenoy, F-75700 Paris, France (Telephone Number in U.S. (212) 963-5981); *Statistical Yearbook*.

SEYCHELLES - NATALITY - See SEYCHELLES - BIRTH RATE

SEYCHELLES - NATIONAL ACCOUNTS

African Development Bank, 01 BP 1387, Abidjan 01, Cote D'Ivoire; *Selected Statistics on Regional Member Countries*.

Federal Statistical Office, Gustav-Stresemann - Ring 11, D-6200, Wiesbaden, Germany; *Seychellen*.

Statistical Office of the United Nations, Publishing Service, New York, New York 10017 (800) 253-9646; *National Accounts Statistics*.

United Nations Economic Commission for Africa, Africa Hall, P.O. Box 3001, Addis Ababa, Ethiopia (Telephone Number in U.S. (800) 253-9646); *African Statistical Yearbook*.

SEYCHELLES - NATIONAL INCOME

Statistical Office of the United Nations, Publishing Service, New York, New York 10017 (800) 253-9646; *Statistical Yearbook.*

SEYCHELLES - NATIONAL PRODUCT

Statistical Office of the United Nations, Publishing Service, New York, New York 10017 (800) 253-9646; *Statistical Yearbook.*

SEYCHELLES - NEWSPAPER PRODUCTION - See SEYCHELLES - FORESTRY AND FOREST PRODUCTS

SEYCHELLES - OCCUPATIONS - See SEYCHELLES - LABOR

SEYCHELLES - PATENTS, TRADEMARKS AND SERVICE MARKS

Statistical Office of the United Nations, Publishing Service, New York, New York 10017 (800) 253-9646; *Statistical Yearbook.*

SEYCHELLES - PERIODICALS

United Nations Educational, Scientific and Cultural Organization (UNESCO), 7 Place de Fontenoy, F-75700 Paris, France (Telephone Number in U.S. (212) 963-5981); *Statistical Yearbook.*

SEYCHELLES - PESTICIDE USE

Food and Agricultural Organization of the United Nations (FAO) Via delle Terme di Caracalla, 00100 Rome, Italy (Telephone Number in U.S. (202) 653-2400); *The State of Food and Agriculture.*

SEYCHELLES - PETROLEUM INDUSTRY

Food and Agricultural Organization of the United Nations (FAO) Via delle Terme di Caracalla, 00100 Rome, Italy (Telephone Number in U.S. (202) 653-2400); *The State of Food and Agriculture.*

United Nations Conference on Trade and Development, Central Statistical Service, Palais des Nations, Geneva, Switzerland (Telephone in U.S. (800) 253-9646); *UNCTAD Commodity Yearbook.*

SEYCHELLES - PIGS - See SEYCHELLES - LIVESTOCK AND POULTRY

SEYCHELLES - POPULATION

African Development Bank, 01 BP 1387, Abidjan 01, Cote D'Ivoire; *Selected Statistics on Regional Member Countries.*

Central Intelligence Agency, Washington, D.C. 20505 (703) 482-1100, www.cia.gov; *The World Factbook.*

The Economist Intelligence Unit, 111 West 57th Street, New York, New York 10019 (800) 938-4685; *Seychelles Country Report;* and *The World Market Atlas.*

Euromonitor International, Inc., 122 South Michigan Avenue, Suite 1200, Chicago, Illinois 60603 (800) 577-EURO; *International Marketing Data and Statistics;* and *The World Economic Factbook.*

Europa Publications Limited, 18 Bedford Square, London, WC1B 3JN, England; *The Europa World Year Book.*

Federal Statistical Office, Gustav-Stresemann - Ring 11, D-6200, Wiesbaden, Germany; *Seychellen.*

Food and Agricultural Organization of the United Nations (FAO), Via delle Terme di Caracalla, 00100 Rome, Italy (Telephone Number in U.S. (202) 653-2400); *Production Yearbook.*

International Labour Office, I.L.O. Publications, 1828 L Street, NW., Suite 801, Washington, D.C. 20036 (301) 638-3152; *Yearbook of Labour Statistics.*

St. Martin's Press, Inc., 175 Fifth Avenue, New York, New York 10010 (800) 221-7945; *The Statesman's Year-Book.*

Statistical Office of the United Nations, Publishing Service, New York, New York 10017 (800) 253-9646; *Demographic Yearbook; Human Development Report; Statistical Yearbook; Survey of Economic and Social Conditions in Africa;* and *World Statistics Pocketbook.*

United Nations Educational, Scientific and Cultural Organization (UNESCO), 7 Place de Fontenoy, F-75700 Paris, France (Telephone Number in U.S. (212) 963-5981); *Statistical Yearbook.*

The World Bank, 1818 H Street, NW, Washington, D.C. 20433 (202) 477-1234; *The World Bank Atlas.*

World Health Organization, Office of Publications, 20 Avenue Appia, CH-1211 Geneva 27, Switzerland (Telephone Number in U.S. (518) 436-9686); *World Health Statistics Annual.*

SEYCHELLES - PRICES

Federal Statistical Office, Gustav-Stresemann - Ring 11, D-6200, Wiesbaden, Germany; *Seychellen.*

Food and Agricultural Organization of the United Nations (FAO), Via delle Terme di Caracalla, 00100 Rome, Italy (Telephone Number in U.S. (202) 653-2400); *Production Yearbook;* and *The State of Food and Agriculture.*

International Labour Office, I.L.O. Publications, 1828 L Street, NW., Suite 801, Washington, D.C. 20036 (301) 638-3152; *Yearbook of Labour Statistics.*

International Monetary Fund, 700 Nineteenth Street, NW, Washington, D.C. 20431 (202) 623-7000; *International Financial Statistics.*

United Nations Economic Commission for Africa, Africa Hall, P.O. Box 3001, Addis Ababa, Ethiopia (Telephone Number in U.S. (800) 253-9646); *African Statistical Yearbook.*

SEYCHELLES - PROPERTY TAXES - See SEYCHELLES - TAXATION

SEYCHELLES - RADIO BROADCASTING - See SEYCHELLES - BROADCASTING

SEYCHELLES - RADIO RECEIVERS

St. Martin's Press, Inc., 175 Fifth Avenue, New York, New York 10010 (800) 221-7945; *The Statesman's Year-Book.*

SEYCHELLES - RAILWAYS

United Nations Economic Commission for Africa, Africa Hall, P.O. Box 3001, Addis Ababa, Ethiopia (Telephone Number in U.S. (800) 253-9646); *African Statistical Yearbook.*

SEYCHELLES - RELIGION

Central Intelligence Agency, Washington, D.C. 20505 (703) 482-1100, www.cia.gov; *The World Factbook.*

St. Martin's Press, Inc., 175 Fifth Avenue, New York, New York 10010 (800) 221-7945; *The Statesman's Year-Book.*

SEYCHELLES - RENT PRICES

International Labour Office, I.L.O. Publications, 1828 L Street, NW., Suite 801, Washington, D.C. 20036 (301) 638-3152; *Yearbook of Labour Statistics.*

SEYCHELLES - RETAIL TRADE

Euromonitor International Inc., 122 South Michigan Avenue, Suite 1200, Chicago, Illinois 60603 (800) 577-EURO; *World Marketing Data and Statistics.*

SEYCHELLES - SCIENCE AND TECHNOLOGY - EXPENDITURE FOR RESEARCH - See SEYCHELLES - SCIENTISTS, TECHNICIANS AND ENGINEERS

SEYCHELLES - SCIENTISTS, TECHNICIANS AND ENGINEERS

Statistical Office of the United Nations, Publishing Service, New York, New York 10017 (800) 253-9646; *Statistical Yearbook.*

SEYCHELLES - SOCIAL DATA

Statistical Office of the United Nations, Publishing Service, New York, New York 10017 (800) 253-9646; *Survey of Economic and Social Conditions in Africa;* and *World Statistics Pocketbook.*

SEYCHELLES - SOCIAL SECURITY

International Monetary Fund, 700 Nineteenth Street, NW, Washington, D.C. 20431 (202) 623-7000; *Government Finance Statistics Yearbook.*

Statistical Office of the United Nations, Publishing Service, New York, New York 10017 (800) 253-9646; *National Accounts Statistics.*

SEYCHELLES - STAMP TAXES AND DUTIES - See SEYCHELLES - TAXATION

SEYCHELLES - STOCKS - COMMODITY - MARKET PRICE - INDEX

Food and Agricultural Organization of the United Nations (FAO) Via delle Terme di Caracalla, 00100 Rome, Italy (Telephone Number in U.S. (202) 653-2400); *The State of Food and Agriculture.*

SEYCHELLES - TAXATION

Europa Publications Limited, 18 Bedford Square, London, WC1B 3JN, England; *The Europa World Year Book.*

International Monetary Fund, 700 Nineteenth Street, NW, Washington, D.C. 20431 (202) 623-7000; *Government Finance Statistics Yearbook.*

The World Bank, 1818 H Street, NW, Washington, D.C. 20433 (202) 477-1234; *World Development Indicators.*

SEYCHELLES - TELEPHONES IN USE

American Telephone and Telegraph Company, 26 Parsippany Road, Whippany, New Jersey 07981 (800) 222-0300; *The World's Telephones.*

Central Intelligence Agency, Washington, D.C. 20505 (703) 482-1100, www.cia.gov; *The World Factbook.*

Europa Publications Limited, 18 Bedford Square, London, WC1B 3JN, England; *The Europa World Year Book.*

St. Martin's Press, Inc., 175 Fifth Avenue, New York, New York 10010 (800) 221-7945; *The Statesman's Year-Book.*

Statistical Office of the United Nations, Publishing Service, New York, New York 10017 (800) 253-9646; *Statistical Yearbook;* and *World Statistics Pocketbook.*

SEYCHELLES - TEXTILE INDUSTRY

United Nations Conference on Trade and Development, Central Statistical Service, Palais des Nations, Geneva, Switzerland (Telephone in U.S. (800) 253-9646); *UNCTAD Commodity Yearbook.*

SEYCHELLES - TOBACCO PRODUCTION

Statistical Office of the United Nations, Publishing Service, New York, New York 10017 (800) 253-9646; *Statistical Yearbook.*

SEYCHELLES - TOURISM

Euromonitor International, Inc., 122 South Michigan Avenue, Suite 1200, Chicago, Illinois 60603 (800) 577-EURO; *The World Economic Factbook*; and *World Marketing Data and Statistics.*

Europa Publications Limited, 18 Bedford Square, London, WC1B 3JN, England; *The Europa World Year Book.*

Federal Statistical Office, Gustav-Stresemann - Ring 11, D-6200, Wiesbaden, Germany; *Seychellen.*

St. Martin's Press, Inc., 175 Fifth Avenue, New York, New York 10010 (800) 221-7945; *The Statesman's Year-Book.*

Statistical Office of the United Nations, Publishing Service, New York, New York 10017 (800) 253-9646; *Statistical Yearbook.*

United Nations Economic Commission for Africa, Africa Hall, P.O. Box 3001, Addis Ababa, Ethiopia (Telephone Number in U.S. (800) 253-9646); *African Statistical Yearbook.*

World Tourism Organization, Calle Capitan Haya 42, E-28020 Madrid, Spain; *Yearbook of Tourism Statistics.*

SEYCHELLES - TRACTORS IN USE

Statistical Office of the United Nations, Publishing Service, New York, New York 10017 (800) 253-9646; *Statistical Yearbook.*

SEYCHELLES - TRADE - See SEYCHELLES - FOREIGN TRADE

SEYCHELLES - TRADEMARKS AND SERVICE MARKS - See SEYCHELLES - PATENTS, TRADEMARKS AND SERVICE MARKS

SEYCHELLES - TRANSPORTATION AND COMMUNICATIONS

Central Intelligence Agency, Washington, D.C. 20505 (703) 482-1100, www.cia.gov; *The World Factbook.*

Euromonitor International, Inc., 122 South Michigan Avenue, Suite 1200, Chicago, Illinois 60603 (800) 577-EURO;

International Marketing Data and Statistics; and *World Marketing Data and Statistics.*

Europa Publications Limited, 18 Bedford Square, London, WC1B 3JN, England; *The Europa World Year Book.*

Federal Statistical Office, Gustav-Stresemann - Ring 11, D-6200, Wiesbaden, Germany; *Seychellen.*

St. Martin's Press, Inc., 175 Fifth Avenue, New York, New York 10010 (800) 221-7945; *The Statesman's Year-Book.*

Statistical Office of the United Nations, Publishing Service, New York, New York 10017 (800) 253-9646; *Human Development Report.*

United Nations Economic Commission for Africa, Africa Hall, P.O. Box 3001, Addis Ababa, Ethiopia (Telephone Number in U.S. (800) 253-9646); *African Statistical Yearbook.*

SEYCHELLES - UNEMPLOYMENT

Central Intelligence Agency, Washington, D.C. 20505 (703) 482-1100, www.cia.gov; *The World Factbook.*

International Labour Office, I.L.O. Publications, 1828 L Street, NW., Suite 801, Washington, D.C. 20036 (301) 638-3152; *Yearbook of Labour Statistics.*

SEYCHELLES - VITAL STATISTICS

St. Martin's Press, Inc., 175 Fifth Avenue, New York, New York 10010 (800) 221-7945; *The Statesman's Year-Book.*

Statistical Office of the United Nations, Publishing Service, New York, New York 10017 (800) 253-9646; *Statistical Yearbook.*

World Health Organization, Office of Publications, 20 Avenue Appia, CH-1211 Geneva 27, Switzerland (Telephone Number in U.S. (518) 436-9686); *World Health Statistics Annual.*

SEYCHELLES - WAGES

Federal Statistical Office, Gustav-Stresemann - Ring 11, D-6200, Wiesbaden, Germany; *Seychellen.*

International Labour Office, I.L.O. Publications, 1828 L Street, NW., Suite 801, Washington, D.C. 20036 (301) 638-3152; *Yearbook of Labour Statistics.*

SEYCHELLES - WEATHER - See SEYCHELLES - CLIMATE

SEYCHELLES - WELFARE

International Monetary Fund, 700 Nineteenth, NW, Washington, D.C. 20431

(202) 623-7000; *Government Finance Statistics Yearbook.*

SHEEP AND LAMBS

U.S. Department of Agriculture, Economic Research Service, 1800 M Street, NW, Washington, D.C. 20036 (202) 694-5050, www.ers.usda.gov; *Agricultural Outlook; Food Consumption, Prices and Expenditures;* and *Farm Business Economic Report.*

U.S. Department of Agriculture, National Agricultural Statistics Service, Fourteenth Street and Independence Avenue, SW, Washington, D.C. 20250 (800) 727-9540, www.usda.gov/nass; *Meat Animals - Production, Disposition, and Income;* and *Agricultural Statistics.*

SHEETS AND PILLOWCASES

U.S. Department of Commerce, Bureau of the Census, Washington, D.C. 20233 (301) 457-4100, www.census.gov; *Current Industrial Reports;* and *Manufacturing Profiles.*

SHELLFISH - CANNED - QUANTITY AND VALUE

U.S. Department of Commerce, National Oceanic and Atmospheric Administration, National Marine Fisheries Service, 1315 East-West Highway, Silver Spring, Maryland 20910 (301) 427-2239, www.nmfs.noaa.gov; *Fisheries of the United States.*

SHELLFISH - CATCH - QUANTITY AND VALUE

U.S. Department of Commerce, National Oceanic and Atmospheric Administration, National Marine Fisheries Service, 1315 East-West Highway, Silver Spring, Maryland 20910 (301) 427-2239, www.nmfs.noaa.gov; *Fisheries of the United States.*

SHELLFISH - CONSUMPTION

U.S. Department of Agriculture, Economic Research Service, 1800 M Street, NW, Washington, D.C. 20036 (202) 694-5050, www.ers.usda.gov; *Food Consumption, Prices, and Expenditures;* and *Agricultural Outlook.*

SHELTER - See also HOUSING AND HOUSING UNITS

SHELTER - CONSUMER PRICE INDEXES

U.S. Department of Labor, Bureau of Labor Statistics, Two Massachusetts Avenue, NE, Washington, D.C. 20212 (202) 691-5200, www.stats.bls.gov; *Monthly Labor Review; Handbook of Labor Statistics;* and *CPI Detailed Report.*

SHIGELLOSIS

U.S. Department of Health and Human Services, Centers for Disease Control and Prevention, 1600 Clifton road, NE, Atlanta, Georgia 30333 (800) 311-3435; *Summary of Notifiable Diseases, United States;* and *Morbidity and Weekly Report.*

SHIP AND BOAT BUILDING, AND REPAIRING

Shipbuilders Council of America, 4301 North Fairfax Drive, Suite 330, Arlington, Virginia 22203 (703) 276-1700; unpublished data.

U.S. Department of Transportation, Maritime Administration, 400 Seventh Street, SW, Washington, D.C. 20590 (202) 366-5807, www.marad.dot.gov; unpublished data.

SHIP AND BOAT BUILDING AND REPAIRING - EARNINGS

Shipbuilders Council of America, 4301 North Fairfax Drive, Suite 330, Arlington, Virginia 22203 (703) 276-1700; unpublished data.

U.S. Department of Commerce, Bureau of the Census, Washington, D.C. 20233 (301) 457-4100, www.census.gov; *Census of Manufactures;* and *Annual Survey of Manufactures.*

U.S. Department of Labor, Bureau of Labor Statistics, Two Massachusetts Avenue, NE, Washington, D.C. 20212 (202) 691-5200, www.stats.bls.gov; *Employment and Earnings;* and Internet site: http://stats.bls.gov/ ceshomehtm.

U.S. Department of Transportation, Maritime Administration, 400 Seventh Street, SW, Washington, D.C. 20590 (202) 366-5807, www.marad.dot.gov; unpublished data.

SHIP AND BOAT BUILDING AND REPAIRING - EMPLOYEES

Shipbuilders Council of America, 4301 North Fairfax Drive, Suite 330, Arlington, Virginia 22203 (703) 276-1700; unpublished data.

U.S. Department of Commerce, Bureau of the Census, Washington, D.C. 20233 (301) 457-4100, www.census.gov; *Census of Manufactures;* and *Annual Survey of Manufactures.*

U.S. Department of Labor, Bureau of Labor Statistics, Two Massachusetts Avenue, NE, Washington, D.C. 20212 (202) 691-5200, www.stats.bls.gov; *Employment and Earnings;* and Internet site: http://stats.bls.gov/ceshome. htm.

U.S. Department of Transportation, Maritime Administration, 400 Seventh Street, SW, Washington, D.C. 20590 (202) 366-5807, www.marad.dot.gov; unpublished data.

SHIP AND BOAT BUILDING AND REPAIRING - OUTPUT

Shipbuilders Council of America, 4301 North Fairfax Drive, Suite 330, Arlington, Virginia 22203 (703) 276-1700; unpublished data.

SHIP AND BOAT BUILDING AND REPAIRING - PRODUCTIVITY

U.S. Department of Labor, Bureau of Labor Statistics, Two Massachusetts Avenue, NE, Washington, D.C. 20212 (202) 691-5200, www.stats.bls.gov; Internet site: http://stats.bls.gov/ iprhome.htm.

SHIP AND BOAT BUILDING AND REPAIRING - SHIPMENTS

U.S. Department of Commerce, Bureau of the Census, Washington, D.C. 20233 (301) 457-4100, www.census.gov; *Census of Manufactures;* and *Annual Survey of Manufactures.*

SHIP AND BOAT BUILDING AND REPAIRING - VALUE ADDED

Shipbuilders Council of America, 4301 North Fairfax Drive, Suite 330, Arlington, Virginia 22203 (703) 276-1700; unpublished data.

U.S. Department of Commerce, Bureau of the Census, Washington, D.C. 20233 (301) 457-4100, www.census.gov; *Census of Manufactures;* and *Annual Survey of Manufactures.*

SHIPMENTS - See also Individual Products or Industries

U.S. Department of Commerce, Bureau of the Census, Washington, D.C. 20233 (301) 457-4100, www.census.gov; *Current Industrial Reports, Manufacturers' Shipments, Inventories, and Orders; 1997 Economic Census: Core Business Statistics Series; Census of Manufactures;* and *Annual Survey of Manufactures.*

SHIPPING - See MERCHANT VESSELS and TONNAGE

SHIPS - MERCHANT VESSELS

Lloyd's Register of Shipping, 71 Fenchurch Street, London EC3, England (Telephone in U.S. (212) 425-050); *World Fleet Statistics;* and *Casualty Return.*

U.S. Department of Transportation, Maritime Administration, 400 Seventh

Street, SW, Washington, D.C. 20590 (202) 366-5807, www.marad.dot.gov; *Merchant Fleets of the World;* and unpublished data.

SHIPS - MERCHANT VESSELS - LOST

Lloyd's Register of Shipping, 71 Fenchurch Street, London EC3, England (Telephone in U.S. (212) 425-8050); *Casualty Return.*

SHIPS - REPAIRS

Shipbuilders Council of America, 4301 North Fairfax Drive, Suite 330, Arlington, Virginia 22203 (703) 276-1700; unpublished data.

U.S. Department of Transportation, Maritime Administration, 400 Seventh Street, SW, Washington, D.C. 20590 (202) 366-5807, www.marad.dot.gov; unpublished data.

SHIPS - TANKER CASUALTIES

Tanker Advisory Center, Incorporated, 10 East End Avenue, New York, New York 10028 (212) 628-7686; *Worldwide Tanker Casualty Returns.*

SHOES - See FOOTWEAR

SHOPLIFTING

U.S. Department of Justice, Federal Bureau of Investigation, 935 Pennsylvania Avenue, NW, Washington, D.C. 20535 (202) 324-3691, www.fbi.gov; *Population-at-Risk Rates and Selected Crime Indicators.*

SHOPPING CENTERS

National Research Bureau, 225 West Wacker Drive, Chicago, Illinois 60606 (312) 346-9097; data published by International Council of Shopping Centers, 1221 Avenue of the Americas, New York, New York 10020 (646) 728-3800; *Shopping Centers Today.*

SHORTENING

U.S. Department of Agriculture, Economic Research Service, 1800 M Street, NW, Washington, D.C. 20036 (202) 694-5050, www.ers.usda.gov; *Food Consumption, Prices and Expenditures;* and *Agricultural Outlook.*

SHRIMP

U.S. Department of Commerce, National Oceanic and Atmospheric Administration, National Marine Fisheries Service, 1315 East-West Highway, Silver Spring, Maryland 20910 (301) 427-2239, www.nmfs.noaa.gov; *Fisheries of the United States.*

SICKNESS - See ILLNESS

Sierra Leone - National Statistical Office

Central Statistics Office, Ministry of Development and Economic Planning, Tower Hill, Freetown, Sierra Leone.

Sierra Leone - Primary Statistics Source

Central Statistics Office, Ministry of Finance, Tower Hill, Freetown, Sierra Leone; *Statistical Bulletin;* and *Annual Statistical Digest.*

SIERRA LEONE - AGRICULTURE

Economist Intelligence Unit, 111 West 57th Street, New York, New York 10019 (800) 938-4685; *Sierra Leone Country Report.*

Euromonitor International, Inc., 122 South Michigan Avenue, Suite 1200, Chicago, Illinois 60603 (800) 577-EURO; *International Marketing Data and Statistics;* and *World Marketing Data and Statistics.*

Europa Publications Limited, 18 Bedford Square, London, WC1B 3JN, England; *The Europa World Year Book.*

Federal Statistical Office, Gustav-Stresemann - Ring 11, D-6200, Wiesbaden, Germany; *Sierra Leone.*

Food and Agricultural Organization of the United Nations (FAO) Via delle Terme di Caracalla, 00100 Rome, Italy (Telephone Number in U.S. (202) 653-2400); *Production Yearbook; The State of Food and Agriculture;* and *Trade Yearbook.*

M.E. Sharpe, 80 Business Park Drive, Armonk, New York 10504 (800) 541-6563; *The Illustrated Book of World Rankings.*

St. Martin's Press, Inc., 175 Fifth Avenue, New York, New York 10010 (800) 221-7945; *The Statesman's Year-Book.*

Statistical Office of the United Nations, Publishing Service, New York, New York 10017 (800) 253-9646; *Statistical Yearbook;* and *Survey of Economic and Social Conditions in Africa.*

United Nations Conference on Trade and Development, Central Statistical Service, Palais des Nations, Geneva, Switzerland (Telephone in U.S. (800) 253-9646); *UNCTAD Commodity Yearbook.*

United Nations Economic Commission for Africa, Africa Hall, P.O. Box 3001, Addis Ababa, Ethiopia (Telephone Number in U.S. (800) 253-9646); *African Statistical*

Yearbook.

The World Bank, 1818 H Street, NW, Washington, D.C. 20433 (202) 477-1234; *World Development Indicators.*

SIERRA LEONE - AIRPORTS

Central Intelligence Agency, Washington, D.C. 20505 (703) 482-1100, www.cia.gov; *The World Factbook.*

SIERRA LEONE - AIRLINE SERVICE

Europa Publications Limited, 18 Bedford Square, London, WC1B 3JN, England; *The Europa World Year Book.*

M.E. Sharpe, 80 Business Park Drive, Armonk, New York 10504 (800) 541-6563; *The Illustrated Book of World Rankings.*

St. Martin's Press, Inc., 175 Fifth Avenue, New York, New York 10010 (800) 221-7945; *The Statesman's Year-Book.*

United Nations Economic Commission for Africa, Africa Hall, P.O. Box 3001, Addis Ababa, Ethiopia (Telephone Number in U.S. (800) 253-9646); *African Statistical Yearbook.*

SIERRA LEONE - ALUMINUM PRODUCTION AND CONSUMPTION - See SIERRA LEONE - MINING AND MINERAL PRODUCTS

SIERRA LEONE - ANIMAL HEALTH

Food and Agricultural Organization of the United Nations (FAO), Via delle Terme di Caracalla, 00100, Rome, Italy (Telephone Number in U.S. (202) 653-2400); *Animal Health Yearbook.*

SIERRA LEONE - AREA AND DENSITY OF POPULATION

African Development Bank, 01 BP 1387, Abidjan 01, Cote D'Ivoire; *Selected Statistics on Regional Member Countries.*

Central Intelligence Agency, Washington, D.C. 20505 (703) 482-1100, www.cia.gov; *The World Factbook.*

Euromonitor International, Inc., 122 South Michigan Avenue, Suite 1200, Chicago, Illinois 60603 (800) 577-EURO; *International Marketing Data and Statistics;* and *The World Economic Factbook.*

Europa Publications Limited, 18 Bedford Square, London, WC1B 3JN, England; *The Europa World Year Book.*

Federal Statistical Office, Gustav-Stresemann - Ring 11, D-6200, Wiesbaden, Germany; *Sierra Leone.*

Food and Agricultural Organization of

the United Nations (FAO) Via delle Terme di Caracalla, 00100 Rome, Italy (Telephone Number in U.S. (202) 653-2400); *The State of Food and Agriculture.*

M.E. Sharpe, 80 Business Park Drive, Armonk, New York 10504 (800) 541-6563; *The Illustrated Book of World Rankings.*

St. Martin's Press, Inc., 175 Fifth Avenue, New York, New York 10010 (800) 221-7945; *The Statesman's Year-Book.*

Statistical Office of the United Nations, Publishing Service, New York, New York 10017 (800) 253-9646; *Statistical Yearbook;* and *Survey of Economic and Social Conditions in Africa.*

United Nations Educational, Scientific and Cultural Organization (UNESCO), 7 Place de Fontenoy, F-75700 Paris, France (Telephone Number in U.S. (212) 963-5981); *Statistical Yearbook.*

The World Bank, 1818 H Street, NW, Washington, D.C. 20433 (202) 477-1234; *World Development Report.*

SIERRA LEONE - ARMS EXPORTS AND IMPORTS - See SIERRA LEONE - MILITARY

SIERRA LEONE - BALANCE OF PAYMENTS

African Development Bank, 01 BP 1387, Abidjan 01, Cote D'Ivoire; *Selected Statistics on Regional Member Countries.*

The Economist Intelligence Unit, 111 West 57th Street, New York, New York 10019 (800) 938-4685; *The World Market Atlas.*

Europa Publications Limited, 18 Bedford Square, London, WC1B 3JN, England; *The Europa World Year Book.*

Federal Statistical Office, Gustav-Stresemann - Ring 11, D-6200, Wiesbaden, Germany; *Sierra Leone.*

International Monetary Fund, 700 Nineteenth Street, NW, Washington, D.C. 20431 (202) 623-7000; *Balance of Payments Yearbook;* and *International Financial Statistics.*

United Nations Conference on Trade and Development (UNCTAD), New York, New York 10017 (800) 253-9646; *Handbook of International Trade and Development Statistics.*

United Nations Economic Commission for Africa, Africa Hall, P.O. Box 3001, Addis Ababa, Ethiopia (Telephone Number in U.S. (800) 253-9646); *African Statistical Yearbook.*

The World Bank, 1818 H Street, NW, Washington, D.C. 20433 (202) 477-1234;

World Development Report; and *World Development Indicators.*

SIERRA LEONE - BANKING

Euromonitor International Inc., 122 South Michigan Avenue, Suite 1200, Chicago, Illinois 60603 (800) 577-EURO; *World Marketing Data and Statistics.*

Europa Publications Limited, 18 Bedford Square, London, WC1B 3JN, England; *The Europa World Year Book.*

International Monetary Fund, 700 Nineteenth Street, NW, Washington, D.C. 20431 (202) 623-7000; *Government Finance Statistics Yearbook;* and *International Financial Statistics.*

M.E. Sharpe, 80 Business Park Drive, Armonk, New York 10504 (800) 541-6563; *The Illustrated Book of World Rankings.*

St. Martin's Press, Inc., 175 Fifth Avenue, New York, New York 10010 (800) 221-7945; *The Statesman's Year-Book.*

United Nations Economic Commission for Africa, Africa Hall, P.O. Box 3001, Addis Ababa, Ethiopia (Telephone Number in U.S. (800) 253-9646); *African Statistical Yearbook.*

SIERRA LEONE - BARLEY PRODUCTION - See SIERRA LEONE - CROPS

SIERRA LEONE - BAUXITE PRODUCTION AND CONSUMPTION - See SIERRA LEONE - MINING AND MINERAL PRODUCTS

SIERRA LEONE - BEER PRODUCTION - See SIERRA LEONE - BEVERAGES

SIERRA LEONE - BEVERAGES

M.E. Sharpe, 80 Business Park Drive, Armonk, New York 10504 (800) 541-6563; *The Illustrated Book of World Rankings.*

Statistical Office of the United Nations, Publishing Service, New York, New York 10017 (800) 253-9646; *Statistical Yearbook.*

SIERRA LEONE - BIRTH RATES

Central Intelligence Agency, Washington, D.C. 20505 (703) 482-1100, www.cia.gov; *The World Factbook.*

Euromonitor International, Inc., 122 South Michigan Avenue, Suite 1200, Chicago, Illinois 60603 (800) 577-EURO; *International Marketing Data and Statistics;* and *The World Economic Factbook.*

Europa Publications Limited, 18 Bedford Square, London, WC1B 3JN, England; *The Europa World Year Book.*

M.E. Sharpe, 80 Business Park Drive,

Armonk, New York 10504 (800) 541-6563; *The Illustrated Book of World Rankings.*

St. Martin's Press, Inc., 175 Fifth Avenue, New York, New York 10010 (800) 221-7945; *The Statesman's Year-Book.*

Statistical Office of the United Nations, Publishing Service, New York, New York 10017 (800) 253-9646; *Demographic Yearbook; Statistical Yearbook;* and *Survey of Economic and Social Conditions in Africa.*

The World Bank, 1818 H Street, NW, Washington, D.C. 20433 (202) 477-1234; *World Development Indicators.*

SIERRA LEONE - BONDS

International Monetary Fund, 700 Nineteenth Street, NW, Washington, D.C. 20431 (202) 623-7000; *Government Finance Statistics Yearbook.*

SIERRA LEONE - BOOK PRODUCTION

Europa Publications Limited, 18 Bedford Square, London, WC1B 3JN, England; *The Europa World Year Book.*

United Nations Educational, Scientific and Cultural Organization (UNESCO), 7 Place de Fontenoy, F-75700 Paris, France (Telephone Number in U.S. (212) 963-5981); *Statistical Yearbook.*

SIERRA LEONE - BROADCASTING

Billboard Limited, P.O. Box 9027, 1006 AA Amsterdam, The Netherlands (Telephone Number in U.S. (212) 764-7300); *World Radio TV Handbook.*

Central Intelligence Agency, Washington, D.C. 20505 (703) 482-1100, www.cia.gov; *The World Factbook.*

Euromonitor International Inc., 122 South Michigan Avenue, Suite 1200, Chicago, Illinois 60603 (800) 577-EURO; *World Marketing Data and Statistics.*

M.E. Sharpe, 80 Business Park Drive, Armonk, New York 10504 (800) 541-6563; *The Illustrated Book of World Rankings.*

St. Martin's Press, Inc., 175 Fifth Avenue, New York, New York 10010 (800) 221-7945; *The Statesman's Year-Book.*

United Nations Educational, Scientific and Cultural Organization (UNESCO), 7 Place de Fontenoy, F-75700 Paris, France (Telephone Number in U.S. (212) 963-5981); *Statistical Yearbook.*

SIERRA LEONE - BUDGET

Central Intelligence Agency, Washington, D.C. 20505 (703) 482-1100,

www.cia.gov; *The World Factbook.*

SIERRA LEONE - BUSINESS AND PROFESSIONAL LICENSES

International Monetary Fund, 700 Nineteenth Street, NW, Washington, D.C. 20431 (202) 623-7000; *Government Finance Statistics Yearbook.*

SIERRA LEONE - CACAO EXPORTS - See SIERRA LEONE - CROPS

SIERRA LEONE - CALORIE SUPPLY

African Development Bank, 01 BP 1387, Abidjan 01, Cote D'Ivoire; *Selected Statistics on Regional Member Countries.*

Food and Agricultural Organization of the United Nations (FAO) Via delle Terme di Caracalla, 00100 Rome, Italy (Telephone Number in U.S. (202) 653-2400); *The State of Food and Agriculture.*

SIERRA LEONE - CAPITAL REVENUE

International Monetary Fund, 700 Nineteenth Street, NW, Washington, D.C. 20431 (202) 623-7000; *Government Finance Statistics Yearbook.*

SIERRA LEONE - CATTLE - See SIERRA LEONE - LIVESTOCK AND POULTRY

SIERRA LEONE - CEMENT PRODUCTION - See SIERRA LEONE - MINING AND MINERAL PRODUCTS

SIERRA LEONE - CHEMICAL (ORGANIC) PRODUCTION - See SIERRA LEONE - MINING AND MINERAL PRODUCTS

SIERRA LEONE - CHICKENS - See SIERRA LEONE - LIVESTOCK AND POULTRY

SIERRA LEONE - CIGARETTE PRODUCTION - See SIERRA LEONE - TOBACCO PRODUCTION

SIERRA LEONE - CLIMATE

M.E. Sharpe, 80 Business Park Drive, Armonk, New York 10504 (800) 541-6563; *The Illustrated Book of World Rankings.*

SIERRA LEONE - COAL PRODUCTION - See SIERRA LEONE - MINING AND MINERAL PRODUCTS

SIERRA LEONE - COCOA (BEANS) PRODUCTION - See SIERRA LEONE - CROPS

SIERRA LEONE - COFFEE - See SIERRA LEONE - CROPS

SIERRA LEONE - COMMERCE

St. Martin's Press, Inc., 175 Fifth Avenue, New York, New York 10010 (800) 221-7945; *The Statesman's Year-Book.*

SIERRA LEONE - COMMUNICATIONS - See SIERRA LEONE - TRANSPORTATION AND COMMUNICATIONS

SIERRA LEONE - CONSTRUCTION INDUSTRY

M.E. Sharpe, 80 Business Park Drive, Armonk, New York 10504 (800) 541-6563; *The Illustrated Book of World Rankings.*

St. Martin's Press, Inc., 175 Fifth Avenue, New York, New York 10010 (800) 221-7945; *The Statesman's Year-Book.*

Statistical Office of the United Nations, Publishing Service, New York, New York 10017 (800) 253-9646; *Statistical Yearbook.*

United Nations Economic Commission for Africa, Africa Hall, P.O. Box 3001, Addis Ababa, Ethiopia (Telephone Number in U.S. (800) 253-9646); *African Statistical Yearbook.*

SIERRA LEONE - CONSUMER PRICE INDEX

African Development Bank, 01 BP 1387, Abidjan 01, Cote D'Ivoire; *Selected Statistics on Regional Member Countries.*

Europa Publications Limited, 18 Bedford Square, London, WC1B 3JN, England; *The Europa World Year Book.*

Statistical Office of the United Nations, Publishing Service, New York, New York 10017 (800) 253-9646; *Statistical Yearbook;* and *Survey of Economic and Social Conditions in Africa.*

United Nations Economic Commission for Africa, Africa Hall, P.O. Box 3001, Addis Ababa, Ethiopia (Telephone Number in U.S. (800) 253-9646); *African Statistical Yearbook.*

SIERRA LEONE - CONSUMER PRICES

Euromonitor International Inc., 122 South Michigan Avenue, Suite 1200, Chicago, Illinois 60603 (800) 577-EURO; *World Marketing Data and Statistics.*

International Labour Office, I.L.O. Publications, 1828 L Street, NW., Suite 801, Washington, D.C. 20036 (301) 638-3152; *Yearbook of Labour Statistics.*

International Monetary Fund, 700 Nineteenth Street, NW, Washington, D.C. 20431 (202) 623-7000; *International Financial Statistics.*

SIERRA LEONE - CONSUMPTION

African Development Bank, 01 BP 1387, Abidjan 01, Cote D'Ivoire; *Selected Statistics on Regional Member Countries.*

Statistical Office of the United Nations, Publishing Service, New York, New York 10017 (800) 253-9646; *Survey of Economic and Social Conditions in Africa.*

The World Bank, 1818 H Street, NW, Washington, D.C. 20433 (202) 477-1234; *World Development Report.*

SIERRA LEONE - COPPER PRODUCTION AND CONSUMPTION - See SIERRA LEONE - MINING AND MINERAL PRODUCTS

SIERRA LEONE - CORN PRODUCTION - See SIERRA LEONE - CROPS

SIERRA LEONE - CORPORATE TAXES - See SIERRA LEONE - TAXATION

SIERRA LEONE - COTTON PRODUCTION - See SIERRA LEONE - CROPS

SIERRA LEONE - CRIME

Yale University Press, Yale Station, New Haven, Connecticut 06520 (800) 987-7323; *Violence and Crime in Cross-National Perspective.*

SIERRA LEONE - CROPS

Europa Publications Limited, 18 Bedford Square, London, WC1B 3JN, England; *The Europa World Year Book.*

Food and Agricultural Organization of the United Nations (FAO) Via delle Terme di Caracalla, 00100 Rome, Italy (Telephone Number in U.S. (202) 653-2400); *The State of Food and Agriculture.*

International Monetary Fund, 700 Nineteenth Street, NW, Washington, D.C. 20431 (202) 623-7000; *International Financial Statistics.*

M.E. Sharpe, 80 Business Park Drive, Armonk, New York 10504 (800) 541-6563; *The Illustrated Book of World Rankings.*

St. Martin's Press, Inc., 175 Fifth Avenue, New York, New York 10010 (800) 221-7945; *The Statesman's Year-Book.*

Statistical Office of the United Nations, Publishing Service, New York, New York 10017 (800) 253-9646; *Statistical Yearbook.*

United Nations Conference on Trade and Development, Central Statistical Service, Palais des Nations, Geneva, Switzerland (Telephone in U.S. (800) 253-9646); *UNCTAD Commodity Yearbook.*

United Nations Economic Commission for Africa, Africa Hall, P.O. Box 3001, Addis Ababa, Ethiopia (Telephone Number in U.S. (800) 253-9646); *African Statistical*

Yearbook.

SIERRA LEONE - CUSTOMS DUTIES

International Monetary Fund, 700 Nineteenth Street, NW, Washington, D.C. 20431 (202) 623-7000; *Government Finance Statistics Yearbook.*

St. Martin's Press, Inc., 175 Fifth Avenue, New York, New York 10010 (800) 221-7945; *The Statesman's Year-Book.*

SIERRA LEONE - DAIRY PRODUCTS

Europa Publications Limited, 18 Bedford Square, London, WC1B 3JN, England; *The Europa World Year Book.*

Food and Agricultural Organization of the United Nations (FAO) Via delle Terme di Caracalla, 00100 Rome, Italy (Telephone Number in U.S. (202) 653-2400); *The State of Food and Agriculture.*

M.E. Sharpe, 80 Business Park Drive, Armonk, New York 10504 (800) 541-6563; *The Illustrated Book of World Rankings.*

St. Martin's Press, Inc., 175 Fifth Avenue, New York, New York 10010 (800) 221-7945; *The Statesman's Year-Book.*

Statistical Office of the United Nations, Publishing Service, New York, New York 10017 (800) 253-9646; *Statistical Yearbook.*

SIERRA LEONE - DEATH RATES - See SIERRA LEONE - MORTALITY

SIERRA LEONE - DEFENSE EXPENDITURES - See SIERRA LEONE - MILITARY

SIERRA LEONE - DEMOGRAPHY

The Economist Intelligence Unit, 111 West 57th Street, New York, New York 10019 (800) 938-4685; *The World Market Atlas.*

Euromonitor International, Inc., 122 South Michigan Avenue, Suite 1200, Chicago, Illinois 60603 (800) 577-EURO; *International Marketing Data and Statistics; World Marketing Data and Statistics;* and *The World Economic Factbook.*

Federal Statistical Office, Gustav-Stresemann - Ring 11, D-6200, Wiesbaden, Germany; *Sierra Leone.*

M.E. Sharpe, 80 Business Park Drive, Armonk, New York 10504 (800) 541-6563; *The Illustrated Book of World Rankings.*

Statistical Office of the United Nations, Publishing Service, New York, New York 10017 (800) 253-9646; *Human Development Report;* and *Survey of Economic and Social Conditions in Africa.*

SIERRA LEONE - DEVELOPMENT ASSISTANCE

Statistical Office of the United Nations, Publishing Service, New York, New York 10017 (800) 253-9646; *Statistical Yearbook.*

SIERRA LEONE - DIAMOND EXPORTS - See SIERRA LEONE - MINING AND MINERAL PRODUCTS

SIERRA LEONE - DIAMOND PRODUCTION - See SIERRA LEONE - MINING AND MINERAL PRODUCTS

SIERRA LEONE - DISEASES - See SIERRA LEONE - HEALTH

SIERRA LEONE - DIVORCE RATES

M.E. Sharpe, 80 Business Park Drive, Armonk, New York 10504 (800) 541-6563; *The Illustrated Book of World Rankings.*

Statistical Office of the United Nations, Publishing Service, New York, New York 10017 (800) 253-9646; *Demographic Yearbook.*

SIERRA LEONE - ECONOMY

African Development Bank, 01 BP 1387, Abidjan 01, Cote D'Ivoire; *Selected Statistics on Regional Member Countries.*

Central Intelligence Agency, Washington, D.C. 20505 (703) 482-1100, www.cia.gov; *The World Factbook.*

Economist Intelligence Unit, 111 West 57th Street, New York, New York 10019 (800) 938-4685; *Sierra Leone Country Report.*

Euromonitor International, Inc., 122 South Michigan Avenue, Suite 1200, Chicago, Illinois 60603 (800) 577-EURO; *International Marketing Data and Statistics; World Marketing Data and Statistics;* and *The World Economic Factbook.*

Europa Publications Limited, 18 Bedford Square, London, WC1B 3JN, England; *The Europa World Year Book.*

Federal Statistical Office, Gustav-Stresemann - Ring 11, D-6200, Wiesbaden, Germany; *Sierra Leone.*

M.E. Sharpe, 80 Business Park Drive, Armonk, New York 10504 (800) 541-6563; *The Illustrated Book of World Rankings.*

St. Martin's Press, Inc., 175 Fifth Avenue, New York, New York 10010 (800) 221-7945; *The Statesman's Year-Book.*

Statistical Office of the United Nations, Publishing Service, New York, New York 10017 (800) 253-9646; *Foreign Trade Statistics for Africa;* and *World Statistics*

Pocketbook.

The World Bank, 1818 H Street, NW, Washington, D.C. 20433 (202) 477-1234; *The World Bank Atlas;* and *World Development Report.*

SIERRA LEONE - EDUCATION

African Development Bank, 01 BP 1387, Abidjan 01, Cote D'Ivoire; *Selected Statistics on Regional Member Countries.*

The Economist Intelligence Unit, 111 West 57th Street, New York, New York 10019 (800) 938-4685; *The World Market Atlas.*

Euromonitor International, Inc., 122 South Michigan Avenue, Suite 1200, Chicago, Illinois 60603 (800) 577-EURO; *International Marketing Data and Statistics;* and *World Marketing Data and Statistics..*

Europa Publications Limited, 18 Bedford Square, London, WC1B 3JN, England; *The Europa World Year Book.*

Federal Statistical Office, Gustav-Stresemann - Ring 11, D-6200, Wiesbaden, Germany; *Sierra Leone.*

International Monetary Fund, 700 Nineteenth Street, NW, Washington, D.C. 20431 (202) 623-7000; *Government Finance Statistics Yearbook.*

M.E. Sharpe, 80 Business Park Drive, Armonk, New York 10504 (800) 541-6563; *The Illustrated Book of World Rankings.*

St. Martin's Press, Inc., 175 Fifth Avenue, New York, New York 10010 (800) 221-7945; *The Statesman's Year-Book.*

Statistical Office of the United Nations, Publishing Service, New York, New York 10017 (800) 253-9646; *Human Development Report;* and *Survey of Economic and Social Conditions in Africa.*

United Nations Economic Commission for Africa, Africa Hall, P.O. Box 3001, Addis Ababa, Ethiopia (Telephone Number in U.S. (800) 253-9646); *African Statistical Yearbook.*

United Nations Educational, Scientific and Cultural Organization (UNESCO), 7 Place de Fontenoy, F-75700 Paris, France (Telephone Number in U.S. (212) 963-5981); *Statistical Yearbook.*

The World Bank, 1818 H Street, NW, Washington, D.C. 20433 (202) 477-1234; *World Development Report;* and *World Development Indicators.*

SIERRA LEONE - EGG PRODUCTION AND CONSUMPTION - See SIERRA LEONE - DAIRY PRODUCTS

SIERRA LEONE - ELECTRICITY

Central Intelligence Agency, Washington, D.C. 20505 (703) 482-1100, www.cia.gov; *The World Factbook.*

M.E. Sharpe, 80 Business Park Drive, Armonk, New York 10504 (800) 541-6563; *The Illustrated Book of World Rankings.*

St. Martin's Press, Inc., 175 Fifth Avenue, New York, New York 10010 (800) 221-7945; *The Statesman's Year-Book.*

Statistical Office of the United Nations, Publishing Service, New York, New York 10017 (800) 253-9646; *Human Development Report; Statistical Yearbook; and Survey of Economic and Social Conditions in Africa.*

United Nations Economic Commission for Africa, Africa Hall, P.O. Box 3001, Addis Ababa, Ethiopia (Telephone Number in U.S. (800) 253-9646); *African Statistical Yearbook.*

SIERRA LEONE - EMPLOYMENT

Euromonitor International, Inc., 122 South Michigan Avenue, Suite 1200, Chicago, Illinois 60603 (800) 577-EURO; *International Marketing Data and Statistics.*

Federal Statistical Office, Gustav-Stresemann - Ring 11, D-6200, Wiesbaden, Germany; *Sierra Leone.*

International Labour Office, I.L.O. Publications, 1828 L Street, NW., Suite 801, Washington, D.C. 20036 (301) 638-3152; *Yearbook of Labour Statistics.*

M.E. Sharpe, 80 Business Park Drive, Armonk, New York 10504 (800) 541-6563; *The Illustrated Book of World Rankings.*

Statistical Office of the United Nations, Publishing Service, New York, New York 10017 (800) 253-9646; *Statistical Yearbook; and Survey of Economic and Social Conditions in Africa.*

SIERRA LEONE - ENERGY

Euromonitor International, Inc., 122 South Michigan Avenue, Suite 1200, Chicago, Illinois 60603 (800) 577-EURO; *International Marketing Data and Statistics; World Marketing Data and Statistics; and The World Economic Factbook.*

Food and Agricultural Organization of the United Nations (FAO) Via delle Terme di Caracalla, 00100 Rome, Italy (Telephone Number in U.S. (202) 653-2400); *The State of Food and Agriculture.*

M.E. Sharpe, 80 Business Park Drive, Armonk, New York 10504 (800) 541-6563; *The Illustrated Book of World Rankings.*

St. Martin's Press, Inc., 175 Fifth Avenue, New York, New York 10010 (800) 221-7945; *The Statesman's Year-Book.*

Statistical Office of the United Nations, Publishing Service, New York, New York 10017 (800) 253-9646; *Energy Statistics Yearbook; Human Development Report; Statistical Yearbook; and World Statistics Pocketbook.*

United Nations Economic Commission for Africa, Africa Hall, P.O. Box 3001, Addis Ababa, Ethiopia (Telephone Number in U.S. (800) 253-9646); *African Statistical Yearbook.*

The World Bank, 1818 H Street, NW, Washington, D.C. 20433 (202) 477-1234; *The World Bank Atlas; and World Development Report.*

SIERRA LEONE - ENVIRONMENT

Economist Intelligence Unit, 111 West 57th Street, New York, New York 10019 (800) 938-4685; *Sierra Leone Country Report.*

Statistical Office of the United Nations, Publishing Service, New York, New York 10017 (800) 253-9646; *World Statistics Pocketbook.*

SIERRA LEONE - EXCHANGE RATES

African Development Bank, 01 BP 1387, Abidjan 01, Cote D'Ivoire; *Selected Statistics on Regional Member Countries.*

Central Intelligence Agency, Washington, D.C. 20505 (703) 482-1100, www.cia.gov; *The World Factbook.*

Euromonitor International, Inc., 122 South Michigan Avenue, Suite 1200, Chicago, Illinois 60603 (800) 577-EURO; *International Marketing Data and Statistics; and The World Economic Factbook.*

Europa Publications Limited, 18 Bedford Square, London, WC1B 3JN, England; *The Europa World Year Book.*

International Monetary Fund, 700 Nineteenth Street, NW, Washington, D.C. 20431 (202) 623-7000; *International Financial Statistics.*

Statistical Office of the United Nations, Publishing Service, New York, New York 10017 (800) 253-9646; *Foreign Trade Statistics for Africa; Statistical Yearbook; and World Statistics Pocketbook.*

SIERRA LEONE - EXCISE TAXES - See SIERRA LEONE - TAXATION

SIERRA LEONE - EXPORTS

African Development Bank, 01 BP 1387,

Abidjan 01, Cote D'Ivoire; *Selected Statistics on Regional Member Countries.*

Central Intelligence Agency, Washington, D.C. 20505 (703) 482-1100, www.cia.gov; *The World Factbook.*

The Economist Intelligence Unit, 111 West 57th Street, New York, New York 10019 (800) 938-4685; *Sierra Leone Country Report; and The World Market Atlas.*

Euromonitor International, Inc., 122 South Michigan Avenue, Suite 1200, Chicago, Illinois 60603 (800) 577-EURO; *International Marketing Data and Statistics; and The World Economic Factbook.*

Europa Publications Limited, 18 Bedford Square, London, WC1B 3JN, England; *The Europa World Year Book.*

Food and Agricultural Organization of the United Nations (FAO) Via delle Terme di Caracalla, 00100 Rome, Italy (Telephone Number in U.S. (202) 653-2400); *The State of Food and Agriculture.*

International Monetary Fund, 700 Nineteenth Street, NW, Washington, D.C. 20431 (202) 623-7000; *Direction of Trade Statistics; Government Finance Statistics Yearbook; and International Financial Statistics.*

St. Martin's Press, Inc., 175 Fifth Avenue, New York, New York 10010 (800) 221-7945; *The Statesman's Year-Book.*

Statistical Office of the United Nations, Publishing Service, New York, New York 10017 (800) 253-9646; *Foreign Trade Statistics for Africa; and Survey of Economic and Social Conditions in Africa.*

United Nations Conference on Trade and Development (UNCTAD), New York, New York 10017 (800) 253-9646; *Handbook of International Trade and Development Statistics.*

United Nations Economic Commission for Africa, Africa Hall, P.O. Box 3001, Addis Ababa, Ethiopia (Telephone Number in U.S. (800) 253-9646); *African Statistical Yearbook.*

The World Bank, 1818 H Street, NW, Washington, D.C. 20433 (202) 477-1234; *World Development Report; and World Development Indicators.*

SIERRA LEONE - EXTERNAL INDEBTEDNESS

Statistical Office of the United Nations, Publishing Service, New York, New York 10017 (800) 253-9646; *Survey of Economic and Social Conditions in Africa.*

The World Bank, 1818 H Street, NW,

Washington, D.C. 20433 (202) 477-1234; *World Development Report;* and *World Development Indicators.*

SIERRA LEONE - EXTERNAL TRADE

African Development Bank, 01 BP 1387, Abidjan 01, Cote D'Ivoire; *Selected Statistics on Regional Member Countries.*

Euromonitor International Inc., 122 South Michigan Avenue, Suite 1200, Chicago, Illinois 60603 (800) 577-EURO; *World Marketing Data and Statistics.*

Food and Agricultural Organization of the United Nations (FAO) Via delle Terme di Caracalla, 00100 Rome, Italy (Telephone Number in U.S. (202) 653-2400); *The State of Food and Agriculture;* and *Trade Yearbook.*

Statistical Office of the United Nations, Publishing Service, New York, New York 10017 (800) 253-9646; *Statistical Yearbook;* and *Survey of Economic and Social Conditions in Africa.*

SIERRA LEONE - FARM CROPS - See SIERRA LEONE - CROPS

SIERRA LEONE - FEMALE WORKING POPULATION - See SIERRA LEONE - EMPLOYMENT

SIERRA LEONE - FERTILITY RATES

Central Intelligence Agency, Washington, D.C. 20505 (703) 482-1100, www.cia.gov; *The World Factbook.*

M.E. Sharpe, 80 Business Park Drive, Armonk, New York 10504 (800) 541-6563; *The Illustrated Book of World Rankings.*

Statistical Office of the United Nations, Publishing Service, New York, New York 10017 (800) 253-9646; *Human Development Report;* and *Survey of Economic and Social Conditions in Africa.*

The World Bank, 1818 H Street, NW, Washington, D.C. 20433 (202) 477-1234; *The World Bank Atlas; World Development Report;* and *World Development Indicators.*

SIERRA LEONE - FERTILIZER

Food and Agricultural Organization of the United Nations (FAO), Via delle Terme di Caracalla, 00100, Rome, Italy (Telephone Number in U.S. (202) 653-2400); *Fertilizer Yearbook;* and *The State of Food and Agriculture.*

Statistical Office of the United Nations, Publishing Service, New York, New York 10017 (800) 253-9646; *Statistical Yearbook.*

SIERRA LEONE - FETAL MORTALITY - See SIERRA LEONE - MORTALITY

SIERRA LEONE - FILM - See SIERRA LEONE - MOTION PICTURES

SIERRA LEONE - FINANCE

African Development Bank, 01 BP 1387, Abidjan 01, Cote D'Ivoire; *Selected Statistics on Regional Member Countries.*

Economist Intelligence Unit, 111 West 57th Street, New York, New York 10019 (800) 938-4685; *Sierra Leone Country Report.*

Europa Publications Limited, 18 Bedford Square, London, WC1B 3JN, England; *The Europa World Year Book.*

Federal Statistical Office, Gustav-Stresemann - Ring 11, D-6200, Wiesbaden, Germany; *Sierra Leone.*

International Monetary Fund, 700 Nineteenth Street, NW, Washington, D.C. 20431 (202) 623-7000; *Government Finance Statistics Yearbook;* and *International Financial Statistics.*

M.E. Sharpe, 80 Business Park Drive, Armonk, New York 10504 (800) 541-6563; *The Illustrated Book of World Rankings.*

St. Martin's Press, Inc., 175 Fifth Avenue, New York, New York 10010 (800) 221-7945; *The Statesman's Year-Book.*

United Nations Economic Commission for Africa, Africa Hall, P.O. Box 3001, Addis Ababa, Ethiopia (Telephone Number in U.S. (800) 253-9646); *African Statistical Yearbook.*

SIERRA LEONE - FISHERIES

Europa Publications Limited, 18 Bedford Square, London, WC1B 3JN, England; *The Europa World Year Book.*

Federal Statistical Office, Gustav-Stresemann - Ring 11, D-6200, Wiesbaden, Germany; *Sierra Leone.*

Food and Agricultural Organization of the United Nations (FAO) Via delle Terme di Caracalla, 00100 Rome, Italy (Telephone Number in U.S. (202) 653-2400); *The State of Food and Agriculture;* and *Yearbook of Fishery Statistics.*

M.E. Sharpe, 80 Business Park Drive, Armonk, New York 10504 (800) 541-6563; *The Illustrated Book of World Rankings.*

St. Martin's Press, Inc., 175 Fifth Avenue, New York, New York 10010 (800) 221-7945; *The Statesman's Year-Book.*

Statistical Office of the United Nations, Publishing Service, New York, New York 10017 (800) 253-9646; *Statistical Yearbook;* and *Survey of Economic and Social*

Conditions in Africa.

United Nations Conference on Trade and Development, Central Statistical Service, Palais des Nations, Geneva, Switzerland (Telephone in U.S. (800) 253-9646); *UNCTAD Commodity Yearbook.*

United Nations Economic Commission for Africa, Africa Hall, P.O. Box 3001, Addis Ababa, Ethiopia (Telephone Number in U.S. (800) 253-9646); *African Statistical Yearbook.*

SIERRA LEONE - FLOUR PRODUCTION

Statistical Office of the United Nations, Publishing Service, New York, New York 10017 (800) 253-9646; *Statistical Yearbook.*

SIERRA LEONE - FOOD

African Development Bank, 01 BP 1387, Abidjan 01, Cote D'Ivoire; *Selected Statistics on Regional Member Countries.*

Food and Agricultural Organization of the United Nations (FAO) Via delle Terme di Caracalla, 00100 Rome, Italy (Telephone Number in U.S. (202) 653-2400); *Production Yearbook;* and *The State of Food and Agriculture.*

Statistical Office of the United Nations, Publishing Service, New York, New York 10017 (800) 253-9646; *Human Development Report.*

United Nations Conference on Trade and Development, Central Statistical Service, Palais des Nations, Geneva, Switzerland (Telephone in U.S. (800) 253-9646); *UNCTAD Commodity Yearbook.*

SIERRA LEONE - FOREIGN DEBT

International Monetary Fund, 700 Nineteenth Street, NW, Washington, D.C. 20431 (202) 623-7000; *Government Finance Statistics Yearbook.*

SIERRA LEONE - FOREIGN TRADE

Economist Intelligence Unit, 111 West 57th Street, New York, New York 10019 (800) 938-4685; *Sierra Leone Country Report.*

Euromonitor International, Inc., 122 South Michigan Avenue, Suite 1200, Chicago, Illinois 60603 (800) 577-EURO; *International Marketing Data and Statistics;* and *The World Economic Factbook.*

Europa Publications Limited, 18 Bedford Square, London, WC1B 3JN, England; *The Europa World Year Book.*

Federal Statistical Office, Gustav-Stresemann - Ring 11, D-6200, Wiesbaden, Germany; *Sierra Leone.*

Food and Agricultural Organization of the United Nations (FAO) Via delle Terme di Caracalla, 00100 Rome, Italy (Telephone Number in U.S. (202) 653-2400); *The State of Food and Agriculture.*

International Monetary Fund, 700 Nineteenth Street, NW, Washington, D.C. 20431 (202) 623-7000; *International Financial Statistics.*

M.E. Sharpe, 80 Business Park Drive, Armonk, New York 10504 (800) 541-6563; *The Illustrated Book of World Rankings.*

St. Martin's Press, Inc., 175 Fifth Avenue, New York, New York 10010 (800) 221-7945; *The Statesman's Year-Book.*

Statistical Office of the United Nations, Publishing Service, New York, New York 10017 (800) 253-9646; *Foreign Trade Statistics for Africa; International Trade Statistics Yearbook;* and *Statistical Yearbook.*

United Nations Conference on Trade and Development, Central Statistical Service, Palais des Nations, Geneva, Switzerland (Telephone in U.S. (800) 253-9646); *UNCTAD Commodity Yearbook.*

United Nations Economic Commission for Africa, Africa Hall, P.O. Box 3001, Addis Ababa, Ethiopia (Telephone Number in U.S. (800) 253-9646); *African Statistical Yearbook.*

The World Bank, 1818 H Street, NW, Washington, D.C. 20433 (202) 477-1234; *World Development Report;* and *World Development Indicators.*

SIERRA LEONE - FORESTRY AND FOREST PRODUCTS

Europa Publications Limited, 18 Bedford Square, London, WC1B 3JN, England; *The Europa World Year Book.*

Federal Statistical Office, Gustav-Stresemann - Ring 11, D-6200, Wiesbaden, Germany; *Sierra Leone.*

Food and Agricultural Organization of the United Nations (FAO) Via delle Terme di Caracalla, 00100 Rome, Italy (Telephone Number in U.S. (202) 653-2400); *The State of Food and Agriculture;* and *Yearbook of Forest Products.*

M.E. Sharpe, 80 Business Park Drive, Armonk, New York 10504 (800) 541-6563; *The Illustrated Book of World Rankings.*

Statistical Office of the United Nations, Publishing Service, New York, New York 10017 (800) 253-9646; *Statistical Yearbook.*

United Nations Conference on Trade and Development, Central Statistical

Service, Palais des Nations, Geneva, Switzerland (Telephone in U.S. (800) 253-9646); *UNCTAD Commodity Yearbook.*

United Nations Economic Commission for Africa, Africa Hall, P.O. Box 3001, Addis Ababa, Ethiopia (Telephone Number in U.S. (800) 253-9646); *African Statistical Yearbook.*

United Nations Educational, Scientific and Cultural Organization (UNESCO), 7 Place de Fontenoy, F-75700 Paris, France (Telephone Number in U.S. (212) 963-5981); *Statistical Yearbook.*

The World Bank, 1818 H Street, NW, Washington, D.C. 20433 (202) 477-1234; *World Development Report.*

SIERRA LEONE - GAS PRODUCTION - See SIERRA LEONE - MINING AND MINERAL PRODUCTS

SIERRA LEONE - GENERAL MORTALITY - See SIERRA LEONE - MORTALITY

SIERRA LEONE - GEOGRAPHIC DATA

M.E. Sharpe, 80 Business Park Drive, Armonk, New York 10504 (800) 541-6563; *The Illustrated Book of World Rankings.*

SIERRA LEONE - GOATS - See SIERRA LEONE - LIVESTOCK AND POULTRY

SIERRA LEONE - GOLD HOLDINGS

International Monetary Fund, 700 Nineteenth Street, NW, Washington, D.C. 20431 (202) 623-7000; *International Financial Statistics.*

Statistical Office of the United Nations, Publishing Service, New York, New York 10017 (800) 253-9646; *Statistical Yearbook.*

The World Bank, 1818 H Street, NW, Washington, D.C. 20433 (202) 477-1234; *World Development Indicators.*

SIERRA LEONE - GOLD PRODUCTION AND CONSUMPTION - See SIERRA LEONE - MINING AND MINERAL PRODUCTS

SIERRA LEONE - GOVERNMENT

Central Intelligence Agency, Washington, D.C. 20505 (703) 482-1100, www.cia.gov; *The World Factbook.*

Europa Publications Limited, 18 Bedford Square, London, WC1B 3JN, England; *The Europa World Year Book.*

International Monetary Fund, 700 Nineteenth Street, NW, Washington, D.C. 20431 (202) 623-7000; *Government Finance Statistics Yearbook;* and *International Financial Statistics.*

St. Martin's Press, Inc., 175 Fifth Avenue, New York, New York 10010 (800) 221-7945; *The Statesman's Year-Book.*

Statistical Office of the United Nations, Publishing Service, New York, New York 10017 (800) 253-9646; *National Accounts Statistics;* and *Survey of Economic and Social Conditions in Africa.*

The World Bank, 1818 H Street, NW, Washington, D.C. 20433 (202) 477-1234; *World Development Report;* and *World Development Indicators.*

SIERRA LEONE - GRAIN PRODUCTION - See SIERRA LEONE - CROPS

SIERRA LEONE - GRANTS

International Monetary Fund, 700 Nineteenth Street, NW, Washington, D.C. 20431 (202) 623-7000; *Government Finance Statistics Yearbook.*

SIERRA LEONE - GROSS DOMESTIC PRODUCT

African Development Bank, 01 BP 1387, Abidjan 01, Cote D'Ivoire; *Selected Statistics on Regional Member Countries.*

The Economist Intelligence Unit, 111 West 57th Street, New York, New York 10019 (800) 938-4685; *Sierra Leone Country Report;* and *The World Market Atlas.*

Euromonitor International, Inc., 122 South Michigan Avenue, Suite 1200, Chicago, Illinois 60603 (800) 577-EURO; *International Marketing Data and Statistics;* and *The World Economic Factbook.*

Europa Publications Limited, 18 Bedford Square, London, WC1B 3JN, England; *The Europa World Year Book.*

M.E. Sharpe, 80 Business Park Drive, Armonk, New York 10504 (800) 541-6563; *The Illustrated Book of World Rankings.*

Statistical Office of the United Nations, Publishing Service, New York, New York 10017 (800) 253-9646; *Human Development Report; National Accounts Statistics; Statistical Yearbook;* and *Survey of Economic and Social Conditions in Africa.*

United Nations Economic Commission for Africa, Africa Hall, P.O. Box 3001, Addis Ababa, Ethiopia (Telephone Number in U.S. (800) 253-9646); *African Statistical Yearbook.*

The World Bank, 1818 H Street, NW, Washington, D.C. 20433 (202) 477-1234; *World Development Report;* and *World Development Indicators.*

SIERRA LEONE - GROSS NATIONAL

PRODUCT

Euromonitor International, Inc., 122 South Michigan Avenue, Suite 1200, Chicago, Illinois 60603 (800) 577-EURO; *International Marketing Data and Statistics.*

Europa Publications Limited, 18 Bedford Square, London, WC1B 3JN, England; *The Europa World Year Book.*

St. Martin's Press, Inc., 175 Fifth Avenue, New York, New York 10010 (800) 221-7945; *The Statesman's Year-Book.*

U.S. Arms Control and Disarmament Agency, 320 Twenty-first Street, NW, Washington, D.C. 20451 (202) 647-8677; *World Military Expenditures and Arms Transfers.*

The World Bank, 1818 H Street, NW, Washington, D.C. 20433 (202) 477-1234; *The World Bank Atlas; World Development Report;* and *World Development Indicators.*

SIERRA LEONE - GROUNDNUTS PRODUCTION - See SIERRA LEONE - CROPS

SIERRA LEONE - HEALTH

African Development Bank, 01 BP 1387, Abidjan 01, Cote D'Ivoire; *Selected Statistics on Regional Member Countries.*

Euromonitor International Inc., 122 South Michigan Avenue, Suite 1200, Chicago, Illinois 60603 (800) 577-EURO; *World Marketing Data and Statistics.*

Federal Statistical Office, Gustav-Stresemann - Ring 11, D-6200, Wiesbaden, Germany; *Sierra Leone.*

International Monetary Fund, 700 Nineteenth Street, NW, Washington, D.C. 20431 (202) 623-7000; *Government Finance Statistics Yearbook.*

M.E. Sharpe, 80 Business Park Drive, Armonk, New York 10504 (800) 541-6563; *The Illustrated Book of World Rankings.*

St. Martin's Press, Inc., 175 Fifth Avenue, New York, New York 10010 (800) 221-7945; *The Statesman's Year-Book.*

Statistical Office of the United Nations, Publishing Service, New York, New York 10017 (800) 253-9646; *Human Development Report;* and *Statistical Yearbook.*

United Nations Children's Fund (UNICEF), 3 United Nations Plaza, New York, New York 10017 (800) 253-9646; *State of the World's Children.*

United Nations Economic Commission for Africa, Africa Hall, P.O. Box 3001, Addis Ababa, Ethiopia (Telephone Number in U.S. (800) 253-9646); *African Statistical Yearbook.*

The World Bank, 1818 H Street, NW, Washington, D.C. 20433 (202) 477-1234; *World Development Report.*

World Health Organization, Office of Publications, 20 Avenue Appia, CH-1211 Geneva 27, Switzerland (Telephone Number in U.S. (518) 436-9686); *World Health Statistics Annual.*

SIERRA LEONE - HIGHWAYS

Central Intelligence Agency, Washington, D.C. 20505 (703) 482-1100, www.cia.gov; *The World Factbook.*

International Road Federation, 2600 Virginia Avenue, NW, Washington, D.C. 20037 (202) 338-4641; *World Road Statistics.*

St. Martin's Press, Inc., 175 Fifth Avenue, New York, New York 10010 (800) 221-7945; *The Statesman's Year-Book.*

Statistical Office of the United Nations, Publishing Service, New York, New York 10017 (800) 253-9646; *Survey of Economic and Social Conditions in Africa.*

United Nations Economic Commission for Africa, Africa Hall, P.O. Box 3001, Addis Ababa, Ethiopia (Telephone Number in U.S. (800) 253-9646); *African Statistical Yearbook.*

SIERRA LEONE - HORSES - See SIERRA LEONE - LIVESTOCK AND POULTRY

SIERRA LEONE - HOURS OF WORK - See SIERRA LEONE - EMPLOYMENT

SIERRA LEONE - HOUSING AND HOUSING UNITS

Euromonitor International Inc., 122 South Michigan Avenue, Suite 1200, Chicago, Illinois 60603 (800) 577-EURO; *World Marketing Data and Statistics.*

SIERRA LEONE - HOUSING EXPENDITURES

International Monetary Fund, 700 Nineteenth Street, NW, Washington, D.C. 20431 (202) 623-7000; *Government Finance Statistics Yearbook.*

M.E. Sharpe, 80 Business Park Drive, Armonk, New York 10504 (800) 541-6563; *The Illustrated Book of World Rankings.*

SIERRA LEONE - ILLITERATE POPULATION

Central Intelligence Agency, Washington, D.C. 20505 (703) 482-1100, www.cia.gov; *The World Factbook.*

The Economist Intelligence Unit, 111 West 57th Street, New York, New York 10019 (800) 938-4685; *The World Market Atlas.*

Euromonitor International, Inc., 122 South Michigan Avenue, Suite 1200, Chicago, Illinois 60603 (800) 577-EURO; *The World Economic Factbook.*

Statistical Office of the United Nations, Publishing Service, New York, New York 10017 (800) 253-9646; *Human Development Report.*

United Nations Educational, Scientific and Cultural Organization (UNESCO), 7 Place de Fontenoy, F-75700 Paris, France (Telephone Number in U.S. (212) 963-5981); *Statistical Yearbook.*

SIERRA LEONE - IMPORTS

African Development Bank, 01 BP 1387, Abidjan 01, Cote D'Ivoire; *Selected Statistics on Regional Member Countries.*

Central Intelligence Agency, Washington, D.C. 20505 (703) 482-1100, www.cia.gov; *The World Factbook.*

The Economist Intelligence Unit, 111 West 57th Street, New York, New York 10019 (800) 938-4685; *Sierra Leone Country Report;* and *The World Market Atlas.*

Euromonitor International, Inc., 122 South Michigan Avenue, Suite 1200, Chicago, Illinois 60603 (800) 577-EURO; *International Marketing Data and Statistics;* and *The World Economic Factbook.*

Europa Publications Limited, 18 Bedford Square, London, WC1B 3JN, England; *The Europa World Year Book.*

Food and Agricultural Organization of the United Nations (FAO) Via delle Terme di Caracalla, 00100 Rome, Italy (Telephone Number in U.S. (202) 653-2400); *The State of Food and Agriculture.*

International Monetary Fund, 700 Nineteenth Street, NW, Washington, D.C. 20431 (202) 623-7000; *Direction of Trade Statistics; Government Finance Statistics Yearbook;* and *International Financial Statistics.*

St. Martin's Press, Inc., 175 Fifth Avenue, New York, New York 10010 (800) 221-7945; *The Statesman's Year-Book.*

Statistical Office of the United Nations, Publishing Service, New York, New York 10017 (800) 253-9646; *Foreign Trade Statistics for Africa;* and *Survey of Economic and Social Conditions in Africa.*

United Nations Conference on Trade and Development (UNCTAD), New York,

New York 10017 (800) 253-9646; *Handbook of International Trade and Development Statistics.*

United Nations Economic Commission for Africa, Africa Hall, P.O. Box 3001, Addis Ababa, Ethiopia (Telephone Number in U.S. (800) 253-9646); *African Statistical Yearbook.*

The World Bank, 1818 H Street, NW, Washington, D.C. 20433 (202) 477-1234; *World Development Report;* and *World Development Indicators.*

SIERRA LEONE - INCOME TAXES - See SIERRA LEONE - TAXATION

SIERRA LEONE - INDUSTRY

Central Intelligence Agency, Washington, D.C. 20505 (703) 482-1100, www.cia.gov; *The World Factbook.*

Economist Intelligence Unit, 111 West 57th Street, New York, New York 10019 (800) 938-4685; *Sierra Leone Country Report.*

Euromonitor International, Inc., 122 South Michigan Avenue, Suite 1200, Chicago, Illinois 60603 (800) 577-EURO; *International Marketing Data and Statistics; World Marketing Data and Statistics;* and *The World Economic Factbook.*

Europa Publications Limited, 18 Bedford Square, London, WC1B 3JN, England; *The Europa World Year Book.*

Federal Statistical Office, Gustav-Stresemann - Ring 11, D-6200, Wiesbaden, Germany; *Sierra Leone.*

International Labour Office, I.L.O. Publications, 1828 L Street, NW., Suite 801, Washington, D.C. 20036 (301) 638-3152; *Yearbook of Labour Statistics.*

M.E. Sharpe, 80 Business Park Drive, Armonk, New York 10504 (800) 541-6563; *The Illustrated Book of World Rankings.*

St. Martin's Press, Inc., 175 Fifth Avenue, New York, New York 10010 (800) 221-7945; *The Statesman's Year-Book.*

Statistical Office of the United Nations, Publishing Service, New York, New York 10017 (800) 253-9646; *Statistical Yearbook;* and *Survey of Economic and Social Conditions in Africa.*

United Nations Economic Commission for Africa, Africa Hall, P.O. Box 3001, Addis Ababa, Ethiopia (Telephone Number in U.S. (800) 253-9646); *African Statistical Yearbook.*

The World Bank, 1818 H Street, NW, Washington, D.C. 20433 (202) 477-1234;

World Development Indicators.

SIERRA LEONE - INFANT AND MATERNAL MORTALITY - See SIERRA LEONE - MORTALITY

SIERRA LEONE - INTERNATIONAL LIQUIDITY

International Monetary Fund, 700 Nineteenth Street, NW, Washington, D.C. 20431 (202) 623-7000; *International Financial Statistics.*

SIERRA LEONE - INTERNATIONAL RESERVES EXCLUDING GOLD

African Development Bank, 01 BP 1387, Abidjan 01, Cote D'Ivoire; *Selected Statistics on Regional Member Countries.*

Statistical Office of the United Nations, Publishing Service, New York, New York 10017 (800) 253-9646; *Statistical Yearbook.*

The World Bank, 1818 H Street, NW, Washington, D.C. 20433 (202) 477-1234; *World Development Indicators.*

SIERRA LEONE - IRON ORE PRODUCTION AND CONSUMPTION - See SIERRA LEONE - MINING AND MINERAL PRODUCTS

SIERRA LEONE - IRRIGATION

Euromonitor International, Inc., 122 South Michigan Avenue, Suite 1200, Chicago, Illinois 60603 (800) 577-EURO; *International Marketing Data and Statistics.*

SIERRA LEONE - LABOR

African Development Bank, 01 BP 1387, Abidjan 01, Cote D'Ivoire; *Selected Statistics on Regional Member Countries.*

Central Intelligence Agency, Washington, D.C. 20505 (703) 482-1100, www.cia.gov; *The World Factbook.*

Euromonitor International, Inc., 122 South Michigan Avenue, Suite 1200, Chicago, Illinois 60603 (800) 577-EURO; *International Marketing Data and Statistics;* and *World Marketing Data and Statistics.*

Europa Publications Limited, 18 Bedford Square, London, WC1B 3JN, England; *The Europa World Year Book.*

Food and Agricultural Organization of the United Nations (FAO) Via delle Terme di Caracalla, 00100 Rome, Italy (Telephone Number in U.S. (202) 653-2400); *The State of Food and Agriculture.*

International Labour Office, I.L.O. Publications, 1828 L Street, NW., Suite 801, Washington, D.C. 20036 (301) 638-3152; *Yearbook of Labour Statistics.*

M.E. Sharpe, 80 Business Park Drive, Armonk, New York 10504 (800) 541-6563; *The Illustrated Book of World Rankings.*

St. Martin's Press, Inc., 175 Fifth Avenue, New York, New York 10010 (800) 221-7945; *The Statesman's Year-Book.*

Statistical Office of the United Nations, Publishing Service, New York, New York 10017 (800) 253-9646; *Human Development Report.*

The World Bank, 1818 H Street, NW, Washington, D.C. 20433 (202) 477-1234; *The World Bank Atlas; World Development Report;* and *World Development Indicators.*

SIERRA LEONE - LAND USE

Central Intelligence Agency, Washington, D.C. 20505 (703) 482-1100, www.cia.gov; *The World Factbook.*

Euromonitor International, Inc., 122 South Michigan Avenue, Suite 1200, Chicago, Illinois 60603 (800) 577-EURO; *International Marketing Data and Statistics.*

Food and Agricultural Organization of the United Nations (FAO), Via delle Terme di Caracalla, 00100 Rome, Italy (Telephone Number in U.S. (202) 653-2400); *Production Yearbook.*

The World Bank, 1818 H Street, NW, Washington, D.C. 20433 (202) 477-1234; *World Development Report.*

SIERRA LEONE - LIBRARIES

M.E. Sharpe, 80 Business Park Drive, Armonk, New York 10504 (800) 541-6563; *The Illustrated Book of World Rankings.*

United Nations Educational, Scientific and Cultural Organization (UNESCO), 7 Place de Fontenoy, F-75700 Paris, France (Telephone Number in U.S. (212) 963-5981); *Statistical Yearbook.*

SIERRA LEONE - LIFE EXPECTANCY

African Development Bank, 01 BP 1387, Abidjan 01, Cote D'Ivoire; *Selected Statistics on Regional Member Countries.*

Central Intelligence Agency, Washington, D.C. 20505 (703) 482-1100, www.cia.gov; *The World Factbook.*

Euromonitor International, Inc., 122 South Michigan Avenue, Suite 1200, Chicago, Illinois 60603 (800) 577-EURO; *The World Economic Factbook.*

St. Martin's Press, Inc., 175 Fifth Avenue, New York, New York 10010 (800) 221-7945; *The Statesman's Year-Book.*

Statistical Office of the United Nations,

Publishing Service, New York, New York 10017 (800) 253-9646; *Human Development Report;* and *World Statistics Pocketbook.*

The World Bank, 1818 H Street, NW, Washington, D.C. 20433 (202) 477-1234; *The World Bank Atlas;* and *World Development Report.*

SIERRA LEONE - LITERACY RATE

Euromonitor International Inc., 122 South Michigan Avenue, Suite 1200, Chicago, Illinois 60603 (800) 577-EURO; *World Marketing Data and Statistics.*

Statistical Office of the United Nations, Publishing Service, New York, New York 10017 (800) 253-9646; *Survey of Economic and Social Conditions in Africa.*

SIERRA LEONE - LIVESTOCK AND POULTRY

Euromonitor International, Inc., 122 South Michigan Avenue, Suite 1200, Chicago, Illinois 60603 (800) 577-EURO; *International Marketing Data and Statistics.*

Europa Publications Limited, 18 Bedford Square, London, WC1B 3JN, England; *The Europa World Year Book.*

Food and Agricultural Organization of the United Nations (FAO), Via delle Terme di Caracalla, 00100 Rome, Italy (Telephone Number in U.S. (202) 653-2400); *Production Yearbook;* and *The State of Food and Agriculture.*

M.E. Sharpe, 80 Business Park Drive, Armonk, New York 10504 (800) 541-6563; *The Illustrated Book of World Rankings.*

St. Martin's Press, Inc., 175 Fifth Avenue, New York, New York 10010 (800) 221-7945; *The Statesman's Year-Book.*

Statistical Office of the United Nations, Publishing Service, New York, New York 10017 (800) 253-9646; *Statistical Yearbook;* and *Survey of Economic and Social Conditions in Africa.*

United Nations Conference on Trade and Development, Central Statistical Service, Palais des Nations, Geneva, Switzerland (Telephone in U.S. (800) 253-9646); *UNCTAD Commodity Yearbook.*

United Nations Economic Commission for Africa, Africa Hall, P.O. Box 3001, Addis Ababa, Ethiopia (Telephone Number in U.S. (800) 253-9646); *African Statistical Yearbook.*

SIERRA LEONE - LIVING LEVELS - See SIERRA LEONE - LIFE EXPECTANCY

SIERRA LEONE - MAIL - NUMBER OF ITEMS

SENT AND RECEIVED

Statistical Office of the United Nations, Publishing Service, New York, New York 10017 (800) 253-9646; *Statistical Yearbook.*

SIERRA LEONE - MANUFACTURING

M.E. Sharpe, 80 Business Park Drive, Armonk, New York 10504 (800) 541-6563; *The Illustrated Book of World Rankings.*

Statistical Office of the United Nations, Publishing Service, New York, New York 10017 (800) 253-9646; *Survey of Economic and Social Conditions in Africa.*

United Nations Economic Commission for Africa, Africa Hall, P.O. Box 3001, Addis Ababa, Ethiopia (Telephone Number in U.S. (800) 253-9646); *African Statistical Yearbook.*

The World Bank, 1818 H Street, NW, Washington, D.C. 20433 (202) 477-1234; *World Development Indicators.*

SIERRA LEONE - MARRIAGE RATES

M.E. Sharpe, 80 Business Park Drive, Armonk, New York 10504 (800) 541-6563; *The Illustrated Book of World Rankings.*

Statistical Office of the United Nations, Publishing Service, New York, New York 10017 (800) 253-9646; *Demographic Yearbook.*

SIERRA LEONE - MEAT PRODUCTION - See SIERRA LEONE - LIVESTOCK AND POULTRY

SIERRA LEONE - MERCHANT SHIPPING

Europa Publications Limited, 18 Bedford Square, London, WC1B 3JN, England; *The Europa World Year Book.*

St. Martin's Press, Inc., 175 Fifth Avenue, New York, New York 10010 (800) 221-7945; *The Statesman's Year-Book.*

Statistical Office of the United Nations, Publishing Service, New York, New York 10017 (800) 253-9646; *Statistical Yearbook.*

United Nations Economic Commission for Africa, Africa Hall, P.O. Box 3001, Addis Ababa, Ethiopia (Telephone Number in U.S. (800) 253-9646); *African Statistical Yearbook.*

U.S. Department of Transportation, Maritime Administration, 400 Seventh Street, SW, Washington, D.C. 20590 (202) 366-5807, www.marad.dot.gov; *A Statistical Analysis of the World's Merchant Fleets.*

SIERRA LEONE - MILITARY

Central Intelligence Agency, Washington, D.C. 20505 (703) 482-1100, www.cia.gov; *The World Factbook.*

Euromonitor International Inc., 122 South Michigan Avenue, Suite 1200, Chicago, Illinois 60603 (800) 577-EURO; *World Marketing Data and Statistics.*

The International Institute for Strategic Studies, 23 Tavistock Street, London WC2E 7NQ, England 44 171 3797676; *The Military Balance.*

International Monetary Fund, 700 Nineteenth Street, NW, Washington, D.C. 20431 (202) 623-7000; *Government Finance Statistics Yearbook.*

St. Martin's Press, Inc., 175 Fifth Avenue, New York, New York 10010 (800) 221-7945; *The Statesman's Year-Book.*

Statistical Office of the United Nations, Publishing Service, New York, New York 10017 (800) 253-9646; *Human Development Report.*

U.S. Arms Control and Disarmament Agency, 320 Twenty-first Street, NW, Washington, D.C. 20451 (202) 647-8677; *World Military Expenditures and Arms Transfers.*

SIERRA LEONE - MILK PRODUCTION - See SIERRA LEONE - DAIRY PRODUCTS

SIERRA LEONE - MINING AND MINERAL PRODUCTS

Europa Publications Limited, 18 Bedford Square, London, WC1B 3JN, England; *The Europa World Year Book.*

International Monetary Fund, 700 Nineteenth Street, NW, Washington, D.C. 20431 (202) 623-7000; *International Financial Statistics.*

M.E. Sharpe, 80 Business Park Drive, Armonk, New York 10504 (800) 541-6563; *The Illustrated Book of World Rankings.*

St. Martin's Press, Inc., 175 Fifth Avenue, New York, New York 10010 (800) 221-7945; *The Statesman's Year-Book.*

Statistical Office of the United Nations, Publishing Service, New York, New York 10017 (800) 253-9646; *Statistical Yearbook.*

United Nations Conference on Trade and Development, Central Statistical Service, Palais des Nations, Geneva, Switzerland (Telephone in U.S. (800) 253-9646); *UNCTAD Commodity Yearbook.*

United Nations Economic Commission for Africa, Africa Hall, P.O. Box 3001, Addis Ababa, Ethiopia (Telephone Number in U.S. (800) 253-9646); *African Statistical*

Yearbook.

SIERRA LEONE - MONEY EXCHANGE RATES - See SIERRA LEONE - EXCHANGE RATES

SIERRA LEONE - MONEY RESERVES

Euromonitor International, Inc., 122 South Michigan Avenue, Suite 1200, Chicago, Illinois 60603 (800) 577-EURO; *International Marketing Data and Statistics.*

Europa Publications Limited, 18 Bedford Square, London, WC1B 3JN, England; *The Europa World Year Book.*

SIERRA LEONE - MONEY SUPPLY

African Development Bank, 01 BP 1387, Abidjan 01, Cote D'Ivoire; *Selected Statistics on Regional Member Countries.*

Economist Intelligence Unit, 111 West 57th Street, New York, New York 10019 (800) 938-4685; *Sierra Leone Country Report.*

Euromonitor International, Inc., 122 South Michigan Avenue, Suite 1200, Chicago, Illinois 60603 (800) 577-EURO; *International Marketing Data and Statistics.*

Federal Statistical Office, Gustav-Stresemann - Ring 11, D-6200, Wiesbaden, Germany; *Sierra Leone.*

International Monetary Fund, 700 Nineteenth Street, NW, Washington, D.C. 20431 (202) 623-7000; *International Financial Statistics.*

The World Bank, 1818 H Street, NW, Washington, D.C. 20433 (202) 477-1234; *World Development Indicators.*

SIERRA LEONE - MONUMENTS AND HISTORICAL SITES

United Nations Educational, Scientific and Cultural Organization (UNESCO), 7 Place de Fontenoy, F-75700 Paris, France (Telephone Number in U.S. (212) 963-5981); *Statistical Yearbook.*

SIERRA LEONE - MORTALITY

Central Intelligence Agency, Washington, D.C. 20505 (703) 482-1100, www.cia.gov; *The World Factbook.*

Euromonitor International, Inc., 122 South Michigan Avenue, Suite 1200, Chicago, Illinois 60603 (800) 577-EURO; *International Marketing Data and Statistics;* and *The World Economic Factbook.*

Europa Publications Limited, 18 Bedford Square, London, WC1B 3JN, England; *The Europa World Year Book.*

St. Martin's Press, Inc., 175 Fifth Avenue, New York, New York 10010 (800) 221-7945; *The Statesman's Year-Book.*

Statistical Office of the United Nations, Publishing Service, New York, New York 10017 (800) 253-9646; *Demographic Yearbook; Human Development Report; Statistical Yearbook; Survey of Economic and Social Conditions in Africa;* and *World Statistics Pocketbook.*

United Nations Children's Fund (UNICEF), 3 United Nations Plaza, New York, New York 10017 (800) 253-9646; *State of the World's Children.*

The World Bank, 1818 H Street, NW, Washington, D.C. 20433 (202) 477-1234; *The World Bank Atlas; World Development Report;* and *World Development Indicators.*

World Health Organization, Office of Publications, 20 Avenue Appia, CH-1211 Geneva 27, Switzerland (Telephone Number in U.S. (518) 436-9686) (Telephone Number in U.S. (518) 436-9686); *World Health Statistics Annual.*

SIERRA LEONE - MOTION PICTURES

United Nations Educational, Scientific and Cultural Organization (UNESCO), 7 Place de Fontenoy, F-75700 Paris, France (Telephone Number in U.S. (212) 963-5981); *Statistical Yearbook.*

SIERRA LEONE - MOTOR VEHICLE TAXES - See SIERRA LEONE - TAXATION

SIERRA LEONE - MOTOR VEHICLES IN USE

Europa Publications Limited, 18 Bedford Square, London, WC1B 3JN, England; *The Europa World Year Book.*

International Road Federation, 2600 Virginia Avenue, NW, Washington, D.C. 20037 (202) 338-4641; *World Road Statistics.*

Statistical Office of the United Nations, Publishing Service, New York, New York 10017 (800) 253-9646; *Statistical Yearbook;* and *Survey of Economic and Social Conditions in Africa.*

SIERRA LEONE - MUSEUMS

M.E. Sharpe, 80 Business Park Drive, Armonk, New York 10504 (800) 541-6563; *The Illustrated Book of World Rankings.*

United Nations Educational, Scientific and Cultural Organization (UNESCO), 7 Place de Fontenoy, F-75700 Paris, France (Telephone Number in U.S. (212) 963-5981); *Statistical Yearbook.*

SIERRA LEONE - NATALITY - See SIERRA LEONE - BIRTH RATE

SIERRA LEONE - NATIONAL ACCOUNTS

African Development Bank, 01 BP 1387, Abidjan 01, Cote D'Ivoire; *Selected Statistics on Regional Member Countries.*

Europa Publications Limited, 18 Bedford Square, London, WC1B 3JN, England; *The Europa World Year Book.*

Federal Statistical Office, Gustav-Stresemann - Ring 11, D-6200, Wiesbaden, Germany; *Sierra Leone.*

Statistical Office of the United Nations, Publishing Service, New York, New York 10017 (800) 253-9646; *National Accounts Statistics;* and *Statistical Yearbook.*

United Nations Economic Commission for Africa, Africa Hall, P.O. Box 3001, Addis Ababa, Ethiopia (Telephone Number in U.S. (800) 253-9646); *African Statistical Yearbook.*

SIERRA LEONE - NATIONAL INCOME

M.E. Sharpe, 80 Business Park Drive, Armonk, New York 10504 (800) 541-6563; *The Illustrated Book of World Rankings.*

Statistical Office of the United Nations, Publishing Service, New York, New York 10017 (800) 253-9646; *National Accounts Statistics;* and *Statistical Yearbook.*

SIERRA LEONE - NATIONAL PRODUCT

M.E. Sharpe, 80 Business Park Drive, Armonk, New York 10504 (800) 541-6563; *The Illustrated Book of World Rankings.*

Statistical Office of the United Nations, Publishing Service, New York, New York 10017 (800) 253-9646; *Statistical Yearbook.*

SIERRA LEONE - NATURAL GAS PRODUCTION - See SIERRA LEONE - MINING AND MINERAL PRODUCTS

SIERRA LEONE - NEWSPAPER PRODUCTION - See SIERRA LEONE - FORESTRY AND FOREST PRODUCTS

SIERRA LEONE - NEWSPRINT - See SIERRA LEONE - FORESTRY AND FOREST PRODUCTS

SIERRA LEONE - OCCUPATIONS - See SIERRA LEONE - LABOR

SIERRA LEONE - PALM KERNELS PRODUCTION - See SIERRA LEONE - CROPS

SIERRA LEONE - PAPER - See SIERRA LEONE - FORESTRY AND FOREST PRODUCTS

SIERRA LEONE - PATENTS, TRADEMARKS AND SERVICE MARKS

Statistical Office of the United Nations, Publishing Service, New York, New York 10017 (800) 253-9646; *Statistical Yearbook.*

SIERRA LEONE - PEANUT PRODUCTION - See SIERRA LEONE - CROPS

SIERRA LEONE - PERIODICALS

United Nations Educational, Scientific and Cultural Organization (UNESCO), 7 Place de Fontenoy, F-75700 Paris, France (Telephone Number in U.S. (212) 963-5981); *Statistical Yearbook.*

SIERRA LEONE - PESTICIDE USE

Food and Agricultural Organization of the United Nations (FAO) Via delle Terme di Caracalla, 00100 Rome, Italy (Telephone Number in U.S. (202) 653-2400); *The State of Food and Agriculture.*

SIERRA LEONE - PETROLEUM INDUSTRY

Food and Agricultural Organization of the United Nations (FAO) Via delle Terme di Caracalla, 00100 Rome, Italy (Telephone Number in U.S. (202) 653-2400); *The State of Food and Agriculture.*

M.E. Sharpe, 80 Business Park Drive, Armonk, New York 10504 (800) 541-6563; *The Illustrated Book of World Rankings.*

Statistical Office of the United Nations, Publishing Service, New York, New York 10017 (800) 253-9646; *Statistical Yearbook.*

United Nations Conference on Trade and Development, Central Statistical Service, Palais des Nations, Geneva, Switzerland (Telephone in U.S. (800) 253-9646); *UNCTAD Commodity Yearbook.*

SIERRA LEONE - PIGS - See SIERRA LEONE - LIVESTOCK AND POULTRY

SIERRA LEONE - POPULATION

African Development Bank, 01 BP 1387, Abidjan 01, Cote D'Ivoire; *Selected Statistics on Regional Member Countries.*

Central Intelligence Agency, Washington, D.C. 20505 (703) 482-1100, www.cia.gov; *The World Factbook.*

The Economist Intelligence Unit, 111 West 57th Street, New York, New York 10019 (800) 938-4685; *Sierra Leone Country Report;* and *The World Market Atlas.*

Euromonitor International, Inc., 122 South Michigan Avenue, Suite 1200, Chicago, Illinois 60603 (800) 577-EURO; *International Marketing Data and Statistics;* and *The World Economic Factbook.*

Europa Publications Limited, 18 Bedford Square, London, WC1B 3JN, England; *The Europa World Year Book.*

Federal Statistical Office, Gustav-Stresemann - Ring 11, D-6200, Wiesbaden, Germany; *Sierra Leone.*

Food and Agricultural Organization of the United Nations (FAO), Via delle Terme di Caracalla, 00100 Rome, Italy (Telephone Number in U.S. (202) 653-2400); *Production Yearbook.*

International Labour Office, I.L.O. Publications, 1828 L Street, NW., Suite 801, Washington, D.C. 20036 (301) 638-3152; *Yearbook of Labour Statistics.*

M.E. Sharpe, 80 Business Park Drive, Armonk, New York 10504 (800) 541-6563; *The Illustrated Book of World Rankings.*

St. Martin's Press, Inc., 175 Fifth Avenue, New York, New York 10010 (800) 221-7945; *The Statesman's Year-Book.*

Statistical Office of the United Nations, Publishing Service, New York, New York 10017 (800) 253-9646; *Demographic Yearbook; Human Development Report; Statistical Yearbook; Survey of Economic and Social Conditions in Africa;* and *World Statistics Pocketbook.*

United Nations Educational, Scientific and Cultural Organization (UNESCO), 7 Place de Fontenoy, F-75700 Paris, France (Telephone Number in U.S. (212) 963-5981); *Statistical Yearbook.*

U.S. Arms Control and Disarmament Agency, 320 Twenty-first Street, NW, Washington, D.C. 20451 (202) 647-8677; *World Military Expenditures and Arms Transfers.*

The World Bank, 1818 H Street, NW, Washington, D.C. 20433 (202) 477-1234; *The World Bank Atlas;* and *World Development Report.*

World Health Organization, Office of Publications, 20 Avenue Appia, CH-1211 Geneva 27, Switzerland (Telephone Number in U.S. (518) 436-9686); *World Health Statistics Annual.*

SIERRA LEONE - POST OFFICES

M.E. Sharpe, 80 Business Park Drive, Armonk, New York 10504 (800) 541-6563; *The Illustrated Book of World Rankings.*

St. Martin's Press, Inc., 175 Fifth Avenue, New York, New York 10010 (800) 221-7945; *The Statesman's Year-Book.*

SIERRA LEONE - POTATO PRODUCTION - See SIERRA LEONE - CROPS

SIERRA LEONE - PRICES

Federal Statistical Office, Gustav-Stresemann - Ring 11, D-6200, Wiesbaden, Germany; *Sierra Leone.*

Food and Agricultural Organization of the United Nations (FAO), Via delle Terme di Caracalla, 00100 Rome, Italy (Telephone Number in U.S. (202) 653-2400); *Production Yearbook;* and *The State of Food and Agriculture.*

International Labour Office, I.L.O. Publications, 1828 L Street, NW., Suite 801, Washington, D.C. 20036 (301) 638-3152; *Yearbook of Labour Statistics;* and *International Financial Statistics.*

M.E. Sharpe, 80 Business Park Drive, Armonk, New York 10504 (800) 541-6563; *The Illustrated Book of World Rankings.*

United Nations Economic Commission for Africa, Africa Hall, P.O. Box 3001, Addis Ababa, Ethiopia (Telephone Number in U.S. (800) 253-9646); *African Statistical Yearbook.*

SIERRA LEONE - PRINTING AND WRITING PAPER - See SIERRA LEONE - FORESTRY AND FOREST PRODUCTS

SIERRA LEONE - PRODUCTION

M.E. Sharpe, 80 Business Park Drive, Armonk, New York 10504 (800) 541-6563; *The Illustrated Book of World Rankings.*

SIERRA LEONE - PRODUCTIVITY

Euromonitor International, Inc., 122 South Michigan Avenue, Suite 1200, Chicago, Illinois 60603 (800) 577-EURO; *International Marketing Data and Statistics.*

SIERRA LEONE - PROPERTY TAXES - See SIERRA LEONE - TAXATION

SIERRA LEONE - PUBLIC FINANCE - See SIERRA LEONE - FINANCE

SIERRA LEONE - RADIO BROADCAST-ING - See SIERRA LEONE - BROADCASTING

SIERRA LEONE - RADIO RECEIVERS

St. Martin's Press, Inc., 175 Fifth Avenue, New York, New York 10010 (800) 221-7945; *The Statesman's Year-Book.*

SIERRA LEONE - RAILWAYS

St. Martin's Press, Inc., 175 Fifth Avenue, New York, New York 10010 (800) 221-7945; *The Statesman's Year-Book.*

United Nations Economic Commission for Africa, Africa Hall, P.O. Box 3001, Addis

Ababa, Ethiopia (Telephone Number in U.S. (800) 253-9646); *African Statistical Yearbook.*

SIERRA LEONE - RELIGION

Central Intelligence Agency, Washington, D.C. 20505 (703) 482-1100, www.cia.gov; *The World Factbook.*

M.E. Sharpe, 80 Business Park Drive, Armonk, New York 10504 (800) 541-6563; *The Illustrated Book of World Rankings.*

St. Martin's Press, Inc., 175 Fifth Avenue, New York, New York 10010 (800) 221-7945; *The Statesman's Year-Book.*

SIERRA LEONE - RENT PRICES

International Labour Office, I.L.O. Publications, 1828 L Street, NW., Suite 801, Washington, D.C. 20036 (301) 638-3152; *Yearbook of Labour Statistics.*

SIERRA LEONE - RETAIL TRADE

Euromonitor International Inc., 122 South Michigan Avenue, Suite 1200, Chicago, Illinois 60603 (800) 577-EURO; *World Marketing Data and Statistics.*

SIERRA LEONE - RICE PRODUCTION - See SIERRA LEONE - CROPS

SIERRA LEONE - ROUNDWOOD PRODUCTION - See SIERRA LEONE - FORESTRY AND FOREST PRODUCTS

SIERRA LEONE - RUBBER PRODUCTION AND CONSUMPTION

M.E. Sharpe, 80 Business Park Drive, Armonk, New York 10504 (800) 541-6563; *The Illustrated Book of World Rankings.*

SIERRA LEONE - SAWNWOOD PRODUCTION - See SIERRA LEONE - FORESTRY AND FOREST PRODUCTS

SIERRA LEONE - SENIOR CITIZENS

M.E. Sharpe, 80 Business Park Drive, Armonk, New York 10504 (800) 541-6563; *The Illustrated Book of World Rankings.*

SIERRA LEONE - SHEEP - See SIERRA LEONE - LIVESTOCK AND POULTRY

SIERRA LEONE - SILVER PRODUCTION AND CONSUMPTION - See SIERRA LEONE - MINING AND MINERAL PRODUCTS

SIERRA LEONE - SOCIAL DATA

African Development Bank, 01 BP 1387, Abidjan 01, Cote D'Ivoire; *Selected Statistics on Regional Member Countries.*

M.E. Sharpe, 80 Business Park Drive, Armonk, New York 10504 (800) 541-6563;

The Illustrated Book of World Rankings.

Statistical Office of the United Nations, Publishing Service, New York, New York 10017 (800) 253-9646; *World Statistics Pocketbook.*

SIERRA LEONE - SOCIAL SECURITY

International Monetary Fund, 700 Nineteenth Street, NW, Washington, D.C. 20431 (202) 623-7000; *Government Finance Statistics Yearbook.*

Statistical Office of the United Nations, Publishing Service, New York, New York 10017 (800) 253-9646; *National Accounts Statistics.*

SIERRA LEONE - STAMP TAXES AND DUTIES - See SIERRA LEONE - TAXATION

SIERRA LEONE - STATE BUDGET REVENUE AND EXPENDITURES

Euromonitor International, Inc., 122 South Michigan Avenue, Suite 1200, Chicago, Illinois 60603 (800) 577-EURO; *International Marketing Data and Statistics.*

SIERRA LEONE - STEEL - See SIERRA LEONE - MINING AND MINERAL PRODUCTS

SIERRA LEONE - STOCKS - COMMODITY - MARKET PRICE - INDEX

Food and Agricultural Organization of the United Nations (FAO) Via delle Terme di Caracalla, 00100 Rome, Italy (Telephone Number in U.S. (202) 653-2400); *The State of Food and Agriculture.*

SIERRA LEONE - SUGAR PRODUCTION AND CONSUMPTION - See SIERRA LEONE - CROPS

SIERRA LEONE - TAXATION

Europa Publications Limited, 18 Bedford Square, London, WC1B 3JN, England; *The Europa World Year Book.*

International Monetary Fund, 700 Nineteenth Street, NW, Washington, D.C. 20431 (202) 623-7000; *Government Finance Statistics Yearbook.*

International Road Federation, 2600 Virginia Avenue, NW, Washington, D.C. 20037 (202) 338-4641; *World Road Statistics.*

The World Bank, 1818 H Street, NW, Washington, D.C. 20433 (202) 477-1234; *World Development Indicators.*

SIERRA LEONE - TELEPHONES IN USE

American Telephone and Telegraph Company, 26 Parsippany Road, Whippany,

New Jersey 07981 (800) 222-0300; *The World's Telephones.*

Central Intelligence Agency, Washington, D.C. 20505 (703) 482-1100, www.cia.gov; *The World Factbook.*

Europa Publications Limited, 18 Bedford Square, London, WC1B 3JN, England; *The Europa World Year Book.*

St. Martin's Press, Inc., 175 Fifth Avenue, New York, New York 10010 (800) 221-7945; *The Statesman's Year-Book.*

Statistical Office of the United Nations, Publishing Service, New York, New York 10017 (800) 253-9646; *Statistical Yearbook;* and *World Statistics Pocketbook.*

SIERRA LEONE - TELEVISION BROADCASTING - See SIERRA LEONE - BROADCASTING

SIERRA LEONE - TEXTILE INDUSTRY

M.E. Sharpe, 80 Business Park Drive, Armonk, New York 10504 (800) 541-6563; *The Illustrated Book of World Rankings.*

United Nations Conference on Trade and Development, Central Statistical Service, Palais des Nations, Geneva, Switzerland (Telephone in U.S. (800) 253-9646); *UNCTAD Commodity Yearbook.*

SIERRA LEONE - TOBACCO PRODUCTION

M.E. Sharpe, 80 Business Park Drive, Armonk, New York 10504 (800) 541-6563; *The Illustrated Book of World Rankings.*

Statistical Office of the United Nations, Publishing Service, New York, New York 10017 (800) 253-9646; *Statistical Yearbook.*

SIERRA LEONE - TOURISM

Euromonitor International, Inc., 122 South Michigan Avenue, Suite 1200, Chicago, Illinois 60603 (800) 577-EURO; *The World Economic Factbook;* and *World Marketing Data and Statistics.*

Europa Publications Limited, 18 Bedford Square, London, WC1B 3JN, England; *The Europa World Year Book.*

Federal Statistical Office, Gustav-Stresemann - Ring 11, D-6200, Wiesbaden, Germany; *Sierra Leone.*

M.E. Sharpe, 80 Business Park Drive, Armonk, New York 10504 (800) 541-6563; *The Illustrated Book of World Rankings.*

St. Martin's Press, Inc., 175 Fifth Avenue, New York, New York 10010 (800) 221-7945; *The Statesman's Year-Book.*

Statistical Office of the United Nations, Publishing Service, New York, New York 10017 (800) 253-9646; *Statistical Yearbook.*

United Nations Economic Commission for Africa, Africa Hall, P.O. Box 3001, Addis Ababa, Ethiopia (Telephone Number in U.S. (800) 253-9646); *African Statistical Yearbook.*

SIERRA LEONE - TRACTORS IN USE

Statistical Office of the United Nations, Publishing Service, New York, New York 10017 (800) 253-9646; *Statistical Yearbook.*

SIERRA LEONE - TRADE - See SIERRA LEONE - FOREIGN TRADE

SIERRA LEONE - TRADEMARKS AND SERVICE MARKS - See SIERRA LEONE - PATENTS, TRADEMARKS AND SERVICE MARKS

SIERRA LEONE - TRANSPORTATION AND COMMUNICATIONS

Central Intelligence Agency, Washington, D.C. 20505 (703) 482-1100, www.cia.gov; *The World Factbook.*

Euromonitor International, Inc., 122 South Michigan Avenue, Suite 1200, Chicago, Illinois 60603 (800) 577-EURO; *International Marketing Data and Statistics;* and *World Marketing Data and Statistics.*

Europa Publications Limited, 18 Bedford Square, London, WC1B 3JN, England; *The Europa World Year Book.*

Federal Statistical Office, Gustav-Stresemann - Ring 11, D-6200, Wiesbaden, Germany; *Sierra Leone.*

M.E. Sharpe, 80 Business Park Drive, Armonk, New York 10504 (800) 541-6563; *The Illustrated Book of World Rankings.*

St. Martin's Press, Inc., 175 Fifth Avenue, New York, New York 10010 (800) 221-7945; *The Statesman's Year-Book.*

Statistical Office of the United Nations, Publishing Service, New York, New York 10017 (800) 253-9646; *Human Development Report.*

United Nations Economic Commission for Africa, Africa Hall, P.O. Box 3001, Addis Ababa, Ethiopia (Telephone Number in U.S. (800) 253-9646); *African Statistical Yearbook.*

SIERRA LEONE - UNEMPLOYMENT

Central Intelligence Agency, Washington, D.C. 20505 (703) 482-1100, www.cia.gov; *The World Factbook.*

Euromonitor International, Inc., 122

South Michigan Avenue, Suite 1200, Chicago, Illinois 60603 (800) 577-EURO; *International Marketing Data and Statistics.*

International Labour Office, I.L.O. Publications, 1828 L Street, NW., Suite 801, Washington, D.C. 20036 (301) 638-3152; *Yearbook of Labour Statistics.*

Statistical Office of the United Nations, Publishing Service, New York, New York 10017 (800) 253-9646; *Statistical Yearbook.*

SIERRA LEONE - VITAL STATISTICS

Euromonitor International, Inc., 122 South Michigan Avenue, Suite 1200, Chicago, Illinois 60603 (800) 577-EURO; *International Marketing Data and Statistics.*

St. Martin's Press, Inc., 175 Fifth Avenue, New York, New York 10010 (800) 221-7945; *The Statesman's Year-Book.*

World Health Organization, Office of Publications, 20 Avenue Appia, CH-1211 Geneva 27, Switzerland (Telephone Number in U.S. (518) 436-9686); *World Health Statistics Annual.*

SIERRA LEONE - WAGES

Federal Statistical Office, Gustav-Stresemann - Ring 11, D-6200, Wiesbaden, Germany; *Sierra Leone.*

International Labour Office, I.L.O. Publications, 1828 L Street, NW., Suite 801, Washington, D.C. 20036 (301) 638-3152; *Yearbook of Labour Statistics.*

SIERRA LEONE - WEATHER - See SIERRA LEONE - CLIMATE

SIERRA LEONE - WELFARE

International Monetary Fund, 700 Nineteenth Street, NW, Washington, D.C. 20431 (202) 623-7000; *Government Finance Statistics Yearbook.*

SIERRA LEONE - WHEAT PRODUCTION AND PRICES - See SIERRA LEONE - CROPS

SIERRA LEONE - WINE PRODUCTION - See SIERRA LEONE - BEVERAGES

SIERRA LEONE - WOOL PRODUCTION - See SIERRA LEONE - TEXTILE INDUSTRY

SILICON

U.S. Department of the Interior, Geological Survey, Office of Minerals Information, 12201 Sunrise Valley Drive, Reston, Virginia 22092 (703) 648-4000, www.minerals.usgs.gov; *Mineral Commodity Summaries.*

SILVER

U.S. Department of the Interior, Geological Survey, Office of Minerals Information, 12201 Sunrise Valley Drive, Reston, Virginia 22092 (703) 648-4000, www.minerals.usgs.gov; *Annual Reports;* and *Mineral Commodity Summaries.*

SILVER - CONSUMPTION

U.S. Department of the Interior, Geological Survey, Office of Minerals Information, 12201 Sunrise Valley Drive, Reston, Virginia 22092 (703) 648-4000, www.minerals.usgs.gov; *Annual Reports;* and *Mineral Commodity Summaries.*

SILVER - EMPLOYMENT

U.S. Department of the Interior, Geological Survey, Office of Minerals Information, 12201 Sunrise Valley Drive, Reston, Virginia 22092 (703) 648-4000, www.minerals.usgs.gov; *Mineral Commodity Summaries.*

SILVER - FOREIGN TRADE

U.S. Department of the Interior, Geological Survey, Office of Minerals Information, 12201 Sunrise Valley Drive, Reston, Virginia 22092 (703) 648-4000, www.minerals.usgs.gov; *Annual Reports;* and *Mineral Commodity Summaries.*

SILVER - PRICES

U.S. Department of the Interior, Geological Survey, Office of Minerals Information, 12201 Sunrise Valley Drive, Reston, Virginia 22092 (703) 648-4000, www.minerals.usgs.gov; *Annual Reports;* and *Mineral Commodity Summaries.*

SILVER - PRODUCTION AND VALUE

U.S. Department of the Interior, Geological Survey, Office of Minerals Information, 12201 Sunrise Valley Drive, Reston, Virginia 22092 (703) 648-4000, www.minerals.usgs.gov; *Annual Reports;* and *Mineral Commodity Summaries.*

SILVER - STRATEGIC AND CRITICAL MATERIAL

U.S. Department of Defense, Defense Logistics Agency, 8725 John J. Kingman Road, Fort Belvoir, Virginia 22060 (703) 767-6666; *Statistical Supplement, Stockpile Report to the Congress.*

SILVER - WORLD PRODUCTION

U.S. Department of the Interior, Geological Survey, Office of Minerals Information, 12201 Sunrise Valley Drive, Reston, Virginia 22092 (703) 648-4000, www.minerals.usgs.gov; *Annual Reports;* and *Mineral Commodity Summaries.*

SILVERWARE - See JEWELRY

Singapore - National Statistical Office

Department of Statistics, Ministry of Trade and Industry, 8 Shenton Way, 10-01 Treasury Building, Singapore 0106.

Singapore - Primary Statistics Source

Department of Statistics, 8 Shenton Way, 10-01 Treasury Building, Singapore 0106; *Monthly Digest of Statistics;* and *Yearbook of Statistics Singapore.*

SINGAPORE - ABORTIONS

Statistical Office of the United Nations, Publishing Service, New York, New York 10017 (800) 253-9646; *Demographic Yearbook.*

SINGAPORE - AGRICULTURE

Asian Development Bank, P.O. Box 789, 1099 Manila, Philippines; *Key Indicators of Developing Asian and Pacific Countries.*

Economist Intelligence Unit, 111 West 57th Street, New York, New York 10019 (800) 938-4685; *Singapore Country Report.*

Euromonitor International, Inc., 122 South Michigan Avenue, Suite 1200, Chicago, Illinois 60603 (800) 577-EURO; *International Marketing Data and Statistics;* and *World Marketing Data and Statistics.*

Europa Publications Limited, 18 Bedford Square, London, WC1B 3JN, England; *The Europa World Year Book.*

Federal Statistical Office, Gustav-Stresemann - Ring 11, D-6200, Wiesbaden, Germany; *Singapur.*

Food and Agricultural Organization of the United Nations (FAO) Via delle Terme di Caracalla, 00100 Rome, Italy (Telephone Number in U.S. (202) 653-2400); *Production Yearbook; The State of Food and Agriculture;* and *Trade Yearbook.*

M.E. Sharpe, 80 Business Park Drive, Armonk, New York 10504 (800) 541-6563; *The Illustrated Book of World Rankings.*

St. Martin's Press, Inc., 175 Fifth Avenue, New York, New York 10010 (800) 221-7945; *The Statesman's Year-Book.*

Statistical Office of the United Nations, Publishing Service, New York, New York 10017 (800) 253-9646; *Asia-Pacific in Figures; Statistical Yearbook;* and *Statistical Yearbook for Asia and the Pacific.*

United Nations Conference on Trade and Development, Central Statistical Service, Palais des Nations, Geneva, Switzerland (Telephone in U.S. (800) 253-9646); *UNCTAD Commodity Yearbook.*

The World Bank, 1818 H Street, NW, Washington, D.C. 20433 (202) 477-1234; *World Development Indicators.*

SINGAPORE - AIRLINE SERVICE

The Economist Intelligence Unit (Asia) Limited, 10th Floor, Luk Kwok Centre, 72 Gloucester Road, Wanchai, Hong Kong (Phone Number in U.S. (800) 938-4685); *Asian Market Atlas.*

Europa Publications Limited, 18 Bedford Square, London, WC1B 3JN, England; *The Europa World Year Book.*

International Civil Aviation Organization, 999 University Street, Montreal, Quebec, Canada H3C 5H7 (514) 954-8219; *Civil Aviation Statistics of the World.*

M.E. Sharpe, 80 Business Park Drive, Armonk, New York 10504 (800) 541-6563; *The Illustrated Book of World Rankings.*

St. Martin's Press, Inc., 175 Fifth Avenue, New York, New York 10010 (800) 221-7945; *The Statesman's Year-Book.*

Statistical Office of the United Nations, Publishing Service, New York, New York 10017 (800) 253-9646; *Statistical Yearbook.*

SINGAPORE - AIRPORTS

Central Intelligence Agency, Washington, D.C. 20505 (703) 482-1100, www.cia.gov; *The World Factbook.*

SINGAPORE - ALUMINUM PRODUCTION AND CONSUMPTION - See SINGAPORE - MINING AND MINERAL PRODUCTS

SINGAPORE - ANIMAL FEEDINGSTUFFS OF AQUATIC ANIMAL ORIGIN

Statistical Office of the United Nations, Publishing Service, New York, New York 10017 (800) 253-9646; *Statistical Yearbook.*

SINGAPORE - ANIMAL HEALTH

Food and Agricultural Organization of the United Nations (FAO), Via delle Terme di Caracalla, 00100, Rome, Italy (Telephone Number in U.S. (202) 653-2400); *Animal Health Yearbook.*

SINGAPORE - AREA AND DENSITY OF POPULATION

Central Intelligence Agency, Washington, D.C. 20505 (703) 482-1100,

www.cia.gov; *The World Factbook.*

Euromonitor International, Inc., 122 South Michigan Avenue, Suite 1200, Chicago, Illinois 60603 (800) 577-EURO; *International Marketing Data and Statistics;* and *The World Economic Factbook.*

Europa Publications Limited, 18 Bedford Square, London, WC1B 3JN, England; *The Europa World Year Book.*

Federal Statistical Office, Gustav-Stresemann - Ring 11, D-6200, Wiesbaden, Germany; *Singapur.*

Food and Agricultural Organization of the United Nations (FAO) Via delle Terme di Caracalla, 00100 Rome, Italy (Telephone Number in U.S. (202) 653-2400); *The State of Food and Agriculture.*

M.E. Sharpe, 80 Business Park Drive, Armonk, New York 10504 (800) 541-6563; *The Illustrated Book of World Rankings.*

St. Martin's Press, Inc., 175 Fifth Avenue, New York, New York 10010 (800) 221-7945; *The Statesman's Year-Book.*

Statistical Office of the United Nations, Publishing Service, New York, New York 10017 (800) 253-9646; *Statistical Yearbook.*

United Nations Educational, Scientific and Cultural Organization (UNESCO), 7 Place de Fontenoy, F-75700 Paris, France (Telephone Number in U.S. (212) 963-5981); *Statistical Yearbook.*

The World Bank, 1818 H Street, NW, Washington, D.C. 20433 (202) 477-1234; *World Development Report.*

SINGAPORE - ARMS EXPORTS AND IMPORTS - See SINGAPORE - MILITARY

SINGAPORE - BALANCE OF PAYMENTS

The Economist Intelligence Unit, 111 West 57th Street, New York, New York 10019 (800) 938-4685; *The World Market Atlas.*

Europa Publications Limited, 18 Bedford Square, London, WC1B 3JN, England; *The Europa World Year Book.*

Federal Statistical Office, Gustav-Stresemann - Ring 11, D-6200, Wiesbaden, Germany; *Singapur.*

International Monetary Fund, 700 Nineteenth Street, NW, Washington, D.C. 20431 (202) 623-7000; *Balance of Payments Yearbook;* and *International Financial Statistics.*

United Nations Conference on Trade and Development (UNCTAD), New York, New York 10017 (800) 253-9646; *Handbook* of International Trade and Development Statistics.

The World Bank, 1818 H Street, NW, Washington, D.C. 20433 (202) 477-1234; *World Development Report;* and *World Development Indicators.*

SINGAPORE - BANKING

Asian Development Bank, P.O. Box 789, 1099 Manila, Philippines; *Key Indicators of Developing Asian and Pacific Countries.*

Euromonitor International Inc., 122 South Michigan Avenue, Suite 1200, Chicago, Illinois 60603 (800) 577-EURO; *World Marketing Data and Statistics.*

Europa Publications Limited, 18 Bedford Square, London, WC1B 3JN, England; *The Europa World Year Book.*

International Monetary Fund, 700 Nineteenth Street, NW, Washington, D.C. 20431 (202) 623-7000; *Government Finance Statistics Yearbook;* and *International Financial Statistics.*

M.E. Sharpe, 80 Business Park Drive, Armonk, New York 10504 (800) 541-6563; *The Illustrated Book of World Rankings.*

St. Martin's Press, Inc., 175 Fifth Avenue, New York, New York 10010 (800) 221-7945; *The Statesman's Year-Book.*

SINGAPORE - BARLEY PRODUCTION - See SINGAPORE - CROPS

SINGAPORE - BEER PRODUCTION - See SINGAPORE - BEVERAGES

SINGAPORE - BEVERAGES

M.E. Sharpe, 80 Business Park Drive, Armonk, New York 10504 (800) 541-6563; *The Illustrated Book of World Rankings.*

Statistical Office of the United Nations, Publishing Service, New York, New York 10017 (800) 253-9646; *Statistical Yearbook.*

SINGAPORE - BIRTH RATES

Central Intelligence Agency, Washington, D.C. 20505 (703) 482-1100, www.cia.gov; *The World Factbook.*

The Economist Intelligence Unit (Asia) Limited, 10th Floor, Luk Kwok Centre, 72 Gloucester Road, Wanchai, Hong Kong (Phone Number in U.S. (800) 938-4685); *Asian Market Atlas.*

Euromonitor International, Inc., 122 South Michigan Avenue, Suite 1200, Chicago, Illinois 60603 (800) 577-EURO; *International Marketing Data and Statistics;* and *The World Economic Factbook.*

Europa Publications Limited, 18 Bedford Square, London, WC1B 3JN, England; *The Europa World Year Book.*

M.E. Sharpe, 80 Business Park Drive, Armonk, New York 10504 (800) 541-6563; *The Illustrated Book of World Rankings.*

St. Martin's Press, Inc., 175 Fifth Avenue, New York, New York 10010 (800) 221-7945; *The Statesman's Year-Book.*

Statistical Office of the United Nations, Publishing Service, New York, New York 10017 (800) 253-9646; *Asia-Pacific in Figures; Demographic Yearbook;* and *Statistical Yearbook.*

The World Bank, 1818 H Street, NW, Washington, D.C. 20433 (202) 477-1234; *World Development Indicators.*

World Health Organization, Office of Publications, 20 Avenue Appia, CH-1211 Geneva 27, Switzerland (Telephone Number in U.S. (518) 436-9686); *World Health Statistics Annual.*

SINGAPORE - BONDS

Asian Development Bank, P.O. Box 789, 1099 Manila, Philippines; *Key Indicators of Developing Asian and Pacific Countries.*

International Monetary Fund, 700 Nineteenth Street, NW, Washington, D.C. 20431 (202) 623-7000; *Government Finance Statistics Yearbook.*

SINGAPORE - BOOK PRODUCTION

St. Martin's Press, Inc., 175 Fifth Avenue, New York, New York 10010 (800) 221-7945; *The Statesman's Year-Book.*

United Nations Educational, Scientific and Cultural Organization (UNESCO), 7 Place de Fontenoy, F-75700 Paris, France (Telephone Number in U.S. (212) 963-5981); *Statistical Yearbook.*

SINGAPORE - BROADCASTING

Billboard Limited, P.O. Box 9027, 1006 AA Amsterdam, The Netherlands (Telephone Number in U.S. (212) 764-7300); *World Radio TV Handbook.*

Central Intelligence Agency, Washington, D.C. 20505 (703) 482-1100, www.cia.gov; *The World Factbook.*

The Economist Intelligence Unit (Asia) Limited, 10th Floor, Luk Kwok Centre, 72 Gloucester Road, Wanchai, Hong Kong (Phone Number in U.S. (800) 938-4685); *Asian Market Atlas.*

Euromonitor International Inc., 122 South Michigan Avenue, Suite 1200, Chicago, Illinois 60603 (800) 577-EURO;

World Marketing Data and Statistics.

Europa Publications Limited, 18 Bedford Square, London, WC1B 3JN, England; *The Europa World Year Book.*

M.E. Sharpe, 80 Business Park Drive, Armonk, New York 10504 (800) 541-6563; *The Illustrated Book of World Rankings.*

St. Martin's Press, Inc., 175 Fifth Avenue, New York, New York 10010 (800) 221-7945; *The Statesman's Year-Book.*

United Nations Educational, Scientific and Cultural Organization (UNESCO), 7 Place de Fontenoy, F-75700 Paris, France (Telephone Number in U.S. (212) 963-5981); *Statistical Yearbook.*

SINGAPORE - BUDGET

Central Intelligence Agency, Washington, D.C. 20505 (703) 482-1100, www.cia.gov; *The World Factbook.*

SINGAPORE - BUSINESS AND PROFESSIONAL LICENSES

International Monetary Fund, 700 Nineteenth Street, NW, Washington, D.C. 20431 (202) 623-7000; *Government Finance Statistics Yearbook.*

SINGAPORE - CALORIE SUPPLY

Asian Development Bank, P.O. Box 789, 1099 Manila, Philippines; *Key Indicators of Developing Asian and Pacific Countries.*

Food and Agricultural Organization of the United Nations (FAO) Via delle Terme di Caracalla, 00100 Rome, Italy (Telephone Number in U.S. (202) 653-2400); *The State of Food and Agriculture.*

SINGAPORE - CAPITAL INVESTMENT

Asian Development Bank, P.O. Box 789, 1099 Manila, Philippines; *Key Indicators of Developing Asian and Pacific Countries.*

SINGAPORE - CAPITAL REVENUE

Asian Development Bank, P.O. Box 789, 1099 Manila, Philippines; *Key Indicators of Developing Asian and Pacific Countries.*

International Monetary Fund, 700 Nineteenth Street, NW, Washington, D.C. 20431 (202) 623-7000; *Government Finance Statistics Yearbook.*

SINGAPORE - CATTLE - See SINGAPORE - LIVESTOCK AND POULTRY

SINGAPORE - CEMENT PRODUCTION - See SINGAPORE - MINING AND MINERAL PRODUCTS

SINGAPORE - CHEMICAL (ORGANIC)

PRODUCTION - See SINGAPORE - MINING AND MINERAL PRODUCTS

SINGAPORE - CHICKENS - See SINGAPORE - LIVESTOCK AND POULTRY

SINGAPORE - CIGAR PRODUCTION - See SINGAPORE - TOBACCO PRODUCTION

SINGAPORE - CIGARETTE PRODUCTION - See SINGAPORE - TOBACCO PRODUCTION

SINGAPORE - CLIMATE

M.E. Sharpe, 80 Business Park Drive, Armonk, New York 10504 (800) 541-6563; *The Illustrated Book of World Rankings*.

St. Martin's Press, Inc., 175 Fifth Avenue, New York, New York 10010 (800) 221-7945; *The Statesman's Year-Book*.

SINGAPORE - COAL PRODUCTION - See SINGAPORE - MINING AND MINERAL PRODUCTS

SINGAPORE - COFFEE - See SINGAPORE - CROPS

SINGAPORE - COMMERCE

St. Martin's Press, Inc., 175 Fifth Avenue, New York, New York 10010 (800) 221-7945; *The Statesman's Year-Book*.

SINGAPORE - COMMUNICATIONS - See SINGAPORE - TRANSPORTATION AND COMMUNICATIONS

SINGAPORE - CONSTRUCTION INDUSTRY

M.E. Sharpe, 80 Business Park Drive, Armonk, New York 10504 (800) 541-6563; *The Illustrated Book of World Rankings*.

Statistical Office of the United Nations, Publishing Service, New York, New York 10017 (800) 253-9646; *Statistical Yearbook*.

SINGAPORE - CONSUMER PRICE INDEX

Asian Development Bank, P.O. Box 789, 1099 Manila, Philippines; *Key Indicators of Developing Asian and Pacific Countries*.

Statistical Office of the United Nations, Publishing Service, New York, New York 10017 (800) 253-9646; *Statistical Yearbook*.

SINGAPORE - CONSUMER PRICES

Euromonitor International Inc., 122 South Michigan Avenue, Suite 1200, Chicago, Illinois 60603 (800) 577-EURO; *World Marketing Data and Statistics*.

International Labour Office, I.L.O. Publications, 1828 L Street, NW., Suite 801, Washington, D.C. 20036 (301) 638-3152; *Yearbook of Labour Statistics*.

International Monetary Fund, 700 Nineteenth Street, NW, Washington, D.C. 20431 (202) 623-7000; *International Financial Statistics*.

SINGAPORE - CONSUMPTION

International Monetary Fund, 700 Nineteenth Street, NW, Washington, D.C. 20431 (202) 623-7000; *International Financial Statistics*.

International Rubber Study Group, York House, Eighth Floor, Empire Way, Wembley, London HA9 0PA, England; *Rubber Statistical Bulletin*.

The World Bank, 1818 H Street, NW, Washington, D.C. 20433 (202) 477-1234; *World Development Report*.

SINGAPORE - COPPER PRODUCTION AND CONSUMPTION - See SINGAPORE - MINING AND MINERAL PRODUCTS

SINGAPORE - CORN PRODUCTION - See SINGAPORE - CROPS

SINGAPORE - CORPORATE TAXES - See SINGAPORE - TAXATION

SINGAPORE - COTTON PRODUCTION - See SINGAPORE - CROPS

SINGAPORE - CRIME

International Criminal Police Organization (INTERPOL), 50 quai Achille Lignon, F-69006 Lyon, France; *International Crime Statistics*.

Yale University Press, Yale Station, New Haven, Connecticut 06520 (800) 987-7323; *Violence and Crime in Cross-National Perspective*.

SINGAPORE - CROPS

Asian Development Bank, P.O. Box 789, 1099 Manila, Philippines; *Key Indicators of Developing Asian and Pacific Countries*.

Commodity Research Bureau, Inc., 30 South Wacker Drive, Chicago Illinois 60606 (312) 454-1801; *Commodity Year Book*.

Europa Publications Limited, 18 Bedford Square, London, WC1B 3JN, England; *The Europa World Year Book*.

Food and Agricultural Organization of the United Nations (FAO) Via delle Terme di Caracalla, 00100 Rome, Italy (Telephone Number in U.S. (202) 653-2400); *The State of Food and Agriculture*.

M.E. Sharpe, 80 Business Park Drive, Armonk, New York 10504 (800) 541-6563; *The Illustrated Book of World Rankings*.

United Nations Conference on Trade and Development, Central Statistical Service, Palais des Nations, Geneva, Switzerland (Telephone in U.S. (800) 253-9646); *UNCTAD Commodity Yearbook*.

SINGAPORE - CUSTOMS DUTIES

St. Martin's Press, Inc., 175 Fifth Avenue, New York, New York 10010 (800) 221-7945; *The Statesman's Year-Book*.

SINGAPORE - DAIRY PRODUCTS

Europa Publications Limited, 18 Bedford Square, London, WC1B 3JN, England; *The Europa World Year Book*.

Food and Agricultural Organization of the United Nations (FAO) Via delle Terme di Caracalla, 00100 Rome, Italy (Telephone Number in U.S. (202) 653-2400); *The State of Food and Agriculture*.

International Monetary Fund, 700 Nineteenth Street, NW, Washington, D.C. 20431 (202) 623-7000; *Government Finance Statistics Yearbook*.

M.E. Sharpe, 80 Business Park Drive, Armonk, New York 10504 (800) 541-6563; *The Illustrated Book of World Rankings*.

Statistical Office of the United Nations, Publishing Service, New York, New York 10017 (800) 253-9646; *Statistical Yearbook*.

SINGAPORE - DEATH RATES - See SINGAPORE - MORTALITY

SINGAPORE - DEFENSE EXPENDITURES - See SINGAPORE - MILITARY

SINGAPORE - DEMOGRAPHY

The Economist Intelligence Unit, 111 West 57th Street, New York, New York 10019 (800) 938-4685; *The World Market Atlas*.

The Economist Intelligence Unit (Asia) Limited, 10th Floor, Luk Kwok Centre, 72 Gloucester Road, Wanchai, Hong Kong (Phone Number in U.S. (800) 938-4685); *Asian Market Atlas*.

Euromonitor International, Inc., 122 South Michigan Avenue, Suite 1200, Chicago, Illinois 60603 (800) 577-EURO; *International Marketing Data and Statistics; World Marketing Data and Statistics;* and *The World Economic Factbook*.

Federal Statistical Office, Gustav-Stresemann - Ring 11, D-6200, Wiesbaden, Germany; *Singapur*.

M.E. Sharpe, 80 Business Park Drive, Armonk, New York 10504 (800) 541-6563; *The Illustrated Book of World Rankings*.

Statistical Office of the United Nations, Publishing Service, New York, New York 10017 (800) 253-9646; *Asia-Pacific in Figures;* and *Human Development Report.*

SINGAPORE - DEVELOPMENT ASSISTANCE

Asian Development Bank, P.O. Box 789, 1099 Manila, Philippines; *Key Indicators of Developing Asian and Pacific Countries.*

SINGAPORE - DIAMOND PRODUCTION - See SINGAPORE - MINING AND MINERAL PRODUCTS

SINGAPORE - DISEASES - See SINGAPORE - HEALTH

SINGAPORE - DIVORCE RATES

M.E. Sharpe, 80 Business Park Drive, Armonk, New York 10504 (800) 541-6563; *The Illustrated Book of World Rankings.*

Statistical Office of the United Nations, Publishing Service, New York, New York 10017 (800) 253-9646; *Demographic Yearbook.*

SINGAPORE - ECONOMY

Asian Development Bank, P.O. Box 789, 1099 Manila, Philippines; *Key Indicators of Developing Asian and Pacific Countries.*

Central Intelligence Agency, Washington, D.C. 20505 (703) 482-1100, www.cia.gov; *The World Factbook.*

Economist Intelligence Unit, 111 West 57th Street, New York, New York 10019 (800) 938-4685; *Singapore Country Report.*

Euromonitor International, Inc., 122 South Michigan Avenue, Suite 1200, Chicago, Illinois 60603 (800) 577-EURO; *International Marketing Data and Statistics; World Marketing Data and Statistics;* and *The World Economic Factbook.*

Europa Publications Limited, 18 Bedford Square, London, WC1B 3JN, England; *The Europa World Year Book.*

Federal Statistical Office, Gustav-Stresemann - Ring 11, D-6200, Wiesbaden, Germany; *Singapur.*

M.E. Sharpe, 80 Business Park Drive, Armonk, New York 10504 (800) 541-6563; *The Illustrated Book of World Rankings.*

St. Martin's Press, Inc., 175 Fifth Avenue, New York, New York 10010 (800) 221-7945; *The Statesman's Year-Book.*

Statistical Office of the United Nations, Publishing Service, New York, New York 10017 (800) 253-9646; *World Statistics*

Pocketbook.

The World Bank, 1818 H Street, NW, Washington, D.C. 20433 (202) 477-1234; *The World Bank Atlas;* and *World Development Report.*

SINGAPORE - EDUCATION

The Economist Intelligence Unit, 111 West 57th Street, New York, New York 10019 (800) 938-4685; *The World Market Atlas.*

The Economist Intelligence Unit (Asia) Limited, 10th Floor, Luk Kwok Centre, 72 Gloucester Road, Wanchai, Hong Kong (Phone Number in U.S. (800) 938-4685); *Asian Market Atlas.*

Euromonitor International, Inc., 122 South Michigan Avenue, Suite 1200, Chicago, Illinois 60603 (800) 577-EURO; *International Marketing Data and Statistics;* and *World Marketing Data and Statistics.*

Europa Publications Limited, 18 Bedford Square, London, WC1B 3JN, England; *The Europa World Year Book.*

Federal Statistical Office, Gustav-Stresemann - Ring 11, D-6200, Wiesbaden, Germany; *Singapur.*

International Monetary Fund, 700 Nineteenth Street, NW, Washington, D.C. 20431 (202) 623-7000; *Government Finance Statistics Yearbook.*

M.E. Sharpe, 80 Business Park Drive, Armonk, New York 10504 (800) 541-6563; *The Illustrated Book of World Rankings.*

St. Martin's Press, Inc., 175 Fifth Avenue, New York, New York 10010 (800) 221-7945; *The Statesman's Year-Book.*

Statistical Office of the United Nations, Publishing Service, New York, New York 10017 (800) 253-9646; *Asia-Pacific in Figures; Human Development Report;* and *Statistical Yearbook for Asia and the Pacific.*

United Nations Educational, Scientific and Cultural Organization (UNESCO), 7 Place de Fontenoy, F-75700 Paris, France (Telephone Number in U.S. (212) 963-5981); *Statistical Yearbook.*

The World Bank, 1818 H Street, NW, Washington, D.C. 20433 (202) 477-1234; *World Development Report;* and *World Development Indicators.*

SINGAPORE - EGG PRODUCTION AND CONSUMPTION - See SINGAPORE - DAIRY PRODUCTS

SINGAPORE - ELECTRICITY

Asian Development Bank, P.O. Box 789, 1099 Manila, Philippines; *Key Indicators of Developing Asian and Pacific Countries.*

Central Intelligence Agency, Washington, D.C. 20505 (703) 482-1100, www.cia.gov; *The World Factbook.*

M.E. Sharpe, 80 Business Park Drive, Armonk, New York 10504 (800) 541-6563; *The Illustrated Book of World Rankings.*

St. Martin's Press, Inc., 175 Fifth Avenue, New York, New York 10010 (800) 221-7945; *The Statesman's Year-Book.*

Statistical Office of the United Nations, Publishing Service, New York, New York 10017 (800) 253-9646; *Electric Power in Asia and the Pacific; Human Development Report;* and *Statistical Yearbook.*

SINGAPORE - EMPLOYMENT

Euromonitor International, Inc., 122 South Michigan Avenue, Suite 1200, Chicago, Illinois 60603 (800) 577-EURO; *International Marketing Data and Statistics.*

Federal Statistical Office, Gustav-Stresemann - Ring 11, D-6200, Wiesbaden, Germany; *Singapur.*

International Labour Office, I.L.O. Publications, 1828 L Street, NW., Suite 801, Washington, D.C. 20036 (301) 638-3152; *Yearbook of Labour Statistics.*

M.E. Sharpe, 80 Business Park Drive, Armonk, New York 10504 (800) 541-6563; *The Illustrated Book of World Rankings.*

Statistical Office of the United Nations, Publishing Service, New York, New York 10017 (800) 253-9646; *Asia-Pacific in Figures;* and *Statistical Yearbook.*

SINGAPORE - ENERGY

Euromonitor International, Inc., 122 South Michigan Avenue, Suite 1200, Chicago, Illinois 60603 (800) 577-EURO; *International Marketing Data and Statistics; World Marketing Data and Statistics;* and *The World Economic Factbook.*

Food and Agricultural Organization of the United Nations (FAO) Via delle Terme di Caracalla, 00100 Rome, Italy (Telephone Number in U.S. (202) 653-2400); *The State of Food and Agriculture.*

M.E. Sharpe, 80 Business Park Drive, Armonk, New York 10504 (800) 541-6563; *The Illustrated Book of World Rankings.*

St. Martin's Press, Inc., 175 Fifth Avenue, New York, New York 10010 (800) 221-7945; *The Statesman's Year-Book.*

Statistical Office of the United Nations,

Publishing Service, New York, New York 10017 (800) 253-9646; *Asia-Pacific in Figures; Energy Statistics Yearbook; Human Development Report; Statistical Yearbook; Statistical Yearbook for Asia and the Pacific;* and *World Statistics Pocketbook.*

The World Bank, 1818 H Street, NW, Washington, D.C. 20433 (202) 477-1234; *The World Bank Atlas;* and *World Development Report.*

SINGAPORE - ENVIRONMENT

Economist Intelligence Unit, 111 West 57th Street, New York, New York 10019 (800) 938-4685; *Singapore Country Report.*

Statistical Office of the United Nations, Publishing Service, New York, New York 10017 (800) 253-9646; *World Statistics Pocketbook.*

SINGAPORE - EXCHANGE RATES

Asian Development Bank, P.O. Box 789, 1099 Manila, Philippines; *Key Indicators of Developing Asian and Pacific Countries.*

Central Intelligence Agency, Washington, D.C. 20505 (703) 482-1100, www.cia.gov; *The World Factbook.*

The Economist Intelligence Unit (Asia) Limited, 10th Floor, Luk Kwok Centre, 72 Gloucester Road, Wanchai, Hong Kong (Phone Number in U.S. (800) 938-4685); *Asian Market Atlas.*

Euromonitor International, Inc., 122 South Michigan Avenue, Suite 1200, Chicago, Illinois 60603 (800) 577-EURO; *International Marketing Data and Statistics;* and *The World Economic Factbook.*

Europa Publications Limited, 18 Bedford Square, London, WC1B 3JN, England; *The Europa World Year Book.*

International Civil Aviation Organization, 999 University Street, Montreal, Quebec, Canada H3C 5H7 (514) 954-8219; *Civil Aviation Statistics of the World.*

International Monetary Fund, 700 Nineteenth Street, NW, Washington, D.C. 20431 (202) 623-7000; *International Financial Statistics.*

Statistical Office of the United Nations, Publishing Service, New York, New York 10017 (800) 253-9646; *Statistical Yearbook;* and *World Statistics Pocketbook.*

Walden Publishing Ltd., Two Market Street, Saffron Walden Essex, CB10 1HZ, England; *The World of Information Asia and Pacific Review.*

SINGAPORE - EXCISE TAXES - See

SINGAPORE - TAXATION

SINGAPORE - EXPORTS

Asian Development Bank, P.O. Box 789, 1099 Manila, Philippines; *Key Indicators of Developing Asian and Pacific Countries.*

Central Intelligence Agency, Washington, D.C. 20505 (703) 482-1100, www.cia.gov; *The World Factbook.*

The Economist Intelligence Unit, 111 West 57th Street, New York, New York 10019 (800) 938-4685; *Singapore Country Report;* and *The World Market Atlas.*

The Economist Intelligence Unit (Asia) Limited, 10th Floor, Luk Kwok Centre, 72 Gloucester Road, Wanchai, Hong Kong (Phone Number in U.S. (800) 938-4685); *Asian Market Atlas.*

Euromonitor International, Inc., 122 South Michigan Avenue, Suite 1200, Chicago, Illinois 60603 (800) 577-EURO; *International Marketing Data and Statistics;* and *The World Economic Factbook.*

Europa Publications Limited, 18 Bedford Square, London, WC1B 3JN, England; *The Europa World Year Book.*

Food and Agricultural Organization of the United Nations (FAO) Via delle Terme di Caracalla, 00100 Rome, Italy (Telephone Number in U.S. (202) 653-2400); *The State of Food and Agriculture.*

International Monetary Fund, 700 Nineteenth Street, NW, Washington, D.C. 20431 (202) 623-7000; *Direction of Trade Statistics;* and *International Financial Statistics.*

International Rubber Study Group, York House, Eighth Floor, Empire Way, Wembley, London HA9 0PA, England; *Rubber Statistical Bulletin.*

St. Martin's Press, Inc., 175 Fifth Avenue, New York, New York 10010 (800) 221-7945; *The Statesman's Year-Book.*

Statistical Office of the United Nations, Publishing Service, New York, New York 10017 (800) 253-9646; *Foreign Trade Statistics of Asia and the Pacific.*

United Nations Conference on Trade and Development (UNCTAD), New York, New York 10017 (800) 253-9646; *Handbook of International Trade and Development Statistics.*

Walden Publishing Ltd., Two Market Street, Saffron Walden Essex, CB10 1HZ, England; *The World of Information Asia and Pacific Review.*

The World Bank, 1818 H Street, NW,

Washington, D.C. 20433 (202) 477-1234; *World Development Report;* and *World Development Indicators.*

SINGAPORE - EXTERNAL FINANCING

Asian Development Bank, P.O. Box 789, 1099 Manila, Philippines; *Key Indicators of Developing Asian and Pacific Countries.*

SINGAPORE - EXTERNAL INDEBTEDNESS

Asian Development Bank, P.O. Box 789, 1099 Manila, Philippines; *Key Indicators of Developing Asian and Pacific Countries.*

The World Bank, 1818 H Street, NW, Washington, D.C. 20433 (202) 477-1234; *World Development Report;* and *World Development Indicators.*

SINGAPORE - EXTERNAL TRADE

Asian Development Bank, P.O. Box 789, 1099 Manila, Philippines; *Key Indicators of Developing Asian and Pacific Countries.*

Euromonitor International Inc., 122 South Michigan Avenue, Suite 1200, Chicago, Illinois 60603 (800) 577-EURO; *World Marketing Data and Statistics.*

Food and Agricultural Organization of the United Nations (FAO) Via delle Terme di Caracalla, 00100 Rome, Italy (Telephone Number in U.S. (202) 653-2400); *The State of Food and Agriculture;* and *Trade Yearbook.*

Statistical Office of the United Nations, Publishing Service, New York, New York 10017 (800) 253-9646; *Asia-Pacific in Figures; Statistical Yearbook;* and *Statistical Yearbook for Asia and the Pacific.*

SINGAPORE - FARM CROPS - See SINGAPORE - CROPS

SINGAPORE - FEMALE WORKING POPULATION - See SINGAPORE - EMPLOYMENT

SINGAPORE - FERTILITY RATES

Central Intelligence Agency, Washington, D.C. 20505 (703) 482-1100, www.cia.gov; *The World Factbook.*

The Economist Intelligence Unit (Asia) Limited, 10th Floor, Luk Kwok Centre, 72 Gloucester Road, Wanchai, Hong Kong (Phone Number in U.S. (800) 938-4685); *Asian Market Atlas.*

M.E. Sharpe, 80 Business Park Drive, Armonk, New York 10504 (800) 541-6563; *The Illustrated Book of World Rankings.*

Statistical Office of the United Nations, Publishing Service, New York, New York

10017 (800) 253-9646; *Human Development Report.*

The World Bank, 1818 H Street, NW, Washington, D.C. 20433 (202) 477-1234; *The World Bank Atlas; World Development Report;* and *World Development Indicators.*

SINGAPORE - FERTILIZER

Food and Agricultural Organization of the United Nations (FAO) Via delle Terme di Caracalla, 00100 Rome, Italy (Telephone Number in U.S. (202) 653-2400); *The State of Food and Agriculture.*

Statistical Office of the United Nations, Publishing Service, New York, New York 10017 (800) 253-9646; *Statistical Yearbook.*

SINGAPORE - FETAL MORTALITY - See SINGAPORE - MORTALITY

SINGAPORE - FILAMENT PRODUCTION - See SINGAPORE - TEXTILE INDUSTRY

SINGAPORE - FILM - See SINGAPORE - MOTION PICTURES

SINGAPORE - FINANCE

Asian Development Bank, P.O. Box 789, 1099 Manila, Philippines; *Key Indicators of Developing Asian and Pacific Countries.*

Economist Intelligence Unit, 111 West 57th Street, New York, New York 10019 (800) 938-4685; *Singapore Country Report.*

Europa Publications Limited, 18 Bedford Square, London, WC1B 3JN, England; *The Europa World Year Book.*

Federal Statistical Office, Gustav-Stresemann - Ring 11, D-6200, Wiesbaden, Germany; *Singapur.*

International Monetary Fund, 700 Nineteenth Street, NW, Washington, D.C. 20431 (202) 623-7000; *Government Finance Statistics Yearbook.*

M.E. Sharpe, 80 Business Park Drive, Armonk, New York 10504 (800) 541-6563; *The Illustrated Book of World Rankings.*

St. Martin's Press, Inc., 175 Fifth Avenue, New York, New York 10010 (800) 221-7945; *The Statesman's Year-Book.*

Statistical Office of the United Nations, Publishing Service, New York, New York 10017 (800) 253-9646; *Statistical Yearbook for Asia and the Pacific.*

SINGAPORE - FISHERIES

Europa Publications Limited, 18 Bedford Square, London, WC1B 3JN, England; *The Europa World Year Book.*

Federal Statistical Office, Gustav-Stresemann - Ring 11, D-6200, Wiesbaden, Germany; *Singapur.*

Food and Agricultural Organization of the United Nations (FAO) Via delle Terme di Caracalla, 00100 Rome, Italy (Telephone Number in U.S. (202) 653-2400); *The State of Food and Agriculture,* and *Yearbook of Fishery Statistics.*

M.E. Sharpe, 80 Business Park Drive, Armonk, New York 10504 (800) 541-6563; *The Illustrated Book of World Rankings.*

St. Martin's Press, Inc., 175 Fifth Avenue, New York, New York 10010 (800) 221-7945; *The Statesman's Year-Book.*

Statistical Office of the United Nations, Publishing Service, New York, New York 10017 (800) 253-9646; *Statistical Yearbook.*

United Nations Conference on Trade and Development, Central Statistical Service, Palais des Nations, Geneva, Switzerland (Telephone in U.S. (800) 253-9646); *UNCTAD Commodity Yearbook.*

SINGAPORE - FOOD

Euromonitor International Inc., 122 South Michigan Avenue, Suite 1200, Chicago, Illinois 60603 (800) 577-EURO; *Retail Trade International.*

Food and Agricultural Organization of the United Nations (FAO) Via delle Terme di Caracalla, 00100 Rome, Italy (Telephone Number in U.S. (202) 653-2400); *Production Yearbook;* and *The State of Food and Agriculture.*

Statistical Office of the United Nations, Publishing Service, New York, New York 10017 (800) 253-9646; *Human Development Report.*

United Nations Conference on Trade and Development, Central Statistical Service, Palais des Nations, Geneva, Switzerland (Telephone in U.S. (800) 253-9646); *UNCTAD Commodity Yearbook.*

SINGAPORE - FOREIGN DEBT

International Monetary Fund, 700 Nineteenth Street, NW, Washington, D.C. 20431 (202) 623-7000; *Government Finance Statistics Yearbook.*

St. Martin's Press, Inc., 175 Fifth Avenue, New York, New York 10010 (800) 221-7945; *The Statesman's Year-Book.*

Walden Publishing Ltd., Two Market Street, Saffron Walden Essex, CB10 1HZ, England; *The World of Information Asia and Pacific Review.*

SINGAPORE - FOREIGN TRADE

Asian Development Bank, P.O. Box 789, 1099 Manila, Philippines; *Key Indicators of Developing Asian and Pacific Countries.*

Economist Intelligence Unit, 111 West 57th Street, New York, New York 10019 (800) 938-4685; *Singapore Country Report.*

The Economist Intelligence Unit (Asia) Limited, 10th Floor, Luk Kwok Centre, 72 Gloucester Road, Wanchai, Hong Kong (Phone Number in U.S. (800) 938-4685); *Asian Market Atlas.*

Euromonitor International, Inc., 122 South Michigan Avenue, Suite 1200, Chicago, Illinois 60603 (800) 577-EURO; *International Marketing Data and Statistics;* and *The World Economic Factbook.*

Europa Publications Limited, 18 Bedford Square, London, WC1B 3JN, England; *The Europa World Year Book.*

Federal Statistical Office, Gustav-Stresemann - Ring 11, D-6200, Wiesbaden, Germany; *Singapur.*

Food and Agricultural Organization of the United Nations (FAO) Via delle Terme di Caracalla, 00100 Rome, Italy (Telephone Number in U.S. (202) 653-2400); *The State of Food and Agriculture.*

International Monetary Fund, 700 Nineteenth Street, NW, Washington, D.C. 20431 (202) 623-7000; *International Financial Statistics.*

M.E. Sharpe, 80 Business Park Drive, Armonk, New York 10504 (800) 541-6563; *The Illustrated Book of World Rankings.*

St. Martin's Press, Inc., 175 Fifth Avenue, New York, New York 10010 (800) 221-7945; *The Statesman's Year-Book.*

Statistical Office of the United Nations, Publishing Service, New York, New York 10017 (800) 253-9646; *International Trade Statistics Yearbook;* and *Statistical Yearbook.*

United Nations Conference on Trade and Development, Central Statistical Service, Palais des Nations, Geneva, Switzerland (Telephone in U.S. (800) 253-9646); *UNCTAD Commodity Yearbook.*

The World Bank, 1818 H Street, NW, Washington, D.C. 20433 (202) 477-1234; *World Development Report;* and *World Development Indicators.*

SINGAPORE - FORESTRY AND FOREST PRODUCTS

The Economist Intelligence Unit (Asia) Limited, 10th Floor, Luk Kwok Centre, 72

Gloucester Road, Wanchai, Hong Kong (Phone Number in U.S. (800) 938-4685); *Asian Market Atlas.*

Federal Statistical Office, Gustav-Stresemann - Ring 11, D-6200, Wiesbaden, Germany; *Singapur.*

Food and Agricultural Organization of the United Nations (FAO) Via delle Terme di Caracalla, 00100 Rome, Italy (Telephone Number in U.S. (202) 653-2400); *The State of Food and Agriculture;* and *Yearbook of Forest Products.*

M.E. Sharpe, 80 Business Park Drive, Armonk, New York 10504 (800) 541-6563; *The Illustrated Book of World Rankings.*

United Nations Conference on Trade and Development, Central Statistical Service, Palais des Nations, Geneva, Switzerland (Telephone in U.S. (800) 253-9646); *UNCTAD Commodity Yearbook.*

United Nations Educational, Scientific and Cultural Organization (UNESCO), 7 Place de Fontenoy, F-75700 Paris, France (Telephone Number in U.S. (212) 963-5981); *Statistical Yearbook.*

The World Bank, 1818 H Street, NW, Washington, D.C. 20433 (202) 477-1234; *World Development Report.*

SINGAPORE - GAS PRODUCTION - See SINGAPORE - MINING AND MINERAL PRODUCTS

SINGAPORE - GENERAL INDUSTRIAL STATISTICS - See SINGAPORE - INDUSTRY

SINGAPORE - GENERAL MORTALITY - See SINGAPORE - MORTALITY

SINGAPORE - GEOGRAPHIC DATA

M.E. Sharpe, 80 Business Park Drive, Armonk, New York 10504 (800) 541-6563; *The Illustrated Book of World Rankings.*

SINGAPORE - GOATS - See SINGAPORE - LIVESTOCK AND POULTRY

SINGAPORE - GOLD HOLDINGS

Statistical Office of the United Nations, Publishing Service, New York, New York 10017 (800) 253-9646; *Statistical Yearbook.*

The World Bank, 1818 H Street, NW, Washington, D.C. 20433 (202) 477-1234; *World Development Indicators.*

SINGAPORE - GOLD PRODUCTION AND CONSUMPTION - See SINGAPORE - MINING AND MINERAL PRODUCTS

SINGAPORE - GOVERNMENT

Asian Development Bank, P.O. Box 789, 1099 Manila, Philippines; *Key Indicators of Developing Asian and Pacific Countries.*

Central Intelligence Agency, Washington, D.C. 20505 (703) 482-1100, www.cia.gov; *The World Factbook.*

Europa Publications Limited, 18 Bedford Square, London, WC1B 3JN, England; *The Europa World Year Book.*

International Monetary Fund, 700 Nineteenth Street, NW, Washington, D.C. 20431 (202) 623-7000; *Government Finance Statistics Yearbook;* and *International Financial Statistics.*

St. Martin's Press, Inc., 175 Fifth Avenue, New York, New York 10010 (800) 221-7945; *The Statesman's Year-Book.*

Statistical Office of the United Nations, Publishing Service, New York, New York 10017 (800) 253-9646; *Asia-Pacific in Figures;* and *National Accounts Statistics.*

The World Bank, 1818 H Street, NW, Washington, D.C. 20433 (202) 477-1234; *World Development Report;* and *World Development Indicators.*

SINGAPORE - GRAIN PRODUCTION - See SINGAPORE - CROPS

SINGAPORE - GRANTS

International Monetary Fund, 700 Nineteenth Street, NW, Washington, D.C. 20431 (202) 623-7000; *Government Finance Statistics Yearbook.*

SINGAPORE - GROSS DOMESTIC PRODUCT

Asian Development Bank, P.O. Box 789, 1099 Manila, Philippines; *Key Indicators of Developing Asian and Pacific Countries.*

The Economist Intelligence Unit, 111 West 57th Street, New York, New York 10019 (800) 938-4685; *Singapore Country Report;* and *The World Market Atlas.*

The Economist Intelligence Unit (Asia) Limited, 10th Floor, Luk Kwok Centre, 72 Gloucester Road, Wanchai, Hong Kong (Phone Number in U.S. (800) 938-4685); *Asian Market Atlas.*

Euromonitor International, Inc., 122 South Michigan Avenue, Suite 1200, Chicago, Illinois 60603 (800) 577-EURO; *International Marketing Data and Statistics;* and *The World Economic Factbook.*

Europa Publications Limited, 18 Bedford Square, London, WC1B 3JN, England; *The Europa World Year Book.*

M.E. Sharpe, 80 Business Park Drive, Armonk, New York 10504 (800) 541-6563;

The Illustrated Book of World Rankings.

Statistical Office of the United Nations, Publishing Service, New York, New York 10017 (800) 253-9646; *Human Development Report; National Accounts Statistics;* and *Statistical Yearbook.*

U.S. Arms Control and Disarmament Agency, 320 Twenty-first Street, NW, Washington, D.C. 20451 (202) 647-8677; *World Military Expenditures and Arms Transfers.*

The World Bank, 1818 H Street, NW, Washington, D.C. 20433 (202) 477-1234; *World Development Report;* and *World Development Indicators.*

SINGAPORE - GROSS NATIONAL PRODUCT

Asian Development Bank, P.O. Box 789, 1099 Manila, Philippines; *Key Indicators of Developing Asian and Pacific Countries.*

Euromonitor International, Inc., 122 South Michigan Avenue, Suite 1200, Chicago, Illinois 60603 (800) 577-EURO; *International Marketing Data and Statistics.*

Europa Publications Limited, 18 Bedford Square, London, WC1B 3JN, England; *The Europa World Year Book.*

St. Martin's Press, Inc., 175 Fifth Avenue, New York, New York 10010 (800) 221-7945; *The Statesman's Year-Book.*

Walden Publishing Ltd., Two Market Street, Saffron Walden Essex, CB10 1HZ, England; *The World of Information Asia and Pacific Review.*

The World Bank, 1818 H Street, NW, Washington, D.C. 20433 (202) 477-1234; *The World Bank Atlas; World Development Report;* and *World Development Indicators.*

SINGAPORE - HEALTH

The Economist Intelligence Unit (Asia) Limited, 10th Floor, Luk Kwok Centre, 72 Gloucester Road, Wanchai, Hong Kong (Phone Number in U.S. (800) 938-4685); *Asian Market Atlas.*

Euromonitor International Inc., 122 South Michigan Avenue, Suite 1200, Chicago, Illinois 60603 (800) 577-EURO; *World Marketing Data and Statistics.*

Federal Statistical Office, Gustav-Stresemann - Ring 11, D-6200, Wiesbaden, Germany; *Singapur.*

M.E. Sharpe, 80 Business Park Drive, Armonk, New York 10504 (800) 541-6563; *The Illustrated Book of World Rankings.*

St. Martin's Press, Inc., 175 Fifth

Avenue, New York, New York 10010 (800) 221-7945; *The Statesman's Year-Book.*

Statistical Office of the United Nations, Publishing Service, New York, New York 10017 (800) 253-9646; *Asia-Pacific in Figures; Human Development Report;* and *Statistical Yearbook.*

United Nations Children's Fund (UNICEF), 3 United Nations Plaza, New York, New York 10017 (800) 253-9646; *State of the World's Children.*

The World Bank, 1818 H Street, NW, Washington, D.C. 20433 (202) 477-1234; *World Development Report.*

World Health Organization, Office of Publications, 20 Avenue Appia, CH-1211 Geneva 27, Switzerland (Telephone Number in U.S. (518) 436-9686); *World Health Statistics Annual.*

SINGAPORE - HEALTH EXPENDITURES

International Monetary Fund, 700 Nineteenth Street, NW, Washington, D.C. 20431 (202) 623-7000; *Government Finance Statistics Yearbook.*

SINGAPORE - HIGHWAYS

Central Intelligence Agency, Washington, D.C. 20505 (703) 482-1100, www.cia.gov; *The World Factbook.*

The Economist Intelligence Unit (Asia) Limited, 10th Floor, Luk Kwok Centre, 72 Gloucester Road, Wanchai, Hong Kong (Phone Number in U.S. (800) 938-4685); *Asian Market Atlas.*

International Road Federation, 2600 Virginia Avenue, NW, Washington, D.C. 20037 (202) 338-4641; *World Road Statistics.*

St. Martin's Press, Inc., 175 Fifth Avenue, New York, New York 10010 (800) 221-7945; *The Statesman's Year-Book.*

SINGAPORE - HORSES - See
SINGAPORE - LIVESTOCK AND POULTRY

SINGAPORE - HOURS OF WORK - See
SINGAPORE - EMPLOYMENT

SINGAPORE - HOUSING AND HOUSING UNITS

Euromonitor International Inc., 122 South Michigan Avenue, Suite 1200, Chicago, Illinois 60603 (800) 577-EURO; *World Marketing Data and Statistics.*

M.E. Sharpe, 80 Business Park Drive, Armonk, New York 10504 (800) 541-6563; *The Illustrated Book of World Rankings.*

Statistical Office of the United Nations, Publishing Service, New York, New York 10017 (800) 253-9646; *Statistical Yearbook.*

SINGAPORE - HOUSING EXPENDITURES

International Monetary Fund, 700 Nineteenth Street, NW, Washington, D.C. 20431 (202) 623-7000; *Government Finance Statistics Yearbook.*

SINGAPORE - ILLITERATE POPULATION

Central Intelligence Agency, Washington, D.C. 20505 (703) 482-1100, www.cia.gov; *The World Factbook.*

The Economist Intelligence Unit, 111 West 57th Street, New York, New York 10019 (800) 938-4685; *The World Market Atlas.*

Euromonitor International, Inc., 122 South Michigan Avenue, Suite 1200, Chicago, Illinois 60603 (800) 577-EURO; *The World Economic Factbook.*

St. Martin's Press, Inc., 175 Fifth Avenue, New York, New York 10010 (800) 221-7945; *The Statesman's Year-Book.*

Statistical Office of the United Nations, Publishing Service, New York, New York 10017 (800) 253-9646; *Asia-Pacific in Figures;* and *Human Development Report.*

United Nations Educational, Scientific and Cultural Organization (UNESCO), 7 Place de Fontenoy, F-75700 Paris, France (Telephone Number in U.S. (212) 963-5981); *Statistical Yearbook.*

SINGAPORE - IMPORTS

Asian Development Bank, P.O. Box 789, 1099 Manila, Philippines; *Key Indicators of Developing Asian and Pacific Countries.*

Central Intelligence Agency, Washington, D.C. 20505 (703) 482-1100, www.cia.gov; *The World Factbook.*

The Economist Intelligence Unit, 111 West 57th Street, New York, New York 10019 (800) 938-4685; *Singapore Country Report;* and *The World Market Atlas.*

The Economist Intelligence Unit (Asia) Limited, 10th Floor, Luk Kwok Centre, 72 Gloucester Road, Wanchai, Hong Kong (Phone Number in U.S. (800) 938-4685); *Asian Market Atlas.*

Euromonitor International, Inc., 122 South Michigan Avenue, Suite 1200, Chicago, Illinois 60603 (800) 577-EURO; *International Marketing Data and Statistics;* and *The World Economic Factbook.*

Europa Publications Limited, 18

Bedford Square, London, WC1B 3JN, England; *The Europa World Year Book.*

Food and Agricultural Organization of the United Nations (FAO) Via delle Terme di Caracalla, 00100 Rome, Italy (Telephone Number in U.S. (202) 653-2400); *The State of Food and Agriculture.*

International Monetary Fund, 700 Nineteenth Street, NW, Washington, D.C. 20431 (202) 623-7000; *Direction of Trade Statistics; Government Finance Statistics Yearbook;* and *International Financial Statistics.*

International Rubber Study Group, York House, Eighth Floor, Empire Way, Wembley, London HA9 0PA, England; *Rubber Statistical Bulletin.*

St. Martin's Press, Inc., 175 Fifth Avenue, New York, New York 10010 (800) 221-7945; *The Statesman's Year-Book.*

Statistical Office of the United Nations, Publishing Service, New York, New York 10017 (800) 253-9646; *Foreign Trade Statistics of Asia and the Pacific.*

United Nations Conference on Trade and Development (UNCTAD), New York, New York 10017 (800) 253-9646; *Handbook of International Trade and Development Statistics.*

Walden Publishing Ltd., Two Market Street, Saffron Walden Essex, CB10 1HZ, England; *The World of Information Asia and Pacific Review.*

The World Bank, 1818 H Street, NW, Washington, D.C. 20433 (202) 477-1234; *World Development Report;* and *World Development Indicators.*

SINGAPORE - INCOME TAXES - See
SINGAPORE - TAXATION

SINGAPORE - INDUSTRY

Central Intelligence Agency, Washington, D.C. 20505 (703) 482-1100, www.cia.gov; *The World Factbook.*

Economist Intelligence Unit, 111 West 57th Street, New York, New York 10019 (800) 938-4685; *Singapore Country Report.*

Euromonitor International, Inc., 122 South Michigan Avenue, Suite 1200, Chicago, Illinois 60603 (800) 577-EURO; *The World Economic Factbook;* and *World Marketing Data and Statistics.*

Europa Publications Limited, 18 Bedford Square, London, WC1B 3JN, England; *The Europa World Year Book.*

Federal Statistical Office, Gustav-Stresemann - Ring 11, D-6200, Wiesbaden,

Germany; *Singapur.*

International Labour Office, I.L.O. Publications, 1828 L Street, NW., Suite 801, Washington, D.C. 20036 (301) 638-3152; *Yearbook of Labour Statistics.*

M.E. Sharpe, 80 Business Park Drive, Armonk, New York 10504 (800) 541-6563; *The Illustrated Book of World Rankings.*

St. Martin's Press, Inc., 175 Fifth Avenue, New York, New York 10010 (800) 221-7945; *The Statesman's Year-Book.*

Statistical Office of the United Nations, Publishing Service, New York, New York 10017 (800) 253-9646; *Asia-Pacific in Figures; Industrial Commodity Statistics; Statistical Yearbook;* and *Statistical Yearbook for Asia and the Pacific.*

The World Bank, 1818 H Street, NW, Washington, D.C. 20433 (202) 477-1234; *World Development Indicators.*

World Intellectual Property Organization, 34 Chemin des Colombettes, CH-1211 Geneva 20. Switzerland; *Industrial Property Statistics.*

SINGAPORE - INFANT AND MATERNAL MORTALITY - See SINGAPORE - MORTALITY

SINGAPORE - INTERNAL TRADE

Statistical Office of the United Nations, Publishing Service, New York, New York 10017 (800) 253-9646; *Statistical Yearbook;* and *Statistical Yearbook for Asia and the Pacific.*

SINGAPORE - INTERNATIONAL LIQUIDITY

International Monetary Fund, 700 Nineteenth Street, NW, Washington, D.C. 20431 (202) 623-7000; *International Financial Statistics.*

SINGAPORE - INTERNATIONAL RESERVES EXCLUDING GOLD

Asian Development Bank, P.O. Box 789, 1099 Manila, Philippines; *Key Indicators of Developing Asian and Pacific Countries.*

Statistical Office of the United Nations, Publishing Service, New York, New York 10017 (800) 253-9646; *Statistical Yearbook.*

The World Bank, 1818 H Street, NW, Washington, D.C. 20433 (202) 477-1234; *World Development Indicators.*

SINGAPORE - INTERNATIONAL STATISTICS

Asian Development Bank, P.O. Box 789, 1099 Manila, Philippines; *Key Indicators of Developing Asian and Pacific Countries.*

SINGAPORE - INVESTMENTS

International Monetary Fund, 700 Nineteenth Street, NW, Washington, D.C. 20431 (202) 623-7000; *International Financial Statistics.*

SINGAPORE - IRON ORE PRODUCTION AND CONSUMPTION - See SINGAPORE - MINING AND MINERAL PRODUCTS

SINGAPORE - IRRIGATION

Euromonitor International, Inc., 122 South Michigan Avenue, Suite 1200, Chicago, Illinois 60603 (800) 577-EURO; *International Marketing Data and Statistics.*

SINGAPORE - LABOR

Central Intelligence Agency, Washington, D.C. 20505 (703) 482-1100, www.cia.gov; *The World Factbook.*

The Economist Intelligence Unit (Asia) Limited, 10th Floor, Luk Kwok Centre, 72 Gloucester Road, Wanchai, Hong Kong (Phone Number in U.S. (800) 938-4685); *Asian Market Atlas.*

Euromonitor International, Inc., 122 South Michigan Avenue, Suite 1200, Chicago, Illinois 60603 (800) 577-EURO; *International Marketing Data and Statistics;* and *World Marketing Data and Statistics.*

Europa Publications Limited, 18 Bedford Square, London, WC1B 3JN, England; *The Europa World Year Book.*

Food and Agricultural Organization of the United Nations (FAO) Via delle Terme di Caracalla, 00100 Rome, Italy (Telephone Number in U.S. (202) 653-2400); *The State of Food and Agriculture.*

International Labour Office, I.L.O. Publications, 1828 L Street, NW., Suite 801, Washington, D.C. 20036 (301) 638-3152; *Yearbook of Labour Statistics.*

M.E. Sharpe, 80 Business Park Drive, Armonk, New York 10504 (800) 541-6563; *The Illustrated Book of World Rankings.*

St. Martin's Press, Inc., 175 Fifth Avenue, New York, New York 10010 (800) 221-7945; *The Statesman's Year-Book.*

Statistical Office of the United Nations, Publishing Service, New York, New York 10017 (800) 253-9646; *Human Development Report.*

The World Bank, 1818 H Street, NW, Washington, D.C. 20433 (202) 477-1234; *The World Bank Atlas; World Development Report;* and *World Development Indicators.*

SINGAPORE - LAND USE

Central Intelligence Agency, Washington, D.C. 20505 (703) 482-1100, www.cia.gov; *The World Factbook.*

Euromonitor International, Inc., 122 South Michigan Avenue, Suite 1200, Chicago, Illinois 60603 (800) 577-EURO; *International Marketing Data and Statistics.*

Food and Agricultural Organization of the United Nations (FAO), Via delle Terme di Caracalla, 00100 Rome, Italy (Telephone Number in U.S. (202) 653-2400); *Production Yearbook.*

The World Bank, 1818 H Street, NW, Washington, D.C. 20433 (202) 477-1234; *World Development Report.*

SINGAPORE - LIBRARIES

M.E. Sharpe, 80 Business Park Drive, Armonk, New York 10504 (800) 541-6563; *The Illustrated Book of World Rankings.*

United Nations Educational, Scientific and Cultural Organization (UNESCO), 7 Place de Fontenoy, F-75700 Paris, France (Telephone Number in U.S. (212) 963-5981); *Statistical Yearbook.*

SINGAPORE - LIFE EXPECTANCY

Central Intelligence Agency, Washington, D.C. 20505 (703) 482-1100, www.cia.gov; *The World Factbook.*

The Economist Intelligence Unit (Asia) Limited, 10th Floor, Luk Kwok Centre, 72 Gloucester Road, Wanchai, Hong Kong (Phone Number in U.S. (800) 938-4685); *Asian Market Atlas.*

Euromonitor International, Inc., 122 South Michigan Avenue, Suite 1200, Chicago, Illinois 60603 (800) 577-EURO; *The World Economic Factbook.*

St. Martin's Press, Inc., 175 Fifth Avenue, New York, New York 10010 (800) 221-7945; *The Statesman's Year-Book.*

Statistical Office of the United Nations, Publishing Service, New York, New York 10017 (800) 253-9646; *Asia-Pacific in Figures; Human Development Report;* and *World Statistics Pocketbook.*

The World Bank, 1818 H Street, NW, Washington, D.C. 20433 (202) 477-1234; *The World Bank Atlas;* and *World Development Report.*

SINGAPORE - LITERACY RATE

Euromonitor International Inc., 122 South Michigan Avenue, Suite 1200, Chicago, Illinois 60603 (800) 577-EURO; *World Marketing Data and Statistics.*

SINGAPORE - LIVESTOCK AND POULTRY

Euromonitor International, Inc., 122 South Michigan Avenue, Suite 1200, Chicago, Illinois 60603 (800) 577-EURO; *International Marketing Data and Statistics.*

Europa Publications Limited, 18 Bedford Square, London, WC1B 3JN, England; *The Europa World Year Book.*

Food and Agricultural Organization of the United Nations (FAO), Via delle Terme di Caracalla, 00100 Rome, Italy (Telephone Number in U.S. (202) 653-2400); *Production Yearbook;* and *The State of Food and Agriculture.*

M.E. Sharpe, 80 Business Park Drive, Armonk, New York 10504 (800) 541-6563; *The Illustrated Book of World Rankings.*

Statistical Office of the United Nations, Publishing Service, New York, New York 10017 (800) 253-9646; *Statistical Yearbook.*

United Nations Conference on Trade and Development, Central Statistical Service, Palais des Nations, Geneva, Switzerland (Telephone in U.S. (800) 253-9646); *UNCTAD Commodity Yearbook.*

SINGAPORE - LIVING LEVELS - See SINGAPORE - LIFE EXPECTANCY

SINGAPORE - MAIL - NUMBER OF ITEMS SENT OR RECEIVED

Statistical Office of the United Nations, Publishing Service, New York, New York 10017 (800) 253-9646; *Statistical Yearbook.*

SINGAPORE - MANPOWER

Statistical Office of the United Nations, Publishing Service, New York, New York 10017 (800) 253-9646; *Statistical Yearbook for Asia and the Pacific.*

SINGAPORE - MANUFACTURING

Asian Development Bank, P.O. Box 789, 1099 Manila, Philippines; *Key Indicators of Developing Asian and Pacific Countries.*

M.E. Sharpe, 80 Business Park Drive, Armonk, New York 10504 (800) 541-6563; *The Illustrated Book of World Rankings.*

Statistical Office of the United Nations, Publishing Service, New York, New York 10017 (800) 253-9646; *Statistical Yearbook.*

The World Bank, 1818 H Street, NW, Washington, D.C. 20433 (202) 477-1234; *World Development Indicators.*

SINGAPORE - MARRIAGE RATES

M.E. Sharpe, 80 Business Park Drive, Armonk, New York 10504 (800) 541-6563; *The Illustrated Book of World Rankings.*

Statistical Office of the United Nations, Publishing Service, New York, New York 10017 (800) 253-9646; *Demographic Yearbook;* and *Statistical Yearbook.*

SINGAPORE - MEAT PRODUCTION - See SINGAPORE - LIVESTOCK AND POULTRY

SINGAPORE - MERCHANT SHIPPING

Europa Publications Limited, 18 Bedford Square, London, WC1B 3JN, England; *The Europa World Year Book.*

Lloyd's Register of Shipping, 17 Battery Place, New York, New York 10004 (212) 425-8050; *Register of Ships.*

St. Martin's Press, Inc., 175 Fifth Avenue, New York, New York 10010 (800) 221-7945; *The Statesman's Year-Book.*

Statistical Office of the United Nations, Publishing Service, New York, New York 10017 (800) 253-9646; *Statistical Yearbook.*

U.S. Department of Transportation, Maritime Administration, 400 Seventh Street, SW, Washington, D.C. 20590 (202) 366-5807, www.marad.dot.gov; *A Statistical Analysis of the World's Merchant Fleets.*

SINGAPORE - MILITARY

Central Intelligence Agency, Washington, D.C. 20505 (703) 482-1100, www.cia.gov; *The World Factbook.*

The Economist Intelligence Unit (Asia) Limited, 10th Floor, Luk Kwok Centre, 72 Gloucester Road, Wanchai, Hong Kong (Phone Number in U.S. (800) 938-4685); *Asian Market Atlas.*

Euromonitor International Inc., 122 South Michigan Avenue, Suite 1200, Chicago, Illinois 60603 (800) 577-EURO; *World Marketing Data and Statistics.*

The International Institute for Strategic Studies, 23 Tavistock Street, London WC2E 7NQ, England 44 171 3797676; *The Military Balance.*

International Monetary Fund, 700 Nineteenth Street, NW, Washington, D.C. 20431 (202) 623-7000; *Government Finance Statistics Yearbook.*

St. Martin's Press, Inc., 175 Fifth Avenue, New York, New York 10010 (800) 221-7945; *The Statesman's Year-Book.*

Statistical Office of the United Nations, Publishing Service, New York, New York 10017 (800) 253-9646; *Human Development Report.*

U.S. Arms Control and Disarmament Agency, 320 Twenty-first Street, NW,

Washington, D.C. 20451 (202) 647-8677; *World Military Expenditures and Arms Transfers.*

SINGAPORE - MILK PRODUCTION - See SINGAPORE - DAIRY PRODUCTS

SINGAPORE - MINING AND MINERAL PRODUCTS

Asian Development Bank, P.O. Box 789, 1099 Manila, Philippines; *Key Indicators of Developing Asian and Pacific Countries.*

M.E. Sharpe, 80 Business Park Drive, Armonk, New York 10504 (800) 541-6563; *The Illustrated Book of World Rankings.*

Statistical Office of the United Nations, Publishing Service, New York, New York 10017 (800) 253-9646; *Statistical Yearbook.*

United Nations Conference on Trade and Development, Central Statistical Service, Palais des Nations, Geneva, Switzerland (Telephone in U.S. (800) 253-9646); *UNCTAD Commodity Yearbook.*

SINGAPORE - MONEY EXCHANGE RATES - See SINGAPORE - EXCHANGE RATES

SINGAPORE - MONEY RESERVES

Euromonitor International, Inc., 122 South Michigan Avenue, Suite 1200, Chicago, Illinois 60603 (800) 577-EURO; *International Marketing Data and Statistics.*

SINGAPORE - MONEY SUPPLY

Asian Development Bank, P.O. Box 789, 1099 Manila, Philippines; *Key Indicators of Developing Asian and Pacific Countries.*

Economist Intelligence Unit, 111 West 57th Street, New York, New York 10019 (800) 938-4685; *Singapore Country Report.*

Euromonitor International, Inc., 122 South Michigan Avenue, Suite 1200, Chicago, Illinois 60603 (800) 577-EURO; *International Marketing Data and Statistics.*

Federal Statistical Office, Gustav-Stresemann - Ring 11, D-6200, Wiesbaden, Germany; *Singapur.*

International Monetary Fund, 700 Nineteenth Street, NW, Washington, D.C. 20431 (202) 623-7000; *International Financial Statistics.*

Statistical Office of the United Nations, Publishing Service, New York, New York 10017 (800) 253-9646; *Statistical Yearbook.*

The World Bank, 1818 H Street, NW, Washington, D.C. 20433 (202) 477-1234; *World Development Indicators.*

SINGAPORE - MONUMENTS AND

HISTORICAL SITES

United Nations Educational, Scientific and Cultural Organization (UNESCO), 7 Place de Fontenoy, F-75700 Paris, France (Telephone Number in U.S. (212) 963-5981); *Statistical Yearbook*.

SINGAPORE - MORTALITY

Central Intelligence Agency, Washington, D.C. 20505 (703) 482-1100, www.cia.gov; *The World Factbook*.

The Economist Intelligence Unit (Asia) Limited, 10th Floor, Luk Kwok Centre, 72 Gloucester Road, Wanchai, Hong Kong (Phone Number in U.S. (800) 938-4685); *Asian Market Atlas*.

Euromonitor International, Inc., 122 South Michigan Avenue, Suite 1200, Chicago, Illinois 60603 (800) 577-EURO; *International Marketing Data and Statistics;* and *The World Economic Factbook*.

Europa Publications Limited, 18 Bedford Square, London, WC1B 3JN, England; *The Europa World Year Book*.

St. Martin's Press, Inc., 175 Fifth Avenue, New York, New York 10010 (800) 221-7945; *The Statesman's Year-Book*.

Statistical Office of the United Nations, Publishing Service, New York, New York 10017 (800) 253-9646; *Asia-Pacific in Figures; Demographic Yearbook; Human Development Report; Statistical Yearbook;* and *World Statistics Pocketbook*.

United Nations Children's Fund (UNICEF), 3 United Nations Plaza, New York, New York 10017 (800) 253-9646; *State of the World's Children*.

The World Bank, 1818 H Street, NW, Washington, D.C. 20433 (202) 477-1234; *The World Bank Atlas; World Development Report;* and *World Development Indicators*.

World Health Organization, Office of Publications, 20 Avenue Appia, CH-1211 Geneva 27, Switzerland (Telephone Number in U.S. (518) 436-9686); *World Health Statistics Annual*.

SINGAPORE - MOTION PICTURES

St. Martin's Press, Inc., 175 Fifth Avenue, New York, New York 10010 (800) 221-7945; *The Statesman's Year-Book*.

Statistical Office of the United Nations, Publishing Service, New York, New York 10017 (800) 253-9646; *Statistical Yearbook*.

United Nations Educational, Scientific and Cultural Organization (UNESCO), 7 Place de Fontenoy, F-75700 Paris, France (Telephone Number in U.S. (212) 963-

5981); *Statistical Yearbook*.

SINGAPORE - MOTOR VEHICLE TAXES -See SINGAPORE - TAXATION

SINGAPORE - MOTOR VEHICLES IN USE

Europa Publications Limited, 18 Bedford Square, London, WC1B 3JN, England; *The Europa World Year Book*.

International Road Federation, 2600 Virginia Avenue, NW, Washington, D.C. 20037 (202) 338-4641; *World Road Statistics*.

Statistical Office of the United Nations, Publishing Service, New York, New York 10017 (800) 253-9646; *Statistical Yearbook*.

SINGAPORE - MUSEUMS

M.E. Sharpe, 80 Business Park Drive, Armonk, New York 10504 (800) 541-6563; *The Illustrated Book of World Rankings*.

United Nations Educational, Scientific and Cultural Organization (UNESCO), 7 Place de Fontenoy, F-75700 Paris, France (Telephone Number in U.S. (212) 963-5981); *Statistical Yearbook*.

SINGAPORE - NATALITY - See SINGAP ORE - BIRTH RATE

SINGAPORE - NATIONAL ACCOUNTS

Europa Publications Limited, 18 Bedford Square, London, WC1B 3JN, England; *The Europa World Year Book*.

Federal Statistical Office, Gustav-Stresemann - Ring 11, D-6200, Wiesbaden, Germany; *Singapur*.

International Monetary Fund, 700 Nineteenth Street, NW, Washington, D.C. 20431 (202) 623-7000; *International Financial Statistics*.

Statistical Office of the United Nations, Publishing Service, New York, New York 10017 (800) 253-9646; *Asia-Pacific in Figures; National Accounts Statistics; Statistical Yearbook;* and *Statistical Yearbook for Asia and the Pacific*.

SINGAPORE - NATIONAL INCOME

M.E. Sharpe, 80 Business Park Drive, Armonk, New York 10504 (800) 541-6563; *The Illustrated Book of World Rankings*.

Statistical Office of the United Nations, Publishing Service, New York, New York 10017 (800) 253-9646; *National Accounts Statistics;* and *Statistical Yearbook*.

SINGAPORE - NATIONAL PRODUCT

M.E. Sharpe, 80 Business Park Drive,

Armonk, New York 10504 (800) 541-6563; *The Illustrated Book of World Rankings*.

Statistical Office of the United Nations, Publishing Service, New York, New York 10017 (800) 253-9646; *Statistical Yearbook*.

SINGAPORE - NATURAL GAS PRODUCTION - See SINGAPORE - MINING AND MINERAL PRODUCTS

SINGAPORE - NATURAL RUBBER PRODUCTION

International Rubber Study Group, York House, Eighth Floor, Empire Way, Wembley, London HA9 0PA, England; *Rubber Statistical Bulletin*.

SINGAPORE - NEWSPAPER PRODUCTION AND CONSUMPTION - See SINGAPORE - FORESTRY AND FOREST PRODUCTS

SINGAPORE - NEWSPRINT - See SINGAPORE - FORESTRY AND FOREST PRODUCTS

SINGAPORE - OCCUPATIONS - See SINGAPORE - LABOR

SINGAPORE - PAPER - See SINGAPORE - FORESTRY AND FOREST PRODUCTS

SINGAPORE - PATENTS, TRADEMARKS AND SERVICE MARKS

Statistical Office of the United Nations, Publishing Service, New York, New York 10017 (800) 253-9646; *Statistical Yearbook*.

World Intellectual Property Organization, 34 Chemin des Colombettes, CH-1211 Geneva 20. Switzerland; *Industrial Property Statistics*.

SINGAPORE - PEANUT PRODUCTION - See SINGAPORE - CROPS

SINGAPORE - PEPPER PRODUCTION - See SINGAPORE - CROPS

SINGAPORE - PERIODICALS

United Nations Educational, Scientific and Cultural Organization (UNESCO), 7 Place de Fontenoy, F-75700 Paris, France (Telephone Number in U.S. (212) 963-5981); *Statistical Yearbook*.

SINGAPORE - PESTICIDE USE

Food and Agricultural Organization of the United Nations (FAO) Via delle Terme di Caracalla, 00100 Rome, Italy (Telephone Number in U.S. (202) 653-2400); *The State of Food and Agriculture*.

SINGAPORE - PETROLEUM INDUSTRY

Asian Development Bank, P.O. Box 789,

1099 Manila, Philippines; *Key Indicators of Developing Asian and Pacific Countries.*

Food and Agricultural Organization of the United Nations (FAO) Via delle Terme di Caracalla, 00100 Rome, Italy (Telephone Number in U.S. (202) 653-2400); *The State of Food and Agriculture.*

M.E. Sharpe, 80 Business Park Drive, Armonk, New York 10504 (800) 541-6563; *The Illustrated Book of World Rankings.*

St. Martin's Press, Inc., 175 Fifth Avenue, New York, New York 10010 (800) 221-7945; *The Statesman's Year-Book.*

Statistical Office of the United Nations, Publishing Service, New York, New York 10017 (800) 253-9646; *Statistical Yearbook.*

United Nations Conference on Trade and Development, Central Statistical Service, Palais des Nations, Geneva, Switzerland (Telephone in U.S. (800) 253-9646); *UNCTAD Commodity Yearbook.*

SINGAPORE - PIGS - See SINGAPORE - LIVESTOCK AND POULTRY

SINGAPORE - POPULATION

Asian Development Bank, P.O. Box 789, 1099 Manila, Philippines; *Key Indicators of Developing Asian and Pacific Countries.*

Central Intelligence Agency, Washington, D.C. 20505 (703) 482-1100, www.cia.gov; *The World Factbook.*

The Economist Intelligence Unit, 111 West 57th Street, New York, New York 10019 (800) 938-4685; *Singapore Country Report;* and *The World Market Atlas.*

The Economist Intelligence Unit (Asia) Limited, 10th Floor, Luk Kwok Centre, 72 Gloucester Road, Wanchai, Hong Kong (Phone Number in U.S. (800) 938-4685); *Asian Market Atlas.*

Euromonitor International, Inc., 122 South Michigan Avenue, Suite 1200, Chicago, Illinois 60603 (800) 577-EURO; *International Marketing Data and Statistics;* and *The World Economic Factbook.*

Europa Publications Limited, 18 Bedford Square, London, WC1B 3JN, England; *The Europa World Year Book.*

Federal Statistical Office, Gustav-Stresemann - Ring 11, D-6200, Wiesbaden, Germany; *Singapur.*

Food and Agricultural Organization of the United Nations (FAO), Via delle Terme di Caracalla, 00100 Rome, Italy (Telephone Number in U.S. (202) 653-2400); *Production Yearbook.*

International Labour Office, I.L.O. Publications, 1828 L Street, NW., Suite 801, Washington, D.C. 20036 (301) 638-3152; *Yearbook of Labour Statistics.*

M.E. Sharpe, 80 Business Park Drive, Armonk, New York 10504 (800) 541-6563; *The Illustrated Book of World Rankings.*

St. Martin's Press, Inc., 175 Fifth Avenue, New York, New York 10010 (800) 221-7945; *The Statesman's Year-Book.*

Statistical Office of the United Nations, Publishing Service, New York, New York 10017 (800) 253-9646; *Asia-Pacific in Figures; Demographic Yearbook; Human Development Report; Statistical Yearbook; Statistical Yearbook for Asia and the Pacific;* and *World Statistics Pocketbook.*

United Nations Educational, Scientific and Cultural Organization (UNESCO), 7 Place de Fontenoy, F-75700 Paris, France (Telephone Number in U.S. (212) 963-5981); *Statistical Yearbook.*

U.S. Arms Control and Disarmament Agency, 320 Twenty-first Street, NW, Washington, D.C. 20451 (202) 647-8677; *World Military Expenditures and Arms Transfers.*

Walden Publishing Ltd., Two Market Street, Saffron Walden Essex, CB10 1HZ, England; *The World of Information Asia and Pacific Review.*

The World Bank, 1818 H Street, NW, Washington, D.C. 20433 (202) 477-1234; *The World Bank Atlas;* and *World Development Report.*

World Health Organization, Office of Publications, 20 Avenue Appia, CH-1211 Geneva 27, Switzerland (Telephone Number in U.S. (518) 436-9686); *World Health Statistics Annual.*

SINGAPORE - POST OFFICES

M.E. Sharpe, 80 Business Park Drive, Armonk, New York 10504 (800) 541-6563; *The Illustrated Book of World Rankings.*

St. Martin's Press, Inc., 175 Fifth Avenue, New York, New York 10010 (800) 221-7945; *The Statesman's Year-Book.*

SINGAPORE - POTATO PRODUCTION - See SINGAPORE - CROPS

SINGAPORE - POWER PRODUCTION INDUSTRY

Statistical Office of the United Nations, Publishing Service, New York, New York 10017 (800) 253-9646; *Electric Power in Asia and the Pacific.*

SINGAPORE - PRICES

Asian Development Bank, P.O. Box 789, 1099 Manila, Philippines; *Key Indicators of Developing Asian and Pacific Countries.*

Federal Statistical Office, Gustav-Stresemann - Ring 11, D-6200, Wiesbaden, Germany; *Singapur.*

Food and Agricultural Organization of the United Nations (FAO), Via delle Terme di Caracalla, 00100 Rome, Italy (Telephone Number in U.S. (202) 653-2400); *Production Yearbook;* and *The State of Food and Agriculture.*

International Labour Office, I.L.O. Publications, 1828 L Street, NW., Suite 801, Washington, D.C. 20036 (301) 638-3152; *Yearbook of Labour Statistics.*

International Monetary Fund, 700 Nineteenth Street, NW, Washington, D.C. 20431 (202) 623-7000; *International Financial Statistics.*

International Rubber Study Group, York House, Eighth Floor, Empire Way, Wembley, London HA9 0PA, England; *Rubber Statistical Bulletin.*

M.E. Sharpe, 80 Business Park Drive, Armonk, New York 10504 (800) 541-6563; *The Illustrated Book of World Rankings.*

SINGAPORE - PRINTING AND WRITING PAPER - See SINGAPORE - FORESTRY AND FOREST PRODUCTS

SINGAPORE - PRODUCTION

International Rubber Study Group, York House, Eighth Floor, Empire Way, Wembley, London HA9 0PA, England; *Rubber Statistical Bulletin.*

M.E. Sharpe, 80 Business Park Drive, Armonk, New York 10504 (800) 541-6563; *The Illustrated Book of World Rankings.*

SINGAPORE - PRODUCTIVITY

Euromonitor International, Inc., 122 South Michigan Avenue, Suite 1200, Chicago, Illinois 60603 (800) 577-EURO; *International Marketing Data and Statistics.*

SINGAPORE - PROPERTY TAXES - See SINGAPORE - TAXATION

SINGAPORE - PUBLIC FINANCE - See SINGAPORE - FINANCE

SINGAPORE - RADIO BROADCASTING - See SINGAPORE - BROADCASTING

SINGAPORE - RADIO RECEIVERS

St. Martin's Press, Inc., 175 Fifth Avenue, New York, New York 10010 (800) 221-7945; *The Statesman's Year-Book.*

SINGAPORE - RAILWAYS

St. Martin's Press, Inc., 175 Fifth Avenue, New York, New York 10010 (800) 221-7945; *The Statesman's Year-Book*.

SINGAPORE - RELIGION

Central Intelligence Agency, Washington, D.C. 20505 (703) 482-1100, www.cia.gov; *The World Factbook*.

M.E. Sharpe, 80 Business Park Drive, Armonk, New York 10504 (800) 541-6563; *The Illustrated Book of World Rankings*.

St. Martin's Press, Inc., 175 Fifth Avenue, New York, New York 10010 (800) 221-7945; *The Statesman's Year-Book*.

SINGAPORE - RENT PRICES

International Labour Office, I.L.O. Publications, 1828 L Street, NW., Suite 801, Washington, D.C. 20036 (301) 638-3152; *Yearbook of Labour Statistics*.

SINGAPORE - RETAIL TRADE

Euromonitor International Inc., 122 South Michigan Avenue, Suite 1200, Chicago, Illinois 60603 (800) 577-EURO; *World Marketing Data and Statistics*; and *Retail Trade International*.

Statistical Office of the United Nations, Publishing Service, New York, New York 10017 (800) 253-9646; *Statistical Yearbook*.

SINGAPORE - RICE PRODUCTION - See SINGAPORE - CROPS

SINGAPORE - ROUNDWOOD PRODUCTION - See SINGAPORE - FORESTRY AND FOREST PRODUCTS

SINGAPORE - RUBBER EXPORTS

International Monetary Fund, 700 Nineteenth Street, NW, Washington, D.C. 20431 (202) 623-7000; *International Financial Statistics*.

SINGAPORE - RUBBER PRODUCTION AND CONSUMPTION

International Rubber Study Group, York House, Eighth Floor, Empire Way, Wembley, London HA9 0PA, England; *Rubber Statistical Bulletin*.

M.E. Sharpe, 80 Business Park Drive, Armonk, New York 10504 (800) 541-6563; *The Illustrated Book of World Rankings*.

SINGAPORE - SAWNWOOD PRODUCTION - See SINGAPORE - FORESTRY AND FOREST PRODUCTS

SINGAPORE - SCIENCE AND TECHNOLOGY - EXPENDITURE

FOR RESEARCH - See SINGAPORE - SCIENTISTS, TECHNICIANS AND ENGINEERS

SINGAPORE - SCIENTISTS, TECHNICIANS AND ENGINEERS

Statistical Office of the United Nations, Publishing Service, New York, New York 10017 (800) 253-9646; *Statistical Yearbook*.

SINGAPORE - SENIOR CITIZENS

M.E. Sharpe, 80 Business Park Drive, Armonk, New York 10504 (800) 541-6563; *The Illustrated Book of World Rankings*.

SINGAPORE - SHEEP - See SINGAPORE - LIVESTOCK AND POULTRY

SINGAPORE - SILVER PRODUCTION AND CONSUMPTION - See SINGAPORE - MINING AND MINERAL PRODUCTS

SINGAPORE - SOCIAL DATA

Asian Development Bank, P.O. Box 789, 1099 Manila, Philippines; *Key Indicators of Developing Asian and Pacific Countries*.

M.E. Sharpe, 80 Business Park Drive, Armonk, New York 10504 (800) 541-6563; *The Illustrated Book of World Rankings*.

Statistical Office of the United Nations, Publishing Service, New York, New York 10017 (800) 253-9646; *World Statistics Pocketbook*.

SINGAPORE - SOCIAL SECURITY

International Monetary Fund, 700 Nineteenth Street, NW, Washington, D.C. 20431 (202) 623-7000; *Government Finance Statistics Yearbook*.

Statistical Office of the United Nations, Publishing Service, New York, New York 10017 (800) 253-9646; *National Accounts Statistics*.

SINGAPORE - STAMP TAXES AND DUTIES - See SINGAPORE - TAXATION

SINGAPORE - STATE BUDGET REVENUE AND EXPENDITURES

Euromonitor International, Inc., 122 South Michigan Avenue, Suite 1200, Chicago, Illinois 60603 (800) 577-EURO; *International Marketing Data and Statistics*.

SINGAPORE - STEEL - See SINGAPORE - MINING AND MINERAL PRODUCTS

SINGAPORE - STOCKS - COMMODITY - MARKET PRICE - INDEX

Food and Agricultural Organization of the United Nations (FAO) Via delle Terme di Caracalla, 00100 Rome, Italy (Telephone Number in U.S. (202) 653-2400); *The State of Food and Agriculture*.

SINGAPORE - SUGAR PRODUCTION AND CONSUMPTION - See SINGAPORE - CROPS

SINGAPORE - TAXATION

Europa Publications Limited, 18 Bedford Square, London, WC1B 3JN, England; *The Europa World Year Book*.

International Monetary Fund, 700 Nineteenth Street, NW, Washington, D.C. 20431 (202) 623-7000; *Government Finance Statistics Yearbook*.

International Road Federation, 2600 Virginia Avenue, NW, Washington, D.C. 20037 (202) 338-4641; *World Road Statistics*.

The World Bank, 1818 H Street, NW, Washington, D.C. 20433 (202) 477-1234; *World Development Indicators*.

SINGAPORE - TELEGRAPH SERVICE

Statistical Office of the United Nations, Publishing Service, New York, New York 10017 (800) 253-9646; *Statistical Yearbook*.

SINGAPORE - TELEPHONES IN USE

American Telephone and Telegraph Company, 26 Parsippany Road, Whippany, New Jersey 07981 (800) 222-0300; *The World's Telephones*.

Central Intelligence Agency, Washington, D.C. 20505 (703) 482-1100, www.cia.gov; *The World Factbook*.

The Economist Intelligence Unit (Asia) Limited, 10th Floor, Luk Kwok Centre, 72 Gloucester Road, Wanchai, Hong Kong (Phone Number in U.S. (800) 938-4685); *Asian Market Atlas*.

Europa Publications Limited, 18 Bedford Square, London, WC1B 3JN, England; *The Europa World Year Book*.

St. Martin's Press, Inc., 175 Fifth Avenue, New York, New York 10010 (800) 221-7945; *The Statesman's Year-Book*.

Statistical Office of the United Nations, Publishing Service, New York, New York 10017 (800) 253-9646; *Statistical Yearbook*; and *World Statistics Pocketbook*.

SINGAPORE - TELEVISION BROADCASTING - See SINGAPORE - BROADCASTING

SINGAPORE - TEXTILE INDUSTRY

Euromonitor International Inc., 122 South Michigan Avenue, Suite 1200,

Chicago, Illinois 60603 (800) 577-EURO; *Retail Trade International.*

M.E. Sharpe, 80 Business Park Drive, Armonk, New York 10504 (800) 541-6563; *The Illustrated Book of World Rankings.*

St. Martin's Press, Inc., 175 Fifth Avenue, New York, New York 10010 (800) 221-7945; *The Statesman's Year-Book.*

Statistical Office of the United Nations, Publishing Service, New York, New York 10017 (800) 253-9646; *Statistical Yearbook.*

United Nations Conference on Trade and Development, Central Statistical Service, Palais des Nations, Geneva, Switzerland (Telephone in U.S. (800) 253-9646); *UNCTAD Commodity Yearbook.*

SINGAPORE - THEATRE

United Nations Educational, Scientific and Cultural Organization (UNESCO), 7 Place de Fontenoy, F-75700 Paris, France (Telephone Number in U.S. (212) 963-5981); *Statistical Yearbook.*

SINGAPORE - TIRE (MOTOR VEHICLE) PRODUCTION

International Rubber Study Group, York House, Eighth Floor, Empire Way, Wembley, London HA9 0PA, England; *Rubber Statistical Bulletin.*

SINGAPORE - TOBACCO PRODUCTION

M.E. Sharpe, 80 Business Park Drive, Armonk, New York 10504 (800) 541-6563; *The Illustrated Book of World Rankings.*

Statistical Office of the United Nations, Publishing Service, New York, New York 10017 (800) 253-9646; *Statistical Yearbook.*

SINGAPORE - TOURISM

Euromonitor International, Inc., 122 South Michigan Avenue, Suite 1200, Chicago, Illinois 60603 (800) 577-EURO; *The World Economic Factbook;* and *World Marketing Data and Statistics.*

Europa Publications Limited, 18 Bedford Square, London, WC1B 3JN, England; *The Europa World Year Book.*

Federal Statistical Office, Gustav-Stresemann - Ring 11, D-6200, Wiesbaden, Germany; *Singapur.*

M.E. Sharpe, 80 Business Park Drive, Armonk, New York 10504 (800) 541-6563; *The Illustrated Book of World Rankings.*

St. Martin's Press, Inc., 175 Fifth Avenue, New York, New York 10010 (800) 221-7945; *The Statesman's Year-Book.*

Statistical Office of the United Nations, Publishing Service, New York, New York 10017 (800) 253-9646; *Statistical Yearbook.*

World Tourism Organization, Calle Capitan Haya 42, E-28020 Madrid, Spain; *Yearbook of Tourism Statistics.*

SINGAPORE - TRACTORS IN USE

Statistical Office of the United Nations, Publishing Service, New York, New York 10017 (800) 253-9646; *Statistical Yearbook.*

SINGAPORE - TRADE - See SINGAPORE - FOREIGN TRADE

SINGAPORE - TRADEMARKS AND SERVICE MARKS - See PATENTS, TRADEMARKS AND SERVICE MARKS

SINGAPORE - TRANSPORTATION AND COMMUNICATIONS

Central Intelligence Agency, Washington, D.C. 20505 (703) 482-1100, www.cia.gov; *The World Factbook.*

The Economist Intelligence Unit (Asia) Limited, 10th Floor, Luk Kwok Centre, 72 Gloucester Road, Wanchai, Hong Kong (Phone Number in U.S. (800) 938-4685); *Asian Market Atlas.*

Euromonitor International, Inc., 122 South Michigan Avenue, Suite 1200, Chicago, Illinois 60603 (800) 577-EURO; *International Marketing Data and Statistics;* and *World Marketing Data and Statistics.*

Europa Publications Limited, 18 Bedford Square, London, WC1B 3JN, England; *The Europa World Year Book.*

Federal Statistical Office, Gustav-Stresemann - Ring 11, D-6200, Wiesbaden, Germany; *Singapur.*

M.E. Sharpe, 80 Business Park Drive, Armonk, New York 10504 (800) 541-6563; *The Illustrated Book of World Rankings.*

St. Martin's Press, Inc., 175 Fifth Avenue, New York, New York 10010 (800) 221-7945; *The Statesman's Year-Book.*

Statistical Office of the United Nations, Publishing Service, New York, New York 10017 (800) 253-9646; *Human Development Report;* and *Statistical Yearbook for Asia and the Pacific.*

SINGAPORE - UNEMPLOYMENT

Central Intelligence Agency, Washington, D.C. 20505 (703) 482-1100, www.cia.gov; *The World Factbook.*

Euromonitor International, Inc., 122 South Michigan Avenue, Suite 1200, Chicago, Illinois 60603 (800) 577-EURO; *International Marketing Data and Statistics.*

International Labour Office, I.L.O. Publications, 1828 L Street, NW., Suite 801, Washington, D.C. 20036 (301) 638-3152; *Yearbook of Labour Statistics.*

St. Martin's Press, Inc., 175 Fifth Avenue, New York, New York 10010 (800) 221-7945; *The Statesman's Year-Book.*

Statistical Office of the United Nations, Publishing Service, New York, New York 10017 (800) 253-9646; *Statistical Yearbook.*

SINGAPORE - UTILITIES

Statistical Office of the United Nations, Publishing Service, New York, New York 10017 (800) 253-9646; *Electric Power in Asia and the Pacific.*

SINGAPORE - VITAL STATISTICS

Euromonitor International, Inc., 122 South Michigan Avenue, Suite 1200, Chicago, Illinois 60603 (800) 577-EURO; *International Marketing Data and Statistics.*

St. Martin's Press, Inc., 175 Fifth Avenue, New York, New York 10010 (800) 221-7945; *The Statesman's Year-Book.*

Statistical Office of the United Nations, Publishing Service, New York, New York 10017 (800) 253-9646; *Statistical Yearbook.*

World Health Organization, Office of Publications, 20 Avenue Appia, CH-1211 Geneva 27, Switzerland (Telephone Number in U.S. (518) 436-9686); *World Health Statistics Annual.*

SINGAPORE - WAGES

Federal Statistical Office, Gustav-Stresemann - Ring 11, D-6200, Wiesbaden, Germany; *Singapur.*

International Labour Office, I.L.O. Publications, 1828 L Street, NW., Suite 801, Washington, D.C. 20036 (301) 638-3152; *Yearbook of Labour Statistics.*

Statistical Office of the United Nations, Publishing Service, New York, New York 10017 (800) 253-9646; *Statistical Yearbook for Asia and the Pacific;* and *Statistical Yearbook.*

SINGAPORE - WEATHER - See SINGAPORE - CLIMATE

SINGAPORE - WELFARE

International Monetary Fund, 700 Nineteenth Street, NW, Washington, D.C. 20431 (202) 623-7000; *Government Finance Statistics Yearbook.*

SINGAPORE - WHEAT PRODUCTION AND

PRICES - See SINGAPORE -CROPS

SINGAPORE - WHOLESALE PRICES

Asian Development Bank, P.O. Box 789, 1099 Manila, Philippines; *Key Indicators of Developing Asian and Pacific Countries.*

International Monetary Fund, 700 Nineteenth Street, NW, Washington, D.C. 20431 (202) 623-7000; *International Financial Statistics.*

Statistical Office of the United Nations, Publishing Service, New York, New York 10017 (800) 253-9646; *Statistical Yearbook.*

SINGAPORE - WHOLESALE TRADE

Statistical Office of the United Nations, Publishing Service, New York, New York 10017 (800) 253-9646; *Statistical Yearbook.*

SINGAPORE - WINE PRODUCTION - See SINGAPORE - BEVERAGES

SINGAPORE - WOOD PULP PRODUCTION - See SINGAPORE - FORESTRY AND FOREST PRODUCTS

SINGAPORE - WOOL PRODUCTION - See SINGAPORE - TEXTILE INDUSTRY

SINGAPORE - ZOOS AND BOTANICAL GARDENS

United Nations Educational, Scientific and Cultural Organization (UNESCO), 7 Place de Fontenoy, F-75700 Paris, France (Telephone Number in U.S. (212) 963-5981); *Statistical Yearbook.*

SINGLE PERSONS - See MARITAL STATUS

SINUSITUS

U.S. Department of Health and Human Services, National Center for Health Statistics, 3700 East-West Highway, Hyattsville, Maryland 20782 (301) 436-8500, www.cdc.gov/nchs; *Vital and Health Statistics*; and unpublished data.

SKATEBOARDING

National Sporting Goods Association, 1601 Feehanville Drive, Suite 300, Mount Prospect, Illinois 66056 (847) 296-6742; *Sports Participation in 1998.*

SKIING

National Sporting Goods Association, 1601 Feehanville Drive, Suite 300, Mount Prospect, Illinois 66056 (847) 296-6742; *The Sporting Goods Market in 1999;* and *Sports Participation in 1998.*

SKINS - See HIDES

SLAUGHTERING AND MEAT PACKING

INDUSTRY - See MEAT AND MEAT PRODUCTS

SLOVAKIA - See also CZECH REPUBLIC

SLOVAKIA - ABORTIONS

Statistical Office of the United Nations, Publishing Service, New York, New York 10017 (800) 253-9646; *Trends in Europe and North America: The Statistical Yearbook of the Economic Commission for Europe.*

SLOVAKIA - AGRICULTURE

Economist Intelligence Unit, 111 West 57th Street, New York, New York 10019 (800) 938-4685; *Slovakia Country Report.*

Euromonitor International Inc., 122 South Michigan Avenue, Suite 1200, Chicago, Illinois 60603 (800) 577-EURO; *World Marketing Data and Statistics.*

Europa Publications Limited, 18 Bedford Square, London, WC1B 3JN, England; *The Europa World Year Book.*

Food and Agriculture Organization of the United Nations (FAO), Via delle Terme di Caracalla, 00100, Rome, Italy (Telephone Number in U.S. (202) 653-2400); *Production Yearbook; The State of Food and Agriculture;* and *Trade Yearbook.*

St. Martin's Press, Inc., 175 Fifth Avenue, New York, New York 10010 (800) 221-7945; *The Statesman's Year-Book.*

Statistical Office of the United Nations, Publishing Service, New York, New York 10017 (800) 253-9646; *Industrial Commodity Statistics Yearbook;* and *Statistical Yearbook.*

United Nations Conference on Trade and Development, Central Statistical Service, Palais des Nations, Geneva, Switzerland (Telephone in U.S. (800) 253-9646); *UNCTAD Commodity Yearbook.*

SLOVAKIA - AIRLINE SERVICE

International Civil Aviation Organization, 999 University Street, Montreal, Quebec, Canada H3C 5H7 (514) 954-8219; *Civil Aviation Statistics of the World.*

St. Martin's Press, Inc., 175 Fifth Avenue, New York, New York 10010 (800) 221-7945; *The Statesman's Year-Book.*

Statistical Office of the United Nations, Publishing Service, New York, New York 10017 (800) 253-9646; *Statistical Yearbook.*

SLOVAKIA - AIRPORTS

Central Intelligence Agency, Washington, D.C. 20505 (703) 482-1100,

www.cia.gov; *The World Factbook.*

SLOVAKIA - ANIMAL HEALTH

Food and Agriculture Organization of the United Nations (FAO), Via delle Terme di Caracalla, 00100, Rome, Italy (Telephone Number in U.S. (202) 653-2400); *Animal Health Yearbook.*

SLOVAKIA - AREA AND DENSITY OF POPULATION

Central Intelligence Agency, Washington, D.C. 20505 (703) 482-1100, www.cia.gov; *The World Factbook.*

Euromonitor International, Inc., 122 South Michigan Avenue, Suite 1200, Chicago, Illinois 60603 (800) 577-EURO; *The World Economic Factbook.*

Europa Publications Limited, 18 Bedford Square, London, WC1B 3JN, England; *The Europa World Year Book.*

St. Martin's Press, Inc., 175 Fifth Avenue, New York, New York 10010 (800) 221-7945; *The Statesman's Year-Book.*

Statistical Office of the United Nations, Publishing Service, New York, New York 10017 (800) 253-9646; *Statistical Yearbook;* and *Trends in Europe and North America: The Statistical Yearbook of the Economic Commission for Europe.*

United Nations Educational, Scientific and Cultural Organization (UNESCO), 7 Place de Fontenoy, F-75700 Paris, France (Telephone Number in U.S. (212) 963-5981); *Statistical Yearbook.*

The World Bank, 1818 H Street, NW, Washington, D.C. 20433 (202) 477-1234; *World Development Report.*

SLOVAKIA - BALANCE OF PAYMENTS

United Nations Conference on Trade and Development (UNCTAD), New York, New York 10017 (800) 253-9646; *Handbook of International Trade and Development Statistics.*

The World Bank, 1818 H Street, NW, Washington, D.C. 20433 (202) 477-1234; *World Development Report.*

SLOVAKIA - BANKING

Euromonitor International Inc., 122 South Michigan Avenue, Suite 1200, Chicago, Illinois 60603 (800) 577-EURO; *World Marketing Data and Statistics.*

St. Martin's Press, Inc., 175 Fifth Avenue, New York, New York 10010 (800) 221-7945; *The Statesman's Year-Book.*

SLOVAKIA - BEVERAGES

Statistical Office of the United Nations, Publishing Service, New York, New York 10017 (800) 253-9646; *Statistical Yearbook.*

SLOVAKIA - BIRTH RATES

Central Intelligence Agency, Washington, D.C. 20505 (703) 482-1100, www.cia.gov; *The World Factbook.*

Euromonitor International, Inc., 122 South Michigan Avenue, Suite 1200, Chicago, Illinois 60603 (800) 577-EURO; *The World Economic Factbook.*

Europa Publications Limited, 18 Bedford Square, London, WC1B 3JN, England; *The Europa World Year Book.*

St. Martin's Press, Inc., 175 Fifth Avenue, New York, New York 10010 (800) 221-7945; *The Statesman's Year-Book.*

Statistical Office of the United Nations, Publishing Service, New York, New York 10017 (800) 253-9646; *Statistical Yearbook.*

SLOVAKIA - BOOK PRODUCTION

Europa Publications Limited, 18 Bedford Square, London, WC1B 3JN, England; *The Europa World Year Book.*

Statistical Office of the United Nations, Publishing Service, New York, New York 10017 (800) 253-9646; *Trends in Europe and North America: The Statistical Yearbook of the Economic Commission for Europe.*

United Nations Educational, Scientific and Cultural Organization (UNESCO), 7 Place de Fontenoy, F-75700 Paris, France (Telephone Number in U.S. (212) 963-5981); *Statistical Yearbook.*

SLOVAKIA - BROADCASTING

Central Intelligence Agency, Washington, D.C. 20505 (703) 482-1100, www.cia.gov; *The World Factbook.*

Euromonitor International Inc., 122 South Michigan Avenue, Suite 1200, Chicago, Illinois 60603 (800) 577-EURO; *World Marketing Data and Statistics.*

St. Martin's Press, Inc., 175 Fifth Avenue, New York, New York 10010 (800) 221-7945; *The Statesman's Year-Book.*

Statistical Office of the United Nations, Publishing Service, New York, New York 10017 (800) 253-9646; *Trends in Europe and North America: The Statistical Yearbook of the Economic Commission for Europe.*

United Nations Educational, Scientific and Cultural Organization (UNESCO), 7 Place de Fontenoy, F-75700 Paris, France (Telephone Number in U.S. (212) 963-5981); *Statistical Yearbook.*

SLOVAKIA - BUDGET

Central Intelligence Agency, Washington, D.C. 20505 (703) 482-1100, www.cia.gov; *The World Factbook.*

SLOVAKIA - CLIMATE

St. Martin's Press, Inc., 175 Fifth Avenue, New York, New York 10010 (800) 221-7945; *The Statesman's Year-Book.*

SLOVAKIA - COMMERCE

St. Martin's Press, Inc., 175 Fifth Avenue, New York, New York 10010 (800) 221-7945; *The Statesman's Year-Book.*

SLOVAKIA - CONSTRUCTION INDUSTRY

St. Martin's Press, Inc., 175 Fifth Avenue, New York, New York 10010 (800) 221-7945; *The Statesman's Year-Book.*

Statistical Office of the United Nations, Publishing Service, New York, New York 10017 (800) 253-9646; *Statistical Yearbook.*

SLOVAKIA - CONSUMER PRICE INDEX

Europa Publications Limited, 18 Bedford Square, London, WC1B 3JN, England; *The Europa World Year Book.*

Statistical Office of the United Nations, Publishing Service, New York, New York 10017 (800) 253-9646; *Statistical Yearbook; and Trends in Europe and North America: The Statistical Yearbook of the Economic Commission for Europe.*

SLOVAKIA - CONSUMER PRICES

Euromonitor International Inc., 122 South Michigan Avenue, Suite 1200, Chicago, Illinois 60603 (800) 577-EURO; *World Marketing Data and Statistics.*

SLOVAKIA - CONSUMPTION

The World Bank, 1818 H Street, NW, Washington, D.C. 20433 (202) 477-1234; *World Development Report.*

SLOVAKIA - CRIME

Statistical Office of the United Nations, Publishing Service, New York, New York 10017 (800) 253-9646; *Trends in Europe and North America: The Statistical Yearbook of the Economic Commission for Europe.*

SLOVAKIA - CROPS

Europa Publications Limited, 18 Bedford Square, London, WC1B 3JN, England; *The Europa World Year Book.*

Food and Agriculture Organization of the United Nations (FAO), Via delle Terme di Caracalla, 00100, Rome, Italy (Telephone Number in U.S. (202) 653-2400); *Production Yearbook; The State of Food and Agriculture;* and *Trade Yearbook.*

St. Martin's Press, Inc., 175 Fifth Avenue, New York, New York 10010 (800) 221-7945; *The Statesman's Year-Book.*

Statistical Office of the United Nations, Publishing Service, New York, New York 10017 (800) 253-9646; *Industrial Commodity Statistics Yearbook;* and *Statistical Yearbook.*

United Nations Conference on Trade and Development, Central Statistical Service, Palais des Nations, Geneva, Switzerland (Telephone in U.S. (800) 253-9646); *UNCTAD Commodity Yearbook.*

SLOVAKIA - DAIRY PRODUCTS

Europa Publications Limited, 18 Bedford Square, London, WC1B 3JN, England; *The Europa World Year Book.*

Food and Agriculture Organization of the United Nations (FAO), Via delle Terme di Caracalla, 00100, Rome, Italy (Telephone Number in U.S. (202) 653-2400); *Production Yearbook; The State of Food and Agriculture;* and *Trade Yearbook.*

St. Martin's Press, Inc., 175 Fifth Avenue, New York, New York 10010 (800) 221-7945; *The Statesman's Year-Book.*

Statistical Office of the United Nations, Publishing Service, New York, New York 10017 (800) 253-9646; *Industrial Commodity Statistics Yearbook;* and *Statistical Yearbook.*

SLOVAKIA - DEATH RATES - See SLOVAKIA - MORTALITY

SLOVAKIA - DEMOGRAPHY

Euromonitor International, Inc., 122 South Michigan Avenue, Suite 1200, Chicago, Illinois 60603 (800) 577-EURO; *The World Economic Factbook; and World Marketing Data and Statistics.*

Statistical Office of the United Nations, Publishing Service, New York, New York 10017 (800) 253-9646; *Demographic Yearbook;* and *Human Development Report.*

SLOVAKIA - DIVORCE RATES

Statistical Office of the United Nations, Publishing Service, New York, New York 10017 (800) 253-9646; *Demographic Yearbook; Statistical Yearbook;* and *Trends in Europe and North America: The Statistical Yearbook of the Economic Commission for Europe.*

SLOVAKIA - ECONOMY

Central Intelligence Agency, Washington, D.C. 20505 (703) 482-1100, www.cia.gov; *The World Factbook.*

Economist Intelligence Unit, 111 West 57th Street, New York, New York 10019 (800) 938-4685; *Slovakia Country Report.*

Euromonitor International, Inc., 122 South Michigan Avenue, Suite 1200, Chicago, Illinois 60603 (800) 577-EURO; *The World Economic Factbook; and World Marketing Data and Statistics.*

Europa Publications Limited, 18 Bedford Square, London, WC1B 3JN, England; *The Europa World Year Book.*

St. Martin's Press, Inc., 175 Fifth Avenue, New York, New York 10010 (800) 221-7945; *The Statesman's Year-Book.*

Statistical Office of the United Nations, Publishing Service, New York, New York 10017 (800) 253-9646; *World Statistics Pocketbook.*

The World Bank, 1818 H Street, NW, Washington, D.C. 20433 (202) 477-1234; *The World Bank Atlas; and World Development Report.*

SLOVAKIA - EDUCATION

Euromonitor International Inc., 122 South Michigan Avenue, Suite 1200, Chicago, Illinois 60603 (800) 577-EURO; *World Marketing Data and Statistics.*

Europa Publications Limited, 18 Bedford Square, London, WC1B 3JN, England; *The Europa World Year Book.*

St. Martin's Press, Inc., 175 Fifth Avenue, New York, New York 10010 (800) 221-7945; *The Statesman's Year-Book.*

Statistical Office of the United Nations, Publishing Service, New York, New York 10017 (800) 253-9646; *Human Development Report; and Trends in Europe and North America: The Statistical Yearbook of the Economic Commission for Europe.*

United Nations Educational, Scientific and Cultural Organization (UNESCO), 7 Place de Fontenoy, F-75700 Paris, France (Telephone Number in U.S. (212) 963-5981); *Statistical Yearbook.*

The World Bank, 1818 H Street, NW, Washington, D.C. 20433 (202) 477-1234; *World Development Report.*

SLOVAKIA - ELECTRICITY

Central Intelligence Agency, Washington, D.C. 20505 (703) 482-1100, www.cia.gov; *The World Factbook.*

St. Martin's Press, Inc., 175 Fifth Avenue, New York, New York 10010 (800) 221-7945; *The Statesman's Year-Book.*

Statistical Office of the United Nations, Publishing Service, New York, New York 10017 (800) 253-9646; *Energy Statistics Yearbook; Human Development Report; Statistical Yearbook; and Trends in Europe and North America: The Statistical Yearbook of the Economic Commission for Europe.*

SLOVAKIA - EMPLOYMENT

Statistical Office of the United Nations, Publishing Service, New York, New York 10017 (800) 253-9646; *Statistical Yearbook; and Trends in Europe and North America: The Statistical Yearbook of the Economic Commission for Europe.*

SLOVAKIA - ENERGY

Euromonitor International, Inc., 122 South Michigan Avenue, Suite 1200, Chicago, Illinois 60603 (800) 577-EURO; *The World Economic Factbook; and World Marketing Data and Statistics.*

St. Martin's Press, Inc., 175 Fifth Avenue, New York, New York 10010 (800) 221-7945; *The Statesman's Year-Book.*

Statistical Office of the United Nations, Publishing Service, New York, New York 10017 (800) 253-9646; *Energy Statistics Yearbook; Human Development Report; Statistical Yearbook; Trends in Europe and North America: The Statistical Yearbook of the Economic Commission for Europe; and World Statistics Pocketbook.*

The World Bank, 1818 H Street, NW, Washington, D.C. 20433 (202) 477-1234; *The World Bank Atlas; and World Development Report.*

SLOVAKIA - ENVIRONMENT

Economist Intelligence Unit, 111 West 57th Street, New York, New York 10019 (800) 938-4685; *Slovakia Country Report.*

Statistical Office of the United Nations, Publishing Service, New York, New York 10017 (800) 253-9646; *Statistical Yearbook; Trends in Europe and North America: The Statistical Yearbook of the Economic Commission for Europe; and World Statistics Pocketbook.*

SLOVAKIA - EXCHANGE RATES

Central Intelligence Agency, Washington, D.C. 20505 (703) 482-1100, www.cia.gov; *The World Factbook.*

Euromonitor International, Inc., 122 South Michigan Avenue, Suite 1200, Chicago, Illinois 60603 (800) 577-EURO;

The World Economic Factbook.

Europa Publications Limited, 18 Bedford Square, London, WC1B 3JN, England; *The Europa World Year Book.*

Statistical Office of the United Nations, Publishing Service, New York, New York 10017 (800) 253-9646; *Statistical Yearbook; Trends in Europe and North America: The Statistical Yearbook of the Economic Commission for Europe; and World Statistics Pocketbook.*

SLOVAKIA - EXPORTS

Central Intelligence Agency, Washington, D.C. 20505 (703) 482-1100, www.cia.gov; *The World Factbook.*

Economist Intelligence Unit, 111 West 57th Street, New York, New York 10019 (800) 938-4685; *Slovakia Country Report.*

Euromonitor International, Inc., 122 South Michigan Avenue, Suite 1200, Chicago, Illinois 60603 (800) 577-EURO; *The World Economic Factbook.*

Europa Publications Limited, 18 Bedford Square, London, WC1B 3JN, England; *The Europa World Year Book.*

St. Martin's Press, Inc., 175 Fifth Avenue, New York, New York 10010 (800) 221-7945; *The Statesman's Year-Book.*

Statistical Office of the United Nations, Publishing Service, New York, New York 10017 (800) 253-9646; *International Trade Statistics Yearbook; and Trends in Europe and North America: The Statistical Yearbook of the Economic Commission for Europe.*

United Nations Conference on Trade and Development (UNCTAD); New York, New York 10017 (800) 253-9646; *Handbook of International Trade and Development Statistics.*

The World Bank, 1818 H Street, NW, Washington, D.C. 20433 (202) 477-1234; *World Development Report.*

SLOVAKIA - EXTERNAL INDEBTEDNESS

The World Bank, 1818 H Street, NW, Washington, D.C. 20433 (202) 477-1234; *World Development Report.*

SLOVAKIA - EXTERNAL TRADE

Euromonitor International Inc., 122 South Michigan Avenue, Suite 1200, Chicago, Illinois 60603 (800) 577-EURO; *World Marketing Data and Statistics.*

Food and Agriculture Organization of the United Nations (FAO), Via delle Terme di Caracalla, 00100, Rome, Italy (Telephone

Number in U.S. (202) 653-2400); *Trade Yearbook.*

Statistical Office of the United Nations, Publishing Service, New York, New York 10017 (800) 253-9646; *Statistical Yearbook.*

SLOVAKIA - FERTILITY RATES

Central Intelligence Agency, Washington, D.C. 20505 (703) 482-1100, www.cia.gov; *The World Factbook.*

Statistical Office of the United Nations, Publishing Service, New York, New York 10017 (800) 253-9646; *Human Development Report;* and *Trends in Europe and North America: The Statistical Yearbook of the Economic Commission for Europe.*

The World Bank, 1818 H Street, NW, Washington, D.C. 20433 (202) 477-1234; *The World Bank Atlas;* and *World Development Report.*

SLOVAKIA - FERTILIZER

Food and Agriculture Organization of the United Nations (FAO), Via delle Terme di Caracalla, 00100, Rome, Italy (Telephone Number in U.S. (202) 653-2400); *Fertilizer Yearbook.*

Statistical Office of the United Nations, Publishing Service, New York, New York 10017 (800) 253-9646; *Industrial Commodity Statistics Yearbook;* and *Statistical Yearbook.*

SLOVAKIA - FINANCE

Economist Intelligence Unit, 111 West 57th Street, New York, New York 10019 (800) 938-4685; *Slovakia Country Report.*

Europa Publications Limited, 18 Bedford Square, London, WC1B 3JN, England; *The Europa World Year Book.*

St. Martin's Press, Inc., 175 Fifth Avenue, New York, New York 10010 (800) 221-7945; *The Statesman's Year-Book.*

SLOVAKIA - FISHERIES

Food and Agriculture Organization of the United Nations (FAO), Via delle Terme di Caracalla, 00100, Rome, Italy (Telephone Number in U.S. (202) 653-2400); *The State of Food and Agriculture;* and *Yearbook of Fisheries.*

Statistical Office of the United Nations, Publishing Service, New York, New York 10017 (800) 253-9646; *Industrial Commodity Statistics Yearbook;* and *Statistical Yearbook.*

United Nations Conference on Trade and Development, Central Statistical

Service, Palais des Nations, Geneva, Switzerland (Telephone in U.S. (800) 253-9646); *UNCTAD Commodity Yearbook.*

SLOVAKIA - FOOD

Euromonitor International Inc., 122 South Michigan Avenue, Suite 1200, Chicago, Illinois 60603 (800) 577-EURO; *Retail Trade International.*

Food and Agriculture Organization of the United Nations (FAO), Via delle Terme di Caracalla, 00100, Rome, Italy (Telephone Number in U.S. (202) 653-2400); *Production Yearbook; The State of Food and Agriculture;* and *Trade Yearbook.*

Statistical Office of the United Nations, Publishing Service, New York, New York 10017 (800) 253-9646; *Human Development Report;* and *Industrial Commodity Statistics Yearbook.*

United Nations Conference on Trade and Development, Central Statistical Service, Palais des Nations, Geneva, Switzerland (Telephone in U.S. (800) 253-9646); *UNCTAD Commodity Yearbook.*

SLOVAKIA - FOREIGN TRADE

Economist Intelligence Unit, 111 West 57th Street, New York, New York 10019 (800) 938-4685; *Slovakia Country Report.*

Euromonitor International, Inc., 122 South Michigan Avenue, Suite 1200, Chicago, Illinois 60603 (800) 577-EURO; *The World Economic Factbook.*

Europa Publications Limited, 18 Bedford Square, London, WC1B 3JN, England; *The Europa World Year Book.*

Food and Agriculture Organization of the United Nations (FAO), Via delle Terme di Caracalla, 00100, Rome, Italy (Telephone Number in U.S. (202) 653-2400); *Trade Yearbook.*

Statistical Office of the United Nations, Publishing Service, New York, New York 10017 (800) 253-9646; *International Trade Statistics Yearbook;* and *Statistical Yearbook.*

The World Bank, 1818 H Street, NW, Washington, D.C. 20433 (202) 477-1234; *World Development Report.*

SLOVAKIA - FORESTRY AND FOREST PRODUCTS

Europa Publications Limited, 18 Bedford Square, London, WC1B 3JN, England; *The Europa World Year Book.*

Food and Agriculture Organization of the United Nations (FAO), Via delle Terme di Caracalla, 00100, Rome, Italy (Telephone

Number in U.S. (202) 653-2400); *The State of Food and Agriculture;* and *Yearbook of Forest Products.*

Statistical Office of the United Nations, Publishing Service, New York, New York 10017 (800) 253-9646; *Industrial Commodity Statistics Yearbook; Statistical Yearbook;* and *Trends in Europe and North America: The Statistical Yearbook of the Economic Commission for Europe.*

United Nations Conference on Trade and Development, Central Statistical Service, Palais des Nations, Geneva, Switzerland (Telephone in U.S. (800) 253-9646); *UNCTAD Commodity Yearbook.*

United Nations Educational, Scientific and Cultural Organization (UNESCO), 7 Place de Fontenoy, F-75700 Paris, France (Telephone Number in U.S. (212) 963-5981); *Statistical Yearbook.*

The World Bank, 1818 H Street, NW, Washington, D.C. 20433 (202) 477-1234; *World Development Report.*

SLOVAKIA - GOVERNMENT

Central Intelligence Agency, Washington, D.C. 20505 (703) 482-1100, www.cia.gov; *The World Factbook.*

Europa Publications Limited, 18 Bedford Square, London, WC1B 3JN, England; *The Europa World Year Book.*

St. Martin's Press, Inc., 175 Fifth Avenue, New York, New York 10010 (800) 221-7945; *The Statesman's Year-Book.*

Statistical Office of the United Nations, Publishing Service, New York, New York 10017 (800) 253-9646; *National Accounts Statistics;* and *Statistical Yearbook.*

The World Bank, 1818 H Street, NW, Washington, D.C. 20433 (202) 477-1234; *World Development Report.*

SLOVAKIA - GROSS DOMESTIC PRODUCT

Economist Intelligence Unit, 111 West 57th Street, New York, New York 10019 (800) 938-4685; *Slovakia Country Report.*

Euromonitor International, Inc., 122 South Michigan Avenue, Suite 1200, Chicago, Illinois 60603 (800) 577-EURO; *The World Economic Factbook.*

Europa Publications Limited, 18 Bedford Square, London, WC1B 3JN, England; *The Europa World Year Book.*

Statistical Office of the United Nations, Publishing Service, New York, New York 10017 (800) 253-9646; *Human Development Report; National Accounts Statistics; Statistical Yearbook;* and *Trends* in Europe and North America: The Statistical Yearbook of the Economic Commission for Europe.

The World Bank, 1818 H Street, NW, Washington, D.C. 20433 (202) 477-1234; World Development Report.

SLOVAKIA - GROSS NATIONAL PRODUCT

The World Bank, 1818 H Street, NW, Washington, D.C. 20433 (202) 477-1234; The World Bank Atlas; and World Development Report.

SLOVAKIA - HEALTH

Euromonitor International Inc., 122 South Michigan Avenue, Suite 1200, Chicago, Illinois 60603 (800) 577-EURO; World Marketing Data and Statistics.

St. Martin's Press, Inc., 175 Fifth Avenue, New York, New York 10010 (800) 221-7945; The Statesman's Year-Book.

Statistical Office of the United Nations, Publishing Service, New York, New York 10017 (800) 253-9646; Human Development Report; Statistical Yearbook; and Trends in Europe and North America: The Statistical Yearbook of the Economic Commission for Europe.

United Nations Children's Fund (UNICEF), 3 United Nations Plaza, New York, New York 10017 (800) 253-9646; State of the World's Children.

The World Bank, 1818 H Street, NW, Washington, D.C. 20433 (202) 477-1234; World Development Report.

SLOVAKIA - HIGHWAYS

Central Intelligence Agency, Washington, D.C. 20505 (703) 482-1100, www.cia.gov; The World Factbook.

St. Martin's Press, Inc., 175 Fifth Avenue, New York, New York 10010 (800) 221-7945; The Statesman's Year-Book.

Statistical Office of the United Nations, Publishing Service, New York, New York 10017 (800) 253-9646; Annual Bulletin of Transport Statistics for Europe; and Trends in Europe and North America: The Statistical Yearbook of the Economic Commission for Europe.

SLOVAKIA - HOUSING AND HOUSING UNITS

Euromonitor International Inc., 122 South Michigan Avenue, Suite 1200, Chicago, Illinois 60603 (800) 577-EURO; World Marketing Data and Statistics.

Statistical Office of the United Nations, Publishing Service, New York, New York

10017 (800) 253-9646; Trends in Europe and North America: The Statistical Yearbook of the Economic Commission for Europe.

SLOVAKIA - ILLITERATE POPULATION

Central Intelligence Agency, Washington, D.C. 20505 (703) 482-1100, www.cia.gov; The World Factbook.

Euromonitor International, Inc., 122 South Michigan Avenue, Suite 1200, Chicago, Illinois 60603 (800) 577-EURO; The World Economic Factbook.

Statistical Office of the United Nations, Publishing Service, New York, New York 10017 (800) 253-9646; Human Development Report.

United Nations Educational, Scientific and Cultural Organization (UNESCO), 7 Place de Fontenoy, F-75700 Paris, France (Telephone Number in U.S. (212) 963-5981); Statistical Yearbook.

SLOVAKIA - IMPORTS

Central Intelligence Agency, Washington, D.C. 20505 (703) 482-1100, www.cia.gov; The World Factbook.

Economist Intelligence Unit, 111 West 57th Street, New York, New York 10019 (800) 938-4685; Slovakia Country Report.

Euromonitor International, Inc., 122 South Michigan Avenue, Suite 1200, Chicago, Illinois 60603 (800) 577-EURO; The World Economic Factbook.

Europa Publications Limited, 18 Bedford Square, London, WC1B 3JN, England; The Europa World Year Book.

St. Martin's Press, Inc., 175 Fifth Avenue, New York, New York 10010 (800) 221-7945; The Statesman's Year-Book.

Statistical Office of the United Nations, Publishing Service, New York, New York 10017 (800) 253-9646; International Trade Statistics Yearbook; and Trends in Europe and North America: The Statistical Yearbook of the Economic Commission for Europe.

United Nations Conference on Trade and Development (UNCTAD), New York, New York 10017 (800) 253-9646; Handbook of International Trade and Development Statistics.

The World Bank, 1818 H Street, NW, Washington, D.C. 20433 (202) 477-1234; World Development Report.

SLOVAKIA - INDUSTRY

Central Intelligence Agency, Washington, D.C. 20505 (703) 482-1100,

www.cia.gov; The World Factbook.

Economist Intelligence Unit, 111 West 57th Street, New York, New York 10019 (800) 938-4685; Slovakia Country Report.

Euromonitor International, Inc., 122 South Michigan Avenue, Suite 1200, Chicago, Illinois 60603 (800) 577-EURO; The World Economic Factbook; and World Marketing Data and Statistics.

Europa Publications Limited, 18 Bedford Square, London, WC1B 3JN, England; The Europa World Year Book.

St. Martin's Press, Inc., 175 Fifth Avenue, New York, New York 10010 (800) 221-7945; The Statesman's Year-Book.

Statistical Office of the United Nations, Publishing Service, New York, New York 10017 (800) 253-9646; Industrial Commodity Statistics Yearbook; Statistical Yearbook; and Trends in Europe and North America: The Statistical Yearbook of the Economic Commission for Europe.

SLOVAKIA - INTERNAL TRADE

Statistical Office of the United Nations, Publishing Service, New York, New York 10017 (800) 253-9646; Statistical Yearbook.

SLOVAKIA - LABOR

Central Intelligence Agency, Washington, D.C. 20505 (703) 482-1100, www.cia.gov; The World Factbook.

Euromonitor International Inc., 122 South Michigan Avenue, Suite 1200, Chicago, Illinois 60603 (800) 577-EURO; World Marketing Data and Statistics.

Europa Publications Limited, 18 Bedford Square, London, WC1B 3JN, England; The Europa World Year Book.

St. Martin's Press, Inc., 175 Fifth Avenue, New York, New York 10010 (800) 221-7945; The Statesman's Year-Book.

Statistical Office of the United Nations, Publishing Service, New York, New York 10017 (800) 253-9646; Human Development Report; and Statistical Yearbook.

The World Bank, 1818 H Street, NW, Washington, D.C. 20433 (202) 477-1234; The World Bank Atlas; and World Development Report.

SLOVAKIA - LAND USE

Central Intelligence Agency, Washington, D.C. 20505 (703) 482-1100, www.cia.gov; The World Factbook.

Food and Agriculture Organization of

the United Nations (FAO), Via delle Terme di Caracalla, 00100, Rome, Italy (Telephone Number in U.S. (202) 653-2400); *Production Yearbook*.

The World Bank, 1818 H Street, NW, Washington, D.C. 20433 (202) 477-1234; *World Development Report*.

SLOVAKIA - LIBRARIES

Statistical Office of the United Nations, Publishing Service, New York, New York 10017 (800) 253-9646; *Trends in Europe and North America: The Statistical Yearbook of the Economic Commission for Europe.*

United Nations Educational, Scientific and Cultural Organization (UNESCO), 7 Place de Fontenoy, F-75700 Paris, France (Telephone Number in U.S. (212) 963-5981); *Statistical Yearbook*.

SLOVAKIA - LIFE EXPECTANCY

Central Intelligence Agency, Washington, D.C. 20505 (703) 482-1100, www.cia.gov; *The World Factbook*.

Euromonitor International, Inc., 122 South Michigan Avenue, Suite 1200, Chicago, Illinois 60603 (800) 577-EURO; *The World Economic Factbook*.

Statistical Office of the United Nations, Publishing Service, New York, New York 10017 (800) 253-9646; *Demographic Yearbook; Human Development Report; Trends in Europe and North America: The Statistical Yearbook of the Economic Commission for Europe; and World Statistics Pocketbook*.

The World Bank, 1818 H Street, NW, Washington, D.C. 20433 (202) 477-1234; *The World Bank Atlas; and World Development Report.*

Euromonitor International Inc., 122 South Michigan Avenue, Suite 1200, Chicago, Illinois 60603 (800) 577-EURO; *World Marketing Data and Statistics.*

SLOVAKIA - LIVESTOCK AND POULTRY

Europa Publications Limited, 18 Bedford Square, London, WC1B 3JN, England; *The Europa World Year Book*.

Food and Agriculture Organization of the United Nations (FAO), Via delle Terme di Caracalla, 00100, Rome, Italy (Telephone Number in U.S. (202) 653-2400); *Production Yearbook; The State of Food and Agriculture; and Trade Yearbook.*

St. Martin's Press, Inc., 175 Fifth Avenue, New York, New York 10010 (800) 221-7945; *The Statesman's Year-Book.*

Statistical Office of the United Nations,

Publishing Service, New York, New York 10017 (800) 253-9646; *Industrial Commodity Statistics Yearbook; and Statistical Yearbook.*

United Nations Conference on Trade and Development, Central Statistical Service, Palais des Nations, Geneva, Switzerland (Telephone in U.S. (800) 253-9646); *UNCTAD Commodity Yearbook.*

SLOVAKIA - MACHINERY

Statistical Office of the United Nations, Publishing Service, New York, New York 10017 (800) 253-9646; *Industrial Commodity Statistics Yearbook.*

SLOVAKIA - MAIL - NUMBER OF PIECES SENT OR RECEIVED

Statistical Office of the United Nations, Publishing Service, New York, New York 10017 (800) 253-9646; *Statistical Yearbook.*

SLOVAKIA - MANUFACTURING

Statistical Office of the United Nations, Publishing Service, New York, New York 10017 (800) 253-9646; *Industrial Commodity Statistics Yearbook; and Statistical Yearbook.*

SLOVAKIA - MARRIAGE RATES

Europa Publications Limited, 18 Bedford Square, London, WC1B 3JN, England; *The Europa World Year Book*.

Statistical Office of the United Nations, Publishing Service, New York, New York 10017 (800) 253-9646; *Demographic Yearbook; Statistical Yearbook; and Trends in Europe and North America: The Statistical Yearbook of the Economic Commission for Europe.*

SLOVAKIA - MERCHANT SHIPPING

Europa Publications Limited, 18 Bedford Square, London, WC1B 3JN, England; *The Europa World Year Book*.

Statistical Office of the United Nations, Publishing Service, New York, New York 10017 (800) 253-9646; *Annual Bulletin of Transport Statistics for Europe; and Statistical Yearbook.*

SLOVAKIA - MILITARY

Central Intelligence Agency, Washington, D.C. 20505 (703) 482-1100, www.cia.gov; *The World Factbook*.

Euromonitor International Inc., 122 South Michigan Avenue, Suite 1200, Chicago, Illinois 60603 (800) 577-EURO; *World Marketing Data and Statistics.*

St. Martin's Press, Inc., 175 Fifth

Avenue, New York, New York 10010 (800) 221-7945; *The Statesman's Year-Book.*

Statistical Office of the United Nations, Publishing Service, New York, New York 10017 (800) 253-9646; *Human Development Report.*

SLOVAKIA - MINING AND MINERAL PRODUCTS

Europa Publications Limited, 18 Bedford Square, London, WC1B 3JN, England; *The Europa World Year Book*.

St. Martin's Press, Inc., 175 Fifth Avenue, New York, New York 10010 (800) 221-7945; *The Statesman's Year-Book.*

Statistical Office of the United Nations, Publishing Service, New York, New York 10017 (800) 253-9646; *Energy Statistics Yearbook; Industrial Commodity Statistics Yearbook; and Statistical Yearbook.*

SLOVAKIA - MONEY SUPPLY

Economist Intelligence Unit, 111 West 57th Street, New York, New York 10019 (800) 938-4685; *Slovakia Country Report.*

SLOVAKIA - MONUMENTS AND HISTORICAL SITES

United Nations Educational, Scientific and Cultural Organization (UNESCO), 7 Place de Fontenoy, F-75700 Paris, France (Telephone Number in U.S. (212) 963-5981); *Statistical Yearbook*.

SLOVAKIA - MORTALITY

Central Intelligence Agency, Washington, D.C. 20505 (703) 482-1100, www.cia.gov; *The World Factbook*.

Euromonitor International, Inc., 122 South Michigan Avenue, Suite 1200, Chicago, Illinois 60603 (800) 577-EURO; *The World Economic Factbook*.

Europa Publications Limited, 18 Bedford Square, London, WC1B 3JN, England; *The Europa World Year Book*.

St. Martin's Press, Inc., 175 Fifth Avenue, New York, New York 10010 (800) 221-7945; *The Statesman's Year-Book.*

Statistical Office of the United Nations, Publishing Service, New York, New York 10017 (800) 253-9646; *Demographic Yearbook; Human Development Report; Statistical Yearbook; Trends in Europe and North America: The Statistical Yearbook of the Economic Commission for Europe; and World Statistics Pocketbook.*

United Nations Children's Fund (UNICEF), 3 United Nations Plaza, New York, New York 10017 (800) 253-9646; *State of the World's Children.*

The World Bank, 1818 H Street, NW, Washington, D.C. 20433 (202) 477-1234; *The World Bank Atlas;* and *World Development Report.*

SLOVAKIA - MOTION PICTURES

St. Martin's Press, Inc., 175 Fifth Avenue, New York, New York 10010 (800) 221-7945; *The Statesman's Year-Book.*

Statistical Office of the United Nations, Publishing Service, New York, New York 10017 (800) 253-9646; *Statistical Yearbook.*

United Nations Educational, Scientific and Cultural Organization (UNESCO), 7 Place de Fontenoy, F-75700 Paris, France (Telephone Number in U.S. (212) 963-5981); *Statistical Yearbook.*

SLOVAKIA - MOTOR VEHICLE PRODUCTION

Europa Publications Limited, 18 Bedford Square, London, WC1B 3JN, England; *The Europa World Year Book.*

Statistical Office of the United Nations, Publishing Service, New York, New York 10017 (800) 253-9646; *Statistical Yearbook.*

SLOVAKIA - MUSEUMS

United Nations Educational, Scientific and Cultural Organization (UNESCO), 7 Place de Fontenoy, F-75700 Paris, France (Telephone Number in U.S. (212) 963-5981); *Statistical Yearbook.*

SLOVAKIA - NATIONAL ACCOUNTS

Europa Publications Limited, 18 Bedford Square, London, WC1B 3JN, England; *The Europa World Year Book.*

Statistical Office of the United Nations, Publishing Service, New York, New York 10017 (800) 253-9646; *National Accounts Statistics;* and *Statistical Yearbook.*

SLOVAKIA - NATIONAL INCOME

Statistical Office of the United Nations, Publishing Service, New York, New York 10017 (800) 253-9646; *National Accounts Statistics;* and *Statistical Yearbook.*

SLOVAKIA - NATIONAL PRODUCT

Statistical Office of the United Nations, Publishing Service, New York, New York 10017 (800) 253-9646; *Statistical Yearbook.*

SLOVAKIA - PATENTS, TRADEMARKS AND SERVICE MARKS

Statistical Office of the United Nations, Publishing Service, New York, New York

10017 (800) 253-9646; *Statistical Yearbook.*

SLOVAKIA - PERIODICALS

United Nations Educational, Scientific and Cultural Organization (UNESCO), 7 Place de Fontenoy, F-75700 Paris, France (Telephone Number in U.S. (212) 963-5981); *Statistical Yearbook.*

SLOVAKIA - PETROLEUM INDUSTRY

Food and Agriculture Organization of the United Nations (FAO), Via delle Terme di Caracalla, 00100, Rome, Italy (Telephone Number in U.S. (202) 653-2400); *The State of Food and Agriculture.*

Statistical Office of the United Nations, Publishing Service, New York, New York 10017 (800) 253-9646; *Energy Statistics Yearbook; Industrial Commodity Statistics Yearbook; Statistical Yearbook;* and *Trends in Europe and North America: The Statistical Yearbook of the Economic Commission for Europe.*

United Nations Conference on Trade and Development, Central Statistical Service, Palais des Nations, Geneva, Switzerland (Telephone in U.S. (800) 253-9646); *UNCTAD Commodity Yearbook.*

SLOVAKIA - POPULATION

Central Intelligence Agency, Washington, D.C. 20505 (703) 482-1100, www.cia.gov; *The World Factbook.*

Economist Intelligence Unit, 111 West 57th Street, New York, New York 10019 (800) 938-4685; *Slovakia Country Report.*

Euromonitor International, Inc., 122 South Michigan Avenue, Suite 1200, Chicago, Illinois 60603 (800) 577-EURO; *The World Economic Factbook.*

Europa Publications Limited, 18 Bedford Square, London, WC1B 3JN, England; *The Europa World Year Book.*

Food and Agriculture Organization of the United Nations (FAO), Via delle Terme di Caracalla, 00100, Rome, Italy (Telephone Number in U.S. (202) 653-2400); *Production Yearbook.*

St. Martin's Press, Inc., 175 Fifth Avenue, New York, New York 10010 (800) 221-7945; *The Statesman's Year-Book.*

Statistical Office of the United Nations, Publishing Service, New York, New York 10017 (800) 253-9646; *Demographic Yearbook; Human Development Report; Statistical Yearbook; Trends in Europe and North America: The Statistical Yearbook of the Economic Commission for Europe;* and *World Statistics Pocketbook.*

United Nations Educational, Scientific and Cultural Organization (UNESCO), 7 Place de Fontenoy, F-75700 Paris, France (Telephone Number in U.S. (212) 963-5981); *Statistical Yearbook.*

The World Bank, 1818 H Street, NW, Washington, D.C. 20433 (202) 477-1234; *The World Bank Atlas;* and *World Development Report.*

SLOVAKIA - POST OFFICES

St. Martin's Press, Inc., 175 Fifth Avenue, New York, New York 10010 (800) 221-7945; *The Statesman's Year-Book.*

Statistical Office of the United Nations, Publishing Service, New York, New York 10017 (800) 253-9646; *Trends in Europe and North America: The Statistical Yearbook of the Economic Commission for Europe.*

SLOVAKIA - PRICES

Food and Agriculture Organization of the United Nations (FAO), Via delle Terme di Caracalla, 00100, Rome, Italy (Telephone Number in U.S. (202) 653-2400); *Production Yearbook.*

SLOVAKIA - RADIO RECEIVER PRODUCTION

Statistical Office of the United Nations, Publishing Service, New York, New York 10017 (800) 253-9646; *Statistical Yearbook.*

SLOVAKIA - RADIO RECEIVERS

St. Martin's Press, Inc., 175 Fifth Avenue, New York, New York 10010 (800) 221-7945; *The Statesman's Year-Book.*

SLOVAKIA - RAILWAYS

Europa Publications Limited, 18 Bedford Square, London, WC1B 3JN, England; *The Europa World Year Book.*

St. Martin's Press, Inc., 175 Fifth Avenue, New York, New York 10010 (800) 221-7945; *The Statesman's Year-Book.*

Statistical Office of the United Nations, Publishing Service, New York, New York 10017 (800) 253-9646; *Annual Bulletin of Transport Statistics for Europe; Statistical Yearbook;* and *Trends in Europe and North America: The Statistical Yearbook of the Economic Commission for Europe.*

SLOVAKIA - RELIGION

Central Intelligence Agency, Washington, D.C. 20505 (703) 482-1100, www.cia.gov; *The World Factbook.*

St. Martin's Press, Inc., 175 Fifth Avenue, New York, New York 10010 (800) 221-7945; *The Statesman's Year-Book.*

SLOVAKIA - RETAIL TRADE

Euromonitor International Inc., 122 South Michigan Avenue, Suite 1200, Chicago, Illinois 60603 (800) 577-EURO; *World Marketing Data and Statistics;* and *Retail Trade International.*

Statistical Office of the United Nations, Publishing Service, New York, New York 10017 (800) 253-9646; *Statistical Yearbook.*

SLOVAKIA - ROADS - See SLOVAKIA - HIGHWAYS

SLOVAKIA - RUBBER PRODUCTION AND CONSUMPTION

Statistical Office of the United Nations, Publishing Service, New York, New York 10017 (800) 253-9646; *Statistical Yearbook.*

SLOVAKIA - SCIENTISTS, TECHNICIANS AND ENGINEERS

Statistical Office of the United Nations, Publishing Service, New York, New York 10017 (800) 253-9646; *Statistical Yearbook.*

SLOVAKIA - SOCIAL DATA

Statistical Office of the United Nations, Publishing Service, New York, New York 10017 (800) 253-9646; *World Statistics Pocketbook.*

SLOVAKIA - SOCIAL SECURITY

Statistical Office of the United Nations, Publishing Service, New York, New York 10017 (800) 253-9646; *National Accounts Statistics.*

SLOVAKIA - TAXATION

Europa Publications Limited, 18 Bedford Square, London, WC1B 3JN, England; *The Europa World Year Book.*

St. Martin's Press, Inc., 175 Fifth Avenue, New York, New York 10010 (800) 221-7945; *The Statesman's Year-Book.*

SLOVAKIA - TELEPHONES IN USE

Central Intelligence Agency, Washington, D.C. 20505 (703) 482-1100, www.cia.gov; *The World Factbook.*

Europa Publications Limited, 18 Bedford Square, London, WC1B 3JN, England; *The Europa World Year Book.*

St. Martin's Press, Inc., 175 Fifth Avenue, New York, New York 10010 (800) 221-7945; *The Statesman's Year-Book.*

Statistical Office of the United Nations, Publishing Service, New York, New York 10017 (800) 253-9646; *Statistical Yearbook; Trends in Europe and North America: The*

Statistical Yearbook of the Economic Commission for Europe; and *World Statistics Pocketbook.*

SLOVAKIA - TEXTILE INDUSTRY

Euromonitor International Inc., 122 South Michigan Avenue, Suite 1200, Chicago, Illinois 60603 (800) 577-EURO; *Retail Trade International.*

St. Martin's Press, Inc., 175 Fifth Avenue, New York, New York 10010 (800) 221-7945; *The Statesman's Year-Book.*

Statistical Office of the United Nations, Publishing Service, New York, New York 10017 (800) 253-9646; *Industrial Commodity Statistics Yearbook;* and *Statistical Yearbook.*

United Nations Conference on Trade and Development, Central Statistical Service, Palais des Nations, Geneva, Switzerland (Telephone in U.S. (800) 253-9646); *UNCTAD Commodity Yearbook.*

SLOVAKIA - THEATRE

United Nations Educational, Scientific and Cultural Organization (UNESCO), 7 Place de Fontenoy, F-75700 Paris, France (Telephone Number in U.S. (212) 963-5981); *Statistical Yearbook.*

SLOVAKIA - TIRE (MOTOR VEHICLE) PRODUCTION

Statistical Office of the United Nations, Publishing Service, New York, New York 10017 (800) 253-9646; *Statistical Yearbook.*

SLOVAKIA - TOBACCO PRODUCTION

Statistical Office of the United Nations, Publishing Service, New York, New York 10017 (800) 253-9646; *Statistical Yearbook.*

SLOVAKIA - TOURISM

Euromonitor International, Inc., 122 South Michigan Avenue, Suite 1200, Chicago, Illinois 60603 (800) 577-EURO; *The World Economic Factbook;* and *World Marketing Data and Statistics.*

Europa Publications Limited, 18 Bedford Square, London, WC1B 3JN, England; *The Europa World Year Book.*

Statistical Office of the United Nations, Publishing Service, New York, New York 10017 (800) 253-9646; *Statistical Yearbook;* and *Trends in Europe and North America: The Statistical Yearbook of the Economic Commission for Europe.*

SLOVAKIA - TRADEMARKS AND SERVICE MARKS - See PATENTS, TRADEMARKS AND SERVICE MARKS

SLOVAKIA - TRANSPORTATION AND COMMUNICATIONS

Central Intelligence Agency, Washington, D.C. 20505 (703) 482-1100, www.cia.gov; *The World Factbook.*

Euromonitor International Inc., 122 South Michigan Avenue, Suite 1200, Chicago, Illinois 60603 (800) 577-EURO; *World Marketing Data and Statistics.*

Europa Publications Limited, 18 Bedford Square, London, WC1B 3JN, England; *The Europa World Year Book.*

St. Martin's Press, Inc., 175 Fifth Avenue, New York, New York 10010 (800) 221-7945; *The Statesman's Year-Book.*

Statistical Office of the United Nations, Publishing Service, New York, New York 10017 (800) 253-9646; *Annual Bulletin of Transport Statistics for Europe; Human Development Report;* and *Trends in Europe and North America: The Statistical Yearbook of the Economic Commission for Europe.*

SLOVAKIA - UNEMPLOYMENT

Central Intelligence Agency, Washington, D.C. 20505 (703) 482-1100, www.cia.gov; *The World Factbook.*

St. Martin's Press, Inc., 175 Fifth Avenue, New York, New York 10010 (800) 221-7945; *The Statesman's Year-Book.*

Statistical Office of the United Nations, Publishing Service, New York, New York 10017 (800) 253-9646; *Statistical Yearbook;* and *Trends in Europe and North America: The Statistical Yearbook of the Economic Commission for Europe.*

SLOVAKIA - VITAL STATISTICS

St. Martin's Press, Inc., 175 Fifth Avenue, New York, New York 10010 (800) 221-7945; *The Statesman's Year-Book.*

Statistical Office of the United Nations, Publishing Service, New York, New York 10017 (800) 253-9646; *Statistical Yearbook.*

SLOVAKIA - WAGES

Statistical Office of the United Nations, Publishing Service, New York, New York 10017 (800) 253-9646; *Statistical Yearbook.*

SLOVAKIA - WHOLESALE PRICES

Statistical Office of the United Nations, Publishing Service, New York, New York 10017 (800) 253-9646; *Statistical Yearbook.*

SLOVAKIA - WHOLESALE TRADE

Statistical Office of the United Nations,

Publishing Service, New York, New York 10017 (800) 253-9646; *Statistical Yearbook.*

SLOVENIA - See also YUGOSLAVIA

SLOVENIA - ABORTIONS

Statistical Office of the United Nations, Publishing Service, New York, New York 10017 (800) 253-9646; *Trends in Europe and North America: The Statistical Yearbook of the Economic Commission for Europe.*

SLOVENIA - AGRICULTURE

Economist Intelligence Unit, 111 West 57th Street, New York, New York 10019 (800) 938-4685; *Slovenia Country Report.*

Euromonitor International Inc., 122 South Michigan Avenue, Suite 1200, Chicago, Illinois 60603 (800) 577-EURO; *World Marketing Data and Statistics.*

Europa Publications Limited, 18 Bedford Square, London, WC1B 3JN, England; *The Europa World Year Book.*

Food and Agriculture Organization of the United Nations (FAO), Via delle Terme di Caracalla, 00100, Rome, Italy (Telephone Number in U.S. (202) 653-2400); *Production Yearbook; The State of Food and Agriculture;* and *Trade Yearbook.*

St. Martin's Press, Inc., 175 Fifth Avenue, New York, New York 10010 (800) 221-7945; *The Statesman's Year-Book.*

Statistical Office of the United Nations, Publishing Service, New York, New York 10017 (800) 253-9646; *Industrial Commodity Statistics Yearbook;* and *Statistical Yearbook.*

SLOVENIA - AIRLINE SERVICE

Europa Publications Limited, 18 Bedford Square, London, WC1B 3JN, England; *The Europa World Year Book.*

International Civil Aviation Organization, 999 University Street, Montreal, Quebec, Canada H3C 5H7 (514) 954-8219; *Civil Aviation Statistics of the World.*

St. Martin's Press, Inc., 175 Fifth Avenue, New York, New York 10010 (800) 221-7945; *The Statesman's Year-Book.*

Statistical Office of the United Nations, Publishing Service, New York, New York 10017 (800) 253-9646; *Statistical Yearbook.*

SLOVENIA - AIRPORTS

Central Intelligence Agency, Washington, D.C. 20505 (703) 482-1100, www.cia.gov; *The World Factbook.*

SLOVENIA - ANIMAL HEALTH

Food and Agriculture Organization of the United Nations (FAO), Via delle Terme di Caracalla, 00100, Rome, Italy (Telephone Number in U.S. (202) 653-2400); *Animal Health Yearbook.*

SLOVENIA - AREA AND DENSITY OF POPULATION

Central Intelligence Agency, Washington, D.C. 20505 (703) 482-1100, www.cia.gov; *The World Factbook.*

Euromonitor International, Inc., 122 South Michigan Avenue, Suite 1200, Chicago, Illinois 60603 (800) 577-EURO; *The World Economic Factbook.*

Europa Publications Limited, 18 Bedford Square, London, WC1B 3JN, England; *The Europa World Year Book.*

St. Martin's Press, Inc., 175 Fifth Avenue, New York, New York 10010 (800) 221-7945; *The Statesman's Year-Book.*

Statistical Office of the United Nations, Publishing Service, New York, New York 10017 (800) 253-9646; *Statistical Yearbook;* and *Trends in Europe and North America: The Statistical Yearbook of the Economic Commission for Europe.*

United Nations Educational, Scientific and Cultural Organization (UNESCO), 7 Place de Fontenoy, F-75700 Paris, France (Telephone Number in U.S. (212) 963-5981); *Statistical Yearbook.*

The World Bank, 1818 H Street, NW, Washington, D.C. 20433 (202) 477-1234; *World Development Report.*

SLOVENIA - BALANCE OF PAYMENTS

Europa Publications Limited, 18 Bedford Square, London, WC1B 3JN, England; *The Europa World Year Book.*

United Nations Conference on Trade and Development (UNCTAD), New York, New York 10017 (800) 253-9646; *Handbook of International Trade and Development Statistics.*

The World Bank, 1818 H Street, NW, Washington, D.C. 20433 (202) 477-1234; *World Development Report.*

SLOVENIA - BANKING

Euromonitor International Inc., 122 South Michigan Avenue, Suite 1200, Chicago, Illinois 60603 (800) 577-EURO; *World Marketing Data and Statistics.*

Europa Publications Limited, 18 Bedford Square, London, WC1B 3JN, England; *The Europa World Year Book.*

St. Martin's Press, Inc., 175 Fifth Avenue, New York, New York 10010 (800) 221-7945; *The Statesman's Year-Book.*

SLOVENIA - BEVERAGES

Statistical Office of the United Nations, Publishing Service, New York, New York 10017 (800) 253-9646; *Statistical Yearbook.*

SLOVENIA - BIRTH RATES

Central Intelligence Agency, Washington, D.C. 20505 (703) 482-1100, www.cia.gov; *The World Factbook.*

Euromonitor International, Inc., 122 South Michigan Avenue, Suite 1200, Chicago, Illinois 60603 (800) 577-EURO; *The World Economic Factbook.*

Europa Publications Limited, 18 Bedford Square, London, WC1B 3JN, England; *The Europa World Year Book.*

St. Martin's Press, Inc., 175 Fifth Avenue, New York, New York 10010 (800) 221-7945; *The Statesman's Year-Book.*

Statistical Office of the United Nations, Publishing Service, New York, New York 10017 (800) 253-9646; *Statistical Yearbook.*

SLOVENIA - BOOK PRODUCTION

Europa Publications Limited, 18 Bedford Square, London, WC1B 3JN, England; *The Europa World Year Book.*

St. Martin's Press, Inc., 175 Fifth Avenue, New York, New York 10010 (800) 221-7945; *The Statesman's Year-Book.*

Statistical Office of the United Nations, Publishing Service, New York, New York 10017 (800) 253-9646; *Trends in Europe and North America: The Statistical Yearbook of the Economic Commission for Europe.*

United Nations Educational, Scientific and Cultural Organization (UNESCO), 7 Place de Fontenoy, F-75700 Paris, France (Telephone Number in U.S. (212) 963-5981); *Statistical Yearbook.*

SLOVENIA - BROADCASTING

Central Intelligence Agency, Washington, D.C. 20505 (703) 482-1100, www.cia.gov; *The World Factbook.*

Euromonitor International Inc., 122 South Michigan Avenue, Suite 1200, Chicago, Illinois 60603 (800) 577-EURO; *World Marketing Data and Statistics.*

Europa Publications Limited, 18 Bedford Square, London, WC1B 3JN, England; *The Europa World Year Book.*

St. Martin's Press, Inc., 175 Fifth

Avenue, New York, New York 10010 (800) 221-7945; *The Statesman's Year-Book.*

Statistical Office of the United Nations, Publishing Service, New York, New York 10017 (800) 253-9646; *Trends in Europe and North America: The Statistical Yearbook of the Economic Commission for Europe.*

United Nations Educational, Scientific and Cultural Organization (UNESCO), 7 Place de Fontenoy, F-75700 Paris, France (Telephone Number in U.S. (212) 963-5981); *Statistical Yearbook.*

SLOVENIA - BUDGET

Central Intelligence Agency, Washington, D.C. 20505 (703) 482-1100, www.cia.gov; *The World Factbook.*

SLOVENIA - COMMERCE

St. Martin's Press, Inc., 175 Fifth Avenue, New York, New York 10010 (800) 221-7945; *The Statesman's Year-Book.*

SLOVENIA - CONSTRUCTION INDUSTRY

Statistical Office of the United Nations, Publishing Service, New York, New York 10017 (800) 253-9646; *Statistical Yearbook.*

SLOVENIA - CONSUMER PRICE INDEX

Statistical Office of the United Nations, Publishing Service, New York, New York 10017 (800) 253-9646; *Statistical Yearbook;* and *Trends in Europe and North America: The Statistical Yearbook of the Economic Commission for Europe.*

SLOVENIA - CONSUMER PRICES

Euromonitor International Inc., 122 South Michigan Avenue, Suite 1200, Chicago, Illinois 60603 (800) 577-EURO; *World Marketing Data and Statistics.*

International Labour Office, I.L.O. Publications, 1828 L Street, NW., Suite 801, Washington, D.C. 20036 (301) 638-3152; *Yearbook of Labour Statistics.*

SLOVENIA - CONSUMPTION

The World Bank, 1818 H Street, NW, Washington, D.C. 20433 (202) 477-1234; *World Development Report.*

SLOVENIA - CRIME

Statistical Office of the United Nations, Publishing Service, New York, New York 10017 (800) 253-9646; *Trends in Europe and North America: The Statistical Yearbook of the Economic Commission for Europe.*

SLOVENIA - CROPS

Europa Publications Limited, 18

Bedford Square, London, WC1B 3JN, England; *The Europa World Year Book.*

Food and Agriculture Organization of the United Nations (FAO), Via delle Terme di Caracalla, 00100, Rome, Italy (Telephone Number in U.S. (202) 653-2400); *Production Yearbook; The State of Food and Agriculture;* and *Trade Yearbook.*

St. Martin's Press, Inc., 175 Fifth Avenue, New York, New York 10010 (800) 221-7945; *The Statesman's Year-Book.*

Statistical Office of the United Nations, Publishing Service, New York, New York 10017 (800) 253-9646; *Industrial Commodity Statistics Yearbook;* and *Statistical Yearbook.*

SLOVENIA - CUSTOMS DUTIES

St. Martin's Press, Inc., 175 Fifth Avenue, New York, New York 10010 (800) 221-7945; *The Statesman's Year-Book.*

SLOVENIA - DAIRY PRODUCTS

Europa Publications Limited, 18 Bedford Square, London, WC1B 3JN, England; *The Europa World Year Book.*

Food and Agriculture Organization of the United Nations (FAO), Via delle Terme di Caracalla, 00100, Rome, Italy (Telephone Number in U.S. (202) 653-2400); *Production Yearbook; The State of Food and Agriculture;* and *Trade Yearbook.*

St. Martin's Press, Inc., 175 Fifth Avenue, New York, New York 10010 (800) 221-7945; *The Statesman's Year-Book.*

Statistical Office of the United Nations, Publishing Service, New York, New York 10017 (800) 253-9646; *Industrial Commodity Statistics Yearbook;* and *Statistical Yearbook.*

SLOVENIA - DEATH RATES - SEE SLOVENIA - MORTALITY

SLOVENIA - DEMOGRAPHY

Euromonitor International, Inc., 122 South Michigan Avenue, Suite 1200, Chicago, Illinois 60603 (800) 577-EURO; *The World Economic Factbook;* and *World Marketing Data and Statistics.*

Statistical Office of the United Nations, Publishing Service, New York, New York 10017 (800) 253-9646; *Demographic Yearbook;* and *Human Development Report.*

SLOVENIA - DIVORCE RATES

Statistical Office of the United Nations, Publishing Service, New York, New York 10017 (800) 253-9646; *Demographic*

Yearbook; Statistical Yearbook; and *Trends in Europe and North America: The Statistical Yearbook of the Economic Commission for Europe.*

SLOVENIA - ECONOMY

Central Intelligence Agency, Washington, D.C. 20505 (703) 482-1100, www.cia.gov; *The World Factbook.*

Economist Intelligence Unit, 111 West 57th Street, New York, New York 10019 (800) 938-4685; *Slovenia Country Report.*

Euromonitor International, Inc., 122 South Michigan Avenue, Suite 1200, Chicago, Illinois 60603 (800) 577-EURO; *The World Economic Factbook;* and *World Marketing Data and Statistics.*

Europa Publications Limited, 18 Bedford Square, London, WC1B 3JN, England; *The Europa World Year Book.*

St. Martin's Press, Inc., 175 Fifth Avenue, New York, New York 10010 (800) 221-7945; *The Statesman's Year-Book.*

Statistical Office of the United Nations, Publishing Service, New York, New York 10017 (800) 253-9646; *World Statistics Pocketbook.*

The World Bank, 1818 H Street, NW, Washington, D.C. 20433 (202) 477-1234; *The World Bank Atlas;* and *World Development Report.*

SLOVENIA - EDUCATION

Euromonitor International Inc., 122 South Michigan Avenue, Suite 1200, Chicago, Illinois 60603 (800) 577-EURO; *World Marketing Data and Statistics.*

Europa Publications Limited, 18 Bedford Square, London, WC1B 3JN, England; *The Europa World Year Book.*

St. Martin's Press, Inc., 175 Fifth Avenue, New York, New York 10010 (800) 221-7945; *The Statesman's Year-Book.*

Statistical Office of the United Nations, Publishing Service, New York, New York 10017 (800) 253-9646; *Human Development Report;* and *Trends in Europe and North America: The Statistical Yearbook of the Economic Commission for Europe.*

United Nations Educational, Scientific and Cultural Organization (UNESCO), 7 Place de Fontenoy, F-75700 Paris, France (Telephone Number in U.S. (212) 963-5981); *Statistical Yearbook.*

The World Bank, 1818 H Street, NW, Washington, D.C. 20433 (202) 477-1234; *World Development Report.*

SLOVENIA - ELECTRICITY

Central Intelligence Agency, Washington, D.C. 20505 (703) 482-1100, www.cia.gov; *The World Factbook*.

St. Martin's Press, Inc., 175 Fifth Avenue, New York, New York 10010 (800) 221-7945; *The Statesman's Year-Book*.

Statistical Office of the United Nations, Publishing Service, New York, New York 10017 (800) 253-9646; *Energy Statistics Yearbook; Human Development Report; Statistical Yearbook;* and *Trends in Europe and North America: The Statistical Yearbook of the Economic Commission for Europe.*

SLOVENIA - EMPLOYMENT

International Labour Office, I.L.O. Publications, 1828 L Street, NW., Suite 801, Washington, D.C. 20036 (301) 638-3152; *Yearbook of Labour Statistics.*

Statistical Office of the United Nations, Publishing Service, New York, New York 10017 (800) 253-9646; *Statistical Yearbook;* and *Trends in Europe and North America: The Statistical Yearbook of the Economic Commission for Europe.*

SLOVENIA - ENERGY

Euromonitor International, Inc., 122 South Michigan Avenue, Suite 1200, Chicago, Illinois 60603 (800) 577-EURO; *The World Economic Factbook;* and *World Marketing Data and Statistics.*

St. Martin's Press, Inc., 175 Fifth Avenue, New York, New York 10010 (800) 221-7945; *The Statesman's Year-Book.*

Statistical Office of the United Nations, Publishing Service, New York, New York 10017 (800) 253-9646; *Energy Statistics Yearbook; Human Development Report; Statistical Yearbook; Trends in Europe and North America: The Statistical Yearbook of the Economic Commission for Europe;* and *World Statistics Pocketbook.*

The World Bank, 1818 H Street, NW, Washington, D.C. 20433 (202) 477-1234; *The World Bank Atlas;* and *World Development Report.*

SLOVENIA - ENVIRONMENT

Economist Intelligence Unit, 111 West 57th Street, New York, New York 10019 (800) 938-4685; *Slovenia Country Report.*

Statistical Office of the United Nations, Publishing Service, New York, New York 10017 (800) 253-9646; *Statistical Yearbook;* and *World Statistics Pocketbook.*

SLOVENIA - EXCHANGE RATES

Central Intelligence Agency, Washington, D.C. 20505 (703) 482-1100, www.cia.gov; *The World Factbook.*

Euromonitor International, Inc., 122 South Michigan Avenue, Suite 1200, Chicago, Illinois 60603 (800) 577-EURO; *The World Economic Factbook.*

Europa Publications Limited, 18 Bedford Square, London, WC1B 3JN, England; *The Europa World Year Book.*

Statistical Office of the United Nations, Publishing Service, New York, New York 10017 (800) 253-9646; *Statistical Yearbook; Trends in Europe and North America: The Statistical Yearbook of the Economic Commission for Europe;* and *World Statistics Pocketbook.*

SLOVENIA - EXPORTS

Central Intelligence Agency, Washington, D.C. 20505 (703) 482-1100, www.cia.gov; *The World Factbook.*

Economist Intelligence Unit, 111 West 57th Street, New York, New York 10019 (800) 938-4685; *Slovenia Country Report.*

Euromonitor International, Inc., 122 South Michigan Avenue, Suite 1200, Chicago, Illinois 60603 (800) 577-EURO; *The World Economic Factbook.*

Europa Publications Limited, 18 Bedford Square, London, WC1B 3JN, England; *The Europa World Year Book.*

St. Martin's Press, Inc., 175 Fifth Avenue, New York, New York 10010 (800) 221-7945; *The Statesman's Year-Book.*

Statistical Office of the United Nations, Publishing Service, New York, New York 10017 (800) 253-9646; *International Trade Statistics Yearbook;* and *Trends in Europe and North America: The Statistical Yearbook of the Economic Commission for Europe.*

United Nations Conference on Trade and Development (UNCTAD), New York, New York 10017 (800) 253-9646; *Handbook of International Trade and Development Statistics.*

The World Bank, 1818 H Street, NW, Washington, D.C. 20433 (202) 477-1234; *World Development Report.*

SLOVENIA - EXTERNAL INDEBTEDNESS

The World Bank, 1818 H Street, NW, Washington, D.C. 20433 (202) 477-1234; *World Development Report.*

SLOVENIA - EXTERNAL TRADE

Euromonitor International Inc., 122

South Michigan Avenue, Suite 1200, Chicago, Illinois 60603 (800) 577-EURO; *World Marketing Data and Statistics.*

Food and Agriculture Organization of the United Nations (FAO), Via delle Terme di Caracalla, 00100, Rome, Italy (Telephone Number in U.S. (202) 653-2400); *Trade Yearbook.*

Statistical Office of the United Nations, Publishing Service, New York, New York 10017 (800) 253-9646; *Statistical Yearbook.*

SLOVENIA - FERTILITY RATES

Central Intelligence Agency, Washington, D.C. 20505 (703) 482-1100, www.cia.gov; *The World Factbook.*

Statistical Office of the United Nations, Publishing Service, New York, New York 10017 (800) 253-9646; *Human Development Report;* and *Trends in Europe and North America: The Statistical Yearbook of the Economic Commission for Europe.*

The World Bank, 1818 H Street, NW, Washington, D.C. 20433 (202) 477-1234; *The World Bank Atlas;* and *World Development Report.*

SLOVENIA - FERTILIZER

Food and Agriculture Organization of the United Nations (FAO), Via delle Terme di Caracalla, 00100, Rome, Italy (Telephone Number in U.S. (202) 653-2400); *Fertilizer Yearbook.*

Statistical Office of the United Nations, Publishing Service, New York, New York 10017 (800) 253-9646; *Industrial Commodity Statistics Yearbook;* and *Statistical Yearbook.*

SLOVENIA - FINANCE

Economist Intelligence Unit, 111 West 57th Street, New York, New York 10019 (800) 938-4685; *Slovenia Country Report.*

Europa Publications Limited, 18 Bedford Square, London, WC1B 3JN, England; *The Europa World Year Book.*

St. Martin's Press, Inc., 175 Fifth Avenue, New York, New York 10010 (800) 221-7945; *The Statesman's Year-Book.*

SLOVENIA - FISHERIES

Europa Publications Limited, 18 Bedford Square, London, WC1B 3JN, England; *The Europa World Year Book.*

Food and Agriculture Organization of the United Nations (FAO), Via delle Terme di Caracalla, 00100, Rome, Italy (Telephone Number in U.S. (202) 653-2400); *The State of Food and Agriculture;* and *Yearbook of*

Fisheries.

St. Martin's Press, Inc., 175 Fifth Avenue, New York, New York 10010 (800) 221-7945; *The Statesman's Year-Book.*

Statistical Office of the United Nations, Publishing Service, New York, New York 10017 (800) 253-9646; *Industrial Commodity Statistics Yearbook;* and *Statistical Yearbook.*

SLOVENIA - FOOD

Food and Agriculture Organization of the United Nations (FAO), Via delle Terme di Caracalla, 00100, Rome, Italy (Telephone Number in U.S. (202) 653-2400); *Production Yearbook; The State of Food and Agriculture;* and *Trade Yearbook.*

Statistical Office of the United Nations, Publishing Service, New York, New York 10017 (800) 253-9646; *Human Development Report;* and *Industrial Commodity Statistics Yearbook.*

SLOVENIA - FOREIGN DEBT

St. Martin's Press, Inc., 175 Fifth Avenue, New York, New York 10010 (800) 221-7945; *The Statesman's Year-Book.*

SLOVENIA - FOREIGN TRADE

Economist Intelligence Unit, 111 West 57th Street, New York, New York 10019 (800) 938-4685; *Slovenia Country Report.*

Euromonitor International, Inc., 122 South Michigan Avenue, Suite 1200, Chicago, Illinois 60603 (800) 577-EURO; *The World Economic Factbook.*

Europa Publications Limited, 18 Bedford Square, London, WC1B 3JN, England; *The Europa World Year Book.*

Food and Agriculture Organization of the United Nations (FAO), Via delle Terme di Caracalla, 00100, Rome, Italy (Telephone Number in U.S. (202) 653-2400); *Trade Yearbook.*

St. Martin's Press, Inc., 175 Fifth Avenue, New York, New York 10010 (800) 221-7945; *The Statesman's Year-Book.*

Statistical Office of the United Nations, Publishing Service, New York, New York 10017 (800) 253-9646; *International Trade Statistics Yearbook;* and *Statistical Yearbook.*

The World Bank, 1818 H Street, NW, Washington, D.C. 20433 (202) 477-1234; *World Development Report.*

SLOVENIA - FORESTRY AND FOREST PRODUCTS

Europa Publications Limited, 18 Bedford Square, London, WC1B 3JN, England; *The Europa World Year Book.*

Food and Agriculture Organization of the United Nations (FAO), Via delle Terme di Caracalla, 00100, Rome, Italy (Telephone Number in U.S. (202) 653-2400); *The State of Food and Agriculture;* and *Yearbook of Forest Products.*

St. Martin's Press, Inc., 175 Fifth Avenue, New York, New York 10010 (800) 221-7945; *The Statesman's Year-Book.*

Statistical Office of the United Nations, Publishing Service, New York, New York 10017 (800) 253-9646; *Industrial Commodity Statistics Yearbook; Statistical Yearbook;* and *Trends in Europe and North America: The Statistical Yearbook of the Economic Commission for Europe.*

United Nations Educational, Scientific and Cultural Organization (UNESCO), 7 Place de Fontenoy, F-75700 Paris, France (Telephone Number in U.S. (212) 963-5981); *Statistical Yearbook.*

The World Bank, 1818 H Street, NW, Washington, D.C. 20433 (202) 477-1234; *World Development Report.*

SLOVENIA - GOVERNMENT

Central Intelligence Agency, Washington, D.C. 20505 (703) 482-1100, www.cia.gov; *The World Factbook.*

Europa Publications Limited, 18 Bedford Square, London, WC1B 3JN, England; *The Europa World Year Book.*

St. Martin's Press, Inc., 175 Fifth Avenue, New York, New York 10010 (800) 221-7945; *The Statesman's Year-Book.*

Statistical Office of the United Nations, Publishing Service, New York, New York 10017 (800) 253-9646; *Statistical Yearbook.*

The World Bank, 1818 H Street, NW, Washington, D.C. 20433 (202) 477-1234; *World Development Report.*

SLOVENIA - GROSS DOMESTIC PRODUCT

Economist Intelligence Unit, 111 West 57th Street, New York, New York 10019 (800) 938-4685; *Slovenia Country Report.*

Euromonitor International, Inc., 122 South Michigan Avenue, Suite 1200, Chicago, Illinois 60603 (800) 577-EURO; *The World Economic Factbook.*

Europa Publications Limited, 18 Bedford Square, London, WC1B 3JN, England; *The Europa World Year Book.*

Statistical Office of the United Nations,

Publishing Service, New York, New York 10017 (800) 253-9646; *Human Development Report; National Accounts Statistics; Statistical Yearbook;* and *Trends in Europe and North America: The Statistical Yearbook of the Economic Commission for Europe.*

The World Bank, 1818 H Street, NW, Washington, D.C. 20433 (202) 477-1234; *World Development Report.*

SLOVENIA - GROSS NATIONAL PRODUCT

St. Martin's Press, Inc., 175 Fifth Avenue, New York, New York 10010 (800) 221-7945; *The Statesman's Year-Book.*

The World Bank, 1818 H Street, NW, Washington, D.C. 20433 (202) 477-1234; *The World Bank Atlas;* and *World Development Report.*

SLOVENIA - HEALTH

Euromonitor International Inc., 122 South Michigan Avenue, Suite 1200, Chicago, Illinois 60603 (800) 577-EURO; *World Marketing Data and Statistics.*

St. Martin's Press, Inc., 175 Fifth Avenue, New York, New York 10010 (800) 221-7945; *The Statesman's Year-Book.*

Statistical Office of the United Nations, Publishing Service, New York, New York 10017 (800) 253-9646; *Human Development Report; Statistical Yearbook;* and *Trends in Europe and North America: The Statistical Yearbook of the Economic Commission for Europe.*

United Nations Children's Fund (UNICEF), 3 United Nations Plaza, New York, New York 10017 (800) 253-9646; *State of the World's Children.*

The World Bank, 1818 H Street, NW, Washington, D.C. 20433 (202) 477-1234; *World Development Report.*

SLOVENIA - HIGHWAYS

Central Intelligence Agency, Washington, D.C. 20505 (703) 482-1100, www.cia.gov; *The World Factbook.*

St. Martin's Press, Inc., 175 Fifth Avenue, New York, New York 10010 (800) 221-7945; *The Statesman's Year-Book.*

Statistical Office of the United Nations, Publishing Service, New York, New York 10017 (800) 253-9646; *Annual Bulletin of Transport Statistics for Europe;* and *Trends in Europe and North America: The Statistical Yearbook of the Economic Commission for Europe.*

SLOVENIA - HOUSING AND HOUSING UNITS

Euromonitor International Inc., 122 South Michigan Avenue, Suite 1200, Chicago, Illinois 60603 (800) 577-EURO; *World Marketing Data and Statistics.*

Statistical Office of the United Nations, Publishing Service, New York, New York 10017 (800) 253-9646; *Trends in Europe and North America: The Statistical Yearbook of the Economic Commission for Europe.*

SLOVENIA - ILLITERATE POPULATION

Central Intelligence Agency, Washington, D.C. 20505 (703) 482-1100, www.cia.gov; *The World Factbook.*

Euromonitor International, Inc., 122 South Michigan Avenue, Suite 1200, Chicago, Illinois 60603 (800) 577-EURO; *The World Economic Factbook.*

Statistical Office of the United Nations, Publishing Service, New York, New York 10017 (800) 253-9646; *Human Development Report.*

United Nations Educational, Scientific and Cultural Organization (UNESCO), 7 Place de Fontenoy, F-75700 Paris, France (Telephone Number in U.S. (212) 963-5981); *Statistical Yearbook.*

SLOVENIA - IMPORTS

Central Intelligence Agency, Washington, D.C. 20505 (703) 482-1100, www.cia.gov; *The World Factbook.*

Economist Intelligence Unit, 111 West 57th Street, New York, New York 10019 (800) 938-4685; *Slovenia Country Report.*

Euromonitor International, Inc., 122 South Michigan Avenue, Suite 1200, Chicago, Illinois 60603 (800) 577-EURO; *The World Economic Factbook.*

Europa Publications Limited, 18 Bedford Square, London, WC1B 3JN, England; *The Europa World Year Book.*

St. Martin's Press, Inc., 175 Fifth Avenue, New York, New York 10010 (800) 221-7945; *The Statesman's Year-Book.*

Statistical Office of the United Nations, Publishing Service, New York, New York 10017 (800) 253-9646; *International Trade Statistics Yearbook;* and *Trends in Europe and North America: The Statistical Yearbook of the Economic Commission for Europe.*

United Nations Conference on Trade and Development (UNCTAD), New York, New York 10017 (800) 253-9646; *Handbook of International Trade and Development Statistics.*

The World Bank, 1818 H Street, NW,

Washington, D.C. 20433 (202) 477-1234; *World Development Report.*

SLOVENIA - INDUSTRY

Central Intelligence Agency, Washington, D.C. 20505 (703) 482-1100, www.cia.gov; *The World Factbook.*

Economist Intelligence Unit, 111 West 57th Street, New York, New York 10019 (800) 938-4685; *Slovenia Country Report.*

Euromonitor International, Inc., 122 South Michigan Avenue, Suite 1200, Chicago, Illinois 60603 (800) 577-EURO; *The World Economic Factbook;* and *World Marketing Data and Statistics.*

Europa Publications Limited, 18 Bedford Square, London, WC1B 3JN, England; *The Europa World Year Book.*

International Labour Office, I.L.O. Publications, 1828 L Street, NW., Suite 801, Washington, D.C. 20036 (301) 638-3152; *Yearbook of Labour Statistics.*

St. Martin's Press, Inc., 175 Fifth Avenue, New York, New York 10010 (800) 221-7945; *The Statesman's Year-Book.*

Statistical Office of the United Nations, Publishing Service, New York, New York 10017 (800) 253-9646; *Industrial Commodity Statistics Yearbook; Statistical Yearbook;* and *Trends in Europe and North America: The Statistical Yearbook of the Economic Commission for Europe.*

SLOVENIA - INTERNAL TRADE

Statistical Office of the United Nations, Publishing Service, New York, New York 10017 (800) 253-9646; *Statistical Yearbook.*

SLOVENIA - LABOR

Central Intelligence Agency, Washington, D.C. 20505 (703) 482-1100, www.cia.gov; *The World Factbook.*

Euromonitor International Inc., 122 South Michigan Avenue, Suite 1200, Chicago, Illinois 60603 (800) 577-EURO; *World Marketing Data and Statistics.*

Europa Publications Limited, 18 Bedford Square, London, WC1B 3JN, England; *The Europa World Year Book.*

International Labour Office, I.L.O. Publications, 1828 L Street, NW., Suite 801, Washington, D.C. 20036 (301) 638-3152; *Yearbook of Labour Statistics.*

St. Martin's Press, Inc., 175 Fifth Avenue, New York, New York 10010 (800) 221-7945; *The Statesman's Year-Book.*

Statistical Office of the United Nations,

Publishing Service, New York, New York 10017 (800) 253-9646; *Human Development Report;* and *Statistical Yearbook.*

The World Bank, 1818 H Street, NW, Washington, D.C. 20433 (202) 477-1234; *The World Bank Atlas;* and *World Development Report.*

SLOVENIA - LAND USE

Central Intelligence Agency, Washington, D.C. 20505 (703) 482-1100, www.cia.gov; *The World Factbook.*

Food and Agriculture Organization of the United Nations (FAO), Via delle Terme di Caracalla, 00100, Rome, Italy (Telephone Number in U.S. (202) 653-2400); *Production Yearbook.*

The World Bank, 1818 H Street, NW, Washington, D.C. 20433 (202) 477-1234; *World Development Report.*

SLOVENIA - LIBRARIES

Statistical Office of the United Nations, Publishing Service, New York, New York 10017 (800) 253-9646; *Trends in Europe and North America: The Statistical Yearbook of the Economic Commission for Europe.*

United Nations Educational, Scientific and Cultural Organization (UNESCO), 7 Place de Fontenoy, F-75700 Paris, France (Telephone Number in U.S. (212) 963-5981); *Statistical Yearbook.*

SLOVENIA - LIFE EXPECTANCY

Central Intelligence Agency, Washington, D.C. 20505 (703) 482-1100, www.cia.gov; *The World Factbook.*

Euromonitor International, Inc., 122 South Michigan Avenue, Suite 1200, Chicago, Illinois 60603 (800) 577-EURO; *The World Economic Factbook.*

Statistical Office of the United Nations, Publishing Service, New York, New York 10017 (800) 253-9646; *Demographic Yearbook; Human Development Report; Trends in Europe and North America: The Statistical Yearbook of the Economic Commission for Europe;* and *World Statistics Pocketbook.*

The World Bank, 1818 H Street, NW, Washington, D.C. 20433 (202) 477-1234; *The World Bank Atlas;* and *World Development Report.*

SLOVENIA - LITERACY RATE

Euromonitor International Inc., 122 South Michigan Avenue, Suite 1200, Chicago, Illinois 60603 (800) 577-EURO; *World Marketing Data and Statistics.*

SLOVENIA - LIVESTOCK AND POULTRY

Europa Publications Limited, 18 Bedford Square, London, WC1B 3JN, England; *The Europa World Year Book.*

Food and Agriculture Organization of the United Nations (FAO), Via delle Terme di Caracalla, 00100, Rome, Italy (Telephone Number in U.S. (202) 653-2400); *Production Yearbook; The State of Food and Agriculture;* and *Trade Yearbook.*

St. Martin's Press, Inc., 175 Fifth Avenue, New York, New York 10010 (800) 221-7945; *The Statesman's Year-Book.*

Statistical Office of the United Nations, Publishing Service, New York, New York 10017 (800) 253-9646; *Industrial Commodity Statistics Yearbook;* and *Statistical Yearbook.*

SLOVENIA - MACHINERY

Statistical Office of the United Nations, Publishing Service, New York, New York 10017 (800) 253-9646; *Industrial Commodity Statistics Yearbook.*

SLOVENIA - MAIL - NUMBER OF PIECES SENT OR RECEIVED

Statistical Office of the United Nations, Publishing Service, New York, New York 10017 (800) 253-9646; *Statistical Yearbook.*

SLOVENIA - MANUFACTURING

Statistical Office of the United Nations, Publishing Service, New York, New York 10017 (800) 253-9646; *Industrial Commodity Statistics Yearbook;* and *Statistical Yearbook.*

SLOVENIA - MARRIAGE RATES

Europa Publications Limited, 18 Bedford Square, London, WC1B 3JN, England; *The Europa World Year Book.*

Statistical Office of the United Nations, Publishing Service, New York, New York 10017 (800) 253-9646; *Demographic Yearbook; Statistical Yearbook;* and *Trends in Europe and North America: The Statistical Yearbook of the Economic Commission for Europe.*

SLOVENIA - MERCHANT SHIPPING

St. Martin's Press, Inc., 175 Fifth Avenue, New York, New York 10010 (800) 221-7945; *The Statesman's Year-Book.*

Statistical Office of the United Nations, Publishing Service, New York, New York 10017 (800) 253-9646; *Statistical Yearbook.*

SLOVENIA - MILITARY

Central Intelligence Agency, Washington, D.C. 20505 (703) 482-1100, www.cia.gov; *The World Factbook.*

Euromonitor International Inc., 122 South Michigan Avenue, Suite 1200, Chicago, Illinois 60603 (800) 577-EURO; *World Marketing Data and Statistics.*

The International Institute for Strategic Studies, 23 Tavistock Street, London WC2E 7NQ, England 44 171 3797676; *The Military Balance.*

St. Martin's Press, Inc., 175 Fifth Avenue, New York, New York 10010 (800) 221-7945; *The Statesman's Year-Book.*

Statistical Office of the United Nations, Publishing Service, New York, New York 10017 (800) 253-9646; *Human Development Report.*

SLOVENIA - MINING AND MINERAL PRODUCTS

Europa Publications Limited, 18 Bedford Square, London, WC1B 3JN, England; *The Europa World Year Book.*

St. Martin's Press, Inc., 175 Fifth Avenue, New York, New York 10010 (800) 221-7945; *The Statesman's Year-Book.*

Statistical Office of the United Nations, Publishing Service, New York, New York 10017 (800) 253-9646; *Energy Statistics Yearbook; Industrial Commodity Statistics Yearbook;* and *Statistical Yearbook.*

SLOVENIA - MONEY SUPPLY

Economist Intelligence Unit, 111 West 57th Street, New York, New York 10019 (800) 938-4685; *Slovenia Country Report.*

Europa Publications Limited, 18 Bedford Square, London, WC1B 3JN, England; *The Europa World Year Book.*

SLOVENIA - MONUMENTS AND HISTORICAL SITES

United Nations Educational, Scientific and Cultural Organization (UNESCO), 7 Place de Fontenoy, F-75700 Paris, France (Telephone Number in U.S. (212) 963-5981); *Statistical Yearbook.*

SLOVENIA - MORTALITY

Central Intelligence Agency, Washington, D.C. 20505 (703) 482-1100, www.cia.gov; *The World Factbook.*

Euromonitor International, Inc., 122 South Michigan Avenue, Suite 1200, Chicago, Illinois 60603 (800) 577-EURO; *The World Economic Factbook.*

Europa Publications Limited, 18

Bedford Square, London, WC1B 3JN, England; *The Europa World Year Book.*

St. Martin's Press, Inc., 175 Fifth Avenue, New York, New York 10010 (800) 221-7945; *The Statesman's Year-Book.*

Statistical Office of the United Nations, Publishing Service, New York, New York 10017 (800) 253-9646; *Demographic Yearbook; Human Development Report; Statistical Yearbook; Trends in Europe and North America: The Statistical Yearbook of the Economic Commission for Europe;* and *World Statistics Pocketbook.*

United Nations Children's Fund (UNICEF), 3 United Nations Plaza, New York, New York 10017 (800) 253-9646; *State of the World's Children.*

The World Bank, 1818 H Street, NW, Washington, D.C. 20433 (202) 477-1234; *The World Bank Atlas;* and *World Development Report.*

SLOVENIA - MOTION PICTURES

St. Martin's Press, Inc., 175 Fifth Avenue, New York, New York 10010 (800) 221-7945; *The Statesman's Year-Book.*

Statistical Office of the United Nations, Publishing Service, New York, New York 10017 (800) 253-9646; *Statistical Yearbook.*

United Nations Educational, Scientific and Cultural Organization (UNESCO), 7 Place de Fontenoy, F-75700 Paris, France (Telephone Number in U.S. (212) 963-5981); *Statistical Yearbook.*

SLOVENIA - MOTOR VEHICLE PRODUCTION

Europa Publications Limited, 18 Bedford Square, London, WC1B 3JN, England; *The Europa World Year Book.*

Statistical Office of the United Nations, Publishing Service, New York, New York 10017 (800) 253-9646; *Statistical Yearbook.*

SLOVENIA - MUSEUMS

United Nations Educational, Scientific and Cultural Organization (UNESCO), 7 Place de Fontenoy, F-75700 Paris, France (Telephone Number in U.S. (212) 963-5981); *Statistical Yearbook.*

SLOVENIA - NATIONAL ACCOUNTS

Statistical Office of the United Nations, Publishing Service, New York, New York 10017 (800) 253-9646; *National Accounts Statistics;* and *Statistical Yearbook.*

SLOVENIA - NATIONAL INCOME

Europa Publications Limited, 18

Bedford Square, London, WC1B 3JN, England; *The Europa World Year Book*.

Statistical Office of the United Nations, Publishing Service, New York, New York 10017 (800) 253-9646; *Statistical Yearbook*.

SLOVENIA - NATIONAL PRODUCT

Statistical Office of the United Nations, Publishing Service, New York, New York 10017 (800) 253-9646; *Statistical Yearbook*.

SLOVENIA - PATENTS, TRADEMARKS AND SERVICE MARKS

Statistical Office of the United Nations, Publishing Service, New York, New York 10017 (800) 253-9646; *Statistical Yearbook*.

SLOVENIA - PERIODICALS

United Nations Educational, Scientific and Cultural Organization (UNESCO), 7 Place de Fontenoy, F-75700 Paris, France (Telephone Number in U.S. (212) 963-5981); *Statistical Yearbook*.

SLOVENIA - PETROLEUM INDUSTRY

Food and Agriculture Organization of the United Nations (FAO), Via delle Terme di Caracalla, 00100, Rome, Italy (Telephone Number in U.S. (202) 653-2400); *The State of Food and Agriculture*.

Statistical Office of the United Nations, Publishing Service, New York, New York 10017 (800) 253-9646; *Energy Statistics Yearbook; Industrial Commodity Statistics Yearbook; Statistical Yearbook;* and *Trends in Europe and North America: The Statistical Yearbook of the Economic Commission for Europe*.

SLOVENIA - POPULATION

Central Intelligence Agency, Washington, D.C. 20505 (703) 482-1100, www.cia.gov; *The World Factbook*.

Economist Intelligence Unit, 111 West 57th Street, New York, New York 10019 (800) 938-4685; *Slovenia Country Report*.

Euromonitor International, Inc., 122 South Michigan Avenue, Suite 1200, Chicago, Illinois 60603 (800) 577-EURO; *The World Economic Factbook*.

Europa Publications Limited, 18 Bedford Square, London, WC1B 3JN, England; *The Europa World Year Book*.

Food and Agriculture Organization of the United Nations (FAO), Via delle Terme di Caracalla, 00100, Rome, Italy (Telephone Number in U.S. (202) 653-2400); *Production Yearbook*.

International Labour Office, I.L.O.

Publications, 1828 L Street, NW., Suite 801, Washington, D.C. 20036 (301) 638-3152; *Yearbook of Labour Statistics*.

St. Martin's Press, Inc., 175 Fifth Avenue, New York, New York 10010 (800) 221-7945; *The Statesman's Year-Book*.

Statistical Office of the United Nations, Publishing Service, New York, New York 10017 (800) 253-9646; *Demographic Yearbook; Human Development Report; Statistical Yearbook; Trends in Europe and North America: The Statistical Yearbook of the Economic Commission for Europe;* and *World Statistics Pocketbook*.

United Nations Educational, Scientific and Cultural Organization (UNESCO), 7 Place de Fontenoy, F-75700 Paris, France (Telephone Number in U.S. (212) 963-5981); *Statistical Yearbook*.

The World Bank, 1818 H Street, NW, Washington, D.C. 20433 (202) 477-1234; *The World Bank Atlas;* and *World Development Report*.

SLOVENIA - POST OFFICES

St. Martin's Press, Inc., 175 Fifth Avenue, New York, New York 10010 (800) 221-7945; *The Statesman's Year-Book*.

Statistical Office of the United Nations, Publishing Service, New York, New York 10017 (800) 253-9646; *Trends in Europe and North America: The Statistical Yearbook of the Economic Commission for Europe*.

SLOVENIA - PRICES

Food and Agriculture Organization of the United Nations (FAO), Via delle Terme di Caracalla, 00100, Rome, Italy (Telephone Number in U.S. (202) 653-2400); *Production Yearbook*.

International Labour Office, I.L.O. Publications, 1828 L Street, NW., Suite 801, Washington, D.C. 20036 (301) 638-3152; *Yearbook of Labour Statistics*.

SLOVENIA - RADIO RECEIVER PRODUCTION

Statistical Office of the United Nations, Publishing Service, New York, New York 10017 (800) 253-9646; *Statistical Yearbook*.

SLOVENIA - RADIO RECEIVERS

St. Martin's Press, Inc., 175 Fifth Avenue, New York, New York 10010 (800) 221-7945; *The Statesman's Year-Book*.

SLOVENIA - RAILWAYS

Europa Publications Limited, 18 Bedford Square, London, WC1B 3JN, England; *The Europa World Year Book*.

St. Martin's Press, Inc., 175 Fifth Avenue, New York, New York 10010 (800) 221-7945; *The Statesman's Year-Book*.

Statistical Office of the United Nations, Publishing Service, New York, New York 10017 (800) 253-9646; *Annual Bulletin of Transport Statistics for Europe; Statistical Yearbook;* and *Trends in Europe and North America: The Statistical Yearbook of the Economic Commission for Europe*.

SLOVENIA - RELIGION

Central Intelligence Agency, Washington, D.C. 20505 (703) 482-1100, www.cia.gov; *The World Factbook*.

St. Martin's Press, Inc., 175 Fifth Avenue, New York, New York 10010 (800) 221-7945; *The Statesman's Year-Book*.

SLOVENIA - RENT PRICES

International Labour Office, I.L.O. Publications, 1828 L Street, NW., Suite 801, Washington, D.C. 20036 (301) 638-3152; *Yearbook of Labour Statistics*.

SLOVENIA - RETAIL PRICE INDEX

Euromonitor International Inc., 122 South Michigan Avenue, Suite 1200, Chicago, Illinois 60603 (800) 577-EURO; *World Marketing Data and Statistics*.

Europa Publications Limited, 18 Bedford Square, London, WC1B 3JN, England; *The Europa World Year Book*.

SLOVENIA - RETAIL TRADE

Statistical Office of the United Nations, Publishing Service, New York, New York 10017 (800) 253-9646; *Statistical Yearbook*.

SLOVENIA - ROADS - See HIGHWAYS

SLOVENIA - RUBBER PRODUCTION AND CONSUMPTION

Statistical Office of the United Nations, Publishing Service, New York, New York 10017 (800) 253-9646; *Statistical Yearbook*.

SLOVENIA - SCIENTISTS, TECHNICIANS AND ENGINEERS

Statistical Office of the United Nations, Publishing Service, New York, New York 10017 (800) 253-9646; *Statistical Yearbook*.

SLOVENIA - SOCIAL DATA

Statistical Office of the United Nations, Publishing Service, New York, New York 10017 (800) 253-9646; *World Statistics Pocketbook*.

SLOVENIA - SOCIAL SECURITY

St. Martin's Press, Inc., 175 Fifth Avenue, New York, New York 10010 (800) 221-7945; *The Statesman's Year-Book*.

Statistical Office of the United Nations, Publishing Service, New York, New York 10017 (800) 253-9646; *National Accounts Statistics.*

SLOVENIA - TAXATION

Europa Publications Limited, 18 Bedford Square, London, WC1B 3JN, England; *The Europa World Year Book.*

SLOVENIA - TELEPHONES IN USE

Central Intelligence Agency, Washington, D.C. 20505 (703) 482-1100, www.cia.gov; *The World Factbook.*

Europa Publications Limited, 18 Bedford Square, London, WC1B 3JN, England; *The Europa World Year Book.*

St. Martin's Press, Inc., 175 Fifth Avenue, New York, New York 10010 (800) 221-7945; *The Statesman's Year-Book.*

Statistical Office of the United Nations, Publishing Service, New York, New York 10017 (800) 253-9646; *Statistical Yearbook; Trends in Europe and North America: The Statistical Yearbook of the Economic Commission for Europe;* and *World Statistics Pocketbook.*

SLOVENIA - TEXTILE INDUSTRY

St. Martin's Press, Inc., 175 Fifth Avenue, New York, New York 10010 (800) 221-7945; *The Statesman's Year-Book.*

Statistical Office of the United Nations, Publishing Service, New York, New York 10017 (800) 253-9646; *Industrial Commodity Statistics Yearbook;* and *Statistical Yearbook.*

SLOVENIA - THEATRE

United Nations Educational, Scientific and Cultural Organization (UNESCO), 7 Place de Fontenoy, F-75700 Paris, France (Telephone Number in U.S. (212) 963-5981); *Statistical Yearbook.*

SLOVENIA - TIRE (MOTOR VEHICLE) PRODUCTION

Statistical Office of the United Nations, Publishing Service, New York, New York 10017 (800) 253-9646; *Statistical Yearbook.*

SLOVENIA - TOBACCO PRODUCTION

Statistical Office of the United Nations, Publishing Service, New York, New York 10017 (800) 253-9646; *Statistical Yearbook.*

SLOVENIA - TOURISM

Euromonitor International, Inc., 122 South Michigan Avenue, Suite 1200, Chicago, Illinois 60603 (800) 577-EURO; *The World Economic Factbook;* and *World Marketing Data and Statistics.*

Europa Publications Limited, 18 Bedford Square, London, WC1B 3JN, England; *The Europa World Year Book.*

St. Martin's Press, Inc., 175 Fifth Avenue, New York, New York 10010 (800) 221-7945; *The Statesman's Year-Book.*

Statistical Office of the United Nations, Publishing Service, New York, New York 10017 (800) 253-9646; *Statistical Yearbook;* and *Trends in Europe and North America: The Statistical Yearbook of the Economic Commission for Europe.*

SLOVENIA - TRADEMARKS AND SERVICE MARKS - See PATENTS, TRADEMARKS AND SERVICE MARKS

SLOVENIA - TRANSPORTATION AND COMMUNICATIONS

Central Intelligence Agency, Washington, D.C. 20505 (703) 482-1100, www.cia.gov; *The World Factbook.*

Euromonitor International Inc., 122 South Michigan Avenue, Suite 1200, Chicago, Illinois 60603 (800) 577-EURO; *World Marketing Data and Statistics.*

Europa Publications Limited, 18 Bedford Square, London, WC1B 3JN, England; *The Europa World Year Book.*

St. Martin's Press, Inc., 175 Fifth Avenue, New York, New York 10010 (800) 221-7945; *The Statesman's Year-Book.*

Statistical Office of the United Nations, Publishing Service, New York, New York 10017 (800) 253-9646; *Annual Bulletin of Transport Statistics for Europe; Human Development Report;* and *Trends in Europe and North America: The Statistical Yearbook of the Economic Commission for Europe.*

SLOVENIA - UNEMPLOYMENT

Central Intelligence Agency, Washington, D.C. 20505 (703) 482-1100, www.cia.gov; *The World Factbook.*

International Labour Office, I.L.O. Publications, 1828 L Street, NW., Suite 801, Washington, D.C. 20036 (301) 638-3152; *Yearbook of Labour Statistics.*

St. Martin's Press, Inc., 175 Fifth Avenue, New York, New York 10010 (800) 221-7945; *The Statesman's Year-Book.*

Statistical Office of the United Nations, Publishing Service, New York, New York

10017 (800) 253-9646; *Statistical Yearbook;* and *Trends in Europe and North America: The Statistical Yearbook of the Economic Commission for Europe.*

SLOVENIA - VITAL STATISTICS

St. Martin's Press, Inc., 175 Fifth Avenue, New York, New York 10010 (800) 221-7945; *The Statesman's Year-Book.*

Statistical Office of the United Nations, Publishing Service, New York, New York 10017 (800) 253-9646; *Statistical Yearbook.*

SLOVENIA - WAGES

Statistical Office of the United Nations, Publishing Service, New York, New York 10017 (800) 253-9646; *Statistical Yearbook.*

SLOVENIA - WHOLESALE PRICES

Statistical Office of the United Nations, Publishing Service, New York, New York 10017 (800) 253-9646; *Statistical Yearbook.*

SLOVENIA - WHOLESALE TRADE

Statistical Office of the United Nations, Publishing Service, New York, New York 10017 (800) 253-9646; *Statistical Yearbook.*

SMALL BUSINESS - BUDGET OUTLAYS

Executive Office of the President, Office of Management and Budget, Executive Office Building, Washington, D.C. 20503 (202) 395-3080, www.whitehouse.gov/omb; *Historical Tables.*

SMALL BUSINESS - EMPLOYEES

U.S. Department of Commerce, Bureau of the Census, Washington, D.C. 20233 (301) 457-4100, www.census.gov; *County Business Patterns.*

SMALL BUSINESS - ESTABLISHMENTS

U.S. Department of Commerce, Bureau of the Census, Washington, D.C. 20233 (301) 457-4100, www.census.gov; *County Business Patterns.*

SMALL BUSINESS - LOANS

Small Business Administration, 409 Third Street, SW, Washington, D.C. 20416 (800) UASK-SBA, www.sbaonline.sba.gov; unpublished data.

SMALL BUSINESS - PAYROLL

U.S. Department of Commerce, Bureau of the Census, Washington, D.C. 20233 (301) 457-4100, www.census.gov; *County Business Patterns.*

SMOKING

U.S. Department of Health and Human Services, Centers for Disease Control and Prevention, 1600 Clifton Road, NE, Atlanta, Georgia 30333 (800) 311-3435, www.cdc.gov; *Morbidity and Mortality Weekly Report.*

U.S. Department of Health and Human Services, National Center for Health Statistics, 3700 East-West Highway, Hyattsville, Maryland 20782 (301) 436-8500, www.cdc.gov/nchs; *National Vital Statistics Report; Injury Checkbook;* and *Health, United States.*

U.S. Department of Health and Human Services, Substance Abuse and Mental Health Services Administration, 5600 Fishers Lane, Rockville, Maryland 20857 (800) 729-6686, www.samhsa.gov; *National Household Survey on Drug Abuse.*

SNAPPER

U.S. Department of Commerce, National Oceanic and Atmospheric Administration, National Marine Fisheries Service, 1315 East-West Highway, Silver Spring, Maryland 20910 (301) 427-2239, www.nmfs.noaa.gov; *Fisheries of the United States.*

SNORKELING

National Sporting Goods Association, 1601 Feehanville Drive, Suite 300, Mount Prospect, Illinois 66056 (847) 296-6742; *Sports Participation in 1998.*

SNOW AND ICE PELLETS - SELECTED CITIES

U.S. Department of Commerce, National Oceanic and Atmospheric Administration, National Climatic Data Center, 151 Patton Avenue, Asheville, North Carolina 28801 (828) 4800, www.ncdc.noaa.gov; *Comparative Climatic Data.*

SNOWBOARDING

National Sporting Goods Association, 1601 Feehanville Drive, Suite 300, Mount Prospect, Illinois 66056 (847) 296-6742; *Sports Participation in 1998.*

SNOWMOBILES

National Sporting Goods Association, 1601 Feehanville Drive, Suite 300, Mount Prospect, Illinois 66056 (847) 296-6742; *The Sporting Goods Market in 1999.*

SOCCER

National Collegiate Athletic Association, 700 West Washington Street, Indianapolis, Indiana 46206 (317) 917-6222; *1997-98 Participation Study.*

National Federation of State High School Associations, Post Office Box 690, Indianapolis, Indiana 46206 (317) 972-6900; *The 1998-99 High School Athletics Participation Study.*

National Sporting Goods Association, 1601 Feehanville Drive, Suite 300, Mount Prospect, Illinois 66056 (847) 296-6742; *Sports Participation in 1998.*

SOCIAL INSURANCE - See also MEDICARE, RETIREMENT SYSTEMS, and SOCIAL SECURITY

SOCIAL INSURANCE - EMPLOYMENT COVERED

Social Security Administration, 6400 Security Boulevard, Baltimore, Maryland 21235 (800) 772-1213, ww.ssa.gov; *Annual Statistical Supplement to the Social Security Bulletin,* and unpublished data.

SOCIAL INSURANCE - EXPENDITURES - PUBLIC

Social Security Administration, 6400 Security Boulevard, Baltimore, Maryland 21235 (800) 772-1213, ww.ssa.gov; *Social Security Bulletin;* and unpublished data.

U.S. Department of Commerce, Bureau of Economic Analysis, Fourteenth Street between Constitution Avenue and E Street, NW, Washington, D.C. 20230 (202) 606-9900, www.bea.doc.gov; *Survey of Current Business.*

SOCIAL INSURANCE - FOREIGN COUNTRIES

Organization for Economic Cooperation and Development, Publication and Information Center, 2001 L Street, NW, Washington, D.C. 20036 (202) 785-6323; *Revenue Statistics of OECD Member Countries;* and *The OECD Observer, No. 214.*

SOCIAL INSURANCE - GOVERNMENT INSURANCE TRUST FUNDS

U.S. Department of Commerce, Bureau of the Census, Washington, D.C. 20233 (301) 457-4608; unpublished data; and Internet site: http://www.census.gov/pub/gov/www/index.html.

SOCIAL INSURANCE - GOVERNMENT INSURANCE TRUST FUNDS - FEDERAL RECEIPTS AND EXPENDITURES

Executive Office of the President, Office of Management and Budget, Executive Office Building, Washington, D.C. 20503 (202) 395-3080, www.whitehouse.gov/omb; *Analytical Perspectives.*

Social Security Administration, 6400 Security Boulevard, Baltimore, Maryland

21235 (800) 772-1213, ww.ssa.gov; *Annual Report of Board of Trustees, OASI, DI, HI, and SMI Trust Funds;* and *Social Security Bulletin.*

SOCIAL INSURANCE - GOVERNMENT INSURANCE TRUST FUNDS - STATE AND LOCAL RECEIPTS - EXPENDITURES

U.S. Department of Commerce, Bureau of the Census, Washington, D.C. 20233 (301) 457-4100, www.census.gov; *Finances of Employee-Retirement Systems of State and Local Government; State Government Finances;* and Internet sites: http://www.census.gov/govs/www/estimate.html; and http://www.census.gov/govs/www/state.html.

SOCIAL INSURANCE - INDIVIDUAL PROGRAMS - BENEFICIARIES AND BENEFITS

Social Security Administration, 6400 Security Boulevard, Baltimore, Maryland 21235 (800) 772-1213, ww.ssa.gov; *Annual Statistical Supplement to the Social Security Bulletin; Social Security Bulletin;* and unpublished data.

SOCIAL INSURANCE - INDIVIDUAL PROGRAMS - COVERAGE

Social Security Administration, 6400 Security Boulevard, Baltimore, Maryland 21235 (800) 772-1213, ww.ssa.gov; *Finances of Employee-Retirement Systems of State and Local Government; Annual Statistical Supplement to the Social Security Bulletin;* and unpublished data.

SOCIAL INSURANCE - INDIVIDUAL PROGRAMS - FEDERAL RETIREMENT INSURANCE

Board of Governors of the Federal Reserve System, Twentieth Street and Constitution Avenue, NW, Washington, D.C. 20551 (202) 452-3000, www.bog.frb.fed.us; *Flow of Funds Accounts.*

Office of Personnel Management, 1900 E Street, NW, Washington, D.C. 20415 (202) 606-1800, www.opm.gov; *Civil Service Retirement and Disability Trust Fund Annual Report.*

Social Security Administration, 6400 Security Boulevard, Baltimore, Maryland 21235 (800) 772-1213, ww.ssa.gov; *Social Security Bulletin; Annual Statistical Supplement to the Social Security Bulletin;* and unpublished data.

SOCIAL INSURANCE - INDIVIDUAL PROGRAMS - OLD-AGE, SURVIVORS, DISABILITY AND HEALTH INSURANCE - CONTRIBUTIONS

Social Security Administration, 6400

Security Boulevard, Baltimore, Maryland 21235 (800) 772-1213, ww.ssa.gov; *Social Security Bulletin;* and *Annual Report of Board of Trustees, OASI, DI, HI, and SMI Trust Funds.*

SOCIAL INSURANCE - INDIVIDUAL PROGRAMS - OLD-AGE, SURVIVORS, DISABILITY AND HEALTH INSURANCE - COVERAGE - WORKERS AND EARNINGS

Social Security Administration, 6400 Security Boulevard, Baltimore, Maryland 21235 (800) 772-1213, ww.ssa.gov; *Annual Statistical Supplement to the Social Security Bulletin;* and unpublished data.

SOCIAL INSURANCE - INDIVIDUAL PROGRAMS - OLD-AGE, SURVIVORS, DISABILITY AND HEALTH SURVIVORS, DISABILITY AND HEALTH INSURANCE - PAYMENTS

Social Security Administration, 6400 Security Boulevard, Baltimore, Maryland 21235 (800) 772-1213, ww.ssa.gov; *Annual Report of Board of Trustees, OASI, DI, HI, and SMI Trust Funds; Social Security Bulletin; Annual Statistical Supplement to the Social Security Bulletin;* and unpublished data.

SOCIAL INSURANCE - INDIVIDUAL PROGRAMS - OLD-AGE, SURVIVORS, DISABILITY AND HEALTH SURVIVORS, DISABILITY AND HEALTH INSURANCE - TAX COLLECTIONS

U.S. Department of the Treasury, Internal Revenue Service, 1111 Constitution Avenue, NW, Washington, D.C. 20224 (202) 874-0410, www.irs.ustreas.gov; Annual Report.

U.S. Department of the Treasury, Bureau of Alcohol, Tobacco and Firearms, 650 Massachusetts Avenue, NW, Washington, D.C. 20226 (202) 927-8500, www.atf.treas.gov; *Alcohol and Tobacco Tax Collections.*

SOCIAL INSURANCE - INDIVIDUAL PROGRAMS - OLD-AGE, SURVIVORS, DISABILITY AND HEALTH INSURANCE - TRUST FUNDS

Executive Office of the President, Office of Management and Budget, Executive Office Building, Washington, D.C. 20503 (202) 395-3080, www.whitehouse.gov/omb; *Analytical Perspectives.*

Social Security Administration, 6400 Security Boulevard, Baltimore, Maryland 21235 (800) 772-1213, ww.ssa.gov; *Social Security Bulletin; and Annual Report of Board of Trustees, OASI, DI, HI and SMI Trust Funds.*

SOCIAL INSURANCE - RAILROAD INSURANCE

Board of Governors of the Federal Reserve System, Twentieth Street and Constitution Avenue, NW, Washington, D.C. 20551 (202) 452-3000, www.bog.frb.fed.us; *Flow of Funds Accounts.*

Social Security Administration, 6400 Security Boulevard, Baltimore, Maryland 21235 (800) 772-1213, ww.ssa.gov; *Social Security Bulletin;* and unpublished data.

SOCIAL INSURANCE - STATE AND LOCAL PUBLIC RETIREMENT SYSTEMS

Social Security Administration, 6400 Security Boulevard, Baltimore, Maryland 21235 (800) 772-1213, ww.ssa.gov; *Social Security Bulletin;* and unpublished data.

U.S. Department of Commerce, Bureau of the Census, Washington, D.C. 20233 (301) 457-4100, www.census.gov; *Finances of Employee-Retirement Systems of State and Local Governments.*

SOCIAL INSURANCE - TRUST FUNDS

Board of Governors of the Federal Reserve System, Twentieth Street and Constitution Avenue, NW, Washington, D.C. 20551 (202) 452-3000, www.bog.frb.fed.us; *Flow of Funds Accounts.*

SOCIAL INSURANCE - UNEMPLOYMENT INSURANCE (FEDERAL AND STATE)

Social Security Administration, 6400 Security Boulevard, Baltimore, Maryland 21235 (800) 772-1213, ww.ssa.gov; *Social Security Bulletin;* and unpublished data.

U.S. Department of Labor, Employment and Training Administration, 200 Constitution Avenue, NW, Washington, D.C. 20210 (202) 219-6871, www.doleta.gov, *Unemployment Insurance Financial Handbook.*

SOCIAL INSURANCE - WORKER'S COMPENSATION

National Academy of Social Insurance, 1776 Massachusetts Avenue, NW, Suite 615, Washington, D.C. 20036-1904 (202) 452-8097; *Workers' Compensation: Benefits, Coverage, and Costs;* and *1996: New Estimates.*

Social Security Administration, 6400 Security Boulevard, Baltimore, Maryland 21235 (800) 772-1213, ww.ssa.gov; *Social Security Bulletin; Annual Statistical Supplement to the Social Security Bulletin;* and unpublished data.

U.S. Department of Health and Human Services, Health Care Financing Administration, 200 Independence Avenue, SW, Washington, D.C. 20201 (202) 690-

6145, www.hcfa.gov; *Health Care Financing Review.*

SOCIAL SCIENCES - DEGREES CONFERRED

National Science Foundation, 4201 Wilson Boulevard, Arlington, Virginia 22230 (703) 306-1234, www.nsf.gov; *Survey of Earned Doctorates, Selected Data on Science and Engineering Doctorate Awards;* and *National Survey of Recent College Graduates.*

U.S. Department of Commerce, Bureau of the Census, Washington, D.C. 20233 (301) 457-4100, www.census.gov; unpublished data.

U.S. Department of Education, National Center for Education Statistics; 555 New Jersey Avenue, NW, Washington, D.C. 20208-5574 (202) 219-1828, http://nces.ed.gov; *Digest of Education Statistics.*

SOCIAL SCIENCES - EMPLOYMENT

U.S. Department of Labor, Bureau of Labor Statistics, Two Massachusetts Avenue, NE, Washington, D.C. 20212 (202) 691-5200, www.stats.bls.gov; *Monthly Labor Review; Employment Earnings;* and unpublished data.

SOCIAL SCIENCES - SALARY OFFERS

College Placement Council, 62 Highland Avenue, Bethlehem, Pennsylvania 18017 (212) 868-1421; *Salary Survey, A Study of Beginning Offers.*

SOCIAL SECURITY - See also SOCIAL INSURANCE

SOCIAL SECURITY - BENEFICIARIES AND PAYMENTS

Social Security Administration, 6400 Security Boulevard, Baltimore, Maryland 21235 (800) 772-1213, ww.ssa.gov; *Annual Statistical Supplement to the Social Security Bulletin;* and unpublished data.

SOCIAL SECURITY - CONTRIBUTIONS - RATES

Social Security Administration, 6400 Security Boulevard, Baltimore, Maryland 21235 (800) 772-1213, ww.ssa.gov; *Annual Statistical Supplement to the Social Security Bulletin;* and unpublished data.

SOCIAL SECURITY - CONTRIBUTIONS - RATES - FOREIGN COUNTRIES

Organization for Economic Cooperation and Development, Publication and Information Center, 2001 L Street, NW, Washington, D.C. 20036 (202) 785-6323; *Revenue Statistics of OECD Member Countries;* and *The OECD Observer, No.*

214.

SOCIAL SECURITY - COVERAGE, WORKERS AND EARNINGS

Social Security Administration, 6400 Security Boulevard, Baltimore, Maryland 21235 (800) 772-1213, ww.ssa.gov; *Annual Statistical Supplement to the Social Security Bulletin;* and unpublished data.

SOCIAL SECURITY - FAMILIES RECEIVING

U.S. Department of Labor, Bureau of Labor Statistics, Two Massachusetts Avenue, NE, Washington, D.C. 20212 (202) 691-5200, www.stats.bls.gov; Internet site: http://ferret.bls.gov/macro/031998/faminc/09000.htm.

SOCIAL SECURITY - OUTLAYS

Executive Office of the President, Office of Management and Budget, Executive Office Building, Washington, D.C. 20503 (202) 395-3080, www.whitehouse.gov/omb; *Historical Tables.*

SOCIAL SECURITY - PAYMENTS

Social Security Administration, 6400 Security Boulevard, Baltimore, Maryland 21235 (800) 772-1213, ww.ssa.gov; *Social Security Bulletin; Annual Statistical Supplement to the Social Security Bulletin; Social Security Bulletin;* and unpublished data.

SOCIAL SECURITY - TRUST FUNDS

Executive Office of the President, Office of Management and Budget, Executive Office Building, Washington, D.C. 20503 (202) 395-3080, www.whitehouse.gov/omb; *Analytical Perspectives.*

Social Security Administration, 6400 Security Boulevard, Baltimore, Maryland 21235 (800) 772-1213, ww.ssa.gov; *Annual Statistical Supplement to the Social Security Bulletin; Annual Report of Board of Trustees, OASI, DI, HI, and SMI Trust Funds; Social Security Bulletin;* and unpublished data.

SOCIAL SERVICES - EARNINGS

U.S. Department of Commerce, Bureau of the Census, Washington, D.C. 20233 (301) 457-4100, www.census.gov; *County Business Patterns; 1997 Economic Census;* and *Census of Service Industries.*

SOCIAL SERVICES - EMPLOYEES

U.S. Department of Commerce, Bureau of the Census, Washington, D.C. 20233 (301) 457-4100, www.census.gov; *County Business Patterns; Census of Service Industries; 1997 Economic Census;* unpublished data.

U.S. Department of Labor, Bureau of Labor Statistics, Two Massachusetts Avenue, NE, Washington, D.C. 20212 (202) 691-5200, www.stats.bls.gov; *Employment and Earnings; Monthly Labor Review;* unpublished data; and Internet site: http://stats.bls.gov/ ceshome.htm.

SOCIAL SERVICES - ESTABLISHMENTS

U.S. Department of Commerce, Bureau of the Census, Washington, D.C. 20233 (301) 457-4100, www.census.gov; *County Business Patterns;* and *Census of Service Industries.*

SOCIAL SERVICES - GROSS DOMESTIC PRODUCT

U.S. Department of Commerce, Bureau of Economic Analysis, Fourteenth Street between Constitution Avenue and E Street, NW, Washington, D.C. 20230 (202) 606-9900, www.bea.doc.gov; *Survey of Current Business.*

SOCIAL SERVICES - OCCUPATIONAL SAFETY

U.S. Department of Labor, Bureau of Labor Statistics, Two Massachusetts Avenue, NE, Washington, D.C. 20212 (202) 691-5200, www.stats.bls.gov; *Occupational Injuries and Illnesses in the United States by Industry.*

SOCIAL SERVICES - RECEIPTS

U.S. Department of Commerce, Bureau of the Census, Washington, D.C. 20233 (301) 457-4100, www.census.gov; *Census of Service Industries; 1997 Economic Census; Service Annual Survey;* and unpublished data.

SOCIAL WELFARE - See also Individual Programs

SOCIAL WELFARE - CHARITABLE CONTRIBUTIONS

Independent Sector, 1200 Eighteenth Street, NW, Suite 200, Washington, D.C. 20036 (202) 467-6161; *Giving and Volunteering in the United States.*

SOCIAL WELFARE - EMPLOYEES - STATE AND LOCAL GOVERNMENT

U.S. Department of Commerce, Bureau of the Census, Washington, D.C. 20233 (301) 457-4100, www.census.gov; Internet site:http://www.census.gov/pub/govs/www/apes.html.

SOCIAL WELFARE - EXPENDITURES - CITY GOVERNMENT

U.S. Department of Commerce, Bureau of the Census, Washington, D.C. 20233 (301) 457-4100, www.census.gov;

unpublished data.

SOCIAL WELFARE - EXPENDITURES - COUNTY GOVERNMENT

U.S. Department of Commerce, Bureau of the Census, Washington, D.C. 20233 (301) 457-4100, www.census.gov; unpublished data.

SOCIAL WELFARE - EXPENDITURES - FEDERAL

Social Security Administration, 6400 Security Boulevard, Baltimore, Maryland 21235 (800) 772-1213, ww.ssa.gov; *Social Security Bulletin;* and unpublished data.

SOCIAL WELFARE - EXPENDITURES - PUBLIC PROGRAMS

Social Security Administration, 6400 Security Boulevard, Baltimore, Maryland 21235 (800) 772-1213, ww.ssa.gov; *Social Security Bulletin;* and unpublished data.

SOCIAL WELFARE - EXPENDITURES - STATE AND LOCAL GOVERNMENT

Social Security Administration, 6400 Security Boulevard, Baltimore, Maryland 21235 (800) 772-1213, ww.ssa.gov, *Social Security Bulletin;* and unpublished data.

U.S. Department of Commerce, Bureau of the Census, Washington, D.C. 20233 (301) 457-4100, www.census.gov; *Government Finances;* and Internet site: http://www.census.gov/govs/www/estimate.html.

SOCIAL WELFARE - EXPENDITURES - STATE GOVERNMENT

U.S. Department of Commerce, Bureau of the Census, Washington, D.C. 20233 (301) 457-4100, www.census.gov; *State Government Finances;* and Internet site: http://www.census.gov/ftp/pub/govs/www/state.htm; http://www.census.gov/govs/www/st97.html.

SOCIAL WELFARE - EXPENDITURES - VOLUNTEERS

Independent Sector, 1200 Eighteenth Street, NW, Suite 200, Washington, D.C. 20036 (202) 467-6161; *Giving and Volunteering in the United States.*

SOCIAL WELFARE ORGANIZATIONS

The Gale Group, 27500 Drake Road, Farmington Hills, Michigan 48331 (800) 877-4253; *Encyclopedia of Association.*

SODIUM CARBONATE

U.S. Department of the Interior, Geological Survey, Office of Minerals

Information, 12201 Sunrise Valley Drive, Reston, Virginia 22092 (703) 648-4000, www.minerals.usgs.gov; *Annual Reports;* and *Mineral Commodity Summaries.*

SODIUM SULFATE

U.S. Department of the Interior, Geological Survey, Office of Minerals Information, 12201 Sunrise Valley Drive, Reston, Virginia 22092 (703) 648-4000, www.minerals.usgs.gov; *Annual Reports;* and *Mineral Commodity Summaries.*

SOFT DRINKS - See also BEVERAGES

U.S. Department of Agriculture, Economic Research Service, 1800 M Street, NW, Washington, D.C. 20036 (202) 694-5050, www.ers.usda.gov; *Food Consumption, Prices, and Expenditures;* and *Agricultural Outlook.*

SOFTBALL

Amateur Softball Association of America, 2801 NE Fiftieth Street, Oklahoma City, Oklahoma 73111-7203 (405) 424-5266.

National Collegiate Athletic Association, 700 West Washington Street, Indianapolis, Indiana 46206 (317) 917-6222; *1997-98 Participation Study.*

National Federation of State High School Associations, Post Office Box 690, Indianapolis, Indiana 46206 (317) 972-6900; *The 1998-99 High School Athletics Participation Study.*

National Sporting Goods Association, 1601 Feehanville Drive, Suite 300, Mount Prospect, Illinois 66056 (847) 296-6742; *Sports Participation in 1998.*

SOFTWARE

Electronic Industries Alliance, 2500 Wilson Boulevard, Arlington, Virginia 22201 (703) 907-7500; *Electronic Market Data Book.*

Veronis, Suhler and Association, 350 Park Avenue, New York, New York 10022 (212) 935-4990; *Communications Industry Report.*

SOLAR ENERGY

U.S. Department of Energy, Energy Information Administration, 1000 Independence Avenue, SW, Washington, D.C. 20585 (202) 586-8800, www.eia.doe.gov; *Solar Collector Manufacturing Activity; Annual Nonutility Producer Report;* and *Annual Energy Review.*

SOLID WASTE - DISPOSAL

Franklin Associates Limited, 4121 West

Eighty-third Street, Suite 108, Prairie Village, Kansas 66208 (913) 649-2225; *Characterization of Municipal Solid Waste in the United States.*

U.S. Department of Commerce, Bureau of the Census, Washington, D.C. 20233 (301) 457-4100, www.census.gov; *Government Finances; State and Local Government Finance Estimates by State;* unpublished data; and Internet site: http://www.census.gov/govs/www/index.html.

SOLID WASTE - EXPENDITURES FOR POLLUTION ABATEMENT

U.S. Department of Commerce, Bureau of the Census, Washington, D.C. 20233 (301) 457-4100, www.census.gov; *Current Industrial Reports.*

SOLID WASTE -INDUSTRY

Environmental Business International, Inc., 4452 Park Boulevard, Suite 306, San Diego, California 92116 (619) 295-7685; *Environmental Business Journal.*

SOLID WASTE - LANDFILLS

Franklin Associates Limited, 4121 West 83rd Street, Suite 108, Prairie Village, Kansas 66208 (913) 649-2225; *Characterization of Municipal Solid Waste in the United States.*

SOLID WASTE - RECYCLING

Franklin Associates, Limited, 4121 West Eighty-third Street, Prairie Village, Kansas 66208 (913) 649-2225; *Characterization of Municipal Solid Waste in the United States.*

Solomon Islands - National Statistical Office

Statistics Office, Ministry of Finance and Economic Planning, Post Office Box G6, Honiara, Solomon Islands.

Solomon Islands - Primary Statistics Sources

Statistics Office, Post Office Box G6, Honiara, Solomon Islands; annual reports, *British Solomon Islands: Annual Abstract of Statistics; Quarterly Digest of Statistics;* and *Statistical Yearbook.*

SOLOMON ISLANDS - AGRICULTURE

Asian Development Bank, P.O. Box 789, 1099 Manila, Philippines; *Key Indicators of Developing Asian and Pacific Countries.*

Economist Intelligence Unit, 111 West 57th Street, New York, New York 10019 (800) 938-4685; *Solomon Islands Country Report.*

Euromonitor International Inc., 122 South Michigan Avenue, Suite 1200, Chicago, Illinois 60603 (800) 577-EURO; *World Marketing Data and Statistics.*

Europa Publications Limited, 18 Bedford Square, London, WC1B 3JN, England; *The Europa World Year Book.*

Food and Agricultural Organization of the United Nations (FAO) Via delle Terme di Caracalla, 00100 Rome, Italy (Telephone Number in U.S. (202) 653-2400); *Production Yearbook; The State of Food and Agriculture;* and *Trade Yearbook.*

St. Martin's Press, Inc., 175 Fifth Avenue, New York, New York 10010 (800) 221-7945; *The Statesman's Year-Book.*

Statistical Office of the United Nations, Publishing Service, New York, New York 10017 (800) 253-9646; *Asia-Pacific in Figures;* and *Statistical Yearbook for Asia and the Pacific.*

United Nations Conference on Trade and Development, Central Statistical Service, Palais des Nations, Geneva, Switzerland (Telephone in U.S. (800) 253-9646); *UNCTAD Commodity Yearbook.*

The World Bank, 1818 H Street, NW, Washington, D.C. 20433 (202) 477-1234; *World Development Indicators.*

SOLOMON ISLANDS - AIRLINE SERVICE

Europa Publications Limited, 18 Bedford Square, London, WC1B 3JN, England; *The Europa World Year Book.*

St. Martin's Press, Inc., 175 Fifth Avenue, New York, New York 10010 (800) 221-7945; *The Statesman's Year-Book.*

SOLOMON ISLANDS - AIRPORTS

Central Intelligence Agency, Washington, D.C. 20505 (703) 482-1100, www.cia.gov; *The World Factbook.*

SOLOMON ISLANDS - ANIMAL HEALTH

Food and Agricultural Organization of the United Nations (FAO), Via delle Terme di Caracalla, 00100, Rome, Italy (Telephone Number in U.S. (202) 653-2400); *Animal Health Yearbook.*

SOLOMON ISLANDS - AREA AND DENSITY OF POPULATION

Central Intelligence Agency, Washington, D.C. 20505 (703) 482-1100, www.cia.gov; *The World Factbook.*

Euromonitor International, Inc., 122 South Michigan Avenue, Suite 1200, Chicago, Illinois 60603 (800) 577-EURO;

The World Economic Factbook.

Europa Publications Limited, 18 Bedford Square, London, WC1B 3JN, England; *The Europa World Year Book.*

Food and Agricultural Organization of the United Nations (FAO) Via delle Terme di Caracalla, 00100 Rome, Italy (Telephone Number in U.S. (202) 653-2400); *The State of Food and Agriculture.*

St. Martin's Press, Inc., 175 Fifth Avenue, New York, New York 10010 (800) 221-7945; *The Statesman's Year-Book.*

Statistical Office of the United Nations, Publishing Service, New York, New York 10017 (800) 253-9646; *Statistical Yearbook.*

SOLOMON ISLANDS - BALANCE OF PAYMENTS

Europa Publications Limited, 18 Bedford Square, London, WC1B 3JN, England; *The Europa World Year Book.*

United Nations Conference on Trade and Development (UNCTAD), New York, New York 10017 (800) 253-9646; *Handbook of International Trade and Development Statistics.*

The World Bank, 1818 H Street, NW, Washington, D.C. 20433 (202) 477-1234; *World Development Indicators.*

SOLOMON ISLANDS - BANKING

Asian Development Bank, P.O. Box 789, 1099 Manila, Philippines; *Key Indicators of Developing Asian and Pacific Countries.*

Euromonitor International Inc., 122 South Michigan Avenue, Suite 1200, Chicago, Illinois 60603 (800) 577-EURO; *World Marketing Data and Statistics.*

Europa Publications Limited, 18 Bedford Square, London, WC1B 3JN, England; *The Europa World Year Book.*

International Monetary Fund, 700 Nineteenth Street, NW, Washington, D.C. 20431 (202) 623-7000; *Government Finance Statistics Yearbook.*

St. Martin's Press, Inc., 175 Fifth Avenue, New York, New York 10010 (800) 221-7945; *The Statesman's Year-Book.*

SOLOMON ISLANDS - BIRTH RATE

Central Intelligence Agency, Washington, D.C. 20505 (703) 482-1100, www.cia.gov; *The World Factbook.*

Euromonitor International, Inc., 122 South Michigan Avenue, Suite 1200, Chicago, Illinois 60603 (800) 577-EURO; *International Marketing Data and Statistics;*

and *The World Economic Factbook.*

Europa Publications Limited, 18 Bedford Square, London, WC1B 3JN, England; *The Europa World Year Book.*

Statistical Office of the United Nations, Publishing Service, New York, New York 10017 (800) 253-9646; *Asia-Pacific in Figures;* and *Statistical Yearbook.*

The World Bank, 1818 H Street, NW, Washington, D.C. 20433 (202) 477-1234; *World Development Indicators.*

SOLOMON ISLANDS - BROADCASTING

Billboard Limited, P.O. Box 9027, 1006 AA Amsterdam, The Netherlands (Telephone Number in U.S. (212) 764-7300); *World Radio TV Handbook.*

Central Intelligence Agency, Washington, D.C. 20505 (703) 482-1100, www.cia.gov; *The World Factbook.*

Euromonitor International Inc., 122 South Michigan Avenue, Suite 1200, Chicago, Illinois 60603 (800) 577-EURO; *World Marketing Data and Statistics.*

St. Martin's Press, Inc., 175 Fifth Avenue, New York, New York 10010 (800) 221-7945; *The Statesman's Year-Book.*

United Nations Educational, Scientific and Cultural Organization (UNESCO), 7 Place de Fontenoy, F-75700 Paris, France (Telephone Number in U.S. (212) 963-5981); *Statistical Yearbook.*

SOLOMON ISLANDS - BUDGET

Central Intelligence Agency, Washington, D.C. 20505 (703) 482-1100, www.cia.gov; *The World Factbook.*

SOLOMON ISLANDS - BUSINESS AND PROFESSIONAL LICENSES

International Monetary Fund, 700 Nineteenth Street, NW, Washington, D.C. 20431 (202) 623-7000; *Government Finance Statistics Yearbook.*

SOLOMON ISLANDS - CALORIE SUPPLY

Asian Development Bank, P.O. Box 789, 1099 Manila, Philippines; *Key Indicators of Developing Asian and Pacific Countries.*

Food and Agricultural Organization of the United Nations (FAO) Via delle Terme di Caracalla, 00100 Rome, Italy (Telephone Number in U.S. (202) 653-2400); *The State of Food and Agriculture.*

SOLOMON ISLANDS - CAPITAL INVESTMENT

Asian Development Bank, P.O. Box 789,

1099 Manila, Philippines; *Key Indicators of Developing Asian and Pacific Countries.*

SOLOMON ISLANDS - CAPITAL REVENUE

Asian Development Bank, P.O. Box 789, 1099 Manila, Philippines; *Key Indicators of Developing Asian and Pacific Countries.*

International Monetary Fund, 700 Nineteenth Street, NW, Washington, D.C. 20431 (202) 623-7000; *Government Finance Statistics Yearbook.*

SOLOMON ISLANDS - CHEMICAL (ORGANIC) PRODUCTION - See SOLOMON ISLANDS - MINING AND MINERAL PRODUCTS

SOLOMON ISLANDS - CLIMATE

St. Martin's Press, Inc., 175 Fifth Avenue, New York, New York 10010 (800) 221-7945; *The Statesman's Year-Book.*

SOLOMON ISLANDS - CLOTHING EXPORTS AND IMPORTS - See SOLOMON ISLANDS - TEXTILE INDUSTRY

SOLOMON ISLANDS - COAL PRODUCTION - See SOLOMON ISLANDS - MINING AND MINERAL PRODUCTS

SOLOMON ISLANDS - COCOA BEAN PRODUCTION - See SOLOMON ISLANDS - CROPS

SOLOMON ISLANDS - COMMERCE

St. Martin's Press, Inc., 175 Fifth Avenue, New York, New York 10010 (800) 221-7945; *The Statesman's Year-Book.*

SOLOMON ISLANDS - COMMUNICATIONS - See SOLOMON ISLANDS - TRANSPORTATION AND COMMUNICATIONS

SOLOMON ISLANDS - CONSUMER PRICE INDEX

Asian Development Bank, P.O. Box 789, 1099 Manila, Philippines; *Key Indicators of Developing Asian and Pacific Countries.*

Europa Publications Limited, 18 Bedford Square, London, WC1B 3JN, England; *The Europa World Year Book.*

Statistical Office of the United Nations, Publishing Service, New York, New York 10017 (800) 253-9646; *Statistical Yearbook.*

SOLOMON ISLANDS - CONSUMER PRICES

Euromonitor International Inc., 122 South Michigan Avenue, Suite 1200, Chicago, Illinois 60603 (800) 577-EURO; *World Marketing Data and Statistics.*

International Labour Office,

I.L.O. Publications, 1828 L Street, NW., Suite 801, Washington, D.C. 20036 (301) 638-3152; *Yearbook of Labour Statistics.*

SOLOMON ISLANDS - CONSUMPTION

South Pacific Commission, Post Box D5, Noumea Cedex, New Caledonia; *Statistical Bulletin of the South Pacific: Retail Price Indexes.*

SOLOMON ISLANDS - CORN PRODUCTION - See SOLOMON ISLANDS - CROPS

SOLOMON ISLANDS - CORPORATE TAXES - See SOLOMON ISLANDS - TAXATION

SOLOMON ISLANDS - CROPS

Asian Development Bank, P.O. Box 789, 1099 Manila, Philippines; *Key Indicators of Developing Asian and Pacific Countries.*

Europa Publications Limited, 18 Bedford Square, London, WC1B 3JN, England; *The Europa World Year Book.*

Food and Agricultural Organization of the United Nations (FAO) Via delle Terme di Caracalla, 00100 Rome, Italy (Telephone Number in U.S. (202) 653-2400); *The State of Food and Agriculture.*

St. Martin's Press, Inc., 175 Fifth Avenue, New York, New York 10010 (800) 221-7945; *The Statesman's Year-Book.*

Statistical Office of the United Nations, Publishing Service, New York, New York 10017 (800) 253-9646; *Statistical Yearbook.*

United Nations Conference on Trade and Development, Central Statistical Service, Palais des Nations, Geneva, Switzerland (Telephone in U.S. (800) 253-9646); *UNCTAD Commodity Yearbook.*

SOLOMON ISLANDS - CUSTOMS DUTIES

St. Martin's Press, Inc., 175 Fifth Avenue, New York, New York 10010 (800) 221-7945; *The Statesman's Year-Book.*

SOLOMON ISLANDS - DAIRY PRODUCTS

Europa Publications Limited, 18 Bedford Square, London, WC1B 3JN, England; *The Europa World Year Book.*

Food and Agricultural Organization of the United Nations (FAO) Via delle Terme di Caracalla, 00100 Rome, Italy (Telephone Number in U.S. (202) 653-2400); *The State of Food and Agriculture.*

St. Martin's Press, Inc., 175 Fifth Avenue, New York, New York 10010 (800) 221-7945; *The Statesman's Year-Book.*

SOLOMON ISLANDS - DEATH RATES - See

SOLOMON ISLANDS - MORTALITY

SOLOMON ISLANDS - DEFENSE EXPENDITURES

International Monetary Fund, 700 Nineteenth Street, NW, Washington, D.C. 20431 (202) 623-7000; *Government Finance Statistics Yearbook.*

SOLOMON ISLANDS - DEMOGRAPHY

Euromonitor International, Inc., 122 South Michigan Avenue, Suite 1200, Chicago, Illinois 60603 (800) 577-EURO; *International Marketing Data and Statistics; World Marketing Data and Statistics;* and *The World Economic Factbook.*

Statistical Office of the United Nations, Publishing Service, New York, New York 10017 (800) 253-9646; *Asia-Pacific in Figures;* and *Human Development Report.*

SOLOMON ISLANDS - DEVELOPMENT ASSISTANCE

Asian Development Bank, P.O. Box 789, 1099 Manila, Philippines; *Key Indicators of Developing Asian and Pacific Countries.*

Statistical Office of the United Nations, Publishing Service, New York, New York 10017 (800) 253-9646; *Statistical Yearbook.*

SOLOMON ISLANDS - ECONOMY

Asian Development Bank, P.O. Box 789, 1099 Manila, Philippines; *Key Indicators of Developing Asian and Pacific Countries.*

Central Intelligence Agency, Washington, D.C. 20505 (703) 482-1100, www.cia.gov; *The World Factbook.*

Economist Intelligence Unit, 111 West 57th Street, New York, New York 10019 (800) 938-4685; *Solomon Islands Country Report.*

Euromonitor International, Inc., 122 South Michigan Avenue, Suite 1200, Chicago, Illinois 60603 (800) 577-EURO; *The World Economic Factbook;* and *World Marketing Data and Statistics.*

Europa Publications Limited, 18 Bedford Square, London, WC1B 3JN, England; *The Europa World Year Book.*

St. Martin's Press, Inc., 175 Fifth Avenue, New York, New York 10010 (800) 221-7945; *The Statesman's Year-Book.*

Statistical Office of the United Nations, Publishing Service, New York, New York 10017 (800) 253-9646; *World Statistics Pocketbook.*

The World Bank, 1818 H Street, NW, Washington, D.C. 20433 (202) 477-1234;

The World Bank Atlas.

SOLOMON ISLANDS - EDUCATION

Euromonitor International, Inc., 122 South Michigan Avenue, Suite 1200, Chicago, Illinois 60603 (800) 577-EURO; *International Marketing Data and Statistics;* and *World Marketing Data and Statistics.*

Europa Publications Limited, 18 Bedford Square, London, WC1B 3JN, England; *The Europa World Year Book.*

International Monetary Fund, 700 Nineteenth Street, NW, Washington, D.C. 20431 (202) 623-7000; *Government Finance Statistics Yearbook.*

St. Martin's Press, Inc., 175 Fifth Avenue, New York, New York 10010 (800) 221-7945; *The Statesman's Year-Book.*

Statistical Office of the United Nations, Publishing Service, New York, New York 10017 (800) 253-9646; *Asia-Pacific in Figures; Human Development Report;* and *Statistical Yearbook for Asia and the Pacific.*

United Nations Educational, Scientific and Cultural Organization (UNESCO), 7 Place de Fontenoy, F-75700 Paris, France (Telephone Number in U.S. (212) 963-5981); *Statistical Yearbook.*

The World Bank, 1818 H Street, NW, Washington, D.C. 20433 (202) 477-1234; *World Development Indicators.*

SOLOMON ISLANDS - EGG PRODUCTION AND CONSUMPTION - See SOLOMON ISLANDS - DAIRY PRODUCTS

SOLOMON ISLANDS - ELECTRICITY

Asian Development Bank, P.O. Box 789, 1099 Manila, Philippines; *Key Indicators of Developing Asian and Pacific Countries.*

Central Intelligence Agency, Washington, D.C. 20505 (703) 482-1100, www.cia.gov; *The World Factbook.*

St. Martin's Press, Inc., 175 Fifth Avenue, New York, New York 10010 (800) 221-7945; *The Statesman's Year-Book.*

Statistical Office of the United Nations, Publishing Service, New York, New York 10017 (800) 253-9646; *Electric Power in Asia and the Pacific; Human Development Report;* and *Statistical Yearbook.*

SOLOMON ISLANDS - EMPLOYMENT

Euromonitor International, Inc., 122 South Michigan Avenue, Suite 1200, Chicago, Illinois 60603 (800) 577-EURO; *International Marketing Data and Statistics.*

International Labour Office, I.L.O. Publications, 1828 L Street, NW., Suite 801, Washington, D.C. 20036 (301) 638-3152; *Yearbook of Labour Statistics.*

Statistical Office of the United Nations, Publishing Service, New York, New York 10017 (800) 253-9646; *Asia-Pacific in Figures.*

SOLOMON ISLANDS - ENERGY

Euromonitor International, Inc., 122 South Michigan Avenue, Suite 1200, Chicago, Illinois 60603 (800) 577-EURO; *International Marketing Data and Statistics; World Marketing Data and Statistics;* and *The World Economic Factbook.*

Food and Agricultural Organization of the United Nations (FAO) Via delle Terme di Caracalla, 00100 Rome, Italy (Telephone Number in U.S. (202) 653-2400); *The State of Food and Agriculture.*

St. Martin's Press, Inc., 175 Fifth Avenue, New York, New York 10010 (800) 221-7945; *The Statesman's Year-Book.*

Statistical Office of the United Nations, Publishing Service, New York, New York 10017 (800) 253-9646; *Asia-Pacific in Figures; Energy Statistics Yearbook; Human Development Report; Statistical Yearbook; Statistical Yearbook for Asia and the Pacific;* and *World Statistics Pocketbook.*

The World Bank, 1818 H Street, NW, Washington, D.C. 20433 (202) 477-1234; *The World Bank Atlas.*

SOLOMON ISLANDS - ENVIRONMENT

Economist Intelligence Unit, 111 West 57th Street, New York, New York 10019 (800) 938-4685; *Solomon Islands Country Report.*

Statistical Office of the United Nations, Publishing Service, New York, New York 10017 (800) 253-9646; *World Statistics Pocketbook.*

SOLOMON ISLANDS - EXCHANGE RATES

Asian Development Bank, P.O. Box 789, 1099 Manila, Philippines; *Key Indicators of Developing Asian and Pacific Countries.*

Central Intelligence Agency, Washington, D.C. 20505 (703) 482-1100, www.cia.gov; *The World Factbook.*

Euromonitor International, Inc., 122 South Michigan Avenue, Suite 1200, Chicago, Illinois 60603 (800) 577-EURO; *International Marketing Data and Statistics;* and *The World Economic Factbook.*

Europa Publications Limited, 18 Bedford Square, London, WC1B 3JN,

England; *The Europa World Year Book.*

Statistical Office of the United Nations, Publishing Service, New York, New York 10017 (800) 253-9646; *World Statistics Pocketbook.*

Walden Publishing Ltd., Two Market Street, Saffron Walden Essex, CB10 1HZ, England; *The World of Information Asia and Pacific Review.*

SOLOMON ISLANDS - EXCISE TAXES - See SOLOMON ISLANDS - TAXATION

SOLOMON ISLANDS - EXPORTS

Asian Development Bank, P.O. Box 789, 1099 Manila, Philippines; *Key Indicators of Developing Asian and Pacific Countries.*

Central Intelligence Agency, Washington, D.C. 20505 (703) 482-1100, www.cia.gov; *The World Factbook.*

Economist Intelligence Unit, 111 West 57th Street, New York, New York 10019 (800) 938-4685; *Solomon Islands Country Report.*

Euromonitor International, Inc., 122 South Michigan Avenue, Suite 1200, Chicago, Illinois 60603 (800) 577-EURO; *International Marketing Data and Statistics;* and *The World Economic Factbook.*

Europa Publications Limited, 18 Bedford Square, London, WC1B 3JN, England; *The Europa World Year Book.*

Food and Agricultural Organization of the United Nations (FAO) Via delle Terme di Caracalla, 00100 Rome, Italy (Telephone Number in U.S. (202) 653-2400); *The State of Food and Agriculture.*

International Monetary Fund, 700 Nineteenth Street, NW, Washington, D.C. 20431 (202) 623-7000; *Direction of Trade Statistics.*

South Pacific Commission, Post Box D5, Noumea Cedex, New Caledonia; *Statistical Bulletin of the South Pacific: Overseas Trade.*

St. Martin's Press, Inc., 175 Fifth Avenue, New York, New York 10010 (800) 221-7945; *The Statesman's Year-Book.*

United Nations Conference on Trade and Development (UNCTAD), New York, New York 10017 (800) 253-9646; *Handbook of International Trade and Development Statistics.*

Walden Publishing Ltd., Two Market Street, Saffron Walden Essex, CB10 1HZ, England; *The World of Information Asia and Pacific Review.*

The World Bank, 1818 H Street, NW, Washington, D.C. 20433 (202) 477-1234; *World Development Indicators.*

SOLOMON ISLANDS - EXTERNAL FINANCING

Asian Development Bank, P.O. Box 789, 1099 Manila, Philippines; *Key Indicators of Developing Asian and Pacific Countries.*

SOLOMON ISLANDS - EXTERNAL INDEBTEDNESS

Asian Development Bank, P.O. Box 789, 1099 Manila, Philippines; *Key Indicators of Developing Asian and Pacific Countries.*

The World Bank, 1818 H Street, NW, Washington, D.C. 20433 (202) 477-1234; *World Development Indicators.*

SOLOMON ISLANDS - EXTERNAL TRADE

Asian Development Bank, P.O. Box 789, 1099 Manila, Philippines; *Key Indicators of Developing Asian and Pacific Countries.*

Euromonitor International Inc., 122 South Michigan Avenue, Suite 1200, Chicago, Illinois 60603 (800) 577-EURO; *World Marketing Data and Statistics.*

Food and Agricultural Organization of the United Nations (FAO) Via delle Terme di Caracalla, 00100 Rome, Italy (Telephone Number in U.S. (202) 653-2400); *The State of Food and Agriculture;* and *Trade Yearbook.*

Statistical Office of the United Nations, Publishing Service, New York, New York 10017 (800) 253-9646; *Asia-Pacific in Figures; Statistical Yearbook;* and *Statistical Yearbook for Asia and the Pacific.*

SOLOMON ISLANDS - FARM CROPS - See SOLOMON ISLANDS - CROPS

SOLOMON ISLANDS - FERTILITY RATES

Central Intelligence Agency, Washington, D.C. 20505 (703) 482-1100, www.cia.gov; *The World Factbook.*

Statistical Office of the United Nations, Publishing Service, New York, New York 10017 (800) 253-9646; *Human Development Report.*

The World Bank, 1818 H Street, NW, Washington, D.C. 20433 (202) 477-1234; *The World Bank Atlas;* and *World Development Indicators.*

SOLOMON ISLANDS - FERTILIZER

Food and Agricultural Organization of the United Nations (FAO) Via delle Terme di Caracalla, 00100 Rome, Italy (Telephone

Number in U.S. (202) 653-2400); *The State of Food and Agriculture.*

Organisation for Economic Co-operation and Development (OECD), 2 rue Andre-Pascal, 75 Paris 16, France (Telephone Number in U.S. (202) 785-6323); *Indicators of Industrial Activity.*

SOLOMON ISLANDS - FINANCE

Asian Development Bank, P.O. Box 789, 1099 Manila, Philippines; *Key Indicators of Developing Asian and Pacific Countries.*

Economist Intelligence Unit, 111 West 57th Street, New York, New York 10019 (800) 938-4685; *Solomon Islands Country Report.*

Europa Publications Limited, 18 Bedford Square, London, WC1B 3JN, England; *The Europa World Year Book.*

Food and Agricultural Organization of the United Nations (FAO) Via delle Terme di Caracalla, 00100 Rome, Italy (Telephone Number in U.S. (202) 653-2400); *The State of Food and Agriculture.*

International Monetary Fund, 700 Nineteenth Street, NW, Washington, D.C. 20431 (202) 623-7000; *Government Finance Statistics Yearbook.*

St. Martin's Press, Inc., 175 Fifth Avenue, New York, New York 10010 (800) 221-7945; *The Statesman's Year-Book.*

Statistical Office of the United Nations, Publishing Service, New York, New York 10017 (800) 253-9646; *Statistical Yearbook for Asia and the Pacific.*

SOLOMON ISLANDS - FISHERIES

Europa Publications Limited, 18 Bedford Square, London, WC1B 3JN, England; *The Europa World Year Book.*

Food and Agricultural Organization of the United Nations (FAO) Via delle Terme di Caracalla, 00100 Rome, Italy (Telephone Number in U.S. (202) 653-2400); *The State of Food and Agriculture;* and *Yearbook of Fishery Statistics.*

St. Martin's Press, Inc., 175 Fifth Avenue, New York, New York 10010 (800) 221-7945; *The Statesman's Year-Book.*

Statistical Office of the United Nations, Publishing Service, New York, New York 10017 (800) 253-9646; *Statistical Yearbook.*

United Nations Conference on Trade and Development, Central Statistical Service, Palais des Nations, Geneva, Switzerland (Telephone in U.S. (800) 253-9646); *UNCTAD Commodity Yearbook.*

SOLOMON ISLANDS - FOOD

Food and Agricultural Organization of the United Nations (FAO) Via delle Terme di Caracalla, 00100 Rome, Italy (Telephone Number in U.S. (202) 653-2400); *The State of Food and Agriculture.*

South Pacific Commission, Post Box D5, Noumea Cedex, New Caledonia; *Statistical Bulletin of the South Pacific: Retail Price Indexes.*

Statistical Office of the United Nations, Publishing Service, New York, New York 10017 (800) 253-9646; *Human Development Report;* and *Statistical Yearbook for Asia and the Pacific.*

United Nations Conference on Trade and Development, Central Statistical Service, Palais des Nations, Geneva, Switzerland (Telephone in U.S. (800) 253-9646); *UNCTAD Commodity Yearbook.*

SOLOMON ISLANDS - FOREIGN DEBT

International Monetary Fund, 700 Nineteenth Street, NW, Washington, D.C. 20431 (202) 623-7000; *Government Finance Statistics Yearbook.*

Walden Publishing Ltd., Two Market Street, Saffron Walden Essex, CB10 1HZ, England; *The World of Information Asia and Pacific Review.*

SOLOMON ISLANDS - FOREIGN TRADE

Asian Development Bank, P.O. Box 789, 1099 Manila, Philippines; *Key Indicators of Developing Asian and Pacific Countries.*

Economist Intelligence Unit, 111 West 57th Street, New York, New York 10019 (800) 938-4685; *Solomon Islands Country Report.*

Euromonitor International, Inc., 122 South Michigan Avenue, Suite 1200, Chicago, Illinois 60603 (800) 577-EURO; *The World Economic Factbook.*

Europa Publications Limited, 18 Bedford Square, London, WC1B 3JN, England; *The Europa World Year Book.*

Food and Agricultural Organization of the United Nations (FAO) Via delle Terme di Caracalla, 00100 Rome, Italy (Telephone Number in U.S. (202) 653-2400); *The State of Food and Agriculture.*

South Pacific Commission, Post Box D5, Noumea Cedex, New Caledonia; *Statistical Bulletin of the South Pacific: Overseas Trade.*

St. Martin's Press, Inc., 175 Fifth Avenue, New York, New York 10010 (800) 221-7945; *The Statesman's Year-Book.*

Statistical Office of the United Nations, Publishing Service, New York, New York 10017 (800) 253-9646; *International Trade Statistics Yearbook;* and *Statistical Yearbook.*

United Nations Conference on Trade and Development, Central Statistical Service, Palais des Nations, Geneva, Switzerland (Telephone in U.S. (800) 253-9646); *UNCTAD Commodity Yearbook.*

The World Bank, 1818 H Street, NW, Washington, D.C. 20433 (202) 477-1234; *World Development Indicators.*

SOLOMON ISLANDS - FORESTRY AND FOREST PRODUCTS

Europa Publications Limited, 18 Bedford Square, London, WC1B 3JN, England; *The Europa World Year Book.*

Food and Agricultural Organization of the United Nations (FAO) Via delle Terme di Caracalla, 00100 Rome, Italy (Telephone Number in U.S. (202) 653-2400); *The State of Food and Agriculture;* and *Yearbook of Forest Products.*

St. Martin's Press, Inc., 175 Fifth Avenue, New York, New York 10010 (800) 221-7945; *The Statesman's Year-Book.*

United Nations Conference on Trade and Development, Central Statistical Service, Palais des Nations, Geneva, Switzerland (Telephone in U.S. (800) 253-9646); *UNCTAD Commodity Yearbook.*

SOLOMON ISLANDS - GAS PRODUCTION - See SOLOMON ISLANDS - MINING AND MINERAL PRODUCTS

SOLOMON ISLANDS - GOLD HOLDINGS

The World Bank, 1818 H Street, NW, Washington, D.C. 20433 (202) 477-1234; *World Development Indicators.*

SOLOMON ISLANDS - GOVERNMENT

Asian Development Bank, P.O. Box 789, 1099 Manila, Philippines; *Key Indicators of Developing Asian and Pacific Countries.*

Central Intelligence Agency, Washington, D.C. 20505 (703) 482-1100, www.cia.gov; *The World Factbook.*

Europa Publications Limited, 18 Bedford Square, London, WC1B 3JN, England; *The Europa World Year Book.*

International Monetary Fund, 700 Nineteenth Street, NW, Washington, D.C. 20431 (202) 623-7000; *Government Finance Statistics Yearbook.*

St. Martin's Press, Inc., 175 Fifth Avenue, New York, New York 10010 (800)

221-7945; *The Statesman's Year-Book.*

Statistical Office of the United Nations, Publishing Service, New York, New York 10017 (800) 253-9646; *Asia-Pacific in Figures;* and *National Accounts Statistics.*

The World Bank, 1818 H Street, NW, Washington, D.C. 20433 (202) 477-1234; *World Development Indicators.*

SOLOMON ISLANDS - GRAIN PRODUCTION - See SOLOMON ISLANDS - CROPS

SOLOMON ISLANDS - GRANTS

International Monetary Fund, 700 Nineteenth Street, NW, Washington, D.C. 20431 (202) 623-7000; *Government Finance Statistics Yearbook.*

SOLOMON ISLANDS - GROSS DOMESTIC PRODUCT

Asian Development Bank, P.O. Box 789, 1099 Manila, Philippines; *Key Indicators of Developing Asian and Pacific Countries.*

Economist Intelligence Unit, 111 West 57th Street, New York, New York 10019 (800) 938-4685; *Solomon Islands Country Report.*

Euromonitor International, Inc., 122 South Michigan Avenue, Suite 1200, Chicago, Illinois 60603 (800) 577-EURO; *International Marketing Data and Statistics;* and *The World Economic Factbook.*

Europa Publications Limited, 18 Bedford Square, London, WC1B 3JN, England; *The Europa World Year Book.*

Statistical Office of the United Nations, Publishing Service, New York, New York 10017 (800) 253-9646; *Human Development Report; National Accounts Statistics;* and *Statistical Yearbook.*

The World Bank, 1818 H Street, NW, Washington, D.C. 20433 (202) 477-1234; *World Development Indicators.*

SOLOMON ISLANDS - GROSS NATIONAL PRODUCT

Asian Development Bank, P.O. Box 789, 1099 Manila, Philippines; *Key Indicators of Developing Asian and Pacific Countries.*

St. Martin's Press, Inc., 175 Fifth Avenue, New York, New York 10010 (800) 221-7945; *The Statesman's Year-Book.*

Walden Publishing Ltd., Two Market Street, Saffron Walden Essex, CB10 1HZ, England; *The World of Information Asia and Pacific Review.*

The World Bank, 1818 H Street, NW,

Washington, D.C. 20433 (202) 477-1234; *The World Bank Atlas;* and *World Development Indicators.*

SOLOMON ISLANDS - HEALTH

Euromonitor International Inc., 122 South Michigan Avenue, Suite 1200, Chicago, Illinois 60603 (800) 577-EURO; *World Marketing Data and Statistics.*

South Pacific Commission, Post Box D5, Noumea Cedex, New Caledonia; *Statistical Bulletin of the South Pacific: Retail Price Indexes.*

St. Martin's Press, Inc., 175 Fifth Avenue, New York, New York 10010 (800) 221-7945; *The Statesman's Year-Book.*

Statistical Office of the United Nations, Publishing Service, New York, New York 10017 (800) 253-9646; *Asia-Pacific in Figures; Human Development Report;* and *Statistical Yearbook.*

SOLOMON ISLANDS - HEALTH EXPENDITURES

International Monetary Fund, 700 Nineteenth Street, NW, Washington, D.C. 20431 (202) 623-7000; *Government Finance Statistics Yearbook.*

SOLOMON ISLANDS - HIGHWAYS

Central Intelligence Agency, Washington, D.C. 20505 (703) 482-1100, www.cia.gov; *The World Factbook.*

St. Martin's Press, Inc., 175 Fifth Avenue, New York, New York 10010 (800) 221-7945; *The Statesman's Year-Book.*

SOLOMON ISLANDS - HOURS OF WORK - See SOLOMON ISLANDS -EMPLOYMENT

SOLOMON ISLANDS - HOUSING AND HOUSING UNITS

Euromonitor International Inc., 122 South Michigan Avenue, Suite 1200, Chicago, Illinois 60603 (800) 577-EURO; *World Marketing Data and Statistics.*

South Pacific Commission, Post Box D5, Noumea Cedex, New Caledonia; *Statistical Bulletin of the South Pacific: Retail Price Indexes.*

SOLOMON ISLANDS - HOUSING EXPENDITURES

International Monetary Fund, 700 Nineteenth Street, NW, Washington, D.C. 20431 (202) 623-7000; *Government Finance Statistics Yearbook.*

South Pacific Commission, Post Box D5, Noumea Cedex, New Caledonia; *Statistical Bulletin of the South Pacific:*

Retail Price Indexes.

SOLOMON ISLANDS - ILLITERATE POPULATION

Central Intelligence Agency, Washington, D.C. 20505 (703) 482-1100, www.cia.gov; *The World Factbook.*

Euromonitor International, Inc., 122 South Michigan Avenue, Suite 1200, Chicago, Illinois 60603 (800) 577-EURO; *The World Economic Factbook.*

Statistical Office of the United Nations, Publishing Service, New York, New York 10017 (800) 253-9646; *Asia-Pacific in Figures;* and *Human Development Report.*

SOLOMON ISLANDS - IMPORTS

Asian Development Bank, P.O. Box 789, 1099 Manila, Philippines; *Key Indicators of Developing Asian and Pacific Countries.*

Central Intelligence Agency, Washington, D.C. 20505 (703) 482-1100, www.cia.gov; *The World Factbook.*

Economist Intelligence Unit, 111 West 57th Street, New York, New York 10019 (800) 938-4685; *Solomon Islands Country Report.*

Euromonitor International, Inc., 122 South Michigan Avenue, Suite 1200, Chicago, Illinois 60603 (800) 577-EURO; *International Marketing Data and Statistics;* and *The World Economic Factbook.*

Europa Publications Limited, 18 Bedford Square, London, WC1B 3JN, England; *The Europa World Year Book.*

Food and Agricultural Organization of the United Nations (FAO) Via delle Terme di Caracalla, 00100 Rome, Italy (Telephone Number in U.S. (202) 653-2400); *The State of Food and Agriculture.*

International Monetary Fund, 700 Nineteenth Street, NW, Washington, D.C. 20431 (202) 623-7000; *Direction of Trade Statistics;* and *Government Finance Statistics Yearbook.*

South Pacific Commission, Post Box D5, Noumea Cedex, New Caledonia; *Statistical Bulletin of the South Pacific: Overseas Trade.*

St. Martin's Press, Inc., 175 Fifth Avenue, New York, New York 10010 (800) 221-7945; *The Statesman's Year-Book.*

United Nations Conference on Trade and Development (UNCTAD), New York, New York 10017 (800) 253-9646; *Handbook of International Trade and Development Statistics.*

Walden Publishing Ltd., Two Market Street, Saffron Walden Essex, CB10 1HZ, England; *The World of Information Asia and Pacific Review.*

The World Bank, 1818 H Street, NW, Washington, D.C. 20433 (202) 477-1234; *World Development Indicators.*

SOLOMON ISLANDS - INCOME TAXES - See SOLOMON ISLANDS - TAXATION

SOLOMON ISLANDS - INDUSTRY

Central Intelligence Agency, Washington, D.C. 20505 (703) 482-1100, www.cia.gov; *The World Factbook.*

Economist Intelligence Unit, 111 West 57th Street, New York, New York 10019 (800) 938-4685; *Solomon Islands Country Report.*

Euromonitor International, Inc., 122 South Michigan Avenue, Suite 1200, Chicago, Illinois 60603 (800) 577-EURO; *The World Economic Factbook;* and *World Marketing Data and Statistics.*

Europa Publications Limited, 18 Bedford Square, London, WC1B 3JN, England; *The Europa World Year Book.*

International Labour Office, I.L.O. Publications, 1828 L Street, NW., Suite 801, Washington, D.C. 20036 (301) 638-3152; *Yearbook of Labour Statistics.*

St. Martin's Press, Inc., 175 Fifth Avenue, New York, New York 10010 (800) 221-7945; *The Statesman's Year-Book.*

Statistical Office of the United Nations, Publishing Service, New York, New York 10017 (800) 253-9646; *Asia-Pacific in Figures;* and *Statistical Yearbook for Asia and the Pacific.*

The World Bank, 1818 H Street, NW, Washington, D.C. 20433 (202) 477-1234; *World Development Indicators.*

SOLOMON ISLANDS - INFANT AND MATERNAL MORTALITY - See SOLOMON ISLANDS - MORTALITY

SOLOMON ISLANDS - INTERNAL TRADE

Statistical Office of the United Nations, Publishing Service, New York, New York 10017 (800) 253-9646; *Statistical Yearbook for Asia and the Pacific.*

SOLOMON ISLANDS - INTERNATIONAL RESERVES EXCLUDING GOLD

Asian Development Bank, P.O. Box 789, 1099 Manila, Philippines; *Key Indicators of Developing Asian and Pacific Countries.*

The World Bank, 1818 H Street, NW,

Washington, D.C. 20433 (202) 477-1234; *World Development Indicators.*

SOLOMON ISLANDS - INTERNATIONAL STATISTICS

Asian Development Bank, P.O. Box 789, 1099 Manila, Philippines; *Key Indicators of Developing Asian and Pacific Countries.*

SOLOMON ISLANDS - LABOR

Central Intelligence Agency, Washington, D.C. 20505 (703) 482-1100, www.cia.gov; *The World Factbook.*

Euromonitor International, Inc., 122 South Michigan Avenue, Suite 1200, Chicago, Illinois 60603 (800) 577-EURO; *International Marketing Data and Statistics;* and *World Marketing Data and Statistics.*

Europa Publications Limited, 18 Bedford Square, London, WC1B 3JN, England; *The Europa World Year Book.*

Food and Agricultural Organization of the United Nations (FAO) Via delle Terme di Caracalla, 00100 Rome, Italy (Telephone Number in U.S. (202) 653-2400); *The State of Food and Agriculture.*

International Labour Office, I.L.O. Publications, 1828 L Street, NW., Suite 801, Washington, D.C. 20036 (301) 638-3152; *Yearbook of Labour Statistics.*

St. Martin's Press, Inc., 175 Fifth Avenue, New York, New York 10010 (800) 221-7945; *The Statesman's Year-Book.*

Statistical Office of the United Nations, Publishing Service, New York, New York 10017 (800) 253-9646; *Human Development Report.*

The World Bank, 1818 H Street, NW, Washington, D.C. 20433 (202) 477-1234; *The World Bank Atlas;* and *World Development Indicators.*

SOLOMON ISLANDS - LAND USE

Central Intelligence Agency, Washington, D.C. 20505 (703) 482-1100, www.cia.gov; *The World Factbook.*

Euromonitor International, Inc., 122 South Michigan Avenue, Suite 1200, Chicago, Illinois 60603 (800) 577-EURO; *International Marketing Data and Statistics.*

Food and Agricultural Organization of the United Nations (FAO) Via delle Terme di Caracalla, 00100 Rome, Italy (Telephone Number in U.S. (202) 653-2400); *Production Yearbook.*

SOLOMON ISLANDS - LIBRARIES

United Nations Educational, Scientific

and Cultural Organization (UNESCO), 7 Place de Fontenoy, F-75700 Paris, France (Telephone Number in U.S. (212) 963-5981); *Statistical Yearbook.*

SOLOMON ISLANDS - LIFE EXPECTANCY

Central Intelligence Agency, Washington, D.C. 20505 (703) 482-1100, www.cia.gov; *The World Factbook.*

Euromonitor International, Inc., 122 South Michigan Avenue, Suite 1200, Chicago, Illinois 60603 (800) 577-EURO; *The World Economic Factbook.*

Statistical Office of the United Nations, Publishing Service, New York, New York 10017 (800) 253-9646; *Asia-Pacific in Figures; Human Development Report;* and *World Statistics Pocketbook.*

The World Bank, 1818 H Street, NW, Washington, D.C. 20433 (202) 477-1234; *The World Bank Atlas.*

SOLOMON ISLANDS - LIVESTOCK AND POULTRY

Europa Publications Limited, 18 Bedford Square, London, WC1B 3JN, England; *The Europa World Year Book.*

Food and Agricultural Organization of the United Nations (FAO), Via delle Terme di Caracalla, 00100 Rome, Italy (Telephone Number in U.S. (202) 653-2400); *Production Yearbook;* and *The State of Food and Agriculture.*

St. Martin's Press, Inc., 175 Fifth Avenue, New York, New York 10010 (800) 221-7945; *The Statesman's Year-Book.*

Statistical Office of the United Nations, Publishing Service, New York, New York 10017 (800) 253-9646; *Statistical Yearbook.*

United Nations Conference on Trade and Development, Central Statistical Service, Palais des Nations, Geneva, Switzerland (Telephone in U.S. (800) 253-9646); *UNCTAD Commodity Yearbook.*

SOLOMON ISLANDS - MAIL - NUMBER OF ITEMS SENT AND RECEIVED

Statistical Office of the United Nations, Publishing Service, New York, New York 10017 (800) 253-9646; *Statistical Yearbook.*

SOLOMON ISLANDS - MANPOWER

Statistical Office of the United Nations, Publishing Service, New York, New York 10017 (800) 253-9646; *Statistical Yearbook for Asia and the Pacific.*

SOLOMON ISLANDS - MANUFACTURING

Asian Development Bank, P.O. Box 789,

1099 Manila, Philippines; *Key Indicators of Developing Asian and Pacific Countries.*

The World Bank, 1818 H Street, NW, Washington, D.C. 20433 (202) 477-1234; *World Development Indicators.*

SOLOMON ISLANDS - MEAT PRODUCTION - See SOLOMON ISLANDS - LIVESTOCK AND POULTRY

SOLOMON ISLANDS - MERCHANT SHIPPING

Europa Publications Limited, 18 Bedford Square, London, WC1B 3JN, England; *The Europa World Year Book.*

St. Martin's Press, Inc., 175 Fifth Avenue, New York, New York 10010 (800) 221-7945; *The Statesman's Year-Book.*

Statistical Office of the United Nations, Publishing Service, New York, New York 10017 (800) 253-9646; *Statistical Yearbook.*

SOLOMON ISLANDS - MILITARY

Central Intelligence Agency, Washington, D.C. 20505 (703) 482-1100, www.cia.gov; *The World Factbook.*

The International Institute for Strategic Studies, 23 Tavistock Street, London WC2E 7NQ, England 44 171 3797676; *The Military Balance.*

St. Martin's Press, Inc., 175 Fifth Avenue, New York, New York 10010 (800) 221-7945; *The Statesman's Year-Book.*

Statistical Office of the United Nations, Publishing Service, New York, New York 10017 (800) 253-9646; *Human Development Report.*

SOLOMON ISLANDS - MINING AND MINERAL PRODUCTS

Europa Publications Limited, 18 Bedford Square, London, WC1B 3JN, England; *The Europa World Year Book.*

M.E. Sharpe, 80 Business Park Drive, Armonk, New York 10504 (800) 541-6563; *The Illustrated Book of World Rankings.*

St. Martin's Press, Inc., 175 Fifth Avenue, New York, New York 10010 (800) 221-7945; *The Statesman's Year-Book.*

Statistical Office of the United Nations, Publishing Service, New York, New York 10017 (800) 253-9646; *Statistical Yearbook.*

United Nations Conference on Trade and Development, Central Statistical Service, Palais des Nations, Geneva, Switzerland (Telephone in U.S. (800) 253-9646); *UNCTAD Commodity Yearbook.*

SOLOMON ISLANDS - MONEY SUPPLY

Asian Development Bank, P.O. Box 789, 1099 Manila, Philippines; *Key Indicators of Developing Asian and Pacific Countries.*

Economist Intelligence Unit, 111 West 57th Street, New York, New York 10019 (800) 938-4685; *Solomon Islands Country Report.*

Europa Publications Limited, 18 Bedford Square, London, WC1B 3JN, England; *The Europa World Year Book.*

The World Bank, 1818 H Street, NW, Washington, D.C. 20433 (202) 477-1234; *World Development Indicators.*

SOLOMON ISLANDS - MORTALITY

Central Intelligence Agency, Washington, D.C. 20505 (703) 482-1100, www.cia.gov; *The World Factbook.*

Euromonitor International, Inc., 122 South Michigan Avenue, Suite 1200, Chicago, Illinois 60603 (800) 577-EURO; *International Marketing Data and Statistics;* and *The World Economic Factbook.*

Europa Publications Limited, 18 Bedford Square, London, WC1B 3JN, England; *The Europa World Year Book.*

Statistical Office of the United Nations, Publishing Service, New York, New York 10017 (800) 253-9646; *Asia-Pacific in Figures; Human Development Report; Statistical Yearbook;* and *World Statistics Pocketbook.*

The World Bank, 1818 H Street, NW, Washington, D.C. 20433 (202) 477-1234; *The World Bank Atlas.*

SOLOMON ISLANDS - MOTOR VEHICLE TAXES - See SOLOMON ISLANDS - TAXATION

SOLOMON ISLANDS - MOTOR VEHICLES IN USE

Europa Publications Limited, 18 Bedford Square, London, WC1B 3JN, England; *The Europa World Year Book.*

SOLOMON ISLANDS - MUSEUMS

United Nations Educational, Scientific and Cultural Organization (UNESCO), 7 Place de Fontenoy, F-75700 Paris, France (Telephone Number in U.S. (212) 963-5981); *Statistical Yearbook.*

SOLOMON ISLANDS - NATIONAL ACCOUNTS

Statistical Office of the United Nations, Publishing Service, New York, New York 10017 (800) 253-9646; *Asia-Pacific in Figures; National Accounts Statistics; Statistical Yearbook;* and *Statistical Yearbook for Asia and the Pacific.*

SOLOMON ISLANDS - NATIONAL INCOME

Statistical Office of the United Nations, Publishing Service, New York, New York 10017 (800) 253-9646; *National Accounts Statistics;* and *Statistical Yearbook.*

SOLOMON ISLANDS - NEWSPAPER PRODUCTION - See SOLOMON ISLANDS - FORESTRY AND FOREST PRODUCTS

SOLOMON ISLANDS - OCCUPATIONS - See SOLOMON ISLANDS - LABOR

SOLOMON ISLANDS - PALM KERNEL AND PALM OIL PRODUCTION - See SOLOMON ISLANDS - CROPS

SOLOMON ISLANDS - PERIODICALS

United Nations Educational, Scientific and Cultural Organization (UNESCO), 7 Place de Fontenoy, F-75700 Paris, France (Telephone Number in U.S. (212) 963-5981); *Statistical Yearbook.*

SOLOMON ISLANDS - PESTICIDE USE

Food and Agricultural Organization of the United Nations (FAO) Via delle Terme di Caracalla, 00100 Rome, Italy (Telephone Number in U.S. (202) 653-2400); *The State of Food and Agriculture.*

SOLOMON ISLANDS - PETROLEUM INDUSTRY

Asian Development Bank, P.O. Box 789, 1099 Manila, Philippines; *Key Indicators of Developing Asian and Pacific Countries.*

Food and Agricultural Organization of the United Nations (FAO) Via delle Terme di Caracalla, 00100 Rome, Italy (Telephone Number in U.S. (202) 653-2400); *The State of Food and Agriculture.*

United Nations Conference on Trade and Development, Central Statistical Service, Palais des Nations, Geneva, Switzerland (Telephone in U.S. (800) 253-9646); *UNCTAD Commodity Yearbook.*

SOLOMON ISLANDS - POPULATION

Asian Development Bank, P.O. Box 789, 1099 Manila, Philippines; *Key Indicators of Developing Asian and Pacific Countries.*

Central Intelligence Agency, Washington, D.C. 20505 (703) 482-1100, www.cia.gov; *The World Factbook.*

Economist Intelligence Unit, 111 West 57th Street, New York, New York 10019 (800) 938-4685; *Solomon Islands Country*

Report.

Euromonitor International, Inc., 122 South Michigan Avenue, Suite 1200, Chicago, Illinois 60603 (800) 577-EURO; *International Marketing Data and Statistics;* and *The World Economic Factbook.*

Europa Publications Limited, 18 Bedford Square, London, WC1B 3JN, England; *The Europa World Year Book.*

Food and Agricultural Organization of the United Nations (FAO), Via delle Terme di Caracalla, 00100 Rome, Italy (Telephone Number in U.S. (202) 653-2400); *Production Yearbook.*

International Labour Office, I.L.O. Publications, 1828 L Street, NW., Suite 801, Washington, D.C. 20036 (301) 638-3152; *Yearbook of Labour Statistics.*

St. Martin's Press, Inc., 175 Fifth Avenue, New York, New York 10010 (800) 221-7945; *The Statesman's Year-Book.*

Statistical Office of the United Nations, Publishing Service, New York, New York 10017 (800) 253-9646; *Asia-Pacific in Figures; Human Development Report; Statistical Yearbook; Statistical Yearbook for Asia and the Pacific;* and *World Statistics Pocketbook.*

United Nations Educational, Scientific and Cultural Organization (UNESCO), 7 Place de Fontenoy, F-75700 Paris, France (Telephone Number in U.S. (212) 963-5981); *Statistical Yearbook.*

Walden Publishing Ltd., Two Market Street, Saffron Walden Essex, CB10 1HZ, England; *The World of Information Asia and Pacific Review.*

The World Bank, 1818 H Street, NW, Washington, D.C. 20433 (202) 477-1234; *The World Bank Atlas.*

World Health Organization, Office of Publications, 20 Avenue Appia, CH-1211 Geneva 27, Switzerland (Telephone Number in U.S. (518) 436-9686); *World Health Statistics Annual.*

SOLOMON ISLANDS - POST OFFICES

St. Martin's Press, Inc., 175 Fifth Avenue, New York, New York 10010 (800) 221-7945; *The Statesman's Year-Book.*

SOLOMON ISLANDS - POWER PRODUCTION INDUSTRY

Statistical Office of the United Nations, Publishing Service, New York, New York 10017 (800) 253-9646; *Electric Power in Asia and the Pacific.*

SOLOMON ISLANDS - PRICES

Asian Development Bank, P.O. Box 789, 1099 Manila, Philippines; *Key Indicators of Developing Asian and Pacific Countries.*

Food and Agricultural Organization of the United Nations (FAO), Via delle Terme di Caracalla, 00100 Rome, Italy (Telephone Number in U.S. (202) 653-2400); *Production Yearbook;* and *The State of Food and Agriculture.*

International Labour Office, I.L.O. Publications, 1828 L Street, NW., Suite 801, Washington, D.C. 20036 (301) 638-3152; *Yearbook of Labour Statistics.*

South Pacific Commission, Post Box D5, Noumea Cedex, New Caledonia; *Statistical Bulletin of the South Pacific: Overseas Trade;* and *Statistical Bulletin of the South Pacific: Retail Price Indexes.*

SOLOMON ISLANDS - PROPERTY TAXES - See SOLOMON ISLANDS - TAXATION

SOLOMON ISLANDS - RADIO BROADCASTING - See SOLOMON ISLANDS - BROADCASTING

SOLOMON ISLANDS - RADIO RECEIVERS

St. Martin's Press, Inc., 175 Fifth Avenue, New York, New York 10010 (800) 221-7945; *The Statesman's Year-Book.*

SOLOMON ISLANDS - RELIGION

Central Intelligence Agency, Washington, D.C. 20505 (703) 482-1100, www.cia.gov; *The World Factbook.*

St. Martin's Press, Inc., 175 Fifth Avenue, New York, New York 10010 (800) 221-7945; *The Statesman's Year-Book.*

SOLOMON ISLANDS - RENT PRICES

International Labour Office, I.L.O. Publications, 1828 L Street, NW., Suite 801, Washington, D.C. 20036 (301) 638-3152; *Yearbook of Labour Statistics.*

SOLOMON ISLANDS - RETAIL TRADE

Euromonitor International, Inc., 12 South Michigan Avenue, Suite 1200, Chicago, Illinois 60603 (800) 577-EURO; *World Marketing Data and Statistics.*

SOLOMON ISLANDS - RICE PRODUCTION - See SOLOMON ISLANDS - CROPS

SOLOMON ISLANDS - ROUNDWOOD PRODUCTION - See SOLOMON ISLANDS - FORESTRY AND FOREST PRODUCTS

SOLOMON ISLANDS - SAWNWOOD PRODUCTION - See SOLOMON ISLANDS - FORESTRY AND FOREST

PRODUCTS

SOLOMON ISLANDS - SCIENTISTS, TECHNICIANS AND ENGINEERS

Statistical Office of the United Nations, Publishing Service, New York, New York 10017 (800) 253-9646; *Statistical Yearbook.*

United Nations Educational, Scientific and Cultural Organization (UNESCO), 7 Place de Fontenoy, F-75700 Paris, France (Telephone Number in U.S. (212) 963-5981); *Statistical Yearbook.*

SOLOMON ISLANDS - SOCIAL DATA

Asian Development Bank, P.O. Box 789, 1099 Manila, Philippines; *Key Indicators of Developing Asian and Pacific Countries.*

Statistical Office of the United Nations, Publishing Service, New York, New York 10017 (800) 253-9646; *World Statistics Pocketbook.*

SOLOMON ISLANDS - SOCIAL SECURITY

International Monetary Fund, 700 Nineteenth Street, NW, Washington, D.C. 20431 (202) 623-7000; *Government Finance Statistics Yearbook.*

Statistical Office of the United Nations, Publishing Service, New York, New York 10017 (800) 253-9646; *National Accounts Statistics.*

SOLOMON ISLANDS - STAMP TAXES AND DUTIES - See SOLOMON ISLANDS - TAXATION

SOLOMON ISLANDS - STOCKS - COMMODITY - MARKET PRICE - INDEX

Food and Agricultural Organization of the United Nations (FAO) Via delle Terme di Caracalla, 00100 Rome, Italy (Telephone Number in U.S. (202) 653-2400); *The State of Food and Agriculture.*

SOLOMON ISLANDS - TAXATION

International Monetary Fund, 700 Nineteenth Street, NW, Washington, D.C. 20431 (202) 623-7000; *Government Finance Statistics Yearbook.*

The World Bank, 1818 H Street, NW, Washington, D.C. 20433 (202) 477-1234; *World Development Indicators.*

SOLOMON ISLANDS - TELEPHONES IN USE

Central Intelligence Agency, Washington, D.C. 20505 (703) 482-1100, www.cia.gov; *The World Factbook.*

Europa Publications Limited, 18 Bedford Square, London, WC1B 3JN,

England; *The Europa World Year Book.*

Statistical Office of the United Nations, Publishing Service, New York, New York 10017 (800) 253-9646; *World Statistics Pocketbook.*

World Health Organization, Office of Publications, 20 Avenue Appia, CH-1211 Geneva 27, Switzerland (Telephone Number in U.S. (518) 436-9686); *World Health Statistics Annual.*

SOLOMON ISLANDS - TEXTILE INDUSTRY

United Nations Conference on Trade and Development, Central Statistical Service, Palais des Nations, Geneva, Switzerland (Telephone in U.S. (800) 253-9646); *UNCTAD Commodity Yearbook.*

SOLOMON ISLANDS - THEATRE

United Nations Educational, Scientific and Cultural Organization (UNESCO), 7 Place de Fontenoy, F-75700 Paris, France (Telephone Number in U.S. (212) 963-5981); *Statistical Yearbook.*

SOLOMON ISLANDS - TOBACCO PRODUCTION

South Pacific Commission, Post Box D5, Noumea Cedex, New Caledonia; *Statistical Bulletin of the South Pacific: Retail Price Indexes.*

Statistical Office of the United Nations, Publishing Service, New York, New York 10017 (800) 253-9646; *Statistical Yearbook.*

SOLOMON ISLANDS - TOURISM

Euromonitor International, Inc., 122 South Michigan Avenue, Suite 1200, Chicago, Illinois 60603 (800) 577-EURO; *The World Economic Factbook;* and *World Marketing Data and Statistics.*

Europa Publications Limited, 18 Bedford Square, London, WC1B 3JN, England; *The Europa World Year Book.*

St. Martin's Press, Inc., 175 Fifth Avenue, New York, New York 10010 (800) 221-7945; *The Statesman's Year-Book.*

World Tourism Organization, Calle Capitan Haya 42, E-28020 Madrid, Spain; *Yearbook of Tourism Statistics.*

SOLOMON ISLANDS - TRADE - See SOLOMON ISLANDS - FOREIGN TRADE

SOLOMON ISLANDS - TRANSPORTATION AND COMMUNICATIONS

Central Intelligence Agency, Washington, D.C. 20505 (703) 482-1100, www.cia.gov; *The World Factbook.*

Euromonitor International, Inc., 122 South Michigan Avenue, Suite 1200, Chicago, Illinois 60603 (800) 577-EURO; *International Marketing Data and Statistics;* and *World Marketing Data and Statistics.*

Europa Publications Limited, 18 Bedford Square, London, WC1B 3JN, England; *The Europa World Year Book.*

South Pacific Commission, Post Box D5, Noumea Cedex, New Caledonia; *Statistical Bulletin of the South Pacific: Retail Price Indexes.*

St. Martin's Press, Inc., 175 Fifth Avenue, New York, New York 10010 (800) 221-7945; *The Statesman's Year-Book.*

Statistical Office of the United Nations, Publishing Service, New York, New York 10017 (800) 253-9646; *Human Development Report;* and *Statistical Yearbook for Asia and the Pacific.*

SOLOMON ISLANDS - UNEMPLOYMENT

Central Intelligence Agency, Washington, D.C. 20505 (703) 482-1100, www.cia.gov; *The World Factbook.*

International Labour Office, I.L.O. Publications, 1828 L Street, NW., Suite 801, Washington, D.C. 20036 (301) 638-3152; *Yearbook of Labour Statistics.*

SOLOMON ISLANDS - UTILITIES

Statistical Office of the United Nations, Publishing Service, New York, New York 10017 (800) 253-9646; *Electric Power in Asia and the Pacific.*

SOLOMON ISLANDS - VITAL STATISTICS

Statistical Office of the United Nations, Publishing Service, New York, New York 10017 (800) 253-9646; *Statistical Yearbook.*

World Health Organization, Office of Publications, 20 Avenue Appia, CH-1211 Geneva 27, Switzerland (Telephone Number in U.S. (518) 436-9686); *World Health Statistics Annual.*

SOLOMON ISLANDS - WAGES

International Labour Office, I.L.O. Publications, 1828 L Street, NW., Suite 801, Washington, D.C. 20036 (301) 638-3152; *Yearbook of Labour Statistics.*

SOLOMON ISLANDS - WAGES AND PRICES

Statistical Office of the United Nations, Publishing Service, New York, New York 10017 (800) 253-9646; *Statistical Yearbook for Asia and the Pacific.*

SOLOMON ISLANDS - WEATHER - See SOLOMON ISLANDS - CLIMATE

SOLOMON ISLANDS - WELFARE

International Monetary Fund, 700 Nineteenth Street, NW, Washington, D.C. 20431 (202) 623-7000; *Government Finance Statistics Yearbook.*

SOLOMON ISLANDS - WHOLESALE PRICES

Asian Development Bank, P.O. Box 789, 1099 Manila, Philippines; *Key Indicators of Developing Asian and Pacific Countries.*

Somalia - National Statistical Office

Statistical Department, State Planning Commission, Post Office Box 1742, Mogadishu, Somalia.

Somalia - Primary Statistics Sources

Central Statistical Department, Post Office Box 1742, Mogadishu, Somalia; *Koobaha Staatistikada* (Statistical Abstract); and *Faafinta Istaatistikada Bisha* (Monthly Statistical Bulletin).

SOMALIA - AGRICULTURE

Economist Intelligence Unit, 111 West 57th Street, New York, New York 10019 (800) 938-4685; *Somalia Country Report.*

Euromonitor International, Inc., 122 South Michigan Avenue, Suite 1200, Chicago, Illinois 60603 (800) 577-EURO; *International Marketing Data and Statistics;* and *World Marketing Data and Statistics.*

Europa Publications Limited, 18 Bedford Square, London, WC1B 3JN, England; *The Europa World Year Book.*

Food and Agricultural Organization of the United Nations (FAO) Via delle Terme di Caracalla, 00100 Rome, Italy (Telephone Number in U.S. (202) 653-2400); *Production Yearbook; The State of Food and Agriculture;* and *Trade Yearbook.*

M.E. Sharpe, 80 Business Park Drive, Armonk, New York 10504 (800) 541-6563; *The Illustrated Book of World Rankings.*

St. Martin's Press, Inc., 175 Fifth Avenue, New York, New York 10010 (800) 221-7945; *The Statesman's Year-Book.*

Statistical Office of the United Nations, Publishing Service, New York, New York 10017 (800) 253-9646; *Statistical Yearbook;* and *Survey of Economic and Social Conditions in Africa.*

United Nations Conference on Trade

and Development, Central Statistical Service, Palais des Nations, Geneva, Switzerland (Telephone in U.S. (800) 253-9646); *UNCTAD Commodity Yearbook.*

United Nations Economic Commission for Africa, Africa Hall, P.O. Box 3001, Addis Ababa, Ethiopia (Telephone Number in U.S. (800) 253-9646); *African Statistical Yearbook.*

The World Bank, 1818 H Street, NW, Washington, D.C. 20433 (202) 477-1234; *World Development Indicators.*

SOMALIA - AIRLINE SERVICE

Europa Publications Limited, 18 Bedford Square, London, WC1B 3JN, England; *The Europa World Year Book.*

International Civil Aviation Organization, 999 University Street, Montreal, Quebec, Canada H3C 5H7 (514) 954-8219; *Civil Aviation Statistics of the World.*

M.E. Sharpe, 80 Business Park Drive, Armonk, New York 10504 (800) 541-6563; *The Illustrated Book of World Rankings.*

St. Martin's Press, Inc., 175 Fifth Avenue, New York, New York 10010 (800) 221-7945; *The Statesman's Year-Book.*

Statistical Office of the United Nations, Publishing Service, New York, New York 10017 (800) 253-9646; *Statistical Yearbook.*

United Nations Economic Commission for Africa, Africa Hall, P.O. Box 3001, Addis Ababa, Ethiopia (Telephone Number in U.S. (800) 253-9646); *African Statistical Yearbook.*

SOMALIA - AIRPORTS

Central Intelligence Agency, Washington, D.C. 20505 (703) 482-1100, www.cia.gov; *The World Factbook.*

SOMALIA - ALUMINUM PRODUCTION AND CONSUMPTION - See SOMALIA - MINING AND MINERAL PRODUCTS

SOMALIA - ANIMAL EXPORTS

International Monetary Fund, 700 Nineteenth Street, NW, Washington, D.C. 20431 (202) 623-7000; *International Financial Statistics.*

SOMALIA - ANIMAL HEALTH

Food and Agricultural Organization of the United Nations (FAO), Via delle Terme di Caracalla, 00100, Rome, Italy (Telephone Number in U.S. (202) 653-2400); *Animal Health Yearbook.*

SOMALIA - AREA AND DENSITY OF

POPULATION

African Development Bank, 01 BP 1387, Abidjan 01, Cote D'Ivoire; *Selected Statistics on Regional Member Countries.*

Euromonitor International, Inc., 122 South Michigan Avenue, Suite 1200, Chicago, Illinois 60603 (800) 577-EURO; *International Marketing Data and Statistics;* and *The World Economic Factbook.*

Europa Publications Limited, 18 Bedford Square, London, WC1B 3JN, England; *The Europa World Year Book.*

Food and Agricultural Organization of the United Nations (FAO) Via delle Terme di Caracalla, 00100 Rome, Italy (Telephone Number in U.S. (202) 653-2400); *The State of Food and Agriculture.*

M.E. Sharpe, 80 Business Park Drive, Armonk, New York 10504 (800) 541-6563; *The Illustrated Book of World Rankings.*

St. Martin's Press, Inc., 175 Fifth Avenue, New York, New York 10010 (800) 221-7945; *The Statesman's Year-Book.*

Statistical Office of the United Nations, Publishing Service, New York, New York 10017 (800) 253-9646; *Statistical Yearbook;* and *Survey of Economic and Social Conditions in Africa.*

United Nations Educational, Scientific and Cultural Organization (UNESCO), 7 Place de Fontenoy, F-75700 Paris, France (Telephone Number in U.S. (212) 963-5981); *Statistical Yearbook.*

SOMALIA - ARMS EXPORTS AND IMPORTS - See SOMALIA - MILITARY

SOMALIA - BALANCE OF PAYMENTS

African Development Bank, 01 BP 1387, Abidjan 01, Cote D'Ivoire; *Selected Statistics on Regional Member Countries.*

The Economist Intelligence Unit, 111 West 57th Street, New York, New York 10019 (800) 938-4685; *The World Market Atlas.*

Europa Publications Limited, 18 Bedford Square, London, WC1B 3JN, England; *The Europa World Year Book.*

International Monetary Fund, 700 Nineteenth Street, NW, Washington, D.C. 20431 (202) 623-7000; *Balance of Payments Yearbook.*

United Nations Conference on Trade and Development (UNCTAD), New York, New York 10017 (800) 253-9646; *Handbook of International Trade and Development Statistics.*

United Nations Economic Commission for Africa, Africa Hall, P.O. Box 3001, Addis Ababa, Ethiopia (Telephone Number in U.S. (800) 253-9646); *African Statistical Yearbook.*

The World Bank, 1818 H Street, NW, Washington, D.C. 20433 (202) 477-1234; *World Development Indicators.*

SOMALIA - BANANA EXPORTS - See SOMALIA - CROPS

SOMALIA - BANKING

Euromonitor International, Inc., 122 South Michigan Avenue, Suite 1200, Chicago, Illinois 60603 (800) 577-EURO: *World Marketing Data and Statistics.*

Europa Publications Limited, 18 Bedford Square, London, WC1B 3JN, England; *The Europa World Year Book.*

International Monetary Fund, 700 Nineteenth Street, NW, Washington, D.C. 20431 (202) 623-7000; *International Financial Statistics.*

M.E. Sharpe, 80 Business Park Drive, Armonk, New York 10504 (800) 541-6563; *The Illustrated Book of World Rankings.*

St. Martin's Press, Inc., 175 Fifth Avenue, New York, New York 10010 (800) 221-7945; *The Statesman's Year-Book.*

United Nations Economic Commission for Africa, Africa Hall, P.O. Box 3001, Addis Ababa, Ethiopia (Telephone Number in U.S. (800) 253-9646); *African Statistical Yearbook.*

SOMALIA - BARLEY PRODUCTION - See SOMALIA - CROPS

SOMALIA - BEER PRODUCTION - See SOMALIA - BEVERAGES

SOMALIA - BEVERAGES

M.E. Sharpe, 80 Business Park Drive, Armonk, New York 10504 (800) 541-6563; *The Illustrated Book of World Rankings.*

SOMALIA - BIRTH RATES

Central Intelligence Agency, Washington, D.C. 20505 (703) 482-1100, www.cia.gov; *The World Factbook.*

Euromonitor International, Inc., 122 South Michigan Avenue, Suite 1200, Chicago, Illinois 60603 (800) 577-EURO; *International Marketing Data and Statistics;* and *The World Economic Factbook.*

Europa Publications Limited, 18 Bedford Square, London, WC1B 3JN, England; *The Europa World Year Book.*

M.E. Sharpe, 80 Business Park Drive, Armonk, New York 10504 (800) 541-6563; *The Illustrated Book of World Rankings.*

St. Martin's Press, Inc., 175 Fifth Avenue, New York, New York 10010 (800) 221-7945; *The Statesman's Year-Book.*

Statistical Office of the United Nations, Publishing Service, New York, New York 10017 (800) 253-9646; *Demographic Yearbook; Statistical Yearbook;* and *Survey of Economic and Social Conditions in Africa.*

The World Bank, 1818 H Street, NW, Washington, D.C. 20433 (202) 477-1234; *World Development Indicators.*

SOMALIA - BROADCASTING

Billboard Limited, P.O. Box 9027, 1006 AA Amsterdam, The Netherlands (Telephone Number in U.S. (212) 764-7300); *World Radio TV Handbook.*

Central Intelligence Agency, Washington, D.C. 20505 (703) 482-1100, www.cia.gov; *The World Factbook.*

Euromonitor International, Inc., 122 South Michigan Avenue, Suite 1200, Chicago, Illinois 60603 (800) 577-EURO: *World Marketing Data and Statistics.*

M.E. Sharpe, 80 Business Park Drive, Armonk, New York 10504 (800) 541-6563; *The Illustrated Book of World Rankings.*

St. Martin's Press, Inc., 175 Fifth Avenue, New York, New York 10010 (800) 221-7945; *The Statesman's Year-Book.*

SOMALIA - BUDGET

Central Intelligence Agency, Washington, D.C. 20505 (703) 482-1100, www.cia.gov; *The World Factbook.*

SOMALIA - BUSINESS AND PROFESSIONAL LICENSES

International Monetary Fund, 700 Nineteenth Street, NW, Washington, D.C. 20431 (202) 623-7000; *Government Finance Statistics Yearbook.*

SOMALIA - BUTTER PRODUCTION - See SOMALIA - DAIRY PRODUCTS

SOMALIA - CALORIE SUPPLY

African Development Bank, 01 BP 1387, Abidjan 01, Cote D'Ivoire; *Selected Statistics on Regional Member Countries.*

Food and Agricultural Organization of the United Nations (FAO) Via delle Terme di Caracalla, 00100 Rome, Italy (Telephone Number in U.S. (202) 653-2400); *The State of Food and Agriculture.*

SOMALIA - CAPITAL REVENUE

International Monetary Fund, 700 Nineteenth Street, NW, Washington, D.C. 20431 (202) 623-7000; *Government Finance Statistics Yearbook.*

SOMALIA - CATTLE - See SOMALIA - LIVESTOCK AND POULTRY

SOMALIA - CEMENT PRODUCTION - See SOMALIA - MINING AND MINERAL PRODUCTS

SOMALIA - CHEMICAL (ORGANIC) PRODUCTION - See SOMALIA - MINING AND MINERAL PRODUCTS

SOMALIA - CHICKENS - See SOMALIA - LIVESTOCK AND POULTRY

SOMALIA - CIGARETTE PRODUCTION - See SOMALIA - TOBACCO PRODUCTION

SOMALIA - CLIMATE

M.E. Sharpe, 80 Business Park Drive, Armonk, New York 10504 (800) 541-6563; *The Illustrated Book of World Rankings.*

St. Martin's Press, Inc., 175 Fifth Avenue, New York, New York 10010 (800) 221-7945; *The Statesman's Year-Book.*

SOMALIA - COAL PRODUCTION - See SOMALIA - MINING AND MINERAL PRODUCTS

SOMALIA - COFFEE PRODUCTION AND CONSUMPTION - See SOMALIA - CROPS

SOMALIA - COMMERCE

St. Martin's Press, Inc., 175 Fifth Avenue, New York, New York 10010 (800) 221-7945; *The Statesman's Year-Book.*

SOMALIA - COMMUNICATIONS - See SOMALIA - TRANSPORTATION AND COMMUNICATIONS

SOMALIA - CONSTRUCTION INDUSTRY

M.E. Sharpe, 80 Business Park Drive, Armonk, New York 10504 (800) 541-6563; *The Illustrated Book of World Rankings.*

United Nations Economic Commission for Africa, Africa Hall, P.O. Box 3001, Addis Ababa, Ethiopia (Telephone Number in U.S. (800) 253-9646); *African Statistical Yearbook.*

SOMALIA - CONSUMER PRICE INDEX

African Development Bank, 01 BP 1387, Abidjan 01, Cote D'Ivoire; *Selected Statistics on Regional Member Countries.*

Europa Publications Limited, 18 Bedford Square, London, WC1B 3JN,

England; *The Europa World Year Book.*

Statistical Office of the United Nations, Publishing Service, New York, New York 10017 (800) 253-9646; *Statistical Yearbook;* and *Survey of Economic and Social Conditions in Africa.*

United Nations Economic Commission for Africa, Africa Hall, P.O. Box 3001, Addis Ababa, Ethiopia (Telephone Number in U.S. (800) 253-9646); *African Statistical Yearbook.*

SOMALIA - CONSUMER PRICES

Euromonitor International, Inc., 122 South Michigan Avenue, Suite 1200, Chicago, Illinois 60603 (800) 577-EURO: *World Marketing Data and Statistics.*

International Labour Office, I.L.O. Publications, 1828 L Street, NW., Suite 801, Washington, D.C. 20036 (301) 638-3152; *Yearbook of Labour Statistics.*

International Monetary Fund, 700 Nineteenth Street, NW, Washington, D.C. 20431 (202) 623-7000; *International Financial Statistics.*

SOMALIA - CONSUMPTION

African Development Bank, 01 BP 1387, Abidjan 01, Cote D'Ivoire; *Selected Statistics on Regional Member Countries.*

Statistical Office of the United Nations, Publishing Service, New York, New York 10017 (800) 253-9646; *Survey of Economic and Social Conditions in Africa.*

SOMALIA - COPPER PRODUCTION AND CONSUMPTION - See SOMALIA - MINING AND MINERAL PRODUCTS

SOMALIA - CORN PRODUCTION - See SOMALIA - CROPS

SOMALIA - CORPORATE TAXES - See SOMALIA - TAXATION

SOMALIA - COTTON PRODUCTION - See SOMALIA - CROPS

SOMALIA - CROPS

Europa Publications Limited, 18 Bedford Square, London, WC1B 3JN, England; *The Europa World Year Book.*

Food and Agricultural Organization of the United Nations (FAO) Via delle Terme di Caracalla, 00100 Rome, Italy (Telephone Number in U.S. (202) 653-2400); *The State of Food and Agriculture.*

International Monetary Fund, 700 Nineteenth Street, NW, Washington, D.C. 20431 (202) 623-7000; *Government Finance Statistics Yearbook.*

M.E. Sharpe, 80 Business Park Drive, Armonk, New York 10504 (800) 541-6563; *The Illustrated Book of World Rankings.*

St. Martin's Press, Inc., 175 Fifth Avenue, New York, New York 10010 (800) 221-7945; *The Statesman's Year-Book.*

Statistical Office of the United Nations, Publishing Service, New York, New York 10017 (800) 253-9646; *Statistical Yearbook.*

United Nations Conference on Trade and Development, Central Statistical Service, Palais des Nations, Geneva, Switzerland (Telephone in U.S. (800) 253-9646); *UNCTAD Commodity Yearbook.*

United Nations Economic Commission for Africa, Africa Hall, P.O. Box 3001, Addis Ababa, Ethiopia (Telephone Number in U.S. (800) 253-9646); *African Statistical Yearbook.*

SOMALIA - CUSTOMS DUTIES

International Monetary Fund, 700 Nineteenth Street, NW, Washington, D.C. 20431 (202) 623-7000; *Government Finance Statistics Yearbook.*

St. Martin's Press, Inc., 175 Fifth Avenue, New York, New York 10010 (800) 221-7945; *The Statesman's Year-Book.*

SOMALIA - DAIRY PRODUCTS

Europa Publications Limited, 18 Bedford Square, London, WC1B 3JN, England; *The Europa World Year Book.*

Food and Agricultural Organization of the United Nations (FAO) Via delle Terme di Caracalla, 00100 Rome, Italy (Telephone Number in U.S. (202) 653-2400); *The State of Food and Agriculture.*

M.E. Sharpe, 80 Business Park Drive, Armonk, New York 10504 (800) 541-6563; *The Illustrated Book of World Rankings.*

St. Martin's Press, Inc., 175 Fifth Avenue, New York, New York 10010 (800) 221-7945; *The Statesman's Year-Book.*

Statistical Office of the United Nations, Publishing Service, New York, New York 10017 (800) 253-9646; *Statistical Yearbook.*

SOMALIA - DEATH RATES - See SOMALIA - MORTALITY

SOMALIA - DEFENSE EXPENDITURES - See SOMALIA - MILITARY

SOMALIA - DEMOGRAPHY

The Economist Intelligence Unit, 111 West 57th Street, New York, New York 10019 (800) 938-4685; *The World Market Atlas.*

Euromonitor International, Inc., 122 South Michigan Avenue, Suite 1200, Chicago, Illinois 60603 (800) 577-EURO; *International Marketing Data and Statistics; World Marketing Data and Statistics;* and *The World Economic Factbook.*

M.E. Sharpe, 80 Business Park Drive, Armonk, New York 10504 (800) 541-6563; *The Illustrated Book of World Rankings.*

Statistical Office of the United Nations, Publishing Service, New York, New York 10017 (800) 253-9646; *Survey of Economic and Social Conditions in Africa.*

SOMALIA - DEVELOPMENT ASSISTANCE

Statistical Office of the United Nations, Publishing Service, New York, New York 10017 (800) 253-9646; *Statistical Yearbook.*

SOMALIA - DIAMOND PRODUCTION - See SOMALIA - MINING AND MINERAL PRODUCTS

SOMALIA - DIVORCE RATES

M.E. Sharpe, 80 Business Park Drive, Armonk, New York 10504 (800) 541-6563; *The Illustrated Book of World Rankings.*

Statistical Office of the United Nations, Publishing Service, New York, New York 10017 (800) 253-9646; *Demographic Yearbook.*

SOMALIA - ECONOMY

African Development Bank, 01 BP 1387, Abidjan 01, Cote D'Ivoire; *Selected Statistics on Regional Member Countries.*

Central Intelligence Agency, Washington, D.C. 20505 (703) 482-1100, www.cia.gov; *The World Factbook.*

Economist Intelligence Unit, 111 West 57th Street, New York, New York 10019 (800) 938-4685; *Somalia Country Report.*

Euromonitor International, Inc., 122 South Michigan Avenue, Suite 1200, Chicago, Illinois 60603 (800) 577-EURO; *International Marketing Data and Statistics; World Marketing Data and Statistics;* and *The World Economic Factbook.*

Europa Publications Limited, 18 Bedford Square, London, WC1B 3JN, England; *The Europa World Year Book.*

M.E. Sharpe, 80 Business Park Drive, Armonk, New York 10504 (800) 541-6563; *The Illustrated Book of World Rankings.*

St. Martin's Press, Inc., 175 Fifth Avenue, New York, New York 10010 (800) 221-7945; *The Statesman's Year-Book.*

Statistical Office of the United Nations,

Publishing Service, New York, New York 10017 (800) 253-9646; *Foreign Trade Statistics for Africa;* and *World Statistics Pocketbook.*

The World Bank, 1818 H Street, NW, Washington, D.C. 20433 (202) 477-1234; *The World Bank Atlas.*

SOMALIA - EDUCATION

African Development Bank, 01 BP 1387, Abidjan 01, Cote D'Ivoire; *Selected Statistics on Regional Member Countries.*

The Economist Intelligence Unit, 111 West 57th Street, New York, New York 10019 (800) 938-4685; *The World Market Atlas.*

Euromonitor International, Inc., 122 South Michigan Avenue, Suite 1200, Chicago, Illinois 60603 (800) 577-EURO; *International Marketing Data and Statistics;* and *World Marketing Data and Statistics..*

Europa Publications Limited, 18 Bedford Square, London, WC1B 3JN, England; *The Europa World Year Book.*

International Monetary Fund, 700 Nineteenth Street, NW, Washington, D.C. 20431 (202) 623-7000; *Government Finance Statistics Yearbook.*

M.E. Sharpe, 80 Business Park Drive, Armonk, New York 10504 (800) 541-6563; *The Illustrated Book of World Rankings.*

St. Martin's Press, Inc., 175 Fifth Avenue, New York, New York 10010 (800) 221-7945; *The Statesman's Year-Book.*

Statistical Office of the United Nations, Publishing Service, New York, New York 10017 (800) 253-9646; *Survey of Economic and Social Conditions in Africa.*

United Nations Economic Commission for Africa, Africa Hall, P.O. Box 3001, Addis Ababa, Ethiopia (Telephone Number in U.S. (800) 253-9646); *African Statistical Yearbook.*

United Nations Educational, Scientific and Cultural Organization (UNESCO), 7 Place de Fontenoy, F-75700 Paris, France (Telephone Number in U.S. (212) 963-5981); *Statistical Yearbook.*

The World Bank, 1818 H Street, NW, Washington, D.C. 20433 (202) 477-1234; *World Development Indicators.*

SOMALIA - EGG PRODUCTION AND CONSUMPTION - See SOMALIA - DAIRY PRODUCTS

SOMALIA - ELECTRICITY

Central Intelligence Agency,

Washington, D.C. 20505 (703) 482-1100, www.cia.gov; *The World Factbook.*

M.E. Sharpe, 80 Business Park Drive, Armonk, New York 10504 (800) 541-6563; *The Illustrated Book of World Rankings.*

St. Martin's Press, Inc., 175 Fifth Avenue, New York, New York 10010 (800) 221-7945; *The Statesman's Year-Book.*

Statistical Office of the United Nations, Publishing Service, New York, New York 10017 (800) 253-9646; *Statistical Yearbook.*

United Nations Economic Commission for Africa, Africa Hall, P.O. Box 3001, Addis Ababa, Ethiopia (Telephone Number in U.S. (800) 253-9646); *African Statistical Yearbook.*

SOMALIA - EMPLOYMENT

Euromonitor International, Inc., 122 South Michigan Avenue, Suite 1200, Chicago, Illinois 60603 (800) 577-EURO; *International Marketing Data and Statistics.*

International Labour Office, I.L.O. Publications, 1828 L Street, NW., Suite 801, Washington, D.C. 20036 (301) 638-3152; *Yearbook of Labour Statistics.*

M.E. Sharpe, 80 Business Park Drive, Armonk, New York 10504 (800) 541-6563; *The Illustrated Book of World Rankings.*

Statistical Office of the United Nations, Publishing Service, New York, New York 10017 (800) 253-9646; *Bulletin of Industrial Statistics for the Arab Countries; Statistical Yearbook;* and *Survey of Economic and Social Conditions in Africa.*

United Nations Economic Commission for Africa, Africa Hall, P.O. Box 3001, Addis Ababa, Ethiopia (Telephone Number in U.S. (800) 253-9646); *African Statistical Yearbook.*

SOMALIA - ENERGY

Euromonitor International, Inc., 122 South Michigan Avenue, Suite 1200, Chicago, Illinois 60603 (800) 577-EURO; *International Marketing Data and Statistics; World Marketing Data and Statistics;* and *The World Economic Factbook.*

Food and Agricultural Organization of the United Nations (FAO) Via delle Terme di Caracalla, 00100 Rome, Italy (Telephone Number in U.S. (202) 653-2400); *The State of Food and Agriculture.*

M.E. Sharpe, 80 Business Park Drive, Armonk, New York 10504 (800) 541-6563; *The Illustrated Book of World Rankings.*

St. Martin's Press, Inc., 175 Fifth Avenue, New York, New York 10010 (800)

221-7945; *The Statesman's Year-Book.*

Statistical Office of the United Nations, Publishing Service, New York, New York 10017 (800) 253-9646; *Energy Statistics Yearbook; Statistical Yearbook;* and *World Statistics Pocketbook.*

United Nations Economic Commission for Africa, Africa Hall, P.O. Box 3001, Addis Ababa, Ethiopia (Telephone Number in U.S. (800) 253-9646); *African Statistical Yearbook.*

The World Bank, 1818 H Street, NW, Washington, D.C. 20433 (202) 477-1234; *The World Bank Atlas.*

SOMALIA - ENVIRONMENT

Economist Intelligence Unit, 111 West 57th Street, New York, New York 10019 (800) 938-4685; *Somalia Country Report.*

Statistical Office of the United Nations, Publishing Service, New York, New York 10017 (800) 253-9646; *World Statistics Pocketbook.*

SOMALIA - EXCHANGE RATES

African Development Bank, 01 BP 1387, Abidjan 01, Cote D'Ivoire; *Selected Statistics on Regional Member Countries.*

Central Intelligence Agency, Washington, D.C. 20505 (703) 482-1100, www.cia.gov; *The World Factbook.*

Euromonitor International, Inc., 122 South Michigan Avenue, Suite 1200, Chicago, Illinois 60603 (800) 577-EURO; *International Marketing Data and Statistics;* and *The World Economic Factbook.*

Europa Publications Limited, 18 Bedford Square, London, WC1B 3JN, England; *The Europa World Year Book.*

International Civil Aviation Organization, 999 University Street, Montreal, Quebec, Canada H3C 5H7 (514) 954-8219; *Civil Aviation Statistics of the World.*

International Monetary Fund, 700 Nineteenth Street, NW, Washington, D.C. 20431 (202) 623-7000; *International Financial Statistics.*

Statistical Office of the United Nations, Publishing Service, New York, New York 10017 (800) 253-9646; *Bulletin of Industrial Statistics for the Arab Countries; Foreign Trade Statistics for Africa; Statistical Yearbook;* and *World Statistics Pocketbook.*

SOMALIA - EXCISE TAXES - See SOMALIA - TAXATION

SOMALIA - EXPORTS

Central Intelligence Agency, Washington, D.C. 20505 (703) 482-1100, www.cia.gov; *The World Factbook.*

The Economist Intelligence Unit, 111 West 57th Street, New York, New York 10019 (800) 938-4685; *Somalia Country Report;* and *The World Market Atlas.*

Euromonitor International, Inc., 122 South Michigan Avenue, Suite 1200, Chicago, Illinois 60603 (800) 577-EURO; *International Marketing Data and Statistics;* and *The World Economic Factbook.*

Europa Publications Limited, 18 Bedford Square, London, WC1B 3JN, England; *The Europa World Year Book.*

Food and Agricultural Organization of the United Nations (FAO) Via delle Terme di Caracalla, 00100 Rome, Italy (Telephone Number in U.S. (202) 653-2400); *The State of Food and Agriculture.*

International Monetary Fund, 700 Nineteenth Street, NW, Washington, D.C. 20431 (202) 623-7000; *Direction of Trade Statistics; Government Finance Statistics Yearbook;* and *International Financial Statistics.*

St. Martin's Press, Inc., 175 Fifth Avenue, New York, New York 10010 (800) 221-7945; *The Statesman's Year-Book.*

Statistical Office of the United Nations, Publishing Service, New York, New York 10017; *Bulletin of Industrial Statistics for the Arab Countries; Foreign Trade Statistics for Africa;* and *Survey of Economic and Social Conditions in Africa.*

United Nations Conference on Trade and Development (UNCTAD), New York, New York 10017 (800) 253-9646; *Handbook of International Trade and Development Statistics.*

United Nations Economic Commission for Africa, Africa Hall, P.O. Box 3001, Addis Ababa, Ethiopia (Telephone Number in U.S. (800) 253-9646); *African Statistical Yearbook.*

The World Bank, 1818 H Street, NW, Washington, D.C. 20433 (202) 477-1234; *World Development Indicators.*

SOMALIA - EXTERNAL INDEBTEDNESS

African Development Bank, 01 BP 1387, Abidjan 01, Cote D'Ivoire; *Selected Statistics on Regional Member Countries.*

Statistical Office of the United Nations, Publishing Service, New York, New York 10017 (800) 253-9646; *Survey of Economic and Social Conditions in Africa.*

The World Bank, 1818 H Street, NW,

Washington, D.C. 20433 (202) 477-1234; *World Development Indicators.*

SOMALIA - EXTERNAL TRADE

African Development Bank, 01 BP 1387, Abidjan 01, Cote D'Ivoire; *Selected Statistics on Regional Member Countries.*

Euromonitor International, Inc., 122 South Michigan Avenue, Suite 1200, Chicago, Illinois 60603 (800) 577-EURO: *World Marketing Data and Statistics.*

Food and Agricultural Organization of the United Nations (FAO) Via delle Terme di Caracalla, 00100 Rome, Italy (Telephone Number in U.S. (202) 653-2400); *The State of Food and Agriculture;* and *Trade Yearbook.*

Statistical Office of the United Nations, Publishing Service, New York, New York 10017 (800) 253-9646; *Statistical Yearbook.*

SOMALIA - FARM CROPS - See SOMALIA - CROPS

SOMALIA - FEMALE WORKING POPULATION - See SOMALIA - EMPLOYMENT

SOMALIA - FERTILITY RATES

Central Intelligence Agency, Washington, D.C. 20505 (703) 482-1100, www.cia.gov; *The World Factbook.*

M.E. Sharpe, 80 Business Park Drive, Armonk, New York 10504 (800) 541-6563; *The Illustrated Book of World Rankings.*

Statistical Office of the United Nations, Publishing Service, New York, New York 10017 (800) 253-9646; *Survey of Economic and Social Conditions in Africa.*

The World Bank, 1818 H Street, NW, Washington, D.C. 20433 (202) 477-1234; *The World Bank Atlas;* and *World Development Indicators.*

SOMALIA - FERTILIZER

Food and Agricultural Organization of the United Nations (FAO), Via delle Terme di Caracalla, 00100, Rome, Italy (Telephone Number in U.S. (202) 653-2400); *Fertilizer Yearbook;* and *The State of Food and Agriculture.*

Statistical Office of the United Nations, Publishing Service, New York, New York 10017 (800) 253-9646; *Statistical Yearbook.*

SOMALIA - FETAL MORTALITY - See SOMALIA - MORTALITY

SOMALIA - FINANCE

African Development Bank, 01 BP 1387,

Abidjan 01, Cote D'Ivoire; *Selected Statistics on Regional Member Countries.*

Economist Intelligence Unit, 111 West 57th Street, New York, New York 10019 (800) 938-4685; *Somalia Country Report.*

Europa Publications Limited, 18 Bedford Square, London, WC1B 3JN, England; *The Europa World Year Book.*

International Monetary Fund, 700 Nineteenth Street, NW, Washington, D.C. 20431 (202) 623-7000; *International Financial Statistics.*

M.E. Sharpe, 80 Business Park Drive, Armonk, New York 10504 (800) 541-6563; *The Illustrated Book of World Rankings.*

St. Martin's Press, Inc., 175 Fifth Avenue, New York, New York 10010 (800) 221-7945; *The Statesman's Year-Book.*

United Nations Economic Commission for Africa, Africa Hall, P.O. Box 3001, Addis Ababa, Ethiopia (Telephone Number in U.S. (800) 253-9646); *African Statistical Yearbook.*

SOMALIA - FISHERIES

Europa Publications Limited, 18 Bedford Square, London, WC1B 3JN, England; *The Europa World Year Book.*

Food and Agricultural Organization of the United Nations (FAO) Via delle Terme di Caracalla, 00100 Rome, Italy (Telephone Number in U.S. (202) 653-2400); *The State of Food and Agriculture;* and *Yearbook of Fishery Statistics.*

M.E. Sharpe, 80 Business Park Drive, Armonk, New York 10504 (800) 541-6563; *The Illustrated Book of World Rankings.*

St. Martin's Press, Inc., 175 Fifth Avenue, New York, New York 10010 (800) 221-7945; *The Statesman's Year-Book.*

Statistical Office of the United Nations, Publishing Service, New York, New York 10017 (800) 253-9646; *Statistical Yearbook;* and *Survey of Economic and Social Conditions in Africa.*

United Nations Conference on Trade and Development, Central Statistical Service, Palais des Nations, Geneva, Switzerland (Telephone in U.S. (800) 253-9646); *UNCTAD Commodity Yearbook.*

United Nations Economic Commission for Africa, Africa Hall, P.O. Box 3001, Addis Ababa, Ethiopia (Telephone Number in U.S. (800) 253-9646); *African Statistical Yearbook.*

SOMALIA - FOOD

African Development Bank, 01 BP 1387, Abidjan 01, Cote D'Ivoire; *Selected Statistics on Regional Member Countries.*

Food and Agricultural Organization of the United Nations (FAO) Via delle Terme di Caracalla, 00100 Rome, Italy (Telephone Number in U.S. (202) 653-2400); *Production Yearbook;* and *The State of Food and Agriculture.*

United Nations Conference on Trade and Development, Central Statistical Service, Palais des Nations, Geneva, Switzerland (Telephone in U.S. (800) 253-9646); *UNCTAD Commodity Yearbook.*

SOMALIA - FOREIGN DEBT

St. Martin's Press, Inc., 175 Fifth Avenue, New York, New York 10010 (800) 221-7945; *The Statesman's Year-Book.*

SOMALIA - FOREIGN TRADE

Economist Intelligence Unit, 111 West 57th Street, New York, New York 10019 (800) 938-4685; *Somalia Country Report.*

Euromonitor International, Inc., 122 South Michigan Avenue, Suite 1200, Chicago, Illinois 60603 (800) 577-EURO; *International Marketing Data and Statistics;* and *The World Economic Factbook.*

Europa Publications Limited, 18 Bedford Square, London, WC1B 3JN, England; *The Europa World Year Book.*

Food and Agricultural Organization of the United Nations (FAO) Via delle Terme di Caracalla, 00100 Rome, Italy (Telephone Number in U.S. (202) 653-2400); *The State of Food and Agriculture.*

International Monetary Fund, 700 Nineteenth Street, NW, Washington, D.C. 20431 (202) 623-7000; *International Financial Statistics.*

M.E. Sharpe, 80 Business Park Drive, Armonk, New York 10504 (800) 541-6563; *The Illustrated Book of World Rankings.*

St. Martin's Press, Inc., 175 Fifth Avenue, New York, New York 10010 (800) 221-7945; *The Statesman's Year-Book.*

Statistical Office of the United Nations, Publishing Service, New York, New York 10017 (800) 253-9646; *Bulletin of Industrial Statistics for the Arab Countries; Foreign Trade Statistics for Africa; International Trade Statistics Yearbook;* and *Statistical Yearbook.*

United Nations Conference on Trade and Development, Central Statistical Service, Palais des Nations, Geneva, Switzerland (Telephone in U.S. (800) 253-9646); *UNCTAD Commodity Yearbook.*

United Nations Economic Commission for Africa, Africa Hall, P.O. Box 3001, Addis Ababa, Ethiopia (Telephone Number in U.S. (800) 253-9646); *African Statistical Yearbook.*

The World Bank, 1818 H Street, NW, Washington, D.C. 20433 (202) 477-1234; *World Development Indicators.*

SOMALIA - FORESTRY AND FOREST PRODUCTS

Europa Publications Limited, 18 Bedford Square, London, WC1B 3JN, England; *The Europa World Year Book.*

Food and Agricultural Organization of the United Nations (FAO) Via delle Terme di Caracalla, 00100 Rome, Italy (Telephone Number in U.S. (202) 653-2400); *The State of Food and Agriculture;* and *Yearbook of Forest Products.*

M.E. Sharpe, 80 Business Park Drive, Armonk, New York 10504 (800) 541-6563; *The Illustrated Book of World Rankings.*

St. Martin's Press, Inc., 175 Fifth Avenue, New York, New York 10010 (800) 221-7945; *The Statesman's Year-Book.*

United Nations Conference on Trade and Development, Central Statistical Service, Palais des Nations, Geneva, Switzerland (Telephone in U.S. (800) 253-9646); *UNCTAD Commodity Yearbook.*

United Nations Economic Commission for Africa, Africa Hall, P.O. Box 3001, Addis Ababa, Ethiopia (Telephone Number in U.S. (800) 253-9646); *African Statistical Yearbook.*

United Nations Educational, Scientific and Cultural Organization (UNESCO), 7 Place de Fontenoy, F-75700 Paris, France (Telephone Number in U.S. (212) 963-5981); *Statistical Yearbook.*

SOMALIA - GAS PRODUCTION - See SOMALIA - MINING AND MINERAL PRODUCTS

SOMALIA - GENERAL INDUSTRIAL STATISTICS - See SOMALIA - INDUSTRY

SOMALIA - GENERAL MORTALITY - See SOMALIA - MORTALITY

SOMALIA - GEOGRAPHIC DATA

M.E. Sharpe, 80 Business Park Drive, Armonk, New York 10504 (800) 541-6563; *The Illustrated Book of World Rankings.*

SOMALIA - GOATS - See SOMALIA - LIVESTOCK AND POULTRY

SOMALIA - GOLD HOLDINGS

International Monetary Fund, 700 Nineteenth Street, NW, Washington, D.C. 20431 (202) 623-7000; *International Financial Statistics.*

Statistical Office of the United Nations, Publishing Service, New York, New York 10017 (800) 253-9646; *Statistical Yearbook.*

The World Bank, 1818 H Street, NW, Washington, D.C. 20433 (202) 477-1234; *World Development Indicators.*

SOMALIA - GOLD PRODUCTION AND CONSUMPTION - See SOMALIA - MINING AND MINERAL PRODUCTS

SOMALIA - GOVERNMENT

Central Intelligence Agency, Washington, D.C. 20505 (703) 482-1100, www.cia.gov; *The World Factbook.*

Europa Publications Limited, 18 Bedford Square, London, WC1B 3JN, England; *The Europa World Year Book.*

International Monetary Fund, 700 Nineteenth Street, NW, Washington, D.C. 20431 (202) 623-7000; *Government Finance Statistics Yearbook;* and *International Financial Statistics.*

St. Martin's Press, Inc., 175 Fifth Avenue, New York, New York 10010 (800) 221-7945; *The Statesman's Year-Book.*

Statistical Office of the United Nations, Publishing Service, New York, New York 10017 (800) 253-9646; *National Accounts Statistics; Statistical Yearbook;* and *Survey of Economic and Social Conditions in Africa.*

The World Bank, 1818 H Street, NW, Washington, D.C. 20433 (202) 477-1234; *World Development Indicators.*

SOMALIA - GRAIN PRODUCTION - See SOMALIA - CROPS

SOMALIA - GRANTS

International Monetary Fund, 700 Nineteenth Street, NW, Washington, D.C. 20431 (202) 623-7000; *Government Finance Statistics Yearbook.*

SOMALIA - GROSS DOMESTIC PRODUCT

African Development Bank, 01 BP 1387, Abidjan 01, Cote D'Ivoire; *Selected Statistics on Regional Member Countries.*

The Economist Intelligence Unit, 111 West 57th Street, New York, New York 10019 (800) 938-4685; *Somalia Country Report;* and *The World Market Atlas.*

Euromonitor International, Inc., 122 South Michigan Avenue, Suite 1200,

Chicago, Illinois 60603 (800) 577-EURO; *International Marketing Data and Statistics;* and *The World Economic Factbook.*

Europa Publications Limited, 18 Bedford Square, London, WC1B 3JN, England; *The Europa World Year Book.*

M.E. Sharpe, 80 Business Park Drive, Armonk, New York 10504 (800) 541-6563; *The Illustrated Book of World Rankings.*

Statistical Office of the United Nations, Publishing Service, New York, New York 10017 (800) 253-9646; *Bulletin of Industrial Statistics for the Arab Countries; National Accounts Statistics; Statistical Yearbook;* and *Survey of Economic and Social Conditions in Africa.*

United Nations Economic Commission for Africa, Africa Hall, P.O. Box 3001, Addis Ababa, Ethiopia (Telephone Number in U.S. (800) 253-9646); *African Statistical Yearbook.*

The World Bank, 1818 H Street, NW, Washington, D.C. 20433 (202) 477-1234; *World Development Indicators.*

SOMALIA - GROSS NATIONAL PRODUCT

Euromonitor International, Inc., 122 South Michigan Avenue, Suite 1200, Chicago, Illinois 60603 (800) 577-EURO; *International Marketing Data and Statistics.*

St. Martin's Press, Inc., 175 Fifth Avenue, New York, New York 10010 (800) 221-7945; *The Statesman's Year-Book.*

U.S. Arms Control and Disarmament Agency, 320 Twenty-first Street, NW, Washington, D.C. 20451 (202) 647-8677; *World Military Expenditures and Arms Transfers.*

The World Bank, 1818 H Street, NW, Washington, D.C. 20433 (202) 477-1234; *The World Bank Atlas;* and *World Development Indicators.*

SOMALIA - GROUNDNUT PRODUCTION - See SOMALIA - CROPS

SOMALIA - HEALTH

African Development Bank, 01 BP 1387, Abidjan 01, Cote D'Ivoire; *Selected Statistics on Regional Member Countries.*

Euromonitor International, Inc., 122 South Michigan Avenue, Suite 1200, Chicago, Illinois 60603 (800) 577-EURO: *World Marketing Data and Statistics.*

M.E. Sharpe, 80 Business Park Drive, Armonk, New York 10504 (800) 541-6563; *The Illustrated Book of World Rankings.*

St. Martin's Press, Inc., 175 Fifth

Avenue, New York, New York 10010 (800) 221-7945; *The Statesman's Year-Book*.

Statistical Office of the United Nations, Publishing Service, New York, New York 10017 (800) 253-9646; *Statistical Yearbook*.

United Nations Children's Fund (UNICEF), 3 United Nations Plaza, New York, New York 10017 (800) 253-9646; *State of the World's Children*.

United Nations Economic Commission for Africa, Africa Hall, P.O. Box 3001, Addis Ababa, Ethiopia (Telephone Number in U.S. (800) 253-9646); *African Statistical Yearbook*.

SOMALIA - HEALTH EXPENDITURES

International Monetary Fund, 700 Nineteenth Street, NW, Washington, D.C. 20431 (202) 623-7000; *Government Finance Statistics Yearbook*.

SOMALIA - HIDES AND SKINS EXPORTS

International Monetary Fund, 700 Nineteenth Street, NW, Washington, D.C. 20431 (202) 623-7000; *International Financial Statistics*.

SOMALIA - HIGHWAYS

Central Intelligence Agency, Washington, D.C. 20505 (703) 482-1100, www.cia.gov; *The World Factbook*.

International Road Federation, 2600 Virginia Avenue, NW, Washington, D.C. 20037 (202) 338-4641; *World Road Statistics*.

St. Martin's Press, Inc., 175 Fifth Avenue, New York, New York 10010 (800) 221-7945; *The Statesman's Year-Book*.

Statistical Office of the United Nations, Publishing Service, New York, New York 10017 (800) 253-9646; *Survey of Economic and Social Conditions in Africa*.

United Nations Economic Commission for Africa, Africa Hall, P.O. Box 3001, Addis Ababa, Ethiopia (Telephone Number in U.S. (800) 253-9646); *African Statistical Yearbook*.

SOMALIA - HORSES - See SOMALIA - LIVESTOCK AND POULTRY

SOMALIA - HOURS OF WORK - See SOMALIA - EMPLOYMENT

SOMALIA - HOUSING AND HOUSING UNITS

Euromonitor International, Inc., 122 South Michigan Avenue, Suite 1200,

Chicago, Illinois 60603 (800) 577-EURO: *World Marketing Data and Statistics*.

SOMALIA - HOUSING EXPENDITURES

International Monetary Fund, 700 Nineteenth Street, NW, Washington, D.C. 20431 (202) 623-7000; *Government Finance Statistics Yearbook*.

M.E. Sharpe, 80 Business Park Drive, Armonk, New York 10504 (800) 541-6563; *The Illustrated Book of World Rankings*.

SOMALIA - ILLITERATE POPULATION

Central Intelligence Agency, Washington, D.C. 20505 (703) 482-1100, www.cia.gov; *The World Factbook*.

The Economist Intelligence Unit, 111 West 57th Street, New York, New York 10019 (800) 938-4685; *The World Market Atlas*.

Euromonitor International, Inc., 122 South Michigan Avenue, Suite 1200, Chicago, Illinois 60603 (800) 577-EURO; *The World Economic Factbook*.

St. Martin's Press, Inc., 175 Fifth Avenue, New York, New York 10010 (800) 221-7945; *The Statesman's Year-Book*.

United Nations Educational, Scientific and Cultural Organization (UNESCO), 7 Place de Fontenoy, F-75700 Paris, France (Telephone Number in U.S. (212) 963-5981); *Statistical Yearbook*.

SOMALIA - IMPORTS

African Development Bank, 01 BP 1387, Abidjan 01, Cote D'Ivoire; *Selected Statistics on Regional Member Countries*.

Central Intelligence Agency, Washington, D.C. 20505 (703) 482-1100, www.cia.gov; *The World Factbook*.

The Economist Intelligence Unit, 111 West 57th Street, New York, New York 10019 (800) 938-4685; *Somalia Country Report*; and *The World Market Atlas*.

Euromonitor International, Inc., 122 South Michigan Avenue, Suite 1200, Chicago, Illinois 60603 (800) 577-EURO; *International Marketing Data and Statistics*; and *The World Economic Factbook*.

Europa Publications Limited, 18 Bedford Square, London, WC1B 3JN, England; *The Europa World Year Book*.

Food and Agricultural Organization of the United Nations (FAO) Via delle Terme di Caracalla, 00100 Rome, Italy (Telephone Number in U.S. (202) 653-2400); *The State of Food and Agriculture*.

International Monetary Fund, 700 Nineteenth Street, NW, Washington, D.C. 20431 (202) 623-7000; *Direction of Trade Statistics; Government Finance Statistics Yearbook*; and *International Financial Statistics*.

St. Martin's Press, Inc., 175 Fifth Avenue, New York, New York 10010 (800) 221-7945; *The Statesman's Year-Book*.

Statistical Office of the United Nations, Publishing Service, New York, New York 10017 (800) 253-9646; *Bulletin of Industrial Statistics for the Arab Countries; Foreign Trade Statistics for Africa*; and *Survey of Economic and Social Conditions in Africa*.

United Nations Conference on Trade and Development (UNCTAD), New York, New York 10017 (800) 253-9646; *Handbook of International Trade and Development Statistics*.

United Nations Economic Commission for Africa, Africa Hall, P.O. Box 3001, Addis Ababa, Ethiopia (Telephone Number in U.S. (800) 253-9646); *African Statistical Yearbook*.

The World Bank, 1818 H Street, NW, Washington, D.C. 20433 (202) 477-1234; *World Development Indicators*.

SOMALIA - INCOME TAXES - See SOMALIA - TAXATION

SOMALIA - INDUSTRY

Central Intelligence Agency, Washington, D.C. 20505 (703) 482-1100, www.cia.gov; *The World Factbook*.

Economist Intelligence Unit, 111 West 57th Street, New York, New York 10019 (800) 938-4685; *Somalia Country Report*.

Euromonitor International, Inc., 122 South Michigan Avenue, Suite 1200, Chicago, Illinois 60603 (800) 577-EURO; *International Marketing Data and Statistics; World Marketing Data and Statistics;* and *The World Economic Factbook*.

Europa Publications Limited, 18 Bedford Square, London, WC1B 3JN, England; *The Europa World Year Book*.

International Labour Office, I.L.O. Publications, 1828 L Street, NW., Suite 801, Washington, D.C. 20036 (301) 638-3152; *Yearbook of Labour Statistics*.

M.E. Sharpe, 80 Business Park Drive, Armonk, New York 10504 (800) 541-6563; *The Illustrated Book of World Rankings*.

St. Martin's Press, Inc., 175 Fifth Avenue, New York, New York 10010 (800) 221-7945; *The Statesman's Year-Book*.

Statistical Office of the United Nations, Publishing Service, New York, New York 10017 (800) 253-9646; *Bulletin of Industrial Statistics for the Arab Countries; Industrial Commodity Statistics Yearbook;* and *Survey of Economic and Social Conditions in Africa.*

United Nations Economic Commission for Africa, Africa Hall, P.O. Box 3001, Addis Ababa, Ethiopia (Telephone Number in U.S. (800) 253-9646); *African Statistical Yearbook.*

The World Bank, 1818 H Street, NW, Washington, D.C. 20433 (202) 477-1234; *World Development Indicators.*

SOMALIA - INFANT AND MATERNAL MORTALITY - See SOMALIA - MORTALITY

SOMALIA - INTERNATIONAL LIQUIDITY

International Monetary Fund, 700 Nineteenth Street, NW, Washington, D.C. 20431 (202) 623-7000; *International Financial Statistics.*

SOMALIA - INTERNATIONAL RESERVES EXCLUDING GOLD

African Development Bank, 01 BP 1387, Abidjan 01, Cote D'Ivoire; *Selected Statistics on Regional Member Countries.*

Statistical Office of the United Nations, Publishing Service, New York, New York 10017 (800) 253-9646; *Statistical Yearbook.*

The World Bank, 1818 H Street, NW, Washington, D.C. 20433 (202) 477-1234; *World Development Indicators.*

SOMALIA - IRON ORE PRODUCTION AND CONSUMPTION - See SOMALIA - MINING AND MINERAL PRODUCTS

SOMALIA - IRRIGATION

Euromonitor International, Inc., 122 South Michigan Avenue, Suite 1200, Chicago, Illinois 60603 (800) 577-EURO; *International Marketing Data and Statistics.*

SOMALIA - LABOR

African Development Bank, 01 BP 1387, Abidjan 01, Cote D'Ivoire; *Selected Statistics on Regional Member Countries.*

Central Intelligence Agency, Washington, D.C. 20505 (703) 482-1100, www.cia.gov; *The World Factbook.*

Euromonitor International, Inc., 122 South Michigan Avenue, Suite 1200, Chicago, Illinois 60603 (800) 577-EURO; *International Marketing Data and Statistics;* and *World Marketing Data and Statistics.*

Europa Publications Limited, 18 Bedford Square, London, WC1B 3JN, England; *The Europa World Year Book.*

Food and Agricultural Organization of the United Nations (FAO) Via delle Terme di Caracalla, 00100 Rome, Italy (Telephone Number in U.S. (202) 653-2400); *The State of Food and Agriculture.*

International Labour Office, I.L.O. Publications, 1828 L Street, NW., Suite 801, Washington, D.C. 20036 (301) 638-3152; *Yearbook of Labour Statistics.*

M.E. Sharpe, 80 Business Park Drive, Armonk, New York 10504 (800) 541-6563; *The Illustrated Book of World Rankings.*

St. Martin's Press, Inc., 175 Fifth Avenue, New York, New York 10010 (800) 221-7945; *The Statesman's Year-Book.*

The World Bank, 1818 H Street, NW, Washington, D.C. 20433 (202) 477-1234; *The World Bank Atlas;* and *World Development Indicators.*

SOMALIA - LAND USE

Central Intelligence Agency, Washington, D.C. 20505 (703) 482-1100, www.cia.gov; *The World Factbook.*

Euromonitor International, Inc., 122 South Michigan Avenue, Suite 1200, Chicago, Illinois 60603 (800) 577-EURO; *International Marketing Data and Statistics.*

Food and Agricultural Organization of the United Nations (FAO), Via delle Terme di Caracalla, 00100 Rome, Italy (Telephone Number in U.S. (202) 653-2400); *Production Yearbook.*

SOMALIA - LIBRARIES

M.E. Sharpe, 80 Business Park Drive, Armonk, New York 10504 (800) 541-6563; *The Illustrated Book of World Rankings.*

United Nations Educational, Scientific and Cultural Organization (UNESCO), 7 Place de Fontenoy, F-75700 Paris, France (Telephone Number in U.S. (212) 963-5981); *Statistical Yearbook.*

SOMALIA - LIFE EXPECTANCY

African Development Bank, 01 BP 1387, Abidjan 01, Cote D'Ivoire; *Selected Statistics on Regional Member Countries.*

Central Intelligence Agency, Washington, D.C. 20505 (703) 482-1100, www.cia.gov; *The World Factbook.*

Euromonitor International, Inc., 122 South Michigan Avenue, Suite 1200, Chicago, Illinois 60603 (800) 577-EURO; *The World Economic Factbook.*

St. Martin's Press, Inc., 175 Fifth Avenue, New York, New York 10010 (800) 221-7945; *The Statesman's Year-Book.*

Statistical Office of the United Nations, Publishing Service, New York, New York 10017 (800) 253-9646; *World Statistics Pocketbook.*

The World Bank, 1818 H Street, NW, Washington, D.C. 20433 (202) 477-1234; *The World Bank Atlas.*

SOMALIA - LITERACY RATE

Euromonitor International Inc., 122 South Michigan Avenue, Suite 1200, Chicago, Illinois 60603 (800) 577-EURO; *World Marketing Data and Statistics.*

Statistical Office of the United Nations, Publishing Service, New York, New York 10017 (800) 253-9646; *Survey of Economic and Social Conditions in Africa.*

SOMALIA - LIVESTOCK AND POULTRY

Commodity Research Bureau, Inc., 30 South Wacker Drive, Chicago Illinois 60606 (312) 454-1801; *Commodity Year Book.*

Euromonitor International, Inc., 122 South Michigan Avenue, Suite 1200, Chicago, Illinois 60603 (800) 577-EURO; *International Marketing Data and Statistics.*

Europa Publications Limited, 18 Bedford Square, London, WC1B 3JN, England; *The Europa World Year Book.*

Food and Agricultural Organization of the United Nations (FAO), Via delle Terme di Caracalla, 00100 Rome, Italy (Telephone Number in U.S. (202) 653-2400); *Production Yearbook;* and *The State of Food and Agriculture.*

M.E. Sharpe, 80 Business Park Drive, Armonk, New York 10504 (800) 541-6563; *The Illustrated Book of World Rankings.*

St. Martin's Press, Inc., 175 Fifth Avenue, New York, New York 10010 (800) 221-7945; *The Statesman's Year-Book.*

Statistical Office of the United Nations, Publishing Service, New York, New York 10017 (800) 253-9646; *Statistical Yearbook;* and *Survey of Economic and Social Conditions in Africa.*

United Nations Conference on Trade and Development, Central Statistical Service, Palais des Nations, Geneva, Switzerland (Telephone in U.S. (800) 253-9646); *UNCTAD Commodity Yearbook.*

United Nations Economic Commission for Africa, Africa Hall, P.O. Box 3001, Addis Ababa, Ethiopia (Telephone Number in U.S. (800) 253-9646); *African Statistical*

Yearbook.

SOMALIA - LIVING LEVELS - See SOMALIA - LIFE EXPECTANCY

SOMALIA - MANUFACTURING

M.E. Sharpe, 80 Business Park Drive, Armonk, New York 10504 (800) 541-6563; *The Illustrated Book of World Rankings.*

Statistical Office of the United Nations, Publishing Service, New York, New York 10017 (800) 253-9646; *Bulletin of Industrial Statistics for the Arab Countries; Statistical Yearbook;* and *Survey of Economic and Social Conditions in Africa.*

United Nations Economic Commission for Africa, Africa Hall, P.O. Box 3001, Addis Ababa, Ethiopia (Telephone Number in U.S. (800) 253-9646); *African Statistical Yearbook.*

The World Bank, 1818 H Street, NW, Washington, D.C. 20433 (202) 477-1234; *World Development Indicators.*

SOMALIA - MARRIAGE RATES

M.E. Sharpe, 80 Business Park Drive, Armonk, New York 10504 (800) 541-6563; *The Illustrated Book of World Rankings.*

Statistical Office of the United Nations, Publishing Service, New York, New York 10017 (800) 253-9646; *Demographic Yearbook.*

SOMALIA - MEAT PRODUCTION - See SOMALIA - LIVESTOCK AND POULTRY

SOMALIA - MERCHANT SHIPPING

Europa Publications Limited, 18 Bedford Square, London, WC1B 3JN, England; *The Europa World Year Book.*

St. Martin's Press, Inc., 175 Fifth Avenue, New York, New York 10010 (800) 221-7945; *The Statesman's Year-Book.*

Statistical Office of the United Nations, Publishing Service, New York, New York 10017 (800) 253-9646; *Statistical Yearbook.*

United Nations Economic Commission for Africa, Africa Hall, P.O. Box 3001, Addis Ababa, Ethiopia (Telephone Number in U.S. (800) 253-9646); *African Statistical Yearbook.*

U.S. Department of Transportation, Maritime Administration, 400 Seventh Street, SW, Washington, D.C. 20590 (202) 366-5807, www.marad.dot.gov; *A Statistical Analysis of the World's Merchant Fleets.*

SOMALIA - MILITARY

Central Intelligence Agency, Washington, D.C. 20505 (703) 482-1100, www.cia.gov; *The World Factbook.*

Euromonitor International Inc., 122 South Michigan Avenue, Suite 1200, Chicago, Illinois 60603 (800) 577-EURO; *World Marketing Data and Statistics.*

International Monetary Fund, 700 Nineteenth Street, NW, Washington, D.C. 20431 (202) 623-7000; *Government Finance Statistics Yearbook.*

St. Martin's Press, Inc., 175 Fifth Avenue, New York, New York 10010 (800) 221-7945; *The Statesman's Year-Book.*

U.S. Arms Control and Disarmament Agency, 320 Twenty-first Street, NW, Washington, D.C. 20451 (202) 647-8677; *World Military Expenditures and Arms Transfers.*

SOMALIA - MILK - See SOMALIA - DAIRY PRODUCTS

SOMALIA - MINING AND MINERAL PRODUCTS

Europa Publications Limited, 18 Bedford Square, London, WC1B 3JN, England; *The Europa World Year Book.*

M.E. Sharpe, 80 Business Park Drive, Armonk, New York 10504 (800) 541-6563; *The Illustrated Book of World Rankings.*

St. Martin's Press, Inc., 175 Fifth Avenue, New York, New York 10010 (800) 221-7945; *The Statesman's Year-Book.*

Statistical Office of the United Nations, Publishing Service, New York, New York 10017 (800) 253-9646; *Bulletin of Industrial Statistics for the Arab Countries;* and *Statistical Yearbook.*

United Nations Conference on Trade and Development, Central Statistical Service, Palais des Nations, Geneva, Switzerland (Telephone in U.S. (800) 253-9646); *UNCTAD Commodity Yearbook.*

United Nations Economic Commission for Africa, Africa Hall, P.O. Box 3001, Addis Ababa, Ethiopia (Telephone Number in U.S. (800) 253-9646); *African Statistical Yearbook.*

SOMALIA - MONEY EXCHANGE RATES - See SOMALIA - EXCHANGE RATES

SOMALIA - MONEY RESERVES

Euromonitor International, Inc., 122 South Michigan Avenue, Suite 1200, Chicago, Illinois 60603 (800) 577-EURO; *International Marketing Data and Statistics.*

SOMALIA - MONEY SUPPLY

African Development Bank, 01 BP 1387, Abidjan 01, Cote D'Ivoire; *Selected Statistics on Regional Member Countries.*

Economist Intelligence Unit, 111 West 57th Street, New York, New York 10019 (800) 938-4685; *Somalia Country Report.*

Euromonitor International, Inc., 122 South Michigan Avenue, Suite 1200, Chicago, Illinois 60603 (800) 577-EURO; *International Marketing Data and Statistics.*

Europa Publications Limited, 18 Bedford Square, London, WC1B 3JN, England; *The Europa World Year Book.*

International Monetary Fund, 700 Nineteenth Street, NW, Washington, D.C. 20431 (202) 623-7000; *International Financial Statistics.*

Statistical Office of the United Nations, Publishing Service, New York, New York 10017 (800) 253-9646; *Statistical Yearbook.*

The World Bank, 1818 H Street, NW, Washington, D.C. 20433 (202) 477-1234; *World Development Indicators.*

SOMALIA - MORTALITY

Central Intelligence Agency, Washington, D.C. 20505 (703) 482-1100, www.cia.gov; *The World Factbook.*

Euromonitor International, Inc., 122 South Michigan Avenue, Suite 1200, Chicago, Illinois 60603 (800) 577-EURO; *International Marketing Data and Statistics;* and *The World Economic Factbook.*

Europa Publications Limited, 18 Bedford Square, London, WC1B 3JN, England; *The Europa World Year Book.*

St. Martin's Press, Inc., 175 Fifth Avenue, New York, New York 10010 (800) 221-7945; *The Statesman's Year-Book.*

Statistical Office of the United Nations, Publishing Service, New York, New York 10017 (800) 253-9646; *Demographic Yearbook; Statistical Yearbook; Survey of Economic and Social Conditions in Africa;* and *World Statistics Pocketbook.*

United Nations Children's Fund (UNICEF), 3 United Nations Plaza, New York, New York 10017 (800) 253-9646; *State of the World's Children.*

The World Bank, 1818 H Street, NW, Washington, D.C. 20433 (202) 477-1234; *The World Bank Atlas;* and *World Development Indicators.*

SOMALIA - MOTOR VEHICLE TAXES - See SOMALIA - TAXATION

SOMALIA - MOTOR VEHICLES IN USE

Europa Publications Limited, 18 Bedford Square, London, WC1B 3JN, England; *The Europa World Year Book.*

International Road Federation, 2600 Virginia Avenue, NW, Washington, D.C. 20037 (202) 338-4641; *World Road Statistics.*

Statistical Office of the United Nations, Publishing Service, New York, New York 10017 (800) 253-9646; *Statistical Yearbook;* and *Survey of Economic and Social Conditions in Africa.*

SOMALIA - MULES - See SOMALIA - LIVESTOCK AND POULTRY

SOMALIA - MUSEUMS

M.E. Sharpe, 80 Business Park Drive, Armonk, New York 10504 (800) 541-6563; *The Illustrated Book of World Rankings.*

SOMALIA - NATALITY - See SOMALIA - BIRTH RATE

SOMALIA - NATIONAL ACCOUNTS

African Development Bank, 01 BP 1387, Abidjan 01, Cote D'Ivoire; *Selected Statistics on Regional Member Countries.*

Europa Publications Limited, 18 Bedford Square, London, WC1B 3JN, England; *The Europa World Year Book.*

Statistical Office of the United Nations, Publishing Service, New York, New York 10017 (800) 253-9646; *Statistical Yearbook.*

United Nations Economic Commission for Africa, Africa Hall, P.O. Box 3001, Addis Ababa, Ethiopia (Telephone Number in U.S. (800) 253-9646); *African Statistical Yearbook.*

SOMALIA - NATIONAL INCOME

M.E. Sharpe, 80 Business Park Drive, Armonk, New York 10504 (800) 541-6563; *The Illustrated Book of World Rankings.*

Statistical Office of the United Nations, Publishing Service, New York, New York 10017 (800) 253-9646; *National Accounts Statistics;* and *Statistical Yearbook.*

SOMALIA - NATIONAL PRODUCT

M.E. Sharpe, 80 Business Park Drive, Armonk, New York 10504 (800) 541-6563; *The Illustrated Book of World Rankings.*

Statistical Office of the United Nations, Publishing Service, New York, New York 10017 (800) 253-9646; *Statistical Yearbook.*

SOMALIA - NATURAL GAS PRODUCTION - See SOMALIA - MINING AND MINERAL PRODUCTS

SOMALIA - NEWSPAPER PRODUCTION - See SOMALIA - FORESTRY AND FOREST PRODUCTS

SOMALIA - NEWSPRINT - See SOMALIA - FORESTRY AND FOREST PRODUCTS

SOMALIA - OCCUPATIONS - See SOMALIA - LABOR

SOMALIA - PAPER - See SOMALIA - FORESTRY AND FOREST PRODUCTS

SOMALIA - PATENTS, TRADEMARKS AND SERVICE MARKS

Statistical Office of the United Nations, Publishing Service, New York, New York 10017 (800) 253-9646; *Statistical Yearbook.*

SOMALIA - PEANUT PRODUCTION - See SOMALIA - CROPS

SOMALIA - PESTICIDE USE

Food and Agricultural Organization of the United Nations (FAO) Via delle Terme di Caracalla, 00100 Rome, Italy (Telephone Number in U.S. (202) 653-2400); *The State of Food and Agriculture.*

SOMALIA - PETROLEUM INDUSTRY

Food and Agricultural Organization of the United Nations (FAO) Via delle Terme di Caracalla, 00100 Rome, Italy (Telephone Number in U.S. (202) 653-2400); *The State of Food and Agriculture.*

M.E. Sharpe, 80 Business Park Drive, Armonk, New York 10504 (800) 541-6563; *The Illustrated Book of World Rankings.*

United Nations Conference on Trade and Development, Central Statistical Service, Palais des Nations, Geneva, Switzerland (Telephone in U.S. (800) 253-9646); *UNCTAD Commodity Yearbook.*

SOMALIA - PIGS - See SOMALIA - LIVESTOCK AND POULTRY

SOMALIA - POPULATION

African Development Bank, 01 BP 1387, Abidjan 01, Cote D'Ivoire; *Selected Statistics on Regional Member Countries.*

Central Intelligence Agency, Washington, D.C. 20505 (703) 482-1100, www.cia.gov; *The World Factbook.*

The Economist Intelligence Unit, 111 West 57th Street, New York, New York 10019 (800) 938-4685; *Somalia Country Report;* and *The World Market Atlas.*

Euromonitor International, Inc., 122 South Michigan Avenue, Suite 1200, Chicago, Illinois 60603 (800) 577-EURO; *International Marketing Data and Statistics;*

and *The World Economic Factbook.*

Europa Publications Limited, 18 Bedford Square, London, WC1B 3JN, England; *The Europa World Year Book.*

Food and Agricultural Organization of the United Nations (FAO), Via delle Terme di Caracalla, 00100 Rome, Italy (Telephone Number in U.S. (202) 653-2400); *Production Yearbook.*

International Labour Office, I.L.O. Publications, 1828 L Street, NW., Suite 801, Washington, D.C. 20036 (301) 638-3152; *Yearbook of Labour Statistics.*

M.E. Sharpe, 80 Business Park Drive, Armonk, New York 10504 (800) 541-6563; *The Illustrated Book of World Rankings.*

St. Martin's Press, Inc., 175 Fifth Avenue, New York, New York 10010 (800) 221-7945; *The Statesman's Year-Book.*

Statistical Office of the United Nations, Publishing Service, New York, New York 10017 (800) 253-9646; *Demographic Yearbook; National Accounts Statistics; Statistical Yearbook; Survey of Economic and Social Conditions in Africa;* and *World Statistics Pocketbook.*

United Nations Educational, Scientific and Cultural Organization (UNESCO), 7 Place de Fontenoy, F-75700 Paris, France (Telephone Number in U.S. (212) 963-5981); *Statistical Yearbook.*

U.S. Arms Control and Disarmament Agency, 320 Twenty-first Street, NW, Washington, D.C. 20451 (202) 647-8677; *World Military Expenditures and Arms Transfers.*

The World Bank, 1818 H Street, NW, Washington, D.C. 20433 (202) 477-1234; *The World Bank Atlas.*

World Health Organization, Office of Publications, 20 Avenue Appia, CH-1211 Geneva 27, Switzerland (Telephone Number in U.S. (518) 436-9686); *World Health Statistics Annual.*

SOMALIA - POST OFFICES

M.E. Sharpe, 80 Business Park Drive, Armonk, New York 10504 (800) 541-6563; *The Illustrated Book of World Rankings.*

SOMALIA - POTATO PRODUCTION - See SOMALIA - CROPS

SOMALIA - POWER PRODUCTION INDUSTRY

Statistical Office of the United Nations, Publishing Service, New York, New York 10017 (800) 253-9646; *Statistical Yearbook.*

SOMALIA - PRICES

Food and Agricultural Organization of the United Nations (FAO), Via delle Terme di Caracalla, 00100 Rome, Italy (Telephone Number in U.S. (202) 653-2400); *Production Yearbook;* and *The State of Food and Agriculture.*

International Labour Office, I.L.O. Publications, 1828 L Street, NW, Washington, D.C. 20036 (301) 638-3152; *Yearbook of Labour Statistics.*

International Monetary Fund, 700 Nineteenth Street, NW, Washington, D.C. 20431 (202) 623-7000; *International Financial Statistics.*

M.E. Sharpe, 80 Business Park Drive, Armonk, New York 10504 (800) 541-6563; *The Illustrated Book of World Rankings.*

United Nations Economic Commission for Africa, Africa Hall, P.O. Box 3001, Addis Ababa, Ethiopia (Telephone Number in U.S. (800) 253-9646); *African Statistical Yearbook.*

SOMALIA - PRINTING AND WRITING PAPER - See SOMALIA - FORESTRY AND FOREST PRODUCTS

SOMALIA - PRODUCTION

M.E. Sharpe, 80 Business Park Drive, Armonk, New York 10504 (800) 541-6563; *The Illustrated Book of World Rankings.*

SOMALIA - PRODUCTIVITY

Euromonitor International, Inc., 122 South Michigan Avenue, Suite 1200, Chicago, Illinois 60603 (800) 577-EURO; *International Marketing Data and Statistics.*

SOMALIA - PROPERTY TAXES - See SOMALIA - TAXATION

SOMALIA - PUBLIC FINANCE - See SOMALIA - FINANCE

SOMALIA - RADIO BROADCASTING - See SOMALIA - BROADCASTING

SOMALIA - RADIO RECEIVERS

St. Martin's Press, Inc., 175 Fifth Avenue, New York, New York 10010 (800) 221-7945; *The Statesman's Year-Book.*

SOMALIA - RAILWAYS

United Nations Economic Commission for Africa, Africa Hall, P.O. Box 3001, Addis Ababa, Ethiopia (Telephone Number in U.S. (800) 253-9646); *African Statistical Yearbook.*

SOMALIA - RELIGION

Central Intelligence Agency, Washington, D.C. 20505 (703) 482-1100, www.cia.gov; *The World Factbook.*

M.E. Sharpe, 80 Business Park Drive, Armonk, New York 10504 (800) 541-6563; *The Illustrated Book of World Rankings.*

St. Martin's Press, Inc., 175 Fifth Avenue, New York, New York 10010 (800) 221-7945; *The Statesman's Year-Book.*

SOMALIA - RENT PRICES

International Labour Office, I.L.O. Publications, 1828 L Street, NW, Washington, D.C. 20036 (301) 638-3152; *Yearbook of Labour Statistics.*

SOMALIA - RETAIL TRADE

Euromonitor International, Inc., 122 South Michigan Avenue, Suite 1200, Chicago, Illinois 60603 (800) 577-EURO; *World Marketing Data and Statistics.*

SOMALIA - RICE PRODUCTION - See SOMALIA - CROPS

SOMALIA - ROUNDWOOD PRODUCTION - See SOMALIA - FORESTRY AND FOREST PRODUCTS

SOMALIA - RUBBER PRODUCTION AND CONSUMPTION

M.E. Sharpe, 80 Business Park Drive, Armonk, New York 10504 (800) 541-6563; *The Illustrated Book of World Rankings.*

SOMALIA - SALT PRODUCTION - See SOMALIA - MINING AND MINERAL PRODUCTS

SOMALIA - SAWNWOOD PRODUCTION - See SOMALIA - FORESTRY AND FOREST PRODUCTS

SOMALIA - SENIOR CITIZENS

M.E. Sharpe, 80 Business Park Drive, Armonk, New York 10504 (800) 541-6563; *The Illustrated Book of World Rankings.*

SOMALIA - SHEEP - See SOMALIA - LIVESTOCK AND POULTRY

SOMALIA - SILVER PRODUCTION AND CONSUMPTION - See SOMALIA - MINING AND MINERAL PRODUCTS

SOMALIA - SOCIAL DATA

African Development Bank, 01 BP 1387, Abidjan 01, Cote D'Ivoire; *Selected Statistics on Regional Member Countries.*

M.E. Sharpe, 80 Business Park Drive, Armonk, New York 10504 (800) 541-6563; *The Illustrated Book of World Rankings*

Statistical Office of the United Nations, Publishing Service, New York, New York 10017 (800) 253-9646; *World Statistics Pocketbook.*

SOMALIA - SOCIAL SECURITY

International Monetary Fund, 700 Nineteenth Street, NW, Washington, D.C. 20431 (202) 623-7000; *Government Finance Statistics Yearbook.*

Statistical Office of the United Nations, Publishing Service, New York, New York 10017 (800) 253-9646; *National Accounts Statistics.*

SOMALIA - STAMP TAXES AND DUTIES -See SOMALIA - TAXATION

SOMALIA - STATE BUDGET REVENUE AND EXPENDITURES

Euromonitor International, Inc., 122 South Michigan Avenue, Suite 1200, Chicago, Illinois 60603 (800) 577-EURO; *International Marketing Data and Statistics.*

SOMALIA - STEEL - See SOMALIA - MINING AND MINERAL PRODUCTS

SOMALIA - STOCKS - COMMODITY - MARKET PRICE - INDEX

Food and Agricultural Organization of the United Nations (FAO) Via delle Terme di Caracalla, 00100 Rome, Italy (Telephone Number in U.S. (202) 653-2400); *The State of Food and Agriculture.*

SOMALIA - SUGAR PRODUCTION AND CONSUMPTION - See SOMALIA - CROPS

SOMALIA - TAXATION

Europa Publications Limited, 18 Bedford Square, London, WC1B 3JN, England; *The Europa World Year Book.*

International Monetary Fund, 700 Nineteenth Street, NW, Washington, D.C. 20431 (202) 623-7000; *Government Finance Statistics Yearbook.*

International Road Federation, 2600 Virginia Avenue, NW, Washington, D.C. 20037 (202) 338-4641; *World Road Statistics.*

The World Bank, 1818 H Street, NW, Washington, D.C. 20433 (202) 477-1234; *World Development Indicators.*

SOMALIA - TELEPHONES IN USE

American Telephone and Telegraph Company, 26 Parsippany Road, Whippany, New Jersey 07981 (800) 222-0300; *The World's Telephones.*

Central Intelligence Agency,

Washington, D.C. 20505 (703) 482-1100, www.cia.gov; *The World Factbook.*

Europa Publications Limited, 18 Bedford Square, London, WC1B 3JN, England; *The Europa World Year Book.*

St. Martin's Press, Inc., 175 Fifth Avenue, New York, New York 10010 (800) 221-7945; *The Statesman's Year-Book.*

Statistical Office of the United Nations, Publishing Service, New York, New York 10017 (800) 253-9646; *Statistical Yearbook;* and *World Statistics Pocketbook.*

SOMALIA - TELEVISION BROADCASTING - See SOMALIA - BROADCASTING

SOMALIA - TEXTILE INDUSTRY

M.E. Sharpe, 80 Business Park Drive, Armonk, New York 10504 (800) 541-6563; *The Illustrated Book of World Rankings.*

South Pacific Commission, Post Box D5, Noumea Cedex, New Caledonia; *Statistical Bulletin of the South Pacific: Retail Price Indexes.*

St. Martin's Press, Inc., 175 Fifth Avenue, New York, New York 10010 (800) 221-7945; *The Statesman's Year-Book.*

United Nations Conference on Trade and Development, Central Statistical Service, Palais des Nations, Geneva, Switzerland (Telephone in U.S. (800) 253-9646); *UNCTAD Commodity Yearbook.*

SOMALIA - TOBACCO PRODUCTION

M.E. Sharpe, 80 Business Park Drive, Armonk, New York 10504 (800) 541-6563; *The Illustrated Book of World Rankings.*

Statistical Office of the United Nations, Publishing Service, New York, New York 10017 (800) 253-9646; *Statistical Yearbook.*

SOMALIA - TOURISM

Euromonitor International, Inc., 122 South Michigan Avenue, Suite 1200, Chicago, Illinois 60603 (800) 577-EURO; *The World Economic Factbook;* and *World Marketing Data and Statistics.*

M.E. Sharpe, 80 Business Park Drive, Armonk, New York 10504 (800) 541-6563; *The Illustrated Book of World Rankings.*

Statistical Office of the United Nations, Publishing Service, New York, New York 10017 (800) 253-9646; *Statistical Yearbook.*

United Nations Economic Commission for Africa, Africa Hall, P.O. Box 3001, Addis Ababa, Ethiopia (Telephone Number in U.S. (800) 253-9646); *African Statistical*

Yearbook.

SOMALIA - TRACTORS IN USE

Statistical Office of the United Nations, Publishing Service, New York, New York 10017 (800) 253-9646; *Statistical Yearbook.*

SOMALIA - TRADE - See SOMALIA - FOREIGN TRADE

SOMALIA - TRADEMARKS AND SERVICE MARKS - See SOMALIA - PATENTS, TRADEMARKS AND SERVICE MARKS

SOMALIA - TRANSPORTATION AND COMMUNICATIONS

Central Intelligence Agency, Washington, D.C. 20505 (703) 482-1100, www.cia.gov; *The World Factbook.*

Euromonitor International, Inc., 122 South Michigan Avenue, Suite 1200, Chicago, Illinois 60603 (800) 577-EURO; *International Marketing Data and Statistics;* and *World Marketing Data and Statistics.*

Europa Publications Limited, 18 Bedford Square, London, WC1B 3JN, England; *The Europa World Year Book.*

M.E. Sharpe, 80 Business Park Drive, Armonk, New York 10504 (800) 541-6563; *The Illustrated Book of World Rankings.*

St. Martin's Press, Inc., 175 Fifth Avenue, New York, New York 10010 (800) 221-7945; *The Statesman's Year-Book.*

United Nations Economic Commission for Africa, Africa Hall, P.O. Box 3001, Addis Ababa, Ethiopia (Telephone Number in U.S. (800) 253-9646); *African Statistical Yearbook.*

SOMALIA - UNEMPLOYMENT

Central Intelligence Agency, Washington, D.C. 20505 (703) 482-1100, www.cia.gov; *The World Factbook.*

Euromonitor International, Inc., 122 South Michigan Avenue, Suite 1200, Chicago, Illinois 60603 (800) 577-EURO; *International Marketing Data and Statistics.*

International Labour Office, I.L.O. Publications, 1828 L Street, NW, Washington, D.C. 20036 (301) 638-3152; *Yearbook of Labour Statistics.*

SOMALIA - VITAL STATISTICS

Euromonitor International, Inc., 122 South Michigan Avenue, Suite 1200, Chicago, Illinois 60603 (800) 577-EURO; *International Marketing Data and Statistics.*

St. Martin's Press, Inc., 175 Fifth

Avenue, New York, New York 10010 (800) 221-7945; *The Statesman's Year-Book.*

World Health Organization, Office of Publications, 20 Avenue Appia, CH-1211 Geneva 27, Switzerland (Telephone Number in U.S. (518) 436-9686); *World Health Statistics Annual.*

SOMALIA - WAGES

International Labour Office, I.L.O. Publications, 1828 L Street, NW, Washington, D.C. 20036 (301) 638-3152; *Yearbook of Labour Statistics.*

SOMALIA - WEATHER - See SOMALIA - CLIMATE

SOMALIA - WELFARE

International Monetary Fund, 700 Nineteenth Street, NW, Washington, D.C. 20431 (202) 623-7000; *Government Finance Statistics Yearbook.*

SOMALIA - WHALES - See SOMALIA - FISHERIES

SOMALIA - WHEAT PRODUCTION AND PRICES - See SOMALIA - CROPS

SOMALIA - WINE PRODUCTION - See SOMALIA - BEVERAGES

SOMALIA - WOOL PRODUCTION - See SOMALIA - TEXTILE INDUSTRY SORORITIES

The Gale Group, 27500 Drake Road, Farmington Hills, Michigan 48331-3535 (800) 877-4253; *Encyclopedia of Associations.*

South Africa - National Statistical Offices

Central Statistical Services, Steyn's Building, 270 Schoeman Street, Pretoria 0002, South Africa.

Central Statistical Services, Private Bag X44, Pretoria 0001, South Africa.

South Africa - Primary Statistics Sources

Central Statistical Services, Steyn's Building, 270 Schoeman Street, Pretoria 0002, South Africa; *South African Statistics* and *Bulletin of Statistics.*

Department of Foreign Affairs and Information, PBX 152, Pretoria 0001, South Africa; *South Africa: Official Yearbook of the Republic of South Africa.*

SOUTH AFRICA - AGRICULTURE

Economist Intelligence Unit, 111 West 57th Street, New York, New York 10019 (800) 938-4685; *South Africa Country Report.*

Euromonitor International, Inc., 122 South Michigan Avenue, Suite 1200, Chicago, Illinois 60603 (800) 577-EURO; *International Marketing Data and Statistics;* and *World Marketing Data and Statistics.*

Europa Publications Limited, 18 Bedford Square, London, WC1B 3JN, England; *The Europa World Year Book.*

Food and Agricultural Organization of the United Nations (FAO) Via delle Terme di Caracalla, 00100 Rome, Italy (Telephone Number in U.S. (202) 653-2400); *Production Yearbook; The State of Food and Agriculture;* and *Trade Yearbook.*

M.E. Sharpe, 80 Business Park Drive, Armonk, New York 10504 (800) 541-6563; *The Illustrated Book of World Rankings.*

St. Martin's Press, Inc., 175 Fifth Avenue, New York, New York 10010 (800) 221-7945; *The Statesman's Year-Book.*

Statistical Office of the United Nations, Publishing Service, New York, New York 10017 (800) 253-9646; *Statistical Yearbook.*

United Nations Conference on Trade and Development, Central Statistical Service, Palais des Nations, Geneva, Switzerland (Telephone in U.S. (800) 253-9646); *UNCTAD Commodity Yearbook.*

The World Bank, 1818 H Street, NW, Washington, D.C. 20433 (202) 477-1234; *World Development Indicators.*

SOUTH AFRICA - AIRLINE SERVICE

Europa Publications Limited, 18 Bedford Square, London, WC1B 3JN, England; *The Europa World Year Book.*

International Civil Aviation Organization, 999 University Street, Montreal, Quebec, Canada H3C 5H7 (514) 954-8219; *Civil Aviation Statistics of the World.*

M.E. Sharpe, 80 Business Park Drive, Armonk, New York 10504 (800) 541-6563; *The Illustrated Book of World Rankings.*

St. Martin's Press, Inc., 175 Fifth Avenue, New York, New York 10010 (800) 221-7945; *The Statesman's Year-Book.*

Statistical Office of the United Nations, Publishing Service, New York, New York 10017 (800) 253-9646; *Statistical Yearbook.*

SOUTH AFRICA - AIRPORTS

Central Intelligence Agency, Washington, D.C. 20505 (703) 482-1100, www.cia.gov; *The World Factbook.*

SOUTH AFRICA - ALUMINUM PRODUCTION AND CONSUMPTION - See SOUTH AFRICA - MINING AND MINERAL PRODUCTS

SOUTH AFRICA - ANIMAL FEEDINGSTUFFS OF AQUATIC ANIMAL ORIGIN

Statistical Office of the United Nations, Publishing Service, New York, New York 10017 (800) 253-9646; *Statistical Yearbook.*

SOUTH AFRICA - ANIMAL HEALTH

Food and Agricultural Organization of the United Nations (FAO), Via delle Terme di Caracalla, 00100 Rome, Italy (Telephone Number in U.S. (202) 653-2400); *Animal Health Yearbook.*

SOUTH AFRICA - ANTIMONY AND ANTIMONY ORE PRODUCTION AND CONSUMPTION - See SOUTH AFRICA - MINING AND MINERAL PRODUCTS

SOUTH AFRICA - AREA AND DENSITY OF POPULATION

Central Intelligence Agency, Washington, D.C. 20505 (703) 482-1100, www.cia.gov; *The World Factbook.*

Euromonitor International, Inc., 122 South Michigan Avenue, Suite 1200, Chicago, Illinois 60603 (800) 577-EURO; *International Marketing Data and Statistics;* and *The World Economic Factbook.*

Europa Publications Limited, 18 Bedford Square, London, WC1B 3JN, England; *The Europa World Year Book.*

Food and Agricultural Organization of the United Nations (FAO) Via delle Terme di Caracalla, 00100 Rome, Italy (Telephone Number in U.S. (202) 653-2400); *The State of Food and Agriculture.*

M.E. Sharpe, 80 Business Park Drive, Armonk, New York 10504 (800) 541-6563; *The Illustrated Book of World Rankings.*

St. Martin's Press, Inc., 175 Fifth Avenue, New York, New York 10010 (800) 221-7945; *The Statesman's Year-Book.*

Statistical Office of the United Nations, Publishing Service, New York, New York 10017 (800) 253-9646; *Statistical Yearbook.*

United Nations Educational, Scientific and Cultural Organization (UNESCO), 7 Place de Fontenoy, F-75700 Paris, France (Telephone Number in U.S. (212) 963-5981); *Statistical Yearbook.*

The World Bank, 1818 H Street, NW, Washington, D.C. 20433 (202) 477-1234; *World Development Report.*

SOUTH AFRICA - ARMS EXPORTS AND IMPORTS - See SOUTH AFRICA - MILITARY

SOUTH AFRICA - BALANCE OF PAYMENTS

The Economist Intelligence Unit, 111 West 57th Street, New York, New York 10019 (800) 938-4685; *The World Market Atlas.*

Europa Publications Limited, 18 Bedford Square, London, WC1B 3JN, England; *The Europa World Year Book.*

International Monetary Fund, 700 Nineteenth Street, NW, Washington, D.C. 20431 (202) 623-7000; *Balance of Payments Yearbook, International Financial Statistics.*

United Nations Conference on Trade and Development (UNCTAD), New York, New York 10017 (800) 253-9646; *Handbook of International Trade and Development Statistics.*

The World Bank, 1818 H Street, NW, Washington, D.C. 20433 (202) 477-1234; *World Development Report;* and *World Development Indicators.*

SOUTH AFRICA - BANKING

Euromonitor International, Inc., 122 South Michigan Avenue, Suite 1200, Chicago, Illinois 60603 (800) 577-EURO: *World Marketing Data and Statistics.*

Europa Publications Limited, 18 Bedford Square, London, WC1B 3JN, England; *The Europa World Year Book.*

International Monetary Fund, 700 Nineteenth Street, NW, Washington, D.C. 20431 (202) 623-7000; *Government Finance Statistics Yearbook;* and *International Financial Statistics.*

M.E. Sharpe, 80 Business Park Drive, Armonk, New York 10504 (800) 541-6563; *The Illustrated Book of World Rankings.*

St. Martin's Press, Inc., 175 Fifth Avenue, New York, New York 10010 (800) 221-7945; *The Statesman's Year-Book.*

Statistical Office of the United Nations, Publishing Service, New York, New York 10017 (800) 253-9646; *Statistical Yearbook.*

SOUTH AFRICA - BARLEY PRODUCTION - See SOUTH AFRICA - CROPS

SOUTH AFRICA - BAUXITE PRODUCTION AND CONSUMPTION - See SOUTH AFRICA - MINING AND MINERAL

PRODUCTS

SOUTH AFRICA - BEER PRODUCTION - See SOUTH AFRICA - BEVERAGES

SOUTH AFRICA - BEVERAGES

M.E. Sharpe, 80 Business Park Drive, Armonk, New York 10504 (800) 541-6563; *The Illustrated Book of World Rankings.*

Statistical Office of the United Nations, Publishing Service, New York, New York 10017 (800) 253-9646; *Statistical Yearbook.*

SOUTH AFRICA - BIRTH RATES

Central Intelligence Agency, Washington, D.C. 20505 (703) 482-1100, www.cia.gov; *The World Factbook.*

Euromonitor International, Inc., 122 South Michigan Avenue, Suite 1200, Chicago, Illinois 60603 (800) 577-EURO; *International Marketing Data and Statistics;* and *The World Economic Factbook.*

Europa Publications Limited, 18 Bedford Square, London, WC1B 3JN, England; *The Europa World Year Book.*

M.E. Sharpe, 80 Business Park Drive, Armonk, New York 10504 (800) 541-6563; *The Illustrated Book of World Rankings.*

St. Martin's Press, Inc., 175 Fifth Avenue, New York, New York 10010 (800) 221-7945; *The Statesman's Year-Book.*

Statistical Office of the United Nations, Publishing Service, New York, New York 10017 (800) 253-9646; *Demographic Yearbook;* and *Statistical Yearbook.*

The World Bank, 1818 H Street, NW, Washington, D.C. 20433 (202) 477-1234; *World Development Indicators.*

SOUTH AFRICA - BONDS

International Monetary Fund, 700 Nineteenth Street, NW, Washington, D.C. 20431 (202) 623-7000; *Government Finance Statistics Yearbook.*

Statistical Office of the United Nations, Publishing Service, New York, New York 10017 (800) 253-9646; *Statistical Yearbook.*

SOUTH AFRICA - BOOK PRODUCTION

St. Martin's Press, Inc., 175 Fifth Avenue, New York, New York 10010 (800) 221-7945; *The Statesman's Year-Book.*

SOUTH AFRICA - BROADCASTING

Billboard Limited, P.O. Box 9027, 1006 AA Amsterdam, The Netherlands (Telephone Number in U.S. (212) 764-7300); *World Radio TV Handbook.*

Central Intelligence Agency, Washington, D.C. 20505 (703) 482-1100, www.cia.gov; *The World Factbook.*

Euromonitor International, Inc., 122 South Michigan Avenue, Suite 1200, Chicago, Illinois 60603 (800) 577-EURO: *World Marketing Data and Statistics.*

M.E. Sharpe, 80 Business Park Drive, Armonk, New York 10504 (800) 541-6563; *The Illustrated Book of World Rankings.*

St. Martin's Press, Inc., 175 Fifth Avenue, New York, New York 10010 (800) 221-7945; *The Statesman's Year-Book.*

SOUTH AFRICA - BUDGET

Central Intelligence Agency, Washington, D.C. 20505 (703) 482-1100, www.cia.gov; *The World Factbook.*

SOUTH AFRICA - BUSINESS AND PROFESSIONAL LICENSES

International Monetary Fund, 700 Nineteenth Street, NW, Washington, D.C. 20431 (202) 623-7000; *Government Finance Statistics Yearbook.*

SOUTH AFRICA - BUTTER - See SOUTH AFRICA - DAIRY PRODUCTS

SOUTH AFRICA - CADMIUM PRODUCTION AND CONSUMPTION - See SOUTH AFRICA - MINING AND MINERAL PRODUCTS

SOUTH AFRICA - CALORIE SUPPLY

Food and Agricultural Organization of the United Nations (FAO) Via delle Terme di Caracalla, 00100 Rome, Italy (Telephone Number in U.S. (202) 653-2400); *The State of Food and Agriculture.*

SOUTH AFRICA - CAPITAL REVENUE

International Monetary Fund, 700 Nineteenth Street, NW, Washington, D.C. 20431 (202) 623-7000; *Government Finance Statistics Yearbook.*

SOUTH AFRICA - CATTLE - See SOUTH AFRICA - LIVESTOCK AND POULTRY

SOUTH AFRICA - CEMENT PRODUCTION - See SOUTH AFRICA - MINING AND MINERAL PRODUCTS

SOUTH AFRICA - CHEESE - See SOUTH AFRICA - DAIRY PRODUCTS

SOUTH AFRICA - CHEMICAL (ORGANIC) PRODUCTION - See SOUTH AFRICA - MINING AND MINERAL PRODUCTS

SOUTH AFRICA - CHICKENS - See SOUTH AFRICA - LIVESTOCK AND POULTRY

SOUTH AFRICA - CHROMITE PRODUCTION AND CONSUMPTION - See SOUTH AFRICA - MINING AND MINERAL PRODUCTS

SOUTH AFRICA - CHROMIUM ORE PRODUCTION AND CONSUMPTION - See SOUTH AFRICA - MINING AND MINERAL PRODUCTS

SOUTH AFRICA - CIGAR AND CIGARETTE PRODUCTION - See SOUTH AFRICA - TOBACCO PRODUCTION

SOUTH AFRICA - CLIMATE

M.E. Sharpe, 80 Business Park Drive, Armonk, New York 10504 (800) 541-6563; *The Illustrated Book of World Rankings.*

St. Martin's Press, Inc., 175 Fifth Avenue, New York, New York 10010 (800) 221-7945; *The Statesman's Year-Book.*

SOUTH AFRICA - COAL PRODUCTION - See SOUTH AFRICA - MINING AND MINERAL PRODUCTS

SOUTH AFRICA - COFFEE PRODUCTION AND CONSUMPTION - See SOUTH AFRICA - CROPS

SOUTH AFRICA - COKE PRODUCTION AND CONSUMPTION - See SOUTH AFRICA - MINING AND MINERAL PRODUCTS

SOUTH AFRICA - COMMERCE

St. Martin's Press, Inc., 175 Fifth Avenue, New York, New York 10010 (800) 221-7945; *The Statesman's Year-Book.*

SOUTH AFRICA - CONSTRUCTION INDUSTRY

M.E. Sharpe, 80 Business Park Drive, Armonk, New York 10504 (800) 541-6563; *The Illustrated Book of World Rankings.*

St. Martin's Press, Inc., 175 Fifth Avenue, New York, New York 10010 (800) 221-7945; *The Statesman's Year-Book.*

Statistical Office of the United Nations, Publishing Service, New York, New York 10017 (800) 253-9646; *Statistical Yearbook.*

SOUTH AFRICA - CONSUMER PRICE INDEX

Europa Publications Limited, 18 Bedford Square, London, WC1B 3JN, England; *The Europa World Year Book.*

Statistical Office of the United Nations, Publishing Service, New York, New York 10017 (800) 253-9646; *Statistical Yearbook.*

SOUTH AFRICA - CONSUMER PRICES

Euromonitor International, Inc., 122 South Michigan Avenue, Suite 1200,

Chicago, Illinois 60603 (800) 577-EURO: *World Marketing Data and Statistics.*

International Labour Office, I.L.O. Publications, 1828 L Street, NW, Washington, D.C. 20036 (301) 638-3152; *Yearbook of Labour Statistics.*

International Monetary Fund, 700 Nineteenth Street, NW, Washington, D.C. 20431 (202) 623-7000; *International Financial Statistics.*

SOUTH AFRICA - CONSUMPTION

International Iron and Steel Institute, 120, rue Colonel Bourg, B-1140, Brussels, Belgium; *Steel Statistical Yearbook.*

International Lead and Zinc Study Group, Metro House, 58 St. James's Street, London SW1A 1LD, England; *Lead and Zinc Statistics.*

International Monetary Fund, 700 Nineteenth Street, NW, Washington, D.C. 20431 (202) 623-7000; *International Financial Statistics.*

The World Bank, 1818 H Street, NW, Washington, D.C. 20433 (202) 477-1234; *World Development Report.*

SOUTH AFRICA - COPPER AND COPPER ORE PRODUCTION AND CONSUMPTION - See SOUTH AFRICA - MINING AND MINERAL PRODUCTS

SOUTH AFRICA - CORN PRODUCTION - See SOUTH AFRICA - CROPS

SOUTH AFRICA - CORPORATE TAXES - See SOUTH AFRICA - TAXATION

SOUTH AFRICA - COTTON - See SOUTH AFRICA - CROPS

SOUTH AFRICA - CROPS

Commodity Research Bureau, Inc., 30 South Wacker Drive, Chicago Illinois 60606 (312) 454-1801; *Commodity Year Book.*

Europa Publications Limited, 18 Bedford Square, London, WC1B 3JN, England; *The Europa World Year Book.*

Food and Agricultural Organization of the United Nations (FAO) Via delle Terme di Caracalla, 00100 Rome, Italy (Telephone Number in U.S. (202) 653-2400); *The State of Food and Agriculture.*

M.E. Sharpe, 80 Business Park Drive, Armonk, New York 10504 (800) 541-6563; *The Illustrated Book of World Rankings.*

St. Martin's Press, Inc., 175 Fifth Avenue, New York, New York 10010 (800) 221-7945; *The Statesman's Year-Book.*

Statistical Office of the United Nations, Publishing Service, New York, New York 10017 (800) 253-9646; *Statistical Yearbook.*

United Nations Conference on Trade and Development, Central Statistical Service, Palais des Nations, Geneva, Switzerland (Telephone in U.S. (800) 253-9646); *UNCTAD Commodity Yearbook.*

SOUTH AFRICA - CUSTOMS DUTIES

International Monetary Fund, 700 Nineteenth Street, NW, Washington, D.C. 20431 (202) 623-7000; *Government Finance Statistics Yearbook.*

St. Martin's Press, Inc., 175 Fifth Avenue, New York, New York 10010 (800) 221-7945; *The Statesman's Year-Book.*

SOUTH AFRICA - DAIRY PRODUCTS

Commodity Research Bureau, Inc., 30 South Wacker Drive, Chicago Illinois 60606 (312) 454-1801; *Commodity Year Book.*

Europa Publications Limited, 18 Bedford Square, London, WC1B 3JN, England; *The Europa World Year Book.*

Food and Agricultural Organization of the United Nations (FAO) Via delle Terme di Caracalla, 00100 Rome, Italy (Telephone Number in U.S. (202) 653-2400); *The State of Food and Agriculture.*

M.E. Sharpe, 80 Business Park Drive, Armonk, New York 10504 (800) 541-6563; *The Illustrated Book of World Rankings.*

St. Martin's Press, Inc., 175 Fifth Avenue, New York, New York 10010 (800) 221-7945; *The Statesman's Year-Book.*

Statistical Office of the United Nations, Publishing Service, New York, New York 10017 (800) 253-9646; *Statistical Yearbook.*

SOUTH AFRICA - DEATH RATES - See SOUTH AFRICA - MORTALITY

SOUTH AFRICA - DEMOGRAPHY

The Economist Intelligence Unit, 111 West 57th Street, New York, New York 10019 (800) 938-4685; *The World Market Atlas.*

Euromonitor International, Inc., 122 South Michigan Avenue, Suite 1200, Chicago, Illinois 60603 (800) 577-EURO; *International Marketing Data and Statistics; World Marketing Data and Statistics;* and *The World Economic Factbook.*

M.E. Sharpe, 80 Business Park Drive, Armonk, New York 10504 (800) 541-6563; *The Illustrated Book of World Rankings.*

Statistical Office of the United Nations,

Publishing Service, New York, New York 10017 (800) 253-9646; *Human Development Report.*

SOUTH AFRICA - DIAMONDS - See SOUTH AFRICA - MINING AND MINERAL PRODUCTS

SOUTH AFRICA - DISCOUNT RATES - See SOUTH AFRICA - BANKING

SOUTH AFRICA - DIVORCE RATES

M.E. Sharpe, 80 Business Park Drive, Armonk, New York 10504 (800) 541-6563; *The Illustrated Book of World Rankings.*

Statistical Office of the United Nations, Publishing Service, New York, New York 10017 (800) 253-9646; *Demographic Yearbook.*

SOUTH AFRICA - ECONOMY

Central Intelligence Agency, Washington, D.C. 20505 (703) 482-1100, www.cia.gov; *The World Factbook.*

Economist Intelligence Unit, 111 West 57th Street, New York, New York 10019 (800) 938-4685; *South Africa Country Report.*

Euromonitor International, Inc., 122 South Michigan Avenue, Suite 1200, Chicago, Illinois 60603 (800) 577-EURO; *International Marketing Data and Statistics; World Marketing Data and Statistics;* and *The World Economic Factbook.*

Europa Publications Limited, 18 Bedford Square, London, WC1B 3JN, England; *The Europa World Year Book.*

M.E. Sharpe, 80 Business Park Drive, Armonk, New York 10504 (800) 541-6563; *The Illustrated Book of World Rankings.*

St. Martin's Press, Inc., 175 Fifth Avenue, New York, New York 10010 (800) 221-7945; *The Statesman's Year-Book.*

Statistical Office of the United Nations, Publishing Service, New York, New York 10017 (800) 253-9646; *Foreign Trade Statistics for Africa;* and *World Statistics Pocketbook.*

The World Bank, 1818 H Street, NW, Washington, D.C. 20433 (202) 477-1234; *The World Bank Atlas;* and *World Development Report.*

SOUTH AFRICA - EDUCATION

The Economist Intelligence Unit, 111 West 57th Street, New York, New York 10019 (800) 938-4685; *The World Market Atlas.*

Euromonitor International, Inc., 122

South Michigan Avenue, Suite 1200, Chicago, Illinois 60603 (800) 577-EURO; *International Marketing Data and Statistics;* and *World Marketing Data and Statistics.*

Europa Publications Limited, 18 Bedford Square, London, WC1B 3JN, England; *The Europa World Year Book.*

M.E. Sharpe, 80 Business Park Drive, Armonk, New York 10504 (800) 541-6563; *The Illustrated Book of World Rankings.*

St. Martin's Press, Inc., 175 Fifth Avenue, New York, New York 10010 (800) 221-7945; *The Statesman's Year-Book.*

Statistical Office of the United Nations, Publishing Service, New York, New York 10017 (800) 253-9646; *Human Development Report.*

United Nations Educational, Scientific and Cultural Organization (UNESCO), 7 Place de Fontenoy, F-75700 Paris, France (Telephone Number in U.S. (212) 963-5981); *Statistical Yearbook.*

The World Bank, 1818 H Street, NW, Washington, D.C. 20433 (202) 477-1234; *World Development Report;* and *World Development Indicators.*

SOUTH AFRICA - EGG PRODUCTION AND CONSUMPTION - See SOUTH AFRICA - DAIRY PRODUCTS

SOUTH AFRICA - ELECTRICITY

Central Intelligence Agency, Washington, D.C. 20505 (703) 482-1100, www.cia.gov; *The World Factbook.*

M.E. Sharpe, 80 Business Park Drive, Armonk, New York 10504 (800) 541-6563; *The Illustrated Book of World Rankings.*

St. Martin's Press, Inc., 175 Fifth Avenue, New York, New York 10010 (800) 221-7945; *The Statesman's Year-Book.*

Statistical Office of the United Nations, Publishing Service, New York, New York 10017 (800) 253-9646; *Human Development Report;* and *Statistical Yearbook.*

SOUTH AFRICA - EMPLOYMENT

Euromonitor International, Inc., 122 South Michigan Avenue, Suite 1200, Chicago, Illinois 60603 (800) 577-EURO; *International Marketing Data and Statistics.*

International Labour Office, I.L.O. Publications, 1828 L Street, NW, Washington, D.C. 20036 (301) 638-3152; *Yearbook of Labour Statistics.*

M.E. Sharpe, 80 Business Park Drive, Armonk, New York 10504 (800) 541-6563;

The Illustrated Book of World Rankings.

Statistical Office of the United Nations, Publishing Service, New York, New York 10017 (800) 253-9646; *Statistical Yearbook.*

SOUTH AFRICA - ENERGY

Euromonitor International, Inc., 122 South Michigan Avenue, Suite 1200, Chicago, Illinois 60603 (800) 577-EURO; *International Marketing Data and Statistics; World Marketing Data and Statistics;* and *The World Economic Factbook.*

Food and Agricultural Organization of the United Nations (FAO) Via delle Terme di Caracalla, 00100 Rome, Italy (Telephone Number in U.S. (202) 653-2400); *The State of Food and Agriculture.*

M.E. Sharpe, 80 Business Park Drive, Armonk, New York 10504 (800) 541-6563; *The Illustrated Book of World Rankings.*

St. Martin's Press, Inc., 175 Fifth Avenue, New York, New York 10010 (800) 221-7945; *The Statesman's Year-Book.*

Statistical Office of the United Nations, Publishing Service, New York, New York 10017 (800) 253-9646; *Energy Statistics Yearbook; Human Development Report; Statistical Yearbook;* and *World Statistics Pocketbook.*

The World Bank, 1818 H Street, NW, Washington, D.C. 20433 (202) 477-1234; *The World Bank Atlas;* and *World Development Report.*

SOUTH AFRICA - ENVIRONMENT

Economist Intelligence Unit, 111 West 57th Street, New York, New York 10019 (800) 938-4685; *South Africa Country Report.*

Statistical Office of the United Nations, Publishing Service, New York, New York 10017 (800) 253-9646; *World Statistics Pocketbook.*

SOUTH AFRICA - EXCHANGE RATES

Central Intelligence Agency, Washington, D.C. 20505 (703) 482-1100, www.cia.gov; *The World Factbook.*

Euromonitor International, Inc., 122 South Michigan Avenue, Suite 1200, Chicago, Illinois 60603 (800) 577-EURO; *International Marketing Data and Statistics;* and *The World Economic Factbook.*

Europa Publications Limited, 18 Bedford Square, London, WC1B 3JN, England; *The Europa World Year Book.*

International Monetary Fund, 700 Nineteenth Street, NW, Washington, D.C.

20431 (202) 623-7000; *International Financial Statistics.*

Statistical Office of the United Nations, Publishing Service, New York, New York 10017 (800) 253-9646; *Foreign Trade Statistics for Africa; Statistical Yearbook;* and *World Statistics Pocketbook.*

SOUTH AFRICA - EXCISE TAXES - See SOUTH AFRICA - TAXATION

SOUTH AFRICA - EXPORTS

Central Intelligence Agency, Washington, D.C. 20505 (703) 482-1100, www.cia.gov; *The World Factbook.*

The Economist Intelligence Unit, 111 West 57th Street, New York, New York 10019 (800) 938-4685; *South Africa Country Report;* and *The World Market Atlas.*

Euromonitor International, Inc., 122 South Michigan Avenue, Suite 1200, Chicago, Illinois 60603 (800) 577-EURO; *International Marketing Data and Statistics;* and *The World Economic Factbook.*

Europa Publications Limited, 18 Bedford Square, London, WC1B 3JN, England; *The Europa World Year Book.*

Food and Agricultural Organization of the United Nations (FAO) Via delle Terme di Caracalla, 00100 Rome, Italy (Telephone Number in U.S. (202) 653-2400); *The State of Food and Agriculture.*

International Iron and Steel Institute, 120, rue Colonel Bourg, B-1140, Brussels, Belgium; *Steel Statistical Yearbook.*

International Lead and Zinc Study Group, Metro House, 58 St. James's Street, London SW1A 1LD, England; *Lead and Zinc Statistics.*

International Monetary Fund, 700 Nineteenth Street, NW, Washington, D.C. 20431 (202) 623-7000; *Government Finance Statistics Yearbook;* and *International Financial Statistics.*

St. Martin's Press, Inc., 175 Fifth Avenue, New York, New York 10010 (800) 221-7945; *The Statesman's Year-Book.*

Statistical Office of the United Nations, Publishing Service, New York, New York 10017 (800) 253-9646; *Foreign Trade Statistics for Africa.*

United Nations Conference on Trade and Development (UNCTAD), New York, New York 10017 (800) 253-9646; *Handbook of International Trade and Development Statistics.*

The World Bank, 1818 H Street, NW, Washington, D.C. 20433 (202) 477-1234;

World Development Report; and *World Development Indicators.*

SOUTH AFRICA - EXTERNAL INDEBTEDNESS

The World Bank, 1818 H Street, NW, Washington, D.C. 20433 (202) 477-1234; *World Development Report;* and *World Development Indicators.*

SOUTH AFRICA - EXTERNAL TRADE

Euromonitor International, Inc., 122 South Michigan Avenue, Suite 1200, Chicago, Illinois 60603 (800) 577-EURO; *The World Economic Factbook;* and *World Marketing Data and Statistics.*

Food and Agricultural Organization of the United Nations (FAO) Via delle Terme di Caracalla, 00100 Rome, Italy (Telephone Number in U.S. (202) 653-2400); *The State of Food and Agriculture;* and *Trade Yearbook.*

Statistical Office of the United Nations, Publishing Service, New York, New York 10017 (800) 253-9646; *Statistical Yearbook.*

SOUTH AFRICA - FABRIC PRODUCTION - See SOUTH AFRICA - TEXTILE INDUSTRY

SOUTH AFRICA - FARM CROPS - See SOUTH AFRICA - CROPS

SOUTH AFRICA - FEMALE WORKING POPULATION - See SOUTH AFRICA - EMPLOYMENT

SOUTH AFRICA - FERTILITY RATES

Central Intelligence Agency, Washington, D.C. 20505 (703) 482-1100, www.cia.gov; *The World Factbook.*

M.E. Sharpe, 80 Business Park Drive, Armonk, New York 10504 (800) 541-6563; *The Illustrated Book of World Rankings.*

Statistical Office of the United Nations, Publishing Service, New York, New York 10017 (800) 253-9646; *Human Development Report.*

The World Bank, 1818 H Street, NW, Washington, D.C. 20433 (202) 477-1234; *The World Bank Atlas; World Development Report;* and *World Development Indicators.*

SOUTH AFRICA - FERTILIZER

Food and Agricultural Organization of the United Nations (FAO), Via delle Terme di Caracalla, 00100, Rome, Italy (Telephone Number in U.S. (202) 653-2400); *Fertilizer Yearbook;* and *The State of Food and Agriculture.*

Statistical Office of the United Nations, Publishing Service, New York, New York

10017 (800) 253-9646; *Statistical Yearbook.*

SOUTH AFRICA - FETAL MORTALITY - See SOUTH AFRICA - MORTALITY

SOUTH AFRICA - FIBRE PRODUCTION - See SOUTH AFRICA - TEXTILE INDUSTRY

SOUTH AFRICA - FILAMENT PRODUCTION - See SOUTH AFRICA - TEXTILE INDUSTRY

SOUTH AFRICA - FINANCE

Economist Intelligence Unit, 111 West 57th Street, New York, New York 10019 (800) 938-4685; *South Africa Country Report.*

Europa Publications Limited, 18 Bedford Square, London, WC1B 3JN, England; *The Europa World Year Book.*

International Monetary Fund, 700 Nineteenth Street, NW, Washington, D.C. 20431 (202) 623-7000; *Government Finance Statistics Yearbook;* and *International Financial Statistics.*

M.E. Sharpe, 80 Business Park Drive, Armonk, New York 10504 (800) 541-6563; *The Illustrated Book of World Rankings.*

St. Martin's Press, Inc., 175 Fifth Avenue, New York, New York 10010 (800) 221-7945; *The Statesman's Year-Book.*

SOUTH AFRICA - FISHERIES

Europa Publications Limited, 18 Bedford Square, London, WC1B 3JN, England; *The Europa World Year Book.*

Food and Agricultural Organization of the United Nations (FAO) Via delle Terme di Caracalla, 00100 Rome, Italy (Telephone Number in U.S. (202) 653-2400); *The State of Food and Agriculture;* and *Yearbook of Fishery Statistics.*

M.E. Sharpe, 80 Business Park Drive, Armonk, New York 10504 (800) 541-6563; *The Illustrated Book of World Rankings.*

St. Martin's Press, Inc., 175 Fifth Avenue, New York, New York 10010 (800) 221-7945; *The Statesman's Year-Book.*

Statistical Office of the United Nations, Publishing Service, New York, New York 10017 (800) 253-9646; *Statistical Yearbook.*

United Nations Conference on Trade and Development, Central Statistical Service, Palais des Nations, Geneva, Switzerland (Telephone in U.S. (800) 253-9646); *UNCTAD Commodity Yearbook.*

SOUTH AFRICA - FLOUR PRODUCTION

Commodity Research Bureau, Inc., 30

South Wacker Drive, Chicago Illinois 60606 (312) 454-1801; *Commodity Year Book.*

Statistical Office of the United Nations, Publishing Service, New York, New York 10017 (800) 253-9646; *Statistical Yearbook.*

SOUTH AFRICA - FOOD

Euromonitor International, Inc., 122 South Michigan Avenue, Suite 1200, Chicago, Illinois 60603 (800) 577-EURO; *Retail Trade International.*

Food and Agricultural Organization of the United Nations (FAO), Via delle Terme di Caracalla, 00100 Rome, Italy (Telephone Number in U.S. (202) 653-2400); *Production Yearbook;* and *The State of Food and Agriculture.*

Statistical Office of the United Nations, Publishing Service, New York, New York 10017 (800) 253-9646; *Human Development Report.*

United Nations Conference on Trade and Development, Central Statistical Service, Palais des Nations, Geneva, Switzerland (Telephone in U.S. (800) 253-9646); *UNCTAD Commodity Yearbook.*

SOUTH AFRICA - FOREIGN DEBT

International Monetary Fund, 700 Nineteenth Street, NW, Washington, D.C. 20431 (202) 623-7000; *Government Finance Statistics Yearbook.*

St. Martin's Press, Inc., 175 Fifth Avenue, New York, New York 10010 (800) 221-7945; *The Statesman's Year-Book.*

SOUTH AFRICA - FOREIGN TRADE

Economist Intelligence Unit, 111 West 57th Street, New York, New York 10019 (800) 938-4685; *South Africa Country Report.*

Euromonitor International, Inc., 122 South Michigan Avenue, Suite 1200, Chicago, Illinois 60603 (800) 577-EURO; *International Marketing Data and Statistics.*

Europa Publications Limited, 18 Bedford Square, London, WC1B 3JN, England; *The Europa World Year Book.*

Food and Agricultural Organization of the United Nations (FAO) Via delle Terme di Caracalla, 00100 Rome, Italy (Telephone Number in U.S. (202) 653-2400); *The State of Food and Agriculture.*

International Iron and Steel Institute, 120, rue Colonel Bourg, B-1140, Brussels, Belgium; *Steel Statistical Yearbook.*

International Monetary Fund, 700 Nineteenth Street, NW, Washington, D.C.

20431 (202) 623-7000; *International Financial Statistics.*

M.E. Sharpe, 80 Business Park Drive, Armonk, New York 10504 (800) 541-6563; *The Illustrated Book of World Rankings.*

St. Martin's Press, Inc., 175 Fifth Avenue, New York, New York 10010 (800) 221-7945; *The Statesman's Year-Book.*

Statistical Office of the United Nations, Publishing Service, New York, New York 10017 (800) 253-9646; *Foreign Trade Statistics for Africa; International Trade Statistics Yearbook;* and *Statistical Yearbook.*

United Nations Conference on Trade and Development, Central Statistical Service, Palais des Nations, Geneva, Switzerland (Telephone in U.S. (800) 253-9646); *UNCTAD Commodity Yearbook.*

The World Bank, 1818 H Street, NW, Washington, D.C. 20433 (202) 477-1234; *World Development Report;* and *World Development Indicators.*

World Bureau of Metal Statistics, 27-A High Street, Ware Hert SG12 9BA, England; *World Metal Statistics.*

SOUTH AFRICA - FORESTRY AND FOREST PRODUCTS

American Forest and Paper Association, 1111 Nineteenth Street, NW, Suite 800, Washington, D.C. 20036 (202) 463-2700; *Wood Pulp and Fiber Statistics.*

Europa Publications Limited, 18 Bedford Square, London, WC1B 3JN, England; *The Europa World Year Book.*

Food and Agricultural Organization of the United Nations (FAO) Via delle Terme di Caracalla, 00100 Rome, Italy (Telephone Number in U.S. (202) 653-2400); *The State of Food and Agriculture;* and *Yearbook of Forest Products.*

M.E. Sharpe, 80 Business Park Drive, Armonk, New York 10504 (800) 541-6563; *The Illustrated Book of World Rankings.*

St. Martin's Press, Inc., 175 Fifth Avenue, New York, New York 10010 (800) 221-7945; *The Statesman's Year-Book.*

Statistical Office of the United Nations, Publishing Service, New York, New York 10017 (800) 253-9646; *Statistical Yearbook.*

United Nations Conference on Trade and Development, Central Statistical Service, Palais des Nations, Geneva, Switzerland (Telephone in U.S. (800) 253-9646); *UNCTAD Commodity Yearbook.*

United Nations Educational, Scientific

and Cultural Organization (UNESCO), 7 Place de Fontenoy, F-75700 Paris, France (Telephone Number in U.S. (212) 963-5981); *Statistical Yearbook.*

The World Bank, 1818 H Street, NW, Washington, D.C. 20433 (202) 477-1234; *World Development Report.*

SOUTH AFRICA - GAS PRODUCTION - See SOUTH AFRICA - MINING AND MINERAL PRODUCTS

SOUTH AFRICA - GENERAL INDUSTRIAL STATISTICS - See SOUTH AFRICA - INDUSTRY

SOUTH AFRICA - GENERAL MORTALITY - See SOUTH AFRICA - MORTALITY

SOUTH AFRICA - GEOGRAPHIC DATA

M.E. Sharpe, 80 Business Park Drive, Armonk, New York 10504 (800) 541-6563; *The Illustrated Book of World Rankings.*

SOUTH AFRICA - GOLD

International Monetary Fund, 700 Nineteenth Street, NW, Washington, D.C. 20431 (202) 623-7000; *International Financial Statistics.*

Statistical Office of the United Nations, Publishing Service, New York, New York 10017 (800) 253-9646; *Statistical Yearbook.*

The World Bank, 1818 H Street, NW, Washington, D.C. 20433 (202) 477-1234; *World Development Indicators.*

SOUTH AFRICA - GOLD PRODUCTION AND CONSUMPTION - See SOUTH AFRICA - MINING AND MINERAL PRODUCTS

SOUTH AFRICA - GOVERNMENT

Central Intelligence Agency, Washington, D.C. 20505 (703) 482-1100, www.cia.gov; *The World Factbook.*

Europa Publications Limited, 18 Bedford Square, London, WC1B 3JN, England; *The Europa World Year Book.*

International Monetary Fund, 700 Nineteenth Street, NW, Washington, D.C. 20431 (202) 623-7000; *Government Finance Statistics Yearbook;* and *International Financial Statistics.*

St. Martin's Press, Inc., 175 Fifth Avenue, New York, New York 10010 (800) 221-7945; *The Statesman's Year-Book.*

Statistical Office of the United Nations, Publishing Service, New York, New York 10017 (800) 253-9646; *National Accounts Statistics.*

The World Bank, 1818 H Street, NW, Washington, D.C. 20433 (202) 477-1234; *World Development Report;* and *World Development Indicators.*

SOUTH AFRICA - GRAIN PRODUCTION - See SOUTH AFRICA - CROPS

SOUTH AFRICA - GRANTS

International Monetary Fund, 700 Nineteenth Street, NW, Washington, D.C. 20431 (202) 623-7000; *Government Finance Statistics Yearbook.*

SOUTH AFRICA - GROSS DOMESTIC PRODUCT

The Economist Intelligence Unit, 111 West 57th Street, New York, New York 10019 (800) 938-4685; *South Africa Country Report;* and *The World Market Atlas.*

Euromonitor International, Inc., 122 South Michigan Avenue, Suite 1200, Chicago, Illinois 60603 (800) 577-EURO; *International Marketing Data and Statistics;* and *The World Economic Factbook.*

Europa Publications Limited, 18 Bedford Square, London, WC1B 3JN, England; *The Europa World Year Book.*

International Monetary Fund, 700 Nineteenth Street, NW, Washington, D.C. 20431 (202) 623-7000; *International Financial Statistics.*

M.E. Sharpe, 80 Business Park Drive, Armonk, New York 10504 (800) 541-6563; *The Illustrated Book of World Rankings.*

Statistical Office of the United Nations, Publishing Service, New York, New York 10017 (800) 253-9646; *Human Development Report; National Accounts Statistics;* and *Statistical Yearbook.*

The World Bank, 1818 H Street, NW, Washington, D.C. 20433 (202) 477-1234; *World Development Report;* and *World Development Indicators.*

SOUTH AFRICA - GROSS NATIONAL PRODUCT

Euromonitor International, Inc., 122 South Michigan Avenue, Suite 1200, Chicago, Illinois 60603 (800) 577-EURO; *International Marketing Data and Statistics.*

Europa Publications Limited, 18 Bedford Square, London, WC1B 3JN, England; *The Europa World Year Book.*

St. Martin's Press, Inc., 175 Fifth Avenue, New York, New York 10010 (800) 221-7945; *The Statesman's Year-Book.*

U.S. Arms Control and Disarmament Agency, 320 Twenty-first Street, NW,

Washington, D.C. 20451 (202) 647-8677; *World Military Expenditures and Arms Transfers.*

The World Bank, 1818 H Street, NW, Washington, D.C. 20433 (202) 477-1234; *The World Bank Atlas; World Development Report;* and *World Development Indicators.*

SOUTH AFRICA - GROUNDNUT PRODUCTION - See SOUTH AFRICA - CROPS

SOUTH AFRICA - HEALTH

Euromonitor International, Inc., 122 South Michigan Avenue, Suite 1200, Chicago, Illinois 60603 (800) 577-EURO: *World Marketing Data and Statistics.*

M.E. Sharpe, 80 Business Park Drive, Armonk, New York 10504 (800) 541-6563; *The Illustrated Book of World Rankings.*

St. Martin's Press, Inc., 175 Fifth Avenue, New York, New York 10010 (800) 221-7945; *The Statesman's Year-Book.*

Statistical Office of the United Nations, Publishing Service, New York, New York 10017 (800) 253-9646; *Human Development Report;* and *Statistical Yearbook.*

United Nations Children's Fund (UNICEF), 3 United Nations Plaza, New York, New York 10017 (800) 253-9646; *State of the World's Children.*

The World Bank, 1818 H Street, NW, Washington, D.C. 20433 (202) 477-1234; *World Development Report.*

SOUTH AFRICA - HIGHWAYS

Central Intelligence Agency, Washington, D.C. 20505 (703) 482-1100, www.cia.gov; *The World Factbook.*

International Road Federation, 2600 Virginia Avenue, NW, Washington, D.C. 20037 (202) 338-4641; *World Road Statistics.*

St. Martin's Press, Inc., 175 Fifth Avenue, New York, New York 10010 (800) 221-7945; *The Statesman's Year-Book.*

SOUTH AFRICA - HORSES - See SOUTH AFRICA - LIVESTOCK AND POULTRY

SOUTH AFRICA - HOURS OF WORK - See SOUTH AFRICA - EMPLOYMENT

SOUTH AFRICA - HOUSING AND HOUSING UNITS

Euromonitor International, Inc., 122 South Michigan Avenue, Suite 1200, Chicago, Illinois 60603 (800) 577-EURO: *World Marketing Data and Statistics.*

M.E. Sharpe, 80 Business Park Drive, Armonk, New York 10504 (800) 541-6563; *The Illustrated Book of World Rankings.*

SOUTH AFRICA - ILLITERATE POPULATION

Central Intelligence Agency, Washington, D.C. 20505 (703) 482-1100, www.cia.gov; *The World Factbook.*

The Economist Intelligence Unit, 111 West 57th Street, New York, New York 10019 (800) 938-4685; *The World Market Atlas.*

Euromonitor International, Inc., 122 South Michigan Avenue, Suite 1200, Chicago, Illinois 60603 (800) 577-EURO; *The World Economic Factbook.*

Statistical Office of the United Nations, Publishing Service, New York, New York 10017 (800) 253-9646; *Human Development Report.*

United Nations Educational, Scientific and Cultural Organization (UNESCO), 7 Place de Fontenoy, F-75700 Paris, France (Telephone Number in U.S. (212) 963-5981); *Statistical Yearbook.*

SOUTH AFRICA - IMPORTS

Central Intelligence Agency, Washington, D.C. 20505 (703) 482-1100, www.cia.gov; *The World Factbook.*

The Economist Intelligence Unit, 111 West 57th Street, New York, New York 10019 (800) 938-4685; *South Africa Country Report;* and *The World Market Atlas.*

Euromonitor International, Inc., 122 South Michigan Avenue, Suite 1200, Chicago, Illinois 60603 (800) 577-EURO; *International Marketing Data and Statistics;* and *The World Economic Factbook.*

Europa Publications Limited, 18 Bedford Square, London, WC1B 3JN, England; *The Europa World Year Book.*

European Commission Office of Press and Public Affairs, 2100 M Street, NW, Washington, D.C. 20037 (202) 862-9500; *Demographic Statistics.*

Food and Agricultural Organization of the United Nations (FAO) Via delle Terme di Caracalla, 00100 Rome, Italy (Telephone Number in U.S. (202) 653-2400); *The State of Food and Agriculture.*

International Iron and Steel Institute, 120, rue Colonel Bourg, B-1140, Brussels, Belgium; *Steel Statistical Yearbook.*

International Lead and Zinc Study Group, Metro House, 58 St. James's Street, London SW1A 1LD, England; *Lead and Zinc Statistics.*

International Monetary Fund, 700 Nineteenth Street, NW, Washington, D.C. 20431 (202) 623-7000; *Government Finance Statistics Yearbook;* and *International Financial Statistics.*

St. Martin's Press, Inc., 175 Fifth Avenue, New York, New York 10010 (800) 221-7945; *The Statesman's Year-Book.*

Statistical Office of the United Nations, Publishing Service, New York, New York 10017 (800) 253-9646; *Foreign Trade Statistics for Africa.*

United Nations Conference on Trade and Development (UNCTAD), New York, New York 10017 (800) 253-9646; *Handbook of International Trade and Development Statistics.*

The World Bank, 1818 H Street, NW, Washington, D.C. 20433 (202) 477-1234; *World Development Report;* and *World Development Indicators.*

SOUTH AFRICA - INCOME TAXES - See SOUTH AFRICA - TAXATION

SOUTH AFRICA - INDUSTRY

Central Intelligence Agency, Washington, D.C. 20505 (703) 482-1100, www.cia.gov; *The World Factbook.*

Economist Intelligence Unit, 111 West 57th Street, New York, New York 10019 (800) 938-4685; *South Africa Country Report.*

Euromonitor International, Inc., 122 South Michigan Avenue, Suite 1200, Chicago, Illinois 60603 (800) 577-EURO; *International Marketing Data and Statistics; World Marketing Data and Statistics;* and *The World Economic Factbook.*

Europa Publications Limited, 18 Bedford Square, London, WC1B 3JN, England; *The Europa World Year Book.*

International Labour Office, I.L.O. Publications, 1828 L Street, NW, Washington, D.C. 20036 (301) 638-3152; *Yearbook of Labour Statistics.*

M.E. Sharpe, 80 Business Park Drive, Armonk, New York 10504 (800) 541-6563; *The Illustrated Book of World Rankings.*

St. Martin's Press, Inc., 175 Fifth Avenue, New York, New York 10010 (800) 221-7945; *The Statesman's Year-Book.*

Statistical Office of the United Nations, Publishing Service, New York, New York 10017 (800) 253-9646; *Industrial Commodity Statistics Yearbook;* and *Statistical Yearbook.*

The World Bank, 1818 H Street, NW,

Washington, D.C. 20433 (202) 477-1234; *World Development Indicators.*

SOUTH AFRICA - INFANT AND MATERNAL MORTALITY - See SOUTH AFRICA - MORTALITY

SOUTH AFRICA - INTERNAL TRADE

Statistical Office of the United Nations, Publishing Service, New York, New York 10017 (800) 253-9646; *Statistical Yearbook.*

SOUTH AFRICA - INTERNATIONAL LIQUIDITY

International Monetary Fund, 700 Nineteenth Street, NW, Washington, D.C. 20431 (202) 623-7000; *International Financial Statistics.*

SOUTH AFRICA - INTERNATIONAL RESERVES EXCLUDING GOLD

Statistical Office of the United Nations, Publishing Service, New York, New York 10017 (800) 253-9646; *Statistical Yearbook.*

The World Bank, 1818 H Street, NW, Washington, D.C. 20433 (202) 477-1234; *World Development Indicators.*

SOUTH AFRICA - INVESTMENTS

International Monetary Fund, 700 Nineteenth Street, NW, Washington, D.C. 20431 (202) 623-7000; *International Financial Statistics.*

SOUTH AFRICA - IRON ORE - See SOUTH AFRICA - MINING AND MINERAL PRODUCTS

SOUTH AFRICA - IRRIGATION

Euromonitor International, Inc., 122 South Michigan Avenue, Suite 1200, Chicago, Illinois 60603 (800) 577-EURO; *International Marketing Data and Statistics.*

SOUTH AFRICA - LABOR

Central Intelligence Agency, Washington, D.C. 20505 (703) 482-1100, www.cia.gov; *The World Factbook.*

Euromonitor International, Inc., 122 South Michigan Avenue, Suite 1200, Chicago, Illinois 60603 (800) 577-EURO; *International Marketing Data and Statistics;* and *World Marketing Data and Statistics.*

Europa Publications Limited, 18 Bedford Square, London, WC1B 3JN, England; *The Europa World Year Book.*

Food and Agricultural Organization of the United Nations (FAO) Via delle Terme di Caracalla, 00100 Rome, Italy (Telephone Number in U.S. (202) 653-2400); *The State of Food and Agriculture.*

International Labour Office, I.L.O. Publications, 1828 L Street, NW, Washington, D.C. 20036 (301) 638-3152; *Yearbook of Labour Statistics.*

M.E. Sharpe, 80 Business Park Drive, Armonk, New York 10504 (800) 541-6563; *The Illustrated Book of World Rankings.*

St. Martin's Press, Inc., 175 Fifth Avenue, New York, New York 10010 (800) 221-7945; *The Statesman's Year-Book.*

Statistical Office of the United Nations, Publishing Service, New York, New York 10017 (800) 253-9646; *Human Development Report.*

The World Bank, 1818 H Street, NW, Washington, D.C. 20433 (202) 477-1234; *The World Bank Atlas; World Development Report;* and *World Development Indicators.*

SOUTH AFRICA - LAND USE

Central Intelligence Agency, Washington, D.C. 20505 (703) 482-1100, www.cia.gov; *The World Factbook.*

Euromonitor International, Inc., 122 South Michigan Avenue, Suite 1200, Chicago, Illinois 60603 (800) 577-EURO; *International Marketing Data and Statistics.*

Food and Agricultural Organization of the United Nations (FAO), Via delle Terme di Caracalla, 00100 Rome, Italy (Telephone Number in U.S. (202) 653-2400); *Production Yearbook.*

The World Bank, 1818 H Street, NW, Washington, D.C. 20433 (202) 477-1234; *World Development Report.*

SOUTH AFRICA - LEAD AND LEAD ORE PRODUCTION AND CONSUMPTION - See SOUTH AFRICA - MINING AND MINERAL PRODUCTS

SOUTH AFRICA - LIBRARIES

M.E. Sharpe, 80 Business Park Drive, Armonk, New York 10504 (800) 541-6563; *The Illustrated Book of World Rankings.*

SOUTH AFRICA - LIFE EXPECTANCY

Central Intelligence Agency, Washington, D.C. 20505 (703) 482-1100, www.cia.gov; *The World Factbook.*

Euromonitor International, Inc., 122 South Michigan Avenue, Suite 1200, Chicago, Illinois 60603 (800) 577-EURO; *The World Economic Factbook.*

Statistical Office of the United Nations, Publishing Service, New York, New York 10017 (800) 253-9646; *Human Development Report;* and *World Statistics Pocketbook.*

The World Bank, 1818 H Street, NW, Washington, D.C. 20433 (202) 477-1234; *The World Bank Atlas;* and *World Development Report.*

SOUTH AFRICA - LITERACY RATE

Euromonitor International, Inc., 122 South Michigan Avenue, Suite 1200, Chicago, Illinois 60603 (800) 577-EURO: *World Marketing Data and Statistics.*

SOUTH AFRICA - LIVESTOCK AND POULTRY

Commodity Research Bureau, Inc., 30 South Wacker Drive, Chicago Illinois 60606 (312) 454-1801; *Commodity Year Book.*

Euromonitor International, Inc., 122 South Michigan Avenue, Suite 1200, Chicago, Illinois 60603 (800) 577-EURO; *International Marketing Data and Statistics.*

Europa Publications Limited, 18 Bedford Square, London, WC1B 3JN, England; *The Europa World Year Book.*

Food and Agricultural Organization of the United Nations (FAO), Via delle Terme di Caracalla, 00100 Rome, Italy (Telephone Number in U.S. (202) 653-2400); *Production Yearbook;* and *The State of Food and Agriculture.*

M.E. Sharpe, 80 Business Park Drive, Armonk, New York 10504 (800) 541-6563; *The Illustrated Book of World Rankings.*

St. Martin's Press, Inc., 175 Fifth Avenue, New York, New York 10010 (800) 221-7945; *The Statesman's Year-Book.*

Statistical Office of the United Nations, Publishing Service, New York, New York 10017 (800) 253-9646; *Statistical Yearbook.*

United Nations Conference on Trade and Development, Central Statistical Service, Palais des Nations, Geneva, Switzerland (Telephone in U.S. (800) 253-9646); *UNCTAD Commodity Yearbook.*

SOUTH AFRICA - LIVING LEVELS - See SOUTH AFRICA - LIFE EXPECTANCY

SOUTH AFRICA - MAIL - NUMBER OF ITEMS SENT AND RECEIVED

Statistical Office of the United Nations, Publishing Service, New York, New York 10017 (800) 253-9646; *Statistical Yearbook.*

SOUTH AFRICA - MANGANESE AND MANGANESE ORE PRODUCTION AND CONSUMPTION - See SOUTH AFRICA - MINING AND MINERAL PRODUCTS

SOUTH AFRICA - MANUFACTURING

American Automobile Manufacturers Association, 1401 H Street, NW, Suite 900, Washington, D.C. 20005 (202) 326-5500; *World Motor Vehicle Data.*

International Monetary Fund, 700 Nineteenth Street, NW, Washington, D.C. 20431 (202) 623-7000; *International Financial Statistics.*

M.E. Sharpe, 80 Business Park Drive, Armonk, New York 10504 (800) 541-6563; *The Illustrated Book of World Rankings.*

Statistical Office of the United Nations, Publishing Service, New York, New York 10017 (800) 253-9646; *Statistical Yearbook.*

The World Bank, 1818 H Street, NW, Washington, D.C. 20433 (202) 477-1234; *World Development Indicators.*

SOUTH AFRICA - MARRIAGE RATES

M.E. Sharpe, 80 Business Park Drive, Armonk, New York 10504 (800) 541-6563; *The Illustrated Book of World Rankings.*

Statistical Office of the United Nations, Publishing Service, New York, New York 10017 (800) 253-9646; *Demographic Yearbook.*

SOUTH AFRICA - MEAT PRODUCTION - See SOUTH AFRICA - LIVESTOCK AND POULTRY

SOUTH AFRICA - MERCHANT SHIPPING

Europa Publications Limited, 18 Bedford Square, London, WC1B 3JN, England; *The Europa World Year Book.*

St. Martin's Press, Inc., 175 Fifth Avenue, New York, New York 10010 (800) 221-7945; *The Statesman's Year-Book.*

Statistical Office of the United Nations, Publishing Service, New York, New York 10017 (800) 253-9646; *Statistical Yearbook.*

U.S. Department of Transportation, Maritime Administration, 400 Seventh Street, SW, Washington, D.C. 20590 (202) 366-5807, www.marad.dot.gov; *A Statistical Analysis of the World's Merchant Fleets.*

SOUTH AFRICA - MILITARY

Central Intelligence Agency, Washington, D.C. 20505 (703) 482-1100, www.cia.gov; *The World Factbook.*

Euromonitor International, Inc., 122 South Michigan Avenue, Suite 1200, Chicago, Illinois 60603 (800) 577-EURO: *World Marketing Data and Statistics.*

The International Institute for Strategic Studies, 23 Tavistock Street, London WC2E

7NQ, England 44 171 3797676; *The Military Balance.*

St. Martin's Press, Inc., 175 Fifth Avenue, New York, New York 10010 (800) 221-7945; *The Statesman's Year-Book.*

Statistical Office of the United Nations, Publishing Service, New York, New York 10017 (800) 253-9646; *Human Development Report.*

U.S. Arms Control and Disarmament Agency, 320 Twenty-first Street, NW, Washington, D.C. 20451 (202) 647-8677; *World Military Expenditures and Arms Transfers.*

SOUTH AFRICA - MILK PRODUCTION - See SOUTH AFRICA - DAIRY PRODUCTS

SOUTH AFRICA - MINING AND MINERAL PRODUCTS

Commodity Research Bureau, Inc., 30 South Wacker Drive, Chicago Illinois 60606 (312) 454-1801; *Commodity Year Book.*

Europa Publications Limited, 18 Bedford Square, London, WC1B 3JN, England; *The Europa World Year Book.*

International Iron and Steel Institute, 120, rue Colonel Bourg, B-1140, Brussels, Belgium; *Steel Statistical Yearbook.*

International Lead and Zinc Study Group, Metro House, 58 St. James's Street, London SW1A 1LD, England; *Lead and Zinc Statistics.*

International Monetary Fund, 700 Nineteenth Street, NW, Washington, D.C. 20431 (202) 623-7000; *International Financial Statistics.*

M.E. Sharpe, 80 Business Park Drive, Armonk, New York 10504 (800) 541-6563; *The Illustrated Book of World Rankings.*

St. Martin's Press, Inc., 175 Fifth Avenue, New York, New York 10010 (800) 221-7945; *The Statesman's Year-Book.*

Statistical Office of the United Nations, Publishing Service, New York, New York 10017 (800) 253-9646; *Statistical Yearbook.*

United Nations Conference on Trade and Development, Central Statistical Service, Palais des Nations, Geneva, Switzerland (Telephone in U.S. (800) 253-9646); *UNCTAD Commodity Yearbook.*

World Bureau of Metal Statistics, 27-A High Street, Ware Hert SG12 9BA, England; *World Metal Statistics.*

SOUTH AFRICA - MOLYBDENUM AND MOLYBDENUM ORE PRODUCTION AND CONSUMPTION - See SOUTH AFRICA -

MINING AND MINERAL PRODUCTS

SOUTH AFRICA - MONEY EXCHANGE RATES - See SOUTH AFRICA - EXCHANGE RATES

SOUTH AFRICA - MONEY RATES - MARKET

Statistical Office of the United Nations, Publishing Service, New York, New York 10017 (800) 253-9646; *Statistical Yearbook.*

SOUTH AFRICA - MONEY RESERVES

Euromonitor International, Inc., 122 South Michigan Avenue, Suite 1200, Chicago, Illinois 60603 (800) 577-EURO; *International Marketing Data and Statistics.*

SOUTH AFRICA - MONEY SUPPLY

Economist Intelligence Unit, 111 West 57th Street, New York, New York 10019 (800) 938-4685; *South Africa Country Report.*

Euromonitor International, Inc., 122 South Michigan Avenue, Suite 1200, Chicago, Illinois 60603 (800) 577-EURO; *International Marketing Data and Statistics.*

Europa Publications Limited, 18 Bedford Square, London, WC1B 3JN, England; *The Europa World Year Book.*

International Monetary Fund, 700 Nineteenth Street, NW, Washington, D.C. 20431 (202) 623-7000; *International Financial Statistics.*

Statistical Office of the United Nations, Publishing Service, New York, New York 10017 (800) 253-9646; *Statistical Yearbook.*

The World Bank, 1818 H Street, NW, Washington, D.C. 20433 (202) 477-1234; *World Development Indicators.*

SOUTH AFRICA - MORTALITY

Central Intelligence Agency, Washington, D.C. 20505 (703) 482-1100, www.cia.gov; *The World Factbook.*

Euromonitor International, Inc., 122 South Michigan Avenue, Suite 1200, Chicago, Illinois 60603 (800) 577-EURO; *International Marketing Data and Statistics;* and *The World Economic Factbook.*

Europa Publications Limited, 18 Bedford Square, London, WC1B 3JN, England; *The Europa World Year Book.*

St. Martin's Press, Inc., 175 Fifth Avenue, New York, New York 10010 (800) 221-7945; *The Statesman's Year-Book.*

Statistical Office of the United Nations, Publishing Service, New York, New York 10017 (800) 253-9646; *Demographic*

Yearbook; Human Development Report; Statistical Yearbook; and *World Statistics Pocketbook.*

United Nations Children's Fund (UNICEF), 3 United Nations Plaza, New York, New York 10017 (800) 253-9646; *State of the World's Children.*

The World Bank, 1818 H Street, NW, Washington, D.C. 20433 (202) 477-1234; *The World Bank Atlas; World Development Report;* and *World Development Indicators.*

SOUTH AFRICA - MOTION PICTURES

St. Martin's Press, Inc., 175 Fifth Avenue, New York, New York 10010 (800) 221-7945; *The Statesman's Year-Book.*

SOUTH AFRICA - MOTOR VEHICLE TAXES - See SOUTH AFRICA - TAXATION

SOUTH AFRICA - MOTOR VEHICLES IN USE

American Automobile Manufacturers Association, 1401 H Street, NW, Suite 900, Washington, D.C. 20005 (202) 326-5500; *World Motor Vehicle Data.*

Europa Publications Limited, 18 Bedford Square, London, WC1B 3JN, England; *The Europa World Year Book.*

International Road Federation, 2600 Virginia Avenue, NW, Washington, D.C. 20037 (202) 338-4641; *World Road Statistics.*

Statistical Office of the United Nations, Publishing Service, New York, New York 10017 (800) 253-9646; *Statistical Yearbook.*

SOUTH AFRICA - MULES - See SOUTH AFRICA - LIVESTOCK AND POULTRY

SOUTH AFRICA - MUSEUMS

M.E. Sharpe, 80 Business Park Drive, Armonk, New York 10504 (800) 541-6563; *The Illustrated Book of World Rankings.*

SOUTH AFRICA - NATALITY - See SOUTH AFRICA - BIRTH RATE

SOUTH AFRICA - NATIONAL ACCOUNTS

Europa Publications Limited, 18 Bedford Square, London, WC1B 3JN, England; *The Europa World Year Book.*

International Monetary Fund, 700 Nineteenth Street, NW, Washington, D.C. 20431 (202) 623-7000; *International Financial Statistics.*

Statistical Office of the United Nations, Publishing Service, New York, New York 10017 (800) 253-9646; *National Accounts Statistics;* and *Statistical Yearbook.*

SOUTH AFRICA - NATIONAL INCOME

M.E. Sharpe, 80 Business Park Drive, Armonk, New York 10504 (800) 541-6563; *The Illustrated Book of World Rankings.*

Statistical Office of the United Nations, Publishing Service, New York, New York 10017 (800) 253-9646; *National Accounts Statistics;* and *Statistical Yearbook.*

SOUTH AFRICA - NATIONAL PRODUCT

M.E. Sharpe, 80 Business Park Drive, Armonk, New York 10504 (800) 541-6563; *The Illustrated Book of World Rankings.*

Statistical Office of the United Nations, Publishing Service, New York, New York 10017 (800) 253-9646; *Statistical Yearbook.*

SOUTH AFRICA - NATURAL GAS PRODUCTION - See SOUTH AFRICA - MINING AND MINERAL PRODUCTS

SOUTH AFRICA - NEWSPAPER PRODUCTION - See SOUTH AFRICA - FORESTRY AND FOREST PRODUCTS

SOUTH AFRICA - NEWSPRINT - See SOUTH AFRICA - FORESTRY AND FOREST PRODUCTS

SOUTH AFRICA - NICKEL AND NICKEL ORE PRODUCTION AND CONSUMPTION - See AFRICA - MINING AND MINERAL PRODUCTS

SOUTH AFRICA - OATS PRODUCTION - See SOUTH AFRICA - CROPS

SOUTH AFRICA - OCCUPATIONS - See SOUTH AFRICA - LABOR

SOUTH AFRICA - ORANGES PRODUCTION - See SOUTH AFRICA - CROPS

SOUTH AFRICA - PAPER - See SOUTH AFRICA - FORESTRY AND FOREST PRODUCTS

SOUTH AFRICA - PATENTS, TRADEMARKS AND SERVICE MARKS

Statistical Office of the United Nations, Publishing Service, New York, New York 10017 (800) 253-9646; *Statistical Yearbook.*

SOUTH AFRICA - PEANUT PRODUCTION - See SOUTH AFRICA - CROPS

SOUTH AFRICA - PESTICIDE USE

Food and Agricultural Organization of the United Nations (FAO) Via delle Terme di Caracalla, 00100 Rome, Italy (Telephone Number in U.S. (202) 653-2400); *The State of Food and Agriculture.*

SOUTH AFRICA - PETROLEUM INDUSTRY

Food and Agricultural Organization of the United Nations (FAO) Via delle Terme di Caracalla, 00100 Rome, Italy (Telephone Number in U.S. (202) 653-2400); *The State of Food and Agriculture.*

M.E. Sharpe, 80 Business Park Drive, Armonk, New York 10504 (800) 541-6563; *The Illustrated Book of World Rankings.*

St. Martin's Press, Inc., 175 Fifth Avenue, New York, New York 10010 (800) 221-7945; *The Statesman's Year-Book.*

Statistical Office of the United Nations, Publishing Service, New York, New York 10017 (800) 253-9646; *Statistical Yearbook.*

United Nations Conference on Trade and Development, Central Statistical Service, Palais des Nations, Geneva, Switzerland (Telephone in U.S. (800) 253-9646); *UNCTAD Commodity Yearbook.*

SOUTH AFRICA - PHOSPHATE ROCK - PRODUCTION - See SOUTH AFRICA - MINING AND MINERAL PRODUCTS

SOUTH AFRICA - PIG-IRON AND FERRO-ALLOYS - PRODUCTION - See SOUTH AFRICA - MINING AND MINERAL PRODUCTS

SOUTH AFRICA - PIGS - See SOUTH AFRICA - LIVESTOCK AND POULTRY

SOUTH AFRICA - PLATINUM PRODUCTION AND CONSUMPTION - See SOUTH AFRICA - MINING AND MINERAL PRODUCTS

SOUTH AFRICA - POPULATION

Central Intelligence Agency, Washington, D.C. 20505 (703) 482-1100, www.cia.gov; *The World Factbook.*

The Economist Intelligence Unit, 111 West 57th Street, New York, New York 10019 (800) 938-4685; *South Africa Country Report;* and *The World Market Atlas.*

Euromonitor International, Inc., 122 South Michigan Avenue, Suite 1200, Chicago, Illinois 60603 (800) 577-EURO; *International Marketing Data and Statistics;* and *The World Economic Factbook.*

Europa Publications Limited, 18 Bedford Square, London, WC1B 3JN, England; *The Europa World Year Book.*

Food and Agricultural Organization of the United Nations (FAO), Via delle Terme di Caracalla, 00100 Rome, Italy (Telephone Number in U.S. (202) 653-2400); *Production Yearbook.*

International Labour Office, I.L.O. Publications, 1828 L Street, NW, Washington, D.C. 20036 (301) 638-3152;

Yearbook of Labour Statistics.

M.E. Sharpe, 80 Business Park Drive, Armonk, New York 10504 (800) 541-6563; *The Illustrated Book of World Rankings.*

St. Martin's Press, Inc., 175 Fifth Avenue, New York, New York 10010 (800) 221-7945; *The Statesman's Year-Book.*

Statistical Office of the United Nations, Publishing Service, New York, New York 10017 (800) 253-9646; *Demographic Yearbook; Human Development Report; Statistical Yearbook;* and *World Statistics Pocketbook.*

United Nations Educational, Scientific and Cultural Organization (UNESCO), 7 Place de Fontenoy, F-75700 Paris, France (Telephone Number in U.S. (212) 963-5981); *Statistical Yearbook.*

U.S. Arms Control and Disarmament Agency, 320 Twenty-first Street, NW, Washington, D.C. 20451 (202) 647-8677; *World Military Expenditures and Arms Transfers.*

The World Bank, 1818 H Street, NW, Washington, D.C. 20433 (202) 477-1234; *The World Bank Atlas;* and *World Development Report.*

World Health Organization, Office of Publications, 20 Avenue Appia, CH-1211 Geneva 27, Switzerland (Telephone Number in U.S. (518) 436-9686); *World Health Statistics Annual.*

SOUTH AFRICA - POST OFFICES

M.E. Sharpe, 80 Business Park Drive, Armonk, New York 10504 (800) 541-6563; *The Illustrated Book of World Rankings.*

St. Martin's Press, Inc., 175 Fifth Avenue, New York, New York 10010 (800) 221-7945; *The Statesman's Year-Book.*

SOUTH AFRICA - POTATO PRODUCTION - See SOUTH AFRICA - CROPS

SOUTH AFRICA - POWER PRODUCTION INDUSTRY

Statistical Office of the United Nations, Publishing Service, New York, New York 10017 (800) 253-9646; *Statistical Yearbook.*

SOUTH AFRICA - PRICES

Food and Agricultural Organization of the United Nations (FAO), Via delle Terme di Caracalla, 00100 Rome, Italy (Telephone Number in U.S. (202) 653-2400); *Production Yearbook;* and *The State of Food and Agriculture.*

International Labour Office, I.L.O. Publications, 1828 L Street, NW,

Washington, D.C. 20036 (301) 638-3152; *Yearbook of Labour Statistics.*

International Lead and Zinc Study Group, Metro House, 58 St. James's Street, London SW1A 1LD, England; *Lead and Zinc Statistics.*

International Monetary Fund, 700 Nineteenth Street, NW, Washington, D.C. 20431 (202) 623-7000; *International Financial Statistics.*

M.E. Sharpe, 80 Business Park Drive, Armonk, New York 10504 (800) 541-6563; *The Illustrated Book of World Rankings.*

World Bureau of Metal Statistics, 27-A High Street, Ware Hert SG12 9BA, England; *World Metal Statistics.*

SOUTH AFRICA - PRINTING AND WRITING PAPER - See SOUTH AFRICA - FORESTRY AND FOREST PRODUCTS

SOUTH AFRICA - PRODUCTION

American Automobile Manufacturers Association, 1401 H Street, NW, Suite 900, Washington, D.C. 20005 (202) 326-5500; *World Motor Vehicle Data.*

International Iron and Steel Institute, 120, rue Colonel Bourg, B-1140, Brussels, Belgium; *Steel Statistical Yearbook.*

International Lead and Zinc Study Group, Metro House, 58 St. James's Street, London SW1A 1LD, England; *Lead and Zinc Statistics.*

M.E. Sharpe, 80 Business Park Drive, Armonk, New York 10504 (800) 541-6563; *The Illustrated Book of World Rankings.*

SOUTH AFRICA - PRODUCTIVITY

Euromonitor International, Inc., 122 South Michigan Avenue, Suite 1200, Chicago, Illinois 60603 (800) 577-EURO; *International Marketing Data and Statistics.*

SOUTH AFRICA - PROPERTY TAXES - See SOUTH AFRICA - TAXATION

SOUTH AFRICA - PUBLIC FINANCE - See SOUTH AFRICA - FINANCE

SOUTH AFRICA - RADIO BROADCASTING - See SOUTH AFRICA - BROADCASTING

SOUTH AFRICA - RADIO RECEIVER PRODUCTION

Statistical Office of the United Nations, Publishing Service, New York, New York 10017 (800) 253-9646; *Statistical Yearbook.*

SOUTH AFRICA - RADIO RECEIVERS

St. Martin's Press, Inc., 175 Fifth

Avenue, New York, New York 10010 (800) 221-7945; *The Statesman's Year-Book.*

SOUTH AFRICA - RAILWAYS

Europa Publications Limited, 18 Bedford Square, London, WC1B 3JN, England; *The Europa World Year Book.*

Jane's Information Group, Sentinel House, 163 Brighton Road, Coulsdon, Surrey CR5 2NH, England (Telephone Number in U.S. (703) 683-3700); *Jane's World Railways.*

St. Martin's Press, Inc., 175 Fifth Avenue, New York, New York 10010 (800) 221-7945; *The Statesman's Year-Book.*

Statistical Office of the United Nations, Publishing Service, New York, New York 10017 (800) 253-9646; *Statistical Yearbook.*

SOUTH AFRICA - RELIGION

Central Intelligence Agency, Washington, D.C. 20505 (703) 482-1100, www.cia.gov; *The World Factbook.*

M.E. Sharpe, 80 Business Park Drive, Armonk, New York 10504 (800) 541-6563; *The Illustrated Book of World Rankings.*

St. Martin's Press, Inc., 175 Fifth Avenue, New York, New York 10010 (800) 221-7945; *The Statesman's Year-Book.*

SOUTH AFRICA - RENT PRICES

International Labour Office, I.L.O. Publications, 1828 L Street, NW, Washington, D.C. 20036 (301) 638-3152; *Yearbook of Labour Statistics.*

SOUTH AFRICA - RETAIL TRADE

Euromonitor International, Inc., 122 South Michigan Avenue, Suite 1200, Chicago, Illinois 60603 (800) 577-EURO: *World Marketing Data and Statistics;* and *Retail Trade International.*

Statistical Office of the United Nations, Publishing Service, New York, New York 10017 (800) 253-9646; *Statistical Yearbook.*

SOUTH AFRICA - RICE PRODUCTION - See SOUTH AFRICA - CROPS

SOUTH AFRICA - ROUNDWOOD PRODUCTION - See SOUTH AFRICA - FORESTRY AND FOREST PRODUCTS

SOUTH AFRICA - RUBBER PRODUCTION AND CONSUMPTION

M.E. Sharpe, 80 Business Park Drive, Armonk, New York 10504 (800) 541-6563; *The Illustrated Book of World Rankings.*

Statistical Office of the United Nations,

Publishing Service, New York, New York 10017 (800) 253-9646; *Statistical Yearbook.*

SOUTH AFRICA - SALT PRODUCTION - See SOUTH AFRICA - MINING AND MINERAL PRODUCTS

SOUTH AFRICA - SAWNWOOD PRODUCTION - See SOUTH AFRICA - FORESTRY AND FOREST PRODUCTS

SOUTH AFRICA - SENIOR CITIZENS

M.E. Sharpe, 80 Business Park Drive, Armonk, New York 10504 (800) 541-6563; *The Illustrated Book of World Rankings.*

SOUTH AFRICA - SHEEP - See SOUTH AFRICA - LIVESTOCK AND POULTRY

SOUTH AFRICA - SILVER PRODUCTION AND CONSUMPTION - See SOUTH AFRICA - MINING AND MINERAL PRODUCTS

SOUTH AFRICA - SOCIAL DATA

M.E. Sharpe, 80 Business Park Drive, Armonk, New York 10504 (800) 541-6563; *The Illustrated Book of World Rankings.*

Statistical Office of the United Nations, Publishing Service, New York, New York 10017 (800) 253-9646; *World Statistics Pocketbook.*

SOUTH AFRICA - SOCIAL SECURITY

Statistical Office of the United Nations, Publishing Service, New York, New York 10017 (800) 253-9646; *National Accounts Statistics.*

SOUTH AFRICA - SOYBEAN PRODUCTION - See SOUTH AFRICA - CROPS

SOUTH AFRICA - STAMP TAXES AND DUTIES - See SOUTH AFRICA -TAXATION

SOUTH AFRICA - STATE BUDGET REVENUE AND EXPENDITURES

Euromonitor International, Inc., 122 South Michigan Avenue, Suite 1200, Chicago, Illinois 60603 (800) 577-EURO; *International Marketing Data and Statistics.*

SOUTH AFRICA - STEEL - See SOUTH AFRICA - MINING AND MINERAL PRODUCTS

SOUTH AFRICA - STOCKS - COMMODITY - MARKET PRICE - INDEXES

Food and Agricultural Organization of the United Nations (FAO) Via delle Terme di Caracalla, 00100 Rome, Italy (Telephone Number in U.S. (202) 653-2400); *The State of Food and Agriculture.*

International Lead and Zinc Study Group, Metro House, 58 St. James's Street, London SW1A 1LD, England; *Lead and Zinc Statistics.*

Statistical Office of the United Nations, Publishing Service, New York, New York 10017 (800) 253-9646; *Statistical Yearbook.*

World Bureau of Metal Statistics, 27-A High Street, Ware Hert SG12 9BA, England; *World Metal Statistics.*

SOUTH AFRICA - SUGAR - See SOUTH AFRICA - CROPS

SOUTH AFRICA - TAXATION

Europa Publications Limited, 18 Bedford Square, London, WC1B 3JN, England; *The Europa World Year Book.*

International Monetary Fund, 700 Nineteenth Street, NW, Washington, D.C. 20431 (202) 623-7000; *Government Finance Statistics Yearbook.*

International Road Federation, 2600 Virginia Avenue, NW, Washington, D.C. 20037 (202) 338-4641; *World Road Statistics.*

St. Martin's Press, Inc., 175 Fifth Avenue, New York, New York 10010 (800) 221-7945; *The Statesman's Year-Book.*

The World Bank, 1818 H Street, NW, Washington, D.C. 20433 (202) 477-1234; *World Development Indicators.*

SOUTH AFRICA - TEA PRODUCTION AND CONSUMPTION - See SOUTH AFRICA - CROPS

SOUTH AFRICA - TELEGRAPH SERVICE

Statistical Office of the United Nations, Publishing Service, New York, New York 10017 (800) 253-9646; *Statistical Yearbook.*

SOUTH AFRICA - TELEPHONES IN USE

American Telephone and Telegraph Company, 26 Parsippany Road, Whippany, New Jersey 07981 (800) 222-0300; *The World's Telephones.*

Central Intelligence Agency, Washington, D.C. 20505 (703) 482-1100, www.cia.gov; *The World Factbook.*

Europa Publications Limited, 18 Bedford Square, London, WC1B 3JN, England; *The Europa World Year Book.*

St. Martin's Press, Inc., 175 Fifth Avenue, New York, New York 10010 (800) 221-7945; *The Statesman's Year-Book.*

Statistical Office of the United Nations, Publishing Service, New York, New York

10017 (800) 253-9646; *Statistical Yearbook;* and *World Statistical Pocketbook.*

SOUTH AFRICA - TELEVISION BROADCASTING - See SOUTH AFRICA - BROADCASTING

SOUTH AFRICA - TEXTILE INDUSTRY

American Forest and Paper Association, 1111 Nineteenth Street, NW, Suite 800, Washington, D.C. 20036 (202) 463-2700; *Wood Pulp and Fiber Statistics.*

Commodity Research Bureau, Inc., 30 South Wacker Drive, Chicago Illinois 60606 (312) 454-1801; *Commodity Year Book.*

Euromonitor International, Inc., 122 South Michigan Avenue, Suite 1200, Chicago, Illinois 60603 (800) 577-EURO; *Retail Trade International.*

M.E. Sharpe, 80 Business Park Drive, Armonk, New York 10504 (800) 541-6563; *The Illustrated Book of World Rankings.*

St. Martin's Press, Inc., 175 Fifth Avenue, New York, New York 10010 (800) 221-7945; *The Statesman's Year-Book.*

Statistical Office of the United Nations, Publishing Service, New York, New York 10017 (800) 253-9646; *Statistical Yearbook.*

United Nations Conference on Trade and Development, Central Statistical Service, Palais des Nations, Geneva, Switzerland (Telephone in U.S. (800) 253-9646); *UNCTAD Commodity Yearbook.*

SOUTH AFRICA - TIN - See SOUTH AFRICA - MINING AND MINERAL PRODUCTS

SOUTH AFRICA - TIRE (MOTOR VEHICLE) PRODUCTION

Statistical Office of the United Nations, Publishing Service, New York, New York 10017 (800) 253-9646; *Statistical Yearbook.*

SOUTH AFRICA - TOBACCO PRODUCTION

M.E. Sharpe, 80 Business Park Drive, Armonk, New York 10504 (800) 541-6563; *The Illustrated Book of World Rankings.*

Statistical Office of the United Nations, Publishing Service, New York, New York 10017 (800) 253-9646; *Statistical Yearbook.*

SOUTH AFRICA - TOURISM

Euromonitor International, Inc., 122 South Michigan Avenue, Suite 1200, Chicago, Illinois 60603 (800) 577-EURO; *The World Economic Factbook;* and *World Marketing Data and Statistics.*

Europa Publications Limited, 18

Bedford Square, London, WC1B 3JN, England; *The Europa World Year Book.*

M.E. Sharpe, 80 Business Park Drive, Armonk, New York 10504 (800) 541-6563; *The Illustrated Book of World Rankings.*

St. Martin's Press, Inc., 175 Fifth Avenue, New York, New York 10010 (800) 221-7945; *The Statesman's Year-Book.*

Statistical Office of the United Nations, Publishing Service, New York, New York 10017 (800) 253-9646; *Statistical Yearbook.*

World Tourism Organization, Calle Capitan Haya 42, E-28020 Madrid, Spain; *Yearbook of Tourism Statistics.*

SOUTH AFRICA - TRACTORS IN USE

Statistical Office of the United Nations, Publishing Service, New York, New York 10017 (800) 253-9646; *Statistical Yearbook.*

SOUTH AFRICA - TRADE - See SOUTH AFRICA - FOREIGN TRADE

SOUTH AFRICA - TRADEMARKS AND SERVICE MARKS - See PATENTS, TRADEMARKS AND SERVICE MARKS

SOUTH AFRICA - TRANSPORTATION AND COMMUNICATIONS

Central Intelligence Agency, Washington, D.C. 20505 (703) 482-1100, www.cia.gov; *The World Factbook.*

Euromonitor International, Inc., 122 South Michigan Avenue, Suite 1200, Chicago, Illinois 60603 (800) 577-EURO; *International Marketing Data and Statistics;* and *World Marketing Data and Statistics.*

Europa Publications Limited, 18 Bedford Square, London, WC1B 3JN, England; *The Europa World Year Book.*

M.E. Sharpe, 80 Business Park Drive, Armonk, New York 10504 (800) 541-6563; *The Illustrated Book of World Rankings.*

St. Martin's Press, Inc., 175 Fifth Avenue, New York, New York 10010 (800) 221-7945; *The Statesman's Year-Book.*

Statistical Office of the United Nations, Publishing Service, New York, New York 10017 (800) 253-9646; *Human Development Report.*

SOUTH AFRICA - TUNGSTEN PRODUCTION AND CONSUMPTION - See SOUTH AFRICA - MINING AND MINERAL PRODUCTS

SOUTH AFRICA - UNEMPLOYMENT

Central Intelligence Agency,

Washington, D.C. 20505 (703) 482-1100, www.cia.gov; *The World Factbook.*

Euromonitor International, Inc., 122 South Michigan Avenue, Suite 1200, Chicago, Illinois 60603 (800) 577-EURO; *International Marketing Data and Statistics.*

International Labour Office, I.L.O. Publications, 1828 L Street, NW, Washington, D.C. 20036 (301) 638-3152; *Yearbook of Labour Statistics.*

St. Martin's Press, Inc., 175 Fifth Avenue, New York, New York 10010 (800) 221-7945; *The Statesman's Year-Book.*

Statistical Office of the United Nations, Publishing Service, New York, New York 10017 (800) 253-9646; *Statistical Yearbook.*

SOUTH AFRICA - URANIUM PRODUCTION AND CONSUMPTION - See SOUTH AFRICA - MINING AND MINERAL PRODUCTS

SOUTH AFRICA - VANADIUM AND VANADIUM ORE PRODUCTION AND CONSUMPTION - See SOUTH AFRICA - MINING AND MINERAL PRODUCTS

SOUTH AFRICA - VITAL STATISTICS

Euromonitor International, Inc., 122 South Michigan Avenue, Suite 1200, Chicago, Illinois 60603 (800) 577-EURO; *International Marketing Data and Statistics.*

St. Martin's Press, Inc., 175 Fifth Avenue, New York, New York 10010 (800) 221-7945; *The Statesman's Year-Book.*

World Health Organization, Office of Publications, 20 Avenue Appia, CH-1211 Geneva 27, Switzerland (Telephone Number in U.S. (518) 436-9686); *World Health Statistics Annual.*

SOUTH AFRICA - WAGES

International Labour Office, I.L.O. Publications, 1828 L Street, NW, Washington, D.C. 20036 (301) 638-3152; *Yearbook of Labour Statistics.*

Statistical Office of the United Nations, Publishing Service, New York, New York 10017 (800) 253-9646; *Statistical Yearbook.*

SOUTH AFRICA - WEATHER - See SOUTH AFRICA - CLIMATE

SOUTH AFRICA - WELFARE

St. Martin's Press, Inc., 175 Fifth Avenue, New York, New York 10010 (800) 221-7945; *The Statesman's Year-Book.*

SOUTH AFRICA - WHALES - See SOUTH AFRICA - FISHERIES

SOUTH AFRICA - WHEAT PRODUCTION AND PRICES - See SOUTH AFRICA - CROPS

SOUTH AFRICA - WHOLESALE PRICES

Statistical Office of the United Nations, Publishing Service, New York, New York 10017 (800) 253-9646; *Statistical Yearbook.*

SOUTH AFRICA - WHOLESALE TRADE

Statistical Office of the United Nations, Publishing Service, New York, New York 10017 (800) 253-9646; *Statistical Yearbook.*

SOUTH AFRICA - WINE PRODUCTION - See SOUTH AFRICA - BEVERAGES

SOUTH AFRICA - WOOD AND WOOD PULP - See SOUTH AFRICA - FORESTRY AND FOREST PRODUCTS

SOUTH AFRICA - WOOL PRODUCTION - See SOUTH AFRICA - TEXTILE INDUSTRY

SOUTH AFRICA - YARN PRODUCTION - See SOUTH AFRICA - TEXTILE INDUSTRY

SOUTH AFRICA - ZINC AND ZINC ORE PRODUCTION AND CONSUMPTION - See SOUTH AFRICA - MINING AND MINERAL PRODUCTS

SOUTH CAROLINA - See also STATE DATA (FOR INDIVIDUAL STATES)

South Carolina - Primary Statistics Source

Division of Research and Statistical Services, Budget and Control Board, R.C. Dennis Building, Room 425, Columbia, South Carolina 29201 (803) 734-3780; *South Carolina Statistical Abstract.*

South Carolina - State Data Centers

Office of Research and Statistics, South Carolina Budget and Control Board, Rembert Dennis Building, Room 425, 1000 Assembly Street, Columbia, South Carolina 29201, Mr. Bobby Bowers and Mr. Mike MacFarlane (803) 734-3780.

South Carolina State Library, Post Office Box 11469, Columbia, South Carolina 29211, Ms. Deborah Hotchkiss (803) 734-8026.

SOUTH DAKOTA - See also STATE DATA (FOR INDIVIDUAL STATES)

South Dakota - Primary Statistics Source

University of South Dakota, State Data

Center, Vermillion, South Dakota 57069 (605) 677-5287; *Selected Social and Economic Characteristics;* and *South Dakota Community Abstracts.*

South Dakota - State Data Centers

South Dakota State Data Center, Business Research Bureau, University of South Dakota, 414 East Clark Street, Vermillion, South Dakota 57069, Ms. Nancy Nelson, Director (605) 677-5287.

Labor Market Information Center, South Dakota Department of Labor, 420 South Roosevelt, Box 4730, Aberdeen, South Dakota 57402-4730, Mr. Phillip George (605) 622-2314.

South Dakota Department of Health, 600 East Capitol Avenue, Pierre, South Dakota 57501-2436, Mr. Jerry Hofer (605) 773-4958.

South Dakota State Library, 800 Governors Drive, Pierre, South Dakota 57501-2294, Ann Eichinger (605) 773-5241.

South Dakota State University, Rural Sociology Department, Post Office Box 504, Brookings, South Dakota 57006-0504, Marcey Moss (605) 688-4132.

SOYBEANS - ACREAGE

U.S. Department of Agriculture, National Agricultural Statistics Service, Fourteenth Street and Independence Avenue, SW, Washington, D.C. 20250 (800) 727-9540, www.usda.gov/nass; *Agricultural Statistics; Crop Production; Field Crops; Crop Values;* and *Agricultural Outlook.*

SOYBEANS - FARM MARKETINGS - SALES

U.S. Department of Agriculture, Economic Research Service, 1800 M Street, NW, Washington, D.C. 20036 (202) 694-5050, www.ers.usda.gov; *Farm Business Economic Report;* and *Agricultural Economic Report, No. 774..*

SOYBEANS - FOREIGN TRADE

U.S. Department of Agriculture, Economic Research Service, 1800 M Street, NW, Washington, D.C. 20036 (202) 694-5050, www.ers.usda.gov; *Agricultural Statistics; U.S. Agricultural Trade Update;* and *Foreign Agricultural Trade of the United States.*

U.S. Department of Agriculture, Foreign Agricultural Service, Fourteenth Street and Independence Avenue, SW, Washington, D.C. 20250 (202) 720-7115, www.fas.usda.gov; *Foreign Agricultural Commodity Circular Series.*

U.S. Department of Commerce, Bureau of the Census, Washington, D.C. 20233 (301) 457-4100, www.census.gov; *U.S. International Trade in Goods and Services.*

SOYBEANS - PRICES

U.S. Department of Agriculture, National Agricultural Statistics Service, Fourteenth Street and Independence Avenue, SW, Washington, D.C. 20250 (800) 727-9540, www.usda.gov/nass; *Agricultural Statistics; Crop Production; Field Crops; Crop Values;* and *Agricultural Outlook.*

SOYBEANS - PRODUCTION

U.S. Department of Agriculture, Economic Research Service, 1800 M Street, NW, Washington, D.C. 20036 (202) 694-5050, www.ers.usda.gov; *Agricultural Outlook.*

U.S. Department of Agriculture, National Agricultural Statistics Service, Fourteenth Street and Independence Avenue, SW, Washington, D.C. 20250 (800) 727-9540, www.usda.gov/nass; *Agricultural Outlook; Crop Production; Crop Values; Field Crops;* and *Agricultural Statistics.*

SOYBEANS - PRODUCTION - WORLD PRODUCTION

U.S. Department of Agriculture, Foreign Agricultural Service, Fourteenth Street and Independence Avenue, SW, Washington, D.C. 20250 (202) 720-7115, www.fas.usda.gov; *Foreign Agricultural Commodity Circular Series.*

SOYBEANS - SUPPLY AND DISAPPEARANCE

U.S. Department of Agriculture, Economic Research Service, 1800 M Street, NW, Washington, D.C. 20036 (202) 694-5050, www.ers.usda.gov; *Agricultural Statistics; Agricultural Outlook;* and *Agricultural Supply and Demand Estimates.*

SPACE EXPENDITURES - PRIVATE

U.S. Department of Commerce, International Trade Administration, 14th Street between Constitution Avenue and E Street, NW, Washington, D.C. 20230 (202) 482-2185, www.ita.doc.gov; *U.S. Industrial Outlook;* and unpublished data.

SPACE PROGRAM - FINANCES

U.S. Department of Commerce, Bureau of the Census, Washington, D.C. 20233 (301) 457-4100, www.census.gov; *Current Industrial Reports, Aerospace Industry (Orders, Sales, and Backlog);* and Internet site: http://www.census.gov/cir/www.

National Aeronautics and Space Administration, 300 E Street, SW,

Washington, D.C. 20546 (202) 358-1000, www.nasa.gov; *NASA Pocket Statistics;* and Internet site: http://ifmp.nasa.gov/codeb/budget/2000html/myb.htm.

SPACE PROGRAM - LAUNCHES

The Congress of the U.S., Congressional Research Service, 10 First Street, SE, Washington, D.C. 20540 (202) 707-5700; *Space Activities of the United States, CIS, and Other Launching Countries/Organizations.*

SPACE PROGRAM - NASA

National Aeronautics and Space Administration, 300 E Street, SW, Washington, D.C. 20546 (202) 358-1000, www.nasa.gov; Internet site: http://ifmp.nasa.gov/codeb/budget/2000html/myb.htm.

SPACE PROGRAM - SPACE SHUTTLE

National Aeronautics and Space Administration, 300 E Street, SW, Washington, D.C. 20546 (202) 358-1000, www.nasa.gov; *NASA Pocket Statistics;* and Internet site: http://www.ksc.nasa.gov/shuttle/missions/missions.html.

SPACE PROGRAM - VEHICLE SYSTEMS

U.S. Department of Commerce, Bureau of the Census, Washington, D.C. 20233 (301) 457-4100, www.census.gov; *Current Industrial Reports, Aerospace Industry (Orders, Sales and Backlog); U.S. International Trade in Goods and Services;* and Internet site: http://www.census.gov/cir/www.

SPACE RESEARCH AND TECHNOLOGY - FEDERAL OUTLAYS

Aerospace Industries Association of America, 1250 Eye Street, NW, Washington, D.C. 20005 (202) 371-8400; *Year End Review and Forecast;* and Internet site: http://www.aia-aerospace.org.

Executive Office of the President, Office of Management and Budget, Executive Office Building, Washington, D.C.20503 (202) 395-3080, www.whitehouse.gov/omb; *Historical Tables.*

National Aeronautics and Space Administration, 300 E Street, SW, Washington, D.C. 20546 (202) 358-1000, www.nasa.gov; *NASA Pocket Statistics;* and Internet site: http://ifmp.hasa.gov/codeb/budget/1000html/myb.htm.

U.S. Department of Commerce, Bureau of the Census, Washington, D.C. 20233 (301) 457-4100, www.census.gov.; *Current Industrial Reports; Aerospace Industry (Orders, Sales and Backlog);* and Internet site: http://www.census.gov/cir.www.

Spain - National Statistical Offices

Instituto Nacional de Estadistica, Ministerio de Economia y Hacienda, Paseo de la Castellana 183, Madrid 28046, Spain.

Ministerio de Economia y Hacienda, Direccion General de Aduanas, Seccion de Estadistica, San Francisco de Sales 6, Madrid 3, Spain.

Spain - Primary Statistics Sources

Instituto Nacional de Estadistica (National Institute of Statistics), Paseo de la Castellana 183, Madrid, Spain; *Anuario estadistico de Espana* (Statistical Yearbook of Spain); and *Boletin mensual de estadistics* (Monthly Bulletin of Statistics).

Spain - Databases

Base de Datos de Entidades de Poblacion, Instituto Geografico Nacional, Calle General Ibanez de Ibero 3, 28003 Madrid, Spain. Subject coverage: Spanish geographic and population data.

ESTACOM, Instituto Espanol de Comercio Exterior-ICEX, Paseo de la Castellana, 14, 28046 Madrid, Spain. Subject coverage: Monthly and annual time series on Spanish import and export activity, including balances of trade figures for trading partners and regions.

SPAIN - ABORTIONS

European Commission Office of Press and Public Affairs, 2100 M Street, NW, Washington, D.C. 20037 (202) 862-9500; *Demographic Statistics.*

Statistical Office of the United Nations, Publishing Service, New York, New York 10017 (800) 253-9646; *Trends in Europe and North America: The Statistical Yearbook of the Economic Commission for Europe.*

SPAIN - AGRICULTURE

Economist Intelligence Unit, 111 West 57th Street, New York, New York 10019 (800) 938-4685; *Spain Country Report.*

Euromonitor International, Inc., 122 South Michigan Avenue, Suite 1200, Chicago, Illinois 60603 (800) 577-EURO: *World Marketing Data and Statistics.*

Europa Publications Limited, 18 Bedford Square, London, WC1B 3JN, England; *The Europa World Year Book.*

European Commission Office of Press and Public Affairs, 2100 M Street, NW,

Washington, D.C. 20037 (202) 862-9500; *Agriculture: Statistical Yearbook; Basic Statistics of the Community; Eurostatistics: Data for Short-Term Economic Analysis;* and *Regions: Statistical Yearbook.*

Federal Statistical Office, Gustav-Stresemann-Ring 11, D-6200 Wiesbaden, Germany; *Spain.*

Food and Agricultural Organization of the United Nations (FAO) Via delle Terme di Caracalla, 00100 Rome, Italy (Telephone Number in U.S. (202) 653-2400); *Production Yearbook; The State of Food and Agriculture;* and *Trade Yearbook.*

M.E. Sharpe, 80 Business Park Drive, Armonk, New York 10504 (800) 541-6563; *The Illustrated Book of World Rankings.*

Organisation for Economic Co-operation and Development (OECD), 2 rue Andre-Pascal, 75 Paris 16, France (Telephone Number in U.S. (202) 785-6323); *Economic Accounts for Agriculture; Indicators of Industrial Activity; Industrial Structure Statistics;* and *OECD Economic Surveys: Spain.*

St. Martin's Press, Inc., 175 Fifth Avenue, New York, New York 10010 (800) 221-7945; *The Statesman's Year-Book.*

Statistical Office of the United Nations, Publishing Service, New York, New York 10017 (800) 253-9646; *Statistical Yearbook.*

United Nations Conference on Trade and Development, Central Statistical Service, Palais des Nations, Geneva, Switzerland (Telephone in U.S. (800) 253-9646); *UNCTAD Commodity Yearbook.*

The World Bank, 1818 H Street, NW, Washington, D.C. 20433 (202) 477-1234; *World Development Indicators.*

SPAIN - AIRLINE SERVICE

Europa Publications Limited, 18 Bedford Square, London, WC1B 3JN, England; *The Europa World Year Book.*

European Commission Office of Press and Public Affairs, 2100 M Street, NW, Washington, D.C. 20037 (202) 862-9500; *Basic Statistics of the Community; Regions: Statistical Yearbook;* and *Transport Annual Statistics.*

International Civil Aviation Organization, 999 University Street, Montreal, Quebec, Canada H3C 5H7 (514) 954-8219; *Civil Aviation Statistics of the World.*

M.E. Sharpe, 80 Business Park Drive, Armonk, New York 10504 (800) 541-6563; *The Illustrated Book of World Rankings.*

Organisation for Economic Co-operation and Development (OECD), 2 rue Andre-Pascal, 75 Paris 16, France (Telephone Number in U.S. (202) 785-6323); *Tourism Policy and International Tourism in OECD Member Countries.*

St. Martin's Press, Inc., 175 Fifth Avenue, New York, New York 10010 (800) 221-7945; *The Statesman's Year-Book.*

Statistical Office of the United Nations, Publishing Service, New York, New York 10017 (800) 253-9646; *Statistical Yearbook.*

SPAIN - AIRPORTS

Central Intelligence Agency, Washington, D.C. 20505 (703) 482-1100, www.cia.gov; *The World Factbook.*

SPAIN - ALUMINUM PRODUCTION AND CONSUMPTION - See SPAIN - MINING AND MINERAL PRODUCTS

SPAIN - ANIMAL FEEDINGSTUFFS

Organisation for Economic Co-operation and Development (OECD), 2 rue Andre-Pascal, 75 Paris 16, France (Telephone Number in U.S. (202) 785-6323); *Foreign Trade by Commodities.*

Statistical Office of the United Nations, Publishing Service, New York, New York 10017 (800) 253-9646; *Statistical Yearbook.*

SPAIN - ANIMAL HEALTH

Food and Agricultural Organization of the United Nations (FAO), Via delle Terme di Caracalla, 00100, Rome, Italy (Telephone Number in U.S. (202) 653-2400); *Animal Health Yearbook.*

SPAIN - ANTIMONY AND ANTIMONY ORE PRODUCTION AND CONSUMPTION - See SPAIN - MINING AND MINERAL PRODUCTS

SPAIN - APPLES PRODUCTION - See SPAIN - CROPS

SPAIN - AREA AND DENSITY OF POPULATION

Central Intelligence Agency, Washington, D.C. 20505 (703) 482-1100, www.cia.gov; *The World Factbook.*

Europa Publications Limited, 18 Bedford Square, London, WC1B 3JN, England; *The Europa World Year Book.*

European Commission Office of Press and Public Affairs, 2100 M Street, NW, Washington, D.C. 20037 (202) 862-9500; *Basic Statistics of the Community; Demographic Statistics;* and *The World Economic Factbook.*

Federal Statistical Office,

Gustav-Stresemann-Ring 11, D-6200 Wiesbaden, Germany; *Spain.*

Food and Agricultural Organization of the United Nations (FAO) Via delle Terme di Caracalla, 00100 Rome, Italy (Telephone Number in U.S. (202) 653-2400); *The State of Food and Agriculture.*

M.E. Sharpe, 80 Business Park Drive, Armonk, New York 10504 (800) 541-6563; *The Illustrated Book of World Rankings.*

St. Martin's Press, Inc., 175 Fifth Avenue, New York, New York 10010 (800) 221-7945; *The Statesman's Year-Book.*

Statistical Office of the United Nations, Publishing Service, New York, New York 10017 (800) 253-9646; *Statistical Yearbook;* and *Trends in Europe and North America: The Statistical Yearbook of the Economic Commission for Europe.*

United Nations Educational, Scientific and Cultural Organization (UNESCO), 7 Place de Fontenoy, F-75700 Paris, France (Telephone Number in U.S. (212) 963-5981); *Statistical Yearbook.*

The World Bank, 1818 H Street, NW, Washington, D.C. 20433 (202) 477-1234; *World Development Report.*

SPAIN - ARMS EXPORTS AND IMPORTS - See SPAIN - MILITARY

SPAIN - ARSENIC PRODUCTION AND CONSUMPTION - See SPAIN - MINING AND MINERAL PRODUCTS

SPAIN - BALANCE OF PAYMENTS

The Economist Intelligence Unit, 111 West 57th Street, New York, New York 10019 (800) 938-4685; *The World Market Atlas.*

Europa Publications Limited, 18 Bedford Square, London, WC1B 3JN, England; *The Europa World Year Book.*

European Commission Office of Press and Public Affairs, 2100 M Street, NW, Washington, D.C. 20037 (202) 862-9500; *ACP: Basic Statistics; Basic Statistics of the Community; Energy Statistics Yearbook;* and *Eurostatistics: Data for Short-Term Economic Analysis.*

Federal Statistical Office, Gustav-Stresemann-Ring 11, D-6200 Wiesbaden, Germany; *Spain.*

International Monetary Fund, 700 Nineteenth Street, NW, Washington, D.C. 20431 (202) 623-7000; *Balance of Payments Yearbook;* and *International Financial Statistics.*

Organisation for Economic Co-

operation and Development (OECD), 2 rue Andre-Pascal, 75 Paris 16, France (Telephone Number in U.S. (202) 785-6323); *Economic Outlook; Geographical Distribution of Financial Flows to Developing Countries; Main Economic Indicators - Historical Statistics;* and *OECD Economic Surveys: Spain.*

United Nations Conference on Trade and Development (UNCTAD), New York, New York 10017 (800) 253-9646; *Handbook of International Trade and Development Statistics.*

The World Bank, 1818 H Street, NW, Washington, D.C. 20433 (202) 477-1234; *World Development Report;* and *World Development Indicators.*

SPAIN - BANKING

Euromonitor International, Inc., 122 South Michigan Avenue, Suite 1200, Chicago, Illinois 60603 (800) 577-EURO: *World Marketing Data and Statistics.*

Europa Publications Limited, 18 Bedford Square, London, WC1B 3JN, England; *The Europa World Year Book.*

European Commission Office of Press and Public Affairs, 2100 M Street, NW, Washington, D.C. 20037 (202) 862-9500; *ACP: Basic Statistics;* and *Eurostatistics: Data for Short-Term Economic Analysis.*

International Monetary Fund, 700 Nineteenth Street, NW, Washington, D.C. 20431 (202) 623-7000; *International Financial Statistics.*

M.E. Sharpe, 80 Business Park Drive, Armonk, New York 10504 (800) 541-6563; *The Illustrated Book of World Rankings.*

Organisation for Economic Co-operation and Development (OECD), 2 rue Andre-Pascal, 75 Paris 16, France (Telephone Number in U.S. (202) 785-6323); *Economic Outlook; Financial Market Trends;* and *OECD Economic Surveys: Spain.*

St. Martin's Press, Inc., 175 Fifth Avenue, New York, New York 10010 (800) 221-7945; *The Statesman's Year-Book.*

Statistical Office of the United Nations, Publishing Service, New York, New York 10017 (800) 253-9646; *Statistical Yearbook.*

SPAIN - BARLEY PRODUCTION - See SPAIN - CROPS

SPAIN - BAUXITE PRODUCTION AND CONSUMPTION - See SPAIN -MINING AND MINERAL PRODUCTS

SPAIN - BEER PRODUCTION - See SPAIN - BEVERAGES

SPAIN - BEVERAGES

European Commission Office of Press and Public Affairs, 2100 M Street, NW, Washington, D.C. 20037 (202) 862-9500; *Basic Statistics of the Community.*

M.E. Sharpe, 80 Business Park Drive, Armonk, New York 10504 (800) 541-6563; *The Illustrated Book of World Rankings.*

Organisation for Economic Co-operation and Development (OECD), 2 rue Andre-Pascal, 75 Paris 16, France (Telephone Number in U.S. (202) 785-6323); *Indicators of Industrial Activity.*

Statistical Office of the United Nations, Publishing Service, New York, New York 10017 (800) 253-9646; *Statistical Yearbook.*

SPAIN - BIRTH RATES

Central Intelligence Agency, Washington, D.C. 20505 (703) 482-1100, www.cia.gov; *The World Factbook.*

Europa Publications Limited, 18 Bedford Square, London, WC1B 3JN, England; *The Europa World Year Book.*

European Commission Office of Press and Public Affairs, 2100 M Street, NW, Washington, D.C. 20037 (202) 862-9500; *Basic Statistics of the Community; Demographic Statistics;* and *The World Economic Factbook.*

M.E. Sharpe, 80 Business Park Drive, Armonk, New York 10504 (800) 541-6563; *The Illustrated Book of World Rankings.*

St. Martin's Press, Inc., 175 Fifth Avenue, New York, New York 10010 (800) 221-7945; *The Statesman's Year-Book.*

Statistical Office of the United Nations, Publishing Service, New York, New York 10017 (800) 253-9646; *Demographic Yearbook;* and *Statistical Yearbook.*

The World Bank, 1818 H Street, NW, Washington, D.C. 20433 (202) 477-1234; *World Development Indicators.*

World Health Organization, Office of Publications, 20 Avenue Appia, CH-1211 Geneva 27, Switzerland (Telephone Number in U.S. (518) 436-9686); *World Health Statistics Annual.*

SPAIN - BISMUTH PRODUCTION AND CONSUMPTION - See SPAIN - MINING AND MINERAL PRODUCTS

SPAIN - BONDS

European Commission Office of Press and Public Affairs, 2100 M Street, NW, Washington, D.C. 20037 (202) 862-9500; *Basic Statistics of the Community.*

Organisation for Economic Co-operation and Development (OECD), 2 rue Andre-Pascal, 75 Paris 16, France (Telephone Number in U.S. (202) 785-6323); *Financial Market Trends.*

SPAIN - BOOK PRODUCTION

Euromonitor International, Inc., 122 South Michigan Avenue, Suite 1200, Chicago, Illinois 60603 (800) 577-EURO; *European Marketing Data and Statistics.*

Europa Publications Limited, 18 Bedford Square, London, WC1B 3JN, England; *The Europa World Year Book.*

Organisation for Economic Co-operation and Development (OECD), 2 rue Andre-Pascal, 75 Paris 16, France (Telephone Number in U.S. (202) 785-6323); *Indicators of Industrial Activity.*

St. Martin's Press, Inc., 175 Fifth Avenue, New York, New York 10010 (800) 221-7945; *The Statesman's Year-Book.*

Statistical Office of the United Nations, Publishing Service, New York, New York 10017 (800) 253-9646; *Trends in Europe and North America: The Statistical Yearbook of the Economic Commission for Europe.*

United Nations Educational, Scientific and Cultural Organization (UNESCO), 7 Place de Fontenoy, F-75700 Paris, France (Telephone Number in U.S. (212) 963-5981); *Statistical Yearbook.*

SPAIN - BROADCASTING

Billboard Limited, P.O. Box 9027, 1006 AA Amsterdam, The Netherlands (Telephone Number in U.S. (212) 764-7300); *World Radio TV Handbook.*

Central Intelligence Agency, Washington, D.C. 20505 (703) 482-1100, www.cia.gov; *The World Factbook.*

Euromonitor International, Inc., 122 South Michigan Avenue, Suite 1200, Chicago, Illinois 60603 (800) 577-EURO: *World Marketing Data and Statistics.*

European Commission Office of Press and Public Affairs, 2100 M Street, NW, Washington, D.C. 20037 (202) 862-9500; *Basic Statistics of the Community.*

M.E. Sharpe, 80 Business Park Drive, Armonk, New York 10504 (800) 541-6563; *The Illustrated Book of World Rankings.*

St. Martin's Press, Inc., 175 Fifth Avenue, New York, New York 10010 (800) 221-7945; *The Statesman's Year-Book.*

Statistical Office of the United Nations, Publishing Service, New York, New York 10017 (800) 253-9646; *Trends in Europe and*

North America: The Statistical Yearbook of the Economic Commission for Europe.

United Nations Educational, Scientific and Cultural Organization (UNESCO), 7 Place de Fontenoy, F-75700 Paris, France (Telephone Number in U.S. (212) 963-5981); *Statistical Yearbook.*

SPAIN - BUDGET

Central Intelligence Agency, Washington, D.C. 20505 (703) 482-1100, www.cia.gov; *The World Factbook.*

SPAIN - BUSINESS

European Commission Office of Press and Public Affairs, 2100 M Street, NW, Washington, D.C. 20037 (202) 862-9500; *Basic Statistics of the Community.*

Organisation for Economic Co-operation and Development (OECD), 2 rue Andre-Pascal, 75 Paris 16, France (Telephone Number in U.S. (202) 785-6323); *Main Economic Indicators - Historical Statistics.*

SPAIN - BUSINESS AND PROFESSIONAL LICENSES

International Monetary Fund, 700 Nineteenth Street, NW, Washington, D.C. 20431 (202) 623-7000; *Government Finance Statistics Yearbook.*

SPAIN - BUTTER - See SPAIN - DAIRY PRODUCTS

SPAIN - CADMIUM PRODUCTION AND CONSUMPTION - See SPAIN - MINING AND MINERAL PRODUCTS

SPAIN - CALORIE SUPPLY

Food and Agricultural Organization of the United Nations (FAO) Via delle Terme di Caracalla, 00100 Rome, Italy (Telephone Number in U.S. (202) 653-2400); *The State of Food and Agriculture.*

SPAIN - CAPITAL INVESTMENT

Organisation for Economic Co-operation and Development (OECD), 2 rue Andre-Pascal, 75 Paris 16, France (Telephone Number in U.S. (202) 785-6323); *Economic Outlook;* and *Financial Market Trends.*

SPAIN - CAPITAL REVENUE

International Monetary Fund, 700 Nineteenth Street, NW, Washington, D.C. 20431 (202) 623-7000; *Government Finance Statistics Yearbook.*

Organisation for Economic Co-operation and Development (OECD), 2 rue Andre-Pascal, 75 Paris 16, France

(Telephone Number in U.S. (202) 785-6323); *Economic Outlook;* and *Financial Market Trends.*

SPAIN - CATTLE - See SPAIN - LIVESTOCK AND POULTRY

SPAIN - CAUSTIC SODA PRODUCTION - See SPAIN - BEVERAGES

SPAIN - CEMENT PRODUCTION - See SPAIN - MINING AND MINERAL PRODUCTS

SPAIN - CEREAL PRODUCTION - See SPAIN - CROPS

SPAIN - CHEESE - See SPAIN - DAIRY PRODUCTS

SPAIN - CHEMICAL INDUSTRY

European Commission Office of Press and Public Affairs, 2100 M Street, NW, Washington, D.C. 20037 (202) 862-9500; *Industrial Production: Quarterly Statistics.*

SPAIN - CHEMICAL (ORGANIC) PRODUCTION - See SPAIN - MINING AND MINERAL PRODUCTS

SPAIN - CHROMITE PRODUCTION AND CONSUMPTION - See SPAIN - MINING AND MINERAL PRODUCTS

SPAIN - CHROMIUM ORE PRODUCTION AND CONSUMPTION - See SPAIN - MINING AND MINERAL PRODUCTS

SPAIN - CIGAR AND CIGARETTE PRODUCTION - See SPAIN - TOBACCO PRODUCTION

SPAIN - CLASS STRUCTURE

European Commission Office of Press and Public Affairs, 2100 M Street, NW, Washington, D.C. 20037 (202) 862-9500; *Basic Statistics of the Community;* and *Labor Force Sample Survey.*

SPAIN - CLIMATE

M.E. Sharpe, 80 Business Park Drive, Armonk, New York 10504 (800) 541-6563; *The Illustrated Book of World Rankings.*

St. Martin's Press, Inc., 175 Fifth Avenue, New York, New York 10010 (800) 221-7945; *The Statesman's Year-Book.*

SPAIN - CLOTHING - PRODUCTION INDEX - See SPAIN - TEXTILE INDUSTRY

SPAIN - CLOTHING EXPORTS AND IMPORTS - See SPAIN - TEXTILE INDUSTRY

SPAIN - COAL PRODUCTION - See SPAIN - MINING AND MINERAL PRODUCTS

SPAIN - COBALT PRODUCTION AND CONSUMPTION - See SPAIN - MINING AND

MINERAL PRODUCTS

SPAIN - COFFEE - See SPAIN - CROPS

SPAIN - COKE AND COKE OVEN ORE PRODUCTION AND CONSUMPTION - See SPAIN - MINING AND MINERAL PRODUCTS

SPAIN - COMMERCE

St. Martin's Press, Inc., 175 Fifth Avenue, New York, New York 10010 (800) 221-7945; *The Statesman's Year-Book.*

SPAIN - COMMUNICATIONS - See SPAIN - TRANSPORTATION AND COMMUNICATIONS

SPAIN - CONSTRUCTION INDUSTRY

European Commission Office of Press and Public Affairs, 2100 M Street, NW, Washington, D.C. 20037 (202) 862-9500; *Basic Statistics of the Community;* and *Labor Force Sample Survey.*

M.E. Sharpe, 80 Business Park Drive, Armonk, New York 10504 (800) 541-6563; *The Illustrated Book of World Rankings.*

Organisation for Economic Co-operation and Development (OECD), 2 rue Andre-Pascal, 75 Paris 16, France (Telephone Number in U.S. (202) 785-6323); *Industrial Structure Statistics; The Iron and Steel Industry; Main Economic Indicators - Historical Statistics;* and *OECD Economic Surveys: Spain.*

St. Martin's Press, Inc., 175 Fifth Avenue, New York, New York 10010 (800) 221-7945; *The Statesman's Year-Book.*

Statistical Office of the United Nations, Publishing Service, New York, New York 10017 (800) 253-9646; *Statistical Yearbook.*

SPAIN - CONSUMER PRICE INDEX

Europa Publications Limited, 18 Bedford Square, London, WC1B 3JN, England; *The Europa World Year Book.*

European Commission Office of Press and Public Affairs, 2100 M Street, NW, Washington, D.C. 20037 (202) 862-9500; *Basic Statistics of the Community;* and *Eurostatistics: Data for Short-Term Economic Analysis.*

Organisation for Economic Co-operation and Development (OECD), 2 rue Andre-Pascal, 75 Paris 16, France (Telephone Number in U.S. (202) 785-6323); *Economic Outlook.*

Statistical Office of the United Nations, Publishing Service, New York, New York 10017 (800) 253-9646; *Statistical Yearbook;* and *Trends in Europe and North America: The Statistical Yearbook of the Economic Commission for Europe.*

SPAIN - CONSUMER PRICES

Euromonitor International, Inc., 122 South Michigan Avenue, Suite 1200, Chicago, Illinois 60603 (800) 577-EURO; *European Marketing Data and Statistics;* and *World Marketing Data and Statistics.*

European Commission Office of Press and Public Affairs, 2100 M Street, NW, Washington, D.C. 20037 (202) 862-9500; *Basic Statistics of the Community; Eurostatistics: Data for Short-Term Economic Analysis;* and *Money and Finance.*

International Labour Office, I.L.O. Publications, 1828 L Street, NW, Washington, D.C. 20036 (301) 638-3152; *Yearbook of Labour Statistics.*

International Monetary Fund, 700 Nineteenth Street, NW, Washington, D.C. 20431 (202) 623-7000; *International Financial Statistics.*

Organisation for Economic Co-operation and Development (OECD), 2 rue Andre-Pascal, 75 Paris 16, France (Telephone Number in U.S. (202) 785-6323); *Economic Outlook.*

SPAIN - CONSUMPTION

European Commission Office of Press and Public Affairs, 2100 M Street, NW, Washington, D.C. 20037 (202) 862-9500; *Basic Statistics of the Community.*

International Iron and Steel Institute, 120, rue Colonel Bourg, B-1140, Brussels, Belgium; *Steel Statistical Yearbook.*

International Lead and Zinc Study Group, Metro House, 58 St. James's Street, London SW1A 1LD, England; *Lead and Zinc Statistics.*

Organisation for Economic Co-operation and Development (OECD), 2 rue Andre-Pascal, 75 Paris 16, France (Telephone Number in U.S. (202) 785-6323); *The Footwear, Raw Hides and Skins, and Leather Industry in OECD Countries; The Iron and Steel Industry; Meat Balances in OECD Member Countries; The Non-Ferrous Metals Industry; The Pulp and Paper Industry;* and *Textile Industry in OECD Countries.*

The World Bank, 1818 H Street, NW, Washington, D.C. 20433 (202) 477-1234; *World Development Report.*

SPAIN - COPPER AND COPPER ORE PRODUCTION AND CONSUMPTION - See SPAIN - MINING AND MINERAL PRODUCTS

SPAIN - CORN PRODUCTION - See

SPAIN - CROPS

SPAIN - CORPORATE INCOME TAXES - See SPAIN - TAXATION

SPAIN - CORPORATE TAXES - See SPAIN - TAXATION

SPAIN - COTTON - See SPAIN - CROPS

SPAIN - CRIME

International Criminal Police Organization (INTERPOL), 50 quai Achille Lignon, F-69006 Lyon, France; *International Crime Statistics.*

Statistical Office of the United Nations, Publishing Service, New York, New York 10017 (800) 253-9646; *Trends in Europe and North America: The Statistical Yearbook of the Economic Commission for Europe.*

SPAIN - CROPS

Commodity Research Bureau, Inc., 30 South Wacker Drive, Chicago Illinois 60606 (312) 454-1801; *Commodity Year Book.*

Euromonitor International, Inc., 122 South Michigan Avenue, Suite 1200, Chicago, Illinois 60603 (800) 577-EURO; *European Marketing Data and Statistics.*

Europa Publications Limited, 18 Bedford Square, London, WC1B 3JN, England; *The Europa World Year Book.*

European Commission Office of Press and Public Affairs, 2100 M Street, NW, Washington, D.C. 20037 (202) 862-9500; *ACP: Basic Statistics; Agriculture: Statistical Yearbook; Basic Statistics of the Community; Crop Production: Quarterly Statistics; Eurostatistics: Data for Short-Term Economic Analysis;* and *Regions: Statistical Yearbook.*

Food and Agricultural Organization of the United Nations (FAO) Via delle Terme di Caracalla, 00100 Rome, Italy (Telephone Number in U.S. (202) 653-2400); *The State of Food and Agriculture.*

M.E. Sharpe, 80 Business Park Drive, Armonk, New York 10504 (800) 541-6563; *The Illustrated Book of World Rankings.*

Organisation for Economic Co-operation and Development (OECD), 2 rue Andre-Pascal, 75 Paris 16, France (Telephone Number in U.S. (202) 785-6323); *Economic Accounts for Agriculture; Foreign Trade by Commodities;* and *Textile Industry in OECD Countries.*

St. Martin's Press, Inc., 175 Fifth Avenue, New York, New York 10010 (800) 221-7945; *The Statesman's Year-Book.*

Statistical Office of the United Nations,

Publishing Service, New York, New York 10017 (800) 253-9646; *Statistical Yearbook.*

United Nations Conference on Trade and Development, Central Statistical Service, Palais des Nations, Geneva, Switzerland (Telephone in U.S. (800) 253-9646); *UNCTAD Commodity Yearbook.*

SPAIN - CUSTOMS DUTIES

European Commission Office of Press and Public Affairs, 2100 M Street, NW, Washington, D.C. 20037 (202) 862-9500; *Basic Statistics of the Community.*

Organisation for Economic Co-operation and Development (OECD), 2 rue Andre-Pascal, 75 Paris 16, France (Telephone Number in U.S. (202) 785-6323); *The Non-Ferrous Metals Industry.*

St. Martin's Press, Inc., 175 Fifth Avenue, New York, New York 10010 (800) 221-7945; *The Statesman's Year-Book.*

SPAIN - DAIRY PRODUCTS

Commodity Research Bureau, Inc., 30 South Wacker Drive, Chicago Illinois 60606 (312) 454-1801; *Commodity Year Book.*

Europa Publications Limited, 18 Bedford Square, London, WC1B 3JN, England; *The Europa World Year Book.*

European Commission Office of Press and Public Affairs, 2100 M Street, NW, Washington, D.C. 20037 (202) 862-9500; *Eurostatistics: Data for Short-Term Economic Analysis.*

Food and Agricultural Organization of the United Nations (FAO) Via delle Terme di Caracalla, 00100 Rome, Italy (Telephone Number in U.S. (202) 653-2400); *The State of Food and Agriculture.*

M.E. Sharpe, 80 Business Park Drive, Armonk, New York 10504 (800) 541-6563; *The Illustrated Book of World Rankings.*

Organisation for Economic Co-operation and Development (OECD), 2 rue Andre-Pascal, 75 Paris 16, France (Telephone Number in U.S. (202) 785-6323); *Economic Accounts for Agriculture;* and *Milk, Milk Products, and Egg Balances in OECD Member Countries.*

St. Martin's Press, Inc., 175 Fifth Avenue, New York, New York 10010 (800) 221-7945; *The Statesman's Year-Book.*

Statistical Office of the United Nations, Publishing Service, New York, New York 10017 (800) 253-9646; *Statistical Yearbook.*

SPAIN - DEATH RATES - See SPAIN - MORTALITY

SPAIN - DEFENSE EXPENDITURES - See SPAIN - MILITARY

SPAIN - DEMOGRAPHY

The Economist Intelligence Unit, 111 West 57th Street, New York, New York 10019 (800) 938-4685; *The World Market Atlas.*

Euromonitor International, Inc., 122 South Michigan Avenue, Suite 1200, Chicago, Illinois 60603 (800) 577-EURO: *World Marketing Data and Statistics.*

European Commission Office of Press and Public Affairs, 2100 M Street, NW, Washington, D.C. 20037 (202) 862-9500; *Basic Statistics of the Community; Demographic Statistics; Employment and Unemployment; Regions: Statistical Yearbook;* and *The World Economic Factbook.*

M.E. Sharpe, 80 Business Park Drive, Armonk, New York 10504 (800) 541-6563; *The Illustrated Book of World Rankings.*

Statistical Office of the United Nations, Publishing Service, New York, New York 10017 (800) 253-9646; *Human Development Report.*

SPAIN - DEVELOPMENT ASSISTANCE

European Commission Office of Press and Public Affairs, 2100 M Street, NW, Washington, D.C. 20037 (202) 862-9500; *ACP: Basic Statistics; Basic Statistics of the Community;* and *Government Financing of Research and Development.*

Organisation for Economic Co-operation and Development (OECD), 2 rue Andre-Pascal, 75 Paris 16, France (Telephone Number in U.S. (202) 785-6323); *Geographical Distribution of Financial Flows to Developing Countries.*

SPAIN - DIAMOND PRODUCTION - See SPAIN - MINING AND MINERAL PRODUCTS

SPAIN - DISCOUNT RATES - See SPAIN - BANKING

SPAIN - DISEASES - See SPAIN - HEALTH

SPAIN - DIVORCE RATES

European Commission Office of Press and Public Affairs, 2100 M Street, NW, Washington, D.C. 20037 (202) 862-9500; *Demographic Statistics.*

M.E. Sharpe, 80 Business Park Drive, Armonk, New York 10504 (800) 541-6563; *The Illustrated Book of World Rankings.*

Statistical Office of the United Nations, Publishing Service, New York, New York 10017 (800) 253-9646; *Demographic*

Yearbook; and *Trends in Europe and North America: The Statistical Yearbook of the Economic Commission for Europe.*

SPAIN - DOMESTIC PRODUCT

European Commission Office of Press and Public Affairs, 2100 M Street, NW, Washington, D.C. 20037 (202) 862-9500; *Basic Statistics of the Community.*

SPAIN - ECONOMY

Central Intelligence Agency, Washington, D.C. 20505 (703) 482-1100, www.cia.gov; *The World Factbook.*

Economist Intelligence Unit, 111 West 57th Street, New York, New York 10019 (800) 938-4685; *Spain Country Report.*

Euromonitor International, Inc., 122 South Michigan Avenue, Suite 1200, Chicago, Illinois 60603 (800) 577-EURO; *European Marketing Data and Statistics; The World Economic Factbook;* and *World Marketing Data and Statistics.*

Europa Publications Limited, 18 Bedford Square, London, WC1B 3JN, England; *The Europa World Year Book.*

European Commission Office of Press and Public Affairs, 2100 M Street, NW, Washington, D.C. 20037 (202) 862-9500; *ACP: Basic Statistics; Basic Statistics of the Community; Energy Statistics Yearbook; Labor Force Sample Survey;* and *Money and Finance.*

M.E. Sharpe, 80 Business Park Drive, Armonk, New York 10504 (800) 541-6563; *The Illustrated Book of World Rankings.*

Organisation for Economic Co-operation and Development (OECD), 2 rue Andre-Pascal, 75 Paris 16, France (Telephone Number in U.S. (202) 785-6323); *Economic Outlook; Geographical Distribution of Financial Flows to Developing Countries; Main Economic Indicators - Historical Statistics; OECD Economic Surveys: Spain;* and *OECD Employment Outlook.*

St. Martin's Press, Inc., 175 Fifth Avenue, New York, New York 10010 (800) 221-7945; *The Statesman's Year-Book.*

Statistical Office of the United Nations, Publishing Service, New York, New York 10017 (800) 253-9646; *World Statistics Pocketbook.*

The World Bank, 1818 H Street, NW, Washington, D.C. 20433 (202) 477-1234; *The World Bank Atlas;* and *World Development Report.*

SPAIN - EDUCATION

The Economist Intelligence Unit, 111 West 57th Street, New York, New York 10019 (800) 938-4685; *The World Market Atlas.*

Euromonitor International, Inc., 122 South Michigan Avenue, Suite 1200, Chicago, Illinois 60603 (800) 577-EURO; *European Marketing Data and Statistics;* and *World Marketing Data and Statistics.*

Europa Publications Limited, 18 Bedford Square, London, WC1B 3JN, England; *The Europa World Year Book.*

European Commission Office of Press and Public Affairs, 2100 M Street, NW, Washington, D.C. 20037 (202) 862-9500; *Basic Statistics of the Community;* and *Regions: Statistical Yearbook.*

Federal Statistical Office, Gustav-Stresemann-Ring 11, D-6200 Wiesbaden, Germany; *Spain.*

International Monetary Fund, 700 Nineteenth Street, NW, Washington, D.C. 20431 (202) 623-7000; *Government Finance Statistics Yearbook.*

M.E. Sharpe, 80 Business Park Drive, Armonk, New York 10504 (800) 541-6563; *The Illustrated Book of World Rankings.*

Organisation for Economic Co-operation and Development (OECD), 2 rue Andre-Pascal, 75 Paris 16, France (Telephone Number in U.S. (202) 785-6323); *Education in OECD Countries.*

St. Martin's Press, Inc., 175 Fifth Avenue, New York, New York 10010 (800) 221-7945; *The Statesman's Year-Book.*

Statistical Office of the United Nations, Publishing Service, New York, New York 10017 (800) 253-9646; *Human Development Report;* and *Trends in Europe and North America: The Statistical Yearbook of the Economic Commission for Europe.*

United Nations Educational, Scientific and Cultural Organization (UNESCO), 7 Place de Fontenoy, F-75700 Paris, France (Telephone Number in U.S. (212) 963-5981); *Statistical Yearbook.*

The World Bank, 1818 H Street, NW, Washington, D.C. 20433 (202) 477-1234; *World Development Report;* and *World Development Indicators.*

SPAIN - EGG PRODUCTION AND CONSUMPTION - See SPAIN - DAIRY PRODUCTS

SPAIN - ELECTRICITY

Central Intelligence Agency, Washington, D.C. 20505 (703) 482-1100,

www.cia.gov; *The World Factbook.*

European Commission Office of Press and Public Affairs, 2100 M Street, NW, Washington, D.C. 20037 (202) 862-9500; *Basic Statistics of the Community; Energy: Monthly Statistics; Energy Statistics Yearbook; Eurostatistics: Data for Short-Term Economic Analysis;* and *Regions: Statistical Yearbook.*

M.E. Sharpe, 80 Business Park Drive, Armonk, New York 10504 (800) 541-6563; *The Illustrated Book of World Rankings.*

Organisation for Economic Co-operation and Development (OECD), 2 rue Andre-Pascal, 75 Paris 16, France (Telephone Number in U.S. (202) 785-6323); *Coal Information; Energy Statistics of OECD Countries; Indicators of Industrial Activity;* and *Industrial Structure Statistics.*

Penn Well Publishing Company, 1421 South Sheridan Road, P.O. Box 1260, Tulsa, Oklahoma 74101 (800) 752-9764; *International Energy Statistics Sourcebook.*

St. Martin's Press, Inc., 175 Fifth Avenue, New York, New York 10010 (800) 221-7945; *The Statesman's Year-Book.*

Statistical Office of the United Nations, Publishing Service, New York, New York 10017 (800) 253-9646; *Human Development Report; Statistical Yearbook;* and *Trends in Europe and North America: The Statistical Yearbook of the Economic Commission for Europe.*

SPAIN - EMPLOYMENT

Euromonitor International, Inc., 122 South Michigan Avenue, Suite 1200, Chicago, Illinois 60603 (800) 577-EURO; *European Marketing Data and Statistics.*

European Commission Office of Press and Public Affairs, 2100 M Street, NW, Washington, D.C. 20037 (202) 862-9500; *Basic Statistics of the Community; Earnings in Agriculture; Employment and Unemployment; Eurostatistics: Data for Short-Term Economic Analysis; Iron and Steel: Statistical Yearbook; Labor Force Sample Survey; OECD Economic Surveys: Spain;* and *Transport Annual Statistics.*

Federal Statistical Office, Gustav-Stresemann-Ring 11, D-6200 Wiesbaden, Germany; *Spain.*

International Labour Office, I.L.O. Publications, 1828 L Street, NW, Washington, D.C. 20036 (301) 638-3152; *Yearbook of Labour Statistics.*

M.E. Sharpe, 80 Business Park Drive, Armonk, New York 10504 (800) 541-6563; *The Illustrated Book of World Rankings.*

Organisation for Economic Co-operation and Development (OECD), 2 rue Andre-Pascal, 75 Paris 16, France (Telephone Number in U.S. (202) 785-6323); *Economic Outlook; The Iron and Steel Industry; Labour Force Statistics; OECD Employment Outlook;* and *Textile Industry in OECD Countries.*

Statistical Office of the United Nations, Publishing Service, New York, New York 10017 (800) 253-9646; *Statistical Yearbook;* and *Trends in Europe and North America: The Statistical Yearbook of the Economic Commission for Europe.*

SPAIN - ENERGY

Euromonitor International, Inc., 122 South Michigan Avenue, Suite 1200, Chicago, Illinois 60603 (800) 577-EURO; *European Marketing Data and Statistics; World Marketing Data and Statistics;* and *The World Economic Factbook.*

European Commission Office of Press and Public Affairs, 2100 M Street, NW, Washington, D.C. 20037 (202) 862-9500; *Basic Statistics of the Community; Energy: Monthly Statistics; Energy Statistics Yearbook; Regions: Statistical Yearbook;* and *Transport Annual Statistics.*

Food and Agricultural Organization of the United Nations (FAO) Via delle Terme di Caracalla, 00100 Rome, Italy (Telephone Number in U.S. (202) 653-2400); *The State of Food and Agriculture.*

M.E. Sharpe, 80 Business Park Drive, Armonk, New York 10504 (800) 541-6563; *The Illustrated Book of World Rankings.*

Organisation for Economic Co-operation and Development (OECD), 2 rue Andre-Pascal, 75 Paris 16, France (Telephone Number in U.S. (202) 785-6323); *Coal Information; Energy Statistics of OECD Countries; OECD Environmental Data;* and *Oil and Gas Information.*

Penn Well Publishing Company, 1421 South Sheridan Road, P.O. Box 1260, Tulsa, Oklahoma 74101 (800) 752-9764; *International Energy Statistics Sourcebook.*

St. Martin's Press, Inc., 175 Fifth Avenue, New York, New York 10010 (800) 221-7945; *The Statesman's Year-Book.*

Statistical Office of the United Nations, Publishing Service, New York, New York 10017 (800) 253-9646; *Energy Statistics Yearbook; Human Development Report; Statistical Yearbook; Trends in Europe and North America: The Statistical Yearbook of the Economic Commission for Europe;* and *World Statistical Pocketbook.*

The World Bank, 1818 H Street, NW, Washington, D.C. 20433 (202) 477-1234;

The World Bank Atlas; and *World Development Report.*

SPAIN - ENGINEERING

European Commission Office of Press and Public Affairs, 2100 M Street, NW, Washington, D.C. 20037 (202) 862-9500; *Basic Statistics of the Community;* and *Industrial Production: Quarterly Statistics.*

SPAIN - ENVIRONMENT

Economist Intelligence Unit, 111 West 57th Street, New York, New York 10019 (800) 938-4685; *Spain Country Report.*

Organization for Economic Co-operation and Development (OECD), 2 rue Andre-Pascal, 75 Paris 16, France (Telephone Number in U.S. (202) 785-6323); *OECD Environmental Data.*

Statistical Office of the United Nations, Publishing Service, New York, New York 10017 (800) 253-9646; *World Statistics Pocketbook.*

SPAIN - EXCHANGE RATES

Central Intelligence Agency, Washington, D.C. 20505 (703) 482-1100, www.cia.gov; *The World Factbook.*

Europa Publications Limited, 18 Bedford Square, London, WC1B 3JN, England; *The Europa World Year Book.*

European Commission Office of Press and Public Affairs, 2100 M Street, NW, Washington, D.C. 20037 (202) 862-9500; *Basic Statistics of the Community; Eurostatistics: Data for Short-Term Economic Analysis; Money and Finance;* and *The World Economic Factbook.*

International Civil Aviation Organization, 999 University Street, Montreal, Quebec, Canada H3C 5H7 (514) 954-8219; *Civil Aviation Statistics of the World.*

International Monetary Fund, 700 Nineteenth Street, NW, Washington, D.C. 20431 (202) 623-7000; *International Financial Statistics.*

Organisation for Economic Co-operation and Development (OECD), 2 rue Andre-Pascal, 75 Paris 16, France (Telephone Number in U.S. (202) 785-6323); *Economic Outlook; Financial Market Trends; OECD Economic Surveys: Spain; Revenue Statistics of OECD Member Countries;* and *Tourism Policy and International Tourism in OECD Member Countries.*

Statistical Office of the United Nations, Publishing Service, New York, New York 10017 (800) 253-9646; *Statistical Yearbook;*

Trends in Europe and North America: The Statistical Yearbook of the Economic Commission for Europe; and *World Statistics Pocketbook.*

SPAIN - EXCISE TAXES - See SPAIN - TAXATION

SPAIN - EXPORTS

Central Intelligence Agency, Washington, D.C. 20505 (703) 482-1100, www.cia.gov; *The World Factbook.*

The Economist Intelligence Unit, 111 West 57th Street, New York, New York 10019 (800) 938-4685; *Spain Country Report;* and *The World Market Atlas.*

Europa Publications Limited, 18 Bedford Square, London, WC1B 3JN, England; *The Europa World Year Book.*

European Commission Office of Press and Public Affairs, 2100 M Street, NW, Washington, D.C. 20037 (202) 862-9500; *Basic Statistics of the Community; Energy: Monthly Statistics; Energy Statistics Yearbook; Eurostatistics: Data for Short-Term Economic Analysis; External Trade: Monthly Statistics; External Trade: Statistical Yearbook; Fisheries: Yearly Statistics;* and *The World Economic Factbook.*

Food and Agricultural Organization of the United Nations (FAO) Via delle Terme di Caracalla, 00100 Rome, Italy (Telephone Number in U.S. (202) 653-2400); *The State of Food and Agriculture.*

International Iron and Steel Institute, 120, rue Colonel Bourg, B-1140, Brussels, Belgium; *Steel Statistical Yearbook.*

International Lead and Zinc Study Group, Metro House, 58 St. James's Street, London SW1A 1LD, England; *Lead and Zinc Statistics.*

International Monetary Fund, 700 Nineteenth Street, NW, Washington, D.C. 20431 (202) 623-7000; *Direction of Trade Statistics;* and *International Financial Statistics.*

Organisation for Economic Co-operation and Development (OECD), 2 rue Andre-Pascal, 75 Paris 16, France (Telephone Number in U.S. (202) 785-6323); *Economic Outlook; The Footwear, Raw Hides and Skins, and Leather Industry in OECD Countries; Foreign Trade by Commodities; Geographical Distribution of Financial Flows to Developing Countries; Industrial Structure Statistics; The Iron and Steel Industry; Milk, Milk Products, and Egg Balances in OECD Member Countries; OECD Economic Surveys: Spain; The Pulp and Paper Industry;* and *Review of Fisheries in OECD Member Countries.*

St. Martin's Press, Inc., 175 Fifth Avenue, New York, New York 10010 (800) 221-7945; *The Statesman's Year-Book.*

Statistical Office of the United Nations, Publishing Service, New York, New York 10017 (800) 253-9646; *Trends in Europe and North America: The Statistical Yearbook of the Economic Commission for Europe.*

United Nations Conference on Trade and Development (UNCTAD), New York, New York 10017 (800) 253-9646; *Handbook of International Trade and Development Statistics.*

The World Bank, 1818 H Street, NW, Washington, D.C. 20433 (202) 477-1234; *World Development Report;* and *World Development Indicators.*

SPAIN - EXTERNAL FINANCING

Organisation for Economic Co-operation and Development (OECD), 2 rue Andre-Pascal, 75 Paris 16, France (Telephone Number in U.S. (202) 785-6323); *Economic Outlook;* and *Financial Market Trends.*

SPAIN - EXTERNAL INDEBTEDNESS

Organisation for Economic Co-operation and Development (OECD), 2 rue Andre-Pascal, 75 Paris 16, France (Telephone Number in U.S. (202) 785-6323); *Financial Market Trends;* and *Geographical Distribution of Financial Flows to Developing Countries.*

The World Bank, 1818 H Street, NW, Washington, D.C. 20433 (202) 477-1234; *World Development Report;* and *World Development Indicators.*

SPAIN - EXTERNAL TRADE

Euromonitor International, Inc., 122 South Michigan Avenue, Suite 1200, Chicago, Illinois 60603 (800) 577-EURO; *World Marketing Data and Statistics.*

European Commission Office of Press and Public Affairs, 2100 M Street, NW, Washington, D.C. 20037 (202) 862-9500; *ACP: Basic Statistics, Basic Statistics of the Community, Eurostatistics: Data for Short-Term Economic Analysis; External Trade: Monthly Statistics; External Trade: Statistical Yearbook;* and *Foreign Trade of the People's Republic of China.*

Food and Agricultural Organization of the United Nations (FAO) Via delle Terme di Caracalla, 00100 Rome, Italy (Telephone Number in U.S. (202) 653-2400); *The State of Food and Agriculture;* and *Trade Yearbook.*

Statistical Office of the United Nations, Publishing Service, New York, New York

10017 (800) 253-9646; *Statistical Yearbook.*

SPAIN - FABRIC PRODUCTION - See SPAIN - TEXTILE INDUSTRY

SPAIN - FARM CROPS - See SPAIN - CROPS

SPAIN - FEMALE WORKING POPULATION - See SPAIN - EMPLOYMENT

SPAIN - FERTILITY RATES

Central Intelligence Agency, Washington, D.C. 20505 (703) 482-1100, www.cia.gov; *The World Factbook.*

European Commission Office of Press and Public Affairs, 2100 M Street, NW, Washington, D.C. 20037 (202) 862-9500; *Demographic Statistics.*

M.E. Sharpe, 80 Business Park Drive, Armonk, New York 10504 (800) 541-6563; *The Illustrated Book of World Rankings.*

Statistical Office of the United Nations, Publishing Service, New York, New York 10017 (800) 253-9646; *Human Development Report;* and *Trends in Europe and North America: The Statistical Yearbook of the Economic Commission for Europe.*

The World Bank, 1818 H Street, NW, Washington, D.C. 20433 (202) 477-1234; *The World Bank Atlas; World Development Report;* and *World Development Indicators.*

SPAIN - FERTILIZER

European Commission Office of Press and Public Affairs, 2100 M Street, NW, Washington, D.C. 20037 (202) 862-9500; *Basic Statistics of the Community.*

Food and Agricultural Organization of the United Nations (FAO) Via delle Terme di Caracalla, 00100 Rome, Italy (Telephone Number in U.S. (202) 653-2400); *The State of Food and Agriculture.*

Organisation for Economic Co-operation and Development (OECD), 2 rue Andre-Pascal, 75 Paris 16, France (Telephone Number in U.S. (202) 785-6323); *Economic Accounts for Agriculture;* and *Foreign Trade by Commodities.*

Statistical Office of the United Nations, Publishing Service, New York, New York 10017 (800) 253-9646; *Statistical Yearbook.*

SPAIN - FETAL MORTALITY - See SPAIN - MORTALITY

SPAIN - FIBRE PRODUCTION - See SPAIN - TEXTILE INDUSTRY

SPAIN - FILAMENT PRODUCTION - See SPAIN - TEXTILE INDUSTRY

SPAIN - FILM - See SPAIN - MOTION PICTURES

SPAIN - FINANCE

Economist Intelligence Unit, 111 West 57th Street, New York, New York 10019 (800) 938-4685; *Spain Country Report.*

Europa Publications Limited, 18 Bedford Square, London, WC1B 3JN, England; *The Europa World Year Book.*

European Commission Office of Press and Public Affairs, 2100 M Street, NW, Washington, D.C. 20037 (202) 862-9500; *ACP: Basic Statistics; Basic Statistics of the Community; Eurostatistics: Data for Short-Term Economic Analysis;* and *Money and Finance.*

Federal Statistical Office, Gustav-Stresemann-Ring 11, D-6200 Wiesbaden, Germany; *Spain.*

International Monetary Fund, 700 Nineteenth Street, NW, Washington, D.C. 20431 (202) 623-7000; *Government Finance Statistics Yearbook;* and *International Financial Statistics.*

M.E. Sharpe, 80 Business Park Drive, Armonk, New York 10504 (800) 541-6563; *The Illustrated Book of World Rankings.*

Organisation for Economic Co-operation and Development (OECD), 2 rue Andre-Pascal, 75 Paris 16, France (Telephone Number in U.S. (202) 785-6323); *Economic Outlook; Financial Market Trends; Geographical Distribution of Financial Flows to Developing Countries; Main Economic Indicators - Historical Statistics; OECD Financial Statistics;* and *Revenue Statistics of OECD Countries.*

St. Martin's Press, Inc., 175 Fifth Avenue, New York, New York 10010 (800) 221-7945; *The Statesman's Year-Book.*

SPAIN - FISHERIES

Euromonitor International, Inc., 122 South Michigan Avenue, Suite 1200, Chicago, Illinois 60603 (800) 577-EURO; *European Marketing Data and Statistics.*

Europa Publications Limited, 18 Bedford Square, London, WC1B 3JN, England; *The Europa World Year Book.*

European Commission Office of Press and Public Affairs, 2100 M Street, NW, Washington, D.C. 20037 (202) 862-9500; *Agriculture: Statistical Yearbook;* and *Fisheries: Yearly Statistics.*

Federal Statistical Office, Gustav-Stresemann-Ring 11, D-6200 Wiesbaden, Germany; *Spain.*

Food and Agricultural Organization of the United Nations (FAO) Via delle Terme di Caracalla, 00100 Rome, Italy (Telephone Number in U.S. (202) 653-2400); *The State of Food and Agriculture;* and *Yearbook of Fishery Statistics.*

M.E. Sharpe, 80 Business Park Drive, Armonk, New York 10504 (800) 541-6563; *The Illustrated Book of World Rankings.*

Organisation for Economic Co-operation and Development (OECD), 2 rue Andre-Pascal, 75 Paris 16, France (Telephone Number in U.S. (202) 785-6323); *Industrial Structure Statistics; Foreign Trade by Commodities;* and *Review of Fisheries in OECD Member Countries.*

St. Martin's Press, Inc., 175 Fifth Avenue, New York, New York 10010 (800) 221-7945; *The Statesman's Year-Book.*

Statistical Office of the United Nations, Publishing Service, New York, New York 10017 (800) 253-9646; *Statistical Yearbook.*

United Nations Conference on Trade and Development, Central Statistical Service, Palais des Nations, Geneva, Switzerland (Telephone in U.S. (800) 253-9646); *UNCTAD Commodity Yearbook.*

SPAIN - FLOUR PRODUCTION

Commodity Research Bureau, Inc., 30 South Wacker Drive, Chicago Illinois 60606 (312) 454-1801; *Commodity Year Book.*

European Commission Office of Press and Public Affairs, 2100 M Street, NW, Washington, D.C. 20037 (202) 862-9500; *Basic Statistics of the Community.*

Statistical Office of the United Nations, Publishing Service, New York, New York 10017 (800) 253-9646; *Statistical Yearbook.*

SPAIN - FOOD

Euromonitor International, Inc., 122 South Michigan Avenue, Suite 1200, Chicago, Illinois 60603 (800) 577-EURO; *Retail Trade International.*

European Commission Office of Press and Public Affairs, 2100 M Street, NW, Washington, D.C. 20037 (202) 862-9500; *Basic Statistics of the Community.*

Food and Agricultural Organization of the United Nations (FAO) Via delle Terme di Caracalla, 00100 Rome, Italy (Telephone Number in U.S. (202) 653-2400); *Production Yearbook;* and *The State of Food and Agriculture.*

Organisation for Economic Co-operation and Development (OECD), 2 rue Andre-Pascal, 75 Paris 16, France

(Telephone Number in U.S. (202) 785-6323); *Food Consumption Statistic;* and *Foreign Trade by Commodities.*

Statistical Office of the United Nations, Publishing Service, New York, New York 10017 (800) 253-9646; *Human Development Report.*

United Nations Conference on Trade and Development, Central Statistical Service, Palais des Nations, Geneva, Switzerland (Telephone in U.S. (800) 253-9646); *UNCTAD Commodity Yearbook.*

SPAIN - FOOTWEAR - PRODUCTION INDEX

Organisation for Economic Co-operation and Development (OECD), 2 rue Andre-Pascal, 75 Paris 16, France (Telephone Number in U.S. (202) 785-6323); *Indicators of Industrial Activity.*

SPAIN - FOREIGN DEBT

International Monetary Fund, 700 Nineteenth Street, NW, Washington, D.C. 20431 (202) 623-7000; *Government Finance Statistics Yearbook.*

Organisation for Economic Co-operation and Development (OECD), 2 rue Andre-Pascal, 75 Paris 16, France (Telephone Number in U.S. (202) 785-6323); *Economic Outlook.*

St. Martin's Press, Inc., 175 Fifth Avenue, New York, New York 10010 (800) 221-7945; *The Statesman's Year-Book.*

SPAIN - FOREIGN INDEBTEDNESS

Organisation for Economic Co-operation and Development (OECD), 2 rue Andre-Pascal, 75 Paris 16, France (Telephone Number in U.S. (202) 785-6323); *Economic Outlook;* and *Financial Market Trends.*

SPAIN - FOREIGN OFFICIAL RESERVES

European Commission Office of Press and Public Affairs, 2100 M Street, NW, Washington, D.C. 20037 (202) 862-9500; *Money and Finance.*

SPAIN - FOREIGN TRADE

Economist Intelligence Unit, 111 West 57th Street, New York, New York 10019 (800) 938-4685; *Spain Country Report.*

Europa Publications Limited, 18 Bedford Square, London, WC1B 3JN, England; *The Europa World Year Book.*

European Commission Office of Press and Public Affairs, 2100 M Street, NW, Washington, D.C. 20037 (202) 862-9500; *Basic Statistics of the Community; Energy Statistics Yearbook; Foreign Trade of the*

People's Republic of China; Iron and Steel: Statistical Yearbook; and The World Economic Factbook.

Federal Statistical Office, Gustav-Stresemann-Ring 11, D-6200 Wiesbaden, Germany; *Spain.*

International Monetary Fund, 700 Nineteenth Street, NW, Washington, D.C. 20431 (202) 623-7000; *International Financial Statistics.*

M.E. Sharpe, 80 Business Park Drive, Armonk, New York 10504 (800) 541-6563; *The Illustrated Book of World Rankings.*

Organisation for Economic Co-operation and Development (OECD), 2 rue Andre-Pascal, 75 Paris 16, France (Telephone Number in U.S. (202) 785-6323); *The Footwear, Raw Hides and Skins, and Leather Industry in OECD Countries; Foreign Trade by Commodities; Main Economic Indicators - Historical Statistics; Meat Balances in OECD Member Countries;* and *OECD Economic Surveys: Spain.*

St. Martin's Press, Inc., 175 Fifth Avenue, New York, New York 10010 (800) 221-7945; *The Statesman's Year-Book.*

Statistical Office of the United Nations, Publishing Service, New York, New York 10017 (800) 253-9646; *International Trade Statistics Yearbook;* and *Statistical Yearbook.*

United Nations Conference on Trade and Development, Central Statistical Service, Palais des Nations, Geneva, Switzerland (Telephone in U.S. (800) 253-9646); *UNCTAD Commodity Yearbook.*

The World Bank, 1818 H Street, NW, Washington, D.C. 20433 (202) 477-1234; *World Development Report;* and *World Development Indicators.*

SPAIN - FORESTRY AND FOREST PRODUCTS

American Forest and Paper Association, 1111 Nineteenth Street, NW, Suite 800, Washington, D.C. 20036 (202) 463-2700; *Wood Pulp and Fiber Statistics.*

Euromonitor International, Inc., 122 South Michigan Avenue, Suite 1200, Chicago, Illinois 60603 (800) 577-EURO; *European Marketing Data and Statistics.*

Europa Publications Limited, 18 Bedford Square, London, WC1B 3JN, England; *The Europa World Year Book.*

European Commission Office of Press and Public Affairs, 2100 M Street, NW, Washington, D.C. 20037 (202) 862-9500; *Agriculture: Statistical Yearbook; Basic*

Statistics of the Community; and Industrial Production: Quarterly Statistics.

Federal Statistical Office, Gustav-Stresemann-Ring 11, D-6200 Wiesbaden, Germany; *Spain.*

Food and Agricultural Organization of the United Nations (FAO) Via delle Terme di Caracalla, 00100 Rome, Italy (Telephone Number in U.S. (202) 653-2400); *The State of Food and Agriculture;* and *Yearbook of Forest Products.*

M.E. Sharpe, 80 Business Park Drive, Armonk, New York 10504 (800) 541-6563; *The Illustrated Book of World Rankings.*

Organisation for Economic Co-operation and Development (OECD), 2 rue Andre-Pascal, 75 Paris 16, France (Telephone Number in U.S. (202) 785-6323); *Foreign Trade by Commodities; Indicators of Industrial Activity; Industrial Structure Statistics;* and *The Pulp and Paper Industry.*

St. Martin's Press, Inc., 175 Fifth Avenue, New York, New York 10010 (800) 221-7945; *The Statesman's Year-Book.*

Statistical Office of the United Nations, Publishing Service, New York, New York 10017 (800) 253-9646; *Statistical Yearbook;* and *Trends in Europe and North America: The Statistical Yearbook of the Economic Commission for Europe.*

United Nations Conference on Trade and Development, Central Statistical Service, Palais des Nations, Geneva, Switzerland (Telephone in U.S. (800) 253-9646); *UNCTAD Commodity Yearbook.*

United Nations Educational, Scientific and Cultural Organization (UNESCO), 7 Place de Fontenoy, F-75700 Paris, France (Telephone Number in U.S. (212) 963-5981); *Statistical Yearbook.*

The World Bank, 1818 H Street, NW, Washington, D.C. 20433 (202) 477-1234; *World Development Report.*

SPAIN - FRUIT PRODUCTION - See SPAIN - CROPS

SPAIN - FURNITURE AND WOOD PRODUCTS - EXPORTS AND IMPORTS

European Commission Office of Press and Public Affairs, 2100 M Street, NW, Washington, D.C. 20037 (202) 862-9500; *Basic Statistics of the Community.*

Organisation for Economic Co-operation and Development (OECD), 2 rue Andre-Pascal, 75 Paris 16, France (Telephone Number in U.S. (202) 785-6323); *Foreign Trade by Commodities;* and *Industrial Structure Statistics.*

SPAIN - GAS - See SPAIN - MINING AND MINERAL PRODUCTS

SPAIN - GENERAL INDUSTRIAL STATISTICS - See SPAIN - INDUSTRY

SPAIN - GENERAL MORTALITY - See SPAIN - MORTALITY

SPAIN - GEOGRAPHIC DATA

European Commission Office of Press and Public Affairs, 2100 M Street, NW, Washington, D.C. 20037 (202) 862-9500; *Basic Statistics of the Community.*

M.E. Sharpe, 80 Business Park Drive, Armonk, New York 10504 (800) 541-6563; *The Illustrated Book of World Rankings.*

SPAIN - GLASS AND GLASS PRODUCTS - PRODUCTION INDEX

Organisation for Economic Co-operation and Development (OECD), 2 rue Andre-Pascal, 75 Paris 16, France (Telephone Number in U.S. (202) 785-6323); *Indicators of Industrial Activity.*

SPAIN - GOATS - See SPAIN - LIVESTOCK AND POULTRY

SPAIN - GOLD HOLDINGS

International Monetary Fund, 700 Nineteenth Street, NW, Washington, D.C. 20431 (202) 623-7000; *International Financial Statistics.*

Statistical Office of the United Nations, Publishing Service, New York, New York 10017 (800) 253-9646; *Statistical Yearbook.*

The World Bank, 1818 H Street, NW, Washington, D.C. 20433 (202) 477-1234; *World Development Indicators.*

SPAIN - GOLD PRODUCTION AND CONSUMPTION - See SPAIN - MINING AND MINERAL PRODUCTS

SPAIN - GOVERNMENT

Central Intelligence Agency, Washington, D.C. 20505 (703) 482-1100, www.cia.gov; *The World Factbook.*

Europa Publications Limited, 18 Bedford Square, London, WC1B 3JN, England; *The Europa World Year Book.*

European Commission Office of Press and Public Affairs, 2100 M Street, NW, Washington, D.C. 20037 (202) 862-9500; *Basic Statistics of the Community; Government Financing of Research and Development;* and *Money and Finance.*

International Monetary Fund, 700 Nineteenth Street, NW, Washington, D.C. 20431 (202) 623-7000; *Government*

Finance Statistics Yearbook; and *International Financial Statistics.*

Organisation for Economic Co-operation and Development (OECD), 2 rue Andre-Pascal, 75 Paris 16, France (Telephone Number in U.S. (202) 785-6323); *Economic Outlook;* and *Revenue Statistics of OECD Member Countries.*

Statistical Office of the United Nations, Publishing Service, New York, New York 10017 (800) 253-9646; *National Accounts Statistics;* and *Statistical Yearbook.*

The World Bank, 1818 H Street, NW, Washington, D.C. 20433 (202) 477-1234; *World Development Report;* and *World Development Indicators.*

SPAIN - GRAIN PRODUCTION - See SPAIN - CROPS

SPAIN - GRANTS

International Monetary Fund, 700 Nineteenth Street, NW, Washington, D.C. 20431 (202) 623-7000; *Government Finance Statistics Yearbook.*

Organisation for Economic Co-operation and Development (OECD), 2 rue Andre-Pascal, 75 Paris 16, France (Telephone Number in U.S. (202) 785-6323); *Geographical Distribution of Financial Flows to Developing Countries.*

SPAIN - GROSS DOMESTIC PRODUCT

The Economist Intelligence Unit, 111 West 57th Street, New York, New York 10019 (800) 938-4685; *Spain Country Report;* and *The World Market Atlas.*

Europa Publications Limited, 18 Bedford Square, London, WC1B 3JN, England; *The Europa World Year Book.*

European Commission Office of Press and Public Affairs, 2100 M Street, NW, Washington, D.C. 20037 (202) 862-9500; *Basic Statistics of the Community; Eurostatistics: Data for Short-Term Economic Analysis; Government Financing for Research and Development; Iron and Steel: Statistical Yearbook; Money and Finance;* and *The World Economic Factbook.*

International Monetary Fund, 700 Nineteenth Street, NW, Washington, D.C. 20431 (202) 623-7000; *International Financial Statistics.*

M.E. Sharpe, 80 Business Park Drive, Armonk, New York 10504 (800) 541-6563; *The Illustrated Book of World Rankings.*

Organisation for Economic Co-operation and Development (OECD), 2 rue Andre-Pascal, 75 Paris 16, France

(Telephone Number in U.S. (202) 785-6323); *Economic Outlook; Geographical Distribution of Financial Flows to Developing Countries;* and *Revenue Statistics of OECD Member Countries.*

Statistical Office of the United Nations, Publishing Service, New York, New York 10017 (800) 253-9646; *Human Development Report; National Accounts Statistics; Statistical Yearbook;* and *Trends in Europe and North America: The Statistical Yearbook of the Economic Commission for Europe.*

The World Bank, 1818 H Street, NW, Washington, D.C. 20433 (202) 477-1234; *World Development Report;* and *World Development Indicators.*

SPAIN - GROSS NATIONAL PRODUCT

Europa Publications Limited, 18 Bedford Square, London, WC1B 3JN, England; *The Europa World Year Book.*

European Commission Office of Press and Public Affairs, 2100 M Street, NW, Washington, D.C. 20037 (202) 862-9500; *ACP: Basic Statistics;* and *Basic Statistics of the Community.*

Organisation for Economic Co-operation and Development (OECD), 2 rue Andre-Pascal, 75 Paris 16, France (Telephone Number in U.S. (202) 785-6323); *Economic Outlook;* and *Geographical Distribution of Financial Flows to Developing Countries.*

St. Martin's Press, Inc., 175 Fifth Avenue, New York, New York 10010 (800) 221-7945; *The Statesman's Year-Book.*

U.S. Arms Control and Disarmament Agency, 320 Twenty-first Street, NW, Washington, D.C. 20451 (202) 647-8677; *World Military Expenditures and Arms Transfers.*

The World Bank, 1818 H Street, NW, Washington, D.C. 20433 (202) 477-1234; *The World Bank Atlas; World Development Report;* and *World Development Indicators.*

SPAIN - GROUNDNUTS PRODUCTION - See SPAIN - CROPS

SPAIN - HEALTH

Euromonitor International, Inc., 122 South Michigan Avenue, Suite 1200, Chicago, Illinois 60603 (800) 577-EURO: *World Marketing Data and Statistics.*

European Commission Office of Press and Public Affairs, 2100 M Street, NW, Washington, D.C. 20037 (202) 862-9500; *Basic Statistics of the Community;* and *Regions: Statistical Yearbook.*

Federal Statistical Office, Gustav-Stresemann-Ring 11, D-6200 Wiesbaden, Germany; *Spain.*

M.E. Sharpe, 80 Business Park Drive, Armonk, New York 10504 (800) 541-6563; *The Illustrated Book of World Rankings.*

Organisation for Economic Co-operation and Development (OECD), 2 rue Andre-Pascal, 75 Paris 16, France (Telephone Number in U.S. (202) 785-6323); *OECD Health Systems: Facts and Trends.*

St. Martin's Press, Inc., 175 Fifth Avenue, New York, New York 10010 (800) 221-7945; *The Statesman's Year-Book.*

Statistical Office of the United Nations, Publishing Service, New York, New York 10017 (800) 253-9646; *Human Development Report; Trends in Europe and North America: The Statistical Yearbook of the Economic Commission for Europe;* and *Statistical Yearbook.*

United Nations Children's Fund (UNICEF), 3 United Nations Plaza, New York, New York 10017 (800) 253-9646; *State of the World's Children.*

The World Bank, 1818 H Street, NW, Washington, D.C. 20433 (202) 477-1234; *World Development Report.*

World Health Organization, Office of Publications, 20 Avenue Appia, CH-1211 Geneva 27, Switzerland (Telephone Number in U.S. (518) 436-9686); *World Health Statistics Annual.*

SPAIN - HEALTH EXPENDITURES

International Monetary Fund, 700 Nineteenth Street, NW, Washington, D.C. 20431 (202) 623-7000; *Government Finance Statistics Yearbook.*

SPAIN - HIDE PRODUCTION

Organisation for Economic Co-operation and Development (OECD), 2 rue Andre-Pascal, 75 Paris 16, France (Telephone Number in U.S. (202) 785-6323); *The Footwear, Raw Hides and Skins, and Leather Industry in OECD Countries; Foreign Trade by Commodities;* and *Indicators of Industrial Activity.*

SPAIN - HIGHWAYS

Central Intelligence Agency, Washington, D.C. 20505 (703) 482-1100, www.cia.gov; *The World Factbook.*

European Commission Office of Press and Public Affairs, 2100 M Street, NW, Washington, D.C. 20037 (202) 862-9500; *Basic Statistics of the Community;* and *Transport Annual Statistics.*

International Road Federation, 2600 Virginia Avenue, NW, Washington, D.C. 20037 (202) 338-4641; *World Road Statistics.*

St. Martin's Press, Inc., 175 Fifth Avenue, New York, New York 10010 (800) 221-7945; *The Statesman's Year-Book.*

Statistical Office of the United Nations, Publishing Service, New York, New York 10017 (800) 253-9646; *Annual Bulletin of Transport Statistics for Europe;* and *Trends in Europe and North America: The Statistical Yearbook of the Economic Commission for Europe.*

SPAIN - HOME FINANCE

Organisation for Economic Co-operation and Development (OECD), 2 rue Andre-Pascal, 75 Paris 16, France (Telephone Number in U.S. (202) 785-6323); *Main Economic Indicators - Historical Statistics.*

SPAIN - HONEY PRODUCTION

Commodity Research Bureau, Inc., 30 South Wacker Drive, Chicago Illinois 60606 (312) 454-1801; *Commodity Year Book.*

SPAIN - HORSES - See SPAIN - LIVESTOCK AND POULTRY

SPAIN - HOURS OF WORK - See SPAIN - EMPLOYMENT

SPAIN - HOUSING AND HOUSING UNITS

Euromonitor International, Inc., 122 South Michigan Avenue, Suite 1200, Chicago, Illinois 60603 (800) 577-EURO: *World Marketing Data and Statistics.*

European Commission Office of Press and Public Affairs, 2100 M Street, NW, Washington, D.C. 20037 (202) 862-9500; *Basic Statistics of the Community; Labor Force Sample Survey;* and *Regions: Statistical Yearbook.*

M.E. Sharpe, 80 Business Park Drive, Armonk, New York 10504 (800) 541-6563; *The Illustrated Book of World Rankings.*

Statistical Office of the United Nations, Publishing Service, New York, New York 10017 (800) 253-9646; *Trends in Europe and North America: The Statistical Yearbook of the Economic Commission for Europe.*

SPAIN - HOUSING CONSTRUCTION - See CONSTRUCTION INDUSTRY

SPAIN - HOUSING EXPENDITURES

European Commission Office of Press and Public Affairs, 2100 M Street, NW, Washington, D.C. 20037 (202) 862-9500; *Basis Statistics of the Community.*

International Monetary Fund, 700 Nineteenth Street, NW, Washington, D.C. 20431 (202) 623-7000; *Government Finance Statistics Yearbook.*

SPAIN - HYDROCHLORIC ACID PRODUCTION

European Commission Office of Press and Public Affairs, 2100 M Street, NW, Washington, D.C. 20037 (202) 862-9500; *Basic Statistics of the Community.*

Statistical Office of the United Nations, Publishing Service, New York, New York 10017 (800) 253-9646; *Statistical Yearbook.*

SPAIN - ILLITERATE POPULATION

Central Intelligence Agency, Washington, D.C. 20505 (703) 482-1100, www.cia.gov; *The World Factbook.*

The Economist Intelligence Unit, 111 West 57th Street, New York, New York 10019 (800) 938-4685; *The World Market Atlas.*

Euromonitor International, Inc., 122 South Michigan Avenue, Suite 1200, Chicago, Illinois 60603 (800) 577-EURO; *The World Economic Factbook.*

Statistical Office of the United Nations, Publishing Service, New York, New York 10017 (800) 253-9646; *Human Development Report.*

United Nations Educational, Scientific and Cultural Organization (UNESCO), 7 Place de Fontenoy, F-75700 Paris, France (Telephone Number in U.S. (212) 963-5981); *Statistical Yearbook.*

SPAIN - IMPORTS

Central Intelligence Agency, Washington, D.C. 20505 (703) 482-1100, www.cia.gov; *The World Factbook.*

The Economist Intelligence Unit, 111 West 57th Street, New York, New York 10019 (800) 938-4685; *Spain Country Report;* and *The World Market Atlas.*

Europa Publications Limited, 18 Bedford Square, London, WC1B 3JN, England; *The Europa World Year Book.*

European Commission Office of Press and Public Affairs, 2100 M Street, NW, Washington, D.C. 20037 (202) 862-9500; *Energy: Monthly Statistics; Eurostatistics: Data for Short-Term Economic Analysis; External Trade: Monthly Statistics; External Trade: Statistical Yearbook;* and *The World Economic Factbook.*

Food and Agricultural Organization of the United Nations (FAO) Via delle Terme di Caracalla, 00100 Rome, Italy (Telephone

Number in U.S. (202) 653-2400); *The State of Food and Agriculture*.

International Iron and Steel Institute, 120, rue Colonel Bourg, B-1140, Brussels, Belgium; *Steel Statistical Yearbook*.

International Lead and Zinc Study Group, Metro House, 58 St. James's Street, London SW1A 1LD, England; *Lead and Zinc Statistics*.

International Monetary Fund, 700 Nineteenth Street, NW, Washington, D.C. 20431 (202) 623-7000; *Direction of Trade Statistics; Government Finance Statistics Yearbook;* and *International Financial Statistics*.

Organisation for Economic Co-operation and Development (OECD), 2 rue Andre-Pascal, 75 Paris 16, France (Telephone Number in U.S. (202) 785-6323); *Economic Outlook; The Footwear, Raw Hides and Skins, and Leather Industry in OECD Countries; Industrial Structure Statistics; The Iron and Steel Industry; Milk, Milk Products, and Egg Balances in OECD Member Countries; OECD Economic Surveys: Spain; The Pulp and Paper Industry;* and *Review of Fisheries in OECD Member Countries*.

St. Martin's Press, Inc., 175 Fifth Avenue, New York, New York 10010 (800) 221-7945; *The Statesman's Year-Book*.

Statistical Office of the United Nations, Publishing Service, New York, New York 10017 (800) 253-9646; *Trends in Europe and North America: The Statistical Yearbook of the Economic Commission for Europe*.

United Nations Conference on Trade and Development (UNCTAD), New York, New York 10017 (800) 253-9646; *Handbook of International Trade and Development Statistics*.

The World Bank, 1818 H Street, NW, Washington, D.C. 20433 (202) 477-1234; *World Development Report;* and *World Development Indicators*.

SPAIN - INCOME TAXES - See SPAIN - TAXATION

SPAIN - INDUSTRIAL METALS PRODUCTION - See SPAIN - MINING AND MINERAL PRODUCTS

SPAIN - INDUSTRY

Central Intelligence Agency, Washington, D.C. 20505 (703) 482-1100, www.cia.gov; *The World Factbook*.

Economist Intelligence Unit, 111 West 57th Street, New York, New York 10019 (800) 938-4685; *Spain Country Report*.

Euromonitor International, Inc., 122 South Michigan Avenue, Suite 1200, Chicago, Illinois 60603 (800) 577-EURO: *World Marketing Data and Statistics*.

Europa Publications Limited, 18 Bedford Square, London, WC1B 3JN, England; *The Europa World Year Book*.

European Commission Office of Press and Public Affairs, 2100 M Street, NW, Washington, D.C. 20037 (202) 862-9500; *Basic Statistics of the Community; Employment and Unemployment; Eurostatistics: Data for Short-Term Economic Analysis; Labor Force Sample Survey;* and *The World Economic Factbook*.

Federal Statistical Office, Gustav-Stresemann-Ring 11, D-6200 Wiesbaden, Germany; *Spain*.

International Labour Office, I.L.O. Publications, 1828 L Street, NW, Washington, D.C. 20036 (301) 638-3152; *Yearbook of Labour Statistics*.

M.E. Sharpe, 80 Business Park Drive, Armonk, New York 10504 (800) 541-6563; *The Illustrated Book of World Rankings*.

Organisation for Economic Co-operation and Development (OECD), 2 rue Andre-Pascal, 75 Paris 16, France (Telephone Number in U.S. (202) 785-6323); *Economic Outlook; Indicators of Industrial Activity; Industrial Structure Statistics; Main Economic Indicators - Historical Statistics;* and *OECD Environmental Data*.

St. Martin's Press, Inc., 175 Fifth Avenue, New York, New York 10010 (800) 221-7945; *The Statesman's Year-Book*.

Statistical Office of the United Nations, Publishing Service, New York, New York 10017 (800) 253-9646; *Industrial Commodity Statistics Yearbook; Statistical Yearbook;* and *Trends in Europe and North America: The Statistical Yearbook of the Economic Commission for Europe*.

The World Bank, 1818 H Street, NW, Washington, D.C. 20433 (202) 477-1234; *World Development Indicators*.

World Intellectual Property Organization, 34 Chemin des Colombettes, CH-1211 Geneva 20. Switzerland; *Industrial Property Statistics*.

SPAIN - INFANT AND MATERNAL MORTALITY - See SPAIN - MORTALITY
SPAIN - INTEREST RATES

European Commission Office of Press and Public Affairs, 2100 M Street, NW, Washington, D.C. 20037 (202) 862-9500; *Money and Finance*.

Organisation for Economic Co-operation and Development (OECD), 2 rue Andre-Pascal, 75 Paris 16, France (Telephone Number in U.S. (202) 785-6323); *Economic Outlook; Financial Market Trends; Main Economic Indicators - Historical Statistics;* and *OECD Financial Statistics*.

SPAIN - INTERNAL TRADE

European Commission Office of Press and Public Affairs, 2100 M Street, NW, Washington, D.C. 20037 (202) 862-9500; *Basic Statistics of the Community*.

Organisation for Economic Co-operation and Development (OECD), 2 rue Andre-Pascal, 75 Paris 16, France (Telephone Number in U.S. (202) 785-6323); *Main Economic Indicators - Historical Statistics*.

SPAIN - INTERNATIONAL FINANCE

European Commission Office of Press and Public Affairs, 2100 M Street, NW, Washington, D.C. 20037 (202) 862-9500; *Basic Statistics of the Community*.

Organisation for Economic Co-operation and Development (OECD), 2 rue Andre-Pascal, 75 Paris 16, France (Telephone Number in U.S. (202) 785-6323); *Economic Outlook;* and *Financial Market Trends*.

SPAIN - INTERNATIONAL LIQUIDITY

International Monetary Fund, 700 Nineteenth Street, NW, Washington, D.C. 20431 (202) 623-7000; *International Financial Statistics*.

Organisation for Economic Co-operation and Development (OECD), 2 rue Andre-Pascal, 75 Paris 16, France (Telephone Number in U.S. (202) 785-6323); *Economic Outlook;* and *Financial Market Trends*.

SPAIN - INTERNATIONAL RESERVES EXCLUDING GOLD

Statistical Office of the United Nations, Publishing Service, New York, New York 10017 (800) 253-9646; *Statistical Yearbook*.

The World Bank, 1818 H Street, NW, Washington, D.C. 20433 (202) 477-1234; *World Development Indicators*.

SPAIN - INTERNATIONAL STATISTICS

Organisation for Economic Co-operation and Development (OECD), 2 rue Andre-Pascal, 75 Paris 16, France (Telephone Number in U.S. (202) 785-6323); *Financial Market Trends;* and *Tourism Policy and International Tourism in OECD Member Countries*.

SPAIN - INVESTMENT

International Monetary Fund, 700 Nineteenth Street, NW, Washington, D.C. 20431 (202) 623-7000; *International Financial Statistics.*

Organisation for Economic Co-operation and Development (OECD), 2 rue Andre-Pascal, 75 Paris 16, France (Telephone Number in U.S. (202) 785-6323); *Economic Outlook; Financial Market Trends; Industrial Structure Statistics; The Iron and Steel Industry; Main Economic Indicators - Historical Statistics;* and *Textile Industry in OECD Countries.*

SPAIN - IRON ORE - See SPAIN - MINING AND MINERAL PRODUCTS

SPAIN - LABOR

Central Intelligence Agency, Washington, D.C. 20505 (703) 482-1100, www.cia.gov; *The World Factbook.*

Euromonitor International, Inc., 122 South Michigan Avenue, Suite 1200, Chicago, Illinois 60603 (800) 577-EURO: *World Marketing Data and Statistics.*

Europa Publications Limited, 18 Bedford Square, London, WC1B 3JN, England; *The Europa World Year Book.*

European Commission Office of Press and Public Affairs, 2100 M Street, NW, Washington, D.C. 20037 (202) 862-9500; *Basic Statistics of the Community; Labor Force Sample Survey;* and *Regions: Statistical Yearbook.*

Food and Agricultural Organization of the United Nations (FAO) Via delle Terme di Caracalla, 00100 Rome, Italy (Telephone Number in U.S. (202) 653-2400); *The State of Food and Agriculture.*

International Labour Office, I.L.O. Publications, 1828 L Street, NW, Washington, D.C. 20036 (301) 638-3152; *Yearbook of Labour Statistics.*

M.E. Sharpe, 80 Business Park Drive, Armonk, New York 10504 (800) 541-6563; *The Illustrated Book of World Rankings.*

Organisation for Economic Co-operation and Development (OECD), 2 rue Andre-Pascal, 75 Paris 16, France (Telephone Number in U.S. (202) 785-6323); *Economic Outlook; The Iron and Steel Industry; Main Economic Indicators - Historical Statistics; Maritime Transport; OECD Economic Surveys: Spain; OECD Employment Outlook;* and *Textile Industry in OECD Countries.*

St. Martin's Press, Inc., 175 Fifth Avenue, New York, New York 10010 (800) 221-7945; *The Statesman's Year-Book.*

Statistical Office of the United Nations, Publishing Service, New York, New York 10017 (800) 253-9646; *Human Development Report.*

The World Bank, 1818 H Street, NW, Washington, D.C. 20433 (202) 477-1234; *The World Bank Atlas; World Development Report;* and *World Development Indicators.*

SPAIN - LAND USE

Central Intelligence Agency, Washington, D.C. 20505 (703) 482-1100, www.cia.gov; *The World Factbook.*

Euromonitor International, Inc., 122 South Michigan Avenue, Suite 1200, Chicago, Illinois 60603 (800) 577-EURO; *European Marketing Data and Statistics.*

European Commission Office of Press and Public Affairs, 2100 M Street, NW, Washington, D.C. 20037 (202) 862-9500; *Agriculture: Statistical Yearbook; Basic Statistics of the Community; Crop Production: Quarterly Statistics;* and *Regions: Statistical Yearbook.*

Food and Agricultural Organization of the United Nations (FAO), Via delle Terme di Caracalla, 00100 Rome, Italy (Telephone Number in U.S. (202) 653-2400); *Production Yearbook.*

The World Bank, 1818 H Street, NW, Washington, D.C. 20433 (202) 477-1234; *World Development Report.*

SPAIN - LEAD AND LEAD ORE PRODUCTION AND CONSUMPTION - See SPAIN - MINING AND MINERAL PRODUCTS

SPAIN - LEATHER - PRODUCTION INDEX

Organisation for Economic Co-operation and Development (OECD), 2 rue Andre-Pascal, 75 Paris 16, France (Telephone Number in U.S. (202) 785-6323); *Indicators of Industrial Activity.*

SPAIN - LEATHER AND FOOTWEAR - EXPORTS AND IMPORTS

European Commission Office of Press and Public Affairs, 2100 M Street, NW, Washington, D.C. 20037 (202) 862-9500; *Basic Statistics of the Community.*

Organisation for Economic Co-operation and Development (OECD), 2 rue Andre-Pascal, 75 Paris 16, France (Telephone Number in U.S. (202) 785-6323); *The Footwear, Raw Hides and Skins, and Leather Industry in OECD Countries.*

SPAIN - LIBRARIES

Euromonitor International, Inc., 122

South Michigan Avenue, Suite 1200, Chicago, Illinois 60603 (800) 577-EURO; *European Marketing Data and Statistics.*

M.E. Sharpe, 80 Business Park Drive, Armonk, New York 10504 (800) 541-6563; *The Illustrated Book of World Rankings.*

Statistical Office of the United Nations, Publishing Service, New York, New York 10017 (800) 253-9646; *Trends in Europe and North America: The Statistical Yearbook of the Economic Commission for Europe.*

United Nations Educational, Scientific and Cultural Organization (UNESCO), 7 Place de Fontenoy, F-75700 Paris, France (Telephone Number in U.S. (212) 963-5981); *Statistical Yearbook.*

SPAIN - LIFE EXPECTANCY

Central Intelligence Agency, Washington, D.C. 20505 (703) 482-1100, www.cia.gov; *The World Factbook.*

Euromonitor International, Inc., 122 South Michigan Avenue, Suite 1200, Chicago, Illinois 60603 (800) 577-EURO; *The World Economic Factbook.*

Organisation for Economic Co-operation and Development (OECD), 2 rue Andre-Pascal, 75 Paris 16, France (Telephone Number in U.S. (202) 785-6323); *Economic Outlook.*

Statistical Office of the United Nations, Publishing Service, New York, New York 10017 (800) 253-9646; *Human Development Report; Trends in Europe and North America: The Statistical Yearbook of the Economic Commission for Europe;* and *World Statistics Pocketbook.*

The World Bank, 1818 H Street, NW, Washington, D.C. 20433 (202) 477-1234; *The World Bank Atlas;* and *World Development Report.*

SPAIN - LIGNITE PRODUCTION - See SPAIN - MINING AND MINERAL PRODUCTS

SPAIN - LITERACY RATE

Euromonitor International, Inc., 122 South Michigan Avenue, Suite 1200, Chicago, Illinois 60603 (800) 577-EURO: *World Marketing Data and Statistics.*

SPAIN - LIVESTOCK AND POULTRY

Commodity Research Bureau, Inc., 30 South Wacker Drive, Chicago Illinois 60606 (312) 454-1801; *Commodity Year Book.*

Euromonitor International, Inc., 122 South Michigan Avenue, Suite 1200, Chicago, Illinois 60603 (800) 577-EURO; *European Marketing Data and Statistics.*

European Commission Office of Press and Public Affairs, 2100 M Street, NW, Washington, D.C. 20037 (202) 862-9500; *Agriculture: Statistical Yearbook; Basic Statistics of the Community; Eurostatistics: Data for Short-Term Economic Analysis;* and *Regions: Statistical Yearbook.*

Food and Agricultural Organization of the United Nations (FAO), Via delle Terme di Caracalla, 00100 Rome, Italy (Telephone Number in U.S. (202) 653-2400); *Production Yearbook;* and *The State of Food and Agriculture.*

M.E. Sharpe, 80 Business Park Drive, Armonk, New York 10504 (800) 541-6563; *The Illustrated Book of World Rankings.*

Organisation for Economic Co-operation and Development (OECD), 2 rue Andre-Pascal, 75 Paris 16, France (Telephone Number in U.S. (202) 785-6323); *Economic Accounts for Agriculture;* and *Meat Balances in OECD Member Countries.*

St. Martin's Press, Inc., 175 Fifth Avenue, New York, New York 10010 (800) 221-7945; *The Statesman's Year-Book.*

Statistical Office of the United Nations, Publishing Service, New York, New York 10017 (800) 253-9646; *Statistical Yearbook.*

United Nations Conference on Trade and Development, Central Statistical Service, Palais des Nations, Geneva, Switzerland (Telephone in U.S. (800) 253-9646); *UNCTAD Commodity Yearbook.*

SPAIN - LIVING LEVELS - See SPAIN - LIFE EXPECTANCY

SPAIN - MACHINERY - PRODUCTION INDEX

Organisation for Economic Co-operation and Development (OECD), 2 rue Andre-Pascal, 75 Paris 16, France (Telephone Number in U.S. (202) 785-6323); *Indicators of Industrial Activity.*

SPAIN - MAGNESIUM PRODUCTION AND CONSUMPTION - See SPAIN - MINING AND MINERAL PRODUCTS

SPAIN - MAIL - NUMBER OF PIECES SENT OR RECEIVED

European Commission Office of Press and Public Affairs, 2100 M Street, NW, Washington, D.C. 20037 (202) 862-9500; *Transport Annual Statistics.*

Statistical Office of the United Nations, Publishing Service, New York, New York 10017 (800) 253-9646; *Statistical Yearbook.*

SPAIN - MANGANESE AND MANGANESE ORE PRODUCTION AND CONSUMPTION -

See SPAIN - MINING AND MINERAL PRODUCTS

SPAIN - MANUFACTURING

American Automobile Manufacturers Association, 1401 H Street, NW, Suite 900, Washington, D.C. 20005 (202) 326-5500; *World Motor Vehicle Data.*

European Commission Office of Press and Public Affairs, 2100 M Street, NW, Washington, D.C. 20037 (202) 862-9500; Basic Statistics of the Community, *Eurostatistics: Data for Short-Term Economic Analysis;* and *Industrial Production: Quarterly Statistics.*

M.E. Sharpe, 80 Business Park Drive, Armonk, New York 10504 (800) 541-6563; *The Illustrated Book of World Rankings.*

Organisation for Economic Co-operation and Development (OECD), 2 rue Andre-Pascal, 75 Paris 16, France (Telephone Number in U.S. (202) 785-6323); *Foreign Trade by Commodities; Indicators of Industrial Activity, Industrial Structure Statistics;* and *OECD Economic Surveys: Spain.*

Statistical Office of the United Nations, Publishing Service, New York, New York 10017 (800) 253-9646; *Statistical Yearbook.*

The World Bank, 1818 H Street, NW, Washington, D.C. 20433 (202) 477-1234; *World Development Indicators.*

SPAIN - MARRIAGE RATES

Europa Publications Limited, 18 Bedford Square, London, WC1B 3JN, England; *The Europa World Year Book.*

European Commission Office of Press and Public Affairs, 2100 M Street, NW, Washington, D.C. 20037 (202) 862-9500; *Basic Statistics of the Community.*

M.E. Sharpe, 80 Business Park Drive, Armonk, New York 10504 (800) 541-6563; *The Illustrated Book of World Rankings.*

Statistical Office of the United Nations, Publishing Service, New York, New York 10017 (800) 253-9646; *Demographic Yearbook; Trends in Europe and North America: The Statistical Yearbook of the Economic Commission for Europe;* and *Statistical Yearbook.*

SPAIN - MEAT PRODUCTION - See SPAIN - LIVESTOCK AND POULTRY

SPAIN - MERCHANT SHIPPING

Europa Publications Limited, 18 Bedford Square, London, WC1B 3JN, England; *The Europa World Year Book.*

European Commission Office of Press and Public Affairs, 2100 M Street, NW, Washington, D.C. 20037 (202) 862-9500; *Basic Statistics of the Community; Fisheries: Yearly Statistics; Regions: Statistical Yearbook;* and *Transport Annual Statistics.*

Lloyd's Register of Shipping, 17 Battery Place, New York, New York 10004 (212) 425-8050; *Register of Ships.*

Organisation for Economic Co-operation and Development (OECD), 2 rue Andre-Pascal, 75 Paris 16, France (Telephone Number in U.S. (202) 785-6323); *Maritime Transport.*

St. Martin's Press, Inc., 175 Fifth Avenue, New York, New York 10010 (800) 221-7945; *The Statesman's Year-Book.*

Statistical Office of the United Nations, Publishing Service, New York, New York 10017 (800) 253-9646; *Statistical Yearbook.*

U.S. Department of Transportation, Maritime Administration, 400 Seventh Street, SW, Washington, D.C. 20590 (202) 366-5807, www.marad.dot.gov; *A Statistical Analysis of the World's Merchant Fleets.*

SPAIN - MERCURY PRODUCTION AND CONSUMPTION - See SPAIN - MINING AND MINERAL PRODUCTS

SPAIN - MILITARY

Central Intelligence Agency, Washington, D.C. 20505 (703) 482-1100, www.cia.gov; *The World Factbook.*

Euromonitor International, Inc., 122 South Michigan Avenue, Suite 1200, Chicago, Illinois 60603 (800) 577-EURO: *World Marketing Data and Statistics.*

European Commission Office of Press and Public Affairs, 2100 M Street, NW, Washington, D.C. 20037 (202) 862-9500; *Government Financing of Research and Development.*

The International Institute for Strategic Studies, 23 Tavistock Street, London WC2E 7NQ, England 44 171 3797676; *The Military Balance.*

International Monetary Fund, 700 Nineteenth Street, NW, Washington, D.C. 20431 (202) 623-7000; *Government Finance Statistics Yearbook.*

St. Martin's Press, Inc., 175 Fifth Avenue, New York, New York 10010 (800) 221-7945; *The Statesman's Year-Book.*

Statistical Office of the United Nations, Publishing Service, New York, New York 10017 (800) 253-9646; *Human*

Development Report.

U.S. Arms Control and Disarmament Agency, 320 Twenty-first Street, NW, Washington, D.C. 20451 (202) 647-8677; *World Military Expenditures and Arms Transfers.*

SPAIN - MILK PRODUCTION - See SPAIN - DAIRY PRODUCTS

SPAIN - MINING AND MINERAL PRODUCTS

Commodity Research Bureau, Inc., 30 South Wacker Drive, Chicago Illinois 60606 (312) 454-1801; *Commodity Year Book.*

Europa Publications Limited, 18 Bedford Square, London, WC1B 3JN, England; *The Europa World Year Book.*

European Commission Office of Press and Public Affairs, 2100 M Street, NW, Washington, D.C. 20037 (202) 862-9500; *ACP: Basic Statistics; Basic Statistics of the Community; Energy: Monthly Statistics; Energy Statistics Yearbook; Eurostatistics: Data for Short-Term Economic Analysis; Industrial Production: Quarterly Statistics; Iron and Steel: Statistical Yearbook; Labor Force Sample Survey; OECD Economic Surveys: Spain; and Regions: Statistical Yearbook.*

International Iron and Steel Institute, 120, rue Colonel Bourg, B-1140, Brussels, Belgium; *Steel Statistical Yearbook.*

International Lead and Zinc Study Group, Metro House, 58 St. James's Street, London SW1A 1LD, England; *Lead and Zinc Statistics.*

M.E. Sharpe, 80 Business Park Drive, Armonk, New York 10504 (800) 541-6563; *The Illustrated Book of World Rankings.*

Organisation for Economic Co-operation and Development (OECD), 2 rue Andre-Pascal, 75 Paris 16, France (Telephone Number in U.S. (202) 785-6323); *Coal Information; Energy Statistics of OECD Countries; Foreign Trade by Commodities; Indicators of Industrial Activity; Industrial Structure Statistics; The Iron and Steel Industry; and The Non-Ferrous Metals Industry.*

Penn Well Publishing Company, 1421 South Sheridan Road, P.O. Box 1260, Tulsa, Oklahoma 74101 (800) 752-9764; *International Energy Statistics Sourcebook.*

St. Martin's Press, Inc., 175 Fifth Avenue, New York, New York 10010 (800) 221-7945; *The Statesman's Year-Book.*

Statistical Office of the United Nations, Publishing Service, New York, New York 10017 (800) 253-9646; *Statistical Yearbook.*

United Nations Conference on Trade and Development, Central Statistical Service, Palais des Nations, Geneva, Switzerland (Telephone in U.S. (800) 253-9646); *UNCTAD Commodity Yearbook.*

World Bureau of Metal Statistics, 27-A High Street, Ware Hert SG12 9BA, England; *World Metal Statistics.*

SPAIN - MOLYBDENUM AND MOLYBDENUM ORE PRODUCTION AND CONSUMPTION - See SPAIN - MINING AND MINERAL PRODUCTS

SPAIN - MONEY EXCHANGE RATES - See SPAIN - EXCHANGE RATES

SPAIN - MONEY RATES - MARKET

European Commission Office of Press and Public Affairs, 2100 M Street, NW, Washington, D.C. 20037 (202) 862-9500; *Basic Statistics of the Community.*

Organisation for Economic Co-operation and Development (OECD), 2 rue Andre-Pascal, 75 Paris 16, France (Telephone Number in U.S. (202) 785-6323); *Economic Outlook;* and *Financial Market Trends.*

SPAIN - MONEY RESERVES

European Commission Office of Press and Public Affairs, 2100 M Street, NW, Washington, D.C. 20037 (202) 862-9500; *Basic Statistics of the Community.*

Organisation for Economic Co-operation and Development (OECD), 2 rue Andre-Pascal, 75 Paris 16, France (Telephone Number in U.S. (202) 785-6323); *Economic Outlook;* and *Financial Market Trends.*

SPAIN - MONEY SUPPLY

Economist Intelligence Unit, 111 West 57th Street, New York, New York 10019 (800) 938-4685; *Spain Country Report.*

Europa Publications Limited, 18 Bedford Square, London, WC1B 3JN, England; *The Europa World Year Book.*

European Commission Office of Press and Public Affairs, 2100 M Street, NW, Washington, D.C. 20037 (202) 862-9500; *Basic Statistics of the Community; Eurostatistics: Data for Short-Term Economic Analysis;* and *Money and Finance.*

International Monetary Fund, 700 Nineteenth Street, NW, Washington, D.C. 20431 (202) 623-7000; *International Financial Statistics.*

Organisation for Economic Co-operation and Development (OECD), 2 rue

Andre-Pascal, 75 Paris 16, France (Telephone Number in U.S. (202) 785-6323); *Economic Outlook.*

Statistical Office of the United Nations, Publishing Service, New York, New York 10017 (800) 253-9646; *Statistical Yearbook.*

The World Bank, 1818 H Street, NW, Washington, D.C. 20433 (202) 477-1234; *World Development Indicators.*

SPAIN - MORTALITY

Central Intelligence Agency, Washington, D.C. 20505 (703) 482-1100, www.cia.gov; *The World Factbook.*

Europa Publications Limited, 18 Bedford Square, London, WC1B 3JN, England; *The Europa World Year Book.*

European Commission Office of Press and Public Affairs, 2100 M Street, NW, Washington, D.C. 20037 (202) 862-9500; *Basic Statistics of the Community; Demographic Statistics;* and *The World Economic Factbook.*

St. Martin's Press, Inc., 175 Fifth Avenue, New York, New York 10010 (800) 221-7945; *The Statesman's Year-Book.*

Statistical Office of the United Nations, Publishing Service, New York, New York 10017 (800) 253-9646; *Demographic Yearbook; Human Development Report; Trends in Europe and North America: The Statistical Yearbook of the Economic Commission for Europe; Statistical Yearbook;* and *World Statistics Pocketbook.*

United Nations Children's Fund (UNICEF), 3 United Nations Plaza, New York, New York 10017 (800) 253-9646; *State of the World's Children.*

The World Bank, 1818 H Street, NW, Washington, D.C. 20433 (202) 477-1234; *The World Bank Atlas; World Development Report;* and *World Development Indicators.*

World Health Organization, Office of Publications, 20 Avenue Appia, CH-1211 Geneva 27, Switzerland (Telephone Number in U.S. (518) 436-9686); *World Health Statistics Annual.*

SPAIN - MOTION PICTURES

St. Martin's Press, Inc., 175 Fifth Avenue, New York, New York 10010 (800) 221-7945; *The Statesman's Year-Book.*

Statistical Office of the United Nations, Publishing Service, New York, New York 10017 (800) 253-9646; *Statistical Yearbook.*

United Nations Educational, Scientific and Cultural Organization (UNESCO), 7 Place de Fontenoy, F-75700 Paris, France

(Telephone Number in U.S. (212) 963-5981); *Statistical Yearbook.*

SPAIN - MOTOR VEHICLE PRODUCTION

American Automobile Manufacturers Association, 1401 H Street, NW, Suite 900, Washington, D.C. 20005 (202) 326-5500; *World Motor Vehicle Data.*

European Commission Office of Press and Public Affairs, 2100 M Street, NW, Washington, D.C. 20037 (202) 862-9500; *Basic Statistics of the Community;* and *Eurostatistics: Data for Short-Term Economic Analysis.*

Organisation for Economic Co-operation and Development (OECD), 2 rue Andre-Pascal, 75 Paris 16, France (Telephone Number in U.S. (202) 785-6323); *Foreign Trade by Commodities;* and *Indicators of Industrial Activity.*

Statistical Office of the United Nations, Publishing Service, New York, New York 10017 (800) 253-9646; *Statistical Yearbook.*

SPAIN - MOTOR VEHICLE TAXES - See SPAIN - TAXATION

SPAIN - MOTOR VEHICLES IN USE

American Automobile Manufacturers Association, 1401 H Street, NW, Suite 900, Washington, D.C. 20005 (202) 326-5500; *World Motor Vehicle Data.*

Europa Publications Limited, 18 Bedford Square, London, WC1B 3JN, England; *The Europa World Year Book.*

European Commission Office of Press and Public Affairs, 2100 M Street, NW, Washington, D.C. 20037 (202) 862-9500; *Basic Statistics of the Community;* and *Transport Annual Statistics.*

International Road Federation, 2600 Virginia Avenue, NW, Washington, D.C. 20037 (202) 338-4641; *World Road Statistics.*

Statistical Office of the United Nations, Publishing Service, New York, New York 10017 (800) 253-9646; *Statistical Yearbook.*

SPAIN - MULES - See SPAIN - LIVESTOCK AND POULTRY

SPAIN - MUSEUMS

Euromonitor International, Inc., 122 South Michigan Avenue, Suite 1200, Chicago, Illinois 60603 (800) 577-EURO; *European Marketing Data and Statistics.*

M.E. Sharpe, 80 Business Park Drive, Armonk, New York 10504 (800) 541-6563; *The Illustrated Book of World Rankings.*

United Nations Educational, Scientific and Cultural Organization (UNESCO), 7 Place de Fontenoy, F-75700 Paris, France (Telephone Number in U.S. (212) 963-5981); *Statistical Yearbook.*

SPAIN - NATALITY - See SPAIN - BIRTH RATE

SPAIN - NATIONAL ACCOUNTS

Europa Publications Limited, 18 Bedford Square, London, WC1B 3JN, England; *The Europa World Year Book.*

European Commission Office of Press and Public Affairs, 2100 M Street, NW, Washington, D.C. 20037 (202) 862-9500; *Basic Statistics of the Community;* and *Eurostatistics: Data for Short-Term Economic Analysis.*

Federal Statistical Office, Gustav-Stresemann-Ring 11, D-6200 Wiesbaden, Germany; *Spain.*

International Monetary Fund, 700 Nineteenth Street, NW, Washington, D.C. 20431 (202) 623-7000; *International Financial Statistics.*

Organisation for Economic Co-operation and Development (OECD), 2 rue Andre-Pascal, 75 Paris 16, France (Telephone Number in U.S. (202) 785-6323); *Economic Outlook.*

Statistical Office of the United Nations, Publishing Service, New York, New York 10017 (800) 253-9646; *National Accounts Statistics;* and *Statistical Yearbook.*

SPAIN - NATIONAL INCOME

M.E. Sharpe, 80 Business Park Drive, Armonk, New York 10504 (800) 541-6563; *The Illustrated Book of World Rankings.*

Organisation for Economic Co-operation and Development (OECD), 2 rue Andre-Pascal, 75 Paris 16, France (Telephone Number in U.S. (202) 785-6323); *Economic Outlook.*

Statistical Office of the United Nations, Publishing Service, New York, New York 10017 (800) 253-9646; *National Accounts Statistics;* and *Statistical Yearbook.*

SPAIN - NATIONAL PRODUCT

European Commission Office of Press and Public Affairs, 2100 M Street, NW, Washington, D.C. 20037 (202) 862-9500; *Basic Statistics of the Community.*

M.E. Sharpe, 80 Business Park Drive, Armonk, New York 10504 (800) 541-6563; *The Illustrated Book of World Rankings.*

Organisation for Economic Co-

operation and Development (OECD), 2 rue Andre-Pascal, 75 Paris 16, France (Telephone Number in U.S. (202) 785-6323); *Economic Outlook.*

Statistical Office of the United Nations, Publishing Service, New York, New York 10017 (800) 253-9646; *Statistical Yearbook.*

SPAIN - NATURAL GAS PRODUCTION - See SPAIN - MINING AND MINERAL PRODUCTS

SPAIN - NEWSPAPER PRODUCTION - See SPAIN - FORESTRY AND FOREST PRODUCTS

SPAIN - NICKEL AND NICKEL ORE PRODUCTION AND CONSUMPTION - See SPAIN - MINING AND MINERAL PRODUCTS

SPAIN - NITRIC ACID PRODUCTION - See SPAIN - MINING AND MINERAL PRODUCTS

SPAIN - OATS PRODUCTION - See SPAIN - CROPS

SPAIN - OCCUPATIONS - See SPAIN - LABOR

SPAIN - OIL PRODUCING CROPS

European Commission Office of Press and Public Affairs, 2100 M Street, NW, Washington, D.C. 20037 (202) 862-9500; *Basic Statistics of the Community.*

Organisation for Economic Co-operation and Development (OECD), 2 rue Andre-Pascal, 75 Paris 16, France (Telephone Number in U.S. (202) 785-6323); *Foreign Trade by Commodities.*

SPAIN - ONION PRODUCTION - See SPAIN - CROPS

SPAIN - ORANGES PRODUCTION - See SPAIN - CROPS

SPAIN - PAPER EXPORTS AND IMPORTS - See SPAIN - FORESTRY AND FOREST PRODUCTS

SPAIN - PATENTS, TRADEMARKS AND SERVICE MARKS

Statistical Office of the United Nations, Publishing Service, New York, New York 10017 (800) 253-9646; *Statistical Yearbook.*

World Intellectual Property Organization, 34 Chemin des Colombettes, CH-1211 Geneva 20. Switzerland; *Industrial Property Statistics.*

SPAIN - PEANUT PRODUCTION - See SPAIN - CROPS

SPAIN - PERIODICALS

United Nations Educational, Scientific and Cultural Organization (UNESCO), 7

Place de Fontenoy, F-75700 Paris, France (Telephone Number in U.S. (212) 963-5981); *Statistical Yearbook*.

SPAIN - PESTICIDE USE

Food and Agricultural Organization of the United Nations (FAO) Via delle Terme di Caracalla, 00100 Rome, Italy (Telephone Number in U.S. (202) 653-2400); *The State of Food and Agriculture*.

SPAIN - PETROLEUM INDUSTRY

Euromonitor International, Inc., 122 South Michigan Avenue, Suite 1200, Chicago, Illinois 60603 (800) 577-EURO; *European Marketing Data and Statistics*.

European Commission Office of Press and Public Affairs, 2100 M Street, NW, Washington, D.C. 20037 (202) 862-9500; *ACP: Basic Statistics; Basic Statistics of the Community;* and *Energy Statistics Yearbook*.

Food and Agricultural Organization of the United Nations (FAO) Via delle Terme di Caracalla, 00100 Rome, Italy (Telephone Number in U.S. (202) 653-2400); *The State of Food and Agriculture*.

M.E. Sharpe, 80 Business Park Drive, Armonk, New York 10504 (800) 541-6563; *The Illustrated Book of World Rankings*.

Organisation for Economic Co-operation and Development (OECD), 2 rue Andre-Pascal, 75 Paris 16, France (Telephone Number in U.S. (202) 785-6323); *Energy Statistics of OECD Countries; Foreign Trade by Commodities; Indicators of Industrial Activity; Oil Statistics;* and *Oil and Gas Information*.

Penn Well Publishing Company, 1421 South Sheridan Road, P.O. Box 1260, Tulsa, Oklahoma 74101 (800) 752-9764; *International Energy Statistics Sourcebook*.

St. Martin's Press, Inc., 175 Fifth Avenue, New York, New York 10010 (800) 221-7945; *The Statesman's Year-Book*.

Statistical Office of the United Nations, Publishing Service, New York, New York 10017 (800) 253-9646; *Statistical Yearbook;* and *Trends in Europe and North America: The Statistical Yearbook of the Economic Commission for Europe*.

United Nations Conference on Trade and Development, Central Statistical Service, Palais des Nations, Geneva, Switzerland (Telephone in U.S. (800) 253-9646); *UNCTAD Commodity Yearbook*.

SPAIN - PHOSPHATES AND PHOSPHATE ROCK PRODUCTION - See SPAIN - MINING AND MINERAL PRODUCTS

SPAIN - PIG-IRON AND FERRO-ALLOY PRODUCTION - See SPAIN - MINING AND MINERAL PRODUCTS

SPAIN - PIGS - See SPAIN - LIVESTOCK AND POULTRY

SPAIN - PIPELINES FOR OIL AND PETROLEUM PRODUCTS

European Commission Office of Press and Public Affairs, 2100 M Street, NW, Washington, D.C. 20037 (202) 862-9500; *Transport Annual Statistics*.

Statistical Office of the United Nations, Publishing Service, New York, New York 10017 (800) 253-9646; *Annual Bulletin of Transport Statistics for Europe*.

SPAIN - PLASTIC AND RESIN PRODUCTION

Commodity Research Bureau, Inc., 30 South Wacker Drive, Chicago Illinois 60606 (312) 454-1801; *Commodity Year Book*.

European Commission Office of Press and Public Affairs, 2100 M Street, NW, Washington, D.C. 20037 (202) 862-9500; *Basic Statistics of the Community*.

Organisation for Economic Co-operation and Development (OECD), 2 rue Andre-Pascal, 75 Paris 16, France (Telephone Number in U.S. (202) 785-6323); *Foreign Trade by Commodities*.

Statistical Office of the United Nations, Publishing Service, New York, New York 10017 (800) 253-9646; *Statistical Yearbook*.

SPAIN - PLATINUM PRODUCTION - See SPAIN - MINING AND MINERAL PRODUCTS

SPAIN - POPULATION

Central Intelligence Agency, Washington, D.C. 20505 (703) 482-1100, www.cia.gov; *The World Factbook*.

Economist Intelligence Unit, 111 West 57th Street, New York, New York 10019 (800) 938-4685; *Spain Country Report*.

Euromonitor International, Inc., 122 South Michigan Avenue, Suite 1200, Chicago, Illinois 60603 (800) 577-EURO; *European Marketing Data and Statistics;* and *The World Economic Factbook*.

Europa Publications Limited, 18 Bedford Square, London, WC1B 3JN, England; *The Europa World Year Book*.

European Commission Office of Press and Public Affairs, 2100 M Street, NW, Washington, D.C. 20037 (202) 862-9500; *ACP: Basic Statistics; Basic Statistics of the Community; Demographic Statistics; Employment and Unemployment; Fisheries: Yearly Statistics; Iron and Steel:*

Statistical Yearbook; Labor Force Sample Survey; and *Regions: Statistical Yearbook*.

Federal Statistical Office, Gustav-Stresemann-Ring 11, D-6200 Wiesbaden, Germany; *Spain*.

Food and Agricultural Organization of the United Nations (FAO), Via delle Terme di Caracalla, 00100 Rome, Italy (Telephone Number in U.S. (202) 653-2400); *Production Yearbook*.

International Labour Office, I.L.O. Publications, 1828 L Street, NW, Washington, D.C. 20036 (301) 638-3152; *Yearbook of Labour Statistics*.

M.E. Sharpe, 80 Business Park Drive, Armonk, New York 10504 (800) 541-6563; *The Illustrated Book of World Rankings*.

St. Martin's Press, Inc., 175 Fifth Avenue, New York, New York 10010 (800) 221-7945; *The Statesman's Year-Book*.

Statistical Office of the United Nations, Publishing Service, New York, New York 10017 (800) 253-9646; *Demographic Yearbook; Human Development Report; Statistical Yearbook; Trends in Europe and North America: The Statistical Yearbook of the Economic Commission for Europe;* and *World Statistics Pocketbook*.

United Nations Educational, Scientific and Cultural Organization (UNESCO), 7 Place de Fontenoy, F-75700 Paris, France (Telephone Number in U.S. (212) 963-5981); *Statistical Yearbook*.

U.S. Arms Control and Disarmament Agency, 320 Twenty-first Street, NW, Washington, D.C. 20451 (202) 647-8677; *World Military Expenditures and Arms Transfers*.

The World Bank, 1818 H Street, NW, Washington, D.C. 20433 (202) 477-1234; *The World Bank Atlas;* and *World Development Report*.

World Health Organization, Office of Publications, 20 Avenue Appia, CH-1211 Geneva 27, Switzerland (Telephone Number in U.S. (518) 436-9686); *World Health Statistics Annual*.

SPAIN - POST OFFICES

M.E. Sharpe, 80 Business Park Drive, Armonk, New York 10504 (800) 541-6563; *The Illustrated Book of World Rankings*.

St. Martin's Press, Inc., 175 Fifth Avenue, New York, New York 10010 (800) 221-7945; *The Statesman's Year-Book*.

Statistical Office of the United Nations, Publishing Service, New York, New York 10017 (800) 253-9646; *Trends in Europe and*

North America: The Statistical Yearbook of the Economic Commission for Europe.

SPAIN - POTATO PRODUCTION - See SPAIN - CROPS

SPAIN - POWER PRODUCTION INDUSTRY

European Commission Office of Press and Public Affairs, 2100 M Street, NW, Washington, D.C. 20037 (202) 862-9500; *Basic Statistics of the Community.*

Statistical Office of the United Nations, Publishing Service, New York, New York 10017 (800) 253-9646; *Statistical Yearbook.*

SPAIN - PRICES

European Commission Office of Press and Public Affairs, 2100 M Street, NW, Washington, D.C. 20037 (202) 862-9500; *Basic Statistics of the Community;* and *Eurostatistics: Data for Short-Term Economic Analysis.*

Federal Statistical Office, Gustav-Stresemann-Ring 11, D-6200 Wiesbaden, Germany; *Spain.*

Food and Agricultural Organization of the United Nations (FAO), Via delle Terme di Caracalla, 00100 Rome, Italy (Telephone Number in U.S. (202) 653-2400); *Production Yearbook;* and *The State of Food and Agriculture.*

International Labour Office, I.L.O. Publications, 1828 L Street, NW, Washington, D.C. 20036 (301) 638-3152; *Yearbook of Labour Statistics.*

International Lead and Zinc Study Group, Metro House, 58 St. James's Street, London SW1A 1LD, England; *Lead and Zinc Statistics.*

International Monetary Fund, 700 Nineteenth Street, NW, Washington, D.C. 20431 (202) 623-7000; *International Financial Statistics.*

M.E. Sharpe, 80 Business Park Drive, Armonk, New York 10504 (800) 541-6563; *The Illustrated Book of World Rankings.*

Organisation for Economic Co-operation and Development (OECD), 2 rue Andre-Pascal, 75 Paris 16, France (Telephone Number in U.S. (202) 785-6323); *Economic Outlook; The Footwear, Raw Hides and Skins, and Leather Industry in OECD Countries; Indicators of Industrial Activity; The Iron and Steel Industry; Main Economic Indicators - Historical Statistics;* and *The Pulp and Paper Industry.*

World Bureau of Metal Statistics, 27-A High Street, Ware Hert SG12 9BA, England; *World Metal Statistics.*

SPAIN - PRINTING AND WRITING PAPER - See SPAIN - FORESTRY AND FOREST PRODUCTS

SPAIN - PRODUCTION

American Automobile Manufacturers Association, 1401 H Street, NW, Suite 900, Washington, D.C. 20005 (202) 326-5500; *World Motor Vehicle Data.*

European Commission Office of Press and Public Affairs, 2100 M Street, NW, Washington, D.C. 20037 (202) 862-9500; *Basic Statistics of the Community; Eurostatistics: Data for Short-Term Economic Analysis;* and *Fisheries: Yearly Statistics.*

International Iron and Steel Institute, 120, rue Colonel Bourg, B-1140, Brussels, Belgium; *Steel Statistical Yearbook.*

International Lead and Zinc Study Group, Metro House, 58 St. James's Street, London SW1A 1LD, England; *Lead and Zinc Statistics.*

M.E. Sharpe, 80 Business Park Drive, Armonk, New York 10504 (800) 541-6563; *The Illustrated Book of World Rankings.*

Organisation for Economic Co-operation and Development (OECD), 2 rue Andre-Pascal, 75 Paris 16, France (Telephone Number in U.S. (202) 785-6323); *Economic Outlook; The Footwear, Raw Hides and Skins, and Leather Industry in OECD Countries; Indicators of Industrial Activity; Industrial Structure Statistics; The Iron and Steel Industry; Meat Balances in OECD Member Countries; Milk, Milk Products, and Egg Balances in OECD Member Countries; The Non-Ferrous Metals Industry; The Pulp and Paper Industry;* and *Textile Industry in OECD Countries.*

SPAIN - PRODUCTIVITY

European Commission Office of Press and Public Affairs, 2100 M Street, NW, Washington, D.C. 20037 (202) 862-9500; *Basic Statistics of the Community.*

Organisation for Economic Co-operation and Development (OECD), 2 rue Andre-Pascal, 75 Paris 16, France (Telephone Number in U.S. (202) 785-6323); *Economic Outlook.*

SPAIN - PROPERTY TAXES - See SPAIN - TAXATION

SPAIN - PUBLIC CONSUMPTION FUND

European Commission Office of Press and Public Affairs, 2100 M Street, NW, Washington, D.C. 20037 (202) 862-9500; *Basic Statistics of the Community.*

Organisation for Economic Co-

operation and Development (OECD), 2 rue Andre-Pascal, 75 Paris 16, France (Telephone Number in U.S. (202) 785-6323); *Revenue Statistics of OECD Member Countries.*

SPAIN - PUBLIC EXPENDITURES

European Commission Office of Press and Public Affairs, 2100 M Street, NW, Washington, D.C. 20037 (202) 862-9500; *Basic Statistics of the Community.*

Organisation for Economic Co-operation and Development (OECD), 2 rue Andre-Pascal, 75 Paris 16, France (Telephone Number in U.S. (202) 785-6323); *Revenue Statistics of OECD Member Countries.*

SPAIN - PUBLIC FINANCE - See SPAIN - FINANCE

SPAIN - PUBLIC HEALTH - See SPAIN - HEALTH

SPAIN - PUBLIC REVENUES

Organisation for Economic Co-operation and Development (OECD), 2 rue Andre-Pascal, 75 Paris 16, France (Telephone Number in U.S. (202) 785-6323); *Revenue Statistics of OECD Member Countries.*

SPAIN - RADIO BROADCASTING - See SPAIN - BROADCASTING

SPAIN - RADIO RECEIVER PRODUCTION

Statistical Office of the United Nations, Publishing Service, New York, New York 10017 (800) 253-9646; *Statistical Yearbook.*

SPAIN - RADIO RECEIVERS

St. Martin's Press, Inc., 175 Fifth Avenue, New York, New York 10010 (800) 221-7945; *The Statesman's Year-Book.*

SPAIN - RAILWAYS

Euromonitor International, Inc., 122 South Michigan Avenue, Suite 1200, Chicago, Illinois 60603 (800) 577-EURO; *European Marketing Data and Statistics.*

Europa Publications Limited, 18 Bedford Square, London, WC1B 3JN, England; *The Europa World Year Book.*

European Commission Office of Press and Public Affairs, 2100 M Street, NW, Washington, D.C. 20037 (202) 862-9500; *Basic Statistics of the Community; Regions: Statistical Yearbook;* and *Transport Annual Statistics.*

Jane's Information Group, Sentinel

House, 163 Brighton Road, Coulsdon, Surrey CR5 2NH, England (Telephone Number in U.S. (703) 683-3700); *Jane's World Railways.*

St. Martin's Press, Inc., 175 Fifth Avenue, New York, New York 10010 (800) 221-7945; *The Statesman's Year-Book.*

Statistical Office of the United Nations, Publishing Service, New York, New York 10017 (800) 253-9646; *Annual Bulletin of Transport Statistics for Europe; Trends in Europe and North America: The Statistical Yearbook of the Economic Commission for Europe;* and *Statistical Yearbook.*

SPAIN - RANCHING

European Commission Office of Press and Public Affairs, 2100 M Street, NW, Washington, D.C. 20037 (202) 862-9500; *Basic Statistics of the Community.*

SPAIN - RELIGION

Central Intelligence Agency, Washington, D.C. 20505 (703) 482-1100, www.cia.gov; *The World Factbook.*

M.E. Sharpe, 80 Business Park Drive, Armonk, New York 10504 (800) 541-6563; *The Illustrated Book of World Rankings.*

St. Martin's Press, Inc., 175 Fifth Avenue, New York, New York 10010 (800) 221-7945; *The Statesman's Year-Book.*

SPAIN - RENT PRICES

International Labour Office, I.L.O. Publications, 1828 L Street, NW, Washington, D.C. 20036 (301) 638-3152; *Yearbook of Labour Statistics.*

SPAIN - RETAIL TRADE

Euromonitor International, Inc., 122 South Michigan Avenue, Suite 1200, Chicago, Illinois 60603 (800) 577-EURO: *World Marketing Data and Statistics;* and *Retail Trade International.*

European Commission Office of Press and Public Affairs, 2100 M Street, NW, Washington, D.C. 20037 (202) 862-9500; *Basic Statistics of the Community;* and *Eurostatistics: Data for Short-Term Economic Analysis.*

SPAIN - RICE PRODUCTION - See SPAIN - CROPS

SPAIN - ROUNDWOOD PRODUCTION - See SPAIN - FORESTRY AND FOREST PRODUCTS

SPAIN - RUBBER PRODUCTION AND CONSUMPTION

European Commission Office of Press

and Public Affairs, 2100 M Street, NW, Washington, D.C. 20037 (202) 862-9500; *Basic Statistics of the Community.*

M.E. Sharpe, 80 Business Park Drive, Armonk, New York 10504 (800) 541-6563; *The Illustrated Book of World Rankings.*

Organisation for Economic Co-operation and Development (OECD), 2 rue Andre-Pascal, 75 Paris 16, France (Telephone Number in U.S. (202) 785-6323); *Foreign Trade by Commodities.*

Statistical Office of the United Nations, Publishing Service, New York, New York 10017 (800) 253-9646; *Statistical Yearbook.*

SPAIN - RYE PRODUCTION - See SPAIN - CROPS

SPAIN - SALT PRODUCTION - See SPAIN - MINING AND MINERAL PRODUCTS

SPAIN - SAVINGS ACCOUNT DEPOSITS - See SPAIN - BANKING

SPAIN - SAWNWOOD PRODUCTION - See SPAIN - FORESTRY AND FOREST PRODUCTS

SPAIN - SCIENCE AND TECHNOLOGY - EXPENDITURE FOR RESEARCH - See SPAIN - SCIENTISTS, TECHNICIANS AND ENGINEERS

SPAIN - SCIENTISTS, TECHNICIANS AND ENGINEERS

European Commission Office of Press and Public Affairs, 2100 M Street, NW, Washington, D.C. 20037 (202) 862-9500; *Basic Statistics of the Community.*

Statistical Office of the United Nations, Publishing Service, New York, New York 10017 (800) 253-9646; *Statistical Yearbook.*

United Nations Educational, Scientific and Cultural Organization (UNESCO), 7 Place de Fontenoy, F-75700 Paris, France (Telephone Number in U.S. (212) 963-5981); *Statistical Yearbook.*

SPAIN - SENIOR CITIZENS

M.E. Sharpe, 80 Business Park Drive, Armonk, New York 10504 (800) 541-6563; *The Illustrated Book of World Rankings.*

SPAIN - SHEEP - See SPAIN - LIVESTOCK AND POULTRY

SPAIN - SHIPBUILDING - PRODUCTION INDEX

Organisation for Economic Co-operation and Development (OECD), 2 rue Andre-Pascal, 75 Paris 16, France (Telephone Number in U.S. (202) 785-6323); *Indicators of Industrial Activity.*

SPAIN - SILVER PRODUCTION AND CONSUMPTION - See SPAIN - MINING AND MINERAL PRODUCTS

SPAIN - SOCIAL DATA

European Commission Office of Press and Public Affairs, 2100 M Street, NW, Washington, D.C. 20037 (202) 862-9500; *ACP: Basic Statistics;* and *Basic Statistics of the Community.*

M.E. Sharpe, 80 Business Park Drive, Armonk, New York 10504 (800) 541-6563; *The Illustrated Book of World Rankings.*

Statistical Office of the United Nations, Publishing Service, New York, New York 10017 (800) 253-9646; *World Statistics Pocketbook.*

SPAIN - SOCIAL SECURITY

European Commission Office of Press and Public Affairs, 2100 M Street, NW, Washington, D.C. 20037 (202) 862-9500; *Basic Statistics of the Community.*

International Monetary Fund, 700 Nineteenth Street, NW, Washington, D.C. 20431 (202) 623-7000; *Government Finance Statistics Yearbook.*

Organisation for Economic Co-operation and Development (OECD), 2 rue Andre-Pascal, 75 Paris 16, France (Telephone Number in U.S. (202) 785-6323); *Revenue Statistics of OECD Member Countries.*

St. Martin's Press, Inc., 175 Fifth Avenue, New York, New York 10010 (800) 221-7945; *The Statesman's Year-Book.*

Statistical Office of the United Nations, Publishing Service, New York, New York 10017 (800) 253-9646; *National Accounts Statistics.*

SPAIN - SOCIOECONOMIC DATA

European Commission Office of Press and Public Affairs, 2100 M Street, NW, Washington, D.C. 20037 (202) 862-9500; *Basic Statistics of the Community.*

Organisation for Economic Co-operation and Development (OECD), 2 rue Andre-Pascal, 75 Paris 16, France (Telephone Number in U.S. (202) 785-6323); *Economic Outlook.*

SPAIN - SOYBEAN PRODUCTION - See SPAIN - CROPS

SPAIN - STAMP TAXES AND DUTIES - See SPAIN - TAXATION

SPAIN - STEEL - See SPAIN - MINING AND MINERAL PRODUCTS

SPAIN - STOCKS - COMMODITY - MARKET PRICE - INDEX

Food and Agricultural Organization of the United Nations (FAO) Via delle Terme di Caracalla, 00100 Rome, Italy (Telephone Number in U.S. (202) 653-2400); *The State of Food and Agriculture.*

International Lead and Zinc Study Group, Metro House, 58 St. James's Street, London SW1A 1LD, England; *Lead and Zinc Statistics.*

Statistical Office of the United Nations, Publishing Service, New York, New York 10017 (800) 253-9646; *Statistical Yearbook.*

World Bureau of Metal Statistics, 27-A High Street, Ware Hert SG12 9BA, England; *World Metal Statistics.*

SPAIN - SUGAR - See SPAIN - CROPS

SPAIN - SULPHUR AND SULPHURIC ACID PRODUCTION - See SPAIN - MINING AND MINERAL PRODUCTS

SPAIN - TAXATION

Europa Publications Limited, 18 Bedford Square, London, WC1B 3JN, England; *The Europa World Year Book.*

European Commission Office of Press and Public Affairs, 2100 M Street, NW, Washington, D.C. 20037 (202) 862-9500; *Basic Statistics of the Community.*

International Monetary Fund, 700 Nineteenth Street, NW, Washington, D.C. 20431 (202) 623-7000; *Government Finance Statistics Yearbook.*

International Road Federation, 2600 Virginia Avenue, NW, Washington, D.C. 20037 (202) 338-4641; *World Road Statistics.*

Organisation for Economic Co-operation and Development (OECD), 2 rue Andre-Pascal, 75 Paris 16, France (Telephone Number in U.S. (202) 785-6323); *Revenue Statistics of OECD Member Countries.*

St. Martin's Press, Inc., 175 Fifth Avenue, New York, New York 10010 (800) 221-7945; *The Statesman's Year-Book.*

The World Bank, 1818 H Street, NW, Washington, D.C. 20433 (202) 477-1234; *World Development Indicators.*

SPAIN - TELEGRAPH SERVICE

European Commission Office of Press and Public Affairs, 2100 M Street, NW, Washington, D.C. 20037 (202) 862-9500; *Transport Annual Statistics.*

Statistical Office of the United Nations, Publishing Service, New York, New York 10017 (800) 253-9646; *Statistical Yearbook.*

SPAIN - TELEPHONES IN USE

American Telephone and Telegraph Company, 26 Parsippany Road, Whippany, New Jersey 07981 (800) 222-0300; *The World's Telephones.*

Central Intelligence Agency, Washington, D.C. 20505 (703) 482-1100, www.cia.gov; *The World Factbook.*

Europa Publications Limited, 18 Bedford Square, London, WC1B 3JN, England; *The Europa World Year Book.*

St. Martin's Press, Inc., 175 Fifth Avenue, New York, New York 10010 (800) 221-7945; *The Statesman's Year-Book.*

Statistical Office of the United Nations, Publishing Service, New York, New York 10017 (800) 253-9646; *Statistical Yearbook; Trends in Europe and North America: The Statistical Yearbook of the Economic Commission for Europe;* and *World Statistics Pocketbook.*

SPAIN - TELEVISION BROADCASTING - See SPAIN - BROADCASTING

SPAIN - TELEVISION RECEIVER PRODUCTION

European Commission Office of Press and Public Affairs, 2100 M Street, NW, Washington, D.C. 20037 (202) 862-9500; *Basic Statistics of the Community.*

Statistical Office of the United Nations, Publishing Service, New York, New York 10017 (800) 253-9646; *Statistical Yearbook.*

SPAIN - TEXTILE INDUSTRY

American Forest and Paper Association, 1111 Nineteenth Street, NW, Suite 800, Washington, D.C. 20036 (202) 463-2700; *Wood Pulp and Fiber Statistics.*

Euromonitor International, Inc., 122 South Michigan Avenue, Suite 1200, Chicago, Illinois 60603 (800) 577-EURO; *Retail Trade International.*

European Commission Office of Press and Public Affairs, 2100 M Street, NW, Washington, D.C. 20037 (202) 862-9500; *Basic Statistics of the Community; Eurostatistics: Data for Short-Term Economic Analysis;* and *Industrial Production: Quarterly Statistics.*

M.E. Sharpe, 80 Business Park Drive, Armonk, New York 10504 (800) 541-6563; *The Illustrated Book of World Rankings.*

Organisation for Economic Co-operation and Development (OECD), 2 rue Andre-Pascal, 75 Paris 16, France (Telephone Number in U.S. (202) 785-6323); *Economic Accounts for Agriculture; Foreign Trade by Commodities; Indicators of Industrial Activity; Industrial Structure Statistics;* and *Textile Industry in OECD Countries.*

St. Martin's Press, Inc., 175 Fifth Avenue, New York, New York 10010 (800) 221-7945; *The Statesman's Year-Book.*

Statistical Office of the United Nations, Publishing Service, New York, New York 10017 (800) 253-9646; *Statistical Yearbook.*

United Nations Conference on Trade and Development, Central Statistical Service, Palais des Nations, Geneva, Switzerland (Telephone in U.S. (800) 253-9646); *UNCTAD Commodity Yearbook.*

SPAIN - THEATRE

United Nations Educational, Scientific and Cultural Organization (UNESCO), 7 Place de Fontenoy, F-75700 Paris, France (Telephone Number in U.S. (212) 963-5981); *Statistical Yearbook.*

SPAIN - TIN - See SPAIN - MINING AND MINERAL PRODUCTS

SPAIN - TOBACCO PRODUCTION

European Commission Office of Press and Public Affairs, 2100 M Street, NW, Washington, D.C. 20037 (202) 862-9500; *Basic Statistics of the Community;* and *Industrial Production: Quarterly Statistics.*

Euromonitor International, Inc., 122 South Michigan Avenue, Suite 1200, Chicago, Illinois 60603 (800) 577-EURO; *European Marketing Data and Statistics.*

M.E. Sharpe, 80 Business Park Drive, Armonk, New York 10504 (800) 541-6563; *The Illustrated Book of World Rankings.*

Organisation for Economic Co-operation and Development (OECD), 2 rue Andre-Pascal, 75 Paris 16, France (Telephone Number in U.S. (202) 785-6323); *Foreign Trade by Commodities; Indicators of Industrial Activity;* and *Industrial Structure Statistics.*

Statistical Office of the United Nations, Publishing Service, New York, New York 10017 (800) 253-9646; *Statistical Yearbook.*

SPAIN - TOURISM

Euromonitor International, Inc., 122 South Michigan Avenue, Suite 1200, Chicago, Illinois 60603 (800) 577-EURO; *European Marketing Data and Statistics; World Marketing Data and Statistics;* and *The World Economic Factbook.*

Europa Publications Limited, 18 Bedford Square, London, WC1B 3JN, England; *The Europa World Year Book.*

European Commission Office of Press and Public Affairs, 2100 M Street, NW, Washington, D.C. 20037 (202) 862-9500; *Transport Annual Statistics.*

Federal Statistical Office, Gustav-Stresemann-Ring 11, D-6200 Wiesbaden, Germany; *Spain.*

M.E. Sharpe, 80 Business Park Drive, Armonk, New York 10504 (800) 541-6563; *The Illustrated Book of World Rankings.*

Organisation for Economic Co-operation and Development (OECD), 2 rue Andre-Pascal, 75 Paris 16, France (Telephone Number in U.S. (202) 785-6323); *Tourism Policy and International Tourism in OECD Member Countries.*

St. Martin's Press, Inc., 175 Fifth Avenue, New York, New York 10010 (800) 221-7945; *The Statesman's Year-Book.*

Statistical Office of the United Nations, Publishing Service, New York, New York 10017 (800) 253-9646; *Statistical Yearbook;* and *Trends in Europe and North America: The Statistical Yearbook of the Economic Commission for Europe.*

World Tourism Organization, Calle Capitan Haya 42, E-28020 Madrid, Spain; *Yearbook of Tourism Statistics.*

SPAIN - TRACTORS IN USE

European Commission Office of Press and Public Affairs, 2100 M Street, NW, Washington, D.C. 20037 (202) 862-9500; *Transport Annual Statistics.*

SPAIN - TRADE

Euromonitor International, Inc., 122 South Michigan Avenue, Suite 1200, Chicago, Illinois 60603 (800) 577-EURO; *European Marketing Data and Statistics.*

Food and Agricultural Organization of the United Nations (FAO) Via delle Terme di Caracalla, 00100 Rome, Italy (Telephone Number in U.S. (202) 653-2400); *The State of Food and Agriculture.*

International Iron and Steel Institute, 120, rue Colonel Bourg, B-1140, Brussels, Belgium; *Steel Statistical Yearbook.*

Organisation for Economic Co-operation and Development (OECD), 2 rue Andre-Pascal, 75 Paris 16, France (Telephone Number in U.S. (202) 785-6323); *Economic Outlook; The Footwear, Raw Hides and Skins, and Leather Industry in OECD Countries; Foreign Trade by Commodities;* and *Maritime Transport.*

World Bureau of Metal Statistics, 27-A High Street, Ware Hert SG12 9BA, England; *World Metal Statistics.*

SPAIN - TRADEMARKS AND SERVICE MARKS - See SPAIN - PATENTS, TRADEMARKS AND SERVICE MARKS

SPAIN - TRANSPORTATION AND COMMUNICATIONS

Central Intelligence Agency, Washington, D.C. 20505 (703) 482-1100, www.cia.gov; *The World Factbook.*

Euromonitor International, Inc., 122 South Michigan Avenue, Suite 1200, Chicago, Illinois 60603 (800) 577-EURO; *World Marketing Data and Statistics.*

Europa Publications Limited, 18 Bedford Square, London, WC1B 3JN, England; *The Europa World Year Book.*

European Commission Office of Press and Public Affairs, 2100 M Street, NW, Washington, D.C. 20037 (202) 862-9500; *Basic Statistics of the Community; Energy Statistics Yearbook; Regions: Statistical Yearbook;* and *Transport Annual Statistics.*

Federal Statistical Office, Gustav-Stresemann-Ring 11, D-6200 Wiesbaden, Germany; *Spain.*

M.E. Sharpe, 80 Business Park Drive, Armonk, New York 10504 (800) 541-6563; *The Illustrated Book of World Rankings.*

St. Martin's Press, Inc., 175 Fifth Avenue, New York, New York 10010 (800) 221-7945; *The Statesman's Year-Book.*

Statistical Office of the United Nations, Publishing Service, New York, New York 10017 (800) 253-9646; *Human Development Report;* and *Trends in Europe and North America: The Statistical Yearbook of the Economic Commission for Europe.*

SPAIN - UNEMPLOYMENT

Central Intelligence Agency, Washington, D.C. 20505 (703) 482-1100, www.cia.gov; *The World Factbook.*

Euromonitor International, Inc., 122 South Michigan Avenue, Suite 1200, Chicago, Illinois 60603 (800) 577-EURO; *European Marketing Data and Statistics.*

European Commission Office of Press and Public Affairs, 2100 M Street, NW, Washington, D.C. 20037 (202) 862-9500; *Basic Statistics of the Community; Employment and Unemployment; Eurostatistics: Data for Short-Term Economic Analysis; Labor Force Sample Survey;* and *Regions: Statistical Yearbook.*

International Labour Office, I.L.O. Publications, 1828 L Street, NW, Suite 801, Washington, D.C. 20036 (301) 638-3152; *Yearbook of Labour Statistics.*

Organisation for Economic Co-operation and Development (OECD), 2 rue Andre-Pascal, 75 Paris 16, France (Telephone Number in U.S. (202) 785-6323); *Economic Outlook; OECD Economic Surveys: Spain;* and *OECD Employment Outlook.*

St. Martin's Press, Inc., 175 Fifth Avenue, New York, New York 10010 (800) 221-7945; *The Statesman's Year-Book.*

Statistical Office of the United Nations, Publishing Service, New York, New York 10017 (800) 253-9646; *Statistical Yearbook;* and *Trends in Europe and North America: The Statistical Yearbook of the Economic Commission for Europe.*

SPAIN - VITAL STATISTICS

European Commission Office of Press and Public Affairs, 2100 M Street, NW, Washington, D.C. 20037 (202) 862-9500; *Basic Statistics of the Community.*

St. Martin's Press, Inc., 175 Fifth Avenue, New York, New York 10010 (800) 221-7945; *The Statesman's Year-Book.*

Statistical Office of the United Nations, Publishing Service, New York, New York 10017 (800) 253-9646; *Statistical Yearbook.*

World Health Organization, Office of Publications, 20 Avenue Appia, CH-1211 Geneva 27, Switzerland (Telephone Number in U.S. (518) 436-9686); *World Health Statistics Annual.*

SPAIN - WAGES

Euromonitor International, Inc., 122 South Michigan Avenue, Suite 1200, Chicago, Illinois 60603 (800) 577-EURO; *European Marketing Data and Statistics.*

European Commission Office of Press and Public Affairs, 2100 M Street, NW, Washington, D.C. 20037 (202) 862-9500; *Basic Statistics of the Community; Earnings in Agriculture;* and *Eurostatistics: Data for Short-Term Economic Analysis.*

Federal Statistical Office, Gustav-Stresemann-Ring 11, D-6200 Wiesbaden, Germany; *Spain.*

International Labour Office, I.L.O. Publications, 1828 L Street, NW, Suite 801, Washington, D.C. 20036 (301) 638-3152; *Yearbook of Labour Statistics.*

Organisation for Economic Co-operation and Development (OECD), 2 rue Andre-Pascal, 75 Paris 16, France

(Telephone Number in U.S. (202) 785-6323); *Economic Outlook; Industrial Structure Statistics;* and *Main Economic Indicators - Historical Statistics.*

Statistical Office of the United Nations, Publishing Service, New York, New York 10017 (800) 253-9646; *Statistical Yearbook.*

SPAIN - WATERWAYS IN USE

European Commission Office of Press and Public Affairs, 2100 M Street, NW, Washington, D.C. 20037 (202) 862-9500; *Basic Statistics of the Community;* and *Transport Annual Statistics.*

Organisation for Economic Co-operation and Development (OECD), 2 rue Andre-Pascal, 75 Paris 16, France (Telephone Number in U.S. (202) 785-6323); *Maritime Transport.*

SPAIN - WEATHER - See SPAIN - CLIMATE

SPAIN - WELFARE

European Commission Office of Press and Public Affairs, 2100 M Street, NW, Washington, D.C. 20037 (202) 862-9500; *Basic Statistics of the Community.*

International Monetary Fund, 700 Nineteenth Street, NW, Washington, D.C. 20431 (202) 623-7000; *Government Finance Statistics Yearbook.*

SPAIN - WHALES - See SPAIN - FISHERIES

SPAIN - WHEAT PRODUCTION AND PRICES - See SPAIN - CROPS

SPAIN - WHOLESALE PRICES

European Commission Office of Press and Public Affairs, 2100 M Street, NW, Washington, D.C. 20037 (202) 862-9500; *Basic Statistics of the Community.*

SPAIN - WINE PRODUCTION - See SPAIN - BEVERAGES

SPAIN - WOOD AND WOOD PULP - See SPAIN - FORESTRY AND FOREST PRODUCTS

SPAIN - WOOL - See SPAIN - TEXTILE INDUSTRY

SPAIN - YARN PRODUCTION - See SPAIN - TEXTILE INDUSTRY

SPAIN - ZINC AND ZINC ORE PRODUCTION AND CONSUMPTION - See SPAIN - MINING AND MINERAL PRODUCTS

SPAIN - ZOOS AND BOTANICAL GARDENS

United Nations Educational, Scientific and Cultural Organization (UNESCO), 7

Place de Fontenoy, F-75700 Paris, France (Telephone Number in U.S. (212) 963-5981); *Statistical Yearbook.*

SPECIAL EDUCATION

U.S. Department of Education, National Center for Education Statistics, 555 New Jersey Avenue, NW, Washington, D.C. 20208-5574 (202) 219-1828, http://nces.ed.gov; *Digest of Education Statistics.*

SPICES - IMPORTS

U.S. Department of Agriculture, Economic Research Service, 1800 M Street, NW, Washington, D.C. 20036 (202) 694-5050, www.ers.usda.gov; *Foreign Agricultural Trade of the United States;* and *U.S. Agricultural Trade Update.*

SPORTING AND ATHLETIC GOODS - See also SPORTS

Marketing Logistics, Inc., 1460 Cloverdale Avenue, Highland Park, Illinois 60035 (847) 831-1575; *Annual Guides to Mail Order Sales.*

National Sporting Goods Association, 1601 Feehanville Drive, Suite 300, Mount Prospect, Illinois 66056 (847) 296-6742; *The Sporting Goods Market in 1999.*

U.S. Department of Commerce, Bureau of the Census, Washington, D.C. 20233 (301) 457-4100, www.census.gov; *U.S. International Trade in Goods and Services.*

SPORTING GOODS - RETAIL STORES

U.S. Department of Commerce, Bureau of the Census, Washington, D.C. 20233 (301) 457-4100, www.census.gov; *County Business Patterns; Current Business Reports;* and *1997 Economic Census.*

SPORTS

Amateur Softball Association, 2801 NE 50th Street, Oklahoma City, Oklahoma 73111-7203 (405) 424-5266.

American Bowling Congress, 5301 South 76th Street, Greendale, Wisconsin 53129 (414) 421-9000.

The American League of Professional Baseball Clubs, 245 Park Avenue, New York, New York 10167 (212) 931-7600; *American League Red Book.*

Association of Racing Commissioners International, Incorporated, Two Paragon Centre, Lexington, Kentucky 40511 (606) 224-7070.

Bicycle Manufactures Association of America, Incorporated, 3050 K Street, NW, Suite 400, Washington, D.C. 20007 (202)

944-9297.

Major League Baseball Players Association, 12 East 49th Street, New York, New York 10017 (212) 826-0808.

National Basketball Association, 645 Fifth Avenue, Tenth, New York, New York 10022 (212) 826-7000.

National Collegiate Athletic Association, 700 West Washington Street, Indianapolis, Indiana 46206 (317) 917-6222; *1997-98 Participation Study.*

National Federation of State High School Associations, Post Office Box 690, Indianapolis, Indiana 46206 (317) 972-6900; *The 1998-99 High School Athletics Participation Study.*

National Football League, 2021 L Street, NW, Sixth Floor, Washington, D.C. 20036 (202) 463-2200.

National Golf Foundation, 1150 South U.S. Highway One, Suite 401, Jupiter, Florida 33477 (561) 744-6006.

National Hockey League, 1800 McGill College Avenue, Suite 2600, Montreal, Quebec, Canada H3A 3J6 (514) 288-9220.

National League of Professional Baseball Clubs, 245 Park Avenue, 28th Floor, New York, New York 10167 (212) 931-7700; *National League Green Book.*

National Sporting Goods Association, 1601 Feehanville Drive, Suite 300, Mount Prospect, Illinois 66056 (847) 296-6742; *Sports Participation in 1998.*

Professional Rodeo Cowboys Association, 101 Prorodeo Drive, Colorado Springs, Colorado 80910 (719) 593-8840; *Official Professional Rodeo Media Guide.*

Tennis Industry Association, 19 Pope Avenue #107, Hilton Head, South Carolina 29928 (843) 686-3036.

U.S. Department of Agriculture, Forest Service, Post Office Box 96090, Washington, D.C. 20090 (202) 205-8333, www.fs.fed.us; *Annual Report.*

SPORTS - EXPENDITURES

National Sporting Goods Association, 1601 Feehanville Drive, Suite 300, Mount Prospect, Illinois 66056 (847) 296-6742; *The Sporting Goods Market in 1999.*

U.S. Department of Commerce, Bureau of Economic Analysis, Fourteenth Street between Constitution Avenue and E Street, NW, Washington, D.C. 20230 (202) 606-9900, www.bea.doc.gov; *The National Income and Product Accounts of the United States;* and *Survey of Current Business.*

SPORTS ASSOCIATIONS

The Gale Group, 27500 Drake Road, Farmington Hills, Michigan 48331-3535 (800) 877-4253; *Encyclopedia of Associations.*

SPORTS INDUSTRY RECEIPTS

U.S. Department of Commerce, Bureau of the Census, Washington, D.C. 20233 (301) 457-4100, www.census.gov; *Current Business Reports, Service Annual Survey.*

SPOT MARKET PRICE INDEX

Commodity Research Bureau, Inc., 30 South Wacker Drive, Chicago Illinois 60606 (312) 454-1801; *Commodity Index Report.*

SQUASH

National Collegiate Athletic Association, 700 West Washington Street, Indianapolis, Indiana 46206 (317) 917-6222; *1997-98 Participation Study.*

SQUID

U.S. Department of Commerce, National Oceanic and Atmospheric Administration, National Marine Fisheries Service, 1315 East-West Highway, Silver Spring, Maryland 20910 (301) 713-2239, www.nmfs.noaa.gov; *Fisheries of the United States.*

Sri Lanka - National Statistical Office

The Director, Department of Census and Statistics, No. 6 Albert Crescent, Colombo 7, Sri Lanka.

Sri Lanka - Primary Statistics Sources

Department of Census and Statistics, No. 6, Albert Crescent, Colombo 7, Sri Lanka; *Statistical Abstract of the Democratic Socialist Republic of Sri Lanka; Statistical Pocketbook of the Democratic Socialist Republic of Sri Lanka;* and *Sri Lanka Yearbook.*

SRI LANKA - AGRICULTURE

Asian Development Bank, P.O. Box 789, 1099 Manila, Philippines; *Key Indicators of Developing Asian and Pacific Countries.*

Economist Intelligence Unit, 111 West 57th Street, New York, New York 10019 (800) 938-4685; *Sri Lanka Country Report.*

Euromonitor International, Inc., 122 South Michigan Avenue, Suite 1200, Chicago, Illinois 60603 (800) 577-EURO; *International Marketing Data and Statistics;* and *World Marketing Data and Statistics.*

Europa Publications Limited, 18 Bedford Square, London, WC1B 3JN, England; *The Europa World Year Book.*

Federal Statistical Office, Gustav-Stresemann-Ring 11, D-6200 Wiesbaden, Germany; *Sri Lanka.*

Food and Agricultural Organization of the United Nations (FAO) Via delle Terme di Caracalla, 00100 Rome, Italy (Telephone Number in U.S. (202) 653-2400); *Production Yearbook; The State of Food and Agriculture;* and *Trade Yearbook.*

M.E. Sharpe, 80 Business Park Drive, Armonk, New York 10504 (800) 541-6563; *The Illustrated Book of World Rankings.*

St. Martin's Press, Inc., 175 Fifth Avenue, New York, New York 10010 (800) 221-7945; *The Statesman's Year-Book.*

Statistical Office of the United Nations, Publishing Service, New York, New York 10017 (800) 253-9646; *Asia-Pacific in Figures; Statistical Yearbook;* and *Statistical Yearbook for Asia and the Pacific.*

United Nations Conference on Trade and Development, Central Statistical Service, Palais des Nations, Geneva, Switzerland (Telephone in U.S. (800) 253-9646); *UNCTAD Commodity Yearbook.*

The World Bank, 1818 H Street, NW, Washington, D.C. 20433 (202) 477-1234; *World Development Indicators.*

SRI LANKA - AIRLINE SERVICE

The Economist Intelligence Unit (Asia) Limited, 10th Floor, Luk Kwok Centre, 72 Gloucester Road, Wanchai, Hong Kong (Phone Number in U.S. (800) 938-4685); *Asian Market Atlas.*

Europa Publications Limited, 18 Bedford Square, London, WC1B 3JN, England; *The Europa World Year Book.*

International Civil Aviation Organization, 999 University Street, Montreal, Quebec, Canada H3C 5H7 (514) 954-8219; *Civil Aviation Statistics of the World.*

M.E. Sharpe, 80 Business Park Drive, Armonk, New York 10504 (800) 541-6563; *The Illustrated Book of World Rankings.*

St. Martin's Press, Inc., 175 Fifth Avenue, New York, New York 10010 (800) 221-7945; *The Statesman's Year-Book.*

Statistical Office of the United Nations, Publishing Service, New York, New York 10017 (800) 253-9646; *Statistical Yearbook.*

SRI LANKA - AIRPORTS

Central Intelligence Agency, Washington, D.C. 20505 (703) 482-1100, www.cia.gov; *The World Factbook.*

SRI LANKA - ALUMINUM PRODUCTION AND CONSUMPTION - See SRI LANKA - MINING AND MINERAL PRODUCTS

SRI LANKA - ANIMAL HEALTH

Food and Agricultural Organization of the United Nations (FAO), Via delle Terme di Caracalla, 00100, Rome, Italy (Telephone Number in U.S. (202) 653-2400); *Animal Health Yearbook.*

SRI LANKA - AREA AND DENSITY OF POPULATION

Central Intelligence Agency, Washington, D.C. 20505 (703) 482-1100, www.cia.gov; *The World Factbook.*

Euromonitor International, Inc., 122 South Michigan Avenue, Suite 1200, Chicago, Illinois 60603 (800) 577-EURO; *International Marketing Data and Statistics;* and *The World Economic Factbook.*

Europa Publications Limited, 18 Bedford Square, London, WC1B 3JN, England; *The Europa World Year Book.*

Federal Statistical Office, Gustav-Stresemann-Ring 11, D-6200 Wiesbaden, Germany; *Sri Lanka.*

Food and Agricultural Organization of the United Nations (FAO) Via delle Terme di Caracalla, 00100 Rome, Italy (Telephone Number in U.S. (202) 653-2400); *The State of Food and Agriculture.*

M.E. Sharpe, 80 Business Park Drive, Armonk, New York 10504 (800) 541-6563; *The Illustrated Book of World Rankings.*

St. Martin's Press, Inc., 175 Fifth Avenue, New York, New York 10010 (800) 221-7945; *The Statesman's Year-Book.*

Statistical Office of the United Nations, Publishing Service, New York, New York 10017 (800) 253-9646; *Statistical Yearbook.*

United Nations Educational, Scientific and Cultural Organization (UNESCO), 7 Place de Fontenoy, F-75700 Paris, France (Telephone Number in U.S. (212) 963-5981); *Statistical Yearbook.*

The World Bank, 1818 H Street, NW, Washington, D.C. 20433 (202) 477-1234; *World Development Report.*

SRI LANKA - ARMS EXPORTS AND IMPORTS - See SRI LANKA - MILITARY

SRI LANKA - BALANCE OF PAYMENTS

The Economist Intelligence Unit, 111 West 57th Street, New York, New York 10019 (800) 938-4685; *The World Market Atlas.*

Europa Publications Limited, 18 Bedford Square, London, WC1B 3JN, England; *The Europa World Year Book.*

Federal Statistical Office, Gustav-Stresemann-Ring 11, D-6200 Wiesbaden, Germany; *Sri Lanka.*

International Monetary Fund, 700 Nineteenth Street, NW, Washington, D.C. 20431 (202) 623-7000; *Balance of Payments Yearbook;* and *International Financial Statistics.*

United Nations Conference on Trade and Development (UNCTAD), New York, New York 10017 (800) 253-9646; *Handbook of International Trade and Development Statistics.*

The World Bank, 1818 H Street, NW, Washington, D.C. 20433 (202) 477-1234; *World Development Report;* and *World Development Indicators.*

SRI LANKA - BANKING

Asian Development Bank, P.O. Box 789, 1099 Manila, Philippines; *Key Indicators of Developing Asian and Pacific Countries.*

Euromonitor International, Inc., 122 South Michigan Avenue, Suite 1200, Chicago, Illinois 60603 (800) 577-EURO; *World Marketing Data and Statistics.*

Europa Publications Limited, 18 Bedford Square, London, WC1B 3JN, England; *The Europa World Year Book.*

International Monetary Fund, 700 Nineteenth Street, NW, Washington, D.C. 20431 (202) 623-7000; *Government Finance Statistics Yearbook;* and *International Financial Statistics.*

M.E. Sharpe, 80 Business Park Drive, Armonk, New York 10504 (800) 541-6563; *The Illustrated Book of World Rankings.*

St. Martin's Press, Inc., 175 Fifth Avenue, New York, New York 10010 (800) 221-7945; *The Statesman's Year-Book.*

Statistical Office of the United Nations, Publishing Service, New York, New York 10017 (800) 253-9646; *Statistical Yearbook.*

SRI LANKA - BARLEY PRODUCTION - See SRI LANKA - CROPS

SRI LANKA - BEER PRODUCTION - See SRI LANKA - BEVERAGES

SRI LANKA - BEVERAGES

M.E. Sharpe, 80 Business Park Drive, Armonk, New York 10504 (800) 541-6563; *The Illustrated Book of World Rankings.*

Statistical Office of the United Nations, Publishing Service, New York, New York 10017 (800) 253-9646; *Statistical Yearbook.*

SRI LANKA - BIRTH RATES

Central Intelligence Agency, Washington, D.C. 20505 (703) 482-1100, www.cia.gov; *The World Factbook.*

The Economist Intelligence Unit (Asia) Limited, 10th Floor, Luk Kwok Centre, 72 Gloucester Road, Wanchai, Hong Kong (Phone Number in U.S. (800) 938-4685); *Asian Market Atlas.*

Euromonitor International, Inc., 122 South Michigan Avenue, Suite 1200, Chicago, Illinois 60603 (800) 577-EURO; *International Marketing Data and Statistics;* and *The World Economic Factbook.*

Europa Publications Limited, 18 Bedford Square, London, WC1B 3JN, England; *The Europa World Year Book.*

M.E. Sharpe, 80 Business Park Drive, Armonk, New York 10504 (800) 541-6563; *The Illustrated Book of World Rankings.*

St. Martin's Press, Inc., 175 Fifth Avenue, New York, New York 10010 (800) 221-7945; *The Statesman's Year-Book.*

Statistical Office of the United Nations, Publishing Service, New York, New York 10017 (800) 253-9646; *Asia-Pacific in Figures; Demographic Yearbook;* and *Statistical Yearbook.*

The World Bank, 1818 H Street, NW, Washington, D.C. 20433 (202) 477-1234; *World Development Indicators.*

World Health Organization, Office of Publications, 20 Avenue Appia, CH-1211 Geneva 27, Switzerland (Telephone Number in U.S. (518) 436-9686); *World Health Statistics Annual.*

SRI LANKA - BONDS

Asian Development Bank, P.O. Box 789, 1099 Manila, Philippines; *Key Indicators of Developing Asian and Pacific Countries.*

International Monetary Fund, 700 Nineteenth Street, NW, Washington, D.C. 20431 (202) 623-7000; *Government Finance Statistics Yearbook.*

Statistical Office of the United Nations, Publishing Service, New York, New York 10017 (800) 253-9646; *Statistical Yearbook.*

SRI LANKA - BOOK PRODUCTION

Europa Publications Limited, 18 Bedford Square, London, WC1B 3JN, England; *The Europa World Year Book.*

United Nations Educational, Scientific and Cultural Organization (UNESCO), 7 Place de Fontenoy, F-75700 Paris, France (Telephone Number in U.S. (212) 963-5981); *Statistical Yearbook.*

SRI LANKA - BROADCASTING

Billboard Limited, P.O. Box 9027, 1006 AA Amsterdam, The Netherlands (Telephone Number in U.S. (212) 764-7300); *World Radio TV Handbook.*

Central Intelligence Agency, Washington, D.C. 20505 (703) 482-1100, www.cia.gov; *The World Factbook.*

Euromonitor International, Inc., 122 South Michigan Avenue, Suite 1200, Chicago, Illinois 60603 (800) 577-EURO; *World Marketing Data and Statistics.*

M.E. Sharpe, 80 Business Park Drive, Armonk, New York 10504 (800) 541-6563; *The Illustrated Book of World Rankings.*

St. Martin's Press, Inc., 175 Fifth Avenue, New York, New York 10010 (800) 221-7945; *The Statesman's Year-Book.*

United Nations Educational, Scientific and Cultural Organization (UNESCO), 7 Place de Fontenoy, F-75700 Paris, France (Telephone Number in U.S. (212) 963-5981); *Statistical Yearbook.*

SRI LANKA - BUDGET

Central Intelligence Agency, Washington, D.C. 20505 (703) 482-1100, www.cia.gov; *The World Factbook.*

SRI LANKA - BUSINESS AND PROFESSIONAL LICENSES

International Monetary Fund, 700 Nineteenth Street, NW, Washington, D.C. 20431 (202) 623-7000; *Government Finance Statistics Yearbook.*

SRI LANKA - CALORIE SUPPLY

Asian Development Bank, P.O. Box 789, 1099 Manila, Philippines; *Key Indicators of Developing Asian and Pacific Countries.*

Food and Agricultural Organization of the United Nations (FAO) Via delle Terme di Caracalla, 00100 Rome, Italy (Telephone Number in U.S. (202) 653-2400); *The State of Food and Agriculture.*

SRI LANKA - CAPITAL INVESTMENT

Asian Development Bank, P.O. Box 789,

1099 Manila, Philippines; *Key Indicators of Developing Asian and Pacific Countries.*

SRI LANKA - CAPITAL REVENUE

Asian Development Bank, P.O. Box 789, 1099 Manila, Philippines; *Key Indicators of Developing Asian and Pacific Countries.*

International Monetary Fund, 700 Nineteenth Street, NW, Washington, D.C. 20431 (202) 623-7000; *Government Finance Statistics Yearbook.*

SRI LANKA - CATTLE - See SRI LANKA - LIVESTOCK AND POULTRY

SRI LANKA - CAUSTIC SODA PRODUCTION - See SRI LANKA - BEVERAGES

SRI LANKA - CEMENT PRODUCTION - See SRI LANKA - MINING AND MINERAL PRODUCTS

SRI LANKA - CHEMICAL (ORGANIC) PRODUCTION - See SRI LANKA - MINING AND MINERAL PRODUCTS

SRI LANKA - CHICKENS - See SRI LANKA - LIVESTOCK AND POULTRY

SRI LANKA - CIGAR PRODUCTION - See SRI LANKA - TOBACCO PRODUCTION

SRI LANKA - CIGARETTE PRODUCTION - See SRI LANKA - TOBACCO PRODUCTION

SRI LANKA - CLIMATE

M.E. Sharpe, 80 Business Park Drive, Armonk, New York 10504 (800) 541-6563; *The Illustrated Book of World Rankings.*

St. Martin's Press, Inc., 175 Fifth Avenue, New York, New York 10010 (800) 221-7945; *The Statesman's Year-Book.*

SRI LANKA - COAL PRODUCTION - See SRI LANKA - MINING AND MINERAL PRODUCTS

SRI LANKA - COCOA (BEANS) PRODUCTION - See SRI LANKA - CROPS

SRI LANKA - COCONUT PRODUCTS EXPORTS - See SRI LANKA - CROPS

SRI LANKA - COFFEE PRODUCTION AND CONSUMPTION - See SRI LANKA - CROPS

SIR LANKA - COMMERCE

St. Martin's Press, Inc., 175 Fifth Avenue, New York, New York 10010 (800) 221-7945; *The Statesman's Year-Book.*

SRI LANKA - COMMUNICATIONS - See SRI LANKA - TRANSPORTATION AND COMMUNICATIONS

SRI LANKA - CONSTRUCTION INDUSTRY

M.E. Sharpe, 80 Business Park Drive, Armonk, New York 10504 (800) 541-6563; *The Illustrated Book of World Rankings.*

Statistical Office of the United Nations, Publishing Service, New York, New York 10017 (800) 253-9646; *Statistical Yearbook.*

SRI LANKA - CONSUMER PRICE INDEX

Asian Development Bank, P.O. Box 789, 1099 Manila, Philippines; *Key Indicators of Developing Asian and Pacific Countries.*

Europa Publications Limited, 18 Bedford Square, London, WC1B 3JN, England; *The Europa World Year Book.*

Statistical Office of the United Nations, Publishing Service, New York, New York 10017 (800) 253-9646; *Statistical Yearbook.*

SRI LANKA - CONSUMER PRICES

Euromonitor International, Inc., 122 South Michigan Avenue, Suite 1200, Chicago, Illinois 60603 (800) 577-EURO; *World Marketing Data and Statistics.*

International Labour Office, I.L.O. Publications, 1828 L Street, NW, Suite 801, Washington, D.C. 20036 (301) 638-3152; *Yearbook of Labour Statistics.*

International Monetary Fund, 700 Nineteenth Street, NW, Washington, D.C. 20431 (202) 623-7000; *International Financial Statistics.*

SRI LANKA - CONSUMPTION

International Rubber Study Group, York House, Eighth Floor, Empire Way, Wembley, London HA9 0PA, England; *Rubber Statistical Handbook.*

The World Bank, 1818 H Street, NW, Washington, D.C. 20433 (202) 477-1234; *World Development Report.*

SRI LANKA - COPPER PRODUCTION AND CONSUMPTION

M.E. Sharpe, 80 Business Park Drive, Armonk, New York 10504 (800) 541-6563; *The Illustrated Book of World Rankings.*

SRI LANKA - CORN PRODUCTION - See SRI LANKA - CROPS

SRI LANKA - CORPORATE TAXES - See SRI LANKA - TAXATION

SRI LANKA - COTTON - See SRI LANKA - CROPS

SRI LANKA - CRIME

International Criminal Police

Organization (INTERPOL), 50 quai Achille Lignon, F-69006 Lyon, France; *International Crime Statistics.*

Yale University Press, Yale Station, New Haven, Connecticut 06520 (800) 987-7323; *Violence and Crime in Cross-National Perspective.*

SRI LANKA - CROPS

Asian Development Bank, P.O. Box 789, 1099 Manila, Philippines; *Key Indicators of Developing Asian and Pacific Countries.*

Commodity Research Bureau, Inc., 30 South Wacker Drive, Chicago Illinois 60606 (312) 454-1801; *Commodity Year Book.*

Europa Publications Limited, 18 Bedford Square, London, WC1B 3JN, England; *The Europa World Year Book.*

Food and Agricultural Organization of the United Nations (FAO) Via delle Terme di Caracalla, 00100 Rome, Italy (Telephone Number in U.S. (202) 653-2400); *The State of Food and Agriculture.*

International Monetary Fund, 700 Nineteenth Street, NW, Washington, D.C. 20431 (202) 623-7000; *International Financial Statistics.*

M.E. Sharpe, 80 Business Park Drive, Armonk, New York 10504 (800) 541-6563; *The Illustrated Book of World Rankings.*

St. Martin's Press, Inc., 175 Fifth Avenue, New York, New York 10010 (800) 221-7945; *The Statesman's Year-Book.*

Statistical Office of the United Nations, Publishing Service, New York, New York 10017 (800) 253-9646; *Statistical Yearbook.*

United Nations Conference on Trade and Development, Central Statistical Service, Palais des Nations, Geneva, Switzerland (Telephone in U.S. (800) 253-9646); *UNCTAD Commodity Yearbook.*

SRI LANKA - CUSTOMS DUTIES

International Monetary Fund, 700 Nineteenth Street, NW, Washington, D.C. 20431 (202) 623-7000; *Government Finance Statistics Yearbook.*

St. Martin's Press, Inc., 175 Fifth Avenue, New York, New York 10010 (800) 221-7945; *The Statesman's Year-Book.*

SRI LANKA - DAIRY PRODUCTS

Europa Publications Limited, 18 Bedford Square, London, WC1B 3JN, England; *The Europa World Year Book.*

Food and Agricultural Organization of the United Nations (FAO) Via delle Terme

di Caracalla, 00100 Rome, Italy (Telephone Number in U.S. (202) 653-2400); *The State of Food and Agriculture.*

M.E. Sharpe, 80 Business Park Drive, Armonk, New York 10504 (800) 541-6563; *The Illustrated Book of World Rankings.*

St. Martin's Press, Inc., 175 Fifth Avenue, New York, New York 10010 (800) 221-7945; *The Statesman's Year-Book.*

Statistical Office of the United Nations, Publishing Service, New York, New York 10017 (800) 253-9646; *Statistical Yearbook.*

SRI LANKA - DEATH RATES - See SRI LANKA - MORTALITY

SRI LANKA - DEFENSE EXPENDITURES - See SRI LANKA - MILITARY

SRI LANKA - DEMOGRAPHY

The Economist Intelligence Unit, 111 West 57th Street, New York, New York 10019 (800) 938-4685; *The World Market Atlas.*

The Economist Intelligence Unit (Asia) Limited, 10th Floor, Luk Kwok Centre, 72 Gloucester Road, Wanchai, Hong Kong (Phone Number in U.S. (800) 938-4685); *Asian Market Atlas.*

Euromonitor International, Inc., 122 South Michigan Avenue, Suite 1200, Chicago, Illinois 60603 (800) 577-EURO; *International Marketing Data and Statistics; World Marketing Data and Statistics;* and *The World Economic Factbook.*

M.E. Sharpe, 80 Business Park Drive, Armonk, New York 10504 (800) 541-6563; *The Illustrated Book of World Rankings.*

Statistical Office of the United Nations, Publishing Service, New York, New York 10017 (800) 253-9646; *Asia-Pacific in Figures;* and *Human Development Report.*

SRI LANKA - DEVELOPMENT ASSISTANCE

Asian Development Bank, P.O. Box 789, 1099 Manila, Philippines; *Key Indicators of Developing Asian and Pacific Countries.*

Statistical Office of the United Nations, Publishing Service, New York, New York 10017 (800) 253-9646; *Statistical Yearbook.*

SRI LANKA - DIAMOND PRODUCTION - See SRI LANKA - MINING AND MINERAL PRODUCTS

SRI LANKA - DISCOUNT RATES - See SRI LANKA - BANKING

SRI LANKA - DISEASES - See SRI LANKA - HEALTH

SRI LANKA - DIVORCE RATES

M.E. Sharpe, 80 Business Park Drive, Armonk, New York 10504 (800) 541-6563; *The Illustrated Book of World Rankings.*

Statistical Office of the United Nations, Publishing Service, New York, New York 10017 (800) 253-9646; *Demographic Yearbook;* and *Statistical Yearbook.*

SRI LANKA - ECONOMY

Asian Development Bank, P.O. Box 789, 1099 Manila, Philippines; *Key Indicators of Developing Asian and Pacific Countries.*

Central Intelligence Agency, Washington, D.C. 20505 (703) 482-1100, www.cia.gov; *The World Factbook.*

Economist Intelligence Unit, 111 West 57th Street, New York, New York 10019 (800) 938-4685; *Sri Lanka Country Report.*

Euromonitor International, Inc., 122 South Michigan Avenue, Suite 1200, Chicago, Illinois 60603 (800) 577-EURO; *International Marketing Data and Statistics; World Marketing Data and Statistics;* and *The World Economic Factbook.*

Europa Publications Limited, 18 Bedford Square, London, WC1B 3JN, England; *The Europa World Year Book.*

M.E. Sharpe, 80 Business Park Drive, Armonk, New York 10504 (800) 541-6563; *The Illustrated Book of World Rankings.*

St. Martin's Press, Inc., 175 Fifth Avenue, New York, New York 10010 (800) 221-7945; *The Statesman's Year-Book.*

Statistical Office of the United Nations, Publishing Service, New York, New York 10017 (800) 253-9646; *World Statistics Pocketbook.*

The World Bank, 1818 H Street, NW, Washington, D.C. 20433 (202) 477-1234; *The World Bank Atlas;* and *World Development Report.*

SRI LANKA - EDUCATION

The Economist Intelligence Unit, 111 West 57th Street, New York, New York 10019 (800) 938-4685; *The World Market Atlas.*

The Economist Intelligence Unit (Asia) Limited, 10th Floor, Luk Kwok Centre, 72 Gloucester Road, Wanchai, Hong Kong (Phone Number in U.S. (800) 938-4685); *Asian Market Atlas.*

Euromonitor International, Inc., 122 South Michigan Avenue, Suite 1200, Chicago, Illinois 60603 (800) 577-EURO; *International Marketing Data and Statistics;*

and *World Marketing Data and Statistics.*

Europa Publications Limited, 18 Bedford Square, London, WC1B 3JN, England; *The Europa World Year Book.*

Federal Statistical Office, Gustav-Stresemann-Ring 11, D-6200 Wiesbaden, Germany; *Sri Lanka.*

International Monetary Fund, 700 Nineteenth Street, NW, Washington, D.C. 20431 (202) 623-7000; *Government Finance Statistics Yearbook.*

M.E. Sharpe, 80 Business Park Drive, Armonk, New York 10504 (800) 541-6563; *The Illustrated Book of World Rankings.*

St. Martin's Press, Inc., 175 Fifth Avenue, New York, New York 10010 (800) 221-7945; *The Statesman's Year-Book.*

Statistical Office of the United Nations, Publishing Service, New York, New York 10017 (800) 253-9646; *Asia-Pacific in Figures; Human Development Report;* and *Statistical Yearbook for Asia and the Pacific.*

United Nations Educational, Scientific and Cultural Organization (UNESCO), 7 Place de Fontenoy, F-75700 Paris, France (Telephone Number in U.S. (212) 963-5981); *Statistical Yearbook.*

The World Bank, 1818 H Street, NW, Washington, D.C. 20433 (202) 477-1234; *World Development Report;* and *World Development Indicators.*

SRI LANKA - EGG PRODUCTION AND CONSUMPTION - See SRI LANKA - DAIRY PRODUCTS

SRI LANKA - ELECTRICITY

Asian Development Bank, P.O. Box 789, 1099 Manila, Philippines; *Key Indicators of Developing Asian and Pacific Countries.*

Central Intelligence Agency, Washington, D.C. 20505 (703) 482-1100, www.cia.gov; *The World Factbook.*

M.E. Sharpe, 80 Business Park Drive, Armonk, New York 10504 (800) 541-6563; *The Illustrated Book of World Rankings.*

St. Martin's Press, Inc., 175 Fifth Avenue, New York, New York 10010 (800) 221-7945; *The Statesman's Year-Book.*

Statistical Office of the United Nations, Publishing Service, New York, New York 10017 (800) 253-9646; *Electric Power in Asia and the Pacific; Human Development Report;* and *Statistical Yearbook.*

SRI LANKA - EMPLOYMENT

Euromonitor International, Inc., 122 South Michigan Avenue, Suite 1200, Chicago, Illinois 60603 (800) 577-EURO; *International Marketing Data and Statistics.*

Federal Statistical Office, Gustav-Stresemann-Ring 11, D-6200 Wiesbaden, Germany; *Sri Lanka.*

International Labour Office, I.L.O. Publications, 1828 L Street, NW, Suite 801, Washington, D.C. 20036 (301) 638-3152; *Yearbook of Labour Statistics.*

M.E. Sharpe, 80 Business Park Drive, Armonk, New York 10504 (800) 541-6563; *The Illustrated Book of World Rankings.*

Statistical Office of the United Nations, Publishing Service, New York, New York 10017 (800) 253-9646; *Asia-Pacific in Figures;* and *Statistical Yearbook.*

SRI LANKA - ENERGY

Euromonitor International, Inc., 122 South Michigan Avenue, Suite 1200, Chicago, Illinois 60603 (800) 577-EURO; *International Marketing Data and Statistics; World Marketing Data and Statistics;* and *The World Economic Factbook.*

Food and Agricultural Organization of the United Nations (FAO) Via delle Terme di Caracalla, 00100 Rome, Italy (Telephone Number in U.S. (202) 653-2400); *The State of Food and Agriculture.*

M.E. Sharpe, 80 Business Park Drive, Armonk, New York 10504 (800) 541-6563; *The Illustrated Book of World Rankings.*

St. Martin's Press, Inc., 175 Fifth Avenue, New York, New York 10010 (800) 221-7945; *The Statesman's Year-Book.*

Statistical Office of the United Nations, Publishing Service, New York, New York 10017 (800) 253-9646; *Asia-Pacific in Figures; Energy Statistics Yearbook; Human Development Report; Statistical Yearbook; Statistical Yearbook for Asia and the Pacific;* and *World Statistics Pocketbook.*

The World Bank, 1818 H Street, NW, Washington, D.C. 20433 (202) 477-1234; *The World Bank Atlas;* and *World Development Report.*

SRI LANKA - ENVIRONMENT

Economist Intelligence Unit, 111 West 57th Street, New York, New York 10019 (800) 938-4685; *Sri Lanka Country Report.*

Statistical Office of the United Nations, Publishing Service, New York, New York 10017 (800) 253-9646; *World Statistics Pocketbook.*

SRI LANKA - EXCHANGE RATES

Asian Development Bank, P.O. Box 789, 1099 Manila, Philippines; *Key Indicators of Developing Asian and Pacific Countries.*

Central Intelligence Agency, Washington, D.C. 20505 (703) 482-1100, www.cia.gov; *The World Factbook.*

The Economist Intelligence Unit (Asia) Limited, 10th Floor, Luk Kwok Centre, 72 Gloucester Road, Wanchai, Hong Kong (Phone Number in U.S. (800) 938-4685); *Asian Market Atlas.*

Euromonitor International, Inc., 122 South Michigan Avenue, Suite 1200, Chicago, Illinois 60603 (800) 577-EURO; *International Marketing Data and Statistics;* and *The World Economic Factbook.*

Europa Publications Limited, 18 Bedford Square, London, WC1B 3JN, England; *The Europa World Year Book.*

International Civil Aviation Organization, 999 University Street, Montreal, Quebec, Canada H3C 5H7 (514) 954-8219; *Civil Aviation Statistics of the World.*

International Monetary Fund, 700 Nineteenth Street, NW, Washington, D.C. 20431 (202) 623-7000; *International Financial Statistics.*

Statistical Office of the United Nations, Publishing Service, New York, New York 10017 (800) 253-9646; *Statistical Yearbook;* and *World Statistics Pocketbook.*

Walden Publishing Ltd., Two Market Street, Saffron Walden Essex, CB10 1HZ, England; *The World of Information Asia and Pacific Review.*

SRI LANKA - EXCISE TAXES - See SRI LANKA - TAXATION

SRI LANKA - EXPORTS

Asian Development Bank, P.O. Box 789, 1099 Manila, Philippines; *Key Indicators of Developing Asian and Pacific Countries.*

Central Intelligence Agency, Washington, D.C. 20505 (703) 482-1100, www.cia.gov; *The World Factbook.*

The Economist Intelligence Unit, 111 West 57th Street, New York, New York 10019 (800) 938-4685; *Sri Lanka Country Report;* and *The World Market Atlas.*

The Economist Intelligence Unit (Asia) Limited, 10th Floor, Luk Kwok Centre, 72 Gloucester Road, Wanchai, Hong Kong (Phone Number in U.S. (800) 938-4685); *Asian Market Atlas.*

Euromonitor International, Inc., 122 South Michigan Avenue, Suite 1200,

Chicago, Illinois 60603 (800) 577-EURO; *International Marketing Data and Statistics;* and *The World Economic Factbook.*

Europa Publications Limited, 18 Bedford Square, London, WC1B 3JN, England; *The Europa World Year Book.*

Food and Agricultural Organization of the United Nations (FAO) Via delle Terme di Caracalla, 00100 Rome, Italy (Telephone Number in U.S. (202) 653-2400); *The State of Food and Agriculture.*

International Monetary Fund, 700 Nineteenth Street, NW, Washington, D.C. 20431 (202) 623-7000; *Direction of Trade Statistics; Government Finance Statistics Yearbook;* and *International Financial Statistics.*

International Rubber Study Group, York House, Eighth Floor, Empire Way, Wembley, London HA9 0PA, England; *Rubber Statistical Handbook.*

St. Martin's Press, Inc., 175 Fifth Avenue, New York, New York 10010 (800) 221-7945; *The Statesman's Year-Book.*

Statistical Office of the United Nations, Publishing Service, New York, New York 10017 (800) 253-9646; *Foreign Trade Statistics of Asia and the Pacific.*

United Nations Conference on Trade and Development (UNCTAD), New York, New York 10017 (800) 253-9646; *Handbook of International Trade and Development Statistics.*

Walden Publishing Ltd., Two Market Street, Saffron Walden Essex, CB10 1HZ, England; *The World of Information Asia and Pacific Review.*

The World Bank, 1818 H Street, NW, Washington, D.C. 20433 (202) 477-1234; *World Development Report;* and *World Development Indicators.*

SRI LANKA - EXTERNAL FINANCING

Asian Development Bank, P.O. Box 789, 1099 Manila, Philippines; *Key Indicators of Developing Asian and Pacific Countries.*

SRI LANKA - EXTERNAL INDEBTEDNESS

Asian Development Bank, P.O. Box 789, 1099 Manila, Philippines; *Key Indicators of Developing Asian and Pacific Countries.*

The World Bank, 1818 H Street, NW, Washington, D.C. 20433 (202) 477-1234; *World Development Report;* and *World Development Indicators.*

SRI LANKA - EXTERNAL TRADE

Asian Development Bank, P.O. Box 789,

1099 Manila, Philippines; *Key Indicators of Developing Asian and Pacific Countries.*

Euromonitor International, Inc., 122 South Michigan Avenue, Suite 1200, Chicago, Illinois 60603 (800) 577-EURO; *World Marketing Data and Statistics.*

Food and Agricultural Organization of the United Nations (FAO) Via delle Terme di Caracalla, 00100 Rome, Italy (Telephone Number in U.S. (202) 653-2400); *The State of Food and Agriculture; and Trade Yearbook.*

Statistical Office of the United Nations, Publishing Service, New York, New York 10017 (800) 253-9646; *Asia-Pacific in Figures; Statistical Yearbook; and Statistical Yearbook for Asia and the Pacific.*

SRI LANKA - FABRIC PRODUCTION - See SRI LANKA - TEXTILE INDUSTRY

SRI LANKA - FARM CROPS - See SRI LANKA - CROPS

SRI LANKA - FEMALE WORKING POPULATION - See SRI LANKA - EMPLOYMENT

SRI LANKA - FERTILITY RATES

The Economist Intelligence Unit (Asia) Limited, 10th Floor, Luk Kwok Centre, 72 Gloucester Road, Wanchai, Hong Kong (Phone Number in U.S. (800) 938-4685); *Asian Market Atlas.*

M.E. Sharpe, 80 Business Park Drive, Armonk, New York 10504 (800) 541-6563; *The Illustrated Book of World Rankings.*

Statistical Office of the United Nations, Publishing Service, New York, New York 10017 (800) 253-9646; *Human Development Report.*

The World Bank, 1818 H Street, NW, Washington, D.C. 20433 (202) 477-1234; *The World Bank Atlas; World Development Report; and World Development Indicators.*

SRI LANKA - FERTILIZER

Food and Agricultural Organization of the United Nations (FAO) Via delle Terme di Caracalla, 00100 Rome, Italy (Telephone Number in U.S. (202) 653-2400); *The State of Food and Agriculture.*

Statistical Office of the United Nations, Publishing Service, New York, New York 10017 (800) 253-9646; *Statistical Yearbook.*

SRI LANKA - FETAL MORTALITY - See SRI LANKA - MORTALITY

SRI LANKA - FILM - See SRI LANKA - MOTION PICTURES

SRI LANKA - FINANCE

Asian Development Bank, P.O. Box 789, 1099 Manila, Philippines; *Key Indicators of Developing Asian and Pacific Countries.*

Economist Intelligence Unit, 111 West 57th Street, New York, New York 10019 (800) 938-4685; *Sri Lanka Country Report.*

Europa Publications Limited, 18 Bedford Square, London, WC1B 3JN, England; *The Europa World Year Book.*

Federal Statistical Office, Gustav-Stresemann-Ring 11, D-6200 Wiesbaden, Germany; *Sri Lanka.*

International Monetary Fund, 700 Nineteenth Street, NW, Washington, D.C. 20431 (202) 623-7000; *Government Finance Statistics Yearbook; and International Financial Statistics.*

M.E. Sharpe, 80 Business Park Drive, Armonk, New York 10504 (800) 541-6563; *The Illustrated Book of World Rankings.*

St. Martin's Press, Inc., 175 Fifth Avenue, New York, New York 10010 (800) 221-7945; *The Statesman's Year-Book.*

Statistical Office of the United Nations, Publishing Service, New York, New York 10017 (800) 253-9646; *Statistical Yearbook for Asia and the Pacific.*

SRI LANKA - FISHERIES

Europa Publications Limited, 18 Bedford Square, London, WC1B 3JN, England; *The Europa World Year Book.*

Federal Statistical Office, Gustav-Stresemann-Ring 11, D-6200 Wiesbaden, Germany; *Sri Lanka.*

Food and Agricultural Organization of the United Nations (FAO) Via delle Terme di Caracalla, 00100 Rome, Italy (Telephone Number in U.S. (202) 653-2400); *The State of Food and Agriculture; and Yearbook of Fishery Statistics.*

M.E. Sharpe, 80 Business Park Drive, Armonk, New York 10504 (800) 541-6563; *The Illustrated Book of World Rankings.*

St. Martin's Press, Inc., 175 Fifth Avenue, New York, New York 10010 (800) 221-7945; *The Statesman's Year-Book.*

Statistical Office of the United Nations, Publishing Service, New York, New York 10017 (800) 253-9646; *Statistical Yearbook.*

United Nations Conference on Trade and Development, Central Statistical Service, Palais des Nations, Geneva, Switzerland (Telephone in U.S. (800) 253-9646); *UNCTAD Commodity Yearbook.*

SRI LANKA - FLOUR PRODUCTION

Statistical Office of the United Nations, Publishing Service, New York, New York 10017 (800) 253-9646; *Statistical Yearbook.*

SRI LANKA - FOOD

Food and Agricultural Organization of the United Nations (FAO), Via delle Terme di Caracalla, 00100 Rome, Italy (Telephone Number in U.S. (202) 653-2400); *Production Yearbook; and The State of Food and Agriculture.*

Statistical Office of the United Nations, Publishing Service, New York, New York 10017 (800) 253-9646; *Human Development Report; and Statistical Yearbook for Asia and the Pacific.*

United Nations Conference on Trade and Development, Central Statistical Service, Palais des Nations, Geneva, Switzerland (Telephone in U.S. (800) 253-9646); *UNCTAD Commodity Yearbook.*

SRI LANKA - FOREIGN DEBT

International Monetary Fund, 700 Nineteenth Street, NW, Washington, D.C. 20431 (202) 623-7000; *Government Finance Statistics Yearbook.*

Walden Publishing Ltd., Two Market Street, Saffron Walden Essex, CB10 1HZ, England; *The World of Information Asia and Pacific Review.*

SRI LANKA - FOREIGN TRADE

Asian Development Bank, P.O. Box 789, 1099 Manila, Philippines; *Key Indicators of Developing Asian and Pacific Countries.*

Economist Intelligence Unit, 111 West 57th Street, New York, New York 10019 (800) 938-4685; *Sri Lanka Country Report.*

The Economist Intelligence Unit (Asia) Limited, 10th Floor, Luk Kwok Centre, 72 Gloucester Road, Wanchai, Hong Kong (Phone Number in U.S. (800) 938-4685); *Asian Market Atlas.*

Euromonitor International, Inc., 122 South Michigan Avenue, Suite 1200, Chicago, Illinois 60603 (800) 577-EURO; *International Marketing Data and Statistics; and The World Economic Factbook.*

Europa Publications Limited, 18 Bedford Square, London, WC1B 3JN, England; *The Europa World Year Book.*

Federal Statistical Office, Gustav-Stresemann-Ring 11, D-6200 Wiesbaden, Germany; *Sri Lanka.*

Food and Agricultural Organization of the United Nations (FAO) Via delle Terme

di Caracalla, 00100 Rome, Italy (Telephone Number in U.S. (202) 653-2400); *The State of Food and Agriculture.*

International Monetary Fund, 700 Nineteenth Street, NW, Washington, D.C. 20431 (202) 623-7000; *International Financial Statistics.*

M.E. Sharpe, 80 Business Park Drive, Armonk, New York 10504 (800) 541-6563; *The Illustrated Book of World Rankings.*

St. Martin's Press, Inc., 175 Fifth Avenue, New York, New York 10010 (800) 221-7945; *The Statesman's Year-Book.*

Statistical Office of the United Nations, Publishing Service, New York, New York 10017 (800) 253-9646; *International Trade Statistics Yearbook;* and *Statistical Yearbook.*

United Nations Conference on Trade and Development, Central Statistical Service, Palais des Nations, Geneva, Switzerland (Telephone in U.S. (800) 253-9646); *UNCTAD Commodity Yearbook.*

The World Bank, 1818 H Street, NW, Washington, D.C. 20433 (202) 477-1234; *World Development Report;* and *World Development Indicators.*

SRI LANKA - FORESTRY AND FOREST PRODUCTS

The Economist Intelligence Unit (Asia) Limited, 10th Floor, Luk Kwok Centre, 72 Gloucester Road, Wanchai, Hong Kong (Phone Number in U.S. (800) 938-4685); *Asian Market Atlas.*

Europa Publications Limited, 18 Bedford Square, London, WC1B 3JN, England; *The Europa World Year Book.*

Federal Statistical Office, Gustav-Stresemann-Ring 11, D-6200 Wiesbaden, Germany; *Sri Lanka.*

Food and Agricultural Organization of the United Nations (FAO) Via delle Terme di Caracalla, 00100 Rome, Italy (Telephone Number in U.S. (202) 653-2400); *The State of Food and Agriculture;* and *Yearbook of Forest Products.*

M.E. Sharpe, 80 Business Park Drive, Armonk, New York 10504 (800) 541-6563; *The Illustrated Book of World Rankings.*

Statistical Office of the United Nations, Publishing Service, New York, New York 10017 (800) 253-9646; *Statistical Yearbook.*

United Nations Conference on Trade and Development, Central Statistical Service, Palais des Nations, Geneva, Switzerland (Telephone in U.S. (800) 253-9646); *UNCTAD Commodity Yearbook.*

United Nations Educational, Scientific and Cultural Organization (UNESCO), 7 Place de Fontenoy, F-75700 Paris, France (Telephone Number in U.S. (212) 963-5981); *Statistical Yearbook.*

The World Bank, 1818 H Street, NW, Washington, D.C. 20433 (202) 477-1234; *World Development Report.*

SRI LANKA - GAS PRODUCTION - See SRI LANKA - MINING AND MINERAL PRODUCTS

SRI LANKA - GENERAL INDUSTRIAL STATISTICS - See SRI LANKA - INDUSTRY

SRI LANKA - GENERAL MORTALITY - See SRI LANKA - MORTALITY

SRI LANKA - GEOGRAPHIC DATA

M.E. Sharpe, 80 Business Park Drive, Armonk, New York 10504 (800) 541-6563; *The Illustrated Book of World Rankings.*

SRI LANKA - GOATS - See SRI LANKA - LIVESTOCK AND POULTRY

SRI LANKA - GOLD HOLDINGS

International Monetary Fund, 700 Nineteenth Street, NW, Washington, D.C. 20431 (202) 623-7000; *International Financial Statistics.*

Statistical Office of the United Nations, Publishing Service, New York, New York 10017 (800) 253-9646; *Statistical Yearbook.*

The World Bank, 1818 H Street, NW, Washington, D.C. 20433 (202) 477-1234; *World Development Indicators.*

SRI LANKA - GOLD PRODUCTION AND CONSUMPTION - See SRI LANKA - MINING AND MINERAL PRODUCTS

SRI LANKA - GOVERNMENT

Asian Development Bank, P.O. Box 789, 1099 Manila, Philippines; *Key Indicators of Developing Asian and Pacific Countries.*

Central Intelligence Agency, Washington, D.C. 20505 (703) 482-1100, www.cia.gov; *The World Factbook.*

Europa Publications Limited, 18 Bedford Square, London, WC1B 3JN, England; *The Europa World Year Book.*

International Monetary Fund, 700 Nineteenth Street, NW, Washington, D.C. 20431 (202) 623-7000; *Government Finance Statistics Yearbook;* and *International Financial Statistics.*

St. Martin's Press, Inc., 175 Fifth Avenue, New York, New York 10010 (800) 221-7945; *The Statesman's Year-Book.*

Statistical Office of the United Nations, Publishing Service, New York, New York 10017 (800) 253-9646; *Asia-Pacific in Figures; National Accounts Statistics;* and *Statistical Yearbook.*

The World Bank, 1818 H Street, NW, Washington, D.C. 20433 (202) 477-1234; *World Development Report;* and *World Development Indicators.*

SRI LANKA - GRAIN PRODUCTION - See SRI LANKA - CROPS

SRI LANKA - GRANTS

International Monetary Fund, 700 Nineteenth Street, NW, Washington, D.C. 20431 (202) 623-7000; *Government Finance Statistics Yearbook.*

SRI LANKA - GROSS DOMESTIC PRODUCT

Asian Development Bank, P.O. Box 789, 1099 Manila, Philippines; *Key Indicators of Developing Asian and Pacific Countries.*

The Economist Intelligence Unit, 111 West 57th Street, New York, New York 10019 (800) 938-4685; *Sri Lanka Country Report;* and *The World Market Atlas.*

The Economist Intelligence Unit (Asia) Limited, 10th Floor, Luk Kwok Centre, 72 Gloucester Road, Wanchai, Hong Kong (Phone Number in U.S. (800) 938-4685); *Asian Market Atlas.*

Euromonitor International, Inc., 122 South Michigan Avenue, Suite 1200, Chicago, Illinois 60603 (800) 577-EURO; *International Marketing Data and Statistics;* and *The World Economic Factbook.*

Europa Publications Limited, 18 Bedford Square, London, WC1B 3JN, England; *The Europa World Year Book.*

M.E. Sharpe, 80 Business Park Drive, Armonk, New York 10504 (800) 541-6563; *The Illustrated Book of World Rankings.*

Statistical Office of the United Nations, Publishing Service, New York, New York 10017 (800) 253-9646; *Human Development Report; National Accounts Statistics;* and *Statistical Yearbook.*

The World Bank, 1818 H Street, NW, Washington, D.C. 20433 (202) 477-1234; *World Development Report;* and *World Development Indicators.*

SRI LANKA - GROSS NATIONAL PRODUCT

Asian Development Bank, P.O. Box 789, 1099 Manila, Philippines; *Key Indicators of Developing Asian and Pacific Countries.*

Euromonitor International, Inc., 122 South Michigan Avenue, Suite 1200,

Chicago, Illinois 60603 (800) 577-EURO; *International Marketing Data and Statistics.*

St. Martin's Press, Inc., 175 Fifth Avenue, New York, New York 10010 (800) 221-7945; *The Statesman's Year-Book.*

U.S. Arms Control and Disarmament Agency, 320 Twenty-first Street, NW, Washington, D.C. 20451 (202) 647-8677; *World Military Expenditures and Arms Transfers.*

Walden Publishing Ltd., Two Market Street, Saffron Walden Essex, CB10 1HZ, England; *The World of Information Asia and Pacific Review.*

The World Bank, 1818 H Street, NW, Washington, D.C. 20433 (202) 477-1234; *The World Bank Atlas; World Development Report;* and *World Development Indicators.*

SRI LANKA - GROUNDNUT PRODUCTION - See SRI LANKA - CROPS

SRI LANKA - HEALTH

The Economist Intelligence Unit (Asia) Limited, 10th Floor, Luk Kwok Centre, 72 Gloucester Road, Wanchai, Hong Kong (Phone Number in U.S. (800) 938-4685); *Asian Market Atlas.*

Euromonitor International, Inc., 122 South Michigan Avenue, Suite 1200, Chicago, Illinois 60603 (800) 577-EURO; *World Marketing Data and Statistics.*

M.E. Sharpe, 80 Business Park Drive, Armonk, New York 10504 (800) 541-6563; *The Illustrated Book of World Rankings.*

St. Martin's Press, Inc., 175 Fifth Avenue, New York, New York 10010 (800) 221-7945; *The Statesman's Year-Book.*

Statistical Office of the United Nations, Publishing Service, New York, New York 10017 (800) 253-9646; *Asia-Pacific in Figures; Human Development Report;* and *Statistical Yearbook.*

United Nations Children's Fund (UNICEF), 3 United Nations Plaza, New York, New York 10017 (800) 253-9646; *State of the World's Children.*

The World Bank, 1818 H Street, NW, Washington, D.C. 20433 (202) 477-1234; *World Development Report.*

World Health Organization, Office of Publications, 20 Avenue Appia, CH-1211 Geneva 27, Switzerland (Telephone Number in U.S. (518) 436-9686); *World Health Statistics Annual.*

SRI LANKA - HEALTH EXPENDITURES

International Monetary Fund, 700 Nineteenth Street, NW, Washington, D.C. 20431 (202) 623-7000; *Government Finance Statistics Yearbook.*

SRI LANKA - HIGHWAYS

Central Intelligence Agency, Washington, D.C. 20505 (703) 482-1100, www.cia.gov; *The World Factbook.*

The Economist Intelligence Unit (Asia) Limited, 10th Floor, Luk Kwok Centre, 72 Gloucester Road, Wanchai, Hong Kong (Phone Number in U.S. (800) 938-4685); *Asian Market Atlas.*

International Road Federation, 2600 Virginia Avenue, NW, Washington, D.C. 20037 (202) 338-4641; *World Road Statistics.*

St. Martin's Press, Inc., 175 Fifth Avenue, New York, New York 10010 (800) 221-7945; *The Statesman's Year-Book.*

SRI LANKA - HORSES - See SRI LANKA - LIVESTOCK AND POULTRY

SRI LANKA - HOURS OF WORK - See SRI LANKA - EMPLOYMENT

SRI LANKA - HOUSING AND HOUSING UNITS

Euromonitor International, Inc., 122 South Michigan Avenue, Suite 1200, Chicago, Illinois 60603 (800) 577-EURO; *World Marketing Data and Statistics.*

SRI LANKA - HOUSING EXPENDITURES

International Monetary Fund, 700 Nineteenth Street, NW, Washington, D.C. 20431 (202) 623-7000; *Government Finance Statistics Yearbook.*

M.E. Sharpe, 80 Business Park Drive, Armonk, New York 10504 (800) 541-6563; *The Illustrated Book of World Rankings.*

SRI LANKA - HYDROCHLORIC ACID PRODUCTION

Statistical Office of the United Nations, Publishing Service, New York, New York 10017 (800) 253-9646; *Statistical Yearbook.*

SRI LANKA - ILLITERATE POPULATION

Central Intelligence Agency, Washington, D.C. 20505 (703) 482-1100, www.cia.gov; *The World Factbook.*

The Economist Intelligence Unit, 111 West 57th Street, New York, New York 10019 (800) 938-4685; *The World Market Atlas.*

Euromonitor International, Inc., 122 South Michigan Avenue, Suite 1200, Chicago, Illinois 60603 (800) 577-EURO;

The World Economic Factbook.

St. Martin's Press, Inc., 175 Fifth Avenue, New York, New York 10010 (800) 221-7945; *The Statesman's Year-Book.*

Statistical Office of the United Nations, Publishing Service, New York, New York 10017 (800) 253-9646; *Asia-Pacific in Figures;* and *Human Development Report.*

United Nations Educational, Scientific and Cultural Organization (UNESCO), 7 Place de Fontenoy, F-75700 Paris, France (Telephone Number in U.S. (212) 963-5981); *Statistical Yearbook.*

SRI LANKA - IMPORTS

Asian Development Bank, P.O. Box 789, 1099 Manila, Philippines; *Key Indicators of Developing Asian and Pacific Countries.*

Central Intelligence Agency, Washington, D.C. 20505 (703) 482-1100, www.cia.gov; *The World Factbook.*

The Economist Intelligence Unit, 111 West 57th Street, New York, New York 10019 (800) 938-4685; *Sri Lanka Country Report;* and *The World Market Atlas.*

The Economist Intelligence Unit (Asia) Limited, 10th Floor, Luk Kwok Centre, 72 Gloucester Road, Wanchai, Hong Kong (Phone Number in U.S. (800) 938-4685); *Asian Market Atlas.*

Euromonitor International, Inc., 122 South Michigan Avenue, Suite 1200, Chicago, Illinois 60603 (800) 577-EURO; *International Marketing Data and Statistics;* and *The World Economic Factbook.*

Europa Publications Limited, 18 Bedford Square, London, WC1B 3JN, England; *The Europa World Year Book.*

Food and Agricultural Organization of the United Nations (FAO) Via delle Terme di Caracalla, 00100 Rome, Italy (Telephone Number in U.S. (202) 653-2400); *The State of Food and Agriculture.*

International Monetary Fund, 700 Nineteenth Street, NW, Washington, D.C. 20431 (202) 623-7000; *Direction of Trade Statistics; Government Finance Statistics Yearbook;* and *International Financial Statistics.*

International Rubber Study Group, York House, Eighth Floor, Empire Way, Wembley, London HA9 0PA, England; *Rubber Statistical Handbook.*

St. Martin's Press, Inc., 175 Fifth Avenue, New York, New York 10010 (800) 221-7945; *The Statesman's Year-Book.*

Statistical Office of the United Nations,

Publishing Service, New York, New York 10017 (800) 253-9646; *Foreign Trade Statistics of Asia and the Pacific.*

United Nations Conference on Trade and Development (UNCTAD), New York, New York 10017 (800) 253-9646; *Handbook of International Trade and Development Statistics.*

Walden Publishing Ltd., Two Market Street, Saffron Walden Essex, CB10 1HZ, England; *The World of Information Asia and Pacific Review.*

The World Bank, 1818 H Street, NW, Washington, D.C. 20433 (202) 477-1234; *World Development Report;* and *World Development Indicators.*

SRI LANKA - INCOME TAXES - See SRI LANKA - TAXATION

SRI LANKA - INDUSTRY

Central Intelligence Agency, Washington, D.C. 20505 (703) 482-1100, www.cia.gov; *The World Factbook.*

Economist Intelligence Unit, 111 West 57th Street, New York, New York 10019 (800) 938-4685; *Sri Lanka Country Report.*

Euromonitor International, Inc., 122 South Michigan Avenue, Suite 1200, Chicago, Illinois 60603 (800) 577-EURO; *International Marketing Data and Statistics; World Marketing Data and Statistics;* and *The World Economic Factbook.*

Europa Publications Limited, 18 Bedford Square, London, WC1B 3JN, England; *The Europa World Year Book.*

Federal Statistical Office, Gustav-Stresemann-Ring 11, D-6200 Wiesbaden, Germany; *Sri Lanka.*

International Labour Office, I.L.O. Publications, 1828 L Street, NW, Suite 801, Washington, D.C. 20036 (301) 638-3152; *Yearbook of Labour Statistics.*

M.E. Sharpe, 80 Business Park Drive, Armonk, New York 10504 (800) 541-6563; *The Illustrated Book of World Rankings.*

St. Martin's Press, Inc., 175 Fifth Avenue, New York, New York 10010 (800) 221-7945; *The Statesman's Year-Book.*

Statistical Office of the United Nations, Publishing Service, New York, New York 10017 (800) 253-9646; *Asia-Pacific in Figures; International Trade Statistics Yearbook; Statistical Yearbook;* and *Statistical Yearbook for Asia and the Pacific.*

The World Bank, 1818 H Street, NW, Washington, D.C. 20433 (202) 477-1234;

World Development Indicators.

World Intellectual Property Organization, 34 Chemin des Colombettes, CH-1211 Geneva 20. Switzerland; *Industrial Property Statistics.*

SRI LANKA - INFANT AND MATERNAL MORTALITY - See SRI LANKA - MORTALITY

SRI LANKA - INTERNAL TRADE

Statistical Office of the United Nations, Publishing Service, New York, New York 10017 (800) 253-9646; *Statistical Yearbook for Asia and the Pacific.*

SRI LANKA - INTERNATIONAL LIQUIDITY

International Monetary Fund, 700 Nineteenth Street, NW, Washington, D.C. 20431 (202) 623-7000; *International Financial Statistics.*

SRI LANKA - INTERNATIONAL RESERVES EXCLUDING GOLD

Asian Development Bank, P.O. Box 789, 1099 Manila, Philippines; *Key Indicators of Developing Asian and Pacific Countries.*

Statistical Office of the United Nations, Publishing Service, New York, New York 10017 (800) 253-9646; *Statistical Yearbook.*

The World Bank, 1818 H Street, NW, Washington, D.C. 20433 (202) 477-1234; *World Development Indicators.*

SRI LANKA - INTERNATIONAL STATISTICS

Asian Development Bank, P.O. Box 789, 1099 Manila, Philippines; *Key Indicators of Developing Asian and Pacific Countries.*

SRI LANKA - INVESTMENTS

International Monetary Fund, 700 Nineteenth Street, NW, Washington, D.C. 20431 (202) 623-7000; *International Financial Statistics.*

SRI LANKA - IRON ORE PRODUCTION AND CONSUMPTION - See SRI LANKA - MINING AND MINERAL PRODUCTS

SRI LANKA - IRRIGATION

Euromonitor International, Inc., 122 South Michigan Avenue, Suite 1200, Chicago, Illinois 60603 (800) 577-EURO; *International Marketing Data and Statistics.*

SRI LANKA - LABOR

Central Intelligence Agency, Washington, D.C. 20505 (703) 482-1100, www.cia.gov; *The World Factbook.*

The Economist Intelligence Unit (Asia) Limited, 10th Floor, Luk Kwok Centre, 72

Gloucester Road, Wanchai, Hong Kong (Phone Number in U.S. (800) 938-4685); *Asian Market Atlas.*

Euromonitor International, Inc., 122 South Michigan Avenue, Suite 1200, Chicago, Illinois 60603 (800) 577-EURO; *International Marketing Data and Statistics;* and *World Marketing Data and Statistics.*

Europa Publications Limited, 18 Bedford Square, London, WC1B 3JN, England; *The Europa World Year Book.*

Food and Agricultural Organization of the United Nations (FAO) Via delle Terme di Caracalla, 00100 Rome, Italy (Telephone Number in U.S. (202) 653-2400); *The State of Food and Agriculture.*

International Labour Office, I.L.O. Publications, 1828 L Street, NW, Suite 801, Washington, D.C. 20036 (301) 638-3152; *Yearbook of Labour Statistics.*

M.E. Sharpe, 80 Business Park Drive, Armonk, New York 10504 (800) 541-6563; *The Illustrated Book of World Rankings.*

St. Martin's Press, Inc., 175 Fifth Avenue, New York, New York 10010 (800) 221-7945; *The Statesman's Year-Book.*

Statistical Office of the United Nations, Publishing Service, New York, New York 10017 (800) 253-9646; *Human Development Report.*

The World Bank, 1818 H Street, NW, Washington, D.C. 20433 (202) 477-1234; *The World Bank Atlas; World Development Report;* and *World Development Indicators.*

SRI LANKA - LAND USE

Central Intelligence Agency, Washington, D.C. 20505 (703) 482-1100, www.cia.gov; *The World Factbook.*

Euromonitor International, Inc., 122 South Michigan Avenue, Suite 1200, Chicago, Illinois 60603 (800) 577-EURO; *International Marketing Data and Statistics.*

Food and Agricultural Organization of the United Nations (FAO), Via delle Terme di Caracalla, 00100 Rome, Italy (Telephone Number in U.S. (202) 653-2400); *Production Yearbook.*

The World Bank, 1818 H Street, NW, Washington, D.C. 20433 (202) 477-1234; *World Development Report.*

SRI LANKA - LIBRARIES

M.E. Sharpe, 80 Business Park Drive, Armonk, New York 10504 (800) 541-6563; *The Illustrated Book of World Rankings.*

United Nations Educational, Scientific

and Cultural Organization (UNESCO), 7 Place de Fontenoy, F-75700 Paris, France (Telephone Number in U.S. (212) 963-5981); *Statistical Yearbook.*

SRI LANKA - LIFE EXPECTANCY

Central Intelligence Agency, Washington, D.C. 20505 (703) 482-1100, www.cia.gov; *The World Factbook.*

The Economist Intelligence Unit (Asia) Limited, 10th Floor, Luk Kwok Centre, 72 Gloucester Road, Wanchai, Hong Kong (Phone Number in U.S. (800) 938-4685); *Asian Market Atlas.*

Euromonitor International, Inc., 122 South Michigan Avenue, Suite 1200, Chicago, Illinois 60603 (800) 577-EURO; *The World Economic Factbook.*

Statistical Office of the United Nations, Publishing Service, New York, New York 10017 (800) 253-9646; *Asia-Pacific in Figures; Human Development Report;* and *World Statistics Pocketbook.*

The World Bank, 1818 H Street, NW, Washington, D.C. 20433 (202) 477-1234; *The World Bank Atlas;* and *World Development Report.*

SRI LANKA - LIVESTOCK AND POULTRY

Euromonitor International, Inc., 122 South Michigan Avenue, Suite 1200, Chicago, Illinois 60603 (800) 577-EURO; *International Marketing Data and Statistics.*

Europa Publications Limited, 18 Bedford Square, London, WC1B 3JN, England; *The Europa World Year Book.*

Food and Agricultural Organization of the United Nations (FAO), Via delle Terme di Caracalla, 00100 Rome, Italy (Telephone Number in U.S. (202) 653-2400); *Production Yearbook;* and *The State of Food and Agriculture.*

M.E. Sharpe, 80 Business Park Drive, Armonk, New York 10504 (800) 541-6563; *The Illustrated Book of World Rankings.*

St. Martin's Press, Inc., 175 Fifth Avenue, New York, New York 10010 (800) 221-7945; *The Statesman's Year-Book.*

Statistical Office of the United Nations, Publishing Service, New York, New York 10017 (800) 253-9646; *Statistical Yearbook.*

United Nations Conference on Trade and Development, Central Statistical Service, Palais des Nations, Geneva, Switzerland (Telephone in U.S. (800) 253-9646); *UNCTAD Commodity Yearbook.*

SRI LANKA - LITERACY RATE

Euromonitor International, Inc., 122 South Michigan Avenue, Suite 1200, Chicago, Illinois 60603 (800) 577-EURO; *World Marketing Data and Statistics.*

SRI LANKA - LIVING LEVELS - See SRI LANKA - LIFE EXPECTANCY

SRI LANKA - MAIL - NUMBER OF PIECES SENT OR RECEIVED

Statistical Office of the United Nations, Publishing Service, New York, New York 10017 (800) 253-9646; *Statistical Yearbook.*

SRI LANKA - MANPOWER

Statistical Office of the United Nations, Publishing Service, New York, New York 10017 (800) 253-9646; *Statistical Yearbook for Asia and the Pacific.*

SRI LANKA - MANUFACTURING

Asian Development Bank, P.O. Box 789, 1099 Manila, Philippines; *Key Indicators of Developing Asian and Pacific Countries.*

M.E. Sharpe, 80 Business Park Drive, Armonk, New York 10504 (800) 541-6563; *The Illustrated Book of World Rankings.*

Statistical Office of the United Nations, Publishing Service, New York, New York 10017 (800) 253-9646; *Statistical Yearbook.*

The World Bank, 1818 H Street, NW, Washington, D.C. 20433 (202) 477-1234; *World Development Indicators.*

SRI LANKA - MARRIAGE RATES

Europa Publications Limited, 18 Bedford Square, London, WC1B 3JN, England; *The Europa World Year Book.*

M.E. Sharpe, 80 Business Park Drive, Armonk, New York 10504 (800) 541-6563; *The Illustrated Book of World Rankings.*

Statistical Office of the United Nations, Publishing Service, New York, New York 10017 (800) 253-9646; *Demographic Yearbook;* and *Statistical Yearbook.*

SRI LANKA - MEAT PRODUCTION - See SRI LANKA - LIVESTOCK AND POULTRY

SRI LANKA - MERCHANT SHIPPING

Europa Publications Limited, 18 Bedford Square, London, WC1B 3JN, England; *The Europa World Year Book.*

Lloyd's Register of Shipping, 17 Battery Place, New York, New York 10004 (212) 425-8050; *Register of Ships.*

St. Martin's Press, Inc., 175 Fifth Avenue, New York, New York 10010 (800) 221-7945; *The Statesman's Year-Book.*

Statistical Office of the United Nations, Publishing Service, New York, New York 10017 (800) 253-9646; *Statistical Yearbook.*

U.S. Department of Transportation, Maritime Administration, 400 Seventh Street, SW, Washington, D.C. 20590 (202) 366-5807, www.marad.dot.gov; *A Statistical Analysis of the World's Merchant Fleets.*

SRI LANKA - MILITARY

Central Intelligence Agency, Washington, D.C. 20505 (703) 482-1100, www.cia.gov; *The World Factbook.*

The Economist Intelligence Unit (Asia) Limited, 10th Floor, Luk Kwok Centre, 72 Gloucester Road, Wanchai, Hong Kong (Phone Number in U.S. (800) 938-4685); *Asian Market Atlas.*

Euromonitor International, Inc., 122 South Michigan Avenue, Suite 1200, Chicago, Illinois 60603 (800) 577-EURO; *World Marketing Data and Statistics.*

The International Institute for Strategic Studies, 23 Tavistock Street, London WC2E 7NQ, England 44 171 3797676; *The Military Balance.*

International Monetary Fund, 700 Nineteenth Street, NW, Washington, D.C. 20431 (202) 623-7000; *Government Finance Statistics Yearbook.*

St. Martin's Press, Inc., 175 Fifth Avenue, New York, New York 10010 (800) 221-7945; *The Statesman's Year-Book.*

Statistical Office of the United Nations, Publishing Service, New York, New York 10017 (800) 253-9646; *Human Development Report.*

U.S. Arms Control and Disarmament Agency, 320 Twenty-first Street, NW, Washington, D.C. 20451 (202) 647-8677; *World Military Expenditures and Arms Transfers.*

SRI LANKA - MILK - See SRI LANKA - DAIRY PRODUCTS

SRI LANKA - MINING AND MINERAL PRODUCTS

Asian Development Bank, P.O. Box 789, 1099 Manila, Philippines; *Key Indicators of Developing Asian and Pacific Countries.*

Europa Publications Limited, 18 Bedford Square, London, WC1B 3JN, England; *The Europa World Year Book.*

M.E. Sharpe, 80 Business Park Drive, Armonk, New York 10504 (800) 541-6563; *The Illustrated Book of World Rankings.*

St. Martin's Press, Inc., 175 Fifth Avenue, New York, New York 10010 (800) 221-7945; *The Statesman's Year-Book.*

Statistical Office of the United Nations, Publishing Service, New York, New York 10017 (800) 253-9646; *Statistical Yearbook.*

United Nations Conference on Trade and Development, Central Statistical Service, Palais des Nations, Geneva, Switzerland (Telephone in U.S. (800) 253-9646); *UNCTAD Commodity Yearbook.*

SRI LANKA - MONEY EXCHANGE RATES - See SRI LANKA - EXCHANGE RATES

SRI LANKA - MONEY RESERVES

Euromonitor International, Inc., 122 South Michigan Avenue, Suite 1200, Chicago, Illinois 60603 (800) 577-EURO; *International Marketing Data and Statistics.*

SRI LANKA - MONEY SUPPLY

Asian Development Bank, P.O. Box 789, 1099 Manila, Philippines; *Key Indicators of Developing Asian and Pacific Countries.*

Economist Intelligence Unit, 111 West 57th Street, New York, New York 10019 (800) 938-4685; *Sri Lanka Country Report.*

Euromonitor International, Inc., 122 South Michigan Avenue, Suite 1200, Chicago, Illinois 60603 (800) 577-EURO; *International Marketing Data and Statistics.*

Europa Publications Limited, 18 Bedford Square, London, WC1B 3JN, England; *The Europa World Year Book.*

International Monetary Fund, 700 Nineteenth Street, NW, Washington, D.C. 20431 (202) 623-7000; *International Financial Statistics.*

Statistical Office of the United Nations, Publishing Service, New York, New York 10017 (800) 253-9646; *Statistical Yearbook.*

The World Bank, 1818 H Street, NW, Washington, D.C. 20433 (202) 477-1234; *World Development Indicators.*

SRI LANKA - MORTALITY

Central Intelligence Agency, Washington, D.C. 20505 (703) 482-1100, www.cia.gov; *The World Factbook.*

The Economist Intelligence Unit (Asia) Limited, 10th Floor, Luk Kwok Centre, 72 Gloucester Road, Wanchai, Hong Kong (Phone Number in U.S. (800) 938-4685); *Asian Market Atlas.*

Euromonitor International, Inc., 122 South Michigan Avenue, Suite 1200,

Chicago, Illinois 60603 (800) 577-EURO; *International Marketing Data and Statistics;* and *The World Economic Factbook.*

Europa Publications Limited, 18 Bedford Square, London, WC1B 3JN, England; *The Europa World Year Book.*

St. Martin's Press, Inc., 175 Fifth Avenue, New York, New York 10010 (800) 221-7945; *The Statesman's Year-Book.*

Statistical Office of the United Nations, Publishing Service, New York, New York 10017 (800) 253-9646; *Asia-Pacific in Figures; Demographic Yearbook; Human Development Report; Statistical Yearbook;* and *World Statistics Pocketbook.*

United Nations Children's Fund (UNICEF), 3 United Nations Plaza, New York, New York 10017 (800) 253-9646; *State of the World's Children.*

The World Bank, 1818 H Street, NW, Washington, D.C. 20433 (202) 477-1234; *The World Bank Atlas; World Development Report;* and *World Development Indicators.*

World Health Organization, Office of Publications, 20 Avenue Appia, CH-1211 Geneva 27, Switzerland (Telephone Number in U.S. (518) 436-9686); *World Health Statistics Annual.*

SRI LANKA - MOTION PICTURES

St. Martin's Press, Inc., 175 Fifth Avenue, New York, New York 10010 (800) 221-7945; *The Statesman's Year-Book.*

Statistical Office of the United Nations, Publishing Service, New York, New York 10017 (800) 253-9646; *Statistical Yearbook.*

United Nations Educational, Scientific and Cultural Organization (UNESCO), 7 Place de Fontenoy, F-75700 Paris, France (Telephone Number in U.S. (212) 963-5981); *Statistical Yearbook.*

SRI LANKA - MOTOR VEHICLE TAXES - See SRI LANKA - TAXATION

SRI LANKA - MOTOR VEHICLES IN USE

Europa Publications Limited, 18 Bedford Square, London, WC1B 3JN, England; *The Europa World Year Book.*

International Road Federation, 2600 Virginia Avenue, NW, Washington, D.C. 20037 (202) 338-4641; *World Road Statistics.*

Statistical Office of the United Nations, Publishing Service, New York, New York 10017 (800) 253-9646; *Statistical Yearbook.*

SRI LANKA - MUSEUMS

M.E. Sharpe, 80 Business Park Drive, Armonk, New York 10504 (800) 541-6563; *The Illustrated Book of World Rankings.*

United Nations Educational, Scientific and Cultural Organization (UNESCO), 7 Place de Fontenoy, F-75700 Paris, France (Telephone Number in U.S. (212) 963-5981); *Statistical Yearbook.*

SRI LANKA - NATALITY - See SRI LANKA - BIRTH RATE

SRI LANKA - NATIONAL ACCOUNTS

Europa Publications Limited, 18 Bedford Square, London, WC1B 3JN, England; *The Europa World Year Book.*

Federal Statistical Office, Gustav-Stresemann-Ring 11, D-6200 Wiesbaden, Germany; *Sri Lanka.*

International Monetary Fund, 700 Nineteenth Street, NW, Washington, D.C. 20431 (202) 623-7000; *International Financial Statistics.*

Statistical Office of the United Nations, Publishing Service, New York, New York 10017 (800) 253-9646; *Asia-Pacific in Figures; National Accounts Statistics; Statistical Yearbook;* and *Statistical Yearbook for Asia and the Pacific.*

SRI LANKA - NATIONAL INCOME

M.E. Sharpe, 80 Business Park Drive, Armonk, New York 10504 (800) 541-6563; *The Illustrated Book of World Rankings.*

Statistical Office of the United Nations, Publishing Service, New York, New York 10017 (800) 253-9646; *Human Development Report;* and *Statistical Yearbook.*

SRI LANKA - NATIONAL PRODUCT

M.E. Sharpe, 80 Business Park Drive, Armonk, New York 10504 (800) 541-6563; *The Illustrated Book of World Rankings.*

Statistical Office of the United Nations, Publishing Service, New York, New York 10017 (800) 253-9646; *Statistical Yearbook.*

SRI LANKA - NATURAL GAS PRODUCTION - See SRI LANKA - MINING AND MINERAL PRODUCTS

SRI LANKA - NATURAL RUBBER PRODUCTION

International Rubber Study Group, York House, Eighth Floor, Empire Way, Wembley, London HA9 0PA, England; *Rubber Statistical Handbook.*

Statistical Office of the United Nations, Publishing Service, New York, New York

10017 (800) 253-9646; *Statistical Yearbook.*

SRI LANKA - NEWSPAPER PRODUCTION AND CONSUMPTION - See SRI LANKA - FORESTRY AND FOREST PRODUCTS

SRI LANKA - NEWSPRINT - See SRI LANKA - FORESTRY AND FOREST PRODUCTS

SRI LANKA - OCCUPATIONS - See SRI LANKA - LABOR

SRI LANKA - PAPER - See SRI LANKA - FORESTRY AND FOREST PRODUCTS

SRI LANKA - PATENTS, TRADEMARKS AND SERVICE MARKS

Statistical Office of the United Nations, Publishing Service, New York, New York 10017 (800) 253-9646; *Statistical Yearbook.*

World Intellectual Property Organization, 34 Chemin des Colombettes, CH-1211 Geneva 20. Switzerland; *Industrial Property Statistics.*

SRI LANKA - PEANUT PRODUCTION - See SRI LANKA - CROPS

SRI LANKA - PEPPER PRODUCTION - See SRI LANKA - CROPS

SRI LANKA - PERIODICALS

United Nations Educational, Scientific and Cultural Organization (UNESCO), 7 Place de Fontenoy, F-75700 Paris, France (Telephone Number in U.S. (212) 963-5981); *Statistical Yearbook.*

SRI LANKA - PESTICIDE USE

Food and Agricultural Organization of the United Nations (FAO) Via delle Terme di Caracalla, 00100 Rome, Italy (Telephone Number in U.S. (202) 653-2400); *The State of Food and Agriculture.*

SRI LANKA - PETROLEUM INDUSTRY

Asian Development Bank, P.O. Box 789, 1099 Manila, Philippines; *Key Indicators of Developing Asian and Pacific Countries.*

Food and Agricultural Organization of the United Nations (FAO) Via delle Terme di Caracalla, 00100 Rome, Italy (Telephone Number in U.S. (202) 653-2400); *The State of Food and Agriculture.*

M.E. Sharpe, 80 Business Park Drive, Armonk, New York 10504 (800) 541-6563; *The Illustrated Book of World Rankings.*

Statistical Office of the United Nations, Publishing Service, New York, New York 10017 (800) 253-9646; *Statistical Yearbook.*

United Nations Conference on Trade

and Development, Central Statistical Service, Palais des Nations, Geneva, Switzerland (Telephone in U.S. (800) 253-9646); *UNCTAD Commodity Yearbook.*

SRI LANKA - PIGS - See SRI LANKA - LIVESTOCK AND POULTRY

SRI LANKA - POPULATION

Asian Development Bank, P.O. Box 789, 1099 Manila, Philippines; *Key Indicators of Developing Asian and Pacific Countries.*

Central Intelligence Agency, Washington, D.C. 20505 (703) 482-1100, www.cia.gov; *The World Factbook.*

The Economist Intelligence Unit, 111 West 57th Street, New York, New York 10019; *Sri Lanka Country Report;* and *The World Market Atlas.*

The Economist Intelligence Unit (Asia) Limited, 10th Floor, Luk Kwok Centre, 72 Gloucester Road, Wanchai, Hong Kong (Phone Number in U.S. (800) 938-4685); *Asian Market Atlas.*

Euromonitor International, Inc., 122 South Michigan Avenue, Suite 1200, Chicago, Illinois 60603 (800) 577-EURO; *International Marketing Data and Statistics;* and *The World Economic Factbook.*

Europa Publications Limited, 18 Bedford Square, London, WC1B 3JN, England; *The Europa World Year Book.*

Federal Statistical Office, Gustav-Stresemann-Ring 11, D-6200 Wiesbaden, Germany; *Sri Lanka.*

Food and Agricultural Organization of the United Nations (FAO) Via delle Terme di Caracalla, 00100 Rome, Italy (Telephone Number in U.S. (202) 653-2400); *Production Yearbook.*

International Labour Office, I.L.O. Publications, 1828 L Street, NW, Suite 801, Washington, D.C. 20036 (301) 638-3152; *Yearbook of Labour Statistics.*

M.E. Sharpe, 80 Business Park Drive, Armonk, New York 10504 (800) 541-6563; *The Illustrated Book of World Rankings.*

St. Martin's Press, Inc., 175 Fifth Avenue, New York, New York 10010 (800) 221-7945; *The Statesman's Year-Book.*

Statistical Office of the United Nations, Publishing Service, New York, New York 10017 (800) 253-9646; *Asia-Pacific in Figures; Demographic Yearbook; Human Development Report; Statistical Yearbook; Statistical Yearbook for Asia and the Pacific;* and *World Statistics Pocketbook.*

United Nations Educational, Scientific

and Cultural Organization (UNESCO), 7 Place de Fontenoy, F-75700 Paris, France (Telephone Number in U.S. (212) 963-5981); *Statistical Yearbook.*

U.S. Arms Control and Disarmament Agency, 320 Twenty-first Street, NW, Washington, D.C. 20451 (202) 647-8677; *World Military Expenditures and Arms Transfers.*

Walden Publishing Ltd., Two Market Street, Saffron Walden Essex, CB10 1HZ, England; *The World of Information Asia and Pacific Review.*

The World Bank, 1818 H Street, NW, Washington, D.C. 20433 (202) 477-1234; *The World Bank Atlas;* and *World Development Report.*

World Health Organization, Office of Publications, 20 Avenue Appia, CH-1211 Geneva 27, Switzerland (Telephone Number in U.S. (518) 436-9686); *World Health Statistics Annual.*

SRI LANKA - POST OFFICES

M.E. Sharpe, 80 Business Park Drive, Armonk, New York 10504 (800) 541-6563; *The Illustrated Book of World Rankings.*

St. Martin's Press, Inc., 175 Fifth Avenue, New York, New York 10010 (800) 221-7945; *The Statesman's Year-Book.*

SRI LANKA - POTATO PRODUCTION - See SRI LANKA - CROPS

SRI LANKA - POWER PRODUCTION INDUSTRY

Statistical Office of the United Nations, Publishing Service, New York, New York 10017 (800) 253-9646; *Electric Power in Asia and the Pacific.*

SRI LANKA - PRICES

Asian Development Bank, P.O. Box 789, 1099 Manila, Philippines; *Key Indicators of Developing Asian and Pacific Countries.*

Federal Statistical Office, Gustav-Stresemann-Ring 11, D-6200 Wiesbaden, Germany; *Sri Lanka.*

Food and Agricultural Organization of the United Nations (FAO), Via delle Terme di Caracalla, 00100 Rome, Italy (Telephone Number in U.S. (202) 653-2400); *Production Yearbook;* and *The State of Food and Agriculture.*

International Labour Office, I.L.O. Publications, 1828 L Street, NW, Suite 801, Washington, D.C. 20036 (301) 638-3152; *Yearbook of Labour Statistics.*

International Monetary Fund, 700

Nineteenth Street, NW, Washington, D.C. 20431 (202) 623-7000; *International Financial Statistics.*

International Rubber Study Group, York House, Eighth Floor, Empire Way, Wembley, London HA9 0PA, England; *Rubber Statistical Handbook.*

M.E. Sharpe, 80 Business Park Drive, Armonk, New York 10504 (800) 541-6563; *The Illustrated Book of World Rankings.*

SRI LANKA - PRINTING AND WRITING PAPER - See SRI LANKA - FORESTRY AND FOREST PRODUCTS

SRI LANKA - PRODUCTION

Asian Development Bank, P.O. Box 789, 1099 Manila, Philippines; *Key Indicators of Developing Asian and Pacific Countries.*

International Rubber Study Group, York House, Eighth Floor, Empire Way, Wembley, London HA9 0PA, England; *Rubber Statistical Handbook.*

M.E. Sharpe, 80 Business Park Drive, Armonk, New York 10504 (800) 541-6563; *The Illustrated Book of World Rankings.*

SRI LANKA - PRODUCTIVITY

Euromonitor International, Inc., 122 South Michigan Avenue, Suite 1200, Chicago, Illinois 60603 (800) 577-EURO; *International Marketing Data and Statistics.*

SRI LANKA - PROPERTY TAXES - See SRI LANKA - TAXATION

SRI LANKA - PUBLIC FINANCE - See SRI LANKA - FINANCE

SRI LANKA - RADIO

The Economist Intelligence Unit (Asia) Limited, 10th Floor, Luk Kwok Centre, 72 Gloucester Road, Wanchai, Hong Kong (Phone Number in U.S. (800) 938-4685); *Asian Market Atlas.*

SRI LANKA - RADIO BROADCASTING - See SRI LANKA - BROADCASTING

SRI LANKA - RADIO RECEIVER PRODUCTION

Statistical Office of the United Nations, Publishing Service, New York, New York 10017 (800) 253-9646; *Statistical Yearbook.*

SRI LANKA - RADIO RECEIVERS

St. Martin's Press, Inc., 175 Fifth Avenue, New York, New York 10010 (800) 221-7945; *The Statesman's Year-Book.*

SRI LANKA - RAILWAYS

Europa Publications Limited, 18 Bedford Square, London, WC1B 3JN, England; *The Europa World Year Book.*

Jane's Information Group, Sentinel House, 163 Brighton Road, Coulsdon, Surrey CR5 2NH, England (Telephone Number in U.S. (703) 683-3700); *Jane's World Railways.*

St. Martin's Press, Inc., 175 Fifth Avenue, New York, New York 10010 (800) 221-7945; *The Statesman's Year-Book.*

Statistical Office of the United Nations, Publishing Service, New York, New York 10017 (800) 253-9646; *Statistical Yearbook.*

SRI LANKA - RELIGION

Central Intelligence Agency, Washington, D.C. 20505 (703) 482-1100, www.cia.gov; *The World Factbook.*

M.E. Sharpe, 80 Business Park Drive, Armonk, New York 10504 (800) 541-6563; *The Illustrated Book of World Rankings.*

St. Martin's Press, Inc., 175 Fifth Avenue, New York, New York 10010 (800) 221-7945; *The Statesman's Year-Book.*

SRI LANKA - RENT PRICES

International Labour Office, I.L.O. Publications, 1828 L Street, NW, Suite 801, Washington, D.C. 20036 (301) 638-3152; *Yearbook of Labour Statistics.*

SRI LANKA - RETAIL TRADE

Euromonitor International, Inc., 122 South Michigan Avenue, Suite 1200, Chicago, Illinois 60603 (800) 577-EURO; *World Marketing Data and Statistics.*

SRI LANKA - RICE PRODUCTION - See SRI LANKA - CROPS

SRI LANKA - ROUNDWOOD PRODUCTION - See SRI LANKA - FORESTRY AND FOREST PRODUCTS

SRI LANKA - RUBBER - INDUSTRIAL CONSUMPTION

International Rubber Study Group, York House, Eighth Floor, Empire Way, Wembley, London HA9 0PA, England; *Rubber Statistical Handbook.*

SRI LANKA - RUBBER EXPORTS

International Monetary Fund, 700 Nineteenth Street, NW, Washington, D.C. 20431 (202) 623-7000; *International Financial Statistics.*

SRI LANKA - RUBBER PRODUCTION AND CONSUMPTION

Commodity Research Bureau, Inc., 30 South Wacker Drive, Chicago Illinois 60606 (312) 454-1801; *Commodity Year Book.*

International Rubber Study Group, York House, Eighth Floor, Empire Way, Wembley, London HA9 0PA, England; *Rubber Statistical Handbook.*

M.E. Sharpe, 80 Business Park Drive, Armonk, New York 10504 (800) 541-6563; *The Illustrated Book of World Rankings.*

SRI LANKA - SALT PRODUCTION - See SRI LANKA - MINING AND MINERAL PRODUCTS

SRI LANKA - SAWNWOOD PRODUCTION - See SRI LANKA - FORESTRY AND FOREST PRODUCTS

SRI LANKA - SCIENCE AND TECHNOLOGY - EXPENDITURE FOR RESEARCH - See SRI LANKA - SCIENTISTS, TECHNICIANS AND ENGINEERS

SRI LANKA - SCIENTISTS, TECHNICIANS AND ENGINEERS

Statistical Office of the United Nations, Publishing Service, New York, New York 10017 (800) 253-9646; *Statistical Yearbook.*

United Nations Educational, Scientific and Cultural Organization (UNESCO), 7 Place de Fontenoy, F-75700 Paris, France (Telephone Number in U.S. (212) 963-5981); *Statistical Yearbook.*

SRI LANKA - SENIOR CITIZENS

M.E. Sharpe, 80 Business Park Drive, Armonk, New York 10504 (800) 541-6563; *The Illustrated Book of World Rankings.*

SRI LANKA - SHEEP - See SRI LANKA - LIVESTOCK AND POULTRY

SRI LANKA - SILVER PRODUCTION AND CONSUMPTION - See SRI LANKA - MINING AND MINERAL PRODUCTS

SRI LANKA - SOCIAL DATA

Asian Development Bank, P.O. Box 789, 1099 Manila, Philippines; *Key Indicators of Developing Asian and Pacific Countries.*

M.E. Sharpe, 80 Business Park Drive, Armonk, New York 10504 (800) 541-6563; *The Illustrated Book of World Rankings.*

Statistical Office of the United Nations, Publishing Service, New York, New York 10017 (800) 253-9646; *World Statistics Pocketbook.*

SRI LANKA - SOCIAL SECURITY

International Monetary Fund, 700

Nineteenth Street, NW, Washington, D.C. 20431 (202) 623-7000; *Government Finance Statistics Yearbook.*

Statistical Office of the United Nations, Publishing Service, New York, New York 10017 (800) 253-9646; *Human Development Report.*

SRI LANKA - SOYBEAN PRODUCTION - See SRI LANKA - CROPS

SRI LANKA - STAMP TAXES AND DUTIES - See SRI LANKA - TAXATION

SRI LANKA - STATE BUDGET REVENUE AND EXPENDITURES

Euromonitor International, Inc., 122 South Michigan Avenue, Suite 1200, Chicago, Illinois 60603 (800) 577-EURO; *International Marketing Data and Statistics.*

SRI LANKA - STEEL - See SRI LANKA - MINING AND MINERAL PRODUCTS

SRI LANKA - STOCKS - COMMODITY - MARKET PRICE - INDEX

Food and Agricultural Organization of the United Nations (FAO) Via delle Terme di Caracalla, 00100 Rome, Italy (Telephone Number in U.S. (202) 653-2400); *The State of Food and Agriculture.*

SRI LANKA - SUGAR PRODUCTION AND CONSUMPTION - See SRI LANKA - CROPS

SRI LANKA - TAXATION

Europa Publications Limited, 18 Bedford Square, London, WC1B 3JN, England; *The Europa World Year Book.*

International Monetary Fund, 700 Nineteenth Street, NW, Washington, D.C. 20431 (202) 623-7000; *Government Finance Statistics Yearbook.*

International Road Federation, 525 School Street, SW, Washington, D.C. 20024 (202) 554-2106; *World Road Statistics.*

St. Martin's Press, Inc., 175 Fifth Avenue, New York, New York 10010 (800) 221-7945; *The Statesman's Year-Book.*

The World Bank, 1818 H Street, NW, Washington, D.C. 20433 (202) 477-1234; *World Development Indicators.*

SRI LANKA - TEA PRODUCTION AND CONSUMPTION - See SRI LANKA - CROPS

SRI LANKA - TELEGRAPH SERVICE

Statistical Office of the United Nations, Publishing Service, New York, New York 10017 (800) 253-9646; *Statistical Yearbook.*

SRI LANKA - TELEPHONES IN USE

American Telephone and Telegraph Company, 26 Parsippany Road, Whippany, New Jersey 07981 (800) 222-0300; *The World's Telephones.*

Central Intelligence Agency, Washington, D.C. 20505 (703) 482-1100, www.cia.gov; *The World Factbook.*

The Economist Intelligence Unit (Asia) Limited, 10th Floor, Luk Kwok Centre, 72 Gloucester Road, Wanchai, Hong Kong (Phone Number in U.S. (800) 938-4685); *Asian Market Atlas.*

Europa Publications Limited, 18 Bedford Square, London, WC1B 3JN, England; *The Europa World Year Book.*

St. Martin's Press, Inc., 175 Fifth Avenue, New York, New York 10010 (800) 221-7945; *The Statesman's Year-Book.*

Statistical Office of the United Nations, Publishing Service, New York, New York 10017 (800) 253-9646; *Statistical Yearbook; and World Statistics Pocketbook.*

SRI LANKA - TELEVISION

The Economist Intelligence Unit (Asia) Limited, 10th Floor, Luk Kwok Centre, 72 Gloucester Road, Wanchai, Hong Kong (Phone Number in U.S. (800) 938-4685); *Asian Market Atlas.*

SRI LANKA - TELEVISION BROADCASTING - See SRI LANKA - BROADCASTING

SRI LANKA - TEXTILE INDUSTRY

M.E. Sharpe, 80 Business Park Drive, Armonk, New York 10504 (800) 541-6563; *The Illustrated Book of World Rankings.*

St. Martin's Press, Inc., 175 Fifth Avenue, New York, New York 10010 (800) 221-7945; *The Statesman's Year-Book.*

Statistical Office of the United Nations, Publishing Service, New York, New York 10017 (800) 253-9646; *Statistical Yearbook.*

United Nations Conference on Trade and Development, Central Statistical Service, Palais des Nations, Geneva, Switzerland (Telephone in U.S. (800) 253-9646); *UNCTAD Commodity Yearbook.*

SRI LANKA - THEATRE

United Nations Educational, Scientific and Cultural Organization (UNESCO), 7 Place de Fontenoy, F-75700 Paris, France (Telephone Number in U.S. (212) 963-5981); *Statistical Yearbook.*

SRI LANKA - TIRE (MOTOR VEHICLE) PRODUCTION

International Rubber Study Group, York House, Eighth Floor, Empire Way, Wembley, London HA9 0PA, England; *Rubber Statistical Handbook.*

Statistical Office of the United Nations, Publishing Service, New York, New York 10017 (800) 253-9646; *Statistical Yearbook.*

SRI LANKA - TOBACCO PRODUCTION

M.E. Sharpe, 80 Business Park Drive, Armonk, New York 10504 (800) 541-6563; *The Illustrated Book of World Rankings.*

Statistical Office of the United Nations, Publishing Service, New York, New York 10017 (800) 253-9646; *Statistical Yearbook.*

SRI LANKA - TOURISM

Euromonitor International, Inc., 122 South Michigan Avenue, Suite 1200, Chicago, Illinois 60603 (800) 577-EURO; *The World Economic Factbook; and World Marketing Data and Statistics.*

Europa Publications Limited, 18 Bedford Square, London, WC1B 3JN, England; *The Europa World Year Book.*

Federal Statistical Office, Gustav-Stresemann-Ring 11, D-6200 Wiesbaden, Germany; *Sri Lanka.*

M.E. Sharpe, 80 Business Park Drive, Armonk, New York 10504 (800) 541-6563; *The Illustrated Book of World Rankings.*

St. Martin's Press, Inc., 175 Fifth Avenue, New York, New York 10010 (800) 221-7945; *The Statesman's Year-Book.*

Statistical Office of the United Nations, Publishing Service, New York, New York 10017 (800) 253-9646; *Statistical Yearbook.*

World Tourism Organization, Calle Capitan Haya 42, E-28020 Madrid, Spain; *Yearbook of Tourism Statistics.*

SRI LANKA - TRACTORS IN USE

Statistical Office of the United Nations, Publishing Service, New York, New York 10017 (800) 253-9646; *Statistical Yearbook.*

SRI LANKA - TRADE - See SRI LANKA - FOREIGN TRADE

SRI LANKA - TRADEMARKS AND SERVICE MARKS - See PATENTS, TRADEMARKS AND SERVICE MARKS

SRI LANKA - TRANSPORTATION AND COMMUNICATIONS

Central Intelligence Agency, Washington, D.C. 20505 (703) 482-1100, www.cia.gov; *The World Factbook.*

The Economist Intelligence Unit (Asia) Limited, 10th Floor, Luk Kwok Centre, 72 Gloucester Road, Wanchai, Hong Kong (Phone Number in U.S. (800) 938-4685); *Asian Market Atlas.*

Euromonitor International, Inc., 122 South Michigan Avenue, Suite 1200, Chicago, Illinois 60603 (800) 577-EURO; *International Marketing Data and Statistics;* and *World Marketing Data and Statistics.*

Europa Publications Limited, 18 Bedford Square, London, WC1B 3JN, England; *The Europa World Year Book.*

Federal Statistical Office, Gustav-Stresemann-Ring 11, D-6200 Wiesbaden, Germany; *Sri Lanka.*

M.E. Sharpe, 80 Business Park Drive, Armonk, New York 10504 (800) 541-6563; *The Illustrated Book of World Rankings.*

St. Martin's Press, Inc., 175 Fifth Avenue, New York, New York 10010 (800) 221-7945; *The Statesman's Year-Book.*

Statistical Office of the United Nations, Publishing Service, New York, New York 10017 (800) 253-9646; *Human Development Report;* and *Statistical Yearbook for Asia and the Pacific.*

SRI LANKA - UNEMPLOYMENT

Central Intelligence Agency, Washington, D.C. 20505 (703) 482-1100, www.cia.gov; *The World Factbook.*

Euromonitor International, Inc., 122 South Michigan Avenue, Suite 1200, Chicago, Illinois 60603 (800) 577-EURO; *International Marketing Data and Statistics.*

International Labour Office, I.L.O. Publications, 1828 L Street, NW, Suite 801, Washington, D.C. 20036 (301) 638-3152; *Yearbook of Labour Statistics.*

Statistical Office of the United Nations, Publishing Service, New York, New York 10017 (800) 253-9646; *Statistical Yearbook.*

SRI LANKA - UTILITIES

Statistical Office of the United Nations, Publishing Service, New York, New York 10017 (800) 253-9646; *Electric Power in Asia and the Pacific.*

SRI LANKA - VITAL STATISTICS

Euromonitor International, Inc., 122 South Michigan Avenue, Suite 1200, Chicago, Illinois 60603 (800) 577-EURO; *International Marketing Data and Statistics.*

St. Martin's Press, Inc., 175 Fifth Avenue, New York, New York 10010 (800) 221-7945; *The Statesman's Year-Book.*

Statistical Office of the United Nations, Publishing Service, New York, New York 10017 (800) 253-9646; *Statistical Yearbook.*

World Health Organization, Office of Publications, 20 Avenue Appia, CH-1211 Geneva 27, Switzerland (Telephone Number in U.S. (518) 436-9686); *World Health Statistics Annual.*

SRI LANKA - WAGES

Federal Statistical Office, Gustav-Stresemann-Ring 11, D-6200 Wiesbaden, Germany; *Sri Lanka.*

International Labour Office, I.L.O. Publications, 1828 L Street, NW, Suite 801, Washington, D.C. 20036 (301) 638-3152; *Yearbook of Labour Statistics.*

Statistical Office of the United Nations, Publishing Service, New York, New York 10017 (800) 253-9646; *Statistical Yearbook for Asia and the Pacific;* and *Statistical Yearbook.*

SRI LANKA - WEATHER - See SRI LANKA - CLIMATE

SRI LANKA - WELFARE

International Monetary Fund, 700 Nineteenth Street, NW, Washington, D.C. 20431 (202) 623-7000; *Government Finance Statistics Yearbook.*

St. Martin's Press, Inc., 175 Fifth Avenue, New York, New York 10010 (800) 221-7945; *The Statesman's Year-Book.*

SRI LANKA - WHEAT PRODUCTION AND PRICES - See SRI LANKA -CROPS

SRI LANKA - WHOLESALE PRICES

Asian Development Bank, P.O. Box 789, 1099 Manila, Philippines; *Key Indicators of Developing Asian and Pacific Countries.*

International Monetary Fund, 700 Nineteenth Street, NW, Washington, D.C. 20431 (202) 623-7000; *International Financial Statistics.*

Statistical Office of the United Nations, Publishing Service, New York, New York 10017 (800) 253-9646; *Statistical Yearbook.*

SRI LANKA - WINE PRODUCTION - See SRI LANKA - BEVERAGES

SRI LANKA - WOOL PRODUCTION - See SRI LANKA - TEXTILE INDUSTRY

SRI LANKA - YARN PRODUCTION - See SRI LANKA - TEXTILE INDUSTRY

SRI LANKA - ZOOS AND BOTANICAL GARDENS

United Nations Educational, Scientific and Cultural Organization (UNESCO), 7 Place de Fontenoy, F-75700 Paris, France (Telephone Number in U.S. (212) 963-5981); *Statistical Yearbook.*

STAMPS - POSTAGE - RECEIPTS FROM

U.S. Postal Service, 475 L'Enfant Plaza West, SW, Washington, D.C. 20260-0010 (202) 268-2000, www.usps.gov; *Annual Report of the Postmaster General; Comprehensive Statement of Postal Operations;* and unpublished data.

STATE AND LOCAL GOVERNMENTS - (COMBINED DATA) - DEBT

U.S. Department of Commerce, Bureau of the Census, Washington, D.C. 20233 (301) 457-4100, www.census.gov; *Government Finances;* and Internet site: http://www.census.gov/ govs/www/estimate.htm.

STATE AND LOCAL GOVERNMENTS - (COMBINED DATA) - DEBT - HIGHWAYS

U.S. Department of Transportation, Federal Highway Administration, 400 Seventh Street, SW, Washington, D.C. 20590 (202) 366-0660, www.fhwa.dot.gov; *Highway Statistics.*

STATE AND LOCAL GOVERNMENTS - (COMBINED DATA) - EMPLOYEES

U.S. Department of Commerce, Bureau of the Census, Washington, D.C. 20233 (301) 457-4100, www.census.gov; *Historical Statistics on Governmental Finances and Employment; Public Employment;* and Internet site: http://www.census.gov/govs/www/apes.html.

STATE AND LOCAL GOVERNMENTS - (COMBINED DATA) - EMPLOYEES - BENEFITS

U.S. Department of Labor, Bureau of Labor Statistics, 2 Massachusetts Avenue, NE, Washington, D.C. 20212 (202) 691-5200, www.stats.bls.gov; *News, Employer Costs for Employee Compensation.*

STATE AND LOCAL GOVERNMENTS - (COMBINED DATA) - EXPENDITURES

U.S. Department of Commerce, Bureau of Economic Analysis, Fourteenth Street between Constitution Avenue and E Street, NW, Washington, D.C. 20230 (202) 606-9900, www.bea.doc.gov; *The National Income and Product Accounts of the United States;* and *Survey of Current Business.*

U.S. Department of Commerce, Bureau of the Census, Washington, D.C. 20233 (301) 457-4100, www.census.gov; *Government Finances; Historical Statistics on Governmental Finances and*

Employment; State and Local Government Finance Estimates by State; unpublished data; and Internet sites: http://www.census.gov/govs/www/index.html; and http://www.census.gov/govs/www/estimate.html.

STATE AND LOCAL GOVERNMENTS - (COMBINED DATA) - EXPENDITURES - BY TYPE

U.S. Department of Commerce, Bureau of the Census, Washington, D.C. 20233 (301) 457-4100, www.census.gov; *Government Finances; Historical Statistics on Governmental Finances and Employment; unpublished data;* and Internet site: http://www.census.gov/pub/govs/www/index.html; and http://www.census.gov/ govs/www/index.html.

STATE AND LOCAL GOVERNMENTS - (COMBINED DATA) - EXPENDITURES - CAPITAL OUTLAY

U.S. Department of Commerce, Bureau of the Census, Washington, D.C. 20233 (301) 457-4100, www.census.gov; *Historical Statistics on Governmental Finances and Employment; Government Finances;* and Internet site: http://www.census.gov/pub/govs/www/index.html; and http://www.census.gov/govs/www/index.html.

STATE AND LOCAL GOVERNMENTS - (COMBINED DATA) - EXPENDITURES - HOSPITALS AND MEDICAL CARE

American Hospital Association, One North Franklin, Suite 27, Chicago, Illinois 60606 (800) 242-2626; *Hospital Statistics.*

U.S. Department of Health and Human Services, Health Care Financing Administration, 200 Independence Avenue, SW, Washington, D.C. 20201 (202) 690-6145, www.hcfa.gov; *Health Care Financing Review.*

STATE AND LOCAL GOVERNMENTS - (COMBINED DATA) - EXPENDITURES - SCHOOLS

U.S. Department of Education, National Center for Education Statistics, 555 New Jersey Avenue, NW, Washington, D.C. 20208-5574 (202) 219-1828, http://nces.ed.gov; *Digest of Education Statistics.*

STATE AND LOCAL GOVERNMENTS - (COMBINED DATA) - EXPENDITURES - SOCIAL INSURANCE, ETC.

Social Security Administration, 6400 Security Boulevard, Baltimore, Maryland 21235 (800) 772-1213, ww.ssa.gov; *Social Security Bulletin;* and unpublished data.

STATE AND LOCAL GOVERNMENTS -

(COMBINED DATA) - FEDERAL AID

Executive Office of the President, Office of Management and Budget, Executive Office Building, Washington, D.C. 20503 (202) 395-3080, www.whitehouse.gov/omb; *Analytical Perspectives;* and *Historical Tables, Budget of the United States Government.*

U.S. Department of Commerce, Bureau of the Census, Washington, D.C. 20233 (301) 457-4100, www.census.gov; *Federal Aid to States for Fiscal Year.*

STATE AND LOCAL GOVERNMENTS - (COMBINED DATA) - FEDERAL AID - BY FUNCTION

Executive Office of the President, Office of Management and Budget, Executive Office Building, Washington, D.C. 20503 (202) 395-3080, www.whitehouse.gov/omb; *Historical Tables.*

U.S. Department of Commerce, Bureau of Economic Analysis, Fourteenth Street between Constitution Avenue and E. Street, NW, Washington, D.C. 20230 (202) 606-9900, www.bea.doc.gov; *National Income and Product Accounts of the U.S.;* and *Survey of Current Business.*

STATE AND LOCAL GOVERNMENTS - (COMBINED DATA) - FINANCES

U.S. Department of Commerce, Bureau of Economic Analysis, Fourteenth Street between Constitution Avenue and E Street, NW, Washington, D.C. 20230 (202) 606-9900, www.bea.doc.gov; *The National Income and Product Accounts of the United States; Survey of Current Business;* and unpublished data.

U.S. Department of Commerce, Bureau of the Census, Washington, D.C. 20233 (301) 457-4100, www.census.gov; *Government Finances;* and Internet site: http://www.census.gov/govs/www/index.htm.

STATE AND LOCAL GOVERNMENTS - (COMBINED DATA) - FINANCES - INTERGOVERNMENTAL

Executive Office of the President, Office of Management and Budget, Executive Office Building, Washington, D.C. 20503 (202) 395-3080, www.whitehouse.gov/omb; *The Budget of the United States;* and *Historical Tables.*

U.S. Department of Commerce, Bureau of the Census, Washington, D.C. 20233 (301) 457-4100, www.census.gov; *Government Finances;* and Internet site: http://www.census.gov/govs/www/index.html.

STATE AND LOCAL GOVERNMENTS - (COMBINED DATA) - FLOW OF FUNDS

Board of Governors of the Federal Reserve System, Twentieth Street and Constitution Avenue, NW, Washington, D.C. 20551 (202) 452-3000, www.bog.frb.fed.us; *Flow of Funds Accounts.*

STATE AND LOCAL GOVERNMENTS - (COMBINED DATA) - FOREST LAND

U.S. Department of Agriculture, Forest Service, Post Office Box 96090, Washington, D.C. 20090 (202) 205-8333, www.fs.fed.us; *Forest Resources of the United States.*

STATE AND LOCAL GOVERNMENTS - (COMBINED DATA) - HOSPITALS

American Hospital Association, One North Franklin, Suite 27, Chicago, Illinois 60606 (800) 242-2626; *Hospital Statistics.*

STATE AND LOCAL GOVERNMENTS - (COMBINED DATA) - NUMBER OF UNITS

U.S. Department of Commerce, Bureau of the Census, Washington, D.C. 20233 (301) 457-4100, www.census.gov; *Census of Governments, Government Organization.*

STATE AND LOCAL GOVERNMENTS - (COMBINED DATA) - PAYROLLS

U.S. Department of Commerce, Bureau of the Census, Washington, D.C. 20233 (301) 457-4100, www.census.gov; *Historical Statistics on Government Finances and Employment; Public Employment;* and Internet site: http://www.census.gov/govs/www/apes.html.

STATE AND LOCAL GOVERNMENTS - (COMBINED DATA) - PURCHASES OF GOODS AND SERVICES

U.S. Department of Commerce, Bureau of Economic Analysis, Fourteenth Street between Constitution Avenue and E Street, NW, Washington, D.C. 20230 (202) 606-9900, www.bea.doc.gov; *The National Income and Product Accounts of the United States;* and *Survey of Current Business.*

STATE AND LOCAL GOVERNMENTS - (COMBINED DATA) - RECEIPTS

U.S. Department of Commerce, Bureau of Economic Analysis, Fourteenth Street between Constitution Avenue and E Street, NW, Washington, D.C. 20230 (202) 606-9900, www.bea.doc.gov; *The National Income and Product Accounts of the United States; Survey of Current Business;* and unpublished data.

STATE AND LOCAL GOVERNMENTS - (COMBINED DATA) - RECEIPTS - BY SOURCE

U.S. Department of Commerce, Bureau of the Census, Washington, D.C. 20233 (301) 457-4100, www.census.gov; unpublished data; and Internet site: http://www.census.gov/pub/govs/www.index.html.

STATE AND LOCAL GOVERNMENTS - (COMBINED DATA) - RETIREMENT SYSTEMS

Board of Governors of the Federal Reserve System, Twentieth Street and Constitution Avenue, NW, Washington, D.C. 20551 (202) 452-3000, www.bog.frb.fed.us; *Flow of Funds Accounts.*

Employee Benefit Research Institute, 2121 K Street, NW, Suite 600, Washington, D.C. 20037 (202) 659-0670; *EBRI Databook on Employee Benefits.*

Social Security Administration, 6400 Security Boulevard, Baltimore, Maryland 21235 (800) 772-1213, ww.ssa.gov; *Social Security Bulletin;* and unpublished data.

U.S. Department of Commerce, Bureau of the Census, Washington, D.C. 20233 (301) 457-4100, www.census.gov; *Finances of Employee-Retirement Systems of State and Local Governments.*

STATE AND LOCAL GOVERNMENTS - (COMBINED DATA) - SECURITIES ISSUED

Thomson Financial Securities Data, Two Gateway Center, Newark, New Jersey 07006 (973) 622-3100; *Municipal New Issues Database.*

STATE AND LOCAL GOVERNMENTS - (COMBINED DATA) - TRUST FUNDS

Executive Office of the President, Office of Management and Budget, Executive Office Building, Washington, D.C. 20503 (202) 395-3080, www.whitehouse.gov/omb; *Analytical Perspectives.*

STATE AND LOCAL GOVERNMENTS - (COMBINED DATA) - WOMEN HOLDING PUBLIC OFFICE

Center for the American Woman and Politics, The Eagleton Institute of Politics, Rutgers University, 191 Ryders Lane, New Brunswick, New Jersey 08901 (732) 932-9384; information releases.

STATE DATA (FOR INDIVIDUAL STATES) - ABORTIONS

Alan Guttmacher Institute, 120 Wall Street, New York, New York 10005 (212) 248-1111; *Abortion Services in the U.S., Family Planning Perspectives;* and unpublished data.

STATE DATA (FOR INDIVIDUAL STATES) - AGRICULTURE - FARMS

U.S. Department of Agriculture, National Agricultural Statistics Service, Fourteenth Street and Independence Avenue, SW, Washington, D.C. 20250 (800) 727-9540, www.usda.gov/nass; *Farm Numbers and Land in Farms;* and *Farms and Land in Farms.*

STATE DATA (FOR INDIVIDUAL STATES) - AGRICULTURE - INCOME - FARM

U.S. Department of Agriculture, Economic Research Service, 1800 M Street, NW, Washington, D.C. 20036 (202) 694-5050, www.ers.usda.gov; *Farm Business Economic Report.*

STATE DATA (FOR INDIVIDUAL STATES) - AIDS

U.S. Department of Health and Human Services, Centers for Disease Control, 2600 Clifton Road, NE, Atlanta, Georgia 30333 (404) 639-3311, www.cdc.gov; *Summary of Notifiable Diseases, U.S.;* and *Morbidity and Mortality Weekly Report.*

STATE DATA (FOR INDIVIDUAL STATES) - ALTITUDES

U.S. Department of the Interior, Geological Survey, National Center, 12201 Sunrise Valley Drive, Reston, Virginia 22092 (703) 648-4000, www.usgs.gov; *Elevations and Distances in the United States.*

STATE DATA (FOR INDIVIDUAL STATES) - AMERICAN INDIAN, ESKIMO, ALEUT POPULATION

U.S. Department of Commerce, Bureau of the Census, Washington, D.C. 20233 (301) 457-4100, www.census.gov; *Population Paper Listings PPL-47;* and Internet site: http://www.census.gov/population/estimates/state/srh/srhus98.txt.

STATE DATA (FOR INDIVIDUAL STATES) - APPAREL AND ACCESSORY STORES - SALES

Market Statistics, 355 Park Avenue, South, New York, New York 10010 (212) 592-6250; *They Survey of Buying Power Data Service.*

STATE DATA (FOR INDIVIDUAL STATES) - AREA

U.S. Department of Commerce, Bureau of the Census, Washington, D.C. 20233 (301) 457-4100, www.census.gov; *Census of Population and Housing; Population Paper Listings PPL-47;* unpublished data; and Internet site: http://www.census.gov/population/estimates/state/srh/srhus98.txt.

STATE DATA (FOR INDIVIDUAL

STATES) - ASSETS AND LIABILITIES - FARM

U.S. Department of Agriculture, Economic Research Service, 1800 M Street, NW, Washington, D.C. 20036 (202) 694-5050, www.ers.usda.gov; *Farm Business Economic Report.*

STATE DATA (FOR INDIVIDUAL STATES) - AUTOMOBILE INSURANCE EXPENDITURES

National Association of Insurance Commissioners, 2301 McGee, Suite 800, Kansas City, Missouri 64108 (816) 842-3600; *State Average Expenditures and Premiums for Personal Automobile Insurance.*

STATE DATA (FOR INDIVIDUAL STATES) - BANKRUPTCIES

Administrative Office of the U.S. Courts, Thurgood Marshall Federal Judiciary Building, 1 Columbus Circle, NE, Washington, D.C. 20544 (202) 502-1455, www.uscourts.gov; unpublished data.

STATE DATA (FOR INDIVIDUAL STATES) - BANKS - COMMERCIAL

Federal Deposit Insurance Corporation, 550 Seventeenth Street, NW, Washington, D.C. 20429 (202) 393-8400, www.fdic.gov; *Statistics on Banking.*

STATE DATA (FOR INDIVIDUAL STATES) - BIRTHS AND BIRTH RATES

U.S. Department of Commerce, Bureau of the Census, Washington, D.C. 20233 (301) 457-4100, www.census.gov; Internet site: http://www.census.gov/population/estimates/state/st-98-2.txt; and http://www.census.gov/population/estimates/state/st-98-7.txt.

U.S. Department of Health and Human Services, National Center for Health Statistics, 3700 East-West Highway, Hyattsville, Maryland 20782 (301) 436-8500, www.cdc.gov/nchs; *Vital Statistics of the United States;* and *National Vital Statistics Report.*

STATE DATA (FOR INDIVIDUAL STATES) - BIRTHS AND BIRTH RATES - BIRTH WEIGHT

U.S. Department of Health and Human Services, National Center for Health Statistics, 3700 East West Highway, Hyattsville, Maryland 20782 (301) 436-8500, www.cdc.gov/nchs; *Vital Statistics of the United States;* and *National Vital Statistics Report.*

STATE DATA (FOR INDIVIDUAL STATES) - BIRTHS AND BIRTH RATES - BIRTHS TO SINGLE OR UNMARRIED

WOMEN

U.S. Department of Health and Human Services, National Center for Health Statistics, 3700 East West Highway, Hyattsville, Maryland 20782 (301) 436-8500, www.cdc.gov/nchs; *Vital Statistics of the United States;* and *National Vital Statistics Report.*

STATE DATA (FOR INDIVIDUAL STATES) - BLACK ELECTED OFFICIALS

Joint Center for Political and Economic Studies, 1090 Vermont Avenue, NW, Suite 1100, Washington, D.C. 20005 (202) 789-3500; *Black Elected Officials, Statistical Summary.*

STATE DATA (FOR INDIVIDUAL STATES) - BLACK POPULATION

U.S. Department of Commerce, Bureau of the Census, Washington, D.C. 20233 (301) 457-4100, www.census.gov; *Population Paper Listing PPL-47;* and Internet site: http://www.census.gov/population/estimates/state/srh/srhus98.txt.

STATE DATA (FOR INDIVIDUAL STATES) - BUILDING MATERIALS AND GARDEN SUPPLIES - SALES

Market Statistics, 355 Park Avenue, South, New York, New York 10010 (212) 592-6250; *The Survey of Buying Power Data Service.*

STATE DATA (FOR INDIVIDUAL STATES) - BUILDING PERMITS

U.S. Department of Commerce, Bureau of the Census, Washington, D.C. 20233 (301) 457-4100, www.census.gov; *Construction Reports.*

STATE DATA (FOR INDIVIDUAL STATES) - BUSINESS ENTERPRISE FAILURES AND STARTS

Dun and Bradstreet, Incorporated, 299 Park Avenue, Twenty-fourth Floor, New York, New York 10171 (212) 593-6800; *A Decade of Business Starts*

STATE DATA (FOR INDIVIDUAL STATES) - CANCER

American Cancer Society, 1599 Clifton Road, NE, Atlanta, Georgia 30329 (404) 320-3333; *Cancer Facts and Figures.*

STATE DATA (FOR INDIVIDUAL STATES) - CAPITAL PUNISHMENT

U.S. Department of Justice, Bureau of Justice Statistics,, 810 Seventh Street, NW, 2nd Floor, Washington, D.C. 20531 (800) 732-3277, www.ojp.usdoj.gov/bjs; *Capital Punishment.*

STATE DATA (FOR INDIVIDUAL STATES) - CHILD ABUSE CASES

U.S. Department of Health and Human Services, National Center on Child Abuse and Neglect, 370 L'Enfant Promenade, SW, Washington, D.C. 20447 (202) 205-8586; *Child Maltreatment: Reports From the States to the National Child Abuse and Neglect System.*

STATE DATA (FOR INDIVIDUAL STATES) - CIGARETTE SMOKING

U.S. Department of Health and Human Services, Centers for Disease Control and Prevention, 1600 Clifton Road, NE, Atlanta, Georgia 30333 (404) 639-3311, www.cdc.gov; *Morbidity and Mortality Weekly Report.*

STATE DATA (FOR INDIVIDUAL STATES) - CIVILIAN LABOR FORCE

U.S. Department of Labor, Bureau of Labor Statistics, Two Massachusetts Avenue, NE, Washington, D.C. 20212 (202) 691-5200, www.stats.bls.gov; Internet site: http://146.142.4.24/cgi-bin/surveymost?gp

STATE DATA (FOR INDIVIDUAL STATES) - CLIMATE

U.S. Department of Commerce, National Oceanic and Atmospheric Administration, National Climatic Data Center, 151 Patton Avenue, Asheville, North Carolina 28801 (828) 271-4800, www.ncdc.noaa.gov; *Climatography of the United States;* and *Comparative Climatic Data.*

STATE DATA (FOR INDIVIDUAL STATES) - COAL AND COKE PRODUCTION

U.S. Department of Energy, Energy Information Administration, 1000 Independence Avenue, SW, Washington, D.C. 20585 (202) 586-8800, www.eia.doe.gov; *Coal Industry; Quarterly Coal Report; Annual Energy Review;* and unpublished data.

STATE DATA (FOR INDIVIDUAL STATES) - CONGRESS, UNITED STATES - COMPOSITION

United States Congress, Joint Committee on Printing, North Capitol and H Streets, NW, Washington, D.C. 20401 (202) 512-0000; *Congressional Directory;* and unpublished data.

STATE DATA (FOR INDIVIDUAL STATES) - CRIME RATES

U.S. Department of Justice, Federal Bureau of Investigation, 935 Pennsylvania Avenue, NW, Washington, D.C. 20535 (202) 324-3691, www.fbi.gov; *Crime in the United States.*

STATE DATA (FOR INDIVIDUAL STATES) - CROPS - PRINCIPAL

U.S. Department of Agriculture, Economic Research Service, 1800 M Street, NW, Washington, D.C. 20036 (202) 694-5050, www.ers.usda.gov; *Foreign Agriculture Trade of the United States; U.S. Agricultural Trade Update; Economic Indicators of the Farm Sector: Production and Efficiency Statistics; Agricultural Resources and Environmental Indicators; AREI Updates: Crop use No. 12;* and *Agricultural Statistics.*

U.S. Department of Agriculture, National Agricultural Statistics Service, Fourteenth Street and Independence Avenue, SW, Washington, D.C. 20250 (800) 727-9540, www.usda.gov/nass; *Crop Production; Crop Values; Non-citrus Fruits and Nuts;* and *Citrus Fruits.*

STATE DATA (FOR INDIVIDUAL STATES) - DEATHS AND DEATH RATES

U.S. Department of Commerce, Bureau of the Census, Washington, D.C. 20233 (301) 457-4100, www.census.gov; Internet sites: http://www.census.gov/population/estimates/state/st-98-2.txt; and http://www.census.gov/population/estimates/state/st-98-7.txt.

U.S. Department of Health and Human Services, National Center for Health Statistics, 3700 East-West Highway, Hyattsville, Maryland 20783 (301) 436-8500, www.cdc.gov/nchs; *Vital Statistics of the United States, National Vital Statistics Report;* and unpublished data.

STATE DATA (FOR INDIVIDUAL STATES) - DEATHS AND DEATH RATES - INFANT

U.S. Department of Health and Human Services, National Center for Health Statistics, 3700 East-West Highway, Hyattsville, Maryland 20783 (301) 436-8500, www.cdc.gov/nchs; *Vital Statistics of the United States;* and unpublished data.

STATE DATA (FOR INDIVIDUAL STATES) - DEFENSE CONTRACTS

U.S. Department of Defense, Office of the Secretary, The Pentagon, Washington, D.C. 20301 (703) 545-6700; *Atlas/Data Abstract for the United States and Selected Areas.*

STATE DATA (FOR INDIVIDUAL STATES) - DEPARTMENT STORES - SALES

Market Statistics, 355 Park Avenue, South, New York, New York 10010 (212) 592-6250; *The Survey of Buying Power Data Service.*

STATE DATA (FOR INDIVIDUAL

STATES) - DOMESTIC TRAVEL EXPENDITURES

Industry Travel Association of America, 1100 New York Avenue, NW, Suite 450, Washington, D.C. 20005 (202) 408-1832; *Impact of Travel on State Economies.*

STATE DATA (FOR INDIVIDUAL STATES) - DRIVERS LICENSES

U.S. Department of Transportation, Federal Highway Administration, 400 Seventh Street, SW, Washington, D.C. 20590 (202) 366-0660, www.fhwa.dot.gov; *Highway Statistics;* and *Selected Highway Statistics and Charts.*

STATE DATA (FOR INDIVIDUAL STATES) - EARNINGS

U.S. Department of Commerce, Bureau of the Census, Washington, D.C. 20233 (301) 457-4100, www.census.gov; *County Business Patterns.*

U.S. Department of Labor, Bureau of Labor Statistics, Two Massachusetts Avenue, NE, Washington, D.C. 20212 (202) 691-5200, www.stats.bls.gov; *News, USDL 99-171;* and *Average Annual Pay by State and Industry.*

STATE DATA (FOR INDIVIDUAL STATES) - EATING AND DRINKING PLACES - SALES

Market Statistics, 355 Park Avenue, South, New York, New York 10010 (212) 592-6250; *The Survey of Buying Power Data Service.*

STATE DATA (FOR INDIVIDUAL STATES) - ELECTIONS

Congressional Quarterly, Inc., 1414 Twenty-second Street, NW, Washington, D.C. 20037 (202) 887-8500; *Congressional Quarterly Weekly Report;* and *America Votes.*

Council of State Governments, P.O. Box 11910, Iron Works Pike, Lexington, Kentucky 40578 (859) 244-8000; *State Elective Officials and the Legislatures.*

National Conference of State Legislatures, 1560 Broadway, Suite 700, Denver, Colorado 80202 (303) 830-2200; unpublished data.

U.S. Congress, Clerk of the House, The Capitol, Washington, D.C. 20515 (202) 224-3121, http://clerkweb.house.gov; *Statistics of the Presidential and Congressional Election.*

U.S. Congress, Joint Committee on Printing, North Capitol and H Streets, NW, Washington, D.C. 20401 (202) 512-0000; *Congressional Directory;* and unpublished

data.

U.S. Department of Commerce, Bureau of the Census, Washington, D.C. 20233 (301) 457-4100, www.census.gov; unpublished data.

STATE DATA (FOR INDIVIDUAL STATES) - ELECTIONS - VOTER REGISTRATION

U.S. Department of Commerce, Bureau of the Census, Washington, D.C. 20233 (301) 457-4100, www.census.gov; unpublished data.

STATE DATA (FOR INDIVIDUAL STATES) - ELECTRICAL POWER

U.S. Department of Energy, Energy Information Administration, 1000 Independence Avenue, SW, Washington, D.C. 20585 (202) 586-8800, www.eia.doe.gov; *Electric Power Annual; Electric Power Monthly;* and *Inventory of Power Plants in the U.S.*

STATE DATA (FOR INDIVIDUAL STATES) - ELEVATIONS

U.S. Department of the Interior, Geological Survey, National Center, 12201 Sunrise Valley Drive, Reston, Virginia 22092 (703) 648-4000, www.usgs.gov; *Elevations and Distances in the United States.*

STATE DATA (FOR INDIVIDUAL STATES) - EMPLOYEES

Office of Personnel Management, 1900 E Street, NW, Washington, D.C. 20415 (202) 606-1800, www.opm.gov; *Biennial Report of Employment by Geographic Area.*

U.S. Department of Commerce, Bureau of the Census, Washington, D.C. 20233 (301) 457-4100, www.census.gov; *County Business Patterns;* and Internet sites: http://www.census.gov/ftp/pub/govs/www/apes/97.html; http://www.census.gov/pub/govs/www/apes.html.

U.S. Department of Labor, Bureau of Labor Statistics, Two Massachusetts Avenue, NE, Washington, D.C. 20212 (202) 691-5200, www.stats.bls.gov; *Employment and Earnings.*

STATE DATA (FOR INDIVIDUAL STATES) - ENERGY CONSUMPTION

U.S. Department of Energy, Energy Information Administration, 1000 Independence Avenue, SW, Washington, D.C. 20585 (202) 586-8800, www.eia.doe.gov; *State Energy Data Report.*

STATE DATA (FOR INDIVIDUAL STATES) - ENERGY EXPENDITURES

U.S. Department of Energy, Energy Information Administration, 1000 Independence Avenue, SW, Washington, D.C. 20585 (202) 586-8800, www.eia.doe.gov; *State Energy Price and Expenditure Report.*

STATE DATA (FOR INDIVIDUAL STATES) - ESTABLISHMENTS

U.S. Department of Commerce, Bureau of the Census, Washington, D.C. 20233 (301) 457-4100, www.census.gov; *County Business Patterns.*

STATE DATA (FOR INDIVIDUAL STATES) - FARMS

U.S. Department of Agriculture, Economic Research Service, 1800 M Street, NW, Washington, D.C. 20036 (202) 694-5050, www.ers.usda.gov; *Farm Business Economic Report.*

U.S. Department of Agriculture, National Agricultural Statistics Service, Fourteenth Street and Independence Avenue, SW, Washington, D.C. 20250 (800) 727-9540, www.usda.gov/nass; *Farms and Land in Farms;* and *1997 Census of Agriculture.*

STATE DATA (FOR INDIVIDUAL STATES) - FARMS - ASSETS AND LIABILITIES

U.S. Department of Agriculture, Economic Research Service, 1800 M Street, NW, Washington, D.C. 20036 (202) 694-5050, www.ers.usda.gov; *Farm Business Economic Report.*

STATE DATA (FOR INDIVIDUAL STATES) - FARMS - INCOME

U.S. Department of Agriculture, Economic Research Service, 1800 M Street, NW, Washington, D.C. 20036 (202) 694-5050, www.ers.usda.gov; *Farm Business Economic Report.*

STATE DATA (FOR INDIVIDUAL STATES) - FARMS - VALUE OF FARM LAND AND BUILDINGS

U.S. Department of Agriculture, National Agricultural Statistics Service, Fourteenth Street and Independence Avenue, SW, Washington, D.C. 20250 (800) 727-9540, www.usda.gov/nass; *Census of Agriculture.*

STATE DATA (FOR INDIVIDUAL STATES) - FEDERAL FUNDS

U.S. Department of Commerce, Bureau of the Census, Washington, D.C. 20233 (301)457-4100, www.census.gov; *Federal Expenditures by State for Fiscal Year.*

STATE DATA (FOR INDIVIDUAL

STATES) - FOOD STAMP PROGRAM

U.S. Department of Agriculture, Food and Nutrition Service, 3101 Park Center Drive, Alexandria, Virginia 22302 (703) 305-2286, www.fns.usda.gov/fns; *Annual Historical Review of FNS Programs*; and unpublished data.

STATE DATA (FOR INDIVIDUAL STATES) - FOOD STORES

Market Statistics, 355 Park Avenue, South, New York, New York 10010 (212) 592-6250; *The Survey of Buying Power Data Service.*

U.S. Department of Commerce, Bureau of the Census, Washington, D.C. 20233 (301)457-4100, www.census.gov; *County Business Patterns.*

STATE DATA (FOR INDIVIDUAL STATES) - FOREIGN INVESTMENT IN THE UNITED STATES

U.S. Department of Commerce, Bureau of Economic Analysis, Fourteenth Street between Constitution Avenue and E Street, NW, Washington, D.C. 20230 (202) 606-9900, www.bea.doc.gov; *Survey of Current Business;* and *Foreign Direct Investment in the United States, Operations of U.S. Affiliates of Foreign Countries.*

STATE DATA (FOR INDIVIDUAL STATES) - FOREIGN TRADE

U.S. Department of Commerce, Bureau of the Census, Washington, D.C. 20233 (301) 457-4100, www.census.gov; *U.S. Merchandise Trade.*

U.S. Department of Agriculture, Economic Research Service, 1800 M Street, NW, Washington, D.C. 20036 (202) 694-5050, www.ers.usda.gov; *Foreign Agricultural Trade of the United States.*

STATE DATA (FOR INDIVIDUAL STATES) - FOREIGN TRAVELING

U.S. Department of Commerce, International Trade Administration, Fourteenth Street between Constitution Avenue and E Street, NW, Washington, D.C. 20230 (202) 482-2185; Internet site: http://www.tinet.ita.gov/

STATE DATA (FOR INDIVIDUAL STATES) - FUEL PRODUCTION

U.S. Department of Energy, Energy Information Administration, Washington, D.C. 20585 (202) 586-8800, www.eia.doe.gov; *Annual Energy Review; U.S. Crude Oil, Natural Gas, and Natural Gas Liquids Reserves; Monthly Energy Review;* and *Petroleum Supply Annual.*

STATE DATA (FOR INDIVIDUAL

STATES) - FURNITURE - HOME FURNISHING STORES

Market Statistics, 355 Park Avenue, South, New York, New York 10010 (212) 592-6250; *The Survey of Buying Power Data Service.*

STATE DATA (FOR INDIVIDUAL STATES) - GAS UTILITY INDUSTRY

American Gas Association, 400 North Capitol Street, NW, Washington, D.C. 20001 (202) 824-7000; *Gas Facts.*

STATE DATA (FOR INDIVIDUAL STATES) - GASOLINE PRICES

U.S. Department of Energy, Energy Information Administration, 1000 Independence Avenue, SW, Washington, D.C. 20585 (202) 586-8800, www.eia.doe.gov; *Petroleum Marketing Monthly.*

STATE DATA (FOR INDIVIDUAL STATES) - GASOLINE SERVICE STATIONS

Market Statistics, 355 Park Avenue, South, New York, New York 10010 (212) 592-6250; *The Survey of Buying Power Data Service.*

STATE DATA (FOR INDIVIDUAL STATES) - GASOLINE TAX RATES

U.S. Department of Transportation, Federal Highway Administration, 400 Seventh Street, SW, Washington, D.C. 20590 (202) 366-0660, www.fhwa.dot.gov; *Highway Statistics.*

STATE DATA (FOR INDIVIDUAL STATES) - GENERAL MERCHANDISE STORES - SALES

Market Statistics, 355 Park Avenue, South, New York, New York 10010 (212) 592-6250; *The Survey of Buying Power Data Service.*

STATE DATA (FOR INDIVIDUAL STATES) - GOVERNMENT FINANCES - FEDERAL AID TO STATE AND LOCAL GOVERNMENTS

U.S. Department of Commerce, Bureau of the Census, Washington, D.C. 20233 (301) 457-4100, www.census.gov; Internet site: http://www.census.gov/govs/ www.esti96.html.

STATE DATA (FOR INDIVIDUAL STATES) - GOVERNMENT FINANCES - FEDERAL INCOME TAX COLLECTIONS

U.S. Department of the Treasury, Internal Revenue Service, 1111 Constitution Avenue, NW, Washington, D.C. 20224 (202) 874-0410, www.irs.ustreas.gov;

Statistics of Income Bulletin.

STATE DATA (FOR INDIVIDUAL STATES) - GOVERNMENT FINANCES - STATE AND LOCAL GOVERNMENTS

U.S. Department of Commerce, Bureau of the Census, Washington, D.C. 20233 (301) 457-4100, www.census.gov; *Government Finances;* and *Federal Expenditures by State for Fiscal Year.*

STATE DATA (FOR INDIVIDUAL STATES) - GOVERNMENT FINANCES - STATE GOVERNMENTS

National Governor's Association, Hall of the States, 444 North Capitol Street, NW, Washington, D.C. 20001 (202) 624-5300; and National Association of State Budget Officers, Hall of the States, 444 North Capitol Street, NW, Suite 642 Washington, D.C. 20001 (202) 624-5382; *State Expenditure Report;* and *Fiscal Survey of the States.*

U.S. Department of Commerce, Bureau of the Census, Washington, D.C. 20233 (301) 457-4100, www.census.gov; *State Government Finances;* and Internet site:http://www.census.gov/ ftp/pub/govs/www/state.html; http://www.census.gov/govs/www/index. html; and http://www.census.gov/ govs/www/st97.html.

STATE DATA (FOR INDIVIDUAL STATES) - GOVERNMENT FINANCES - TAX COLLECTIONS

U.S. Department of Commerce, Bureau of the Census, Washington, D.C. 20233 (301) 457-4100, www.census.gov; Internet site: http://www.census.gov/govs/ www/index.html.

STATE DATA (FOR INDIVIDUAL STATES) - GOVERNORS - VOTE CAST

Elections Research Center, 5508 Greystone Street, Chevy Chase, Maryland 20815; *America Votes;* and unpublished data.

STATE DATA (FOR INDIVIDUAL STATES) - GROSS DOMESTIC PRODUCT

U.S. Department of Commerce, Bureau of Economic Analysis, Fourteenth Street between Constitution Avenue and E Street, NW, Washington, D.C. 20230 (202) 606-9900, www.bea.doc.gov; *Survey of Current Business.*

STATE DATA (FOR INDIVIDUAL STATES) - HAZARDOUS WASTE SITES

Environmental Protection Agency, 1200 Pennsylvania Avenue, NW, Washington, D.C. 20460 (888) 372-8255, www.epa.gov; *Supplementary Materials: National*

Priorities List, Proposed Rule.

STATE DATA (FOR INDIVIDUAL STATES) - HEALTH INSURANCE COVERAGE

U.S. Department of Commerce, Bureau of the Census, Washington, D.C. 20233 (301) 457-4100, www.census.gov; unpublished data; and Internet site: http://www.census.gov/hhes/hlthins/hlthin97/hi97t8.html.

STATE DATA (FOR INDIVIDUAL STATES) - HIGHWAY FUNDS

U.S. Department of Transportation, Federal Highway Administration, 400 Seventh Street, SW, Washington, D.C. 20590 (202) 366-0660, www.fhwa.dot.gov; *Highway Statistics.*

STATE DATA (FOR INDIVIDUAL STATES) - HIGHWAY MILEAGE

U.S. Department of Transportation, Federal Highway Administration, 400 Seventh Street, SW, Washington, D.C. 20590 (202) 366-0660, www.fhwa.dot.gov; *Highway Statistics.*

STATE DATA (FOR INDIVIDUAL STATES) - HIGHWAY TRUST FUND

U.S. Department of Commerce, Bureau of the Census, Washington, D.C. 20233 (301) 457-4100, www.census.gov; *Federal Expenditures by State for Fiscal Year.*

STATE DATA (FOR INDIVIDUAL STATES) - HISPANIC ELECTED OFFICIALS

National Association of Latino Elected and Appointed Officials, NALEO Education Fund, 5800 South Eastern Avenue, Suite 365, Los Angeles, California 90040 (213) 262-8503; *National Roster of Hispanic Elected Officials.*

STATE DATA (FOR INDIVIDUAL STATES) - HISPANIC POPULATION

U.S. Department of Commerce, Bureau of the Census, Washington, D.C. 20233 (301) 457-4100, www.census.gov; *Population Paper Listings PPL-47;* and Internet site:http://www.census.gov/population/estimates/state/srh/srhus98.txt.

STATE DATA (FOR INDIVIDUAL STATES) - HOSPITALS - COST TO PATIENT

American Hospital Association, One North Franklin, Suite 27, Chicago, Illinois 60606 (800) 242-2626; *Hospital Statistics.*

STATE DATA (FOR INDIVIDUAL STATES) - HOUSEHOLDS OR FAMILIES

U.S. Department of Commerce, Bureau of the Census, Washington, D.C. 20233 (301) 457-4100, www.census.gov; *Census of Population, General Population Characteristics, United States;* unpublished data; and Internet site: http://www.census.gov/population/estimates/housing/prhuhh1.txt.

STATE DATA (FOR INDIVIDUAL STATES) - HOUSING

National Association of Home Builders of the U.S., 1201 15th Street, NW, Washington, D.C. 20005 (202) 822-0200; data provided by Econometric Forecasting Service.

National Association of Realtors, 430 North Michigan Avenue, Chicago, Illinois 60611-4087 (800) 874-6500; *Real Estate Outlook: Market Trends and Insights.*

U.S. Department of Commerce, Bureau of the Census, Washington, D.C. 20233 (301) 457-4100, www.census.gov; *Construction Reports;* and Internet site: http://www.census.gov/hhes/www/hus.html.

STATE DATA (FOR INDIVIDUAL STATES) - HOUSING - SOLD

National Association of Realtors, 430 North Michigan Avenue, Chicago, Illinois 60611-4087 (800) 874-6500; *Real Estate Outlook: Market Trends and Insights.*

STATE DATA (FOR INDIVIDUAL STATES) - IMMIGRANTS ADMITTED

U.S. Department of Justice, Immigration and Naturalization Service, 425 I Street, NW, Washington, D.C. 20536 (202) 305-1613, www.ins.usdoj.gov; *Statistical Yearbook.*

STATE DATA (FOR INDIVIDUAL STATES) - INCOME

U.S. Department of Commerce, Bureau of the Census, Washington, D.C. 20233 (301) 457-4100, www.census.gov; *Current Population Reports;* and Internet site: http://www.census.gov/hhes/income/histinc/inchhdet.html.

STATE DATA (FOR INDIVIDUAL STATES) - INCOME - DISPOSABLE PERSONAL

U.S. Department of Commerce, Bureau of Economic Analysis, Fourteenth Street between Constitution Avenue and E Street, NW, Washington, D.C. 20230 (202) 606-9900, www.bea.doc.gov; *Survey of Current Business;* and unpublished data.

STATE DATA (FOR INDIVIDUAL STATES) - INCOME - HOUSEHOLD

U.S. Department of Commerce, Bureau of the Census, Washington, D.C. 20233 (301) 457-4100, www.census.gov; *Current Population Report;* and Internet site: http://www.census.gov/hhes/income/histinc/inchhdet.html.

STATE DATA (FOR INDIVIDUAL STATES) - INCOME - PERSONAL

U.S. Department of Commerce, Bureau of Economic Analysis, Fourteenth Street between Constitution Avenue and E Street, NW, Washington, D.C. 20230 (202) 606-9900, www.bea.doc.gov; *Survey of Current Business;* and unpublished data.

STATE DATA (FOR INDIVIDUAL STATES) - INCORPORATIONS

Dun and Bradstreet Corporation, 299 Park Avenue, Twenty-fourth Floor, New York, New York 10171 (212) 593-6800; *A Decade of Business Starts;* and *Business Failure Record.*

STATE DATA (FOR INDIVIDUAL STATES) - LAND

General Services Administration, General Services Building, Eighteenth and F Streets, NW, Washington, D.C. 20405 (202) 708-5082, www.gsa.gov; *Inventory Report on Real Property Owned by the United States Throughout the World.*

STATE DATA (FOR INDIVIDUAL STATES) - LAND - FEDERAL

General Services Administration, General Services Building, Eighteenth and F Streets, NW, Washington, D.C. 20405 (202) 708-5082, www.gsa.gov; *Inventory Report on Real Property Owned by the United States Throughout the World.*

STATE DATA (FOR INDIVIDUAL STATES) - LEGISLATURES - COMPOSITION

Council of State Governments, Post Office Box 11910, Iron Works Pike, Lexington, Kentucky 40578 (859) 244-8000; *State Elective Officials and the Legislatures.*

National Conference of State Legislatures, 1560 Broadway, Suite 700, Denver, Colorado 80202 (303) 830-2200; *unpublished data.*

STATE DATA (FOR INDIVIDUAL STATES) - LIFE EXPECTANCY

U.S. Department of Health and Human Services, National Center for Health Statistics, 3700 East-West Highway, Hyattsville, Maryland 20782 (301) 436-8500, www.cdc.gov/nchs; *U.S. Decennial Life Tables for 1989-91, Vol. II.*

STATE DATA (FOR INDIVIDUAL STATES) - LIVESTOCK

U.S. Department of Agriculture,

National Agricultural Statistics Service, Fourteenth Street and Independence Avenue, SW, Washington, D.C. 20250 (800) 727-9540, www.usda.gov/nass; *Meat Animals - Production, Disposition and Income; Dairy Products;* and *Milk Production, Disposition, and Income.*

STATE DATA (FOR INDIVIDUAL STATES) - LOCAL GOVERNMENT UNITS

U.S. Department of Commerce, Bureau of the Census, Washington, D.C. 20233 (301) 457-4100, www.census.gov; *Census of Governments;* and *Government Organization.*

STATE DATA (FOR INDIVIDUAL STATES) - LOTTERIES - REVENUE FROM

U.S. Department of Commerce, Bureau of the Census, Washington, D.C. 20233 (301) 457-4100, www.census.gov; unpublished data.

STATE DATA (FOR INDIVIDUAL STATES) - MANUFACTURES - SUMMARY STATISTICS

U.S. Department of Commerce, Bureau of the Census, Washington, D.C. 20233 (301) 457-4100, www.census.gov; *Annual Survey of Manufactures, Geographic Area Statistics;* and *1997 Economic Census.*

STATE DATA (FOR INDIVIDUAL STATES) - MARRIAGE AND DIVORCE

U.S. Department of Health and Human Services, Public Health Service, 200 Independence Avenue, SW, Washington, D.C. 20201 (202) 690-7694, www.hhs.gov/phs; *Vital Statistics of the United States;* and *National Vital Statistics Report.*

STATE DATA (FOR INDIVIDUAL STATES) - MEDICARE

U.S. Department of Health and Human Services, Health Care Financing Administration, 200 Independence Avenue, SW, Washington, D.C. 20201 (202) 690-6145, www.hcfa.gov; *Statistical Report on Medical Care: Eligibles, Recipients, Payments, and Services;* and Internet sites: http://www.hcfa.gov/medicaid/trends97.html; and http://www.hcfa.gov/medicaid/master97.htm.

STATE DATA (FOR INDIVIDUAL STATES) - MEDICARE

U.S. Department of Health and Human Services, Health Care Financing Administration, 200 Independence Avenue, SW, Washington, D.C. 20201 (202) 690-6145, www.hcfa.gov; unpublished data.

STATE DATA (FOR INDIVIDUAL STATES) - METROPOLITAN AREA

POPULATION

U.S. Department of Commerce, Bureau of the Census, Washington, D.C. 20233 (301) 457-4100, www.census.gov; *Census of Population and Housing, Supplementary Reports, Metropolitan Areas as Defined by the Office of Management and Budget; U.S. Census of Population and Housing, Population and Housing Unit Counts;* and unpublished data.

STATE DATA (FOR INDIVIDUAL STATES) - MILK PRODUCTION

U.S. Department of Agriculture, National Agricultural Statistics Service, Fourteenth Street and Independence Avenue, SW, Washington, D.C. 20250 (800) 727-9540, www.usda.gov/nass; *Milk Production, Disposition, and Income;* and *Dairy Products.*

STATE DATA (FOR INDIVIDUAL STATES) - MINERAL PRODUCTION AND VALUE

U.S. Department of the Interior, Geological Survey, Office of Minerals Information, 12201 Sunrise Valley Drive, Reston, Virginia 22092 (703) 648-4000, www.minerals.usgs.gov; *Annual Reports;* and *Mineral Commodities Summaries.*

STATE DATA (FOR INDIVIDUAL STATES) - MOTORCYCLES

U.S. Department of Transportation, Federal Highway Administration, 400 Seventh Street, SW, Washington, D.C. 20590 (202) 366-0660, www.fhwa.dot.gov; *Highway Statistics;* and *Selected Highway Statistics and Charts.*

STATE DATA (FOR INDIVIDUAL STATES) - MOTOR FUEL TAX

U.S. Department of Transportation, Federal Highway Administration, 400 Seventh Street, SW, Washington, D.C. 20590 (202) 366-0660, www.fhwa.dot.gov; *Highway Statistics.*

STATE DATA (FOR INDIVIDUAL STATES) - MOTOR VEHICLE DEALERS

Market Statistics, 355 Park Avenue, South, New York, New York 10010 (212) 592-6250; *The Survey of Buying Power Data Service.*

STATE DATA (FOR INDIVIDUAL STATES) - MOTOR VEHICLE REGISTRATIONS

U.S. Department of Transportation, Federal Highway Administration, 400 Seventh Street, SW, Washington, D.C. 20590 (202) 366-0660, www.fhwa.dot.gov; *Highway Statistics;* and *Selected Highway Statistics and Charts.*

STATE DATA (FOR INDIVIDUAL STATES) - NATIONAL FORESTS

U.S. Department of Agriculture, Forest Service, Post Office Box 96090, Washington, D.C. 20090 (202) 205-8333, www.fs.fed.us; *Annual Report.*

STATE DATA (FOR INDIVIDUAL STATES) - NEWSPAPERS - NUMBER AND CIRCULATION

Editor and Publisher, 11 West Nineteenth Street, New York, New York 10011 (212) 675-4380; *Editor and Publisher International Year Book.*

STATE DATA (FOR INDIVIDUAL STATES) - NURSES

U.S. Department of Health and Human Services, Health Resources and Services Administration, 5600 Fishers Lane, Rockville, Maryland 20857 (301) 443-3376, www.hrsa.gov; unpublished data.

STATE DATA (FOR INDIVIDUAL STATES) - PARKS

National Association of State Park Directors, 9894 East Holden Place, Tucson, Arizona 85748 (520) 298-4924; *Annual Information Exchange.*

U.S. Department of the Interior, National Park Service, C Street between Eighteenth and Nineteenth Streets, NW, Washington, D.C. 20240 (202) 208-6843, www.nps.gov; *National Park Statistical Abstract;* and unpublished data.

STATE DATA (FOR INDIVIDUAL STATES) - PATENTS

U.S. Department of Commerce, Patent and Trademark Office, 2121 Crystal Drive, Arlington, Virginia 22202 (703) 305-8341, www.uspto.gov; Technology Assessment and Forecast Database.

STATE DATA (FOR INDIVIDUAL STATES) - PHYSICIANS

U.S. Department of Health and Human Services, Health Resources and Services Administration, 5600 Fishers Lane, Rockville, Maryland 20857 (301) 443-3376, www.hrsa.gov; unpublished data.

STATE DATA (FOR INDIVIDUAL STATES) - POLICE PROTECTION

U.S. Department of Justice, Bureau of Justice Statistics, 810 Seventh Street, NW, 2nd Floor, Washington, D.C. 20531 (800) 732-3277, www.ojp.usdoj.gov/bjs; *Census of State and Local Law Enforcement Agencies.*

STATE DATA (FOR INDIVIDUAL STATES) - POPULATION

U.S. Department of Commerce, Bureau of the Census, Washington, D.C. 20233 (301) 457-4100, www.census.gov; *Current Population Reports; Census of Population and Housing; Population and Housing Unit Counts;* and unpublished data.

STATE DATA (FOR INDIVIDUAL STATES) - POPULATION - AGE DISTRIBUTION

U.S. Department of Commerce, Bureau of the Census, Washington, D.C. 20233 (301) 457-4100, www.census.gov; unpublished data.

STATE DATA (FOR INDIVIDUAL STATES) - POPULATION - BLACK

U.S. Department of Commerce, Bureau of the Census, Washington, D.C. 20233 (301) 457-4100, www.census.gov; *Current Population Reports.*

STATE DATA (FOR INDIVIDUAL STATES) - POPULATION - DENSITY

U.S. Department of Commerce, Bureau of the Census, Washington, D.C. 20233 (301) 457-4100, www.census.gov; *Current Population Reports; Census of Population and Housing; Population and Housing Unit Counts;* and unpublished data.

STATE DATA (FOR INDIVIDUAL STATES) - POPULATION - METROPOLITAN AREAS

U.S. Department of Commerce, Bureau of the Census, Washington, D.C. 20233 (301) 457-4100, www.census.gov; *Census of Population and Housing, Supplementary Reports, Metropolitan Areas as Defined by the Office of Management and Budget;* and *Census of Population and Housing, Population and Housing Unit Counts.*

STATE DATA (FOR INDIVIDUAL STATES) - POULTRY

U.S. Department of Agriculture, National Agricultural Statistics Service, Fourteenth Street and Independence Avenue, SW, Washington, D.C. 20250 (800) 727-9540, www.usda.gov/nass; *Poultry - Production and Value;* and *Turkeys.*

STATE DATA (FOR INDIVIDUAL STATES) - POVERTY

U.S. Department of Commerce, Bureau of the Census, Washington, D.C. 20233 (301) 457-4100, www.census.gov; *Current Population Reports;* and Internet site: http://www.census.gov/hhes/poverty/hist pov/hstpov21.html.

STATE DATA (FOR INDIVIDUAL STATES) - PRESIDENT - VOTE CAST

Congressional Quarterly, Inc., 1414

22nd Street, NW, Washington, D.C. 20037 (202) 887-8500; *America Votes.*

STATE DATA (FOR INDIVIDUAL STATES) - PRISONS AND PRISONERS

U.S. Department of Justice, Bureau of Justice Statistics, 810 Seventh Street, NW, 2nd Floor, Washington, D.C. 20531 (800) 732-3277, www.ojp.usdoj.gov/bjs; *Prisoners in 1997.*

STATE DATA (FOR INDIVIDUAL STATES) - PUBLIC AID

Social Security Administration, 6400 Security Boulevard, Baltimore, Maryland 21235 (800) 772-1213, ww.ssa.gov; *Social Security Bulletin;* and *Annual Statistical Supplement to the Social Security Bulletin.*

STATE DATA (FOR INDIVIDUAL STATES) - RECREATIONAL AREAS

National Association of State Park Directors, 9894 East Holden Place, Tucson, Arizona 85748 (520) 298-4924; *Annual Information Exchange.*

U.S. Department of Agriculture, Forest Service, Post Office Box 96090, Washington, D.C. 20090 (202) 205-8333, www.fs.fed.us; *Annual Report.*

STATE DATA (FOR INDIVIDUAL STATES) - REPRESENTATIVES, UNITED STATES - VOTE CAST

Congressional Quarterly, Inc., 1414 22nd Street, NW, Washington, D.C. 20037 (202) 887-8500; *America Votes.*

STATE DATA (FOR INDIVIDUAL STATES) - RESEARCH AND DEVELOPMENT

National Science Foundation, 4201 Wilson Boulevard, Arlington, Virginia 22230 (703) 306-1234, www.nsf.gov; *National Patterns of R&D Resources.*

STATE DATA (FOR INDIVIDUAL STATES) - RETAIL TRADE - SALES

Market Statistics, 355 Park Avenue, New York, New York 10010 (212) 592-6250; *The Survey of Buying Power Data Service.*

U.S. Department of Commerce, Bureau of the Census, Washington, D.C. 20233 (301) 457-4100, www.census.gov; *County Business Patterns.*

STATE DATA (FOR INDIVIDUAL STATES) - ROADS AND HIGHWAYS

U.S. Department of Commerce, Bureau of the Census, Washington, D.C. 20233 (301) 457-4100, www.census.gov; *Federal Expenditures by State for Fiscal Year.*

U.S. Department of Transportation, Federal Highway Administration, 400 Seventh Street, SW, Washington, D.C. 20590 (202) 366-0660, www.fhwa.dot.gov; *Highway Statistics.*

STATE DATA (FOR INDIVIDUAL STATES) - SALES

Market Statistics, 355 Park Avenue, New York, New York 10010 (212) 592-6250; *The Survey of Buying Power Data Service.*

National Research Bureau, 225 West Wacker Drive, Chicago, Illinois 60606 (312) 346-9097; data published by International Council of Shopping Centers, 1221 Avenue of the Americas, New York, New York 10020 (646) 728-3800; *Shopping Centers Today.*

U.S. Department of Commerce, Bureau of the Census, Washington, D.C. 20233 (301) 606-9900; *County Business Patterns.*

STATE DATA (FOR INDIVIDUAL STATES) - SCHOOLS AND EDUCATION - COLLEGES - NUMBER

U.S. Department of Education, National Center for Education Statistics, 555 New Jersey Avenue, NW, Washington, D.C. 20208-5574 (202) 219-1828, http://nces.ed.gov; *Digest of Education Statistics.*

STATE DATA (FOR INDIVIDUAL STATES) - SCHOOLS AND EDUCATION - EDUCATIONAL ATTAINMENT

U.S. Department of Commerce, Bureau of the Census, Washington, D.C. 20233 (301) 606-9900; *Census of Population*; and *Current Population Reports.*

STATE DATA (FOR INDIVIDUAL STATES) - SCHOOLS AND EDUCATION - ELEMENTARY AND SECONDARY TEACHERS - PUBLIC

National Education Association, 1201 Sixteenth Street, NW, Washington, D.C. 20036 (202) 833-4000; *Estimates of School Statistics.*

STATE DATA (FOR INDIVIDUAL STATES) - SCHOOLS AND EDUCATION - ENROLLMENT - ELEMENTARY AND SECONDARY

U.S. Department of Education, National Center for Education Statistics, 555 New Jersey Avenue, NW, Washington, D.C. 20208-5574 (202) 219-1828, http://nces.ed.gov; *Digest of Education Statistics.*

STATE DATA (FOR INDIVIDUAL STATES) - SCHOOLS AND EDUCATION - ENROLLMENT - HIGHER EDUCATION

U.S. Department of Education, National Center for Education Statistics, 555 New Jersey Avenue, NW, Washington, D.C. 20208-5574 (202) 219-1828, http://nces.ed.gov; *Digest of Education Statistics.*

STATE DATA (FOR INDIVIDUAL STATES) - SCHOOLS AND EDUCATION - FINANCES - ELEMENTARY AND SECONDARY - PUBLIC

National Education Association, 1201 Sixteenth Street, NW, Washington, D.C. 20036 (202) 833-4000; *Estimates of School Statistics.*

STATE DATA (FOR INDIVIDUAL STATES) - SCHOOLS AND EDUCATION - FINANCES - HIGHER EDUCATION - PUBLIC

Research Associates of Washington, 1200 North Nash Street #225, Arlington, Virginia 22209 (703) 243-3399; *State Profiles: Financing Public Higher Education.*

STATE DATA (FOR INDIVIDUAL STATES) - SCHOOLS AND EDUCATION - HIGH SCHOOL GRADUATES - PUBLIC

U.S. Department of Education, National Center for Education 555 New Jersey Avenue, NW, Washington, D.C. 20208-5574 (202) 219-1828, http://nces.ed.gov; *Digest of Education Statistics.*

STATE DATA (FOR INDIVIDUAL STATES) - SCHOOLS AND EDUCATION - TEACHERS

National Education Association, 1201 Sixteenth Street, NW, Washington, D.C. 20016 (202) 833-4000; *Estimates of School Statistics.*

STATE DATA (FOR INDIVIDUAL STATES) - SENATORS - VOTE CAST

Congressional Quarterly, Inc., 1414 22nd Street, NW, Washington, D.C. 20037 (202) 887-8500; *America Votes.*

STATE DATA (FOR INDIVIDUAL STATES) - SHOPPING CENTERS

National Research Bureau, 225 West Wacker Drive, Suite 2275, Chicago, Illinois 60606 (312) 346-9097; data published by International Council of Shopping Centers, 1221 Avenue of the Americas, New York, New York 10020 (646) 728-3800; *Shopping Centers Today.*

STATE DATA (FOR INDIVIDUAL STATES) - SOCIAL SECURITY PROGRAM

Social Security Administration, 6400 Security Boulevard, Baltimore, Maryland 21235 (800) 772-1213, ww.ssa.gov; *Social Security Bulletin.*

U.S. Department of Health and Human Services, Health Care Financing Administration, 200 Independence Avenue, SW, Washington, D.C. 20201 (202) 690-6145, www.hcfa.gov; unpublished data.

STATE DATA (FOR INDIVIDUAL STATES) - SUPPLEMENTAL SECURITY INCOME

Social Security Administration, 6400 Security Boulevard, Baltimore, Maryland 21235 (800) 772-1213, ww.ssa.gov; *Social Security Bulletin;* and *Annual Statistical Supplement to the Social Security Bulletin.*

STATE DATA (FOR INDIVIDUAL STATES) - TAXATION

U.S. Department of Commerce, Bureau of the Census, Washington, D.C. 20233 (301) 457-4100, www.census.gov; *State Government Finances.*

U.S. Department of the Treasury, Internal Revenue Service, 1111 Constitution Avenue, NW, Washington, D.C. 20224 (202) 874-0410, www.irs.ustreas.gov; *Statistics of Income Bulletin.*

STATE DATA (FOR INDIVIDUAL STATES) - TRANSPORTATION TO WORK

U.S. Department of Commerce, Bureau of the Census, Washington, D.C. 20233 (301) 457-4100, www.census.gov; *Census of Population and Housing.*

STATE DATA (FOR INDIVIDUAL STATES) - UNEMPLOYMENT

U.S. Department of Labor, Bureau of Labor Statistics, Two Massachusetts Avenue, NE, Washington, D.C. 20212 (202) 691-5200, www.stats.bls.gov; *Geographic Profile of Employment and Unemployment.*

STATE DATA (FOR INDIVIDUAL STATES) - UNEMPLOYMENT INSURANCE

U.S. Department of Labor, Employment and Training Administration, 200 Constitution Avenue, NW, Washington, D.C. 20210 (202) 219-6871, www.doleta.gov; *Unemployment Insurance Data Summary.*

STATE DATA (FOR INDIVIDUAL STATES) - UNION MEMBERSHIP

Bureau of National Affairs, 1231 Twenty-fifth Street, NW, Washington, D.C. 20037 (800) 372-1033, www.bna.com; *Union Membership and Earnings Data Book: Compilations from the Current Population Survey.*

STATE DATA (FOR INDIVIDUAL STATES) - VETERANS - NUMBER AND EXPENDITURES

U.S. Department of Veterans Affairs, 810 Vermont Avenue, NW, Washington, D.C. 20420 (202) 273-5400, www.va.gov; *Annual Report of the Secretary of Veterans Affairs.*

STATE DATA (FOR INDIVIDUAL STATES) - VOTER TURNOUT

Congressional Quarterly, Inc., 1414 22nd Street, NW, Washington, D.C. 20037 (202) 887-8500; *Congressional Quarterly Weekly Report.*

Elections Research Center, 5508 Greystone Street, Chevy Chase, Maryland 20815; *America Votes.*

U.S. Department of Commerce, Bureau of the Census, Washington, D.C. 20233 (301) 457-4100, www.census.gov; *Current Population Reports.*

STATE DATA (FOR INDIVIDUAL STATES) - VOTES CAST

Congressional Quarterly, Inc., 1414 22nd Street, NW, Washington, D.C. 20037 (202) 887-8500; *Congressional Quarterly Weekly Report.*

Election Research Center, 5508 Greystone Street, Chevy Chase, Maryland 20815 (202) 659-9490; *America Votes;* and unpublished data.

United States Congress, Clerk of the House, The Capitol, Washington, D.C. 20515 (202) 224-3121, http://clerkweb.house.gov; *Statistics of the Presidential and Congressional Election.*

U.S. Department of Commerce, Bureau of the Census, Washington, D.C. 20233 (301) 457-4100, www.census.gov; *Current Population Reports.*

STATE DATA (FOR INDIVIDUAL STATES) - VOTING AGE POPULATION

Elections Research Center, 5508 Greystone Street, Chevy Chase, Maryland 20815; *America Votes.*

U.S. Department of Commerce, Bureau of the Census, Washington, D.C. 20233 (301) 457-4100, www.census.gov; *Current Population Reports.*

STATE DATA (FOR INDIVIDUAL STATES) - WOMEN HOLDING PUBLIC OFFICE

Center for the American Woman and Politics, The Eagleton Institute of Politics, Rutgers University, 191 Ryders Lane, New Brunswick, New Jersey 08901 (732) 932-9384; information releases.

STATE DATA (FOR INDIVIDUAL STATES) - YEAR OF ADMISSION TO STATEHOOD

U.S. Department of Commerce, Bureau of the Census, Washington, D.C. 20233 (301) 457-4100, www.census.gov; *Census of Population and Housing;* and unpublished data.

STATE GOVERNMENT - See also STATE AND LOCAL GOVERNMENTS

STATE GOVERNMENT - DEBT

U.S. Department of Commerce, Bureau of the Census, Washington, D.C. 20233 (301) 457-4100, www.census.gov; *State Government Finances;* and unpublished data.

STATE GOVERNMENT - DEBT - PUBLIC HIGHWAYS

U.S. Department of Transportation, Federal Highway Administration, 400 Seventh Street, SW, Washington, D.C. 20590 (202) 366-0660, www.fhwa.dot.gov; *Highway Statistics.*

STATE GOVERNMENT - EMPLOYEES AND PAYROLLS

U.S. Department of Commerce, Bureau of the Census, Washington, D.C. 20233 (301) 457-4100, www.census.gov; *Public Employment; Historical Statistics on Governmental Finances and Employment;* and unpublished data.

STATE GOVERNMENT - FINANCES

National Association of State Budget Officers, Hall of the States, 444 North Capitol Street, Suite 642, Washington, D.C. 20001 (202) 624-5382; *Fiscal Survey of the States;* and *NASBO State Expenditure Report.*

U.S. Department of Commerce, Bureau of Economic Analysis, Fourteenth Street between Constitution Avenue and E Street, NW, Washington, D.C. 20230 (202) 606-9900, www.bea.doc.gov; *The National Income and Product Accounts of the United States;* and *Survey of Current Business.*

U.S. Department of Commerce, Bureau of the Census, Washington, D.C. 20233 (301) 457-4100, www.census.gov; *Government Finances State Government Finances; State Government Tax Collections;* and unpublished data.

STATE GOVERNMENT - FINANCES - REVENUE FROM LOTTERIES

U.S. Department of Commerce, Bureau of the Census, Washington, D.C. 20233 (301) 457-4100, www.census.gov; *State Government Finances.*

STATE GOVERNMENT - FINANCES - TAX COLLECTIONS

U.S. Department of Commerce, Bureau of the Census, Washington, D.C. 20233 (301) 457-4100, www.census.gov; *State Government Tax Collections;* and *State Government Finances.*

STATE GOVERNMENT - HIGHWAY FUNDS - DISBURSEMENTS OF

U.S. Department of Transportation, Federal Highway Administration, 400 Seventh Street, SW, Washington, D.C. 20590 (202) 366-0660, www.fhwa.dot.gov; *Highway Statistics.*

STATE GOVERNMENT - PARK SYSTEMS

National Association of State Park Directors, 9894 East Holden Place, Tucson, Arizona 85748 (520) 298-4924; *Annual Information Exchange.*

STATE GOVERNMENT - PAYMENTS FOR PUBLIC ASSISTANCE

Social Security Administration, 6400 Security Boulevard, Baltimore, Maryland 21235 (800) 772-1213, ww.ssa.gov; *Annual Statistical Supplement to the Social Security Bulletin;* and *Social Security Bulletin.*

U.S. Department of Health and Human Services, Administration for Children and Families, 370 L'Enfant Promenade, SW, Washington, D.C. 20447 (202) 401-9200, www.acf.dhhs.gov; *Quarterly Public Assistance Statistics.*

STATE GOVERNMENT - RECEIPTS - HIGHWAYS

U.S. Department of Transportation, Federal Highway Administration, 400 Seventh Street, SW, Washington, D.C. 20590 (202) 366-0660, www.fhwa.dot.gov; *Highway Statistics.*

STATE GOVERNMENT - TAXES

U.S. Department of Commerce, Bureau of the Census, Washington, D.C. 20233 (301) 457-4100, www.census.gov; *Historical Statistics on Governmental Finances and Employment; Government Finances; State Government Finances;* and *State Government Tax Collections.*

STATE HIGHWAYS - See HIGHWAYS

STATE PARK SYSTEMS

National Association of State Park Directors, 9894 East Holden Place, Tucson, Arizona 85748 (520) 298-4924; *Annual Information Exchange.*

STATEHOOD - ADMISSION TO

U.S. Department of Commerce, Bureau of the Census, Washington, D.C. 20233 (301) 457-4100, www.census.gov; *Census of Population and Housing;* and unpublished data from the TIGER/Geographic Information Control System.

STEAM ENGINES AND TURBINES, ELECTRIC - LOCOMOTIVE (RAILROAD)

Association of American Railroads, American Railroads Building, 50 F Street, NW, Washington, D.C. 20001 (202) 639-2100; *Railroad Facts; Statistics of Railroads of Class I;* and *Analysis of Class I Railroads.*

STEEL - See also IRON AND STEEL

American Iron and Steel Institute, 1101 Seventeenth Street, NW, Washington, D.C. 20036 (202) 452-7100; *Annual Statistical Report.*

U.S. Department of the Interior, Geological Survey, Office of Minerals Information, 12201 Sunrise Valley Drive, Reston, Virginia 22092 (703) 648-4000, www.minerals.usgs.gov; *Annual Reports;* and *Mineral Commodity Summaries.*

STEEL - SCRAP

American Iron and Steel Institute, 1101 Seventeenth Street, NW, Washington, D.C. 20036 (202) 452-7100; *Annual Statistical Report.*

STEEL - WORLD PRODUCTION

U.S. Department of the Interior, Geological Survey, Office of Minerals Information, 12201 Sunrise Valley Drive, Reston, Virginia 22092 (703) 648-4000, www.minerals.usgs.gov; *Annual Reports;* and *Mineral Commodities Summaries.*

STEEL WORKS AND ROLLING MILLS - See IRON AND STEEL

STIMULANTS - PERSONS USING

U.S. Department of Health and Human Services, Substance Abuse and Mental Health Administration, 5600 Fishers Lane, Rockville, Maryland 20857 (800) 729-6686, www.samhsa.gov; *National Household Survey on Drug Abuse.*

STOCK EXCHANGES - PRICES

New York Stock Exchange, 11 Wall Street, New York, New York 10005 (212) 656-3000; *Fact Book.*

STOCK EXCHANGES - VOLUME OF TRADING

National Association of Securities Dealers, 1735 K Street, NW, Washington, D.C. 20006 (202) 728-8000; *Fact Book.*

New York Stock Exchange, 11 Wall Street, New York, New York 10005 (212)

656-3000; *Fact Book.*

U.S. Securities and Exchange Commission, 450 Fifth Street, NW, Washington, D.C. 20549 (202) 942-4040, www.sec.gov; unpublished data.

STOCKHOLDERS' EQUITY - PROFIT RATES ON

Federal Deposit Insurance Corporation, 550 Seventeenth Street, NW, Washington, D.C. 20429 (202) 393-8400, www.fdic.gov; *Annual Report; The FDIC Quarterly Banking Profile; Statistics on Banking;* and unpublished data.

STOCKPILES - GOVERNMENT - STRATEGIC AND CRITICAL MATERIALS

U.S. Department of Defense, Defense Logistics Agency, 8725 John J. Kingman Road, Fort Belvoir, Virginia 22060 (703) 767-6666; *Statistical Supplement, Stockpile Report to the Congress.*

STOCKS - CORPORATE - FLOW OF FUNDS

Board of Governors of the Federal Reserve System, Twentieth Street and Constitution Avenue, NW, Washington, D.C. 20551 (202) 452-3000, www.bog.frb.fed.us; *Flow of Funds Accounts.*

STOCKS - FOREIGN - UNITED STATES PURCHASES AND SALES OF

U.S. Department of the Treasury, Fifteenth Street and Pennsylvania Avenue, NW, Washington, D.C. 20220 (202) 622-2000; *Treasury Bulletin.*

STOCKS - HOLDINGS BY SECTOR

Board of Governors of the Federal Reserve System, Twentieth Street and Constitution Avenue, NW, Washington, D.C. 20235 (202) 884-7799; *Flow of Funds Accounts.*

STOCKS - LIFE INSURANCE

American Council of Life Insurance, 1001 Pennsylvania Avenue, NW, Washington, D.C. 20004-2599 (202) 624-2000; *Life Insurance Fact Book.*

STOCKS - NEW ISSUES

Board of Governors of the Federal Reserve System, Twentieth Street and Constitution Avenue, NW, Washington, D.C. 20551 (202) 452-3000, www.bog.frb.fed.us; *Federal Reserve Bulletin;* and *Flow of Funds Accounts;* and *Annual Statistical Digest.*

STOCKS - OWNERSHIP

Board of Governors of the Federal

Reserve System, Twentieth Street and Constitution Avenue, NW, Washington, D.C. 20235 (202) 884-7799; *Federal Reserve Bulletin.*

STOCKS - PRICES, YIELD, SALES, ISSUES, ETC.

Board of Governors of the Federal Reserve System, Twentieth Street and Constitution Avenue, NW, Washington, D.C. 20551 (202) 452-3000, www.bog.frb.fed.us; *Annual Statistical Digest;* and *Federal Reserve Bulletin.*

Commodity Futures Trading Commission, 2033 K Street, NW, Washington, D.C. 20581 (202) 254-6387; *Annual Report.*

Dow Jones and Company, Inc., 200 Liberty Street, New York, New York 10006 (212) 597-5600; *Wall Street Journal.*

International Finance Corporation, 1818 H Street, NW, Washington, D.C. 20006 (202) 477-1234; *Emerging Stock Markets Factbook.*

Morgan Stanley Capital International, 1585 Broadway, New York, New York 10036 (212) 761-4000; unpublished data.

National Association of Securities Dealers, 1735 K Street, NW, Washington, D.C. 20006 (202) 728-8000; *Fact Book.*

New York Stock Exchange, 11 Wall Street, New York, New York 10005 (212) 656-3000; *Fact Book.*

Securities and Exchange Commission, 450 Fifth Street, NW, Washington, D.C. 20549 (202) 942-4040, www.sec.gov; unpublished data.

STONE

U.S. Department of the Interior, Geological Survey, Office of Minerals Information, 12201 Sunrise Valley Drive, Reston, Virginia 22092 (703) 648-4000, www.minerals.usgs.gov; *Annual Reports;* and *Mineral Commodities Summaries.*

STONE - CLAY - AND GLASS PRODUCTS

Association of American Railroads, American Railroads Building, 50 F Street, NW, Washington, D.C. 20001 (202) 639-2100; *Freight Commodity Statistics;* and *Weekly Railroad Traffic.*

STONE - CLAY - AND GLASS PRODUCTS - MANUFACTURING - EARNINGS

U.S. Department of Commerce, Bureau of the Census, Washington, D.C. 20233 (301) 457-4100, www.census.gov; *Census of Manufactures;* and *Annual Survey of*

Manufactures.

U.S. Department of Labor, Bureau of Labor Statistics, Two Massachusetts Avenue, NE, Washington, D.C. 20212 (202) 691-5200, www.stats.bls.gov; *Employment and Earnings;* and Internet site: http://stats.bls.gov/ ceshome.htm.

STONE - CLAY - AND GLASS PRODUCTS - MANUFACTURING - EMPLOYEES

U.S. Department of Commerce, Bureau of the Census, Washington, D.C. 20233 (301) 457-4100, www.census.gov; *Census of Manufactures;* and *Annual Survey of Manufactures.*

U.S. Department of Labor, Bureau of Labor Statistics, Two Massachusetts Avenue, NE, Washington, D.C. 20212 (202) 691-5200, www.stats.bls.gov; *Employment and Earnings; Monthly Labor Review;* and Internet site: http://stats.bls.gov/ ceshome.htm.

STONE - CLAY - AND GLASS PRODUCTS - MANUFACTURING - ENERGY CONSUMPTION

U.S. Department of Energy, Energy Information Administration, 1000 Independence Avenue, SW, Washington, D.C. 20585 (202) 586-8800, www.eia.doe.gov; *Manufacturing Energy Consumption.*

STONE - CLAY - AND GLASS PRODUCTS - MANUFACTURING -FOREIGN TRADE

U.S. Department of Commerce, Bureau of the Census, Washington, D.C. 20233 (301) 457-4100, www.census.gov; *U.S. International Trade in Goods and Services.*

STONE - CLAY - AND GLASS PRODUCTS - MANUFACTURING - GROSS DOMESTIC PRODUCT

U.S. Department of Commerce, Bureau of Economic Analysis, Fourteenth Street between Constitution Avenue and E Street, NW, Washington, D.C. 20230 (202) 606-9900, www.bea.doc.gov; *Survey of Current Business.*

STONE - CLAY - AND GLASS PRODUCTS - MANUFACTURING - OCCUPATIONAL SAFETY

U.S. Department of Labor, Bureau of Labor Statistics, Two Massachusetts Avenue, NE, Washington, D.C. 20212 (202) 691-5200, www.stats.bls.gov; *Occupational Injuries and Illnesses in the United States by Industry.*

STONE - CLAY - AND GLASS PRODUCTS - MANUFACTURING -PATENTS

U.S. Department of Commerce, Patent and Trademark Office, 2011 Crystal Avenue, Arlington, Virginia 22202 (703) 305-8341, www.uspto.gov; *Patenting Trends in the United States, State Country Report.*

STONE - CLAY - AND GLASS PRODUCTS - MANUFACTURING - PRODUCTIVITY

Board of Governors of the Federal Reserve System, Twentieth Street and Constitution Avenue, NW, Washington, D.C. 20551 (202) 452-3000, www.bog.frb.fed.us; *Federal Reserve Bulletin;* and *Industrial Production and Capacity Utilization.*

U.S. Department of Labor, Bureau of Labor Statistics, Two Massachusetts Avenue, NE, Washington, D.C. 20212 (202) 691-5200, www.stats.bls.gov; Internet site: http://stats.bls.gov/iprhome.htm.

STONE - CLAY - AND GLASS PRODUCTS - MANUFACTURING - PROFITS

Executive Office of the President, Council of Economic Advisors, Old Executive Office Building, Washington, D.C. 20500 (202) 395-5084, www.whitehouse. gov/cea; *Economic Report of the President.*

U.S. Department of Commerce, Bureau of the Census, Washington, D.C. 20233 (301) 457-4100, www.census.gov; *Quarterly Financial Report for Manufacturing, Mining and Trade Corporations.*

STONE - CLAY - AND GLASS PRODUCTS - MANUFACTURING - RESEARCH AND DEVELOPMENT

National Science Foundation, 4201 Wilson Boulevard, Arlington, Virginia 22230 (703) 306-1234, www.nsf.gov; *Research and Development in Industry.*

STONE - CLAY - AND GLASS PRODUCTS - MANUFACTURING - SALES, SHIPMENTS, RECEIPTS

U.S. Department of Commerce, Bureau of the Census, Washington, D.C. 20233 (301) 457-4100, www.census.gov; *Census of Manufactures; Annual Survey of Manufactures;* and *Current Industrial Reports, Manufactures' Shipments, Inventories and Orders.*

STONE - CLAY - AND GLASS PRODUCTS - MANUFACTURING - TOXIC CHEMICAL RELEASES

Environmental Protection Agency, 1200 Pennsylvania Avenue, NW, Washington, D.C. 20460 (888) 372-8255, www.epa.gov; *Toxics Release Inventory.*

STONE - CLAY - AND GLASS PRODUCTS - MANUFACTURING - VALUE ADDED

U.S. Department of Commerce, Bureau of the Census, Washington, D.C. 20233 (301) 457-4100, www.census.gov; *Census of Manufactures;* and *Annual Survey of Manufactures.*

STONE - CRUSHED

U.S. Department of the Interior, Geological Survey, Office of Minerals Information, 12201 Sunrise Valley Drive, Reston, Virginia 22092 (703) 648-4000, www.minerals.usgs.gov; *Mineral Commodity Summaries.*

STOVES AND RANGES

Euromonitor International, Inc., 122 South Michigan Avenue, Suite 1200, Chicago, Illinois 60603 (800) 577-EURO; *European Marketing Data and Statistics.*

STRATEGIC AND CRITICAL MATERIALS

U.S. Department of Defense, Defense Logistics Agency, 8725 John J. Kingman Road, Fort Belvoir, Virginia 22060 (703) 767-6666; *Statistical Supplement, Stockpile Report to the Congress.*

STRATEGIC FORCES

Executive Office of the President, Office of Management and Budget, Executive Office Building, Washington, D.C.20503 (202) 395-3080, www.whitehouse.gov/ omb; *Budget of the United States Government.*

STRATEGIC PETROLEUM RESERVES

U.S. Department of Energy, Energy Information Administration, 1000 Independence Avenue, SW, Washington, D.C. 20585 (202) 586-8800, www.eia.doe.gov; *Petroleum Supply Annual; Annual Energy Review;* and *U.S. Crude Oil, Natural Gas, and Natural Gas Liquids Reserves.*

STRAWBERRIES

U.S. Department of Agriculture, National Agricultural Statistics Service, Fourteenth Street and Independence Avenue, SW, Washington, D.C. 20250 (800) 727-9540, www.usda.gov/nass; *Agricultural Statistics;* and *Farm Business Economic Report.*

STROKE - See also CEREBROVASCULAR DISEASES

STRONTIUM

U.S. Department of the Interior, Geological Survey, Office of Minerals Information, 12201 Sunrise Valley Drive, Reston, Virginia 22092 (703) 648-4000, www.minerals.usgs.gov; *Mineral Commodity Summaries.*

STUDENTS - See EDUCATION - ENROLLMENT

SUBWAYS AND URBAN RAILWAYS

American Public Transportation Association, 1201 New York Avenue, NW, Suite 400, Washington, D.C. 20005 (202) 898-4000; *Transit Fact Book;* and Internet site: http://www.apta.com/pubs/ pubs/stats/index.htm.

Sudan - National Statistical Office

Department of Statistics, Ministry of Finance and Economic Planning, Post Office Box 700, Khartoum, Sudan.

Sudan - Primary Statistics Sources

Department of Statistics, Post Office Box 700, Khartoum, Sudan; *Statistical Abstract for the Democratic Republic of the Sudan;* and *Statistical Yearbook.*

SUDAN - AGRICULTURE

Economist Intelligence Unit, 111 West 57th Street, New York, New York 10019 (800) 938-4685; *Sudan Country Report.*

Euromonitor International, Inc., 122 South Michigan Avenue, Suite 1200, Chicago, Illinois 60603 (800) 577-EURO; *International Marketing Data and Statistics;* and *World Marketing Data and Statistics.*

Europa Publications Limited, 18 Bedford Square, London, WC1B 3JN, England; *The Europa World Year Book.*

Food and Agricultural Organization of the United Nations (FAO) Via delle Terme di Caracalla, 00100 Rome, Italy (Telephone Number in U.S. (202) 653-2400); *Production Yearbook; The State of Food and Agriculture;* and *Trade Yearbook.*

M.E. Sharpe, 80 Business Park Drive, Armonk, New York 10504 (800) 541-6563; *The Illustrated Book of World Rankings.*

St. Martin's Press, Inc., 175 Fifth Avenue, New York, New York 10010 (800) 221-7945; *The Statesman's Year-Book.*

Statistical Office of the United Nations, Publishing Service, New York, New York 10017 (800) 253-9646; *Statistical Yearbook;* and *Survey of Economic and Social Conditions in Africa.*

United Nations Conference on Trade and Development, Central Statistical Service, Palais des Nations, Geneva, Switzerland (Telephone in U.S. (800) 253-9646); *UNCTAD Commodity Yearbook*.

United Nations Economic Commission for Africa, Africa Hall, P.O. Box 3001, Addis Ababa, Ethiopia (Telephone Number in U.S. (800) 253-9646); *African Statistical Yearbook*.

The World Bank, 1818 H Street, NW, Washington, D.C. 20433 (202) 477-1234; *World Development Indicators*.

Statistical Office of the United Nations, Publishing Service, New York, New York 10017 (800) 253-9646; *Survey of Economic and Social Conditions in Africa*.

The World Bank, 1818 H Street, NW, Washington, D.C. 20433 (202) 477-1234; *World Development Indicators*.

SUDAN - AIRLINE SERVICE

Europa Publications Limited, 18 Bedford Square, London, WC1B 3JN, England; *The Europa World Year Book*.

International Civil Aviation Organization, 999 University Street, Montreal, Quebec, Canada H3C 5H7 (514) 954-8219; *Civil Aviation Statistics of the World*.

M.E. Sharpe, 80 Business Park Drive, Armonk, New York 10504 (800) 541-6563; *The Illustrated Book of World Rankings*.

St. Martin's Press, Inc., 175 Fifth Avenue, New York, New York 10010 (800) 221-7945; *The Statesman's Year-Book*.

Statistical Office of the United Nations, Publishing Service, New York, New York 10017 (800) 253-9646; *Statistical Yearbook*.

United Nations Economic Commission for Africa, Africa Hall, P.O. Box 3001, Addis Ababa, Ethiopia (Telephone Number in U.S. (800) 253-9646); *African Statistical Yearbook*.

SUDAN - AIRPORTS

Central Intelligence Agency, Washington, D.C. 20505 (703) 482-1100, www.cia.gov; *The World Factbook*.

SUDAN - ALUMINUM PRODUCTION AND CONSUMPTION - See SUDAN - MINING AND MINERAL PRODUCTS

SUDAN - ANIMAL HEALTH

Food and Agricultural Organization of the United Nations (FAO), Via delle Terme di Caracalla, 00100, Rome, Italy (Telephone Number in U.S. (202) 653-2400); *Animal Health Yearbook*.

SUDAN - AREA AND DENSITY OF POPULATION

African Development Bank, 01 BP 1387, Abidjan 01, Cote D'Ivoire; *Selected Statistics on Regional Member Countries*.

Central Intelligence Agency, Washington, D.C. 20505 (703) 482-1100, www.cia.gov; *The World Factbook*.

Euromonitor International, Inc., 122 South Michigan Avenue, Suite 1200, Chicago, Illinois 60603 (800) 577-EURO; *International Marketing Data and Statistics; and The World Economic Factbook*.

Europa Publications Limited, 18 Bedford Square, London, WC1B 3JN, England; *The Europa World Year Book*.

Food and Agricultural Organization of the United Nations (FAO) Via delle Terme di Caracalla, 00100 Rome, Italy (Telephone Number in U.S. (202) 653-2400); *The State of Food and Agriculture*.

M.E. Sharpe, 80 Business Park Drive, Armonk, New York 10504 (800) 541-6563; *The Illustrated Book of World Rankings*.

St. Martin's Press, Inc., 175 Fifth Avenue, New York, New York 10010 (800) 221-7945; *The Statesman's Year-Book*.

Statistical Office of the United Nations, Publishing Service, New York, New York 10017 (800) 253-9646; *Statistical Yearbook; and Survey of Economic and Social Conditions in Africa*.

United Nations Educational, Scientific and Cultural Organization (UNESCO), 7 Place de Fontenoy, F-75700 Paris, France (Telephone Number in U.S. (212) 963-5981); *Statistical Yearbook*.

SUDAN - ARMS EXPORTS AND IMPORTS - See SUDAN - MILITARY

SUDAN - BALANCE OF PAYMENTS

African Development Bank, 01 BP 1387, Abidjan 01, Cote D'Ivoire; *Selected Statistics on Regional Member Countries*.

The Economist Intelligence Unit, 111 West 57th Street, New York, New York 10019 (800) 938-4685; *The World Market Atlas*.

Europa Publications Limited, 18 Bedford Square, London, WC1B 3JN, England; *The Europa World Year Book*.

International Monetary Fund, 700 Nineteenth Street, NW, Washington, D.C. 20431 (202) 623-7000; *Balance of Payments Yearbook; and International Financial Statistics*.

United Nations Conference on Trade and Development (UNCTAD), New York, New York 10017 (800) 253-9646; *Handbook of International Trade and Development Statistics*.

United Nations Economic Commission for Africa, Africa Hall, P.O. Box 3001, Addis Ababa, Ethiopia (Telephone Number in U.S. (800) 253-9646); *African Statistical Yearbook*.

The World Bank, 1818 H Street, NW, Washington, D.C. 20433 (202) 477-1234; *World Development Indicators*.

SUDAN - BANKING

Euromonitor International, Inc., 122 South Michigan Avenue, Suite 1200, Chicago, Illinois 60603 (800) 577-EURO; *World Marketing Data and Statistics*.

Europa Publications Limited, 18 Bedford Square, London, WC1B 3JN, England; *The Europa World Year Book*.

International Monetary Fund, 700 Nineteenth Street, NW, Washington, D.C. 20431 (202) 623-7000; *International Financial Statistics*.

M.E. Sharpe, 80 Business Park Drive, Armonk, New York 10504 (800) 541-6563; *The Illustrated Book of World Rankings*.

St. Martin's Press, Inc., 175 Fifth Avenue, New York, New York 10010 (800) 221-7945; *The Statesman's Year-Book*.

United Nations Economic Commission for Africa, Africa Hall, P.O. Box 3001, Addis Ababa, Ethiopia (Telephone Number in U.S. (800) 253-9646); *African Statistical Yearbook*.

SUDAN - BARLEY PRODUCTION - See SUDAN - CROPS
SUDAN - BEER PRODUCTION - See SUDAN - BEVERAGES

SUDAN - BEVERAGES

M.E. Sharpe, 80 Business Park Drive, Armonk, New York 10504 (800) 541-6563; *The Illustrated Book of World Rankings*.

Statistical Office of the United Nations, Publishing Service, New York, New York 10017 (800) 253-9646; *Statistical Yearbook*.

SUDAN - BIRTH RATES

Central Intelligence Agency, Washington, D.C. 20505 (703) 482-1100, www.cia.gov; *The World Factbook*.

Euromonitor International, Inc., 122 South Michigan Avenue, Suite 1200,

Chicago, Illinois 60603 (800) 577-EURO; *International Marketing Data and Statistics;* and *The World Economic Factbook.*

Europa Publications Limited, 18 Bedford Square, London, WC1B 3JN, England; *The Europa World Year Book.*

M.E. Sharpe, 80 Business Park Drive, Armonk, New York 10504 (800) 541-6563; *The Illustrated Book of World Rankings.*

Statistical Office of the United Nations, Publishing Service, New York, New York 10017 (800) 253-9646; *Demographic Yearbook; Statistical Yearbook;* and *Survey of Economic and Social Conditions in Africa.*

The World Bank, 1818 H Street, NW, Washington, D.C. 20433 (202) 477-1234; *World Development Indicators.*

SUDAN - BONDS

International Monetary Fund, 700 Nineteenth Street, NW, Washington, D.C. 20431 (202) 623-7000; *Government Finance Statistics Yearbook.*

SUDAN - BOOK PRODUCTION

United Nations Educational, Scientific and Cultural Organization (UNESCO), 7 Place de Fontenoy, F-75700 Paris, France (Telephone Number in U.S. (212) 963-5981); *Statistical Yearbook.*

SUDAN - BROADCASTING

Billboard Limited, P.O. Box 9027, 1006 AA Amsterdam, The Netherlands (Telephone Number in U.S. (212) 764-7300); *World Radio TV Handbook.*

Central Intelligence Agency, Washington, D.C. 20505 (703) 482-1100, www.cia.gov; *The World Factbook.*

Euromonitor International, Inc., 122 South Michigan Avenue, Suite 1200, Chicago, Illinois 60603 (800) 577-EURO; *World Marketing Data and Statistics.*

M.E. Sharpe, 80 Business Park Drive, Armonk, New York 10504 (800) 541-6563; *The Illustrated Book of World Rankings.*

St. Martin's Press, Inc., 175 Fifth Avenue, New York, New York 10010 (800) 221-7945; *The Statesman's Year-Book.*

United Nations Educational, Scientific and Cultural Organization (UNESCO), 7 Place de Fontenoy, F-75700 Paris, France (Telephone Number in U.S. (212) 963-5981); *Statistical Yearbook.*

SUDAN - BUDGET

Central Intelligence Agency, Washington, D.C. 20505 (703) 482-1100, www.cia.gov; *The World Factbook.*

SUDAN - BUSINESS AND PROFESSIONAL LICENSES

International Monetary Fund, 700 Nineteenth Street, NW, Washington, D.C. 20431 (202) 623-7000; *Government Finance Statistics Yearbook.*

SUDAN - BUTTER PRODUCTION - See SUDAN - DAIRY PRODUCTS

SUDAN - CALORIE SUPPLY

African Development Bank, 01 BP 1387, Abidjan 01, Cote D'Ivoire; *Selected Statistics on Regional Member Countries.*

Food and Agricultural Organization of the United Nations (FAO) Via delle Terme di Caracalla, 00100 Rome, Italy (Telephone Number in U.S. (202) 653-2400); *The State of Food and Agriculture.*

SUDAN - CAPITAL REVENUE

International Monetary Fund, 700 Nineteenth Street, NW, Washington, D.C. 20431 (202) 623-7000; *Government Finance Statistics Yearbook.*

SUDAN - CATTLE - See SUDAN - LIVESTOCK AND POULTRY

SUDAN - CEMENT PRODUCTION - See SUDAN - MINING AND MINERAL PRODUCTS

SUDAN - CHEESE PRODUCTION AND CONSUMPTION - See SUDAN DAIRY PRODUCTS

SUDAN - CHEMICAL (ORGANIC) PRODUCTION - See SUDAN - MINING AND MINERAL PRODUCTS

SUDAN - CHICKENS - See SUDAN - LIVESTOCK AND POULTRY

SUDAN - CHROMIUM ORE PRODUCTION AND CONSUMPTION - See SUDAN - MINING AND MINERAL PRODUCTS

SUDAN - CIGARETTE PRODUCTION - See SUDAN - TOBACCO PRODUCTION

SUDAN - CLIMATE

M.E. Sharpe, 80 Business Park Drive, Armonk, New York 10504 (800) 541-6563; *The Illustrated Book of World Rankings.*

St. Martin's Press, Inc., 175 Fifth Avenue, New York, New York 10010 (800) 221-7945; *The Statesman's Year-Book.*

SUDAN - COAL PRODUCTION - See SUDAN - MINING AND MINERAL

PRODUCTS

SUDAN - COFFEE PRODUCTION AND CONSUMPTION - See SUDAN -CROPS

SUDAN - COMMERCE

St. Martin's Press, Inc., 175 Fifth Avenue, New York, New York 10010 (800) 221-7945; *The Statesman's Year-Book.*

SUDAN - COMMUNICATIONS - See SUDAN - TRANSPORTATION AND COMMUNICATIONS

SUDAN - CONSTRUCTION INDUSTRY

M.E. Sharpe, 80 Business Park Drive, Armonk, New York 10504 (800) 541-6563; *The Illustrated Book of World Rankings.*

United Nations Economic Commission for Africa, Africa Hall, P.O. Box 3001, Addis Ababa, Ethiopia (Telephone Number in U.S. (800) 253-9646); *African Statistical Yearbook.*

SUDAN - CONSUMER PRICE INDEX

African Development Bank, 01 BP 1387, Abidjan 01, Cote D'Ivoire; *Selected Statistics on Regional Member Countries.*

Europa Publications Limited, 18 Bedford Square, London, WC1B 3JN, England; *The Europa World Year Book.*

Statistical Office of the United Nations, Publishing Service, New York, New York 10017 (800) 253-9646; *Statistical Yearbook;* and *Survey of Economic and Social Conditions in Africa.*

United Nations Economic Commission for Africa, Africa Hall, P.O. Box 3001, Addis Ababa, Ethiopia (Telephone Number in U.S. (800) 253-9646); *African Statistical Yearbook.*

SUDAN - CONSUMER PRICES

Euromonitor International, Inc., 122 South Michigan Avenue, Suite 1200, Chicago, Illinois 60603 (800) 577-EURO; *World Marketing Data and Statistics.*

International Labour Office, I.L.O. Publications, 1828 L Street, NW, Suite 801, Washington, D.C. 20036 (301) 638-3152; *Yearbook of Labour Statistics.*

International Monetary Fund, 700 Nineteenth Street, NW, Washington, D.C. 20431 (202) 623-7000; *International Financial Statistics.*

SUDAN - CONSUMER RATES

M.E. Sharpe, 80 Business Park Drive, Armonk, New York 10504 (800) 541-6563; *The Illustrated Book of World Rankings.*

SUDAN - CONSUMPTION

African Development Bank, 01 BP 1387, Abidjan 01, Cote D'Ivoire; *Selected Statistics on Regional Member Countries.*

Statistical Office of the United Nations, Publishing Service, New York, New York 10017 (800) 253-9646; *Survey of Economic and Social Conditions in Africa.*

SUDAN - COPPER PRODUCTION AND CONSUMPTION - See SUDAN - MINING AND MINERAL PRODUCTS

SUDAN - CORN PRODUCTION - See SUDAN - CROPS

SUDAN - CORPORATE TAXES - See SUDAN - TAXATION

SUDAN - COTTON - See SUDAN - CROPS

SUDAN - CRIME

International Criminal Police Organization (INTERPOL), 50 quai Achille Lignon, F-69006 Lyon, France; *International Crime Statistics.*

Yale University Press, Yale Station, New Haven, Connecticut 06520 (800) 987-7323; *Violence and Crime in Cross-National Perspective.*

SUDAN - CROPS

Commodity Research Bureau, Inc., 30 South Wacker Drive, Chicago Illinois 60606 (312) 454-1801; *Commodity Year Book.*

Europa Publications Limited, 18 Bedford Square, London, WC1B 3JN, England; *The Europa World Year Book.*

Food and Agricultural Organization of the United Nations (FAO) Via delle Terme di Caracalla, 00100 Rome, Italy (Telephone Number in U.S. (202) 653-2400); *The State of Food and Agriculture.*

International Monetary Fund, 700 Nineteenth Street, NW, Washington, D.C. 20431 (202) 623-7000; *International Financial Statistics.*

M.E. Sharpe, 80 Business Park Drive, Armonk, New York 10504 (800) 541-6563; *The Illustrated Book of World Rankings.*

St. Martin's Press, Inc., 175 Fifth Avenue, New York, New York 10010 (800) 221-7945; *The Statesman's Year-Book.*

Statistical Office of the United Nations, Publishing Service, New York, New York 10017 (800) 253-9646; *Statistical Yearbook.*

United Nations Conference on Trade and Development, Central Statistical Service, Palais des Nations, Geneva,

Switzerland (Telephone in U.S. (800) 253-9646); *UNCTAD Commodity Yearbook.*

United Nations Economic Commission for Africa, Africa Hall, P.O. Box 3001, Addis Ababa, Ethiopia (Telephone Number in U.S. (800) 253-9646); *African Statistical Yearbook.*

SUDAN - CUSTOMS DUTIES

International Monetary Fund, 700 Nineteenth Street, NW, Washington, D.C. 20431 (202) 623-7000; *Government Finance Statistics Yearbook.*

SUDAN - DAIRY PRODUCTS

Europa Publications Limited, 18 Bedford Square, London, WC1B 3JN, England; *The Europa World Year Book.*

Food and Agricultural Organization of the United Nations (FAO) Via delle Terme di Caracalla, 00100 Rome, Italy (Telephone Number in U.S. (202) 653-2400); *The State of Food and Agriculture.*

M.E. Sharpe, 80 Business Park Drive, Armonk, New York 10504 (800) 541-6563; *The Illustrated Book of World Rankings.*

St. Martin's Press, Inc., 175 Fifth Avenue, New York, New York 10010 (800) 221-7945; *The Statesman's Year-Book.*

Statistical Office of the United Nations, Publishing Service, New York, New York 10017 (800) 253-9646; *Statistical Yearbook.*

SUDAN - DEATH RATES - See SUDAN - MORTALITY

SUDAN - DEFENSE EXPENDITURES - See SUDAN - MILITARY

SUDAN - DEMOGRAPHY

The Economist Intelligence Unit, 111 West 57th Street, New York, New York 10019 (800) 938-4685; *The World Market Atlas.*

Euromonitor International, Inc., 122 South Michigan Avenue, Suite 1200, Chicago, Illinois 60603 (800) 577-EURO; *International Marketing Data and Statistics; World Marketing Data and Statistics;* and *The World Economic Factbook.*

M.E. Sharpe, 80 Business Park Drive, Armonk, New York 10504 (800) 541-6563; *The Illustrated Book of World Rankings.*

Statistical Office of the United Nations, Publishing Service, New York, New York 10017 (800) 253-9646; *Human Development Report;* and *Survey of Economic and Social Conditions in Africa.*

SUDAN - DEVELOPMENT ASSISTANCE

Statistical Office of the United Nations, Publishing Service, New York, New York 10017 (800) 253-9646; *Statistical Yearbook.*

SUDAN - DIAMOND PRODUCTION - See SUDAN - MINING AND MINERAL PRODUCTS

SUDAN - DISEASES - See SUDAN - HEALTH

SUDAN - DIVORCE RATES

M.E. Sharpe, 80 Business Park Drive, Armonk, New York 10504 (800) 541-6563; *The Illustrated Book of World Rankings.*

Statistical Office of the United Nations, Publishing Service, New York, New York 10017 (800) 253-9646; *Demographic Yearbook.*

SUDAN - ECONOMY

African Development Bank, 01 BP 1387, Abidjan 01, Cote D'Ivoire; *Selected Statistics on Regional Member Countries.*

Central Intelligence Agency, Washington, D.C. 20505 (703) 482-1100, www.cia.gov; *The World Factbook.*

Economist Intelligence Unit, 111 West 57th Street, New York, New York 10019 (800) 938-4685; *Sudan Country Report.*

Euromonitor International, Inc., 122 South Michigan Avenue, Suite 1200, Chicago, Illinois 60603 (800) 577-EURO; *International Marketing Data and Statistics; World Marketing Data and Statistics;* and *The World Economic Factbook.*

Europa Publications Limited, 18 Bedford Square, London, WC1B 3JN, England; *The Europa World Year Book.*

M.E. Sharpe, 80 Business Park Drive, Armonk, New York 10504 (800) 541-6563; *The Illustrated Book of World Rankings.*

St. Martin's Press, Inc., 175 Fifth Avenue, New York, New York 10010 (800) 221-7945; *The Statesman's Year-Book.*

Statistical Office of the United Nations, Publishing Service, New York, New York 10017 (800) 253-9646; *Foreign Trade Statistics for Africa;* and *World Statistics Pocketbook.*

The World Bank, 1818 H Street, NW, Washington, D.C. 20433 (202) 477-1234; *The World Bank Atlas.*

SUDAN - EDUCATION

African Development Bank, 01 BP 1387, Abidjan 01, Cote D'Ivoire; *Selected Statistics on Regional Member Countries.*

The Economist Intelligence Unit, 111

West 57th Street, New York, New York 10019 (800) 938-4685; *The World Market Atlas.*

Euromonitor International, Inc., 122 South Michigan Avenue, Suite 1200, Chicago, Illinois 60603 (800) 577-EURO; *International Marketing Data and Statistics;* and *World Marketing Data and Statistics.*

Europa Publications Limited, 18 Bedford Square, London, WC1B 3JN, England; *The Europa World Year Book.*

International Monetary Fund, 700 Nineteenth Street, NW, Washington, D.C. 20431 (202) 623-7000; *Government Finance Statistics Yearbook.*

M.E. Sharpe, 80 Business Park Drive, Armonk, New York 10504 (800) 541-6563; *The Illustrated Book of World Rankings.*

St. Martin's Press, Inc., 175 Fifth Avenue, New York, New York 10010 (800) 221-7945; *The Statesman's Year-Book.*

Statistical Office of the United Nations, Publishing Service, New York, New York 10017 (800) 253-9646; *Human Development Report;* and *Survey of Economic and Social Conditions in Africa.*

United Nations Economic Commission for Africa, Africa Hall, P.O. Box 3001, Addis Ababa, Ethiopia (Telephone Number in U.S. (800) 253-9646); *African Statistical Yearbook.*

United Nations Educational, Scientific and Cultural Organization (UNESCO), 7 Place de Fontenoy, F-75700 Paris, France (Telephone Number in U.S. (212) 963-5981); *Statistical Yearbook.*

The World Bank, 1818 H Street, NW, Washington, D.C. 20433 (202) 477-1234; *World Development Indicators.*

SUDAN - EGG PRODUCTION AND CONSUMPTION - See SUDAN - DAIRY PRODUCTS

SUDAN - ELECTRICITY

Central Intelligence Agency, Washington, D.C. 20505 (703) 482-1100, www.cia.gov; *The World Factbook.*

M.E. Sharpe, 80 Business Park Drive, Armonk, New York 10504 (800) 541-6563; *The Illustrated Book of World Rankings.*

Penn Well Publishing Company, 1421 South Sheridan Road, P.O. Box 1260, Tulsa, Oklahoma 74101 (800) 752-9764; *International Energy Statistics Sourcebook.*

St. Martin's Press, Inc., 175 Fifth Avenue, New York, New York 10010 (800) 221-7945; *The Statesman's Year-Book.*

Statistical Office of the United Nations, Publishing Service, New York, New York 10017 (800) 253-9646; *Human Development Report; Statistical Yearbook;* and *Survey of Economic and Social Conditions in Africa.*

United Nations Economic Commission for Africa, Africa Hall, P.O. Box 3001, Addis Ababa, Ethiopia (Telephone Number in U.S. (800) 253-9646); *African Statistical Yearbook.*

SUDAN - EMPLOYMENT

Euromonitor International, Inc., 122 South Michigan Avenue, Suite 1200, Chicago, Illinois 60603 (800) 577-EURO; *International Marketing Data and Statistics.*

International Labour Office, I.L.O. Publications, 1828 L Street, NW, Suite 801, Washington, D.C. 20036 (301) 638-3152; *Yearbook of Labour Statistics.*

M.E. Sharpe, 80 Business Park Drive, Armonk, New York 10504 (800) 541-6563; *The Illustrated Book of World Rankings.*

Statistical Office of the United Nations, Publishing Service, New York, New York 10017 (800) 253-9646; *Bulletin of Industrial Statistics for the Arab Countries; Statistical Yearbook;* and *Survey of Economic and Social Conditions in Africa.*

United Nations Economic Commission for Africa, Africa Hall, P.O. Box 3001, Addis Ababa, Ethiopia (Telephone Number in U.S. (800) 253-9646); *African Statistical Yearbook.*

SUDAN - ENERGY

Euromonitor International, Inc., 122 South Michigan Avenue, Suite 1200, Chicago, Illinois 60603 (800) 577-EURO; *International Marketing Data and Statistics; World Marketing Data and Statistics;* and *The World Economic Factbook.*

Food and Agricultural Organization of the United Nations (FAO) Via delle Terme di Caracalla, 00100 Rome, Italy (Telephone Number in U.S. (202) 653-2400); *The State of Food and Agriculture.*

M.E. Sharpe, 80 Business Park Drive, Armonk, New York 10504 (800) 541-6563; *The Illustrated Book of World Rankings.*

Penn Well Publishing Company, 1421 South Sheridan Road, P.O. Box 1260, Tulsa, Oklahoma 74101 (800) 752-9764; *International Energy Statistics Sourcebook.*

St. Martin's Press, Inc., 175 Fifth Avenue, New York, New York 10010 (800) 221-7945; *The Statesman's Year-Book.*

Statistical Office of the United Nations,

Publishing Service, New York, New York 10017 (800) 253-9646; *Human Development Report; Statistical Yearbook; Yearbook on World Energy Statistics;* and *World Statistics Pocketbook.*

United Nations Economic Commission for Africa, Africa Hall, P.O. Box 3001, Addis Ababa, Ethiopia (Telephone Number in U.S. (800) 253-9646); *African Statistical Yearbook.*

The World Bank, 1818 H Street, NW, Washington, D.C. 20433 (202) 477-1234; *The World Bank Atlas.*

SUDAN - ENVIRONMENT

Economist Intelligence Unit, 111 West 57th Street, New York, New York 10019 (800) 938-4685; *Sudan Country Report.*

Statistical Office of the United Nations, Publishing Service, New York, New York 10017 (800) 253-9646; *World Statistics Pocketbook.*

SUDAN - EXCHANGE RATES

African Development Bank, 01 BP 1387, Abidjan 01, Cote D'Ivoire; *Selected Statistics on Regional Member Countries.*

Central Intelligence Agency, Washington, D.C. 20505 (703) 482-1100, www.cia.gov; *The World Factbook.*

Euromonitor International, Inc., 122 South Michigan Avenue, Suite 1200, Chicago, Illinois 60603 (800) 577-EURO; *International Marketing Data and Statistics;* and *The World Economic Factbook.*

Europa Publications Limited, 18 Bedford Square, London, WC1B 3JN, England; *The Europa World Year Book.*

International Civil Aviation Organization, 999 University Street, Montreal, Quebec, Canada H3C 5H7 (514) 954-8219; *Civil Aviation Statistics of the World.*

International Monetary Fund, 700 Nineteenth Street, NW, Washington, D.C. 20431 (202) 623-7000; *International Financial Statistics.*

Statistical Office of the United Nations, Publishing Service, New York, New York 10017 (800) 253-9646; *Bulletin of Industrial Statistics for the Arab Countries; Foreign Trade Statistics for Africa; Statistical Yearbook;* and *World Statistics Pocketbook.*

SUDAN - EXCISE TAXES - See SUDAN - TAXATION

SUDAN - EXPORTS

African Development Bank, 01 BP 1387,

Abidjan 01, Cote D'Ivoire; *Selected Statistics on Regional Member Countries.*

Central Intelligence Agency, Washington, D.C. 20505 (703) 482-1100, www.cia.gov; *The World Factbook.*

The Economist Intelligence Unit, 111 West 57th Street, New York, New York 10019 (800) 938-4685; *Sudan Country Report;* and *The World Market Atlas.*

Euromonitor International, Inc., 122 South Michigan Avenue, Suite 1200, Chicago, Illinois 60603 (800) 577-EURO; *International Marketing Data and Statistics; and The World Economic Factbook.*

Europa Publications Limited, 18 Bedford Square, London, WC1B 3JN, England; *The Europa World Year Book.*

Food and Agricultural Organization of the United Nations (FAO) Via delle Terme di Caracalla, 00100 Rome, Italy (Telephone Number in U.S. (202) 653-2400); *The State of Food and Agriculture.*

International Monetary Fund, 700 Nineteenth Street, NW, Washington, D.C. 20431 (202) 623-7000; *Direction of Trade Statistics; Government Finance Statistics Yearbook;* and *International Financial Statistics.*

St. Martin's Press, Inc., 175 Fifth Avenue, New York, New York 10010 (800) 221-7945; *The Statesman's Year-Book.*

Statistical Office of the United Nations, Publishing Service, New York, New York 10017 (800) 253-9646; *Bulletin of Industrial Statistics for the Arab Countries; Foreign Trade Statistics for Africa;* and *Survey of Economic and Social Conditions in Africa.*

United Nations Conference on Trade and Development (UNCTAD), New York, New York 10017 (800) 253-9646; *Handbook of International Trade and Development Statistics.*

United Nations Economic Commission for Africa, Africa Hall, P.O. Box 3001, Addis Ababa, Ethiopia (Telephone Number in U.S. (800) 253-9646); *African Statistical Yearbook.*

The World Bank, 1818 H Street, NW, Washington, D.C. 20433 (202) 477-1234; *World Development Indicators.*

SUDAN - EXTERNAL INDEBTEDNESS

Statistical Office of the United Nations, Publishing Service, New York, New York 10017 (800) 253-9646; *Survey of Economic and Social Conditions in Africa.*

The World Bank, 1818 H Street, NW, Washington, D.C. 20433 (202) 477-1234;

World Development Indicators.

SUDAN - EXTERNAL TRADE

African Development Bank, 01 BP 1387, Abidjan 01, Cote D'Ivoire; *Selected Statistics on Regional Member Countries.*

Euromonitor International, Inc., 122 South Michigan Avenue, Suite 1200, Chicago, Illinois 60603 (800) 577-EURO; *World Marketing Data and Statistics.*

Food and Agricultural Organization of the United Nations (FAO) Via delle Terme di Caracalla, 00100 Rome, Italy (Telephone Number in U.S. (202) 653-2400); *The State of Food and Agriculture;* and *Trade Yearbook.*

Statistical Office of the United Nations, Publishing Service, New York, New York 10017 (800) 253-9646; *Statistical Yearbook.*

SUDAN - FABRIC PRODUCTION - See SUDAN - TEXTILE INDUSTRY

SUDAN - FARM CROPS - See SUDAN - CROPS

SUDAN - FEMALE WORKING POPULATION - See SUDAN - EMPLOYMENT

SUDAN - FERTILITY RATES

Central Intelligence Agency, Washington, D.C. 20505 (703) 482-1100, www.cia.gov; *The World Factbook.*

M.E. Sharpe, 80 Business Park Drive, Armonk, New York 10504 (800) 541-6563; *The Illustrated Book of World Rankings.*

Statistical Office of the United Nations, Publishing Service, New York, New York 10017 (800) 253-9646; *Human Development Report;* and *Survey of Economic and Social Conditions in Africa.*

The World Bank, 1818 H Street, NW, Washington, D.C. 20433 (202) 477-1234; *The World Bank Atlas;* and *World Development Indicators.*

SUDAN - FERTILIZER

Food and Agricultural Organization of the United Nations (FAO), Via delle Terme di Caracalla, 00100, Rome, Italy (Telephone Number in U.S. (202) 653-2400); *Fertilizer Yearbook;* and *The State of Food and Agriculture.*

Statistical Office of the United Nations, Publishing Service, New York, New York 10017 (800) 253-9646; *Statistical Yearbook.*

SUDAN - FETAL MORTALITY - See SUDAN - MORTALITY

SUDAN - FINANCE

African Development Bank, 01 BP 1387, Abidjan 01, Cote D'Ivoire; *Selected Statistics on Regional Member Countries.*

Economist Intelligence Unit, 111 West 57th Street, New York, New York 10019 (800) 938-4685; *Sudan Country Report.*

Europa Publications Limited, 18 Bedford Square, London, WC1B 3JN, England; *The Europa World Year Book.*

International Monetary Fund, 700 Nineteenth Street, NW, Washington, D.C. 20431 (202) 623-7000; *Government Finance Statistics Yearbook;* and *International Financial Statistics.*

M.E. Sharpe, 80 Business Park Drive, Armonk, New York 10504 (800) 541-6563; *The Illustrated Book of World Rankings.*

St. Martin's Press, Inc., 175 Fifth Avenue, New York, New York 10010 (800) 221-7945; *The Statesman's Year-Book.*

United Nations Economic Commission for Africa, Africa Hall, P.O. Box 3001, Addis Ababa, Ethiopia (Telephone Number in U.S. (800) 253-9646); *African Statistical Yearbook.*

SUDAN - FISHERIES

Europa Publications Limited, 18 Bedford Square, London, WC1B 3JN, England; *The Europa World Year Book.*

Food and Agricultural Organization of the United Nations (FAO) Via delle Terme di Caracalla, 00100 Rome, Italy (Telephone Number in U.S. (202) 653-2400); *The State of Food and Agriculture;* and *Yearbook of Fishery Statistics.*

M.E. Sharpe, 80 Business Park Drive, Armonk, New York 10504 (800) 541-6563; *The Illustrated Book of World Rankings.*

Statistical Office of the United Nations, Publishing Service, New York, New York 10017 (800) 253-9646; *Survey of Economic and Social Conditions in Africa.*

United Nations Conference on Trade and Development, Central Statistical Service, Palais des Nations, Geneva, Switzerland (Telephone in U.S. (800) 253-9646); *UNCTAD Commodity Yearbook.*

United Nations Economic Commission for Africa, Africa Hall, P.O. Box 3001, Addis Ababa, Ethiopia (Telephone Number in U.S. (800) 253-9646); *African Statistical Yearbook.*

SUDAN - FLOUR PRODUCTION

Statistical Office of the United Nations,

Publishing Service, New York, New York 10017 (800) 253-9646; *Statistical Yearbook.*

SUDAN - FOOD

African Development Bank, 01 BP 1387, Abidjan 01, Cote D'Ivoire; *Selected Statistics on Regional Member Countries.*

Food and Agricultural Organization of the United Nations (FAO) Via delle Terme di Caracalla, 00100 Rome, Italy (Telephone Number in U.S. (202) 653-2400); *Production Yearbook;* and *The State of Food and Agriculture.*

Statistical Office of the United Nations, Publishing Service, New York, New York 10017 (800) 253-9646; *Human Development Report.*

United Nations Conference on Trade and Development, Central Statistical Service, Palais des Nations, Geneva, Switzerland (Telephone in U.S. (800) 253-9646); *UNCTAD Commodity Yearbook.*

SUDAN - FOREIGN DEBT

International Monetary Fund, 700 Nineteenth Street, NW, Washington, D.C. 20431 (202) 623-7000; *Government Finance Statistics Yearbook.*

SUDAN - FOREIGN TRADE

Economist Intelligence Unit, 111 West 57th Street, New York, New York 10019 (800) 938-4685; *Sudan Country Report.*

Euromonitor International, Inc., 122 South Michigan Avenue, Suite 1200, Chicago, Illinois 60603 (800) 577-EURO; *International Marketing Data and Statistics;* and *The World Economic Factbook.*

Europa Publications Limited, 18 Bedford Square, London, WC1B 3JN, England; *The Europa World Year Book.*

Food and Agricultural Organization of the United Nations (FAO) Via delle Terme di Caracalla, 00100 Rome, Italy (Telephone Number in U.S. (202) 653-2400); *The State of Food and Agriculture.*

International Monetary Fund, 700 Nineteenth Street, NW, Washington, D.C. 20431 (202) 623-7000; *International Financial Statistics.*

M.E. Sharpe, 80 Business Park Drive, Armonk, New York 10504 (800) 541-6563; *The Illustrated Book of World Rankings.*

St. Martin's Press, Inc., 175 Fifth Avenue, New York, New York 10010 (800) 221-7945; *The Statesman's Year-Book.*

Statistical Office of the United Nations,

Publishing Service, New York, New York 10017 (800) 253-9646; *Bulletin of Industrial Statistics for the Arab Countries; Foreign Trade Statistics for Africa; International Trade Statistics Yearbook;* and *Statistical Yearbook.*

United Nations Conference on Trade and Development, Central Statistical Service, Palais des Nations, Geneva, Switzerland (Telephone in U.S. (800) 253-9646); *UNCTAD Commodity Yearbook.*

United Nations Economic Commission for Africa, Africa Hall, P.O. Box 3001, Addis Ababa, Ethiopia (Telephone Number in U.S. (800) 253-9646); *African Statistical Yearbook.*

The World Bank, 1818 H Street, NW, Washington, D.C. 20433 (202) 477-1234; *World Development Indicators.*

SUDAN - FORESTRY AND FOREST PRODUCTS

Europa Publications Limited, 18 Bedford Square, London, WC1B 3JN, England; *The Europa World Year Book.*

Food and Agricultural Organization of the United Nations (FAO) Via delle Terme di Caracalla, 00100 Rome, Italy (Telephone Number in U.S. (202) 653-2400); *The State of Food and Agriculture;* and *Yearbook of Forest Products.*

M.E. Sharpe, 80 Business Park Drive, Armonk, New York 10504 (800) 541-6563; *The Illustrated Book of World Rankings.*

St. Martin's Press, Inc., 175 Fifth Avenue, New York, New York 10010 (800) 221-7945; *The Statesman's Year-Book.*

Statistical Office of the United Nations, Publishing Service, New York, New York 10017 (800) 253-9646; *Statistical Yearbook.*

United Nations Conference on Trade and Development, Central Statistical Service, Palais des Nations, Geneva, Switzerland (Telephone in U.S. (800) 253-9646); *UNCTAD Commodity Yearbook.*

United Nations Economic Commission for Africa, Africa Hall, P.O. Box 3001, Addis Ababa, Ethiopia (Telephone Number in U.S. (800) 253-9646); *African Statistical Yearbook.*

United Nations Educational, Scientific and Cultural Organization (UNESCO), 7 Place de Fontenoy, F-75700 Paris, France (Telephone Number in U.S. (212) 963-5981); *Statistical Yearbook.*

SUDAN - GAS PRODUCTION - See SUDAN - MINING AND MINERAL PRODUCTS

SUDAN - GENERAL MORTALITY - See

SUDAN - MORTALITY

SUDAN - GEOGRAPHIC DATA

M.E. Sharpe, 80 Business Park Drive, Armonk, New York 10504 (800) 541-6563; *The Illustrated Book of World Rankings.*

SUDAN - GOATS - See SUDAN - LIVESTOCK AND POULTRY

SUDAN - GOLD HOLDINGS

International Monetary Fund, 700 Nineteenth Street, NW, Washington, D.C. 20431 (202) 623-7000; *International Financial Statistics.*

Statistical Office of the United Nations, Publishing Service, New York, New York 10017 (800) 253-9646; *Statistical Yearbook.*

The World Bank, 1818 H Street, NW, Washington, D.C. 20433 (202) 477-1234; *World Development Indicators.*

SUDAN - GOLD PRODUCTION AND CONSUMPTION - See SUDAN - MINING AND MINERAL PRODUCTS

SUDAN - GOVERNMENT

Central Intelligence Agency, Washington, D.C. 20505 (703) 482-1100, www.cia.gov; *The World Factbook.*

Europa Publications Limited, 18 Bedford Square, London, WC1B 3JN, England; *The Europa World Year Book.*

International Monetary Fund, 700 Nineteenth Street, NW, Washington, D.C. 20431 (202) 623-7000; *Government Finance Statistics Yearbook;* and *International Financial Statistics.*

St. Martin's Press, Inc., 175 Fifth Avenue, New York, New York 10010 (800) 221-7945; *The Statesman's Year-Book.*

Statistical Office of the United Nations, Publishing Service, New York, New York 10017 (800) 253-9646; *National Accounts Statistics;* and *Survey of Economic and Social Conditions in Africa.*

The World Bank, 1818 H Street, NW, Washington, D.C. 20433 (202) 477-1234; *World Development Indicators.*

SUDAN - GRAIN PRODUCTION - See SUDAN - CROPS

SUDAN - GRANTS

International Monetary Fund, 700 Nineteenth Street, NW, Washington, D.C. 20431 (202) 623-7000; *Government Finance Statistics Yearbook.*

SUDAN - GROSS DOMESTIC PRODUCT

African Development Bank, 01 BP 1387, Abidjan 01, Cote D'Ivoire; *Selected Statistics on Regional Member Countries.*

The Economist Intelligence Unit, 111 West 57th Street, New York, New York 10019 (800) 938-4685; *Sudan Country Report;* and *The World Market Atlas.*

Euromonitor International, Inc., 122 South Michigan Avenue, Suite 1200, Chicago, Illinois 60603 (800) 577-EURO; *International Marketing Data and Statistics;* and *The World Economic Factbook.*

M.E. Sharpe, 80 Business Park Drive, Armonk, New York 10504 (800) 541-6563; *The Illustrated Book of World Rankings.*

Statistical Office of the United Nations, Publishing Service, New York, New York 10017 (800) 253-9646; *Bulletin of Industrial Statistics for the Arab Countries; Human Development Report; National Accounts Statistics; Statistical Yearbook;* and *Survey of Economic and Social Conditions in Africa.*

United Nations Economic Commission for Africa, Africa Hall, P.O. Box 3001, Addis Ababa, Ethiopia (Telephone Number in U.S. (800) 253-9646); *African Statistical Yearbook.*

The World Bank, 1818 H Street, NW, Washington, D.C. 20433 (202) 477-1234; *World Development Indicators.*

SUDAN - GROSS NATIONAL PRODUCT

Euromonitor International, Inc., 122 South Michigan Avenue, Suite 1200, Chicago, Illinois 60603 (800) 577-EURO; *International Marketing Data and Statistics.*

St. Martin's Press, Inc., 175 Fifth Avenue, New York, New York 10010 (800) 221-7945; *The Statesman's Year-Book.*

U.S. Arms Control and Disarmament Agency, 320 Twenty-first Street, NW, Washington, D.C. 20451 (202) 647-8677; *World Military Expenditures and Arms Transfers.*

The World Bank, 1818 H Street, NW, Washington, D.C. 20433 (202) 477-1234; *The World Bank Atlas;* and *World Development Indicators.*

SUDAN - GROUNDNUTS - See SUDAN - CROPS

SUDAN - HEALTH

African Development Bank, 01 BP 1387, Abidjan 01, Cote D'Ivoire; *Selected Statistics on Regional Member Countries.*

Euromonitor International, Inc., 122 South Michigan Avenue, Suite 1200, Chicago, Illinois 60603 (800) 577-EURO; *World Marketing Data and Statistics.*

M.E. Sharpe, 80 Business Park Drive, Armonk, New York 10504 (800) 541-6563; *The Illustrated Book of World Rankings.*

St. Martin's Press, Inc., 175 Fifth Avenue, New York, New York 10010 (800) 221-7945; *The Statesman's Year-Book.*

Statistical Office of the United Nations, Publishing Service, New York, New York 10017 (800) 253-9646; *Human Development Report;* and *Statistical Yearbook.*

United Nations Children's Fund (UNICEF), 3 United Nations Plaza, New York, New York 10017 (800) 253-9646; *State of the World's Children.*

United Nations Economic Commission for Africa, Africa Hall, P.O. Box 3001, Addis Ababa, Ethiopia (Telephone Number in U.S. (800) 253-9646); *African Statistical Yearbook.*

World Health Organization, Office of Publications, 20 Avenue Appia, CH-1211 Geneva 27, Switzerland (Telephone Number in U.S. (518) 436-9686); *World Health Statistics Annual.*

SUDAN - HEALTH EXPENDITURES

International Monetary Fund, 700 Nineteenth Street, NW, Washington, D.C. 20431 (202) 623-7000; *Government Finance Statistics Yearbook.*

SUDAN - HIGHWAYS

Central Intelligence Agency, Washington, D.C. 20505 (703) 482-1100, www.cia.gov; *The World Factbook.*

International Road Federation, 2600 Virginia Avenue, NW, Washington, D.C. 20037 (202) 338-4641; *World Road Statistics.*

St. Martin's Press, Inc., 175 Fifth Avenue, New York, New York 10010 (800) 221-7945; *The Statesman's Year-Book.*

Statistical Office of the United Nations, Publishing Service, New York, New York 10017 (800) 253-9646; *Survey of Economic and Social Conditions in Africa.*

United Nations Economic Commission for Africa, Africa Hall, P.O. Box 3001, Addis Ababa, Ethiopia (Telephone Number in U.S. (800) 253-9646); *African Statistical Yearbook.*

SUDAN - HORSES - See SUDAN - LIVESTOCK AND POULTRY

SUDAN - HOURS OF WORK - See SUDAN - EMPLOYMENT

SUDAN - HOUSING AND HOUSING UNITS

Euromonitor International, Inc., 122 South Michigan Avenue, Suite 1200, Chicago, Illinois 60603 (800) 577-EURO; *World Marketing Data and Statistics.*

SUDAN - HOUSING EXPENDITURES

International Monetary Fund, 700 Nineteenth Street, NW, Washington, D.C. 20431 (202) 623-7000; *Government Finance Statistics Yearbook.*

M.E. Sharpe, 80 Business Park Drive, Armonk, New York 10504 (800) 541-6563; *The Illustrated Book of World Rankings.*

SUDAN - ILLITERATE POPULATION

Central Intelligence Agency, Washington, D.C. 20505 (703) 482-1100, www.cia.gov; *The World Factbook.*

The Economist Intelligence Unit, 111 West 57th Street, New York, New York 10019; *The World Market Atlas.*

Euromonitor International, Inc., 122 South Michigan Avenue, Suite 1200, Chicago, Illinois 60603 (800) 577-EURO; *The World Economic Factbook.*

Statistical Office of the United Nations, Publishing Service, New York, New York 10017 (800) 253-9646; *Human Development Report.*

United Nations Educational, Scientific and Cultural Organization (UNESCO), 7 Place de Fontenoy, F-75700 Paris, France (Telephone Number in U.S. (212) 963-5981); *Statistical Yearbook.*

SUDAN - IMPORTS

African Development Bank, 01 BP 1387, Abidjan 01, Cote D'Ivoire; *Selected Statistics on Regional Member Countries.*

Central Intelligence Agency, Washington, D.C. 20505 (703) 482-1100, www.cia.gov; *The World Factbook.*

The Economist Intelligence Unit, 111 West 57th Street, New York, New York 10019 (800) 938-4685; *Sudan Country Report;* and *The World Market Atlas.*

Euromonitor International, Inc., 122 South Michigan Avenue, Suite 1200, Chicago, Illinois 60603 (800) 577-EURO; *International Marketing Data and Statistics;* and *The World Economic Factbook.*

Europa Publications Limited, 18 Bedford Square, London, WC1B 3JN, England; *The Europa World Year Book.*

Food and Agricultural Organization of the United Nations (FAO) Via delle Terme di Caracalla, 00100 Rome, Italy (Telephone Number in U.S. (202) 653-2400); *The State of Food and Agriculture.*

International Monetary Fund, 700 Nineteenth Street, NW, Washington, D.C. 20431 (202) 623-7000; *Direction of Trade Statistics; Government Finance Statistics Yearbook;* and *International Financial Statistics.*

St. Martin's Press, Inc., 175 Fifth Avenue, New York, New York 10010 (800) 221-7945; *The Statesman's Year-Book.*

Statistical Office of the United Nations, Publishing Service, New York, New York 10017 (800) 253-9646; *Bulletin of Industrial Statistics for the Arab Countries; Foreign Trade Statistics for Africa;* and *Survey of Economic and Social Conditions in Africa.*

United Nations Conference on Trade and Development (UNCTAD), New York, New York 10017 (800) 253-9646; *Handbook of International Trade and Development Statistics.*

United Nations Economic Commission for Africa, Africa Hall, P.O. Box 3001, Addis Ababa, Ethiopia (Telephone Number in U.S. (800) 253-9646); *African Statistical Yearbook.*

The World Bank, 1818 H Street, NW, Washington, D.C. 20433 (202) 477-1234; *World Development Indicators.*

SUDAN - INCOME TAXES - See SUDAN - TAXATION

SUDAN - INDUSTRY

Central Intelligence Agency, Washington, D.C. 20505 (703) 482-1100, www.cia.gov; *The World Factbook.*

Economist Intelligence Unit, 111 West 57th Street, New York, New York 10019 (800) 938-4685; *Sudan Country Report.*

Euromonitor International, Inc., 122 South Michigan Avenue, Suite 1200, Chicago, Illinois 60603 (800) 577-EURO; *International Marketing Data and Statistics; World Marketing Data and Statistics;* and *The World Economic Factbook.*

Europa Publications Limited, 18 Bedford Square, London, WC1B 3JN, England; *The Europa World Year Book.*

International Labour Office, I.L.O. Publications, 1828 L Street, NW, Suite 801, Washington, D.C. 20036 (301) 638-3152; *Yearbook of Labour Statistics.*

M.E. Sharpe, 80 Business Park Drive, Armonk, New York 10504 (800) 541-6563; *The Illustrated Book of World Rankings.*

St. Martin's Press, Inc., 175 Fifth Avenue, New York, New York 10010 (800) 221-7945; *The Statesman's Year-Book.*

Statistical Office of the United Nations, Publishing Service, New York, New York 10017 (800) 253-9646; *Bulletin of Industrial Statistics for the Arab Countries.*

United Nations Economic Commission for Africa, Africa Hall, P.O. Box 3001, Addis Ababa, Ethiopia (Telephone Number in U.S. (800) 253-9646); *African Statistical Yearbook.*

The World Bank, 1818 H Street, NW, Washington, D.C. 20433 (202) 477-1234; *World Development Indicators.*

World Intellectual Property Organization, 34 Chemin des Colombettes, CH-1211 Geneva 20. Switzerland; *Industrial Property Statistics.*

SUDAN - INFANT AND MATERNAL MORTALITY - See SUDAN - MORTALITY

SUDAN - INTERNATIONAL LIQUIDITY

International Monetary Fund, 700 Nineteenth Street, NW, Washington, D.C. 20431 (202) 623-7000; *International Financial Statistics.*

SUDAN - INTERNATIONAL RESERVES EXCLUDING GOLD

African Development Bank, 01 BP 1387, Abidjan 01, Cote D'Ivoire; *Selected Statistics on Regional Member Countries.*

Statistical Office of the United Nations, Publishing Service, New York, New York 10017 (800) 253-9646; *Statistical Yearbook.*

The World Bank, 1818 H Street, NW, Washington, D.C. 20433 (202) 477-1234; *World Development Indicators.*

SUDAN - INVESTMENTS

International Monetary Fund, 700 Nineteenth Street, NW, Washington, D.C. 20431 (202) 623-7000; *International Financial Statistics.*

SUDAN - IRON ORE PRODUCTION AND CONSUMPTION - See SUDAN - MINING AND MINERAL PRODUCTS

SUDAN - IRRIGATION

Euromonitor International, Inc., 122 South Michigan Avenue, Suite 1200, Chicago, Illinois 60603 (800) 577-EURO; *International Marketing Data and Statistics.*

SUDAN - LABOR

African Development Bank, 01 BP 1387, Abidjan 01, Cote D'Ivoire; *Selected*

Statistics on Regional Member Countries.

Central Intelligence Agency, Washington, D.C. 20505 (703) 482-1100, www.cia.gov; *The World Factbook.*

Euromonitor International, Inc., 122 South Michigan Avenue, Suite 1200, Chicago, Illinois 60603 (800) 577-EURO; *International Marketing Data and Statistics;* and *World Marketing Data and Statistics.*

Europa Publications Limited, 18 Bedford Square, London, WC1B 3JN, England; *The Europa World Year Book.*

Food and Agricultural Organization of the United Nations (FAO) Via delle Terme di Caracalla, 00100 Rome, Italy (Telephone Number in U.S. (202) 653-2400); *The State of Food and Agriculture.*

International Labour Office, I.L.O. Publications, 1828 L Street, NW, Suite 801, Washington, D.C. 20036 (301) 638-3152; *Yearbook of Labour Statistics.*

M.E. Sharpe, 80 Business Park Drive, Armonk, New York 10504 (800) 541-6563; *The Illustrated Book of World Rankings.*

St. Martin's Press, Inc., 175 Fifth Avenue, New York, New York 10010 (800) 221-7945; *The Statesman's Year-Book.*

Statistical Office of the United Nations, Publishing Service, New York, New York 10017 (800) 253-9646; *Human Development Report.*

The World Bank, 1818 H Street, NW, Washington, D.C. 20433 (202) 477-1234; *The World Bank Atlas;* and *World Development Indicators.*

SUDAN - LAND USE

Central Intelligence Agency, Washington, D.C. 20505 (703) 482-1100, www.cia.gov; *The World Factbook.*

Euromonitor International, Inc., 122 South Michigan Avenue, Suite 1200, Chicago, Illinois 60603 (800) 577-EURO; *International Marketing Data and Statistics.*

Food and Agricultural Organization of the United Nations (FAO), Via delle Terme di Caracalla, 00100 Rome, Italy (Telephone Number in U.S. (202) 653-2400); *Production Yearbook.*

SUDAN - LIBRARIES

M.E. Sharpe, 80 Business Park Drive, Armonk, New York 10504 (800) 541-6563; *The Illustrated Book of World Rankings.*

SUDAN - LIFE EXPECTANCY

African Development Bank, 01 BP 1387,

Abidjan 01, Cote D'Ivoire; *Selected Statistics on Regional Member Countries.*

Central Intelligence Agency, Washington, D.C. 20505 (703) 482-1100, www.cia.gov; *The World Factbook.*

Euromonitor International, Inc., 122 South Michigan Avenue, Suite 1200, Chicago, Illinois 60603 (800) 577-EURO; *The World Economic Factbook.*

Statistical Office of the United Nations, Publishing Service, New York, New York 10017 (800) 253-9646; *Human Development Report; and World Statistics Pocketbook.*

The World Bank, 1818 H Street, NW, Washington, D.C. 20433 (202) 477-1234; *The World Bank Atlas.*

SUDAN - LITERACY RATE

Euromonitor International, Inc., 122 South Michigan Avenue, Suite 1200, Chicago, Illinois 60603 (800) 577-EURO; *World Marketing Data and Statistics.*

Statistical Office of the United Nations, Publishing Service, New York, New York 10017 (800) 253-9646; *Survey of Economic and Social Conditions in Africa.*

SUDAN - LIVESTOCK AND POULTRY

Euromonitor International, Inc., 122 South Michigan Avenue, Suite 1200, Chicago, Illinois 60603 (800) 577-EURO; *International Marketing Data and Statistics.*

Europa Publications Limited, 18 Bedford Square, London, WC1B 3JN, England; *The Europa World Year Book.*

Food and Agricultural Organization of the United Nations (FAO), Via delle Terme di Caracalla, 00100 Rome, Italy (Telephone Number in U.S. (202) 653-2400); *Production Yearbook; and The State of Food and Agriculture.*

M.E. Sharpe, 80 Business Park Drive, Armonk, New York 10504 (800) 541-6563; *The Illustrated Book of World Rankings.*

St. Martin's Press, Inc., 175 Fifth Avenue, New York, New York 10010 (800) 221-7945; *The Statesman's Year-Book.*

Statistical Office of the United Nations, Publishing Service, New York, New York 10017 (800) 253-9646; *Statistical Yearbook; and Survey of Economic and Social Conditions in Africa.*

United Nations Conference on Trade and Development, Central Statistical Service, Palais des Nations, Geneva, Switzerland (Telephone in U.S. (800) 253-9646); *UNCTAD Commodity Yearbook.*

United Nations Economic Commission for Africa, Africa Hall, P.O. Box 3001, Addis Ababa, Ethiopia (Telephone Number in U.S. (800) 253-9646); *African Statistical Yearbook.*

SUDAN - LIVING LEVELS - See SUDAN - LIFE EXPECTANCY

SUDAN - MAIL - NUMBER OF ITEMS SENT OR RECEIVED

Statistical Office of the United Nations, Publishing Service, New York, New York 10017 (800) 253-9646; *Statistical Yearbook.*

SUDAN - MANGANESE ORE PRODUCTION AND CONSUMPTION - See SUDAN - MINING AND MINERAL PRODUCTS

SUDAN - MANUFACTURING

M.E. Sharpe, 80 Business Park Drive, Armonk, New York 10504 (800) 541-6563; *The Illustrated Book of World Rankings.*

Statistical Office of the United Nations, Publishing Service, New York, New York 10017 (800) 253-9646; *Bulletin of Industrial Statistics for the Arab Countries; Statistical Yearbook; and Survey of Economic and Social Conditions in Africa.*

United Nations Economic Commission for Africa, Africa Hall, P.O. Box 3001, Addis Ababa, Ethiopia (Telephone Number in U.S. (800) 253-9646); *African Statistical Yearbook.*

The World Bank, 1818 H Street, NW, Washington, D.C. 20433 (202) 477-1234; *World Development Indicators.*

SUDAN - MARRIAGE RATES

M.E. Sharpe, 80 Business Park Drive, Armonk, New York 10504 (800) 541-6563; *The Illustrated Book of World Rankings.*

Statistical Office of the United Nations, Publishing Service, New York, New York 10017 (800) 253-9646; *Demographic Yearbook.*

SUDAN - MEAT PRODUCTION - See SUDAN - LIVESTOCK AND POULTRY

SUDAN - MERCHANT SHIPPING

Europa Publications Limited, 18 Bedford Square, London, WC1B 3JN, England; *The Europa World Year Book.*

Lloyd's Register of Shipping, 17 Battery Place, New York, New York 10004 (212) 425-8050; *Register of Ships.*

St. Martin's Press, Inc., 175 Fifth Avenue, New York, New York 10010 (800) 221-7945; *The Statesman's Year-Book.*

Statistical Office of the United Nations, Publishing Service, New York, New York 10017 (800) 253-9646; *Statistical Yearbook.*

United Nations Economic Commission for Africa, Africa Hall, P.O. Box 3001, Addis Ababa, Ethiopia (Telephone Number in U.S. (800) 253-9646); *African Statistical Yearbook.*

U.S. Department of Transportation, Maritime Administration, 400 Seventh Street, SW, Washington, D.C. 20590 (202) 366-5807, www.marad.dot.gov; *A Statistical Analysis of the World's Merchant Fleets.*

SUDAN - MILITARY

Central Intelligence Agency, Washington, D.C. 20505 (703) 482-1100, www.cia.gov; *The World Factbook.*

Euromonitor International, Inc., 122 South Michigan Avenue, Suite 1200, Chicago, Illinois 60603 (800) 577-EURO; *World Marketing Data and Statistics.*

The International Institute for Strategic Studies, 23 Tavistock Street, London WC2E 7NQ, England 44 171 3797676; *The Military Balance.*

International Monetary Fund, 700 Nineteenth Street, NW, Washington, D.C. 20431 (202) 623-7000; *Government Finance Statistics Yearbook.*

St. Martin's Press, Inc., 175 Fifth Avenue, New York, New York 10010 (800) 221-7945; *The Statesman's Year-Book.*

Statistical Office of the United Nations, Publishing Service, New York, New York 10017 (800) 253-9646; *Human Development Report.*

U.S. Arms Control and Disarmament Agency, 320 Twenty-first Street, NW, Washington, D.C. 20451 (202) 647-8677; *World Military Expenditures and Arms Transfers.*

SUDAN - MILK - See SUDAN - DAIRY PRODUCTS

SUDAN - MINING AND MINERAL PRODUCTS

Europa Publications Limited, 18 Bedford Square, London, WC1B 3JN, England; *The Europa World Year Book.*

M.E. Sharpe, 80 Business Park Drive, Armonk, New York 10504 (800) 541-6563; *The Illustrated Book of World Rankings.*

Penn Well Publishing Company, 1421 South Sheridan Road, P.O. Box 1260, Tulsa, Oklahoma 74101 (800) 752-9764; *International Energy Statistics Sourcebook.*

St. Martin's Press, Inc., 175 Fifth Avenue, New York, New York 10010 (800) 221-7945; *The Statesman's Year-Book.*

Statistical Office of the United Nations, Publishing Service, New York, New York 10017 (800) 253-9646; *Bulletin of Industrial Statistics for the Arab Countries;* and *Statistical Yearbook.*

United Nations Conference on Trade and Development, Central Statistical Service, Palais des Nations, Geneva, Switzerland (Telephone in U.S. (800) 253-9646); *UNCTAD Commodity Yearbook.*

United Nations Economic Commission for Africa, Africa Hall, P.O. Box 3001, Addis Ababa, Ethiopia (Telephone Number in U.S. (800) 253-9646); *African Statistical Yearbook.*

SUDAN - MONEY EXCHANGE RATES - See SUDAN - EXCHANGE RATES

SUDAN - MONEY RESERVES

Euromonitor International, Inc., 122 South Michigan Avenue, Suite 1200, Chicago, Illinois 60603 (800) 577-EURO; *International Marketing Data and Statistics.*

SUDAN - MONEY SUPPLY

African Development Bank, 01 BP 1387, Abidjan 01, Cote D'Ivoire; *Selected Statistics on Regional Member Countries.*

Economist Intelligence Unit, 111 West 57th Street, New York, New York 10019 (800) 938-4685; *Sudan Country Report.*

Euromonitor International, Inc., 122 South Michigan Avenue, Suite 1200, Chicago, Illinois 60603 (800) 577-EURO; *International Marketing Data and Statistics.*

Europa Publications Limited, 18 Bedford Square, London, WC1B 3JN, England; *The Europa World Year Book.*

International Monetary Fund, 700 Nineteenth Street, NW, Washington, D.C. 20431 (202) 623-7000; *International Financial Statistics.*

Statistical Office of the United Nations, Publishing Service, New York, New York 10017 (800) 253-9646; *Statistical Yearbook.*

The World Bank, 1818 H Street, NW, Washington, D.C. 20433 (202) 477-1234; *World Development Indicators.*

SUDAN - MORTALITY

Central Intelligence Agency, Washington, D.C. 20505 (703) 482-1100, www.cia.gov; *The World Factbook.*

Euromonitor International, Inc., 122

South Michigan Avenue, Suite 1200, Chicago, Illinois 60603 (800) 577-EURO; *International Marketing Data and Statistics;* and *The World Economic Factbook.*

Statistical Office of the United Nations, Publishing Service, New York, New York 10017 (800) 253-9646; *Democratic Yearbook; Human Development Report; Statistical Yearbook; Survey of Economic and Social Conditions in Africa;* and *World Statistics Pocketbook.*

United Nations Children's Fund (UNICEF), 3 United Nations Plaza, New York, New York 10017 (800) 253-9646; *State of the World's Children.*

The World Bank, 1818 H Street, NW, Washington, D.C. 20433 (202) 477-1234; *The World Bank Atlas;* and *World Development Indicators.*

World Health Organization, Office of Publications, 20 Avenue Appia, CH-1211 Geneva 27, Switzerland (Telephone Number in U.S. (518) 436-9686); *World Health Statistics Annual.*

SUDAN - MOTION PICTURES

St. Martin's Press, Inc., 175 Fifth Avenue, New York, New York 10010 (800) 221-7945; *The Statesman's Year-Book.*

Statistical Office of the United Nations, Publishing Service, New York, New York 10017 (800) 253-9646; *Statistical Yearbook.*

SUDAN - MOTOR VEHICLE TAXES - See SUDAN - TAXATION

SUDAN - MOTOR VEHICLES IN USE

Europa Publications Limited, 18 Bedford Square, London, WC1B 3JN, England; *The Europa World Year Book.*

International Road Federation, 2600 Virginia Avenue, NW, Washington, D.C. 20037 (202) 338-4641; *World Road Statistics.*

Statistical Office of the United Nations, Publishing Service, New York, New York 10017 (800) 253-9646; *Statistical Yearbook;* and *Survey of Economic and Social Conditions in Africa.*

SUDAN - MULES - See SUDAN - LIVESTOCK AND POULTRY

SUDAN - MUSEUMS

M.E. Sharpe, 80 Business Park Drive, Armonk, New York 10504 (800) 541-6563; *The Illustrated Book of World Rankings.*

United Nations Educational, Scientific and Cultural Organization (UNESCO), 7 Place de Fontenoy, F-75700 Paris, France

(Telephone Number in U.S. (212) 963-5981); *Statistical Yearbook.*

SUDAN - NATALITY - See SUDAN - BIRTH RATES

SUDAN - NATIONAL ACCOUNTS

African Development Bank, 01 BP 1387, Abidjan 01, Cote D'Ivoire; *Selected Statistics on Regional Member Countries.*

Europa Publications Limited, 18 Bedford Square, London, WC1B 3JN, England; *The Europa World Year Book.*

International Monetary Fund, 700 Nineteenth Street, NW, Washington, D.C. 20431 (202) 623-7000; *International Financial Statistics.*

Statistical Office of the United Nations, Publishing Service, New York, New York 10017 (800) 253-9646; *National Accounts Statistics;* and *Statistical Yearbook.*

United Nations Economic Commission for Africa, Africa Hall, P.O. Box 3001, Addis Ababa, Ethiopia (Telephone Number in U.S. (800) 253-9646); *African Statistical Yearbook.*

SUDAN - NATIONAL INCOME

M.E. Sharpe, 80 Business Park Drive, Armonk, New York 10504 (800) 541-6563; *The Illustrated Book of World Rankings.*

Statistical Office of the United Nations, Publishing Service, New York, New York 10017 (800) 253-9646; *National Accounts Statistics;* and *Statistical Yearbook.*

SUDAN - NATIONAL PRODUCT

M.E. Sharpe, 80 Business Park Drive, Armonk, New York 10504 (800) 541-6563; *The Illustrated Book of World Rankings.*

Statistical Office of the United Nations, Publishing Service, New York, New York 10017 (800) 253-9646; *Statistical Yearbook.*

SUDAN - NATURAL GAS PRODUCTION - See SUDAN - MINING AND MINERAL PRODUCTS

SUDAN - NEWSPAPER PRODUCTION - See SUDAN - FORESTRY AND FOREST PRODUCTS

SUDAN - NEWSPRINT - See SUDAN - FORESTRY AND FOREST PRODUCTS

SUDAN - OCCUPATIONS - See SUDAN - LABOR

SUDAN - PAPER - See SUDAN - FORESTRY AND FOREST PRODUCTS

SUDAN - PATENTS, TRADEMARKS AND

SERVICE MARKS

World Intellectual Property Organization, 34 Chemin des Colombettes, CH-1211 Geneva 20. Switzerland; *Industrial Property Statistics.*

SUDAN - PEANUT PRODUCTION - See SUDAN - CROPS

SUDAN - PERIODICALS

United Nations Educational, Scientific and Cultural Organization (UNESCO), 7 Place de Fontenoy, F-75700 Paris, France (Telephone Number in U.S. (212) 963-5981); *Statistical Yearbook.*

SUDAN - PESTICIDE USE

Food and Agricultural Organization of the United Nations (FAO) Via delle Terme di Caracalla, 00100 Rome, Italy (Telephone Number in U.S. (202) 653-2400); *The State of Food and Agriculture.*

SUDAN - PETROLEUM INDUSTRY

Food and Agricultural Organization of the United Nations (FAO) Via delle Terme di Caracalla, 00100 Rome, Italy (Telephone Number in U.S. (202) 653-2400); *The State of Food and Agriculture.*

M.E. Sharpe, 80 Business Park Drive, Armonk, New York 10504 (800) 541-6563; *The Illustrated Book of World Rankings.*

Penn Well Publishing Company, 1421 South Sheridan Road, P.O. Box 1260, Tulsa, Oklahoma 74101 (800) 752-9764; *International Energy Statistics Sourcebook.*

St. Martin's Press, Inc., 175 Fifth Avenue, New York, New York 10010 (800) 221-7945; *The Statesman's Year-Book.*

Statistical Office of the United Nations, Publishing Service, New York, New York 10017 (800) 253-9646; *Statistical Yearbook.*

United Nations Conference on Trade and Development, Central Statistical Service, Palais des Nations, Geneva, Switzerland (Telephone in U.S. (800) 253-9646); *UNCTAD Commodity Yearbook.*

SUDAN - PIGS - See SUDAN - LIVESTOCK AND POULTRY

SUDAN - POPULATION

African Development Bank, 01 BP 1387, Abidjan 01, Cote D'Ivoire; *Selected Statistics on Regional Member Countries.*

Central Intelligence Agency, Washington, D.C. 20505 (703) 482-1100, www.cia.gov; *The World Factbook.*

The Economist Intelligence Unit, 111 West 57th Street, New York, New York 10019 (800) 938-4685; *Sudan Country Report;* and *The World Market Atlas.*

Euromonitor International, Inc., 122 South Michigan Avenue, Suite 1200, Chicago, Illinois 60603 (800) 577-EURO; *International Marketing Data and Statistics;* and *The World Economic Factbook.*

Europa Publications Limited, 18 Bedford Square, London, WC1B 3JN, England; *The Europa World Year Book.*

Food and Agricultural Organization of the United Nations (FAO), Via delle Terme di Caracalla, 00100 Rome, Italy (Telephone Number in U.S. (202) 653-2400); *Production Yearbook.*

International Labour Office, I.L.O. Publications, 1828 L Street, NW, Suite 801, Washington, D.C. 20036 (301) 638-3152; *Yearbook of Labour Statistics.*

M.E. Sharpe, 80 Business Park Drive, Armonk, New York 10504 (800) 541-6563; *The Illustrated Book of World Rankings.*

St. Martin's Press, Inc., 175 Fifth Avenue, New York, New York 10010 (800) 221-7945; *The Statesman's Year-Book.*

Statistical Office of the United Nations, Publishing Service, New York, New York 10017 (800) 253-9646; *Demographic Yearbook; Human Development Report; Statistical Yearbook; Survey of Economic and Social Conditions in Africa;* and *World Statistics Pocketbook.*

United Nations Educational, Scientific and Cultural Organization (UNESCO), 7 Place de Fontenoy, F-75700 Paris, France (Telephone Number in U.S. (212) 963-5981); *Statistical Yearbook.*

U.S. Arms Control and Disarmament Agency, 320 Twenty-first Street, NW, Washington, D.C. 20451 (202) 647-8677; *World Military Expenditures and Arms Transfers.*

The World Bank, 1818 H Street, NW, Washington, D.C. 20433 (202) 477-1234; *The World Bank Atlas.*

World Health Organization, Office of Publications, 20 Avenue Appia, CH-1211 Geneva 27, Switzerland (Telephone Number in U.S. (518) 436-9686); *World Health Statistics Annual.*

SUDAN - POST OFFICES

M.E. Sharpe, 80 Business Park Drive, Armonk, New York 10504 (800) 541-6563; *The Illustrated Book of World Rankings.*

SUDAN - POTATO PRODUCTION - See SUDAN - CROPS

SUDAN - PRICES

Food and Agricultural Organization of the United Nations (FAO), Via delle Terme di Caracalla, 00100 Rome, Italy (Telephone Number in U.S. (202) 653-2400); *Production Yearbook;* and *The State of Food and Agriculture.*

International Labour Office, I.L.O. Publications, 1828 L Street, NW, Suite 801, Washington, D.C. 20036 (301) 638-3152; *Yearbook of Labour Statistics.*

International Monetary Fund, 700 Nineteenth Street, NW, Washington, D.C. 20431 (202) 623-7000; *International Financial Statistics.*

M.E. Sharpe, 80 Business Park Drive, Armonk, New York 10504 (800) 541-6563; *The Illustrated Book of World Rankings.*

United Nations Economic Commission for Africa, Africa Hall, P.O. Box 3001, Addis Ababa, Ethiopia (Telephone Number in U.S. (800) 253-9646); *African Statistical Yearbook.*

SUDAN - PRINTING AND WRITING PAPER - See SUDAN - FORESTRY AND FOREST PRODUCTS

SUDAN - PRODUCTION

M.E. Sharpe, 80 Business Park Drive, Armonk, New York 10504 (800) 541-6563; *The Illustrated Book of World Rankings.*

SUDAN - PRODUCTIVITY

Euromonitor International, Inc., 122 Michigan Avenue, Suite 1200, Chicago, Illinois 60603 (800) 577-EURO; *International Marketing Data and Statistics.*

SUDAN - PROPERTY TAXES - SUDAN - TAXATION

SUDAN - PUBLIC FINANCE - See SUDAN - FINANCE

SUDAN - RADIO BROADCASTING - See SUDAN - BROADCASTING

SUDAN - RADIO RECEIVERS

St. Martin's Press, Inc., 175 Fifth Avenue, New York, New York 10010 (800) 221-7945; *The Statesman's Year-Book.*

SUDAN - RAILWAYS

Europa Publications Limited, 18 Bedford Square, London, WC1B 3JN, England; *The Europa World Year Book.*

Jane's Information Group, Sentinel House, 163 Brighton Road, Coulsdon, Surrey CR5 2NH, England (Telephone Number in U.S. (703) 683-3700); *Jane's*

World Railways.

St. Martin's Press, Inc., 175 Fifth Avenue, New York, New York 10010 (800) 221-7945; *The Statesman's Year-Book.*

Statistical Office of the United Nations, Publishing Service, New York, New York 10017 (800) 253-9646; *Statistical Yearbook;* and *Survey of Economic and Social Conditions in Africa.*

United Nations Economic Commission for Africa, Africa Hall, P.O. Box 3001, Addis Ababa, Ethiopia (Telephone Number in U.S. (800) 253-9646); *African Statistical Yearbook.*

SUDAN - RELIGION

Central Intelligence Agency, Washington, D.C. 20505 (703) 482-1100, www.cia.gov; *The World Factbook.*

M.E. Sharpe, 80 Business Park Drive, Armonk, New York 10504 (800) 541-6563; *The Illustrated Book of World Rankings.*

St. Martin's Press, Inc., 175 Fifth Avenue, New York, New York 10010 (800) 221-7945; *The Statesman's Year-Book.*

SUDAN - RENT PRICES

International Labour Office, I.L.O. Publications, 1828 L Street, NW, Suite 801, Washington, D.C. 20036 (301) 638-3152; *Yearbook of Labour Statistics.*

SUDAN - RETAIL TRADE

Euromonitor International, Inc., 122 South Michigan Avenue, Suite 1200, Chicago, Illinois 60603 (800) 577-EURO; *World Marketing Data and Statistics.*

SUDAN - RICE PRODUCTION - See SUDAN - CROPS

SUDAN - ROUNDWOOD PRODUCTION - See SUDAN - FORESTRY AND FOREST PRODUCTS

SUDAN - RUBBER PRODUCTION AND CONSUMPTION

M.E. Sharpe, 80 Business Park Drive, Armonk, New York 10504 (800) 541-6563; *The Illustrated Book of World Rankings.*

SUDAN - SALT PRODUCTION - See SUDAN - MINING AND MINERAL PRODUCTS

SUDAN - SAWNWOOD PRODUCTION - See SUDAN - FORESTRY AND FOREST PRODUCTS

SUDAN - SCIENCE AND TECHNOLOGY - EXPENDITURE FOR RESEARCH - See SUDAN - SCIENTISTS, TECHNICIANS AND ENGINEERS

SUDAN - SCIENTISTS, TECHNICIANS AND ENGINEERS

Statistical Office of the United Nations, Publishing Service, New York, New York 10017 (800) 253-9646; *Statistical Yearbook.*

United Nations Educational, Scientific and Cultural Organization (UNESCO), 7 Place de Fontenoy, F-75700 Paris, France (Telephone Number in U.S. (212) 963-5981); *Statistical Yearbook.*

SUDAN - SENIOR CITIZENS

M.E. Sharpe, 80 Business Park Drive, Armonk, New York 10504 (800) 541-6563; *The Illustrated Book of World Rankings.*

SUDAN - SESAME - See SUDAN - CROPS

SUDAN - SHEEP - See SUDAN - LIVESTOCK AND POULTRY

SUDAN - SILVER PRODUCTION AND CONSUMPTION - See SUDAN - MINING AND MINERAL PRODUCTS

SUDAN - SOCIAL DATA

African Development Bank, 01 BP 1387, Abidjan 01, Cote D'Ivoire; *Selected Statistics on Regional Member Countries.*

M.E. Sharpe, 80 Business Park Drive, Armonk, New York 10504 (800) 541-6563; *The Illustrated Book of World Rankings.*

Statistical Office of the United Nations, Publishing Service, New York, New York 10017 (800) 253-9646; *World Statistics Pocketbook.*

SUDAN - SOCIAL SECURITY

International Monetary Fund, 700 Nineteenth Street, NW, Washington, D.C. 20431 (202) 623-7000; *Government Finance Statistics Yearbook.*

Statistical Office of the United Nations, Publishing Service, New York, New York 10017 (800) 253-9646; *National Accounts Statistics.*

SUDAN - STAMP TAXES AND DUTIES - See SUDAN - TAXATION

SUDAN - STATE BUDGET REVENUE AND EXPENDITURES

Euromonitor International, Inc., 122 Michigan Avenue, Suite 1200, Chicago, Illinois 60603 (800) 577-EURO; *International Marketing Data and Statistics.*

SUDAN - STEEL - See SUDAN - MINING AND MINERAL PRODUCTS

SUDAN - STOCKS - COMMODITY - MARKET PRICE - INDEX

Food and Agricultural Organization of the United Nations (FAO) Via delle Terme di Caracalla, 00100 Rome, Italy (Telephone Number in U.S. (202) 653-2400); *The State of Food and Agriculture.*

SUDAN - SUGAR PRODUCTION AND CONSUMPTION - See SUDAN -CROPS

SUDAN - TAXATION

International Monetary Fund, 700 Nineteenth Street, NW, Washington, D.C. 20431 (202) 623-7000; *Government Finance Statistics Yearbook.*

International Road Federation, 2600 Virginia Avenue, NW, Washington, D.C. 20037 (202) 338-4641; *World Road Statistics.*

The World Bank, 1818 H Street, NW, Washington, D.C. 20433 (202) 477-1234; *World Development Indicators.*

SUDAN - TEA CONSUMPTION - See SUDAN - CROPS

SUDAN - TELEGRAPH SERVICE

Statistical Office of the United Nations, Publishing Service, New York, New York 10017 (800) 253-9646; *Statistical Yearbook.*

SUDAN - TELEPHONES IN USE

American Telephone and Telegraph Company, 26 Parsippany Road, Whippany, New Jersey 07981 (800) 222-0300; *The World's Telephones.*

Central Intelligence Agency, Washington, D.C. 20505 (703) 482-1100, www.cia.gov; *The World Factbook.*

St. Martin's Press, Inc., 175 Fifth Avenue, New York, New York 10010 (800) 221-7945; *The Statesman's Year-Book.*

Statistical Office of the United Nations, Publishing Service, New York, New York 10017 (800) 253-9646; *Statistical Yearbook;* and *World Statistics Pocketbook.*

SUDAN - TELEVISION BROADCASTING - See SUDAN - BROADCASTING

SUDAN - TEXTILE INDUSTRY

M.E. Sharpe, 80 Business Park Drive, Armonk, New York 10504 (800) 541-6563; *The Illustrated Book of World Rankings.*

Statistical Office of the United Nations, Publishing Service, New York, New York 10017 (800) 253-9646; *Statistical Yearbook.*

United Nations Conference on Trade and Development, Central Statistical Service, Palais des Nations, Geneva, Switzerland (Telephone in U.S. (800) 253-

9646); *UNCTAD Commodity Yearbook*.

SUDAN - TOBACCO PRODUCTION

M.E. Sharpe, 80 Business Park Drive, Armonk, New York 10504 (800) 541-6563; *The Illustrated Book of World Rankings*.

Statistical Office of the United Nations, Publishing Service, New York, New York 10017 (800) 253-9646; *Statistical Yearbook*.

SUDAN - TOURISM

Euromonitor International, Inc., 122 Michigan Avenue, Suite 1200, Chicago, Illinois 60603 (800) 577-EURO; *The World Economic Factbook;* and *World Marketing Data and Statistics*.

M.E. Sharpe, 80 Business Park Drive, Armonk, New York 10504 (800) 541-6563; *The Illustrated Book of World Rankings*.

St. Martin's Press, Inc., 175 Fifth Avenue, New York, New York 10010 (800) 221-7945; *The Statesman's Year-Book*.

Statistical Office of the United Nations, Publishing Service, New York, New York 10017 (800) 253-9646; *Statistical Yearbook*.

United Nations Economic Commission for Africa, Africa Hall, P.O. Box 3001, Addis Ababa, Ethiopia (Telephone Number in U.S. (800) 253-9646); *African Statistical Yearbook*.

World Tourism Organization, Calle Capitan Haya 42, E-28020 Madrid, Spain; *Yearbook of Tourism Statistics*.

SUDAN - TRACTORS IN USE

Statistical Office of the United Nations, Publishing Service, New York, New York 10017 (800) 253-9646; *Statistical Yearbook*.

SUDAN - TRADE - See SUDAN - FOREIGN TRADE

SUDAN - TRADEMARKS AND SERVICE MARKS - See TRADEMARKS AND SERVICE MARKS - PATENTS, TRADEMARKS AND SERVICE MARKS

SUDAN - TRANSPORTATION AND COMMUNICATIONS

Central Intelligence Agency, Washington, D.C. 20505 (703) 482-1100, www.cia.gov; *The World Factbook*.

Euromonitor International, Inc., 122 Michigan Avenue, Suite 1200, Chicago, Illinois 60603 (800) 577-EURO; *International Marketing Data and Statistics;* and *World Marketing Data and Statistics*.

M.E. Sharpe, 80 Business Park Drive, Armonk, New York 10504 (800) 541-6563;

The Illustrated Book of World Rankings.

St. Martin's Press, Inc., 175 Fifth Avenue, New York, New York 10010 (800) 221-7945; *The Statesman's Year-Book*.

Statistical Office of the United Nations, Publishing Service, New York, New York 10017 (800) 253-9646; *Human Development Report*.

United Nations Economic Commission for Africa, Africa Hall, P.O. Box 3001, Addis Ababa, Ethiopia (Telephone Number in U.S. (800) 253-9646); *African Statistical Yearbook*.

SUDAN - UNEMPLOYMENT

Central Intelligence Agency, Washington, D.C. 20505 (703) 482-1100, www.cia.gov; *The World Factbook*.

Euromonitor International, Inc., 122 Michigan Avenue, Suite 1200, Chicago, Illinois 60603 (800) 577-EURO; *International Marketing Data and Statistics*.

International Labour Office, I.L.O. Publications, 1828 L Street, NW, Suite 801, Washington, D.C. 20036 (301) 638-3152; *Yearbook of Labour Statistics*.

Statistical Office of the United Nations, Publishing Service, New York, New York 10017 (800) 253-9646; *Statistical Yearbook*.

SUDAN - VITAL STATISTICS

Euromonitor International, Inc., 122 Michigan Avenue, Suite 1200, Chicago, Illinois 60603 (800) 577-EURO; *International Marketing Data and Statistics*.

Statistical Office of the United Nations, Publishing Service, New York, New York 10017 (800) 253-9646; *Statistical Yearbook*.

World Health Organization, Office of Publications, 20 Avenue Appia, CH-1211 Geneva 27, Switzerland (Telephone Number in U.S. (518) 436-9686); *World Health Statistics Annual*.

SUDAN - WAGES

International Labour Office, I.L.O. Publications, 1828 L Street, NW, Suite 801, Washington, D.C. 20036 (301) 638-3152; *Yearbook of Labour Statistics*.

SUDAN - WEATHER - See SUDAN - CLIMATE

SUDAN - WELFARE

International Monetary Fund, 700 Nineteenth Street, NW, Washington, D.C. 20431 (202) 623-7000; *Government Finance Statistics Yearbook*.

SUDAN - WHEAT PRODUCTION AND PRICES - See SUDAN - CROPS

SUDAN - WHOLESALE PRICES

Statistical Office of the United Nations, Publishing Service, New York, New York 10017 (800) 253-9646; *Statistical Yearbook*.

SUDAN - WINE PRODUCTION - See SUDAN - BEVERAGES

SUDAN - WOOL PRODUCTION - See SUDAN - TEXTILE INDUSTRY

SUGAR AND SUGAR CANE - See also FOOD AND KINDRED PRODUCTS

SUGAR AND SUGAR CANE - BEET

U.S. Department of Agriculture, Economic Research Service, 1800 M Street, NW, Washington, D.C. 20036 (202) 694-5050, www.ers.usda.gov; *Managing Risk in Farming: Concepts, Research, and Analysis, Agricultural Economic Report No. 774*.

U.S. Department of Agriculture, National Agricultural Statistics Service, Fourteenth Street and Independence Avenue, SW, Washington, D.C. 20250 (800) 727-9540, www.usda.gov/nass; *Farm Business Economic Report*.

SUGAR AND SUGAR CANE - CONSUMPTION

U.S. Department of Agriculture, Economic Research Service, 1800 M Street, NW, Washington, D.C. 20036 (202) 694-5050, www.ers.usda.gov; *Food Consumption, Prices, and Expenditures;* and *Agricultural Outlook*.

SUGAR AND SUGAR CANE - FARM MARKETINGS

U.S. Department of Agriculture, Economic Research Service, 1800 M Street, NW, Washington, D.C. 20036 (202) 694-5050, www.ers.usda.gov; *Farm Business Economic Report*.

SUGAR AND SUGAR CANE - FOREIGN TRADE

U.S. Department of Agriculture, Economic Research Service, 1800 M Street, NW, Washington, D.C. 20036 (202) 694-5050, www.ers.usda.gov; *Food Consumption, Prices, and Expenditures; U.S. Agricultural Trade Update;* and *Foreign Agricultural Trade of the United States*.

U.S. Department of Commerce, Bureau of the Census, Washington, D.C. 20233 (301) 457-4100, www.census.gov; *U.S. International Trade in Goods and Services*.

SUGAR AND SUGAR CANE - MANUFACTURE

U.S. Department of Commerce, Bureau of the Census, Washington, D.C. 20233 (301) 457-4100, www.census.gov; *Census of Manufactures;* and *Annual Survey of Manufactures.*

SUGAR AND SUGAR CANE - PRICES

U.S. Department of Agriculture, National Agricultural Statistics Service, Fourteenth Street and Independence Avenue, SW, Washington, D.C. 20250 (800) 727-9540, www.usda.gov/nass; *Field Crops; Crop Production;* and *Crop Values.*

U.S. Department of Labor, Bureau of Labor Statistics, Two Massachusetts Avenue, NE, Washington, D.C. 20212 (202) 691-5200, www.stats.bls.gov; *Producer Price Indexes.*

SUGAR AND SUGAR CANE - PRODUCTION

U.S. Department of Agriculture, Economic Research Service, 1800 M Street, NW, Washington, D.C. 20036 (202) 694-5050, www.ers.usda.gov; *Agricultural Outlook.*

SUGAR AND SUGAR CANE - PRODUCTION - WORLD

Statistical Office of the United Nations, Publishing Service, New York, New York 10017 (800) 253-9646; *Monthly Bulletin of Statistics.*

SUICIDES

U.S. Department of Health and Human Services, National Center for Health Statistics, 3700 East-West Highay, Hyattsville, Maryland 20782 (301) 436-8500, www.cdc.gov/nchs; *Vital Statistics of the United States; National Vital Statistics Report; Advance Data from Vital and Health Statistics No. 23; Public Health;* and unpublished data.

World Health Organization, Office of Publications, 20 Avenue Appia, CH-1211 Geneva 27, Switzerland (Telephone Number in U.S. (518) 436-9686); *World Health Statistics Annual.*

SULFUR - CONSUMPTION

U.S. Department of the Interior, Geological Survey, Office of Minerals Information, 12201 Sunrise Valley Drive, Reston, Virginia 22092 (703) 648-4000, www.minerals.usgs.gov; *Mineral Commodity Summaries.*

SULFUR - EMPLOYMENT

U.S. Department of the Interior, Geological Survey, Office of Minerals Information, 12201 Sunrise Valley Drive, Reston, Virginia 22092 (703) 648-4000,

www.minerals.usgs.gov; *Mineral Commodity Summaries.*

SULFUR - FOREIGN TRADE

U.S. Department of the Interior, Geological Survey, Office of Minerals Information, 12201 Sunrise Valley Drive, Reston, Virginia 22092 (703) 648-4000, www.minerals.usgs.gov; *Mineral Commodity Summaries.*

SULFUR - PRICES

U.S. Department of the Interior, Geological Survey, Office of Minerals Information, 12201 Sunrise Valley Drive, Reston, Virginia 22092 (703) 648-4000, www.minerals.usgs.gov; *Annual Reports;* and *Mineral Commodity Summaries.*

SULFUR - PRODUCTION AND VALUE

U.S. Department of the Interior, Geological Survey, Office of Minerals Information, 12201 Sunrise Valley Drive, Reston, Virginia 22092 (703) 648-4000, www.minerals.usgs.gov; *Annual Reports;* and *Mineral Commodity Summaries.*

SULFUR - WORLD PRODUCTION

U.S. Department of the Interior, Geological Survey, Office of Minerals Information, 12201 Sunrise Valley Drive, Reston, Virginia 22092 (703) 648-4000, www.minerals.usgs.gov; *Annual Reports;* and *Mineral Commodity Summaries.*

SUNFLOWER

U.S. Department of Agriculture, Economic Research Service, 1800 M Street, NW, Washington, D.C. 20036 (202) 694-5050, www.ers.usda.gov; *Farm Business Economic Report.*

SUPERMARKETS - See GROCERY STORES

SUPPLEMENTAL SECURITY INCOME

The Congress of the U.S., Congressional Research Service, 10 First Street, SE, Washington, D.C. 20540 (202) 707-5700; *Cash and Non-Cash Benefits for Persons with Limited Income: Eligibility Rules, Recipient and Expenditure Data.*

Social Security Administration, 6400 Security Boulevard, Baltimore, Maryland 21235 (800) 772-1213, ww.ssa.gov; *Social Security Bulletin; Annual Statistical Supplement to the Social Security Bulletin;* unpublished data; and Internet site: http://ferret.bls.gov/ macro/031998/faminc/09000.html.

SUPPLEMENTAL SECURITY INCOME - STATES

Social Security Administration,6400

Security Boulevard, Baltimore, Maryland 21235 (800) 772-1213, ww.ssa.gov; *Social Security Bulletin;* and *Annual Statistical Supplement to the Social Security Bulletin.*

SURGEONS - See also PHYSICIANS

American Medical Association, 515 North State Street, Chicago, Illinois 60610 (312) 464-5000; *Socioeconomic Characteristics of Medical Practice.*

SURGICAL PROCEDURES

U.S. Department of Health and Human Services, National Center for Health Statistics, 3700 East-West Highway, Hyattsville, Maryland 20782 (301) 436-8500, www.cdc.gov/nchs; *Vital and Health Statistics.*

SURGICAL PROCEDURES - ORGAN TRANSPLANTS - FACILITIES

American Association of Tissue Banks, 1350 Beverly Road, Suite 220-A, McLean, Virginia 22101 (703) 827-9582.

Eye Bank Association of America, 1001 Connecticut Avenue, NW, Suite 601, Washington, D.C. 20036-5504 (202) 775-4999.

United Network for Organ Sharing, 1100 Boulders Parkway, Suite 500, Richmond, Virginia 23225 (804) 330-8620.

Suriname - National Statistical Office

Algemeen Bureau Voor de Statistiek, Post Office Box 244, Paramaribo, Suriname.

Suriname - Primary Statistics Source

General Bureau of Statistics, Post Office Box 244, Paramaribo, Suriname; *Jaacijfers voor Suriname* (Statistical Yearbook of Suriname).

SURINAME - AGRICULTURE

Economist Intelligence Unit, 111 West 57th Street, New York, New York 10019 (800) 938-4685; *Suriname Country Report.*

Euromonitor International, Inc., 122 South Michigan Avenue, Suite 1200, Chicago, Illinois 60603 (800) 577-EURO; *World Marketing Data and Statistics.*

Europa Publications Limited, 18 Bedford Square, London, WC1B 3JN, England; *The Europa World Year Book.*

Food and Agricultural Organization of the United Nations (FAO) Via delle Terme

di Caracalla, 00100 Rome, Italy (Telephone Number in U.S. (202) 653-2400); *Production Yearbook; The State of Food and Agriculture;* and *Trade Yearbook.*

Inter-American Development Bank, 1300 New York Avenue, NW, Washington, D.C. 20577 (202) 623-1753; *Economic and Social Progress in Latin America.*

M.E. Sharpe, 80 Business Park Drive, Armonk, New York 10504 (800) 541-6563; *The Illustrated Book of World Rankings.*

St. Martin's Press, Inc., 175 Fifth Avenue, New York, New York 10010 (800) 221-7945; *The Statesman's Year-Book.*

Statistical Office of the United Nations, Publishing Service, New York, New York 10017 (800) 253-9646; *Statistical Yearbook.*

United Nations Conference on Trade and Development, Central Statistical Service, Palais des Nations, Geneva, Switzerland (Telephone in U.S. (800) 253-9646); *UNCTAD Commodity Yearbook.*

The World Bank, 1818 H Street, NW, Washington, D.C. 20433 (202) 477-1234; *World Development Indicators.*

SURINAME - AIRLINE SERVICE

Europa Publications Limited, 18 Bedford Square, London, WC1B 3JN, England; *The Europa World Year Book.*

M.E. Sharpe, 80 Business Park Drive, Armonk, New York 10504 (800) 541-6563; *The Illustrated Book of World Rankings.*

St. Martin's Press, Inc., 175 Fifth Avenue, New York, New York 10010 (800) 221-7945; *The Statesman's Year-Book.*

SURINAME - AIRPORTS

Central Intelligence Agency, Washington, D.C. 20505 (703) 482-1100, www.cia.gov; *The World Factbook.*

SURINAME - ALUMINUM - See SURINAME - MINING AND MINERAL PRODUCTS

SURINAME - ANIMAL HEALTH

Food and Agricultural Organization of the United Nations (FAO), Via delle Terme di Caracalla, 00100, Rome, Italy (Telephone Number in U.S. (202) 653-2400); *Animal Health Yearbook.*

SURINAME - AREA AND DENSITY OF POPULATION

Central Intelligence Agency, Washington, D.C. 20505 (703) 482-1100, www.cia.gov; *The World Factbook.*

Euromonitor International, Inc., 122

Michigan Avenue, Suite 1200, Chicago, Illinois 60603 (800) 577-EURO; *The World Economic Factbook.*

Europa Publications Limited, 18 Bedford Square, London, WC1B 3JN, England; *The Europa World Year Book.*

Food and Agricultural Organization of the United Nations (FAO) Via delle Terme di Caracalla, 00100 Rome, Italy (Telephone Number in U.S. (202) 653-2400); *The State of Food and Agriculture.*

Inter-American Development Bank, 1300 New York Avenue, NW, Washington, D.C. 20577 (202) 623-1753; *Economic and Social Progress in Latin America.*

M.E. Sharpe, 80 Business Park Drive, Armonk, New York 10504 (800) 541-6563; *The Illustrated Book of World Rankings.*

St. Martin's Press, Inc., 175 Fifth Avenue, New York, New York 10010 (800) 221-7945; *The Statesman's Year-Book.*

Statistical Office of the United Nations, Publishing Service, New York, New York 10017 (800) 253-9646; *Statistical Yearbook.*

United Nations Educational, Scientific and Cultural Organization (UNESCO), 7 Place de Fontenoy, F-75700 Paris, France (Telephone Number in U.S. (212) 963-5981); *Statistical Yearbook.*

SURINAME - ARMS EXPORTS AND IMPORTS - See SURINAME - MILITARY

SURINAME - BALANCE OF PAYMENTS

The Economist Intelligence Unit, 111 West 57th Street, New York, New York 10019 (800) 938-4685; *The World Market Atlas.*

Europa Publications Limited, 18 Bedford Square, London, WC1B 3JN, England; *The Europa World Year Book.*

Inter-American Development Bank, 1300 New York Avenue, NW, Washington, D.C. 20577 (202) 623-1753; *Economic and Social Progress in Latin America.*

International Monetary Fund, 700 Nineteenth Street, NW, Washington, D.C. 20431 (202) 623-7000; *Balance of Payments Yearbook;* and *International Financial Statistics.*

Organization of American States (OAS), General Secretariat, Washington, D.C. 20006 (202) 458-3533; *Statistical Bulletin of the OAS.*

Statistical Office of the United Nations, Publishing Service, New York, New York 10017 (800) 253-9646; *Economic Survey of Latin America and the Caribbean.*

United Nations Conference on Trade and Development (UNCTAD), New York, New York 10017 (800) 253-9646; *Handbook of International Trade and Development Statistics.*

The World Bank, 1818 H Street, NW, Washington, D.C. 20433 (202) 477-1234; *World Development Indicators.*

SURINAME - BANANA PRODUCTION - See SURINAME - CROPS

SURINAME - BANKING

Euromonitor International, Inc., 122 South Michigan Avenue, Suite 1200, Chicago, Illinois 60603 (800) 577-EURO; *World Marketing Data and Statistics.*

Europa Publications Limited, 18 Bedford Square, London, WC1B 3JN, England; *The Europa World Year Book.*

Inter-American Development Bank, 1300 New York Avenue, NW, Washington, D.C. 20577 (202) 623-1753; *Economic and Social Progress in Latin America.*

International Monetary Fund, 700 Nineteenth Street, NW, Washington, D.C. 20431 (202) 623-7000; *Government Finance Statistics Yearbook;* and *International Financial Statistics.*

M.E. Sharpe, 80 Business Park Drive, Armonk, New York 10504 (800) 541-6563; *The Illustrated Book of World Rankings.*

St. Martin's Press, Inc., 175 Fifth Avenue, New York, New York 10010 (800) 221-7945; *The Statesman's Year-Book.*

SURINAME - BARLEY PRODUCTION - See SURINAME - CROPS

SURINAME - BAUXITE - See SURINAME - MINING AND MINERAL PRODUCTS

SURINAME - BEER PRODUCTION - See SURINAME - BEVERAGES

SURINAME - BEVERAGES

M.E. Sharpe, 80 Business Park Drive, Armonk, New York 10504 (800) 541-6563; *The Illustrated Book of World Rankings.*

Statistical Office of the United Nations, Publishing Service, New York, New York 10017 (800) 253-9646; *Statistical Yearbook.*

SURINAME - BIRTH RATES

Central Intelligence Agency, Washington, D.C. 20505 (703) 482-1100, www.cia.gov; *The World Factbook.*

Euromonitor International, Inc., 122 Michigan Avenue, Suite 1200, Chicago, Illinois 60603 (800) 577-EURO;

International Marketing Data and Statistics; and *The World Economic Factbook.*

Europa Publications Limited, 18 Bedford Square, London, WC1B 3JN, England; *The Europa World Year Book.*

M.E. Sharpe, 80 Business Park Drive, Armonk, New York 10504 (800) 541-6563; *The Illustrated Book of World Rankings.*

Statistical Office of the United Nations, Publishing Service, New York, New York 10017 (800) 253-9646; *Demographic Yearbook;* and *Statistical Yearbook.*

The World Bank, 1818 H Street, NW, Washington, D.C. 20433 (202) 477-1234; *World Development Indicators.*

SURINAME - BONDS

Inter-American Development Bank, 1300 New York Avenue, NW, Washington, D.C. 20577 (202) 623-1753; *Economic and Social Progress in Latin America.*

International Monetary Fund, 700 Nineteenth Street, NW, Washington, D.C. 20431 (202) 623-7000; *Government Finance Statistics Yearbook.*

SURINAME - BROADCASTING

Billboard Limited, P.O. Box 9027, 1006 AA Amsterdam, The Netherlands (Telephone Number in U.S. (212) 764-7300); *World Radio TV Handbook.*

Central Intelligence Agency, Washington, D.C. 20505 (703) 482-1100, www.cia.gov; *The World Factbook.*

Euromonitor International, Inc., 122 South Michigan Avenue, Suite 1200, Chicago, Illinois 60603 (800) 577-EURO; *World Marketing Data and Statistics.*

St. Martin's Press, Inc., 175 Fifth Avenue, New York, New York 10010 (800) 221-7945; *The Statesman's Year-Book.*

SURINAME - BUDGET

Central Intelligence Agency, Washington, D.C. 20505 (703) 482-1100, www.cia.gov; *The World Factbook.*

SURINAME - BUSINESS

Inter-American Development Bank, 1300 New York Avenue, NW, Washington, D.C. 20577 (202) 623-1753; *Economic and Social Progress in Latin America.*

SURINAME - BUSINESS AND PROFESSIONAL LICENSES

International Monetary Fund, 700 Nineteenth Street, NW, Washington, D.C. 20431 (202) 623-7000; *Government Finance Statistics Yearbook.*

SURINAME - BUTTER PRODUCTION - See SURINAME - DAIRY PRODUCTS

SURINAME - CALORIE SUPPLY

Food and Agricultural Organization of the United Nations (FAO) Via delle Terme di Caracalla, 00100 Rome, Italy (Telephone Number in U.S. (202) 653-2400); *The State of Food and Agriculture.*

SURINAME - CAPITAL INVESTMENT

Inter-American Development Bank, 1300 New York Avenue, NW, Washington, D.C. 20577 (202) 623-1753; *Economic and Social Progress in Latin America.*

SURINAME - CAPITAL REVENUE

Inter-American Development Bank, 1300 New York Avenue, NW, Washington, D.C. 20577 (202) 623-1753; *Economic and Social Progress in Latin America.*

International Monetary Fund, 700 Nineteenth Street, NW, Washington, D.C. 20431 (202) 623-7000; *Government Finance Statistics Yearbook.*

SURINAME - CATTLE - See SURINAME - LIVESTOCK AND POULTRY

SURINAME - CEMENT PRODUCTION - See SURINAME - MINING AND MINERAL PRODUCTS

SURINAME - CHEESE PRODUCTION AND CONSUMPTION - See SURINAME - DAIRY PRODUCTS

SURINAME - CHEMICAL (ORGANIC) PRODUCTION - See SURINAME - MINING AND MINERAL PRODUCTS

SURINAME - CIGARETTE PRODUCTION - See SURINAME - TOBACCO PRODUCTION

SURINAME - CLIMATE

M.E. Sharpe, 80 Business Park Drive, Armonk, New York 10504 (800) 541-6563; *The Illustrated Book of World Rankings.*

St. Martin's Press, Inc., 175 Fifth Avenue, New York, New York 10010 (800) 221-7945; *The Statesman's Year-Book.*

SURINAME - COAL PRODUCTION - See SURINAME - MINING AND MINERAL PRODUCTS

SURINAME - COCOA PRODUCTION

Statistical Office of the United Nations, Publishing Service, New York, New York 10017 (800) 253-9646; *Statistical Yearbook.*

U.C.L.A. Latin American Center Publications, University of California, Los Angeles, California 90024 (310) 825-6634; *Statistical Abstract of Latin America.*

SURINAME - COFFEE - See SURINAME - CROPS

SURINAME - COMMERCE

St. Martin's Press, Inc., 175 Fifth Avenue, New York, New York 10010 (800) 221-7945; *The Statesman's Year-Book.*

SURINAME - COMMUNICATIONS - See SURINAME - TRANSPORTATION AND COMMUNICATIONS

SURINAME - CONSTRUCTION INDUSTRY

Inter-American Development Bank, 1300 New York Avenue, NW, Washington, D.C. 20577 (202) 623-1753; *Economic and Social Progress in Latin America.*

M.E. Sharpe, 80 Business Park Drive, Armonk, New York 10504 (800) 541-6563; *The Illustrated Book of World Rankings.*

SURINAME - CONSUMER PRICE INDEX

Europa Publications Limited, 18 Bedford Square, London, WC1B 3JN, England; *The Europa World Year Book.*

Statistical Office of the United Nations, Publishing Service, New York, New York 10017 (800) 253-9646; *Statistical Yearbook.*

SURINAME - CONSUMER PRICES

Euromonitor International, Inc., 122 South Michigan Avenue, Suite 1200, Chicago, Illinois 60603 (800) 577-EURO; *World Marketing Data and Statistics.*

International Labour Office, I.L.O. Publications, 1828 L Street, NW, Suite 801, Washington, D.C. 20036 (301) 638-3152; *Yearbook of Labour Statistics.*

International Monetary Fund, 700 Nineteenth Street, NW, Washington, D.C. 20431 (202) 623-7000; *International Financial Statistics.*

Organization of American States (OAS), General Secretariat, Washington, D.C. 20006 (202) 458-3533; *Statistical Bulletin of the OAS.*

SURINAME - CONSUMPTION

Inter-American Development Bank, 1300 New York Avenue, NW, Washington, D.C. 20577 (202) 623-1753; *Economic and Social Progress in Latin America.*

SURINAME - COPPER PRODUCTION AND CONSUMPTION - See SURINAME - MINING AND MINERAL PRODUCTS

SURINAME - CORN PRODUCTION - See SURINAME - CROPS

SURINAME - CORPORATE INCOME TAXES - See SURINAME - TAXATION

SURINAME - CORPORATE TAXES - See SURINAME - TAXATION

SURINAME - COTTON PRODUCTION - See SURINAME - CROPS

SURINAME - CRIME

Yale University Press, Yale Station, New Haven, Connecticut 06520 (800) 987-7323; *Violence and Crime in Cross-National Perspective.*

SURINAME - CROPS

Europa Publications Limited, 18 Bedford Square, London, WC1B 3JN, England; *The Europa World Year Book.*

Food and Agricultural Organization of the United Nations (FAO) Via delle Terme di Caracalla, 00100 Rome, Italy (Telephone Number in U.S. (202) 653-2400); *The State of Food and Agriculture.*

M.E. Sharpe, 80 Business Park Drive, Armonk, New York 10504 (800) 541-6563; *The Illustrated Book of World Rankings.*

St. Martin's Press, Inc., 175 Fifth Avenue, New York, New York 10010 (800) 221-7945; *The Statesman's Year-Book.*

U.C.L.A. Latin American Center Publications, University of California, Los Angeles, California 90024 (310) 825-6634; *Statistical Abstract of Latin America.*

United Nations Conference on Trade and Development, Central Statistical Service, Palais des Nations, Geneva, Switzerland (Telephone in U.S. (800) 253-9646); *UNCTAD Commodity Yearbook.*

SURINAME - CUSTOMS DUTIES

Inter-American Development Bank, 1300 New York Avenue, NW, Washington, D.C. 20577 (202) 623-1753; *Economic and Social Progress in Latin America.*

International Monetary Fund, 700 Nineteenth Street, NW, Washington, D.C. 20431 (202) 623-7000; *Government Finance Statistics Yearbook.*

St. Martin's Press, Inc., 175 Fifth Avenue, New York, New York 10010 (800) 221-7945; *The Statesman's Year-Book.*

SURINAME - DAIRY PRODUCTS

Food and Agricultural Organization of the United Nations (FAO) Via delle Terme di Caracalla, 00100 Rome, Italy (Telephone Number in U.S. (202) 653-2400); *The State of Food and Agriculture.*

M.E. Sharpe, 80 Business Park Drive, Armonk, New York 10504 (800) 541-6563; *The Illustrated Book of World Rankings.*

St. Martin's Press, Inc., 175 Fifth Avenue, New York, New York 10010 (800) 221-7945; *The Statesman's Year-Book.*

U.C.L.A. Latin American Center Publications, University of California, Los Angeles, California 90024 (310) 825-6634; *Statistical Abstract of Latin America.*

SURINAME - DEATH RATES - See SURINAME - MORTALITY

SURINAME - DEFENSE EXPENDITURES - See SURINAME - MILITARY

SURINAME - DEMOGRAPHY

The Economist Intelligence Unit, 111 West 57th Street, New York, New York 10019 (800) 938-4685; *The World Market Atlas.*

Euromonitor International, Inc., 122 Michigan Avenue, Suite 1200, Chicago, Illinois 60603 (800) 577-EURO; *International Marketing Data and Statistics; World Marketing Data and Statistics;* and *The World Economic Factbook.*

M.E. Sharpe, 80 Business Park Drive, Armonk, New York 10504 (800) 541-6563; *The Illustrated Book of World Rankings.*

Statistical Office of the United Nations, Publishing Service, New York, New York 10017 (800) 253-9646; *Human Development Report.*

SURINAME - DEVELOPMENT ASSISTANCE

Inter-American Development Bank, 1300 New York Avenue, NW, Washington, D.C. 20577 (202) 623-1753; *Economic and Social Progress in Latin America.*

Statistical Office of the United Nations, Publishing Service, New York, New York 10017 (800) 253-9646; *Statistical Yearbook.*

SURINAME - DIAMOND PRODUCTION - See SURINAME - MINING AND MINERAL PRODUCTS

SURINAME - DISCOUNT RATES - See SURINAME - BANKING

SURINAME - DISEASES - See SURINAME - HEALTH

SURINAME - DIVORCE RATES

M.E. Sharpe, 80 Business Park Drive, Armonk, New York 10504 (800) 541-6563; *The Illustrated Book of World Rankings.*

Statistical Office of the United Nations, Publishing Service, New York, New York 10017 (800) 253-9646; *Demographic Yearbook;* and *Statistical Yearbook.*

SURINAME - ECONOMY

Central Intelligence Agency, Washington, D.C. 20505 (703) 482-1100, www.cia.gov; *The World Factbook.*

Economist Intelligence Unit, 111 West 57th Street, New York, New York 10019 (800) 938-4685; *Suriname Country Report.*

Euromonitor International, Inc., 122 Michigan Avenue, Suite 1200, Chicago, Illinois 60603 (800) 577-EURO; *The World Economic Factbook;* and *World Marketing Data and Statistics.*

Europa Publications Limited, 18 Bedford Square, London, WC1B 3JN, England; *The Europa World Year Book.*

Inter-American Development Bank, 1300 New York Avenue, NW, Washington, D.C. 20577 (202) 623-1753; *Economic and Social Progress in Latin America.*

M.E. Sharpe, 80 Business Park Drive, Armonk, New York 10504 (800) 541-6563; *The Illustrated Book of World Rankings.*

Organization of American States (OAS), General Secretariat, Washington, D.C. 20006 (202) 458-3533; *Statistical Bulletin of the OAS.*

St. Martin's Press, Inc., 175 Fifth Avenue, New York, New York 10010 (800) 221-7945; *The Statesman's Year-Book.*

Statistical Office of the United Nations, Publishing Service, New York, New York 10017 (800) 253-9646; *Economic Survey of Latin America and the Caribbean;* and *World Statistics Pocketbook.*

The World Bank, 1818 H Street, NW, Washington, D.C. 20433 (202) 477-1234; *The World Bank Atlas.*

SURINAME - EDUCATION

The Economist Intelligence Unit, 111 West 57th Street, New York, New York 10019 (800) 938-4685; *The World Market Atlas.*

Euromonitor International, Inc., 122 Michigan Avenue, Suite 1200, Chicago, Illinois 60603 (800) 577-EURO; *International Marketing Data and Statistics;* and *World Marketing Data and Statistics.*

Europa Publications Limited, 18 Bedford Square, London, WC1B 3JN, England; *The Europa World Year Book.*

International Monetary Fund, 700 Nineteenth Street, NW, Washington, D.C. 20431 (202) 623-7000; *Government Finance Statistics Yearbook.*

M.E. Sharpe, 80 Business Park Drive, Armonk, New York 10504 (800) 541-6563; *The Illustrated Book of World Rankings.*

St. Martin's Press, Inc., 175 Fifth Avenue, New York, New York 10010 (800) 221-7945; *The Statesman's Year-Book.*

Statistical Office of the United Nations, Publishing Service, New York, New York 10017 (800) 253-9646; *Human Development Report.*

United Nations Educational, Scientific and Cultural Organization (UNESCO), 7 Place de Fontenoy, F-75700 Paris, France (Telephone Number in U.S. (212) 963-5981); *Statistical Yearbook.*

The World Bank, 1818 H Street, NW, Washington, D.C. 20433 (202) 477-1234; *World Development Indicators.*

SURINAME - EGG PRODUCTION AND CONSUMPTION - See SURINAME - DAIRY PRODUCTS

SURINAME - ELECTRICITY

Central Intelligence Agency, Washington, D.C. 20505 (703) 482-1100, www.cia.gov; *The World Factbook.*

Inter-American Development Bank, 1300 New York Avenue, NW, Washington, D.C. 20577 (202) 623-1753; *Economic and Social Progress in Latin America.*

M.E. Sharpe, 80 Business Park Drive, Armonk, New York 10504 (800) 541-6563; *The Illustrated Book of World Rankings.*

Organization of American States (OAS), General Secretariat, Washington, D.C. 20006 (202) 458-3533; *Statistical Bulletin of the OAS.*

Penn Well Publishing Company, 1421 South Sheridan Road, P.O. Box 1260, Tulsa, Oklahoma 74101 (800) 752-9764; *International Energy Statistics Sourcebook.*

St. Martin's Press, Inc., 175 Fifth Avenue, New York, New York 10010 (800) 221-7945; *The Statesman's Year-Book.*

Statistical Office of the United Nations, Publishing Service, New York, New York 10017 (800) 253-9646; *Human Development Report;* and *Statistical Yearbook.*

SURINAME - EMPLOYMENT

Euromonitor International, Inc., 122 Michigan Avenue, Suite 1200, Chicago,

Illinois 60603 (800) 577-EURO; *International Marketing Data and Statistics.*

International Labour Office, I.L.O. Publications, 1828 L Street, NW, Suite 801, Washington, D.C. 20036 (301) 638-3152; *Yearbook of Labour Statistics.*

M.E. Sharpe, 80 Business Park Drive, Armonk, New York 10504 (800) 541-6563; *The Illustrated Book of World Rankings.*

Organization of American States (OAS), General Secretariat, Washington, D.C. 20006 (202) 458-3533; *Statistical Bulletin of the OAS.*

Statistical Office of the United Nations, Publishing Service, New York, New York 10017 (800) 253-9646; *Statistical Yearbook.*

SURINAME - ENERGY

Euromonitor International, Inc., 122 Michigan Avenue, Suite 1200, Chicago, Illinois 60603 (800) 577-EURO; *International Marketing Data and Statistics; World Marketing Data and Statistics;* and *The World Economic Factbook.*

Food and Agricultural Organization of the United Nations (FAO) Via delle Terme di Caracalla, 00100 Rome, Italy (Telephone Number in U.S. (202) 653-2400); *The State of Food and Agriculture.*

M.E. Sharpe, 80 Business Park Drive, Armonk, New York 10504 (800) 541-6563; *The Illustrated Book of World Rankings.*

Penn Well Publishing Company, 1421 South Sheridan Road, P.O. Box 1260, Tulsa, Oklahoma 74101 (800) 752-9764; *International Energy Statistics Sourcebook.*

St. Martin's Press, Inc., 175 Fifth Avenue, New York, New York 10010 (800) 221-7945; *The Statesman's Year-Book.*

Statistical Office of the United Nations, Publishing Service, New York, New York 10017 (800) 253-9646; *Energy Statistics Yearbook; Human Development Report; Statistical Yearbook;* and *World Statistics Pocketbook.*

The World Bank, 1818 H Street, NW, Washington, D.C. 20433 (202) 477-1234; *The World Bank Atlas.*

SURINAME - ENVIRONMENT

Economist Intelligence Unit, 111 West 57th Street, New York, New York 10019 (800) 938-4685; *Suriname Country Report.*

Statistical Office of the United Nations, Publishing Service, New York, New York 10017 (800) 253-9646; *World Statistics Pocketbook.*

SURINAME - EXCHANGE RATES

Central Intelligence Agency, Washington, D.C. 20505 (703) 482-1100, www.cia.gov; *The World Factbook.*

Euromonitor International, Inc., 122 Michigan Avenue, Suite 1200, Chicago, Illinois 60603 (800) 577-EURO; *International Marketing Data and Statistics;* and *The World Economic Factbook.*

Europa Publications Limited, 18 Bedford Square, London, WC1B 3JN, England; *The Europa World Year Book.*

Inter-American Development Bank, 1300 New York Avenue, NW, Washington, D.C. 20577 (202) 623-1753; *Economic and Social Progress in Latin America.*

International Monetary Fund, 700 Nineteenth Street, NW, Washington, D.C. 20431 (202) 623-7000; *International Financial Statistics.*

Organization of American States (OAS), General Secretariat, Washington, D.C. 20006 (202) 458-3533; *Statistical Bulletin of the OAS.*

Statistical Office of the United Nations, Publishing Service, New York, New York 10017 (800) 253-9646; *Statistical Yearbook;* and *World Statistics Pocketbook.*

SURINAME - EXCISE TAXES - See SURINAME - TAXATION

SURINAME - EXPORTS

Central Intelligence Agency, Washington, D.C. 20505 (703) 482-1100, www.cia.gov; *The World Factbook.*

The Economist Intelligence Unit, 111 West 57th Street, New York, New York 10019 (800) 938-4685; *Suriname Country Report;* and *The World Market Atlas.*

Euromonitor International, Inc., 122 Michigan Avenue, Suite 1200, Chicago, Illinois 60603 (800) 577-EURO; *International Marketing Data and Statistics;* and *The World Economic Factbook.*

Europa Publications Limited, 18 Bedford Square, London, WC1B 3JN, England; *The Europa World Year Book.*

Food and Agricultural Organization of the United Nations (FAO) Via delle Terme di Caracalla, 00100 Rome, Italy (Telephone Number in U.S. (202) 653-2400); *The State of Food and Agriculture.*

Inter-American Development Bank, 1300 New York Avenue, NW, Washington, D.C. 20577 (202) 623-1753; *Economic and Social Progress in Latin America.*

International Monetary Fund, 700 Nineteenth Street, NW, Washington, D.C. 20431 (202) 623-7000; *Direction of Trade Statistics; Government Finance Statistics Yearbook;* and *International Financial Statistics.*

St. Martin's Press, Inc., 175 Fifth Avenue, New York, New York 10010 (800) 221-7945; *The Statesman's Year-Book.*

United Nations Conference on Trade and Development (UNCTAD), New York, New York 10017 (800) 253-9646; *Handbook of International Trade and Development Statistics.*

The World Bank, 1818 H Street, NW, Washington, D.C. 20433 (202) 477-1234; *World Development Indicators.*

SURINAME - EXTERNAL FINANCING

Inter-American Development Bank, 1300 New York Avenue, NW, Washington, D.C. 20577 (202) 623-1753; *Economic and Social Progress in Latin America.*

SURINAME - EXTERNAL INDEBTEDNESS

Inter-American Development Bank, 1300 New York Avenue, NW, Washington, D.C. 20577 (202) 623-1753; *Economic and Social Progress in Latin America.*

The World Bank, 1818 H Street, NW, Washington, D.C. 20433 (202) 477-1234; *World Development Indicators.*

SURINAME - EXTERNAL TRADE

Euromonitor International, Inc., 122 South Michigan Avenue, Suite 1200, Chicago, Illinois 60603 (800) 577-EURO; *World Marketing Data and Statistics.*

Food and Agricultural Organization of the United Nations (FAO) Via delle Terme di Caracalla, 00100 Rome, Italy (Telephone Number in U.S. (202) 653-2400); *The State of Food and Agriculture;* and *Trade Yearbook.*

Inter-American Development Bank, 1300 New York Avenue, NW, Washington, D.C. 20577 (202) 623-1753; *Economic and Social Progress in Latin America.*

Statistical Office of the United Nations, Publishing Service, New York, New York 10017 (800) 253-9646; *Statistical Yearbook.*

SURINAME - FARM CROPS - See SURINAME - CROPS

SURINAME - FERTILITY RATES

Central Intelligence Agency, Washington, D.C. 20505 (703) 482-1100, www.cia.gov; *The World Factbook.*

M.E. Sharpe, 80 Business Park Drive, Armonk, New York 10504 (800) 541-6563; *The Illustrated Book of World Rankings.*

Statistical Office of the United Nations, Publishing Service, New York, New York 10017 (800) 253-9646; *Human Development Report.*

The World Bank, 1818 H Street, NW, Washington, D.C. 20433 (202) 477-1234; *The World Bank Atlas;* and *World Development Indicators.*

SURINAME - FERTILIZER

Food and Agricultural Organization of the United Nations (FAO) Via delle Terme di Caracalla, 00100 Rome, Italy (Telephone Number in U.S. (202) 653-2400); *The State of Food and Agriculture.*

SURINAME - FETAL MORTALITY - See SURINAME - MORTALITY

SURINAME - FINANCE

Economist Intelligence Unit, 111 West 57th Street, New York, New York 10019 (800) 938-4685; *Suriname Country Report.*

Europa Publications Limited, 18 Bedford Square, London, WC1B 3JN, England; *The Europa World Year Book.*

Inter-American Development Bank, 1300 New York Avenue, NW, Washington, D.C. 20577 (202) 623-1753; *Economic and Social Progress in Latin America.*

International Monetary Fund, 700 Nineteenth Street, NW, Washington, D.C. 20431 (202) 623-7000; *Government Finance Statistics Yearbook.*

M.E. Sharpe, 80 Business Park Drive, Armonk, New York 10504 (800) 541-6563; *The Illustrated Book of World Rankings.*

St. Martin's Press, Inc., 175 Fifth Avenue, New York, New York 10010 (800) 221-7945; *The Statesman's Year-Book.*

SURINAME - FISHERIES

Europa Publications Limited, 18 Bedford Square, London, WC1B 3JN, England; *The Europa World Year Book.*

Food and Agricultural Organization of the United Nations (FAO) Via delle Terme di Caracalla, 00100 Rome, Italy (Telephone Number in U.S. (202) 653-2400); *The State of Food and Agriculture;* and *Yearbook of Fishery Statistics.*

Inter-American Development Bank, 1300 New York Avenue, NW, Washington, D.C. 20577 (202) 623-1753; *Economic and Social Progress in Latin America.*

M.E. Sharpe, 80 Business Park Drive, Armonk, New York 10504 (800) 541-6563; *The Illustrated Book of World Rankings.*

St. Martin's Press, Inc., 175 Fifth Avenue, New York, New York 10010 (800) 221-7945; *The Statesman's Year-Book.*

Statistical Office of the United Nations, Publishing Service, New York, New York 10017 (800) 253-9646; *Statistical Yearbook.*

United Nations Conference on Trade and Development, Central Statistical Service, Palais des Nations, Geneva, Switzerland (Telephone in U.S. (800) 253-9646); *UNCTAD Commodity Yearbook.*

SURINAME - FOOD

Food and Agricultural Organization of the United Nations (FAO) Via delle Terme di Caracalla, 00100 Rome, Italy (Telephone Number in U.S. (202) 653-2400); *Production Yearbook;* and *The State of Food and Agriculture.*

Statistical Office of the United Nations, Publishing Service, New York, New York 10017 (800) 253-9646; *Human Development Report.*

United Nations Conference on Trade and Development, Central Statistical Service, Palais des Nations, Geneva, Switzerland (Telephone in U.S. (800) 253-9646); *UNCTAD Commodity Yearbook.*

SURINAME - FOREIGN AID

Inter-American Development Bank, 1300 New York Avenue, NW, Washington, D.C. 20577 (202) 623-1753; *Economic and Social Progress in Latin America.*

SURINAME - FOREIGN DEBT

Inter-American Development Bank, 1300 New York Avenue, NW, Washington, D.C. 20577 (202) 623-1753; *Economic and Social Progress in Latin America.*

International Monetary Fund, 700 Nineteenth Street, NW, Washington, D.C. 20431 (202) 623-7000; *Government Finance Statistics Yearbook.*

SURINAME - FOREIGN INDEBTEDNESS

Inter-American Development Bank, 1300 New York Avenue, NW, Washington, D.C. 20577 (202) 623-1753; *Economic and Social Progress in Latin America.*

Statistical Office of the United Nations, Publishing Service, New York, New York 10017 (800) 253-9646; *Economic Survey of Latin America and the Caribbean.*

SURINAME - FOREIGN TRADE

Economist Intelligence Unit, 111 West 57th Street, New York, New York 10019 (800) 938-4685; *Suriname Country Report.*

Euromonitor International, Inc., 122 Michigan Avenue, Suite 1200, Chicago, Illinois 60603 (800) 577-EURO; *The World Economic Factbook.*

Europa Publications Limited, 18 Bedford Square, London, WC1B 3JN, England; *The Europa World Year Book.*

Food and Agricultural Organization of the United Nations (FAO) Via delle Terme di Caracalla, 00100 Rome, Italy (Telephone Number in U.S. (202) 653-2400); *The State of Food and Agriculture.*

Inter-American Development Bank, 1300 New York Avenue, NW, Washington, D.C. 20577 (202) 623-1753; *Economic and Social Progress in Latin America.*

M.E. Sharpe, 80 Business Park Drive, Armonk, New York 10504 (800) 541-6563; *The Illustrated Book of World Rankings.*

St. Martin's Press, Inc., 175 Fifth Avenue, New York, New York 10010 (800) 221-7945; *The Statesman's Year-Book.*

Statistical Office of the United Nations, Publishing Service, New York, New York 10017 (800) 253-9646; *Economic Survey of Latin America and the Caribbean; International Trade Statistics Yearbook;* and *Statistical Yearbook.*

The World Bank, 1818 H Street, NW, Washington, D.C. 20433 (202) 477-1234; *World Development Indicators.*

SURINAME - FORESTRY AND FOREST PRODUCTS

Europa Publications Limited, 18 Bedford Square, London, WC1B 3JN, England; *The Europa World Year Book.*

Food and Agricultural Organization of the United Nations (FAO) Via delle Terme di Caracalla, 00100 Rome, Italy (Telephone Number in U.S. (202) 653-2400); *The State of Food and Agriculture;* and *Yearbook of Forest Products.*

Inter-American Development Bank, 1300 New York Avenue, NW, Washington, D.C. 20577 (202) 623-1753; *Economic and Social Progress in Latin America.*

M.E. Sharpe, 80 Business Park Drive, Armonk, New York 10504 (800) 541-6563; *The Illustrated Book of World Rankings.*

St. Martin's Press, Inc., 175 Fifth Avenue, New York, New York 10010 (800) 221-7945; *The Statesman's Year-Book.*

Statistical Office of the United Nations,

Publishing Service, New York, New York 10017 (800) 253-9646; *Statistical Yearbook.*

U.C.L.A. Latin American Center Publications, University of California, Los Angeles, California 90024 (310) 825-6634; *Statistical Abstract of Latin America.*

United Nations Conference on Trade and Development, Central Statistical Service, Palais des Nations, Geneva, Switzerland (Telephone in U.S. (800) 253-9646); *UNCTAD Commodity Yearbook.*

United Nations Educational, Scientific and Cultural Organization (UNESCO), 7 Place de Fontenoy, F-75700 Paris, France (Telephone Number in U.S. (212) 963-5981); *Statistical Yearbook.*

SURINAME - GAS PRODUCTION - See SURINAME - MINING AND MINERAL PRODUCTS

SURINAME - GENERAL MORTALITY - See SURINAME - MORTALITY

SURINAME - GEOGRAPHIC DATA

M.E. Sharpe, 80 Business Park Drive, Armonk, New York 10504 (800) 541-6563; *The Illustrated Book of World Rankings.*

SURINAME - GOLD HOLDINGS

International Monetary Fund, 700 Nineteenth Street, NW, Washington, D.C. 20431 (202) 623-7000; *International Financial Statistics.*

Statistical Office of the United Nations, Publishing Service, New York, New York 10017 (800) 253-9646; *Statistical Yearbook.*

The World Bank, 1818 H Street, NW, Washington, D.C. 20433 (202) 477-1234; *World Development Indicators.*

SURINAME - GOLD PRODUCTION AND CONSUMPTION - See SURINAME - MINING AND MINERAL PRODUCTS

SURINAME - GOVERNMENT

Central Intelligence Agency, Washington, D.C. 20505 (703) 482-1100, www.cia.gov; *The World Factbook.*

Europa Publications Limited, 18 Bedford Square, London, WC1B 3JN, England; *The Europa World Year Book.*

Inter-American Development Bank, 1300 New York Avenue, NW, Washington, D.C. 20577 (202) 623-1753; *Economic and Social Progress in Latin America.*

International Monetary Fund, 700 Nineteenth Street, NW, Washington, D.C. 20431 (202) 623-7000; *Government Finance Statistics Yearbook;* and

International Financial Statistics.

St. Martin's Press, Inc., 175 Fifth Avenue, New York, New York 10010 (800) 221-7945; *The Statesman's Year-Book.*

Statistical Office of the United Nations, Publishing Service, New York, New York 10017 (800) 253-9646; *National Accounts Statistics.*

The World Bank, 1818 H Street, NW, Washington, D.C. 20433 (202) 477-1234; *World Development Indicators.*

SURINAME - GRAIN PRODUCTION - See SURINAME - CROPS

SURINAME - GRANTS

International Monetary Fund, 700 Nineteenth Street, NW, Washington, D.C. 20431 (202) 623-7000; *Government Finance Statistics Yearbook.*

SURINAME - GROSS DOMESTIC PRODUCT

The Economist Intelligence Unit, 111 West 57th Street, New York, New York 10019 (800) 938-4685; *Suriname Country Report;* and *The World Market Atlas.*

Euromonitor International, Inc., 122 Michigan Avenue, Suite 1200, Chicago, Illinois 60603 (800) 577-EURO; *International Marketing Data and Statistics;* and *The World Economic Factbook.*

Europa Publications Limited, 18 Bedford Square, London, WC1B 3JN, England; *The Europa World Year Book.*

Inter-American Development Bank, 1300 New York Avenue, NW, Washington, D.C. 20577 (202) 623-1753; *Economic and Social Progress in Latin America.*

M.E. Sharpe, 80 Business Park Drive, Armonk, New York 10504 (800) 541-6563; *The Illustrated Book of World Rankings.*

Statistical Office of the United Nations, Publishing Service, New York, New York 10017 (800) 253-9646; *Human Development Report; National Accounts Statistics;* and *Statistical Yearbook.*

The World Bank, 1818 H Street, NW, Washington, D.C. 20433 (202) 477-1234; *World Development Indicators.*

SURINAME - GROSS NATIONAL PRODUCT

Inter-American Development Bank, 1300 New York Avenue, NW, Washington, D.C. 20577 (202) 623-1753; *Economic and Social Progress in Latin America.*

St. Martin's Press, Inc., 175 Fifth

Avenue, New York, New York 10010 (800) 221-7945; *The Statesman's Year-Book.*

The World Bank, 1818 H Street, NW, Washington, D.C. 20433 (202) 477-1234; *World Development Indicators.*

U.S. Arms Control and Disarmament Agency, 320 Twenty-first Street, NW, Washington, D.C. 20451 (202) 647-8677; *World Military Expenditures and Arms Transfers.*

The World Bank, 1818 H Street, NW, Washington, D.C. 20433 (202) 477-1234; *The World Bank Atlas.*

SURINAME - GROUNDNUT PRODUCTION - See SURINAME - CROPS

SURINAME - HEALTH

Euromonitor International, Inc., 122 South Michigan Avenue, Suite 1200, Chicago, Illinois 60603 (800) 577-EURO; *World Marketing Data and Statistics.*

M.E. Sharpe, 80 Business Park Drive, Armonk, New York 10504 (800) 541-6563; *The Illustrated Book of World Rankings.*

St. Martin's Press, Inc., 175 Fifth Avenue, New York, New York 10010 (800) 221-7945; *The Statesman's Year-Book.*

Statistical Office of the United Nations, Publishing Service, New York, New York 10017 (800) 253-9646; *Human Development Report;* and *Statistical Yearbook.*

World Health Organization, Office of Publications, 20 Avenue Appia, CH-1211 Geneva 27, Switzerland (Telephone Number in U.S. (518) 436-9686); *World Health Statistics Annual.*

SURINAME - HEALTH EXPENDITURES

International Monetary Fund, 700 Nineteenth Street, NW, Washington, D.C. 20431 (202) 623-7000; *Government Finance Statistics Yearbook.*

SURINAME - HIGHWAYS

Central Intelligence Agency, Washington, D.C. 20505 (703) 482-1100, www.cia.gov; *The World Factbook.*

St. Martin's Press, Inc., 175 Fifth Avenue, New York, New York 10010 (800) 221-7945; *The Statesman's Year-Book.*

SURINAME - HORSES - See SURINAME - LIVESTOCK AND POULTRY

SURINAME - HOURS OF WORK - See SURINAME - EMPLOYMENT

SURINAME - HOUSING AND HOUSING

UNITS

Euromonitor International, Inc., 122 South Michigan Avenue, Suite 1200, Chicago, Illinois 60603 (800) 577-EURO; *World Marketing Data and Statistics.*

SURINAME - HOUSING EXPENDITURES

International Monetary Fund, 700 Nineteenth Street, NW, Washington, D.C. 20431 (202) 623-7000; *Government Finance Statistics Yearbook.*

M.E. Sharpe, 80 Business Park Drive, Armonk, New York 10504 (800) 541-6563; *The Illustrated Book of World Rankings.*

SURINAME - ILLITERATE POPULATION

Central Intelligence Agency, Washington, D.C. 20505 (703) 482-1100, www.cia.gov; *The World Factbook.*

The Economist Intelligence Unit, 111 West 57th Street, New York, New York 10019 (800) 938-4685; *The World Market Atlas.*

Euromonitor International, Inc., 122 Michigan Avenue, Suite 1200, Chicago, Illinois 60603 (800) 577-EURO; *The World Economic Factbook.*

Statistical Office of the United Nations, Publishing Service, New York, New York 10017 (800) 253-9646; *Human Development Report.*

United Nations Educational, Scientific and Cultural Organization (UNESCO), 7 Place de Fontenoy, F-75700 Paris, France (Telephone Number in U.S. (212) 963-5981); *Statistical Yearbook.*

SURINAME - IMPORTS

Central Intelligence Agency, Washington, D.C. 20505 (703) 482-1100, www.cia.gov; *The World Factbook.*

The Economist Intelligence Unit, 111 West 57th Street, New York, New York 10019 (800) 938-4685; *Suriname Country Report;* and *The World Market Atlas.*

Euromonitor International, Inc., 122 Michigan Avenue, Suite 1200, Chicago, Illinois 60603 (800) 577-EURO; *International Marketing Data and Statistics;* and *The World Economic Factbook.*

Food and Agricultural Organization of the United Nations (FAO) Via delle Terme di Caracalla, 00100 Rome, Italy (Telephone Number in U.S. (202) 653-2400); *The State of Food and Agriculture.*

Inter-American Development Bank, 1300 New York Avenue, NW, Washington, D.C. 20577 (202) 623-1753; *Economic and*

Social Progress in Latin America.

International Monetary Fund, 700 Nineteenth Street, NW, Washington, D.C. 20431 (202) 623-7000; *Direction of Trade Statistics; Government Finance Statistics Yearbook;* and *International Financial Statistics.*

St. Martin's Press, Inc., 175 Fifth Avenue, New York, New York 10010 (800) 221-7945; *The Statesman's Year-Book.*

United Nations Conference on Trade and Development (UNCTAD), New York, New York 10017 (800) 253-9646; *Handbook of International Trade and Development Statistics.*

The World Bank, 1818 H Street, NW, Washington, D.C. 20433 (202) 477-1234; *World Development Indicators.*

SURINAME - INCOME TAXES - See SURINAME - TAXATION

SURINAME - INDUSTRIAL METALS PRODUCTION - See SURINAME - MINING AND MINERAL PRODUCTS

SURINAME - INDUSTRY

Central Intelligence Agency, Washington, D.C. 20505 (703) 482-1100, www.cia.gov; *The World Factbook.*

Economist Intelligence Unit, 111 West 57th Street, New York, New York 10019 (800) 938-4685; *Suriname Country Report.*

Euromonitor International, Inc., 122 Michigan Avenue, Suite 1200, Chicago, Illinois 60603 (800) 577-EURO; *The World Economic Factbook;* and *World Marketing Data and Statistics.*

Europa Publications Limited, 18 Bedford Square, London, WC1B 3JN, England; *The Europa World Year Book.*

International Labour Office, I.L.O. Publications, 1828 L Street, NW, Suite 801, Washington, D.C. 20036 (301) 638-3152; *Yearbook of Labour Statistics.*

M.E. Sharpe, 80 Business Park Drive, Armonk, New York 10504 (800) 541-6563; *The Illustrated Book of World Rankings.*

St. Martin's Press, Inc., 175 Fifth Avenue, New York, New York 10010 (800) 221-7945; *The Statesman's Year-Book.*

Statistical Office of the United Nations, Publishing Service, New York, New York 10017 (800) 253-9646; *Economic Survey of Latin America and the Caribbean.*

The World Bank, 1818 H Street, NW, Washington, D.C. 20433 (202) 477-1234; *World Development Indicators.*

SURINAME - INFANT AND MATERNAL
MORTALITY - See SURINAME - MORTALITY

SURINAME - INFLATIONARY FACTORS

Statistical Office of the United Nations,
Publishing Service, New York, New York
10017 (800) 253-9646; *Economic Survey of
Latin America and the Caribbean.*

SURINAME - INTEREST RATES

Inter-American Development Bank,
1300 New York Avenue, NW, Washington,
D.C. 20577 (202) 623-1753; *Economic and
Social Progress in Latin America.*

SURINAME - INTERNATIONAL FINANCE

Inter-American Development Bank,
1300 New York Avenue, NW, Washington,
D.C. 20577 (202) 623-1753; *Economic and
Social Progress in Latin America.*

SURINAME - INTERNATIONAL
LIQUIDITY

Inter-American Development Bank,
1300 New York Avenue, NW, Washington,
D.C. 20577 (202) 623-1753; *Economic and
Social Progress in Latin America.*

International Monetary Fund, 700
Nineteenth Street, NW, Washington, D.C.
20431 (202) 623-7000; *International
Financial Statistics.*

SURINAME - INTERNATIONAL
RESERVES

Organization of American States (OAS),
General Secretariat, Washington, D.C.
20006 (202) 458-3533; *Statistical Bulletin of
the OAS.*

SURINAME - INTERNATIONAL
RESERVES EXCLUDING GOLD

Inter-American Development Bank,
1300 New York Avenue, NW, Washington,
D.C. 20577 (202) 623-1753; *Economic and
Social Progress in Latin America.*

Statistical Office of the United Nations,
Publishing Service, New York, New York
10017 (800) 253-9646; *Statistical Yearbook.*

The World Bank, 1818 H Street, NW,
Washington, D.C. 20433 (202) 477-1234;
World Development Indicators.

SURINAME - INTERNATIONAL
STATISTICS

Inter-American Development Bank,
1300 New York Avenue, NW, Washington,
D.C. 20577 (202) 623-1753; *Economic and
Social Progress in Latin America.*

SURINAME - INVESTMENTS

Inter-American Development Bank,
1300 New York Avenue, NW, Washington,
D.C. 20577 (202) 623-1753; *Economic and
Social Progress in Latin America.*

International Monetary Fund, 700
Nineteenth Street, NW, Washington, D.C.
20431 (202) 623-7000; *International
Financial Statistics.*

SURINAME - IRON ORE PRODUCTION AND
CONSUMPTION - See SURINAME - MINING
AND MINERAL PRODUCTS

SURINAME - IRRIGATION

Inter-American Development Bank,
1300 New York Avenue, NW, Washington,
D.C. 20577 (202) 623-1753; *Economic and
Social Progress in Latin America.*

SURINAME - LABOR

Central Intelligence Agency,
Washington, D.C. 20505 (703) 482-1100,
www.cia.gov; *The World Factbook.*

Euromonitor International, Inc., 122
Michigan Avenue, Suite 1200, Chicago,
Illinois 60603 (800) 577-EURO;
International Marketing Data and Statistics;
and *World Marketing Data and Statistics.*

Europa Publications Limited, 18
Bedford Square, London, WC1B 3JN,
England; *The Europa World Year Book.*

Food and Agricultural Organization of
the United Nations (FAO) Via delle Terme
di Caracalla, 00100 Rome, Italy (Telephone
Number in U.S. (202) 653-2400); *The State
of Food and Agriculture.*

International Labour Office,
I.L.O. Publications, 1828 L Street, NW, Suite
801, Washington, D.C. 20036 (301) 638-
3152; *Yearbook of Labour Statistics.*

M.E. Sharpe, 80 Business Park Drive,
Armonk, New York 10504 (800) 541-6563;
The Illustrated Book of World Rankings.

St. Martin's Press, Inc., 175 Fifth
Avenue, New York, New York 10010 (800)
221-7945; *The Statesman's Year-Book.*

Statistical Office of the United Nations,
Publishing Service, New York, New York
10017 (800) 253-9646; *Human
Development Report.*

The World Bank, 1818 H Street, NW,
Washington, D.C. 20433 (202) 477-1234;
The World Bank Atlas; and *World
Development Indicators.*

SURINAME - LAND USE

Central Intelligence Agency,
Washington, D.C. 20505 (703) 482-1100,
www.cia.gov; *The World Factbook.*

Euromonitor International, Inc., 122
Michigan Avenue, Suite 1200, Chicago,
Illinois 60603 (800) 577-EURO;
International Marketing Data and Statistics.

Food and Agricultural Organization of
the United Nations (FAO), Via delle Terme
di Caracalla, 00100 Rome, Italy (Telephone
Number in U.S. (202) 653-2400);
Production Yearbook.

Inter-American Development Bank,
1300 New York Avenue, NW, Washington,
D.C. 20577 (202) 623-1753; *Economic and
Social Progress in Latin America.*

SURINAME - LIBRARIES

M.E. Sharpe, 80 Business Park Drive,
Armonk, New York 10504 (800) 541-6563;
The Illustrated Book of World Rankings.

United Nations Educational, Scientific
and Cultural Organization (UNESCO), 7
Place de Fontenoy, F-75700 Paris, France
(Telephone Number in U.S. (212) 963-
5981); *Statistical Yearbook.*

SURINAME - LIFE EXPECTANCY

Central Intelligence Agency,
Washington, D.C. 20505 (703) 482-1100,
www.cia.gov; *The World Factbook.*

Euromonitor International, Inc., 122
Michigan Avenue, Suite 1200, Chicago,
Illinois 60603 (800) 577-EURO; *The World
Economic Factbook.*

Statistical Office of the United Nations,
Publishing Service, New York, New York
10017 (800) 253-9646; *Human
Development Report;* and *World Statistics
Pocketbook.*

The World Bank, 1818 H Street, NW,
Washington, D.C. 20433 (202) 477-1234;
The World Bank Atlas.

SURINAME - LITERACY RATE

Euromonitor International, Inc., 122
South Michigan Avenue, Suite 1200,
Chicago, Illinois 60603 (800) 577-EURO;
World Marketing Data and Statistics.

SURINAME - LIVESTOCK AND POULTRY

Europa Publications Limited, 18
Bedford Square, London, WC1B 3JN,
England; *The Europa World Year Book.*

Food and Agricultural Organization of
the United Nations (FAO), Via delle Terme
di Caracalla, 00100 Rome, Italy (Telephone
Number in U.S. (202) 653-2400);
Production Yearbook; and *The State of
Food and Agriculture.*

M.E. Sharpe, 80 Business Park Drive,
Armonk, New York 10504 (800) 541-6563;

The Illustrated Book of World Rankings.

St. Martin's Press, Inc., 175 Fifth Avenue, New York, New York 10010 (800) 221-7945; *The Statesman's Year-Book.*

Statistical Office of the United Nations, Publishing Service, New York, New York 10017 (800) 253-9646; *Statistical Yearbook.*

United Nations Conference on Trade and Development, Central Statistical Service, Palais des Nations, Geneva, Switzerland (Telephone in U.S. (800) 253-9646); *UNCTAD Commodity Yearbook.*

SURINAME - MAIN ECONOMIC INDICATORS - See SURINAME - ECONOMY

SURINAME - MAIN INDICATORS - See SURINAME - ECONOMY

SURINAME - MANUFACTURING

Inter-American Development Bank, 1300 New York Avenue, NW, Washington, D.C. 20577 (202) 623-1753; *Economic and Social Progress in Latin America.*

M.E. Sharpe, 80 Business Park Drive, Armonk, New York 10504 (800) 541-6563; *The Illustrated Book of World Rankings.*

Statistical Office of the United Nations, Publishing Service, New York, New York 10017 (800) 253-9646; *Statistical Yearbook.*

The World Bank, 1818 H Street, NW, Washington, D.C. 20433 (202) 477-1234; *World Development Indicators.*

SURINAME - MARRIAGE RATES

M.E. Sharpe, 80 Business Park Drive, Armonk, New York 10504 (800) 541-6563; *The Illustrated Book of World Rankings.*

Statistical Office of the United Nations, Publishing Service, New York, New York 10017 (800) 253-9646; *Demographic Yearbook;* and *Statistical Yearbook.*

SURINAME - MEAT PRODUCTION - See SURINAME - LIVESTOCK AND POULTRY

SURINAME - MERCHANT SHIPPING

Europa Publications Limited, 18 Bedford Square, London, WC1B 3JN, England; *The Europa World Year Book.*

Statistical Office of the United Nations, Publishing Service, New York, New York 10017 (800) 253-9646; *Statistical Yearbook.*

U.S. Department of Transportation, Maritime Administration, 400 Seventh Street, SW, Washington, D.C. 20590 (202) 366-5807, www.marad.dot.gov; *A Statistical Analysis of the World's Merchant Fleets.*

SURINAME - MILITARY

Central Intelligence Agency, Washington, D.C. 20505 (703) 482-1100, www.cia.gov; *The World Factbook.*

Euromonitor International, Inc., 122 South Michigan Avenue, Suite 1200, Chicago, Illinois 60603 (800) 577-EURO; *World Marketing Data and Statistics.*

The International Institute for Strategic Studies, 23 Tavistock Street, London WC2E 7NQ, England 44 171 3797676; *The Military Balance.*

International Monetary Fund, 700 Nineteenth Street, NW, Washington, D.C. 20431 (202) 623-7000; *Government Finance Statistics Yearbook.*

St. Martin's Press, Inc., 175 Fifth Avenue, New York, New York 10010 (800) 221-7945; *The Statesman's Year-Book.*

Statistical Office of the United Nations, Publishing Service, New York, New York 10017 (800) 253-9646; *Human Development Report.*

U.S. Arms Control and Disarmament Agency, 320 Twenty-first Street, NW, Washington, D.C. 20451 (202) 647-8677; *World Military Expenditures and Arms Transfers.*

SURINAME - MILK PRODUCTION - See SURINAME - DAIRY PRODUCTS

SURINAME - MINING AND MINERAL PRODUCTS

Commodity Research Bureau, Inc., 30 South Wacker Drive, Chicago Illinois 60606 (312) 454-1801; *Commodity Year Book.*

Europa Publications Limited, 18 Bedford Square, London, WC1B 3JN, England; *The Europa World Year Book.*

Inter-American Development Bank, 1300 New York Avenue, NW, Washington, D.C. 20577 (202) 623-1753; *Economic and Social Progress in Latin America.*

International Monetary Fund, 700 Nineteenth Street, NW, Washington, D.C. 20431 (202) 623-7000; *International Financial Statistics.*

M.E. Sharpe, 80 Business Park Drive, Armonk, New York 10504 (800) 541-6563; *The Illustrated Book of World Rankings.*

Organization of American States (OAS), General Secretariat, Washington, D.C. 20006 (202) 458-3533; *Statistical Bulletin of the OAS.*

Penn Well Publishing Company, 1421 South Sheridan Road, P.O. Box 1260, Tulsa,

Oklahoma 74101 (800) 752-9764; *International Energy Statistics Sourcebook.*

St. Martin's Press, Inc., 175 Fifth Avenue, New York, New York 10010 (800) 221-7945; *The Statesman's Year-Book.*

Statistical Office of the United Nations, Publishing Service, New York, New York 10017 (800) 253-9646; *Statistical Yearbook.*

U.C.L.A. Latin American Center Publications, University of California, Los Angeles, California 90024 (310) 825-6634; *Statistical Abstract of Latin America.*

United Nations Conference on Trade and Development, Central Statistical Service, Palais des Nations, Geneva, Switzerland (Telephone in U.S. (800) 253-9646); *UNCTAD Commodity Yearbook.*

SURINAME - MONEY EXCHANGE RATES - See SURINAME - EXCHANGE RATES

SURINAME - MONEY RATES - MARKET

Inter-American Development Bank, 1300 New York Avenue, NW, Washington, D.C. 20577 (202) 623-1753; *Economic and Social Progress in Latin America.*

SURINAME - MONEY RESERVES

Inter-American Development Bank, 1300 New York Avenue, NW, Washington, D.C. 20577 (202) 623-1753; *Economic and Social Progress in Latin America.*

SURINAME - MONEY SUPPLY

Economist Intelligence Unit, 111 West 57th Street, New York, New York 10019 (800) 938-4685; *Suriname Country Report.*

Europa Publications Limited, 18 Bedford Square, London, WC1B 3JN, England; *The Europa World Year Book.*

Inter-American Development Bank, 1300 New York Avenue, NW, Washington, D.C. 20577 (202) 623-1753; *Economic and Social Progress in Latin America.*

International Monetary Fund, 700 Nineteenth Street, NW, Washington, D.C. 20431 (202) 623-7000; *International Financial Statistics.*

Statistical Office of the United Nations, Publishing Service, New York, New York 10017 (800) 253-9646; *Statistical Yearbook.*

The World Bank, 1818 H Street, NW, Washington, D.C. 20433 (202) 477-1234; *World Development Indicators.*

SURINAME - MORTALITY

Central Intelligence Agency, Washington, D.C. 20505 (703) 482-1100, www.cia.gov; *The World Factbook.*

Euromonitor International, Inc., 122 Michigan Avenue, Suite 1200, Chicago, Illinois 60603 (800) 577-EURO; *International Marketing Data and Statistics;* and *The World Economic Factbook.*

Europa Publications Limited, 18 Bedford Square, London, WC1B 3JN, England; *The Europa World Year Book.*

Statistical Office of the United Nations, Publishing Service, New York, New York 10017 (800) 253-9646; *Demographic Yearbook; Human Development Report; Statistical Yearbook;* and *World Statistics Pocketbook.*

The World Bank, 1818 H Street, NW, Washington, D.C. 20433 (202) 477-1234; *The World Bank Atlas;* and *World Development Indicators.*

World Health Organization, Office of Publications, 20 Avenue Appia, CH-1211 Geneva 27, Switzerland (Telephone Number in U.S. (518) 436-9686); *World Health Statistics Annual.*

SURINAME - MOTION PICTURES

St. Martin's Press, Inc., 175 Fifth Avenue, New York, New York 10010 (800) 221-7945; *The Statesman's Year-Book.*

SURINAME - MOTOR VEHICLE TAXES - See SURINAME - TAXATION

SURINAME - MOTOR VEHICLES IN USE

Europa Publications Limited, 18 Bedford Square, London, WC1B 3JN, England; *The Europa World Year Book.*

Statistical Office of the United Nations, Publishing Service, New York, New York 10017 (800) 253-9646; *Statistical Yearbook.*

SURINAME - MUSEUMS

M.E. Sharpe, 80 Business Park Drive, Armonk, New York 10504 (800) 541-6563; *The Illustrated Book of World Rankings.*

SURINAME - NATALITY - See SURINAME - BIRTH RATE

SURINAME - NATIONAL ACCOUNTS

Europa Publications Limited, 18 Bedford Square, London, WC1B 3JN, England; *The Europa World Year Book.*

Inter-American Development Bank, 1300 New York Avenue, NW, Washington, D.C. 20577 (202) 623-1753; *Economic and Social Progress in Latin America.*

Organization of American States (OAS), General Secretariat, Washington, D.C. 20006 (202) 458-3533; *Statistical Bulletin of the OAS.*

Statistical Office of the United Nations, Publishing Service, New York, New York 10017 (800) 253-9646; *National Accounts Statistics;* and *Statistical Yearbook.*

SURINAME - NATIONAL INCOME

Inter-American Development Bank, 1300 New York Avenue, NW, Washington, D.C. 20577 (202) 623-1753; *Economic and Social Progress in Latin America.*

M.E. Sharpe, 80 Business Park Drive, Armonk, New York 10504 (800) 541-6563; *The Illustrated Book of World Rankings.*

Statistical Office of the United Nations, Publishing Service, New York, New York 10017 (800) 253-9646; *National Accounts Statistics;* and *Statistical Yearbook.*

SURINAME - NATIONAL PRODUCT

M.E. Sharpe, 80 Business Park Drive, Armonk, New York 10504 (800) 541-6563; *The Illustrated Book of World Rankings.*

SURINAME - NATURAL GAS PRODUCTION - See SURINAME - MINING AND MINERAL PRODUCTS

SURINAME - NEWSPAPER PRODUCTION - See SURINAME - FORESTRY AND FOREST PRODUCTS

SURINAME - NEWSPRINT EXPORTS AND IMPORTS - See SURINAME - FORESTRY AND FOREST PRODUCTS

SURINAME - OCCUPATIONS - See SURINAME - LABOR

SURINAME - ORANGES PRODUCTION - See SURINAME - CROPS

SURINAME - PALM KERNELS AND PALM OIL PRODUCTION - See SURINAME - CROPS

SURINAME - PAPER - See SURINAME - FORESTRY AND FOREST PRODUCTS

SURINAME - PATENTS, TRADEMARKS AND SERVICE MARKS

Statistical Office of the United Nations, Publishing Service, New York, New York 10017 (800) 253-9646; *Statistical Yearbook.*

SURINAME - PEANUT PRODUCTION - See SURINAME - CROPS

SURINAME - PERIODICALS

United Nations Educational, Scientific and Cultural Organization (UNESCO), 7

Place de Fontenoy, F-75700 Paris, France (Telephone Number in U.S. (212) 963-5981); *Statistical Yearbook.*

SURINAME - PESTICIDE USE

Food and Agricultural Organization of the United Nations (FAO) Via delle Terme di Caracalla, 00100 Rome, Italy (Telephone Number in U.S. (202) 653-2400); *The State of Food and Agriculture.*

SURINAME - PETROLEUM INDUSTRY

Food and Agricultural Organization of the United Nations (FAO) Via delle Terme di Caracalla, 00100 Rome, Italy (Telephone Number in U.S. (202) 653-2400); *The State of Food and Agriculture.*

Inter-American Development Bank, 1300 New York Avenue, NW, Washington, D.C. 20577 (202) 623-1753; *Economic and Social Progress in Latin America.*

M.E. Sharpe, 80 Business Park Drive, Armonk, New York 10504 (800) 541-6563; *The Illustrated Book of World Rankings.*

Penn Well Publishing Company, 1421 South Sheridan Road, P.O. Box 1260, Tulsa, Oklahoma 74101 (800) 752-9764; *International Energy Statistics Sourcebook.*

St. Martin's Press, Inc., 175 Fifth Avenue, New York, New York 10010 (800) 221-7945; *The Statesman's Year-Book.*

United Nations Conference on Trade and Development, Central Statistical Service, Palais des Nations, Geneva, Switzerland (Telephone in U.S. (800) 253-9646); *UNCTAD Commodity Yearbook.*

SURINAME - PIG-IRON AND FERRO-ALLOY PRODUCTION - See SURINAME - MINING AND MINERAL PRODUCTS

SURINAME - PIGS - See SURINAME - LIVESTOCK AND POULTRY

SURINAME - POPULATION

Central Intelligence Agency, Washington, D.C. 20505 (703) 482-1100, www.cia.gov; *The World Factbook.*

The Economist Intelligence Unit, 111 West 57th Street, New York, New York 10019 (800) 938-4685; *Suriname Country Report;* and *The World Market Atlas.*

Euromonitor International, Inc., 122 Michigan Avenue, Suite 1200, Chicago, Illinois 60603 (800) 577-EURO; *International Marketing Data and Statistics;* and *The World Economic Factbook.*

Europa Publications Limited, 18 Bedford Square, London, WC1B 3JN, England; *The Europa World Year Book.*

Food and Agricultural Organization of the United Nations (FAO), Via delle Terme di Caracalla, 00100 Rome, Italy (Telephone Number in U.S. (202) 653-2400); *Production Yearbook.*

Inter-American Development Bank, 1300 New York Avenue, NW, Washington, D.C. 20577 (202) 623-1753; *Economic and Social Progress in Latin America.*

International Labour Office, I.L.O. Publications, 1828 L Street, NW, Suite 801, Washington, D.C. 20036 (301) 638-3152; *Yearbook of Labour Statistics.*

M.E. Sharpe, 80 Business Park Drive, Armonk, New York 10504 (800) 541-6563; *The Illustrated Book of World Rankings.*

Organization of American States (OAS), General Secretariat, Washington, D.C. 20006 (202) 458-3533; *Statistical Bulletin of the OAS.*

St. Martin's Press, Inc., 175 Fifth Avenue, New York, New York 10010 (800) 221-7945; *The Statesman's Year-Book.*

Statistical Office of the United Nations, Publishing Service, New York, New York 10017 (800) 253-9646; *Demographic Yearbook; Human Development Report; Statistical Yearbook;* and *World Statistics Pocketbook.*

United Nations Educational, Scientific and Cultural Organization (UNESCO), 7 Place de Fontenoy, F-75700 Paris, France (Telephone Number in U.S. (212) 963-5981); *Statistical Yearbook.*

U.S. Arms Control and Disarmament Agency, 320 Twenty-first Street, NW, Washington, D.C. 20451 (202) 647-8677; *World Military Expenditures and Arms Transfers.*

The World Bank, 1818 H Street, NW, Washington, D.C. 20433 (202) 477-1234; *The World Bank Atlas.*

World Health Organization, Office of Publications, 20 Avenue Appia, CH-1211 Geneva 27, Switzerland (Telephone Number in U.S. (518) 436-9686); *World Health Statistics Annual.*

SURINAME - POST OFFICES

M.E. Sharpe, 80 Business Park Drive, Armonk, New York 10504 (800) 541-6563; *The Illustrated Book of World Rankings.*

SURINAME - POTATO PRODUCTION - See SURINAME - CROPS

SURINAME - PRICES

Food and Agricultural Organization of the United Nations (FAO), Via delle Terme di Caracalla, 00100 Rome, Italy (Telephone Number in U.S. (202) 653-2400); *Production Yearbook;* and *The State of Food and Agriculture.*

International Labour Office, I.L.O. Publications, 1828 L Street, NW, Suite 801, Washington, D.C. 20036 (301) 638-3152; *Yearbook of Labour Statistics.*

International Monetary Fund, 700 Nineteenth Street, NW, Washington, D.C. 20431 (202) 623-7000; *International Financial Statistics.*

M.E. Sharpe, 80 Business Park Drive, Armonk, New York 10504 (800) 541-6563; *The Illustrated Book of World Rankings.*

Statistical Office of the United Nations, Publishing Service, New York, New York 10017 (800) 253-9646; *Economic Survey of Latin America and the Caribbean.*

SURINAME - PRINTING AND WRITING PAPER EXPORTS AND IMPORTS - See SURINAME - FORESTRY AND FOREST PRODUCTS

SURINAME - PRODUCTION

M.E. Sharpe, 80 Business Park Drive, Armonk, New York 10504 (800) 541-6563; *The Illustrated Book of World Rankings.*

SURINAME - PROPERTY TAXES - See SURINAME - TAXATION

SURINAME - PUBLIC CONSUMPTION FUND

Inter-American Development Bank, 1300 New York Avenue, NW, Washington, D.C. 20577 (202) 623-1753; *Economic and Social Progress in Latin America.*

SURINAME - PUBLIC EXPENDITURES

Inter-American Development Bank, 1300 New York Avenue, NW, Washington, D.C. 20577 (202) 623-1753; *Economic and Social Progress in Latin America.*

SURINAME - PUBLIC FINANCE - See SURINAME - FINANCE

SURINAME - PUBLIC REVENUES

Inter-American Development Bank, 1300 New York Avenue, NW, Washington, D.C. 20577 (202) 623-1753; *Economic and Social Progress in Latin America.*

SURINAME - RADIO BROADCASTING

M.E. Sharpe, 80 Business Park Drive, Armonk, New York 10504 (800) 541-6563; *The Illustrated Book of World Rankings.*

SURINAME - RADIO RECEIVERS

St. Martin's Press, Inc., 175 Fifth Avenue, New York, New York 10010 (800) 221-7945; *The Statesman's Year-Book.*

SURINAME - RAILWAYS

St. Martin's Press, Inc., 175 Fifth Avenue, New York, New York 10010 (800) 221-7945; *The Statesman's Year-Book.*

SURINAME - RELIGION

Central Intelligence Agency, Washington, D.C. 20505 (703) 482-1100, www.cia.gov; *The World Factbook.*

M.E. Sharpe, 80 Business Park Drive, Armonk, New York 10504 (800) 541-6563; *The Illustrated Book of World Rankings.*

St. Martin's Press, Inc., 175 Fifth Avenue, New York, New York 10010 (800) 221-7945; *The Statesman's Year-Book.*

SURINAME - RENT PRICES

International Labour Office, I.L.O. Publications, 1828 L Street, NW, Suite 801, Washington, D.C. 20036 (301) 638-3152; *Yearbook of Labour Statistics.*

SURINAME - RETAIL TRADE

Euromonitor International, Inc., 122 South Michigan Avenue, Suite 1200, Chicago, Illinois 60603 (800) 577-EURO; *World Marketing Data and Statistics.*

Inter-American Development Bank, 1300 New York Avenue, NW, Washington, D.C. 20577 (202) 623-1753; *Economic and Social Progress in Latin America.*

SURINAME - RICE PRODUCTION - See SURINAME - CROPS

SURINAME - ROUNDWOOD PRODUCTION - See SURINAME - FORESTRY AND FOREST PRODUCTS

SURINAME - RUBBER PRODUCTION AND CONSUMPTION

M.E. Sharpe, 80 Business Park Drive, Armonk, New York 10504 (800) 541-6563; *The Illustrated Book of World Rankings.*

SURINAME - SAWNWOOD PRODUCTION - See SURINAME - FORESTRY AND FOREST PRODUCTS

SURINAME - SENIOR CITIZENS

M.E. Sharpe, 80 Business Park Drive, Armonk, New York 10504 (800) 541-6563; *The Illustrated Book of World Rankings.*

SURINAME - SHEEP - See SURINAME - LIVESTOCK AND POULTRY

SURINAME - SILVER PRODUCTION AND CONSUMPTION - See SURINAME - MINING

AND MINERAL PRODUCTS

SURINAME - SOCIAL DATA

M.E. Sharpe, 80 Business Park Drive, Armonk, New York 10504 (800) 541-6563; *The Illustrated Book of World Rankings.*

Statistical Office of the United Nations, Publishing Service, New York, New York 10017 (800) 253-9646; *World Statistics Pocketbook.*

SURINAME - SOCIAL SECURITY

Inter-American Development Bank, 1300 New York Avenue, NW, Washington, D.C. 20577 (202) 623-1753; *Economic and Social Progress in Latin America.*

International Monetary Fund, 700 Nineteenth Street, NW, Washington, D.C. 20431 (202) 623-7000; *Government Finance Statistics Yearbook.*

Statistical Office of the United Nations, Publishing Service, New York, New York 10017 (800) 253-9646; *National Accounts Statistics.*

SURINAME - SOCIOECONOMIC DATA

Inter-American Development Bank, 1300 New York Avenue, NW, Washington, D.C. 20577 (202) 623-1753; *Economic and Social Progress in Latin America.*

SURINAME - STAMP TAXES AND DUTIES - See SURINAME - TAXATION

SURINAME - STATE BUDGET REVENUE AND EXPENDITURES

Inter-American Development Bank, 1300 New York Avenue, NW, Washington, D.C. 20577 (202) 623-1753; *Economic and Social Progress in Latin America.*

SURINAME - STEEL - See SURINAME - MINING AND MINERAL PRODUCTS

SURINAME - STOCKS - COMMODITY - MARKET PRICE - INDEX

Food and Agricultural Organization of the United Nations (FAO) Via delle Terme di Caracalla, 00100 Rome, Italy (Telephone Number in U.S. (202) 653-2400); *The State of Food and Agriculture.*

SURINAME - SUGAR PRODUCTION AND CONSUMPTION - See SURINAME - CROPS

SURINAME - TAXATION

Europa Publications Limited, 18 Bedford Square, London, WC1B 3JN, England; *The Europa World Year Book.*

Inter-American Development Bank, 1300 New York Avenue, NW, Washington,

D.C. 20577 (202) 623-1753; *Economic and Social Progress in Latin America.*

International Monetary Fund, 700 Nineteenth Street, NW, Washington, D.C. 20431 (202) 623-7000; *Government Finance Statistics Yearbook.*

The World Bank, 1818 H Street, NW, Washington, D.C. 20433 (202) 477-1234; *World Development Indicators.*

SURINAME - TELEGRAPH SERVICE

Statistical Office of the United Nations, Publishing Service, New York, New York 10017 (800) 253-9646; *Statistical Yearbook.*

SURINAME - TELEPHONES IN USE

American Telephone and Telegraph Company, 26 Parsippany Road, Whippany, New Jersey 07981 (800) 222-0300; *The World's Telephones.*

Central Intelligence Agency, Washington, D.C. 20505 (703) 482-1100, www.cia.gov; *The World Factbook.*

Europa Publications Limited, 18 Bedford Square, London, WC1B 3JN, England; *The Europa World Year Book.*

St. Martin's Press, Inc., 175 Fifth Avenue, New York, New York 10010 (800) 221-7945; *The Statesman's Year-Book.*

Statistical Office of the United Nations, Publishing Service, New York, New York 10017 (800) 253-9646; *Statistical Yearbook;* and *World Statistics Pocketbook.*

SURINAME - TELEVISION BROADCASTING

M.E. Sharpe, 80 Business Park Drive, Armonk, New York 10504 (800) 541-6563; *The Illustrated Book of World Rankings.*

SURINAME - TEXTILE INDUSTRY

M.E. Sharpe, 80 Business Park Drive, Armonk, New York 10504 (800) 541-6563; *The Illustrated Book of World Rankings.*

United Nations Conference on Trade and Development, Central Statistical Service, Palais des Nations, Geneva, Switzerland (Telephone in U.S. (800) 253-9646); *UNCTAD Commodity Yearbook.*

SURINAME - TOBACCO PRODUCTION

M.E. Sharpe, 80 Business Park Drive, Armonk, New York 10504 (800) 541-6563; *The Illustrated Book of World Rankings.*

Statistical Office of the United Nations, Publishing Service, New York, New York 10017 (800) 253-9646; *Statistical Yearbook.*

U.C.L.A. Latin American Center Publications, University of California, Los Angeles, California 90024 (310) 825-6634; *Statistical Abstract of Latin America.*

SURINAME - TOURISM

Euromonitor International, Inc., 122 Michigan Avenue, Suite 1200, Chicago, Illinois 60603 (800) 577-EURO; *The World Economic Factbook;* and *World Marketing Data and Statistics.*

Europa Publications Limited, 18 Bedford Square, London, WC1B 3JN, England; *The Europa World Year Book.*

M.E. Sharpe, 80 Business Park Drive, Armonk, New York 10504 (800) 541-6563; *The Illustrated Book of World Rankings.*

St. Martin's Press, Inc., 175 Fifth Avenue, New York, New York 10010 (800) 221-7945; *The Statesman's Year-Book.*

Statistical Office of the United Nations, Publishing Service, New York, New York 10017 (800) 253-9646; *Statistical Yearbook.*

World Tourism Organization, Calle Capitan Haya 42, E-28020 Madrid, Spain; *Yearbook of Tourism Statistics.*

SURINAME - TRACTORS IN USE

Statistical Office of the United Nations, Publishing Service, New York, New York 10017 (800) 253-9646; *Statistical Yearbook.*

SURINAME - TRADE - See SURINAME - FOREIGN TRADE

SURINAME - TRADEMARKS AND SERVICE MARKS - See SURINAME - PATENTS, TRADEMARKS AND SERVICE MARKS

SURINAME - TRANSPORTATION AND COMMUNICATIONS

Central Intelligence Agency, Washington, D.C. 20505 (703) 482-1100, www.cia.gov; *The World Factbook.*

Euromonitor International, Inc., 122 Michigan Avenue, Suite 1200, Chicago, Illinois 60603 (800) 577-EURO; *International Marketing Data and Statistics;* and *World Marketing Data and Statistics.*

Europa Publications Limited, 18 Bedford Square, London, WC1B 3JN, England; *The Europa World Year Book.*

Inter-American Development Bank, 1300 New York Avenue, NW, Washington, D.C. 20577 (202) 623-1753; *Economic and Social Progress in Latin America.*

M.E. Sharpe, 80 Business Park Drive, Armonk, New York 10504 (800) 541-6563;

The Illustrated Book of World Rankings.

St. Martin's Press, Inc., 175 Fifth Avenue, New York, New York 10010 (800) 221-7945; *The Statesman's Year-Book.*

Statistical Office of the United Nations, Publishing Service, New York, New York 10017 (800) 253-9646; *Human Development Report.*

SURINAME - UNEMPLOYMENT

Central Intelligence Agency, Washington, D.C. 20505 (703) 482-1100, www.cia.gov; *The World Factbook.*

International Labour Office, I.L.O. Publications, 1828 L Street, NW, Suite 801, Washington, D.C. 20036 (301) 638-3152; *Yearbook of Labour Statistics.*

Statistical Office of the United Nations, Publishing Service, New York, New York 10017 (800) 253-9646; *Statistical Yearbook.*

SURINAME - VITAL STATISTICS

Statistical Office of the United Nations, Publishing Service, New York, New York 10017 (800) 253-9646; *Statistical Yearbook.*

World Health Organization, Office of Publications, 20 Avenue Appia, CH-1211 Geneva 27, Switzerland (Telephone Number in U.S. (518) 436-9686); *World Health Statistics Annual.*

SURINAME - WAGES

International Labour Office, I.L.O. Publications, 1828 L Street, NW, Suite 801, Washington, D.C. 20036 (301) 638-3152; *Yearbook of Labour Statistics.*

Statistical Office of the United Nations, Publishing Service, New York, New York 10017 (800) 253-9646; *Statistical Yearbook.*

SURINAME - WEATHER - See SURINAME - CLIMATE

SURINAME - WELFARE

Inter-American Development Bank, 1300 New York Avenue, NW, Washington, D.C. 20577 (202) 623-1753; *Economic and Social Progress in Latin America.*

International Monetary Fund, 700 Nineteenth Street, NW, Washington, D.C. 20431 (202) 623-7000; *Government Finance Statistics Yearbook.*

SURINAME - WHEAT PRODUCTION AND PRICES - See SURINAME - CROPS

SURINAME - WHOLESALE PRICES

Inter-American Development Bank, 1300 New York Avenue, NW, Washington,

D.C. 20577 (202) 623-1753; *Economic and Social Progress in Latin America.*

SURINAME - WHOLESALE TRADE

Inter-American Development Bank, 1300 New York Avenue, NW, Washington, D.C. 20577 (202) 623-1753; *Economic and Social Progress in Latin America.*

SURINAME - WINE PRODUCTION - See SURINAME - BEVERAGES

SURINAME - WOOD PULP PRODUCTION - See SURINAME - FORESTRY AND FOREST PRODUCTS

SURINAME - WOOL PRODUCTION - See SURINAME - TEXTILE

SVALBARD AND JAN MAYEN ISLANDS - AIRPORTS

Central Intelligence Agency, Washington, D.C. 20505 (703) 482-1100, www.cia.gov; *The World Factbook.*

SVALBARD AND JAN MAYEN ISLANDS - AREA AND DENSITY OF POPULATION

Central Intelligence Agency, Washington, D.C. 20505 (703) 482-1100, www.cia.gov; *The World Factbook.*

Europa Publications Limited, 18 Bedford Square, London, WC1B 3JN, England; *The Europa World Year Book.*

SVALBARD AND JAN MAYEN ISLANDS - BIRTH RATES

Central Intelligence Agency, Washington, D.C. 20505 (703) 482-1100, www.cia.gov; *The World Factbook.*

SVALBARD AND JAN MAYEN ISLANDS - BROADCASTING

Central Intelligence Agency, Washington, D.C. 20505 (703) 482-1100, www.cia.gov; *The World Factbook.*

SVALBARD AND JAN MAYEN ISLANDS - BUDGET

Central Intelligence Agency, Washington, D.C. 20505 (703) 482-1100, www.cia.gov; *The World Factbook.*

SVALBARD AND JAN MAYEN ISLANDS - ECONOMY

Central Intelligence Agency, Washington, D.C. 20505 (703) 482-1100, www.cia.gov; *The World Factbook.*

SVALBARD AND JAN MAYEN ISLANDS - ELECTRICITY

Central Intelligence Agency,

Washington, D.C. 20505 (703) 482-1100, www.cia.gov; *The World Factbook.*

SVALBARD AND JAN MAYEN ISLANDS - EXCHANGE RATES

Central Intelligence Agency, Washington, D.C. 20505 (703) 482-1100, www.cia.gov; *The World Factbook.*

SVALBARD AND JAN MAYEN ISLANDS - EXPORTS

Central Intelligence Agency, Washington, D.C. 20505 (703) 482-1100, www.cia.gov; *The World Factbook.*

SVALBARD AND JAN MAYEN ISLANDS - FERTILITY RATES

Central Intelligence Agency, Washington, D.C. 20505 (703) 482-1100, www.cia.gov; *The World Factbook.*

SVALBARD AND JAN MAYEN ISLANDS - FINANCE

Europa Publications Limited, 18 Bedford Square, London, WC1B 3JN, England; *The Europa World Year Book.*

SVALBARD AND JAN MAYEN ISLANDS - FISHERIES

Food and Agricultural Organization of the United Nations (FAO), Via delle Terme di Caracalla, 00100, Rome, Italy (Telephone Number in U.S. (202) 653-2400); *Yearbook of Fishery Statistics.*

SVALBARD AND JAN MAYEN ISLANDS - GOVERNMENT

Central Intelligence Agency, Washington, D.C. 20505 (703) 482-1100, www.cia.gov; *The World Factbook.*

Europa Publications Limited, 18 Bedford Square, London, WC1B 3JN, England; *The Europa World Year Book.*

SVALBARD AND JAN MAYEN ISLANDS - HIGHWAYS

Central Intelligence Agency, Washington, D.C. 20505 (703) 482-1100, www.cia.gov; *The World Factbook.*

SVALBARD AND JAN MAYEN ISLANDS - ILLITERATE POPULATION

Central Intelligence Agency, Washington, D.C. 20505 (703) 482-1100, www.cia.gov; *The World Factbook.*

SVALBARD AND JAN MAYEN ISLANDS - IMPORTS

Central Intelligence Agency, Washington, D.C. 20505 (703) 482-1100, www.cia.gov; *The World Factbook.*

SVALBARD AND JAN MAYEN
ISLANDS - INDUSTRY

Central Intelligence Agency, Washington, D.C. 20505 (703) 482-1100, www.cia.gov; *The World Factbook.*

SVALBARD AND JAN MAYEN
ISLANDS - LABOR

Central Intelligence Agency, Washington, D.C. 20505 (703) 482-1100, www.cia.gov; *The World Factbook.*

SVALBARD AND JAN MAYEN
ISLANDS - LAND USE

Central Intelligence Agency, Washington, D.C. 20505 (703) 482-1100, www.cia.gov; *The World Factbook.*

SVALBARD AND JAN MAYEN
ISLANDS - LIFE EXPECTANCY

Central Intelligence Agency, Washington, D.C. 20505 (703) 482-1100, www.cia.gov; *The World Factbook.*

SVALBARD AND JAN MAYEN
ISLANDS - MILITARY

Central Intelligence Agency, Washington, D.C. 20505 (703) 482-1100, www.cia.gov; *The World Factbook.*

SVALBARD AND JAN MAYEN
ISLANDS - MINING AND MINERAL
PRODUCTS

Europa Publications Limited, 18 Bedford Square, London, WC1B 3JN, England; *The Europa World Year Book.*

SVALBARD AND JAN MAYEN
ISLANDS - MORTALITY

Central Intelligence Agency, Washington, D.C. 20505 (703) 482-1100, www.cia.gov; *The World Factbook.*

SVALBARD AND JAN MAYEN
ISLANDS - POPULATION

Central Intelligence Agency, Washington, D.C. 20505 (703) 482-1100, www.cia.gov; *The World Factbook.*

Europa Publications Limited, 18 Bedford Square, London, WC1B 3JN, England; *The Europa World Year Book.*

Statistical Office of the United Nations, Publishing Service, New York, New York 10017 (800) 253-9646; *Statistical Yearbook.*

World Health Organization, Office of Publications, 20 Avenue Appia, CH-1211 Geneva 27, Switzerland (Telephone Number in U.S. (518) 436-9686); *World Health Statistics Annual.*

SVALBARD AND JAN MAYEN
ISLANDS - RELIGION

Central Intelligence Agency, Washington, D.C. 20505 (703) 482-1100, www.cia.gov; *The World Factbook.*

SVALBARD AND JAN MAYEN
ISLANDS - TELEPHONES IN USE

Central Intelligence Agency, Washington, D.C. 20505 (703) 482-1100, www.cia.gov; *The World Factbook.*

SVALBARD AND JAN MAYEN
ISLANDS - TOURISM

Europa Publications Limited, 18 Bedford Square, London, WC1B 3JN, England; *The Europa World Year Book.*

SVALBARD AND JAN MAYEN
ISLANDS - TRANSPORTATION AND
COMMUNICATIONS

Central Intelligence Agency, Washington, D.C. 20505 (703) 482-1100, www.cia.gov; *The World Factbook.*

SVALBARD AND JAN MAYEN
ISLANDS - UNEMPLOYMENT RATE

Central Intelligence Agency, Washington, D.C. 20505 (703) 482-1100, www.cia.gov; *The World Factbook.*

SVALBARD AND JAN MAYEN
ISLANDS - VITAL STATISTICS

World Health Organization, Office of Publications, 20 Avenue Appia, CH-1211 Geneva 27, Switzerland (Telephone Number in U.S. (518) 436-9686); *World Health Statistics Annual.*

Swaziland - National Statistical Office

Central Statistical Office, Post Office Box 456, Mbabane, Swaziland.

Swaziland - Primary Statistics Source

Central Statistical Office, Post Office Box 456, Mbabane, Swaziland; *Annual Statistical Bulletin;* and *Quarterly Digest of Statistics.*

SWAZILAND - AGRICULTURE

Economist Intelligence Unit, 111 West 57th Street, New York, New York 10019 (800) 938-4685; *Swaziland Country Report.*

Euromonitor International, Inc., 122 South Michigan Avenue, Suite 1200, Chicago, Illinois 60603 (800) 577-EURO; *World Marketing Data and Statistics.*

Europa Publications Limited, 18 Bedford Square, London, WC1B 3JN, England; *The Europa World Year Book.*

Food and Agricultural Organization of the United Nations (FAO) Via delle Terme di Caracalla, 00100 Rome, Italy (Telephone Number in U.S. (202) 653-2400); *Production Yearbook; The State of Food and Agriculture;* and *Trade Yearbook.*

M.E. Sharpe, 80 Business Park Drive, Armonk, New York 10504 (800) 541-6563; *The Illustrated Book of World Rankings.*

St. Martin's Press, Inc., 175 Fifth Avenue, New York, New York 10010 (800) 221-7945; *The Statesman's Year-Book.*

Statistical Office of the United Nations, Publishing Service, New York, New York 10017 (800) 253-9646; *Statistical Yearbook;* and *Survey of Economic and Social Conditions in Africa.*

United Nations Conference on Trade and Development, Central Statistical Service, Palais des Nations, Geneva, Switzerland (Telephone in U.S. (800) 253-9646); *UNCTAD Commodity Yearbook.*

United Nations Economic Commission for Africa, Africa Hall, P.O. Box 3001, Addis Ababa, Ethiopia (Telephone Number in U.S. (800) 253-9646); *African Statistical Yearbook.*

The World Bank, 1818 H Street, NW, Washington, D.C. 20433 (202) 477-1234; *World Development Indicators.*

SWAZILAND - AIRLINE SERVICE

Europa Publications Limited, 18 Bedford Square, London, WC1B 3JN, England; *The Europa World Year Book.*

M.E. Sharpe, 80 Business Park Drive, Armonk, New York 10504 (800) 541-6563; *The Illustrated Book of World Rankings.*

St. Martin's Press, Inc., 175 Fifth Avenue, New York, New York 10010 (800) 221-7945; *The Statesman's Year-Book.*

United Nations Economic Commission for Africa, Africa Hall, P.O. Box 3001, Addis Ababa, Ethiopia (Telephone Number in U.S. (800) 253-9646); *African Statistical Yearbook.*

SWAZILAND - AIRPORTS

Central Intelligence Agency, Washington, D.C. 20505 (703) 482-1100, www.cia.gov; *The World Factbook.*

SWAZILAND - ALUMINUM PRODUCTION AND CONSUMPTION - See SWAZILAND - MINING AND MINERAL PRODUCTS

SWAZILAND - ANIMAL HEALTH

Food and Agricultural Organization of the United Nations (FAO), Via delle Terme di Caracalla, 00100, Rome, Italy (Telephone Number in U.S. (202) 653-2400); *Animal Health Yearbook.*

SWAZILAND - AREA AND DENSITY OF POPULATION

African Development Bank, 01 BP 1387, Abidjan 01, Cote D'Ivoire; *Selected Statistics on Regional Member Countries.*

Central Intelligence Agency, Washington, D.C. 20505 (703) 482-1100, www.cia.gov; *The World Factbook.*

Euromonitor International, Inc., 122 Michigan Avenue, Suite 1200, Chicago, Illinois 60603 (800) 577-EURO; *The World Economic Factbook.*

Europa Publications Limited, 18 Bedford Square, London, WC1B 3JN, England; *The Europa World Year Book.*

Food and Agricultural Organization of the United Nations (FAO) Via delle Terme di Caracalla, 00100 Rome, Italy (Telephone Number in U.S. (202) 653-2400); *The State of Food and Agriculture.*

M.E. Sharpe, 80 Business Park Drive, Armonk, New York 10504 (800) 541-6563; *The Illustrated Book of World Rankings.*

St. Martin's Press, Inc., 175 Fifth Avenue, New York, New York 10010 (800) 221-7945; *The Statesman's Year-Book.*

Statistical Office of the United Nations, Publishing Service, New York, New York 10017 (800) 253-9646; *Statistical Yearbook;* and *Survey of Economic and Social Conditions in Africa.*

United Nations Educational, Scientific and Cultural Organization (UNESCO), 7 Place de Fontenoy, F-75700 Paris, France (Telephone Number in U.S. (212) 963-5981); *Statistical Yearbook.*

SWAZILAND - ARMS EXPORTS AND IMPORTS - See SWAZILAND - MILITARY

SWAZILAND - BALANCE OF PAYMENTS

African Development Bank, 01 BP 1387, Abidjan 01, Cote D'Ivoire; *Selected Statistics on Regional Member Countries.*

The Economist Intelligence Unit, 111 West 57th Street, New York, New York 10019 (800) 938-4685; *The World Market Atlas.*

Europa Publications Limited, 18 Bedford Square, London, WC1B 3JN, England; *The Europa World Year Book.*

International Monetary Fund, 700 Nineteenth Street, NW, Washington, D.C. 20431 (202) 623-7000; *Balance of Payments Yearbook.*

United Nations Conference on Trade and Development (UNCTAD), New York, New York 10017 (800) 253-9646; *Handbook of International Trade and Development Statistics.*

United Nations Economic Commission for Africa, Africa Hall, P.O. Box 3001, Addis Ababa, Ethiopia (Telephone Number in U.S. (800) 253-9646); *African Statistical Yearbook.*

The World Bank, 1818 H Street, NW, Washington, D.C. 20433 (202) 477-1234; *World Development Indicators.*

SWAZILAND - BANKING

Euromonitor International, Inc., 122 South Michigan Avenue, Suite 1200, Chicago, Illinois 60603 (800) 577-EURO; *World Marketing Data and Statistics.*

Europa Publications Limited, 18 Bedford Square, London, WC1B 3JN, England; *The Europa World Year Book.*

International Monetary Fund, 700 Nineteenth Street, NW, Washington, D.C. 20431 (202) 623-7000; *Government Finance Statistics Yearbook;* and *International Financial Statistics.*

M.E. Sharpe, 80 Business Park Drive, Armonk, New York 10504 (800) 541-6563; *The Illustrated Book of World Rankings.*

St. Martin's Press, Inc., 175 Fifth Avenue, New York, New York 10010 (800) 221-7945; *The Statesman's Year-Book.*

United Nations Economic Commission for Africa, Africa Hall, P.O. Box 3001, Addis Ababa, Ethiopia (Telephone Number in U.S. (800) 253-9646); *African Statistical Yearbook.*

SWAZILAND - BARLEY PRODUCTION - See SWAZILAND - CROPS

SWAZILAND - BEER PRODUCTION - See SWAZILAND - BEVERAGES

SWAZILAND - BEVERAGES

M.E. Sharpe, 80 Business Park Drive, Armonk, New York 10504 (800) 541-6563; *The Illustrated Book of World Rankings.*

SWAZILAND - BIRTH RATES

Central Intelligence Agency, Washington, D.C. 20505 (703) 482-1100, www.cia.gov; *The World Factbook.*

Euromonitor International, Inc., 122

Michigan Avenue, Suite 1200, Chicago, Illinois 60603 (800) 577-EURO; *International Marketing Data and Statistics;* and *The World Economic Factbook.*

Europa Publications Limited, 18 Bedford Square, London, WC1B 3JN, England; *The Europa World Year Book.*

M.E. Sharpe, 80 Business Park Drive, Armonk, New York 10504 (800) 541-6563; *The Illustrated Book of World Rankings.*

Statistical Office of the United Nations, Publishing Service, New York, New York 10017 (800) 253-9646; *Demographic Yearbook; Statistical Yearbook;* and *Survey of Economic and Social Conditions in Africa.*

The World Bank, 1818 H Street, NW, Washington, D.C. 20433 (202) 477-1234; *World Development Indicators.*

SWAZILAND - BONDS

International Monetary Fund, 700 Nineteenth Street, NW, Washington, D.C. 20431 (202) 623-7000; *Government Finance Statistics Yearbook.*

SWAZILAND - BROADCASTING

Billboard Limited, P.O. Box 9027, 1006 AA Amsterdam, The Netherlands (Telephone Number in U.S. (212) 764-7300); *World Radio TV Handbook.*

Central Intelligence Agency, Washington, D.C. 20505 (703) 482-1100, www.cia.gov; *The World Factbook.*

Euromonitor International, Inc., 122 South Michigan Avenue, Suite 1200, Chicago, Illinois 60603 (800) 577-EURO; *World Marketing Data and Statistics.*

St. Martin's Press, Inc., 175 Fifth Avenue, New York, New York 10010 (800) 221-7945; *The Statesman's Year-Book.*

SWAZILAND - BUDGET

Central Intelligence Agency, Washington, D.C. 20505 (703) 482-1100, www.cia.gov; *The World Factbook.*

SWAZILAND - BUSINESS AND PROFESSIONAL LICENSES

International Monetary Fund, 700 Nineteenth Street, NW, Washington, D.C. 20431 (202) 623-7000; *Government Finance Statistics Yearbook.*

SWAZILAND - CALORIE SUPPLY

African Development Bank, 01 BP 1387, Abidjan 01, Cote D'Ivoire; *Selected Statistics on Regional Member Countries.*

Food and Agricultural Organization of the United Nations (FAO) Via delle Terme di Caracalla, 00100 Rome, Italy (Telephone Number in U.S. (202) 653-2400); *The State of Food and Agriculture.*

SWAZILAND - CAPITAL REVENUE

International Monetary Fund, 700 Nineteenth Street, NW, Washington, D.C. 20431 (202) 623-7000; *Government Finance Statistics Yearbook.*

SWAZILAND - CATTLE - See SWAZILAND - LIVESTOCK AND POULTRY

SWAZILAND - CEMENT PRODUCTION - See SWAZILAND - MINING AND MINERAL PRODUCTS

SWAZILAND - CHEMICAL (ORGANIC) PRODUCTION - See SWAZILAND - MINING AND MINERAL PRODUCTS

SWAZILAND - CHICKENS - See SWAZILAND - LIVESTOCK AND POULTRY

SWAZILAND - CIGARETTE PRODUCTION - See SWAZILAND - TOBACCO PRODUCTION

SWAZILAND - CLIMATE

M.E. Sharpe, 80 Business Park Drive, Armonk, New York 10504 (800) 541-6563; *The Illustrated Book of World Rankings.*

St. Martin's Press, Inc., 175 Fifth Avenue, New York, New York 10010 (800) 221-7945; *The Statesman's Year-Book.*

SWAZILAND - COAL PRODUCTION - See SWAZILAND - MINING AND MINERAL PRODUCTS

SWAZILAND - COFFEE PRODUCTION AND CONSUMPTION - See SWAZILAND -CROPS

SWAZILAND - COMMERCE

St. Martin's Press, Inc., 175 Fifth Avenue, New York, New York 10010 (800) 221-7945; *The Statesman's Year-Book.*

SWAZILAND - COMMUNICATIONS - See SWAZILAND - TRANSPORTATION AND COMMUNICATIONS

SWAZILAND - CONSTRUCTION INDUSTRY

M.E. Sharpe, 80 Business Park Drive, Armonk, New York 10504 (800) 541-6563; *The Illustrated Book of World Rankings.*

Statistical Office of the United Nations, Publishing Service, New York, New York 10017 (800) 253-9646; *Statistical Yearbook.*

United Nations Economic Commission for Africa, Africa Hall, P.O. Box 3001, Addis Ababa, Ethiopia (Telephone Number in

U.S. (800) 253-9646); *African Statistical Yearbook.*

SWAZILAND - CONSUMER PRICE INDEX

African Development Bank, 01 BP 1387, Abidjan 01, Cote D'Ivoire; *Selected Statistics on Regional Member Countries.*

Statistical Office of the United Nations, Publishing Service, New York, New York 10017 (800) 253-9646; *Statistical Yearbook;* and *Survey of Economic and Social Conditions in Africa.*

United Nations Economic Commission for Africa, Africa Hall, P.O. Box 3001, Addis Ababa, Ethiopia (Telephone Number in U.S. (800) 253-9646); *African Statistical Yearbook.*

SWAZILAND - CONSUMER PRICES

Euromonitor International, Inc., 122 South Michigan Avenue, Suite 1200, Chicago, Illinois 60603 (800) 577-EURO; *World Marketing Data and Statistics.*

International Labour Office, I.L.O. Publications, 1828 L Street, NW, Suite 801, Washington, D.C. 20036 (301) 638-3152; *Yearbook of Labour Statistics.*

International Monetary Fund, 700 Nineteenth Street, NW, Washington, D.C. 20431 (202) 623-7000; *International Financial Statistics.*

SWAZILAND - CONSUMPTION

African Development Bank, 01 BP 1387, Abidjan 01, Cote D'Ivoire; *Selected Statistics on Regional Member Countries.*

Statistical Office of the United Nations, Publishing Service, New York, New York 10017 (800) 253-9646; *Survey of Economic and Social Conditions in Africa.*

SWAZILAND - COPPER PRODUCTION AND CONSUMPTION - See SWAZILAND -MINING AND MINERAL PRODUCTS

SWAZILAND - CORN PRODUCTION - See SWAZILAND - CROPS

SWAZILAND - CORPORATE TAXES - See SWAZILAND - TAXATION

SWAZILAND - COTTON PRODUCTION - See SWAZILAND - CROPS

SWAZILAND - CRIME

Yale University Press, Yale Station, New Haven, Connecticut 06520 (800) 987-7323; *Violence and Crime in Cross-National Perspective.*

SWAZILAND - CROPS

Europa Publications Limited, 18 Bedford Square, London, WC1B 3JN, England; *The Europa World Year Book.*

Food and Agricultural Organization of the United Nations (FAO) Via delle Terme di Caracalla, 00100 Rome, Italy (Telephone Number in U.S. (202) 653-2400); *The State of Food and Agriculture.*

International Monetary Fund, 700 Nineteenth Street, NW, Washington, D.C. 20431 (202) 623-7000; *International Financial Statistics.*

M.E. Sharpe, 80 Business Park Drive, Armonk, New York 10504 (800) 541-6563; *The Illustrated Book of World Rankings.*

St. Martin's Press, Inc., 175 Fifth Avenue, New York, New York 10010 (800) 221-7945; *The Statesman's Year-Book.*

Statistical Office of the United Nations, Publishing Service, New York, New York 10017 (800) 253-9646; *Statistical Yearbook.*

United Nations Conference on Trade and Development, Central Statistical Service, Palais des Nations, Geneva, Switzerland (Telephone in U.S. (800) 253-9646); *UNCTAD Commodity Yearbook.*

United Nations Economic Commission for Africa, Africa Hall, P.O. Box 3001, Addis Ababa, Ethiopia (Telephone Number in U.S. (800) 253-9646); *African Statistical Yearbook.*

SWAZILAND - CUSTOMS DUTIES

International Monetary Fund, 700 Nineteenth Street, NW, Washington, D.C. 20431 (202) 623-7000; *Government Finance Statistics Yearbook.*

St. Martin's Press, Inc., 175 Fifth Avenue, New York, New York 10010 (800) 221-7945; *The Statesman's Year-Book.*

SWAZILAND - DAIRY PRODUCTS

Europa Publications Limited, 18 Bedford Square, London, WC1B 3JN, England; *The Europa World Year Book.*

Food and Agricultural Organization of the United Nations (FAO) Via delle Terme di Caracalla, 00100 Rome, Italy (Telephone Number in U.S. (202) 653-2400); *The State of Food and Agriculture.*

M.E. Sharpe, 80 Business Park Drive, Armonk, New York 10504 (800) 541-6563; *The Illustrated Book of World Rankings.*

St. Martin's Press, Inc., 175 Fifth Avenue, New York, New York 10010 (800) 221-7945; *The Statesman's Year-Book.*

SWAZILAND - DEATH RATES - See

SWAZILAND - MORTALITY

SWAZILAND - DEFENSE
EXPENDITURES - See SWAZILAND - MILITARY

SWAZILAND - DEMOGRAPHY

The Economist Intelligence Unit, 111 West 57th Street, New York, New York 10019 (800) 938-4685; *The World Market Atlas.*

Euromonitor International, Inc., 122 Michigan Avenue, Suite 1200, Chicago, Illinois 60603 (800) 577-EURO; *International Marketing Data and Statistics; World Marketing Data and Statistics;* and *The World Economic Factbook.*

M.E. Sharpe, 80 Business Park Drive, Armonk, New York 10504 (800) 541-6563; *The Illustrated Book of World Rankings.*

Statistical Office of the United Nations, Publishing Service, New York, New York 10017 (800) 253-9646; *Human Development Report;* and *Survey of Economic and Social Conditions in Africa.*

SWAZILAND - DEVELOPMENT ASSISTANCE

Statistical Office of the United Nations, Publishing Service, New York, New York 10017 (800) 253-9646; *Statistical Yearbook.*

SWAZILAND - DIAMOND PRODUCTION - See SWAZILAND - MINING AND MINERAL PRODUCTS

SWAZILAND - DISEASES - See SWAZILAND - HEALTH

SWAZILAND - DIVORCE RATES

M.E. Sharpe, 80 Business Park Drive, Armonk, New York 10504 (800) 541-6563; *The Illustrated Book of World Rankings.*

Statistical Office of the United Nations, Publishing Service, New York, New York 10017 (800) 253-9646; *Demographic Yearbook.*

SWAZILAND - ECONOMY

African Development Bank, 01 BP 1387, Abidjan 01, Cote D'Ivoire; *Selected Statistics on Regional Member Countries.*

Central Intelligence Agency, Washington, D.C. 20505 (703) 482-1100, www.cia.gov; *The World Factbook.*

Economist Intelligence Unit, 111 West 57th Street, New York, New York 10019 (800) 938-4685; *Swaziland Country Report.*

Euromonitor International, Inc., 122 Michigan Avenue, Suite 1200, Chicago,

Illinois 60603 (800) 577-EURO; *The World Economic Factbook;* and *World Marketing Data and Statistics.*

M.E. Sharpe, 80 Business Park Drive, Armonk, New York 10504 (800) 541-6563; *The Illustrated Book of World Rankings.*

St. Martin's Press, Inc., 175 Fifth Avenue, New York, New York 10010 (800) 221-7945; *The Statesman's Year-Book.*

Statistical Office of the United Nations, Publishing Service, New York, New York 10017 (800) 253-9646; *World Statistics Pocketbook.*

The World Bank, 1818 H Street, NW, Washington, D.C. 20433 (202) 477-1234; *The World Bank Atlas.*

SWAZILAND - EDUCATION

African Development Bank, 01 BP 1387, Abidjan 01, Cote D'Ivoire; *Selected Statistics on Regional Member Countries.*

The Economist Intelligence Unit, 111 West 57th Street, New York, New York 10019 (800) 938-4685; *The World Market Atlas.*

Euromonitor International, Inc., 122 Michigan Avenue, Suite 1200, Chicago, Illinois 60603 (800) 577-EURO; *International Marketing Data and Statistics;* and *World Marketing Data and Statistics.*

Europa Publications Limited, 18 Bedford Square, London, WC1B 3JN, England; *The Europa World Year Book.*

International Monetary Fund, 700 Nineteenth Street, NW, Washington, D.C. 20431 (202) 623-7000; *Government Finance Statistics Yearbook.*

M.E. Sharpe, 80 Business Park Drive, Armonk, New York 10504 (800) 541-6563; *The Illustrated Book of World Rankings.*

St. Martin's Press, Inc., 175 Fifth Avenue, New York, New York 10010 (800) 221-7945; *The Statesman's Year-Book.*

Statistical Office of the United Nations, Publishing Service, New York, New York 10017 (800) 253-9646; *Human Development Report;* and *Survey of Economic and Social Conditions in Africa.*

United Nations Economic Commission for Africa, Africa Hall, P.O. Box 3001, Addis Ababa, Ethiopia (Telephone Number in U.S. (800) 253-9646); *African Statistical Yearbook.*

United Nations Educational, Scientific and Cultural Organization (UNESCO), 7 Place de Fontenoy, F-75700 Paris, France (Telephone Number in U.S. (212) 963-

5981); *Statistical Yearbook.*

The World Bank, 1818 H Street, NW, Washington, D.C. 20433 (202) 477-1234; *World Development Indicators.*

SWAZILAND - EGG PRODUCTION AND CONSUMPTION - See SWAZILAND - DAIRY PRODUCTS

SWAZILAND - ELECTRICITY

Central Intelligence Agency, Washington, D.C. 20505 (703) 482-1100, www.cia.gov; *The World Factbook.*

M.E. Sharpe, 80 Business Park Drive, Armonk, New York 10504 (800) 541-6563; *The Illustrated Book of World Rankings.*

St. Martin's Press, Inc., 175 Fifth Avenue, New York, New York 10010 (800) 221-7945; *The Statesman's Year-Book.*

Statistical Office of the United Nations, Publishing Service, New York, New York 10017 (800) 253-9646; *Human Development Report;* and *Survey of Economic and Social Conditions in Africa.*

United Nations Economic Commission for Africa, Africa Hall, P.O. Box 3001, Addis Ababa, Ethiopia (Telephone Number in U.S. (800) 253-9646); *African Statistical Yearbook.*

SWAZILAND - EMPLOYMENT

Euromonitor International, Inc., 122 Michigan Avenue, Suite 1200, Chicago, Illinois 60603 (800) 577-EURO; *International Marketing Data and Statistics.*

International Labour Office, I.L.O. Publications, 1828 L Street, NW, Suite 801, Washington, D.C. 20036 (301) 638-3152; *Yearbook of Labour Statistics.*

M.E. Sharpe, 80 Business Park Drive, Armonk, New York 10504 (800) 541-6563; *The Illustrated Book of World Rankings.*

Statistical Office of the United Nations, Publishing Service, New York, New York 10017 (800) 253-9646; *Statistical Yearbook;* and *Survey of Economic and Social Conditions in Africa.*

United Nations Economic Commission for Africa, Africa Hall, P.O. Box 3001, Addis Ababa, Ethiopia (Telephone Number in U.S. (800) 253-9646); *African Statistical Yearbook.*

SWAZILAND - ENERGY

Euromonitor International, Inc., 122 Michigan Avenue, Suite 1200, Chicago, Illinois 60603 (800) 577-EURO; *International Marketing Data and Statistics; World Marketing Data and Statistics;* and

The World Economic Factbook.

Food and Agricultural Organization of the United Nations (FAO) Via delle Terme di Caracalla, 00100 Rome, Italy (Telephone Number in U.S. (202) 653-2400); *The State of Food and Agriculture.*

M.E. Sharpe, 80 Business Park Drive, Armonk, New York 10504 (800) 541-6563; *The Illustrated Book of World Rankings.*

St. Martin's Press, Inc., 175 Fifth Avenue, New York, New York 10010 (800) 221-7945; *The Statesman's Year-Book.*

Statistical Office of the United Nations, Publishing Service, New York, New York 10017 (800) 253-9646; *Energy Statistics Yearbook; Human Development Report; Statistical Yearbook;* and *World Statistics Pocketbook.*

United Nations Economic Commission for Africa, Africa Hall, P.O. Box 3001, Addis Ababa, Ethiopia (Telephone Number in U.S. (800) 253-9646); *African Statistical Yearbook.*

The World Bank, 1818 H Street, NW, Washington, D.C. 20433 (202) 477-1234; *The World Bank Atlas.*

SWAZILAND - ENVIRONMENT

Economist Intelligence Unit, 111 West 57th Street, New York, New York 10019 (800) 938-4685; *Swaziland Country Report.*

Statistical Office of the United Nations, Publishing Service, New York, New York 10017 (800) 253-9646; *World Statistics Pocketbook.*

SWAZILAND - EXCHANGE RATES

Central Intelligence Agency, Washington, D.C. 20505 (703) 482-1100, www.cia.gov; *The World Factbook.*

Euromonitor International, Inc., 122 Michigan Avenue, Suite 1200, Chicago, Illinois 60603 (800) 577-EURO; *International Marketing Data and Statistics;* and *The World Economic Factbook.*

Europa Publications Limited, 18 Bedford Square, London, WC1B 3JN, England; *The Europa World Year Book.*

International Monetary Fund, 700 Nineteenth Street, NW, Washington, D.C. 20431 (202) 623-7000; *International Financial Statistics.*

Statistical Office of the United Nations, Publishing Service, New York, New York 10017 (800) 253-9646; *Statistical Yearbook;* and *World Statistics Pocketbook.*

SWAZILAND - EXCISE TAXES - See

SWAZILAND - TAXATION

SWAZILAND - EXPORTS

African Development Bank, 01 BP 1387, Abidjan 01, Cote D'Ivoire; *Selected Statistics on Regional Member Countries.*

Central Intelligence Agency, Washington, D.C. 20505 (703) 482-1100, www.cia.gov; *The World Factbook.*

The Economist Intelligence Unit, 111 West 57th Street, New York, New York 10019 (800) 938-4685; *Swaziland Country Report;* and *The World Market Atlas.*

Euromonitor International, Inc., 122 Michigan Avenue, Suite 1200, Chicago, Illinois 60603 (800) 577-EURO; *International Marketing Data and Statistics;* and *The World Economic Factbook.*

Europa Publications Limited, 18 Bedford Square, London, WC1B 3JN, England; *The Europa World Year Book.*

Food and Agricultural Organization of the United Nations (FAO) Via delle Terme di Caracalla, 00100 Rome, Italy (Telephone Number in U.S. (202) 653-2400); *The State of Food and Agriculture.*

International Monetary Fund, 700 Nineteenth Street, NW, Washington, D.C. 20431 (202) 623-7000; *Direction of Trade Statistics; Government Finance Statistics Yearbook;* and *International Financial Statistics.*

St. Martin's Press, Inc., 175 Fifth Avenue, New York, New York 10010 (800) 221-7945; *The Statesman's Year-Book.*

Statistical Office of the United Nations, Publishing Service, New York, New York 10017 (800) 253-9646; *Survey of Economic and Social Conditions in Africa.*

United Nations Conference on Trade and Development (UNCTAD), New York, New York 10017 (800) 253-9646; *Handbook of International Trade and Development Statistics.*

United Nations Economic Commission for Africa, Africa Hall, P.O. Box 3001, Addis Ababa, Ethiopia (Telephone Number in U.S. (800) 253-9646); *African Statistical Yearbook.*

The World Bank, 1818 H Street, NW, Washington, D.C. 20433 (202) 477-1234; *World Development Indicators.*

SWAZILAND - EXTERNAL INDEBTEDNESS

African Development Bank, 01 BP 1387, Abidjan 01, Cote D'Ivoire; *Selected Statistics on Regional Member Countries.*

Statistical Office of the United Nations, Publishing Service, New York, New York 10017 (800) 253-9646; *Survey of Economic and Social Conditions in Africa.*

The World Bank, 1818 H Street, NW, Washington, D.C. 20433 (202) 477-1234; *World Development Indicators.*

SWAZILAND - EXTERNAL TRADE

Euromonitor International, Inc., 122 South Michigan Avenue, Suite 1200, Chicago, Illinois 60603 (800) 577-EURO; *World Marketing Data and Statistics.*

Food and Agricultural Organization of the United Nations (FAO) Via delle Terme di Caracalla, 00100 Rome, Italy (Telephone Number in U.S. (202) 653-2400); *The State of Food and Agriculture;* and *Trade Yearbook.*

Statistical Office of the United Nations, Publishing Service, New York, New York 10017 (800) 253-9646; *Survey of Economic and Social Conditions in Africa.*

SWAZILAND - FARM CROPS - See SWAZILAND - CROPS

SWAZILAND - FERTILITY RATES

Central Intelligence Agency, Washington, D.C. 20505 (703) 482-1100, www.cia.gov; *The World Factbook.*

M.E. Sharpe, 80 Business Park Drive, Armonk, New York 10504 (800) 541-6563; *The Illustrated Book of World Rankings.*

Statistical Office of the United Nations, Publishing Service, New York, New York 10017 (800) 253-9646; *Human Development Report;* and *Survey of Economic and Social Conditions in Africa.*

The World Bank, 1818 H Street, NW, Washington, D.C. 20433 (202) 477-1234; *The World Bank Atlas;* and *World Development Indicators.*

SWAZILAND - FERTILIZER

Food and Agricultural Organization of the United Nations (FAO), Via delle Terme di Caracalla, 00100, Rome, Italy (Telephone Number in U.S. (202) 653-2400); *Fertilizer Yearbook;* and *The State of Food and Agriculture.*

Statistical Office of the United Nations, Publishing Service, New York, New York 10017 (800) 253-9646; *Statistical Yearbook.*

SWAZILAND - FETAL MORTALITY - See SWAZILAND - MORTALITY

SWAZILAND - FIBRE PRODUCTION - See SWAZILAND - TEXTILE INDUSTRY

SWAZILAND - FINANCE

African Development Bank, 01 BP 1387, Abidjan 01, Cote D'Ivoire; *Selected Statistics on Regional Member Countries.*

Economist Intelligence Unit, 111 West 57th Street, New York, New York 10019 (800) 938-4685; *Swaziland Country Report.*

Europa Publications Limited, 18 Bedford Square, London, WC1B 3JN, England; *The Europa World Year Book.*

International Monetary Fund, 700 Nineteenth Street, NW, Washington, D.C. 20431 (202) 623-7000; *Government Finance Statistics Yearbook;* and *International Financial Statistics.*

M.E. Sharpe, 80 Business Park Drive, Armonk, New York 10504 (800) 541-6563; *The Illustrated Book of World Rankings.*

St. Martin's Press, Inc., 175 Fifth Avenue, New York, New York 10010 (800) 221-7945; *The Statesman's Year-Book.*

United Nations Economic Commission for Africa, Africa Hall, P.O. Box 3001, Addis Ababa, Ethiopia (Telephone Number in U.S. (800) 253-9646); *African Statistical Yearbook.*

SWAZILAND - FISHERIES

Food and Agricultural Organization of the United Nations (FAO) Via delle Terme di Caracalla, 00100 Rome, Italy (Telephone Number in U.S. (202) 653-2400); *The State of Food and Agriculture;* and *Yearbook of Fishery Statistics.*

M.E. Sharpe, 80 Business Park Drive, Armonk, New York 10504 (800) 541-6563; *The Illustrated Book of World Rankings.*

United Nations Conference on Trade and Development, Central Statistical Service, Palais des Nations, Geneva, Switzerland (Telephone in U.S. (800) 253-9646); *UNCTAD Commodity Yearbook.*

United Nations Economic Commission for Africa, Africa Hall, P.O. Box 3001, Addis Ababa, Ethiopia (Telephone Number in U.S. (800) 253-9646); *African Statistical Yearbook.*

SWAZILAND - FOOD

African Development Bank, 01 BP 1387, Abidjan 01, Cote D'Ivoire; *Selected Statistics on Regional Member Countries.*

Food and Agricultural Organization of the United Nations (FAO) Via delle Terme di Caracalla, 00100 Rome, Italy (Telephone Number in U.S. (202) 653-2400); *Production Yearbook;* and *The State of Food and Agriculture.*

Statistical Office of the United Nations, Publishing Service, New York, New York 10017 (800) 253-9646; *Human Development Report.*

United Nations Conference on Trade and Development, Central Statistical Service, Palais des Nations, Geneva, Switzerland (Telephone in U.S. (800) 253-9646); *UNCTAD Commodity Yearbook.*

SWAZILAND - FOREIGN DEBT

International Monetary Fund, 700 Nineteenth Street, NW, Washington, D.C. 20431 (202) 623-7000; *Government Finance Statistics Yearbook.*

SWAZILAND - FOREIGN TRADE

Economist Intelligence Unit, 111 West 57th Street, New York, New York 10019 (800) 938-4685; *Swaziland Country Report.*

Euromonitor International, Inc., 122 Michigan Avenue, Suite 1200, Chicago, Illinois 60603 (800) 577-EURO; *The World Economic Factbook.*

Europa Publications Limited, 18 Bedford Square, London, WC1B 3JN, England; *The Europa World Year Book.*

Food and Agricultural Organization of the United Nations (FAO) Via delle Terme di Caracalla, 00100 Rome, Italy (Telephone Number in U.S. (202) 653-2400); *The State of Food and Agriculture.*

M.E. Sharpe, 80 Business Park Drive, Armonk, New York 10504 (800) 541-6563; *The Illustrated Book of World Rankings.*

St. Martin's Press, Inc., 175 Fifth Avenue, New York, New York 10010 (800) 221-7945; *The Statesman's Year-Book.*

United Nations Conference on Trade and Development, Central Statistical Service, Palais des Nations, Geneva, Switzerland (Telephone in U.S. (800) 253-9646); *UNCTAD Commodity Yearbook.*

United Nations Economic Commission for Africa, Africa Hall, P.O. Box 3001, Addis Ababa, Ethiopia (Telephone Number in U.S. (800) 253-9646); *African Statistical Yearbook.*

The World Bank, 1818 H Street, NW, Washington, D.C. 20433 (202) 477-1234; *World Development Indicators.*

SWAZILAND - FORESTRY AND FOREST PRODUCTS

American Forest and Paper Association, 1111 Nineteenth Street, NW, Suite 800, Washington, D.C. 20036 (202) 463-2700; *Wood Pulp and Fiber Statistics.*

Europa Publications Limited, 18 Bedford Square, London, WC1B 3JN, England; *The Europa World Year Book.*

Food and Agricultural Organization of the United Nations (FAO) Via delle Terme di Caracalla, 00100 Rome, Italy (Telephone Number in U.S. (202) 653-2400); *The State of Food and Agriculture;* and *Yearbook of Forest Products.*

International Monetary Fund, 700 Nineteenth Street, NW, Washington, D.C. 20431 (202) 623-7000; *International Financial Statistics.*

M.E. Sharpe, 80 Business Park Drive, Armonk, New York 10504 (800) 541-6563; *The Illustrated Book of World Rankings.*

St. Martin's Press, Inc., 175 Fifth Avenue, New York, New York 10010 (800) 221-7945; *The Statesman's Year-Book.*

Statistical Office of the United Nations, Publishing Service, New York, New York 10017 (800) 253-9646; *Statistical Yearbook.*

United Nations Conference on Trade and Development, Central Statistical Service, Palais des Nations, Geneva, Switzerland (Telephone in U.S. (800) 253-9646); *UNCTAD Commodity Yearbook.*

United Nations Economic Commission for Africa, Africa Hall, P.O. Box 3001, Addis Ababa, Ethiopia (Telephone Number in U.S. (800) 253-9646); *African Statistical Yearbook.*

United Nations Educational, Scientific and Cultural Organization (UNESCO), 7 Place de Fontenoy, F-75700 Paris, France (Telephone Number in U.S. (212) 963-5981); *Statistical Yearbook.*

SWAZILAND - GAS PRODUCTION - See SWAZILAND - MINING AND MINERAL PRODUCTS

SWAZILAND - GENERAL INDUSTRIAL STATISTICS - See SWAZILAND - INDUSTRY

SWAZILAND - GENERAL MORTALITY - See SWAZILAND - MORTALITY

SWAZILAND - GEOGRAPHIC DATA

M.E. Sharpe, 80 Business Park Drive, Armonk, New York 10504 (800) 541-6563; *The Illustrated Book of World Rankings.*

SWAZILAND - GOATS - See SWAZILAND - LIVESTOCK AND POULTRY

SWAZILAND - GOLD HOLDINGS

The World Bank, 1818 H Street, NW, Washington, D.C. 20433 (202) 477-1234; *World Development Indicators.*

SWAZILAND - GOLD PRODUCTION AND CONSUMPTION - See SWAZILAND - MINING AND MINERAL PRODUCTS

SWAZILAND - GOVERNMENT

Central Intelligence Agency, Washington, D.C. 20505 (703) 482-1100, www.cia.gov; *The World Factbook.*

Europa Publications Limited, 18 Bedford Square, London, WC1B 3JN, England; *The Europa World Year Book.*

International Monetary Fund, 700 Nineteenth Street, NW, Washington, D.C. 20431 (202) 623-7000; *Government Finance Statistics Yearbook;* and *International Financial Statistics.*

St. Martin's Press, Inc., 175 Fifth Avenue, New York, New York 10010 (800) 221-7945; *The Statesman's Year-Book.*

Statistical Office of the United Nations, Publishing Service, New York, New York 10017 (800) 253-9646; *National Accounts Statistics; Statistical Yearbook;* and *Survey of Economic and Social Conditions in Africa.*

The World Bank, 1818 H Street, NW, Washington, D.C. 20433 (202) 477-1234; *World Development Indicators.*

SWAZILAND - GRAIN PRODUCTION - See SWAZILAND - CROPS

SWAZILAND - GRANTS

International Monetary Fund, 700 Nineteenth Street, NW, Washington, D.C. 20431 (202) 623-7000; *Government Finance Statistics Yearbook.*

SWAZILAND - GROSS DOMESTIC PRODUCT

African Development Bank, 01 BP 1387, Abidjan 01, Cote D'Ivoire; *Selected Statistics on Regional Member Countries.*

The Economist Intelligence Unit, 111 West 57th Street, New York, New York 10019 (800) 938-4685; *Swaziland Country Report;* and *The World Market Atlas.*

Euromonitor International, Inc., 122 Michigan Avenue, Suite 1200, Chicago, Illinois 60603 (800) 577-EURO; *International Marketing Data and Statistics;* and *The World Economic Factbook.*

Europa Publications Limited, 18 Bedford Square, London, WC1B 3JN, England; *The Europa World Year Book.*

M.E. Sharpe, 80 Business Park Drive, Armonk, New York 10504 (800) 541-6563; *The Illustrated Book of World Rankings.*

Statistical Office of the United Nations, Publishing Service, New York, New York 10017 (800) 253-9646; *National Accounts Statistics; Human Development Report; Statistical Yearbook;* and *Survey of Economic and Social Conditions in Africa.*

United Nations Economic Commission for Africa, Africa Hall, P.O. Box 3001, Addis Ababa, Ethiopia (Telephone Number in U.S. (800) 253-9646); *African Statistical Yearbook.*

U.S. Arms Control and Disarmament Agency, 320 Twenty-first Street, NW, Washington, D.C. 20451 (202) 647-8677; *World Military Expenditures and Arms Transfers.*

The World Bank, 1818 H Street, NW, Washington, D.C. 20433 (202) 477-1234; *World Development Indicators.*

SWAZILAND - GROSS NATIONAL PRODUCT

St. Martin's Press, Inc., 175 Fifth Avenue, New York, New York 10010 (800) 221-7945; *The Statesman's Year-Book.*

The World Bank, 1818 H Street, NW, Washington, D.C. 20433 (202) 477-1234; *The World Bank Atlas;* and *World Development Indicators.*

SWAZILAND - HEALTH

African Development Bank, 01 BP 1387, Abidjan 01, Cote D'Ivoire; *Selected Statistics on Regional Member Countries.*

Euromonitor International, Inc., 122 South Michigan Avenue, Suite 1200, Chicago, Illinois 60603 (800) 577-EURO; *World Marketing Data and Statistics.*

M.E. Sharpe, 80 Business Park Drive, Armonk, New York 10504 (800) 541-6563; *The Illustrated Book of World Rankings.*

St. Martin's Press, Inc., 175 Fifth Avenue, New York, New York 10010 (800) 221-7945; *The Statesman's Year-Book.*

Statistical Office of the United Nations, Publishing Service, New York, New York 10017 (800) 253-9646; *Human Development Report;* and *Statistical Yearbook.*

United Nations Economic Commission for Africa, Africa Hall, P.O. Box 3001, Addis Ababa, Ethiopia (Telephone Number in U.S. (800) 253-9646); *African Statistical Yearbook.*

World Health Organization, Office of Publications, 20 Avenue Appia, CH-1211 Geneva 27, Switzerland (Telephone Number in U.S. (518) 436-9686); *World Health Statistics Annual.*

SWAZILAND - HIGHWAYS

Central Intelligence Agency, Washington, D.C. 20505 (703) 482-1100, www.cia.gov; *The World Factbook.*

International Road Federation, 2600 Virginia Avenue, NW, Washington, D.C. 20037 (202) 338-4641; *World Road Statistics.*

St. Martin's Press, Inc., 175 Fifth Avenue, New York, New York 10010 (800) 221-7945; *The Statesman's Year-Book.*

Statistical Office of the United Nations, Publishing Service, New York, New York 10017 (800) 253-9646; *Survey of Economic and Social Conditions in Africa.*

United Nations Economic Commission for Africa, Africa Hall, P.O. Box 3001, Addis Ababa, Ethiopia (Telephone Number in U.S. (800) 253-9646); *African Statistical Yearbook.*

SWAZILAND - HORSES - See SWAZILAND - LIVESTOCK AND POULTRY

SWAZILAND - HOURS OF WORK - See SWAZILAND - EMPLOYMENT

SWAZILAND - HOUSING AND HOUSING UNITS

Euromonitor International, Inc., 122 South Michigan Avenue, Suite 1200, Chicago, Illinois 60603 (800) 577-EURO; *World Marketing Data and Statistics.*

SWAZILAND - HOUSING EXPENDITURES

International Monetary Fund, 700 Nineteenth Street, NW, Washington, D.C. 20431 (202) 623-7000; *Government Finance Statistics Yearbook.*

M.E. Sharpe, 80 Business Park Drive, Armonk, New York 10504 (800) 541-6563; *The Illustrated Book of World Rankings.*

SWAZILAND - ILLITERATE POPULATION

Central Intelligence Agency, Washington, D.C. 20505 (703) 482-1100, www.cia.gov; *The World Factbook.*

The Economist Intelligence Unit, 111 West 57th Street, New York, New York 10019 (800) 938-4685; *The World Market Atlas.*

Euromonitor International, Inc., 122 Michigan Avenue, Suite 1200, Chicago, Illinois 60603 (800) 577-EURO; *The World Economic Factbook.*

Statistical Office of the United Nations, Publishing Service, New York, New York 10017 (800) 253-9646; *Human Development Report.*

United Nations Educational, Scientific and Cultural Organization (UNESCO), 7 Place de Fontenoy, F-75700 Paris, France (Telephone Number in U.S. (212) 963-5981); *Statistical Yearbook.*

SWAZILAND - IMPORTS

African Development Bank, 01 BP 1387, Abidjan 01, Cote D'Ivoire; *Selected Statistics on Regional Member Countries.*

Central Intelligence Agency, Washington, D.C. 20505 (703) 482-1100, www.cia.gov; *The World Factbook.*

The Economist Intelligence Unit, 111 West 57th Street, New York, New York 10019 (800) 938-4685; *Swaziland Country Report;* and *The World Market Atlas.*

Euromonitor International, Inc., 122 Michigan Avenue, Suite 1200, Chicago, Illinois 60603 (800) 577-EURO; *International Marketing Data and Statistics;* and *The World Economic Factbook.*

Europa Publications Limited, 18 Bedford Square, London, WC1B 3JN, England; *The Europa World Year Book.*

Food and Agricultural Organization of the United Nations (FAO) Via delle Terme di Caracalla, 00100 Rome, Italy (Telephone Number in U.S. (202) 653-2400); *The State of Food and Agriculture.*

International Monetary Fund, 700 Nineteenth Street, NW, Washington, D.C. 20431 (202) 623-7000; *Direction of Trade Statistics; Government Finance Statistics Yearbook;* and *International Financial Statistics.*

St. Martin's Press, Inc., 175 Fifth Avenue, New York, New York 10010 (800) 221-7945; *The Statesman's Year-Book.*

Statistical Office of the United Nations, Publishing Service, New York, New York 10017 (800) 253-9646; *Survey of Economic and Social Conditions in Africa.*

United Nations Conference on Trade and Development (UNCTAD), New York, New York 10017 (800) 253-9646; *Handbook of International Trade and Development Statistics.*

United Nations Economic Commission for Africa, Africa Hall, P.O. Box 3001, Addis Ababa, Ethiopia (Telephone Number in U.S. (800) 253-9646); *African Statistical Yearbook.*

The World Bank, 1818 H Street, NW, Washington, D.C. 20433 (202) 477-1234; *World Development Indicators.*

SWAZILAND - INCOME TAXES - See SWAZILAND - TAXATION

SWAZILAND - INDUSTRY

Central Intelligence Agency, Washington, D.C. 20505 (703) 482-1100, www.cia.gov; *The World Factbook.*

Economist Intelligence Unit, 111 West 57th Street, New York, New York 10019 (800) 938-4685; *Swaziland Country Report.*

Euromonitor International, Inc., 122 Michigan Avenue, Suite 1200, Chicago, Illinois 60603 (800) 577-EURO; *The World Economic Factbook;* and *World Marketing Data and Statistics.*

Europa Publications Limited, 18 Bedford Square, London, WC1B 3JN, England; *The Europa World Year Book.*

International Labour Office, I.L.O. Publications, 1828 L Street, NW, Suite 801, Washington, D.C. 20036 (301) 638-3152; *Yearbook of Labour Statistics.*

M.E. Sharpe, 80 Business Park Drive, Armonk, New York 10504 (800) 541-6563; *The Illustrated Book of World Rankings.*

St. Martin's Press, Inc., 175 Fifth Avenue, New York, New York 10010 (800) 221-7945; *The Statesman's Year-Book.*

Statistical Office of the United Nations, Publishing Service, New York, New York 10017 (800) 253-9646; *Industrial Commodity Statistics Yearbook;* and *Survey of Economic and Social Conditions in Africa.*

United Nations Economic Commission for Africa, Africa Hall, P.O. Box 3001, Addis Ababa, Ethiopia (Telephone Number in U.S. (800) 253-9646); *African Statistical Yearbook.*

The World Bank, 1818 H Street, NW, Washington, D.C. 20433 (202) 477-1234; *World Development Indicators.*

World Intellectual Property Organization, 34 Chemin des Colombettes, CH-1211 Geneva 20. Switzerland; *Industrial Property Statistics.*

SWAZILAND - INFANT AND MATERNAL MORTALITY - See SWAZILAND - MORTALITY

SWAZILAND - INTERNAL TRADE

Statistical Office of the United Nations, Publishing Service, New York, New York 10017 (800) 253-9646; *Statistical Yearbook.*

SWAZILAND - INTERNATIONAL RESERVES EXCLUDING GOLD

African Development Bank, 01 BP 1387, Abidjan 01, Cote D'Ivoire; *Selected Statistics on Regional Member Countries.*

Statistical Office of the United Nations, Publishing Service, New York, New York 10017 (800) 253-9646; *Statistical Yearbook.*

The World Bank, 1818 H Street, NW, Washington, D.C. 20433 (202) 477-1234; *World Development Indicators.*

SWAZILAND - IRON ORE - See SWAZILAND - MINING AND MINERAL PRODUCTS

SWAZILAND - LABOR

African Development Bank, 01 BP 1387, Abidjan 01, Cote D'Ivoire; *Selected Statistics on Regional Member Countries.*

Central Intelligence Agency, Washington, D.C. 20505 (703) 482-1100, www.cia.gov; *The World Factbook.*

Euromonitor International, Inc., 122 Michigan Avenue, Suite 1200, Chicago, Illinois 60603 (800) 577-EURO; *International Marketing Data and Statistics;* and *World Marketing Data and Statistics.*

Europa Publications Limited, 18 Bedford Square, London, WC1B 3JN, England; *The Europa World Year Book.*

Food and Agricultural Organization of the United Nations (FAO) Via delle Terme di Caracalla, 00100 Rome, Italy (Telephone Number in U.S. (202) 653-2400); *The State of Food and Agriculture.*

International Labour Office, I.L.O. Publications, 1828 L Street, NW, Suite 801, Washington, D.C. 20036 (301) 638-3152; *Yearbook of Labour Statistics.*

M.E. Sharpe, 80 Business Park Drive, Armonk, New York 10504 (800) 541-6563; *The Illustrated Book of World Rankings.*

St. Martin's Press, Inc., 175 Fifth Avenue, New York, New York 10010 (800) 221-7945; *The Statesman's Year-Book.*

Statistical Office of the United Nations, Publishing Service, New York, New York 10017 (800) 253-9646; *Human Development Report.*

The World Bank, 1818 H Street, NW, Washington, D.C. 20433 (202) 477-1234; *The World Bank Atlas;* and *World Development Indicators.*

SWAZILAND - LAND USE

Central Intelligence Agency, Washington, D.C. 20505 (703) 482-1100, www.cia.gov; *The World Factbook.*

Euromonitor International, Inc., 122 Michigan Avenue, Suite 1200, Chicago, Illinois 60603 (800) 577-EURO; *International Marketing Data and Statistics.*

Food and Agricultural Organization of the United Nations (FAO), Via delle Terme di Caracalla, 00100 Rome, Italy (Telephone Number in U.S. (202) 653-2400); *Production Yearbook.*

SWAZILAND - LIBRARIES

M.E. Sharpe, 80 Business Park Drive, Armonk, New York 10504 (800) 541-6563; *The Illustrated Book of World Rankings.*

United Nations Educational, Scientific and Cultural Organization (UNESCO), 7 Place de Fontenoy, F-75700 Paris, France (Telephone Number in U.S. (212) 963-5981); *Statistical Yearbook.*

SWAZILAND - LIFE EXPECTANCY

African Development Bank, 01 BP 1387, Abidjan 01, Cote D'Ivoire; *Selected Statistics on Regional Member Countries.*

Central Intelligence Agency, Washington, D.C. 20505 (703) 482-1100, www.cia.gov; *The World Factbook.*

Euromonitor International, Inc., 122 Michigan Avenue, Suite 1200, Chicago, Illinois 60603 (800) 577-EURO; *The World Economic Factbook.*

Statistical Office of the United Nations, Publishing Service, New York, New York 10017 (800) 253-9646; *Human Development Report;* and *World Statistics Pocketbook.*

The World Bank, 1818 H Street, NW, Washington, D.C. 20433 (202) 477-1234; *The World Bank Atlas.*

SWAZILAND - LITERACY RATE

Euromonitor International, Inc., 122 South Michigan Avenue, Suite 1200, Chicago, Illinois 60603 (800) 577-EURO; *World Marketing Data and Statistics.*

Statistical Office of the United Nations, Publishing Service, New York, New York 10017 (800) 253-9646; *Survey of Economic and Social Conditions in Africa.*

SWAZILAND - LIVESTOCK AND POULTRY

Europa Publications Limited, 18 Bedford Square, London, WC1B 3JN, England; *The Europa World Year Book.*

Food and Agricultural Organization of the United Nations (FAO), Via delle Terme di Caracalla, 00100 Rome, Italy (Telephone Number in U.S. (202) 653-2400); *Production Yearbook;* and *The State of Food and Agriculture.*

M.E. Sharpe, 80 Business Park Drive, Armonk, New York 10504 (800) 541-6563; *The Illustrated Book of World Rankings.*

St. Martin's Press, Inc., 175 Fifth Avenue, New York, New York 10010 (800) 221-7945; *The Statesman's Year-Book.*

Statistical Office of the United Nations, Publishing Service, New York, New York 10017 (800) 253-9646; *Statistical Yearbook;* and *Survey of Economic and Social Conditions in Africa.*

United Nations Conference on Trade and Development, Central Statistical Service, Palais des Nations, Geneva, Switzerland (Telephone in U.S. (800) 253-9646); *UNCTAD Commodity Yearbook.*

United Nations Economic Commission for Africa, Africa Hall, P.O. Box 3001, Addis Ababa, Ethiopia (Telephone Number in U.S. (800) 253-9646); *African Statistical Yearbook.*

SWAZILAND - LIVING LEVELS - See SWAZILAND - LIFE EXPECTANCY

SWAZILAND - MAIL - NUMBER OF ITEMS SENT AND RECEIVED

Statistical Office of the United Nations, Publishing Service, New York, New York 10017 (800) 253-9646; *Statistical Yearbook.*

SWAZILAND - MANUFACTURING

M.E. Sharpe, 80 Business Park Drive, Armonk, New York 10504 (800) 541-6563; *The Illustrated Book of World Rankings.*

Statistical Office of the United Nations, Publishing Service, New York, New York 10017 (800) 253-9646; *Statistical Yearbook;* and *Survey of Economic and Social Conditions in Africa.*

United Nations Economic Commission for Africa, Africa Hall, P.O. Box 3001, Addis Ababa, Ethiopia (Telephone Number in U.S. (800) 253-9646); *African Statistical Yearbook.*

The World Bank, 1818 H Street, NW, Washington, D.C. 20433 (202) 477-1234; *World Development Indicators.*

SWAZILAND - MARRIAGE RATES

M.E. Sharpe, 80 Business Park Drive, Armonk, New York 10504 (800) 541-6563; *The Illustrated Book of World Rankings.*

Statistical Office of the United Nations, Publishing Service, New York, New York 10017 (800) 253-9646; *Demographic Yearbook.*

SWAZILAND - MEAT PRODUCTION - See SWAZILAND - LIVESTOCK AND POULTRY

SWAZILAND - MERCHANT SHIPPING

Europa Publications Limited, 18

Bedford Square, London, WC1B 3JN, England; *The Europa World Year Book.*

United Nations Economic Commission for Africa, Africa Hall, P.O. Box 3001, Addis Ababa, Ethiopia (Telephone Number in U.S. (800) 253-9646); *African Statistical Yearbook.*

SWAZILAND - MILITARY

Central Intelligence Agency, Washington, D.C. 20505 (703) 482-1100, www.cia.gov; *The World Factbook.*

Euromonitor International, Inc., 122 South Michigan Avenue, Suite 1200, Chicago, Illinois 60603 (800) 577-EURO; *World Marketing Data and Statistics.*

International Monetary Fund, 700 Nineteenth Street, NW, Washington, D.C. 20431 (202) 623-7000; *Government Finance Statistics Yearbook.*

St. Martin's Press, Inc., 175 Fifth Avenue, New York, New York 10010 (800) 221-7945; *The Statesman's Year-Book.*

Statistical Office of the United Nations, Publishing Service, New York, New York 10017 (800) 253-9646; *Human Development Report.*

U.S. Arms Control and Disarmament Agency, 320 Twenty-first Street, NW, Washington, D.C. 20451 (202) 647-8677; *World Military Expenditures and Arms Transfers.*

SWAZILAND - MILK PRODUCTION - See SWAZILAND - DAIRY PRODUCTS

SWAZILAND - MINING AND MINERAL PRODUCTS

Europa Publications Limited, 18 Bedford Square, London, WC1B 3JN, England; *The Europa World Year Book.*

International Monetary Fund, 700 Nineteenth Street, NW, Washington, D.C. 20431 (202) 623-7000; *International Financial Statistics.*

M.E. Sharpe, 80 Business Park Drive, Armonk, New York 10504 (800) 541-6563; *The Illustrated Book of World Rankings.*

St. Martin's Press, Inc., 175 Fifth Avenue, New York, New York 10010 (800) 221-7945; *The Statesman's Year-Book.*

Statistical Office of the United Nations, Publishing Service, New York, New York 10017 (800) 253-9646; *Statistical Yearbook.*

United Nations Conference on Trade and Development, Central Statistical Service, Palais des Nations, Geneva, Switzerland (Telephone in U.S. (800) 253-

9646); *UNCTAD Commodity Yearbook.*

United Nations Economic Commission for Africa, Africa Hall, P.O. Box 3001, Addis Ababa, Ethiopia (Telephone Number in U.S. (800) 253-9646); *African Statistical Yearbook.*

SWAZILAND - MONEY EXCHANGE RATES - See SWAZILAND - EXCHANGE RATES

SWAZILAND - MONEY SUPPLY

African Development Bank, 01 BP 1387, Abidjan 01, Cote D'Ivoire; *Selected Statistics on Regional Member Countries.*

Economist Intelligence Unit, 111 West 57th Street, New York, New York 10019 (800) 938-4685; *Swaziland Country Report.*

Europa Publications Limited, 18 Bedford Square, London, WC1B 3JN, England; *The Europa World Year Book.*

International Monetary Fund, 700 Nineteenth Street, NW, Washington, D.C. 20431 (202) 623-7000; *International Financial Statistics.*

The World Bank, 1818 H Street, NW, Washington, D.C. 20433 (202) 477-1234; *World Development Indicators.*

SWAZILAND - MORTALITY

Central Intelligence Agency, Washington, D.C. 20505 (703) 482-1100, www.cia.gov; *The World Factbook.*

Euromonitor International, Inc., 122 Michigan Avenue, Suite 1200, Chicago, Illinois 60603 (800) 577-EURO; *International Marketing Data and Statistics;* and *The World Economic Factbook.*

Europa Publications Limited, 18 Bedford Square, London, WC1B 3JN, England; *The Europa World Year Book.*

Statistical Office of the United Nations, Publishing Service, New York, New York 10017 (800) 253-9646; *Demographic Yearbook; Human Development Report; Statistical Yearbook; Survey of Economic and Social Conditions in Africa;* and *World Statistics Pocketbook.*

The World Bank, 1818 H Street, NW, Washington, D.C. 20433 (202) 477-1234; *The World Bank Atlas;* and *World Development Indicators.*

World Health Organization, Office of Publications, 20 Avenue Appia, CH-1211 Geneva 27, Switzerland (Telephone Number in U.S. (518) 436-9686); *World Health Statistics Annual.*

SWAZILAND - MOTION PICTURES

St. Martin's Press, Inc., 175 Fifth Avenue, New York, New York 10010 (800) 221-7945; *The Statesman's Year-Book.*

Statistical Office of the United Nations, Publishing Service, New York, New York 10017 (800) 253-9646; *Statistical Yearbook.*

SWAZILAND - MOTOR VEHICLE TAXES - See SWAZILAND - TAXATION

SWAZILAND - MOTOR VEHICLES IN USE

Europa Publications Limited, 18 Bedford Square, London, WC1B 3JN, England; *The Europa World Year Book.*

International Road Federation, 2600 Virginia Avenue, NW, Washington, D.C. 20037 (202) 338-4641; *World Road Statistics.*

Statistical Office of the United Nations, Publishing Service, New York, New York 10017 (800) 253-9646; *Statistical Yearbook;* and *Survey of Economic and Social Conditions in Africa.*

SWAZILAND - MULES - See
SWAZILAND - LIVESTOCK AND POULTRY

SWAZILAND - MUSEUMS

M.E. Sharpe, 80 Business Park Drive, Armonk, New York 10504 (800) 541-6563; *The Illustrated Book of World Rankings.*

SWAZILAND - NATALITY - See
SWAZILAND - BIRTH RATE

SWAZILAND - NATIONAL ACCOUNTS

African Development Bank, 01 BP 1387, Abidjan 01, Cote D'Ivoire; *Selected Statistics on Regional Member Countries.*

Europa Publications Limited, 18 Bedford Square, London, WC1B 3JN, England; *The Europa World Year Book.*

Statistical Office of the United Nations, Publishing Service, New York, New York 10017 (800) 253-9646; *National Accounts Statistics;* and *Statistical Yearbook.*

United Nations Economic Commission for Africa, Africa Hall, P.O. Box 3001, Addis Ababa, Ethiopia (Telephone Number in U.S. (800) 253-9646); *African Statistical Yearbook.*

SWAZILAND - NATIONAL INCOME

M.E. Sharpe, 80 Business Park Drive, Armonk, New York 10504 (800) 541-6563; *The Illustrated Book of World Rankings.*

Statistical Office of the United Nations, Publishing Service, New York, New York 10017 (800) 253-9646; *National Accounts Statistics;* and *Statistical Yearbook.*

SWAZILAND - NATIONAL PRODUCT

M.E. Sharpe, 80 Business Park Drive, Armonk, New York 10504 (800) 541-6563; *The Illustrated Book of World Rankings.*

SWAZILAND - NATURAL GAS PRODUCTION - See SWAZILAND - MINING AND MINERAL PRODUCTS

SWAZILAND - NEWSPAPER PRODUCTION - See SWAZILAND - FORESTRY AND FOREST PRODUCTS

SWAZILAND - OCCUPATIONS - See SWAZILAND - LABOR

SWAZILAND - PATENTS, TRADEMARKS AND SERVICE MARKS

Statistical Office of the United Nations, Publishing Service, New York, New York 10017 (800) 253-9646; *Statistical Yearbook.*

World Intellectual Property Organization, 34 Chemin des Colombettes, CH-1211 Geneva 20. Switzerland; *Industrial Property Statistics.*

SWAZILAND - PEANUT PRODUCTION - See SWAZILAND - CROPS

SWAZILAND - PESTICIDE USE

Food and Agricultural Organization of the United Nations (FAO) Via delle Terme di Caracalla, 00100 Rome, Italy (Telephone Number in U.S. (202) 653-2400); *The State of Food and Agriculture.*

SWAZILAND - PETROLEUM INDUSTRY

Food and Agricultural Organization of the United Nations (FAO) Via delle Terme di Caracalla, 00100 Rome, Italy (Telephone Number in U.S. (202) 653-2400); *The State of Food and Agriculture.*

M.E. Sharpe, 80 Business Park Drive, Armonk, New York 10504 (800) 541-6563; *The Illustrated Book of World Rankings.*

United Nations Conference on Trade and Development, Central Statistical Service, Palais des Nations, Geneva, Switzerland (Telephone in U.S. (800) 253-9646); *UNCTAD Commodity Yearbook.*

SWAZILAND - PIGS - See SWAZILAND - LIVESTOCK AND POULTRY

SWAZILAND - POPULATION

African Development Bank, 01 BP 1387, Abidjan 01, Cote D'Ivoire; *Selected Statistics on Regional Member Countries.*

Central Intelligence Agency, Washington, D.C. 20505 (703) 482-1100, www.cia.gov; *The World Factbook.*

The Economist Intelligence Unit, 111 West 57th Street, New York, New York 10019 (800) 938-4685; *Swaziland Country Report;* and *The World Market Atlas.*

Euromonitor International, Inc., 122 Michigan Avenue, Suite 1200, Chicago, Illinois 60603 (800) 577-EURO; *International Marketing Data and Statistics;* and *The World Economic Factbook.*

Europa Publications Limited, 18 Bedford Square, London, WC1B 3JN, England; *The Europa World Year Book.*

Food and Agricultural Organization of the United Nations (FAO), Via delle Terme di Caracalla, 00100 Rome, Italy (Telephone Number in U.S. (202) 653-2400); *Production Yearbook.*

International Labour Office, I.L.O. Publications, 1828 L Street, NW, Suite 801, Washington, D.C. 20036 (301) 638-3152; *Yearbook of Labour Statistics.*

M.E. Sharpe, 80 Business Park Drive, Armonk, New York 10504 (800) 541-6563; *The Illustrated Book of World Rankings.*

St. Martin's Press, Inc., 175 Fifth Avenue, New York, New York 10010 (800) 221-7945; *The Statesman's Year-Book.*

Statistical Office of the United Nations, Publishing Service, New York, New York 10017 (800) 253-9646; *Demographic Yearbook; Human Development Report; Statistical Yearbook; Survey of Economic and Social Conditions in Africa;* and *World Statistics Pocketbook.*

United Nations Educational, Scientific and Cultural Organization (UNESCO), 7 Place de Fontenoy, F-75700 Paris, France (Telephone Number in U.S. (212) 963-5981); *Statistical Yearbook.*

U.S. Arms Control and Disarmament Agency, 320 Twenty-first Street, NW, Washington, D.C. 20451 (202) 647-8677; *World Military Expenditures and Arms Transfers.*

The World Bank, 1818 H Street, NW, Washington, D.C. 20433 (202) 477-1234; *The World Bank Atlas.*

World Health Organization, Office of Publications, 20 Avenue Appia, CH-1211 Geneva 27, Switzerland (Telephone Number in U.S. (518) 436-9686); *World Health Statistics Annual.*

SWAZILAND - POST OFFICES

M.E. Sharpe, 80 Business Park Drive, Armonk, New York 10504 (800) 541-6563; *The Illustrated Book of World Rankings.*

St. Martin's Press, Inc., 175 Fifth Avenue, New York, New York 10010 (800) 221-7945; *The Statesman's Year-Book.*

SWAZILAND - POTATO PRODUCTION - See SWAZILAND - CROPS

SWAZILAND - PRICES

Food and Agricultural Organization of the United Nations (FAO), Via delle Terme di Caracalla, 00100 Rome, Italy (Telephone Number in U.S. (202) 653-2400); *Production Yearbook;* and *The State of Food and Agriculture.*

International Labour Office, I.L.O. Publications, 1828 L Street, NW, Suite 801, Washington, D.C. 20036 (301) 638-3152; *Yearbook of Labour Statistics.*

International Monetary Fund, 700 Nineteenth Street, NW, Washington, D.C. 20431 (202) 623-7000; *International Financial Statistics.*

M.E. Sharpe, 80 Business Park Drive, Armonk, New York 10504 (800) 541-6563; *The Illustrated Book of World Rankings.*

United Nations Economic Commission for Africa, Africa Hall, P.O. Box 3001, Addis Ababa, Ethiopia (Telephone Number in U.S. (800) 253-9646); *African Statistical Yearbook.*

SWAZILAND - PRODUCTION

M.E. Sharpe, 80 Business Park Drive, Armonk, New York 10504 (800) 541-6563; *The Illustrated Book of World Rankings.*

SWAZILAND - PROPERTY TAXES - See SWAZILAND - TAXATION

SWAZILAND - PUBLIC FINANCE - See SWAZILAND - FINANCE

SWAZILAND - RADIO BROADCASTING

M.E. Sharpe, 80 Business Park Drive, Armonk, New York 10504 (800) 541-6563; *The Illustrated Book of World Rankings.*

SWAZILAND - RADIO RECEIVERS

St. Martin's Press, Inc., 175 Fifth Avenue, New York, New York 10010 (800) 221-7945; *The Statesman's Year-Book.*

SWAZILAND - RAILWAYS

Europa Publications Limited, 18 Bedford Square, London, WC1B 3JN, England; *The Europa World Year Book.*

Jane's Information Group, Sentinel House, 163 Brighton Road, Coulsdon, Surrey CR5 2NH, England (Telephone Number in U.S. (703) 683-3700); *Jane's World Railways.*

St. Martin's Press, Inc., 175 Fifth Avenue, New York, New York 10010 (800) 221-7945; *The Statesman's Year-Book.*

Statistical Office of the United Nations, Publishing Service, New York, New York 10017 (800) 253-9646; *Survey of Economic and Social Conditions in Africa.*

United Nations Economic Commission for Africa, Africa Hall, P.O. Box 3001, Addis Ababa, Ethiopia (Telephone Number in U.S. (800) 253-9646); *African Statistical Yearbook.*

SWAZILAND - RELIGION

Central Intelligence Agency, Washington, D.C. 20505 (703) 482-1100, www.cia.gov; *The World Factbook.*

M.E. Sharpe, 80 Business Park Drive, Armonk, New York 10504 (800) 541-6563; *The Illustrated Book of World Rankings.*

St. Martin's Press, Inc., 175 Fifth Avenue, New York, New York 10010 (800) 221-7945; *The Statesman's Year-Book.*

SWAZILAND - RETAIL PRICE INDEX

Europa Publications Limited, 18 Bedford Square, London, WC1B 3JN, England; *The Europa World Year Book.*

SWAZILAND - RETAIL TRADE

Euromonitor International, Inc., 122 South Michigan Avenue, Suite 1200, Chicago, Illinois 60603 (800) 577-EURO; *World Marketing Data and Statistics.*

Statistical Office of the United Nations, Publishing Service, New York, New York 10017 (800) 253-9646; *Statistical Yearbook.*

SWAZILAND - RICE PRODUCTION - See SWAZILAND - CROPS

SWAZILAND - ROUNDWOOD PRODUCTION - See SWAZILAND - FORESTRY AND FOREST PRODUCTS

SWAZILAND - RUBBER PRODUCTION AND CONSUMPTION

M.E. Sharpe, 80 Business Park Drive, Armonk, New York 10504 (800) 541-6563; *The Illustrated Book of World Rankings.*

SWAZILAND - SAWNWOOD PRODUCTION - See SWAZILAND - FORESTRY AND FOREST PRODUCTS

SWAZILAND - SOCIAL DATA

Statistical Office of the United Nations, Publishing Service, New York, New York 10017 (800) 253-9646; *World Statistics Pocketbook.*

SWAZILAND - SOCIAL SECURITY

Statistical Office of the United Nations, Publishing Service, New York, New York 10017 (800) 253-9646; *National Accounts Statistics.*

SWAZILAND - SENIOR CITIZENS

M.E. Sharpe, 80 Business Park Drive, Armonk, New York 10504 (800) 541-6563; *The Illustrated Book of World Rankings.*

SWAZILAND - SHEEP - See SWAZILAND - LIVESTOCK AND POULTRY

SWAZILAND - SILVER PRODUCTION AND CONSUMPTION - See RWANDA - MINING AND MINERAL PRODUCTS

SWAZILAND - SOCIAL DATA

African Development Bank, 01 BP 1387, Abidjan 01, Cote D'Ivoire; *Selected Statistics on Regional Member Countries.*

M.E. Sharpe, 80 Business Park Drive, Armonk, New York 10504 (800) 541-6563; *The Illustrated Book of World Rankings.*

SWAZILAND - STAMP TAXES AND DUTIES - See SWAZILAND - TAXATION

SWAZILAND - STEEL PRODUCTION - See SWAZILAND - MINING AND MINERAL PRODUCTS

SWAZILAND - STOCKS - COMMODITY - MARKET PRICE - INDEX

Food and Agricultural Organization of the United Nations (FAO) Via delle Terme di Caracalla, 00100 Rome, Italy (Telephone Number in U.S. (202) 653-2400); *The State of Food and Agriculture.*

SWAZILAND - SUGAR - See SWAZILAND - CROPS

SWAZILAND - TAXATION

Europa Publications Limited, 18 Bedford Square, London, WC1B 3JN, England; *The Europa World Year Book.*

International Monetary Fund, 700 Nineteenth Street, NW, Washington, D.C. 20431 (202) 623-7000; *Government Finance Statistics Yearbook.*

International Road Federation, 2600 Virginia Avenue, NW, Washington, D.C. 20037 (202) 338-4641; *World Road Statistics.*

The World Bank, 1818 H Street, NW, Washington, D.C. 20433 (202) 477-1234; *World Development Indicators.*

SWAZILAND - TELEPHONES IN USE

American Telephone and Telegraph Company, 26 Parsippany Road, Whippany, New Jersey 07981 (800) 222-0300; *The World's Telephones.*

Central Intelligence Agency, Washington, D.C. 20505 (703) 482-1100, www.cia.gov; *The World Factbook.*

Europa Publications Limited, 18 Bedford Square, London, WC1B 3JN, England; *The Europa World Year Book.*

St. Martin's Press, Inc., 175 Fifth Avenue, New York, New York 10010 (800) 221-7945; *The Statesman's Year-Book.*

Statistical Office of the United Nations, Publishing Service, New York, New York 10017 (800) 253-9646; *Statistical Yearbook;* and *World Statistics Pocketbook.*

SWAZILAND - TELEVISION BROADCASTING

M.E. Sharpe, 80 Business Park Drive, Armonk, New York 10504 (800) 541-6563; *The Illustrated Book of World Rankings.*

SWAZILAND - TEXTILE INDUSTRY

American Forest and Paper Association, 1111 Nineteenth Street, NW, Suite 800, Washington, D.C. 20036 (202) 463-2700; *Wood Pulp and Fiber Statistics.*

M.E. Sharpe, 80 Business Park Drive, Armonk, New York 10504 (800) 541-6563; *The Illustrated Book of World Rankings.*

United Nations Conference on Trade and Development, Central Statistical Service, Palais des Nations, Geneva, Switzerland (Telephone in U.S. (800) 253-9646); *UNCTAD Commodity Yearbook.*

SWAZILAND - TIN PRODUCTION AND CONSUMPTION - See SWAZILAND - MINING AND MINERAL PRODUCTS

SWAZILAND - TOBACCO PRODUCTION

M.E. Sharpe, 80 Business Park Drive, Armonk, New York 10504 (800) 541-6563; *The Illustrated Book of World Rankings.*

Statistical Office of the United Nations, Publishing Service, New York, New York 10017 (800) 253-9646; *Statistical Yearbook.*

SWAZILAND - TOURISM

Euromonitor International, Inc., 122 Michigan Avenue, Suite 1200, Chicago, Illinois 60603 (800) 577-EURO; *The World Economic Factbook;* and *World Marketing Data and Statistics.*

Europa Publications Limited, 18 Bedford Square, London, WC1B 3JN, England; *The Europa World Year Book.*

M.E. Sharpe, 80 Business Park Drive, Armonk, New York 10504 (800) 541-6563; *The Illustrated Book of World Rankings.*

St. Martin's Press, Inc., 175 Fifth Avenue, New York, New York 10010 (800) 221-7945; *The Statesman's Year-Book.*

United Nations Economic Commission for Africa, Africa Hall, P.O. Box 3001, Addis Ababa, Ethiopia (Telephone Number in U.S. (800) 253-9646); *African Statistical Yearbook.*

SWAZILAND - TRACTORS IN USE

Statistical Office of the United Nations, Publishing Service, New York, New York 10017 (800) 253-9646; *Statistical Yearbook.*

SWAZILAND - TRADE - See SWAZILAND - FOREIGN TRADE

SWAZILAND - TRADEMARKS AND SERVICE MARKS - See SWAZILAND - PATENTS, TRADEMARKS AND SERVICE MARKS

SWAZILAND - TRANSPORTATION AND COMMUNICATIONS

Central Intelligence Agency, Washington, D.C. 20505 (703) 482-1100, www.cia.gov; *The World Factbook.*

Euromonitor International, Inc., 122 Michigan Avenue, Suite 1200, Chicago, Illinois 60603 (800) 577-EURO; *International Marketing Data and Statistics;* and *World Marketing Data and Statistics.*

Europa Publications Limited, 18 Bedford Square, London, WC1B 3JN, England; *The Europa World Year Book.*

M.E. Sharpe, 80 Business Park Drive, Armonk, New York 10504 (800) 541-6563; *The Illustrated Book of World Rankings.*

St. Martin's Press, Inc., 175 Fifth Avenue, New York, New York 10010 (800) 221-7945; *The Statesman's Year-Book.*

Statistical Office of the United Nations, Publishing Service, New York, New York 10017 (800) 253-9646; *Human Development Report.*

United Nations Economic Commission for Africa, Africa Hall, P.O. Box 3001, Addis Ababa, Ethiopia (Telephone Number in U.S. (800) 253-9646); *African Statistical Yearbook.*

SWAZILAND - UNEMPLOYMENT

Central Intelligence Agency, Washington, D.C. 20505 (703) 482-1100, www.cia.gov; *The World Factbook.*

International Labour Office, I.L.O. Publications, 1828 L Street, NW, Suite

801, Washington, D.C. 20036 (301) 638-3152; *Yearbook of Labour Statistics.*

SWAZILAND - VITAL STATISTICS

World Health Organization, Office of Publications, 20 Avenue Appia, CH-1211 Geneva 27, Switzerland (Telephone Number in U.S. (518) 436-9686); *World Health Statistics Annual.*

SWAZILAND - WAGES

International Labour Office, I.L.O. Publications, 1828 L Street, NW, Suite 801, Washington, D.C. 20036 (301) 638-3152; *Yearbook of Labour Statistics.*

Statistical Office of the United Nations, Publishing Service, New York, New York 10017 (800) 253-9646; *Statistical Yearbook.*

SWAZILAND - WEATHER - See SWAZILAND - CLIMATE

SWAZILAND - WHEAT PRODUCTION AND PRICES - See SWAZILAND - CROPS

SWAZILAND - WHOLESALE TRADE

Statistical Office of the United Nations, Publishing Service, New York, New York 10017 (800) 253-9646; *Statistical Yearbook.*

SWAZILAND - WINE PRODUCTION - See SWAZILAND - BEVERAGES

SWAZILAND - WOOD AND WOOD PULP - See SWAZILAND - FORESTRY AND FOREST PRODUCTS

SWAZILAND - WOOL PRODUCTION - See SWAZILAND - TEXTILE INDUSTRY

Sweden - National Statistical Office

Statistiska Central Byran, Karlavagen 100, S-115 81 Stockholm, Sweden.

Sweden - Primary Statistics Sources

Statistiska Centralbyran (National Bureau of Statistics), Karlavagen 100, S-115 81, Stockholm, Sweden; *Statistisk arsbok for Sverige* (Statistical Yearbook of Sweden); *Allman manadsstatistik* (Monthly Digest of Swedish Statistics); and *Statistiska meddelanden* (Statistical Reports).

Sweden - Databases

Statistical Data Bases Division, Statistics Sweden, S-115 81 Stockholm, Sweden. Offers the following data bases: (1)

Regional Statistics Data Base; (2) Sub-Area Statistical Data Base; and (3) Time Series Data Base. Subject coverage: Population, employment, economic, and social statistics for international, national, regional, and local area.

SWEDEN - ABORTIONS

Nordic Council of Ministers, Store Strandstraede 18, DK-1255 Copenhagen K, Denmark and the Nordic Statistical Secretariat, Postboks 2550, DK-2100 Copenhagen 0, Denmark; *The Yearbook of Nordic Statistics.*

Statistical Office of the United Nations, Publishing Service, New York, New York 10017 (800) 253-9646; *Demographic Yearbook;* and *Trends in Europe and North America: The Statistical Yearbook of the Economic Commission for Europe.*

SWEDEN - AGRICULTURE

Economist Intelligence Unit, 111 West 57th Street, New York, New York 10019 (800) 938-4685; *Sweden Country Report.*

Euromonitor International, Inc., 122 South Michigan Avenue, Suite 1200, Chicago, Illinois 60603 (800) 577-EURO; *World Marketing Data and Statistics.*

Europa Publications Limited, 18 Bedford Square, London, WC1B 3JN, England; *The Europa World Year Book.*

Food and Agricultural Organization of the United Nations (FAO) Via delle Terme di Caracalla, 00100 Rome, Italy (Telephone Number in U.S. (202) 653-2400); *Production Yearbook; The State of Food and Agriculture;* and *Trade Yearbook.*

M.E. Sharpe, 80 Business Park Drive, Armonk, New York 10504 (800) 541-6563; *The Illustrated Book of World Rankings.*

Nordic Council of Ministers, Store Strandstraede 18, DK-1255 Copenhagen K, Denmark and the Nordic Statistical Secretariat, Postboks 2550, DK-2100 Copenhagen 0, Denmark; *The Yearbook of Nordic Statistics.*

Organisation for Economic Co-operation and Development (OECD), 2 rue Andre-Pascal, 75 Paris 16, France (Telephone Number in U.S. (202) 785-6323); *Economic Accounts for Agriculture; Indicators of Industrial Activity; Industrial Structure Statistics;* and *OECD Economic Surveys: Sweden.*

St. Martin's Press, Inc., 175 Fifth Avenue, New York, New York 10010 (800) 221-7945; *The Statesman's Year-Book.*

Statistical Office of the United Nations,

Publishing Service, New York, New York 10017 (800) 253-9646; *Statistical Yearbook.*

United Nations Conference on Trade and Development, Central Statistical Service, Palais des Nations, Geneva, Switzerland (Telephone in U.S. (800) 253-9646); *UNCTAD Commodity Yearbook.*

The World Bank, 1818 H Street, NW, Washington, D.C. 20433 (202) 477-1234; *World Development Indicators.*

SWEDEN - AIRLINE SERVICE

Europa Publications Limited, 18 Bedford Square, London, WC1B 3JN, England; *The Europa World Year Book.*

M.E. Sharpe, 80 Business Park Drive, Armonk, New York 10504 (800) 541-6563; *The Illustrated Book of World Rankings.*

Nordic Council of Ministers, Store Strandstraede 18, DK-1255 Copenhagen K, Denmark and the Nordic Statistical Secretariat, Postboks 2550, DK-2100 Copenhagen 0, Denmark; *The Yearbook of Nordic Statistics.*

Organisation for Economic Co-operation and Development (OECD), 2 rue Andre-Pascal, 75 Paris 16, France (Telephone Number in U.S. (202) 785-6323); *Tourism Policy and International Tourism in OECD Member Countries.*

St. Martin's Press, Inc., 175 Fifth Avenue, New York, New York 10010 (800) 221-7945; *The Statesman's Year-Book.*

Statistical Office of the United Nations, Publishing Service, New York, New York 10017 (800) 253-9646; *Statistical Yearbook.*

SWEDEN - AIRPORTS

Central Intelligence Agency, Washington, D.C. 20505 (703) 482-1100, www.cia.gov; *The World Factbook.*

SWEDEN - ALUMINUM PRODUCTION AND CONSUMPTION - See SWEDEN - MINING AND MINERAL PRODUCTS

SWEDEN - ANIMAL FEEDINGSTUFFS

Organisation for Economic Co-operation and Development (OECD), 2 rue Andre-Pascal, 75 Paris 16, France (Telephone Number in U.S. (202) 785-6323); *Foreign Trade by Commodities.*

Statistical Office of the United Nations, Publishing Service, New York, New York 10017 (800) 253-9646; *Statistical Yearbook.*

SWEDEN - ANIMAL HEALTH

Food and Agricultural Organization of the United Nations (FAO), Via delle Terme

di Caracalla, 00100, Rome, Italy (Telephone Number in U.S. (202) 653-2400); *Animal Health Yearbook.*

SWEDEN - ANTIMONY AND ANTIMONY ORE PRODUCTION AND CONSUMPTION - See SWEDEN - MINING AND MINERAL PRODUCTS

SWEDEN - AREA AND DENSITY OF POPULATION

Central Intelligence Agency, Washington, D.C. 20505 (703) 482-1100, www.cia.gov; *The World Factbook.*

Euromonitor International, Inc., 122 Michigan Avenue, Suite 1200, Chicago, Illinois 60603 (800) 577-EURO; *The World Economic Factbook.*

Europa Publications Limited, 18 Bedford Square, London, WC1B 3JN, England; *The Europa World Year Book.*

Food and Agricultural Organization of the United Nations (FAO) Via delle Terme di Caracalla, 00100 Rome, Italy (Telephone Number in U.S. (202) 653-2400); *The State of Food and Agriculture.*

M.E. Sharpe, 80 Business Park Drive, Armonk, New York 10504 (800) 541-6563; *The Illustrated Book of World Rankings.*

Nordic Council of Ministers, Store Strandstraede 18, DK-1255 Copenhagen K, Denmark and the Nordic Statistical Secretariat, Postboks 2550, DK-2100 Copenhagen 0, Denmark; *The Yearbook of Nordic Statistics.*

St. Martin's Press, Inc., 175 Fifth Avenue, New York, New York 10010 (800) 221-7945; *The Statesman's Year-Book.*

Statistical Office of the United Nations, Publishing Service, New York, New York 10017 (800) 253-9646; *Statistical Yearbook; and Trends in Europe and North America: The Statistical Yearbook of the Economic Commission for Europe.*

United Nations Educational, Scientific and Cultural Organization (UNESCO), 7 Place de Fontenoy, F-75700 Paris, France (Telephone Number in U.S. (212) 963-5981); *Statistical Yearbook.*

The World Bank, 1818 H Street, NW, Washington, D.C. 20433 (202) 477-1234; *World Development Report.*

SWEDEN - ARMS EXPORTS AND IMPORTS - See SWEDEN - MILITARY

SWEDEN - ARSENIC PRODUCTION AND CONSUMPTION - See SWEDEN - MINING AND MINERAL PRODUCTS

SWEDEN - BALANCE OF PAYMENTS

The Economist Intelligence Unit, 111 West 57th Street, New York, New York 10019 (800) 938-4685; *The World Market Atlas.*

Europa Publications Limited, 18 Bedford Square, London, WC1B 3JN, England; *The Europa World Year Book.*

International Monetary Fund, 700 Nineteenth Street, NW, Washington, D.C. 20431 (202) 623-7000; *Balance of Payments Yearbook; and International Financial Statistics.*

Nordic Council of Ministers, Store Strandstraede 18, DK-1255 Copenhagen K, Denmark and the Nordic Statistical Secretariat, Postboks 2550, DK-2100 Copenhagen 0, Denmark; *The Yearbook of Nordic Statistics.*

Organisation for Economic Co-operation and Development (OECD), 2 rue Andre-Pascal, 75 Paris 16, France (Telephone Number in U.S. (202) 785-6323); *Economic Outlook; Geographical Distribution of Financial Flows to Developing Countries; Main Economic Indicators - Historical Statistics; and OECD Economic Surveys: Sweden.*

United Nations Conference on Trade and Development (UNCTAD), New York, New York 10017 (800) 253-9646; *Handbook of International Trade and Development Statistics.*

The World Bank, 1818 H Street, NW, Washington, D.C. 20433 (202) 477-1234; *World Development Report; and World Development Indicators.*

SWEDEN - BANKING

Euromonitor International, Inc., 122 South Michigan Avenue, Suite 1200, Chicago, Illinois 60603 (800) 577-EURO; *World Marketing Data and Statistics.*

Europa Publications Limited, 18 Bedford Square, London, WC1B 3JN, England; *The Europa World Year Book.*

International Monetary Fund, 700 Nineteenth Street, NW, Washington, D.C. 20431 (202) 623-7000; *Government Finance Statistics Yearbook; and International Financial Statistics.*

M.E. Sharpe, 80 Business Park Drive, Armonk, New York 10504 (800) 541-6563; *The Illustrated Book of World Rankings.*

Nordic Council of Ministers, Store Strandstraede 18, DK-1255 Copenhagen K, Denmark and the Nordic Statistical Secretariat, Postboks 2550, DK-2100 Copenhagen 0, Denmark; *The Yearbook of Nordic Statistics.*

Organisation for Economic Co-operation and Development (OECD), 2 rue Andre-Pascal, 75 Paris 16, France (Telephone Number in U.S. (202) 785-6323); *Economic Outlook; Financial Market Trends;* and *OECD Economic Surveys: Sweden.*

St. Martin's Press, Inc., 175 Fifth Avenue, New York, New York 10010 (800) 221-7945; *The Statesman's Year-Book.*

Statistical Office of the United Nations, Publishing Service, New York, New York 10017 (800) 253-9646; *Statistical Yearbook.*

SWEDEN - BARLEY PRODUCTION - See SWEDEN - CROPS

SWEDEN - BAUXITE PRODUCTION AND CONSUMPTION - See SWEDEN - MINING AND MINERAL PRODUCTS

SWEDEN - BEER PRODUCTION - See SWEDEN - BEVERAGES

SWEDEN - BEVERAGES

M.E. Sharpe, 80 Business Park Drive, Armonk, New York 10504 (800) 541-6563; *The Illustrated Book of World Rankings.*

Organisation for Economic Co-operation and Development (OECD), 2 rue Andre-Pascal, 75 Paris 16, France (Telephone Number in U.S. (202) 785-6323); *Indicators of Industrial Activity.*

Statistical Office of the United Nations, Publishing Service, New York, New York 10017 (800) 253-9646; *Statistical Yearbook.*

SWEDEN - BIRTH RATES

Central Intelligence Agency, Washington, D.C. 20505 (703) 482-1100, www.cia.gov; *The World Factbook.*

Euromonitor International, Inc., 122 Michigan Avenue, Suite 1200, Chicago, Illinois 60603 (800) 577-EURO; *The World Economic Factbook.*

Europa Publications Limited, 18 Bedford Square, London, WC1B 3JN, England; *The Europa World Year Book.*

M.E. Sharpe, 80 Business Park Drive, Armonk, New York 10504 (800) 541-6563; *The Illustrated Book of World Rankings.*

Nordic Council of Ministers, Store Strandstraede 18, DK-1255 Copenhagen K, Denmark and the Nordic Statistical Secretariat, Postboks 2550, DK-2100 Copenhagen 0, Denmark; *The Yearbook of Nordic Statistics.*

St. Martin's Press, Inc., 175 Fifth Avenue, New York, New York 10010 (800) 221-7945; *The Statesman's Year-Book.*

Statistical Office of the United Nations, Publishing Service, New York, New York 10017 (800) 253-9646; *Demographic Yearbook;* and *Statistical Yearbook.*

The World Bank, 1818 H Street, NW, Washington, D.C. 20433 (202) 477-1234; *World Development Indicators.*

World Health Organization, Office of Publications, 20 Avenue Appia, CH-1211 Geneva 27, Switzerland (Telephone Number in U.S. (518) 436-9686); *World Health Statistics Annual.*

SWEDEN - BISMUTH PRODUCTION AND CONSUMPTION - See SWEDEN - MINING AND MINERAL PRODUCTS

SWEDEN - BONDS

International Monetary Fund, 700 Nineteenth Street, NW, Washington, D.C. 20431 (202) 623-7000; *Government Finance Statistics Yearbook.*

Organisation for Economic Co-operation and Development (OECD), 2 rue Andre-Pascal, 75 Paris 16, France (Telephone Number in U.S. (202) 785-6323); *Financial Market Trends.*

Statistical Office of the United Nations, Publishing Service, New York, New York 10017 (800) 253-9646; *Statistical Yearbook.*

SWEDEN - BOOK PRODUCTION

Euromonitor International, Inc., 122 Michigan Avenue, Suite 1200, Chicago, Illinois 60603 (800) 577-EURO; *European Marketing Data and Statistics.*

Europa Publications Limited, 18 Bedford Square, London, WC1B 3JN, England; *The Europa World Year Book.*

Nordic Council of Ministers, Store Strandstraede 18, DK-1255 Copenhagen K, Denmark and the Nordic Statistical Secretariat, Postboks 2550, DK-2100 Copenhagen 0, Denmark; *The Yearbook of Nordic Statistics.*

Organisation for Economic Co-operation and Development (OECD), 2 rue Andre-Pascal, 75 Paris 16, France (Telephone Number in U.S. (202) 785-6323); *Indicators of Industrial Activity.*

St. Martin's Press, Inc., 175 Fifth Avenue, New York, New York 10010 (800) 221-7945; *The Statesman's Year-Book.*

Statistical Office of the United Nations, Publishing Service, New York, New York 10017 (800) 253-9646; *Trends in Europe and North America: The Statistical Yearbook of the Economic Commission for Europe.*

United Nations Educational, Scientific and Cultural Organization (UNESCO), 7 Place de Fontenoy, F-75700 Paris, France (Telephone Number in U.S. (212) 963-5981); *Statistical Yearbook.*

SWEDEN - BROADCASTING

Billboard Limited, P.O. Box 9027, 1006 AA Amsterdam, The Netherlands (Telephone Number in U.S. (212) 764-7300); *World Radio TV Handbook.*

Central Intelligence Agency, Washington, D.C. 20505 (703) 482-1100, www.cia.gov; *The World Factbook.*

Euromonitor International, Inc., 122 South Michigan Avenue, Suite 1200, Chicago, Illinois 60603 (800) 577-EURO; *World Marketing Data and Statistics.*

Europa Publications Limited, 18 Bedford Square, London, WC1B 3JN, England; *The Europa World Year Book.*

Nordic Council of Ministers, Store Strandstraede 18, DK-1255 Copenhagen K, Denmark and the Nordic Statistical Secretariat, Postboks 2550, DK-2100 Copenhagen 0, Denmark; *The Yearbook of Nordic Statistics.*

St. Martin's Press, Inc., 175 Fifth Avenue, New York, New York 10010 (800) 221-7945; *The Statesman's Year-Book.*

Statistical Office of the United Nations, Publishing Service, New York, New York 10017 (800) 253-9646; *Trends in Europe and North America: The Statistical Yearbook of the Economic Commission for Europe.*

United Nations Educational, Scientific and Cultural Organization (UNESCO), 7 Place de Fontenoy, F-75700 Paris, France (Telephone Number in U.S. (212) 963-5981); *Statistical Yearbook.*

SWEDEN - BUDGET

Central Intelligence Agency, Washington, D.C. 20505 (703) 482-1100, www.cia.gov; *The World Factbook.*

SWEDEN - BUSINESS

Organisation for Economic Co-operation and Development (OECD), 2 rue Andre-Pascal, 75 Paris 16, France (Telephone Number in U.S. (202) 785-6323); *Main Economic Indicators - Historical Statistics.*

SWEDEN - BUTTER - See SWEDEN - DAIRY PRODUCTS

SWEDEN - CADMIUM PRODUCTION AND CONSUMPTION - See SWEDEN - MINING AND MINERAL PRODUCTS

SWEDEN - CALORIE SUPPLY

Food and Agricultural Organization of the United Nations (FAO) Via delle Terme di Caracalla, 00100 Rome, Italy (Telephone Number in U.S. (202) 653-2400); *The State of Food and Agriculture.*

SWEDEN - CAPITAL INVESTMENT

Organisation for Economic Co-operation and Development (OECD), 2 rue Andre-Pascal, 75 Paris 16, France (Telephone Number in U.S. (202) 785-6323); *Economic Outlook;* and *Financial Market Trends.*

SWEDEN - CAPITAL REVENUE

International Monetary Fund, 700 Nineteenth Street, NW, Washington, D.C. 20431 (202) 623-7000; *Government Finance Statistics Yearbook.*

Organisation for Economic Co-operation and Development (OECD), 2 rue Andre-Pascal, 75 Paris 16, France (Telephone Number in U.S. (202) 785-6323); *Economic Outlook;* and *Financial Market Trends.*

SWEDEN - CATTLE - See SWEDEN - LIVESTOCK AND POULTRY

SWEDEN - CAUSTIC SODA PRODUCTION - See SWEDEN - BEVERAGES

SWEDEN - CEMENT PRODUCTION - See SWEDEN - MINING AND MINERAL PRODUCTS

SWEDEN - CEREAL PRODUCTION - See SWEDEN - CROPS

SWEDEN - CHEESE - See SWEDEN - DAIRY PRODUCTS

SWEDEN - CHEMICAL (ORGANIC) PRODUCTION - See SWEDEN - MINING AND MINERAL PRODUCTS

SWEDEN - CHROMITE PRODUCTION AND CONSUMPTION - See SWEDEN - MINING AND MINERAL PRODUCTS

SWEDEN - CHROMIUM ORE PRODUCTION AND CONSUMPTION - See SWEDEN - MINING AND MINERAL PRODUCTS

SWEDEN - CIGAR PRODUCTION - See SWEDEN - TOBACCO PRODUCTION

SWEDEN - CIGARETTE PRODUCTION - See SWEDEN - TOBACCO PRODUCTION

SWEDEN - CLIMATE

M.E. Sharpe, 80 Business Park Drive, Armonk, New York 10504 (800) 541-6563; *The Illustrated Book of World Rankings.*

Nordic Council of Ministers, Store

Strandstraede 18, DK-1255 Copenhagen K, Denmark and the Nordic Statistical Secretariat, Postboks 2550, DK-2100 Copenhagen 0, Denmark; *The Yearbook of Nordic Statistics.*

St. Martin's Press, Inc., 175 Fifth Avenue, New York, New York 10010 (800) 221-7945; *The Statesman's Year-Book.*

SWEDEN - CLOTHING - PRODUCTION INDEX - See SWEDEN - TEXTILE INDUSTRY

SWEDEN - CLOTHING EXPORTS AND IMPORTS - See SWEDEN - TEXTILE INDUSTRY

SWEDEN - COAL PRODUCTION - See SWEDEN - MINING AND MINERAL PRODUCTS

SWEDEN - COBALT PRODUCTION AND CONSUMPTION - See SWEDEN - MINING AND MINERAL PRODUCTS

SWEDEN - COFFEE PRODUCTION AND CONSUMPTION

M.E. Sharpe, 80 Business Park Drive, Armonk, New York 10504 (800) 541-6563; *The Illustrated Book of World Rankings.*

Statistical Office of the United Nations, Publishing Service, New York, New York 10017 (800) 253-9646; *Statistical Yearbook.*

SWEDEN - COKE AND COKE OVEN ORE PRODUCTION AND CONSUMPTION - See SWEDEN - MINING AND MINERAL PRODUCTS

SWEDEN - COMMERCE

St. Martin's Press, Inc., 175 Fifth Avenue, New York, New York 10010 (800) 221-7945; *The Statesman's Year-Book.*

SWEDEN - CONSTRUCTION INDUSTRY

M.E. Sharpe, 80 Business Park Drive, Armonk, New York 10504 (800) 541-6563; *The Illustrated Book of World Rankings.*

Organisation for Economic Co-operation and Development/ (OECD), 2 rue Andre-Pascal, 75 Paris 16, France (Telephone Number in U.S. (202) 785-6323); *Industrial Structure Statistics; Main Economic Indicators - Historical Statistics;* and *OECD Economic Surveys: Sweden.*

St. Martin's Press, Inc., 175 Fifth Avenue, New York, New York 10010 (800) 221-7945; *The Statesman's Year-Book.*

Statistical Office of the United Nations, Publishing Service, New York, New York 10017 (800) 253-9646; *Statistical Yearbook.*

SWEDEN - CONSUMER PRICE INDEX

Europa Publications Limited, 18 Bedford Square, London, WC1B 3JN, England; *The Europa World Year Book.*

Nordic Council of Ministers, Store Strandstraede 18, DK-1255 Copenhagen K, Denmark and the Nordic Statistical Secretariat, Postboks 2550, DK-2100 Copenhagen 0, Denmark; *The Yearbook of Nordic Statistics.*

Organisation for Economic Co-operation and Development (OECD), 2 rue Andre-Pascal, 75 Paris 16, France (Telephone Number in U.S. (202) 785-6323); *Economic Outlook.*

Statistical Office of the United Nations, Publishing Service, New York, New York 10017 (800) 253-9646; *Statistical Yearbook;* and *Trends in Europe and North America: The Statistical Yearbook of the Economic Commission for Europe.*

SWEDEN - CONSUMER PRICES

Euromonitor International, Inc., 122 Michigan Avenue, Suite 1200, Chicago, Illinois 60603 (800) 577-EURO; *European Marketing Data and Statistics;* and *World Marketing Data and Statistics.*

International Labour Office, I.L.O. Publications, 1828 L Street, NW, Suite 801, Washington, D.C. 20036 (301) 638-3152; *Yearbook of Labour Statistics.*

International Monetary Fund, 700 Nineteenth Street, NW, Washington, D.C. 20431 (202) 623-7000; *International Financial Statistics.*

Organisation for Economic Co-operation and Development (OECD), 2 rue Andre-Pascal, 75 Paris 16, France (Telephone Number in U.S. (202) 785-6323); *Economic Outlook.*

SWEDEN - CONSUMPTION

International Lead and Zinc Study Group, Metro House, 58 St. James's Street, London SW1A 1LD, England; *Lead and Zinc Statistics.*

International Rubber Study Group, York House, Eighth Floor, Empire Way, Wembley, London HA9 0PA, England; *Rubber Statistical Bulletin.*

Nordic Council of Ministers, Store Strandstraede 18, DK-1255 Copenhagen K, Denmark and the Nordic Statistical Secretariat, Postboks 2550, DK-2100 Copenhagen 0, Denmark; *The Yearbook of Nordic Statistics.*

Organisation for Economic Co-operation and Development (OECD), 2 rue Andre-Pascal, 75 Paris 16, France (Telephone Number in U.S. (202) 785-

6323); *The Footwear, Raw Hides and Skins, and Leather Industry in OECD Countries; The Iron and Steel Industry; Meat Balances in OECD Member Countries; The Non-Ferrous Metals Industry; The Pulp and Paper Industry;* and *Textile Industry in OECD Countries.*

The World Bank, 1818 H Street, NW, Washington, D.C. 20433 (202) 477-1234; *World Development Report.*

SWEDEN - COPPER AND COPPER ORE PRODUCTION AND CONSUMPTION - See SWEDEN - MINING AND MINERAL PRODUCTS

SWEDEN - CORN PRODUCTION

Food and Agricultural Organization of the United Nations (FAO) Via delle Terme di Caracalla, 00100 Rome, Italy (Telephone Number in U.S. (202) 653-2400); *The State of Food and Agriculture.*

M.E. Sharpe, 80 Business Park Drive, Armonk, New York 10504 (800) 541-6563; *The Illustrated Book of World Rankings.*

SWEDEN - CORPORATE INCOME TAXES - See SWEDEN - TAXATION

SWEDEN - CORPORATE TAXES - See SWEDEN - TAXATION

SWEDEN - COTTON - See SWEDEN - CROPS

SWEDEN - CRIME

International Criminal Police Organization (INTERPOL), 50 quai Achille Lignon, F-69006 Lyon, France; *International Crime Statistics.*

Nordic Council of Ministers, Store Strandstraede 18, DK-1255 Copenhagen K, Denmark and the Nordic Statistical Secretariat, Postboks 2550, DK-2100 Copenhagen 0, Denmark; *The Yearbook of Nordic Statistics.*

Statistical Office of the United Nations, Publishing Service, New York, New York 10017 (800) 253-9646; *Trends in Europe and North America: The Statistical Yearbook of the Economic Commission for Europe.*

Yale University Press, Yale Station, New Haven, Connecticut 06520 (800) 987-7323; *Violence and Crime in Cross-National Perspective.*

SWEDEN - CROPS

Commodity Research Bureau, Inc., 30 South Wacker Drive, Chicago Illinois 60606 (312) 454-1801; *Commodity Year Book.*

Euromonitor International, Inc., 122 Michigan Avenue, Suite 1200, Chicago,

Illinois 60603 (800) 577-EURO; *European Marketing Data and Statistics.*

Europa Publications Limited, 18 Bedford Square, London, WC1B 3JN, England; *The Europa World Year Book.*

Food and Agricultural Organization of the United Nations (FAO) Via delle Terme di Caracalla, 00100 Rome, Italy (Telephone Number in U.S. (202) 653-2400); *The State of Food and Agriculture.*

M.E. Sharpe, 80 Business Park Drive, Armonk, New York 10504 (800) 541-6563; *The Illustrated Book of World Rankings.*

Organisation for Economic Co-operation and Development (OECD), 2 rue Andre-Pascal, 75 Paris 16, France (Telephone Number in U.S. (202) 785-6323); *Economic Accounts for Agriculture; Foreign Trade by Commodities;* and *Textile Industry in OECD Countries.*

St. Martin's Press, Inc., 175 Fifth Avenue, New York, New York 10010 (800) 221-7945; *The Statesman's Year-Book.*

Statistical Office of the United Nations, Publishing Service, New York, New York 10017 (800) 253-9646; *Statistical Yearbook.*

United Nations Conference on Trade and Development, Central Statistical Service, Palais des Nations, Geneva, Switzerland (Telephone in U.S. (800) 253-9646); *UNCTAD Commodity Yearbook.*

SWEDEN - CUSTOMS DUTIES

International Monetary Fund, 700 Nineteenth Street, NW, Washington, D.C. 20431 (202) 623-7000; *Government Finance Statistics Yearbook.*

Organisation for Economic Co-operation and Development (OECD), 2 rue Andre-Pascal, 75 Paris 16, France (Telephone Number in U.S. (202) 785-6323); *The Non-Ferrous Metals Industry.*

St. Martin's Press, Inc., 175 Fifth Avenue, New York, New York 10010 (800) 221-7945; *The Statesman's Year-Book.*

SWEDEN - DAIRY PRODUCTS

Commodity Research Bureau, Inc., 30 South Wacker Drive, Chicago Illinois 60606 (312) 454-1801; *Commodity Year Book.*

Europa Publications Limited, 18 Bedford Square, London, WC1B 3JN, England; *The Europa World Year Book.*

Food and Agricultural Organization of the United Nations (FAO) Via delle Terme di Caracalla, 00100 Rome, Italy (Telephone Number in U.S. (202) 653-2400); *The State of Food and Agriculture.*

M.E. Sharpe, 80 Business Park Drive, Armonk, New York 10504 (800) 541-6563; *The Illustrated Book of World Rankings.*

Nordic Council of Ministers, Store Strandstraede 18, DK-1255 Copenhagen K, Denmark and the Nordic Statistical Secretariat, Postboks 2550, DK-2100 Copenhagen 0, Denmark; *The Yearbook of Nordic Statistics.*

Organisation for Economic Co-operation and Development (OECD), 2 rue Andre-Pascal, 75 Paris 16, France (Telephone Number in U.S. (202) 785-6323); *Economic Accounts for Agriculture;* and *Milk, Milk Products, and Egg Balances in OECD Member Countries.*

St. Martin's Press, Inc., 175 Fifth Avenue, New York, New York 10010 (800) 221-7945; *The Statesman's Year-Book.*

Statistical Office of the United Nations, Publishing Service, New York, New York 10017 (800) 253-9646; *Statistical Yearbook.*

SWEDEN - DEATH RATES - See SWEDEN - MORTALITY

SWEDEN - DEFENSE EXPENDITURES - See SWEDEN - MILITARY

SWEDEN - DEMOGRAPHY

The Economist Intelligence Unit, 111 West 57th Street, New York, New York 10019 (800) 938-4685; *The World Market Atlas.*

Euromonitor International, Inc., 122 Michigan Avenue, Suite 1200, Chicago, Illinois 60603 (800) 577-EURO; *The World Economic Factbook;* and *World Marketing Data and Statistics.*

M.E. Sharpe, 80 Business Park Drive, Armonk, New York 10504 (800) 541-6563; *The Illustrated Book of World Rankings.*

Nordic Council of Ministers, Store Strandstraede 18, DK-1255 Copenhagen K, Denmark and the Nordic Statistical Secretariat, Postboks 2550, DK-2100 Copenhagen 0, Denmark; *The Yearbook of Nordic Statistics.*

Statistical Office of the United Nations, Publishing Service, New York, New York 10017 (800) 253-9646; *Human Development Report.*

SWEDEN - DEVELOPMENT ASSISTANCE

Organisation for Economic Co-operation and Development (OECD), 2 rue Andre-Pascal, 75 Paris 16, France (Telephone Number in U.S. (202) 785-6323); *Geographical Distribution of Financial Flows to Developing Countries.*

Statistical Office of the United Nations, Publishing Service, New York, New York 10017 (800) 253-9646; *Statistical Yearbook.*

SWEDEN - DIAMOND PRODUCTION - See SWEDEN - MINING AND MINERAL PRODUCTS

SWEDEN - DISCOUNT RATES - See SWEDEN - BANKING

SWEDEN - DISEASES - See SWEDEN - HEALTH

SWEDEN - DIVORCE RATES

M.E. Sharpe, 80 Business Park Drive, Armonk, New York 10504 (800) 541-6563; *The Illustrated Book of World Rankings.*

Nordic Council of Ministers, Store Strandstraede 18, DK-1255 Copenhagen K, Denmark and the Nordic Statistical Secretariat, Postboks 2550, DK-2100 Copenhagen 0, Denmark; *The Yearbook of Nordic Statistics.*

Statistical Office of the United Nations, Publishing Service, New York, New York 10017 (800) 253-9646; *Demographic Yearbook; Trends in Europe and North America: The Statistical Yearbook of the Economic Commission for Europe;* and *Statistical Yearbook.*

SWEDEN - ECONOMY

Central Intelligence Agency, Washington, D.C. 20505 (703) 482-1100, www.cia.gov; *The World Factbook.*

Economist Intelligence Unit, 111 West 57th Street, New York, New York 10019 (800) 938-4685; *Sweden Country Report.*

Euromonitor International, Inc., 122 Michigan Avenue, Suite 1200, Chicago, Illinois 60603 (800) 577-EURO; *European Marketing Data and Statistics; World Marketing Data and Statistics;* and *The World Economic Factbook.*

Europa Publications Limited, 18 Bedford Square, London, WC1B 3JN, England; *The Europa World Year Book.*

M.E. Sharpe, 80 Business Park Drive, Armonk, New York 10504 (800) 541-6563; *The Illustrated Book of World Rankings.*

Organisation for Economic Co-operation and Development (OECD), 2 rue Andre-Pascal, 75 Paris 16, France (Telephone Number in U.S. (202) 785-6323); *Economic Outlook; Geographical Distribution of Financial Flows to Developing Countries; Main Economic Indicators - Historical Statistics, OECD Economic Surveys: Sweden;* and *OECD Employment Outlook.*

St. Martin's Press, Inc., 175 Fifth Avenue, New York, New York 10010 (800) 221-7945; *The Statesman's Year-Book.*

Statistical Office of the United Nations, Publishing Service, New York, New York 10017 (800) 253-9646; *World Statistics Pocketbook.*

The World Bank, 1818 H Street, NW, Washington, D.C. 20433 (202) 477-1234; *The World Bank Atlas;* and *World Development Report.*

SWEDEN - EDUCATION

The Economist Intelligence Unit, 111 West 57th Street, New York, New York 10019 (800) 938-4685; *The World Market Atlas.*

Euromonitor International, Inc., 122 Michigan Avenue, Suite 1200, Chicago, Illinois 60603 (800) 577-EURO; *European Marketing Data and Statistics;* and *World Marketing Data and Statistics.*

Europa Publications Limited, 18 Bedford Square, London, WC1B 3JN, England; *The Europa World Year Book.*

International Monetary Fund, 700 Nineteenth Street, NW, Washington, D.C. 20431 (202) 623-7000; *Government Finance Statistics Yearbook.*

M.E. Sharpe, 80 Business Park Drive, Armonk, New York 10504 (800) 541-6563; *The Illustrated Book of World Rankings.*

Nordic Council of Ministers, Store Strandstraede 18, DK-1255 Copenhagen K, Denmark and the Nordic Statistical Secretariat, Postboks 2550, DK-2100 Copenhagen 0, Denmark; *The Yearbook of Nordic Statistics.*

Organisation for Economic Co-operation and Development (OECD), 2 rue Andre-Pascal, 75 Paris 16, France (Telephone Number in U.S. (202) 785-6323); *Education in OECD Countries.*

St. Martin's Press, Inc., 175 Fifth Avenue, New York, New York 10010 (800) 221-7945; *The Statesman's Year-Book.*

Statistical Office of the United Nations, Publishing Service, New York, New York 10017 (800) 253-9646; *Human Development Report;* and *Trends in Europe and North America: The Statistical Yearbook of the Economic Commission for Europe.*

United Nations Educational, Scientific and Cultural Organization (UNESCO), 7 Place de Fontenoy, F-75700 Paris, France (Telephone Number in U.S. (212) 963-5981); *Statistical Yearbook.*

The World Bank, 1818 H Street, NW, Washington, D.C. 20433 (202) 477-1234; *World Development Report;* and *World Development Indicators.*

SWEDEN - EGG PRODUCTION AND CONSUMPTION - See SWEDEN - DAIRY PRODUCTS

SWEDEN - ELECTRICITY

Central Intelligence Agency, Washington, D.C. 20505 (703) 482-1100, www.cia.gov; *The World Factbook.*

Commodity Research Bureau, Inc., 30 South Wacker Drive, Chicago Illinois 60606 (312) 454-1801; *Commodity Year Book.*

M.E. Sharpe, 80 Business Park Drive, Armonk, New York 10504 (800) 541-6563; *The Illustrated Book of World Rankings.*

Nordic Council of Ministers, Store Strandstraede 18, DK-1255 Copenhagen K, Denmark and the Nordic Statistical Secretariat, Postboks 2550, DK-2100 Copenhagen 0, Denmark; *The Yearbook of Nordic Statistics.*

Organisation for Economic Co-operation and Development (OECD), 2 rue Andre-Pascal, 75 Paris 16, France (Telephone Number in U.S. (202) 785-6323); *Coal Information; Energy Statistics of OECD Countries;* and *Industrial Structure Statistics.*

St. Martin's Press, Inc., 175 Fifth Avenue, New York, New York 10010 (800) 221-7945; *The Statesman's Year-Book.*

Statistical Office of the United Nations, Publishing Service, New York, New York 10017 (800) 253-9646; *Human Development Report; Statistical Yearbook;* and *Trends in Europe and North America: The Statistical Yearbook of the Economic Commission for Europe.*

SWEDEN - EMPLOYMENT

Euromonitor International, Inc., 122 Michigan Avenue, Suite 1200, Chicago, Illinois 60603 (800) 577-EURO; *European Marketing Data and Statistics.*

International Labour Office, I.L.O. Publications, 1828 L Street, NW, Suite 801, Washington, D.C. 20036 (301) 638-3152; *Yearbook of Labour Statistics.*

M.E. Sharpe, 80 Business Park Drive, Armonk, New York 10504 (800) 541-6563; *The Illustrated Book of World Rankings.*

Nordic Council of Ministers, Store Strandstraede 18, DK-1255 Copenhagen K, Denmark and the Nordic Statistical Secretariat, Postboks 2550, DK-2100 Copenhagen 0, Denmark; *The Yearbook of*

Nordic Statistics.

Organisation for Economic Co-operation and Development (OECD), 2 rue Andre-Pascal, 75 Paris 16, France (Telephone Number in U.S. (202) 785-6323); *Economic Outlook; The Iron and Steel Industry; OECD Economic Surveys: Sweden; OECD Employment Outlook;* and *Textile Industry in OECD Countries.*

Statistical Office of the United Nations, Publishing Service, New York, New York 10017 (800) 253-9646; *Statistical Yearbook;* and *Trends in Europe and North America: The Statistical Yearbook of the Economic Commission for Europe.*

SWEDEN - ENERGY

Euromonitor International, Inc., 122 Michigan Avenue, Suite 1200, Chicago, Illinois 60603 (800) 577-EURO; *European Marketing Data and Statistics; World Marketing Data and Statistics;* and *The World Economic Factbook.*

Food and Agricultural Organization of the United Nations (FAO) Via delle Terme di Caracalla, 00100 Rome, Italy (Telephone Number in U.S. (202) 653-2400); *The State of Food and Agriculture.*

M.E. Sharpe, 80 Business Park Drive, Armonk, New York 10504 (800) 541-6563; *The Illustrated Book of World Rankings.*

Nordic Council of Ministers, Store Strandstraede 18, DK-1255 Copenhagen K, Denmark and the Nordic Statistical Secretariat, Postboks 2550, DK-2100 Copenhagen 0, Denmark; *The Yearbook of Nordic Statistics.*

Organisation for Economic Co-operation and Development (OECD), 2 rue Andre-Pascal, 75 Paris 16, France (Telephone Number in U.S. (202) 785-6323); *Coal Information; Energy Statistics of OECD Countries; OECD Environmental Data;* and *Oil and Gas Information.*

St. Martin's Press, Inc., 175 Fifth Avenue, New York, New York 10010 (800) 221-7945; *The Statesman's Year-Book.*

Statistical Office of the United Nations, Publishing Service, New York, New York 10017 (800) 253-9646; *Energy Statistics Yearbook; Human Development Report; Statistical Yearbook; Trends in Europe and North America: The Statistical Yearbook of the Economic Commission for Europe;* and *World Statistics Pocketbook.*

The World Bank, 1818 H Street, NW, Washington, D.C. 20433 (202) 477-1234; *The World Bank Atlas;* and *World Development Report.*

SWEDEN - ENGINEERING AND METAL

PRODUCTS - EXPORTS AND IMPORTS

SWEDEN - ENVIRONMENT

Economist Intelligence Unit, 111 West 57th Street, New York, New York 10019 (800) 938-4685; *Sweden Country Report.*

Organization for Economic Co-operation and Development (OECD), 2 rue Andre-Pascal, 75 Paris 16, France (Telephone Number in U.S. (202) 785-6323); *OECD Environmental Data.*

Statistical Office of the United Nations, Publishing Service, New York, New York 10017 (800) 253-9646; *Trends in Europe and North America: The Statistical Yearbook of the Economic Commission for Europe;* and *World Statistics Pocketbook.*

SWEDEN - EXCHANGE RATES

Central Intelligence Agency, Washington, D.C. 20505 (703) 482-1100, www.cia.gov; *The World Factbook.*

Euromonitor International, Inc., 122 Michigan Avenue, Suite 1200, Chicago, Illinois 60603 (800) 577-EURO; *The World Economic Factbook.*

Europa Publications Limited, 18 Bedford Square, London, WC1B 3JN, England; *The Europa World Year Book.*

International Monetary Fund, 700 Nineteenth Street, NW, Washington, D.C. 20431 (202) 623-7000; *International Financial Statistics.*

Nordic Council of Ministers, Store Strandstraede 18, DK-1255 Copenhagen K, Denmark and the Nordic Statistical Secretariat, Postboks 2550, DK-2100 Copenhagen 0, Denmark; *The Yearbook of Nordic Statistics.*

Organisation for Economic Co-operation and Development (OECD), 2 rue Andre-Pascal, 75 Paris 16, France (Telephone Number in U.S. (202) 785-6323); *Economic Outlook; Financial Market Trends; Revenue Statistics of OECD Member Countries;* and *Tourism Policy and International Tourism in OECD Member Countries.*

Statistical Office of the United Nations, Publishing Service, New York, New York 10017 (800) 253-9646; *Statistical Yearbook; Trends in Europe and North America: The Statistical Yearbook of the Economic Commission for Europe;* and *World Statistics Pocketbook.*

SWEDEN - EXCISE TAXES - See SWEDEN - TAXATION

SWEDEN - EXPORTS

Central Intelligence Agency, Washington, D.C. 20505 (703) 482-1100, www.cia.gov; *The World Factbook.*

The Economist Intelligence Unit, 111 West 57th Street, New York, New York 10019 (800) 938-4685; *Sweden Country Report;* and *The World Market Atlas.*

Euromonitor International, Inc., 122 Michigan Avenue, Suite 1200, Chicago, Illinois 60603 (800) 577-EURO; *The World Economic Factbook.*

Europa Publications Limited, 18 Bedford Square, London, WC1B 3JN, England; *The Europa World Year Book.*

Food and Agricultural Organization of the United Nations (FAO) Via delle Terme di Caracalla, 00100 Rome, Italy (Telephone Number in U.S. (202) 653-2400); *The State of Food and Agriculture.*

International Lead and Zinc Study Group, Metro House, 58 St. James's Street, London SW1A 1LD, England; *Lead and Zinc Statistics.*

International Monetary Fund, 700 Nineteenth Street, NW, Washington, D.C. 20431 (202) 623-7000; *Direction of Trade Statistics;* and *International Financial Statistics.*

International Rubber Study Group, York House, Eighth Floor, Empire Way, Wembley, London HA9 0PA, England; *Rubber Statistical Bulletin.*

Nordic Council of Ministers, Store Strandstraede 18, DK-1255 Copenhagen K, Denmark and the Nordic Statistical Secretariat, Postboks 2550, DK-2100 Copenhagen 0, Denmark; *The Yearbook of Nordic Statistics.*

Organisation for Economic Co-operation and Development (OECD), 2 rue Andre-Pascal, 75 Paris 16, France (Telephone Number in U.S. (202) 785-6323); *Economic Outlook; The Footwear, Raw Hides and Skins, and Leather Industry in OECD Countries; Foreign Trade by Commodities; Geographical Distribution of Financial Flows to Developing Countries; Industrial Structure Statistics; The Iron and Steel Industry; Milk, Milk Products, and Egg Balances in OECD Member Countries; OECD Economic Surveys: Sweden; The Pulp and Paper Industry;* and *Review of Fisheries in OECD Member Countries.*

St. Martin's Press, Inc., 175 Fifth Avenue, New York, New York 10010 (800) 221-7945; *The Statesman's Year-Book.*

Statistical Office of the United Nations, Publishing Service, New York, New York 10017 (800) 253-9646; *Trends in Europe and North America: The Statistical Yearbook of*

the Economic Commission for Europe.

United Nations Conference on Trade and Development (UNCTAD), New York, New York 10017 (800) 253-9646; *Handbook of International Trade and Development Statistics.*

The World Bank, 1818 H Street, NW, Washington, D.C. 20433 (202) 477-1234; *World Development Report;* and *World Development Indicators.*

SWEDEN - EXTERNAL FINANCING

Organisation for Economic Co-operation and Development (OECD), 2 rue Andre-Pascal, 75 Paris 16, France (Telephone Number in U.S. (202) 785-6323); *Economic Outlook;* and *Financial Market Trends.*

SWEDEN - EXTERNAL INDEBTEDNESS

Organisation for Economic Co-operation and Development (OECD), 2 rue Andre-Pascal, 75 Paris 16, France (Telephone Number in U.S. (202) 785-6323); *Financial Market Trends;* and *Geographical Distribution of Financial Flows to Developing Countries.*

The World Bank, 1818 H Street, NW, Washington, D.C. 20433 (202) 477-1234; *World Development Report;* and *World Development Indicators.*

SWEDEN - EXTERNAL TRADE

Euromonitor International, Inc., 122 South Michigan Avenue, Suite 1200, Chicago, Illinois 60603 (800) 577-EURO; *World Marketing Data and Statistics.*

Food and Agricultural Organization of the United Nations (FAO) Via delle Terme di Caracalla, 00100 Rome, Italy (Telephone Number in U.S. (202) 653-2400); *The State of Food and Agriculture;* and *Trade Yearbook.*

Nordic Council of Ministers, Store Strandstraede 18, DK-1255 Copenhagen K, Denmark and the Nordic Statistical Secretariat, Postboks 2550, DK-2100 Copenhagen 0, Denmark; *The Yearbook of Nordic Statistics.*

Statistical Office of the United Nations, Publishing Service, New York, New York 10017 (800) 253-9646; *Statistical Yearbook.*

SWEDEN - FABRIC PRODUCTION - See SWEDEN - TEXTILE INDUSTRY

SWEDEN - FARM CROPS - See SWEDEN - CROPS

SWEDEN - FEMALE WORKING POPULATION - See SWEDEN - EMPLOYMENT

SWEDEN - FERTILITY RATES

Central Intelligence Agency, Washington, D.C. 20505 (703) 482-1100, www.cia.gov; *The World Factbook.*

M.E. Sharpe, 80 Business Park Drive, Armonk, New York 10504 (800) 541-6563; *The Illustrated Book of World Rankings.*

Nordic Council of Ministers, Store Strandstraede 18, DK-1255 Copenhagen K, Denmark and the Nordic Statistical Secretariat, Postboks 2550, DK-2100 Copenhagen 0, Denmark; *The Yearbook of Nordic Statistics.*

Statistical Office of the United Nations, Publishing Service, New York, New York 10017 (800) 253-9646; *Human Development Report;* and *Trends in Europe and North America: The Statistical Yearbook of the Economic Commission for Europe.*

The World Bank, 1818 H Street, NW, Washington, D.C. 20433 (202) 477-1234; *The World Bank Atlas; World Development Report;* and *World Development Indicators.*

SWEDEN - FERTILIZER

Food and Agricultural Organization of the United Nations (FAO) Via delle Terme di Caracalla, 00100 Rome, Italy (Telephone Number in U.S. (202) 653-2400); *The State of Food and Agriculture.*

Organisation for Economic Co-operation and Development (OECD), 2 rue Andre-Pascal, 75 Paris 16, France (Telephone Number in U.S. (202) 785-6323); *Economic Accounts for Agriculture;* and *Foreign Trade by Commodities.*

Statistical Office of the United Nations, Publishing Service, New York, New York 10017 (800) 253-9646; *Statistical Yearbook.*

SWEDEN - FETAL MORTALITY - See SWEDEN - MORTALITY

SWEDEN - FILAMENT PRODUCTION - See SWEDEN - TEXTILE INDUSTRY

SWEDEN - FILM - See SWEDEN - MOTION PICTURES

SWEDEN - FINANCE

Economist Intelligence Unit, 111 West 57th Street, New York, New York 10019 (800) 938-4685; *Sweden Country Report.*

Europa Publications Limited, 18 Bedford Square, London, WC1B 3JN, England; *The Europa World Year Book.*

International Monetary Fund, 700 Nineteenth Street, NW, Washington, D.C. 20431 (202) 623-7000; *Government Finance Statistics Yearbook;* and *International Financial Statistics.*

M.E. Sharpe, 80 Business Park Drive, Armonk, New York 10504 (800) 541-6563; *The Illustrated Book of World Rankings.*

Nordic Council of Ministers, Store Strandstraede 18, DK-1255 Copenhagen K, Denmark and the Nordic Statistical Secretariat, Postboks 2550, DK-2100 Copenhagen 0, Denmark; *The Yearbook of Nordic Statistics.*

Organisation for Economic Co-operation and Development (OECD), 2 rue Andre-Pascal, 75 Paris 16, France (Telephone Number in U.S. (202) 785-6323); *Economic Outlook; Financial Market Trends; Geographical Distribution of Financial Flows to Developing Countries; Main Economic Indicators - Historical Statistics; OECD Financial Statistics;* and *Revenue Statistics of OECD Member Countries.*

St. Martin's Press, Inc., 175 Fifth Avenue, New York, New York 10010 (800) 221-7945; *The Statesman's Year-Book.*

SWEDEN - FISHERIES

Euromonitor International, Inc., 122 Michigan Avenue, Suite 1200, Chicago, Illinois 60603 (800) 577-EURO; *European Marketing Data and Statistics.*

Europa Publications Limited, 18 Bedford Square, London, WC1B 3JN, England; *The Europa World Year Book.*

Food and Agricultural Organization of the United Nations (FAO) Via delle Terme di Caracalla, 00100 Rome, Italy (Telephone Number in U.S. (202) 653-2400); *The State of Food and Agriculture;* and *Yearbook of Fishery Statistics.*

M.E. Sharpe, 80 Business Park Drive, Armonk, New York 10504 (800) 541-6563; *The Illustrated Book of World Rankings.*

Nordic Council of Ministers, Store Strandstraede 18, DK-1255 Copenhagen K, Denmark and the Nordic Statistical Secretariat, Postboks 2550, DK-2100 Copenhagen 0, Denmark; *The Yearbook of Nordic Statistics.*

Organisation for Economic Co-operation and Development (OECD), 2 rue Andre-Pascal, 75 Paris 16, France (Telephone Number in U.S. (202) 785-6323); *Foreign Trade by Commodities; Industrial Structure Statistics;* and *Review of Fisheries in OECD Member Countries.*

St. Martin's Press, Inc., 175 Fifth Avenue, New York, New York 10010 (800) 221-7945; *The Statesman's Year-Book.*

Statistical Office of the United Nations, Publishing Service, New York, New York 10017 (800) 253-9646; *Statistical Yearbook.*

United Nations Conference on Trade and Development, Central Statistical Service, Palais des Nations, Geneva, Switzerland (Telephone in U.S. (800) 253-9646); *UNCTAD Commodity Yearbook.*

SWEDEN - FLOUR PRODUCTION

Statistical Office of the United Nations, Publishing Service, New York, New York 10017 (800) 253-9646; *Statistical Yearbook.*

SWEDEN - FOOD

Euromonitor International, Inc., 122 South Michigan Avenue, Suite 1200, Chicago, Illinois 60603 (800) 577-EURO; *Retail Trade International.*

Food and Agricultural Organization of the United Nations (FAO) Via delle Terme di Caracalla, 00100 Rome, Italy (Telephone Number in U.S. (202) 653-2400); *Production Yearbook;* and *The State of Food and Agriculture.*

Organisation for Economic Co-operation and Development (OECD), 2 rue Andre-Pascal, 75 Paris 16, France (Telephone Number in U.S. (202) 785-6323); *Foreign Trade by Commodities;* and *Main Economic Indicators- Historical Statistics.*

Statistical Office of the United Nations, Publishing Service, New York, New York 10017 (800) 253-9646; *Human Development Report.*

SWEDEN - FOOTWEAR - PRODUCTION INDEX

Organisation for Economic Co-operation and Development (OECD), 2 rue Andre-Pascal, 75 Paris 16, France (Telephone Number in U.S. (202) 785-6323); *Indicators of Industrial Activity.*

SWEDEN - FOREIGN DEBT

International Monetary Fund, 700 Nineteenth Street, NW, Washington, D.C. 20431 (202) 623-7000; *Government Finance Statistics Yearbook.*

Organisation for Economic Co-operation and Development (OECD), 2 rue Andre-Pascal, 75 Paris 16, France (Telephone Number in U.S. (202) 785-6323); *Economic Outlook.*

St. Martin's Press, Inc., 175 Fifth Avenue, New York, New York 10010 (800) 221-7945; *The Statesman's Year-Book.*

SWEDEN - FOREIGN INDEBTEDNESS

Organisation for Economic Co-operation and Development (OECD), 2 rue Andre-Pascal, 75 Paris 16, France (Telephone Number in U.S. (202) 785-6323); *Economic Outlook;* and *Financial Market Trends.*

SWEDEN - FOREIGN TRADE

Economist Intelligence Unit, 111 West 57th Street, New York, New York 10019 (800) 938-4685; *Sweden Country Report.*

Euromonitor International, Inc., 122 Michigan Avenue, Suite 1200, Chicago, Illinois 60603 (800) 577-EURO; *European Marketing Data and Statistics;* and *The World Economic Factbook.*

Europa Publications Limited, 18 Bedford Square, London, WC1B 3JN, England; *The Europa World Year Book.*

Food and Agricultural Organization of the United Nations (FAO) Via delle Terme di Caracalla, 00100 Rome, Italy (Telephone Number in U.S. (202) 653-2400); *The State of Food and Agriculture.*

International Monetary Fund, 700 Nineteenth Street, NW, Washington, D.C. 20431 (202) 623-7000; *International Financial Statistics.*

M.E. Sharpe, 80 Business Park Drive, Armonk, New York 10504 (800) 541-6563; *The Illustrated Book of World Rankings.*

Organisation for Economic Co-operation and Development (OECD), 2 rue Andre-Pascal, 75 Paris 16, France (Telephone Number in U.S. (202) 785-6323); *Economic Outlook; The Footwear, Raw Hides and Skins, and Leather Industry in OECD Countries; Foreign Trade by Commodities; Main Economic Indicators - Historical Statistics; Maritime Transport; Meat Balances in OECD Member Countries;* and *OECD Economic Surveys: Sweden.*

St. Martin's Press, Inc., 175 Fifth Avenue, New York, New York 10010 (800) 221-7945; *The Statesman's Year-Book.*

Statistical Office of the United Nations, Publishing Service, New York, New York 10017 (800) 253-9646; *International Trade Statistics Yearbook, Statistical Yearbook;* and *Trade Manufactures of Developing Countries.*

United Nations Conference on Trade and Development, Central Statistical Service, Palais des Nations, Geneva, Switzerland (Telephone in U.S. (800) 253-9646); *UNCTAD Commodity Yearbook.*

The World Bank, 1818 H Street, NW, Washington, D.C. 20433 (202) 477-1234; *World Development Report;* and *World Development Indicators.*

World Bureau of Metal Statistics, 27-A High Street, Ware Hert SG12 9BA, England; *World Metal Statistics.*

SWEDEN - FORESTRY AND FOREST INDUSTRY

Euromonitor International, Inc., 122 Michigan Avenue, Suite 1200, Chicago, Illinois 60603 (800) 577-EURO; *European Marketing Data and Statistics.*

Europa Publications Limited, 18 Bedford Square, London, WC1B 3JN, England; *The Europa World Year Book.*

Food and Agricultural Organization of the United Nations (FAO) Via delle Terme di Caracalla, 00100 Rome, Italy (Telephone Number in U.S. (202) 653-2400); *The State of Food and Agriculture;* and *Yearbook of Forest Products.*

International Monetary Fund, 700 Nineteenth Street, NW, Washington, D.C. 20431 (202) 623-7000; *International Financial Statistics.*

M.E. Sharpe, 80 Business Park Drive, Armonk, New York 10504 (800) 541-6563; *The Illustrated Book of World Rankings.*

Nordic Council of Ministers, Store Strandstraede 18, DK-1255 Copenhagen K, Denmark and the Nordic Statistical Secretariat, Postboks 2550, DK-2100 Copenhagen 0, Denmark; *The Yearbook of Nordic Statistics.*

Organisation for Economic Co-operation and Development (OECD), 2 rue Andre-Pascal, 75 Paris 16, France (Telephone Number in U.S. (202) 785-6323); *Indicators of Industrial Activity; Industrial Structure Statistics;* and *The Pulp and Paper Industry.*

St. Martin's Press, Inc., 175 Fifth Avenue, New York, New York 10010 (800) 221-7945; *The Statesman's Year-Book.*

Statistical Office of the United Nations, Publishing Service, New York, New York 10017 (800) 253-9646; *Statistical Yearbook;* and *Trends in Europe and North America: The Statistical Yearbook of the Economic Commission for Europe.*

United Nations Conference on Trade and Development, Central Statistical Service, Palais des Nations, Geneva, Switzerland (Telephone in U.S. (800) 253-9646); *UNCTAD Commodity Yearbook.*

United Nations Educational, Scientific and Cultural Organization (UNESCO), 7 Place de Fontenoy, F-75700 Paris, France (Telephone Number in U.S. (212) 963-5981); *Statistical Yearbook.*

The World Bank, 1818 H Street, NW,

Washington, D.C. 20433 (202) 477-1234; *World Development Report.*

SWEDEN - FRUIT PRODUCTION - See SWEDEN - CROPS

SWEDEN - FURNITURE AND WOOD PRODUCTS - EXPORTS AND IMPORTS

Organisation for Economic Co-operation and Development (OECD), 2 rue Andre-Pascal, 75 Paris 16, France (Telephone Number in U.S. (202) 785-6323); *Foreign Trade by Commodities;* and *Industrial Structure Statistics.*

SWEDEN - GAS - See SWEDEN - MINING AND MINERAL PRODUCTS

SWEDEN - GENERAL INDUSTRIAL STATISTICS - See SWEDEN - INDUSTRY

SWEDEN - GENERAL MORTALITY - See SWEDEN - MORTALITY

SWEDEN - GEOGRAPHIC DATA

M.E. Sharpe, 80 Business Park Drive, Armonk, New York 10504 (800) 541-6563; *The Illustrated Book of World Rankings.*

SWEDEN - GLASS AND GLASS PRODUCTS - PRODUCTION INDEX - See SWEDEN - MINING AND MINERAL PRODUCTS

SWEDEN - GOATS - See SWEDEN - LIVESTOCK AND POULTRY

SWEDEN - GOLD HOLDINGS

International Monetary Fund, 700 Nineteenth Street, NW, Washington, D.C. 20431 (202) 623-7000; *International Financial Statistics.*

Statistical Office of the United Nations, Publishing Service, New York, New York 10017 (800) 253-9646; *Statistical Yearbook.*

The World Bank, 1818 H Street, NW, Washington, D.C. 20433 (202) 477-1234; *World Development Indicators.*

SWEDEN - GOLD PRODUCTION AND CONSUMPTION - See SWEDEN - MINING AND MINERAL PRODUCTS

SWEDEN - GOVERNMENT

Central Intelligence Agency, Washington, D.C. 20505 (703) 482-1100, www.cia.gov; *The World Factbook.*

Europa Publications Limited, 18 Bedford Square, London, WC1B 3JN, England; *The Europa World Year Book.*

International Monetary Fund, 700 Nineteenth Street, NW, Washington, D.C. 20431 (202) 623-7000; *Government Finance Statistics Yearbook;* and

International Financial Statistics.

Nordic Council of Ministers, Store Strandstraede 18, DK-1255 Copenhagen K, Denmark and the Nordic Statistical Secretariat, Postboks 2550, DK-2100 Copenhagen 0, Denmark; *The Yearbook of Nordic Statistics.*

Organisation for Economic Co-operation and Development (OECD), 2 rue Andre-Pascal, 75 Paris 16, France (Telephone Number in U.S. (202) 785-6323); *Economic Outlook;* and *Revenue Statistics of OECD Member Countries.*

St. Martin's Press, Inc., 175 Fifth Avenue, New York, New York 10010 (800) 221-7945; *The Statesman's Year-Book.*

Statistical Office of the United Nations, Publishing Service, New York, New York 10017 (800) 253-9646; *National Accounts Statistics;* and *Statistical Yearbook.*

The World Bank, 1818 H Street, NW, Washington, D.C. 20433 (202) 477-1234; *World Development Report;* and *World Development Indicators.*

SWEDEN - GRAIN PRODUCTION - See SWEDEN - CROPS

SWEDEN - GRANTS

International Monetary Fund, 700 Nineteenth Street, NW, Washington, D.C. 20431 (202) 623-7000; *Government Finance Statistics Yearbook.*

Organisation for Economic Co-operation and Development (OECD), 2 rue Andre-Pascal, 75 Paris 16, France (Telephone Number in U.S. (202) 785-6323); *Geographical Distribution of Financial Flows to Developing Countries.*

SWEDEN - GROSS DOMESTIC PRODUCT

The Economist Intelligence Unit, 111 West 57th Street, New York, New York 10019 (800) 938-4685; *Sweden Country Report;* and *The World Market Atlas.*

Euromonitor International, Inc., 122 Michigan Avenue, Suite 1200, Chicago, Illinois 60603 (800) 577-EURO; *The World Economic Factbook.*

Europa Publications Limited, 18 Bedford Square, London, WC1B 3JN, England; *The Europa World Year Book.*

International Monetary Fund, 700 Nineteenth Street, NW, Washington, D.C. 20431 (202) 623-7000; *International Financial Statistics.*

M.E. Sharpe, 80 Business Park Drive, Armonk, New York 10504 (800) 541-6563; *The Illustrated Book of World Rankings.*

Nordic Council of Ministers, Store Strandstraede 18, DK-1255 Copenhagen K, Denmark and the Nordic Statistical Secretariat, Postboks 2550, DK-2100 Copenhagen 0, Denmark; *The Yearbook of Nordic Statistics.*

Organisation for Economic Co-operation and Development (OECD), 2 rue Andre-Pascal, 75 Paris 16, France (Telephone Number in U.S. (202) 785-6323); *Economic Outlook, Geographical Distribution of Financial Flows to Developing Countries, Revenue Statistics of OECD Member Countries.*

Statistical Office of the United Nations, Publishing Service, New York, New York 10017 (800) 253-9646; *Human Development Report; National Accounts Statistics; Statistical Yearbook;* and *Trends in Europe and North America: The Statistical Yearbook of the Economic Commission for Europe.*

The World Bank, 1818 H Street, NW, Washington, D.C. 20433 (202) 477-1234; *World Development Report;* and *World Development Indicators.*

SWEDEN - GROSS NATIONAL PRODUCT

Europa Publications Limited, 18 Bedford Square, London, WC1B 3JN, England; *The Europa World Year Book.*

Organisation for Economic Co-operation and Development (OECD), 2 rue Andre-Pascal, 75 Paris 16, France (Telephone Number in U.S. (202) 785-6323); *Economic Outlook;* and *Geographical Distribution of Financial Flows to Developing Countries.*

St. Martin's Press, Inc., 175 Fifth Avenue, New York, New York 10010 (800) 221-7945; *The Statesman's Year-Book.*

U.S. Arms Control and Disarmament Agency, 320 Twenty-first Street, NW, Washington, D.C. 20451 (202) 647-8677; *World Military Expenditures and Arms Transfers.*

The World Bank, 1818 H Street, NW, Washington, D.C. 20433 (202) 477-1234; *The World Bank Atlas; World Development Report;* and *World Development Indicators.*

SWEDEN - HEALTH

Euromonitor International, Inc., 122 South Michigan Avenue, Suite 1200, Chicago, Illinois 60603 (800) 577-EURO; *World Marketing Data and Statistics.*

M.E. Sharpe, 80 Business Park Drive, Armonk, New York 10504 (800) 541-6563; *The Illustrated Book of World Rankings.*

Nordic Council of Ministers, Store Strandstraede 18, DK-1255 Copenhagen K, Denmark and the Nordic Statistical Secretariat, Postboks 2550, DK-2100 Copenhagen 0, Denmark; *The Yearbook of Nordic Statistics.*

Organisation for Economic Co-operation and Development (OECD), 2 rue Andre-Pascal, 75 Paris 16, France (Telephone Number in U.S. (202) 785-6323); *OECD Health Systems: Facts and Trends.*

St. Martin's Press, Inc., 175 Fifth Avenue, New York, New York 10010 (800) 221-7945; *The Statesman's Year-Book.*

Statistical Office of the United Nations, Publishing Service, New York, New York 10017 (800) 253-9646; *Human Development Report; Trends in Europe and North America: The Statistical Yearbook of the Economic Commission for Europe;* and *Statistical Yearbook.*

United Nations Children's Fund (UNICEF), 3 United Nations Plaza, New York, New York 10017 (800) 253-9646; *State of the World's Children.*

The World Bank, 1818 H Street, NW, Washington, D.C. 20433 (202) 477-1234; *World Development Report.*

World Health Organization, Office of Publications, 20 Avenue Appia, CH-1211 Geneva 27, Switzerland (Telephone Number in U.S. (518) 436-9686); *World Health Statistics Annual.*

SWEDEN - HEALTH EXPENDITURES

International Monetary Fund, 700 Nineteenth Street, NW, Washington, D.C. 20431 (202) 623-7000; *Government Finance Statistics Yearbook.*

SWEDEN - HIDE PRODUCTION

Organisation for Economic Co-operation and Development (OECD), 2 rue Andre-Pascal, 75 Paris 16, France (Telephone Number in U.S. (202) 785-6323); *The Footwear, Raw Hides and Skins, and Leather Industry in OECD Countries; Foreign Trade by Commodities;* and *Indicators of Industrial Activity.*

SWEDEN - HIGHWAYS

Central Intelligence Agency, Washington, D.C. 20505 (703) 482-1100, www.cia.gov; *The World Factbook.*

International Road Federation, 2600 Virginia Avenue, NW, Washington, D.C. 20037 (202) 338-4641; *World Road Statistics.*

Nordic Council of Ministers, Store Strandstraede 18, DK-1255 Copenhagen K,

Denmark and the Nordic Statistical Secretariat, Postboks 2550, DK-2100 Copenhagen 0, Denmark; *The Yearbook of Nordic Statistics.*

St. Martin's Press, Inc., 175 Fifth Avenue, New York, New York 10010 (800) 221-7945; *The Statesman's Year-Book.*

Statistical Office of the United Nations, Publishing Service, New York, New York 10017 (800) 253-9646; *Annual Bulletin of Transport Statistics for Europe;* and *Trends in Europe and North America: The Statistical Yearbook of the Economic Commission for Europe.*

SWEDEN - HOME FINANCE

Organisation for Economic Co-operation and Development (OECD), 2 rue Andre-Pascal, 75 Paris 16, France (Telephone Number in U.S. (202) 785-6323); *Main Economic Indicators - Historical Statistics.*

SWEDEN - HORSES - See SWEDEN - LIVESTOCK AND POULTRY

SWEDEN - HOURS OF WORK - See SWEDEN - EMPLOYMENT

SWEDEN - HOUSING AND HOUSING UNITS

Euromonitor International, Inc., 122 South Michigan Avenue, Suite 1200, Chicago, Illinois 60603 (800) 577-EURO; *World Marketing Data and Statistics.*

M.E. Sharpe, 80 Business Park Drive, Armonk, New York 10504 (800) 541-6563; *The Illustrated Book of World Rankings.*

Nordic Council of Ministers, Store Strandstraede 18, DK-1255 Copenhagen K, Denmark and the Nordic Statistical Secretariat, Postboks 2550, DK-2100 Copenhagen 0, Denmark; *The Yearbook of Nordic Statistics.*

Statistical Office of the United Nations, Publishing Service, New York, New York 10017 (800) 253-9646; *Statistical Yearbook;* and *Trends in Europe and North America: The Statistical Yearbook of the Economic Commission for Europe.*

SWEDEN - HOUSING CONSTRUCTION

Nordic Council of Ministers, Store Strandstraede 18, DK-1255 Copenhagen K, Denmark and the Nordic Statistical Secretariat, Postboks 2550, DK-2100 Copenhagen 0, Denmark; *The Yearbook of Nordic Statistics.*

Organisation for Economic Co-operation and Development (OECD), 2 rue Andre-Pascal, 75 Paris 16, France (Telephone Number in U.S. (202) 785-6323); *The Iron and Steel Industry.*

SWEDEN - HOUSING EXPENDITURES

International Monetary Fund, 700 Nineteenth Street, NW, Washington, D.C. 20431 (202) 623-7000; *Government Finance Statistics Yearbook.*

SWEDEN - HYDROCHLORIC ACID PRODUCTION

Statistical Office of the United Nations, Publishing Service, New York, New York 10017 (800) 253-9646; *Statistical Yearbook.*

SWEDEN - ILLITERATE POPULATION

Central Intelligence Agency, Washington, D.C. 20505 (703) 482-1100, www.cia.gov; *The World Factbook.*

The Economist Intelligence Unit, 111 West 57th Street, New York, New York 10019 (800) 938-4685; *The World Market Atlas.*

Euromonitor International, Inc., 122 Michigan Avenue, Suite 1200, Chicago, Illinois 60603 (800) 577-EURO; *The World Economic Factbook.*

Statistical Office of the United Nations, Publishing Service, New York, New York 10017 (800) 253-9646; *Human Development Report.*

SWEDEN - IMPORTS

Central Intelligence Agency, Washington, D.C. 20505 (703) 482-1100, www.cia.gov; *The World Factbook.*

The Economist Intelligence Unit, 111 West 57th Street, New York, New York 10019 (800) 938-4685; *Sweden Country Report;* and *The World Market Atlas.*

Euromonitor International, Inc., 122 Michigan Avenue, Suite 1200, Chicago, Illinois 60603 (800) 577-EURO; *The World Economic Factbook.*

Europa Publications Limited, 18 Bedford Square, London, WC1B 3JN, England; *The Europa World Year Book.*

Food and Agricultural Organization of the United Nations (FAO) Via delle Terme di Caracalla, 00100 Rome, Italy (Telephone Number in U.S. (202) 653-2400); *The State of Food and Agriculture.*

International Lead and Zinc Study Group, Metro House, 58 St. James's Street, London SW1A 1LD, England; *Lead and Zinc Statistics.*

International Monetary Fund, 700 Nineteenth Street, NW, Washington, D.C. 20431 (202) 623-7000; *Direction of Trade Statistics; Government Finance Statistics Yearbook;* and *International Financial Statistics.*

International Rubber Study Group, York House, Eighth Floor, Empire Way, Wembley, London HA9 0PA, England; *Rubber Statistical Bulletin.*

Nordic Council of Ministers, Store Strandstraede 18, DK-1255 Copenhagen K, Denmark and the Nordic Statistical Secretariat, Postboks 2550, DK-2100 Copenhagen 0, Denmark; *The Yearbook of Nordic Statistics.*

Organisation for Economic Co-operation and Development (OECD), 2 rue Andre-Pascal, 75 Paris 16, France (Telephone Number in U.S. (202) 785-6323); *Economic Outlook; The Footwear, Raw Hides and Skins, and Leather Industry in OECD Countries; Industrial Structure Statistics; The Iron and Steel Industry; Milk, Milk Products, and Egg Balances in OECD Member Countries; OECD Economic Surveys: Sweden; The Pulp and Paper Industry;* and *Review of Fisheries in OECD Member Countries.*

St. Martin's Press, Inc., 175 Fifth Avenue, New York, New York 10010 (800) 221-7945; *The Statesman's Year-Book.*

Statistical Office of the United Nations, Publishing Service, New York, New York 10017 (800) 253-9646; *Trends in Europe and North America: The Statistical Yearbook of the Economic Commission for Europe.*

United Nations Conference on Trade and Development (UNCTAD), New York, New York 10017 (800) 253-9646; *Handbook of International Trade and Development Statistics.*

The World Bank, 1818 H Street, NW, Washington, D.C. 20433 (202) 477-1234; *World Development Report;* and *World Development Indicators.*

SWEDEN - INCOME TAXES - See SWEDEN - TAXATION

SWEDEN - INDUSTRIAL METALS PRODUCTION - See SWEDEN - MINING AND MINERAL PRODUCTS

SWEDEN - INDUSTRY

Central Intelligence Agency, Washington, D.C. 20505 (703) 482-1100, www.cia.gov; *The World Factbook.*

Economist Intelligence Unit, 111 West 57th Street, New York, New York 10019 (800) 938-4685; *Sweden Country Report.*

Euromonitor International, Inc., 122 Michigan Avenue, Suite 1200, Chicago, Illinois 60603 (800) 577-EURO; *The World Economic Factbook;* and *World Marketing Data and Statistics.*

Europa Publications Limited, 18 Bedford Square, London, WC1B 3JN, England; *The Europa World Year Book.*

International Labour Office, I.L.O. Publications, 1828 L Street, NW, Suite 801, Washington, D.C. 20036 (301) 638-3152; *Yearbook of Labour Statistics.*

M.E. Sharpe, 80 Business Park Drive, Armonk, New York 10504 (800) 541-6563; *The Illustrated Book of World Rankings.*

Nordic Council of Ministers, Store Strandstraede 18, DK-1255 Copenhagen K, Denmark and the Nordic Statistical Secretariat, Postboks 2550, DK-2100 Copenhagen 0, Denmark; *The Yearbook of Nordic Statistics.*

Organisation for Economic Co-operation and Development (OECD), 2 rue Andre-Pascal, 75 Paris 16, France (Telephone Number in U.S. (202) 785-6323); *Economic Outlook; Industrial Structure Statistics; Indicators of Industrial Activity; Main Economic Indicators - Historical Statistics;* and *OECD Environmental Data.*

St. Martin's Press, Inc., 175 Fifth Avenue, New York, New York 10010 (800) 221-7945; *The Statesman's Year-Book.*

Statistical Office of the United Nations, Publishing Service, New York, New York 10017 (800) 253-9646; *Industrial Commodity Statistics Yearbook; Statistical Yearbook;* and *Trends in Europe and North America: The Statistical Yearbook of the Economic Commission for Europe.*

The World Bank, 1818 H Street, NW, Washington, D.C. 20433 (202) 477-1234; *World Development Indicators.*

World Intellectual Property Organization, 34 Chemin des Colombettes, CH-1211 Geneva 20. Switzerland; *Industrial Property Statistics.*

SWEDEN - INFANT AND MATERNAL MORTALITY - See SWEDEN - MORTALITY

SWEDEN - INTEREST RATES

Organisation for Economic Co-operation and Development (OECD), 2 rue Andre-Pascal, 75 Paris 16, France (Telephone Number in U.S. (202) 785-6323); *Economic Outlook; Financial Market Trends; Main Economic Indicators - Historical Statistics;* and *OECD Financial Statistics.*

SWEDEN - INTERNAL TRADE

Nordic Council of Ministers, Store Strandstraede 18, DK-1255 Copenhagen K, Denmark and the Nordic Statistical Secretariat, Postboks 2550, DK-2100

Copenhagen 0, Denmark; *The Yearbook of Nordic Statistics.*

Organisation for Economic Co-operation and Development (OECD), 2 rue Andre-Pascal, 75 Paris 16, France (Telephone Number in U.S. (202) 785-6323); *Main Economic Indicators - Historical Statistics.*

Statistical Office of the United Nations, Publishing Service, New York, New York 10017 (800) 253-9646; *Statistical Yearbook.*

SWEDEN - INTERNATIONAL FINANCE

Organisation for Economic Co-operation and Development (OECD), 2 rue Andre-Pascal, 75 Paris 16, France (Telephone Number in U.S. (202) 785-6323); *Economic Outlook;* and *Financial Market Trends.*

SWEDEN - INTERNATIONAL LIQUIDITY

International Monetary Fund, 700 Nineteenth Street, NW, Washington, D.C. 20431 (202) 623-7000; *International Financial Statistics.*

Organisation for Economic Co-operation and Development (OECD), 2 rue Andre-Pascal, 75 Paris 16, France (Telephone Number in U.S. (202) 785-6323); *Economic Outlook;* and *Financial Market Trends.*

SWEDEN - INTERNATIONAL RESERVES EXCLUDING GOLD

Statistical Office of the United Nations, Publishing Service, New York, New York 10017 (800) 253-9646; *Statistical Yearbook.*

The World Bank, 1818 H Street, NW, Washington, D.C. 20433 (202) 477-1234; *World Development Indicators.*

SWEDEN - INTERNATIONAL STATISTICS

Organisation for Economic Co-operation and Development (OECD), 2 rue Andre-Pascal, 75 Paris 16, France (Telephone Number in U.S. (202) 785-6323); *Financial Market Trends;* and *Tourism Policy and International Tourism in OECD Member Countries.*

SWEDEN - INVESTMENTS

International Monetary Fund, 700 Nineteenth Street, NW, Washington, D.C. 20431 (202) 623-7000; *International Financial Statistics.*

Organisation for Economic Co-operation and Development (OECD), 2 rue Andre-Pascal, 75 Paris 16, France (Telephone Number in U.S. (202) 785-6323); *Economic Outlook; Financial Market Trends; Industrial Structure*

Statistics; The Iron and Steel Industry; and *Textile Industry in OECD Countries.*

SWEDEN - IRON ORE PRODUCTION AND CONSUMPTION - See SWEDEN - MINING AND MINERAL PRODUCTS

SWEDEN - LABOR

Central Intelligence Agency, Washington, D.C. 20505 (703) 482-1100, www.cia.gov; *The World Factbook.*

Euromonitor International, Inc., 122 South Michigan Avenue, Suite 1200, Chicago, Illinois 60603 (800) 577-EURO; *World Marketing Data and Statistics.*

Europa Publications Limited, 18 Bedford Square, London, WC1B 3JN, England; *The Europa World Year Book.*

Food and Agricultural Organization of the United Nations (FAO) Via delle Terme di Caracalla, 00100 Rome, Italy (Telephone Number in U.S. (202) 653-2400); *The State of Food and Agriculture.*

International Labour Office, I.L.O. Publications, 1828 L Street, NW, Suite 801, Washington, D.C. 20036 (301) 638-3152; *Yearbook of Labour Statistics.*

M.E. Sharpe, 80 Business Park Drive, Armonk, New York 10504 (800) 541-6563; *The Illustrated Book of World Rankings.*

Nordic Council of Ministers, Store Strandstraede 18, DK-1255 Copenhagen K, Denmark and the Nordic Statistical Secretariat, Postboks 2550, DK-2100 Copenhagen 0, Denmark; *The Yearbook of Nordic Statistics.*

Organisation for Economic Co-operation and Development (OECD), 2 rue Andre-Pascal, 75 Paris 16, France (Telephone Number in U.S. (202) 785-6323); *Economic Outlook; The Iron and Steel Industry; Main Economic Indicators - Historical Statistics; Maritime Transport; OECD Employment Outlook; OECD Economic Surveys: Sweden;* and *Textile Industry in OECD Countries.*

St. Martin's Press, Inc., 175 Fifth Avenue, New York, New York 10010 (800) 221-7945; *The Statesman's Year-Book.*

Statistical Office of the United Nations, Publishing Service, New York, New York 10017 (800) 253-9646; *Human Development Report.*

The World Bank, 1818 H Street, NW, Washington, D.C. 20433 (202) 477-1234; *The World Bank Atlas; World Development Report;* and *World Development Indicators.*

SWEDEN - LAND USE

Central Intelligence Agency, Washington, D.C. 20505 (703) 482-1100, www.cia.gov; *The World Factbook.*

Euromonitor International, Inc., 122 Michigan Avenue, Suite 1200, Chicago, Illinois 60603 (800) 577-EURO; *European Marketing Data and Statistics.*

Food and Agricultural Organization of the United Nations (FAO), Via delle Terme di Caracalla, 00100 Rome, Italy (Telephone Number in U.S. (202) 653-2400); *Production Yearbook.*

The World Bank, 1818 H Street, NW, Washington, D.C. 20433 (202) 477-1234; *World Development Report.*

SWEDEN - LEAD AND LEAD ORE PRODUCTION AND CONSUMPTION - See SWEDEN - MINING AND MINERAL PRODUCTS

SWEDEN - LEATHER - PRODUCTION INDEX

Organisation for Economic Co-operation and Development (OECD), 2 rue Andre-Pascal, 75 Paris 16, France (Telephone Number in U.S. (202) 785-6323); *Indicators of Industrial Activity.*

SWEDEN - LEATHER AND FOOTWEAR - EXPORTS AND IMPORTS

Organisation for Economic Co-operation and Development (OECD), 2 rue Andre-Pascal, 75 Paris 16, France (Telephone Number in U.S. (202) 785-6323); *The Footwear, Raw Hides and Skins, and Leather Industry in OECD Countries.*

SWEDEN - LIBRARIES

Euromonitor International, Inc., 122 Michigan Avenue, Suite 1200, Chicago, Illinois 60603 (800) 577-EURO; *European Marketing Data and Statistics.*

M.E. Sharpe, 80 Business Park Drive, Armonk, New York 10504 (800) 541-6563; *The Illustrated Book of World Rankings.*

Nordic Council of Ministers, Store Strandstraede 18, DK-1255 Copenhagen K, Denmark and the Nordic Statistical Secretariat, Postboks 2550, DK-2100 Copenhagen 0, Denmark; *The Yearbook of Nordic Statistics.*

Statistical Office of the United Nations, Publishing Service, New York, New York 10017 (800) 253-9646; *Trends in Europe and North America: The Statistical Yearbook of the Economic Commission for Europe.*

United Nations Educational, Scientific and Cultural Organization (UNESCO), 7 Place de Fontenoy, F-75700 Paris, France

(Telephone Number in U.S. (212) 963-5981); *Statistical Yearbook.*

SWEDEN - LIFE EXPECTANCY

Central Intelligence Agency, Washington, D.C. 20505 (703) 482-1100, www.cia.gov; *The World Factbook.*

Euromonitor International, Inc., 122 Michigan Avenue, Suite 1200, Chicago, Illinois 60603 (800) 577-EURO; *The World Economic Factbook.*

Organisation for Economic Co-operation and Development (OECD), 2 rue Andre-Pascal, 75 Paris 16, France (Telephone Number in U.S. (202) 785-6323); *Economic Outlook.*

St. Martin's Press, Inc., 175 Fifth Avenue, New York, New York 10010 (800) 221-7945; *The Statesman's Year-Book.*

Statistical Office of the United Nations, Publishing Service, New York, New York 10017 (800) 253-9646; *Human Development Report; Trends in Europe and North America: The Statistical Yearbook of the Economic Commission for Europe;* and *World Statistics Pocketbook.*

The World Bank, 1818 H Street, NW, Washington, D.C. 20433 (202) 477-1234; *The World Bank Atlas;* and *World Development Report.*

SWEDEN - LIGNITE PRODUCTION - See SWEDEN - MINING AND MINERAL PRODUCTS

SWEDEN - LITERACY RATE

Euromonitor International, Inc., 122 South Michigan Avenue, Suite 1200, Chicago, Illinois 60603 (800) 577-EURO; *World Marketing Data and Statistics.*

SWEDEN - LIVESTOCK AND POULTRY

Euromonitor International, Inc., 122 Michigan Avenue, Suite 1200, Chicago, Illinois 60603 (800) 577-EURO; *European Marketing Data and Statistics.*

Europa Publications Limited, 18 Bedford Square, London, WC1B 3JN, England; *The Europa World Year Book.*

Food and Agricultural Organization of the United Nations (FAO), Via delle Terme di Caracalla, 00100 Rome, Italy (Telephone Number in U.S. (202) 653-2400); *Production Yearbook;* and *The State of Food and Agriculture.*

M.E. Sharpe, 80 Business Park Drive, Armonk, New York 10504 (800) 541-6563; *The Illustrated Book of World Rankings.*

Nordic Council of Ministers, Store

Strandstraede 18, DK-1255 Copenhagen K, Denmark and the Nordic Statistical Secretariat, Postboks 2550, DK-2100 Copenhagen 0, Denmark; *The Yearbook of Nordic Statistics.*

Organisation for Economic Co-operation and Development (OECD), 2 rue Andre-Pascal, 75 Paris 16, France (Telephone Number in U.S. (202) 785-6323); *Economic Accounts for Agriculture;* and *Meat Balances in OECD Member Countries.*

St. Martin's Press, Inc., 175 Fifth Avenue, New York, New York 10010 (800) 221-7945; *The Statesman's Year-Book.*

Statistical Office of the United Nations, Publishing Service, New York, New York 10017 (800) 253-9646; *Statistical Yearbook.*

United Nations Conference on Trade and Development, Central Statistical Service, Palais des Nations, Geneva, Switzerland (Telephone in U.S. (800) 253-9646); *UNCTAD Commodity Yearbook.*

SWEDEN - LIVING LEVELS - See SWEDEN - LIFE EXPECTANCY

SWEDEN - MACHINERY - PRODUCTION INDEX

Organisation for Economic Co-operation and Development (OECD), 2 rue Andre-Pascal, 75 Paris 16, France (Telephone Number in U.S. (202) 785-6323); *Indicators of Industrial Activity.*

SWEDEN - MAGNESIUM PRODUCTION AND CONSUMPTION - See SWEDEN - MINING AND MINERAL PRODUCTS

SWEDEN - MAIL - NUMBER OF PIECES SENT OR RECEIVED

Nordic Council of Ministers, Store Strandstraede 18, DK-1255 Copenhagen K, Denmark and the Nordic Statistical Secretariat, Postboks 2550, DK-2100 Copenhagen 0, Denmark; *The Yearbook of Nordic Statistics.*

Statistical Office of the United Nations, Publishing Service, New York, New York 10017 (800) 253-9646; *Statistical Yearbook.*

SWEDEN - MAIN ECONOMIC INDICATORS - See SWEDEN - ECONOMY

SWEDEN - MAIN INDICATORS - See SWEDEN - ECONOMY

SWEDEN - MANGANESE AND MANGANESE ORE PRODUCTION AND CONSUMPTION - See SWEDEN - MINING AND MINERAL PRODUCTS

SWEDEN - MANUFACTURING

American Automobile Manufacturers Association, 1401 H Street, NW, Suite 900, Washington, D.C. 20005 (202) 326-5500; *World Motor Vehicle Data.*

M.E. Sharpe, 80 Business Park Drive, Armonk, New York 10504 (800) 541-6563; *The Illustrated Book of World Rankings.*

Nordic Council of Ministers, Store Strandstraede 18, DK-1255 Copenhagen K, Denmark and the Nordic Statistical Secretariat, Postboks 2550, DK-2100 Copenhagen 0, Denmark; *The Yearbook of Nordic Statistics.*

Organisation for Economic Co-operation and Development (OECD), 2 rue Andre-Pascal, 75 Paris 16, France (Telephone Number in U.S. (202) 785-6323); *Foreign Trade by Commodities; Indicators of Industrial Activity; Industrial Structure Statistics;* and *OECD Economic Surveys: Sweden.*

Statistical Office of the United Nations, Publishing Service, New York, New York 10017 (800) 253-9646; *Statistical Yearbook.*

The World Bank, 1818 H Street, NW, Washington, D.C. 20433 (202) 477-1234; *World Development Indicators.*

SWEDEN - MARRIAGE RATE

Europa Publications Limited, 18 Bedford Square, London, WC1B 3JN, England; *The Europa World Year Book.*

M.E. Sharpe, 80 Business Park Drive, Armonk, New York 10504 (800) 541-6563; *The Illustrated Book of World Rankings.*

Nordic Council of Ministers, Store Strandstraede 18, DK-1255 Copenhagen K, Denmark and the Nordic Statistical Secretariat, Postboks 2550, DK-2100 Copenhagen 0, Denmark; *The Yearbook of Nordic Statistics.*

Statistical Office of the United Nations, Publishing Service, New York, New York 10017 (800) 253-9646; *Demographic Yearbook; Statistical Yearbook;* and *Trends in Europe and North America: The Statistical Yearbook of the Economic Commission for Europe.*

SWEDEN - MEAT PRODUCTION - See SWEDEN - LIVESTOCK AND POULTRY

SWEDEN - MERCHANT SHIPPING

Europa Publications Limited, 18 Bedford Square, London, WC1B 3JN, England; *The Europa World Year Book.*

International Criminal Police Organization (INTERPOL), 50 quai Achille Lignon, F-69006, Lyon, France; *International Crime Statistics.*

Nordic Council of Ministers, Store Strandstraede 18, DK-1255 Copenhagen K, Denmark and the Nordic Statistical Secretariat, Postboks 2550, DK-2100 Copenhagen 0, Denmark; *The Yearbook of Nordic Statistics.*

Organisation for Economic Co-operation and Development (OECD), 2 rue Andre-Pascal, 75 Paris 16, France (Telephone Number in U.S. (202) 785-6323); *Maritime Transport.*

St. Martin's Press, Inc., 175 Fifth Avenue, New York, New York 10010 (800) 221-7945; *The Statesman's Year-Book.*

Statistical Office of the United Nations, Publishing Service, New York, New York 10017 (800) 253-9646; *Statistical Yearbook.*

U.S. Department of Transportation, Maritime Administration, 400 Seventh Street, SW, Washington, D.C. 20590 (202) 366-5807, www.marad.dot.gov; *A Statistical Analysis of the World's Merchant Fleets.*

SWEDEN - MERCURY PRODUCTION AND CONSUMPTION - See SWEDEN - MINING AND MINERAL PRODUCTS

SWEDEN - MILITARY

Central Intelligence Agency, Washington, D.C. 20505 (703) 482-1100, www.cia.gov; *The World Factbook.*

Euromonitor International, Inc., 122 South Michigan Avenue, Suite 1200, Chicago, Illinois 60603 (800) 577-EURO; *World Marketing Data and Statistics.*

The International Institute for Strategic Studies, 23 Tavistock Street, London WC2E 7NQ, England 44 171 3797676; *The Military Balance.*

International Monetary Fund, 700 Nineteenth Street, NW, Washington, D.C. 20431 (202) 623-7000; *Government Finance Statistics Yearbook.*

Nordic Council of Ministers, Store Strandstraede 18, DK-1255 Copenhagen K, Denmark and the Nordic Statistical Secretariat, Postboks 2550, DK-2100 Copenhagen 0, Denmark; *The Yearbook of Nordic Statistics.*

St. Martin's Press, Inc., 175 Fifth Avenue, New York, New York 10010 (800) 221-7945; *The Statesman's Year-Book.*

Statistical Office of the United Nations, Publishing Service, New York, New York 10017 (800) 253-9646; *Human Development Report.*

U.S. Arms Control and Disarmament Agency, 320 Twenty-first Street, NW, Washington, D.C. 20451 (202) 647-8677; *World Military Expenditures and Arms Transfers.*

SWEDEN - MILK PRODUCTION - See SWEDEN - DAIRY PRODUCTS

SWEDEN - MINING AND MINERAL PRODUCTS

Commodity Research Bureau, Inc., 30 South Wacker Drive, Chicago Illinois 60606 (312) 454-1801; *Commodity Year Book.*

Europa Publications Limited, 18 Bedford Square, London, WC1B 3JN, England; *The Europa World Year Book.*

International Lead and Zinc Study Group, Metro House, 58 St. James's Street, London SW1A 1LD, England; *Lead and Zinc Statistics.*

M.E. Sharpe, 80 Business Park Drive, Armonk, New York 10504 (800) 541-6563; *The Illustrated Book of World Rankings.*

Nordic Council of Ministers, Store Strandstraede 18, DK-1255 Copenhagen K, Denmark and the Nordic Statistical Secretariat, Postboks 2550, DK-2100 Copenhagen 0, Denmark; *The Yearbook of Nordic Statistics.*

Organisation for Economic Co-operation and Development (OECD), 2 rue Andre-Pascal, 75 Paris 16, France (Telephone Number in U.S. (202) 785-6323); *Coal Information; Energy Statistics of OECD Countries; Foreign Trade by Commodities; Indicators of Industrial Activity; Industrial Structure Statistics; The Iron and Steel Industry; The Non-Ferrous Metals Industry;* and *OECD Economic Surveys: Sweden.*

St. Martin's Press, Inc., 175 Fifth Avenue, New York, New York 10010 (800) 221-7945; *The Statesman's Year-Book.*

Statistical Office of the United Nations, Publishing Service, New York, New York 10017 (800) 253-9646; *Statistical Yearbook.*

United Nations Conference on Trade and Development, Central Statistical Service, Palais des Nations, Geneva, Switzerland (Telephone in U.S. (800) 253-9646); *UNCTAD Commodity Yearbook.*

World Bureau of Metal Statistics, 27-A High Street, Ware Hert SG12 9BA, England; *World Metal Statistics.*

SWEDEN - MOLYBDENUM AND MOLYBDENUM ORE PRODUCTION AND CONSUMPTION - See SWEDEN - MINING AND MINERAL PRODUCTS

SWEDEN - MONEY AND CREDIT

Organisation for Economic Cooperation and Development (OECD), 2 rue Andre-Pascal, 75 Paris 16, France (Telephone Number in U.S. (202) 785-6323); *OECD Economic Surveys: Sweden.*

SWEDEN - MONEY EXCHANGE RATES - See SWEDEN - EXCHANGE RATES

SWEDEN - MONEY RATES - MARKET

Organisation for Economic Co-operation and Development (OECD), 2 rue Andre-Pascal, 75 Paris 16, France (Telephone Number in U.S. (202) 785-6323); *Economic Outlook;* and *Financial Market Trends.*

SWEDEN - MONEY RESERVES

Organisation for Economic Co-operation and Development (OECD), 2 rue Andre-Pascal, 75 Paris 16, France (Telephone Number in U.S. (202) 785-6323); *Economic Outlook;* and *Financial Market Trends.*

SWEDEN - MONEY SUPPLY

Economist Intelligence Unit, 111 West 57th Street, New York, New York 10019 (800) 938-4685; *Sweden Country Report.*

International Monetary Fund, 700 Nineteenth Street, NW, Washington, D.C. 20431 (202) 623-7000; *International Financial Statistics.*

Nordic Council of Ministers, Store Strandstraede 18, DK-1255 Copenhagen K, Denmark and the Nordic Statistical Secretariat, Postboks 2550, DK-2100 Copenhagen 0, Denmark; *The Yearbook of Nordic Statistics.*

Organisation for Economic Co-operation and Development (OECD), 2 rue Andre-Pascal, 75 Paris 16, France (Telephone Number in U.S. (202) 785-6323); *Economic Outlook.*

Statistical Office of the United Nations, Publishing Service, New York, New York 10017 (800) 253-9646; *Statistical Yearbook.*

The World Bank, 1818 H Street, NW, Washington, D.C. 20433 (202) 477-1234; *World Development Indicators.*

SWEDEN - MONUMENTS AND HISTORICAL SITES

United Nations Educational, Scientific and Cultural Organization (UNESCO), 7 Place de Fontenoy, F-75700 Paris, France (Telephone Number in U.S. (212) 963-5981); *Statistical Yearbook.*

SWEDEN - MORTALITY

Central Intelligence Agency,

Washington, D.C. 20505 (703) 482-1100, www.cia.gov; *The World Factbook.*

Euromonitor International, Inc., 122 Michigan Avenue, Suite 1200, Chicago, Illinois 60603 (800) 577-EURO; *The World Economic Factbook.*

Europa Publications Limited, 18 Bedford Square, London, WC1B 3JN, England; *The Europa World Year Book.*

Nordic Council of Ministers, Store Strandstraede 18, DK-1255 Copenhagen K, Denmark and the Nordic Statistical Secretariat, Postboks 2550, DK-2100 Copenhagen 0, Denmark; *The Yearbook of Nordic Statistics.*

St. Martin's Press, Inc., 175 Fifth Avenue, New York, New York 10010 (800) 221-7945; *The Statesman's Year-Book.*

Statistical Office of the United Nations, Publishing Service, New York, New York 10017 (800) 253-9646; *Demographic Yearbook; Human Development Report; Statistical Yearbook; Trends in Europe and North America: The Statistical Yearbook of the Economic Commission for Europe;* and *World Statistics Pocketbook.*

United Nations Children's Fund (UNICEF), 3 United Nations Plaza, New York, New York 10017 (800) 253-9646; *State of the World's Children.*

The World Bank, 1818 H Street, NW, Washington, D.C. 20433 (202) 477-1234; *The World Bank Atlas; World Development Report;* and *World Development Indicators.*

World Health Organization, Office of Publications, 20 Avenue Appia, CH-1211 Geneva 27, Switzerland (Telephone Number in U.S. (518) 436-9686); *World Health Statistics Annual.*

SWEDEN - MOTION PICTURES

St. Martin's Press, Inc., 175 Fifth Avenue, New York, New York 10010 (800) 221-7945; *The Statesman's Year-Book.*

Statistical Office of the United Nations, Publishing Service, New York, New York 10017 (800) 253-9646; *Statistical Yearbook.*

United Nations Educational, Scientific and Cultural Organization (UNESCO), 7 Place de Fontenoy, F-75700 Paris, France (Telephone Number in U.S. (212) 963-5981); *Statistical Yearbook.*

SWEDEN - MOTOR VEHICLE PRODUCTION

American Automobile Manufacturers Association, 1401 H Street, NW, Suite 900, Washington, D.C. 20005 (202) 326-5500; *World Motor Vehicle Data.*

Organisation for Economic Co-operation and Development (OECD), 2 rue Andre-Pascal, 75 Paris 16, France (Telephone Number in U.S. (202) 785-6323); *Foreign Trade by Commodities;* and *Indicators of Industrial Activity.*

Statistical Office of the United Nations, Publishing Service, New York, New York 10017 (800) 253-9646; *Statistical Yearbook.*

SWEDEN - MOTOR VEHICLE TAXES - See SWEDEN - TAXATION

SWEDEN - MOTOR VEHICLES IN USE

American Automobile Manufacturers Association, 1401 H Street, NW, Suite 900, Washington, D.C. 20005 (202) 326-5500; *World Motor Vehicle Data.*

Europa Publications Limited, 18 Bedford Square, London, WC1B 3JN, England; *The Europa World Year Book.*

International Road Federation, 2600 Virginia Avenue, NW, Washington, D.C. 20037 (202) 338-4641; *World Road Statistics.*

Nordic Council of Ministers, Store Strandstraede 18, DK-1255 Copenhagen K, Denmark and the Nordic Statistical Secretariat, Postboks 2550, DK-2100 Copenhagen 0, Denmark; *The Yearbook of Nordic Statistics.*

Statistical Office of the United Nations, Publishing Service, New York, New York 10017 (800) 253-9646; *Statistical Yearbook.*

SWEDEN - MUSEUMS

Euromonitor International, Inc., 122 Michigan Avenue, Suite 1200, Chicago, Illinois 60603 (800) 577-EURO; *European Marketing Data and Statistics.*

M.E. Sharpe, 80 Business Park Drive, Armonk, New York 10504 (800) 541-6563; *The Illustrated Book of World Rankings.*

Nordic Council of Ministers, Store Strandstraede 18, DK-1255 Copenhagen K, Denmark and the Nordic Statistical Secretariat, Postboks 2550, DK-2100 Copenhagen 0, Denmark; *The Yearbook of Nordic Statistics.*

United Nations Educational, Scientific and Cultural Organization (UNESCO), 7 Place de Fontenoy, F-75700 Paris, France (Telephone Number in U.S. (212) 963-5981); *Statistical Yearbook.*

SWEDEN - NATALITY - See SWEDEN - BIRTH RATE

SWEDEN - NATIONAL ACCOUNTS

Europa Publications Limited, 18

Bedford Square, London, WC1B 3JN, England; *The Europa World Year Book.*

International Monetary Fund, 700 Nineteenth Street, NW, Washington, D.C. 20431 (202) 623-7000; *International Financial Statistics.*

Nordic Council of Ministers, Store Strandstraede 18, DK-1255 Copenhagen K, Denmark and the Nordic Statistical Secretariat, Postboks 2550, DK-2100 Copenhagen 0, Denmark; *The Yearbook of Nordic Statistics.*

Organisation for Economic Co-operation and Development (OECD), 2 rue Andre-Pascal, 75 Paris 16, France (Telephone Number in U.S. (202) 785-6323); *Economic Outlook.*

Statistical Office of the United Nations, Publishing Service, New York, New York 10017 (800) 253-9646; *National Accounts Statistics;* and *Statistical Yearbook.*

SWEDEN - NATIONAL INCOME

M.E. Sharpe, 80 Business Park Drive, Armonk, New York 10504 (800) 541-6563; *The Illustrated Book of World Rankings.*

Nordic Council of Ministers, Store Strandstraede 18, DK-1255 Copenhagen K, Denmark and the Nordic Statistical Secretariat, Postboks 2550, DK-2100 Copenhagen 0, Denmark; *The Yearbook of Nordic Statistics.*

Organisation for Economic Co-operation and Development (OECD), 2 rue Andre-Pascal, 75 Paris 16, France (Telephone Number in U.S. (202) 785-6323); *Economic Outlook.*

Statistical Office of the United Nations, Publishing Service, New York, New York 10017 (800) 253-9646; *National Accounts Statistics;* and *Statistical Yearbook.*

SWEDEN - NATIONAL PRODUCT

M.E. Sharpe, 80 Business Park Drive, Armonk, New York 10504 (800) 541-6563; *The Illustrated Book of World Rankings.*

Organisation for Economic Co-operation and Development (OECD), 2 rue Andre-Pascal, 75 Paris 16, France (Telephone Number in U.S. (202) 785-6323); *Economic Outlook;* and *Main Economic Indicators - Historical Statistics.*

Statistical Office of the United Nations, Publishing Service, New York, New York 10017 (800) 253-9646; *Statistical Yearbook.*

SWEDEN - NATURAL GAS PRODUCTION - See SWEDEN - MINING AND MINERAL PRODUCTS

SWEDEN - NATURAL RUBBER PRODUCTION

International Rubber Study Group, York House, Eighth Floor, Empire Way, Wembley, London HA9 0PA, England; *Rubber Statistical Bulletin.*

SWEDEN - NEWSPAPER - See SWEDEN - FORESTRY AND FOREST PRODUCTS

SWEDEN - NEWSPRINT PRODUCTION AND CONSUMPTION - See SWEDEN - FORESTRY AND FOREST PRODUCTS

SWEDEN - NICKEL AND NICKEL ORE PRODUCTION AND CONSUMPTION - See SWEDEN - MINING AND MINERAL PRODUCTS

SWEDEN - NITRIC ACID PRODUCTION - See SWEDEN - MINING AND MINERAL PRODUCTS

SWEDEN - OATS PRODUCTION - See SWEDEN - CROPS

SWEDEN - OCCUPATIONS - See SWEDEN - LABOR

SWEDEN - OIL PRODUCING CROPS

Organisation for Economic Co-operation and Development (OECD), 2 rue Andre-Pascal, 75 Paris 16, France (Telephone Number in U.S. (202) 785-6323); *Foreign Trade by Commodities.*

SWEDEN - PAPER - See SWEDEN - FORESTRY AND FOREST PRODUCTS

SWEDEN - PATENTS, TRADEMARKS AND SERVICE MARKS

Nordic Council of Ministers, Store Strandstraede 18, DK-1255 Copenhagen K, Denmark and the Nordic Statistical Secretariat, Postboks 2550, DK-2100 Copenhagen 0, Denmark; *The Yearbook of Nordic Statistics.*

Statistical Office of the United Nations, Publishing Service, New York, New York 10017 (800) 253-9646; *Statistical Yearbook.*

World Intellectual Property Organization, 34 Chemin des Colombettes, CH-1211 Geneva 20. Switzerland; *Industrial Property Statistics.*

SWEDEN - PEANUT PRODUCTION - See SWEDEN - CROPS

SWEDEN - PERIODICALS

United Nations Educational, Scientific and Cultural Organization (UNESCO), 7 Place de Fontenoy, F-75700 Paris, France (Telephone Number in U.S. (212) 963-5981); *Statistical Yearbook.*

SWEDEN - PESTICIDE USE

Food and Agricultural Organization of the United Nations (FAO) Via delle Terme di Caracalla, 00100 Rome, Italy (Telephone Number in U.S. (202) 653-2400); *The State of Food and Agriculture.*

SWEDEN - PETROLEUM INDUSTRY

Euromonitor International, Inc., 122 Michigan Avenue, Suite 1200, Chicago, Illinois 60603 (800) 577-EURO; *European Marketing Data and Statistics.*

Food and Agricultural Organization of the United Nations (FAO) Via delle Terme di Caracalla, 00100 Rome, Italy (Telephone Number in U.S. (202) 653-2400); *The State of Food and Agriculture.*

M.E. Sharpe, 80 Business Park Drive, Armonk, New York 10504 (800) 541-6563; *The Illustrated Book of World Rankings.*

Organisation for Economic Co-operation and Development (OECD), 2 rue Andre-Pascal, 75 Paris 16, France (Telephone Number in U.S. (202) 785-6323); *Energy Statistics of OECD Countries; Foreign Trade by Commodities; Indicators of Industrial Activity;* and *Oil and Gas Information.*

St. Martin's Press, Inc., 175 Fifth Avenue, New York, New York 10010 (800) 221-7945; *The Statesman's Year-Book.*

Statistical Office of the United Nations, Publishing Service, New York, New York 10017 (800) 253-9646; *Statistical Yearbook;* and *Trends in Europe and North America: The Statistical Yearbook of the Economic Commission for Europe.*

United Nations Conference on Trade and Development, Central Statistical Service, Palais des Nations, Geneva, Switzerland (Telephone in U.S. (800) 253-9646); *UNCTAD Commodity Yearbook.*

SWEDEN - PHOSPHATE ROCK PRODUCTION - See SWEDEN - MINING AND MINERAL PRODUCTS

SWEDEN - PHOSPHATES PRODUCTION - See SWEDEN - MINING AND MINERAL PRODUCTS

SWEDEN - PIG-IRON AND FERRO-ALLOY PRODUCTION - See SWEDEN - MINING AND MINERAL PRODUCTS

SWEDEN - PIGS - See SWEDEN - LIVESTOCK AND POULTRY

SWEDEN - PLASTIC AND RESIN PRODUCTION

Organisation for Economic Co-operation and Development (OECD), 2 rue

Andre-Pascal, 75 Paris 16, France (Telephone Number in U.S. (202) 785-6323); *Foreign Trade by Commodities.*

Statistical Office of the United Nations, Publishing Service, New York, New York 10017 (800) 253-9646; *Statistical Yearbook.*

SWEDEN - PLATINUM PRODUCTION AND CONSUMPTION - See SWEDEN - MINING AND MINERAL PRODUCTS

SWEDEN - POPULATION

Central Intelligence Agency, Washington, D.C. 20505 (703) 482-1100, www.cia.gov; *The World Factbook.*

The Economist Intelligence Unit, 111 West 57th Street, New York, New York 10019 (800) 938-4685; *Sweden Country Report;* and *The World Market Atlas.*

Euromonitor International, Inc., 122 Michigan Avenue, Suite 1200, Chicago, Illinois 60603 (800) 577-EURO; *European Marketing Data and Statistics;* and *The World Economic Factbook.*

Europa Publications Limited, 18 Bedford Square, London, WC1B 3JN, England; *The Europa World Year Book.*

Food and Agricultural Organization of the United Nations (FAO), Via delle Terme di Caracalla, 00100 Rome, Italy (Telephone Number in U.S. (202) 653-2400); *Production Yearbook.*

International Labour Office, I.L.O. Publications, 1828 L Street, NW, Suite 801, Washington, D.C. 20036 (301) 638-3152; *Yearbook of Labour Statistics.*

M.E. Sharpe, 80 Business Park Drive, Armonk, New York 10504 (800) 541-6563; *The Illustrated Book of World Rankings.*

Nordic Council of Ministers, Store Strandstraede 18, DK-1255 Copenhagen K, Denmark and the Nordic Statistical Secretariat, Postboks 2550, DK-2100 Copenhagen 0, Denmark; *The Yearbook of Nordic Statistics.*

St. Martin's Press, Inc., 175 Fifth Avenue, New York, New York 10010 (800) 221-7945; *The Statesman's Year-Book.*

Statistical Office of the United Nations, Publishing Service, New York, New York 10017 (800) 253-9646; *Demographic Yearbook; Human Development Report; Statistical Yearbook; Trends in Europe and North America: The Statistical Yearbook of the Economic Commission for Europe;* and *World Statistics Pocketbook.*

United Nations Educational, Scientific and Cultural Organization (UNESCO), 7 Place de Fontenoy, F-75700 Paris, France

(Telephone Number in U.S. (212) 963-5981); *Statistical Yearbook.*

U.S. Arms Control and Disarmament Agency, 320 Twenty-first Street, NW, Washington, D.C. 20451 (202) 647-8677; *World Military Expenditures and Arms Transfers.*

The World Bank, 1818 H Street, NW, Washington, D.C. 20433 (202) 477-1234; *The World Bank Atlas;* and *World Development Report.*

World Health Organization, Office of Publications, 20 Avenue Appia, CH-1211 Geneva 27, Switzerland (Telephone Number in U.S. (518) 436-9686); *World Health Statistics Annual.*

SWEDEN - POST OFFICES

M.E. Sharpe, 80 Business Park Drive, Armonk, New York 10504 (800) 541-6563; *The Illustrated Book of World Rankings.*

St. Martin's Press, Inc., 175 Fifth Avenue, New York, New York 10010 (800) 221-7945; *The Statesman's Year-Book.*

Statistical Office of the United Nations, Publishing Service, New York, New York 10017 (800) 253-9646; *Trends in Europe and North America: The Statistical Yearbook of the Economic Commission for Europe.*

SWEDEN - POTATO PRODUCTION - See SWEDEN - CROPS

SWEDEN - POWER PRODUCTION INDUSTRY

Statistical Office of the United Nations, Publishing Service, New York, New York 10017 (800) 253-9646; *Statistical Yearbook.*

SWEDEN - PRICES

Food and Agricultural Organization of the United Nations (FAO), Via delle Terme di Caracalla, 00100 Rome, Italy (Telephone Number in U.S. (202) 653-2400); *Production Yearbook;* and *The State of Food and Agriculture.*

International Labour Office, I.L.O. Publications, 1828 L Street, NW, Suite 801, Washington, D.C. 20036 (301) 638-3152; *Yearbook of Labour Statistics.*

International Lead and Zinc Study Group, Metro House, 58 St. James's Street, London SW1A 1LD, England; *Lead and Zinc Statistics.*

International Monetary Fund, 700 Nineteenth Street, NW, Washington, D.C. 20431 (202) 623-7000; *International Financial Statistics.*

International Rubber Study Group, York

House, Eighth Floor, Empire Way, Wembley, London HA9 0PA, England; *Rubber Statistical Bulletin.*

M.E. Sharpe, 80 Business Park Drive, Armonk, New York 10504 (800) 541-6563; *The Illustrated Book of World Rankings.*

Nordic Council of Ministers, Store Strandstraede 18, DK-1255 Copenhagen K, Denmark and the Nordic Statistical Secretariat, Postboks 2550, DK-2100 Copenhagen 0, Denmark; *The Yearbook of Nordic Statistics.*

Organisation for Economic Co-operation and Development (OECD), 2 rue Andre-Pascal, 75 Paris 16, France (Telephone Number in U.S. (202) 785-6323); *Economic Outlook; The Footwear, Raw Hides and Skins, and Leather Industry in OECD Countries; Indicators of Industrial Activity; The Iron and Steel Industry; Main Economic Indicators - Historical Statistics;* and *The Pulp and Paper Industry.*

World Bureau of Metal Statistics, 27-A High Street, Ware Hert SG12 9BA, England; *World Metal Statistics.*

SWEDEN - PRINTING AND WRITING PAPER - See SWEDEN - FORESTRY AND FOREST PRODUCTS

SWEDEN - PRODUCTION

American Automobile Manufacturers Association, 1401 H Street, NW, Suite 900, Washington, D.C. 20005 (202) 326-5500; *World Motor Vehicle Data.*

International Lead and Zinc Study Group, Metro House, 58 St. James's Street, London SW1A 1LD, England; *Lead and Zinc Statistics.*

International Rubber Study Group, York House, Eighth Floor, Empire Way, Wembley, London HA9 0PA, England; *Rubber Statistical Bulletin.*

M.E. Sharpe, 80 Business Park Drive, Armonk, New York 10504 (800) 541-6563; *The Illustrated Book of World Rankings.*

Organisation for Economic Co-operation and Development (OECD), 2 rue Andre-Pascal, 75 Paris 16, France (Telephone Number in U.S. (202) 785-6323); *Economic Outlook; The Footwear, Raw Hides and Skins, and Leather Industry in OECD Countries; Indicators of Industrial Activity; Industrial Structure Statistics; The Iron and Steel Industry; Meat Balances in OECD Member Countries; Milk, Milk Products, and Egg Balances in OECD Member Countries; The Non-Ferrous Metals Industry; The Pulp and Paper Industry;* and *Textile Industry in OECD Countries.*

SWEDEN - PRODUCTIVITY

Organisation for Economic Co-operation and Development (OECD), 2 rue Andre-Pascal, 75 Paris 16, France (Telephone Number in U.S. (202) 785-6323); *Economic Outlook.*

SWEDEN - PROPERTY TAXES - See SWEDEN - TAXATION

SWEDEN - PUBLIC CONSUMPTION FUND

Organisation for Economic Co-operation and Development (OECD), 2 rue Andre-Pascal, 75 Paris 16, France (Telephone Number in U.S. (202) 785-6323); *Revenue Statistics of OECD Member Countries.*

SWEDEN - PUBLIC EXPENDITURES

Organisation for Economic Co-operation and Development (OECD), 2 rue Andre-Pascal, 75 Paris 16, France (Telephone Number in U.S. (202) 785-6323); *Revenue Statistics of OECD Member Countries.*

SWEDEN - PUBLIC FINANCE - See SWEDEN - FINANCE

SWEDEN - PUBLIC REVENUES

Organisation for Economic Co-operation and Development (OECD), 2 rue Andre-Pascal, 75 Paris 16, France (Telephone Number in U.S. (202) 785-6323); *Revenue Statistics of OECD Member Countries.*

SWEDEN - RADIO BROADCASTING

M.E. Sharpe, 80 Business Park Drive, Armonk, New York 10504 (800) 541-6563; *The Illustrated Book of World Rankings.*

Nordic Council of Ministers, Store Strandstraede 18, DK-1255 Copenhagen K, Denmark and the Nordic Statistical Secretariat, Postboks 2550, DK-2100 Copenhagen 0, Denmark; *The Yearbook of Nordic Statistics.*

United Nations Educational, Scientific and Cultural Organization (UNESCO), 7 Place de Fontenoy, F-75700 Paris, France (Telephone Number in U.S. (212) 963-5981); *Statistical Yearbook.*

SWEDEN - RADIO RECEIVER PRODUCTION

Statistical Office of the United Nations, Publishing Service, New York, New York 10017 (800) 253-9646; *Statistical Yearbook.*

SWEDEN - RADIO RECEIVERS

St. Martin's Press, Inc., 175 Fifth Avenue, New York, New York 10010 (800) 221-7945; *The Statesman's Year-Book.*

SWEDEN - RAILWAYS

Euromonitor International, Inc., 122 Michigan Avenue, Suite 1200, Chicago, Illinois 60603 (800) 577-EURO; *European Marketing Data and Statistics.*

Europa Publications Limited, 18 Bedford Square, London, WC1B 3JN, England; *The Europa World Year Book.*

Jane's Information Group, Sentinel House, 163 Brighton Road, Coulsdon, Surrey CR5 2NH, England (Telephone Number in U.S. (703) 683-3700); *Jane's World Railways.*

Nordic Council of Ministers, Store Strandstraede 18, DK-1255 Copenhagen K, Denmark and the Nordic Statistical Secretariat, Postboks 2550, DK-2100 Copenhagen 0, Denmark; *The Yearbook of Nordic Statistics.*

St. Martin's Press, Inc., 175 Fifth Avenue, New York, New York 10010 (800) 221-7945; *The Statesman's Year-Book.*

Statistical Office of the United Nations, Publishing Service, New York, New York 10017 (800) 253-9646; *Annual Bulletin of Transport Statistics for Europe; Trends in Europe and North America: The Statistical Yearbook of the Economic Commission for Europe;* and *Statistical Yearbook.*

SWEDEN - RELIGION

Central Intelligence Agency, Washington, D.C. 20505 (703) 482-1100, www.cia.gov; *The World Factbook.*

M.E. Sharpe, 80 Business Park Drive, Armonk, New York 10504 (800) 541-6563; *The Illustrated Book of World Rankings.*

St. Martin's Press, Inc., 175 Fifth Avenue, New York, New York 10010 (800) 221-7945; *The Statesman's Year-Book.*

SWEDEN - RENT PRICES

International Labour Office, I.L.O. Publications, 1828 L Street, NW, Suite 801, Washington, D.C. 20036 (301) 638-3152; *Yearbook of Labour Statistics.*

SWEDEN - RETAIL TRADE

Euromonitor International, Inc., 122 South Michigan Avenue, Suite 1200, Chicago, Illinois 60603 (800) 577-EURO; *World Marketing Data and Statistics;* and *Retail Trade International.*

Statistical Office of the United Nations, Publishing Service, New York, New York 10017 (800) 253-9646; *Statistical Yearbook.*

SWEDEN - RICE PRODUCTION - See SWEDEN - CROPS

SWEDEN - ROUNDWOOD PRODUCTION - See SWEDEN - FORESTRY AND FOREST PRODUCTS

SWEDEN - RUBBER PRODUCTION AND CONSUMPTION

International Rubber Study Group, York House, Eighth Floor, Empire Way, Wembley, London HA9 0PA, England; *Rubber Statistical Bulletin.*

M.E. Sharpe, 80 Business Park Drive, Armonk, New York 10504 (800) 541-6563; *The Illustrated Book of World Rankings.*

Organisation for Economic Co-operation and Development (OECD), 2 rue Andre-Pascal, 75 Paris 16, France (Telephone Number in U.S. (202) 785-6323); *Foreign Trade by Commodities.*

Statistical Office of the United Nations, Publishing Service, New York, New York 10017 (800) 253-9646; *Statistical Yearbook.*

SWEDEN - SALT PRODUCTION - See SWEDEN - MINING AND MINERAL PRODUCTS

SWEDEN - SAWNWOOD PRODUCTION - See SWEDEN - FORESTRY AND FOREST PRODUCTS

SWEDEN - SCIENCE AND TECHNOLOGY - EXPENDITURE FOR RESEARCH - See SCIENCE, TECHNICIANS AND ENGINEERS

SWEDEN - SCIENTISTS, TECHNICIANS AND ENGINEERS

Statistical Office of the United Nations, Publishing Service, New York, New York 10017 (800) 253-9646; *Statistical Yearbook.*

United Nations Educational, Scientific and Cultural Organization (UNESCO), 7 Place de Fontenoy, F-75700 Paris, France (Telephone Number in U.S. (212) 963-5981); *Statistical Yearbook.*

SWEDEN - SENIOR CITIZENS

M.E. Sharpe, 80 Business Park Drive, Armonk, New York 10504 (800) 541-6563; *The Illustrated Book of World Rankings.*

SWEDEN - SHEEP - See SWEDEN - LIVESTOCK AND POULTRY

SWEDEN - SHIPBUILDING - PRODUCTION INDEX

Organisation for Economic Co-operation and Development (OECD), 2 rue Andre-Pascal, 75 Paris 16, France (Telephone Number in U.S. (202) 785-6323); *Indicators of Industrial Activity.*

SWEDEN - SILVER PRODUCTION AND CONSUMPTION - See SWEDEN - MINING AND MINERAL PRODUCTS

SWEDEN - SOCIAL DATA

M.E. Sharpe, 80 Business Park Drive, Armonk, New York 10504 (800) 541-6563; *The Illustrated Book of World Rankings.*

Statistical Office of the United Nations, Publishing Service, New York, New York 10017 (800) 253-9646; *World Statistics Pocketbook.*

SWEDEN - SOCIAL SECURITY

International Monetary Fund, 700 Nineteenth Street, NW, Washington, D.C. 20431 (202) 623-7000; *Government Finance Statistics Yearbook.*

Nordic Council of Ministers, Store Strandstraede 18, DK-1255 Copenhagen K, Denmark and the Nordic Statistical Secretariat, Postboks 2550, DK-2100 Copenhagen 0, Denmark; *The Yearbook of Nordic Statistics.*

Organisation for Economic Co-operation and Development (OECD), 2 rue Andre-Pascal, 75 Paris 16, France (Telephone Number in U.S. (202) 785-6323); *Revenue Statistics of OECD Member Countries.*

St. Martin's Press, Inc., 175 Fifth Avenue, New York, New York 10010 (800) 221-7945; *The Statesman's Year-Book.*

Statistical Office of the United Nations, Publishing Service, New York, New York 10017 (800) 253-9646; *National Accounts Statistics.*

SWEDEN - SOCIOECONOMIC DATA

Organisation for Economic Co-operation and Development (OECD), 2 rue Andre-Pascal, 75 Paris 16, France (Telephone Number in U.S. (202) 785-6323); *Economic Outlook.*

SWEDEN - STAMP TAXES AND DUTIES - See SWEDEN - TAXATION

SWEDEN - STEEL - See SWEDEN - MINING AND MINERAL PRODUCTS

SWEDEN - STOCKS - COMMODITY - MARKET PRICE - INDEXES

Food and Agricultural Organization of the United Nations (FAO) Via delle Terme di Caracalla, 00100 Rome, Italy (Telephone Number in U.S. (202) 653-2400); *The State of Food and Agriculture.*

International Lead and Zinc Study Group, Metro House, 58 St. James's Street, London SW1A 1LD, England; *Lead and Zinc Statistics.*

Statistical Office of the United Nations, Publishing Service, New York, New York 10017 (800) 253-9646; *Statistical Yearbook.*

World Bureau of Metal Statistics, 27-A High Street, Ware Hert SG12 9BA, England; *World Metal Statistics.*

SWEDEN - SUGAR EXPORTS - See SWEDEN - CROPS

SWEDEN - SULPHUR AND SULPHURIC ACID PRODUCTION - See SWEDEN - MINING AND MINERAL PRODUCTS

SWEDEN - TAXATION

Europa Publications Limited, 18 Bedford Square, London, WC1B 3JN, England; *The Europa World Year Book.*

International Monetary Fund, 700 Nineteenth Street, NW, Washington, D.C. 20431 (202) 623-7000; *Government Finance Statistics Yearbook.*

International Road Federation, 2600 Virginia Avenue, NW, Washington, D.C. 20037 (202) 338-4641; *World Road Statistics.*

Nordic Council of Ministers, Store Strandstraede 18, DK-1255 Copenhagen K, Denmark and the Nordic Statistical Secretariat, Postboks 2550, DK-2100 Copenhagen 0, Denmark; *The Yearbook of Nordic Statistics.*

Organisation for Economic Co-operation and Development (OECD), 2 rue Andre-Pascal, 75 Paris 16, France (Telephone Number in U.S. (202) 785-6323); *Revenue Statistics of OECD Member Countries.*

St. Martin's Press, Inc., 175 Fifth Avenue, New York, New York 10010 (800) 221-7945; *The Statesman's Year-Book.*

The World Bank, 1818 H Street, NW, Washington, D.C. 20433 (202) 477-1234; *World Development Indicators.*

SWEDEN - TEA CONSUMPTION

Statistical Office of the United Nations, Publishing Service, New York, New York 10017 (800) 253-9646; *Statistical Yearbook.*

SWEDEN - TELEGRAPH SERVICE

Nordic Council of Ministers, Store Strandstraede 18, DK-1255 Copenhagen K, Denmark and the Nordic Statistical Secretariat, Postboks 2550, DK-2100 Copenhagen 0, Denmark; *The Yearbook of Nordic Statistics.*

Statistical Office of the United Nations,

Publishing Service, New York, New York 10017 (800) 253-9646; *Statistical Yearbook.*

SWEDEN - TELEPHONES IN USE

American Telephone and Telegraph Company, 26 Parsippany Road, Whippany, New Jersey 07981 (800) 222-0300; *The World's Telephones.*

Central Intelligence Agency, Washington, D.C. 20505 (703) 482-1100, www.cia.gov; *The World Factbook.*

Nordic Council of Ministers, Store Strandstraede 18, DK-1255 Copenhagen K, Denmark and the Nordic Statistical Secretariat, Postboks 2550, DK-2100 Copenhagen 0, Denmark; *The Yearbook of Nordic Statistics.*

Statistical Office of the United Nations, Publishing Service, New York, New York 10017 (800) 253-9646; *Statistical Yearbook; Trends in Europe and North America: The Statistical Yearbook of the Economic Commission for Europe;* and *World Statistics Pocketbook.*

SWEDEN - TELEVISION BROADCASTING

M.E. Sharpe, 80 Business Park Drive, Armonk, New York 10504 (800) 541-6563; *The Illustrated Book of World Rankings.*

Nordic Council of Ministers, Store Strandstraede 18, DK-1255 Copenhagen K, Denmark and the Nordic Statistical Secretariat, Postboks 2550, DK-2100 Copenhagen 0, Denmark; *The Yearbook of Nordic Statistics.*

United Nations Educational, Scientific and Cultural Organization (UNESCO), 7 Place de Fontenoy, F-75700 Paris, France (Telephone Number in U.S. (212) 963-5981); *Statistical Yearbook.*

SWEDEN - TELEVISION RECEIVER PRODUCTION

Statistical Office of the United Nations, Publishing Service, New York, New York 10017 (800) 253-9646; *Statistical Yearbook.*

SWEDEN - TEXTILE INDUSTRY

Euromonitor International, Inc., 122 South Michigan Avenue, Suite 1200, Chicago, Illinois 60603 (800) 577-EURO; *Retail Trade International.*

M.E. Sharpe, 80 Business Park Drive, Armonk, New York 10504 (800) 541-6563; *The Illustrated Book of World Rankings.*

Organisation for Economic Co-operation and Development (OECD), 2 rue Andre-Pascal, 75 Paris 16, France (Telephone Number in U.S. (202) 785-6323); *Economic Accounts for Agriculture;*

Foreign Trade by Commodities; Indicators of Industrial Activity; Industrial Structure Statistics; and *Textile Industry in OECD Countries.*

St. Martin's Press, Inc., 175 Fifth Avenue, New York, New York 10010 (800) 221-7945; *The Statesman's Year-Book.*

Statistical Office of the United Nations, Publishing Service, New York, New York 10017 (800) 253-9646; *Statistical Yearbook.*

United Nations Conference on Trade and Development, Central Statistical Service, Palais des Nations, Geneva, Switzerland (Telephone in U.S. (800) 253-9646); *UNCTAD Commodity Yearbook.*

SWEDEN - THEATRE

United Nations Educational, Scientific and Cultural Organization (UNESCO), 7 Place de Fontenoy, F-75700 Paris, France (Telephone Number in U.S. (212) 963-5981); *Statistical Yearbook.*

SWEDEN - TIN - See SWEDEN - MINING AND MINERAL PRODUCTS

SWEDEN - TIRE (MOTOR VEHICLE) PRODUCTION

International Rubber Study Group, York House, Eighth Floor, Empire Way, Wembley, London HA9 0PA, England; *Rubber Statistical Bulletin.*

Statistical Office of the United Nations, Publishing Service, New York, New York 10017 (800) 253-9646; *Statistical Yearbook.*

SWEDEN - TOBACCO PRODUCTION

Euromonitor International, Inc., 122 South Michigan Avenue, Suite 1200, Chicago, Illinois 60603 (800) 577-EURO; *European Marketing Data and Statistics.*

M.E. Sharpe, 80 Business Park Drive, Armonk, New York 10504 (800) 541-6563; *The Illustrated Book of World Rankings.*

Organisation for Economic Co-operation and Development (OECD), 2 rue Andre-Pascal, 75 Paris 16, France (Telephone Number in U.S. (202) 785-6323); *Foreign Trade by Commodities; Indicators of Industrial Activity;* and *Industrial Structure Statistics.*

Statistical Office of the United Nations, Publishing Service, New York, New York 10017 (800) 253-9646; *Statistical Yearbook.*

SWEDEN - TOURISM

Euromonitor International, Inc., 122 South Michigan Avenue, Suite 1200, Chicago, Illinois 60603 (800) 577-EURO; *European Marketing Data and Statistics;*

World Marketing Data and Statistics; and *The World Economic Factbook.*

Europa Publications Limited, 18 Bedford Square, London, WC1B 3JN, England; *The Europa World Year Book.*

M.E. Sharpe, 80 Business Park Drive, Armonk, New York 10504 (800) 541-6563; *The Illustrated Book of World Rankings.*

Organisation for Economic Co-operation and Development (OECD), 2 rue Andre-Pascal, 75 Paris 16, France (Telephone Number in U.S. (202) 785-6323); *Tourism Policy and International Tourism in OECD Member Countries.*

St. Martin's Press, Inc., 175 Fifth Avenue, New York, New York 10010 (800) 221-7945; *The Statesman's Year-Book.*

Statistical Office of the United Nations, Publishing Service, New York, New York 10017 (800) 253-9646; *Statistical Yearbook;* and *Trends in Europe and North America: The Statistical Yearbook of the Economic Commission for Europe.*

World Tourism Organization, Calle Capitan Haya 42, E-28020 Madrid, Spain; *Yearbook of Tourism Statistics.*

SWEDEN - TRACTORS IN USE

Statistical Office of the United Nations, Publishing Service, New York, New York 10017 (800) 253-9646; *Statistical Yearbook.*

SWEDEN - TRADE - See SWEDEN - FOREIGN TRADE

SWEDEN - TRADEMARKS AND SERVICE MARKS - See SWEDEN - PATENTS, TRADEMARKS AND SERVICE MARKS

SWEDEN - TRANSPORTATION AND COMMUNICATIONS

Central Intelligence Agency, Washington, D.C. 20505 (703) 482-1100, www.cia.gov; *The World Factbook.*

Euromonitor International, Inc., 122 South Michigan Avenue, Suite 1200, Chicago, Illinois 60603 9800) 577-EURO; *World Marketing Data and Statistics.*

Europa Publications Limited, 18 Bedford Square, London, WC1B 3JN, England; *The Europa World Year Book.*

M.E. Sharpe, 80 Business Park Drive, Armonk, New York 10504 (800) 541-6563; *The Illustrated Book of World Rankings.*

Nordic Council of Ministers, Store Strandstraede 18, DK-1255 Copenhagen K, Denmark and the Nordic Statistical Secretariat, Postboks 2550, DK-2100 Copenhagen 0, Denmark; *The Yearbook of*

Nordic Statistics.

St. Martin's Press, Inc., 175 Fifth Avenue, New York, New York 10010 (800) 221-7945; *The Statesman's Year-Book.*

Statistical Office of the United Nations, Publishing Service, New York, New York 10017 (800) 253-9646; *Human Development Report;* and *Trends in Europe and North America: The Statistical Yearbook of the Economic Commission for Europe.*

SWEDEN - TUNGSTEN PRODUCTION AND CONSUMPTION - See SWEDEN - MINING AND MINERAL PRODUCTS

SWEDEN - UNEMPLOYMENT

Central Intelligence Agency, Washington, D.C. 20505 (703) 482-1100, www.cia.gov; *The World Factbook.*

Euromonitor International, Inc., 122 South Michigan Avenue, Suite 1200, Chicago, Illinois 60603 (800) 577-EURO; *European Marketing Data and Statistics.*

International Labour Office, I.L.O. Publications, 1828 L Street, NW, Suite 801, Washington, D.C. 20036 (301) 638-3152; *Yearbook of Labour Statistics.*

Nordic Council of Ministers, Store Strandstraede 18, DK-1255 Copenhagen K, Denmark and the Nordic Statistical Secretariat, Postboks 2550, DK-2100 Copenhagen 0, Denmark; *The Yearbook of Nordic Statistics.*

Organisation for Economic Co-operation and Development (OECD), 2 rue Andre-Pascal, 75 Paris 16, France (Telephone Number in U.S. (202) 785-6323); *Economic Outlook; OECD Economic Surveys: Sweden;* and *OECD Employment Outlook.*

St. Martin's Press, Inc., 175 Fifth Avenue, New York, New York 10010 (800) 221-7945; *The Statesman's Year-Book.*

Statistical Office of the United Nations, Publishing Service, New York, New York 10017 (800) 253-9646; *Statistical Yearbook;* and *Trends in Europe and North America: The Statistical Yearbook of the Economic Commission for Europe.*

SWEDEN - URANIUM PRODUCTION AND CONSUMPTION - See SWEDEN - MINING AND MINERAL PRODUCTS

SWEDEN - VANADIUM AND VANADIUM ORE PRODUCTION AND CONSUMPTION - See SWEDEN - MINING AND MINERAL PRODUCTS

SWEDEN - VITAL STATISTICS

Nordic Council of Ministers, Store Strandstraede 18, DK-1255 Copenhagen K, Denmark and the Nordic Statistical Secretariat, Postboks 2550, DK-2100 Copenhagen 0, Denmark; *The Yearbook of Nordic Statistics.*

St. Martin's Press, Inc., 175 Fifth Avenue, New York, New York 10010 (800) 221-7945; *The Statesman's Year-Book.*

Statistical Office of the United Nations, Publishing Service, New York, New York 10017 (800) 253-9646; *Statistical Yearbook.*

World Health Organization, Office of Publications, 20 Avenue Appia, CH-1211 Geneva 27, Switzerland (Telephone Number in U.S. (518) 436-9686); *World Health Statistics Annual.*

SWEDEN - WAGES

Euromonitor International, Inc., 122 South Michigan Avenue, Suite 1200, Chicago, Illinois 60603 (800) 577-EURO; *European Marketing Data and Statistics.*

International Labour Office, I.L.O. Publications, 1828 L Street, NW, Suite 801, Washington, D.C. 20036 (301) 638-3152; *Yearbook of Labour Statistics.*

Nordic Council of Ministers, Store Strandstraede 18, DK-1255 Copenhagen K, Denmark and the Nordic Statistical Secretariat, Postboks 2550, DK-2100 Copenhagen 0, Denmark; *The Yearbook of Nordic Statistics.*

Organisation for Economic Co-operation and Development (OECD), 2 rue Andre-Pascal, 75 Paris 16, France (Telephone Number in U.S. (202) 785-6323); *Economic Outlook; Industrial Structure Statistics;* and *Main Economic Indicators - Historical Statistics.*

Statistical Office of the United Nations, Publishing Service, New York, New York 10017 (800) 253-9646; *Statistical Yearbook.*

SWEDEN - WATERWAYS IN USE

Organisation for Economic Co-operation and Development (OECD), 2 rue Andre-Pascal, 75 Paris 16, France (Telephone Number in U.S. (202) 785-6323); *Maritime Transport.*

Statistical Office of the United Nations, Publishing Service, New York, New York 10017 (800) 253-9646; *Annual Bulletin of Transport Statistics for Europe.*

SWEDEN - WEATHER - See SWEDEN - CLIMATE

SWEDEN - WELFARE

International Monetary Fund, 700

Nineteenth Street, NW, Washington, D.C. 20431 (202) 623-7000; *Government Finance Statistics Yearbook.*

Nordic Council of Ministers, Store Strandstraede 18, DK-1255 Copenhagen K, Denmark and the Nordic Statistical Secretariat, Postboks 2550, DK-2100 Copenhagen 0, Denmark; *The Yearbook of Nordic Statistics.*

St. Martin's Press, Inc., 175 Fifth Avenue, New York, New York 10010 (800) 221-7945; *The Statesman's Year-Book.*

SWEDEN - WHEAT PRODUCTION AND PRICES - See SWEDEN - CROPS

SWEDEN - WHOLESALE PRICES

Nordic Council of Ministers, Store Strandstraede 18, DK-1255 Copenhagen K, Denmark and the Nordic Statistical Secretariat, Postboks 2550, DK-2100 Copenhagen 0, Denmark; *The Yearbook of Nordic Statistics.*

Statistical Office of the United Nations, Publishing Service, New York, New York 10017 (800) 253-9646; *Statistical Yearbook.*

SWEDEN - WHOLESALE TRADE

Statistical Office of the United Nations, Publishing Service, New York, New York 10017 (800) 253-9646; *Statistical Yearbook.*

SWEDEN - WINE PRODUCTION - See SWEDEN - BEVERAGES

SWEDEN - WOOD AND WOOD PULP - See SWEDEN - FORESTRY AND FOREST PRODUCTS

SWEDEN - WOOL PRODUCTION AND CONSUMPTION - See SWEDEN - TEXTILE INDUSTRY

SWEDEN - YARN PRODUCTION - See SWEDEN - TEXTILE INDUSTRY

SWEDEN - ZINC AND ZINC ORE PRODUCTION AND CONSUMPTION -See SWEDEN - MINING AND MINERAL PRODUCTS

SWEET POTATOES

U.S. Department of Agriculture, Economic Research Service, 1800 M Street, NW, Washington, D.C. 20036 (202) 694-5050, www.ers.usda.gov; *Food Consumption, Prices, and Expenditures;* and *Agricultural Outlook.*

U.S. Department of Agriculture, National Agricultural Statistics Service, Fourteenth Street and Independence Avenue, SW, Washington, D.C. 20250 (800) 727-9540, www.usda.gov/nass; *Vegetables;* and *Agricultural Statistics.*

SWIMMING

National Collegiate Athletic Association, 700 West Washington Street, Indianapolis, Indiana 46206 (317) 917-6222; *1997-98 Participation Study.*

National Sporting Goods Association, 1601 Feehanville Drive, Suite 300, Mount Prospect, Illinois 66056 (847) 296-6742; *Sports Participation in 1998.*

SWINE - See HOGS

SWITCHBOARD AND SWITCHGEAR APPARATUS

U.S. Department of Commerce, Bureau of the Census, Washington, D.C. 20233 (301) 457-4100, www.census.gov; *Current Industrial Reports;* and *Manufacturing Profiles.*

Switzerland - National Statistical Offices

Division de la Statistique du Commerce, Direction Generale des Douanes, Monbijoustrasse 40, CH-3011 Berne, Switzerland.

Office Federale de la Statistique, Hallwylstrasse 15, CH-3003 Berne, Switzerland.

Switzerland - Primary Statistics Sources

Office Federale de la Statistique, Hallwylstrasse 15, CH-3003 Berne, Switzerland; *Statistiches Jahrbuch der Schweiz: Annuaire statistique de la Suisse* (Statistical Yearbook of Switzerland); and *La Vie Economique: Rapports Economiques etde Statostoqie Sociale* (Economic Life: Economic Reports and Social Statistics).

Switzerland - Databases

Federal Statistical Office, Schwarz forstrasse 96, CH-3003 Berne, Switzerland. Offers the following databases: (1) Statistical Information Systems (STATINF); and (2) GEOSTAT. Subject coverage: Swiss statistical information.

SWITZERLAND - ABORTIONS

Statistical Office of the United Nations, Publishing Service, New York, New York 10017 (800) 253-9646; *Trends in Europe and North America: The Statistical Yearbook of the Economic Commission for Europe.*

SWITZERLAND - AGRICULTURE

Economist Intelligence Unit, 111 West

57th Street, New York, New York 10019 (800) 938-4685; *Switzerland Country Report.*

Euromonitor International, Inc., 122 South Michigan Avenue, Suite 1200, Chicago, Illinois 60603 9800) 577-EURO; *World Marketing Data and Statistics.*

Europa Publications Limited, 18 Bedford Square, London, WC1B 3JN, England; *The Europa World Year Book.*

Food and Agricultural Organization of the United Nations (FAO) Via delle Terme di Caracalla, 00100 Rome, Italy (Telephone Number in U.S. (202) 653-2400); *Production Yearbook; The State of Food and Agriculture;* and *Trade Yearbook.*

M.E. Sharpe, 80 Business Park Drive, Armonk, New York 10504 (800) 541-6563; *The Illustrated Book of World Rankings.*

Organisation for Economic Co-operation and Development (OECD), 2 rue Andre-Pascal, 75 Paris 16, France (Telephone Number in U.S. (202) 785-6323); *Economic Accounts for Agriculture; Indicators of Industrial Activity; Industrial Structure Statistics;* and *OECD Economic Surveys: Switzerland.*

St. Martin's Press, Inc., 175 Fifth Avenue, New York, New York 10010 (800) 221-7945; *The Statesman's Year-Book.*

Statistical Office of the United Nations, Publishing Service, New York, New York 10017 (800) 253-9646; *Statistical Yearbook.*

United Nations Conference on Trade and Development, Central Statistical Service, Palais des Nations, Geneva, Switzerland (Telephone in U.S. (800) 253-9646); *UNCTAD Commodity Yearbook.*

The World Bank, 1818 H Street, NW, Washington, D.C. 20433 (202) 477-1234; *World Development Indicators.*

SWITZERLAND - AIRLINE SERVICE

Europa Publications Limited, 18 Bedford Square, London, WC1B 3JN, England; *The Europa World Year Book.*

International Civil Aviation Organization, 999 University Street, Montreal, Quebec, Canada H3C 5H7 (514) 954-8219; *Civil Aviation Statistics of the World.*

M.E. Sharpe, 80 Business Park Drive, Armonk, New York 10504 (800) 541-6563; *The Illustrated Book of World Rankings.*

Organisation for Economic Co-operation and Development (OECD), 2 rue Andre-Pascal, 75 Paris 16, France (Telephone Number in U.S. (202) 785-

6323); *Tourism Policy and International Tourism in OECD Member Countries.*

St. Martin's Press, Inc., 175 Fifth Avenue, New York, New York 10010 (800) 221-7945; *The Statesman's Year-Book.*

Statistical Office of the United Nations, Publishing Service, New York, New York 10017 (800) 253-9646; *Statistical Yearbook.*

SWITZERLAND - AIRPORTS

Central Intelligence Agency, Washington, D.C. 20505 (703) 482-1100, www.cia.gov; *The World Factbook.*

SWITZERLAND - ALUMINUM PRODUCTION AND CONSUMPTION - See SWITZERLAND - MINING AND MINERAL PRODUCTS

SWITZERLAND - ANIMAL FEEDINGSTUFFS - EXPORTS

Organisation for Economic Co-operation and Development (OECD), 2 rue Andre-Pascal, 75 Paris 16, France (Telephone Number in U.S. (202) 785-6323); *Foreign Trade by Commodities.*

SWITZERLAND - ANIMAL HEALTH

Food and Agricultural Organization of the United Nations (FAO), Via delle Terme di Caracalla, 00100, Rome, Italy (Telephone Number in U.S. (202) 653-2400); *Animal Health Yearbook.*

SWITZERLAND - ANTIMONY AND ANTIMONY ORE PRODUCTION AND CONSUMPTION - See SWITZERLAND - MINING AND MINERAL PRODUCTS

SWITZERLAND - AREA AND DENSITY OF POPULATION

Central Intelligence Agency, Washington, D.C. 20505 (703) 482-1100, www.cia.gov; *The World Factbook.*

Euromonitor International, Inc., 122 South Michigan Avenue, Suite 1200, Chicago, Illinois 60603 (800) 577-EURO; *The World Economic Factbook.*

Europa Publications Limited, 18 Bedford Square, London, WC1B 3JN, England; *The Europa World Year Book.*

Food and Agricultural Organization of the United Nations (FAO) Via delle Terme di Caracalla, 00100 Rome, Italy (Telephone Number in U.S. (202) 653-2400); *The State of Food and Agriculture.*

M.E. Sharpe, 80 Business Park Drive, Armonk, New York 10504 (800) 541-6563; *The Illustrated Book of World Rankings.*

St. Martin's Press, Inc., 175 Fifth Avenue, New York, New York 10010 (800)

221-7945; *The Statesman's Year-Book.*

Statistical Office of the United Nations, Publishing Service, New York, New York 10017 (800) 253-9646; *Statistical Yearbook;* and *Trends in Europe and North America: The Statistical Yearbook of the Economic Commission for Europe.*

United Nations Educational, Scientific and Cultural Organization (UNESCO), 7 Place de Fontenoy, F-75700 Paris, France (Telephone Number in U.S. (212) 963-5981); *Statistical Yearbook.*

The World Bank, 1818 H Street, NW, Washington, D.C. 20433 (202) 477-1234; *World Development Report.*

SWITZERLAND - ARMS EXPORTS AND IMPORTS - See SWITZERLAND - MILITARY

SWITZERLAND - ARSENIC PRODUCTION AND CONSUMPTION - See SWITZERLAND - MINING AND MINERAL PRODUCTS

SWITZERLAND - BALANCE OF PAYMENTS

The Economist Intelligence Unit, 111 West 57th Street, New York, New York 10019; *The World Market Atlas.*

Europa Publications Limited, 18 Bedford Square, London, WC1B 3JN, England; *The Europa World Year Book.*

International Monetary Fund, 700 Nineteenth Street, NW, Washington, D.C. 20431 (202) 623-7000; *Balance of Payments Yearbook;* and *International Financial Statistics.*

Organisation for Economic Co-operation and Development (OECD), 2 rue Andre-Pascal, 75 Paris 16, France (Telephone Number in U.S. (202) 785-6323); *Economic Outlook; Geographical Distribution of Financial Flows to Developing Countries;* and *OECD Economic Surveys: Switzerland.*

United Nations Conference on Trade and Development (UNCTAD), New York, New York 10017 (800) 253-9646; *Handbook of International Trade and Development Statistics.*

The World Bank, 1818 H Street, NW, Washington, D.C. 20433 (202) 477-1234; *World Development Report;* and *World Development Indicators.*

SWITZERLAND - BANKING

Euromonitor International, Inc., 122 South Michigan Avenue, Suite 1200, Chicago, Illinois 60603 9800) 577-EURO; *World Marketing Data and Statistics.*

Europa Publications Limited, 18 Bedford Square, London, WC1B 3JN,

England; *The Europa World Year Book.*

International Monetary Fund, 700 Nineteenth Street, NW, Washington, D.C. 20431 (202) 623-7000; *International Financial Statistics.*

M.E. Sharpe, 80 Business Park Drive, Armonk, New York 10504 (800) 541-6563; *The Illustrated Book of World Rankings.*

Organisation for Economic Co-operation and Development (OECD), 2 rue Andre-Pascal, 75 Paris 16, France (Telephone Number in U.S. (202) 785-6323); *Economic Outlook; Financial Market Trends;* and *OECD Economic Surveys: Switzerland.*

St. Martin's Press, Inc., 175 Fifth Avenue, New York, New York 10010 (800) 221-7945; *The Statesman's Year-Book.*

Statistical Office of the United Nations, Publishing Service, New York, New York 10017 (800) 253-9646; *Statistical Yearbook.*

SWITZERLAND - BARLEY PRODUCTION -
See SWITZERLAND - CROPS

SWITZERLAND - BAUXITE
PRODUCTION AND CONSUMPTION - See SWITZERLAND - MINING AND MINERAL PRODUCTS

SWITZERLAND - BEER PRODUCTION - See
SWITZERLAND - BEVERAGES

SWITZERLAND - BEVERAGES

M.E. Sharpe, 80 Business Park Drive, Armonk, New York 10504 (800) 541-6563; *The Illustrated Book of World Rankings.*

Organisation for Economic Co-operation and Development (OECD), 2 rue Andre-Pascal, 75 Paris 16, France (Telephone Number in U.S. (202) 785-6323); *Indicators of Industrial Activity.*

Statistical Office of the United Nations, Publishing Service, New York, New York 10017 (800) 253-9646; *Statistical Yearbook.*

SWITZERLAND - BIRTH RATE

Central Intelligence Agency, Washington, D.C. 20505 (703) 482-1100, www.cia.gov; *The World Factbook.*

Euromonitor International, Inc., 122 South Michigan Avenue, Suite 1200, Chicago, Illinois 60603 (800) 577-EURO; *The World Economic Factbook.*

Europa Publications Limited, 18 Bedford Square, London, WC1B 3JN, England; *The Europa World Year Book.*

M.E. Sharpe, 80 Business Park Drive, Armonk, New York 10504 (800) 541-6563;

The Illustrated Book of World Rankings.

St. Martin's Press, Inc., 175 Fifth Avenue, New York, New York 10010 (800) 221-7945; *The Statesman's Year-Book.*

Statistical Office of the United Nations, Publishing Service, New York, New York 10017 (800) 253-9646; *Demographic Yearbook;* and *Statistical Yearbook.*

The World Bank, 1818 H Street, NW, Washington, D.C. 20433 (202) 477-1234; *World Development Indicators.*

World Health Organization, Office of Publications, 20 Avenue Appia, CH-1211 Geneva 27, Switzerland (Telephone Number in U.S. (518) 436-9686); *World Health Statistics Annual.*

SWITZERLAND - BISMUTH
PRODUCTION AND CONSUMPTION - See SWITZERLAND - MINING AND MINERAL PRODUCTS

SWITZERLAND - BONDS

Organisation for Economic Co-operation and Development (OECD), 2 rue Andre-Pascal, 75 Paris 16, France (Telephone Number in U.S. (202) 785-6323); *Financial Market Trends.*

Statistical Office of the United Nations, Publishing Service, New York, New York 10017 (800) 253-9646; *Statistical Yearbook.*

SWITZERLAND - BOOK PRODUCTION

Euromonitor International, Inc., 122 South Michigan Avenue, Suite 1200, Chicago, Illinois 60603 (800) 577-EURO; *European Marketing Data and Statistics.*

Europa Publications Limited, 18 Bedford Square, London, WC1B 3JN, England; *The Europa World Year Book.*

Organisation for Economic Co-operation and Development (OECD), 2 rue Andre-Pascal, 75 Paris 16, France (Telephone Number in U.S. (202) 785-6323); *Indicators of Industrial Activity.*

St. Martin's Press, Inc., 175 Fifth Avenue, New York, New York 10010 (800) 221-7945; *The Statesman's Year-Book.*

Statistical Office of the United Nations, Publishing Service, New York, New York 10017 (800) 253-9646; *Trends in Europe and North America: The Statistical Yearbook of the Economic Commission for Europe.*

United Nations Educational, Scientific and Cultural Organization (UNESCO), 7 Place de Fontenoy, F-75700 Paris, France (Telephone Number in U.S. (212) 963-5981); *Statistical Yearbook.*

SWITZERLAND - BROADCASTING

Billboard Limited, P.O. Box 9027, 1006 AA Amsterdam, The Netherlands (Telephone Number in U.S. (212) 764-7300); *World Radio TV Handbook.*

Central Intelligence Agency, Washington, D.C. 20505 (703) 482-1100, www.cia.gov; *The World Factbook.*

Euromonitor International, Inc., 122 South Michigan Avenue, Suite 1200, Chicago, Illinois 60603 9800) 577-EURO; *World Marketing Data and Statistics.*

Europa Publications Limited, 18 Bedford Square, London, WC1B 3JN, England; *The Europa World Year Book.*

M.E. Sharpe, 80 Business Park Drive, Armonk, New York 10504 (800) 541-6563; *The Illustrated Book of World Rankings.*

St. Martin's Press, Inc., 175 Fifth Avenue, New York, New York 10010 (800) 221-7945; *The Statesman's Year-Book.*

Statistical Office of the United Nations, Publishing Service, New York, New York 10017 (800) 253-9646; *Trends in Europe and North America: The Statistical Yearbook of the Economic Commission for Europe.*

United Nations Educational, Scientific and Cultural Organization (UNESCO), 7 Place de Fontenoy, F-75700 Paris, France (Telephone Number in U.S. (212) 963-5981); *Statistical Yearbook.*

SWITZERLAND - BUDGET

Central Intelligence Agency, Washington, D.C. 20505 (703) 482-1100, www.cia.gov; *The World Factbook.*

SWITZERLAND - BUSINESS

Organisation for Economic Co-operation and Development (OECD), 2 rue Andre-Pascal, 75 Paris 16, France (Telephone Number in U.S. (202) 785-6323); *Main Economic Indicators - Historical Statistics.*

SWITZERLAND - BUTTER
CONSUMPTION - See SWITZERLAND - DAIRY PRODUCTS

SWITZERLAND - CADMIUM
PRODUCTION AND CONSUMPTION - See SWITZERLAND - MINING AND MINERAL PRODUCTS

SWITZERLAND - CALORIE SUPPLY

Food and Agricultural Organization of the United Nations (FAO) Via delle Terme di Caracalla, 00100 Rome, Italy (Telephone Number in U.S. (202) 653-2400); *The State of Food and Agriculture.*

SWITZERLAND - CAPITAL INVESTMENT

Organisation for Economic Co-operation and Development (OECD), 2 rue Andre-Pascal, 75 Paris 16, France (Telephone Number in U.S. (202) 785-6323); *Economic Outlook;* and *Financial Market Trends.*

SWITZERLAND - CAPITAL REVENUE

International Monetary Fund, 700 Nineteenth Street, NW, Washington, D.C. 20431 (202) 623-7000; *Government Finance Statistics Yearbook.*

Organisation for Economic Co-operation and Development (OECD), 2 rue Andre-Pascal, 75 Paris 16, France (Telephone Number in U.S. (202) 785-6323); *Economic Outlook;* and *Financial Market Trends.*

SWITZERLAND - CATTLE - See SWITZERLAND - LIVESTOCK AND POULTRY

SWITZERLAND - CAUSTIC SODA PRODUCTION - See SWITZERLAND - BEVERAGES

SWITZERLAND - CEMENT PRODUCTION - See SWITZERLAND - MINING AND MINERAL PRODUCTS

SWITZERLAND - CEREAL PRODUCTION - See SWITZERLAND - CROPS

SWITZERLAND - CHEESE - See SWITZERLAND - DAIRY PRODUCTS

SWITZERLAND - CHEMICAL (ORGANIC) PRODUCTION - See SWITZERLAND - MINING AND MINERAL PRODUCTS

SWITZERLAND - CHROMITE PRODUCTION AND CONSUMPTION - See SWITZERLAND - MINING AND MINERAL PRODUCTS

SWITZERLAND - CHROMIUM ORE PRODUCTION AND CONSUMPTION - See SWITZERLAND - MINING AND MINERAL PRODUCTS

SWITZERLAND - CIGAR PRODUCTION - See SWITZERLAND - TOBACCO PRODUCTION

SWITZERLAND - CIGARETTE PRODUCTION - See SWITZERLAND - TOBACCO PRODUCTION

SWITZERLAND - CLIMATE

M.E. Sharpe, 80 Business Park Drive, Armonk, New York 10504 (800) 541-6563; *The Illustrated Book of World Rankings.*

St. Martin's Press, Inc., 175 Fifth Avenue, New York, New York 10010 (800) 221-7945; *The Statesman's Year-Book.*

SWITZERLAND - CLOTHING - PRODUCTION INDEX - See SWITZERLAND - TEXTILE INDUSTRY

SWITZERLAND - CLOTHING EXPORTS AND IMPORTS - See SWITZERLAND - TEXTILE INDUSTRY

SWITZERLAND - COAL PRODUCTION - See SWITZERLAND - MINING AND MINERAL PRODUCTS

SWITZERLAND - COBALT PRODUCTION AND CONSUMPTION - See SWITZERLAND - MINING AND MINERAL PRODUCTS

SWITZERLAND - COFFEE PRODUCTION AND CONSUMPTION - See SWITZERLAND - CROPS

SWITZERLAND - COKE AND COKE OVEN ORE PRODUCTION AND CONSUMPTION - See SWITZERLAND - MINING AND MINERAL PRODUCTS

SWITZERLAND - COMMERCE

St. Martin's Press, Inc., 175 Fifth Avenue, New York, New York 10010 (800) 221-7945; *The Statesman's Year-Book.*

SWITZERLAND - COMMUNICATIONS - See SWITZERLAND - TRANSPORTATION AND COMMUNICATIONS

SWITZERLAND - CONSTRUCTION INDUSTRY

M.E. Sharpe, 80 Business Park Drive, Armonk, New York 10504 (800) 541-6563; *The Illustrated Book of World Rankings.*

Organisation for Economic Co-operation and Development (OECD), 2 rue Andre-Pascal, 75 Paris 16, France (Telephone Number in U.S. (202) 785-6323); *Industrial Structure Statistics; The Iron and Steel Industry; Main Economic Indicators - Historical Statistics;* and *OECD Economic Surveys: Switzerland.*

St. Martin's Press, Inc., 175 Fifth Avenue, New York, New York 10010 (800) 221-7945; *The Statesman's Year-Book.*

Statistical Office of the United Nations, Publishing Service, New York, New York 10017 (800) 253-9646; *Statistical Yearbook.*

SWITZERLAND - CONSUMER PRICE INDEX

Europa Publications Limited, 18 Bedford Square, London, WC1B 3JN, England; *The Europa World Year Book.*

Organisation for Economic Co-operation and Development (OECD), 2 rue Andre-Pascal, 75 Paris 16, France (Telephone Number in U.S. (202) 785-6323); *Economic Outlook.*

Statistical Office of the United Nations, Publishing Service, New York, New York 10017 (800) 253-9646; *Statistical Yearbook; and Trends in Europe and North America: The Statistical Yearbook of the Economic Commission for Europe.*

SWITZERLAND - CONSUMER PRICES

Euromonitor International, Inc., 122 South Michigan Avenue, Suite 1200, Chicago, Illinois 60603 (800) 577-EURO; *European Marketing Data and Statistics;* and *World Marketing Data and Statistics.*

International Labour Office, I.L.O. Publications, 1828 L Street, NW, Suite 801, Washington, D.C. 20036 (301) 638-3152; *Yearbook of Labour Statistics.*

International Monetary Fund, 700 Nineteenth Street, NW, Washington, D.C. 20431 (202) 623-7000; *International Financial Statistics.*

Organisation for Economic Co-operation and Development (OECD), 2 rue Andre-Pascal, 75 Paris 16, France (Telephone Number in U.S. (202) 785-6323); *Economic Outlook.*

SWITZERLAND - CONSUMPTION

Organisation for Economic Co-operation and Development (OECD), 2 rue Andre-Pascal, 75 Paris 16, France (Telephone Number in U.S. (202) 785-6323); *The Footwear, Raw Hides and Skins, and Leather Industry in OECD Countries; The Iron and Steel Industry; Meat Balances in OECD Member Countries; The Non-Ferrous Metals Industry; The Pulp and Paper Industry;* and *Textile Industry in OECD Countries.*

The World Bank, 1818 H Street, NW, Washington, D.C. 20433 (202) 477-1234; *World Development Report.*

SWITZERLAND - COPPER AND COPPER ORE PRODUCTION AND CONSUMPTION - See SWITZERLAND - MINING AND MINERAL PRODUCTS

SWITZERLAND - CORN PRODUCTION - See SWITZERLAND - CROPS

SWITZERLAND - CORPORATE INCOME TAXES - See SWITZERLAND - TAXATION

SWITZERLAND - CORPORATE TAXES - See SWITZERLAND - TAXATION

SWITZERLAND - COTTON - See SWITZERLAND - CROPS

SWITZERLAND - CRIME

Statistical Office of the United Nations, Publishing Service, New York, New York 10017 (800) 253-9646; *Trends in Europe and*

North America: The Statistical Yearbook of the Economic Commission for Europe.

Yale University Press, Yale Station, New Haven, Connecticut 06520 (800) 987-7323; *Violence and Crime in Cross-National Perspective.*

SWITZERLAND - CROPS

American Forest and Paper Association, 1111 Nineteenth Street, NW, Suite 800, Washington, D.C. 20036 (202) 463-2700; *Wood Pulp and Fiber Statistics.*

Euromonitor International, Inc., 122 South Michigan Avenue, Suite 1200, Chicago, Illinois 60603 (800) 577-EURO; *European Marketing Data and Statistics.*

Europa Publications Limited, 18 Bedford Square, London, WC1B 3JN, England; *The Europa World Year Book.*

Food and Agricultural Organization of the United Nations (FAO) Via delle Terme di Caracalla, 00100 Rome, Italy (Telephone Number in U.S. (202) 653-2400); *The State of Food and Agriculture.*

M.E. Sharpe, 80 Business Park Drive, Armonk, New York 10504 (800) 541-6563; *The Illustrated Book of World Rankings.*

Organisation for Economic Co-operation and Development (OECD), 2 rue Andre-Pascal, 75 Paris 16, France (Telephone Number in U.S. (202) 785-6323); *Economic Accounts for Agriculture; Foreign Trade by Commodities;* and *Textile Industry in OECD Countries.*

St. Martin's Press, Inc., 175 Fifth Avenue, New York, New York 10010 (800) 221-7945; *The Statesman's Year-Book.*

Statistical Office of the United Nations, Publishing Service, New York, New York 10017 (800) 253-9646; *Statistical Yearbook.*

United Nations Conference on Trade and Development, Central Statistical Service, Palais des Nations, Geneva, Switzerland (Telephone in U.S. (800) 253-9646); *UNCTAD Commodity Yearbook.*

SWITZERLAND - CUSTOMS DUTIES

International Monetary Fund, 700 Nineteenth Street, NW, Washington, D.C. 20431 (202) 623-7000; *Government Finance Statistics Yearbook.*

Organisation for Economic Co-operation and Development (OECD), 2 rue Andre-Pascal, 75 Paris 16, France (Telephone Number in U.S. (202) 785-6323); *The Non-Ferrous Metals Industry.*

SWITZERLAND - DAIRY PRODUCTS

Commodity Research Bureau, Inc., 30 South Wacker Drive, Chicago Illinois 60606 (312) 454-1801; *Commodity Year Book.*

Europa Publications Limited, 18 Bedford Square, London, WC1B 3JN, England; *The Europa World Year Book.*

Food and Agricultural Organization of the United Nations (FAO) Via delle Terme di Caracalla, 00100 Rome, Italy (Telephone Number in U.S. (202) 653-2400); *The State of Food and Agriculture.*

M.E. Sharpe, 80 Business Park Drive, Armonk, New York 10504 (800) 541-6563; *The Illustrated Book of World Rankings.*

Organisation for Economic Co-operation and Development (OECD), 2 rue Andre-Pascal, 75 Paris 16, France (Telephone Number in U.S. (202) 785-6323); *Economic Accounts for Agriculture;* and *Milk, Milk Products, and Egg Balances in OECD Member Countries.*

St. Martin's Press, Inc., 175 Fifth Avenue, New York, New York 10010 (800) 221-7945; *The Statesman's Year-Book.*

Statistical Office of the United Nations, Publishing Service, New York, New York 10017 (800) 253-9646; *Statistical Yearbook.*

SWITZERLAND - DEATH RATES - See SWITZERLAND - MORTALITY

SWITZERLAND - DEFENSE EXPENDITURES - See SWITZERLAND - MILITARY

SWITZERLAND - DEMOGRAPHY

The Economist Intelligence Unit, 111 West 57th Street, New York, New York 10019 (800) 938-4685; *The World Market Atlas.*

Euromonitor International, Inc., 122 South Michigan Avenue, Suite 1200, Chicago, Illinois 60603 (800) 577-EURO; *The World Economic Factbook;* and *World Marketing Data and Statistics.*

M.E. Sharpe, 80 Business Park Drive, Armonk, New York 10504 (800) 541-6563; *The Illustrated Book of World Rankings.*

Statistical Office of the United Nations, Publishing Service, New York, New York 10017 (800) 253-9646; *Human Development Report.*

SWITZERLAND - DEVELOPMENT ASSISTANCE

Organisation for Economic Co-operation and Development (OECD), 2 rue Andre-Pascal, 75 Paris 16, France (Telephone Number in U.S. (202) 785-6323); *Geographical Distribution of Financial Flows to Developing Countries.*

Statistical Office of the United Nations, Publishing Service, New York, New York 10017 (800) 253-9646; *Statistical Yearbook.*

SWITZERLAND - DIAMOND PRODUCTION - See SWITZERLAND - MINING AND MINERAL PRODUCTS

SWITZERLAND - DISCOUNT RATES - See SWITZERLAND - BANKING

SWITZERLAND - DISEASES - See SWITZERLAND - HEALTH

SWITZERLAND - DIVORCE RATES

M.E. Sharpe, 80 Business Park Drive, Armonk, New York 10504 (800) 541-6563; *The Illustrated Book of World Rankings.*

Statistical Office of the United Nations, Publishing Service, New York, New York 10017 (800) 253-9646; *Demographic Yearbook; Trends in Europe and North America: The Statistical Yearbook of the Economic Commission for Europe;* and *Statistical Yearbook.*

SWITZERLAND - ECONOMY

Central Intelligence Agency, Washington, D.C. 20505 (703) 482-1100, www.cia.gov; *The World Factbook.*

Economist Intelligence Unit, 111 West 57th Street, New York, New York 10019 (800) 938-4685; *Switzerland Country Report.*

Euromonitor International, Inc., 122 South Michigan Avenue, Suite 1200, Chicago, Illinois 60603 (800) 577-EURO; *European Marketing Data and Statistics; World Marketing Data and Statistics;* and *The World Economic Factbook.*

Europa Publications Limited, 18 Bedford Square, London, WC1B 3JN, England; *The Europa World Year Book.*

M.E. Sharpe, 80 Business Park Drive, Armonk, New York 10504 (800) 541-6563; *The Illustrated Book of World Rankings.*

Organisation for Economic Co-operation and Development (OECD), 2 rue Andre-Pascal, 75 Paris 16, France (Telephone Number in U.S. (202) 785-6323); *Economic Outlook; Geographical Distribution of Financial Flows to Developing Countries; Main Economic Indicators - Historical Statistics; OECD Economic Surveys: Switzerland;* and *OECD Employment Outlook.*

St. Martin's Press, Inc., 175 Fifth Avenue, New York, New York 10010 (800)

221-7945; *The Statesman's Year-Book.*

Statistical Office of the United Nations, Publishing Service, New York, New York 10017 (800) 253-9646; *World Statistics Pocketbook.*

The World Bank, 1818 H Street, NW, Washington, D.C. 20433 (202) 477-1234; *The World Bank Atlas;* and *World Development Report.*

SWITZERLAND - EDUCATION

The Economist Intelligence Unit, 111 West 57th Street, New York, New York 10019 (800) 938-4685; *The World Market Atlas.*

Euromonitor International, Inc., 122 South Michigan Avenue, Suite 1200, Chicago, Illinois 60603 (800) 577-EURO; *European Marketing Data and Statistics;* and *World Marketing Data and Statistics.*

Europa Publications Limited, 18 Bedford Square, London, WC1B 3JN, England; *The Europa World Year Book.*

International Monetary Fund, 700 Nineteenth Street, NW, Washington, D.C. 20431 (202) 623-7000; *Government Finance Statistics Yearbook.*

M.E. Sharpe, 80 Business Park Drive, Armonk, New York 10504 (800) 541-6563; *The Illustrated Book of World Rankings.*

Organisation for Economic Co-operation and Development (OECD), 2 rue Andre-Pascal, 75 Paris 16, France (Telephone Number in U.S. (202) 785-6323); *Education in OECD Countries.*

St. Martin's Press, Inc., 175 Fifth Avenue, New York, New York 10010 (800) 221-7945; *The Statesman's Year-Book.*

Statistical Office of the United Nations, Publishing Service, New York, New York 10017 (800) 253-9646; *Human Development Report;* and *Trends in Europe and North America: The Statistical Yearbook of the Economic Commission for Europe.*

United Nations Educational, Scientific and Cultural Organization (UNESCO), 7 Place de Fontenoy, F-75700 Paris, France (Telephone Number in U.S. (212) 963-5981); *Statistical Yearbook.*

The World Bank, 1818 H Street, NW, Washington, D.C. 20433 (202) 477-1234; *World Development Report;* and *World Development Indicators.*

SWITZERLAND - EGG PRODUCTION AND CONSUMPTION - See SWITZERLAND - DAIRY PRODUCTS

SWITZERLAND - ELECTRICITY

Central Intelligence Agency, Washington, D.C. 20505 (703) 482-1100, www.cia.gov; *The World Factbook.*

Commodity Research Bureau, Inc., 30 South Wacker Drive, Chicago Illinois 60606 (312) 454-1801; *Commodity Year Book.*

M.E. Sharpe, 80 Business Park Drive, Armonk, New York 10504 (800) 541-6563; *The Illustrated Book of World Rankings.*

Organisation for Economic Co-operation and Development (OECD), 2 rue Andre-Pascal, 75 Paris 16, France (Telephone Number in U.S. (202) 785-6323); *Coal Information; Energy Statistics of OECD Countries; Indicators of Industrial Activity;* and *Industrial Structure Statistics.*

St. Martin's Press, Inc., 175 Fifth Avenue, New York, New York 10010 (800) 221-7945; *The Statesman's Year-Book.*

Statistical Office of the United Nations, Publishing Service, New York, New York 10017 (800) 253-9646; *Human Development Report; Trends in Europe and North America: The Statistical Yearbook of the Economic Commission for Europe;* and *Statistical Yearbook.*

SWITZERLAND - EMPLOYMENT

Euromonitor International, Inc., 122 South Michigan Avenue, Suite 1200, Chicago, Illinois 60603 (800) 577-EURO; *European Marketing Data and Statistics.*

International Labour Office, I.L.O. Publications, 1828 L Street, NW, Suite 801, Washington, D.C. 20036 (301) 638-3152; *Yearbook of Labour Statistics.*

M.E. Sharpe, 80 Business Park Drive, Armonk, New York 10504 (800) 541-6563; *The Illustrated Book of World Rankings.*

Organisation for Economic Co-operation and Development (OECD), 2 rue Andre-Pascal, 75 Paris 16, France (Telephone Number in U.S. (202) 785-6323); *Economic Outlook; The Iron and Steel Industry; OECD Economic Surveys: Switzerland; OECD Employment Outlook;* and *Textile Industry in OECD Countries.*

Statistical Office of the United Nations, Publishing Service, New York, New York 10017 (800) 253-9646; *Statistical Yearbook;* and *Trends in Europe and North America: The Statistical Yearbook of the Economic Commission for Europe.*

SWITZERLAND - ENERGY

Euromonitor International, Inc., 122 South Michigan Avenue, Suite 1200, Chicago, Illinois 60603 (800) 577-EURO;

European Marketing Data and Statistics; World Marketing Data and Statistics; and *The World Economic Factbook.*

Food and Agricultural Organization of the United Nations (FAO) Via delle Terme di Caracalla, 00100 Rome, Italy (Telephone Number in U.S. (202) 653-2400); *The State of Food and Agriculture.*

M.E. Sharpe, 80 Business Park Drive, Armonk, New York 10504 (800) 541-6563; *The Illustrated Book of World Rankings.*

Organisation for Economic Co-operation and Development (OECD), 2 rue Andre-Pascal, 75 Paris 16, France (Telephone Number in U.S. (202) 785-6323); *Coal Information; Energy Statistics of OECD Countries; OECD Environmental Data;* and *Oil and Gas Information.*

St. Martin's Press, Inc., 175 Fifth Avenue, New York, New York 10010 (800) 221-7945; *The Statesman's Year-Book.*

Statistical Office of the United Nations, Publishing Service, New York, New York 10017 (800) 253-9646; *Energy Statistics Yearbook; Human Development Report; Trends in Europe and North America: The Statistical Yearbook of the Economic Commission for Europe; Statistical Yearbook;* and *World Statistics Pocketbook.*

The World Bank, 1818 H Street, NW, Washington, D.C. 20433 (202) 477-1234; *The World Bank Atlas;* and *World Development Report.*

SWITZERLAND - ENVIRONMENT

Economist Intelligence Unit, 111 West 57th Street, New York, New York 10019 (800) 938-4685; *Switzerland Country Report.*

Organization for Economic Co-operation and Development (OECD), 2 rue Andre-Pascal, 75 Paris 16, France (Telephone Number in U.S. (202) 785-6323); *OECD Environmental Data.*

Statistical Office of the United Nations, Publishing Service, New York, New York 10017 (800) 253-9646; *Trends in Europe and North America: The Statistical Yearbook of the Economic Commission for Europe;* and *World Statistics Pocketbook.*

SWITZERLAND - EXCHANGE RATES

Central Intelligence Agency, Washington, D.C. 20505 (703) 482-1100, www.cia.gov; *The World Factbook.*

Euromonitor International, Inc., 122 South Michigan Avenue, Suite 1200, Chicago, Illinois 60603 (800) 577-EURO; *The World Economic Factbook.*

Europa Publications Limited, 18 Bedford Square, London, WC1B 3JN, England; *The Europa World Year Book.*

International Civil Aviation Organization, 999 University Street, Montreal, Quebec, Canada H3C 5H7 (514) 954-8219; *Civil Aviation Statistics of the World.*

International Monetary Fund, 700 Nineteenth Street, NW, Washington, D.C. 20431 (202) 623-7000; *International Financial Statistics.*

Organisation for Economic Co-operation and Development (OECD), 2 rue Andre-Pascal, 75 Paris 16, France (Telephone Number in U.S. (202) 785-6323); *Economic Outlook; Financial Market Trends; OECD Economic Surveys: Switzerland; Revenue Statistics of OECD Member Countries;* and *Tourism Policy and International Tourism in OECD Member Countries.*

Statistical Office of the United Nations, Publishing Service, New York, New York 10017 (800) 253-9646; *Statistical Yearbook; Trends in Europe and North America: The Statistical Yearbook of the Economic Commission for Europe;* and *World Statistics Pocketbook.*

SWITZERLAND - EXCISE TAXES - See SWITZERLAND - TAXATION

SWITZERLAND - EXPORTS

Central Intelligence Agency, Washington, D.C. 20505 (703) 482-1100, www.cia.gov; *The World Factbook.*

The Economist Intelligence Unit, 111 West 57th Street, New York, New York 10019 (800) 938-4685; *Switzerland Country Report;* and *The World Market Atlas.*

Euromonitor International, Inc., 122 South Michigan Avenue, Suite 1200, Chicago, Illinois 60603 (800) 577-EURO; *The World Economic Factbook.*

Europa Publications Limited, 18 Bedford Square, London, WC1B 3JN, England; *The Europa World Year Book.*

Food and Agricultural Organization of the United Nations (FAO) Via delle Terme di Caracalla, 00100 Rome, Italy (Telephone Number in U.S. (202) 653-2400); *The State of Food and Agriculture.*

International Monetary Fund, 700 Nineteenth Street, NW, Washington, D.C. 20431 (202) 623-7000; *Direction of Trade Statistics;* and *International Financial Statistics.*

Organisation for Economic Co-operation and Development (OECD), 2 rue

Andre-Pascal, 75 Paris 16, France (Telephone Number in U.S. (202) 785-6323); *Economic Outlook; The Footwear, Raw Hides and Skins, and Leather Industry in OECD Countries; Foreign Trade by Commodities; Geographical Distribution of Financial Flows to Developing Countries; Industrial Structure Statistics; The Iron and Steel Industry; Milk, Milk Products, and Egg Balances in OECD Member Countries; OECD Economic Surveys: Switzerland;* and *The Pulp and Paper Industry.*

St. Martin's Press, Inc., 175 Fifth Avenue, New York, New York 10010 (800) 221-7945; *The Statesman's Year-Book.*

Statistical Office of the United Nations, Publishing Service, New York, New York 10017 (800) 253-9646; *Trends in Europe and North America: The Statistical Yearbook of the Economic Commission for Europe.*

United Nations Conference on Trade and Development (UNCTAD), New York, New York 10017 (800) 253-9646; *Handbook of International Trade and Development Statistics.*

The World Bank, 1818 H Street, NW, Washington, D.C. 20433 (202) 477-1234; *World Development Report;* and *World Development Indicators.*

SWITZERLAND - EXTERNAL FINANCING

Organisation for Economic Co-operation and Development (OECD), 2 rue Andre-Pascal, 75 Paris 16, France (Telephone Number in U.S. (202) 785-6323); *Economic Outlook;* and *Financial Market Trends.*

SWITZERLAND - EXTERNAL INDEBTEDNESS

Organisation for Economic Co-operation and Development (OECD), 2 rue Andre-Pascal, 75 Paris 16, France (Telephone Number in U.S. (202) 785-6323); *Financial Market Trends;* and *Geographical Distribution of Financial Flows to Developing Countries.*

The World Bank, 1818 H Street, NW, Washington, D.C. 20433 (202) 477-1234; *World Development Report;* and *World Development Indicators.*

SWITZERLAND - EXTERNAL TRADE

Euromonitor International, Inc., 122 South Michigan Avenue, Suite 1200, Chicago, Illinois 60603 9800) 577-EURO; *World Marketing Data and Statistics.*

Food and Agricultural Organization of the United Nations (FAO) Via delle Terme di Caracalla, 00100 Rome, Italy (Telephone Number in U.S. (202) 653-2400); *The State of Food and Agriculture;* and *Trade*

Yearbook.

Statistical Office of the United Nations, Publishing Service, New York, New York 10017 (800) 253-9646; *Statistical Yearbook.*

SWITZERLAND - FABRIC PRODUCTION - See SWITZERLAND - TEXTILE INDUSTRY

SWITZERLAND - FARM CROPS - See SWITZERLAND - CROPS

SWITZERLAND - FERTILITY RATES

Central Intelligence Agency, Washington, D.C. 20505 (703) 482-1100, www.cia.gov; *The World Factbook.*

M.E. Sharpe, 80 Business Park Drive, Armonk, New York 10504 (800) 541-6563; *The Illustrated Book of World Rankings.*

Statistical Office of the United Nations, Publishing Service, New York, New York 10017 (800) 253-9646; *Human Development Report;* and *Trends in Europe and North America: The Statistical Yearbook of the Economic Commission for Europe.*

The World Bank, 1818 H Street, NW, Washington, D.C. 20433 (202) 477-1234; *The World Bank Atlas; World Development Report;* and *World Development Indicators.*

SWITZERLAND - FERTILIZER

Food and Agricultural Organization of the United Nations (FAO) Via delle Terme di Caracalla, 00100 Rome, Italy (Telephone Number in U.S. (202) 653-2400); *The State of Food and Agriculture.*

Organisation for Economic Co-operation and Development (OECD), 2 rue Andre-Pascal, 75 Paris 16, France (Telephone Number in U.S. (202) 785-6323); *Economic Accounts for Agriculture;* and *Foreign Trade by Commodities.*

Statistical Office of the United Nations, Publishing Service, New York, New York 10017 (800) 253-9646; *Statistical Yearbook.*

SWITZERLAND - FETAL MORTALITY - See SWITZERLAND - MORTALITY

SWITZERLAND - FIBRE PRODUCTION - See SWITZERLAND - TEXTILE INDUSTRY

SWITZERLAND - FILAMENT PRODUCTION - See SWITZERLAND - TEXTILE INDUSTRY

SWITZERLAND - FILM - See SWITZERLAND - MOTION PICTURES

SWITZERLAND - FINANCE

Economist Intelligence Unit, 111 West 57th Street, New York, New York 10019 (800) 938-4685; *Switzerland Country*

Report.

Europa Publications Limited, 18 Bedford Square, London, WC1B 3JN, England; *The Europa World Year Book.*

M.E. Sharpe, 80 Business Park Drive, Armonk, New York 10504 (800) 541-6563; *The Illustrated Book of World Rankings.*

Organisation for Economic Co-operation and Development (OECD), 2 rue Andre-Pascal, 75 Paris 16, France (Telephone Number in U.S. (202) 785-6323); *Economic Outlook; Financial Market Trends; Geographical Distribution of Financial Flows to Developing Countries; Main Economic Indicators - Historical Statistics; OECD Financial Statistics;* and *Revenue Statistics of OECD Member Countries.*

St. Martin's Press, Inc., 175 Fifth Avenue, New York, New York 10010 (800) 221-7945; *The Statesman's Year-Book.*

SWITZERLAND - FISHERIES

Euromonitor International, Inc., 122 South Michigan Avenue, Suite 1200, Chicago, Illinois 60603 (800) 577-EURO; *European Marketing Data and Statistics.*

Europa Publications Limited, 18 Bedford Square, London, WC1B 3JN, England; *The Europa World Year Book.*

Food and Agricultural Organization of the United Nations (FAO) Via delle Terme di Caracalla, 00100 Rome, Italy (Telephone Number in U.S. (202) 653-2400); *The State of Food and Agriculture;* and *Yearbook of Fishery Statistics.*

M.E. Sharpe, 80 Business Park Drive, Armonk, New York 10504 (800) 541-6563; *The Illustrated Book of World Rankings.*

Organisation for Economic Co-operation and Development (OECD), 2 rue Andre-Pascal, 75 Paris 16, France (Telephone Number in U.S. (202) 785-6323); *Foreign Trade by Commodities;* and *Industrial Structure Statistics.*

Statistical Office of the United Nations, Publishing Service, New York, New York 10017 (800) 253-9646; *Statistical Yearbook.*

United Nations Conference on Trade and Development, Central Statistical Service, Palais des Nations, Geneva, Switzerland (Telephone in U.S. (800) 253-9646); *UNCTAD Commodity Yearbook.*

SWITZERLAND - FLOUR PRODUCTION

Statistical Office of the United Nations, Publishing Service, New York, New York 10017 (800) 253-9646; *Statistical Yearbook.*

SWITZERLAND - FOOD

Euromonitor International, Inc., 122 South Michigan Avenue, Suite 1200, Chicago, Illinois 60603 (800) 577-EURO; *Retail Trade International.*

Food and Agricultural Organization of the United Nations (FAO) Via delle Terme di Caracalla, 00100 Rome, Italy (Telephone Number in U.S. (202) 653-2400); *The State of Food and Agriculture.*

Organisation for Economic Co-operation and Development (OECD), 2 rue Andre-Pascal, 75 Paris 16, France (Telephone Number in U.S. (202) 785-6323); *Food Consumption Statistics;* and *Foreign Trade by Commodities.*

Statistical Office of the United Nations, Publishing Service, New York, New York 10017 (800) 253-9646; *Human Development Report.*

United Nations Conference on Trade and Development, Central Statistical Service, Palais des Nations, Geneva, Switzerland (Telephone in U.S. (800) 253-9646); *UNCTAD Commodity Yearbook.*

SWITZERLAND - FOOTWEAR - PRODUCTION INDEX

Organisation for Economic Co-operation and Development (OECD), 2 rue Andre-Pascal, 75 Paris 16, France (Telephone Number in U.S. (202) 785-6323); *Indicators of Industrial Activity.*

SWITZERLAND - FOREIGN DEBT

Organisation for Economic Co-operation and Development (OECD), 2 rue Andre-Pascal, 75 Paris 16, France (Telephone Number in U.S. (202) 785-6323); *Economic Outlook.*

SWITZERLAND - FOREIGN INDEBTEDNESS

Organisation for Economic Co-operation and Development (OECD), 2 rue Andre-Pascal, 75 Paris 16, France (Telephone Number in U.S. (202) 785-6323); *Economic Outlook;* and *Financial Market Trends.*

SWITZERLAND - FOREIGN TRADE

Economist Intelligence Unit, 111 West 57th Street, New York, New York 10019 (800) 938-4685; *Switzerland Country Report.*

Euromonitor International, Inc., 122 South Michigan Avenue, Suite 1200, Chicago, Illinois 60603 (800) 577-EURO; *European Marketing Data and Statistics;* and *The World Economic Factbook.*

Europa Publications Limited, 18 Bedford Square, London, WC1B 3JN, England; *The Europa World Year Book.*

Food and Agricultural Organization of the United Nations (FAO) Via delle Terme di Caracalla, 00100 Rome, Italy (Telephone Number in U.S. (202) 653-2400); *The State of Food and Agriculture.*

International Monetary Fund, 700 Nineteenth Street, NW, Washington, D.C. 20431 (202) 623-7000; *International Financial Statistics.*

M.E. Sharpe, 80 Business Park Drive, Armonk, New York 10504 (800) 541-6563; *The Illustrated Book of World Rankings.*

Organisation for Economic Co-operation and Development (OECD), 2 rue Andre-Pascal, 75 Paris 16, France (Telephone Number in U.S. (202) 785-6323); *Economic Outlook; The Footwear, Raw Hides and Skins, and Leather Industry in OECD Countries; Foreign Trade by Commodities; Main Economic Indicators - Historical Statistics; Maritime Transport; Meat Balances in OECD Member Countries;* and *OECD Economic Surveys: Switzerland.*

St. Martin's Press, Inc., 175 Fifth Avenue, New York, New York 10010 (800) 221-7945; *The Statesman's Year-Book.*

Statistical Office of the United Nations, Publishing Service, New York, New York 10017 (800) 253-9646; *International Trade Statistics Yearbook;* and *Statistical Yearbook.*

United Nations Conference on Trade and Development, Central Statistical Service, Palais des Nations, Geneva, Switzerland (Telephone in U.S. (800) 253-9646); *UNCTAD Commodity Yearbook.*

The World Bank, 1818 H Street, NW, Washington, D.C. 20433 (202) 477-1234; *World Development Report; World Metal Statistics;* and *World Development Indicators.*

SWITZERLAND - FORESTRY AND FOREST PRODUCTS

Euromonitor International, Inc., 122 South Michigan Avenue, Suite 1200, Chicago, Illinois 60603 (800) 577-EURO; *European Marketing Data and Statistics.*

Europa Publications Limited, 18 Bedford Square, London, WC1B 3JN, England; *The Europa World Year Book.*

Food and Agricultural Organization of the United Nations (FAO) Via delle Terme di Caracalla, 00100 Rome, Italy (Telephone Number in U.S. (202) 653-2400); *The State of Food and Agriculture;* and *Yearbook of Forest Products.*

M.E. Sharpe, 80 Business Park Drive, Armonk, New York 10504 (800) 541-6563; *The Illustrated Book of World Rankings.*

Organisation for Economic Co-operation and Development (OECD), 2 rue Andre-Pascal, 75 Paris 16, France (Telephone Number in U.S. (202) 785-6323); *Indicators of Industrial Activity; Industrial Structure Statistics;* and *The Pulp and Paper Industry.*

Statistical Office of the United Nations, Publishing Service, New York, New York 10017 (800) 253-9646; *Statistical Yearbook;* and *Trends in Europe and North America: The Statistical Yearbook of the Economic Commission for Europe.*

United Nations Conference on Trade and Development, Central Statistical Service, Palais des Nations, Geneva, Switzerland (Telephone in U.S. (800) 253-9646); *UNCTAD Commodity Yearbook.*

United Nations Educational, Scientific and Cultural Organization (UNESCO), 7 Place de Fontenoy, F-75700 Paris, France (Telephone Number in U.S. (212) 963-5981); *Statistical Yearbook.*

The World Bank, 1818 H Street, NW, Washington, D.C. 20433 (202) 477-1234; *World Development Report.*

SWITZERLAND - FRUIT PRODUCTION - See SWITZERLAND - CROPS

SWITZERLAND - FURNITURE AND WOOD PRODUCTS - EXPORTS AND IMPORTS

Organisation for Economic Co-operation and Development (OECD), 2 rue Andre-Pascal, 75 Paris 16, France (Telephone Number in U.S. (202) 785-6323); *Foreign Trade by Commodities;* and *Industrial Structure Statistics.*

SWITZERLAND - GAS AND GAS LIQUIDS PRODUCTION - See SWITZERLAND - MINING AND MINERAL PRODUCTS

SWITZERLAND - GENERAL INDUSTRIAL STATISTICS - See SWITZERLAND - INDUSTRY

SWITZERLAND - GENERAL MORTALITY - See SWITZERLAND - MORTALITY

SWITZERLAND - GEOGRAPHIC DATA

M.E. Sharpe, 80 Business Park Drive, Armonk, New York 10504 (800) 541-6563; *The Illustrated Book of World Rankings.*

SWITZERLAND - GLASS AND GLASS PRODUCTS - PRODUCTION INDEX - See SWITZERLAND - MINING AND MINERAL PRODUCTS

SWITZERLAND - GOATS - See SWITZERLAND - LIVESTOCK AND POULTRY

SWITZERLAND - GOLD HOLDINGS

International Monetary Fund, 700 Nineteenth Street, NW, Washington, D.C. 20431 (202) 623-7000; *International Financial Statistics.*

Statistical Office of the United Nations, Publishing Service, New York, New York 10017 (800) 253-9646; *Statistical Yearbook.*

The World Bank, 1818 H Street, NW, Washington, D.C. 20433 (202) 477-1234; *World Development Indicators.*

SWITZERLAND - GOLD PRODUCTION AND CONSUMPTION - See SWITZERLAND - MINING AND MINERAL PRODUCTS

SWITZERLAND - GOVERNMENT

Central Intelligence Agency, Washington, D.C. 20505 (703) 482-1100, www.cia.gov; *The World Factbook.*

Europa Publications Limited, 18 Bedford Square, London, WC1B 3JN, England; *The Europa World Year Book.*

International Monetary Fund, 700 Nineteenth Street, NW, Washington, D.C. 20431 (202) 623-7000; *Government Finance Statistics Yearbook;* and *International Financial Statistics.*

Organisation for Economic Co-operation and Development (OECD), 2 rue Andre-Pascal, 75 Paris 16, France (Telephone Number in U.S. (202) 785-6323); *Economic Outlook;* and *Revenue Statistics of OECD Member Countries.*

St. Martin's Press, Inc., 175 Fifth Avenue, New York, New York 10010 (800) 221-7945; *The Statesman's Year-Book.*

Statistical Office of the United Nations, Publishing Service, New York, New York 10017 (800) 253-9646; *National Accounts Statistics;* and *Statistical Yearbook.*

The World Bank, 1818 H Street, NW, Washington, D.C. 20433 (202) 477-1234; *World Development Report;* and *World Development Indicators.*

SWITZERLAND - GRAIN PRODUCTION - See SWITZERLAND - CROPS

SWITZERLAND - GRANTS

International Monetary Fund, 700 Nineteenth Street, NW, Washington, D.C. 20431 (202) 623-7000; *Government Finance Statistics Yearbook.*

Organisation for Economic Co-operation and Development (OECD), 2 rue Andre-Pascal, 75 Paris 16, France (Telephone Number in U.S. (202) 785-6323); *Geographical Distribution of Financial Flows to Developing Countries.*

SWITZERLAND - GROSS DOMESTIC PRODUCT

The Economist Intelligence Unit, 111 West 57th Street, New York, New York 10019 (800) 938-4685; *Switzerland Country Report;* and *The World Market Atlas.*

Euromonitor International, Inc., 122 South Michigan Avenue, Suite 1200, Chicago, Illinois 60603 (800) 577-EURO; *The World Economic Factbook.*

Europa Publications Limited, 18 Bedford Square, London, WC1B 3JN, England; *The Europa World Year Book.*

M.E. Sharpe, 80 Business Park Drive, Armonk, New York 10504 (800) 541-6563; *The Illustrated Book of World Rankings.*

Organisation for Economic Co-operation and Development (OECD), 2 rue Andre-Pascal, 75 Paris 16, France (Telephone Number in U.S. (202) 785-6323); *Economic Outlook; Geographical Distribution of Financial Flows to Developing Countries;* and *Revenue Statistics of OECD Member Countries.*

Statistical Office of the United Nations, Publishing Service, New York, New York 10017 (800) 253-9646; *Human Development Report; National Accounts Statistics; Trends in Europe and North America: The Statistical Yearbook of the Economic Commission for Europe;* and *Statistical Yearbook.*

The World Bank, 1818 H Street, NW, Washington, D.C. 20433 (202) 477-1234; *World Development Report;* and *World Development Indicators.*

SWITZERLAND - GROSS NATIONAL PRODUCT

Organisation for Economic Co-operation and Development (OECD), 2 rue Andre-Pascal, 75 Paris 16, France (Telephone Number in U.S. (202) 785-6323); *Economic Outlook;* and *Geographical Distribution of Financial Flows to Developing Countries.*

St. Martin's Press, Inc., 175 Fifth Avenue, New York, New York 10010 (800) 221-7945; *The Statesman's Year-Book.*

Statistical Office of the United Nations, Publishing Service, New York, New York 10017 (800) 253-9646; *National Accounts Statistics.*

U.S. Arms Control and Disarmament Agency, 320 Twenty-first Street, NW, Washington, D.C. 20451 (202) 647-8677; *World Military Expenditures and Arms Transfers.*

The World Bank, 1818 H Street, NW, Washington, D.C. 20433 (202) 477-1234; *The World Bank Atlas; World Development Report;* and *World Development Indicators.*

SWITZERLAND - HEALTH

Euromonitor International, Inc., 122 South Michigan Avenue, Suite 1200, Chicago, Illinois 60603 9800) 577-EURO; *World Marketing Data and Statistics.*

M.E. Sharpe, 80 Business Park Drive, Armonk, New York 10504 (800) 541-6563; *The Illustrated Book of World Rankings.*

Organisation for Economic Co-operation and Development (OECD), 2 rue Andre-Pascal, 75 Paris 16, France (Telephone Number in U.S. (202) 785-6323); *OECD Health Systems: Facts and Trends.*

St. Martin's Press, Inc., 175 Fifth Avenue, New York, New York 10010 (800) 221-7945; *The Statesman's Year-Book.*

Statistical Office of the United Nations, Publishing Service, New York, New York 10017 (800) 253-9646; *Human Development Report; Trends in Europe and North America: The Statistical Yearbook of the Economic Commission for Europe;* and *Statistical Yearbook.*

United Nations Children's Fund (UNICEF), 3 United Nations Plaza, New York, New York 10017 (800) 253-9646; *State of the World's Children.*

The World Bank, 1818 H Street, NW, Washington, D.C. 20433 (202) 477-1234; *World Development Report.*

World Health Organization, Office of Publications, 20 Avenue Appia, CH-1211 Geneva 27, Switzerland (Telephone Number in U.S. (518) 436-9686); *World Health Statistics Annual.*

SWITZERLAND - HEALTH EXPENDITURES

International Monetary Fund, 700 Nineteenth Street, NW, Washington, D.C. 20431 (202) 623-7000; *Government Finance Statistics Yearbook.*

SWITZERLAND - HIDE PRODUCTION

Organisation for Economic Co-operation and Development (OECD), 2 rue Andre-Pascal, 75 Paris 16, France (Telephone Number in U.S. (202) 785-6323); *The Footwear, Raw Hides and Skins, and Leather Industry in OECD Countries; Foreign Trade by Commodities;* and *Indicators of Industrial Activity.*

SWITZERLAND - HIGHWAYS

Central Intelligence Agency, Washington, D.C. 20505 (703) 482-1100, www.cia.gov; *The World Factbook.*

International Road Federation, 2600 Virginia Avenue, NW, Washington, D.C. 20037 (202) 338-4641; *World Road Statistics.*

St. Martin's Press, Inc., 175 Fifth Avenue, New York, New York 10010 (800) 221-7945; *The Statesman's Year-Book.*

Statistical Office of the United Nations, Publishing Service, New York, New York 10017 (800) 253-9646; *Annual Bulletin of Transport Statistics for Europe;* and *Trends in Europe and North America: The Statistical Yearbook of the Economic Commission for Europe.*

SWITZERLAND - HOME FINANCE

Organisation for Economic Co-operation and Development (OECD), 2 rue Andre-Pascal, 75 Paris 16, France (Telephone Number in U.S. (202) 785-6323); *Main Economic Indicators - Historical Statistics.*

SWITZERLAND - HORSES - See SWITZERLAND - LIVESTOCK AND POULTRY

SWITZERLAND - HOURS OF WORK - See SWITZERLAND - EMPLOYMENT

SWITZERLAND - HOUSING AND HOUSING UNITS

Euromonitor International, Inc., 122 South Michigan Avenue, Suite 1200, Chicago, Illinois 60603 9800) 577-EURO; *World Marketing Data and Statistics.*

M.E. Sharpe, 80 Business Park Drive, Armonk, New York 10504 (800) 541-6563; *The Illustrated Book of World Rankings.*

Statistical Office of the United Nations, Publishing Service, New York, New York 10017 (800) 253-9646; *Trends in Europe and North America: The Statistical Yearbook of the Economic Commission for Europe.*

SWITZERLAND - HOUSING EXPENDITURES

International Monetary Fund, 700 Nineteenth Street, NW, Washington, D.C. 20431 (202) 623-7000; *Government Finance Statistics Yearbook.*

SWITZERLAND - ILLITERATE

POPULATION

Central Intelligence Agency, Washington, D.C. 20505 (703) 482-1100, www.cia.gov; *The World Factbook.*

The Economist Intelligence Unit, 111 West 57th Street, New York, New York 10019 (800) 938-4685; *The World Market Atlas.*

Euromonitor International, Inc., 122 South Michigan Avenue, Suite 1200, Chicago, Illinois 60603 (800) 577-EURO; *The World Economic Factbook.*

Statistical Office of the United Nations, Publishing Service, New York, New York 10017 (800) 253-9646; *Human Development Report.*

SWITZERLAND - IMPORTS

Central Intelligence Agency, Washington, D.C. 20505 (703) 482-1100, www.cia.gov; *The World Factbook.*

The Economist Intelligence Unit, 111 West 57th Street, New York, New York 10019 (800) 938-4685; *Switzerland Country Report;* and *The World Market Atlas.*

Euromonitor International, Inc., 122 South Michigan Avenue, Suite 1200, Chicago, Illinois 60603 (800) 577-EURO; *The World Economic Factbook.*

Europa Publications Limited, 18 Bedford Square, London, WC1B 3JN, England; *The Europa World Year Book.*

Food and Agricultural Organization of the United Nations (FAO) Via delle Terme di Caracalla, 00100 Rome, Italy (Telephone Number in U.S. (202) 653-2400); *The State of Food and Agriculture.*

International Monetary Fund, 700 Nineteenth Street, NW, Washington, D.C. 20431 (202) 623-7000; *Direction of Trade Statistics; International Financial Statistics;* and *Government Finance Statistics Yearbook,*

Organisation for Economic Co-operation and Development (OECD), 2 rue Andre-Pascal, 75 Paris 16, France (Telephone Number in U.S. (202) 785-6323); *Economic Outlook; The Footwear, Raw Hides and Skins, and Leather Industry in OECD Countries; Industrial Structure Statistics; The Iron and Steel Industry; Milk, Milk Products, and Egg Balances in OECD Member Countries; OECD Economic Surveys: Switzerland;* and *The Pulp and Paper Industry.*

St. Martin's Press, Inc., 175 Fifth Avenue, New York, New York 10010 (800) 221-7945; *The Statesman's Year-Book.*

Statistical Office of the United Nations, Publishing Service, New York, New York 10017 (800) 253-9646; *Trends in Europe and North America: The Statistical Yearbook of the Economic Commission for Europe.*

United Nations Conference on Trade and Development (UNCTAD), New York, New York 10017 (800) 253-9646; *Handbook of International Trade and Development Statistics.*

The World Bank, 1818 H Street, NW, Washington, D.C. 20433 (202) 477-1234; *World Development Report;* and *World Development Indicators.*

SWITZERLAND - INCOME TAXES - See SWITZERLAND - TAXATION

SWITZERLAND - INDUSTRIAL METALS PRODUCTION - See SWITZERLAND - MINING AND MINERAL PRODUCTS

SWITZERLAND - INDUSTRY

Central Intelligence Agency, Washington, D.C. 20505 (703) 482-1100, www.cia.gov; *The World Factbook.*

Economist Intelligence Unit, 111 West 57th Street, New York, New York 10019 (800) 938-4685; *Switzerland Country Report.*

Euromonitor International, Inc., 122 South Michigan Avenue, Suite 1200, Chicago, Illinois 60603 (800) 577-EURO; *The World Economic Factbook;* and *World Marketing Data and Statistics.*

Europa Publications Limited, 18 Bedford Square, London, WC1B 3JN, England; *The Europa World Year Book.*

International Labour Office, I.L.O. Publications, 1828 L Street, NW, Suite 801, Washington, D.C. 20036 (301) 638-3152; *Yearbook of Labour Statistics.*

M.E. Sharpe, 80 Business Park Drive, Armonk, New York 10504 (800) 541-6563; *The Illustrated Book of World Rankings.*

Organisation for Economic Co-operation and Development (OECD), 2 rue Andre-Pascal, 75 Paris 16, France (Telephone Number in U.S. (202) 785-6323); *Economic Outlook; Industrial Structure Statistics; Indicators of Industrial Activity; Main Economic Indicators - Historical Statistics;* and *OECD Environmental Data.*

St. Martin's Press, Inc., 175 Fifth Avenue, New York, New York 10010 (800) 221-7945; *The Statesman's Year-Book.*

Statistical Office of the United Nations, Publishing Service, New York, New York 10017 (800) 253-9646; *Industrial*

Commodity Statistics Yearbook; Trends in Europe and North America: The Statistical Yearbook of the Economic Commission for Europe; and *Statistical Yearbook.*

The World Bank, 1818 H Street, NW, Washington, D.C. 20433 (202) 477-1234; *World Development Indicators.*

World Intellectual Property Organization, 34 Chemin des Colombettes, CH-1211 Geneva 20, Switzerland; *Industrial Property Statistics.*

SWITZERLAND - INFANT AND MATERNAL MORTALITY - See SWITZERLAND - MORTALITY

SWITZERLAND - INTEREST RATES

Organisation for Economic Co-operation and Development (OECD), 2 rue Andre-Pascal, 75 Paris 16, France (Telephone Number in U.S. (202) 785-6323); *Economic Outlook; Financial Market Trends; Main Economic Indicators - Historical Statistics;* and *OECD Financial Statistics.*

SWITZERLAND - INTERNAL TRADE

Organisation for Economic Co-operation and Development (OECD), 2 rue Andre-Pascal, 75 Paris 16, France (Telephone Number in U.S. (202) 785-6323); *Main Economic Indicators - Historical Statistics.*

SWITZERLAND - INTERNATIONAL FINANCE

Organisation for Economic Co-operation and Development (OECD), 2 rue Andre-Pascal, 75 Paris 16, France (Telephone Number in U.S. (202) 785-6323); *Economic Outlook;* and *Financial Market Trends.*

SWITZERLAND - INTERNATIONAL LIQUIDITY

International Monetary Fund, 700 Nineteenth Street, NW, Washington, D.C. 20431 (202) 623-7000; *International Financial Statistics.*

Organisation for Economic Co-operation and Development (OECD), 2 rue Andre-Pascal, 75 Paris 16, France (Telephone Number in U.S. (202) 785-6323); *Economic Outlook;* and *Financial Market Trends.*

SWITZERLAND - INTERNATIONAL RESERVES EXCLUDING GOLD

Statistical Office of the United Nations, Publishing Service, New York, New York 10017 (800) 253-9646; *Statistical Yearbook.*

The World Bank, 1818 H Street, NW,

Washington, D.C. 20433 (202) 477-1234; *World Development Indicators.*

SWITZERLAND - INTERNATIONAL STATISTICS

Organisation for Economic Co-operation and Development (OECD), 2 rue Andre-Pascal, 75 Paris 16, France (Telephone Number in U.S. (202) 785-6323); *Financial Market Trends;* and *Tourism Policy and International Tourism in OECD Member Countries.*

SWITZERLAND - INVESTMENTS

Organisation for Economic Co-operation and Development (OECD), 2 rue Andre-Pascal, 75 Paris 16, France (Telephone Number in U.S. (202) 785-6323); *Economic Outlook; Financial Market Trends; Industrial Structure Statistics; The Iron and Steel Industry;* and *Textile Industry in OECD Countries.*

SWITZERLAND - IRON ORE PRODUCTION AND CONSUMPTION - See SWITZERLAND - MINING AND MINERAL PRODUCTS

SWITZERLAND - LABOR

Central Intelligence Agency, Washington, D.C. 20505 (703) 482-1100, www.cia.gov; *The World Factbook.*

Euromonitor International, Inc., 122 South Michigan Avenue, Suite 1200, Chicago, Illinois 60603 9800) 577-EURO; *World Marketing Data and Statistics.*

Europa Publications Limited, 18 Bedford Square, London, WC1B 3JN, England; *The Europa World Year Book.*

Food and Agricultural Organization of the United Nations (FAO) Via delle Terme di Caracalla, 00100 Rome, Italy (Telephone Number in U.S. (202) 653-2400); *The State of Food and Agriculture.*

International Labour Office, I.L.O. Publications, 1828 L Street, NW, Suite 801, Washington, D.C. 20036 (301) 638-3152; *Yearbook of Labour Statistics.*

M.E. Sharpe, 80 Business Park Drive, Armonk, New York 10504 (800) 541-6563; *The Illustrated Book of World Rankings.*

Organisation for Economic Co-operation and Development (OECD), 2 rue Andre-Pascal, 75 Paris 16, France (Telephone Number in U.S. (202) 785-6323); *Economic Outlook; The Iron and Steel Industry; Maritime Transport; OECD Economic Surveys: Switzerland; OECD Employment Outlook;* and *Textile Industry in OECD Countries.*

St. Martin's Press, Inc., 175 Fifth Avenue, New York, New York 10010 (800) 221-7945; *The Statesman's Year-Book.*

Statistical Office of the United Nations, Publishing Service, New York, New York 10017 (800) 253-9646; *Human Development Report.*

The World Bank, 1818 H Street, NW, Washington, D.C. 20433 (202) 477-1234; *The World Bank Atlas; World Development Report;* and *World Development Indicators.*

SWITZERLAND - LAND USE

Central Intelligence Agency, Washington, D.C. 20505 (703) 482-1100, www.cia.gov; *The World Factbook.*

Euromonitor International, Inc., 122 South Michigan Avenue, Suite 1200, Chicago, Illinois 60603 (800) 577-EURO; *European Marketing Data and Statistics.*

Food and Agricultural Organization of the United Nations (FAO), Via delle Terme di Caracalla, 00100 Rome, Italy (Telephone Number in U.S. (202) 653-2400); *Production Yearbook.*

The World Bank, 1818 H Street, NW, Washington, D.C. 20433 (202) 477-1234; *World Development Report.*

SWITZERLAND - LEAD AND LEAD ORE PRODUCTION AND CONSUMPTION - See SWITZERLAND - MINING AND MINERAL PRODUCTS

SWITZERLAND - LEATHER - PRODUCTION INDEX

Organisation for Economic Co-operation and Development (OECD), 2 rue Andre-Pascal, 75 Paris 16, France (Telephone Number in U.S. (202) 785-6323); *Indicators of Industrial Activity.*

SWITZERLAND - LEATHER AND FOOTWEAR - EXPORTS AND IMPORTS

Organisation for Economic Co-operation and Development (OECD), 2 rue Andre-Pascal, 75 Paris 16, France (Telephone Number in U.S. (202) 785-6323); *The Footwear, Raw Hides and Skins, and Leather Industry in OECD Countries.*

SWITZERLAND - LIBRARIES

Euromonitor International, Inc., 122 South Michigan Avenue, Suite 1200, Chicago, Illinois 60603 (800) 577-EURO; *European Marketing Data and Statistics.*

M.E. Sharpe, 80 Business Park Drive, Armonk, New York 10504 (800) 541-6563; *The Illustrated Book of World Rankings.*

Statistical Office of the United Nations, Publishing Service, New York, New York 10017 (800) 253-9646; *Trends in Europe and North America: The Statistical Yearbook of*

the Economic Commission for Europe.

United Nations Educational, Scientific and Cultural Organization (UNESCO), 7 Place de Fontenoy, F-75700 Paris, France (Telephone Number in U.S. (212) 963-5981); *Statistical Yearbook.*

SWITZERLAND - LIFE EXPECTANCY

Central Intelligence Agency, Washington, D.C. 20505 (703) 482-1100, www.cia.gov; *The World Factbook.*

Euromonitor International, Inc., 122 South Michigan Avenue, Suite 1200, Chicago, Illinois 60603 (800) 577-EURO; *The World Economic Factbook.*

Organisation for Economic Co-operation and Development (OECD), 2 rue Andre-Pascal, 75 Paris 16, France (Telephone Number in U.S. (202) 785-6323); *Economic Outlook.*

St. Martin's Press, Inc., 175 Fifth Avenue, New York, New York 10010 (800) 221-7945; *The Statesman's Year-Book.*

Statistical Office of the United Nations, Publishing Service, New York, New York 10017 (800) 253-9646; *Human Development Report;* and *Trends in Europe and North America: The Statistical Yearbook of the Economic Commission for Europe.*

The World Bank, 1818 H Street, NW, Washington, D.C. 20433 (202) 477-1234; *The World Bank Atlas;* and *World Development Report.*

SWITZERLAND - LIGNITE PRODUCTION - See SWITZERLAND - MINING AND MINERAL PRODUCTS

SWITZERLAND - LITERACY RATE

Euromonitor International, Inc., 122 South Michigan Avenue, Suite 1200, Chicago, Illinois 60603 9800) 577-EURO; *World Marketing Data and Statistics.*

SWITZERLAND - LIVESTOCK AND POULTRY

Euromonitor International, Inc., 122 South Michigan Avenue, Suite 1200, Chicago, Illinois 60603 (800) 577-EURO; *European Marketing Data and Statistics.*

Europa Publications Limited, 18 Bedford Square, London, WC1B 3JN, England; *The Europa World Year Book.*

Food and Agricultural Organization of the United Nations (FAO), Via delle Terme di Caracalla, 00100 Rome, Italy (Telephone Number in U.S. (202) 653-2400); *Production Yearbook;* and *The State of Food and Agriculture.*

M.E. Sharpe, 80 Business Park Drive, Armonk, New York 10504 (800) 541-6563; *The Illustrated Book of World Rankings.*

Organisation for Economic Co-operation and Development (OECD), 2 rue Andre-Pascal, 75 Paris 16, France (Telephone Number in U.S. (202) 785-6323); *Economic Accounts for Agriculture;* and *Meat Balances in OECD Member Countries.*

St. Martin's Press, Inc., 175 Fifth Avenue, New York, New York 10010 (800) 221-7945; *The Statesman's Year-Book.*

Statistical Office of the United Nations, Publishing Service, New York, New York 10017 (800) 253-9646; *Statistical Yearbook.*

United Nations Conference on Trade and Development, Central Statistical Service, Palais des Nations, Geneva, Switzerland (Telephone in U.S. (800) 253-9646); *UNCTAD Commodity Yearbook.*

SWITZERLAND - LIVING LEVELS - See SWITZERLAND - LIFE EXPECTANCY

SWITZERLAND - MACHINERY - PRODUCTION INDEX

Organisation for Economic Co-operation and Development (OECD), 2 rue Andre-Pascal, 75 Paris 16, France (Telephone Number in U.S. (202) 785-6323); *Indicators of Industrial Activity.*

SWITZERLAND - MAGNESIUM PRODUCTION AND CONSUMPTION - See SWITZERLAND - MINING AND MINERAL PRODUCTS

SWITZERLAND - MAIL - NUMBER OF PIECES SENT OR RECEIVED

Statistical Office of the United Nations, Publishing Service, New York, New York 10017 (800) 253-9646; *Statistical Yearbook.*

SWITZERLAND - MANGANESE PRODUCTION AND CONSUMPTION -See SWITZERLAND - MINING AND MINERAL PRODUCTS

SWITZERLAND - MANUFACTURING

American Automobile Manufacturers Association, 1401 H Street, NW, Suite 900, Washington, D.C. 20005 (202) 326-5500; *World Motor Vehicle Data.*

M.E. Sharpe, 80 Business Park Drive, Armonk, New York 10504 (800) 541-6563; *The Illustrated Book of World Rankings.*

Organisation for Economic Co-operation and Development (OECD), 2 rue Andre-Pascal, 75 Paris 16, France (Telephone Number in U.S. (202) 785-6323); *Foreign Trade by Commodities;*

Indicators of Industrial Activity; Industrial Structure Statistics; and *Economic Surveys: Switzerland.*

Statistical Office of the United Nations, Publishing Service, New York, New York 10017 (800) 253-9646; *Statistical Yearbook.*

The World Bank, 1818 H Street, NW, Washington, D.C. 20433 (202) 477-1234; *World Development Indicators.*

SWITZERLAND - MARRIAGE RATES

Europa Publications Limited, 18 Bedford Square, London, WC1B 3JN, England; *The Europa World Year Book.*

M.E. Sharpe, 80 Business Park Drive, Armonk, New York 10504 (800) 541-6563; *The Illustrated Book of World Rankings.*

Statistical Office of the United Nations, Publishing Service, New York, New York 10017 (800) 253-9646; *Demographic Yearbook; Trends in Europe and North America: The Statistical Yearbook of the Economic Commission for Europe;* and *Statistical Yearbook.*

SWITZERLAND - MEAT PRODUCTION - See SWITZERLAND - LIVESTOCK AND POULTRY

SWITZERLAND - MERCHANT SHIPPING

Lloyd's Register of Shipping, 17 Battery Place, New York, New York 10004 (212) 425-8050; *Register of Ships.*

Organisation for Economic Co-operation and Development (OECD), 2 rue Andre-Pascal, 75 Paris 16, France (Telephone Number in U.S. (202) 785-6323); *Maritime Transport.*

St. Martin's Press, Inc., 175 Fifth Avenue, New York, New York 10010 (800) 221-7945; *The Statesman's Year-Book.*

Statistical Office of the United Nations, Publishing Service, New York, New York 10017 (800) 253-9646; *Annual Bulletin of Transport Statistics for Europe;* and *Statistical Yearbook.*

U.S. Department of Transportation, Maritime Administration, 400 Seventh Avenue, SW, Washington, D.C. 20590 (202) 366-5807, www.marad.dot.gov; *A Statistical Analysis of the World's Merchant Fleets.*

SWITZERLAND - MERCURY PRODUCTION AND CONSUMPTION - See SWITZERLAND - MINING AND MINERAL PRODUCTS

SWITZERLAND - MILITARY

Central Intelligence Agency, Washington, D.C. 20505 (703) 482-1100, www.cia.gov; *The World Factbook.*

Euromonitor International, Inc., 122 South Michigan Avenue, Suite 1200, Chicago, Illinois 60603 9800) 577-EURO; *World Marketing Data and Statistics.*

The International Institute for Strategic Studies, 23 Tavistock Street, London WC2E 7NQ, England 44 171 3797676; *The Military Balance.*

International Monetary Fund, 700 Nineteenth Street, NW, Washington, D.C. 20431 (202) 623-7000; *Government Finance Statistics Yearbook.*

St. Martin's Press, Inc., 175 Fifth Avenue, New York, New York 10010 (800) 221-7945; *The Statesman's Year-Book.*

Statistical Office of the United Nations, Publishing Service, New York, New York 10017 (800) 253-9646; *Human Development Report.*

U.S. Arms Control and Disarmament Agency, 320 Twenty-first Street, NW, Washington, D.C. 20451 (202) 647-8677; *World Military Expenditures and Arms Transfers.*

SWITZERLAND - MILK PRODUCTION - See SWITZERLAND - DAIRY PRODUCTS

SWITZERLAND - MINING AND MINERAL PRODUCTS

Commodity Research Bureau, Inc., 30 South Wacker Drive, Chicago Illinois 60606 (312) 454-1801; *Commodity Year Book.*

M.E. Sharpe, 80 Business Park Drive, Armonk, New York 10504 (800) 541-6563; *The Illustrated Book of World Rankings.*

Organisation for Economic Co-operation and Development (OECD), 2 rue Andre-Pascal, 75 Paris 16, France (Telephone Number in U.S. (202) 785-6323); *Coal Information; Energy Statistics of OECD Countries; Foreign Trade by Commodities; Indicators of Industrial Activity; Industrial Structure Statistics; The Iron and Steel Industry; The Non-Ferrous Metals Industry;* and *OECD Economic Surveys: Switzerland.*

St. Martin's Press, Inc., 175 Fifth Avenue, New York, New York 10010 (800) 221-7945; *The Statesman's Year-Book.*

Statistical Office of the United Nations, Publishing Service, New York, New York 10017 (800) 253-9646; *Statistical Yearbook.*

United Nations Conference on Trade and Development, Central Statistical Service, Palais des Nations, Geneva, Switzerland (Telephone in U.S. (800) 253-

9646); *UNCTAD Commodity Yearbook.*

World Bureau of Metal Statistics, 27-A High Street, Ware Hert SG12 9BA, England; *World Metal Statistics.*

SWITZERLAND - MOLYBDENUM AND MOLYBDENUM ORE PRODUCTION AND CONSUMPTION - See SWITZERLAND - MINING AND MINERAL PRODUCTS

SWITZERLAND - MONEY EXCHANGE RATES - See SWITZERLAND - EXCHANGE RATES

SWITZERLAND - MONEY RATES - MARKET

Organisation for Economic Co-operation and Development (OECD), 2 rue Andre-Pascal, 75 Paris 16, France (Telephone Number in U.S. (202) 785-6323); *Economic Outlook;* and *Financial Market Trends.*

SWITZERLAND - MONEY RESERVES

Organisation for Economic Co-operation and Development (OECD), 2 rue Andre-Pascal, 75 Paris 16, France (Telephone Number in U.S. (202) 785-6323); *Economic Outlook;* and *Financial Market Trends.*

SWITZERLAND - MONEY SUPPLY

Economist Intelligence Unit, 111 West 57th Street, New York, New York 10019 (800) 938-4685; *Switzerland Country Report.*

Europa Publications Limited, 18 Bedford Square, London, WC1B 3JN, England; *The Europa World Year Book.*

International Monetary Fund, 700 Nineteenth Street, NW, Washington, D.C. 20431 (202) 623-7000; *International Financial Statistics.*

Organisation for Economic Co-operation and Development (OECD), 2 rue Andre-Pascal, 75 Paris 16, France (Telephone Number in U.S. (202) 785-6323); *Economic Outlook.*

Statistical Office of the United Nations, Publishing Service, New York, New York 10017 (800) 253-9646; *Statistical Yearbook.*

The World Bank, 1818 H Street, NW, Washington, D.C. 20433 (202) 477-1234; *World Development Indicators.*

SWITZERLAND - MORTALITY

Central Intelligence Agency, Washington, D.C. 20505 (703) 482-1100, www.cia.gov; *The World Factbook.*

Euromonitor International, Inc., 122 South Michigan Avenue, Suite 1200,

Chicago, Illinois 60603 (800) 577-EURO; *The World Economic Factbook.*

St. Martin's Press, Inc., 175 Fifth Avenue, New York, New York 10010 (800) 221-7945; *The Statesman's Year-Book.*

Statistical Office of the United Nations, Publishing Service, New York, New York 10017 (800) 253-9646; *Demographic Yearbook; Human Development Report; Trends in Europe and North America: The Statistical Yearbook of the Economic Commission for Europe; Statistical Yearbook;* and *World Statistics Pocketbook.*

United Nations Children's Fund (UNICEF), 3 United Nations Plaza, New York, New York 10017 (800) 253-9646; *State of the World's Children.*

The World Bank, 1818 H Street, NW, Washington, D.C. 20433 (202) 477-1234; *The World Bank Atlas; World Development Report;* and *World Development Indicators.*

World Health Organization, Office of Publications, 20 Avenue Appia, CH-1211 Geneva 27, Switzerland (Telephone Number in U.S. (518) 436-9686); *World Health Statistics Annual.*

SWITZERLAND - MOTION PICTURES

St. Martin's Press, Inc., 175 Fifth Avenue, New York, New York 10010 (800) 221-7945; *The Statesman's Year-Book.*

Statistical Office of the United Nations, Publishing Service, New York, New York 10017 (800) 253-9646; *Statistical Yearbook.*

United Nations Educational, Scientific and Cultural Organization (UNESCO), 7 Place de Fontenoy, F-75700 Paris, France (Telephone Number in U.S. (212) 963-5981); *Statistical Yearbook.*

SWITZERLAND - MOTOR VEHICLE ASSEMBLY

American Automobile Manufacturers Association, 1401 H Street, NW, Suite 900, Washington, D.C. 20005 (202) 326-5500; *World Motor Vehicle Data.*

Statistical Office of the United Nations, Publishing Service, New York, New York 10017 (800) 253-9646; *Statistical Yearbook.*

SWITZERLAND - MOTOR VEHICLE PRODUCTION

Organisation for Economic Co-operation and Development (OECD), 2 rue Andre-Pascal, 75 Paris 16, France (Telephone Number in U.S. (202) 785-6323); *Foreign Trade by Commodities;* and *Indicators of Industrial Activity.*

SWITZERLAND - MOTOR VEHICLES IN USE

American Automobile Manufacturers Association, 1401 H Street, NW, Suite 900, Washington, D.C. 20005 (202) 326-5500; *World Motor Vehicle Data.*

Europa Publications Limited, 18 Bedford Square, London, WC1B 3JN, England; *The Europa World Year Book.*

International Road Federation, 2600 Virginia Avenue, NW, Washington, D.C. 20037 (202) 338-4641; *World Road Statistics.*

Statistical Office of the United Nations, Publishing Service, New York, New York 10017 (800) 253-9646; *Statistical Yearbook.*

SWITZERLAND - MULES - See SWITZERLAND - LIVESTOCK AND POULTRY

SWITZERLAND - MUSEUMS

Euromonitor International, Inc., 122 South Michigan Avenue, Suite 1200, Chicago, Illinois 60603 (800) 577-EURO; *European Marketing Data and Statistics.*

M.E. Sharpe, 80 Business Park Drive, Armonk, New York 10504 (800) 541-6563; *The Illustrated Book of World Rankings.*

SWITZERLAND - NATALITY - See SWITZERLAND - BIRTH RATE

SWITZERLAND - NATIONAL ACCOUNTS

Europa Publications Limited, 18 Bedford Square, London, WC1B 3JN, England; *The Europa World Year Book.*

International Monetary Fund, 700 Nineteenth Street, NW, Washington, D.C. 20431 (202) 623-7000; *International Financial Statistics.*

Organisation for Economic Co-operation and Development (OECD), 2 rue Andre-Pascal, 75 Paris 16, France (Telephone Number in U.S. (202) 785-6323); *Economic Outlook.*

Statistical Office of the United Nations, Publishing Service, New York, New York 10017 (800) 253-9646; *National Accounts Statistics;* and *Statistical Yearbook.*

SWITZERLAND - NATIONAL INCOME

M.E. Sharpe, 80 Business Park Drive, Armonk, New York 10504 (800) 541-6563; *The Illustrated Book of World Rankings.*

Organisation for Economic Co-operation and Development (OECD), 2 rue Andre-Pascal, 75 Paris 16, France (Telephone Number in U.S. (202) 785-6323); *Economic Outlook.*

Statistical Office of the United Nations,

Publishing Service, New York, New York 10017 (800) 253-9646; *Statistical Yearbook.*

SWITZERLAND - NATIONAL PRODUCT

M.E. Sharpe, 80 Business Park Drive, Armonk, New York 10504 (800) 541-6563; *The Illustrated Book of World Rankings.*

Organisation for Economic Co-operation and Development (OECD), 2 rue Andre-Pascal, 75 Paris 16, France (Telephone Number in U.S. (202) 785-6323); *Economic Outlook.*

Statistical Office of the United Nations, Publishing Service, New York, New York 10017 (800) 253-9646; *Statistical Yearbook.*

SWITZERLAND - NATURAL GAS PRODUCTION - See SWITZERLAND - MINING AND MINERAL PRODUCTS

SWITZERLAND - NEWSPAPER PRODUCTION - See SWITZERLAND - FORESTRY AND FOREST PRODUCTS

SWITZERLAND - NEWSPRINT PRODUCTION AND CONSUMPTION - See SWITZERLAND - FORESTRY AND FOREST PRODUCTS

SWITZERLAND - NICKEL AND NICKEL ORE PRODUCTION AND CONSUMPTION - See SWITZERLAND - MINING AND MINERAL PRODUCTS

SWITZERLAND - NITRIC ACID PRODUCTION - See SWITZERLAND - MINING AND MINERAL PRODUCTS

SWITZERLAND - OATS PRODUCTION - See SWITZERLAND - CROPS

SWITZERLAND - OCCUPATIONS - See SWITZERLAND - LABOR

SWITZERLAND - OIL PRODUCING CROPS

Organisation for Economic Co-operation and Development (OECD), 2 rue Andre-Pascal, 75 Paris 16, France (Telephone Number in U.S. (202) 785-6323); *Foreign Trade by Commodities.*

SWITZERLAND - PAPER - See SWITZERLAND - FORESTRY AND FOREST PRODUCTS

SWITZERLAND - PATENTS, TRADEMARKS AND SERVICE MARKS

Statistical Office of the United Nations, Publishing Service, New York, New York 10017 (800) 253-9646; *Statistical Yearbook.*

World Intellectual Property Organization, 34 Chemin des Colombettes, CH-1211 Geneva 20, Switzerland; *Industrial Property Statistics.*

SWITZERLAND - PEANUT PRODUCTION - See SWITZERLAND - CROPS

SWITZERLAND - PERIODICALS

United Nations Educational, Scientific and Cultural Organization (UNESCO), 7 Place de Fontenoy, F-75700 Paris, France (Telephone Number in U.S. (212) 963-5981); *Statistical Yearbook.*

SWITZERLAND - PESTICIDE USE

Food and Agricultural Organization of the United Nations (FAO) Via delle Terme di Caracalla, 00100 Rome, Italy (Telephone Number in U.S. (202) 653-2400); *The State of Food and Agriculture.*

SWITZERLAND - PETROLEUM INDUSTRY

Euromonitor International, Inc., 122 South Michigan Avenue, Suite 1200, Chicago, Illinois 60603 (800) 577-EURO; *European Marketing Data and Statistics.*

Food and Agricultural Organization of the United Nations (FAO) Via delle Terme di Caracalla, 00100 Rome, Italy (Telephone Number in U.S. (202) 653-2400); *The State of Food and Agriculture.*

M.E. Sharpe, 80 Business Park Drive, Armonk, New York 10504 (800) 541-6563; *The Illustrated Book of World Rankings.*

Organisation for Economic Co-operation and Development (OECD), 2 rue Andre-Pascal, 75 Paris 16, France (Telephone Number in U.S. (202) 785-6323); *Energy Statistics of OECD Countries; Foreign Trade by Commodities; Indicators of Industrial Activity;* and *Oil and Gas Information.*

St. Martin's Press, Inc., 175 Fifth Avenue, New York, New York 10010 (800) 221-7945; *The Statesman's Year-Book.*

Statistical Office of the United Nations, Publishing Service, New York, New York 10017 (800) 253-9646; *Statistical Yearbook;* and *Trends in Europe and North America: The Statistical Yearbook of the Economic Commission for Europe.*

United Nations Conference on Trade and Development, Central Statistical Service, Palais des Nations, Geneva, Switzerland (Telephone in U.S. (800) 253-9646); *UNCTAD Commodity Yearbook.*

SWITZERLAND - PHOSPHATE ROCK PRODUCTION - See SWITZERLAND - MINING AND MINERAL PRODUCTS

SWITZERLAND - PHOSPHATES PRODUCTION - See SWITZERLAND - MINING AND MINERAL PRODUCTS

SWITZERLAND - PIG-IRON AND FERRO-ALLOY PRODUCTION - See SWITZERLAND - MINING AND MINERAL PRODUCTS

SWITZERLAND - PIGS - See SWITZERLAND - LIVESTOCK AND POULTRY

SWITZERLAND - PIPELINES FOR OIL AND PETROLEUM PRODUCTS

Statistical Office of the United Nations, Publishing Service, New York, New York 10017 (800) 253-9646; *Annual Bulletin of Transport Statistics for Europe.*

SWITZERLAND - PLASTIC AND RESIN PRODUCTION

Organisation for Economic Co-operation and Development (OECD), 2 rue Andre-Pascal, 75 Paris 16, France (Telephone Number in U.S. (202) 785-6323); *Foreign Trade by Commodities.*

SWITZERLAND - PLATINUM PRODUCTION AND CONSUMPTION - See SWITZERLAND - MINING AND MINERAL PRODUCTS

SWITZERLAND - POPULATION

Central Intelligence Agency, Washington, D.C. 20505 (703) 482-1100, www.cia.gov; *The World Factbook.*

The Economist Intelligence Unit, 111 West 57th Street, New York, New York 10019 (800) 938-4685; *Switzerland Country Report;* and *The World Market Atlas.*

Euromonitor International, Inc., 122 South Michigan Avenue, Suite 1200, Chicago, Illinois 60603 (800) 577-EURO; *European Marketing Data and Statistics;* and *The World Economic Factbook.*

Europa Publications Limited, 18 Bedford Square, London, WC1B 3JN, England; *The Europa World Year Book.*

Food and Agricultural Organization of the United Nations (FAO), Via delle Terme di Caracalla, 00100 Rome, Italy (Telephone Number in U.S. (202) 653-2400); *Production Yearbook.*

International Labour Office, I.L.O. Publications, 1828 L Street, NW, Suite 801, Washington, D.C. 20036 (301) 638-3152; *Yearbook of Labour Statistics.*

M.E. Sharpe, 80 Business Park Drive, Armonk, New York 10504 (800) 541-6563; *The Illustrated Book of World Rankings.*

St. Martin's Press, Inc., 175 Fifth Avenue, New York, New York 10010 (800) 221-7945; *The Statesman's Year-Book.*

Statistical Office of the United Nations,

Publishing Service, New York, New York 10017 (800) 253-9646; *Demographic Yearbook; Human Development Report; Statistical Yearbook; Trends in Europe and North America: The Statistical Yearbook of the Economic Commission for Europe;* and *World Statistics Pocketbook.*

United Nations Educational, Scientific and Cultural Organization (UNESCO), 7 Place de Fontenoy, F-75700 Paris, France (Telephone Number in U.S. (212) 963-5981); *Statistical Yearbook.*

U.S. Arms Control and Disarmament Agency, 320 Twenty-first Street, NW, Washington, D.C. 20451 (202) 647-8677; *World Military Expenditures and Arms Transfers.*

The World Bank, 1818 H Street, NW, Washington, D.C. 20433 (202) 477-1234; *The World Bank Atlas;* and *World Development Report.*

World Health Organization, Office of Publications, 20 Avenue Appia, CH-1211 Geneva 27, Switzerland (Telephone Number in U.S. (518) 436-9686); *World Health Statistics Annual.*

SWITZERLAND - POST OFFICES

M.E. Sharpe, 80 Business Park Drive, Armonk, New York 10504 (800) 541-6563; *The Illustrated Book of World Rankings.*

St. Martin's Press, Inc., 175 Fifth Avenue, New York, New York 10010 (800) 221-7945; *The Statesman's Year-Book.*

Statistical Office of the United Nations, Publishing Service, New York, New York 10017 (800) 253-9646; *Trends in Europe and North America: The Statistical Yearbook of the Economic Commission for Europe.*

SWITZERLAND - POTATO PRODUCTION - See SWITZERLAND - CROPS

SWITZERLAND - POWER PRODUCTION INDUSTRY

Statistical Office of the United Nations, Publishing Service, New York, New York 10017 (800) 253-9646; *Statistical Yearbook.*

SWITZERLAND - PRICES

Food and Agricultural Organization of the United Nations (FAO), Via delle Terme di Caracalla, 00100 Rome, Italy (Telephone Number in U.S. (202) 653-2400); *Production Yearbook;* and *The State of Food and Agriculture.*

International Labour Office, I.L.O. Publications, 1828 L Street, NW, Suite 801, Washington, D.C. 20036 (301) 638-3152; *Yearbook of Labour Statistics.*

International Monetary Fund, 700 Nineteenth Street, NW, Washington, D.C. 20431 (202) 623-7000; *International Financial Statistics*.

M.E. Sharpe, 80 Business Park Drive, Armonk, New York 10504 (800) 541-6563; *The Illustrated Book of World Rankings*.

Organisation for Economic Co-operation and Development (OECD), 2 rue Andre-Pascal, 75 Paris 16, France (Telephone Number in U.S. (202) 785-6323); *Economic Outlook; The Footwear, Raw Hides and Skins, and Leather Industry in OECD Countries; Indicators of Industrial Activity; The Iron and Steel Industry; Main Economic Indicators - Historical Statistics; and The Pulp and Paper Industry*.

World Bureau of Metal Statistics, 27-A High Street, Ware Hert SG12 9BA, England; *World Metal Statistics*.

SWITZERLAND - PRINTING AND WRITING PAPER - See SWITZERLAND - FORESTRY AND FOREST PRODUCTS

SWITZERLAND - PRODUCTION

American Automobile Manufacturers Association, 1401 H Street, NW, Suite 900, Washington, D.C. 20005 (202) 326-5500; *World Motor Vehicle Data*.

M.E. Sharpe, 80 Business Park Drive, Armonk, New York 10504 (800) 541-6563; *The Illustrated Book of World Rankings*.

Organisation for Economic Co-operation and Development (OECD), 2 rue Andre-Pascal, 75 Paris 16, France (Telephone Number in U.S. (202) 785-6323); *Economic Outlook; The Footwear, Raw Hides and Skins, and Leather Industry in OECD Countries; Indicators of Industrial Activity; Industrial Structure Statistics; The Iron and Steel Industry; Meat Balances in OECD Member Countries; Milk, Milk Products, and Egg Balances in OECD Member Countries; The Non-Ferrous Metals Industry; The Pulp and Paper Industry; and Textile Industry in OECD Countries*.

SWITZERLAND - PRODUCTIVITY

Organisation for Economic Co-operation and Development (OECD), 2 rue Andre-Pascal, 75 Paris 16, France (Telephone Number in U.S. (202) 785-6323); *Economic Outlook*.

SWITZERLAND - PROPERTY TAXES - See SWITZERLAND - TAXATION

SWITZERLAND - PUBLIC CONSUMPTION FUND

Organisation for Economic Co-operation and Development (OECD), 2 rue Andre-Pascal, 75 Paris 16, France

(Telephone Number in U.S. (202) 785-6323); *Revenue Statistics of OECD Member Countries*.

SWITZERLAND - PUBLIC EXPENDITURES

Organisation for Economic Co-operation and Development (OECD), 2 rue Andre-Pascal, 75 Paris 16, France (Telephone Number in U.S. (202) 785-6323); *Revenue Statistics of OECD Member Countries*.

SWITZERLAND - PUBLIC FINANCE - See SWITZERLAND - FINANCE

SWITZERLAND - PUBLIC REVENUES

Organisation for Economic Co-operation and Development (OECD), 2 rue Andre-Pascal, 75 Paris 16, France (Telephone Number in U.S. (202) 785-6323); *Revenue Statistics of OECD Member Countries*.

SWITZERLAND - RADIO BROADCASTING - See SWITZERLAND - BROADCASTING

SWITZERLAND - RADIO RECEIVERS

St. Martin's Press, Inc., 175 Fifth Avenue, New York, New York 10010 (800) 221-7945; *The Statesman's Year-Book*.

SWITZERLAND - RAILWAYS

Euromonitor International, Inc., 122 South Michigan Avenue, Suite 1200, Chicago, Illinois 60603 (800) 577-EURO; *European Marketing Data and Statistics*.

Europa Publications Limited, 18 Bedford Square, London, WC1B 3JN, England; *The Europa World Year Book*.

Jane's Information Group, Sentinel House, 163 Brighton Road, Coulsdon, Surrey CR5 2NH, England (Telephone Number in U.S. (703) 683-3700); *Jane's World Railways*.

St. Martin's Press, Inc., 175 Fifth Avenue, New York, New York 10010 (800) 221-7945; *The Statesman's Year-Book*.

Statistical Office of the United Nations, Publishing Service, New York, New York 10017 (800) 253-9646; *Annual Bulletin of Transport Statistics for Europe; Trends in Europe and North America: The Statistical Yearbook of the Economic Commission for Europe; and Statistical Yearbook*.

SWITZERLAND - RELIGION

Central Intelligence Agency, Washington, D.C. 20505 (703) 482-1100, www.cia.gov; *The World Factbook*.

M.E. Sharpe, 80 Business Park Drive,

Armonk, New York 10504 (800) 541-6563; *The Illustrated Book of World Rankings*.

St. Martin's Press, Inc., 175 Fifth Avenue, New York, New York 10010 (800) 221-7945; *The Statesman's Year-Book*.

SWITZERLAND - RENT PRICES

International Labour Office, I.L.O. Publications, 1828 L Street, NW, Suite 801, Washington, D.C. 20036 (301) 638-3152; *Yearbook of Labour Statistics*.

SWITZERLAND - RETAIL TRADE

Euromonitor International, Inc., 122 South Michigan Avenue, Suite 1200, Chicago, Illinois 60603 9800) 577-EURO; *World Marketing Data and Statistics; and Retail Trade International*.

SWITZERLAND - RICE PRODUCTION - See SWITZERLAND - CROPS

SWITZERLAND - ROUNDWOOD PRODUCTION - See SWITZERLAND - FORESTRY AND FOREST PRODUCTS

SWITZERLAND - RUBBER PRODUCTION AND CONSUMPTION

M.E. Sharpe, 80 Business Park Drive, Armonk, New York 10504 (800) 541-6563; *The Illustrated Book of World Rankings*.

Organisation for Economic Co-operation and Development (OECD), 2 rue Andre-Pascal, 75 Paris 16, France (Telephone Number in U.S. (202) 785-6323); *Foreign Trade by Commodities*.

SWITZERLAND - SALES

Organisation for Economic Co-operation and Development (OECD), 2 rue Andre-Pascal, 75 Paris 16, France (Telephone Number in U.S. (202) 785-6323); *Main Economic Indicators - Historical Statistics*.

SWITZERLAND - SALT PRODUCTION - See SWITZERLAND - MINING AND MINERAL PRODUCTS

SWITZERLAND - SAWNWOOD PRODUCTION - See SWITZERLAND - FORESTRY AND FOREST PRODUCTS

SWITZERLAND - SCIENCE AND TECHNOLOGY - EXPENDITURES FOR RESEARCH - See SWITZERLAND - SCIENTISTS, TECHNICIANS AND ENGINEERS

SWITZERLAND - SCIENTISTS, TECHNICIANS AND ENGINEERS

Statistical Office of the United Nations, Publishing Service, New York, New York 10017 (800) 253-9646; *Statistical Yearbook*.

United Nations Educational, Scientific and Cultural Organization (UNESCO), 7 Place de Fontenoy, F-75700 Paris, France (Telephone Number in U.S. (212) 963-5981); *Statistical Yearbook.*

SWITZERLAND - SENIOR CITIZENS

M.E. Sharpe, 80 Business Park Drive, Armonk, New York 10504 (800) 541-6563; *The Illustrated Book of World Rankings.*

SWITZERLAND - SHEEP - See SWITZERLAND - LIVESTOCK AND POULTRY

SWITZERLAND - SHIPBUILDING - PRODUCTION INDEX

Organisation for Economic Co-operation and Development (OECD), 2 rue Andre-Pascal, 75 Paris 16, France (Telephone Number in U.S. (202) 785-6323); *Indicators of Industrial Activity.*

SWITZERLAND - SILVER PRODUCTION AND CONSUMPTION - See SWITZERLAND - MINING AND MINERAL PRODUCTS

SWITZERLAND - SOCIAL DATA

M.E. Sharpe, 80 Business Park Drive, Armonk, New York 10504 (800) 541-6563; *The Illustrated Book of World Rankings.*

Statistical Office of the United Nations, Publishing Service, New York, New York 10017 (800) 253-9646; *World Statistics Pocketbook.*

SWITZERLAND - SOCIAL SECURITY

International Monetary Fund, 700 Nineteenth Street, NW, Washington, D.C. 20431 (202) 623-7000; *Government Finance Statistics Yearbook.*

Organisation for Economic Co-operation and Development (OECD), 2 rue Andre-Pascal, 75 Paris 16, France (Telephone Number in U.S. (202) 785-6323); *Revenue Statistics of OECD Member Countries.*

St. Martin's Press, Inc., 175 Fifth Avenue, New York, New York 10010 (800) 221-7945; *The Statesman's Year-Book.*

Statistical Office of the United Nations, Publishing Service, New York, New York 10017 (800) 253-9646; *National Accounts Statistics.*

SWITZERLAND - SOCIOECONOMIC DATA

Organisation for Economic Co-operation and Development (OECD), 2 rue Andre-Pascal, 75 Paris 16, France (Telephone Number in U.S. (202) 785-6323); *Economic Outlook.*

SWITZERLAND - STEEL - See SWITZERLAND - MINING AND MINERAL PRODUCTS

SWITZERLAND - STOCKS - COMMODITY - MARKET PRICE - INDEXES

Food and Agricultural Organization of the United Nations (FAO) Via delle Terme di Caracalla, 00100 Rome, Italy (Telephone Number in U.S. (202) 653-2400); *The State of Food and Agriculture.*

Statistical Office of the United Nations, Publishing Service, New York, New York 10017 (800) 253-9646; *Statistical Yearbook.*

World Bureau of Metal Statistics, 27-A High Street, Ware Hert SG12 9BA, England; *World Metal Statistics.*

SWITZERLAND - SUGAR - See SWITZERLAND - CROPS

SWITZERLAND - SULPHUR PRODUCTION - See SWITZERLAND - MINING AND MINERAL PRODUCTS

SWITZERLAND - SULPHURIC ACID PRODUCTION - See SWITZERLAND - MINING AND MINERAL PRODUCTS

SWITZERLAND - TAXATION

Europa Publications Limited, 18 Bedford Square, London, WC1B 3JN, England; *The Europa World Year Book.*

International Monetary Fund, 700 Nineteenth Street, NW, Washington, D.C. 20431 (202) 623-7000; *Government Finance Statistics Yearbook.*

International Road Federation, 2600 Virginia Avenue, NW, Washington, D.C. 20037 (202) 338-4641; *World Road Statistics.*

Organisation for Economic Co-operation and Development (OECD), 2 rue Andre-Pascal, 75 Paris 16, France (Telephone Number in U.S. (202) 785-6323); *Revenue Statistics of OECD Member Countries.*

The World Bank, 1818 H Street, NW, Washington, D.C. 20433 (202) 477-1234; *World Development Indicators.*

SWITZERLAND - TEA CONSUMPTION

Statistical Office of the United Nations, Publishing Service, New York, New York 10017 (800) 253-9646; *Statistical Yearbook.*

SWITZERLAND - TELEGRAPH SERVICE

Statistical Office of the United Nations, Publishing Service, New York, New York 10017 (800) 253-9646; *Statistical Yearbook.*

SWITZERLAND - TELEPHONES IN USE

American Telephone and Telegraph Company, 26 Parsippany Road, Whippany, New Jersey 07981 (800) 222-0300; *The World's Telephones.*

Central Intelligence Agency, Washington, D.C. 20505 (703) 482-1100, www.cia.gov; *The World Factbook.*

Europa Publications Limited, 18 Bedford Square, London, WC1B 3JN, England; *The Europa World Year Book.*

St. Martin's Press, Inc., 175 Fifth Avenue, New York, New York 10010 (800) 221-7945; *The Statesman's Year-Book.*

Statistical Office of the United Nations, Publishing Service, New York, New York 10017 (800) 253-9646; *Statistical Yearbook; Trends in Europe and North America: The Statistical Yearbook of the Economic Commission for Europe;* and *World Statistics Pocketbook.*

SWITZERLAND - TELEVISION BROADCASTING - See SWITZERLAND - BROADCASTING

SWITZERLAND - TEXTILE INDUSTRY

American Forest and Paper Association, 1111 Nineteenth Street, NW, Suite 800, Washington, D.C. 20036 (202) 463-2700; *Wood Pulp and Fiber Statistics.*

Euromonitor International, Inc., 122 South Michigan Avenue, Suite 1200, Chicago, Illinois 60603 (800) 577-EURO; *Retail Trade International.*

M.E. Sharpe, 80 Business Park Drive, Armonk, New York 10504 (800) 541-6563; *The Illustrated Book of World Rankings.*

Organisation for Economic Co-operation and Development (OECD), 2 rue Andre-Pascal, 75 Paris 16, France (Telephone Number in U.S. (202) 785-6323); *Economic Accounts for Agriculture; Foreign Trade by Commodities; Indicators of Industrial Activity; Industrial Structure Statistics;* and *Textile Industry in OECD Countries.*

St. Martin's Press, Inc., 175 Fifth Avenue, New York, New York 10010 (800) 221-7945; *The Statesman's Year-Book.*

Statistical Office of the United Nations, Publishing Service, New York, New York 10017 (800) 253-9646; *Statistical Yearbook.*

United Nations Conference on Trade and Development, Central Statistical Service, Palais des Nations, Geneva, Switzerland (Telephone in U.S. (800) 253-9646); *UNCTAD Commodity Yearbook.*

SWITZERLAND - THEATRE

United Nations Educational, Scientific and Cultural Organization (UNESCO), 7 Place de Fontenoy, F-75700 Paris, France (Telephone Number in U.S. (212) 963-5981); *Statistical Yearbook.*

SWITZERLAND - TIN - See SWITZERLAND - MINING AND MINERAL PRODUCTS

SWITZERLAND - TOBACCO PRODUCTION

Euromonitor International, Inc., 122 South Michigan Avenue, Suite 1200, Chicago, Illinois 60603 (800) 577-EURO; *European Marketing Data and Statistics.*

M.E. Sharpe, 80 Business Park Drive, Armonk, New York 10504 (800) 541-6563; *The Illustrated Book of World Rankings.*

Organisation for Economic Co-operation and Development (OECD), 2 rue Andre-Pascal, 75 Paris 16, France (Telephone Number in U.S. (202) 785-6323); *Foreign Trade by Commodities; Indicators of Industrial Activity;* and *Industrial Structure Statistics.*

Statistical Office of the United Nations, Publishing Service, New York, New York 10017 (800) 253-9646; *Statistical Yearbook.*

SWITZERLAND - TOURISM

Euromonitor International, Inc., 122 South Michigan Avenue, Suite 1200, Chicago, Illinois 60603 (800) 577-EURO; *European Marketing Data and Statistics; World Marketing Data and Statistics;* and *The World Economic Factbook.*

Europa Publications Limited, 18 Bedford Square, London, WC1B 3JN, England; *The Europa World Year Book.*

M.E. Sharpe, 80 Business Park Drive, Armonk, New York 10504 (800) 541-6563; *The Illustrated Book of World Rankings.*

Organisation for Economic Co-operation and Development (OECD), 2 rue Andre-Pascal, 75 Paris 16, France (Telephone Number in U.S. (202) 785-6323); *Tourism Policy and International Tourism in OECD Member Countries.*

St. Martin's Press, Inc., 175 Fifth Avenue, New York, New York 10010 (800) 221-7945; *The Statesman's Year-Book.*

Statistical Office of the United Nations, Publishing Service, New York, New York 10017 (800) 253-9646; *Statistical Yearbook;* and *Trends in Europe and North America: The Statistical Yearbook of the Economic Commission for Europe.*

World Tourism Organization, Calle Capitan Haya 42, E-28020 Madrid, Spain;

Yearbook of Tourism Statistics.

SWITZERLAND - TRACTORS IN USE

Statistical Office of the United Nations, Publishing Service, New York, New York 10017 (800) 253-9646; *Statistical Yearbook.*

SWITZERLAND - TRADE - See SWITZERLAND - FOREIGN TRADE

SWITZERLAND - TRADEMARKS AND SERVICE MARKS - See SWITZERLAND - PATENTS, TRADEMARKS AND SERVICE MARKS

SWITZERLAND - TRANSPORTATION AND COMMUNICATIONS

Central Intelligence Agency, Washington, D.C. 20505 (703) 482-1100, www.cia.gov; *The World Factbook.*

Euromonitor International, Inc., 122 South Michigan Avenue, Suite 1200, Chicago, Illinois 60603 9800) 577-EURO; *World Marketing Data and Statistics.*

Europa Publications Limited, 18 Bedford Square, London, WC1B 3JN, England; *The Europa World Year Book.*

M.E. Sharpe, 80 Business Park Drive, Armonk, New York 10504 (800) 541-6563; *The Illustrated Book of World Rankings.*

St. Martin's Press, Inc., 175 Fifth Avenue, New York, New York 10010 (800) 221-7945; *The Statesman's Year-Book.*

Statistical Office of the United Nations, Publishing Service, New York, New York 10017 (800) 253-9646; *Human Development Report;* and *Trends in Europe and North America: The Statistical Yearbook of the Economic Commission for Europe.*

SWITZERLAND - TUNGSTEN PRODUCTION AND CONSUMPTION - See SWITZERLAND - MINING AND MINERAL PRODUCTS

SWITZERLAND - UNEMPLOYMENT

Central Intelligence Agency, Washington, D.C. 20505 (703) 482-1100, www.cia.gov; *The World Factbook.*

Euromonitor International, Inc., 122 South Michigan Avenue, Suite 1200, Chicago, Illinois 60603 (800) 577-EURO; *European Marketing Data and Statistics.*

International Labour Office, I.L.O. Publications, 1828 L Street, NW, Suite 801, Washington, D.C. 20036 (301) 638-3152; *Yearbook of Labour Statistics.*

Organisation for Economic Co-operation and Development (OECD), 2 rue Andre-Pascal, 75 Paris 16, France

(Telephone Number in U.S. (202) 785-6323); *Economic Outlook; OECD Economic Surveys: Switzerland;* and *OECD Employment Outlook.*

St. Martin's Press, Inc., 175 Fifth Avenue, New York, New York 10010 (800) 221-7945; *The Statesman's Year-Book.*

Statistical Office of the United Nations, Publishing Service, New York, New York 10017 (800) 253-9646; *Statistical Yearbook;* and *Trends in Europe and North America: The Statistical Yearbook of the Economic Commission for Europe.*

SWITZERLAND - URANIUM PRODUCTION AND CONSUMPTION - See SWITZERLAND - MINING AND MINERAL PRODUCTS

SWITZERLAND - VANADIUM AND VANADIUM ORE PRODUCTION AND CONSUMPTION - See SWITZERLAND - MINING AND MINERAL PRODUCTS

SWITZERLAND - VITAL STATISTICS

St. Martin's Press, Inc., 175 Fifth Avenue, New York, New York 10010 (800) 221-7945; *The Statesman's Year-Book.*

Statistical Office of the United Nations, Publishing Service, New York, New York 10017 (800) 253-9646; *Statistical Yearbook.*

World Health Organization, Office of Publications, 20 Avenue Appia, CH-1211 Geneva 27, Switzerland (Telephone Number in U.S. (518) 436-9686); *World Health Statistics Annual.*

SWITZERLAND - WAGES

Euromonitor International, Inc., 122 South Michigan Avenue, Suite 1200, Chicago, Illinois 60603 (800) 577-EURO; *European Marketing Data and Statistics.*

International Labour Office, I.L.O. Publications, 1828 L Street, NW, Suite 801, Washington, D.C. 20036 (301) 638-3152; *Yearbook of Labour Statistics.*

Organisation for Economic Co-operation and Development (OECD), 2 rue Andre-Pascal, 75 Paris 16, France (Telephone Number in U.S. (202) 785-6323); *Economic Outlook; Industrial Structure Statistics;* and *Main Economic Indicators - Historical Statistics.*

Statistical Office of the United Nations, Publishing Service, New York, New York 10017 (800) 253-9646; *Statistical Yearbook.*

SWITZERLAND - WATERWAYS IN USE

Organisation for Economic Co-operation and Development (OECD), 2 rue Andre-Pascal, 75 Paris 16, France

(Telephone Number in U.S. (202) 785-6323); *Maritime Transport.*

Statistical Office of the United Nations, Publishing Service, New York, New York 10017 (800) 253-9646; *Annual Bulletin of Transport Statistics for Europe.*

SWITZERLAND - WEATHER - See SWITZERLAND - CLIMATE

SWITZERLAND - WELFARE

International Monetary Fund, 700 Nineteenth Street, NW, Washington, D.C. 20431 (202) 623-7000; *Government Finance Statistics Yearbook.*

St. Martin's Press, Inc., 175 Fifth Avenue, New York, New York 10010 (800) 221-7945; *The Statesman's Year-Book.*

SWITZERLAND - WHEAT - See SWITZERLAND - CROPS

SWITZERLAND - WHOLESALE PRICES

Statistical Office of the United Nations, Publishing Service, New York, New York 10017 (800) 253-9646; *Statistical Yearbook.*

SWITZERLAND - WINE PRODUCTION - See SWITZERLAND - BEVERAGES

SWITZERLAND - WOOD AND WOOD PULP - See SWITZERLAND - FORESTRY AND FOREST PRODUCTS

SWITZERLAND - WOOL PRODUCTION AND CONSUMPTION - See SWITZERLAND - TEXTILE INDUSTRY

SWITZERLAND - YARN PRODUCTION - See SWITZERLAND - TEXTILE INDUSTRY

SWITZERLAND - ZINC AND ZINC ORE PRODUCTION AND CONSUMPTION - See SWITZERLAND - MINING AND MINERAL PRODUCTS

SWORDFISH - IMPORTS

U.S. Department of Commerce, National Oceanic and Atmospheric Administration, National Marine Fisheries Service, 1335 East-West Highway, Silver Spring, Maryland 20910 (301) 427-2239; *Fisheries of the United States.*

SYMPHONY ORCHESTRAS

American Symphony Orchestra League, 33 West 60th Street, 5th Floor, New York, New York 10023 (212) 262-5161.

SYNAGOGUES - See RELIGION

SYPHILIS

U.S. Department of Health and Human Services, Centers for Disease Control, 1600

Clifton Road, NE, Atlanta, Georgia 30333 (404) 639-3311, www.cdc.gov; *Summary of Notifiable Diseases, United States, Morbidity and Mortality Weekly Reports.*

Syrian Arab Republic - National Statistical Office

Central Bureau of Statistics, Abel-Malek Bin Marwan Street, Malki Quarter, Damascus, Syrian Arab Republic.

Syrian Arab Republic - Primary Statistics Source

Central Bureau of Statistics, Abel-Malek Bin Marwan Street, Malki Quarter, Damascus, Syrian Arab Republic; *Statistical Abstract.*

SYRIAN ARAB REPUBLIC - AGRICULTURE

Economic Commission for Western Asia, Post Office Box 27, Baghdad, Iraq; *Statistical Abstract of Western Asia.*

Economist Intelligence Unit, 111 West 57th Street, New York, New York 10019 (800) 938-4685; *Syria Country Report.*

Euromonitor International, Inc., 122 South Michigan Avenue, Suite 1200, Chicago, Illinois 60603 (800) 577-EURO; *International Marketing Data and Statistics;* and *World Marketing Data and Statistics.*

Europa Publications Limited, 18 Bedford Square, London, WC1B 3JN, England; *The Europa World Year Book.*

Food and Agricultural Organization of the United Nations (FAO) Via delle Terme di Caracalla, 00100 Rome, Italy (Telephone Number in U.S. (202) 653-2400); *Production Yearbook;* and *The State of Food and Agriculture,* and *Trade Yearbook.*

Federal Statistical Office, Gustav-Stresemann-Ring 11, D-6200 Wiesbaden, Germany; *Syrien.*

M.E. Sharpe, 80 Business Park Drive, Armonk, New York 10504 (800) 541-6563; *The Illustrated Book of World Rankings.*

St. Martin's Press, Inc., 175 Fifth Avenue, New York, New York 10010 (800) 221-7945; *The Statesman's Year-Book.*

Statistical Office of the United Nations, Publishing Service, New York, New York 10017 (800) 253-9646; *Statistical Yearbook.*

United Nations Conference on Trade and Development, Central Statistical Service, Palais des Nations, Geneva, Switzerland (Telephone in U.S. (800) 253-9646); *UNCTAD Commodity Yearbook.*

The World Bank, 1818 H Street, NW, Washington, D.C. 20433 (202) 477-1234; *World Development Indicators.*

SYRIAN ARAB REPUBLIC - AIRLINE SERVICE

Economic Commission for Western Asia, Post Office Box 27, Baghdad, Iraq; *Statistical Abstract of Western Asia.*

Europa Publications Limited, 18 Bedford Square, London, WC1B 3JN, England; *The Europa World Year Book.*

M.E. Sharpe, 80 Business Park Drive, Armonk, New York 10504 (800) 541-6563; *The Illustrated Book of World Rankings.*

St. Martin's Press, Inc., 175 Fifth Avenue, New York, New York 10010 (800) 221-7945; *The Statesman's Year-Book.*

Statistical Office of the United Nations, Publishing Service, New York, New York 10017 (800) 253-9646; *Statistical Yearbook.*

SYRIAN ARAB REPUBLIC - AIRPORTS

Central Intelligence Agency, Washington, D.C. 20505 (703) 482-1100, www.cia.gov; *The World Factbook.*

SYRIAN ARAB REPUBLIC - ALUMINUM PRODUCTION AND CONSUMPTION - See SYRIAN ARAB REPUBLIC - MINING AND MINERAL PRODUCTS

SYRIAN ARAB REPUBLIC - ANIMAL HEALTH

Food and Agricultural Organization of the United Nations (FAO), Via delle Terme di Caracalla, 00100, Rome, Italy (Telephone Number in U.S. (202) 653-2400); *Animal Health Yearbook.*

SYRIAN ARAB REPUBLIC - AREA AND DENSITY OF POPULATION

Central Intelligence Agency, Washington, D.C. 20505 (703) 482-1100, www.cia.gov; *The World Factbook.*

Economic Commission for Western Asia, Post Office Box 27, Baghdad, Iraq; *Statistical Abstract of Western Asia.*

Euromonitor International, Inc., 122 South Michigan Avenue, Suite 1200, Chicago, Illinois 60603 (800) 577-EURO; *International Marketing Data and Statistics;* and *The World Economic Factbook.*

Europa Publications Limited, 18 Bedford Square, London, WC1B 3JN, England; *The Europa World Year Book.*

Federal Statistical Office, Gustav-Stresemann-Ring 11, D-6200 Wiesbaden, Germany; *Syrien.*

Food and Agricultural Organization of the United Nations (FAO) Via delle Terme di Caracalla, 00100 Rome, Italy (Telephone Number in U.S. (202) 653-2400); *The State of Food and Agriculture.*

M.E. Sharpe, 80 Business Park Drive, Armonk, New York 10504 (800) 541-6563; *The Illustrated Book of World Rankings.*

St. Martin's Press, Inc., 175 Fifth Avenue, New York, New York 10010 (800) 221-7945; *The Statesman's Year-Book.*

Statistical Office of the United Nations, Publishing Service, New York, New York 10017 (800) 253-9646; *Statistical Yearbook.*

United Nations Educational, Scientific and Cultural Organization (UNESCO), 7 Place de Fontenoy, F-75700 Paris, France (Telephone Number in U.S. (212) 963-5981); *Statistical Yearbook.*

SYRIAN ARAB REPUBLIC - ARMS EXPORTS AND IMPORTS - See SYRIAN ARAB REPUBLIC - MILITARY

SYRIAN ARAB REPUBLIC - BALANCE OF PAYMENTS

Economic Commission for Western Asia, Post Office Box 27, Baghdad, Iraq; *Statistical Abstract of Western Asia.*

The Economist Intelligence Unit, 111 West 57th Street, New York, New York 10019 (800) 938-4685; *The World Market Atlas.*

Europa Publications Limited, 18 Bedford Square, London, WC1B 3JN, England; *The Europa World Year Book.*

Federal Statistical Office, Gustav-Stresemann - Ring 11, D-6200, Wiesbaden, Germany; *Syrien.*

International Monetary Fund, 700 Nineteenth Street, NW, Washington, D.C. 20431 (202) 623-7000; *Balance of Payments Yearbook.*

United Nations Conference on Trade and Development (UNCTAD), New York, New York 10017 (800) 253-9646; *Handbook of International Trade and Development Statistics.*

The World Bank, 1818 H Street, NW, Washington, D.C. 20433 (202) 477-1234; *World Development Indicators.*

SYRIAN ARAB REPUBLIC - BALANCE OF TRADE

Economic Commission for Western Asia, Post Office Box 27, Baghdad, Iraq; *Statistical Abstract of Western Asia.*

SYRIAN ARAB REPUBLIC - BANKING

Economic Commission for Western Asia, Post Office Box 27, Baghdad, Iraq; *Statistical Abstract of Western Asia.*

Euromonitor International, Inc., 122 South Michigan Avenue, Suite 1200, Chicago, Illinois 60603 9800) 577-EURO; *World Marketing Data and Statistics.*

Europa Publications Limited, 18 Bedford Square, London, WC1B 3JN, England; *The Europa World Year Book.*

International Monetary Fund, 700 Nineteenth Street, NW, Washington, D.C. 20431 (202) 623-7000; *International Financial Statistics.*

M.E. Sharpe, 80 Business Park Drive, Armonk, New York 10504 (800) 541-6563; *The Illustrated Book of World Rankings.*

St. Martin's Press, Inc., 175 Fifth Avenue, New York, New York 10010 (800) 221-7945; *The Statesman's Year-Book.*

Statistical Office of the United Nations, Publishing Service, New York, New York 10017 (800) 253-9646; *Statistical Yearbook.*

SYRIAN ARAB REPUBLIC - BARLEY PRODUCTION - See SYRIAN ARAB REPUBLIC - CROPS

SYRIAN ARAB REPUBLIC - BEER PRODUCTION - See SYRIAN ARAB REPUBLIC - BEVERAGES

SYRIAN ARAB REPUBLIC - BEVERAGES

M.E. Sharpe, 80 Business Park Drive, Armonk, New York 10504 (800) 541-6563; *The Illustrated Book of World Rankings.*

Statistical Office of the United Nations, Publishing Service, New York, New York 10017 (800) 253-9646; *Statistical Yearbook.*

SYRIAN ARAB REPUBLIC - BIRTH RATES

Central Intelligence Agency, Washington, D.C. 20505 (703) 482-1100, www.cia.gov; *The World Factbook.*

Euromonitor International, Inc., 122 South Michigan Avenue, Suite 1200, Chicago, Illinois 60603 (800) 577-EURO; *International Marketing Data and Statistics;* and *The World Economic Factbook.*

Europa Publications Limited, 18 Bedford Square, London, WC1B 3JN, England; *The Europa World Year Book.*

M.E. Sharpe, 80 Business Park Drive, Armonk, New York 10504 (800) 541-6563; *The Illustrated Book of World Rankings.*

St. Martin's Press, Inc., 175 Fifth Avenue, New York, New York 10010 (800)

221-7945; *The Statesman's Year-Book.*

Statistical Office of the United Nations, Publishing Service, New York, New York 10017 (800) 253-9646; *Demographic Yearbook;* and *Statistical Yearbook.*

The World Bank, 1818 H Street, NW, Washington, D.C. 20433 (202) 477-1234; *World Development Indicators.*

World Health Organization, Office of Publications, 20 Avenue Appia, CH-1211 Geneva 27, Switzerland (Telephone Number in U.S. (518) 436-9686); *World Health Statistics Annual.*

SYRIAN ARAB REPUBLIC - BOOK PRODUCTION

United Nations Educational, Scientific and Cultural Organization (UNESCO), 7 Place de Fontenoy, F-75700 Paris, France (Telephone Number in U.S. (212) 963-5981); *Statistical Yearbook.*

SYRIAN ARAB REPUBLIC - BROADCASTING

Billboard Limited, P.O. Box 9027, 1006 AA Amsterdam, The Netherlands (Telephone Number in U.S. (212) 764-7300); *World Radio TV Handbook.*

Central Intelligence Agency, Washington, D.C. 20505 (703) 482-1100, www.cia.gov; *The World Factbook.*

Euromonitor International, Inc., 122 South Michigan Avenue, Suite 1200, Chicago, Illinois 60603 9800) 577-EURO; *World Marketing Data and Statistics.*

M.E. Sharpe, 80 Business Park Drive, Armonk, New York 10504 (800) 541-6563; *The Illustrated Book of World Rankings.*

St. Martin's Press, Inc., 175 Fifth Avenue, New York, New York 10010 (800) 221-7945; *The Statesman's Year-Book.*

SYRIAN ARAB REPUBLIC - BUDGET

Central Intelligence Agency, Washington, D.C. 20505 (703) 482-1100, www.cia.gov; *The World Factbook.*

SYRIAN ARAB REPUBLIC - BUSINESS AND PROFESSIONAL LICENSES

International Monetary Fund, 700 Nineteenth Street, NW, Washington, D.C. 20431 (202) 623-7000; *Government Finance Statistics Yearbook.*

SYRIAN ARAB REPUBLIC - BUTTER PRODUCTION - See SYRIAN ARAB REPUBLIC - DAIRY PRODUCTS

SYRIAN ARAB REPUBLIC - CALORIE SUPPLY

Food and Agricultural Organization of the United Nations (FAO) Via delle Terme di Caracalla, 00100 Rome, Italy (Telephone Number in U.S. (202) 653-2400); *The State of Food and Agriculture.*

SYRIAN ARAB REPUBLIC - CAPITAL REVENUE

International Monetary Fund, 700 Nineteenth Street, NW, Washington, D.C. 20431 (202) 623-7000; *Government Finance Statistics Yearbook.*

SYRIAN ARAB REPUBLIC - CATTLE - See SYRIAN ARAB REPUBLIC - LIVESTOCK AND POULTRY

SYRIAN ARAB REPUBLIC - CEMENT PRODUCTION - See SYRIAN ARAB REPUBLIC - MINING AND MINERAL PRODUCTS

SYRIAN ARAB REPUBLIC - CHEESE PRODUCTION AND CONSUMPTION - See SYRIAN ARAB REPUBLIC - DAIRY PRODUCTS

SYRIAN ARAB REPUBLIC - CHEMICAL (ORGANIC) PRODUCTION - See SYRIAN ARAB REPUBLIC - MINING AND MINERAL PRODUCTS

SYRIAN ARAB REPUBLIC - CHICKENS - See SYRIAN ARAB REPUBLIC - LIVESTOCK AND POULTRY

SYRIAN ARAB REPUBLIC - CIGARETTE PRODUCTION - See SYRIAN ARAB REPUBLIC - TOBACCO PRODUCTION

SYRIAN ARAB REPUBLIC - CLIMATE

M.E. Sharpe, 80 Business Park Drive, Armonk, New York 10504 (800) 541-6563; *The Illustrated Book of World Rankings.*

St. Martin's Press, Inc., 175 Fifth Avenue, New York, New York 10010 (800) 221-7945; *The Statesman's Year-Book.*

SYRIAN ARAB REPUBLIC - COAL PRODUCTION - See SYRIAN ARAB REPUBLIC - MINING AND MINERAL PRODUCTS

SYRIAN ARAB REPUBLIC - COFFEE PRODUCTION AND CONSUMPTION

M.E. Sharpe, 80 Business Park Drive, Armonk, New York 10504 (800) 541-6563; *The Illustrated Book of World Rankings.*

SYRIAN ARAB REPUBLIC - COMMERCE

St. Martin's Press, Inc., 175 Fifth Avenue, New York, New York 10010 (800) 221-7945; *The Statesman's Year-Book.*

SYRIAN ARAB REPUBLIC - COMMUNICATIONS - See SYRIAN ARAB

REPUBLIC - TRANSPORTATION AND COMMUNICATIONS

SYRIAN ARAB REPUBLIC - CONSTRUCTION INDUSTRY

M.E. Sharpe, 80 Business Park Drive, Armonk, New York 10504 (800) 541-6563; *The Illustrated Book of World Rankings.*

Statistical Office of the United Nations, Publishing Service, New York, New York 10017 (800) 253-9646; *Statistical Yearbook.*

SYRIAN ARAB REPUBLIC - CONSUMER PRICE INDEX

Europa Publications Limited, 18 Bedford Square, London, WC1B 3JN, England; *The Europa World Year Book.*

Statistical Office of the United Nations, Publishing Service, New York, New York 10017 (800) 253-9646; *Statistical Yearbook.*

SYRIAN ARAB REPUBLIC - CONSUMER PRICES

Euromonitor International, Inc., 122 South Michigan Avenue, Suite 1200, Chicago, Illinois 60603 9800) 577-EURO; *World Marketing Data and Statistics.*

International Labour Office, I.L.O. Publications, 1828 L Street, NW, Suite 801, Washington, D.C. 20036 (301) 638-3152; *Yearbook of Labour Statistics.*

International Monetary Fund, 700 Nineteenth Street, NW, Washington, D.C. 20431 (202) 623-7000; *International Financial Statistics.*

SYRIAN ARAB REPUBLIC - COPPER PRODUCTION AND CONSUMPTION - See SYRIAN ARAB REPUBLIC - MINING AND MINERAL PRODUCTS

SYRIAN ARAB REPUBLIC - CORN PRODUCTION - See SYRIAN ARAB REPUBLIC - CROPS

SYRIAN ARAB REPUBLIC - CORPORATE TAXES - See SYRIAN ARAB REPUBLIC

SYRIAN ARAB REPUBLIC - COTTON - See SYRIAN ARAB REPUBLIC - CROPS

SYRIAN ARAB REPUBLIC - CRIME

International Criminal Police Organization (INTERPOL), 50 quai Achille Lignon, F-69006 Lyon, France; *International Crime Statistics.*

Yale University Press, Yale Station, New Haven, Connecticut 06520 (800) 987-7323; *Violence and Crime in Cross-National Perspective.*

SYRIAN ARAB REPUBLIC - CROPS

Europa Publications Limited, 18 Bedford Square, London, WC1B 3JN, England; *The Europa World Year Book.*

Food and Agricultural Organization of the United Nations (FAO) Via delle Terme di Caracalla, 00100 Rome, Italy (Telephone Number in U.S. (202) 653-2400); *The State of Food and Agriculture.*

International Monetary Fund, 700 Nineteenth Street, NW, Washington, D.C. 20431 (202) 623-7000; *International Financial Statistics.*

M.E. Sharpe, 80 Business Park Drive, Armonk, New York 10504 (800) 541-6563; *The Illustrated Book of World Rankings.*

St. Martin's Press, Inc., 175 Fifth Avenue, New York, New York 10010 (800) 221-7945; *The Statesman's Year-Book.*

Statistical Office of the United Nations, Publishing Service, New York, New York 10017 (800) 253-9646; *Statistical Yearbook.*

United Nations Conference on Trade and Development, Central Statistical Service, Palais des Nations, Geneva, Switzerland (Telephone in U.S. (800) 253-9646); *UNCTAD Commodity Yearbook.*

SYRIAN ARAB REPUBLIC - CUSTOMS DUTIES

International Monetary Fund, 700 Nineteenth Street, NW, Washington, D.C. 20431 (202) 623-7000; *Government Finance Statistics Yearbook.*

St. Martin's Press, Inc., 175 Fifth Avenue, New York, New York 10010 (800) 221-7945; *The Statesman's Year-Book.*

SYRIAN ARAB REPUBLIC - DAIRY PRODUCTS

Economic Commission for Western Asia, Post Office Box 27, Baghdad, Iraq; *Statistical Abstract of Western Asia.*

Europa Publications Limited, 18 Bedford Square, London, WC1B 3JN, England; *The Europa World Year Book.*

M.E. Sharpe, 80 Business Park Drive, Armonk, New York 10504 (800) 541-6563; *The Illustrated Book of World Rankings.*

St. Martin's Press, Inc., 175 Fifth Avenue, New York, New York 10010 (800) 221-7945; *The Statesman's Year-Book.*

Statistical Office of the United Nations, Publishing Service, New York, New York 10017 (800) 253-9646; *Statistical Yearbook.*

SYRIAN ARAB REPUBLIC - DEATH RATES - See SYRIAN ARAB REPUBLIC - MORTALITY

SYRIAN ARAB REPUBLIC - DEFENSE EXPENDITURES - See SYRIAN ARAB REPUBLIC - MILITARY

SYRIAN ARAB REPUBLIC - DEMOGRAPHY

The Economist Intelligence Unit, 111 West 57th Street, New York, New York 10019 (800) 938-4685; *The World Market Atlas.*

Euromonitor International, Inc., 122 South Michigan Avenue, Suite 1200, Chicago, Illinois 60603 (800) 577-EURO; *International Marketing Data and Statistics; World Marketing Data and Statistics;* and *The World Economic Factbook.*

Federal Statistical Office, Gustav-Stresemann - Ring 11, D-6200, Wiesbaden, Germany; *Syrien.*

M.E. Sharpe, 80 Business Park Drive, Armonk, New York 10504 (800) 541-6563; *The Illustrated Book of World Rankings.*

Statistical Office of the United Nations, Publishing Service, New York, New York 10017 (800) 253-9646; *Human Development Report.*

SYRIAN ARAB REPUBLIC - DEVELOPMENT ASSISTANCE

Statistical Office of the United Nations, Publishing Service, New York, New York 10017 (800) 253-9646; *Statistical Yearbook.*

SYRIAN ARAB REPUBLIC - DIAMOND PRODUCTION - See SYRIAN ARAB REPUBLIC - MINING AND MINERAL PRODUCTS

SYRIAN ARAB REPUBLIC - DISCOUNT RATES - See SYRIAN ARAB REPUBLIC - BANKING

SYRIAN ARAB REPUBLIC - DISEASES - See SYRIAN ARAB REPUBLIC - HEALTH

SYRIAN ARAB REPUBLIC - DIVORCE RATES

M.E. Sharpe, 80 Business Park Drive, Armonk, New York 10504 (800) 541-6563; *The Illustrated Book of World Rankings.*

Statistical Office of the United Nations, Publishing Service, New York, New York 10017 (800) 253-9646; *Demographic Yearbook;* and *Statistical Yearbook.*

SYRIAN ARAB REPUBLIC - ECONOMY

Central Intelligence Agency, Washington, D.C. 20505 (703) 482-1100, www.cia.gov; *The World Factbook.*

Economist Intelligence Unit, 111 West 57th Street, New York, New York 10019 (800) 938-4685; *Syria Country Report.*

Euromonitor International, Inc., 122 South Michigan Avenue, Suite 1200, Chicago, Illinois 60603 (800) 577-EURO; *International Marketing Data and Statistics; World Marketing Data and Statistics;* and *The World Economic Factbook.*

Europa Publications Limited, 18 Bedford Square, London, WC1B 3JN, England; *The Europa World Year Book.*

Federal Statistical Office, Gustav-Stresemann - Ring 11, D-6200, Wiesbaden, Germany; *Syrien.*

M.E. Sharpe, 80 Business Park Drive, Armonk, New York 10504 (800) 541-6563; *The Illustrated Book of World Rankings.*

St. Martin's Press, Inc., 175 Fifth Avenue, New York, New York 10010 (800) 221-7945; *The Statesman's Year-Book.*

Statistical Office of the United Nations, Publishing Service, New York, New York 10017 (800) 253-9646; *World Statistics Pocketbook.*

The World Bank, 1818 H Street, NW, Washington, D.C. 20433 (202) 477-1234; *The World Bank Atlas.*

SYRIAN ARAB REPUBLIC - EDUCATION

Economic Commission for Western Asia, Post Office Box 27, Baghdad, Iraq; *Statistical Abstract of Western Asia.*

The Economist Intelligence Unit, 111 West 57th Street, New York, New York 10019 (800) 938-4685; *The World Market Atlas.*

Euromonitor International, Inc., 122 South Michigan Avenue, Suite 1200, Chicago, Illinois 60603 (800) 577-EURO; *International Marketing Data and Statistics;* and *World Marketing Data and Statistics.*

Europa Publications Limited, 18 Bedford Square, London, WC1B 3JN, England; *The Europa World Year Book.*

Federal Statistical Office, Gustav-Stresemann-Ring 11, D-6200 Wiesbaden, Germany; *Syrien.*

International Monetary Fund, 700 Nineteenth Street, NW, Washington, D.C. 20431 (202) 623-7000; *Government Finance Statistics Yearbook.*

M.E. Sharpe, 80 Business Park Drive, Armonk, New York 10504 (800) 541-6563; *The Illustrated Book of World Rankings.*

St. Martin's Press, Inc., 175 Fifth Avenue, New York, New York 10010 (800) 221-7945; *The Statesman's Year-Book.*

Statistical Office of the United Nations,

Publishing Service, New York, New York 10017 (800) 253-9646; *Human Development Report.*

United Nations Educational, Scientific and Cultural Organization (UNESCO), 7 Place de Fontenoy, F-75700 Paris, France (Telephone Number in U.S. (212) 963-5981); *Statistical Yearbook.*

The World Bank, 1818 H Street, NW, Washington, D.C. 20433 (202) 477-1234; *World Development Indicators.*

SYRIAN ARAB REPUBLIC - EGG PRODUCTION AND CONSUMPTION -See SYRIAN ARAB REPUBLIC - DAIRY PRODUCTS

SYRIAN ARAB REPUBLIC - ELECTRICITY

Central Intelligence Agency, Washington, D.C. 20505 (703) 482-1100, www.cia.gov; *The World Factbook.*

M.E. Sharpe, 80 Business Park Drive, Armonk, New York 10504 (800) 541-6563; *The Illustrated Book of World Rankings.*

Penn Well Publishing Company, 1421 South Sheridan Road, P.O. Box 1260, Tulsa, Oklahoma 74101 (800) 752-9764; *International Energy Statistics Sourcebook.*

St. Martin's Press, Inc., 175 Fifth Avenue, New York, New York 10010 (800) 221-7945; *The Statesman's Year-Book.*

Statistical Office of the United Nations, Publishing Service, New York, New York 10017 (800) 253-9646; *Human Development Report;* and *Statistical Yearbook.*

SYRIAN ARAB REPUBLIC - EMPLOYMENT

Economic Commission for Western Asia, Post Office Box 27, Baghdad, Iraq; *Statistical Abstract of Western Asia.*

Euromonitor International, Inc., 122 South Michigan Avenue, Suite 1200, Chicago, Illinois 60603 (800) 577-EURO; *International Marketing Data and Statistics.*

Federal Statistical Office, Gustav-Stresemann-Ring 11, D-6200 Wiesbaden, Germany; *Syrien.*

International Labour Office, I.L.O. Publications, 1828 L Street, NW, Suite 801, Washington, D.C. 20036 (301) 638-3152; *Yearbook of Labour Statistics.*

M.E. Sharpe, 80 Business Park Drive, Armonk, New York 10504 (800) 541-6563; *The Illustrated Book of World Rankings.*

Statistical Office of the United Nations, Publishing Service, New York, New York

10017 (800) 253-9646; *Bulletin of Industrial Statistics for the Arab Countries;* and *Statistical Yearbook.*

SYRIAN ARAB REPUBLIC - ENERGY

Economic Commission for Western Asia, Post Office Box 27, Baghdad, Iraq; *Statistical Abstract of Western Asia.*

Euromonitor International, Inc., 122 South Michigan Avenue, Suite 1200, Chicago, Illinois 60603 (800) 577-EURO; *International Marketing Data and Statistics; World Marketing Data and Statistics;* and *The World Economic Factbook.*

Food and Agricultural Organization of the United Nations (FAO) Via delle Terme di Caracalla, 00100 Rome, Italy (Telephone Number in U.S. (202) 653-2400); *The State of Food and Agriculture.*

M.E. Sharpe, 80 Business Park Drive, Armonk, New York 10504 (800) 541-6563; *The Illustrated Book of World Rankings.*

Penn Well Publishing Company, 1421 South Sheridan Road, P.O. Box 1260, Tulsa, Oklahoma 74101 (800) 752-9764; *International Energy Statistics Sourcebook.*

St. Martin's Press, Inc., 175 Fifth Avenue, New York, New York 10010 (800) 221-7945; *The Statesman's Year-Book.*

Statistical Office of the United Nations, Publishing Service, New York, New York 10017 (800) 253-9646; *Energy Statistics Yearbook; Human Development Report; Statistical Yearbook;* and *World Statistics Pocketbook.*

The World Bank, 1818 H Street, NW, Washington, D.C. 20433 (202) 477-1234; *The World Bank Atlas.*

SYRIAN ARAB REPUBLIC - ENVIRONMENT

Economist Intelligence Unit, 111 West 57th Street, New York, New York 10019 (800) 938-4685; *Syria Country Report.*

Statistical Office of the United Nations, Publishing Service, New York, New York 10017 (800) 253-9646; *World Statistics Pocketbook.*

SYRIAN ARAB REPUBLIC - EXCHANGE RATES

Central Intelligence Agency, Washington, D.C. 20505 (703) 482-1100, www.cia.gov; *The World Factbook.*

Economic Commission for Western Asia, Post Office Box 27, Baghdad, Iraq; *Statistical Abstract of Western Asia.*

Euromonitor International, Inc., 122 South Michigan Avenue, Suite 1200,

Chicago, Illinois 60603 (800) 577-EURO; *International Marketing Data and Statistics;* and *The World Economic Factbook.*

Europa Publications Limited, 18 Bedford Square, London, WC1B 3JN, England; *The Europa World Year Book.*

International Monetary Fund, 700 Nineteenth Street, NW, Washington, D.C. 20431 (202) 623-7000; *International Financial Statistics.*

Statistical Office of the United Nations, Publishing Service, New York, New York 10017 (800) 253-9646; *Bulletin of Industrial Statistics for the Arab Countries; Statistical Yearbook;* and *World Statistics Pocketbook.*

SYRIAN ARAB REPUBLIC - EXCISE TAXES - See SYRIAN ARAB REPUBLIC - TAXATION

SYRIAN ARAB REPUBLIC - EXPORTS

Central Intelligence Agency, Washington, D.C. 20505 (703) 482-1100, www.cia.gov; *The World Factbook.*

Economic Commission for Western Asia, Post Office Box 27, Baghdad, Iraq; *Statistical Abstract of Western Asia.*

The Economist Intelligence Unit, 111 West 57th Street, New York, New York 10019 (800) 938-4685; *Syria Country Report;* and *The World Market Atlas.*

Euromonitor International, Inc., 122 South Michigan Avenue, Suite 1200, Chicago, Illinois 60603 (800) 577-EURO; *International Marketing Data and Statistics;* and *The World Economic Factbook.*

Europa Publications Limited, 18 Bedford Square, London, WC1B 3JN, England; *The Europa World Year Book.*

Food and Agricultural Organization of the United Nations (FAO) Via delle Terme di Caracalla, 00100 Rome, Italy (Telephone Number in U.S. (202) 653-2400); *The State of Food and Agriculture.*

International Monetary Fund, 700 Nineteenth Street, NW, Washington, D.C. 20431 (202) 623-7000; *Direction of Trade Statistics; Government Finance Statistics Yearbook;* and *International Financial Statistics.*

St. Martin's Press, Inc., 175 Fifth Avenue, New York, New York 10010 (800) 221-7945; *The Statesman's Year-Book.*

Statistical Office of the United Nations, Publishing Service, New York, New York 10017 (800) 253-9646; *Bulletin of Industrial Statistics for the Arab Countries.*

United Nations Conference on Trade and Development (UNCTAD), New York,

New York 10017 (800) 253-9646; *Handbook of International Trade and Development Statistics.*

The World Bank, 1818 H Street, NW, Washington, D.C. 20433 (202) 477-1234; *World Development Indicators.*

SYRIAN ARAB REPUBLIC - EXTERNAL INDEBTEDNESS

The World Bank, 1818 H Street, NW, Washington, D.C. 20433 (202) 477-1234; *World Development Indicators.*

SYRIAN ARAB REPUBLIC - EXTERNAL TRADE

Euromonitor International, Inc., 122 South Michigan Avenue, Suite 1200, Chicago, Illinois 60603 9800) 577-EURO; *World Marketing Data and Statistics.*

Food and Agricultural Organization of the United Nations (FAO) Via delle Terme di Caracalla, 00100 Rome, Italy (Telephone Number in U.S. (202) 653-2400); *The State of Food and Agriculture;* and *Trade Yearbook.*

Statistical Office of the United Nations, Publishing Service, New York, New York 10017 (800) 253-9646; *Statistical Yearbook.*

SYRIAN ARAB REPUBLIC - FABRIC PRODUCTION - See SYRIAN ARAB REPUBLIC - TEXTILE INDUSTRY

SYRIAN ARAB REPUBLIC - FARM CROPS - See SYRIAN ARAB REPUBLIC - CROPS

SYRIAN ARAB REPUBLIC - FEMALE WORKING POPULATION - See SYRIAN ARAB REPUBLIC - EMPLOYMENT

SYRIAN ARAB REPUBLIC - FERTILITY RATES

Central Intelligence Agency, Washington, D.C. 20505 (703) 482-1100, www.cia.gov; *The World Factbook.*

M.E. Sharpe, 80 Business Park Drive, Armonk, New York 10504 (800) 541-6563; *The Illustrated Book of World Rankings.*

Statistical Office of the United Nations, Publishing Service, New York, New York 10017 (800) 253-9646; *Human Development Report.*

The World Bank, 1818 H Street, NW, Washington, D.C. 20433 (202) 477-1234; *The World Bank Atlas;* and *World Development Indicators.*

SYRIAN ARAB REPUBLIC - FERTILIZER

Food and Agricultural Organization of the United Nations (FAO) Via delle Terme

di Caracalla, 00100 Rome, Italy (Telephone Number in U.S. (202) 653-2400); *The State of Food and Agriculture.*

Statistical Office of the United Nations, Publishing Service, New York, New York 10017 (800) 253-9646; *Statistical Yearbook.*

SYRIAN ARAB REPUBLIC - FETAL MORTALITY - See SYRIAN ARAB REPUBLIC - MORTALITY

SYRIAN ARAB REPUBLIC - FILM - See SYRIAN ARAB REPUBLIC - MOTION PICTURES

SYRIAN ARAB REPUBLIC - FINANCE

Economic Commission for Western Asia, Post Office Box 27, Baghdad, Iraq; *Statistical Abstract of Western Asia.*

Economist Intelligence Unit, 111 West 57th Street, New York, New York 10019 (800) 938-4685; *Syria Country Report.*

Europa Publications Limited, 18 Bedford Square, London, WC1B 3JN, England; *The Europa World Year Book.*

Federal Statistical Office, Gustav-Stresemann - Ring 11, D-6200, Wiesbaden, Germany; *Syrien.*

International Monetary Fund, 700 Nineteenth Street, NW, Washington, D.C. 20431 (202) 623-7000; *International Financial Statistics.*

M.E. Sharpe, 80 Business Park Drive, Armonk, New York 10504 (800) 541-6563; *The Illustrated Book of World Rankings.*

St. Martin's Press, Inc., 175 Fifth Avenue, New York, New York 10010 (800) 221-7945; *The Statesman's Year-Book.*

SYRIAN ARAB REPUBLIC - FISHERIES

Economic Commission for Western Asia, Post Office Box 27, Baghdad, Iraq; *Statistical Abstract of Western Asia.*

Europa Publications Limited, 18 Bedford Square, London, WC1B 3JN, England; *The Europa World Year Book.*

Federal Statistical Office, Gustav-Stresemann - Ring 11, D-6200, Wiesbaden, Germany; *Syrien.*

Food and Agricultural Organization of the United Nations (FAO) Via delle Terme di Caracalla, 00100 Rome, Italy (Telephone Number in U.S. (202) 653-2400); *The State of Food and Agriculture;* and *Yearbook of Fishery Statistics.*

M.E. Sharpe, 80 Business Park Drive, Armonk, New York 10504 (800) 541-6563; *The Illustrated Book of World Rankings.*

St. Martin's Press, Inc., 175 Fifth Avenue, New York, New York 10010 (800) 221-7945; *The Statesman's Year-Book.*

Statistical Office of the United Nations, Publishing Service, New York, New York 10017 (800) 253-9646; *Statistical Yearbook.*

United Nations Conference on Trade and Development, Central Statistical Service, Palais des Nations, Geneva, Switzerland (Telephone in U.S. (800) 253-9646); *UNCTAD Commodity Yearbook.*

SYRIAN ARAB REPUBLIC - FLOUR PRODUCTION

Statistical Office of the United Nations, Publishing Service, New York, New York 10017 (800) 253-9646; *Statistical Yearbook.*

SYRIAN ARAB REPUBLIC - FOOD

Food and Agricultural Organization of the United Nations (FAO) Via delle Terme di Caracalla, 00100 Rome, Italy (Telephone Number in U.S. (202) 653-2400); *Production Yearbook;* and *The State of Food and Agriculture.*

Statistical Office of the United Nations, Publishing Service, New York, New York 10017 (800) 253-9646; *Human Development Report.*

United Nations Conference on Trade and Development, Central Statistical Service, Palais des Nations, Geneva, Switzerland (Telephone in U.S. (800) 253-9646); *UNCTAD Commodity Yearbook.*

SYRIAN ARAB REPUBLIC - FOREIGN DEBT

St. Martin's Press, Inc., 175 Fifth Avenue, New York, New York 10010 (800) 221-7945; *The Statesman's Year-Book.*

SYRIAN ARAB REPUBLIC - FOREIGN TRADE

Economic Commission for Western Asia, Post Office Box 27, Baghdad, Iraq; *Statistical Abstract of Western Asia.*

Economist Intelligence Unit, 111 West 57th Street, New York, New York 10019 (800) 938-4685; *Syria Country Report.*

Euromonitor International, Inc., 122 South Michigan Avenue, Suite 1200, Chicago, Illinois 60603 (800) 577-EURO; *International Marketing Data and Statistics;* and *The World Economic Factbook.*

Europa Publications Limited, 18 Bedford Square, London, WC1B 3JN, England; *The Europa World Year Book.*

Federal Statistical Office, Gustav-Stresemann - Ring 11, D-6200, Wiesbaden, Germany; *Syrien.*

Food and Agricultural Organization of the United Nations (FAO) Via delle Terme di Caracalla, 00100 Rome, Italy (Telephone Number in U.S. (202) 653-2400); *The State of Food and Agriculture.*

M.E. Sharpe, 80 Business Park Drive, Armonk, New York 10504 (800) 541-6563; *The Illustrated Book of World Rankings.*

St. Martin's Press, Inc., 175 Fifth Avenue, New York, New York 10010 (800) 221-7945; *The Statesman's Year-Book.*

Statistical Office of the United Nations, Publishing Service, New York, New York 10017 (800) 253-9646; *Bulletin of Industrial Statistics for the Arab Countries; International Trade Statistics Yearbook;* and *Statistical Yearbook.*

United Nations Conference on Trade and Development, Central Statistical Service, Palais des Nations, Geneva, Switzerland (Telephone in U.S. (800) 253-9646); *UNCTAD Commodity Yearbook.*

The World Bank, 1818 H Street, NW, Washington, D.C. 20433 (202) 477-1234; *World Development Indicators.*

SYRIAN ARAB REPUBLIC - FORESTRY AND FOREST PRODUCTS

Europa Publications Limited, 18 Bedford Square, London, WC1B 3JN, England; *The Europa World Year Book.*

Federal Statistical Office, Gustav-Stresemann - Ring 11, D-6200, Wiesbaden, Germany; *Syrien.*

Food and Agricultural Organization of the United Nations (FAO) Via delle Terme di Caracalla, 00100 Rome, Italy (Telephone Number in U.S. (202) 653-2400); *The State of Food and Agriculture.*

M.E. Sharpe, 80 Business Park Drive, Armonk, New York 10504 (800) 541-6563; *The Illustrated Book of World Rankings.*

St. Martin's Press, Inc., 175 Fifth Avenue, New York, New York 10010 (800) 221-7945; *The Statesman's Year-Book.*

Statistical Office of the United Nations, Publishing Service, New York, New York 10017 (800) 253-9646; *Statistical Yearbook.*

United Nations Conference on Trade and Development, Central Statistical Service, Palais des Nations, Geneva, Switzerland (Telephone in U.S. (800) 253-9646); *UNCTAD Commodity Yearbook.*

United Nations Educational, Scientific and Cultural Organization (UNESCO), 7 Place de Fontenoy, F-75700 Paris, France (Telephone Number in U.S. (212) 963-5981); *Statistical Yearbook.*

SYRIAN ARAB REPUBLIC - GAS PRODUCTION - See SYRIAN ARAB REPUBLIC - MINING AND MINERAL PRODUCTS

SYRIAN ARAB REPUBLIC - GENERAL INDUSTRIAL STATISTICS - See SYRIAN ARAB REPUBLIC - INDUSTRY

SYRIAN ARAB REPUBLIC - GENERAL MORTALITY - See SYRIAN ARAB REPUBLIC - MORTALITY

SYRIAN ARAB REPUBLIC - GEOGRAPHIC DATA

M.E. Sharpe, 80 Business Park Drive, Armonk, New York 10504 (800) 541-6563; *The Illustrated Book of World Rankings.*

SYRIAN ARAB REPUBLIC - GOATS - See SYRIAN ARAB REPUBLIC - LIVESTOCK AND POULTRY

SYRIAN ARAB REPUBLIC - GOLD HOLDINGS

International Monetary Fund, 700 Nineteenth Street, NW, Washington, D.C. 20431 (202) 623-7000; *International Financial Statistics.*

Statistical Office of the United Nations, Publishing Service, New York, New York 10017 (800) 253-9646; *Statistical Yearbook.*

The World Bank, 1818 H Street, NW, Washington, D.C. 20433 (202) 477-1234; *World Development Indicators.*

SYRIAN ARAB REPUBLIC - GOLD PRODUCTION AND CONSUMPTION - See SYRIAN ARAB REPUBLIC - MINING AND MINERAL PRODUCTS

SYRIAN ARAB REPUBLIC - GOVERNMENT

Central Intelligence Agency, Washington, D.C. 20505 (703) 482-1100, www.cia.gov; *The World Factbook.*

Economic Commission for Western Asia, Post Office Box 27, Baghdad, Iraq; *Statistical Abstract of Western Asia.*

Europa Publications Limited, 18 Bedford Square, London, WC1B 3JN, England; *The Europa World Year Book.*

International Monetary Fund, 700 Nineteenth Street, NW, Washington, D.C. 20431 (202) 623-7000; *Government Finance Statistics Yearbook.*

St. Martin's Press, Inc., 175 Fifth Avenue, New York, New York 10010 (800) 221-7945; *The Statesman's Year-Book.*

Statistical Office of the United Nations, Publishing Service, New York, New York

10017 (800) 253-9646; *National Accounts Statistics;* and *Statistical Yearbook.*

The World Bank, 1818 H Street, NW, Washington, D.C. 20433 (202) 477-1234; *World Development Indicators.*

SYRIAN ARAB REPUBLIC - GRAIN PRODUCTION - See SYRIAN ARAB REPUBLIC - CROPS

SYRIAN ARAB REPUBLIC - GRANTS

International Monetary Fund, 700 Nineteenth Street, NW, Washington, D.C. 20431 (202) 623-7000; *Government Finance Statistics Yearbook.*

SYRIAN ARAB REPUBLIC - GROSS DOMESTIC PRODUCT

Economic Commission for Western Asia, Post Office Box 27, Baghdad, Iraq; *Statistical Abstract of Western Asia.*

The Economist Intelligence Unit, 111 West 57th Street, New York, New York 10019 (800) 938-4685; *Syria Country Report;* and *The World Market Atlas.*

Euromonitor International, Inc., 122 South Michigan Avenue, Suite 1200, Chicago, Illinois 60603 (800) 577-EURO; *International Marketing Data and Statistics;* and *The World Economic Factbook.*

Europa Publications Limited, 18 Bedford Square, London, WC1B 3JN, England; *The Europa World Year Book.*

M.E. Sharpe, 80 Business Park Drive, Armonk, New York 10504 (800) 541-6563; *The Illustrated Book of World Rankings.*

Statistical Office of the United Nations, Publishing Service, New York, New York 10017 (800) 253-9646; *Bulletin of Industrial Statistics for the Arab Countries; Human Development Report; National Accounts Statistics;* and *Statistical Yearbook.*

The World Bank, 1818 H Street, NW, Washington, D.C. 20433 (202) 477-1234; *World Development Indicators.*

SYRIAN ARAB REPUBLIC - GROSS NATIONAL PRODUCT

Euromonitor International, Inc., 122 South Michigan Avenue, Suite 1200, Chicago, Illinois 60603 (800) 577-EURO; *International Marketing Data and Statistics.*

St. Martin's Press, Inc., 175 Fifth Avenue, New York, New York 10010 (800) 221-7945; *The Statesman's Year-Book.*

U.S. Arms Control and Disarmament Agency, 320 Twenty-first Street, NW, Washington, D.C. 20451 (202) 647-8677; *World Military Expenditures and Arms*

Transfers.

The World Bank, 1818 H Street, NW, Washington, D.C. 20433 (202) 477-1234; *The World Bank Atlas;* and *World Development Indicators.*

SYRIAN ARAB REPUBLIC - GROUNDNUT PRODUCTION

Statistical Office of the United Nations, Publishing Service, New York, New York 10017 (800) 253-9646; *Statistical Yearbook.*

SYRIAN ARAB REPUBLIC - HEALTH

Economic Commission for Western Asia, Post Office Box 27, Baghdad, Iraq; *Statistical Abstract of Western Asia.*

Euromonitor International, Inc., 122 South Michigan Avenue, Suite 1200, Chicago, Illinois 60603 9800) 577-EURO; *World Marketing Data and Statistics.*

Federal Statistical Office, Gustav-Stresemann-Ring 11, D-6200 Wiesbaden, Germany; *Syrien.*

M.E. Sharpe, 80 Business Park Drive, Armonk, New York 10504 (800) 541-6563; *The Illustrated Book of World Rankings.*

St. Martin's Press, Inc., 175 Fifth Avenue, New York, New York 10010 (800) 221-7945; *The Statesman's Year-Book.*

Statistical Office of the United Nations, Publishing Service, New York, New York 10017 (800) 253-9646; *Human Development Report;* and *Statistical Yearbook.*

United Nations Children's Fund (UNICEF), 3 United Nations Plaza, New York, New York 10017 (800) 253-9646; *State of the World's Children.*

World Health Organization, Office of Publications, 20 Avenue Appia, CH-1211 Geneva 27, Switzerland (Telephone Number in U.S. (518) 436-9686); *World Health Statistics Annual.*

SYRIAN ARAB REPUBLIC - HEALTH EXPENDITURES

International Monetary Fund, 700 Nineteenth Street, NW, Washington, D.C. 20431 (202) 623-7000; *Government Finance Statistics Yearbook.*

SYRIAN ARAB REPUBLIC - HIGHWAYS

Central Intelligence Agency, Washington, D.C. 20505 (703) 482-1100, www.cia.gov; *The World Factbook.*

Economic Commission for Western Asia, Post Office Box 27, Baghdad, Iraq; *Statistical Abstract of Western Asia.*

International Road Federation, 2600 Virginia Avenue, NW, Washington, D.C. 20037 (202) 338-4641; *World Road Statistics.*

St. Martin's Press, Inc., 175 Fifth Avenue, New York, New York 10010 (800) 221-7945; *The Statesman's Year-Book.*

SYRIAN ARAB REPUBLIC - HORSES - See SYRIAN ARAB REPUBLIC - LIVESTOCK AND POULTRY

SYRIAN ARAB REPUBLIC - HOURS OF WORK - See SYRIAN ARAB REPUBLIC - EMPLOYMENT

SYRIAN ARAB REPUBLIC - HOUSING AND HOUSING UNITS

Euromonitor International, Inc., 122 South Michigan Avenue, Suite 1200, Chicago, Illinois 60603 9800) 577-EURO; *World Marketing Data and Statistics.*

M.E. Sharpe, 80 Business Park Drive, Armonk, New York 10504 (800) 541-6563; *The Illustrated Book of World Rankings.*

SYRIAN ARAB REPUBLIC - HOUSING EXPENDITURES

International Monetary Fund, 700 Nineteenth Street, NW, Washington, D.C. 20431 (202) 623-7000; *Government Finance Statistics Yearbook.*

SYRIAN ARAB REPUBLIC - ILLITERATE POPULATION

Central Intelligence Agency, Washington, D.C. 20505 (703) 482-1100, www.cia.gov; *The World Factbook.*

The Economist Intelligence Unit, 111 West 57th Street, New York, New York 10019 (800) 938-4685; *The World Market Atlas.*

Euromonitor International, Inc., 122 South Michigan Avenue, Suite 1200, Chicago, Illinois 60603 (800) 577-EURO; *The World Economic Factbook.*

Statistical Office of the United Nations, Publishing Service, New York, New York 10017 (800) 253-9646; *Human Development Report.*

United Nations Educational, Scientific and Cultural Organization (UNESCO), 7 Place de Fontenoy, F-75700 Paris, France (Telephone Number in U.S. (212) 963-5981); *Statistical Yearbook.*

SYRIAN ARAB REPUBLIC - IMPORTS

Central Intelligence Agency, Washington, D.C. 20505 (703) 482-1100, www.cia.gov; *The World Factbook.*

Economic Commission for Western Asia, Post Office Box 27, Baghdad, Iraq; *Statistical Abstract of Western Asia.*

The Economist Intelligence Unit, 111 West 57th Street, New York, New York 10019 (800) 938-4685; *Syria Country Report;* and *The World Market Atlas.*

Euromonitor International, Inc., 122 South Michigan Avenue, Suite 1200, Chicago, Illinois 60603 (800) 577-EURO; *International Marketing Data and Statistics;* and *The World Economic Factbook.*

Europa Publications Limited, 18 Bedford Square, London, WC1B 3JN, England; *The Europa World Year Book.*

Food and Agricultural Organization of the United Nations (FAO) Via delle Terme di Caracalla, 00100 Rome, Italy (Telephone Number in U.S. (202) 653-2400); *The State of Food and Agriculture.*

International Monetary Fund, 700 Nineteenth Street, NW, Washington, D.C. 20431 (202) 623-7000; *Direction of Trade Statistics; International Financial Statistics;* and *Government Finance Statistics Yearbook.*

St. Martin's Press, Inc., 175 Fifth Avenue, New York, New York 10010 (800) 221-7945; *The Statesman's Year-Book.*

Statistical Office of the United Nations, Publishing Service, New York, New York 10017 (800) 253-9646; *Bulletin of Industrial Statistics for the Arab Countries.*

United Nations Conference on Trade and Development (UNCTAD), New York, New York 10017 (800) 253-9646; *Handbook of International Trade and Development Statistics.*

The World Bank, 1818 H Street, NW, Washington, D.C. 20433 (202) 477-1234; *World Development Indicators.*

SYRIAN ARAB REPUBLIC - INCOME TAXES - See SYRIAN ARAB REPUBLIC - TAXATION

SYRIAN ARAB REPUBLIC - INDUSTRY

Central Intelligence Agency, Washington, D.C. 20505 (703) 482-1100, www.cia.gov; *The World Factbook.*

Economist Intelligence Unit, 111 West 57th Street, New York, New York 10019 (800) 938-4685; *Syria Country Report.*

Euromonitor International, Inc., 122 South Michigan Avenue, Suite 1200, Chicago, Illinois 60603 (800) 577-EURO; *International Marketing Data and Statistics; World Marketing Data and Statistics;* and *The World Economic Factbook.*

Europa Publications Limited, 18 Bedford Square, London, WC1B 3JN, England; *The Europa World Year Book.*

Federal Statistical Office, Gustav-Stresemann - Ring 11, D-6200, Wiesbaden, Germany; *Syrien.*

International Labour Office, I.L.O. Publications, 1828 L Street, NW, Suite 801, Washington, D.C. 20036 (301) 638-3152; *Yearbook of Labour Statistics.*

M.E. Sharpe, 80 Business Park Drive, Armonk, New York 10504 (800) 541-6563; *The Illustrated Book of World Rankings.*

St. Martin's Press, Inc., 175 Fifth Avenue, New York, New York 10010 (800) 221-7945; *The Statesman's Year-Book.*

Statistical Office of the United Nations, Publishing Service, New York, New York 10017 (800) 253-9646; *Bulletin of Industrial Statistics for the Arab Countries; Industrial Commodity Statistics Yearbook;* and *Statistical Yearbook.*

The World Bank, 1818 H Street, NW, Washington, D.C. 20433 (202) 477-1234; *World Development Indicators.*

SYRIAN ARAB REPUBLIC - INFANT AND MATERNAL MORTALITY - See SYRIAN ARAB REPUBLIC - MORTALITY

SYRIAN ARAB REPUBLIC - INTERNATIONAL LIQUIDITY

International Monetary Fund, 700 Nineteenth Street, NW, Washington, D.C. 20431 (202) 623-7000; *International Financial Statistics.*

SYRIAN ARAB REPUBLIC - INTERNATIONAL RESERVES EXCLUDING GOLD

Statistical Office of the United Nations, Publishing Service, New York, New York 10017 (800) 253-9646; *Statistical Yearbook.*

The World Bank, 1818 H Street, NW, Washington, D.C. 20433 (202) 477-1234; *World Development Indicators.*

SYRIAN ARAB REPUBLIC - IRON ORE PRODUCTION AND CONSUMPTION - See SYRIAN ARAB REPUBLIC - MINING AND MINERAL PRODUCTS

SYRIAN ARAB REPUBLIC - IRRIGATION

Euromonitor International, Inc., 122 South Michigan Avenue, Suite 1200, Chicago, Illinois 60603 (800) 577-EURO; *International Marketing Data and Statistics.*

SYRIAN ARAB REPUBLIC - LABOR

Central Intelligence Agency,

Washington, D.C. 20505 (703) 482-1100, www.cia.gov; *The World Factbook.*

Economic Commission for Western Asia, Post Office Box 27, Baghdad, Iraq; *Statistical Abstract of Western Asia.*

Euromonitor International, Inc., 122 South Michigan Avenue, Suite 1200, Chicago, Illinois 60603 (800) 577-EURO; *International Marketing Data and Statistics;* and *World Marketing Data and Statistics.*

Europa Publications Limited, 18 Bedford Square, London, WC1B 3JN, England; *The Europa World Year Book.*

Food and Agricultural Organization of the United Nations (FAO) Via delle Terme di Caracalla, 00100 Rome, Italy (Telephone Number in U.S. (202) 653-2400); *The State of Food and Agriculture.*

International Labour Office, I.L.O. Publications, 1828 L Street, NW, Suite 801, Washington, D.C. 20036 (301) 638-3152; *Yearbook of Labour Statistics.*

M.E. Sharpe, 80 Business Park Drive, Armonk, New York 10504 (800) 541-6563; *The Illustrated Book of World Rankings.*

St. Martin's Press, Inc., 175 Fifth Avenue, New York, New York 10010 (800) 221-7945; *The Statesman's Year-Book.*

Statistical Office of the United Nations, Publishing Service, New York, New York 10017 (800) 253-9646; *Human Development Report.*

The World Bank, 1818 H Street, NW, Washington, D.C. 20433 (202) 477-1234; *The World Bank Atlas;* and *World Development Indicators.*

SYRIAN ARAB REPUBLIC - LAND USE

Central Intelligence Agency, Washington, D.C. 20505 (703) 482-1100, www.cia.gov; *The World Factbook.*

Economic Commission for Western Asia, Post Office Box 27, Baghdad, Iraq; *Statistical Abstract of Western Asia.*

Euromonitor International, Inc., 122 South Michigan Avenue, Suite 1200, Chicago, Illinois 60603 (800) 577-EURO; *International Marketing Data and Statistics.*

Food and Agricultural Organization of the United Nations (FAO), Via delle Terme di Caracalla, 00100 Rome, Italy (Telephone Number in U.S. (202) 653-2400); *Production Yearbook.*

SYRIAN ARAB REPUBLIC - LIBRARIES

M.E. Sharpe, 80 Business Park Drive,

Armonk, New York 10504 (800) 541-6563; *The Illustrated Book of World Rankings.*

United Nations Educational, Scientific and Cultural Organization (UNESCO), 7 Place de Fontenoy, F-75700 Paris, France (Telephone Number in U.S. (212) 963-5981); *Statistical Yearbook.*

SYRIAN ARAB REPUBLIC - LIFE EXPECTANCY

Central Intelligence Agency, Washington, D.C. 20505 (703) 482-1100, www.cia.gov; *The World Factbook.*

Euromonitor International, Inc., 122 South Michigan Avenue, Suite 1200, Chicago, Illinois 60603 (800) 577-EURO; *The World Economic Factbook.*

St. Martin's Press, Inc., 175 Fifth Avenue, New York, New York 10010 (800) 221-7945; *The Statesman's Year-Book.*

Statistical Office of the United Nations, Publishing Service, New York, New York 10017 (800) 253-9646; *Human Development Report;* and *World Statistics Pocketbook.*

The World Bank, 1818 H Street, NW, Washington, D.C. 20433 (202) 477-1234; *The World Bank Atlas.*

SYRIAN ARAB REPUBLIC - LITERACY RATE

Euromonitor International, Inc., 122 South Michigan Avenue, Suite 1200, Chicago, Illinois 60603 9800) 577-EURO; *World Marketing Data and Statistics.*

SYRIAN ARAB REPUBLIC - LIVESTOCK AND POULTRY

Economic Commission for Western Asia, Post Office Box 27, Baghdad, Iraq; *Statistical Abstract of Western Asia.*

Euromonitor International, Inc., 122 South Michigan Avenue, Suite 1200, Chicago, Illinois 60603 (800) 577-EURO; *International Marketing Data and Statistics.*

Europa Publications Limited, 18 Bedford Square, London, WC1B 3JN, England; *The Europa World Year Book.*

Food and Agricultural Organization of the United Nations (FAO), Via delle Terme di Caracalla, 00100 Rome, Italy (Telephone Number in U.S. (202) 653-2400); *Production Yearbook;* and *The State of Food and Agriculture.*

M.E. Sharpe, 80 Business Park Drive, Armonk, New York 10504 (800) 541-6563; *The Illustrated Book of World Rankings.*

St. Martin's Press, Inc., 175 Fifth Avenue, New York, New York 10010 (800)

221-7945; *The Statesman's Year-Book.*

Statistical Office of the United Nations, Publishing Service, New York, New York 10017 (800) 253-9646; *Statistical Yearbook.*

United Nations Conference on Trade and Development, Central Statistical Service, Palais des Nations, Geneva, Switzerland (Telephone in U.S. (800) 253-9646); *UNCTAD Commodity Yearbook.*

SYRIAN ARAB REPUBLIC - LIVING LEVELS - See SYRIAN ARAB REPUBLIC - LIFE EXPECTANCY

SYRIAN ARAB REPUBLIC - MAIL - NUMBER OF PIECES SENT OR RECEIVED

Statistical Office of the United Nations, Publishing Service, New York, New York 10017 (800) 253-9646; *Statistical Yearbook.*

SYRIAN ARAB REPUBLIC - MANUFACTURING

M.E. Sharpe, 80 Business Park Drive, Armonk, New York 10504 (800) 541-6563; *The Illustrated Book of World Rankings.*

Statistical Office of the United Nations, Publishing Service, New York, New York 10017 (800) 253-9646; *Bulletin of Industrial Statistics for the Arab Countries;* and *Statistical Yearbook.*

The World Bank, 1818 H Street, NW, Washington, D.C. 20433 (202) 477-1234; *World Development Indicators.*

SYRIAN ARAB REPUBLIC - MARRIAGE RATES

Europa Publications Limited, 18 Bedford Square, London, WC1B 3JN, England; *The Europa World Year Book.*

M.E. Sharpe, 80 Business Park Drive, Armonk, New York 10504 (800) 541-6563; *The Illustrated Book of World Rankings.*

Statistical Office of the United Nations, Publishing Service, New York, New York 10017 (800) 253-9646; *Demographic Yearbook;* and *Statistical Yearbook.*

SYRIAN ARAB REPUBLIC - MEAT PRODUCTION - See SYRIAN ARAB REPUBLIC - LIVESTOCK AND POULTRY

SYRIAN ARAB REPUBLIC - MERCHANT SHIPPING

Economic Commission for Western Asia, Post Office Box 27, Baghdad, Iraq; *Statistical Abstract of Western Asia.*

Europa Publications Limited, 18 Bedford Square, London, WC1B 3JN, England; *The Europa World Year Book.*

Lloyd's Register of Shipping, 17 Battery Place, New York, New York 10004 (212) 425-8050; *Register of Ships.*

United Nations Educational, Scientific and Cultural Organization (UNESCO), 7 Place de Fontenoy, F-75700 Paris, France (Telephone Number in U.S. (212) 963-5981); *Statistical Yearbook.*

U.S. Department of Transportation, Maritime Administration, 400 Seventh Street, SW, Washington, D.C. 20590 (202) 366-5807, www.marad.dot.gov; *A Statistical Analysis of the World's Merchant Fleets.*

SYRIAN ARAB REPUBLIC - MILITARY

Central Intelligence Agency, Washington, D.C. 20505 (703) 482-1100, www.cia.gov; *The World Factbook.*

Euromonitor International, Inc., 122 South Michigan Avenue, Suite 1200, Chicago, Illinois 60603 9800) 577-EURO; *World Marketing Data and Statistics.*

The International Institute for Strategic Studies, 23 Tavistock Street, London WC2E 7NQ, England 44 171 3797676; *The Military Balance.*

International Monetary Fund, 700 Nineteenth Street, NW, Washington, D.C. 20431 (202) 623-7000; *Government Finance Statistics Yearbook.*

St. Martin's Press, Inc., 175 Fifth Avenue, New York, New York 10010 (800) 221-7945; *The Statesman's Year-Book.*

Statistical Office of the United Nations, Publishing Service, New York, New York 10017 (800) 253-9646; *Human Development Report.*

U.S. Arms Control and Disarmament Agency, 320 Twenty-first Street, NW, Washington, D.C. 20451 (202) 647-8677; *World Military Expenditures and Arms Transfers.*

SYRIAN ARAB REPUBLIC - MILK PRODUCTION - See SYRIAN ARAB REPUBLIC - DAIRY PRODUCTS

SYRIAN ARAB REPUBLIC - MINING AND MINERAL PRODUCTS

Economic Commission for Western Asia, Post Office Box 27, Baghdad, Iraq; *Statistical Abstract of Western Asia.*

Europa Publications Limited, 18 Bedford Square, London, WC1B 3JN, England; *The Europa World Year Book.*

M.E. Sharpe, 80 Business Park Drive, Armonk, New York 10504 (800) 541-6563; *The Illustrated Book of World Rankings.*

Penn Well Publishing Company, 1421 South Sheridan Road, P.O. Box 1260, Tulsa, Oklahoma 74101 (800) 752-9764; *International Energy Statistics Sourcebook.*

St. Martin's Press, Inc., 175 Fifth Avenue, New York, New York 10010 (800) 221-7945; *The Statesman's Year-Book.*

Statistical Office of the United Nations, Publishing Service, New York, New York 10017 (800) 253-9646; *Bulletin of Industrial Statistics for the Arab Countries;* and *Statistical Yearbook.*

United Nations Conference on Trade and Development, Central Statistical Service, Palais des Nations, Geneva, Switzerland (Telephone in U.S. (800) 253-9646); *UNCTAD Commodity Yearbook.*

SYRIAN ARAB REPUBLIC - MONEY EXCHANGE RATES - See SYRIAN ARAB REPUBLIC - EXCHANGE RATES

SYRIAN ARAB REPUBLIC - MONEY RESERVES

Euromonitor International, Inc., 122 South Michigan Avenue, Suite 1200, Chicago, Illinois 60603 (800) 577-EURO; *International Marketing Data and Statistics.*

SYRIAN ARAB REPUBLIC - MONEY SUPPLY

Economic Commission for Western Asia, Post Office Box 27, Baghdad, Iraq; *Statistical Abstract of Western Asia.*

Economist Intelligence Unit, 111 West 57th Street, New York, New York 10019 (800) 938-4685; *Syria Country Report.*

Euromonitor International, Inc., 122 South Michigan Avenue, Suite 1200, Chicago, Illinois 60603 (800) 577-EURO; *International Marketing Data and Statistics.*

Europa Publications Limited, 18 Bedford Square, London, WC1B 3JN, England; *The Europa World Year Book.*

Federal Statistical Office, Gustav-Stresemann - Ring 11, D-6200, Wiesbaden, Germany; *Syrien.*

International Monetary Fund, 700 Nineteenth Street, NW, Washington, D.C. 20431 (202) 623-7000; *International Financial Statistics.*

Statistical Office of the United Nations, Publishing Service, New York, New York 10017 (800) 253-9646; *Statistical Yearbook.*

The World Bank, 1818 H Street, NW, Washington, D.C. 20433 (202) 477-1234; *World Development Indicators.*

SYRIAN ARAB REPUBLIC - MONUMENTS AND HISTORICAL SITES

United Nations Educational, Scientific and Cultural Organization (UNESCO), 7 Place de Fontenoy, F-75700 Paris, France (Telephone Number in U.S. (212) 963-5981); *Statistical Yearbook.*

SYRIAN ARAB REPUBLIC - MORTALITY

Central Intelligence Agency, Washington, D.C. 20505 (703) 482-1100, www.cia.gov; *The World Factbook.*

Euromonitor International, Inc., 122 South Michigan Avenue, Suite 1200, Chicago, Illinois 60603 (800) 577-EURO; *International Marketing Data and Statistics;* and *The World Economic Factbook.*

St. Martin's Press, Inc., 175 Fifth Avenue, New York, New York 10010 (800) 221-7945; *The Statesman's Year-Book.*

Statistical Office of the United Nations, Publishing Service, New York, New York 10017 (800) 253-9646; *Demographic Yearbook; Human Development Report; Statistical Yearbook;* and *World Statistics Pocketbook*

United Nations Children's Fund (UNICEF), 3 United Nations Plaza, New York, New York 10017 (800) 253-9646; *State of the World's Children.*

The World Bank, 1818 H Street, NW, Washington, D.C. 20433 (202) 477-1234; *The World Bank Atlas;* and *World Development Indicators.*

World Health Organization, Office of Publications, 20 Avenue Appia, CH-1211 Geneva 27, Switzerland (Telephone Number in U.S. (518) 436-9686); *World Health Statistics Annual.*

SYRIAN ARAB REPUBLIC - MOTION PICTURES

St. Martin's Press, Inc., 175 Fifth Avenue, New York, New York 10010 (800) 221-7945; *The Statesman's Year-Book.*

Statistical Office of the United Nations, Publishing Service, New York, New York 10017 (800) 253-9646; *Statistical Yearbook.*

United Nations Educational, Scientific and Cultural Organization (UNESCO), 7 Place de Fontenoy, F-75700 Paris, France (Telephone Number in U.S. (212) 963-5981); *Statistical Yearbook.*

SYRIAN ARAB REPUBLIC - MOTOR VEHICLES IN USE

Economic Commission for Western Asia, Post Office Box 27, Baghdad, Iraq; *Statistical Abstract of Western Asia.*

Europa Publications Limited, 18 Bedford Square, London, WC1B 3JN,

England; *The Europa World Year Book.*

International Road Federation, 2600 Virginia Avenue, NW, Washington, D.C. 20037 (202) 338-4641; *World Road Statistics.*

Statistical Office of the United Nations, Publishing Service, New York, New York 10017 (800) 253-9646; *Statistical Yearbook.*

SYRIAN ARAB REPUBLIC - MOTOR VEHICLES TAXES - See SYRIAN ARAB REPUBLIC - TAXATION

SYRIAN ARAB REPUBLIC - MULES - See SYRIAN ARAB REPUBLIC - LIVESTOCK AND POULTRY

SYRIAN ARAB REPUBLIC - MUSEUMS

M.E. Sharpe, 80 Business Park Drive, Armonk, New York 10504 (800) 541-6563; *The Illustrated Book of World Rankings.*

United Nations Educational, Scientific and Cultural Organization (UNESCO), 7 Place de Fontenoy, F-75700 Paris, France (Telephone Number in U.S. (212) 963-5981); *Statistical Yearbook.*

SYRIAN ARAB REPUBLIC - NATALITY - See SYRIAN ARAB REPUBLIC - BIRTH RATE

SYRIAN ARAB REPUBLIC - NATIONAL ACCOUNTS

Economic Commission for Western Asia, Post Office Box 27, Baghdad, Iraq; *Statistical Abstract of Western Asia.*

Europa Publications Limited, 18 Bedford Square, London, WC1B 3JN, England; *The Europa World Year Book.*

Federal Statistical Office, Gustav-Stresemann - Ring 11, D-6200, Wiesbaden, Germany; *Syrien.*

Statistical Office of the United Nations, Publishing Service, New York, New York 10017 (800) 253-9646; *National Accounts Statistics;* and *Statistical Yearbook.*

SYRIAN ARAB REPUBLIC - NATIONAL INCOME

M.E. Sharpe, 80 Business Park Drive, Armonk, New York 10504 (800) 541-6563; *The Illustrated Book of World Rankings.*

Statistical Office of the United Nations, Publishing Service, New York, New York 10017 (800) 253-9646; *National Accounts Statistics;* and *Statistical Yearbook.*

SYRIAN ARAB REPUBLIC - NATIONAL PRODUCT

M.E. Sharpe, 80 Business Park Drive, Armonk, New York 10504 (800) 541-6563;

The Illustrated Book of World Rankings.

Statistical Office of the United Nations, Publishing Service, New York, New York 10017 (800) 253-9646; *Statistical Yearbook.*

SYRIAN ARAB REPUBLIC - NATURAL GAS PRODUCTION - See SYRIAN ARAB REPUBLIC - MINING AND MINERAL PRODUCTS

M.E. Sharpe, 80 Business Park Drive, Armonk, New York 10504 (800) 541-6563; *The Illustrated Book of World Rankings.*

SYRIAN ARAB REPUBLIC - NEWSPAPER PRODUCTION AND CONSUMPTION - SYRIAN ARAB REPUBLIC - FORESTRY AND FOREST PRODUCTS

SYRIAN ARAB REPUBLIC - NEWSPRINT PRODUCTION AND CONSUMPTION - See SYRIAN ARAB REPUBLIC - FORESTRY AND FOREST PRODUCTS

SYRIAN ARAB REPUBLIC - OATS PRODUCTION - See SYRIAN ARAB REPUBLIC - CROPS

SYRIAN ARAB REPUBLIC - OCCUPATIONS - See SYRIAN ARAB REPUBLIC - LABOR

SYRIAN ARAB REPUBLIC - PAPER - See SYRIAN ARAB REPUBLIC - FORESTRY AND FOREST PRODUCTS

SYRIAN ARAB REPUBLIC - PATENTS, TRADEMARKS AND SERVICE MARKS

Statistical Office of the United Nations, Publishing Service, New York, New York 10017 (800) 253-9646; *Statistical Yearbook.*

SYRIAN ARAB REPUBLIC - PEANUT PRODUCTION - See SYRIAN ARAB REPUBLIC - CROPS

SYRIAN ARAB REPUBLIC - PERIODICALS

United Nations Educational, Scientific and Cultural Organization (UNESCO), 7 Place de Fontenoy, F-75700 Paris, France (Telephone Number in U.S. (212) 963-5981); *Statistical Yearbook.*

SYRIAN ARAB REPUBLIC - PESTICIDE USE

Food and Agricultural Organization of the United Nations (FAO) Via delle Terme di Caracalla, 00100 Rome, Italy (Telephone Number in U.S. (202) 653-2400); *The State of Food and Agriculture.*

SYRIAN ARAB REPUBLIC - PETROLEUM INDUSTRY

Food and Agricultural Organization of the United Nations (FAO) Via delle Terme di Caracalla, 00100 Rome, Italy (Telephone Number in U.S. (202) 653-2400); *The State of Food and Agriculture.*

M.E. Sharpe, 80 Business Park Drive, Armonk, New York 10504 (800) 541-6563; *The Illustrated Book of World Rankings.*

Penn Well Publishing Company, 1421 South Sheridan Road, P.O. Box 1260, Tulsa, Oklahoma 74101 (800) 752-9764; *International Energy Statistics Sourcebook.*

St. Martin's Press, Inc., 175 Fifth Avenue, New York, New York 10010 (800) 221-7945; *The Statesman's Year-Book.*

Statistical Office of the United Nations, Publishing Service, New York, New York 10017 (800) 253-9646; *Statistical Yearbook.*

United Nations Conference on Trade and Development, Central Statistical Service, Palais des Nations, Geneva, Switzerland (Telephone in U.S. (800) 253-9646); *UNCTAD Commodity Yearbook.*

SYRIAN ARAB REPUBLIC - PHOSPHATE ROCK PRODUCTION - See SYRIAN ARAB REPUBLIC - MINING AND MINERAL PRODUCTS

SYRIAN ARAB REPUBLIC - PIGS - See SYRIAN ARAB REPUBLIC - LIVESTOCK AND POULTRY

SYRIAN ARAB REPUBLIC - POPULATION

Central Intelligence Agency, Washington, D.C. 20505 (703) 482-1100, www.cia.gov; *The World Factbook.*

Economic Commission for Western Asia, Post Office Box 27, Baghdad, Iraq; *Statistical Abstract of Western Asia.*

The Economist Intelligence Unit, 111 West 57th Street, New York, New York 10019 (800) 938-4685; *Syria Country Report;* and *The World Market Atlas.*

Euromonitor International, Inc., 122 South Michigan Avenue, Suite 1200, Chicago, Illinois 60603 (800) 577-EURO; *International Marketing Data and Statistics; Middle East Economic Handbook;* and *The World Economic Factbook.*

Europa Publications Limited, 18 Bedford Square, London, WC1B 3JN, England; *The Europa World Year Book.*

Federal Statistical Office, Gustav-Stresemann-Ring 11, D-6200 Wiesbaden, Germany; *Syrien.*

Food and Agricultural Organization of the United Nations (FAO), Via delle Terme di Caracalla, 00100 Rome, Italy (Telephone Number in U.S. (202) 653-2400); *Production Yearbook.*

International Labour Office, I.L.O. Publications, 1828 L Street, NW, Suite 801, Washington, D.C. 20036 (301) 638-

3152; *Yearbook of Labour Statistics.*

M.E. Sharpe, 80 Business Park Drive, Armonk, New York 10504 (800) 541-6563; *The Illustrated Book of World Rankings.*

St. Martin's Press, Inc., 175 Fifth Avenue, New York, New York 10010 (800) 221-7945; *The Statesman's Year-Book.*

Statistical Office of the United Nations, Publishing Service, New York, New York 10017 (800) 253-9646; *Demographic Yearbook; Human Development Report; Statistical Yearbook;* and *World Statistics Pocketbook.*

United Nations Educational, Scientific and Cultural Organization (UNESCO), 7 Place de Fontenoy, F-75700 Paris, France (Telephone Number in U.S. (212) 963-5981); *Statistical Yearbook.*

U.S. Arms Control and Disarmament Agency, 320 Twenty-first Street, NW, Washington, D.C. 20451 (202) 647-8677; *World Military Expenditures and Arms Transfers.*

The World Bank, 1818 H Street, NW, Washington, D.C. 20433 (202) 477-1234; *The World Bank Atlas.*

World Health Organization, Office of Publications, 20 Avenue Appia, CH-1211 Geneva 27, Switzerland (Telephone Number in U.S. (518) 436-9686); *World Health Statistics Annual.*

SYRIAN ARAB REPUBLIC - POST OFFICES

M.E. Sharpe, 80 Business Park Drive, Armonk, New York 10504 (800) 541-6563; *The Illustrated Book of World Rankings.*

SYRIAN ARAB REPUBLIC - POTATO PRODUCTION - See SYRIAN ARAB REPUBLIC - CROPS

SYRIAN ARAB REPUBLIC - POWER PRODUCTION INDUSTRY

Statistical Office of the United Nations, Publishing Service, New York, New York 10017 (800) 253-9646; *Statistical Yearbook.*

SYRIAN ARAB REPUBLIC - PRICES

Economic Commission for Western Asia, Post Office Box 27, Baghdad, Iraq; *Statistical Abstract of Western Asia.*

Federal Statistical Office, Gustav-Stresemann - Ring 11, D-6200, Wiesbaden, Germany; *Syrien.*

Food and Agricultural Organization of the United Nations (FAO), Via delle Terme di Caracalla, 00100 Rome, Italy (Telephone Number in U.S. (202) 653-2400); *Production Yearbook;* and *The State of*

Food and Agriculture.

International Labour Office, I.L.O. Publications, 1828 L Street, NW, Suite 801, Washington, D.C. 20036 (301) 638-3152; *Yearbook of Labour Statistics.*

International Monetary Fund, 700 Nineteenth Street, NW, Washington, D.C. 20431 (202) 623-7000; *International Financial Statistics.*

M.E. Sharpe, 80 Business Park Drive, Armonk, New York 10504 (800) 541-6563; *The Illustrated Book of World Rankings.*

SYRIAN ARAB REPUBLIC - PRINTING AND WRITING PAPER - See SYRIAN ARAB REPUBLIC - FORESTRY AND FOREST PRODUCTS

SYRIAN ARAB REPUBLIC - PRODUCTION

M.E. Sharpe, 80 Business Park Drive, Armonk, New York 10504 (800) 541-6563; *The Illustrated Book of World Rankings.*

SYRIAN ARAB REPUBLIC - PRODUCTIVITY

Euromonitor International, Inc., 122 South Michigan Avenue, Suite 1200, Chicago, Illinois 60603 (800) 577-EURO; *International Marketing Data and Statistics.*

SYRIAN ARAB REPUBLIC - PROPERTY TAXES - See SYRIAN ARAB REPUBLIC - TAXATION

SYRIAN ARAB REPUBLIC - PUBLIC FINANCE - See SYRIAN ARAB REPUBLIC - FINANCE

SYRIAN ARAB REPUBLIC - RADIO BROADCASTING - See SYRIAN ARAB REPUBLIC - BROADCASTING

SYRIAN ARAB REPUBLIC - RADIO RECEIVERS

St. Martin's Press, Inc., 175 Fifth Avenue, New York, New York 10010 (800) 221-7945; *The Statesman's Year-Book.*

SYRIAN ARAB REPUBLIC - RAILWAYS

Europa Publications Limited, 18 Bedford Square, London, WC1B 3JN, England; *The Europa World Year Book.*

Jane's Information Group, Sentinel House, 163 Brighton Road, Coulsdon, Surrey CR5 2NH, England (Telephone Number in U.S. (703) 683-3700); *Jane's World Railways.*

St. Martin's Press, Inc., 175 Fifth Avenue, New York, New York 10010 (800) 221-7945; *The Statesman's Year-Book.*

Statistical Office of the United Nations,

Publishing Service, New York, New York 10017 (800) 253-9646; *Statistical Yearbook.*

SYRIAN ARAB REPUBLIC - RELIGION

Central Intelligence Agency, Washington, D.C. 20505 (703) 482-1100, www.cia.gov; *The World Factbook.*

M.E. Sharpe, 80 Business Park Drive, Armonk, New York 10504 (800) 541-6563; *The Illustrated Book of World Rankings.*

St. Martin's Press, Inc., 175 Fifth Avenue, New York, New York 10010 (800) 221-7945; *The Statesman's Year-Book.*

SYRIAN ARAB REPUBLIC - RENT PRICES

International Labour Office, I.L.O. Publications, 1828 L Street, NW, Suite 801, Washington, D.C. 20036 (301) 638-3152; *Yearbook of Labour Statistics.*

SYRIAN ARAB REPUBLIC - RETAIL TRADE

Euromonitor International, Inc., 122 South Michigan Avenue, Suite 1200, Chicago, Illinois 60603 9800) 577-EURO; *World Marketing Data and Statistics.*

SYRIAN ARAB REPUBLIC - RUBBER PRODUCTION AND CONSUMPTION

M.E. Sharpe, 80 Business Park Drive, Armonk, New York 10504 (800) 541-6563; *The Illustrated Book of World Rankings.*

SYRIAN ARAB REPUBLIC - SALT PRODUCTION - See SYRIAN ARAB REPUBLIC - MINING AND MINERAL PRODUCTS

SYRIAN ARAB REPUBLIC - SAWNWOOD PRODUCTION - See SYRIAN ARAB REPUBLIC - FORESTRY AND FOREST PRODUCTS

SYRIAN ARAB REPUBLIC - SCIENTISTS, TECHNICIANS AND ENGINEERS

Statistical Office of the United Nations, Publishing Service, New York, New York 10017 (800) 253-9646; *Statistical Yearbook.*

SYRIAN ARAB REPUBLIC - SENIOR CITIZENS

M.E. Sharpe, 80 Business Park Drive, Armonk, New York 10504 (800) 541-6563; *The Illustrated Book of World Rankings.*

SYRIAN ARAB REPUBLIC - SHEEP - See SYRIAN ARAB REPUBLIC - LIVESTOCK AND POULTRY

SYRIAN ARAB REPUBLIC - SILVER PRODUCTION AND CONSUMPTION - See SYRIAN ARAB REPUBLIC - MINING AND MINERAL PRODUCTS

SYRIAN ARAB REPUBLIC - SOCIAL DATA

M.E. Sharpe, 80 Business Park Drive, Armonk, New York 10504 (800) 541-6563; *The Illustrated Book of World Rankings.*

Statistical Office of the United Nations, Publishing Service, New York, New York 10017 (800) 253-9646; *World Statistics Pocketbook.*

SYRIAN ARAB REPUBLIC - SOCIAL SECURITY

International Monetary Fund, 700 Nineteenth Street, NW, Washington, D.C. 20431 (202) 623-7000; *Government Finance Statistics Yearbook.*

Statistical Office of the United Nations, Publishing Service, New York, New York 10017 (800) 253-9646; *National Accounts Statistics.*

SYRIAN ARAB REPUBLIC - STATE BUDGET REVENUE AND EXPENDITURES

Euromonitor International, Inc., 122 South Michigan Avenue, Suite 1200, Chicago, Illinois 60603 (800) 577-EURO; *International Marketing Data and Statistics.*

SYRIAN ARAB REPUBLIC - STEEL - See SYRIAN ARAB REPUBLIC - MINING AND MINERAL PRODUCTS

SYRIAN ARAB REPUBLIC - STOCKS - COMMODITY - MARKET PRICE - INDEX

Food and Agricultural Organization of the United Nations (FAO) Via delle Terme di Caracalla, 00100 Rome, Italy (Telephone Number in U.S. (202) 653-2400); *The State of Food and Agriculture.*

SYRIAN ARAB REPUBLIC - SUGAR PRODUCTION AND CONSUMPTION - See SYRIAN ARAB REPUBLIC - CROPS

SYRIAN ARAB REPUBLIC - TAXATION

Europa Publications Limited, 18 Bedford Square, London, WC1B 3JN, England; *The Europa World Year Book.*

International Monetary Fund, 700 Nineteenth Street, NW, Washington, D.C. 20431 (202) 623-7000; *Government Finance Statistics Yearbook.*

International Road Federation, 2600 Virginia Avenue, NW, Washington, D.C. 20037 (202) 338-4641; *World Road Statistics.*

The World Bank, 1818 H Street, NW, Washington, D.C. 20433 (202) 477-1234; *World Development Indicators.*

SYRIAN ARAB REPUBLIC - TEA CONSUMPTION

Statistical Office of the United Nations, Publishing Service, New York, New York 10017 (800) 253-9646; *Statistical Yearbook.*

SYRIAN ARAB REPUBLIC - TELEGRAPH SERVICE

Statistical Office of the United Nations, Publishing Service, New York, New York 10017 (800) 253-9646; *Statistical Yearbook.*

SYRIAN ARAB REPUBLIC - TELEPHONES IN USE

American Telephone and Telegraph Company, 26 Parsippany Road, Whippany, New Jersey 07981 (800) 222-0300; *The World's Telephones.*

Central Intelligence Agency, Washington, D.C. 20505 (703) 482-1100, www.cia.gov; *The World Factbook.*

St. Martin's Press, Inc., 175 Fifth Avenue, New York, New York 10010 (800) 221-7945; *The Statesman's Year-Book.*

Statistical Office of the United Nations, Publishing Service, New York, New York 10017 (800) 253-9646; *Statistical Yearbook;* and *World Statistics Pocketbook.*

SYRIAN ARAB REPUBLIC - TELEVISION BROADCASTING - See SYRIAN ARAB REPUBLIC - BROADCASTING

SYRIAN ARAB REPUBLIC - TELEVISION RECEIVER PRODUCTION

Statistical Office of the United Nations, Publishing Service, New York, New York 10017 (800) 253-9646; *Statistical Yearbook.*

SYRIAN ARAB REPUBLIC - TEXTILE INDUSTRY

M.E. Sharpe, 80 Business Park Drive, Armonk, New York 10504 (800) 541-6563; *The Illustrated Book of World Rankings.*

St. Martin's Press, Inc., 175 Fifth Avenue, New York, New York 10010 (800) 221-7945; *The Statesman's Year-Book.*

Statistical Office of the United Nations, Publishing Service, New York, New York 10017 (800) 253-9646; *Statistical Yearbook.*

United Nations Conference on Trade and Development, Central Statistical Service, Palais des Nations, Geneva, Switzerland (Telephone in U.S. (800) 253-9646); *UNCTAD Commodity Yearbook.*

SYRIAN ARAB REPUBLIC - THEATRE

United Nations Educational, Scientific and Cultural Organization (UNESCO), 7 Place de Fontenoy, F-75700 Paris, France (Telephone Number in U.S. (212) 963-5981); *Statistical Yearbook.*

SYRIAN ARAB REPUBLIC - TIN - INDUSTRIAL CONSUMPTION - See SYRIAN ARAB REPUBLIC - MINING AND MINERAL PRODUCTS

SYRIAN ARAB REPUBLIC - TOBACCO PRODUCTION

M.E. Sharpe, 80 Business Park Drive, Armonk, New York 10504 (800) 541-6563; *The Illustrated Book of World Rankings.*

Statistical Office of the United Nations, Publishing Service, New York, New York 10017 (800) 253-9646; *Statistical Yearbook.*

SYRIAN ARAB REPUBLIC - TOURISM

Economic Commission for Western Asia, Post Office Box 27, Baghdad, Iraq; *Statistical Abstract of Western Asia.*

Euromonitor International, Inc., 122 South Michigan Avenue, Suite 1200, Chicago, Illinois 60603 (800) 577-EURO; *The World Economic Factbook;* and *World Marketing Data and Statistics.*

Europa Publications Limited, 18 Bedford Square, London, WC1B 3JN, England; *The Europa World Year Book.*

Federal Statistical Office, Gustav-Stresemann - Ring 11, D-6200, Wiesbaden, Germany; *Syrien.*

M.E. Sharpe, 80 Business Park Drive, Armonk, New York 10504 (800) 541-6563; *The Illustrated Book of World Rankings.*

St. Martin's Press, Inc., 175 Fifth Avenue, New York, New York 10010 (800) 221-7945; *The Statesman's Year-Book.*

Statistical Office of the United Nations, Publishing Service, New York, New York 10017 (800) 253-9646; *Statistical Yearbook.*

World Tourism Organization, Calle Capitan Haya 42, E-28020 Madrid, Spain; *Yearbook of Tourism Statistics.*

SYRIAN ARAB REPUBLIC - TRACTORS IN USE

Statistical Office of the United Nations, Publishing Service, New York, New York 10017 (800) 253-9646; *Statistical Yearbook.*

SYRIAN ARAB REPUBLIC - TRADE - See SYRIAN ARAB REPUBLIC - FOREIGN TRADE

SYRIAN ARAB REPUBLIC - TRADEMARKS AND SERVICE MARKS - See SYRIAN ARAB REPUBLIC - PATENTS, TRADEMARKS AND SERVICE MARKS

SYRIAN ARAB REPUBLIC - TRANSPORTATION AND

COMMUNICATIONS

Central Intelligence Agency, Washington, D.C. 20505 (703) 482-1100, www.cia.gov; *The World Factbook*.

Economic Commission for Western Asia, Post Office Box 27, Baghdad, Iraq; *Statistical Abstract of Western Asia*.

Euromonitor International, Inc., 122 South Michigan Avenue, Suite 1200, Chicago, Illinois 60603 (800) 577-EURO; *International Marketing Data and Statistics; and World Marketing Data and Statistics*.

Europa Publications Limited, 18 Bedford Square, London, WC1B 3JN, England; *The Europa World Year Book*.

Federal Statistical Office, Gustav-Stresemann - Ring 11, D-6200, Wiesbaden, Germany; *Syrien*.

M.E. Sharpe, 80 Business Park Drive, Armonk, New York 10504 (800) 541-6563; *The Illustrated Book of World Rankings*.

St. Martin's Press, Inc., 175 Fifth Avenue, New York, New York 10010 (800) 221-7945; *The Statesman's Year-Book*.

Statistical Office of the United Nations, Publishing Service, New York, New York 10017 (800) 253-9646; *Human Development Report*.

SYRIAN ARAB REPUBLIC - UNEMPLOYMENT

Central Intelligence Agency, Washington, D.C. 20505 (703) 482-1100, www.cia.gov; *The World Factbook*.

Euromonitor International, Inc., 122 South Michigan Avenue, Suite 1200, Chicago, Illinois 60603 (800) 577-EURO; *International Marketing Data and Statistics*.

International Labour Office, I.L.O. Publications, 1828 L Street, NW, Suite 801, Washington, D.C. 20036 (301) 638-3152; *Yearbook of Labour Statistics*.

Statistical Office of the United Nations, Publishing Service, New York, New York 10017 (800) 253-9646; *Statistical Yearbook*.

SYRIAN ARAB REPUBLIC - VITAL STATISTICS

Euromonitor International, Inc., 122 South Michigan Avenue, Suite 1200, Chicago, Illinois 60603 (800) 577-EURO; *International Marketing Data and Statistics*.

St. Martin's Press, Inc., 175 Fifth Avenue, New York, New York 10010 (800) 221-7945; *The Statesman's Year-Book*.

Statistical Office of the United Nations, Publishing Service, New York, New York 10017 (800) 253-9646; *Statistical Yearbook*.

World Health Organization, Office of Publications, 20 Avenue Appia, CH-1211 Geneva 27, Switzerland (Telephone Number in U.S. (518) 436-9686); *World Health Statistics Annual*.

SYRIAN ARAB REPUBLIC - WAGES

Federal Statistical Office, Gustav-Stresemann - Ring 11, D-6200, Wiesbaden, Germany; *Syrien*.

International Labour Office, I.L.O. Publications, 1828 L Street, NW, Suite 801, Washington, D.C. 20036 (301) 638-3152; *Yearbook of Labour Statistics*.

Statistical Office of the United Nations, Publishing Service, New York, New York 10017 (800) 253-9646; *Statistical Yearbook*.

SYRIAN ARAB REPUBLIC - WEATHER - See SYRIAN ARAB REPUBLIC - CLIMATE

SYRIAN ARAB REPUBLIC - WELFARE

International Monetary Fund, 700 Nineteenth Street, NW, Washington, D.C. 20431 (202) 623-7000; *Government Finance Statistics Yearbook*.

SYRIAN ARAB REPUBLIC - WHEAT PRODUCTION AND PRICES - See SYRIAN ARAB REPUBLIC - CROPS

SYRIAN ARAB REPUBLIC - WHOLESALE PRICES

International Monetary Fund, 700 Nineteenth Street, NW, Washington, D.C. 20431 (202) 623-7000; *International Financial Statistics.*

Statistical Office of the United Nations, Publishing Service, New York, New York 10017 (800) 253-9646; *Statistical Yearbook.*

SYRIAN ARAB REPUBLIC - WINE PRODUCTION - See SYRIAN ARAB REPUBLIC - BEVERAGES

SYRIAN ARAB REPUBLIC - WOOL

PRODUCTION - See SYRIAN ARAB REPUBLIC - TEXTILE INDUSTRY

SYRIAN ARAB REPUBLIC - YARN PRODUCTION - See SYRIAN ARAB REPUBLIC - TEXTILE INDUSTRY

T

Taiwan - National Statistical Office

Inspectorate General of Customs, Ministry of Finance, 85 Hsim-Hseng South Road, Section 1, Taipei, Republic of China.

Taiwan - Primary Statistics Sources

Council for Economic Planning and Development, Ninth Floor, 87 Nanking East Road, Section 2, Taipei, Republic of China; *Taiwan Statistical Data Book.*

Directorate - General of Budget, Accounting and Statistics, Executive Yuan, Republic of China; *Monthly Bulletin of Statistics; Monthly Statistics of the Republic of China; Republic of China in Figures;* and *Statistical Yearbook of the Republic of China.*

TAIWAN - AGRICULTURE

Council for Economic Planning and Development, Ninth Floor, 87 Nanking East Road, Section 2, Taipei, Republic of China; *Taiwan Statistical Data Book.*

Department of Agriculture and Forestry, Taiwan Provincial Government, Chunghsing Village, Nantou, Nantou Hsien, Taiwan, Republic of China; *Taiwan Agricultural Yearbook.*

Directorate - General of Budget, Accounting and Statistics, Executive Yuan, Republic of China; *Monthly Statistics of the Republic of China;* and *Statistical Yearbook of Republic of China.*

Economist Intelligence Unit, 111 West 57th Street, New York, New York 10019 (800) 938-4685; *Taiwan Country Report.*

Euromonitor International, Inc., 122 South Michigan Avenue, Suite 1200, Chicago, Illinois 60603 (800) 577-EURO; *International Marketing Data and Statistics;* and *World Marketing Data and Statistics.*

Europa Publications Limited, 18 Bedford Square, London, WC1B 3JN, England; *The Europa World Year Book.*

Federal Statistical Office, Gustav - Stresemann - Ring 11, D-6200 Wiesbaden, Germany; *China (Taiwan).*

M.E. Sharpe, 80 Business Park Drive, Armonk, New York 10504 (800) 541-6563; *The Illustrated Book of World Rankings.*

St. Martin's Press, Inc., 175 Fifth Avenue, New York, New York 10010 (800) 221-7945; *The Statesman's Year-Book.*

United Nations Conference on Trade and Development, Central Statistical Service, Palais des Nations, Geneva, Switzerland (Telephone in U.S. (800) 253-9646); *UNCTAD Commodity Yearbook.*

TAIWAN - AIRLINE SERVICE

Council for Economic Planning and Development, Ninth Floor, 87 Nanking East Road, Section 2, Taipei, Republic of China; *Taiwan Statistical Data Book.*

Directorate - General of Budget, Accounting and Statistics, Executive Yuan, The Republic of China; *Monthly Statistics of the Republic of China;* and *Statistical Yearbook of The Republic of China.*

The Economist Intelligence Unit (Asia) Limited, 10th Floor, Luk Kwok Centre, 72 Gloucester Road, Wanchai, Hong Kong (Phone Number in U.S. (800) 938-4685); *Asian Market Atlas.*

Europa Publications Limited, 18 Bedford Square, London, WC1B 3JN, England; *The Europa World Year Book.*

M.E. Sharpe, 80 Business Park Drive, Armonk, New York 10504 (800) 541-6563; *The Illustrated Book of World Rankings.*

St. Martin's Press, Inc., 175 Fifth Avenue, New York, New York 10010 (800) 221-7945; *The Statesman's Year-Book.*

TAIWAN - AIRPORTS

Central Intelligence Agency, Washington, D.C. 20505 (703) 482-1100, www.cia.gov; *The World Factbook.*

TAIWAN - ALUMINUM PRODUCTION AND CONSUMPTION - See TAIWAN - MINING AND MINERAL PRODUCTS

TAIWAN - ANTIMONY AND ANTIMONY ORE - See TAIWAN - MINING AND MINERAL PRODUCTS

TAIWAN - AQUATIC PRODUCTS - WHOLESALE PRICES

Directorate - General of Budget, Accounting and Statistics, Executive Yuan, The Republic of China; *Statistical Yearbook of The Republic of China.*

TAIWAN - AREA AND DENSITY OF POPULATION

Central Intelligence Agency, Washington, D.C. 20505 (703) 482-1100, www.cia.gov; *The World Factbook.*

Council for Economic Planning and Development, Ninth Floor, 87 Nanking East Road, Section 2, Taipei, Republic of China; *Taiwan Statistical Data Book.*

Directorate - General of Budget, Accounting and Statistics, Executive Yuan, Republic of China; *Monthly Statistics of the Republic of China.*

Euromonitor International, Inc., 122 South Michigan Avenue, Suite 1200, Chicago, Illinois 60603 (800) 577-EURO; *International Marketing Data and Statistics;* and *The World Economic Factbook.*

Europa Publications Limited, 18 Bedford Square, London, WC1B 3JN, England; *The Europa World Year Book.*

Federal Statistical Office, Gustav - Stresemann - Ring 11, D-6200 Wiesbaden, Germany; *China (Taiwan).*

M.E. Sharpe, 80 Business Park Drive, Armonk, New York 10504 (800) 541-6563; *The Illustrated Book of World Rankings*.

St. Martin's Press, Inc., 175 Fifth Avenue, New York, New York 10010 (800) 221-7945; *The Statesman's Year-Book*.

TAIWAN - ARMS EXPORTS AND IMPORTS - See TAIWAN - MILITARY

TAIWAN - ASBESTOS PRODUCTION

Council for Economic Planning and Development, Ninth Floor, 87 Nanking East Road, Section 2, Taipei, Republic of China; *Taiwan Statistical Data Book*.

Directorate - General of Budget, Accounting and Statistics, Executive Yuan, The Republic of China; *Statistical Yearbook of The Republic of China*.

TAIWAN - BALANCE OF PAYMENTS

Council for Economic Planning and Development, Ninth Floor, 87 Nanking East Road, Section 2, Taipei, Republic of China; *Taiwan Statistical Data Book*.

Department of Statistics, Ministry of Finance, 2, Aikuo West Road, Taipei, Republic of China; *The Republic of China Monthly of Financial Statistics*.

Directorate - General of Budget, Accounting and Statistics, Executive Yuan, The Republic of China; *Monthly Statistics of the Republic of China; and Statistical Yearbook of The Republic of China*.

Economic Research Department, The Central Bank of China, 2, Roosevelt Road, Section 1, Taipei 10757, Republic of China; *Financial Statistics Monthly Taiwan District, The Republic of China*.

The Economist Intelligence Unit, 111 West 57th Street, New York, New York 10019 (800) 938-4685; *The World Market Atlas*.

Europa Publications Limited, 18 Bedford Square, London, WC1B 3JN, England; *The Europa World Year Book*.

Federal Statistical Office, Gustav - Stresemann - Ring 11, D-6200 Wiesbaden, Germany; *China (Taiwan)*.

United Nations Conference on Trade and Development (UNCTAD), New York, New York 10017 (800) 253-9646; *Handbook of International Trade and Development Statistics*.

TAIWAN - BANKING

Council for Economic Planning and Development, Ninth Floor, 87 Nanking East Road, Section 2, Taipei, Republic of China;

Taiwan Statistical Data Book.

Department of Statistics, Ministry of Finance, 2, Aikuo West Road, Taipei, Republic of China; *The Republic of China Monthly of Financial Statistics*.

Directorate - General of Budget, Accounting and Statistics, Executive Yuan, The Republic of China; *Monthly Statistics of the Republic of China; and Statistical Yearbook of The Republic of China*.

Economic Research Department, The Central Bank of China, 2, Roosevelt Road, Section 1, Taipei 10757, Republic of China; *Financial Statistics Monthly Taiwan District, The Republic of China*.

Euromonitor International, Inc., 122 South Michigan Avenue, Suite 1200, Chicago, Illinois 60603 (800) 577-EURO; *World Marketing Data and Statistics*.

M.E. Sharpe, 80 Business Park Drive, Armonk, New York 10504 (800) 541-6563; *The Illustrated Book of World Rankings*.

St. Martin's Press, Inc., 175 Fifth Avenue, New York, New York 10010 (800) 221-7945; *The Statesman's Year-Book*.

TAIWAN - BARLEY PRODUCTION - See TAIWAN - CROPS

TAIWAN - BAUXITE PRODUCTION AND CONSUMPTION - See TAIWAN - MINING AND MINERAL PRODUCTS

TAIWAN - BEER PRODUCTION - See TAIWAN - BEVERAGES

TAIWAN - BEVERAGES

Council for Economic Planning and Development, Ninth Floor, 87 Nanking East Road, Section 2, Taipei, Republic of China; *Taiwan Statistical Data Book*.

Directorate - General of Budget, Accounting and Statistics, Executive Yuan, The Republic of China; *Statistical Yearbook of The Republic of China*.

M.E. Sharpe, 80 Business Park Drive, Armonk, New York 10504 (800) 541-6563; *The Illustrated Book of World Rankings*.

TAIWAN - BIRTH RATES

Central Intelligence Agency, Washington, D.C. 20505 (703) 482-1100, www.cia.gov; *The World Factbook*.

Council for Economic Planning and Development, Ninth Floor, 87 Nanking East Road, Section 2, Taipei, Republic of China; *Taiwan Statistical Data Book*.

Directorate - General of Budget, Accounting and Statistics, Executive Yuan,

Republic of China; *Monthly Statistics of the Republic of China*.

The Economist Intelligence Unit (Asia) Limited, 10th Floor, Luk Kwok Centre, 72 Gloucester Road, Wanchai, Hong Kong (Phone Number in U.S. (800) 938-4685); *Asian Market Atlas*.

Euromonitor International, Inc., 122 South Michigan Avenue, Suite 1200, Chicago, Illinois 60603 (800) 577-EURO; *International Marketing Data and Statistics; and The World Economic Factbook*.

Europa Publications Limited, 18 Bedford Square, London, WC1B 3JN, England; *The Europa World Year Book*.

M.E. Sharpe, 80 Business Park Drive, Armonk, New York 10504 (800) 541-6563; *The Illustrated Book of World Rankings*.

St. Martin's Press, Inc., 175 Fifth Avenue, New York, New York 10010 (800) 221-7945; *The Statesman's Year-Book*.

TAIWAN - BISMUTH PRODUCTION AND CONSUMPTION - See TAIWAN - MINING AND MINERAL PRODUCTS

TAIWAN - BONDS

Council for Economic Planning and Development, Ninth Floor, 87 Nanking East Road, Section 2, Taipei, Republic of China; *Taiwan Statistical Data Book*.

Department of Statistics, Ministry of Finance, 2, Aikuo West Road, Taipei, Republic of China; *The Republic of China Monthly of Financial Statistics*.

Directorate - General of Budget, Accounting and Statistics, Executive Yuan, The Republic of China; *Monthly Statistics of the Republic of China; and Statistical Yearbook of The Republic of China*.

TAIWAN - BOOK PRODUCTION

Council for Economic Planning and Development, Ninth Floor, 87 Nanking East Road, Section 2, Taipei, Republic of China; *Taiwan Statistical Data Book*.

Directorate - General of Budget, Accounting and Statistics, Executive Yuan, The Republic of China; *Statistical Yearbook of The Republic of China*.

St. Martin's Press, Inc., 175 Fifth Avenue, New York, New York 10010 (800) 221-7945; *The Statesman's Year-Book*.

TAIWAN - BROADCASTING

Billboard Limited, P.O. Box 9027, 1006 AA Amsterdam, The Netherlands (Telephone Number in U.S. (212) 764-7300); *World Radio TV Handbook*.

Central Intelligence Agency, Washington, D.C. 20505 (703) 482-1100, www.cia.gov; *The World Factbook*.

Euromonitor International, Inc., 122 South Michigan Avenue, Suite 1200, Chicago, Illinois 60603 (800) 577-EURO; *World Marketing Data and Statistics*.

M.E. Sharpe, 80 Business Park Drive, Armonk, New York 10504 (800) 541-6563; *The Illustrated Book of World Rankings*.

St. Martin's Press, Inc., 175 Fifth Avenue, New York, New York 10010 (800) 221-7945; *The Statesman's Year-Book*.

TAIWAN - BUDGET ACCOUNTS

Central Intelligence Agency, Washington, D.C. 20505 (703) 482-1100, www.cia.gov; *The World Factbook*.

Council for Economic Planning and Development, Ninth Floor, 87 Nanking East Road, Section 2, Taipei, Republic of China; *Taiwan Statistical Data Book*.

Department of Statistics, Ministry of Finance, 2, Aikuo West Road, Taipei, Republic of China; *The Republic of China Monthly of Financial Statistics*.

Directorate - General of Budget, Accounting and Statistics, Executive Yuan, The Republic of China; *Monthly Statistics of the Republic of China*; and *Statistical Yearbook of The Republic of China*.

Economic Research Department, The Central Bank of China, 2, Roosevelt Road, Section 1, Taipei 10757, Republic of China; *Financial Statistics Monthly Taiwan District, The Republic of China*.

TAIWAN - BUSINESS - COMPANIES BY TYPE OF COMPANY

Council for Economic Planning and Development, Ninth Floor, 87 Nanking East Road, Section 2, Taipei, Republic of China; *Taiwan Statistical Data Book*.

Directorate - General of Budget, Accounting and Statistics, Executive Yuan, The Republic of China; *Statistical Yearbook of The Republic of China*.

TAIWAN - BUTTER PRODUCTION - See TAIWAN - DAIRY PRODUCTS

TAIWAN - CABBAGE PRODUCTION - See TAIWAN - CROPS

TAIWAN - CAPITAL FLOW DISTRIBUTION

Directorate - General of Budget, Accounting and Statistics, Executive Yuan, The Republic of China; *Statistical Yearbook of The Republic of China*.

TAIWAN - CASTOR BEAN PRODUCTION - See TAIWAN - CROPS

TAIWAN - CATTLE - See TAIWAN - LIVESTOCK AND POULTRY

TAIWAN - CAULIFLOWER PRODUCTION - See TAIWAN - CROPS

TAIWAN - CAUSTIC SODA PRODUCTION - See TAIWAN - BEVERAGES

TAIWAN - CEMENT PRODUCTION - See TAIWAN - MINING AND MINERAL PRODUCTS

TAIWAN - CHEESE PRODUCTION AND CONSUMPTION - See TAIWAN - DAIRY PRODUCTS

TAIWAN - CHEMICAL (ORGANIC) PRODUCTION - See TAIWAN - MINING AND MINERAL PRODUCTS

TAIWAN - CHESTNUT PRODUCTION - See TAIWAN - CROPS

TAIWAN - CHICKENS - See TAIWAN - LIVESTOCK AND POULTRY

TAIWAN - CIGARETTE PRODUCTION - See TAIWAN - TOBACCO PRODUCTION

TAIWAN - CLIMATE

M.E. Sharpe, 80 Business Park Drive, Armonk, New York 10504 (800) 541-6563; *The Illustrated Book of World Rankings*.

St. Martin's Press, Inc., 175 Fifth Avenue, New York, New York 10010 (800) 221-7945; *The Statesman's Year-Book*.

TAIWAN - CLOTHING EXPORTS AND IMPORTS - See TAIWAN - TEXTILE INDUSTRY

TAIWAN - COAL PRODUCTION - See TAIWAN - MINING AND MINERAL PRODUCTS

TAIWAN - COFFEE - See TAIWAN - CROPS

TAIWAN - COKE OVEN COKE - See TAIWAN - MINING AND MINERAL PRODUCTS

TAIWAN - COMMERCE

St. Martin's Press, Inc., 175 Fifth Avenue, New York, New York 10010 (800) 221-7945; *The Statesman's Year-Book*.

TAIWAN - COMMUNICATIONS - See TAIWAN - TRANSPORTATION AND COMMUNICATIONS

TAIWAN - CONSTRUCTION INDUSTRY

Council for Economic Planning and Development, Ninth Floor, 87 Nanking East

Road, Section 2, Taipei, Republic of China; *Taiwan Statistical Data Book*.

Directorate - General of Budget, Accounting and Statistics, Executive Yuan, The Republic of China; *Monthly Statistics of the Republic of China*; and *Statistical Yearbook of The Republic of China*.

M.E. Sharpe, 80 Business Park Drive, Armonk, New York 10504 (800) 541-6563; *The Illustrated Book of World Rankings*.

St. Martin's Press, Inc., 175 Fifth Avenue, New York, New York 10010 (800) 221-7945; *The Statesman's Year-Book*.

TAIWAN - CONSUMER PRICE INDEX

Council for Economic Planning and Development, Ninth Floor, 87 Nanking East Road, Section 2, Taipei, Republic of China; *Taiwan Statistical Data Book*.

Department of Statistics, Ministry of Finance, 2, Aikuo West Road, Taipei, Republic of China; *The Republic of China Monthly of Financial Statistics*.

Directorate - General of Budget, Accounting and Statistics, Executive Yuan, The Republic of China; *Monthly Statistics of the Republic of China*; and *Statistical Yearbook of The Republic of China*.

Economic Research Department, The Central Bank of China, 2, Roosevelt Road, Section 1, Taipei 10757, Republic of China; *Financial Statistics Monthly Taiwan District, The Republic of China*.

Europa Publications Limited, 18 Bedford Square, London, WC1B 3JN, England; *The Europa World Year Book*.

Federal Statistical Office, Gustav - Stresemann - Ring 11, D-6200 Wiesbaden, Germany; *China (Taiwan)*.

TAIWAN - CONSUMER PRICES

Euromonitor International, Inc., 122 South Michigan Avenue, Suite 1200, Chicago, Illinois 60603 (800) 577-EURO; *World Marketing Data and Statistics*.

Federal Statistical Office, Gustav - Stresemann - Ring 11, D-6200 Wiesbaden, Germany; *China (Taiwan)*.

TAIWAN - COPPER AND COPPER ORE - See TAIWAN - MINING AND MINERAL PRODUCTS

TAIWAN - CORN PRODUCTION - See TAIWAN - CROPS

TAIWAN - CORPORATE TAXES - See TAIWAN - TAXATION

TAIWAN - COTTON - See TAIWAN - CROPS

TAIWAN - CRIME - ALL TYPES

International Criminal Police Organization (INTERPOL), 50 quai Achille Lignon, F-69006 Lyon, France; *International Crime Statistics.*

Yale University Press, Yale Station, New Haven, Connecticut 06520 (800) 987-7323; *Violence and Crime in Cross-National Perspective.*

TAIWAN - CRIMINAL RESEARCH

Yale University Press, Yale Station, New Haven, Connecticut 06520 (800) 987-7323; *Violence and Crime in Cross-National Perspective.*

TAIWAN - CROPS

Commodity Research Bureau, Inc., 30 South Wacker Drive, Chicago, Illinois 60606 (312) 454-1801; *Commodity Year Book.*

Council for Economic Planning and Development, Ninth Floor, 87 Nanking East Road, Section 2, Taipei, Republic of China; *Taiwan Statistical Data Book.*

Department of Agriculture and Forestry, Taiwan Provincial Government, Chunghsing Village, Nantou, Nantou Hsien, Taiwan, Republic of China; *Taiwan Agricultural Yearbook.*

Directorate - General of Budget, Accounting and Statistics, Executive Yuan, The Republic of China; *Monthly Statistics of the Republic of China;* and *Statistical Yearbook of The Republic of China.*

Europa Publications Limited, 18 Bedford Square, London, WC1B 3JN, England; *The Europa World Year Book.*

Food and Agricultural Organization of the United Nations (FAO), Via delle Terme di Caracalla, 00100 Rome, Italy (Telephone Number in U.S. (202) 653-2400); *Production Yearbook.*

M.E. Sharpe, 80 Business Park Drive, Armonk, New York 10504 (800) 541-6563; *The Illustrated Book of World Rankings.*

St. Martin's Press, Inc., 175 Fifth Avenue, New York, New York 10010 (800) 221-7945; *The Statesman's Year-Book.*

United Nations Conference on Trade and Development, Central Statistical Service, Palais des Nations, Geneva, Switzerland (Telephone in U.S. (800) 253-9646); *UNCTAD Commodity Yearbook.*

TAIWAN - CUSTOMS DUTIES

St. Martin's Press, Inc., 175 Fifth Avenue, New York, New York 10010 (800) 221-7945; *The Statesman's Year-Book.*

TAIWAN - DAIRY PRODUCTS

Commodity Research Bureau, Inc., 30 South Wacker Drive, Chicago, Illinois 60606 (312) 454-1801; *Commodity Year Book.*

Council for Economic Planning and Development, Ninth Floor, 87 Nanking East Road, Section 2, Taipei, Republic of China; *Taiwan Statistical Data Book.*

Department of Agriculture and Forestry, Taiwan Provincial Government, Chunghsing Village, Nantou, Nantou Hsien, Taiwan, Republic of China; *Taiwan Agricultural Yearbook.*

Directorate - General of Budget, Accounting and Statistics, Executive Yuan, The Republic of China; *Monthly Statistics of the Republic of China;* and *Statistical Yearbook of The Republic of China.*

Europa Publications Limited, 18 Bedford Square, London, WC1B 3JN, England; *The Europa World Year Book.*

M.E. Sharpe, 80 Business Park Drive, Armonk, New York 10504 (800) 541-6563; *The Illustrated Book of World Rankings.*

St. Martin's Press, Inc., 175 Fifth Avenue, New York, New York 10010 (800) 221-7945; *The Statesman's Year-Book.*

TAIWAN - DEATH RATE - See TAIWAN - MORTALITY

TAIWAN - DEFENSE EXPENDITURES - See TAIWAN - MILITARY

TAIWAN - DEMOGRAPHY

The Economist Intelligence Unit, 111 West 57th Street, New York, New York 10019 (800) 938-4685; *The World Market Atlas.*

The Economist Intelligence Unit (Asia) Limited, 10th Floor, Luk Kwok Centre, 72 Gloucester Road, Wanchai, Hong Kong (Phone Number in U.S. (800) 938-4685); *Asian Market Atlas.*

Euromonitor International, Inc., 122 South Michigan Avenue, Suite 1200, Chicago, Illinois 60603 (800) 577-EURO; *International Marketing Data and Statistics; World Marketing Data and Statistics;* and *The World Economic Factbook.*

Federal Statistical Office, Gustav - Stresemann - Ring 11, D-6200 Wiesbaden, Germany; *China (Taiwan).*

M.E. Sharpe, 80 Business Park Drive, Armonk, New York 10504 (800) 541-6563; *The Illustrated Book of World Rankings.*

TAIWAN - DEVELOPMENT ASSISTANCE

Directorate - General of Budget, Accounting and Statistics, Executive Yuan, The Republic of China; *Monthly Statistics of the Republic of China;* and *Statistical Yearbook of The Republic of China.*

TAIWAN - DIAMOND PRODUCTION - See TAIWAN - MINING AND MINERAL PRODUCTS

TAIWAN - DISCOUNT RATES - See TAIWAN - BANKING

TAIWAN - DISEASE - See TAIWAN - HEALTH

TAIWAN - DIVORCE RATES

Council for Economic Planning and Development, Ninth Floor, 87 Nanking East Road, Section 2, Taipei, Republic of China; *Taiwan Statistical Data Book.*

Directorate - General of Budget, Accounting and Statistics, Executive Yuan, Republic of China; *Monthly Statistics of the Republic of China.*

M.E. Sharpe, 80 Business Park Drive, Armonk, New York 10504 (800) 541-6563; *The Illustrated Book of World Rankings.*

TAIWAN - ECONOMY

Central Intelligence Agency, Washington, D.C. 20505 (703) 482-1100, www.cia.gov; *The World Factbook.*

Council for Economic Planning and Development, Ninth Floor, 87 Nanking East Road, Section 2, Taipei, Republic of China; *Taiwan Statistical Data Book.*

Department of Statistics, Ministry of Finance, 2, Aikuo West Road, Taipei, Republic of China; *The Republic of China Monthly of Financial Statistics.*

Directorate - General of Budget, Accounting and Statistics, Executive Yuan, Republic of China; *Monthly Statistics of the Republic of China.*

Economic Research Department, The Central Bank of China, 2, Roosevelt Road, Section 1, Taipei 10757, Republic of China; *Financial Statistics Monthly Taiwan District, The Republic of China.*

Economist Intelligence Unit, 111 West 57th Street, New York, New York 10019 (800) 938-4685; *Taiwan Country Report.*

Euromonitor International, Inc., 122 South Michigan Avenue, Suite 1200, Chicago, Illinois 60603 (800) 577-EURO; *International Marketing Data and Statistics; World Marketing Data and Statistics;* and *The World Economic Factbook.*

Europa Publications Limited, 18

Bedford Square, London, WC1B 3JN, England; *The Europa World Year Book.*

Federal Statistical Office, Gustav - Stresemann - Ring 11, D-6200 Wiesbaden, Germany; *China (Taiwan).*

M.E. Sharpe, 80 Business Park Drive, Armonk, New York 10504 (800) 541-6563; *The Illustrated Book of World Rankings.*

St. Martin's Press, Inc., 175 Fifth Avenue, New York, New York 10010 (800) 221-7945; *The Statesman's Year-Book.*

TAIWAN - EDUCATION

Council for Economic Planning and Development, Ninth Floor, 87 Nanking East Road, Section 2, Taipei, Republic of China; *Taiwan Statistical Data Book.*

Directorate - General of Budget, Accounting and Statistics, Executive Yuan, The Republic of China; *Statistical Yearbook of The Republic of China.*

The Economist Intelligence Unit, 111 West 57th Street, New York, New York 10019 (800) 938-4685; *The World Market Atlas.*

The Economist Intelligence Unit (Asia) Limited, 10th Floor, Luk Kwok Centre, 72 Gloucester Road, Wanchai, Hong Kong (Phone Number in U.S. (800) 938-4685); *Asian Market Atlas.*

Euromonitor International, Inc., 122 South Michigan Avenue, Suite 1200, Chicago, Illinois 60603 (800) 577-EURO; *International Marketing Data and Statistics;* and *World Marketing Data and Statistics.*

Europa Publications Limited, 18 Bedford Square, London, WC1B 3JN, England; *The Europa World Year Book.*

Federal Statistical Office, Gustav - Stresemann - Ring 11, D-6200 Wiesbaden, Germany; *China (Taiwan).*

M.E. Sharpe, 80 Business Park Drive, Armonk, New York 10504 (800) 541-6563; *The Illustrated Book of World Rankings.*

Ministry of Education, 5, Chungshan South Road, Taipei, Republic of China; *Educational Statistics of the Republic of China.*

St. Martin's Press, Inc., 175 Fifth Avenue, New York, New York 10010 (800) 221-7945; *The Statesman's Year-Book.*

TAIWAN - EGG PRODUCTION AND CONSUMPTION - See TAIWAN -DAIRY PRODUCTS

TAIWAN - EGGPLANT PRODUCTION - See TAIWAN - CROPS

TAIWAN - ELECTRICITY

Central Intelligence Agency, Washington, D.C. 20505 (703) 482-1100, www.cia.gov; *The World Factbook.*

Council for Economic Planning and Development, Ninth Floor, 87 Nanking East Road, Section 2, Taipei, Republic of China; *Taiwan Statistical Data Book.*

Directorate - General of Budget, Accounting and Statistics, Executive Yuan, The Republic of China; *Statistical Yearbook of The Republic of China.*

M.E. Sharpe, 80 Business Park Drive, Armonk, New York 10504 (800) 541-6563; *The Illustrated Book of World Rankings.*

Penn Well Publishing Company, 1421 South Sheridan Road, P.O. Box 1260, Tulsa, Oklahoma 74101 (800) 752-9764; *International Energy Statistics Sourcebook.*

TAIWAN - EMPLOYMENT

Council for Economic Planning and Development, Ninth Floor, 87 Nanking East Road, Section 2, Taipei, Republic of China; *Taiwan Statistical Data Book.*

Directorate - General of Budget, Accounting and Statistics, Executive Yuan, Republic of China; *Monthly Statistics of the Republic of China;* and *Statistical Yearbook of The Republic of China.*

Euromonitor International, Inc., 122 South Michigan Avenue, Suite 1200, Chicago, Illinois 60603 (800) 577-EURO; *International Marketing Data and Statistics.*

Federal Statistical Office, Gustav - Stresemann - Ring 11, D-6200 Wiesbaden, Germany; *China (Taiwan).*

M.E. Sharpe, 80 Business Park Drive, Armonk, New York 10504 (800) 541-6563; *The Illustrated Book of World Rankings.*

St. Martin's Press, Inc., 175 Fifth Avenue, New York, New York 10010 (800) 221-7945; *The Statesman's Year-Book.*

TAIWAN - ENERGY

Council for Economic Planning and Development, Ninth Floor, 87 Nanking East Road, Section 2, Taipei, Republic of China; *Taiwan Statistical Data Book.*

Directorate - General of Budget, Accounting and Statistics, Executive Yuan, Republic of China; *Monthly Statistics of the Republic of China;* and *Statistical Yearbook of The Republic of China.*

Euromonitor International, Inc., 122 South Michigan Avenue, Suite 1200, Chicago, Illinois 60603 (800) 577-EURO;

International Marketing Data and Statistics; World Marketing Data and Statistics; and *The World Economic Factbook.*

M.E. Sharpe, 80 Business Park Drive, Armonk, New York 10504 (800) 541-6563; *The Illustrated Book of World Rankings.*

Penn Well Publishing Company, 1421 South Sheridan Road, P.O. Box 1260, Tulsa, Oklahoma 74101 (800) 752-9764; *International Energy Statistics Sourcebook.*

St. Martin's Press, Inc., 175 Fifth Avenue, New York, New York 10010 (800) 221-7945; *The Statesman's Year-Book.*

TAIWAN - ENVIRONMENT

Economist Intelligence Unit, 111 West 57th Street, New York, New York 10019 (800) 938-4685; *Taiwan Country Report.*

TAIWAN - EXCHANGE RATES

Central Intelligence Agency, Washington, D.C. 20505 (703) 482-1100, www.cia.gov; *The World Factbook.*

Council for Economic Planning and Development, Ninth Floor, 87 Nanking East Road, Section 2, Taipei, Republic of China; *Taiwan Statistical Data Book.*

Department of Statistics, Ministry of Finance, 2, Aikuo West Road, Taipei, Republic of China; *The Republic of China Monthly of Financial Statistics.*

Directorate - General of Budget, Accounting and Statistics, Executive Yuan, The Republic of China; *Monthly Statistics of the Republic of China;* and *Statistical Yearbook of The Republic of China.*

Economic Research Department, The Central Bank of China, 2, Roosevelt Road, Section 1, Taipei 10757, Republic of China; *Financial Statistics Monthly Taiwan District, The Republic of China.*

The Economist Intelligence Unit (Asia) Limited, 10th Floor, Luk Kwok Centre, 72 Gloucester Road, Wanchai, Hong Kong (Phone Number in U.S. (800) 938-4685); *Asian Market Atlas.*

Euromonitor International, Inc., 122 South Michigan Avenue, Suite 1200, Chicago, Illinois 60603 (800) 577-EURO; *International Marketing Data and Statistics;* and *The World Economic Factbook.*

Europa Publications Limited, 18 Bedford Square, London, WC1B 3JN, England; *The Europa World Year Book.*

Walden Publishing Ltd., Two Market Street, Saffron Walden Essex, CB10 1HZ, England; *The World of Information Asia and Pacific Review.*

TAIWAN - EXPORTS

Central Intelligence Agency, Washington, D.C. 20505 (703) 482-1100, www.cia.gov; *The World Factbook*.

Council for Economic Planning and Development, Ninth Floor, 87 Nanking East Road, Section 2, Taipei, Republic of China; *Taiwan Statistical Data Book*.

Department of Statistics, Ministry of Finance, 2, Aikuo West Road, Taipei, Republic of China; *The Republic of China Monthly of Financial Statistics*.

Directorate - General of Budget, Accounting and Statistics, Executive Yuan, Republic of China; *Monthly Statistics of the Republic of China*.

Economic Research Department, The Central Bank of China, 2, Roosevelt Road, Section 1, Taipei 10757, Republic of China; *Financial Statistics Monthly Taiwan District, The Republic of China*.

The Economist Intelligence Unit, 111 West 57th Street, New York, New York 10019; *Taiwan Country Report;* and *The World Market Atlas*.

The Economist Intelligence Unit (Asia) Limited, 10th Floor, Luk Kwok Centre, 72 Gloucester Road, Wanchai, Hong Kong (Phone Number in U.S. (800) 938-4685); *Asian Market Atlas*.

Euromonitor International, Inc., 122 South Michigan Avenue, Suite 1200, Chicago, Illinois 60603 (800) 577-EURO; *International Marketing Data and Statistics;* and *The World Economic Factbook*.

Europa Publications Limited, 18 Bedford Square, London, WC1B 3JN, England; *The Europa World Year Book*.

St. Martin's Press, Inc., 175 Fifth Avenue, New York, New York 10010 (800) 221-7945; *The Statesman's Year-Book*.

United Nations Conference on Trade and Development (UNCTAD), New York, New York 10017 (800) 253-9646; *Handbook of International Trade and Development Statistics*.

Walden Publishing Ltd., Two Market Street, Saffron Walden Essex, CB10 1HZ, England; *The World of Information Asia and Pacific Review*.

TAIWAN - EXTERNAL INDEBTEDNESS

Council for Economic Planning and Development, Ninth Floor, 87 Nanking East Road, Section 2, Taipei, Republic of China; *Taiwan Statistical Data Book*.

TAIWAN - EXTERNAL TRADE

Council for Economic Planning and Development, Ninth Floor, 87 Nanking East Road, Section 2, Taipei, Republic of China; *Taiwan Statistical Data Book*.

Directorate - General of Budget, Accounting and Statistics, Executive Yuan, The Republic of China; *Monthly Statistics of the Republic of China;* and *Statistical Yearbook of The Republic of China*.

Euromonitor International, Inc., 122 South Michigan Avenue, Suite 1200, Chicago, Illinois 60603 (800) 577-EURO; *World Marketing Data and Statistics*.

TAIWAN - FABRIC PRODUCTION - See TAIWAN - TEXTILE INDUSTRY

TAIWAN - FARM CROPS - See TAIWAN - CROPS

TAIWAN - FEMALE WORKING POPULATION - TAIWAN - EMPLOYMENT

TAIWAN - FERTILITY RATES

Central Intelligence Agency, Washington, D.C. 20505 (703) 482-1100, www.cia.gov; *The World Factbook*.

The Economist Intelligence Unit (Asia) Limited, 10th Floor, Luk Kwok Centre, 72 Gloucester Road, Wanchai, Hong Kong (Phone Number in U.S. (800) 938-4685); *Asian Market Atlas*.

M.E. Sharpe, 80 Business Park Drive, Armonk, New York 10504 (800) 541-6563; *The Illustrated Book of World Rankings*.

TAIWAN - FERTILIZER

Council for Economic Planning and Development, Ninth Floor, 87 Nanking East Road, Section 2, Taipei, Republic of China; *Taiwan Statistical Data Book*.

Department of Agriculture and Forestry, Taiwan Provincial Government, Chunghsing Village, Nantou, Nantou Hsien, Taiwan, Republic of China; *Taiwan Agricultural Yearbook*.

Directorate - General of Budget, Accounting and Statistics, Executive Yuan, The Republic of China; *Monthly Statistics of the Republic of China;* and *Statistical Yearbook of The Republic of China*.

TAIWAN - FETAL MORTALITY - See TAIWAN - MORTALITY

TAIWAN - FIBRE PRODUCTION - See TAIWAN - TEXTILE INDUSTRY

TAIWAN - FINANCE

Economist Intelligence Unit, 111 West 57th Street, New York, New York 10019 (800) 938-4685; *Taiwan Country Report*.

Europa Publications Limited, 18 Bedford Square, London, WC1B 3JN, England; *The Europa World Year Book*.

Federal Statistical Office, Gustav - Stresemann - Ring 11, D-6200 Wiesbaden, Germany; *China (Taiwan)*.

M.E. Sharpe, 80 Business Park Drive, Armonk, New York 10504 (800) 541-6563; *The Illustrated Book of World Rankings*.

St. Martin's Press, Inc., 175 Fifth Avenue, New York, New York 10010 (800) 221-7945; *The Statesman's Year-Book*.

TAIWAN - FINANCIAL INSTITUTIONS

Council for Economic Planning and Development, Ninth Floor, 87 Nanking East Road, Section 2, Taipei, Republic of China; *Taiwan Statistical Data Book*.

Department of Statistics, Ministry of Finance, 2, Aikuo West Road, Taipei, Republic of China; *The Republic of China Monthly of Financial Statistics*.

Directorate - General of Budget, Accounting and Statistics, Executive Yuan, The Republic of China; *Monthly Statistics of the Republic of China;* and *Statistical Yearbook of The Republic of China*.

Economic Research Department, The Central Bank of China, 2, Roosevelt Road, Section 1, Taipei 10757, Republic of China; *Financial Statistics Monthly Taiwan District, The Republic of China*.

TAIWAN - FIREWOOD PRODUCTION

Department of Agriculture and Forestry, Taiwan Provincial Government, Chunghsing Village, Nantou, Nantou Hsien, Taiwan, Republic of China; *Taiwan Agricultural Yearbook*.

Directorate - General of Budget, Accounting and Statistics, Executive Yuan, The Republic of China; *Statistical Yearbook of The Republic of China*.

TAIWAN - FISHERIES

Council for Economic Planning and Development, Ninth Floor, 87 Nanking East Road, Section 2, Taipei, Republic of China; *Taiwan Statistical Data Book*.

Department of Agriculture and Forestry, Taiwan Provincial Government, Chunghsing Village, Nantou, Nantou Hsien, Taiwan, Republic of China; *Taiwan Agricultural Yearbook*.

Directorate - General of Budget, Accounting and Statistics, Executive Yuan, The Republic of China; *Monthly Statistics of the Republic of China;* and *Statistical Yearbook of The Republic of China*.

Europa Publications Limited, 18 Bedford Square, London, WC1B 3JN, England; *The Europa World Year Book*.

Federal Statistical Office, Gustav - Stresemann - Ring 11, D-6200 Wiesbaden, Germany; *China (Taiwan)*.

M.E. Sharpe, 80 Business Park Drive, Armonk, New York 10504 (800) 541-6563; *The Illustrated Book of World Rankings*.

St. Martin's Press, Inc., 175 Fifth Avenue, New York, New York 10010 (800) 221-7945; *The Statesman's Year-Book*.

United Nations Conference on Trade and Development, Central Statistical Service, Palais des Nations, Geneva, Switzerland (Telephone in U.S. (800) 253-9646); *UNCTAD Commodity Yearbook*.

TAIWAN - FLOUR PRODUCTION

Department of Agriculture and Forestry, Taiwan Provincial Government, Chunghsing Village, Nantou, Nantou Hsien, Taiwan, Republic of China; *Taiwan Agricultural Yearbook*.

Directorate - General of Budget, Accounting and Statistics, Executive Yuan, The Republic of China; *Statistical Yearbook of The Republic of China*.

TAIWAN - FOOD

Council for Economic Planning and Development, Ninth Floor, 87 Nanking East Road, Section 2, Taipei, Republic of China; *Taiwan Statistical Data Book*.

Department of Agriculture and Forestry, Taiwan Provincial Government, Chunghsing Village, Nantou, Nantou Hsien, Taiwan, Republic of China; *Taiwan Agricultural Yearbook*.

Directorate - General of Budget, Accounting and Statistics, Executive Yuan, The Republic of China; *Monthly Statistics of the Republic of China; and Statistical Yearbook of The Republic of China*.

Euromonitor International, Inc., 122 South Michigan Avenue, Suite 1200, Chicago, Illinois 60603 (800) 577-EURO; *Retail Trade International*.

United Nations Conference on Trade and Development, Central Statistical Service, Palais des Nations, Geneva, Switzerland (Telephone in U.S. (800) 253-9646); *UNCTAD Commodity Yearbook*.

TAIWAN - FOREIGN DEBT

St. Martin's Press, Inc., 175 Fifth Avenue, New York, New York 10010 (800) 221-7945; *The Statesman's Year-Book*.

Walden Publishing Ltd., Two Market Street, Saffron Walden Essex, CB10 1HZ, England; *The World of Information Asia and Pacific Review*.

TAIWAN - FOREIGN TRADE

Council for Economic Planning and Development, Ninth Floor, 87 Nanking East Road, Section 2, Taipei, Republic of China; *Taiwan Statistical Data Book*.

Department of Agriculture and Forestry, Taiwan Provincial Government, Chunghsing Village, Nantou, Nantou Hsien, Taiwan, Republic of China; *Taiwan Agricultural Yearbook*.

Department of Statistics, Ministry of Finance, 2, Aikuo West Road, Taipei, Republic of China; *The Republic of China Monthly of Financial Statistics*.

Directorate - General of Budget, Accounting and Statistics, Executive Yuan, Republic of China; *Monthly Statistics of the Republic of China*.

Economic Research Department, The Central Bank of China, 2, Roosevelt Road, Section 1, Taipei 10757, Republic of China; *Financial Statistics Monthly Taiwan District, The Republic of China*.

Economist Intelligence Unit, 111 West 57th Street, New York, New York 10019 (800) 938-4685; *Taiwan Country Report*.

The Economist Intelligence Unit (Asia) Limited, 10th Floor, Luk Kwok Centre, 72 Gloucester Road, Wanchai, Hong Kong (Phone Number in U.S. (800) 938-4685); *Asian Market Atlas*.

Euromonitor International, Inc., 122 South Michigan Avenue, Suite 1200, Chicago, Illinois 60603 (800) 577-EURO; *International Marketing Data and Statistics; and The World Economic Factbook*.

Europa Publications Limited, 18 Bedford Square, London, WC1B 3JN, England; *The Europa World Year Book*.

Federal Statistical Office, Gustav - Stresemann - Ring 11, D-6200 Wiesbaden, Germany; *China (Taiwan)*.

M.E. Sharpe, 80 Business Park Drive, Armonk, New York 10504 (800) 541-6563; *The Illustrated Book of World Rankings*.

St. Martin's Press, Inc., 175 Fifth Avenue, New York, New York 10010 (800) 221-7945; *The Statesman's Year-Book*.

TAIWAN - FORESTRY AND FOREST PRODUCTS

American Forest and Paper Association, 1111 Nineteenth Street, NW,

Washington, D.C. 20036 (202) 463-2700; *Wood Pulp and Fiber Statistics*.

Council for Economic Planning and Development, Ninth Floor, 87 Nanking East Road, Section 2, Taipei, Republic of China; *Taiwan Statistical Data Book*.

Department of Agriculture and Forestry, Taiwan Provincial Government, Chunghsing Village, Nantou, Nantou Hsien, Taiwan, Republic of China; *Taiwan Agricultural Yearbook*.

Directorate - General of Budget, Accounting and Statistics, Executive Yuan, The Republic of China; *Monthly Statistics of the Republic of China; and Statistical Yearbook of The Republic of China*.

The Economist Intelligence Unit (Asia) Limited, 10th Floor, Luk Kwok Centre, 72 Gloucester Road, Wanchai, Hong Kong (Phone Number in U.S. (800) 938-4685); *Asian Market Atlas*.

Europa Publications Limited, 18 Bedford Square, London, WC1B 3JN, England; *The Europa World Year Book*.

Federal Statistical Office, Gustav - Stresemann - Ring 11, D-6200 Wiesbaden, Germany; *China (Taiwan)*.

M.E. Sharpe, 80 Business Park Drive, Armonk, New York 10504 (800) 541-6563; *The Illustrated Book of World Rankings*.

St. Martin's Press, Inc., 175 Fifth Avenue, New York, New York 10010 (800) 221-7945; *The Statesman's Year-Book*.

United Nations Conference on Trade and Development, Central Statistical Service, Palais des Nations, Geneva, Switzerland (Telephone in U.S. (800) 253-9646); *UNCTAD Commodity Yearbook*.

TAIWAN - FRUIT PRODUCTION - See TAIWAN - CROPS

TAIWAN - GARLIC PRODUCTION - See TAIWAN - CROPS

TAIWAN - GAS PRODUCTION - See TAIWAN - MINING AND MINERAL PRODUCTS

TAIWAN - GENERAL INDUSTRIAL STATISTICS - See TAIWAN - INDUSTRY

TAIWAN - GENERAL MORTALITY - See TAIWAN - MORTALITY

TAIWAN - GEOGRAPHIC DATA

Federal Statistical Office, Gustav - Stresemann - Ring 11, D-6200 Wiesbaden, Germany; *China (Taiwan)*.

M.E. Sharpe, 80 Business Park Drive,

Armonk, New York 10504 (800) 541-6563; *The Illustrated Book of World Rankings.*

TAIWAN - GOATS - See TAIWAN - LIVESTOCK AND POULTRY

TAIWAN - GOLD PRODUCTION AND CONSUMPTION - See TAIWAN - MINING AND MINERAL PRODUCTS

TAIWAN - GOVERNMENT

Central Intelligence Agency, Washington, D.C. 20505 (703) 482-1100, www.cia.gov; *The World Factbook.*

Council for Economic Planning and Development, Ninth Floor, 87 Nanking East Road, Section 2, Taipei, Republic of China; *Taiwan Statistical Data Book.*

Department of Statistics, Ministry of Finance, 2, Aikuo West Road, Taipei, Republic of China; *The Republic of China Monthly of Financial Statistics.*

Directorate - General of Budget, Accounting and Statistics, Executive Yuan, Republic of China; *Monthly Statistics of the Republic of China.*

Economic Research Department, The Central Bank of China, 2, Roosevelt Road, Section 1, Taipei 10757, Republic of China; *Financial Statistics Monthly Taiwan District, The Republic of China.*

Europa Publications Limited, 18 Bedford Square, London, WC1B 3JN, England; *The Europa World Year Book.*

St. Martin's Press, Inc., 175 Fifth Avenue, New York, New York 10010 (800) 221-7945; *The Statesman's Year-Book.*

TAIWAN - GRAIN PRODUCTION - See TAIWAN - CROPS

TAIWAN - GREEN PEPPER AND CHILIE PRODUCTION - See TAIWAN - CROPS

TAIWAN - GROSS DOMESTIC PRODUCT

Council for Economic Planning and Development, Ninth Floor, 87 Nanking East Road, Section 2, Taipei, Republic of China; *Taiwan Statistical Data Book.*

Department of Statistics, Ministry of Finance, 2, Aikuo West Road, Taipei, Republic of China; *The Republic of China Monthly of Financial Statistics.*

Directorate - General of Budget, Accounting and Statistics, Executive Yuan, The Republic of China; *Monthly Statistics of the Republic of China; and Statistical Yearbook of The Republic of China.*

Economic Research Department, The Central Bank of China, 2, Roosevelt Road,

Section 1, Taipei 10757, Republic of China; *Financial Statistics Monthly Taiwan District, The Republic of China.*

The Economist Intelligence Unit, 111 West 57th Street, New York, New York 10019 (800) 938-4685; *Taiwan Country Report;* and *The World Market Atlas.*

The Economist Intelligence Unit (Asia) Limited, 10th Floor, Luk Kwok Centre, 72 Gloucester Road, Wanchai, Hong Kong (Phone Number in U.S. (800) 938-4685); *Asian Market Atlas.*

Euromonitor International, Inc., 122 South Michigan Avenue, Suite 1200, Chicago, Illinois 60603 (800) 577-EURO; *International Marketing Data and Statistics;* and *The World Economic Factbook.*

Europa Publications Limited, 18 Bedford Square, London, WC1B 3JN, England; *The Europa World Year Book.*

M.E. Sharpe, 80 Business Park Drive, Armonk, New York 10504 (800) 541-6563; *The Illustrated Book of World Rankings.*

TAIWAN - GROSS NATIONAL PRODUCT

Council for Economic Planning and Development, Ninth Floor, 87 Nanking East Road, Section 2, Taipei, Republic of China; *Taiwan Statistical Data Book.*

Department of Statistics, Ministry of Finance, 2, Aikuo West Road, Taipei, Republic of China; *The Republic of China Monthly of Financial Statistics.*

Directorate - General of Budget, Accounting and Statistics, Executive Yuan, Republic of China; *Monthly Statistics of the Republic of China.*

Economic Research Department, The Central Bank of China, 2, Roosevelt Road, Section 1, Taipei 10757, Republic of China; *Financial Statistics Monthly Taiwan District, The Republic of China.*

Euromonitor International, Inc., 122 South Michigan Avenue, Suite 1200, Chicago, Illinois 60603 (800) 577-EURO; *International Marketing Data and Statistics.*

Europa Publications Limited, 18 Bedford Square, London, WC1B 3JN, England; *The Europa World Year Book.*

St. Martin's Press, Inc., 175 Fifth Avenue, New York, New York 10010 (800) 221-7945; *The Statesman's Year-Book.*

U.S. Arms Control and Disarmament Agency, 320 Twenty-first Street, NW, Washington, D.C. 20451 (202) 647-8677; *World Military Expenditures and Arms Transfers.*

Walden Publishing Ltd., Two Market Street, Saffron Walden Essex, CB10 1HZ, England; *The World of Information Asia and Pacific Review.*

TAIWAN - GROUNDNUTS PRODUCTION - See TAIWAN - CROPS

TAIWAN - HEALTH

Council for Economic Planning and Development, Ninth Floor, 87 Nanking East Road, Section 2, Taipei, Republic of China; *Taiwan Statistical Data Book.*

Directorate - General of Budget, Accounting and Statistics, Executive Yuan, The Republic of China; *Monthly Statistics of the Republic of China; and Statistical Yearbook of The Republic of China.*

The Economist Intelligence Unit (Asia) Limited, 10th Floor, Luk Kwok Centre, 72 Gloucester Road, Wanchai, Hong Kong (Phone Number in U.S. (800) 938-4685); *Asian Market Atlas.*

Euromonitor International, Inc., 122 South Michigan Avenue, Suite 1200, Chicago, Illinois 60603 (800) 577-EURO; *World Marketing Data and Statistics.*

Federal Statistical Office, Gustav - Stresemann - Ring 11, D-6200 Wiesbaden, Germany; *China (Taiwan).*

M.E. Sharpe, 80 Business Park Drive, Armonk, New York 10504 (800) 541-6563; *The Illustrated Book of World Rankings.*

St. Martin's Press, Inc., 175 Fifth Avenue, New York, New York 10010 (800) 221-7945; *The Statesman's Year-Book.*

TAIWAN - HEMP FIBRE PRODUCTION - See TAIWAN - TEXTILE INDUSTRY

TAIWAN - HIDE PRODUCTION

Council for Economic Planning and Development, Ninth Floor, 87 Nanking East Road, Section 2, Taipei, Republic of China; *Taiwan Statistical Data Book.*

Department of Agriculture and Forestry, Taiwan Provincial Government, Chunghsing Village, Nantou, Nantou Hsien, Taiwan, Republic of China; *Taiwan Agricultural Yearbook.*

TAIWAN - HIGHWAYS

Central Intelligence Agency, Washington, D.C. 20505 (703) 482-1100, www.cia.gov; *The World Factbook.*

The Economist Intelligence Unit (Asia) Limited, 10th Floor, Luk Kwok Centre, 72 Gloucester Road, Wanchai, Hong Kong (Phone Number in U.S. (800) 938-4685); *Asian Market Atlas.*

International Road Federation, 2600 Virginia Avenue, NW, Washington, D.C. 20037 (202) 338-4641; *World Road Statistics.*

St. Martin's Press, Inc., 175 Fifth Avenue, New York, New York 10010 (800) 221-7945; *The Statesman's Year-Book.*

TAIWAN - HONEY PRODUCTION

Commodity Research Bureau, Inc., 30 South Wacker Drive, Chicago, Illinois 60606 (312) 454-1801; *Commodity Year Book.*

Department of Agriculture and Forestry, Taiwan Provincial Government, Chunghsing Village, Nantou, Nantou Hsien, Taiwan, Republic of China; *Taiwan Agricultural Yearbook.*

TAIWAN - HORSES - See TAIWAN - LIVESTOCK AND POULTRY

TAIWAN - HOURS OF WORK - See TAIWAN - EMPLOYMENT

TAIWAN - HOUSING AND HOUSING UNITS

Council for Economic Planning and Development, Ninth Floor, 87 Nanking East Road, Section 2, Taipei, Republic of China; *Taiwan Statistical Data Book.*

Directorate - General of Budget, Accounting and Statistics, Executive Yuan, The Republic of China; *Monthly Statistics of the Republic of China;* and *Statistical Yearbook of The Republic of China.*

Euromonitor International, Inc., 122 South Michigan Avenue, Suite 1200, Chicago, Illinois 60603 (800) 577-EURO; *World Marketing Data and Statistics.*

M.E. Sharpe, 80 Business Park Drive, Armonk, New York 10504 (800) 541-6563; *The Illustrated Book of World Rankings.*

TAIWAN - HYDROCHLORIC ACID PRODUCTION

Directorate - General of Budget, Accounting and Statistics, Executive Yuan, The Republic of China; *Statistical Yearbook of The Republic of China.*

TAIWAN - ILLITERATE POPULATION

Central Intelligence Agency, Washington, D.C. 20505 (703) 482-1100, www.cia.gov; *The World Factbook.*

The Economist Intelligence Unit, 111 West 57th Street, New York, New York 10019 (800) 938-4685; *The World Market Atlas.*

TAIWAN - IMPORT TRANSACTIONS

Council for Economic Planning and

Development, Ninth Floor, 87 Nanking East Road, Section 2, Taipei, Republic of China; *Taiwan Statistical Data Book.*

Directorate - General of Budget, Accounting and Statistics, Executive Yuan, The Republic of China; *Statistical Yearbook of The Republic of China.*

TAIWAN - IMPORTS

Central Intelligence Agency, Washington, D.C. 20505 (703) 482-1100, www.cia.gov; *The World Factbook.*

Council for Economic Planning and Development, Ninth Floor, 87 Nanking East Road, Section 2, Taipei, Republic of China; *Taiwan Statistical Data Book.*

Department of Statistics, Ministry of Finance, 2, Aikuo West Road, Taipei, Republic of China; *The Republic of China Monthly of Financial Statistics.*

Directorate - General of Budget, Accounting and Statistics, Executive Yuan, Republic of China; *Monthly Statistics of the Republic of China.*

Economic Research Department, The Central Bank of China, 2, Roosevelt Road, Section 1, Taipei 10757, Republic of China; *Financial Statistics Monthly Taiwan District, The Republic of China.*

Economist Intelligence Unit, 111 West 57th Street, New York, New York 10019 (800) 938-4685; *Taiwan Country Report.*

The Economist Intelligence Unit (Asia) Limited, 10th Floor, Luk Kwok Centre, 72 Gloucester Road, Wanchai, Hong Kong (Phone Number in U.S. (800) 938-4685); *Asian Market Atlas;* and *The World Market Atlas.*

Euromonitor International, Inc., 122 South Michigan Avenue, Suite 1200, Chicago, Illinois 60603 (800) 577-EURO; *International Marketing Data and Statistics;* and *The World Economic Factbook.*

Europa Publications Limited, 18 Bedford Square, London, WC1B 3JN, England; *The Europa World Year Book.*

St. Martin's Press, Inc., 175 Fifth Avenue, New York, New York 10010 (800) 221-7945; *The Statesman's Year-Book.*

United Nations Conference on Trade and Development (UNCTAD), New York, New York 10017 (800) 253-9646; *Handbook of International Trade and Development Statistics.*

Walden Publishing Ltd., Two Market Street, Saffron Walden Essex, CB10 1HZ, England; *The World of Information Asia and Pacific Review.*

TAIWAN - INCOME AVERAGES

Council for Economic Planning and Development, Ninth Floor, 87 Nanking East Road, Section 2, Taipei, Republic of China; *Taiwan Statistical Data Book.*

Directorate - General of Budget, Accounting and Statistics, Executive Yuan, The Republic of China; *Statistical Yearbook of The Republic of China.*

TAIWAN - INCOME DISTRIBUTION

Council for Economic Planning and Development, Ninth Floor, 87 Nanking East Road, Section 2, Taipei, Republic of China; *Taiwan Statistical Data Book.*

TAIWAN - INDUSTRY

Central Intelligence Agency, Washington, D.C. 20505 (703) 482-1100, www.cia.gov; *The World Factbook.*

Council for Economic Planning and Development, Ninth Floor, 87 Nanking East Road, Section 2, Taipei, Republic of China; *Taiwan Statistical Data Book.*

Directorate - General of Budget, Accounting and Statistics, Executive Yuan, The Republic of China; *Monthly Statistics of the Republic of China;* and *Statistical Yearbook of The Republic of China.*

Economist Intelligence Unit, 111 West 57th Street, New York, New York 10019 (800) 938-4685; *Taiwan Country Report.*

Euromonitor International, Inc., 122 South Michigan Avenue, Suite 1200, Chicago, Illinois 60603 (800) 577-EURO; *The World Economic Factbook;* and *World Marketing Data and Statistics.*

Europa Publications Limited, 18 Bedford Square, London, WC1B 3JN, England; *The Europa World Year Book.*

Federal Statistical Office, Gustav - Stresemann - Ring 11, D-6200 Wiesbaden, Germany; *China (Taiwan).*

M.E. Sharpe, 80 Business Park Drive, Armonk, New York 10504 (800) 541-6563; *The Illustrated Book of World Rankings.*

St. Martin's Press, Inc., 175 Fifth Avenue, New York, New York 10010 (800) 221-7945; *The Statesman's Year-Book.*

TAIWAN - INFANT AND MATERNAL MORTALITY - See TAIWAN - MORTALITY

TAIWAN - INTERNATIONAL RESERVES

Council for Economic Planning and Development, Ninth Floor, 87 Nanking East Road, Section 2, Taipei, Republic of China; *Taiwan Statistical Data Book.*

Directorate - General of Budget, Accounting and Statistics, Executive Yuan, The Republic of China; *Monthly Statistics of the Republic of China;* and *Statistical Yearbook of The Republic of China.*

TAIWAN - IRON ORE PRODUCTION AND CONSUMPTION - See TAIWAN - MINING AND MINERAL PRODUCTS

TAIWAN - IRRIGATION

Department of Agriculture and Forestry, Taiwan Provincial Government, Chunghsing Village, Nantou, Nantou Hsien, Taiwan, Republic of China; *Taiwan Agricultural Yearbook.*

Euromonitor International, Inc., 122 South Michigan Avenue, Suite 1200, Chicago, Illinois 60603 (800) 577-EURO; *International Marketing Data and Statistics.*

TAIWAN - JUTE PRODUCTION - See TAIWAN - CROPS

TAIWAN - LABOR

Central Intelligence Agency, Washington, D.C. 20505 (703) 482-1100, www.cia.gov; *The World Factbook.*

Council for Economic Planning and Development, Ninth Floor, 87 Nanking East Road, Section 2, Taipei, Republic of China; *Taiwan Statistical Data Book.*

Directorate - General of Budget, Accounting and Statistics, Executive Yuan, Republic of China; *Monthly Statistics of the Republic of China;* and *Statistical Yearbook of the Republic of China.*

The Economist Intelligence Unit (Asia) Limited, 10th Floor, Luk Kwok Centre, 72 Gloucester Road, Wanchai, Hong Kong (Phone Number in U.S. (800) 938-4685); *Asian Market Atlas.*

Euromonitor International, Inc., 122 South Michigan Avenue, Suite 1200, Chicago, Illinois 60603 (800) 577-EURO; *International Marketing Data and Statistics;* and *World Marketing Data and Statistics.*

Europa Publications Limited, 18 Bedford Square, London, WC1B 3JN, England; *The Europa World Year Book.*

M.E. Sharpe, 80 Business Park Drive, Armonk, New York 10504 (800) 541-6563; *The Illustrated Book of World Rankings.*

St. Martin's Press, Inc., 175 Fifth Avenue, New York, New York 10010 (800) 221-7945; *The Statesman's Year-Book.*

TAIWAN - LAND USE

Central Intelligence Agency, Washington, D.C. 20505 (703) 482-1100,

www.cia.gov; *The World Factbook.*

Council for Economic Planning and Development, Ninth Floor, 87 Nanking East Road, Section 2, Taipei, Republic of China; *Taiwan Statistical Data Book.*

Department of Agriculture and Forestry, Taiwan Provincial Government, Chunghsing Village, Nantou, Nantou Hsien, Taiwan, Republic of China; *Taiwan Agricultural Yearbook.*

Directorate - General of Budget, Accounting and Statistics, Executive Yuan, Republic of China; *Monthly Statistics of the Republic of China.*

Euromonitor International, Inc., 122 South Michigan Avenue, Suite 1200, Chicago, Illinois 60603 (800) 577-EURO; *International Marketing Data and Statistics.*

TAIWAN - LEAD PRODUCTION AND CONSUMPTION - See TAIWAN -MINING AND MINERAL PRODUCTS

TAIWAN - LIBRARIES

M.E. Sharpe, 80 Business Park Drive, Armonk, New York 10504 (800) 541-6563; *The Illustrated Book of World Rankings.*

TAIWAN - LIFE EXPECTANCY

Central Intelligence Agency, Washington, D.C. 20505 (703) 482-1100, www.cia.gov; *The World Factbook.*

The Economist Intelligence Unit (Asia) Limited, 10th Floor, Luk Kwok Centre, 72 Gloucester Road, Wanchai, Hong Kong (Phone Number in U.S. (800) 938-4685); *Asian Market Atlas.*

Euromonitor International, Inc., 122 South Michigan Avenue, Suite 1200, Chicago, Illinois 60603 (800) 577-EURO; *The World Economic Factbook.*

St. Martin's Press, Inc., 175 Fifth Avenue, New York, New York 10010 (800) 221-7945; *The Statesman's Year-Book.*

TAIWAN - LIGNITE PRODUCTION - See TAIWAN - MINING AND MINERAL PRODUCTS

TAIWAN - LITERACY RATE

Euromonitor International, Inc., 122 South Michigan Avenue, Suite 1200, Chicago, Illinois 60603 (800) 577-EURO; *World Marketing Data and Statistics.*

TAIWAN - LIVESTOCK AND POULTRY

Commodity Research Bureau, Inc., 30 South Wacker Drive, Chicago, Illinois 60606 (312) 454-1801; *Commodity Year Book.*

Council for Economic Planning and Development, Ninth Floor, 87 Nanking East Road, Section 2, Taipei, Republic of China; *Taiwan Statistical Data Book.*

Department of Agriculture and Forestry, Taiwan Provincial Government, Chunghsing Village, Nantou, Nantou Hsien, Taiwan, Republic of China; *Taiwan Agricultural Yearbook.*

Directorate - General of Budget, Accounting and Statistics, Executive Yuan, The Republic of China; *Monthly Statistics of the Republic of China;* and *Statistical Yearbook of The Republic of China.*

Euromonitor International, Inc., 122 South Michigan Avenue, Suite 1200, Chicago, Illinois 60603 (800) 577-EURO; *International Marketing Data and Statistics.*

Europa Publications Limited, 18 Bedford Square, London, WC1B 3JN, England; *The Europa World Year Book.*

M.E. Sharpe, 80 Business Park Drive, Armonk, New York 10504 (800) 541-6563; *The Illustrated Book of World Rankings.*

St. Martin's Press, Inc., 175 Fifth Avenue, New York, New York 10010 (800) 221-7945; *The Statesman's Year-Book.*

United Nations Conference on Trade and Development, Central Statistical Service, Palais des Nations, Geneva, Switzerland (Telephone in U.S. (800) 253-9646); *UNCTAD Commodity Yearbook.*

TAIWAN - MAGAZINES

Council for Economic Planning and Development, Ninth Floor, 87 Nanking East Road, Section 2, Taipei, Republic of China; *Taiwan Statistical Data Book.*

Directorate - General of Budget, Accounting and Statistics, Executive Yuan, The Republic of China; *Monthly Statistics of the Republic of China;* and *Statistical Yearbook of The Republic of China.*

TAIWAN - MAGNESIUM PRODUCTION AND CONSUMPTION - See TAIWAN - MINING AND MINERAL PRODUCTS

TAIWAN - MAIL TRAFFIC

Council for Economic Planning and Development, Ninth Floor, 87 Nanking East Road, Section 2, Taipei, Republic of China; *Taiwan Statistical Data Book.*

Directorate - General of Budget, Accounting and Statistics, Executive Yuan, The Republic of China; *Monthly Statistics of the Republic of China;* and *Statistical Yearbook of The Republic of China.*

TAIWAN - MANGANESE PRODUCTION AND

CONSUMPTION - See TAIWAN - MINING AND MINERAL PRODUCTS

TAIWAN - MANUFACTURING

American Automobile Manufacturers Association, 1401 H Street, NW, Suite 900, Washington, D.C. 20005 (202) 326-5500; *World Motor Vehicle Data.*

Council for Economic Planning and Development, Ninth Floor, 87 Nanking East Road, Section 2, Taipei, Republic of China; *Taiwan Statistical Data Book.*

Department of Statistics, Ministry of Finance, 2, Aikuo West Road, Taipei, Republic of China; *The Republic of China Monthly of Financial Statistics.*

Directorate - General of Budget, Accounting and Statistics, Executive Yuan, The Republic of China; *Monthly Statistics of the Republic of China; and Statistical Yearbook of The Republic of China.*

M.E. Sharpe, 80 Business Park Drive, Armonk, New York 10504 (800) 541-6563; *The Illustrated Book of World Rankings.*

TAIWAN - MARRIAGE RATES

Council for Economic Planning and Development, Ninth Floor, 87 Nanking East Road, Section 2, Taipei, Republic of China; *Taiwan Statistical Data Book.*

Directorate - General of Budget, Accounting and Statistics, Executive Yuan, Republic of China; *Monthly Statistics of the Republic of China.*

Europa Publications Limited, 18 Bedford Square, London, WC1B 3JN, England; *The Europa World Year Book.*

M.E. Sharpe, 80 Business Park Drive, Armonk, New York 10504 (800) 541-6563; *The Illustrated Book of World Rankings.*

TAIWAN - MEAT PRODUCTION - See TAIWAN - LIVESTOCK AND POULTRY

TAIWAN - MERCHANT SHIPPING

Council for Economic Planning and Development, Ninth Floor, 87 Nanking East Road, Section 2, Taipei, Republic of China; *Taiwan Statistical Data Book.*

Directorate - General of Budget, Accounting and Statistics, Executive Yuan, The Republic of China; *Monthly Statistics of the Republic of China; and Statistical Yearbook of The Republic of China.*

Europa Publications Limited, 18 Bedford Square, London, WC1B 3JN, England; *The Europa World Year Book.*

Lloyd's Register of Shipping, 17 Battery Place, New York, New York 10004 (212) 425-8050; *Register of Ships.*

St. Martin's Press, Inc., 175 Fifth Avenue, New York, New York 10010 (800) 221-7945; *The Statesman's Year-Book.*

U.S. Department of Transportation, Maritime Administration, 400 Seventh Street, SW, Washington, D.C. 20590 (202) 366-5807; *A Statistical Analysis of the World's Merchant Fleets.*

TAIWAN - MERCURY PRODUCTION AND CONSUMPTION - See TAIWAN - MINING AND MINERAL PRODUCTS

TAIWAN - MILITARY

Central Intelligence Agency, Washington, D.C. 20505 (703) 482-1100, www.cia.gov; *The World Factbook.*

The Economist Intelligence Unit (Asia) Limited, 10th Floor, Luk Kwok Centre, 72 Gloucester Road, Wanchai, Hong Kong (Phone Number in U.S. (800) 938-4685); *Asian Market Atlas.*

Euromonitor International, Inc., 122 South Michigan Avenue, Suite 1200, Chicago, Illinois 60603 (800) 577-EURO; *World Marketing Data and Statistics.*

The International Institute for Strategic Studies, 23 Tavistock Street, London WC2E 7NQ, England 44 171 3797676; *The Military Balance.*

St. Martin's Press, Inc., 175 Fifth Avenue, New York, New York 10010 (800) 221-7945; *The Statesman's Year-Book.*

U.S. Arms Control and Disarmament Agency, 320 Twenty-first Street, NW, Washington, D.C. 20451 (202) 647-8677; *World Military Expenditures and Arms Transfers.*

TAIWAN - MILK PRODUCTION - See TAIWAN - DAIRY PRODUCTS

TAIWAN - MILLET PRODUCTION - See TAIWAN - CROPS

TAIWAN - MINING AND MINERAL PRODUCTS

Commodity Research Bureau, Inc., 30 South Wacker Drive, Chicago, Illinois 60606 (312) 454-1801; *Commodity Year Book.*

Council for Economic Planning and Development, Ninth Floor, 87 Nanking East Road, Section 2, Taipei, Republic of China; *Taiwan Statistical Data Book.*

Directorate - General of Budget, Accounting and Statistics, Executive Yuan, The Republic of China; *Monthly Statistics*

of the Republic of China; and *Statistical Yearbook of The Republic of China.*

Europa Publications Limited, 18 Bedford Square, London, WC1B 3JN, England; *The Europa World Year Book.*

M.E. Sharpe, 80 Business Park Drive, Armonk, New York 10504 (800) 541-6563; *The Illustrated Book of World Rankings.*

Penn Well Publishing Company, 1421 South Sheridan Road, P.O. Box 1260, Tulsa, Oklahoma 74101 (800) 752-9764; *International Energy Statistics Sourcebook.*

St. Martin's Press, Inc., 175 Fifth Avenue, New York, New York 10010 (800) 221-7945; *The Statesman's Year-Book.*

United Nations Conference on Trade and Development, Central Statistical Service, Palais des Nations, Geneva, Switzerland (Telephone in U.S. (800) 253-9646); *UNCTAD Commodity Yearbook.*

TAIWAN - MOLYBDENUM PRODUCTION AND CONSUMPTION - See TAIWAN - MINING AND MINERAL PRODUCTS

TAIWAN - MONEY EXCHANGE RATE - See TAIWAN - EXCHANGE RATES

TAIWAN - MONEY RESERVES

Council for Economic Planning and Development, Ninth Floor, 87 Nanking East Road, Section 2, Taipei, Republic of China; *Taiwan Statistical Data Book.*

Directorate - General of Budget, Accounting and Statistics, Executive Yuan, Republic of China; *Monthly Statistics of the Republic of China.*

Economic Research Department, The Central Bank of China, 2, Roosevelt Road, Section 1, Taipei 10757, Republic of China; *Financial Statistics Monthly Taiwan District, The Republic of China.*

Euromonitor International, Inc., 122 South Michigan Avenue, Suite 1200, Chicago, Illinois 60603 (800) 577-EURO; *International Marketing Data and Statistics.*

TAIWAN - MONEY SUPPLY

Council for Economic Planning and Development, Ninth Floor, 87 Nanking East Road, Section 2, Taipei, Republic of China; *Taiwan Statistical Data Book.*

Department of Statistics, Ministry of Finance, 2, Aikuo West Road, Taipei, Republic of China; *The Republic of China Monthly of Financial Statistics.*

Directorate - General of Budget, Accounting and Statistics, Executive Yuan,

The Republic of China; *Monthly Statistics of the Republic of China;* and *Statistical Yearbook of The Republic of China.*

Economic Research Department, The Central Bank of China, 2, Roosevelt Road, Section 1, Taipei 10757, Republic of China; *Financial Statistics Monthly Taiwan District, The Republic of China.*

Economist Intelligence Unit, 111 West 57th Street, New York, New York 10019 (800) 938-4685; *Taiwan Country Report.*

Euromonitor International, Inc., 122 South Michigan Avenue, Suite 1200, Chicago, Illinois 60603 (800) 577-EURO; *International Marketing Data and Statistics.*

Europa Publications Limited, 18 Bedford Square, London, WC1B 3JN, England; *The Europa World Year Book.*

Federal Statistical Office, Gustav - Stresemann - Ring 11, D-6200 Wiesbaden, Germany; *China (Taiwan).*

TAIWAN - MORTALITY

Central Intelligence Agency, Washington, D.C. 20505 (703) 482-1100, www.cia.gov; *The World Factbook.*

Council for Economic Planning and Development, Ninth Floor, 87 Nanking East Road, Section 2, Taipei, Republic of China; *Taiwan Statistical Data Book.*

Directorate - General of Budget, Accounting and Statistics, Executive Yuan, The Republic of China; *Monthly Statistics of the Republic of China;* and *Statistical Yearbook of The Republic of China.*

The Economist Intelligence Unit (Asia) Limited, 10th Floor, Luk Kwok Centre, 72 Gloucester Road, Wanchai, Hong Kong (Phone Number in U.S. (800) 938-4685); *Asian Market Atlas.*

Euromonitor International, Inc., 122 South Michigan Avenue, Suite 1200, Chicago, Illinois 60603 (800) 577-EURO; *International Marketing Data and Statistics;* and *The World Economic Factbook.*

Europa Publications Limited, 18 Bedford Square, London, WC1B 3JN, England; *The Europa World Year Book.*

St. Martin's Press, Inc., 175 Fifth Avenue, New York, New York 10010 (800) 221-7945; *The Statesman's Year-Book.*

TAIWAN - MOTION PICTURES

Council for Economic Planning and Development, Ninth Floor, 87 Nanking East Road, Section 2, Taipei, Republic of China; *Taiwan Statistical Data Book.*

Directorate - General of Budget, Accounting and Statistics, Executive Yuan, The Republic of China; *Monthly Statistics of the Republic of China;* and *Statistical Yearbook of The Republic of China.*

St. Martin's Press, Inc., 175 Fifth Avenue, New York, New York 10010 (800) 221-7945; *The Statesman's Year-Book.*

TAIWAN - MOTOR VEHICLE PRODUCTION

American Automobile Manufacturers Association, 1401 H Street, NW, Suite 900, Washington, D.C. 20005 (202) 326-5500; *World Motor Vehicle Data.*

Council for Economic Planning and Development, Ninth Floor, 87 Nanking East Road, Section 2, Taipei, Republic of China; *Taiwan Statistical Data Book.*

Directorate - General of Budget, Accounting and Statistics, Executive Yuan, The Republic of China; *Monthly Statistics of the Republic of China;* and *Statistical Yearbook of The Republic of China.*

TAIWAN - MOTOR VEHICLE TAXES - See TAIWAN - TAXATION

TAIWAN - MOTOR VEHICLES IN USE

American Automobile Manufacturers Association, 1401 H Street, NW, Suite 900, Washington, D.C. 20005 (202) 326-5500; *World Motor Vehicle Data.*

Council for Economic Planning and Development, Ninth Floor, 87 Nanking East Road, Section 2, Taipei, Republic of China; *Taiwan Statistical Data Book.*

Directorate - General of Budget, Accounting and Statistics, Executive Yuan, The Republic of China; *Monthly Statistics of the Republic of China;* and *Statistical Yearbook of The Republic of China.*

Europa Publications Limited, 18 Bedford Square, London, WC1B 3JN, England; *The Europa World Year Book.*

International Road Federation, 2600 Virginia Avenue, NW, Washington, D.C. 20037 (202) 338-4641; *World Road Statistics.*

TAIWAN - MULES - See TAIWAN - LIVESTOCK AND POULTRY

TAIWAN - MUSEUMS

M.E. Sharpe, 80 Business Park Drive, Armonk, New York 10504 (800) 541-6563; *The Illustrated Book of World Rankings.*

TAIWAN - NATALITY - See TAIWAN - BIRTH RATES

TAIWAN - NATIONAL ACCOUNTS

Council for Economic Planning and Development, Ninth Floor, 87 Nanking East Road, Section 2, Taipei, Republic of China; *Taiwan Statistical Data Book.*

Department of Statistics, Ministry of Finance, 2, Aikuo West Road, Taipei, Republic of China; *The Republic of China Monthly of Financial Statistics.*

Directorate - General of Budget, Accounting and Statistics, Executive Yuan, The Republic of China; *Monthly Statistics of the Republic of China;* and *Statistical Yearbook of The Republic of China.*

Economic Research Department, The Central Bank of China, 2, Roosevelt Road, Section 1, Taipei 10757, Republic of China; *Financial Statistics Monthly Taiwan District, The Republic of China.*

Europa Publications Limited, 18 Bedford Square, London, WC1B 3JN, England; *The Europa World Year Book.*

Federal Statistical Office, Gustav - Stresemann - Ring 11, D-6200 Wiesbaden, Germany; *China (Taiwan).*

TAIWAN - NATIONAL INCOME

Council for Economic Planning and Development, Ninth Floor, 87 Nanking East Road, Section 2, Taipei, Republic of China; *Taiwan Statistical Data Book.*

Department of Statistics, Ministry of Finance, 2, Aikuo West Road, Taipei, Republic of China; *The Republic of China Monthly of Financial Statistics.*

Directorate - General of Budget, Accounting and Statistics, Executive Yuan, The Republic of China; *Monthly Statistics of the Republic of China;* and *Statistical Yearbook of The Republic of China.*

Economic Research Department, The Central Bank of China, 2, Roosevelt Road, Section 1, Taipei 10757, Republic of China; *Financial Statistics Monthly Taiwan District, The Republic of China.*

M.E. Sharpe, 80 Business Park Drive, Armonk, New York 10504 (800) 541-6563; *The Illustrated Book of World Rankings.*

TAIWAN - NATIONAL PRODUCT

M.E. Sharpe, 80 Business Park Drive, Armonk, New York 10504 (800) 541-6563; *The Illustrated Book of World Rankings.*

TAIWAN - NATURAL GAS PRODUCTION - See TAIWAN - MINING AND MINERAL PRODUCTS

TAIWAN - NEWS AGENCIES

Council for Economic Planning and

Development, Ninth Floor, 87 Nanking East Road, Section 2, Taipei, Republic of China; *Taiwan Statistical Data Book.*

Directorate - General of Budget, Accounting and Statistics, Executive Yuan, The Republic of China; *Monthly Statistics of the Republic of China;* and *Statistical Yearbook of The Republic of China.*

TAIWAN - NEWSPAPERS - See TAIWAN - FORESTRY AND FOREST PRODUCTS

TAIWAN - NITRIC ACID PRODUCTION - See TAIWAN - MINING AND MINERAL PRODUCTS

TAIWAN - OATS PRODUCTION - See TAIWAN - CROPS

TAIWAN - OCCUPATIONS - See TAIWAN - LABOR

TAIWAN - PAPER - See TAIWAN - FORESTRY AND FOREST PRODUCTS

TAIWAN - PEANUT PRODUCTION - See TAIWAN - CROPS

TAIWAN - PETROLEUM INDUSTRY

Commodity Research Bureau, Inc., 30 South Wacker Drive, Suite 1810, Chicago, Illinois 60606 (800) 621-5271 Inc., 30 South Wacker Drive, Chicago, Illinois 60606 (312) 454-1801; *Commodity Year Book.*

Council for Economic Planning and Development, Ninth Floor, 87 Nanking East Road, Section 2, Taipei, Republic of China; *Taiwan Statistical Data Book.*

Directorate - General of Budget, Accounting and Statistics, Executive Yuan, The Republic of China; *Monthly Statistics of the Republic of China;* and *Statistical Yearbook of The Republic of China.*

M.E. Sharpe, 80 Business Park Drive, Armonk, New York 10504 (800) 541-6563; *The Illustrated Book of World Rankings.*

Penn Well Publishing Company, 1421 South Sheridan Road, P.O. Box 1260, Tulsa, Oklahoma 74101 (800) 752-9764; *International Energy Statistics Sourcebook.*

St. Martin's Press, Inc., 175 Fifth Avenue, New York, New York 10010 (800) 221-7945; *The Statesman's Year-Book.*

United Nations Conference on Trade and Development, Central Statistical Service, Palais des Nations, Geneva, Switzerland (Telephone in U.S. (800) 253-9646); *UNCTAD Commodity Yearbook.*

TAIWAN - PIG-IRON AND FERRO-ALLOY PRODUCTION - See TAIWAN - MINING AND MINERAL PRODUCTS

TAIWAN - PIGS - See TAIWAN - LIVESTOCK AND POULTRY

TAIWAN - PLASTICS AND RESINS PRODUCTION

Council for Economic Planning and Development, Ninth Floor, 87 Nanking East Road, Section 2, Taipei, Republic of China; *Taiwan Statistical Data Book.*

Directorate - General of Budget, Accounting and Statistics, Executive Yuan, The Republic of China; *Statistical Yearbook of The Republic of China.*

TAIWAN - POPULATION

Central Intelligence Agency, Washington, D.C. 20505 (703) 482-1100, www.cia.gov; *The World Factbook.*

Council for Economic Planning and Development, Ninth Floor, 87 Nanking East Road, Section 2, Taipei, Republic of China; *Taiwan Statistical Data Book.*

Directorate - General of Budget, Accounting and Statistics, Executive Yuan, The Republic of China; *Monthly Statistics of the Republic of China;* and *Statistical Yearbook of The Republic of China.*

The Economist Intelligence Unit, 111 West 57th Street, New York, New York 10019 (800) 938-4685; *Taiwan Country Report;* and *The World Market Atlas.*

The Economist Intelligence Unit (Asia) Limited, 10th Floor, Luk Kwok Centre, 72 Gloucester Road, Wanchai, Hong Kong (Phone Number in U.S. (800) 938-4685); *Asian Market Atlas.*

Euromonitor International, Inc., 122 South Michigan Avenue, Suite 1200, Chicago, Illinois 60603 (800) 577-EURO; *International Marketing Data and Statistics;* and *The World Economic Factbook.*

Europa Publications Limited, 18 Bedford Square, London, WC1B 3JN, England; *The Europa World Year Book.*

Federal Statistical Office, Gustav - Stresemann - Ring 11, D-6200 Wiesbaden, Germany; *China (Taiwan).*

M.E. Sharpe, 80 Business Park Drive, Armonk, New York 10504 (800) 541-6563; *The Illustrated Book of World Rankings.*

St. Martin's Press, Inc., 175 Fifth Avenue, New York, New York 10010 (800) 221-7945; *The Statesman's Year-Book.*

U.S. Arms Control and Disarmament Agency, 320 Twenty-first Street, NW, Washington, D.C. 20451 (202) 647-8677; *World Military Expenditures and Arms Transfers.*

Walden Publishing Ltd., Two Market Street, Saffron Walden Essex, CB10 1HZ, England; *The World of Information Asia and Pacific Review.*

TAIWAN - POST OFFICES

M.E. Sharpe, 80 Business Park Drive, Armonk, New York 10504 (800) 541-6563; *The Illustrated Book of World Rankings.*

St. Martin's Press, Inc., 175 Fifth Avenue, New York, New York 10010 (800) 221-7945; *The Statesman's Year-Book.*

TAIWAN - POTATO PRODUCTION - See TAIWAN - CROPS

TAIWAN - PRICES

Council for Economic Planning and Development, Ninth Floor, 87 Nanking East Road, Section 2, Taipei, Republic of China; *Taiwan Statistical Data Book.*

Department of Statistics, Ministry of Finance, 2, Aikuo West Road, Taipei, Republic of China; *The Republic of China Monthly of Financial Statistics.*

Directorate - General of Budget, Accounting and Statistics, Executive Yuan, Republic of China; *Monthly Statistics of the Republic of China.*

Economic Research Department, The Central Bank of China, 2, Roosevelt Road, Section 1, Taipei 10757, Republic of China; *Financial Statistics Monthly Taiwan District, The Republic of China.*

Federal Statistical Office, Gustav - Stresemann - Ring 11, D-6200 Wiesbaden, Germany; *China (Taiwan).*

M.E. Sharpe, 80 Business Park Drive, Armonk, New York 10504 (800) 541-6563; *The Illustrated Book of World Rankings.*

TAIWAN - PRINTING AND WRITING PAPER - See TAIWAN - FORESTRY AND FOREST PRODUCTS

TAIWAN - PRODUCTION

American Automobile Manufacturers Association, 1401 H Street, NW, Suite 900, Washington, D.C. 20005 (202) 326-5500; *World Motor Vehicle Data.*

Council for Economic Planning and Development, Ninth Floor, 87 Nanking East Road, Section 2, Taipei, Republic of China; *Taiwan Statistical Data Book.*

Directorate - General of Budget, Accounting and Statistics, Executive Yuan, Republic of China; *Monthly Statistics of the Republic of China.*

M.E. Sharpe, 80 Business Park Drive,

Armonk, New York 10504 (800) 541-6563; *The Illustrated Book of World Rankings.*

TAIWAN - PRODUCTIVITY

Council for Economic Planning and Development, Ninth Floor, 87 Nanking East Road, Section 2, Taipei, Republic of China; *Taiwan Statistical Data Book.*

Euromonitor International, Inc., 122 South Michigan Avenue, Suite 1200, Chicago, Illinois 60603 (800) 577-EURO; *International Marketing Data and Statistics.*

TAIWAN - PUBLIC FINANCE - See
TAIWAN - FINANCE

TAIWAN - RADIO BROADCASTING - See
TAIWAN - BROADCASTING

TAIWAN - RADIO RECEIVERS

Council for Economic Planning and Development, Ninth Floor, 87 Nanking East Road, Section 2, Taipei, Republic of China; *Taiwan Statistical Data Book.*

Directorate - General of Budget, Accounting and Statistics, Executive Yuan, The Republic of China; *Monthly Statistics of the Republic of China;* and *Statistical Yearbook of The Republic of China.*

The Economist Intelligence Unit (Asia) Limited, 10th Floor, Luk Kwok Centre, 72 Gloucester Road, Wanchai, Hong Kong (Phone Number in U.S. (800) 938-4685); *Asian Market Atlas.*

St. Martin's Press, Inc., 175 Fifth Avenue, New York, New York 10010 (800) 221-7945; *The Statesman's Year-Book.*

TAIWAN - RAILWAYS

Council for Economic Planning and Development, Ninth Floor, 87 Nanking East Road, Section 2, Taipei, Republic of China; *Taiwan Statistical Data Book.*

Directorate - General of Budget, Accounting and Statistics, Executive Yuan, The Republic of China; *Monthly Statistics of the Republic of China;* and *Statistical Yearbook of The Republic of China.*

Europa Publications Limited, 18 Bedford Square, London, WC1B 3JN, England; *The Europa World Year Book.*

Jane's Information Group, Sentinel House, 163 Brighton Road, Coulsdon, Surrey CR5 2NH, England (Telephone Number in U.S. (703) 683-3700); *Jane's World Railways.*

St. Martin's Press, Inc., 175 Fifth Avenue, New York, New York 10010 (800) 221-7945; *The Statesman's Year-Book.*

TAIWAN - RELIGION

Central Intelligence Agency, Washington, D.C. 20505 (703) 482-1100, www.cia.gov; *The World Factbook.*

M.E. Sharpe, 80 Business Park Drive, Armonk, New York 10504 (800) 541-6563; *The Illustrated Book of World Rankings.*

St. Martin's Press, Inc., 175 Fifth Avenue, New York, New York 10010 (800) 221-7945; *The Statesman's Year-Book.*

TAIWAN - RETAIL TRADE

Council for Economic Planning and Development, Ninth Floor, 87 Nanking East Road, Section 2, Taipei, Republic of China; *Taiwan Statistical Data Book.*

Directorate - General of Budget, Accounting and Statistics, Executive Yuan, The Republic of China; *Monthly Statistics of the Republic of China;* and *Statistical Yearbook of The Republic of China.*

Euromonitor International, Inc., 122 South Michigan Avenue, Suite 1200, Chicago, Illinois 60603 (800) 577-EURO; *World Marketing Data and Statistics;* and *Retail Trade International.*

TAIWAN - RICE PRODUCTION - See
TAIWAN - CROPS

TAIWAN - ROOT AND TUBER PRODUCTION - See TAIWAN - CROPS

TAIWAN - ROUNDWOOD PRODUCTION - See TAIWAN - FORESTRY AND FOREST PRODUCTS

TAIWAN - RUBBER PRODUCTION AND CONSUMPTION

Department of Agriculture and Forestry, Taiwan Provincial Government, Chunghsing Village, Nantou, Nantou Hsien, Taiwan, Republic of China; *Taiwan Agricultural Yearbook.*

Directorate - General of Budget, Accounting and Statistics, Executive Yuan, The Republic of China; *Statistical Yearbook of The Republic of China.*

M.E. Sharpe, 80 Business Park Drive, Armonk, New York 10504 (800) 541-6563; *The Illustrated Book of World Rankings.*

TAIWAN - SALT PRODUCTION - See TAIWAN - MINING AND MINERAL PRODUCTS

TAIWAN - SAWNWOOD PRODUCTION - See TAIWAN - FORESTRY AND FOREST PRODUCTS

TAIWAN - SENIOR CITIZENS

M.E. Sharpe, 80 Business Park Drive, Armonk, New York 10504 (800) 541-6563; *The Illustrated Book of World Rankings.*

TAIWAN - SESAME SEED PRODUCTION - See TAIWAN - CROPS

TAIWAN - SHEEP - See TAIWAN - LIVESTOCK AND POULTRY

TAIWAN - SILVER PRODUCTION AND CONSUMPTION - See TAIWAN - MINING AND MINERAL PRODUCTS

TAIWAN - SISAL PRODUCTION - See TAIWAN - CROPS

TAIWAN - SOCIAL DATA

Council for Economic Planning and Development, Ninth Floor, 87 Nanking East Road, Section 2, Taipei, Republic of China; *Taiwan Statistical Data Book.*

Directorate - General of Budget, Accounting and Statistics, Executive Yuan, Republic of China; *Monthly Statistics of the Republic of China.*

M.E. Sharpe, 80 Business Park Drive, Armonk, New York 10504 (800) 541-6563; *The Illustrated Book of World Rankings.*

TAIWAN - SOCIAL SECURITY

St. Martin's Press, Inc., 175 Fifth Avenue, New York, New York 10010 (800) 221-7945; *The Statesman's Year-Book.*

TAIWAN - SOYBEAN PRODUCTION - See TAIWAN - CROPS

TAIWAN - STATE BUDGET REVENUE AND EXPENDITURES

Euromonitor International, Inc., 122 South Michigan Avenue, Suite 1200, Chicago, Illinois 60603 (800) 577-EURO; *International Marketing Data and Statistics.*

TAIWAN - STEEL - See TAIWAN - MINING AND MINERAL PRODUCTS

TAIWAN - SUGAR PRODUCTION AND CONSUMPTION - See TAIWAN - CROPS

TAIWAN - SULPHUR AND SULPHURIC ACID - See TAIWAN - MINING AND MINERAL PRODUCTS

TAIWAN - TAXATION

Department of Statistics, Ministry of Finance, 2, Aikuo West Road, Taipei, Republic of China; *The Republic of China Monthly of Financial Statistics.*

Directorate - General of Budget, Accounting and Statistics, Executive Yuan, The Republic of China; *Statistical*

Yearbook of The Republic of China.

Europa Publications Limited, 18 Bedford Square, London, WC1B 3JN, England; *The Europa World Year Book.*

International Road Federation, 2600 Virginia Avenue, NW, Washington, D.C. 20037 (202) 338-4641; *World Road Statistics.*

St. Martin's Press, Inc., 175 Fifth Avenue, New York, New York 10010 (800) 221-7945; *The Statesman's Year-Book.*

TAIWAN - TEA PRODUCTION AND CONSUMPTION - See TAIWAN - CROPS

TAIWAN - TELEGRAPH SERVICE

Council for Economic Planning and Development, Ninth Floor, 87 Nanking East Road, Section 2, Taipei, Republic of China; *Taiwan Statistical Data Book.*

Directorate - General of Budget, Accounting and Statistics, Executive Yuan, The Republic of China; *Monthly Statistics of the Republic of China; and Statistical Yearbook of The Republic of China.*

TAIWAN - TELEPHONES IN USE

American Telephone and Telegraph Company, 26 Parsippany Road, Whippany, New Jersey 07981 (800) 222-0300; *The World's Telephones.*

Central Intelligence Agency, Washington, D.C. 20505 (703) 482-1100, www.cia.gov; *The World Factbook.*

Council for Economic Planning and Development, Ninth Floor, 87 Nanking East Road, Section 2, Taipei, Republic of China; *Taiwan Statistical Data Book.*

Directorate - General of Budget, Accounting and Statistics, Executive Yuan, The Republic of China; *Statistical Yearbook of The Republic of China.*

The Economist Intelligence Unit (Asia) Limited, 10th Floor, Luk Kwok Centre, 72 Gloucester Road, Wanchai, Hong Kong (Phone Number in U.S. (800) 938-4685); *Asian Market Atlas.*

Europa Publications Limited, 18 Bedford Square, London, WC1B 3JN, England; *The Europa World Year Book.*

St. Martin's Press, Inc., 175 Fifth Avenue, New York, New York 10010 (800) 221-7945; *The Statesman's Year-Book.*

TAIWAN - TELEVISION BROADCASTING - See TAIWAN - BROADCASTING

TAIWAN - TELEVISION RECEIVERS

Directorate - General of Budget, Accounting and Statistics, Executive Yuan, The Republic of China; *Statistical Yearbook of The Republic of China.*

The Economist Intelligence Unit (Asia) Limited, 10th Floor, Luk Kwok Centre, 72 Gloucester Road, Wanchai, Hong Kong (Phone Number in U.S. (800) 938-4685); *Asian Market Atlas.*

TAIWAN - TEXTILE INDUSTRY

American Forest and Paper Association, 1111 Nineteenth Street, NW, Washington, D.C. 20036 (202) 463-2700; *Wood Pulp and Fiber Statistics.*

Council for Economic Planning and Development, Ninth Floor, 87 Nanking East Road, Section 2, Taipei, Republic of China; *Taiwan Statistical Data Book.*

Department of Agriculture and Forestry, Taiwan Provincial Government, Chunghsing Village, Nantou, Nantou Hsien, Taiwan, Republic of China; *Taiwan Agricultural Yearbook.*

Directorate - General of Budget, Accounting and Statistics, Executive Yuan, The Republic of China; *Monthly Statistics of the Republic of China; and Statistical Yearbook of The Republic of China.*

Euromonitor International, Inc., 122 South Michigan Avenue, Suite 1200, Chicago, Illinois 60603 (800) 577-EURO; *Retail Trade International.*

M.E. Sharpe, 80 Business Park Drive, Armonk, New York 10504 (800) 541-6563; *The Illustrated Book of World Rankings.*

St. Martin's Press, Inc., 175 Fifth Avenue, New York, New York 10010 (800) 221-7945; *The Statesman's Year-Book.*

United Nations Conference on Trade and Development, Central Statistical Service, Palais des Nations, Geneva, Switzerland (Telephone in U.S. (800) 253-9646); *UNCTAD Commodity Yearbook.*

TAIWAN - TIRE (MOTOR VEHICLE) PRODUCTION

Directorate - General of Budget, Accounting and Statistics, Executive Yuan, The Republic of China; *Statistical Yearbook of The Republic of China.*

TAIWAN - TOBACCO PRODUCTION

Commodity Research Bureau, Inc., 30 South Wacker Drive, Chicago, Illinois 60606 (312) 454-1801; *Commodity Year Book.*

Department of Agriculture and Forestry, Taiwan Provincial Government, Chunghsing Village, Nantou, Nantou Hsien,

Taiwan, Republic of China; *Taiwan Agricultural Yearbook.*

Directorate - General of Budget, Accounting and Statistics, Executive Yuan, The Republic of China; *Statistical Yearbook of The Republic of China.*

M.E. Sharpe, 80 Business Park Drive, Armonk, New York 10504 (800) 541-6563; *The Illustrated Book of World Rankings.*

TAIWAN - TOURISM

Council for Economic Planning and Development, Ninth Floor, 87 Nanking East Road, Section 2, Taipei, Republic of China; *Taiwan Statistical Data Book.*

Directorate - General of Budget, Accounting and Statistics, Executive Yuan, The Republic of China; *Monthly Statistics of the Republic of China; and Statistical Yearbook of The Republic of China.*

Euromonitor International, Inc., 122 South Michigan Avenue, Suite 1200, Chicago, Illinois 60603 (800) 577-EURO; *The World Economic Factbook; and World Marketing Data and Statistics.*

Europa Publications Limited, 18 Bedford Square, London, WC1B 3JN, England; *The Europa World Year Book.*

Federal Statistical Office, Gustav - Stresemann - Ring 11, D-6200 Wiesbaden, Germany; *China (Taiwan).*

M.E. Sharpe, 80 Business Park Drive, Armonk, New York 10504 (800) 541-6563; *The Illustrated Book of World Rankings.*

St. Martin's Press, Inc., 175 Fifth Avenue, New York, New York 10010 (800) 221-7945; *The Statesman's Year-Book.*

TAIWAN - TRACTORS IN USE

Department of Agriculture and Forestry, Taiwan Provincial Government, Chunghsing Village, Nantou, Nantou Hsien, Taiwan, Republic of China; *Taiwan Agricultural Yearbook.*

TAIWAN - TRADE - See TAIWAN - FOREIGN TRADE

TAIWAN - TRANSPORTATION AND COMMUNICATIONS

Central Intelligence Agency, Washington, D.C. 20505 (703) 482-1100, www.cia.gov; *The World Factbook.*

Council for Economic Planning and Development, Ninth Floor, 87 Nanking East Road, Section 2, Taipei, Republic of China; *Taiwan Statistical Data Book.*

Directorate - General of Budget,

Accounting and Statistics, Executive Yuan, Republic of China; *Monthly Statistics of the Republic of China.*

The Economist Intelligence Unit (Asia) Limited, 10th Floor, Luk Kwok Centre, 72 Gloucester Road, Wanchai, Hong Kong (Phone Number in U.S. (800) 938-4685); *Asian Market Atlas.*

Euromonitor International, Inc., 122 South Michigan Avenue, Suite 1200, Chicago, Illinois 60603 (800) 577-EURO; *International Marketing Data and Statistics;* and *World Marketing Data and Statistics.*

Europa Publications Limited, 18 Bedford Square, London, WC1B 3JN, England; *The Europa World Year Book.*

Federal Statistical Office, Gustav - Stresemann - Ring 11, D-6200 Wiesbaden, Germany; *China (Taiwan).*

M.E. Sharpe, 80 Business Park Drive, Armonk, New York 10504 (800) 541-6563; *The Illustrated Book of World Rankings.*

St. Martin's Press, Inc., 175 Fifth Avenue, New York, New York 10010 (800) 221-7945; *The Statesman's Year-Book.*

TAIWAN - TUNGSTEN PRODUCTION AND CONSUMPTION - See TAIWAN - MINING AND MINERAL PRODUCTS

TAIWAN - TURKEYS - See TAIWAN - LIVESTOCK AND POULTRY

TAIWAN - UNEMPLOYMENT

Central Intelligence Agency, Washington, D.C. 20505 (703) 482-1100, www.cia.gov; *The World Factbook.*

Council for Economic Planning and Development, Ninth Floor, 87 Nanking East Road, Section 2, Taipei, Republic of China; *Taiwan Statistical Data Book.*

Directorate - General of Budget, Accounting and Statistics, Executive Yuan, The Republic of China; *Monthly Statistics of the Republic of China;* and *Statistical Yearbook of The Republic of China.*

Euromonitor International, Inc., 122 South Michigan Avenue, Suite 1200, Chicago, Illinois 60603 (800) 577-EURO; *International Marketing Data and Statistics.*

St. Martin's Press, Inc., 175 Fifth Avenue, New York, New York 10010 (800) 221-7945; *The Statesman's Year-Book.*

TAIWAN - UTILITIES

Council for Economic Planning and Development, Ninth Floor, 87 Nanking East Road, Section 2, Taipei, Republic of China; *Taiwan Statistical Data Book.*

TAIWAN - VANADIUM PRODUCTION AND CONSUMPTION - See TAIWAN - MINING AND MINERAL PRODUCTS

TAIWAN - VEGETABLE PRODUCTION - See TAIWAN - CROPS

TAIWAN - VITAL STATISTICS

Council for Economic Planning and Development, Ninth Floor, 87 Nanking East Road, Section 2, Taipei, Republic of China; *Taiwan Statistical Data Book.*

Directorate - General of Budget, Accounting and Statistics, Executive Yuan, Republic of China; *Monthly Statistics of the Republic of China.*

Euromonitor International, Inc., 122 South Michigan Avenue, Suite 1200, Chicago, Illinois 60603 (800) 577-EURO; *International Marketing Data and Statistics.*

St. Martin's Press, Inc., 175 Fifth Avenue, New York, New York 10010 (800) 221-7945; *The Statesman's Year-Book.*

TAIWAN - WAGES

Council for Economic Planning and Development, Ninth Floor, 87 Nanking East Road, Section 2, Taipei, Republic of China; *Taiwan Statistical Data Book.*

Directorate - General of Budget, Accounting and Statistics, Executive Yuan, The Republic of China; *Monthly Statistics of the Republic of China;* and *Statistical Yearbook of The Republic of China.*

Federal Statistical Office, Gustav - Stresemann - Ring 11, D-6200 Wiesbaden, Germany; *China (Taiwan).*

TAIWAN - WATERMELON PRODUCTION - See TAIWAN - CROPS

TAIWAN - WEATHER - See TAIWAN - CLIMATE

TAIWAN - WHALES - See TAIWAN - FISHERIES

TAIWAN - WHEAT PRODUCTION AND PRICES - See TAIWAN - CROPS

TAIWAN - WHOLESALE PRICE

Council for Economic Planning and Development, Ninth Floor, 87 Nanking East Road, Section 2, Taipei, Republic of China; *Taiwan Statistical Data Book.*

Directorate - General of Budget, Accounting and Statistics, Executive Yuan, The Republic of China; *Statistical Yearbook of The Republic of China.*

TAIWAN - WHOLESALE TRADE

Council for Economic Planning and Development, Ninth Floor, 87 Nanking East Road, Section 2, Taipei, Republic of China; *Taiwan Statistical Data Book.*

Directorate - General of Budget, Accounting and Statistics, Executive Yuan, The Republic of China; *Statistical Yearbook of The Republic of China.*

TAIWAN - WINE PRODUCTION - See TAIWAN - BEVERAGES

TAIWAN - WOOD - See TAIWAN - FORESTRY AND FOREST PRODUCTS

TAIWAN - WOOL - See TAIWAN - TEXTILE INDUSTRY

TAIWAN - WORKING DAYS

Council for Economic Planning and Development, Ninth Floor, 87 Nanking East Road, Section 2, Taipei, Republic of China; *Taiwan Statistical Data Book.*

Directorate - General of Budget, Accounting and Statistics, Executive Yuan, The Republic of China; *Statistical Yearbook of The Republic of China.*

TAIWAN - YARN PRODUCTION - See TAIWAN - TEXTILE INDUSTRY

Tajikistan - National Statistical Office

State Committee of Republic of Tajikistan on Statistics, 127 Ayini Street, Dushanbe - 29, 734029, Tajikistan.

TAJIKISTAN - ABORTIONS

Statistical Office of the United Nations, Publishing Service, New York, New York 10017 (800) 253-9646; *Trends in Europe and North America: The Statistical Yearbook of the Economic Commission for Europe.*

TAJIKISTAN - AGRICULTURE

Academic International Press, Box 1111, Gulf Breeze, Florida 32562; *Russia and Eurasia Facts and Figures Annual.*

Business International Moscow, 23 Profsoyuznaya Ulitsa, 117859, Moscow (Telephone Number in U.S. (800) 938-4685); *The CIS Market Atlas.*

Economist Intelligence Unit, 111 West 57th Street, New York, New York 10019 (800) 938-4685; *Tajikistan Country Report.*

Euromonitor International, Inc., 122 South Michigan Avenue, Suite 1200, Chicago, Illinois 60603 (800) 577-EURO; *World Marketing Data and Statistics.*

Europa Publications Limited, 18

Bedford Square, London, WC1B 3JN, England; *The Europa World Year Book.*

Food and Agriculture Organization of the United Nations (FAO), Via delle Terme di Caracalla, 00100, Rome, Italy (Telephone Number in U.S. (202) 653-2400); *Production Yearbook; The State of Food and Agriculture;* and *Trade Yearbook.*

St. Martin's Press, Inc., 175 Fifth Avenue, New York, New York 10010 (800) 221-7945; *The Statesman's Year-Book.*

Statistical Office of the United Nations, Publishing Service, New York, New York 10017 (800) 253-9646; *Industrial Commodity Statistics Yearbook;* and *Statistical Yearbook.*

The World Bank, 1818 H Street, NW, Washington, D.C. 20433 (202) 477-1234; *Statistical Handbook: States of the Former USSR;* and *World Development Indicators.*

TAJIKISTAN - AIRLINE SERVICE

Business International Moscow, 23 Profsoyuznaya Ulitsa, 117859, Moscow (Telephone Number in U.S. (800) 938-4685); *The CIS Market Atlas.*

International Civil Aviation Organization, 999 University Street, Montreal, Quebec, Canada H3C 5H7 (514) 954-8219; *Civil Aviation Statistics of the World.*

St. Martin's Press, Inc., 175 Fifth Avenue, New York, New York 10010 (800) 221-7945; *The Statesman's Year-Book.*

Statistical Office of the United Nations, Publishing Service, New York, New York 10017 (800) 253-9646; *Statistical Yearbook.*

TAJIKISTAN - AIRPORTS

Central Intelligence Agency, Washington, D.C. 20505 (703) 482-1100, www.cia.gov; *The World Factbook.*

TAJIKISTAN - ANIMAL HEALTH

Statistical Office of the United Nations, Publishing Service, New York, New York 10017 (800) 253-9646; *Statistical Yearbook.*

TAJIKISTAN - AREA AND DENSITY OF POPULATION

Academic International Press, Box 1111, Gulf Breeze, Florida 32562; *Russia and Eurasia Facts and Figures Annual.*

Business International Moscow, 23 Profsoyuznaya Ulitsa, 117859, Moscow (Telephone Number in U.S. (800) 938-4685); *The CIS Market Atlas.*

Central Intelligence Agency,

Washington, D.C. 20505 (703) 482-1100, www.cia.gov; *The World Factbook.*

Euromonitor International, Inc., 122 South Michigan Avenue, Suite 1200, Chicago, Illinois 60603 (800) 577-EURO; *The World Economic Factbook.*

Europa Publications Limited, 18 Bedford Square, London, WC1B 3JN, England; *The Europa World Year Book.*

St. Martin's Press, Inc., 175 Fifth Avenue, New York, New York 10010 (800) 221-7945; *The Statesman's Year-Book.*

Statistical Office of the United Nations, Publishing Service, New York, New York 10017 (800) 253-9646; *Statistical Yearbook;* and *Trends in Europe and North America: The Statistical Yearbook of the Economic Commission for Europe.*

United Nations Educational, Scientific and Cultural Organization (UNESCO), 7 Place de Fontenoy, F-75700 Paris, France (Telephone Number in U.S. (212) 963-5981); *Statistical Yearbook.*

The World Bank, 1818 H Street, NW, Washington, D.C. 20433 (202) 477-1234; *World Development Report.*

TAJIKISTAN - BALANCE OF PAYMENTS

Europa Publications Limited, 18 Bedford Square, London, WC1B 3JN, England; *The Europa World Year Book.*

The World Bank, 1818 H Street, NW, Washington, D.C. 20433 (202) 477-1234; *World Development Report;* and *World Development Indicators.*

TAJIKISTAN - BANKING

Business International Moscow, 23 Profsoyuznaya Ulitsa, 117859, Moscow (Telephone Number in U.S. (800) 938-4685); *The CIS Market Atlas.*

Euromonitor International, Inc., 122 South Michigan Avenue, Suite 1200, Chicago, Illinois 60603 (800) 577-EURO; *World Marketing Data and Statistics.*

TAJIKISTAN - BEVERAGES

Statistical Office of the United Nations, Publishing Service, New York, New York 10017 (800) 253-9646; *Statistical Yearbook.*

TAJIKISTAN - BIRTH RATES

Academic International Press, Box 1111, Gulf Breeze, Florida 32562; *Russia and Eurasia Facts and Figures Annual.*

Business International Moscow, 23 Profsoyuznaya Ulitsa, 117859, Moscow

(Telephone Number in U.S. (800) 938-4685); *The CIS Market Atlas.*

Central Intelligence Agency, Washington, D.C. 20505 (703) 482-1100, www.cia.gov; *The World Factbook.*

Euromonitor International, Inc., 122 South Michigan Avenue, Suite 1200, Chicago, Illinois 60603 (800) 577-EURO; *International Marketing Data and Statistics;* and *The World Economic Factbook.*

Europa Publications Limited, 18 Bedford Square, London, WC1B 3JN, England; *The Europa World Year Book.*

St. Martin's Press, Inc., 175 Fifth Avenue, New York, New York 10010 (800) 221-7945; *The Statesman's Year-Book.*

Statistical Office of the United Nations, Publishing Service, New York, New York 10017 (800) 253-9646; *Statistical Yearbook.*

World Health Organization, Office of Publications, 20 Avenue Appia, CH-1211 Geneva 27, Switzerland (Telephone Number in U.S. (518) 436-9686); *World Health Statistics Annual.*

TAJIKISTAN - BOOK PRODUCTION

Statistical Office of the United Nations, Publishing Service, New York, New York 10017 (800) 253-9646; *Trends in Europe and North America: The Statistical Yearbook of the Economic Commission for Europe.*

United Nations Educational, Scientific and Cultural Organization (UNESCO), 7 Place de Fontenoy, F-75700 Paris, France (Telephone Number in U.S. (212) 963-5981); *Statistical Yearbook.*

TAJIKISTAN - BROADCASTING

Central Intelligence Agency, Washington, D.C. 20505 (703) 482-1100, www.cia.gov; *The World Factbook.*

Euromonitor International, Inc., 122 South Michigan Avenue, Suite 1200, Chicago, Illinois 60603 (800) 577-EURO; *World Marketing Data and Statistics.*

St. Martin's Press, Inc., 175 Fifth Avenue, New York, New York 10010 (800) 221-7945; *The Statesman's Year-Book.*

Statistical Office of the United Nations, Publishing Service, New York, New York 10017 (800) 253-9646; *Trends in Europe and North America: The Statistical Yearbook of the Economic Commission for Europe.*

United Nations Educational, Scientific and Cultural Organization (UNESCO), 7 Place de Fontenoy, F-75700 Paris, France (Telephone Number in U.S. (212) 963-5981); *Statistical Yearbook.*

TAJIKISTAN - BUDGET

Business International Moscow, 23 Profsoyuznaya Ulitsa, 117859, Moscow (Telephone Number in U.S. (800) 938-4685); *The CIS Market Atlas.*

Central Intelligence Agency, Washington, D.C. 20505 (703) 482-1100, www.cia.gov; *The World Factbook.*

TAJIKISTAN - CAPITAL INVESTMENT

The World Bank, 1818 H Street, NW, Washington, D.C. 20433 (202) 477-1234; *Statistical Handbook: States of the Former USSR.*

TAJIKISTAN - CATTLE - See
TAJIKISTAN - LIVESTOCK AND POULTRY

TAJIKISTAN - CHEMICALS

Business International Moscow, 23 Profsoyuznaya Ulitsa, 117859, Moscow (Telephone Number in U.S. (800) 938-4685); *The CIS Market Atlas.*

TAJIKISTAN - COAL PRODUCTION AND CONSUMPTION - See TAJIKISTAN - MINING AND MINERAL PRODUCTIONS

TAJIKISTAN - COMMERCE

St. Martin's Press, Inc., 175 Fifth Avenue, New York, New York 10010 (800) 221-7945; *The Statesman's Year-Book.*

TAJIKISTAN - COMMUNICATIONS - See TAJIKISTAN - TRANSPORTATION AND COMMUNICATIONS

TAJIKISTAN - CONSTRUCTION INDUSTRY

Academic International Press, Box 1111, Gulf Breeze, Florida 32562; *Russia and Eurasia Facts and Figures Annual.*

Business International Moscow, 23 Profsoyuznaya Ulitsa, 117859, Moscow (Telephone Number in U.S. (800) 938-4685); *The CIS Market Atlas.*

Statistical Office of the United Nations, Publishing Service, New York, New York 10017 (800) 253-9646; *Statistical Yearbook.*

TAJIKISTAN - CONSUMER PRICE INDEX

Europa Publications Limited, 18 Bedford Square, London, WC1B 3JN, England; *The Europa World Year Book.*

Statistical Office of the United Nations, Publishing Service, New York, New York 10017 (800) 253-9646; *Statistical Yearbook;* and *Trends in Europe and North America: The Statistical Yearbook of the Economic Commission for Europe.*

TAJIKISTAN - CONSUMER PRICES

Euromonitor International, Inc., 122 South Michigan Avenue, Suite 1200, Chicago, Illinois 60603 (800) 577-EURO; *World Marketing Data and Statistics.*

TAJIKISTAN - CONSUMER PRODUCTS

Business International Moscow, 23 Profsoyuznaya Ulitsa, 117859, Moscow (Telephone Number in U.S. (800) 938-4685); *The CIS Market Atlas.*

TAJIKISTAN - CONSUMPTION

Business International Moscow, 23 Profsoyuznaya Ulitsa, 117859, Moscow (Telephone Number in U.S. (800) 938-4685); *The CIS Market Atlas.*

The World Bank, 1818 H Street, NW, Washington, D.C. 20433 (202) 477-1234; *Statistical Handbook: States of the Former USSR;* and *World Development Report;*

TAJIKISTAN - COTTON PRODUCTION AND CONSUMPTION - See TAJIKISTAN -CROPS

TAJIKISTAN - CRIME

Academic International Press, Box 1111, Gulf Breeze, Florida 32562; *Russia and Eurasia Facts and Figures Annual.*

Statistical Office of the United Nations, Publishing Service, New York, New York 10017 (800) 253-9646; *Trends in Europe and North America: The Statistical Yearbook of the Economic Commission for Europe.*

TAJIKISTAN - CROPS

Academic International Press, Box 1111, Gulf Breeze, Florida 32562; *Russia and Eurasia Facts and Figures Annual.*

Europa Publications Limited, 18 Bedford Square, London, WC1B 3JN, England; *The Europa World Year Book.*

Food and Agriculture Organization of the United Nations (FAO), Via delle Terme di Caracalla, 00100, Rome, Italy (Telephone Number in U.S. (202) 653-2400); *Production Yearbook; The State of Food and Agriculture;* and *Trade Yearbook.*

St. Martin's Press, Inc., 175 Fifth Avenue, New York, New York 10010 (800) 221-7945; *The Statesman's Year-Book.*

Statistical Office of the United Nations, Publishing Service, New York, New York 10017 (800) 253-9646; *Industrial Commodity Statistics Yearbook;* and *Statistical Yearbook.*

The World Bank, 1818 H Street, NW, Washington, D.C. 20433 (202) 477-1234; *Statistical Handbook: States of the Former USSR.*

TAJIKISTAN - DAIRY PRODUCTS

Europa Publications Limited, 18 Bedford Square, London, WC1B 3JN, England; *The Europa World Year Book.*

Food and Agriculture Organization of the United Nations (FAO), Via delle Terme di Caracalla, 00100, Rome, Italy (Telephone Number in U.S. (202) 653-2400); *Production Yearbook; The State of Food and Agriculture;* and *Trade Yearbook.*

St. Martin's Press, Inc., 175 Fifth Avenue, New York, New York 10010 (800) 221-7945; *The Statesman's Year-Book.*

Statistical Office of the United Nations, Publishing Service, New York, New York 10017 (800) 253-9646; *Industrial Commodity Statistics Yearbook;* and *Statistical Yearbook.*

TAJIKISTAN - DEATH RATES - See TAJIKISTAN - MORTALITY

TAJIKISTAN - DEMOGRAPHY

Business International Moscow, 23 Profsoyuznaya Ulitsa, 117859, Moscow (Telephone Number in U.S. (800) 938-4685); *The CIS Market Atlas.*

The Economist Intelligence Unit, 111 West 57th Street, New York, New York 10019 (800) 938-4685; *The World Market Atlas.*

Euromonitor International, Inc., 122 South Michigan Avenue, Suite 1200, Chicago, Illinois 60603 (800) 577-EURO; *International Marketing Data and Statistics; World Marketing Data and Statistics;* and *The World Economic Factbook.*

Statistical Office of the United Nations, Publishing Service, New York, New York 10017 (800) 253-9646; *Demographic Yearbook;* and *Human Development Report.*

The World Bank, 1818 H Street, NW, Washington, D.C. 20433 (202) 477-1234; *Statistical Handbook: States of the Former USSR.*

TAJIKISTAN - DISEASES - See TAJIKISTAN - HEALTH

TAJIKISTAN - DIVORCE RATES

Academic International Press, Box 1111, Gulf Breeze, Florida 32562; *Russia and Eurasia Facts and Figures Annual.*

Statistical Office of the United Nations, Publishing Service, New York, New York 10017 (800) 253-9646; *Demographic Yearbook; Statistical Yearbook;* and *Trends in Europe and North America: The*

Statistical Yearbook of the Economic Commission for Europe.

TAJIKISTAN - DOMESTIC INVESTMENT

Business International Moscow, 23 Profsoyuznaya Ulitsa, 117859, Moscow (Telephone Number in U.S. (800) 938-4685); *The CIS Market Atlas.*

TAJIKISTAN - ECONOMY

Academic International Press, Box 1111, Gulf Breeze, Florida 32562; *Russia and Eurasia Facts and Figures Annual.*

Business International Moscow, 23 Profsoyuznaya Ulitsa, 117859, Moscow (Telephone Number in U.S. (800) 938-4685); *The CIS Market Atlas.*

Central Intelligence Agency, Washington, D.C. 20505 (703) 482-1100, www.cia.gov; *The World Factbook.*

Economist Intelligence Unit, 111 West 57th Street, New York, New York 10019 (800) 938-4685; *Tajikistan Country Report.*

Euromonitor International, Inc., 122 South Michigan Avenue, Suite 1200, Chicago, Illinois 60603 (800) 577-EURO; *The World Economic Factbook;* and *World Marketing Data and Statistics.*

Europa Publications Limited, 18 Bedford Square, London, WC1B 3JN, England; *The Europa World Year Book.*

St. Martin's Press, Inc., 175 Fifth Avenue, New York, New York 10010 (800) 221-7945; *The Statesman's Year-Book.*

Statistical Office of the United Nations, Publishing Service, New York, New York 10017 (800) 253-9646; *World Statistics Pocketbook.*

The World Bank, 1818 H Street, NW, Washington, D.C. 20433 (202) 477-1234; *The World Bank Atlas;* and *World Development Report.*

TAJIKISTAN - EDUCATION

Academic International Press, Box 1111, Gulf Breeze, Florida 32562; *Russia and Eurasia Facts and Figures Annual.*

Business International Moscow, 23 Profsoyuznaya Ulitsa, 117859, Moscow (Telephone Number in U.S. (800) 938-4685); *The CIS Market Atlas.*

Euromonitor International, Inc., 122 South Michigan Avenue, Suite 1200, Chicago, Illinois 60603 (800) 577-EURO; *International Marketing Data and Statistics;* and *World Marketing Data and Statistics.*

Europa Publications Limited, 18

Bedford Square, London, WC1B 3JN, England; *The Europa World Year Book.*

St. Martin's Press, Inc., 175 Fifth Avenue, New York, New York 10010 (800) 221-7945; *The Statesman's Year-Book.*

Statistical Office of the United Nations, Publishing Service, New York, New York 10017 (800) 253-9646; *Human Development Report;* and *Trends in Europe and North America: The Statistical Yearbook of the Economic Commission for Europe.*

United Nations Educational, Scientific and Cultural Organization (UNESCO), 7 Place de Fontenoy, F-75700 Paris, France (Telephone Number in U.S. (212) 963-5981); *Statistical Yearbook.*

The World Bank, 1818 H Street, NW, Washington, D.C. 20433 (202) 477-1234; *World Development Report.*

TAJIKISTAN - ELECTRICITY

Academic International Press, Box 1111, Gulf Breeze, Florida 32562; *Russia and Eurasia Facts and Figures Annual.*

Business International Moscow, 23 Profsoyuznaya Ulitsa, 117859, Moscow (Telephone Number in U.S. (800) 938-4685); *The CIS Market Atlas.*

Central Intelligence Agency, Washington, D.C. 20505 (703) 482-1100, www.cia.gov; *The World Factbook.*

St. Martin's Press, Inc., 175 Fifth Avenue, New York, New York 10010 (800) 221-7945; *The Statesman's Year-Book.*

Statistical Office of the United Nations, Publishing Service, New York, New York 10017 (800) 253-9646; *Energy Statistics Yearbook; Human Development Report; Statistical Yearbook;* and *Trends in Europe and North America: The Statistical Yearbook of the Economic Commission for Europe.*

The World Bank, 1818 H Street, NW, Washington, D.C. 20433 (202) 477-1234; *Statistical Handbook: States of the Former USSR.*

TAJIKISTAN - EMPLOYMENT

Euromonitor International, Inc., 122 South Michigan Avenue, Suite 1200, Chicago, Illinois 60603 (800) 577-EURO; *International Marketing Data and Statistics.*

Statistical Office of the United Nations, Publishing Service, New York, New York 10017 (800) 253-9646; *Statistical Yearbook;* and *Trends in Europe and North America: The Statistical Yearbook of the Economic Commission for Europe.*

The World Bank, 1818 H Street, NW, Washington, D.C. 20433 (202) 477-1234; *Statistical Handbook: States of the Former USSR.*

TAJIKISTAN - ENERGY

Academic International Press, Box 1111, Gulf Breeze, Florida 32562; *Russia and Eurasia Facts and Figures Annual.*

Business International Moscow, 23 Profsoyuznaya Ulitsa, 117859, Moscow (Telephone Number in U.S. (800) 938-4685); *The CIS Market Atlas.*

Euromonitor International, Inc., 122 South Michigan Avenue, Suite 1200, Chicago, Illinois 60603 (800) 577-EURO; *International Marketing Data and Statistics; World Marketing Data and Statistics;* and *The World Economic Factbook.*

St. Martin's Press, Inc., 175 Fifth Avenue, New York, New York 10010 (800) 221-7945; *The Statesman's Year-Book.*

Statistical Office of the United Nations, Publishing Service, New York, New York 10017 (800) 253-9646; *Energy Statistics Yearbook; Human Development Report; Statistical Yearbook; Trends in Europe and North America: The Statistical Yearbook of the Economic Commission for Europe;* and *World Statistics Pocketbook.*

The World Bank, 1818 H Street, NW, Washington, D.C. 20433 (202) 477-1234; *Statistical Handbook: States of the Former USSR; The World Bank Atlas;* and *World Development Report.*

TAJIKISTAN - ENVIRONMENT

Business International Moscow, 23 Profsoyuznaya Ulitsa, 117859, Moscow (Telephone Number in U.S. (800) 938-4685); *The CIS Market Atlas.*

Economist Intelligence Unit, 111 West 57th Street, New York, New York 10019 (800) 938-4685; *Tajikistan Country Report.*

Statistical Office of the United Nations, Publishing Service, New York, New York 10017 (800) 253-9646; *Statistical Yearbook; Trends in Europe and North America: The Statistical Yearbook of the Economic Commission for Europe;* and *World Statistics Pocketbook.*

TAJIKISTAN - ENVIRONMENT

Economist Intelligence Unit, 111 West 57th Street, New York, New York 10019 (800) 938-4685; *Tajikistan Country Report.*

TAJIKISTAN - EXCHANGE RATES

Central Intelligence Agency, Washington, D.C. 20505 (703) 482-1100,

www.cia.gov; *The World Factbook.*

Euromonitor International, Inc., 122 South Michigan Avenue, Suite 1200, Chicago, Illinois 60603 (800) 577-EURO; *International Marketing Data and Statistics;* and *The World Economic Factbook.*

Europa Publications Limited, 18 Bedford Square, London, WC1B 3JN, England; *The Europa World Year Book.*

Statistical Office of the United Nations, Publishing Service, New York, New York 10017 (800) 253-9646; *Statistical Yearbook; Trends in Europe and North America: The Statistical Yearbook of the Economic Commission for Europe;* and *World Statistics Pocketbook.*

Walden Publishing Ltd., Two Market Street, Saffron Walden Essex, CB10 1HZ, England; *The World of Information Asia and Pacific Review.*

TAJIKISTAN - EXPORTS

Academic International Press, Box 1111, Gulf Breeze, Florida 32562; *Russia and Eurasia Facts and Figures Annual.*

Business International Moscow, 23 Profsoyuznaya Ulitsa, 117859, Moscow (Telephone Number in U.S. (800) 938-4685); *The CIS Market Atlas.*

Central Intelligence Agency, Washington, D.C. 20505 (703) 482-1100, www.cia.gov; *The World Factbook.*

The Economist Intelligence Unit, 111 West 57th Street, New York, New York 10019 (800) 938-4685; *Tajikistan Country Report;* and *The World Market Atlas.*

Euromonitor International, Inc., 122 South Michigan Avenue, Suite 1200, Chicago, Illinois 60603 (800) 577-EURO; *International Marketing Data and Statistics;* and *The World Economic Factbook.*

Europa Publications Limited, 18 Bedford Square, London, WC1B 3JN, England; *The Europa World Year Book.*

International Monetary Fund, 700 Nineteenth Street, NW, Washington, D.C. 20431 (202) 623-7000; *Direction of Trade Statistics.*

St. Martin's Press, Inc., 175 Fifth Avenue, New York, New York 10010 (800) 221-7945; *The Statesman's Year-Book.*

Statistical Office of the United Nations, Publishing Service, New York, New York 10017 (800) 253-9646; *International Trade Statistics Yearbook;* and *Trends in Europe and North America: The Statistical Yearbook of the Economic Commission for Europe.*

Walden Publishing Ltd., Two Market Street, Saffron Walden Essex, CB10 1HZ, England; *The World of Information Asia and Pacific Review.*

The World Bank, 1818 H Street, NW, Washington, D.C. 20433 (202) 477-1234; *Statistical Handbook: States of the Former USSR; World Development Report;* and *World Development Indicators.*

TAJIKISTAN - EXTERNAL DEBT

Food and Agriculture Organization of the United Nations (FAO), Via delle Terme di Caracalla, 00100, Rome, Italy (Telephone Number in U.S. (202) 653-2400); *Trade Yearbook.*

The World Bank, 1818 H Street, NW, Washington, D.C. 20433 (202) 477-1234; *World Development Report;* and *World Development Indicators.*

TAJIKISTAN - EXTERNAL TRADE

Academic International Press, Box 1111, Gulf Breeze, Florida 32562; *Russia and Eurasia Facts and Figures Annual.*

Euromonitor International, Inc., 122 South Michigan Avenue, Suite 1200, Chicago, Illinois 60603 (800) 577-EURO; *World Marketing Data and Statistics.*

Statistical Office of the United Nations, Publishing Service, New York, New York 10017 (800) 253-9646; *Statistical Yearbook.*

The World Bank, 1818 H Street, NW, Washington, D.C. 20433 (202) 477-1234; *Statistical Handbook: States of the Former USSR.*

TAJIKISTAN - FABRIC PRODUCTION AND CONSUMPTION - See TAJIKISTAN - TEXTILE INDUSTRY

TAJIKISTAN - FERTILITY RATES

Central Intelligence Agency, Washington, D.C. 20505 (703) 482-1100, www.cia.gov; *The World Factbook.*

Statistical Office of the United Nations, Publishing Service, New York, New York 10017 (800) 253-9646; *Human Development Report;* and *Trends in Europe and North America: The Statistical Yearbook of the Economic Commission for Europe.*

The World Bank, 1818 H Street, NW, Washington, D.C. 20433 (202) 477-1234; *Statistical Handbook: States of the Former USSR; The World Bank Atlas; World Development Report;* and *World Development Indicators.*

World Health Organization, Office of Publications, 20 Avenue Appia, CH-1211

Geneva 27, Switzerland (Telephone Number in U.S. (518) 436-9686); *World Health Statistics Annual.*

TAJIKISTAN - FERTILIZER

Food and Agriculture Organization of the United Nations (FAO), Via delle Terme di Caracalla, 00100, Rome, Italy (Telephone Number in U.S. (202) 653-2400); *Fertilizer Yearbook.*

Statistical Office of the United Nations, Publishing Service, New York, New York 10017 (800) 253-9646; *Industrial Commodity Statistics Yearbook;* and *Statistical Yearbook.*

TAJIKISTAN - FINANCE

Economist Intelligence Unit, 111 West 57th Street, New York, New York 10019 (800) 938-4685; *Tajikistan Country Report.*

Europa Publications Limited, 18 Bedford Square, London, WC1B 3JN, England; *The Europa World Year Book.*

The World Bank, 1818 H Street, NW, Washington, D.C. 20433 (202) 477-1234; *Statistical Handbook: States of the Former USSR.*

TAJIKISTAN - FISHERIES

Europa Publications Limited, 18 Bedford Square, London, WC1B 3JN, England; *The Europa World Year Book.*

Food and Agriculture Organization of the United Nations (FAO), Via delle Terme di Caracalla, 00100, Rome, Italy (Telephone Number in U.S. (202) 653-2400); *The State of Food and Agriculture;* and *Yearbook of Fishery Statistics.*

Statistical Office of the United Nations, Publishing Service, New York, New York 10017 (800) 253-9646; *Industrial Commodity Statistics Yearbook;* and *Statistical Yearbook.*

TAJIKISTAN - FOOD

Food and Agriculture Organization of the United Nations (FAO), Via delle Terme di Caracalla, 00100, Rome, Italy (Telephone Number in U.S. (202) 653-2400); *Production Yearbook; The State of Food and Agriculture;* and *Trade Yearbook.*

Statistical Office of the United Nations, Publishing Service, New York, New York 10017 (800) 253-9646; *Human Development Report;* and *Industrial Commodity Statistics Yearbook.*

TAJIKISTAN - FOOTWEAR PRODUCTION AND CONSUMPTION - See TAJIKISTAN - TEXTILE INDUSTRY

TAJIKISTAN - FOREIGN DEBT

Walden Publishing Ltd., Two Market Street, Saffron Walden Essex, CB10 1HZ, England; *The World of Information Asia and Pacific Review.*

TAJIKISTAN - FOREIGN INVESTMENT

Business International Moscow, 23 Profsoyuznaya Ulitsa, 117859, Moscow (Telephone Number in U.S. (800) 938-4685); *The CIS Market Atlas.*

TAJIKISTAN - FOREIGN TRADE

Business International Moscow, 23 Profsoyuznaya Ulitsa, 117859, Moscow (Telephone Number in U.S. (800) 938-4685); *The CIS Market Atlas.*

Economist Intelligence Unit, 111 West 57th Street, New York, New York 10019 (800) 938-4685; *Tajikistan Country Report.*

Euromonitor International, Inc., 122 South Michigan Avenue, Suite 1200, Chicago, Illinois 60603 (800) 577-EURO; *The World Economic Factbook.*

Europa Publications Limited, 18 Bedford Square, London, WC1B 3JN, England; *The Europa World Year Book.*

Food and Agriculture Organization of the United Nations (FAO), Via delle Terme di Caracalla, 00100, Rome, Italy (Telephone Number in U.S. (202) 653-2400); *Trade Yearbook.*

International Monetary Fund, 700 Nineteenth Street, NW, Washington, D.C. 20431 (202) 623-7000; *Direction of Trade Statistics.*

St. Martin's Press, Inc., 175 Fifth Avenue, New York, New York 10010 (800) 221-7945; *The Statesman's Year-Book.*

Statistical Office of the United Nations, Publishing Service, New York, New York 10017 (800) 253-9646; *International Trade Statistics Yearbook;* and *Statistical Yearbook.*

The World Bank, 1818 H Street, NW, Washington, D.C. 20433 (202) 477-1234; *Statistical Handbook: States of the Former USSR; World Development Report;* and *World Development Indicators.*

TAJIKISTAN - FORESTRY AND FOREST PRODUCTS

Academic International Press, Box 1111, Gulf Breeze, Florida 32562; *Russia and Eurasia Facts and Figures Annual.*

Business International Moscow, 23 Profsoyuznaya Ulitsa, 117859, Moscow (Telephone Number in U.S. (800) 938-

4685); *The CIS Market Atlas.*

Food and Agriculture Organization of the United Nations (FAO), Via delle Terme di Caracalla, 00100, Rome, Italy (Telephone Number in U.S. (202) 653-2400); *The State of Food and Agriculture;* and *Yearbook of Forest Products.*

Statistical Office of the United Nations, Publishing Service, New York, New York 10017 (800) 253-9646; *Industrial Commodity Statistics Yearbook; Statistical Yearbook;* and *Trends in Europe and North America: The Statistical Yearbook of the Economic Commission for Europe.*

United Nations Educational, Scientific and Cultural Organization (UNESCO), 7 Place de Fontenoy, F-75700 Paris, France (Telephone Number in U.S. (212) 963-5981); *Statistical Yearbook.*

The World Bank, 1818 H Street, NW, Washington, D.C. 20433 (202) 477-1234; *World Development Report.*

TAJIKISTAN - GOATS - See TAJIKISTAN - LIVESTOCK AND POULTRY

TAJIKISTAN - GOVERNMENT

Academic International Press, Box 1111, Gulf Breeze, Florida 32562; *Russia and Eurasia Facts and Figures Annual.*

Central Intelligence Agency, Washington, D.C. 20505 (703) 482-1100, www.cia.gov; *The World Factbook.*

Europa Publications Limited, 18 Bedford Square, London, WC1B 3JN, England; *The Europa World Year Book.*

St. Martin's Press, Inc., 175 Fifth Avenue, New York, New York 10010 (800) 221-7945; *The Statesman's Year-Book.*

Statistical Office of the United Nations, Publishing Service, New York, New York 10017 (800) 253-9646; *National Accounts Statistics;* and *Statistical Yearbook.*

The World Bank, 1818 H Street, NW, Washington, D.C. 20433 (202) 477-1234; *Statistical Handbook: States of the Former USSR;* and *World Development Report.*

TAJIKISTAN - GROSS DOMESTIC PRODUCT

Academic International Press, Box 1111, Gulf Breeze, Florida 32562; *Russia and Eurasia Facts and Figures Annual.*

Economist Intelligence Unit, 111 West 57th Street, New York, New York 10019 (800) 938-4685; *Tajikistan Country Report.*

Euromonitor International, Inc., 122 South Michigan Avenue, Suite 1200, Chicago, Illinois 60603 (800) 577-EURO;

International Marketing Data and Statistics; and *The World Economic Factbook.*

Statistical Office of the United Nations, Publishing Service, New York, New York 10017 (800) 253-9646; *Human Development Report; National Accounts Statistics; Statistical Yearbook;* and *Trends in Europe and North America: The Statistical Yearbook of the Economic Commission for Europe.*

The World Bank, 1818 H Street, NW, Washington, D.C. 20433 (202) 477-1234; *Statistical Handbook: States of the Former USSR; World Development Report;* and *World Development Indicators.*

TAJIKISTAN - GROSS NATIONAL PRODUCT

St. Martin's Press, Inc., 175 Fifth Avenue, New York, New York 10010 (800) 221-7945; *The Statesman's Year-Book.*

Walden Publishing Ltd., Two Market Street, Saffron Walden Essex, CB10 1HZ, England; *The World of Information Asia and Pacific Review.*

The World Bank, 1818 H Street, NW, Washington, D.C. 20433 (202) 477-1234; *The World Bank Atlas; World Development Report;* and *World Development Indicators.*

TAJIKISTAN - HEALTH

Academic International Press, Box 1111, Gulf Breeze, Florida 32562; *Russia and Eurasia Facts and Figures Annual.*

Business International Moscow, 23 Profsoyuznaya Ulitsa, 117859, Moscow (Telephone Number in U.S. (800) 938-4685); *The CIS Market Atlas.*

Euromonitor International, Inc., 122 South Michigan Avenue, Suite 1200, Chicago, Illinois 60603 (800) 577-EURO; *World Marketing Data and Statistics.*

St. Martin's Press, Inc., 175 Fifth Avenue, New York, New York 10010 (800) 221-7945; *The Statesman's Year-Book.*

Statistical Office of the United Nations, Publishing Service, New York, New York 10017 (800) 253-9646; *Human Development Report; Statistical Yearbook;* and *Trends in Europe and North America: The Statistical Yearbook of the Economic Commission for Europe.*

United Nations Children's Fund (UNICEF), 3 United Nations Plaza, New York, New York 10017 (800) 253-9646; *State of the World's Children.*

The World Bank, 1818 H Street, NW, Washington, D.C. 20433 (202) 477-1234; *World Development Report.*

World Health Organization, Office of Publications, 20 Avenue Appia, CH-1211 Geneva 27, Switzerland (Telephone Number in U.S. (518) 436-9686); *World Health Statistics Annual.*

TAJIKISTAN - HIGHWAYS

Academic International Press, Box 1111, Gulf Breeze, Florida 32562; *Russia and Eurasia Facts and Figures Annual.*

Business International Moscow, 23 Profsoyuznaya Ulitsa, 117859, Moscow (Telephone Number in U.S. (800) 938-4685); *The CIS Market Atlas.*

Central Intelligence Agency, Washington, D.C. 20505 (703) 482-1100, www.cia.gov; *The World Factbook.*

St. Martin's Press, Inc., 175 Fifth Avenue, New York, New York 10010 (800) 221-7945; *The Statesman's Year-Book.*

Statistical Office of the United Nations, Publishing Service, New York, New York 10017 (800) 253-9646; *Trends in Europe and North America: The Statistical Yearbook of the Economic Commission for Europe.*

TAJIKISTAN - HOUSING AND HOUSING UNITS

Business International Moscow, 23 Profsoyuznaya Ulitsa, 117859, Moscow (Telephone Number in U.S. (800) 938-4685); *The CIS Market Atlas.*

Euromonitor International, Inc., 122 South Michigan Avenue, Suite 1200, Chicago, Illinois 60603 (800) 577-EURO; *World Marketing Data and Statistics.*

Statistical Office of the United Nations, Publishing Service, New York, New York 10017 (800) 253-9646; *Trends in Europe and North America: The Statistical Yearbook of the Economic Commission for Europe.*

TAJIKISTAN - ILLITERATE POPULATION

Central Intelligence Agency, Washington, D.C. 20505 (703) 482-1100, www.cia.gov; *The World Factbook.*

Euromonitor International, Inc., 122 South Michigan Avenue, Suite 1200, Chicago, Illinois 60603 (800) 577-EURO; *The World Economic Factbook.*

Statistical Office of the United Nations, Publishing Service, New York, New York 10017 (800) 253-9646; *Human Development Report.*

United Nations Educational, Scientific and Cultural Organization (UNESCO), 7 Place de Fontenoy, F-75700 Paris, France (Telephone Number in U.S. (212) 963-5981); *Statistical Yearbook.*

TAJIKISTAN - IMPORTS

Academic International Press, Box 1111, Gulf Breeze, Florida 32562; *Russia and Eurasia Facts and Figures Annual.*

Business International Moscow, 23 Profsoyuznaya Ulitsa, 117859, Moscow (Telephone Number in U.S. (800) 938-4685); *The CIS Market Atlas.*

Central Intelligence Agency, Washington, D.C. 20505 (703) 482-1100, www.cia.gov; *The World Factbook.*

The Economist Intelligence Unit, 111 West 57th Street, New York, New York 10019 (800) 938-4685; *Tajikistan Country Report;* and *The World Market Atlas.*

Euromonitor International, Inc., 122 South Michigan Avenue, Suite 1200, Chicago, Illinois 60603 (800) 577-EURO; *International Marketing Data and Statistics;* and *The World Economic Factbook.*

Europa Publications Limited, 18 Bedford Square, London, WC1B 3JN, England; *The Europa World Year Book.*

International Monetary Fund, 700 Nineteenth Street, NW, Washington, D.C. 20431 (202) 623-7000; *Direction of Trade Statistics.*

St. Martin's Press, Inc., 175 Fifth Avenue, New York, New York 10010 (800) 221-7945; *The Statesman's Year-Book.*

Statistical Office of the United Nations, Publishing Service, New York, New York 10017 (800) 253-9646; *International Trade Statistics Yearbook;* and *Trends in Europe and North America: The Statistical Yearbook of the Economic Commission for Europe.*

Walden Publishing Ltd., Two Market Street, Saffron Walden Essex, CB10 1HZ, England; *The World of Information Asia and Pacific Review.*

The World Bank, 1818 H Street, NW, Washington, D.C. 20433 (202) 477-1234; *Statistical Handbook: States of the Former USSR; World Development Report;* and *World Development Indicators.*

TAJIKISTAN - INDUSTRY

Academic International Press, Box 1111, Gulf Breeze, Florida 32562; *Russia and Eurasia Facts and Figures Annual.*

Business International Moscow, 23 Profsoyuznaya Ulitsa, 117859, Moscow (Telephone Number in U.S. (800) 938-4685); *The CIS Market Atlas.*

Central Intelligence Agency, Washington, D.C. 20505 (703) 482-1100,

www.cia.gov; *The World Factbook.*

Economist Intelligence Unit, 111 West 57th Street, New York, New York 10019 (800) 938-4685; *Tajikistan Country Report.*

Euromonitor International, Inc., 122 South Michigan Avenue, Suite 1200, Chicago, Illinois 60603 (800) 577-EURO; *The World Economic Factbook;* and *World Marketing Data and Statistics.*

Europa Publications Limited, 18 Bedford Square, London, WC1B 3JN, England; *The Europa World Year Book.*

St. Martin's Press, Inc., 175 Fifth Avenue, New York, New York 10010 (800) 221-7945; *The Statesman's Year-Book.*

Statistical Office of the United Nations, Publishing Service, New York, New York 10017 (800) 253-9646; *Industrial Commodity Statistics Yearbook; Statistical Yearbook;* and *Trends in Europe and North America: The Statistical Yearbook of the Economic Commission for Europe.*

The World Bank, 1818 H Street, NW, Washington, D.C. 20433 (202) 477-1234; *Statistical Handbook: States of the Former USSR;* and *World Development Indicators.*

TAJIKISTAN - INFANT MORTALITY RATES - See TAJIKISTAN - MORTALITY

TAJIKISTAN - INTERNAL TRADE

Statistical Office of the United Nations, Publishing Service, New York, New York 10017 (800) 253-9646; *Statistical Yearbook.*

TAJIKISTAN - LABOR

Academic International Press, Box 1111, Gulf Breeze, Florida 32562; *Russia and Eurasia Facts and Figures Annual.*

Business International Moscow, 23 Profsoyuznaya Ulitsa, 117859, Moscow (Telephone Number in U.S. (800) 938-4685); *The CIS Market Atlas.*

Central Intelligence Agency, Washington, D.C. 20505 (703) 482-1100, www.cia.gov; *The World Factbook.*

Euromonitor International, Inc., 122 South Michigan Avenue, Suite 1200, Chicago, Illinois 60603 (800) 577-EURO; *International Marketing Data and Statistics;* and *World Marketing Data and Statistics.*

Europa Publications Limited, 18 Bedford Square, London, WC1B 3JN, England; *The Europa World Year Book.*

St. Martin's Press, Inc., 175 Fifth Avenue, New York, New York 10010 (800) 221-7945; *The Statesman's Year-Book.*

Statistical Office of the United Nations, Publishing Service, New York, New York 10017 (800) 253-9646; *Human Development Report;* and *Statistical Yearbook.*

The World Bank, 1818 H Street, NW, Washington, D.C. 20433 (202) 477-1234; *Statistical Handbook: States of the Former USSR; The World Bank Atlas; World Development Report;* and *World Development Indicators.*

TAJIKISTAN - LAND USE

Central Intelligence Agency, Washington, D.C. 20505 (703) 482-1100, www.cia.gov; *The World Factbook.*

Euromonitor International, Inc., 122 South Michigan Avenue, Suite 1200, Chicago, Illinois 60603 (800) 577-EURO; *International Marketing Data and Statistics.*

Food and Agriculture Organization of the United Nations (FAO), Via delle Terme di Caracalla, 00100, Rome, Italy (Telephone Number in U.S. (202) 653-2400); *Production Yearbook.*

The World Bank, 1818 H Street, NW, Washington, D.C. 20433 (202) 477-1234; *World Development Report.*

TAJIKISTAN - LIBRARIES

Statistical Office of the United Nations, Publishing Service, New York, New York 10017 (800) 253-9646; *Trends in Europe and North America: The Statistical Yearbook of the Economic Commission for Europe.*

United Nations Educational, Scientific and Cultural Organization (UNESCO), 7 Place de Fontenoy, F-75700 Paris, France (Telephone Number in U.S. (212) 963-5981); *Statistical Yearbook.*

TAJIKISTAN - LIFE EXPECTANCY

Academic International Press, Box 1111, Gulf Breeze, Florida 32562; *Russia and Eurasia Facts and Figures Annual.*

Business International Moscow, 23 Profsoyuznaya Ulitsa, 117859, Moscow (Telephone Number in U.S. (800) 938-4685); *The CIS Market Atlas.*

Central Intelligence Agency, Washington, D.C. 20505 (703) 482-1100, www.cia.gov; *The World Factbook.*

Euromonitor International, Inc., 122 South Michigan Avenue, Suite 1200, Chicago, Illinois 60603 (800) 577-EURO; *The World Economic Factbook.*

Statistical Office of the United Nations, Publishing Service, New York, New York 10017 (800) 253-9646; *Demographic*

Yearbook; Human Development Report; Trends in Europe and North America: The Statistical Yearbook of the Economic Commission for Europe; and *World Statistics Pocketbook.*

The World Bank, 1818 H Street, NW, Washington, D.C. 20433 (202) 477-1234; *The World Bank Atlas; World Development Report;* and *World Development Indicators.*

World Health Organization, Office of Publications, 20 Avenue Appia, CH-1211 Geneva 27, Switzerland (Telephone Number in U.S. (518) 436-9686); *World Health Statistics Annual.*

TAJIKISTAN - LITERACY RATE

Euromonitor International, Inc., 122 South Michigan Avenue, Suite 1200, Chicago, Illinois 60603 (800) 577-EURO; *World Marketing Data and Statistics.*

TAJIKISTAN - LIVESTOCK AND POULTRY

Academic International Press, Box 1111, Gulf Breeze, Florida 32562; *Russia and Eurasia Facts and Figures Annual.*

Business International Moscow, 23 Profsoyuznaya Ulitsa, 117859, Moscow (Telephone Number in U.S. (800) 938-4685); *The CIS Market Atlas.*

Europa Publications Limited, 18 Bedford Square, London, WC1B 3JN, England; *The Europa World Year Book.*

Food and Agriculture Organization of the United Nations (FAO), Via delle Terme di Caracalla, 00100, Rome, Italy (Telephone Number in U.S. (202) 653-2400); *Production Yearbook; The State of Food and Agriculture;* and *Trade Yearbook.*

St. Martin's Press, Inc., 175 Fifth Avenue, New York, New York 10010 (800) 221-7945; *The Statesman's Year-Book.*

Statistical Office of the United Nations, Publishing Service, New York, New York 10017 (800) 253-9646; *Industrial Commodity Statistics Yearbook;* and *Statistical Yearbook.*

TAJIKISTAN - MACHINERY

Statistical Office of the United Nations, Publishing Service, New York, New York 10017 (800) 253-9646; *Industrial Commodity Statistics Yearbook.*

TAJIKISTAN - MAIL - NUMBER OF PIECES SENT OR RECEIVED

Statistical Office of the United Nations, Publishing Service, New York, New York 10017 (800) 253-9646; *Statistical Yearbook.*

TAJIKISTAN - MANUFACTURING

Statistical Office of the United Nations, Publishing Service, New York, New York 10017 (800) 253-9646; *Industrial Commodity Statistics Yearbook;* and *Statistical Yearbook.*

The World Bank, 1818 H Street, NW, Washington, D.C. 20433 (202) 477-1234; *World Development Indicators.*

TAJIKISTAN - MARRIAGE RATES

Academic International Press, Box 1111, Gulf Breeze, Florida 32562; *Russia and Eurasia Facts and Figures Annual.*

Europa Publications Limited, 18 Bedford Square, London, WC1B 3JN, England; *The Europa World Year Book.*

Statistical Office of the United Nations, Publishing Service, New York, New York 10017 (800) 253-9646; *Demographic Yearbook; Statistical Yearbook;* and *Trends in Europe and North America: The Statistical Yearbook of the Economic Commission for Europe.*

TAJIKISTAN - MEAT PRODUCTION - See TAJIKISTAN - LIVESTOCK AND POULTRY

TAJIKISTAN - MERCHANT SHIPPING

St. Martin's Press, Inc., 175 Fifth Avenue, New York, New York 10010 (800) 221-7945; *The Statesman's Year-Book.*

Statistical Office of the United Nations, Publishing Service, New York, New York 10017 (800) 253-9646; *Statistical Yearbook.*

TAJIKISTAN - MILITARY

Academic International Press, Box 1111, Gulf Breeze, Florida 32562; *Russia and Eurasia Facts and Figures Annual.*

Central Intelligence Agency, Washington, D.C. 20505 (703) 482-1100, www.cia.gov; *The World Factbook.*

Euromonitor International, Inc., 122 South Michigan Avenue, Suite 1200, Chicago, Illinois 60603 (800) 577-EURO; *World Marketing Data and Statistics.*

The International Institute for Strategic Studies, 23 Tavistock Street, London WC2E 7NQ, England 44 171 3797676; *The Military Balance.*

Statistical Office of the United Nations, Publishing Service, New York, New York 10017 (800) 253-9646; *Human Development Report.*

TAJIKISTAN - MINING AND MINERAL PRODUCTS

Academic International Press, Box 1111, Gulf Breeze, Florida 32562; *Russia and Eurasia Facts and Figures Annual.*

Business International Moscow, 23 Profsoyuznaya Ulitsa, 117859, Moscow (Telephone Number in U.S. (800) 938-4685); *The CIS Market Atlas.*

Europa Publications Limited, 18 Bedford Square, London, WC1B 3JN, England; *The Europa World Year Book.*

St. Martin's Press, Inc., 175 Fifth Avenue, New York, New York 10010 (800) 221-7945; *The Statesman's Year-Book.*

Statistical Office of the United Nations, Publishing Service, New York, New York 10017 (800) 253-9646; *Energy Statistics Yearbook; Industrial Commodity Statistics Yearbook;* and *Statistical Yearbook.*

TAJIKISTAN - MONEY SUPPLY

Economist Intelligence Unit, 111 West 57th Street, New York, New York 10019 (800) 938-4685; *Tajikistan Country Report.*

Europa Publications Limited, 18 Bedford Square, London, WC1B 3JN, England; *The Europa World Year Book.*

TAJIKISTAN - MONUMENTS AND HISTORICAL SITES

United Nations Educational, Scientific and Cultural Organization (UNESCO), 7 Place de Fontenoy, F-75700 Paris, France (Telephone Number in U.S. (212) 963-5981); *Statistical Yearbook.*

TAJIKISTAN - MORTALITY

Academic International Press, Box 1111, Gulf Breeze, Florida 32562; *Russia and Eurasia Facts and Figures Annual.*

Business International Moscow, 23 Profsoyuznaya Ulitsa, 117859, Moscow (Telephone Number in U.S. (800) 938-4685); *The CIS Market Atlas.*

Central Intelligence Agency, Washington, D.C. 20505 (703) 482-1100, www.cia.gov; *The World Factbook.*

Euromonitor International, Inc., 122 South Michigan Avenue, Suite 1200, Chicago, Illinois 60603 (800) 577-EURO; *International Marketing Data and Statistics;* and *The World Economic Factbook.*

Europa Publications Limited, 18 Bedford Square, London, WC1B 3JN, England; *The Europa World Year Book.*

St. Martin's Press, Inc., 175 Fifth Avenue, New York, New York 10010 (800) 221-7945; *The Statesman's Year-Book.*

Statistical Office of the United Nations, Publishing Service, New York, New York

10017 (800) 253-9646; *Demographic Yearbook; Human Development Report; Statistical Yearbook; Trends in Europe and North America: The Statistical Yearbook of the Economic Commission for Europe;* and *World Statistics Pocketbook.*

United Nations Children's Fund (UNICEF), 3 United Nations Plaza, New York, New York 10017 (800) 253-9646; *State of the World's Children.*

The World Bank, 1818 H Street, NW, Washington, D.C. 20433 (202) 477-1234; *The World Bank Atlas; World Development Report;* and *World Development Indicators.*

World Health Organization, Office of Publications, 20 Avenue Appia, CH-1211 Geneva 27, Switzerland (Telephone Number in U.S. (518) 436-9686); *World Health Statistics Annual.*

TAJIKISTAN - MOTION PICTURES

Statistical Office of the United Nations, Publishing Service, New York, New York 10017 (800) 253-9646; *Statistical Yearbook.*

United Nations Educational, Scientific and Cultural Organization (UNESCO), 7 Place de Fontenoy, F-75700 Paris, France (Telephone Number in U.S. (212) 963-5981); *Statistical Yearbook.*

TAJIKISTAN - MOTOR VEHICLES

Business International Moscow, 23 Profsoyuznaya Ulitsa, 117859, Moscow (Telephone Number in U.S. (800) 938-4685); *The CIS Market Atlas.*

Statistical Office of the United Nations, Publishing Service, New York, New York 10017 (800) 253-9646; *Statistical Yearbook.*

TAJIKISTAN - MUSEUMS

United Nations Educational, Scientific and Cultural Organization (UNESCO), 7 Place de Fontenoy, F-75700 Paris, France (Telephone Number in U.S. (212) 963-5981); *Statistical Yearbook.*

TAJIKISTAN - NATIONAL ACCOUNTS

Europa Publications Limited, 18 Bedford Square, London, WC1B 3JN, England; *The Europa World Year Book.*

Statistical Office of the United Nations, Publishing Service, New York, New York 10017 (800) 253-9646; *National Accounts Statistics;* and *Statistical Yearbook.*

The World Bank, 1818 H Street, NW, Washington, D.C. 20433 (202) 477-1234; *Statistical Handbook: States of the Former USSR.*

TAJIKISTAN - NATIONAL INCOME

Business International Moscow, 23 Profsoyuznaya Ulitsa, 117859, Moscow (Telephone Number in U.S. (800) 938-4685); *The CIS Market Atlas.*

Statistical Office of the United Nations, Publishing Service, New York, New York 10017 (800) 253-9646; *National Accounts Statistics;* and *Statistical Yearbook.*

TAJIKISTAN - NATIONAL PRODUCT

Statistical Office of the United Nations, Publishing Service, New York, New York 10017 (800) 253-9646; *Statistical Yearbook.*

TAJIKISTAN - PATENTS, TRADEMARKS AND SERVICE MARKS

Statistical Office of the United Nations, Publishing Service, New York, New York 10017 (800) 253-9646; *Statistical Yearbook.*

TAJIKISTAN - PERIODICALS

United Nations Educational, Scientific and Cultural Organization (UNESCO), 7 Place de Fontenoy, F-75700 Paris, France (Telephone Number in U.S. (212) 963-5981); *Statistical Yearbook.*

TAJIKISTAN - PETROLEUM INDUSTRY

Food and Agriculture Organization of the United Nations (FAO), Via delle Terme di Caracalla, 00100, Rome, Italy (Telephone Number in U.S. (202) 653-2400); *The State of Food and Agriculture.*

Statistical Office of the United Nations, Publishing Service, New York, New York 10017 (800) 253-9646; *Energy Statistics Yearbook; Industrial Commodity Statistics Yearbook; Statistical Yearbook;* and *Trends in Europe and North America: The Statistical Yearbook of the Economic Commission for Europe.*

TAJIKISTAN - PIGS - See TAJIKISTAN - LIVESTOCK AND POULTRY

TAJIKISTAN - POPULATION

Academic International Press, Box 1111, Gulf Breeze, Florida 32562; *Russia and Eurasia Facts and Figures Annual.*

Business International Moscow, 23 Profsoyuznaya Ulitsa, 117859, Moscow (Telephone Number in U.S. (800) 938-4685); *The CIS Market Atlas.*

Central Intelligence Agency, Washington, D.C. 20505 (703) 482-1100, www.cia.gov; *The World Factbook.*

The Economist Intelligence Unit, 111 West 57th Street, New York, New York 10019 (800) 938-4685; *Tajikistan Country Report;* and *The World Market Atlas.*

Euromonitor International, Inc., 122 South Michigan Avenue, Suite 1200, Chicago, Illinois 60603 (800) 577-EURO; *International Marketing Data and Statistics;* and *The World Economic Factbook.*

Europa Publications Limited, 18 Bedford Square, London, WC1B 3JN, England; *The Europa World Year Book.*

Food and Agriculture Organization of the United Nations (FAO), Via delle Terme di Caracalla, 00100, Rome, Italy (Telephone Number in U.S. (202) 653-2400); *Production Yearbook.*

St. Martin's Press, Inc., 175 Fifth Avenue, New York, New York 10010 (800) 221-7945; *The Statesman's Year-Book.*

Statistical Office of the United Nations, Publishing Service, New York, New York 10017 (800) 253-9646; *Demographic Yearbook; Human Development Report; Statistical Yearbook; Trends in Europe and North America: The Statistical Yearbook of the Economic Commission for Europe;* and *World Statistics Pocketbook.*

United Nations Educational, Scientific and Cultural Organization (UNESCO), 7 Place de Fontenoy, F-75700 Paris, France (Telephone Number in U.S. (212) 963-5981); *Statistical Yearbook.*

Walden Publishing Ltd., Two Market Street, Saffron Walden Essex, CB10 1HZ, England; *The World of Information Asia and Pacific Review.*

The World Bank, 1818 H Street, NW, Washington, D.C. 20433 (202) 477-1234; *Statistical Handbook: States of the Former USSR; The World Bank Atlas; World Development Report;* and *World Development Indicators.*

World Health Organization, Office of Publications, 20 Avenue Appia, CH-1211 Geneva 27, Switzerland (Telephone Number in U.S. (518) 436-9686); *World Health Statistics Annual.*

TAJIKISTAN - POST OFFICES

Statistical Office of the United Nations, Publishing Service, New York, New York 10017 (800) 253-9646; *Trends in Europe and North America: The Statistical Yearbook of the Economic Commission for Europe.*

TAJIKISTAN - POULTRY - See TAJIKISTAN - LIVESTOCK AND POULTRY

TAJIKISTAN - PRICES

Food and Agriculture Organization of the United Nations (FAO), Via delle Terme di Caracalla, 00100, Rome, Italy (Telephone Number in U.S. (202) 653-2400); *Production Yearbook.*

The World Bank, 1818 H Street, NW, Washington, D.C. 20433 (202) 477-1234; *Statistical Handbook: States of the Former USSR.*

TAJIKISTAN - PRODUCTION

The World Bank, 1818 H Street, NW, Washington, D.C. 20433 (202) 477-1234; *Statistical Handbook: States of the Former USSR.*

TAJIKISTAN - PUBLIC FINANCE - See TAJIKISTAN - FINANCE

TAJIKISTAN - RADIO RECEIVER PRODUCTION

Statistical Office of the United Nations, Publishing Service, New York, New York 10017 (800) 253-9646; *Statistical Yearbook.*

TAJIKISTAN - RADIO RECEIVERS

St. Martin's Press, Inc., 175 Fifth Avenue, New York, New York 10010 (800) 221-7945; *The Statesman's Year-Book.*

TAJIKISTAN - RAILWAYS

Academic International Press, Box 1111, Gulf Breeze, Florida 32562; *Russia and Eurasia Facts and Figures Annual.*

Business International Moscow, 23 Profsoyuznaya Ulitsa, 117859, Moscow (Telephone Number in U.S. (800) 938-4685); *The CIS Market Atlas.*

St. Martin's Press, Inc., 175 Fifth Avenue, New York, New York 10010 (800) 221-7945; *The Statesman's Year-Book.*

Statistical Office of the United Nations, Publishing Service, New York, New York 10017 (800) 253-9646; *Statistical Yearbook;* and *Trends in Europe and North America: The Statistical Yearbook of the Economic Commission for Europe.*

TAJIKISTAN - RELIGION

Academic International Press, Box 1111, Gulf Breeze, Florida 32562; *Russia and Eurasia Facts and Figures Annual.*

Central Intelligence Agency, Washington, D.C. 20505 (703) 482-1100, www.cia.gov; *The World Factbook.*

St. Martin's Press, Inc., 175 Fifth Avenue, New York, New York 10010 (800) 221-7945; *The Statesman's Year-Book.*

TAJIKISTAN - RETAIL TRADE

Business International Moscow, 23 Profsoyuznaya Ulitsa, 117859, Moscow (Telephone Number in U.S. (800) 938-4685); *The CIS Market Atlas.*

Euromonitor International, Inc., 122 South Michigan Avenue, Suite 1200, Chicago, Illinois 60603 (800) 577-EURO; *World Marketing Data and Statistics.*

Statistical Office of the United Nations, Publishing Service, New York, New York 10017 (800) 253-9646; *Statistical Yearbook.*

TAJIKISTAN - ROADS - See TAJIKISTAN - HIGHWAYS

TAJIKISTAN - ROUNDWOOD PRODUCTION AND CONSUMPTION - See TAJIKISTAN - FORESTRY AND FOREST PRODUCTS

TAJIKISTAN - RUBBER PRODUCTION AND CONSUMPTION

Statistical Office of the United Nations, Publishing Service, New York, New York 10017 (800) 253-9646; *Statistical Yearbook.*

TAJIKISTAN - SCIENTISTS, TECHNICIANS AND ENGINEERS

Statistical Office of the United Nations, Publishing Service, New York, New York 10017 (800) 253-9646; *Statistical Yearbook.*

TAJIKISTAN - SHEEP - See TAJIKISTAN - LIVESTOCK AND POULTRY

TAJIKISTAN - SOCIAL DATA

Statistical Office of the United Nations, Publishing Service, New York, New York 10017 (800) 253-9646; *World Statistics Pocketbook.*

TAJIKISTAN - STEEL PRODUCTION AND CONSUMPTION - See TAJIKISTAN - MINING AND MINERAL PRODUCTS

TAJIKISTAN - TAXATION

Europa Publications Limited, 18 Bedford Square, London, WC1B 3JN, England; *The Europa World Year Book.*

TAJIKISTAN - TELEPHONES IN USE

Academic International Press, Box 1111, Gulf Breeze, Florida 32562; *Russia and Eurasia Facts and Figures Annual.*

Central Intelligence Agency, Washington, D.C. 20505 (703) 482-1100, www.cia.gov; *The World Factbook.*

Statistical Office of the United Nations, Publishing Service, New York, New York 10017 (800) 253-9646; *Statistical Yearbook; Trends in Europe and North America: The Statistical Yearbook of the Economic Commission for Europe;* and *World Statistics Pocketbook.*

TAJIKISTAN - TEXTILE INDUSTRY

Business International Moscow, 23 Profsoyuznaya Ulitsa, 117859, Moscow (Telephone Number in U.S. (800) 938-4685); *The CIS Market Atlas.*

Statistical Office of the United Nations, Publishing Service, New York, New York 10017 (800) 253-9646; *Industrial Commodity Statistics Yearbook;* and *Statistical Yearbook.*

TAJIKISTAN - THEATRE

United Nations Educational, Scientific and Cultural Organization (UNESCO), 7 Place de Fontenoy, F-75700 Paris, France (Telephone Number in U.S. (212) 963-5981); *Statistical Yearbook.*

TAJIKISTAN - TIRE (MOTOR VEHICLE) PRODUCTION

Statistical Office of the United Nations, Publishing Service, New York, New York 10017 (800) 253-9646; *Statistical Yearbook.*

TAJIKISTAN - TOBACCO PRODUCTION

Statistical Office of the United Nations, Publishing Service, New York, New York 10017 (800) 253-9646; *Statistical Yearbook.*

TAJIKISTAN - TOURISM

Business International Moscow, 23 Profsoyuznaya Ulitsa, 117859, Moscow (Telephone Number in U.S. (800) 938-4685); *The CIS Market Atlas.*

Euromonitor International, Inc., 122 South Michigan Avenue, Suite 1200, Chicago, Illinois 60603 (800) 577-EURO; *The World Economic Factbook;* and *World Marketing Data and Statistics.*

Statistical Office of the United Nations, Publishing Service, New York, New York 10017 (800) 253-9646; *Statistical Yearbook;* and *Trends in Europe and North America: The Statistical Yearbook of the Economic Commission for Europe.*

TAJIKISTAN - TRADEMARKS AND SERVICE MARKS - See TAJIKISTAN - PATENTS, TRADEMARKS AND SERVICE MARKS

TAJIKISTAN - TRANSPORTATION AND COMMUNICATIONS

Academic International Press, Box 1111, Gulf Breeze, Florida 32562; *Russia and Eurasia Facts and Figures Annual.*

Business International Moscow, 23 Profsoyuznaya Ulitsa, 117859, Moscow (Telephone Number in U.S. (800) 938-4685); *The CIS Market Atlas.*

Central Intelligence Agency, Washington, D.C. 20505 (703) 482-1100,

www.cia.gov; *The World Factbook.*

Euromonitor International, Inc., 122 South Michigan Avenue, Suite 1200, Chicago, Illinois 60603 (800) 577-EURO; *International Marketing Data and Statistics;* and *World Marketing Data and Statistics.*

St. Martin's Press, Inc., 175 Fifth Avenue, New York, New York 10010 (800) 221-7945; *The Statesman's Year-Book.*

Statistical Office of the United Nations, Publishing Service, New York, New York 10017 (800) 253-9646; *Human Development Report;* and *Trends in Europe and North America: The Statistical Yearbook of the Economic Commission for Europe.*

TAJIKISTAN - UNEMPLOYMENT

Central Intelligence Agency, Washington, D.C. 20505 (703) 482-1100, www.cia.gov; *The World Factbook.*

St. Martin's Press, Inc., 175 Fifth Avenue, New York, New York 10010 (800) 221-7945; *The Statesman's Year-Book.*

Statistical Office of the United Nations, Publishing Service, New York, New York 10017 (800) 253-9646; *Statistical Yearbook;* and *Trends in Europe and North America: The Statistical Yearbook of the Economic Commission for Europe.*

TAJIKISTAN - VITAL STATISTICS

St. Martin's Press, Inc., 175 Fifth Avenue, New York, New York 10010 (800) 221-7945; *The Statesman's Year-Book.*

Statistical Office of the United Nations, Publishing Service, New York, New York 10017 (800) 253-9646; *Statistical Yearbook.*

World Health Organization, Office of Publications, 20 Avenue Appia, CH-1211 Geneva 27, Switzerland (Telephone Number in U.S. (518) 436-9686); *World Health Statistics Annual.*

TAJIKISTAN - WAGES

Business International Moscow, 23 Profsoyuznaya Ulitsa, 117859, Moscow (Telephone Number in U.S. (800) 938-4685); *The CIS Market Atlas.*

Statistical Office of the United Nations, Publishing Service, New York, New York 10017 (800) 253-9646; *Statistical Yearbook.*

The World Bank, 1818 H Street, NW, Washington, D.C. 20433 (202) 477-1234; *Statistical Handbook: States of the Former USSR.*

TAJIKISTAN - WELFARE

Academic International Press, Box 1111, Gulf Breeze, Florida 32562; *Russia and Eurasia Facts and Figures Annual.*

St. Martin's Press, Inc., 175 Fifth Avenue, New York, New York 10010 (800) 221-7945; *The Statesman's Year-Book.*

TAJIKISTAN - WHOLESALE PRICES

Academic International Press, Box 1111, Gulf Breeze, Florida 32562; *Russia and Eurasia Facts and Figures Annual.*

Statistical Office of the United Nations, Publishing Service, New York, New York 10017 (800) 253-9646; *Statistical Yearbook.*

TAJIKISTAN - WHOLESALE TRADE

Statistical Office of the United Nations, Publishing Service, New York, New York 10017 (800) 253-9646; *Statistical Yearbook.*

TAJIKISTAN - WOOL PRODUCTION AND CONSUMPTION - See TAJIKISTAN - TEXTILE INDUSTRY

TALC, PYROPHYLLITE, AND SOAPSTONE

U.S. Department of the Interior, Geological Survey, Office of Minerals Information, 12201 Sunrise Valley Drive, Reston, Virginia 22092 (703) 648-4000, www.minerals.usgs.gov; *Minerals Yearbook;* and *Mineral Commodities Summaries.*

TANGELOS AND TANGERINES

U.S. Department of Agriculture, National Agricultural Statistics Service, Fourteenth Street and Independence Avenue, SW, Washington, D.C. 20250 (800) 727-9540, www.usda.gov/nass; *Citrus Fruits;* and unpublished data.

TANTALUM

U.S. Department of the Interior, Geological Survey, Office of Minerals Information, 12201 Sunrise Valley Drive, Reston, Virginia 22092 (703) 648-4000, www.minerals.usgs.gov; *Mineral Commodity Summaries.*

Tanzania (United Republic Of) - National Statistical Office

Bureau of Statistics, Post Office Box 796, Dar es Salaam, United Republic of Tanzania.

Tanzania (United Republic Of) - Primary Statistics Sources

Bureau of Statistics, Government Publications Agency, Post Office Box 1801, Dar es Salaam, Tanzania; *Statistical Abstract;* and *Quarterly Statistical Bulletin.*

TANZANIA (UNITED REPUBLIC OF) - AGRICULTURE

Economist Intelligence Unit, 111 West 57th Street, New York, New York 10019 (800) 938-4685; *Tanzania Country Report.*

Euromonitor International, Inc., 122 South Michigan Avenue, Suite 1200, Chicago, Illinois 60603 (800) 577-EURO; *International Marketing Data and Statistics;* and *World Marketing Data and Statistics.*

Europa Publications Limited, 18 Bedford Square, London, WC1B 3JN, England; *The Europa World Year Book.*

Food and Agricultural Organization of the United Nations (FAO) Via delle Terme di Caracalla, 00100 Rome, Italy (Telephone Number in U.S. (202) 653-2400); *Production Yearbook; The State of Food and Agriculture;* and *Trade Yearbook.*

M.E. Sharpe, 80 Business Park Drive, Armonk, New York 10504 (800) 541-6563; *The Illustrated Book of World Rankings.*

St. Martin's Press, Inc., 175 Fifth Avenue, New York, New York 10010 (800) 221-7945; *The Statesman's Year-Book.*

Statistical Office of the United Nations, Publishing Service, New York, New York 10017 (800) 253-9646; *Statistical Yearbook;* and *Survey of Economic and Social Conditions in Africa.*

United Nations Conference on Trade and Development, Central Statistical Service, Palais des Nations, Geneva, Switzerland (Telephone in U.S. (800) 253-9646); *UNCTAD Commodity Yearbook.*

United Nations Economic Commission for Africa, Africa Hall, P.O. Box 3001, Addis Ababa, Ethiopia (Telephone Number in U.S. (800) 253-9646); *African Statistical Yearbook.*

The World Bank, 1818 H Street, NW, Washington, D.C. 20433 (202) 477-1234; *World Development Indicators.*

TANZANIA (UNITED REPUBLIC OF) - AIRLINE SERVICE

Europa Publications Limited, 18 Bedford Square, London, WC1B 3JN, England; *The Europa World Year Book.*

International Civil Aviation Organization, 999 University Street, Montreal, Quebec, Canada H3C 5H7 (514) 954-8219; *Civil Aviation Statistics of the World.*

M.E. Sharpe, 80 Business Park Drive, Armonk, New York 10504 (800) 541-6563; *The Illustrated Book of World Rankings.*

St. Martin's Press, Inc., 175 Fifth Avenue, New York, New York 10010 (800) 221-7945; *The Statesman's Year-Book.*

Statistical Office of the United Nations, Publishing Service, New York, New York 10017 (800) 253-9646; *Statistical Yearbook.*

United Nations Economic Commission for Africa, Africa Hall, P.O. Box 3001, Addis Ababa, Ethiopia (Telephone Number in U.S. (800) 253-9646); *African Statistical Yearbook.*

TANZANIA - AIRPORTS

Central Intelligence Agency, Washington, D.C. 20505 (703) 482-1100, www.cia.gov; *The World Factbook.*

TANZANIA (UNITED REPUBLIC OF) - ALUMINUM PRODUCTION AND CONSUMPTION - See TANZANIA (UNITED REPUBLIC OF) - MINING AND MINERAL PRODUCTS

TANZANIA (UNITED REPUBLIC OF) - ANIMAL HEALTH

Food and Agricultural Organization of the United Nations (FAO), Via delle Terme di Caracalla, 00100, Rome, Italy (Telephone Number in U.S. (202) 653-2400); *Animal Health Yearbook.*

TANZANIA (UNITED REPUBLIC OF) - AREA AND DENSITY OF POPULATION

African Development Bank, 01 BP 1387, Abidjan 01, Cote D'Ivoire; *Selected Statistics on Regional Member Countries.*

Central Intelligence Agency, Washington, D.C. 20505 (703) 482-1100, www.cia.gov; *The World Factbook.*

Commodity Research Bureau, Inc., 30 South Wacker Drive, Chicago, Illinois 60606 (312) 454-1801; *Commodity Year Book.*

Euromonitor International, Inc., 122 South Michigan Avenue, Suite 1200, Chicago, Illinois 60603 (800) 577-EURO; *The World Economic Factbook.*

Europa Publications Limited, 18 Bedford Square, London, WC1B 3JN, England; *The Europa World Year Book.*

Food and Agricultural Organization of the United Nations (FAO) Via delle Terme di Caracalla, 00100 Rome, Italy (Telephone Number in U.S. (202) 653-2400); *The State of Food and Agriculture.*

M.E. Sharpe, 80 Business Park Drive, Armonk, New York 10504 (800) 541-6563; *The Illustrated Book of World Rankings.*

St. Martin's Press, Inc., 175 Fifth Avenue, New York, New York 10010 (800) 221-7945; *The Statesman's Year-Book.*

Statistical Office of the United Nations, Publishing Service, New York, New York 10017 (800) 253-9646; *Statistical Yearbook;* and *Survey of Economic and Social Conditions in Africa.*

United Nations Educational, Scientific and Cultural Organization (UNESCO), 7 Place de Fontenoy, F-75700 Paris, France (Telephone Number in U.S. (212) 963-5981); *Statistical Yearbook.*

The World Bank, 1818 H Street, NW, Washington, D.C. 20433 (202) 477-1234; *World Development Report.*

TANZANIA (UNITED REPUBLIC OF) - ARMS EXPORTS AND IMPORTS - See TANZANIA (UNITED REPUBLIC OF) - MILITARY

TANZANIA (UNITED REPUBLIC OF) - BALANCE OF PAYMENTS

African Development Bank, 01 BP 1387, Abidjan 01, Cote D'Ivoire; *Selected Statistics on Regional Member Countries.*

The Economist Intelligence Unit, 111 West 57th Street, New York, New York 10019 (800) 938-4685; *The World Market Atlas.*

Europa Publications Limited, 18 Bedford Square, London, WC1B 3JN, England; *The Europa World Year Book.*

International Monetary Fund, 700 Nineteenth Street, NW, Washington, D.C. 20431 (202) 623-7000; *Balance of Payments Yearbook.*

United Nations Conference on Trade and Development (UNCTAD), New York, New York 10017 (800) 253-9646; *Handbook of International Trade and Development Statistics.*

United Nations Economic Commission for Africa, Africa Hall, P.O. Box 3001, Addis Ababa, Ethiopia (Telephone Number in U.S. (800) 253-9646); *African Statistical Yearbook.*

The World Bank, 1818 H Street, NW, Washington, D.C. 20433 (202) 477-1234; *World Development Report;* and *World Development Indicators.*

TANZANIA (UNITED REPUBLIC OF) - BANKING

Euromonitor International, Inc., 122

South Michigan Avenue, Suite 1200, Chicago, Illinois 60603 (800) 577-EURO; *World Marketing Data and Statistics*.

Europa Publications Limited, 18 Bedford Square, London, WC1B 3JN, England; *The Europa World Year Book*.

International Monetary Fund, 700 Nineteenth Street, NW, Washington, D.C. 20431 (202) 623-7000; *International Financial Statistics*.

M.E. Sharpe, 80 Business Park Drive, Armonk, New York 10504 (800) 541-6563; *The Illustrated Book of World Rankings*.

St. Martin's Press, Inc., 175 Fifth Avenue, New York, New York 10010 (800) 221-7945; *The Statesman's Year-Book*.

United Nations Economic Commission for Africa, Africa Hall, P.O. Box 3001, Addis Ababa, Ethiopia (Telephone Number in U.S. (800) 253-9646); *African Statistical Yearbook*.

TANZANIA (UNITED REPUBLIC OF) - BARLEY PRODUCTION - See TANZANIA (UNITED REPUBLIC OF) - CROPS

TANZANIA (UNITED REPUBLIC OF) - BEER PRODUCTION - See TANZANIA (UNITED REPUBLIC OF) - BEVERAGES

TANZANIA (UNITED REPUBLIC OF) - BEVERAGES

M.E. Sharpe, 80 Business Park Drive, Armonk, New York 10504 (800) 541-6563; *The Illustrated Book of World Rankings*.

Statistical Office of the United Nations, Publishing Service, New York, New York 10017 (800) 253-9646; *Statistical Yearbook*.

TANZANIA (UNITED REPUBLIC OF) - BIRTH RATES

Central Intelligence Agency, Washington, D.C. 20505 (703) 482-1100, www.cia.gov; *The World Factbook*.

Euromonitor International, Inc., 122 South Michigan Avenue, Suite 1200, Chicago, Illinois 60603 (800) 577-EURO; *International Marketing Data and Statistics; and The World Economic Factbook*.

Europa Publications Limited, 18 Bedford Square, London, WC1B 3JN, England; *The Europa World Year Book*.

M.E. Sharpe, 80 Business Park Drive, Armonk, New York 10504 (800) 541-6563; *The Illustrated Book of World Rankings*.

Statistical Office of the United Nations, Publishing Service, New York, New York 10017 (800) 253-9646; *Demographic Yearbook; Statistical Yearbook;* and *Survey*

of Economic and Social Conditions in Africa.

The World Bank, 1818 H Street, NW, Washington, D.C. 20433 (202) 477-1234; *World Development Indicators*.

TANZANIA (UNITED REPUBLIC OF) - BONDS

International Monetary Fund, 700 Nineteenth Street, NW, Washington, D.C. 20431 (202) 623-7000; *Government Finance Statistics Yearbook*.

TANZANIA (UNITED REPUBLIC OF) - BROADCASTING

Billboard Limited, P.O. Box 9027, 1006 AA Amsterdam, The Netherlands (Telephone Number in U.S. (212) 764-7300); *World Radio TV Handbook*.

Central Intelligence Agency, Washington, D.C. 20505 (703) 482-1100, www.cia.gov; *The World Factbook*.

Euromonitor International, Inc., 122 South Michigan Avenue, Suite 1200, Chicago, Illinois 60603 (800) 577-EURO; *World Marketing Data and Statistics*.

M.E. Sharpe, 80 Business Park Drive, Armonk, New York 10504 (800) 541-6563; *The Illustrated Book of World Rankings*.

St. Martin's Press, Inc., 175 Fifth Avenue, New York, New York 10010 (800) 221-7945; *The Statesman's Year-Book*.

TANZANIA (UNITED REPUBLIC OF) - BUDGET

Central Intelligence Agency, Washington, D.C. 20505 (703) 482-1100, www.cia.gov; *The World Factbook*.

TANZANIA (UNITED REPUBLIC OF) - BUSINESS AND PROFESSIONAL LICENSES

International Monetary Fund, 700 Nineteenth Street, NW, Washington, D.C. 20431 (202) 623-7000; *Government Finance Statistics Yearbook*.

TANZANIA (UNITED REPUBLIC OF) - BUTTER PRODUCTION - See TANZANIA (UNITED REPUBLIC OF) - DAIRY PRODUCTS

TANZANIA (UNITED REPUBLIC OF) - CALORIE SUPPLY

African Development Bank, 01 BP 1387, Abidjan 01, Cote D'Ivoire; *Selected Statistics on Regional Member Countries*.

Food and Agricultural Organization of the United Nations (FAO) Via delle Terme di Caracalla, 00100 Rome, Italy (Telephone Number in U.S. (202) 653-2400); *The State*

of Food and Agriculture.

TANZANIA (UNITED REPUBLIC OF) - CAPITAL REVENUE

International Monetary Fund, 700 Nineteenth Street, NW, Washington, D.C. 20431 (202) 623-7000; *Government Finance Statistics Yearbook*.

TANZANIA (UNITED REPUBLIC OF) - CASHEW NUTS EXPORTS - See TANZANIA (UNITED REPUBLIC OF) - CROPS

TANZANIA (UNITED REPUBLIC OF) - CATTLE - See TANZANIA (UNITED REPUBLIC OF) - LIVESTOCK AND POULTRY

TANZANIA (UNITED REPUBLIC OF) - CEMENT PRODUCTION - See TANZANIA (UNITED REPUBLIC OF) - MINING AND MINERAL PRODUCTS

TANZANIA (UNITED REPUBLIC OF) - CHEMICAL (ORGANIC) PRODUCTION - See TANZANIA (UNITED REPUBLIC OF) - MINING AND MINERAL PRODUCTS

TANZANIA (UNITED REPUBLIC OF) - CHICKENS - See TANZANIA (UNITED REPUBLIC OF) - LIVESTOCK AND POULTRY

TANZANIA (UNITED REPUBLIC OF) - CIGARETTE PRODUCTION - See TANZANIA (UNITED REPUBLIC OF) - TOBACCO PRODUCTION

TANZANIA (UNITED REPUBLIC OF) - CLIMATE

M.E. Sharpe, 80 Business Park Drive, Armonk, New York 10504 (800) 541-6563; *The Illustrated Book of World Rankings*.

St. Martin's Press, Inc., 175 Fifth Avenue, New York, New York 10010 (800) 221-7945; *The Statesman's Year-Book*.

TANZANIA (UNITED REPUBLIC OF) - COAL PRODUCTION - See TANZANIA (UNITED REPUBLIC OF) - MINING AND MINERAL PRODUCTS

TANZANIA (UNITED REPUBLIC OF) - COCOA PRODUCTION - See TANZANIA (UNITED REPUBLIC OF) - CROPS

TANZANIA (UNITED REPUBLIC OF) - COFFEE EXPORTS AND IMPORTS - See TANZANIA (UNITED REPUBLIC OF) - CROPS

TANZANIA (UNITED REPUBLIC OF) - COMMERCE

St. Martin's Press, Inc., 175 Fifth Avenue, New York, New York 10010 (800) 221-7945; *The Statesman's Year-Book*.

TANZANIA (UNITED REPUBLIC OF) - COMMUNICATIONS - See TANZANIA (UNITED REPUBLIC OF) - TRANSPORTATION AND COMMUNICATIONS

TANZANIA (UNITED REPUBLIC OF) - CONSTRUCTION INDUSTRY

M.E. Sharpe, 80 Business Park Drive, Armonk, New York 10504 (800) 541-6563; *The Illustrated Book of World Rankings.*

Statistical Office of the United Nations, Publishing Service, New York, New York 10017 (800) 253-9646; *Construction Statistics Yearbook;* and *Statistical Yearbook.*

United Nations Economic Commission for Africa, Africa Hall, P.O. Box 3001, Addis Ababa, Ethiopia (Telephone Number in U.S. (800) 253-9646; *African Statistical Yearbook.*

TANZANIA (UNITED REPUBLIC OF) - CONSUMER PRICE INDEX

African Development Bank, 01 BP 1387, Abidjan 01, Cote D'Ivoire; *Selected Statistics on Regional Member Countries.*

Europa Publications Limited, 18 Bedford Square, London, WC1B 3JN, England; *The Europa World Year Book.*

Statistical Office of the United Nations, Publishing Service, New York, New York 10017 (800) 253-9646; *Statistical Yearbook;* and *Survey of Economic and Social Conditions in Africa.*

United Nations Economic Commission for Africa, Africa Hall, P.O. Box 3001, Addis Ababa, Ethiopia (Telephone Number in U.S. (800) 253-9646; *African Statistical Yearbook.*

TANZANIA (UNITED REPUBLIC OF) - CONSUMER PRICES

Euromonitor International, Inc., 122 South Michigan Avenue, Suite 1200, Chicago, Illinois 60603 (800) 577-EURO; *World Marketing Data and Statistics.*

International Labour Office, I.L.O. Publications, 1828 L Street, NW, Washington, D.C. 20036 (301) 638-3152; *Yearbook of Labour Statistics.*

International Monetary Fund, 700 Nineteenth Street, NW, Washington, D.C. 20431 (202) 623-7000; *International Financial Statistics.*

TANZANIA (UNITED REPUBLIC OF) - CONSUMPTION

African Development Bank, 01 BP 1387, Abidjan 01, Cote D'Ivoire; *Selected Statistics on Regional Member Countries.*

Statistical Office of the United Nations, Publishing Service, New York, New York 10017 (800) 253-9646; *Survey of Economic and Social Conditions in Africa.*

The World Bank, 1818 H Street, NW, Washington, D.C. 20433 (202) 477-1234; *World Development Report.*

TANZANIA (UNITED REPUBLIC OF) - COPPER PRODUCTION AND CONSUMPTION - See TANZANIA (UNITED REPUBLIC OF) - MINING AND MINERAL PRODUCTS

TANZANIA (UNITED REPUBLIC OF) - CORN PRODUCTION - See TANZANIA (UNITED REPUBLIC OF) - CROPS

TANZANIA (UNITED REPUBLIC OF) - CORPORATE TAXES - See TANZANIA (UNITED REPUBLIC OF) - TAXATION

TANZANIA (UNITED REPUBLIC OF) - COTTON - See TANZANIA (UNITED REPUBLIC OF) - CROPS

TANZANIA (UNITED REPUBLIC OF) - CRIME

International Criminal Police Organization (INTERPOL), 50 quai Achille Lignon, F-69006 Lyon, France; *International Crime Statistics.*

Yale University Press, Yale Station, New Haven, Connecticut 06520 (800) 987-7323; *Violence and Crime in Cross-National Perspective.*

TANZANIA (UNITED REPUBLIC OF) - CROPS

Europa Publications Limited, 18 Bedford Square, London, WC1B 3JN, England; *The Europa World Year Book.*

Food and Agricultural Organization of the United Nations (FAO) Via delle Terme di Caracalla, 00100 Rome, Italy (Telephone Number in U.S. (202) 653-2400); *The State of Food and Agriculture.*

International Monetary Fund, 700 Nineteenth Street, NW, Washington, D.C. 20431 (202) 623-7000; *Government Finance Statistics Yearbook.*

M.E. Sharpe, 80 Business Park Drive, Armonk, New York 10504 (800) 541-6563; *The Illustrated Book of World Rankings.*

St. Martin's Press, Inc., 175 Fifth Avenue, New York, New York 10010 (800) 221-7945; *The Statesman's Year-Book.*

Statistical Office of the United Nations, Publishing Service, New York, New York 10017 (800) 253-9646; *Statistical Yearbook.*

United Nations Conference on Trade and Development, Central Statistical Service, Palais des Nations, Geneva, Switzerland (Telephone in U.S. (800) 253-9646); *UNCTAD Commodity Yearbook.*

United Nations Economic Commission for Africa, Africa Hall, P.O. Box 3001, Addis Ababa, Ethiopia (Telephone Number in U.S. (800) 253-9646); *African Statistical Yearbook.*

TANZANIA (UNITED REPUBLIC OF) - CUSTOMS DUTIES

International Monetary Fund, 700 Nineteenth Street, NW, Washington, D.C. 20431 (202) 623-7000; *Government Finance Statistics Yearbook.*

TANZANIA (UNITED REPUBLIC OF) - DAIRY PRODUCTS

Europa Publications Limited, 18 Bedford Square, London, WC1B 3JN, England; *The Europa World Year Book.*

Food and Agricultural Organization of the United Nations (FAO) Via delle Terme di Caracalla, 00100 Rome, Italy (Telephone Number in U.S. (202) 653-2400); *The State of Food and Agriculture.*

M.E. Sharpe, 80 Business Park Drive, Armonk, New York 10504 (800) 541-6563; *The Illustrated Book of World Rankings.*

St. Martin's Press, Inc., 175 Fifth Avenue, New York, New York 10010 (800) 221-7945; *The Statesman's Year-Book.*

Statistical Office of the United Nations, Publishing Service, New York, New York 10017 (800) 253-9646; *Statistical Yearbook.*

TANZANIA (UNITED REPUBLIC OF) - DEATH RATE - See TANZANIA (UNITED REPUBLIC OF) - MORTALITY

TANZANIA (UNITED REPUBLIC OF) - DEFENSE EXPENDITURES - See TANZANIA (UNITED REPUBLIC OF) - MILITARY

TANZANIA (UNITED REPUBLIC OF) - DEMOGRAPHY

Euromonitor International, Inc., 122 South Michigan Avenue, Suite 1200, Chicago, Illinois 60603 (800) 577-EURO; *International Marketing Data and Statistics; World Marketing Data and Statistics;* and *The World Economic Factbook.*

M.E. Sharpe, 80 Business Park Drive, Armonk, New York 10504 (800) 541-6563; *The Illustrated Book of World Rankings.*

Statistical Office of the United Nations,

Publishing Service, New York, New York 10017 (800) 253-9646; *Human Development Report;* and *Survey of Economic and Social Conditions in Africa.*

TANZANIA (UNITED REPUBLIC OF) - DEVELOPMENT ASSISTANCE

Statistical Office of the United Nations, Publishing Service, New York, New York 10017 (800) 253-9646; *Statistical Yearbook.*

TANZANIA (UNITED REPUBLIC OF) - DIAMOND PRODUCTION - See TANZANIA (UNITED REPUBLIC OF) - MINING AND MINERAL PRODUCTS

TANZANIA (UNITED REPUBLIC OF) - DIVORCE RATES

M.E. Sharpe, 80 Business Park Drive, Armonk, New York 10504 (800) 541-6563; *The Illustrated Book of World Rankings.*

Statistical Office of the United Nations, Publishing Service, New York, New York 10017 (800) 253-9646; *Demographic Yearbook.*

TANZANIA (UNITED REPUBLIC OF) - ECONOMY

African Development Bank, 01 BP 1387, Abidjan 01, Cote D'Ivoire; *Selected Statistics on Regional Member Countries.*

Central Intelligence Agency, Washington, D.C. 20505 (703) 482-1100, www.cia.gov; *The World Factbook.*

Economist Intelligence Unit, 111 West 57th Street, New York, New York 10019 (800) 938-4685; *Tanzania Country Report.*

Euromonitor International, Inc., 122 South Michigan Avenue, Suite 1200, Chicago, Illinois 60603 (800) 577-EURO; *International Marketing Data and Statistics; World Marketing Data and Statistics;* and *The World Economic Factbook.*

Europa Publications Limited, 18 Bedford Square, London, WC1B 3JN, England; *The Europa World Year Book.*

M.E. Sharpe, 80 Business Park Drive, Armonk, New York 10504 (800) 541-6563; *The Illustrated Book of World Rankings.*

St. Martin's Press, Inc., 175 Fifth Avenue, New York, New York 10010 (800) 221-7945; *The Statesman's Year-Book.*

Statistical Office of the United Nations, Publishing Service, New York, New York 10017 (800) 253-9646; *Foreign Trade Statistics for Africa;* and *World Statistics Pocketbook.*

The World Bank, 1818 H Street, NW, Washington, D.C. 20433 (202) 477-1234;

The World Bank Atlas; and *World Development Report.*

TANZANIA (UNITED REPUBLIC OF) - EDUCATION

African Development Bank, 01 BP 1387, Abidjan 01, Cote D'Ivoire; *Selected Statistics on Regional Member Countries.*

Euromonitor International, Inc., 122 South Michigan Avenue, Suite 1200, Chicago, Illinois 60603 (800) 577-EURO; *International Marketing Data and Statistics;* and *World Marketing Data and Statistics.*

Europa Publications Limited, 18 Bedford Square, London, WC1B 3JN, England; *The Europa World Year Book.*

International Monetary Fund, 700 Nineteenth Street, NW, Washington, D.C. 20431 (202) 623-7000; *Government Finance Statistics Yearbook.*

M.E. Sharpe, 80 Business Park Drive, Armonk, New York 10504 (800) 541-6563; *The Illustrated Book of World Rankings.*

St. Martin's Press, Inc., 175 Fifth Avenue, New York, New York 10010 (800) 221-7945; *The Statesman's Year-Book.*

Statistical Office of the United Nations, Publishing Service, New York, New York 10017 (800) 253-9646; *Human Development Report;* and *Survey of Economic and Social Conditions in Africa.*

United Nations Economic Commission for Africa, Africa Hall, P.O. Box 3001, Addis Ababa, Ethiopia (Telephone Number in U.S. (800) 253-9646); *African Statistical Yearbook.*

United Nations Educational, Scientific and Cultural Organization (UNESCO), 7 Place de Fontenoy, F-75700 Paris, France (Telephone Number in U.S. (212) 963-5981); *Statistical Yearbook.*

The World Bank, 1818 H Street, NW, Washington, D.C. 20433 (202) 477-1234; *World Development Report;* and *World Development Indicators.*

TANZANIA (UNITED REPUBLIC OF) - EGG PRODUCTION AND CONSUMPTION - See TANZANIA (UNITED REPUBLIC OF) - DAIRY PRODUCTS

TANZANIA (UNITED REPUBLIC OF) - ELECTRICITY

Central Intelligence Agency, Washington, D.C. 20505 (703) 482-1100, www.cia.gov; *The World Factbook.*

M.E. Sharpe, 80 Business Park Drive, Armonk, New York 10504 (800) 541-6563; *The Illustrated Book of World Rankings.*

St. Martin's Press, Inc., 175 Fifth Avenue, New York, New York 10010 (800) 221-7945; *The Statesman's Year-Book.*

Statistical Office of the United Nations, Publishing Service, New York, New York 10017 (800) 253-9646; *Human Development Report; Statistical Yearbook;* and *Survey of Economic and Social Conditions in Africa.*

United Nations Economic Commission for Africa, Africa Hall, P.O. Box 3001, Addis Ababa, Ethiopia (Telephone Number in U.S. (800) 253-9646); *African Statistical Yearbook.*

TANZANIA (UNITED REPUBLIC OF) - EMPLOYMENT

Euromonitor International, Inc., 122 South Michigan Avenue, Suite 1200, Chicago, Illinois 60603 (800) 577-EURO; *International Marketing Data and Statistics.*

International Labour Office, I.L.O. Publications, 1828 L Street, NW, Washington, D.C. 20036 (301) 638-3152; *Yearbook of Labour Statistics.*

M.E. Sharpe, 80 Business Park Drive, Armonk, New York 10504 (800) 541-6563; *The Illustrated Book of World Rankings.*

Statistical Office of the United Nations, Publishing Service, New York, New York 10017 (800) 253-9646; *Statistical Yearbook;* and *Survey of Economic and Social Conditions in Africa.*

United Nations Economic Commission for Africa, Africa Hall, P.O. Box 3001, Addis Ababa, Ethiopia (Telephone Number in U.S. (800) 253-9646); *African Statistical Yearbook.*

TANZANIA (UNITED REPUBLIC OF) - ENERGY

Euromonitor International, Inc., 122 South Michigan Avenue, Suite 1200, Chicago, Illinois 60603 (800) 577-EURO; *International Marketing Data and Statistics; World Marketing Data and Statistics;* and *The World Economic Factbook.*

Food and Agricultural Organization of the United Nations (FAO) Via delle Terme di Caracalla, 00100 Rome, Italy (Telephone Number in U.S. (202) 653-2400); *The State of Food and Agriculture.*

M.E. Sharpe, 80 Business Park Drive, Armonk, New York 10504 (800) 541-6563; *The Illustrated Book of World Rankings.*

St. Martin's Press, Inc., 175 Fifth Avenue, New York, New York 10010 (800) 221-7945; *The Statesman's Year-Book.*

Statistical Office of the United Nations,

Publishing Service, New York, New York 10017 (800) 253-9646; *Energy Statistics Yearbook; Human Development Report; Statistical Yearbook;* and *World Statistics Pocketbook.*

United Nations Economic Commission for Africa, Africa Hall, P.O. Box 3001, Addis Ababa, Ethiopia (Telephone Number in U.S. (800) 253-9646); *African Statistical Yearbook.*

The World Bank, 1818 H Street, NW, Washington, D.C. 20433 (202) 477-1234; *The World Bank Atlas;* and *World Development Report.*

TANZANIA (UNITED REPUBLIC OF) - ENVIRONMENT

Economist Intelligence Unit, 111 West 57th Street, New York, New York 10019 (800) 938-4685; *Tanzania Country Report.*

Statistical Office of the United Nations, Publishing Service, New York, New York 10017 (800) 253-9646; *World Statistics Pocketbook.*

TANZANIA (UNITED REPUBLIC OF) - EXCHANGE RATES

African Development Bank, 01 BP 1387, Abidjan 01, Cote D'Ivoire; *Selected Statistics on Regional Member Countries.*

Central Intelligence Agency, Washington, D.C. 20505 (703) 482-1100, www.cia.gov; *The World Factbook.*

Euromonitor International, Inc., 122 South Michigan Avenue, Suite 1200, Chicago, Illinois 60603 (800) 577-EURO; *International Marketing Data and Statistics;* and *The World Economic Factbook.*

Europa Publications Limited, 18 Bedford Square, London, WC1B 3JN, England; *The Europa World Year Book.*

International Civil Aviation Organization, 999 University Street, Montreal, Quebec, Canada H3C 5H7 (514) 954-8219; *Civil Aviation Statistics of the World.*

International Monetary Fund, 700 Nineteenth Street, NW, Washington, D.C. 20431 (202) 623-7000; *International Financial Statistics.*

Statistical Office of the United Nations, Publishing Service, New York, New York 10017 (800) 253-9646; *Foreign Trade Statistics for Africa; Statistical Yearbook;* and *World Statistics Pocketbook.*

TANZANIA (UNITED REPUBLIC OF) - EXCISE TAXES - See TANZANIA (UNITED REPUBLIC OF) - TAXATION

TANZANIA (UNITED REPUBLIC OF) - EXPORTS

Central Intelligence Agency, Washington, D.C. 20505 (703) 482-1100, www.cia.gov; *The World Factbook.*

Economist Intelligence Unit, 111 West 57th Street, New York, New York 10019 (800) 938-4685; *Tanzania Country Report.*

Euromonitor International, Inc., 122 South Michigan Avenue, Suite 1200, Chicago, Illinois 60603 (800) 577-EURO; *International Marketing Data and Statistics;* and *The World Economic Factbook.*

Europa Publications Limited, 18 Bedford Square, London, WC1B 3JN, England; *The Europa World Year Book.*

Food and Agricultural Organization of the United Nations (FAO) Via delle Terme di Caracalla, 00100 Rome, Italy (Telephone Number in U.S. (202) 653-2400); *The State of Food and Agriculture.*

International Monetary Fund, 700 Nineteenth Street, NW, Washington, D.C. 20431 (202) 623-7000; *Direction of Trade Statistics; Government Finance Statistics Yearbook;* and *International Financial Statistics.*

St. Martin's Press, Inc., 175 Fifth Avenue, New York, New York 10010 (800) 221-7945; *The Statesman's Year-Book.*

Statistical Office of the United Nations, Publishing Service, New York, New York 10017 (800) 253-9646; *Foreign Trade Statistics for Africa;* and *Survey of Economic and Social Conditions in Africa.*

United Nations Conference on Trade and Development (UNCTAD), New York, New York 10017 (800) 253-9646; *Handbook of International Trade and Development Statistics.*

United Nations Economic Commission for Africa, Africa Hall, P.O. Box 3001, Addis Ababa, Ethiopia (Telephone Number in U.S. (800) 253-9646); *African Statistical Yearbook.*

The World Bank, 1818 H Street, NW, Washington, D.C. 20433 (202) 477-1234; *World Development Report;* and *World Development Indicators.*

TANZANIA (UNITED REPUBLIC OF) - EXTERNAL INDEBTEDNESS

African Development Bank, 01 BP 1387, Abidjan 01, Cote D'Ivoire; *Selected Statistics on Regional Member Countries.*

Statistical Office of the United Nations, Publishing Service, New York, New York 10017 (800) 253-9646; *Survey of Economic*

and Social Conditions in Africa.

The World Bank, 1818 H Street, NW, Washington, D.C. 20433 (202) 477-1234; *World Development Report;* and *World Development Indicators.*

TANZANIA (UNITED REPUBLIC OF) - EXTERNAL TRADE

Euromonitor International, Inc., 122 South Michigan Avenue, Suite 1200, Chicago, Illinois 60603 (800) 577-EURO; *World Marketing Data and Statistics.*

Food and Agricultural Organization of the United Nations (FAO) Via delle Terme di Caracalla, 00100 Rome, Italy (Telephone Number in U.S. (202) 653-2400); *The State of Food and Agriculture;* and *Trade Yearbook.*

Statistical Office of the United Nations, Publishing Service, New York, New York 10017 (800) 253-9646; *Statistical Yearbook;* and *Survey of Economic and Social Conditions in Africa.*

TANZANIA (UNITED REPUBLIC OF) - FABRIC PRODUCTION - See TANZANIA (UNITED REPUBLIC OF) - TEXTILE INDUSTRY

TANZANIA (UNITED REPUBLIC OF) - FARM CROPS - See TANZANIA (UNITED REPUBLIC OF) - CROPS

TANZANIA (UNITED REPUBLIC OF) - FEMALE WORKING POPULATION - See TANZANIA (UNITED REPUBLIC OF) - EMPLOYMENT

TANZANIA (UNITED REPUBLIC OF) - FERTILITY RATES

Central Intelligence Agency, Washington, D.C. 20505 (703) 482-1100, www.cia.gov; *The World Factbook.*

M.E. Sharpe, 80 Business Park Drive, Armonk, New York 10504 (800) 541-6563; *The Illustrated Book of World Rankings.*

Statistical Office of the United Nations, Publishing Service, New York, New York 10017 (800) 253-9646; *Human Development Report;* and *Survey of Economic and Social Conditions in Africa.*

The World Bank, 1818 H Street, NW, Washington, D.C. 20433 (202) 477-1234; *The World Bank Atlas; World Development Report;* and *World Development Indicators.*

TANZANIA (UNITED REPUBLIC OF) - FERTILIZER PRODUCTION AND CONSUMPTION

Food and Agricultural Organization of the United Nations (FAO), Via delle Terme

di Caracalla, 00100, Rome, Italy (Telephone Number in U.S. (202) 653-2400); *Fertilizer Yearbook;* and *The State of Food and Agriculture.*

Statistical Office of the United Nations, Publishing Service, New York, New York 10017 (800) 253-9646; *Statistical Yearbook.*

TANZANIA (UNITED REPUBLIC OF) - FETAL MORTALITY - See TANZANIA (UNITED REPUBLIC OF) - MORTALITY

TANZANIA (UNITED REPUBLIC OF) - FINANCE

African Development Bank, 01 BP 1387, Abidjan 01, Cote D'Ivoire; *Selected Statistics on Regional Member Countries.*

Economist Intelligence Unit, 111 West 57th Street, New York, New York 10019 (800) 938-4685; *Tanzania Country Report.*

Europa Publications Limited, 18 Bedford Square, London, WC1B 3JN, England; *The Europa World Year Book.*

International Monetary Fund, 700 Nineteenth Street, NW, Washington, D.C. 20431 (202) 623-7000; *Government Finance Statistics Yearbook.*

M.E. Sharpe, 80 Business Park Drive, Armonk, New York 10504 (800) 541-6563; *The Illustrated Book of World Rankings.*

St. Martin's Press, Inc., 175 Fifth Avenue, New York, New York 10010 (800) 221-7945; *The Statesman's Year-Book.*

United Nations Economic Commission for Africa, Africa Hall, P.O. Box 3001, Addis Ababa, Ethiopia (Telephone Number in U.S. (800) 253-9646); *African Statistical Yearbook.*

TANZANIA (UNITED REPUBLIC OF) - FISHERIES

Europa Publications Limited, 18 Bedford Square, London, WC1B 3JN, England; *The Europa World Year Book.*

Food and Agricultural Organization of the United Nations (FAO) Via delle Terme di Caracalla, 00100 Rome, Italy (Telephone Number in U.S. (202) 653-2400); *The State of Food and Agriculture;* and *Yearbook of Fishery Statistics.*

M.E. Sharpe, 80 Business Park Drive, Armonk, New York 10504 (800) 541-6563; *The Illustrated Book of World Rankings.*

St. Martin's Press, Inc., 175 Fifth Avenue, New York, New York 10010 (800) 221-7945; *The Statesman's Year-Book.*

Statistical Office of the United Nations, Publishing Service, New York, New York

10017 (800) 253-9646; *Statistical Yearbook;* and *Survey of Economic and Social Conditions in Africa.*

United Nations Conference on Trade and Development, Central Statistical Service, Palais des Nations, Geneva, Switzerland (Telephone in U.S. (800) 253-9646); *UNCTAD Commodity Yearbook.*

United Nations Economic Commission for Africa, Africa Hall, P.O. Box 3001, Addis Ababa, Ethiopia (Telephone Number in U.S. (800) 253-9646); *African Statistical Yearbook.*

TANZANIA (UNITED REPUBLIC OF) - FLOUR PRODUCTION

Statistical Office of the United Nations, Publishing Service, New York, New York 10017 (800) 253-9646; *Statistical Yearbook.*

TANZANIA (UNITED REPUBLIC OF) - FOOD

African Development Bank, 01 BP 1387, Abidjan 01, Cote D'Ivoire; *Selected Statistics on Regional Member Countries.*

Food and Agricultural Organization of the United Nations (FAO) Via delle Terme di Caracalla, 00100 Rome, Italy (Telephone Number in U.S. (202) 653-2400); *Production Yearbook;* and *The State of Food and Agriculture.*

Statistical Office of the United Nations, Publishing Service, New York, New York 10017 (800) 253-9646; *Human Development Report.*

United Nations Conference on Trade and Development, Central Statistical Service, Palais des Nations, Geneva, Switzerland (Telephone in U.S. (800) 253-9646); *UNCTAD Commodity Yearbook.*

TANZANIA (UNITED REPUBLIC OF) - FOREIGN TRADE

Economist Intelligence Unit, 111 West 57th Street, New York, New York 10019 (800) 938-4685; *Tanzania Country Report.*

Euromonitor International, Inc., 122 South Michigan Avenue, Suite 1200, Chicago, Illinois 60603 (800) 577-EURO; *International Marketing Data and Statistics;* and *The World Economic Factbook.*

Europa Publications Limited, 18 Bedford Square, London, WC1B 3JN, England; *The Europa World Year Book.*

Food and Agricultural Organization of the United Nations (FAO), Via delle Terme di Caracalla, 00100 Rome, Italy (Telephone Number in U.S. (202) 653-2400); *The State of Food and Agriculture.*

International Monetary Fund, 700

Nineteenth Street, NW, Washington, D.C. 20431 (202) 623-7000; *International Financial Statistics.*

M.E. Sharpe, 80 Business Park Drive, Armonk, New York 10504 (800) 541-6563; *The Illustrated Book of World Rankings.*

St. Martin's Press, Inc., 175 Fifth Avenue, New York, New York 10010 (800) 221-7945; *The Statesman's Year-Book.*

Statistical Office of the United Nations, Publishing Service, New York, New York 10017 (800) 253-9646; *Foreign Trade Statistics for Africa; International Trade Statistics Yearbook;* and *Statistical Yearbook.*

United Nations Conference on Trade and Development, Central Statistical Service, Palais des Nations, Geneva, Switzerland (Telephone in U.S. (800) 253-9646); *UNCTAD Commodity Yearbook.*

United Nations Economic Commission for Africa, Africa Hall, P.O. Box 3001, Addis Ababa, Ethiopia (Telephone Number in U.S. (800) 253-9646); *African Statistical Yearbook.*

The World Bank, 1818 H Street, NW, Washington, D.C. 20433 (202) 477-1234; *World Development Report;* and *World Development Indicators.*

TANZANIA (UNITED REPUBLIC OF) - FORESTRY AND FOREST PRODUCTS

Europa Publications Limited, 18 Bedford Square, London, WC1B 3JN, England; *The Europa World Year Book.*

Food and Agricultural Organization of the United Nations (FAO) Via delle Terme di Caracalla, 00100 Rome, Italy (Telephone Number in U.S. (202) 653-2400); *The State of Food and Agriculture;* and *Yearbook of Forest Products.*

M.E. Sharpe, 80 Business Park Drive, Armonk, New York 10504 (800) 541-6563; *The Illustrated Book of World Rankings.*

St. Martin's Press, Inc., 175 Fifth Avenue, New York, New York 10010 (800) 221-7945; *The Statesman's Year-Book.*

Statistical Office of the United Nations, Publishing Service, New York, New York 10017 (800) 253-9646; *Statistical Yearbook.*

United Nations Conference on Trade and Development, Central Statistical Service, Palais des Nations, Geneva, Switzerland (Telephone in U.S. (800) 253-9646); *UNCTAD Commodity Yearbook.*

United Nations Economic Commission for Africa, Africa Hall, P.O. Box 3001, Addis Ababa, Ethiopia (Telephone Number in

U.S. (800) 253-9646; *African Statistical Yearbook.*

United Nations Educational, Scientific and Cultural Organization (UNESCO), 7 Place de Fontenoy, F-75700 Paris, France (Telephone Number in U.S. (212) 963-5981); *Statistical Yearbook.*

The World Bank, 1818 H Street, NW, Washington, D.C. 20433 (202) 477-1234; *World Development Report.*

TANZANIA (UNITED REPUBLIC OF) - GAS PRODUCTION - See TANZANIA (UNITED REPUBLIC OF) - MINING AND MINERAL PRODUCTS

TANZANIA (UNITED REPUBLIC OF) - GENERAL INDUSTRIAL STATISTICS - See TANZANIA (UNITED REPUBLIC OF) - INDUSTRY

TANZANIA (UNITED REPUBLIC OF) - GENERAL MORTALITY - See TANZANIA (UNITED REPUBLIC OF) - MORTALITY

TANZANIA (UNITED REPUBLIC OF) - GEOGRAPHIC DATA

M.E. Sharpe, 80 Business Park Drive, Armonk, New York 10504 (800) 541-6563; *The Illustrated Book of World Rankings.*

TANZANIA (UNITED REPUBLIC OF) - GOATS - See TANZANIA (UNITED REPUBLIC OF) - LIVESTOCK AND POULTRY

TANZANIA (UNITED REPUBLIC OF) - GOLD HOLDINGS

Statistical Office of the United Nations, Publishing Service, New York, New York 10017 (800) 253-9646; *Statistical Yearbook.*

The World Bank, 1818 H Street, NW, Washington, D.C. 20433 (202) 477-1234; *World Development Indicators.*

TANZANIA (UNITED REPUBLIC OF) - GOLD PRODUCTION AND CONSUMPTION - See TANZANIA (UNITED REPUBLIC OF) - MINING AND MINERAL PRODUCTS

TANZANIA (UNITED REPUBLIC OF) - GOVERNMENT

Central Intelligence Agency, Washington, D.C. 20505 (703) 482-1100, www.cia.gov; *The World Factbook.*

Europa Publications Limited, 18 Bedford Square, London, WC1B 3JN, England; *The Europa World Year Book.*

International Monetary Fund, 700 Nineteenth Street, NW, Washington, D.C. 20431 (202) 623-7000; *Government Finance Statistics Yearbook.*

St. Martin's Press, Inc., 175 Fifth Avenue, New York, New York 10010 (800) 221-7945; *The Statesman's Year-Book.*

Statistical Office of the United Nations, Publishing Service, New York, New York 10017 (800) 253-9646; *National Accounts Statistics; Statistical Yearbook;* and *Survey of Economic and Social Conditions in Africa.*

The World Bank, 1818 H Street, NW, Washington, D.C. 20433 (202) 477-1234; *World Development Report;* and *World Development Indicators.*

TANZANIA (UNITED REPUBLIC OF) - GRAIN PRODUCTION - See TANZANIA (UNITED REPUBLIC OF) - CROPS

TANZANIA (UNITED REPUBLIC OF) - GRANTS

International Monetary Fund, 700 Nineteenth Street, NW, Washington, D.C. 20431 (202) 623-7000; *Government Finance Statistics Yearbook.*

TANZANIA (UNITED REPUBLIC OF) - GROSS DOMESTIC PRODUCT

African Development Bank, 01 BP 1387, Abidjan 01, Cote D'Ivoire; *Selected Statistics on Regional Member Countries.*

The Economist Intelligence Unit, 111 West 57th Street, New York, New York 10019 (800) 938-4685; *Tanzania Country Report;* and *The World Market Atlas.*

Euromonitor International, Inc., 122 South Michigan Avenue, Suite 1200, Chicago, Illinois 60603 (800) 577-EURO; *International Marketing Data and Statistics;* and *The World Economic Factbook.*

Europa Publications Limited, 18 Bedford Square, London, WC1B 3JN, England; *The Europa World Year Book.*

M.E. Sharpe, 80 Business Park Drive, Armonk, New York 10504 (800) 541-6563; *The Illustrated Book of World Rankings.*

Statistical Office of the United Nations, Publishing Service, New York, New York 10017 (800) 253-9646; *Human Development Report; National Accounts Statistics; Statistical Yearbook;* and *Survey of Economic and Social Conditions in Africa.*

United Nations Economic Commission for Africa, Africa Hall, P.O. Box 3001, Addis Ababa, Ethiopia (Telephone Number in U.S. (800) 253-9646); *African Statistical Yearbook.*

The World Bank, 1818 H Street, NW, Washington, D.C. 20433 (202) 477-1234; World Development Report; and *World*

Development Indicators.

TANZANIA (UNITED REPUBLIC OF) - GROSS NATIONAL PRODUCT

Euromonitor International, Inc., 122 South Michigan Avenue, Suite 1200, Chicago, Illinois 60603 (800) 577-EURO; *International Marketing Data and Statistics.*

Europa Publications Limited, 18 Bedford Square, London, WC1B 3JN, England; *The Europa World Year Book.*

St. Martin's Press, Inc., 175 Fifth Avenue, New York, New York 10010 (800) 221-7945; *The Statesman's Year-Book.*

U.S. Arms Control and Disarmament Agency, 320 Twenty-first Street, NW, Washington, D.C. 20451 (202) 647-8677; *World Military Expenditures and Arms Transfers.*

The World Bank, 1818 H Street, NW, Washington, D.C. 20433 (202) 477-1234; *The World Bank Atlas; World Development Report;* and *World Development Indicators.*

TANZANIA (UNITED REPUBLIC OF) - GROUNDNUTS PRODUCTION - See TANZANIA (UNITED REPUBLIC OF) - CROPS

TANZANIA (UNITED REPUBLIC OF) - HEALTH

African Development Bank, 01 BP 1387, Abidjan 01, Cote D'Ivoire; *Selected Statistics on Regional Member Countries.*

Euromonitor International, Inc., 122 South Michigan Avenue, Suite 1200, Chicago, Illinois 60603 (800) 577-EURO; *World Marketing Data and Statistics.*

M.E. Sharpe, 80 Business Park Drive, Armonk, New York 10504 (800) 541-6563; *The Illustrated Book of World Rankings.*

St. Martin's Press, Inc., 175 Fifth Avenue, New York, New York 10010 (800) 221-7945; *The Statesman's Year-Book.*

Statistical Office of the United Nations, Publishing Service, New York, New York 10017 (800) 253-9646; *Human Development Report;* and *Statistical Yearbook.*

United Nations Children's Fund (UNICEF), 3 United Nations Plaza, New York, New York 10017 (800) 253-9646; *State of the World's Children.*

United Nations Economic Commission for Africa, Africa Hall, P.O. Box 3001, Addis Ababa, Ethiopia (Telephone Number in U.S. (800) 253-9646); *African Statistical Yearbook.*

The World Bank, 1818 H Street, NW, Washington, D.C. 20433 (202) 477-1234; *World Development Report.*

TANZANIA (UNITED REPUBLIC OF) - HEALTH EXPENDITURES

International Monetary Fund, 700 Nineteenth Street, NW, Washington, D.C. 20431 (202) 623-7000; *Government Finance Statistics Yearbook.*

TANZANIA (UNITED REPUBLIC OF) - HIGHWAYS

Central Intelligence Agency, Washington, D.C. 20505 (703) 482-1100, www.cia.gov; *The World Factbook.*

International Road Federation, 2600 Virginia Avenue, NW, Washington, D.C. 20037 (202) 338-4641; *World Road Statistics.*

St. Martin's Press, Inc., 175 Fifth Avenue, New York, New York 10010 (800) 221-7945; *The Statesman's Year-Book.*

Statistical Office of the United Nations, Publishing Service, New York, New York 10017 (800) 253-9646; *Survey of Economic and Social Conditions in Africa.*

United Nations Economic Commission for Africa, Africa Hall, P.O. Box 3001, Addis Ababa, Ethiopia (Telephone Number in U.S. (800) 253-9646); *African Statistical Yearbook.*

TANZANIA (UNITED REPUBLIC OF) - HOURS OF WORK - See TANZANIA (UNITED REPUBLIC OF) - EMPLOYMENT

TANZANIA (UNITED REPUBLIC OF) - HOUSING AND HOUSING UNITS

Euromonitor International, Inc., 122 South Michigan Avenue, Suite 1200, Chicago, Illinois 60603 (800) 577-EURO; *World Marketing Data and Statistics.*

M.E. Sharpe, 80 Business Park Drive, Armonk, New York 10504 (800) 541-6563; *The Illustrated Book of World Rankings.*

TANZANIA (UNITED REPUBLIC OF) - HOUSING EXPENDITURES

International Monetary Fund, 700 Nineteenth Street, NW, Washington, D.C. 20431 (202) 623-7000; *Government Finance Statistics Yearbook.*

TANZANIA (UNITED REPUBLIC OF) - ILLITERATE POPULATION

Central Intelligence Agency, Washington, D.C. 20505 (703) 482-1100, www.cia.gov; *The World Factbook.*

The Economist Intelligence Unit, 111

West 57th Street, New York, New York 10019 (800) 938-4685; *The World Market Atlas.*

Euromonitor International, Inc., 122 South Michigan Avenue, Suite 1200, Chicago, Illinois 60603 (800) 577-EURO; *The World Economic Factbook.*

Statistical Office of the United Nations, Publishing Service, New York, New York 10017 (800) 253-9646; *Human Development Report.*

United Nations Educational, Scientific and Cultural Organization (UNESCO), 7 Place de Fontenoy, F-75700 Paris, France (Telephone Number in U.S. (212) 963-5981); *Statistical Yearbook.*

TANZANIA (UNITED REPUBLIC OF) - IMPORTS

African Development Bank, 01 BP 1387, Abidjan 01, Cote D'Ivoire; *Selected Statistics on Regional Member Countries.*

Central Intelligence Agency, Washington, D.C. 20505 (703) 482-1100, www.cia.gov; *The World Factbook.*

Economist Intelligence Unit, 111 West 57th Street, New York, New York 10019 (800) 938-4685; *Tanzania Country Report.*

Euromonitor International, Inc., 122 South Michigan Avenue, Suite 1200, Chicago, Illinois 60603 (800) 577-EURO; *International Marketing Data and Statistics;* and *The World Economic Factbook.*

Europa Publications Limited, 18 Bedford Square, London, WC1B 3JN, England; *The Europa World Year Book.*

Food and Agricultural Organization of the United Nations (FAO) Via delle Terme di Caracalla, 00100 Rome, Italy (Telephone Number in U.S. (202) 653-2400); *The State of Food and Agriculture.*

International Monetary Fund, 700 Nineteenth Street, NW, Washington, D.C. 20431 (202) 623-7000; *Direction of Trade Statistics; Government Finance Statistics Yearbook;* and *International Financial Statistics.*

St. Martin's Press, Inc., 175 Fifth Avenue, New York, New York 10010 (800) 221-7945; *The Statesman's Year-Book.*

Statistical Office of the United Nations, Publishing Service, New York, New York 10017 (800) 253-9646; *Foreign Trade Statistics for Africa;* and *Survey of Economic and Social Conditions in Africa.*

United Nations Conference on Trade and Development (UNCTAD), New York, New York 10017 (800) 253-9646; *Handbook of International Trade and Development Statistics.*

United Nations Economic Commission for Africa, Africa Hall, P.O. Box 3001, Addis Ababa, Ethiopia (Telephone Number in U.S. (800) 253-9646); *African Statistical Yearbook.*

The World Bank, 1818 H Street, NW, Washington, D.C. 20433 (202) 477-1234; *World Development Report;* and *World Development Indicators.*

TANZANIA (UNITED REPUBLIC OF) - INCOME TAXES - See TANZANIA (UNITED REPUBLIC OF) - TAXATION

TANZANIA (UNITED REPUBLIC OF) - INDUSTRY

Central Intelligence Agency, Washington, D.C. 20505 (703) 482-1100, www.cia.gov; *The World Factbook.*

Economist Intelligence Unit, 111 West 57th Street, New York, New York 10019 (800) 938-4685; *Tanzania Country Report.*

Euromonitor International, Inc., 122 South Michigan Avenue, Suite 1200, Chicago, Illinois 60603 (800) 577-EURO; *International Marketing Data and Statistics; World Marketing Data and Statistics;* and *The World Economic Factbook.*

Europa Publications Limited, 18 Bedford Square, London, WC1B 3JN, England; *The Europa World Year Book.*

International Labour Office, I.L.O. Publications, 1828 L Street, NW, Washington, D.C. 20036 (301) 638-3152; *Yearbook of Labour Statistics.*

M.E. Sharpe, 80 Business Park Drive, Armonk, New York 10504 (800) 541-6563; *The Illustrated Book of World Rankings.*

St. Martin's Press, Inc., 175 Fifth Avenue, New York, New York 10010 (800) 221-7945; *The Statesman's Year-Book.*

Statistical Office of the United Nations, Publishing Service, New York, New York 10017 (800) 253-9646; *Industrial Commodity Statistics Yearbook.*

United Nations Economic Commission for Africa, Africa Hall, P.O. Box 3001, Addis Ababa, Ethiopia (Telephone Number in U.S. (800) 253-9646); *African Statistical Yearbook.*

The World Bank, 1818 H Street, NW, Washington, D.C. 20433 (202) 477-1234; *World Development Indicators.*

TANZANIA (UNITED REPUBLIC OF) - INFANT AND MATERNAL MORTALITY - See TANZANIA (UNITED REPUBLIC OF) -

MORTALITY

TANZANIA (UNITED REPUBLIC OF) - INTERNATIONAL LIQUIDITY

International Monetary Fund, 700 Nineteenth Street, NW, Washington, D.C. 20431 (202) 623-7000; *International Financial Statistics.*

TANZANIA (UNITED REPUBLIC OF) - INTERNATIONAL RESERVES EXCLUDING GOLD

African Development Bank, 01 BP 1387, Abidjan 01, Cote D'Ivoire; *Selected Statistics on Regional Member Countries.*

Statistical Office of the United Nations, Publishing Service, New York, New York 10017 (800) 253-9646; *Statistical Yearbook.*

The World Bank, 1818 H Street, NW, Washington, D.C. 20433 (202) 477-1234; *World Development Indicators.*

TANZANIA (UNITED REPUBLIC OF) - IRON ORE PRODUCTION AND CONSUMPTION - See TANZANIA (UNITED REPUBLIC OF) - MINING AND MINERAL PRODUCTS

TANZANIA (UNITED REPUBLIC OF) - IRRIGATION

Euromonitor International, Inc., 122 South Michigan Avenue, Suite 1200, Chicago, Illinois 60603 (800) 577-EURO; *International Marketing Data and Statistics.*

TANZANIA (UNITED REPUBLIC OF) - LABOR

African Development Bank, 01 BP 1387, Abidjan 01, Cote D'Ivoire; *Selected Statistics on Regional Member Countries.*

Central Intelligence Agency, Washington, D.C. 20505 (703) 482-1100, www.cia.gov; *The World Factbook.*

Euromonitor International, Inc., 122 South Michigan Avenue, Suite 1200, Chicago, Illinois 60603 (800) 577-EURO; *International Marketing Data and Statistics;* and *World Marketing Data and Statistics.*

Europa Publications Limited, 18 Bedford Square, London, WC1B 3JN, England; *The Europa World Year Book.*

Food and Agricultural Organization of the United Nations (FAO) Via delle Terme di Caracalla, 00100 Rome, Italy (Telephone Number in U.S. (202) 653-2400); *The State of Food and Agriculture.*

International Labour Office, I.L.O. Publications, 1828 L Street, NW, Washington, D.C. 20036 (301) 638-3152; *Yearbook of Labour Statistics.*

M.E. Sharpe, 80 Business Park Drive, Armonk, New York 10504 (800) 541-6563; *The Illustrated Book of World Rankings.*

St. Martin's Press, Inc., 175 Fifth Avenue, New York, New York 10010 (800) 221-7945; *The Statesman's Year-Book.*

Statistical Office of the United Nations, Publishing Service, New York, New York 10017 (800) 253-9646; *Human Development Report.*

The World Bank, 1818 H Street, NW, Washington, D.C. 20433 (202) 477-1234; *The World Bank Atlas; World Development Report;* and *World Development Indicators.*

TANZANIA (UNITED REPUBLIC OF) - LAND USE

Central Intelligence Agency, Washington, D.C. 20505 (703) 482-1100, www.cia.gov; *The World Factbook.*

Euromonitor International, Inc., 122 South Michigan Avenue, Suite 1200, Chicago, Illinois 60603 (800) 577-EURO; *International Marketing Data and Statistics.*

Food and Agricultural Organization of the United Nations (FAO), Via delle Terme di Caracalla, 00100 Rome, Italy (Telephone Number in U.S. (202) 653-2400); *Production Yearbook.*

The World Bank, 1818 H Street, NW, Washington, D.C. 20433 (202) 477-1234; *World Development Report.*

TANZANIA (UNITED REPUBLIC OF) - LIBRARIES

M.E. Sharpe, 80 Business Park Drive, Armonk, New York 10504 (800) 541-6563; *The Illustrated Book of World Rankings.*

United Nations Educational, Scientific and Cultural Organization (UNESCO), 7 Place de Fontenoy, F-75700 Paris, France (Telephone Number in U.S. (212) 963-5981); *Statistical Yearbook.*

TANZANIA (UNITED REPUBLIC OF) - LIFE EXPECTANCY

African Development Bank, 01 BP 1387, Abidjan 01, Cote D'Ivoire; *Selected Statistics on Regional Member Countries.*

Central Intelligence Agency, Washington, D.C. 20505 (703) 482-1100, www.cia.gov; *The World Factbook.*

Euromonitor International, Inc., 122 South Michigan Avenue, Suite 1200, Chicago, Illinois 60603 (800) 577-EURO; *The World Economic Factbook.*

Statistical Office of the United Nations, Publishing Service, New York, New York

10017 (800) 253-9646; *Human Development Report;* and *World Statistics Pocketbook.*

The World Bank, 1818 H Street, NW, Washington, D.C. 20433 (202) 477-1234; *The World Bank Atlas;* and *World Development Report.*

TANZANIA (UNITED REPUBLIC OF) - LITERACY RATE

Euromonitor International, Inc., 122 South Michigan Avenue, Suite 1200, Chicago, Illinois 60603 (800) 577-EURO; *World Marketing Data and Statistics.*

Statistical Office of the United Nations, Publishing Service, New York, New York 10017 (800) 253-9646; *Survey of Economic and Social Conditions in Africa.*

TANZANIA (UNITED REPUBLIC OF) - LIVESTOCK AND POULTRY

Euromonitor International, Inc., 122 South Michigan Avenue, Suite 1200, Chicago, Illinois 60603 (800) 577-EURO; *International Marketing Data and Statistics.*

Europa Publications Limited, 18 Bedford Square, London, WC1B 3JN, England; *The Europa World Year Book.*

Food and Agricultural Organization of the United Nations (FAO), Via delle Terme di Caracalla, 00100 Rome, Italy (Telephone Number in U.S. (202) 653-2400); *Production Yearbook;* and *The State of Food and Agriculture.*

M.E. Sharpe, 80 Business Park Drive, Armonk, New York 10504 (800) 541-6563; *The Illustrated Book of World Rankings.*

St. Martin's Press, Inc., 175 Fifth Avenue, New York, New York 10010 (800) 221-7945; *The Statesman's Year-Book.*

Statistical Office of the United Nations, Publishing Service, New York, New York 10017 (800) 253-9646; *Statistical Yearbook;* and *Survey of Economic and Social Conditions in Africa.*

United Nations Conference on Trade and Development, Central Statistical Service, Palais des Nations, Geneva, Switzerland (Telephone in U.S. (800) 253-9646); *UNCTAD Commodity Yearbook.*

United Nations Economic Commission for Africa, Africa Hall, P.O. Box 3001, Addis Ababa, Ethiopia (Telephone Number in U.S. (800) 253-9646); *African Statistical Yearbook.*

TANZANIA (UNITED REPUBLIC OF) - LIVING LEVELS - See TANZANIA (UNITED REPUBLIC OF) - LIFE EXPECTANCY

TANZANIA (UNITED REPUBLIC OF) - MAIL - NUMBER OF PIECES SENT OR RECEIVED

Statistical Office of the United Nations, Publishing Service, New York, New York 10017 (800) 253-9646; *Statistical Yearbook.*

TANZANIA (UNITED REPUBLIC OF) - MANUFACTURING

M.E. Sharpe, 80 Business Park Drive, Armonk, New York 10504 (800) 541-6563; *The Illustrated Book of World Rankings.*

Statistical Office of the United Nations, Publishing Service, New York, New York 10017 (800) 253-9646; *Statistical Yearbook; and Survey of Economic and Social Conditions in Africa.*

United Nations Economic Commission for Africa, Africa Hall, P.O. Box 3001, Addis Ababa, Ethiopia (Telephone Number in U.S. (800) 253-9646); *African Statistical Yearbook.*

The World Bank, 1818 H Street, NW, Washington, D.C. 20433 (202) 477-1234; *World Development Indicators.*

TANZANIA (UNITED REPUBLIC OF) - MARRIAGE RATES

M.E. Sharpe, 80 Business Park Drive, Armonk, New York 10504 (800) 541-6563; *The Illustrated Book of World Rankings.*

Statistical Office of the United Nations, Publishing Service, New York, New York 10017 (800) 253-9646; *Demographic Yearbook.*

TANZANIA (UNITED REPUBLIC OF) - MEAT PRODUCTION - See TANZANIA (UNITED REPUBLIC OF) - LIVESTOCK AND POULTRY

TANZANIA (UNITED REPUBLIC OF) - MERCHANT SHIPPING

Europa Publications Limited, 18 Bedford Square, London, WC1B 3JN, England; *The Europa World Year Book.*

St. Martin's Press, Inc., 175 Fifth Avenue, New York, New York 10010 (800) 221-7945; *The Statesman's Year-Book.*

Statistical Office of the United Nations, Publishing Service, New York, New York 10017 (800) 253-9646; *Statistical Yearbook.*

United Nations Economic Commission for Africa, Africa Hall, P.O. Box 3001, Addis Ababa, Ethiopia (Telephone Number in U.S. (800) 253-9646); *African Statistical Yearbook.*

U.S. Department of Transportation, Maritime Administration, 400 Seventh Street, SW, Washington, D.C. 20590 (202) 366-5807, www.marad.dot.gov; *A Statistical Analysis of the World's Merchant Fleets.*

TANZANIA (UNITED REPUBLIC OF) - MILITARY

Central Intelligence Agency, Washington, D.C. 20505 (703) 482-1100, www.cia.gov; *The World Factbook.*

Euromonitor International, Inc., 122 South Michigan Avenue, Suite 1200, Chicago, Illinois 60603 (800) 577-EURO; *World Marketing Data and Statistics.*

The International Institute for Strategic Studies, 23 Tavistock Street, London WC2E 7NQ, England 44 171 3797676; *The Military Balance.*

International Monetary Fund, 700 Nineteenth Street, NW, Washington, D.C. 20431 (202) 623-7000; *Government Finance Statistics Yearbook.*

St. Martin's Press, Inc., 175 Fifth Avenue, New York, New York 10010 (800) 221-7945; *The Statesman's Year-Book.*

Statistical Office of the United Nations, Publishing Service, New York, New York 10017 (800) 253-9646; *Human Development Report.*

U.S. Arms Control and Disarmament Agency, 320 Twenty-first Street, NW, Washington, D.C. 20451 (202) 647-8677; *World Military Expenditures and Arms Transfers.*

TANZANIA (UNITED REPUBLIC OF) - MILK PRODUCTION - See TANZANIA (UNITED REPUBLIC OF) - DAIRY PRODUCTS

TANZANIA (UNITED REPUBLIC OF) - MINING AND MINERAL PRODUCTS

Europa Publications Limited, 18 Bedford Square, London, WC1B 3JN, England; *The Europa World Year Book.*

M.E. Sharpe, 80 Business Park Drive, Armonk, New York 10504 (800) 541-6563; *The Illustrated Book of World Rankings.*

St. Martin's Press, Inc., 175 Fifth Avenue, New York, New York 10010 (800) 221-7945; *The Statesman's Year-Book.*

Statistical Office of the United Nations, Publishing Service, New York, New York 10017 (800) 253-9646; *Statistical Yearbook.*

United Nations Conference on Trade and Development, Central Statistical Service, Palais des Nations, Geneva, Switzerland (Telephone in U.S. (800) 253-9646); *UNCTAD Commodity Yearbook.*

United Nations Economic Commission for Africa, Africa Hall, P.O. Box 3001, Addis Ababa, Ethiopia (Telephone Number in U.S. (800) 253-9646); *African Statistical Yearbook.*

TANZANIA (UNITED REPUBLIC OF) - MONEY EXCHANGE RATE - See TANZANIA (UNITED REPUBLIC OF) - EXCHANGE RATES

TANZANIA (UNITED REPUBLIC OF) - MONEY RESERVES

Euromonitor International, Inc., 122 South Michigan Avenue, Suite 1200, Chicago, Illinois 60603 (800) 577-EURO; *International Marketing Data and Statistics.*

TANZANIA (UNITED REPUBLIC OF) - MONEY SUPPLY

African Development Bank, 01 BP 1387, Abidjan 01, Cote D'Ivoire; *Selected Statistics on Regional Member Countries.*

Economist Intelligence Unit, 111 West 57th Street, New York, New York 10019 (800) 938-4685; *Tanzania Country Report.*

Euromonitor International, Inc., 122 South Michigan Avenue, Suite 1200, Chicago, Illinois 60603 (800) 577-EURO; *International Marketing Data and Statistics.*

Europa Publications Limited, 18 Bedford Square, London, WC1B 3JN, England; *The Europa World Year Book.*

International Monetary Fund, 700 Nineteenth Street, NW, Washington, D.C. 20431 (202) 623-7000; *International Financial Statistics.*

Statistical Office of the United Nations, Publishing Service, New York, New York 10017 (800) 253-9646; *Statistical Yearbook.*

The World Bank, 1818 H Street, NW, Washington, D.C. 20433 (202) 477-1234; *World Development Indicators.*

TANZANIA (UNITED REPUBLIC OF) - MONUMENTS AND HISTORICAL SITES

United Nations Educational, Scientific and Cultural Organization (UNESCO), 7 Place de Fontenoy, F-75700 Paris, France (Telephone Number in U.S. (212) 963-5981); *Statistical Yearbook.*

TANZANIA (UNITED REPUBLIC OF) - MORTALITY

Central Intelligence Agency, Washington, D.C. 20505 (703) 482-1100, www.cia.gov; *The World Factbook.*

Euromonitor International, Inc., 122 South Michigan Avenue, Suite 1200, Chicago, Illinois 60603 (800) 577-EURO;

International Marketing Data and Statistics; and *The World Economic Factbook.*

Europa Publications Limited, 18 Bedford Square, London, WC1B 3JN, England; *The Europa World Year Book.*

Statistical Office of the United Nations, Publishing Service, New York, New York 10017 (800) 253-9646; *Demographic Yearbook; Human Development Report; Statistical Yearbook; Survey of Economic and Social Conditions in Africa;* and *World Statistics Pocketbook.*

United Nations Children's Fund (UNICEF), 3 United Nations Plaza, New York, New York 10017 (800) 253-9646; *State of the World's Children.*

The World Bank, 1818 H Street, NW, Washington, D.C. 20433 (202) 477-1234; *The World Bank Atlas; World Development Report;* and *World Development Indicators.*

TANZANIA (UNITED REPUBLIC OF) - MOTION PICTURES

Statistical Office of the United Nations, Publishing Service, New York, New York 10017 (800) 253-9646; *Statistical Yearbook.*

TANZANIA (UNITED REPUBLIC OF) - MOTOR VEHICLE PRODUCTION

Statistical Office of the United Nations, Publishing Service, New York, New York 10017 (800) 253-9646; *Statistical Yearbook.*

TANZANIA (UNITED REPUBLIC OF) - MOTOR VEHICLE TAXES - See TANZANIA (UNITED REPUBLIC OF) - TAXATION

TANZANIA (UNITED REPUBLIC OF) - MOTOR VEHICLES IN USE

Europa Publications Limited, 18 Bedford Square, London, WC1B 3JN, England; *The Europa World Year Book.*

International Road Federation, 2600 Virginia Avenue, NW, Washington, D.C. 20037 (202) 338-4641; *World Road Statistics.*

Statistical Office of the United Nations, Publishing Service, New York, New York 10017 (800) 253-9646; *Statistical Yearbook;* and *Survey of Economic and Social Conditions in Africa.*

TANZANIA (UNITED REPUBLIC OF) - MUSEUMS

M.E. Sharpe, 80 Business Park Drive, Armonk, New York 10504 (800) 541-6563; *The Illustrated Book of World Rankings.*

United Nations Educational, Scientific and Cultural Organization (UNESCO), 7 Place de Fontenoy, F-75700 Paris, France

(Telephone Number in U.S. (212) 963-5981); *Statistical Yearbook.*

TANZANIA (UNITED REPUBLIC OF) - NATALITY - See TANZANIA (UNITED REPUBLIC OF) - BIRTH RATE

TANZANIA (UNITED REPUBLIC OF) - NATIONAL ACCOUNTS

Europa Publications Limited, 18 Bedford Square, London, WC1B 3JN, England; *The Europa World Year Book.*

Statistical Office of the United Nations, Publishing Service, New York, New York 10017 (800) 253-9646; *National Accounts Statistics; Statistical Yearbook;* and *Survey of Economic and Social Conditions in Africa.*

United Nations Economic Commission for Africa, Africa Hall, P.O. Box 3001, Addis Ababa, Ethiopia (Telephone Number in U.S. (800) 253-9646); *African Statistical Yearbook.*

TANZANIA (UNITED REPUBLIC OF) - NATIONAL INCOME

M.E. Sharpe, 80 Business Park Drive, Armonk, New York 10504 (800) 541-6563; *The Illustrated Book of World Rankings.*

Statistical Office of the United Nations, Publishing Service, New York, New York 10017 (800) 253-9646; *National Accounts Statistics;* and *Statistical Yearbook.*

TANZANIA (UNITED REPUBLIC OF) - NATIONAL PRODUCT

M.E. Sharpe, 80 Business Park Drive, Armonk, New York 10504 (800) 541-6563; *The Illustrated Book of World Rankings.*

Statistical Office of the United Nations, Publishing Service, New York, New York 10017 (800) 253-9646; *Statistical Yearbook.*

TANZANIA (UNITED REPUBLIC OF) - NATURAL GAS PRODUCTION - See TANZANIA (UNITED REPUBLIC OF) - MINING AND MINERAL PRODUCTS

TANZANIA (UNITED REPUBLIC OF) - NEWSPAPER PRODUCTION - See TANZANIA (UNITED REPUBLIC OF) - FORESTRY AND FOREST PRODUCTS

TANZANIA (UNITED REPUBLIC OF) - NEWSPRINT - See TANZANIA (UNITED REPUBLIC OF) - FORESTRY AND FOREST PRODUCTS

TANZANIA (UNITED REPUBLIC OF) - OCCUPATIONS - See TANZANIA (UNITED REPUBLIC OF) - LABOR

TANZANIA (UNITED REPUBLIC OF) - PALM KERNELS AND PALM OIL - See TANZANIA

(UNITED REPUBLIC OF) - CROPS

TANZANIA (UNITED REPUBLIC OF) - PAPER - See TANZANIA (UNITED REPUBLIC OF) - FORESTRY AND FOREST PRODUCTS

TANZANIA (UNITED REPUBLIC OF) - PATENTS, TRADEMARKS AND SERVICE MARKS

Statistical Office of the United Nations, Publishing Service, New York, New York 10017 (800) 253-9646; *Statistical Yearbook.*

TANZANIA (UNITED REPUBLIC OF) - PEANUT PRODUCTION - See TANZANIA (UNITED REPUBLIC OF) - CROPS

TANZANIA (UNITED REPUBLIC OF) - PESTICIDE USE

Food and Agricultural Organization of the United Nations (FAO) Via delle Terme di Caracalla, 00100 Rome, Italy (Telephone Number in U.S. (202) 653-2400); *The State of Food and Agriculture.*

TANZANIA (UNITED REPUBLIC OF) - PETROLEUM INDUSTRY

Food and Agricultural Organization of the United Nations (FAO) Via delle Terme di Caracalla, 00100 Rome, Italy (Telephone Number in U.S. (202) 653-2400); *The State of Food and Agriculture.*

M.E. Sharpe, 80 Business Park Drive, Armonk, New York 10504 (800) 541-6563; *The Illustrated Book of World Rankings.*

Statistical Office of the United Nations, Publishing Service, New York, New York 10017 (800) 253-9646; *Statistical Yearbook.*

United Nations Conference on Trade and Development, Central Statistical Service, Palais des Nations, Geneva, Switzerland (Telephone in U.S. (800) 253-9646); *UNCTAD Commodity Yearbook.*

TANZANIA (UNITED REPUBLIC OF) - PIGS - See TANZANIA (UNITED REPUBLIC OF) - LIVESTOCK AND POULTRY

TANZANIA (UNITED REPUBLIC OF) - POPULATION

African Development Bank, 01 BP 1387, Abidjan 01, Cote D'Ivoire; *Selected Statistics on Regional Member Countries.*

Central Intelligence Agency, Washington, D.C. 20505 (703) 482-1100, www.cia.gov; *The World Factbook.*

Economist Intelligence Unit, 111 West 57th Street, New York, New York 10019 (800) 938-4685; *Tanzania Country Report.*

Euromonitor International, Inc., 122

South Michigan Avenue, Suite 1200, Chicago, Illinois 60603 (800) 577-EURO; *International Marketing Data and Statistics; and The World Economic Factbook.*

Europa Publications Limited, 18 Bedford Square, London, WC1B 3JN, England; *The Europa World Year Book.*

Food and Agricultural Organization of the United Nations (FAO), Via delle Terme di Caracalla, 00100 Rome, Italy (Telephone Number in U.S. (202) 653-2400); *Production Yearbook.*

International Labour Office, I.L.O. Publications, 1828 L Street, NW, Washington, D.C. 20036 (301) 638-3152; *Yearbook of Labour Statistics.*

M.E. Sharpe, 80 Business Park Drive, Armonk, New York 10504 (800) 541-6563; *The Illustrated Book of World Rankings.*

St. Martin's Press, Inc., 175 Fifth Avenue, New York, New York 10010 (800) 221-7945; *The Statesman's Year-Book.*

Statistical Office of the United Nations, Publishing Service, New York, New York 10017 (800) 253-9646; *Demographic Yearbook; Human Development Report; Statistical Yearbook; Survey of Economic and Social Conditions in Africa; and World Statistics Pocketbook.*

United Nations Educational, Scientific and Cultural Organization (UNESCO), 7 Place de Fontenoy, F-75700 Paris, France (Telephone Number in U.S. (212) 963-5981); *Statistical Yearbook.*

U.S. Arms Control and Disarmament Agency, 320 Twenty-first Street, NW, Washington, D.C. 20451 (202) 647-8677; *World Military Expenditures and Arms Transfers.*

The World Bank, 1818 H Street, NW, Washington, D.C. 20433 (202) 477-1234; *The World Bank Atlas;* and *World Development Report.*

World Health Organization, Office of Publications, 20 Avenue Appia, CH-1211 Geneva 27, Switzerland (Telephone Number in U.S. (518) 436-9686); *World Health Statistics Annual.*

TANZANIA (UNITED REPUBLIC OF) - POST OFFICES

M.E. Sharpe, 80 Business Park Drive, Armonk, New York 10504 (800) 541-6563; *The Illustrated Book of World Rankings.*

TANZANIA (UNITED REPUBLIC OF) - POTATO PRODUCTION - See TANZANIA (UNITED REPUBLIC OF) - CROPS

TANZANIA (UNITED REPUBLIC OF) -

POWER PRODUCTION INDUSTRY

Statistical Office of the United Nations, Publishing Service, New York, New York 10017 (800) 253-9646; *Statistical Yearbook.*

TANZANIA (UNITED REPUBLIC OF) - PRICES

Food and Agricultural Organization of the United Nations (FAO), Via delle Terme di Caracalla, 00100 Rome, Italy (Telephone Number in U.S. (202) 653-2400); *Production Yearbook;* and *The State of Food and Agriculture.*

International Labour Office, I.L.O. Publications, 1828 L Street, NW, Washington, D.C. 20036 (301) 638-3152; *Yearbook of Labour Statistics.*

International Monetary Fund, 700 Nineteenth Street, NW, Washington, D.C. 20431 (202) 623-7000; *International Financial Statistics.*

M.E. Sharpe, 80 Business Park Drive, Armonk, New York 10504 (800) 541-6563; *The Illustrated Book of World Rankings.*

Statistical Office of the United Nations, Publishing Service, New York, New York 10017 (800) 253-9646; *Statistical Yearbook.*

United Nations Economic Commission for Africa, Africa Hall, P.O. Box 3001, Addis Ababa, Ethiopia (Telephone Number in U.S. (800) 253-9646); *African Statistical Yearbook.*

TANZANIA (UNITED REPUBLIC OF) - PRINTING AND WRITING PAPER - See TANZANIA (UNITED REPUBLIC OF) - FORESTRY AND FOREST PRODUCTS

TANZANIA (UNITED REPUBLIC OF) - PRODUCTION

M.E. Sharpe, 80 Business Park Drive, Armonk, New York 10504 (800) 541-6563; *The Illustrated Book of World Rankings.*

TANZANIA (UNITED REPUBLIC OF) - PRODUCTIVITY

Euromonitor International, Inc., 122 South Michigan Avenue, Suite 1200, Chicago, Illinois 60603 (800) 577-EURO; *International Marketing Data and Statistics.*

TANZANIA (UNITED REPUBLIC OF) - PROPERTY TAXES - See TANZANIA (UNITED REPUBLIC OF) - TAXATION

TANZANIA (UNITED REPUBLIC OF) - PUBLIC FINANCE - See TANZANIA (UNITED REPUBLIC OF) - FINANCE

TANZANIA (UNITED REPUBLIC OF) - RADIO BROADCASTING - See TANZANIA (UNITED REPUBLIC OF) - BROADCASTING

TANZANIA (UNITED REPUBLIC OF) - RADIO RECEIVER PRODUCTION

Statistical Office of the United Nations, Publishing Service, New York, New York 10017 (800) 253-9646; *Statistical Yearbook.*

TANZANIA (UNITED REPUBLIC OF) - RADIO RECEIVERS

St. Martin's Press, Inc., 175 Fifth Avenue, New York, New York 10010 (800) 221-7945; *The Statesman's Year-Book.*

TANZANIA (UNITED REPUBLIC OF) - RAILWAYS

Europa Publications Limited, 18 Bedford Square, London, WC1B 3JN, England; *The Europa World Year Book.*

Jane's Information Group, Sentinel House, 163 Brighton Road, Coulsdon, Surrey CR5 2NH, England (Telephone Number in U.S. (703) 683-3700); *Jane's World Railways.*

St. Martin's Press, Inc., 175 Fifth Avenue, New York, New York 10010 (800) 221-7945; *The Statesman's Year-Book.*

Statistical Office of the United Nations, Publishing Service, New York, New York 10017 (800) 253-9646; *Survey of Economic and Social Conditions in Africa.*

United Nations Economic Commission for Africa, Africa Hall, P.O. Box 3001, Addis Ababa, Ethiopia (Telephone Number in U.S. (800) 253-9646); *African Statistical Yearbook.*

TANZANIA (UNITED REPUBLIC OF) - RELIGION

Central Intelligence Agency, Washington, D.C. 20505 (703) 482-1100, www.cia.gov; *The World Factbook.*

M.E. Sharpe, 80 Business Park Drive, Armonk, New York 10504 (800) 541-6563; *The Illustrated Book of World Rankings.*

St. Martin's Press, Inc., 175 Fifth Avenue, New York, New York 10010 (800) 221-7945; *The Statesman's Year-Book.*

TANZANIA (UNITED REPUBLIC OF) - RENT PRICES

International Monetary Fund, 700 Nineteenth Street, NW, Washington, D.C. 20431 (202) 623-7000; *Yearbook of Labour Statistics.*

TANZANIA (UNITED REPUBLIC OF) - RETAIL TRADE

Euromonitor International, Inc., 122 South Michigan Avenue, Suite 1200, Chicago, Illinois 60603 (800) 577-EURO;

World Marketing Data and Statistics.

TANZANIA (UNITED REPUBLIC OF) - RICE PRODUCTION - See TANZANIA (UNITED REPUBLIC OF) - CROPS

TANZANIA (UNITED REPUBLIC OF) - ROUNDWOOD PRODUCTION - See TANZANIA (UNITED REPUBLIC OF) - FORESTRY AND FOREST PRODUCTS

TANZANIA (UNITED REPUBLIC OF) - RUBBER PRODUCTION AND CONSUMPTION

M.E. Sharpe, 80 Business Park Drive, Armonk, New York 10504 (800) 541-6563; *The Illustrated Book of World Rankings.*

TANZANIA (UNITED REPUBLIC OF) - SALT PRODUCTION - See TANZANIA (UNITED REPUBLIC OF) - MINING AND MINERAL PRODUCTS

TANZANIA (UNITED REPUBLIC OF) - SAWNWOOD PRODUCTION - See TANZANIA (UNITED REPUBLIC OF) - FORESTRY AND FOREST PRODUCTS

TANZANIA (UNITED REPUBLIC OF) - SCIENTISTS AND TECHNICIANS

United Nations Educational, Scientific and Cultural Organization (UNESCO), 7 Place de Fontenoy, F-75700 Paris, France (Telephone Number in U.S. (212) 963-5981); *Statistical Yearbook.*

TANZANIA (UNITED REPUBLIC OF) - SENIOR CITIZENS

M.E. Sharpe, 80 Business Park Drive, Armonk, New York 10504 (800) 541-6563; *The Illustrated Book of World Rankings.*

TANZANIA (UNITED REPUBLIC OF) - SHEEP - See TANZANIA (UNITED REPUBLIC OF) - LIVESTOCK AND POULTRY

TANZANIA (UNITED REPUBLIC OF) - SILVER PRODUCTION AND CONSUMPTION - See TANZANIA (UNITED REPUBLIC OF) - MINING AND MINERAL PRODUCTS

TANZANIA (UNITED REPUBLIC OF) - SISAL EXPORTS - See TANZANIA (UNITED REPUBLIC OF) - CROPS

TANZANIA (UNITED REPUBLIC OF) - SOCIAL DATA

African Development Bank, 01 BP 1387, Abidjan 01, Cote D'Ivoire; *Selected Statistics on Regional Member Countries.*

M.E. Sharpe, 80 Business Park Drive, Armonk, New York 10504 (800) 541-6563; *The Illustrated Book of World Rankings.*

Statistical Office of the United Nations, Publishing Service, New York, New York 10017 (800) 253-9646; *World Statistics Pocketbook.*

TANZANIA (UNITED REPUBLIC OF) - SOCIAL SECURITY

International Monetary Fund, 700 Nineteenth Street, NW, Washington, D.C. 20431 (202) 623-7000; *Government Finance Statistics Yearbook.*

Statistical Office of the United Nations, Publishing Service, New York, New York 10017 (800) 253-9646; *National Accounts Statistics.*

TANZANIA (UNITED REPUBLIC OF) - SOYBEAN PRODUCTION - See TANZANIA (UNITED REPUBLIC OF) - CROPS

TANZANIA (UNITED REPUBLIC OF) - STAMP TAXES AND DUTIES - See TANZANIA (UNITED REPUBLIC OF) - TAXATION

TANZANIA (UNITED REPUBLIC OF) - STATE BUDGET REVENUE AND EXPENDITURES

Euromonitor International, Inc., 122 South Michigan Avenue, Suite 1200, Chicago, Illinois 60603 (800) 577-EURO; *International Marketing Data and Statistics.*

TANZANIA (UNITED REPUBLIC OF) - STEEL - See TANZANIA (UNITED REPUBLIC OF) - MINING AND MINERAL PRODUCTS

TANZANIA (UNITED REPUBLIC OF) - STOCKS - COMMODITY - MARKET PRICE - INDEX

Food and Agricultural Organization of the United Nations (FAO), Via delle Terme di Caracalla, 00100 Rome, Italy (Telephone Number in U.S. (202) 653-2400); *The State of Food and Agriculture.*

TANZANIA (UNITED REPUBLIC OF) - SUGAR PRODUCTION AND CONSUMPTION - See TANZANIA (UNITED REPUBLIC OF) - CROPS

TANZANIA (UNITED REPUBLIC OF) - TAXATION

Europa Publications Limited, 18 Bedford Square, London, WC1B 3JN, England; *The Europa World Year Book.*

International Monetary Fund, 700 Nineteenth Street, NW, Washington, D.C. 20431 (202) 623-7000; *Government Finance Statistics Yearbook.*

International Road Federation, 2600 Virginia Avenue, NW, Washington, D.C. 20037 (202) 338-4641; *World Road Statistics.*

The World Bank, 1818 H Street, NW, Washington, D.C. 20433 (202) 477-1234; *World Development Indicators.*

TANZANIA (UNITED REPUBLIC OF) - TEA PRODUCTION AND CONSUMPTION - See TANZANIA (UNITED REPUBLIC OF) - CROPS

TANZANIA (UNITED REPUBLIC OF) - TELEGRAPH SERVICE

Statistical Office of the United Nations, Publishing Service, New York, New York 10017 (800) 253-9646; *Statistical Yearbook.*

TANZANIA (UNITED REPUBLIC OF) - TELEPHONES IN USE

American Telephone and Telegraph Company, 26 Parsippany Road, Whippany, New Jersey 07981 (800) 222-0300; *The World's Telephones.*

Central Intelligence Agency, Washington, D.C. 20505 (703) 482-1100, www.cia.gov; *The World Factbook.*

Europa Publications Limited, 18 Bedford Square, London, WC1B 3JN, England; *The Europa World Year Book.*

St. Martin's Press, Inc., 175 Fifth Avenue, New York, New York 10010 (800) 221-7945; *The Statesman's Year-Book.*

Statistical Office of the United Nations, Publishing Service, New York, New York 10017 (800) 253-9646; *Statistical Yearbook;* and *World Statistics Pocketbook.*

TANZANIA (UNITED REPUBLIC OF) - TELEVISION BROADCASTING - See TANZANIA (UNITED REPUBLIC OF) - BROADCASTING

TANZANIA (UNITED REPUBLIC OF) - TEXTILE INDUSTRY

St. Martin's Press, Inc., 175 Fifth Avenue, New York, New York 10010 (800) 221-7945; *The Statesman's Year-Book.*

Statistical Office of the United Nations, Publishing Service, New York, New York 10017 (800) 253-9646; *Statistical Yearbook.*

United Nations Conference on Trade and Development, Central Statistical Service, Palais des Nations, Geneva, Switzerland (Telephone in U.S. (800) 253-9646); *UNCTAD Commodity Yearbook.*

TANZANIA (UNITED REPUBLIC OF) - THEATRE

United Nations Educational, Scientific and Cultural Organization (UNESCO), 7 Place de Fontenoy, F-75700 Paris, France (Telephone Number in U.S. (212) 963-5981); *Statistical Yearbook.*

TANZANIA (UNITED REPUBLIC OF) - TIN PRODUCTION AND CONSUMPTION - See TANZANIA (UNITED REPUBLIC OF) - MINING AND MINERAL PRODUCTS

TANZANIA (UNITED REPUBLIC OF) - TOBACCO PRODUCTION

M.E. Sharpe, 80 Business Park Drive, Armonk, New York 10504 (800) 541-6563; *The Illustrated Book of World Rankings.*

Statistical Office of the United Nations, Publishing Service, New York, New York 10017 (800) 253-9646; *Statistical Yearbook.*

TANZANIA (UNITED REPUBLIC OF) - TOURISM

Euromonitor International, Inc., 122 South Michigan Avenue, Suite 1200, Chicago, Illinois 60603 (800) 577-EURO; *The World Economic Factbook;* and *World Marketing Data and Statistics.*

Europa Publications Limited, 18 Bedford Square, London, WC1B 3JN, England; *The Europa World Year Book.*

M.E. Sharpe, 80 Business Park Drive, Armonk, New York 10504 (800) 541-6563; *The Illustrated Book of World Rankings.*

St. Martin's Press, Inc., 175 Fifth Avenue, New York, New York 10010 (800) 221-7945; *The Statesman's Year-Book.*

Statistical Office of the United Nations, Publishing Service, New York, New York 10017 (800) 253-9646; *Statistical Yearbook.*

United Nations Economic Commission for Africa, Africa Hall, P.O. Box 3001, Addis Ababa, Ethiopia (Telephone Number in U.S. (800) 253-9646); *African Statistical Yearbook.*

World Tourism Organization, Calle Capitan Haya 42, E-28020 Madrid, Spain; *Yearbook of Tourism Statistics.*

TANZANIA (UNITED REPUBLIC OF) - TRACTORS IN USE

Statistical Office of the United Nations, Publishing Service, New York, New York 10017 (800) 253-9646; *Statistical Yearbook.*

TANZANIA (UNITED REPUBLIC OF) - TRADE - See TANZANIA (UNITED REPUBLIC OF) - FOREIGN TRADE

TANZANIA (UNITED REPUBLIC OF) - TRADEMARKS AND SERVICE MARKS - See TANZANIA (UNITED REPUBLIC OF) - PATENTS, TRADEMARKS AND SERVICE MARKS

TANZANIA (UNITED REPUBLIC OF) - TRANSPORTATION AND COMMUNICATIONS

Central Intelligence Agency, Washington, D.C. 20505 (703) 482-1100, www.cia.gov; *The World Factbook.*

Euromonitor International, Inc., 122 South Michigan Avenue, Suite 1200, Chicago, Illinois 60603 (800) 577-EURO; *International Marketing Data and Statistics;* and *World Marketing Data and Statistics.*

Europa Publications Limited, 18 Bedford Square, London, WC1B 3JN, England; *The Europa World Year Book.*

M.E. Sharpe, 80 Business Park Drive, Armonk, New York 10504 (800) 541-6563; *The Illustrated Book of World Rankings.*

St. Martin's Press, Inc., 175 Fifth Avenue, New York, New York 10010 (800) 221-7945; *The Statesman's Year-Book.*

Statistical Office of the United Nations, Publishing Service, New York, New York 10017 (800) 253-9646; *Human Development Report.*

United Nations Economic Commission for Africa, Africa Hall, P.O. Box 3001, Addis Ababa, Ethiopia (Telephone Number in U.S. (800) 253-9646); *African Statistical Yearbook.*

TANZANIA (UNITED REPUBLIC OF) - TUNGSTEN PRODUCTION AND CONSUMPTION - See TANZANIA (UNITED REPUBLIC OF) - MINING AND MINERAL PRODUCTS

TANZANIA (UNITED REPUBLIC OF) - UNEMPLOYMENT

Central Intelligence Agency, Washington, D.C. 20505 (703) 482-1100, www.cia.gov; *The World Factbook.*

Euromonitor International, Inc., 122 South Michigan Avenue, Suite 1200, Chicago, Illinois 60603 (800) 577-EURO; *International Marketing Data and Statistics.*

International Monetary Fund, 700 Nineteenth Street, NW, Washington, D.C. 20431 (202) 623-7000; *Yearbook of Labour Statistics.*

TANZANIA (UNITED REPUBLIC OF) - VITAL STATISTICS

Euromonitor International, Inc., 122 South Michigan Avenue, Suite 1200, Chicago, Illinois 60603 (800) 577-EURO; *International Marketing Data and Statistics.*

Statistical Office of the United Nations, Publishing Service, New York, New York 10017 (800) 253-9646; *Statistical Yearbook.*

World Health Organization, Office of Publications, 20 Avenue Appia, CH-1211 Geneva 27, Switzerland (Telephone

Number in U.S. (518) 436-9686); *World Health Statistics Annual.*

TANZANIA (UNITED REPUBLIC OF) - WAGES

International Monetary Fund, 700 Nineteenth Street, NW, Washington, D.C. 20431 (202) 623-7000; *Yearbook of Labour Statistics.*

Statistical Office of the United Nations, Publishing Service, New York, New York 10017 (800) 253-9646; *Statistical Yearbook.*

TANZANIA (UNITED REPUBLIC OF) - WEATHER

M.E. Sharpe, 80 Business Park Drive, Armonk, New York 10504 (800) 541-6563; *The Illustrated Book of World Rankings.*

TANZANIA (UNITED REPUBLIC OF) - WELFARE

International Monetary Fund, 700 Nineteenth Street, NW, Washington, D.C. 20431 (202) 623-7000; *Government Finance Statistics Yearbook.*

TANZANIA (UNITED REPUBLIC OF) - WHEAT PRODUCTION AND PRICES - See TANZANIA (UNITED REPUBLIC OF) - CROPS

TANZANIA (UNITED REPUBLIC OF) - WINE PRODUCTION - See TANZANIA (UNITED REPUBLIC OF) - BEVERAGES

TANZANIA (UNITED REPUBLIC OF) - WOOL PRODUCTION - See TANZANIA (UNITED REPUBLIC OF) - TEXTILE INDUSTRY

TARGET SHOOTING

National Sporting Goods Association, 1601 Feehanville Drive, Suite 300, Mount Prospect, Illinois 60056 (847) 296-6742; *Sports Participation in 1998.*

TARIFF - See CUSTOMS RECEIPTS

TAX EXPENDITURES - REVENUE LOSS ESTIMATES

Executive Office of the President, Office of Management and Budget, Executive Office Building, Washington, D.C. 20503 (202) 395-3080, www.whitehouse.gov/omb; *Analytical Perspectives.*

TAX RECEIPTS - FOREIGN COUNTRIES

Organization for Economic Cooperation and Development, Publication and Information Center, 2001 L Street, NW, Washington, D.C. 20036-4095 (202) 785-6323; *Revenue Statistics of OECD Member Countries.*

TAX RECEIPTS - GOVERNMENTAL REVENUE - BY TYPE OF TAX

U.S. Department of Commerce, Bureau of the Census, Washington, D.C. 20233 (301) 457-4100, www.census.gov; *Government Finances;* and Internet sites http://www.census.gov/ftp/pub/govs/www/index.html and http://www.census.gov/pub/govs/www/index.html.

TAX RECEIPTS - MOTOR-FUEL TAXES AND MOTOR-VEHICLE FEES

U.S. Department of Commerce, Bureau of the Census, Washington, D.C. 20233 (301) 457-4100, www.census.gov; Internet site: http://www.census.gov/govs/www/state.html.

U.S. Department of Transportation, Federal Highway Administration, 400 Seventh Street, SW, Washington, D.C. 20590 (202) 366-0660; *Highway Statistics;* and *Price Trends for Federal Aid Highway Construction.*

TAX RECEIPTS - NATIONAL (INTERNAL REVENUE)

U.S. Department of Commerce, Bureau of the Census, Washington, D.C. 20233 (301)457-4100, www.census.gov; *Government Finances*; and Internet sites http://www.census.gov/ftp/pub/govs/www/index.html;and http://www.census.gov/pub/govs/www/index.html.

U.S. Department of the Treasury, Bureau of Alcohol, Tobacco, and Firearms, 650 Massachusetts Avenue, NW, Washington, D.C. 20226 (202) 927-8500, www.atf.treas.gov; *Alcohol and Tobacco Tax Collections.*

U.S. Department of the Treasury, Internal Revenue Service, 1111 Constitution Avenue, NW, Washington, D.C. 20224 (202) 874-0410, www.irs.ustreas.gov; *Annual Report.*

TAX RECEIPTS - NATIONAL (INTERNAL REVENUE) - ADJUSTED GROSS INCOME

U.S. Department of the Treasury, Internal Revenue Service, 1111 Constitution Avenue, NW, Washington, D.C. 20224 (202) 874-0410, www.irs.ustreas.gov; *Statistics of Income Bulletin;* and *Statistics of Income, Individual Income Tax Returns.*

TAX RECEIPTS - NATIONAL (INTERNAL REVENUE) - BY TYPE OF TAX

U.S. Department of Commerce, Bureau of the Census, Washington, D.C. 20233 (301) 457-4100, www.census.gov; *Government Finances;* and Internet sites http://www.census.gov/ftp/pub/govs/www/index.html;and

http://www.census.gov/pub/govs/www/index.html.

TAX RECEIPTS - NATIONAL (INTERNAL REVENUE) - COLLECTIONS BY SOURCE

U.S. Department of the Treasury, Bureau of Alcohol, Tobacco, and Firearms, 650 Massachusetts Avenue, NW, Washington, D.C. 20226 (202) 927-8500, www.atf.treas.gov; *Alcohol and Tobacco Tax Collections.*

U.S. Department of the Treasury, Internal Revenue Service, 1111 Constitution Avenue, NW, Washington, D.C. 20224 (202) 874-0410, www.irs.ustreas.gov; *Annual Report.*

TAX RECEIPTS - NATIONAL (INTERNAL REVENUE) - CORPORATION INCOME TAX - FEDERAL BUDGET RECEIPTS

Executive Office of the President, Office of Management and Budget, Executive Office Building, Washington, D.C. 20503 (202) 395-3080, www.whitehouse.gov/omb; *Historical Tables.*

TAX RECEIPTS - NATIONAL (INTERNAL REVENUE) - CORPORATION INCOME TAX - INTERNAL REVENUE COLLECTIONS

U.S. Department of the Treasury, Bureau of Alcohol, Tobacco, and Firearms, 650 Massachusetts Avenue, NW, Washington, D.C. 20226 (202) 927-8500, www.atf.treas.gov; *Alcohol and Tobacco Tax Collections.*

U.S. Department of the Treasury, Internal Revenue Service, 1111 Constitution Avenue, NW, Washington, D.C. 20224 (202) 874-0410, www.irs.ustreas.gov, *Annual Report of the Commissioner and Chief Counsel of the Internal Revenue Service;* and *IRS Data Book.*

TAX RECEIPTS - NATIONAL (INTERNAL REVENUE) - CORPORATION INCOME TAX - TAX LIABILITIES

U.S. Department of the Treasury, Internal Revenue Service, 1111 Constitution Avenue, NW, Washington, D.C. 20224 (202) 874-0410, www.irs.ustreas.gov; *Statistics of Income, Corporation Income Tax Returns.*

TAX RECEIPTS - NATIONAL (INTERNAL REVENUE) - CORPORATION INCOME TAX - TAX RETURNS FILED

U.S. Department of the Treasury, Internal Revenue Service, 1111 Constitution Avenue, NW, Washington, D.C. 20224 (202) 874-0410, www.irs.ustreas.gov; *Annual Report of the Commissioner and Chief Counsel of the Internal Revenue Service; IRS Data Book;* and *Statistics of Income, Corporation Income Tax Returns.*

TAX RECEIPTS - NATIONAL (INTERNAL REVENUE) - EMPLOYMENT TAXES

Executive Office of the President, Office of Management and Budget, Executive Office Building, Washington, D.C. 20503 (202) 395-3080, www.whitehouse.gov/omb; *Historical Tables.*

U.S. Department of the Treasury, Bureau of Alcohol, Tobacco, and Firearms, 650 Massachusetts Avenue, NW, Washington, D.C. 20226 (202) 927-8500, www.atf.treas.gov; *Alcohol and Tobacco Tax Collections.*

U.S. Department of the Treasury, Internal Revenue Service, 1111 Constitution Avenue, NW, Washington, D.C. 20224 (202) 874-0410, www.irs.ustreas.gov; *Annual Report of the Commissioner and Chief Counsel of the Internal Revenue Service;* and *IRS Data Book.*

TAX RECEIPTS - NATIONAL (INTERNAL REVENUE) - ESTATE AND GIFT TAXES

Executive Office of the President, Office of Management and Budget, Executive Office Building, Washington, D.C. 20503 (202) 395-3080, www.whitehouse.gov/omb; *Historical Tables.*

U.S. Department of the Treasury, Bureau of Alcohol, Tobacco, and Firearms, 650 Massachusetts Avenue, NW, Washington, D.C. 20226 (202) 927-8500, www.atf.treas.gov; *Alcohol and Tobacco Tax Collections.*

U.S. Department of the Treasury, Internal Revenue Service, 1111 Constitution Avenue, NW, Washington, D.C. 20224 (202) 874-0410, www.irs.ustreas.gov; *Annual Report of the Commissioner and Chief Counsel of the Internal Revenue Service;* and *IRS Data Book.*

TAX RECEIPTS - NATIONAL (INTERNAL REVENUE) - EXCISE TAXES

Executive Office of the President, Office of Management and Budget, Executive Office Building, Washington, D.C. 20503 (202) 395-3080, www.whitehouse.gov/omb; *Historical Tables.*

U.S. Department of the Treasury, Bureau of Alcohol, Tobacco, and Firearms, 650 Massachusetts Avenue, NW, Washington, D.C. 20226 (202) 927-8500, www.atf.treas.gov; *Alcohol and Tobacco Tax Collections.*

U.S. Department of the Treasury, Internal Revenue Service, 1111 Constitution Avenue, NW, Washington, D.C. 20224 (202) 874-0410, www.irs.ustreas.gov; *Annual Report of the Commissioner and Chief Counsel of the Internal Revenue Service;* and *IRS Data Book.*

TAX RECEIPTS - NATIONAL (INTERNAL REVENUE) - INDIVIDUAL INCOME TAX

Executive Office of the President, Office of Management and Budget, Executive Office Building, Washington, D.C. 20503 (202) 395-3080, www.whitehouse.gov/omb; *Historical Tables.*

U.S. Department of Commerce, Bureau of the Census, Washington, D.C. 20233 (301)457-4100, www.census.gov; *Government Finances;* and Internet sites http://www.census.gov/ftp/pub/govs/www/index.html; and http://www.census.gov/pub/govs/www/index.html.

U.S. Department of the Treasury, Bureau of Alcohol, Tobacco, and Firearms, 650 Massachusetts Avenue, NW, Washington, D.C. 20226 (202) 927-8500, www.atf.treas.gov; *Alcohol and Tobacco Tax Collections.*

U.S. Department of the Treasury, Internal Revenue Service, 1111 Constitution Avenue, NW, Washington, D.C. 20224 (202) 874-0410, www.irs.ustreas.gov; *Annual Report of the Commissioner and Chief Counsel of the Internal Revenue Service; Statistics of Income, Individual Income Tax Returns; Statistics of Income Bulletin;* and *IRS Data Book.*

TAX RECEIPTS - NATIONAL (INTERNAL REVENUE) - INDIVIDUAL INCOME TAX - AVERAGE TAX BY INCOME LEVEL

U.S. Department of the Treasury, Internal Revenue Service, 1111 Constitution Avenue, NW, Washington, D.C. 20224 (202) 874-0410, www.irs.ustreas.gov; *Statistics of Income, Individual Income Tax Returns;* and *Statistics of Income Bulletin.*

TAX RECEIPTS - NATIONAL (INTERNAL REVENUE) - INDIVIDUAL INCOME TAX - RATES

U.S. Department of the Treasury, Fifteenth Street and Pennsylvania Avenue, NW, Washington, D.C. 20220 (202) 622-2000; unpublished data.

TAX RECEIPTS - PROPERTY TAX - CITY GOVERNMENT

U.S. Department of Commerce, Bureau of the Census, Washington, D.C. 20233 (301) 457-4100, www.census.gov; *City Government Finances;* and Internet site: http://www.census.gov/ftp/pub/govs/www/city94.html.

TAX RECEIPTS - PROPERTY TAX - RATES - SELECTED CITIES

Government of the District of Columbia, Department of Finances and Revenue, 441 Fourth Street, NW, Washington, D.C. 20001

(202) 727-6103; *Tax Rates and Tax Burdens in the District of Columbia: A Nationwide Comparison.*

TAX RECEIPTS - PROPERTY TAX - STATE AND LOCAL GOVERNMENT

U.S. Department of Commerce, Bureau of the Census, Washington, D.C. 20233 (301)457-4100, www.census.gov; *Government Finances;* and Internet sites: http://www.census.gov/ftp/pub/govs/www/index.html and http://www.census.gov/pub/govs/www/index.html.

TAX RECEIPTS - STATE AND LOCAL GOVERNMENT - BY HOUSEHOLD INCOME

Government of the District of Columbia, Department of Finance and Revenue, 441 Fourth Street, NW, Washington, D.C. 20001 (202) 727-6103; *Tax Rates and Tax Burdens in the District of Columbia: A Nationwide Comparison.*

TAX RECEIPTS - STATE AND LOCAL GOVERNMENT - BY TYPE OF TAX

U.S. Department of Commerce, Bureau of the Census, Washington, D.C. 20233 (301) 457-4100, www.census.gov; *Government Finances;* and Internet sites http://www.census.gov/ftp/pub/govs/www/index.html and http://www.census.gov/pub/govs/www.index.html.

TAX RECEIPTS - STATE AND LOCAL GOVERNMENT - CITY GOVERNMENT

Government of the District of Columbia, Department of Finance and Revenue, 441 Fourth Street, NW, Washington, D.C. 20001 (202) 727-6103; *Tax Rates and Tax Burdens in the District of Columbia: A Nationwide Comparison.*

U.S. Department of Commerce, Bureau of the Census, Washington, D.C. 20233 (301) 457-4100, www.census.gov; *City Government Finances;* and Internet site http://www.census.gov/ftp/pub/govs/www/city94.html.

TAX RECEIPTS - STATE AND LOCAL GOVERNMENT - STATE GOVERNMENT

U.S. Department of Commerce, Bureau of the Census, Washington, D.C. 20233 (301) 457-4100, www.census.gov; *State Government Finances; State Government Tax Collections; Historical Statistics on Governmental Finances and Employment;* and Internet site: http://www.census.gov/govs/ www/state.html.

TEA

U.S. Department of Agriculture, Economic Research Service, 1800 M Street,

NW, Washington, D.C. 20036 (202) 694-5050, www.ers.usda.gov; *Food Consumption, Prices, and Expenditures.*

TEACHERS - CATHOLIC SCHOOLS

National Catholic Education Association, 1077 Thirtieth Street, Suite 100, NW Washington, D.C. 20007 (202) 337-6232; *U.S. Catholic Elementary and Secondary Schools Annual Statistical Report on Schools Enrollment and Staffing.*

TEACHERS - DEGREES CONFERRED

U.S. Department of Education, National Center for Education Statistics, 555 New Jersey Avenue, NW, Washington, D.C. 20208-1828, http://nces.ed.gov; *Digest of Education Statistics.*

TEACHERS - EMPLOYMENT

National Education Association, 1201 Sixteenth Street, NW, Washington, D.C. 20036 (202) 833-4000; *Estimates of School Statistics Database.*

U.S. Department of Education, National Center for Education Statistics; 555 New Jersey Avenue, NW, Washington, D.C. 20208-1828, http://nces.ed.gov; *Digest of Education Statistics; Projections of Education Statistics; Fall Staff in Postsecondary Institutions;* and unpublished data.

U.S. Department of Labor, Bureau of Labor Statistics, Two Massachusetts Avenue, NE, Washington, D.C. 20212 (202) 691-5200, www.stats.bls.gov; *Employment and Earnings;* and unpublished data.

TEACHERS - EMPLOYMENT - NEWLY HIRED

U.S. Department of Education, National Center for Education Statistics, 555 New Jersey Avenue, NW, Washington, D.C. 20208-1828, http://nces.ed.gov; *Condition of Education.*

TEACHERS - EMPLOYMENT - PROJECTIONS

U.S. Department of Labor, Bureau of Labor Statistics, Two Massachusetts Avenue, NE, Washington, D.C. 20212 (202) 691-5200, www.stats.bls.gov; *Monthly Labor Review.*

TEACHERS - PRIVATE SCHOOLS

U.S. Department of Education, National Center for Education Statistics; 555 New Jersey Avenue, NW, Washington, D.C. 20208-1828, http://nces.ed.gov; *Digest of Education Statistics.*

TEACHERS - PUBLIC SCHOOLS

National Education Association, 1201 Sixteenth Street, NW, Washington, D.C. 20036 (202) 833-4000; *Estimates of School Statistics Database.*

U.S. Department of Education, National Center for Education Statistics, 555 New Jersey Avenue, NW, Washington, D.C. 20208-1828, http://nces.ed.gov; *Digest of Education Statistics;* and *Projections of Educational Statistics.*

TEACHERS - PUBLIC SCHOOLS - EXPERIENCE AND DEGREES HELD

U.S. Department of Education, National Center for Education Statistics, 555 New Jersey Avenue, NW, Washington, D.C. 20208-1828, http://nces.ed.gov; *Digest of Education Statistics; and unpublished data.*

TEACHERS - PUBLIC SCHOOLS - HIGHER EDUCATION INSTITUTIONS

U.S. Department of Education, National Center for Education Statistics, 555 New Jersey Avenue, NW, Washington, D.C. 20208-1828, http://nces.ed.gov; *Digest of Education Statistics; Projections of Education Statistics;* and unpublished data.

TEACHERS - PUBLIC SCHOOLS - NUMBER

National Education Association, 1201 Sixteenth Street, NW, Washington, D.C. 20036 (202) 833-4000; *Estimates of School Statistics.*

U.S. Department of Education, National Center for Education Statistics, 555 New Jersey Avenue, NW, Washington, D.C. 20208-1828, http://nces.ed.gov; *Projections of Education Statistics; Digest of Education Statistics;* and unpublished data.

TEACHERS - PUBLIC SCHOOLS - SALARIES

American Association of University Professors, 1012 Fourteenth Street, NW, Suite 500, Washington, D.C. 20005 (202) 737-5900; *Annual Report on the Economic Status of the Profession.*

TEACHERS - RESOURCES

National Education Association, 1201 Sixteenth Street, NW, Washington, D.C. 20036 (202) 833-4000; *Status of the American Public School Teacher.*

TEACHERS - STATES

National Education Association, 1201 Sixteenth Street, NW, Washington, D.C. 20036 (202) 833-4000; *Estimates of School Statistics Database.*

TEACHERS - WORKPLACE VIOLENCE

U.S. Department of Justice, Bureau of Justice Statistics, 810 Seventh Street, NW,

2nd Floor, Washington, D.C. 20531 (800) 732-3277, www.ojp.usdoj.gov/bjs; *Workplace Violence.*

TECHNICIANS

U.S. Department of Labor, Bureau of Labor Statistics, Two Massachusetts Avenue, NE, Washington, D.C. 20212 (202) 691-5200, www.stats.bls.gov; *Employment and Earnings.*

TECHNOLOGY IN SCHOOL

Quality Education Data, Inc., 1600 Broadway, 12th Floor, Denver, Colorado 80202 (303) 860-1832; *National Education Database.*

TELECOMMUNICATIONS

Federal Communications Commission, 445 Twelfth Street, SW, Washington, D.C. 20554 (888) 225-5322, www.fcc.gov; *Trends in Telephone Service.*

U.S. Department of Commerce, Bureau of the Census, Washington, D.C. 20233 (301) 457-4100, www.census.gov; *Manufacturing Profile; U.S. International Trade in Goods and Services;* and Internet site: http://www.census.gov/ftp/pub/industry/1/ma36p97.pdf.

TELEGRAPH AND OTHER COMMUNICATIONS

Federal Communications Commission, 445 Twelfth Street, SW, Washington, D.C. 20554 (888) 225-5322, www.fcc.gov; *Statistics of Communications Common Carriers;* and *Trends in Telephone Service.*

TELEPHONE COMMUNICATION - CARRIERS

Federal Communications Commission, 445 Twelfth Street, SW, Washington, D.C. 20554 (888) 225-5322, www.fcc.gov; *Trends in Telephone Service.*

TELEPHONE COMMUNICATION - CELLULAR

Cellular Telecommunications Industry Association, 1250 Connecticut Avenue, NW, Suite 800, Washington, D.C. 20036 (202) 785-0081; *Semi-annual Wireless Survey.*

International Telecommunications Union, Palais des Nations, CH-1211 Geneva 20, Switzerland; *World Telecommunication Indicators.*

The World Bank, 1818 H Street, NW, Washington, D.C. 20043 (202) 477-1234; *World Development Indicators.*

TELEPHONE COMMUNICATION - EARNINGS

Federal Communications Commission, 445 Twelfth Street, SW, Washington, D.C. 20554 (888) 225-5322, www.fcc.gov; *Statistics of Communications Common Carriers;* and *Trends in Telephone Service.*

U.S. Department of Labor, Bureau of Labor Statistics, Two Massachusetts Avenue, NE, Washington, D.C. 20212 (202) 691-5200, www.stats.bls.gov; *Employment and Earnings;* and Internet site: http://stats.bls.gov/ceshome.htm.

TELEPHONE COMMUNICATION - EMPLOYEES

Cellular Telecommunications Industry Association, 1250 Connecticut Avenue, NW, Suite 800, Washington, D.C. 20036 (202) 785-0081; *Semi-annual Wireless Survey.*

Federal Communications Commission, 445 Twelfth Street, SW, Washington, D.C. 20554 (888) 225-5322, www.fcc.gov; *Statistics of Communication Common Carriers.*

U.S. Department of Labor, Bureau of Labor Statistics, Two Massachusetts Avenue, NE, Washington, D.C. 20212 (202) 691-5200, www.stats.bls.gov; *Employment and Earnings;* and Internet site: http://stats.bls.gov/ceshome.htm.

TELEPHONE COMMUNICATION - FINANCES

Cellular Telecommunications Industry Association, 1250 Connecticut Avenue, NW, Suite 800, Washington, D.C. 20036 (202) 785-0081; *Semi-annual Wireless Survey.*

Federal Communications Commission, 445 Twelfth Street, SW, Washington, D.C. 20554 (888) 225-5322, www.fcc.gov; *Statistics of Communication Common Carriers.*

U.S. Department of Commerce, Bureau of the Census, Washington, D.C. 20233 (301) 457-4100, www.census.gov; *Annual Survey of Communications Services.*

TELEPHONE COMMUNICATIONS - PRODUCTIVITY

U.S. Department of Labor, Bureau of Labor Statistics, Two Massachusetts Avenue, NE, Washington, D.C. 20212 (202) 691-5200, www.stats.bls.gov; Internet site http://stats.bls.gov/iprhome.htm.

TELEPHONE COMMUNICATIONS - RECEIPTS

Federal Communications Commission, 445 Twelfth Street, SW, Washington, D.C. 20554 (888) 225-5322, www.fcc.gov;

Statistics of Communication Common Carriers.; *Statistics of Communications Common Carriers.*

TELEPHONES - See also TELEGRAPH, ETC.

TELEPHONES - ACCESS LINES

Federal Communications Commission, 445 Twelfth Street, SW, Washington, D.C. 20554 (888) 225-5322, www.fcc.gov; *Statistics of Communication Common Carriers.*; *Statistics of Communication Carriers.*

TELEPHONES - CALLS

Federal Communications Commission, 445 Twelfth Street, SW, Washington, D.C. 20554 (888) 225-5322, www.fcc.gov; *Statistics of Communication Common Carriers.*; *Statistics of Communication Common Carriers.*

TELEPHONES - CONSUMER EXPENDITURES

U.S. Department of Labor, Bureau of Labor Statistics, Two Massachusetts Avenue, NE, Washington, D.C. 20212 (202) 691-5200, www.stats.bls.gov; *Consumer Expenditures*; and unpublished data.

TELEPHONES - CONSUMER PRICE INDEX

U.S. Department of Labor, Bureau of Labor Statistics, Two Massachusetts Avenue, NE, Washington, D.C. 20212 (202) 691-5200, www.stats.bls.gov; *Monthly Labor Review;* and *Handbook of Labor Statistics.*

TELEPHONES - HOUSEHOLDS WITH SERVICE

Federal Communications Commission, 445 Twelfth Street, SW, Washington, D.C. 20554 (888) 225-5322, www.fcc.gov; *Statistics of Communication Common Carriers.*; *Trends in Telephone Service.*

U.S. Department of Commerce, Bureau of the Census, Washington, D.C. 20233 (301) 457-4100, www.census.gov; *Census of Housing; Current Housing Reports*; and unpublished data.

TELEPHONES - NUMBER

Federal Communications Commission, 445 Twelfth Street, SW, Washington, D.C. 20554 (888) 225-5322, www.fcc.gov; *Statistics of Communications Common Carriers.*

TELEPHONES - NUMBER - FOREIGN COUNTRIES

International Telecommunication Union, Palais des Nations, CH-1211 Geneva 20, Switzerland 41 22 7305111, *World Telecommunication Indicators.*

TELEPHONES - SHIPMENTS

U.S. Department of Commerce, Bureau of the Census, Washington, D.C. 20233 (301) 457-4100, www.census.gov; Manufacturing Profile; and Internet site: http://www.census.gov/ ftp/pub/industry/1/mg36p97.pdf.

TELEVISION BROADCASTING - See also CABLE AND OTHER PAY TV SERVICES, PUBLIC BROADCASTING STATIONS and RADIO

TELEVISION BROADCASTING - ADVERTISING EXPENDITURES

McCann-Erickson, Inc., 750 Third Avenue, New York, New York 10017 (212) 697-6000; compiled for Crain Communications, Inc., 740 North Rush Street, Chicago, Illinois 60611 (312) 649-5200; in *Advertising Age.*

Television Bureau of Advertising, Inc. 3 East 54th Street, New York, New York 10022 (212) 486-1111; data compiled by Competitive Media Reporting, 11 West 42nd Street, New York, New York 10036 (212) 789-1400.

TELEVISION BROADCASTING - EARNINGS

U.S. Department of Commerce, Bureau of the Census, Washington, D.C. 20233 (301) 457-4100, www.census.gov; *Census of Transportation, Communications and Utilities.*

U.S. Department of Commerce, Economics and Statistics Administration, Fourteenth Street and Constitution Avenue, NW, Room 4858, Washington, D.C. 20230 (800) 782-8872, www.esa.doc.gov; *The Emerging Digital Economy II.*

U.S. Department of Labor, Bureau of Labor Statistics, Two Massachusetts Avenue, NE, Washington, D.C. 20212 (202) 691-5200, www.stats.bls.gov; *Employment and Earnings;* and Internet site: http://stats.bls.gov/ ceshome.htm.

TELEVISION BROADCASTING - EMPLOYEES

U.S. Department of Commerce, Economics and Statistics Administration, Fourteenth Street and Constitution Avenue, NW, Room 4858, Washington, D.C. 20230 (800) 782-8872, www.esa.doc.gov; *The Emerging Digital Economy II.*

U.S. Department of Labor, Bureau of Labor Statistics, Two Massachusetts Avenue, NE, Washington, D.C. 20212 (202) 691-5200, www.stats.bls.gov; *Employment and Earnings;* and Internet site: stats.bls.gov/ceshome.htm.

TELEVISION BROADCASTING - FINANCES

U.S. Department of Commerce, Bureau of the Census, Washington, D.C. 20233 (301) 457-4100, www.census.gov; *Annual Survey of Communication Services.*

Veronis, Suhler and Associates, 350 Park Avenue, New York, New York 10022 (212) 935-4990; *Communications Industry Report.*

TELEVISION BROADCASTING - GROSS DOMESTIC PRODUCT

U.S. Department of Commerce, Economics and Statistics Administration, Fourteenth Street and Constitution Avenue, NW, Room 4858, Washington, D.C. 20230 (800) 782-8872, www.esa.doc.gov; *The Emerging Digital Economy II.*

TELEVISION BROADCASTING - MERGERS AND ACQUISITIONS

Thomson Financial Securities Data, Two Gateway Center, Newark, New Jersey 07006 (973) 622-3100; *Merger and Corporate Transactions Database.*

TELEVISIONS - CONSUMER EXPENDITURES

U.S. Department of Commerce, Bureau of Economic Analysis, Fourteenth Street between Constitution Avenue and E Street, NW, Washington, D.C. 20230 (202) 606-9900, www.bea.doc.gov; *The National Income and Product Accounts of the U.S.;* and *Survey of Current Business.*

U.S. Department of Labor, Bureau of Labor Statistics, Two Massachusetts Avenue, NE, Washington, D.C. 20212 (202) 691-5200, www.stats.bls.gov; *Consumer Expenditure Survey.*

TELEVISIONS - HOUSEHOLDS WITH

Television Bureau of Advertising, Inc., 3 East 54th Street, New York, New York 10022 (212) 486-1111; *Trends in Television.*

TELEVISIONS - VIEWING

Mediamark Research, Incorporated, 708 Third Avenue, New York, New York 10017 (212) 599-0444; *Multimedia Audiences.*

Veronis, Suhler and Associates, 350 Park Avenue, New York, New York 10022 (212) 935-4990; *Communications Industry Report.*

TEMPERATURE - CITIES

U.S. Department of Commerce,

National Oceanic and Atmospheric Administration, National Climatic Data Center, 151 Patton Avenue, Asheville, North Carolina 28801 (828) 271-4800, www.ncdc.noaa.gov; *Climatography of the United States;* and *Comparative Climatic Data.*

TEMPERATURE - STATES (HIGHS AND LOWS)

U.S. Department of Commerce, National Oceanic and Atmospheric Administration, National Climatic Data Center, 151 Patton Avenue, Asheville, North Carolina 28801 (828) 271-4800, www.ncdc.noaa.gov; Internet site: http://www.ncdc.noaa.gov/climate/

TEMPLES (FRUIT)

U.S. Department of Agriculture, National Agricultural Statistics Service, Fourteenth Street and Independence Avenue, SW, Washington, D.C. 20250 (800) 727-9540, www.usda.gov/nass; *Citrus Fruits.*

TENNESSEE - See also STATE DATA (FOR INDIVIDUAL STATES)

Tennessee - Primary Statistics Source

Center for Business and Economic Research, College of Business Administration, University of Tennessee, 100 Glocker Business Building, Knoxville, Tennessee 37996-4170 (615) 974-6080; *Tennessee Statistical Abstract.*

Tennessee - State Data Centers

Center for Business and Economic Research, University of Tennessee-Knoxville, 100 Glocker Business Building, Knoxville, Tennessee 37996-4170, Ms. Betty Vickers (615) 974-6080.

Tennessee Department of Economic and Community Development, Research Division, 320 Sixth Avenue, North, Rachel Jackson Building, 8th Floor, Nashville, Tennessee 37243-0405, Mr. Don Waller (615) 974-6080.

TENNIS

National Collegiate Athletic Association, 700 West Washington Street, Indianapolis, Indiana 46206 (317) 917-6222; *1997-98 Participation Study.*

National Sporting Goods Association, 1601 Feehanville Drive, Suite 300, Mount Prospect, Illinois 60056 (847) 296-6742; *The Sporting Goods Market in 1999;* and *Sports Participation in 1998.*

Tennis Industry Association, 19 Pope Avenue #107, Hilton Head, South Carolina 29928 (843) 686-3036.

United States Tennis Association, Post Office Box 5046, White Plains, New York 10602 (914) 696-7000.

TENURE - See HOUSING AND HOUSING UNITS and FARMS

TETANUS

U.S. Department of Health and Human Services, Centers for Disease Control and Prevention, 1600 Clifton Road, NE, Atlanta, Georgia 30333 (800) 311-3435, www.cdc.gov; *Summary of Notifiable Diseases, United States, Morbidity and Mortality Weekly Report.*

TEXAS - See also STATE DATA (FOR INDIVIDUAL STATES)

Texas - Primary Statistics Sources

Dallas Morning News, Incorporated, Communications Center, Post Office Box 655237, Dallas, Texas 75265 (214) 977-8261; *Texas Almanac.*

Texas - State Data Centers

Department of Rural Sociology, Texas A&M University System, Special Services Building, College Station, Texas 77843-2125, Dr. Steve Murdock (409) 845-5115.

Texas Department of Economic Development, 1700 North Congress, Post Office box 12728, Austin, Texas 78701, Ms. Donna Osborne (512) 936-0223.

Texas Natural Resources Information System (TNRIS), Post Office Box 13231, Austin, Texas 78711, Mr. Charles Palmer (512) 463-8399.

Texas State Library, Lorenzo de Zavala Building, Post Office Box 12927, Capitol Station, Austin, Texas 78711, Ms. Diana Houston (512) 463-5455.

TEXTILE MILL PRODUCTS - END - USE

Fiber Economics Bureau, Incorporated, 101 Eisenhower Parkway, Roseland, New Jersey 07068 (201) 228-1107; *Textile Organon.*

TEXTILE MILL PRODUCTS - FOREIGN TRADE

U.S. Department of Commerce, Bureau of the Census, Washington, D.C. 20233 (301) 457-4100, www.census.gov; *U.S. International Trade in Goods and Services;* and *Manufacturing Profiles.*

TEXTILE MILL PRODUCTS MANUFACTURING - CAPITAL

U.S. Department of Commerce, Bureau of Economic Analysis, Fourteenth Street between Constitution Avenue and E Street, NW, Washington, D.C. 20230 (202) 606-9900, www.bea.doc.gov; *Survey of Current Business.*

TEXTILE MILL PRODUCTS - MANUFACTURING - EARNINGS

U.S. Department of Commerce, Bureau of the Census, Washington, D.C. 20233 (301) 457-4100, www.census.gov; *County Business Patterns; Census of Manufactures; 1997 Economic Census, Core Business Statistics Series;* and *Annual Survey of Manufactures.*

U.S. Department of Labor, Bureau of Labor Statistics, Two Massachusetts Avenue, NE, Washington, D.C. 20212 (202) 691-5200, www.stats.bls.gov; *Employment and Earnings;* and Internet site: http://stats.bls.gov/ceshome. htm.

TEXTILE MILL PRODUCTS - MANUFACTURING - EMPLOYEES

U.S. Department of Commerce, Bureau of the Census, Washington, D.C. 20233 (301) 457-4100, www.census.gov; *Census of Manufactures; Annual Survey of Manufactures; Exports from Manufacturing Establishments; 1997 Economic Census, Core Business Statistics Series;* and *County Business Patterns.*

U.S. Department of Labor, Bureau of Labor Statistics, Two Massachusetts Avenue, NE, Washington, D.C. 20212 (202) 691-5200, www.stats.bls.gov; *Employment and Earnings; Monthly Labor Review;* and Internet site: http://stats.bls.gov/ceshome.htm.

TEXTILE MILL PRODUCTS - MANUFACTURING - ENERGY CONSUMPTION

U.S. Department of Energy, Energy Information Administration, 1000 Independence Avenue, SW, Washington, D.C. 20585 (202) 586-8800, www.eia.doe.gov; *Manufacturing Energy Consumption.*

TEXTILE MILL PRODUCTS - MANUFACTURING - ESTABLISHMENTS

U.S. Department of Commerce, Bureau of the Census, Washington, D.C. 20233 (301) 457-4100, www.census.gov; *County Business Patterns;* and *1997 Economic Census, Core Business Statistics Series.*

TEXTILE MILL PRODUCTS - MANUFACTURING - FOREIGN TRADE

U.S. Department of Commerce, Bureau of the Census, Washington, D.C. 20233 (301) 457-4100, www.census.gov; *U.S. International Trade in Goods and Services.*

TEXTILE MILL PRODUCTS - MANUFACTURING - GROSS DOMESTIC PRODUCT

U.S. Department of Commerce, Bureau of Economic Analysis, Fourteenth Street between Constitution Avenue and E Street, NW, Washington, D.C. 20230 (202) 606-9900, www.bea.doc.gov; *Survey of Current Business.*

TEXTILE MILL PRODUCTS - MANUFACTURING - INVENTORIES

U.S. Department of Commerce, Bureau of the Census, Washington, D.C. 20233 (301) 457-4100, www.census.gov; *Current Industrial Reports, Manufacture Shipments, Inventories, and Orders.*

TEXTILE MILL PRODUCTS - MANUFACTURING - MERGERS AND ACQUISITIONS

Thomson Financial Securities Data, 2 Gateway Center, Newark, New Jersey 07006 (973) 622-3100; *Merger and Corporate Transactions Database.*

TEXTILE MILL PRODUCTS - MANUFACTURING - OCCUPATIONAL SAFETY

U.S. Department of Labor, Bureau of Labor Statistics, Two Massachusetts Avenue, NE, Washington, D.C. 20212 (202) 691-5200, www.stats.bls.gov; *Occupational Injuries and Illnesses in the United States by Industry.*

TEXTILE MILL PRODUCTS - MANUFACTURING - OUTPUT

Board of Governors of the Federal Reserve System, Twentieth Street and Constitution Avenue, NW, Washington, D.C. 20551 (202) 452-3000, www.bog.frb.fed.us; *Federal Reserve Bulletin;* and *Industrial Production and Capacity Utilization, Statistical Release G-17.*

TEXTILE MILL PRODUCTS - MANUFACTURING - PATENTS

U.S. Department of Commerce, Patent and Trademark Office, 2011 Crystal Drive, Arlington, Virginia 22202 (703) 305-8341, www.uspto.gov; *Patenting Trends in the United States, State Country Report.*

TEXTILE MILL PRODUCTS - MANUFACTURING - PRODUCTIVITY

Board of Governors of the Federal Reserve System, Twentieth Street and Constitution Avenue, NW, Washington, D.C. 20551 (202) 452-3000, www.bog.frb.fed.us; *Federal Reserve Bulletin;* and *Industrial Production and Capacity Utilization, Statistical Release G-17.*

U.S. Department of Labor, Bureau of Labor Statistics, Two Massachusetts Avenue, NE, Washington, D.C. 20212 (202) 691-5200, www.stats.bls.gov; Internet site http://stats.bls.gov/irphomr.htm.

TEXTILE MILL PRODUCTS - MANUFACTURING - SHIPMENTS

U.S. Department of Commerce, Bureau of the Census, Washington, D.C. 20233 (301) 457-4100, www.census.gov; *Current Industrial Reports, Manufactures' Shipments, Inventories and Orders; Annual Survey of Manufactures; 1997 Economic Census, Core Business Statistics Series;* and *Census of Manufactures.*

TEXTILE MILL PRODUCTS - MANUFACTURING - TOXIC CHEMICAL RELEASES

Environmental Protection Agency, 1200 Pennsylvania Avenue, NW, Washington, D.C. 20460 (888) 372-8255, www.epa.gov; *Toxics Release Inventory.*

TEXTILE MILL PRODUCTS - MANUFACTURING - VALUE ADDED

U.S. Department of Commerce, Bureau of the Census, Washington, D.C. 20233 (301) 457-4100, www.census.gov; *Census of Manufactures;* and *Annual Survey of Manufactures.*

TEXTILE MILLS - MANUFACTURING

U.S. Department of Commerce, Bureau of the Census, Washington, D.C. 20233 (301) 457-4100, www.census.gov; *1997 Economic Census, Core Business Statistics Series.*

THAI POPULATION

U.S. Department of Commerce, Bureau of the Census, Washington, D.C. 20233 (301) 457-4100, www.census.gov; *Census of Population, General Population Characteristics, U.S.*

Thailand - National Statistical Offices

Bank of Thailand, Bangkhunprom, Bangkok 10200, Thailand; for economics statistics.

Centre for Industrial Statistics, Information and Research, Industrial Economics and Planning Division, Ministry of Industry, Rama 6 Road, Bangkok 10400, Thailand; for industrial statistics.

National Statistical Office, Larn Luang Road, Bangkok 10100, Thailand; for general statistics.

Techniques and Statistics Division, Customs Department, Sunthornkosa Road, Klong Toey, Bangkok 10110, Thailand; for foreign statistics.

Thailand - Primary Statistics Sources

National Statistical Office, Bangkok, Thailand; *Statistical Yearbook Thailand; Quarterly Bulletin of Statistics;* and *Statistical Handbook.*

THAILAND - AGRICULTURE

Asian Development Bank, P.O. Box 789, 1099 Manila, Philippines; *Key Indicators of Developing Asian and Pacific Countries.*

Economist Intelligence Unit, 111 West 57th Street, New York, New York 10019 (800) 938-4685; *Thailand Country Report.*

Euromonitor International, Inc., 122 South Michigan Avenue, Suite 1200, Chicago, Illinois 60603 (800) 577-EURO; *International Marketing Data and Statistics;* and *World Marketing Data and Statistics.*

Europa Publications Limited, 18 Bedford Square, London, WC1B 3JN, England; *The Europa World Year Book.*

Food and Agricultural Organization of the United Nations (FAO) Via delle Terme di Caracalla, 00100 Rome, Italy (Telephone Number in U.S. (202) 653-2400); *Production Yearbook; The State of Food and Agriculture;* and *Trade Yearbook.*

M.E. Sharpe, 80 Business Park Drive, Armonk, New York 10504 (800) 541-6563; *The Illustrated Book of World Rankings.*

National Statistical Office, Office of the Prime Minister, Bangkok Metropolis 10100, Thailand; *Statistical Yearbook Thailand.*

St. Martin's Press, Inc., 175 Fifth Avenue, New York, New York 10010 (800) 221-7945; *The Statesman's Year-Book.*

Statistical Office of the United Nations, Publishing Service, New York, New York 10017 (800) 253-9646; *Asia-Pacific in Figures; Statistical Yearbook;* and *Statistical Yearbook for Asia and the Pacific.*

United Nations Conference on Trade and Development, Central Statistical Service, Palais des Nations, Geneva, Switzerland (Telephone in U.S. (800) 253-9646); *UNCTAD Commodity Yearbook.*

The World Bank, 1818 H Street, NW, Washington, D.C. 20433 (202) 477-1234; *World Development Indicators.*

THAILAND - AIRLINE SERVICE

The Economist Intelligence Unit (Asia) Limited, 10th Floor, Luk Kwok Centre, 72 Gloucester Road, Wanchai, Hong Kong (Phone Number in U.S. (800) 938-4685); *Asian Market Atlas.*

Europa Publications Limited, 18 Bedford Square, London, WC1B 3JN, England; *The Europa World Year Book.*

International Civil Aviation Organization, 999 University Street, Montreal, Quebec, Canada H3C 5H7 (514) 954-8219; *Civil Aviation Statistics of the World.*

M.E. Sharpe, 80 Business Park Drive, Armonk, New York 10504 (800) 541-6563; *The Illustrated Book of World Rankings.*

St. Martin's Press, Inc., 175 Fifth Avenue, New York, New York 10010 (800) 221-7945; *The Statesman's Year-Book.*

Statistical Office of the United Nations, Publishing Service, New York, New York 10017 (800) 253-9646; *Statistical Yearbook.*

THAILAND - AIRPORTS

Central Intelligence Agency, Washington, D.C. 20505 (703) 482-1100, www.cia.gov; *The World Factbook.*

THAILAND - ALUMINUM PRODUCTION AND CONSUMPTION - See THAILAND - MINING AND MINERAL PRODUCTS

THAILAND - ANIMAL HEALTH

Food and Agricultural Organization of the United Nations (FAO), Via delle Terme di Caracalla, 00100, Rome, Italy (Telephone Number in U.S. (202) 653-2400); *Animal Health Yearbook.*

National Statistical Office, Office of the Prime Minister, Bangkok Metropolis 10100, Thailand; *Statistical Yearbook Thailand.*

THAILAND - ANTIMONY ORE PRODUCTION AND CONSUMPTION - See THAILAND - MINING AND MINERAL PRODUCTS

THAILAND - AREA AND DENSITY OF POPULATION

Central Intelligence Agency, Washington, D.C. 20505 (703) 482-1100, www.cia.gov; *The World Factbook.*

Euromonitor International, Inc., 122 South Michigan Avenue, Suite 1200, Chicago, Illinois 60603 (800) 577-EURO; *International Marketing Data and Statistics;*

and *The World Economic Factbook.*

Europa Publications Limited, 18 Bedford Square, London, WC1B 3JN, England; *The Europa World Year Book.*

Food and Agricultural Organization of the United Nations (FAO) Via delle Terme di Caracalla, 00100 Rome, Italy (Telephone Number in U.S. (202) 653-2400); *The State of Food and Agriculture.*

M.E. Sharpe, 80 Business Park Drive, Armonk, New York 10504 (800) 541-6563; *The Illustrated Book of World Rankings.*

National Statistical Office, Office of the Prime Minister, Bangkok Metropolis 10100, Thailand; *Statistical Yearbook Thailand.*

St. Martin's Press, Inc., 175 Fifth Avenue, New York, New York 10010 (800) 221-7945; *The Statesman's Year-Book.*

Statistical Office of the United Nations, Publishing Service, New York, New York 10017 (800) 253-9646; *Statistical Yearbook.*

United Nations Educational, Scientific and Cultural Organization (UNESCO), 7 Place de Fontenoy, F-75700 Paris, France (Telephone Number in U.S. (212) 963-5981); *Statistical Yearbook.*

The World Bank, 1818 H Street, NW, Washington, D.C. 20433 (202) 477-1234; *World Development Report.*

THAILAND - ARMS EXPORTS AND IMPORTS - See THAILAND - MILITARY

THAILAND - BALANCE OF PAYMENTS

The Economist Intelligence Unit, 111 West 57th Street, New York, New York 10019 (800) 938-4685; *The World Market Atlas.*

Europa Publications Limited, 18 Bedford Square, London, WC1B 3JN, England; *The Europa World Year Book.*

International Monetary Fund, 700 Nineteenth Street, NW, Washington, D.C. 20431 (202) 623-7000; *Balance of Payments Yearbook;* and *International Financial Statistics.*

National Statistical Office, Office of the Prime Minister, Bangkok Metropolis 10100, Thailand; *Statistical Yearbook Thailand.*

United Nations Conference on Trade and Development (UNCTAD), New York, New York 10017 (800) 253-9646; *Handbook of International Trade and Development.*

The World Bank, 1818 H Street, NW, Washington, D.C. 20433 (202) 477-1234; *World Development Report;* and *World Development Indicators.*

THAILAND - BANKING

Asian Development Bank, P.O. Box 789, 1099 Manila, Philippines; *Key Indicators of Developing Asian and Pacific Countries.*

Euromonitor International, Inc., 122 South Michigan Avenue, Suite 1200, Chicago, Illinois 60603 (800) 577-EURO; *World Marketing Data and Statistics.*

Europa Publications Limited, 18 Bedford Square, London, WC1B 3JN, England; *The Europa World Year Book.*

International Monetary Fund, 700 Nineteenth Street, NW, Washington, D.C. 20431 (202) 623-7000; *Government Finance Statistics Yearbook;* and *International Financial Statistics.*

M.E. Sharpe, 80 Business Park Drive, Armonk, New York 10504 (800) 541-6563; *The Illustrated Book of World Rankings.*

National Statistical Office, Office of the Prime Minister, Bangkok Metropolis 10100, Thailand; *Statistical Yearbook Thailand.*

St. Martin's Press, Inc., 175 Fifth Avenue, New York, New York 10010 (800) 221-7945; *The Statesman's Year-Book.*

Statistical Office of the United Nations, Publishing Service, New York, New York 10017 (800) 253-9646; *Statistical Yearbook.*

THAILAND - BARLEY PRODUCTION - See THAILAND - CROPS

THAILAND - BEER PRODUCTION - See THAILAND - BEVERAGES

THAILAND - BEVERAGES

M.E. Sharpe, 80 Business Park Drive, Armonk, New York 10504 (800) 541-6563; *The Illustrated Book of World Rankings.*

Statistical Office of the United Nations, Publishing Service, New York, New York 10017 (800) 253-9646; *Statistical Yearbook.*

THAILAND - BIRTH RATES

Central Intelligence Agency, Washington, D.C. 20505 (703) 482-1100, www.cia.gov; *The World Factbook.*

The Economist Intelligence Unit (Asia) Limited, 10th Floor, Luk Kwok Centre, 72 Gloucester Road, Wanchai, Hong Kong (Phone Number in U.S. (800) 938-4685); *Asian Market Atlas.*

Euromonitor International, Inc., 122 South Michigan Avenue, Suite 1200, Chicago, Illinois 60603 (800) 577-EURO; *International Marketing Data and Statistics;* and *The World Economic Factbook.*

Europa Publications Limited, 18 Bedford Square, London, WC1B 3JN, England; *The Europa World Year Book*.

M.E. Sharpe, 80 Business Park Drive, Armonk, New York 10504 (800) 541-6563; *The Illustrated Book of World Rankings*.

National Statistical Office, Office of the Prime Minister, Bangkok Metropolis 10100, Thailand; *Statistical Yearbook Thailand*.

St. Martin's Press, Inc., 175 Fifth Avenue, New York, New York 10010 (800) 221-7945; *The Statesman's Year-Book*.

Statistical Office of the United Nations, Publishing Service, New York, New York 10017 (800) 253-9646; *Asia-Pacific in Figures; Demographic Yearbook;* and *Statistical Yearbook*.

The World Bank, 1818 H Street, NW, Washington, D.C. 20433 (202) 477-1234; *World Development Indicators*.

World Health Organization, Office of Publications, 20 Avenue Appia, CH-1211 Geneva 27, Switzerland (Telephone Number in U.S. (518) 436-9686); *World Health Statistics Annual*.

THAILAND - BONDS

Asian Development Bank, P.O. Box 789, 1099 Manila, Philippines; *Key Indicators of Developing Asian and Pacific Countries*.

International Monetary Fund, 700 Nineteenth Street, NW, Washington, D.C. 20431 (202) 623-7000; *Government Finance Statistics Yearbook*.

THAILAND - BOOK PRODUCTION

Europa Publications Limited, 18 Bedford Square, London, WC1B 3JN, England; *The Europa World Year Book*.

United Nations Educational, Scientific and Cultural Organization (UNESCO), 7 Place de Fontenoy, F-75700 Paris, France (Telephone Number in U.S. (212) 963-5981); *Statistical Yearbook*.

THAILAND - BROADCASTING

Billboard Limited, P.O. Box 9027, 1006 AA Amsterdam, The Netherlands (Telephone Number in U.S. (212) 764-7300); *World Radio TV Handbook*.

Central Intelligence Agency, Washington, D.C. 20505 (703) 482-1100, www.cia.gov; *The World Factbook*.

Euromonitor International, Inc., 122 South Michigan Avenue, Suite 1200, Chicago, Illinois 60603 (800) 577-EURO; *World Marketing Data and Statistics*.

M.E. Sharpe, 80 Business Park Drive, Armonk, New York 10504 (800) 541-6563; *The Illustrated Book of World Rankings*.

St. Martin's Press, Inc., 175 Fifth Avenue, New York, New York 10010 (800) 221-7945; *The Statesman's Year-Book*.

THAILAND - BUSINESS AND PROFESSIONAL LICENSES

International Monetary Fund, 700 Nineteenth Street, NW, Washington, D.C. 20431 (202) 623-7000; *Government Finance Statistics Yearbook*.

THAILAND - CALORIE SUPPLY

Asian Development Bank, P.O. Box 789, 1099 Manila, Philippines; *Key Indicators of Developing Asian and Pacific Countries*.

Food and Agricultural Organization of the United Nations (FAO) Via delle Terme di Caracalla, 00100 Rome, Italy (Telephone Number in U.S. (202) 653-2400); *The State of Food and Agriculture*.

THAILAND - CAPITAL INVESTMENT

Asian Development Bank, P.O. Box 789, 1099 Manila, Philippines; *Key Indicators of Developing Asian and Pacific Countries*.

THAILAND - CAPITAL REVENUE

Asian Development Bank, P.O. Box 789, 1099 Manila, Philippines; *Key Indicators of Developing Asian and Pacific Countries*.

International Monetary Fund, 700 Nineteenth Street, NW, Washington, D.C. 20431 (202) 623-7000; *Government Finance Statistics Yearbook*.

THAILAND - CATTLE - See THAILAND - LIVESTOCK AND POULTRY

THAILAND - CAUSTIC ACID PRODUCTION

Statistical Office of the United Nations, Publishing Service, New York, New York 10017 (800) 253-9646; *Statistical Yearbook*.

THAILAND - CEMENT PRODUCTION - See THAILAND - MINING AND MINERAL PRODUCTS

THAILAND - CHEMICAL (ORGANIC) PRODUCTION - See THAILAND - MINING AND MINERAL PRODUCTS

THAILAND - CHICKENS - See THAILAND - LIVESTOCK AND POULTRY

THAILAND - CIGAR PRODUCTION - See THAILAND - TOBACCO PRODUCTION

THAILAND - CIGARETTE PRODUCTION - See THAILAND - TOBACCO PRODUCTION

THAILAND - CLIMATE

M.E. Sharpe, 80 Business Park Drive, Armonk, New York 10504 (800) 541-6563; *The Illustrated Book of World Rankings*.

National Statistical Office, Office of the Prime Minister, Bangkok Metropolis 10100, Thailand; *Statistical Yearbook Thailand*.

St. Martin's Press, Inc., 175 Fifth Avenue, New York, New York 10010 (800) 221-7945; *The Statesman's Year-Book*.

THAILAND - COAL PRODUCTION - See THAILAND - MINING AND MINERAL PRODUCTS

THAILAND - COFFEE - See THAILAND - CROPS

THAILAND - COMMERCE

St. Martin's Press, Inc., 175 Fifth Avenue, New York, New York 10010 (800) 221-7945; *The Statesman's Year-Book*.

THAILAND - COMMUNICATIONS - See THAILAND - TRANSPORTATION AND COMMUNICATIONS

THAILAND - CONSTRUCTION INDUSTRY

M.E. Sharpe, 80 Business Park Drive, Armonk, New York 10504 (800) 541-6563; *The Illustrated Book of World Rankings*.

Statistical Office of the United Nations, Publishing Service, New York, New York 10017 (800) 253-9646; *Statistical Yearbook*.

THAILAND - CONSUMER PRICE INDEX

Asian Development Bank, P.O. Box 789, 1099 Manila, Philippines; *Key Indicators of Developing Asian and Pacific Countries*.

Europa Publications Limited, 18 Bedford Square, London, WC1B 3JN, England; *The Europa World Year Book*.

National Statistical Office, Office of the Prime Minister, Bangkok Metropolis 10100, Thailand; *Statistical Yearbook Thailand*.

Statistical Office of the United Nations, Publishing Service, New York, New York 10017 (800) 253-9646; *Statistical Yearbook*.

THAILAND - CONSUMER PRICES

Euromonitor International, Inc., 122 South Michigan Avenue, Suite 1200, Chicago, Illinois 60603 (800) 577-EURO; *World Marketing Data and Statistics*.

International Labour Office, I.L.O. Publications, 1828 L Street, NW, Suite 801, Washington, D.C. 20036 (301) 638-3152; *Yearbook of Labour Statistics*.

International Monetary Fund, 700 Nineteenth Street, NW, Washington, D.C. 20431 (202) 623-7000; *International Financial Statistics.*

National Statistical Office, Office of the Prime Minister, Bangkok Metropolis 10100, Thailand; *Statistical Yearbook Thailand.*

THAILAND - CONSUMPTION

International Rubber Study Group, York House, Eighth Floor, Empire Way, Wembley, London HA9 0PA, England; *Rubber Statistical Handbook.*

National Statistical Office, Office of the Prime Minister, Bangkok Metropolis 10100, Thailand; *Statistical Yearbook Thailand.*

The World Bank, 1818 H Street, NW, Washington, D.C. 20433 (202) 477-1234; *World Development Report.*

THAILAND - COPPER PRODUCTION AND CONSUMPTION - See THAILAND - MINING AND MINERAL PRODUCTS

THAILAND - CORN - See THAILAND - CROPS

THAILAND - CORPORATE TAXES - See THAILAND - TAXATION

THAILAND - COTTON - See THAILAND - CROPS

THAILAND - CRIME

National Statistical Office, Office of the Prime Minister, Bangkok Metropolis 10100, Thailand; *Statistical Yearbook Thailand.*

Yale University Press, Yale Station, New Haven, Connecticut 06520 (800) 987-7323; *Violence and Crime in Cross-National Perspective.*

THAILAND - CROPS

Asian Development Bank, P.O. Box 789, 1099 Manila, Philippines; *Key Indicators of Developing Asian and Pacific Countries.*

Commodity Research Bureau, Inc., 30 South Wacker Drive, Chicago, Illinois 60606 (312) 454-1801; *Commodity Year Book.*

Europa Publications Limited, 18 Bedford Square, London, WC1B 3JN, England; *The Europa World Year Book.*

International Monetary Fund, 700 Nineteenth Street, NW, Washington, D.C. 20431 (202) 623-7000; *International Financial Statistics.*

Food and Agricultural Organization of the United Nations (FAO) Via delle Terme di Caracalla, 00100 Rome, Italy (Telephone Number in U.S. (202) 653-2400); *The State of Food and Agriculture.*

M.E. Sharpe, 80 Business Park Drive, Armonk, New York 10504 (800) 541-6563; *The Illustrated Book of World Rankings.*

National Statistical Office, Office of the Prime Minister, Bangkok Metropolis 10100, Thailand; *Statistical Yearbook Thailand.*

St. Martin's Press, Inc., 175 Fifth Avenue, New York, New York 10010 (800) 221-7945; *The Statesman's Year-Book.*

Statistical Office of the United Nations, Publishing Service, New York, New York 10017 (800) 253-9646; *Statistical Yearbook.*

United Nations Conference on Trade and Development, Central Statistical Service, Palais des Nations, Geneva, Switzerland (Telephone in U.S. (800) 253-9646); *UNCTAD Commodity Yearbook.*

THAILAND - CUSTOMS DUTIES

International Monetary Fund, 700 Nineteenth Street, NW, Washington, D.C. 20431 (202) 623-7000; *Government Finance Statistics Yearbook.*

St. Martin's Press, Inc., 175 Fifth Avenue, New York, New York 10010 (800) 221-7945; *The Statesman's Year-Book.*

THAILAND - DAIRY PRODUCTS

Europa Publications Limited, 18 Bedford Square, London, WC1B 3JN, England; *The Europa World Year Book.*

Food and Agricultural Organization of the United Nations (FAO) Via delle Terme di Caracalla, 00100 Rome, Italy (Telephone Number in U.S. (202) 653-2400); *The State of Food and Agriculture.*

M.E. Sharpe, 80 Business Park Drive, Armonk, New York 10504 (800) 541-6563; *The Illustrated Book of World Rankings.*

St. Martin's Press, Inc., 175 Fifth Avenue, New York, New York 10010 (800) 221-7945; *The Statesman's Year-Book.*

Statistical Office of the United Nations, Publishing Service, New York, New York 10017 (800) 253-9646; *Statistical Yearbook.*

THAILAND - DEATH RATES - See THAILAND - MORTALITY

THAILAND - DEFENSE EXPENDITURES - See THAILAND - MILITARY

THAILAND - DEMOGRAPHY

The Economist Intelligence Unit (Asia) Limited, 10th Floor, Luk Kwok Centre, 72 Gloucester Road, Wanchai, Hong Kong (Phone Number in U.S. (800) 938-4685); *Asian Market Atlas.*

The Economist Intelligence Unit, 111 West 57th Street, New York, New York 10019 (800) 938-4685; *The World Market Atlas.*

Euromonitor International, Inc., 122 South Michigan Avenue, Suite 1200, Chicago, Illinois 60603 (800) 577-EURO; *International Marketing Data and Statistics; World Marketing Data and Statistics;* and *The World Economic Factbook.*

M.E. Sharpe, 80 Business Park Drive, Armonk, New York 10504 (800) 541-6563; *The Illustrated Book of World Rankings.*

Statistical Office of the United Nations, Publishing Service, New York, New York 10017 (800) 253-9646; *Asia-Pacific in Figures;* and *Human Development Report.*

THAILAND - DEVELOPMENT ASSISTANCE

Asian Development Bank, P.O. Box 789, 1099 Manila, Philippines; *Key Indicators of Developing Asian and Pacific Countries.*

Statistical Office of the United Nations, Publishing Service, New York, New York 10017 (800) 253-9646; *Statistical Yearbook.*

THAILAND - DIAMOND PRODUCTION - See THAILAND - MINING AND MINERAL PRODUCTS

THAILAND - DISCOUNT RATES - See THAILAND - BANKING

THAILAND - DISEASES - See THAILAND - HEALTH

THAILAND - DIVORCE RATES

M.E. Sharpe, 80 Business Park Drive, Armonk, New York 10504 (800) 541-6563; *The Illustrated Book of World Rankings.*

National Statistical Office, Office of the Prime Minister, Bangkok Metropolis 10100, Thailand; *Statistical Yearbook Thailand.*

Statistical Office of the United Nations, Publishing Service, New York, New York 10017 (800) 253-9646; *Demographic Yearbook;* and *Statistical Yearbook.*

THAILAND - ECONOMY

Asian Development Bank, P.O. Box 789, 1099 Manila, Philippines; *Key Indicators of Developing Asian and Pacific Countries.*

Central Intelligence Agency, Washington, D.C. 20505 (703) 482-1100, www.cia.gov; *The World Factbook.*

Economist Intelligence Unit, 111 West 57th Street, New York, New York 10019

(800) 938-4685; *Thailand Country Report.*

Euromonitor International, Inc., 122 South Michigan Avenue, Suite 1200, Chicago, Illinois 60603 (800) 577-EURO; *International Marketing Data and Statistics; World Marketing Data and Statistics;* and *The World Economic Factbook.*

Europa Publications Limited, 18 Bedford Square, London, WC1B 3JN, England; *The Europa World Year Book.*

M.E. Sharpe, 80 Business Park Drive, Armonk, New York 10504 (800) 541-6563; *The Illustrated Book of World Rankings.*

St. Martin's Press, Inc., 175 Fifth Avenue, New York, New York 10010 (800) 221-7945; *The Statesman's Year-Book.*

Statistical Office of the United Nations, Publishing Service, New York, New York 10017 (800) 253-9646; *World Statistics Pocketbook.*

The World Bank, 1818 H Street, NW, Washington, D.C. 20433 (202) 477-1234; *The World Bank Atlas;* and *World Development Report.*

THAILAND - EDUCATION

The Economist Intelligence Unit, 111 West 57th Street, New York, New York 10019 (800) 938-4685; *The World Market Atlas.*

The Economist Intelligence Unit (Asia) Limited, 10th Floor, Luk Kwok Centre, 72 Gloucester Road, Wanchai, Hong Kong (Phone Number in U.S. (800) 938-4685); *Asian Market Atlas.*

Euromonitor International, Inc., 122 South Michigan Avenue, Suite 1200, Chicago, Illinois 60603 (800) 577-EURO; *International Marketing Data and Statistics;* and *World Marketing Data and Statistics.*

Europa Publications Limited, 18 Bedford Square, London, WC1B 3JN, England; *The Europa World Year Book.*

International Monetary Fund, 700 Nineteenth Street, NW, Washington, D.C. 20431 (202) 623-7000; *Government Finance Statistics Yearbook.*

M.E. Sharpe, 80 Business Park Drive, Armonk, New York 10504 (800) 541-6563; *The Illustrated Book of World Rankings.*

National Statistical Office, Office of the Prime Minister, Bangkok Metropolis 10100, Thailand; *Statistical Yearbook Thailand.*

St. Martin's Press, Inc., 175 Fifth Avenue, New York, New York 10010 (800) 221-7945; *The Statesman's Year-Book.*

Statistical Office of the United Nations, Publishing Service, New York, New York 10017 (800) 253-9646; *Asia-Pacific in Figures;* and *Human Development Report.*

United Nations Educational, Scientific and Cultural Organization (UNESCO), 7 Place de Fontenoy, F-75700 Paris, France (Telephone Number in U.S. (212) 963-5981); *Statistical Yearbook.*

The World Bank, 1818 H Street, NW, Washington, D.C. 20433 (202) 477-1234; *World Development Report;* and *World Development Indicators.*

THAILAND - EGG PRODUCTION - See THAILAND - DAIRY PRODUCTS

THAILAND - ELECTRICITY

Asian Development Bank, P.O. Box 789, 1099 Manila, Philippines; *Key Indicators of Developing Asian and Pacific Countries.*

Central Intelligence Agency, Washington, D.C. 20505 (703) 482-1100, www.cia.gov; *The World Factbook.*

M.E. Sharpe, 80 Business Park Drive, Armonk, New York 10504 (800) 541-6563; *The Illustrated Book of World Rankings.*

National Statistical Office, Office of the Prime Minister, Bangkok Metropolis 10100, Thailand; *Statistical Yearbook Thailand.*

Penn Well Publishing Company, 1421 South Sheridan Road, P.O. Box 1260, Tulsa, Oklahoma 74101 (800) 752-9764; *International Energy Statistics Sourcebook.*

St. Martin's Press, Inc., 175 Fifth Avenue, New York, New York 10010 (800) 221-7945; *The Statesman's Year-Book.*

Statistical Office of the United Nations, Publishing Service, New York, New York 10017 (800) 253-9646; *Electric Power in Asia and the Pacific; Human Development Report;* and *Statistical Yearbook.*

THAILAND - EMPLOYMENT

Euromonitor International, Inc., 122 South Michigan Avenue, Suite 1200, Chicago, Illinois 60603 (800) 577-EURO; *International Marketing Data and Statistics.*

International Labour Office, I.L.O. Publications, 1828 L Street, NW, Suite 801, Washington, D.C. 20036 (301) 638-3152; *Yearbook of Labour Statistics.*

M.E. Sharpe, 80 Business Park Drive, Armonk, New York 10504 (800) 541-6563; *The Illustrated Book of World Rankings.*

National Statistical Office, Office of the Prime Minister, Bangkok Metropolis 10100, Thailand; *Statistical Yearbook Thailand.*

Statistical Office of the United Nations, Publishing Service, New York, New York 10017 (800) 253-9646; *Asia-Pacific in Figures;* and *Statistical Yearbook*

THAILAND - ENERGY

Euromonitor International, Inc., 122 South Michigan Avenue, Suite 1200, Chicago, Illinois 60603 (800) 577-EURO; *International Marketing Data and Statistics; World Marketing Data and Statistics;* and *The World Economic Factbook.*

Food and Agricultural Organization of the United Nations (FAO) Via delle Terme di Caracalla, 00100 Rome, Italy (Telephone Number in U.S. (202) 653-2400); *The State of Food and Agriculture.*

M.E. Sharpe, 80 Business Park Drive, Armonk, New York 10504 (800) 541-6563; *The Illustrated Book of World Rankings.*

National Statistical Office, Office of the Prime Minister, Bangkok Metropolis 10100, Thailand; *Statistical Yearbook Thailand.*

Penn Well Publishing Company, 1421 South Sheridan Road, P.O. Box 1260, Tulsa, Oklahoma 74101 (800) 752-9764; *International Energy Statistics Sourcebook.*

St. Martin's Press, Inc., 175 Fifth Avenue, New York, New York 10010 (800) 221-7945; *The Statesman's Year-Book.*

Statistical Office of the United Nations, Publishing Service, New York, New York 10017 (800) 253-9646; *Asia-Pacific in Figures; Energy Statistics Yearbook; Human Development Report; Statistical Yearbook for Asia and the Pacific;* and *World Statistics Pocketbook.*

The World Bank, 1818 H Street, NW, Washington, D.C. 20433 (202) 477-1234; *The World Bank Atlas;* and *World Development Report.*

THAILAND - ENVIRONMENT

Economist Intelligence Unit, 111 West 57th Street, New York, New York 10019 (800) 938-4685; *Thailand Country Report.*

THAILAND - EXCHANGE RATES

Asian Development Bank, P.O. Box 789, 1099 Manila, Philippines; *Key Indicators of Developing Asian and Pacific Countries.*

Central Intelligence Agency, Washington, D.C. 20505 (703) 482-1100, www.cia.gov; *The World Factbook.*

The Economist Intelligence Unit (Asia) Limited, 10th Floor, Luk Kwok Centre, 72 Gloucester Road, Wanchai, Hong Kong (Phone Number in U.S. (800) 938-4685); *Asian Market Atlas.*

Euromonitor International, Inc., 122 South Michigan Avenue, Suite 1200, Chicago, Illinois 60603 (800) 577-EURO; *International Marketing Data and Statistics;* and *The World Economic Factbook.*

Europa Publications Limited, 18 Bedford Square, London, WC1B 3JN, England; *The Europa World Year Book.*

International Civil Aviation Organization, 999 University Street, Montreal, Quebec, Canada H3C 5H7 (514) 954-8219; *Civil Aviation Statistics of the World.*

International Monetary Fund, 700 Nineteenth Street, NW, Washington, D.C. 20431 (202) 623-7000; *International Financial Statistics.*

National Statistical Office, Office of the Prime Minister, Bangkok Metropolis 10100, Thailand; *Statistical Yearbook Thailand.*

Statistical Office of the United Nations, Publishing Service, New York, New York 10017 (800) 253-9646; *Statistical Yearbook.*

Walden Publishing Ltd., Two Market Street, Saffron Walden Essex, CB10 1HZ, England; *The World of Information Asia and Pacific Review.*

THAILAND - EXCISE TAXES - See THAILAND - TAXATION

THAILAND - EXPORTS

Asian Development Bank, P.O. Box 789, 1099 Manila, Philippines; *Key Indicators of Developing Asian and Pacific Countries.*

Central Intelligence Agency, Washington, D.C. 20505 (703) 482-1100, www.cia.gov; *The World Factbook.*

The Economist Intelligence Unit, 111 West 57th Street, New York, New York 10019 (800) 938-4685; *Thailand Country Report;* and *The World Market Atlas.*

The Economist Intelligence Unit (Asia) Limited, 10th Floor, Luk Kwok Centre, 72 Gloucester Road, Wanchai, Hong Kong (Phone Number in U.S. (800) 938-4685); *Asian Market Atlas.*

Euromonitor International, Inc., 122 South Michigan Avenue, Suite 1200, Chicago, Illinois 60603 (800) 577-EURO; *International Marketing Data and Statistics;* and *The World Economic Factbook.*

Europa Publications Limited, 18 Bedford Square, London, WC1B 3JN, England; *The Europa World Year Book.*

Food and Agricultural Organization of the United Nations (FAO) Via delle Terme di Caracalla, 00100 Rome, Italy (Telephone

Number in U.S. (202) 653-2400); *The State of Food and Agriculture.*

International Monetary Fund, 700 Nineteenth Street, NW, Washington, D.C. 20431 (202) 623-7000; *Direction of Trade Statistics; Government Finance Statistics Yearbook;* and *International Financial Statistics.*

International Rubber Study Group, York House, Eighth Floor, Empire Way, Wembley, London HA9 0PA, England; *Rubber Statistical Handbook.*

National Statistical Office, Office of the Prime Minister, Bangkok Metropolis 10100, Thailand; *Statistical Yearbook Thailand.*

St. Martin's Press, Inc., 175 Fifth Avenue, New York, New York 10010 (800) 221-7945; *The Statesman's Year-Book.*

Statistical Office of the United Nations, Publishing Service, New York, New York 10017 (800) 253-9646; *Foreign Trade Statistics of Asia and the Pacific.*

United Nations Conference on Trade and Development (UNCTAD), New York, New York 10017 (800) 253-9646; *Handbook of International Trade and Development.*

Walden Publishing Ltd., Two Market Street, Saffron Walden Essex, CB10 1HZ, England; *The World of Information Asia and Pacific Review.*

The World Bank, 1818 H Street, NW, Washington, D.C. 20433 (202) 477-1234; *World Development Report;* and *World Development Indicators.*

THAILAND - EXTERNAL FINANCING

Asian Development Bank, P.O. Box 789, 1099 Manila, Philippines; *Key Indicators of Developing Asian and Pacific Countries.*

THAILAND - EXTERNAL INDEBTEDNESS

Asian Development Bank, P.O. Box 789, 1099 Manila, Philippines; *Key Indicators of Developing Asian and Pacific Countries.*

The World Bank, 1818 H Street, NW, Washington, D.C. 20433 (202) 477-1234; *World Development Report;* and *World Development Indicators.*

THAILAND - EXTERNAL TRADE

Asian Development Bank, P.O. Box 789, 1099 Manila, Philippines; *Key Indicators of Developing Asian and Pacific Countries.*

Euromonitor International, Inc., 122 South Michigan Avenue, Suite 1200, Chicago, Illinois 60603 (800) 577-EURO; *World Marketing Data and Statistics.*

Food and Agricultural Organization of the United Nations (FAO) Via delle Terme di Caracalla, 00100 Rome, Italy (Telephone Number in U.S. (202) 653-2400); *The State of Food and Agriculture;* and *Trade Yearbook.*

Statistical Office of the United Nations, Publishing Service, New York, New York 10017 (800) 253-9646; *Asia-Pacific in Figures; Statistical Yearbook;* and *Statistical Yearbook for Asia and the Pacific.*

THAILAND - FABRIC PRODUCTION - See THAILAND - TEXTILE INDUSTRY

THAILAND - FARM CROPS - See THAILAND - CROPS

THAILAND - FEMALE WORKING POPULATION - See THAILAND - EMPLOYMENT

THAILAND - FERTILITY RATES

Central Intelligence Agency, Washington, D.C. 20505 (703) 482-1100, www.cia.gov; *The World Factbook.*

The Economist Intelligence Unit (Asia) Limited, 10th Floor, Luk Kwok Centre, 72 Gloucester Road, Wanchai, Hong Kong (Phone Number in U.S. (800) 938-4685); *Asian Market Atlas.*

M.E. Sharpe, 80 Business Park Drive, Armonk, New York 10504 (800) 541-6563; *The Illustrated Book of World Rankings.*

Statistical Office of the United Nations, Publishing Service, New York, New York 10017 (800) 253-9646; *Human Development Report.*

The World Bank, 1818 H Street, NW, Washington, D.C. 20433 (202) 477-1234; *The World Bank Atlas; World Development Report;* and *World Development Indicators.*

THAILAND - FERTILIZER

Food and Agricultural Organization of the United Nations (FAO), Via delle Terme di Caracalla, 00100, Rome, Italy (Telephone Number in U.S. (202) 653-2400); *Fertilizer Yearbook;* and *The State of Food and Agriculture.*

Statistical Office of the United Nations, Publishing Service, New York, New York 10017 (800) 253-9646; *Statistical Yearbook.*

THAILAND - FETAL MORTALITY - See THAILAND - MORTALITY

THAILAND - FIBRE PRODUCTION - See THAILAND - TEXTILE INDUSTRY

THAILAND - FILAMENT PRODUCTION - See THAILAND - TEXTILE INDUSTRY

THAILAND - FILM - See THAILAND - MOTION PICTURES

THAILAND - FINANCE

Asian Development Bank, P.O. Box 789, 1099 Manila, Philippines; *Key Indicators of Developing Asian and Pacific Countries.*

Economist Intelligence Unit, 111 West 57th Street, New York, New York 10019 (800) 938-4685; *Thailand Country Report.*

Europa Publications Limited, 18 Bedford Square, London, WC1B 3JN, England; *The Europa World Year Book.*

International Monetary Fund, 700 Nineteenth Street, NW, Washington, D.C. 20431 (202) 623-7000; *Government Finance Statistics Yearbook.*

M.E. Sharpe, 80 Business Park Drive, Armonk, New York 10504 (800) 541-6563; *The Illustrated Book of World Rankings.*

National Statistical Office, Office of the Prime Minister, Bangkok Metropolis 10100, Thailand; *Statistical Yearbook Thailand.*

St. Martin's Press, Inc., 175 Fifth Avenue, New York, New York 10010 (800) 221-7945; *The Statesman's Year-Book.*

Statistical Office of the United Nations, Publishing Service, New York, New York 10017 (800) 253-9646; *Statistical Yearbook for Asia and the Pacific.*

THAILAND - FISHERIES

Europa Publications Limited, 18 Bedford Square, London, WC1B 3JN, England; *The Europa World Year Book.*

Food and Agricultural Organization of the United Nations (FAO) Via delle Terme di Caracalla, 00100 Rome, Italy (Telephone Number in U.S. (202) 653-2400); *The State of Food and Agriculture; and Yearbook of Fishery Statistics.*

M.E. Sharpe, 80 Business Park Drive, Armonk, New York 10504 (800) 541-6563; *The Illustrated Book of World Rankings.*

National Statistical Office, Office of the Prime Minister, Bangkok Metropolis 10100, Thailand; *Statistical Yearbook Thailand.*

St. Martin's Press, Inc., 175 Fifth Avenue, New York, New York 10010 (800) 221-7945; *The Statesman's Year-Book.*

Statistical Office of the United Nations, Publishing Service, New York, New York 10017 (800) 253-9646; *Statistical Yearbook.*

United Nations Conference on Trade and Development, Central Statistical Service, Palais des Nations, Geneva,

Switzerland (Telephone in U.S. (800) 253-9646); *UNCTAD Commodity Yearbook.*

THAILAND - FLOUR PRODUCTION

Statistical Office of the United Nations, Publishing Service, New York, New York 10017 (800) 253-9646; *Statistical Yearbook.*

THAILAND - FOOD

Euromonitor International, Inc., 122 South Michigan Avenue, Suite 1200, Chicago, Illinois 60603 (800) 577-EURO; *Retail Trade International.*

Food and Agricultural Organization of the United Nations (FAO) Via delle Terme di Caracalla, 00100 Rome, Italy (Telephone Number in U.S. (202) 653-2400); *Production Yearbook; and The State of Food and Agriculture.*

Statistical Office of the United Nations, Publishing Service, New York, New York 10017 (800) 253-9646; *Human Development Report; and Statistical Yearbook for Asia and the Pacific.*

United Nations Conference on Trade and Development, Central Statistical Service, Palais des Nations, Geneva, Switzerland (Telephone in U.S. (800) 253-9646); *UNCTAD Commodity Yearbook.*

THAILAND - FOREIGN DEBT

International Monetary Fund, 700 Nineteenth Street, NW, Washington, D.C. 20431 (202) 623-7000; *Government Finance Statistics Yearbook.*

Walden Publishing Ltd., Two Market Street, Saffron Walden Essex, CB10 1HZ, England; *The World of Information Asia and Pacific Review.*

THAILAND - FOREIGN TRADE

Asian Development Bank, P.O. Box 789, 1099 Manila, Philippines; *Key Indicators of Developing Asian and Pacific Countries.*

Economist Intelligence Unit, 111 West 57th Street, New York, New York 10019 (800) 938-4685; *Thailand Country Report.*

The Economist Intelligence Unit (Asia) Limited, 10th Floor, Luk Kwok Centre, 72 Gloucester Road, Wanchai, Hong Kong (Phone Number in U.S. (800) 938-4685); *Asian Market Atlas.*

Euromonitor International, Inc., 122 South Michigan Avenue, Suite 1200, Chicago, Illinois 60603 (800) 577-EURO; *International Marketing Data and Statistics; and The World Economic Factbook.*

Europa Publications Limited, 18 Bedford Square, London, WC1B 3JN,

England; *The Europa World Year Book.*

Food and Agricultural Organization of the United Nations (FAO) Via delle Terme di Caracalla, 00100 Rome, Italy (Telephone Number in U.S. (202) 653-2400); *The State of Food and Agriculture.*

International Monetary Fund, 700 Nineteenth Street, NW, Washington, D.C. 20431 (202) 623-7000; *International Financial Statistics.*

M.E. Sharpe, 80 Business Park Drive, Armonk, New York 10504 (800) 541-6563; *The Illustrated Book of World Rankings.*

National Statistical Office, Office of the Prime Minister, Bangkok Metropolis 10100, Thailand; *Statistical Yearbook Thailand.*

St. Martin's Press, Inc., 175 Fifth Avenue, New York, New York 10010 (800) 221-7945; *The Statesman's Year-Book.*

Statistical Office of the United Nations, Publishing Service, New York, New York 10017 (800) 253-9646; *International Trade Statistics Yearbook; and Statistical Yearbook.*

United Nations Conference on Trade and Development, Central Statistical Service, Palais des Nations, Geneva, Switzerland (Telephone in U.S. (800) 253-9646); *UNCTAD Commodity Yearbook.*

The World Bank, 1818 H Street, NW, Washington, D.C. 20433 (202) 477-1234; *World Development Report.*

THAILAND - FORESTRY AND FOREST PRODUCTS

American Forest and Paper Association, 1111 Nineteenth Street, NW, Washington, D.C. 20036 (202) 463-2700; *Wood Pulp and Fiber Statistics.*

The Economist Intelligence Unit (Asia) Limited, 10th Floor, Luk Kwok Centre, 72 Gloucester Road, Wanchai, Hong Kong (Phone Number in U.S. (800) 938-4685); *Asian Market Atlas.*

Europa Publications Limited, 18 Bedford Square, London, WC1B 3JN, England; *The Europa World Year Book.*

Food and Agricultural Organization of the United Nations (FAO) Via delle Terme di Caracalla, 00100 Rome, Italy (Telephone Number in U.S. (202) 653-2400); *The State of Food and Agriculture; and Yearbook of Forest Products.*

M.E. Sharpe, 80 Business Park Drive, Armonk, New York 10504 (800) 541-6563; *The Illustrated Book of World Rankings.*

National Statistical Office, Office of the Prime Minister, Bangkok Metropolis 10100, Thailand; *Statistical Yearbook Thailand.*

St. Martin's Press, Inc., 175 Fifth Avenue, New York, New York 10010 (800) 221-7945; *The Statesman's Year-Book.*

Statistical Office of the United Nations, Publishing Service, New York, New York 10017 (800) 253-9646; *Statistical Yearbook.*

United Nations Conference on Trade and Development, Central Statistical Service, Palais des Nations, Geneva, Switzerland (Telephone in U.S. (800) 253-9646); *UNCTAD Commodity Yearbook.*

United Nations Educational, Scientific and Cultural Organization (UNESCO), 7 Place de Fontenoy, F-75700 Paris, France (Telephone Number in U.S. (212) 963-5981); *Statistical Yearbook.*

The World Bank, 1818 H Street, NW, Washington, D.C. 20433 (202) 477-1234; *World Development Report.*

THAILAND - GAS PRODUCTION - See THAILAND - MINING AND MINERAL PRODUCTS

THAILAND - GENERAL MORTALITY - See THAILAND - MORTALITY

THAILAND - GEOGRAPHIC DATA

M.E. Sharpe, 80 Business Park Drive, Armonk, New York 10504 (800) 541-6563; *The Illustrated Book of World Rankings.*

THAILAND - GOLD HOLDINGS

International Monetary Fund, 700 Nineteenth Street, NW, Washington, D.C. 20431 (202) 623-7000; *International Financial Statistics.*

Statistical Office of the United Nations, Publishing Service, New York, New York 10017 (800) 253-9646; *Statistical Yearbook.*

The World Bank, 1818 H Street, NW, Washington, D.C. 20433 (202) 477-1234; *World Development Indicators.*

THAILAND - GOLD PRODUCTION AND CONSUMPTION - See THAILAND - MINING AND MINERAL PRODUCTS

THAILAND - GOVERNMENT

Asian Development Bank, P.O. Box 789, 1099 Manila, Philippines; *Key Indicators of Developing Asian and Pacific Countries.*

Central Intelligence Agency, Washington, D.C. 20505 (703) 482-1100, www.cia.gov; *The World Factbook.*

Europa Publications Limited, 18

Bedford Square, London, WC1B 3JN, England; *The Europa World Year Book.*

International Monetary Fund, 700 Nineteenth Street, NW, Washington, D.C. 20431 (202) 623-7000; *Government Finance Statistics Yearbook;* and *International Financial Statistics.*

National Statistical Office, Office of the Prime Minister, Bangkok Metropolis 10100, Thailand; *Statistical Yearbook Thailand.*

St. Martin's Press, Inc., 175 Fifth Avenue, New York, New York 10010 (800) 221-7945; *The Statesman's Year-Book.*

Statistical Office of the United Nations, Publishing Service, New York, New York 10017 (800) 253-9646; *Asia-Pacific in Figures; National Accounts Statistics;* and *Statistical Yearbook.*

The World Bank, 1818 H Street, NW, Washington, D.C. 20433 (202) 477-1234; *World Development Report;* and *World Development Indicators.*

THAILAND - GRAIN PRODUCTION - See THAILAND - CROPS

THAILAND - GRANTS

International Monetary Fund, 700 Nineteenth Street, NW, Washington, D.C. 20431 (202) 623-7000; *Government Finance Statistics Yearbook.*

THAILAND - GROSS DOMESTIC PRODUCT

Asian Development Bank, P.O. Box 789, 1099 Manila, Philippines; *Key Indicators of Developing Asian and Pacific Countries.*

The Economist Intelligence Unit, 111 West 57th Street, New York, New York 10019 (800) 938-4685; *Thailand Country Report;* and *The World Market Atlas.*

The Economist Intelligence Unit (Asia) Limited, 10th Floor, Luk Kwok Centre, 72 Gloucester Road, Wanchai, Hong Kong (Phone Number in U.S. (800) 938-4685); *Asian Market Atlas.*

Euromonitor International, Inc., 122 South Michigan Avenue, Suite 1200, Chicago, Illinois 60603 (800) 577-EURO; *International Marketing Data and Statistics;* and *The World Economic Factbook.*

Europa Publications Limited, 18 Bedford Square, London, WC1B 3JN, England; *The Europa World Year Book.*

M.E. Sharpe, 80 Business Park Drive, Armonk, New York 10504 (800) 541-6563; *The Illustrated Book of World Rankings.*

National Statistical Office, Office of the Prime Minister, Bangkok Metropolis 10100,

Thailand; *Statistical Yearbook Thailand.*

Statistical Office of the United Nations, Publishing Service, New York, New York 10017 (800) 253-9646; *Human Development Report; National Accounts Statistics;* and *Statistical Yearbook.*

The World Bank, 1818 H Street, NW, Washington, D.C. 20433 (202) 477-1234; *World Development Report;* and *World Development Indicators.*

THAILAND - GROSS NATIONAL PRODUCT

Asian Development Bank, P.O. Box 789, 1099 Manila, Philippines; *Key Indicators of Developing Asian and Pacific Countries.*

Euromonitor International, Inc., 122 South Michigan Avenue, Suite 1200, Chicago, Illinois 60603 (800) 577-EURO; *International Marketing Data and Statistics.*

Europa Publications Limited, 18 Bedford Square, London, WC1B 3JN, England; *The Europa World Year Book.*

National Statistical Office, Office of the Prime Minister, Bangkok Metropolis 10100, Thailand; *Statistical Yearbook Thailand.*

St. Martin's Press, Inc., 175 Fifth Avenue, New York, New York 10010 (800) 221-7945; *The Statesman's Year-Book.*

U.S. Arms Control and Disarmament Agency, 320 Twenty-first Street, NW, Washington, D.C. 20451 (202) 647-8677; *World Military Expenditures and Arms Transfers.*

Walden Publishing Ltd., Two Market Street, Saffron Walden Essex, CB10 1HZ, England; *The World of Information Asia and Pacific Review.*

The World Bank, 1818 H Street, NW, Washington, D.C. 20433 (202) 477-1234; *The World Bank Atlas; World Development Report;* and *World Development Indicators.*

THAILAND - GROUNDNUTS PRODUCTION - See THAILAND - CROPS

THAILAND - HEALTH

The Economist Intelligence Unit (Asia) Limited, 10th Floor, Luk Kwok Centre, 72 Gloucester Road, Wanchai, Hong Kong (Phone Number in U.S. (800) 938-4685); *Asian Market Atlas.*

Euromonitor International, Inc., 122 South Michigan Avenue, Suite 1200, Chicago, Illinois 60603 (800) 577-EURO; *World Marketing Data and Statistics.*

M.E. Sharpe, 80 Business Park Drive, Armonk, New York 10504 (800) 541-6563; *The Illustrated Book of World Rankings.*

National Statistical Office, Office of the Prime Minister, Bangkok Metropolis 10100, Thailand; *Statistical Yearbook Thailand.*

St. Martin's Press, Inc., 175 Fifth Avenue, New York, New York 10010 (800) 221-7945; *The Statesman's Year-Book.*

Statistical Office of the United Nations, Publishing Service, New York, New York 10017 (800) 253-9646; *Asia-Pacific in Figures; Human Development Report;* and *Statistical Yearbook.*

United Nations Children's Fund (UNICEF), 3 United Nations Plaza, New York, New York 10017 (800) 253-9646; *State of the World's Children.*

The World Bank, 1818 H Street, NW, Washington, D.C. 20433 (202) 477-1234; *World Development Report.*

World Health Organization, Office of Publications, 20 Avenue Appia, CH-1211 Geneva 27, Switzerland (Telephone Number in U.S. (518) 436-9686); *World Health Statistics Annual.*

THAILAND - HEALTH EXPENDITURES

International Monetary Fund, 700 Nineteenth Street, NW, Washington, D.C. 20431 (202) 623-7000; *Government Finance Statistics Yearbook.*

THAILAND - HIGHWAYS

Central Intelligence Agency, Washington, D.C. 20505 (703) 482-1100, www.cia.gov; *The World Factbook.*

The Economist Intelligence Unit (Asia) Limited, 10th Floor, Luk Kwok Centre, 72 Gloucester Road, Wanchai, Hong Kong (Phone Number in U.S. (800) 938-4685); *Asian Market Atlas.*

International Road Federation, 2600 Virginia Avenue, NW, Washington, D.C. 20037 (202) 338-4641; *World Road Statistics.*

St. Martin's Press, Inc., 175 Fifth Avenue, New York, New York 10010 (800) 221-7945; *The Statesman's Year-Book.*

THAILAND - HORSES - See THAILAND - LIVESTOCK AND POULTRY

THAILAND - HOURS OF WORK - See THAILAND - EMPLOYMENT

THAILAND - HOUSING AND HOUSING UNITS

Euromonitor International, Inc., 122 South Michigan Avenue, Suite 1200, Chicago, Illinois 60603 (800) 577-EURO; *World Marketing Data and Statistics.*

M.E. Sharpe, 80 Business Park Drive, Armonk, New York 10504 (800) 541-6563; *The Illustrated Book of World Rankings.*

THAILAND - HOUSING EXPENDITURES

International Monetary Fund, 700 Nineteenth Street, NW, Washington, D.C. 20431 (202) 623-7000; *Government Finance Statistics Yearbook.*

THAILAND - HYDROCHLORIC ACID PRODUCTION

Statistical Office of the United Nations, Publishing Service, New York, New York 10017 (800) 253-9646; *Statistical Yearbook.*

THAILAND - ILLITERATE POPULATION

Central Intelligence Agency, Washington, D.C. 20505 (703) 482-1100, www.cia.gov; *The World Factbook.*

The Economist Intelligence Unit, 111 West 57th Street, New York, New York 10019 (800) 938-4685; *The World Market Atlas.*

Euromonitor International, Inc., 122 South Michigan Avenue, Suite 1200, Chicago, Illinois 60603 (800) 577-EURO; *The World Economic Factbook.*

Statistical Office of the United Nations, Publishing Service, New York, New York 10017 (800) 253-9646; *Asia-Pacific in Figures;* and *Human Development Report.*

United Nations Educational, Scientific and Cultural Organization (UNESCO), 7 Place de Fontenoy, F-75700 Paris, France (Telephone Number in U.S. (212) 963-5981); *Statistical Yearbook.*

THAILAND - IMPORTS

Asian Development Bank, P.O. Box 789, 1099 Manila, Philippines; *Key Indicators of Developing Asian and Pacific Countries.*

Central Intelligence Agency, Washington, D.C. 20505 (703) 482-1100, www.cia.gov; *The World Factbook.*

The Economist Intelligence Unit, 111 West 57th Street, New York, New York 10019 (800) 938-4685; *Thailand Country Report;* and *The World Market Atlas.*

The Economist Intelligence Unit (Asia) Limited, 10th Floor, Luk Kwok Centre, 72 Gloucester Road, Wanchai, Hong Kong (Phone Number in U.S. (800) 938-4685); *Asian Market Atlas.*

Euromonitor International, Inc., 122 South Michigan Avenue, Suite 1200, Chicago, Illinois 60603 (800) 577-EURO; *International Marketing Data and Statistics;* and *The World Economic Factbook.*

Europa Publications Limited, 18 Bedford Square, London, WC1B 3JN, England; *The Europa World Year Book.*

Food and Agricultural Organization of the United Nations (FAO) Via delle Terme di Caracalla, 00100 Rome, Italy (Telephone Number in U.S. (202) 653-2400); *The State of Food and Agriculture.*

International Monetary Fund, 700 Nineteenth Street, NW, Washington, D.C. 20431 (202) 623-7000; *Direction of Trade Statistics; Government Finance Statistics Yearbook;* and *International Financial Statistics.*

International Rubber Study Group, York House, Eighth Floor, Empire Way, Wembley, London HA9 0PA, England; *Rubber Statistical Handbook.*

National Statistical Office, Office of the Prime Minister, Bangkok Metropolis 10100, Thailand; *Statistical Yearbook Thailand.*

St. Martin's Press, Inc., 175 Fifth Avenue, New York, New York 10010 (800) 221-7945; *The Statesman's Year-Book.*

Statistical Office of the United Nations, Publishing Service, New York, New York 10017 (800) 253-9646; *Foreign Trade Statistics of Asia and the Pacific.*

United Nations Conference on Trade and Development (UNCTAD), New York, New York 10017 (800) 253-9646; *Handbook of International Trade and Development.*

Walden Publishing Ltd., Two Market Street, Saffron Walden Essex, CB10 1HZ, England; *The World of Information Asia and Pacific Review.*

The World Bank, 1818 H Street, NW, Washington, D.C. 20433 (202) 477-1234; *World Development Report;* and *World Development Indicators.*

THAILAND - INCOME TAXES - See THAILAND - TAXATION

THAILAND - INDUSTRIAL METALS PRODUCTION - See THAILAND - MINING AND MINERAL PRODUCTS

THAILAND - INDUSTRY

Central Intelligence Agency, Washington, D.C. 20505 (703) 482-1100, www.cia.gov; *The World Factbook.*

Economist Intelligence Unit, 111 West 57th Street, New York, New York 10019 (800) 938-4685; *Thailand Country Report.*

Euromonitor International, Inc., 122 South Michigan Avenue, Suite 1200, Chicago, Illinois 60603 (800) 577-EURO; *The World Economic Factbook;* and *World*

Marketing Data and Statistics.

Europa Publications Limited, 18 Bedford Square, London, WC1B 3JN, England; *The Europa World Year Book.*

International Labour Office, I.L.O. Publications, 1828 L Street, NW, Suite 801, Washington, D.C. 20036 (301) 638-3152; *Yearbook of Labour Statistics.*

M.E. Sharpe, 80 Business Park Drive, Armonk, New York 10504 (800) 541-6563; *The Illustrated Book of World Rankings.*

National Statistical Office, Office of the Prime Minister, Bangkok Metropolis 10100, Thailand; *Statistical Yearbook Thailand.*

St. Martin's Press, Inc., 175 Fifth Avenue, New York, New York 10010 (800) 221-7945; *The Statesman's Year-Book.*

Statistical Office of the United Nations, Publishing Service, New York, New York 10017 (800) 253-9646; *Asia-Pacific in Figures;* and *Statistical Yearbook for Asia and the Pacific.*

The World Bank, 1818 H Street, NW, Washington, D.C. 20433 (202) 477-1234; *World Development Indicators.*

World Intellectual Property Organization, 34 Chemin des Colombettes, CH-1211 Geneva 20. Switzerland; *Industrial Property Statistics.*

THAILAND - INFANT AND MATERNAL MORTALITY - See THAILAND - MORTALITY

THAILAND - INTERNAL TRADE

Statistical Office of the United Nations, Publishing Service, New York, New York 10017 (800) 253-9646; *Statistical Yearbook for Asia and the Pacific.*

THAILAND - INTERNATIONAL LIQUIDITY

International Monetary Fund, 700 Nineteenth Street, NW, Washington, D.C. 20431 (202) 623-7000; *International Financial Statistics.*

THAILAND - INTERNATIONAL RESERVES EXCLUDING GOLD

Asian Development Bank, P.O. Box 789, 1099 Manila, Philippines; *Key Indicators of Developing Asian and Pacific Countries.*

Statistical Office of the United Nations, Publishing Service, New York, New York 10017 (800) 253-9646; *Statistical Yearbook.*

The World Bank, 1818 H Street, NW, Washington, D.C. 20433 (202) 477-1234; *World Development Indicators.*

THAILAND - INTERNATIONAL STATISTICS

Asian Development Bank, P.O. Box 789, 1099 Manila, Philippines; *Key Indicators of Developing Asian and Pacific Countries.*

THAILAND - INVESTMENTS

International Monetary Fund, 700 Nineteenth Street, NW, Washington, D.C. 20431 (202) 623-7000; *International Financial Statistics.*

THAILAND - IRON ORE PRODUCTION AND CONSUMPTION - See THAILAND - MINING AND MINERAL PRODUCTS

THAILAND - IRRIGATION

Euromonitor International, Inc., 122 South Michigan Avenue, Suite 1200, Chicago, Illinois 60603 (800) 577-EURO; *International Marketing Data and Statistics.*

THAILAND - LABOR

Central Intelligence Agency, Washington, D.C. 20505 (703) 482-1100, www.cia.gov; *The World Factbook.*

The Economist Intelligence Unit (Asia) Limited, 10th Floor, Luk Kwok Centre, 72 Gloucester Road, Wanchai, Hong Kong (Phone Number in U.S. (800) 938-4685); *Asian Market Atlas.*

Euromonitor International, Inc., 122 South Michigan Avenue, Suite 1200, Chicago, Illinois 60603 (800) 577-EURO; *International Marketing Data and Statistics;* and *World Marketing Data and Statistics.*

Europa Publications Limited, 18 Bedford Square, London, WC1B 3JN, England; *The Europa World Year Book.*

Food and Agricultural Organization of the United Nations (FAO) Via delle Terme di Caracalla, 00100 Rome, Italy (Telephone Number in U.S. (202) 653-2400); *The State of Food and Agriculture.*

International Labour Office, I.L.O. Publications, 1828 L Street, NW, Suite 801, Washington, D.C. 20036 (301) 638-3152; *Yearbook of Labour Statistics.*

M.E. Sharpe, 80 Business Park Drive, Armonk, New York 10504 (800) 541-6563; *The Illustrated Book of World Rankings.*

National Statistical Office, Office of the Prime Minister, Bangkok Metropolis 10100, Thailand; *Statistical Yearbook Thailand.*

St. Martin's Press, Inc., 175 Fifth Avenue, New York, New York 10010 (800) 221-7945; *The Statesman's Year-Book.*

Statistical Office of the United Nations, Publishing Service, New York, New York 10017 (800) 253-9646; *Human Development Report.*

The World Bank, 1818 H Street, NW, Washington, D.C. 20433 (202) 477-1234; *The World Bank Atlas; World Development Report;* and *World Development Indicators.*

THAILAND - LAND USE

Central Intelligence Agency, Washington, D.C. 20505 (703) 482-1100, www.cia.gov; *The World Factbook.*

Euromonitor International, Inc., 122 South Michigan Avenue, Suite 1200, Chicago, Illinois 60603 (800) 577-EURO; *International Marketing Data and Statistics.*

Food and Agricultural Organization of the United Nations (FAO), Via delle Terme di Caracalla, 00100 Rome, Italy (Telephone Number in U.S. (202) 653-2400); *Production Yearbook.*

The World Bank, 1818 H Street, NW, Washington, D.C. 20433 (202) 477-1234; *World Development Report.*

THAILAND - LEAD ORE PRODUCTION AND CONSUMPTION - See THAILAND - MINING AND MINERAL PRODUCTS

THAILAND - LIBRARIES

M.E. Sharpe, 80 Business Park Drive, Armonk, New York 10504 (800) 541-6563; *The Illustrated Book of World Rankings.*

United Nations Educational, Scientific and Cultural Organization (UNESCO), 7 Place de Fontenoy, F-75700 Paris, France (Telephone Number in U.S. (212) 963-5981); *Statistical Yearbook.*

THAILAND - LIFE EXPECTANCY

Central Intelligence Agency, Washington, D.C. 20505 (703) 482-1100, www.cia.gov; *The World Factbook.*

The Economist Intelligence Unit (Asia) Limited, 10th Floor, Luk Kwok Centre, 72 Gloucester Road, Wanchai, Hong Kong (Phone Number in U.S. (800) 938-4685); *Asian Market Atlas.*

Euromonitor International, Inc., 122 South Michigan Avenue, Suite 1200, Chicago, Illinois 60603 (800) 577-EURO; *The World Economic Factbook.*

St. Martin's Press, Inc., 175 Fifth Avenue, New York, New York 10010 (800) 221-7945; *The Statesman's Year-Book.*

Statistical Office of the United Nations, Publishing Service, New York, New York 10017 (800) 253-9646; *Asia-Pacific in Figures; Human Development Report;* and *World Statistics Pocketbook.*

The World Bank, 1818 H Street, NW, Washington, D.C. 20433 (202) 477-1234;

The World Bank Atlas; and *World Development Report.*

THAILAND - LIGNITE PRODUCTION - See THAILAND - MINING AND MINERAL PRODUCTS

THAILAND - LITERACY RATE

Euromonitor International, Inc., 122 South Michigan Avenue, Suite 1200, Chicago, Illinois 60603 (800) 577-EURO; *World Marketing Data and Statistics.*

THAILAND - LIVESTOCK AND POULTRY

Euromonitor International, Inc., 122 South Michigan Avenue, Suite 1200, Chicago, Illinois 60603 (800) 577-EURO; *International Marketing Data and Statistics.*

Europa Publications Limited, 18 Bedford Square, London, WC1B 3JN, England; *The Europa World Year Book.*

Food and Agricultural Organization of the United Nations (FAO), Via delle Terme di Caracalla, 00100 Rome, Italy (Telephone Number in U.S. (202) 653-2400); *Production Yearbook;* and *The State of Food and Agriculture.*

M.E. Sharpe, 80 Business Park Drive, Armonk, New York 10504 (800) 541-6563; *The Illustrated Book of World Rankings.*

National Statistical Office, Office of the Prime Minister, Bangkok Metropolis 10100, Thailand; *Statistical Yearbook Thailand.*

St. Martin's Press, Inc., 175 Fifth Avenue, New York, New York 10010 (800) 221-7945; *The Statesman's Year-Book.*

Statistical Office of the United Nations, Publishing Service, New York, New York 10017 (800) 253-9646; *Statistical Yearbook.*

United Nations Conference on Trade and Development, Central Statistical Service, Palais des Nations, Geneva, Switzerland (Telephone in U.S. (800) 253-9646); *UNCTAD Commodity Yearbook.*

THAILAND - LIVING LEVELS - See THAILAND - LIFE EXPECTANCY

THAILAND - MAIL - NUMBER OF PIECES SENT OR RECEIVED

Statistical Office of the United Nations, Publishing Service, New York, New York 10017 (800) 253-9646; *Statistical Yearbook.*

THAILAND - MANGANESE ORE PRODUCTION AND CONSUMPTION - See THAILAND - MINING AND MINERAL PRODUCTS

THAILAND - MANPOWER

Statistical Office of the United Nations, Publishing Service, New York, New York 10017 (800) 253-9646; *Statistical Yearbook for Asia and the Pacific.*

THAILAND - MANUFACTURING

Asian Development Bank, P.O. Box 789, 1099 Manila, Philippines; *Key Indicators of Developing Asian and Pacific Countries.*

M.E. Sharpe, 80 Business Park Drive, Armonk, New York 10504 (800) 541-6563; *The Illustrated Book of World Rankings.*

National Statistical Office, Office of the Prime Minister, Bangkok Metropolis 10100, Thailand; *Statistical Yearbook Thailand.*

Statistical Office of the United Nations, Publishing Service, New York, New York 10017 (800) 253-9646; *Statistical Yearbook.*

The World Bank, 1818 H Street, NW, Washington, D.C. 20433 (202) 477-1234; *World Development Indicators.*

THAILAND - MARRIAGE RATES

Europa Publications Limited, 18 Bedford Square, London, WC1B 3JN, England; *The Europa World Year Book.*

M.E. Sharpe, 80 Business Park Drive, Armonk, New York 10504 (800) 541-6563; *The Illustrated Book of World Rankings.*

National Statistical Office, Office of the Prime Minister, Bangkok Metropolis 10100, Thailand; *Statistical Yearbook Thailand.*

Statistical Office of the United Nations, Publishing Service, New York, New York 10017 (800) 253-9646; *Demographic Yearbook;* and *Statistical Yearbook.*

THAILAND - MEAT PRODUCTION - See THAILAND - LIVESTOCK AND POULTRY

THAILAND - MERCHANT SHIPPING

Europa Publications Limited, 18 Bedford Square, London, WC1B 3JN, England; *The Europa World Year Book.*

Lloyd's Register of Shipping, 17 Battery Place, New York, New York 10004 (212) 425-8050; *Register of Ships.*

St. Martin's Press, Inc., 175 Fifth Avenue, New York, New York 10010 (800) 221-7945; *The Statesman's Year-Book.*

Statistical Office of the United Nations, Publishing Service, New York, New York 10017 (800) 253-9646; *Statistical Yearbook.*

U.S. Department of Transportation, Maritime Administration, 400 Seventh Street, SW, Washington, D.C. 20590 (202) 366-5807; *A Statistical Analysis of the World's Merchant Fleets.*

THAILAND - MILITARY

Central Intelligence Agency, Washington, D.C. 20505 (703) 482-1100, www.cia.gov; *The World Factbook.*

The Economist Intelligence Unit (Asia) Limited, 10th Floor, Luk Kwok Centre, 72 Gloucester Road, Wanchai, Hong Kong (Phone Number in U.S. (800) 938-4685); *Asian Market Atlas.*

Euromonitor International, Inc., 122 South Michigan Avenue, Suite 1200, Chicago, Illinois 60603 (800) 577-EURO; *World Marketing Data and Statistics.*

The International Institute for Strategic Studies, 23 Tavistock Street, London WC2E 7NQ, England 44 171 3797676; *The Military Balance.*

International Monetary Fund, 700 Nineteenth Street, NW, Washington, D.C. 20431 (202) 623-7000; *Government Finance Statistics Yearbook.*

St. Martin's Press, Inc., 175 Fifth Avenue, New York, New York 10010 (800) 221-7945; *The Statesman's Year-Book.*

Statistical Office of the United Nations, Publishing Service, New York, New York 10017 (800) 253-9646; *Human Development Report.*

U.S. Arms Control and Disarmament Agency, 320 Twenty-first Street, NW, Washington, D.C. 20451 (202) 647-8677; *World Military Expenditures and Arms Transfers.*

THAILAND - MILK - See THAILAND - DAIRY PRODUCTS

THAILAND - MINING AND MINERAL PRODUCTS

Asian Development Bank, P.O. Box 789, 1099 Manila, Philippines; *Key Indicators of Developing Asian and Pacific Countries.*

Europa Publications Limited, 18 Bedford Square, London, WC1B 3JN, England; *The Europa World Year Book.*

International Monetary Fund, 700 Nineteenth Street, NW, Washington, D.C. 20431 (202) 623-7000; *International Financial Statistics.*

M.E. Sharpe, 80 Business Park Drive, Armonk, New York 10504 (800) 541-6563; *The Illustrated Book of World Rankings.*

National Statistical Office, Office of the Prime Minister, Bangkok Metropolis 10100, Thailand; *Statistical Yearbook Thailand.*

Penn Well Publishing Company, 1421 South Sheridan Road, P.O. Box 1260, Tulsa, Oklahoma 74101 (800) 752-9764; *International Energy Statistics Sourcebook.*

St. Martin's Press, Inc., 175 Fifth Avenue, New York, New York 10010 (800) 221-7945; *The Statesman's Year-Book.*

Statistical Office of the United Nations, Publishing Service, New York, New York 10017 (800) 253-9646; *Statistical Yearbook.*

United Nations Conference on Trade and Development, Central Statistical Service, Palais des Nations, Geneva, Switzerland (Telephone in U.S. (800) 253-9646); *UNCTAD Commodity Yearbook.*

THAILAND - MONEY EXCHANGE RATE - See THAILAND - EXCHANGE RATE

THAILAND - MONEY RESERVES

Euromonitor International, Inc., 122 South Michigan Avenue, Suite 1200, Chicago, Illinois 60603 (800) 577-EURO; *International Marketing Data and Statistics.*

THAILAND - MONEY SUPPLY

Asian Development Bank, P.O. Box 789, 1099 Manila, Philippines; *Key Indicators of Developing Asian and Pacific Countries.*

Economist Intelligence Unit, 111 West 57th Street, New York, New York 10019 (800) 938-4685; *Thailand Country Report.*

Euromonitor International, Inc., 122 South Michigan Avenue, Suite 1200, Chicago, Illinois 60603 (800) 577-EURO; *International Marketing Data and Statistics.*

Europa Publications Limited, 18 Bedford Square, London, WC1B 3JN, England; *The Europa World Year Book.*

International Monetary Fund, 700 Nineteenth Street, NW, Washington, D.C. 20431 (202) 623-7000; *International Financial Statistics.*

Statistical Office of the United Nations, Publishing Service, New York, New York 10017 (800) 253-9646; *Statistical Yearbook.*

The World Bank, 1818 H Street, NW, Washington, D.C. 20433 (202) 477-1234; *World Development Indicators.*

THAILAND - MONUMENTS AND HISTORICAL SITES

United Nations Educational, Scientific and Cultural Organization (UNESCO), 7 Place de Fontenoy, F-75700 Paris, France (Telephone Number in U.S. (212) 963-5981); *Statistical Yearbook.*

THAILAND - MORTALITY

Central Intelligence Agency, Washington, D.C. 20505 (703) 482-1100, www.cia.gov; *The World Factbook.*

The Economist Intelligence Unit (Asia) Limited, 10th Floor, Luk Kwok Centre, 72 Gloucester Road, Wanchai, Hong Kong (Phone Number in U.S. (800) 938-4685); *Asian Market Atlas.*

Euromonitor International, Inc., 122 South Michigan Avenue, Suite 1200, Chicago, Illinois 60603 (800) 577-EURO; *International Marketing Data and Statistics;* and *The World Economic Factbook.*

Europa Publications Limited, 18 Bedford Square, London, WC1B 3JN, England; *The Europa World Year Book.*

National Statistical Office, Office of the Prime Minister, Bangkok Metropolis 10100, Thailand; *Statistical Yearbook Thailand.*

St. Martin's Press, Inc., 175 Fifth Avenue, New York, New York 10010 (800) 221-7945; *The Statesman's Year-Book.*

Statistical Office of the United Nations, Publishing Service, New York, New York 10017 (800) 253-9646; *Asia-Pacific in Figures; Demographic Yearbook; Human Development Report; Statistical Yearbook;* and *World Statistics Pocketbook.*

United Nations Children's Fund (UNICEF), 3 United Nations Plaza, New York, New York 10017 (800) 253-9646; *State of the World's Children.*

The World Bank, 1818 H Street, NW, Washington, D.C. 20433 (202) 477-1234; *The World Bank Atlas; World Development Report;* and *World Development Indicators.*

World Health Organization, Office of Publications, 20 Avenue Appia, CH-1211 Geneva 27, Switzerland (Telephone Number in U.S. (518) 436-9686); *World Health Statistics Annual.*

THAILAND - MOTION PICTURES

St. Martin's Press, Inc., 175 Fifth Avenue, New York, New York 10010 (800) 221-7945; *The Statesman's Year-Book.*

Statistical Office of the United Nations, Publishing Service, New York, New York 10017 (800) 253-9646; *Statistical Yearbook.*

United Nations Educational, Scientific and Cultural Organization (UNESCO), 7 Place de Fontenoy, F-75700 Paris, France (Telephone Number in U.S. (212) 963-5981); *Statistical Yearbook.*

THAILAND - MOTOR VEHICLE PRODUCTION

Statistical Office of the United Nations,

Publishing Service, New York, New York 10017 (800) 253-9646; *Statistical Yearbook.*

THAILAND - MOTOR VEHICLE TAXES - See THAILAND - TAXATION

THAILAND - MOTOR VEHICLES IN USE

Europa Publications Limited, 18 Bedford Square, London, WC1B 3JN, England; *The Europa World Year Book.*

International Road Federation, 2600 Virginia Avenue, NW, Washington, D.C. 20037 (202) 338-4641; *World Road Statistics.*

National Statistical Office, Office of the Prime Minister, Bangkok Metropolis 10100, Thailand; *Statistical Yearbook Thailand.*

Statistical Office of the United Nations, Publishing Service, New York, New York 10017 (800) 253-9646; *Statistical Yearbook.*

THAILAND - MUSEUMS

M.E. Sharpe, 80 Business Park Drive, Armonk, New York 10504 (800) 541-6563; *The Illustrated Book of World Rankings.*

United Nations Educational, Scientific and Cultural Organization (UNESCO), 7 Place de Fontenoy, F-75700 Paris, France (Telephone Number in U.S. (212) 963-5981); *Statistical Yearbook.*

THAILAND - NATALITY - See THAILAND - BIRTH RATE

THAILAND - NATIONAL ACCOUNTS

Europa Publications Limited, 18 Bedford Square, London, WC1B 3JN, England; *The Europa World Year Book.*

Statistical Office of the United Nations, Publishing Service, New York, New York 10017 (800) 253-9646; *Asia-Pacific in Figures; National Accounts Statistics; Statistical Yearbook;* and *Statistical Yearbook for Asia and the Pacific.*

THAILAND - NATIONAL INCOME

M.E. Sharpe, 80 Business Park Drive, Armonk, New York 10504 (800) 541-6563; *The Illustrated Book of World Rankings.*

Statistical Office of the United Nations, Publishing Service, New York, New York 10017 (800) 253-9646; *National Accounts Statistics;* and *Statistical Yearbook.*

THAILAND - NATIONAL PRODUCT

M.E. Sharpe, 80 Business Park Drive, Armonk, New York 10504 (800) 541-6563; *The Illustrated Book of World Rankings.*

Statistical Office of the United Nations,

Publishing Service, New York, New York 10017 (800) 253-9646; *Statistical Yearbook.*

THAILAND - NATURAL GAS PRODUCTION - See THAILAND - MINING AND MINERAL PRODUCTS

THAILAND - NATURAL RUBBER PRODUCTION

International Rubber Study Group, York House, Eighth Floor, Empire Way, Wembley, London HA9 0PA, England; *Rubber Statistical Handbook.*

National Statistical Office, Office of the Prime Minister, Bangkok Metropolis 10100, Thailand; *Statistical Yearbook Thailand.*

Statistical Office of the United Nations, Publishing Service, New York, New York 10017 (800) 253-9646; *Statistical Yearbook.*

THAILAND - NEWSPAPER PRODUCTION - See THAILAND - FORESTRY AND FOREST PRODUCTS

THAILAND - NEWSPRINT - See THAILAND - CROPS

THAILAND - OCCUPATIONS - See THAILAND - LABOR

THAILAND - PALM KERNELS AND PALM OIL - See THAILAND - CROPS

THAILAND - PAPER - See THAILAND - FORESTRY AND FOREST PRODUCTS

THAILAND - PATENTS, TRADEMARKS AND SERVICE MARKS

World Intellectual Property Organization, 34 Chemin des Colombettes, CH-1211 Geneva 20. Switzerland; *Industrial Property Statistics.*

THAILAND - PEANUT PRODUCTION - See THAILAND - CROPS

THAILAND - PERIODICALS

United Nations Educational, Scientific and Cultural Organization (UNESCO), 7 Place de Fontenoy, F-75700 Paris, France (Telephone Number in U.S. (212) 963-5981); *Statistical Yearbook.*

THAILAND - PESTICIDE USE

Food and Agricultural Organization of the United Nations (FAO) Via delle Terme di Caracalla, 00100 Rome, Italy (Telephone Number in U.S. (202) 653-2400); *The State of Food and Agriculture.*

THAILAND - PETROLEUM INDUSTRY

Asian Development Bank, P.O. Box 789, 1099 Manila, Philippines; *Key Indicators of Developing Asian and Pacific Countries.*

Food and Agricultural Organization of the United Nations (FAO) Via delle Terme di Caracalla, 00100 Rome, Italy (Telephone Number in U.S. (202) 653-2400); *The State of Food and Agriculture.*

M.E. Sharpe, 80 Business Park Drive, Armonk, New York 10504 (800) 541-6563; *The Illustrated Book of World Rankings.*

Penn Well Publishing Company, 1421 South Sheridan Road, P.O. Box 1260, Tulsa, Oklahoma 74101 (800) 752-9764; *International Energy Statistics Sourcebook.*

St. Martin's Press, Inc., 175 Fifth Avenue, New York, New York 10010 (800) 221-7945; *The Statesman's Year-Book.*

Statistical Office of the United Nations, Publishing Service, New York, New York 10017 (800) 253-9646; *Statistical Yearbook.*

United Nations Conference on Trade and Development, Central Statistical Service, Palais des Nations, Geneva, Switzerland (Telephone in U.S. (800) 253-9646); *UNCTAD Commodity Yearbook.*

THAILAND - PHOSPHATE ROCK PRODUCTION - See THAILAND - MINING AND MINERAL PRODUCTS

THAILAND - PIG-IRON AND FERRO-ALLOY PRODUCTION - See THAILAND - MINING AND MINERAL PRODUCTS

THAILAND - PIGS - See THAILAND - LIVESTOCK AND POULTRY

THAILAND - POPULATION

Asian Development Bank, P.O. Box 789, 1099 Manila, Philippines; *Key Indicators of Developing Asian and Pacific Countries.*

Central Intelligence Agency, Washington, D.C. 20505 (703) 482-1100, www.cia.gov; *The World Factbook.*

The Economist Intelligence Unit, 111 West 57th Street, New York, New York 10019 (800) 938-4685; *Thailand Country Report;* and *The World Market Atlas.*

The Economist Intelligence Unit (Asia) Limited, 10th Floor, Luk Kwok Centre, 72 Gloucester Road, Wanchai, Hong Kong (Phone Number in U.S. (800) 938-4685); *Asian Market Atlas.*

Euromonitor International, Inc., 122 South Michigan Avenue, Suite 1200, Chicago, Illinois 60603 (800) 577-EURO; *International Marketing Data and Statistics;* and *The World Economic Factbook.*

Europa Publications Limited, 18 Bedford Square, London, WC1B 3JN, England; *The Europa World Year Book.*

Food and Agricultural Organization of the United Nations (FAO), Via delle Terme di Caracalla, 00100 Rome, Italy (Telephone Number in U.S. (202) 653-2400); *Production Yearbook.*

International Labour Office, I.L.O. Publications, 1828 L Street, NW, Suite 801, Washington, D.C. 20036 (301) 638-3152; *Yearbook of Labour Statistics.*

M.E. Sharpe, 80 Business Park Drive, Armonk, New York 10504 (800) 541-6563; *The Illustrated Book of World Rankings.*

National Statistical Office, Office of the Prime Minister, Bangkok Metropolis 10100, Thailand; *Statistical Yearbook Thailand.*

St. Martin's Press, Inc., 175 Fifth Avenue, New York, New York 10010 (800) 221-7945; *The Statesman's Year-Book.*

Statistical Office of the United Nations, Publishing Service, New York, New York 10017 (800) 253-9646; *Asia-Pacific in Figures; Demographic Yearbook; Human Development Report; Statistical Yearbook; Statistical Yearbook for Asia and the Pacific;* and *Trends in Europe and North America: The Statistical Yearbook of the Economic Commission for Europe.*

United Nations Educational, Scientific and Cultural Organization (UNESCO), 7 Place de Fontenoy, F-75700 Paris, France (Telephone Number in U.S. (212) 963-5981); *Statistical Yearbook.*

U.S. Arms Control and Disarmament Agency, 320 Twenty-first Street, NW, Washington, D.C. 20451 (202) 647-8677; *World Military Expenditures and Arms Transfers.*

Walden Publishing Ltd., Two Market Street, Saffron Walden Essex, CB10 1HZ, England; *The World of Information Asia and Pacific Review.*

The World Bank, 1818 H Street, NW, Washington, D.C. 20433 (202) 477-1234; *The World Bank Atlas;* and *World Development Report.*

World Health Organization, Office of Publications, 20 Avenue Appia, CH-1211 Geneva 27, Switzerland (Telephone Number in U.S. (518) 436-9686); *World Health Statistics Annual.*

THAILAND - POST OFFICES

M.E. Sharpe, 80 Business Park Drive, Armonk, New York 10504 (800) 541-6563; *The Illustrated Book of World Rankings.*

THAILAND - POTATO PRODUCTION - See THAILAND - CROPS

THAILAND - POWER PRODUCTION INDUSTRY

Statistical Office of the United Nations, Publishing Service, New York, New York 10017 (800) 253-9646; *Electric Power in Asia and the Pacific.*

THAILAND - PRICES

Asian Development Bank, P.O. Box 789, 1099 Manila, Philippines; *Key Indicators of Developing Asian and Pacific Countries.*

Food and Agricultural Organization of the United Nations (FAO), Via delle Terme di Caracalla, 00100 Rome, Italy (Telephone Number in U.S. (202) 653-2400); *Production Yearbook;* and *The State of Food and Agriculture.*

International Labour Office, I.L.O. Publications, 1828 L Street, NW, Suite 801, Washington, D.C. 20036 (301) 638-3152; *Yearbook of Labour Statistics.*

International Monetary Fund, 700 Nineteenth Street, NW, Washington, D.C. 20431 (202) 623-7000; *International Financial Statistics.*

International Rubber Study Group, York House, Eighth Floor, Empire Way, Wembley, London HA9 0PA, England; *Rubber Statistical Handbook.*

M.E. Sharpe, 80 Business Park Drive, Armonk, New York 10504 (800) 541-6563; *The Illustrated Book of World Rankings.*

National Statistical Office, Office of the Prime Minister, Bangkok Metropolis 10100, Thailand; *Statistical Yearbook Thailand.*

THAILAND - PRINTING AND WRITING PAPER - See THAILAND - FORESTRY AND FOREST PRODUCTS

THAILAND - PRODUCTION

International Rubber Study Group, York House, Eighth Floor, Empire Way, Wembley, London HA9 0PA, England; *Rubber Statistical Handbook.*

M.E. Sharpe, 80 Business Park Drive, Armonk, New York 10504 (800) 541-6563; *The Illustrated Book of World Rankings.*

National Statistical Office, Office of the Prime Minister, Bangkok Metropolis 10100, Thailand; *Statistical Yearbook Thailand.*

THAILAND - PRODUCTIVITY

Euromonitor International, Inc., 122 South Michigan Avenue, Suite 1200, Chicago, Illinois 60603 (800) 577-EURO; *International Marketing Data and Statistics.*

THAILAND - PROPERTY TAXES - See THAILAND - TAXATION

THAILAND - PUBLIC FINANCE - See THAILAND - FINANCE

THAILAND - RADIO

The Economist Intelligence Unit (Asia) Limited, 10th Floor, Luk Kwok Centre, 72 Gloucester Road, Wanchai, Hong Kong (Phone Number in U.S. (800) 938-4685); *Asian Market Atlas.*

THAILAND - RADIO BROADCASTING - See THAILAND - BROADCASTING

THAILAND - RADIO RECEIVERS

St. Martin's Press, Inc., 175 Fifth Avenue, New York, New York 10010 (800) 221-7945; *The Statesman's Year-Book.*

THAILAND - RAILWAYS

Europa Publications Limited, 18 Bedford Square, London, WC1B 3JN, England; *The Europa World Year Book.*

Jane's Information Group, Sentinel House, 163 Brighton Road, Coulsdon, Surrey CR5 2NH, England (Telephone Number in U.S. (703) 683-3700); *Jane's World Railways.*

National Statistical Office, Office of the Prime Minister, Bangkok Metropolis 10100, Thailand; *Statistical Yearbook Thailand.*

St. Martin's Press, Inc., 175 Fifth Avenue, New York, New York 10010 (800) 221-7945; *The Statesman's Year-Book.*

Statistical Office of the United Nations, Publishing Service, New York, New York 10017 (800) 253-9646; *Statistical Yearbook.*

THAILAND - RELIGION

Central Intelligence Agency, Washington, D.C. 20505 (703) 482-1100, www.cia.gov; *The World Factbook.*

M.E. Sharpe, 80 Business Park Drive, Armonk, New York 10504 (800) 541-6563; *The Illustrated Book of World Rankings.*

St. Martin's Press, Inc., 175 Fifth Avenue, New York, New York 10010 (800) 221-7945; *The Statesman's Year-Book.*

THAILAND - RENT PRICES

International Labour Office, I.L.O. Publications, 1828 L Street, NW, Suite 801, Washington, D.C. 20036 (301) 638-3152; *Yearbook of Labour Statistics.*

THAILAND - RETAIL TRADE

Euromonitor International, Inc., 122

South Michigan Avenue, Suite 1200, Chicago, Illinois 60603 (800) 577-EURO; *World Marketing Data and Statistics;* and *Retail Trade International.*

THAILAND - RICE - See THAILAND - CROPS

THAILAND - ROUNDWOOD PRODUCTION - See THAILAND - FORESTRY AND FOREST PRODUCTS

THAILAND - RUBBER EXPORTS

International Monetary Fund, 700 Nineteenth Street, NW, Washington, D.C. 20431 (202) 623-7000; *International Financial Statistics.*

THAILAND - RUBBER PRODUCTION AND CONSUMPTION

Commodity Research Bureau, Inc., 30 South Wacker Drive, Chicago, Illinois 60606 (312) 454-1801; *Commodity Year Book.*

International Rubber Study Group, York House, Eighth Floor, Empire Way, Wembley, London HA9 0PA, England; *Rubber Statistical Handbook.*

M.E. Sharpe, 80 Business Park Drive, Armonk, New York 10504 (800) 541-6563; *The Illustrated Book of World Rankings.*

National Statistical Office, Office of the Prime Minister, Bangkok Metropolis 10100, Thailand; *Statistical Yearbook Thailand.*

THAILAND - SALT PRODUCTION

Statistical Office of the United Nations, Publishing Service, New York, New York 10017 (800) 253-9646; *Statistical Yearbook.*

THAILAND - SAWNWOOD PRODUCTION - See THAILAND - FORESTRY AND FOREST PRODUCTS

THAILAND - SCIENTISTS, TECHNICIANS AND ENGINEERS

Statistical Office of the United Nations, Publishing Service, New York, New York 10017 (800) 253-9646; *Statistical Yearbook.*

THAILAND - SENIOR CITIZENS

M.E. Sharpe, 80 Business Park Drive, Armonk, New York 10504 (800) 541-6563; *The Illustrated Book of World Rankings.*

THAILAND - SHEEP - See THAILAND - LIVESTOCK AND POULTRY

THAILAND - SILVER PRODUCTION AND CONSUMPTION - See THAILAND - MINING AND MINERAL PRODUCTS

THAILAND - SOCIAL DATA

Asian Development Bank, P.O. Box 789,

1099 Manila, Philippines; *Key Indicators of Developing Asian and Pacific Countries.*

M.E. Sharpe, 80 Business Park Drive, Armonk, New York 10504 (800) 541-6563; *The Illustrated Book of World Rankings.*

Statistical Office of the United Nations, Publishing Service, New York, New York 10017 (800) 253-9646; *World Statistics Pocketbook.*

THAILAND - SOCIAL SECURITY

International Monetary Fund, 700 Nineteenth Street, NW, Washington, D.C. 20431 (202) 623-7000; *Government Finance Statistics Yearbook.*

Statistical Office of the United Nations, Publishing Service, New York, New York 10017 (800) 253-9646; *National Accounts Statistics.*

THAILAND - SOYBEAN PRODUCTION - See THAILAND - CROPS

THAILAND - STAMP TAXES AND DUTIES - See THAILAND - TAXATION

THAILAND - STATE BUDGET REVENUE AND EXPENDITURES

Euromonitor International, Inc., 122 South Michigan Avenue, Suite 1200, Chicago, Illinois 60603 (800) 577-EURO; *International Marketing Data and Statistics.*

THAILAND - STEEL - See THAILAND - MINING AND MINERAL PRODUCTS

THAILAND - STOCKS - COMMODITY - MARKET PRICE - INDEX

Food and Agricultural Organization of the United Nations (FAO) Via delle Terme di Caracalla, 00100 Rome, Italy (Telephone Number in U.S. (202) 653-2400); *The State of Food and Agriculture.*

THAILAND - SUGAR - See THAILAND - CROPS

THAILAND - SULPHURIC ACID PRODUCTION - See THAILAND - MINING AND MINERAL PRODUCTS

THAILAND - TAXATION

Europa Publications Limited, 18 Bedford Square, London, WC1B 3JN, England; *The Europa World Year Book.*

International Monetary Fund, 700 Nineteenth Street, NW, Washington, D.C. 20431 (202) 623-7000; *Government Finance Statistics Yearbook.*

International Road Federation, 2600 Virginia Avenue, NW, Washington, D.C. 20037 (202) 338-4641; *World Road Statistics.*

The World Bank, 1818 H Street, NW, Washington, D.C. 20433 (202) 477-1234; *World Development Indicators.*

THAILAND - TEA CONSUMPTION - See THAILAND - CROPS

THAILAND - TELEGRAPH SERVICE

Statistical Office of the United Nations, Publishing Service, New York, New York 10017 (800) 253-9646; *Statistical Yearbook.*

THAILAND - TELEPHONES IN USE

American Telephone and Telegraph Company, 26 Parsippany Road, Whippany, New Jersey 07981 (800) 222-0300; *The World's Telephones.*

Central Intelligence Agency, Washington, D.C. 20505 (703) 482-1100, www.cia.gov; *The World Factbook.*

The Economist Intelligence Unit (Asia) Limited, 10th Floor, Luk Kwok Centre, 72 Gloucester Road, Wanchai, Hong Kong (Phone Number in U.S. (800) 938-4685); *Asian Market Atlas.*

Europa Publications Limited, 18 Bedford Square, London, WC1B 3JN, England; *The Europa World Year Book.*

National Statistical Office, Office of the Prime Minister, Bangkok Metropolis 10100, Thailand; *Statistical Yearbook Thailand.*

St. Martin's Press, Inc., 175 Fifth Avenue, New York, New York 10010 (800) 221-7945; *The Statesman's Year-Book.*

Statistical Office of the United Nations, Publishing Service, New York, New York 10017 (800) 253-9646; *Statistical Yearbook;* and *World Statistics Pocketbook.*

THAILAND - TELEVISION

The Economist Intelligence Unit (Asia) Limited, 10th Floor, Luk Kwok Centre, 72 Gloucester Road, Wanchai, Hong Kong (Phone Number in U.S. (800) 938-4685); *Asian Market Atlas.*

THAILAND - TELEVISION BROADCASTING - See THAILAND - BROADCASTING

THAILAND - TELEVISION RECEIVER PRODUCTION

Statistical Office of the United Nations, Publishing Service, New York, New York 10017 (800) 253-9646; *Statistical Yearbook.*

THAILAND - TEXTILE INDUSTRY

American Forest and Paper Association, 1111 Nineteenth Street, NW,

Washington, D.C. 20036 (202) 463-2700; *Wood Pulp and Fiber Statistics.*

Euromonitor International, Inc., 122 South Michigan Avenue, Suite 1200, Chicago, Illinois 60603 (800) 577-EURO; *Retail Trade International.*

M.E. Sharpe, 80 Business Park Drive, Armonk, New York 10504 (800) 541-6563; *The Illustrated Book of World Rankings.*

Statistical Office of the United Nations, Publishing Service, New York, New York 10017 (800) 253-9646; *Statistical Yearbook.*

THAILAND - TIN - See THAILAND - MINING AND MINERAL PRODUCTS

THAILAND - TIRE (MOTOR VEHICLE) PRODUCTION

International Rubber Study Group, York House, Eighth Floor, Empire Way, Wembley, London HA9 0PA, England; *Rubber Statistical Handbook.*

Statistical Office of the United Nations, Publishing Service, New York, New York 10017 (800) 253-9646; *Statistical Yearbook.*

THAILAND - TOBACCO PRODUCTION

M.E. Sharpe, 80 Business Park Drive, Armonk, New York 10504 (800) 541-6563; *The Illustrated Book of World Rankings.*

Statistical Office of the United Nations, Publishing Service, New York, New York 10017 (800) 253-9646; *Statistical Yearbook.*

THAILAND - TOURISM

Euromonitor International, Inc., 122 South Michigan Avenue, Suite 1200, Chicago, Illinois 60603 (800) 577-EURO; *The World Economic Factbook;* and *World Marketing Data and Statistics.*

Europa Publications Limited, 18 Bedford Square, London, WC1B 3JN, England; *The Europa World Year Book.*

M.E. Sharpe, 80 Business Park Drive, Armonk, New York 10504 (800) 541-6563; *The Illustrated Book of World Rankings.*

National Statistical Office, Office of the Prime Minister, Bangkok Metropolis 10100, Thailand; *Statistical Yearbook Thailand.*

St. Martin's Press, Inc., 175 Fifth Avenue, New York, New York 10010 (800) 221-7945; *The Statesman's Year-Book.*

Statistical Office of the United Nations, Publishing Service, New York, New York 10017 (800) 253-9646; *Statistical Yearbook.*

World Tourism Organization, Calle Capitan Haya 42, E-28020 Madrid, Spain;

Yearbook of Tourism Statistics.

THAILAND - TRACTORS IN USE

Statistical Office of the United Nations, Publishing Service, New York, New York 10017 (800) 253-9646; *Statistical Yearbook.*

THAILAND - TRADE - See THAILAND - FOREIGN TRADE

THAILAND - TRADEMARKS AND SERVICE MARKS - See THAILAND - PATENTS, TRADEMARKS AND SERVICE MARKS

THAILAND - TRANSPORTATION AND COMMUNICATIONS

Central Intelligence Agency, Washington, D.C. 20505 (703) 482-1100, www.cia.gov; *The World Factbook.*

The Economist Intelligence Unit (Asia) Limited, 10th Floor, Luk Kwok Centre, 72 Gloucester Road, Wanchai, Hong Kong (Phone Number in U.S. (800) 938-4685); *Asian Market Atlas.*

Euromonitor International, Inc., 122 South Michigan Avenue, Suite 1200, Chicago, Illinois 60603 (800) 577-EURO; *International Marketing Data and Statistics;* and *World Marketing Data and Statistics.*

M.E. Sharpe, 80 Business Park Drive, Armonk, New York 10504 (800) 541-6563; *The Illustrated Book of World Rankings.*

National Statistical Office, Office of the Prime Minister, Bangkok Metropolis 10100, Thailand; *Statistical Yearbook Thailand.*

St. Martin's Press, Inc., 175 Fifth Avenue, New York, New York 10010 (800) 221-7945; *The Statesman's Year-Book.*

Statistical Office of the United Nations, Publishing Service, New York, New York 10017 (800) 253-9646; *Human Development Report;* and *Statistical Yearbook for Asia and the Pacific.*

United Nations Economic Commission for Africa, Africa Hall, P.O. Box 3001, Addis Ababa, Ethiopia (Telephone Number in U.S. (800) 253-9646); *African Statistical Yearbook.*

THAILAND - TUNGSTEN PRODUCTION AND CONSUMPTION - See THAILAND - MINING AND MINERAL PRODUCTS

THAILAND - UNEMPLOYMENT

Central Intelligence Agency, Washington, D.C. 20505 (703) 482-1100, www.cia.gov; *The World Factbook.*

Euromonitor International, Inc., 122 South Michigan Avenue, Suite 1200, Chicago, Illinois 60603 (800) 577-EURO;

International Marketing Data and Statistics.

International Labour Office, I.L.O. Publications, 1828 L Street, NW, Suite 801, Washington, D.C. 20036 (301) 638-3152; *Yearbook of Labour Statistics.*

St. Martin's Press, Inc., 175 Fifth Avenue, New York, New York 10010 (800) 221-7945; *The Statesman's Year-Book.*

Statistical Office of the United Nations, Publishing Service, New York, New York 10017 (800) 253-9646; *Statistical Yearbook.*

THAILAND - UTILITIES

Statistical Office of the United Nations, Publishing Service, New York, New York 10017 (800) 253-9646; *Electric Power in Asia and the Pacific.*

THAILAND - VITAL STATISTICS

Euromonitor International, Inc., 122 South Michigan Avenue, Suite 1200, Chicago, Illinois 60603 (800) 577-EURO; *International Marketing Data and Statistics.*

National Statistical Office, Office of the Prime Minister, Bangkok Metropolis 10100, Thailand; *Statistical Yearbook Thailand.*

St. Martin's Press, Inc., 175 Fifth Avenue, New York, New York 10010 (800) 221-7945; *The Statesman's Year-Book.*

Statistical Office of the United Nations, Publishing Service, New York, New York 10017 (800) 253-9646; *Statistical Yearbook.*

World Health Organization, Office of Publications, 20 Avenue Appia, CH-1211 Geneva 27, Switzerland (Telephone Number in U.S. (518) 436-9686); *World Health Statistics Annual.*

THAILAND - WAGES

International Labour Office, I.L.O. Publications, 1828 L Street, NW, Suite 801, Washington, D.C. 20036 (301) 638-3152; *Yearbook of Labour Statistics.*

National Statistical Office, Office of the Prime Minister, Bangkok Metropolis 10100, Thailand; *Statistical Yearbook Thailand.*

Statistical Office of the United Nations, Publishing Service, New York, New York 10017 (800) 253-9646; *Statistical Yearbook for Asia and the Pacific.*

THAILAND - WEATHER - See THAILAND - CLIMATE

THAILAND - WELFARE

International Monetary Fund, 700 Nineteenth Street, NW, Washington, D.C. 20431 (202) 623-7000; *Government Finance*

Statistics Yearbook.

THAILAND - WHEAT - See THAILAND - CROPS

THAILAND - WHOLESALE PRICES

Asian Development Bank, P.O. Box 789, 1099 Manila, Philippines; *Key Indicators of Developing Asian and Pacific Countries.*

International Monetary Fund, 700 Nineteenth Street, NW, Washington, D.C. 20431 (202) 623-7000; *International Financial Statistics.*

Statistical Office of the United Nations, Publishing Service, New York, New York 10017 (800) 253-9646; *Statistical Yearbook.*

THAILAND - WINE PRODUCTION - See THAILAND - BEVERAGES

THAILAND - WOOD - See THAILAND - FORESTRY AND FOREST PRODUCTS

THAILAND - WOOL PRODUCTION - See THAILAND - TEXTILE INDUSTRY

THAILAND - YARN PRODUCTION - See THAILAND - TEXTILE INDUSTRY

THAILAND - ZINC ORE PRODUCTION AND CONSUMPTION - See THAILAND - MINING AND MINERAL PRODUCTS

THAILAND - ZOOS AND BOTANICAL GARDENS

United Nations Educational, Scientific and Cultural Organization (UNESCO), 7 Place de Fontenoy, F-75700 Paris, France (Telephone Number in U.S. (212) 963-5981); *Statistical Yearbook.*

THEATERS - ATTENDANCE AND RECEIPTS

League of American Theaters and Producers, Inc., 226 West 47th Street, New York, New York 10036 (212) 764-1122.

THEATERS - FEDERAL AID

National Endowment for the Arts, 1100 Pennsylvania Avenue, NW, Washington, D.C. 20506 (202) 682-5400, www.arts.gov; *Annual Report.*

THEATERS - PERSONAL EXPENDITURES

U.S. Department of Commerce, Bureau of Economic Analysis, Fourteenth Street between Constitution Avenue and E Street, NW, Washington, D.C. 20230 (202) 606-9900, www.bea.doc.gov; *The National Income and Product Accounts of the United States;* and *Survey of Current Business.*

Veronis Suhler and Associates, 350 Park Avenue, New York, New York 10022 (212) 935-4990; *Communications Industry*

Report.

THEATERS - THEATER INDUSTRY RECEIPTS

U.S. Department of Commerce, Bureau of the Census, Washington, D.C. 20233 (301) 457-4100, www.census.gov; *Current Business Reports, Service Annual Survey.*

THEFT - See CRIME AND CRIMINALS

THEOLOGY - DEGREES CONFERRED

U.S. Department of Commerce, Bureau of the Census, Washington, D.C. 20233 (301) 457-4100, www.census.gov; unpublished data.

U.S. Department of Education, National Center for Education Statistics, 555 New Jersey Avenue, NW, Washington, D.C. 20208-1828, http://nces.ed.gov; *Digest of Education Statistics.*

THREAD - See YARN, THREAD, etc.

THRIFT SAVINGS PLAN

Employee Benefit Research Institute 2121 K Street, NW, Suite 600, Washington, D.C. 20037 (202) 659-0670; *EBRI Databook on Employee Benefits.*

TIMBER - See also LUMBER AND WOOD PRODUCTS

TIMBER - CONSUMPTION

U.S. Department of Agriculture, Forest Service, Post Office Box 96090, Washington, D.C. 20090 (202) 205-8333, www.fs.fed.us; *Timber Demand and Technology Assessment.*

TIMBER - FOREIGN TRADE

U.S. Department of Agriculture, Forest Service, Post Office Box 96090, Washington, D.C. 20090 (202) 205-8333, www.fs.fed.us; *Timber Demand and Technology Assessment;* and *Agricultural Statistics.*

TIMBER - PRODUCER PRICES

U.S. Department of Agriculture, Forest Service, Post Office Box 96090, Washington, D.C. 20090 (202) 205-8333, www.fs.fed.us; *Timber Demand and Technology Assessment;* and *Agricultural Statistics.*

U.S. Department of Labor, Bureau of Labor Statistics, Two Massachusetts Avenue, NE, Washington, D.C. 20212 (202) 691-5200, www.stats.bls.gov; *Producer Price Indexes.*

TIMBER - PRODUCTION

U.S. Department of Agriculture, Forest Service, Post Office Box 96090, Washington, D.C. 20090 (202) 205-8333, www.fs.fed.us; *Timber Demand and Technology Assessment;* and *Agricultural Statistics.*

TIMBER - PRODUCTION - WORLD (ROUNDWOOD)

Food and Agriculture Organization of the United Nations, Via delle Terme di Caracalla, 00100 Rome, Italy (Telephone Number in U.S. (202) 653-2400: *State of the World's Forest.*

Statistical Office of the United Nations, New York, New York 10017 (800) 253-9646; *Monthly Bulletin of Statistics.*

TIMBER - REMOVED FROM NATIONAL FORESTS

U.S. Department of Agriculture, Forest Service, Post Office Box 96090, Washington, D.C. 20090 (202) 205-8333, www.fs.fed.us; *Timber Demand and Technology Assessment;* and *Agricultural Statistics.*

TIMBER - ROUNDWOOD PRODUCTS

U.S. Department of Agriculture, Forest Service, Post Office Box 96090, Washington, D.C. 20090 (202) 205-8333, www.fs.fed.us; *Timber Demand and Technology Assessment.*

TIMBER - VOLUME - GROWTH AND CUT

U.S. Department of Agriculture, Forest Service, Post Office Box 96090, Washington, D.C. 20090 (202) 205-8333, www.fs.fed.us; *Forest Resources of the United States.*

TIN - FOREIGN TRADE

U.S. Department of the Interior, Geological Survey, Office of Minerals Information, 12201 Sunrise Valley Drive, Reston, Virginia 22092 (703) 648-4000, www.minerals.usgs.gov; *Mineral Commodity Summaries.*

TIN - PRICES

U.S. Department of the Interior, Geological Survey, Office of Minerals Information, 12201 Sunrise Valley Drive, Reston, Virginia 22092 (703) 648-4000, www.minerals.usgs.gov; *Mineral Commodity Summaries.*

TIN - PRODUCTION

U.S. Department of the Interior, Geological Survey, Office of Minerals Information, 12201 Sunrise Valley Drive, Reston, Virginia 22092 (703)648-4000, www.minerals.usgs.gov; *Mineral Commodity Summaries.*

TIN - PRODUCTION - WORLD

U.S. Department of the Interior, Geological Survey, Office of Minerals Information, 12201 Sunrise Valley Drive, Reston, Virginia 22092 (703) 648-4000, www.minerals.usgs.gov; *Mineral Commodity Summaries.*

TIN - STRATEGIC AND CRITICAL MATERIALS

U.S. Department of Defense, Defense Logistics Agency, 8725 John J. Kingman Road, Fort Belvoir, Virginia 22060 (703) 767-6666; *Statistical Supplement, Stockpile Report to the Congress.*

TIRES AND TUBES

The Rubber Manufacturers Association, Incorporated, 1400 K Street, NW, Washington, D.C. 20005 (202) 682-4800; *RMA Monthly Tire Report.*

U.S. Department of Commerce, Bureau of the Census, Washington, D.C. 20233 (301) 457-4100, www.census.gov; *Annual Survey of Manufactures; U.S. International Trade in Goods and Services;* and *Census of Manufactures.*

U.S. Department of Transportation, National Highway Traffic Safety Administration, 400 Seventh Street, SW, Washington, D.C. 20590 (202) 366-9550; *Motor Vehicles Recall Campaigns.*

TITANIUM - PRODUCTION

U.S. Department of the Interior, Geological Survey, Office of Minerals Information, 12201 Sunrise Valley Drive, Reston, Virginia 22092 (703)648-4000, www.minerals.usgs.gov; *Mineral Commodity Summaries.*

TITANIUM - STRATEGIC AND CRITICAL MATERIAL

U.S. Department of Defense, Defense Logistics Agency, 8725 John J. Kingman Road, Fort Belvoir, Virginia 22060 (703) 767-6666; *Statistical Supplement, Stockpile Report to the Congress.*

TITANIUM - WORLD PRODUCTION

U.S. Department of the Interior, Geological Survey, Office of Minerals Information, 12201 Sunrise Valley Drive, Reston, Virginia 22092 (703) 648-4000, www.minerals.usgs.gov; *Mineral Commodity Summaries.*

TOBACCO - See also TOBACCO PRODUCTS, MANUFACTURING and CIGARETTES

TOBACCO - ACREAGE HARVESTED

U.S. Department of Agriculture, Economic Research Service, 1800 M Street, NW, Washington, D.C. 20036 (202) 694-5050, www.ers.usda.gov; *Agricultural Statistics; Agricultural Outlook;* and *Tobacco Situation.*

U.S. Department of Agriculture, National Agricultural Statistics Service, Fourteenth Street and Independence Avenue, SW, Washington, D.C. 20250 (800) 727-9540, www.usda.gov/nass; *Crop Production; Crop Values;* and *Field Crops.*

TOBACCO - ADVERTISING EXPENDITURES

Television Bureau of Advertising, Incorporated, 3 East 54th Street, New York, New York 10022 (212) 486-1111; from data compiled by Competitive Media Reporting, 11 West 42nd Street, New York, New York 10036 (212) 789-1400.

TOBACCO - CONSUMER EXPENDITURES

U.S. Department of Labor, Bureau of Labor Statistics, Two Massachusetts Avenue, NE, Washington, D.C. 20212 (202) 691-5200, www.stats.bls.gov; *Consumer Expenditures*; and unpublished data.

TOBACCO - CONSUMPTION AND USE

U.S. Department of Health and Human Services, Centers for Disease Control and Prevention, 1600 Clifton Road, NE, Atlanta, Georgia 30333 (800) 311-3435, www.cdc.gov; *Morbidity and Mortality Weekly Report.*

U.S. Department of Health and Human Services, National Center for Health Statistics, 3700 East-West Highway, Hyattsville, Maryland 20782 (301) 436-8500, www.cdc.gov/nchs; *Health, United States.*

U.S. Department of Health and Human Services, Substance Abuse and Mental Health Services Administration, 5600 Fishers Lane, Rockville, Maryland 20857 (800) 729-6686, www.samhsa.gov; *National Household Survey on Drug Abuse.*

TOBACCO - FARM MARKETINGS - SALES

U.S. Department of Agriculture, Economic Research Service, 1800 M Street, NW, Washington, D.C. 20036 (202) 694-5050, www.ers.usda.gov; *Farm Business Economic Report.*

TOBACCO - FOREIGN COUNTRIES

U.S. Department of Agriculture, Foreign Agricultural Service, Fourteenth Street and Independence Avenue, SW, Washington, D.C. 20250 (202) 720-7115, www.fas.usda.gov; *Tobacco: World Markets and Trade.*

TOBACCO - FOREIGN TRADE

U.S. Department of Agriculture, Economic Research Service, 1800 M Street, NW, Washington, D.C. 20036 (202) 694-5050, www.ers.usda.gov; *Foreign Agricultural Trade of the United States;* and *U.S. Agricultural Trade Update.*

U.S. Department of Agriculture, Foreign Agricultural Service, Fourteenth Street and Independence Avenue, SW, Washington, D.C. 20250 (202) 720-7115, www.fas.usda.gov; *Tobacco: World Markets and Trade.*

U.S. Department of Agriculture, National Agricultural Statistics Service, Fourteenth Street and Independence Avenue, SW, Washington, D.C. 20250 (800) 727-9540, www.usda.gov/nass; *Crop Production; Field Crops;* and *Crop Values.*

U.S. Department of Commerce, Bureau of the Census, Washington, D.C. 20233 (301) 457-4100, www.census.gov; *U.S. International Trade in Goods and Services.*

TOBACCO - PRICES

U.S. Department of Agriculture, National Agricultural Statistics Service, Fourteenth Street and Independence Avenue, SW, Washington, D.C. 20250 (800) 727-9540, www.usda.gov/nass; *Agricultural Prices: Annual Summary; Crop Production;* and *Crop Values.*

U.S. Department of Labor, Bureau of Labor Statistics, Two Massachusetts Avenue, NE, Washington, D.C. 20212 (202) 691-5200, www.stats.bls.gov; *Monthly Labor Review;* and *CPI Detailed Report.*

TOBACCO - PRODUCTION

Statistical Office of the United Nations, Publishing Service, New York, New York 10017 (800) 253-9646; *Monthly Bulletin of Statistics.*

U.S. Department of Agriculture, Economic Research Service, 1800 M Street, NW, Washington, D.C. 20036 (202) 694-5050, www.ers.usda.gov; *Agricultural Outlook;* and *Agricultural Statistics.*

U.S. Department of Agriculture, Foreign Agricultural Service, Fourteenth Street and Independence Avenue, SW, Washington, D.C. 20250 (202) 720-7115, www.fas.usda.gov; *Foreign Agricultural Commodity Circular Series;* and *Tobacco: World Markets and Trade.*

U.S. Department of Agriculture, National Agricultural Statistics Service, Fourteenth Street and Independence Avenue, SW, Washington, D.C. 20250 (800) 727-9540, www.usda.gov/nass; *Crop Production;* and *Crop Values.*

TOBACCO - TAXES

U.S. Department of Commerce, Bureau of the Census, Washington, D.C. 20233 (301) 457-4100, www.census.gov; *State Government Finances;* and Internet site http://www.census.gov/ftp/pub/govs/www/state/html.

U.S. Department of Treasury, Bureau of Alcohol, Tobacco and Firearms, 650 Massachusetts Avenue, NW, Washington, D.C. 20226 (202) 927-8500, www.atf.treas.gov; *Alcohol and Tobacco Tax Collections.*

U.S. Department of Treasury, Internal Revenue Service, 1111 Constitution Avenue, NW, Washington, D.C. 20224 (202) 874-0410, www.irs.ustreas.gov; *Annual Report.*

TOBACCO PRODUCTS - MANUFACTURING - CAPITAL

U.S. Department of Commerce, Bureau of Economic Analysis, Fourteenth Street between Constitution Avenue and E Street, NW, Washington, D.C. 20230 (202) 606-9900, www.bea.doc.gov; *Survey of Current Business;* and unpublished data.

TOBACCO PRODUCTS - MANUFACTURING - EARNINGS

U.S. Department of Commerce, Bureau of the Census, Washington, D.C. 20233 (301) 457-4100, www.census.gov; *Census of Manufactures;* and *Annual Survey of Manufactures.*

U.S. Department of Labor, Bureau of Labor Statistics, Two Massachusetts Avenue, NE, Washington, D.C. 20212 (202) 691-5200, www.stats.bls.gov; *Employment and Earnings;* and Internet site: http://stats.bls.gov/ ceshome.htm.

TOBACCO PRODUCTS - MANUFACTURING - EMPLOYEES

U.S. Department of Commerce, Bureau of the Census, Washington, D.C. 20233 (301) 457-4100, www.census.gov; *Census of Manufactures;* and *Annual Survey of Manufactures.*

U.S. Department of Labor, Bureau of Labor Statistics, Two Massachusetts Avenue, NE, Washington, D.C. 20212 (202) 691-5200, www.stats.bls.gov; *Employment and Earnings; Monthly Labor Review;* and Internet site: http://stats.bls.gov/ceshome.htm.

TOBACCO PRODUCTS - MANUFACTURING - ENERGY CONSUMPTION

U.S. Department of Energy, Energy Information Administration, 1000 Independence Avenue, SW, Washington, D.C. 20585 (202) 586-8800, www. eia.doe.gov; *Manufacturing Energy Consumption.*

TOBACCO PRODUCTS - FOREIGN TRADE

U.S. Department of Commerce, Bureau of the Census, Washington, D.C. 20233 (301) 457-4100, www.census.gov; *U.S. International Trade in Goods and Services.*

TOBACCO PRODUCTS - GROSS DOMESTIC PRODUCT

U.S. Department of Commerce, Bureau of Economic Analysis, Fourteenth Street between Constitution Avenue and E Street, NW, Washington, D.C. 20230 (202) 606-9900, www.bea.doc.gov; *Survey of Current Business.*

TOBACCO PRODUCTS - MANUFACTURING - INVENTORIES

U.S. Department of Commerce, Bureau of the Census, Washington, D.C. 20233 (301) 457-4100, www.census.gov; *Current Industrial Reports, Manufactures' Shipments, Inventories, and Orders.*

TOBACCO PRODUCTS - MANUFACTURING - OCCUPATIONAL SAFETY

U.S. Department of Labor, Bureau of Labor Statistics, Two Massachusetts Avenue, NE, Washington, D.C. 20212 (202) 691-5200, www.stats.bls.gov; *Occupational Injuries and Illnesses in the United States by Industry.*

TOBACCO PRODUCTS - PRICE INDEXES

U.S. Department of Labor, Bureau of Labor Statistics, Two Massachusetts Avenue, NE, Washington, D.C. 20212 (202) 691-5200, www.stats.bls.gov; *Monthly Labor Review*; and *CPI Detailed Report.*

TOBACCO PRODUCTS - MANUFACTURING - PRODUCTIVITY

U.S. Department of Labor, Bureau of Labor Statistics, Two Massachusetts Avenue, NE, Washington, D.C. 20212 (202) 691-5200, www.stats.bls.gov; Internet site http://stats.bls.gov/iprhome.htm.

TOBACCO PRODUCTS - MANUFACTURING - PROFIT

Time Warner, Time and Life Building, Rockefeller Center, New York, New York 10020 (212) 522-1212; *The Fortune Directories.*

TOBACCO PRODUCTS - MANUFACTURING - SHIPMENTS

Time Warner, Time and Life Building, Rockefeller Center, New York, New York 10020 (212) 522-1212; *The Fortune Directories.*

U.S. Department of Commerce, Bureau of the Census, Washington, D.C. 20233 (301) 457-4100, www.census.gov; *Current Industrial Reports; Manufactures' Shipments, Inventories, and Orders; Census of Manufactures;* and *Annual Survey of Manufactures.*

TOBACCO PRODUCTS - MANUFACTURING - TOXIC CHEMICAL RELEASES

Environmental Protection Agency, 1200 Pennsylvania Avenue, NW, Washington, D.C. 20460 (888) 372-8255, www.epa.gov; *Toxics Release Inventory.*

TOBACCO PRODUCTS - MANUFACTURING - VALUE ADDED

U.S. Department of Commerce, Bureau of the Census, Washington, D.C. 20233 (301) 457-4100, www.census.gov; *Census of Manufactures;* and *Annual Survey of Manufactures.*

Togo - National Statistical Office

Direction de la Statistique, BP 118, Lome, Togo.

Togo - Primary Statistics Sources

Direction de la Statistique (Department of Statistics), BP 118, Lome, Togo; *Bulletin mensuel de statistique* (Monthly Bulletin of Statistics); and *Annuaire statistique du Togo* (Statistical Yearbook of Togo).

TOGO - AGRICULTURE

Economist Intelligence Unit, 111 West 57th Street, New York, New York 10019 (800) 938-4685; *Togo Country Report.*

Euromonitor International, Inc., 122 South Michigan Avenue, Suite 1200, Chicago, Illinois 60603 (800) 577-EURO; *International Marketing Data and Statistics;* and *World Marketing Data and Statistics.*

Europa Publications Limited, 18 Bedford Square, London, WC1B 3JN, England; *The Europa World Year Book.*

Food and Agricultural Organization of the United Nations (FAO) Via delle Terme di Caracalla, 00100 Rome, Italy (Telephone Number in U.S. (202) 653-2400); *Production Yearbook; The State of Food and Agriculture,* and *Trade Yearbook.*

M.E. Sharpe, 80 Business Park Drive, Armonk, New York 10504 (800) 541-6563; *The Illustrated Book of World Rankings.*

St. Martin's Press, Inc., 175 Fifth Avenue, New York, New York 10010 (800) 221-7945; *The Statesman's Year-Book.*

Statistical Office of the United Nations, Publishing Service, New York, New York 10017 (800) 253-9646; *Statistical Yearbook;* and *Survey of Economic and Social Conditions in Africa.*

United Nations Conference on Trade and Development, Central Statistical Service, Palais des Nations, Geneva, Switzerland (Telephone in U.S. (800) 253-9646); *UNCTAD Commodity Yearbook.*

United Nations Economic Commission for Africa, Africa Hall, P.O. Box 3001, Addis Ababa, Ethiopia (Telephone Number in U.S. (800) 253-9646); *African Statistical Yearbook.*

The World Bank, 1818 H Street, NW, Washington, D.C. 20433 (202) 477-1234; *World Development Indicators.*

TOGO - AIRLINE SERVICE

Europa Publications Limited, 18 Bedford Square, London, WC1B 3JN, England; *The Europa World Year Book.*

M.E. Sharpe, 80 Business Park Drive, Armonk, New York 10504 (800) 541-6563; *The Illustrated Book of World Rankings.*

St. Martin's Press, Inc., 175 Fifth Avenue, New York, New York 10010 (800) 221-7945; *The Statesman's Year-Book.*

Statistical Office of the United Nations, Publishing Service, New York, New York 10017 (800) 253-9646; *Statistical Yearbook.*

United Nations Economic Commission for Africa, Africa Hall, P.O. Box 3001, Addis Ababa, Ethiopia (Telephone Number in U.S. (800) 253-9646); *African Statistical Yearbook.*

TOGO - AIRPORTS

Central Intelligence Agency, Washington, D.C. 20505 (703) 482-1100, www.cia.gov; *The World Factbook.*

TOGO - ALUMINUM PRODUCTION AND CONSUMPTION - See TOGO - MINING AND MINERAL PRODUCTS

TOGO - ANIMAL HEALTH

Food and Agricultural Organization of the United Nations (FAO), Via delle Terme di Caracalla, 00100, Rome, Italy (Telephone Number in U.S. (202) 653-2400); *Animal Health Yearbook.*

TOGO - AREA AND DENSITY OF POPULATION

African Development Bank, 01 BP 1387, Abidjan 01, Cote D'Ivoire; *Selected Statistics on Regional Member Countries.*

Central Intelligence Agency, Washington, D.C. 20505 (703) 482-1100, www.cia.gov; *The World Factbook.*

Euromonitor International, Inc., 122 South Michigan Avenue, Suite 1200, Chicago, Illinois 60603 (800) 577-EURO; *International Marketing Data and Statistics;* and *The World Economic Factbook.*

Europa Publications Limited, 18 Bedford Square, London, WC1B 3JN, England; *The Europa World Year Book.*

Food and Agricultural Organization of the United Nations (FAO) Via delle Terme di Caracalla, 00100 Rome, Italy (Telephone Number in U.S. (202) 653-2400); *The State of Food and Agriculture.*

M.E. Sharpe, 80 Business Park Drive, Armonk, New York 10504 (800) 541-6563; *The Illustrated Book of World Rankings.*

St. Martin's Press, Inc., 175 Fifth Avenue, New York, New York 10010 (800) 221-7945; *The Statesman's Year-Book.*

Statistical Office of the United Nations, Publishing Service, New York, New York 10017 (800) 253-9646; *Statistical Yearbook;* and *Survey of Economic and Social Conditions in Africa.*

United Nations Educational, Scientific and Cultural Organization (UNESCO), 7 Place de Fontenoy, F-75700 Paris, France (Telephone Number in U.S. (212) 963-5981); *Statistical Yearbook.*

The World Bank, 1818 H Street, NW, Washington, D.C. 20433 (202) 477-1234; *World Development Report.*

TOGO - ARMS EXPORTS AND IMPORTS - See TOGO - MILITARY

TOGO - BALANCE OF PAYMENTS

African Development Bank, 01 BP 1387, Abidjan 01, Cote D'Ivoire; *Selected Statistics on Regional Member Countries.*

The Economist Intelligence Unit, 111 West 57th Street, New York, New York 10019 (800) 938-4685; *The World Market Atlas.*

Europa Publications Limited, 18 Bedford Square, London, WC1B 3JN, England; *The Europa World Year Book.*

International Monetary Fund, 700 Nineteenth Street, NW, Washington, D.C. 20431 (202) 623-7000; *Balance of Payments Yearbook.*

United Nations Conference on Trade and Development (UNCTAD), New York, New York 10017 (800) 253-9646; *Handbook of International Trade and Development Statistics.*

United Nations Economic Commission for Africa, Africa Hall, P.O. Box 3001, Addis Ababa, Ethiopia (Telephone Number in U.S. (800) 253-9646); *African Statistical Yearbook.*

The World Bank, 1818 H Street, NW, Washington, D.C. 20433 (202) 477-1234; *World Development Report;* and *World Development Indicators.*

TOGO - BANKING

Euromonitor International, Inc., 122 South Michigan Avenue, Suite 1200, Chicago, Illinois 60603 (800) 577-EURO; *World Marketing Data and Statistics.*

Europa Publications Limited, 18 Bedford Square, London, WC1B 3JN, England; *The Europa World Year Book.*

International Monetary Fund, 700 Nineteenth Street, NW, Washington, D.C. 20431 (202) 623-7000; *International Financial Statistics.*

M.E. Sharpe, 80 Business Park Drive, Armonk, New York 10504 (800) 541-6563; *The Illustrated Book of World Rankings.*

St. Martin's Press, Inc., 175 Fifth Avenue, New York, New York 10010 (800) 221-7945; *The Statesman's Year-Book.*

Statistical Office of the United Nations, Publishing Service, New York, New York 10017 (800) 253-9646; *Statistical Yearbook.*

United Nations Economic Commission for Africa, Africa Hall, P.O. Box 3001, Addis Ababa, Ethiopia (Telephone Number in U.S. (800) 253-9646); *African Statistical Yearbook.*

TOGO - BARLEY PRODUCTION - See TOGO - CROPS

TOGO - BEER PRODUCTION - See TOGO - BEVERAGES

TOGO - BEVERAGES

M.E. Sharpe, 80 Business Park Drive, Armonk, New York 10504 (800) 541-6563; *The Illustrated Book of World Rankings.*

Statistical Office of the United Nations, Publishing Service, New York, New York 10017 (800) 253-9646; *Statistical Yearbook.*

TOGO - BIRTH RATES

Central Intelligence Agency, Washington, D.C. 20505 (703) 482-1100, www.cia.gov; *The World Factbook.*

Euromonitor International, Inc., 122 South Michigan Avenue, Suite 1200, Chicago, Illinois 60603 (800) 577-EURO; *International Marketing Data and Statistics;* and *The World Economic Factbook.*

Europa Publications Limited, 18 Bedford Square, London, WC1B 3JN, England; *The Europa World Year Book.*

M.E. Sharpe, 80 Business Park Drive, Armonk, New York 10504 (800) 541-6563; *The Illustrated Book of World Rankings.*

Statistical Office of the United Nations, Publishing Service, New York, New York 10017 (800) 253-9646; *Demographic Yearbook; Statistical Yearbook;* and *Survey of Economic and Social Conditions in Africa.*

The World Bank, 1818 H Street, NW, Washington, D.C. 20433 (202) 477-1234; *World Development Indicators.*

TOGO - BROADCASTING

Billboard Limited, P.O. Box 9027, 1006 AA Amsterdam, The Netherlands (Telephone Number in U.S. (212) 764-7300); *World Radio TV Handbook.*

Central Intelligence Agency, Washington, D.C. 20505 (703) 482-1100, www.cia.gov; *The World Factbook.*

Euromonitor International, Inc., 122 South Michigan Avenue, Suite 1200, Chicago, Illinois 60603 (800) 577-EURO; *World Marketing Data and Statistics.*

M.E. Sharpe, 80 Business Park Drive, Armonk, New York 10504 (800) 541-6563; *The Illustrated Book of World Rankings.*

St. Martin's Press, Inc., 175 Fifth Avenue, New York, New York 10010 (800) 221-7945; *The Statesman's Year-Book.*

United Nations Educational, Scientific and Cultural Organization (UNESCO), 7 Place de Fontenoy, F-75700 Paris, France (Telephone Number in U.S. (212) 963-5981); *Statistical Yearbook.*

TOGO - BUDGET

Central Intelligence Agency, Washington, D.C. 20505 (703) 482-1100, www.cia.gov; *The World Factbook.*

TOGO - BUSINESS AND PROFESSIONAL LICENSES

International Monetary Fund, 700 Nineteenth Street, NW, Washington, D.C. 20431 (202) 623-7000; *Government Finance*

Statistics Yearbook.

TOGO - CACAO EXPORTS - See TOGO - CROPS

TOGO - CALORIE SUPPLY

African Development Bank, 01 BP 1387, Abidjan 01, Cote D'Ivoire; *Selected Statistics on Regional Member Countries.*

Food and Agricultural Organization of the United Nations (FAO) Via delle Terme di Caracalla, 00100 Rome, Italy (Telephone Number in U.S. (202) 653-2400); *The State of Food and Agriculture.*

TOGO - CATTLE - See TOGO - LIVESTOCK AND POULTRY

TOGO - CEMENT PRODUCTION - See TOGO - MINING AND MINERAL PRODUCTS

TOGO - CHEMICAL (ORGANIC) PRODUCTION - See TOGO - MINING AND MINERAL PRODUCTS

TOGO - CHICKENS - See TOGO - LIVESTOCK AND POULTRY

TOGO - CIGARETTE PRODUCTION - See TOGO - TOBACCO PRODUCTION

TOGO - CLIMATE

M.E. Sharpe, 80 Business Park Drive, Armonk, New York 10504 (800) 541-6563; *The Illustrated Book of World Rankings.*

St. Martin's Press, Inc., 175 Fifth Avenue, New York, New York 10010 (800) 221-7945; *The Statesman's Year-Book.*

TOGO - COAL PRODUCTION - See TOGO - MINING AND MINERAL PRODUCTS

TOGO - COCOA (BEANS) PRODUCTION - See TOGO - CROPS

TOGO - COFFEE - See TOGO - CROPS

TOGO - COMMERCE

St. Martin's Press, Inc., 175 Fifth Avenue, New York, New York 10010 (800) 221-7945; *The Statesman's Year-Book.*

TOGO - COMMUNICATIONS - See TOGO - TRANSPORTATION AND COMMUNICATIONS

TOGO - CONSTRUCTION INDUSTRY

M.E. Sharpe, 80 Business Park Drive, Armonk, New York 10504 (800) 541-6563; *The Illustrated Book of World Rankings.*

St. Martin's Press, Inc., 175 Fifth Avenue, New York, New York 10010 (800) 221-7945; *The Statesman's Year-Book.*

Statistical Office of the United Nations, Publishing Service, New York, New York 10017 (800) 253-9646; *Statistical Yearbook.*

United Nations Economic Commission for Africa, Africa Hall, P.O. Box 3001, Addis Ababa, Ethiopia (Telephone Number in U.S. (800) 253-9646); *African Statistical Yearbook.*

TOGO - CONSUMER PRICE INDEX

African Development Bank, 01 BP 1387, Abidjan 01, Cote D'Ivoire; *Selected Statistics on Regional Member Countries.*

Europa Publications Limited, 18 Bedford Square, London, WC1B 3JN, England; *The Europa World Year Book.*

Statistical Office of the United Nations, Publishing Service, New York, New York 10017 (800) 253-9646; *Statistical Yearbook;* and *Survey of Economic and Social Conditions in Africa.*

United Nations Economic Commission for Africa, Africa Hall, P.O. Box 3001, Addis Ababa, Ethiopia (Telephone Number in U.S. (800) 253-9646); *African Statistical Yearbook.*

TOGO - CONSUMER PRICES

Euromonitor International, Inc., 122 South Michigan Avenue, Suite 1200, Chicago, Illinois 60603 (800) 577-EURO; *World Marketing Data and Statistics.*

International Labour Office, I.L.O. Publications, 1828 L Street, NW, Suite 801, Washington, D.C. 20036 (301) 638-3152; *Yearbook of Labour Statistics.*

International Monetary Fund, 700 Nineteenth Street, NW, Washington, D.C. 20431 (202) 623-7000; *International Financial Statistics.*

TOGO - CONSUMPTION

African Development Bank, 01 BP 1387, Abidjan 01, Cote D'Ivoire; *Selected Statistics on Regional Member Countries.*

Statistical Office of the United Nations, Publishing Service, New York, New York 10017 (800) 253-9646; *Survey of Economic and Social Conditions in Africa.*

The World Bank, 1818 H Street, NW, Washington, D.C. 20433 (202) 477-1234; *World Development Report.*

TOGO - COPPER PRODUCTION AND CONSUMPTION - See TOGO - MINING AND MINERAL PRODUCTS

TOGO - CORN PRODUCTION - See TOGO - CROPS

TOGO - CORPORATE TAXES - See TOGO - TAXATION

TOGO - COTTON - See TOGO - CROPS

TOGO - CROPS

Europa Publications Limited, 18 Bedford Square, London, WC1B 3JN, England; *The Europa World Year Book.*

Food and Agricultural Organization of the United Nations (FAO) Via delle Terme di Caracalla, 00100 Rome, Italy (Telephone Number in U.S. (202) 653-2400); *The State of Food and Agriculture.*

International Monetary Fund, 700 Nineteenth Street, NW, Washington, D.C. 20431 (202) 623-7000; *International Financial Statistics.*

M.E. Sharpe, 80 Business Park Drive, Armonk, New York 10504 (800) 541-6563; *The Illustrated Book of World Rankings.*

St. Martin's Press, Inc., 175 Fifth Avenue, New York, New York 10010 (800) 221-7945; *The Statesman's Year-Book.*

Statistical Office of the United Nations, Publishing Service, New York, New York 10017 (800) 253-9646; *Statistical Yearbook.*

United Nations Conference on Trade and Development, Central Statistical Service, Palais des Nations, Geneva, Switzerland (Telephone in U.S. (800) 253-9646); *UNCTAD Commodity Yearbook.*

United Nations Economic Commission for Africa, Africa Hall, P.O. Box 3001, Addis Ababa, Ethiopia (Telephone Number in U.S. (800) 253-9646); *African Statistical Yearbook.*

TOGO - CUSTOMS DUTIES

International Monetary Fund, 700 Nineteenth Street, NW, Washington, D.C. 20431 (202) 623-7000; *Government Finance Statistics Yearbook.*

St. Martin's Press, Inc., 175 Fifth Avenue, New York, New York 10010 (800) 221-7945; *The Statesman's Year-Book.*

TOGO - DAIRY PRODUCTS

Europa Publications Limited, 18 Bedford Square, London, WC1B 3JN, England; *The Europa World Year Book.*

Food and Agricultural Organization of the United Nations (FAO) Via delle Terme di Caracalla, 00100 Rome, Italy (Telephone Number in U.S. (202) 653-2400); *The State of Food and Agriculture.*

M.E. Sharpe, 80 Business Park Drive, Armonk, New York 10504 (800) 541-6563;

The Illustrated Book of World Rankings.

St. Martin's Press, Inc., 175 Fifth Avenue, New York, New York 10010 (800) 221-7945; *The Statesman's Year-Book.*

TOGO - DEATH RATES - See TOGO - MORTALITY

TOGO - DEFENSE EXPENDITURES - See TOGO - MILITARY

TOGO - DEMOGRAPHY

The Economist Intelligence Unit, 111 West 57th Street, New York, New York 10019 (800) 938-4685; *The World Market Atlas.*

Euromonitor International, Inc., 122 South Michigan Avenue, Suite 1200, Chicago, Illinois 60603 (800) 577-EURO; *International Marketing Data and Statistics; World Marketing Data and Statistics;* and *The World Economic Factbook.*

M.E. Sharpe, 80 Business Park Drive, Armonk, New York 10504 (800) 541-6563; *The Illustrated Book of World Rankings.*

Statistical Office of the United Nations, Publishing Service, New York, New York 10017 (800) 253-9646; *Human Development Report;* and *Survey of Economic and Social Conditions in Africa.*

TOGO - DEVELOPMENT ASSISTANCE

Statistical Office of the United Nations, Publishing Service, New York, New York 10017 (800) 253-9646; *Statistical Yearbook.*

TOGO - DIAMOND PRODUCTION - See TOGO - MINING AND MINERAL PRODUCTS

TOGO - DISCOUNT RATES - See TOGO - BANKING

TOGO - DISEASES - See TOGO - HEALTH

TOGO - DIVORCE RATES

M.E. Sharpe, 80 Business Park Drive, Armonk, New York 10504 (800) 541-6563; *The Illustrated Book of World Rankings.*

Statistical Office of the United Nations, Publishing Service, New York, New York 10017 (800) 253-9646; *Demographic Yearbook.*

TOGO - ECONOMY

African Development Bank, 01 BP 1387, Abidjan 01, Cote D'Ivoire; *Selected Statistics on Regional Member Countries.*

Central Intelligence Agency, Washington, D.C. 20505 (703) 482-1100, www.cia.gov; *The World Factbook.*

Economist Intelligence Unit, 111 West 57th Street, New York, New York 10019 (800) 938-4685; *Togo Country Report.*

Euromonitor International, Inc., 122 South Michigan Avenue, Suite 1200, Chicago, Illinois 60603 (800) 577-EURO; *International Marketing Data and Statistics; World Marketing Data and Statistics;* and *The World Economic Factbook.*

Europa Publications Limited, 18 Bedford Square, London, WC1B 3JN, England; *The Europa World Year Book.*

M.E. Sharpe, 80 Business Park Drive, Armonk, New York 10504 (800) 541-6563; *The Illustrated Book of World Rankings.*

St. Martin's Press, Inc., 175 Fifth Avenue, New York, New York 10010 (800) 221-7945; *The Statesman's Year-Book.*

Statistical Office of the United Nations, Publishing Service, New York, New York 10017 (800) 253-9646; *Foreign Trade Statistics for Africa;* and *World Statistics Pocketbook.*

The World Bank, 1818 H Street, NW, Washington, D.C. 20433 (202) 477-1234; *The World Bank Atlas;* and *World Development Report.*

TOGO - EDUCATION

African Development Bank, 01 BP 1387, Abidjan 01, Cote D'Ivoire; *Selected Statistics on Regional Member Countries.*

The Economist Intelligence Unit, 111 West 57th Street, New York, New York 10019 (800) 938-4685; *The World Market Atlas.*

Euromonitor International, Inc., 122 South Michigan Avenue, Suite 1200, Chicago, Illinois 60603 (800) 577-EURO; *International Marketing Data and Statistics;* and *World Marketing Data and Statistics.*

Europa Publications Limited, 18 Bedford Square, London, WC1B 3JN, England; *The Europa World Year Book.*

International Monetary Fund, 700 Nineteenth Street, NW, Washington, D.C. 20431 (202) 623-7000; *Government Finance Statistics Yearbook.*

M.E. Sharpe, 80 Business Park Drive, Armonk, New York 10504 (800) 541-6563; *The Illustrated Book of World Rankings.*

St. Martin's Press, Inc., 175 Fifth Avenue, New York, New York 10010 (800) 221-7945; *The Statesman's Year-Book.*

Statistical Office of the United Nations, Publishing Service, New York, New York 10017 (800) 253-9646; *Human*

Development Report; and *Survey of Economic and Social Conditions in Africa.*

United Nations Economic Commission for Africa, Africa Hall, P.O. Box 3001, Addis Ababa, Ethiopia (Telephone Number in U.S. (800) 253-9646); *African Statistical Yearbook.*

United Nations Educational, Scientific and Cultural Organization (UNESCO), 7 Place de Fontenoy, F-75700 Paris, France (Telephone Number in U.S. (212) 963-5981); *Statistical Yearbook.*

The World Bank, 1818 H Street, NW, Washington, D.C. 20433 (202) 477-1234; *World Development Report;* and *World Development Indicators.*

TOGO - EGG PRODUCTION AND CONSUMPTION - See TOGO - DAIRY PRODUCTS

TOGO - ELECTRICITY

Central Intelligence Agency, Washington, D.C. 20505 (703) 482-1100, www.cia.gov; *The World Factbook.*

M.E. Sharpe, 80 Business Park Drive, Armonk, New York 10504 (800) 541-6563; *The Illustrated Book of World Rankings.*

St. Martin's Press, Inc., 175 Fifth Avenue, New York, New York 10010 (800) 221-7945; *The Statesman's Year-Book.*

Statistical Office of the United Nations, Publishing Service, New York, New York 10017 (800) 253-9646; *Human Development Report; Statistical Yearbook;* and *Survey of Economic and Social Conditions in Africa.*

United Nations Economic Commission for Africa, Africa Hall, P.O. Box 3001, Addis Ababa, Ethiopia (Telephone Number in U.S. (800) 253-9646); *African Statistical Yearbook.*

TOGO - EMPLOYMENT

Euromonitor International, Inc., 122 South Michigan Avenue, Suite 1200, Chicago, Illinois 60603 (800) 577-EURO; *International Marketing Data and Statistics.*

International Labour Office, I.L.O. Publications, 1828 L Street, NW, Suite 801, Washington, D.C. 20036 (301) 638-3152; *Yearbook of Labour Statistics.*

M.E. Sharpe, 80 Business Park Drive, Armonk, New York 10504 (800) 541-6563; *The Illustrated Book of World Rankings.*

Statistical Office of the United Nations, Publishing Service, New York, New York 10017 (800) 253-9646; *Statistical Yearbook;* and *Survey of Economic and Social*

Conditions in Africa.

United Nations Economic Commission for Africa, Africa Hall, P.O. Box 3001, Addis Ababa, Ethiopia (Telephone Number in U.S. (800) 253-9646); *African Statistical Yearbook.*

TOGO - ENERGY

Euromonitor International, Inc., 122 South Michigan Avenue, Suite 1200, Chicago, Illinois 60603 (800) 577-EURO; *International Marketing Data and Statistics; World Marketing Data and Statistics;* and *The World Economic Factbook.*

Food and Agricultural Organization of the United Nations (FAO) Via delle Terme di Caracalla, 00100 Rome, Italy (Telephone Number in U.S. (202) 653-2400); *The State of Food and Agriculture.*

M.E. Sharpe, 80 Business Park Drive, Armonk, New York 10504 (800) 541-6563; *The Illustrated Book of World Rankings.*

St. Martin's Press, Inc., 175 Fifth Avenue, New York, New York 10010 (800) 221-7945; *The Statesman's Year-Book.*

Statistical Office of the United Nations, Publishing Service, New York, New York 10017 (800) 253-9646; *Energy Statistics Yearbook; Human Development Report; Statistical Yearbook;* and *World Statistics Pocketbook.*

United Nations Economic Commission for Africa, Africa Hall, P.O. Box 3001, Addis Ababa, Ethiopia (Telephone Number in U.S. (800) 253-9646); *African Statistical Yearbook.*

The World Bank, 1818 H Street, NW, Washington, D.C. 20433 (202) 477-1234; *The World Bank Atlas;* and *World Development Report.*

TOGO - ENVIRONMENT

Economist Intelligence Unit, 111 West 57th Street, New York, New York 10019 (800) 938-4685; *Togo Country Report.*

Statistical Office of the United Nations, Publishing Service, New York, New York 10017 (800) 253-9646; *World Statistics Pocketbook.*

TOGO - EXCHANGE RATES

Central Intelligence Agency, Washington, D.C. 20505 (703) 482-1100, www.cia.gov; *The World Factbook.*

Euromonitor International, Inc., 122 South Michigan Avenue, Suite 1200, Chicago, Illinois 60603 (800) 577-EURO; *International Marketing Data and Statistics;* and *The World Economic Factbook.*

Europa Publications Limited, 18 Bedford Square, London, WC1B 3JN, England; *The Europa World Year Book.*

International Monetary Fund, 700 Nineteenth Street, NW, Washington, D.C. 20431 (202) 623-7000; *International Financial Statistics.*

Statistical Office of the United Nations, Publishing Service, New York, New York 10017 (800) 253-9646; *Foreign Trade Statistics for Africa; Statistical Yearbook;* and *World Statistics Pocketbook.*

TOGO - EXCISE TAXES - See TOGO - TAXATION

TOGO - EXPORTS

African Development Bank, 01 BP 1387, Abidjan 01, Cote D'Ivoire; *Selected Statistics on Regional Member Countries.*

Central Intelligence Agency, Washington, D.C. 20505 (703) 482-1100, www.cia.gov; *The World Factbook.*

The Economist Intelligence Unit, 111 West 57th Street, New York, New York 10019 (800) 938-4685; *Togo Country Report;* and *The World Market Atlas.*

Euromonitor International, Inc., 122 South Michigan Avenue, Suite 1200, Chicago, Illinois 60603 (800) 577-EURO; *International Marketing Data and Statistics;* and *The World Economic Factbook.*

Europa Publications Limited, 18 Bedford Square, London, WC1B 3JN, England; *The Europa World Year Book.*

Food and Agricultural Organization of the United Nations (FAO) Via delle Terme di Caracalla, 00100 Rome, Italy (Telephone Number in U.S. (202) 653-2400); *The State of Food and Agriculture.*

International Monetary Fund, 700 Nineteenth Street, NW, Washington, D.C. 20431 (202) 623-7000; *Direction of Trade Statistics; Government Finance Statistics Yearbook;* and *International Financial Statistics.*

St. Martin's Press, Inc., 175 Fifth Avenue, New York, New York 10010 (800) 221-7945; *The Statesman's Year-Book.*

Statistical Office of the United Nations, Publishing Service, New York, New York 10017 (800) 253-9646; *Foreign Trade Statistics for Africa;* and *Survey of Economic and Social Conditions in Africa.*

United Nations Conference on Trade and Development (UNCTAD), New York, New York 10017 (800) 253-9646; *Handbook of International Trade and Development Statistics.*

United Nations Economic Commission for Africa, Africa Hall, P.O. Box 3001, Addis Ababa, Ethiopia (Telephone Number in U.S. (800) 253-9646); *African Statistical Yearbook.*

The World Bank, 1818 H Street, NW, Washington, D.C. 20433 (202) 477-1234; *World Development Report;* and *World Development Indicators.*

TOGO - EXTERNAL INDEBTEDNESS

African Development Bank, 01 BP 1387, Abidjan 01, Cote D'Ivoire; *Selected Statistics on Regional Member Countries.*

Statistical Office of the United Nations, Publishing Service, New York, New York 10017 (800) 253-9646; *Survey of Economic and Social Conditions in Africa.*

The World Bank, 1818 H Street, NW, Washington, D.C. 20433 (202) 477-1234; *World Development Report;* and *World Development Indicators.*

TOGO - EXTERNAL TRADE

African Development Bank, 01 BP 1387, Abidjan 01, Cote D'Ivoire; *Selected Statistics on Regional Member Countries.*

Euromonitor International, Inc., 122 South Michigan Avenue, Suite 1200, Chicago, Illinois 60603 (800) 577-EURO; *World Marketing Data and Statistics.*

Food and Agricultural Organization of the United Nations (FAO) Via delle Terme di Caracalla, 00100 Rome, Italy (Telephone Number in U.S. (202) 653-2400); *The State of Food and Agriculture;* and *Trade Yearbook.*

Statistical Office of the United Nations, Publishing Service, New York, New York 10017 (800) 253-9646; *Statistical Yearbook.*

TOGO - FABRIC PRODUCTION - See TOGO - TEXTILE INDUSTRY

TOGO - FARM CROPS - See TOGO - CROPS

TOGO - FEMALE WORKING POPULATION - See TOGO - EMPLOYMENT

TOGO - FERTILITY RATES

Central Intelligence Agency, Washington, D.C. 20505 (703) 482-1100, www.cia.gov; *The World Factbook.*

M.E. Sharpe, 80 Business Park Drive, Armonk, New York 10504 (800) 541-6563; *The Illustrated Book of World Rankings.*

Statistical Office of the United Nations, Publishing Service, New York, New York 10017 (800) 253-9646; *Human Development Report;* and *Survey of*

Economic and Social Conditions in Africa.

The World Bank, 1818 H Street, NW, Washington, D.C. 20433 (202) 477-1234; *The World Bank Atlas; World Development Report;* and *World Development Indicators.*

TOGO - FERTILIZER

Food and Agricultural Organization of the United Nations (FAO), Via delle Terme di Caracalla, 00100, Rome, Italy (Telephone Number in U.S. (202) 653-2400); *Fertilizer Yearbook;* and *The State of Food and Agriculture.*

Statistical Office of the United Nations, Publishing Service, New York, New York 10017 (800) 253-9646; *Statistical Yearbook.*

TOGO - FETAL MORTALITY - See TOGO - MORTALITY

TOGO - FINANCE

African Development Bank, 01 BP 1387, Abidjan 01, Cote D'Ivoire; *Selected Statistics on Regional Member Countries.*

Economist Intelligence Unit, 111 West 57th Street, New York, New York 10019 (800) 938-4685; *Togo Country Report.*

Europa Publications Limited, 18 Bedford Square, London, WC1B 3JN, England; *The Europa World Year Book.*

M.E. Sharpe, 80 Business Park Drive, Armonk, New York 10504 (800) 541-6563; *The Illustrated Book of World Rankings.*

St. Martin's Press, Inc., 175 Fifth Avenue, New York, New York 10010 (800) 221-7945; *The Statesman's Year-Book.*

United Nations Economic Commission for Africa, Africa Hall, P.O. Box 3001, Addis Ababa, Ethiopia (Telephone Number in U.S. (800) 253-9646); *African Statistical Yearbook.*

TOGO - FISHERIES

Europa Publications Limited, 18 Bedford Square, London, WC1B 3JN, England; *The Europa World Year Book.*

Food and Agricultural Organization of the United Nations (FAO) Via delle Terme di Caracalla, 00100 Rome, Italy (Telephone Number in U.S. (202) 653-2400); *The State of Food and Agriculture;* and *Yearbook of Fishery Statistics.*

M.E. Sharpe, 80 Business Park Drive, Armonk, New York 10504 (800) 541-6563; *The Illustrated Book of World Rankings.*

St. Martin's Press, Inc., 175 Fifth Avenue, New York, New York 10010 (800) 221-7945; *The Statesman's Year-Book.*

Statistical Office of the United Nations, Publishing Service, New York, New York 10017 (800) 253-9646; *Statistical Yearbook;* and *Survey of Economic and Social Conditions in Africa.*

United Nations Conference on Trade and Development, Central Statistical Service, Palais des Nations, Geneva, Switzerland (Telephone in U.S. (800) 253-9646); *UNCTAD Commodity Yearbook.*

United Nations Economic Commission for Africa, Africa Hall, P.O. Box 3001, Addis Ababa, Ethiopia (Telephone Number in U.S. (800) 253-9646); *African Statistical Yearbook.*

TOGO - FOOD

African Development Bank, 01 BP 1387, Abidjan 01, Cote D'Ivoire; *Selected Statistics on Regional Member Countries.*

Food and Agricultural Organization of the United Nations (FAO) Via delle Terme di Caracalla, 00100 Rome, Italy (Telephone Number in U.S. (202) 653-2400); *Production Yearbook;* and *The State of Food and Agriculture.*

Statistical Office of the United Nations, Publishing Service, New York, New York 10017 (800) 253-9646; *Human Development Report.*

United Nations Conference on Trade and Development, Central Statistical Service, Palais des Nations, Geneva, Switzerland (Telephone in U.S. (800) 253-9646); *UNCTAD Commodity Yearbook.*

TOGO - FOREIGN TRADE

Economist Intelligence Unit, 111 West 57th Street, New York, New York 10019 (800) 938-4685; *Togo Country Report.*

Euromonitor International, Inc., 122 South Michigan Avenue, Suite 1200, Chicago, Illinois 60603 (800) 577-EURO; *International Marketing Data and Statistics;* and *The World Economic Factbook.*

Europa Publications Limited, 18 Bedford Square, London, WC1B 3JN, England; *The Europa World Year Book.*

Food and Agricultural Organization of the United Nations (FAO) Via delle Terme di Caracalla, 00100 Rome, Italy (Telephone Number in U.S. (202) 653-2400); *The State of Food and Agriculture.*

International Monetary Fund, 700 Nineteenth Street, NW, Washington, D.C. 20431 (202) 623-7000; *International Financial Statistics.*

M.E. Sharpe, 80 Business Park Drive, Armonk, New York 10504 (800) 541-6563;

The Illustrated Book of World Rankings.

St. Martin's Press, Inc., 175 Fifth Avenue, New York, New York 10010 (800) 221-7945; *The Statesman's Year-Book.*

Statistical Office of the United Nations, Publishing Service, New York, New York 10017 (800) 253-9646; *Foreign Trade Statistics for Africa; International Trade Statistics Yearbook;* and *Statistical Yearbook.*

United Nations Conference on Trade and Development, Central Statistical Service, Palais des Nations, Geneva, Switzerland (Telephone in U.S. (800) 253-9646); *UNCTAD Commodity Yearbook.*

United Nations Economic Commission for Africa, Africa Hall, P.O. Box 3001, Addis Ababa, Ethiopia (Telephone Number in U.S. (800) 253-9646); *African Statistical Yearbook.*

The World Bank, 1818 H Street, NW, Washington, D.C. 20433 (202) 477-1234; *World Development Report;* and *World Development Indicators.*

TOGO - FORESTRY AND FOREST PRODUCTS

Europa Publications Limited, 18 Bedford Square, London, WC1B 3JN, England; *The Europa World Year Book.*

Food and Agricultural Organization of the United Nations (FAO) Via delle Terme di Caracalla, 00100 Rome, Italy (Telephone Number in U.S. (202) 653-2400); *The State of Food and Agriculture;* and *Yearbook of Forest Products.*

M.E. Sharpe, 80 Business Park Drive, Armonk, New York 10504 (800) 541-6563; *The Illustrated Book of World Rankings.*

St. Martin's Press, Inc., 175 Fifth Avenue, New York, New York 10010 (800) 221-7945; *The Statesman's Year-Book.*

Statistical Office of the United Nations, Publishing Service, New York, New York 10017 (800) 253-9646; *Statistical Yearbook.*

United Nations Economic Commission for Africa, Africa Hall, P.O. Box 3001, Addis Ababa, Ethiopia (Telephone Number in U.S. (800) 253-9646); *African Statistical Yearbook.*

United Nations Educational, Scientific and Cultural Organization (UNESCO), 7 Place de Fontenoy, F-75700 Paris, France (Telephone Number in U.S. (212) 963-5981); *Statistical Yearbook.*

The World Bank, 1818 H Street, NW, Washington, D.C. 20433 (202) 477-1234; *World Development Report.*

TOGO - GAS PRODUCTION - See TOGO - MINING AND MINERAL PRODUCTS

TOGO - GENERAL INDUSTRIAL STATISTICS - See TOGO - INDUSTRY

TOGO - GENERAL MORTALITY - See TOGO - MORTALITY

TOGO - GEOGRAPHIC DATA

M.E. Sharpe, 80 Business Park Drive, Armonk, New York 10504 (800) 541-6563; *The Illustrated Book of World Rankings.*

TOGO - GOATS - See TOGO - LIVESTOCK AND POULTRY

TOGO - GOLD HOLDINGS

International Monetary Fund, 700 Nineteenth Street, NW, Washington, D.C. 20431 (202) 623-7000; *International Financial Statistics.*

Statistical Office of the United Nations, Publishing Service, New York, New York 10017 (800) 253-9646; *Statistical Yearbook.*

The World Bank, 1818 H Street, NW, Washington, D.C. 20433 (202) 477-1234; *World Development Indicators.*

TOGO - GOLD PRODUCTION AND CONSUMPTION - See TOGO - MINING AND MINERAL PRODUCTS

TOGO - GOVERNMENT

Central Intelligence Agency, Washington, D.C. 20505 (703) 482-1100, www.cia.gov; *The World Factbook.*

Europa Publications Limited, 18 Bedford Square, London, WC1B 3JN, England; *The Europa World Year Book.*

International Monetary Fund, 700 Nineteenth Street, NW, Washington, D.C. 20431 (202) 623-7000; *Government Finance Statistics Yearbook;* and *International Financial Statistics.*

St. Martin's Press, Inc., 175 Fifth Avenue, New York, New York 10010 (800) 221-7945; *The Statesman's Year-Book.*

Statistical Office of the United Nations, Publishing Service, New York, New York 10017 (800) 253-9646; *National Accounts Statistics; Statistical Yearbook;* and *Survey of Economic and Social Conditions in Africa.*

The World Bank, 1818 H Street, NW, Washington, D.C. 20433 (202) 477-1234; *World Development Report;* and *World Development Indicators.*

TOGO - GRAIN PRODUCTION - See TOGO - CROPS

TOGO - GROSS DOMESTIC PRODUCT

African Development Bank, 01 BP 1387, Abidjan 01, Cote D'Ivoire; *Selected Statistics on Regional Member Countries.*

The Economist Intelligence Unit, 111 West 57th Street, New York, New York 10019 (800) 938-4685; *Togo Country Report;* and *The World Market Atlas.*

Euromonitor International, Inc., 122 South Michigan Avenue, Suite 1200, Chicago, Illinois 60603 (800) 577-EURO; *International Marketing Data and Statistics;* and *The World Economic Factbook.*

Europa Publications Limited, 18 Bedford Square, London, WC1B 3JN, England; *The Europa World Year Book.*

M.E. Sharpe, 80 Business Park Drive, Armonk, New York 10504 (800) 541-6563; *The Illustrated Book of World Rankings.*

Statistical Office of the United Nations, Publishing Service, New York, New York 10017 (800) 253-9646; *Human Development Report; National Accounts Statistics; Statistical Yearbook;* and *Survey of Economic and Social Conditions in Africa.*

United Nations Economic Commission for Africa, Africa Hall, P.O. Box 3001, Addis Ababa, Ethiopia (Telephone Number in U.S. (800) 253-9646); *African Statistical Yearbook.*

The World Bank, 1818 H Street, NW, Washington, D.C. 20433 (202) 477-1234; *World Development Report;* and *World Development Indicators.*

TOGO - GROSS NATIONAL PRODUCT

Euromonitor International, Inc., 122 South Michigan Avenue, Suite 1200, Chicago, Illinois 60603 (800) 577-EURO; *International Marketing Data and Statistics.*

St. Martin's Press, Inc., 175 Fifth Avenue, New York, New York 10010 (800) 221-7945; *The Statesman's Year-Book.*

U.S. Arms Control and Disarmament Agency, 320 Twenty-first Street, NW, Washington, D.C. 20451 (202) 647-8677; *World Military Expenditures and Arms Transfers.*

The World Bank, 1818 H Street, NW, Washington, D.C. 20433 (202) 477-1234; *The World Bank Atlas; World Development Report;* and *World Development Indicators.*

TOGO - GROUNDNUTS PRODUCTION - See TOGO - CROPS

TOGO - HEALTH

African Development Bank, 01 BP 1387, Abidjan 01, Cote D'Ivoire; *Selected Statistics on Regional Member Countries.*

Euromonitor International, Inc., 122 South Michigan Avenue, Suite 1200, Chicago, Illinois 60603 (800) 577-EURO; *World Marketing Data and Statistics.*

M.E. Sharpe, 80 Business Park Drive, Armonk, New York 10504 (800) 541-6563; *The Illustrated Book of World Rankings.*

St. Martin's Press, Inc., 175 Fifth Avenue, New York, New York 10010 (800) 221-7945; *The Statesman's Year-Book.*

Statistical Office of the United Nations, Publishing Service, New York, New York 10017 (800) 253-9646; *Human Development Report;* and *Statistical Yearbook.*

United Nations Children's Fund (UNICEF), 3 United Nations Plaza, New York, New York 10017 (800) 253-9646; *State of the World's Children.*

United Nations Economic Commission for Africa, Africa Hall, P.O. Box 3001, Addis Ababa, Ethiopia (Telephone Number in U.S. (800) 253-9646); *African Statistical Yearbook.*

The World Bank, 1818 H Street, NW, Washington, D.C. 20433 (202) 477-1234; *World Development Report.*

World Health Organization, Office of Publications, 20 Avenue Appia, CH-1211 Geneva 27, Switzerland (Telephone Number in U.S. (518) 436-9686); *World Health Statistics Annual.*

TOGO - HEALTH EXPENDITURES

International Monetary Fund, 700 Nineteenth Street, NW, Washington, D.C. 20431 (202) 623-7000; *Government Finance Statistics Yearbook.*

TOGO - HIGHWAYS

Central Intelligence Agency, Washington, D.C. 20505 (703) 482-1100, www.cia.gov; *The World Factbook.*

International Road Federation, 2600 Virginia Avenue, NW, Washington, D.C. 20037 (202) 338-4641; *World Road Statistics.*

St. Martin's Press, Inc., 175 Fifth Avenue, New York, New York 10010 (800) 221-7945; *The Statesman's Year-Book.*

Statistical Office of the United Nations, Publishing Service, New York, New York 10017 (800) 253-9646; *Survey of Economic and Social Conditions in Africa.*

United Nations Economic Commission for Africa, Africa Hall, P.O. Box 3001, Addis Ababa, Ethiopia (Telephone Number in U.S. (800) 253-9646); *African Statistical Yearbook.*

TOGO - HORSES - See TOGO - LIVESTOCK AND POULTRY

TOGO - HOURS OF WORK - See TOGO - EMPLOYMENT

TOGO - HOUSING AND HOUSING UNITS

Euromonitor International, Inc., 122 South Michigan Avenue, Suite 1200, Chicago, Illinois 60603 (800) 577-EURO; *World Marketing Data and Statistics.*

M.E. Sharpe, 80 Business Park Drive, Armonk, New York 10504 (800) 541-6563; *The Illustrated Book of World Rankings.*

TOGO - HOUSING EXPENDITURES

International Monetary Fund, 700 Nineteenth Street, NW, Washington, D.C. 20431 (202) 623-7000; *Government Finance Statistics Yearbook.*

TOGO - ILLITERATE POPULATION

Central Intelligence Agency, Washington, D.C. 20505 (703) 482-1100, www.cia.gov; *The World Factbook.*

The Economist Intelligence Unit, 111 West 57th Street, New York, New York 10019 (800) 938-4685; *The World Market Atlas.*

Euromonitor International, Inc., 122 South Michigan Avenue, Suite 1200, Chicago, Illinois 60603 (800) 577-EURO; *The World Economic Factbook.*

St. Martin's Press, Inc., 175 Fifth Avenue, New York, New York 10010 (800) 221-7945; *The Statesman's Year-Book.*

Statistical Office of the United Nations, Publishing Service, New York, New York 10017 (800) 253-9646; *Human Development Report.*

United Nations Educational, Scientific and Cultural Organization (UNESCO), 7 Place de Fontenoy, F-75700 Paris, France (Telephone Number in U.S. (212) 963-5981); *Statistical Yearbook.*

TOGO - IMPORTS

African Development Bank, 01 BP 1387, Abidjan 01, Cote D'Ivoire; *Selected Statistics on Regional Member Countries.*

Central Intelligence Agency, Washington, D.C. 20505 (703) 482-1100, www.cia.gov; *The World Factbook.*

The Economist Intelligence Unit, 111 West 57th Street, New York, New York 10019 (800) 938-4685; *Togo Country Report;* and *The World Market Atlas.*

Euromonitor International, Inc., 122 South Michigan Avenue, Suite 1200, Chicago, Illinois 60603 (800) 577-EURO; *International Marketing Data and Statistics;* and *The World Economic Factbook.*

Europa Publications Limited, 18 Bedford Square, London, WC1B 3JN, England; *The Europa World Year Book.*

Food and Agricultural Organization of the United Nations (FAO) Via delle Terme di Caracalla, 00100 Rome, Italy (Telephone Number in U.S. (202) 653-2400); *The State of Food and Agriculture.*

International Monetary Fund, 700 Nineteenth Street, NW, Washington, D.C. 20431 (202) 623-7000; *Direction of Trade Statistics; Government Finance Statistics Yearbook;* and *International Financial Statistics.*

St. Martin's Press, Inc., 175 Fifth Avenue, New York, New York 10010 (800) 221-7945; *The Statesman's Year-Book.*

Statistical Office of the United Nations, Publishing Service, New York, New York 10017 (800) 253-9646; *Foreign Trade Statistics for Africa, Survey of Economic and Social Conditions in Africa.*

United Nations Conference on Trade and Development (UNCTAD), New York, New York 10017 (800) 253-9646; *Handbook of International Trade and Development Statistics.*

United Nations Economic Commission for Africa, Africa Hall, P.O. Box 3001, Addis Ababa, Ethiopia (Telephone Number in U.S. (800) 253-9646); *African Statistical Yearbook.*

The World Bank, 1818 H Street, NW, Washington, D.C. 20433 (202) 477-1234; *World Development Report;* and *World Development Indicators.*

TOGO - INCOME TAXES - See TOGO - TAXATION

TOGO - INDUSTRY

Central Intelligence Agency, Washington, D.C. 20505 (703) 482-1100, www.cia.gov; *The World Factbook.*

Economist Intelligence Unit, 111 West 57th Street, New York, New York 10019 (800) 938-4685; *Togo Country Report.*

Euromonitor International, Inc., 122 South Michigan Avenue, Suite 1200, Chicago, Illinois 60603 (800) 577-EURO;

International Marketing Data and Statistics; World Marketing Data and Statistics; and *The World Economic Factbook.*

Europa Publications Limited, 18 Bedford Square, London, WC1B 3JN, England; *The Europa World Year Book.*

International Labour Office, I.L.O. Publications, 1828 L Street, NW, Suite 801, Washington, D.C. 20036 (301) 638-3152; *Yearbook of Labour Statistics.*

M.E. Sharpe, 80 Business Park Drive, Armonk, New York 10504 (800) 541-6563; *The Illustrated Book of World Rankings.*

St. Martin's Press, Inc., 175 Fifth Avenue, New York, New York 10010 (800) 221-7945; *The Statesman's Year-Book.*

Statistical Office of the United Nations, Publishing Service, New York, New York 10017 (800) 253-9646; *Industrial Commodity Statistics Yearbook;* and *Survey of Economic and Social Conditions in Africa.*

United Nations Economic Commission for Africa, Africa Hall, P.O. Box 3001, Addis Ababa, Ethiopia (Telephone Number in U.S. (800) 253-9646); *African Statistical Yearbook.*

The World Bank, 1818 H Street, NW, Washington, D.C. 20433 (202) 477-1234; *World Development Indicators.*

TOGO - INFANT AND MATERNAL MORTALITY - See TOGO - MORTALITY

TOGO - INTERNAL TRADE

Statistical Office of the United Nations, Publishing Service, New York, New York 10017 (800) 253-9646; *Statistical Yearbook.*

TOGO - INTERNATIONAL LIQUIDITY

International Monetary Fund, 700 Nineteenth Street, NW, Washington, D.C. 20431 (202) 623-7000; *International Financial Statistics.*

TOGO - INTERNATIONAL RESERVES EXCLUDING GOLD

African Development Bank, 01 BP 1387, Abidjan 01, Cote D'Ivoire; *Selected Statistics on Regional Member Countries.*

Statistical Office of the United Nations, Publishing Service, New York, New York 10017 (800) 253-9646; *Statistical Yearbook.*

The World Bank, 1818 H Street, NW, Washington, D.C. 20433 (202) 477-1234; *World Development Indicators.*

TOGO - IRON ORE PRODUCTION AND

CONSUMPTION - See TOGO - MINING AND MINERAL PRODUCTS

TOGO - IRRIGATION

Euromonitor International, Inc., 122 South Michigan Avenue, Suite 1200, Chicago, Illinois 60603 (800) 577-EURO; *International Marketing Data and Statistics.*

TOGO - LABOR

African Development Bank, 01 BP 1387, Abidjan 01, Cote D'Ivoire; *Selected Statistics on Regional Member Countries.*

Central Intelligence Agency, Washington, D.C. 20505 (703) 482-1100, www.cia.gov; *The World Factbook.*

Euromonitor International, Inc., 122 South Michigan Avenue, Suite 1200, Chicago, Illinois 60603 (800) 577-EURO; *International Marketing Data and Statistics;* and *World Marketing Data and Statistics.*

Europa Publications Limited, 18 Bedford Square, London, WC1B 3JN, England; *The Europa World Year Book.*

Food and Agricultural Organization of the United Nations (FAO) Via delle Terme di Caracalla, 00100 Rome, Italy (Telephone Number in U.S. (202) 653-2400); *The State of Food and Agriculture.*

International Labour Office, I.L.O. Publications, 1828 L Street, NW, Suite 801, Washington, D.C. 20036 (301) 638-3152; *Yearbook of Labour Statistics.*

M.E. Sharpe, 80 Business Park Drive, Armonk, New York 10504 (800) 541-6563; *The Illustrated Book of World Rankings.*

St. Martin's Press, Inc., 175 Fifth Avenue, New York, New York 10010 (800) 221-7945; *The Statesman's Year-Book.*

Statistical Office of the United Nations, Publishing Service, New York, New York 10017 (800) 253-9646; *Human Development Report.*

The World Bank, 1818 H Street, NW, Washington, D.C. 20433 (202) 477-1234; *The World Bank Atlas; World Development Report;* and *World Development Indicators.*

TOGO - LAND USE

Central Intelligence Agency, Washington, D.C. 20505 (703) 482-1100, www.cia.gov; *The World Factbook.*

Euromonitor International, Inc., 122 South Michigan Avenue, Suite 1200, Chicago, Illinois 60603 (800) 577-EURO; *International Marketing Data and Statistics.*

Food and Agricultural Organization of

the United Nations (FAO), Via delle Terme di Caracalla, 00100 Rome, Italy (Telephone Number in U.S. (202) 653-2400); *Production Yearbook.*

The World Bank, 1818 H Street, NW, Washington, D.C. 20433 (202) 477-1234; *World Development Report.*

TOGO - LIBRARIES

M.E. Sharpe, 80 Business Park Drive, Armonk, New York 10504 (800) 541-6563; *The Illustrated Book of World Rankings.*

United Nations Educational, Scientific and Cultural Organization (UNESCO), 7 Place de Fontenoy, F-75700 Paris, France (Telephone Number in U.S. (212) 963-5981); *Statistical Yearbook.*

TOGO - LIFE EXPECTANCY

African Development Bank, 01 BP 1387, Abidjan 01, Cote D'Ivoire; *Selected Statistics on Regional Member Countries.*

Central Intelligence Agency, Washington, D.C. 20505 (703) 482-1100, www.cia.gov; *The World Factbook.*

Euromonitor International, Inc., 122 South Michigan Avenue, Suite 1200, Chicago, Illinois 60603 (800) 577-EURO; *The World Economic Factbook.*

Statistical Office of the United Nations, Publishing Service, New York, New York 10017 (800) 253-9646; *Human Development Report;* and *World Statistics Pocketbook.*

The World Bank, 1818 H Street, NW, Washington, D.C. 20433 (202) 477-1234; *The World Bank Atlas;* and *World Development Report.*

TOGO - LITERACY RATE

Euromonitor International, Inc., 122 South Michigan Avenue, Suite 1200, Chicago, Illinois 60603 (800) 577-EURO; *World Marketing Data and Statistics.*

Statistical Office of the United Nations, Publishing Service, New York, New York 10017 (800) 253-9646; *Survey of Economic and Social Conditions in Africa.*

TOGO - LIVESTOCK AND POULTRY

Euromonitor International, Inc., 122 South Michigan Avenue, Suite 1200, Chicago, Illinois 60603 (800) 577-EURO; *International Marketing Data and Statistics.*

Europa Publications Limited, 18 Bedford Square, London, WC1B 3JN, England; *The Europa World Year Book.*

Food and Agricultural Organization of

the United Nations (FAO), Via delle Terme di Caracalla, 00100 Rome, Italy (Telephone Number in U.S. (202) 653-2400); *Production Yearbook;* and *The State of Food and Agriculture.*

M.E. Sharpe, 80 Business Park Drive, Armonk, New York 10504 (800) 541-6563; *The Illustrated Book of World Rankings.*

St. Martin's Press, Inc., 175 Fifth Avenue, New York, New York 10010 (800) 221-7945; *The Statesman's Year-Book.*

Statistical Office of the United Nations, Publishing Service, New York, New York 10017 (800) 253-9646; *Statistical Yearbook;* and *Survey of Economic and Social Conditions in Africa.*

United Nations Conference on Trade and Development, Central Statistical Service, Palais des Nations, Geneva, Switzerland (Telephone in U.S. (800) 253-9646); *UNCTAD Commodity Yearbook.*

United Nations Economic Commission for Africa, Africa Hall, P.O. Box 3001, Addis Ababa, Ethiopia (Telephone Number in U.S. (800) 253-9646); *African Statistical Yearbook.*

TOGO - MAIL - PIECES SENT OR RECEIVED

Statistical Office of the United Nations, Publishing Service, New York, New York 10017 (800) 253-9646; *Statistical Yearbook.*

TOGO - MANUFACTURING

M.E. Sharpe, 80 Business Park Drive, Armonk, New York 10504 (800) 541-6563; *The Illustrated Book of World Rankings.*

Statistical Office of the United Nations, Publishing Service, New York, New York 10017 (800) 253-9646; *Statistical Yearbook;* and *Survey of Economic and Social Conditions in Africa.*

United Nations Economic Commission for Africa, Africa Hall, P.O. Box 3001, Addis Ababa, Ethiopia (Telephone Number in U.S. (800) 253-9646); *African Statistical Yearbook.*

The World Bank, 1818 H Street, NW, Washington, D.C. 20433 (202) 477-1234; *World Development Indicators.*

TOGO - MARRIAGE RATES

M.E. Sharpe, 80 Business Park Drive, Armonk, New York 10504 (800) 541-6563; *The Illustrated Book of World Rankings.*

Statistical Office of the United Nations, Publishing Service, New York, New York 10017 (800) 253-9646; *Demographic Yearbook;* and *Statistical Yearbook.*

TOGO - MEAT PRODUCTION - See
TOGO - LIVESTOCK AND POULTRY

TOGO - MERCHANT SHIPPING

Europa Publications Limited, 18
Bedford Square, London, WC1B 3JN,
England; *The Europa World Year Book*.

St. Martin's Press, Inc., 175 Fifth
Avenue, New York, New York 10010 (800)
221-7945; *The Statesman's Year-Book*.

Statistical Office of the United Nations,
Publishing Service, New York, New York
10017 (800) 253-9646; *Statistical Yearbook*.

United Nations Economic Commission
for Africa, Africa Hall, P.O. Box 3001, Addis
Ababa, Ethiopia (Telephone Number in
U.S. (800) 253-9646); *African Statistical
Yearbook*.

TOGO - MILITARY

Central Intelligence Agency,
Washington, D.C. 20505 (703) 482-1100,
www.cia.gov; *The World Factbook*.

Euromonitor International, Inc., 122
South Michigan Avenue, Suite 1200,
Chicago, Illinois 60603 (800) 577-EURO;
World Marketing Data and Statistics.

The International Institute for Strategic
Studies, 23 Tavistock Street, London WC2E
7NQ, England 44 171 3797676; *The Military
Balance*.

International Monetary Fund, 700
Nineteenth Street, NW, Washington, D.C.
20431 (202) 623-7000; *Government Finance
Statistics Yearbook*.

St. Martin's Press, Inc., 175 Fifth
Avenue, New York, New York 10010 (800)
221-7945; *The Statesman's Year-Book*.

Statistical Office of the United Nations,
Publishing Service, New York, New York
10017 (800) 253-9646; *Human
Development Report*.

U.S. Arms Control and Disarmament
Agency, 320 Twenty-first Street, NW,
Washington, D.C. 20451 (202) 647-8677;
*World Military Expenditures and Arms
Transfers*.

TOGO - MILK - See TOGO - DAIRY
PRODUCTS

TOGO - MINING AND MINERAL PRODUCTS

Europa Publications Limited, 18
Bedford Square, London, WC1B 3JN,
England; *The Europa World Year Book*.

International Monetary Fund, 700
Nineteenth Street, NW, Washington, D.C.
20431 (202) 623-7000; *International*

Financial Statistics.

M.E. Sharpe, 80 Business Park Drive,
Armonk, New York 10504 (800) 541-6563;
The Illustrated Book of World Rankings.

St. Martin's Press, Inc., 175 Fifth
Avenue, New York, New York 10010 (800)
221-7945; *The Statesman's Year-Book*.

Statistical Office of the United Nations,
Publishing Service, New York, New York
10017 (800) 253-9646; *Statistical Yearbook*.

United Nations Conference on Trade
and Development, Central Statistical
Service, Palais des Nations, Geneva,
Switzerland (Telephone in U.S. (800) 253-
9646); *UNCTAD Commodity Yearbook*.

United Nations Economic Commission
for Africa, Africa Hall, P.O. Box 3001, Addis
Ababa, Ethiopia (Telephone Number in
U.S. (800) 253-9646); *African Statistical
Yearbook*.

TOGO - MONEY EXCHANGE RATE - See
TOGO - EXCHANGE RATES

TOGO - MONEY RESERVES

Euromonitor International, Inc., 122
South Michigan Avenue, Suite 1200,
Chicago, Illinois 60603 (800) 577-EURO;
International Marketing Data and Statistics.

TOGO - MONEY SUPPLY

African Development Bank, 01 BP 1387,
Abidjan 01, Cote D'Ivoire; *Selected
Statistics on Regional Member Countries*.

Economist Intelligence Unit, 111 West
57th Street, New York, New York 10019
(800) 938-4685; *Togo Country Report*.

Euromonitor International, Inc., 122
South Michigan Avenue, Suite 1200,
Chicago, Illinois 60603 (800) 577-EURO;
International Marketing Data and Statistics.

Europa Publications Limited, 18
Bedford Square, London, WC1B 3JN,
England; *The Europa World Year Book*.

International Monetary Fund, 700
Nineteenth Street, NW, Washington, D.C.
20431 (202) 623-7000; *International
Financial Statistics*.

Statistical Office of the United Nations,
Publishing Service, New York, New York
10017 (800) 253-9646; *Statistical Yearbook*.

The World Bank, 1818 H Street, NW,
Washington, D.C. 20433 (202) 477-1234;
World Development Indicators.

TOGO - MORTALITY

Central Intelligence Agency,

Washington, D.C. 20505 (703) 482-1100,
www.cia.gov; *The World Factbook*.

Euromonitor International, Inc., 122
South Michigan Avenue, Suite 1200,
Chicago, Illinois 60603 (800) 577-EURO;
International Marketing Data and Statistics;
and *The World Economic Factbook*.

Europa Publications Limited, 18
Bedford Square, London, WC1B 3JN,
England; *The Europa World Year Book*.

St. Martin's Press, Inc., 175 Fifth
Avenue, New York, New York 10010 (800)
221-7945; *The Statesman's Year-Book*.

Statistical Office of the United Nations,
Publishing Service, New York, New York
10017 (800) 253-9646; *Demographic
Yearbook; Human Development Report;
Statistical Yearbook; Survey of Economic
and Social Conditions in Africa;* and *World
Statistics Pocketbook*.

United Nations Children's Fund
(UNICEF), 3 United Nations Plaza, New
York, New York 10017 (800) 253-9646; *State
of the World's Children*.

The World Bank, 1818 H Street, NW,
Washington, D.C. 20433 (202) 477-1234;
*The World Bank Atlas; World Development
Report;* and *World Development Indicators*.

World Health Organization, Office of
Publications, 20 Avenue Appia, CH-1211
Geneva 27, Switzerland (Telephone
Number in U.S. (518) 436-9686); *World
Health Statistics Annual*.

TOGO - MOTOR VEHICLE TAXES - See
TOGO - TAXATION

TOGO - MOTOR VEHICLES IN USE

Europa Publications Limited, 18
Bedford Square, London, WC1B 3JN,
England; *The Europa World Year Book*.

International Road Federation, 2600
Virginia Avenue, NW, Washington, D.C.
20037 (202) 338-4641; *World Road
Statistics*.

Statistical Office of the United Nations,
Publishing Service, New York, New York
10017 (800) 253-9646; *Statistical Yearbook;*
and *Survey of Economic and Social
Conditions in Africa*.

TOGO - MUSEUMS

M.E. Sharpe, 80 Business Park Drive,
Armonk, New York 10504 (800) 541-6563;
The Illustrated Book of World Rankings.

United Nations Educational, Scientific
and Cultural Organization (UNESCO), 7
Place de Fontenoy, F-75700 Paris, France
(Telephone Number in U.S. (212) 963-

5981); *Statistical Yearbook.*

TOGO - NATALITY - See TOGO - BIRTH RATES

TOGO - NATIONAL ACCOUNTS

African Development Bank, 01 BP 1387, Abidjan 01, Cote D'Ivoire; *Selected Statistics on Regional Member Countries.*

Europa Publications Limited, 18 Bedford Square, London, WC1B 3JN, England; *The Europa World Year Book.*

Statistical Office of the United Nations, Publishing Service, New York, New York 10017 (800) 253-9646; *National Accounts Statistics;* and *Statistical Yearbook.*

United Nations Economic Commission for Africa, Africa Hall, P.O. Box 3001, Addis Ababa, Ethiopia (Telephone Number in U.S. (800) 253-9646); *African Statistical Yearbook.*

TOGO - NATIONAL INCOME

M.E. Sharpe, 80 Business Park Drive, Armonk, New York 10504 (800) 541-6563; *The Illustrated Book of World Rankings.*

Statistical Office of the United Nations, Publishing Service, New York, New York 10017 (800) 253-9646; *National Accounts Statistics;* and *Statistical Yearbook.*

TOGO - NATIONAL PRODUCT

M.E. Sharpe, 80 Business Park Drive, Armonk, New York 10504 (800) 541-6563; *The Illustrated Book of World Rankings.*

TOGO - NATURAL GAS PRODUCTION - See TOGO - MINING AND MINERAL PRODUCTS

TOGO - NEWSPAPER PRODUCTION - See TOGO - FORESTRY AND FOREST PRODUCTS

TOGO - NEWSPRINT PRODUCTION AND CONSUMPTION - See TOGO - FORESTRY AND FOREST PRODUCTS

TOGO - OCCUPATIONS - See TOGO - LABOR

TOGO - PALM KERNELS PRODUCTION - See TOGO - CROPS

TOGO - PAPER - See TOGO - FORESTRY AND FOREST PRODUCTS

TOGO - PEANUT PRODUCTION - See TOGO - CROPS

TOGO - PESTICIDE USE

Food and Agricultural Organization of the United Nations (FAO) Via delle Terme di Caracalla, 00100 Rome, Italy (Telephone Number in U.S. (202) 653-2400); *The State of Food and Agriculture.*

TOGO - PETROLEUM INDUSTRY

Food and Agricultural Organization of the United Nations (FAO) Via delle Terme di Caracalla, 00100 Rome, Italy (Telephone Number in U.S. (202) 653-2400); *The State of Food and Agriculture.*

M.E. Sharpe, 80 Business Park Drive, Armonk, New York 10504 (800) 541-6563; *The Illustrated Book of World Rankings.*

United Nations Conference on Trade and Development, Central Statistical Service, Palais des Nations, Geneva, Switzerland (Telephone in U.S. (800) 253-9646); *UNCTAD Commodity Yearbook.*

TOGO - PHOSPHATE ROCK PRODUCTION - See TOGO - MINING AND MINERAL PRODUCTS

TOGO - PHOSPHATES EXPORTS - See TOGO - MINING AND MINERAL PRODUCTS

TOGO - PIGS - See TOGO - LIVESTOCK AND POULTRY

TOGO - POPULATION

African Development Bank, 01 BP 1387, Abidjan 01, Cote D'Ivoire; *Selected Statistics on Regional Member Countries.*

Central Intelligence Agency, Washington, D.C. 20505 (703) 482-1100, www.cia.gov; *The World Factbook.*

The Economist Intelligence Unit, 111 West 57th Street, New York, New York 10019 (800) 938-4685; *Togo Country Report;* and *The World Market Atlas.*

Euromonitor International, Inc., 122 South Michigan Avenue, Suite 1200, Chicago, Illinois 60603 (800) 577-EURO; *International Marketing Data and Statistics;* and *The World Economic Factbook.*

Europa Publications Limited, 18 Bedford Square, London, WC1B 3JN, England; *The Europa World Year Book.*

Food and Agricultural Organization of the United Nations (FAO), Via delle Terme di Caracalla, 00100 Rome, Italy (Telephone Number in U.S. (202) 653-2400); *Production Yearbook.*

International Labour Office, I.L.O. Publications, 1828 L Street, NW, Suite 801, Washington, D.C. 20036 (301) 638-3152; *Yearbook of Labour Statistics.*

M.E. Sharpe, 80 Business Park Drive, Armonk, New York 10504 (800) 541-6563; *The Illustrated Book of World Rankings.*

St. Martin's Press, Inc., 175 Fifth Avenue, New York, New York 10010 (800) 221-7945; *The Statesman's Year-Book.*

Statistical Office of the United Nations, Publishing Service, New York, New York 10017 (800) 253-9646; *Demographic Yearbook; Human Development Report; Statistical Yearbook; Survey of Economic and Social Conditions in Africa;* and *World Statistics Pocketbook.*

United Nations Educational, Scientific and Cultural Organization (UNESCO), 7 Place de Fontenoy, F-75700 Paris, France (Telephone Number in U.S. (212) 963-5981); *Statistical Yearbook.*

U.S. Arms Control and Disarmament Agency, 320 Twenty-first Street, NW, Washington, D.C. 20451 (202) 647-8677; *World Military Expenditures and Arms Transfers.*

The World Bank, 1818 H Street, NW, Washington, D.C. 20433 (202) 477-1234; *The World Bank Atlas;* and *World Development Report.*

World Health Organization, Office of Publications, 20 Avenue Appia, CH-1211 Geneva 27, Switzerland (Telephone Number in U.S. (518) 436-9686); *World Health Statistics Annual.*

TOGO - POST OFFICES

M.E. Sharpe, 80 Business Park Drive, Armonk, New York 10504 (800) 541-6563; *The Illustrated Book of World Rankings.*

St. Martin's Press, Inc., 175 Fifth Avenue, New York, New York 10010 (800) 221-7945; *The Statesman's Year-Book.*

TOGO - POTATO PRODUCTION - See TOGO - CROPS

TOGO - PRICES

Food and Agricultural Organization of the United Nations (FAO), Via delle Terme di Caracalla, 00100 Rome, Italy (Telephone Number in U.S. (202) 653-2400); *Production Yearbook;* and *The State of Food and Agriculture.*

International Labour Office, I.L.O. Publications, 1828 L Street, NW, Suite 801, Washington, D.C. 20036 (301) 638-3152; *Yearbook of Labour Statistics.*

International Monetary Fund, 700 Nineteenth Street, NW, Washington, D.C. 20431 (202) 623-7000; *International Financial Statistics.*

M.E. Sharpe, 80 Business Park Drive, Armonk, New York 10504 (800) 541-6563; *The Illustrated Book of World Rankings.*

United Nations Economic Commission for Africa, Africa Hall, P.O. Box 3001, Addis Ababa, Ethiopia (Telephone Number in U.S. (800) 253-9646); *African Statistical Yearbook*.

TOGO - PRODUCTION

M.E. Sharpe, 80 Business Park Drive, Armonk, New York 10504 (800) 541-6563; *The Illustrated Book of World Rankings*.

TOGO - PRODUCTIVITY

Euromonitor International, Inc., 122 South Michigan Avenue, Suite 1200, Chicago, Illinois 60603 (800) 577-EURO; *International Marketing Data and Statistics*.

TOGO - PROPERTY TAXES - See TOGO - TAXATION

TOGO - PUBLIC FINANCE - See TOGO - FINANCE

TOGO - RADIO BROADCASTING - See TOGO - BROADCASTING

TOGO - RADIO RECEIVERS

St. Martin's Press, Inc., 175 Fifth Avenue, New York, New York 10010 (800) 221-7945; *The Statesman's Year-Book*.

TOGO - RAILWAYS

Europa Publications Limited, 18 Bedford Square, London, WC1B 3JN, England; *The Europa World Year Book*.

Jane's Information Group, Sentinel House, 163 Brighton Road, Coulsdon, Surrey CR5 2NH, England (Telephone Number in U.S. (703) 683-3700); *Jane's World Railways*.

St. Martin's Press, Inc., 175 Fifth Avenue, New York, New York 10010 (800) 221-7945; *The Statesman's Year-Book*.

Statistical Office of the United Nations, Publishing Service, New York, New York 10017 (800) 253-9646; *Statistical Yearbook; and Survey of Economic and Social Conditions in Africa*.

United Nations Economic Commission for Africa, Africa Hall, P.O. Box 3001, Addis Ababa, Ethiopia (Telephone Number in U.S. (800) 253-9646); *African Statistical Yearbook*.

TOGO - RELIGION

Central Intelligence Agency, Washington, D.C. 20505 (703) 482-1100, www.cia.gov; *The World Factbook*.

M.E. Sharpe, 80 Business Park Drive, Armonk, New York 10504 (800) 541-6563; *The Illustrated Book of World Rankings*.

St. Martin's Press, Inc., 175 Fifth Avenue, New York, New York 10010 (800) 221-7945; *The Statesman's Year-Book*.

TOGO - RENT PRICES

International Labour Office, I.L.O. Publications, 1828 L Street, NW, Suite 801, Washington, D.C. 20036 (301) 638-3152; *Yearbook of Labour Statistics*.

TOGO - RETAIL TRADE

Euromonitor International, Inc., 122 South Michigan Avenue, Suite 1200, Chicago, Illinois 60603 (800) 577-EURO; *World Marketing Data and Statistics*.

Statistical Office of the United Nations, Publishing Service, New York, New York 10017 (800) 253-9646; *Statistical Yearbook*.

TOGO - RETAIL TRADE EMPLOYMENT - MALE AND FEMALE - See TOGO - EMPLOYMENT

TOGO - RICE PRODUCTION - See TOGO - CROPS

TOGO - ROUNDWOOD PRODUCTION - See TOGO - FORESTRY AND FOREST PRODUCTS

TOGO - RUBBER PRODUCTION AND CONSUMPTION

M.E. Sharpe, 80 Business Park Drive, Armonk, New York 10504 (800) 541-6563; *The Illustrated Book of World Rankings*.

TOGO - SAWNWOOD PRODUCTION - See TOGO - FORESTRY AND FOREST PRODUCTS

TOGO - SCIENCE AND TECHNOLOGY - EXPENDITURE FOR RESEARCH - See TOGO - SCIENTISTS, TECHNICIANS AND ENGINEERS

TOGO - SCIENTISTS, TECHNICIANS AND ENGINEERS

Statistical Office of the United Nations, Publishing Service, New York, New York 10017 (800) 253-9646; *Statistical Yearbook*.

United Nations Educational, Scientific and Cultural Organization (UNESCO), 7 Place de Fontenoy, F-75700 Paris, France (Telephone Number in U.S. (212) 963-5981); *Statistical Yearbook*.

TOGO - SENIOR CITIZENS

M.E. Sharpe, 80 Business Park Drive, Armonk, New York 10504 (800) 541-6563; *The Illustrated Book of World Rankings*.

TOGO - SHEEP - See TOGO - LIVESTOCK AND POULTRY

TOGO - SILVER PRODUCTION AND CONSUMPTION - See TOGO - MINING AND MINERAL PRODUCTS

TOGO - SOCIAL DATA

African Development Bank, 01 BP 1387, Abidjan 01, Cote D'Ivoire; *Selected Statistics on Regional Member Countries*.

M.E. Sharpe, 80 Business Park Drive, Armonk, New York 10504 (800) 541-6563; *The Illustrated Book of World Rankings*.

Statistical Office of the United Nations, Publishing Service, New York, New York 10017 (800) 253-9646; *World Statistics Pocketbook*.

TOGO - SOCIAL SECURITY

International Monetary Fund, 700 Nineteenth Street, NW, Washington, D.C. 20431 (202) 623-7000; *Government Finance Statistics Yearbook*.

Statistical Office of the United Nations, Publishing Service, New York, New York 10017 (800) 253-9646; *National Accounts Statistics*.

TOGO - STAMP TAXES AND DUTIES - See TOGO - TAXATION

TOGO - STATE BUDGET REVENUE AND EXPENDITURES

Euromonitor International, Inc., 122 South Michigan Avenue, Suite 1200, Chicago, Illinois 60603 (800) 577-EURO; *International Marketing Data and Statistics*.

TOGO - STEEL - See TOGO - MINING AND MINERAL PRODUCTS

TOGO - STOCKS - COMMODITY - MARKET PRICE - INDEX

Food and Agricultural Organization of the United Nations (FAO) Via delle Terme di Caracalla, 00100 Rome, Italy (Telephone Number in U.S. (202) 653-2400); *The State of Food and Agriculture*.

TOGO - SUGAR PRODUCTION AND CONSUMPTION - See TOGO - CROPS

TOGO - TAXATION

Europa Publications Limited, 18 Bedford Square, London, WC1B 3JN, England; *The Europa World Year Book*.

International Monetary Fund, 700 Nineteenth Street, NW, Washington, D.C. 20431 (202) 623-7000; *Government Finance Statistics Yearbook*.

International Road Federation, 2600 Virginia Avenue, NW, Washington, D.C. 20037 (202) 338-4641; *World Road*

Statistics.

The World Bank, 1818 H Street, NW, Washington, D.C. 20433 (202) 477-1234; *World Development Indicators.*

TOGO - TELEGRAPH SERVICE

Statistical Office of the United Nations, Publishing Service, New York, New York 10017 (800) 253-9646; *Statistical Yearbook.*

TOGO - TELEPHONES IN USE

American Telephone and Telegraph Company, 26 Parsippany Road, Whippany, New Jersey 07981 (800) 222-0300; *The World's Telephones.*

Central Intelligence Agency, Washington, D.C. 20505 (703) 482-1100, www.cia.gov; *The World Factbook.*

Europa Publications Limited, 18 Bedford Square, London, WC1B 3JN, England; *The Europa World Year Book.*

St. Martin's Press, Inc., 175 Fifth Avenue, New York, New York 10010 (800) 221-7945; *The Statesman's Year-Book.*

Statistical Office of the United Nations, Publishing Service, New York, New York 10017 (800) 253-9646; *Statistical Yearbook;* and *World Statistics Pocketbook.*

TOGO - TELEVISION BROADCASTING - See TOGO - BROADCASTING

TOGO - TEXTILE INDUSTRY

M.E. Sharpe, 80 Business Park Drive, Armonk, New York 10504 (800) 541-6563; *The Illustrated Book of World Rankings.*

St. Martin's Press, Inc., 175 Fifth Avenue, New York, New York 10010 (800) 221-7945; *The Statesman's Year-Book.*

Statistical Office of the United Nations, Publishing Service, New York, New York 10017 (800) 253-9646; *Statistical Yearbook.*

United Nations Conference on Trade and Development, Central Statistical Service, Palais des Nations, Geneva, Switzerland (Telephone in U.S. (800) 253-9646); *UNCTAD Commodity Yearbook.*

TOGO - TOBACCO PRODUCTION

M.E. Sharpe, 80 Business Park Drive, Armonk, New York 10504 (800) 541-6563; *The Illustrated Book of World Rankings.*

Statistical Office of the United Nations, Publishing Service, New York, New York 10017 (800) 253-9646; *Statistical Yearbook.*

TOGO - TOURISM

Euromonitor International, Inc., 122 South Michigan Avenue, Suite 1200, Chicago, Illinois 60603 (800) 577-EURO; *The World Economic Factbook;* and *World Marketing Data and Statistics.*

Europa Publications Limited, 18 Bedford Square, London, WC1B 3JN, England; *The Europa World Year Book.*

M.E. Sharpe, 80 Business Park Drive, Armonk, New York 10504 (800) 541-6563; *The Illustrated Book of World Rankings.*

St. Martin's Press, Inc., 175 Fifth Avenue, New York, New York 10010 (800) 221-7945; *The Statesman's Year-Book.*

Statistical Office of the United Nations, Publishing Service, New York, New York 10017 (800) 253-9646; *Statistical Yearbook.*

United Nations Economic Commission for Africa, Africa Hall, P.O. Box 3001, Addis Ababa, Ethiopia (Telephone Number in U.S. (800) 253-9646); *African Statistical Yearbook.*

World Tourism Organization, Calle Capitan Haya 42, E-28020 Madrid, Spain; *Yearbook of Tourism Statistics.*

TOGO - TRACTORS IN USE

Statistical Office of the United Nations, Publishing Service, New York, New York 10017 (800) 253-9646; *Statistical Yearbook.*

TOGO - TRADE - See TOGO - FOREIGN TRADE

TOGO - TRANSPORTATION AND COMMUNICATIONS

Central Intelligence Agency, Washington, D.C. 20505 (703) 482-1100, www.cia.gov; *The World Factbook.*

Euromonitor International, Inc., 122 South Michigan Avenue, Suite 1200, Chicago, Illinois 60603 (800) 577-EURO; *International Marketing Data and Statistics;* and *World Marketing Data and Statistics.*

Europa Publications Limited, 18 Bedford Square, London, WC1B 3JN, England; *The Europa World Year Book.*

M.E. Sharpe, 80 Business Park Drive, Armonk, New York 10504 (800) 541-6563; *The Illustrated Book of World Rankings.*

St. Martin's Press, Inc., 175 Fifth Avenue, New York, New York 10010 (800) 221-7945; *The Statesman's Year-Book.*

Statistical Office of the United Nations, Publishing Service, New York, New York 10017 (800) 253-9646; *Human Development Report.*

United Nations Economic Commission for Africa, Africa Hall, P.O. Box 3001, Addis Ababa, Ethiopia (Telephone Number in U.S. (800) 253-9646); *African Statistical Yearbook.*

TOGO - UNEMPLOYMENT

Central Intelligence Agency, Washington, D.C. 20505 (703) 482-1100, www.cia.gov; *The World Factbook.*

Euromonitor International, Inc., 122 South Michigan Avenue, Suite 1200, Chicago, Illinois 60603 (800) 577-EURO; *International Marketing Data and Statistics.*

International Labour Office, I.L.O. Publications, 1828 L Street, NW, Suite 801, Washington, D.C. 20036 (301) 638-3152; *Yearbook of Labour Statistics.*

Statistical Office of the United Nations, Publishing Service, New York, New York 10017 (800) 253-9646; *Statistical Yearbook.*

TOGO - VITAL STATISTICS

Euromonitor International, Inc., 122 South Michigan Avenue, Suite 1200, Chicago, Illinois 60603 (800) 577-EURO; *International Marketing Data and Statistics.*

Statistical Office of the United Nations, Publishing Service, New York, New York 10017 (800) 253-9646; *Statistical Yearbook.*

World Health Organization, Office of Publications, 20 Avenue Appia, CH-1211 Geneva 27, Switzerland (Telephone Number in U.S. (518) 436-9686); *World Health Statistics Annual.*

TOGO - WAGES

International Labour Office, I.L.O. Publications, 1828 L Street, NW, Suite 801, Washington, D.C. 20036 (301) 638-3152; *Yearbook of Labour Statistics.*

TOGO - WEATHER

M.E. Sharpe, 80 Business Park Drive, Armonk, New York 10504 (800) 541-6563; *The Illustrated Book of World Rankings.*

TOGO - WELFARE

International Monetary Fund, 700 Nineteenth Street, NW, Washington, D.C. 20431 (202) 623-7000; *Government Finance Statistics Yearbook.*

TOGO - WHEAT PRODUCTION AND PRICES - See TOGO - CROPS

TOGO - WHOLESALE TRADE

Statistical Office of the United Nations, Publishing Service, New York, New York 10017 (800) 253-9646; *Statistical Yearbook.*

TOGO - WINE PRODUCTION - See
TOGO - BEVERAGES

TOGO - WOOL PRODUCTION - See
TOGO - TEXTILE INDUSTRY

TOKELAU ISLANDS - AGRICULTURE

Europa Publications Limited, 18 Bedford Square, London, WC1B 3JN, England; *The Europa World Year Book.*

Food and Agricultural Organization of the United Nations (FAO) Via delle Terme di Caracalla, 00100 Rome, Italy (Telephone Number in U.S. (202) 653-2400); *Production Yearbook; The State of Food and Agriculture;* and *Trade Yearbook.*

United Nations Conference on Trade and Development, Central Statistical Service, Palais des Nations, Geneva, Switzerland (Telephone in U.S. (800) 253-9646); *UNCTAD Commodity Yearbook.*

TOKELAU ISLANDS - AIRPORTS

Central Intelligence Agency, Washington, D.C. 20505 (703) 482-1100, www.cia.gov; *The World Factbook.*

TOKELAU ISLANDS - ANIMAL HEALTH

Food and Agricultural Organization of the United Nations (FAO), Via delle Terme di Caracalla, 00100, Rome, Italy (Telephone Number in U.S. (202) 653-2400); *Animal Health Yearbook.*

TOKELAU ISLANDS - AREA AND DENSITY OF POPULATION

Central Intelligence Agency, Washington, D.C. 20505 (703) 482-1100, www.cia.gov; *The World Factbook.*

Europa Publications Limited, 18 Bedford Square, London, WC1B 3JN, England; *The Europa World Year Book.*

Food and Agricultural Organization of the United Nations (FAO) Via delle Terme di Caracalla, 00100 Rome, Italy (Telephone Number in U.S. (202) 653-2400); *The State of Food and Agriculture.*

St. Martin's Press, Inc., 175 Fifth Avenue, New York, New York 10010 (800) 221-7945; *The Statesman's Year-Book.*

Statistical Office of the United Nations, Publishing Service, New York, New York 10017 (800) 253-9646; *Statistical Yearbook.*

TOKELAU ISLANDS - BIRTH RATES

Central Intelligence Agency, Washington, D.C. 20505 (703) 482-1100, www.cia.gov; *The World Factbook.*

Europa Publications Limited, 18 Bedford Square, London, WC1B 3JN, England; *The Europa World Year Book.*

Statistical Office of the United Nations, Publishing Service, New York, New York 10017 (800) 253-9646; *Demographic Yearbook;* and *Statistical Yearbook.*

TOKELAU ISLANDS - BROADCASTING

Central Intelligence Agency, Washington, D.C. 20505 (703) 482-1100, www.cia.gov; *The World Factbook.*

TOKELAU ISLANDS - BUDGET

Central Intelligence Agency, Washington, D.C. 20505 (703) 482-1100, www.cia.gov; *The World Factbook.*

TOKELAU ISLANDS - CALORIE SUPPLY

Food and Agricultural Organization of the United Nations (FAO) Via delle Terme di Caracalla, 00100 Rome, Italy (Telephone Number in U.S. (202) 653-2400); *The State of Food and Agriculture.*

TOKELAU ISLANDS - CORN PRODUCTION - See TOKELAU ISLANDS - CROPS

TOKELAU ISLANDS - CORPORATE TAXES - See TOKELAU ISLANDS - TAXATION

TOKELAU ISLANDS - CROPS

Europa Publications Limited, 18 Bedford Square, London, WC1B 3JN, England; *The Europa World Year Book.*

Food and Agricultural Organization of the United Nations (FAO) Via delle Terme di Caracalla, 00100 Rome, Italy (Telephone Number in U.S. (202) 653-2400); *The State of Food and Agriculture.*

St. Martin's Press, Inc., 175 Fifth Avenue, New York, New York 10010 (800) 221-7945; *The Statesman's Year-Book.*

United Nations Conference on Trade and Development, Central Statistical Service, Palais des Nations, Geneva, Switzerland (Telephone in U.S. (800) 253-9646); *UNCTAD Commodity Yearbook.*

TOKELAU ISLANDS - DAIRY PRODUCTS

Food and Agricultural Organization of the United Nations (FAO) Via delle Terme di Caracalla, 00100 Rome, Italy (Telephone Number in U.S. (202) 653-2400); *The State of Food and Agriculture.*

TOKELAU ISLANDS - DEATH RATES - See TOKELAU ISLANDS - MORTALITY

TOKELAU ISLANDS - DEVELOPMENT ASSISTANCE

Statistical Office of the United Nations,

Publishing Service, New York, New York 10017 (800) 253-9646; *Statistical Yearbook.*

TOKELAU ISLANDS - DISEASES - See TOKELAU ISLANDS - HEALTH

TOKELAU ISLANDS - DIVORCE RATES

Statistical Office of the United Nations, Publishing Service, New York, New York 10017 (800) 253-9646; *Demographic Yearbook.*

TOKELAU ISLANDS - ECONOMY

Central Intelligence Agency, Washington, D.C. 20505 (703) 482-1100, www.cia.gov; *The World Factbook.*

St. Martin's Press, Inc., 175 Fifth Avenue, New York, New York 10010 (800) 221-7945; *The Statesman's Year-Book.*

TOKELAU ISLANDS - EDUCATION

Europa Publications Limited, 18 Bedford Square, London, WC1B 3JN, England; *The Europa World Year Book.*

TOKELAU ISLANDS - EGG PRODUCTION AND CONSUMPTION - See TOKELAU ISLANDS - DAIRY PRODUCTS

TOKELAU ISLANDS - ELECTRICITY

Central Intelligence Agency, Washington, D.C. 20505 (703) 482-1100, www.cia.gov; *The World Factbook.*

TOKELAU ISLANDS - ENERGY

Food and Agricultural Organization of the United Nations (FAO) Via delle Terme di Caracalla, 00100 Rome, Italy (Telephone Number in U.S. (202) 653-2400); *The State of Food and Agriculture.*

TOKELAU ISLANDS - EXCHANGE RATES

Central Intelligence Agency, Washington, D.C. 20505 (703) 482-1100, www.cia.gov; *The World Factbook.*

Europa Publications Limited, 18 Bedford Square, London, WC1B 3JN, England; *The Europa World Year Book.*

Walden Publishing Ltd., Two Market Street, Saffron Walden Essex, CB10 1HZ, England; *The World of Information Asia and Pacific Review.*

TOKELAU ISLANDS - EXPORTS

Central Intelligence Agency, Washington, D.C. 20505 (703) 482-1100, www.cia.gov; *The World Factbook.*

Europa Publications Limited, 18 Bedford Square, London, WC1B 3JN, England; *The Europa World Year Book.*

Food and Agricultural Organization of the United Nations (FAO) Via delle Terme di Caracalla, 00100 Rome, Italy (Telephone Number in U.S. (202) 653-2400); *The State of Food and Agriculture.*

South Pacific Commission, Post Box D5, Noumea Cedex, New Caledonia; *Statistical Bulletin of the South Pacific: Overseas Trade.*

Walden Publishing Ltd., Two Market Street, Saffron Walden Essex, CB10 1HZ, England; *The World of Information Asia and Pacific Review.*

TOKELAU ISLANDS - EXTERNAL TRADE

Food and Agricultural Organization of the United Nations (FAO), Via delle Terme di Caracalla, 00100, Rome, Italy (Telephone Number in U.S. (202) 653-2400); *Trade Yearbook;* and *The State of Food and Agriculture.*

TOKELAU ISLANDS - FARM CROPS - See TOKELAU ISLANDS - CROPS

TOKELAU ISLANDS - FERTILITY RATES

Central Intelligence Agency, Washington, D.C. 20505 (703) 482-1100, www.cia.gov; *The World Factbook.*

TOKELAU ISLANDS - FERTILIZER

Food and Agricultural Organization of the United Nations (FAO) Via delle Terme di Caracalla, 00100, Rome, Italy (Telephone Number in U.S. (202) 653-2400); *Fertilizer Yearbook;* and *The State of Food and Agriculture.*

TOKELAU ISLANDS - FETAL MORTALITY - See TOKELAU ISLANDS - MORTALITY

TOKELAU ISLANDS - FINANCE

Europa Publications Limited, 18 Bedford Square, London, WC1B 3JN, England; *The Europa World Year Book.*

TOKELAU ISLANDS - FISHERIES

Europa Publications Limited, 18 Bedford Square, London, WC1B 3JN, England; *The Europa World Year Book.*

Food and Agricultural Organization of the United Nations (FAO) Via delle Terme di Caracalla, 00100 Rome, Italy (Telephone Number in U.S. (202) 653-2400); *The State of Food and Agriculture;* and *Yearbook of Fishery Statistics.*

St. Martin's Press, Inc., 175 Fifth Avenue, New York, New York 10010 (800) 221-7945; *The Statesman's Year-Book.*

United Nations Conference on Trade and Development, Central Statistical Service, Palais des Nations, Geneva, Switzerland (Telephone in U.S. (800) 253-9646); *UNCTAD Commodity Yearbook.*

TOKELAU ISLANDS - FOOD

Food and Agricultural Organization of the United Nations (FAO) Via delle Terme di Caracalla, 00100 Rome, Italy (Telephone Number in U.S. (202) 653-2400); *Production Yearbook;* and *The State of Food and Agriculture.*

United Nations Conference on Trade and Development, Central Statistical Service, Palais des Nations, Geneva, Switzerland (Telephone in U.S. (800) 253-9646); *UNCTAD Commodity Yearbook.*

TOKELAU ISLANDS - FOREIGN DEBT

Walden Publishing Ltd., Two Market Street, Saffron Walden Essex, CB10 1HZ, England; *The World of Information Asia and Pacific Review.*

TOKELAU ISLANDS - FOREIGN TRADE

Food and Agricultural Organization of the United Nations (FAO) Via delle Terme di Caracalla, 00100 Rome, Italy (Telephone Number in U.S. (202) 653-2400); *The State of Food and Agriculture.*

South Pacific Commission, Post Box D5, Noumea Cedex, New Caledonia; *Statistical Bulletin of the South Pacific: Overseas Trade.*

United Nations Conference on Trade and Development, Central Statistical Service, Palais des Nations, Geneva, Switzerland (Telephone in U.S. (800) 253-9646); *UNCTAD Commodity Yearbook.*

TOKELAU ISLANDS - FORESTRY AND FOREST PRODUCTS

Food and Agricultural Organization of the United Nations (FAO) Via delle Terme di Caracalla, 00100 Rome, Italy (Telephone Number in U.S. (202) 653-2400); *The State of Food and Agriculture.*

Statistical Office of the United Nations, Publishing Service, New York, New York 10017 (800) 253-9646; *Statistical Yearbook.*

United Nations Conference on Trade and Development, Central Statistical Service, Palais des Nations, Geneva, Switzerland (Telephone in U.S. (800) 253-9646); *UNCTAD Commodity Yearbook.*

TOKELAU ISLANDS - GENERAL MORTALITY - See TOKELAU ISLANDS - MORTALITY

TOKELAU ISLANDS - GOVERNMENT

Central Intelligence Agency, Washington, D.C. 20505 (703) 482-1100, www.cia.gov; *The World Factbook.*

Europa Publications Limited, 18 Bedford Square, London, WC1B 3JN, England; *The Europa World Year Book.*

St. Martin's Press, Inc., 175 Fifth Avenue, New York, New York 10010 (800) 221-7945; *The Statesman's Year-Book.*

TOKELAU ISLANDS - GRAIN PRODUCTION - See TOKELAU ISLANDS - CROPS

TOKELAU ISLANDS - GROSS NATIONAL PRODUCT

Walden Publishing Ltd., Two Market Street, Saffron Walden Essex, CB10 1HZ, England; *The World of Information Asia and Pacific Review.*

TOKELAU ISLANDS - HEALTH

St. Martin's Press, Inc., 175 Fifth Avenue, New York, New York 10010 (800) 221-7945; *The Statesman's Year-Book.*

World Health Organization, Office of Publications, 20 Avenue Appia, CH-1211 Geneva 27, Switzerland (Telephone Number in U.S. (518) 436-9686); *World Health Statistics Annual.*

TOKELAU ISLANDS - HIGHWAYS

Central Intelligence Agency, Washington, D.C. 20505 (703) 482-1100, www.cia.gov; *The World Factbook.*

TOKELAU ISLANDS - ILLITERATE POPULATION

Central Intelligence Agency, Washington, D.C. 20505 (703) 482-1100, www.cia.gov; *The World Factbook.*

TOKELAU ISLANDS - IMPORTS

Central Intelligence Agency, Washington, D.C. 20505 (703) 482-1100, www.cia.gov; *The World Factbook.*

Europa Publications Limited, 18 Bedford Square, London, WC1B 3JN, England; *The Europa World Year Book.*

Food and Agricultural Organization of the United Nations (FAO) Via delle Terme di Caracalla, 00100 Rome, Italy (Telephone Number in U.S. (202) 653-2400); *The State of Food and Agriculture.*

South Pacific Commission, Post Box D5, Noumea Cedex, New Caledonia; *Statistical Bulletin of the South Pacific: Overseas Trade.*

Walden Publishing Ltd., Two Market

Street, Saffron Walden Essex, CB10 1HZ, England; *The World of Information Asia and Pacific Review*.

TOKELAU ISLANDS - INDUSTRY

Central Intelligence Agency, Washington, D.C. 20505 (703) 482-1100, www.cia.gov; *The World Factbook*.

TOKELAU ISLANDS - INFANT AND MATERNAL MORTALITY - See TOKELAU ISLANDS - MORTALITY

TOKELAU ISLANDS - LABOR

Central Intelligence Agency, Washington, D.C. 20505 (703) 482-1100, www.cia.gov; *The World Factbook*.

Food and Agricultural Organization of the United Nations (FAO) Via delle Terme di Caracalla, 00100 Rome, Italy (Telephone Number in U.S. (202) 653-2400); *The State of Food and Agriculture*.

TOKELAU ISLANDS - LAND USE

Central Intelligence Agency, Washington, D.C. 20505 (703) 482-1100, www.cia.gov; *The World Factbook*.

Food and Agricultural Organization of the United Nations (FAO), Via delle Terme di Caracalla, 00100 Rome, Italy (Telephone Number in U.S. (202) 653-2400); *Production Yearbook*.

TOKELAU ISLANDS - LIBRARIES

United Nations Educational, Scientific and Cultural Organization (UNESCO), 7 Place de Fontenoy, F-75700 Paris, France (Telephone Number in U.S. (212) 963-5981); *Statistical Yearbook*.

TOKELAU ISLANDS - LIFE EXPECTANCY

Central Intelligence Agency, Washington, D.C. 20505 (703) 482-1100, www.cia.gov; *The World Factbook*.

TOKELAU ISLANDS - LIVESTOCK AND POULTRY

Europa Publications Limited, 18 Bedford Square, London, WC1B 3JN, England; *The Europa World Year Book*.

Food and Agricultural Organization of the United Nations (FAO), Via delle Terme di Caracalla, 00100 Rome, Italy (Telephone Number in U.S. (202) 653-2400); *Production Yearbook;* and *The State of Food and Agriculture*.

St. Martin's Press, Inc., 175 Fifth Avenue, New York, New York 10010 (800) 221-7945; *The Statesman's Year-Book*.

Statistical Office of the United Nations,

Publishing Service, New York, New York 10017 (800) 253-9646; *Statistical Yearbook*.

United Nations Conference on Trade and Development, Central Statistical Service, Palais des Nations, Geneva, Switzerland (Telephone in U.S. (800) 253-9646); *UNCTAD Commodity Yearbook*.

TOKELAU ISLANDS - MARRIAGE RATES

Statistical Office of the United Nations, Publishing Service, New York, New York 10017 (800) 253-9646; *Demographic Yearbook;* and *Statistical Yearbook*.

TOKELAU ISLANDS - MEAT PRODUCTION - See TOKELAU ISLANDS - LIVESTOCK AND POULTRY

TOKELAU ISLANDS - MILITARY

Central Intelligence Agency, Washington, D.C. 20505 (703) 482-1100, www.cia.gov; *The World Factbook*.

TOKELAU ISLANDS - MINING AND MINERAL PRODUCTS

United Nations Conference on Trade and Development, Central Statistical Service, Palais des Nations, Geneva, Switzerland (Telephone in U.S. (800) 253-9646); *UNCTAD Commodity Yearbook*.

TOKELAU ISLANDS - MORTALITY

Central Intelligence Agency, Washington, D.C. 20505 (703) 482-1100, www.cia.gov; *The World Factbook*.

Europa Publications Limited, 18 Bedford Square, London, WC1B 3JN, England; *The Europa World Year Book*.

Statistical Office of the United Nations, Publishing Service, New York, New York 10017 (800) 253-9646; *Demographic Yearbook;* and *Statistical Yearbook*.

World Health Organization, Office of Publications, 20 Avenue Appia, CH-1211 Geneva 27, Switzerland (Telephone Number in U.S. (518) 436-9686); *World Health Statistics Annual*.

TOKELAU ISLANDS - NATALITY - See TOKELAU ISLANDS - BIRTH RATES

TOKELAU ISLANDS - NEWSPAPER PRODUCTION - See TOKELAU ISLANDS - FORESTRY AND FOREST PRODUCTS

TOKELAU ISLANDS - OCCUPATIONS - See TOKELAU ISLANDS - LABOR

TOKELAU ISLANDS - PERIODICALS

United Nations Educational, Scientific and Cultural Organization (UNESCO), 7 Place de Fontenoy, F-75700 Paris, France

(Telephone Number in U.S. (212) 963-5981); *Statistical Yearbook*.

TOKELAU ISLANDS - PESTICIDE USE

Food and Agricultural Organization of the United Nations (FAO) Via delle Terme di Caracalla, 00100 Rome, Italy (Telephone Number in U.S. (202) 653-2400); *The State of Food and Agriculture*.

TOKELAU ISLANDS - PETROLEUM INDUSTRY

Food and Agricultural Organization of the United Nations (FAO) Via delle Terme di Caracalla, 00100 Rome, Italy (Telephone Number in U.S. (202) 653-2400); *The State of Food and Agriculture*.

United Nations Conference on Trade and Development, Central Statistical Service, Palais des Nations, Geneva, Switzerland (Telephone in U.S. (800) 253-9646); *UNCTAD Commodity Yearbook*.

TOKELAU ISLANDS - PIGS - See TOKELAU ISLANDS - LIVESTOCK AND POULTRY

TOKELAU ISLANDS - POPULATION

Central Intelligence Agency, Washington, D.C. 20505 (703) 482-1100, www.cia.gov; *The World Factbook*.

Europa Publications Limited, 18 Bedford Square, London, WC1B 3JN, England; *The Europa World Year Book*.

Food and Agricultural Organization of the United Nations (FAO), Via delle Terme di Caracalla, 00100 Rome, Italy (Telephone Number in U.S. (202) 653-2400); *Production Yearbook*.

St. Martin's Press, Inc., 175 Fifth Avenue, New York, New York 10010 (800) 221-7945; *The Statesman's Year-Book*.

Statistical Office of the United Nations, Publishing Service, New York, New York 10017 (800) 253-9646; *Demographic Yearbook;* and *Statistical Yearbook*.

Walden Publishing Ltd., Two Market Street, Saffron Walden Essex, CB10 1HZ, England; *The World of Information Asia and Pacific Review*.

World Health Organization, Office of Publications, 20 Avenue Appia, CH-1211 Geneva 27, Switzerland (Telephone Number in U.S. (518) 436-9686); *World Health Statistics Annual*.

TOKELAU ISLANDS - PRICES

Food and Agricultural Organization of the United Nations (FAO), Via delle Terme di Caracalla, 00100 Rome, Italy (Telephone Number in U.S. (202) 653-2400); *Production*

Yearbook; and *The State of Food and Agriculture.*

South Pacific Commission, Post Box D5, Noumea Cedex, New Caledonia; *Statistical Bulletin of the South Pacific: Overseas Trade.*

TOKELAU ISLANDS - RELIGION

Central Intelligence Agency, Washington, D.C. 20505 (703) 482-1100, www.cia.gov; *The World Factbook.*

TOKELAU ISLANDS - SCIENTISTS, TECHNICIANS AND ENGINEERS

Statistical Office of the United Nations, Publishing Service, New York, New York 10017 (800) 253-9646; *Statistical Yearbook.*

TOKELAU ISLANDS - STOCKS - COMMODITY - MARKET PRICE - INDEX

Food and Agricultural Organization of the United Nations (FAO) Via delle Terme di Caracalla, 00100 Rome, Italy (Telephone Number in U.S. (202) 653-2400); *The State of Food and Agriculture.*

TOKELAU ISLANDS - TELEPHONES IN USE

American Telephone and Telegraph Company, 26 Parsippany Road, Whippany, New Jersey 07981 (800) 222-0300; *The World's Telephones.*

Central Intelligence Agency, Washington, D.C. 20505 (703) 482-1100, www.cia.gov; *The World Factbook.*

TOKELAU ISLANDS - TEXTILE INDUSTRY

United Nations Conference on Trade and Development, Central Statistical Service, Palais des Nations, Geneva, Switzerland (Telephone in U.S. (800) 253-9646); *UNCTAD Commodity Yearbook.*

TOKELAU ISLANDS - TRADE - See TOKELAU ISLANDS - FOREIGN TRADE

TOKELAU ISLANDS - TRANSPORTATION AND COMMUNICATIONS

Central Intelligence Agency, Washington, D.C. 20505 (703) 482-1100, www.cia.gov; *The World Factbook.*

Europa Publications Limited, 18 Bedford Square, London, WC1B 3JN, England; *The Europa World Year Book.*

TOKELAU ISLANDS - UNEMPLOYMENT RATE

Central Intelligence Agency, Washington, D.C. 20505 (703) 482-1100, www.cia.gov; *The World Factbook.*

TOKELAU ISLANDS - VITAL STATISTICS

World Health Organization, Office of Publications, 20 Avenue Appia, CH-1211 Geneva 27, Switzerland (Telephone Number in U.S. (518) 436-9686); *World Health Statistics Annual.*

TOMATOES

U.S. Department of Agriculture, Economic Research Service, 1800 M Street, NW, Washington, D.C. 20036 (202) 694-5050, www.ers.usda.gov; *Food Consumption, Prices and Expenditures; Agricultural Outlook;* and *Farm Business Economic Report.*

U.S. Department of Agriculture, National Agricultural Statistics Service, Fourteenth Street and Independence Avenue, SW, Washington, D.C. 20250 (800) 727-9540, www.usda.gov.nass; *Agricultural Statistics;* and *Vegetables.*

U.S. Department of Labor, Bureau of Labor Statistics, Two Massachusetts Avenue, NE, Washington, D.C. 20212 (202) 691-5200, www.stats.bls.gov; *CPI Detailed Report;* and *Monthly Labor Review.*

Tonga - National Statistical Office

Statistics Department, Ministry of Finance, Post Office Box 149, Nuku'alofa, Tonga.

Tonga - Primary Statistics Source

Statistics Department, P.O. Box 149, Nuku'alofa, Tonga; *Statistical Abstract.*

TONGA - AGRICULTURE

Asian Development Bank, P.O. Box 789, 1099 Manila, Philippines; *Key Indicators of Developing Asian and Pacific Countries.*

Central Intelligence Agency, Washington, D.C. 20505 (703) 482-1100, www.cia.gov; *The World Factbook.*

Economist Intelligence Unit, 111 West 57th Street, New York, New York 10019 (800) 938-4685; *Tonga Country Report.*

Euromonitor International, Inc., 122 South Michigan Avenue, Suite 1200, Chicago, Illinois 60603 (800) 577-EURO; *World Marketing Data and Statistics.*

Europa Publications Limited, 18 Bedford Square, London, WC1B 3JN, England; *The Europa World Year Book.*

Food and Agricultural Organization of the United Nations (FAO) Via delle Terme di Caracalla, 00100 Rome, Italy (Telephone Number in U.S. (202) 653-2400);

Production Yearbook; The State of Food and Agriculture, and *Trade Yearbook.*

St. Martin's Press, Inc., 175 Fifth Avenue, New York, New York 10010 (800) 221-7945; *The Statesman's Year-Book.*

Statistical Office of the United Nations, Publishing Service, New York, New York 10017 (800) 253-9646; *Asia-Pacific in Figures; Statistical Yearbook;* and *Statistical Yearbook for Asia and the Pacific.*

United Nations Conference on Trade and Development, Central Statistical Service, Palais des Nations, Geneva, Switzerland (Telephone in U.S. (800) 253-9646); *UNCTAD Commodity Yearbook.*

The World Bank, 1818 H Street, NW, Washington, D.C. 20433 (202) 477-1234; *World Development Indicators.*

TONGA - AIRLINE SERVICE

Europa Publications Limited, 18 Bedford Square, London, WC1B 3JN, England; *The Europa World Year Book.*

St. Martin's Press, Inc., 175 Fifth Avenue, New York, New York 10010 (800) 221-7945; *The Statesman's Year-Book.*

TONGA - ANIMAL HEALTH

Food and Agricultural Organization of the United Nations (FAO), Via delle Terme di Caracalla, 00100, Rome, Italy (Telephone Number in U.S. (202) 653-2400); *Animal Health Yearbook.*

TONGA - AREA AND DENSITY OF POPULATION

Central Intelligence Agency, Washington, D.C. 20505 (703) 482-1100, www.cia.gov; *The World Factbook.*

Euromonitor International, Inc., 122 South Michigan Avenue, Suite 1200, Chicago, Illinois 60603 (800) 577-EURO; *The World Economic Factbook.*

Europa Publications Limited, 18 Bedford Square, London, WC1B 3JN, England; *The Europa World Year Book.*

Food and Agricultural Organization of the United Nations (FAO) Via delle Terme di Caracalla, 00100 Rome, Italy (Telephone Number in U.S. (202) 653-2400); *The State of Food and Agriculture.*

St. Martin's Press, Inc., 175 Fifth Avenue, New York, New York 10010 (800) 221-7945; *The Statesman's Year-Book.*

Statistical Office of the United Nations, Publishing Service, New York, New York 10017 (800) 253-9646; *Statistical Yearbook.*

TONGA - BALANCE OF PAYMENTS

Europa Publications Limited, 18 Bedford Square, London, WC1B 3JN, England; *The Europa World Year Book.*

International Monetary Fund, 700 Nineteenth Street, NW, Washington, D.C. 20431 (202) 623-7000; *Balance of Payments Yearbook.*

The World Bank, 1818 H Street, NW, Washington, D.C. 20433 (202) 477-1234; *World Development Indicators.*

TONGA - BANKING

Asian Development Bank, P.O. Box 789, 1099 Manila, Philippines; *Key Indicators of Developing Asian and Pacific Countries.*

Euromonitor International, Inc., 122 South Michigan Avenue, Suite 1200, Chicago, Illinois 60603 (800) 577-EURO; *World Marketing Data and Statistics.*

Europa Publications Limited, 18 Bedford Square, London, WC1B 3JN, England; *The Europa World Year Book.*

St. Martin's Press, Inc., 175 Fifth Avenue, New York, New York 10010 (800) 221-7945; *The Statesman's Year-Book.*

TONGA - BIRTH RATES

Central Intelligence Agency, Washington, D.C. 20505 (703) 482-1100, www.cia.gov; *The World Factbook.*

Euromonitor International, Inc., 122 South Michigan Avenue, Suite 1200, Chicago, Illinois 60603 (800) 577-EURO; *International Marketing Data and Statistics; and The World Economic Factbook.*

Europa Publications Limited, 18 Bedford Square, London, WC1B 3JN, England; *The Europa World Year Book.*

Statistical Office of the United Nations, Publishing Service, New York, New York 10017 (800) 253-9646; *Asia-Pacific in Figures; Demographic Yearbook; and Statistical Yearbook.*

The World Bank, 1818 H Street, NW, Washington, D.C. 20433 (202) 477-1234; *World Development Indicators.*

TONGA - BONDS

Asian Development Bank, P.O. Box 789, 1099 Manila, Philippines; *Key Indicators of Developing Asian and Pacific Countries.*

TONGA - BOOK PRODUCTION

United Nations Educational, Scientific and Cultural Organization (UNESCO), 7

Place de Fontenoy, F-75700 Paris, France (Telephone Number in U.S. (212) 963-5981); *Statistical Yearbook.*

The World Bank, 1818 H Street, NW, Washington, D.C. 20433 (202) 477-1234; *World Development Indicators.*

TONGA - BROADCASTING

Billboard Limited, P.O. Box 9027, 1006 AA Amsterdam, The Netherlands (Telephone Number in U.S. (212) 764-7300); *World Radio TV Handbook.*

Central Intelligence Agency, Washington, D.C. 20505 (703) 482-1100, www.cia.gov; *The World Factbook.*

Euromonitor International, Inc., 122 South Michigan Avenue, Suite 1200, Chicago, Illinois 60603 (800) 577-EURO; *World Marketing Data and Statistics.*

St. Martin's Press, Inc., 175 Fifth Avenue, New York, New York 10010 (800) 221-7945; *The Statesman's Year-Book.*

TONGA - BUDGET

Central Intelligence Agency, Washington, D.C. 20505 (703) 482-1100, www.cia.gov; *The World Factbook.*

TONGA - CALORIE SUPPLY

Asian Development Bank, P.O. Box 789, 1099 Manila, Philippines; *Key Indicators of Developing Asian and Pacific Countries.*

Food and Agricultural Organization of the United Nations (FAO) Via delle Terme di Caracalla, 00100 Rome, Italy (Telephone Number in U.S. (202) 653-2400); *The State of Food and Agriculture.*

TONGA - CAPITAL INVESTMENT

Asian Development Bank, P.O. Box 789, 1099 Manila, Philippines; *Key Indicators of Developing Asian and Pacific Countries.*

TONGA - CAPITAL REVENUE

Asian Development Bank, P.O. Box 789, 1099 Manila, Philippines; *Key Indicators of Developing Asian and Pacific Countries.*

TONGA - CATTLE - See TONGA - LIVESTOCK AND POULTRY

TONGA - CHEMICAL (ORGANIC) PRODUCTION - See TONGA - MINING AND MINERAL PRODUCTS

TONGA - CLIMATE

St. Martin's Press, Inc., 175 Fifth Avenue, New York, New York 10010 (800) 221-7945; *The Statesman's Year-Book.*

TONGA - CLOTHING EXPORTS AND IMPORTS - See TONGA - TEXTILE INDUSTRY

TONGA - COAL PRODUCTION - See TONGA - MINING AND MINERAL PRODUCTS

TONGA - COMMERCE

St. Martin's Press, Inc., 175 Fifth Avenue, New York, New York 10010 (800) 221-7945; *The Statesman's Year-Book.*

TONGA - COMMUNICATIONS - See TRANSPORTATION AND COMMUNICATIONS

TONGA - CONSUMER PRICE INDEX

Asian Development Bank, P.O. Box 789, 1099 Manila, Philippines; *Key Indicators of Developing Asian and Pacific Countries.*

Europa Publications Limited, 18 Bedford Square, London, WC1B 3JN, England; *The Europa World Year Book.*

Statistical Office of the United Nations, Publishing Service, New York, New York 10017 (800) 253-9646; *Statistical Yearbook.*

TONGA - CONSUMER PRICES

Euromonitor International, Inc., 122 South Michigan Avenue, Suite 1200, Chicago, Illinois 60603 (800) 577-EURO; *World Marketing Data and Statistics.*

International Labour Office, I.L.O. Publications, 1828 L Street, NW, Suite 801, Washington, D.C. 20036 (301) 638-3152; *Yearbook of Labour Statistics.*

TONGA - CONSUMPTION

South Pacific Commission, Post Box D5, Noumea Cedex, New Caledonia; *Statistical Bulletin of the South Pacific: Retail Price Indexes.*

TONGA - CORN PRODUCTION - See TONGA - CROPS

TONGA - CORPORATE TAXES - See TONGA - TAXATION

TONGA - CROPS

Asian Development Bank, P.O. Box 789, 1099 Manila, Philippines; *Key Indicators of Developing Asian and Pacific Countries.*

Europa Publications Limited, 18 Bedford Square, London, WC1B 3JN, England; *The Europa World Year Book.*

Food and Agricultural Organization of the United Nations (FAO) Via delle Terme di Caracalla, 00100 Rome, Italy (Telephone Number in U.S. (202) 653-2400); *The State*

of Food and Agriculture.

Statistical Office of the United Nations, Publishing Service, New York, New York 10017 (800) 253-9646; *Statistical Yearbook.*

United Nations Conference on Trade and Development, Central Statistical Service, Palais des Nations, Geneva, Switzerland (Telephone in U.S. (800) 253-9646); *UNCTAD Commodity Yearbook.*

TONGA - CUSTOMS DUTIES

St. Martin's Press, Inc., 175 Fifth Avenue, New York, New York 10010 (800) 221-7945; *The Statesman's Year-Book.*

TONGA - DAIRY PRODUCTS

Europa Publications Limited, 18 Bedford Square, London, WC1B 3JN, England; *The Europa World Year Book.*

Food and Agricultural Organization of the United Nations (FAO) Via delle Terme di Caracalla, 00100 Rome, Italy (Telephone Number in U.S. (202) 653-2400); *The State of Food and Agriculture.*

TONGA - DEATH RATES - See TONGA - MORTALITY

TONGA - DEMOGRAPHY

Euromonitor International, Inc., 122 South Michigan Avenue, Suite 1200, Chicago, Illinois 60603 (800) 577-EURO; *International Marketing Data and Statistics; World Marketing Data and Statistics;* and *The World Economic Factbook.*

Statistical Office of the United Nations, Publishing Service, New York, New York 10017 (800) 253-9646; *Asia-Pacific in Figures.*

TONGA - DEVELOPMENT ASSISTANCE

Asian Development Bank, P.O. Box 789, 1099 Manila, Philippines; *Key Indicators of Developing Asian and Pacific Countries.*

Statistical Office of the United Nations, Publishing Service, New York, New York 10017 (800) 253-9646; *Statistical Yearbook.*

TONGA - DISEASES - See TONGA - HEALTH

TONGA - DIVORCE RATES

Statistical Office of the United Nations, Publishing Service, New York, New York 10017 (800) 253-9646; *Demographic Yearbook;* and *Statistical Yearbook.*

TONGA - ECONOMY

Asian Development Bank, P.O. Box 789, 1099 Manila, Philippines; *Key Indicators of Developing Asian and Pacific Countries.*

Central Intelligence Agency, Washington, D.C. 20505 (703) 482-1100, www.cia.gov; *The World Factbook.*

Economist Intelligence Unit, 111 West 57th Street, New York, New York 10019 (800) 938-4685; *Tonga Country Report.*

Euromonitor International, Inc., 122 South Michigan Avenue, Suite 1200, Chicago, Illinois 60603 (800) 577-EURO; *The World Economic Factbook;* and *World Marketing Data and Statistics.*

Europa Publications Limited, 18 Bedford Square, London, WC1B 3JN, England; *The Europa World Year Book.*

St. Martin's Press, Inc., 175 Fifth Avenue, New York, New York 10010 (800) 221-7945; *The Statesman's Year-Book.*

Statistical Office of the United Nations, Publishing Service, New York, New York 10017 (800) 253-9646; *World Statistics Pocketbook.*

The World Bank, 1818 H Street, NW, Washington, D.C. 20433 (202) 477-1234; *The World Bank Atlas.*

TONGA - EDUCATION

Euromonitor International, Inc., 122 South Michigan Avenue, Suite 1200, Chicago, Illinois 60603 (800) 577-EURO; *International Marketing Data and Statistics;* and *World Marketing Data and Statistics.*

Europa Publications Limited, 18 Bedford Square, London, WC1B 3JN, England; *The Europa World Year Book.*

St. Martin's Press, Inc., 175 Fifth Avenue, New York, New York 10010 (800) 221-7945; *The Statesman's Year-Book.*

Statistical Office of the United Nations, Publishing Service, New York, New York 10017 (800) 253-9646; *Asia-Pacific in Figures.*

United Nations Educational, Scientific and Cultural Organization (UNESCO), 7 Place de Fontenoy, F-75700 Paris, France (Telephone Number in U.S. (212) 963-5981); *Statistical Yearbook.*

The World Bank, 1818 H Street, NW, Washington, D.C. 20433 (202) 477-1234; *World Development Indicators.*

TONGA - EGG PRODUCTION AND CONSUMPTION - See TONGA - DAIRY PRODUCTS

TONGA - ELECTRICITY

Asian Development Bank, P.O. Box 789, 1099 Manila, Philippines; *Key Indicators of Developing Asian and Pacific Countries.*

Central Intelligence Agency, Washington, D.C. 20505 (703) 482-1100, www.cia.gov; *The World Factbook.*

St. Martin's Press, Inc., 175 Fifth Avenue, New York, New York 10010 (800) 221-7945; *The Statesman's Year-Book.*

Statistical Office of the United Nations, Publishing Service, New York, New York 10017 (800) 253-9646; *Electric Power in Asia and the Pacific.*

TONGA - EMPLOYMENT

Euromonitor International, Inc., 122 South Michigan Avenue, Suite 1200, Chicago, Illinois 60603 (800) 577-EURO; *International Marketing Data and Statistics.*

International Labour Office, I.L.O. Publications, 1828 L Street, NW, Suite 801, Washington, D.C. 20036 (301) 638-3152; *Yearbook of Labour Statistics.*

Statistical Office of the United Nations, Publishing Service, New York, New York 10017 (800) 253-9646; *Asia-Pacific in Figures.*

TONGA - ENERGY

Euromonitor International, Inc., 122 South Michigan Avenue, Suite 1200, Chicago, Illinois 60603 (800) 577-EURO; *International Marketing Data and Statistics; World Marketing Data and Statistics;* and *The World Economic Factbook.*

Food and Agricultural Organization of the United Nations (FAO) Via delle Terme di Caracalla, 00100 Rome, Italy (Telephone Number in U.S. (202) 653-2400); *The State of Food and Agriculture.*

St. Martin's Press, Inc., 175 Fifth Avenue, New York, New York 10010 (800) 221-7945; *The Statesman's Year-Book.*

Statistical Office of the United Nations, Publishing Service, New York, New York 10017 (800) 253-9646; *Asia-Pacific in Figures; Energy Statistics Yearbook; Statistical Yearbook for Asia and the Pacific;* and *World Statistics Pocketbook.*

The World Bank, 1818 H Street, NW, Washington, D.C. 20433 (202) 477-1234; *The World Bank Atlas.*

TONGA - ENVIRONMENT

Economist Intelligence Unit, 111 West 57th Street, New York, New York 10019 (800) 938-4685; *Tonga Country Report.*

Statistical Office of the United Nations, Publishing Service, New York, New York 10017 (800) 253-9646; *World Statistics Pocketbook.*

TONGA - EXCHANGE RATES

Asian Development Bank, P.O. Box 789, 1099 Manila, Philippines; *Key Indicators of Developing Asian and Pacific Countries.*

Central Intelligence Agency, Washington, D.C. 20505 (703) 482-1100, www.cia.gov; *The World Factbook.*

Euromonitor International, Inc., 122 South Michigan Avenue, Suite 1200, Chicago, Illinois 60603 (800) 577-EURO; *International Marketing Data and Statistics;* and *The World Economic Factbook.*

Europa Publications Limited, 18 Bedford Square, London, WC1B 3JN, England; *The Europa World Year Book.*

Statistical Office of the United Nations, Publishing Service, New York, New York 10017 (800) 253-9646; *World Statistics Pocketbook.*

Walden Publishing Ltd., Two Market Street, Saffron Walden Essex, CB10 1HZ, England; *The World of Information Asia and Pacific Review.*

TONGA - EXPORTS

Asian Development Bank, P.O. Box 789, 1099 Manila, Philippines; *Key Indicators of Developing Asian and Pacific Countries.*

Central Intelligence Agency, Washington, D.C. 20505 (703) 482-1100, www.cia.gov; *The World Factbook.*

Economist Intelligence Unit, 111 West 57th Street, New York, New York 10019 (800) 938-4685; *Tonga Country Report.*

Euromonitor International, Inc., 122 South Michigan Avenue, Suite 1200, Chicago, Illinois 60603 (800) 577-EURO; *International Marketing Data and Statistics;* and *The World Economic Factbook.*

Europa Publications Limited, 18 Bedford Square, London, WC1B 3JN, England; *The Europa World Year Book.*

Food and Agricultural Organization of the United Nations (FAO) Via delle Terme di Caracalla, 00100 Rome, Italy (Telephone Number in U.S. (202) 653-2400); *The State of Food and Agriculture.*

International Monetary Fund, 700 Nineteenth Street, NW, Washington, D.C. 20431 (202) 623-7000; *Direction of Trade Statistics.*

South Pacific Commission, Post Box D5, Noumea Cedex, New Caledonia; *Statistical Bulletin of the South Pacific: Overseas Trade.*

St. Martin's Press, Inc., 175 Fifth

Avenue, New York, New York 10010 (800) 221-7945; *The Statesman's Year-Book.*

Statistical Office of the United Nations, Publishing Service, New York, New York 10017 (800) 253-9646; *Foreign Trade Statistics of Asia and the Pacific.*

Walden Publishing Ltd., Two Market Street, Saffron Walden Essex, CB10 1HZ, England; *The World of Information Asia and Pacific Review.*

The World Bank, 1818 H Street, NW, Washington, D.C. 20433 (202) 477-1234; *World Development Indicators.*

TONGA - EXTERNAL FINANCING

Asian Development Bank, P.O. Box 789, 1099 Manila, Philippines; *Key Indicators of Developing Asian and Pacific Countries.*

Statistical Office of the United Nations, Publishing Service, New York, New York 10017 (800) 253-9646; *Asia-Pacific in Figures.*

TONGA - EXTERNAL INDEBTEDNESS

Asian Development Bank, P.O. Box 789, 1099 Manila, Philippines; *Key Indicators of Developing Asian and Pacific Countries.*

The World Bank, 1818 H Street, NW, Washington, D.C. 20433 (202) 477-1234; *World Development Indicators.*

TONGA - EXTERNAL TRADE

Asian Development Bank, P.O. Box 789, 1099 Manila, Philippines; *Key Indicators of Developing Asian and Pacific Countries.*

Euromonitor International, Inc., 122 South Michigan Avenue, Suite 1200, Chicago, Illinois 60603 (800) 577-EURO; *World Marketing Data and Statistics.*

Food and Agricultural Organization of the United Nations (FAO) Via delle Terme di Caracalla, 00100 Rome, Italy (Telephone Number in U.S. (202) 653-2400); *The State of Food and Agriculture;* and *Trade Yearbook.*

Statistical Office of the United Nations, Publishing Service, New York, New York 10017 (800) 253-9646; *Statistical Yearbook for Asia and the Pacific.*

TONGA - FARM CROPS - See TONGA - CROPS

TONGA - FERTILITY RATES

Central Intelligence Agency, Washington, D.C. 20505 (703) 482-1100, www.cia.gov; *The World Factbook.*

The World Bank, 1818 H Street, NW,

Washington, D.C. 20433 (202) 477-1234; *The World Bank Atlas;* and *World Development Indicators.*

TONGA - FERTILIZER

Food and Agricultural Organization of the United Nations (FAO), Via delle Terme di Caracalla, 00100, Rome, Italy (Telephone Number in U.S. (202) 653-2400); *Fertilizer Yearbook;* and *The State of Food and Agriculture.*

TONGA - FETAL MORTALITY - See TONGA - MORTALITY

TONGA - FINANCE

Asian Development Bank, P.O. Box 789, 1099 Manila, Philippines; *Key Indicators of Developing Asian and Pacific Countries.*

Economist Intelligence Unit, 111 West 57th Street, New York, New York 10019 (800) 938-4685; *Tonga Country Report.*

Europa Publications Limited, 18 Bedford Square, London, WC1B 3JN, England; *The Europa World Year Book.*

St. Martin's Press, Inc., 175 Fifth Avenue, New York, New York 10010 (800) 221-7945; *The Statesman's Year-Book.*

Statistical Office of the United Nations, Publishing Service, New York, New York 10017 (800) 253-9646; *Statistical Yearbook for Asia and the Pacific.*

TONGA - FISHERIES

Europa Publications Limited, 18 Bedford Square, London, WC1B 3JN, England; *The Europa World Year Book.*

Food and Agricultural Organization of the United Nations (FAO) Via delle Terme di Caracalla, 00100 Rome, Italy (Telephone Number in U.S. (202) 653-2400); *The State of Food and Agriculture.*

St. Martin's Press, Inc., 175 Fifth Avenue, New York, New York 10010 (800) 221-7945; *The Statesman's Year-Book.*

Statistical Office of the United Nations, Publishing Service, New York, New York 10017 (800) 253-9646; *Statistical Yearbook;* and *Yearbook of Fishery Statistics.*

United Nations Conference on Trade and Development, Central Statistical Service, Palais des Nations, Geneva, Switzerland (Telephone in U.S. (800) 253-9646); *UNCTAD Commodity Yearbook.*

TONGA - FOOD

Food and Agricultural Organization of the United Nations (FAO) Via delle Terme di Caracalla, 00100 Rome, Italy (Telephone

Number in U.S. (202) 653-2400); *The State of Food and Agriculture.*

South Pacific Commission, Post Box D5, Noumea Cedex, New Caledonia; *Statistical Bulletin of the South Pacific: Retail Price Indexes.*

Statistical Office of the United Nations, Publishing Service, New York, New York 10017 (800) 253-9646; *Statistical Yearbook for Asia and the Pacific.*

United Nations Conference on Trade and Development, Central Statistical Service, Palais des Nations, Geneva, Switzerland (Telephone in U.S. (800) 253-9646); *UNCTAD Commodity Yearbook.*

TONGA - FOREIGN DEBT

Walden Publishing Ltd., Two Market Street, Saffron Walden Essex, CB10 1HZ, England; *The World of Information Asia and Pacific Review.*

TONGA - FOREIGN TRADE

Asian Development Bank, P.O. Box 789, 1099 Manila, Philippines; *Key Indicators of Developing Asian and Pacific Countries.*

Economist Intelligence Unit, 111 West 57th Street, New York, New York 10019 (800) 938-4685; *Tonga Country Report.*

Euromonitor International, Inc., 122 South Michigan Avenue, Suite 1200, Chicago, Illinois 60603 (800) 577-EURO; *The World Economic Factbook.*

Europa Publications Limited, 18 Bedford Square, London, WC1B 3JN, England; *The Europa World Year Book.*

Food and Agricultural Organization of the United Nations (FAO) Via delle Terme di Caracalla, 00100 Rome, Italy (Telephone Number in U.S. (202) 653-2400); *The State of Food and Agriculture.*

South Pacific Commission, Post Box D5, Noumea Cedex, New Caledonia; *Statistical Bulletin of the South Pacific: Overseas Trade.*

St. Martin's Press, Inc., 175 Fifth Avenue, New York, New York 10010 (800) 221-7945; *The Statesman's Year-Book.*

Statistical Office of the United Nations, Publishing Service, New York, New York 10017 (800) 253-9646; *International Trade Statistics Yearbook;* and *Statistical Yearbook.*

United Nations Conference on Trade and Development, Central Statistical Service, Palais des Nations, Geneva, Switzerland (Telephone in U.S. (800) 253-9646); *UNCTAD Commodity Yearbook.*

The World Bank, 1818 H Street, NW, Washington, D.C. 20433 (202) 477-1234; *World Development Indicators.*

TONGA - FORESTRY AND FOREST PRODUCTS

Europa Publications Limited, 18 Bedford Square, London, WC1B 3JN, England; *The Europa World Year Book.*

Food and Agricultural Organization of the United Nations (FAO) Via delle Terme di Caracalla, 00100 Rome, Italy (Telephone Number in U.S. (202) 653-2400); *The State of Food and Agriculture.*

United Nations Conference on Trade and Development, Central Statistical Service, Palais des Nations, Geneva, Switzerland (Telephone in U.S. (800) 253-9646); *UNCTAD Commodity Yearbook.*

TONGA - GENERAL INDUSTRIAL STATISTICS - See TONGA - INDUSTRY

TONGA - GENERAL MORTALITY - See TONGA - MORTALITY

TONGA - GOVERNMENT

Asian Development Bank, P.O. Box 789, 1099 Manila, Philippines; *Key Indicators of Developing Asian and Pacific Countries.*

Central Intelligence Agency, Washington, D.C. 20505 (703) 482-1100, www.cia.gov; *The World Factbook.*

Europa Publications Limited, 18 Bedford Square, London, WC1B 3JN, England; *The Europa World Year Book.*

St. Martin's Press, Inc., 175 Fifth Avenue, New York, New York 10010 (800) 221-7945; *The Statesman's Year-Book.*

Statistical Office of the United Nations, Publishing Service, New York, New York 10017 (800) 253-9646; *Asia-Pacific in Figures; National Accounts Statistics;* and *Statistical Yearbook.*

The World Bank, 1818 H Street, NW, Washington, D.C. 20433 (202) 477-1234; *World Development Indicators.*

TONGA - GRAIN PRODUCTION - See TONGA - CROPS

TONGA - GROSS DOMESTIC PRODUCT

Asian Development Bank, P.O. Box 789, 1099 Manila, Philippines; *Key Indicators of Developing Asian and Pacific Countries.*

Economist Intelligence Unit, 111 West 57th Street, New York, New York 10019 (800) 938-4685; *Tonga Country Report.*

Euromonitor International, Inc., 122

South Michigan Avenue, Suite 1200, Chicago, Illinois 60603 (800) 577-EURO; *International Marketing Data and Statistics;* and *The World Economic Factbook.*

Europa Publications Limited, 18 Bedford Square, London, WC1B 3JN, England; *The Europa World Year Book.*

Statistical Office of the United Nations, Publishing Service, New York, New York 10017 (800) 253-9646; *National Accounts Statistics;* and *Statistical Yearbook.*

The World Bank, 1818 H Street, NW, Washington, D.C. 20433 (202) 477-1234; *World Development Indicators.*

TONGA - GROSS NATIONAL PRODUCT

Asian Development Bank, P.O. Box 789, 1099 Manila, Philippines; *Key Indicators of Developing Asian and Pacific Countries.*

St. Martin's Press, Inc., 175 Fifth Avenue, New York, New York 10010 (800) 221-7945; *The Statesman's Year-Book.*

Walden Publishing Ltd., Two Market Street, Saffron Walden Essex, CB10 1HZ, England; *The World of Information Asia and Pacific Review.*

The World Bank, 1818 H Street, NW, Washington, D.C. 20433 (202) 477-1234; *The World Bank Atlas;* and *World Development Indicators.*

TONGA - GROUNDNUT PRODUCTION - See TONGA - CROPS

TONGA - HEALTH

Euromonitor International, Inc., 122 South Michigan Avenue, Suite 1200, Chicago, Illinois 60603 (800) 577-EURO; *World Marketing Data and Statistics.*

South Pacific Commission, Post Box D5, Noumea Cedex, New Caledonia; *Statistical Bulletin of the South Pacific: Retail Price Indexes.*

St. Martin's Press, Inc., 175 Fifth Avenue, New York, New York 10010 (800) 221-7945; *The Statesman's Year-Book.*

Statistical Office of the United Nations, Publishing Service, New York, New York 10017 (800) 253-9646; *Asia-Pacific in Figures;* and *Statistical Yearbook.*

World Health Organization, Office of Publications, 20 Avenue Appia, CH-1211 Geneva 27, Switzerland (Telephone Number in U.S. (518) 436-9686); *World Health Statistics Annual.*

TONGA - HIGHWAYS

Central Intelligence Agency,

Washington, D.C. 20505 (703) 482-1100, www.cia.gov; *The World Factbook.*

St. Martin's Press, Inc., 175 Fifth Avenue, New York, New York 10010 (800) 221-7945; *The Statesman's Year-Book.*

TONGA - HORSES - See TONGA - LIVESTOCK AND POULTRY

TONGA - HOURS OF WORK - See TONGA - EMPLOYMENT

TONGA - HOUSING AND HOUSING UNITS

Euromonitor International, Inc., 122 South Michigan Avenue, Suite 1200, Chicago, Illinois 60603 (800) 577-EURO; *World Marketing Data and Statistics.*

South Pacific Commission, Post Box D5, Noumea Cedex, New Caledonia; *Statistical Bulletin of the South Pacific: Retail Price Indexes.*

TONGA - HOUSING EXPENDITURES

South Pacific Commission, Post Box D5, Noumea Cedex, New Caledonia; *Statistical Bulletin of the South Pacific: Retail Price Indexes.*

TONGA - ILLITERATE POPULATION

Central Intelligence Agency, Washington, D.C. 20505 (703) 482-1100, www.cia.gov; *The World Factbook.*

Euromonitor International, Inc., 122 South Michigan Avenue, Suite 1200, Chicago, Illinois 60603 (800) 577-EURO; *The World Economic Factbook.*

Statistical Office of the United Nations, Publishing Service, New York, New York 10017 (800) 253-9646; *Asia-Pacific in Figures.*

TONGA - IMPORTS

Asian Development Bank, P.O. Box 789, 1099 Manila, Philippines; *Key Indicators of Developing Asian and Pacific Countries.*

Central Intelligence Agency, Washington, D.C. 20505 (703) 482-1100, www.cia.gov; *The World Factbook.*

Economist Intelligence Unit, 111 West 57th Street, New York, New York 10019 (800) 938-4685; *Tonga Country Report.*

Euromonitor International, Inc., 122 South Michigan Avenue, Suite 1200, Chicago, Illinois 60603 (800) 577-EURO; *International Marketing Data and Statistics;* and *The World Economic Factbook.*

Europa Publications Limited, 18 Bedford Square, London, WC1B 3JN, England; *The Europa World Year Book.*

Food and Agricultural Organization of the United Nations (FAO) Via delle Terme di Caracalla, 00100 Rome, Italy (Telephone Number in U.S. (202) 653-2400); *The State of Food and Agriculture.*

International Monetary Fund, 700 Nineteenth Street, NW, Washington, D.C. 20431 (202) 623-7000; *Direction of Trade Statistics.*

South Pacific Commission, Post Box D5, Noumea Cedex, New Caledonia; *Statistical Bulletin of the South Pacific: Overseas Trade.*

St. Martin's Press, Inc., 175 Fifth Avenue, New York, New York 10010 (800) 221-7945; *The Statesman's Year-Book.*

Statistical Office of the United Nations, Publishing Service, New York, New York 10017 (800) 253-9646; *Foreign Trade Statistics of Asia and the Pacific.*

Walden Publishing Ltd., Two Market Street, Saffron Walden Essex, CB10 1HZ, England; *The World of Information Asia and Pacific Review.*

The World Bank, 1818 H Street, NW, Washington, D.C. 20433 (202) 477-1234; *World Development Indicators.*

TONGA - INDUSTRY

Central Intelligence Agency, Washington, D.C. 20505 (703) 482-1100, www.cia.gov; *The World Factbook.*

Economist Intelligence Unit, 111 West 57th Street, New York, New York 10019 (800) 938-4685; *Tonga Country Report.*

Euromonitor International, Inc., 122 South Michigan Avenue, Suite 1200, Chicago, Illinois 60603 (800) 577-EURO; *The World Economic Factbook;* and *World Marketing Data and Statistics.*

International Labour Office, I.L.O. Publications, 1828 L Street, NW, Suite 801, Washington, D.C. 20036 (301) 638-3152; *Yearbook of Labour Statistics.*

Statistical Office of the United Nations, Publishing Service, New York, New York 10017 (800) 253-9646; *Asia-Pacific in Figures; Industrial Commodity Statistics Yearbook;* and *Statistical Yearbook for Asia and the Pacific.*

TONGA - INFANT AND MATERNAL MORTALITY - See TONGA - MORTALITY

TONGA - INTERNAL TRADE

Statistical Office of the United Nations, Publishing Service, New York, New York 10017 (800) 253-9646; *Statistical Yearbook for Asia and the Pacific.*

TONGA - INTERNATIONAL RESERVES EXCLUDING GOLD

Asian Development Bank, P.O. Box 789, 1099 Manila, Philippines; *Key Indicators of Developing Asian and Pacific Countries.*

TONGA - INTERNATIONAL STATISTICS

Asian Development Bank, P.O. Box 789, 1099 Manila, Philippines; *Key Indicators of Developing Asian and Pacific Countries.*

TONGA - LABOR

Central Intelligence Agency, Washington, D.C. 20505 (703) 482-1100, www.cia.gov; *The World Factbook.*

Euromonitor International, Inc., 122 South Michigan Avenue, Suite 1200, Chicago, Illinois 60603 (800) 577-EURO; *International Marketing Data and Statistics;* and *World Marketing Data and Statistics.*

Europa Publications Limited, 18 Bedford Square, London, WC1B 3JN, England; *The Europa World Year Book.*

Food and Agricultural Organization of the United Nations (FAO) Via delle Terme di Caracalla, 00100 Rome, Italy (Telephone Number in U.S. (202) 653-2400); *The State of Food and Agriculture.*

International Labour Office, I.L.O. Publications, 1828 L Street, NW, Suite 801, Washington, D.C. 20036 (301) 638-3152; *Yearbook of Labour Statistics.*

The World Bank, 1818 H Street, NW, Washington, D.C. 20433 (202) 477-1234; *The World Bank Atlas;* and *World Development Indicators.*

TONGA - LAND USE

Central Intelligence Agency, Washington, D.C. 20505 (703) 482-1100, www.cia.gov; *The World Factbook.*

Euromonitor International, Inc., 122 South Michigan Avenue, Suite 1200, Chicago, Illinois 60603 (800) 577-EURO; *International Marketing Data and Statistics.*

Food and Agricultural Organization of the United Nations (FAO), Via delle Terme di Caracalla, 00100 Rome, Italy (Telephone Number in U.S. (202) 653-2400); *Production Yearbook.*

TONGA - LIBRARIES

United Nations Educational, Scientific and Cultural Organization (UNESCO), 7 Place de Fontenoy, F-75700 Paris, France (Telephone Number in U.S. (212) 963-5981); *Statistical Yearbook.*

TONGA - LIFE EXPECTANCY

Central Intelligence Agency, Washington, D.C. 20505 (703) 482-1100, www.cia.gov; *The World Factbook*.

Euromonitor International, Inc., 122 South Michigan Avenue, Suite 1200, Chicago, Illinois 60603 (800) 577-EURO; *The World Economic Factbook*.

Statistical Office of the United Nations, Publishing Service, New York, New York 10017 (800) 253-9646; *Asia-Pacific in Figures;* and *World Statistics Pocketbook*.

The World Bank, 1818 H Street, NW, Washington, D.C. 20433 (202) 477-1234; *The World Bank Atlas*.

TONGA - LITERACY RATE

Euromonitor International, Inc., 122 South Michigan Avenue, Suite 1200, Chicago, Illinois 60603 (800) 577-EURO; *World Marketing Data and Statistics*.

TONGA - LIVESTOCK AND POULTRY

Europa Publications Limited, 18 Bedford Square, London, WC1B 3JN, England; *The Europa World Year Book*.

Food and Agricultural Organization of the United Nations (FAO), Via delle Terme di Caracalla, 00100 Rome, Italy (Telephone Number in U.S. (202) 653-2400); *Production Yearbook;* and *The State of Food and Agriculture*.

St. Martin's Press, Inc., 175 Fifth Avenue, New York, New York 10010 (800) 221-7945; *The Statesman's Year-Book*.

Statistical Office of the United Nations, Publishing Service, New York, New York 10017 (800) 253-9646; *Statistical Yearbook*.

United Nations Conference on Trade and Development, Central Statistical Service, Palais des Nations, Geneva, Switzerland (Telephone in U.S. (800) 253-9646); *UNCTAD Commodity Yearbook*.

TONGA - MAIL - NUMBER OF ITEMS SENT AND RECEIVED

Statistical Office of the United Nations, Publishing Service, New York, New York 10017 (800) 253-9646; *Statistical Yearbook*.

TONGA - MANPOWER

Statistical Office of the United Nations, Publishing Service, New York, New York 10017 (800) 253-9646; *Statistical Yearbook for Asia and the Pacific*.

TONGA - MANUFACTURING

Asian Development Bank, P.O. Box 789, 1099 Manila, Philippines; *Key Indicators of Developing Asian and Pacific Countries*.

The World Bank, 1818 H Street, NW, Washington, D.C. 20433 (202) 477-1234; *World Development Indicators*.

TONGA - MARRIAGE RATES

Statistical Office of the United Nations, Publishing Service, New York, New York 10017 (800) 253-9646; *Demographic Yearbook;* and *Statistical Yearbook*.

TONGA - MEAT PRODUCTION - See TONGA - LIVESTOCK AND POULTRY

TONGA - MERCHANT SHIPPING

Europa Publications Limited, 18 Bedford Square, London, WC1B 3JN, England; *The Europa World Year Book*.

St. Martin's Press, Inc., 175 Fifth Avenue, New York, New York 10010 (800) 221-7945; *The Statesman's Year-Book*.

Statistical Office of the United Nations, Publishing Service, New York, New York 10017 (800) 253-9646; *Statistical Yearbook*.

U.S. Department of Transportation, Maritime Administration, 400 Seventh Street, SW, Washington, D.C. 20590 (202) 366-5807; *A Statistical Analysis of the World's Merchant Fleets*.

TONGA - MILITARY

Central Intelligence Agency, Washington, D.C. 20505 (703) 482-1100, www.cia.gov; *The World Factbook*.

Euromonitor International, Inc., 122 South Michigan Avenue, Suite 1200, Chicago, Illinois 60603 (800) 577-EURO; *World Marketing Data and Statistics*.

TONGA - MINING AND MINERAL PRODUCTS

Asian Development Bank, P.O. Box 789, 1099 Manila, Philippines; *Key Indicators of Developing Asian and Pacific Countries*.

United Nations Conference on Trade and Development, Central Statistical Service, Palais des Nations, Geneva, Switzerland (Telephone in U.S. (800) 253-9646); *UNCTAD Commodity Yearbook*.

TONGA - MONEY SUPPLY

Asian Development Bank, P.O. Box 789, 1099 Manila, Philippines; *Key Indicators of Developing Asian and Pacific Countries*.

Economist Intelligence Unit, 111 West 57th Street, New York, New York 10019 (800) 938-4685; *Tonga Country Report*.

Europa Publications Limited, 18 Bedford Square, London, WC1B 3JN, England; *The Europa World Year Book*.

The World Bank, 1818 H Street, NW, Washington, D.C. 20433 (202) 477-1234; *World Development Indicators*.

TONGA - MORTALITY

Central Intelligence Agency, Washington, D.C. 20505 (703) 482-1100, www.cia.gov; *The World Factbook*.

Euromonitor International, Inc., 122 South Michigan Avenue, Suite 1200, Chicago, Illinois 60603 (800) 577-EURO; *International Marketing Data and Statistics;* and *The World Economic Factbook*.

Europa Publications Limited, 18 Bedford Square, London, WC1B 3JN, England; *The Europa World Year Book*.

Statistical Office of the United Nations, Publishing Service, New York, New York 10017 (800) 253-9646; *Asia-Pacific in Figures; Demographic Yearbook; Statistical Yearbook;* and *World Statistics Pocketbook*.

The World Bank, 1818 H Street, NW, Washington, D.C. 20433 (202) 477-1234; *The World Bank Atlas*.

World Health Organization, Office of Publications, 20 Avenue Appia, CH-1211 Geneva 27, Switzerland (Telephone Number in U.S. (518) 436-9686); *World Health Statistics Annual*.

TONGA - MOTION PICTURES

Statistical Office of the United Nations, Publishing Service, New York, New York 10017 (800) 253-9646; *Statistical Yearbook*.

TONGA - MOTOR VEHICLES IN USE

Europa Publications Limited, 18 Bedford Square, London, WC1B 3JN, England; *The Europa World Year Book*.

Statistical Office of the United Nations, Publishing Service, New York, New York 10017 (800) 253-9646; *Statistical Yearbook*.

TONGA - NATALITY - See TONGA - BIRTH RATES

TONGA - NATIONAL ACCOUNTS

Statistical Office of the United Nations, Publishing Service, New York, New York 10017 (800) 253-9646; *Asia-Pacific in Figures; National Accounts Statistics;* and *Statistical Yearbook for Asia and the Pacific*.

TONGA - NATIONAL INCOME

Statistical Office of the United Nations, Publishing Service, New York, New York 10017 (800) 253-9646; *National Accounts Statistics;* and *Statistical Yearbook*.

TONGA - NEWSPAPER PRODUCTION - See TONGA - FORESTRY AND FOREST PRODUCTS

TONGA - OCCUPATIONS - See TONGA - OCCUPATIONS

TONGA - PERIODICALS

United Nations Educational, Scientific and Cultural Organization (UNESCO), 7 Place de Fontenoy, F-75700 Paris, France (Telephone Number in U.S. (212) 963-5981); *Statistical Yearbook.*

TONGA - PESTICIDE USE

Food and Agricultural Organization of the United Nations (FAO) Via delle Terme di Caracalla, 00100 Rome, Italy (Telephone Number in U.S. (202) 653-2400); *The State of Food and Agriculture.*

TONGA - PETROLEUM INDUSTRY

Asian Development Bank, P.O. Box 789, 1099 Manila, Philippines; *Key Indicators of Developing Asian and Pacific Countries.*

Food and Agricultural Organization of the United Nations (FAO) Via delle Terme di Caracalla, 00100 Rome, Italy (Telephone Number in U.S. (202) 653-2400); *The State of Food and Agriculture.*

United Nations Conference on Trade and Development, Central Statistical Service, Palais des Nations, Geneva, Switzerland (Telephone in U.S. (800) 253-9646); *UNCTAD Commodity Yearbook.*

TONGA - PIGS - See TONGA - LIVESTOCK AND POULTRY

TONGA - POPULATION

Asian Development Bank, P.O. Box 789, 1099 Manila, Philippines; *Key Indicators of Developing Asian and Pacific Countries.*

Central Intelligence Agency, Washington, D.C. 20505 (703) 482-1100, www.cia.gov; *The World Factbook.*

Economist Intelligence Unit, 111 West 57th Street, New York, New York 10019 (800) 938-4685; *Tonga Country Report.*

Euromonitor International, Inc., 122 South Michigan Avenue, Suite 1200, Chicago, Illinois 60603 (800) 577-EURO; *International Marketing Data and Statistics;* and *The World Economic Factbook.*

Europa Publications Limited, 18 Bedford Square, London, WC1B 3JN, England; *The Europa World Year Book.*

Food and Agricultural Organization of the United Nations (FAO), Via delle Terme di Caracalla, 00100 Rome, Italy (Telephone

Number in U.S. (202) 653-2400); *Production Yearbook.*

International Labour Office, I.L.O. Publications, 1828 L Street, NW, Suite 801, Washington, D.C. 20036 (301) 638-3152; *Yearbook of Labour Statistics.*

St. Martin's Press, Inc., 175 Fifth Avenue, New York, New York 10010 (800) 221-7945; *The Statesman's Year-Book.*

Statistical Office of the United Nations, Publishing Service, New York, New York 10017 (800) 253-9646; *Asia-Pacific in Figures; Demographic Yearbook; Statistical Yearbook; Statistical Yearbook for Asia and the Pacific;* and *World Statistics Pocketbook.*

Walden Publishing Ltd., Two Market Street, Saffron Walden Essex, CB10 1HZ, England; *The World of Information Asia and Pacific Review.*

The World Bank, 1818 H Street, NW, Washington, D.C. 20433 (202) 477-1234; *The World Bank Atlas.*

TONGA - POWER PRODUCTION INDUSTRY

Statistical Office of the United Nations, Publishing Service, New York, New York 10017 (800) 253-9646; *Electric Power in Asia and the Pacific.*

TONGA - PRICES

Asian Development Bank, P.O. Box 789, 1099 Manila, Philippines; *Key Indicators of Developing Asian and Pacific Countries.*

Food and Agricultural Organization of the United Nations (FAO), Via delle Terme di Caracalla, 00100 Rome, Italy (Telephone Number in U.S. (202) 653-2400); *Production Yearbook;* and *The State of Food and Agriculture.*

International Labour Office, I.L.O. Publications, 1828 L Street, NW, Suite 801, Washington, D.C. 20036 (301) 638-3152; *Yearbook of Labour Statistics.*

South Pacific Commission, Post Box D5, Noumea Cedex, New Caledonia; *Statistical Bulletin of the South Pacific: Overseas Trade;* and *Statistical Bulletin of the South Pacific: Retail Price Indexes.*

TONGA - RADIO RECEIVERS

St. Martin's Press, Inc., 175 Fifth Avenue, New York, New York 10010 (800) 221-7945; *The Statesman's Year-Book.*

TONGA - RELIGION

Central Intelligence Agency, Washington, D.C. 20505 (703) 482-1100,

www.cia.gov; *The World Factbook.*

St. Martin's Press, Inc., 175 Fifth Avenue, New York, New York 10010 (800) 221-7945; *The Statesman's Year-Book.*

TONGA - RETAIL TRADE

Euromonitor International, Inc., 122 South Michigan Avenue, Suite 1200, Chicago, Illinois 60603 (800) 577-EURO; *World Marketing Data and Statistics.*

TONGA - RICE PRODUCTION - See TONGA - CROPS

TONGA - SOCIAL DATA

Asian Development Bank, P.O. Box 789, 1099 Manila, Philippines; *Key Indicators of Developing Asian and Pacific Countries.*

Statistical Office of the United Nations, Publishing Service, New York, New York 10017 (800) 253-9646; *World Statistics Pocketbook.*

TONGA - SOCIAL SECURITY

Statistical Office of the United Nations, Publishing Service, New York, New York 10017 (800) 253-9646; *National Accounts Statistics.*

TONGA - STOCKS - COMMODITY - MARKET PRICE - INDEX

Food and Agricultural Organization of the United Nations (FAO) Via delle Terme di Caracalla, 00100 Rome, Italy (Telephone Number in U.S. (202) 653-2400); *The State of Food and Agriculture.*

TONGA - TAXATION

Europa Publications Limited, 18 Bedford Square, London, WC1B 3JN, England; *The Europa World Year Book.*

The World Bank, 1818 H Street, NW, Washington, D.C. 20433 (202) 477-1234; *World Development Indicators.*

TONGA - TELEPHONES IN USE

American Telephone and Telegraph Company, 26 Parsippany Road, Whippany, New Jersey 07981 (800) 222-0300; *The World's Telephones.*

Central Intelligence Agency, Washington, D.C. 20505 (703) 482-1100, www.cia.gov; *The World Factbook.*

St. Martin's Press, Inc., 175 Fifth Avenue, New York, New York 10010 (800) 221-7945; *The Statesman's Year-Book.*

Statistical Office of the United Nations, Publishing Service, New York, New York 10017 (800) 253-9646; *World Statistics*

Pocketbook.

TONGA - TEXTILE INDUSTRY

South Pacific Commission, Post Box D5, Noumea Cedex, New Caledonia; *Statistical Bulletin of the South Pacific: Retail Price Indexes.*

United Nations Conference on Trade and Development, Central Statistical Service, Palais des Nations, Geneva, Switzerland (Telephone in U.S. (800) 253-9646); *UNCTAD Commodity Yearbook.*

TONGA - TOBACCO PRODUCTION

South Pacific Commission, Post Box D5, Noumea Cedex, New Caledonia; *Statistical Bulletin of the South Pacific: Retail Price Indexes.*

TONGA - TOURISM

Euromonitor International, Inc., 122 South Michigan Avenue, Suite 1200, Chicago, Illinois 60603 (800) 577-EURO; *The World Economic Factbook;* and *World Marketing Data and Statistics.*

Europa Publications Limited, 18 Bedford Square, London, WC1B 3JN, England; *The Europa World Year Book.*

St. Martin's Press, Inc., 175 Fifth Avenue, New York, New York 10010 (800) 221-7945; *The Statesman's Year-Book.*

Statistical Office of the United Nations, Publishing Service, New York, New York 10017 (800) 253-9646; *Statistical Yearbook.*

World Tourism Organization, Calle Capitan Haya 42, E-28020 Madrid, Spain; *Yearbook of Tourism Statistics.*

TONGA - TRACTORS IN USE

Statistical Office of the United Nations, Publishing Service, New York, New York 10017 (800) 253-9646; *Statistical Yearbook.*

TONGA - TRADE - See TONGA - FOREIGN TRADE

TONGA - TRANSPORTATION AND COMMUNICATIONS

Central Intelligence Agency, Washington, D.C. 20505 (703) 482-1100, www.cia.gov; *The World Factbook.*

Euromonitor International, Inc., 122 South Michigan Avenue, Suite 1200, Chicago, Illinois 60603 (800) 577-EURO; *International Marketing Data and Statistics;* and *World Marketing Data and Statistics.*

Europa Publications Limited, 18 Bedford Square, London, WC1B 3JN, England; *The Europa World Year Book.*

South Pacific Commission, Post Box D5, Noumea Cedex, New Caledonia; *Statistical Bulletin of the South Pacific: Retail Price Indexes.*

St. Martin's Press, Inc., 175 Fifth Avenue, New York, New York 10010 (800) 221-7945; *The Statesman's Year-Book.*

Statistical Office of the United Nations, Publishing Service, New York, New York 10017 (800) 253-9646; *Statistical Yearbook for Asia and the Pacific.*

TONGA - UNEMPLOYMENT

Central Intelligence Agency, Washington, D.C. 20505 (703) 482-1100, www.cia.gov; *The World Factbook.*

International Labour Office, I.L.O. Publications, 1828 L Street, NW, Suite 801, Washington, D.C. 20036 (301) 638-3152; *Yearbook of Labour Statistics.*

TONGA - UTILITIES

Statistical Office of the United Nations, Publishing Service, New York, New York 10017 (800) 253-9646; *Electric Power in Asia and the Pacific.*

TONGA - VITAL STATISTICS

Statistical Office of the United Nations, Publishing Service, New York, New York 10017 (800) 253-9646; *Statistical Yearbook.*

TONGA - WAGES

International Labour Office, I.L.O. Publications, 1828 L Street, NW, Suite 801, Washington, D.C. 20036 (301) 638-3152; *Yearbook of Labour Statistics.*

Statistical Office of the United Nations, Publishing Service, New York, New York 10017 (800) 253-9646; *Statistical Yearbook for Asia and the Pacific.*

TONGA - WHOLESALE PRICES

Asian Development Bank, P.O. Box 789, 1099 Manila, Philippines; *Key Indicators of Developing Asian and Pacific Countries.*

TONNAGE - VESSELS - ENTERED AND CLEARED IN FOREIGN TRADE

U.S. Department of Commerce, Bureau of the Census, Washington, D.C. 20233 (301) 457-4100, www.census.gov; TA 987.

TONNAGE - VESSELS - MERCHANT

Lloyd's Register of Shipping, 71 Fenchurch Street, London EC3, England; *Statistical Tables; Annual Summary of Merchant Ships Completed in the World;* and *World Fleet Statistics.*

TONNAGE - VESSELS - SHIPS AND TONNAGE LOST

Lloyd's Register of Shipping, 71 Fenchurch Street, London EC3, England; *Casualty Return.*

TOOLS - See CUTLERY AND MACHINE TOOLS

TORNADOES

U.S. Department of Commerce, National Oceanic and Atmospheric Administration, National Climatic Data Center, 151 Patton Avenue, Asheville, North Carolina 28801 (704) 271-4800, www.ncdc.noaa.gov; *Storm Data.*

TOURISM - FOREIGN - See also TRAVEL

U.S. Department of Commerce, International Trade Administration, Fourteenth Street between Constitution Avenue and E Street, NW, Washington, D.C. 20230 (202) 482-2185, www.ita.doc.gov; Internet site http://www.tinet.ita.doc.gov.

U.S. Department of Justice, Immigration and Naturalization Service, 425 I Street, NW, Washington, D.C. 20536 (202) 305-1613, www.ins.usdoj.gov; *Statistical Yearbook.*

TOWNSHIPS AND SPECIAL DISTRICTS

U.S. Department of Commerce, Bureau of the Census, Washington, D.C. 20233 (301) 457-4100, www.census.gov; *Census of Governments;* and *Government Organization.*

TOXIC-SHOCK SYNDROME

U.S. Department of Health and Human Services, Centers for Disease Control, 1600 Clifton Road, NE, Atlanta, Georgia 30333 (800) 311-3435, www.cdc.gov; *Summary of Notifiable Diseases, United States, Morbidity and Mortality Weekly Report.*

TOYS AND SPORTING GOODS - ADVERTISING EXPENDITURES

Television Bureau of Advertising, Inc., 3 East 54th Street, New York, New York 10022 (212) 486-1111; from data compiled by Competitive Media Reporting, 11 West 42nd Street, New York, New York 10036 (212) 789-1400.

TOYS AND SPORTING GOODS - CONSUMER EXPENDITURES

U.S. Department of Commerce, Bureau of Economic Analysis, Fourteenth Street between Constitution Avenue and E Street, NW, Washington, D.C. 20230 (202) 606-9900, www.bea.doc.gov; *The National Income and Product Accounts of the United*

States; and *Survey of Current Business.*

TOYS AND SPORTING GOODS - FOREIGN TRADE

U.S. Department of Commerce, Bureau of the Census, Washington, D.C. 20233 (301) 457-4100, www.census.gov; *U.S. International Trade in Goods and Services.*

TOYS AND SPORTING GOODS - MANUFACTURING - EARNINGS

U.S. Department of Labor, Bureau of Labor Statistics, Two Massachusetts Avenue, NE, Washington, D.C. 20212 (202) 691-5200, www.stats.bls.gov; *Employment and Earnings*; and Internet site: http://stats.bls.gov/ceshome.htm.

TOYS AND SPORTING GOODS - MANUFACTURING - EMPLOYEES

U.S. Department of Labor, Bureau of Labor Statistics, Two Massachusetts Avenue, NE, Washington, D.C. 20212 (202) 691-5200, www.stats.bls.gov; *Employment and Earnings*; and Internet site: http://stats.bls.gov/ceshome.htm.

TOYS AND SPORTING GOODS - MANUFACTURING - PRODUCTIVITY

U.S. Department of Labor, Bureau of Labor Statistics, Two Massachusetts Avenue, NE, Washington, D.C. 20212 (202) 691-5200, www.stats.bls.gov; Internet site: http://stats.bls.gov/ iprhome.htm.

TOYS AND SPORTING GOODS - MANUFACTURING - SHIPMENTS

U.S. Department of Commerce, Bureau of the Census, Washington, D.C. 20233 (301) 457-4100, www.census.gov; *Census of Manufactures*; and *Annual Survey of Manufactures.*

TOYS AND SPORTING GOODS - PRICE INDEXES

U.S. Department of Labor, Bureau of Labor Statistics, Two Massachusetts Avenue, NE, Washington, D.C. 20212 (202) 691-5200, www.stats.bls.gov; *Monthly Labor Review*; and *CPI Detailed Report.*

TRACK

National Collegiate Athletics Association, 700 West Washington Street, Indianapolis, Indiana 46206 (317) 917-6222; *1997-98 Participation Study.*

National Federation of State High School Associations, Post Office Box 690, Indianapolis, Indiana 46206 (317) 972-6900; *The 1998-99 High School Athletics Participation Survey.*

TRADE (BUSINESS) - See: COMMERCE, FOREIGN TRADE, RETAIL TRADE and WHOLESALE TRADE

TRADE, BUSINESS AND COMMERCIAL ASSOCIATIONS

The Gale Group, 27500 Drake Road, Farmington Hills, Michigan 48331-3535 (800) 877-4253; *Encyclopedia of Associations.*

TRAILERS (CAMPERS)

American Automobile Manufacturers Association, 1401 H Street, NW, Suite 900, Washington, D.C. 20005 (202) 326-5500; *Motor Vehicle Facts and Figures.*

Recreation Vehicle Industry Association, Post Office Box 2999, 1896 Preston White Drive, Reston, Virginia 22090 (703) 620-6003; *RVIA Industry Profile.*

TRANQUILIZERS

U.S. Department of Health and Human Services, Substance Abuse and Mental Health Services Administration, 5600 Fishers Lane, Rockville, Maryland 20857 (800) 729-6686, www.samhsa.gov; *National Household Survey on Drug Abuse.*

TRANSIT INDUSTRY - See PASSENGER TRANSIT INDUSTRY

TRANSPORTATION - See also MOTOR VEHICLES and Individual Modes

TRANSPORTATION - ACCIDENTS

International Civil Aviation Organization, 999 University Street, Montreal, Quebec, Canada H3C 5H7 (514) 954-8219; *Civil Aviation Statistics of the World.*

U.S. Department of Transportation, Bureau of Transportation Statistics, 400 Seventh Street, SW, Washington, D.C. 20590 (202) 366-DATA; *National Transportation Statistics.*

TRANSPORTATION - CARRIERS OF PASSENGERS

Air Transport Association of America, 1301 Pennsylvania Avenue, NW, Washington, D.C. 20004 (202) 626-4000; *Air Transport*; and *Air Transport, Facts and Figures.*

American Public Transit Association, 1201 New York Avenue, NW, Suite 400, Washington, D.C. 20005 (202) 898-4000; *Transit Fact Book;* and Internet site: http://www.apta.com/pubs/stats/index.htm.

Association of American Railroads,

American Railroads Building, 50 F Street, NW, Washington, D.C. 20001 (202) 639-2100; *Railroad Facts; Statistics of Railroads of Class I;* and *Analysis of Class I Railroads.*

Eno Transportation Foundation, One Farragut Square, South, Suite 500, Washington, D.C. 20006 (202) 879-4700; *Transportation in America.*

U.S. Department of Transportation, Bureau of Transportation Statistics, 400 Seventh Street, SW, Washington, D.C. 20590 (202) 366-DATA; *Selected Earnings Data, Class I Motor Carriers of Passengers.*

TRANSPORTATION - CARRIERS OF PROPERTY

Association of American Railroads, American Railroads Building, 50 F Street, NW, Washington, D.C. 20001 (202) 639-2100; *Weekly Railroad Traffic;* and *Freight Commodity Statistics.*

Eno Transportation Foundation, One Farragut Square, South, Suite 500, Washington, D.C. 20006 (202) 879-4700; *Transportation in America.*

U.S. Department of Commerce, Bureau of the Census, Washington, D.C. 20233 (301) 457-4100, www.census.gov; *Transportation Annual Survey.*

U.S. Department of Transportation, Bureau of Transportation Statistics, 400 Seventh Street, SW, Washington, D.C. 20590 (202) 366-DATA; *National Transportation Statistics.*

TRANSPORTATION - COMMODITY FLOW

U.S. Department of Transportation, Bureau of Transportation Statistics, 400 Seventh Street, SW, Washington, D.C. 20590 (202) 366-DATA; National Transportation Statistics based on data from U.S. Bureau of the Census *Commodity Flow Survey, U.S. Preliminary Report.*

TRANSPORTATION - CONSUMER COMPLAINTS

U.S. Department of Transportation, Office of Consumer Affairs, 400 Seventh Street, SW, Washington, D.C. 20590 (202) 366-4000; *Air Travel Consumer Report.*

TRANSPORTATION - CONSUMER EXPENDITURES

U.S. Department of Labor, Bureau of Labor Statistics, Two Massachusetts Avenue, NE, Washington, D.C. 20212 (202) 691-5200, www.stats.bls.gov; *Consumer Expenditures in 1997;* unpublished data; and Internet site: http:// stats.bls.gov/csxmsa.html.

TRANSPORTATION - CONSUMER PRICE

INDEXES

U.S. Department of Labor, Bureau of Labor Statistics, Two Massachusetts Avenue, NE, Washington, D.C. 20212 (202) 691-5200, www.stats.bls.gov; *Consumer Price Indexes, Detailed Report; Monthly Labor Review;* and *Handbook of Labor Statistics.*

TRANSPORTATION - CONSUMER PRICE INDEXES - MOTOR FUEL

U.S. Department of Labor, Bureau of Labor Statistics, Two Massachusetts Avenue, NE, Washington, D.C. 20212 (202) 691-5200, www.stats.bls.gov; *Monthly Labor Review;* and *CPI Detailed Report.*

TRANSPORTATION - CONSUMER PRICE INDEXES - NEW CARS AND NEW TRUCKS

U.S. Department of Labor, Bureau of Labor Statistics, Two Massachusetts Avenue, NE, Washington, D.C. 20212 (202) 691-5200, www.stats.bls.gov; *Monthly Labor Review;* and *CPI Detailed Report.*

TRANSPORTATION - COST INDEXES - AIRLINES

Air Transport Association of America, 1301 Pennsylvania Avenue, NW, Washington, D.C. 20004 (202) 626-4000; *Air Transport;* and unpublished data.

TRANSPORTATION - COST INDEXES - RAILROAD

U.S. Department of Labor, Bureau of Labor Statistics, Two Massachusetts Avenue, NE, Washington, D.C. 20212 (202) 691-5200, www.stats.bls.gov; *Producer Price Indexes.*

TRANSPORTATION - ENERGY CONSUMPTION

U.S. Department of Energy, Energy Information Administration, Washington, D.C. 20585 (202) 586-8800, www. eia.doe.gov; *State Energy Data Report; Monthly Energy Review; Annual Energy Review;* and *State Energy Price and Expenditure Report.*

TRANSPORTATION - EXPENDITURES

Eno Transportation Foundation, One Farragut Square, South, Suite 500, Washington, D.C. 20006 (202) 879-4700; *Transportation in America.*

U.S. Department of Commerce, Bureau of Economic Analysis, Fourteenth Street between Constitution Avenue and E Street, NW, Washington, D.C. 20230 (202) 606-9900, www.bea.doc.gov; *National Income and Product Accounts of the U.S.,* and *Survey of Current Business.*

U.S. Department of Commerce, Bureau of the Census, Washington, D.C. 20233 (301) 457-4100, www.census.gov; *Service Annual Survey.*

TRANSPORTATION - FEDERAL GOVERNMENT - AID TO STATE AND LOCAL GOVERNMENTS

Executive Office of the President, Office of Management and Budget, Executive Office Building, Washington, D.C. 20503 (202) 395-3080, www.whitehouse.gov/ omb; *Historical Tables,* and *Budget of the United States Government.*

TRANSPORTATION - FEDERAL GOVERNMENT - OUTLAYS

Executive Office of the President, Office of Management and Budget, Executive Office Building, Washington, D.C. 20503 (202)395-3080, www.whitehouse.gov/ omb; *Historical Tables,* and *Budget of the United States Government.*

National Science Foundation, 4201 Wilson Boulevard, Arlington, Virginia 22230 (703) 306-1234, www.nsf.gov; *Federal R & D Funding by Budget Function.*

TRANSPORTATION - FREIGHT

Eno Transportation Foundation, One Farragut Square, South, Suite 500, Washington, D.C. 20006 (202) 879-4700; *Transportation in America.*

TRANSPORTATION - GOVERNMENT EMPLOYEES AND PAYROLLS

U.S. Department of Commerce, Bureau of the Census, Washington, D.C. 20233 (301) 457-4100, www.census.gov; Internet site: http://www.census.gov/pub/ govs/apes.html.

TRANSPORTATION - GOVERNMENT FINANCES

Executive Office of the President, Office of Management and Budget, Executive Office Building, Washington, D.C. 20503 (202) 395-3080, www.whitehouse.gov/ omb; *Historical Tables.*

U.S. Department of Commerce, Bureau of the Census, Washington, D.C. 20233 (301) 457-4100, www.census.gov; *Government Finances;* and Internet sites: http://www.census.gov/pub/govs/www/in dex.html; http://www.census.gov/ govs/www/estimate.html; http://www.census.gov/govs/www/st97.ht ml; and http://www.census.gov/ftp/ pub/govs/estimate.html.

TRANSPORTATION - OCCUPATIONS

Air Transport Association of America, 1301 Pennsylvania Avenue, NW,

Washington, D.C. 20004 (202) 626-4000; *Air Transport;* and *Air Transport, Facts and Figures.*

U.S. Department of Commerce, Bureau of the Census, Washington, D.C. 20233 (301) 457-4100, www.census.gov; *Current Population Reports.*

U.S. Department of Labor, Bureau of Labor Statistics, Two Massachusetts Avenue, NE, Washington, D.C. 20212 (202) 691-5200, www.stats.bls.gov; *Employment and Earnings; Monthly Labor Review;* Bulletin 2307; and unpublished data.

TRANSPORTATION - OUTLAYS - BY TYPE OF TRANSPORT

Eno Transportation Foundation, One Farragut Square, South, Suite 500, Washington, D.C. 20006 (202) 879-4700; *Transportation in America.*

TRANSPORTATION - RECEIPTS

U.S. Department of Commerce, Bureau of the Census, Washington, D.C. 20233 (301) 457-4100, www.census.gov; *Service Annual Survey.*

TRANSPORTATION - STOCK

Board of Governors of the Federal Reserve System, Twentieth Street and Constitution Avenue, NW, Washington, D.C. 20551 (202) 452-3000, www.bog.frb.fed.us; *Federal Reserve Bulletin;* and *Annual Statistical Digest.*

TRANSPORTATION - TRANSPORTATION TO WORK

U.S. Department of Commerce, Bureau of the Census, Washington, D.C. 20233 (301) 457-4100, www.census.gov; *Census of Population and Housing.*

TRANSPORTATION - TRAVEL TRENDS

U.S. Department of Transportation, Federal Highway Administration, 400 Seventh Street, SW, Washington, D.C. 20590 (202) 366-0660; *National Personal Transportation Survey, Summary of Travel Trends.*

TRANSPORTATION - TRAVEL VOLUME

Eno Transportation Foundation, One Farragut Square, South, Suite 500, Washington, D.C. 20006 (202) 879-4700; *Transportation in America.*

Regional Airline Association, 2025 M Street, NW, Suite 800, Washington, D.C. 20036 (202) 367-1170; *Annual Report of the Regional Airline Industry.*

U.S. Department of Commerce, Bureau of the Census, Washington, D.C. 20233

(301) 457-4100, www.census.gov; *Census of Population and Housing.*

TRANSPORTATION - WORKPLACE VIOLENCE

U.S. Department of Justice, Bureau of Justice Statistics, 810 Seventh Street, NW, 2nd Floor, Washington, D.C. 20531 (800) 732-3277, www.ojp.usdoj.gov/bjs; *Workplace Violence.*

TRANSPORTATION AND PUBLIC UTILITIES INDUSTRY - See also Individual Industries

TRANSPORTATION, COMMUNICATIONS, AND PUBLIC UTILITIES INDUSTRY - CAPITAL

U.S. Department of Commerce, Bureau of Economic Analysis, Fourteenth Street between Constitution Avenue and E Street, NW, Washington, D.C. 20230 (202) 606-9900, www.bea.doc.gov; *National Income and Product Accounts; Fixed Reproducible Tangible Wealth in the United States;* and *Survey of Current Business.*

TRANSPORTATION, COMMUNICATIONS, AND PUBLIC UTILITIES INDUSTRY - CONSTRUCTION

U.S. Department of Commerce, Bureau of the Census, Washington, D.C. 20233 (301) 457-4100, www.census.gov; *Current Construction Reports, Value of New Construction.*

TRANSPORTATION, COMMUNICATIONS, AND PUBLIC UTILITIES INDUSTRY - CONSTRUCTION - COST INDEXES

U.S. Department of Commerce, Bureau of the Census, Washington, D.C. 20233 (301) 457-4100, www.census.gov; *Current Construction Review.*

TRANSPORTATION, COMMUNICATIONS, AND PUBLIC UTILITIES INDUSTRY - EARNINGS

U.S. Department of Commerce, Bureau of the Census, Washington, D.C. 20233 (301) 457-4100, www.census.gov; *County Business Patterns; 1997 Economic Census: Advance Summary Statistics for the U.S. 1997 NAICS Basis; Statistics of U.S. Businesses;* and *Census of Transportation, Communications and Utilities.*

U.S. Department of Labor, Bureau of Labor Statistics, Two Massachusetts Avenue, NE, Washington, D.C. 20212 (202) 691-5200, www.stats.bls.gov; *Employment and Earnings;* Bulletins 2445 and 2481; and Internet site: http://stats.bls.gov/ceshome.htm.

TRANSPORTATION, COMMUNICATIONS, AND PUBLIC UTILITIES INDUSTRY - EMPLOYEES

U.S. Department of Commerce, Bureau of the Census, Washington, D.C. 20233 (301) 457-4100, www.census.gov; *1997 Economic Census: Advance Summary Statistics for the U.S. 1997 NAICS Basis;* and *County Business Patterns.*

U.S. Department of Labor, Bureau of Labor Statistics, Two Massachusetts Avenue, NE, Washington, D.C. 20212 (202) 691-5200, www.stats.bls.gov; *Employment and Earnings; Monthly Labor Review; News, USDL 98-93,* published data; and Internet site: http://stats.bls.gov/ceshome.htm.

TRANSPORTATION, COMMUNICATIONS, AND PUBLIC UTILITIES INDUSTRY - ESTABLISHMENTS

U.S. Department of Commerce, Bureau of the Census, Washington, D.C. 20233 (301) 457-4100, www.census.gov; *County Business Patterns; Census of Transportation, Communication and Utilities;* and *1997 Economic Census: Advance Summary Statistics for the U.S. NAICS Basis.*

TRANSPORTATION, COMMUNICATIONS, AND PUBLIC UTILITIES INDUSTRY - FAILURES

Dun and Bradstreet Corporation, One Diamond Hill Road, Murray Hill, New Jersey 07974 (908) 665-5000; *Business Failure Record.*

TRANSPORTATION, COMMUNICATIONS, AND PUBLIC UTILITIES INDUSTRY - FINANCES

U.S. Department of Commerce, Bureau of the Census, Washington, D.C. 20233 (301) 457-4100, www.census.gov; *Census of Transportation, Communication and Utilities.*

U.S. Department of the Treasury, Internal Revenue Service, 1111 Constitution Avenue, NW, Washington, D.C. 20224 (202) 874-0410, www.irs.ustreas.gov; *Statistics of Income,* various publications and unpublished data.

TRANSPORTATION, COMMUNICATIONS, AND PUBLIC UTILITIES INDUSTRY - GROSS DOMESTIC PRODUCT

U.S. Department of Commerce, Bureau of Economic Analysis, Fourteenth Street between Constitution Avenue and E Street, NW, Washington, D.C. 20230 (202) 606-9900, www.bea.doc.gov; *Survey of Current Business.*

TRANSPORTATION, COMMUNICATIONS, AND PUBLIC UTILITIES INDUSTRY - HEALTH INSURANCE COVERAGE - EMPLOYEES

U.S. Department of Health and Human Services, National Center for Health Statistics, 3700 East-West Highway, Hyattsville, Maryland 20782 (301) 436-8500, www.cdc.gov/nchs; *Employer-Sponsored Health Insurance, State and National Estimates.*

TRANSPORTATION, COMMUNICATIONS, AND PUBLIC UTILITIES INDUSTRY - MERGERS AND ACQUISITION

Thomson Financial Securities Data, Two Gateway Center, Newark, New Jersey 07006 (973) 622-3100; *Merger and Corporate Transaction Database.*

TRANSPORTATION, COMMUNICATIONS, AND PUBLIC UTILITIES INDUSTRY - OCCUPATIONAL SAFETY

National Safety Council, 1121 Spring Lake Drive, Itasca, Illinois 60143-3201 (630) 285-1121; *Accident Facts.*

TRANSPORTATION, COMMUNICATIONS, AND PUBLIC UTILITIES INDUSTRY - PRODUCTIVITY

U.S. Department of Labor, Bureau of Labor Statistics, Two Massachusetts Avenue, NE, Washington, D.C. 20212 (202) 691-5200, www.stats.bls.gov; Internet site: http://stats.bls.gov/iprhome.htm.

TRANSPORTATION, COMMUNICATIONS, AND PUBLIC UTILITIES INDUSTRY - PROFITS

Forbes, Inc., 60 Fifth Avenue, New York, New York 10011 (212) 691-6130; *Forbes Annual Report on American Industry.*

U.S. Department of Commerce, Bureau of Economic Analysis, Fourteenth Street between Constitution Avenue and E Street, NW, Washington, D.C. 20230 (202) 606-9900, www.bea.doc.gov; *The National Income and Product Accounts of the United States;* and *Survey of Current Business.*

U.S. Department of the Treasury, Internal Revenue Service, 1111 Constitution Avenue, NW, Washington, D.C. 20224 (202) 874-0410, www.irs.ustreas.gov; *Statistics of Income.*

TRANSPORTATION, COMMUNICATIONS, AND PUBLIC UTILITIES INDUSTRY - UNION MEMBERSHIP

U.S. Department of Labor, Bureau of Labor Statistics, Two Massachusetts Avenue, NE, Washington, D.C. 20212 (202) 691-5200, www.stats.bls.gov; *Employment and Earnings.*

TRANSPORTATION EQUIPMENT - MANUFACTURING - CAPITAL

U.S. Department of Commerce, Bureau

of Economic Analysis, Fourteenth Street between Constitution Avenue and E Street, NW, Washington, D.C. 20230 (202) 606-9900, www.bea.doc.gov; *Survey of Current Business.*

TRANSPORTATION EQUIPMENT - MANUFACTURING - EARNINGS

U.S. Department of Commerce, Bureau of the Census, Washington, D.C. 20233 (301) 457-4100, www.census.gov; *Census of Manufactures;* and *Annual Survey of Manufactures.*

U.S. Department of Commerce, Bureau of the Census, Washington, D.C. 20233 (301) 457-4100, www.census.gov; *1997 Economic Census: Core Business Statistics Series.*

U.S. Department of Labor, Bureau of Labor Statistics, Two Massachusetts Avenue, NE, Washington, D.C. 20212 (202) 691-5200, www.stats.bls.gov; *Employment and Earnings;* and Internet site: http://stats.bls.gov/ceshome. htm.

TRANSPORTATION EQUIPMENT - MANUFACTURING - EMPLOYEES

U.S. Department of Commerce, Bureau of the Census, Washington, D.C. 20233 (301) 457-4100, www.census.gov; *Census of Manufactures;* and *Annual Survey of Manufactures.*

U.S. Department of Commerce, Bureau of the Census, Washington, D.C. 20233 (301) *457-4100, www.census.gov;1997 Economic Census, Core Business Statistics Series.*

U.S. Department of Labor, Bureau of Labor Statistics, Two Massachusetts Avenue, NE, Washington, D.C. 20212 (202) 691-5200, www.stats.bls.gov; *Employment and Earnings; Monthly Labor Review;* and Internet site: http://stats.bls.gov/ceshome.htm.

TRANSPORTATION EQUIPMENT - MANUFACTURING - ENERGY CONSUMPTION

U.S. Department of Energy, Energy Information Administration, 1000 Independence Avenue, SW, Washington, D.C. 20585 (202) 586-8800, www.eia.doe.gov; *Manufacturing Energy Consumption.*

TRANSPORTATION EQUIPMENT - MANUFACTURING - ESTABLISHMENTS

U.S. Department of Commerce, Bureau of the Census, Washington, D.C. 20233 (301) 457-4100, www.census.gov; *1997 Economic Census, Core Business Statistics Series.*

TRANSPORTATION EQUIPMENT - MANUFACTURING - FOREIGN TRADE

U.S. Department of Commerce, Bureau of the Census, Washington, D.C. 20233 (301) 457-4100, www.census.gov; *U.S. International Trade in Goods and Services.*

TRANSPORTATION EQUIPMENT - MANUFACTURING - GROSS DOMESTIC PRODUCT

U.S. Department of Commerce, Bureau of Economic Analysis, Fourteenth Street between Constitution Avenue and E Street, SW, Washington, D.C. 20230 (202) 606-9900, www.bea.doc.gov; *The National Income and Product Accounts of the United States;* and *Survey of Current Business.*

TRANSPORTATION EQUIPMENT - MANUFACTURING - INVENTORIES

U.S. Department of Commerce, Bureau of the Census, Washington, D.C. 20233 (301) 457-4100, www.census.gov; *Current Industrial Reports, Manufactures' Shipments, Inventories, and Orders.*

TRANSPORTATION EQUIPMENT - MANUFACTURING - MERGERS AND ACQUISITIONS

Thomson Financial Securities Data, Two Gateway Center, Newark, New Jersey 07006 (973) 622-3100; *Merger and Corporate Transactions Database.*

TRANSPORTATION EQUIPMENT - MANUFACTURING - OCCUPATIONAL SAFETY

U.S. Department of Labor, Bureau of Labor Statistics, Two Massachusetts Avenue, NE, Washington, D.C. 20212 (202) 691-5200, www.stats.bls.gov; *Occupational Injuries and Illnesses in the U.S. by Industry.*

TRANSPORTATION EQUIPMENT - MANUFACTURING - PRODUCER PRICES

U.S. Department of Labor, Bureau of Labor Statistics, Two Massachusetts Avenue, NE, Washington, D.C. 20212 (202) 691-5200, www.stats.bls.gov; *Producer Price Indexes.*

TRANSPORTATION EQUIPMENT - MANUFACTURING - PRODUCTIVITY

Board of Governors of the Federal Reserve System, Twentieth Street and Constitution Avenue, NW, Washington, D.C. 20551 (202) 452-3000, www.bog.frb.fed.us; *Federal Reserve Bulletin;* and *Industrial Production and Capacity Utilization.*

U.S. Department of Labor, Bureau of Labor Statistics, Two Massachusetts Avenue, NE, Washington, D.C. 20212 (202)

691-5200, www.stats.bls.gov; Internet site: http://stats.bls.gov/iprhome.htm.

TRANSPORTATION EQUIPMENT - MANUFACTURING - PROFITS

Forbes, Inc., 60 Fifth Avenue, New York, New York 10011 (212) 691-4230; *Forbes Annual Report on American Industry.*

Time Warner, Time and Life Building, Rockefeller Center, New York, New York 10020 (212) 522-1212; *The Fortune Directories.*

TRANSPORTATION EQUIPMENT - MANUFACTURING - RESEARCH AND DEVELOPMENT

National Science Foundation, 4201 Wilson Boulevard, Arlington, Virginia 22230 (703) 306-1234, www.nsf.gov; *Research and Development in Industry.*

TRANSPORTATION EQUIPMENT - MANUFACTURING - SHIPMENTS

U.S. Department of Commerce, Bureau of the Census, Washington, D.C. 20233 (301) 457-4100, www.census.gov; *Current Industrial Reports, Manufactures' Shipments, Inventories, and Orders; Census of Manufactures;* and *Annual Survey of Manufactures.*

U.S. Department of Commerce, Bureau of the Census, Washington, D.C. 20233 (301) 457-4100, www.census.gov; and International Trade Administration, 14th Street between Constitution Avenue and E Street, NW, Washington, D.C. 20230 (202) 482-3809; estimates.

TRANSPORTATION EQUIPMENT - MANUFACTURING - TOXIC CHEMICAL RELEASES

Environmental Protection Agency, 1200 Pennsylvania Avenue, NW, Washington, D.C. 20460 (888) 372-8255, www.epa.gov; *Toxics Release Inventory.*

TRANSPORTATION EQUIPMENT - MANUFACTURING - VALUE ADDED

U.S. Department of Commerce, Bureau of the Census, Washington, D.C. 20233 (301) 457-4100, www.census.gov; *Census of Manufactures;* and *Annual Survey of Manufactures.*

TRAVEL - ACCIDENTS

U.S. Department of Health and Human Services, National Center for Health Statistics, 3700 East-West Highway, Hyattsville, Maryland 20782 (301) 436-8500, www.cdc.gov/nchs; *Vital Statistics of the United States.*

U.S. Department of Transportation, Bureau of Transportation Statistics, 400 Seventh Street, SW, Washington, D.C. 20590 (202) 366-DATA; *National Transportation Statistics.*

TRAVEL - ACCIDENTS - AIR CARRIERS

International Civil Aviation Organization, 999 University Street, Montreal, Quebec, H3C 5H7, Canada (514) 954-8219; *Civil Aviation Statistics of the World.*

TRAVEL - ADVERTISING EXPENDITURES

Television Bureau of Advertising, Incorporated, 3 East 54th Street, New York, New York 10022 (212) 486-1111; from data compiled by Competitive Media Reporting, 11 West 42nd Street, New York, New York 10036 (212) 789-1400.

TRAVEL - BUSINESS - PLEASURE TRAVELERS

United States Travel Data Center, 1100 New York Avenue, NW, Suite 450, Washington, D.C. 20005 (202) 408-8422; *National Travel Survey.*

TRAVEL - DOMESTIC EXPENDITURES BY STATE

United States Travel Data Center, 1100 New York Avenue, NW, Suite 450, Washington, D.C. 20005 (202) 408-8422; *Impact of Travel on State Economies.*

TRAVEL - FOREIGN

U.S. Department of Commerce, International Trade Administration, Fourteenth Street between Constitution Avenue and E Street, NW, Washington, D.C. 20230 (202) 482-2185, www.ita.doc.gov; Internet site http://www.tinet.ita.doc.gov.

U.S. Department of Justice, Immigration and Naturalization Service, 425 Eye Street, NW, Washington, D.C. 20536 (202) 305-1613, www.ins.usdoj.gov; *Statistical Yearbook.*

World Tourism Organization, Madrid, Spain; unpublished data.

TRAVEL - HIGHWAY MILEAGE

U.S. Department of Transportation, Federal Highway Administration, 400 Seventh Street, NW, Washington, D.C. 20590 (202) 366-0660; *Highway Statistics;* and *Fatal and Injury Accident Rates on Public Roads in the United States.*

TRAVEL - HOUSEHOLD TRIPS

U.S. Department of Transportation, Bureau of Transportation Statistics, 400

Seventh Street, NW, Washington, D.C. 20590 (202) 366-DATA; *American Travel Survey.*

TRAVEL - NONIMMIGRANTS

U.S. Department of Justice, Immigration and Naturalization Service, 425 I Street, NW, Washington, D.C. 20536 (202) 305-1613, www.ins.usdoj.gov; *Statistical Yearbook.*

TRAVEL - PASSENGERS

Air Transport Association of America, 1301 Pennsylvania Avenue, NW, Washington, D.C. 20004 (202) 626-4000; *Air Transport;* and *Air Transport, Facts and Figures.*

Regional Airline Association, 2025 M Street, NW, Suite 800, Washington, D.C. 20036 (202) 367-1170; *Annual Report.*

U.S. Department of Commerce, International Trade Administration, Fourteenth Street between Constitution Avenue and E Street, NW, Washington, D.C. 20230 (202) 482-2185, www.ita.doc.gov/; Internet site: http://www.tinet.ita.doc.gov.

TRAVEL - PERSON MILES AND PERSON TRIPS

U.S. Department of Transportation, Bureau of Transportation Statistics, 400 Seventh Street, SW, Washington, D.C. 20590 (202) 366-DATA; *American Travel Survey.*

TRAVEL - RECREATION

United States Travel Data Center, 1100 New York Avenue, NW, Suite 450, Washington, D.C. 20005 (202) 408-8422; *National Travel Survey.*

TRAVEL - SERVICES

U.S. Department of Commerce, Bureau of the Census, Washington, D.C. 20233 (301) 457-4100, www.census.gov; *U.S. International Trade in Goods and Services.*

TRAVEL - TOURISTS

U.S. Department of Commerce, International Trade Administration, Fourteenth Street between Constitution Avenue and E Street, NW, Washington, D.C. 20230 (202) 482-2185, www.ita.doc.gov; Internet site: http://www.tinet.ita.doc.gov/

U.S. Department of Justice, Immigration and Naturalization Service, 425 Eye Street, NW, Washington, D.C. 20536 (202) 305-1613, www.ins.usdoj.gov; *Statistical Yearbook.*

TRAVEL - VOLUME

Air Transport Association of America, 1301 Pennsylvania Avenue, NW, Washington, D.C. 20004 (202) 626-4000; *Air Transport;* and *Air Transport, Facts and Figures.*

Eno Transportation Foundation, One Farragut Square, South, Suite 500, Washington, D.C. 20006 (202) 879-4700; *Transportation in America.*

Regional Airline Association, 2025 M Street, NW, Suite 800, Washington, D.C. 20036 (202) 367-1170; *Annual Report.*

TRAVEL ARRANGEMENTS

U.S. Department of Commerce, Bureau of the Census, Washington, D.C. 20233 (301) 457-4100, www.census.gov; *Current Business Reports, Service Annual Survey: 1997;* and *Service Annual Survey.*

TRAVEL IN THE UNITED STATES

U.S. Department of Transportation, Bureau of Transportation Statistics, 400 Seventh Street, SW, Washington, D.C. 20590 (202) 366-DATA; *American Travel Survey.*

TRAVELERS CHECKS

Board of Governors of the Federal Reserve System, Twentieth Street and Constitution Avenue, NW, Washington, D.C. 20551 (202) 452-3000, www.bog.frb.fed.us; *Federal Reserve Bulletin; Money Stock, Liquid Assets and Debt Measures;* and *Federal Reserve Statistical Release H.6.*

TREASURY BONDS - FOREIGN PURCHASES AND SALES

U.S. Department of the Treasury, 15th Street and Pennsylvania Avenue, NW, Washington, D.C. 20220 (202) 622-2000; *Treasury Bulletin.*

TREASURY BONDS - SALES, PRICES, AND YIELDS

Board of Governors of the Federal Reserve System, Twentieth Street and Constitution Avenue, NW, Washington, D.C. 20551 (202) 452-3000, www.bog.frb.fed.us; *Federal Reserve Bulletin.*

TRIBES - AMERICAN INDIAN

U.S. Department of Commerce, Bureau of the Census, Washington, D.C. 20233 (301) 457-4100, www.census.gov; *Census of Population, General Population Characteristics, American Indian and Alaska Native Areas.*

TRICHINOSIS

U.S. Department of Health and Human Services, Centers for Disease Control and Prevention, 1600 Clifton Road, NE, Atlanta, Georgia 30333 (800) 311-3435, www.cdc.gov; *Summary of Notifiable Diseases, U.S.*; and *Morbidity and Mortality Weekly Report*.

Trinidad and Tobago - National Statistical Office

Central Statistical Office, 23 Park Street, Post Office Box 98, Port of Spain, Trinidad.

Trinidad and Tobago - Primary Statistics Sources

Central Statistical Office, Post Office Box 98, Port of Spain, Trinidad; *Annual Statistical Digest*.

TRINIDAD AND TOBAGO - AGRICULTURE

The Economist Intelligence Unit, 111 West 57th Street, New York, New York 10019 (800) 938-4685; *Trinidad and Tobago Country Report*; and *The New Latin America Market Atlas*.

Euromonitor International, Inc., 122 South Michigan Avenue, Suite 1200, Chicago, Illinois 60603 (800) 577-EURO; *International Marketing Data and Statistics*; and *World Marketing Data and Statistics*.

Europa Publications Limited, 18 Bedford Square, London, WC1B 3JN, England; *The Europa World Year Book*.

Federal Statistical Office, Gustav-Stresemann - Ring 11, D-6200, Wiesbaden, Germany; *Trinidad and Tobago*.

Food and Agricultural Organization of the United Nations (FAO) Via delle Terme di Caracalla, 00100 Rome, Italy (Telephone Number in U.S. (202) 653-2400); *Production Yearbook; The State of Food and Agriculture;* and *Trade Yearbook*.

Inter-American Development Bank, 1300 New York Avenue, NW, Washington, D.C. 20577 (202) 623-1753; *Economic and Social Progress in Latin America*.

M.E. Sharpe, 80 Business Park Drive, Armonk, New York 10504 (800) 541-6563; *The Illustrated Book of World Rankings*.

St. Martin's Press, Inc., 175 Fifth Avenue, New York, New York 10010 (800) 221-7945; *The Statesman's Year-Book*.

Statistical Office of the United Nations, Publishing Service, New York, New York 10017 (800) 253-9646; *Statistical Yearbook*.

United Nations Conference on Trade and Development, Central Statistical Service, Palais des Nations, Geneva, Switzerland (Telephone in U.S. (800) 253-9646); *UNCTAD Commodity Yearbook*.

The World Bank, 1818 H Street, NW, Washington, D.C. 20433 (202) 477-1234; *World Development Indicators*.

TRINIDAD AND TOBAGO - AIRLINE SERVICE

The Economist Intelligence Unit, 111 West 57th Street, New York, New York 10019 (800) 938-4685; *The New Latin America Market Atlas*.

Europa Publications Limited, 18 Bedford Square, London, WC1B 3JN, England; *The Europa World Year Book*.

M.E. Sharpe, 80 Business Park Drive, Armonk, New York 10504 (800) 541-6563; *The Illustrated Book of World Rankings*.

St. Martin's Press, Inc., 175 Fifth Avenue, New York, New York 10010 (800) 221-7945; *The Statesman's Year-Book*.

Statistical Office of the United Nations, Publishing Service, New York, New York 10017 (800) 253-9646; *Statistical Yearbook*.

TRINIDAD AND TOBAGO - AIRPORTS

Central Intelligence Agency, Washington, D.C. 20505 (703) 482-1100, www.cia.gov; *The World Factbook*.

TRINIDAD AND TOBAGO - ALUMINUM PRODUCTION AND CONSUMPTION - See TRINIDAD AND TOBAGO - MINING AND MINERAL PRODUCTS

TRINIDAD AND TOBAGO - ANIMAL HEALTH

Food and Agricultural Organization of the United Nations (FAO), Via delle Terme di Caracalla, 00100, Rome, Italy (Telephone Number in U.S. (202) 653-2400); *Animal Health Yearbook*.

TRINIDAD AND TOBAGO - AREA AND DENSITY OF POPULATION

Central Intelligence Agency, Washington, D.C. 20505 (703) 482-1100, www.cia.gov; *The World Factbook*.

Euromonitor International, Inc., 122 South Michigan Avenue, Suite 1200, Chicago, Illinois 60603 (800) 577-EURO; *International Marketing Data and Statistics*; and *The World Economic Factbook*.

Europa Publications Limited, 18 Bedford Square, London, WC1B 3JN, England; *The Europa World Year Book*.

Federal Statistical Office, Gustav-Stresemann - Ring 11, D-6200, Wiesbaden, Germany; *Trinidad and Tobago*.

Food and Agricultural Organization of the United Nations (FAO) Via delle Terme di Caracalla, 00100 Rome, Italy (Telephone Number in U.S. (202) 653-2400); *The State of Food and Agriculture*.

Inter-American Development Bank, 1300 New York Avenue, NW, Washington, D.C. 20577 (202) 623-1753; *Economic and Social Progress in Latin America*.

M.E. Sharpe, 80 Business Park Drive, Armonk, New York 10504 (800) 541-6563; *The Illustrated Book of World Rankings*.

St. Martin's Press, Inc., 175 Fifth Avenue, New York, New York 10010 (800) 221-7945; *The Statesman's Year-Book*.

Statistical Office of the United Nations, Publishing Service, New York, New York 10017 (800) 253-9646; *Statistical Yearbook*.

United Nations Educational, Scientific and Cultural Organization (UNESCO), 7 Place de Fontenoy, F-75700 Paris, France (Telephone Number in U.S. (212) 963-5981); *Statistical Yearbook*.

The World Bank, 1818 H Street, NW, Washington, D.C. 20433 (202) 477-1234; *World Development Report*.

TRINIDAD AND TOBAGO - ARMS EXPORTS AND IMPORTS - See TRINIDAD AND TOBAGO - MILITARY

TRINIDAD AND TOBAGO - BALANCE OF PAYMENTS

The Economist Intelligence Unit, 111 West 57th Street, New York, New York 10019 (800) 938-4685; *The New Latin America Market Atlas;* and *The World Market Atlas*.

Europa Publications Limited, 18 Bedford Square, London, WC1B 3JN, England; *The Europa World Year Book*.

Federal Statistical Office, Gustav-Stresemann - Ring 11, D-6200, Wiesbaden, Germany; *Trinidad and Tobago*.

Inter-American Development Bank, 1300 New York Avenue, NW, Washington, D.C. 20577 (202) 623-1753; *Economic and Social Progress in Latin America*.

International Monetary Fund, 700 Nineteenth Street, NW, Washington, D.C. 20431 (202) 623-7000; *Balance of Payments Yearbook;* and *International Financial Statistics*.

Organization of American States (OAS), General Secretariat, Washington, D.C.

20006 (202) 458-3533; *Statistical Bulletin of the OAS.*

Statistical Office of the United Nations, Publishing Service, New York, New York 10017 (800) 253-9646; *Economic Survey of Latin America and the Caribbean.*

United Nations Conference on Trade and Development (UNCTAD), New York, New York 10017 (800) 253-9646; *Handbook of International Trade and Development Statistics.*

The World Bank, 1818 H Street, NW, Washington, D.C. 20433 (202) 477-1234; *World Development Report;* and *World Development Indicators.*

TRINIDAD AND TOBAGO - BANANA PRODUCTION - See TRINIDAD AND TOBAGO - CROPS

TRINIDAD AND TOBAGO - BANKING

Euromonitor International, Inc., 122 South Michigan Avenue, Suite 1200, Chicago, Illinois 60603 (800) 577-EURO; *World Marketing Data and Statistics.*

Europa Publications Limited, 18 Bedford Square, London, WC1B 3JN, England; *The Europa World Year Book.*

Inter-American Development Bank, 1300 New York Avenue, NW, Washington, D.C. 20577 (202) 623-1753; *Economic and Social Progress in Latin America.*

International Monetary Fund, 700 Nineteenth Street, NW, Washington, D.C. 20431 (202) 623-7000; *International Financial Statistics.*

M.E. Sharpe, 80 Business Park Drive, Armonk, New York 10504 (800) 541-6563; *The Illustrated Book of World Rankings.*

St. Martin's Press, Inc., 175 Fifth Avenue, New York, New York 10010 (800) 221-7945; *The Statesman's Year-Book.*

TRINIDAD AND TOBAGO - BARLEY PRODUCTION - See TRINIDAD AND TOBAGO - CROPS

TRINIDAD AND TOBAGO - BEER PRODUCTION - See TRINIDAD AND TOBAGO - BEVERAGES

TRINIDAD AND TOBAGO - BEVERAGES

M.E. Sharpe, 80 Business Park Drive, Armonk, New York 10504 (800) 541-6563; *The Illustrated Book of World Rankings.*

Statistical Office of the United Nations, Publishing Service, New York, New York 10017 (800) 253-9646; *Statistical Yearbook.*

TRINIDAD AND TOBAGO - BIRTH RATES

Central Intelligence Agency, Washington, D.C. 20505 (703) 482-1100, www.cia.gov; *The World Factbook.*

Euromonitor International, Inc., 122 South Michigan Avenue, Suite 1200, Chicago, Illinois 60603 (800) 577-EURO; *International Marketing Data and Statistics;* and *The World Economic Factbook.*

Europa Publications Limited, 18 Bedford Square, London, WC1B 3JN, England; *The Europa World Year Book.*

M.E. Sharpe, 80 Business Park Drive, Armonk, New York 10504 (800) 541-6563; *The Illustrated Book of World Rankings.*

St. Martin's Press, Inc., 175 Fifth Avenue, New York, New York 10010 (800) 221-7945; *The Statesman's Year-Book.*

Statistical Office of the United Nations, Publishing Service, New York, New York 10017 (800) 253-9646; *Demographic Yearbook;* and *Statistical Yearbook.*

The World Bank, 1818 H Street, NW, Washington, D.C. 20433 (202) 477-1234; *World Development Indicators.*

World Health Organization, Office of Publications, 20 Avenue Appia, CH-1211 Geneva 27, Switzerland (Telephone Number in U.S. (518) 436-9686); *World Health Statistics Annual.*

TRINIDAD AND TOBAGO - BONDS

Inter-American Development Bank, 1300 New York Avenue, NW, Washington, D.C. 20577 (202) 623-1753; *Economic and Social Progress in Latin America.*

International Monetary Fund, 700 Nineteenth Street, NW, Washington, D.C. 20431 (202) 623-7000; *Government Finance Statistics Yearbook.*

Statistical Office of the United Nations, Publishing Service, New York, New York 10017 (800) 253-9646; *Statistical Yearbook.*

TRINIDAD AND TOBAGO - BOOK PRODUCTION

United Nations Educational, Scientific and Cultural Organization (UNESCO), 7 Place de Fontenoy, F-75700 Paris, France (Telephone Number in U.S. (212) 963-5981); *Statistical Yearbook.*

TRINIDAD AND TOBAGO - BROADCASTING

Billboard Limited, P.O. Box 9027, 1006 AA Amsterdam, The Netherlands (Telephone Number in U.S. (212) 764-7300); *World Radio TV Handbook.*

Central Intelligence Agency,

Washington, D.C. 20505 (703) 482-1100, www.cia.gov; *The World Factbook.*

Euromonitor International, Inc., 122 South Michigan Avenue, Suite 1200, Chicago, Illinois 60603 (800) 577-EURO; *World Marketing Data and Statistics.*

M.E. Sharpe, 80 Business Park Drive, Armonk, New York 10504 (800) 541-6563; *The Illustrated Book of World Rankings.*

St. Martin's Press, Inc., 175 Fifth Avenue, New York, New York 10010 (800) 221-7945; *The Statesman's Year-Book.*

United Nations Educational, Scientific and Cultural Organization (UNESCO), 7 Place de Fontenoy, F-75700 Paris, France (Telephone Number in U.S. (212) 963-5981); *Statistical Yearbook.*

TRINIDAD AND TOBAGO - BUDGET

Central Intelligence Agency, Washington, D.C. 20505 (703) 482-1100, www.cia.gov; *The World Factbook.*

TRINIDAD AND TOBAGO - BUSINESS

Inter-American Development Bank, 1300 New York Avenue, NW, Washington, D.C. 20577 (202) 623-1753; *Economic and Social Progress in Latin America.*

TRINIDAD AND TOBAGO - BUSINESS AND PROFESSIONAL LICENSES

International Monetary Fund, 700 Nineteenth Street, NW, Washington, D.C. 20431 (202) 623-7000; *Government Finance Statistics Yearbook.*

TRINIDAD AND TOBAGO - BUTTER PRODUCTION - See TRINIDAD AND TOBAGO - DAIRY PRODUCTS

TRINIDAD AND TOBAGO - CALORIE SUPPLY

Food and Agricultural Organization of the United Nations (FAO) Via delle Terme di Caracalla, 00100 Rome, Italy (Telephone Number in U.S. (202) 653-2400); *The State of Food and Agriculture.*

TRINIDAD AND TOBAGO - CAPITAL INVESTMENT

Inter-American Development Bank, 1300 New York Avenue, NW, Washington, D.C. 20577 (202) 623-1753; *Economic and Social Progress in Latin America.*

TRINIDAD AND TOBAGO - CAPITAL REVENUE

Inter-American Development Bank, 1300 New York Avenue, NW, Washington, D.C. 20577 (202) 623-1753; *Economic and Social Progress in Latin America.*

International Monetary Fund, 700 Nineteenth Street, NW, Washington, D.C. 20431 (202) 623-7000; *Government Finance Statistics Yearbook*.

TRINIDAD AND TOBAGO - CATTLE - See TRINIDAD AND TOBAGO - LIVESTOCK AND POULTRY

TRINIDAD AND TOBAGO - CEMENT PRODUCTION - See TRINIDAD AND TOBAGO - MINING AND MINERAL PRODUCTS

TRINIDAD AND TOBAGO - CHEESE PRODUCTION AND CONSUMPTION - See TRINIDAD AND TOBAGO - DAIRY PRODUCTS

TRINIDAD AND TOBAGO - CHEMICAL (ORGANIC) PRODUCTION - See TRINIDAD AND TOBAGO - MINING AND MINERAL PRODUCTS

TRINIDAD AND TOBAGO - CHICKENS - See TRINIDAD AND TOBAGO - LIVESTOCK AND POULTRY

TRINIDAD AND TOBAGO - CIGARETTE PRODUCTION - See TRINIDAD AND TOBAGO - TOBACCO PRODUCTION

TRINIDAD AND TOBAGO - CLIMATE

M.E. Sharpe, 80 Business Park Drive, Armonk, New York 10504 (800) 541-6563; *The Illustrated Book of World Rankings*.

St. Martin's Press, Inc., 175 Fifth Avenue, New York, New York 10010 (800) 221-7945; *The Statesman's Year-Book*.

TRINIDAD AND TOBAGO - COAL PRODUCTION - See TRINIDAD AND TOBAGO - MINING AND MINERAL PRODUCTS

TRINIDAD AND TOBAGO - COCOA (BEANS) PRODUCTION - See TRINIDAD AND TOBAGO - CROPS

TRINIDAD AND TOBAGO - COFFEE - See TRINIDAD AND TOBAGO - CROPS

TRINIDAD AND TOBAGO - COMMERCE

St. Martin's Press, Inc., 175 Fifth Avenue, New York, New York 10010 (800) 221-7945; *The Statesman's Year-Book*.

TRINIDAD AND TOBAGO - COMMUNICATIONS - See TRINIDAD AND TOBAGO - TRANSPORTATION AND COMMUNICATIONS

TRINIDAD AND TOBAGO - CONSTRUCTION INDUSTRY

The Economist Intelligence Unit, 111 West 57th Street, New York, New York 10019 (800) 938-4685; *The New Latin America Market Atlas*.

Inter-American Development Bank, 1300 New York Avenue, NW, Washington, D.C. 20577 (202) 623-1753; *Economic and Social Progress in Latin America*.

M.E. Sharpe, 80 Business Park Drive, Armonk, New York 10504 (800) 541-6563; *The Illustrated Book of World Rankings*.

Statistical Office of the United Nations, Publishing Service, New York, New York 10017 (800) 253-9646; *Statistical Yearbook*.

TRINIDAD AND TOBAGO - CONSUMER PRICE INDEX

Europa Publications Limited, 18 Bedford Square, London, WC1B 3JN, England; *The Europa World Year Book*.

Statistical Office of the United Nations, Publishing Service, New York, New York 10017 (800) 253-9646; *Statistical Yearbook*.

TRINIDAD AND TOBAGO - CONSUMER PRICES

The Economist Intelligence Unit, 111 West 57th Street, New York, New York 10019 (800) 938-4685; *The New Latin America Market Atlas*.

Euromonitor International, Inc., 122 South Michigan Avenue, Suite 1200, Chicago, Illinois 60603 (800) 577-EURO; *World Marketing Data and Statistics*.

International Labour Office, I.L.O. Publications, 1828 L Street, NW, Suite 801, Washington, D.C. 20036 (301) 638-3152; *Yearbook of Labour Statistics*.

International Monetary Fund, 700 Nineteenth Street, NW, Washington, D.C. 20431 (202) 623-7000; *International Financial Statistics*.

Organization of American States (OAS), General Secretariat, Washington, D.C. 20006 (202) 458-3533; *Statistical Bulletin of the OAS*.

TRINIDAD AND TOBAGO - CONSUMPTION

The Economist Intelligence Unit, 111 West 57th Street, New York, New York 10019 (800) 938-4685; *The New Latin America Market Atlas*.

Inter-American Development Bank, 1300 New York Avenue, NW, Washington, D.C. 20577 (202) 623-1753; *Economic and Social Progress in Latin America*.

The World Bank, 1818 H Street, NW, Washington, D.C. 20433 (202) 477-1234; *World Development Report*.

TRINIDAD AND TOBAGO - COPPER PRODUCTION AND CONSUMPTION - See TRINIDAD AND TOBAGO - MINING AND MINERAL PRODUCTS

TRINIDAD AND TOBAGO - CORN PRODUCTION - See TRINIDAD AND TOBAGO - CROPS

TRINIDAD AND TOBAGO - CORPORATE INCOME TAXES - See TRINIDAD AND TOBAGO - TAXATION

TRINIDAD AND TOBAGO - CORPORATE TAXES - See TRINIDAD AND TOBAGO - TAXATION

TRINIDAD AND TOBAGO - COTTON - See TRINIDAD AND TOBAGO - CROPS

TRINIDAD AND TOBAGO - CRIME

Yale University Press, Yale Station, New Haven, Connecticut 06520 (800) 987-7323; *Violence and Crime in Cross-National Perspective*.

TRINIDAD AND TOBAGO - CROPS

Commodity Research Bureau, Inc., 30 South Wacker Drive, Chicago, Illinois 60606 (312) 454-1801; *Commodity Year Book*.

The Economist Intelligence Unit, 111 West 57th Street, New York, New York 10019 (800) 938-4685; *The New Latin America Market Atlas*.

Europa Publications Limited, 18 Bedford Square, London, WC1B 3JN, England; *The Europa World Year Book*.

Food and Agricultural Organization of the United Nations (FAO) Via delle Terme di Caracalla, 00100 Rome, Italy (Telephone Number in U.S. (202) 653-2400); *The State of Food and Agriculture*.

International Monetary Fund, 700 Nineteenth Street, NW, Washington, D.C. 20431 (202) 623-7000; *International Financial Statistics*.

M.E. Sharpe, 80 Business Park Drive, Armonk, New York 10504 (800) 541-6563; *The Illustrated Book of World Rankings*.

Organization of American States (OAS), General Secretariat, Washington, D.C. 20006 (202) 458-3533; *Statistical Bulletin of the OAS*.

St. Martin's Press, Inc., 175 Fifth Avenue, New York, New York 10010 (800) 221-7945; *The Statesman's Year-Book*.

Statistical Office of the United Nations, Publishing Service, New York, New York 10017 (800) 253-9646; *Statistical Yearbook*.

U.C.L.A. Latin American Center

Publications, University of California, Los Angeles, California 90024 (310) 825-6634; *Statistical Abstract of Latin America.*

United Nations Conference on Trade and Development, Central Statistical Service, Palais des Nations, Geneva, Switzerland (Telephone in U.S. (800) 253-9646); *UNCTAD Commodity Yearbook.*

TRINIDAD AND TOBAGO - CUSTOMS DUTIES

Inter-American Development Bank, 1300 New York Avenue, NW, Washington, D.C. 20577 (202) 623-1753; *Economic and Social Progress in Latin America.*

International Monetary Fund, 700 Nineteenth Street, NW, Washington, D.C. 20431 (202) 623-7000; *Government Finance Statistics Yearbook.*

St. Martin's Press, Inc., 175 Fifth Avenue, New York, New York 10010 (800) 221-7945; *The Statesman's Year-Book.*

TRINIDAD AND TOBAGO - DAIRY PRODUCTS

Europa Publications Limited, 18 Bedford Square, London, WC1B 3JN, England; *The Europa World Year Book.*

Food and Agricultural Organization of the United Nations (FAO) Via delle Terme di Caracalla, 00100 Rome, Italy (Telephone Number in U.S. (202) 653-2400); *The State of Food and Agriculture.*

M.E. Sharpe, 80 Business Park Drive, Armonk, New York 10504 (800) 541-6563; *The Illustrated Book of World Rankings.*

Statistical Office of the United Nations, Publishing Service, New York, New York 10017 (800) 253-9646; *Statistical Yearbook.*

U.C.L.A. Latin American Center Publications, University of California, Los Angeles, California 90024 (310) 825-6634; *Statistical Abstract of Latin America.*

TRINIDAD AND TOBAGO - DEATH RATES - See TRINIDAD AND TOBAGO - MORTALITY

TRINIDAD AND TOBAGO - DEBT

The Economist Intelligence Unit, 111 West 57th Street, New York, New York 10019 (800) 938-4685; *The New Latin America Market Atlas.*

TRINIDAD AND TOBAGO - DEFENSE

The Economist Intelligence Unit, 111 West 57th Street, New York, New York 10019 (800) 938-4685; *The New Latin America Market Atlas.*

U.S. Arms Control and Disarmament Agency, 320 Twenty-first Street, NW, Washington, D.C. 20451 (202) 647-8677; *World Military Expenditures and Arms Transfers.*

TRINIDAD AND TOBAGO - DEFENSE EXPENDITURES - See TRINIDAD AND TOBAGO - MILITARY

TRINIDAD AND TOBAGO - DEMOGRAPHY

The Economist Intelligence Unit, 111 West 57th Street, New York, New York 10019 (800) 938-4685; *The World Market Atlas.*

Euromonitor International, Inc., 122 South Michigan Avenue, Suite 1200, Chicago, Illinois 60603 (800) 577-EURO; *International Marketing Data and Statistics; World Marketing Data and Statistics* and *The World Economic Factbook.*

Federal Statistical Office, Gustav-Stresemann - Ring 11, D-6200, Wiesbaden, Germany; *Trinidad and Tobago.*

M.E. Sharpe, 80 Business Park Drive, Armonk, New York 10504 (800) 541-6563; *The Illustrated Book of World Rankings.*

Statistical Office of the United Nations, Publishing Service, New York, New York 10017 (800) 253-9646; *Human Development Report.*

TRINIDAD AND TOBAGO - DEVELOPMENT ASSISTANCE

Inter-American Development Bank, 1300 New York Avenue, NW, Washington, D.C. 20577 (202) 623-1753; *Economic and Social Progress in Latin America.*

Statistical Office of the United Nations, Publishing Service, New York, New York 10017 (800) 253-9646; *Statistical Yearbook.*

TRINIDAD AND TOBAGO - DIAMOND PRODUCTION - See TRINIDAD AND TOBAGO - MINING AND MINERAL PRODUCTS

TRINIDAD AND TOBAGO - DISCOUNT RATES - See TRINIDAD AND TOBAGO - BANKING

TRINIDAD AND TOBAGO - DIVORCE RATES

M.E. Sharpe, 80 Business Park Drive, Armonk, New York 10504 (800) 541-6563; *The Illustrated Book of World Rankings.*

Statistical Office of the United Nations, Publishing Service, New York, New York 10017 (800) 253-9646; *Demographic Yearbook;* and *Statistical Yearbook.*

TRINIDAD AND TOBAGO - ECONOMY

Central Intelligence Agency, Washington, D.C. 20505 (703) 482-1100, www.cia.gov; *The World Factbook.*

The Economist Intelligence Unit, 111 West 57th Street, New York, New York 10019 (800) 938-4685; *Trinidad and Tobago Country Report.*

Euromonitor International, Inc., 122 South Michigan Avenue, Suite 1200, Chicago, Illinois 60603 (800) 577-EURO; *International Marketing Data and Statistics; World Marketing Data and Statistics;* and *The World Economic Factbook.*

Europa Publications Limited, 18 Bedford Square, London, WC1B 3JN, England; *The Europa World Year Book.*

Federal Statistical Office, Gustav-Stresemann - Ring 11, D-6200, Wiesbaden, Germany; *Trinidad and Tobago.*

Inter-American Development Bank, 1300 New York Avenue, NW, Washington, D.C. 20577 (202) 623-1753; *Economic and Social Progress in Latin America.*

M.E. Sharpe, 80 Business Park Drive, Armonk, New York 10504 (800) 541-6563; *The Illustrated Book of World Rankings.*

Organization of American States (OAS), General Secretariat, Washington, D.C. 20006 (202) 458-3533; *Statistical Bulletin of the OAS.*

St. Martin's Press, Inc., 175 Fifth Avenue, New York, New York 10010 (800) 221-7945; *The Statesman's Year-Book.*

Statistical Office of the United Nations, Publishing Service, New York, New York 10017 (800) 253-9646; *Economic Survey of Latin America and the Caribbean;* and *World Statistics Pocketbook.*

The World Bank, 1818 H Street, NW, Washington, D.C. 20433 (202) 477-1234; *The World Bank Atlas;* and *World Development Report.*

TRINIDAD AND TOBAGO - EDUCATION

The Economist Intelligence Unit, 111 West 57th Street, New York, New York 10019 (800) 938-4685; *The New Latin America Market Atlas;* and *The World Market Atlas.*

Euromonitor International, Inc., 122 South Michigan Avenue, Suite 1200, Chicago, Illinois 60603 (800) 577-EURO; *International Marketing Data and Statistics;* and *World Marketing Data an d Statistics.*

Europa Publications Limited, 18 Bedford Square, London, WC1B 3JN, England; *The Europa World Year Book.*

Federal Statistical Office, Gustav-Stresemann - Ring 11, D-6200, Wiesbaden, Germany; *Trinidad and Tobago.*

International Monetary Fund, 700 Nineteenth Street, NW, Washington, D.C. 20431 (202) 623-7000; *Government Finance Statistics Yearbook.*

M.E. Sharpe, 80 Business Park Drive, Armonk, New York 10504 (800) 541-6563; *The Illustrated Book of World Rankings.*

St. Martin's Press, Inc., 175 Fifth Avenue, New York, New York 10010 (800) 221-7945; *The Statesman's Year-Book.*

Statistical Office of the United Nations, Publishing Service, New York, New York 10017 (800) 253-9646; *Human Development Report.*

United Nations Educational, Scientific and Cultural Organization (UNESCO), 7 Place de Fontenoy, F-75700 Paris, France (Telephone Number in U.S. (212) 963-5981); *Statistical Yearbook.*

The World Bank, 1818 H Street, NW, Washington, D.C. 20433 (202) 477-1234; *World Development Report;* and *World Development Indicators.*

TRINIDAD AND TOBAGO - EGG PRODUCTION AND CONSUMPTION -See TRINIDAD AND TOBAGO - DAIRY PRODUCTS

TRINIDAD AND TOBAGO - ELECTRICITY

Central Intelligence Agency, Washington, D.C. 20505 (703) 482-1100, www.cia.gov; *The World Factbook.*

The Economist Intelligence Unit, 111 West 57th Street, New York, New York 10019 (800) 938-4685; *The New Latin America Market Atlas.*

Inter-American Development Bank, 1300 New York Avenue, NW, Washington, D.C. 20577 (202) 623-1753; *Economic and Social Progress in Latin America.*

M.E. Sharpe, 80 Business Park Drive, Armonk, New York 10504 (800) 541-6563; *The Illustrated Book of World Rankings.*

Penn Well Publishing Company, 1421 South Sheridan Road, P.O. Box 1260, Tulsa, Oklahoma 74101 (800) 752-9764; *International Energy Statistics Sourcebook.*

St. Martin's Press, Inc., 175 Fifth Avenue, New York, New York 10010 (800) 221-7945; *The Statesman's Year-Book.*

Statistical Office of the United Nations, Publishing Service, New York, New York 10017 (800) 253-9646; *Human Development Report;* and *Statistical*

Yearbook.

TRINIDAD AND TOBAGO - EMPLOYMENT

Euromonitor International, Inc., 122 South Michigan Avenue, Suite 1200, Chicago, Illinois 60603 (800) 577-EURO; *International Marketing Data and Statistics.*

Federal Statistical Office, Gustav-Stresemann - Ring 11, D-6200, Wiesbaden, Germany; *Trinidad and Tobago.*

International Labour Office, I.L.O. Publications, 1828 L Street, NW, Suite 801, Washington, D.C. 20036 (301) 638-3152; *Yearbook of Labour Statistics.*

M.E. Sharpe, 80 Business Park Drive, Armonk, New York 10504 (800) 541-6563; *The Illustrated Book of World Rankings.*

Organization of American States (OAS), General Secretariat, Washington, D.C. 20006 (202) 458-3533; *Statistical Bulletin of the OAS.*

Statistical Office of the United Nations, Publishing Service, New York, New York 10017 (800) 253-9646; *Statistical Yearbook.*

TRINIDAD AND TOBAGO - ENERGY

The Economist Intelligence Unit, 111 West 57th Street, New York, New York 10019 (800) 938-4685; *The New Latin America Market Atlas.*

Euromonitor International, Inc., 122 South Michigan Avenue, Suite 1200, Chicago, Illinois 60603 (800) 577-EURO; *International Marketing Data and Statistics; World Marketing Data and Statistics;* and *The World Economic Factbook.*

Food and Agricultural Organization of the United Nations (FAO) Via delle Terme di Caracalla, 00100 Rome, Italy (Telephone Number in U.S. (202) 653-2400); *The State of Food and Agriculture.*

M.E. Sharpe, 80 Business Park Drive, Armonk, New York 10504 (800) 541-6563; *The Illustrated Book of World Rankings.*

Penn Well Publishing Company, 1421 South Sheridan Road, P.O. Box 1260, Tulsa, Oklahoma 74101 (800) 752-9764; *International Energy Statistics Sourcebook.*

St. Martin's Press, Inc., 175 Fifth Avenue, New York, New York 10010 (800) 221-7945; *The Statesman's Year-Book.*

Statistical Office of the United Nations, Publishing Service, New York, New York 10017 (800) 253-9646; *Energy Statistics Yearbook; Human Development Report;* and *World Statistics Pocketbook.*

The World Bank, 1818 H Street, NW, Washington, D.C. 20433 (202) 477-1234; *The World Bank Atlas;* and *World Development Report.*

TRINIDAD AND TOBAGO - ENVIRONMENT

The Economist Intelligence Unit, 111 West 57th Street, New York, New York 10019 (800) 938-4685; *Trinidad and Tobago Country Report.*

Statistical Office of the United Nations, Publishing Service, New York, New York 10017 (800) 253-9646; *World Statistics Pocketbook.*

TRINIDAD AND TOBAGO - EXCHANGE RATES

Central Intelligence Agency, Washington, D.C. 20505 (703) 482-1100, www.cia.gov; *The World Factbook.*

Euromonitor International, Inc., 122 South Michigan Avenue, Suite 1200, Chicago, Illinois 60603 (800) 577-EURO; *International Marketing Data and Statistics;* and *The World Economic Factbook.*

Europa Publications Limited, 18 Bedford Square, London, WC1B 3JN, England; *The Europa World Year Book.*

Inter-American Development Bank, 1300 New York Avenue, NW, Washington, D.C. 20577 (202) 623-1753; *Economic and Social Progress in Latin America.*

International Monetary Fund, 700 Nineteenth Street, NW, Washington, D.C. 20431 (202) 623-7000; *International Financial Statistics.*

Organization of American States (OAS), General Secretariat, Washington, D.C. 20006 (202) 458-3533; *Statistical Bulletin of the OAS.*

Statistical Office of the United Nations, Publishing Service, New York, New York 10017 (800) 253-9646; *Statistical Yearbook;* and *World Statistics Pocketbook.*

TRINIDAD AND TOBAGO - EXCISE TAXES - See TRINIDAD AND TOBAGO - TAXATION

TRINIDAD AND TOBAGO - EXPORTS

Central Intelligence Agency, Washington, D.C. 20505 (703) 482-1100, www.cia.gov; *The World Factbook.*

The Economist Intelligence Unit, 111 West 57th Street, New York, New York 10019 (800) 938-4685; *The New Latin America Market Atlas; Trinidad and Tobago Country Report; The World Market Atlas;* and *The World Economic Factbook.*

Euromonitor International, Inc., 122

South Michigan Avenue, Suite 1200, Chicago, Illinois 60603 (800) 577-EURO; *International Marketing Data and Statistics.*

Europa Publications Limited, 18 Bedford Square, London, WC1B 3JN, England; *The Europa World Year Book.*

Food and Agricultural Organization of the United Nations (FAO) Via delle Terme di Caracalla, 00100 Rome, Italy (Telephone Number in U.S. (202) 653-2400); *The State of Food and Agriculture.*

Inter-American Development Bank, 1300 New York Avenue, NW, Washington, D.C. 20577 (202) 623-1753; *Economic and Social Progress in Latin America.*

International Monetary Fund, 700 Nineteenth Street, NW, Washington, D.C. 20431 (202) 623-7000; *Direction of Trade Statistics; Government Finance Statistics Yearbook;* and *International Financial Statistics.*

Organization of American States (OAS), General Secretariat, Washington, D.C. 20006 (202) 458-3533; *Statistical Bulletin of the OAS.*

St. Martin's Press, Inc., 175 Fifth Avenue, New York, New York 10010 (800) 221-7945; *The Statesman's Year-Book.*

United Nations Conference on Trade and Development (UNCTAD), New York, New York 10017 (800) 253-9646; *Handbook of International Trade and Development Statistics.*

The World Bank, 1818 H Street, NW, Washington, D.C. 20433 (202) 477-1234; *World Development Report;* and *World Development Indicators.*

TRINIDAD AND TOBAGO - EXTERNAL FINANCING

Inter-American Development Bank, 1300 New York Avenue, NW, Washington, D.C. 20577 (202) 623-1753; *Economic and Social Progress in Latin America.*

TRINIDAD AND TOBAGO - EXTERNAL INDEBTEDNESS

Inter-American Development Bank, 1300 New York Avenue, NW, Washington, D.C. 20577 (202) 623-1753; *Economic and Social Progress in Latin America.*

The World Bank, 1818 H Street, NW, Washington, D.C. 20433 (202) 477-1234; *World Development Report;* and *World Development Indicators.*

TRINIDAD AND TOBAGO - EXTERNAL TRADE

Euromonitor International, Inc., 122

South Michigan Avenue, Suite 1200, Chicago, Illinois 60603 (800) 577-EURO; *World Marketing Data and Statistics.*

Food and Agricultural Organization of the United Nations (FAO) Via delle Terme di Caracalla, 00100 Rome, Italy (Telephone Number in U.S. (202) 653-2400); *The State of Food and Agriculture;* and *Trade Yearbook.*

Inter-American Development Bank, 1300 New York Avenue, NW, Washington, D.C. 20577 (202) 623-1753; *Economic and Social Progress in Latin America.*

Statistical Office of the United Nations, Publishing Service, New York, New York 10017 (800) 253-9646; *Statistical Yearbook.*

TRINIDAD AND TOBAGO - FARM CROPS - See TRINIDAD AND TOBAGO - CROPS

TRINIDAD AND TOBAGO - FEMALE WORKING POPULATION - See TRINIDAD AND TOBAGO - EMPLOYMENT

TRINIDAD AND TOBAGO - FERTILITY RATES

Central Intelligence Agency, Washington, D.C. 20505 (703) 482-1100, www.cia.gov; *The World Factbook.*

M.E. Sharpe, 80 Business Park Drive, Armonk, New York 10504 (800) 541-6563; *The Illustrated Book of World Rankings.*

Statistical Office of the United Nations, Publishing Service, New York, New York 10017 (800) 253-9646; *Human Development Report.*

The World Bank, 1818 H Street, NW, Washington, D.C. 20433 (202) 477-1234; *The World Bank Atlas; World Development Report;* and *World Development Indicators.*

TRINIDAD AND TOBAGO - FERTILIZER

The Economist Intelligence Unit, 111 West 57th Street, New York, New York 10019 (800) 938-4685; *The New Latin America Market Atlas.*

Food and Agricultural Organization of the United Nations (FAO), Via delle Terme di Caracalla, 00100, Rome, Italy (Telephone Number in U.S. (202) 653-2400); *Fertilizer Yearbook;* and *The State of Food and Agriculture.*

Statistical Office of the United Nations, Publishing Service, New York, New York 10017 (800) 253-9646; *Statistical Yearbook.*

TRINIDAD AND TOBAGO - FETAL MORTALITY - See TRINIDAD AND TOBAGO - MORTALITY

TRINIDAD AND TOBAGO - FINANCE

The Economist Intelligence Unit, 111 West 57th Street, New York, New York 10019 (800) 938-4685; *Trinidad and Tobago Country Report.*

Europa Publications Limited, 18 Bedford Square, London, WC1B 3JN, England; *The Europa World Year Book.*

Federal Statistical Office, Gustav-Stresemann - Ring 11, D-6200, Wiesbaden, Germany; *Trinidad and Tobago.*

Inter-American Development Bank, 1300 New York Avenue, NW, Washington, D.C. 20577 (202) 623-1753; *Economic and Social Progress in Latin America.*

International Monetary Fund, 700 Nineteenth Street, NW, Washington, D.C. 20431 (202) 623-7000; *Government Finance Statistics Yearbook.*

M.E. Sharpe, 80 Business Park Drive, Armonk, New York 10504 (800) 541-6563; *The Illustrated Book of World Rankings.*

Organization of American States (OAS), General Secretariat, Washington, D.C. 20006 (202) 458-3533; *Statistical Bulletin of the OAS.*

St. Martin's Press, Inc., 175 Fifth Avenue, New York, New York 10010 (800) 221-7945; *The Statesman's Year-Book.*

TRINIDAD AND TOBAGO - FISHERIES

Europa Publications Limited, 18 Bedford Square, London, WC1B 3JN, England; *The Europa World Year Book.*

Federal Statistical Office, Gustav-Stresemann - Ring 11, D-6200, Wiesbaden, Germany; *Trinidad and Tobago.*

Food and Agricultural Organization of the United Nations (FAO) Via delle Terme di Caracalla, 00100 Rome, Italy (Telephone Number in U.S. (202) 653-2400); *The State of Food and Agriculture;* and *Yearbook of Fishery Statistics.*

Inter-American Development Bank, 1300 New York Avenue, NW, Washington, D.C. 20577 (202) 623-1753; *Economic and Social Progress in Latin America.*

M.E. Sharpe, 80 Business Park Drive, Armonk, New York 10504 (800) 541-6563; *The Illustrated Book of World Rankings.*

St. Martin's Press, Inc., 175 Fifth Avenue, New York, New York 10010 (800) 221-7945; *The Statesman's Year-Book.*

Statistical Office of the United Nations, Publishing Service, New York, New York 10017 (800) 253-9646; *Statistical Yearbook.*

United Nations Conference on Trade and Development, Central Statistical Service, Palais des Nations, Geneva, Switzerland (Telephone in U.S. (800) 253-9646); *UNCTAD Commodity Yearbook*.

TRINIDAD AND TOBAGO - FOOD

Food and Agricultural Organization of the United Nations (FAO) Via delle Terme di Caracalla, 00100 Rome, Italy (Telephone Number in U.S. (202) 653-2400); *The State of Food and Agriculture*.

Statistical Office of the United Nations, Publishing Service, New York, New York 10017 (800) 253-9646; *Human Development Report*.

United Nations Conference on Trade and Development, Central Statistical Service, Palais des Nations, Geneva, Switzerland (Telephone in U.S. (800) 253-9646); *UNCTAD Commodity Yearbook*.

TRINIDAD AND TOBAGO - FOREIGN AID

Inter-American Development Bank, 1300 New York Avenue, NW, Washington, D.C. 20577 (202) 623-1753; *Economic and Social Progress in Latin America*.

TRINIDAD AND TOBAGO - FOREIGN DEBT

The Economist Intelligence Unit, 111 West 57th Street, New York, New York 10019 (800) 938-4685; *The New Latin America Market Atlas*.

Inter-American Development Bank, 1300 New York Avenue, NW, Washington, D.C. 20577 (202) 623-1753; *Economic and Social Progress in Latin America*.

International Monetary Fund, 700 Nineteenth Street, NW, Washington, D.C. 20431 (202) 623-7000; *Government Finance Statistics Yearbook*.

TRINIDAD AND TOBAGO - FOREIGN INDEBTEDNESS

Inter-American Development Bank, 1300 New York Avenue, NW, Washington, D.C. 20577 (202) 623-1753; *Economic and Social Progress in Latin America*.

Statistical Office of the United Nations, Publishing Service, New York, New York 10017 (800) 253-9646; *Economic Survey of Latin America and the Caribbean*.

TRINIDAD AND TOBAGO - FOREIGN INVESTMENT

The Economist Intelligence Unit, 111 West 57th Street, New York, New York 10019 (800) 938-4685; *The New Latin America Market Atlas*.

TRINIDAD AND TOBAGO - FOREIGN TRADE

The Economist Intelligence Unit, 111 West 57th Street, New York, New York 10019 (800) 938-4685; *The New Latin America Market Atlas;* and *Trinidad and Tobago Country Report*.

Euromonitor International, Inc., 122 South Michigan Avenue, Suite 1200, Chicago, Illinois 60603 (800) 577-EURO; *International Marketing Data and Statistics;* and *The World Economic Factbook*.

Europa Publications Limited, 18 Bedford Square, London, WC1B 3JN, England; *The Europa World Year Book*.

Federal Statistical Office, Gustav-Stresemann - Ring 11, D-6200, Wiesbaden, Germany; *Trinidad and Tobago*.

Food and Agricultural Organization of the United Nations (FAO) Via delle Terme di Caracalla, 00100 Rome, Italy (Telephone Number in U.S. (202) 653-2400); *The State of Food and Agriculture*.

Inter-American Development Bank, 1300 New York Avenue, NW, Washington, D.C. 20577 (202) 623-1753; *Economic and Social Progress in Latin America*.

International Monetary Fund, 700 Nineteenth Street, NW, Washington, D.C. 20431 (202) 623-7000; *International Financial Statistics*.

M.E. Sharpe, 80 Business Park Drive, Armonk, New York 10504 (800) 541-6563; *The Illustrated Book of World Rankings*.

St. Martin's Press, Inc., 175 Fifth Avenue, New York, New York 10010 (800) 221-7945; *The Statesman's Year-Book*.

Statistical Office of the United Nations, Publishing Service, New York, New York 10017 (800) 253-9646; *Economic Survey of Latin America and the Caribbean; International Trade Statistics Yearbook;* and *Statistical Yearbook*.

United Nations Conference on Trade and Development, Central Statistical Service, Palais des Nations, Geneva, Switzerland (Telephone in U.S. (800) 253-9646); *UNCTAD Commodity Yearbook*.

The World Bank, 1818 H Street, NW, Washington, D.C. 20433 (202) 477-1234; *World Development Report;* and *World Development Indicators*.

TRINIDAD AND TOBAGO - FORESTRY AND FOREST PRODUCTS

The Economist Intelligence Unit, 111 West 57th Street, New York, New York 10019 (800) 938-4685; *The New Latin America Market Atlas*.

Europa Publications Limited, 18 Bedford Square, London, WC1B 3JN, England; *The Europa World Year Book*.

Federal Statistical Office, Gustav-Stresemann - Ring 11, D-6200, Wiesbaden, Germany; *Trinidad and Tobago*.

Food and Agricultural Organization of the United Nations (FAO) Via delle Terme di Caracalla, 00100 Rome, Italy (Telephone Number in U.S. (202) 653-2400); *The State of Food and Agriculture;* and *Yearbook of Forest Products*.

Inter-American Development Bank, 1300 New York Avenue, NW, Washington, D.C. 20577 (202) 623-1753; *Economic and Social Progress in Latin America*.

M.E. Sharpe, 80 Business Park Drive, Armonk, New York 10504 (800) 541-6563; *The Illustrated Book of World Rankings*.

Statistical Office of the United Nations, Publishing Service, New York, New York 10017 (800) 253-9646; *Statistical Yearbook*.

U.C.L.A. Latin American Center Publications, University of California, Los Angeles, California 90024 (310) 825-6634; *Statistical Abstract of Latin America*.

United Nations Conference on Trade and Development, Central Statistical Service, Palais des Nations, Geneva, Switzerland (Telephone in U.S. (800) 253-9646); *UNCTAD Commodity Yearbook*.

United Nations Educational, Scientific and Cultural Organization (UNESCO), 7 Place de Fontenoy, F-75700 Paris, France (Telephone Number in U.S. (212) 963-5981); *Statistical Yearbook*.

The World Bank, 1818 H Street, NW, Washington, D.C. 20433 (202) 477-1234; *World Development Report*.

TRINIDAD AND TOBAGO - GAS AND GAS LIQUIDS (NATURAL) PRODUCTION - See TRINIDAD AND TOBAGO - MINING AND MINERAL PRODUCTS

TRINIDAD AND TOBAGO - GENERAL INDUSTRIAL STATISTICS - See TRINIDAD AND TOBAGO - INDUSTRY

TRINIDAD AND TOBAGO - GENERAL MORTALITY - See TRINIDAD AND TOBAGO - MORTALITY

TRINIDAD AND TOBAGO - GEOGRAPHIC DATA

M.E. Sharpe, 80 Business Park Drive, Armonk, New York 10504 (800) 541-6563; *The Illustrated Book of World Rankings*.

TRINIDAD AND TOBAGO - GOLD HOLDINGS

International Monetary Fund, 700 Nineteenth Street, NW, Washington, D.C. 20431 (202) 623-7000; *International Financial Statistics.*

Statistical Office of the United Nations, Publishing Service, New York, New York 10017 (800) 253-9646; *Statistical Yearbook.*

The World Bank, 1818 H Street, NW, Washington, D.C. 20433 (202) 477-1234; *World Development Indicators.*

TRINIDAD AND TOBAGO - GOLD PRODUCTION AND CONSUMPTION - See TRINIDAD AND TOBAGO - MINING AND MINERAL PRODUCTS

TRINIDAD AND TOBAGO - GOLD RESERVES

The Economist Intelligence Unit, 111 West 57th Street, New York, New York 10019 (800) 938-4685; *The New Latin America Market Atlas.*

TRINIDAD AND TOBAGO - GOVERNMENT

Central Intelligence Agency, Washington, D.C. 20505 (703) 482-1100, www.cia.gov; *The World Factbook.*

Europa Publications Limited, 18 Bedford Square, London, WC1B 3JN, England; *The Europa World Year Book.*

Inter-American Development Bank, 1300 New York Avenue, NW, Washington, D.C. 20577 (202) 623-1753; *Economic and Social Progress in Latin America.*

International Monetary Fund, 700 Nineteenth Street, NW, Washington, D.C. 20431 (202) 623-7000; *Government Finance Statistics Yearbook.*

St. Martin's Press, Inc., 175 Fifth Avenue, New York, New York 10010 (800) 221-7945; *The Statesman's Year-Book.*

Statistical Office of the United Nations, Publishing Service, New York, New York 10017 (800) 253-9646; *National Accounts Statistics.*

The World Bank, 1818 H Street, NW, Washington, D.C. 20433 (202) 477-1234; *World Development Report;* and *World Development Indicators.*

TRINIDAD AND TOBAGO - GRAIN PRODUCTION - See TRINIDAD AND TOBAGO - CROPS

TRINIDAD AND TOBAGO - GRANTS

International Monetary Fund, 700 Nineteenth Street, NW, Washington, D.C. 20431 (202) 623-7000; *Government Finance Statistics Yearbook.*

TRINIDAD AND TOBAGO - GROSS DOMESTIC PRODUCT

The Economist Intelligence Unit, 111 West 57th Street, New York, New York 10019 (800) 938-4685; *The New Latin America Market Atlas; The World Market Atlas;* and *Trinidad and Tobago Country Report.*

Euromonitor International, Inc., 122 South Michigan Avenue, Suite 1200, Chicago, Illinois 60603 (800) 577-EURO; *International Marketing Data and Statistics;* and *The World Economic Factbook.*

Europa Publications Limited, 18 Bedford Square, London, WC1B 3JN, England; *The Europa World Year Book.*

Inter-American Development Bank, 1300 New York Avenue, NW, Washington, D.C. 20577 (202) 623-1753; *Economic and Social Progress in Latin America.*

M.E. Sharpe, 80 Business Park Drive, Armonk, New York 10504 (800) 541-6563; *The Illustrated Book of World Rankings.*

Organization of American States (OAS), General Secretariat, Washington, D.C. 20006 (202) 458-3533; *Statistical Bulletin of the OAS.*

Statistical Office of the United Nations, Publishing Service, New York, New York 10017 (800) 253-9646; *Human Development Report; National Accounts Statistics;* and *Statistical Yearbook.*

The World Bank, 1818 H Street, NW, Washington, D.C. 20433 (202) 477-1234; *World Development Report;* and *World Development Indicators.*

TRINIDAD AND TOBAGO - GROSS NATIONAL PRODUCT

Euromonitor International, Inc., 122 South Michigan Avenue, Suite 1200, Chicago, Illinois 60603 (800) 577-EURO; *International Marketing Data and Statistics.*

Inter-American Development Bank, 1300 New York Avenue, NW, Washington, D.C. 20577 (202) 623-1753; *Economic and Social Progress in Latin America.*

St. Martin's Press, Inc., 175 Fifth Avenue, New York, New York 10010 (800) 221-7945; *The Statesman's Year-Book.*

U.S. Arms Control and Disarmament Agency, 320 Twenty-first Street, NW, Washington, D.C. 20451 (202) 647-8677; *World Military Expenditures and Arms Transfers.*

The World Bank, 1818 H Street, NW, Washington, D.C. 20433 (202) 477-1234; *The World Bank Atlas; World Development*

Report; and *World Development Indicators.*

TRINIDAD AND TOBAGO - HEALTH

The Economist Intelligence Unit, 111 West 57th Street, New York, New York 10019 (800) 938-4685; *The New Latin America Market Atlas.*

Euromonitor International, Inc., 122 South Michigan Avenue, Suite 1200, Chicago, Illinois 60603 (800) 577-EURO; *World Marketing Data and Statistics.*

Federal Statistical Office, Gustav-Stresemann - Ring 11, D-6200, Wiesbaden, Germany; *Trinidad and Tobago.*

M.E. Sharpe, 80 Business Park Drive, Armonk, New York 10504 (800) 541-6563; *The Illustrated Book of World Rankings.*

St. Martin's Press, Inc., 175 Fifth Avenue, New York, New York 10010 (800) 221-7945; *The Statesman's Year-Book.*

Statistical Office of the United Nations, Publishing Service, New York, New York 10017 (800) 253-9646; *Human Development Report;* and *Statistical Yearbook.*

United Nations Children's Fund (UNICEF), 3 United Nations Plaza, New York, New York 10017 (800) 253-9646; *State of the World's Children.*

The World Bank, 1818 H Street, NW, Washington, D.C. 20433 (202) 477-1234; *World Development Report.*

TRINIDAD AND TOBAGO - HEALTH EXPENDITURES

International Monetary Fund, 700 Nineteenth Street, NW, Washington, D.C. 20431 (202) 623-7000; *Government Finance Statistics Yearbook.*

TRINIDAD AND TOBAGO - HIGHWAYS

Central Intelligence Agency, Washington, D.C. 20505 (703) 482-1100, www.cia.gov; *The World Factbook.*

The Economist Intelligence Unit, 111 West 57th Street, New York, New York 10019 (800) 938-4685; *The New Latin America Market Atlas.*

St. Martin's Press, Inc., 175 Fifth Avenue, New York, New York 10010 (800) 221-7945; *The Statesman's Year-Book.*

TRINIDAD AND TOBAGO - HORSES - See TRINIDAD AND TOBAGO - LIVESTOCK AND POULTRY

TRINIDAD AND TOBAGO - HOURS OF WORK - See TRINIDAD AND TOBAGO - EMPLOYMENT

TRINIDAD AND TOBAGO - HOUSING AND HOUSING UNITS

Euromonitor International, Inc., 122 South Michigan Avenue, Suite 1200, Chicago, Illinois 60603 (800) 577-EURO; *World Marketing Data and Statistics*.

M.E. Sharpe, 80 Business Park Drive, Armonk, New York 10504 (800) 541-6563; *The Illustrated Book of World Rankings*.

TRINIDAD AND TOBAGO - HOUSING EXPENDITURES

International Monetary Fund, 700 Nineteenth Street, NW, Washington, D.C. 20431 (202) 623-7000; *Government Finance Statistics Yearbook*.

TRINIDAD AND TOBAGO - ILLITERATE POPULATION

Central Intelligence Agency, Washington, D.C. 20505 (703) 482-1100, www.cia.gov; *The World Factbook*.

The Economist Intelligence Unit, 111 West 57th Street, New York, New York 10019 (800) 938-4685; *The New Latin America Market Atlas;* and *The World Market Atlas*.

Euromonitor International, Inc., 122 South Michigan Avenue, Suite 1200, Chicago, Illinois 60603 (800) 577-EURO; *The World Economic Factbook*.

Statistical Office of the United Nations, Publishing Service, New York, New York 10017 (800) 253-9646; *Human Development Report*.

United Nations Educational, Scientific and Cultural Organization (UNESCO), 7 Place de Fontenoy, F-75700 Paris, France (Telephone Number in U.S. (212) 963-5981); *Statistical Yearbook*.

TRINIDAD AND TOBAGO - IMPORTS

Central Intelligence Agency, Washington, D.C. 20505 (703) 482-1100, www.cia.gov; *The World Factbook*.

The Economist Intelligence Unit, 111 West 57th Street, New York, New York 10019 (800) 938-4685; *The New Latin America Market Atlas; The World Market Atlas;* and *Trinidad and Tobago Country Report*.

Euromonitor International, Inc., 122 South Michigan Avenue, Suite 1200, Chicago, Illinois 60603 (800) 577-EURO; *International Marketing Data and Statistics;* and *The World Economic Factbook*.

Europa Publications Limited, 18 Bedford Square, London, WC1B 3JN, England; *The Europa World Year Book*.

Food and Agricultural Organization of the United Nations (FAO) Via delle Terme di Caracalla, 00100 Rome, Italy (Telephone Number in U.S. (202) 653-2400); *The State of Food and Agriculture*.

Inter-American Development Bank, 1300 New York Avenue, NW, Washington, D.C. 20577 (202) 623-1753; *Economic and Social Progress in Latin America*.

International Monetary Fund, 700 Nineteenth Street, NW, Washington, D.C. 20431 (202) 623-7000; *Direction of Trade Statistics; Government Finance Statistics Yearbook;* and *International Financial Statistics*.

Organization of American States (OAS), General Secretariat, Washington, D.C. 20006 (202) 458-3533; *Statistical Bulletin of the OAS*.

St. Martin's Press, Inc., 175 Fifth Avenue, New York, New York 10010 (800) 221-7945; *The Statesman's Year-Book*.

United Nations Conference on Trade and Development (UNCTAD), New York, New York 10017 (800) 253-9646; *Handbook of International Trade and Development Statistics*.

The World Bank, 1818 H Street, NW, Washington, D.C. 20433 (202) 477-1234; *World Development Report;* and *World Development Indicators*.

TRINIDAD AND TOBAGO - INCOME TAXES - See TRINIDAD AND TOBAGO - TAXATION

TRINIDAD AND TOBAGO - INDUSTRY

Central Intelligence Agency, Washington, D.C. 20505 (703) 482-1100, www.cia.gov; *The World Factbook*.

The Economist Intelligence Unit, 111 West 57th Street, New York, New York 10019 (800) 938-4685; *Trinidad and Tobago Country Report*.

Euromonitor International, Inc., 122 South Michigan Avenue, Suite 1200, Chicago, Illinois 60603 (800) 577-EURO; *International Marketing Data and Statistics; World Marketing Data and Statistics;* and *The World Economic Factbook*.

Europa Publications Limited, 18 Bedford Square, London, WC1B 3JN, England; *The Europa World Year Book*.

Federal Statistical Office, Gustav-Stresemann - Ring 11, D-6200, Wiesbaden, Germany; *Trinidad and Tobago*.

International Labour Office, I.L.O. Publications, 1828 L Street, NW, Suite 801, Washington, D.C. 20036 (301) 638-3152; *Yearbook of Labour Statistics*.

M.E. Sharpe, 80 Business Park Drive, Armonk, New York 10504 (800) 541-6563; *The Illustrated Book of World Rankings*.

St. Martin's Press, Inc., 175 Fifth Avenue, New York, New York 10010 (800) 221-7945; *The Statesman's Year-Book*.

Statistical Office of the United Nations, Publishing Service, New York, New York 10017 (800) 253-9646; *Economic Survey of Latin America and the Caribbean;* and *Industrial Commodity Statistics Yearbook*.

The World Bank, 1818 H Street, NW, Washington, D.C. 20433 (202) 477-1234; *World Development Indicators*.

TRINIDAD AND TOBAGO - INFANT AND MATERNAL MORTALITY - See TRINIDAD AND TOBAGO - MORTALITY

TRINIDAD AND TOBAGO - INFLATIONARY FACTORS

Statistical Office of the United Nations, Publishing Service, New York, New York 10017 (800) 253-9646; *Economic Survey of Latin America and the Caribbean*.

TRINIDAD AND TOBAGO - INTEREST RATES

Inter-American Development Bank, 1300 New York Avenue, NW, Washington, D.C. 20577 (202) 623-1753; *Economic and Social Progress in Latin America*.

Organization of American States (OAS), General Secretariat, Washington, D.C. 20006 (202) 458-3533; *Statistical Bulletin of the OAS*.

TRINIDAD AND TOBAGO - INTERNATIONAL FINANCE

Inter-American Development Bank, 1300 New York Avenue, NW, Washington, D.C. 20577 (202) 623-1753; *Economic and Social Progress in Latin America*.

TRINIDAD AND TOBAGO - INTERNATIONAL LIQUIDITY

Inter-American Development Bank, 1300 New York Avenue, NW, Washington, D.C. 20577 (202) 623-1753; *Economic and Social Progress in Latin America*.

International Monetary Fund, 700 Nineteenth Street, NW, Washington, D.C. 20431 (202) 623-7000; *International Financial Statistics*.

TRINIDAD AND TOBAGO - INTERNATIONAL RESERVES

Organization of American States (OAS), General Secretariat, Washington, D.C. 20006 (202) 458-3533; *Statistical Bulletin of the OAS*.

TRINIDAD AND TOBAGO - INTERNATIONAL RESERVES EXCLUDING GOLD

Inter-American Development Bank, 1300 New York Avenue, NW, Washington, D.C. 20577 (202) 623-1753; *Economic and Social Progress in Latin America*.

Statistical Office of the United Nations, Publishing Service, New York, New York 10017 (800) 253-9646; *Statistical Yearbook*.

The World Bank, 1818 H Street, NW, Washington, D.C. 20433 (202) 477-1234; *World Development Indicators*.

TRINIDAD AND TOBAGO - INTERNATIONAL STATISTICS

Inter-American Development Bank, 1300 New York Avenue, NW, Washington, D.C. 20577 (202) 623-1753; *Economic and Social Progress in Latin America*.

TRINIDAD AND TOBAGO - INVESTMENTS

Inter-American Development Bank, 1300 New York Avenue, NW, Washington, D.C. 20577 (202) 623-1753; *Economic and Social Progress in Latin America*.

TRINIDAD AND TOBAGO - IRON ORE PRODUCTION AND CONSUMPTION - See TRINIDAD AND TOBAGO - MINING AND MINERAL PRODUCTS

TRINIDAD AND TOBAGO - IRRIGATION

Euromonitor International, Inc., 122 South Michigan Avenue, Suite 1200, Chicago, Illinois 60603 (800) 577-EURO; *International Marketing Data and Statistics*.

Inter-American Development Bank, 1300 New York Avenue, NW, Washington, D.C. 20577 (202) 623-1753; *Economic and Social Progress in Latin America*.

TRINIDAD AND TOBAGO - LABOR

Central Intelligence Agency, Washington, D.C. 20505 (703) 482-1100, www.cia.gov; *The World Factbook*.

The Economist Intelligence Unit, 111 West 57th Street, New York, New York 10019 (800) 938-4685; *The New Latin America Market Atlas*.

Euromonitor International, Inc., 122 South Michigan Avenue, Suite 1200, Chicago, Illinois 60603 (800) 577-EURO; *International Marketing Data and Statistics; and World Marketing Data and Statistics*.

Europa Publications Limited, 18 Bedford Square, London, WC1B 3JN, England; *The Europa World Year Book*.

Food and Agricultural Organization of the United Nations (FAO) Via delle Terme di Caracalla, 00100 Rome, Italy (Telephone Number in U.S. (202) 653-2400); *The State of Food and Agriculture*.

International Labour Office, I.L.O. Publications, 1828 L Street, NW, Suite 801, Washington, D.C. 20036 (301) 638-3152; *Yearbook of Labour Statistics*.

M.E. Sharpe, 80 Business Park Drive, Armonk, New York 10504 (800) 541-6563; *The Illustrated Book of World Rankings*.

St. Martin's Press, Inc., 175 Fifth Avenue, New York, New York 10010 (800) 221-7945; *The Statesman's Year-Book*.

Statistical Office of the United Nations, Publishing Service, New York, New York 10017 (800) 253-9646; *Human Development Report*.

The World Bank, 1818 H Street, NW, Washington, D.C. 20433 (202) 477-1234; *The World Bank Atlas; World Development Report; and World Development Indicators*.

TRINIDAD AND TOBAGO - LAND AREA

The Economist Intelligence Unit, 111 West 57th Street, New York, New York 10019 (800) 938-4685; *The New Latin America Market Atlas*.

TRINIDAD AND TOBAGO - LAND USE

Central Intelligence Agency, Washington, D.C. 20505 (703) 482-1100, www.cia.gov; *The World Factbook*.

Euromonitor International, Inc., 122 South Michigan Avenue, Suite 1200, Chicago, Illinois 60603 (800) 577-EURO; *International Marketing Data and Statistics*.

Food and Agricultural Organization of the United Nations (FAO), Via delle Terme di Caracalla, 00100 Rome, Italy (Telephone Number in U.S. (202) 653-2400); *Production Yearbook*.

Inter-American Development Bank, 1300 New York Avenue, NW, Washington, D.C. 20577 (202) 623-1753; *Economic and Social Progress in Latin America*.

The World Bank, 1818 H Street, NW, Washington, D.C. 20433 (202) 477-1234; *World Development Report*.

TRINIDAD AND TOBAGO - LIBRARIES

M.E. Sharpe, 80 Business Park Drive, Armonk, New York 10504 (800) 541-6563; *The Illustrated Book of World Rankings*.

United Nations Educational, Scientific and Cultural Organization (UNESCO), 7

Place de Fontenoy, F-75700 Paris, France (Telephone Number in U.S. (212) 963-5981); *Statistical Yearbook*.

TRINIDAD AND TOBAGO - LIFE EXPECTANCY

Central Intelligence Agency, Washington, D.C. 20505 (703) 482-1100, www.cia.gov; *The World Factbook*.

The Economist Intelligence Unit, 111 West 57th Street, New York, New York 10019 (800) 938-4685; *The New Latin America Market Atlas*.

Euromonitor International, Inc., 122 South Michigan Avenue, Suite 1200, Chicago, Illinois 60603 (800) 577-EURO; *The World Economic Factbook*.

St. Martin's Press, Inc., 175 Fifth Avenue, New York, New York 10010 (800) 221-7945; *The Statesman's Year-Book*.

Statistical Office of the United Nations, Publishing Service, New York, New York 10017 (800) 253-9646; *Human Development Report; and World Statistics Pocketbook*.

The World Bank, 1818 H Street, NW, Washington, D.C. 20433 (202) 477-1234; *The World Bank Atlas; and World Development Report*.

TRINIDAD AND TOBAGO - LITERACY RATE

Euromonitor International, Inc., 122 South Michigan Avenue, Suite 1200, Chicago, Illinois 60603 (800) 577-EURO; *World Marketing Data and Statistics*.

TRINIDAD AND TOBAGO - LIVESTOCK AND POULTRY

Euromonitor International, Inc., 122 South Michigan Avenue, Suite 1200, Chicago, Illinois 60603 (800) 577-EURO; *International Marketing Data and Statistics*.

Europa Publications Limited, 18 Bedford Square, London, WC1B 3JN, England; *The Europa World Year Book*.

Food and Agricultural Organization of the United Nations (FAO), Via delle Terme di Caracalla, 00100 Rome, Italy (Telephone Number in U.S. (202) 653-2400); *Production Yearbook; and The State of Food and Agriculture*.

M.E. Sharpe, 80 Business Park Drive, Armonk, New York 10504 (800) 541-6563; *The Illustrated Book of World Rankings*.

St. Martin's Press, Inc., 175 Fifth Avenue, New York, New York 10010 (800) 221-7945; *The Statesman's Year-Book*.

Statistical Office of the United Nations,

Publishing Service, New York, New York 10017 (800) 253-9646; *Statistical Yearbook.*

United Nations Conference on Trade and Development, Central Statistical Service, Palais des Nations, Geneva, Switzerland (Telephone in U.S. (800) 253-9646); *UNCTAD Commodity Yearbook.*

TRINIDAD AND TOBAGO - LIVING LEVELS - See TRINIDAD AND TOBAGO - LIFE EXPECTANCY

TRINIDAD AND TOBAGO - MAIL - NUMBER OF ITEMS SENT AND RECEIVED

Statistical Office of the United Nations, Publishing Service, New York, New York 10017 (800) 253-9646; *Statistical Yearbook.*

TRINIDAD AND TOBAGO - MAIN ECONOMIC INDICATORS - See TRINIDAD AND TOBAGO - ECONOMY

TRINIDAD AND TOBAGO - MANUFACTURING

The Economist Intelligence Unit, 111 West 57th Street, New York, New York 10019 (800) 938-4685; *The New Latin America Market Atlas.*

Inter-American Development Bank, 1300 New York Avenue, NW, Washington, D.C. 20577 (202) 623-1753; *Economic and Social Progress in Latin America.*

M.E. Sharpe, 80 Business Park Drive, Armonk, New York 10504 (800) 541-6563; *The Illustrated Book of World Rankings.*

Statistical Office of the United Nations, Publishing Service, New York, New York 10017 (800) 253-9646; *Statistical Yearbook.*

The World Bank, 1818 H Street, NW, Washington, D.C. 20433 (202) 477-1234; *World Development Indicators.*

TRINIDAD AND TOBAGO - MARRIAGE RATES

M.E. Sharpe, 80 Business Park Drive, Armonk, New York 10504 (800) 541-6563; *The Illustrated Book of World Rankings.*

Statistical Office of the United Nations, Publishing Service, New York, New York 10017 (800) 253-9646; *Demographic Yearbook;* and *Statistical Yearbook.*

TRINIDAD AND TOBAGO - MEAT PRODUCTION - See TRINIDAD AND TOBAGO - LIVESTOCK AND POULTRY

TRINIDAD AND TOBAGO - MERCHANT SHIPPING

Europa Publications Limited, 18 Bedford Square, London, WC1B 3JN, England; *The Europa World Year Book.*

Lloyd's Register of Shipping, 17 Battery Place, New York, New York 10004 (212) 425-8050; *Register of Ships.*

St. Martin's Press, Inc., 175 Fifth Avenue, New York, New York 10010 (800) 221-7945; *The Statesman's Year-Book.*

Statistical Office of the United Nations, Publishing Service, New York, New York 10017 (800) 253-9646; *Statistical Yearbook.*

U.S. Department of Transportation, Maritime Administration, 400 Seventh Street, SW, Washington, D.C. 20590 (202) 366-5807, www.marad.dot.gov; *A Statistical Analysis of the World's Merchant Fleets.*

TRINIDAD AND TOBAGO - MILITARY

Central Intelligence Agency, Washington, D.C. 20505 (703) 482-1100, www.cia.gov; *The World Factbook.*

The Economist Intelligence Unit, 111 West 57th Street, New York, New York 10019 (800) 938-4685; *The New Latin America Market Atlas.*

Euromonitor International, Inc., 122 South Michigan Avenue, Suite 1200, Chicago, Illinois 60603 (800) 577-EURO; *World Marketing Data and Statistics.*

The International Institute for Strategic Studies, 23 Tavistock Street, London WC2E 7NQ, England 44 171 3797676; *The Military Balance.*

International Monetary Fund, 700 Nineteenth Street, NW, Washington, D.C. 20431 (202) 623-7000; *Government Finance Statistics Yearbook.*

St. Martin's Press, Inc., 175 Fifth Avenue, New York, New York 10010 (800) 221-7945; *The Statesman's Year-Book.*

Statistical Office of the United Nations, Publishing Service, New York, New York 10017 (800) 253-9646; *Human Development Report.*

U.S. Arms Control and Disarmament Agency, 320 Twenty-first Street, NW, Washington, D.C. 20451 (202) 647-8677; *World Military Expenditures and Arms Transfers.*

TRINIDAD AND TOBAGO - MILK PRODUCTION - See TRINIDAD AND TOBAGO - DAIRY PRODUCTS

TRINIDAD AND TOBAGO - MINING AND MINERAL PRODUCTS

The Economist Intelligence Unit, 111 West 57th Street, New York, New York 10019 (800) 938-4685; *The New Latin America Market Atlas.*

Europa Publications Limited, 18 Bedford Square, London, WC1B 3JN, England; *The Europa World Year Book.*

Inter-American Development Bank, 1300 New York Avenue, NW, Washington, D.C. 20577 (202) 623-1753; *Economic and Social Progress in Latin America.*

M.E. Sharpe, 80 Business Park Drive, Armonk, New York 10504 (800) 541-6563; *The Illustrated Book of World Rankings.*

Penn Well Publishing Company, 1421 South Sheridan Road, P.O. Box 1260, Tulsa, Oklahoma 74101 (800) 752-9764; *International Energy Statistics Sourcebook.*

St. Martin's Press, Inc., 175 Fifth Avenue, New York, New York 10010 (800) 221-7945; *The Statesman's Year-Book.*

Statistical Office of the United Nations, Publishing Service, New York, New York 10017 (800) 253-9646; *Statistical Yearbook.*

U.C.L.A. Latin American Center Publications, University of California, Los Angeles, California 90024 (310) 825-6634; *Statistical Abstract of Latin America.*

United Nations Conference on Trade and Development, Central Statistical Service, Palais des Nations, Geneva, Switzerland (Telephone in U.S. (800) 253-9646); *UNCTAD Commodity Yearbook.*

TRINIDAD AND TOBAGO - MONEY EXCHANGE RATE - See TRINIDAD AND TOBAGO - EXCHANGE RATES

TRINIDAD AND TOBAGO - MONEY MARKET RATES

Inter-American Development Bank, 1300 New York Avenue, NW, Washington, D.C. 20577 (202) 623-1753; *Economic and Social Progress in Latin America.*

Statistical Office of the United Nations, Publishing Service, New York, New York 10017 (800) 253-9646; *Statistical Yearbook.*

TRINIDAD AND TOBAGO - MONEY RESERVES

Euromonitor International, Inc., 122 South Michigan Avenue, Suite 1200, Chicago, Illinois 60603 (800) 577-EURO; *International Marketing Data and Statistics.*

Inter-American Development Bank, 1300 New York Avenue, NW, Washington, D.C. 20577 (202) 623-1753; *Economic and Social Progress in Latin America.*

TRINIDAD AND TOBAGO - MONEY SUPPLY

The Economist Intelligence Unit, 111 West 57th Street, New York, New York

10019 (800) 938-4685; *Trinidad and Tobago Country Report.*

Euromonitor International, Inc., 122 South Michigan Avenue, Suite 1200, Chicago, Illinois 60603 (800) 577-EURO; *International Marketing Data and Statistics.*

Europa Publications Limited, 18 Bedford Square, London, WC1B 3JN, England; *The Europa World Year Book.*

Federal Statistical Office, Gustav-Stresemann - Ring 11, D-6200, Wiesbaden, Germany; *Trinidad and Tobago.*

Inter-American Development Bank, 1300 New York Avenue, NW, Washington, D.C. 20577 (202) 623-1753; *Economic and Social Progress in Latin America.*

International Monetary Fund, 700 Nineteenth Street, NW, Washington, D.C. 20431 (202) 623-7000; *International Financial Statistics.*

Statistical Office of the United Nations, Publishing Service, New York, New York 10017 (800) 253-9646; *Statistical Yearbook.*

The World Bank, 1818 H Street, NW, Washington, D.C. 20433 (202) 477-1234; *World Development Indicators.*

TRINIDAD AND TOBAGO - MORTALITY

Central Intelligence Agency, Washington, D.C. 20505 (703) 482-1100, www.cia.gov; *The World Factbook.*

The Economist Intelligence Unit, 111 West 57th Street, New York, New York 10019 (800) 938-4685; *The New Latin America Market Atlas.*

Euromonitor International, Inc., 122 South Michigan Avenue, Suite 1200, Chicago, Illinois 60603 (800) 577-EURO; *International Marketing Data and Statistics;* and *The World Economic Factbook.*

Europa Publications Limited, 18 Bedford Square, London, WC1B 3JN, England; *The Europa World Year Book.*

St. Martin's Press, Inc., 175 Fifth Avenue, New York, New York 10010 (800) 221-7945; *The Statesman's Year-Book.*

Statistical Office of the United Nations, Publishing Service, New York, New York 10017 (800) 253-9646; *Demographic Yearbook; Human Development Report; Statistical Yearbook;* and *World Statistics Pocketbook.*

United Nations Children's Fund (UNICEF), 3 United Nations Plaza, New York, New York 10017 (800) 253-9646; *State of the World's Children.*

The World Bank, 1818 H Street, NW, Washington, D.C. 20433 (202) 477-1234; *The World Bank Atlas; World Development Report;* and *World Development Indicators.*

World Health Organization, Office of Publications, 20 Avenue Appia, CH-1211 Geneva 27, Switzerland (Telephone Number in U.S. (518) 436-9686); *World Health Statistics Annual.*

TRINIDAD AND TOBAGO - MOTION PICTURES

St. Martin's Press, Inc., 175 Fifth Avenue, New York, New York 10010 (800) 221-7945; *The Statesman's Year-Book.*

Statistical Office of the United Nations, Publishing Service, New York, New York 10017 (800) 253-9646; *Statistical Yearbook.*

TRINIDAD AND TOBAGO - MOTOR VEHICLE PRODUCTION

Statistical Office of the United Nations, Publishing Service, New York, New York 10017 (800) 253-9646; *Statistical Yearbook.*

TRINIDAD AND TOBAGO - MOTOR VEHICLE TAXES - See TRINIDAD AND TOBAGO - TAXATION

TRINIDAD AND TOBAGO - MOTOR VEHICLES

The Economist Intelligence Unit, 111 West 57th Street, New York, New York 10019 (800) 938-4685; *The New Latin America Market Atlas.*

TRINIDAD AND TOBAGO - MOTOR VEHICLES IN USE

Europa Publications Limited, 18 Bedford Square, London, WC1B 3JN, England; *The Europa World Year Book.*

Statistical Office of the United Nations, Publishing Service, New York, New York 10017 (800) 253-9646; *Statistical Yearbook.*

TRINIDAD AND TOBAGO - MULES - See TRINIDAD AND TOBAGO - LIVESTOCK AND POULTRY

TRINIDAD AND TOBAGO - MUSEUMS

M.E. Sharpe, 80 Business Park Drive, Armonk, New York 10504 (800) 541-6563; *The Illustrated Book of World Rankings.*

United Nations Educational, Scientific and Cultural Organization (UNESCO), 7 Place de Fontenoy, F-75700 Paris, France (Telephone Number in U.S. (212) 963-5981); *Statistical Yearbook.*

TRINIDAD AND TOBAGO - NATALITY - See TRINIDAD AND TOBAGO - BIRTH RATE

TRINIDAD AND TOBAGO - NATIONAL ACCOUNTS

Europa Publications Limited, 18 Bedford Square, London, WC1B 3JN, England; *The Europa World Year Book.*

Federal Statistical Office, Gustav-Stresemann - Ring 11, D-6200, Wiesbaden, Germany; *Trinidad and Tobago.*

Inter-American Development Bank, 1300 New York Avenue, NW, Washington, D.C. 20577 (202) 623-1753; *Economic and Social Progress in Latin America.*

Organization of American States (OAS), General Secretariat, Washington, D.C. 20006 (202) 458-3533; *Statistical Bulletin of the OAS.*

Statistical Office of the United Nations, Publishing Service, New York, New York 10017 (800) 253-9646; *National Accounts Statistics;* and *Statistical Yearbook.*

TRINIDAD AND TOBAGO - NATIONAL INCOME

Inter-American Development Bank, 1300 New York Avenue, NW, Washington, D.C. 20577 (202) 623-1753; *Economic and Social Progress in Latin America.*

M.E. Sharpe, 80 Business Park Drive, Armonk, New York 10504 (800) 541-6563; *The Illustrated Book of World Rankings.*

Statistical Office of the United Nations, Publishing Service, New York, New York 10017 (800) 253-9646; *National Accounts Statistics;* and *Statistical Yearbook.*

TRINIDAD AND TOBAGO - NATIONAL PRODUCT

M.E. Sharpe, 80 Business Park Drive, Armonk, New York 10504 (800) 541-6563; *The Illustrated Book of World Rankings.*

Statistical Office of the United Nations, Publishing Service, New York, New York 10017 (800) 253-9646; *Statistical Yearbook.*

TRINIDAD AND TOBAGO - NATURAL GAS PRODUCTION - See TRINIDAD AND TOBAGO - MINING AND MINERAL PRODUCTS

TRINIDAD AND TOBAGO - NEWSPAPER PRODUCTION - See TRINIDAD AND TOBAGO - FORESTRY AND FOREST PRODUCTS

TRINIDAD AND TOBAGO - NEWSPRINT EXPORTS AND IMPORTS - See TRINIDAD AND TOBAGO - FORESTRY AND FOREST PRODUCTS

TRINIDAD AND TOBAGO - OCCUPATIONS - See TRINIDAD AND

TOBAGO - LABOR

TRINIDAD AND TOBAGO - ORANGES PRODUCTION - See TRINIDAD AND TOBAGO - CROPS

TRINIDAD AND TOBAGO - PAPER - See TRINIDAD AND TOBAGO - FORESTRY AND FOREST PRODUCTS

TRINIDAD AND TOBAGO - PATENTS, TRADEMARKS AND SERVICE MARKS

Statistical Office of the United Nations, Publishing Service, New York, New York 10017 (800) 253-9646; *Statistical Yearbook.*

TRINIDAD AND TOBAGO - PEANUT PRODUCTION - See TRINIDAD AND TOBAGO - CROPS

TRINIDAD AND TOBAGO - PESTICIDE USE

Food and Agricultural Organization of the United Nations (FAO) Via delle Terme di Caracalla, 00100 Rome, Italy (Telephone Number in U.S. (202) 653-2400); *The State of Food and Agriculture.*

TRINIDAD AND TOBAGO - PETROLEUM INDUSTRY

The Economist Intelligence Unit, 111 West 57th Street, New York, New York 10019 (800) 938-4685; *The New Latin America Market Atlas.*

Food and Agricultural Organization of the United Nations (FAO) Via delle Terme di Caracalla, 00100 Rome, Italy (Telephone Number in U.S. (202) 653-2400); *The State of Food and Agriculture.*

Inter-American Development Bank, 1300 New York Avenue, NW, Washington, D.C. 20577 (202) 623-1753; *Economic and Social Progress in Latin America.*

International Monetary Fund, 700 Nineteenth Street, NW, Washington, D.C. 20431 (202) 623-7000; *International Financial Statistics.*

M.E. Sharpe, 80 Business Park Drive, Armonk, New York 10504 (800) 541-6563; *The Illustrated Book of World Rankings.*

Organization of American States (OAS), General Secretariat, Washington, D.C. 20006 (202) 458-3533; *Statistical Bulletin of the OAS.*

Penn Well Publishing Company, 1421 South Sheridan Road, P.O. Box 1260, Tulsa, Oklahoma 74101 (800) 752-9764; *International Energy Statistics Sourcebook.*

St. Martin's Press, Inc., 175 Fifth Avenue, New York, New York 10010 (800) 221-7945; *The Statesman's Year-Book.*

Statistical Office of the United Nations, Publishing Service, New York, New York 10017 (800) 253-9646; *Statistical Yearbook.*

United Nations Conference on Trade and Development, Central Statistical Service, Palais des Nations, Geneva, Switzerland (Telephone in U.S. (800) 253-9646); *UNCTAD Commodity Yearbook.*

TRINIDAD AND TOBAGO - PIG-IRON AND FERRO-ALLOY PRODUCTION - See TRINIDAD AND TOBAGO - MINING AND MINERAL PRODUCTS

TRINIDAD AND TOBAGO - PIGS - See TRINIDAD AND TOBAGO - LIVESTOCK AND POULTRY

TRINIDAD AND TOBAGO - POPULATION

Central Intelligence Agency, Washington, D.C. 20505 (703) 482-1100, www.cia.gov; *The World Factbook.*

The Economist Intelligence Unit, 111 West 57th Street, New York, New York 10019 (800) 938-4685; *The New Latin America Market Atlas; The World Market Atlas;* and *Trinidad and Tobago Country Report.*

Euromonitor International, Inc., 122 South Michigan Avenue, Suite 1200, Chicago, Illinois 60603 (800) 577-EURO; *International Marketing Data and Statistics;* and *The World Economic Factbook.*

Europa Publications Limited, 18 Bedford Square, London, WC1B 3JN, England; *The Europa World Year Book.*

Federal Statistical Office, Gustav-Stresemann - Ring 11, D-6200, Wiesbaden, Germany; *Trinidad and Tobago.*

Food and Agricultural Organization of the United Nations (FAO), Via delle Terme di Caracalla, 00100 Rome, Italy (Telephone Number in U.S. (202) 653-2400); *Production Yearbook.*

Inter-American Development Bank, 1300 New York Avenue, NW, Washington, D.C. 20577 (202) 623-1753; *Economic and Social Progress in Latin America.*

International Labour Office, I.L.O. Publications, 1828 L Street, NW, Suite 801, Washington, D.C. 20036 (301) 638-3152; *Yearbook of Labour Statistics.*

M.E. Sharpe, 80 Business Park Drive, Armonk, New York 10504 (800) 541-6563; *The Illustrated Book of World Rankings.*

Organization of American States (OAS), General Secretariat, Washington, D.C. 20006 (202) 458-3533; *Statistical Bulletin of the OAS.*

St. Martin's Press, Inc., 175 Fifth Avenue, New York, New York 10010 (800) 221-7945; *The Statesman's Year-Book.*

Statistical Office of the United Nations, Publishing Service, New York, New York 10017 (800) 253-9646; *Demographic Yearbook; Human Development Report; Statistical Yearbook;* and *World Statistics Pocketbook.*

United Nations Educational, Scientific and Cultural Organization (UNESCO), 7 Place de Fontenoy, F-75700 Paris, France (Telephone Number in U.S. (212) 963-5981); *Statistical Yearbook.*

U.S. Arms Control and Disarmament Agency, 320 Twenty-first Street, NW, Washington, D.C. 20451 (202) 647-8677; *World Military Expenditures and Arms Transfers.*

The World Bank, 1818 H Street, NW, Washington, D.C. 20433 (202) 477-1234; *The World Bank Atlas;* and *World Development Report.*

World Health Organization, Office of Publications, 20 Avenue Appia, CH-1211 Geneva 27, Switzerland (Telephone Number in U.S. (518) 436-9686); *World Health Statistics Annual.*

TRINIDAD AND TOBAGO - POST OFFICES

M.E. Sharpe, 80 Business Park Drive, Armonk, New York 10504 (800) 541-6563; *The Illustrated Book of World Rankings.*

St. Martin's Press, Inc., 175 Fifth Avenue, New York, New York 10010 (800) 221-7945; *The Statesman's Year-Book.*

TRINIDAD AND TOBAGO - POTATO PRODUCTION - See TRINIDAD AND TOBAGO - CROPS

TRINIDAD AND TOBAGO - POWER PRODUCTION INDUSTRY

Statistical Office of the United Nations, Publishing Service, New York, New York 10017 (800) 253-9646; *Statistical Yearbook.*

TRINIDAD AND TOBAGO - PRICES

Federal Statistical Office, Gustav-Stresemann - Ring 11, D-6200, Wiesbaden, Germany; *Trinidad and Tobago.*

Food and Agricultural Organization of the United Nations (FAO), Via delle Terme di Caracalla, 00100 Rome, Italy (Telephone Number in U.S. (202) 653-2400); *Production Yearbook;* and *The State of Food and Agriculture.*

International Labour Office, I.L.O. Publications, 1828 L Street, NW, Suite 801, Washington, D.C. 20036 (301) 638-

3152; *Yearbook of Labour Statistics.*

International Monetary Fund, 700 Nineteenth Street, NW, Washington, D.C. 20431 (202) 623-7000; *International Financial Statistics.*

M.E. Sharpe, 80 Business Park Drive, Armonk, New York 10504 (800) 541-6563; *The Illustrated Book of World Rankings.*

Statistical Office of the United Nations, Publishing Service, New York, New York 10017 (800) 253-9646; *Economic Survey of Latin America and the Caribbean.*

TRINIDAD AND TOBAGO - PRINTING AND WRITING PAPER - See TRINIDAD AND TOBAGO - FORESTRY AND FOREST PRODUCTS

TRINIDAD AND TOBAGO - PRODUCTION

M.E. Sharpe, 80 Business Park Drive, Armonk, New York 10504 (800) 541-6563; *The Illustrated Book of World Rankings.*

TRINIDAD AND TOBAGO - PRODUCTIVITY

Euromonitor International, Inc., 122 South Michigan Avenue, Suite 1200, Chicago, Illinois 60603 (800) 577-EURO; *International Marketing Data and Statistics.*

TRINIDAD AND TOBAGO - PROPERTY TAXES - See TRINIDAD AND TOBAGO - TAXATION

TRINIDAD AND TOBAGO - PUBLIC CONSUMPTION FUND

Inter-American Development Bank, 1300 New York Avenue, NW, Washington, D.C. 20577 (202) 623-1753; *Economic and Social Progress in Latin America.*

TRINIDAD AND TOBAGO - PUBLIC EXPENDITURES

Inter-American Development Bank, 1300 New York Avenue, NW, Washington, D.C. 20577 (202) 623-1753; *Economic and Social Progress in Latin America.*

Organization of American States (OAS), General Secretariat, Washington, D.C. 20006 (202) 458-3533; *Statistical Bulletin of the OAS.*

TRINIDAD AND TOBAGO - PUBLIC FINANCE - See TRINIDAD AND TOBAGO - FINANCE

TRINIDAD AND TOBAGO - PUBLIC REVENUE

Inter-American Development Bank, 1300 New York Avenue, NW, Washington, D.C. 20577 (202) 623-1753; *Economic and Social Progress in Latin America.*

Organization of American States (OAS), General Secretariat, Washington, D.C. 20006 (202) 458-3533; *Statistical Bulletin of the OAS.*

TRINIDAD AND TOBAGO - RADIO BROADCASTING - See TRINIDAD AND TOBAGO - BROADCASTING

TRINIDAD AND TOBAGO - RADIO RECEIVER PRODUCTION

Statistical Office of the United Nations, Publishing Service, New York, New York 10017 (800) 253-9646; *Statistical Yearbook.*

TRINIDAD AND TOBAGO - RADIO RECEIVERS

St. Martin's Press, Inc., 175 Fifth Avenue, New York, New York 10010 (800) 221-7945; *The Statesman's Year-Book.*

TRINIDAD AND TOBAGO - RAILWAYS

The Economist Intelligence Unit, 111 West 57th Street, New York, New York 10019 (800) 938-4685; *The New Latin America Market Atlas.*

TRINIDAD AND TOBAGO - RELIGION

Central Intelligence Agency, Washington, D.C. 20505 (703) 482-1100, www.cia.gov; *The World Factbook.*

M.E. Sharpe, 80 Business Park Drive, Armonk, New York 10504 (800) 541-6563; *The Illustrated Book of World Rankings.*

St. Martin's Press, Inc., 175 Fifth Avenue, New York, New York 10010 (800) 221-7945; *The Statesman's Year-Book.*

TRINIDAD AND TOBAGO - RENT PRICES

International Labour Office, I.L.O. Publications, 1828 L Street, NW, Suite 801, Washington, D.C. 20036 (301) 638-3152; *Yearbook of Labour Statistics.*

TRINIDAD AND TOBAGO - RESERVES EXCLUDING GOLD

The Economist Intelligence Unit, 111 West 57th Street, New York, New York 10019 (800) 938-4685; *The New Latin America Market Atlas.*

TRINIDAD AND TOBAGO - RETAIL TRADE

Euromonitor International, Inc., 122 South Michigan Avenue, Suite 1200, Chicago, Illinois 60603 (800) 577-EURO; *World Marketing Data and Statistics.*

Inter-American Development Bank, 1300 New York Avenue, NW, Washington, D.C. 20577 (202) 623-1753; *Economic and Social Progress in Latin America.*

TRINIDAD AND TOBAGO - RICE PRODUCTION - See TRINIDAD AND TOBAGO - CROPS

TRINIDAD AND TOBAGO - ROUNDWOOD PRODUCTION - See TRINIDAD AND TOBAGO - FORESTRY AND FOREST PRODUCTS

TRINIDAD AND TOBAGO - RUBBER PRODUCTION AND CONSUMPTION

M.E. Sharpe, 80 Business Park Drive, Armonk, New York 10504 (800) 541-6563; *The Illustrated Book of World Rankings.*

TRINIDAD AND TOBAGO - SAWNWOOD PRODUCTION - See TRINIDAD AND TOBAGO - FORESTRY AND FOREST PRODUCTS

TRINIDAD AND TOBAGO - SCIENCE AND TECHNOLOGY - EXPENDITURE FOR RESEARCH

Statistical Office of the United Nations, Publishing Service, New York, New York 10017 (800) 253-9646; *Statistical Yearbook.*

TRINIDAD AND TOBAGO - SCIENTISTS AND TECHNICIANS

Statistical Office of the United Nations, Publishing Service, New York, New York 10017 (800) 253-9646; *Statistical Yearbook.*

TRINIDAD AND TOBAGO - SENIOR CITIZENS

M.E. Sharpe, 80 Business Park Drive, Armonk, New York 10504 (800) 541-6563; *The Illustrated Book of World Rankings.*

TRINIDAD AND TOBAGO - SHEEP - See TRINIDAD AND TOBAGO - LIVESTOCK AND POULTRY

TRINIDAD AND TOBAGO - SILVER PRODUCTION AND CONSUMPTION - See TRINIDAD AND TOBAGO - MINING AND MINERAL PRODUCTS

TRINIDAD AND TOBAGO - SOCIAL DATA

M.E. Sharpe, 80 Business Park Drive, Armonk, New York 10504 (800) 541-6563; *The Illustrated Book of World Rankings.*

Statistical Office of the United Nations, Publishing Service, New York, New York 10017 (800) 253-9646; *World Statistics Pocketbook.*

TRINIDAD AND TOBAGO - SOCIAL SECURITY

Inter-American Development Bank, 1300 New York Avenue, NW, Washington, D.C. 20577 (202) 623-1753; *Economic and Social Progress in Latin America.*

International Monetary Fund, 700 Nineteenth Street, NW, Washington, D.C. 20431 (202) 623-7000; *Government Finance Statistics Yearbook.*

Statistical Office of the United Nations, Publishing Service, New York, New York 10017 (800) 253-9646; *National Accounts Statistics.*

TRINIDAD AND TOBAGO - SOCIOECONOMIC DATA

Inter-American Development Bank, 1300 New York Avenue, NW, Washington, D.C. 20577 (202) 623-1753; *Economic and Social Progress in Latin America.*

TRINIDAD AND TOBAGO - SOYBEAN PRODUCTION - See TRINIDAD AND TOBAGO - CROPS

TRINIDAD AND TOBAGO - STAMP TAXES AND DUTIES - See TRINIDAD AND TOBAGO - TAXATION

TRINIDAD AND TOBAGO - STATE BUDGET REVENUE AND EXPENDITURES

Euromonitor International, Inc., 122 South Michigan Avenue, Suite 1200, Chicago, Illinois 60603 (800) 577-EURO; *International Marketing Data and Statistics.*

Inter-American Development Bank, 1300 New York Avenue, NW, Washington, D.C. 20577 (202) 623-1753; *Economic and Social Progress in Latin America.*

TRINIDAD AND TOBAGO - STEEL - See TRINIDAD AND TOBAGO - MINING AND MINERAL PRODUCTS

TRINIDAD AND TOBAGO - STOCKS - COMMODITY - MARKET PRICE - INDEX

Food and Agricultural Organization of the United Nations (FAO) Via delle Terme di Caracalla, 00100 Rome, Italy (Telephone Number in U.S. (202) 653-2400); *The State of Food and Agriculture.*

TRINIDAD AND TOBAGO - SUGAR - See TRINIDAD AND TOBAGO - CROPS

TRINIDAD AND TOBAGO - SULPHURIC ACID PRODUCTION - See TRINIDAD AND TOBAGO - MINING AND MINERAL PRODUCTS

TRINIDAD AND TOBAGO - TAXATION

Inter-American Development Bank, 1300 New York Avenue, NW, Washington, D.C. 20577 (202) 623-1753; *Economic and Social Progress in Latin America.*

International Monetary Fund, 700 Nineteenth Street, NW, Washington, D.C. 20431 (202) 623-7000; *Government Finance Statistics Yearbook.*

The World Bank, 1818 H Street, NW, Washington, D.C. 20433 (202) 477-1234; *World Development Indicators.*

TRINIDAD AND TOBAGO - TELEPHONES IN USE

American Telephone and Telegraph Company, 26 Parsippany Road, Whippany, New Jersey 07981 (800) 222-0300; *The World's Telephones.*

Central Intelligence Agency, Washington, D.C. 20505 (703) 482-1100, www.cia.gov; *The World Factbook.*

The Economist Intelligence Unit, 111 West 57th Street, New York, New York 10019 (800) 938-4685; *The New Latin America Market Atlas.*

St. Martin's Press, Inc., 175 Fifth Avenue, New York, New York 10010 (800) 221-7945; *The Statesman's Year-Book.*

Statistical Office of the United Nations, Publishing Service, New York, New York 10017 (800) 253-9646; *Statistical Yearbook;* and *World Statistics Pocketbook.*

TRINIDAD AND TOBAGO - TELEVISION BROADCASTING - See TRINIDAD AND TOBAGO - BROADCASTING

TRINIDAD AND TOBAGO - TELEVISION RECEIVER PRODUCTION

Statistical Office of the United Nations, Publishing Service, New York, New York 10017 (800) 253-9646; *Statistical Yearbook.*

TRINIDAD AND TOBAGO - TEXTILE INDUSTRY

M.E. Sharpe, 80 Business Park Drive, Armonk, New York 10504 (800) 541-6563; *The Illustrated Book of World Rankings.*

United Nations Conference on Trade and Development, Central Statistical Service, Palais des Nations, Geneva, Switzerland (Telephone in U.S. (800) 253-9646); *UNCTAD Commodity Yearbook.*

TRINIDAD AND TOBAGO - THEATRE PERFORMANCES

United Nations Educational, Scientific and Cultural Organization (UNESCO), 7 Place de Fontenoy, F-75700 Paris, France (Telephone Number in U.S. (212) 963-5981); *Statistical Yearbook.*

TRINIDAD AND TOBAGO - TOBACCO PRODUCTION

M.E. Sharpe, 80 Business Park Drive, Armonk, New York 10504 (800) 541-6563; *The Illustrated Book of World Rankings.*

Statistical Office of the United Nations,

Publishing Service, New York, New York 10017 (800) 253-9646; *Statistical Yearbook.*

U.C.L.A. Latin American Center Publications, University of California, Los Angeles, California 90024 (310) 825-6634; *Statistical Abstract of Latin America.*

TRINIDAD AND TOBAGO - TOURISM

The Economist Intelligence Unit, 111 West 57th Street, New York, New York 10019 (800) 938-4685; *The New Latin America Market Atlas.*

Euromonitor International, Inc., 122 South Michigan Avenue, Suite 1200, Chicago, Illinois 60603 (800) 577-EURO; *The World Economic Factbook;* and *World Marketing Data and Statistics.*

Europa Publications Limited, 18 Bedford Square, London, WC1B 3JN, England; *The Europa World Year Book.*

Federal Statistical Office, Gustav-Stresemann - Ring 11, D-6200, Wiesbaden, Germany; *Trinidad and Tobago.*

M.E. Sharpe, 80 Business Park Drive, Armonk, New York 10504 (800) 541-6563; *The Illustrated Book of World Rankings.*

Organization of American States (OAS), General Secretariat, Washington, D.C. 20006 (202) 458-3533; *Statistical Bulletin of the OAS.*

St. Martin's Press, Inc., 175 Fifth Avenue, New York, New York 10010 (800) 221-7945; *The Statesman's Year-Book.*

Statistical Office of the United Nations, Publishing Service, New York, New York 10017 (800) 253-9646; *Statistical Yearbook.*

World Tourism Organization, Calle Capitan Haya 42, E-28020 Madrid, Spain; *Yearbook of Tourism Statistics.*

TRINIDAD AND TOBAGO - TRACTORS IN USE

The Economist Intelligence Unit, 111 West 57th Street, New York, New York 10019 (800) 938-4685; *The New Latin America Market Atlas.*

Statistical Office of the United Nations, Publishing Service, New York, New York 10017 (800) 253-9646; *Statistical Yearbook.*

TRINIDAD AND TOBAGO - TRADE - See TRINIDAD AND TOBAGO - FOREIGN TRADE

TRINIDAD AND TOBAGO -TRADEMARKS AND SERVICE MARKS - See TRINIDAD AND TOBAGO - PATENTS, TRADEMARKS AND SERVICE MARKS

TRINIDAD AND TOBAGO -

TRANSPORTATION AND COMMUNICATIONS

Central Intelligence Agency, Washington, D.C. 20505 (703) 482-1100, www.cia.gov; *The World Factbook*.

The Economist Intelligence Unit, 111 West 57th Street, New York, New York 10019 (800) 938-4685; *The New Latin America Market Atlas*.

Euromonitor International, Inc., 122 South Michigan Avenue, Suite 1200, Chicago, Illinois 60603 (800) 577-EURO; *International Marketing Data and Statistics; and World Marketing Data and Statistics*.

Europa Publications Limited, 18 Bedford Square, London, WC1B 3JN, England; *The Europa World Year Book*.

Federal Statistical Office, Gustav-Stresemann - Ring 11, D-6200, Wiesbaden, Germany; *Trinidad and Tobago*.

Inter-American Development Bank, 1300 New York Avenue, NW, Washington, D.C. 20577 (202) 623-1753; *Economic and Social Progress in Latin America*.

M.E. Sharpe, 80 Business Park Drive, Armonk, New York 10504 (800) 541-6563; *The Illustrated Book of World Rankings*.

St. Martin's Press, Inc., 175 Fifth Avenue, New York, New York 10010 (800) 221-7945; *The Statesman's Year-Book*.

Statistical Office of the United Nations, Publishing Service, New York, New York 10017 (800) 253-9646; *Human Development Report*.

TRINIDAD AND TOBAGO - UNEMPLOYMENT

Central Intelligence Agency, Washington, D.C. 20505 (703) 482-1100, www.cia.gov; *The World Factbook*.

The Economist Intelligence Unit, 111 West 57th Street, New York, New York 10019 (800) 938-4685; *The New Latin America Market Atlas*.

Euromonitor International, Inc., 122 South Michigan Avenue, Suite 1200, Chicago, Illinois 60603 (800) 577-EURO; *International Marketing Data and Statistics*.

Organization of American States (OAS), General Secretariat, Washington, D.C. 20006 (202) 458-3533; *Statistical Bulletin of the OAS*.

St. Martin's Press, Inc., 175 Fifth Avenue, New York, New York 10010 (800) 221-7945; *The Statesman's Year-Book*.

Statistical Office of the United Nations,

Publishing Service, New York, New York 10017 (800) 253-9646; *Statistical Yearbook*.

TRINIDAD AND TOBAGO - VITAL STATISTICS

Euromonitor International, Inc., 122 South Michigan Avenue, Suite 1200, Chicago, Illinois 60603 (800) 577-EURO; *International Marketing Data and Statistics*.

St. Martin's Press, Inc., 175 Fifth Avenue, New York, New York 10010 (800) 221-7945; *The Statesman's Year-Book*.

Statistical Office of the United Nations, Publishing Service, New York, New York 10017 (800) 253-9646; *Statistical Yearbook*.

World Health Organization, Office of Publications, 20 Avenue Appia, CH-1211 Geneva 27, Switzerland (Telephone Number in U.S. (518) 436-9686); *World Health Statistics Annual*.

TRINIDAD AND TOBAGO - WAGES

Federal Statistical Office, Gustav-Stresemann - Ring 11, D-6200, Wiesbaden, Germany; *Trinidad and Tobago*.

International Labour Office, I.L.O. Publications, 1828 L Street, NW, Suite 801, Washington, D.C. 20036 (301) 638-3152; *Yearbook of Labour Statistics*.

Organization of American States (OAS), General Secretariat, Washington, D.C. 20006 (202) 458-3533; *Statistical Bulletin of the OAS*.

TRINIDAD AND TOBAGO - WEATHER - See TRINIDAD AND TOBAGO - CLIMATE

TRINIDAD AND TOBAGO - WELFARE

Inter-American Development Bank, 1300 New York Avenue, NW, Washington, D.C. 20577 (202) 623-1753; *Economic and Social Progress in Latin America*.

International Monetary Fund, 700 Nineteenth Street, NW, Washington, D.C. 20431 (202) 623-7000; *Government Finance Statistics Yearbook*.

TRINIDAD AND TOBAGO - WHEAT - See TRINIDAD AND TOBAGO - CROPS

TRINIDAD AND TOBAGO - WHOLESALE PRICES

Inter-American Development Bank, 1300 New York Avenue, NW, Washington, D.C. 20577 (202) 623-1753; *Economic and Social Progress in Latin America*.

TRINIDAD AND TOBAGO - WHOLESALE TRADE

Inter-American Development Bank,

1300 New York Avenue, NW, Washington, D.C. 20577 (202) 623-1753; *Economic and Social Progress in Latin America*.

TRINIDAD AND TOBAGO - WINE PRODUCTION - See TRINIDAD AND TOBAGO - BEVERAGES

TRINIDAD AND TOBAGO - WOOD PULP PRODUCTION - See TRINIDAD AND TOBAGO - FORESTRY AND FOREST PRODUCTS

TRINIDAD AND TOBAGO - WOOL PRODUCTION - See TRINIDAD AND TOBAGO - TEXTILE INDUSTRY

TRINIDAD AND TOBAGO - ZOOS AND BOTANICAL GARDENS

United Nations Educational, Scientific and Cultural Organization (UNESCO), 7 Place de Fontenoy, F-75700 Paris, France (Telephone Number in U.S. (212) 963-5981); *Statistical Yearbook*.

TRIPOLI

U.S. Department of the Interior, Geological Survey, Office of Minerals Information, 12201 Sunrise Valley Drive, Reston, Virginia 22092 (703) 648-4000, www.minerals.usgs.gov; *Annual Reports; and Mineral Commodities Summaries*.

TRIPS - See TRAVEL

TRUCK PROFILE

U.S. Department of Transportation, Federal Highway Administration, 400 Seventh Street, SW, Washington, D.C. 20590 (202) 366-0660, www.fhwa.dot.gov; *Highway Statistics Summary*.

TRUCKING AND WAREHOUSING - See also MOTOR VEHICLES and TRANSPORTATION AND TRUCKS

TRUCKING AND WAREHOUSING - EARNINGS

U.S. Department of Commerce, Bureau of the Census, Washington, D.C. 20233 (301) 457-4100, www.census.gov; *County Business Patterns*.

U.S. Department of Labor, Bureau of Labor Statistics, Two Massachusetts Avenue, NE, Washington, D.C. 20212 (202) 691-5200, www.stats.bls.gov; *Employment and Earnings*; Bulletins 2445 and 2481; and Internet site: http://stats.bls.gov/ceshome.htm.

TRUCKING AND WAREHOUSING - EMPLOYEES

U.S. Department of Commerce, Bureau of the Census, Washington, D.C. 20233 (301) 457-4100, www.census.gov; *County*

Business Patterns.

U.S. Department of Labor, Bureau of Labor Statistics, Two Massachusetts Avenue, NE, Washington, D.C. 20212 (202) 691-5200, www.stats.bls.gov; *Employment and Earnings;* Bulletins 2445 and 2481; and Internet site: http://stats.bls.gov/ceshome.htm.

TRUCKING AND WAREHOUSING - FINANCES

U.S. Department of Commerce, Bureau of the Census, Washington, D.C. 20233 (301) 457-4100, www.census.gov; *Current Business Reports, Motor Freight Transportation and Warehousing Survey.*

TRUCKING AND WAREHOUSING - OCCUPATIONAL SAFETY

U.S. Department of Labor, Bureau of Labor Statistics, Two Massachusetts Avenue, NE, Washington, D.C. 20212 (202) 691-5200, www.stats.bls.gov; *Occupational Injuries and Illnesses in the United States by Industry.*

TRUCKING AND WAREHOUSING - PRODUCTIVITY

U.S. Department of Labor, Bureau of Labor Statistics, Two Massachusetts Avenue, NE, Washington, D.C. 20212 (202) 691-5200, www.stats.bls.gov; Internet site http://stats.bls.gov/iprhome.htm.

TRUCKS - FACTORY SALES (TRUCKS AND BUSES)

American Automobile Manufacturers Association, 1401 H Street, NW, Suite 900, Washington, D.C. 20005 (202) 326-5500; *Motor Vehicle Facts and Figures;* and *World Motor Vehicle Data.*

TRUCKS - MOTOR FUEL CONSUMPTION

U.S. Department of Commerce, Bureau of Economic Analysis, Fourteen Street between Constitution Avenue and E Street, NW, Washington, D.C. 20230 (202) 606-9900, www.bea.doc.gov; *Survey of Current Business.*

TRUCKS - FOREIGN COUNTRIES

U.S. Department of Transportation, Federal Highway Administration, 800 Independence Avenue, SW, Washington, D.C. 20590 (202) 366-0660, www.fhwa.dot.gov; *Highway Statistics.*

TRUCKS - IMPORTS

U.S. Department of Commerce, Bureau of Economic Analysis, Fourteen Street between Constitution Avenue and E Street, NW, Washington, D.C. 20230 (202) 606-9900, www.bea.doc.gov; *Survey of Current Business.*

TRUCKS - MOTOR FUEL CONSUMPTION

U.S. Department of Transportation, Federal Highway Administration, 800 Independence Avenue, SW, Washington, D.C. 20590 (202) 366-0660, www.fhwa.dot.gov; *Highway Statistics;* and *Highway Statistics Summary.*

TRUCKS - REGISTRATION (TRUCKS AND BUSES)

U.S. Department of Transportation, Federal Highway Administration, 400 Seventh Street, SW, Washington, D.C. 20590 (202) 366-0660, www.fhwa.dot.gov; *Highway Statistics;* and *Selected Highway Statistics and Charts.*

TRUCKS - TRAFFIC FATALITIES

U.S. Department of Transportation, National Highway Traffic Safety Administration, 400 Seventh Street, SW, Washington, D.C. 20590 (202) 366-8892, www.nhtsa.dot.gov; *Traffic Safety Facts.*

TRUCKS - TRAVEL AND SPEED

U.S. Department of Transportation, Federal Highway Administration, 400 Seventh Street, SW, Washington, D.C. 20590 (202) 366-0660, www.fhwa.dot.gov; *Highway Statistics Summary.*

TRUST FUNDS - UNITED STATES GOVERNMENT

Executive Office of the President, Office of Management and Budget, Executive Office Building, Washington, D.C. 20503 (202) 395-3080, www.whitehouse.gov/omb; *Analytical Perspectives.*

TUBERCULOSIS

U.S. Department of Health and Human Services, Center for Disease Control, 1600 Clifton Road, NE, Atlanta, Georgia 30333 (800) 311-3435, www.cdc.gov; *Summary of Notifiable Diseases, United States,* and *Morbidity and Mortality Weekly Report.*

TUBERCULOSIS - DEATHS

U.S. Department of Health and Human Services, National Center for Health Statistics 3700 East West Highway, Hyattsville, Maryland 20782 (301) 436-8500, www.cdc.gov/nchs; *Vital Statistics of the United States;* and *National Vital Statistics Reports.*

TUBERCULOSIS - HOSPITALS

American Hospital Association, One North Franklin, Suite 27, Chicago, Illinois 60606 (800) 242-2626; *Hospital Statistics.*

TUITION

U.S. Department of Education, National Center for Education Statistics, 555 New Jersey Avenue, NW, Washington, D.C. 20208-1828, http://nces.ed.gov; *Digest of Education Statistics.*

TUITION - CONSUMER PRICE INDEXES

U.S. Department of Labor, Bureau of Labor Statistics, Two Massachusetts Avenue, NE, Washington, D.C. 20212 (202) 691-5200, www.stats.bls.gov; *Monthly Labor Review;* and *CPI Detailed Report.*

TULAREMIA

U.S. Department of Health and Human Services, Centers for Disease Control, 1600 Clifton Road, NE, Atlanta, Georgia 30333 (800) 311-3435, www.cdc.gov; *Summary of Notifiable Diseases, United States, Morbidity and Mortality Weekly Report.*

TUNA

U.S. Department of Commerce, National Oceanic and Atmospheric Administration, National Marine Fisheries Service, 1315 East-West Highway, Silver Spring, Maryland 20910 (301) 427-2239, www.nmfs.noaa.gov; *Fisheries of the United States.*

TUNA - CATCH

U.S. Department of Commerce, National Oceanic and Atmospheric Administration, National Marine Fisheries Service, 1315 East-West Highway, Silver Spring, Maryland 20910 (301) 427-2239, www.nmfs.noaa.gov; *Fishery Statistics of the United States;* and *Fisheries of the United States.*

TUNA - PRICES

U.S. Department of Labor, Bureau of Labor Statistics, Two Massachusetts Avenue, NE, Washington, D.C. 20212 (202) 691-5200, www.stats.bls.gov; *Monthly Labor Review;* and *CPI Detailed Report.*

TUNA - SUPPLY

U.S. Department of Commerce, National Oceanic and Atmospheric Administration, National Marine Fisheries Service, 1315 East-West Highway, Silver Spring, Maryland 20910 (301) 427-2239, www.nmfs.noaa.gov; *Fisheries of the United States.*

TUNGSTEN - FOREIGN TRADE

U.S. Department of the Interior, Geological Survey, Office of Minerals Information, 12201 Sunrise Valley Drive, Reston, Virginia 22092 (703) 648-4000, www.minerals.usgs.gov; *Annual Reports;*

and *Mineral Commodity Summaries.*

TUNGSTEN - PRODUCTION AND VALUE

U.S. Department of the Interior, Geological Survey, Office of Minerals Information, 12201 Sunrise Valley Drive, Reston, Virginia 22092 (703) 648-4000, www.minerals.usgs.gov; *Annual Reports;* and *Mineral Commodities Summaries.*

TUNGSTEN - STRATEGIC AND CRITICAL MATERIAL

U.S. Department of Defense, Defense Logistics Agency, 8725 John J. Kingman Road, Fort Belvoir, Virginia 22060 (703) 767-6666; *Statistical Supplement, Stockpile Report to the Congress.*

TUNGSTEN - WORLD PRODUCTION

U.S. Department of the Interior, Geological Survey, Office of Minerals Information, 12201 Sunrise Valley Drive, Reston, Virginia 22092 (703)648-4000, www.minerals.usgs.gov; *Annual Report;* and *Mineral Commodities Summary.*

Tunisia - National Statistical Office

Institut National de Statistique, 27 rue du Liban, 1002 Tunis-Belvedere, Tunis, Tunisia.

Tunisia - Primary Statistics Sources

Institut National de la Statistique, 27 rue du Liban, 1002 Tunis-Belvedere, Tunis, Tunisia; *Annuaire statistique de la Tunisie* (Statistical Yearbook of Tunisia); *Bulletin mensuel de statistique* (Monthly Bulletin of Statistics); and *L'Economie de la Tunisie en Chiffres* (The Tunisian Economy in Figures).

TUNISIA - ABORTIONS

Statistical Office of the United Nations, Publishing Service, New York, New York 10017 (800) 253-9646; *Demographic Yearbook.*

TUNISIA - AGRICULTURE

The Economist Intelligence Unit, 111 West 57th Street, New York, New York 10019 (800) 938-4685; *Tunisia Country Report.*

Euromonitor International, Inc., 122 South Michigan Avenue, Suite 1200, Chicago, Illinois 60603 (800) 577-EURO; *International Marketing Data and Statistics;* and *World Marketing Data and Statistics.*

Europa Publications Limited, 18 Bedford Square, London, WC1B 3JN, England; *The Europa World Year Book.*

Federal Statistical Office, Gustav-Stresemann - Ring 11, D-6200, Wiesbaden, Germany; *Tunesien.*

Food and Agricultural Organization of the United Nations (FAO) Via delle Terme di Caracalla, 00100 Rome, Italy (Telephone Number in U.S. (202) 653-2400); *Production Yearbook; The State of Food and Agriculture;* and *Trade Yearbook.*

M.E. Sharpe, 80 Business Park Drive, Armonk, New York 10504 (800) 541-6563; *The Illustrated Book of World Rankings.*

St. Martin's Press, Inc., 175 Fifth Avenue, New York, New York 10010 (800) 221-7945; *The Statesman's Year-Book.*

Statistical Office of the United Nations, Publishing Service, New York, New York 10017 (800) 253-9646; *Statistical Yearbook;* and *Survey of Economic and Social Conditions in Africa.*

United Nations Conference on Trade and Development, Central Statistical Service, Palais des Nations, Geneva, Switzerland (Telephone in U.S. (800) 253-9646); *UNCTAD Commodity Yearbook.*

United Nations Economic Commission for Africa, Africa Hall, P.O. Box 3001, Addis Ababa, Ethiopia (Telephone Number in U.S. (800) 253-9646); *African Statistical Yearbook.*

The World Bank, 1818 H Street, NW, Washington, D.C. 20433 (202) 477-1234; *World Development Indicators.*

TUNISIA - AIRLINE SERVICE

Europa Publications Limited, 18 Bedford Square, London, WC1B 3JN, England; *The Europa World Year Book.*

International Civil Aviation Organization, 999 University Street, Montreal, Quebec, Canada H3C 5H7 (514) 954-8219; *Civil Aviation Statistics of the World.*

M.E. Sharpe, 80 Business Park Drive, Armonk, New York 10504 (800) 541-6563; *The Illustrated Book of World Rankings.*

St. Martin's Press, Inc., 175 Fifth Avenue, New York, New York 10010 (800) 221-7945; *The Statesman's Year-Book.*

Statistical Office of the United Nations, Publishing Service, New York, New York 10017 (800) 253-9646; *Statistical Yearbook.*

United Nations Economic Commission for Africa, Africa Hall, P.O. Box 3001, Addis Ababa, Ethiopia (Telephone Number in

U.S. (800) 253-9646); *African Statistical Yearbook.*

TUNISIA - ALUMINUM PRODUCTION AND CONSUMPTION - See TUNISIA - MINING AND MINERAL PRODUCTS

TUNISIA - ANIMAL HEALTH

Food and Agricultural Organization of the United Nations (FAO), Via delle Terme di Caracalla, 00100, Rome, Italy (Telephone Number in U.S. (202) 653-2400); *Animal Health Yearbook.*

TUNISIA - AREA AND DENSITY OF POPULATION

African Development Bank, 01 BP 1387, Abidjan 01, Cote D'Ivoire; *Selected Statistics on Regional Member Countries.*

Central Intelligence Agency, Washington, D.C. 20505 (703) 482-1100, www.cia.gov; *The World Factbook.*

Euromonitor International, Inc., 122 South Michigan Avenue, Suite 1200, Chicago, Illinois 60603 (800) 577-EURO; *International Marketing Data and Statistics;* and *The World Economic Factbook.*

Europa Publications Limited, 18 Bedford Square, London, WC1B 3JN, England; *The Europa World Year Book.*

Federal Statistical Office, Gustav-Stresemann - Ring 11, D-6200, Wiesbaden, Germany; *Tunesien.*

Food and Agricultural Organization of the United Nations (FAO) Via delle Terme di Caracalla, 00100 Rome, Italy (Telephone Number in U.S. (202) 653-2400); *The State of Food and Agriculture.*

M.E. Sharpe, 80 Business Park Drive, Armonk, New York 10504 (800) 541-6563; *The Illustrated Book of World Rankings.*

St. Martin's Press, Inc., 175 Fifth Avenue, New York, New York 10010 (800) 221-7945; *The Statesman's Year-Book.*

Statistical Office of the United Nations, Publishing Service, New York, New York 10017 (800) 253-9646; *Statistical Yearbook;* and *Survey of Economic and Social Conditions in Africa.*

United Nations Educational, Scientific and Cultural Organization (UNESCO), 7 Place de Fontenoy, F-75700 Paris, France (Telephone Number in U.S. (212) 963-5981); *Statistical Yearbook.*

The World Bank, 1818 H Street, NW, Washington, D.C. 20433 (202) 477-1234; *World Development Report.*

TUNISIA - ARMS EXPORTS AND IMPORTS -

See TUNISIA - MILITARY

TUNISIA - BALANCE OF PAYMENTS

African Development Bank, 01 BP 1387, Abidjan 01, Cote D'Ivoire; *Selected Statistics on Regional Member Countries.*

The Economist Intelligence Unit, 111 West 57th Street, New York, New York 10019 (800) 938-4685; *The World Market Atlas.*

Europa Publications Limited, 18 Bedford Square, London, WC1B 3JN, England; *The Europa World Year Book.*

Federal Statistical Office, Gustav-Stresemann - Ring 11, D-6200, Wiesbaden, Germany; *Tunesien.*

International Monetary Fund, 700 Nineteenth Street, NW, Washington, D.C. 20431 (202) 623-7000; *Balance of Payments Yearbook.*

United Nations Conference on Trade and Development (UNCTAD), New York, New York 10017 (800) 253-9646; *Handbook of International Trade and Development.*

United Nations Economic Commission for Africa, Africa Hall, P.O. Box 3001, Addis Ababa, Ethiopia (Telephone Number in U.S. (800) 253-9646); *African Statistical Yearbook.*

The World Bank, 1818 H Street, NW, Washington, D.C. 20433 (202) 477-1234; *World Development Report;* and *World Development Indicators.*

TUNISIA - BANKING

Euromonitor International, Inc., 122 South Michigan Avenue, Suite 1200, Chicago, Illinois 60603 (800) 577-EURO; *World Marketing Data and Statistics.*

Europa Publications Limited, 18 Bedford Square, London, WC1B 3JN, England; *The Europa World Year Book.*

International Monetary Fund, 700 Nineteenth Street, NW, Washington, D.C. 20431 (202) 623-7000; *Government Finance Statistics Yearbook;* and *International Financial Statistics.*

M.E. Sharpe, 80 Business Park Drive, Armonk, New York 10504 (800) 541-6563; *The Illustrated Book of World Rankings.*

St. Martin's Press, Inc., 175 Fifth Avenue, New York, New York 10010 (800) 221-7945; *The Statesman's Year-Book.*

Statistical Office of the United Nations, Publishing Service, New York, New York 10017 (800) 253-9646; *Statistical Yearbook.*

United Nations Economic Commission for Africa, Africa Hall, P.O. Box 3001, Addis Ababa, Ethiopia (Telephone Number in U.S. (800) 253-9646); *African Statistical Yearbook.*

TUNISIA - BARLEY PRODUCTION - See TUNISIA - CROPS

TUNISIA - BEER PRODUCTION - See TUNISIA - BEVERAGES

TUNISIA - BEVERAGES

M.E. Sharpe, 80 Business Park Drive, Armonk, New York 10504 (800) 541-6563; *The Illustrated Book of World Rankings.*

Statistical Office of the United Nations, Publishing Service, New York, New York 10017 (800) 253-9646; *Statistical Yearbook.*

TUNISIA - BIRTH RATES

Central Intelligence Agency, Washington, D.C. 20505 (703) 482-1100, www.cia.gov; *The World Factbook.*

Euromonitor International, Inc., 122 South Michigan Avenue, Suite 1200, Chicago, Illinois 60603 (800) 577-EURO; *International Marketing Data and Statistics;* and *The World Economic Factbook.*

Europa Publications Limited, 18 Bedford Square, London, WC1B 3JN, England; *The Europa World Year Book.*

M.E. Sharpe, 80 Business Park Drive, Armonk, New York 10504 (800) 541-6563; *The Illustrated Book of World Rankings.*

St. Martin's Press, Inc., 175 Fifth Avenue, New York, New York 10010 (800) 221-7945; *The Statesman's Year-Book.*

Statistical Office of the United Nations, Publishing Service, New York, New York 10017 (800) 253-9646; *Demographic Yearbook; Statistical Yearbook;* and *Survey of Economic and Social Conditions in Africa.*

The World Bank, 1818 H Street, NW, Washington, D.C. 20433 (202) 477-1234; *World Development Indicators.*

TUNISIA - BONDS

International Monetary Fund, 700 Nineteenth Street, NW, Washington, D.C. 20431 (202) 623-7000; *Government Finance Statistics Yearbook.*

TUNISIA - BOOK PRODUCTION

Europa Publications Limited, 18 Bedford Square, London, WC1B 3JN, England; *The Europa World Year Book.*

United Nations Educational, Scientific

and Cultural Organization (UNESCO), 7 Place de Fontenoy, F-75700 Paris, France (Telephone Number in U.S. (212) 963-5981); *Statistical Yearbook.*

TUNISIA - BROADCASTING

Billboard Limited, P.O. Box 9027, 1006 AA Amsterdam, The Netherlands (Telephone Number in U.S. (212) 764-7300); *World Radio TV Handbook.*

Central Intelligence Agency, Washington, D.C. 20505 (703) 482-1100, www.cia.gov; *The World Factbook.*

Euromonitor International, Inc., 122 South Michigan Avenue, Suite 1200, Chicago, Illinois 60603 (800) 577-EURO; *World Marketing Data and Statistics.*

M.E. Sharpe, 80 Business Park Drive, Armonk, New York 10504 (800) 541-6563; *The Illustrated Book of World Rankings.*

St. Martin's Press, Inc., 175 Fifth Avenue, New York, New York 10010 (800) 221-7945; *The Statesman's Year-Book.*

TUNISIA - BUDGET

Central Intelligence Agency, Washington, D.C. 20505 (703) 482-1100, www.cia.gov; *The World Factbook.*

TUNISIA - BUSINESS AND PROFESSIONAL LICENSES

International Monetary Fund, 700 Nineteenth Street, NW, Washington, D.C. 20431 (202) 623-7000; *Government Finance Statistics Yearbook.*

TUNISIA - BUTTER PRODUCTION - See TUNISIA - DAIRY PRODUCTS

TUNISIA - CALORIE SUPPLY

African Development Bank, 01 BP 1387, Abidjan 01, Cote D'Ivoire; *Selected Statistics on Regional Member Countries.*

Food and Agricultural Organization of the United Nations (FAO) Via delle Terme di Caracalla, 00100 Rome, Italy (Telephone Number in U.S. (202) 653-2400); *The State of Food and Agriculture.*

TUNISIA - CAPITAL REVENUE

International Monetary Fund, 700 Nineteenth Street, NW, Washington, D.C. 20431 (202) 623-7000; *Government Finance Statistics Yearbook.*

TUNISIA - CATTLE - See TUNISIA - LIVESTOCK AND POULTRY

TUNISIA - CEMENT PRODUCTION - See TUNISIA - MINING AND MINERAL PRODUCTS

TUNISIA - CHEESE PRODUCTION AND CONSUMPTION - See TUNISIA - DAIRY PRODUCTS

TUNISIA - CHEMICAL (ORGANIC) PRODUCTION - See TUNISIA - MINING AND MINERAL PRODUCTS

TUNISIA - CHICKENS - See TUNISIA - LIVESTOCK AND POULTRY

TUNISIA - CIGAR PRODUCTION - See TUNISIA - TOBACCO PRODUCTION

TUNISIA - CIGARETTE PRODUCTION - See TUNISIA - TOBACCO PRODUCTION

TUNISIA - CLIMATE

M.E. Sharpe, 80 Business Park Drive, Armonk, New York 10504 (800) 541-6563; *The Illustrated Book of World Rankings.*

St. Martin's Press, Inc., 175 Fifth Avenue, New York, New York 10010 (800) 221-7945; *The Statesman's Year-Book.*

TUNISIA - COAL PRODUCTION - See TUNISIA - MINING AND MINERAL PRODUCTS

TUNISIA - COFFEE PRODUCTION AND CONSUMPTION - See TUNISIA - CROPS

TUNISIA - COMMERCE

St. Martin's Press, Inc., 175 Fifth Avenue, New York, New York 10010 (800) 221-7945; *The Statesman's Year-Book.*

TUNISIA - COMMUNICATIONS - See TUNISIA - TRANSPORTATION AND COMMUNICATIONS

TUNISIA - CONSTRUCTION INDUSTRY

M.E. Sharpe, 80 Business Park Drive, Armonk, New York 10504 (800) 541-6563; *The Illustrated Book of World Rankings.*

Statistical Office of the United Nations, Publishing Service, New York, New York 10017 (800) 253-9646; *Statistical Yearbook.*

United Nations Economic Commission for Africa, Africa Hall, P.O. Box 3001, Addis Ababa, Ethiopia (Telephone Number in U.S. (800) 253-9646); *African Statistical Yearbook.*

TUNISIA - CONSUMER PRICE INDEX

African Development Bank, 01 BP 1387, Abidjan 01, Cote D'Ivoire; *Selected Statistics on Regional Member Countries.*

Europa Publications Limited, 18 Bedford Square, London, WC1B 3JN, England; *The Europa World Year Book.*

Statistical Office of the United Nations,

Publishing Service, New York, New York 10017 (800) 253-9646; *Statistical Yearbook;* and *Survey of Economic and Social Conditions in Africa.*

United Nations Economic Commission for Africa, Africa Hall, P.O. Box 3001, Addis Ababa, Ethiopia (Telephone Number in U.S. (800) 253-9646); *African Statistical Yearbook.*

TUNISIA - CONSUMER PRICES

Euromonitor International, Inc., 122 South Michigan Avenue, Suite 1200, Chicago, Illinois 60603 (800) 577-EURO; *World Marketing Data and Statistics.*

International Labour Office, I.L.O. Publications, 1828 L Street, NW, Suite 801, Washington, D.C. 20036 (301) 638-3152; *Yearbook of Labour Statistics.*

International Monetary Fund, 700 Nineteenth Street, NW, Washington, D.C. 20431 (202) 623-7000; *International Financial Statistics.*

TUNISIA - CONSUMPTION

African Development Bank, 01 BP 1387, Abidjan 01, Cote D'Ivoire; *Selected Statistics on Regional Member Countries.*

International Lead and Zinc Study Group, Metro House, 58 St. James's Street, London SW1A 1LD, England; *Lead and Zinc Statistics.*

Statistical Office of the United Nations, Publishing Service, New York, New York 10017 (800) 253-9646; *Survey of Economic and Social Conditions in Africa.*

The World Bank, 1818 H Street, NW, Washington, D.C. 20433 (202) 477-1234; *World Development Report.*

TUNISIA - COPPER PRODUCTION AND CONSUMPTION - See TUNISIA - MINING AND MINERAL PRODUCTS

TUNISIA - CORN PRODUCTION - See TUNISIA - CROPS

TUNISIA - CORPORATE TAXES - See TUNISIA - TAXATION

TUNISIA - COTTON PRODUCTION AND CONSUMPTION - See TUNISIA - CROPS

TUNISIA - CRIME

International Criminal Police Organization (INTERPOL), 50 quai Achille Lignon, F-69006 Lyon, France; *International Crime Statistics.*

Yale University Press, Yale Station, New Haven, Connecticut 06520 (800) 987-7323; *Violence and Crime in Cross-National*

Perspective.

TUNISIA - CROPS

Europa Publications Limited, 18 Bedford Square, London, WC1B 3JN, England; *The Europa World Year Book.*

Food and Agricultural Organization of the United Nations (FAO) Via delle Terme di Caracalla, 00100 Rome, Italy (Telephone Number in U.S. (202) 653-2400); *The State of Food and Agriculture.*

M.E. Sharpe, 80 Business Park Drive, Armonk, New York 10504 (800) 541-6563; *The Illustrated Book of World Rankings.*

St. Martin's Press, Inc., 175 Fifth Avenue, New York, New York 10010 (800) 221-7945; *The Statesman's Year-Book.*

Statistical Office of the United Nations, Publishing Service, New York, New York 10017 (800) 253-9646; *Statistical Yearbook.*

United Nations Conference on Trade and Development, Central Statistical Service, Palais des Nations, Geneva, Switzerland (Telephone in U.S. (800) 253-9646); *UNCTAD Commodity Yearbook.*

United Nations Economic Commission for Africa, Africa Hall, P.O. Box 3001, Addis Ababa, Ethiopia (Telephone Number in U.S. (800) 253-9646); *African Statistical Yearbook.*

TUNISIA - CUSTOMS DUTIES

International Monetary Fund, 700 Nineteenth Street, NW, Washington, D.C. 20431 (202) 623-7000; *Government Finance Statistics Yearbook.*

St. Martin's Press, Inc., 175 Fifth Avenue, New York, New York 10010 (800) 221-7945; *The Statesman's Year-Book.*

TUNISIA - DAIRY PRODUCTS

Europa Publications Limited, 18 Bedford Square, London, WC1B 3JN, England; *The Europa World Year Book.*

Food and Agricultural Organization of the United Nations (FAO) Via delle Terme di Caracalla, 00100 Rome, Italy (Telephone Number in U.S. (202) 653-2400); *The State of Food and Agriculture.*

M.E. Sharpe, 80 Business Park Drive, Armonk, New York 10504 (800) 541-6563; *The Illustrated Book of World Rankings.*

St. Martin's Press, Inc., 175 Fifth Avenue, New York, New York 10010 (800) 221-7945; *The Statesman's Year-Book.*

Statistical Office of the United Nations, Publishing Service, New York, New York

10017 (800) 253-9646; *Statistical Yearbook.*

TUNISIA - DEATH RATES - See TUNISIA - MORTALITY

TUNISIA - DEFENSE EXPENDITURES - See TUNISIA - MILITARY

TUNISIA - DEMOGRAPHY

The Economist Intelligence Unit, 111 West 57th Street, New York, New York 10019 (800) 938-4685; *The World Market Atlas.*

Euromonitor International, Inc., 122 South Michigan Avenue, Suite 1200, Chicago, Illinois 60603 (800) 577-EURO; *International Marketing Data and Statistics; World Marketing Data and Statistics;* and *The World Economic Factbook.*

Federal Statistical Office, Gustav-Stresemann - Ring 11, D-6200, Wiesbaden, Germany; *Tunesien.*

M.E. Sharpe, 80 Business Park Drive, Armonk, New York 10504 (800) 541-6563; *The Illustrated Book of World Rankings.*

Statistical Office of the United Nations, Publishing Service, New York, New York 10017 (800) 253-9646; *Human Development Report;* and *Survey of Economic and Social Conditions in Africa.*

TUNISIA - DEVELOPMENT ASSISTANCE

Statistical Office of the United Nations, Publishing Service, New York, New York 10017 (800) 253-9646; *Statistical Yearbook.*

TUNISIA - DIAMOND PRODUCTION - See TUNISIA - MINING AND MINERAL PRODUCTS

TUNISIA - DISCOUNT RATES - See TUNISIA - BANKING

TUNISIA - DISEASES - See TUNISIA - HEALTH

TUNISIA - DIVORCE RATES

M.E. Sharpe, 80 Business Park Drive, Armonk, New York 10504 (800) 541-6563; *The Illustrated Book of World Rankings.*

Statistical Office of the United Nations, Publishing Service, New York, New York 10017 (800) 253-9646; *Demographic Yearbook;* and *Statistical Yearbook.*

TUNISIA - ECONOMY

African Development Bank, 01 BP 1387, Abidjan 01, Cote D'Ivoire; *Selected Statistics on Regional Member Countries.*

Central Intelligence Agency, Washington, D.C. 20505 (703) 482-1100,

www.cia.gov; *The World Factbook.*

The Economist Intelligence Unit, 111 West 57th Street, New York, New York 10019 (800) 938-4685; *Tunisia Country Report.*

Euromonitor International, Inc., 122 South Michigan Avenue, Suite 1200, Chicago, Illinois 60603 (800) 577-EURO; *International Marketing Data and Statistics; World Marketing Data and Statistics;* and *The World Economic Factbook.*

Europa Publications Limited, 18 Bedford Square, London, WC1B 3JN, England; *The Europa World Year Book.*

Federal Statistical Office, Gustav-Stresemann - Ring 11, D-6200, Wiesbaden, Germany; *Tunesien.*

M.E. Sharpe, 80 Business Park Drive, Armonk, New York 10504 (800) 541-6563; *The Illustrated Book of World Rankings.*

St. Martin's Press, Inc., 175 Fifth Avenue, New York, New York 10010 (800) 221-7945; *The Statesman's Year-Book.*

Statistical Office of the United Nations, Publishing Service, New York, New York 10017 (800) 253-9646; *Foreign Trade Statistics for Africa;* and *World Statistics Pocketbook.*

The World Bank, 1818 H Street, NW, Washington, D.C. 20433 (202) 477-1234; *The World Bank Atlas;* and *World Development Report.*

TUNISIA - EDUCATION

African Development Bank, 01 BP 1387, Abidjan 01, Cote D'Ivoire; *Selected Statistics on Regional Member Countries.*

The Economist Intelligence Unit, 111 West 57th Street, New York, New York 10019 (800) 938-4685; *The World Market Atlas.*

Euromonitor International, Inc., 122 South Michigan Avenue, Suite 1200, Chicago, Illinois 60603 (800) 577-EURO; *International Marketing Data and Statistics;* and *World Marketing Data and Statistics.*

Europa Publications Limited, 18 Bedford Square, London, WC1B 3JN, England; *The Europa World Year Book.*

Federal Statistical Office, Gustav-Stresemann - Ring 11, D-6200, Wiesbaden, Germany; *Tunesien.*

International Monetary Fund, 700 Nineteenth Street, NW, Washington, D.C. 20431 (202) 623-7000; *Government Finance Statistics Yearbook.*

M.E. Sharpe, 80 Business Park Drive, Armonk, New York 10504 (800) 541-6563; *The Illustrated Book of World Rankings.*

St. Martin's Press, Inc., 175 Fifth Avenue, New York, New York 10010 (800) 221-7945; *The Statesman's Year-Book.*

Statistical Office of the United Nations, Publishing Service, New York, New York 10017 (800) 253-9646; *Human Development Report;* and *Survey of Economic and Social Conditions in Africa.*

United Nations Economic Commission for Africa, Africa Hall, P.O. Box 3001, Addis Ababa, Ethiopia (Telephone Number in U.S. (800) 253-9646); *African Statistical Yearbook.*

United Nations Educational, Scientific and Cultural Organization (UNESCO), 7 Place de Fontenoy, F-75700 Paris, France (Telephone Number in U.S. (212) 963-5981); *Statistical Yearbook.*

The World Bank, 1818 H Street, NW, Washington, D.C. 20433 (202) 477-1234; *World Development Report;* and *World Development Indicators.*

TUNISIA - EGG PRODUCTION AND CONSUMPTION - See TUNISIA - DAIRY PRODUCTS

TUNISIA - ELECTRICITY

Central Intelligence Agency, Washington, D.C. 20505 (703) 482-1100, www.cia.gov; *The World Factbook.*

M.E. Sharpe, 80 Business Park Drive, Armonk, New York 10504 (800) 541-6563; *The Illustrated Book of World Rankings.*

Penn Well Publishing Company, 1421 South Sheridan Road, P.O. Box 1260, Tulsa, Oklahoma 74101 (800) 752-9764; *International Energy Statistics Sourcebook.*

St. Martin's Press, Inc., 175 Fifth Avenue, New York, New York 10010 (800) 221-7945; *The Statesman's Year-Book.*

Statistical Office of the United Nations, Publishing Service, New York, New York 10017 (800) 253-9646; *Human Development Report; Statistical Yearbook;* and *Survey of Economic and Social Conditions in Africa.*

United Nations Economic Commission for Africa, Africa Hall, P.O. Box 3001, Addis Ababa, Ethiopia (Telephone Number in U.S. (800) 253-9646); *African Statistical Yearbook.*

TUNISIA - EMPLOYMENT

Euromonitor International, Inc., 122 South Michigan Avenue, Suite 1200,

Chicago, Illinois 60603 (800) 577-EURO; *International Marketing Data and Statistics.*

Federal Statistical Office, Gustav-Stresemann - Ring 11, D-6200, Wiesbaden, Germany; *Tunesien.*

International Labour Office, I.L.O. Publications, 1828 L Street, NW, Suite 801, Washington, D.C. 20036 (301) 638-3152; *Yearbook of Labour Statistics.*

M.E. Sharpe, 80 Business Park Drive, Armonk, New York 10504 (800) 541-6563; *The Illustrated Book of World Rankings.*

Statistical Office of the United Nations, Publishing Service, New York, New York 10017 (800) 253-9646; *Bulletin of Industrial Statistics for the Arab Countries; Statistical Yearbook;* and *Survey of Economic and Social Conditions in Africa.*

United Nations Economic Commission for Africa, Africa Hall, P.O. Box 3001, Addis Ababa, Ethiopia (Telephone Number in U.S. (800) 253-9646); *African Statistical Yearbook.*

TUNISIA - ENERGY

Euromonitor International, Inc., 122 South Michigan Avenue, Suite 1200, Chicago, Illinois 60603 (800) 577-EURO; *International Marketing Data and Statistics; World Marketing Data and Statistics;* and *The World Economic Factbook.*

Food and Agricultural Organization of the United Nations (FAO) Via delle Terme di Caracalla, 00100 Rome, Italy (Telephone Number in U.S. (202) 653-2400); *The State of Food and Agriculture.*

M.E. Sharpe, 80 Business Park Drive, Armonk, New York 10504 (800) 541-6563; *The Illustrated Book of World Rankings.*

Penn Well Publishing Company, 1421 South Sheridan Road, P.O. Box 1260, Tulsa, Oklahoma 74101 (800) 752-9764; *International Energy Statistics Sourcebook.*

St. Martin's Press, Inc., 175 Fifth Avenue, New York, New York 10010 (800) 221-7945; *The Statesman's Year-Book.*

Statistical Office of the United Nations, Publishing Service, New York, New York 10017 (800) 253-9646; *Energy Statistics Yearbook; Human Development Report;* and *World Statistics Pocketbook.*

United Nations Economic Commission for Africa, Africa Hall, P.O. Box 3001, Addis Ababa, Ethiopia (Telephone Number in U.S. (800) 253-9646); *African Statistical Yearbook.*

The World Bank, 1818 H Street, NW, Washington, D.C. 20433 (202) 477-1234;

The World Bank Atlas; and *World Development Report.*

TUNISIA - ENVIRONMENT

The Economist Intelligence Unit, 111 West 57th Street, New York, New York 10019 (800) 938-4685; *Tunisia Country Report.*

Statistical Office of the United Nations, Publishing Service, New York, New York 10017 (800) 253-9646; *World Statistics Pocketbook.*

TUNISIA - EXCHANGE RATES

African Development Bank, 01 BP 1387, Abidjan 01, Cote D'Ivoire; *Selected Statistics on Regional Member Countries.*

Central Intelligence Agency, Washington, D.C. 20505 (703) 482-1100, www.cia.gov; *The World Factbook.*

Euromonitor International, Inc., 122 South Michigan Avenue, Suite 1200, Chicago, Illinois 60603 (800) 577-EURO; *International Marketing Data and Statistics;* and *The World Economic Factbook.*

Europa Publications Limited, 18 Bedford Square, London, WC1B 3JN, England; *The Europa World Year Book.*

International Civil Aviation Organization, 999 University Street, Montreal, Quebec, Canada H3C 5H7 (514) 954-8219; *Civil Aviation Statistics of the World.*

International Monetary Fund, 700 Nineteenth Street, NW, Washington, D.C. 20431 (202) 623-7000; *International Financial Statistics.*

Statistical Office of the United Nations, Publishing Service, New York, New York 10017 (800) 253-9646; *Bulletin of Industrial Statistics for the Arab Countries; Foreign Trade Statistics for Africa; Statistical Yearbook;* and *World Statistics Pocketbook.*

TUNISIA - EXCISE TAXES - See
TUNISIA - TAXATION

TUNISIA - EXPORTS

African Development Bank, 01 BP 1387, Abidjan 01, Cote D'Ivoire; *Selected Statistics on Regional Member Countries.*

Central Intelligence Agency, Washington, D.C. 20505 (703) 482-1100, www.cia.gov; *The World Factbook.*

The Economist Intelligence Unit, 111 West 57th Street, New York, New York 10019 (800) 938-4685; *The World Market Atlas; and Tunisia Country Report.*

Euromonitor International, Inc., 122 South Michigan Avenue, Suite 1200, Chicago, Illinois 60603 (800) 577-EURO; *International Marketing Data and Statistics;* and *The World Economic Factbook.*

Europa Publications Limited, 18 Bedford Square, London, WC1B 3JN, England; *The Europa World Year Book.*

Food and Agricultural Organization of the United Nations (FAO) Via delle Terme di Caracalla, 00100 Rome, Italy (Telephone Number in U.S. (202) 653-2400); *The State of Food and Agriculture.*

International Lead and Zinc Study Group, Metro House, 58 St. James's Street, London SW1A 1LD, England; *Lead and Zinc Statistics.*

International Monetary Fund, 700 Nineteenth Street, NW, Washington, D.C. 20431 (202) 623-7000; *Direction of Trade Statistics; Government Finance Statistics Yearbook;* and *International Financial Statistics.*

St. Martin's Press, Inc., 175 Fifth Avenue, New York, New York 10010 (800) 221-7945; *The Statesman's Year-Book.*

Statistical Office of the United Nations, Publishing Service, New York, New York 10017 (800) 253-9646; *Bulletin of Industrial Statistics for the Arab Countries; Foreign Trade Statistics for Africa;* and *Survey of Economic and Social Conditions in Africa.*

United Nations Conference on Trade and Development (UNCTAD), New York, New York 10017 (800) 253-9646; *Handbook of International Trade and Development.*

United Nations Economic Commission for Africa, Africa Hall, P.O. Box 3001, Addis Ababa, Ethiopia (Telephone Number in U.S. (800) 253-9646); *African Statistical Yearbook.*

The World Bank, 1818 H Street, NW, Washington, D.C. 20433 (202) 477-1234; *World Development Report;* and *World Development Indicators.*

TUNISIA - EXTERNAL INDEBTEDNESS

African Development Bank, 01 BP 1387, Abidjan 01, Cote D'Ivoire; *Selected Statistics on Regional Member Countries.*

Statistical Office of the United Nations, Publishing Service, New York, New York 10017 (800) 253-9646; *Survey of Economic and Social Conditions in Africa.*

The World Bank, 1818 H Street, NW, Washington, D.C. 20433 (202) 477-1234; *World Development Report;* and *World Development Indicators.*

TUNISIA - EXTERNAL TRADE

African Development Bank, 01 BP 1387, Abidjan 01, Cote D'Ivoire; *Selected Statistics on Regional Member Countries.*

Euromonitor International, Inc., 122 South Michigan Avenue, Suite 1200, Chicago, Illinois 60603 (800) 577-EURO; *World Marketing Data and Statistics.*

Food and Agricultural Organization of the United Nations (FAO) Via delle Terme di Caracalla, 00100 Rome, Italy (Telephone Number in U.S. (202) 653-2400); *The State of Food and Agriculture;* and *Trade Yearbook.*

Statistical Office of the United Nations, Publishing Service, New York, New York 10017 (800) 253-9646; *Statistical Yearbook.*

TUNISIA - FABRIC PRODUCTION - TUNISIA - TEXTILE INDUSTRY

TUNISIA - FARM CROPS - See TUNISIA - CROPS

TUNISIA - FEMALE WORKING POPULATION - See TUNISIA - EMPLOYMENT

TUNISIA - FERTILITY RATES

Central Intelligence Agency, Washington, D.C. 20505 (703) 482-1100, www.cia.gov; *The World Factbook.*

M.E. Sharpe, 80 Business Park Drive, Armonk, New York 10504 (800) 541-6563; *The Illustrated Book of World Rankings.*

Statistical Office of the United Nations, Publishing Service, New York, New York 10017 (800) 253-9646; *Human Development Report;* and *Survey of Economic and Social Conditions in Africa.*

The World Bank, 1818 H Street, NW, Washington, D.C. 20433 (202) 477-1234; *The World Bank Atlas; World Development Report;* and *World Development Indicators.*

TUNISIA - FERTILIZER

Food and Agricultural Organization of the United Nations (FAO), Via delle Terme di Caracalla, 00100, Rome, Italy (Telephone Number in U.S. (202) 653-2400); *Fertilizer Yearbook;* and *The State of Food and Agriculture.*

Statistical Office of the United Nations, Publishing Service, New York, New York 10017 (800) 253-9646; *Statistical Yearbook.*

TUNISIA - FETAL MORTALITY - See TUNISIA - MORTALITY

TUNISIA - FILM - See TUNISIA - MOTION PICTURES

TUNISIA - FINANCE

African Development Bank, 01 BP 1387, Abidjan 01, Cote D'Ivoire; *Selected Statistics on Regional Member Countries.*

The Economist Intelligence Unit, 111 West 57th Street, New York, New York 10019 (800) 938-4685; *Tunisia Country Report.*

Europa Publications Limited, 18 Bedford Square, London, WC1B 3JN, England; *The Europa World Year Book.*

Federal Statistical Office, Gustav-Stresemann - Ring 11, D-6200, Wiesbaden, Germany; *Tunesien.*

International Monetary Fund, 700 Nineteenth Street, NW, Washington, D.C. 20431 (202) 623-7000; *Government Finance Statistics Yearbook.*

M.E. Sharpe, 80 Business Park Drive, Armonk, New York 10504 (800) 541-6563; *The Illustrated Book of World Rankings.*

St. Martin's Press, Inc., 175 Fifth Avenue, New York, New York 10010 (800) 221-7945; *The Statesman's Year-Book.*

United Nations Economic Commission for Africa, Africa Hall, P.O. Box 3001, Addis Ababa, Ethiopia (Telephone Number in U.S. (800) 253-9646); *African Statistical Yearbook.*

TUNISIA - FISHERIES

Europa Publications Limited, 18 Bedford Square, London, WC1B 3JN, England; *The Europa World Year Book.*

Federal Statistical Office, Gustav-Stresemann - Ring 11, D-6200, Wiesbaden, Germany; *Tunesien.*

Food and Agricultural Organization of the United Nations (FAO) Via delle Terme di Caracalla, 00100 Rome, Italy (Telephone Number in U.S. (202) 653-2400); *The State of Food and Agriculture;* and *Yearbook of Fishery Statistics.*

M.E. Sharpe, 80 Business Park Drive, Armonk, New York 10504 (800) 541-6563; *The Illustrated Book of World Rankings.*

St. Martin's Press, Inc., 175 Fifth Avenue, New York, New York 10010 (800) 221-7945; *The Statesman's Year-Book.*

Statistical Office of the United Nations, Publishing Service, New York, New York 10017 (800) 253-9646; *Statistical Yearbook;* and *Survey of Economic and Social Conditions in Africa.*

United Nations Conference on Trade and Development, Central Statistical Service, Palais des Nations, Geneva, Switzerland (Telephone in U.S. (800) 253-9646); *UNCTAD Commodity Yearbook.*

United Nations Economic Commission for Africa, Africa Hall, P.O. Box 3001, Addis Ababa, Ethiopia (Telephone Number in U.S. (800) 253-9646); *African Statistical Yearbook.*

TUNISIA - FLOUR PRODUCTION

Statistical Office of the United Nations, Publishing Service, New York, New York 10017 (800) 253-9646; *Statistical Yearbook.*

TUNISIA - FOOD

African Development Bank, 01 BP 1387, Abidjan 01, Cote D'Ivoire; *Selected Statistics on Regional Member Countries.*

Food and Agricultural Organization of the United Nations (FAO) Via delle Terme di Caracalla, 00100 Rome, Italy (Telephone Number in U.S. (202) 653-2400); *Production Yearbook;* and *The State of Food and Agriculture.*

Statistical Office of the United Nations, Publishing Service, New York, New York 10017 (800) 253-9646; *Human Development Report.*

United Nations Conference on Trade and Development, Central Statistical Service, Palais des Nations, Geneva, Switzerland (Telephone in U.S. (800) 253-9646); *UNCTAD Commodity Yearbook.*

TUNISIA - FOREIGN DEBT

International Monetary Fund, 700 Nineteenth Street, NW, Washington, D.C. 20431 (202) 623-7000; *Government Finance Statistics Yearbook.*

TUNISIA - FOREIGN TRADE

The Economist Intelligence Unit, 111 West 57th Street, New York, New York 10019 (800) 938-4685; *Tunisia Country Report.*

Euromonitor International, Inc., 122 South Michigan Avenue, Suite 1200, Chicago, Illinois 60603 (800) 577-EURO; *International Marketing Data and Statistics;* and *The World Economic Factbook.*

Europa Publications Limited, 18 Bedford Square, London, WC1B 3JN, England; *The Europa World Year Book.*

Federal Statistical Office, Gustav-Stresemann - Ring 11, D-6200, Wiesbaden, Germany; *Tunesien.*

Food and Agricultural Organization of the United Nations (FAO) Via delle Terme di Caracalla, 00100 Rome, Italy (Telephone

Number in U.S. (202) 653-2400); *The State of Food and Agriculture.*

M.E. Sharpe, 80 Business Park Drive, Armonk, New York 10504 (800) 541-6563; *The Illustrated Book of World Rankings.*

St. Martin's Press, Inc., 175 Fifth Avenue, New York, New York 10010 (800) 221-7945; *The Statesman's Year-Book.*

Statistical Office of the United Nations, Publishing Service, New York, New York 10017 (800) 253-9646; *Bulletin of Industrial Statistics for the Arab Countries; Foreign Trade Statistics for Africa; International Trade Statistics Yearbook;* and *Statistical Yearbook.*

United Nations Conference on Trade and Development, Central Statistical Service, Palais des Nations, Geneva, Switzerland (Telephone in U.S. (800) 253-9646); *UNCTAD Commodity Yearbook.*

United Nations Economic Commission for Africa, Africa Hall, P.O. Box 3001, Addis Ababa, Ethiopia (Telephone Number in U.S. (800) 253-9646); *African Statistical Yearbook.*

The World Bank, 1818 H Street, NW, Washington, D.C. 20433 (202) 477-1234; *World Development Report;* and *World Development Indicators.*

TUNISIA - FORESTRY AND FOREST PRODUCTS

Europa Publications Limited, 18 Bedford Square, London, WC1B 3JN, England; *The Europa World Year Book.*

Federal Statistical Office, Gustav-Stresemann - Ring 11, D-6200, Wiesbaden, Germany; *Tunesien.*

Food and Agricultural Organization of the United Nations (FAO) Via delle Terme di Caracalla, 00100 Rome, Italy (Telephone Number in U.S. (202) 653-2400); *The State of Food and Agriculture;* and *Yearbook of Forest Products.*

M.E. Sharpe, 80 Business Park Drive, Armonk, New York 10504 (800) 541-6563; *The Illustrated Book of World Rankings.*

Statistical Office of the United Nations, Publishing Service, New York, New York 10017 (800) 253-9646; *Statistical Yearbook.*

United Nations Conference on Trade and Development, Central Statistical Service, Palais des Nations, Geneva, Switzerland (Telephone in U.S. (800) 253-9646); *UNCTAD Commodity Yearbook.*

United Nations Economic Commission for Africa, Africa Hall, P.O. Box 3001, Addis Ababa, Ethiopia (Telephone Number in

U.S. (800) 253-9646); *African Statistical Yearbook.*

United Nations Educational, Scientific and Cultural Organization (UNESCO), 7 Place de Fontenoy, F-75700 Paris, France (Telephone Number in U.S. (212) 963-5981); *Statistical Yearbook.*

The World Bank, 1818 H Street, NW, Washington, D.C. 20433 (202) 477-1234; *World Development Report.*

TUNISIA - GAS AND GAS LIQUIDS (NATURAL) PRODUCTION - See TUNISIA - MINING AND MINERAL PRODUCTS

TUNISIA - GENERAL INDUSTRIAL STATISTICS - See TUNISIA - INDUSTRY

TUNISIA - GENERAL MORTALITY - See TUNISIA - MORTALITY

TUNISIA - GEOGRAPHIC DATA

M.E. Sharpe, 80 Business Park Drive, Armonk, New York 10504 (800) 541-6563; *The Illustrated Book of World Rankings.*

TUNISIA - GOATS - See TUNISIA - LIVESTOCK AND POULTRY

TUNISIA - GOLD HOLDINGS

International Monetary Fund, 700 Nineteenth Street, NW, Washington, D.C. 20431 (202) 623-7000; *International Financial Statistics.*

Statistical Office of the United Nations, Publishing Service, New York, New York 10017 (800) 253-9646; *Statistical Yearbook.*

The World Bank, 1818 H Street, NW, Washington, D.C. 20433 (202) 477-1234; *World Development Indicators.*

TUNISIA - GOLD PRODUCTION AND CONSUMPTION - See TUNISIA - MINING AND MINERAL PRODUCTS

TUNISIA - GOVERNMENT

Central Intelligence Agency, Washington, D.C. 20505 (703) 482-1100, www.cia.gov; *The World Factbook.*

Europa Publications Limited, 18 Bedford Square, London, WC1B 3JN, England; *The Europa World Year Book.*

International Monetary Fund, 700 Nineteenth Street, NW, Washington, D.C. 20431 (202) 623-7000; *Government Finance Statistics Yearbook.*

St. Martin's Press, Inc., 175 Fifth Avenue, New York, New York 10010 (800) 221-7945; *The Statesman's Year-Book.*

Statistical Office of the United Nations,

Publishing Service, New York, New York 10017 (800) 253-9646; *National Accounts Statistics;* and *Survey of Economic and Social Conditions in Africa.*

The World Bank, 1818 H Street, NW, Washington, D.C. 20433 (202) 477-1234; *World Development Report;* and *World Development Indicators.*

TUNISIA - GRAIN PRODUCTION - See TUNISIA - CROPS

TUNISIA - GRANTS

International Monetary Fund, 700 Nineteenth Street, NW, Washington, D.C. 20431 (202) 623-7000; *Government Finance Statistics Yearbook.*

TUNISIA - GROSS DOMESTIC PRODUCT

African Development Bank, 01 BP 1387, Abidjan 01, Cote D'Ivoire; *Selected Statistics on Regional Member Countries.*

The Economist Intelligence Unit, 111 West 57th Street, New York, New York 10019 (800) 938-4685; *The World Market Atlas;* and *Tunisia Country Report.*

Euromonitor International, Inc., 122 South Michigan Avenue, Suite 1200, Chicago, Illinois 60603 (800) 577-EURO; *International Marketing Data and Statistics;* and *The World Economic Factbook.*

Europa Publications Limited, 18 Bedford Square, London, WC1B 3JN, England; *The Europa World Year Book.*

M.E. Sharpe, 80 Business Park Drive, Armonk, New York 10504 (800) 541-6563; *The Illustrated Book of World Rankings.*

Statistical Office of the United Nations, Publishing Service, New York, New York 10017 (800) 253-9646; *Bulletin of Industrial Statistics for the Arab Countries; Human Development Report; National Accounts Statistics; Statistical Yearbook;* and *Survey of Economic and Social Conditions in Africa.*

United Nations Economic Commission for Africa, Africa Hall, P.O. Box 3001, Addis Ababa, Ethiopia (Telephone Number in U.S. (800) 253-9646); *African Statistical Yearbook.*

The World Bank, 1818 H Street, NW, Washington, D.C. 20433 (202) 477-1234; *World Development Report;* and *World Development Indicators.*

TUNISIA - GROSS NATIONAL PRODUCT

Euromonitor International, Inc., 122 South Michigan Avenue, Suite 1200, Chicago, Illinois 60603 (800) 577-EURO; *International Marketing Data and Statistics.*

St. Martin's Press, Inc., 175 Fifth Avenue, New York, New York 10010 (800) 221-7945; *The Statesman's Year-Book.*

U.S. Arms Control and Disarmament Agency, 320 Twenty-first Street, NW, Washington, D.C. 20451 (202) 647-8677; *World Military Expenditures and Arms Transfers.*

The World Bank, 1818 H Street, NW, Washington, D.C. 20433 (202) 477-1234; *The World Bank Atlas; World Development Report;* and *World Development Indicators.*

TUNISIA - HEALTH

African Development Bank, 01 BP 1387, Abidjan 01, Cote D'Ivoire; *Selected Statistics on Regional Member Countries.*

Euromonitor International, Inc., 122 South Michigan Avenue, Suite 1200, Chicago, Illinois 60603 (800) 577-EURO; *World Marketing Data and Statistics.*

Federal Statistical Office, Gustav-Stresemann - Ring 11, D-6200, Wiesbaden, Germany; *Tunesien.*

M.E. Sharpe, 80 Business Park Drive, Armonk, New York 10504 (800) 541-6563; *The Illustrated Book of World Rankings.*

St. Martin's Press, Inc., 175 Fifth Avenue, New York, New York 10010 (800) 221-7945; *The Statesman's Year-Book.*

Statistical Office of the United Nations, Publishing Service, New York, New York 10017 (800) 253-9646; *Human Development Report;* and *Statistical Yearbook.*

United Nations Children's Fund (UNICEF), 3 United Nations Plaza, New York, New York 10017 (800) 253-9646; *State of the World's Children.*

United Nations Economic Commission for Africa, Africa Hall, P.O. Box 3001, Addis Ababa, Ethiopia (Telephone Number in U.S. (800) 253-9646); *African Statistical Yearbook.*

The World Bank, 1818 H Street, NW, Washington, D.C. 20433 (202) 477-1234; *World Development Report.*

World Health Organization, Office of Publications, 20 Avenue Appia, CH-1211 Geneva 27, Switzerland (Telephone Number in U.S. (518) 436-9686); *World Health Statistics Annual.*

TUNISIA - HEALTH EXPENDITURES

International Monetary Fund, 700 Nineteenth Street, NW, Washington, D.C. 20431 (202) 623-7000; *Government Finance Statistics Yearbook.*

TUNISIA - HIGHWAYS

Central Intelligence Agency, Washington, D.C. 20505 (703) 482-1100, www.cia.gov; *The World Factbook.*

International Road Federation, 2600 Virginia Avenue, NW, Washington, D.C. 20037 (202) 338-4641; *World Road Statistics.*

St. Martin's Press, Inc., 175 Fifth Avenue, New York, New York 10010 (800) 221-7945; *The Statesman's Year-Book.*

Statistical Office of the United Nations, Publishing Service, New York, New York 10017 (800) 253-9646; *Survey of Economic and Social Conditions in Africa.*

United Nations Economic Commission for Africa, Africa Hall, P.O. Box 3001, Addis Ababa, Ethiopia (Telephone Number in U.S. (800) 253-9646); *African Statistical Yearbook.*

TUNISIA - HORSES - See TUNISIA - LIVESTOCK AND POULTRY

TUNISIA - HOURS OF WORK - See TUNISIA - EMPLOYMENT

TUNISIA - HOUSING AND HOUSING UNITS

Euromonitor International, Inc., 122 South Michigan Avenue, Suite 1200, Chicago, Illinois 60603 (800) 577-EURO; *World Marketing Data and Statistics.*

M.E. Sharpe, 80 Business Park Drive, Armonk, New York 10504 (800) 541-6563; *The Illustrated Book of World Rankings.*

TUNISIA - HOUSING EXPENDITURES

International Monetary Fund, 700 Nineteenth Street, NW, Washington, D.C. 20431 (202) 623-7000; *Government Finance Statistics Yearbook.*

TUNISIA - ILLITERATE POPULATION

Central Intelligence Agency, Washington, D.C. 20505 (703) 482-1100, www.cia.gov; *The World Factbook.*

The Economist Intelligence Unit, 111 West 57th Street, New York, New York 10019 (800) 938-4685; *The World Market Atlas.*

Euromonitor International, Inc., 122 South Michigan Avenue, Suite 1200, Chicago, Illinois 60603 (800) 577-EURO; *The World Economic Factbook.*

Statistical Office of the United Nations, Publishing Service, New York, New York 10017 (800) 253-9646; *Human Development Report.*

United Nations Educational, Scientific and Cultural Organization (UNESCO), 7 Place de Fontenoy, F-75700 Paris, France (Telephone Number in U.S. (212) 963-5981); *Statistical Yearbook.*

TUNISIA - IMPORTS

African Development Bank, 01 BP 1387, Abidjan 01, Cote D'Ivoire; *Selected Statistics on Regional Member Countries.*

Central Intelligence Agency, Washington, D.C. 20505 (703) 482-1100, www.cia.gov; *The World Factbook.*

The Economist Intelligence Unit, 111 West 57th Street, New York, New York 10019 (800) 938-4685; *The World Market Atlas;* and *Tunisia Country Report.*

Euromonitor International, Inc., 122 South Michigan Avenue, Suite 1200, Chicago, Illinois 60603 (800) 577-EURO; *International Marketing Data and Statistics;* and *The World Economic Factbook.*

Europa Publications Limited, 18 Bedford Square, London, WC1B 3JN, England; *The Europa World Year Book.*

Food and Agricultural Organization of the United Nations (FAO) Via delle Terme di Caracalla, 00100 Rome, Italy (Telephone Number in U.S. (202) 653-2400); *The State of Food and Agriculture.*

International Lead and Zinc Study Group, Metro House, 58 St. James's Street, London SW1A 1LD, England; *Lead and Zinc Statistics.*

International Monetary Fund, 700 Nineteenth Street, NW, Washington, D.C. 20431 (202) 623-7000; *Direction of Trade Statistics; Government Finance Statistics Yearbook;* and *International Financial Statistics.*

St. Martin's Press, Inc., 175 Fifth Avenue, New York, New York 10010 (800) 221-7945; *The Statesman's Year-Book.*

Statistical Office of the United Nations, Publishing Service, New York, New York 10017 (800) 253-9646; *Bulletin of Industrial Statistics for the Arab Countries; Foreign Trade Statistics for Africa;* and *Survey of Economic and Social Conditions in Africa.*

United Nations Conference on Trade and Development (UNCTAD), New York, New York 10017 (800) 253-9646; *Handbook of International Trade and Development.*

United Nations Economic Commission for Africa, Africa Hall, P.O. Box 3001, Addis Ababa, Ethiopia (Telephone Number in U.S. (800) 253-9646); *African Statistical Yearbook.*

The World Bank, 1818 H Street, NW, Washington, D.C. 20433 (202) 477-1234; *World Development Report;* and *World Development Indicators.*

TUNISIA - INCOME TAXES - See TUNISIA - TAXATION

TUNISIA - INDUSTRIAL METALS PRODUCTION - See TUNISIA - MINING AND MINERAL PRODUCTS

TUNISIA - INDUSTRY

Central Intelligence Agency, Washington, D.C. 20505 (703) 482-1100, www.cia.gov; *The World Factbook.*

The Economist Intelligence Unit, 111 West 57th Street, New York, New York 10019 (800) 938-4685; *Tunisia Country Report.*

Euromonitor International, Inc., 122 South Michigan Avenue, Suite 1200, Chicago, Illinois 60603 (800) 577-EURO; *International Marketing Data and Statistics; World Marketing Data and Statistics;* and *The World Economic Factbook.*

Europa Publications Limited, 18 Bedford Square, London, WC1B 3JN, England; *The Europa World Year Book.*

Federal Statistical Office, Gustav-Stresemann - Ring 11, D-6200, Wiesbaden, Germany; *Tunesien.*

International Labour Office, I.L.O. Publications, 1828 L Street, NW, Suite 801, Washington, D.C. 20036 (301) 638-3152; *Yearbook of Labour Statistics.*

M.E. Sharpe, 80 Business Park Drive, Armonk, New York 10504 (800) 541-6563; *The Illustrated Book of World Rankings.*

St. Martin's Press, Inc., 175 Fifth Avenue, New York, New York 10010 (800) 221-7945; *The Statesman's Year-Book.*

Statistical Office of the United Nations, Publishing Service, New York, New York 10017 (800) 253-9646; *Bulletin of Industrial Statistics for the Arab Countries; Industrial Commodity Statistics Yearbook, Statistical Yearbook;* and *Survey of Economic and Social Conditions in Africa.*

United Nations Economic Commission for Africa, Africa Hall, P.O. Box 3001, Addis Ababa, Ethiopia (Telephone Number in U.S. (800) 253-9646); *African Statistical Yearbook.*

The World Bank, 1818 H Street, NW, Washington, D.C. 20433 (202) 477-1234; *World Development Indicators.*

World Intellectual Property Organization, 34 Chemin des Colombettes,

CH-1211 Geneva 20. Switzerland; *Industrial Property Statistics.*

TUNISIA - INFANT AND MATERNAL MORTALITY - See TUNISIA - MORTALITY

TUNISIA - INTERNATIONAL LIQUIDITY

International Monetary Fund, 700 Nineteenth Street, NW, Washington, D.C. 20431 (202) 623-7000; *International Financial Statistics.*

TUNISIA - INTERNATIONAL RESERVES EXCLUDING GOLD

African Development Bank, 01 BP 1387, Abidjan 01, Cote D'Ivoire; *Selected Statistics on Regional Member Countries.*

Statistical Office of the United Nations, Publishing Service, New York, New York 10017 (800) 253-9646; *Statistical Yearbook.*

The World Bank, 1818 H Street, NW, Washington, D.C. 20433 (202) 477-1234; *World Development Indicators.*

TUNISIA - IRON ORE PRODUCTION AND CONSUMPTION - See TUNISIA - MINING AND MINERAL PRODUCTS

TUNISIA - IRRIGATION

Euromonitor International, Inc., 122 South Michigan Avenue, Suite 1200, Chicago, Illinois 60603 (800) 577-EURO; *International Marketing Data and Statistics.*

TUNISIA - LABOR

African Development Bank, 01 BP 1387, Abidjan 01, Cote D'Ivoire; *Selected Statistics on Regional Member Countries.*

Central Intelligence Agency, Washington, D.C. 20505 (703) 482-1100, www.cia.gov; *The World Factbook.*

Euromonitor International, Inc., 122 South Michigan Avenue, Suite 1200, Chicago, Illinois 60603 (800) 577-EURO; *International Marketing Data and Statistics;* and *World Marketing Data and Statistics.*

Europa Publications Limited, 18 Bedford Square, London, WC1B 3JN, England; *The Europa World Year Book.*

Food and Agricultural Organization of the United Nations (FAO) Via delle Terme di Caracalla, 00100 Rome, Italy (Telephone Number in U.S. (202) 653-2400); *The State of Food and Agriculture.*

International Labour Office, I.L.O. Publications, 1828 L Street, NW, Suite 801, Washington, D.C. 20036 (301) 638-3152; *Yearbook of Labour Statistics.*

M.E. Sharpe, 80 Business Park Drive,

Armonk, New York 10504 (800) 541-6563; *The Illustrated Book of World Rankings.*

St. Martin's Press, Inc., 175 Fifth Avenue, New York, New York 10010 (800) 221-7945; *The Statesman's Year-Book.*

Statistical Office of the United Nations, Publishing Service, New York, New York 10017 (800) 253-9646; *Human Development Report.*

The World Bank, 1818 H Street, NW, Washington, D.C. 20433 (202) 477-1234; *The World Bank Atlas; World Development Report;* and *World Development Indicators.*

TUNISIA - LAND USE

Central Intelligence Agency, Washington, D.C. 20505 (703) 482-1100, www.cia.gov; *The World Factbook.*

Euromonitor International, Inc., 122 South Michigan Avenue, Suite 1200, Chicago, Illinois 60603 (800) 577-EURO; *International Marketing Data and Statistics.*

Food and Agricultural Organization of the United Nations (FAO), Via delle Terme di Caracalla, 00100 Rome, Italy (Telephone Number in U.S. (202) 653-2400); *Production Yearbook.*

The World Bank, 1818 H Street, NW, Washington, D.C. 20433 (202) 477-1234; *World Development Report.*

TUNISIA - LEAD AND LEAD ORE - See TUNISIA - MINING AND MINERAL PRODUCTS

TUNISIA - LIBRARIES

M.E. Sharpe, 80 Business Park Drive, Armonk, New York 10504 (800) 541-6563; *The Illustrated Book of World Rankings.*

United Nations Educational, Scientific and Cultural Organization (UNESCO), 7 Place de Fontenoy, F-75700 Paris, France (Telephone Number in U.S. (212) 963-5981); *Statistical Yearbook.*

TUNISIA - LIFE EXPECTANCY

African Development Bank, 01 BP 1387, Abidjan 01, Cote D'Ivoire; *Selected Statistics on Regional Member Countries.*

Central Intelligence Agency, Washington, D.C. 20505 (703) 482-1100, www.cia.gov; *The World Factbook.*

Euromonitor International, Inc., 122 South Michigan Avenue, Suite 1200, Chicago, Illinois 60603 (800) 577-EURO; *The World Economic Factbook.*

St. Martin's Press, Inc., 175 Fifth Avenue, New York, New York 10010 (800)

221-7945; *The Statesman's Year-Book.*

Statistical Office of the United Nations, Publishing Service, New York, New York 10017 (800) 253-9646; *Human Development Report;* and *World Statistics Pocketbook.*

The World Bank, 1818 H Street, NW, Washington, D.C. 20433 (202) 477-1234; *The World Bank Atlas;* and *World Development Report.*

TUNISIA - LITERACY RATE

Euromonitor International, Inc., 122 South Michigan Avenue, Suite 1200, Chicago, Illinois 60603 (800) 577-EURO; *World Marketing Data and Statistics.*

Statistical Office of the United Nations, Publishing Service, New York, New York 10017 (800) 253-9646; *Survey of Economic and Social Conditions in Africa.*

TUNISIA - LIVESTOCK AND POULTRY

Euromonitor International, Inc., 122 South Michigan Avenue, Suite 1200, Chicago, Illinois 60603 (800) 577-EURO; *International Marketing Data and Statistics.*

Europa Publications Limited, 18 Bedford Square, London, WC1B 3JN, England; *The Europa World Year Book.*

Food and Agricultural Organization of the United Nations (FAO), Via delle Terme di Caracalla, 00100 Rome, Italy (Telephone Number in U.S. (202) 653-2400); *Production Yearbook;* and *The State of Food and Agriculture.*

M.E. Sharpe, 80 Business Park Drive, Armonk, New York 10504 (800) 541-6563; *The Illustrated Book of World Rankings.*

St. Martin's Press, Inc., 175 Fifth Avenue, New York, New York 10010 (800) 221-7945; *The Statesman's Year-Book.*

Statistical Office of the United Nations, Publishing Service, New York, New York 10017 (800) 253-9646; *Statistical Yearbook;* and *Survey of Economic and Social Conditions in Africa.*

United Nations Conference on Trade and Development, Central Statistical Service, Palais des Nations, Geneva, Switzerland (Telephone in U.S. (800) 253-9646); *UNCTAD Commodity Yearbook.*

United Nations Economic Commission for Africa, Africa Hall, P.O. Box 3001, Addis Ababa, Ethiopia (Telephone Number in U.S. (800) 253-9646); *African Statistical Yearbook.*

TUNISIA - LIVING LEVELS - See TUNISIA - LIFE EXPECTANCY

TUNISIA - MAIL - NUMBER OF PIECES SENT OR RECEIVED

Statistical Office of the United Nations, Publishing Service, New York, New York 10017 (800) 253-9646; *Statistical Yearbook.*

TUNISIA - MANUFACTURING

M.E. Sharpe, 80 Business Park Drive, Armonk, New York 10504 (800) 541-6563; *The Illustrated Book of World Rankings.*

Statistical Office of the United Nations, Publishing Service, New York, New York 10017 (800) 253-9646; *Bulletin of Industrial Statistics for the Arab Countries; Statistical Yearbook;* and *Survey of Economic and Social Conditions in Africa.*

United Nations Economic Commission for Africa, Africa Hall, P.O. Box 3001, Addis Ababa, Ethiopia (Telephone Number in U.S. (800) 253-9646); *African Statistical Yearbook.*

The World Bank, 1818 H Street, NW, Washington, D.C. 20433 (202) 477-1234; *World Development Indicators.*

TUNISIA - MARRIAGE RATES

Europa Publications Limited, 18 Bedford Square, London, WC1B 3JN, England; *The Europa World Year Book.*

M.E. Sharpe, 80 Business Park Drive, Armonk, New York 10504 (800) 541-6563; *The Illustrated Book of World Rankings.*

Statistical Office of the United Nations, Publishing Service, New York, New York 10017 (800) 253-9646; *Demographic Yearbook;* and *Statistical Yearbook.*

TUNISIA - MEAT PRODUCTION - See TUNISIA - LIVESTOCK AND POULTRY

TUNISIA - MERCHANT SHIPPING

Europa Publications Limited, 18 Bedford Square, London, WC1B 3JN, England; *The Europa World Year Book.*

St. Martin's Press, Inc., 175 Fifth Avenue, New York, New York 10010 (800) 221-7945; *The Statesman's Year-Book.*

Statistical Office of the United Nations, Publishing Service, New York, New York 10017 (800) 253-9646; *Statistical Yearbook.*

United Nations Economic Commission for Africa, Africa Hall, P.O. Box 3001, Addis Ababa, Ethiopia (Telephone Number in U.S. (800) 253-9646); *African Statistical Yearbook.*

U.S. Department of Transportation, Maritime Administration, 400 Seventh Street, SW, Washington, D.C. 20590 (202) 366-5807, www.marad.dot.gov; *A Statistical Analysis of the World's Merchant Fleets.*

TUNISIA - MERCURY PRODUCTION - See TUNISIA - MINING AND MINERAL PRODUCTS

TUNISIA - MILITARY

Central Intelligence Agency, Washington, D.C. 20505 (703) 482-1100, www.cia.gov; *The World Factbook.*

Euromonitor International, Inc., 122 South Michigan Avenue, Suite 1200, Chicago, Illinois 60603 (800) 577-EURO; *World Marketing Data and Statistics.*

The International Institute for Strategic Studies, 23 Tavistock Street, London WC2E 7NQ, England 44 171 3797676; *The Military Balance.*

International Monetary Fund, 700 Nineteenth Street, NW, Washington, D.C. 20431 (202) 623-7000; *Government Finance Statistics Yearbook.*

St. Martin's Press, Inc., 175 Fifth Avenue, New York, New York 10010 (800) 221-7945; *The Statesman's Year-Book.*

Statistical Office of the United Nations, Publishing Service, New York, New York 10017 (800) 253-9646; *Human Development Report.*

U.S. Arms Control and Disarmament Agency, 320 Twenty-first Street, NW, Washington, D.C. 20451 (202) 647-8677; *World Military Expenditures and Arms Transfers.*

TUNISIA - MILK PRODUCTION - See TUNISIA - DAIRY PRODUCTS

TUNISIA - MINING AND MINERAL PRODUCTS

Europa Publications Limited, 18 Bedford Square, London, WC1B 3JN, England; *The Europa World Year Book.*

International Lead and Zinc Study Group, Metro House, 58 St. James's Street, London SW1A 1LD, England; *Lead and Zinc Statistics.*

International Monetary Fund, 700 Nineteenth Street, NW, Washington, D.C. 20431 (202) 623-7000; *International Financial Statistics.*

M.E. Sharpe, 80 Business Park Drive, Armonk, New York 10504 (800) 541-6563; *The Illustrated Book of World Rankings.*

Penn Well Publishing Company, 1421 South Sheridan Road, P.O. Box 1260, Tulsa,

Oklahoma 74101 (800) 752-9764; *International Energy Statistics Sourcebook.*

St. Martin's Press, Inc., 175 Fifth Avenue, New York, New York 10010 (800) 221-7945; *The Statesman's Year-Book.*

Statistical Office of the United Nations, Publishing Service, New York, New York 10017 (800) 253-9646; *Bulletin of Industrial Statistics for the Arab Countries;* and *Statistical Yearbook.*

United Nations Conference on Trade and Development, Central Statistical Service, Palais des Nations, Geneva, Switzerland (Telephone in U.S. (800) 253-9646); *UNCTAD Commodity Yearbook.*

United Nations Economic Commission for Africa, Africa Hall, P.O. Box 3001, Addis Ababa, Ethiopia (Telephone Number in U.S. (800) 253-9646); *African Statistical Yearbook.*

TUNISIA - MONEY EXCHANGE RATE - See TUNISIA - EXCHANGE RATES

TUNISIA - MONEY RESERVES

Euromonitor International, Inc., 122 South Michigan Avenue, Suite 1200, Chicago, Illinois 60603 (800) 577-EURO; *International Marketing Data and Statistics.*

TUNISIA - MONEY SUPPLY

African Development Bank, 01 BP 1387, Abidjan 01, Cote D'Ivoire; *Selected Statistics on Regional Member Countries.*

The Economist Intelligence Unit, 111 West 57th Street, New York, New York 10019 (800) 938-4685; *Tunisia Country Report.*

Euromonitor International, Inc., 122 South Michigan Avenue, Suite 1200, Chicago, Illinois 60603 (800) 577-EURO; *International Marketing Data and Statistics.*

Europa Publications Limited, 18 Bedford Square, London, WC1B 3JN, England; *The Europa World Year Book.*

Federal Statistical Office, Gustav-Stresemann - Ring 11, D-6200, Wiesbaden, Germany; *Tunesien.*

International Monetary Fund, 700 Nineteenth Street, NW, Washington, D.C. 20431 (202) 623-7000; *International Financial Statistics.*

Statistical Office of the United Nations, Publishing Service, New York, New York 10017 (800) 253-9646; *Statistical Yearbook.*

The World Bank, 1818 H Street, NW, Washington, D.C. 20433 (202) 477-1234; *World Development Indicators.*

TUNISIA - MORTALITY

Central Intelligence Agency, Washington, D.C. 20505 (703) 482-1100, www.cia.gov; *The World Factbook.*

Euromonitor International, Inc., 122 South Michigan Avenue, Suite 1200, Chicago, Illinois 60603 (800) 577-EURO; *International Marketing Data and Statistics;* and *The World Economic Factbook.*

Europa Publications Limited, 18 Bedford Square, London, WC1B 3JN, England; *The Europa World Year Book.*

St. Martin's Press, Inc., 175 Fifth Avenue, New York, New York 10010 (800) 221-7945; *The Statesman's Year-Book.*

Statistical Office of the United Nations, Publishing Service, New York, New York 10017 (800) 253-9646; *Demographic Yearbook; Human Development Report; Statistical Yearbook; Survey of Economic and Social Conditions in Africa;* and *World Statistics Pocketbook.*

United Nations Children's Fund (UNICEF), 3 United Nations Plaza, New York, New York 10017 (800) 253-9646; *State of the World's Children.*

The World Bank, 1818 H Street, NW, Washington, D.C. 20433 (202) 477-1234; *The World Bank Atlas; World Development Report;* and *World Development Indicators.*

World Health Organization, Office of Publications, 20 Avenue Appia, CH-1211 Geneva 27, Switzerland (Telephone Number in U.S. (518) 436-9686); *World Health Statistics Annual.*

TUNISIA - MOTION PICTURES

St. Martin's Press, Inc., 175 Fifth Avenue, New York, New York 10010 (800) 221-7945; *The Statesman's Year-Book.*

Statistical Office of the United Nations, Publishing Service, New York, New York 10017 (800) 253-9646; *Statistical Yearbook.*

United Nations Educational, Scientific and Cultural Organization (UNESCO), 7 Place de Fontenoy, F-75700 Paris, France (Telephone Number in U.S. (212) 963-5981); *Statistical Yearbook.*

TUNISIA - MOTOR VEHICLE ASSEMBLY

Statistical Office of the United Nations, Publishing Service, New York, New York 10017 (800) 253-9646; *Statistical Yearbook.*

TUNISIA - MOTOR VEHICLE PRODUCTION

American Automobile Manufacturers Association, 1401 H Street, NW, Suite 900,

Washington, D.C. 20005 (202) 326-5500; *World Motor Vehicle Data.*

TUNISIA - MOTOR VEHICLE TAXES - See TUNISIA - TAXATION

TUNISIA - MOTOR VEHICLES IN USE

American Automobile Manufacturers Association, 1401 H Street, NW, Suite 900, Washington, D.C. 20005 (202) 326-5500; *World Motor Vehicle Data.*

Europa Publications Limited, 18 Bedford Square, London, WC1B 3JN, England; *The Europa World Year Book.*

International Road Federation, 2600 Virginia Avenue, NW, Washington, D.C. 20037 (202) 338-4641; *World Road Statistics.*

Statistical Office of the United Nations, Publishing Service, New York, New York 10017 (800) 253-9646; *Statistical Yearbook;* and *Survey of Economic and Social Conditions in Africa.*

TUNISIA - MULES - See TUNISIA - LIVESTOCK AND POULTRY

TUNISIA - MUSEUMS

M.E. Sharpe, 80 Business Park Drive, Armonk, New York 10504 (800) 541-6563; *The Illustrated Book of World Rankings.*

United Nations Educational, Scientific and Cultural Organization (UNESCO), 7 Place de Fontenoy, F-75700 Paris, France (Telephone Number in U.S. (212) 963-5981); *Statistical Yearbook.*

TUNISIA - NATALITY - See TUNISIA - BIRTH RATE

TUNISIA - NATIONAL ACCOUNTS

African Development Bank, 01 BP 1387, Abidjan 01, Cote D'Ivoire; *Selected Statistics on Regional Member Countries.*

Europa Publications Limited, 18 Bedford Square, London, WC1B 3JN, England; *The Europa World Year Book.*

Federal Statistical Office, Gustav-Stresemann - Ring 11, D-6200, Wiesbaden, Germany; *Tunesien.*

Statistical Office of the United Nations, Publishing Service, New York, New York 10017 (800) 253-9646; *National Accounts Statistics;* and *Statistical Yearbook.*

United Nations Economic Commission for Africa, Africa Hall, P.O. Box 3001, Addis Ababa, Ethiopia (Telephone Number in U.S. (800) 253-9646); *African Statistical Yearbook.*

TUNISIA - NATIONAL INCOME

M.E. Sharpe, 80 Business Park Drive, Armonk, New York 10504 (800) 541-6563; *The Illustrated Book of World Rankings.*

Statistical Office of the United Nations, Publishing Service, New York, New York 10017 (800) 253-9646; *National Accounts Statistics;* and *Statistical Yearbook.*

TUNISIA - NATIONAL PRODUCT

M.E. Sharpe, 80 Business Park Drive, Armonk, New York 10504 (800) 541-6563; *The Illustrated Book of World Rankings.*

Statistical Office of the United Nations, Publishing Service, New York, New York 10017 (800) 253-9646; *Statistical Yearbook.*

TUNISIA - NATURAL GAS PRODUCTION - See TUNISIA - MINING AND MINERAL PRODUCTS

TUNISIA - NEWSPAPER PRODUCTION - See TUNISIA - FORESTRY AND FOREST PRODUCTS

TUNISIA - NEWSPRINT - See TUNISIA - FORESTRY AND FOREST PRODUCTS

TUNISIA - OATS PRODUCTION - See TUNISIA - CROPS

TUNISIA - OCCUPATIONS - See TUNISIA - LABOR

TUNISIA - OLIVE OIL EXPORTS

International Monetary Fund, 700 Nineteenth Street, NW, Washington, D.C. 20431 (202) 623-7000; *International Financial Statistics.*

TUNISIA - PAPER - See TUNISIA - FORESTRY AND FOREST PRODUCTS

TUNISIA - PATENTS, TRADEMARKS AND SERVICE MARKS

Statistical Office of the United Nations, Publishing Service, New York, New York 10017 (800) 253-9646; *Statistical Yearbook.*

World Intellectual Property Organization, 34 Chemin des Colombettes, CH-1211 Geneva 20. Switzerland; *Industrial Property Statistics.*

TUNISIA - PEANUT PRODUCTION - See TUNISIA - CROPS

TUNISIA - PERIODICALS

United Nations Educational, Scientific and Cultural Organization (UNESCO), 7 Place de Fontenoy, F-75700 Paris, France (Telephone Number in U.S. (212) 963-5981); *Statistical Yearbook.*

TUNISIA - PESTICIDE USE

Food and Agricultural Organization of the United Nations (FAO) Via delle Terme di Caracalla, 00100 Rome, Italy (Telephone Number in U.S. (202) 653-2400); *The State of Food and Agriculture.*

TUNISIA - PETROLEUM INDUSTRY

Food and Agricultural Organization of the United Nations (FAO) Via delle Terme di Caracalla, 00100 Rome, Italy (Telephone Number in U.S. (202) 653-2400); *The State of Food and Agriculture.*

M.E. Sharpe, 80 Business Park Drive, Armonk, New York 10504 (800) 541-6563; *The Illustrated Book of World Rankings.*

Penn Well Publishing Company, 1421 South Sheridan Road, P.O. Box 1260, Tulsa, Oklahoma 74101 (800) 752-9764; *International Energy Statistics Sourcebook.*

St. Martin's Press, Inc., 175 Fifth Avenue, New York, New York 10010 (800) 221-7945; *The Statesman's Year-Book.*

Statistical Office of the United Nations, Publishing Service, New York, New York 10017 (800) 253-9646; *Statistical Yearbook.*

United Nations Conference on Trade and Development, Central Statistical Service, Palais des Nations, Geneva, Switzerland (Telephone in U.S. (800) 253-9646); *UNCTAD Commodity Yearbook.*

TUNISIA - PHOSPHATE ROCK PRODUCTION - See TUNISIA - MINING AND MINERAL PRODUCTS

TUNISIA - PHOSPHATES EXPORTS - See TUNISIA - MINING AND MINERAL PRODUCTS

TUNISIA - PIG-IRON AND FERRO-ALLOY PRODUCTION - See TUNISIA - MINING AND MINERAL PRODUCTS

TUNISIA - PIGS - See TUNISIA - LIVESTOCK AND POULTRY

TUNISIA - POPULATION

African Development Bank, 01 BP 1387, Abidjan 01, Cote D'Ivoire; *Selected Statistics on Regional Member Countries.*

Central Intelligence Agency, Washington, D.C. 20505 (703) 482-1100, www.cia.gov; *The World Factbook.*

The Economist Intelligence Unit, 111 West 57th Street, New York, New York 10019 (800) 938-4685; *The World Market Atlas;* and *Tunisia Country Report.*

Euromonitor International, Inc., 122 South Michigan Avenue, Suite 1200, Chicago, Illinois 60603 (800) 577-EURO; *International Marketing Data and Statistics;* and *The World Economic Factbook.*

Europa Publications Limited, 18 Bedford Square, London, WC1B 3JN, England; *The Europa World Year Book.*

Federal Statistical Office, Gustav-Stresemann - Ring 11, D-6200, Wiesbaden, Germany; *Tunesien.*

Food and Agricultural Organization of the United Nations (FAO), Via delle Terme di Caracalla, 00100 Rome, Italy (Telephone Number in U.S. (202) 653-2400); *Production Yearbook.*

International Labour Office, I.L.O. Publications, 1828 L Street, NW, Suite 801, Washington, D.C. 20036 (301) 638-3152; *Yearbook of Labour Statistics.*

M.E. Sharpe, 80 Business Park Drive, Armonk, New York 10504 (800) 541-6563; *The Illustrated Book of World Rankings.*

St. Martin's Press, Inc., 175 Fifth Avenue, New York, New York 10010 (800) 221-7945; *The Statesman's Year-Book.*

Statistical Office of the United Nations, Publishing Service, New York, New York 10017 (800) 253-9646; *Demographic Yearbook; Human Development Report; Statistical Yearbook; Survey of Economic and Social Conditions in Africa;* and *World Statistics Pocketbook.*

United Nations Educational, Scientific and Cultural Organization (UNESCO), 7 Place de Fontenoy, F-75700 Paris, France (Telephone Number in U.S. (212) 963-5981); *Statistical Yearbook.*

U.S. Arms Control and Disarmament Agency, 320 Twenty-first Street, NW, Washington, D.C. 20451 (202) 647-8677; *World Military Expenditures and Arms Transfers.*

The World Bank, 1818 H Street, NW, Washington, D.C. 20433 (202) 477-1234; *The World Bank Atlas;* and *World Development Report.*

World Health Organization, Office of Publications, 20 Avenue Appia, CH-1211 Geneva 27, Switzerland (Telephone Number in U.S. (518) 436-9686); *World Health Statistics Annual.*

TUNISIA - POST OFFICES

M.E. Sharpe, 80 Business Park Drive, Armonk, New York 10504 (800) 541-6563; *The Illustrated Book of World Rankings.*

TUNISIA - POTATO PRODUCTION - See TUNISIA - CROPS

TUNISIA - POWER PRODUCTION INDUSTRY

Statistical Office of the United Nations, Publishing Service, New York, New York 10017 (800) 253-9646; *Statistical Yearbook.*

TUNISIA - PRICES

Federal Statistical Office, Gustav-Stresemann - Ring 11, D-6200, Wiesbaden, Germany; *Tunesien.*

Food and Agricultural Organization of the United Nations (FAO), Via delle Terme di Caracalla, 00100 Rome, Italy (Telephone Number in U.S. (202) 653-2400); *Production Yearbook;* and *The State of Food and Agriculture.*

International Labour Office, I.L.O. Publications, 1828 L Street, NW, Suite 801, Washington, D.C. 20036 (301) 638-3152; *Yearbook of Labour Statistics.*

International Lead and Zinc Study Group, Metro House, 58 St. James's Street, London SW1A 1LD, England; *Lead and Zinc Statistics.*

International Monetary Fund, 700 Nineteenth Street, NW, Washington, D.C. 20431 (202) 623-7000; *International Financial Statistics.*

M.E. Sharpe, 80 Business Park Drive, Armonk, New York 10504 (800) 541-6563; *The Illustrated Book of World Rankings.*

United Nations Economic Commission for Africa, Africa Hall, P.O. Box 3001, Addis Ababa, Ethiopia (Telephone Number in U.S. (800) 253-9646); *African Statistical Yearbook.*

TUNISIA - PRINTING AND WRITING PAPER - See TUNISIA - FORESTRY AND FOREST PRODUCTS

TUNISIA - PRODUCTION

American Automobile Manufacturers Association, 1401 H Street, NW, Suite 900, Washington, D.C. 20005 (202) 326-5500; *World Motor Vehicle Data.*

International Lead and Zinc Study Group, Metro House, 58 St. James's Street, London SW1A 1LD, England; *Lead and Zinc Statistics.*

M.E. Sharpe, 80 Business Park Drive, Armonk, New York 10504 (800) 541-6563; *The Illustrated Book of World Rankings.*

TUNISIA - PRODUCTIVITY

Euromonitor International, Inc., 122 South Michigan Avenue, Suite 1200, Chicago, Illinois 60603 (800) 577-EURO; *International Marketing Data and Statistics.*

TUNISIA - PROPERTY TAXES - See TUNISIA - TAXATION

TUNISIA - PUBLIC FINANCE - See TUNISIA - FINANCE

TUNISIA - RADIO BROADCASTING - See TUNISIA - BROADCASTING

TUNISIA - RADIO RECEIVER PRODUCTION

Statistical Office of the United Nations, Publishing Service, New York, New York 10017 (800) 253-9646; *Statistical Yearbook.*

TUNISIA - RADIO RECEIVERS

St. Martin's Press, Inc., 175 Fifth Avenue, New York, New York 10010 (800) 221-7945; *The Statesman's Year-Book.*

TUNISIA - RAILWAYS

Europa Publications Limited, 18 Bedford Square, London, WC1B 3JN, England; *The Europa World Year Book.*

Jane's Information Group, Sentinel House, 163 Brighton Road, Coulsdon, Surrey CR5 2NH, England (Telephone Number in U.S. (703) 683-3700); *Jane's World Railways.*

St. Martin's Press, Inc., 175 Fifth Avenue, New York, New York 10010 (800) 221-7945; *The Statesman's Year-Book.*

Statistical Office of the United Nations, Publishing Service, New York, New York 10017 (800) 253-9646; *Statistical Yearbook;* and *Survey of Economic and Social Conditions in Africa.*

United Nations Economic Commission for Africa, Africa Hall, P.O. Box 3001, Addis Ababa, Ethiopia (Telephone Number in U.S. (800) 253-9646); *African Statistical Yearbook.*

TUNISIA - RELIGION

Central Intelligence Agency, Washington, D.C. 20505 (703) 482-1100, www.cia.gov; *The World Factbook.*

M.E. Sharpe, 80 Business Park Drive, Armonk, New York 10504 (800) 541-6563; *The Illustrated Book of World Rankings.*

St. Martin's Press, Inc., 175 Fifth Avenue, New York, New York 10010 (800) 221-7945; *The Statesman's Year-Book.*

TUNISIA - RENT PRICES

International Labour Office, I.L.O. Publications, 1828 L Street, NW, Suite 801, Washington, D.C. 20036 (301) 638-3152; *Yearbook of Labour Statistics.*

TUNISIA - RETAIL TRADE

Euromonitor International, Inc., 122 South Michigan Avenue, Suite 1200, Chicago, Illinois 60603 (800) 577-EURO; *World Marketing Data and Statistics.*

TUNISIA - RICE PRODUCTION - See TUNISIA - CROPS

TUNISIA - ROUNDWOOD PRODUCTION - See TUNISIA - FORESTRY AND FOREST PRODUCTS

TUNISIA - RUBBER PRODUCTION AND CONSUMPTION

M.E. Sharpe, 80 Business Park Drive, Armonk, New York 10504 (800) 541-6563; *The Illustrated Book of World Rankings.*

TUNISIA - SALT PRODUCTION - See TUNISIA - MINING AND MINERAL PRODUCTS

TUNISIA - SAWNWOOD PRODUCTION - See TUNISIA - FORESTRY AND FOREST PRODUCTS

TUNISIA - SCIENTISTS, TECHNICIANS AND ENGINEERS

Statistical Office of the United Nations, Publishing Service, New York, New York 10017 (800) 253-9646; *Statistical Yearbook.*

United Nations Educational, Scientific and Cultural Organization (UNESCO), 7 Place de Fontenoy, F-75700 Paris, France (Telephone Number in U.S. (212) 963-5981); *Statistical Yearbook.*

TUNISIA - SENIOR CITIZENS

M.E. Sharpe, 80 Business Park Drive, Armonk, New York 10504 (800) 541-6563; *The Illustrated Book of World Rankings.*

TUNISIA - SHEEP - See TUNISIA - LIVESTOCK AND POULTRY

TUNISIA - SILVER PRODUCTION AND CONSUMPTION - See TUNISIA - MINING AND MINERAL PRODUCTS

TUNISIA - SOCIAL DATA

African Development Bank, 01 BP 1387, Abidjan 01, Cote D'Ivoire; *Selected Statistics on Regional Member Countries.*

M.E. Sharpe, 80 Business Park Drive, Armonk, New York 10504 (800) 541-6563; *The Illustrated Book of World Rankings.*

St. Martin's Press, Inc., 175 Fifth Avenue, New York, New York 10010 (800) 221-7945; *The Statesman's Year-Book.*

Statistical Office of the United Nations, Publishing Service, New York, New York 10017 (800) 253-9646; *World Statistics Pocketbook.*

TUNISIA - SOCIAL SECURITY

International Monetary Fund, 700 Nineteenth Street, NW, Washington, D.C. 20431 (202) 623-7000; *Government Finance Statistics Yearbook*.

Statistical Office of the United Nations, Publishing Service, New York, New York 10017 (800) 253-9646; *National Accounts Statistics*.

TUNISIA - STAMP TAXES AND DUTIES - See TUNISIA - TAXATION

TUNISIA - STATE BUDGET REVENUE AND EXPENDITURES

Euromonitor International, Inc., 122 South Michigan Avenue, Suite 1200, Chicago, Illinois 60603 (800) 577-EURO; *International Marketing Data and Statistics*.

TUNISIA - STEEL - See TUNISIA - MINING AND MINERAL PRODUCTS

TUNISIA - STOCKS - COMMODITY - MARKET PRICE - INDEX

Food and Agricultural Organization of the United Nations (FAO) Via delle Terme di Caracalla, 00100 Rome, Italy (Telephone Number in U.S. (202) 653-2400); *The State of Food and Agriculture*.

International Lead and Zinc Study Group, Metro House, 58 St. James's Street, London SW1A 1LD, England; *Lead and Zinc Statistics*.

TUNISIA - SUGAR PRODUCTION AND CONSUMPTION - See TUNISIA - CROPS

TUNISIA - SULPHURIC ACID PRODUCTION - See TUNISIA - MINING AND MINERAL PRODUCTS

TUNISIA - TAXATION

Europa Publications Limited, 18 Bedford Square, London, WC1B 3JN, England; *The Europa World Year Book*.

International Monetary Fund, 700 Nineteenth Street, NW, Washington, D.C. 20431 (202) 623-7000; *Government Finance Statistics Yearbook*.

International Road Federation, 2600 Virginia Avenue, NW, Washington, D.C. 20037 (202) 338-4641; *World Road Statistics*.

The World Bank, 1818 H Street, NW, Washington, D.C. 20433 (202) 477-1234; *World Development Indicators*.

TUNISIA - TEA - See TUNISIA - CROPS

TUNISIA - TELEGRAPH SERVICE

Statistical Office of the United Nations, Publishing Service, New York, New York 10017 (800) 253-9646; *Statistical Yearbook*.

TUNISIA - TELEPHONES IN USE

American Telephone and Telegraph Company, 26 Parsippany Road, Whippany, New Jersey 07981 (800) 222-0300; *The World's Telephones*.

Central Intelligence Agency, Washington, D.C. 20505 (703) 482-1100, www.cia.gov; *The World Factbook*.

St. Martin's Press, Inc., 175 Fifth Avenue, New York, New York 10010 (800) 221-7945; *The Statesman's Year-Book*.

Statistical Office of the United Nations, Publishing Service, New York, New York 10017 (800) 253-9646; *Statistical Yearbook; and World Statistics Pocketbook*.

TUNISIA - TELEVISION BROADCASTING - See TUNISIA - BROADCASTING

TUNISIA - TELEVISION RECEIVER PRODUCTION

Statistical Office of the United Nations, Publishing Service, New York, New York 10017 (800) 253-9646; *Statistical Yearbook*.

TUNISIA - TEXTILE INDUSTRY

M.E. Sharpe, 80 Business Park Drive, Armonk, New York 10504 (800) 541-6563; *The Illustrated Book of World Rankings*.

St. Martin's Press, Inc., 175 Fifth Avenue, New York, New York 10010 (800) 221-7945; *The Statesman's Year-Book*.

Statistical Office of the United Nations, Publishing Service, New York, New York 10017 (800) 253-9646; *Statistical Yearbook*.

United Nations Conference on Trade and Development, Central Statistical Service, Palais des Nations, Geneva, Switzerland (Telephone in U.S. (800) 253-9646); *UNCTAD Commodity Yearbook*.

TUNISIA - THEATRE

United Nations Educational, Scientific and Cultural Organization (UNESCO), 7 Place de Fontenoy, F-75700 Paris, France (Telephone Number in U.S. (212) 963-5981); *Statistical Yearbook*.

TUNISIA - TIRE (MOTOR VEHICLE) PRODUCTION

Statistical Office of the United Nations, Publishing Service, New York, New York 10017 (800) 253-9646; *Statistical Yearbook*.

TUNISIA - TOBACCO PRODUCTION

M.E. Sharpe, 80 Business Park Drive, Armonk, New York 10504 (800) 541-6563; *The Illustrated Book of World Rankings*.

Statistical Office of the United Nations, Publishing Service, New York, New York 10017 (800) 253-9646; *Statistical Yearbook*.

TUNISIA - TOURISM

Euromonitor International, Inc., 122 South Michigan Avenue, Suite 1200, Chicago, Illinois 60603 (800) 577-EURO; *The World Economic Factbook; and World Marketing Data and Statistics*.

Europa Publications Limited, 18 Bedford Square, London, WC1B 3JN, England; *The Europa World Year Book*.

Federal Statistical Office, Gustav-Stresemann - Ring 11, D-6200, Wiesbaden, Germany; *Tunesien*.

M.E. Sharpe, 80 Business Park Drive, Armonk, New York 10504 (800) 541-6563; *The Illustrated Book of World Rankings*.

St. Martin's Press, Inc., 175 Fifth Avenue, New York, New York 10010 (800) 221-7945; *The Statesman's Year-Book*.

Statistical Office of the United Nations, Publishing Service, New York, New York 10017 (800) 253-9646; *Statistical Yearbook*.

United Nations Economic Commission for Africa, Africa Hall, P.O. Box 3001, Addis Ababa, Ethiopia (Telephone Number in U.S. (800) 253-9646); *African Statistical Yearbook*.

World Tourism Organization, Calle Capitan Haya 42, E-28020 Madrid, Spain; *Yearbook of Tourism Statistics*.

TUNISIA - TRACTORS IN USE

Statistical Office of the United Nations, Publishing Service, New York, New York 10017 (800) 253-9646; *Statistical Yearbook*.

TUNISIA - TRADE - See TUNISIA - FOREIGN TRADE

TUNISIA - TRADEMARKS AND SERVICE MARKS - See TUNISIA - PATENTS, TRADEMARKS AND SERVICE MARKS

TUNISIA - TRANSPORTATION AND COMMUNICATIONS

Central Intelligence Agency, Washington, D.C. 20505 (703) 482-1100, www.cia.gov; *The World Factbook*.

Euromonitor International, Inc., 122 South Michigan Avenue, Suite 1200, Chicago, Illinois 60603 (800) 577-EURO; *International Marketing Data and Statistics; and World Marketing Data and Statistics*.

Europa Publications Limited, 18 Bedford Square, London, WC1B 3JN, England; *The Europa World Year Book.*

Federal Statistical Office, Gustav-Stresemann - Ring 11, D-6200, Wiesbaden, Germany; *Tunesien.*

M.E. Sharpe, 80 Business Park Drive, Armonk, New York 10504 (800) 541-6563; *The Illustrated Book of World Rankings.*

St. Martin's Press, Inc., 175 Fifth Avenue, New York, New York 10010 (800) 221-7945; *The Statesman's Year-Book.*

Statistical Office of the United Nations, Publishing Service, New York, New York 10017 (800) 253-9646; *Human Development Report.*

United Nations Economic Commission for Africa, Africa Hall, P.O. Box 3001, Addis Ababa, Ethiopia (Telephone Number in U.S. (800) 253-9646); *African Statistical Yearbook.*

TUNISIA - UNEMPLOYMENT

Central Intelligence Agency, Washington, D.C. 20505 (703) 482-1100, www.cia.gov; *The World Factbook.*

Euromonitor International, Inc., 122 South Michigan Avenue, Suite 1200, Chicago, Illinois 60603 (800) 577-EURO; *International Marketing Data and Statistics.*

International Labour Office, I.L.O. Publications, 1828 L Street, NW, Suite 801, Washington, D.C. 20036 (301) 638-3152; *Yearbook of Labour Statistics.*

St. Martin's Press, Inc., 175 Fifth Avenue, New York, New York 10010 (800) 221-7945; *The Statesman's Year-Book.*

Statistical Office of the United Nations, Publishing Service, New York, New York 10017 (800) 253-9646; *Statistical Yearbook.*

TUNISIA - VITAL STATISTICS

St. Martin's Press, Inc., 175 Fifth Avenue, New York, New York 10010 (800) 221-7945; *The Statesman's Year-Book.*

Statistical Office of the United Nations, Publishing Service, New York, New York 10017 (800) 253-9646; *Statistical Yearbook.*

World Health Organization, Office of Publications, 20 Avenue Appia, CH-1211 Geneva 27, Switzerland (Telephone Number in U.S. (518) 436-9686); *World Health Statistics Annual.*

TUNISIA - WAGES

Federal Statistical Office, Gustav-Stresemann - Ring 11, D-6200, Wiesbaden,

Germany; *Tunesien.*

International Labour Office, I.L.O. Publications, 1828 L Street, NW, Suite 801, Washington, D.C. 20036 (301) 638-3152; *Yearbook of Labour Statistics.*

TUNISIA - WEATHER - See TUNISIA - CLIMATE

TUNISIA - WELFARE

International Monetary Fund, 700 Nineteenth Street, NW, Washington, D.C. 20431 (202) 623-7000; *Government Finance Statistics Yearbook.*

TUNISIA - WHEAT PRODUCTION AND PRICES - See TUNISIA - CROPS

TUNISIA - WHOLESALE PRICES

International Monetary Fund, 700 Nineteenth Street, NW, Washington, D.C. 20431 (202) 623-7000; *International Financial Statistics.*

TUNISIA - WINE PRODUCTION - See TUNISIA - BEVERAGES

TUNISIA - WOOL PRODUCTION - See TUNISIA - TEXTILE INDUSTRY

TUNISIA - YARN PRODUCTION - See TUNISIA - TEXTILE INDUSTRY

TUNISIA - ZINC AND ZINC ORE PRODUCTION AND CONSUMPTION -See TUNISIA - MINING AND MINERAL PRODUCTS

TURBINES - See STEAM ENGINES

Turkey - National Statistical Office

Devlet Istatistik Enstitusu (State Institute of Statistics), Necatibey Caddesi, 114 Ankara, Turkey.

Turkey - Primary Statistics Sources

Devlet Istatistik Enstitusu, Necati bey Caddesi, 114 Ankara, Turkey; *Aylik Istratistik bulteni* (Monthly Bulletin of Statistics) and *Turkiye Istatistik yilligi* (Statistical Yearbook of Turkey).

TURKEY - ABORTIONS

Statistical Office of the United Nations, Publishing Service, New York, New York 10017 (800) 253-9646; *Trends in Europe and North America: The Statistical Yearbook of the Economic Commission for Europe.*

TURKEY - AGRICULTURE

The Economist Intelligence Unit, 111

West 57th Street, New York, New York 10019 (800) 938-4685; *Turkey Country Report.*

Euromonitor International, Inc., 122 South Michigan Avenue, Suite 1200, Chicago, Illinois 60603 (800) 577-EURO; *World Marketing Data and Statistics.*

Europa Publications Limited, 18 Bedford Square, London, WC1B 3JN, England; *The Europa World Year Book.*

Food and Agricultural Organization of the United Nations (FAO) Via delle Terme di Caracalla, 00100 Rome, Italy (Telephone Number in U.S. (202) 653-2400); *Production Yearbook; The State of Food and Agriculture;* and *Trade Yearbook.*

M.E. Sharpe, 80 Business Park Drive, Armonk, New York 10504 (800) 541-6563; *The Illustrated Book of World Rankings.*

Organisation for Economic Co-operation and Development (OECD), 2 rue Andre-Pascal, 75 Paris 16, France (Telephone Number in U.S. (202) 785-6323); *Economic Accounts for Agriculture; Industrial Structure Statistics;* and *OECD Economic Surveys: Turkey.*

St. Martin's Press, Inc., 175 Fifth Avenue, New York, New York 10010 (800) 221-7945; *The Statesman's Year-Book.*

Statistical Office of the United Nations, Publishing Service, New York, New York 10017 (800) 253-9646; *Statistical Yearbook.*

United Nations Conference on Trade and Development, Central Statistical Service, Palais des Nations, Geneva, Switzerland (Telephone in U.S. (800) 253-9646); *UNCTAD Commodity Yearbook.*

The World Bank, 1818 H Street, NW, Washington, D.C. 20433 (202) 477-1234; *World Development Indicators.*

TURKEY - AIRLINE SERVICE

Europa Publications Limited, 18 Bedford Square, London, WC1B 3JN, England; *The Europa World Year Book.*

International Civil Aviation Organization, 999 University Street, Montreal, Quebec, Canada H3C 5H7 (514) 954-8219; *Civil Aviation Statistics of the World.*

M.E. Sharpe, 80 Business Park Drive, Armonk, New York 10504 (800) 541-6563; *The Illustrated Book of World Rankings.*

Organisation for Economic Co-operation and Development (OECD), 2 rue Andre-Pascal, 75 Paris 16, France (Telephone Number in U.S. (202) 785-6323); *Tourism Policy and International*

Tourism in OECD Member Countries.

St. Martin's Press, Inc., 175 Fifth Avenue, New York, New York 10010 (800) 221-7945; *The Statesman's Year-Book.*

Statistical Office of the United Nations, Publishing Service, New York, New York 10017 (800) 253-9646; *Statistical Yearbook.*

TURKEY - AIRPORTS

Central Intelligence Agency, Washington, D.C. 20505 (703) 482-1100, www.cia.gov; *The World Factbook.*

TURKEY - ALMOND PRODUCTION - See TURKEY - CROPS

TURKEY - ALUMINUM PRODUCTION AND CONSUMPTION - See TURKEY - MINING AND MINERAL PRODUCTS

TURKEY - ANIMAL FEEDINGSTUFFS - EXPORTS

Organisation for Economic Co-operation and Development (OECD), 2 rue Andre-Pascal, 75 Paris 16, France (Telephone Number in U.S. (202) 785-6323); *Foreign Trade by Commodities.*

TURKEY - ANIMAL HEALTH

Food and Agricultural Organization of the United Nations (FAO), Via delle Terme di Caracalla, 00100, Rome, Italy (Telephone Number in U.S. (202) 653-2400); *Animal Health Yearbook.*

TURKEY - ANTIMONY AND ANTIMONY ORE - See TURKEY - MINING AND MINERAL PRODUCTS

TURKEY - APPLES - See TURKEY - CROPS

TURKEY - AREA AND DENSITY OF POPULATION

Central Intelligence Agency, Washington, D.C. 20505 (703) 482-1100, www.cia.gov; *The World Factbook.*

Euromonitor International, Inc., 122 South Michigan Avenue, Suite 1200, Chicago, Illinois 60603 (800) 577-EURO; *The World Economic Factbook.*

Europa Publications Limited, 18 Bedford Square, London, WC1B 3JN, England; *The Europa World Year Book.*

Food and Agricultural Organization of the United Nations (FAO) Via delle Terme di Caracalla, 00100 Rome, Italy (Telephone Number in U.S. (202) 653-2400); *The State of Food and Agriculture.*

M.E. Sharpe, 80 Business Park Drive, Armonk, New York 10504 (800) 541-6563; *The Illustrated Book of World Rankings.*

St. Martin's Press, Inc., 175 Fifth Avenue, New York, New York 10010 (800) 221-7945; *The Statesman's Year-Book.*

Statistical Office of the United Nations, Publishing Service, New York, New York 10017 (800) 253-9646; *Statistical Yearbook;* and *Trends in Europe and North America: The Statistical Yearbook of the Economic Commission for Europe.*

United Nations Educational, Scientific and Cultural Organization (UNESCO), 7 Place de Fontenoy, F-75700 Paris, France (Telephone Number in U.S. (212) 963-5981); *Statistical Yearbook.*

The World Bank, 1818 H Street, NW, Washington, D.C. 20433 (202) 477-1234; *World Development Report.*

TURKEY - ARMS EXPORTS AND IMPORTS - See TURKEY - MILITARY

TURKEY - BALANCE OF PAYMENTS

The Economist Intelligence Unit, 111 West 57th Street, New York, New York 10019 (800) 938-4685; *The World Market Atlas.*

Europa Publications Limited, 18 Bedford Square, London, WC1B 3JN, England; *The Europa World Year Book.*

International Monetary Fund, 700 Nineteenth Street, NW, Washington, D.C. 20431 (202) 623-7000; *Balance of Payments Yearbook;* and *International Financial Statistics.*

Organisation for Economic Co-operation and Development (OECD), 2 rue Andre-Pascal, 75 Paris 16, France (Telephone Number in U.S. (202) 785-6323); *Economic Outlook; Geographical Distribution of Financial Flows to Developing Countries; Main Economic Indicators - Historical Statistics;* and *OECD Economic Surveys: Turkey.*

United Nations Conference on Trade and Development (UNCTAD), New York, New York 10017 (800) 253-9646; *Handbook of International Trade and Development.*

The World Bank, 1818 H Street, NW, Washington, D.C. 20433 (202) 477-1234; *World Development Report;* and *World Development Indicators.*

TURKEY - BANKING

Euromonitor International, Inc., 122 South Michigan Avenue, Suite 1200, Chicago, Illinois 60603 (800) 577-EURO; *World Marketing Data and Statistics.*

Europa Publications Limited, 18 Bedford Square, London, WC1B 3JN, England; *The Europa World Year Book.*

International Monetary Fund, 700 Nineteenth Street, NW, Washington, D.C. 20431 (202) 623-7000; *International Financial Statistics.*

M.E. Sharpe, 80 Business Park Drive, Armonk, New York 10504 (800) 541-6563; *The Illustrated Book of World Rankings.*

Organisation for Economic Co-operation and Development (OECD), 2 rue Andre-Pascal, 75 Paris 16, France (Telephone Number in U.S. (202) 785-6323); *Economic Outlook; Financial Market Trends;* and *OECD Economic Surveys: Turkey.*

St. Martin's Press, Inc., 175 Fifth Avenue, New York, New York 10010 (800) 221-7945; *The Statesman's Year-Book.*

Statistical Office of the United Nations, Publishing Service, New York, New York 10017 (800) 253-9646; *Statistical Yearbook.*

TURKEY - BARLEY PRODUCTION - See TURKEY - CROPS

TURKEY - BAUXITE PRODUCTION AND CONSUMPTION - See TURKEY - MINING AND MINERAL PRODUCTS

TURKEY - BEER PRODUCTION - See TURKEY - BEVERAGES

TURKEY - BEVERAGES

M.E. Sharpe, 80 Business Park Drive, Armonk, New York 10504 (800) 541-6563; *The Illustrated Book of World Rankings.*

Statistical Office of the United Nations, Publishing Service, New York, New York 10017 (800) 253-9646; *Statistical Yearbook.*

TURKEY - BIRTH RATES

Central Intelligence Agency, Washington, D.C. 20505 (703) 482-1100, www.cia.gov; *The World Factbook.*

Euromonitor International, Inc., 122 South Michigan Avenue, Suite 1200, Chicago, Illinois 60603 (800) 577-EURO; *The World Economic Factbook.*

Europa Publications Limited, 18 Bedford Square, London, WC1B 3JN, England; *The Europa World Year Book.*

M.E. Sharpe, 80 Business Park Drive, Armonk, New York 10504 (800) 541-6563; *The Illustrated Book of World Rankings.*

St. Martin's Press, Inc., 175 Fifth Avenue, New York, New York 10010 (800) 221-7945; *The Statesman's Year-Book.*

Statistical Office of the United Nations, Publishing Service, New York, New York 10017 (800) 253-9646; *Demographic*

Yearbook; and *Statistical Yearbook.*

The World Bank, 1818 H Street, NW, Washington, D.C. 20433 (202) 477-1234; *World Development Indicators.*

TURKEY - BONDS

International Monetary Fund, 700 Nineteenth Street, NW, Washington, D.C. 20431 (202) 623-7000; *Government Finance Statistics Yearbook.*

Organisation for Economic Co-operation and Development (OECD), 2 rue Andre-Pascal, 75 Paris 16, France (Telephone Number in U.S. (202) 785-6323); *Financial Market Trends.*

TURKEY - BOOK PRODUCTION

Euromonitor International, Inc., 122 South Michigan Avenue, Suite 1200, Chicago, Illinois 60603 (800) 577-EURO; *European Marketing Data and Statistics.*

Europa Publications Limited, 18 Bedford Square, London, WC1B 3JN, England; *The Europa World Year Book.*

St. Martin's Press, Inc., 175 Fifth Avenue, New York, New York 10010 (800) 221-7945; *The Statesman's Year-Book.*

Statistical Office of the United Nations, Publishing Service, New York, New York 10017 (800) 253-9646; *Trends in Europe and North America: The Statistical Yearbook of the Economic Commission for Europe.*

TURKEY - BROADCASTING

Billboard Limited, P.O. Box 9027, 1006 AA Amsterdam, The Netherlands (Telephone Number in U.S. (212) 764-7300); *World Radio TV Handbook.*

Central Intelligence Agency, Washington, D.C. 20505 (703) 482-1100, www.cia.gov; *The World Factbook.*

Euromonitor International, Inc., 122 South Michigan Avenue, Suite 1200, Chicago, Illinois 60603 (800) 577-EURO; *World Marketing Data and Statistics.*

M.E. Sharpe, 80 Business Park Drive, Armonk, New York 10504 (800) 541-6563; *The Illustrated Book of World Rankings.*

St. Martin's Press, Inc., 175 Fifth Avenue, New York, New York 10010 (800) 221-7945; *The Statesman's Year-Book.*

Statistical Office of the United Nations, Publishing Service, New York, New York 10017 (800) 253-9646; *Trends in Europe and North America: The Statistical Yearbook of the Economic Commission for Europe.*

United Nations Educational, Scientific

and Cultural Organization (UNESCO), 7 Place de Fontenoy, F-75700 Paris, France (Telephone Number in U.S. (212) 963-5981); *Statistical Yearbook.*

TURKEY - BUDGET

Central Intelligence Agency, Washington, D.C. 20505 (703) 482-1100, www.cia.gov; *The World Factbook.*

TURKEY - BUTTER - See TURKEY - DAIRY PRODUCTS

TURKEY - CALORIE SUPPLY

Food and Agricultural Organization of the United Nations (FAO) Via delle Terme di Caracalla, 00100 Rome, Italy (Telephone Number in U.S. (202) 653-2400); *The State of Food and Agriculture.*

TURKEY - CAPITAL INVESTMENT

Organisation for Economic Co-operation and Development (OECD), 2 rue Andre-Pascal, 75 Paris 16, France (Telephone Number in U.S. (202) 785-6323); *Economic Outlook;* and *Financial Market Trends.*

TURKEY - CAPITAL REVENUE

International Monetary Fund, 700 Nineteenth Street, NW, Washington, D.C. 20431 (202) 623-7000; *Government Finance Statistics Yearbook.*

Organisation for Economic Co-operation and Development (OECD), 2 rue Andre-Pascal, 75 Paris 16, France (Telephone Number in U.S. (202) 785-6323); *Economic Outlook;* and *Financial Market Trends.*

TURKEY - CATTLE - See TURKEY - LIVESTOCK AND POULTRY

TURKEY - CAULIFLOWER PRODUCTION - See TURKEY - CROPS

TURKEY - CAUSTIC SODA PRODUCTION - See TURKEY - BEVERAGES

TURKEY - CEMENT PRODUCTION - See TURKEY - MINING AND MINERAL PRODUCTS

TURKEY - CEREAL PRODUCTION - See TURKEY - CROPS

TURKEY - CHEESE - See TURKEY - DAIRY PRODUCTS

TURKEY - CHEMICAL (ORGANIC) PRODUCTION - See TURKEY - MINING AND MINERAL PRODUCTS

TURKEY - CHESTNUT PRODUCTION - See TURKEY - CROPS

TURKEY - CHICK PEA PRODUCTION - See TURKEY - CROPS

TURKEY - CHROMITE PRODUCTION AND CONSUMPTION - See TURKEY - MINING AND MINERAL PRODUCTS

TURKEY - CHROMIUM ORE PRODUCTION AND CONSUMPTION - See TURKEY - MINING AND MINERAL PRODUCTS

TURKEY - CIGAR PRODUCTION - See TURKEY - TOBACCO PRODUCTION

TURKEY - CIGARETTE PRODUCTION - See TURKEY - TOBACCO PRODUCTION

TURKEY - CLIMATE

M.E. Sharpe, 80 Business Park Drive, Armonk, New York 10504 (800) 541-6563; *The Illustrated Book of World Rankings.*

St. Martin's Press, Inc., 175 Fifth Avenue, New York, New York 10010 (800) 221-7945; *The Statesman's Year-Book.*

TURKEY - CLOTHING EXPORTS AND IMPORTS - See TURKEY - TEXTILE INDUSTRY

TURKEY - COAL PRODUCTION - See TURKEY - MINING AND MINERAL PRODUCTS

TURKEY - COBALT PRODUCTION AND CONSUMPTION - See TURKEY - MINING AND MINERAL PRODUCTS

TURKEY - COFFEE PRODUCTION - See TURKEY - CROPS

TURKEY - COKE AND COKE OVEN COKE PRODUCTION AND CONSUMPTION - See TURKEY - MINING AND MINERAL PRODUCTS

TURKEY - COMMERCE

St. Martin's Press, Inc., 175 Fifth Avenue, New York, New York 10010 (800) 221-7945; *The Statesman's Year-Book.*

TURKEY - CONSTRUCTION INDUSTRY

M.E. Sharpe, 80 Business Park Drive, Armonk, New York 10504 (800) 541-6563; *The Illustrated Book of World Rankings.*

Organisation for Economic Co-operation and Development (OECD), 2 rue Andre-Pascal, 75 Paris 16, France (Telephone Number in U.S. (202) 785-6323); *Industrial Structure Statistics; The Iron and Steel Industry; Main Economic Indicators - Historical Statistics;* and *OECD Economic Surveys: Turkey.*

St. Martin's Press, Inc., 175 Fifth Avenue, New York, New York 10010 (800)

221-7945; *The Statesman's Year-Book.*

Statistical Office of the United Nations, Publishing Service, New York, New York 10017 (800) 253-9646; *Statistical Yearbook.*

TURKEY - CONSUMER PRICE INDEX

Europa Publications Limited, 18 Bedford Square, London, WC1B 3JN, England; *The Europa World Year Book.*

Organisation for Economic Co-operation and Development (OECD), 2 rue Andre-Pascal, 75 Paris 16, France (Telephone Number in U.S. (202) 785-6323); *Economic Outlook.*

Statistical Office of the United Nations, Publishing Service, New York, New York 10017 (800) 253-9646; *Statistical Yearbook; and Trends in Europe and North America: The Statistical Yearbook of the Economic Commission for Europe.*

TURKEY - CONSUMER PRICES

Euromonitor International, Inc., 122 South Michigan Avenue, Suite 1200, Chicago, Illinois 60603 (800) 577-EURO; *European Marketing Data and Statistics; and World Marketing Data and Statistics.*

International Labour Office, I.L.O. Publications, 1828 L Street, NW, Suite 801, Washington, D.C. 20036 (301) 638-3152; *Yearbook of Labour Statistics.*

International Monetary Fund, 700 Nineteenth Street, NW, Washington, D.C. 20431 (202) 623-7000; *International Financial Statistics.*

Organisation for Economic Co-operation and Development (OECD), 2 rue Andre-Pascal, 75 Paris 16, France (Telephone Number in U.S. (202) 785-6323); *Economic Outlook.*

TURKEY - CONSUMPTION

Organisation for Economic Co-operation and Development (OECD), 2 rue Andre-Pascal, 75 Paris 16, France (Telephone Number in U.S. (202) 785-6323); *The Footwear, Raw Hides and Skins, and Leather Industry in OECD Countries; The Iron and Steel Industry; Meat Balances in OECD Member Countries; The Non-Ferrous Metals Industry; The Pulp and Paper Industry; and Textile Industry in OECD Countries.*

The World Bank, 1818 H Street, NW, Washington, D.C. 20433 (202) 477-1234; *World Development Report.*

TURKEY - COPPER AND COPPER ORE PRODUCTION AND CONSUMPTION - See TURKEY - MINING AND MINERAL PRODUCTS

TURKEY - CORN PRODUCTION - See TURKEY - CROPS

TURKEY - CORPORATE INCOME TAXES - See TURKEY - TAXATION

TURKEY - CORPORATE TAXES - See TURKEY - TAXATION

TURKEY - COTTON - See TURKEY - CROPS

TURKEY - CRIME

International Criminal Police Organization (INTERPOL), 50 quai Achille Lignon, F-69006 Lyon, France; *International Crime Statistics.*

Statistical Office of the United Nations, Publishing Service, New York, New York 10017 (800) 253-9646; *Trends in Europe and North America: The Statistical Yearbook of the Economic Commission for Europe.*

Yale University Press, Yale Station, New Haven, Connecticut 06520 (800) 987-7323; *Violence and Crime in Cross-National Perspective.*

TURKEY - CROPS

Commodity Research Bureau, Inc., 30 South Wacker Drive, Chicago, Illinois 60606 (312) 454-1801; *Commodity Year Book.*

Euromonitor International, Inc., 122 South Michigan Avenue, Suite 1200, Chicago, Illinois 60603 (800) 577-EURO; *European Marketing Data and Statistics.*

Europa Publications Limited, 18 Bedford Square, London, WC1B 3JN, England; *The Europa World Year Book.*

Food and Agricultural Organization of the United Nations (FAO) Via delle Terme di Caracalla, 00100 Rome, Italy (Telephone Number in U.S. (202) 653-2400); *Production Yearbook; and The State of Food and Agriculture.*

International Monetary Fund, 700 Nineteenth Street, NW, Washington, D.C. 20431 (202) 623-7000; *Government Finance Statistics Yearbook.*

M.E. Sharpe, 80 Business Park Drive, Armonk, New York 10504 (800) 541-6563; *The Illustrated Book of World Rankings.*

Organisation for Economic Co-operation and Development (OECD), 2 rue Andre-Pascal, 75 Paris 16, France (Telephone Number in U.S. (202) 785-6323); *Economic Accounts for Agriculture; Foreign Trade by Commodities; and Textile Industries in OECD Countries.*

St. Martin's Press, Inc., 175 Fifth Avenue, New York, New York 10010 (800) 221-7945; *The Statesman's Year-Book.*

Statistical Office of the United Nations, Publishing Service, New York, New York 10017 (800) 253-9646; *Statistical Yearbook.*

United Nations Conference on Trade and Development, Central Statistical Service, Palais des Nations, Geneva, Switzerland (Telephone in U.S. (800) 253-9646); *UNCTAD Commodity Yearbook.*

TURKEY - CUSTOMS DUTIES

International Monetary Fund, 700 Nineteenth Street, NW, Washington, D.C. 20431 (202) 623-7000; *Government Finance Statistics Yearbook.*

Organisation for Economic Co-operation and Development (OECD), 2 rue Andre-Pascal, 75 Paris 16, France (Telephone Number in U.S. (202) 785-6323); *The Non-Ferrous Metals Industry.*

St. Martin's Press, Inc., 175 Fifth Avenue, New York, New York 10010 (800) 221-7945; *The Statesman's Year-Book.*

TURKEY - DAIRY PRODUCTS

Europa Publications Limited, 18 Bedford Square, London, WC1B 3JN, England; *The Europa World Year Book.*

Food and Agricultural Organization of the United Nations (FAO) Via delle Terme di Caracalla, 00100 Rome, Italy (Telephone Number in U.S. (202) 653-2400); *Production Yearbook; and The State of Food and Agriculture.*

M.E. Sharpe, 80 Business Park Drive, Armonk, New York 10504 (800) 541-6563; *The Illustrated Book of World Rankings.*

Organisation for Economic Co-operation and Development (OECD), 2 rue Andre-Pascal, 75 Paris 16, France (Telephone Number in U.S. (202) 785-6323); *Economic Accounts for Agriculture; and Milk, Milk Products, and Egg Balances in OECD Member Countries.*

St. Martin's Press, Inc., 175 Fifth Avenue, New York, New York 10010 (800) 221-7945; *The Statesman's Year-Book.*

Statistical Office of the United Nations, Publishing Service, New York, New York 10017 (800) 253-9646; *Statistical Yearbook.*

TURKEY - DEATH RATES - See TURKEY - MORTALITY

TURKEY - DEFENSE EXPENDITURES - See TURKEY - MILITARY

TURKEY - DEMOGRAPHY

Euromonitor International, Inc., 122 South Michigan Avenue, Suite 1200, Chicago, Illinois 60603 (800) 577-EURO;

The World Economic Factbook; and *World Marketing Data and Statistics.*

M.E. Sharpe, 80 Business Park Drive, Armonk, New York 10504 (800) 541-6563; *The Illustrated Book of World Rankings.*

Statistical Office of the United Nations, Publishing Service, New York, New York 10017 (800) 253-9646; *Human Development Report.*

TURKEY - DEVELOPMENT ASSISTANCE

Organisation for Economic Co-operation and Development (OECD), 2 rue Andre-Pascal, 75 Paris 16, France (Telephone Number in U.S. (202) 785-6323); *Geographical Distribution of Financial Flows to Developing Countries.*

Statistical Office of the United Nations, Publishing Service, New York, New York 10017 (800) 253-9646; *Statistical Yearbook.*

TURKEY - DIAMOND PRODUCTION - See TURKEY - MINING AND MINERAL PRODUCTS

TURKEY - DISCOUNT RATES - See TURKEY - BANKING

TURKEY - DISEASES - See TURKEY - HEALTH

TURKEY - DIVORCE RATES

M.E. Sharpe, 80 Business Park Drive, Armonk, New York 10504 (800) 541-6563; *The Illustrated Book of World Rankings.*

Statistical Office of the United Nations, Publishing Service, New York, New York 10017 (800) 253-9646; *Demographic Yearbook; Statistical Yearbook;* and *Trends in Europe and North America: The Statistical Yearbook of the Economic Commission for Europe.*

TURKEY - ECONOMY

Central Intelligence Agency, Washington, D.C. 20505 (703) 482-1100, www.cia.gov; *The World Factbook.*

The Economist Intelligence Unit, 111 West 57th Street, New York, New York 10019 (800) 938-4685; *Turkey Country Report.*

Euromonitor International, Inc., 122 South Michigan Avenue, Suite 1200, Chicago, Illinois 60603 (800) 577-EURO; *European Marketing Data and Statistics; World Marketing Data and Statistics;* and *The World Economic Factbook.*

Europa Publications Limited, 18 Bedford Square, London, WC1B 3JN, England; *The Europa World Year Book.*

M.E. Sharpe, 80 Business Park Drive, Armonk, New York 10504 (800) 541-6563; *The Illustrated Book of World Rankings.*

Organisation for Economic Co-operation and Development (OECD), 2 rue Andre-Pascal, 75 Paris 16, France (Telephone Number in U.S. (202) 785-6323); *Economic Outlook; Geographical Distribution of Financial Flows to Developing Countries; OECD Economic Surveys: Turkey;* and *OECD Employment Outlook.*

St. Martin's Press, Inc., 175 Fifth Avenue, New York, New York 10010 (800) 221-7945; *The Statesman's Year-Book.*

Statistical Office of the United Nations, Publishing Service, New York, New York 10017 (800) 253-9646; *World Statistics Pocketbook.*

The World Bank, 1818 H Street, NW, Washington, D.C. 20433 (202) 477-1234; *The World Bank Atlas;* and *World Development Report.*

TURKEY - EDUCATION

The Economist Intelligence Unit, 111 West 57th Street, New York, New York 10019 (800) 938-4685; *The World Market Atlas.*

Euromonitor International, Inc., 122 South Michigan Avenue, Suite 1200, Chicago, Illinois 60603 (800) 577-EURO; *European Marketing Data and Statistics;* and *World Marketing Data and Statistics.*

Europa Publications Limited, 18 Bedford Square, London, WC1B 3JN, England; *The Europa World Year Book.*

International Monetary Fund, 700 Nineteenth Street, NW, Washington, D.C. 20431 (202) 623-7000; *Government Finance Statistics Yearbook.*

M.E. Sharpe, 80 Business Park Drive, Armonk, New York 10504 (800) 541-6563; *The Illustrated Book of World Rankings.*

Organisation for Economic Co-operation and Development (OECD), 2 rue Andre-Pascal, 75 Paris 16, France (Telephone Number in U.S. (202) 785-6323); *Education in OECD Countries.*

St. Martin's Press, Inc., 175 Fifth Avenue, New York, New York 10010 (800) 221-7945; *The Statesman's Year-Book.*

Statistical Office of the United Nations, Publishing Service, New York, New York 10017 (800) 253-9646; *Human Development Report;* and *Trends in Europe and North America: The Statistical Yearbook of the Economic Commission for Europe.*

M.E. Sharpe, 80 Business Park Drive, Armonk, New York 10504 (800) 541-6563; *The Illustrated Book of World Rankings.*

Organisation for Economic Co-operation and Development (OECD), 2 rue Andre-Pascal, 75 Paris 16, France (Telephone Number in U.S. (202) 785-6323); *The Illustrated Book of World Rankings.*

United Nations Educational, Scientific and Cultural Organization (UNESCO), 7 Place de Fontenoy, F-75700 Paris, France (Telephone Number in U.S. (212) 963-5981); *Statistical Yearbook.*

The World Bank, 1818 H Street, NW, Washington, D.C. 20433 (202) 477-1234; *World Development Report;* and *World Development Indicators.*

TURKEY - EGG PRODUCTION AND CONSUMPTION - See TURKEY - DAIRY PRODUCTS

TURKEY - EGGPLANT PRODUCTION - See TURKEY - CROPS

TURKEY - ELECTRICITY

Central Intelligence Agency, Washington, D.C. 20505 (703) 482-1100, www.cia.gov; *The World Factbook.*

M.E. Sharpe, 80 Business Park Drive, Armonk, New York 10504 (800) 541-6563; *The Illustrated Book of World Rankings.*

Organisation for Economic Co-operation and Development (OECD), 2 rue Andre-Pascal, 75 Paris 16, France (Telephone Number in U.S. (202) 785-6323); *Coal Information; Energy Statistics of OECD Countries;* and *Industrial Structure Statistics.*

Penn Well Publishing Company, 1421 South Sheridan Road, P.O. Box 1260, Tulsa, Oklahoma 74101 (800) 752-9764; *International Energy Statistics Sourcebook.*

St. Martin's Press, Inc., 175 Fifth Avenue, New York, New York 10010 (800) 221-7945; *The Statesman's Year-Book.*

Statistical Office of the United Nations, Publishing Service, New York, New York 10017 (800) 253-9646; *Human Development Report; Statistical Yearbook;* and *Trends in Europe and North America: The Statistical Yearbook of the Economic Commission for Europe.*

TURKEY - EMPLOYMENT

Euromonitor International, Inc., 122 South Michigan Avenue, Suite 1200, Chicago, Illinois 60603 (800) 577-EURO; *European Marketing Data and Statistics.*

International Labour Office, I.L.O. Publications, 1828 L Street, NW, Suite 801, Washington, D.C. 20036 (301) 638-3152; *Yearbook of Labour Statistics.*

M.E. Sharpe, 80 Business Park Drive, Armonk, New York 10504 (800) 541-6563; *The Illustrated Book of World Rankings.*

Organisation for Economic Co-operation and Development (OECD), 2 rue

Andre-Pascal, 75 Paris 16, France (Telephone Number in U.S. (202) 785-6323); *Economic Outlook; The Iron and Steel Industry; OECD Economic Surveys: Turkey; OECD Employment Outlook;* and *Textile Industry in OECD Countries.*

Statistical Office of the United Nations, Publishing Service, New York, New York 10017 (800) 253-9646; *Statistical Yearbook;* and *Trends in Europe and North America: The Statistical Yearbook of the Economic Commission for Europe.*

TURKEY - ENERGY

Euromonitor International, Inc., 122 South Michigan Avenue, Suite 1200, Chicago, Illinois 60603 (800) 577-EURO; *European Marketing Data and Statistics; World Marketing Data and Statistics;* and *The World Economic Factbook.*

Food and Agricultural Organization of the United Nations (FAO) Via delle Terme di Caracalla, 00100 Rome, Italy (Telephone Number in U.S. (202) 653-2400); *The State of Food and Agriculture.*

M.E. Sharpe, 80 Business Park Drive, Armonk, New York 10504 (800) 541-6563; *The Illustrated Book of World Rankings.*

Organisation for Economic Co-operation and Development (OECD), 2 rue Andre-Pascal, 75 Paris 16, France (Telephone Number in U.S. (202) 785-6323); *Coal Information; Energy Statistics of OECD Countries; Oil and Gas Information;* and *OECD Environmental Data.*

Penn Well Publishing Company, 1421 South Sheridan Road, P.O. Box 1260, Tulsa, Oklahoma 74101 (800) 752-9764; *International Energy Statistics Sourcebook.*

St. Martin's Press, Inc., 175 Fifth Avenue, New York, New York 10010 (800) 221-7945; *The Statesman's Year-Book.*

Statistical Office of the United Nations, Publishing Service, New York, New York 10017 (800) 253-9646; *Energy Statistics Yearbook; Human Development Report; Statistical Yearbook; Trends in Europe and North America: The Statistical Yearbook of the Economic Commission for Europe;* and *World Statistics Pocketbook.*

The World Bank, 1818 H Street, NW, Washington, D.C. 20433 (202) 477-1234; *The World Bank Atlas;* and *World Development Report.*

TURKEY - ENVIRONMENT

The Economist Intelligence Unit, 111 West 57th Street, New York, New York 10019 (800) 938-4685; *Turkey Country Report.*

Organization for Economic Co-operation and Development (OECD), 2 rue Andre-Pascal, 75 Paris 16, France (Telephone Number in U.S. (202) 785-6323); *OECD Environmental Data.*

Statistical Office of the United Nations, Publishing Service, New York, New York 10017 (800) 253-9646; *Trends in Europe and North America: The Statistical Yearbook of the Economic Commission for Europe;* and *World Statistics Pocketbook.*

TURKEY - EXCHANGE RATES

Central Intelligence Agency, Washington, D.C. 20505 (703) 482-1100, www.cia.gov; *The World Factbook.*

Euromonitor International, Inc., 122 South Michigan Avenue, Suite 1200, Chicago, Illinois 60603 (800) 577-EURO; *The World Economic Factbook.*

Europa Publications Limited, 18 Bedford Square, London, WC1B 3JN, England; *The Europa World Year Book.*

International Civil Aviation Organization, 999 University Street, Montreal, Quebec, Canada H3C 5H7 (514) 954-8219; *Civil Aviation Statistics of the World;* and *International Financial Statistics.*

International Monetary Fund, 700 Nineteenth Street, NW, Washington, D.C. 20431 (202) 623-7000; *International Financial Statistics.*

Organisation for Economic Co-operation and Development (OECD), 2 rue Andre-Pascal, 75 Paris 16, France (Telephone Number in U.S. (202) 785-6323); *Economic Outlook; Financial Market Trends; Revenue Statistics of OECD Member Countries;* and *Tourism Policy and International Tourism in OECD Member Countries.*

Statistical Office of the United Nations, Publishing Service, New York, New York 10017 (800) 253-9646; *Statistical Yearbook; Trends in Europe and North America: The Statistical Yearbook of the Economic Commission for Europe;* and *World Statistics Pocketbook.*

TURKEY - EXCISE TAXES - See TURKEY - TAXATION

TURKEY - EXPORTS

Central Intelligence Agency, Washington, D.C. 20505 (703) 482-1100, www.cia.gov; *The World Factbook.*

The Economist Intelligence Unit, 111 West 57th Street, New York, New York 10019 (800) 938-4685; *The World Market Atlas;* and *Turkey Country Report.*

Euromonitor International, Inc., 122 South Michigan Avenue, Suite 1200, Chicago, Illinois 60603 (800) 577-EURO; *The World Economic Factbook.*

Europa Publications Limited, 18 Bedford Square, London, WC1B 3JN, England; *The Europa World Year Book.*

Food and Agricultural Organization of the United Nations (FAO) Via delle Terme di Caracalla, 00100 Rome, Italy (Telephone Number in U.S. (202) 653-2400); *The State of Food and Agriculture.*

International Monetary Fund, 700 Nineteenth Street, NW, Washington, D.C. 20431 (202) 623-7000; *Direction of Trade Statistics;* and *International Financial Statistics.*

Organisation for Economic Co-operation and Development (OECD), 2 rue Andre-Pascal, 75 Paris 16, France (Telephone Number in U.S. (202) 785-6323); *Economic Outlook; The Footwear, Raw Hides and Skins, and Leather Industry in OECD Countries; Foreign Trade by Commodities; Geographical Distribution of Financial Flows to Developing Countries; Industrial Structure Statistics; The Iron and Steel Industry; Milk, Milk Products, and Egg Balances in OECD Member Countries; OECD Economic Surveys: Turkey; The Pulp and Paper Industry;* and *Review of Fisheries in OECD Member Countries.*

St. Martin's Press, Inc., 175 Fifth Avenue, New York, New York 10010 (800) 221-7945; *The Statesman's Year-Book.*

Statistical Office of the United Nations, Publishing Service, New York, New York 10017 (800) 253-9646; *Trends in Europe and North America: The Statistical Yearbook of the Economic Commission for Europe.*

United Nations Conference on Trade and Development (UNCTAD), New York, New York 10017 (800) 253-9646; *Handbook of International Trade and Development.*

The World Bank, 1818 H Street, NW, Washington, D.C. 20433 (202) 477-1234; *World Development Report;* and *World Development Indicators.*

TURKEY - EXTERNAL FINANCING

Organisation for Economic Co-operation and Development (OECD), 2 rue Andre-Pascal, 75 Paris 16, France (Telephone Number in U.S. (202) 785-6323); *Economic Outlook;* and *Financial Market Trends.*

TURKEY - EXTERNAL INDEBTEDNESS

Organisation for Economic Co-operation and Development (OECD), 2 rue Andre-Pascal, 75 Paris 16, France

(Telephone Number in U.S. (202) 785-6323); *Financial Market Trends;* and *Geographical Distribution of Financial Flows to Developing Countries.*

The World Bank, 1818 H Street, NW, Washington, D.C. 20433 (202) 477-1234; *World Development Report;* and *World Development Indicators.*

TURKEY - EXTERNAL TRADE

Euromonitor International, Inc., 122 South Michigan Avenue, Suite 1200, Chicago, Illinois 60603 (800) 577-EURO; *World Marketing Data and Statistics.*

Food and Agricultural Organization of the United Nations (FAO) Via delle Terme di Caracalla, 00100 Rome, Italy (Telephone Number in U.S. (202) 653-2400); *The State of Food and Agriculture;* and *Trade Yearbook.*

Statistical Office of the United Nations, Publishing Service, New York, New York 10017 (800) 253-9646; *Statistical Yearbook.*

TURKEY - FABRIC PRODUCTION - See TURKEY - TEXTILE INDUSTRY

TURKEY - FARM CROPS - See TURKEY - CROPS

TURKEY - FERTILITY RATES

Central Intelligence Agency, Washington, D.C. 20505 (703) 482-1100, www.cia.gov; *The World Factbook.*

M.E. Sharpe, 80 Business Park Drive, Armonk, New York 10504 (800) 541-6563; *The Illustrated Book of World Rankings.*

Statistical Office of the United Nations, Publishing Service, New York, New York 10017 (800) 253-9646; *Human Development Report;* and *Trends in Europe and North America: The Statistical Yearbook of the Economic Commission for Europe.*

The World Bank, 1818 H Street, NW, Washington, D.C. 20433 (202) 477-1234; *The World Bank Atlas; World Development Report;* and *World Development Indicators.*

TURKEY - FERTILIZER

Food and Agricultural Organization of the United Nations (FAO), Via delle Terme di Caracalla, 00100, Rome, Italy (Telephone Number in U.S. (202) 653-2400); *Fertilizer Yearbook;* and *The State of Food and Agriculture.*

Organisation for Economic Co-operation and Development (OECD), 2 rue Andre-Pascal, 75 Paris 16, France (Telephone Number in U.S. (202) 785-6323); *Economic Accounts for Agriculture;*

and *Foreign Trade by Commodities.*

Statistical Office of the United Nations, Publishing Service, New York, New York 10017 (800) 253-9646; *Statistical Yearbook.*

TURKEY - FETAL MORTALITY - See TURKEY - MORTALITY

TURKEY - FIBRE PRODUCTION - See TURKEY - TEXTILE INDUSTRY

TURKEY - FILAMENT PRODUCTION - See TURKEY - TEXTILE INDUSTRY

TURKEY - FILM - See TURKEY - MOTION PICTURES

TURKEY - FINANCE

The Economist Intelligence Unit, 111 West 57th Street, New York, New York 10019 (800) 938-4685; *Turkey Country Report.*

Europa Publications Limited, 18 Bedford Square, London, WC1B 3JN, England; *The Europa World Year Book.*

International Monetary Fund, 700 Nineteenth Street, NW, Washington, D.C. 20431 (202) 623-7000; *Government Finance Statistics Yearbook.*

M.E. Sharpe, 80 Business Park Drive, Armonk, New York 10504 (800) 541-6563; *The Illustrated Book of World Rankings.*

Organisation for Economic Co-operation and Development (OECD), 2 rue Andre-Pascal, 75 Paris 16, France (Telephone Number in U.S. (202) 785-6323); *Economic Outlook; Financial Market Trends; Geographical Distribution of Financial Flows to Developing Countries; OECD Financial Statistics;* and *Revenue Statistics of OECD Member Countries.*

St. Martin's Press, Inc., 175 Fifth Avenue, New York, New York 10010 (800) 221-7945; *The Statesman's Year-Book.*

TURKEY - FISHERIES

Euromonitor International, Inc., 122 South Michigan Avenue, Suite 1200, Chicago, Illinois 60603 (800) 577-EURO; *European Marketing Data and Statistics.*

Europa Publications Limited, 18 Bedford Square, London, WC1B 3JN, England; *The Europa World Year Book.*

Food and Agricultural Organization of the United Nations (FAO) Via delle Terme di Caracalla, 00100 Rome, Italy (Telephone Number in U.S. (202) 653-2400); *The State of Food and Agriculture.*

M.E. Sharpe, 80 Business Park Drive, Armonk, New York 10504 (800) 541-6563;

The Illustrated Book of World Rankings.

Organisation for Economic Co-operation and Development (OECD), 2 rue Andre-Pascal, 75 Paris 16, France (Telephone Number in U.S. (202) 785-6323); *Foreign Trade by Commodities;* and *Review of Fisheries in OECD Member Countries.*

St. Martin's Press, Inc., 175 Fifth Avenue, New York, New York 10010 (800) 221-7945; *The Statesman's Year-Book.*

Statistical Office of the United Nations, Publishing Service, New York, New York 10017 (800) 253-9646; *Statistical Yearbook.*

United Nations Conference on Trade and Development, Central Statistical Service, Palais des Nations, Geneva, Switzerland (Telephone in U.S. (800) 253-9646); *UNCTAD Commodity Yearbook.*

TURKEY - FLAX FIBRE PRODUCTION - See TURKEY - TEXTILE INDUSTRY

TURKEY - FLOUR PRODUCTION

Statistical Office of the United Nations, Publishing Service, New York, New York 10017 (800) 253-9646; *Statistical Yearbook.*

TURKEY - FOOD

Euromonitor International, Inc., 122 South Michigan Avenue, Suite 1200, Chicago, Illinois 60603 (800) 577-EURO; *Retail Trade International.*

Food and Agricultural Organization of the United Nations (FAO) Via delle Terme di Caracalla, 00100 Rome, Italy (Telephone Number in U.S. (202) 653-2400); *Production Yearbook;* and *The State of Food and Agriculture.*

Organisation for Economic Co-operation and Development (OECD), 2 rue Andre-Pascal, 75 Paris 16, France (Telephone Number in U.S. (202) 785-6323); *Foreign Trade by Commodities.*

Statistical Office of the United Nations, Publishing Service, New York, New York 10017 (800) 253-9646; *Human Development Report.*

United Nations Conference on Trade and Development, Central Statistical Service, Palais des Nations, Geneva, Switzerland (Telephone in U.S. (800) 253-9646); *UNCTAD Commodity Yearbook.*

TURKEY - FOREIGN DEBT

Organisation for Economic Co-operation and Development (OECD), 2 rue Andre-Pascal, 75 Paris 16, France (Telephone Number in U.S. (202) 785-6323); *Economic Outlook.*

St. Martin's Press, Inc., 175 Fifth Avenue, New York, New York 10010 (800) 221-7945; *The Statesman's Year-Book.*

TURKEY - FOREIGN TRADE

The Economist Intelligence Unit, 111 West 57th Street, New York, New York 10019 (800) 938-4685; *Turkey Country Report.*

Euromonitor International, Inc., 122 South Michigan Avenue, Suite 1200, Chicago, Illinois 60603 (800) 577-EURO; *European Marketing Data and Statistics;* and *The World Economic Factbook.*

Europa Publications Limited, 18 Bedford Square, London, WC1B 3JN, England; *The Europa World Year Book.*

Food and Agricultural Organization of the United Nations (FAO) Via delle Terme di Caracalla, 00100 Rome, Italy (Telephone Number in U.S. (202) 653-2400); *The State of Food and Agriculture.*

International Monetary Fund, 700 Nineteenth Street, NW, Washington, D.C. 20431 (202) 623-7000; *International Financial Statistics.*

M.E. Sharpe, 80 Business Park Drive, Armonk, New York 10504 (800) 541-6563; *The Illustrated Book of World Rankings.*

Organisation for Economic Co-operation and Development (OECD), 2 rue Andre-Pascal, 75 Paris 16, France (Telephone Number in U.S. (202) 785-6323); *Economic Outlook; The Footwear, Raw Hides and Skins, and Leather Industry in OECD Countries; Foreign Trade by Commodities; Main Economic Indicators - Historical Statistics; Maritime Transport; Meat Balances in OECD Member Countries;* and *OECD Economic Surveys: Turkey.*

St. Martin's Press, Inc., 175 Fifth Avenue, New York, New York 10010 (800) 221-7945; *The Statesman's Year-Book.*

Statistical Office of the United Nations, Publishing Service, New York, New York 10017 (800) 253-9646; *International Trade Statistics Yearbook;* and *Statistical Yearbook.*

United Nations Conference on Trade and Development, Central Statistical Service, Palais des Nations, Geneva, Switzerland (Telephone in U.S. (800) 253-9646); *UNCTAD Commodity Yearbook.*

The World Bank, 1818 H Street, NW, Washington, D.C. 20433 (202) 477-1234; *World Development Report;* and *World Development Indicators.*

TURKEY - FORESTRY AND FOREST PRODUCTS

Euromonitor International, Inc., 122 South Michigan Avenue, Suite 1200, Chicago, Illinois 60603 (800) 577-EURO; *European Marketing Data and Statistics.*

Europa Publications Limited, 18 Bedford Square, London, WC1B 3JN, England; *The Europa World Year Book.*

Food and Agricultural Organization of the United Nations (FAO) Via delle Terme di Caracalla, 00100 Rome, Italy (Telephone Number in U.S. (202) 653-2400); *The State of Food and Agriculture;* and *Yearbook of Forest Products.*

M.E. Sharpe, 80 Business Park Drive, Armonk, New York 10504 (800) 541-6563; *The Illustrated Book of World Rankings.*

Organisation for Economic Co-operation and Development (OECD), 2 rue Andre-Pascal, 75 Paris 16, France (Telephone Number in U.S. (202) 785-6323); *Foreign Trade by Commodities; Industrial Structure Statistics;* and *The Pulp and Paper Industry.*

St. Martin's Press, Inc., 175 Fifth Avenue, New York, New York 10010 (800) 221-7945; *The Statesman's Year-Book.*

Statistical Office of the United Nations, Publishing Service, New York, New York 10017 (800) 253-9646; *Statistical Yearbook;* and *Trends in Europe and North America: The Statistical Yearbook of the Economic Commission for Europe.*

United Nations Conference on Trade and Development, Central Statistical Service, Palais des Nations, Geneva, Switzerland (Telephone in U.S. (800) 253-9646); *UNCTAD Commodity Yearbook.*

United Nations Educational, Scientific and Cultural Organization (UNESCO), 7 Place de Fontenoy, F-75700 Paris, France (Telephone Number in U.S. (212) 963-5981); *Statistical Yearbook.*

The World Bank, 1818 H Street, NW, Washington, D.C. 20433 (202) 477-1234; *World Development Report.*

TURKEY - FRUIT PRODUCTION - See TURKEY - CROPS

Organisation for Economic Co-operation and Development (OECD), 2 rue Andre-Pascal, 75 Paris 16, France (Telephone Number in U.S. (202) 785-6323); *Economic Accounts for Agriculture;* and *Foreign Trade by Commodities.*

TURKEY - FURNITURE AND WOOD PRODUCTS - EXPORTS AND IMPORTS

Organisation for Economic Co-operation and Development (OECD), 2 rue Andre-Pascal, 75 Paris 16, France

(Telephone Number in U.S. (202) 785-6323); *Foreign Trade by Commodities; Industrial Structure Statistics;* and *OECD Economic Surveys: Turkey.*

TURKEY - GARLIC PRODUCTION - See TURKEY - CROPS

TURKEY - GAS PRODUCTION - See TURKEY - MINING AND MINERAL PRODUCTS

TURKEY - GENERAL INDUSTRIAL STATISTICS - See TURKEY - INDUSTRY

TURKEY - GENERAL MORTALITY - See TURKEY - MORTALITY

TURKEY - GEOGRAPHIC DATA

M.E. Sharpe, 80 Business Park Drive, Armonk, New York 10504 (800) 541-6563; *The Illustrated Book of World Rankings.*

TURKEY - GOATS - See TURKEY - LIVESTOCK AND POULTRY

TURKEY - GOLD HOLDINGS

International Monetary Fund, 700 Nineteenth Street, NW, Washington, D.C. 20431 (202) 623-7000; *International Financial Statistics.*

The World Bank, 1818 H Street, NW, Washington, D.C. 20433 (202) 477-1234; *World Development Indicators.*

TURKEY - GOLD PRODUCTION AND CONSUMPTION - See TURKEY - MINING AND MINERAL PRODUCTS

TURKEY - GOVERNMENT

Central Intelligence Agency, Washington, D.C. 20505 (703) 482-1100, www.cia.gov; *The World Factbook.*

Europa Publications Limited, 18 Bedford Square, London, WC1B 3JN, England; *The Europa World Year Book.*

International Monetary Fund, 700 Nineteenth Street, NW, Washington, D.C. 20431 (202) 623-7000; *Government Finance Statistics Yearbook;* and *International Financial Statistics.*

Organisation for Economic Co-operation and Development (OECD), 2 rue Andre-Pascal, 75 Paris 16, France (Telephone Number in U.S. (202) 785-6323); *Economic Outlook;* and *Revenue Statistics of OECD Member Countries.*

St. Martin's Press, Inc., 175 Fifth Avenue, New York, New York 10010 (800) 221-7945; *The Statesman's Year-Book.*

Statistical Office of the United Nations,

Publishing Service, New York, New York 10017 (800) 253-9646; *National Accounts Statistics;* and *Statistical Yearbook.*

The World Bank, 1818 H Street, NW, Washington, D.C. 20433 (202) 477-1234; *World Development Report;* and *World Development Indicators.*

TURKEY - GRAIN PRODUCTION - See TURKEY - CROPS

TURKEY - GRANTS

International Monetary Fund, 700 Nineteenth Street, NW, Washington, D.C. 20431 (202) 623-7000; *Government Finance Statistics Yearbook.*

Organisation for Economic Co-operation and Development (OECD), 2 rue Andre-Pascal, 75 Paris 16, France (Telephone Number in U.S. (202) 785-6323); *Geographical Distribution of Financial Flows to Developing Countries.*

TURKEY - GREEN PEPPER AND CHILIE PRODUCTION - See TURKEY - CROPS

TURKEY - GROSS DOMESTIC PRODUCT

The Economist Intelligence Unit, 111 West 57th Street, New York, New York 10019 (800) 938-4685; *The World Market Atlas;* and *Turkey Country Report.*

Euromonitor International, Inc., 122 South Michigan Avenue, Suite 1200, Chicago, Illinois 60603 (800) 577-EURO; *The World Economic Factbook.*

Europa Publications Limited, 18 Bedford Square, London, WC1B 3JN, England; *The Europa World Year Book.*

M.E. Sharpe, 80 Business Park Drive, Armonk, New York 10504 (800) 541-6563; *The Illustrated Book of World Rankings.*

Organisation for Economic Co-operation and Development (OECD), 2 rue Andre-Pascal, 75 Paris 16, France (Telephone Number in U.S. (202) 785-6323); *Economic Outlook; Geographical Distribution of Financial Flows to Developing Countries;* and *Revenue Statistics of OECD Member Countries.*

Statistical Office of the United Nations, Publishing Service, New York, New York 10017 (800) 253-9646; *Human Development Report; National Accounts Statistics; Statistical Yearbook;* and *Trends in Europe and North America: The Statistical Yearbook of the Economic Commission for Europe.*

The World Bank, 1818 H Street, NW, Washington, D.C. 20433 (202) 477-1234; *World Development Report;* and *World Development Indicators.*

TURKEY - GROSS NATIONAL PRODUCT

Europa Publications Limited, 18 Bedford Square, London, WC1B 3JN, England; *The Europa World Year Book.*

Organisation for Economic Co-operation and Development (OECD), 2 rue Andre-Pascal, 75 Paris 16, France (Telephone Number in U.S. (202) 785-6323); *Economic Outlook;* and *Geographical Distribution of Financial Flows to Developing Countries.*

St. Martin's Press, Inc., 175 Fifth Avenue, New York, New York 10010 (800) 221-7945; *The Statesman's Year-Book.*

U.S. Arms Control and Disarmament Agency, 320 Twenty-first Street, NW, Washington, D.C. 20451 (202) 647-8677; *World Military Expenditures and Arms Transfers.*

The World Bank, 1818 H Street, NW, Washington, D.C. 20433 (202) 477-1234; *The World Bank Atlas; World Development Report;* and *World Development Indicators.*

TURKEY - GROUNDNUTS PRODUCTION - See TURKEY - CROPS

TURKEY - HAZELNUT PRODUCTION - See TURKEY - CROPS

TURKEY - HEALTH

Euromonitor International, Inc., 122 South Michigan Avenue, Suite 1200, Chicago, Illinois 60603 (800) 577-EURO; *World Marketing Data and Statistics.*

M.E. Sharpe, 80 Business Park Drive, Armonk, New York 10504 (800) 541-6563; *The Illustrated Book of World Rankings.*

Organisation for Economic Co-operation and Development (OECD), 2 rue Andre-Pascal, 75 Paris 16, France (Telephone Number in U.S. (202) 785-6323); *OECD Health Systems: Facts and Trends.*

St. Martin's Press, Inc., 175 Fifth Avenue, New York, New York 10010 (800) 221-7945; *The Statesman's Year-Book.*

Statistical Office of the United Nations, Publishing Service, New York, New York 10017 (800) 253-9646; *Human Development Report; Statistical Yearbook;* and *Trends in Europe and North America: The Statistical Yearbook of the Economic Commission for Europe.*

United Nations Children's Fund (UNICEF), 3 United Nations Plaza, New York, New York 10017 (800) 253-9646; *State of the World's Children.*

The World Bank, 1818 H Street, NW,

Washington, D.C. 20433 (202) 477-1234; *World Development Report.*

World Health Organization, Office of Publications, 20 Avenue Appia, CH-1211 Geneva 27, Switzerland (Telephone Number in U.S. (518) 436-9686); *World Health Statistics Annual.*

TURKEY - HEALTH EXPENDITURES

International Monetary Fund, 700 Nineteenth Street, NW, Washington, D.C. 20431 (202) 623-7000; *Government Finance Statistics Yearbook.*

TURKEY - HEMP FIBRE PRODUCTION - See TURKEY - TEXTILE INDUSTRY

TURKEY - HIDE PRODUCTION

Food and Agricultural Organization of the United Nations (FAO), Via delle Terme di Caracalla, 00100 Rome, Italy (Telephone Number in U.S. (202) 653-2400); *Production Yearbook.*

Organisation for Economic Co-operation and Development (OECD), 2 rue Andre-Pascal, 75 Paris 16, France (Telephone Number in U.S. (202) 785-6323); *The Footwear, Raw Hides and Skins, and Leather Industry in OECD Countries;* and *Foreign Trade by Commodities.*

TURKEY - HIGHWAYS

Central Intelligence Agency, Washington, D.C. 20505 (703) 482-1100, www.cia.gov; *The World Factbook.*

International Road Federation, 2600 Virginia Avenue, NW, Washington, D.C. 20037 (202) 338-4641; *World Road Statistics.*

St. Martin's Press, Inc., 175 Fifth Avenue, New York, New York 10010 (800) 221-7945; *The Statesman's Year-Book.*

Statistical Office of the United Nations, Publishing Service, New York, New York 10017 (800) 253-9646; *Annual Bulletin of Transport Statistics for Europe;* and *Trends in Europe and North America: The Statistical Yearbook of the Economic Commission for Europe.*

TURKEY - HOME FINANCE

Organisation for Economic Co-operation and Development (OECD), 2 rue Andre-Pascal, 75 Paris 16, France (Telephone Number in U.S. (202) 785-6323); *Main Economic Indicators - Historical Statistics.*

TURKEY - HONEY PRODUCTION

Commodity Research Bureau, Inc., 30

South Wacker Drive, Chicago, Illinois 60606 (312) 454-1801; *Commodity Year Book.*

TURKEY - HORSES - See TURKEY - LIVESTOCK AND POULTRY

TURKEY - HOURS OF WORK - See TURKEY - EMPLOYMENT

TURKEY - HOUSING AND HOUSING UNITS

Euromonitor International, Inc., 122 South Michigan Avenue, Suite 1200, Chicago, Illinois 60603 (800) 577-EURO; *World Marketing Data and Statistics.*

M.E. Sharpe, 80 Business Park Drive, Armonk, New York 10504 (800) 541-6563; *The Illustrated Book of World Rankings.*

Statistical Office of the United Nations, Publishing Service, New York, New York 10017 (800) 253-9646; *Trends in Europe and North America: The Statistical Yearbook of the Economic Commission for Europe.*

TURKEY - HOUSING CONSTRUCTION - See TURKEY - CONSTRUCTION INDUSTRY

TURKEY - HOUSING EXPENDITURES

International Monetary Fund, 700 Nineteenth Street, NW, Washington, D.C. 20431 (202) 623-7000; *Government Finance Statistics Yearbook.*

TURKEY - HYDROCHLORIC ACID PRODUCTION

Statistical Office of the United Nations, Publishing Service, New York, New York 10017 (800) 253-9646; *Statistical Yearbook.*

TURKEY - ILLITERATE POPULATION

Central Intelligence Agency, Washington, D.C. 20505 (703) 482-1100, www.cia.gov; *The World Factbook.*

The Economist Intelligence Unit, 111 West 57th Street, New York, New York 10019 (800) 938-4685; *The World Market Atlas.*

Euromonitor International, Inc., 122 South Michigan Avenue, Suite 1200, Chicago, Illinois 60603 (800) 577-EURO; *The World Economic Factbook.*

Statistical Office of the United Nations, Publishing Service, New York, New York 10017 (800) 253-9646; *Human Development Report.*

United Nations Educational, Scientific and Cultural Organization (UNESCO), 7 Place de Fontenoy, F-75700 Paris, France (Telephone Number in U.S. (212) 963-5981); *Statistical Yearbook.*

TURKEY - IMPORTS

Central Intelligence Agency, Washington, D.C. 20505 (703) 482-1100, www.cia.gov; *The World Factbook.*

The Economist Intelligence Unit, 111 West 57th Street, New York, New York 10019 (800) 938-4685; *The World Market Atlas;* and *Turkey Country Report.*

Euromonitor International, Inc., 122 South Michigan Avenue, Suite 1200, Chicago, Illinois 60603 (800) 577-EURO; *The World Economic Factbook.*

Europa Publications Limited, 18 Bedford Square, London, WC1B 3JN, England; *The Europa World Year Book.*

Food and Agricultural Organization of the United Nations (FAO) Via delle Terme di Caracalla, 00100 Rome, Italy (Telephone Number in U.S. (202) 653-2400); *The State of Food and Agriculture.*

International Monetary Fund, 700 Nineteenth Street, NW, Washington, D.C. 20431 (202) 623-7000; *Direction of Trade Statistics; Government Finance Statistics Yearbook;* and *International Financial Statistics.*

Organisation for Economic Co-operation and Development (OECD), 2 rue Andre-Pascal, 75 Paris 16, France (Telephone Number in U.S. (202) 785-6323); *Economic Outlook; The Footwear, Raw Hides and Skins, and Leather Industry in OECD Countries; Industrial Structure Statistics; The Iron and Steel Industry; Milk, Milk Products, and Egg Balances in OECD Member Countries; OECD Economic Surveys: Turkey; The Pulp and Paper Industry;* and *Review of Fisheries in OECD Member Countries.*

St. Martin's Press, Inc., 175 Fifth Avenue, New York, New York 10010 (800) 221-7945; *The Statesman's Year-Book.*

Statistical Office of the United Nations, Publishing Service, New York, New York 10017 (800) 253-9646; *Trends in Europe and North America: The Statistical Yearbook of the Economic Commission for Europe.*

United Nations Conference on Trade and Development (UNCTAD), New York, New York 10017 (800) 253-9646; *Handbook of International Trade and Development.*

The World Bank, 1818 H Street, NW, Washington, D.C. 20433 (202) 477-1234; *World Development Report;* and *World Development Indicators.*

TURKEY - INCOME TAXES - See TURKEY - TAXATION

TURKEY - INDUSTRIAL METALS PRODUCTION - See TURKEY - MINING AND MINERAL PRODUCTS

TURKEY - INDUSTRY

Central Intelligence Agency, Washington, D.C. 20505 (703) 482-1100, www.cia.gov; *The World Factbook.*

The Economist Intelligence Unit, 111 West 57th Street, New York, New York 10019 (800) 938-4685; *Turkey Country Report.*

Euromonitor International, Inc., 122 South Michigan Avenue, Suite 1200, Chicago, Illinois 60603 (800) 577-EURO; *The World Economic Factbook;* and *World Marketing Data and Statistics.*

Europa Publications Limited, 18 Bedford Square, London, WC1B 3JN, England; *The Europa World Year Book.*

International Labour Office, I.L.O. Publications, 1828 L Street, NW, Suite 801, Washington, D.C. 20036 (301) 638-3152; *Yearbook of Labour Statistics.*

M.E. Sharpe, 80 Business Park Drive, Armonk, New York 10504 (800) 541-6563; *The Illustrated Book of World Rankings.*

Organisation for Economic Co-operation and Development (OECD), 2 rue Andre-Pascal, 75 Paris 16, France (Telephone Number in U.S. (202) 785-6323); *Economic Outlook, Industrial Structure Statistics* and *OECD Environmental Data.*

St. Martin's Press, Inc., 175 Fifth Avenue, New York, New York 10010 (800) 221-7945; *The Statesman's Year-Book.*

Statistical Office of the United Nations, Publishing Service, New York, New York 10017 (800) 253-9646; *Industrial Commodity Statistics Yearbook, Statistical Yearbook;* and *Trends in Europe and North America: The Statistical Yearbook of the Economic Commission for Europe.*

The World Bank, 1818 H Street, NW, Washington, D.C. 20433 (202) 477-1234; *World Development Indicators.*

World Intellectual Property Organization, 34 Chemin des Colombettes, CH-1211 Geneva 20. Switzerland; *Industrial Property Statistics.*

TURKEY - INFANT AND MATERNAL MORTALITY - See TURKEY - MORTALITY

TURKEY - INTEREST RATES

Organisation for Economic Co-operation and Development (OECD), 2 rue Andre-Pascal, 75 Paris 16, France (Telephone Number in U.S. (202) 785-6323); *Economic Outlook; Financial Market Trends;* and *OECD Financial Statistics.*

TURKEY - INTERNAL TRADE

Statistical Office of the United Nations, Publishing Service, New York, New York 10017 (800) 253-9646; *Statistical Yearbook.*

TURKEY - INTERNATIONAL FINANCE

Organisation for Economic Co-operation and Development (OECD), 2 rue Andre-Pascal, 75 Paris 16, France (Telephone Number in U.S. (202) 785-6323); *Economic Outlook;* and *Financial Market Trends.*

TURKEY - INTERNATIONAL LIQUIDITY

International Monetary Fund, 700 Nineteenth Street, NW, Washington, D.C. 20431 (202) 623-7000; *International Financial Statistics.*

Organisation for Economic Co-operation and Development (OECD), 2 rue Andre-Pascal, 75 Paris 16, France (Telephone Number in U.S. (202) 785-6323); *Economic Outlook;* and *Financial Market Trends.*

TURKEY - INTERNATIONAL RESERVES EXCLUDING GOLD

Statistical Office of the United Nations, Publishing Service, New York, New York 10017 (800) 253-9646; *Statistical Yearbook.*

The World Bank, 1818 H Street, NW, Washington, D.C. 20433 (202) 477-1234; *World Development Indicators.*

TURKEY - INTERNATIONAL STATISTICS

Organisation for Economic Co-operation and Development (OECD), 2 rue Andre-Pascal, 75 Paris 16, France (Telephone Number in U.S. (202) 785-6323); *Financial Market Trends;* and *Tourism Policy and International Tourism in OECD Member Countries.*

TURKEY - INVESTMENTS

International Monetary Fund, 700 Nineteenth Street, NW, Washington, D.C. 20431 (202) 623-7000; *International Financial Statistics.*

Organisation for Economic Co-operation and Development (OECD), 2 rue Andre-Pascal, 75 Paris 16, France (Telephone Number in U.S. (202) 785-6323); *Economic Outlook; Financial Market Trends; Industrial Structure Statistics; The Iron and Steel Industry;* and *Textile Industry in OECD Countries.*

TURKEY - IRON ORE PRODUCTION AND CONSUMPTION - See TURKEY - MINING AND MINERAL PRODUCTS

TURKEY - LABOR

Central Intelligence Agency, Washington, D.C. 20505 (703) 482-1100, www.cia.gov; *The World Factbook.*

Euromonitor International, Inc., 122 South Michigan Avenue, Suite 1200, Chicago, Illinois 60603 (800) 577-EURO; *World Marketing Data and Statistics.*

Europa Publications Limited, 18 Bedford Square, London, WC1B 3JN, England; *The Europa World Year Book.*

Food and Agricultural Organization of the United Nations (FAO) Via delle Terme di Caracalla, 00100 Rome, Italy (Telephone Number in U.S. (202) 653-2400); *The State of Food and Agriculture.*

International Labour Office, I.L.O. Publications, 1828 L Street, NW, Suite 801, Washington, D.C. 20036 (301) 638-3152; *Yearbook of Labour Statistics.*

M.E. Sharpe, 80 Business Park Drive, Armonk, New York 10504 (800) 541-6563; *The Illustrated Book of World Rankings.*

Organisation for Economic Co-operation and Development (OECD), 2 rue Andre-Pascal, 75 Paris 16, France (Telephone Number in U.S. (202) 785-6323); *Economic Outlook; The Iron and Steel Industry; Maritime Transport; OECD Economic Surveys: Turkey; OECD Employment Outlook;* and *Textile Industry in OECD Countries.*

St. Martin's Press, Inc., 175 Fifth Avenue, New York, New York 10010 (800) 221-7945; *The Statesman's Year-Book.*

Statistical Office of the United Nations, Publishing Service, New York, New York 10017 (800) 253-9646; *The World Bank Atlas;* and *Human Development Report.*

The World Bank, 1818 H Street, NW, Washington, D.C. 20433 (202) 477-1234; *World Development Report;* and *World Development Indicators.*

TURKEY - LAND USE

Central Intelligence Agency, Washington, D.C. 20505 (703) 482-1100, www.cia.gov; *The World Factbook.*

Euromonitor International, Inc., 122 South Michigan Avenue, Suite 1200, Chicago, Illinois 60603 (800) 577-EURO; *European Marketing Data and Statistics.*

Food and Agricultural Organization of the United Nations (FAO), Via delle Terme di Caracalla, 00100 Rome, Italy (Telephone Number in U.S. (202) 653-2400); *Production Yearbook.*

The World Bank, 1818 H Street, NW, Washington, D.C. 20433 (202) 477-1234; *World Development Report.*

TURKEY - LEAD AND LEAD ORE - See TURKEY - MINING AND MINERAL PRODUCTS

TURKEY - LEATHER AND FOOTWEAR EXPORTS AND IMPORTS

Organisation for Economic Co-operation and Development (OECD), 2 rue Andre-Pascal, 75 Paris 16, France (Telephone Number in U.S. (202) 785-6323); *The Footwear, Raw Hides and Skins, and Leather Industry in OECD Countries.*

TURKEY - LIBRARIES

Euromonitor International, Inc., 122 South Michigan Avenue, Suite 1200, Chicago, Illinois 60603 (800) 577-EURO; *European Marketing Data and Statistics.*

M.E. Sharpe, 80 Business Park Drive, Armonk, New York 10504 (800) 541-6563; *The Illustrated Book of World Rankings.*

Statistical Office of the United Nations, Publishing Service, New York, New York 10017 (800) 253-9646; *Trends in Europe and North America: The Statistical Yearbook of the Economic Commission for Europe.*

United Nations Educational, Scientific and Cultural Organization (UNESCO), 7 Place de Fontenoy, F-75700 Paris, France (Telephone Number in U.S. (212) 963-5981); *Statistical Yearbook.*

TURKEY - LIFE EXPECTANCY

Central Intelligence Agency, Washington, D.C. 20505 (703) 482-1100, www.cia.gov; *The World Factbook.*

Euromonitor International, Inc., 122 South Michigan Avenue, Suite 1200, Chicago, Illinois 60603 (800) 577-EURO; *The World Economic Factbook.*

Organisation for Economic Co-operation and Development (OECD), 2 rue Andre-Pascal, 75 Paris 16, France (Telephone Number in U.S. (202) 785-6323); *Economic Outlook.*

St. Martin's Press, Inc., 175 Fifth Avenue, New York, New York 10010 (800) 221-7945; *The Statesman's Year-Book.*

Statistical Office of the United Nations, Publishing Service, New York, New York 10017 (800) 253-9646; *Human Development Report; Trends in Europe and North America: The Statistical Yearbook of the Economic Commission for Europe;* and *World Statistics Pocketbook.*

The World Bank, 1818 H Street, NW, Washington, D.C. 20433 (202) 477-1234; *The World Bank Atlas;* and *World Development Report.*

TURKEY - LIGNITE PRODUCTION - See TURKEY - MINING AND MINERAL PRODUCTS

TURKEY - LITERACY RATE

Euromonitor International, Inc., 122 South Michigan Avenue, Suite 1200, Chicago, Illinois 60603 (800) 577-EURO; *World Marketing Data and Statistics.*

TURKEY - LIVESTOCK AND POULTRY

Commodity Research Bureau, Inc., 30 South Wacker Drive, Chicago, Illinois 60606 (312) 454-1801; *Commodity Year Book.*

Euromonitor International, Inc., 122 South Michigan Avenue, Suite 1200, Chicago, Illinois 60603 (800) 577-EURO; *European Marketing Data and Statistics.*

Europa Publications Limited, 18 Bedford Square, London, WC1B 3JN, England; *The Europa World Year Book.*

Food and Agricultural Organization of the United Nations (FAO), Via delle Terme di Caracalla, 00100 Rome, Italy (Telephone Number in U.S. (202) 653-2400); *Production Yearbook;* and *The State of Food and Agriculture.*

M.E. Sharpe, 80 Business Park Drive, Armonk, New York 10504 (800) 541-6563; *The Illustrated Book of World Rankings.*

Organisation for Economic Co-operation and Development (OECD), 2 rue Andre-Pascal, 75 Paris 16, France (Telephone Number in U.S. (202) 785-6323); *Economic Accounts for Agriculture;* and *Meat Balances in OECD Member Countries.*

St. Martin's Press, Inc., 175 Fifth Avenue, New York, New York 10010 (800) 221-7945; *The Statesman's Year-Book.*

Statistical Office of the United Nations, Publishing Service, New York, New York 10017 (800) 253-9646; *Statistical Yearbook.*

United Nations Conference on Trade and Development, Central Statistical Service, Palais des Nations, Geneva, Switzerland (Telephone in U.S. (800) 253-9646); *UNCTAD Commodity Yearbook.*

TURKEY - LIVING LEVELS - See TURKEY - LIFE EXPECTANCY

TURKEY - MAIL - NUMBER OF PIECES SENT OR RECEIVED

Statistical Office of the United Nations,

Publishing Service, New York, New York 10017 (800) 253-9646; *Statistical Yearbook.*

TURKEY - MANGANESE ORE PRODUCTION AND CONSUMPTION - See TURKEY - MINING AND MINERAL PRODUCTS

TURKEY - MANUFACTURING

American Automobile Manufacturers Association, 1401 H Street, NW, Suite 900, Washington, D.C. 20005 (202) 326-5500; *World Motor Vehicle Data.*

Organisation for Economic Co-operation and Development (OECD), 2 rue Andre-Pascal, 75 Paris 16, France (Telephone Number in U.S. (202) 785-6323); *Foreign Trade by Commodities; Industrial Structure Statistics;* and *OECD Economic Surveys: Turkey.*

Statistical Office of the United Nations, Publishing Service, New York, New York 10017 (800) 253-9646; *Statistical Yearbook.*

The World Bank, 1818 H Street, NW, Washington, D.C. 20433 (202) 477-1234; *World Development Indicators.*

TURKEY - MARRIAGE RATES

M.E. Sharpe, 80 Business Park Drive, Armonk, New York 10504 (800) 541-6563; *The Illustrated Book of World Rankings.*

Statistical Office of the United Nations, Publishing Service, New York, New York 10017 (800) 253-9646; *Demographic Yearbook;* and *Trends in Europe and North America: The Statistical Yearbook of the Economic Commission for Europe.*

TURKEY - MEAT PRODUCTION - See TURKEY - LIVESTOCK AND POULTRY

TURKEY - MERCHANT SHIPPING

Europa Publications Limited, 18 Bedford Square, London, WC1B 3JN, England; *The Europa World Year Book.*

Lloyd's Register of Shipping, 17 Battery Place, New York, New York 10004 (212) 425-8050; *Register of Ships.*

Organisation for Economic Co-operation and Development (OECD), 2 rue Andre-Pascal, 75 Paris 16, France (Telephone Number in U.S. (202) 785-6323); *Maritime Transport.*

St. Martin's Press, Inc., 175 Fifth Avenue, New York, New York 10010 (800) 221-7945; *The Statesman's Year-Book.*

Statistical Office of the United Nations, Publishing Service, New York, New York 10017 (800) 253-9646; *Statistical Yearbook.*

U.S. Department of Transportation,

Maritime Administration, 400 Seventh Street, SW, Washington, D.C. 20590 (202) 366-5807, www.marad.dot.gov; *A Statistical Analysis of the World's Merchant Fleets.*

TURKEY - MERCURY PRODUCTION AND CONSUMPTION - See TURKEY - MINING AND MINERAL PRODUCTS

TURKEY - MILITARY

Central Intelligence Agency, Washington, D.C. 20505 (703) 482-1100, www.cia.gov; *The World Factbook.*

Euromonitor International, Inc., 122 South Michigan Avenue, Suite 1200, Chicago, Illinois 60603 (800) 577-EURO; *World Marketing Data and Statistics.*
The International Institute for Strategic Studies, 23 Tavistock Street, London WC2E 7NQ, England 44 171 3797676; *The Military Balance.*

International Monetary Fund, 700 Nineteenth Street, NW, Washington, D.C. 20431 (202) 623-7000; *Government Finance Statistics Yearbook.*

St. Martin's Press, Inc., 175 Fifth Avenue, New York, New York 10010 (800) 221-7945; *The Statesman's Year-Book.*

Statistical Office of the United Nations, Publishing Service, New York, New York 10017 (800) 253-9646; *Human Development Report.*

U.S. Arms Control and Disarmament Agency, 320 Twenty-first Street, NW, Washington, D.C. 20451 (202) 647-8677; *World Military Expenditures and Arms Transfers.*

TURKEY - MILK PRODUCTION - See TURKEY - DAIRY PRODUCTS

TURKEY - MILLET PRODUCTION

Food and Agricultural Organization of the United Nations (FAO), Via delle Terme di Caracalla, 00100 Rome, Italy (Telephone Number in U.S. (202) 653-2400); *Production Yearbook.*

TURKEY - MINING AND MINERAL PRODUCTS

Commodity Research Bureau, Inc., 30 South Wacker Drive, Suite 1810, Chicago, Illinois 60606 (800) 621-5271 Inc., 30 South Wacker Drive, Chicago, Illinois 60606 (312) 454-1801; *Commodity Year Book.*

Europa Publications Limited, 18 Bedford Square, London, WC1B 3JN, England; *The Europa World Year Book.*

M.E. Sharpe, 80 Business Park Drive, Armonk, New York 10504 (800) 541-6563;

The Illustrated Book of World Rankings.

Organisation for Economic Co-operation and Development (OECD), 2 rue Andre-Pascal, 75 Paris 16, France (Telephone Number in U.S. (202) 785-6323); *Coal Information; Energy Statistics of OECD Countries; Foreign Trade by Commodities; Industrial Structure Statistics; The Iron and Steel Industry; Main Economic Indicators - Historical Statistics; The Non-Ferrous Metals Industry;* and *OECD Economic Surveys: Turkey.*

Penn Well Publishing Company, 1421 South Sheridan Road, P.O. Box 1260, Tulsa, Oklahoma 74101 (800) 752-9764; *International Energy Statistics Sourcebook.*

St. Martin's Press, Inc., 175 Fifth Avenue, New York, New York 10010 (800) 221-7945; *The Statesman's Year-Book.*

Statistical Office of the United Nations, Publishing Service, New York, New York 10017 (800) 253-9646; *Statistical Yearbook.*

United Nations Conference on Trade and Development, Central Statistical Service, Palais des Nations, Geneva, Switzerland (Telephone in U.S. (800) 253-9646); *UNCTAD Commodity Yearbook.*

TURKEY - MONEY AND CREDIT

Organisation for Economic Cooperation and Development (OECD), 2 rue Andre-Pascal, 75 Paris 16, France (Telephone Number in U.S. (202) 785-6323); *OECD Economic Surveys: Turkey.*

TURKEY - MONEY EXCHANGE RATE - See TURKEY - EXCHANGE RATE

TURKEY - MONEY RATES - MARKET

Organisation for Economic Co-operation and Development (OECD), 2 rue Andre-Pascal, 75 Paris 16, France (Telephone Number in U.S. (202) 785-6323); *Economic Outlook;* and *Financial Market Trends.*

TURKEY - MONEY RESERVES

Organisation for Economic Co-operation and Development (OECD), 2 rue Andre-Pascal, 75 Paris 16, France (Telephone Number in U.S. (202) 785-6323); *Economic Outlook;* and *Financial Market Trends.*

TURKEY - MONEY SUPPLY

The Economist Intelligence Unit, 111 West 57th Street, New York, New York 10019 (800) 938-4685; *Turkey Country Report.*

Europa Publications Limited, 18 Bedford Square, London, WC1B 3JN,

England; *The Europa World Year Book.*

International Monetary Fund, 700 Nineteenth Street, NW, Washington, D.C. 20431 (202) 623-7000; *International Financial Statistics.*

Organisation for Economic Co-operation and Development (OECD), 2 rue Andre-Pascal, 75 Paris 16, France (Telephone Number in U.S. (202) 785-6323); *Economic Outlook.*

Statistical Office of the United Nations, Publishing Service, New York, New York 10017 (800) 253-9646; *Statistical Yearbook.*

The World Bank, 1818 H Street, NW, Washington, D.C. 20433 (202) 477-1234; *World Development Indicators.*

TURKEY - MORTALITY

Central Intelligence Agency, Washington, D.C. 20505 (703) 482-1100, www.cia.gov; *The World Factbook.*

Euromonitor International, Inc., 122 South Michigan Avenue, Suite 1200, Chicago, Illinois 60603 (800) 577-EURO; *The World Economic Factbook.*

Europa Publications Limited, 18 Bedford Square, London, WC1B 3JN, England; *The Europa World Year Book.*

St. Martin's Press, Inc., 175 Fifth Avenue, New York, New York 10010 (800) 221-7945; *The Statesman's Year-Book.*

Statistical Office of the United Nations, Publishing Service, New York, New York 10017 (800) 253-9646; *Demographic Yearbook; Human Development Report; Statistical Yearbook; Trends in Europe and North America: The Statistical Yearbook of the Economic Commission for Europe;* and *World Statistics Pocketbook.*

United Nations Children's Fund (UNICEF), 3 United Nations Plaza, New York, New York 10017 (800) 253-9646; *State of the World's Children.*

The World Bank, 1818 H Street, NW, Washington, D.C. 20433 (202) 477-1234; *The World Bank Atlas; World Development Report;* and *World Development Indicators.*

World Health Organization, Office of Publications, 20 Avenue Appia, CH-1211 Geneva 27, Switzerland (Telephone Number in U.S. (518) 436-9686); *World Health Statistics Annual.*

TURKEY - MOTION PICTURES

United Nations Educational, Scientific and Cultural Organization (UNESCO), 7 Place de Fontenoy, F-75700 Paris, France (Telephone Number in U.S. (212) 963-

5981); *Statistical Yearbook.*

TURKEY - MOTOR VEHICLE ASSEMBLY

Statistical Office of the United Nations, Publishing Service, New York, New York 10017 (800) 253-9646; *Statistical Yearbook.*

TURKEY - MOTOR VEHICLE PRODUCTION

American Automobile Manufacturers Association, 1401 H Street, NW, Suite 900, Washington, D.C. 20005 (202) 326-5500; *World Motor Vehicle Data.*

Organisation for Economic Co-operation and Development (OECD), 2 rue Andre-Pascal, 75 Paris 16, France (Telephone Number in U.S. (202) 785-6323); *Foreign Trade by Commodities.*

TURKEY - MOTOR VEHICLE TAXES - See TURKEY - TAXATION

TURKEY - MOTOR VEHICLES IN USE

American Automobile Manufacturers Association, 1401 H Street, NW, Suite 900, Washington, D.C. 20005 (202) 326-5500; *World Motor Vehicle Data.*

Europa Publications Limited, 18 Bedford Square, London, WC1B 3JN, England; *The Europa World Year Book.*

International Road Federation, 2600 Virginia Avenue, NW, Washington, D.C. 20037 (202) 338-4641; *World Road Statistics.*

Statistical Office of the United Nations, Publishing Service, New York, New York 10017 (800) 253-9646; *Statistical Yearbook.*

TURKEY - MULES - See TURKEY - LIVESTOCK AND POULTRY

TURKEY - MUSEUMS

Euromonitor International, Inc., 122 South Michigan Avenue, Suite 1200, Chicago, Illinois 60603 (800) 577-EURO; *European Marketing Data and Statistics.*

M.E. Sharpe, 80 Business Park Drive, Armonk, New York 10504 (800) 541-6563; *The Illustrated Book of World Rankings.*

United Nations Educational, Scientific and Cultural Organization (UNESCO), 7 Place de Fontenoy, F-75700 Paris, France (Telephone Number in U.S. (212) 963-5981); *Statistical Yearbook.*

TURKEY - NATALITY - See TURKEY - BIRTH RATES

TURKEY - NATIONAL ACCOUNTS

Europa Publications Limited, 18

Bedford Square, London, WC1B 3JN, England; *The Europa World Year Book*.

International Monetary Fund, 700 Nineteenth Street, NW, Washington, D.C. 20431 (202) 623-7000; *International Financial Statistics*.

Organisation for Economic Co-operation and Development (OECD), 2 rue Andre-Pascal, 75 Paris 16, France (Telephone Number in U.S. (202) 785-6323); *Economic Outlook*.

Statistical Office of the United Nations, Publishing Service, New York, New York 10017 (800) 253-9646; *National Accounts Statistics;* and *Statistical Yearbook*.

TURKEY - NATIONAL INCOME

M.E. Sharpe, 80 Business Park Drive, Armonk, New York 10504 (800) 541-6563; *The Illustrated Book of World Rankings*.

Organisation for Economic Co-operation and Development (OECD), 2 rue Andre-Pascal, 75 Paris 16, France (Telephone Number in U.S. (202) 785-6323); *Economic Outlook*.

Statistical Office of the United Nations, Publishing Service, New York, New York 10017 (800) 253-9646; *National Accounts Statistics;* and *Statistical Yearbook*.

TURKEY - NATIONAL PRODUCT

M.E. Sharpe, 80 Business Park Drive, Armonk, New York 10504 (800) 541-6563; *The Illustrated Book of World Rankings*.

Organisation for Economic Co-operation and Development (OECD), 2 rue Andre-Pascal, 75 Paris 16, France (Telephone Number in U.S. (202) 785-6323); *Economic Outlook*.

Statistical Office of the United Nations, Publishing Service, New York, New York 10017 (800) 253-9646; *Statistical Yearbook*.

TURKEY - NATURAL GAS PRODUCTION - See TURKEY - MINING AND MINERAL PRODUCTS

TURKEY - NEWSPAPER PRODUCTION - See TURKEY - FORESTRY AND FOREST PRODUCTS

TURKEY - NEWSPRINT - See TURKEY - FORESTRY AND FOREST PRODUCTS

TURKEY - NICKEL PRODUCTION AND CONSUMPTION - See TURKEY - MINING AND MINERAL PRODUCTS

TURKEY - NITRIC ACID PRODUCTION - See TURKEY - MINING AND MINERAL PRODUCTS

TURKEY - OATS PRODUCTION - See TURKEY - CROPS

TURKEY - OCCUPATIONS - See TURKEY - LABOR

TURKEY - OIL PRODUCING CROPS

Organisation for Economic Co-operation and Development (OECD), 2 rue Andre-Pascal, 75 Paris 16, France (Telephone Number in U.S. (202) 785-6323); *Foreign Trade by Commodities*.

TURKEY - ONION PRODUCTION - See TURKEY - CROPS

TURKEY - ORANGES PRODUCTION - See TURKEY - CROPS

TURKEY - PAPER - See TURKEY - FORESTRY AND FOREST PRODUCTS

TURKEY - PATENTS, TRADEMARKS AND SERVICE MARKS

Statistical Office of the United Nations, Publishing Service, New York, New York 10017 (800) 253-9646; *Statistical Yearbook*.

World Intellectual Property Organization, 34 Chemin des Colombettes, CH-1211 Geneva 20. Switzerland; *Industrial Property Statistics*.

TURKEY - PEANUT PRODUCTION - See TURKEY - CROPS

TURKEY - PERIODICALS

United Nations Educational, Scientific and Cultural Organization (UNESCO), 7 Place de Fontenoy, F-75700 Paris, France (Telephone Number in U.S. (212) 963-5981); *Statistical Yearbook*.

TURKEY - PESTICIDE USE

Food and Agricultural Organization of the United Nations (FAO) Via delle Terme di Caracalla, 00100 Rome, Italy (Telephone Number in U.S. (202) 653-2400); *The State of Food and Agriculture*.

TURKEY - PETROLEUM INDUSTRY

Euromonitor International, Inc., 122 South Michigan Avenue, Suite 1200, Chicago, Illinois 60603 (800) 577-EURO; *European Marketing Data and Statistics*.

Food and Agricultural Organization of the United Nations (FAO) Via delle Terme di Caracalla, 00100 Rome, Italy (Telephone Number in U.S. (202) 653-2400); *The State of Food and Agriculture*.

M.E. Sharpe, 80 Business Park Drive, Armonk, New York 10504 (800) 541-6563; *The Illustrated Book of World Rankings*.

Organisation for Economic Co-operation and Development (OECD), 2 rue Andre-Pascal, 75 Paris 16, France (Telephone Number in U.S. (202) 785-6323); *Energy Statistics of OECD Countries; Foreign Trade by Commodities;* and *Oil and Gas Information*.

Penn Well Publishing Company, 1421 South Sheridan Road, P.O. Box 1260, Tulsa, Oklahoma 74101 (800) 752-9764; *International Energy Statistics Sourcebook*.

St. Martin's Press, Inc., 175 Fifth Avenue, New York, New York 10010 (800) 221-7945; *The Statesman's Year-Book*.

Statistical Office of the United Nations, Publishing Service, New York, New York 10017 (800) 253-9646; *Statistical Yearbook;* and *Trends in Europe and North America: The Statistical Yearbook of the Economic Commission for Europe*.

United Nations Conference on Trade and Development, Central Statistical Service, Palais des Nations, Geneva, Switzerland (Telephone in U.S. (800) 253-9646); *UNCTAD Commodity Yearbook*.

TURKEY - PIG-IRON AND FERRO-ALLOY PRODUCTION - See TURKEY - MINING AND MINERAL PRODUCTS

TURKEY - PIGS - See TURKEY - LIVESTOCK AND POULTRY

TURKEY - PIPELINES FOR OIL AND PETROLEUM PRODUCTS

Statistical Office of the United Nations, Publishing Service, New York, New York 10017 (800) 253-9646; *Annual Bulletin of Transport Statistics for Europe*.

TURKEY - PISTACHIO PRODUCTION - See TURKEY - CROPS

TURKEY - PLASTIC AND RESIN PRODUCTION

Organisation for Economic Co-operation and Development (OECD), 2 rue Andre-Pascal, 75 Paris 16, France (Telephone Number in U.S. (202) 785-6323); *Foreign Trade by Commodities*.

TURKEY - POPULATION

Central Intelligence Agency, Washington, D.C. 20505 (703) 482-1100, www.cia.gov; *The World Factbook*.

The Economist Intelligence Unit, 111 West 57th Street, New York, New York 10019 (800) 938-4685; *The World Market Atlas;* and *Turkey Country Report*.

Euromonitor International, Inc., 122 South Michigan Avenue, Suite 1200,

Chicago, Illinois 60603 (800) 577-EURO; *European Marketing Data and Statistics;* and *The World Economic Factbook.*

Europa Publications Limited, 18 Bedford Square, London, WC1B 3JN, England; *The Europa World Year Book.*

Food and Agricultural Organization of the United Nations (FAO), Via delle Terme di Caracalla, 00100 Rome, Italy (Telephone Number in U.S. (202) 653-2400); *Production Yearbook.*

International Labour Office, I.L.O. Publications, 1828 L Street, NW, Suite 801, Washington, D.C. 20036 (301) 638-3152; *Yearbook of Labour Statistics.*

M.E. Sharpe, 80 Business Park Drive, Armonk, New York 10504 (800) 541-6563; *The Illustrated Book of World Rankings.*

St. Martin's Press, Inc., 175 Fifth Avenue, New York, New York 10010 (800) 221-7945; *The Statesman's Year-Book.*

Statistical Office of the United Nations, Publishing Service, New York, New York 10017 (800) 253-9646; *Demographic Yearbook; Human Development Report; Statistical Yearbook; Trends in Europe and North America: The Statistical Yearbook of the Economic Commission for Europe;* and *World Statistics Pocketbook.*

United Nations Educational, Scientific and Cultural Organization (UNESCO), 7 Place de Fontenoy, F-75700 Paris, France (Telephone Number in U.S. (212) 963-5981); *Statistical Yearbook.*

U.S. Arms Control and Disarmament Agency, 320 Twenty-first Street, NW, Washington, D.C. 20451 (202) 647-8677; *World Military Expenditures and Arms Transfers.*

The World Bank, 1818 H Street, NW, Washington, D.C. 20433 (202) 477-1234; *The World Bank Atlas;* and *World Development Report.*

World Health Organization, Office of Publications, 20 Avenue Appia, CH-1211 Geneva 27, Switzerland (Telephone Number in U.S. (518) 436-9686); *World Health Statistics Annual.*

TURKEY - POST OFFICES

M.E. Sharpe, 80 Business Park Drive, Armonk, New York 10504 (800) 541-6563; *The Illustrated Book of World Rankings.*

St. Martin's Press, Inc., 175 Fifth Avenue, New York, New York 10010 (800) 221-7945; *The Statesman's Year-Book.*

Statistical Office of the United Nations, Publishing Service, New York, New York 10017 (800) 253-9646; *Trends in Europe and North America: The Statistical Yearbook of the Economic Commission for Europe.*

TURKEY - POTATO PRODUCTION - See TURKEY - CROPS

TURKEY - POWER PRODUCTION INDUSTRY

Statistical Office of the United Nations, Publishing Service, New York, New York 10017 (800) 253-9646; *Statistical Yearbook.*

TURKEY - PRICES

Food and Agricultural Organization of the United Nations (FAO), Via delle Terme di Caracalla, 00100 Rome, Italy (Telephone Number in U.S. (202) 653-2400); *Production Yearbook;* and *The State of Food and Agriculture.*

International Labour Office, I.L.O. Publications, 1828 L Street, NW, Suite 801, Washington, D.C. 20036 (301) 638-3152; *Yearbook of Labour Statistics.*

International Monetary Fund, 700 Nineteenth Street, NW, Washington, D.C. 20431 (202) 623-7000; *International Financial Statistics.*

M.E. Sharpe, 80 Business Park Drive, Armonk, New York 10504 (800) 541-6563; *The Illustrated Book of World Rankings.*

Organisation for Economic Co-operation and Development (OECD), 2 rue Andre-Pascal, 75 Paris 16, France (Telephone Number in U.S. (202) 785-6323); *Economic Outlook; The Footwear, Raw Hides and Skins, and Leather Industry in OECD Countries; The Iron and Steel Industry; Main Economic Indicators - Historical Statistics;* and *The Pulp and Paper Industry.*

TURKEY - PRINTING AND WRITING PAPER - See TURKEY - FORESTRY AND FOREST PRODUCTS

TURKEY - PRODUCTION

American Automobile Manufacturers Association, 1401 H Street, NW, Suite 900, Washington, D.C. 20005 (202) 326-5500; *World Motor Vehicle Data.*

M.E. Sharpe, 80 Business Park Drive, Armonk, New York 10504 (800) 541-6563; *The Illustrated Book of World Rankings.*

Organisation for Economic Co-operation and Development (OECD), 2 rue Andre-Pascal, 75 Paris 16, France (Telephone Number in U.S. (202) 785-6323); *Economic Outlook; The Footwear, Raw Hides and Skins, and Leather Industry in OECD Countries; Industrial Structure Statistics; The Iron and Steel Industry; Meat*

Balances in OECD Member Countries; Milk, Milk Products, and Egg Balances in OECD Member Countries; The Non-Ferrous Metals Industry; The Pulp and Paper Industry;* and *Textile Industry in OECD Countries.*

TURKEY - PRODUCTIVITY

Organisation for Economic Co-operation and Development (OECD), 2 rue Andre-Pascal, 75 Paris 16, France (Telephone Number in U.S. (202) 785-6323); *Economic Outlook.*

TURKEY - PROPERTY TAXES - See TURKEY - TAXATION

TURKEY - PUBLIC CONSUMPTION FUND

Organisation for Economic Co-operation and Development (OECD), 2 rue Andre-Pascal, 75 Paris 16, France (Telephone Number in U.S. (202) 785-6323); *Revenue Statistics of OECD Member Countries.*

TURKEY - PUBLIC EXPENDITURES

Organisation for Economic Co-operation and Development (OECD), 2 rue Andre-Pascal, 75 Paris 16, France (Telephone Number in U.S. (202) 785-6323); *Revenue Statistics of OECD Member Countries.*

TURKEY - PUBLIC FINANCE - See TURKEY - FINANCE

TURKEY - RADIO BROADCASTING - See TURKEY - BROADCASTING

TURKEY - RADIO RECEIVER PRODUCTION

Statistical Office of the United Nations, Publishing Service, New York, New York 10017 (800) 253-9646; *Statistical Yearbook.*

TURKEY - RADIO RECEIVERS

St. Martin's Press, Inc., 175 Fifth Avenue, New York, New York 10010 (800) 221-7945; *The Statesman's Year-Book.*

TURKEY - RAILWAYS

Euromonitor International, Inc., 122 South Michigan Avenue, Suite 1200, Chicago, Illinois 60603 (800) 577-EURO; *European Marketing Data and Statistics.*

Europa Publications Limited, 18 Bedford Square, London, WC1B 3JN, England; *The Europa World Year Book.*

Jane's Information Group, Sentinel House, 163 Brighton Road, Coulsdon, Surrey CR5 2NH, England (Telephone Number in U.S. (703) 683-3700); *Jane's World Railways.*

St. Martin's Press, Inc., 175 Fifth Avenue, New York, New York 10010 (800) 221-7945; *The Statesman's Year-Book.*

Statistical Office of the United Nations, Publishing Service, New York, New York 10017 (800) 253-9646; *Annual Bulletin of Transport Statistics for Europe; Statistical Yearbook;* and *Trends in Europe and North America: The Statistical Yearbook of the Economic Commission for Europe.*

TURKEY - RAPESEED PRODUCTION - See TURKEY - CROPS

TURKEY - RELIGION

Central Intelligence Agency, Washington, D.C. 20505 (703) 482-1100, www.cia.gov; *The World Factbook.*

M.E. Sharpe, 80 Business Park Drive, Armonk, New York 10504 (800) 541-6563; *The Illustrated Book of World Rankings.*

St. Martin's Press, Inc., 175 Fifth Avenue, New York, New York 10010 (800) 221-7945; *The Statesman's Year-Book.*

TURKEY - RENT PRICES

International Labour Office, I.L.O. Publications, 1828 L Street, NW, Suite 801, Washington, D.C. 20036 (301) 638-3152; *Yearbook of Labour Statistics.*

TURKEY - RETAIL TRADE

Euromonitor International, Inc., 122 South Michigan Avenue, Suite 1200, Chicago, Illinois 60603 (800) 577-EURO; *World Marketing Data and Statistics;* and *Retail Trade International.*

Statistical Office of the United Nations, Publishing Service, New York, New York 10017 (800) 253-9646; *Statistical Yearbook.*

TURKEY - RICE PRODUCTION - See TURKEY - CROPS

TURKEY - ROOT AND TUBER PRODUCTION

Food and Agricultural Organization of the United Nations (FAO), Via delle Terme di Caracalla, 00100 Rome, Italy (Telephone Number in U.S. (202) 653-2400); *Production Yearbook.*

TURKEY - ROUNDWOOD PRODUCTION - See TURKEY - FORESTRY AND FOREST PRODUCTS

TURKEY - RUBBER PRODUCTION AND CONSUMPTION

M.E. Sharpe, 80 Business Park Drive, Armonk, New York 10504 (800) 541-6563; *The Illustrated Book of World Rankings.*

Organisation for Economic Co-operation and Development (OECD), 2 rue Andre-Pascal, 75 Paris 16, France (Telephone Number in U.S. (202) 785-6323); *Foreign Trade by Commodities.*

Statistical Office of the United Nations, Publishing Service, New York, New York 10017 (800) 253-9646; *Statistical Yearbook.*

TURKEY - RYE PRODUCTION - See TURKEY - CROPS

TURKEY - SAFFLOWER SEED PRODUCTION - See TURKEY - CROPS

TURKEY - SALT PRODUCTION - See TURKEY - MINING AND MINERAL PRODUCTS

TURKEY - SAWNWOOD PRODUCTION - See TURKEY - FORESTRY AND FOREST PRODUCTS

TURKEY - SCIENCE AND TECHNOLOGY - EXPENDITURE FOR RESEARCH - See TURKEY - SCIENTISTS, TECHNICIANS AND ENGINEERS

TURKEY - SCIENTISTS, TECHNICIANS AND ENGINEERS

Statistical Office of the United Nations, Publishing Service, New York, New York 10017 (800) 253-9646; *Statistical Yearbook.*

TURKEY - SENIOR CITIZENS

M.E. Sharpe, 80 Business Park Drive, Armonk, New York 10504 (800) 541-6563; *The Illustrated Book of World Rankings.*

TURKEY - SERVICE INDUSTRY EMPLOYMENT - MALE AND FEMALE - See TURKEY - EMPLOYMENT

TURKEY - SESAME SEED PRODUCTION

Food and Agricultural Organization of the United Nations (FAO), Via delle Terme di Caracalla, 00100 Rome, Italy (Telephone Number in U.S. (202) 653-2400); *Production Yearbook.*

TURKEY - SHEEP - See TURKEY - LIVESTOCK AND POULTRY

TURKEY - SILVER PRODUCTION AND CONSUMPTION - See TURKEY - MINING AND MINERAL PRODUCTS

TURKEY - SOCIAL DATA

M.E. Sharpe, 80 Business Park Drive, Armonk, New York 10504 (800) 541-6563; *The Illustrated Book of World Rankings.*

Statistical Office of the United Nations, Publishing Service, New York, New York 10017 (800) 253-9646; *World Statistics*

Pocketbook.

TURKEY - SOCIAL SECURITY

International Monetary Fund, 700 Nineteenth Street, NW, Washington, D.C. 20431 (202) 623-7000; *Government Finance Statistics Yearbook.*

Organisation for Economic Co-operation and Development (OECD), 2 rue Andre-Pascal, 75 Paris 16, France (Telephone Number in U.S. (202) 785-6323); *Revenue Statistics of OECD Member Countries.*

St. Martin's Press, Inc., 175 Fifth Avenue, New York, New York 10010 (800) 221-7945; *The Statesman's Year-Book.*

Statistical Office of the United Nations, Publishing Service, New York, New York 10017 (800) 253-9646; *National Accounts Statistics.*

TURKEY - SOCIOECONOMIC DATA

Organisation for Economic Co-operation and Development (OECD), 2 rue Andre-Pascal, 75 Paris 16, France (Telephone Number in U.S. (202) 785-6323); *Economic Outlook.*

TURKEY - SOYBEAN PRODUCTION - See TURKEY - CROPS

TURKEY - STAMP TAXES AND DUTIES - See TURKEY - TAXATION

TURKEY - STEEL - See TURKEY - MINING AND MINERAL PRODUCTS

TURKEY - STOCKS - COMMODITY - MARKET PRICE - INDEX

Food and Agricultural Organization of the United Nations (FAO) Via delle Terme di Caracalla, 00100 Rome, Italy (Telephone Number in U.S. (202) 653-2400); *The State of Food and Agriculture.*

TURKEY - SUGAR - See TURKEY - CROPS

TURKEY - SULPHUR AND SULPHURIC ACID PRODUCTION - See TURKEY - MINING AND MINERAL PRODUCTS

TURKEY - TAXATION

Europa Publications Limited, 18 Bedford Square, London, WC1B 3JN, England; *The Europa World Year Book.*

International Monetary Fund, 700 Nineteenth Street, NW, Washington, D.C. 20431 (202) 623-7000; *Government Finance Statistics Yearbook.*

International Road Federation, 2600 Virginia Avenue, NW, Washington, D.C.

20037 (202) 338-4641; *World Road Statistics.*

Organisation for Economic Co-operation and Development (OECD), 2 rue Andre-Pascal, 75 Paris 16, France (Telephone Number in U.S. (202) 785-6323); *Revenue Statistics of OECD Member Countries.*

The World Bank, 1818 H Street, NW, Washington, D.C. 20433 (202) 477-1234; *World Development Indicators.*

TURKEY - TEA - See TURKEY - CROPS

TURKEY - TELEGRAPH SERVICE

Statistical Office of the United Nations, Publishing Service, New York, New York 10017 (800) 253-9646; *Statistical Yearbook.*

TURKEY - TELEPHONES IN USE

American Telephone and Telegraph Company, 26 Parsippany Road, Whippany, New Jersey 07981 (800) 222-0300; *The World's Telephones.*

Central Intelligence Agency, Washington, D.C. 20505 (703) 482-1100, www.cia.gov; *The World Factbook.*

Europa Publications Limited, 18 Bedford Square, London, WC1B 3JN, England; *The Europa World Year Book.*

St. Martin's Press, Inc., 175 Fifth Avenue, New York, New York 10010 (800) 221-7945; *The Statesman's Year-Book.*

Statistical Office of the United Nations, Publishing Service, New York, New York 10017 (800) 253-9646; *Statistical Yearbook; Trends in Europe and North America: The Statistical Yearbook of the Economic Commission for Europe; and World Statistics Pocketbook.*

TURKEY - TELEVISION BROADCASTING - See TURKEY - BROADCASTING

TURKEY - TELEVISION RECEIVER PRODUCTION

Statistical Office of the United Nations, Publishing Service, New York, New York 10017 (800) 253-9646; *Statistical Yearbook.*

TURKEY - TEXTILE INDUSTRY

Euromonitor International, Inc., 122 South Michigan Avenue, Suite 1200, Chicago, Illinois 60603 (800) 577-EURO; *Retail Trade International.*

Food and Agricultural Organization of the United Nations (FAO), Via delle Terme di Caracalla, 00100 Rome, Italy (Telephone Number in U.S. (202) 653-2400); *Production Yearbook.*

M.E. Sharpe, 80 Business Park Drive, Armonk, New York 10504 (800) 541-6563; *The Illustrated Book of World Rankings.*

Organisation for Economic Co-operation and Development (OECD), 2 rue Andre-Pascal, 75 Paris 16, France (Telephone Number in U.S. (202) 785-6323); *Economic Accounts for Agriculture; Foreign Trade by Commodities; Industrial Structure Statistics;* and *Textile Industry in OECD Countries.*

St. Martin's Press, Inc., 175 Fifth Avenue, New York, New York 10010 (800) 221-7945; *The Statesman's Year-Book.*

Statistical Office of the United Nations, Publishing Service, New York, New York 10017 (800) 253-9646; *Statistical Yearbook.*

United Nations Conference on Trade and Development, Central Statistical Service, Palais des Nations, Geneva, Switzerland (Telephone in U.S. (800) 253-9646); *UNCTAD Commodity Yearbook.*

TURKEY - THEATRE

United Nations Educational, Scientific and Cultural Organization (UNESCO), 7 Place de Fontenoy, F-75700 Paris, France (Telephone Number in U.S. (212) 963-5981); *Statistical Yearbook.*

TURKEY - TIN - See TURKEY - MINING AND MINERAL PRODUCTS

TURKEY - TIRE (MOTOR VEHICLE) PRODUCTION

Statistical Office of the United Nations, Publishing Service, New York, New York 10017 (800) 253-9646; *Statistical Yearbook.*

TURKEY - TOBACCO PRODUCTION

Commodity Research Bureau, Inc., 30 South Wacker Drive, Chicago, Illinois 60606 (312) 454-1801; *Commodity Year Book.*

Euromonitor International, Inc., 122 South Michigan Avenue, Suite 1200, Chicago, Illinois 60603 (800) 577-EURO; *European Marketing Data and Statistics.*

International Monetary Fund, 700 Nineteenth Street, NW, Washington, D.C. 20431 (202) 623-7000; *International Financial Statistics.*

M.E. Sharpe, 80 Business Park Drive, Armonk, New York 10504 (800) 541-6563; *The Illustrated Book of World Rankings.*

Organisation for Economic Co-operation and Development (OECD), 2 rue Andre-Pascal, 75 Paris 16, France (Telephone Number in U.S. (202) 785-6323); *Foreign Trade by Commodities;* and *Industrial Structure Statistics.*

Statistical Office of the United Nations, Publishing Service, New York, New York 10017 (800) 253-9646; *Statistical Yearbook.*

TURKEY - TOURISM

Euromonitor International, Inc., 122 South Michigan Avenue, Suite 1200, Chicago, Illinois 60603 (800) 577-EURO; *European Marketing Data and Statistics; World Marketing Data and Statistics;* and *The World Economic Factbook.*

Europa Publications Limited, 18 Bedford Square, London, WC1B 3JN, England; *The Europa World Year Book.*

M.E. Sharpe, 80 Business Park Drive, Armonk, New York 10504 (800) 541-6563; *The Illustrated Book of World Rankings.*

Organisation for Economic Co-operation and Development (OECD), 2 rue Andre-Pascal, 75 Paris 16, France (Telephone Number in U.S. (202) 785-6323); *Tourism Policy and International Tourism in OECD Member Countries.*

St. Martin's Press, Inc., 175 Fifth Avenue, New York, New York 10010 (800) 221-7945; *The Statesman's Year-Book.*

Statistical Office of the United Nations, Publishing Service, New York, New York 10017 (800) 253-9646; *Statistical Yearbook; and Trends in Europe and North America: The Statistical Yearbook of the Economic Commission for Europe.*

World Tourism Organization, Calle Capitan Haya 42, E-28020 Madrid, Spain; *Yearbook of Tourism Statistics.*

TURKEY - TRACTORS IN USE

Statistical Office of the United Nations, Publishing Service, New York, New York 10017 (800) 253-9646; *Statistical Yearbook.*

TURKEY - TRADE - See TURKEY - FOREIGN TRADE

TURKEY - TRADEMARKS AND SERVICE MARKS - See TURKEY - PATENTS, TRADEMARKS AND SERVICE MARKS

TURKEY - TRANSPORTATION AND COMMUNICATIONS

Central Intelligence Agency, Washington, D.C. 20505 (703) 482-1100, www.cia.gov; *The World Factbook.*

Euromonitor International, Inc., 122 South Michigan Avenue, Suite 1200, Chicago, Illinois 60603 (800) 577-EURO; *World Marketing Data and Statistics.*

Europa Publications Limited, 18 Bedford Square, London, WC1B 3JN,

England; *The Europa World Year Book.*

M.E. Sharpe, 80 Business Park Drive, Armonk, New York 10504 (800) 541-6563; *The Illustrated Book of World Rankings.*

St. Martin's Press, Inc., 175 Fifth Avenue, New York, New York 10010 (800) 221-7945; *The Statesman's Year-Book.*

Statistical Office of the United Nations, Publishing Service, New York, New York 10017 (800) 253-9646; *Human Development Report;* and *Trends in Europe and North America: The Statistical Yearbook of the Economic Commission for Europe.*

TURKEY - TURKEYS - See TURKEY - LIVESTOCK AND POULTRY

TURKEY - UNEMPLOYMENT

Central Intelligence Agency, Washington, D.C. 20505 (703) 482-1100, www.cia.gov; *The World Factbook.*

Euromonitor International, Inc., 122 South Michigan Avenue, Suite 1200, Chicago, Illinois 60603 (800) 577-EURO; *European Marketing Data and Statistics.*

International Labour Office, I.L.O. Publications, 1828 L Street, NW, Suite 801, Washington, D.C. 20036 (301) 638-3152; *Yearbook of Labour Statistics.*

Organisation for Economic Co-operation and Development (OECD), 2 rue Andre-Pascal, 75 Paris 16, France (Telephone Number in U.S. (202) 785-6323); *Economic Outlook; OECD Economic Surveys: Turkey;* and *OECD Employment Outlook.*

St. Martin's Press, Inc., 175 Fifth Avenue, New York, New York 10010 (800) 221-7945; *The Statesman's Year-Book.*

Statistical Office of the United Nations, Publishing Service, New York, New York 10017 (800) 253-9646; *Statistical Yearbook;* and *Trends in Europe and North America: The Statistical Yearbook of the Economic Commission for Europe.*

TURKEY - URANIUM PRODUCTION AND CONSUMPTION - See TURKEY - MINING AND MINERAL PRODUCTS

TURKEY - VITAL STATISTICS

St. Martin's Press, Inc., 175 Fifth Avenue, New York, New York 10010 (800) 221-7945; *The Statesman's Year-Book.*

World Health Organization, Office of Publications, 20 Avenue Appia, CH-1211 Geneva 27, Switzerland (Telephone Number in U.S. (518) 436-9686); *World Health Statistics Annual.*

TURKEY - WAGES

Euromonitor International, Inc., 122 South Michigan Avenue, Suite 1200, Chicago, Illinois 60603 (800) 577-EURO; *European Marketing Data and Statistics.*

International Labour Office, I.L.O. Publications, 1828 L Street, NW, Suite 801, Washington, D.C. 20036 (301) 638-3152; *Yearbook of Labour Statistics.*

Organisation for Economic Co-operation and Development (OECD), 2 rue Andre-Pascal, 75 Paris 16, France (Telephone Number in U.S. (202) 785-6323); *Economic Outlook;* and *Industrial Structure Statistics.*

Statistical Office of the United Nations, Publishing Service, New York, New York 10017 (800) 253-9646; *Statistical Yearbook.*

TURKEY - WALNUT PRODUCTION - See TURKEY - CROPS

TURKEY - WATERMELON PRODUCTION - See TURKEY - CROPS

TURKEY - WATERWAYS IN USE

Organisation for Economic Co-operation and Development (OECD), 2 rue Andre-Pascal, 75 Paris 16, France (Telephone Number in U.S. (202) 785-6323); *Maritime Transport.*

TURKEY - WEATHER - See TURKEY - CLIMATE

TURKEY - WELFARE

International Monetary Fund, 700 Nineteenth Street, NW, Washington, D.C. 20431 (202) 623-7000; *Government Finance Statistics Yearbook.*

TURKEY - WHEAT PRODUCTION AND PRICES - See TURKEY - CROPS

TURKEY - WHOLESALE PRICES

International Monetary Fund, 700 Nineteenth Street, NW, Washington, D.C. 20431 (202) 623-7000; *International Financial Statistics.*

Statistical Office of the United Nations, Publishing Service, New York, New York 10017 (800) 253-9646; *Statistical Yearbook.*

TURKEY - WHOLESALE TRADE

Statistical Office of the United Nations, Publishing Service, New York, New York 10017 (800) 253-9646; *Statistical Yearbook.*

TURKEY - WINE PRODUCTION

M.E. Sharpe, 80 Business Park Drive,

Armonk, New York 10504 (800) 541-6563; *The Illustrated Book of World Rankings.*

Statistical Office of the United Nations, Publishing Service, New York, New York 10017 (800) 253-9646; *Statistical Yearbook.*

TURKEY - WOOD AND WOOD PULP - See TURKEY - FORESTRY AND FOREST PRODUCTS

TURKEY - WOOL - See TURKEY - TEXTILE INDUSTRY

TURKEY - YARN PRODUCTION - See TURKEY - TEXTILE INDUSTRY

TURKEY - ZINC ORE PRODUCTION AND CONSUMPTION - See TURKEY - MINING AND MINERAL PRODUCTS

TURKEY - ZINC PRODUCTION AND CONSUMPTION - See TURKEY - MINING AND MINERAL PRODUCTS

TURKEYS

U.S. Department of Agriculture, Economic Research Service, 1800 M Street, NW, Washington, D.C. 20036 (202) 694-5050, www.ers.usda.gov; *Farm Business Economic Report; Food Consumption, Prices and Expenditures;* and *Agricultural Outlook.*

U.S. Department of Agriculture, National Agricultural Statistics Service, Fourteenth Street and Independence Avenue, SW, Washington, D.C. 20250 (800) 727-9540, www.usda.gov/nass; *Poultry-Production and Value;* and *Turkeys.*

U.S. Department of Labor, Bureau of Labor Statistics, Two Massachusetts Avenue, NE, Washington, D.C. 20212 (202) 691-5200, www.stats.bls.gov; *Monthly Labor Review;* and *CPI Detailed Report.*

Turkmenistan - National Statistical Office

State Committee of Republic of Turkmenistan on Statistics, 72 Makhtumkuli Avenue, Ashkhabad 744000, Turkmenistan.

TURKMENISTAN - ABORTIONS

Statistical Office of the United Nations, Publishing Service, New York, New York 10017 (800) 253-9646; *Trends in Europe and North America: The Statistical Yearbook of the Economic Commission for Europe.*

TURKMENISTAN - AGRICULTURE

Academic International Press, Box 1111, Gulf Breeze, Florida 32562; *Russia and Eurasia Facts and Figures Annual.*

Business International Moscow, 23

Profsoyuznaya Ulitsa, 117859, Moscow (Telephone Number in U.S. (800) 938-4685); *The CIS Market Atlas*.

The Economist Intelligence Unit, 111 West 57th Street, New York, New York 10019 (800) 938-4685; *Turkmenistan Country Report*.

Euromonitor International, Inc., 122 South Michigan Avenue, Suite 1200, Chicago, Illinois 60603 (800) 577-EURO; *World Marketing Data and Statistics*.

Europa Publications Limited, 18 Bedford Square, London, WC1B 3JN, England; *The Europa World Year Book*.

Food and Agriculture Organization of the United Nations (FAO), Via delle Terme di Caracalla, 00100, Rome, Italy (Telephone Number in U.S. (202) 653-2400); *Production Yearbook; The State of Food and Agriculture;* and *Trade Yearbook*.

St. Martin's Press, Inc., 175 Fifth Avenue, New York, New York 10010 (800) 221-7945; *The Statesman's Year-Book*.

Statistical Office of the United Nations, Publishing Service, New York, New York 10017 (800) 253-9646; *Industrial Commodity Statistics Yearbook;* and *Statistical Yearbook*.

The World Bank, 1818 H Street, NW, Washington, D.C. 20433 (202) 477-1234; *Statistical Handbook: States of the Former USSR;* and *World Development Indicators*.

TURKMENISTAN - AIRLINE SERVICE

Business International Moscow, 23 Profsoyuznaya Ulitsa, 117859, Moscow (Telephone Number in U.S. (800) 938-4685); *The CIS Market Atlas*.

International Civil Aviation Organization, 999 University Street, Montreal, Quebec, Canada H3C 5H7 (514) 954-8219; *Civil Aviation Statistics of the World*.

St. Martin's Press, Inc., 175 Fifth Avenue, New York, New York 10010 (800) 221-7945; *The Statesman's Year-Book*.

Statistical Office of the United Nations, Publishing Service, New York, New York 10017 (800) 253-9646; *Statistical Yearbook*.

TURKMENISTAN - AIRPORTS

Central Intelligence Agency, Washington, D.C. 20505 (703) 482-1100, www.cia.gov; *The World Factbook*.

TURKMENISTAN - ANIMAL HEALTH

Food and Agriculture Organization of the United Nations (FAO), Via delle Terme

di Caracalla, 00100, Rome, Italy (Telephone Number in U.S. (202) 653-2400); *Animal Health Yearbook*.

TURKMENISTAN - AREA AND DENSITY OF POPULATION

Academic International Press, Box 1111, Gulf Breeze, Florida 32562; *Russia and Eurasia Facts and Figures Annual*.

Business International Moscow, 23 Profsoyuznaya Ulitsa, 117859, Moscow (Telephone Number in U.S. (800) 938-4685); *The CIS Market Atlas*.

Central Intelligence Agency, Washington, D.C. 20505 (703) 482-1100, www.cia.gov; *The World Factbook*.

Euromonitor International, Inc., 122 South Michigan Avenue, Suite 1200, Chicago, Illinois 60603 (800) 577-EURO; *The World Economic Factbook*.

Europa Publications Limited, 18 Bedford Square, London, WC1B 3JN, England; *The Europa World Year Book*.

St. Martin's Press, Inc., 175 Fifth Avenue, New York, New York 10010 (800) 221-7945; *The Statesman's Year-Book*.

Statistical Office of the United Nations, Publishing Service, New York, New York 10017 (800) 253-9646; *Statistical Yearbook;* and *Trends in Europe and North America: The Statistical Yearbook of the Economic Commission for Europe*.

United Nations Educational, Scientific and Cultural Organization (UNESCO), 7 Place de Fontenoy, F-75700 Paris, France (Telephone Number in U.S. (212) 963-5981); *Statistical Yearbook*.

The World Bank, 1818 H Street, NW, Washington, D.C. 20433 (202) 477-1234; *World Development Report*.

TURKMENISTAN - BALANCE OF PAYMENT

Europa Publications Limited, 18 Bedford Square, London, WC1B 3JN, England; *The Europa World Year Book*.

The World Bank, 1818 H Street, NW, Washington, D.C. 20433 (202) 477-1234; *World Development Report;* and *World Development Indicators*.

TURKMENISTAN - BANKING

Business International Moscow, 23 Profsoyuznaya Ulitsa, 117859, Moscow (Telephone Number in U.S. (800) 938-4685); *The CIS Market Atlas*.

Euromonitor International, Inc., 122 South Michigan Avenue, Suite 1200, Chicago, Illinois 60603 (800) 577-EURO;

World Marketing Data and Statistics.

St. Martin's Press, Inc., 175 Fifth Avenue, New York, New York 10010 (800) 221-7945; *The Statesman's Year-Book*.

TURKMENISTAN - BEVERAGES

Statistical Office of the United Nations, Publishing Service, New York, New York 10017 (800) 253-9646; *Statistical Yearbook*.

TURKMENISTAN - BIRTH RATES

Academic International Press, Box 1111, Gulf Breeze, Florida 32562; *Russia and Eurasia Facts and Figures Annual*.

Business International Moscow, 23 Profsoyuznaya Ulitsa, 117859, Moscow (Telephone Number in U.S. (800) 938-4685); *The CIS Market Atlas*.

Central Intelligence Agency, Washington, D.C. 20505 (703) 482-1100, www.cia.gov; *The World Factbook*.

Euromonitor International, Inc., 122 South Michigan Avenue, Suite 1200, Chicago, Illinois 60603 (800) 577-EURO; *International Marketing Data and Statistics;* and *The World Economic Factbook*.

Europa Publications Limited, 18 Bedford Square, London, WC1B 3JN, England; *The Europa World Year Book*.

Statistical Office of the United Nations, Publishing Service, New York, New York 10017 (800) 253-9646; *Statistical Yearbook*.

World Health Organization, Office of Publications, 20 Avenue Appia, CH-1211 Geneva 27, Switzerland (Telephone Number in U.S. (518) 436-9686); *World Health Statistics Annual*.

TURKMENISTAN - BOOK PRODUCTION

Statistical Office of the United Nations, Publishing Service, New York, New York 10017 (800) 253-9646; *Trends in Europe and North America: The Statistical Yearbook of the Economic Commission for Europe*.

United Nations Educational, Scientific and Cultural Organization (UNESCO), 7 Place de Fontenoy, F-75700 Paris, France (Telephone Number in U.S. (212) 963-5981); *Statistical Yearbook*.

TURKMENISTAN - BROADCASTING

Central Intelligence Agency, Washington, D.C. 20505 (703) 482-1100, www.cia.gov; *The World Factbook*.

Euromonitor International, Inc., 122 South Michigan Avenue, Suite 1200, Chicago, Illinois 60603 (800) 577-EURO;

World Marketing Data and Statistics.

St. Martin's Press, Inc., 175 Fifth Avenue, New York, New York 10010 (800) 221-7945; *The Statesman's Year-Book.*

Statistical Office of the United Nations, Publishing Service, New York, New York 10017 (800) 253-9646; *Trends in Europe and North America: The Statistical Yearbook of the Economic Commission for Europe.*

United Nations Educational, Scientific and Cultural Organization (UNESCO), 7 Place de Fontenoy, F-75700 Paris, France (Telephone Number in U.S. (212) 963-5981); *Statistical Yearbook.*

TURKMENISTAN - BUDGET

Business International Moscow, 23 Profsoyuznaya Ulitsa, 117859, Moscow (Telephone Number in U.S. (800) 938-4685); *The CIS Market Atlas.*

Central Intelligence Agency, Washington, D.C. 20505 (703) 482-1100, www.cia.gov; *The World Factbook.*

TURKMENISTAN - CAPITAL INVESTMENTS

The World Bank, 1818 H Street, NW, Washington, D.C. 20433 (202) 477-1234; *Statistical Handbook: States of the Former USSR.*

TURKMENISTAN - CATTLE - See TURKMENISTAN - LIVESTOCK AND POULTRY

TURKMENISTAN - CHEMICALS

Business International Moscow, 23 Profsoyuznaya Ulitsa, 117859, Moscow (Telephone Number in U.S. (800) 938-4685); *The CIS Market Atlas.*

TURKMENISTAN - COAL PRODUCTION AND CONSUMPTION - See TURKMENISTAN - MINING AND MINERAL PRODUCTS

TURKMENISTAN - COMMERCE

St. Martin's Press, Inc., 175 Fifth Avenue, New York, New York 10010 (800) 221-7945; *The Statesman's Year-Book.*

TURKMENISTAN - COMMUNICATIONS - See TURKMENISTAN - TRANSPORTATION AND COMMUNICATIONS

TURKMENISTAN - CONSTRUCTION INDUSTRY

Academic International Press, Box 1111, Gulf Breeze, Florida 32562; *Russia and Eurasia Facts and Figures Annual.*

Business International Moscow, 23

Profsoyuznaya Ulitsa, 117859, Moscow (Telephone Number in U.S. (800) 938-4685); *The CIS Market Atlas.*

Statistical Office of the United Nations, Publishing Service, New York, New York 10017 (800) 253-9646; *Statistical Yearbook.*

TURKMENISTAN - CONSUMER PRICE INDEX

Statistical Office of the United Nations, Publishing Service, New York, New York 10017 (800) 253-9646; *Statistical Yearbook;* and *Trends in Europe and North America: The Statistical Yearbook of the Economic Commission for Europe.*

TURKMENISTAN - CONSUMER PRICES

Euromonitor International, Inc., 122 South Michigan Avenue, Suite 1200, Chicago, Illinois 60603 (800) 577-EURO; *World Marketing Data and Statistics.*

TURKMENISTAN - CONSUMER PRODUCTS

Business International Moscow, 23 Profsoyuznaya Ulitsa, 117859, Moscow (Telephone Number in U.S. (800) 938-4685); *The CIS Market Atlas.*

TURKMENISTAN - CONSUMPTION

Business International Moscow, 23 Profsoyuznaya Ulitsa, 117859, Moscow (Telephone Number in U.S. (800) 938-4685); *The CIS Market Atlas.*

The World Bank, 1818 H Street, NW, Washington, D.C. 20433 (202) 477-1234; *World Development Report;* and *Statistical Handbook: States of the Former USSR.*

TURKMENISTAN - COTTON PRODUCTION AND CONSUMPTION - See TURKMENISTAN - CROPS

TURKMENISTAN - CRIME

Academic International Press, Box 1111, Gulf Breeze, Florida 32562; *Russia and Eurasia Facts and Figures Annual.*

Statistical Office of the United Nations, Publishing Service, New York, New York 10017 (800) 253-9646; *Trends in Europe and North America: The Statistical Yearbook of the Economic Commission for Europe.*

TURKMENISTAN - CROPS

Academic International Press, Box 1111, Gulf Breeze, Florida 32562; *Russia and Eurasia Facts and Figures Annual.*

Business International Moscow, 23 Profsoyuznaya Ulitsa, 117859, Moscow (Telephone Number in U.S. (800) 938-4685); *The CIS Market Atlas.*

Europa Publications Limited, 18 Bedford Square, London, WC1B 3JN, England; *The Europa World Year Book.*

Food and Agriculture Organization of the United Nations (FAO), Via delle Terme di Caracalla, 00100, Rome, Italy (Telephone Number in U.S. (202) 653-2400); *Production Yearbook;* and *The State of Food and Agriculture.*

St. Martin's Press, Inc., 175 Fifth Avenue, New York, New York 10010 (800) 221-7945; *The Statesman's Year-Book.*

Statistical Office of the United Nations, Publishing Service, New York, New York 10017 (800) 253-9646; *Industrial Commodity Statistics Yearbook; Statistical Yearbook;* and *Trade Yearbook.*

The World Bank, 1818 H Street, NW, Washington, D.C. 20433 (202) 477-1234; *Statistical Handbook: States of the Former USSR.*

TURKMENISTAN - DAIRY PRODUCTS

Europa Publications Limited, 18 Bedford Square, London, WC1B 3JN, England; *The Europa World Year Book.*

Food and Agriculture Organization of the United Nations (FAO), Via delle Terme di Caracalla, 00100, Rome, Italy (Telephone Number in U.S. (202) 653-2400); *Production Yearbook; The State of Food and Agriculture;* and *Trade Yearbook.*

St. Martin's Press, Inc., 175 Fifth Avenue, New York, New York 10010 (800) 221-7945; *The Statesman's Year-Book.*

Statistical Office of the United Nations, Publishing Service, New York, New York 10017 (800) 253-9646; *Industrial Commodity Statistics Yearbook;* and *Statistical Yearbook.*

TURKMENISTAN - DEATH RATES - See TURKMENISTAN - MORTALITY

TURKMENISTAN - DEMOGRAPHY

Business International Moscow, 23 Profsoyuznaya Ulitsa, 117859, Moscow (Telephone Number in U.S. (800) 938-4685); *The CIS Market Atlas.*

Euromonitor International, Inc., 122 South Michigan Avenue, Suite 1200, Chicago, Illinois 60603 (800) 577-EURO; *International Marketing Data and Statistics; World Marketing Data and Statistics;* and *The World Economic Factbook.*

Statistical Office of the United Nations, Publishing Service, New York, New York 10017 (800) 253-9646; *Demographic Yearbook;* and *Human Development Report.*

The World Bank, 1818 H Street, NW, Washington, D.C. 20433 (202) 477-1234; *Statistical Handbook: States of the Former USSR.*

TURKMENISTAN - DISEASES - See TURKMENISTAN - HEALTH

TURKMENISTAN - DIVORCE RATES

Academic International Press, Box 1111, Gulf Breeze, Florida 32562; *Russia and Eurasia Facts and Figures Annual.*

Statistical Office of the United Nations, Publishing Service, New York, New York 10017 (800) 253-9646; *Demographic Yearbook; Statistical Yearbook;* and *Trends in Europe and North America: The Statistical Yearbook of the Economic Commission for Europe.*

TURKMENISTAN - DOMESTIC INVESTMENT

Business International Moscow, 23 Profsoyuznaya Ulitsa, 117859, Moscow (Telephone Number in U.S. (800) 938-4685); *The CIS Market Atlas.*

TURKMENISTAN - ECONOMY

Academic International Press, Box 1111, Gulf Breeze, Florida 32562; *Russia and Eurasia Facts and Figures Annual.*

Business International Moscow, 23 Profsoyuznaya Ulitsa, 117859, Moscow (Telephone Number in U.S. (800) 938-4685); *The CIS Market Atlas.*

Central Intelligence Agency, Washington, D.C. 20505 (703) 482-1100, www.cia.gov; *The World Factbook.*

The Economist Intelligence Unit, 111 West 57th Street, New York, New York 10019 (800) 938-4685; *Turkmenistan Country Report.*

Euromonitor International, Inc., 122 South Michigan Avenue, Suite 1200, Chicago, Illinois 60603 (800) 577-EURO; *The World Economic Factbook;* and *World Marketing Data and Statistics.*

Europa Publications Limited, 18 Bedford Square, London, WC1B 3JN, England; *The Europa World Year Book.*

St. Martin's Press, Inc., 175 Fifth Avenue, New York, New York 10010 (800) 221-7945; *The Statesman's Year-Book.*

Statistical Office of the United Nations, Publishing Service, New York, New York 10017 (800) 253-9646; *World Statistics Pocketbook.*

The World Bank, 1818 H Street, NW, Washington, D.C. 20433 (202) 477-1234;

The World Bank Atlas; and *World Development Report.*

TURKMENISTAN - EDUCATION

Academic International Press, Box 1111, Gulf Breeze, Florida 32562; *Russia and Eurasia Facts and Figures Annual.*

Business International Moscow, 23 Profsoyuznaya Ulitsa, 117859, Moscow (Telephone Number in U.S. (800) 938-4685); *The CIS Market Atlas.*

Euromonitor International, Inc., 122 South Michigan Avenue, Suite 1200, Chicago, Illinois 60603 (800) 577-EURO; *International Marketing Data and Statistics;* and *World Marketing Data and Statistics.*

Europa Publications Limited, 18 Bedford Square, London, WC1B 3JN, England; *The Europa World Year Book.*

St. Martin's Press, Inc., 175 Fifth Avenue, New York, New York 10010 (800) 221-7945; *The Statesman's Year-Book.*

Statistical Office of the United Nations, Publishing Service, New York, New York 10017 (800) 253-9646; *Human Development Report;* and *Trends in Europe and North America: The Statistical Yearbook of the Economic Commission for Europe.*

United Nations Educational, Scientific and Cultural Organization (UNESCO), 7 Place de Fontenoy, F-75700 Paris, France (Telephone Number in U.S. (212) 963-5981); *Statistical Yearbook.*

The World Bank, 1818 H Street, NW, Washington, D.C. 20433 (202) 477-1234; *World Development Report.*

TURKMENISTAN - ELECTRICITY

Academic International Press, Box 1111, Gulf Breeze, Florida 32562; *Russia and Eurasia Facts and Figures Annual.*

Business International Moscow, 23 Profsoyuznaya Ulitsa, 117859, Moscow (Telephone Number in U.S. (800) 938-4685); *The CIS Market Atlas.*

Central Intelligence Agency, Washington, D.C. 20505 (703) 482-1100, www.cia.gov; *The World Factbook.*

St. Martin's Press, Inc., 175 Fifth Avenue, New York, New York 10010 (800) 221-7945; *The Statesman's Year-Book.*

Statistical Office of the United Nations, Publishing Service, New York, New York 10017 (800) 253-9646; *Energy Statistics Yearbook; Human Development Report; Statistical Yearbook;* and *Trends in Europe and North America: The Statistical*

Yearbook of the Economic Commission for Europe.

The World Bank, 1818 H Street, NW, Washington, D.C. 20433 (202) 477-1234; *Statistical Handbook: States of the Former USSR.*

TURKMENISTAN - EMPLOYMENT

Euromonitor International, Inc., 122 South Michigan Avenue, Suite 1200, Chicago, Illinois 60603 (800) 577-EURO; *International Marketing Data and Statistics.*

Statistical Office of the United Nations, Publishing Service, New York, New York 10017 (800) 253-9646; *Statistical Yearbook;* and *Trends in Europe and North America: The Statistical Yearbook of the Economic Commission for Europe.*

The World Bank, 1818 H Street, NW, Washington, D.C. 20433 (202) 477-1234; *Statistical Handbook: States of the Former USSR.*

TURKMENISTAN - ENERGY

Academic International Press, Box 1111, Gulf Breeze, Florida 32562; *Russia and Eurasia Facts and Figures Annual.*

Business International Moscow, 23 Profsoyuznaya Ulitsa, 117859, Moscow (Telephone Number in U.S. (800) 938-4685); *The CIS Market Atlas.*

Euromonitor International, Inc., 122 South Michigan Avenue, Suite 1200, Chicago, Illinois 60603 (800) 577-EURO; *International Marketing Data and Statistics; World Marketing Data and Statistics;* and *The World Economic Factbook.*

St. Martin's Press, Inc., 175 Fifth Avenue, New York, New York 10010 (800) 221-7945; *The Statesman's Year-Book.*

Statistical Office of the United Nations, Publishing Service, New York, New York 10017 (800) 253-9646; *Energy Statistics Yearbook; Human Development Report; Statistical Yearbook; Trends in Europe and North America: The Statistical Yearbook of the Economic Commission for Europe;* and *World Statistics Pocketbook.*

The World Bank, 1818 H Street, NW, Washington, D.C. 20433 (202) 477-1234; *The World Bank Atlas; World Development Report;* and *Statistical Handbook: States of the Former USSR.*

TURKMENISTAN - ENVIRONMENT

Business International Moscow, 23 Profsoyuznaya Ulitsa, 117859, Moscow (Telephone Number in U.S. (800) 938-4685); *The CIS Market Atlas.*

The Economist Intelligence Unit, 111 West 57th Street, New York, New York 10019 (800) 938-4685; *Turkmenistan Country Report.*

Statistical Office of the United Nations, Publishing Service, New York, New York 10017 (800) 253-9646; *Statistical Yearbook; Trends in Europe and North America: The Statistical Yearbook of the Economic Commission for Europe;* and *World Statistics Pocketbook.*

TURKMENISTAN - EXCHANGE RATES

Central Intelligence Agency, Washington, D.C. 20505 (703) 482-1100, www.cia.gov; *The World Factbook.*

Euromonitor International, Inc., 122 South Michigan Avenue, Suite 1200, Chicago, Illinois 60603 (800) 577-EURO; *International Marketing Data and Statistics;* and *The World Economic Factbook.*

Europa Publications Limited, 18 Bedford Square, London, WC1B 3JN, England; *The Europa World Year Book.*

Statistical Office of the United Nations, Publishing Service, New York, New York 10017 (800) 253-9646; *Statistical Yearbook; Trends in Europe and North America: The Statistical Yearbook of the Economic Commission for Europe;* and *World Statistics Pocketbook.*

TURKMENISTAN - EXPORTS

Academic International Press, Box 1111, Gulf Breeze, Florida 32562; *Russia and Eurasia Facts and Figures Annual.*

Business International Moscow, 23 Profsoyuznaya Ulitsa, 117859, Moscow (Telephone Number in U.S. (800) 938-4685); *The CIS Market Atlas.*

Central Intelligence Agency, Washington, D.C. 20505 (703) 482-1100, www.cia.gov; *The World Factbook.*

The Economist Intelligence Unit, 111 West 57th Street, New York, New York 10019 (800) 938-4685; *Turkmenistan Country Report.*

Euromonitor International, Inc., 122 South Michigan Avenue, Suite 1200, Chicago, Illinois 60603 (800) 577-EURO; *International Marketing Data and Statistics;* and *The World Economic Factbook.*

Europa Publications Limited, 18 Bedford Square, London, WC1B 3JN, England; *The Europa World Year Book.*

International Monetary Fund, 700 Nineteenth Street, NW, Washington, D.C. 20431 (202) 623-7000; *Direction of Trade Statistics.*

St. Martin's Press, Inc., 175 Fifth Avenue, New York, New York 10010 (800) 221-7945; *The Statesman's Year-Book.*

Statistical Office of the United Nations, Publishing Service, New York, New York 10017 (800) 253-9646; *International Trade Statistics Yearbook;* and *Trends in Europe and North America: The Statistical Yearbook of the Economic Commission for Europe.*

The World Bank, 1818 H Street, NW, Washington, D.C. 20433 (202) 477-1234; *Statistical Handbook: States of the Former USSR; World Development Report;* and *World Development Indicators.*

TURKMENISTAN - EXTERNAL INDEBTEDNESS

The World Bank, 1818 H Street, NW, Washington, D.C. 20433 (202) 477-1234; *World Development Report.*

TURKMENISTAN - EXTERNAL TRADE

Academic International Press, Box 1111, Gulf Breeze, Florida 32562; *Russia and Eurasia Facts and Figures Annual.*

Euromonitor International, Inc., 122 South Michigan Avenue, Suite 1200, Chicago, Illinois 60603 (800) 577-EURO; *World Marketing Data and Statistics.*

Food and Agriculture Organization of the United Nations (FAO), Via delle Terme di Caracalla, 00100, Rome, Italy (Telephone Number in U.S. (202) 653-2400); *Trade Yearbook.*

Statistical Office of the United Nations, Publishing Service, New York, New York 10017 (800) 253-9646; *Statistical Yearbook.*

The World Bank, 1818 H Street, NW, Washington, D.C. 20433 (202) 477-1234; *Statistical Handbook: States of the Former USSR;* and *World Development Indicators.*

TURKMENISTAN - FABRIC PRODUCTION AND CONSUMPTION - See TURKMENISTAN - TEXTILE INDUSTRY

TURKMENISTAN - FERTILITY RATES

Central Intelligence Agency, Washington, D.C. 20505 (703) 482-1100, www.cia.gov; *The World Factbook.*

Statistical Office of the United Nations, Publishing Service, New York, New York 10017 (800) 253-9646; *Human Development Report;* and *Trends in Europe and North America: The Statistical Yearbook of the Economic Commission for Europe.*

The World Bank, 1818 H Street, NW, Washington, D.C. 20433 (202) 477-1234;

Statistical Handbook: States of the Former USSR; The World Bank Atlas; World Development Report; and *World Development Indicators.*

World Health Organization, Office of Publications, 20 Avenue Appia, CH-1211 Geneva 27, Switzerland (Telephone Number in U.S. (518) 436-9686); *World Health Statistics Annual.*

TURKMENISTAN - FERTILIZER

Food and Agriculture Organization of the United Nations (FAO), Via delle Terme di Caracalla, 00100, Rome, Italy (Telephone Number in U.S. (202) 653-2400); *Fertilizer Yearbook.*

Statistical Office of the United Nations, Publishing Service, New York, New York 10017 (800) 253-9646; *Industrial Commodity Statistics Yearbook;* and *Statistical Yearbook.*

TURKMENISTAN - FINANCE

The Economist Intelligence Unit, 111 West 57th Street, New York, New York 10019 (800) 938-4685; *Turkmenistan Country Report.*

Europa Publications Limited, 18 Bedford Square, London, WC1B 3JN, England; *The Europa World Year Book.*

St. Martin's Press, Inc., 175 Fifth Avenue, New York, New York 10010 (800) 221-7945; *The Statesman's Year-Book.*

The World Bank, 1818 H Street, NW, Washington, D.C. 20433 (202) 477-1234; *Statistical Handbook: States of the Former USSR.*

TURKMENISTAN - FISHERIES

Food and Agriculture Organization of the United Nations (FAO), Via delle Terme di Caracalla, 00100, Rome, Italy (Telephone Number in U.S. (202) 653-2400); *The State of Food and Agriculture;* and *Yearbook of Fishery Statistics.*

St. Martin's Press, Inc., 175 Fifth Avenue, New York, New York 10010 (800) 221-7945; *The Statesman's Year-Book.*

Statistical Office of the United Nations, Publishing Service, New York, New York 10017 (800) 253-9646; *Industrial Commodity Statistics Yearbook;* and *Statistical Yearbook.*

TURKMENISTAN - FOOD

Food and Agriculture Organization of the United Nations (FAO), Via delle Terme di Caracalla, 00100, Rome, Italy (Telephone Number in U.S. (202) 653-2400); *Production Yearbook; The State of Food and Agriculture;* and *Trade Yearbook.*

Statistical Office of the United Nations, Publishing Service, New York, New York 10017 (800) 253-9646; *Human Development Report;* and *Industrial Commodity Statistics Yearbook.*

TURKMENISTAN - FOOTWEAR PRODUCTION AND CONSUMPTION - See TURKMENISTAN - TEXTILE INDUSTRY

TURKMENISTAN - FOREIGN INVESTMENT

Business International Moscow, 23 Profsoyuznaya Ulitsa, 117859, Moscow (Telephone Number in U.S. (800) 938-4685); *The CIS Market Atlas.*

TURKMENISTAN - FOREIGN TRADE

Business International Moscow, 23 Profsoyuznaya Ulitsa, 117859, Moscow (Telephone Number in U.S. (800) 938-4685); *The CIS Market Atlas.*

The Economist Intelligence Unit, 111 West 57th Street, New York, New York 10019 (800) 938-4685; *Turkmenistan Country Report.*

Euromonitor International, Inc., 122 South Michigan Avenue, Suite 1200, Chicago, Illinois 60603 (800) 577-EURO; *The World Economic Factbook.*

Europa Publications Limited, 18 Bedford Square, London, WC1B 3JN, England; *The Europa World Year Book.*

International Monetary Fund, 700 Nineteenth Street, NW, Washington, D.C. 20431 (202) 623-7000; *Direction of Trade Statistics.*

St. Martin's Press, Inc., 175 Fifth Avenue, New York, New York 10010 (800) 221-7945; *The Statesman's Year-Book.*

Statistical Office of the United Nations, Publishing Service, New York, New York 10017 (800) 253-9646; *International Trade Statistics Yearbook; Statistical Yearbook;* and *Trade Yearbook.*

The World Bank, 1818 H Street, NW, Washington, D.C. 20433 (202) 477-1234; *World Development Report;* and *World Development Indicators.*

TURKMENISTAN - FORESTRY AND FOREST PRODUCTS

Academic International Press, Box 1111, Gulf Breeze, Florida 32562; *Russia and Eurasia Facts and Figures Annual.*

Business International Moscow, 23 Profsoyuznaya Ulitsa, 117859, Moscow (Telephone Number in U.S. (800) 938-

4685); *The CIS Market Atlas.*

Food and Agriculture Organization of the United Nations (FAO), Via delle Terme di Caracalla, 00100, Rome, Italy (Telephone Number in U.S. (202) 653-2400); *The State of Food and Agriculture;* and *Yearbook of Forest Products.*

St. Martin's Press, Inc., 175 Fifth Avenue, New York, New York 10010 (800) 221-7945; *The Statesman's Year-Book.*

Statistical Office of the United Nations, Publishing Service, New York, New York 10017 (800) 253-9646; *Industrial Commodity Statistics Yearbook; Statistical Yearbook;* and *Trends in Europe and North America: The Statistical Yearbook of the Economic Commission for Europe.*

United Nations Educational, Scientific and Cultural Organization (UNESCO), 7 Place de Fontenoy, F-75700 Paris, France (Telephone Number in U.S. (212) 963-5981); *Statistical Yearbook.*

The World Bank, 1818 H Street, NW, Washington, D.C. 20433 (202) 477-1234; *World Development Report.*

TURKMENISTAN - GOATS - See TURKMENISTAN - LIVESTOCK AND POULTRY

TURKMENISTAN - GOVERNMENT

Academic International Press, Box 1111, Gulf Breeze, Florida 32562; *Russia and Eurasia Facts and Figures Annual.*

Central Intelligence Agency, Washington, D.C. 20505 (703) 482-1100, www.cia.gov; *The World Factbook.*

Europa Publications Limited, 18 Bedford Square, London, WC1B 3JN, England; *The Europa World Year Book.*

St. Martin's Press, Inc., 175 Fifth Avenue, New York, New York 10010 (800) 221-7945; *The Statesman's Year-Book.*

Statistical Office of the United Nations, Publishing Service, New York, New York 10017 (800) 253-9646; *Statistical Yearbook.*

The World Bank, 1818 H Street, NW, Washington, D.C. 20433 (202) 477-1234; *World Development Report;* and *Statistical Handbook: States of the Former USSR.*

TURKMENISTAN - GROSS DOMESTIC PRODUCT

Academic International Press, Box 1111, Gulf Breeze, Florida 32562; *Russia and Eurasia Facts and Figures Annual.*

The Economist Intelligence Unit, 111 West 57th Street, New York, New York

10019 (800) 938-4685; *Turkmenistan Country Report.*

Euromonitor International, Inc., 122 South Michigan Avenue, Suite 1200, Chicago, Illinois 60603 (800) 577-EURO; *International Marketing Data and Statistics;* and *The World Economic Factbook.*

Statistical Office of the United Nations, Publishing Service, New York, New York 10017 (800) 253-9646; *Human Development Report; National Accounts Statistics; Statistical Yearbook;* and *Trends in Europe and North America: The Statistical Yearbook of the Economic Commission for Europe.*

The World Bank, 1818 H Street, NW, Washington, D.C. 20433 (202) 477-1234; *World Development Report; Statistical Handbook: States of the Former USSR;* and *World Development Indicators.*

TURKMENISTAN - GROSS NATIONAL PRODUCT

St. Martin's Press, Inc., 175 Fifth Avenue, New York, New York 10010 (800) 221-7945; *The Statesman's Year-Book.*

The World Bank, 1818 H Street, NW, Washington, D.C. 20433 (202) 477-1234; *The World Bank Atlas; World Development Report;* and *World Development Indicators.*

TURKMENISTAN - HEALTH

Academic International Press, Box 1111, Gulf Breeze, Florida 32562; *Russia and Eurasia Facts and Figures Annual.*

Business International Moscow, 23 Profsoyuznaya Ulitsa, 117859, Moscow (Telephone Number in U.S. (800) 938-4685); *The CIS Market Atlas.*

Euromonitor International, Inc., 122 South Michigan Avenue, Suite 1200, Chicago, Illinois 60603 (800) 577-EURO; *World Marketing Data and Statistics.*

St. Martin's Press, Inc., 175 Fifth Avenue, New York, New York 10010 (800) 221-7945; *The Statesman's Year-Book.*

Statistical Office of the United Nations, Publishing Service, New York, New York 10017 (800) 253-9646; *Human Development Report; Statistical Yearbook;* and *Trends in Europe and North America: The Statistical Yearbook of the Economic Commission for Europe.*

United Nations Children's Fund (UNICEF), 3 United Nations Plaza, New York, New York 10017 (800) 253-9646; *State of the World's Children.*

The World Bank, 1818 H Street, NW, Washington, D.C. 20433 (202) 477-1234;

World Development Report.

World Health Organization, Office of Publications, 20 Avenue Appia, CH-1211 Geneva 27, Switzerland (Telephone Number in U.S. (518) 436-9686); *World Health Statistics Annual.*

TURKMENISTAN - HIGHWAYS

Academic International Press, Box 1111, Gulf Breeze, Florida 32562; *Russia and Eurasia Facts and Figures Annual.*

Business International Moscow, 23 Profsoyuznaya Ulitsa, 117859, Moscow (Telephone Number in U.S. (800) 938-4685); *The CIS Market Atlas.*

Central Intelligence Agency, Washington, D.C. 20505 (703) 482-1100, www.cia.gov; *The World Factbook.*

St. Martin's Press, Inc., 175 Fifth Avenue, New York, New York 10010 (800) 221-7945; *The Statesman's Year-Book.*

Statistical Office of the United Nations, Publishing Service, New York, New York 10017 (800) 253-9646; *Trends in Europe and North America: The Statistical Yearbook of the Economic Commission for Europe.*

TURKMENISTAN - HOUSING AND HOUSING UNITS

Business International Moscow, 23 Profsoyuznaya Ulitsa, 117859, Moscow (Telephone Number in U.S. (800) 938-4685); *The CIS Market Atlas.*

Euromonitor International, Inc., 122 South Michigan Avenue, Suite 1200, Chicago, Illinois 60603 (800) 577-EURO; *World Marketing Data and Statistics.*

Statistical Office of the United Nations, Publishing Service, New York, New York 10017 (800) 253-9646; *Trends in Europe and North America: The Statistical Yearbook of the Economic Commission for Europe.*

TURKMENISTAN - ILLITERATE POPULATION

Central Intelligence Agency, Washington, D.C. 20505 (703) 482-1100, www.cia.gov; *The World Factbook.*

Euromonitor International, Inc., 122 South Michigan Avenue, Suite 1200, Chicago, Illinois 60603 (800) 577-EURO; *The World Economic Factbook.*

Statistical Office of the United Nations, Publishing Service, New York, New York 10017 (800) 253-9646; *Human Development Report.*

United Nations Educational, Scientific and Cultural Organization (UNESCO), 7

Place de Fontenoy, F-75700 Paris, France (Telephone Number in U.S. (212) 963-5981); *Statistical Yearbook.*

TURKMENISTAN - IMPORTS

Academic International Press, Box 1111, Gulf Breeze, Florida 32562; *Russia and Eurasia Facts and Figures Annual.*

Business International Moscow, 23 Profsoyuznaya Ulitsa, 117859, Moscow (Telephone Number in U.S. (800) 938-4685); *The CIS Market Atlas.*

Central Intelligence Agency, Washington, D.C. 20505 (703) 482-1100, www.cia.gov; *The World Factbook.*

The Economist Intelligence Unit, 111 West 57th Street, New York, New York 10019 (800) 938-4685; *Turkmenistan Country Report.*

Euromonitor International, Inc., 122 South Michigan Avenue, Suite 1200, Chicago, Illinois 60603 (800) 577-EURO; *International Marketing Data and Statistics;* and *The World Economic Factbook.*

Europa Publications Limited, 18 Bedford Square, London, WC1B 3JN, England; *The Europa World Year Book.*

International Monetary Fund, 700 Nineteenth Street, NW, Washington, D.C. 20431 (202) 623-7000; *Direction of Trade Statistics.*

St. Martin's Press, Inc., 175 Fifth Avenue, New York, New York 10010 (800) 221-7945; *The Statesman's Year-Book.*

Statistical Office of the United Nations, Publishing Service, New York, New York 10017 (800) 253-9646; *International Trade Statistics Yearbook;* and *Trends in Europe and North America: The Statistical Yearbook of the Economic Commission for Europe.*

The World Bank, 1818 H Street, NW, Washington, D.C. 20433 (202) 477-1234; *World Development Report; Statistical Handbook: States of the Former USSR;* and *World Development Indicators.*

TURKMENISTAN - INDUSTRY

Academic International Press, Box 1111, Gulf Breeze, Florida 32562; *Russia and Eurasia Facts and Figures Annual.*

Business International Moscow, 23 Profsoyuznaya Ulitsa, 117859, Moscow (Telephone Number in U.S. (800) 938-4685); *The CIS Market Atlas.*

Central Intelligence Agency, Washington, D.C. 20505 (703) 482-1100, www.cia.gov; *The World Factbook.*

The Economist Intelligence Unit, 111 West 57th Street, New York, New York 10019 (800) 938-4685; *Turkmenistan Country Report.*

Euromonitor International, Inc., 122 South Michigan Avenue, Suite 1200, Chicago, Illinois 60603 (800) 577-EURO; *The World Economic Factbook;* and *World Marketing Data and Statistics.*

Europa Publications Limited, 18 Bedford Square, London, WC1B 3JN, England; *The Europa World Year Book.*

St. Martin's Press, Inc., 175 Fifth Avenue, New York, New York 10010 (800) 221-7945; *The Statesman's Year-Book.*

Statistical Office of the United Nations, Publishing Service, New York, New York 10017 (800) 253-9646; *Industrial Commodity Statistics Yearbook; Statistical Yearbook;* and *Trends in Europe and North America: The Statistical Yearbook of the Economic Commission for Europe.*

The World Bank, 1818 H Street, NW, Washington, D.C. 20433 (202) 477-1234; *Statistical Handbook: States of the Former USSR;* and *World Development Indicators.*

TURKMENISTAN - INFANT MORTALITY RATES - See TURKMENISTAN - MORTALITY

TURKMENISTAN - INTERNAL TRADE

Statistical Office of the United Nations, Publishing Service, New York, New York 10017 (800) 253-9646; *Statistical Yearbook.*

TURKMENISTAN - LABOR

Academic International Press, Box 1111, Gulf Breeze, Florida 32562; *Russia and Eurasia Facts and Figures Annual.*

Business International Moscow, 23 Profsoyuznaya Ulitsa, 117859, Moscow (Telephone Number in U.S. (800) 938-4685); *The CIS Market Atlas.*

Central Intelligence Agency, Washington, D.C. 20505 (703) 482-1100, www.cia.gov; *The World Factbook.*

Euromonitor International, Inc., 122 South Michigan Avenue, Suite 1200, Chicago, Illinois 60603 (800) 577-EURO; *International Marketing Data and Statistics;* and *World Marketing Data and Statistics.*

Europa Publications Limited, 18 Bedford Square, London, WC1B 3JN, England; *The Europa World Year Book.*

St. Martin's Press, Inc., 175 Fifth Avenue, New York, New York 10010 (800) 221-7945; *The Statesman's Year-Book.*

Statistical Office of the United Nations,

Publishing Service, New York, New York 10017 (800) 253-9646; *Human Development Report;* and *Statistical Yearbook.*

The World Bank, 1818 H Street, NW, Washington, D.C. 20433 (202) 477-1234; *Statistical Handbook: States of the Former USSR; The World Bank Atlas; World Development Report;* and *World Development Indicators.*

TURKMENISTAN - LAND USE

Central Intelligence Agency, Washington, D.C. 20505 (703) 482-1100, www.cia.gov; *The World Factbook.*

Euromonitor International, Inc., 122 South Michigan Avenue, Suite 1200, Chicago, Illinois 60603 (800) 577-EURO; *International Marketing Data and Statistics.*

Food and Agriculture Organization of the United Nations (FAO), Via delle Terme di Caracalla, 00100, Rome, Italy (Telephone Number in U.S. (202) 653-2400); *Production Yearbook.*

The World Bank, 1818 H Street, NW, Washington, D.C. 20433 (202) 477-1234; *World Development Report.*

TURKMENISTAN - LIBRARIES

Statistical Office of the United Nations, Publishing Service, New York, New York 10017 (800) 253-9646; *Trends in Europe and North America: The Statistical Yearbook of the Economic Commission for Europe.*

United Nations Educational, Scientific and Cultural Organization (UNESCO), 7 Place de Fontenoy, F-75700 Paris, France (Telephone Number in U.S. (212) 963-5981); *Statistical Yearbook.*

TURKMENISTAN - LIFE EXPECTANCY

Academic International Press, Box 1111, Gulf Breeze, Florida 32562; *Russia and Eurasia Facts and Figures Annual.*

Business International Moscow, 23 Profsoyuznaya Ulitsa, 117859, Moscow (Telephone Number in U.S. (800) 938-4685); *The CIS Market Atlas.*

Central Intelligence Agency, Washington, D.C. 20505 (703) 482-1100, www.cia.gov; *The World Factbook.*

Euromonitor International, Inc., 122 South Michigan Avenue, Suite 1200, Chicago, Illinois 60603 (800) 577-EURO; *The World Economic Factbook.*

Statistical Office of the United Nations, Publishing Service, New York, New York 10017 (800) 253-9646; *Demographic*

Yearbook; Human Development Report; Trends in Europe and North America: The Statistical Yearbook of the Economic Commission for Europe; and *World Statistics Pocketbook.*

The World Bank, 1818 H Street, NW, Washington, D.C. 20433 (202) 477-1234; *The World Bank Atlas; World Development Report;* and *World Development Indicators.*

World Health Organization, Office of Publications, 20 Avenue Appia, CH-1211 Geneva 27, Switzerland (Telephone Number in U.S. (518) 436-9686); *World Health Statistics Annual.*

TURKMENISTAN - LITERACY RATE

Euromonitor International, Inc., 122 South Michigan Avenue, Suite 1200, Chicago, Illinois 60603 (800) 577-EURO; *World Marketing Data and Statistics.*

TURKMENISTAN - LIVESTOCK AND POULTRY

Academic International Press, Box 1111, Gulf Breeze, Florida 32562; *Russia and Eurasia Facts and Figures Annual.*

Business International Moscow, 23 Profsoyuznaya Ulitsa, 117859, Moscow (Telephone Number in U.S. (800) 938-4685); *The CIS Market Atlas.*

Europa Publications Limited, 18 Bedford Square, London, WC1B 3JN, England; *The Europa World Year Book.*

Food and Agriculture Organization of the United Nations (FAO), Via delle Terme di Caracalla, 00100, Rome, Italy (Telephone Number in U.S. (202) 653-2400); *Production Yearbook; The State of Food and Agriculture;* and *Trade Yearbook.*

St. Martin's Press, Inc., 175 Fifth Avenue, New York, New York 10010 (800) 221-7945; *The Statesman's Year-Book.*

Statistical Office of the United Nations, Publishing Service, New York, New York 10017 (800) 253-9646; *Industrial Commodity Statistics Yearbook;* and *Statistical Yearbook.*

TURKMENISTAN - MACHINERY

Statistical Office of the United Nations, Publishing Service, New York, New York 10017 (800) 253-9646; *Industrial Commodity Statistics Yearbook.*

TURKMENISTAN - MAIL-NUMBER OF PIECES SENT OR RECEIVED

Statistical Office of the United Nations, Publishing Service, New York, New York 10017 (800) 253-9646; *Statistical Yearbook.*

TURKMENISTAN - MANUFACTURING

Statistical Office of the United Nations, Publishing Service, New York, New York 10017 (800) 253-9646; *Industrial Commodity Statistics Yearbook;* and *Statistical Yearbook.*

The World Bank, 1818 H Street, NW, Washington, D.C. 20433 (202) 477-1234; *World Development Indicators.*

TURKMENISTAN - MARRIAGE RATES

Academic International Press, Box 1111, Gulf Breeze, Florida 32562; *Russia and Eurasia Facts and Figures Annual.*

Europa Publications Limited, 18 Bedford Square, London, WC1B 3JN, England; *The Europa World Year Book.*

Statistical Office of the United Nations, Publishing Service, New York, New York 10017 (800) 253-9646; *Demographic Yearbook; Statistical Yearbook;* and *Trends in Europe and North America: The Statistical Yearbook of the Economic Commission for Europe.*

TURKMENISTAN - MEAT PRODUCTION - See TURKMENISTAN - LIVESTOCK AND POULTRY

TURKMENISTAN - MERCHANT SHIPPING

Statistical Office of the United Nations, Publishing Service, New York, New York 10017 (800) 253-9646; *Statistical Yearbook.*

TURKMENISTAN - MILITARY

Academic International Press, Box 1111, Gulf Breeze, Florida 32562; *Russia and Eurasia Facts and Figures Annual.*

Central Intelligence Agency, Washington, D.C. 20505 (703) 482-1100, www.cia.gov; *The World Factbook.*

Euromonitor International, Inc., 122 South Michigan Avenue, Suite 1200, Chicago, Illinois 60603 (800) 577-EURO; *World Marketing Data and Statistics.*

The International Institute for Strategic Studies, 23 Tavistock Street, London WC2E 7NQ, England 44 171 3797676; *The Military Balance.*

St. Martin's Press, Inc., 175 Fifth Avenue, New York, New York 10010 (800) 221-7945; *The Statesman's Year-Book.*

Statistical Office of the United Nations, Publishing Service, New York, New York 10017 (800) 253-9646; *Human Development Report.*

TURKMENISTAN - MINING AND MINERAL PRODUCTS

Academic International Press, Box 1111, Gulf Breeze, Florida 32562; *Russia and Eurasia Facts and Figures Annual*.

Business International Moscow, 23 Profsoyuznaya Ulitsa, 117859, Moscow (Telephone Number in U.S. (800) 938-4685); *The CIS Market Atlas*.

Europa Publications Limited, 18 Bedford Square, London, WC1B 3JN, England; *The Europa World Year Book*.

St. Martin's Press, Inc., 175 Fifth Avenue, New York, New York 10010 (800) 221-7945; *The Statesman's Year-Book*.

Statistical Office of the United Nations, Publishing Service, New York, New York 10017 (800) 253-9646; *Energy Statistics Yearbook; Industrial Commodity Statistics Yearbook;* and *Statistical Yearbook*.

TURKMENISTAN - MONEY SUPPLY

The Economist Intelligence Unit, 111 West 57th Street, New York, New York 10019 (800) 938-4685; *Turkmenistan Country Report*.

TURKMENISTAN - MONUMENTS

United Nations Educational, Scientific and Cultural Organization (UNESCO), 7 Place de Fontenoy, F-75700 Paris, France (Telephone Number in U.S. (212) 963-5981); *Statistical Yearbook*.

TURKMENISTAN - MORTALITY

Academic International Press, Box 1111, Gulf Breeze, Florida 32562; *Russia and Eurasia Facts and Figures Annual*.

Business International Moscow, 23 Profsoyuznaya Ulitsa, 117859, Moscow (Telephone Number in U.S. (800) 938-4685); *The CIS Market Atlas*.

Central Intelligence Agency, Washington, D.C. 20505 (703) 482-1100, www.cia.gov; *The World Factbook*.

Euromonitor International, Inc., 122 South Michigan Avenue, Suite 1200, Chicago, Illinois 60603 (800) 577-EURO; *International Marketing Data and Statistics;* and *The World Economic Factbook*.

Europa Publications Limited, 18 Bedford Square, London, WC1B 3JN, England; *The Europa World Year Book*.

St. Martin's Press, Inc., 175 Fifth Avenue, New York, New York 10010 (800) 221-7945; *The Statesman's Year-Book*.

Statistical Office of the United Nations, Publishing Service, New York, New York 10017 (800) 253-9646; *Demographic Yearbook; Human Development Report;*

Statistical Yearbook; Trends in Europe and North America: The Statistical Yearbook of the Economic Commission for Europe; and *World Statistics Pocketbook*.

United Nations Children's Fund (UNICEF), 3 United Nations Plaza, New York, New York 10017 (800) 253-9646; *State of the World's Children*.

The World Bank, 1818 H Street, NW, Washington, D.C. 20433 (202) 477-1234; *The World Bank Atlas; World Development Report;* and *World Development Indicators*.

World Health Organization, Office of Publications, 20 Avenue Appia, CH-1211 Geneva 27, Switzerland (Telephone Number in U.S. (518) 436-9686); *World Health Statistics Annual*.

TURKMENISTAN - MOTION PICTURES

Statistical Office of the United Nations, Publishing Service, New York, New York 10017 (800) 253-9646; *Statistical Yearbook*.

United Nations Educational, Scientific and Cultural Organization (UNESCO), 7 Place de Fontenoy, F-75700 Paris, France (Telephone Number in U.S. (212) 963-5981); *Statistical Yearbook*.

TURKMENISTAN - MOTOR VEHICLES

Business International Moscow, 23 Profsoyuznaya Ulitsa, 117859, Moscow (Telephone Number in U.S. (800) 938-4685); *The CIS Market Atlas*.

Statistical Office of the United Nations, Publishing Service, New York, New York 10017 (800) 253-9646; *Statistical Yearbook*.

TURKMENISTAN - MUSEUMS

United Nations Educational, Scientific and Cultural Organization (UNESCO), 7 Place de Fontenoy, F-75700 Paris, France (Telephone Number in U.S. (212) 963-5981); *Statistical Yearbook*.

TURKMENISTAN - NATIONAL ACCOUNTS

Europa Publications Limited, 18 Bedford Square, London, WC1B 3JN, England; *The Europa World Year Book*.

Statistical Office of the United Nations, Publishing Service, New York, New York 10017 (800) 253-9646; *National Accounts Statistics;* and *Statistical Yearbook*.

The World Bank, 1818 H Street, NW, Washington, D.C. 20433 (202) 477-1234; *Statistical Handbook: States of the Former USSR*.

TURKMENISTAN - NATIONAL INCOME

Business International Moscow, 23 Profsoyuznaya Ulitsa, 117859, Moscow (Telephone Number in U.S. (800) 938-4685); *The CIS Market Atlas*.

Statistical Office of the United Nations, Publishing Service, New York, New York 10017 (800) 253-9646; *Statistical Yearbook*.

TURKMENISTAN - NATIONAL PRODUCT

Statistical Office of the United Nations, Publishing Service, New York, New York 10017 (800) 253-9646; *Statistical Yearbook*.

TURKMENISTAN - PATENTS, TRADEMARKS AND SERVICE MARKS

Statistical Office of the United Nations, Publishing Service, New York, New York 10017 (800) 253-9646; *Statistical Yearbook*.

TURKMENISTAN - PERIODICALS

United Nations Educational, Scientific and Cultural Organization (UNESCO), 7 Place de Fontenoy, F-75700 Paris, France (Telephone Number in U.S. (212) 963-5981); *Statistical Yearbook*.

TURKMENISTAN - PETROLEUM INDUSTRY

St. Martin's Press, Inc., 175 Fifth Avenue, New York, New York 10010 (800) 221-7945; *The Statesman's Year-Book*.

Statistical Office of the United Nations, Publishing Service, New York, New York 10017 (800) 253-9646; *Energy Statistics Yearbook; Industrial Commodity Statistics Yearbook; The State of Food and Agriculture; Statistical Yearbook;* and *Trends in Europe and North America: The Statistical Yearbook of the Economic Commission for Europe*.

TURKMENISTAN - PIGS - See TURKMENISTAN - LIVESTOCK AND POULTRY

TURKMENISTAN - POPULATION

Academic International Press, Box 1111, Gulf Breeze, Florida 32562; *Russia and Eurasia Facts and Figures Annual*.

Business International Moscow, 23 Profsoyuznaya Ulitsa, 117859, Moscow (Telephone Number in U.S. (800) 938-4685); *The CIS Market Atlas*.

Central Intelligence Agency, Washington, D.C. 20505 (703) 482-1100, www.cia.gov; *The World Factbook*.

The Economist Intelligence Unit, 111 West 57th Street, New York, New York 10019 (800) 938-4685; *Turkmenistan Country Report*.

Euromonitor International, Inc., 122 South Michigan Avenue, Suite 1200, Chicago, Illinois 60603 (800) 577-EURO; *International Marketing Data and Statistics;* and *The World Economic Factbook*.

Europa Publications Limited, 18 Bedford Square, London, WC1B 3JN, England; *The Europa World Year Book*.

Food and Agriculture Organization of the United Nations (FAO), Via delle Terme di Caracalla, 00100, Rome, Italy (Telephone Number in U.S. (202) 653-2400); *Production Yearbook*.

St. Martin's Press, Inc., 175 Fifth Avenue, New York, New York 10010 (800) 221-7945; *The Statesman's Year-Book*.

Statistical Office of the United Nations, Publishing Service, New York, New York 10017 (800) 253-9646; *Demographic Yearbook; Human Development Report; Statistical Yearbook; Trends in Europe and North America: The Statistical Yearbook of the Economic Commission for Europe;* and *World Statistics Pocketbook*.

United Nations Educational, Scientific and Cultural Organization (UNESCO), 7 Place de Fontenoy, F-75700 Paris, France (Telephone Number in U.S. (212) 963-5981); *Statistical Yearbook*.

The World Bank, 1818 H Street, NW, Washington, D.C. 20433 (202) 477-1234; *Statistical Handbook: States of the Former USSR; The World Bank Atlas; World Development Report;* and *World Development Indicators*.

World Health Organization, Office of Publications, 20 Avenue Appia, CH-1211 Geneva 27, Switzerland (Telephone Number in U.S. (518) 436-9686); *World Health Statistics Annual*.

TURKMENISTAN - POST OFFICES

Statistical Office of the United Nations, Publishing Service, New York, New York 10017 (800) 253-9646; *Trends in Europe and North America: The Statistical Yearbook of the Economic Commission for Europe*.

TURKMENISTAN - POULTRY - See TURKMENISTAN - LIVESTOCK AND POULTRY

TURKMENISTAN - PRICES

Food and Agriculture Organization of the United Nations (FAO), Via delle Terme di Caracalla, 00100, Rome, Italy (Telephone Number in U.S. (202) 653-2400); *Production Yearbook*.

The World Bank, 1818 H Street, NW, Washington, D.C. 20433 (202) 477-1234; *Statistical Handbook: States of the Former USSR*.

TURKMENISTAN - PRODUCTION

The World Bank, 1818 H Street, NW, Washington, D.C. 20433 (202) 477-1234; *Statistical Handbook: States of the Former USSR*.

TURKMENISTAN - PUBLIC FINANCE - See TURKMENISTAN - FINANCE

TURKMENISTAN - RADIO RECEIVER PRODUCTION

Statistical Office of the United Nations, Publishing Service, New York, New York 10017 (800) 253-9646; *Statistical Yearbook*.

TURKMENISTAN - RADIO RECEIVERS

St. Martin's Press, Inc., 175 Fifth Avenue, New York, New York 10010 (800) 221-7945; *The Statesman's Year-Book*.

TURKMENISTAN - RAILWAYS

Academic International Press, Box 1111, Gulf Breeze, Florida 32562; *Russia and Eurasia Facts and Figures Annual*.

Business International Moscow, 23 Profsoyuznaya Ulitsa, 117859, Moscow (Telephone Number in U.S. (800) 938-4685); *The CIS Market Atlas*.

St. Martin's Press, Inc., 175 Fifth Avenue, New York, New York 10010 (800) 221-7945; *The Statesman's Year-Book*.

Statistical Office of the United Nations, Publishing Service, New York, New York 10017 (800) 253-9646; *Statistical Yearbook;* and *Trends in Europe and North America: The Statistical Yearbook of the Economic Commission for Europe*.

TURKMENISTAN - RELIGION

Academic International Press, Box 1111, Gulf Breeze, Florida 32562; *Russia and Eurasia Facts and Figures Annual*.

Central Intelligence Agency, Washington, D.C. 20505 (703) 482-1100, www.cia.gov; *The World Factbook*.

St. Martin's Press, Inc., 175 Fifth Avenue, New York, New York 10010 (800) 221-7945; *The Statesman's Year-Book*.

TURKMENISTAN - RETAIL TRADE

Business International Moscow, 23 Profsoyuznaya Ulitsa, 117859, Moscow (Telephone Number in U.S. (800) 938-4685); *The CIS Market Atlas*.

Euromonitor International, Inc., 122 South Michigan Avenue, Suite 1200, Chicago, Illinois 60603 (800) 577-EURO;

World Marketing Data and Statistics.

Europa Publications Limited, 18 Bedford Square, London, WC1B 3JN, England; *The Europa World Year Book*.

Statistical Office of the United Nations, Publishing Service, New York, New York 10017 (800) 253-9646; *Statistical Yearbook*.

TURKMENISTAN - ROADS - See TURKMENISTAN - HIGHWAYS

TURKMENISTAN - ROUNDWOOD PRODUCTION AND CONSUMPTION - See TURKMENISTAN - FORESTRY AND FOREST PRODUCTS

TURKMENISTAN - RUBBER PRODUCTION AND CONSUMPTION

Statistical Office of the United Nations, Publishing Service, New York, New York 10017 (800) 253-9646; *Statistical Yearbook*.

TURKMENISTAN - SCIENTISTS, TECHNICIANS AND ENGINEERS

Statistical Office of the United Nations, Publishing Service, New York, New York 10017 (800) 253-9646; *Statistical Yearbook*.

TURKMENISTAN - SHEEP - See TURKMENISTAN - LIVESTOCK AND POULTRY

TURKMENISTAN - SOCIAL DATA

Statistical Office of the United Nations, Publishing Service, New York, New York 10017 (800) 253-9646; *World Statistics Pocketbook*.

TURKMENISTAN - STEEL PRODUCTION AND CONSUMPTION - See TURKMENISTAN - MINING AND MINERAL PRODUCTS

TURKMENISTAN - TAXATION

Europa Publications Limited, 18 Bedford Square, London, WC1B 3JN, England; *The Europa World Year Book*.

TURKMENISTAN - TELEPHONES IN USE

Academic International Press, Box 1111, Gulf Breeze, Florida 32562; *Russia and Eurasia Facts and Figures Annual*.

Central Intelligence Agency, Washington, D.C. 20505 (703) 482-1100, www.cia.gov; *The World Factbook*.

Statistical Office of the United Nations, Publishing Service, New York, New York 10017 (800) 253-9646; *Statistical Yearbook; Trends in Europe and North America: The Statistical Yearbook of the Economic Commission for Europe;* and *World Statistics Pocketbook*.

TURKMENISTAN - TEXTILE INDUSTRY

Business International Moscow, 23 Profsoyuznaya Ulitsa, 117859, Moscow (Telephone Number in U.S. (800) 938-4685); *The CIS Market Atlas.*

Statistical Office of the United Nations, Publishing Service, New York, New York 10017 (800) 253-9646; *Industrial Commodity Statistics Yearbook;* and *Statistical Yearbook.*

TURKMENISTAN - THEATRE

United Nations Educational, Scientific and Cultural Organization (UNESCO), 7 Place de Fontenoy, F-75700 Paris, France (Telephone Number in U.S. (212) 963-5981); *Statistical Yearbook.*

TURKMENISTAN - TIRE (MOTOR VEHICLE) PRODUCTION

Statistical Office of the United Nations, Publishing Service, New York, New York 10017 (800) 253-9646; *Statistical Yearbook.*

TURKMENISTAN - TOBACCO PRODUCTION

Statistical Office of the United Nations, Publishing Service, New York, New York 10017 (800) 253-9646; *Statistical Yearbook.*

TURKMENISTAN - TOURISM

Business International Moscow, 23 Profsoyuznaya Ulitsa, 117859, Moscow (Telephone Number in U.S. (800) 938-4685); *The CIS Market Atlas.*

Euromonitor International, Inc., 122 South Michigan Avenue, Suite 1200, Chicago, Illinois 60603 (800) 577-EURO; *The World Economic Factbook;* and *World Marketing Data and Statistics.*

Statistical Office of the United Nations, Publishing Service, New York, New York 10017 (800) 253-9646; *Statistical Yearbook;* and *Trends in Europe and North America: The Statistical Yearbook of the Economic Commission for Europe.*

TURKMENISTAN - TRADEMARKS AND SERVICE MARKS - See TURKMENISTAN - PATENTS, TRADEMARKS AND SERVICE MARKS

TURKMENISTAN - TRANSPORTATION AND COMMUNICATIONS

Academic International Press, Box 1111, Gulf Breeze, Florida 32562; *Russia and Eurasia Facts and Figures Annual.*

Business International Moscow, 23 Profsoyuznaya Ulitsa, 117859, Moscow (Telephone Number in U.S. (800) 938-4685); *The CIS Market Atlas.*

Central Intelligence Agency, Washington, D.C. 20505 (703) 482-1100, www.cia.gov; *The World Factbook.*

Euromonitor International, Inc., 122 South Michigan Avenue, Suite 1200, Chicago, Illinois 60603 (800) 577-EURO; *International Marketing Data and Statistics;* and *World Marketing Data and Statistics.*

St. Martin's Press, Inc., 175 Fifth Avenue, New York, New York 10010 (800) 221-7945; *The Statesman's Year-Book.*

Statistical Office of the United Nations, Publishing Service, New York, New York 10017 (800) 253-9646; *Human Development Report;* and *Trends in Europe and North America: The Statistical Yearbook of the Economic Commission for Europe.*

TURKMENISTAN - UNEMPLOYMENT

Central Intelligence Agency, Washington, D.C. 20505 (703) 482-1100, www.cia.gov; *The World Factbook.*

St. Martin's Press, Inc., 175 Fifth Avenue, New York, New York 10010 (800) 221-7945; *The Statesman's Year-Book.*

Statistical Office of the United Nations, Publishing Service, New York, New York 10017 (800) 253-9646; *Trends in Europe and North America: The Statistical Yearbook of the Economic Commission for Europe.*

TURKMENISTAN - VITAL STATISTICS

St. Martin's Press, Inc., 175 Fifth Avenue, New York, New York 10010 (800) 221-7945; *The Statesman's Year-Book.*

Statistical Office of the United Nations, Publishing Service, New York, New York 10017 (800) 253-9646; *Statistical Yearbook.*

World Health Organization, Office of Publications, 20 Avenue Appia, CH-1211 Geneva 27, Switzerland (Telephone Number in U.S. (518) 436-9686); *World Health Statistics Annual.*

TURKMENISTAN - WAGES

Business International Moscow, 23 Profsoyuznaya Ulitsa, 117859, Moscow (Telephone Number in U.S. (800) 938-4685); *The CIS Market Atlas.*

Statistical Office of the United Nations, Publishing Service, New York, New York 10017 (800) 253-9646; *Statistical Yearbook.*

The World Bank, 1818 H Street, NW, Washington, D.C. 20433 (202) 477-1234; *Statistical Handbook: States of the Former USSR.*

TURKMENISTAN - WELFARE

Academic International Press, Box 1111, Gulf Breeze, Florida 32562; *Russia and Eurasia Facts and Figures Annual.*

St. Martin's Press, Inc., 175 Fifth Avenue, New York, New York 10010 (800) 221-7945; *The Statesman's Year-Book.*

TURKMENISTAN - WHOLESALE PRICES

Academic International Press, Box 1111, Gulf Breeze, Florida 32562; *Russia and Eurasia Facts and Figures Annual.*

Statistical Office of the United Nations, Publishing Service, New York, New York 10017 (800) 253-9646; *Statistical Yearbook.*

TURKMENISTAN - WHOLESALE TRADE

Statistical Office of the United Nations, Publishing Service, New York, New York 10017 (800) 253-9646; *Statistical Yearbook.*

TURKMENISTAN - WOOL PRODUCTION AND CONSUMPTION - See TURKMENISTAN - TEXTILE INDUSTRY

Turks and Caicos Islands - National Statistical Office

The Chief Secretary, Chief Secretary's Office, Grand Turk, Turks and Caicos Islands.

Turks and Caicos Islands - Primary Statistics Source

Foreign and Commonwealth Office, HM Stationery Office, Post Office Box 569, London SE1 9NH; Turks and Caicos Islands: Report for the Year.

TURKS AND CAICOS ISLANDS - AGRICULTURE

The Economist Intelligence Unit, 111 West 57th Street, New York, New York 10019 (800) 938-4685; *Turks and Caicos Islands Country Report.*

Europa Publications Limited, 18 Bedford Square, London, WC1B 3JN, England; *The Europa World Year Book.*

Food and Agricultural Organization of the United Nations (FAO) Via delle Terme di Caracalla, 00100 Rome, Italy (Telephone Number in U.S. (202) 653-2400); *Production Yearbook;* and *The State of Food and Agriculture,* and *Trade Yearbook.*

United Nations Conference on Trade and Development, Central Statistical Service, Palais des Nations, Geneva, Switzerland (Telephone in U.S. (800) 253-9646); *UNCTAD Commodity Yearbook.*

TURKS AND CAICOS ISLANDS - AIRLINE SERVICE

St. Martin's Press, Inc., 175 Fifth Avenue, New York, New York 10010 (800) 221-7945; *The Statesman's Year-Book.*

TURKS AND CAICOS ISLANDS - AIRPORTS

Central Intelligence Agency, Washington, D.C. 20505 (703) 482-1100, www.cia.gov; *The World Factbook.*

TURKS AND CAICOS ISLANDS - ANIMAL HEALTH

Food and Agricultural Organization of the United Nations (FAO), Via delle Terme di Caracalla, 00100, Rome, Italy (Telephone Number in U.S. (202) 653-2400); *Animal Health Yearbook.*

TURKS AND CAICOS ISLANDS - AREA AND DENSITY OF POPULATION

Central Intelligence Agency, Washington, D.C. 20505 (703) 482-1100, www.cia.gov; *The World Factbook.*

Europa Publications Limited, 18 Bedford Square, London, WC1B 3JN, England; *The Europa World Year Book.*

Food and Agricultural Organization of the United Nations (FAO) Via delle Terme di Caracalla, 00100 Rome, Italy (Telephone Number in U.S. (202) 653-2400); *The State of Food and Agriculture.*

St. Martin's Press, Inc., 175 Fifth Avenue, New York, New York 10010 (800) 221-7945; *The Statesman's Year-Book.*

Statistical Office of the United Nations, Publishing Service, New York, New York 10017 (800) 253-9646; *Statistical Yearbook.*

TURKS AND CAICOS ISLANDS - BANKING

St. Martin's Press, Inc., 175 Fifth Avenue, New York, New York 10010 (800) 221-7945; *The Statesman's Year-Book.*

TURKS AND CAICOS ISLANDS - BIRTH RATES

Central Intelligence Agency, Washington, D.C. 20505 (703) 482-1100, www.cia.gov; *The World Factbook.*

Europa Publications Limited, 18 Bedford Square, London, WC1B 3JN, England; *The Europa World Year Book.*

St. Martin's Press, Inc., 175 Fifth Avenue, New York, New York 10010 (800) 221-7945; *The Statesman's Year-Book.*

Statistical Office of the United Nations,

Publishing Service, New York, New York 10017 (800) 253-9646; *Demographic Yearbook;* and *Statistical Yearbook.*

TURKS AND CAICOS ISLANDS - BROADCASTING

Billboard Limited, P.O. Box 9027, 1006 AA Amsterdam, The Netherlands (Telephone Number in U.S. (212) 764-7300); *World Radio TV Handbook.*

Central Intelligence Agency, Washington, D.C. 20505 (703) 482-1100, www.cia.gov; *The World Factbook.*

St. Martin's Press, Inc., 175 Fifth Avenue, New York, New York 10010 (800) 221-7945; *The Statesman's Year-Book.*

United Nations Educational, Scientific and Cultural Organization (UNESCO), 7 Place de Fontenoy, F-75700 Paris, France (Telephone Number in U.S. (212) 963-5981); *Statistical Yearbook.*

TURKS AND CAICOS ISLANDS - BUDGET

Central Intelligence Agency, Washington, D.C. 20505 (703) 482-1100, www.cia.gov; *The World Factbook.*

TURKS AND CAICOS ISLANDS - CALORIE SUPPLY

Food and Agricultural Organization of the United Nations (FAO) Via delle Terme di Caracalla, 00100 Rome, Italy (Telephone Number in U.S. (202) 653-2400); *The State of Food and Agriculture.*

TURKS AND CAICOS ISLANDS - CHEMICAL (ORGANIC) PRODUCTION - See TURKS AND CAICOS ISLANDS - MINING AND MINERAL PRODUCTS

TURKS AND CAICOS ISLANDS - CLIMATE

St. Martin's Press, Inc., 175 Fifth Avenue, New York, New York 10010 (800) 221-7945; *The Statesman's Year-Book.*

TURKS AND CAICOS ISLANDS - COMMERCE

St. Martin's Press, Inc., 175 Fifth Avenue, New York, New York 10010 (800) 221-7945; *The Statesman's Year-Book.*

TURKS AND CAICOS ISLANDS - CORN PRODUCTION - See TURKS AND CAICOS ISLANDS - CROPS

TURKS AND CAICOS ISLANDS - CORPORATE TAXES - See TURKS AND CAICOS ISLANDS - TAXATION

TURKS AND CAICOS ISLANDS - CROPS

Food and Agricultural Organization of

the United Nations (FAO) Via delle Terme di Caracalla, 00100 Rome, Italy (Telephone Number in U.S. (202) 653-2400); *The State of Food and Agriculture.*

United Nations Conference on Trade and Development, Central Statistical Service, Palais des Nations, Geneva, Switzerland (Telephone in U.S. (800) 253-9646); *UNCTAD Commodity Yearbook.*

TURKS AND CAICOS ISLANDS - CUSTOMS DUTIES

St. Martin's Press, Inc., 175 Fifth Avenue, New York, New York 10010 (800) 221-7945; *The Statesman's Year-Book.*

TURKS AND CAICOS ISLANDS - DAIRY PRODUCTS

Food and Agricultural Organization of the United Nations (FAO) Via delle Terme di Caracalla, 00100 Rome, Italy (Telephone Number in U.S. (202) 653-2400); *The State of Food and Agriculture.*

TURKS AND CAICOS ISLANDS - DEATH RATES - See TURKS AND CAICOS ISLANDS - MORTALITY

TURKS AND CAICOS ISLANDS - DIVORCE RATES

Statistical Office of the United Nations, Publishing Service, New York, New York 10017 (800) 253-9646; *Demographic Yearbook;* and *Statistical Yearbook.*

TURKS AND CAICOS ISLANDS - ECONOMY

Central Intelligence Agency, Washington, D.C. 20505 (703) 482-1100, www.cia.gov; *The World Factbook.*

The Economist Intelligence Unit, 111 West 57th Street, New York, New York 10019 (800) 938-4685; *Turks and Caicos Islands Country Report.*

St. Martin's Press, Inc., 175 Fifth Avenue, New York, New York 10010 (800) 221-7945; *The Statesman's Year-Book.*

TURKS AND CAICOS ISLANDS - EDUCATION

Europa Publications Limited, 18 Bedford Square, London, WC1B 3JN, England; *The Europa World Year Book.*

St. Martin's Press, Inc., 175 Fifth Avenue, New York, New York 10010 (800) 221-7945; *The Statesman's Year-Book.*

United Nations Educational, Scientific and Cultural Organization (UNESCO), 7 Place de Fontenoy, F-75700 Paris, France (Telephone Number in U.S. (212) 963-5981); *Statistical Yearbook.*

TURKS AND CAICOS ISLANDS - EGG PRODUCTION AND CONSUMPTION - See TURKS AND CAICOS ISLANDS - DAIRY PRODUCTS

TURKS AND CAICOS ISLANDS - ELECTRICITY

Central Intelligence Agency, Washington, D.C. 20505 (703) 482-1100, www.cia.gov; *The World Factbook*.

TURKS AND CAICOS ISLANDS - ENERGY

Food and Agricultural Organization of the United Nations (FAO) Via delle Terme di Caracalla, 00100 Rome, Italy (Telephone Number in U.S. (202) 653-2400); *The State of Food and Agriculture*.

TURKS AND CAICOS ISLANDS - ENVIRONMENT

The Economist Intelligence Unit, 111 West 57th Street, New York, New York 10019 (800) 938-4685; *Turks and Caicos Islands Country Report*.

TURKS AND CAICOS ISLANDS - EXCHANGE RATES

Central Intelligence Agency, Washington, D.C. 20505 (703) 482-1100, www.cia.gov; *The World Factbook*.

Europa Publications Limited, 18 Bedford Square, London, WC1B 3JN, England; *The Europa World Year Book*.

TURKS AND CAICOS ISLANDS - EXPORTS

Central Intelligence Agency, Washington, D.C. 20505 (703) 482-1100, www.cia.gov; *The World Factbook*.

The Economist Intelligence Unit, 111 West 57th Street, New York, New York 10019 (800) 938-4685; *Turks and Caicos Islands Country Report*.

Europa Publications Limited, 18 Bedford Square, London, WC1B 3JN, England; *The Europa World Year Book*.

Food and Agricultural Organization of the United Nations (FAO) Via delle Terme di Caracalla, 00100 Rome, Italy (Telephone Number in U.S. (202) 653-2400); *The State of Food and Agriculture*.

St. Martin's Press, Inc., 175 Fifth Avenue, New York, New York 10010 (800) 221-7945; *The Statesman's Year-Book*.

TURKS AND CAICOS ISLANDS - EXTERNAL TRADE

Food and Agricultural Organization of the United Nations (FAO) Via delle Terme

di Caracalla, 00100 Rome, Italy (Telephone Number in U.S. (202) 653-2400); *The State of Food and Agriculture*.

TURKS AND CAICOS ISLANDS - FARM CROPS - See TURKS AND CAICOS ISLANDS - CROPS

TURKS AND CAICOS ISLANDS - FERTILITY RATES

Central Intelligence Agency, Washington, D.C. 20505 (703) 482-1100, www.cia.gov; *The World Factbook*.

TURKS AND CAICOS ISLANDS - FERTILIZER

Food and Agricultural Organization of the United Nations (FAO), Via delle Terme di Caracalla, 00100, Rome, Italy (Telephone Number in U.S. (202) 653-2400); *Fertilizer Yearbook;* and *The State of Food and Agriculture*.

TURKS AND CAICOS ISLANDS - FETAL MORTALITY - See TURKS AND CAICOS ISLANDS - MORTALITY

TURKS AND CAICOS ISLANDS - FINANCE

The Economist Intelligence Unit, 111 West 57th Street, New York, New York 10019 (800) 938-4685; *Turks and Caicos Islands Country Report*.

Europa Publications Limited, 18 Bedford Square, London, WC1B 3JN, England; *The Europa World Year Book*.

St. Martin's Press, Inc., 175 Fifth Avenue, New York, New York 10010 (800) 221-7945; *The Statesman's Year-Book*.

TURKS AND CAICOS ISLANDS - FISHERIES

Europa Publications Limited, 18 Bedford Square, London, WC1B 3JN, England; *The Europa World Year Book*.

Food and Agricultural Organization of the United Nations (FAO) Via delle Terme di Caracalla, 00100 Rome, Italy (Telephone Number in U.S. (202) 653-2400); *The State of Food and Agriculture;* and *Yearbook of Fishery Statistics*.

United Nations Conference on Trade and Development, Central Statistical Service, Palais des Nations, Geneva, Switzerland (Telephone in U.S. (800) 253-9646); *UNCTAD Commodity Yearbook*.

TURKS AND CAICOS ISLANDS - FOOD

United Nations Conference on Trade and Development, Central Statistical Service, Palais des Nations, Geneva, Switzerland (Telephone in U.S. (800) 253-

9646); *UNCTAD Commodity Yearbook*.

TURKS AND CAICOS ISLANDS - FOREIGN TRADE

The Economist Intelligence Unit, 111 West 57th Street, New York, New York 10019 (800) 938-4685; *Turks and Caicos Islands Country Report*.

Food and Agricultural Organization of the United Nations (FAO) Via delle Terme di Caracalla, 00100 Rome, Italy (Telephone Number in U.S. (202) 653-2400); *The State of Food and Agriculture*.

St. Martin's Press, Inc., 175 Fifth Avenue, New York, New York 10010 (800) 221-7945; *The Statesman's Year-Book*.

United Nations Conference on Trade and Development, Central Statistical Service, Palais des Nations, Geneva, Switzerland (Telephone in U.S. (800) 253-9646); *UNCTAD Commodity Yearbook*.

TURKS AND CAICOS ISLANDS - FORESTRY AND FOREST PRODUCTS

Statistical Office of the United Nations, Publishing Service, New York, New York 10017 (800) 253-9646; *Statistical Yearbook*.

United Nations Conference on Trade and Development, Central Statistical Service, Palais des Nations, Geneva, Switzerland (Telephone in U.S. (800) 253-9646); *UNCTAD Commodity Yearbook*.

TURKS AND CAICOS ISLANDS - GENERAL MORTALITY - See TURKS AND CAICOS ISLANDS - MORTALITY

TURKS AND CAICOS ISLANDS - GOVERNMENT

Central Intelligence Agency, Washington, D.C. 20505 (703) 482-1100, www.cia.gov; *The World Factbook*.

Europa Publications Limited, 18 Bedford Square, London, WC1B 3JN, England; *The Europa World Year Book*.

TURKS AND CAICOS ISLANDS - GRAIN PRODUCTION - See TURKS AND CAICOS ISLANDS - CROPS

TURKS AND CAICOS ISLANDS - GROSS DOMESTIC PRODUCT

The Economist Intelligence Unit, 111 West 57th Street, New York, New York 10019 (800) 938-4685; *Turks and Caicos Islands Country Report*.

Statistical Office of the United Nations, Publishing Service, New York, New York 10017 (800) 253-9646; *Statistical Yearbook*.

TURKS AND CAICOS ISLANDS - HEALTH

St. Martin's Press, Inc., 175 Fifth Avenue, New York, New York 10010 (800) 221-7945; *The Statesman's Year-Book.*

Statistical Office of the United Nations, Publishing Service, New York, New York 10017 (800) 253-9646; *Statistical Yearbook.*

TURKS AND CAICOS ISLANDS - HIGHWAYS

Central Intelligence Agency, Washington, D.C. 20505 (703) 482-1100, www.cia.gov; *The World Factbook.*

TURKS AND CAICOS ISLANDS - ILLITERATE POPULATION

Central Intelligence Agency, Washington, D.C. 20505 (703) 482-1100, www.cia.gov; *The World Factbook.*

United Nations Educational, Scientific and Cultural Organization (UNESCO), 7 Place de Fontenoy, F-75700 Paris, France (Telephone Number in U.S. (212) 963-5981); *Statistical Yearbook.*

TURKS AND CAICOS ISLANDS - IMPORTS

Central Intelligence Agency, Washington, D.C. 20505 (703) 482-1100, www.cia.gov; *The World Factbook.*

The Economist Intelligence Unit, 111 West 57th Street, New York, New York 10019 (800) 938-4685; *Turks and Caicos Islands Country Report.*

Europa Publications Limited, 18 Bedford Square, London, WC1B 3JN, England; *The Europa World Year Book.*

Food and Agricultural Organization of the United Nations (FAO) Via delle Terme di Caracalla, 00100 Rome, Italy (Telephone Number in U.S. (202) 653-2400); *The State of Food and Agriculture.*

St. Martin's Press, Inc., 175 Fifth Avenue, New York, New York 10010 (800) 221-7945; *The Statesman's Year-Book.*

TURKS AND CAICOS ISLANDS - INDUSTRY

Central Intelligence Agency, Washington, D.C. 20505 (703) 482-1100, www.cia.gov; *The World Factbook.*

The Economist Intelligence Unit, 111 West 57th Street, New York, New York 10019 (800) 938-4685; *Turks and Caicos Islands Country Report.*

Europa Publications Limited, 18 Bedford Square, London, WC1B 3JN, England; *The Europa World Year Book.*

St. Martin's Press, Inc., 175 Fifth Avenue, New York, New York 10010 (800) 221-7945; *The Statesman's Year-Book.*

TURKS AND CAICOS ISLANDS - INFANT AND MATERNAL MORTALITY - See TURKS AND CAICOS ISLANDS - MORTALITY

TURKS AND CAICOS ISLANDS - LABOR

Central Intelligence Agency, Washington, D.C. 20505 (703) 482-1100, www.cia.gov; *The World Factbook.*

Europa Publications Limited, 18 Bedford Square, London, WC1B 3JN, England; *The Europa World Year Book.*

Food and Agricultural Organization of the United Nations (FAO) Via delle Terme di Caracalla, 00100 Rome, Italy (Telephone Number in U.S. (202) 653-2400); *The State of Food and Agriculture.*

St. Martin's Press, Inc., 175 Fifth Avenue, New York, New York 10010 (800) 221-7945; *The Statesman's Year-Book.*

TURKS AND CAICOS ISLANDS - LAND USE

Central Intelligence Agency, Washington, D.C. 20505 (703) 482-1100, www.cia.gov; *The World Factbook.*

TURKS AND CAICOS ISLANDS - LIFE EXPECTANCY

Central Intelligence Agency, Washington, D.C. 20505 (703) 482-1100, www.cia.gov; *The World Factbook.*

TURKS AND CAICOS ISLANDS - LIVESTOCK AND POULTRY

Food and Agricultural Organization of the United Nations (FAO) Via delle Terme di Caracalla, 00100 Rome, Italy (Telephone Number in U.S. (202) 653-2400); *The State of Food and Agriculture.*

United Nations Conference on Trade and Development, Central Statistical Service, Palais des Nations, Geneva, Switzerland (Telephone in U.S. (800) 253-9646); *UNCTAD Commodity Yearbook.*

TURKS AND CAICOS ISLANDS - MARRIAGE RATES

Statistical Office of the United Nations, Publishing Service, New York, New York 10017 (800) 253-9646; *Demographic Yearbook;* and *Statistical Yearbook.*

TURKS AND CAICOS ISLANDS - MEAT PRODUCTION - See TURKS AND CAICOS ISLANDS - LIVESTOCK AND POULTRY

TURKS AND CAICOS ISLANDS - MERCHANT SHIPPING

Europa Publications Limited, 18 Bedford Square, London, WC1B 3JN, England; *The Europa World Year Book.*

St. Martin's Press, Inc., 175 Fifth Avenue, New York, New York 10010 (800) 221-7945; *The Statesman's Year-Book.*

Statistical Office of the United Nations, Publishing Service, New York, New York 10017 (800) 253-9646; *Statistical Yearbook.*

TURKS AND CAICOS ISLANDS - MINING AND MINERAL PRODUCTS

Statistical Office of the United Nations, Publishing Service, New York, New York 10017 (800) 253-9646; *Statistical Yearbook.*

United Nations Conference on Trade and Development, Central Statistical Service, Palais des Nations, Geneva, Switzerland (Telephone in U.S. (800) 253-9646); *UNCTAD Commodity Yearbook.*

TURKS AND CAICOS ISLANDS - MONEY SUPPLY

The Economist Intelligence Unit, 111 West 57th Street, New York, New York 10019 (800) 938-4685; *Turks and Caicos Islands Country Report.*

TURKS AND CAICOS ISLANDS - MORTALITY

Central Intelligence Agency, Washington, D.C. 20505 (703) 482-1100, www.cia.gov; *The World Factbook.*

Europa Publications Limited, 18 Bedford Square, London, WC1B 3JN, England; *The Europa World Year Book.*

St. Martin's Press, Inc., 175 Fifth Avenue, New York, New York 10010 (800) 221-7945; *The Statesman's Year-Book.*

Statistical Office of the United Nations, Publishing Service, New York, New York 10017 (800) 253-9646; *Demographic Yearbook;* and *Statistical Yearbook.*

TURKS AND CAICOS ISLANDS - MOTION PICTURES

Statistical Office of the United Nations, Publishing Service, New York, New York 10017 (800) 253-9646; *Statistical Yearbook.*

TURKS AND CAICOS ISLANDS - NATALITY - See TURKS AND CAICOS ISLANDS - BIRTH RATES

TURKS AND CAICOS ISLANDS - NATIONAL ACCOUNTS

Statistical Office of the United Nations, Publishing Service, New York, New York 10017 (800) 253-9646; *Statistical Yearbook.*

TURKS AND CAICOS ISLANDS - NATIONAL INCOME

Statistical Office of the United Nations,

Publishing Service, New York, New York 10017 (800) 253-9646; *Statistical Yearbook.*

TURKS AND CAICOS ISLANDS - NEWSPAPER PRODUCTION - See TURKS AND CAICOS ISLANDS - FORESTRY AND FOREST PRODUCTS

TURKS AND CAICOS ISLANDS - OCCUPATIONS - See TURKS AND CAICOS ISLANDS - LABOR

TURKS AND CAICOS ISLANDS - PERIODICALS

United Nations Educational, Scientific and Cultural Organization (UNESCO), 7 Place de Fontenoy, F-75700 Paris, France (Telephone Number in U.S. (212) 963-5981); *Statistical Yearbook.*

TURKS AND CAICOS ISLANDS - PESTICIDE USE

Food and Agricultural Organization of the United Nations (FAO) Via delle Terme di Caracalla, 00100 Rome, Italy (Telephone Number in U.S. (202) 653-2400); *The State of Food and Agriculture.*

TURKS AND CAICOS ISLANDS - PETROLEUM INDUSTRY

Food and Agricultural Organization of the United Nations (FAO) Via delle Terme di Caracalla, 00100 Rome, Italy (Telephone Number in U.S. (202) 653-2400); *The State of Food and Agriculture.*

United Nations Conference on Trade and Development, Central Statistical Service, Palais des Nations, Geneva, Switzerland (Telephone in U.S. (800) 253-9646); *UNCTAD Commodity Yearbook.*

TURKS AND CAICOS ISLANDS - POPULATION

Central Intelligence Agency, Washington, D.C. 20505 (703) 482-1100, www.cia.gov; *The World Factbook.*

The Economist Intelligence Unit, 111 West 57th Street, New York, New York 10019 (800) 938-4685; *Turks and Caicos Islands Country Report.*

Europa Publications Limited, 18 Bedford Square, London, WC1B 3JN, England; *The Europa World Year Book.*

St. Martin's Press, Inc., 175 Fifth Avenue, New York, New York 10010 (800) 221-7945; *The Statesman's Year-Book.*

Statistical Office of the United Nations, Publishing Service, New York, New York 10017 (800) 253-9646; *Demographic Yearbook;* and *Statistical Yearbook.*

World Health Organization, Office of

Publications, 20 Avenue Appia, CH-1211 Geneva 27, Switzerland (Telephone Number in U.S. (518) 436-9686); *World Health Statistics Annual.*

TURKS AND CAICOS ISLANDS - PRICES

Food and Agricultural Organization of the United Nations (FAO) Via delle Terme di Caracalla, 00100 Rome, Italy (Telephone Number in U.S. (202) 653-2400); *The State of Food and Agriculture.*

TURKS AND CAICOS ISLANDS - RADIO BROADCASTING - See TURKS AND CAICOS ISLANDS - BROADCASTING

TURKS AND CAICOS ISLANDS - RADIO RECEIVERS

St. Martin's Press, Inc., 175 Fifth Avenue, New York, New York 10010 (800) 221-7945; *The Statesman's Year-Book.*

TURKS AND CAICOS ISLANDS - RELIGION

Central Intelligence Agency, Washington, D.C. 20505 (703) 482-1100, www.cia.gov; *The World Factbook.*

St. Martin's Press, Inc., 175 Fifth Avenue, New York, New York 10010 (800) 221-7945; *The Statesman's Year-Book.*

TURKS AND CAICOS ISLANDS - SALT PRODUCTION - See TURKS AND CAICOS ISLANDS - MINING AND MINERAL PRODUCTS

TURKS AND CAICOS ISLANDS - SCIENCE AND TECHNOLOGY - EXPENDITURE FOR RESEARCH - See TURKS AND CAICOS ISLANDS - SCIENTISTS, TECHNICIANS AND ENGINEERS

TURKS AND CAICOS ISLANDS - SCIENTISTS, TECHNICIANS AND ENGINEERS

Statistical Office of the United Nations, Publishing Service, New York, New York 10017 (800) 253-9646; *Statistical Yearbook.*

TURKS AND CAICOS ISLANDS - STOCKS - COMMODITY - MARKET PRICE - INDEX

Food and Agricultural Organization of the United Nations (FAO) Via delle Terme di Caracalla, 00100 Rome, Italy (Telephone Number in U.S. (202) 653-2400); *The State of Food and Agriculture.*

TURKS AND CAICOS ISLANDS - TAXATION

Europa Publications Limited, 18 Bedford Square, London, WC1B 3JN, England; *The Europa World Year Book.*

TURKS AND CAICOS ISLANDS -

TELEPHONES IN USE

American Telephone and Telegraph Company, 26 Parsippany Road, Whippany, New Jersey 07981 (800) 222-0300; *The World's Telephones.*

Central Intelligence Agency, Washington, D.C. 20505 (703) 482-1100, www.cia.gov; *The World Factbook.*

Europa Publications Limited, 18 Bedford Square, London, WC1B 3JN, England; *The Europa World Year Book.*

St. Martin's Press, Inc., 175 Fifth Avenue, New York, New York 10010 (800) 221-7945; *The Statesman's Year-Book.*

TURKS AND CAICOS ISLANDS - TEXTILE INDUSTRY

United Nations Conference on Trade and Development, Central Statistical Service, Palais des Nations, Geneva, Switzerland (Telephone in U.S. (800) 253-9646); *UNCTAD Commodity Yearbook.*

TURKS AND CAICOS ISLANDS - THEATRE

United Nations Educational, Scientific and Cultural Organization (UNESCO), 7 Place de Fontenoy, F-75700 Paris, France (Telephone Number in U.S. (212) 963-5981); *Statistical Yearbook.*

TURKS AND CAICOS ISLANDS - TOURISM

Europa Publications Limited, 18 Bedford Square, London, WC1B 3JN, England; *The Europa World Year Book.*

St. Martin's Press, Inc., 175 Fifth Avenue, New York, New York 10010 (800) 221-7945; *The Statesman's Year-Book.*

World Tourism Organization, Calle Capitan Haya 42, E-28020 Madrid, Spain; *Yearbook of Tourism Statistics.*

TURKS AND CAICOS ISLANDS - TRADE - See TURKS AND CAICOS ISLANDS - FOREIGN TRADE

TURKS AND CAICOS ISLANDS - TRANSPORTATION AND COMMUNICATIONS

Central Intelligence Agency, Washington, D.C. 20505 (703) 482-1100, www.cia.gov; *The World Factbook.*

Europa Publications Limited, 18 Bedford Square, London, WC1B 3JN, England; *The Europa World Year Book.*

St. Martin's Press, Inc., 175 Fifth Avenue, New York, New York 10010 (800) 221-7945; *The Statesman's Year-Book.*

TURKS AND CAICOS ISLANDS -
UNEMPLOYMENT

Central Intelligence Agency,
Washington, D.C. 20505 (703) 482-1100,
www.cia.gov; *The World Factbook.*

St. Martin's Press, Inc., 175 Fifth
Avenue, New York, New York 10010 (800)
221-7945; *The Statesman's Year-Book.*

TURKS AND CAICOS ISLANDS - VITAL
STATISTICS

St. Martin's Press, Inc., 175 Fifth
Avenue, New York, New York 10010 (800)
221-7945; *The Statesman's Year-Book.*

Statistical Office of the United Nations,
Publishing Service, New York, New York
10017 (800) 253-9646; *Statistical Yearbook.*

World Health Organization, Office of
Publications, 20 Avenue Appia, CH-1211
Geneva 27, Switzerland (Telephone
Number in U.S. (518) 436-9686); *World
Health Statistics Annual.*

Tuvalu - National Statistical Office

Planning and Statistics Division,
Ministry of Finance, P.O. Box 33, Viaku,
Funafuti Island, Tuvalu.

TUVALU - AGRICULTURE

Euromonitor International, Inc., 122
South Michigan Avenue, Suite 1200,
Chicago, Illinois 60603 (800) 577-EURO;
World Marketing Data and Statistics.

Europa Publications Limited, 18
Bedford Square, London, WC1B 3JN,
England; *The Europa World Year Book.*

Food and Agricultural Organization of
the United Nations (FAO) Via delle Terme
di Caracalla, 00100 Rome, Italy (Telephone
Number in U.S. (202) 653-2400); *The State
of Food and Agriculture.*

St. Martin's Press, Inc., 175 Fifth
Avenue, New York, New York 10010 (800)
221-7945; *The Statesman's Year-Book.*

Statistical Office of the United Nations,
Publishing Service, New York, New York
10017 (800) 253-9646; *Asia-Pacific in
Figures;* and *Statistical Yearbook for Asia
and the Pacific.*

United Nations Conference on Trade
and Development, Central Statistical
Service, Palais des Nations, Geneva,
Switzerland (Telephone in U.S. (800) 253-
9646); *UNCTAD Commodity Yearbook.*

TUVALU - AIRLINE SERVICE

St. Martin's Press, Inc., 175 Fifth
Avenue, New York, New York 10010 (800)
221-7945; *The Statesman's Year-Book.*

TUVALU - AIRPORTS

Central Intelligence Agency,
Washington, D.C. 20505 (703) 482-1100,
www.cia.gov; *The World Factbook.*

TUVALU - AREA AND DENSITY OF
POPULATION

Central Intelligence Agency,
Washington, D.C. 20505 (703) 482-1100,
www.cia.gov; *The World Factbook.*

Euromonitor International, Inc., 122
South Michigan Avenue, Suite 1200,
Chicago, Illinois 60603 (800) 577-EURO;
The World Economic Factbook.

Europa Publications Limited, 18
Bedford Square, London, WC1B 3JN,
England; *The Europa World Year Book.*

Food and Agricultural Organization of
the United Nations (FAO) Via delle Terme
di Caracalla, 00100 Rome, Italy (Telephone
Number in U.S. (202) 653-2400); *The State
of Food and Agriculture.*

St. Martin's Press, Inc., 175 Fifth
Avenue, New York, New York 10010 (800)
221-7945; *The Statesman's Year-Book.*

TUVALU - BANKING

Euromonitor International, Inc., 122
South Michigan Avenue, Suite 1200,
Chicago, Illinois 60603 (800) 577-EURO;
World Marketing Data and Statistics.

St. Martin's Press, Inc., 175 Fifth
Avenue, New York, New York 10010 (800)
221-7945; *The Statesman's Year-Book.*

TUVALU - BIRTH RATES

Central Intelligence Agency,
Washington, D.C. 20505 (703) 482-1100,
www.cia.gov; *The World Factbook.*

Euromonitor International, Inc., 122
South Michigan Avenue, Suite 1200,
Chicago, Illinois 60603 (800) 577-EURO;
International Marketing Data and Statistics;
and *The World Economic Factbook.*

Europa Publications Limited, 18
Bedford Square, London, WC1B 3JN,
England; *The Europa World Year Book.*

Statistical Office of the United Nations,
Publishing Service, New York, New York
10017 (800) 253-9646; *Asia-Pacific in
Figures;* and *Demographic Yearbook.*

TUVALU - BROADCASTING

Billboard Limited, P.O. Box 9027, 1006

AA Amsterdam, The Netherlands
(Telephone Number in U.S. (212) 764-
7300); *World Radio TV Handbook.*

Central Intelligence Agency,
Washington, D.C. 20505 (703) 482-1100,
www.cia.gov; *The World Factbook.*

Euromonitor International, Inc., 122
South Michigan Avenue, Suite 1200,
Chicago, Illinois 60603 (800) 577-EURO;
World Marketing Data and Statistics.

St. Martin's Press, Inc., 175 Fifth
Avenue, New York, New York 10010 (800)
221-7945; *The Statesman's Year-Book.*

TUVALU - BUDGET

Central Intelligence Agency,
Washington, D.C. 20505 (703) 482-1100,
www.cia.gov; *The World Factbook.*

TUVALU - CALORIE SUPPLY

Food and Agricultural Organization of
the United Nations (FAO) Via delle Terme
di Caracalla, 00100 Rome, Italy (Telephone
Number in U.S. (202) 653-2400); *The State
of Food and Agriculture.*

TUVALU - CHEMICAL (ORGANIC)
PRODUCTION - See TUVALU - MINING AND
MINERAL PRODUCTS

TUVALU - CLIMATE

St. Martin's Press, Inc., 175 Fifth
Avenue, New York, New York 10010 (800)
221-7945; *The Statesman's Year-Book.*

TUVALU - CLOTHING EXPORTS AND
IMPORTS - See TUVALU - TEXTILE
INDUSTRY

TUVALU - COAL PRODUCTION - See
TUVALU - MINING AND MINERAL
PRODUCTS

TUVALU - COMMERCE

St. Martin's Press, Inc., 175 Fifth
Avenue, New York, New York 10010 (800)
221-7945; *The Statesman's Year-Book.*

TUVALU - COMMUNICATIONS - See
TUVALU - TRANSPORTATION AND
COMMUNICATIONS

TUVALU - CONSUMER PRICES

Euromonitor International, Inc., 122
South Michigan Avenue, Suite 1200,
Chicago, Illinois 60603 (800) 577-EURO;
World Marketing Data and Statistics.

TUVALU - CONSUMPTION

Europa Publications Limited, 18
Bedford Square, London, WC1B 3JN,
England; *The Europa World Year Book.*

South Pacific Commission, Post Box D5, Noumea Cedex, New Caledonia; *Statistical Bulletin of the South Pacific: Retail Price Indexes.*

TUVALU - CORN PRODUCTION - See TUVALU - CROPS

TUVALU - CORPORATE TAXES - See TUVALU - TAXATION

TUVALU - CROPS

Europa Publications Limited, 18 Bedford Square, London, WC1B 3JN, England; *The Europa World Year Book.*

Food and Agricultural Organization of the United Nations (FAO), Via delle Terme di Caracalla, 00100, Rome, Italy (Telephone Number in U.S. (202) 653-2400); *The State of Food and Agriculture.*

St. Martin's Press, Inc., 175 Fifth Avenue, New York, New York 10010 (800) 221-7945; *The Statesman's Year-Book.*

United Nations Conference on Trade and Development, Central Statistical Service, Palais des Nations, Geneva, Switzerland (Telephone in U.S. (800) 253-9646); *UNCTAD Commodity Yearbook.*

TUVALU - DAIRY PRODUCTS

Europa Publications Limited, 18 Bedford Square, London, WC1B 3JN, England; *The Europa World Year Book.*

Food and Agricultural Organization of the United Nations (FAO) Via delle Terme di Caracalla, 00100 Rome, Italy (Telephone Number in U.S. (202) 653-2400); *The State of Food and Agriculture.*

TUVALU - DEMOGRAPHY

Euromonitor International, Inc., 122 South Michigan Avenue, Suite 1200, Chicago, Illinois 60603 (800) 577-EURO; *International Marketing Data and Statistics; World Marketing Data and Statistics;* and *The World Economic Factbook.*

Statistical Office of the United Nations, Publishing Service, New York, New York 10017 (800) 253-9646; *Asia-Pacific in Figures.*

TUVALU - DIVORCE RATES

Statistical Office of the United Nations, Publishing Service, New York, New York 10017 (800) 253-9646; *Demographic Yearbook.*

TUVALU - ECONOMY

Central Intelligence Agency, Washington, D.C. 20505 (703) 482-1100, www.cia.gov; *The World Factbook.*

Euromonitor International, Inc., 122 South Michigan Avenue, Suite 1200, Chicago, Illinois 60603 (800) 577-EURO; *The World Economic Factbook;* and *World Marketing Data and Statistics.*

Europa Publications Limited, 18 Bedford Square, London, WC1B 3JN, England; *The Europa World Year Book.*

TUVALU - EDUCATION

Euromonitor International, Inc., 122 South Michigan Avenue, Suite 1200, Chicago, Illinois 60603 (800) 577-EURO; *International Marketing Data and Statistics;* and *World Marketing Data and Statistics.*

Europa Publications Limited, 18 Bedford Square, London, WC1B 3JN, England; *The Europa World Year Book.*

St. Martin's Press, Inc., 175 Fifth Avenue, New York, New York 10010 (800) 221-7945; *The Statesman's Year-Book.*

Statistical Office of the United Nations, Publishing Service, New York, New York 10017 (800) 253-9646; *Asia-Pacific in Figures.*

TUVALU - EGG PRODUCTION AND CONSUMPTION - See TUVALU -DAIRY PRODUCTS

TUVALU - ELECTRICITY

Central Intelligence Agency, Washington, D.C. 20505 (703) 482-1100, www.cia.gov; *The World Factbook.*

St. Martin's Press, Inc., 175 Fifth Avenue, New York, New York 10010 (800) 221-7945; *The Statesman's Year-Book.*

TUVALU - EMPLOYMENT

Euromonitor International, Inc., 122 South Michigan Avenue, Suite 1200, Chicago, Illinois 60603 (800) 577-EURO; *International Marketing Data and Statistics.*

Statistical Office of the United Nations, Publishing Service, New York, New York 10017 (800) 253-9646; *Asia-Pacific in Figures.*

TUVALU - ENERGY

Euromonitor International, Inc., 122 South Michigan Avenue, Suite 1200, Chicago, Illinois 60603 (800) 577-EURO; *International Marketing Data and Statistics; World Marketing Data and Statistics;* and *The World Economic Factbook.*

Food and Agricultural Organization of the United Nations (FAO) Via delle Terme di Caracalla, 00100 Rome, Italy (Telephone Number in U.S. (202) 653-2400); *The State of Food and Agriculture.*

St. Martin's Press, Inc., 175 Fifth Avenue, New York, New York 10010 (800) 221-7945; *The Statesman's Year-Book.*

Statistical Office of the United Nations, Publishing Service, New York, New York 10017 (800) 253-9646; *Asia-Pacific in Figures;* and *Statistical Yearbook for Asia and the Pacific.*

TUVALU - EXCHANGE RATES

Central Intelligence Agency, Washington, D.C. 20505 (703) 482-1100, www.cia.gov; *The World Factbook.*

Euromonitor International, Inc., 122 South Michigan Avenue, Suite 1200, Chicago, Illinois 60603 (800) 577-EURO; *International Marketing Data and Statistics;* and *The World Economic Factbook.*

Europa Publications Limited, 18 Bedford Square, London, WC1B 3JN, England; *The Europa World Year Book.*

Walden Publishing Ltd., Two Market Street, Saffron Walden Essex, CB10 1HZ, England; *The World of Information Asia and Pacific Review.*

TUVALU - EXPORTS

Central Intelligence Agency, Washington, D.C. 20505 (703) 482-1100, www.cia.gov; *The World Factbook.*

Euromonitor International, Inc., 122 South Michigan Avenue, Suite 1200, Chicago, Illinois 60603 (800) 577-EURO; *International Marketing Data and Statistics;* and *The World Economic Factbook.*

Europa Publications Limited, 18 Bedford Square, London, WC1B 3JN, England; *The Europa World Year Book.*

Food and Agricultural Organization of the United Nations (FAO) Via delle Terme di Caracalla, 00100 Rome, Italy (Telephone Number in U.S. (202) 653-2400); *The State of Food and Agriculture.*

South Pacific Commission, Post Box D5, Noumea Cedex, New Caledonia; *Statistical Bulletin of the South Pacific: Overseas Trade.*

St. Martin's Press, Inc., 175 Fifth Avenue, New York, New York 10010 (800) 221-7945; *The Statesman's Year-Book.*

Walden Publishing Ltd., Two Market Street, Saffron Walden Essex, CB10 1HZ, England; *The World of Information Asia and Pacific Review.*

TUVALU - EXTERNAL TRADE

Euromonitor International, Inc., 122 South Michigan Avenue, Suite 1200,

Chicago, Illinois 60603 (800) 577-EURO; *World Marketing Data and Statistics*.

Food and Agricultural Organization of the United Nations (FAO) Via delle Terme di Caracalla, 00100 Rome, Italy (Telephone Number in U.S. (202) 653-2400); *The State of Food and Agriculture.*

Statistical Office of the United Nations, Publishing Service, New York, New York 10017 (800) 253-9646; *Asia-Pacific in Figures;* and *Statistical Yearbook for Asia and the Pacific.*

TUVALU - FARM CROPS - See TUVALU - CROPS

TUVALU - FERTILITY RATE

Central Intelligence Agency, Washington, D.C. 20505 (703) 482-1100, www.cia.gov; *The World Factbook.*

TUVALU - FERTILIZER

Food and Agricultural Organization of the United Nations (FAO) Via delle Terme di Caracalla, 00100 Rome, Italy (Telephone Number in U.S. (202) 653-2400); *The State of Food and Agriculture.*

TUVALU - FETAL MORTALITY - See TUVALU - MORTALITY

TUVALU - FINANCE

Europa Publications Limited, 18 Bedford Square, London, WC1B 3JN, England; *The Europa World Year Book.*

St. Martin's Press, Inc., 175 Fifth Avenue, New York, New York 10010 (800) 221-7945; *The Statesman's Year-Book.*

Statistical Office of the United Nations, Publishing Service, New York, New York 10017 (800) 253-9646; *Statistical Yearbook for Asia and the Pacific.*

TUVALU - FISHERIES

Europa Publications Limited, 18 Bedford Square, London, WC1B 3JN, England; *The Europa World Year Book.*

Food and Agricultural Organization of the United Nations (FAO) Via delle Terme di Caracalla, 00100 Rome, Italy (Telephone Number in U.S. (202) 653-2400); *The State of Food and Agriculture.*

St. Martin's Press, Inc., 175 Fifth Avenue, New York, New York 10010 (800) 221-7945; *The Statesman's Year-Book.*

United Nations Conference on Trade and Development, Central Statistical Service, Palais des Nations, Geneva, Switzerland (Telephone in U.S. (800) 253-9646); *UNCTAD Commodity Yearbook.*

TUVALU - FOOD

Food and Agricultural Organization of the United Nations (FAO) Via delle Terme di Caracalla, 00100 Rome, Italy (Telephone Number in U.S. (202) 653-2400); *The State of Food and Agriculture.*

South Pacific Commission, Post Box D5, Noumea Cedex, New Caledonia; *Statistical Bulletin of the South Pacific: Retail Price Indexes.*

Statistical Office of the United Nations, Publishing Service, New York, New York 10017 (800) 253-9646; *Statistical Yearbook for Asia and the Pacific.*

United Nations Conference on Trade and Development, Central Statistical Service, Palais des Nations, Geneva, Switzerland (Telephone in U.S. (800) 253-9646); *UNCTAD Commodity Yearbook.*

TUVALU - FOREIGN DEBT

Walden Publishing Ltd., Two Market Street, Saffron Walden Essex, CB10 1HZ, England; *The World of Information Asia and Pacific Review.*

TUVALU - FOREIGN TRADE

Euromonitor International, Inc., 122 South Michigan Avenue, Suite 1200, Chicago, Illinois 60603 (800) 577-EURO; *The World Economic Factbook.*

Europa Publications Limited, 18 Bedford Square, London, WC1B 3JN, England; *The Europa World Year Book.*

Food and Agricultural Organization of the United Nations (FAO) Via delle Terme di Caracalla, 00100 Rome, Italy (Telephone Number in U.S. (202) 653-2400); *The State of Food and Agriculture.*

South Pacific Commission, Post Box D5, Noumea Cedex, New Caledonia; *Statistical Bulletin of the South Pacific: Overseas Trade.*

St. Martin's Press, Inc., 175 Fifth Avenue, New York, New York 10010 (800) 221-7945; *The Statesman's Year-Book.*

Statistical Office of the United Nations, Publishing Service, New York, New York 10017 (800) 253-9646; *International Trade Statistics Yearbook.*

United Nations Conference on Trade and Development, Central Statistical Service, Palais des Nations, Geneva, Switzerland (Telephone in U.S. (800) 253-9646); *UNCTAD Commodity Yearbook.*

TUVALU - FORESTRY AND FOREST PRODUCTS

Food and Agricultural Organization of the United Nations (FAO) Via delle Terme di Caracalla, 00100 Rome, Italy (Telephone Number in U.S. (202) 653-2400); *The State of Food and Agriculture.*

United Nations Conference on Trade and Development, Central Statistical Service, Palais des Nations, Geneva, Switzerland (Telephone in U.S. (800) 253-9646); *UNCTAD Commodity Yearbook.*

TUVALU - GENERAL MORTALITY - See TUVALU - MORTALITY

TUVALU - GOVERNMENT

Central Intelligence Agency, Washington, D.C. 20505 (703) 482-1100, www.cia.gov; *The World Factbook.*

Europa Publications Limited, 18 Bedford Square, London, WC1B 3JN, England; *The Europa World Year Book.*

St. Martin's Press, Inc., 175 Fifth Avenue, New York, New York 10010 (800) 221-7945; *The Statesman's Year-Book.*

Statistical Office of the United Nations, Publishing Service, New York, New York 10017 (800) 253-9646; *Asia-Pacific in Figures.*

TUVALU - GRAIN PRODUCTION - See TUVALU - CROPS

TUVALU - GROSS DOMESTIC PRODUCT

Euromonitor International, Inc., 122 South Michigan Avenue, Suite 1200, Chicago, Illinois 60603 (800) 577-EURO; *International Marketing Data and Statistics;* and *The World Economic Factbook.*

TUVALU - GROSS NATIONAL PRODUCT

Walden Publishing Ltd., Two Market Street, Saffron Walden Essex, CB10 1HZ, England; *The World of Information Asia and Pacific Review.*

TUVALU - HEALTH

Euromonitor International, Inc., 122 South Michigan Avenue, Suite 1200, Chicago, Illinois 60603 (800) 577-EURO; *World Marketing Data and Statistics.*

South Pacific Commission, Post Box D5, Noumea Cedex, New Caledonia; *Statistical Bulletin of the South Pacific: Retail Price Indexes.*

St. Martin's Press, Inc., 175 Fifth Avenue, New York, New York 10010 (800) 221-7945; *The Statesman's Year-Book.*

Statistical Office of the United Nations, Publishing Service, New York, New York 10017 (800) 253-9646; *Asia-Pacific in*

Figures.

TUVALU - HIGHWAYS

Central Intelligence Agency, Washington, D.C. 20505 (703) 482-1100, www.cia.gov; *The World Factbook.*

TUVALU - HOUSING AND HOUSING UNITS

Euromonitor International, Inc., 122 South Michigan Avenue, Suite 1200, Chicago, Illinois 60603 (800) 577-EURO; *World Marketing Data and Statistics.*

South Pacific Commission, Post Box D5, Noumea Cedex, New Caledonia; *Statistical Bulletin of the South Pacific: Retail Price Indexes.*

TUVALU - ILLITERATE POPULATION

Central Intelligence Agency, Washington, D.C. 20505 (703) 482-1100, www.cia.gov; *The World Factbook.*

Euromonitor International, Inc., 122 South Michigan Avenue, Suite 1200, Chicago, Illinois 60603 (800) 577-EURO; *The World Economic Factbook.*

Statistical Office of the United Nations, Publishing Service, New York, New York 10017 (800) 253-9646; *Asia-Pacific in Figures.*

TUVALU - IMPORTS

Central Intelligence Agency, Washington, D.C. 20505 (703) 482-1100, www.cia.gov; *The World Factbook.*

Euromonitor International, Inc., 122 South Michigan Avenue, Suite 1200, Chicago, Illinois 60603 (800) 577-EURO; *International Marketing Data and Statistics;* and *The World Economic Factbook.*

Europa Publications Limited, 18 Bedford Square, London, WC1B 3JN, England; *The Europa World Year Book.*

Food and Agricultural Organization of the United Nations (FAO) Via delle Terme di Caracalla, 00100 Rome, Italy (Telephone Number in U.S. (202) 653-2400); *The State of Food and Agriculture.*

South Pacific Commission, Post Box D5, Noumea Cedex, New Caledonia; *Statistical Bulletin of the South Pacific: Overseas Trade.*

St. Martin's Press, Inc., 175 Fifth Avenue, New York, New York 10010 (800) 221-7945; *The Statesman's Year-Book.*

Walden Publishing Ltd., Two Market Street, Saffron Walden Essex, CB10 1HZ, England; *The World of Information Asia and Pacific Review.*

TUVALU - INDUSTRY

Central Intelligence Agency, Washington, D.C. 20505 (703) 482-1100, www.cia.gov; *The World Factbook.*

Euromonitor International, Inc., 122 South Michigan Avenue, Suite 1200, Chicago, Illinois 60603 (800) 577-EURO; *The World Economic Factbook;* and *World Marketing Data and Statistics.*

St. Martin's Press, Inc., 175 Fifth Avenue, New York, New York 10010 (800) 221-7945; *The Statesman's Year-Book.*

Statistical Office of the United Nations, Publishing Service, New York, New York 10017 (800) 253-9646; *Asia-Pacific in Figures;* and *Statistical Yearbook for Asia and the Pacific.*

TUVALU - INFANT AND MATERNAL MORTALITY - See TUVALU - MORTALITY

TUVALU - INTERNAL TRADE

Statistical Office of the United Nations, Publishing Service, New York, New York 10017 (800) 253-9646; *Statistical Yearbook for Asia and the Pacific.*

TUVALU - LABOR

Central Intelligence Agency, Washington, D.C. 20505 (703) 482-1100, www.cia.gov; *The World Factbook.*

Euromonitor International, Inc., 122 South Michigan Avenue, Suite 1200, Chicago, Illinois 60603 (800) 577-EURO; *International Marketing Data and Statistics;* and *World Marketing Data and Statistics.*

Europa Publications Limited, 18 Bedford Square, London, WC1B 3JN, England; *The Europa World Year Book.*

Food and Agricultural Organization of the United Nations (FAO) Via delle Terme di Caracalla, 00100 Rome, Italy (Telephone Number in U.S. (202) 653-2400); *The State of Food and Agriculture.*

TUVALU - LAND USE

Central Intelligence Agency, Washington, D.C. 20505 (703) 482-1100, www.cia.gov; *The World Factbook.*

Euromonitor International, Inc., 122 South Michigan Avenue, Suite 1200, Chicago, Illinois 60603 (800) 577-EURO; *International Marketing Data and Statistics.*

TUVALU - LIFE EXPECTANCY

Central Intelligence Agency, Washington, D.C. 20505 (703) 482-1100, www.cia.gov; *The World Factbook.*

Euromonitor International, Inc., 122 South Michigan Avenue, Suite 1200, Chicago, Illinois 60603 (800) 577-EURO; *The World Economic Factbook.*

Statistical Office of the United Nations, Publishing Service, New York, New York 10017 (800) 253-9646; *Asia-Pacific in Figures.*

TUVALU - LITERACY RATE

Euromonitor International, Inc., 122 South Michigan Avenue, Suite 1200, Chicago, Illinois 60603 (800) 577-EURO; *World Marketing Data and Statistics.*

TUVALU - LIVESTOCK AND POULTRY

Europa Publications Limited, 18 Bedford Square, London, WC1B 3JN, England; *The Europa World Year Book.*

Food and Agricultural Organization of the United Nations (FAO) Via delle Terme di Caracalla, 00100 Rome, Italy (Telephone Number in U.S. (202) 653-2400); *The State of Food and Agriculture.*

United Nations Conference on Trade and Development, Central Statistical Service, Palais des Nations, Geneva, Switzerland (Telephone in U.S. (800) 253-9646); *UNCTAD Commodity Yearbook.*

TUVALU - MAIL - NUMBER OF ITEMS SENT AND RECEIVED

Statistical Office of the United Nations, Publishing Service, New York, New York 10017 (800) 253-9646; *Statistical Yearbook.*

TUVALU - MANPOWER

Statistical Office of the United Nations, Publishing Service, New York, New York 10017 (800) 253-9646; *Statistical Yearbook for Asia and the Pacific.*

TUVALU - MARRIAGE RATES

Statistical Office of the United Nations, Publishing Service, New York, New York 10017 (800) 253-9646; *Demographic Yearbook.*

TUVALU - MEAT PRODUCTION - See TUVALU - LIVESTOCK AND POULTRY

TUVALU - MERCHANT SHIPPING

St. Martin's Press, Inc., 175 Fifth Avenue, New York, New York 10010 (800) 221-7945; *The Statesman's Year-Book.*

TUVALU - MILITARY

Central Intelligence Agency, Washington, D.C. 20505 (703) 482-1100, www.cia.gov; *The World Factbook.*

Euromonitor International, Inc., 122 South Michigan Avenue, Suite 1200, Chicago, Illinois 60603 (800) 577-EURO; *World Marketing Data and Statistics.*

TUVALU - MINING AND MINERAL PRODUCTS

United Nations Conference on Trade and Development, Central Statistical Service, Palais des Nations, Geneva, Switzerland (Telephone in U.S. (800) 253-9646); *UNCTAD Commodity Yearbook.*

TUVALU - MORTALITY

Central Intelligence Agency, Washington, D.C. 20505 (703) 482-1100, www.cia.gov; *The World Factbook.*

Euromonitor International, Inc., 122 South Michigan Avenue, Suite 1200, Chicago, Illinois 60603 (800) 577-EURO; *International Marketing Data and Statistics;* and *The World Economic Factbook.*

Europa Publications Limited, 18 Bedford Square, London, WC1B 3JN, England; *The Europa World Year Book.*

Statistical Office of the United Nations, Publishing Service, New York, New York 10017 (800) 253-9646; *Asia-Pacific in Figures;* and *Demographic Yearbook.*

TUVALU - NATALITY - See TUVALU - BIRTH RATES

TUVALU - NATIONAL ACCOUNTS

Statistical Office of the United Nations, Publishing Service, New York, New York 10017 (800) 253-9646; *Asia-Pacific in Figures;* and *Statistical Yearbook for Asia and the Pacific.*

TUVALU - NEWSPAPER PRODUCTION - See TUVALU - FORESTRY AND FOREST PRODUCTS

TUVALU - OCCUPATIONS - See TUVALU - LABOR

TUVALU - PESTICIDE USE

Food and Agricultural Organization of the United Nations (FAO) Via delle Terme di Caracalla, 00100 Rome, Italy (Telephone Number in U.S. (202) 653-2400); *The State of Food and Agriculture.*

TUVALU - PETROLEUM INDUSTRY

Food and Agricultural Organization of the United Nations (FAO) Via delle Terme di Caracalla, 00100 Rome, Italy (Telephone Number in U.S. (202) 653-2400); *The State of Food and Agriculture.*

United Nations Conference on Trade and Development, Central Statistical Service, Palais des Nations, Geneva, Switzerland (Telephone in U.S. (800) 253-9646); *UNCTAD Commodity Yearbook.*

TUVALU - POPULATION

Central Intelligence Agency, Washington, D.C. 20505 (703) 482-1100, www.cia.gov; *The World Factbook.*

Euromonitor International, Inc., 122 South Michigan Avenue, Suite 1200, Chicago, Illinois 60603 (800) 577-EURO; *International Marketing Data and Statistics;* and *The World Economic Factbook.*

Europa Publications Limited, 18 Bedford Square, London, WC1B 3JN, England; *The Europa World Year Book.*

St. Martin's Press, Inc., 175 Fifth Avenue, New York, New York 10010 (800) 221-7945; *The Statesman's Year-Book.*

Statistical Office of the United Nations, Publishing Service, New York, New York 10017 (800) 253-9646; *Asia-Pacific in Figures; Demographic Yearbook;* and *Statistical Yearbook for Asia and the Pacific.*

Walden Publishing Ltd., Two Market Street, Saffron Walden Essex, CB10 1HZ, England; *The World of Information Asia and Pacific Review.*

World Health Organization, Office of Publications, 20 Avenue Appia, CH-1211 Geneva 27, Switzerland (Telephone Number in U.S. (518) 436-9686); *World Health Statistics Annual.*

TUVALU - PRICES

Food and Agricultural Organization of the United Nations (FAO) Via delle Terme di Caracalla, 00100 Rome, Italy (Telephone Number in U.S. (202) 653-2400); *The State of Food and Agriculture.*

South Pacific Commission, Post Box D5, Noumea Cedex, New Caledonia; *Statistical Bulletin of the South Pacific: Overseas Trade;* and *Statistical Bulletin of the South Pacific: Retail Price Indexes.*

TUVALU - RADIO RECEIVERS

St. Martin's Press, Inc., 175 Fifth Avenue, New York, New York 10010 (800) 221-7945; *The Statesman's Year-Book.*

TUVALU - RELIGION

Central Intelligence Agency, Washington, D.C. 20505 (703) 482-1100, www.cia.gov; *The World Factbook.*

St. Martin's Press, Inc., 175 Fifth Avenue, New York, New York 10010 (800) 221-7945; *The Statesman's Year-Book.*

TUVALU - RETAIL TRADE

Euromonitor International, Inc., 122 South Michigan Avenue, Suite 1200, Chicago, Illinois 60603 (800) 577-EURO; *World Marketing Data and Statistics.*

TUVALU - STOCKS - COMMODITY - MARKET PRICE - INDEX

Food and Agricultural Organization of the United Nations (FAO) Via delle Terme di Caracalla, 00100 Rome, Italy (Telephone Number in U.S. (202) 653-2400); *The State of Food and Agriculture.*

TUVALU - TELEPHONES IN USE

American Telephone and Telegraph Company, 26 Parsippany Road, Whippany, New Jersey 07981 (800) 222-0300; *The World's Telephones.*

Central Intelligence Agency, Washington, D.C. 20505 (703) 482-1100, www.cia.gov; *The World Factbook.*

TUVALU - TEXTILE INDUSTRY

South Pacific Commission, Post Box D5, Noumea Cedex, New Caledonia; *Statistical Bulletin of the South Pacific: Retail Price Indexes.*

United Nations Conference on Trade and Development, Central Statistical Service, Palais des Nations, Geneva, Switzerland (Telephone in U.S. (800) 253-9646); *UNCTAD Commodity Yearbook.*

TUVALU - TOBACCO PRODUCTION

South Pacific Commission, Post Box D5, Noumea Cedex, New Caledonia; *Statistical Bulletin of the South Pacific: Retail Price Indexes.*

TUVALU - TOURISM

Euromonitor International, Inc., 122 South Michigan Avenue, Suite 1200, Chicago, Illinois 60603 (800) 577-EURO; *The World Economic Factbook;* and *World Marketing Data and Statistics.*

World Tourism Organization, Calle Capitan Haya 42, E-28020 Madrid, Spain; *Yearbook of Tourism Statistics.*

TUVALU - TRADE - See TUVALU - FOREIGN TRADE

TUVALU - TRANSPORTATION AND COMMUNICATIONS

Central Intelligence Agency, Washington, D.C. 20505 (703) 482-1100, www.cia.gov; *The World Factbook*.

Euromonitor International, Inc., 122 South Michigan Avenue, Suite 1200, Chicago, Illinois 60603 (800) 577-EURO; *International Marketing Data and Statistics;* and *World Marketing Data and Statistics.*

South Pacific Commission, Post Box D5, Noumea Cedex, New Caledonia; *Statistical Bulletin of the South Pacific: Retail Price Indexes.*

St. Martin's Press, Inc., 175 Fifth Avenue, New York, New York 10010 (800) 221-7945; *The Statesman's Year-Book.*

Statistical Office of the United Nations, Publishing Service, New York, New York 10017 (800) 253-9646; *Statistical Yearbook for Asia and the Pacific.*

TUVALU - UNEMPLOYMENT RATE

Central Intelligence Agency, Washington, D.C. 20505 (703) 482-1100, www.cia.gov; *The World Factbook*.

TUVALU - VITAL STATISTICS

World Health Organization, Office of Publications, 20 Avenue Appia, CH-1211 Geneva 27, Switzerland (Telephone Number in U.S. (518) 436-9686); *World Health Statistics Annual.*

TUVALU - WAGES

Statistical Office of the United Nations, Publishing Service, New York, New York 10017 (800) 253-9646; *Statistical Yearbook for Asia and the Pacific.*

TYPHOID FEVER

U.S. Department of Health and Human Services, Centers for Disease Control, 1600 Clifton Road, NE, Atlanta, Georgia 30333 (800) 311-3435, www.cdc.gov; *Summary of Notifiable Diseases, United States, Morbidity and Mortality Weekly Report.*

TYPHUS FEVER

U.S. Department of Health and Human Services, Centers for Disease Control, 1600 Clifton Road, NE, Atlanta, Georgia 30333 (800) 311-3435, www.cdc.gov; *Summary of Notifiable Diseases, United States, Morbidity and Mortality Weekly Report.*

U

Uganda - National Statistical Office

Chief Government Statistician, Department of Statistics, Ministry of Planning and Economic Development, Post Office Box 13, Entebbe, Uganda.

Uganda - Primary Statistics Source

Statistics Division, Ministry of Planning, Government Printer, Post Office Box 33, Entebbe, Uganda; *Quarterly Economic and Statistical Bulletin.*

UGANDA - AGRICULTURE

Economist Intelligence Unit, 111 West 57th Street, New York, New York 10019 (800) 938-4685; *Uganda Country Report.*

Euromonitor International, Inc., 122 South Michigan Avenue, Suite 1200, Chicago, Illinois 60603 (800) 577-EURO; *International Marketing Data and Statistics;* and *World Marketing Data and Statistics.*

Europa Publications Limited, 18 Bedford Square, London, WC1B 3JN, England; *The Europa World Year Book.*

Food and Agricultural Organization of the United Nations (FAO) Via delle Terme di Caracalla, 00100 Rome, Italy (Telephone Number in U.S. (202) 653-2400); *The State of Food and Agriculture;* and *Trade Yearbook.*

M.E. Sharpe, 80 Business Park Drive, Armonk, New York 10504 (800) 541-6563; *The Illustrated Book of World Rankings.*

St. Martin's Press, Inc., 175 Fifth Avenue, New York, New York 10010 (800) 221-7945; *The Statesman's Year-Book.*

Statistical Office of the United Nations, Publishing Service, New York, New York 10017 (800) 253-9646; *Statistical Yearbook;* and *Survey of Economic and Social*

Conditions in Africa.

United Nations Conference on Trade and Development, Central Statistical Service, Palais des Nations, Geneva, Switzerland (Telephone in U.S. (800) 253-9646); *UNCTAD Commodity Yearbook.*

United Nations Economic Commission for Africa, Africa Hall, P.O. Box 3001, Addis Ababa, Ethiopia (Telephone Number in U.S. (800) 253-9646); *African Statistical Yearbook.*

The World Bank, 1818 H Street, NW, Washington, D.C. 20433 (202) 477-1234; *World Development Indicators.*

UGANDA - AIRLINE SERVICE

Europa Publications Limited, 18 Bedford Square, London, WC1B 3JN, England; *The Europa World Year Book.*

International Civil Aviation Organization, 999 University Street, Montreal, Quebec, Canada H3C 5H7 (514) 954-8219; *Civil Aviation Statistics of the World.*

M.E. Sharpe, 80 Business Park Drive, Armonk, New York 10504 (800) 541-6563; *The Illustrated Book of World Rankings.*

St. Martin's Press, Inc., 175 Fifth Avenue, New York, New York 10010 (800) 221-7945; *The Statesman's Year-Book.*

Statistical Office of the United Nations, Publishing Service, New York, New York 10017 (800) 253-9646; *Statistical Yearbook.*

United Nations Economic Commission for Africa, Africa Hall, P.O. Box 3001, Addis Ababa, Ethiopia (Telephone Number in U.S. (800) 253-9646); *African Statistical Yearbook.*

UGANDA - AIRPORTS

Central Intelligence Agency, Washington, D.C. 20505 (703) 482-1100, www.cia.gov; *The World Factbook.*

UGANDA - ALUMINUM PRODUCTION AND CONSUMPTION - See UGANDA - MINING AND MINERAL PRODUCTS

UGANDA - AREA AND DENSITY OF POPULATION

African Development Bank, 01 BP 1387, Abidjan 01, Cote D'Ivoire; *Selected Statistics on Regional Member Countries.*

Central Intelligence Agency, Washington, D.C. 20505 (703) 482-1100, www.cia.gov; *The World Factbook.*

Euromonitor International, Inc., 122 South Michigan Avenue, Suite 1200, Chicago, Illinois 60603 (800) 577-EURO; *International Marketing Data and Statistics;* and *The World Economic Factbook.*

Europa Publications Limited, 18 Bedford Square, London, WC1B 3JN, England; *The Europa World Year Book.*

Food and Agricultural Organization of the United Nations (FAO) Via delle Terme di Caracalla, 00100 Rome, Italy (Telephone Number in U.S. (202) 653-2400); *The State of Food and Agriculture.*

M.E. Sharpe, 80 Business Park Drive, Armonk, New York 10504 (800) 541-6563; *The Illustrated Book of World Rankings.*

St. Martin's Press, Inc., 175 Fifth Avenue, New York, New York 10010 (800) 221-7945; *The Statesman's Year-Book.*

Statistical Office of the United Nations, Publishing Service, New York, New York 10017 (800) 253-9646; *Statistical Yearbook;* and *Survey of Economic and Social Conditions in Africa.*

United Nations Educational, Scientific and Cultural Organization (UNESCO), 7 Place de Fontenoy, F-75700 Paris, France (Telephone Number in U.S. (212) 963-5981); *Statistical Yearbook.*

The World Bank, 1818 H Street, NW, Washington, D.C. 20433 (202) 477-1234;

World Development Report.

UGANDA - ARMS EXPORTS AND IMPORTS - See UGANDA - MILITARY

UGANDA - BALANCE OF PAYMENTS

African Development Bank, 01 BP 1387, Abidjan 01, Cote D'Ivoire; *Selected Statistics on Regional Member Countries.*

The Economist Intelligence Unit, 111 West 57th Street, New York, New York 10019 (800) 938-4685; *The World Market Atlas.*

Europa Publications Limited, 18 Bedford Square, London, WC1B 3JN, England; *The Europa World Year Book.*

International Monetary Fund, 700 Nineteenth Street, NW, Washington, D.C. 20431; *Balance of Payments Yearbook.*

United Nations Conference on Trade and Development (UNCTAD), New York, New York 10017 (800) 253-9646; *Handbook of International Trade and Development Statistics.*

United Nations Economic Commission for Africa, Africa Hall, P.O. Box 3001, Addis Ababa, Ethiopia (Telephone Number in U.S. (800) 253-9646); *African Statistical Yearbook.*

The World Bank, 1818 H Street, NW, Washington, D.C. 20433 (202) 477-1234; *World Development Report;* and *World Development Indicators.*

UGANDA - BANKING

Euromonitor International, Inc., 122 South Michigan Avenue, Suite 1200, Chicago, Illinois 60603 (800) 577-EURO; *World Marketing Data and Statistics.*

Europa Publications Limited, 18 Bedford Square, London, WC1B 3JN, England; *The Europa World Year Book.*

International Monetary Fund, 700 Nineteenth Street, NW, Washington, D.C. 20431 (202) 623-7000; *International Financial Statistics.*

M.E. Sharpe, 80 Business Park Drive, Armonk, New York 10504 (800) 541-6563; *The Illustrated Book of World Rankings.*

St. Martin's Press, Inc., 175 Fifth Avenue, New York, New York 10010 (800) 221-7945; *The Statesman's Year-Book.*

United Nations Economic Commission for Africa, Africa Hall, P.O. Box 3001, Addis Ababa, Ethiopia (Telephone Number in U.S. (800) 253-9646); *African Statistical Yearbook.*

UGANDA - BARLEY PRODUCTION - See UGANDA - CROPS

UGANDA - BEER PRODUCTION - See UGANDA - BEVERAGES

UGANDA - BEVERAGES

M.E. Sharpe, 80 Business Park Drive, Armonk, New York 10504 (800) 541-6563; *The Illustrated Book of World Rankings.*

Statistical Office of the United Nations, Publishing Service, New York, New York 10017 (800) 253-9646; *Statistical Yearbook.*

UGANDA - BIRTH RATES

Central Intelligence Agency, Washington, D.C. 20505 (703) 482-1100, www.cia.gov; *The World Factbook.*

Euromonitor International, Inc., 122 South Michigan Avenue, Suite 1200, Chicago, Illinois 60603 (800) 577-EURO; *International Marketing Data and Statistics;* and *The World Economic Factbook.*

Europa Publications Limited, 18 Bedford Square, London, WC1B 3JN, England; *The Europa World Year Book.*

M.E. Sharpe, 80 Business Park Drive, Armonk, New York 10504 (800) 541-6563; *The Illustrated Book of World Rankings.*

St. Martin's Press, Inc., 175 Fifth Avenue, New York, New York 10010 (800) 221-7945; *The Statesman's Year-Book.*

Statistical Office of the United Nations, Publishing Service, New York, New York 10017 (800) 253-9646; *Demographic Yearbook; Statistical Yearbook;* and *Survey of Economic and Social Conditions in Africa.*

The World Bank, 1818 H Street, NW, Washington, D.C. 20433 (202) 477-1234; *World Development Indicators.*

UGANDA - BROADCASTING

Billboard Limited, P.O. Box 9027, 1006 AA Amsterdam, The Netherlands (Telephone Number in U.S. (212) 764-7300); *World Radio TV Handbook.*

Central Intelligence Agency, Washington, D.C. 20505 (703) 482-1100, www.cia.gov; *The World Factbook.*

Euromonitor International, Inc., 122 South Michigan Avenue, Suite 1200, Chicago, Illinois 60603 (800) 577-EURO; *World Marketing Data and Statistics.*

M.E. Sharpe, 80 Business Park Drive, Armonk, New York 10504 (800) 541-6563; *The Illustrated Book of World Rankings.*

St. Martin's Press, Inc., 175 Fifth Avenue, New York, New York 10010 (800) 221-7945; *The Statesman's Year-Book.*

UGANDA - BUDGET

Central Intelligence Agency, Washington, D.C. 20505 (703) 482-1100, www.cia.gov; *The World Factbook.*

UGANDA - CALORIE SUPPLY

African Development Bank, 01 BP 1387, Abidjan 01, Cote D'Ivoire; *Selected Statistics on Regional Member Countries.*

Food and Agricultural Organization of the United Nations (FAO) Via delle Terme di Caracalla, 00100 Rome, Italy (Telephone Number in U.S. (202) 653-2400); *The State of Food and Agriculture.*

UGANDA - CASTOR BEAN PRODUCTION - See UGANDA - CROPS

UGANDA - CATTLE - See UGANDA - LIVESTOCK AND POULTRY

UGANDA - CEMENT PRODUCTION - See UGANDA - MINING AND MINERAL PRODUCTS

UGANDA - CHEMICAL (ORGANIC) PRODUCTION - See UGANDA - MINING AND MINERAL PRODUCTS

UGANDA - CHICK PEA PRODUCTION - See UGANDA - CROPS

UGANDA - CHICKENS - See UGANDA - LIVESTOCK AND POULTRY

UGANDA - CIGARETTE PRODUCTION - See UGANDA - TOBACCO PRODUCTION

UGANDA - CLIMATE

M.E. Sharpe, 80 Business Park Drive, Armonk, New York 10504 (800) 541-6563; *The Illustrated Book of World Rankings.*

St. Martin's Press, Inc., 175 Fifth Avenue, New York, New York 10010 (800) 221-7945; *The Statesman's Year-Book.*

UGANDA - COAL PRODUCTION - See UGANDA - MINING AND MINERAL PRODUCTS

UGANDA - COCOA PRODUCTION - See UGANDA - CROPS

UGANDA - COFFEE - See UGANDA - CROPS

UGANDA - COMMERCE

St. Martin's Press, Inc., 175 Fifth Avenue, New York, New York 10010 (800) 221-7945; *The Statesman's Year-Book.*

UGANDA - COMMUNICATIONS - See UGANDA - TRANSPORTATION AND COMMUNICATIONS

UGANDA - CONSTRUCTION INDUSTRY

M.E. Sharpe, 80 Business Park Drive, Armonk, New York 10504 (800) 541-6563; *The Illustrated Book of World Rankings.*

Statistical Office of the United Nations, Publishing Service, New York, New York 10017 (800) 253-9646; *Statistical Yearbook.*

United Nations Economic Commission for Africa, Africa Hall, P.O. Box 3001, Addis Ababa, Ethiopia (Telephone Number in U.S. (800) 253-9646); *African Statistical Yearbook.*

UGANDA - CONSUMER PRICE INDEX

African Development Bank, 01 BP 1387, Abidjan 01, Cote D'Ivoire; *Selected Statistics on Regional Member Countries.*

Europa Publications Limited, 18 Bedford Square, London, WC1B 3JN, England; *The Europa World Year Book.*

Statistical Office of the United Nations, Publishing Service, New York, New York 10017 (800) 253-9646; *Statistical Yearbook;* and *Survey of Economic and Social Conditions in Africa.*

United Nations Economic Commission for Africa, Africa Hall, P.O. Box 3001, Addis Ababa, Ethiopia (Telephone Number in U.S. (800) 253-9646); *African Statistical Yearbook.*

UGANDA - CONSUMER PRICES

Euromonitor International, Inc., 122 South Michigan Avenue, Suite 1200, Chicago, Illinois 60603 (800) 577-EURO; *World Marketing Data and Statistics.*

International Labour Office, I.L.O. Publications, 1828 L Street, NW, Suite 801, Washington, D.C. 20036 (301) 638-3152; *Yearbook of Labour Statistics.*

International Monetary Fund, 700 Nineteenth Street, NW, Washington, D.C. 20431 (202) 623-7000; *International Financial Statistics.*

UGANDA - CONSUMPTION

African Development Bank, 01 BP 1387, Abidjan 01, Cote D'Ivoire; *Selected Statistics on Regional Member Countries.*

Statistical Office of the United Nations, Publishing Service, New York, New York 10017 (800) 253-9646; *Survey of Economic and Social Conditions in Africa.*

The World Bank, 1818 H Street, NW, Washington, D.C. 20433 (202) 477-1234; *World Development Report.*

UGANDA - COPPER AND COPPER ORE PRODUCTION AND CONSUMPTION - See UGANDA - MINING AND MINERAL PRODUCTS

UGANDA - CORN PRODUCTION - See UGANDA - CROPS

UGANDA - CORPORATE TAXES - See UGANDA - TAXATION

UGANDA - COTTON - See UGANDA - CROPS

UGANDA - CRIME

Yale University Press, Yale Station, New Haven, Connecticut 06520 (800) 987-7323; *Violence and Crime in Cross-National Perspective.*

UGANDA - CROPS

Commodity Research Bureau, Inc., 30 South Wacker Drive, Chicago, Illinois 60606 (312) 454-1801; *Commodity Year Book.*

Europa Publications Limited, 18 Bedford Square, London, WC1B 3JN, England; *The Europa World Year Book.*

Food and Agricultural Organization of the United Nations (FAO) Via delle Terme di Caracalla, 00100 Rome, Italy (Telephone Number in U.S. (202) 653-2400); *The State of Food and Agriculture.*

International Monetary Fund, 700 Nineteenth Street, NW, Washington, D.C. 20431 (202) 623-7000; *International Financial Statistics.*

M.E. Sharpe, 80 Business Park Drive, Armonk, New York 10504 (800) 541-6563; *The Illustrated Book of World Rankings.*

St. Martin's Press, Inc., 175 Fifth Avenue, New York, New York 10010 (800) 221-7945; *The Statesman's Year-Book.*

Statistical Office of the United Nations, Publishing Service, New York, New York 10017 (800) 253-9646; *Statistical Yearbook.*

United Nations Conference on Trade and Development, Central Statistical Service, Palais des Nations, Geneva, Switzerland (Telephone in U.S. (800) 253-9646); *UNCTAD Commodity Yearbook.*

United Nations Economic Commission for Africa, Africa Hall, P.O. Box 3001, Addis Ababa, Ethiopia (Telephone Number in U.S. (800) 253-9646); *African Statistical Yearbook.*

UGANDA - CUSTOMS DUTIES

St. Martin's Press, Inc., 175 Fifth Avenue, New York, New York 10010 (800) 221-7945; *The Statesman's Year-Book.*

UGANDA - DAIRY PRODUCTS

Europa Publications Limited, 18 Bedford Square, London, WC1B 3JN, England; *The Europa World Year Book.*

Food and Agricultural Organization of the United Nations (FAO) Via delle Terme di Caracalla, 00100 Rome, Italy (Telephone Number in U.S. (202) 653-2400); *The State of Food and Agriculture.*

M.E. Sharpe, 80 Business Park Drive, Armonk, New York 10504 (800) 541-6563; *The Illustrated Book of World Rankings.*

St. Martin's Press, Inc., 175 Fifth Avenue, New York, New York 10010 (800) 221-7945; *The Statesman's Year-Book.*

Statistical Office of the United Nations, Publishing Service, New York, New York 10017 (800) 253-9646; *Statistical Yearbook.*

UGANDA - DEATH RATES - See UGANDA - MORTALITY

UGANDA - DEFENSE EXPENDITURES - See UGANDA - MILITARY

UGANDA - DEVELOPMENT ASSISTANCE

Statistical Office of the United Nations, Publishing Service, New York, New York 10017 (800) 253-9646; *Statistical Yearbook.*

UGANDA - DEMOGRAPHY

The Economist Intelligence Unit, 111 West 57th Street, New York, New York 10019 (800) 938-4685; *The World Market Atlas.*

Euromonitor International, Inc., 122 South Michigan Avenue, Suite 1200, Chicago, Illinois 60603 (800) 577-EURO; *International Marketing Data and Statistics; World Marketing Data and Statistics;* and *The World Economic Factbook.*

M.E. Sharpe, 80 Business Park Drive, Armonk, New York 10504 (800) 541-6563; *The Illustrated Book of World Rankings.*

Statistical Office of the United Nations, Publishing Service, New York, New York 10017 (800) 253-9646; *Human Development Report;* and *Survey of Economic and Social Conditions in Africa.*

UGANDA - DIAMOND PRODUCTION - See UGANDA - MINING AND MINERAL PRODUCTS

UGANDA - DIVORCE RATES

M.E. Sharpe, 80 Business Park Drive, Armonk, New York 10504 (800) 541-6563; *The Illustrated Book of World Rankings.*

Statistical Office of the United Nations, Publishing Service, New York, New York 10017 (800) 253-9646; *Demographic Yearbook.*

UGANDA - ECONOMY

African Development Bank, 01 BP 1387, Abidjan 01, Cote D'Ivoire; *Selected Statistics on Regional Member Countries.*

Central Intelligence Agency, Washington, D.C. 20505 (703) 482-1100, www.cia.gov; *The World Factbook.*

Economist Intelligence Unit, 111 West 57th Street, New York, New York 10019 (800) 938-4685; *Uganda Country Report.*

Euromonitor International, Inc., 122 South Michigan Avenue, Suite 1200, Chicago, Illinois 60603 (800) 577-EURO; *International Marketing Data and Statistics; World Marketing Data and Statistics;* and *The World Economic Factbook.*

Europa Publications Limited, 18 Bedford Square, London, WC1B 3JN, England; *The Europa World Year Book.*

M.E. Sharpe, 80 Business Park Drive, Armonk, New York 10504 (800) 541-6563; *The Illustrated Book of World Rankings.*

St. Martin's Press, Inc., 175 Fifth Avenue, New York, New York 10010 (800) 221-7945; *The Statesman's Year-Book.*

Statistical Office of the United Nations, Publishing Service, New York, New York 10017 (800) 253-9646; *Foreign Trade Statistics for Africa;* and *World Statistics Pocketbook.*

The World Bank, 1818 H Street, NW, Washington, D.C. 20433 (202) 477-1234; *The World Bank Atlas;* and *World Development Report.*

UGANDA - EDUCATION

African Development Bank, 01 BP 1387, Abidjan 01, Cote D'Ivoire; *Selected Statistics on Regional Member Countries.*

The Economist Intelligence Unit, 111 West 57th Street, New York, New York 10019 (800) 938-4685; *The World Market Atlas.*

Euromonitor International, Inc., 122 South Michigan Avenue, Suite 1200, Chicago, Illinois 60603 (800) 577-EURO; *International Marketing Data and Statistics;* and *World Marketing Data and Statistics.*

Europa Publications Limited, 18 Bedford Square, London, WC1B 3JN, England; *The Europa World Year Book.*

M.E. Sharpe, 80 Business Park Drive, Armonk, New York 10504 (800) 541-6563; *The Illustrated Book of World Rankings.*

St. Martin's Press, Inc., 175 Fifth Avenue, New York, New York 10010 (800) 221-7945; *The Statesman's Year-Book.*

Statistical Office of the United Nations, Publishing Service, New York, New York 10017 (800) 253-9646; *Human Development Report;* and *Survey of Economic and Social Conditions in Africa.*

United Nations Economic Commission for Africa, Africa Hall, P.O. Box 3001, Addis Ababa, Ethiopia (Telephone Number in U.S. (800) 253-9646); *African Statistical Yearbook.*

United Nations Educational, Scientific and Cultural Organization (UNESCO), 7 Place de Fontenoy, F-75700 Paris, France (Telephone Number in U.S. (212) 963-5981); *Statistical Yearbook.*

The World Bank, 1818 H Street, NW, Washington, D.C. 20433 (202) 477-1234; *World Development Report;* and *World Development Indicators.*

UGANDA - EGG PRODUCTION AND CONSUMPTION - See UGANDA -DAIRY PRODUCTS

UGANDA - ELECTRICITY

Central Intelligence Agency, Washington, D.C. 20505 (703) 482-1100, www.cia.gov; *The World Factbook.*

M.E. Sharpe, 80 Business Park Drive, Armonk, New York 10504 (800) 541-6563; *The Illustrated Book of World Rankings.*

St. Martin's Press, Inc., 175 Fifth Avenue, New York, New York 10010 (800) 221-7945; *The Statesman's Year-Book.*

Statistical Office of the United Nations, Publishing Service, New York, New York 10017 (800) 253-9646; *Human Development Report; Statistical Yearbook;* and *Survey of Economic and Social Conditions in Africa.*

United Nations Economic Commission for Africa, Africa Hall, P.O. Box 3001, Addis Ababa, Ethiopia (Telephone Number in U.S. (800) 253-9646); *African Statistical Yearbook.*

UGANDA - EMPLOYMENT

Euromonitor International, Inc., 122 South Michigan Avenue, Suite 1200, Chicago, Illinois 60603 (800) 577-EURO;

International Marketing Data and Statistics.

International Labour Office, I.L.O. Publications, 1828 L Street, NW, Suite 801, Washington, D.C. 20036 (301) 638-3152; *Yearbook of Labour Statistics.*

M.E. Sharpe, 80 Business Park Drive, Armonk, New York 10504 (800) 541-6563; *The Illustrated Book of World Rankings.*

Statistical Office of the United Nations, Publishing Service, New York, New York 10017 (800) 253-9646; *Statistical Yearbook;* and *Survey of Economic and Social Conditions in Africa.*

United Nations Economic Commission for Africa, Africa Hall, P.O. Box 3001, Addis Ababa, Ethiopia (Telephone Number in U.S. (800) 253-9646); *African Statistical Yearbook.*

UGANDA - ENERGY

Euromonitor International, Inc., 122 South Michigan Avenue, Suite 1200, Chicago, Illinois 60603 (800) 577-EURO; *International Marketing Data and Statistics; World Marketing Data and Statistics;* and *The World Economic Factbook.*

Food and Agricultural Organization of the United Nations (FAO) Via delle Terme di Caracalla, 00100 Rome, Italy (Telephone Number in U.S. (202) 653-2400); *The State of Food and Agriculture.*

M.E. Sharpe, 80 Business Park Drive, Armonk, New York 10504 (800) 541-6563; *The Illustrated Book of World Rankings.*

St. Martin's Press, Inc., 175 Fifth Avenue, New York, New York 10010 (800) 221-7945; *The Statesman's Year-Book.*

Statistical Office of the United Nations, Publishing Service, New York, New York 10017 (800) 253-9646; *Energy Statistics Yearbook; Human Development Report;* and *World Statistics Pocketbook.*

United Nations Economic Commission for Africa, Africa Hall, P.O. Box 3001, Addis Ababa, Ethiopia (Telephone Number in U.S. (800) 253-9646); *African Statistical Yearbook.*

The World Bank, 1818 H Street, NW, Washington, D.C. 20433 (202) 477-1234; *The World Bank Atlas;* and *World Development Report.*

UGANDA - ENVIRONMENT

Economist Intelligence Unit, 111 West 57th Street, New York, New York 10019 (800) 938-4685; *Uganda Country Report.*

Statistical Office of the United Nations, Publishing Service, New York, New York

10017 (800) 253-9646; *World Statistics Pocketbook.*

UGANDA - EXCHANGE RATE

African Development Bank, 01 BP 1387, Abidjan 01, Cote D'Ivoire; *Selected Statistics on Regional Member Countries.*

Central Intelligence Agency, Washington, D.C. 20505 (703) 482-1100, www.cia.gov; *The World Factbook.*

Euromonitor International, Inc., 122 South Michigan Avenue, Suite 1200, Chicago, Illinois 60603 (800) 577-EURO; *International Marketing Data and Statistics; and The World Economic Factbook.*

Europa Publications Limited, 18 Bedford Square, London, WC1B 3JN, England; *The Europa World Year Book.*

International Civil Aviation Organization, 999 University Street, Montreal, Quebec, Canada H3C 5H7 (514) 954-8219; *Civil Aviation Statistics of the World.*

International Monetary Fund, 700 Nineteenth Street, NW, Washington, D.C. 20431 (202) 623-7000; *International Financial Statistics.*

Statistical Office of the United Nations, Publishing Service, New York, New York 10017 (800) 253-9646; *Foreign Trade Statistics for Africa; Statistical Yearbook; and World Statistics Pocketbook.*

UGANDA - EXPORTS

African Development Bank, 01 BP 1387, Abidjan 01, Cote D'Ivoire; *Selected Statistics on Regional Member Countries.*

Central Intelligence Agency, Washington, D.C. 20505 (703) 482-1100, www.cia.gov; *The World Factbook.*

The Economist Intelligence Unit, 111 West 57th Street, New York, New York 10019 (800) 938-4685; *Uganda Country Report; and The World Market Atlas.*

Euromonitor International, Inc., 122 South Michigan Avenue, Suite 1200, Chicago, Illinois 60603 (800) 577-EURO; *International Marketing Data and Statistics; and The World Economic Factbook.*

Europa Publications Limited, 18 Bedford Square, London, WC1B 3JN, England; *The Europa World Year Book.*

Food and Agricultural Organization of the United Nations (FAO) Via delle Terme di Caracalla, 00100 Rome, Italy (Telephone Number in U.S. (202) 653-2400); *The State of Food and Agriculture.*

International Monetary Fund, 700 Nineteenth Street, NW, Washington, D.C. 20431 (202) 623-7000; *Direction of Trade Statistics;* and *International Financial Statistics.*

St. Martin's Press, Inc., 175 Fifth Avenue, New York, New York 10010 (800) 221-7945; *The Statesman's Year-Book.*

Statistical Office of the United Nations, Publishing Service, New York, New York 10017 (800) 253-9646; *Foreign Trade Statistics for Africa;* and *Survey of Economic and Social Conditions in Africa.*

United Nations Conference on Trade and Development (UNCTAD), New York, New York 10017 (800) 253-9646; *Handbook of International Trade and Development Statistics.*

United Nations Economic Commission for Africa, Africa Hall, P.O. Box 3001, Addis Ababa, Ethiopia (Telephone Number in U.S. (800) 253-9646); *African Statistical Yearbook.*

The World Bank, 1818 H Street, NW, Washington, D.C. 20433 (202) 477-1234; *World Development Report; and World Development Indicators.*

UGANDA - EXTERNAL INDEBTEDNESS

African Development Bank, 01 BP 1387, Abidjan 01, Cote D'Ivoire; *Selected Statistics on Regional Member Countries.*

Statistical Office of the United Nations, Publishing Service, New York, New York 10017 (800) 253-9646; *Survey of Economic and Social Conditions in Africa.*

The World Bank, 1818 H Street, NW, Washington, D.C. 20433 (202) 477-1234; *World Development Report; and World Development Indicators.*

UGANDA - EXTERNAL TRADE

African Development Bank, 01 BP 1387, Abidjan 01, Cote D'Ivoire; *Selected Statistics on Regional Member Countries.*

Euromonitor International, Inc., 122 South Michigan Avenue, Suite 1200, Chicago, Illinois 60603 (800) 577-EURO; *World Marketing Data and Statistics.*

Food and Agricultural Organization of the United Nations (FAO) Via delle Terme di Caracalla, 00100 Rome, Italy (Telephone Number in U.S. (202) 653-2400); *The State of Food and Agriculture.*

Statistical Office of the United Nations, Publishing Service, New York, New York 10017 (800) 253-9646; *Statistical Yearbook.*

UGANDA - FABRIC PRODUCTION

Statistical Office of the United Nations, Publishing Service, New York, New York 10017 (800) 253-9646; *Statistical Yearbook.*

UGANDA - FARM CROPS - See
UGANDA - CROPS

UGANDA - FEMALE WORKING POPULATION - See UGANDA - EMPLOYMENT

UGANDA - FERTILITY RATES

Central Intelligence Agency, Washington, D.C. 20505 (703) 482-1100, www.cia.gov; *The World Factbook.*

M.E. Sharpe, 80 Business Park Drive, Armonk, New York 10504 (800) 541-6563; *The Illustrated Book of World Rankings.*

Statistical Office of the United Nations, Publishing Service, New York, New York 10017 (800) 253-9646; *Human Development Report;* and *Survey of Economic and Social Conditions in Africa.*

The World Bank, 1818 H Street, NW, Washington, D.C. 20433 (202) 477-1234; *The World Bank Atlas; World Development Report;* and *World Development Indicators.*

UGANDA - FERTILIZER

Food and Agricultural Organization of the United Nations (FAO), Via delle Terme di Caracalla, 00100 Rome, Italy (Telephone Number in U.S. (202) 653-2400); *Fertilizer Yearbook;* and *The State of Food and Agriculture.*

Statistical Office of the United Nations, Publishing Service, New York, New York 10017 (800) 253-9646; *Statistical Yearbook.*

UGANDA - FETAL MORTALITY - See
UGANDA - MORTALITY

UGANDA - FINANCE

African Development Bank, 01 BP 1387, Abidjan 01, Cote D'Ivoire; *Selected Statistics on Regional Member Countries.*

Economist Intelligence Unit, 111 West 57th Street, New York, New York 10019 (800) 938-4685; *Uganda Country Report.*

Europa Publications Limited, 18 Bedford Square, London, WC1B 3JN, England; *The Europa World Year Book.*

M.E. Sharpe, 80 Business Park Drive, Armonk, New York 10504 (800) 541-6563; *The Illustrated Book of World Rankings.*

St. Martin's Press, Inc., 175 Fifth Avenue, New York, New York 10010 (800) 221-7945; *The Statesman's Year-Book.*

United Nations Economic Commission

for Africa, Africa Hall, P.O. Box 3001, Addis Ababa, Ethiopia (Telephone Number in U.S. (800) 253-9646); *African Statistical Yearbook*.

UGANDA - FISHERIES

Europa Publications Limited, 18 Bedford Square, London, WC1B 3JN, England; *The Europa World Year Book*.

Food and Agricultural Organization of the United Nations (FAO) Via delle Terme di Caracalla, 00100 Rome, Italy (Telephone Number in U.S. (202) 653-2400); *The State of Food and Agriculture;* and *Yearbook of Fishery Statistics*.

M.E. Sharpe, 80 Business Park Drive, Armonk, New York 10504 (800) 541-6563; *The Illustrated Book of World Rankings*.

St. Martin's Press, Inc., 175 Fifth Avenue, New York, New York 10010 (800) 221-7945; *The Statesman's Year-Book*.

Statistical Office of the United Nations, Publishing Service, New York, New York 10017 (800) 253-9646; *Statistical Yearbook;* and *Survey of Economic and Social Conditions in Africa*.

United Nations Conference on Trade and Development, Central Statistical Service, Palais des Nations, Geneva, Switzerland (Telephone in U.S. (800) 253-9646); *UNCTAD Commodity Yearbook*.

United Nations Economic Commission for Africa, Africa Hall, P.O. Box 3001, Addis Ababa, Ethiopia (Telephone Number in U.S. (800) 253-9646); *African Statistical Yearbook*.

UGANDA - FLOUR PRODUCTION

Statistical Office of the United Nations, Publishing Service, New York, New York 10017 (800) 253-9646; *Statistical Yearbook*.

UGANDA - FOOD

African Development Bank, 01 BP 1387, Abidjan 01, Cote D'Ivoire; *Selected Statistics on Regional Member Countries*.

Food and Agricultural Organization of the United Nations (FAO) Via delle Terme di Caracalla, 00100 Rome, Italy (Telephone Number in U.S. (202) 653-2400); *The State of Food and Agriculture*.

Statistical Office of the United Nations, Publishing Service, New York, New York 10017 (800) 253-9646; *Human Development Report*.

United Nations Conference on Trade and Development, Central Statistical Service, Palais des Nations, Geneva, Switzerland (Telephone in U.S. (800) 253-

9646); *UNCTAD Commodity Yearbook*.

UGANDA - FOREIGN TRADE

Economist Intelligence Unit, 111 West 57th Street, New York, New York 10019 (800) 938-4685; *Uganda Country Report*.

Euromonitor International, Inc., 122 South Michigan Avenue, Suite 1200, Chicago, Illinois 60603 (800) 577-EURO; *International Marketing Data and Statistics;* and *The World Economic Factbook*.

Europa Publications Limited, 18 Bedford Square, London, WC1B 3JN, England; *The Europa World Year Book*.

Food and Agricultural Organization of the United Nations (FAO) Via delle Terme di Caracalla, 00100 Rome, Italy (Telephone Number in U.S. (202) 653-2400); *The State of Food and Agriculture*.

International Monetary Fund, 700 Nineteenth Street, NW, Washington, D.C. 20431 (202) 623-7000; *International Financial Statistics*.

M.E. Sharpe, 80 Business Park Drive, Armonk, New York 10504 (800) 541-6563; *The Illustrated Book of World Rankings*.

St. Martin's Press, Inc., 175 Fifth Avenue, New York, New York 10010 (800) 221-7945; *The Statesman's Year-Book*.

Statistical Office of the United Nations, Publishing Service, New York, New York 10017 (800) 253-9646; *Foreign Trade Statistics for Africa; International Trade Statistics Yearbook; Statistical Yearbook;* and *Trade in Manufactures of Development Countries*.

United Nations Conference on Trade and Development, Central Statistical Service, Palais des Nations, Geneva, Switzerland (Telephone in U.S. (800) 253-9646); *UNCTAD Commodity Yearbook*.

United Nations Economic Commission for Africa, Africa Hall, P.O. Box 3001, Addis Ababa, Ethiopia (Telephone Number in U.S. (800) 253-9646); *African Statistical Yearbook*.

The World Bank, 1818 H Street, NW, Washington, D.C. 20433 (202) 477-1234; *World Development Report;* and *World Development Indicators*.

UGANDA - FORESTRY AND FOREST PRODUCTS

Europa Publications Limited, 18 Bedford Square, London, WC1B 3JN, England; *The Europa World Year Book*.

Food and Agricultural Organization of the United Nations (FAO) Via delle Terme

di Caracalla, 00100 Rome, Italy (Telephone Number in U.S. (202) 653-2400); *The State of Food and Agriculture;* and *Yearbook of Forest Products*.

M.E. Sharpe, 80 Business Park Drive, Armonk, New York 10504 (800) 541-6563; *The Illustrated Book of World Rankings*.

St. Martin's Press, Inc., 175 Fifth Avenue, New York, New York 10010 (800) 221-7945; *The Statesman's Year-Book*.

Statistical Office of the United Nations, Publishing Service, New York, New York 10017 (800) 253-9646; *Statistical Yearbook*.

United Nations Conference on Trade and Development, Central Statistical Service, Palais des Nations, Geneva, Switzerland (Telephone in U.S. (800) 253-9646); *UNCTAD Commodity Yearbook*.

United Nations Economic Commission for Africa, Africa Hall, P.O. Box 3001, Addis Ababa, Ethiopia (Telephone Number in U.S. (800) 253-9646); *African Statistical Yearbook*.

United Nations Educational, Scientific and Cultural Organization (UNESCO), 7 Place de Fontenoy, F-75700 Paris, France (Telephone Number in U.S. (212) 963-5981); *Statistical Yearbook*.

The World Bank, 1818 H Street, NW, Washington, D.C. 20433 (202) 477-1234; *World Development Report*.

UGANDA - GAS PRODUCTION - See UGANDA - MINING AND MINERAL PRODUCTS

UGANDA - GENERAL MORTALITY - See UGANDA - MORTALITY

UGANDA - GEOGRAPHIC DATA

M.E. Sharpe, 80 Business Park Drive, Armonk, New York 10504 (800) 541-6563; *The Illustrated Book of World Rankings*.

UGANDA - GOATS - See UGANDA - LIVESTOCK AND POULTRY

UGANDA - GOLD HOLDINGS

International Monetary Fund, 700 Nineteenth Street, NW, Washington, D.C. 20431 (202) 623-7000; *International Financial Statistics*.

Statistical Office of the United Nations, Publishing Service, New York, New York 10017 (800) 253-9646; *Statistical Yearbook*.

The World Bank, 1818 H Street, NW, Washington, D.C. 20433 (202) 477-1234; *World Development Indicators*.

UGANDA - GOLD PRODUCTION AND

CONSUMPTION - See UGANDA - MINING AND MINERAL PRODUCTS

UGANDA - GOVERNMENT

Central Intelligence Agency, Washington, D.C. 20505 (703) 482-1100, www.cia.gov; *The World Factbook*.

Europa Publications Limited, 18 Bedford Square, London, WC1B 3JN, England; *The Europa World Year Book*.

International Monetary Fund, 700 Nineteenth Street, NW, Washington, D.C. 20431 (202) 623-7000; *International Financial Statistics*.

St. Martin's Press, Inc., 175 Fifth Avenue, New York, New York 10010 (800) 221-7945; *The Statesman's Year-Book*.

Statistical Office of the United Nations, Publishing Service, New York, New York 10017 (800) 253-9646; *National Accounts Statistics; Statistical Yearbook;* and *Survey of Economic and Social Conditions in Africa*.

The World Bank, 1818 H Street, NW, Washington, D.C. 20433 (202) 477-1234; *World Development Report;* and *World Development Indicators*.

UGANDA - GRAIN PRODUCTION - See UGANDA - CROPS

UGANDA - GROSS DOMESTIC PRODUCT

African Development Bank, 01 BP 1387, Abidjan 01, Cote D'Ivoire; *Selected Statistics on Regional Member Countries*.

The Economist Intelligence Unit, 111 West 57th Street, New York, New York 10019 (800) 938-4685; *Uganda Country Report;* and *The World Market Atlas*.

Euromonitor International, Inc., 122 South Michigan Avenue, Suite 1200, Chicago, Illinois 60603 (800) 577-EURO; *International Marketing Data and Statistics;* and *The World Economic Factbook*.

M.E. Sharpe, 80 Business Park Drive, Armonk, New York 10504 (800) 541-6563; *The Illustrated Book of World Rankings*.

Statistical Office of the United Nations, Publishing Service, New York, New York 10017 (800) 253-9646; *Human Development Report; National Accounts Statistics; Statistical Yearbook;* and *Survey of Economic and Social Conditions in Africa*.

United Nations Economic Commission for Africa, Africa Hall, P.O. Box 3001, Addis Ababa, Ethiopia (Telephone Number in U.S. (800) 253-9646); *African Statistical Yearbook*.

The World Bank, 1818 H Street, NW, Washington, D.C. 20433 (202) 477-1234; *World Development Report;* and *World Development Indicators*.

UGANDA - GROSS NATIONAL PRODUCT

Euromonitor International, Inc., 122 South Michigan Avenue, Suite 1200, Chicago, Illinois 60603 (800) 577-EURO; *International Marketing Data and Statistics*.

St. Martin's Press, Inc., 175 Fifth Avenue, New York, New York 10010 (800) 221-7945; *The Statesman's Year-Book*.

U.S. Arms Control and Disarmament Agency, 320 Twenty-first Street, NW, Washington, D.C. 20451 (202) 647-8677; *World Military Expenditures and Arms Transfers*.

The World Bank, 1818 H Street, NW, Washington, D.C. 20433 (202) 477-1234; *The World Bank Atlas; World Development Report;* and *World Development Indicators*.

UGANDA - GROUNDNUTS PRODUCTION - See UGANDA - CROPS

UGANDA - HEALTH

African Development Bank, 01 BP 1387, Abidjan 01, Cote D'Ivoire; *Selected Statistics on Regional Member Countries*.

Euromonitor International, Inc., 122 South Michigan Avenue, Suite 1200, Chicago, Illinois 60603 (800) 577-EURO; *World Marketing Data and Statistics*.

M.E. Sharpe, 80 Business Park Drive, Armonk, New York 10504 (800) 541-6563; *The Illustrated Book of World Rankings*.

St. Martin's Press, Inc., 175 Fifth Avenue, New York, New York 10010 (800) 221-7945; *The Statesman's Year-Book*.

Statistical Office of the United Nations, Publishing Service, New York, New York 10017 (800) 253-9646; *Human Development Report;* and *Statistical Yearbook*.

United Nations Children's Fund (UNICEF), 3 United Nations Plaza, New York, New York 10017 (800) 253-9646; *State of the World's Children*.

United Nations Economic Commission for Africa, Africa Hall, P.O. Box 3001, Addis Ababa, Ethiopia (Telephone Number in U.S. (800) 253-9646); *African Statistical Yearbook*.

The World Bank, 1818 H Street, NW, Washington, D.C. 20433 (202) 477-1234; *World Development Report*.

UGANDA - HIDE PRODUCTION

Food and Agricultural Organization of the United Nations (FAO), Via delle Terme di Caracalla, 00100 Rome, Italy (Telephone Number in U.S. (202) 653-2400); *Production Yearbook*.

UGANDA - HIGHWAYS

Central Intelligence Agency, Washington, D.C. 20505 (703) 482-1100, www.cia.gov; *The World Factbook*.

International Road Federation, 2600 Virginia Avenue, NW, Washington, D.C. 20037 (202) 338-4641; *World Road Statistics*.

St. Martin's Press, Inc., 175 Fifth Avenue, New York, New York 10010 (800) 221-7945; *The Statesman's Year-Book*.

Statistical Office of the United Nations, Publishing Service, New York, New York 10017 (800) 253-9646; *Survey of Economic and Social Conditions in Africa*.

United Nations Economic Commission for Africa, Africa Hall, P.O. Box 3001, Addis Ababa, Ethiopia (Telephone Number in U.S. (800) 253-9646); *African Statistical Yearbook*.

UGANDA - HORSES - See UGANDA - LIVESTOCK AND POULTRY

UGANDA - HOURS OF WORK - See UGANDA - EMPLOYMENT

UGANDA - HOUSING AND HOUSING UNITS

Euromonitor International, Inc., 122 South Michigan Avenue, Suite 1200, Chicago, Illinois 60603 (800) 577-EURO; *World Marketing Data and Statistics*.

M.E. Sharpe, 80 Business Park Drive, Armonk, New York 10504 (800) 541-6563; *The Illustrated Book of World Rankings*.

UGANDA - ILLITERATE POPULATION

Central Intelligence Agency, Washington, D.C. 20505 (703) 482-1100, www.cia.gov; *The World Factbook*.

The Economist Intelligence Unit, 111 West 57th Street, New York, New York 10019 (800) 938-4685; *The World Market Atlas*.

Euromonitor International, Inc., 122 South Michigan Avenue, Suite 1200, Chicago, Illinois 60603 (800) 577-EURO; *The World Economic Factbook*.

St. Martin's Press, Inc., 175 Fifth Avenue, New York, New York 10010 (800) 221-7945; *The Statesman's Year-Book*.

Statistical Office of the United Nations, Publishing Service, New York, New York

10017 (800) 253-9646; *Human Development Report.*

United Nations Educational, Scientific and Cultural Organization (UNESCO), 7 Place de Fontenoy, F-75700 Paris, France (Telephone Number in U.S. (212) 963-5981); *Statistical Yearbook.*

UGANDA - IMPORTS

African Development Bank, 01 BP 1387, Abidjan 01, Cote D'Ivoire; *Selected Statistics on Regional Member Countries.*

Central Intelligence Agency, Washington, D.C. 20505 (703) 482-1100, www.cia.gov; *The World Factbook.*

The Economist Intelligence Unit, 111 West 57th Street, New York, New York 10019 (800) 938-4685; *Uganda Country Report;* and *The World Market Atlas.*

Euromonitor International, Inc., 122 South Michigan Avenue, Suite 1200, Chicago, Illinois 60603 (800) 577-EURO; *International Marketing Data and Statistics;* and *The World Economic Factbook.*

Europa Publications Limited, 18 Bedford Square, London, WC1B 3JN, England; *The Europa World Year Book.*

Food and Agricultural Organization of the United Nations (FAO) Via delle Terme di Caracalla, 00100 Rome, Italy (Telephone Number in U.S. (202) 653-2400); *The State of Food and Agriculture.*

International Monetary Fund, 700 Nineteenth Street, NW, Washington, D.C. 20431 (202) 623-7000; *Direction of Trade Statistics;* and *International Financial Statistics.*

St. Martin's Press, Inc., 175 Fifth Avenue, New York, New York 10010 (800) 221-7945; *The Statesman's Year-Book.*

Statistical Office of the United Nations, Publishing Service, New York, New York 10017 (800) 253-9646; *Foreign Trade Statistics for Africa;* and *Survey of Economic and Social Conditions in Africa.*

United Nations Conference on Trade and Development (UNCTAD), New York, New York 10017 (800) 253-9646; *Handbook of International Trade and Development Statistics.*

United Nations Economic Commission for Africa, Africa Hall, P.O. Box 3001, Addis Ababa, Ethiopia (Telephone Number in U.S. (800) 253-9646); *African Statistical Yearbook.*

The World Bank, 1818 H Street, NW, Washington, D.C. 20433 (202) 477-1234; *World Development Report;* and *World Development Indicators.*

UGANDA - INDUSTRIAL METALS PRODUCTION - See UGANDA - MINING AND MINERAL PRODUCTS

UGANDA - INDUSTRY

Central Intelligence Agency, Washington, D.C. 20505 (703) 482-1100, www.cia.gov; *The World Factbook.*

Economist Intelligence Unit, 111 West 57th Street, New York, New York 10019 (800) 938-4685; *Uganda Country Report.*

Euromonitor International, Inc., 122 South Michigan Avenue, Suite 1200, Chicago, Illinois 60603 (800) 577-EURO; *International Marketing Data and Statistics; World Marketing Data and Statistics;* and *The World Economic Factbook.*

Europa Publications Limited, 18 Bedford Square, London, WC1B 3JN, England; *The Europa World Year Book.*

International Labour Office, I.L.O. Publications, 1828 L Street, NW, Suite 801, Washington, D.C. 20036 (301) 638-3152; *Yearbook of Labour Statistics.*

M.E. Sharpe, 80 Business Park Drive, Armonk, New York 10504 (800) 541-6563; *The Illustrated Book of World Rankings.*

St. Martin's Press, Inc., 175 Fifth Avenue, New York, New York 10010 (800) 221-7945; *The Statesman's Year-Book.*

Statistical Office of the United Nations, Publishing Service, New York, New York 10017 (800) 253-9646; *Survey of Economic and Social Conditions in Africa.*

United Nations Economic Commission for Africa, Africa Hall, P.O. Box 3001, Addis Ababa, Ethiopia (Telephone Number in U.S. (800) 253-9646); *African Statistical Yearbook.*

The World Bank, 1818 H Street, NW, Washington, D.C. 20433 (202) 477-1234; *World Development Indicators.*

UGANDA - INFANT AND MATERNAL MORTALITY - See UGANDA - MORTALITY

UGANDA - INTERNAL TRADE

Statistical Office of the United Nations, Publishing Service, New York, New York 10017 (800) 253-9646; *Statistical Yearbook.*

UGANDA - INTERNATIONAL LIQUIDITY

International Monetary Fund, 700 Nineteenth Street, NW, Washington, D.C. 20431 (202) 623-7000; *International Financial Statistics.*

UGANDA - INTERNATIONAL RESERVES - EXCLUDING GOLD

African Development Bank, 01 BP 1387, Abidjan 01, Cote D'Ivoire; *Selected Statistics on Regional Member Countries.*

Statistical Office of the United Nations, Publishing Service, New York, New York 10017 (800) 253-9646; *Statistical Yearbook.*

The World Bank, 1818 H Street, NW, Washington, D.C. 20433 (202) 477-1234; *World Development Indicators.*

UGANDA - IRON ORE PRODUCTION AND CONSUMPTION - See UGANDA - MINING AND MINERAL PRODUCTS

UGANDA - IRRIGATION

Euromonitor International, Inc., 122 South Michigan Avenue, Suite 1200, Chicago, Illinois 60603 (800) 577-EURO; *International Marketing Data and Statistics.*

UGANDA - LABOR

African Development Bank, 01 BP 1387, Abidjan 01, Cote D'Ivoire; *Selected Statistics on Regional Member Countries.*

Central Intelligence Agency, Washington, D.C. 20505 (703) 482-1100, www.cia.gov; *The World Factbook.*

Euromonitor International, Inc., 122 South Michigan Avenue, Suite 1200, Chicago, Illinois 60603 (800) 577-EURO; *International Marketing Data and Statistics;* and *World Marketing Data and Statistics.*

Europa Publications Limited, 18 Bedford Square, London, WC1B 3JN, England; *The Europa World Year Book.*

Food and Agricultural Organization of the United Nations (FAO) Via delle Terme di Caracalla, 00100 Rome, Italy (Telephone Number in U.S. (202) 653-2400); *The State of Food and Agriculture.*

International Labour Office, I.L.O. Publications, 1828 L Street, NW, Suite 801, Washington, D.C. 20036 (301) 638-3152; *Yearbook of Labour Statistics.*

M.E. Sharpe, 80 Business Park Drive, Armonk, New York 10504 (800) 541-6563; *The Illustrated Book of World Rankings.*

St. Martin's Press, Inc., 175 Fifth Avenue, New York, New York 10010 (800) 221-7945; *The Statesman's Year-Book.*

Statistical Office of the United Nations, Publishing Service, New York, New York 10017 (800) 253-9646; *Human Development Report.*

The World Bank, 1818 H Street, NW, Washington, D.C. 20433 (202) 477-1234; *The World Bank Atlas; World Development Report;* and *World Development Indicators.*

UGANDA - LAND USE

Central Intelligence Agency, Washington, D.C. 20505 (703) 482-1100, www.cia.gov; *The World Factbook.*

Euromonitor International, Inc., 122 South Michigan Avenue, Suite 1200, Chicago, Illinois 60603 (800) 577-EURO; *International Marketing Data and Statistics.*

The World Bank, 1818 H Street, NW, Washington, D.C. 20433 (202) 477-1234; *World Development Report.*

UGANDA - LIBRARIES

M.E. Sharpe, 80 Business Park Drive, Armonk, New York 10504 (800) 541-6563; *The Illustrated Book of World Rankings.*

United Nations Educational, Scientific and Cultural Organization (UNESCO), 7 Place de Fontenoy, F-75700 Paris, France (Telephone Number in U.S. (212) 963-5981); *Statistical Yearbook.*

UGANDA - LIFE EXPECTANCY

African Development Bank, 01 BP 1387, Abidjan 01, Cote D'Ivoire; *Selected Statistics on Regional Member Countries.*

Central Intelligence Agency, Washington, D.C. 20505 (703) 482-1100, www.cia.gov; *The World Factbook.*

Euromonitor International, Inc., 122 South Michigan Avenue, Suite 1200, Chicago, Illinois 60603 (800) 577-EURO; *The World Economic Factbook.*

St. Martin's Press, Inc., 175 Fifth Avenue, New York, New York 10010 (800) 221-7945; *The Statesman's Year-Book.*

Statistical Office of the United Nations, Publishing Service, New York, New York 10017 (800) 253-9646; *Human Development Report;* and *World Statistics Pocketbook.*

The World Bank, 1818 H Street, NW, Washington, D.C. 20433 (202) 477-1234; *The World Bank Atlas;* and *World Development Report.*

UGANDA - LITERACY RATE

Euromonitor International, Inc., 122 South Michigan Avenue, Suite 1200, Chicago, Illinois 60603 (800) 577-EURO; *World Marketing Data and Statistics.*

Statistical Office of the United Nations, Publishing Service, New York, New York

10017 (800) 253-9646; *Survey of Economic and Social Conditions in Africa.*

UGANDA - LIVESTOCK AND POULTRY

Euromonitor International, Inc., 122 South Michigan Avenue, Suite 1200, Chicago, Illinois 60603 (800) 577-EURO; *International Marketing Data and Statistics.*

Europa Publications Limited, 18 Bedford Square, London, WC1B 3JN, England; *The Europa World Year Book.*

Food and Agricultural Organization of the United Nations (FAO) Via delle Terme di Caracalla, 00100 Rome, Italy (Telephone Number in U.S. (202) 653-2400); *The State of Food and Agriculture.*

M.E. Sharpe, 80 Business Park Drive, Armonk, New York 10504 (800) 541-6563; *The Illustrated Book of World Rankings.*

St. Martin's Press, Inc., 175 Fifth Avenue, New York, New York 10010 (800) 221-7945; *The Statesman's Year-Book.*

Statistical Office of the United Nations, Publishing Service, New York, New York 10017 (800) 253-9646; *Statistical Yearbook;* and *Survey of Economic and Social Conditions in Africa.*

United Nations Conference on Trade and Development, Central Statistical Service, Palais des Nations, Geneva, Switzerland (Telephone in U.S. (800) 253-9646); *UNCTAD Commodity Yearbook.*

United Nations Economic Commission for Africa, Africa Hall, P.O. Box 3001, Addis Ababa, Ethiopia (Telephone Number in U.S. (800) 253-9646); *African Statistical Yearbook.*

UGANDA - LIVING LEVELS - See UGANDA - LIFE EXPECTANCY

UGANDA - MAIL - NUMBER OF PIECES SENT OR RECEIVED

Statistical Office of the United Nations, Publishing Service, New York, New York 10017 (800) 253-9646; *Statistical Yearbook.*

UGANDA - MANUFACTURING

M.E. Sharpe, 80 Business Park Drive, Armonk, New York 10504 (800) 541-6563; *The Illustrated Book of World Rankings.*

Statistical Office of the United Nations, Publishing Service, New York, New York 10017 (800) 253-9646; *Survey of Economic and Social Conditions in Africa.*

United Nations Economic Commission for Africa, Africa Hall, P.O. Box 3001, Addis Ababa, Ethiopia (Telephone Number in U.S. (800) 253-9646); *African Statistical*

Yearbook.

The World Bank, 1818 H Street, NW, Washington, D.C. 20433 (202) 477-1234; *World Development Indicators.*

UGANDA - MARRIAGE RATES

M.E. Sharpe, 80 Business Park Drive, Armonk, New York 10504 (800) 541-6563; *The Illustrated Book of World Rankings.*

Statistical Office of the United Nations, Publishing Service, New York, New York 10017 (800) 253-9646; *Demographic Yearbook.*

UGANDA - MEAT PRODUCTION - See UGANDA - LIVESTOCK AND POULTRY

UGANDA - MERCHANT SHIPPING

United Nations Economic Commission for Africa, Africa Hall, P.O. Box 3001, Addis Ababa, Ethiopia (Telephone Number in U.S. (800) 253-9646); *African Statistical Yearbook.*

U.S. Department of Transportation, Maritime Administration, 400 Seventh Street, SW, Washington, D.C. 20590 (202) 366-5807, www.marad.dot.gov; *A Statistical Analysis of the World's Merchant Fleets.*

UGANDA - MILITARY

Central Intelligence Agency, Washington, D.C. 20505 (703) 482-1100, www.cia.gov; *The World Factbook.*

Euromonitor International, Inc., 122 South Michigan Avenue, Suite 1200, Chicago, Illinois 60603 (800) 577-EURO; *World Marketing Data and Statistics.*

The International Institute for Strategic Studies, 23 Tavistock Street, London WC2E 7NQ, England 44 171 3797676; *The Military Balance.*

St. Martin's Press, Inc., 175 Fifth Avenue, New York, New York 10010 (800) 221-7945; *The Statesman's Year-Book.*

Statistical Office of the United Nations, Publishing Service, New York, New York 10017 (800) 253-9646; *Human Development Report.*

United Nations Economic Commission for Africa, Africa Hall, P.O. Box 3001, Addis Ababa, Ethiopia (Telephone Number in U.S. (800) 253-9646); *African Statistical Yearbook.*

U.S. Arms Control and Disarmament Agency, 320 Twenty-first Street, NW, Washington, D.C. 20451 (202) 647-8677; *World Military Expenditures and Arms Transfers.*

UGANDA - MILK PRODUCTION - See UGANDA - DAIRY PRODUCTS

UGANDA - MILLET PRODUCTION - See UGANDA - CROPS

UGANDA - MINING AND MINERAL PRODUCTS

Europa Publications Limited, 18 Bedford Square, London, WC1B 3JN, England; *The Europa World Year Book.*

M.E. Sharpe, 80 Business Park Drive, Armonk, New York 10504 (800) 541-6563; *The Illustrated Book of World Rankings.*

Statistical Office of the United Nations, Publishing Service, New York, New York 10017 (800) 253-9646; *Statistical Yearbook.*

United Nations Conference on Trade and Development, Central Statistical Service, Palais des Nations, Geneva, Switzerland (Telephone in U.S. (800) 253-9646); *UNCTAD Commodity Yearbook.*

United Nations Economic Commission for Africa, Africa Hall, P.O. Box 3001, Addis Ababa, Ethiopia (Telephone Number in U.S. (800) 253-9646); *African Statistical Yearbook.*

UGANDA - MONEY EXCHANGE RATE - See UGANDA - EXCHANGE RATES

UGANDA - MONEY RESERVES

Euromonitor International, Inc., 122 South Michigan Avenue, Suite 1200, Chicago, Illinois 60603 (800) 577-EURO; *International Marketing Data and Statistics.*

UGANDA - MONEY SUPPLY

African Development Bank, 01 BP 1387, Abidjan 01, Cote D'Ivoire; *Selected Statistics on Regional Member Countries.*

Economist Intelligence Unit, 111 West 57th Street, New York, New York 10019 (800) 938-4685; *Uganda Country Report.*

Euromonitor International, Inc., 122 South Michigan Avenue, Suite 1200, Chicago, Illinois 60603 (800) 577-EURO; *International Marketing Data and Statistics.*

Europa Publications Limited, 18 Bedford Square, London, WC1B 3JN, England; *The Europa World Year Book.*

International Monetary Fund, 700 Nineteenth Street, NW, Washington, D.C. 20431 (202) 623-7000; *International Financial Statistics.*

Statistical Office of the United Nations, Publishing Service, New York, New York 10017 (800) 253-9646; *Statistical Yearbook.*

The World Bank, 1818 H Street, NW, Washington, D.C. 20433 (202) 477-1234; *World Development Indicators.*

UGANDA - MORTALITY

Central Intelligence Agency, Washington, D.C. 20505 (703) 482-1100, www.cia.gov; *The World Factbook.*

Euromonitor International, Inc., 122 South Michigan Avenue, Suite 1200, Chicago, Illinois 60603 (800) 577-EURO; *International Marketing Data and Statistics;* and *The World Economic Factbook.*

Europa Publications Limited, 18 Bedford Square, London, WC1B 3JN, England; *The Europa World Year Book.*

St. Martin's Press, Inc., 175 Fifth Avenue, New York, New York 10010 (800) 221-7945; *The Statesman's Year-Book.*

Statistical Office of the United Nations, Publishing Service, New York, New York 10017 (800) 253-9646; *Demographic Yearbook; Human Development Report; Statistical Yearbook; Survey of Economic and Social Conditions in Africa;* and *World Statistics Pocketbook.*

United Nations Children's Fund (UNICEF), 3 United Nations Plaza, New York, New York 10017 (800) 253-9646; *State of the World's Children.*

The World Bank, 1818 H Street, NW, Washington, D.C. 20433 (202) 477-1234; *The World Bank Atlas;* and *World Development Report.*

UGANDA - MOTION PICTURES

Statistical Office of the United Nations, Publishing Service, New York, New York 10017 (800) 253-9646; *Statistical Yearbook.*

UGANDA - MOTOR VEHICLES IN USE

Europa Publications Limited, 18 Bedford Square, London, WC1B 3JN, England; *The Europa World Year Book.*

International Road Federation, 2600 Virginia Avenue, NW, Washington, D.C. 20037 (202) 338-4641; *World Road Statistics.*

Statistical Office of the United Nations, Publishing Service, New York, New York 10017 (800) 253-9646; *Statistical Yearbook;* and *Survey of Economic and Social Conditions in Africa.*

UGANDA - MUSEUMS

M.E. Sharpe, 80 Business Park Drive, Armonk, New York 10504 (800) 541-6563; *The Illustrated Book of World Rankings.*

UGANDA - NATALITY

Statistical Office of the United Nations, Publishing Service, New York, New York 10017 (800) 253-9646; *Demographic Yearbook.*

UGANDA - NATIONAL ACCOUNTS

African Development Bank, 01 BP 1387, Abidjan 01, Cote D'Ivoire; *Selected Statistics on Regional Member Countries.*

Europa Publications Limited, 18 Bedford Square, London, WC1B 3JN, England; *The Europa World Year Book.*

Statistical Office of the United Nations, Publishing Service, New York, New York 10017 (800) 253-9646; *National Accounts Statistics;* and *Statistical Yearbook.*

United Nations Economic Commission for Africa, Africa Hall, P.O. Box 3001, Addis Ababa, Ethiopia (Telephone Number in U.S. (800) 253-9646); *African Statistical Yearbook.*

UGANDA - NATIONAL INCOME

M.E. Sharpe, 80 Business Park Drive, Armonk, New York 10504 (800) 541-6563; *The Illustrated Book of World Rankings.*

Statistical Office of the United Nations, Publishing Service, New York, New York 10017 (800) 253-9646; *National Accounts Statistics;* and *Statistical Yearbook.*

UGANDA - NATIONAL PRODUCT

M.E. Sharpe, 80 Business Park Drive, Armonk, New York 10504 (800) 541-6563; *The Illustrated Book of World Rankings.*

Statistical Office of the United Nations, Publishing Service, New York, New York 10017 (800) 253-9646; *Statistical Yearbook.*

UGANDA - NATURAL GAS PRODUCTION - See UGANDA - MINING AND MINERAL PRODUCTS

UGANDA - NEWSPAPER PRODUCTION - See UGANDA - FORESTRY AND FOREST PRODUCTS

UGANDA - NEWSPRINT - See UGANDA - FORESTRY AND FOREST PRODUCTS

UGANDA - OCCUPATIONS - See UGANDA - LABOR

UGANDA - PAPER - See UGANDA - FORESTRY AND FOREST PRODUCTS

UGANDA - PATENTS, TRADEMARKS AND SERVICE MARKS

Statistical Office of the United Nations, Publishing Service, New York, New York

10017 (800) 253-9646; *Statistical Yearbook.*

UGANDA - PEANUT PRODUCTION - See
UGANDA - CROPS

UGANDA - PESTICIDE USE

Food and Agricultural Organization of
the United Nations (FAO) Via delle Terme
di Caracalla, 00100 Rome, Italy (Telephone
Number in U.S. (202) 653-2400); *The State
of Food and Agriculture.*

UGANDA - PETROLEUM INDUSTRY

Food and Agricultural Organization of
the United Nations (FAO) Via delle Terme
di Caracalla, 00100 Rome, Italy (Telephone
Number in U.S. (202) 653-2400); *The State
of Food and Agriculture.*

M.E. Sharpe, 80 Business Park Drive,
Armonk, New York 10504 (800) 541-6563;
The Illustrated Book of World Rankings.

United Nations Conference on Trade
and Development, Central Statistical
Service, Palais des Nations, Geneva,
Switzerland (Telephone in U.S. (800) 253-
9646); *UNCTAD Commodity Yearbook.*

UGANDA - PHOSPHATE ROCK
PRODUCTION - See UGANDA - MINING
AND MINERAL PRODUCTS

UGANDA - PIGS - See UGANDA -
LIVESTOCK AND POULTRY

UGANDA - POPULATION

Central Intelligence Agency,
Washington, D.C. 20505 (703) 482-1100,
www.cia.gov; *The World Factbook.*

The Economist Intelligence Unit, 111
West 57th Street, New York, New York
10019 (800) 938-4685; *Uganda Country
Report;* and *The World Market Atlas.*

Euromonitor International, Inc., 122
South Michigan Avenue, Suite 1200,
Chicago, Illinois 60603 (800) 577-EURO;
International Marketing Data and Statistics;
and *The World Economic Factbook.*

Europa Publications Limited, 18
Bedford Square, London, WC1B 3JN,
England; *The Europa World Year Book.*

International Labour Office,
I.L.O. Publications, 1828 L Street, NW, Suite
801, Washington, D.C. 20036 (301) 638-
3152; *Yearbook of Labour Statistics.*

M.E. Sharpe, 80 Business Park Drive,
Armonk, New York 10504 (800) 541-6563;
The Illustrated Book of World Rankings.

St. Martin's Press, Inc., 175 Fifth
Avenue, New York, New York 10010 (800)
221-7945; *The Statesman's Year-Book.*

Statistical Office of the United Nations,
Publishing Service, New York, New York
10017 (800) 253-9646; *Demographic
Yearbook; Human Development Report;
Statistical Yearbook; Survey of Economic
and Social Conditions in Africa;* and *World
Statistics Pocketbook.*

United Nations Educational, Scientific
and Cultural Organization (UNESCO), 7
Place de Fontenoy, F-75700 Paris, France
(Telephone Number in U.S. (212) 963-
5981); *Statistical Yearbook.*

U.S. Arms Control and Disarmament
Agency, 320 Twenty-first Street, NW,
Washington, D.C. 20451 (202) 647-8677;
*World Military Expenditures and Arms
Transfers.*

The World Bank, 1818 H Street, NW,
Washington, D.C. 20433 (202) 477-1234;
The World Bank Atlas; and *World
Development Report.*

World Health Organization, Office of
Publications, 20 Avenue Appia, CH-1211
Geneva 27, Switzerland (Telephone
Number in U.S. (518) 436-9686); *World
Health Statistics Annual.*

UGANDA - POST OFFICES

M.E. Sharpe, 80 Business Park Drive,
Armonk, New York 10504 (800) 541-6563;
The Illustrated Book of World Rankings.

UGANDA - POTATO PRODUCTION - See
UGANDA - CROPS

UGANDA - PRICES

Food and Agricultural Organization of
the United Nations (FAO) Via delle Terme
di Caracalla, 00100 Rome, Italy (Telephone
Number in U.S. (202) 653-2400); *The State
of Food and Agriculture.*

International Labour Office,
I.L.O. Publications, 1828 L Street, NW, Suite
801, Washington, D.C. 20036 (301) 638-
3152; *Yearbook of Labour Statistics.*

International Monetary Fund, 700
Nineteenth Street, NW, Washington, D.C.
20431 (202) 623-7000; *International
Financial Statistics.*

M.E. Sharpe, 80 Business Park Drive,
Armonk, New York 10504 (800) 541-6563;
The Illustrated Book of World Rankings.

United Nations Economic Commission
for Africa, Africa Hall, P.O. Box 3001, Addis
Ababa, Ethiopia (Telephone Number in
U.S. (800) 253-9646); *African Statistical
Yearbook.*

UGANDA - PRINTING AND WRITING
PAPER - See UGANDA - FORESTRY AND
FOREST PRODUCTS

UGANDA - PRODUCTION

M.E. Sharpe, 80 Business Park Drive,
Armonk, New York 10504 (800) 541-6563;
The Illustrated Book of World Rankings.

UGANDA - PRODUCTIVITY

Euromonitor International, Inc., 122
South Michigan Avenue, Suite 1200,
Chicago, Illinois 60603 (800) 577-EURO;
International Marketing Data and Statistics.

UGANDA - PUBLIC FINANCE - See
UGANDA - FINANCE

UGANDA - RADIO BROADCASTING - See
UGANDA - BROADCASTING

UGANDA - RADIO RECEIVERS

St. Martin's Press, Inc., 175 Fifth
Avenue, New York, New York 10010 (800)
221-7945; *The Statesman's Year-Book.*

UGANDA - RAILWAYS

Europa Publications Limited, 18
Bedford Square, London, WC1B 3JN,
England; *The Europa World Year Book.*

Jane's Information Group, Sentinel
House, 163 Brighton Road, Coulsdon,
Surrey CR5 2NH, England (Telephone
Number in U.S. (703) 683-3700); *Jane's
World Railways.*

St. Martin's Press, Inc., 175 Fifth
Avenue, New York, New York 10010 (800)
221-7945; *The Statesman's Year-Book.*

Statistical Office of the United Nations,
Publishing Service, New York, New York
10017 (800) 253-9646; *Survey of Economic
and Social Conditions in Africa.*

United Nations Economic Commission
for Africa, Africa Hall, P.O. Box 3001, Addis
Ababa, Ethiopia (Telephone Number in
U.S. (800) 253-9646); *African Statistical
Yearbook.*

UGANDA - RELIGION

Central Intelligence Agency,
Washington, D.C. 20505 (703) 482-1100,
www.cia.gov; *The World Factbook.*

M.E. Sharpe, 80 Business Park Drive,
Armonk, New York 10504 (800) 541-6563;
The Illustrated Book of World Rankings.

St. Martin's Press, Inc., 175 Fifth
Avenue, New York, New York 10010 (800)
221-7945; *The Statesman's Year-Book.*

UGANDA - RETAIL TRADE

Euromonitor International, Inc., 122
South Michigan Avenue, Suite 1200,
Chicago, Illinois 60603 (800) 577-EURO;

World Marketing Data and Statistics.

Statistical Office of the United Nations, Publishing Service, New York, New York 10017 (800) 253-9646; *Statistical Yearbook.*

UGANDA - RICE PRODUCTION - See UGANDA - CROPS

UGANDA - ROOT AND TUBER PRODUCTION - See UGANDA - CROPS

UGANDA - ROUNDWOOD PRODUCTION - See UGANDA - FORESTRY AND FOREST PRODUCTS

UGANDA - RUBBER PRODUCTION AND CONSUMPTION

M.E. Sharpe, 80 Business Park Drive, Armonk, New York 10504 (800) 541-6563; *The Illustrated Book of World Rankings.*

UGANDA - SALT PRODUCTION - See UGANDA - MINING AND MINERALS

UGANDA - SAWNWOOD PRODUCTION - See UGANDA - FORESTRY AND FOREST PRODUCTS

UGANDA - SENIOR CITIZENS

M.E. Sharpe, 80 Business Park Drive, Armonk, New York 10504 (800) 541-6563; *The Illustrated Book of World Rankings.*

UGANDA - SESAME SEED PRODUCTION - See UGANDA - CROPS

UGANDA - SHEEP - See UGANDA - LIVESTOCK AND POULTRY

UGANDA - SILVER PRODUCTION AND CONSUMPTION - See UGANDA - MINING AND MINERAL PRODUCTS

UGANDA - SISAL PRODUCTION - See UGANDA - CROPS

UGANDA - SOCIAL DATA

M.E. Sharpe, 80 Business Park Drive, Armonk, New York 10504 (800) 541-6563; *The Illustrated Book of World Rankings.*

Statistical Office of the United Nations, Publishing Service, New York, New York 10017 (800) 253-9646; *World Statistics Pocketbook.*

UGANDA - SOCIAL SECURITY

Statistical Office of the United Nations, Publishing Service, New York, New York 10017 (800) 253-9646; *National Accounts Statistics.*

UGANDA - SOYBEAN PRODUCTION - See UGANDA - CROPS

UGANDA - STATE BUDGET REVENUE AND EXPENDITURES

Euromonitor International, Inc., 122 South Michigan Avenue, Suite 1200, Chicago, Illinois 60603 (800) 577-EURO; *International Marketing Data and Statistics.*

UGANDA - STEEL - See UGANDA - MINING AND MINERAL PRODUCTS

UGANDA - STOCKS - COMMODITY - MARKET PRICE - INDEX

Food and Agricultural Organization of the United Nations (FAO) Via delle Terme di Caracalla, 00100 Rome, Italy (Telephone Number in U.S. (202) 653-2400); *The State of Food and Agriculture.*

UGANDA - SUGAR PRODUCTION AND CONSUMPTION - See UGANDA - CROPS

UGANDA - SULPHURIC ACID PRODUCTION - See UGANDA - MINING AND MINERAL PRODUCTS

UGANDA - TAXATION

Europa Publications Limited, 18 Bedford Square, London, WC1B 3JN, England; *The Europa World Year Book.*

International Road Federation, 2600 Virginia Avenue, NW, Washington, D.C. 20037 (202) 338-4641; *World Road Statistics.*

The World Bank, 1818 H Street, NW, Washington, D.C. 20433 (202) 477-1234; *World Development Indicators.*

UGANDA - TEA PRODUCTION AND CONSUMPTION - See UGANDA - CROPS

UGANDA - TELEGRAPH SERVICE

Statistical Office of the United Nations, Publishing Service, New York, New York 10017 (800) 253-9646; *Statistical Yearbook.*

UGANDA - TELEPHONES IN USE

American Telephone and Telegraph Company, 26 Parsippany Road, Whippany, New Jersey 07981 (800) 222-0300; *The World's Telephones.*

Central Intelligence Agency, Washington, D.C. 20505 (703) 482-1100, www.cia.gov; *The World Factbook.*

Europa Publications Limited, 18 Bedford Square, London, WC1B 3JN, England; *The Europa World Year Book.*

St. Martin's Press, Inc., 175 Fifth Avenue, New York, New York 10010 (800) 221-7945; *The Statesman's Year-Book.*

Statistical Office of the United Nations, Publishing Service, New York, New York 10017 (800) 253-9646; *Statistical Yearbook;* and *World Statistics Pocketbook.*

UGANDA - TELEVISION BROADCASTING - See UGANDA - BROADCASTING

UGANDA - TEXTILE INDUSTRY

M.E. Sharpe, 80 Business Park Drive, Armonk, New York 10504 (800) 541-6563; *The Illustrated Book of World Rankings.*

United Nations Conference on Trade and Development, Central Statistical Service, Palais des Nations, Geneva, Switzerland (Telephone in U.S. (800) 253-9646); *UNCTAD Commodity Yearbook.*

UGANDA - TIN PRODUCTION AND CONSUMPTION - See UGANDA - MINING AND MINERAL PRODUCTS

UGANDA - TOBACCO PRODUCTION

M.E. Sharpe, 80 Business Park Drive, Armonk, New York 10504 (800) 541-6563; *The Illustrated Book of World Rankings.*

Statistical Office of the United Nations, Publishing Service, New York, New York 10017 (800) 253-9646; *Statistical Yearbook.*

UGANDA - TOURISM

Euromonitor International, Inc., 122 South Michigan Avenue, Suite 1200, Chicago, Illinois 60603 (800) 577-EURO; *The World Economic Factbook;* and *World Marketing Data and Statistics.*

Europa Publications Limited, 18 Bedford Square, London, WC1B 3JN, England; *The Europa World Year Book.*

M.E. Sharpe, 80 Business Park Drive, Armonk, New York 10504 (800) 541-6563; *The Illustrated Book of World Rankings.*

St. Martin's Press, Inc., 175 Fifth Avenue, New York, New York 10010 (800) 221-7945; *The Statesman's Year-Book.*

Statistical Office of the United Nations, Publishing Service, New York, New York 10017 (800) 253-9646; *Statistical Yearbook.*

United Nations Economic Commission for Africa, Africa Hall, P.O. Box 3001, Addis Ababa, Ethiopia (Telephone Number in U.S. (800) 253-9646); *African Statistical Yearbook.*

UGANDA - TRACTORS IN USE

Statistical Office of the United Nations, Publishing Service, New York, New York 10017 (800) 253-9646; *Statistical Yearbook.*

UGANDA - TRADE - See UGANDA - FOREIGN TRADE

UGANDA - TRADEMARKS AND SERVICE MARKS - See UGANDA - PATENTS, TRADEMARKS AND SERVICE MARKS

UGANDA - TRANSPORTATION AND COMMUNICATIONS

Central Intelligence Agency, Washington, D.C. 20505 (703) 482-1100, www.cia.gov; *The World Factbook.*

Euromonitor International, Inc., 122 South Michigan Avenue, Suite 1200, Chicago, Illinois 60603 (800) 577-EURO; *International Marketing Data and Statistics;* and *World Marketing Data and Statistics.*

Europa Publications Limited, 18 Bedford Square, London, WC1B 3JN, England; *The Europa World Year Book.*

M.E. Sharpe, 80 Business Park Drive, Armonk, New York 10504 (800) 541-6563; *The Illustrated Book of World Rankings.*

St. Martin's Press, Inc., 175 Fifth Avenue, New York, New York 10010 (800) 221-7945; *The Statesman's Year-Book.*

Statistical Office of the United Nations, Publishing Service, New York, New York 10017 (800) 253-9646; *Human Development Report.*

United Nations Economic Commission for Africa, Africa Hall, P.O. Box 3001, Addis Ababa, Ethiopia (Telephone Number in U.S. (800) 253-9646); *African Statistical Yearbook.*

UGANDA - TUNGSTEN PRODUCTION AND CONSUMPTION - See UGANDA - MINING AND MINERAL PRODUCTS

UGANDA - UNEMPLOYMENT

Central Intelligence Agency, Washington, D.C. 20505 (703) 482-1100, www.cia.gov; *The World Factbook.*

Euromonitor International, Inc., 122 South Michigan Avenue, Suite 1200, Chicago, Illinois 60603 (800) 577-EURO; *International Marketing Data and Statistics.*

International Labour Office, I.L.O. Publications, 1828 L Street, NW, Suite 801, Washington, D.C. 20036 (301) 638-3152; *Yearbook of Labour Statistics.*

UGANDA - VITAL STATISTICS

Euromonitor International, Inc., 122 South Michigan Avenue, Suite 1200, Chicago, Illinois 60603 (800) 577-EURO; *International Marketing Data and Statistics.*

St. Martin's Press, Inc., 175 Fifth

Avenue, New York, New York 10010 (800) 221-7945; *The Statesman's Year-Book.*

Statistical Office of the United Nations, Publishing Service, New York, New York 10017 (800) 253-9646; *Statistical Yearbook.*

World Health Organization, Office of Publications, 20 Avenue Appia, CH-1211 Geneva 27, Switzerland (Telephone Number in U.S. (518) 436-9686); *World Health Statistics Annual.*

UGANDA - WAGES

International Labour Office, I.L.O. Publications, 1828 L Street, NW, Suite 801, Washington, D.C. 20036 (301) 638-3152; *Yearbook of Labour Statistics.*

UGANDA - WEATHER

M.E. Sharpe, 80 Business Park Drive, Armonk, New York 10504 (800) 541-6563; *The Illustrated Book of World Rankings.*

UGANDA - WHEAT PRODUCTION AND PRICES - See UGANDA - CROPS

UGANDA - WHOLESALE TRADE

Statistical Office of the United Nations, Publishing Service, New York, New York 10017 (800) 253-9646; *Statistical Yearbook.*

UGANDA - WINE PRODUCTION - See UGANDA - BEVERAGES

UGANDA - WOOL PRODUCTION - See UGANDA - TEXTILE INDUSTRY

UKRAINE - ABORTIONS

Statistical Office of the United Nations, Publishing Service, New York, New York 10017 (800) 253-9646; *Demographic Yearbook;* and *Trends in Europe and North America: The Statistical Yearbook of the Economic Commission for Europe.*

UKRAINE - AGRICULTURE

Academic International Press, Box 1111, Gulf Breeze, Florida 32562; *Russia and Eurasia Facts and Figures Annual.*

Business International Moscow, 23 Profsoyuznaya Ulitsa, 117859, Moscow (Telephone Number in U.S. (800) 938-4685); *The CIS Market Atlas.*

Economist Intelligence Unit, 111 West 57th Street, New York, New York 10019 (800) 938-4685; *Ukraine Country Report.*

Euromonitor International, Inc., 122 South Michigan Avenue, Suite 1200, Chicago, Illinois 60603 (800) 577-EURO; *World Marketing Data and Statistics.*

Europa Publications Limited, 18

Bedford Square, London, WC1B 3JN, England; *The Europa World Year Book.*

Federal Statistical Office, Gustav-Stresemann - Ring 11, D-6200, Wiesbaden, Germany; *Ukraine.*

Food and Agriculture Organization of the United Nations (FAO), Via delle Terme di Caracalla, 00100, Rome, Italy (Telephone Number in U.S. (202) 653-2400); *Production Yearbook; The State of Food and Agriculture;* and *Trade Yearbook.*

St. Martin's Press, Inc., 175 Fifth Avenue, New York, New York 10010 (800) 221-7945; *The Statesman's Year-Book.*

Statistical Office of the United Nations, Publishing Service, New York, New York 10017 (800) 253-9646; *Industrial Commodity Statistics Yearbook;* and *Statistical Yearbook.*

The World Bank, 1818 H Street, NW, Washington, D.C. 20433 (202) 477-1234; *Statistical Handbook: States of the Former USSR;* and *World Development Indicators.*

UKRAINE - AIRLINE SERVICE

Business International Moscow, 23 Profsoyuznaya Ulitsa, 117859, Moscow (Telephone Number in U.S. (800) 938-4685); *The CIS Market Atlas.*

International Civil Aviation Organization, 999 University Street, Montreal, Quebec, Canada H3C 5H7 (514) 954-8219; *Civil Aviation Statistics of the World.*

St. Martin's Press, Inc., 175 Fifth Avenue, New York, New York 10010 (800) 221-7945; *The Statesman's Year-Book.*

Statistical Office of the United Nations, Publishing Service, New York, New York 10017 (800) 253-9646; *Statistical Yearbook.*

UKRAINE - AIRPORTS

Central Intelligence Agency, Washington, D.C. 20505 (703) 482-1100, www.cia.gov; *The World Factbook.*

UKRAINE - ANIMAL HEALTH

Food and Agriculture Organization of the United Nations (FAO), Via delle Terme di Caracalla, 00100, Rome, Italy (Telephone Number in U.S. (202) 653-2400); *Animal Health Yearbook.*

UKRAINE - AREA AND DENSITY OF POPULATION

Academic International Press, Box 1111, Gulf Breeze, Florida 32562; *Russia and Eurasia Facts and Figures Annual.*

Business International Moscow, 23 Profsoyuznaya Ulitsa, 117859, Moscow (Telephone Number in U.S. (800) 938-4685); *The CIS Market Atlas*.

Central Intelligence Agency, Washington, D.C. 20505 (703) 482-1100, www.cia.gov; *The World Factbook*.

Euromonitor International, Inc., 122 South Michigan Avenue, Suite 1200, Chicago, Illinois 60603 (800) 577-EURO; *The World Economic Factbook*.

Europa Publications Limited, 18 Bedford Square, London, WC1B 3JN, England; *The Europa World Year Book*.

Federal Statistical Office, Gustav-Stresemann - Ring 11, D-6200, Wiesbaden, Germany; *Ukraine*.

St. Martin's Press, Inc., 175 Fifth Avenue, New York, New York 10010 (800) 221-7945; *The Statesman's Year-Book*.

Statistical Office of the United Nations, Publishing Service, New York, New York 10017 (800) 253-9646; *Statistical Yearbook; and Trends in Europe and North America: The Statistical Yearbook of the Economic Commission for Europe*.

United Nations Educational, Scientific and Cultural Organization (UNESCO), 7 Place de Fontenoy, F-75700 Paris, France (Telephone Number in U.S. (212) 963-5981); *Statistical Yearbook*.

The World Bank, 1818 H Street, NW, Washington, D.C. 20433 (202) 477-1234; *World Development Report*.

UKRAINE - BALANCE OF PAYMENTS

Federal Statistical Office, Gustav-Stresemann - Ring 11, D-6200, Wiesbaden, Germany; *Ukraine*.

United Nations Conference on Trade and Development (UNCTAD), New York, New York 10017 (800) 253-9646; *Handbook of International Trade and Development Statistics*.

The World Bank, 1818 H Street, NW, Washington, D.C. 20433 (202) 477-1234; *World Development Report; and World Development Indicators*.

UKRAINE - BANKING

Business International Moscow, 23 Profsoyuznaya Ulitsa, 117859, Moscow (Telephone Number in U.S. (800) 938-4685); *The CIS Market Atlas*.

Euromonitor International, Inc., 122 South Michigan Avenue, Suite 1200, Chicago, Illinois 60603 (800) 577-EURO; *World Marketing Data and Statistics*.

St. Martin's Press, Inc., 175 Fifth Avenue, New York, New York 10010 (800) 221-7945; *The Statesman's Year-Book*.

UKRAINE - BEER PRODUCTION - See UKRAINE - BEVERAGES

UKRAINE - BEVERAGES

Statistical Office of the United Nations, Publishing Service, New York, New York 10017 (800) 253-9646; *Statistical Yearbook*.

UKRAINE - BIRTH RATES

Academic International Press, Box 1111, Gulf Breeze, Florida 32562; *Russia and Eurasia Facts and Figures Annual*.

Business International Moscow, 23 Profsoyuznaya Ulitsa, 117859, Moscow (Telephone Number in U.S. (800) 938-4685); *The CIS Market Atlas*.

Central Intelligence Agency, Washington, D.C. 20505 (703) 482-1100, www.cia.gov; *The World Factbook*.

Euromonitor International, Inc., 122 South Michigan Avenue, Suite 1200, Chicago, Illinois 60603 (800) 577-EURO; *The World Economic Factbook*.

Europa Publications Limited, 18 Bedford Square, London, WC1B 3JN, England; *The Europa World Year Book*.

St. Martin's Press, Inc., 175 Fifth Avenue, New York, New York 10010 (800) 221-7945; *The Statesman's Year-Book*.

Statistical Office of the United Nations, Publishing Service, New York, New York 10017 (800) 253-9646; *Demographic Yearbook; and Statistical Yearbook*.

World Health Organization, Office of Publications, 20 Avenue Appia, CH-1211 Geneva 27, Switzerland (Telephone Number in U.S. (518) 436-9686); *World Health Statistics Annual*.

UKRAINE - BOOK PRODUCTION

Europa Publications Limited, 18 Bedford Square, London, WC1B 3JN, England; *The Europa World Year Book*.

Statistical Office of the United Nations, Publishing Service, New York, New York 10017 (800) 253-9646; *Trends in Europe and North America: The Statistical Yearbook of the Economic Commission for Europe*.

United Nations Educational, Scientific and Cultural Organization (UNESCO), 7 Place de Fontenoy, F-75700 Paris, France (Telephone Number in U.S. (212) 963-5981); *Statistical Yearbook*.

UKRAINE - BROADCASTING

Central Intelligence Agency, Washington, D.C. 20505 (703) 482-1100, www.cia.gov; *The World Factbook*.

Euromonitor International, Inc., 122 South Michigan Avenue, Suite 1200, Chicago, Illinois 60603 (800) 577-EURO; *World Marketing Data and Statistics*.

St. Martin's Press, Inc., 175 Fifth Avenue, New York, New York 10010 (800) 221-7945; *The Statesman's Year-Book*.

Statistical Office of the United Nations, Publishing Service, New York, New York 10017 (800) 253-9646; *Trends in Europe and North America: The Statistical Yearbook of the Economic Commission for Europe*.

United Nations Educational, Scientific and Cultural Organization (UNESCO), 7 Place de Fontenoy, F-75700 Paris, France (Telephone Number in U.S. (212) 963-5981); *Statistical Yearbook*.

UKRAINE - BUDGET

Central Intelligence Agency, Washington, D.C. 20505 (703) 482-1100, www.cia.gov; *The World Factbook*.

UKRAINE - BUTTER PRODUCTION AND CONSUMPTION - See UKRAINE - DAIRY PRODUCTS

UKRAINE - CAPITAL INVESTMENT

The World Bank, 1818 H Street, NW, Washington, D.C. 20433 (202) 477-1234; *Statistical Handbook: States of the Former USSR*.

UKRAINE - CATTLE - See UKRAINE - LIVESTOCK AND POULTRY

UKRAINE - CAUSTIC SODA PRODUCTION - See UKRAINE - BEVERAGES

UKRAINE - CEMENT PRODUCTION - See UKRAINE - MINING AND MINERAL PRODUCTS

UKRAINE - CHEESE PRODUCTION AND CONSUMPTION - See UKRAINE - DAIRY PRODUCTS

UKRAINE - CHEMICAL (ORGANIC) PRODUCTION - See UKRAINE - MINING AND MINERAL PRODUCTS

UKRAINE - CHEMICALS

Business International Moscow, 23 Profsoyuznaya Ulitsa, 117859, Moscow (Telephone Number in U.S. (800) 938-4685); *The CIS Market Atlas*.

UKRAINE - COAL PRODUCTION - See UKRAINE - MINING AND MINERAL PRODUCTS

UKRAINE - COKE OVEN COKE PRODUCTION AND CONSUMPTION - See UKRAINE - MINING AND MINERAL PRODUCTS

UKRAINE - COMMERCE

St. Martin's Press, Inc., 175 Fifth Avenue, New York, New York 10010 (800) 221-7945; *The Statesman's Year-Book.*

UKRAINE - COMMUNICATIONS - See UKRAINE - TRANSPORTATION AND COMMUNICATIONS

UKRAINE - CONSTRUCTION INDUSTRY

Academic International Press, Box 1111, Gulf Breeze, Florida 32562; *Russia and Eurasia Facts and Figures Annual.*

Business International Moscow, 23 Profsoyuznaya Ulitsa, 117859, Moscow (Telephone Number in U.S. (800) 938-4685); *The CIS Market Atlas.*

Statistical Office of the United Nations, Publishing Service, New York, New York 10017 (800) 253-9646; *Statistical Yearbook.*

UKRAINE - CONSUMER PRICE INDEX

Statistical Office of the United Nations, Publishing Service, New York, New York 10017 (800) 253-9646; *Statistical Yearbook;* and *Trends in Europe and North America: The Statistical Yearbook of the Economic Commission for Europe.*

UKRAINE - CONSUMER PRICES

Euromonitor International, Inc., 122 South Michigan Avenue, Suite 1200, Chicago, Illinois 60603 (800) 577-EURO; *World Marketing Data and Statistics.*

International Labour Office, I.L.O. Publications, 1828 L Street, NW, Suite 801, Washington, D.C. 20036 (301) 638-3152; *Yearbook of Labour Statistics.*

UKRAINE - CONSUMER PRODUCTS

Business International Moscow, 23 Profsoyuznaya Ulitsa, 117859, Moscow (Telephone Number in U.S. (800) 938-4685); *The CIS Market Atlas.*

UKRAINE - CONSUMPTION

Business International Moscow, 23 Profsoyuznaya Ulitsa, 117859, Moscow (Telephone Number in U.S. (800) 938-4685); *The CIS Market Atlas.*

The World Bank, 1818 H Street, NW, Washington, D.C. 20433 (202) 477-1234; *Statistical Handbook: States of the Former USSR;* and *World Development Report.*

UKRAINE - CORN PRODUCTION - See

UKRAINE - CROPS

UKRAINE - COTTON PRODUCTION AND CONSUMPTION - See UKRAINE - CROPS

UKRAINE - CRIME

Academic International Press, Box 1111, Gulf Breeze, Florida 32562; *Russia and Eurasia Facts and Figures Annual.*

Statistical Office of the United Nations, Publishing Service, New York, New York 10017 (800) 253-9646; *Trends in Europe and North America: The Statistical Yearbook of the Economic Commission for Europe.*

UKRAINE - CROPS

Academic International Press, Box 1111, Gulf Breeze, Florida 32562; *Russia and Eurasia Facts and Figures Annual.*

Europa Publications Limited, 18 Bedford Square, London, WC1B 3JN, England; *The Europa World Year Book.*

Food and Agriculture Organization of the United Nations (FAO), Via delle Terme di Caracalla, 00100, Rome, Italy (Telephone Number in U.S. (202) 653-2400); *Production Yearbook; The State of Food and Agriculture;* and *Trade Yearbook.*

St. Martin's Press, Inc., 175 Fifth Avenue, New York, New York 10010 (800) 221-7945; *The Statesman's Year-Book.*

Statistical Office of the United Nations, Publishing Service, New York, New York 10017 (800) 253-9646; *Industrial Commodity Statistics Yearbook;* and *Statistical Yearbook.*

The World Bank, 1818 H Street, NW, Washington, D.C. 20433 (202) 477-1234; *Statistical Handbook: States of the Former USSR.*

UKRAINE - DAIRY PRODUCTS

Europa Publications Limited, 18 Bedford Square, London, WC1B 3JN, England; *The Europa World Year Book.*

Food and Agriculture Organization of the United Nations (FAO), Via delle Terme di Caracalla, 00100, Rome, Italy (Telephone Number in U.S. (202) 653-2400); *Production Yearbook; The State of Food and Agriculture;* and *Trade Yearbook.*

St. Martin's Press, Inc., 175 Fifth Avenue, New York, New York 10010 (800) 221-7945; *The Statesman's Year-Book.*

Statistical Office of the United Nations, Publishing Service, New York, New York 10017 (800) 253-9646; *Industrial Commodity Statistics Yearbook;* and *Statistical Yearbook.*

UKRAINE - DEATH RATES - See UKRAINE - MORTALITY

UKRAINE - DEMOGRAPHY

Business International Moscow, 23 Profsoyuznaya Ulitsa, 117859, Moscow (Telephone Number in U.S. (800) 938-4685); *The CIS Market Atlas.*

Euromonitor International, Inc., 122 South Michigan Avenue, Suite 1200, Chicago, Illinois 60603 (800) 577-EURO; *The World Economic Factbook;* and *World Marketing Data and Statistics.*

Federal Statistical Office, Gustav-Stresemann - Ring 11, D-6200, Wiesbaden, Germany; *Ukraine.*

Statistical Office of the United Nations, Publishing Service, New York, New York 10017 (800) 253-9646; *Demographic Yearbook;* and *Human Development Report.*

The World Bank, 1818 H Street, NW, Washington, D.C. 20433 (202) 477-1234; *Statistical Handbook: States of the Former USSR.*

UKRAINE - DISEASES - See UKRAINE - HEALTH

UKRAINE - DIVORCE RATES

Academic International Press, Box 1111, Gulf Breeze, Florida 32562; *Russia and Eurasia Facts and Figures Annual.*

Statistical Office of the United Nations, Publishing Service, New York, New York 10017 (800) 253-9646; *Demographic Yearbook; Statistical Yearbook;* and *Trends in Europe and North America: The Statistical Yearbook of the Economic Commission for Europe.*

UKRAINE - DOMESTIC INVESTMENT

Business International Moscow, 23 Profsoyuznaya Ulitsa, 117859, Moscow (Telephone Number in U.S. (800) 938-4685); *The CIS Market Atlas.*

UKRAINE - ECONOMY

Academic International Press, Box 1111, Gulf Breeze, Florida 32562; *Russia and Eurasia Facts and Figures Annual.*

Business International Moscow, 23 Profsoyuznaya Ulitsa, 117859, Moscow (Telephone Number in U.S. (800) 938-4685); *The CIS Market Atlas.*

Central Intelligence Agency, Washington, D.C. 20505 (703) 482-1100, www.cia.gov; *The World Factbook.*

Economist Intelligence Unit, 111 West

57th Street, New York, New York 10019 (800) 938-4685; *Ukraine Country Report.*

Euromonitor International, Inc., 122 South Michigan Avenue, Suite 1200, Chicago, Illinois 60603 (800) 577-EURO; *The World Economic Factbook;* and *World Marketing Data and Statistics.*

Europa Publications Limited, 18 Bedford Square, London, WC1B 3JN, England; *The Europa World Year Book.*

Federal Statistical Office, Gustav-Stresemann - Ring 11, D-6200, Wiesbaden, Germany; *Ukraine.*

St. Martin's Press, Inc., 175 Fifth Avenue, New York, New York 10010 (800) 221-7945; *The Statesman's Year-Book.*

Statistical Office of the United Nations, Publishing Service, New York, New York 10017 (800) 253-9646; *World Statistics Pocketbook.*

The World Bank, 1818 H Street, NW, Washington, D.C. 20433 (202) 477-1234; *The World Bank Atlas;* and *World Development Report.*

UKRAINE - EDUCATION

Academic International Press, Box 1111, Gulf Breeze, Florida 32562; *Russia and Eurasia Facts and Figures Annual.*

Business International Moscow, 23 Profsoyuznaya Ulitsa, 117859, Moscow (Telephone Number in U.S. (800) 938-4685); *The CIS Market Atlas.*

Euromonitor International, Inc., 122 South Michigan Avenue, Suite 1200, Chicago, Illinois 60603 (800) 577-EURO; *World Marketing Data and Statistics.*

Europa Publications Limited, 18 Bedford Square, London, WC1B 3JN, England; *The Europa World Year Book.*

Federal Statistical Office, Gustav-Stresemann - Ring 11, D-6200, Wiesbaden, Germany; *Ukraine.*

St. Martin's Press, Inc., 175 Fifth Avenue, New York, New York 10010 (800) 221-7945; *The Statesman's Year-Book.*

Statistical Office of the United Nations, Publishing Service, New York, New York 10017 (800) 253-9646; *Human Development Report;* and *Trends in Europe and North America: The Statistical Yearbook of the Economic Commission for Europe.*

United Nations Educational, Scientific and Cultural Organization (UNESCO), 7 Place de Fontenoy, F-75700 Paris, France (Telephone Number in U.S. (212) 963-

5981); *Statistical Yearbook.*

The World Bank, 1818 H Street, NW, Washington, D.C. 20433 (202) 477-1234; *World Development Report.*

UKRAINE - ELECTRICITY

Academic International Press, Box 1111, Gulf Breeze, Florida 32562; *Russia and Eurasia Facts and Figures Annual.*

Business International Moscow, 23 Profsoyuznaya Ulitsa, 117859, Moscow (Telephone Number in U.S. (800) 938-4685); *The CIS Market Atlas.*

Central Intelligence Agency, Washington, D.C. 20505 (703) 482-1100, www.cia.gov; *The World Factbook.*

St. Martin's Press, Inc., 175 Fifth Avenue, New York, New York 10010 (800) 221-7945; *The Statesman's Year-Book.*

Statistical Office of the United Nations, Publishing Service, New York, New York 10017 (800) 253-9646; *Energy Statistics Yearbook; Human Development Report; Trends in Europe and North America: The Statistical Yearbook of the Economic Commission for Europe;* and *Statistical Yearbook.*

The World Bank, 1818 H Street, NW, Washington, D.C. 20433 (202) 477-1234; *Statistical Handbook: States of the Former USSR.*

UKRAINE - EMPLOYMENT

Federal Statistical Office, Gustav-Stresemann - Ring 11, D-6200, Wiesbaden, Germany; *Ukraine.*

International Labour Office, I.L.O. Publications, 1828 L Street, NW, Suite 801, Washington, D.C. 20036 (301) 638-3152; *Yearbook of Labour Statistics.*

Statistical Office of the United Nations, Publishing Service, New York, New York 10017 (800) 253-9646; *Statistical Yearbook;* and *Trends in Europe and North America: The Statistical Yearbook of the Economic Commission for Europe.*

The World Bank, 1818 H Street, NW, Washington, D.C. 20433 (202) 477-1234; *Statistical Handbook: States of the Former USSR.*

UKRAINE - ENERGY

Academic International Press, Box 1111, Gulf Breeze, Florida 32562; *Russia and Eurasia Facts and Figures Annual.*

Business International Moscow, 23 Profsoyuznaya Ulitsa, 117859, Moscow (Telephone Number in U.S. (800) 938-

4685); *The CIS Market Atlas.*

Euromonitor International, Inc., 122 South Michigan Avenue, Suite 1200, Chicago, Illinois 60603 (800) 577-EURO; *The World Economic Factbook;* and *World Marketing Data and Statistics.*

St. Martin's Press, Inc., 175 Fifth Avenue, New York, New York 10010 (800) 221-7945; *The Statesman's Year-Book.*

Statistical Office of the United Nations, Publishing Service, New York, New York 10017 (800) 253-9646; *Energy Statistics Yearbook; Human Development Report; Trends in Europe and North America: The Statistical Yearbook of the Economic Commission for Europe; Statistical Yearbook;* and *World Statistics Pocketbook.*

The World Bank, 1818 H Street, NW, Washington, D.C. 20433 (202) 477-1234; *The World Bank Atlas; Statistical Handbook: States of the Former USSR;* and *World Development Report.*

UKRAINE - ENVIRONMENT

Business International Moscow, 23 Profsoyuznaya Ulitsa, 117859, Moscow (Telephone Number in U.S. (800) 938-4685); *The CIS Market Atlas.*

Economist Intelligence Unit, 111 West 57th Street, New York, New York 10019 (800) 938-4685; *Ukraine Country Report.*

Statistical Office of the United Nations, Publishing Service, New York, New York 10017 (800) 253-9646; *Statistical Yearbook; Trends in Europe and North America: The Statistical Yearbook of the Economic Commission for Europe;* and *World Statistics Pocketbook.*

UKRAINE - EXCHANGE RATE

Central Intelligence Agency, Washington, D.C. 20505 (703) 482-1100, www.cia.gov; *The World Factbook.*

Euromonitor International, Inc., 122 South Michigan Avenue, Suite 1200, Chicago, Illinois 60603 (800) 577-EURO; *The World Economic Factbook.*

Europa Publications Limited, 18 Bedford Square, London, WC1B 3JN, England; *The Europa World Year Book.*

Statistical Office of the United Nations, Publishing Service, New York, New York 10017 (800) 253-9646; *Statistical Yearbook; Trends in Europe and North America: The Statistical Yearbook of the Economic Commission for Europe;* and *World Statistics Pocketbook.*

UKRAINE - EXPORTS

Academic International Press, Box 1111, Gulf Breeze, Florida 32562; *Russia and Eurasia Facts and Figures Annual*.

Business International Moscow, 23 Profsoyuznaya Ulitsa, 117859, Moscow (Telephone Number in U.S. (800) 938-4685); *The CIS Market Atlas*.

Central Intelligence Agency, Washington, D.C. 20505 (703) 482-1100, www.cia.gov; *The World Factbook*.

Economist Intelligence Unit, 111 West 57th Street, New York, New York 10019 (800) 938-4685; *Ukraine Country Report*.

Euromonitor International, Inc., 122 South Michigan Avenue, Suite 1200, Chicago, Illinois 60603 (800) 577-EURO; *The World Economic Factbook*.

International Monetary Fund, 700 Nineteenth Street, NW, Washington, D.C. 20431 (202) 623-7000; *Direction of Trade Statistics*.

St. Martin's Press, Inc., 175 Fifth Avenue, New York, New York 10010 (800) 221-7945; *The Statesman's Year-Book*.

Statistical Office of the United Nations, Publishing Service, New York, New York 10017 (800) 253-9646; *International Trade Statistics Yearbook;* and *Trends in Europe and North America: The Statistical Yearbook of the Economic Commission for Europe*.

United Nations Conference on Trade and Development (UNCTAD), New York, New York 10017 (800) 253-9646; *Handbook of International Trade and Development Statistics*.

The World Bank, 1818 H Street, NW, Washington, D.C. 20433 (202) 477-1234; *Statistical Handbook: States of the Former USSR; World Development Report;* and *World Development Indicators*.

UKRAINE - EXTERNAL DEBT

The World Bank, 1818 H Street, NW, Washington, D.C. 20433 (202) 477-1234; *World Development Indicators*.

UKRAINE - EXTERNAL INDEBTEDNESS

The World Bank, 1818 H Street, NW, Washington, D.C. 20433 (202) 477-1234; *World Development Report*.

UKRAINE - EXTERNAL TRADE

Academic International Press, Box 1111, Gulf Breeze, Florida 32562; *Russia and Eurasia Facts and Figures Annual*.

Euromonitor International, Inc., 122

South Michigan Avenue, Suite 1200, Chicago, Illinois 60603 (800) 577-EURO; *World Marketing Data and Statistics*.

Food and Agriculture Organization of the United Nations (FAO), Via delle Terme di Caracalla, 00100, Rome, Italy (Telephone Number in U.S. (202) 653-2400); *Trade Yearbook*.

Statistical Office of the United Nations, Publishing Service, New York, New York 10017 (800) 253-9646; *Statistical Yearbook*.

The World Bank, 1818 H Street, NW, Washington, D.C. 20433 (202) 477-1234; *Statistical Handbook: States of the Former USSR,*

UKRAINE - FABRIC PRODUCTION - See UKRAINE - TEXTILE INDUSTRY

UKRAINE - FERTILITY RATES

Central Intelligence Agency, Washington, D.C. 20505 (703) 482-1100, www.cia.gov; *The World Factbook*.

Statistical Office of the United Nations, Publishing Service, New York, New York 10017 (800) 253-9646; *Human Development Report;* and *Trends in Europe and North America: The Statistical Yearbook of the Economic Commission for Europe*.

The World Bank, 1818 H Street, NW, Washington, D.C. 20433 (202) 477-1234; *The World Bank Atlas; Statistical Handbook: States of the Former USSR; World Development Report;* and *World Development Indicators*.

World Health Organization, Office of Publications, 20 Avenue Appia, CH-1211 Geneva 27, Switzerland (Telephone Number in U.S. (518) 436-9686); *World Health Statistics Annual*.

UKRAINE - FERTILIZER

Food and Agriculture Organization of the United Nations (FAO), Via delle Terme di Caracalla, 00100, Rome, Italy (Telephone Number in U.S. (202) 653-2400); *Fertilizer Yearbook*.

Statistical Office of the United Nations, Publishing Service, New York, New York 10017 (800) 253-9646; *Industrial Commodity Statistics Yearbook;* and *Statistical Yearbook*.

UKRAINE - FETAL MORTALITY - See UKRAINE - MORTALITY

UKRAINE - FIBRE PRODUCTION - See UKRAINE - TEXTILE INDUSTRY

UKRAINE - FILAMENT PRODUCTION - See UKRAINE - TEXTILE INDUSTRY

UKRAINE - FINANCE

Economist Intelligence Unit, 111 West 57th Street, New York, New York 10019 (800) 938-4685; *Ukraine Country Report*.

Europa Publications Limited, 18 Bedford Square, London, WC1B 3JN, England; *The Europa World Year Book*.

Federal Statistical Office, Gustav-Stresemann - Ring 11, D-6200, Wiesbaden, Germany; *Ukraine*.

St. Martin's Press, Inc., 175 Fifth Avenue, New York, New York 10010 (800) 221-7945; *The Statesman's Year-Book*.

The World Bank, 1818 H Street, NW, Washington, D.C. 20433 (202) 477-1234; *Statistical Handbook: States of the Former USSR*.

UKRAINE - FISHERIES

Federal Statistical Office, Gustav-Stresemann - Ring 11, D-6200, Wiesbaden, Germany; *Ukraine*.

Food and Agriculture Organization of the United Nations (FAO), Via delle Terme di Caracalla, 00100, Rome, Italy (Telephone Number in U.S. (202) 653-2400); *The State of Food and Agriculture;* and *Yearbook of Fishery Statistics*.

Statistical Office of the United Nations, Publishing Service, New York, New York 10017 (800) 253-9646; *Industrial Commodity Statistics Yearbook;* and *Statistical Yearbook*.

UKRAINE - FLOUR PRODUCTION

Statistical Office of the United Nations, Publishing Service, New York, New York 10017 (800) 253-9646; *Statistical Yearbook*.

UKRAINE - FOOD

Euromonitor International, Inc., 122 South Michigan Avenue, Suite 1200, Chicago, Illinois 60603 (800) 577-EURO; *Retail Trade International*.

Food and Agriculture Organization of the United Nations (FAO), Via delle Terme di Caracalla, 00100, Rome, Italy (Telephone Number in U.S. (202) 653-2400); *Production Yearbook; The State of Food and Agriculture;* and *Trade Yearbook*.

Statistical Office of the United Nations, Publishing Service, New York, New York 10017 (800) 253-9646; *Human Development Report;* and *Industrial Commodity Statistics Yearbook*.

UKRAINE - FOOTWEAR PRODUCTION AND CONSUMPTION - See UKRAINE - TEXTILE INDUSTRY

UKRAINE - FOREIGN INVESTMENT

Business International Moscow, 23 Profsoyuznaya Ulitsa, 117859, Moscow (Telephone Number in U.S. (800) 938-4685); *The CIS Market Atlas.*

UKRAINE - FOREIGN TRADE

Business International Moscow, 23 Profsoyuznaya Ulitsa, 117859, Moscow (Telephone Number in U.S. (800) 938-4685); *The CIS Market Atlas.*

Economist Intelligence Unit, 111 West 57th Street, New York, New York 10019 (800) 938-4685; *Ukraine Country Report.*

Euromonitor International, Inc., 122 South Michigan Avenue, Suite 1200, Chicago, Illinois 60603 (800) 577-EURO; *The World Economic Factbook.*

Europa Publications Limited, 18 Bedford Square, London, WC1B 3JN, England; *The Europa World Year Book.*

Federal Statistical Office, Gustav-Stresemann - Ring 11, D-6200, Wiesbaden, Germany; *Ukraine.*

International Monetary Fund, 700 Nineteenth Street, NW, Washington, D.C. 20431 (202) 623-7000; *Direction of Trade Statistics.*

St. Martin's Press, Inc., 175 Fifth Avenue, New York, New York 10010 (800) 221-7945; *The Statesman's Year-Book.*

Statistical Office of the United Nations, Publishing Service, New York, New York 10017 (800) 253-9646; *International Trade Statistics Yearbook; Statistical Yearbook;* and *Trade Yearbook.*

The World Bank, 1818 H Street, NW, Washington, D.C. 20433 (202) 477-1234; *Statistical Handbook: States of the Former USSR; World Development Report;* and *World Development Indicators.*

UKRAINE - FORESTRY AND FOREST PRODUCTS

Academic International Press, Box 1111, Gulf Breeze, Florida 32562; *Russia and Eurasia Facts and Figures Annual.*

Business International Moscow, 23 Profsoyuznaya Ulitsa, 117859, Moscow (Telephone Number in U.S. (800) 938-4685); *The CIS Market Atlas.*

Federal Statistical Office, Gustav-Stresemann - Ring 11, D-6200, Wiesbaden, Germany; *Ukraine.*

Food and Agriculture Organization of the United Nations (FAO), Via delle Terme di Caracalla, 00100, Rome, Italy (Telephone Number in U.S. (202) 653-2400); *The State of Food and Agriculture;* and *Yearbook of Forest Products.*

St. Martin's Press, Inc., 175 Fifth Avenue, New York, New York 10010 (800) 221-7945; *The Statesman's Year-Book.*

Statistical Office of the United Nations, Publishing Service, New York, New York 10017 (800) 253-9646; *Industrial Commodity Statistics Yearbook; Trends in Europe and North America: The Statistical Yearbook of the Economic Commission for Europe;* and *Statistical Yearbook.*

United Nations Educational, Scientific and Cultural Organization (UNESCO), 7 Place de Fontenoy, F-75700 Paris, France (Telephone Number in U.S. (212) 963-5981); *Statistical Yearbook.*

The World Bank, 1818 H Street, NW, Washington, D.C. 20433 (202) 477-1234; *World Development Report.*

UKRAINE - GAS PRODUCTION - See UKRAINE - MINING AND MINERAL PRODUCTS

UKRAINE - GENERAL MORTALITY - See UKRAINE - MORTALITY

UKRAINE - GOATS - See UKRAINE - LIVESTOCK AND POULTRY

UKRAINE - GOVERNMENT

Academic International Press, Box 1111, Gulf Breeze, Florida 32562; *Russia and Eurasia Facts and Figures Annual.*

Central Intelligence Agency, Washington, D.C. 20505 (703) 482-1100, www.cia.gov; *The World Factbook.*

Europa Publications Limited, 18 Bedford Square, London, WC1B 3JN, England; *The Europa World Year Book.*

St. Martin's Press, Inc., 175 Fifth Avenue, New York, New York 10010 (800) 221-7945; *The Statesman's Year-Book.*

Statistical Office of the United Nations, Publishing Service, New York, New York 10017 (800) 253-9646; *National Accounts Statistics;* and *Statistical Yearbook.*

The World Bank, 1818 H Street, NW, Washington, D.C. 20433 (202) 477-1234; *Statistical Handbook: States of the Former USSR;* and *World Development Report.*

UKRAINE - GROSS DOMESTIC PRODUCT

Academic International Press, Box 1111, Gulf Breeze, Florida 32562; *Russia and Eurasia Facts and Figures Annual.*

Economist Intelligence Unit, 111 West 57th Street, New York, New York 10019 (800) 938-4685; *Ukraine Country Report.*

Euromonitor International, Inc., 122 South Michigan Avenue, Suite 1200, Chicago, Illinois 60603 (800) 577-EURO; *The World Economic Factbook.*

Statistical Office of the United Nations, Publishing Service, New York, New York 10017 (800) 253-9646; *Human Development Report; National Accounts Statistics; Trends in Europe and North America: The Statistical Yearbook of the Economic Commission for Europe;* and *Statistical Yearbook.*

The World Bank, 1818 H Street, NW, Washington, D.C. 20433 (202) 477-1234; *Statistical Handbook: States of the Former USSR; World Development Report;* and *World Development Indicators.*

UKRAINE - GROSS NATIONAL PRODUCT

St. Martin's Press, Inc., 175 Fifth Avenue, New York, New York 10010 (800) 221-7945; *The Statesman's Year-Book.*

The World Bank, 1818 H Street, NW, Washington, D.C. 20433 (202) 477-1234; *The World Bank Atlas; World Development Report;* and *World Development Indicators.*

UKRAINE - HEALTH

Academic International Press, Box 1111, Gulf Breeze, Florida 32562; *Russia and Eurasia Facts and Figures Annual.*

Business International Moscow, 23 Profsoyuznaya Ulitsa, 117859, Moscow (Telephone Number in U.S. (800) 938-4685); *The CIS Market Atlas.*

Euromonitor International, Inc., 122 South Michigan Avenue, Suite 1200, Chicago, Illinois 60603 (800) 577-EURO; *World Marketing Data and Statistics.*

Federal Statistical Office, Gustav-Stresemann - Ring 11, D-6200, Wiesbaden, Germany; *Ukraine.*

St. Martin's Press, Inc., 175 Fifth Avenue, New York, New York 10010 (800) 221-7945; *The Statesman's Year-Book.*

Statistical Office of the United Nations, Publishing Service, New York, New York 10017 (800) 253-9646; *Human Development Report; Trends in Europe and North America: The Statistical Yearbook of the Economic Commission for Europe;* and *Statistical Yearbook.*

United Nations Children's Fund (UNICEF), 3 United Nations Plaza, New York, New York 10017 (800) 253-9646; *State of the World's Children.*

The World Bank, 1818 H Street, NW, Washington, D.C. 20433 (202) 477-1234; *World Development Report.*

World Health Organization, Office of Publications, 20 Avenue Appia, CH-1211 Geneva 27, Switzerland (Telephone Number in U.S. (518) 436-9686); *World Health Statistics Annual.*

UKRAINE - HIGHWAYS

Academic International Press, Box 1111, Gulf Breeze, Florida 32562; *Russia and Eurasia Facts and Figures Annual.*

Business International Moscow, 23 Profsoyuznaya Ulitsa, 117859, Moscow (Telephone Number in U.S. (800) 938-4685); *The CIS Market Atlas.*

Central Intelligence Agency, Washington, D.C. 20505 (703) 482-1100, www.cia.gov; *The World Factbook.*

St. Martin's Press, Inc., 175 Fifth Avenue, New York, New York 10010 (800) 221-7945; *The Statesman's Year-Book.*

Statistical Office of the United Nations, Publishing Service, New York, New York 10017 (800) 253-9646; *Annual Bulletin of Transport Statistics for Europe;* and *Trends in Europe and North America: The Statistical Yearbook of the Economic Commission for Europe.*

UKRAINE - HOUSING AND HOUSING UNITS

Business International Moscow, 23 Profsoyuznaya Ulitsa, 117859, Moscow (Telephone Number in U.S. (800) 938-4685); *The CIS Market Atlas.*

Euromonitor International, Inc., 122 South Michigan Avenue, Suite 1200, Chicago, Illinois 60603 (800) 577-EURO; *World Marketing Data and Statistics.*

Statistical Office of the United Nations, Publishing Service, New York, New York 10017 (800) 253-9646; *Trends in Europe and North America: The Statistical Yearbook of the Economic Commission for Europe.*

UKRAINE - ILLITERATE POPULATION

Central Intelligence Agency, Washington, D.C. 20505 (703) 482-1100, www.cia.gov; *The World Factbook.*

Euromonitor International, Inc., 122 South Michigan Avenue, Suite 1200, Chicago, Illinois 60603 (800) 577-EURO; *The World Economic Factbook.*

Statistical Office of the United Nations, Publishing Service, New York, New York 10017 (800) 253-9646; *Human Development Report.*

United Nations Educational, Scientific and Cultural Organization (UNESCO), 7 Place de Fontenoy, F-75700 Paris, France (Telephone Number in U.S. (212) 963-5981); *Statistical Yearbook.*

UKRAINE - IMPORTS

Academic International Press, Box 1111, Gulf Breeze, Florida 32562; *Russia and Eurasia Facts and Figures Annual.*

Business International Moscow, 23 Profsoyuznaya Ulitsa, 117859, Moscow (Telephone Number in U.S. (800) 938-4685); *The CIS Market Atlas.*

Central Intelligence Agency, Washington, D.C. 20505 (703) 482-1100, www.cia.gov; *The World Factbook.*

Economist Intelligence Unit, 111 West 57th Street, New York, New York 10019 (800) 938-4685; *Ukraine Country Report.*

Euromonitor International, Inc., 122 South Michigan Avenue, Suite 1200, Chicago, Illinois 60603 (800) 577-EURO; *The World Economic Factbook.*

Europa Publications Limited, 18 Bedford Square, London, WC1B 3JN, England; *The Europa World Year Book.*

International Monetary Fund, 700 Nineteenth Street, NW, Washington, D.C. 20431 (202) 623-7000; *Direction of Trade Statistics.*

St. Martin's Press, Inc., 175 Fifth Avenue, New York, New York 10010 (800) 221-7945; *The Statesman's Year-Book.*

Statistical Office of the United Nations, Publishing Service, New York, New York 10017 (800) 253-9646; *International Trade Statistics Yearbook;* and *Trends in Europe and North America: The Statistical Yearbook of the Economic Commission for Europe.*

United Nations Conference on Trade and Development (UNCTAD), New York, New York 10017 (800) 253-9646; *Handbook of International Trade and Development Statistics.*

The World Bank, 1818 H Street, NW, Washington, D.C. 20433 (202) 477-1234; *Statistical Handbook: States of the Former USSR; World Development Report;* and *World Development Indicators.*

UKRAINE - INDUSTRY

Academic International Press, Box 1111, Gulf Breeze, Florida 32562; *Russia and Eurasia Facts and Figures Annual.*

Business International Moscow, 23 Profsoyuznaya Ulitsa, 117859, Moscow

(Telephone Number in U.S. (800) 938-4685); *The CIS Market Atlas.*

Central Intelligence Agency, Washington, D.C. 20505 (703) 482-1100, www.cia.gov; *The World Factbook.*

Economist Intelligence Unit, 111 West 57th Street, New York, New York 10019 (800) 938-4685; *Ukraine Country Report.*

Euromonitor International, Inc., 122 South Michigan Avenue, Suite 1200, Chicago, Illinois 60603 (800) 577-EURO; *The World Economic Factbook;* and *World Marketing Data and Statistics.*

Europa Publications Limited, 18 Bedford Square, London, WC1B 3JN, England; *The Europa World Year Book.*

Federal Statistical Office, Gustav-Stresemann - Ring 11, D-6200, Wiesbaden, Germany; *Ukraine.*

International Labour Office, I.L.O. Publications, 1828 L Street, NW, Suite 801, Washington, D.C. 20036 (301) 638-3152; *Yearbook of Labour Statistics.*

St. Martin's Press, Inc., 175 Fifth Avenue, New York, New York 10010 (800) 221-7945; *The Statesman's Year-Book.*

Statistical Office of the United Nations, Publishing Service, New York, New York 10017 (800) 253-9646; *Industrial Commodity Statistics Yearbook; Trends in Europe and North America: The Statistical Yearbook of the Economic Commission for Europe;* and *Statistical Yearbook.*

The World Bank, 1818 H Street, NW, Washington, D.C. 20433 (202) 477-1234; *Statistical Handbook: States of the Former USSR;* and *World Development Indicators.*

UKRAINE - INFANT AND MATERNAL MORTALITY - See UKRAINE - MORTALITY

UKRAINE - INTERNAL TRADE

Statistical Office of the United Nations, Publishing Service, New York, New York 10017 (800) 253-9646; *Statistical Yearbook.*

UKRAINE - IRON ORE PRODUCTION AND CONSUMPTION - See UKRAINE - MINING AND MINERAL PRODUCTS

UKRAINE - LABOR

Academic International Press, Box 1111, Gulf Breeze, Florida 32562; *Russia and Eurasia Facts and Figures Annual.*

Business International Moscow, 23 Profsoyuznaya Ulitsa, 117859, Moscow (Telephone Number in U.S. (800) 938-4685); *The CIS Market Atlas.*

Central Intelligence Agency, Washington, D.C. 20505 (703) 482-1100, www.cia.gov; *The World Factbook.*

Euromonitor International, Inc., 122 South Michigan Avenue, Suite 1200, Chicago, Illinois 60603 (800) 577-EURO; *World Marketing Data and Statistics.*

Europa Publications Limited, 18 Bedford Square, London, WC1B 3JN, England; *The Europa World Year Book.*

International Labour Office, I.L.O. Publications, 1828 L Street, NW, Suite 801, Washington, D.C. 20036 (301) 638-3152; *Yearbook of Labour Statistics.*

St. Martin's Press, Inc., 175 Fifth Avenue, New York, New York 10010 (800) 221-7945; *The Statesman's Year-Book.*

Statistical Office of the United Nations, Publishing Service, New York, New York 10017 (800) 253-9646; *Human Development Report;* and *Statistical Yearbook.*

The World Bank, 1818 H Street, NW, Washington, D.C. 20433 (202) 477-1234; *Statistical Handbook: States of the Former USSR; The World Bank Atlas; World Development Report;* and *World Development Indicators.*

UKRAINE - LAND USE

Central Intelligence Agency, Washington, D.C. 20505 (703) 482-1100, www.cia.gov; *The World Factbook.*

Food and Agriculture Organization of the United Nations (FAO), Via delle Terme di Caracalla, 00100, Rome, Italy (Telephone Number in U.S. (202) 653-2400); *Production Yearbook.*

The World Bank, 1818 H Street, NW, Washington, D.C. 20433 (202) 477-1234; *World Development Report.*

UKRAINE - LIBRARIES

Statistical Office of the United Nations, Publishing Service, New York, New York 10017 (800) 253-9646; *Trends in Europe and North America: The Statistical Yearbook of the Economic Commission for Europe.*

United Nations Educational, Scientific and Cultural Organization (UNESCO), 7 Place de Fontenoy, F-75700 Paris, France (Telephone Number in U.S. (212) 963-5981); *Statistical Yearbook.*

UKRAINE - LIFE EXPECTANCY

Academic International Press, Box 1111, Gulf Breeze, Florida 32562; *Russia and Eurasia Facts and Figures Annual.*

Business International Moscow, 23 Profsoyuznaya Ulitsa, 117859, Moscow (Telephone Number in U.S. (800) 938-4685); *The CIS Market Atlas.*

Central Intelligence Agency, Washington, D.C. 20505 (703) 482-1100, www.cia.gov; *The World Factbook.*

Euromonitor International, Inc., 122 South Michigan Avenue, Suite 1200, Chicago, Illinois 60603 (800) 577-EURO; *The World Economic Factbook.*

Statistical Office of the United Nations, Publishing Service, New York, New York 10017 (800) 253-9646; *Demographic Yearbook; Trends in Europe and North America: The Statistical Yearbook of the Economic Commission for Europe; Human Development Report;* and *World Statistics Pocketbook.*

The World Bank, 1818 H Street, NW, Washington, D.C. 20433 (202) 477-1234; *The World Bank Atlas; World Development Report;* and *World Development Indicators.*

World Health Organization, Office of Publications, 20 Avenue Appia, CH-1211 Geneva 27, Switzerland (Telephone Number in U.S. (518) 436-9686); *World Health Statistics Annual.*

UKRAINE - LIGNITE PRODUCTION - See UKRAINE - MINING AND MINERAL PRODUCTS

UKRAINE - LITERACY RATE

Euromonitor International, Inc., 122 South Michigan Avenue, Suite 1200, Chicago, Illinois 60603 (800) 577-EURO; *World Marketing Data and Statistics.*

UKRAINE - LIVESTOCK AND POULTRY

Academic International Press, Box 1111, Gulf Breeze, Florida 32562; *Russia and Eurasia Facts and Figures Annual.*

Business International Moscow, 23 Profsoyuznaya Ulitsa, 117859, Moscow (Telephone Number in U.S. (800) 938-4685); *The CIS Market Atlas.*

Food and Agriculture Organization of the United Nations (FAO), Via delle Terme di Caracalla, 00100, Rome, Italy (Telephone Number in U.S. (202) 653-2400); *Production Yearbook; The State of Food and Agriculture;* and *Trade Yearbook.*

St. Martin's Press, Inc., 175 Fifth Avenue, New York, New York 10010 (800) 221-7945; *The Statesman's Year-Book.*

Statistical Office of the United Nations, Publishing Service, New York, New York 10017 (800) 253-9646; *Industrial Commodity Statistics Yearbook;* and *Statistical Yearbook.*

UKRAINE - MACHINERY

Statistical Office of the United Nations, Publishing Service, New York, New York 10017 (800) 253-9646; *Industrial Commodity Statistics Yearbook.*

UKRAINE - MAIL - NUMBER OF ITEMS SENT AND RECEIVED

Statistical Office of the United Nations, Publishing Service, New York, New York 10017 (800) 253-9646; *Statistical Yearbook.*

UKRAINE - MANGANESE ORE PRODUCTION AND CONSUMPTION - See UKRAINE - MINING AND MINERAL PRODUCTS

UKRAINE - MANUFACTURING

Statistical Office of the United Nations, Publishing Service, New York, New York 10017 (800) 253-9646; *Industrial Commodity Statistics Yearbook;* and *Statistical Yearbook.*

The World Bank, 1818 H Street, NW, Washington, D.C. 20433 (202) 477-1234; *World Development Indicators.*

UKRAINE - MARRIAGE RATES

Academic International Press, Box 1111, Gulf Breeze, Florida 32562; *Russia and Eurasia Facts and Figures Annual.*

Europa Publications Limited, 18 Bedford Square, London, WC1B 3JN, England; *The Europa World Year Book.*

Statistical Office of the United Nations, Publishing Service, New York, New York 10017 (800) 253-9646; *Demographic Yearbook; Trends in Europe and North America: The Statistical Yearbook of the Economic Commission for Europe;* and *Statistical Yearbook.*

UKRAINE - MEAT PRODUCTION - See UKRAINE - LIVESTOCK AND POULTRY

UKRAINE - MERCHANT SHIPPING

St. Martin's Press, Inc., 175 Fifth Avenue, New York, New York 10010 (800) 221-7945; *The Statesman's Year-Book.*

Statistical Office of the United Nations, Publishing Service, New York, New York 10017 (800) 253-9646; *Annual Bulletin of Transport Statistics for Europe;* and *Statistical Yearbook.*

UKRAINE - MILITARY

Academic International Press, Box 1111, Gulf Breeze, Florida 32562; *Russia and Eurasia Facts and Figures Annual.*

Central Intelligence Agency, Washington, D.C. 20505 (703) 482-1100, www.cia.gov; *The World Factbook*.

Euromonitor International, Inc., 122 South Michigan Avenue, Suite 1200, Chicago, Illinois 60603 (800) 577-EURO; *World Marketing Data and Statistics*.

The International Institute for Strategic Studies, 23 Tavistock Street, London WC2E 7NQ, England 44 171 3797676; *The Military Balance*.

St. Martin's Press, Inc., 175 Fifth Avenue, New York, New York 10010 (800) 221-7945; *The Statesman's Year-Book*.

Statistical Office of the United Nations, Publishing Service, New York, New York 10017 (800) 253-9646; *Human Development Report*.

UKRAINE - MILK PRODUCTION - See UKRAINE - DAIRY PRODUCTS

UKRAINE - MINING AND MINERAL PRODUCTS

Academic International Press, Box 1111, Gulf Breeze, Florida 32562; *Russia and Eurasia Facts and Figures Annual*.

Business International Moscow, 23 Profsoyuznaya Ulitsa, 117859, Moscow (Telephone Number in U.S. (800) 938-4685); *The CIS Market Atlas*.

Europa Publications Limited, 18 Bedford Square, London, WC1B 3JN, England; *The Europa World Year Book*.

St. Martin's Press, Inc., 175 Fifth Avenue, New York, New York 10010 (800) 221-7945; *The Statesman's Year-Book*.

Statistical Office of the United Nations, Publishing Service, New York, New York 10017 (800) 253-9646; *Energy Statistics Yearbook; Industrial Commodity Statistics Yearbook;* and *Statistical Yearbook*.

UKRAINE - MONEY SUPPLY

Economist Intelligence Unit, 111 West 57th Street, New York, New York 10019 (800) 938-4685; *Ukraine Country Report*.

Europa Publications Limited, 18 Bedford Square, London, WC1B 3JN, England; *The Europa World Year Book*.

Federal Statistical Office, Gustav-Stresemann - Ring 11, D-6200, Wiesbaden, Germany; *Ukraine*.

UKRAINE - MORTALITY

Academic International Press, Box 1111, Gulf Breeze, Florida 32562; *Russia and Eurasia Facts and Figures Annual*.

Business International Moscow, 23 Profsoyuznaya Ulitsa, 117859, Moscow (Telephone Number in U.S. (800) 938-4685); *The CIS Market Atlas*.

Central Intelligence Agency, Washington, D.C. 20505 (703) 482-1100, www.cia.gov; *The World Factbook*.

Euromonitor International, Inc., 122 South Michigan Avenue, Suite 1200, Chicago, Illinois 60603 (800) 577-EURO; *The World Economic Factbook*.

Europa Publications Limited, 18 Bedford Square, London, WC1B 3JN, England; *The Europa World Year Book*.

St. Martin's Press, Inc., 175 Fifth Avenue, New York, New York 10010 (800) 221-7945; *The Statesman's Year-Book*.

Statistical Office of the United Nations, Publishing Service, New York, New York 10017 (800) 253-9646; *Demographic Yearbook; Human Development Report; Trends in Europe and North America: The Statistical Yearbook of the Economic Commission for Europe; Statistical Yearbook;* and *World Statistics Pocketbook*.

The World Bank, 1818 H Street, NW, Washington, D.C. 20433 (202) 477-1234; *The World Bank Atlas; World Development Report;* and *World Development Indicators*.

United Nations Children's Fund (UNICEF), 3 United Nations Plaza, New York, New York 10017 (800) 253-9646; *State of the World's Children*.

World Health Organization, Office of Publications, 20 Avenue Appia, CH-1211 Geneva 27, Switzerland (Telephone Number in U.S. (518) 436-9686); *World Health Statistics Annual*.

UKRAINE - MOTION PICTURES

Statistical Office of the United Nations, Publishing Service, New York, New York 10017 (800) 253-9646; *Statistical Yearbook*.

United Nations Educational, Scientific and Cultural Organization (UNESCO), 7 Place de Fontenoy, F-75700 Paris, France (Telephone Number in U.S. (212) 963-5981); *Statistical Yearbook*.

UKRAINE - MOTOR VEHICLE PRODUCTION

Statistical Office of the United Nations, Publishing Service, New York, New York 10017 (800) 253-9646; *Statistical Yearbook*.

UKRAINE - MOTOR VEHICLES

Business International Moscow, 23 Profsoyuznaya Ulitsa, 117859, Moscow (Telephone Number in U.S. (800) 938-

4685); *The CIS Market Atlas*.

UKRAINE - MUSEUMS

United Nations Educational, Scientific and Cultural Organization (UNESCO), 7 Place de Fontenoy, F-75700 Paris, France (Telephone Number in U.S. (212) 963-5981); *Statistical Yearbook*.

UKRAINE - NATALITY

Statistical Office of the United Nations, Publishing Service, New York, New York 10017 (800) 253-9646; *Demographic Yearbook;* and *National Accounts Statistics*.

World Health Organization, Office of Publications, 20 Avenue Appia, CH-1211 Geneva 27, Switzerland (Telephone Number in U.S. (518) 436-9686); *World Health Statistics Annual*.

UKRAINE - NATIONAL ACCOUNTS

Europa Publications Limited, 18 Bedford Square, London, WC1B 3JN, England; *The Europa World Year Book*.

Federal Statistical Office, Gustav-Stresemann - Ring 11, D-6200, Wiesbaden, Germany; *Ukraine*.

Statistical Office of the United Nations, Publishing Service, New York, New York 10017 (800) 253-9646; *Statistical Yearbook*.

The World Bank, 1818 H Street, NW, Washington, D.C. 20433 (202) 477-1234; *Statistical Handbook: States of the Former USSR*.

UKRAINE - NATIONAL INCOME

Business International Moscow, 23 Profsoyuznaya Ulitsa, 117859, Moscow (Telephone Number in U.S. (800) 938-4685); *The CIS Market Atlas*.

Statistical Office of the United Nations, Publishing Service, New York, New York 10017 (800) 253-9646; *National Accounts Statistics;* and *Statistical Yearbook*.

UKRAINE - NATIONAL PRODUCT

Statistical Office of the United Nations, Publishing Service, New York, New York 10017 (800) 253-9646; *Statistical Yearbook*.

UKRAINE - NET MATERIAL PRODUCT

Statistical Office of the United Nations, Publishing Service, New York, New York 10017 (800) 253-9646; *Statistical Yearbook*.

UKRAINE - NEWSPAPER PRODUCTION - See UKRAINE - FORESTRY AND FOREST PRODUCTS

UKRAINE - OATS PRODUCTION - See UKRAINE - CROPS

UKRAINE - PAPER PRODUCTION - See UKRAINE - FORESTRY AND FOREST PRODUCTS

UKRAINE - PATENTS, TRADEMARKS AND SERVICE MARKS

Statistical Office of the United Nations, Publishing Service, New York, New York 10017 (800) 253-9646; *Statistical Yearbook.*

UKRAINE - PERIODICALS

United Nations Educational, Scientific and Cultural Organization (UNESCO), 7 Place de Fontenoy, F-75700 Paris, France (Telephone Number in U.S. (212) 963-5981); *Statistical Yearbook.*

UKRAINE - PETROLEUM INDUSTRY

Food and Agriculture Organization of the United Nations (FAO), Via delle Terme di Caracalla, 00100, Rome, Italy (Telephone Number in U.S. (202) 653-2400); *The State of Food and Agriculture.*

St. Martin's Press, Inc., 175 Fifth Avenue, New York, New York 10010 (800) 221-7945; *The Statesman's Year-Book.*

Statistical Office of the United Nations, Publishing Service, New York, New York 10017 (800) 253-9646; *Energy Statistics Yearbook; Industrial Commodity Statistics Yearbook; Trends in Europe and North America: The Statistical Yearbook of the Economic Commission for Europe;* and *Statistical Yearbook.*

UKRAINE - PIG-IRON AND FERRO-ALLOY PRODUCTION - See UKRAINE - MINING AND MINERAL PRODUCTS

UKRAINE - PIGS - See UKRAINE - LIVESTOCK AND POULTRY

UKRAINE - PIPELINES FOR OIL AND PETROLEUM PRODUCTS

Statistical Office of the United Nations, Publishing Service, New York, New York 10017 (800) 253-9646; *Annual Bulletin of Transport Statistics for Europe.*

UKRAINE - POPULATION

Academic International Press, Box 1111, Gulf Breeze, Florida 32562; *Russia and Eurasia Facts and Figures Annual.*

Business International Moscow, 23 Profsoyuznaya Ulitsa, 117859, Moscow (Telephone Number in U.S. (800) 938-4685); *The CIS Market Atlas.*

Central Intelligence Agency, Washington, D.C. 20505 (703) 482-1100, www.cia.gov; *The World Factbook.*

Economist Intelligence Unit, 111 West 57th Street, New York, New York 10019 (800) 938-4685; *Ukraine Country Report.*

Euromonitor International, Inc., 122 South Michigan Avenue, Suite 1200, Chicago, Illinois 60603 (800) 577-EURO; *The World Economic Factbook.*

Federal Statistical Office, Gustav-Stresemann - Ring 11, D-6200, Wiesbaden, Germany; *Ukraine.*

Food and Agriculture Organization of the United Nations (FAO), Via delle Terme di Caracalla, 00100, Rome, Italy (Telephone Number in U.S. (202) 653-2400); *Production Yearbook.*

International Labour Office, I.L.O. Publications, 1828 L Street, NW, Suite 801, Washington, D.C. 20036 (301) 638-3152; *Yearbook of Labour Statistics.*

St. Martin's Press, Inc., 175 Fifth Avenue, New York, New York 10010 (800) 221-7945; *The Statesman's Year-Book.*

Statistical Office of the United Nations, Publishing Service, New York, New York 10017 (800) 253-9646; *Demographic Yearbook; Human Development Report; Trends in Europe and North America: The Statistical Yearbook of the Economic Commission for Europe; Statistical Yearbook;* and *World Statistics Pocketbook.*

United Nations Educational, Scientific and Cultural Organization (UNESCO), 7 Place de Fontenoy, F-75700 Paris, France (Telephone Number in U.S. (212) 963-5981); *Statistical Yearbook.*

The World Bank, 1818 H Street, NW, Washington, D.C. 20433 (202) 477-1234; *Statistical Handbook: States of the Former USSR; The World Bank Atlas; World Development Report;* and *World Development Indicators.*

World Health Organization, Office of Publications, 20 Avenue Appia, CH-1211 Geneva 27, Switzerland (Telephone Number in U.S. (518) 436-9686); *World Health Statistics Annual.*

UKRAINE - POST OFFICES

Statistical Office of the United Nations, Publishing Service, New York, New York 10017 (800) 253-9646; *Trends in Europe and North America: The Statistical Yearbook of the Economic Commission for Europe.*

UKRAINE - POTATO PRODUCTION - See UKRAINE - CROPS

UKRAINE - POULTRY - See UKRAINE - LIVESTOCK AND POULTRY

UKRAINE - PRICES

Federal Statistical Office, Gustav-Stresemann - Ring 11, D-6200, Wiesbaden, Germany; *Ukraine.*

Food and Agriculture Organization of the United Nations (FAO), Via delle Terme di Caracalla, 00100, Rome, Italy (Telephone Number in U.S. (202) 653-2400); *Production Yearbook.*

International Labour Office, I.L.O. Publications, 1828 L Street, NW, Suite 801, Washington, D.C. 20036 (301) 638-3152; *Yearbook of Labour Statistics.*

The World Bank, 1818 H Street, NW, Washington, D.C. 20433 (202) 477-1234; *Statistical Handbook: States of the Former USSR.*

UKRAINE - PRODUCTION

The World Bank, 1818 H Street, NW, Washington, D.C. 20433 (202) 477-1234; *Statistical Handbook: States of the Former USSR.*

UKRAINE - PUBLIC FINANCE - See UKRAINE - FINANCE

UKRAINE - RADIO RECEIVER PRODUCTION

Statistical Office of the United Nations, Publishing Service, New York, New York 10017 (800) 253-9646; *Statistical Yearbook.*

UKRAINE - RADIO RECEIVERS

St. Martin's Press, Inc., 175 Fifth Avenue, New York, New York 10010 (800) 221-7945; *The Statesman's Year-Book.*

UKRAINE - RAILWAYS

Academic International Press, Box 1111, Gulf Breeze, Florida 32562; *Russia and Eurasia Facts and Figures Annual.*

Business International Moscow, 23 Profsoyuznaya Ulitsa, 117859, Moscow (Telephone Number in U.S. (800) 938-4685); *The CIS Market Atlas.*

St. Martin's Press, Inc., 175 Fifth Avenue, New York, New York 10010 (800) 221-7945; *The Statesman's Year-Book.*

Statistical Office of the United Nations, Publishing Service, New York, New York 10017 (800) 253-9646; *Annual Bulletin of Transport Statistics for Europe; Trends in Europe and North America: The Statistical Yearbook of the Economic Commission for Europe;* and *Statistical Yearbook.*

UKRAINE - RELIGION

Academic International Press, Box 1111, Gulf Breeze, Florida 32562; *Russia and Eurasia Facts and Figures Annual.*

St. Martin's Press, Inc., 175 Fifth Avenue, New York, New York 10010 (800) 221-7945; *The Statesman's Year-Book.*

UKRAINE - RENT PRICES

International Labour Office, I.L.O. Publications, 1828 L Street, NW, Suite 801, Washington, D.C. 20036 (301) 638-3152; *Yearbook of Labour Statistics.*

UKRAINE - RETAIL PRICE INDEX

Europa Publications Limited, 18 Bedford Square, London, WC1B 3JN, England; *The Europa World Year Book.*

UKRAINE - RETAIL TRADE

Business International Moscow, 23 Profsoyuznaya Ulitsa, 117859, Moscow (Telephone Number in U.S. (800) 938-4685); *The CIS Market Atlas.*

Euromonitor International, Inc., 122 South Michigan Avenue, Suite 1200, Chicago, Illinois 60603 (800) 577-EURO; *World Marketing Data and Statistics;* and *World Marketing Data and Statistics.*

Statistical Office of the United Nations, Publishing Service, New York, New York 10017 (800) 253-9646; *Statistical Yearbook.*

UKRAINE - RICE PRODUCTION - See UKRAINE - CROPS

UKRAINE - ROADS - See UKRAINE - HIGHWAYS

UKRAINE - ROUNDWOOD PRODUCTION AND CONSUMPTION - See UKRAINE - FORESTRY AND FOREST PRODUCTS

UKRAINE - RUBBER PRODUCTION AND CONSUMPTION

Statistical Office of the United Nations, Publishing Service, New York, New York 10017 (800) 253-9646; *Statistical Yearbook.*

UKRAINE - SALT PRODUCTION - See UKRAINE - MINING AND MINERALS

UKRAINE - SCIENCE AND TECHNOLOGY - EXPENDITURE FOR RESEARCH - See UKRAINE - SCIENTISTS, TECHNICIANS AND ENGINEERS

UKRAINE - SCIENTISTS, TECHNICIANS AND ENGINEERS

Statistical Office of the United Nations, Publishing Service, New York, New York 10017 (800) 253-9646; *Statistical Yearbook.*

UKRAINE - SHEEP - See UKRAINE - LIVESTOCK AND POULTRY

UKRAINE - SOCIAL DATA

Statistical Office of the United Nations, Publishing Service, New York, New York 10017 (800) 253-9646; *World Statistics Pocketbook.*

UKRAINE - SOCIAL SECURITY

Statistical Office of the United Nations, Publishing Service, New York, New York 10017 (800) 253-9646; *National Accounts Statistics.*

UKRAINE - STEEL - See UKRAINE - MINING AND MINERAL PRODUCTS

UKRAINE - SUGAR PRODUCTION - See UKRAINE - CROP

UKRAINE - TELEGRAPH SERVICE

Statistical Office of the United Nations, Publishing Service, New York, New York 10017 (800) 253-9646; *Statistical Yearbook.*

UKRAINE - TAXATION

Europa Publications Limited, 18 Bedford Square, London, WC1B 3JN, England; *The Europa World Year Book.*

UKRAINE - TELEPHONES IN USE

Academic International Press, Box 1111, Gulf Breeze, Florida 32562; *Russia and Eurasia Facts and Figures Annual.*

Statistical Office of the United Nations, Publishing Service, New York, New York 10017 (800) 253-9646; *Statistical Yearbook; Trends in Europe and North America: The Statistical Yearbook of the Economic Commission for Europe;* and *World Statistics Pocketbook.*

UKRAINE - TELEVISION RECEIVER PRODUCTION

Statistical Office of the United Nations, Publishing Service, New York, New York 10017 (800) 253-9646; *Statistical Yearbook.*

UKRAINE - TEXTILE INDUSTRY

Business International Moscow, 23 Profsoyuznaya Ulitsa, 117859, Moscow (Telephone Number in U.S. (800) 938-4685); *The CIS Market Atlas.*

Euromonitor International, Inc., 122 South Michigan Avenue, Suite 1200, Chicago, Illinois 60603 (800) 577-EURO; *Retail Trade International.*

St. Martin's Press, Inc., 175 Fifth Avenue, New York, New York 10010 (800) 221-7945; *The Statesman's Year-Book.*

Statistical Office of the United Nations, Publishing Service, New York, New York 10017 (800) 253-9646; *Industrial Commodity Statistics Yearbook;* and

Statistical Yearbook.

UKRAINE - THEATRE

United Nations Educational, Scientific and Cultural Organization (UNESCO), 7 Place de Fontenoy, F-75700 Paris, France (Telephone Number in U.S. (212) 963-5981); *Statistical Yearbook.*

UKRAINE - TIRE (MOTOR VEHICLE) PRODUCTION

Statistical Office of the United Nations, Publishing Service, New York, New York 10017 (800) 253-9646; *Statistical Yearbook.*

UKRAINE - TOBACCO PRODUCTION

Statistical Office of the United Nations, Publishing Service, New York, New York 10017 (800) 253-9646; *Statistical Yearbook.*

UKRAINE - TOURISM

Business International Moscow, 23 Profsoyuznaya Ulitsa, 117859, Moscow (Telephone Number in U.S. (800) 938-4685); *The CIS Market Atlas.*

Euromonitor International, Inc., 122 South Michigan Avenue, Suite 1200, Chicago, Illinois 60603 (800) 577-EURO; *The World Economic Factbook;* and *World Marketing Data and Statistics.*

Federal Statistical Office, Gustav-Stresemann - Ring 11, D-6200, Wiesbaden, Germany; *Ukraine.*

Statistical Office of the United Nations, Publishing Service, New York, New York 10017 (800) 253-9646; *Statistical Yearbook;* and *Trends in Europe and North America: The Statistical Yearbook of the Economic Commission for Europe.*

UKRAINE - TRADEMARKS AND SERVICE MARKS - See UKRAINE - PATENTS, TRADEMARKS AND SERVICE MARKS

UKRAINE - TRANSPORTATION AND COMMUNICATIONS

Academic International Press, Box 1111, Gulf Breeze, Florida 32562; *Russia and Eurasia Facts and Figures Annual.*

Business International Moscow, 23 Profsoyuznaya Ulitsa, 117859, Moscow (Telephone Number in U.S. (800) 938-4685); *The CIS Market Atlas.*

Euromonitor International, Inc., 122 South Michigan Avenue, Suite 1200, Chicago, Illinois 60603 (800) 577-EURO; *World Marketing Data and Statistics.*

Federal Statistical Office, Gustav-Stresemann - Ring 11, D-6200, Wiesbaden, Germany; *Ukraine.*

St. Martin's Press, Inc., 175 Fifth Avenue, New York, New York 10010 (800) 221-7945; *The Statesman's Year-Book.*

Statistical Office of the United Nations, Publishing Service, New York, New York 10017 (800) 253-9646; *Annual Bulletin of Transport Statistics for Europe; Human Development Report;* and *Trends in Europe and North America: The Statistical Yearbook of the Economic Commission for Europe.*

UKRAINE - UNEMPLOYMENT

International Labour Office, I.L.O. Publications, 1828 L Street, NW, Suite 801, Washington, D.C. 20036 (301) 638-3152; *Yearbook of Labour Statistics.*

St. Martin's Press, Inc., 175 Fifth Avenue, New York, New York 10010 (800) 221-7945; *The Statesman's Year-Book.*

Statistical Office of the United Nations, Publishing Service, New York, New York 10017 (800) 253-9646; *Statistical Yearbook;* and *Trends in Europe and North America: The Statistical Yearbook of the Economic Commission for Europe.*

UKRAINE - VITAL STATISTICS

St. Martin's Press, Inc., 175 Fifth Avenue, New York, New York 10010 (800) 221-7945; *The Statesman's Year-Book.*

Statistical Office of the United Nations, Publishing Service, New York, New York 10017 (800) 253-9646; *Statistical Yearbook.*

World Health Organization, Office of Publications, 20 Avenue Appia, CH-1211 Geneva 27, Switzerland (Telephone Number in U.S. (518) 436-9686); *World Health Statistics Annual.*

UKRAINE - WAGES

Business International Moscow, 23 Profsoyuznaya Ulitsa, 117859, Moscow (Telephone Number in U.S. (800) 938-4685); *The CIS Market Atlas.*

Federal Statistical Office, Gustav-Stresemann - Ring 11, D-6200, Wiesbaden, Germany; *Ukraine.*

International Labour Office, I.L.O. Publications, 1828 L Street, NW, Suite 801, Washington, D.C. 20036 (301) 638-3152; *Yearbook of Labour Statistics.*

Statistical Office of the United Nations, Publishing Service, New York, New York 10017 (800) 253-9646; *Statistical Yearbook.*

The World Bank, 1818 H Street, NW, Washington, D.C. 20433 (202) 477-1234; *Statistical Handbook: States of the Former USSR.*

UKRAINE - WATERWAYS IN USE

Statistical Office of the United Nations, Publishing Service, New York, New York 10017 (800) 253-9646; *Annual Bulletin of Transport Statistics for Europe.*

UKRAINE - WELFARE

Academic International Press, Box 1111, Gulf Breeze, Florida 32562; *Russia and Eurasia Facts and Figures Annual.*

St. Martin's Press, Inc., 175 Fifth Avenue, New York, New York 10010 (800) 221-7945; *The Statesman's Year-Book.*

UKRAINE - WHEAT PRODUCTION AND PRICES - See UKRAINE - CROPS

UKRAINE - WHOLESALE PRICES

Academic International Press, Box 1111, Gulf Breeze, Florida 32562; *Russia and Eurasia Facts and Figures Annual.*

Statistical Office of the United Nations, Publishing Service, New York, New York 10017 (800) 253-9646; *Statistical Yearbook.*

UKRAINE - WHOLESALE TRADE

Statistical Office of the United Nations, Publishing Service, New York, New York 10017 (800) 253-9646; *Statistical Yearbook.*

UKRAINE - WINE PRODUCTION - See UKRAINE - BEVERAGES

UKRAINE - WOOL PRODUCTION AND CONSUMPTION - See UKRAINE - TEXTILE INDUSTRY

UKRAINE - YARN PRODUCTION - See UKRAINE - TEXTILE INDUSTRY

UKRAINIAN SSR - See UKRAINE

ULCER OF STOMACH AND DUODENUM - DEATHS

U.S. Department of Health and Human Services, National Center for Health Statistics, 3700 East-West Highway, Hyattsville, Maryland 20782 (301) 436-8500, www.cdc.gov/nchs; *Vital Statistics of the United States; National Vital Statistics Report;* and unpublished data.

ULTRASOUND DIAGNOSIS

U.S. Department of Health and Human Services, National Center for Health Statistics, 3700 East-West Highway, Hyattsville, Maryland 20782 (301) 436-8500, www.cdc.gov/nchs; *Vital and Health Statistics.*

UNEMPLOYMENT - See LABOR FORCE - UNEMPLOYED WORKERS

UNEMPLOYMENT INSURANCE - BENEFICIARIES

U.S. Department of Labor, Employment and Training Administration, 200 Constitution Avenue, NW, Washington, D.C. 20210 (202) 219-6871, www.doleta.gov; *Unemployment Insurance Financial Handbook.*

UNEMPLOYMENT INSURANCE - COVERAGE - WORKERS AND EARNINGS

U.S. Department of Labor, Employment and Training Administration, 200 Constitution Avenue, NW, Washington, D.C. 20210 (202) 219-6871, www.doleta.gov; *Unemployment Insurance Financial Handbook.*

UNEMPLOYMENT INSURANCE - GOVERNMENTAL FINANCES

Executive Office of the President, Office of Management and Budget, Executive Office Building, Washington, D.C. 20503 (202) 395-3080, www.whitehouse.gov/omb; *Historical Tables;* and *Analytical Perspectives.*

U.S. Department of Commerce, Bureau of the Census, Washington, D.C. 20233 (301) 457-4100, www.census.gov; *Government Finances;* and Internet sites: http://www.census.gov/govs/www/estimate.html; and http://www.census.gov/ftp/pub/govs/www/state.html.

UNEMPLOYMENT INSURANCE - PAYMENTS

Social Security Administration, 6400 Security Boulevard, Baltimore, Maryland 21235 (800) 772-1213, www.ssa.gov; *Social Security Bulletin;* and unpublished data.

U.S. Department of Labor, Employment and Training Administration, 200 Constitution Avenue, NW, Washington, D.C. 20210 (202) 219-6871, www.doleta.gov; *Unemployment Insurance Financial Handbook.*

UNINCORPORATED ENTERPRISES - FLOW OF FUNDS

Board of Governors of the Federal Reserve System, Twentieth Street and Constitution Avenue, NW, Washington, D.C. 20551 (202) 452-3000, www.bog.frb.fed.us; *Flow of Funds Accounts.*

UNIONS - See LABOR ORGANIZATIONS OR UNIONS

United Arab Emirates - National Statistical Offices

International Criminal Police Organization (INTERPOL), 50 quai Achille Lignon, F-69006 Lyon, France; *International Crime Statistics.*

UNITED ARAB EMIRATES - CROPS

Europa Publications Limited, 18 Bedford Square, London, WC1B 3JN, England; *The Europa World Year Book.*

Food and Agricultural Organization of the United Nations (FAO) Via delle Terme di Caracalla, 00100 Rome, Italy (Telephone Number in U.S. (202) 653-2400); *The State of Food and Agriculture.*

M.E. Sharpe, 80 Business Park Drive, Armonk, New York 10504 (800) 541-6563; *The Illustrated Book of World Rankings.*

St. Martin's Press, Inc., 175 Fifth Avenue, New York, New York 10010 (800) 221-7945; *The Statesman's Year-Book.*

United Nations Conference on Trade and Development, Central Statistical Service, Palais des Nations, Geneva, Switzerland (Telephone in U.S. (800) 253-9646); *UNCTAD Commodity Yearbook.*

UNITED ARAB EMIRATES - DAIRY PRODUCTS

Economic Commission for Western Asia, Post Office Box 27, Baghdad, Iraq; *Statistical Abstract of Western Asia.*

Europa Publications Limited, 18 Bedford Square, London, WC1B 3JN, England; *The Europa World Year Book.*

Food and Agricultural Organization of the United Nations (FAO) Via delle Terme di Caracalla, 00100 Rome, Italy (Telephone Number in U.S. (202) 653-2400); *Production Yearbook;* and *The State of Food and Agriculture.*

M.E. Sharpe, 80 Business Park Drive, Armonk, New York 10504 (800) 541-6563; *The Illustrated Book of World Rankings.*

St. Martin's Press, Inc., 175 Fifth Avenue, New York, New York 10010 (800) 221-7945; *The Statesman's Year-Book.*

UNITED ARAB EMIRATES - DEATH RATES - See UNITED ARAB EMIRATES - MORTALITY

UNITED ARAB EMIRATES - DEFENSE EXPENDITURES - See UNITED ARAB EMIRATES - MILITARY

UNITED ARAB EMIRATES - DEMOGRAPHY

Central Intelligence Agency, Washington, D.C. 20505 (703) 482-1100, www.cia.gov; *The World Factbook.*

The Economist Intelligence Unit, 111 West 57th Street, New York, New York 10019 (800) 938-4685; *The World Market Atlas.*

Euromonitor International, Inc., 122 South Michigan Avenue, Suite 1200, Chicago, Illinois 60603 (800) 577-EURO; *International Marketing Data and Statistics; World Marketing Data and Statistics;* and *The World Economic Factbook.*

M.E. Sharpe, 80 Business Park Drive, Armonk, New York 10504 (800) 541-6563; *The Illustrated Book of World Rankings.*

Statistical Office of the United Nations, Publishing Service, New York, New York 10017 (800) 253-9646; *Human Development Report.*

UNITED ARAB EMIRATES - DEVELOPMENT ASSISTANCE

Statistical Office of the United Nations, Publishing Service, New York, New York 10017 (800) 253-9646; *Statistical Yearbook.*

UNITED ARAB EMIRATES - DIAMOND PRODUCTION - See UNITED ARAB EMIRATES - MINING AND MINERAL PRODUCTS

UNITED ARAB EMIRATES - DIVORCE RATES

M.E. Sharpe, 80 Business Park Drive, Armonk, New York 10504 (800) 541-6563; *The Illustrated Book of World Rankings.*

Statistical Office of the United Nations, Publishing Service, New York, New York 10017 (800) 253-9646; *Demographic Yearbook.*

UNITED ARAB EMIRATES - ECONOMY

Central Intelligence Agency, Washington, D.C. 20505 (703) 482-1100, www.cia.gov; *The World Factbook.*

Economist Intelligence Unit, 111 West 57th Street, New York, New York 10019 (800) 938-4685; *United Arab Emirates Country Report.*

Euromonitor International, Inc., 122 South Michigan Avenue, Suite 1200, Chicago, Illinois 60603 (800) 577-EURO; *International Marketing Data and Statistics; World Marketing Data and Statistics;* and *The World Economic Factbook.*

Europa Publications Limited, 18 Bedford Square, London, WC1B 3JN, England; *The Europa World Year Book.*

Federal Statistical Office, Gustav-Stresemann - Ring 11, D-6200, Wiesbaden, Germany; *Vereinigte Arabische Emirate.*

M.E. Sharpe, 80 Business Park Drive,

Armonk, New York 10504 (800) 541-6563; *The Illustrated Book of World Rankings.*

St. Martin's Press, Inc., 175 Fifth Avenue, New York, New York 10010 (800) 221-7945; *The Statesman's Year-Book.*

Statistical Office of the United Nations, Publishing Service, New York, New York 10017 (800) 253-9646; *World Statistics Pocketbook.*

The World Bank, 1818 H Street, NW, Washington, D.C. 20433 (202) 477-1234; *The World Bank Atlas;* and *World Development Report.*

UNITED ARAB EMIRATES - EDUCATION

Economic Commission for Western Asia, Post Office Box 27, Baghdad, Iraq; *Statistical Abstract of Western Asia.*

The Economist Intelligence Unit, 111 West 57th Street, New York, New York 10019 (800) 938-4685; *The World Market Atlas.*

Euromonitor International, Inc., 122 South Michigan Avenue, Suite 1200, Chicago, Illinois 60603 (800) 577-EURO; *International Marketing Data and Statistics;* and *World Marketing Data and Statistics.*

Europa Publications Limited, 18 Bedford Square, London, WC1B 3JN, England; *The Europa World Year Book.*

Federal Statistical Office, Gustav-Stresemann - Ring 11, D-6200, Wiesbaden, Germany; *Vereinigte Arabische Emirate.*

International Monetary Fund, 700 Nineteenth Street, NW, Washington, D.C. 20431 (202) 623-7000; *Government Finance Statistics Yearbook.*

M.E. Sharpe, 80 Business Park Drive, Armonk, New York 10504 (800) 541-6563; *The Illustrated Book of World Rankings.*

St. Martin's Press, Inc., 175 Fifth Avenue, New York, New York 10010 (800) 221-7945; *The Statesman's Year-Book.*

Statistical Office of the United Nations, Publishing Service, New York, New York 10017 (800) 253-9646; *Human Development Report.*

United Nations Educational, Scientific and Cultural Organization (UNESCO), 7 Place de Fontenoy, F-75700 Paris, France (Telephone Number in U.S. (212) 963-5981); *Statistical Yearbook.*

The World Bank, 1818 H Street, NW, Washington, D.C. 20433 (202) 477-1234; *World Development Report;* and *World Development Indicators.*

UNITED ARAB EMIRATES - EGG PRODUCTION AND CONSUMPTION - See UNITED ARAB EMIRATES - DAIRY PRODUCTS

UNITED ARAB EMIRATES - ELECTRICITY

Central Intelligence Agency, Washington, D.C. 20505 (703) 482-1100, www.cia.gov; *The World Factbook.*

M.E. Sharpe, 80 Business Park Drive, Armonk, New York 10504 (800) 541-6563; *The Illustrated Book of World Rankings.*

Penn Well Publishing Company, 1421 South Sheridan Road, P.O. Box 1260, Tulsa, Oklahoma 74101 (800) 752-9764; *International Energy Statistics Sourcebook.*

St. Martin's Press, Inc., 175 Fifth Avenue, New York, New York 10010 (800) 221-7945; *The Statesman's Year-Book.*

Statistical Office of the United Nations, Publishing Service, New York, New York 10017 (800) 253-9646; *Human Development Report;* and *Statistical Yearbook.*

UNITED ARAB EMIRATES - EMPLOYMENT

Economic Commission for Western Asia, Post Office Box 27, Baghdad, Iraq; *Statistical Abstract of Western Asia.*

Euromonitor International, Inc., 122 South Michigan Avenue, Suite 1200, Chicago, Illinois 60603 (800) 577-EURO; *International Marketing Data and Statistics.*

Federal Statistical Office, Gustav-Stresemann - Ring 11, D-6200, Wiesbaden, Germany; *Vereinigte Arabische Emirate.*

International Labour Office, I.L.O. Publications, 1828 L Street, NW, Suite 801, Washington, D.C. 20036 (301) 638-3152; *Yearbook of Labour Statistics.*

M.E. Sharpe, 80 Business Park Drive, Armonk, New York 10504 (800) 541-6563; *The Illustrated Book of World Rankings.*

Statistical Office of the United Nations, Publishing Service, New York, New York 10017 (800) 253-9646; *Bulletin of Industrial Statistics for the Arab Countries.*

UNITED ARAB EMIRATES - ENERGY

Economic Commission for Western Asia, Post Office Box 27, Baghdad, Iraq; *Statistical Abstract of Western Asia.*

Euromonitor International, Inc., 122 South Michigan Avenue, Suite 1200, Chicago, Illinois 60603 (800) 577-EURO; *International Marketing Data and Statistics;*

World Marketing Data and Statistics; and *The World Economic Factbook.*

Food and Agricultural Organization of the United Nations (FAO) Via delle Terme di Caracalla, 00100 Rome, Italy (Telephone Number in U.S. (202) 653-2400); *The State of Food and Agriculture.*

M.E. Sharpe, 80 Business Park Drive, Armonk, New York 10504 (800) 541-6563; *The Illustrated Book of World Rankings.*

Penn Well Publishing Company, 1421 South Sheridan Road, P.O. Box 1260, Tulsa, Oklahoma 74101 (800) 752-9764; *International Energy Statistics Sourcebook.*

St. Martin's Press, Inc., 175 Fifth Avenue, New York, New York 10010 (800) 221-7945; *The Statesman's Year-Book.*

Statistical Office of the United Nations, Publishing Service, New York, New York 10017 (800) 253-9646; *Energy Statistics Yearbook; Human Development Report; Statistical Yearbook;* and *World Statistics Pocketbook.*

The World Bank, 1818 H Street, NW, Washington, D.C. 20433 (202) 477-1234; *The World Bank Atlas;* and *World Development Report.*

UNITED ARAB EMIRATES - ENVIRONMENT

Economist Intelligence Unit, 111 West 57th Street, New York, New York 10019 (800) 938-4685; *United Arab Emirates Country Report.*

Statistical Office of the United Nations, Publishing Service, New York, New York 10017 (800) 253-9646; *World Statistics Pocketbook.*

UNITED ARAB EMIRATES - EXCHANGE RATES

Central Intelligence Agency, Washington, D.C. 20505 (703) 482-1100, www.cia.gov; *The World Factbook.*

Euromonitor International, Inc., 122 South Michigan Avenue, Suite 1200, Chicago, Illinois 60603 (800) 577-EURO; *International Marketing Data and Statistics;* and *The World Economic Factbook.*

Europa Publications Limited, 18 Bedford Square, London, WC1B 3JN, England; *The Europa World Year Book.*

International Monetary Fund, 700 Nineteenth Street, NW, Washington, D.C. 20431 (202) 623-7000; *International Financial Statistics.*

Organization of Petroleum Exporting Countries, Obere Donaustrasse 93, 1020 Vienna 2, Austria; *OPEC Annual Statistical*

Bulletin.

Statistical Office of the United Nations, Publishing Service, New York, New York 10017 (800) 253-9646; *Bulletin of Industrial Statistics for the Arab Countries; Statistical Yearbook;* and *World Statistics Pocketbook.*

UNITED ARAB EMIRATES - EXPORTS

Central Intelligence Agency, Washington, D.C. 20505 (703) 482-1100, www.cia.gov; *The World Factbook.*

Economic Commission for Western Asia, Post Office Box 27, Baghdad, Iraq; *Statistical Abstract of Western Asia.*

The Economist Intelligence Unit, 111 West 57th Street, New York, New York 10019 (800) 938-4685; *United Arab Emirates;* and *The World Market Atlas.*

Euromonitor International, Inc., 122 South Michigan Avenue, Suite 1200, Chicago, Illinois 60603 (800) 577-EURO; *International Marketing Data and Statistics;* and *The World Economic Factbook.*

Europa Publications Limited, 18 Bedford Square, London, WC1B 3JN, England; *The Europa World Year Book.*

Food and Agricultural Organization of the United Nations (FAO) Via delle Terme di Caracalla, 00100 Rome, Italy (Telephone Number in U.S. (202) 653-2400); *The State of Food and Agriculture.*

International Monetary Fund, 700 Nineteenth Street, NW, Washington, D.C. 20431 (202) 623-7000; *Direction of Trade Statistics;* and *International Financial Statistics.*

Organization of Petroleum Exporting Countries, Obere Donaustrasse 93, 1020 Vienna 2, Austria; *OPEC Annual Statistical Bulletin.*

St. Martin's Press, Inc., 175 Fifth Avenue, New York, New York 10010 (800) 221-7945; *The Statesman's Year-Book.*

Statistical Office of the United Nations, Publishing Service, New York, New York 10017 (800) 253-9646; *Bulletin of Industrial Statistics for the Arab Countries.*

The World Bank, 1818 H Street, NW, Washington, D.C. 20433 (202) 477-1234; *World Development Report;* and *World Development Indicators.*

UNITED ARAB EMIRATES - EXTERNAL INDEBTEDNESS

The World Bank, 1818 H Street, NW, Washington, D.C. 20433 (202) 477-1234; *World Development Report;* and *World Development Indicators.*

UNITED ARAB EMIRATES - EXTERNAL TRADE

Euromonitor International, Inc., 122 South Michigan Avenue, Suite 1200, Chicago, Illinois 60603 (800) 577-EURO; *World Marketing Data and Statistics.*

Food and Agricultural Organization of the United Nations (FAO) Via delle Terme di Caracalla, 00100 Rome, Italy (Telephone Number in U.S. (202) 653-2400); *The State of Food and Agriculture;* and *Trade Yearbook.*

UNITED ARAB EMIRATES - FARM CROPS - See UNITED ARAB EMIRATES - CROPS

UNITED ARAB EMIRATES - FEMALE WORKING POPULATION - See UNITED ARAB EMIRATES - EMPLOYMENT

UNITED ARAB EMIRATES - FERTILITY RATES

Central Intelligence Agency, Washington, D.C. 20505 (703) 482-1100, www.cia.gov; *The World Factbook.*

M.E. Sharpe, 80 Business Park Drive, Armonk, New York 10504 (800) 541-6563; *The Illustrated Book of World Rankings.*

Statistical Office of the United Nations, Publishing Service, New York, New York 10017 (800) 253-9646; *Human Development Report.*

The World Bank, 1818 H Street, NW, Washington, D.C. 20433 (202) 477-1234; *The World Bank Atlas; World Development Report;* and *World Development Indicators.*

UNITED ARAB EMIRATES - FERTILIZER

Food and Agricultural Organization of the United Nations (FAO), Via delle Terme di Caracalla, 00100 Rome, Italy (Telephone Number in U.S. (202) 653-2400); *Fertilizer Yearbook;* and *The State of Food and Agriculture.*

Statistical Office of the United Nations, Publishing Service, New York, New York 10017 (800) 253-9646; *Statistical Yearbook.*

UNITED ARAB EMIRATES - FETAL MORTALITY - See UNITED ARAB EMIRATES - MORTALITY

UNITED ARAB EMIRATES - FINANCE

Economic Commission for Western Asia, Post Office Box 27, Baghdad, Iraq; *Statistical Abstract of Western Asia.*

Economist Intelligence Unit, 111 West 57th Street, New York, New York 10019 (800) 938-4685; *United Arab Emirates Country Report.*

Europa Publications Limited, 18 Bedford Square, London, WC1B 3JN, England; *The Europa World Year Book.*

Federal Statistical Office, Gustav-Stresemann - Ring 11, D-6200, Wiesbaden, Germany; *Vereinigte Arabische Emirate.*

International Monetary Fund, 700 Nineteenth Street, NW, Washington, D.C. 20431 (202) 623-7000; *Government Finance Statistics Yearbook.*

M.E. Sharpe, 80 Business Park Drive, Armonk, New York 10504 (800) 541-6563; *The Illustrated Book of World Rankings.*

St. Martin's Press, Inc., 175 Fifth Avenue, New York, New York 10010 (800) 221-7945; *The Statesman's Year-Book.*

UNITED ARAB EMIRATES - FISHERIES

Economic Commission for Western Asia, Post Office Box 27, Baghdad, Iraq; *Statistical Abstract of Western Asia.*

Europa Publications Limited, 18 Bedford Square, London, WC1B 3JN, England; *The Europa World Year Book.*

Federal Statistical Office, Gustav-Stresemann - Ring 11, D-6200, Wiesbaden, Germany; *Vereinigte Arabische Emirate.*

Food and Agricultural Organization of the United Nations (FAO) Via delle Terme di Caracalla, 00100 Rome, Italy (Telephone Number in U.S. (202) 653-2400); *The State of Food and Agriculture;* and *Yearbook of Fishery Statistics.*

M.E. Sharpe, 80 Business Park Drive, Armonk, New York 10504 (800) 541-6563; *The Illustrated Book of World Rankings.*

St. Martin's Press, Inc., 175 Fifth Avenue, New York, New York 10010 (800) 221-7945; *The Statesman's Year-Book.*

Statistical Office of the United Nations, Publishing Service, New York, New York 10017 (800) 253-9646; *Statistical Yearbook.*

United Nations Conference on Trade and Development, Central Statistical Service, Palais des Nations, Geneva, Switzerland (Telephone in U.S. (800) 253-9646); *UNCTAD Commodity Yearbook.*

UNITED ARAB EMIRATES - FOOD

Food and Agricultural Organization of the United Nations (FAO) Via delle Terme di Caracalla, 00100 Rome, Italy (Telephone Number in U.S. (202) 653-2400); *Production Yearbook;* and *The State of Food and Agriculture.*

Statistical Office of the United Nations, Publishing Service, New York, New York

10017 (800) 253-9646; *Human Development Report.*

United Nations Conference on Trade and Development, Central Statistical Service, Palais des Nations, Geneva, Switzerland (Telephone in U.S. (800) 253-9646); *UNCTAD Commodity Yearbook.*

UNITED ARAB EMIRATES - FOREIGN TRADE

Economic Commission for Western Asia, Post Office Box 27, Baghdad, Iraq; *Statistical Abstract of Western Asia.*

Economist Intelligence Unit, 111 West 57th Street, New York, New York 10019 (800) 938-4685; *United Arab Emirates Country Report.*

Euromonitor International, Inc., 122 South Michigan Avenue, Suite 1200, Chicago, Illinois 60603 (800) 577-EURO; *International Marketing Data and Statistics;* and *The World Economic Factbook.*

Europa Publications Limited, 18 Bedford Square, London, WC1B 3JN, England; *The Europa World Year Book.*

Federal Statistical Office, Gustav-Stresemann - Ring 11, D-6200, Wiesbaden, Germany; *Vereinigte Arabische Emirate.*

Food and Agricultural Organization of the United Nations (FAO) Via delle Terme di Caracalla, 00100 Rome, Italy (Telephone Number in U.S. (202) 653-2400); *The State of Food and Agriculture.*

M.E. Sharpe, 80 Business Park Drive, Armonk, New York 10504 (800) 541-6563; *The Illustrated Book of World Rankings.*

St. Martin's Press, Inc., 175 Fifth Avenue, New York, New York 10010 (800) 221-7945; *The Statesman's Year-Book.*

Statistical Office of the United Nations, Publishing Service, New York, New York 10017 (800) 253-9646; *Bulletin of Industrial Statistics for the Arab Countries; International Trade Statistics Yearbook;* and *Statistical Yearbook.*

United Nations Conference on Trade and Development, Central Statistical Service, Palais des Nations, Geneva, Switzerland (Telephone in U.S. (800) 253-9646); *UNCTAD Commodity Yearbook.*

The World Bank, 1818 H Street, NW, Washington, D.C. 20433 (202) 477-1234; *World Development Report;* and *World Development Indicators.*

UNITED ARAB EMIRATES - FORESTRY AND FOREST PRODUCTS

Federal Statistical Office, Gustav-

Stresemann - Ring 11, D-6200, Wiesbaden, Germany; *Vereinigte Arabische Emirate.*

Food and Agricultural Organization of the United Nations (FAO) Via delle Terme di Caracalla, 00100 Rome, Italy (Telephone Number in U.S. (202) 653-2400); *The State of Food and Agriculture.*

M.E. Sharpe, 80 Business Park Drive, Armonk, New York 10504 (800) 541-6563; *The Illustrated Book of World Rankings.*

Statistical Office of the United Nations, Publishing Service, New York, New York 10017 (800) 253-9646; *Statistical Yearbook.*

United Nations Conference on Trade and Development, Central Statistical Service, Palais des Nations, Geneva, Switzerland (Telephone in U.S. (800) 253-9646); *UNCTAD Commodity Yearbook.*

United Nations Educational, Scientific and Cultural Organization (UNESCO), 7 Place de Fontenoy, F-75700 Paris, France (Telephone Number in U.S. (212) 963-5981); *Statistical Yearbook.*

The World Bank, 1818 H Street, NW, Washington, D.C. 20433 (202) 477-1234; *World Development Report.*

UNITED ARAB EMIRATES - GAS AND GAS LIQUIDS PRODUCTION - See UNITED ARAB EMIRATES - MINING AND MINERAL PRODUCTS

UNITED ARAB EMIRATES - GENERAL MORTALITY - See UNITED ARAB EMIRATES - MORTALITY

UNITED ARAB EMIRATES - GEOGRAPHIC DATA

M.E. Sharpe, 80 Business Park Drive, Armonk, New York 10504 (800) 541-6563; *The Illustrated Book of World Rankings.*

UNITED ARAB EMIRATES - GOLD HOLDINGS

International Monetary Fund, 700 Nineteenth Street, NW, Washington, D.C. 20431 (202) 623-7000; *International Financial Statistics.*

Statistical Office of the United Nations, Publishing Service, New York, New York 10017 (800) 253-9646; *Statistical Yearbook.*

The World Bank, 1818 H Street, NW, Washington, D.C. 20433 (202) 477-1234; *World Development Indicators.*

UNITED ARAB EMIRATES - GOLD PRODUCTION AND CONSUMPTION - See UNITED ARAB EMIRATES - MINING AND MINERAL PRODUCTS

UNITED ARAB EMIRATES -GOVERNMENT

Central Intelligence Agency, Washington, D.C. 20505 (703) 482-1100, www.cia.gov; *The World Factbook.*

Economic Commission for Western Asia, Post Office Box 27, Baghdad, Iraq; *Statistical Abstract of Western Asia.*

Europa Publications Limited, 18 Bedford Square, London, WC1B 3JN, England; *The Europa World Year Book.*

International Monetary Fund, 700 Nineteenth Street, NW, Washington, D.C. 20431 (202) 623-7000; *Government Finance Statistics Yearbook.*

St. Martin's Press, Inc., 175 Fifth Avenue, New York, New York 10010 (800) 221-7945; *The Statesman's Year-Book.*

Statistical Office of the United Nations, Publishing Service, New York, New York 10017 (800) 253-9646; *National Accounts Statistics.*

The World Bank, 1818 H Street, NW, Washington, D.C. 20433 (202) 477-1234; *World Development Report;* and *World Development Indicators.*

UNITED ARAB EMIRATES - GRAIN PRODUCTION - See UNITED ARAB EMIRATES - CROPS

UNITED ARAB EMIRATES - GRANTS

International Monetary Fund, 700 Nineteenth Street, NW, Washington, D.C. 20431 (202) 623-7000; *Government Finance Statistics Yearbook.*

UNITED ARAB EMIRATES - GROSS DOMESTIC PRODUCT

Economic Commission for Western Asia, Post Office Box 27, Baghdad, Iraq; *Statistical Abstract of Western Asia.*

Economist Intelligence Unit, 111 West 57th Street, New York, New York 10019 (800) 938-4685; *United Arab Emirates Country Report.*

Euromonitor International, Inc., 122 South Michigan Avenue, Suite 1200, Chicago, Illinois 60603 (800) 577-EURO; *International Marketing Data and Statistics;* and *The World Economic Factbook.*

Europa Publications Limited, 18 Bedford Square, London, WC1B 3JN, England; *The Europa World Year Book.*

M.E. Sharpe, 80 Business Park Drive, Armonk, New York 10504 (800) 541-6563; *The Illustrated Book of World Rankings.*

Statistical Office of the United Nations, Publishing Service, New York, New York 10017 (800) 253-9646; *Bulletin of Industrial*

Statistics for the Arab Countries; Human Development Report; and *National Accounts Statistics.*

The World Bank, 1818 H Street, NW, Washington, D.C. 20433 (202) 477-1234; *World Development Report;* and *World Development Indicators.*

UNITED ARAB EMIRATES - GROSS NATIONAL PRODUCT

Euromonitor International, Inc., 122 South Michigan Avenue, Suite 1200, Chicago, Illinois 60603 (800) 577-EURO; *International Marketing Data and Statistics.*

Europa Publications Limited, 18 Bedford Square, London, WC1B 3JN, England; *The Europa World Year Book.*

Organization of Petroleum Exporting Countries, Obere Donaustrasse 93, 1020 Vienna 2, Austria; *OPEC Annual Statistical Bulletin.*

St. Martin's Press, Inc., 175 Fifth Avenue, New York, New York 10010 (800) 221-7945; *The Statesman's Year-Book.*

U.S. Arms Control and Disarmament Agency, 320 Twenty-first Street, NW, Washington, D.C. 20451 (202) 647-8677; *World Military Expenditures and Arms Transfers.*

The World Bank, 1818 H Street, NW, Washington, D.C. 20433 (202) 477-1234; *The World Bank Atlas; World Development Report;* and *World Development Indicators.*

UNITED ARAB EMIRATES - HEALTH

Economic Commission for Western Asia, Post Office Box 27, Baghdad, Iraq; *Statistical Abstract of Western Asia.*

Euromonitor International, Inc., 122 South Michigan Avenue, Suite 1200, Chicago, Illinois 60603 (800) 577-EURO; *World Marketing Data and Statistics.*

Federal Statistical Office, Gustav-Stresemann - Ring 11, D-6200, Wiesbaden, Germany; *Vereinigte Arabische Emirate.*

M.E. Sharpe, 80 Business Park Drive, Armonk, New York 10504 (800) 541-6563; *The Illustrated Book of World Rankings.*

St. Martin's Press, Inc., 175 Fifth Avenue, New York, New York 10010 (800) 221-7945; *The Statesman's Year-Book.*

Statistical Office of the United Nations, Publishing Service, New York, New York 10017 (800) 253-9646; *Human Development Report;* and *Statistical Yearbook.*

United Nations Children's Fund

(UNICEF), 3 United Nations Plaza, New York, New York 10017 (800) 253-9646; *State of the World's Children*.

The World Bank, 1818 H Street, NW, Washington, D.C. 20433 (202) 477-1234; *World Development Report*.

UNITED ARAB EMIRATES - HEALTH EXPENDITURES

International Monetary Fund, 700 Nineteenth Street, NW, Washington, D.C. 20431 (202) 623-7000; *Government Finance Statistics Yearbook*.

UNITED ARAB EMIRATES - HIDE PRODUCTION

Food and Agricultural Organization of the United Nations (FAO), Via delle Terme di Caracalla, 00100 Rome, Italy (Telephone Number in U.S. (202) 653-2400); *Production Yearbook*.

UNITED ARAB EMIRATES - HIGHWAYS

Central Intelligence Agency, Washington, D.C. 20505 (703) 482-1100, www.cia.gov; *The World Factbook*.

Economic Commission for Western Asia, Post Office Box 27, Baghdad, Iraq; *Statistical Abstract of Western Asia*.

St. Martin's Press, Inc., 175 Fifth Avenue, New York, New York 10010 (800) 221-7945; *The Statesman's Year-Book*.

UNITED ARAB EMIRATES - HORSES - See UNITED ARAB EMIRATES - LIVESTOCK AND POULTRY

UNITED ARAB EMIRATES - HOURS OF WORK - See UNITED ARAB EMIRATES - EMPLOYMENT

UNITED ARAB EMIRATES - HOUSING AND HOUSING UNITS

Euromonitor International, Inc., 122 South Michigan Avenue, Suite 1200, Chicago, Illinois 60603 (800) 577-EURO; *World Marketing Data and Statistics*.

M.E. Sharpe, 80 Business Park Drive, Armonk, New York 10504 (800) 541-6563; *The Illustrated Book of World Rankings*.

UNITED ARAB EMIRATES - HOUSING EXPENDITURES

International Monetary Fund, 700 Nineteenth Street, NW, Washington, D.C. 20431 (202) 623-7000; *Government Finance Statistics Yearbook*.

UNITED ARAB EMIRATES - ILLITERATE POPULATION

Central Intelligence Agency,

Washington, D.C. 20505 (703) 482-1100, www.cia.gov; *The World Factbook*.

The Economist Intelligence Unit, 111 West 57th Street, New York, New York 10019 (800) 938-4685; *The World Market Atlas*.

Euromonitor International, Inc., 122 South Michigan Avenue, Suite 1200, Chicago, Illinois 60603 (800) 577-EURO; *The World Economic Factbook*.

St. Martin's Press, Inc., 175 Fifth Avenue, New York, New York 10010 (800) 221-7945; *The Statesman's Year-Book*.

Statistical Office of the United Nations, Publishing Service, New York, New York 10017 (800) 253-9646; *Human Development Report*.

United Nations Educational, Scientific and Cultural Organization (UNESCO), 7 Place de Fontenoy, F-75700 Paris, France (Telephone Number in U.S. (212) 963-5981); *Statistical Yearbook*.

UNITED ARAB EMIRATES - IMPORTS

Central Intelligence Agency, Washington, D.C. 20505 (703) 482-1100, www.cia.gov; *The World Factbook*.

Economic Commission for Western Asia, Post Office Box 27, Baghdad, Iraq; *Statistical Abstract of Western Asia*.

The Economist Intelligence Unit, 111 West 57th Street, New York, New York 10019 (800) 938-4685; *United Arab Emirates Country Report*; and *The World Market Atlas*.

Euromonitor International, Inc., 122 South Michigan Avenue, Suite 1200, Chicago, Illinois 60603 (800) 577-EURO; *International Marketing Data and Statistics*; and *The World Economic Factbook*.

Europa Publications Limited, 18 Bedford Square, London, WC1B 3JN, England; *The Europa World Year Book*.

Food and Agricultural Organization of the United Nations (FAO) Via delle Terme di Caracalla, 00100 Rome, Italy (Telephone Number in U.S. (202) 653-2400); *The State of Food and Agriculture*.

International Monetary Fund, 700 Nineteenth Street, NW, Washington, D.C. 20431 (202) 623-7000; *Direction of Trade Statistics*; and *International Financial Statistics*.

St. Martin's Press, Inc., 175 Fifth Avenue, New York, New York 10010 (800) 221-7945; *The Statesman's Year-Book*.

Statistical Office of the United Nations,

Publishing Service, New York, New York 10017 (800) 253-9646; *Bulletin of Industrial Statistics for the Arab Countries*.

The World Bank, 1818 H Street, NW, Washington, D.C. 20433 (202) 477-1234; *World Development Report*; and *World Development Indicators*.

UNITED ARAB EMIRATES - INCOME TAXES - See UNITED ARAB EMIRATES - TAXATION

UNITED ARAB EMIRATES - INDUSTRY

Central Intelligence Agency, Washington, D.C. 20505 (703) 482-1100, www.cia.gov; *The World Factbook*.

Economist Intelligence Unit, 111 West 57th Street, New York, New York 10019 (800) 938-4685; *United Arab Emirates Country Report*.

Euromonitor International, Inc., 122 South Michigan Avenue, Suite 1200, Chicago, Illinois 60603 (800) 577-EURO; *International Marketing Data and Statistics*; *World Marketing Data and Statistics*; and *The World Economic Factbook*.

Europa Publications Limited, 18 Bedford Square, London, WC1B 3JN, England; *The Europa World Year Book*.

Federal Statistical Office, Gustav-Stresemann - Ring 11, D-6200, Wiesbaden, Germany; *Vereinigte Arabische Emirate*.

International Labour Office, I.L.O. Publications, 1828 L Street, NW, Suite 801, Washington, D.C. 20036 (301) 638-3152; *Yearbook of Labour Statistics*.

M.E. Sharpe, 80 Business Park Drive, Armonk, New York 10504 (800) 541-6563; *The Illustrated Book of World Rankings*.

St. Martin's Press, Inc., 175 Fifth Avenue, New York, New York 10010 (800) 221-7945; *The Statesman's Year-Book*.

Statistical Office of the United Nations, Publishing Service, New York, New York 10017 (800) 253-9646; *Bulletin of Industrial Statistics for the Arab Countries*.

The World Bank, 1818 H Street, NW, Washington, D.C. 20433 (202) 477-1234; *World Development Indicators*.

UNITED ARAB EMIRATES - INFANT AND MATERNAL MORTALITY - See UNITED ARAB EMIRATES - MORTALITY

UNITED ARAB EMIRATES - INTERNATIONAL LIQUIDITY

International Monetary Fund, 700 Nineteenth Street, NW, Washington, D.C. 20431 (202) 623-7000; *International*

Financial Statistics.

UNITED ARAB EMIRATES - INTERNATIONAL RESERVES EXCLUDING GOLD

Statistical Office of the United Nations, Publishing Service, New York, New York 10017 (800) 253-9646; *Statistical Yearbook.*

The World Bank, 1818 H Street, NW, Washington, D.C. 20433 (202) 477-1234; *World Development Indicators.*

UNITED ARAB EMIRATES - IRON ORE PRODUCTION AND CONSUMPTION - See UNITED ARAB EMIRATES - MINING AND MINERAL PRODUCTS

UNITED ARAB EMIRATES - IRRIGATION

Euromonitor International, Inc., 122 South Michigan Avenue, Suite 1200, Chicago, Illinois 60603 (800) 577-EURO; *International Marketing Data and Statistics.*

UNITED ARAB EMIRATES - LABOR

Central Intelligence Agency, Washington, D.C. 20505 (703) 482-1100, www.cia.gov; *The World Factbook.*

Economic Commission for Western Asia, Post Office Box 27, Baghdad, Iraq; *Statistical Abstract of Western Asia.*

Euromonitor International, Inc., 122 South Michigan Avenue, Suite 1200, Chicago, Illinois 60603 (800) 577-EURO; *International Marketing Data and Statistics;* and *World Marketing Data and Statistics.*

Europa Publications Limited, 18 Bedford Square, London, WC1B 3JN, England; *The Europa World Year Book.*

Food and Agricultural Organization of the United Nations (FAO) Via delle Terme di Caracalla, 00100 Rome, Italy (Telephone Number in U.S. (202) 653-2400); *The State of Food and Agriculture.*

International Labour Office, I.L.O. Publications, 1828 L Street, NW, Suite 801, Washington, D.C. 20036 (301) 638-3152; *Yearbook of Labour Statistics.*

M.E. Sharpe, 80 Business Park Drive, Armonk, New York 10504 (800) 541-6563; *The Illustrated Book of World Rankings.*

St. Martin's Press, Inc., 175 Fifth Avenue, New York, New York 10010 (800) 221-7945; *The Statesman's Year-Book.*

Statistical Office of the United Nations, Publishing Service, New York, New York 10017 (800) 253-9646; *Human Development Report.*

The World Bank, 1818 H Street, NW,

Washington, D.C. 20433 (202) 477-1234; *The World Bank Atlas; World Development Report;* and *World Development Indicators.*

UNITED ARAB EMIRATES - LAND USE

Central Intelligence Agency, Washington, D.C. 20505 (703) 482-1100, www.cia.gov; *The World Factbook.*

Economic Commission for Western Asia, Post Office Box 27, Baghdad, Iraq; *Statistical Abstract of Western Asia.*

Euromonitor International, Inc., 122 South Michigan Avenue, Suite 1200, Chicago, Illinois 60603 (800) 577-EURO; *International Marketing Data and Statistics.*

Food and Agricultural Organization of the United Nations (FAO), Via delle Terme di Caracalla, 00100 Rome, Italy (Telephone Number in U.S. (202) 653-2400); *Production Yearbook.*

The World Bank, 1818 H Street, NW, Washington, D.C. 20433 (202) 477-1234; *World Development Report.*

UNITED ARAB EMIRATES - LIBRARIES

M.E. Sharpe, 80 Business Park Drive, Armonk, New York 10504 (800) 541-6563; *The Illustrated Book of World Rankings.*

United Nations Educational, Scientific and Cultural Organization (UNESCO), 7 Place de Fontenoy, F-75700 Paris, France (Telephone Number in U.S. (212) 963-5981); *Statistical Yearbook.*

UNITED ARAB EMIRATES - LIFE EXPECTANCY

Central Intelligence Agency, Washington, D.C. 20505 (703) 482-1100, www.cia.gov; *The World Factbook.*

Euromonitor International, Inc., 122 South Michigan Avenue, Suite 1200, Chicago, Illinois 60603 (800) 577-EURO; *The World Economic Factbook.*

St. Martin's Press, Inc., 175 Fifth Avenue, New York, New York 10010 (800) 221-7945; *The Statesman's Year-Book.*

Statistical Office of the United Nations, Publishing Service, New York, New York 10017 (800) 253-9646; *Human Development Report;* and *World Statistics Pocketbook.*

The World Bank, 1818 H Street, NW, Washington, D.C. 20433 (202) 477-1234; *The World Bank Atlas;* and *World Development Report.*

UNITED ARAB EMIRATES - LITERACY RATE

Euromonitor International, Inc., 122

South Michigan Avenue, Suite 1200, Chicago, Illinois 60603 (800) 577-EURO; *World Marketing Data and Statistics.*

UNITED ARAB EMIRATES - LIVESTOCK AND POULTRY

Economic Commission for Western Asia, Post Office Box 27, Baghdad, Iraq; *Statistical Abstract of Western Asia.*

Europa Publications Limited, 18 Bedford Square, London, WC1B 3JN, England; *The Europa World Year Book.*

Food and Agricultural Organization of the United Nations (FAO), Via delle Terme di Caracalla, 00100 Rome, Italy (Telephone Number in U.S. (202) 653-2400); *Production Yearbook;* and *The State of Food and Agriculture.*

M.E. Sharpe, 80 Business Park Drive, Armonk, New York 10504 (800) 541-6563; *The Illustrated Book of World Rankings.*

St. Martin's Press, Inc., 175 Fifth Avenue, New York, New York 10010 (800) 221-7945; *The Statesman's Year-Book.*

United Nations Conference on Trade and Development, Central Statistical Service, Palais des Nations, Geneva, Switzerland (Telephone in U.S. (800) 253-9646); *UNCTAD Commodity Yearbook.*

UNITED ARAB EMIRATES - LIVING LEVELS - See UNITED ARAB EMIRATES -LIFE EXPECTANCY

UNITED ARAB EMIRATES - MAIL - NUMBER OF ITEMS SENT AND RECEIVED

Statistical Office of the United Nations, Publishing Service, New York, New York 10017 (800) 253-9646; *Statistical Yearbook.*

UNITED ARAB EMIRATES - MANUFACTURING

M.E. Sharpe, 80 Business Park Drive, Armonk, New York 10504 (800) 541-6563; *The Illustrated Book of World Rankings.*

Statistical Office of the United Nations, Publishing Service, New York, New York 10017 (800) 253-9646; *Bulletin of Industrial Statistics for the Arab Countries.*

The World Bank, 1818 H Street, NW, Washington, D.C. 20433 (202) 477-1234; *World Development Indicators.*

UNITED ARAB EMIRATES - MARRIAGE RATES

Europa Publications Limited, 18 Bedford Square, London, WC1B 3JN, England; *The Europa World Year Book.*

M.E. Sharpe, 80 Business Park Drive,

Armonk, New York 10504 (800) 541-6563; *The Illustrated Book of World Rankings.*

Statistical Office of the United Nations, Publishing Service, New York, New York 10017 (800) 253-9646; *Demographic Yearbook.*

UNITED ARAB EMIRATES - MEAT PRODUCTION - See UNITED ARAB EMIRATES - LIVESTOCK AND POULTRY

UNITED ARAB EMIRATES - MERCHANT SHIPPING

Economic Commission for Western Asia, Post Office Box 27, Baghdad, Iraq; *Statistical Abstract of Western Asia.*

Europa Publications Limited, 18 Bedford Square, London, WC1B 3JN, England; *The Europa World Year Book.*

Lloyd's Register of Shipping, 17 Battery Place, New York, New York 10004 (212) 425-8050; *Register of Ships.*

Organization of Petroleum Exporting Countries, Obere Donaustrasse 93, 1020 Vienna 2, Austria; *OPEC Annual Statistical Bulletin.*

St. Martin's Press, Inc., 175 Fifth Avenue, New York, New York 10010 (800) 221-7945; *The Statesman's Year-Book.*

Statistical Office of the United Nations, Publishing Service, New York, New York 10017 (800) 253-9646; *Statistical Yearbook.*

U.S. Department of Transportation, Maritime Administration, 400 Seventh Street, SW, Washington, D.C. 20590 (202) 366-5807, www.marad.dot.gov; *A Statistical Analysis of the World's Merchant Fleets.*

UNITED ARAB EMIRATES - MILITARY

Central Intelligence Agency, Washington, D.C. 20505 (703) 482-1100, www.cia.gov; *The World Factbook.*

Euromonitor International, Inc., 122 South Michigan Avenue, Suite 1200, Chicago, Illinois 60603 (800) 577-EURO; *World Marketing Data and Statistics.*

The International Institute for Strategic Studies, 23 Tavistock Street, London WC2E 7NQ, England 44 171 3797676 ; *The Military Balance.*

International Monetary Fund, 700 Nineteenth Street, NW, Washington, D.C. 20431 (202) 623-7000; *Government Finance Statistics Yearbook.*

St. Martin's Press, Inc., 175 Fifth Avenue, New York, New York 10010 (800) 221-7945; *The Statesman's Year-Book.*

Statistical Office of the United Nations, Publishing Service, New York, New York 10017 (800) 253-9646; *Human Development Report.*

U.S. Arms Control and Disarmament Agency, 320 Twenty-first Street, NW, Washington, D.C. 20451 (202) 647-8677; *World Military Expenditures and Arms Transfers.*

UNITED ARAB EMIRATES - MILK PRODUCTION - See UNITED ARAB EMIRATES - DAIRY PRODUCTS

UNITED ARAB EMIRATES - MINING AND MINERAL PRODUCTS

Economic Commission for Western Asia, Post Office Box 27, Baghdad, Iraq; *Statistical Abstract of Western Asia.*

Europa Publications Limited, 18 Bedford Square, London, WC1B 3JN, England; *The Europa World Year Book.*

M.E. Sharpe, 80 Business Park Drive, Armonk, New York 10504 (800) 541-6563; *The Illustrated Book of World Rankings.*

Organization of Petroleum Exporting Countries, Obere Donaustrasse 93, 1020 Vienna 2, Austria; *OPEC Annual Statistical Bulletin.*

Penn Well Publishing Company, 1421 South Sheridan Road, P.O. Box 1260, Tulsa, Oklahoma 74101 (800) 752-9764; *International Energy Statistics Sourcebook.*

Statistical Office of the United Nations, Publishing Service, New York, New York 10017 (800) 253-9646; *Bulletin of Industrial Statistics for the Arab Countries;* and *Statistical Yearbook.*

United Nations Conference on Trade and Development, Central Statistical Service, Palais des Nations, Geneva, Switzerland (Telephone in U.S. (800) 253-9646); *UNCTAD Commodity Yearbook.*

UNITED ARAB EMIRATES - MONEY EXCHANGE RATES - See UNITED ARAB EMIRATES - EXCHANGE RATES

UNITED ARAB EMIRATES - MONEY RESERVES

Euromonitor International, Inc., 122 South Michigan Avenue, Suite 1200, Chicago, Illinois 60603 (800) 577-EURO; *International Marketing Data and Statistics.*

UNITED ARAB EMIRATES - MONEY SUPPLY

Economic Commission for Western Asia, Post Office Box 27, Baghdad, Iraq; *Statistical Abstract of Western Asia.*

Economist Intelligence Unit, 111 West

57th Street, New York, New York 10019 (800) 938-4685; *United Arab Emirates Country Report.*

Euromonitor International, Inc., 122 South Michigan Avenue, Suite 1200, Chicago, Illinois 60603 (800) 577-EURO; *International Marketing Data and Statistics.*

Europa Publications Limited, 18 Bedford Square, London, WC1B 3JN, England; *The Europa World Year Book.*

Federal Statistical Office, Gustav-Stresemann - Ring 11, D-6200, Wiesbaden, Germany; *Vereinigte Arabische Emirate.*

Statistical Office of the United Nations, Publishing Service, New York, New York 10017 (800) 253-9646; *Statistical Yearbook.*

The World Bank, 1818 H Street, NW, Washington, D.C. 20433 (202) 477-1234; *World Development Indicators.*

UNITED ARAB EMIRATES - MORTALITY

Central Intelligence Agency, Washington, D.C. 20505 (703) 482-1100, www.cia.gov; *The World Factbook.*

Euromonitor International, Inc., 122 South Michigan Avenue, Suite 1200, Chicago, Illinois 60603 (800) 577-EURO; *International Marketing Data and Statistics;* and *The World Economic Factbook.*

Europa Publications Limited, 18 Bedford Square, London, WC1B 3JN, England; *The Europa World Year Book.*

St. Martin's Press, Inc., 175 Fifth Avenue, New York, New York 10010 (800) 221-7945; *The Statesman's Year-Book.*

Statistical Office of the United Nations, Publishing Service, New York, New York 10017 (800) 253-9646; *Demographic Yearbook; Human Development Report; Statistical Yearbook;* and *World Statistics Pocketbook.*

United Nations Children's Fund (UNICEF), 3 United Nations Plaza, New York, New York 10017 (800) 253-9646; *State of the World's Children.*

The World Bank, 1818 H Street, NW, Washington, D.C. 20433 (202) 477-1234; *The World Bank Atlas;* and *World Development Report.*

UNITED ARAB EMIRATES - MOTION PICTURES

Statistical Office of the United Nations, Publishing Service, New York, New York 10017 (800) 253-9646; *Statistical Yearbook.*

UNITED ARAB EMIRATES - MOTOR VEHICLES

Economic Commission for Western Asia, Post Office Box 27, Baghdad, Iraq; *Statistical Abstract of Western Asia.*

UNITED ARAB EMIRATES - MUSEUMS

M.E. Sharpe, 80 Business Park Drive, Armonk, New York 10504 (800) 541-6563; *The Illustrated Book of World Rankings.*

United Nations Educational, Scientific and Cultural Organization (UNESCO), 7 Place de Fontenoy, F-75700 Paris, France (Telephone Number in U.S. (212) 963-5981); *Statistical Yearbook.*

UNITED ARAB EMIRATES - NATALITY

Statistical Office of the United Nations, Publishing Service, New York, New York 10017 (800) 253-9646; *Demographic Yearbook.*

UNITED ARAB EMIRATES - NATIONAL ACCOUNTS

Economic Commission for Western Asia, Post Office Box 27, Baghdad, Iraq; *Statistical Abstract of Western Asia.*

Europa Publications Limited, 18 Bedford Square, London, WC1B 3JN, England; *The Europa World Year Book.*

Federal Statistical Office, Gustav-Stresemann - Ring 11, D-6200, Wiesbaden, Germany; *Vereinigte Arabische Emirate.*

Statistical Office of the United Nations, Publishing Service, New York, New York 10017 (800) 253-9646; *National Accounts Statistics.*

UNITED ARAB EMIRATES - NATIONAL INCOME

M.E. Sharpe, 80 Business Park Drive, Armonk, New York 10504 (800) 541-6563; *The Illustrated Book of World Rankings.*

Statistical Office of the United Nations, Publishing Service, New York, New York 10017 (800) 253-9646; *National Accounts Statistics.*

UNITED ARAB EMIRATES - NATIONAL PRODUCT

M.E. Sharpe, 80 Business Park Drive, Armonk, New York 10504 (800) 541-6563; *The Illustrated Book of World Rankings.*

UNITED ARAB EMIRATES - NATURAL GAS PRODUCTION - See UNITED ARAB EMIRATES - MINING AND MINERAL PRODUCTS

UNITED ARAB EMIRATES - NEWSPAPER PRODUCTION - See UNITED ARAB EMIRATES - FORESTRY AND FOREST PRODUCTS

UNITED ARAB EMIRATES - OCCUPATIONS - See UNITED ARAB EMIRATES - LABOR

UNITED ARAB EMIRATES - PEANUT PRODUCTION - See UNITED ARAB EMIRATES - CROPS

UNITED ARAB EMIRATES - PERIODICALS

United Nations Educational, Scientific and Cultural Organization (UNESCO), 7 Place de Fontenoy, F-75700 Paris, France (Telephone Number in U.S. (212) 963-5981); *Statistical Yearbook.*

UNITED ARAB EMIRATES - PESTICIDE USE

Food and Agricultural Organization of the United Nations (FAO) Via delle Terme di Caracalla, 00100 Rome, Italy (Telephone Number in U.S. (202) 653-2400); *The State of Food and Agriculture.*

UNITED ARAB EMIRATES - PETROLEUM INDUSTRY

Food and Agricultural Organization of the United Nations (FAO) Via delle Terme di Caracalla, 00100 Rome, Italy (Telephone Number in U.S. (202) 653-2400); *The State of Food and Agriculture.*

M.E. Sharpe, 80 Business Park Drive, Armonk, New York 10504 (800) 541-6563; *The Illustrated Book of World Rankings.*

Organization of Petroleum Exporting Countries, Obere Donaustrasse 93, 1020 Vienna 2, Austria; *OPEC Annual Statistical Bulletin.*

Penn Well Publishing Company, 1421 South Sheridan Road, P.O. Box 1260, Tulsa, Oklahoma 74101 (800) 752-9764; *International Energy Statistics Sourcebook.*

St. Martin's Press, Inc., 175 Fifth Avenue, New York, New York 10010 (800) 221-7945; *The Statesman's Year-Book.*

Statistical Office of the United Nations, Publishing Service, New York, New York 10017 (800) 253-9646; *Statistical Yearbook.*

United Nations Conference on Trade and Development, Central Statistical Service, Palais des Nations, Geneva, Switzerland (Telephone in U.S. (800) 253-9646); *UNCTAD Commodity Yearbook.*

UNITED ARAB EMIRATES - PIGS - See UNITED ARAB EMIRATES - LIVESTOCK AND POULTRY

UNITED ARAB EMIRATES - PIPELINES FOR OIL AND PETROLEUM PRODUCTS

Organization of Petroleum Exporting Countries, Obere Donaustrasse 93, 1020 Vienna 2, Austria; *OPEC Annual Statistical Bulletin.*

UNITED ARAB EMIRATES - POPULATION

Central Intelligence Agency, Washington, D.C. 20505 (703) 482-1100, www.cia.gov; *The World Factbook.*

Economic Commission for Western Asia, Post Office Box 27, Baghdad, Iraq; *Statistical Abstract of Western Asia.*

The Economist Intelligence Unit, 111 West 57th Street, New York, New York 10019 (800) 938-4685; *United Arab Emirates Country Report;* and *The World Market Atlas.*

Euromonitor International, Inc., 122 South Michigan Avenue, Suite 1200, Chicago, Illinois 60603 (800) 577-EURO; *International Marketing Data and Statistics;* and *The World Economic Factbook.*

Europa Publications Limited, 18 Bedford Square, London, WC1B 3JN, England; *The Europa World Year Book.*

Federal Statistical Office, Gustav-Stresemann - Ring 11, D-6200, Wiesbaden, Germany; *Vereinigte Arabische Emirate.*

Food and Agricultural Organization of the United Nations (FAO), Via delle Terme di Caracalla, 00100 Rome, Italy (Telephone Number in U.S. (202) 653-2400); *Production Yearbook.*

International Labour Office, I.L.O. Publications, 1828 L Street, NW, Suite 801, Washington, D.C. 20036 (301) 638-3152; *Yearbook of Labour Statistics.*

M.E. Sharpe, 80 Business Park Drive, Armonk, New York 10504 (800) 541-6563; *The Illustrated Book of World Rankings.*

St. Martin's Press, Inc., 175 Fifth Avenue, New York, New York 10010 (800) 221-7945; *The Statesman's Year-Book.*

Statistical Office of the United Nations, Publishing Service, New York, New York 10017 (800) 253-9646; *Demographic Yearbook; Human Development Report; Statistical Yearbook;* and *World Statistics Pocketbook.*

U.S. Arms Control and Disarmament Agency, 320 Twenty-first Street, NW, Washington, D.C. 20451 (202) 647-8677; *World Military Expenditures and Arms Transfers.*

Statistical Office of the United Nations, Publishing Service, New York, New York 10017 (800) 253-9646; *Human Development Report.*

The World Bank, 1818 H Street, NW, Washington, D.C. 20433 (202) 477-1234; *The World Bank Atlas.*

World Health Organization, Office of Publications, 20 Avenue Appia, CH-1211 Geneva 27, Switzerland (Telephone Number in U.S. (518) 436-9686); *World Health Statistics Annual.*

UNITED ARAB EMIRATES - POST OFFICES

M.E. Sharpe, 80 Business Park Drive, Armonk, New York 10504 (800) 541-6563; *The Illustrated Book of World Rankings.*

St. Martin's Press, Inc., 175 Fifth Avenue, New York, New York 10010 (800) 221-7945; *The Statesman's Year-Book.*

UNITED ARAB EMIRATES - POTATO PRODUCTION - See UNITED ARAB EMIRATES - CROPS

UNITED ARAB EMIRATES - PRICES

Economic Commission for Western Asia, Post Office Box 27, Baghdad, Iraq; *Statistical Abstract of Western Asia.*

Federal Statistical Office, Gustav-Stresemann - Ring 11, D-6200, Wiesbaden, Germany; *Vereinigte Arabische Emirate.*

Food and Agricultural Organization of the United Nations (FAO), Via delle Terme di Caracalla, 00100 Rome, Italy (Telephone Number in U.S. (202) 653- 2400); *Production Yearbook*; and *The State of Food and Agriculture.*

International Labour Office, I.L.O. Publications, 1828 L Street, NW, Suite 801, Washington, D.C. 20036 (301) 638-3152; *Yearbook of Labour Statistics.*

UNITED ARAB EMIRATES - PRODUCTION

M.E. Sharpe, 80 Business Park Drive, Armonk, New York 10504 (800) 541-6563; *The Illustrated Book of World Rankings.*

UNITED ARAB EMIRATES - PRODUCTIVITY

Euromonitor International, Inc., 122 South Michigan Avenue, Suite 1200, Chicago, Illinois 60603 (800) 577-EURO; *International Marketing Data and Statistics.*

UNITED ARAB EMIRATES - PUBLIC FINANCE - See UNITED ARAB EMIRATES - FINANCE

UNITED ARAB EMIRATES - RADIO BROADCASTING - See UNITED ARAB EMIRATES - BROADCASTING

UNITED ARAB EMIRATES - RADIO RECEIVERS

St. Martin's Press, Inc., 175 Fifth Avenue, New York, New York 10010 (800) 221-7945; *The Statesman's Year-Book.*

UNITED ARAB EMIRATES - RELIGION

M.E. Sharpe, 80 Business Park Drive, Armonk, New York 10504 (800) 541-6563; *The Illustrated Book of World Rankings.*

St. Martin's Press, Inc., 175 Fifth Avenue, New York, New York 10010 (800) 221-7945; *The Statesman's Year-Book.*

UNITED ARAB EMIRATES - RETAIL TRADE

Euromonitor International, Inc., 122 South Michigan Avenue, Suite 1200, Chicago, Illinois 60603 (800) 577-EURO; *World Marketing Data and Statistics.*

UNITED ARAB EMIRATES - RICE PRODUCTION - See UNITED ARAB EMIRATES - CROPS

UNITED ARAB EMIRATES - RUBBER PRODUCTION AND CONSUMPTION

M.E. Sharpe, 80 Business Park Drive, Armonk, New York 10504 (800) 541-6563; *The Illustrated Book of World Rankings.*

UNITED ARAB EMIRATES - SENIOR CITIZENS

M.E. Sharpe, 80 Business Park Drive, Armonk, New York 10504 (800) 541-6563; *The Illustrated Book of World Rankings.*

UNITED ARAB EMIRATES - SHEEP - See UNITED ARAB EMIRATES - LIVESTOCK AND POULTRY

UNITED ARAB EMIRATES - SILVER PRODUCTION AND CONSUMPTION - See UNITED ARAB EMIRATES - MINING AND MINERAL PRODUCTS

UNITED ARAB EMIRATES - SOCIAL DATA

M.E. Sharpe, 80 Business Park Drive, Armonk, New York 10504 (800) 541-6563; *The Illustrated Book of World Rankings.*

Statistical Office of the United Nations, Publishing Service, New York, New York 10017 (800) 253-9646; *World Statistics Pocketbook.*

UNITED ARAB EMIRATES - SOCIAL SECURITY

International Monetary Fund, 700 Nineteenth Street, NW, Washington, D.C. 20431 (202) 623-7000; *Government Finance Statistics Yearbook.*

Statistical Office of the United Nations, Publishing Service, New York, New York 10017 (800) 253-9646; *National Accounts Statistics.*

UNITED ARAB EMIRATES - STATE BUDGET REVENUE AND EXPENDITURES

Euromonitor International, Inc., 122 South Michigan Avenue, Suite 1200, Chicago, Illinois 60603 (800) 577-EURO; *International Marketing Data and Statistics.*

UNITED ARAB EMIRATES - STEEL PRODUCTION - See UNITED ARAB EMIRATES - MINING AND MINERAL PRODUCTS

UNITED ARAB EMIRATES - STOCKS - COMMODITY - MARKET PRICE - INDEX

Food and Agricultural Organization of the United Nations (FAO) Via delle Terme di Caracalla, 00100 Rome, Italy (Telephone Number in U.S. (202) 653-2400); *The State of Food and Agriculture.*

UNITED ARAB EMIRATES - SUGAR PRODUCTION AND CONSUMPTION - See UNITED ARAB EMIRATES - CROPS

UNITED ARAB EMIRATES - TAXATION

Europa Publications Limited, 18 Bedford Square, London, WC1B 3JN, England; *The Europa World Year Book.*

International Monetary Fund, 700 Nineteenth Street, NW, Washington, D.C. 20431 (202) 623-7000; *Government Finance Statistics Yearbook.*

The World Bank, 1818 H Street, NW, Washington, D.C. 20433 (202) 477-1234; *World Development Indicators.*

UNITED ARAB EMIRATES - TELEPHONES IN USE

American Telephone and Telegraph Company, 26 Parsippany Road, Whippany, New Jersey 07981 (800) 222-0300; *The World's Telephones.*

Europa Publications Limited, 18 Bedford Square, London, WC1B 3JN, England; *The Europa World Year Book.*

St. Martin's Press, Inc., 175 Fifth Avenue, New York, New York 10010 (800) 221-7945; *The Statesman's Year-Book.*

Statistical Office of the United Nations, Publishing Service, New York, New York 10017 (800) 253-9646; *Statistical Yearbook;* and *World Statistics Pocketbook.*

UNITED ARAB EMIRATES - TELEVISION BROADCASTING - See UNITED ARAB EMIRATES - BROADCASTING

UNITED ARAB EMIRATES - TEXTILE INDUSTRY

M.E. Sharpe, 80 Business Park Drive, Armonk, New York 10504 (800) 541-6563;

The Illustrated Book of World Rankings.

St. Martin's Press, Inc., 175 Fifth Avenue, New York, New York 10010 (800) 221-7945; *The Statesman's Year-Book.*

United Nations Conference on Trade and Development, Central Statistical Service, Palais des Nations, Geneva, Switzerland (Telephone in U.S. (800) 253-9646); *UNCTAD Commodity Yearbook.*

UNITED ARAB EMIRATES - THEATRE

United Nations Educational, Scientific and Cultural Organization (UNESCO), 7 Place de Fontenoy, F-75700 Paris, France (Telephone Number in U.S. (212) 963-5981); *Statistical Yearbook.*

UNITED ARAB EMIRATES - TOBACCO PRODUCTION

M.E. Sharpe, 80 Business Park Drive, Armonk, New York 10504 (800) 541-6563; *The Illustrated Book of World Rankings.*

UNITED ARAB EMIRATES - TOURISM

Economic Commission for Western Asia, Post Office Box 27, Baghdad, Iraq; *Statistical Abstract of Western Asia.*

Euromonitor International, Inc., 122 South Michigan Avenue, Suite 1200, Chicago, Illinois 60603 (800) 577-EURO; *The World Economic Factbook;* and *World Marketing Data and Statistics.*

St. Martin's Press, Inc., 175 Fifth Avenue, New York, New York 10010 (800) 221-7945; *The Statesman's Year-Book.*

UNITED ARAB EMIRATES - TRADE - See UNITED ARAB EMIRATES - FOREIGN TRADE

UNITED ARAB EMIRATES - TRANSPORTATION AND COMMUNICATIONS

Economic Commission for Western Asia, Post Office Box 27, Baghdad, Iraq; *Statistical Abstract of Western Asia.*

Euromonitor International, Inc., 122 South Michigan Avenue, Suite 1200, Chicago, Illinois 60603 (800) 577-EURO; *International Marketing Data and Statistics;* and *World Marketing Data and Statistics.*

Europa Publications Limited, 18 Bedford Square, London, WC1B 3JN, England; *The Europa World Year Book.*

M.E. Sharpe, 80 Business Park Drive, Armonk, New York 10504 (800) 541-6563; *The Illustrated Book of World Rankings.*

St. Martin's Press, Inc., 175 Fifth Avenue, New York, New York 10010 (800)

221-7945; *The Statesman's Year-Book.*

Statistical Office of the United Nations, Publishing Service, New York, New York 10017 (800) 253-9646; *Human Development Report.*

UNITED ARAB EMIRATES - UNEMPLOYMENT

Euromonitor International, Inc., 122 South Michigan Avenue, Suite 1200, Chicago, Illinois 60603 (800) 577-EURO; *International Marketing Data and Statistics.*

International Labour Office, I.L.O. Publications, 1828 L Street, NW, Suite 801, Washington, D.C. 20036 (301) 638-3152; *Yearbook of Labour Statistics.*

UNITED ARAB EMIRATES - VITAL STATISTICS

Euromonitor International, Inc., 122 South Michigan Avenue, Suite 1200, Chicago, Illinois 60603 (800) 577-EURO; *International Marketing Data and Statistics.*

St. Martin's Press, Inc., 175 Fifth Avenue, New York, New York 10010 (800) 221-7945; *The Statesman's Year-Book.*

World Health Organization, Office of Publications, 20 Avenue Appia, CH-1211 Geneva 27, Switzerland (Telephone Number in U.S. (518) 436-9686); *World Health Statistics Annual.*

UNITED ARAB EMIRATES - WAGES

International Labour Office, I.L.O. Publications, 1828 L Street, NW, Suite 801, Washington, D.C. 20036 (301) 638-3152; *Yearbook of Labour Statistics.*

UNITED ARAB EMIRATES - WEATHER - See UNITED ARAB EMIRATES - CLIMATE

UNITED ARAB EMIRATES - WELFARE

International Monetary Fund, 700 Nineteenth Street, NW, Washington, D.C. 20431 (202) 623-7000; *Government Finance Statistics Yearbook.*

UNITED ARAB EMIRATES - WHEAT PRODUCTION AND PRICES - See UNITED ARAB EMIRATES - CROPS

UNITED ARAB EMIRATES - WINE PRODUCTION - See UNITED ARAB EMIRATES - BEVERAGES

UNITED ARAB EMIRATES - WOOL PRODUCTION - See UNITED ARAB EMIRATES - TEXTILE INDUSTRY

UNITED ARAB EMIRATES - ZOOS AND BOTANICAL GARDENS

United Nations Educational, Scientific and Cultural Organization (UNESCO), 7 Place de Fontenoy, F-75700 Paris, France (Telephone Number in U.S. (212) 963-5981); *Statistical Yearbook.*

United Kingdom - National Statistical Offices

Business Statistics Office, Government Buildings, Cardiff Road, Newport, Gwent NP9 1XC, England.

Central Statistical Office, Great George Street, London SW1P 3AQ, England.

Office of Population Censuses and Surveys, Head Office, Saint Catherine's House, 10 Kingsway, London WC2B 6JP, England.

United Kingdom - Primary Statistics Sources

HM Stationery Office, Post Office Box 276, London SW8 5DT, England; *Annual Abstract of Statistics;* and *Monthly Digest of Statistics.*

United Kingdom - Databases

CSO Macro-Economic Data Bank, Great Britain Central Statistical Office, Room 52/4, Great George Street, London SW1P 3AQ, England. Subject coverage: United Kingdom economics and demographics.

Financial Statistics Division, Bank of England, Threadneedle Street, London EC2R 8AH, England. Subject coverage: Data of United Kingdom financial indicator statistics.

National Online Manpower Information System (NOMIS), University of Durham, Mountjoy Research Centre, Unit 3P, Durham DH1 35W, England. Subject coverage: Employment and census data for the United Kingdom.

Town Focus, Property Intelligence Plc., Ingram House, 13-15 John Adam Street, London WC2N 6LD, England. Subject coverage: Demographic and socioeconomic statistics on urban areas in the United Kingdom.

UNITED KINGDOM - ABORTIONS

European Commission Office of Press and Public Affairs Information Service, 2100 M Street, NW, Washington, D.C. 20037 (202) 862-9500; *Demographic Statistics.*

Statistical Office of the United Nations, Publishing Service, New York, New York 10017 (800) 253-9646; *Demographic*

Yearbook; and *Trends in Europe and North America: The Statistical Yearbook of the Economic Commission for Europe.*

UNITED KINGDOM - AGRICULTURE

Economist Intelligence Unit, 111 West 57th Street, New York, New York 10019 (800) 938-4685; *United Kingdom Country Report.*

Euromonitor International, Inc., 122 South Michigan Avenue, Suite 1200, Chicago, Illinois 60603 (800) 577-EURO; *World Marketing Data and Statistics.*

Europa Publications Limited, 18 Bedford Square, London, WC1B 3JN, England; *The Europa World Year Book.*

European Commission Office of Press and Public Affairs, 2100 M Street, NW, Washington, D.C. 20037 (202) 862-9500; *Agriculture: Statistical Yearbook; Basic Statistics of the Community; Eurostatistics: Data for Short-Term Economic Analysis; Labor Force Sample Survey;* and *Regions: Statistical Yearbook.*

Food and Agricultural Organization of the United Nations (FAO) Via delle Terme di Caracalla, 00100 Rome, Italy (Telephone Number in U.S. (202) 653-2400); *Production Yearbook;* and *The State of Food and Agriculture.*

M.E. Sharpe, 80 Business Park Drive, Armonk, New York 10504 (800) 541-6563; *The Illustrated Book of World Rankings.*

National Technical Information Service, 5285 Port Royal Road, Springfield, Virginia 22161 (703) 487-4600; *Handbook of Economic Statistics.*

Organisation for Economic Co-operation and Development (OECD), 2 rue Andre-Pascal, 75 Paris 16, France (Telephone Number in U.S. (202) 785-6323); *Economic Accounts for Agriculture; Indicators of Industrial Activity; Industrial Structure Statistics;* and *OECD Economic Surveys: United Kingdom.*

St. Martin's Press, Inc., 175 Fifth Avenue, New York, New York 10010 (800) 221-7945; *The Statesman's Year-Book.*

Statistical Office of the United Nations, Publishing Service, New York, New York 10017 (800) 253-9646; *Statistical Yearbook.*

United Nations Conference on Trade and Development, Central Statistical Service, Palais des Nations, Geneva, Switzerland (Telephone in U.S. (800) 253-9646); *UNCTAD Commodity Yearbook.*

The World Bank, 1818 H Street, NW, Washington, D.C. 20433 (202) 477-1234; *World Development Indicators.*

UNITED KINGDOM - AIRLINE SERVICE

Europa Publications Limited, 18 Bedford Square, London, WC1B 3JN, England; *The Europa World Year Book.*

European Commission Office of Press and Public Affairs, 2100 M Street, NW, Washington, D.C. 20037 (202) 862-9500; *Basic Statistics of the Community; Regions: Statistical Yearbook;* and *Transport Annual Statistics.*

International Civil Aviation Organization, 999 University Street, Montreal, Quebec, Canada H3C 5H7 (514) 954-8219; *Civil Aviation Statistics of the World.*

M.E. Sharpe, 80 Business Park Drive, Armonk, New York 10504 (800) 541-6563; *The Illustrated Book of World Rankings.*

National Technical Information Service, 5285 Port Royal Road, Springfield, Virginia 22161 (703) 487-4600; *Handbook of Economic Statistics.*

Organisation for Economic Co-operation and Development (OECD), 2 rue Andre-Pascal, 75 Paris 16, France (Telephone Number in U.S. (202) 785-6323); *Tourism Policy and International Tourism in OECD Member Countries.*

St. Martin's Press, Inc., 175 Fifth Avenue, New York, New York 10010 (800) 221-7945; *The Statesman's Year-Book.*

Statistical Office of the United Nations, Publishing Service, New York, New York 10017 (800) 253-9646; *Statistical Yearbook.*

UNITED KINGDOM - AIRPORTS

Central Intelligence Agency, Washington, D.C. 20505 (703) 482-1100, www.cia.gov; *The World Factbook.*

UNITED KINGDOM - ALMOND PRODUCTION - See UNITED KINGDOM - CROPS

UNITED KINGDOM - ALUMINUM PRODUCTION AND CONSUMPTION - See UNITED KINGDOM - MINING AND MINERAL PRODUCTS

UNITED KINGDOM - ANIMAL FEEDINGSTUFFS

Organisation for Economic Co-operation and Development (OECD), 2 rue Andre-Pascal, 75 Paris 16, France (Telephone Number in U.S. (202) 785-6323); *Foreign Trade by Commodities.*

Statistical Office of the United Nations, Publishing Service, New York, New York 10017 (800) 253-9646; *Statistical Yearbook.*

UNITED KINGDOM - ANIMAL HEALTH

Food and Agricultural Organization of the United Nations (FAO), Via delle Terme di Caracalla, 00100 Rome, Italy (Telephone Number in U.S. (202) 653-2400); *Animal Health Yearbook.*

UNITED KINGDOM - ANTIMONY AND ANTIMONY ORE PRODUCTION AND CONSUMPTION - See UNITED KINGDOM - MINING AND MINERAL PRODUCTS

UNITED KINGDOM - APPLES PRODUCTION - See UNITED KINGDOM - CROPS

UNITED KINGDOM - AREA AND DENSITY OF POPULATION

Central Intelligence Agency, Washington, D.C. 20505 (703) 482-1100, www.cia.gov; *The World Factbook.*

Euromonitor International, Inc., 122 South Michigan Avenue, Suite 1200, Chicago, Illinois 60603 (800) 577-EURO; *The World Economic Factbook.*

Europa Publications Limited, 18 Bedford Square, London, WC1B 3JN, England; *The Europa World Year Book.*

European Commission Office of Press and Public Affairs, 2100 M Street, NW, Washington, D.C. 20037 (202) 862-9500; *Demographic Statistics, Basic Statistics of the Community.*

Food and Agricultural Organization of the United Nations (FAO) Via delle Terme di Caracalla, 00100 Rome, Italy (Telephone Number in U.S. (202) 653-2400); *The State of Food and Agriculture.*

M.E. Sharpe, 80 Business Park Drive, Armonk, New York 10504 (800) 541-6563; *The Illustrated Book of World Rankings.*

National Technical Information Service, 5285 Port Royal Road, Springfield, Virginia 22161 (703) 487-4600; *Handbook of Economic Statistics.*

St. Martin's Press, Inc., 175 Fifth Avenue, New York, New York 10010 (800) 221-7945; *The Statesman's Year-Book.*

Statistical Office of the United Nations, Publishing Service, New York, New York 10017 (800) 253-9646; *Statistical Yearbook;* and *Trends in Europe and North America: The Statistical Yearbook of the Economic Commission for Europe.*

United Nations Educational, Scientific and Cultural Organization (UNESCO), 7 Place de Fontenoy, F-75700 Paris, France (Telephone Number in U.S. (212) 963-5981); *Statistical Yearbook.*

STATISTICS SOURCES, Twenty-sixth Edition - 2003

The World Bank, 1818 H Street, NW, Washington, D.C. 20433 (202) 477-1234; *World Development Report.*

UNITED KINGDOM - ARMS EXPORTS AND IMPORTS - See UNITED KINGDOM - MILITARY

UNITED KINGDOM - ARSENIC PRODUCTION AND CONSUMPTION - See UNITED KINGDOM - MINING AND MINERAL PRODUCTS

UNITED KINGDOM - BALANCE OF PAYMENTS

The Economist Intelligence Unit, 111 West 57th Street, New York, New York 10019 (800) 938-4685; *The World Market Atlas.*

Europa Publications Limited, 18 Bedford Square, London, WC1B 3JN, England; *The Europa World Year Book.*

European Commission Office of Press and Public Affairs, 2100 M Street, NW, Washington, D.C. 20037 (202) 862-9500; *ACP: Basic Statistics; Basic Statistics of the Community; Energy Statistics Yearbook;* and *Eurostatistics: Data for Short-Term Economic Analysis.*

International Monetary Fund, 700 Nineteenth Street, NW, Washington, D.C. 20431 (202) 623-7000; *Balance of Payments Yearbook;* and *International Financial Statistics.*

National Technical Information Service, 5285 Port Royal Road, Springfield, Virginia 22161 (703) 487-4600; *Handbook of Economic Statistics.*

Organisation for Economic Co-operation and Development (OECD), 2 rue Andre-Pascal, 75 Paris 16, France (Telephone Number in U.S. (202) 785-6323); *Economic Outlook; Geographical Distribution of Financial Flows to Developing Countries; Main Economic Indicators - Historical Statistics;* and *OECD Economic Surveys: United Kingdom.*

United Nations Conference on Trade and Development (UNCTAD), New York, New York 10017 (800) 253-9646; *Handbook of International Trade and Development Statistics.*

The World Bank, 1818 H Street, NW, Washington, D.C. 20433 (202) 477-1234; *World Development Report;* and *World Development Indicators.*

UNITED KINGDOM - BANANA PRODUCTION - See UNITED KINGDOM - CROPS

UNITED KINGDOM - BANKING

Euromonitor International, Inc., 122 South Michigan Avenue, Suite 1200, Chicago, Illinois 60603 (800) 577-EURO; *World Marketing Data and Statistics.*

Europa Publications Limited, 18 Bedford Square, London, WC1B 3JN, England; *The Europa World Year Book.*

European Commission Office of Press and Public Affairs, 2100 M Street, NW, Washington, D.C. 20037 (202) 862-9500; *ACP: Basic Statistics* and *Eurostatistics: Data for Short-Term Economic Analysis.*

International Monetary Fund, 700 Nineteenth Street, NW, Washington, D.C. 20431 (202) 623-7000; *Government Finance Statistics Yearbook; International Financial Statistics;* and *International Financial Statistics.*

M.E. Sharpe, 80 Business Park Drive, Armonk, New York 10504 (800) 541-6563; *The Illustrated Book of World Rankings.*

National Technical Information Service, 5285 Port Royal Road, Springfield, Virginia 22161 (703) 487-4600; *Handbook of Economic Statistics.*

Organisation for Economic Co-operation and Development (OECD), 2 rue Andre-Pascal, 75 Paris 16, France (Telephone Number in U.S. (202) 785-6323); *Economic Outlook; Financial Market Trends;* and *OECD Economic Surveys: United Kingdom.*

St. Martin's Press, Inc., 175 Fifth Avenue, New York, New York 10010 (800) 221-7945; *The Statesman's Year-Book.*

Statistical Office of the United Nations, Publishing Service, New York, New York 10017 (800) 253-9646; *Statistical Yearbook.*

UNITED KINGDOM - BARLEY PRODUCTION - See UNITED KINGDOM - CROPS

UNITED KINGDOM - BAUXITE PRODUCTION AND CONSUMPTION - See UNITED KINGDOM - MINING AND MINERAL PRODUCTS

UNITED KINGDOM - BEER PRODUCTION - See UNITED KINGDOM - BEVERAGES

UNITED KINGDOM - BEVERAGES

European Commission Office of Press and Public Affairs, 2100 M Street, NW, Washington, D.C. 20037 (202) 862-9500; *Basic Statistics of the Community.*

M.E. Sharpe, 80 Business Park Drive, Armonk, New York 10504 (800) 541-6563; *The Illustrated Book of World Rankings.*

National Technical Information Service,

5285 Port Royal Road, Springfield, Virginia 22161 (703) 487-4600; *Handbook of Economic Statistics.*

Organisation for Economic Co-operation and Development (OECD), 2 rue Andre-Pascal, 75 Paris 16, France (Telephone Number in U.S. (202) 785-6323); *Indicators of Industrial Activity.*

Statistical Office of the United Nations, Publishing Service, New York, New York 10017 (800) 253-9646; *Statistical Yearbook.*

UNITED KINGDOM - BIRTH RATES

Central Intelligence Agency, Washington, D.C. 20505 (703) 482-1100, www.cia.gov; *The World Factbook.*

Euromonitor International, Inc., 122 South Michigan Avenue, Suite 1200, Chicago, Illinois 60603 (800) 577-EURO; *The World Economic Factbook.*

Europa Publications Limited, 18 Bedford Square, London, WC1B 3JN, England; *The Europa World Year Book.*

European Commission Office of Press and Public Affairs, 2100 M Street, NW, Washington, D.C. 20037 (202) 862-9500; *Basic Statistics of the Community;* and *Demographic Statistics.*

M.E. Sharpe, 80 Business Park Drive, Armonk, New York 10504 (800) 541-6563; *The Illustrated Book of World Rankings.*

St. Martin's Press, Inc., 175 Fifth Avenue, New York, New York 10010 (800) 221-7945; *The Statesman's Year-Book.*

Statistical Office of the United Nations, Publishing Service, New York, New York 10017 (800) 253-9646; *Demographic Yearbook;* and *Statistical Yearbook.*

The World Bank, 1818 H Street, NW, Washington, D.C. 20433 (202) 477-1234; *World Development Indicators.*

World Health Organization, Office of Publications, 20 Avenue Appia, CH-1211 Geneva 27, Switzerland (Telephone Number in U.S. (518) 436-9686); *World Health Statistics Annual.*

UNITED KINGDOM - BISMUTH PRODUCTION AND CONSUMPTION - See UNITED KINGDOM - MINING AND MINERAL PRODUCTS

UNITED KINGDOM - BONDS

European Commission Office of Press and Public Affairs, 2100 M Street, NW, Washington, D.C. 20037 (202) 862-9500; *Basic Statistics of the Community.*

International Monetary Fund, 700 Nineteenth Street, NW, Washington, D.C. 20431 (202) 623-7000; *Government Finance Statistics Yearbook.*

Organisation for Economic Co-operation and Development (OECD), 2 rue Andre-Pascal, 75 Paris 16, France (Telephone Number in U.S. (202) 785-6323); *Financial Market Trends.*

Statistical Office of the United Nations, Publishing Service, New York, New York 10017 (800) 253-9646; *Statistical Yearbook.*

UNITED KINGDOM - BOOK PRODUCTION

Euromonitor International, Inc., 122 South Michigan Avenue, Suite 1200, Chicago, Illinois 60603 (800) 577-EURO; *European Marketing Data and Statistics.*

Europa Publications Limited, 18 Bedford Square, London, WC1B 3JN, England; *The Europa World Year Book.*

Organisation for Economic Co-operation and Development (OECD), 2 rue Andre-Pascal, 75 Paris 16, France (Telephone Number in U.S. (202) 785-6323); *Indicators of Industrial Activity.*

St. Martin's Press, Inc., 175 Fifth Avenue, New York, New York 10010 (800) 221-7945; *The Statesman's Year-Book.*

Statistical Office of the United Nations, Publishing Service, New York, New York 10017 (800) 253-9646; *Trends in Europe and North America: The Statistical Yearbook of the Economic Commission for Europe.*

United Nations Educational, Scientific and Cultural Organization (UNESCO), 7 Place de Fontenoy, F-75700 Paris, France (Telephone Number in U.S. (212) 963-5981); *Statistical Yearbook.*

UNITED KINGDOM - BROADCASTING

Billboard Limited, P.O. Box 9027, 1006 AA Amsterdam, The Netherlands (Telephone Number in U.S. (212) 764-7300); *World Radio TV Handbook.*

Central Intelligence Agency, Washington, D.C. 20505 (703) 482-1100, www.cia.gov; *The World Factbook.*

Euromonitor International, Inc., 122 South Michigan Avenue, Suite 1200, Chicago, Illinois 60603 (800) 577-EURO; *World Marketing Data and Statistics.*

European Commission Office of Press and Public Affairs, 2100 M Street, NW, Washington, D.C. 20037 (202) 862-9500; *Basic Statistics of the Community.*

M.E. Sharpe, 80 Business Park Drive, Armonk, New York 10504 (800) 541-6563;

The Illustrated Book of World Rankings.

St. Martin's Press, Inc., 175 Fifth Avenue, New York, New York 10010 (800) 221-7945; *The Statesman's Year-Book.*

Statistical Office of the United Nations, Publishing Service, New York, New York 10017 (800) 253-9646; *Trends in Europe and North America: The Statistical Yearbook of the Economic Commission for Europe.*

United Nations Educational, Scientific and Cultural Organization (UNESCO), 7 Place de Fontenoy, F-75700 Paris, France (Telephone Number in U.S. (212) 963-5981); *Statistical Yearbook.*

UNITED KINGDOM - BUDGET

Central Intelligence Agency, Washington, D.C. 20505 (703) 482-1100, www.cia.gov; *The World Factbook.*

UNITED KINGDOM - BUSINESS

European Commission Office of Press and Public Affairs, 2100 M Street, NW, Washington, D.C. 20037 (202) 862-9500; *Basic Statistics of the Community.*

Organisation for Economic Co-operation and Development (OECD), 2 rue Andre-Pascal, 75 Paris 16, France (Telephone Number in U.S. (202) 785-6323); *Main Economic Indicators - Historical Statistics.*

UNITED KINGDOM - BUTTER - See UNITED KINGDOM - DAIRY PRODUCTS

UNITED KINGDOM - CABBAGE PRODUCTION - See UNITED KINGDOM - CROPS

UNITED KINGDOM - CADMIUM PRODUCTION AND CONSUMPTION - See UNITED KINGDOM - MINING AND MINERAL PRODUCTS

UNITED KINGDOM - CALORIE SUPPLY

Food and Agricultural Organization of the United Nations (FAO) Via delle Terme di Caracalla, 00100 Rome, Italy (Telephone Number in U.S. (202) 653-2400); *The State of Food and Agriculture.*

UNITED KINGDOM - CAPITAL INVESTMENT

National Technical Information Service, 5285 Port Royal Road, Springfield, Virginia 22161 (703) 487-4600; *Handbook of Economic Statistics.*

Organisation for Economic Co-operation and Development (OECD), 2 rue Andre-Pascal, 75 Paris 16, France (Telephone Number in U.S. (202) 785-6323); *Economic Outlook;* and *Financial Market Trends.*

UNITED KINGDOM - CAPITAL REVENUE

International Monetary Fund, 700 Nineteenth Street, NW, Washington, D.C. 20431 (202) 623-7000; *Government Finance Statistics Yearbook.*

Organisation for Economic Co-operation and Development (OECD), 2 rue Andre-Pascal, 75 Paris 16, France (Telephone Number in U.S. (202) 785-6323); *Economic Outlook;* and *Financial Market Trends.*

UNITED KINGDOM - CASHEW NUT PRODUCTION - See UNITED KINGDOM - CROPS

UNITED KINGDOM - CASTOR BEAN PRODUCTION - See UNITED KINGDOM - CROPS

UNITED KINGDOM - CATTLE - See UNITED KINGDOM - LIVESTOCK AND POULTRY

UNITED KINGDOM - CAULIFLOWER PRODUCTION - See UNITED KINGDOM - CROPS

UNITED KINGDOM - CAUSTIC SODA PRODUCTION - See UNITED KINGDOM - BEVERAGES

UNITED KINGDOM - CEMENT PRODUCTION - See UNITED KINGDOM - MINING AND MINERAL PRODUCTS

UNITED KINGDOM - CEREAL PRODUCTION - See UNITED KINGDOM - CROPS

UNITED KINGDOM - CHEESE - See UNITED KINGDOM - DAIRY PRODUCTS

UNITED KINGDOM - CHEMICAL INDUSTRY

European Commission Office of Press and Public Affairs, 2100 M Street, NW, Washington, D.C. 20037 (202) 862-9500; *Industrial Production: Quarterly Statistics.*

UNITED KINGDOM - CHEMICAL (ORGANIC) PRODUCTION - See UNITED KINGDOM - MINING AND MINERAL PRODUCTS

UNITED KINGDOM - CHESTNUT PRODUCTION - See UNITED KINGDOM - CROPS

UNITED KINGDOM - CHICKENS - See UNITED KINGDOM - LIVESTOCK AND POULTRY

UNITED KINGDOM - CHROMITE PRODUCTION AND CONSUMPTION - See UNITED KINGDOM - MINING AND MINERAL PRODUCTS

UNITED KINGDOM - CHROMIUM ORE PRODUCTION AND CONSUMPTION - See

UNITED KINGDOM - MINING AND MINERAL PRODUCTS

UNITED KINGDOM - CIGAR PRODUCTION - See UNITED KINGDOM - TOBACCO PRODUCTION

UNITED KINGDOM - CIGARETTE PRODUCTION - See UNITED KINGDOM - TOBACCO PRODUCTION

UNITED KINGDOM - CLASS STRUCTURE

European Commission Office of Press and Public Affairs, 2100 M Street, NW, Washington, D.C. 20037 (202) 862-9500; *Basis Statistics of the Community;* and *Labor Force Sample Survey.*

UNITED KINGDOM - CLIMATE

M.E. Sharpe, 80 Business Park Drive, Armonk, New York 10504 (800) 541-6563; *The Illustrated Book of World Rankings.*

St. Martin's Press, Inc., 175 Fifth Avenue, New York, New York 10010 (800) 221-7945; *The Statesman's Year-Book.*

UNITED KINGDOM - CLOTHING - See UNITED KINGDOM - TEXTILE INDUSTRY

UNITED KINGDOM - COAL PRODUCTION - See UNITED KINGDOM - MINING AND MINERAL PRODUCTS

UNITED KINGDOM - COBALT PRODUCTION AND CONSUMPTION - See UNITED KINGDOM - MINING AND MINERAL PRODUCTS

UNITED KINGDOM - COCOA (BEANS) PRODUCTION - See UNITED KINGDOM - CROPS

UNITED KINGDOM - COFFEE - See UNITED KINGDOM - CROPS

UNITED KINGDOM - COKE AND COKE OVEN ORE PRODUCTION AND CONSUMPTION - See UNITED KINGDOM - MINING AND MINERAL PRODUCTS

UNITED KINGDOM - COMMERCE

St. Martin's Press, Inc., 175 Fifth Avenue, New York, New York 10010 (800) 221-7945; *The Statesman's Year-Book.*

UNITED KINGDOM - COMMUNICATIONS - See UNITED KINGDOM - TRANSPORTATION AND COMMUNICATIONS

UNITED KINGDOM - CONSTRUCTION INDUSTRY

European Commission Office of Press and Public Affairs, 2100 M Street, NW, Washington, D.C. 20037 (202) 862-9500; *Basic Statistics of the Community;* and

Labor Force Sample Survey.

M.E. Sharpe, 80 Business Park Drive, Armonk, New York 10504 (800) 541-6563; *The Illustrated Book of World Rankings.*

Organisation for Economic Co-operation and Development (OECD), 2 rue Andre-Pascal, 75 Paris 16, France (Telephone Number in U.S. (202) 785-6323); *Industrial Structure Statistics; The Iron and Steel Industry; Main Economic Indicators - Historical Statistics;* and *OECD Economic Surveys: United Kingdom.*

St. Martin's Press, Inc., 175 Fifth Avenue, New York, New York 10010 (800) 221-7945; *The Statesman's Year-Book.*

Statistical Office of the United Nations, Publishing Service, New York, New York 10017 (800) 253-9646; *Statistical Yearbook.*

UNITED KINGDOM - CONSUMER PRICE INDEX

European Commission Office of Press and Public Affairs, 2100 M Street, NW, Washington, D.C. 20037 (202) 862-9500; *Basic Statistics of the Community;* and *Eurostatistics: Data for Short-Term Economic Analysis.*

National Technical Information Service, 5285 Port Royal Road, Springfield, Virginia 22161 (703) 487-4600; *Handbook of Economic Statistics.*

Organisation for Economic Co-operation and Development (OECD), 2 rue Andre-Pascal, 75 Paris 16, France (Telephone Number in U.S. (202) 785-6323); *Economic Outlook.*

Statistical Office of the United Nations, Publishing Service, New York, New York 10017 (800) 253-9646; *Statistical Yearbook;* and *Trends in Europe and North America: The Statistical Yearbook of the Economic Commission for Europe.*

UNITED KINGDOM - CONSUMER PRICES

Euromonitor International, Inc., 122 South Michigan Avenue, Suite 1200, Chicago, Illinois 60603 (800) 577-EURO; *European Marketing Data and Statistics;* and *World Marketing Data and Statistics.*

European Commission Office of Press and Public Affairs, 2100 M Street, NW, Washington, D.C. 20037 (202) 862-9500; *Basic Statistics of the Community;* and *Money and Finance.*

International Labour Office, I.L.O. Publications, 1828 L Street, NW, Suite 801, Washington, D.C. 20036 (301) 638-3152; *Yearbook of Labour Statistics.*

International Monetary Fund, 700

Nineteenth Street, NW, Washington, D.C. 20431 (202) 623-7000; *International Financial Statistics.*

Organisation for Economic Co-operation and Development (OECD), 2 rue Andre-Pascal, 75 Paris 16, France (Telephone Number in U.S. (202) 785-6323); *Economic Outlook.*

UNITED KINGDOM - CONSUMPTION

European Commission Office of Press and Public Affairs, 2100 M Street, NW, Washington, D.C. 20037 (202) 862-9500; *Basic Statistics of the Community.*

International Iron and Steel Institute, 120, rue Colonel Bourg, B-1140, Belgium; *Steel Statistical Yearbook.*

International Lead and Zinc Study Group, Metro House, 58 St. James's Street, London SW1A 1LD England; *Lead and Zinc Statistics.*

International Rubber Study Group, York House, Eighth Floor, Empire Way, Wembley, London HA9 0PA, England; *Rubber Statistical Bulletin.*

National Technical Information Service, 5285 Port Royal Road, Springfield, Virginia 22161 (703) 487-4600; *Handbook of Economic Statistics.*

Organisation for Economic Co-operation and Development (OECD), 2 rue Andre-Pascal, 75 Paris 16, France (Telephone Number in U.S. (202) 785-6323); *The Footwear, Raw Hides and Skins, and Leather Industry in OECD Countries; The Iron and Steel Industry; Meat Balances in OECD Member Countries; The Non-Ferrous Metals Industry; The Pulp and Paper Industry;* and *Textile Industry in OECD Countries.*

The World Bank, 1818 H Street, NW, Washington, D.C. 20433 (202) 477-1234; *World Development Report.*

UNITED KINGDOM - COPPER AND COPPER ORE PRODUCTION AND CONSUMPTION - See UNITED KINGDOM - MINING AND MINERAL PRODUCTS

UNITED KINGDOM - CORN PRODUCTION - See UNITED KINGDOM - CROPS

UNITED KINGDOM - CORPORATE INCOME TAXES - See UNITED KINGDOM - TAXATION

UNITED KINGDOM - CORPORATE TAXES - See UNITED KINGDOM - TAXATION

UNITED KINGDOM - COTTON - See UNITED KINGDOM - CROPS

UNITED KINGDOM - CRIME

International Criminal Police Organization (INTERPOL), 50 quai Achille Lignon, F-69006 Lyon, France; *International Crime Statistics.*

Statistical Office of the United Nations, Publishing Service, New York, New York 10017 (800) 253-9646; *Trends in Europe and North America: The Statistical Yearbook of the Economic Commission for Europe.*

Yale University Press, Yale Station, New Haven, Connecticut 06520 (800) 987-7323; *Violence and Crime in Cross-National Perspective.*

UNITED KINGDOM - CROPS

Commodity Research Bureau, Inc., 30 South Wacker Drive, Chicago, Illinois 60606 (312) 454-1801; *Commodity Year Book.*

Europa Publications Limited, 18 Bedford Square, London, WC1B 3JN, England; *The Europa World Year Book.*

European Commission Office of Press and Public Affairs, 2100 M Street, NW, Washington, D.C. 20037 (202) 862-9500; *ACP: Basic Statistics; Agriculture: Statistical Yearbook; Basic Statistics of the Community; Crop Production: Quarterly Statistics; Eurostatistics: Data for Short-Term Economic Analysis;* and *Regions: Statistical Yearbook.*

Food and Agricultural Organization of the United Nations (FAO) Via delle Terme di Caracalla, 00100 Rome, Italy (Telephone Number in U.S. (202) 653-2400); *Production Yearbook;* and *The State of Food and Agriculture.*

M.E. Sharpe, 80 Business Park Drive, Armonk, New York 10504 (800) 541-6563; *The Illustrated Book of World Rankings.*

National Technical Information Service, 5285 Port Royal Road, Springfield, Virginia 22161 (703) 487-4600; *Handbook of Economic Statistics.*

Organisation for Economic Co-operation and Development (OECD), 2 rue Andre-Pascal, 75 Paris 16, France (Telephone Number in U.S. (202) 785-6323); *Economic Accounts for Agriculture; Foreign Trade by Commodities;* and *Textile Industry in OECD Countries.*

St. Martin's Press, Inc., 175 Fifth Avenue, New York, New York 10010 (800) 221-7945; *The Statesman's Year-Book.*

Statistical Office of the United Nations, Publishing Service, New York, New York 10017 (800) 253-9646; *Statistical Yearbook.*

United Nations Conference on Trade and Development, Central Statistical Service, Palais des Nations, Geneva, Switzerland (Telephone in U.S. (800) 253-9646); *UNCTAD Commodity Yearbook.*

UNITED KINGDOM - CUSTOMS DUTIES

European Commission Office of Press and Public Affairs, 2100 M Street, NW, Washington, D.C. 20037 (202) 862-9500; *Basic Statistics of the Community.*

International Monetary Fund, 700 Nineteenth Street, NW, Washington, D.C. 20431 (202) 623-7000; *Government Finance Statistics Yearbook.*

Organisation for Economic Co-operation and Development (OECD), 2 rue Andre-Pascal, 75 Paris 16, France (Telephone Number in U.S. (202) 785-6323); *The Non-Ferrous Metals Industry.*

St. Martin's Press, Inc., 175 Fifth Avenue, New York, New York 10010 (800) 221-7945; *The Statesman's Year-Book.*

UNITED KINGDOM - DAIRY PRODUCTS

Commodity Research Bureau, Inc., 30 South Wacker Drive, Chicago, Illinois 60606 (312) 454-1801; *Commodity Year Book.*

Europa Publications Limited, 18 Bedford Square, London, WC1B 3JN, England; *The Europa World Year Book.*

European Commission Office of Press and Public Affairs, 2100 M Street, NW, Washington, D.C. 20037 (202) 862-9500; *Basic Statistics of the Community;* and *Eurostatistics: Data for Short-Term Economic Analysis.*

Food and Agricultural Organization of the United Nations (FAO), Via delle Terme di Caracalla, 00100 Rome, Italy (Telephone Number in U.S. (202) 653-2400); *Production Yearbook;* and *The State of Food and Agriculture.*

National Technical Information Service, 5285 Port Royal Road, Springfield, Virginia 22161 (703) 487-4600; *Handbook of Economic Statistics.*

Organisation for Economic Co-operation and Development (OECD), 2 rue Andre-Pascal, 75 Paris 16, France (Telephone Number in U.S. (202) 785-6323); *Economic Accounts for Agriculture;* and *Milk, Milk Products, and Egg Balances in OECD Member Countries.*

St. Martin's Press, Inc., 175 Fifth Avenue, New York, New York 10010 (800) 221-7945; *The Statesman's Year-Book.*

Statistical Office of the United Nations, Publishing Service, New York, New York 10017 (800) 253-9646; *Statistical Yearbook.*

UNITED KINGDOM - DEATH RATES - See UNITED KINGDOM - MORTALITY

UNITED KINGDOM - DEFENSE EXPENDITURES - See UNITED KINGDOM - MILITARY

UNITED KINGDOM - DEMOGRAPHY

The Economist Intelligence Unit, 111 West 57th Street, New York, New York 10019 (800) 938-4685; *The World Market Atlas.*

Euromonitor International, Inc., 122 South Michigan Avenue, Suite 1200, Chicago, Illinois 60603 (800) 577-EURO; *The World Economic Factbook;* and *World Marketing Data and Statistics.*

European Commission Office of Press and Public Affairs, 2100 M Street, NW, Washington, D.C. 20037 (202) 862-9500; *Basic Statistics of the Community; Demographic Statistics; Employment and Unemployment;* and *Regions: Statistical Yearbook.*

M.E. Sharpe, 80 Business Park Drive, Armonk, New York 10504 (800) 541-6563; *The Illustrated Book of World Rankings.*

Statistical Office of the United Nations, Publishing Service, New York, New York 10017 (800) 253-9646; *Human Development Report.*

UNITED KINGDOM - DEVELOPMENT ASSISTANCE

European Commission Office of Press and Public Affairs, 2100 M Street, NW, Washington, D.C. 20037 (202) 862-9500; *ACP: Basic Statistics; Basic Statistics of the Community;* and *Government Financing of Research and Development.*

Organisation for Economic Co-operation and Development (OECD), 2 rue Andre-Pascal, 75 Paris 16, France (Telephone Number in U.S. (202) 785-6323); *Geographical Distribution of Financial Flows to Developing Countries.*

Statistical Office of the United Nations, Publishing Service, New York, New York 10017 (800) 253-9646; *Statistical Yearbook.*

UNITED KINGDOM - DIAMOND PRODUCTION AND EXPORTS - See UNITED KINGDOM - MINING AND MINERAL PRODUCTS

UNITED KINGDOM - DISCOUNT RATES - See UNITED KINGDOM - BANKING

UNITED KINGDOM - DIVORCE RATES

European Commission Office of Press and Public Affairs, 2100 M Street, NW, Washington, D.C. 20037 (202) 862-9500;

Demographic Statistics.

M.E. Sharpe, 80 Business Park Drive, Armonk, New York 10504 (800) 541-6563; *The Illustrated Book of World Rankings.*

Statistical Office of the United Nations, Publishing Service, New York, New York 10017 (800) 253-9646; *Demographic Yearbook; Trends in Europe and North America: The Statistical Yearbook of the Economic Commission for Europe;* and *Statistical Yearbook.*

UNITED KINGDOM - DOMESTIC PRODUCT

European Commission Office of Press and Public Affairs, 2100 M Street, NW, Washington, D.C. 20037 (202) 862-9500; *Basic Statistics of the Community.*

UNITED KINGDOM - DUCKS - See UNITED KINGDOM - LIVESTOCK AND POULTRY

UNITED KINGDOM - ECONOMY

Central Intelligence Agency, Washington, D.C. 20505 (703) 482-1100, www.cia.gov; *The World Factbook.*

Economist Intelligence Unit, 111 West 57th Street, New York, New York 10019 (800) 938-4685; *United Kingdom Country Report.*

Euromonitor International, Inc., 122 South Michigan Avenue, Suite 1200, Chicago, Illinois 60603 (800) 577-EURO; *European Marketing Data and Statistics; World Marketing Data and Statistics;* and *The World Economic Factbook.*

Europa Publications Limited, 18 Bedford Square, London, WC1B 3JN, England; *The Europa World Year Book.*

European Commission Office of Press and Public Affairs, 2100 M Street, NW, Washington, D.C. 20037 (202) 862-9500; *ACP: Basic Statistics; Basic Statistics of the Community; Energy Statistics Yearbook; Labor Force Sample Survey;* and *Money and Finance.*

M.E. Sharpe, 80 Business Park Drive, Armonk, New York 10504 (800) 541-6563; *The Illustrated Book of World Rankings.*

National Technical Information Service, 5285 Port Royal Road, Springfield, Virginia 22161 (703) 487-4600; *Handbook of Economic Statistics.*

Organisation for Economic Co-operation and Development (OECD), 2 rue Andre-Pascal, 75 Paris 16, France (Telephone Number in U.S. (202) 785-6323); *Economic Outlook; Geographical Distribution of Financial Flows to Developing Countries; Main Economic Indicators - Historical Statistics; OECD*

Economic Surveys: United Kingdom; and *OECD Employment Outlook.*

St. Martin's Press, Inc., 175 Fifth Avenue, New York, New York 10010 (800) 221-7945; *The Statesman's Year-Book.*

Statistical Office of the United Nations, Publishing Service, New York, New York 10017 (800) 253-9646; *World Statistics Pocketbook.*

The World Bank, 1818 H Street, NW, Washington, D.C. 20433 (202) 477-1234; *The World Bank Atlas;* and *World Development Report.*

UNITED KINGDOM - EDUCATION

The Economist Intelligence Unit, 111 West 57th Street, New York, New York 10019 (800) 938-4685; *The World Market Atlas.*

Euromonitor International, Inc., 122 South Michigan Avenue, Suite 1200, Chicago, Illinois 60603 (800) 577-EURO; *European Marketing Data and Statistics;* and *World Marketing Data and Statistics.*

Europa Publications Limited, 18 Bedford Square, London, WC1B 3JN, England; *The Europa World Year Book.*

European Commission Office of Press and Public Affairs, 2100 M Street, NW, Washington, D.C. 20037 (202) 862-9500; *Basic Statistics of the Community;* and *Regions: Statistical Yearbook.*

International Monetary Fund, 700 Nineteenth Street, NW, Washington, D.C. 20431 (202) 623-7000; *Government Finance Statistics Yearbook.*

M.E. Sharpe, 80 Business Park Drive, Armonk, New York 10504 (800) 541-6563; *The Illustrated Book of World Rankings.*

Organisation for Economic Co-operation and Development (OECD), 2 rue Andre-Pascal, 75 Paris 16, France (Telephone Number in U.S. (202) 785-6323); *Education in OECD Countries.*

St. Martin's Press, Inc., 175 Fifth Avenue, New York, New York 10010 (800) 221-7945; *The Statesman's Year-Book.*

Statistical Office of the United Nations, Publishing Service, New York, New York 10017 (800) 253-9646; *Human Development Report;* and *Trends in Europe and North America: The Statistical Yearbook of the Economic Commission for Europe.*

United Nations Educational, Scientific and Cultural Organization (UNESCO), 7 Place de Fontenoy, F-75700 Paris, France (Telephone Number in U.S. (212) 963-

5981); *Statistical Yearbook.*

The World Bank, 1818 H Street, NW, Washington, D.C. 20433 (202) 477-1234; *World Development Report;* and *World Development Indicators.*

UNITED KINGDOM - EGG PRODUCTION AND CONSUMPTION - See UNITED KINGDOM - DAIRY PRODUCTS

UNITED KINGDOM - ELECTRICITY

Central Intelligence Agency, Washington, D.C. 20505 (703) 482-1100, www.cia.gov; *The World Factbook.*

Commodity Research Bureau, Inc., 30 South Wacker Drive, Chicago, Illinois 60606 (312) 454-1801; *Commodity Year Book.*

European Commission Office of Press and Public Affairs, 2100 M Street, NW, Washington, D.C. 20037 (202) 862-9500; *Basic Statistics of the Community; Energy: Monthly Statistics; Energy Statistics Yearbook;* and *Eurostatistics: Data for Short-Term Economic Analysis.*

M.E. Sharpe, 80 Business Park Drive, Armonk, New York 10504 (800) 541-6563; *The Illustrated Book of World Rankings.*

National Technical Information Service, 5285 Port Royal Road, Springfield, Virginia 22161 (703) 487-4600; *Handbook of Economic Statistics.*

Organisation for Economic Co-operation and Development (OECD), 2 rue Andre-Pascal, 75 Paris 16, France (Telephone Number in U.S. (202) 785-6323); *Coal Information; Energy Statistics of OECD Countries; Indicators of Industrial Activity; Industrial Structure Statistics;* and *Regions: Statistical Yearbook.*

Penn Well Publishing Company, 1421 South Sheridan Road, P.O. Box 1260, Tulsa, Oklahoma 74101 (800) 752-9764; *International Energy Statistics Sourcebook.*

St. Martin's Press, Inc., 175 Fifth Avenue, New York, New York 10010 (800) 221-7945; *The Statesman's Year-Book.*

Statistical Office of the United Nations, Publishing Service, New York, New York 10017 (800) 253-9646; *Human Development Report; Trends in Europe and North America: The Statistical Yearbook of the Economic Commission for Europe;* and *Statistical Yearbook.*

UNITED KINGDOM - EMPLOYMENT

Euromonitor International, Inc., 122 South Michigan Avenue, Suite 1200, Chicago, Illinois 60603 (800) 577-EURO; *European Marketing Data and Statistics.*

European Commission Office of Press and Public Affairs, 2100 M Street, NW, Washington, D.C. 20037 (202) 862-9500; *Basic Statistics of the Community; Earnings in Agriculture; Employment and Unemployment; Eurostatistics: Data for Short-Term Economic Analysis; Labor Force Sample Survey;* and *Transport Annual Statistics.*

International Labour Office, I.L.O. Publications, 1828 L Street, NW, Suite 801, Washington, D.C. 20036 (301) 638-3152; *Yearbook of Labour Statistics.*

M.E. Sharpe, 80 Business Park Drive, Armonk, New York 10504 (800) 541-6563; *The Illustrated Book of World Rankings.*

National Technical Information Service, 5285 Port Royal Road, Springfield, Virginia 22161 (703) 487-4600; *Handbook of Economic Statistics.*

Organisation for Economic Co-operation and Development (OECD), 2 rue Andre-Pascal, 75 Paris 16, France (Telephone Number in U.S. (202) 785-6323); *Economic Outlook; Foreign Trade by Commodities; Indicators of Industrial Activity; Industrial Structure Statistics; The Iron and Steel Industry; Iron and Steel: Statistical Yearbook; OECD Economic Surveys: United Kingdom; OECD Employment Outlook;* and *Textile Industry in OECD Countries.*

Statistical Office of the United Nations, Publishing Service, New York, New York 10017 (800) 253-9646; *Statistical Yearbook;* and *Trends in Europe and North America: The Statistical Yearbook of the Economic Commission for Europe.*

UNITED KINGDOM - ENERGY

Euromonitor International, Inc., 122 South Michigan Avenue, Suite 1200, Chicago, Illinois 60603 (800) 577-EURO; *European Marketing Data and Statistics; World Marketing Data and Statistics;* and *The World Economic Factbook.*

European Commission Office of Press and Public Affairs, 2100 M Street, NW, Washington, D.C. 20037 (202) 862-9500; *Basic Statistics of the Community; Energy: Monthly Statistics; Energy Statistics Yearbook; Regions: Statistical Yearbook;* and *Transport Annual Statistics.*

Food and Agricultural Organization of the United Nations (FAO) Via delle Terme di Caracalla, 00100 Rome, Italy (Telephone Number in U.S. (202) 653-2400); *The State of Food and Agriculture.*

M.E. Sharpe, 80 Business Park Drive, Armonk, New York 10504 (800) 541-6563; *The Illustrated Book of World Rankings.*

National Technical Information Service, 5285 Port Royal Road, Springfield, Virginia 22161 (703) 487-4600; *Handbook of Economic Statistics.*

Organisation for Economic Co-operation and Development (OECD), 2 rue Andre-Pascal, 75 Paris 16, France (Telephone Number in U.S. (202) 785-6323); *Coal Information; Energy Statistics of OECD Countries; OECD Environmental Data;* and *Oil and Gas Information.*

Penn Well Publishing Company, 1421 South Sheridan Road, P.O. Box 1260, Tulsa, Oklahoma 74101 (800) 752-9764; *International Energy Statistics Sourcebook.*

St. Martin's Press, Inc., 175 Fifth Avenue, New York, New York 10010 (800) 221-7945; *The Statesman's Year-Book.*

Statistical Office of the United Nations, Publishing Service, New York, New York 10017 (800) 253-9646; *Energy Statistics Yearbook; Human Development Report; Trends in Europe and North America: The Statistical Yearbook of the Economic Commission for Europe; Statistical Yearbook;* and *World Statistics Pocketbook.*

The World Bank, 1818 H Street, NW, Washington, D.C. 20433 (202) 477-1234; *The World Bank Atlas;* and *World Development Report.*

UNITED KINGDOM - ENGINEERING AND METAL PRODUCTS - EXPORTS AND IMPORTS

European Commission Office of Press and Public Affairs, 2100 M Street, NW, Washington, D.C. 20037 (202) 862-9500; *Basic Statistics of the Community;* and *Industrial Production: Quarterly Statistics.*

UNITED KINGDOM - ENVIRONMENT

Economist Intelligence Unit, 111 West 57th Street, New York, New York 10019 (800) 938-4685; *United Kingdom Country Report.*

Organization for Economic Co-operation and Development (OECD), 2 rue Andre-Pascal, 75 Paris 16, France (Telephone Number in U.S. (202) 785-6323); *OECD Environmental Data.*

Statistical Office of the United Nations, Publishing Service, New York, New York 10017 (800) 253-9646; *Trends in Europe and North America: The Statistical Yearbook of the Economic Commission for Europe;* and *World Statistics Pocketbook.*

UNITED KINGDOM - EXCHANGE RATES

Central Intelligence Agency, Washington, D.C. 20505 (703) 482-1100, www.cia.gov; *The World Factbook.*

Euromonitor International, Inc., 122 South Michigan Avenue, Suite 1200, Chicago, Illinois 60603 (800) 577-EURO; *The World Economic Factbook.*

Europa Publications Limited, 18 Bedford Square, London, WC1B 3JN, England; *The Europa World Year Book.*

European Commission Office of Press and Public Affairs, 2100 M Street, NW, Washington, D.C. 20037 (202) 862-9500; *Basic Statistics of the Community; Eurostatistics: Data for Short-Term Economic Analysis;* and *Money and Finance.*

International Civil Aviation Organization, 999 University Street, Montreal, Quebec, Canada H3C 5H7 (514) 954-8219; *Civil Aviation Statistics of the World.*

International Monetary Fund, 700 Nineteenth Street, NW, Washington, D.C. 20431 (202) 623-7000; *International Financial Statistics.*

National Technical Information Service, 5285 Port Royal Road, Springfield, Virginia 22161 (703) 487-4600; *Handbook of Economic Statistics.*

Organisation for Economic Co-operation and Development (OECD), 2 rue Andre-Pascal, 75 Paris 16, France (Telephone Number in U.S. (202) 785-6323); *Economic Outlook; Financial Market Trends; Revenue Statistics of OECD Member Countries;* and *Tourism Policy and International Tourism in OECD Member Countries.*

Statistical Office of the United Nations, Publishing Service, New York, New York 10017 (800) 253-9646; *Statistical Yearbook; Trends in Europe and North America: The Statistical Yearbook of the Economic Commission for Europe;* and *World Statistics Pocketbook.*

UNITED KINGDOM - EXCISE TAXES - See UNITED KINGDOM - TAXATION

UNITED KINGDOM - EXPORTS

Central Intelligence Agency, Washington, D.C. 20505 (703) 482-1100, www.cia.gov; *The World Factbook.*

The Economist Intelligence Unit, 111 West 57th Street, New York, New York 10019 (800) 938-4685; *United Kingdom Country Report;* and *The World Market Atlas.*

Euromonitor International, Inc., 122 South Michigan Avenue, Suite 1200, Chicago, Illinois 60603 (800) 577-EURO; *The World Economic Factbook.*

Europa Publications Limited, 18 Bedford Square, London, WC1B 3JN, England; *The Europa World Year Book.*

European Commission Office of Press and Public Affairs, 2100 M Street, NW, Washington, D.C. 20037 (202) 862-9500; *Basic Statistics of the Community; Energy: Monthly Statistics; Energy Statistics Yearbook; Eurostatistics: Data for Short-Term Economic Analysis; External Trade: Monthly Statistics; External Trade: Statistical Yearbook;* and *Fisheries: Yearly Statistics.*

Food and Agricultural Organization of the United Nations (FAO) Via delle Terme di Caracalla, 00100 Rome, Italy (Telephone Number in U.S. (202) 653-2400); *The State of Food and Agriculture.*

International Iron and Steel Institute, 120, rue Colonel Bourg, B-1140, Belgium; *Steel Statistical Yearbook.*

International Lead and Zinc Study Group, Metro House, 58 St. James's Street, London SW1A 1LD England; *Lead and Zinc Statistics.*

International Monetary Fund, 700 Nineteenth Street, NW, Washington, D.C. 20431 (202) 623-7000; *Direction of Trade Statistics; Government Finance Statistics Yearbook;* and *International Financial Statistics.*

International Rubber Study Group, York House, Eighth Floor, Empire Way, Wembley, London HA9 0PA, England; *Rubber Statistical Bulletin.*

National Technical Information Service, 5285 Port Royal Road, Springfield, Virginia 22161 (703) 487-4600; *Handbook of Economic Statistics.*

Organisation for Economic Co-operation and Development (OECD), 2 rue Andre-Pascal, 75 Paris 16, France (Telephone Number in U.S. (202) 785-6323); *Economic Outlook; The Footwear, Raw Hides and Skins, and Leather Industry in OECD Countries; Foreign Trade by Commodities; Geographical Distribution of Financial Flows to Developing Countries; Industrial Structure Statistics; The Iron and Steel Industry; Milk, Milk Products, and Egg Balances in OECD Member Countries; OECD Economic Surveys: United Kingdom; The Pulp and Paper Industry;* and *Review of Fisheries in OECD Member Countries.*

St. Martin's Press, Inc., 175 Fifth Avenue, New York, New York 10010 (800) 221-7945; *The Statesman's Year-Book.*

Statistical Office of the United Nations, Publishing Service, New York, New York 10017 (800) 253-9646; *Trends in Europe and North America: The Statistical Yearbook of the Economic Commission for Europe.*

United Nations Conference on Trade and Development (UNCTAD), New York, New York 10017 (800) 253-9646; *Handbook of International Trade and Development Statistics.*

The World Bank, 1818 H Street, NW, Washington, D.C. 20433 (202) 477-1234; *World Development Report;* and *World Development Indicators.*

UNITED KINGDOM - EXTERNAL FINANCING

Organisation for Economic Co-operation and Development (OECD), 2 rue Andre-Pascal, 75 Paris 16, France (Telephone Number in U.S. (202) 785-6323); *Economic Outlook;* and *Financial Market Trends.*

UNITED KINGDOM - EXTERNAL INDEBTEDNESS

National Technical Information Service, 5285 Port Royal Road, Springfield, Virginia 22161 (703) 487-4600; *Handbook of Economic Statistics.*

Organisation for Economic Co-operation and Development (OECD), 2 rue Andre-Pascal, 75 Paris 16, France (Telephone Number in U.S. (202) 785-6323); *Financial Market Trends;* and *Geographical Distribution of Financial Flows to Developing Countries.*

The World Bank, 1818 H Street, NW, Washington, D.C. 20433 (202) 477-1234; *World Development Report;* and *World Development Indicators.*

UNITED KINGDOM - EXTERNAL TRADE

Euromonitor International, Inc., 122 South Michigan Avenue, Suite 1200, Chicago, Illinois 60603 (800) 577-EURO; *World Marketing Data and Statistics.*

European Commission Office of Press and Public Affairs, 2100 M Street, NW, Washington, D.C. 20037 (202) 862-9500; *ACP: Basic Statistics; Basic Statistics of the Community; Eurostatistics: Data for Short-Term Economic Analysis; External Trade: Monthly Statistics; External Trade: Statistical Yearbook;* and *Foreign Trade of the People's Republic of China.*

Food and Agricultural Organization of the United Nations (FAO) Via delle Terme di Caracalla, 00100 Rome, Italy (Telephone Number in U.S. (202) 653-2400); *The State of Food and Agriculture;* and *Trade Yearbook.*

National Technical Information Service, 5285 Port Royal Road, Springfield, Virginia 22161 (703) 487-4600; *Handbook of*

Economic Statistics.

Statistical Office of the United Nations, Publishing Service, New York, New York 10017 (800) 253-9646; *Statistical Yearbook.*

UNITED KINGDOM - FABRIC PRODUCTION - See UNITED KINGDOM - TEXTILE INDUSTRY

UNITED KINGDOM - FARM CROPS - See UNITED KINGDOM - CROPS

UNITED KINGDOM - FEMALE WORKING POPULATION - See UNITED KINGDOM - EMPLOYMENT

UNITED KINGDOM - FERTILITY RATES

Central Intelligence Agency, Washington, D.C. 20505 (703) 482-1100, www.cia.gov; *The World Factbook.*

European Commission Office of Press and Public Affairs, 2100 M Street, NW, Washington, D.C. 20037 (202) 862-9500; *Demographic Statistics.*

M.E. Sharpe, 80 Business Park Drive, Armonk, New York 10504 (800) 541-6563; *The Illustrated Book of World Rankings.*

Statistical Office of the United Nations, Publishing Service, New York, New York 10017 (800) 253-9646; *Human Development Report;* and *Trends in Europe and North America: The Statistical Yearbook of the Economic Commission for Europe.*

The World Bank, 1818 H Street, NW, Washington, D.C. 20433 (202) 477-1234; *The World Bank Atlas; World Development Report;* and *World Development Indicators.*

UNITED KINGDOM - FERTILIZER

European Commission Office of Press and Public Affairs, 2100 M Street, NW, Washington, D.C. 20037 (202) 862-9500; *Basic Statistics of the Community.*

Food and Agricultural Organization of the United Nations (FAO) Via delle Terme di Caracalla, 00100 Rome, Italy (Telephone Number in U.S. (202) 653-2400); *The State of Food and Agriculture.*

National Technical Information Service, 5285 Port Royal Road, Springfield, Virginia 22161 (703) 487-4600; *Handbook of Economic Statistics.*

Organisation for Economic Co-operation and Development (OECD), 2 rue Andre-Pascal, 75 Paris 16, France (Telephone Number in U.S. (202) 785-6323); *Economic Accounts for Agriculture;* and *Foreign Trade by Commodities.*

Statistical Office of the United Nations,

Publishing Service, New York, New York 10017 (800) 253-9646; *Statistical Yearbook.*

UNITED KINGDOM - FETAL MORTALITY - See UNITED KINGDOM - MORTALITY

UNITED KINGDOM - FIBRE PRODUCTION - See UNITED KINGDOM - TEXTILE INDUSTRY

UNITED KINGDOM - FILAMENT PRODUCTION - See UNITED KINGDOM - TEXTILE INDUSTRY

UNITED KINGDOM - FILM - See UNITED KINGDOM - MOTION PICTURES

UNITED KINGDOM - FINANCE

Economist Intelligence Unit, 111 West 57th Street, New York, New York 10019 (800) 938-4685; *United Kingdom Country Report.*

Europa Publications Limited, 18 Bedford Square, London, WC1B 3JN, England; *The Europa World Year Book.*

European Commission Office of Press and Public Affairs, 2100 M Street, NW, Washington, D.C. 20037 (202) 862-9500; *ACP: Basic Statistics; Basic Statistics of the Community; Eurostatistics: Data for Short-Term Economic Analysis;* and *Money and Finance.*

International Monetary Fund, 700 Nineteenth Street, NW, Washington, D.C. 20431 (202) 623-7000; *Government Finance Statistics Yearbook.*

M.E. Sharpe, 80 Business Park Drive, Armonk, New York 10504 (800) 541-6563; *The Illustrated Book of World Rankings.*

National Technical Information Service, 5285 Port Royal Road, Springfield, Virginia 22161 (703) 487-4600; *Handbook of Economic Statistics.*

Organisation for Economic Co-operation and Development (OECD), 2 rue Andre-Pascal, 75 Paris 16, France (Telephone Number in U.S. (202) 785-6323); *Economic Outlook; Financial Market Trends; Geographical Distribution of Financial Flows to Developing Countries; Main Economic Indicators - Historical Statistics; OECD Financial Statistics;* and *Revenue Statistics of OECD Member Countries.*

St. Martin's Press, Inc., 175 Fifth Avenue, New York, New York 10010 (800) 221-7945; *The Statesman's Year-Book.*

UNITED KINGDOM - FISHERIES

Euromonitor International, Inc., 122 South Michigan Avenue, Suite 1200,

Chicago, Illinois 60603 (800) 577-EURO; *European Marketing Data and Statistics.*

Europa Publications Limited, 18 Bedford Square, London, WC1B 3JN, England; *The Europa World Year Book.*

European Commission Office of Press and Public Affairs, 2100 M Street, NW, Washington, D.C. 20037 (202) 862-9500; *Agriculture: Statistical Yearbook;* and *Fisheries: Yearly Statistics.*

Food and Agricultural Organization of the United Nations (FAO) Via delle Terme di Caracalla, 00100 Rome, Italy (Telephone Number in U.S. (202) 653-2400); *The State of Food and Agriculture;* and *Yearbook of Fishery Statistics.*

M.E. Sharpe, 80 Business Park Drive, Armonk, New York 10504 (800) 541-6563; *The Illustrated Book of World Rankings.*

National Technical Information Service, 5285 Port Royal Road, Springfield, Virginia 22161 (703) 487-4600; *Handbook of Economic Statistics.*

Organisation for Economic Co-operation and Development (OECD), 2 rue Andre-Pascal, 75 Paris 16, France (Telephone Number in U.S. (202) 785-6323); *Foreign Trade by Commodities; Industrial Structure Statistics;* and *Review of Fisheries in OECD Member Countries.*

St. Martin's Press, Inc., 175 Fifth Avenue, New York, New York 10010 (800) 221-7945; *The Statesman's Year-Book.*

Statistical Office of the United Nations, Publishing Service, New York, New York 10017 (800) 253-9646; *Statistical Yearbook.*

United Nations Conference on Trade and Development, Central Statistical Service, Palais des Nations, Geneva, Switzerland (Telephone in U.S. (800) 253-9646); *UNCTAD Commodity Yearbook.*

UNITED KINGDOM - FLAX AND FLAX FIBRE PRODUCTION - See UNITED KINGDOM - TEXTILE INDUSTRY

UNITED KINGDOM - FLOUR PRODUCTION

Commodity Research Bureau, Inc., 30 South Wacker Drive, Chicago, Illinois 60606 (312) 454-1801; *Commodity Year Book.*

European Commission Office of Press and Public Affairs, 2100 M Street, NW, Washington, D.C. 20037 (202) 862-9500; *Basic Statistics of the Community.*

Statistical Office of the United Nations, Publishing Service, New York, New York 10017 (800) 253-9646; *Statistical Yearbook.*

UNITED KINGDOM - FOOD

Euromonitor International, Inc., 122 South Michigan Avenue, Suite 1200, Chicago, Illinois 60603 (800) 577-EURO; *Retail Trade International.*

European Commission Office of Press and Public Affairs, 2100 M Street, NW, Washington, D.C. 20037 (202) 862-9500; *Basic Statistics of the Community.*

Food and Agricultural Organization of the United Nations (FAO) Via delle Terme di Caracalla, 00100 Rome, Italy (Telephone Number in U.S. (202) 653-2400); *Production Yearbook;* and *The State of Food and Agriculture.*

Organisation for Economic Co-operation and Development (OECD), 2 rue Andre-Pascal, 75 Paris 16, France (Telephone Number in U.S. (202) 785-6323); *Foreign Trade by Commodities;* and *Main Economic Indicators - Historical Statistics.*

Statistical Office of the United Nations, Publishing Service, New York, New York 10017 (800) 253-9646; *Human Development Report.*

United Nations Conference on Trade and Development, Central Statistical Service, Palais des Nations, Geneva, Switzerland (Telephone in U.S. (800) 253-9646); *UNCTAD Commodity Yearbook.*

UNITED KINGDOM - FOOTWEAR - PRODUCTION INDEX

Organisation for Economic Co-operation and Development (OECD), 2 rue Andre-Pascal, 75 Paris 16, France (Telephone Number in U.S. (202) 785-6323); *Indicators of Industrial Activity.*

UNITED KINGDOM - FOREIGN AID

National Technical Information Service, 5285 Port Royal Road, Springfield, Virginia 22161 (703) 487-4600; *Handbook of Economic Statistics.*

UNITED KINGDOM - FOREIGN DEBT

International Monetary Fund, 700 Nineteenth Street, NW, Washington, D.C. 20431 (202) 623-7000; *Government Finance Statistics Yearbook.*

Organisation for Economic Co-operation and Development (OECD), 2 rue Andre-Pascal, 75 Paris 16, France (Telephone Number in U.S. (202) 785-6323); *Economic Outlook.*

St. Martin's Press, Inc., 175 Fifth Avenue, New York, New York 10010 (800) 221-7945; *The Statesman's Year-Book.*

UNITED KINGDOM - FOREIGN INDEBTEDNESS

Organisation for Economic Co-operation and Development (OECD), 2 rue Andre-Pascal, 75 Paris 16, France (Telephone Number in U.S. (202) 785-6323); *Economic Outlook;* and *Financial Market Trends.*

UNITED KINGDOM - FOREIGN OFFICIAL RESERVES

European Commission Office of Press and Public Affairs, 2100 M Street, NW, Washington, D.C. 20037 (202) 862-9500; *Money and Finance.*

UNITED KINGDOM - FOREIGN TRADE

Economist Intelligence Unit, 111 West 57th Street, New York, New York 10019 (800) 938-4685; *United Kingdom Country Report.*

Euromonitor International, Inc., 122 South Michigan Avenue, Suite 1200, Chicago, Illinois 60603 (800) 577-EURO; *European Marketing Data and Statistics;* and *The World Economic Factbook.*

Europa Publications Limited, 18 Bedford Square, London, WC1B 3JN, England; *The Europa World Year Book.*

European Commission Office of Press and Public Affairs, 2100 M Street, NW, Washington, D.C. 20037 (202) 862-9500; *Basic Statistics of the Community; Energy Statistics Yearbook;* and *Foreign Trade of the People's Republic of China.*

Food and Agricultural Organization of the United Nations (FAO) Via delle Terme di Caracalla, 00100 Rome, Italy (Telephone Number in U.S. (202) 653-2400); *The State of Food and Agriculture;* and *The State of Food and Agriculture.*

International Iron and Steel Institute, 120, rue Colonel Bourg, B-1140, Belgium; *Steel Statistical Yearbook.*

International Monetary Fund, 700 Nineteenth Street, NW, Washington, D.C. 20431 (202) 623-7000; *International Financial Statistics.*

M.E. Sharpe, 80 Business Park Drive, Armonk, New York 10504 (800) 541-6563; *The Illustrated Book of World Rankings.*

National Technical Information Service, 5285 Port Royal Road, Springfield, Virginia 22161 (703) 487-4600; *Handbook of Economic Statistics.*

Organisation for Economic Co-operation and Development (OECD), 2 rue Andre-Pascal, 75 Paris 16, France (Telephone Number in U.S. (202) 785-6323); *Economic Outlook; The Footwear, Raw Hides and Skins, and Leather Industry in OECD Countries; Foreign Trade by*

Commodities; Iron and Steel: Statistical Yearbook; Main Economic Indicators - Historical Statistics; Maritime Transport; Meat Balances in OECD Member Countries; and *OECD Economic Surveys: United Kingdom.*

St. Martin's Press, Inc., 175 Fifth Avenue, New York, New York 10010 (800) 221-7945; *The Statesman's Year-Book.*

Statistical Office of the United Nations, Publishing Service, New York, New York 10017 (800) 253-9646; *International Trade Statistics Yearbook;* and *Statistical Yearbook.*

United Nations Conference on Trade and Development, Central Statistical Service, Palais des Nations, Geneva, Switzerland (Telephone in U.S. (800) 253-9646); *UNCTAD Commodity Yearbook.*

The World Bank, 1818 H Street, NW, Washington, D.C. 20433 (202) 477-1234; *World Development Report;* and *World Development Indicators.*

World Bureau of Metal Statistics, 27-A High Street, Ware Hert SG12 9BA, England; *World Metal Statistics.*

UNITED KINGDOM - FORESTRY AND FOREST PRODUCTS

American Forest and Paper Association, 1111 Nineteenth Street, NW, Washington, D.C. 20036 (202) 463-2700; *Wood Pulp and Fiber Statistics.*

Euromonitor International, Inc., 122 South Michigan Avenue, Suite 1200, Chicago, Illinois 60603 (800) 577-EURO; *European Marketing Data and Statistics.*

Europa Publications Limited, 18 Bedford Square, London, WC1B 3JN, England; *The Europa World Year Book.*

European Commission Office of Press and Public Affairs, 2100 M Street, NW, Washington, D.C. 20037 (202) 862-9500; *Agriculture: Statistical Yearbook; Basic Statistics of the Community;* and *Industrial Production: Quarterly Statistics.*

Food and Agricultural Organization of the United Nations (FAO) Via delle Terme di Caracalla, 00100 Rome, Italy (Telephone Number in U.S. (202) 653-2400); *The State of Food and Agriculture;* and *Yearbook of Forest Products.*

M.E. Sharpe, 80 Business Park Drive, Armonk, New York 10504 (800) 541-6563; *The Illustrated Book of World Rankings.*

National Technical Information Service, 5285 Port Royal Road, Springfield, Virginia 22161 (703) 487-4600; *Handbook of Economic Statistics.*

Organisation for Economic Co-operation and Development (OECD), 2 rue Andre-Pascal, 75 Paris 16, France (Telephone Number in U.S. (202) 785-6323); *Foreign Trade by Commodities; Indicators of Industrial Activity; Industrial Structure Statistics;* and *The Pulp and Paper Industry.*

St. Martin's Press, Inc., 175 Fifth Avenue, New York, New York 10010 (800) 221-7945; *The Statesman's Year-Book.*

Statistical Office of the United Nations, Publishing Service, New York, New York 10017 (800) 253-9646; *Statistical Yearbook;* and *Trends in Europe and North America: The Statistical Yearbook of the Economic Commission for Europe.*

United Nations Conference on Trade and Development, Central Statistical Service, Palais des Nations, Geneva, Switzerland (Telephone in U.S. (800) 253-9646); *UNCTAD Commodity Yearbook.*

United Nations Educational, Scientific and Cultural Organization (UNESCO), 7 Place de Fontenoy, F-75700 Paris, France (Telephone Number in U.S. (212) 963-5981); *Statistical Yearbook.*

The World Bank, 1818 H Street, NW, Washington, D.C. 20433 (202) 477-1234; *World Development Report.*

UNITED KINGDOM - FRUIT PRODUCTION - See UNITED KINGDOM - CROPS

UNITED KINGDOM - FURNITURE AND WOOD PRODUCTS - EXPORTS AND IMPORTS

European Commission Office of Press and Public Affairs, 2100 M Street, NW, Washington, D.C. 20037 (202) 862-9500; *Basic Statistics of the Community.*

Organisation for Economic Co-operation and Development (OECD), 2 rue Andre-Pascal, 75 Paris 16, France (Telephone Number in U.S. (202) 785-6323); *Foreign Trade by Commodities;* and *Industrial Structure Statistics.*

UNITED KINGDOM - GARLIC PRODUCTION - See UNITED KINGDOM - CROPS

UNITED KINGDOM - GAS AND GAS LIQUIDS PRODUCTION - See UNITED KINGDOM - MINING AND MINERAL PRODUCTS

UNITED KINGDOM - GENERAL INDUSTRIAL STATISTICS - See UNITED KINGDOM - INDUSTRY

UNITED KINGDOM - GENERAL MORTALITY - See UNITED KINGDOM -

MORTALITY

UNITED KINGDOM - GEOGRAPHIC DATA

European Commission Office of Press and Public Affairs, 2100 M Street, NW, Washington, D.C. 20037 (202) 862-9500; *Basic Statistics of the Community.*

M.E. Sharpe, 80 Business Park Drive, Armonk, New York 10504 (800) 541-6563; *The Illustrated Book of World Rankings.*

UNITED KINGDOM - GLASS AND GLASS PRODUCTS - PRODUCTION INDEX

Organisation for Economic Co-operation and Development (OECD), 2 rue Andre-Pascal, 75 Paris 16, France (Telephone Number in U.S. (202) 785-6323); *Indicators of Industrial Activity.*

UNITED KINGDOM - GOATS - See UNITED KINGDOM - LIVESTOCK AND POULTRY

UNITED KINGDOM - GOLD HOLDINGS

Statistical Office of the United Nations, Publishing Service, New York, New York 10017 (800) 253-9646; *Statistical Yearbook.*

The World Bank, 1818 H Street, NW, Washington, D.C. 20433 (202) 477-1234; *World Development Indicators.*

UNITED KINGDOM - GOLD PRODUCTION AND CONSUMPTION - See UNITED KINGDOM - MINING AND MINERAL PRODUCTS

UNITED KINGDOM - GOVERNMENT

Central Intelligence Agency, Washington, D.C. 20505 (703) 482-1100, www.cia.gov; *The World Factbook.*

Europa Publications Limited, 18 Bedford Square, London, WC1B 3JN, England; *The Europa World Year Book.*

European Commission Office of Press and Public Affairs, 2100 M Street, NW, Washington, D.C. 20037 (202) 862-9500; *Basic Statistics of the Community; Government Financing of Research and Development;* and *Money and Finance.*

International Monetary Fund, 700 Nineteenth Street, NW, Washington, D.C. 20431 (202) 623-7000; *Government Finance Statistics Yearbook;* and *International Financial Statistics.*

Organisation for Economic Co-operation and Development (OECD), 2 rue Andre-Pascal, 75 Paris 16, France (Telephone Number in U.S. (202) 785-6323); *Economic Outlook;* and *Revenue Statistics of OECD Member Countries.*

St. Martin's Press, Inc., 175 Fifth Avenue, New York, New York 10010 (800) 221-7945; *The Statesman's Year-Book.*

Statistical Office of the United Nations, Publishing Service, New York, New York 10017 (800) 253-9646; *National Accounts Statistics;* and *Statistical Yearbook.*

The World Bank, 1818 H Street, NW, Washington, D.C. 20433 (202) 477-1234; *World Development Report;* and *World Development Indicators.*

UNITED KINGDOM - GRAIN PRODUCTION - See UNITED KINGDOM - CROPS

UNITED KINGDOM - GRANTS

International Monetary Fund, 700 Nineteenth Street, NW, Washington, D.C. 20431 (202) 623-7000; *Government Finance Statistics Yearbook.*

National Technical Information Service, 5285 Port Royal Road, Springfield, Virginia 22161 (703) 487-4600; *Handbook of Economic Statistics.*

Organisation for Economic Co-operation and Development (OECD), 2 rue Andre-Pascal, 75 Paris 16, France (Telephone Number in U.S. (202) 785-6323); *Geographical Distribution of Financial Flows to Developing Countries.*

UNITED KINGDOM - GREEN PEPPER AND CHILIE PRODUCTION - See UNITED KINGDOM - CROPS

UNITED KINGDOM - GROSS DOMESTIC PRODUCT

The Economist Intelligence Unit, 111 West 57th Street, New York, New York 10019 (800) 938-4685; *United Kingdom Country Report;* and *The World Market Atlas.*

Euromonitor International, Inc., 122 South Michigan Avenue, Suite 1200, Chicago, Illinois 60603 (800) 577-EURO; *The World Economic Factbook.*

Europa Publications Limited, 18 Bedford Square, London, WC1B 3JN, England; *The Europa World Year Book.*

European Commission Office of Press and Public Affairs, 2100 M Street, NW, Washington, D.C. 20037 (202) 862-9500; *Basic Statistics of the Community; Eurostatistics: Data for Short-Term Economic Analysis; Government Financing of Research and Development; Iron and Steel: Statistical Yearbook;* and *Money and Finance.*

International Monetary Fund, 700 Nineteenth Street, NW, Washington, D.C. 20431 (202) 623-7000; *International Financial Statistics.*

M.E. Sharpe, 80 Business Park Drive, Armonk, New York 10504 (800) 541-6563; *The Illustrated Book of World Rankings.*

National Technical Information Service, 5285 Port Royal Road, Springfield, Virginia 22161 (703) 487-4600; *Handbook of Economic Statistics.*

Organisation for Economic Co-operation and Development (OECD), 2 rue Andre-Pascal, 75 Paris 16, France (Telephone Number in U.S. (202) 785-6323); *Economic Outlook; Geographical Distribution of Financial Flows to Developing Countries;* and *Revenue Statistics of OECD Member Countries.*

Statistical Office of the United Nations, Publishing Service, New York, New York 10017 (800) 253-9646; *Human Development Report; National Accounts Statistics; Trends in Europe and North America: The Statistical Yearbook of the Economic Commission for Europe;* and *Statistical Yearbook.*

The World Bank, 1818 H Street, NW, Washington, D.C. 20433 (202) 477-1234; *World Development Report;* and *World Development Indicators.*

UNITED KINGDOM - GROSS INDUSTRIAL PRODUCT - GROWTH RATES

European Commission Office of Press and Public Affairs, 2100 M Street, NW, Washington, D.C. 20037 (202) 862-9500; *Government Financing of Research and Development.*

UNITED KINGDOM - GROSS NATIONAL PRODUCT

Europa Publications Limited, 18 Bedford Square, London, WC1B 3JN, England; *The Europa World Year Book.*

European Commission Office of Press and Public Affairs, 2100 M Street, NW, Washington, D.C. 20037 (202) 862-9500; *ACP: Basic Statistics;* and *Basic Statistics of the Community.*

National Technical Information Service, 5285 Port Royal Road, Springfield, Virginia 22161 (703) 487-4600; *Handbook of Economic Statistics.*

Organisation for Economic Co-operation and Development (OECD), 2 rue Andre-Pascal, 75 Paris 16, France (Telephone Number in U.S. (202) 785-6323); *Economic Outlook;* and *Geographical Distribution of Financial Flows to Developing Countries.*

St. Martin's Press, Inc., 175 Fifth Avenue, New York, New York 10010 (800)

221-7945; *The Statesman's Year-Book.*

U.S. Arms Control and Disarmament Agency, 320 Twenty-first Street, NW, Washington, D.C. 20451 (202) 647-8677; *World Military Expenditures and Arms Transfers.*

The World Bank, 1818 H Street, NW, Washington, D.C. 20433 (202) 477-1234; *The World Bank Atlas; World Development Report;* and *World Development Indicators.*

UNITED KINGDOM - GROUNDNUT PRODUCTION - See UNITED KINGDOM - CROPS

UNITED KINGDOM - HAY PRODUCTION - See UNITED KINGDOM - CROPS

UNITED KINGDOM - HAZELNUT PRODUCTION - See UNITED KINGDOM - CROPS

UNITED KINGDOM - HEALTH

Euromonitor International, Inc., 122 South Michigan Avenue, Suite 1200, Chicago, Illinois 60603 (800) 577-EURO; *World Marketing Data and Statistics.*

European Commission Office of Press and Public Affairs, 2100 M Street, NW, Washington, D.C. 20037 (202) 862-9500; *Basic Statistics of the Community;* and *Regions: Statistical Yearbook.*

M.E. Sharpe, 80 Business Park Drive, Armonk, New York 10504 (800) 541-6563; *The Illustrated Book of World Rankings.*

Organisation for Economic Co-operation and Development (OECD), 2 rue Andre-Pascal, 75 Paris 16, France (Telephone Number in U.S. (202) 785-6323); *OECD Health Systems: Facts and Trends.*

St. Martin's Press, Inc., 175 Fifth Avenue, New York, New York 10010 (800) 221-7945; *The Statesman's Year-Book.*

Statistical Office of the United Nations, Publishing Service, New York, New York 10017 (800) 253-9646; *Human Development Report; Trends in Europe and North America: The Statistical Yearbook of the Economic Commission for Europe;* and *Statistical Yearbook.*

United Nations Children's Fund (UNICEF), 3 United Nations Plaza, New York, New York 10017 (800) 253-9646; *State of the World's Children.*

The World Bank, 1818 H Street, NW, Washington, D.C. 20433 (202) 477-1234; *World Development Report.*

UNITED KINGDOM - HEALTH EXPENDITURES

International Monetary Fund, 700 Nineteenth Street, NW, Washington, D.C. 20431 (202) 623-7000; *Government Finance Statistics Yearbook.*

UNITED KINGDOM - HEMP FIBRE PRODUCTION - See UNITED KINGDOM - TEXTILE INDUSTRY

UNITED KINGDOM - HIDE PRODUCTION

Food and Agricultural Organization of the United Nations (FAO), Via delle Terme di Caracalla, 00100 Rome, Italy (Telephone Number in U.S. (202) 653-2400); *Production Yearbook.*

Organisation for Economic Co-operation and Development (OECD), 2 rue Andre-Pascal, 75 Paris 16, France (Telephone Number in U.S. (202) 785-6323); *The Footwear, Raw Hides and Skins, and Leather Industry in OECD Countries; Foreign Trade by Commodities;* and *Indicators of Industrial Activity.*

UNITED KINGDOM - HIGHWAYS

Central Intelligence Agency, Washington, D.C. 20505 (703) 482-1100, www.cia.gov; *The World Factbook.*

European Commission Office of Press and Public Affairs, 2100 M Street, NW, Washington, D.C. 20037 (202) 862-9500; *Basic Statistics of the Community;* and *Transport Annual Statistics.*

International Road Federation, 2600 Virginia Avenue, NW, Washington, D.C. 20037 (202) 338-4641; *World Road Statistics.*

St. Martin's Press, Inc., 175 Fifth Avenue, New York, New York 10010 (800) 221-7945; *The Statesman's Year-Book.*

Statistical Office of the United Nations, Publishing Service, New York, New York 10017 (800) 253-9646; *Annual Bulletin of Transport Statistics for Europe;* and *Trends in Europe and North America: The Statistical Yearbook of the Economic Commission for Europe.*

UNITED KINGDOM - HOME FINANCE

Organisation for Economic Co-operation and Development (OECD), 2 rue Andre-Pascal, 75 Paris 16, France (Telephone Number in U.S. (202) 785-6323); *Main Economic Indicators - Historical Statistics.*

UNITED KINGDOM - HOPS PRODUCTION - See UNITED KINGDOM - CROPS

UNITED KINGDOM - HORSES - See UNITED KINGDOM - LIVESTOCK AND POULTRY

UNITED KINGDOM - HOURS OF WORK - See UNITED KINGDOM - EMPLOYMENT

UNITED KINGDOM - HOUSING AND HOUSING UNITS

Euromonitor International, Inc., 122 South Michigan Avenue, Suite 1200, Chicago, Illinois 60603 (800) 577-EURO; *World Marketing Data and Statistics.*

European Commission Office of Press and Public Affairs, 2100 M Street, NW, Washington, D.C. 20037 (202) 862-9500; *Basic Statistics of the Community; Labor Force Sample Survey;* and *Regions: Statistical Yearbook.*

M.E. Sharpe, 80 Business Park Drive, Armonk, New York 10504 (800) 541-6563; *The Illustrated Book of World Rankings.*

National Technical Information Service, 5285 Port Royal Road, Springfield, Virginia 22161 (703) 487-4600; *Handbook of Economic Statistics.*

Statistical Office of the United Nations, Publishing Service, New York, New York 10017 (800) 253-9646; *Trends in Europe and North America: The Statistical Yearbook of the Economic Commission for Europe.*

UNITED KINGDOM - HOUSING CONSTRUCTION - See UNITED KINGDOM - CONSTRUCTION INDUSTRY

UNITED KINGDOM - HOUSING EXPENDITURES

European Commission Office of Press and Public Affairs, 2100 M Street, NW, Washington, D.C. 20037 (202) 862-9500; *Basic Statistics of the Community.*

International Monetary Fund, 700 Nineteenth Street, NW, Washington, D.C. 20431 (202) 623-7000; *Government Finance Statistics Yearbook.*

UNITED KINGDOM - HYDROCHLORIC ACID PRODUCTION

European Commission Office of Press and Public Affairs, 2100 M Street, NW, Washington, D.C. 20037 (202) 862-9500; *Basic Statistics of the Community.*

Statistical Office of the United Nations, Publishing Service, New York, New York 10017 (800) 253-9646; *Statistical Yearbook.*

UNITED KINGDOM - ILLITERATE POPULATION

Central Intelligence Agency, Washington, D.C. 20505 (703) 482-1100, www.cia.gov; *The World Factbook.*

The Economist Intelligence Unit, 111 West 57th Street, New York, New York

10019 (800) 938-4685; *The World Market Atlas.*

Euromonitor International, Inc., 122 South Michigan Avenue, Suite 1200, Chicago, Illinois 60603 (800) 577-EURO; *The World Economic Factbook.*

St. Martin's Press, Inc., 175 Fifth Avenue, New York, New York 10010 (800) 221-7945; *The Statesman's Year-Book.*

Statistical Office of the United Nations, Publishing Service, New York, New York 10017 (800) 253-9646; *Human Development Report.*

UNITED KINGDOM - IMPORTS

Central Intelligence Agency, Washington, D.C. 20505 (703) 482-1100, www.cia.gov; *The World Factbook.*

The Economist Intelligence Unit, 111 West 57th Street, New York, New York 10019 (800) 938-4685; *United Kingdom Country Report;* and *The World Market Atlas.*

Euromonitor International, Inc., 122 South Michigan Avenue, Suite 1200, Chicago, Illinois 60603 (800) 577-EURO; *The World Economic Factbook.*

Europa Publications Limited, 18 Bedford Square, London, WC1B 3JN, England; *The Europa World Year Book.*

European Commission Office of Press and Public Affairs, 2100 M Street, NW, Washington, D.C. 20037 (202) 862-9500; *Basic Statistics of the Community; Energy: Monthly Statistics; Energy Statistics Yearbook; Eurostatistics: Data for Short-Term Economic Analysis; External Trade: Monthly Statistics; External Trade: Statistical Yearbook;* and *Fisheries: Yearly Statistics.*

Food and Agricultural Organization of the United Nations (FAO) Via delle Terme di Caracalla, 00100 Rome, Italy (Telephone Number in U.S. (202) 653-2400); *The State of Food and Agriculture.*

International Iron and Steel Institute, 120, rue Colonel Bourg, B-1140, Belgium; *Steel Statistical Yearbook.*

International Lead and Zinc Study Group, Metro House, 58 St. James's Street, London SW1A 1LD England; *Lead and Zinc Statistics.*

International Monetary Fund, 700 Nineteenth Street, NW, Washington, D.C. 20431 (202) 623-7000; *Direction of Trade Statistics; Government Finance Statistics Yearbook;* and *International Financial Statistics.*

International Rubber Study Group, York House, Eighth Floor, Empire Way, Wembley, London HA9 0PA, England; *Rubber Statistical Bulletin.*

National Technical Information Service, 5285 Port Royal Road, Springfield, Virginia 22161 (703) 487-4600; *Handbook of Economic Statistics.*

Organisation for Economic Co-operation and Development (OECD), 2 rue Andre-Pascal, 75 Paris 16, France (Telephone Number in U.S. (202) 785-6323); *Economic Outlook; The Footwear, Raw Hides and Skins, and Leather Industry in OECD Countries; Industrial Structure Statistics; The Iron and Steel Industry; Milk, Milk Products, and Egg Balances in OECD Member Countries; The Pulp and Paper Industry; OECD Economic Surveys: United Kingdom;* and *Review of Fisheries in OECD Member Countries.*

St. Martin's Press, Inc., 175 Fifth Avenue, New York, New York 10010 (800) 221-7945; *The Statesman's Year-Book.*

Statistical Office of the United Nations, Publishing Service, New York, New York 10017 (800) 253-9646; *Trends in Europe and North America: The Statistical Yearbook of the Economic Commission for Europe.*

United Nations Conference on Trade and Development (UNCTAD), New York, New York 10017 (800) 253-9646; *Handbook of International Trade and Development Statistics.*

The World Bank, 1818 H Street, NW, Washington, D.C. 20433 (202) 477-1234; *World Development Report;* and *World Development Indicators.*

UNITED KINGDOM - INCOME TAXES - See UNITED KINGDOM - TAXATION

UNITED KINGDOM - INDUSTRIAL METALS PRODUCTION - See UNITED KINGDOM - MINING AND MINERAL PRODUCTS

UNITED KINGDOM - INDUSTRY

Central Intelligence Agency, Washington, D.C. 20505 (703) 482-1100, www.cia.gov; *The World Factbook.*

Economist Intelligence Unit, 111 West 57th Street, New York, New York 10019 (800) 938-4685; *United Kingdom Country Report.*

Euromonitor International, Inc., 122 South Michigan Avenue, Suite 1200, Chicago, Illinois 60603 (800) 577-EURO; *The World Economic Factbook;* and *World Marketing Data and Statistics.*

Europa Publications Limited, 18 Bedford Square, London, WC1B 3JN,

England; *The Europa World Year Book.*

European Commission Office of Press and Public Affairs, 2100 M Street, NW, Washington, D.C. 20037 (202) 862-9500; *Basic Statistics of the Community; Employment and Unemployment; Eurostatistics: Data for Short-Term Economic Analysis;* and *Labor Force Sample Survey.*

International Labour Office, I.L.O. Publications, 1828 L Street, NW, Suite 801, Washington, D.C. 20036 (301) 638-3152; *Yearbook of Labour Statistics.*

M.E. Sharpe, 80 Business Park Drive, Armonk, New York 10504 (800) 541-6563; *The Illustrated Book of World Rankings.*

National Technical Information Service, 5285 Port Royal Road, Springfield, Virginia 22161 (703) 487-4600; *Handbook of Economic Statistics.*

Organisation for Economic Co-operation and Development (OECD), 2 rue Andre-Pascal, 75 Paris 16, France (Telephone Number in U.S. (202) 785-6323); *Economic Outlook; Indicators of Industrial Activity; Industrial Structure Statistics; Main Economic Indicators - Historical Statistics;* and *OECD Environmental Data.*

St. Martin's Press, Inc., 175 Fifth Avenue, New York, New York 10010 (800) 221-7945; *The Statesman's Year-Book.*

Statistical Office of the United Nations, Publishing Service, New York, New York 10017 (800) 253-9646; *Industrial Commodity Statistics Yearbook; Trends in Europe and North America: The Statistical Yearbook of the Economic Commission for Europe;* and *Statistical Yearbook.*

The World Bank, 1818 H Street, NW, Washington, D.C. 20433 (202) 477-1234; *World Development Indicators.*

World Intellectual Property Organization, 34 Chemin des Colombettes, CH-1211 Geneva 20. Switzerland; *Industrial Property Statistics.*

UNITED KINGDOM - INFANT AND MATERNAL MORTALITY - See UNITED KINGDOM - MORTALITY

UNITED KINGDOM - INFLATIONARY FACTORS

National Technical Information Service, 5285 Port Royal Road, Springfield, Virginia 22161 (703) 487-4600; *Handbook of Economic Statistics.*

UNITED KINGDOM - INTEREST RATES

National Technical Information Service,

5285 Port Royal Road, Springfield, Virginia 22161 (703) 487-4600; *Handbook of Economic Statistics.*

Organisation for Economic Co-operation and Development (OECD), 2 rue Andre-Pascal, 75 Paris 16, France (Telephone Number in U.S. (202) 785-6323); *Economic Outlook; Financial Market Trends; Main Economic Indicators - Historical Statistics; Money and Finance;* and *OECD Financial Statistics.*

UNITED KINGDOM - INTERNAL TRADE

European Commission Office of Press and Public Affairs, 2100 M Street, NW, Washington, D.C. 20037 (202) 862-9500; *Basic Statistics of the Community.*

Organisation for Economic Co-operation and Development (OECD), 2 rue Andre-Pascal, 75 Paris 16, France (Telephone Number in U.S. (202) 785-6323); *Main Economic Indicators - Historical Statistics.*

UNITED KINGDOM - INTERNATIONAL FINANCE

European Commission Office of Press and Public Affairs, 2100 M Street, NW, Washington, D.C. 20037 (202) 862-9500; *Basic Statistics of the Community.*

Organisation for Economic Co-operation and Development (OECD), 2 rue Andre-Pascal, 75 Paris 16, France (Telephone Number in U.S. (202) 785-6323); *Economic Outlook;* and *Financial Market Trends.*

UNITED KINGDOM - INTERNATIONAL LIQUIDITY

International Monetary Fund, 700 Nineteenth Street, NW, Washington, D.C. 20431 (202) 623-7000; *International Financial Statistics.*

Organisation for Economic Co-operation and Development (OECD), 2 rue Andre-Pascal, 75 Paris 16, France (Telephone Number in U.S. (202) 785-6323); *Economic Outlook;* and *Financial Market Trends.*

UNITED KINGDOM - INTERNATIONAL RESERVES EXCLUDING GOLD

National Technical Information Service, 5285 Port Royal Road, Springfield, Virginia 22161 (703) 487-4600; *Handbook of Economic Statistics.*

Statistical Office of the United Nations, Publishing Service, New York, New York 10017 (800) 253-9646; *Statistical Yearbook.*

The World Bank, 1818 H Street, NW, Washington, D.C. 20433 (202) 477-1234;

World Development Indicators.

UNITED KINGDOM - INTERNATIONAL STATISTICS

Organisation for Economic Co-operation and Development (OECD), 2 rue Andre-Pascal, 75 Paris 16, France (Telephone Number in U.S. (202) 785-6323); *Financial Market Trends;* and *Tourism Policy and International Tourism in OECD Member Countries.*

UNITED KINGDOM - INVESTMENTS

International Monetary Fund, 700 Nineteenth Street, NW, Washington, D.C. 20431 (202) 623-7000; *International Financial Statistics.*

Organisation for Economic Co-operation and Development (OECD), 2 rue Andre-Pascal, 75 Paris 16, France (Telephone Number in U.S. (202) 785-6323); *Economic Outlook; Financial Market Trends; Industrial Structure Statistics; The Iron and Steel Industry;* and *Textile Industry in OECD Countries.*

UNITED KINGDOM - IRON ORE - See UNITED KINGDOM - MINING AND MINERAL PRODUCTS

UNITED KINGDOM - JUTE PRODUCTION - See UNITED KINGDOM - CROPS

UNITED KINGDOM - LABOR

Central Intelligence Agency, Washington, D.C. 20505 (703) 482-1100, www.cia.gov; *The World Factbook.*

Euromonitor International, Inc., 122 South Michigan Avenue, Suite 1200, Chicago, Illinois 60603 (800) 577-EURO; *World Marketing Data and Statistics.*

Europa Publications Limited, 18 Bedford Square, London, WC1B 3JN, England; *The Europa World Year Book.*

European Commission Office of Press and Public Affairs, 2100 M Street, NW, Washington, D.C. 20037 (202) 862-9500; *Basic Statistics of the Community; Labor Force Sample Survey;* and *Regions: Statistical Yearbook.*

Food and Agricultural Organization of the United Nations (FAO) Via delle Terme di Caracalla, 00100 Rome, Italy (Telephone Number in U.S. (202) 653-2400); *The State of Food and Agriculture.*

International Labour Office, I.L.O. Publications, 1828 L Street, NW, Suite 801, Washington, D.C. 20036 (301) 638-3152; *Yearbook of Labour Statistics.*

M.E. Sharpe, 80 Business Park Drive, Armonk, New York 10504 (800) 541-6563;

The Illustrated Book of World Rankings.

National Technical Information Service, 5285 Port Royal Road, Springfield, Virginia 22161 (703) 487-4600; *Handbook of Economic Statistics.*

Organisation for Economic Co-operation and Development (OECD), 2 rue Andre-Pascal, 75 Paris 16, France (Telephone Number in U.S. (202) 785-6323); *Economic Outlook; The Iron and Steel Industry; Main Economic Indicators - Historical Statistics; Maritime Transport; OECD Employment Outlook; OECD Economic Surveys: United Kingdom;* and *Textile Industry in OECD Countries.*

St. Martin's Press, Inc., 175 Fifth Avenue, New York, New York 10010 (800) 221-7945; *The Statesman's Year-Book.*

Statistical Office of the United Nations, Publishing Service, New York, New York 10017 (800) 253-9646; *Human Development Report.*

The World Bank, 1818 H Street, NW, Washington, D.C. 20433 (202) 477-1234; *The World Bank Atlas; World Development Report;* and *World Development Indicators.*

UNITED KINGDOM - LAND USE

Central Intelligence Agency, Washington, D.C. 20505 (703) 482-1100, www.cia.gov; *The World Factbook.*

Euromonitor International, Inc., 122 South Michigan Avenue, Suite 1200, Chicago, Illinois 60603 (800) 577-EURO; *European Marketing Data and Statistics.*

European Commission Office of Press and Public Affairs, 2100 M Street, NW, Washington, D.C. 20037 (202) 862-9500; *Agriculture: Statistical Yearbook; Basic Statistics of the Community; Crop Production: Quarterly Statistics;* and *Regions: Statistical Yearbook.*

Food and Agricultural Organization of the United Nations (FAO), Via delle Terme di Caracalla, 00100 Rome, Italy (Telephone Number in U.S. (202) 653-2400); *Production Yearbook.*

The World Bank, 1818 H Street, NW, Washington, D.C. 20433 (202) 477-1234; *World Development Report.*

UNITED KINGDOM - LEAD AND LEAD ORE PRODUCTION AND CONSUMPTION - See UNITED KINGDOM - MINING AND MINERAL PRODUCTS

UNITED KINGDOM - LEATHER - PRODUCTION INDEX

Organisation for Economic Co-operation and Development (OECD), 2 rue

Andre-Pascal, 75 Paris 16, France (Telephone Number in U.S. (202) 785-6323); *Indicators of Industrial Activity.*

UNITED KINGDOM - LEATHER AND FOOTWEAR - EXPORTS AND IMPORTS

European Commission Office of Press and Public Affairs, 2100 M Street, NW, Washington, D.C. 20037 (202) 862-9500; *Basic Statistics of the Community.*

Organisation for Economic Co-operation and Development (OECD), 2 rue Andre-Pascal, 75 Paris 16, France (Telephone Number in U.S. (202) 785-6323); *The Footwear, Raw Hides and Skins, and Leather Industry in OECD Countries.*

UNITED KINGDOM - LIBRARIES

Euromonitor International, Inc., 122 South Michigan Avenue, Suite 1200, Chicago, Illinois 60603 (800) 577-EURO; *European Marketing Data and Statistics.*

M.E. Sharpe, 80 Business Park Drive, Armonk, New York 10504 (800) 541-6563; *The Illustrated Book of World Rankings.*

Statistical Office of the United Nations, Publishing Service, New York, New York 10017 (800) 253-9646; *Trends in Europe and North America: The Statistical Yearbook of the Economic Commission for Europe.*

United Nations Educational, Scientific and Cultural Organization (UNESCO), 7 Place de Fontenoy, F-75700 Paris, France (Telephone Number in U.S. (212) 963-5981); *Statistical Yearbook.*

UNITED KINGDOM - LIFE EXPECTANCY

Central Intelligence Agency, Washington, D.C. 20505 (703) 482-1100, www.cia.gov; *The World Factbook.*

Euromonitor International, Inc., 122 South Michigan Avenue, Suite 1200, Chicago, Illinois 60603 (800) 577-EURO; *The World Economic Factbook.*

Organisation for Economic Co-operation and Development (OECD), 2 rue Andre-Pascal, 75 Paris 16, France (Telephone Number in U.S. (202) 785-6323); *Economic Outlook.*

St. Martin's Press, Inc., 175 Fifth Avenue, New York, New York 10010 (800) 221-7945; *The Statesman's Year-Book.*

Statistical Office of the United Nations, Publishing Service, New York, New York 10017 (800) 253-9646; *Human Development Report; Trends in Europe and North America: The Statistical Yearbook of the Economic Commission for Europe;* and *World Statistics Pocketbook.*

The World Bank, 1818 H Street, NW, Washington, D.C. 20433 (202) 477-1234; *The World Bank Atlas;* and *World Development Report.*

UNITED KINGDOM - LIGNITE PRODUCTION - See UNITED KINGDOM - MINING AND MINERAL PRODUCTS

UNITED KINGDOM - LITERACY RATE

Euromonitor International, Inc., 122 South Michigan Avenue, Suite 1200, Chicago, Illinois 60603 (800) 577-EURO; *World Marketing Data and Statistics.*

UNITED KINGDOM - LIVESTOCK AND POULTRY

Commodity Research Bureau, Inc., 30 South Wacker Drive, Chicago, Illinois 60606 (312) 454-1801; *Commodity Year Book.*

Euromonitor International, Inc., 122 South Michigan Avenue, Suite 1200, Chicago, Illinois 60603 (800) 577-EURO; *European Marketing Data and Statistics.*

Europa Publications Limited, 18 Bedford Square, London, WC1B 3JN, England; *The Europa World Year Book.*

European Commission Office of Press and Public Affairs, 2100 M Street, NW, Washington, D.C. 20037 (202) 862-9500; *Agriculture: Statistical Yearbook; Basic Statistics of the Community; Eurostatistics: Data for Short-Term Economic Analysis;* and *Regions: Statistical Yearbook.*

Food and Agricultural Organization of the United Nations (FAO), Via delle Terme di Caracalla, 00100 Rome, Italy (Telephone Number in U.S. (202) 653-2400); *Production Yearbook;* and *The State of Food and Agriculture.*

M.E. Sharpe, 80 Business Park Drive, Armonk, New York 10504 (800) 541-6563; *The Illustrated Book of World Rankings.*

National Technical Information Service, 5285 Port Royal Road, Springfield, Virginia 22161 (703) 487-4600; *Handbook of Economic Statistics.*

Organisation for Economic Co-operation and Development (OECD), 2 rue Andre-Pascal, 75 Paris 16, France (Telephone Number in U.S. (202) 785-6323); *Economic Accounts for Agriculture;* and *Meat Balances in OECD Member Countries.*

St. Martin's Press, Inc., 175 Fifth Avenue, New York, New York 10010 (800) 221-7945; *The Statesman's Year-Book.*

Statistical Office of the United Nations, Publishing Service, New York, New York 10017 (800) 253-9646; *Statistical Yearbook.*

UNITED KINGDOM - LIVING LEVELS - See UNITED KINGDOM - LIFE EXPECTANCY

UNITED KINGDOM - MACHINERY - PRODUCTION INDEX

Organisation for Economic Co-operation and Development (OECD), 2 rue Andre-Pascal, 75 Paris 16, France (Telephone Number in U.S. (202) 785-6323); *Indicators of Industrial Activity.*

UNITED KINGDOM - MAGNESIUM PRODUCTION AND CONSUMPTION - See UNITED KINGDOM - MINING AND MINERAL PRODUCTS

UNITED KINGDOM - MAIL - NUMBER OF PIECES SENT OR RECEIVED

European Commission Office of Press and Public Affairs, 2100 M Street, NW, Washington, D.C. 20037 (202) 862-9500; *Transport Annual Statistics.*

Statistical Office of the United Nations, Publishing Service, New York, New York 10017 (800) 253-9646; *Statistical Yearbook.*

UNITED KINGDOM - MAIN ECONOMIC INDICATORS - See UNITED KINGDOM - ECONOMY

UNITED KINGDOM - MANGANESE PRODUCTION AND CONSUMPTION - See UNITED KINGDOM - MINING AND MINERAL PRODUCTS

UNITED KINGDOM - MANUFACTURING

European Commission Office of Press and Public Affairs, 2100 M Street, NW, Washington, D.C. 20037 (202) 862-9500; *Basic Statistics of the Community; Eurostatistics: Data for Short-Term Economic Analysis;* and *Industrial Production: Quarterly Statistics.*

M.E. Sharpe, 80 Business Park Drive, Armonk, New York 10504 (800) 541-6563; *The Illustrated Book of World Rankings.*

Organisation for Economic Co-operation and Development (OECD), 2 rue Andre-Pascal, 75 Paris 16, France (Telephone Number in U.S. (202) 785-6323); *Indicators of Industrial Activity; Industrial Structure Statistics;* and *OECD Economic Surveys: United Kingdom.*

Statistical Office of the United Nations, Publishing Service, New York, New York 10017 (800) 253-9646; *Statistical Yearbook.*

The World Bank, 1818 H Street, NW, Washington, D.C. 20433 (202) 477-1234; *World Development Indicators.*

UNITED KINGDOM - MARRIAGE RATES

Europa Publications Limited, 18

Bedford Square, London, WC1B 3JN, England; *The Europa World Year Book*.

European Commission Office of Press and Public Affairs, 2100 M Street, NW, Washington, D.C. 20037 (202) 862-9500; *Basic Statistics of the Community*.

M.E. Sharpe, 80 Business Park Drive, Armonk, New York 10504 (800) 541-6563; *The Illustrated Book of World Rankings*.

Statistical Office of the United Nations, Publishing Service, New York, New York 10017 (800) 253-9646; *Demographic Yearbook; Trends in Europe and North America: The Statistical Yearbook of the Economic Commission for Europe;* and *Statistical Yearbook*.

UNITED KINGDOM - MEAT PRODUCTION - See UNITED KINGDOM -LIVESTOCK AND POULTRY

UNITED KINGDOM - MERCHANT SHIPPING

Europa Publications Limited, 18 Bedford Square, London, WC1B 3JN, England; *The Europa World Year Book*.

European Commission Office of Press and Public Affairs, 2100 M Street, NW, Washington, D.C. 20037 (202) 862-9500; *Basic Statistics of the Community; Fisheries: Yearly Statistics; Regions: Statistical Yearbook;* and *Transport Annual Statistics*.

National Technical Information Service, 5285 Port Royal Road, Springfield, Virginia 22161 (703) 487-4600; *Handbook of Economic Statistics*.

Organisation for Economic Co-operation and Development (OECD), 2 rue Andre-Pascal, 75 Paris 16, France (Telephone Number in U.S. (202) 785-6323); *Maritime Transport*.

St. Martin's Press, Inc., 175 Fifth Avenue, New York, New York 10010 (800) 221-7945; *The Statesman's Year-Book*.

Statistical Office of the United Nations, Publishing Service, New York, New York 10017 (800) 253-9646; *Annual Bulletin of Transport Statistics for Europe;* and *Statistical Yearbook*.

U.S. Department of Transportation, Maritime Administration, 400 Seventh Street, SW, Washington, D.C. 20590 (202) 366-5807, www.marad.dot.gov; *A Statistical Analysis of the World's Merchant Fleets*.

UNITED KINGDOM - MERCURY PRODUCTION AND CONSUMPTION - See UNITED KINGDOM - MINING AND MINERAL PRODUCTS

UNITED KINGDOM - MILITARY

Central Intelligence Agency, Washington, D.C. 20505 (703) 482-1100, www.cia.gov; *The World Factbook*.

Euromonitor International, Inc., 122 South Michigan Avenue, Suite 1200, Chicago, Illinois 60603 (800) 577-EURO; *World Marketing Data and Statistics*.

European Commission Office of Press and Public Affairs, 2100 M Street, NW, Washington, D.C. 20037 (202) 862-9500; *Government Financing of Research and Development*.

The International Institute for Strategic Studies, 23 Tavistock Street, London WC2E 7NQ, England 44 171 3797676; *The Military Balance*.

International Monetary Fund, 700 Nineteenth Street, NW, Washington, D.C. 20431 (202) 623-7000; *Government Finance Statistics Yearbook*.

National Technical Information Service, 5285 Port Royal Road, Springfield, Virginia 22161 (703) 487-4600; *Handbook of Economic Statistics*.

St. Martin's Press, Inc., 175 Fifth Avenue, New York, New York 10010 (800) 221-7945; *The Statesman's Year-Book*.

Statistical Office of the United Nations, Publishing Service, New York, New York 10017 (800) 253-9646; *Human Development Report*.

U.S. Arms Control and Disarmament Agency, 320 Twenty-first Street, NW, Washington, D.C. 20451 (202) 647-8677; *World Military Expenditures and Arms Transfers*.

UNITED KINGDOM - MILK PRODUCTION - See UNITED KINGDOM - DAIRY PRODUCTS

UNITED KINGDOM - MILLET PRODUCTION - See UNITED KINGDOM - CROPS

UNITED KINGDOM - MINING AND MINERAL PRODUCTS

Commodity Research Bureau, Inc., 30 South Wacker Drive, Chicago, Illinois 60606 (312) 454-1801; *Commodity Year Book*.

Europa Publications Limited, 18 Bedford Square, London, WC1B 3JN, England; *The Europa World Year Book*.

European Commission Office of Press and Public Affairs, 2100 M Street, NW, Washington, D.C. 20037 (202) 862-9500; *ACP: Basic Statistics; Basic Statistics of the Community; Energy: Monthly Statistics; Energy Statistics Yearbook; Eurostatistics:*

Data for Short-Term Economic Analysis; Industrial Production: Quarterly Statistics; Iron and Steel: Statistical Yearbook; Labor Force Sample Survey; and *Regions: Statistical Yearbook*.

International Iron and Steel Institute, 120, rue Colonel Bourg, B-1140, Belgium; *Steel Statistical Yearbook*.

International Lead and Zinc Study Group, Metro House, 58 St. James's Street, London SW1A 1LD England; *Lead and Zinc Statistics*.

International Monetary Fund, 700 Nineteenth Street, NW, Washington, D.C. 20431 (202) 623-7000; *International Financial Statistics*.

M.E. Sharpe, 80 Business Park Drive, Armonk, New York 10504 (800) 541-6563; *The Illustrated Book of World Rankings*.

National Technical Information Service, 5285 Port Royal Road, Springfield, Virginia 22161 (703) 487-4600; *Handbook of Economic Statistics*.

Organisation for Economic Co-operation and Development (OECD), 2 rue Andre-Pascal, 75 Paris 16, France (Telephone Number in U.S. (202) 785-6323); *Coal Information; Energy Statistics of OECD Countries; Foreign Trade by Commodities; Indicators of Industrial Activity; Industrial Structure Statistics; The Iron and Steel Industry;* and *The Non-Ferrous Metals Industry*.

Penn Well Publishing Company, 1421 South Sheridan Road, P.O. Box 1260, Tulsa, Oklahoma 74101 (800) 752-9764; *International Energy Statistics Sourcebook*.

St. Martin's Press, Inc., 175 Fifth Avenue, New York, New York 10010 (800) 221-7945; *The Statesman's Year-Book*.

Statistical Office of the United Nations, Publishing Service, New York, New York 10017 (800) 253-9646; *Statistical Yearbook*.

United Nations Conference on Trade and Development, Central Statistical Service, Palais des Nations, Geneva, Switzerland (Telephone in U.S. (800) 253-9646); *UNCTAD Commodity Yearbook*.

World Bureau of Metal Statistics, 27-A High Street, Ware Hert SG12 9BA, England; *World Metal Statistics*.

UNITED KINGDOM - MOLASSES PRODUCTION - See UNITED KINGDOM - CROPS

UNITED KINGDOM - MOLYBDENUM AND MOLYBDENUM ORE PRODUCTION AND CONSUMPTION - See UNITED KINGDOM - MINING AND MINERAL PRODUCTS

UNITED KINGDOM - MONEY AND CREDIT

Organisation for Economic Cooperation and Development (OECD), 2 rue Andre-Pascal, 75 Paris 16, France (Telephone Number in U.S. (202) 785-6323); *OECD Economic Surveys: United Kingdom.*

UNITED KINGDOM - MONEY EXCHANGE RATE - See UNITED KINGDOM - EXCHANGE RATE

UNITED KINGDOM - MONEY RATES - MARKET

European Commission Office of Press and Public Affairs, 2100 M Street, NW, Washington, D.C. 20037 (202) 862-9500; *Basic Statistics of the Community.*

Organisation for Economic Co-operation and Development (OECD), 2 rue Andre-Pascal, 75 Paris 16, France (Telephone Number in U.S. (202) 785-6323); *Economic Outlook;* and *Financial Market Trends.*

Statistical Office of the United Nations, Publishing Service, New York, New York 10017 (800) 253-9646; *Statistical Yearbook.*

UNITED KINGDOM - MONEY RESERVES

European Commission Office of Press and Public Affairs, 2100 M Street, NW, Washington, D.C. 20037 (202) 862-9500; *Basic Statistics of the Community.*

Organisation for Economic Co-operation and Development (OECD), 2 rue Andre-Pascal, 75 Paris 16, France (Telephone Number in U.S. (202) 785-6323); *Economic Outlook;* and *Financial Market Trends.*

UNITED KINGDOM - MONEY SUPPLY

Economist Intelligence Unit, 111 West 57th Street, New York, New York 10019 (800) 938-4685; *United Kingdom Country Report.*

Europa Publications Limited, 18 Bedford Square, London, WC1B 3JN, England; *The Europa World Year Book.*

European Commission Office of Press and Public Affairs, 2100 M Street, NW, Washington, D.C. 20037 (202) 862-9500; *Basic Statistics of the Community; Eurostatistics: Data for Short-Term Economic Analysis;* and *Money and Finance.*

International Monetary Fund, 700 Nineteenth Street, NW, Washington, D.C. 20431 (202) 623-7000; *International Financial Statistics.*

Organisation for Economic Co-operation and Development (OECD), 2 rue

Andre-Pascal, 75 Paris 16, France (Telephone Number in U.S. (202) 785-6323); *Economic Outlook.*

Statistical Office of the United Nations, Publishing Service, New York, New York 10017 (800) 253-9646; *Statistical Yearbook.*

The World Bank, 1818 H Street, NW, Washington, D.C. 20433 (202) 477-1234; *World Development Indicators.*

UNITED KINGDOM - MORTALITY

Central Intelligence Agency, Washington, D.C. 20505 (703) 482-1100, www.cia.gov; *The World Factbook.*

Europa Publications Limited, 18 Bedford Square, London, WC1B 3JN, England; *The Europa World Year Book.*

European Commission Office of Press and Public Affairs, 2100 M Street, NW, Washington, D.C. 20037 (202) 862-9500; *Basic Statistics of the Community; Demographic Statistics;* and *The World Economic Factbook.*

St. Martin's Press, Inc., 175 Fifth Avenue, New York, New York 10010 (800) 221-7945; *The Statesman's Year-Book.*

Statistical Office of the United Nations, Publishing Service, New York, New York 10017 (800) 253-9646; *Demographic Yearbook; Human Development Report; Trends in Europe and North America: The Statistical Yearbook of the Economic Commission for Europe; Statistical Yearbook;* and *World Statistics Pocketbook.*

United Nations Children's Fund (UNICEF), 3 United Nations Plaza, New York, New York 10017 (800) 253-9646; *State of the World's Children.*

The World Bank, 1818 H Street, NW, Washington, D.C. 20433 (202) 477-1234; *The World Bank Atlas;* and *World Development Report.*

World Health Organization, Office of Publications, 20 Avenue Appia, CH-1211 Geneva 27, Switzerland (Telephone Number in U.S. (518) 436-9686); *World Health Statistics Annual.*

UNITED KINGDOM - MOTION PICTURES

St. Martin's Press, Inc., 175 Fifth Avenue, New York, New York 10010 (800) 221-7945; *The Statesman's Year-Book.*

Statistical Office of the United Nations, Publishing Service, New York, New York 10017 (800) 253-9646; *Statistical Yearbook.*

United Nations Educational, Scientific and Cultural Organization (UNESCO), 7 Place de Fontenoy, F-75700 Paris, France

(Telephone Number in U.S. (212) 963-5981); *Statistical Yearbook.*

UNITED KINGDOM - MOTOR VEHICLE PRODUCTION

Europa Publications Limited, 18 Bedford Square, London, WC1B 3JN, England; *The Europa World Year Book.*

European Commission Office of Press and Public Affairs, 2100 M Street, NW, Washington, D.C. 20037 (202) 862-9500; *Basic Statistics of the Community;* and *Eurostatistics: Data for Short-Term Economic Analysis.*

National Technical Information Service, 5285 Port Royal Road, Springfield, Virginia 22161 (703) 487-4600; *Handbook of Economic Statistics.*

Organisation for Economic Co-operation and Development (OECD), 2 rue Andre-Pascal, 75 Paris 16, France (Telephone Number in U.S. (202) 785-6323); *Foreign Trade by Commodities.*

Statistical Office of the United Nations, Publishing Service, New York, New York 10017 (800) 253-9646; *Statistical Yearbook.*

UNITED KINGDOM - MOTOR VEHICLE TAXES - See UNITED KINGDOM - TAXATION

UNITED KINGDOM - MOTOR VEHICLES IN USE

European Commission Office of Press and Public Affairs, 2100 M Street, NW, Washington, D.C. 20037 (202) 862-9500; *Basic Statistics of the Community;* and *Transport Annual Statistics.*

International Road Federation, 2600 Virginia Avenue, NW, Washington, D.C. 20037 (202) 338-4641; *World Road Statistics.*

Statistical Office of the United Nations, Publishing Service, New York, New York 10017 (800) 253-9646; *Statistical Yearbook.*

UNITED KINGDOM - MULES - See UNITED KINGDOM - LIVESTOCK AND POULTRY

UNITED KINGDOM - MUSEUMS

Euromonitor International, Inc., 122 South Michigan Avenue, Suite 1200, Chicago, Illinois 60603 (800) 577-EURO; *European Marketing Data and Statistics.*

M.E. Sharpe, 80 Business Park Drive, Armonk, New York 10504 (800) 541-6563; *The Illustrated Book of World Rankings.*

UNITED KINGDOM - NATALITY - See UNITED KINGDOM - BIRTH RATE

UNITED KINGDOM - NATIONAL ACCOUNTS

Europa Publications Limited, 18 Bedford Square, London, WC1B 3JN, England; *The Europa World Year Book.*

European Commission Office of Press and Public Affairs, 2100 M Street, NW, Washington, D.C. 20037 (202) 862-9500; *Basic Statistics of the Community;* and *Eurostatistics: Data for Short-Term Economic Analysis.*

International Monetary Fund, 700 Nineteenth Street, NW, Washington, D.C. 20431 (202) 623-7000; *International Financial Statistics.*

Organisation for Economic Co-operation and Development (OECD), 2 rue Andre-Pascal, 75 Paris 16, France (Telephone Number in U.S. (202) 785-6323); *Economic Outlook.*

Statistical Office of the United Nations, Publishing Service, New York, New York 10017 (800) 253-9646; *National Accounts Statistics;* and *Statistical Yearbook.*

UNITED KINGDOM - NATIONAL INCOME

M.E. Sharpe, 80 Business Park Drive, Armonk, New York 10504 (800) 541-6563; *The Illustrated Book of World Rankings.*

Organisation for Economic Co-operation and Development (OECD), 2 rue Andre-Pascal, 75 Paris 16, France (Telephone Number in U.S. (202) 785-6323); *Economic Outlook.*

Statistical Office of the United Nations, Publishing Service, New York, New York 10017 (800) 253-9646; *National Accounts Statistics;* and *Statistical Yearbook.*

UNITED KINGDOM - NATIONAL PRODUCT

European Commission Office of Press and Public Affairs, 2100 M Street, NW, Washington, D.C. 20037 (202) 862-9500; *Basic Statistics of the Community.*

M.E. Sharpe, 80 Business Park Drive, Armonk, New York 10504 (800) 541-6563; *The Illustrated Book of World Rankings.*

Organisation for Economic Co-operation and Development (OECD), 2 rue Andre-Pascal, 75 Paris 16, France (Telephone Number in U.S. (202) 785-6323); *Economic Outlook;* and *Main Economic Indicators - Historical Statistics.*

Statistical Office of the United Nations, Publishing Service, New York, New York 10017 (800) 253-9646; *Statistical Yearbook.*

UNITED KINGDOM - NATURAL GAS PRODUCTION - See UNITED KINGDOM - MINING AND MINERAL PRODUCTS

UNITED KINGDOM - NEWSPAPER PRODUCTION - See UNITED KINGDOM - FORESTRY AND FOREST PRODUCTS

UNITED KINGDOM - NEWSPRINT - See UNITED KINGDOM - FORESTRY AND FOREST PRODUCTS

UNITED KINGDOM - NICKEL AND NICKEL ORE PRODUCTION AND CONSUMPTION - See UNITED KINGDOM - MINING AND MINERAL PRODUCTS

UNITED KINGDOM - NITRIC ACID PRODUCTION - See UNITED KINGDOM - MINING AND MINERAL PRODUCTS

UNITED KINGDOM - OATS PRODUCTION - See UNITED KINGDOM - CROPS

UNITED KINGDOM - OCCUPATIONS - See UNITED KINGDOM - LABOR

UNITED KINGDOM - OIL PRODUCING CROPS

European Commission Office of Press and Public Affairs, 2100 M Street, NW, Washington, D.C. 20037 (202) 862-9500; *Basic Statistics of the Community.*

Organisation for Economic Co-operation and Development (OECD), 2 rue Andre-Pascal, 75 Paris 16, France (Telephone Number in U.S. (202) 785-6323); *Foreign Trade by Commodities.*

UNITED KINGDOM - ONION PRODUCTION - See UNITED KINGDOM - CROPS

UNITED KINGDOM - PALM KERNEL PRODUCTION - See UNITED KINGDOM - CROPS

UNITED KINGDOM - PAPER - See UNITED KINGDOM - FORESTRY AND FOREST PRODUCTS

UNITED KINGDOM - PATENTS, TRADEMARKS AND SERVICE MARKS

Statistical Office of the United Nations, Publishing Service, New York, New York 10017 (800) 253-9646; *Statistical Yearbook.*

World Intellectual Property Organization, 34 Chemin des Colombettes, CH-1211 Geneva 20. Switzerland; *Industrial Property Statistics.*

UNITED KINGDOM - PEANUT PRODUCTION - See UNITED KINGDOM - CROPS

UNITED KINGDOM - PEPPER PRODUCTION - See UNITED KINGDOM - CROPS

UNITED KINGDOM - PERIODICALS

United Nations Educational, Scientific and Cultural Organization (UNESCO), 7 Place de Fontenoy, F-75700 Paris, France (Telephone Number in U.S. (212) 963-5981); *Statistical Yearbook.*

UNITED KINGDOM - PESTICIDE USE

Food and Agricultural Organization of the United Nations (FAO) Via delle Terme di Caracalla, 00100 Rome, Italy (Telephone Number in U.S. (202) 653-2400); *The State of Food and Agriculture.*

UNITED KINGDOM - PETROLEUM INDUSTRY

Euromonitor International, Inc., 122 South Michigan Avenue, Suite 1200, Chicago, Illinois 60603 (800) 577-EURO; *European Marketing Data and Statistics.*

European Commission Office of Press and Public Affairs, 2100 M Street, NW, Washington, D.C. 20037 (202) 862-9500; *ACP: Basic Statistics; Basic Statistics of the Community;* and *Energy Statistics Yearbook.*

Food and Agricultural Organization of the United Nations (FAO) Via delle Terme di Caracalla, 00100 Rome, Italy (Telephone Number in U.S. (202) 653-2400); *The State of Food and Agriculture.*

M.E. Sharpe, 80 Business Park Drive, Armonk, New York 10504 (800) 541-6563; *The Illustrated Book of World Rankings.*

National Technical Information Service, 5285 Port Royal Road, Springfield, Virginia 22161 (703) 487-4600; *Handbook of Economic Statistics.*

Organisation for Economic Co-operation and Development (OECD), 2 rue Andre-Pascal, 75 Paris 16, France (Telephone Number in U.S. (202) 785-6323); *Energy Statistics of OECD Countries; Foreign Trade by Commodities; Indicators of Industrial Activity;* and *Oil and Gas Information.*

Penn Well Publishing Company, 1421 South Sheridan Road, P.O. Box 1260, Tulsa, Oklahoma 74101 (800) 752-9764; *International Energy Statistics Sourcebook.*

St. Martin's Press, Inc., 175 Fifth Avenue, New York, New York 10010 (800) 221-7945; *The Statesman's Year-Book.*

Statistical Office of the United Nations, Publishing Service, New York, New York 10017 (800) 253-9646; *Statistical Yearbook;* and *Trends in Europe and North America: The Statistical Yearbook of the Economic Commission for Europe.*

United Nations Conference on Trade and Development, Central Statistical

Service, Palais des Nations, Geneva, Switzerland (Telephone in U.S. (800) 253-9646); *UNCTAD Commodity Yearbook*.

UNITED KINGDOM - PHOSPHATE ROCK PRODUCTION - See UNITED KINGDOM - MINING AND MINERAL PRODUCTS

UNITED KINGDOM - PHOSPHATES PRODUCTION - See UNITED KINGDOM - MINING AND MINERAL PRODUCTS

UNITED KINGDOM - PIG-IRON AND FERRO-ALLOY PRODUCTION - See UNITED KINGDOM - MINING AND MINERAL PRODUCTS

UNITED KINGDOM - PIGS - See UNITED KINGDOM - LIVESTOCK AND POULTRY

UNITED KINGDOM - PIPELINES FOR OIL AND PETROLEUM PRODUCTS

European Commission Office of Press and Public Affairs, 2100 M Street, NW, Washington, D.C. 20037 (202) 862-9500; *Transport Annual Statistics*.

National Technical Information Service, 5285 Port Royal Road, Springfield, Virginia 22161 (703) 487-4600; *Handbook of Economic Statistics*.

Statistical Office of the United Nations, Publishing Service, New York, New York 10017 (800) 253-9646; *Annual Bulletin of Transport Statistics for Europe*.

UNITED KINGDOM - PLASTIC AND RESIN PRODUCTION

Commodity Research Bureau, Inc., 30 South Wacker Drive, Suite 1810, Chicago, Illinois 60606 (312) 454-1801; *Commodity Year Book*.

European Commission Office of Press and Public Affairs, 2100 M Street, NW, Washington, D.C. 20037 (202) 862-9500; *Basic Statistics of the Community*.

Organisation for Economic Co-operation and Development (OECD), 2 rue Andre-Pascal, 75 Paris 16, France (Telephone Number in U.S. (202) 785-6323); *Foreign Trade by Commodities*.

Statistical Office of the United Nations, Publishing Service, New York, New York 10017 (800) 253-9646; *Statistical Yearbook*.

UNITED KINGDOM - PLATINUM PRODUCTION - See UNITED KINGDOM - MINING AND MINERAL PRODUCTS

UNITED KINGDOM - POPULATION

Central Intelligence Agency, Washington, D.C. 20505 (703) 482-1100, www.cia.gov; *The World Factbook*.

The Economist Intelligence Unit, 111 West 57th Street, New York, New York 10019 (800) 938-4685; *United Kingdom Country Report;* and *The World Market Atlas*.

Euromonitor International, Inc., 122 South Michigan Avenue, Suite 1200, Chicago, Illinois 60603 (800) 577-EURO; *European Marketing Data and Statistics;* and *The World Economic Factbook*.

Europa Publications Limited, 18 Bedford Square, London, WC1B 3JN, England; *The Europa World Year Book*.

European Commission Office of Press and Public Affairs, 2100 M Street, NW, Washington, D.C. 20037 (202) 862-9500; *ACP: Basic Statistics; Basic Statistics of the Community; Demographic Statistics; Employment and Unemployment; Fisheries: Yearly Statistics; Iron and Steel: Statistical Yearbook; Labor Force Sample Survey;* and *Regions: Statistical Yearbook*.

Food and Agricultural Organization of the United Nations (FAO), Via delle Terme di Caracalla, 00100 Rome, Italy (Telephone Number in U.S. (202) 653-2400); *Production Yearbook*.

International Labour Office, I.L.O. Publications, 1828 L Street, NW, Suite 801, Washington, D.C. 20036 (301) 638-3152; *Yearbook of Labour Statistics*.

M.E. Sharpe, 80 Business Park Drive, Armonk, New York 10504 (800) 541-6563; *The Illustrated Book of World Rankings*.

National Technical Information Service, 5285 Port Royal Road, Springfield, Virginia 22161 (703) 487-4600; *Handbook of Economic Statistics*.

St. Martin's Press, Inc., 175 Fifth Avenue, New York, New York 10010 (800) 221-7945; *The Statesman's Year-Book*.

Statistical Office of the United Nations, Publishing Service, New York, New York 10017 (800) 253-9646; *Demographic Yearbook; Human Development Report; Trends in Europe and North America: The Statistical Yearbook of the Economic Commission for Europe; Statistical Yearbook;* and *World Statistics Pocketbook*.

United Nations Educational, Scientific and Cultural Organization (UNESCO), 7 Place de Fontenoy, F-75700 Paris, France (Telephone Number in U.S. (212) 963-5981); *Statistical Yearbook*.

U.S. Arms Control and Disarmament Agency, 320 Twenty-first Street, NW, Washington, D.C. 20451 (202) 647-8677; *World Military Expenditures and Arms Transfers*.

The World Bank, 1818 H Street, NW, Washington, D.C. 20433 (202) 477-1234; *The World Bank Atlas;* and *World Development Report*.

World Health Organization, Office of Publications, 20 Avenue Appia, CH-1211 Geneva 27, Switzerland (Telephone Number in U.S. (518) 436-9686); *World Health Statistics Annual*.

UNITED KINGDOM - POST OFFICES

M.E. Sharpe, 80 Business Park Drive, Armonk, New York 10504 (800) 541-6563; *The Illustrated Book of World Rankings*.

St. Martin's Press, Inc., 175 Fifth Avenue, New York, New York 10010 (800) 221-7945; *The Statesman's Year-Book*.

Statistical Office of the United Nations, Publishing Service, New York, New York 10017 (800) 253-9646; *Trends in Europe and North America: The Statistical Yearbook of the Economic Commission for Europe*.

UNITED KINGDOM - POTATO PRODUCTION - See UNITED KINGDOM - CROPS

UNITED KINGDOM - POWER PRODUCTION INDUSTRY

European Commission Office of Press and Public Affairs, 2100 M Street, NW, Washington, D.C. 20037 (202) 862-9500; *Basic Statistics of the Community*.

Statistical Office of the United Nations, Publishing Service, New York, New York 10017 (800) 253-9646; *Statistical Yearbook*.

UNITED KINGDOM - PRICES

European Commission Office of Press and Public Affairs, 2100 M Street, NW, Washington, D.C. 20037 (202) 862-9500; *Basic Statistics of the Community;* and *Eurostatistics: Data for Short-Term Economic Analysis*.

Food and Agricultural Organization of the United Nations (FAO), Via delle Terme di Caracalla, 00100 Rome, Italy (Telephone Number in U.S. (202) 653-2400); *Production Yearbook;* and *The State of Food and Agriculture*.

International Labour Office, I.L.O. Publications, 1828 L Street, NW, Suite 801, Washington, D.C. 20036 (301) 638-3152; *Yearbook of Labour Statistics*.

International Lead and Zinc Study Group, Metro House, 58 St. James's Street, London SW1A 1LD England; *Lead and Zinc Statistics*.

International Monetary Fund, 700 Nineteenth Street, NW, Washington, D.C.

20431 (202) 623-7000; *International Financial Statistics.*

International Rubber Study Group, York House, Eighth Floor, Empire Way, Wembley, London HA9 0PA, England; *Rubber Statistical Bulletin.*

M.E. Sharpe, 80 Business Park Drive, Armonk, New York 10504 (800) 541-6563; *The Illustrated Book of World Rankings.*

National Technical Information Service, 5285 Port Royal Road, Springfield, Virginia 22161 (703) 487-4600; *Handbook of Economic Statistics.*

Organisation for Economic Co-operation and Development (OECD), 2 rue Andre-Pascal, 75 Paris 16, France (Telephone Number in U.S. (202) 785-6323); *Economic Outlook; The Footwear, Raw Hides and Skins, and Leather Industry in OECD Countries; Indicators of Industrial Activity; The Iron and Steel Industry; Main Economic Indicators - Historical Statistics; and The Pulp and Paper Industry.*

World Bureau of Metal Statistics, 27-A High Street, Ware Hert SG12 9BA, England; *World Metal Statistics.*

UNITED KINGDOM - PRINTING AND WRITING PAPER - See UNITED KINGDOM - FORESTRY AND FOREST PRODUCTS

UNITED KINGDOM - PRODUCTION

European Commission Office of Press and Public Affairs, 2100 M Street, NW, Washington, D.C. 20037 (202) 862-9500; *Basic Statistics of the Community; Eurostatistics: Data for Short-Term Economic Analysis; and Fisheries: Yearly Statistics.*

International Iron and Steel Institute, 120, rue Colonel Bourg, B-1140, Belgium; *Steel Statistical Yearbook.*

International Lead and Zinc Study Group, Metro House, 58 St. James's Street, London SW1A 1LD England; *Lead and Zinc Statistics.*

International Rubber Study Group, York House, Eighth Floor, Empire Way, Wembley, London HA9 0PA, England; *Rubber Statistical Bulletin.*

National Technical Information Service, 5285 Port Royal Road, Springfield, Virginia 22161 (703) 487-4600; *Handbook of Economic Statistics.*

Organisation for Economic Co-operation and Development (OECD), 2 rue Andre-Pascal, 75 Paris 16, France (Telephone Number in U.S. (202) 785-6323); *Economic Outlook; The Footwear, Raw Hides and Skins, and Leather Industry in OECD Countries; Indicators of Industrial Activity; Industrial Structure Statistics; The Iron and Steel Industry; Meat Balances in OECD Member Countries; Milk, Milk Products, and Egg Balances in OECD Member Countries; The Non-Ferrous Metals Industry; The Pulp and Paper Industry; and Textile Industry in OECD Countries.*

UNITED KINGDOM - PRODUCTIVITY

European Commission Office of Press and Public Affairs, 2100 M Street, NW, Washington, D.C. 20037 (202) 862-9500; *Basic Statistics of the Community.*

Organisation for Economic Co-operation and Development (OECD), 2 rue Andre-Pascal, 75 Paris 16, France (Telephone Number in U.S. (202) 785-6323); *Economic Outlook.*

UNITED KINGDOM - PROPERTY TAXES - See UNITED KINGDOM - TAXATION

UNITED KINGDOM - PUBLIC CONSUMPTION FUND

European Commission Office of Press and Public Affairs, 2100 M Street, NW, Washington, D.C. 20037 (202) 862-9500; *Basic Statistics of the Community.*

Organisation for Economic Co-operation and Development (OECD), 2 rue Andre-Pascal, 75 Paris 16, France (Telephone Number in U.S. (202) 785-6323); *Revenue Statistics of OECD Member Countries.*

UNITED KINGDOM - PUBLIC EXPENDITURES

European Commission Office of Press and Public Affairs, 2100 M Street, NW, Washington, D.C. 20037 (202) 862-9500; *Basic Statistics of the Community.*

National Technical Information Service, 5285 Port Royal Road, Springfield, Virginia 22161 (703) 487-4600; *Handbook of Economic Statistics.*

Organisation for Economic Co-operation and Development (OECD), 2 rue Andre-Pascal, 75 Paris 16, France (Telephone Number in U.S. (202) 785-6323); *Revenue Statistics of OECD Member Countries.*

UNITED KINGDOM - PUBLIC FINANCE - See UNITED KINGDOM - FINANCE

UNITED KINGDOM - PUBLIC HEALTH - See UNITED KINGDOM - HEALTH

UNITED KINGDOM - PUBLIC REVENUES

National Technical Information Service, 5285 Port Royal Road, Springfield, Virginia 22161 (703) 487-4600; *Handbook of Economic Statistics.*

Organisation for Economic Co-operation and Development (OECD), 2 rue Andre-Pascal, 75 Paris 16, France (Telephone Number in U.S. (202) 785-6323); *Revenue Statistics of OECD Member Countries.*

UNITED KINGDOM - RADIO BROADCASTING - See UNITED KINGDOM - BROADCASTING

UNITED KINGDOM - RADIO RECEIVER PRODUCTION

Statistical Office of the United Nations, Publishing Service, New York, New York 10017 (800) 253-9646; *Statistical Yearbook.*

UNITED KINGDOM - RADIO RECEIVERS

St. Martin's Press, Inc., 175 Fifth Avenue, New York, New York 10010 (800) 221-7945; *The Statesman's Year-Book.*

UNITED KINGDOM - RAILWAYS

Euromonitor International, Inc., 122 South Michigan Avenue, Suite 1200, Chicago, Illinois 60603 (800) 577-EURO; *European Marketing Data and Statistics.*

Europa Publications Limited, 18 Bedford Square, London, WC1B 3JN, England; *The Europa World Year Book.*

European Commission Office of Press and Public Affairs, 2100 M Street, NW, Washington, D.C. 20037 (202) 862-9500; *Basic Statistics of the Community; Regions: Statistical Yearbook; and Transport Annual Statistics.*

Jane's Information Group, Sentinel House, 163 Brighton Road, Coulsdon, Surrey CR5 2NH, England (Telephone Number in U.S. (703) 683-3700); *Jane's World Railways.*

National Technical Information Service, 5285 Port Royal Road, Springfield, Virginia 22161 (703) 487-4600; *Handbook of Economic Statistics.*

St. Martin's Press, Inc., 175 Fifth Avenue, New York, New York 10010 (800) 221-7945; *The Statesman's Year-Book.*

Statistical Office of the United Nations, Publishing Service, New York, New York 10017 (800) 253-9646; *Annual Bulletin of Transport Statistics for Europe; Trends in Europe and North America: The Statistical Yearbook of the Economic Commission for Europe; and Statistical Yearbook.*

UNITED KINGDOM - RANCHING

European Commission Office of Press and Public Affairs, 2100 M Street, NW,

Washington, D.C. 20037 (202) 862-9500; *Basic Statistics of the Community.*

UNITED KINGDOM - RAPESEED PRODUCTION - See UNITED KINGDOM - CROPS

UNITED KINGDOM - RELIGION

Central Intelligence Agency, Washington, D.C. 20505 (703) 482-1100, www.cia.gov; *The World Factbook.*

M.E. Sharpe, 80 Business Park Drive, Armonk, New York 10504 (800) 541-6563; *The Illustrated Book of World Rankings.*

St. Martin's Press, Inc., 175 Fifth Avenue, New York, New York 10010 (800) 221-7945; *The Statesman's Year-Book.*

UNITED KINGDOM - RENT PRICES

International Labour Office, I.L.O. Publications, 1828 L Street, NW, Suite 801, Washington, D.C. 20036 (301) 638-3152; *Yearbook of Labour Statistics.*

UNITED KINGDOM - RETAIL PRICE INDEX

Europa Publications Limited, 18 Bedford Square, London, WC1B 3JN, England; *The Europa World Year Book.*

UNITED KINGDOM - RETAIL TRADE

Euromonitor International, Inc., 122 South Michigan Avenue, Suite 1200, Chicago, Illinois 60603 (800) 577-EURO; *World Marketing Data and Statistics;* and *Retail Trade International.*

European Commission Office of Press and Public Affairs, 2100 M Street, NW, Washington, D.C. 20037 (202) 862-9500; *Basic Statistics of the Community;* and *Eurostatistics: Data for Short-Term Economic Analysis.*

Statistical Office of the United Nations, Publishing Service, New York, New York 10017 (800) 253-9646; *Statistical Yearbook.*

UNITED KINGDOM - RICE PRODUCTION - See UNITED KINGDOM - CROPS

UNITED KINGDOM - ROOT AND TUBER PRODUCTION - See UNITED KINGDOM - CROPS

UNITED KINGDOM - ROUNDWOOD PRODUCTION - See UNITED KINGDOM - FORESTRY AND FOREST PRODUCTS

UNITED KINGDOM - RUBBER PRODUCTION AND CONSUMPTION

Commodity Research Bureau, Inc., 30 South Wacker Drive, Chicago, Illinois 60606 (312) 454-1801; *Commodity Year Book.*

European Commission Office of Press and Public Affairs, 2100 M Street, NW, Washington, D.C. 20037 (202) 862-9500; *Basic Statistics of the Community.*

International Rubber Study Group, York House, Eighth Floor, Empire Way, Wembley, London HA9 0PA, England; *Rubber Statistical Bulletin.*

M.E. Sharpe, 80 Business Park Drive, Armonk, New York 10504 (800) 541-6563; *The Illustrated Book of World Rankings.*

National Technical Information Service, 5285 Port Royal Road, Springfield, Virginia 22161 (703) 487-4600; *Handbook of Economic Statistics.*

Organisation for Economic Co-operation and Development (OECD), 2 rue Andre-Pascal, 75 Paris 16, France (Telephone Number in U.S. (202) 785-6323); *Foreign Trade by Commodities.*

Statistical Office of the United Nations, Publishing Service, New York, New York 10017 (800) 253-9646; *Statistical Yearbook.*

UNITED KINGDOM - RYE PRODUCTION - See UNITED KINGDOM - CROPS

UNITED KINGDOM - SAFFLOWER SEED PRODUCTION - See UNITED KINGDOM - CROPS

UNITED KINGDOM - SALT PRODUCTION - See UNITED KINGDOM - MINING AND MINERAL PRODUCTS

UNITED KINGDOM - SAVINGS ACCOUNT DEPOSITS - See UNITED KINGDOM - BANKING

UNITED KINGDOM - SAWNWOOD PRODUCTION - See UNITED KINGDOM - FORESTRY AND FOREST PRODUCTS

UNITED KINGDOM - SCIENCE AND TECHNOLOGY - EXPENDITURE FOR RESEARCH - See UNITED KINGDOM - SCIENCE, TECHNICIANS AND ENGINEERS

UNITED KINGDOM - SCIENTISTS, TECHNICIANS AND ENGINEERS

European Commission Office of Press and Public Affairs, 2100 M Street, NW, Washington, D.C. 20037 (202) 862-9500; *Basic Statistics of the Community.*

Statistical Office of the United Nations, Publishing Service, New York, New York 10017 (800) 253-9646; *Statistical Yearbook.*

United Nations Educational, Scientific and Cultural Organization (UNESCO), 7 Place de Fontenoy, F-75700 Paris, France (Telephone Number in U.S. (212) 963-5981); *Statistical Yearbook.*

UNITED KINGDOM - SENIOR CITIZENS

M.E. Sharpe, 80 Business Park Drive, Armonk, New York 10504 (800) 541-6563; *The Illustrated Book of World Rankings.*

UNITED KINGDOM - SESAME SEED PRODUCTION - See UNITED KINGDOM - CROPS

UNITED KINGDOM - SHEEP - See UNITED KINGDOM - LIVESTOCK AND POULTRY

UNITED KINGDOM - SHIPBUILDING - PRODUCTION INDEX

Organisation for Economic Co-operation and Development (OECD), 2 rue Andre-Pascal, 75 Paris 16, France (Telephone Number in U.S. (202) 785-6323); *Indicators of Industrial Activity.*

UNITED KINGDOM - SILVER PRODUCTION AND CONSUMPTION - See UNITED KINGDOM - MINING AND MINERAL PRODUCTS

UNITED KINGDOM - SISAL PRODUCTION - See UNITED KINGDOM -CROPS

UNITED KINGDOM - SOCIAL DATA

European Commission Office of Press and Public Affairs, 2100 M Street, NW, Washington, D.C. 20037 (202) 862-9500; *ACP: Basic Statistics;* and *Basic Statistics of the Community.*

M.E. Sharpe, 80 Business Park Drive, Armonk, New York 10504 (800) 541-6563; *The Illustrated Book of World Rankings.*

Statistical Office of the United Nations, Publishing Service, New York, New York 10017 (800) 253-9646; *World Statistics Pocketbook.*

UNITED KINGDOM - SOCIAL SECURITY

European Commission Office of Press and Public Affairs, 2100 M Street, NW, Washington, D.C. 20037 (202) 862-9500; *Basic Statistics of the Community.*

International Monetary Fund, 700 Nineteenth Street, NW, Washington, D.C. 20431 (202) 623-7000; *Government Finance Statistics Yearbook.*

Organisation for Economic Co-operation and Development (OECD), 2 rue Andre-Pascal, 75 Paris 16, France (Telephone Number in U.S. (202) 785-6323); *Revenue Statistics of OECD Member Countries.*

St. Martin's Press, Inc., 175 Fifth Avenue, New York, New York 10010 (800) 221-7945; *The Statesman's Year-Book.*

Statistical Office of the United Nations,

Publishing Service, New York, New York 10017 (800) 253-9646; *National Accounts Statistics.*

UNITED KINGDOM - SOCIOECONOMIC DATA

European Commission Office of Press and Public Affairs, 2100 M Street, NW, Washington, D.C. 20037 (202) 862-9500; *Basic Statistics of the Community.*

Organisation for Economic Co-operation and Development (OECD), 2 rue Andre-Pascal, 75 Paris 16, France (Telephone Number in U.S. (202) 785-6323); *Economic Outlook.*

UNITED KINGDOM - SOYBEAN PRODUCTION - See UNITED KINGDOM - CROPS

UNITED KINGDOM - STAMP TAXES AND DUTIES - See UNITED KINGDOM - TAXATION

UNITED KINGDOM - STEEL - See UNITED KINGDOM - MINING AND MINERAL PRODUCTS

UNITED KINGDOM - STOCKS - COMMODITY - MARKET PRICE - INDEXES

Food and Agricultural Organization of the United Nations (FAO) Via delle Terme di Caracalla, 00100 Rome, Italy (Telephone Number in U.S. (202) 653-2400); *The State of Food and Agriculture.*

International Lead and Zinc Study Group, Metro House, 58 St. James's Street, London SW1A 1LD England; *Lead and Zinc Statistics.*

Statistical Office of the United Nations, Publishing Service, New York, New York 10017 (800) 253-9646; *Statistical Yearbook.*

World Bureau of Metal Statistics, 27-A High Street, Ware Hert SG12 9BA, England; *World Metal Statistics.*

UNITED KINGDOM - STRAW PRODUCTION - See UNITED KINGDOM - CROPS

UNITED KINGDOM - SUGAR - See UNITED KINGDOM - CROPS

UNITED KINGDOM - SUGARBEET PRODUCTION - See UNITED KINGDOM - CROPS

UNITED KINGDOM - SULPHUR AND SULPHURIC ACID PRODUCTION - See UNITED KINGDOM - MINING AND MINERAL PRODUCTS

UNITED KINGDOM - SUNFLOWER PRODUCTION - See UNITED KINGDOM - CROPS

UNITED KINGDOM - TAXATION

Europa Publications Limited, 18 Bedford Square, London, WC1B 3JN, England; *The Europa World Year Book.*

European Commission Office of Press and Public Affairs, 2100 M Street, NW, Washington, D.C. 20037 (202) 862-9500; *Basic Statistics of the Community.*

International Monetary Fund, 700 Nineteenth Street, NW, Washington, D.C. 20431 (202) 623-7000; *Government Finance Statistics Yearbook.*

International Road Federation, 2600 Virginia Avenue, NW, Washington, D.C. 20037 (202) 338-4641; *World Road Statistics.*

Organisation for Economic Co-operation and Development (OECD), 2 rue Andre-Pascal, 75 Paris 16, France (Telephone Number in U.S. (202) 785-6323); *Indicators of Industrial Activity;* and *Revenue Statistics of OECD Member Countries.*

St. Martin's Press, Inc., 175 Fifth Avenue, New York, New York 10010 (800) 221-7945; *The Statesman's Year-Book.*

The World Bank, 1818 H Street, NW, Washington, D.C. 20433 (202) 477-1234; *World Development Indicators.*

UNITED KINGDOM - TEA PRODUCTION AND CONSUMPTION - See UNITED KINGDOM - CROPS

UNITED KINGDOM - TELEGRAMS SERVICES

European Commission Office of Press and Public Affairs, 2100 M Street, NW, Washington, D.C. 20037 (202) 862-9500; *Transport Annual Statistics.*

Statistical Office of the United Nations, Publishing Service, New York, New York 10017 (800) 253-9646; *Statistical Yearbook.*

UNITED KINGDOM - TELEPHONES IN USE

American Telephone and Telegraph Company, 26 Parsippany Road, Whippany, New Jersey 07981 (800) 222-0300; *The World's Telephones.*

Central Intelligence Agency, Washington, D.C. 20505 (703) 482-1100, www.cia.gov; *The World Factbook.*

Europa Publications Limited, 18 Bedford Square, London, WC1B 3JN, England; *The Europa World Year Book.*

European Commission Office of Press and Public Affairs, 2100 M Street, NW, Washington, D.C. 20037 (202) 862-9500; *Basic Statistics of the Community;* and

Transport Annual Statistics.

St. Martin's Press, Inc., 175 Fifth Avenue, New York, New York 10010 (800) 221-7945; *The Statesman's Year-Book.*

Statistical Office of the United Nations, Publishing Service, New York, New York 10017 (800) 253-9646; *Statistical Yearbook; Trends in Europe and North America: The Statistical Yearbook of the Economic Commission for Europe;* and *World Statistics Pocketbook.*

UNITED KINGDOM - TELEVISION BROADCASTING - See UNITED KINGDOM - BROADCASTING

UNITED KINGDOM - TELEVISION RECEIVER PRODUCTION

European Commission Office of Press and Public Affairs, 2100 M Street, NW, Washington, D.C. 20037 (202) 862-9500; *Basic Statistics of the Community.*

National Technical Information Service, 5285 Port Royal Road, Springfield, Virginia 22161 (703) 487-4600; *Handbook of Economic Statistics.*

Statistical Office of the United Nations, Publishing Service, New York, New York 10017 (800) 253-9646; *Statistical Yearbook.*

UNITED KINGDOM - TEXTILE INDUSTRY

American Forest and Paper Association, 1111 Nineteenth Street, NW, Washington, D.C. 20036 (202) 463-2700; *Wood Pulp and Fiber Statistics.*

Commodity Research Bureau, Inc., 30 South Wacker Drive, Chicago, Illinois 60606 (312) 454-1801; *Commodity Year Book.*

Euromonitor International, Inc., 122 South Michigan Avenue, Suite 1200, Chicago, Illinois 60603 (800) 577-EURO; *Retail Trade International.*

European Commission Office of Press and Public Affairs, 2100 M Street, NW, Washington, D.C. 20037 (202) 862-9500; *Basic Statistics of the Community; Eurostatistics: Data for Short-Term Economic Analysis;* and *Industrial Production: Quarterly Statistics.*

M.E. Sharpe, 80 Business Park Drive, Armonk, New York 10504 (800) 541-6563; *The Illustrated Book of World Rankings.*

National Technical Information Service, 5285 Port Royal Road, Springfield, Virginia 22161 (703) 487-4600; *Handbook of Economic Statistics.*

Organisation for Economic Co-operation and Development (OECD), 2 rue Andre-Pascal, 75 Paris 16, France

(Telephone Number in U.S. (202) 785-6323); *Economic Accounts for Agriculture; Foreign Trade by Commodities; Indicators of Industrial Activity; Industrial Structure Statistics;* and *Textile Industry in OECD Countries.*

St. Martin's Press, Inc., 175 Fifth Avenue, New York, New York 10010 (800) 221-7945; *The Statesman's Year-Book.*

Statistical Office of the United Nations, Publishing Service, New York, New York 10017 (800) 253-9646; *Statistical Yearbook.*

United Nations Conference on Trade and Development, Central Statistical Service, Palais des Nations, Geneva, Switzerland (Telephone in U.S. (800) 253-9646); *UNCTAD Commodity Yearbook.*

UNITED KINGDOM - THEATRE

United Nations Educational, Scientific and Cultural Organization (UNESCO), 7 Place de Fontenoy, F-75700 Paris, France (Telephone Number in U.S. (212) 963-5981); *Statistical Yearbook.*

UNITED KINGDOM - TIMBER - RESOURCE FORESTS - See UNITED KINGDOM - FORESTRY AND FOREST PRODUCTS

UNITED KINGDOM - TIMBER PRODUCTION - See UNITED KINGDOM - FORESTRY AND FOREST PRODUCTS

UNITED KINGDOM - TIN PRODUCTION - See UNITED KINGDOM - MINING AND MINERAL PRODUCTS

UNITED KINGDOM - TIRE (MOTOR VEHICLE) PRODUCTION

International Rubber Study Group, York House, Eighth Floor, Empire Way, Wembley, London HA9 0PA, England; *Rubber Statistical Bulletin.*

National Technical Information Service, 5285 Port Royal Road, Springfield, Virginia 22161 (703) 487-4600; *Handbook of Economic Statistics.*

Statistical Office of the United Nations, Publishing Service, New York, New York 10017 (800) 253-9646; *Statistical Yearbook.*

UNITED KINGDOM - TOBACCO PRODUCTION

Euromonitor International, Inc., 122 South Michigan Avenue, Suite 1200, Chicago, Illinois 60603 (800) 577-EURO; *European Marketing Data and Statistics.*

European Commission Office of Press and Public Affairs, 2100 M Street, NW, Washington, D.C. 20037 (202) 862-9500; *Basic Statistics of the Community;* and *Industrial Production: Quarterly Statistics.*

M.E. Sharpe, 80 Business Park Drive, Armonk, New York 10504 (800) 541-6563; *The Illustrated Book of World Rankings.*

Organisation for Economic Co-operation and Development (OECD), 2 rue Andre-Pascal, 75 Paris 16, France (Telephone Number in U.S. (202) 785-6323); *Indicators of Industrial Activity; Industrial Structure Statistics;* and *Foreign Trade by Commodities.*

Statistical Office of the United Nations, Publishing Service, New York, New York 10017 (800) 253-9646; *Statistical Yearbook.*

UNITED KINGDOM - TOURISM

Euromonitor International, Inc., 122 South Michigan Avenue, Suite 1200, Chicago, Illinois 60603 (800) 577-EURO; *European Marketing Data and Statistics; World Marketing Data and Statistics;* and *The World Economic Factbook.*

Europa Publications Limited, 18 Bedford Square, London, WC1B 3JN, England; *The Europa World Year Book.*

European Commission Office of Press and Public Affairs, 2100 M Street, NW, Washington, D.C. 20037 (202) 862-9500; *Transport Annual Statistics.*

M.E. Sharpe, 80 Business Park Drive, Armonk, New York 10504 (800) 541-6563; *The Illustrated Book of World Rankings.*

Organisation for Economic Co-operation and Development (OECD), 2 rue Andre-Pascal, 75 Paris 16, France (Telephone Number in U.S. (202) 785-6323); *Tourism Policy and International Tourism in OECD Member Countries.*

St. Martin's Press, Inc., 175 Fifth Avenue, New York, New York 10010 (800) 221-7945; *The Statesman's Year-Book.*

Statistical Office of the United Nations, Publishing Service, New York, New York 10017 (800) 253-9646; *Statistical Yearbook;* and *Trends in Europe and North America: The Statistical Yearbook of the Economic Commission for Europe.*

World Tourism Organization, Calle Capitan Haya 42, E-28020 Madrid, Spain; *Yearbook of Tourism Statistics.*

UNITED KINGDOM - TRACTORS IN USE

European Commission Office of Press and Public Affairs, 2100 M Street, NW, Washington, D.C. 20037 (202) 862-9500; *Transport Annual Statistics.*

Statistical Office of the United Nations, Publishing Service, New York, New York 10017 (800) 253-9646; *Statistical Yearbook.*

UNITED KINGDOM - TRADE - See UNITED KINGDOM - FOREIGN TRADE

UNITED KINGDOM - TRADEMARKS AND SERVICE MARKS - See UNITED KINGDOM - PATENTS, TRADEMARKS AND SERVICE MARKS

UNITED KINGDOM - TRANSPORTATION AND COMMUNICATIONS

Central Intelligence Agency, Washington, D.C. 20505 (703) 482-1100, www.cia.gov; *The World Factbook.*

Euromonitor International, Inc., 122 South Michigan Avenue, Suite 1200, Chicago, Illinois 60603 (800) 577-EURO; *World Marketing Data and Statistics.*

Europa Publications Limited, 18 Bedford Square, London, WC1B 3JN, England; *The Europa World Year Book.*

European Commission Office of Press and Public Affairs, 2100 M Street, NW, Washington, D.C. 20037 (202) 862-9500; *Basic Statistics of the Community; Energy Statistics Yearbook; Regions: Statistical Yearbook;* and *Transport Annual Statistics.*

M.E. Sharpe, 80 Business Park Drive, Armonk, New York 10504 (800) 541-6563; *The Illustrated Book of World Rankings.*

St. Martin's Press, Inc., 175 Fifth Avenue, New York, New York 10010 (800) 221-7945; *The Statesman's Year-Book.*

Statistical Office of the United Nations, Publishing Service, New York, New York 10017 (800) 253-9646; *Human Development Report;* and *Trends in Europe and North America: The Statistical Yearbook of the Economic Commission for Europe.*

UNITED KINGDOM - TUNGSTEN PRODUCTION AND CONSUMPTION - See UNITED KINGDOM - MINING AND MINERAL PRODUCTS

UNITED KINGDOM - TURKEYS - See UNITED KINGDOM - LIVESTOCK AND POULTRY

UNITED KINGDOM - UNEMPLOYMENT

Central Intelligence Agency, Washington, D.C. 20505 (703) 482-1100, www.cia.gov; *The World Factbook.*

Euromonitor International, Inc., 122 South Michigan Avenue, Suite 1200, Chicago, Illinois 60603 (800) 577-EURO; *European Marketing Data and Statistics.*

European Commission Office of Press and Public Affairs, 2100 M Street, NW, Washington, D.C. 20037 (202) 862-9500; *Basic Statistics of the Community;*

Employment and Unemployment; Eurostatistics: Data for Short-Term Economic Analysis; Labor Force Sample Survey; and *Regions: Statistical Yearbook.*

International Labour Office, I.L.O. Publications, 1828 L Street, NW, Suite 801, Washington, D.C. 20036 (301) 638-3152; *Yearbook of Labour Statistics.*

National Technical Information Service, 5285 Port Royal Road, Springfield, Virginia 22161 (703) 487-4600; *Handbook of Economic Statistics.*

Organisation for Economic Co-operation and Development (OECD), 2 rue Andre-Pascal, 75 Paris 16, France (Telephone Number in U.S. (202) 785-6323); *Economic Outlook; OECD Economic Surveys: United Kingdom;* and *OECD Employment Outlook.*

St. Martin's Press, Inc., 175 Fifth Avenue, New York, New York 10010 (800) 221-7945; *The Statesman's Year-Book.*

Statistical Office of the United Nations, Publishing Service, New York, New York 10017 (800) 253-9646; *Statistical Yearbook;* and *Trends in Europe and North America: The Statistical Yearbook of the Economic Commission for Europe.*

UNITED KINGDOM - URANIUM PRODUCTION AND CONSUMPTION - See UNITED KINGDOM - MINING AND MINERAL PRODUCTS

UNITED KINGDOM - VANADIUM AND VANADIUM ORE PRODUCTION AND CONSUMPTION - See UNITED KINGDOM - MINING AND MINERAL PRODUCTS

UNITED KINGDOM - VITAL STATISTICS

European Commission Office of Press and Public Affairs, 2100 M Street, NW, Washington, D.C. 20037 (202) 862-9500; *Basic Statistics of the Community.*

St. Martin's Press, Inc., 175 Fifth Avenue, New York, New York 10010 (800) 221-7945; *The Statesman's Year-Book.*

Statistical Office of the United Nations, Publishing Service, New York, New York 10017 (800) 253-9646; *Statistical Yearbook.*

World Health Organization, Office of Publications, 20 Avenue Appia, CH-1211 Geneva 27, Switzerland (Telephone Number in U.S. (518) 436-9686); *World Health Statistics Annual.*

UNITED KINGDOM - WAGES

Euromonitor International, Inc., 122 South Michigan Avenue, Suite 1200, Chicago, Illinois 60603 (800) 577-EURO; *European Marketing Data and Statistics.*

European Commission Office of Press and Public Affairs, 2100 M Street, NW, Washington, D.C. 20037 (202) 862-9500; *Basic Statistics of the Community; Earnings in Agriculture;* and *Eurostatistics: Data for Short-Term Economic Analysis.*

International Labour Office, I.L.O. Publications, 1828 L Street, NW, Suite 801, Washington, D.C. 20036 (301) 638-3152; *Yearbook of Labour Statistics.*

Organisation for Economic Co-operation and Development (OECD), 2 rue Andre-Pascal, 75 Paris 16, France (Telephone Number in U.S. (202) 785-6323); *Economic Outlook; Industrial Structure Statistics;* and *Main Economic Indicators - Historical Statistics.*

Statistical Office of the United Nations, Publishing Service, New York, New York 10017 (800) 253-9646; *Statistical Yearbook.*

UNITED KINGDOM - WALNUT PRODUCTION - See UNITED KINGDOM - CROPS

UNITED KINGDOM - WATERWAYS IN USE

European Commission Office of Press and Public Affairs, 2100 M Street, NW, Washington, D.C. 20037 (202) 862-9500; *Basic Statistics of the Community;* and *Transport Annual Statistics.*

National Technical Information Service, 5285 Port Royal Road, Springfield, Virginia 22161 (703) 487-4600; *Handbook of Economic Statistics.*

Organisation for Economic Co-operation and Development (OECD), 2 rue Andre-Pascal, 75 Paris 16, France (Telephone Number in U.S. (202) 785-6323); *Maritime Transport.*

Statistical Office of the United Nations, Publishing Service, New York, New York 10017 (800) 253-9646; *Annual Bulletin of Transport Statistics for Europe.*

UNITED KINGDOM - WEATHER - See UNITED KINGDOM - CLIMATE

UNITED KINGDOM - WELFARE

European Commission Office of Press and Public Affairs, 2100 M Street, NW, Washington, D.C. 20037 (202) 862-9500; *Basic Statistics of the Community.*

International Monetary Fund, 700 Nineteenth Street, NW, Washington, D.C. 20431 (202) 623-7000; *Government Finance Statistics Yearbook.*

St. Martin's Press, Inc., 175 Fifth Avenue, New York, New York 10010 (800) 221-7945; *The Statesman's Year-Book.*

UNITED KINGDOM - WHEAT PRODUCTION AND PRICES - See UNITED KINGDOM - CROPS

UNITED KINGDOM - WHOLESALE PRICES

European Commission Office of Press and Public Affairs, 2100 M Street, NW, Washington, D.C. 20037 (202) 862-9500; *Basic Statistics of the Community.*

National Technical Information Service, 5285 Port Royal Road, Springfield, Virginia 22161 (703) 487-4600; *Handbook of Economic Statistics.*

Statistical Office of the United Nations, Publishing Service, New York, New York 10017 (800) 253-9646; *Statistical Yearbook.*

UNITED KINGDOM - WINE PRODUCTION - See UNITED KINGDOM - BEVERAGES

UNITED KINGDOM - WOOD AND WOOD PULP - See UNITED KINGDOM - FORESTRY AND FOREST PRODUCTS

UNITED KINGDOM - WOOL - See UNITED KINGDOM - TEXTILE INDUSTRY

UNITED KINGDOM - YARN PRODUCTION - See UNITED KINGDOM - TEXTILE INDUSTRY

UNITED KINGDOM - ZINC AND ZINC ORE PRODUCTION AND CONSUMPTION - See UNITED KINGDOM - MINING AND MINERAL PRODUCTS

UNITED STATES SECURITIES - See also DEBT

UNITED STATES SECURITIES - FOREIGN PURCHASES AND SALES

U.S. Department of the Treasury, Fifteenth Street and Pennsylvania Avenue, NW, Washington, D.C. 20220 (202) 622-2000; *Treasury Bulletin.*

UNITED STATES SECURITIES - HELD BY BANKS

Board of Governors of the Federal Reserve System, Twentieth Street and Constitution Avenue, NW, Washington, D.C. 20551 (202) 452-3000, www.bog.frb.fed.us; *Flow of Funds Accounts.*

Federal Deposit Insurance Corporation, 550 Seventeenth Street, NW, Washington, D.C. 20429 (202) 393-8400, www.fdic.gov; *Annual Report; The FDIC Quarterly Banking Profile;* and *Statistics on Banking.*

U.S. Department of the Treasury, Fifteenth Street and Pennsylvania Avenue, NW, Washington, D.C. 20220 (202) 622-2000; *Treasury Bulletin.*

UNITED STATES SECURITIES - HOLDINGS BY HOUSEHOLDS

Board of Governors of the Federal Reserve System, Twentieth Street and Constitution Avenue, NW, Washington, D.C. 20551 (202) 452-3000, www.bog.frb.fed.us; *Flow of Funds Accounts.*

UNITED STATES SECURITIES - PRICES, SALES, AND YIELDS

Board of Governors of the Federal Reserve System, Twentieth Street and Constitution Avenue, NW, Washington, D.C. 20551 (202) 452-3000, www.bog.frb.fed.us; *Federal Reserve Bulletin.*

UNITED STATES SECURITIES - TAXABLE YIELDS

Board of Governors of the Federal Reserve System, Twentieth Street and Constitution Avenue, NW, Washington, D.C. 20551 (202) 452-3000, www.bog.frb.fed.us; *Federal Reserve Bulletin;* and *Annual Statistical Digest.*

UNIVERSITIES - See EDUCATION, HIGHER EDUCATION INSTITUTIONS

URANIUM - See also NUCLEAR POWER

U.S. Department of Energy, Energy Information Administration, 1000 Independence Avenue, SW, Washington, D.C. 20585 (202) 586-5000; *Annual Energy Review;* and unpublished data.

U.S. Department of the Interior, Geological Survey, National Center, Office of Minerals Information, 12201 Sunrise Valley Drive, Reston, Virginia 22092 (703) 648-4000, www.minerals.usgs.gov; *Annual Report*; and *Mineral Commodities Summary.*

URBAN POPULATION - See POPULATION

Uruguay - National Statistical Offices

CENCI Uruguay, Misiones 1361 Esc 14, Casilla de Correo 1510, Montevideo, Uruguay; for foreign trade statistics.

Direccion General de Estadistica y Censos, Cuareim 2052, Montevideo, Uruguay; for other statistics.

Uruguay - Primary Statistics Source

Direccion General de Estadisticas, Cuareim, 2052, Montivideo, Uruguay;

Anuario Estadistico.

URUGUAY - AGRICULTURE

The Economist Intelligence Unit, 111 West 57th Street, New York, New York 10019 (800) 938-4685; *Uruguay Country Report;* and *The New Latin America Market Atlas.*

Euromonitor International, Inc., 122 South Michigan Avenue, Suite 1200, Chicago, Illinois 60603 (800) 577-EURO; *International Marketing Data and Statistics;* and *World Marketing Data and Statistics.*

Europa Publications Limited, 18 Bedford Square, London, WC1B 3JN, England; *The Europa World Year Book.*

Federal Statistical Office, Gustav-Stresemann-Ring 11, D-6200 Wiesbaden, Germany; *Uruguay.*

Food and Agricultural Organization of the United Nations (FAO), Via delle Terme di Caracalla, 00100 Rome, Italy (Telephone Number in U.S. (202) 653-2400); *Production Yearbook; The State of Food and Agriculture;* and *Trade Yearbook.*

Inter-American Development Bank, 1300 New York Avenue, NW, Washington, D.C. 20577 (202) 623-1753; *Economic and Social Progress in Latin America.*

M.E. Sharpe, 80 Business Park Drive, Armonk, New York 10504 (800) 541-6563; *The Illustrated Book of World Rankings.*

St. Martin's Press, Inc., 175 Fifth Avenue, New York, New York 10010 (800) 221-7945; *The Statesman's Year-Book.*

Statistical Office of the United Nations, Publishing Service, New York, New York 10017 (800) 253-9646; *Statistical Yearbook;* and *Statistical Yearbook for Latin America and the Caribbean.*

Time Books, 201 East 50th Street, New York, New York 10022 (800) 726-0600; *The Economist Book of Vital World Statistics.*

U.C.L.A. Latin American Center Publications, University of California, Los Angeles, California 90024 (310) 825-6634; *Statistical Abstract of Latin America.*

United Nations Conference on Trade and Development, Central Statistical Service, Palais des Nations, Geneva, Switzerland (Telephone in U.S. (800) 253-9646); *UNCTAD Commodity Yearbook.*

The World Bank, 1818 H Street, NW, Washington, D.C. 20433 (202) 477-1234; *World Development Indicators.*

URUGUAY - AIRLINE SERVICE

The Economist Intelligence Unit, 111 West 57th Street, New York, New York 10019 (800) 938-4685; *The New Latin America Market Atlas.*

Europa Publications Limited, 18 Bedford Square, London, WC1B 3JN, England; *The Europa World Year Book.*

International Civil Aviation Organization, 999 University Street, Montreal, Quebec, Canada H3C 5H7 (514) 954-8219; *Civil Aviation Statistics of the World.*

M.E. Sharpe, 80 Business Park Drive, Armonk, New York 10504 (800) 541-6563; *The Illustrated Book of World Rankings.*

St. Martin's Press, Inc., 175 Fifth Avenue, New York, New York 10010 (800) 221-7945; *The Statesman's Year-Book.*

Statistical Office of the United Nations, Publishing Service, New York, New York 10017 (800) 253-9646; *Statistical Yearbook.*

Time Books, 201 East 50th Street, New York, New York 10022 (800) 726-0600; *The Economist Book of Vital World Statistics.*

URUGUAY - AIRPORTS

Central Intelligence Agency, Washington, D.C. 20505 (703) 482-1100, www.cia.gov; *The World Factbook.*

URUGUAY - ALUMINUM PRODUCTION AND CONSUMPTION - See URUGUAY - MINING AND MINERAL PRODUCTS

URUGUAY - ANIMAL HEALTH

Food and Agricultural Organization of the United Nations (FAO), Via delle Terme di Caracalla, 00100 Rome, Italy (Telephone Number in U.S. (202) 653-2400); *Animal Health Yearbook.*

URUGUAY - AREA AND DENSITY OF POPULATION

Central Intelligence Agency, Washington, D.C. 20505 (703) 482-1100, www.cia.gov; *The World Factbook.*

Euromonitor International, Inc., 122 South Michigan Avenue, Suite 1200, Chicago, Illinois 60603 (800) 577-EURO; *International Marketing Data and Statistics;* and *The World Economic Factbook.*

Europa Publications Limited, 18 Bedford Square, London, WC1B 3JN, England; *The Europa World Year Book.*

Federal Statistical Office, Gustav-Stresemann-Ring 11, D-6200 Wiesbaden, Germany; *Uruguay.*

Food and Agricultural Organization of the United Nations (FAO) Via delle Terme di Caracalla, 00100 Rome, Italy (Telephone Number in U.S. (202) 653-2400); *The State of Food and Agriculture.*

Inter-American Development Bank, 1300 New York Avenue, NW, Washington, D.C. 20577 (202) 623-1753; *Economic and Social Progress in Latin America.*

M.E. Sharpe, 80 Business Park Drive, Armonk, New York 10504 (800) 541-6563; *The Illustrated Book of World Rankings.*

St. Martin's Press, Inc., 175 Fifth Avenue, New York, New York 10010 (800) 221-7945; *The Statesman's Year-Book.*

Statistical Office of the United Nations, Publishing Service, New York, New York 10017 (800) 253-9646; *Statistical Yearbook.*

Time Books, 201 East 50th Street, New York, New York 10022 (800) 726-0600; *The Economist Book of Vital World Statistics.*

United Nations Educational, Scientific and Cultural Organization (UNESCO), 7 Place de Fontenoy, F-75700 Paris, France (Telephone Number in U.S. (212) 963-5981); *Statistical Yearbook.*

The World Bank, 1818 H Street, NW, Washington, D.C. 20433 (202) 477-1234; *World Development Report.*

URUGUAY - ARMS EXPORTS AND IMPORTS - See URUGUAY - MILITARY

URUGUAY - BALANCE OF PAYMENTS

The Economist Intelligence Unit, 111 West 57th Street, New York, New York 10019 (800) 938-4685; *The New Latin America Market Atlas;* and *The World Market Atlas.*

Europa Publications Limited, 18 Bedford Square, London, WC1B 3JN, England; *The Europa World Year Book.*

Federal Statistical Office, Gustav-Stresemann-Ring 11, D-6200 Wiesbaden, Germany; *Uruguay.*

Inter-American Development Bank, 1300 New York Avenue, NW, Washington, D.C. 20577 (202) 623-1753; *Economic and Social Progress in Latin America.*

International Monetary Fund, 700 Nineteenth Street, NW, Washington, D.C. 20431 (202) 623-7000; *Balance of Payments Yearbook.*

Organization of American States (OAS), General Secretariat, Washington, D.C. 20006 (202) 458-3533; *Statistical Bulletin of the OAS.*

Statistical Office of the United Nations, Publishing Service, New York, New York 10017 (800) 253-9646; *Economic Survey of Latin America and the Caribbean;* and *Statistical Yearbook for Latin America and the Caribbean.*

Time Books, 201 East 50th Street, New York, New York 10022 (800) 726-0600; *The Economist Book of Vital World Statistics.*

U.C.L.A. Latin American Center Publications, University of California, Los Angeles, California 90024 (310) 825-6634; *Statistical Abstract of Latin America.*

United Nations Conference on Trade and Development (UNCTAD), New York, New York 10017 (800) 253-9646; *Handbook of International Trade and Development Statistics.*

The World Bank, 1818 H Street, NW, Washington, D.C. 20433 (202) 477-1234; *World Development Report;* and *World Development Indicators.*

URUGUAY - BANANA PRODUCTION - See URUGUAY - CROPS

URUGUAY - BANKING

Euromonitor International, Inc., 122 South Michigan Avenue, Suite 1200, Chicago, Illinois 60603 (800) 577-EURO; *World Marketing Data and Statistics.*

Europa Publications Limited, 18 Bedford Square, London, WC1B 3JN, England; *The Europa World Year Book.*

Inter-American Development Bank, 1300 New York Avenue, NW, Washington, D.C. 20577 (202) 623-1753; *Economic and Social Progress in Latin America.*

International Monetary Fund, 700 Nineteenth Street, NW, Washington, D.C. 20431 (202) 623-7000; *Government Finance Statistics Yearbook;* and *International Financial Statistics.*

M.E. Sharpe, 80 Business Park Drive, Armonk, New York 10504 (800) 541-6563; *The Illustrated Book of World Rankings.*

St. Martin's Press, Inc., 175 Fifth Avenue, New York, New York 10010 (800) 221-7945; *The Statesman's Year-Book.*

Statistical Office of the United Nations, Publishing Service, New York, New York 10017 (800) 253-9646; *Statistical Yearbook for Latin America and the Caribbean.*

URUGUAY - BARLEY PRODUCTION - See URUGUAY - CROPS

URUGUAY - BEER PRODUCTION - See URUGUAY - BEVERAGES

URUGUAY - BEVERAGES

M.E. Sharpe, 80 Business Park Drive, Armonk, New York 10504 (800) 541-6563; *The Illustrated Book of World Rankings.*

Statistical Office of the United Nations, Publishing Service, New York, New York 10017 (800) 253-9646; *Statistical Yearbook.*

URUGUAY - BIRTH RATES

Central Intelligence Agency, Washington, D.C. 20505 (703) 482-1100, www.cia.gov; *The World Factbook.*

Euromonitor International, Inc., 122 South Michigan Avenue, Suite 1200, Chicago, Illinois 60603 (800) 577-EURO; *International Marketing Data and Statistics;* and *The World Economic Factbook.*

Europa Publications Limited, 18 Bedford Square, London, WC1B 3JN, England; *The Europa World Year Book.*

M.E. Sharpe, 80 Business Park Drive, Armonk, New York 10504 (800) 541-6563; *The Illustrated Book of World Rankings.*

St. Martin's Press, Inc., 175 Fifth Avenue, New York, New York 10010 (800) 221-7945; *The Statesman's Year-Book.*

Statistical Office of the United Nations, Publishing Service, New York, New York 10017 (800) 253-9646; *Demographic Yearbook; Statistical Yearbook;* and *Statistical Yearbook for Latin America and the Caribbean.*

Time Books, 201 East 50th Street, New York, New York 10022 (800) 726-0600; *The Economist Book of Vital World Statistics.*

The World Bank, 1818 H Street, NW, Washington, D.C. 20433 (202) 477-1234; *World Development Indicators.*

World Health Organization, Office of Publications, 20 Avenue Appia, CH-1211 Geneva 27, Switzerland (Telephone Number in U.S. (518) 436-9686); *World Health Statistics Annual.*

URUGUAY - BONDS

Inter-American Development Bank, 1300 New York Avenue, NW, Washington, D.C. 20577 (202) 623-1753; *Economic and Social Progress in Latin America.*

International Monetary Fund, 700 Nineteenth Street, NW, Washington, D.C. 20431 (202) 623-7000; *Government Finance Statistics Yearbook.*

Statistical Office of the United Nations, Publishing Service, New York, New York 10017 (800) 253-9646; *Statistical Yearbook.*

URUGUAY - BOOK PRODUCTION

Europa Publications Limited, 18 Bedford Square, London, WC1B 3JN, England; *The Europa World Year Book.*

United Nations Educational, Scientific and Cultural Organization (UNESCO), 7 Place de Fontenoy, F-75700 Paris, France (Telephone Number in U.S. (212) 963-5981); *Statistical Yearbook.*

URUGUAY - BROADCASTING

Billboard Limited, P.O. Box 9027, 1006 AA Amsterdam, The Netherlands (Telephone Number in U.S. (212) 764-7300); *World Radio TV Handbook.*

Central Intelligence Agency, Washington, D.C. 20505 (703) 482-1100, www.cia.gov; *The World Factbook.*

Euromonitor International, Inc., 122 South Michigan Avenue, Suite 1200, Chicago, Illinois 60603 (800) 577-EURO; *World Marketing Data and Statistics.*

M.E. Sharpe, 80 Business Park Drive, Armonk, New York 10504 (800) 541-6563; *The Illustrated Book of World Rankings.*

St. Martin's Press, Inc., 175 Fifth Avenue, New York, New York 10010 (800) 221-7945; *The Statesman's Year-Book.*

Time Books, 201 East 50th Street, New York, New York 10022 (800) 726-0600; *The Economist Book of Vital World Statistics.*

URUGUAY - BUDGET

Central Intelligence Agency, Washington, D.C. 20505 (703) 482-1100, www.cia.gov; *The World Factbook.*

URUGUAY - BUSINESS

Inter-American Development Bank, 1300 New York Avenue, NW, Washington, D.C. 20577 (202) 623-1753; *Economic and Social Progress in Latin America.*

URUGUAY - BUSINESS AND PROFESSIONAL LICENSES

International Monetary Fund, 700 Nineteenth Street, NW, Washington, D.C. 20431 (202) 623-7000; *Government Finance Statistics Yearbook.*

URUGUAY - BUTTER PRODUCTION - See URUGUAY - DAIRY PRODUCTS

URUGUAY - CALORIE SUPPLY

Food and Agricultural Organization of the United Nations (FAO) Via delle Terme di Caracalla, 00100 Rome, Italy (Telephone Number in U.S. (202) 653-2400); *The State of Food and Agriculture.*

Statistical Office of the United Nations, Publishing Service, New York, New York 10017 (800) 253-9646; *Statistical Yearbook for Latin America and the Caribbean.*

URUGUAY - CAPITAL INVESTMENT

Inter-American Development Bank, 1300 New York Avenue, NW, Washington, D.C. 20577 (202) 623-1753; *Economic and Social Progress in Latin America.*

URUGUAY - CAPITAL REVENUE

Inter-American Development Bank, 1300 New York Avenue, NW, Washington, D.C. 20577 (202) 623-1753; *Economic and Social Progress in Latin America.*

International Monetary Fund, 700 Nineteenth Street, NW, Washington, D.C. 20431 (202) 623-7000; *Government Finance Statistics Yearbook.*

URUGUAY - CATTLE - See URUGUAY - LIVESTOCK AND POULTRY

URUGUAY - CEMENT PRODUCTION - See URUGUAY - MINING AND MINERAL PRODUCTS

URUGUAY - CHEESE PRODUCTION AND CONSUMPTION - See URUGUAY - DAIRY PRODUCTS

URUGUAY - CHEMICAL (ORGANIC) PRODUCTION - See URUGUAY - MINING AND MINERAL PRODUCTS

URUGUAY - CHICKENS - See URUGUAY - LIVESTOCK AND POULTRY

URUGUAY - CIGARETTE PRODUCTION - See URUGUAY - TOBACCO PRODUCTION

URUGUAY - CLIMATE

M.E. Sharpe, 80 Business Park Drive, Armonk, New York 10504 (800) 541-6563; *The Illustrated Book of World Rankings.*

St. Martin's Press, Inc., 175 Fifth Avenue, New York, New York 10010 (800) 221-7945; *The Statesman's Year-Book.*

URUGUAY - COAL PRODUCTION - See URUGUAY - MINING AND MINERAL PRODUCTS

URUGUAY - COCOA (BEANS) PRODUCTION - See URUGUAY - CROPS

URUGUAY - COFFEE - See URUGUAY - CROPS

URUGUAY - COMMERCE

St. Martin's Press, Inc., 175 Fifth Avenue, New York, New York 10010 (800) 221-7945; *The Statesman's Year-Book.*

URUGUAY - COMMUNICATIONS - See URUGUAY - TRANSPORTATION AND COMMUNICATIONS

URUGUAY - CONSTRUCTION INDUSTRY

The Economist Intelligence Unit, 111 West 57th Street, New York, New York 10019 (800) 938-4685; *The New Latin America Market Atlas.*

Inter-American Development Bank, 1300 New York Avenue, NW, Washington, D.C. 20577 (202) 623-1753; *Economic and Social Progress in Latin America.*

M.E. Sharpe, 80 Business Park Drive, Armonk, New York 10504 (800) 541-6563; *The Illustrated Book of World Rankings.*

St. Martin's Press, Inc., 175 Fifth Avenue, New York, New York 10010 (800) 221-7945; *The Statesman's Year-Book.*

Statistical Office of the United Nations, Publishing Service, New York, New York 10017 (800) 253-9646; *Statistical Yearbook.*

U.C.L.A. Latin American Center Publications, University of California, Los Angeles, California 90024 (310) 825-6634; *Statistical Abstract of Latin America.*

URUGUAY - CONSUMER PRICE INDEX

Europa Publications Limited, 18 Bedford Square, London, WC1B 3JN, England; *The Europa World Year Book.*

Statistical Office of the United Nations, Publishing Service, New York, New York 10017 (800) 253-9646; *Statistical Yearbook.*

Time Books, 201 East 50th Street, New York, New York 10022 (800) 726-0600; *The Economist Book of Vital World Statistics.*

U.C.L.A. Latin American Center Publications, University of California, Los Angeles, California 90024 (310) 825-6634; *Statistical Abstract of Latin America.*

URUGUAY - CONSUMER PRICES

The Economist Intelligence Unit, 111 West 57th Street, New York, New York 10019 (800) 938-4685; *The New Latin America Market Atlas.*

Euromonitor International, Inc., 122 South Michigan Avenue, Suite 1200, Chicago, Illinois 60603 (800) 577-EURO; *World Marketing Data and Statistics.*

International Labour Office, I.L.O. Publications, 1828 L Street, NW, Suite 801, Washington, D.C. 20036 (301) 638-3152; *Yearbook of Labour Statistics.*

International Monetary Fund, 700 Nineteenth Street, NW, Washington, D.C.

20431 (202) 623-7000; *International Financial Statistics.*

Organization of American States (OAS), General Secretariat, Washington, D.C. 20006 (202) 458-3533; *Statistical Bulletin of the OAS.*

URUGUAY - CONSUMPTION

The Economist Intelligence Unit, 111 West 57th Street, New York, New York 10019 (800) 938-4685; *The New Latin America Market Atlas.*

Inter-American Development Bank, 1300 New York Avenue, NW, Washington, D.C. 20577 (202) 623-1753; *Economic and Social Progress in Latin America.*

Statistical Office of the United Nations, Publishing Service, New York, New York 10017 (800) 253-9646; *Statistical Yearbook for Latin America and the Caribbean.*

The World Bank, 1818 H Street, NW, Washington, D.C. 20433 (202) 477-1234; *World Development Report.*

URUGUAY - COOPERATIVES

U.C.L.A. Latin American Center Publications, University of California, Los Angeles, California 90024 (310) 825-6634; *Statistical Abstract of Latin America.*

URUGUAY - COPPER PRODUCTION AND CONSUMPTION - See URUGUAY - MINING AND MINERAL PRODUCTS

URUGUAY - CORN PRODUCTION - See URUGUAY - CROPS

URUGUAY - CORPORATE INCOME TAXES - See URUGUAY - TAXATION

URUGUAY - CORPORATE TAXES - See URUGUAY - TAXATION

URUGUAY - COTTON - See URUGUAY - CROPS

URUGUAY - CROPS

The Economist Intelligence Unit, 111 West 57th Street, New York, New York 10019 (800) 938-4685; *The New Latin America Market Atlas.*

Europa Publications Limited, 18 Bedford Square, London, WC1B 3JN, England; *The Europa World Year Book.*

Food and Agricultural Organization of the United Nations (FAO) Via delle Terme di Caracalla, 00100 Rome, Italy (Telephone Number in U.S. (202) 653-2400); *Production Yearbook;* and *The State of Food and Agriculture.*

M.E. Sharpe, 80 Business Park Drive,

Armonk, New York 10504 (800) 541-6563; *The Illustrated Book of World Rankings.*

St. Martin's Press, Inc., 175 Fifth Avenue, New York, New York 10010 (800) 221-7945; *The Statesman's Year-Book.*

Statistical Office of the United Nations, Publishing Service, New York, New York 10017 (800) 253-9646; *Statistical Yearbook.*

U.C.L.A. Latin American Center Publications, University of California, Los Angeles, California 90024 (310) 825-6634; *Statistical Abstract of Latin America.*

United Nations Conference on Trade and Development, Central Statistical Service, Palais des Nations, Geneva, Switzerland (Telephone in U.S. (800) 253-9646); *UNCTAD Commodity Yearbook.*

URUGUAY - CUSTOMS DUTIES

Inter-American Development Bank, 1300 New York Avenue, NW, Washington, D.C. 20577 (202) 623-1753; *Economic and Social Progress in Latin America.*

International Monetary Fund, 700 Nineteenth Street, NW, Washington, D.C. 20431 (202) 623-7000; *Government Finance Statistics Yearbook.*

St. Martin's Press, Inc., 175 Fifth Avenue, New York, New York 10010 (800) 221-7945; *The Statesman's Year-Book.*

URUGUAY - DAIRY PRODUCTS

Europa Publications Limited, 18 Bedford Square, London, WC1B 3JN, England; *The Europa World Year Book.*

Food and Agricultural Organization of the United Nations (FAO) Via delle Terme di Caracalla, 00100 Rome, Italy (Telephone Number in U.S. (202) 653-2400); *The State of Food and Agriculture.*

M.E. Sharpe, 80 Business Park Drive, Armonk, New York 10504 (800) 541-6563; *The Illustrated Book of World Rankings.*

St. Martin's Press, Inc., 175 Fifth Avenue, New York, New York 10010 (800) 221-7945; *The Statesman's Year-Book.*

Statistical Office of the United Nations, Publishing Service, New York, New York 10017 (800) 253-9646; *Statistical Yearbook.*

U.C.L.A. Latin American Center Publications, University of California, Los Angeles, California 90024 (310) 825-6634; *Statistical Abstract of Latin America.*

URUGUAY - DEATH RATES - See URUGUAY - MORTALITY

URUGUAY - DEBT

The Economist Intelligence Unit, 111 West 57th Street, New York, New York 10019 (800) 938-4685; *The New Latin America Market Atlas.*

URUGUAY - DEFENSE EXPENDITURES - See URUGUAY - MILITARY

URUGUAY - DEFENSE EXPENDITURES

International Monetary Fund, 700 Nineteenth Street, NW, Washington, D.C. 20431 (202) 623-7000; *Government Finance Statistics Yearbook.*

URUGUAY - DEMOGRAPHY

The Economist Intelligence Unit, 111 West 57th Street, New York, New York 10019 (800) 938-4685; *The World Market Atlas.*

Euromonitor International, Inc., 122 South Michigan Avenue, Suite 1200, Chicago, Illinois 60603 (800) 577-EURO; *International Marketing Data and Statistics; World Marketing Data and Statistics;* and *The World Economic Factbook.*

M.E. Sharpe, 80 Business Park Drive, Armonk, New York 10504 (800) 541-6563; *The Illustrated Book of World Rankings.*

Statistical Office of the United Nations, Publishing Service, New York, New York 10017 (800) 253-9646; *Human Development Report.*

URUGUAY - DEVELOPMENT ASSISTANCE

Inter-American Development Bank, 1300 New York Avenue, NW, Washington, D.C. 20577 (202) 623-1753; *Economic and Social Progress in Latin America.*

Statistical Office of the United Nations, Publishing Service, New York, New York 10017 (800) 253-9646; *Statistical Yearbook.*

URUGUAY - DIAMOND PRODUCTION - See URUGUAY - MINING AND MINERAL PRODUCTS

URUGUAY - DISCOUNT RATES - See URUGUAY - BANKING

URUGUAY - DIVORCE RATES

M.E. Sharpe, 80 Business Park Drive, Armonk, New York 10504 (800) 541-6563; *The Illustrated Book of World Rankings.*

Statistical Office of the United Nations, Publishing Service, New York, New York 10017 (800) 253-9646; *Demographic Yearbook;* and *Statistical Yearbook.*

URUGUAY - DUCKS - See URUGUAY - LIVESTOCK AND POULTRY

URUGUAY - ECONOMY

Central Intelligence Agency, Washington, D.C. 20505 (703) 482-1100, www.cia.gov; *The World Factbook*.

Economist Intelligence Unit, 111 West 57th Street, New York, New York 10019 (800) 938-4685; *Uruguay Country Report*.

Euromonitor International, Inc., 122 South Michigan Avenue, Suite 1200, Chicago, Illinois 60603 (800) 577-EURO; *International Marketing Data and Statistics; World Marketing Data and Statistics;* and *The World Economic Factbook*.

Europa Publications Limited, 18 Bedford Square, London, WC1B 3JN, England; *The Europa World Year Book*.

Inter-American Development Bank, 1300 New York Avenue, NW, Washington, D.C. 20577 (202) 623-1753; *Economic and Social Progress in Latin America*.

M.E. Sharpe, 80 Business Park Drive, Armonk, New York 10504 (800) 541-6563; *The Illustrated Book of World Rankings*.

Organization of American States (OAS), General Secretariat, Washington, D.C. 20006 (202) 458-3533; *Statistical Bulletin of the OAS*.

St. Martin's Press, Inc., 175 Fifth Avenue, New York, New York 10010 (800) 221-7945; *The Statesman's Year-Book*.

Statistical Office of the United Nations, Publishing Service, New York, New York 10017 (800) 253-9646; *Economic Survey of Latin America and the Caribbean;* and *World Statistics Pocketbook*.

U.C.L.A. Latin American Center Publications, University of California, Los Angeles, California 90024 (310) 825-6634; *Statistical Abstract of Latin America*.

The World Bank, 1818 H Street, NW, Washington, D.C. 20433 (202) 477-1234; *The World Bank Atlas;* and *World Development Report*.

URUGUAY - EDUCATION

The Economist Intelligence Unit, 111 West 57th Street, New York, New York 10019 (800) 938-4685; *The New Latin America Market Atlas;* and *The World Market Atlas*.

Euromonitor International, Inc., 122 South Michigan Avenue, Suite 1200, Chicago, Illinois 60603 (800) 577-EURO; *International Marketing Data and Statistics;* and *World Marketing Data and Statistics*.

Europa Publications Limited, 18 Bedford Square, London, WC1B 3JN,

England; *The Europa World Year Book*.

Federal Statistical Office, Gustav-Stresemann-Ring 11, D-6200 Wiesbaden, Germany; *Uruguay*.

International Monetary Fund, 700 Nineteenth Street, NW, Washington, D.C. 20431 (202) 623-7000; *Government Finance Statistics Yearbook*.

M.E. Sharpe, 80 Business Park Drive, Armonk, New York 10504 (800) 541-6563; *The Illustrated Book of World Rankings*.

St. Martin's Press, Inc., 175 Fifth Avenue, New York, New York 10010 (800) 221-7945; *The Statesman's Year-Book*.

Statistical Office of the United Nations, Publishing Service, New York, New York 10017 (800) 253-9646; *Human Development Report;* and *Statistical Yearbook for Latin America and the Caribbean*.

Time Books, 201 East 50th Street, New York, New York 10022 (800) 726-0600; *The Economist Book of Vital World Statistics*.

U.C.L.A. Latin American Center Publications, University of California, Los Angeles, California 90024 (310) 825-6634; *Statistical Abstract of Latin America*.

United Nations Educational, Scientific and Cultural Organization (UNESCO), 7 Place de Fontenoy, F-75700 Paris, France (Telephone Number in U.S. (212) 963-5981); *Statistical Yearbook*.

The World Bank, 1818 H Street, NW, Washington, D.C. 20433 (202) 477-1234; *World Development Report;* and *World Development Indicators*.

URUGUAY - EGG PRODUCTION AND CONSUMPTION - See URUGUAY - DAIRY PRODUCTS

URUGUAY - ELECTRICITY

Central Intelligence Agency, Washington, D.C. 20505 (703) 482-1100, www.cia.gov; *The World Factbook*.

The Economist Intelligence Unit, 111 West 57th Street, New York, New York 10019 (800) 938-4685; *The New Latin America Market Atlas*.

Inter-American Development Bank, 1300 New York Avenue, NW, Washington, D.C. 20577 (202) 623-1753; *Economic and Social Progress in Latin America*.

M.E. Sharpe, 80 Business Park Drive, Armonk, New York 10504 (800) 541-6563; *The Illustrated Book of World Rankings*.

Organization of American States (OAS),

General Secretariat, Washington, D.C. 20006 (202) 458-3533; *Statistical Bulletin of the OAS*.

St. Martin's Press, Inc., 175 Fifth Avenue, New York, New York 10010 (800) 221-7945; *The Statesman's Year-Book*.

Statistical Office of the United Nations, Publishing Service, New York, New York 10017 (800) 253-9646; *Human Development Report;* and *Statistical Yearbook*.

Time Books, 201 East 50th Street, New York, New York 10022 (800) 726-0600; *The Economist Book of Vital World Statistics*.

URUGUAY - EMPLOYMENT

Euromonitor International, Inc., 122 South Michigan Avenue, Suite 1200, Chicago, Illinois 60603 (800) 577-EURO; *International Marketing Data and Statistics*.

Federal Statistical Office, Gustav-Stresemann-Ring 11, D-6200 Wiesbaden, Germany; *Uruguay*.

International Labour Office, I.L.O. Publications, 1828 L Street, NW, Suite 801, Washington, D.C. 20036 (301) 638-3152; *Yearbook of Labour Statistics*.

M.E. Sharpe, 80 Business Park Drive, Armonk, New York 10504 (800) 541-6563; *The Illustrated Book of World Rankings*.

Statistical Office of the United Nations, Publishing Service, New York, New York 10017 (800) 253-9646; *Statistical Yearbook;* and *Statistical Yearbook for Latin America and the Caribbean*.

U.C.L.A. Latin American Center Publications, University of California, Los Angeles, California 90024 (310) 825-6634; *Statistical Abstract of Latin America*.

URUGUAY - ENERGY

The Economist Intelligence Unit, 111 West 57th Street, New York, New York 10019 (800) 938-4685; *The New Latin America Market Atlas*.

Euromonitor International, Inc., 122 South Michigan Avenue, Suite 1200, Chicago, Illinois 60603 (800) 577-EURO; *International Marketing Data and Statistics; World Marketing Data and Statistics;* and *The World Economic Factbook*.

M.E. Sharpe, 80 Business Park Drive, Armonk, New York 10504 (800) 541-6563; *The Illustrated Book of World Rankings*.

St. Martin's Press, Inc., 175 Fifth Avenue, New York, New York 10010 (800) 221-7945; *The Statesman's Year-Book*.

Statistical Office of the United Nations, Publishing Service, New York, New York 10017 (800) 253-9646; *Energy Statistics Yearbook; Human Development Report; Statistical Yearbook; Statistical Yearbook for Latin America and the Caribbean;* and *World Statistics Pocketbook.*

Time Books, 201 East 50th Street, New York, New York 10022 (800) 726-0600; *The Economist Book of Vital World Statistics.*

U.C.L.A. Latin American Center Publications, University of California, Los Angeles, California 90024 (310) 825-6634; *Statistical Abstract of Latin America.*

The World Bank, 1818 H Street, NW, Washington, D.C. 20433 (202) 477-1234; *The World Bank Atlas;* and *World Development Report.*

URUGUAY - ENVIRONMENT

Economist Intelligence Unit, 111 West 57th Street, New York, New York 10019 (800) 938-4685; *Uruguay Country Report.*

Statistical Office of the United Nations, Publishing Service, New York, New York 10017 (800) 253-9646; *World Statistics Pocketbook.*

URUGUAY - EXCHANGE RATES

Central Intelligence Agency, Washington, D.C. 20505 (703) 482-1100, www.cia.gov; *The World Factbook.*

Euromonitor International, Inc., 122 South Michigan Avenue, Suite 1200, Chicago, Illinois 60603 (800) 577-EURO; *International Marketing Data and Statistics;* and *The World Economic Factbook.*

Europa Publications Limited, 18 Bedford Square, London, WC1B 3JN, England; *The Europa World Year Book.*

Inter-American Development Bank, 1300 New York Avenue, NW, Washington, D.C. 20577 (202) 623-1753; *Economic and Social Progress in Latin America.*

International Civil Aviation Organization, 999 University Street, Montreal, Quebec, Canada H3C 5H7 (514) 954-8219; *Civil Aviation Statistics of the World.*

International Monetary Fund, 700 Nineteenth Street, NW, Washington, D.C. 20431 (202) 623-7000; *International Financial Statistics.*

Organization of American States (OAS), General Secretariat, Washington, D.C. 20006 (202) 458-3533; *Statistical Bulletin of the OAS.*

Statistical Office of the United Nations,

Publishing Service, New York, New York 10017 (800) 253-9646; *Statistical Yearbook;* and *World Statistics Pocketbook.*

U.C.L.A. Latin American Center Publications, University of California, Los Angeles, California 90024 (310) 825-6634; *Statistical Abstract of Latin America.*

URUGUAY - EXCISE TAXES - See URUGUAY - TAXATION

URUGUAY - EXPORTS

Central Intelligence Agency, Washington, D.C. 20505 (703) 482-1100, www.cia.gov; *The World Factbook.*

The Economist Intelligence Unit, 111 West 57th Street, New York, New York 10019 (800) 938-4685; *The New Latin America Market Atlas; Uruguay Country Report;* and *The World Market Atlas.*

Euromonitor International, Inc., 122 South Michigan Avenue, Suite 1200, Chicago, Illinois 60603 (800) 577-EURO; *International Marketing Data and Statistics;* and *The World Economic Factbook.*

Europa Publications Limited, 18 Bedford Square, London, WC1B 3JN, England; *The Europa World Year Book.*

Food and Agricultural Organization of the United Nations (FAO) Via delle Terme di Caracalla, 00100 Rome, Italy (Telephone Number in U.S. (202) 653-2400); *The State of Food and Agriculture.*

Inter-American Development Bank, 1300 New York Avenue, NW, Washington, D.C. 20577 (202) 623-1753; *Economic and Social Progress in Latin America.*

International Monetary Fund, 700 Nineteenth Street, NW, Washington, D.C. 20431 (202) 623-7000; *Direction of Trade Statistics; Government Finance Statistics Yearbook;* and *International Financial Statistics.*

Organization of American States (OAS), General Secretariat, Washington, D.C. 20006 (202) 458-3533; *Statistical Bulletin of the OAS.*

St. Martin's Press, Inc., 175 Fifth Avenue, New York, New York 10010 (800) 221-7945; *The Statesman's Year-Book.*

Statistical Office of the United Nations, Publishing Service, New York, New York 10017 (800) 253-9646; *Statistical Yearbook for Latin America and the Caribbean.*

Time Books, 201 East 50th Street, New York, New York 10022 (800) 726-0600; *The Economist Book of Vital World Statistics.*

United Nations Conference on Trade

and Development (UNCTAD), New York, New York 10017 (800) 253-9646; *Handbook of International Trade and Development Statistics.*

The World Bank, 1818 H Street, NW, Washington, D.C. 20433 (202) 477-1234; *World Development Report;* and *World Development Indicators.*

URUGUAY - EXTERNAL FINANCING

Inter-American Development Bank, 1300 New York Avenue, NW, Washington, D.C. 20577 (202) 623-1753; *Economic and Social Progress in Latin America.*

Statistical Office of the United Nations, Publishing Service, New York, New York 10017 (800) 253-9646; *Statistical Yearbook for Latin America and the Caribbean.*

URUGUAY - EXTERNAL INDEBTEDNESS

Inter-American Development Bank, 1300 New York Avenue, NW, Washington, D.C. 20577 (202) 623-1753; *Economic and Social Progress in Latin America.*

Statistical Office of the United Nations, Publishing Service, New York, New York 10017 (800) 253-9646; *Statistical Yearbook for Latin America and the Caribbean.*

The World Bank, 1818 H Street, NW, Washington, D.C. 20433 (202) 477-1234; *World Development Report;* and *World Development Indicators.*

URUGUAY - EXTERNAL TRADE

Euromonitor International, Inc., 122 South Michigan Avenue, Suite 1200, Chicago, Illinois 60603 (800) 577-EURO; *World Marketing Data and Statistics.*

Food and Agricultural Organization of the United Nations (FAO) Via delle Terme di Caracalla, 00100 Rome, Italy (Telephone Number in U.S. (202) 653-2400); *The State of Food and Agriculture.*

Inter-American Development Bank, 1300 New York Avenue, NW, Washington, D.C. 20577 (202) 623-1753; *Economic and Social Progress in Latin America.*

Statistical Office of the United Nations, Publishing Service, New York, New York 10017 (800) 253-9646; *Statistical Yearbook;* and *Statistical Yearbook for Latin America and the Caribbean.*

URUGUAY - FAMILY PLANNING

U.C.L.A. Latin American Center Publications, University of California, Los Angeles, California 90024 (310) 825-6634; *Statistical Abstract of Latin America.*

URUGUAY - FARM CROPS - See URUGUAY

- CROPS

URUGUAY - FEMALE WORKING POPULATION - See URUGUAY - EMPLOYMENT

URUGUAY - FERTILITY RATES

Central Intelligence Agency, Washington, D.C. 20505 (703) 482-1100, www.cia.gov; *The World Factbook*.

M.E. Sharpe, 80 Business Park Drive, Armonk, New York 10504 (800) 541-6563; *The Illustrated Book of World Rankings*.

Statistical Office of the United Nations, Publishing Service, New York, New York 10017 (800) 253-9646; *Human Development Report*.

Time Books, 201 East 50th Street, New York, New York 10022 (800) 726-0600; *The Economist Book of Vital World Statistics*.

The World Bank, 1818 H Street, NW, Washington, D.C. 20433 (202) 477-1234; *The World Bank Atlas; World Development Report*; and *World Development Indicators*.

URUGUAY - FERTILIZER

The Economist Intelligence Unit, 111 West 57th Street, New York, New York 10019 (800) 938-4685; *The New Latin America Market Atlas*.

Food and Agricultural Organization of the United Nations (FAO), Via delle Terme di Caracalla, 00100 Rome, Italy (Telephone Number in U.S. (202) 653-2400); *Annual Fertilizer Review;* and *The State of Food and Agriculture*.

Statistical Office of the United Nations, Publishing Service, New York, New York 10017 (800) 253-9646; *Statistical Yearbook*.

URUGUAY - FETAL MORTALITY - See URUGUAY - MORTALITY

URUGUAY - FIBRE PRODUCTION - See URUGUAY - TEXTILE INDUSTRY

URUGUAY - FILAMENT PRODUCTION - See URUGUAY - TEXTILE INDUSTRY

URUGUAY - FINANCE

Economist Intelligence Unit, 111 West 57th Street, New York, New York 10019 (800) 938-4685; *Uruguay Country Report*.

Europa Publications Limited, 18 Bedford Square, London, WC1B 3JN, England; *The Europa World Year Book*.

Federal Statistical Office, Gustav-Stresemann-Ring 11, D-6200 Wiesbaden, Germany; *Uruguay*.

Inter-American Development Bank, 1300 New York Avenue, NW, Washington, D.C. 20577 (202) 623-1753; *Economic and Social Progress in Latin America*.

International Monetary Fund, 700 Nineteenth Street, NW, Washington, D.C. 20431 (202) 623-7000; *Government Finance Statistics Yearbook*.

M.E. Sharpe, 80 Business Park Drive, Armonk, New York 10504 (800) 541-6563; *The Illustrated Book of World Rankings*.

Organization of American States (OAS), General Secretariat, Washington, D.C. 20006 (202) 458-3533; *Statistical Bulletin of the OAS*.

St. Martin's Press, Inc., 175 Fifth Avenue, New York, New York 10010 (800) 221-7945; *The Statesman's Year-Book*.

U.C.L.A. Latin American Center Publications, University of California, Los Angeles, California 90024 (310) 825-6634; *Statistical Abstract of Latin America*.

URUGUAY - FISHERIES

Europa Publications Limited, 18 Bedford Square, London, WC1B 3JN, England; *The Europa World Year Book*.

Federal Statistical Office, Gustav-Stresemann-Ring 11, D-6200 Wiesbaden, Germany; *Uruguay*.

Food and Agricultural Organization of the United Nations (FAO) Via delle Terme di Caracalla, 00100 Rome, Italy (Telephone Number in U.S. (202) 653-2400); *The State of Food and Agriculture;* and *Yearbook of Fishery Statistics*.

Inter-American Development Bank, 1300 New York Avenue, NW, Washington, D.C. 20577 (202) 623-1753; *Economic and Social Progress in Latin America*.

M.E. Sharpe, 80 Business Park Drive, Armonk, New York 10504 (800) 541-6563; *The Illustrated Book of World Rankings*.

St. Martin's Press, Inc., 175 Fifth Avenue, New York, New York 10010 (800) 221-7945; *The Statesman's Year-Book*.

Statistical Office of the United Nations, Publishing Service, New York, New York 10017 (800) 253-9646; *Statistical Yearbook*.

U.C.L.A. Latin American Center Publications, University of California, Los Angeles, California 90024 (310) 825-6634; *Statistical Abstract of Latin America*.

United Nations Conference on Trade and Development, Central Statistical Service, Palais des Nations, Geneva, Switzerland (Telephone in U.S. (800) 253-9646); *UNCTAD Commodity Yearbook*.

URUGUAY - FLOUR PRODUCTION

Statistical Office of the United Nations, Publishing Service, New York, New York 10017 (800) 253-9646; *Statistical Yearbook*.

URUGUAY - FOOD

Food and Agricultural Organization of the United Nations (FAO) Via delle Terme di Caracalla, 00100 Rome, Italy (Telephone Number in U.S. (202) 653-2400); *The State of Food and Agriculture*.

Statistical Office of the United Nations, Publishing Service, New York, New York 10017 (800) 253-9646; *Human Development Report*.

United Nations Conference on Trade and Development, Central Statistical Service, Palais des Nations, Geneva, Switzerland (Telephone in U.S. (800) 253-9646); *UNCTAD Commodity Yearbook*.

URUGUAY - FOREIGN AID

Inter-American Development Bank, 1300 New York Avenue, NW, Washington, D.C. 20577 (202) 623-1753; *Economic and Social Progress in Latin America*.

URUGUAY - FOREIGN DEBT

The Economist Intelligence Unit, 111 West 57th Street, New York, New York 10019 (800) 938-4685; *The New Latin America Market Atlas*.

Inter-American Development Bank, 1300 New York Avenue, NW, Washington, D.C. 20577 (202) 623-1753; *Economic and Social Progress in Latin America*.

International Monetary Fund, 700 Nineteenth Street, NW, Washington, D.C. 20431 (202) 623-7000; *Government Finance Statistics Yearbook*.

St. Martin's Press, Inc., 175 Fifth Avenue, New York, New York 10010 (800) 221-7945; *The Statesman's Year-Book*.

URUGUAY - FOREIGN INDEBTEDNESS

Inter-American Development Bank, 1300 New York Avenue, NW, Washington, D.C. 20577 (202) 623-1753; *Economic and Social Progress in Latin America*.

Statistical Office of the United Nations, Publishing Service, New York, New York 10017 (800) 253-9646; *Economic Survey of Latin America and the Caribbean*.

URUGUAY - FOREIGN INVESTMENT

The Economist Intelligence Unit, 111 West 57th Street, New York, New York

10019 (800) 938-4685; *The New Latin America Market Atlas.*

URUGUAY - FOREIGN TRADE

The Economist Intelligence Unit, 111 West 57th Street, New York, New York 10019 (800) 938-4685; *The New Latin America Market Atlas;* and *Uruguay Country Report.*

Euromonitor International, Inc., 122 South Michigan Avenue, Suite 1200, Chicago, Illinois 60603 (800) 577-EURO; *International Marketing Data and Statistics;* and *The World Economic Factbook.*

Europa Publications Limited, 18 Bedford Square, London, WC1B 3JN, England; *The Europa World Year Book.*

Federal Statistical Office, Gustav-Stresemann-Ring 11, D-6200 Wiesbaden, Germany; *Uruguay.*

Food and Agricultural Organization of the United Nations (FAO) Via delle Terme di Caracalla, 00100 Rome, Italy (Telephone Number in U.S. (202) 653-2400); *The State of Food and Agriculture.*

Inter-American Development Bank, 1300 New York Avenue, NW, Washington, D.C. 20577 (202) 623-1753; *Economic and Social Progress in Latin America.*

International Monetary Fund, 700 Nineteenth Street, NW, Washington, D.C. 20431 (202) 623-7000; *International Financial Statistics.*

M.E. Sharpe, 80 Business Park Drive, Armonk, New York 10504 (800) 541-6563; *The Illustrated Book of World Rankings.*

St. Martin's Press, Inc., 175 Fifth Avenue, New York, New York 10010 (800) 221-7945; *The Statesman's Year-Book.*

Statistical Office of the United Nations, Publishing Service, New York, New York 10017 (800) 253-9646; *Economic Survey of Latin America and the Caribbean; International Trade Statistics Yearbook;* and *Statistical Yearbook.*

U.C.L.A. Latin American Center Publications, University of California, Los Angeles, California 90024 (310) 825-6634; *Statistical Abstract of Latin America.*

United Nations Conference on Trade and Development, Central Statistical Service, Palais des Nations, Geneva, Switzerland (Telephone in U.S. (800) 253-9646); *UNCTAD Commodity Yearbook.*

The World Bank, 1818 H Street, NW, Washington, D.C. 20433 (202) 477-1234; *World Development Report;* and *World Development Indicators.*

URUGUAY - FORESTRY AND FOREST PRODUCTS

American Forest and Paper Association, 1111 Nineteenth Street, NW, Washington, D.C. 20036 (202) 463-2700; *Wood Pulp and Fiber Statistics.*

Europa Publications Limited, 18 Bedford Square, London, WC1B 3JN, England; *The Europa World Year Book.*

Federal Statistical Office, Gustav-Stresemann-Ring 11, D-6200 Wiesbaden, Germany; *Uruguay.*

Food and Agricultural Organization of the United Nations (FAO) Via delle Terme di Caracalla, 00100 Rome, Italy (Telephone Number in U.S. (202) 653-2400); *The State of Food and Agriculture;* and *Yearbook of Forest Products.*

Inter-American Development Bank, 1300 New York Avenue, NW, Washington, D.C. 20577 (202) 623-1753; *Economic and Social Progress in Latin America.*

M.E. Sharpe, 80 Business Park Drive, Armonk, New York 10504 (800) 541-6563; *The Illustrated Book of World Rankings.*

St. Martin's Press, Inc., 175 Fifth Avenue, New York, New York 10010 (800) 221-7945; *The Statesman's Year-Book.*

Statistical Office of the United Nations, Publishing Service, New York, New York 10017 (800) 253-9646; *Statistical Yearbook.*

U.C.L.A. Latin American Center Publications, University of California, Los Angeles, California 90024 (310) 825-6634; *Statistical Abstract of Latin America.*

United Nations Conference on Trade and Development, Central Statistical Service, Palais des Nations, Geneva, Switzerland (Telephone in U.S. (800) 253-9646); *UNCTAD Commodity Yearbook.*

United Nations Educational, Scientific and Cultural Organization (UNESCO), 7 Place de Fontenoy, F-75700 Paris, France (Telephone Number in U.S. (212) 963-5981); *Statistical Yearbook.*

The World Bank, 1818 H Street, NW, Washington, D.C. 20433 (202) 477-1234; *World Development Report.*

URUGUAY - GARLIC PRODUCTION - See URUGUAY - CROPS

URUGUAY - GAS PRODUCTION - See URUGUAY - MINING AND MINERAL PRODUCTS

URUGUAY - GENERAL INDUSTRIAL STATISTICS - See URUGUAY - INDUSTRY

URUGUAY - GENERAL MORTALITY - See URUGUAY - MORTALITY

URUGUAY - GEOGRAPHIC DATA

M.E. Sharpe, 80 Business Park Drive, Armonk, New York 10504 (800) 541-6563; *The Illustrated Book of World Rankings.*

U.C.L.A. Latin American Center Publications, University of California, Los Angeles, California 90024 (310) 825-6634; *Statistical Abstract of Latin America.*

URUGUAY - GOATS - See URUGUAY - LIVESTOCK AND POULTRY

URUGUAY - GOLD HOLDINGS

International Monetary Fund, 700 Nineteenth Street, NW, Washington, D.C. 20431 (202) 623-7000; *International Financial Statistics.*

Statistical Office of the United Nations, Publishing Service, New York, New York 10017 (800) 253-9646; *Statistical Yearbook.*

The World Bank, 1818 H Street, NW, Washington, D.C. 20433 (202) 477-1234; *World Development Indicators.*

URUGUAY - GOLD PRODUCTION AND CONSUMPTION - See URUGUAY - MINING AND MINERAL PRODUCTS

URUGUAY - GOLD RESERVES

The Economist Intelligence Unit, 111 West 57th Street, New York, New York 10019 (800) 938-4685; *The New Latin America Market Atlas.*

URUGUAY - GOVERNMENT

Central Intelligence Agency, Washington, D.C. 20505 (703) 482-1100, www.cia.gov; *The World Factbook.*

Europa Publications Limited, 18 Bedford Square, London, WC1B 3JN, England; *The Europa World Year Book.*

Inter-American Development Bank, 1300 New York Avenue, NW, Washington, D.C. 20577 (202) 623-1753; *Economic and Social Progress in Latin America.*

International Monetary Fund, 700 Nineteenth Street, NW, Washington, D.C. 20431 (202) 623-7000; *Government Finance Statistics Yearbook;* and *International Financial Statistics.*

St. Martin's Press, Inc., 175 Fifth Avenue, New York, New York 10010 (800) 221-7945; *The Statesman's Year-Book.*

Statistical Office of the United Nations, Publishing Service, New York, New York 10017 (800) 253-9646; *National Accounts*

Statistics.

Time Books, 201 East 50th Street, New York, New York 10022 (800) 726-0600; *The Economist Book of Vital World Statistics.*

The World Bank, 1818 H Street, NW, Washington, D.C. 20433 (202) 477-1234; *World Development Report;* and *World Development Indicators.*

URUGUAY - GRAIN PRODUCTION - See URUGUAY - CROPS

URUGUAY - GREEN PEPPER AND CHILIE PRODUCTION - See URUGUAY - CROPS

URUGUAY - GROSS DOMESTIC PRODUCT

The Economist Intelligence Unit, 111 West 57th Street, New York, New York 10019 (800) 938-4685; *The New Latin America Market Atlas; Uruguay Country Report;* and *The World Market Atlas.*

Euromonitor International, Inc., 122 South Michigan Avenue, Suite 1200, Chicago, Illinois 60603 (800) 577-EURO; *International Marketing Data and Statistics;* and *The World Economic Factbook.*

Europa Publications Limited, 18 Bedford Square, London, WC1B 3JN, England; *The Europa World Year Book.*

Inter-American Development Bank, 1300 New York Avenue, NW, Washington, D.C. 20577 (202) 623-1753; *Economic and Social Progress in Latin America.*

M.E. Sharpe, 80 Business Park Drive, Armonk, New York 10504 (800) 541-6563; *The Illustrated Book of World Rankings.*

Organization of American States (OAS), General Secretariat, Washington, D.C. 20006 (202) 458-3533; *Statistical Bulletin of the OAS.*

Statistical Office of the United Nations, Publishing Service, New York, New York 10017 (800) 253-9646; *Human Development Report; National Accounts Statistics; Statistical Yearbook;* and *Statistical Yearbook for Latin America and the Caribbean.*

Time Books, 201 East 50th Street, New York, New York 10022 (800) 726-0600; *The Economist Book of Vital World Statistics.*

U.C.L.A. Latin American Center Publications, University of California, Los Angeles, California 90024 (310) 825-6634; *Statistical Abstract of Latin America.*

The World Bank, 1818 H Street, NW, Washington, D.C. 20433 (202) 477-1234; *World Development Report;* and *World Development Indicators.*

URUGUAY - GROSS NATIONAL PRODUCT

Euromonitor International, Inc., 122 South Michigan Avenue, Suite 1200, Chicago, Illinois 60603 (800) 577-EURO; *International Marketing Data and Statistics.*

Inter-American Development Bank, 1300 New York Avenue, NW, Washington, D.C. 20577 (202) 623-1753; *Economic and Social Progress in Latin America.*

St. Martin's Press, Inc., 175 Fifth Avenue, New York, New York 10010 (800) 221-7945; *The Statesman's Year-Book.*

U.S. Arms Control and Disarmament Agency, 320 Twenty-first Street, NW, Washington, D.C. 20451 (202) 647-8677; *World Military Expenditures and Arms Transfers.*

The World Bank, 1818 H Street, NW, Washington, D.C. 20433 (202) 477-1234; *The World Bank Atlas; World Development Report;* and *World Development Indicators.*

URUGUAY - HEALTH

The Economist Intelligence Unit, 111 West 57th Street, New York, New York 10019 (800) 938-4685; *The New Latin America Market Atlas.*

Euromonitor International, Inc., 122 South Michigan Avenue, Suite 1200, Chicago, Illinois 60603 (800) 577-EURO; *World Marketing Data and Statistics.*

Federal Statistical Office, Gustav-Stresemann-Ring 11, D-6200 Wiesbaden, Germany; *Uruguay.*

M.E. Sharpe, 80 Business Park Drive, Armonk, New York 10504 (800) 541-6563; *The Illustrated Book of World Rankings.*

St. Martin's Press, Inc., 175 Fifth Avenue, New York, New York 10010 (800) 221-7945; *The Statesman's Year-Book.*

Statistical Office of the United Nations, Publishing Service, New York, New York 10017 (800) 253-9646; *Human Development Report; Statistical Yearbook;* and *Statistical Yearbook for Latin America and the Caribbean.*

Time Books, 201 East 50th Street, New York, New York 10022 (800) 726-0600; *The Economist Book of Vital World Statistics.*

U.C.L.A. Latin American Center Publications, University of California, Los Angeles, California 90024 (310) 825-6634; *Statistical Abstract of Latin America.*

United Nations Children's Fund (UNICEF), 3 United Nations Plaza, New York, New York 10017 (800) 253-9646; *State of the World's Children.*

The World Bank, 1818 H Street, NW, Washington, D.C. 20433 (202) 477-1234; *World Development Report.*

URUGUAY - HEALTH EXPENDITURES

International Monetary Fund, 700 Nineteenth Street, NW, Washington, D.C. 20431 (202) 623-7000; *Government Finance Statistics Yearbook.*

URUGUAY - HIDE PRODUCTION

Food and Agricultural Organization of the United Nations (FAO), Via delle Terme di Caracalla, 00100 Rome, Italy (Telephone Number in U.S. (202) 653-2400); *Production Yearbook.*

URUGUAY - HIDES EXPORTS

International Monetary Fund, 700 Nineteenth Street, NW, Washington, D.C. 20431 (202) 623-7000; *International Financial Statistics.*

URUGUAY - HIGHWAYS

Central Intelligence Agency, Washington, D.C. 20505 (703) 482-1100, www.cia.gov; *The World Factbook.*

The Economist Intelligence Unit, 111 West 57th Street, New York, New York 10019 (800) 938-4685; *The New Latin America Market Atlas.*

St. Martin's Press, Inc., 175 Fifth Avenue, New York, New York 10010 (800) 221-7945; *The Statesman's Year-Book.*

URUGUAY - HORSES - See URUGUAY - LIVESTOCK AND POULTRY

URUGUAY - HOURS OF WORK - See URUGUAY - EMPLOYMENT

URUGUAY - HOUSING AND HOUSING UNITS

Euromonitor International, Inc., 122 South Michigan Avenue, Suite 1200, Chicago, Illinois 60603 (800) 577-EURO; *World Marketing Data and Statistics.*

M.E. Sharpe, 80 Business Park Drive, Armonk, New York 10504 (800) 541-6563; *The Illustrated Book of World Rankings.*

Statistical Office of the United Nations, Publishing Service, New York, New York 10017 (800) 253-9646; *Statistical Yearbook for Latin America and the Caribbean.*

U.C.L.A. Latin American Center Publications, University of California, Los Angeles, California 90024 (310) 825-6634; *Statistical Abstract of Latin America.*

URUGUAY - HOUSING EXPENDITURES

International Monetary Fund, 700 Nineteenth Street, NW, Washington, D.C. 20431 (202) 623-7000; *Government Finance Statistics Yearbook.*

URUGUAY - ILLITERATE POPULATION

Central Intelligence Agency, Washington, D.C. 20505 (703) 482-1100, www.cia.gov; *The World Factbook.*

The Economist Intelligence Unit, 111 West 57th Street, New York, New York 10019 (800) 938-4685; *The New Latin America Market Atlas;* and *The World Market Atlas.*

Euromonitor International, Inc., 122 South Michigan Avenue, Suite 1200, Chicago, Illinois 60603 (800) 577-EURO; *The World Economic Factbook.*

Statistical Office of the United Nations, Publishing Service, New York, New York 10017 (800) 253-9646; *Human Development Report;* and *Statistical Yearbook for Latin America and the Caribbean.*

United Nations Educational, Scientific and Cultural Organization (UNESCO), 7 Place de Fontenoy, F-75700 Paris, France (Telephone Number in U.S. (212) 963-5981); *Statistical Yearbook.*

URUGUAY - IMMIGRATION

U.C.L.A. Latin American Center Publications, University of California, Los Angeles, California 90024 (310) 825-6634; *Statistical Abstract of Latin America.*

URUGUAY - IMPORTS

Central Intelligence Agency, Washington, D.C. 20505 (703) 482-1100, www.cia.gov; *The World Factbook.*

The Economist Intelligence Unit, 111 West 57th Street, New York, New York 10019 (800) 938-4685; *The New Latin America Market Atlas; Uruguay Country Report;* and *The World Market Atlas.*

Euromonitor International, Inc., 122 South Michigan Avenue, Suite 1200, Chicago, Illinois 60603 (800) 577-EURO; *International Marketing Data and Statistics;* and *The World Economic Factbook.*

Europa Publications Limited, 18 Bedford Square, London, WC1B 3JN, England; *The Europa World Year Book.*

Food and Agricultural Organization of the United Nations (FAO) Via delle Terme di Caracalla, 00100 Rome, Italy (Telephone Number in U.S. (202) 653-2400); *The State of Food and Agriculture.*

Inter-American Development Bank,

1300 New York Avenue, NW, Washington, D.C. 20577 (202) 623-1753; *Economic and Social Progress in Latin America.*

International Monetary Fund, 700 Nineteenth Street, NW, Washington, D.C. 20431 (202) 623-7000; *Direction of Trade Statistics; Government Finance Statistics Yearbook;* and *International Financial Statistics.*

Organization of American States (OAS), General Secretariat, Washington, D.C. 20006 (202) 458-3533; *Statistical Bulletin of the OAS.*

St. Martin's Press, Inc., 175 Fifth Avenue, New York, New York 10010 (800) 221-7945; *The Statesman's Year-Book.*

Statistical Office of the United Nations, Publishing Service, New York, New York 10017 (800) 253-9646; *Statistical Yearbook for Latin America and the Caribbean.*

Time Books, 201 East 50th Street, New York, New York 10022 (800) 726-0600; *The Economist Book of Vital World Statistics.*

United Nations Conference on Trade and Development (UNCTAD), New York, New York 10017 (800) 253-9646; *Handbook of International Trade and Development Statistics.*

The World Bank, 1818 H Street, NW, Washington, D.C. 20433 (202) 477-1234; *World Development Report;* and *World Development Indicators.*

URUGUAY - INCOME DISTRIBUTION

Statistical Office of the United Nations, Publishing Service, New York, New York 10017 (800) 253-9646; *Statistical Yearbook for Latin America and the Caribbean.*

U.C.L.A. Latin American Center Publications, University of California, Los Angeles, California 90024 (310) 825-6634; *Statistical Abstract of Latin America.*

URUGUAY - INCOME TAXES - See URUGUAY - TAXATION

URUGUAY - INDUSTRIAL METALS PRODUCTION - See URUGUAY - MINING AND MINERAL PRODUCTS

URUGUAY - INDUSTRY

Central Intelligence Agency, Washington, D.C. 20505 (703) 482-1100, www.cia.gov; *The World Factbook.*

Economist Intelligence Unit, 111 West 57th Street, New York, New York 10019 (800) 938-4685; *Uruguay Country Report.*

Euromonitor International, Inc., 122 South Michigan Avenue, Suite 1200,

Chicago, Illinois 60603 (800) 577-EURO; *International Marketing Data and Statistics; World Marketing Data and Statistics;* and *The World Economic Factbook.*

Europa Publications Limited, 18 Bedford Square, London, WC1B 3JN, England; *The Europa World Year Book.*

Federal Statistical Office, Gustav-Stresemann-Ring 11, D-6200 Wiesbaden, Germany; *Uruguay.*

International Labour Office, I.L.O. Publications, 1828 L Street, NW, Suite 801, Washington, D.C. 20036 (301) 638-3152; *Yearbook of Labour Statistics.*

M.E. Sharpe, 80 Business Park Drive, Armonk, New York 10504 (800) 541-6563; *The Illustrated Book of World Rankings.*

St. Martin's Press, Inc., 175 Fifth Avenue, New York, New York 10010 (800) 221-7945; *The Statesman's Year-Book.*

Statistical Office of the United Nations, Publishing Service, New York, New York 10017 (800) 253-9646; *Industrial Commodity Statistics Yearbook;* and *Statistical Yearbook.*

Time Books, 201 East 50th Street, New York, New York 10022 (800) 726-0600; *The Economist Book of Vital World Statistics.*

U.C.L.A. Latin American Center Publications, University of California, Los Angeles, California 90024 (310) 825-6634; *Statistical Abstract of Latin America.*

The World Bank, 1818 H Street, NW, Washington, D.C. 20433 (202) 477-1234; *World Development Indicators.*

World Intellectual Property Organization, 34 Chemin des Colombettes, CH-1211 Geneva 20. Switzerland; *Industrial Property Statistics.*

URUGUAY - INFANT AND MATERNAL MORTALITY - See URUGUAY -MORTALITY

URUGUAY - INFLATIONARY FACTORS

Statistical Office of the United Nations, Publishing Service, New York, New York 10017 (800) 253-9646; *Economic Survey of Latin America and the Caribbean.*

URUGUAY - INTEREST RATES

Inter-American Development Bank, 1300 New York Avenue, NW, Washington, D.C. 20577 (202) 623-1753; *Economic and Social Progress in Latin America.*

URUGUAY - INTERNATIONAL FINANCE

Inter-American Development Bank, 1300 New York Avenue, NW, Washington,

D.C. 20577 (202) 623-1753; *Economic and Social Progress in Latin America.*

U.C.L.A. Latin American Center Publications, University of California, Los Angeles, California 90024 (310) 825-6634; *Statistical Abstract of Latin America.*

URUGUAY - INTERNATIONAL LIQUIDITY

Inter-American Development Bank, 1300 New York Avenue, NW, Washington, D.C. 20577 (202) 623-1753; *Economic and Social Progress in Latin America.*

International Monetary Fund, 700 Nineteenth Street, NW, Washington, D.C. 20431 (202) 623-7000; *International Financial Statistics.*

URUGUAY - INTERNATIONAL RESERVES

Inter-American Development Bank, 1300 New York Avenue, NW, Washington, D.C. 20577 (202) 623-1753; *Economic and Social Progress in Latin America.*

Organization of American States (OAS), General Secretariat, Washington, D.C. 20006 (202) 458-3533; *Statistical Bulletin of the OAS.*

URUGUAY - INTERNATIONAL RESERVES EXCLUDING GOLD

Statistical Office of the United Nations, Publishing Service, New York, New York 10017 (800) 253-9646; *Statistical Yearbook.*

The World Bank, 1818 H Street, NW, Washington, D.C. 20433 (202) 477-1234; *World Development Indicators.*

URUGUAY - INTERNATIONAL STATISTICS

Inter-American Development Bank, 1300 New York Avenue, NW, Washington, D.C. 20577 (202) 623-1753; *Economic and Social Progress in Latin America.*

U.C.L.A. Latin American Center Publications, University of California, Los Angeles, California 90024 (310) 825-6634; *Statistical Abstract of Latin America.*

URUGUAY - INVESTMENT

Inter-American Development Bank, 1300 New York Avenue, NW, Washington, D.C. 20577 (202) 623-1753; *Economic and Social Progress in Latin America.*

Statistical Office of the United Nations, Publishing Service, New York, New York 10017 (800) 253-9646; *Statistical Yearbook for Latin America and the Caribbean.*

URUGUAY - IRON ORE PRODUCTION AND CONSUMPTION - See URUGUAY - MINING AND MINERAL PRODUCTS

URUGUAY - IRRIGATION

Euromonitor International, Inc., 122 South Michigan Avenue, Suite 1200, Chicago, Illinois 60603 (800) 577-EURO; *International Marketing Data and Statistics.*

Inter-American Development Bank, 1300 New York Avenue, NW, Washington, D.C. 20577 (202) 623-1753; *Economic and Social Progress in Latin America.*

URUGUAY - LABOR

Central Intelligence Agency, Washington, D.C. 20505 (703) 482-1100, www.cia.gov; *The World Factbook.*

The Economist Intelligence Unit, 111 West 57th Street, New York, New York 10019 (800) 938-4685; *The New Latin America Market Atlas.*

Euromonitor International, Inc., 122 South Michigan Avenue, Suite 1200, Chicago, Illinois 60603 (800) 577-EURO; *International Marketing Data and Statistics;* and *World Marketing Data and Statistics.*

Europa Publications Limited, 18 Bedford Square, London, WC1B 3JN, England; *The Europa World Year Book.*

Food and Agricultural Organization of the United Nations (FAO) Via delle Terme di Caracalla, 00100 Rome, Italy (Telephone Number in U.S. (202) 653-2400); *The State of Food and Agriculture.*

International Labour Office, I.L.O. Publications, 1828 L Street, NW, Suite 801, Washington, D.C. 20036 (301) 638-3152; *Yearbook of Labour Statistics.*

M.E. Sharpe, 80 Business Park Drive, Armonk, New York 10504 (800) 541-6563; *The Illustrated Book of World Rankings.*

St. Martin's Press, Inc., 175 Fifth Avenue, New York, New York 10010 (800) 221-7945; *The Statesman's Year-Book.*

Statistical Office of the United Nations, Publishing Service, New York, New York 10017 (800) 253-9646; *Human Development Report.*

Time Books, 201 East 50th Street, New York, New York 10022 (800) 726-0600; *The Economist Book of Vital World Statistics.*

The World Bank, 1818 H Street, NW, Washington, D.C. 20433 (202) 477-1234; *The World Bank Atlas; World Development Report;* and *World Development Indicators.*

URUGUAY - LAND AREA

The Economist Intelligence Unit, 111 West 57th Street, New York, New York 10019 (800) 938-4685; *The New Latin America Market Atlas.*

URUGUAY - LAND USE

Central Intelligence Agency, Washington, D.C. 20505 (703) 482-1100, www.cia.gov; *The World Factbook.*

Euromonitor International, Inc., 122 South Michigan Avenue, Suite 1200, Chicago, Illinois 60603 (800) 577-EURO; *International Marketing Data and Statistics.*

Inter-American Development Bank, 1300 New York Avenue, NW, Washington, D.C. 20577 (202) 623-1753; *Economic and Social Progress in Latin America.*

The World Bank, 1818 H Street, NW, Washington, D.C. 20433 (202) 477-1234; *World Development Report.*

URUGUAY - LIBRARIES

M.E. Sharpe, 80 Business Park Drive, Armonk, New York 10504 (800) 541-6563; *The Illustrated Book of World Rankings.*

United Nations Educational, Scientific and Cultural Organization (UNESCO), 7 Place de Fontenoy, F-75700 Paris, France (Telephone Number in U.S. (212) 963-5981); *Statistical Yearbook.*

URUGUAY - LIFE EXPECTANCY

Central Intelligence Agency, Washington, D.C. 20505 (703) 482-1100, www.cia.gov; *The World Factbook.*

The Economist Intelligence Unit, 111 West 57th Street, New York, New York 10019 (800) 938-4685; *The New Latin America Market Atlas.*

Euromonitor International, Inc., 122 South Michigan Avenue, Suite 1200, Chicago, Illinois 60603 (800) 577-EURO; *The World Economic Factbook.*

St. Martin's Press, Inc., 175 Fifth Avenue, New York, New York 10010 (800) 221-7945; *The Statesman's Year-Book.*

Statistical Office of the United Nations, Publishing Service, New York, New York 10017 (800) 253-9646; *Human Development Report; Statistical Yearbook for Latin America and the Caribbean;* and *World Statistics Pocketbook.*

Time Books, 201 East 50th Street, New York, New York 10022 (800) 726-0600; *The Economist Book of Vital World Statistics.*

The World Bank, 1818 H Street, NW, Washington, D.C. 20433 (202) 477-1234; *The World Bank Atlas;* and *World Development Report.*

URUGUAY - LITERACY RATE

Euromonitor International, Inc., 122 South Michigan Avenue, Suite 1200, Chicago, Illinois 60603 (800) 577-EURO; *World Marketing Data and Statistics*.

URUGUAY - LIVESTOCK AND POULTRY

Commodity Research Bureau, Inc., 30 South Wacker Drive, Chicago, Illinois 60606 (312) 454-1801; *Commodity Year Book*.

Euromonitor International, Inc., 122 South Michigan Avenue, Suite 1200, Chicago, Illinois 60603 (800) 577-EURO; *International Marketing Data and Statistics*.

Europa Publications Limited, 18 Bedford Square, London, WC1B 3JN, England; *The Europa World Year Book*.

Food and Agricultural Organization of the United Nations (FAO) Via delle Terme di Caracalla, 00100 Rome, Italy (Telephone Number in U.S. (202) 653-2400); *Production Yearbook;* and *The State of Food and Agriculture*.

M.E. Sharpe, 80 Business Park Drive, Armonk, New York 10504 (800) 541-6563; *The Illustrated Book of World Rankings*.

St. Martin's Press, Inc., 175 Fifth Avenue, New York, New York 10010 (800) 221-7945; *The Statesman's Year-Book*.

Statistical Office of the United Nations, Publishing Service, New York, New York 10017 (800) 253-9646; *Statistical Yearbook*.

United Nations Conference on Trade and Development, Central Statistical Service, Palais des Nations, Geneva, Switzerland (Telephone in U.S. (800) 253-9646); *UNCTAD Commodity Yearbook*.

URUGUAY - LIVING LEVELS - See URUGUAY - LIFE EXPECTANCY

URUGUAY - MAIL - NUMBER OF ITEMS SENT AND RECEIVED

Statistical Office of the United Nations, Publishing Service, New York, New York 10017 (800) 253-9646; *Statistical Yearbook*.

URUGUAY - MAIN ECONOMIC INDICATORS - See URUGUAY - ECONOMY

URUGUAY - MANUFACTURING

The Economist Intelligence Unit, 111 West 57th Street, New York, New York 10019 (800) 938-4685; *The New Latin America Market Atlas*.

Inter-American Development Bank, 1300 New York Avenue, NW, Washington, D.C. 20577 (202) 623-1753; *Economic and Social Progress in Latin America*.

M.E. Sharpe, 80 Business Park Drive,

Armonk, New York 10504 (800) 541-6563; *The Illustrated Book of World Rankings*.

Statistical Office of the United Nations, Publishing Service, New York, New York 10017 (800) 253-9646; *Statistical Yearbook;* and *Statistical Yearbook for Latin America and the Caribbean*.

Time Books, 201 East 50th Street, New York, New York 10022 (800) 726-0600; *The Economist Book of Vital World Statistics*.

The World Bank, 1818 H Street, NW, Washington, D.C. 20433 (202) 477-1234; *World Development Indicators*.

URUGUAY - MARRIAGE RATES

Europa Publications Limited, 18 Bedford Square, London, WC1B 3JN, England; *The Europa World Year Book*.

M.E. Sharpe, 80 Business Park Drive, Armonk, New York 10504 (800) 541-6563; *The Illustrated Book of World Rankings*.

Statistical Office of the United Nations, Publishing Service, New York, New York 10017 (800) 253-9646; *Demographic Yearbook;* and *Statistical Yearbook*.

URUGUAY - MEAT EXPORTS

International Monetary Fund, 700 Nineteenth Street, NW, Washington, D.C. 20431 (202) 623-7000; *International Financial Statistics*.

Organization of American States (OAS), General Secretariat, Washington, D.C. 20006 (202) 458-3533; *Statistical Bulletin of the OAS*.

URUGUAY - MEAT PRODUCTION - See URUGUAY - LIVESTOCK AND POULTRY

URUGUAY - MEDICAL PERSONNEL

U.C.L.A. Latin American Center Publications, University of California, Los Angeles, California 90024 (310) 825-6634; *Statistical Abstract of Latin America*.

URUGUAY - MERCHANT SHIPPING

Europa Publications Limited, 18 Bedford Square, London, WC1B 3JN, England; *The Europa World Year Book*.

Lloyd's Register of Shipping, 17 Battery Place, New York, New York 10004 (212) 425-8050; *Register of Ships*.

St. Martin's Press, Inc., 175 Fifth Avenue, New York, New York 10010 (800) 221-7945; *The Statesman's Year-Book*.

Statistical Office of the United Nations, Publishing Service, New York, New York 10017 (800) 253-9646; *Statistical Yearbook*.

Time Books, 201 East 50th Street, New York, New York 10022 (800) 726-0600; *The Economist Book of Vital World Statistics*.

U.S. Department of Transportation, Maritime Administration, 400 Seventh Street, SW, Washington, D.C. 20590 (202) 366-5807; www.marad.dot.gov; *A Statistical Analysis of the World's Merchant Fleets*.

URUGUAY - MILITARY

Central Intelligence Agency, Washington, D.C. 20505 (703) 482-1100, www.cia.gov; *The World Factbook*.

The Economist Intelligence Unit, 111 West 57th Street, New York, New York 10019 (800) 938-4685; *The New Latin America Market Atlas*.

Euromonitor International, Inc., 122 South Michigan Avenue, Suite 1200, Chicago, Illinois 60603 (800) 577-EURO; *World Marketing Data and Statistics*.

The International Institute for Strategic Studies, 23 Tavistock Street, London WC2E 7NQ, England 44 171 3797676; *The Military Balance*.

St. Martin's Press, Inc., 175 Fifth Avenue, New York, New York 10010 (800) 221-7945; *The Statesman's Year-Book*.

Statistical Office of the United Nations, Publishing Service, New York, New York 10017 (800) 253-9646; *Human Development Report*.

U.C.L.A. Latin American Center Publications, University of California, Los Angeles, California 90024 (310) 825-6634; *Statistical Abstract of Latin America*.

U.S. Arms Control and Disarmament Agency, 320 Twenty-first Street, NW, Washington, D.C. 20451 (202) 647-8677; *World Military Expenditures and Arms Transfers*.

URUGUAY - MILK PRODUCTION - See URUGUAY - DAIRY PRODUCTS

URUGUAY - MINING AND MINERAL PRODUCTS

The Economist Intelligence Unit, 111 West 57th Street, New York, New York 10019 (800) 938-4685; *The New Latin America Market Atlas*.

Inter-American Development Bank, 1300 New York Avenue, NW, Washington, D.C. 20577 (202) 623-1753; *Economic and Social Progress in Latin America*.

M.E. Sharpe, 80 Business Park Drive, Armonk, New York 10504 (800) 541-6563; *The Illustrated Book of World Rankings*.

Statistical Office of the United Nations, Publishing Service, New York, New York 10017 (800) 253-9646; *Statistical Yearbook;* and *Statistical Yearbook for Latin America and the Caribbean.*

U.C.L.A. Latin American Center Publications, University of California, Los Angeles, California 90024 (310) 825-6634; *Statistical Abstract of Latin America.*

United Nations Conference on Trade and Development, Central Statistical Service, Palais des Nations, Geneva, Switzerland (Telephone in U.S. (800) 253-9646); *UNCTAD Commodity Yearbook.*

URUGUAY - MONEY EXCHANGE RATE - See URUGUAY - EXCHANGE RATES

URUGUAY - MONEY RATES - MARKET

Inter-American Development Bank, 1300 New York Avenue, NW, Washington, D.C. 20577 (202) 623-1753; *Economic and Social Progress in Latin America.*

URUGUAY - MONEY RESERVES

Euromonitor International, Inc., 122 South Michigan Avenue, Suite 1200, Chicago, Illinois 60603 (800) 577-EURO; *International Marketing Data and Statistics.*

Inter-American Development Bank, 1300 New York Avenue, NW, Washington, D.C. 20577 (202) 623-1753; *Economic and Social Progress in Latin America.*

URUGUAY - MONEY SUPPLY

Economist Intelligence Unit, 111 West 57th Street, New York, New York 10019 (800) 938-4685; *Uruguay Country Report.*

Euromonitor International, Inc., 122 South Michigan Avenue, Suite 1200, Chicago, Illinois 60603 (800) 577-EURO; *International Marketing Data and Statistics.*

Europa Publications Limited, 18 Bedford Square, London, WC1B 3JN, England; *The Europa World Year Book.*

Inter-American Development Bank, 1300 New York Avenue, NW, Washington, D.C. 20577 (202) 623-1753; *Economic and Social Progress in Latin America.*

International Monetary Fund, 700 Nineteenth Street, NW, Washington, D.C. 20431 (202) 623-7000; *International Financial Statistics.*

Statistical Office of the United Nations, Publishing Service, New York, New York 10017 (800) 253-9646; *Statistical Yearbook.*

U.C.L.A. Latin American Center Publications, University of California, Los Angeles, California 90024 (310) 825-6634;

Statistical Abstract of Latin America.

The World Bank, 1818 H Street, NW, Washington, D.C. 20433 (202) 477-1234; *World Development Indicators.*

URUGUAY - MORTALITY

Central Intelligence Agency, Washington, D.C. 20505 (703) 482-1100, www.cia.gov; *The World Factbook.*

The Economist Intelligence Unit, 111 West 57th Street, New York, New York 10019 (800) 938-4685; *The New Latin America Market Atlas.*

Euromonitor International, Inc., 122 South Michigan Avenue, Suite 1200, Chicago, Illinois 60603 (800) 577-EURO; *International Marketing Data and Statistics;* and *The World Economic Factbook.*

Europa Publications Limited, 18 Bedford Square, London, WC1B 3JN, England; *The Europa World Year Book.*

St. Martin's Press, Inc., 175 Fifth Avenue, New York, New York 10010 (800) 221-7945; *The Statesman's Year-Book.*

Statistical Office of the United Nations, Publishing Service, New York, New York 10017 (800) 253-9646; *Demographic Yearbook; Human Development Report; Statistical Yearbook; Statistical Yearbook for Latin America and the Caribbean;* and *World Statistics Pocketbook.*

Time Books, 201 East 50th Street, New York, New York 10022 (800) 726-0600; *The Economist Book of Vital World Statistics.*

United Nations Children's Fund (UNICEF), 3 United Nations Plaza, New York, New York 10017 (800) 253-9646; *State of the World's Children.*

The World Bank, 1818 H Street, NW, Washington, D.C. 20433 (202) 477-1234; *The World Bank Atlas; World Development Report;* and *World Development Indicators.*

World Health Organization, Office of Publications, 20 Avenue Appia, CH-1211 Geneva 27, Switzerland (Telephone Number in U.S. (518) 436-9686); *World Health Statistics Annual.*

URUGUAY - MOTION PICTURES

St. Martin's Press, Inc., 175 Fifth Avenue, New York, New York 10010 (800) 221-7945; *The Statesman's Year-Book.*

URUGUAY - MOTOR VEHICLE TAXES - See URUGUAY - TAXATION

URUGUAY - MOTOR VEHICLES IN USE

The Economist Intelligence Unit, 111

West 57th Street, New York, New York 10019 (800) 938-4685; *The New Latin America Market Atlas.*

Europa Publications Limited, 18 Bedford Square, London, WC1B 3JN, England; *The Europa World Year Book.*

Statistical Office of the United Nations, Publishing Service, New York, New York 10017 (800) 253-9646; *Statistical Yearbook.*

Time Books, 201 East 50th Street, New York, New York 10022 (800) 726-0600; *The Economist Book of Vital World Statistics.*

URUGUAY - MULES - See URUGUAY - LIVESTOCK AND POULTRY

URUGUAY - MUSEUMS

M.E. Sharpe, 80 Business Park Drive, Armonk, New York 10504 (800) 541-6563; *The Illustrated Book of World Rankings.*

United Nations Educational, Scientific and Cultural Organization (UNESCO), 7 Place de Fontenoy, F-75700 Paris, France (Telephone Number in U.S. (212) 963-5981); *Statistical Yearbook.*

URUGUAY - NATALITY - See URUGUAY - BIRTH RATE

URUGUAY - NATIONAL ACCOUNTS

Europa Publications Limited, 18 Bedford Square, London, WC1B 3JN, England; *The Europa World Year Book.*

Federal Statistical Office, Gustav-Stresemann-Ring 11, D-6200 Wiesbaden, Germany; *Uruguay.*

Inter-American Development Bank, 1300 New York Avenue, NW, Washington, D.C. 20577 (202) 623-1753; *Economic and Social Progress in Latin America.*

International Monetary Fund, 700 Nineteenth Street, NW, Washington, D.C. 20431 (202) 623-7000; *International Financial Statistics.*

Organization of American States (OAS), General Secretariat, Washington, D.C. 20006 (202) 458-3533; *Statistical Bulletin of the OAS.*

Statistical Office of the United Nations, Publishing Service, New York, New York 10017 (800) 253-9646; *National Accounts Statistics;* and *Statistical Yearbook.*

U.C.L.A. Latin American Center Publications, University of California, Los Angeles, California 90024 (310) 825-6634; *Statistical Abstract of Latin America.*

URUGUAY - NATIONAL INCOME

Inter-American Development Bank, 1300 New York Avenue, NW, Washington, D.C. 20577 (202) 623-1753; *Economic and Social Progress in Latin America.*

M.E. Sharpe, 80 Business Park Drive, Armonk, New York 10504 (800) 541-6563; *The Illustrated Book of World Rankings.*

Statistical Office of the United Nations, Publishing Service, New York, New York 10017 (800) 253-9646; *Human Development Report; Statistical Yearbook;* and *Statistical Yearbook for Latin America and the Caribbean.*

URUGUAY - NATIONAL PRODUCT

M.E. Sharpe, 80 Business Park Drive, Armonk, New York 10504 (800) 541-6563; *The Illustrated Book of World Rankings.*

Statistical Office of the United Nations, Publishing Service, New York, New York 10017 (800) 253-9646; *Statistical Yearbook.*

URUGUAY - NATURAL GAS PRODUCTION - See URUGUAY - MINING AND MINERAL PRODUCTS

URUGUAY - NEWSPAPER PRODUCTION - See URUGUAY - FORESTRY AND FOREST PRODUCTS

URUGUAY - NEWSPRINT - See URUGUAY - FORESTRY AND FOREST PRODUCTS

URUGUAY - NUTRITION

Statistical Office of the United Nations, Publishing Service, New York, New York 10017 (800) 253-9646; *Statistical Yearbook for Latin America and the Caribbean.*

URUGUAY - OATS PRODUCTION - See URUGUAY - CROPS

URUGUAY - OCCUPATIONS - See URUGUAY - LABOR

URUGUAY - ORANGES PRODUCTION - See URUGUAY - CROPS

URUGUAY - PAPER - See URUGUAY - FORESTRY AND FOREST PRODUCTS

URUGUAY - PATENTS, TRADEMARKS AND SERVICE MARKS

Statistical Office of the United Nations, Publishing Service, New York, New York 10017 (800) 253-9646; *Statistical Yearbook.*

World Intellectual Property Organization, 34 Chemin des Colombettes, CH-1211 Geneva 20. Switzerland; *Industrial Property Statistics.*

URUGUAY - PEANUT PRODUCTION - See URUGUAY - CROPS

URUGUAY - PERIODICALS

United Nations Educational, Scientific and Cultural Organization (UNESCO), 7 Place de Fontenoy, F-75700 Paris, France (Telephone Number in U.S. (212) 963-5981); *Statistical Yearbook.*

URUGUAY - PESTICIDE USE

Food and Agricultural Organization of the United Nations (FAO) Via delle Terme di Caracalla, 00100 Rome, Italy (Telephone Number in U.S. (202) 653-2400); *The State of Food and Agriculture.*

URUGUAY - PETROLEUM INDUSTRY

The Economist Intelligence Unit, 111 West 57th Street, New York, New York 10019 (800) 938-4685; *The New Latin America Market Atlas.*

Food and Agricultural Organization of the United Nations (FAO) Via delle Terme di Caracalla, 00100 Rome, Italy (Telephone Number in U.S. (202) 653-2400); *The State of Food and Agriculture.*

Inter-American Development Bank, 1300 New York Avenue, NW, Washington, D.C. 20577 (202) 623-1753; *Economic and Social Progress in Latin America.*

M.E. Sharpe, 80 Business Park Drive, Armonk, New York 10504 (800) 541-6563; *The Illustrated Book of World Rankings.*

St. Martin's Press, Inc., 175 Fifth Avenue, New York, New York 10010 (800) 221-7945; *The Statesman's Year-Book.*

Statistical Office of the United Nations, Publishing Service, New York, New York 10017 (800) 253-9646; *Statistical Yearbook.*

United Nations Conference on Trade and Development, Central Statistical Service, Palais des Nations, Geneva, Switzerland (Telephone in U.S. (800) 253-9646); *UNCTAD Commodity Yearbook.*

URUGUAY - PIG-IRON AND FERRO-ALLOY PRODUCTION - See URUGUAY - MINING AND MINERAL PRODUCTS

URUGUAY - PIGS - See URUGUAY - LIVESTOCK AND POULTRY

URUGUAY - POLITICAL DATA

U.C.L.A. Latin American Center Publications, University of California, Los Angeles, California 90024 (310) 825-6634; *Statistical Abstract of Latin America.*

URUGUAY - POPULATION

Central Intelligence Agency, Washington, D.C. 20505 (703) 482-1100, www.cia.gov; *The World Factbook.*

The Economist Intelligence Unit, 111 West 57th Street, New York, New York 10019 (800) 938-4685; *The New Latin America Market Atlas; Uruguay Country Report;* and *The World Market Atlas.*

Euromonitor International, Inc., 122 South Michigan Avenue, Suite 1200, Chicago, Illinois 60603 (800) 577-EURO; *International Marketing Data and Statistics;* and *The World Economic Factbook.*

Europa Publications Limited, 18 Bedford Square, London, WC1B 3JN, England; *The Europa World Year Book.*

Federal Statistical Office, Gustav-Stresemann-Ring 11, D-6200 Wiesbaden, Germany; *Uruguay.*

Inter-American Development Bank, 1300 New York Avenue, NW, Washington, D.C. 20577 (202) 623-1753; *Economic and Social Progress in Latin America.*

International Labour Office, I.L.O. Publications, 1828 L Street, NW, Suite 801, Washington, D.C. 20036 (301) 638-3152; *Yearbook of Labour Statistics.*

M.E. Sharpe, 80 Business Park Drive, Armonk, New York 10504 (800) 541-6563; *The Illustrated Book of World Rankings.*

Organization of American States (OAS), General Secretariat, Washington, D.C. 20006 (202) 458-3533; *Statistical Bulletin of the OAS.*

St. Martin's Press, Inc., 175 Fifth Avenue, New York, New York 10010 (800) 221-7945; *The Statesman's Year-Book.*

Statistical Office of the United Nations, Publishing Service, New York, New York 10017 (800) 253-9646; *Demographic Yearbook; Human Development Report; Statistical Yearbook; Statistical Yearbook for Latin America and the Caribbean;* and *World Statistics Pocketbook.*

Time Books, 201 East 50th Street, New York, New York 10022 (800) 726-0600; *The Economist Book of Vital World Statistics.*

U.C.L.A. Latin American Center Publications, University of California, Los Angeles, California 90024 (310) 825-6634; *Statistical Abstract of Latin America.*

United Nations Educational, Scientific and Cultural Organization (UNESCO), 7 Place de Fontenoy, F-75700 Paris, France (Telephone Number in U.S. (212) 963-5981); *Statistical Yearbook.*

U.S. Arms Control and Disarmament Agency, 320 Twenty-first Street, NW, Washington, D.C. 20451 (202) 647-8677; *World Military Expenditures and Arms*

Transfers.

The World Bank, 1818 H Street, NW, Washington, D.C. 20433 (202) 477-1234; *The World Bank Atlas;* and *World Development Report.*

World Health Organization, Office of Publications, 20 Avenue Appia, CH-1211 Geneva 27, Switzerland (Telephone Number in U.S. (518) 436-9686); *World Health Statistics Annual.*

URUGUAY - POST OFFICES

M.E. Sharpe, 80 Business Park Drive, Armonk, New York 10504 (800) 541-6563; *The Illustrated Book of World Rankings.*

St. Martin's Press, Inc., 175 Fifth Avenue, New York, New York 10010 (800) 221-7945; *The Statesman's Year-Book.*

URUGUAY - POTATO PRODUCTION - See URUGUAY - CROPS

URUGUAY - PRICES

Federal Statistical Office, Gustav-Stresemann-Ring 11, D-6200 Wiesbaden, Germany; *Uruguay.*

Food and Agricultural Organization of the United Nations (FAO) Via delle Terme di Caracalla, 00100 Rome, Italy (Telephone Number in U.S. (202) 653-2400); *The State of Food and Agriculture.*

International Labour Office, I.L.O. Publications, 1828 L Street, NW, Suite 801, Washington, D.C. 20036 (301) 638-3152; *Yearbook of Labour Statistics.*

International Monetary Fund, 700 Nineteenth Street, NW, Washington, D.C. 20431 (202) 623-7000; *International Financial Statistics.*

M.E. Sharpe, 80 Business Park Drive, Armonk, New York 10504 (800) 541-6563; *The Illustrated Book of World Rankings.*

Statistical Office of the United Nations, Publishing Service, New York, New York 10017 (800) 253-9646; *Statistical Yearbook for Latin America and the Caribbean.*

URUGUAY - PRINTING AND WRITING PAPER - See URUGUAY - FORESTRY AND FOREST PRODUCTS

URUGUAY - PRODUCTION

M.E. Sharpe, 80 Business Park Drive, Armonk, New York 10504 (800) 541-6563; *The Illustrated Book of World Rankings.*

URUGUAY - PRODUCTIVITY

Euromonitor International, Inc., 122 South Michigan Avenue, Suite 1200, Chicago, Illinois 60603 (800) 577-EURO; *International Marketing Data and Statistics.*

URUGUAY - PROPERTY TAXES - See URUGUAY - TAXATION URUGUAY - PUBLIC CONSUMPTION FUND

Inter-American Development Bank, 1300 New York Avenue, NW, Washington, D.C. 20577 (202) 623-1753; *Economic and Social Progress in Latin America.*

M.E. Sharpe, 80 Business Park Drive, Armonk, New York 10504 (800) 541-6563; *The Illustrated Book of World Rankings.*

URUGUAY - PUBLIC EXPENDITURE

Inter-American Development Bank, 1300 New York Avenue, NW, Washington, D.C. 20577 (202) 623-1753; *Economic and Social Progress in Latin America.*

Statistical Office of the United Nations, Publishing Service, New York, New York 10017 (800) 253-9646; *Statistical Yearbook for Latin America and the Caribbean.*

URUGUAY - PUBLIC FINANCES - See URUGUAY - FINANCES

URUGUAY - PUBLIC REVENUES

Inter-American Development Bank, 1300 New York Avenue, NW, Washington, D.C. 20577 (202) 623-1753; *Economic and Social Progress in Latin America.*

URUGUAY - RADIO BROADCASTING - See URUGUAY - BROADCASTING

URUGUAY - RADIO RECEIVERS

St. Martin's Press, Inc., 175 Fifth Avenue, New York, New York 10010 (800) 221-7945; *The Statesman's Year-Book.*

URUGUAY - RAILWAYS

The Economist Intelligence Unit, 111 West 57th Street, New York, New York 10019 (800) 938-4685; *The New Latin America Market Atlas.*

Europa Publications Limited, 18 Bedford Square, London, WC1B 3JN, England; *The Europa World Year Book.*

Jane's Information Group, Sentinel House, 163 Brighton Road, Coulsdon, Surrey CR5 2NH, England (Telephone Number in U.S. (703) 683-3700); *Jane's World Railways.*

St. Martin's Press, Inc., 175 Fifth Avenue, New York, New York 10010 (800) 221-7945; *The Statesman's Year-Book.*

Statistical Office of the United Nations, Publishing Service, New York, New York 10017 (800) 253-9646; *Statistical Yearbook.*

URUGUAY - RANCHING

U.C.L.A. Latin American Center Publications, University of California, Los Angeles, California 90024 (310) 825-6634; *Statistical Abstract of Latin America.*

URUGUAY - RELIGION

Central Intelligence Agency, Washington, D.C. 20505 (703) 482-1100, www.cia.gov; *The World Factbook.*

M.E. Sharpe, 80 Business Park Drive, Armonk, New York 10504 (800) 541-6563; *The Illustrated Book of World Rankings.*

St. Martin's Press, Inc., 175 Fifth Avenue, New York, New York 10010 (800) 221-7945; *The Statesman's Year-Book.*

U.C.L.A. Latin American Center Publications, University of California, Los Angeles, California 90024 (310) 825-6634; *Statistical Abstract of Latin America.*

URUGUAY - RENT PRICES

International Labour Office, I.L.O. Publications, 1828 L Street, NW, Suite 801, Washington, D.C. 20036 (301) 638-3152; *Yearbook of Labour Statistics.*

URUGUAY - RESERVES EXCLUDING GOLD

The Economist Intelligence Unit, 111 West 57th Street, New York, New York 10019 (800) 938-4685; *The New Latin America Market Atlas.*

URUGUAY - RETAIL TRADE

Euromonitor International, Inc., 122 South Michigan Avenue, Suite 1200, Chicago, Illinois 60603 (800) 577-EURO; *World Marketing Data and Statistics.*

Inter-American Development Bank, 1300 New York Avenue, NW, Washington, D.C. 20577 (202) 623-1753; *Economic and Social Progress in Latin America.*

URUGUAY - RICE PRODUCTION - See URUGUAY - CROPS

URUGUAY - ROOT AND TUBER PRODUCTION - See URUGUAY - CROPS

URUGUAY - ROUNDWOOD PRODUCTION - See URUGUAY - FORESTRY AND FOREST PRODUCTS

URUGUAY - RUBBER PRODUCTION AND CONSUMPTION

M.E. Sharpe, 80 Business Park Drive, Armonk, New York 10504 (800) 541-6563; *The Illustrated Book of World Rankings.*

URUGUAY - SAWNWOOD PRODUCTION - See URUGUAY - FORESTRY AND FOREST

PRODUCTS

URUGUAY - SCIENTISTS, TECHNICIANS AND ENGINEERS

Statistical Office of the United Nations, Publishing Service, New York, New York 10017 (800) 253-9646; *Statistical Yearbook.*

U.C.L.A. Latin American Center Publications, University of California, Los Angeles, California 90024 (310) 825-6634; *Statistical Abstract of Latin America.*

United Nations Educational, Scientific and Cultural Organization (UNESCO), 7 Place de Fontenoy, F-75700 Paris, France (Telephone Number in U.S. (212) 963-5981); *Statistical Yearbook.*

URUGUAY - SENIOR CITIZENS

M.E. Sharpe, 80 Business Park Drive, Armonk, New York 10504 (800) 541-6563; *The Illustrated Book of World Rankings.*

URUGUAY - SHEEP - See URUGUAY - LIVESTOCK AND POULTRY

URUGUAY - SILVER PRODUCTION AND CONSUMPTION - See URUGUAY - MINING AND MINERAL PRODUCTS

URUGUAY - SOCIAL DATA

M.E. Sharpe, 80 Business Park Drive, Armonk, New York 10504 (800) 541-6563; *The Illustrated Book of World Rankings.*

Statistical Office of the United Nations, Publishing Service, New York, New York 10017 (800) 253-9646; *World Statistics Pocketbook.*

U.C.L.A. Latin American Center Publications, University of California, Los Angeles, California 90024 (310) 825-6634; *Statistical Abstract of Latin America.*

URUGUAY - SOCIAL SECURITY

Inter-American Development Bank, 1300 New York Avenue, NW, Washington, D.C. 20577 (202) 623-1753; *Economic and Social Progress in Latin America.*

International Monetary Fund, 700 Nineteenth Street, NW, Washington, D.C. 20431 (202) 623-7000; *Government Finance Statistics Yearbook.*

St. Martin's Press, Inc., 175 Fifth Avenue, New York, New York 10010 (800) 221-7945; *The Statesman's Year-Book.*

Statistical Office of the United Nations, Publishing Service, New York, New York 10017 (800) 253-9646; *National Accounts Statistics.*

URUGUAY - SOCIOECONOMIC DATA

Inter-American Development Bank, 1300 New York Avenue, NW, Washington, D.C. 20577 (202) 623-1753; *Economic and Social Progress in Latin America.*

U.C.L.A. Latin American Center Publications, University of California, Los Angeles, California 90024 (310) 825-6634; *Statistical Abstract of Latin America.*

URUGUAY - SOYBEAN PRODUCTION - See URUGUAY - CROPS

URUGUAY - STAMP TAXES AND DUTIES - See URUGUAY - TAXATION

URUGUAY - STATE BUDGET REVENUE AND EXPENDITURES

Euromonitor International, Inc., 122 South Michigan Avenue, Suite 1200, Chicago, Illinois 60603 (800) 577-EURO; *International Marketing Data and Statistics.*

Inter-American Development Bank, 1300 New York Avenue, NW, Washington, D.C. 20577 (202) 623-1753; *Economic and Social Progress in Latin America.*

URUGUAY - STEEL - See URUGUAY - MINING AND MINERAL PRODUCTS

URUGUAY - STOCKS - COMMODITY - MARKET PRICE - INDEX

Food and Agricultural Organization of the United Nations (FAO) Via delle Terme di Caracalla, 00100 Rome, Italy (Telephone Number in U.S. (202) 653-2400); *The State of Food and Agriculture.*

URUGUAY - SUGAR PRODUCTION AND CONSUMPTION - See URUGUAY - CROPS

URUGUAY - SULPHURIC ACID PRODUCTION - See URUGUAY - MINING AND MINERAL PRODUCTS

URUGUAY - TAXATION

Europa Publications Limited, 18 Bedford Square, London, WC1B 3JN, England; *The Europa World Year Book.*

Inter-American Development Bank, 1300 New York Avenue, NW, Washington, D.C. 20577 (202) 623-1753; *Economic and Social Progress in Latin America.*

International Monetary Fund, 700 Nineteenth Street, NW, Washington, D.C. 20431 (202) 623-7000; *Government Finance Statistics Yearbook.*

Statistical Office of the United Nations, Publishing Service, New York, New York 10017 (800) 253-9646; *Statistical Yearbook for Latin America and the Caribbean.*

The World Bank, 1818 H Street, NW, Washington, D.C. 20433 (202) 477-1234; *World Development Indicators.*

URUGUAY - TELEGRAPH SERVICE

Statistical Office of the United Nations, Publishing Service, New York, New York 10017 (800) 253-9646; *Statistical Yearbook.*

URUGUAY - TELEPHONES IN USE

American Telephone and Telegraph Company, 26 Parsippany Road, Whippany, New Jersey 07981 (800) 222-0300; *The World's Telephones.*

Central Intelligence Agency, Washington, D.C. 20505 (703) 482-1100, www.cia.gov; *The World Factbook.*

The Economist Intelligence Unit, 111 West 57th Street, New York, New York 10019 (800) 938-4685; *The New Latin America Market Atlas.*

Europa Publications Limited, 18 Bedford Square, London, WC1B 3JN, England; *The Europa World Year Book.*

St. Martin's Press, Inc., 175 Fifth Avenue, New York, New York 10010 (800) 221-7945; *The Statesman's Year-Book.*

Statistical Office of the United Nations, Publishing Service, New York, New York 10017 (800) 253-9646; *Statistical Yearbook;* and *World Statistics Pocketbook.*

URUGUAY - TELEVISION BROADCASTING - See URUGUAY - BROADCASTING

URUGUAY - TEXTILE INDUSTRY

American Forest and Paper Association, 1111 Nineteenth Street, NW, Washington, D.C. 20036 (202) 463-2700; *Wood Pulp and Fiber Statistics.*

Commodity Research Bureau, Inc., 30 South Wacker Drive, Chicago, Illinois 60606 (312) 454-1801; *Commodity Year Book.*

International Monetary Fund, 700 Nineteenth Street, NW, Washington, D.C. 20431 (202) 623-7000; *International Financial Statistics.*

M.E. Sharpe, 80 Business Park Drive, Armonk, New York 10504 (800) 541-6563; *The Illustrated Book of World Rankings.*

St. Martin's Press, Inc., 175 Fifth Avenue, New York, New York 10010 (800) 221-7945; *The Statesman's Year-Book.*

Statistical Office of the United Nations, Publishing Service, New York, New York 10017 (800) 253-9646; *Statistical Yearbook.*

United Nations Conference on Trade and Development, Central Statistical

Service, Palais des Nations, Geneva, Switzerland (Telephone in U.S. (800) 253-9646); *UNCTAD Commodity Yearbook*.

URUGUAY - THEATRE

United Nations Educational, Scientific and Cultural Organization (UNESCO), 7 Place de Fontenoy, F-75700 Paris, France (Telephone Number in U.S. (212) 963-5981); *Statistical Yearbook*.

URUGUAY - TIN - INDUSTRIAL CONSUMPTION - See URUGUAY - MINING AND MINERAL PRODUCTS

URUGUAY - TOBACCO PRODUCTION

M.E. Sharpe, 80 Business Park Drive, Armonk, New York 10504 (800) 541-6563; *The Illustrated Book of World Rankings*.

Statistical Office of the United Nations, Publishing Service, New York, New York 10017 (800) 253-9646; *Statistical Yearbook*.

U.C.L.A. Latin American Center Publications, University of California, Los Angeles, California 90024 (310) 825-6634; *Statistical Abstract of Latin America*.

URUGUAY - TOURISM

The Economist Intelligence Unit, 111 West 57th Street, New York, New York 10019 (800) 938-4685; *The New Latin America Market Atlas*.

Euromonitor International, Inc., 122 South Michigan Avenue, Suite 1200, Chicago, Illinois 60603 (800) 577-EURO; *The World Economic Factbook;* and *World Marketing Data and Statistics*.

Europa Publications Limited, 18 Bedford Square, London, WC1B 3JN, England; *The Europa World Year Book*.

Federal Statistical Office, Gustav-Stresemann-Ring 11, D-6200 Wiesbaden, Germany; *Uruguay*.

M.E. Sharpe, 80 Business Park Drive, Armonk, New York 10504 (800) 541-6563; *The Illustrated Book of World Rankings*.

St. Martin's Press, Inc., 175 Fifth Avenue, New York, New York 10010 (800) 221-7945; *The Statesman's Year-Book*.

Statistical Office of the United Nations, Publishing Service, New York, New York 10017 (800) 253-9646; *Statistical Yearbook;* and *Statistical Yearbook for Latin America and the Caribbean*.

Time Books, 201 East 50th Street, New York, New York 10022 (800) 726-0600; *The Economist Book of Vital World Statistics*.

U.C.L.A. Latin American Center

Publications, University of California, Los Angeles, California 90024 (310) 825-6634; *Statistical Abstract of Latin America*.

World Tourism Organization, Calle Capitan Haya 42, E-28020 Madrid, Spain; *Yearbook of Tourism Statistics*.

URUGUAY - TRACTORS IN USE

The Economist Intelligence Unit, 111 West 57th Street, New York, New York 10019 (800) 938-4685; *The New Latin America Market Atlas*.

Statistical Office of the United Nations, Publishing Service, New York, New York 10017 (800) 253-9646; *Statistical Yearbook*.

URUGUAY - TRADE - See URUGUAY - FOREIGN TRADE

URUGUAY - TRADEMARKS AND SERVICE MARKS - See URUGUAY - PATENTS, TRADEMARKS AND SERVICE MARKS

URUGUAY - TRANSPORTATION AND COMMUNICATIONS

Central Intelligence Agency, Washington, D.C. 20505 (703) 482-1100, www.cia.gov; *The World Factbook*.

The Economist Intelligence Unit, 111 West 57th Street, New York, New York 10019 (800) 938-4685; *The New Latin America Market Atlas*.

Euromonitor International, Inc., 122 South Michigan Avenue, Suite 1200, Chicago, Illinois 60603 (800) 577-EURO; *International Marketing Data and Statistics;* and *World Marketing Data and Statistics*.

Europa Publications Limited, 18 Bedford Square, London, WC1B 3JN, England; *The Europa World Year Book*.

Federal Statistical Office, Gustav-Stresemann-Ring 11, D-6200 Wiesbaden, Germany; *Uruguay*.

Inter-American Development Bank, 1300 New York Avenue, NW, Washington, D.C. 20577 (202) 623-1753; *Economic and Social Progress in Latin America*.

M.E. Sharpe, 80 Business Park Drive, Armonk, New York 10504 (800) 541-6563; *The Illustrated Book of World Rankings*.

St. Martin's Press, Inc., 175 Fifth Avenue, New York, New York 10010 (800) 221-7945; *The Statesman's Year-Book*.

Statistical Office of the United Nations, Publishing Service, New York, New York 10017 (800) 253-9646; *Human Development Report;* and *Statistical Yearbook for Latin America and the Caribbean*.

U.C.L.A. Latin American Center Publications, University of California, Los Angeles, California 90024 (310) 825-6634; *Statistical Abstract of Latin America*.

URUGUAY - TURKEYS - See URUGUAY - LIVESTOCK AND POULTRY

URUGUAY - UNEMPLOYMENT

Central Intelligence Agency, Washington, D.C. 20505 (703) 482-1100, www.cia.gov; *The World Factbook*.

The Economist Intelligence Unit, 111 West 57th Street, New York, New York 10019 (800) 938-4685; *The New Latin America Market Atlas*.

Euromonitor International, Inc., 122 South Michigan Avenue, Suite 1200, Chicago, Illinois 60603 (800) 577-EURO; *International Marketing Data and Statistics*.

International Labour Office, I.L.O. Publications, 1828 L Street, NW, Suite 801, Washington, D.C. 20036 (301) 638-3152; *Yearbook of Labour Statistics*.

Organization of American States (OAS), General Secretariat, Washington, D.C. 20006 (202) 458-3533; *Statistical Bulletin of the OAS*.

Statistical Office of the United Nations, Publishing Service, New York, New York 10017 (800) 253-9646; *Statistical Yearbook*.

U.C.L.A. Latin American Center Publications, University of California, Los Angeles, California 90024 (310) 825-6634; *Statistical Abstract of Latin America*.

URUGUAY - UTILITIES

U.C.L.A. Latin American Center Publications, University of California, Los Angeles, California 90024 (310) 825-6634; *Statistical Abstract of Latin America*.

URUGUAY - VITAL STATISTICS

Euromonitor International, Inc., 122 South Michigan Avenue, Suite 1200, Chicago, Illinois 60603 (800) 577-EURO; *International Marketing Data and Statistics*.

St. Martin's Press, Inc., 175 Fifth Avenue, New York, New York 10010 (800) 221-7945; *The Statesman's Year-Book*.

URUGUAY - WAGES

Federal Statistical Office, Gustav-Stresemann-Ring 11, D-6200 Wiesbaden, Germany; *Uruguay*.

International Labour Office, I.L.O. Publications, 1828 L Street, NW, Suite 801, Washington, D.C. 20036 (301) 638-3152; *Yearbook of Labour Statistics*.

Organization of American States (OAS), General Secretariat, Washington, D.C. 20006 (202) 458-3533; *Statistical Bulletin of the OAS.*

Statistical Office of the United Nations, Publishing Service, New York, New York 10017 (800) 253-9646; *Statistical Yearbook.*

U.C.L.A. Latin American Center Publications, University of California, Los Angeles, California 90024 (310) 825-6634; *Statistical Abstract of Latin America.*

URUGUAY - WEATHER - See URUGUAY - CLIMATE

URUGUAY - WELFARE

Inter-American Development Bank, 1300 New York Avenue, NW, Washington, D.C. 20577 (202) 623-1753; *Economic and Social Progress in Latin America.*

International Monetary Fund, 700 Nineteenth Street, NW, Washington, D.C. 20431 (202) 623-7000; *Government Finance Statistics Yearbook.*

URUGUAY - WHEAT PRODUCTION AND PRICES - See URUGUAY - CROPS

URUGUAY - WHOLESALE PRICES

Inter-American Development Bank, 1300 New York Avenue, NW, Washington, D.C. 20577 (202) 623-1753; *Economic and Social Progress in Latin America.*

International Monetary Fund, 700 Nineteenth Street, NW, Washington, D.C. 20431 (202) 623-7000; *International Financial Statistics.*

Organization of American States (OAS), General Secretariat, Washington, D.C. 20006 (202) 458-3533; *Statistical Bulletin of the OAS.*

Statistical Office of the United Nations, Publishing Service, New York, New York 10017 (800) 253-9646; *Statistical Yearbook.*

URUGUAY - WHOLESALE TRADE

Inter-American Development Bank, 1300 New York Avenue, NW, Washington, D.C. 20577 (202) 623-1753; *Economic and Social Progress in Latin America.*

URUGUAY - WINE PRODUCTION - See URUGUAY - BEVERAGES

URUGUAY - WOOD AND WOOD PULP - See URUGUAY - FORESTRY AND FOREST PRODUCTS

URUGUAY - WOOL - See URUGUAY - TEXTILE INDUSTRY

UTAH - See also STATE DATA (FOR INDIVIDUAL STATES)

Utah - Primary Statistics Sources

University of Utah, Bureau of Economic and Business Research, 401 Kendall Graff Building, Salt Lake City, Utah 84112 (801) 581-6333; *Statistical Abstract of Utah.*

Utah Foundation, 10 West 100 South 323, Salt Lake City, Utah 84101 (801) 364-1837; *Statistical Review of Government in Utah.*

Utah - State Data Centers

Governor's Office of Planning and Budget, State Capitol, Room 116, Salt Lake City, Utah 84114, Ms. Lisa Hillman (801) 537-9013.

Department of Community and Economic Development, 324 South State Street, Suite 500, Salt Lake City, Utah 84111, Mr. Doug Jex (801) 538-8897.

Department of Employment Security, 140 East 300 South, Post Office Box 11249, Salt Lake City, Utah 84147, Mr. Ken Jensen (801) 536-7813.

University of Utah, Bureau of Economic and Business Research 401 KDGB, Salt Lake City, Utah 84112, Mr. Frank Hachman (801) 581-3353.

UTILITIES - See also GAS UTILITY INDUSTRY and ELECTRIC LIGHT AND POWER INDUSTRY

UTILITIES - ADVERTISING EXPENDITURES

Television Bureau of Advertising, Inc., 3 East 54th Street, New York, New York 10022 (212) 486-1111; from data compiled by Competitive Media Reporting, 11 West 42nd Street, New York, New York 10036 (212) 789-1400.

UTILITIES - ELECTRIC SUPPLY SYSTEMS AND GENERATING PLANTS - STATES

U.S. Department of Energy, Energy Information Administration, Washington, D.C. 20585 (202) 586-5000; *Electric Power Annual; Electric Power Monthly;* and *Inventory of Power Plants in the U.S.*

UTILITIES - PRODUCTION INDEXES - MANUFACTURE

Board of Governors of the Federal Reserve System, Twentieth Street and Constitution Avenue, NW, Washington, D.C. 20551 (202) 452-3000, www.bog.frb.fed.us; *Federal Reserve Bulletin;* and *Industrial Production and Capacity Utilization.*

UZBEKISTAN - ABORTIONS

Statistical Office of the United Nations, Publishing Service, New York, New York 10017 (800) 253-9646; *Trends in Europe and North America: The Statistical Yearbook of the Economic Commission for Europe.*

UZBEKISTAN - AGRICULTURE

Academic International Press, Box 1111, Gulf Breeze, Florida 32562; *Russia and Eurasia Facts and Figures Annual.*

Business International Moscow, 23 Profsoyuznaya Ulitsa, 117859, Moscow (Telephone Number in U.S. (800) 938-4685); *The CIS Market Atlas.*

Economist Intelligence Unit, 111 West 57th Street, New York, New York 10019 (800) 938-4685; *Uzbekistan Country Report.*

Euromonitor International, Inc., 122 South Michigan Avenue, Suite 1200, Chicago, Illinois 60603 (800) 577-EURO; *World Marketing Data and Statistics.*

Europa Publications Limited, 18 Bedford Square, London, WC1B 3JN, England; *The Europa World Year Book.*

Food and Agriculture Organization of the United Nations (FAO), Via delle Terme di Caracalla, 00100, Rome, Italy (Telephone Number in U.S. (202) 653-2400); *Production Yearbook; The State of Food and Agriculture;* and *Trade Yearbook.*

St. Martin's Press, Inc., 175 Fifth Avenue, New York, New York 10010 (800) 221-7945; *The Statesman's Year-Book.*

Statistical Office of the United Nations, Publishing Service, New York, New York 10017 (800) 253-9646; *Industrial Commodity Statistics Yearbook;* and *Statistical Yearbook.*

The World Bank, 1818 H Street, NW, Washington, D.C. 20433 (202) 477-1234; *Statistical Handbook: States of the Former USSR;* and *World Development Indicators.*

UZBEKISTAN - AIRLINE SERVICE

Business International Moscow, 23 Profsoyuznaya Ulitsa, 117859, Moscow (Telephone Number in U.S. (800) 938-4685); *The CIS Market Atlas.*

International Civil Aviation Organization, 999 University Street, Montreal, Quebec, Canada H3C 5H7 (514) 954-8219; *Civil Aviation Statistics of the World.*

St. Martin's Press, Inc., 175 Fifth Avenue, New York, New York 10010 (800)

221-7945; *The Statesman's Year-Book.*

Statistical Office of the United Nations, Publishing Service, New York, New York 10017 (800) 253-9646; *Statistical Yearbook.*

UZBEKISTAN - AIRPORTS

Central Intelligence Agency, Washington, D.C. 20505 (703) 482-1100, www.cia.gov; *The World Factbook.*

UZBEKISTAN - ANIMAL HEALTH

Food and Agriculture Organization of the United Nations (FAO), Via delle Terme di Caracalla, 00100, Rome, Italy (Telephone Number in U.S. (202) 653-2400); *Animal Health Yearbook.*

UZBEKISTAN - AREA AND DENSITY OF POPULATION

Academic International Press, Box 1111, Gulf Breeze, Florida 32562; *Russia and Eurasia Facts and Figures Annual.*

Business International Moscow, 23 Profsoyuznaya Ulitsa, 117859, Moscow (Telephone Number in U.S. (800) 938-4685); *The CIS Market Atlas.*

Central Intelligence Agency, Washington, D.C. 20505 (703) 482-1100, www.cia.gov; *The World Factbook.*

Euromonitor International, Inc., 122 South Michigan Avenue, Suite 1200, Chicago, Illinois 60603 (800) 577-EURO; *The World Economic Factbook.*

Europa Publications Limited, 18 Bedford Square, London, WC1B 3JN, England; *The Europa World Year Book.*

St. Martin's Press, Inc., 175 Fifth Avenue, New York, New York 10010 (800) 221-7945; *The Statesman's Year-Book.*

Statistical Office of the United Nations, Publishing Service, New York, New York 10017 (800) 253-9646; *Statistical Yearbook;* and *Trends in Europe and North America: The Statistical Yearbook of the Economic Commission for Europe.*

United Nations Educational, Scientific and Cultural Organization (UNESCO), 7 Place de Fontenoy, F-75700 Paris, France (Telephone Number in U.S. (212) 963-5981); *Statistical Yearbook.*

The World Bank, 1818 H Street, NW, Washington, D.C. 20433 (202) 477-1234; *World Development Report.*

UZBEKISTAN - BALANCE OF PAYMENTS

Europa Publications Limited, 18 Bedford Square, London, WC1B 3JN, England; *The Europa World Year Book.*

United Nations Conference on Trade and Development (UNCTAD), New York, New York 10017 (800) 253-9646; *Handbook of International Trade and Development Statistics.*

The World Bank, 1818 H Street, NW, Washington, D.C. 20433 (202) 477-1234; *World Development Report;* and *World Development Indicators.*

UZBEKISTAN - BANKING

Business International Moscow, 23 Profsoyuznaya Ulitsa, 117859, Moscow (Telephone Number in U.S. (800) 938-4685); *The CIS Market Atlas.*

Euromonitor International, Inc., 122 South Michigan Avenue, Suite 1200, Chicago, Illinois 60603 (800) 577-EURO; *World Marketing Data and Statistics.*

UZBEKISTAN - BEVERAGES

Statistical Office of the United Nations, Publishing Service, New York, New York 10017 (800) 253-9646; *Statistical Yearbook.*

UZBEKISTAN - BIRTH RATES

Academic International Press, Box 1111, Gulf Breeze, Florida 32562; *Russia and Eurasia Facts and Figures Annual.*

Business International Moscow, 23 Profsoyuznaya Ulitsa, 117859, Moscow (Telephone Number in U.S. (800) 938-4685); *The CIS Market Atlas.*

Central Intelligence Agency, Washington, D.C. 20505 (703) 482-1100, www.cia.gov; *The World Factbook.*

Euromonitor International, Inc., 122 South Michigan Avenue, Suite 1200, Chicago, Illinois 60603 (800) 577-EURO; *International Marketing Data and Statistics;* and *The World Economic Factbook.*

Europa Publications Limited, 18 Bedford Square, London, WC1B 3JN, England; *The Europa World Year Book.*

Statistical Office of the United Nations, Publishing Service, New York, New York 10017 (800) 253-9646; *Statistical Yearbook.*

World Health Organization, Office of Publications, 20 Avenue Appia, CH-1211 Geneva 27, Switzerland (Telephone Number in U.S. (518) 436-9686); *World Health Statistics Annual.*

UZBEKISTAN - BOOK PRODUCTION

Statistical Office of the United Nations, Publishing Service, New York, New York 10017 (800) 253-9646; *Trends in Europe and North America: The Statistical Yearbook of the Economic Commission for Europe.*

United Nations Educational, Scientific and Cultural Organization (UNESCO), 7 Place de Fontenoy, F-75700 Paris, France (Telephone Number in U.S. (212) 963-5981); *Statistical Yearbook.*

UZBEKISTAN - BROADCASTING

Central Intelligence Agency, Washington, D.C. 20505 (703) 482-1100, www.cia.gov; *The World Factbook.*

Euromonitor International, Inc., 122 South Michigan Avenue, Suite 1200, Chicago, Illinois 60603 (800) 577-EURO; *World Marketing Data and Statistics.*

St. Martin's Press, Inc., 175 Fifth Avenue, New York, New York 10010 (800) 221-7945; *The Statesman's Year-Book.*

Statistical Office of the United Nations, Publishing Service, New York, New York 10017 (800) 253-9646; *Trends in Europe and North America: The Statistical Yearbook of the Economic Commission for Europe.*

United Nations Educational, Scientific and Cultural Organization (UNESCO), 7 Place de Fontenoy, F-75700 Paris, France (Telephone Number in U.S. (212) 963-5981); *Statistical Yearbook.*

UZBEKISTAN - BUDGET

Business International Moscow, 23 Profsoyuznaya Ulitsa, 117859, Moscow (Telephone Number in U.S. (800) 938-4685); *The CIS Market Atlas.*

Central Intelligence Agency, Washington, D.C. 20505 (703) 482-1100, www.cia.gov; *The World Factbook.*

UZBEKISTAN - CAPITAL INVESTMENT

The World Bank, 1818 H Street, NW, Washington, D.C. 20433 (202) 477-1234; *Statistical Handbook: States of the Former USSR.*

UZBEKISTAN - CATTLE

Business International Moscow, 23 Profsoyuznaya Ulitsa, 117859, Moscow (Telephone Number in U.S. (800) 938-4685); *The CIS Market Atlas.*

UZBEKISTAN - CHEMICALS

Business International Moscow, 23 Profsoyuznaya Ulitsa, 117859, Moscow (Telephone Number in U.S. (800) 938-4685); *The CIS Market Atlas.*

UZBEKISTAN - COAL PRODUCTION AND CONSUMPTION - See UZBEKISTAN - MINING AND MINERAL PRODUCTS

UZBEKISTAN - COMMERCE

St. Martin's Press, Inc., 175 Fifth Avenue, New York, New York 10010 (800) 221-7945; *The Statesman's Year-Book.*

UZBEKISTAN - COMMUNICATIONS - See UZBEKISTAN - TRANSPORTATION AND COMMUNICATIONS

UZBEKISTAN - CONSTRUCTION INDUSTRY

Academic International Press, Box 1111, Gulf Breeze, Florida 32562; *Russia and Eurasia Facts and Figures Annual.*

Business International Moscow, 23 Profsoyuznaya Ulitsa, 117859, Moscow (Telephone Number in U.S. (800) 938-4685); *The CIS Market Atlas.*

Statistical Office of the United Nations, Publishing Service, New York, New York 10017 (800) 253-9646; *Statistical Yearbook.*

UZBEKISTAN - CONSUMER PRICE INDEX

Statistical Office of the United Nations, Publishing Service, New York, New York 10017 (800) 253-9646; *Statistical Yearbook;* and *Trends in Europe and North America: The Statistical Yearbook of the Economic Commission for Europe.*

UZBEKISTAN - CONSUMER PRICES

Euromonitor International, Inc., 122 South Michigan Avenue, Suite 1200, Chicago, Illinois 60603 (800) 577-EURO; *World Marketing Data and Statistics.*

UZBEKISTAN - CONSUMER PRODUCTS

Business International Moscow, 23 Profsoyuznaya Ulitsa, 117859, Moscow (Telephone Number in U.S. (800) 938-4685); *The CIS Market Atlas.*

UZBEKISTAN - CONSUMPTION

Business International Moscow, 23 Profsoyuznaya Ulitsa, 117859, Moscow (Telephone Number in U.S. (800) 938-4685); *The CIS Market Atlas.*

The World Bank, 1818 H Street, NW, Washington, D.C. 20433 (202) 477-1234; *World Development Report;* and *Statistical Handbook: States of the Former USSR.*

UZBEKISTAN - COTTON PRODUCTION AND CONSUMPTION - See UZBEKISTAN - CROPS

UZBEKISTAN - CRIME

Academic International Press, Box 1111, Gulf Breeze, Florida 32562; *Russia and Eurasia Facts and Figures Annual.*

Statistical Office of the United Nations, Publishing Service, New York, New York

10017 (800) 253-9646; *Trends in Europe and North America: The Statistical Yearbook of the Economic Commission for Europe.*

UZBEKISTAN - CROPS

Academic International Press, Box 1111, Gulf Breeze, Florida 32562; *Russia and Eurasia Facts and Figures Annual.*

Europa Publications Limited, 18 Bedford Square, London, WC1B 3JN, England; *The Europa World Year Book.*

Food and Agriculture Organization of the United Nations (FAO), Via delle Terme di Caracalla, 00100, Rome, Italy (Telephone Number in U.S. (202) 653-2400); *Production Yearbook; The State of Food and Agriculture;* and *Trade Yearbook.*

St. Martin's Press, Inc., 175 Fifth Avenue, New York, New York 10010 (800) 221-7945; *The Statesman's Year-Book.*

Statistical Office of the United Nations, Publishing Service, New York, New York 10017 (800) 253-9646; *Industrial Commodity Statistics Yearbook;* and *Statistical Yearbook.*

The World Bank, 1818 H Street, NW, Washington, D.C. 20433 (202) 477-1234; *Statistical Handbook: States of the Former USSR.*

UZBEKISTAN - DAIRY PRODUCTS

Europa Publications Limited, 18 Bedford Square, London, WC1B 3JN, England; *The Europa World Year Book.*

Food and Agriculture Organization of the United Nations (FAO), Via delle Terme di Caracalla, 00100, Rome, Italy (Telephone Number in U.S. (202) 653-2400); *Production Yearbook; The State of Food and Agriculture;* and *Trade Yearbook.*

St. Martin's Press, Inc., 175 Fifth Avenue, New York, New York 10010 (800) 221-7945; *The Statesman's Year-Book.*

Statistical Office of the United Nations, Publishing Service, New York, New York 10017 (800) 253-9646; *Industrial Commodity Statistics Yearbook;* and *Statistical Yearbook.*

UZBEKISTAN - DEATH RATES - See UZBEKISTAN - MORTALITY

UZBEKISTAN - DEMOGRAPHY

Business International Moscow, 23 Profsoyuznaya Ulitsa, 117859, Moscow (Telephone Number in U.S. (800) 938-4685); *The CIS Market Atlas.*

Euromonitor International, Inc., 122 South Michigan Avenue, Suite 1200,

Chicago, Illinois 60603 (800) 577-EURO; *International Marketing Data and Statistics; World Marketing Data and Statistics;* and *The World Economic Factbook.*

Statistical Office of the United Nations, Publishing Service, New York, New York 10017 (800) 253-9646; *Demographic Yearbook;* and *Human Development Report.*

The World Bank, 1818 H Street, NW, Washington, D.C. 20433 (202) 477-1234; *Statistical Handbook: States of the Former USSR.*

UZBEKISTAN - DISEASES - See UZBEKISTAN - HEALTH

UZBEKISTAN - DIVORCE RATES

Academic International Press, Box 1111, Gulf Breeze, Florida 32562; *Russia and Eurasia Facts and Figures Annual.*

Statistical Office of the United Nations, Publishing Service, New York, New York 10017 (800) 253-9646; *Demographic Yearbook; Trends in Europe and North America: The Statistical Yearbook of the Economic Commission for Europe;* and *Statistical Yearbook.*

UZBEKISTAN - DOMESTIC INVESTMENT

Business International Moscow, 23 Profsoyuznaya Ulitsa, 117859, Moscow (Telephone Number in U.S. (800) 938-4685); *The CIS Market Atlas.*

UZBEKISTAN - ECONOMY

Academic International Press, Box 1111, Gulf Breeze, Florida 32562; *Russia and Eurasia Facts and Figures Annual.*

Business International Moscow, 23 Profsoyuznaya Ulitsa, 117859, Moscow (Telephone Number in U.S. (800) 938-4685); *The CIS Market Atlas.*

Central Intelligence Agency, Washington, D.C. 20505 (703) 482-1100, www.cia.gov; *The World Factbook.*

Economist Intelligence Unit, 111 West 57th Street, New York, New York 10019 (800) 938-4685; *Uzbekistan Country Report.*

Euromonitor International, Inc., 122 South Michigan Avenue, Suite 1200, Chicago, Illinois 60603 (800) 577-EURO; *The World Economic Factbook;* and *World Marketing Data and Statistics.*

Europa Publications Limited, 18 Bedford Square, London, WC1B 3JN, England; *The Europa World Year Book.*

St. Martin's Press, Inc., 175 Fifth Avenue, New York, New York 10010 (800)

221-7945; *The Statesman's Year-Book.*

Statistical Office of the United Nations, Publishing Service, New York, New York 10017 (800) 253-9646; *World Statistics Pocketbook.*

The World Bank, 1818 H Street, NW, Washington, D.C. 20433 (202) 477-1234; *The World Bank Atlas; and World Development Report.*

UZBEKISTAN - EDUCATION

Academic International Press, Box 1111, Gulf Breeze, Florida 32562; *Russia and Eurasia Facts and Figures Annual.*

Business International Moscow, 23 Profsoyuznaya Ulitsa, 117859, Moscow (Telephone Number in U.S. (800) 938-4685); *The CIS Market Atlas.*

Euromonitor International, Inc., 122 South Michigan Avenue, Suite 1200, Chicago, Illinois 60603 (800) 577-EURO; *International Marketing Data and Statistics; and World Marketing Data and Statistics.*

Europa Publications Limited, 18 Bedford Square, London, WC1B 3JN, England; *The Europa World Year Book.*

St. Martin's Press, Inc., 175 Fifth Avenue, New York, New York 10010 (800) 221-7945; *The Statesman's Year-Book.*

Statistical Office of the United Nations, Publishing Service, New York, New York 10017 (800) 253-9646; *Human Development Report; and Trends in Europe and North America: The Statistical Yearbook of the Economic Commission for Europe.*

United Nations Educational, Scientific and Cultural Organization (UNESCO), 7 Place de Fontenoy, F-75700 Paris, France (Telephone Number in U.S. (212) 963-5981); *Statistical Yearbook.*

The World Bank, 1818 H Street, NW, Washington, D.C. 20433 (202) 477-1234; *World Development Report.*

UZBEKISTAN - ELECTRICITY

Academic International Press, Box 1111, Gulf Breeze, Florida 32562; *Russia and Eurasia Facts and Figures Annual.*

Business International Moscow, 23 Profsoyuznaya Ulitsa, 117859, Moscow (Telephone Number in U.S. (800) 938-4685); *The CIS Market Atlas.*

Central Intelligence Agency, Washington, D.C. 20505 (703) 482-1100, www.cia.gov; *The World Factbook.*

St. Martin's Press, Inc., 175 Fifth

Avenue, New York, New York 10010 (800) 221-7945; *The Statesman's Year-Book.*

Statistical Office of the United Nations, Publishing Service, New York, New York 10017 (800) 253-9646; *Energy Statistics Yearbook; Human Development Report; Trends in Europe and North America: The Statistical Yearbook of the Economic Commission for Europe; and Statistical Yearbook.*

The World Bank, 1818 H Street, NW, Washington, D.C. 20433 (202) 477-1234; *Statistical Handbook: States of the Former USSR.*

UZBEKISTAN - EMPLOYMENT

Euromonitor International, Inc., 122 South Michigan Avenue, Suite 1200, Chicago, Illinois 60603 (800) 577-EURO; *International Marketing Data and Statistics.*

Statistical Office of the United Nations, Publishing Service, New York, New York 10017 (800) 253-9646; *Statistical Yearbook; and Trends in Europe and North America: The Statistical Yearbook of the Economic Commission for Europe.*

The World Bank, 1818 H Street, NW, Washington, D.C. 20433 (202) 477-1234; *Statistical Handbook: States of the Former USSR.*

UZBEKISTAN - ENERGY

Academic International Press, Box 1111, Gulf Breeze, Florida 32562; *Russia and Eurasia Facts and Figures Annual.*

Business International Moscow, 23 Profsoyuznaya Ulitsa, 117859, Moscow (Telephone Number in U.S. (800) 938-4685); *The CIS Market Atlas.*

Euromonitor International, Inc., 122 South Michigan Avenue, Suite 1200, Chicago, Illinois 60603 (800) 577-EURO; *International Marketing Data and Statistics; World Marketing Data and Statistics; and The World Economic Factbook.*

St. Martin's Press, Inc., 175 Fifth Avenue, New York, New York 10010 (800) 221-7945; *The Statesman's Year-Book.*

Statistical Office of the United Nations, Publishing Service, New York, New York 10017 (800) 253-9646; *Energy Statistics Yearbook; Human Development Report; Trends in Europe and North America: The Statistical Yearbook of the Economic Commission for Europe; Statistical Yearbook; and World Statistics Pocketbook.*

The World Bank, 1818 H Street, NW, Washington, D.C. 20433 (202) 477-1234; *The World Bank Atlas; World Development Report; and Statistical Handbook: States of*

the Former USSR.

UZBEKISTAN - ENVIRONMENT

Business International Moscow, 23 Profsoyuznaya Ulitsa, 117859, Moscow (Telephone Number in U.S. (800) 938-4685); *The CIS Market Atlas.*

Economist Intelligence Unit, 111 West 57th Street, New York, New York 10019 (800) 938-4685; *Uzbekistan Country Report.*

Statistical Office of the United Nations, Publishing Service, New York, New York 10017 (800) 253-9646; *Statistical Yearbook; World Statistics Pocketbook; and Trends in Europe and North America: The Statistical Yearbook of the Economic Commission for Europe.*

UZBEKISTAN - EXCHANGE RATES

Central Intelligence Agency, Washington, D.C. 20505 (703) 482-1100, www.cia.gov; *The World Factbook.*

Euromonitor International, Inc., 122 South Michigan Avenue, Suite 1200, Chicago, Illinois 60603 (800) 577-EURO; *International Marketing Data and Statistics; and The World Economic Factbook.*

Europa Publications Limited, 18 Bedford Square, London, WC1B 3JN, England; *The Europa World Year Book.*

Statistical Office of the United Nations, Publishing Service, New York, New York 10017 (800) 253-9646; *Statistical Yearbook; World Statistics Pocketbook; and Trends in Europe and North America: The Statistical Yearbook of the Economic Commission for Europe.*

UZBEKISTAN - EXPORTS

Academic International Press, Box 1111, Gulf Breeze, Florida 32562; *Russia and Eurasia Facts and Figures Annual.*

Business International Moscow, 23 Profsoyuznaya Ulitsa, 117859, Moscow (Telephone Number in U.S. (800) 938-4685); *The CIS Market Atlas.*

Central Intelligence Agency, Washington, D.C. 20505 (703) 482-1100, www.cia.gov; *The World Factbook.*

Economist Intelligence Unit, 111 West 57th Street, New York, New York 10019 (800) 938-4685; *Uzbekistan Country Report.*

Euromonitor International, Inc., 122 South Michigan Avenue, Suite 1200, Chicago, Illinois 60603 (800) 577-EURO; *International Marketing Data and Statistics; and The World Economic Factbook.*

Europa Publications Limited, 18

Bedford Square, London, WC1B 3JN, England; *The Europa World Year Book.*

International Monetary Fund, 700 Nineteenth Street, NW, Washington, D.C. 20431 (202) 623-7000; *Direction of Trade Statistics.*

St. Martin's Press, Inc., 175 Fifth Avenue, New York, New York 10010 (800) 221-7945; *The Statesman's Year-Book.*

Statistical Office of the United Nations, Publishing Service, New York, New York 10017 (800) 253-9646; *International Trade Statistics Yearbook;* and *Trends in Europe and North America: The Statistical Yearbook of the Economic Commission for Europe.*

United Nations Conference on Trade and Development (UNCTAD), New York, New York 10017 (800) 253-9646; *Handbook of International Trade and Development Statistics.*

The World Bank, 1818 H Street, NW, Washington, D.C. 20433 (202) 477-1234; *Statistical Handbook: States of the Former USSR; World Development Report;* and *World Development Indicators.*

UZBEKISTAN - EXTERNAL DEBT

The World Bank, 1818 H Street, NW, Washington, D.C. 20433 (202) 477-1234; *World Development Indicators.*

UZBEKISTAN - EXTERNAL INDEBTEDNESS

The World Bank, 1818 H Street, NW, Washington, D.C. 20433 (202) 477-1234; *World Development Report.*

UZBEKISTAN - EXTERNAL TRADE

Academic International Press, Box 1111, Gulf Breeze, Florida 32562; *Russia and Eurasia Facts and Figures Annual.*

Euromonitor International, Inc., 122 South Michigan Avenue, Suite 1200, Chicago, Illinois 60603 (800) 577-EURO; *World Marketing Data and Statistics.*

Food and Agriculture Organization of the United Nations (FAO), Via delle Terme di Caracalla, 00100, Rome, Italy (Telephone Number in U.S. (202) 653-2400); *Trade Yearbook.*

Statistical Office of the United Nations, Publishing Service, New York, New York 10017 (800) 253-9646; *Statistical Yearbook.*

The World Bank, 1818 H Street, NW, Washington, D.C. 20433 (202) 477-1234; *Statistical Handbook: States of the Former USSR.*

UZBEKISTAN - FABRIC PRODUCTION AND

CONSUMPTION - See UZBEKISTAN - TEXTILE INDUSTRY

UZBEKISTAN - FERTILITY RATES

Central Intelligence Agency, Washington, D.C. 20505 (703) 482-1100, www.cia.gov; *The World Factbook.*

Statistical Office of the United Nations, Publishing Service, New York, New York 10017 (800) 253-9646; *Human Development Report;* and *Trends in Europe and North America: The Statistical Yearbook of the Economic Commission for Europe.*

The World Bank, 1818 H Street, NW, Washington, D.C. 20433 (202) 477-1234; *The World Bank Atlas; World Development Report;* and *Statistical Handbook: States of the Former USSR.*

World Health Organization, Office of Publications, 20 Avenue Appia, CH-1211 Geneva 27, Switzerland (Telephone Number in U.S. (518) 436-9686); *World Health Statistics Annual.*

UZBEKISTAN - FERTILIZER

Food and Agriculture Organization of the United Nations (FAO), Via delle Terme di Caracalla, 00100, Rome, Italy (Telephone Number in U.S. (202) 653-2400); *Fertilizer Yearbook.*

Statistical Office of the United Nations, Publishing Service, New York, New York 10017 (800) 253-9646; *Industrial Commodity Statistics Yearbook;* and *Statistical Yearbook.*

UZBEKISTAN - FINANCE

Economist Intelligence Unit, 111 West 57th Street, New York, New York 10019 (800) 938-4685; *Uzbekistan Country Report.*

Europa Publications Limited, 18 Bedford Square, London, WC1B 3JN, England; *The Europa World Year Book.*

The World Bank, 1818 H Street, NW, Washington, D.C. 20433 (202) 477-1234; *Statistical Handbook: States of the Former USSR.*

UZBEKISTAN - FISHERIES

Food and Agriculture Organization of the United Nations (FAO), Via delle Terme di Caracalla, 00100, Rome, Italy (Telephone Number in U.S. (202) 653-2400); *The State of Food and Agriculture;* and *Yearbook of Fishery Statistics.*

Statistical Office of the United Nations, Publishing Service, New York, New York 10017 (800) 253-9646; *Industrial Commodity Statistics Yearbook;* and

Statistical Yearbook.

UZBEKISTAN - FOOD

Food and Agriculture Organization of the United Nations (FAO), Via delle Terme di Caracalla, 00100, Rome, Italy (Telephone Number in U.S. (202) 653-2400); *Production Yearbook; The State of Food and Agriculture;* and *Trade Yearbook.*

Statistical Office of the United Nations, Publishing Service, New York, New York 10017 (800) 253-9646; *Human Development Report;* and *Industrial Commodity Statistics Yearbook.*

UZBEKISTAN - FOOTWEAR
PRODUCTION AND CONSUMPTION - See
UZBEKISTAN - TEXTILE INDUSTRY

UZBEKISTAN - FOREIGN INVESTMENT

Business International Moscow, 23 Profsoyuznaya Ulitsa, 117859, Moscow (Telephone Number in U.S. (800) 938-4685); *The CIS Market Atlas.*

UZBEKISTAN - FOREIGN TRADE

Business International Moscow, 23 Profsoyuznaya Ulitsa, 117859, Moscow (Telephone Number in U.S. (800) 938-4685); *The CIS Market Atlas.*

Economist Intelligence Unit, 111 West 57th Street, New York, New York 10019 (800) 938-4685; *Uzbekistan Country Report.*

Euromonitor International, Inc., 122 South Michigan Avenue, Suite 1200, Chicago, Illinois 60603 (800) 577-EURO; *The World Economic Factbook.*

Europa Publications Limited, 18 Bedford Square, London, WC1B 3JN, England; *The Europa World Year Book.*

Food and Agriculture Organization of the United Nations (FAO), Via delle Terme di Caracalla, 00100, Rome, Italy (Telephone Number in U.S. (202) 653-2400); *Trade Yearbook.*

International Monetary Fund, 700 Nineteenth Street, NW, Washington, D.C. 20431 (202) 623-7000; *Direction of Trade Statistics.*

St. Martin's Press, Inc., 175 Fifth Avenue, New York, New York 10010 (800) 221-7945; *The Statesman's Year-Book.*

Statistical Office of the United Nations, Publishing Service, New York, New York 10017 (800) 253-9646; *International Trade Statistics Yearbook;* and *Statistical Yearbook.*

The World Bank, 1818 H Street, NW, Washington, D.C. 20433 (202) 477-1234;

Statistical Handbook: States of the Former USSR; World Development Report; and *World Development Indicators.*

UZBEKISTAN - FORESTRY AND FOREST PRODUCTS

Academic International Press, Box 1111, Gulf Breeze, Florida 32562; *Russia and Eurasia Facts and Figures Annual.*

Business International Moscow, 23 Profsoyuznaya Ulitsa, 117859, Moscow (Telephone Number in U.S. (800) 938-4685); *The CIS Market Atlas.*

Food and Agriculture Organization of the United Nations (FAO), Via delle Terme di Caracalla, 00100, Rome, Italy (Telephone Number in U.S. (202) 653-2400); *The State of Food and Agriculture;* and *Yearbook of Forest Products.*

St. Martin's Press, Inc., 175 Fifth Avenue, New York, New York 10010 (800) 221-7945; *The Statesman's Year-Book.*

Statistical Office of the United Nations, Publishing Service, New York, New York 10017 (800) 253-9646; *Industrial Commodity Statistics Yearbook; Trends in Europe and North America: The Statistical Yearbook of the Economic Commission for Europe;* and *Statistical Yearbook.*

United Nations Educational, Scientific and Cultural Organization (UNESCO), 7 Place de Fontenoy, F-75700 Paris, France (Telephone Number in U.S. (212) 963-5981); *Statistical Yearbook.*

The World Bank, 1818 H Street, NW, Washington, D.C. 20433 (202) 477-1234; *World Development Report.*

UZBEKISTAN - GOATS - See UZBEKISTAN - LIVESTOCK AND POULTRY

UZBEKISTAN - GOVERNMENT

Academic International Press, Box 1111, Gulf Breeze, Florida 32562; *Russia and Eurasia Facts and Figures Annual.*

Central Intelligence Agency, Washington, D.C. 20505 (703) 482-1100, www.cia.gov; *The World Factbook.*

Europa Publications Limited, 18 Bedford Square, London, WC1B 3JN, England; *The Europa World Year Book.*

St. Martin's Press, Inc., 175 Fifth Avenue, New York, New York 10010 (800) 221-7945; *The Statesman's Year-Book.*

Statistical Office of the United Nations, Publishing Service, New York, New York 10017 (800) 253-9646; *Statistical Yearbook.*

The World Bank, 1818 H Street, NW,

Washington, D.C. 20433 (202) 477-1234; *Statistical Handbook: States of the Former USSR;* and *World Development Report.*

UZBEKISTAN - GROSS DOMESTIC PRODUCT

Economist Intelligence Unit, 111 West 57th Street, New York, New York 10019 (800) 938-4685; *Uzbekistan Country Report.*

Euromonitor International, Inc., 122 South Michigan Avenue, Suite 1200, Chicago, Illinois 60603 (800) 577-EURO; *International Marketing Data and Statistics;* and *The World Economic Factbook.*

Statistical Office of the United Nations, Publishing Service, New York, New York 10017 (800) 253-9646; *Human Development Report; National Accounts Statistics; Trends in Europe and North America: The Statistical Yearbook of the Economic Commission for Europe;* and *Statistical Yearbook.*

The World Bank, 1818 H Street, NW, Washington, D.C. 20433 (202) 477-1234; *Statistical Handbook: States of the Former USSR; World Development Report;* and *World Development Indicators.*

UZBEKISTAN - GROSS NATIONAL PRODUCT

Europa Publications Limited, 18 Bedford Square, London, WC1B 3JN, England; *The Europa World Year Book.*

St. Martin's Press, Inc., 175 Fifth Avenue, New York, New York 10010 (800) 221-7945; *The Statesman's Year-Book.*

The World Bank, 1818 H Street, NW, Washington, D.C. 20433 (202) 477-1234; *The World Bank Atlas; World Development Report;* and *World Development Indicators.*

UZBEKISTAN - HEALTH

Academic International Press, Box 1111, Gulf Breeze, Florida 32562; *Russia and Eurasia Facts and Figures Annual.*

Business International Moscow, 23 Profsoyuznaya Ulitsa, 117859, Moscow (Telephone Number in U.S. (800) 938-4685); *The CIS Market Atlas.*

Euromonitor International, Inc., 122 South Michigan Avenue, Suite 1200, Chicago, Illinois 60603 (800) 577-EURO; *World Marketing Data and Statistics.*

St. Martin's Press, Inc., 175 Fifth Avenue, New York, New York 10010 (800) 221-7945; *The Statesman's Year-Book.*

Statistical Office of the United Nations, Publishing Service, New York, New York 10017 (800) 253-9646; *Human*

Development Report; Trends in Europe and North America: The Statistical Yearbook of the Economic Commission for Europe; and *Statistical Yearbook.*

United Nations Children's Fund (UNICEF), 3 United Nations Plaza, New York, New York 10017 (800) 253-9646; *State of the World's Children.*

The World Bank, 1818 H Street, NW, Washington, D.C. 20433 (202) 477-1234; *World Development Report.*

World Health Organization, Office of Publications, 20 Avenue Appia, CH-1211 Geneva 27, Switzerland (Telephone Number in U.S. (518) 436-9686); *World Health Statistics Annual.*

UZBEKISTAN - HIGHWAYS

Academic International Press, Box 1111, Gulf Breeze, Florida 32562; *Russia and Eurasia Facts and Figures Annual.*

Business International Moscow, 23 Profsoyuznaya Ulitsa, 117859, Moscow (Telephone Number in U.S. (800) 938-4685); *The CIS Market Atlas.*

Central Intelligence Agency, Washington, D.C. 20505 (703) 482-1100, www.cia.gov; *The World Factbook.*

St. Martin's Press, Inc., 175 Fifth Avenue, New York, New York 10010 (800) 221-7945; *The Statesman's Year-Book.*

Statistical Office of the United Nations, Publishing Service, New York, New York 10017 (800) 253-9646; *Trends in Europe and North America: The Statistical Yearbook of the Economic Commission for Europe.*

UZBEKISTAN - HOUSING AND HOUSING UNITS

Business International Moscow, 23 Profsoyuznaya Ulitsa, 117859, Moscow (Telephone Number in U.S. (800) 938-4685); *The CIS Market Atlas.*

Euromonitor International, Inc., 122 South Michigan Avenue, Suite 1200, Chicago, Illinois 60603 (800) 577-EURO; *World Marketing Data and Statistics.*

Statistical Office of the United Nations, Publishing Service, New York, New York 10017 (800) 253-9646; *Trends in Europe and North America: The Statistical Yearbook of the Economic Commission for Europe.*

UZBEKISTAN - ILLITERATE POPULATION

Central Intelligence Agency, Washington, D.C. 20505 (703) 482-1100, www.cia.gov; *The World Factbook.*

Euromonitor International, Inc., 122

South Michigan Avenue, Suite 1200, Chicago, Illinois 60603 (800) 577-EURO; *The World Economic Factbook*.

Statistical Office of the United Nations, Publishing Service, New York, New York 10017 (800) 253-9646; *Human Development Report*.

United Nations Educational, Scientific and Cultural Organization (UNESCO), 7 Place de Fontenoy, F-75700 Paris, France (Telephone Number in U.S. (212) 963-5981); *Statistical Yearbook*.

UZBEKISTAN - IMPORTS

Academic International Press, Box 1111, Gulf Breeze, Florida 32562; *Russia and Eurasia Facts and Figures Annual*.

Business International Moscow, 23 Profsoyuznaya Ulitsa, 117859, Moscow (Telephone Number in U.S. (800) 938-4685); *The CIS Market Atlas*.

Central Intelligence Agency, Washington, D.C. 20505 (703) 482-1100, www.cia.gov; *The World Factbook*.

Economist Intelligence Unit, 111 West 57th Street, New York, New York 10019 (800) 938-4685; *Uzbekistan Country Report*.

Euromonitor International, Inc., 122 South Michigan Avenue, Suite 1200, Chicago, Illinois 60603 (800) 577-EURO; *International Marketing Data and Statistics;* and *The World Economic Factbook*.

Europa Publications Limited, 18 Bedford Square, London, WC1B 3JN, England; *The Europa World Year Book*.

International Monetary Fund, 700 Nineteenth Street, NW, Washington, D.C. 20431 (202) 623-7000; *Direction of Trade Statistics*.

St. Martin's Press, Inc., 175 Fifth Avenue, New York, New York 10010 (800) 221-7945; *The Statesman's Year-Book*.

Statistical Office of the United Nations, Publishing Service, New York, New York 10017 (800) 253-9646; *International Trade Statistics Yearbook;* and *Trends in Europe and North America: The Statistical Yearbook of the Economic Commission for Europe*.

United Nations Conference on Trade and Development (UNCTAD), New York, New York 10017 (800) 253-9646; *Handbook of International Trade and Development Statistics*.

The World Bank, 1818 H Street, NW, Washington, D.C. 20433 (202) 477-1234; *Statistical Handbook: States of the Former USSR; World Development Report;* and

World Development Indicators.

UZBEKISTAN - INDUSTRY

Academic International Press, Box 1111, Gulf Breeze, Florida 32562; *Russia and Eurasia Facts and Figures Annual*.

Business International Moscow, 23 Profsoyuznaya Ulitsa, 117859, Moscow (Telephone Number in U.S. (800) 938-4685); *The CIS Market Atlas*.

Central Intelligence Agency, Washington, D.C. 20505 (703) 482-1100, www.cia.gov; *The World Factbook*.

Economist Intelligence Unit, 111 West 57th Street, New York, New York 10019 (800) 938-4685; *Uzbekistan Country Report*.

Euromonitor International, Inc., 122 South Michigan Avenue, Suite 1200, Chicago, Illinois 60603 (800) 577-EURO; *The World Economic Factbook;* and *World Marketing Data and Statistics*.

Europa Publications Limited, 18 Bedford Square, London, WC1B 3JN, England; *The Europa World Year Book*.

St. Martin's Press, Inc., 175 Fifth Avenue, New York, New York 10010 (800) 221-7945; *The Statesman's Year-Book*.

Statistical Office of the United Nations, Publishing Service, New York, New York 10017 (800) 253-9646; *Industrial Commodity Statistics Yearbook; Trends in Europe and North America: The Statistical Yearbook of the Economic Commission for Europe;* and *Statistical Yearbook*.

The World Bank, 1818 H Street, NW, Washington, D.C. 20433 (202) 477-1234; *Statistical Handbook: States of the Former USSR;* and *World Development Indicators*.

UZBEKISTAN - INFANT MORTALITY - See UZBEKISTAN - MORTALITY

UZBEKISTAN - INTERNAL TRADE

Statistical Office of the United Nations, Publishing Service, New York, New York 10017 (800) 253-9646; *Statistical Yearbook*.

UZBEKISTAN - LABOR

Academic International Press, Box 1111, Gulf Breeze, Florida 32562; *Russia and Eurasia Facts and Figures Annual*.

Business International Moscow, 23 Profsoyuznaya Ulitsa, 117859, Moscow (Telephone Number in U.S. (800) 938-4685); *The CIS Market Atlas*.

Central Intelligence Agency, Washington, D.C. 20505 (703) 482-1100, www.cia.gov; *The World Factbook*.

Euromonitor International, Inc., 122 South Michigan Avenue, Suite 1200, Chicago, Illinois 60603 (800) 577-EURO; *International Marketing Data and Statistics;* and *World Marketing Data and Statistics*.

Europa Publications Limited, 18 Bedford Square, London, WC1B 3JN, England; *The Europa World Year Book*.

St. Martin's Press, Inc., 175 Fifth Avenue, New York, New York 10010 (800) 221-7945; *The Statesman's Year-Book*.

Statistical Office of the United Nations, Publishing Service, New York, New York 10017 (800) 253-9646; *Human Development Report;* and *Statistical Yearbook*.

The World Bank, 1818 H Street, NW, Washington, D.C. 20433 (202) 477-1234; *Statistical Handbook: States of the Former USSR; The World Bank Atlas; World Development Report;* and *World Development Indicators*.

UZBEKISTAN - LAND USE

Central Intelligence Agency, Washington, D.C. 20505 (703) 482-1100, www.cia.gov; *The World Factbook*.

Euromonitor International, Inc., 122 South Michigan Avenue, Suite 1200, Chicago, Illinois 60603 (800) 577-EURO; *International Marketing Data and Statistics*.

Food and Agriculture Organization of the United Nations (FAO), Via delle Terme di Caracalla, 00100, Rome, Italy (Telephone Number in U.S. (202) 653-2400); *Production Yearbook*.

The World Bank, 1818 H Street, NW, Washington, D.C. 20433 (202) 477-1234; *World Development Report*.

UZBEKISTAN - LIBRARIES

Statistical Office of the United Nations, Publishing Service, New York, New York 10017 (800) 253-9646; *Trends in Europe and North America: The Statistical Yearbook of the Economic Commission for Europe*.

United Nations Educational, Scientific and Cultural Organization (UNESCO), 7 Place de Fontenoy, F-75700 Paris, France (Telephone Number in U.S. (212) 963-5981); *Statistical Yearbook*.

UZBEKISTAN - LIFE EXPECTANCY

Academic International Press, Box 1111, Gulf Breeze, Florida 32562; *Russia and Eurasia Facts and Figures Annual*.

Business International Moscow, 23 Profsoyuznaya Ulitsa, 117859, Moscow (Telephone Number in U.S. (800) 938-

4685); *The CIS Market Atlas.*

Central Intelligence Agency, Washington, D.C. 20505 (703) 482-1100, www.cia.gov; *The World Factbook.*

Euromonitor International, Inc., 122 South Michigan Avenue, Suite 1200, Chicago, Illinois 60603 (800) 577-EURO; *The World Economic Factbook.*

Statistical Office of the United Nations, Publishing Service, New York, New York 10017 (800) 253-9646; *Demographic Yearbook; Human Development Report; World Statistics Pocketbook;* and *Trends in Europe and North America: The Statistical Yearbook of the Economic Commission for Europe.*

The World Bank, 1818 H Street, NW, Washington, D.C. 20433 (202) 477-1234; *The World Bank Atlas; World Development Report;* and *World Development Indicators.*

World Health Organization, Office of Publications, 20 Avenue Appia, CH-1211 Geneva 27, Switzerland (Telephone Number in U.S. (518) 436-9686); *World Health Statistics Annual.*

UZBEKISTAN - LITERACY RATE

Euromonitor International, Inc., 122 South Michigan Avenue, Suite 1200, Chicago, Illinois 60603 (800) 577-EURO; *World Marketing Data and Statistics.*

UZBEKISTAN - LIVESTOCK AND POULTRY

Academic International Press, Box 1111, Gulf Breeze, Florida 32562; *Russia and Eurasia Facts and Figures Annual.*

Business International Moscow, 23 Profsoyuznaya Ulitsa, 117859, Moscow (Telephone Number in U.S. (800) 938-4685); *The CIS Market Atlas.*

Europa Publications Limited, 18 Bedford Square, London, WC1B 3JN, England; *The Europa World Year Book.*

Food and Agriculture Organization of the United Nations (FAO), Via delle Terme di Caracalla, 00100, Rome, Italy (Telephone Number in U.S. (202) 653-2400); *Production Yearbook; The State of Food and Agriculture;* and *Trade Yearbook.*

St. Martin's Press, Inc., 175 Fifth Avenue, New York, New York 10010 (800) 221-7945; *The Statesman's Year-Book.*

Statistical Office of the United Nations, Publishing Service, New York, New York 10017 (800) 253-9646; *Industrial Commodity Statistics Yearbook;* and *Statistical Yearbook.*

UZBEKISTAN - MACHINERY

Statistical Office of the United Nations, Publishing Service, New York, New York 10017 (800) 253-9646; *Industrial Commodity Statistics Yearbook.*

UZBEKISTAN - MAIL-NUMBER OF PIECES SENT OR RECEIVED

Statistical Office of the United Nations, Publishing Service, New York, New York 10017 (800) 253-9646; *Statistical Yearbook.*

UZBEKISTAN - MANUFACTURING

Statistical Office of the United Nations, Publishing Service, New York, New York 10017 (800) 253-9646; *Industrial Commodity Statistics Yearbook;* and *Statistical Yearbook.*

The World Bank, 1818 H Street, NW, Washington, D.C. 20433 (202) 477-1234; *World Development Indicators.*

UZBEKISTAN - MARRIAGE RATES

Academic International Press, Box 1111, Gulf Breeze, Florida 32562; *Russia and Eurasia Facts and Figures Annual.*

Statistical Office of the United Nations, Publishing Service, New York, New York 10017 (800) 253-9646; *Demographic Yearbook; Statistical Yearbook;* and *Trends in Europe and North America: The Statistical Yearbook of the Economic Commission for Europe.*

UZBEKISTAN - MERCHANT SHIPPING

Statistical Office of the United Nations, Publishing Service, New York, New York 10017 (800) 253-9646; *Statistical Yearbook.*

UZBEKISTAN - MILITARY

Academic International Press, Box 1111, Gulf Breeze, Florida 32562; *Russia and Eurasia Facts and Figures Annual.*

Central Intelligence Agency, Washington, D.C. 20505 (703) 482-1100, www.cia.gov; *The World Factbook.*

Euromonitor International, Inc., 122 South Michigan Avenue, Suite 1200, Chicago, Illinois 60603 (800) 577-EURO; *World Marketing Data and Statistics.*

The International Institute for Strategic Studies, 23 Tavistock Street, London WC2E 7NQ, England 44 171 3797676; *The Military Balance.*

St. Martin's Press, Inc., 175 Fifth Avenue, New York, New York 10010 (800) 221-7945; *The Statesman's Year-Book.*

Statistical Office of the United Nations, Publishing Service, New York, New York 10017 (800) 253-9646; *Human*

Development Report.

UZBEKISTAN - MINING AND MINERAL PRODUCTS

Academic International Press, Box 1111, Gulf Breeze, Florida 32562; *Russia and Eurasia Facts and Figures Annual.*

Business International Moscow, 23 Profsoyuznaya Ulitsa, 117859, Moscow (Telephone Number in U.S. (800) 938-4685); *The CIS Market Atlas.*

Europa Publications Limited, 18 Bedford Square, London, WC1B 3JN, England; *The Europa World Year Book.*

St. Martin's Press, Inc., 175 Fifth Avenue, New York, New York 10010 (800) 221-7945; *The Statesman's Year-Book.*

Statistical Office of the United Nations, Publishing Service, New York, New York 10017 (800) 253-9646; *Energy Statistics Yearbook; Industrial Commodity Statistics Yearbook;* and *Statistical Yearbook.*

UZBEKISTAN - MONEY SUPPLY

Economist Intelligence Unit, 111 West 57th Street, New York, New York 10019 (800) 938-4685; *Uzbekistan Country Report.*

UZBEKISTAN - MONUMENTS AND HISTORICAL SITES

United Nations Educational, Scientific and Cultural Organization (UNESCO), 7 Place de Fontenoy, F-75700 Paris, France (Telephone Number in U.S. (212) 963-5981); *Statistical Yearbook.*

UZBEKISTAN - MORTALITY

Academic International Press, Box 1111, Gulf Breeze, Florida 32562; *Russia and Eurasia Facts and Figures Annual.*

Business International Moscow, 23 Profsoyuznaya Ulitsa, 117859, Moscow (Telephone Number in U.S. (800) 938-4685); *The CIS Market Atlas.*

Central Intelligence Agency, Washington, D.C. 20505 (703) 482-1100, www.cia.gov; *The World Factbook.*

Euromonitor International, Inc., 122 South Michigan Avenue, Suite 1200, Chicago, Illinois 60603 (800) 577-EURO; *International Marketing Data and Statistics;* and *The World Economic Factbook.*

Europa Publications Limited, 18 Bedford Square, London, WC1B 3JN, England; *The Europa World Year Book.*

Statistical Office of the United Nations, Publishing Service, New York, New York 10017 (800) 253-9646; *Demographic*

Yearbook; Human Development Report; Statistical Yearbook; World Statistics Pocketbook; and *Trends in Europe and North America: The Statistical Yearbook of the Economic Commission for Europe.*

United Nations Children's Fund (UNICEF), 3 United Nations Plaza, New York, New York 10017 (800) 253-9646; *State of the World's Children.*

The World Bank, 1818 H Street, NW, Washington, D.C. 20433 (202) 477-1234; *The World Bank Atlas; World Development Report;* and *World Development Indicators.*

World Health Organization, Office of Publications, 20 Avenue Appia, CH-1211 Geneva 27, Switzerland (Telephone Number in U.S. (518) 436-9686); *World Health Statistics Annual.*

UZBEKISTAN - MOTION PICTURES

Statistical Office of the United Nations, Publishing Service, New York, New York 10017 (800) 253-9646; *Statistical Yearbook.*

United Nations Educational, Scientific and Cultural Organization (UNESCO), 7 Place de Fontenoy, F-75700 Paris, France (Telephone Number in U.S. (212) 963-5981); *Statistical Yearbook.*

UZBEKISTAN - MOTOR VEHICLES

Business International Moscow, 23 Profsoyuznaya Ulitsa, 117859, Moscow (Telephone Number in U.S. (800) 938-4685); *The CIS Market Atlas.*

Statistical Office of the United Nations, Publishing Service, New York, New York 10017 (800) 253-9646; *Statistical Yearbook.*

UZBEKISTAN - NATIONAL ACCOUNTS

Europa Publications Limited, 18 Bedford Square, London, WC1B 3JN, England; *The Europa World Year Book.*

Statistical Office of the United Nations, Publishing Service, New York, New York 10017 (800) 253-9646; *National Accounts Statistics;* and *Statistical Yearbook.*

The World Bank, 1818 H Street, NW, Washington, D.C. 20433 (202) 477-1234; *Statistical Handbook: States of the Former USSR.*

UZBEKISTAN - NATIONAL INCOME

Business International Moscow, 23 Profsoyuznaya Ulitsa, 117859, Moscow (Telephone Number in U.S. (800) 938-4685); *The CIS Market Atlas.*

Statistical Office of the United Nations, Publishing Service, New York, New York 10017 (800) 253-9646; *Statistical Yearbook.*

UZBEKISTAN - NATIONAL PRODUCT

Statistical Office of the United Nations, Publishing Service, New York, New York 10017 (800) 253-9646; *Statistical Yearbook.*

UZBEKISTAN - PATENTS, TRADEMARKS AND SERVICE MARKS

Statistical Office of the United Nations, Publishing Service, New York, New York 10017 (800) 253-9646; *Statistical Yearbook.*

UZBEKISTAN - PERIODICALS

United Nations Educational, Scientific and Cultural Organization (UNESCO), 7 Place de Fontenoy, F-75700 Paris, France (Telephone Number in U.S. (212) 963-5981); *Statistical Yearbook.*

UZBEKISTAN - PETROLEUM INDUSTRY

Food and Agriculture Organization of the United Nations (FAO), Via delle Terme di Caracalla, 00100, Rome, Italy (Telephone Number in U.S. (202) 653-2400); *The State of Food and Agriculture.*

Statistical Office of the United Nations, Publishing Service, New York, New York 10017 (800) 253-9646; *Energy Statistics Yearbook; Industrial Commodity Statistics Yearbook; Statistical Yearbook;* and *Trends in Europe and North America: The Statistical Yearbook of the Economic Commission for Europe.*

UZBEKISTAN - PIGS - See UZBEKISTAN - LIVESTOCK AND POULTRY

UZBEKISTAN - POPULATION

Academic International Press, Box 1111, Gulf Breeze, Florida 32562; *Russia and Eurasia Facts and Figures Annual.*

Business International Moscow, 23 Profsoyuznaya Ulitsa, 117859, Moscow (Telephone Number in U.S. (800) 938-4685); *The CIS Market Atlas.*

Central Intelligence Agency, Washington, D.C. 20505 (703) 482-1100, www.cia.gov; *The World Factbook.*

Economist Intelligence Unit, 111 West 57th Street, New York, New York 10019 (800) 938-4685; *Uzbekistan Country Report.*

Euromonitor International, Inc., 122 South Michigan Avenue, Suite 1200, Chicago, Illinois 60603 (800) 577-EURO; *International Marketing Data and Statistics;* and *The World Economic Factbook.*

Europa Publications Limited, 18 Bedford Square, London, WC1B 3JN, England; *The Europa World Year Book.*

Food and Agriculture Organization of

the United Nations (FAO), Via delle Terme di Caracalla, 00100, Rome, Italy (Telephone Number in U.S. (202) 653-2400); *Production Yearbook.*

St. Martin's Press, Inc., 175 Fifth Avenue, New York, New York 10010 (800) 221-7945; *The Statesman's Year-Book.*

Statistical Office of the United Nations, Publishing Service, New York, New York 10017 (800) 253-9646; *Demographic Yearbook; Human Development Report; Statistical Yearbook; World Statistics Pocketbook;* and *Trends in Europe and North America: The Statistical Yearbook of the Economic Commission for Europe.*

United Nations Educational, Scientific and Cultural Organization (UNESCO), 7 Place de Fontenoy, F-75700 Paris, France (Telephone Number in U.S. (212) 963-5981); *Statistical Yearbook.*

The World Bank, 1818 H Street, NW, Washington, D.C. 20433 (202) 477-1234; *Statistical Handbook: States of the Former USSR; The World Bank Atlas; World Development Report;* and *World Development Indicators.*

World Health Organization, Office of Publications, 20 Avenue Appia, CH-1211 Geneva 27, Switzerland (Telephone Number in U.S. (518) 436-9686); *World Health Statistics Annual.*

UZBEKISTAN - POST OFFICES

Statistical Office of the United Nations, Publishing Service, New York, New York 10017 (800) 253-9646; *Trends in Europe and North America: The Statistical Yearbook of the Economic Commission for Europe.*

UZBEKISTAN - POULTRY - See UZBEKISTAN - LIVESTOCK AND POULTRY

UZBEKISTAN - PRICES

Food and Agriculture Organization of the United Nations (FAO), Via delle Terme di Caracalla, 00100, Rome, Italy (Telephone Number in U.S. (202) 653-2400); *Production Yearbook.*

The World Bank, 1818 H Street, NW, Washington, D.C. 20433 (202) 477-1234; *Statistical Handbook: States of the Former USSR.*

UZBEKISTAN - PRODUCTION

The World Bank, 1818 H Street, NW, Washington, D.C. 20433 (202) 477-1234; *Statistical Handbook: States of the Former USSR.*

UZBEKISTAN - PUBLIC FINANCE - See UZBEKISTAN - FINANCE

UZBEKISTAN - RADIO RECEIVER PRODUCTION

Statistical Office of the United Nations, Publishing Service, New York, New York 10017 (800) 253-9646; *Statistical Yearbook.*

UZBEKISTAN - RADIO RECEIVERS

St. Martin's Press, Inc., 175 Fifth Avenue, New York, New York 10010 (800) 221-7945; *The Statesman's Year-Book.*

UZBEKISTAN - RAILWAYS

Academic International Press, Box 1111, Gulf Breeze, Florida 32562; *Russia and Eurasia Facts and Figures Annual.*

Business International Moscow, 23 Profsoyuznaya Ulitsa, 117859, Moscow (Telephone Number in U.S. (800) 938-4685); *The CIS Market Atlas.*

St. Martin's Press, Inc., 175 Fifth Avenue, New York, New York 10010 (800) 221-7945; *The Statesman's Year-Book.*

Statistical Office of the United Nations, Publishing Service, New York, New York 10017 (800) 253-9646; *Statistical Yearbook; and Trends in Europe and North America: The Statistical Yearbook of the Economic Commission for Europe.*

UZBEKISTAN - RELIGION

Academic International Press, Box 1111, Gulf Breeze, Florida 32562; *Russia and Eurasia Facts and Figures Annual.*

Central Intelligence Agency, Washington, D.C. 20505 (703) 482-1100, www.cia.gov; *The World Factbook.*

St. Martin's Press, Inc., 175 Fifth Avenue, New York, New York 10010 (800) 221-7945; *The Statesman's Year-Book.*

UZBEKISTAN - RETAIL PRICE INDEX

Europa Publications Limited, 18 Bedford Square, London, WC1B 3JN, England; *The Europa World Year Book.*

UZBEKISTAN - RETAIL TRADE

Business International Moscow, 23 Profsoyuznaya Ulitsa, 117859, Moscow (Telephone Number in U.S. (800) 938-4685); *The CIS Market Atlas.*

Euromonitor International, Inc., 122 South Michigan Avenue, Suite 1200, Chicago, Illinois 60603 (800) 577-EURO; *World Marketing Data and Statistics.*

Statistical Office of the United Nations, Publishing Service, New York, New York 10017 (800) 253-9646; *Statistical Yearbook.*

UZBEKISTAN - ROADS - See UZBEKISTAN - HIGHWAYS

UZBEKISTAN - ROUNDWOOD PRODUCTION AND CONSUMPTION - See UZBEKISTAN - FORESTRY AND FOREST PRODUCTS

UZBEKISTAN - RUBBER PRODUCTION AND CONSUMPTION

Statistical Office of the United Nations, Publishing Service, New York, New York 10017 (800) 253-9646; *Statistical Yearbook.*

UZBEKISTAN - SCIENTISTS, TECHNICIANS AND ENGINEERS

Statistical Office of the United Nations, Publishing Service, New York, New York 10017 (800) 253-9646; *Statistical Yearbook.*

UZBEKISTAN - SHEEP - See UZBEKISTAN - LIVESTOCK AND POULTRY

UZBEKISTAN - SOCIAL DATA

Statistical Office of the United Nations, Publishing Service, New York, New York 10017 (800) 253-9646; *World Statistics Pocketbook.*

UZBEKISTAN - STEEL PRODUCTION AND CONSUMPTION - See UZBEKISTAN - MINING AND MINERAL PRODUCTS

UZBEKISTAN - TAXATION

Europa Publications Limited, 18 Bedford Square, London, WC1B 3JN, England; *The Europa World Year Book.*

UZBEKISTAN - TELEPHONES IN USE

Academic International Press, Box 1111, Gulf Breeze, Florida 32562; *Russia and Eurasia Facts and Figures Annual.*

Central Intelligence Agency, Washington, D.C. 20505 (703) 482-1100, www.cia.gov; *The World Factbook.*

Statistical Office of the United Nations, Publishing Service, New York, New York 10017 (800) 253-9646; *Statistical Yearbook; World Statistics Pocketbook; and Trends in Europe and North America: The Statistical Yearbook of the Economic Commission for Europe.*

UZBEKISTAN - TEXTILE INDUSTRY

Business International Moscow, 23 Profsoyuznaya Ulitsa, 117859, Moscow (Telephone Number in U.S. (800) 938-4685); *The CIS Market Atlas.*

Statistical Office of the United Nations, Publishing Service, New York, New York 10017 (800) 253-9646; *Industrial Commodity Statistics Yearbook;* and

Statistical Yearbook.

UZBEKISTAN - THEATRE

United Nations Educational, Scientific and Cultural Organization (UNESCO), 7 Place de Fontenoy, F-75700 Paris, France (Telephone Number in U.S. (212) 963-5981); *Statistical Yearbook.*

UZBEKISTAN - TIRE (MOTOR VEHICLE) PRODUCTION

Statistical Office of the United Nations, Publishing Service, New York, New York 10017 (800) 253-9646; *Statistical Yearbook.*

UZBEKISTAN - TOBACCO PRODUCTION

Statistical Office of the United Nations, Publishing Service, New York, New York 10017 (800) 253-9646; *Statistical Yearbook.*

UZBEKISTAN - TOURISM

Business International Moscow, 23 Profsoyuznaya Ulitsa, 117859, Moscow (Telephone Number in U.S. (800) 938-4685); *The CIS Market Atlas.*

Euromonitor International, Inc., 122 South Michigan Avenue, Suite 1200, Chicago, Illinois 60603 (800) 577-EURO; *The World Economic Factbook;* and *World Marketing Data and Statistics.*

Statistical Office of the United Nations, Publishing Service, New York, New York 10017 (800) 253-9646; *Statistical Yearbook; and Trends in Europe and North America: The Statistical Yearbook of the Economic Commission for Europe.*

UZBEKISTAN - TRADEMARKS AND SERVICE MARKS - See UZBEKISTAN - PATENTS, TRADEMARKS AND SERVICE MARKS

UZBEKISTAN - TRANSPORTATION AND COMMUNICATION

Academic International Press, Box 1111, Gulf Breeze, Florida 32562; *Russia and Eurasia Facts and Figures Annual.*

Business International Moscow, 23 Profsoyuznaya Ulitsa, 117859, Moscow (Telephone Number in U.S. (800) 938-4685); *The CIS Market Atlas.*

Central Intelligence Agency, Washington, D.C. 20505 (703) 482-1100, www.cia.gov; *The World Factbook.*

Euromonitor International, Inc., 122 South Michigan Avenue, Suite 1200, Chicago, Illinois 60603 (800) 577-EURO; *International Marketing Data and Statistics;* and *World Marketing Data and Statistics.*

St. Martin's Press, Inc., 175 Fifth Avenue, New York, New York 10010 (800)

221-7945; *The Statesman's Year-Book.*

Statistical Office of the United Nations, Publishing Service, New York, New York 10017 (800) 253-9646; *Human Development Report;* and *Trends in Europe and North America: The Statistical Yearbook of the Economic Commission for Europe.*

UZBEKISTAN - UNEMPLOYMENT

Central Intelligence Agency, Washington, D.C. 20505 (703) 482-1100, www.cia.gov; *The World Factbook.*

St. Martin's Press, Inc., 175 Fifth Avenue, New York, New York 10010 (800) 221-7945; *The Statesman's Year-Book.*

Statistical Office of the United Nations, Publishing Service, New York, New York 10017 (800) 253-9646; *Statistical Yearbook;* and *Trends in Europe and North America: The Statistical Yearbook of the Economic Commission for Europe.*

UZBEKISTAN - VITAL STATISTICS

Statistical Office of the United Nations, Publishing Service, New York, New York 10017 (800) 253-9646; *Statistical Yearbook.*

World Health Organization, Office of Publications, 20 Avenue Appia, CH-1211 Geneva 27, Switzerland (Telephone Number in U.S. (518) 436-9686); *World Health Statistics Annual.*

UZBEKISTAN - WAGES

Business International Moscow, 23 Profsoyuznaya Ulitsa, 117859, Moscow (Telephone Number in U.S. (800) 938-4685); *The CIS Market Atlas.*

Statistical Office of the United Nations, Publishing Service, New York, New York 10017 (800) 253-9646; *Statistical Yearbook.*

The World Bank, 1818 H Street, NW, Washington, D.C. 20433 (202) 477-1234; *Statistical Handbook: States of the Former USSR.*

UZBEKISTAN - WELFARE

Academic International Press, Box 1111, Gulf Breeze, Florida 32562; *Russia and Eurasia Facts and Figures Annual.*

St. Martin's Press, Inc., 175 Fifth Avenue, New York, New York 10010 (800) 221-7945; *The Statesman's Year-Book.*

UZBEKISTAN - WHOLESALE PRICES

Academic International Press, Box 1111, Gulf Breeze, Florida 32562; *Russia and Eurasia Facts and Figures Annual.*

Statistical Office of the United Nations, Publishing Service, New York, New York 10017 (800) 253-9646; *Statistical Yearbook.*

UZBEKISTAN - WHOLESALE TRADE

Statistical Office of the United Nations, Publishing Service, New York, New York 10017 (800) 253-9646; *Statistical Yearbook.*

UZBEKISTAN - WOOL PRODUCTION AND CONSUMPTION - See UZBEKISTAN - TEXTILE INDUSTRY

V

VACANCY RATES - HOUSING

Oncor International, 1747 Pennsylvania Avenue, NW, Suite 350, Washington, D.C. 20006 (800) 231-7224; *Electronic Market Data Book*.

VACANCY RATES - OFFICE BUILDINGS

Oncor International, 1747 Pennsylvania Avenue, NW, Suite 350, Washington, D.C. 20006 (800) 231-7224; *Year-end Market Data Book*.

Society of Industrial and Office Realtors, 700 Eleventh Street, NW, Suite 510, Washington, D.C. 20001 (202) 383-1150; *Comparative Statistics of Industrial and Office Real Estate Markets*.

VALUE ADDED - See also Individual Manufacturing and Mining Industries

VALUE ADDED BY MANUFACTURE - ALL INDUSTRIES

U.S. Department of Commerce, Bureau of the Census, Washington, D.C. 20233 (301) 457-4100, www.census.gov; *Census of Manufactures;* and *Annual Survey of Manufactures*.

VALUE ADDED BY MANUFACTURE - STATES

U.S. Department of Labor, Bureau of Labor Statistics, Two Massachusetts Avenue, NE, Washington, D.C. 20212 (202) 691-5200, www.stats.bls.gov; *Employment and Earnings*.

VANADIUM

U.S. Department of the Interior, Geological Survey, Office of Minerals Information, 12201 Sunrise Valley Drive, Reston, Virginia 22092 (703) 648-4000, www.minerals.usgs.gov; *Annual Reports;* and *Mineral Commodity Summaries*.

Vanuatu - National Statistical Office

Bureau of Statistics, Census Administrator and Principal Statistician, Vanuatu Government, Private Mail Bag 19, Port Vila, Vanuatu.

Vanuatu - Primary Statistics Source

HM Stationery Office, Post Office Box 569, London SE1, England; *Vanuatu Anglo-French Condominium: Report for the Year*.

VANUATU - AGRICULTURE

Economist Intelligence Unit, 111 West 57th Street, New York, New York 10019 (800) 938-4685; *Vanuatu Country Report*.

Euromonitor International, Inc., 122 South Michigan Avenue, Suite 1200, Chicago, Illinois 60603 (800) 577-EURO; *World Marketing Data and Statistics*.

Europa Publications Limited, 18 Bedford Square, London, WC1B 3JN, England; *The Europa World Year Book*.

Food and Agricultural Organization of the United Nations (FAO) Via delle Terme di Caracalla, 00100 Rome, Italy (Telephone Number in U.S. (202) 653-2400); *Production Yearbook; The State of Food and Agriculture;* and *Trade Yearbook*.

St. Martin's Press, Inc., 175 Fifth Avenue, New York, New York 10010 (800) 221-7945; *The Statesman's Year-Book*.

Statistical Office of the United Nations, Publishing Service, New York, New York 10017 (800) 253-9646; *Asia-Pacific in Figures;* and *Statistical Yearbook*.

United Nations Conference on Trade and Development, Central Statistical Service, Palais des Nations, Geneva, Switzerland (Telephone in U.S. (800) 253-9646); *UNCTAD Commodity Yearbook*.

The World Bank, 1818 H Street, NW, Washington, D.C. 20433 (202) 477-1234; *World Development Indicators*.

VANUATU - AIRLINE SERVICE

St. Martin's Press, Inc., 175 Fifth Avenue, New York, New York 10010 (800) 221-7945; *The Statesman's Year-Book*.

VANUATU - AIRPORTS

Central Intelligence Agency, Washington, D.C. 20505 (703) 482-1100, www.cia.gov; *The World Factbook*.

VANUATU - ANIMAL HEALTH

Food and Agricultural Organization of the United Nations (FAO), Via delle Terme di Caracalla, 00100 Rome, Italy (Telephone Number in U.S. (202) 653-2400); *Animal Health Yearbook*.

VANUATU - AREA AND DENSITY OF POPULATION

Central Intelligence Agency, Washington, D.C. 20505 (703) 482-1100, www.cia.gov; *The World Factbook*.

Euromonitor International, Inc., 122 South Michigan Avenue, Suite 1200, Chicago, Illinois 60603 (800) 577-EURO; *The World Economic Factbook*.

Europa Publications Limited, 18 Bedford Square, London, WC1B 3JN, England; *The Europa World Year Book*.

Food and Agricultural Organization of the United Nations (FAO) Via delle Terme di Caracalla, 00100 Rome, Italy (Telephone Number in U.S. (202) 653-2400); *The State of Food and Agriculture*.

St. Martin's Press, Inc., 175 Fifth Avenue, New York, New York 10010 (800) 221-7945; *The Statesman's Year-Book*.

Statistical Office of the United Nations, Publishing Service, New York, New York 10017 (800) 253-9646; *Statistical Yearbook*.

United Nations Educational, Scientific and Cultural Organization (UNESCO), 7 Place de Fontenoy, F-75700 Paris, France (Telephone Number in U.S. (212) 963-5981); *Statistical Yearbook.*

VANUATU - BALANCE OF PAYMENTS

Europa Publications Limited, 18 Bedford Square, London, WC1B 3JN, England; *The Europa World Year Book.*

United Nations Conference on Trade and Development (UNCTAD), New York, New York 10017 (800) 253-9646; *Handbook of International Trade and Development Statistics.*

The World Bank, 1818 H Street, NW, Washington, D.C. 20433 (202) 477-1234; *World Development Indicators.*

VANUATU - BANKING

Euromonitor International, Inc., 122 South Michigan Avenue, Suite 1200, Chicago, Illinois 60603 (800) 577-EURO; *World Marketing Data and Statistics.*

St. Martin's Press, Inc., 175 Fifth Avenue, New York, New York 10010 (800) 221-7945; *The Statesman's Year-Book.*

VANUATU - BIRTH RATES

Central Intelligence Agency, Washington, D.C. 20505 (703) 482-1100, www.cia.gov; *The World Factbook.*

Euromonitor International, Inc., 122 South Michigan Avenue, Suite 1200, Chicago, Illinois 60603 (800) 577-EURO; *International Marketing Data and Statistics;* and *The World Economic Factbook.*

Europa Publications Limited, 18 Bedford Square, London, WC1B 3JN, England; *The Europa World Year Book.*

Statistical Office of the United Nations, Publishing Service, New York, New York 10017 (800) 253-9646; *Asia-Pacific in Figures; Demographic Yearbook;* and *Statistical Yearbook.*

The World Bank, 1818 H Street, NW, Washington, D.C. 20433 (202) 477-1234; *World Development Indicators.*

VANUATU - BROADCASTING

Billboard Limited, P.O. Box 9027, 1006 AA Amsterdam, The Netherlands (Telephone Number in U.S. (212) 764-7300); *World Radio TV Handbook.*

Central Intelligence Agency, Washington, D.C. 20505 (703) 482-1100, www.cia.gov; *The World Factbook.*

Euromonitor International, Inc., 122

South Michigan Avenue, Suite 1200, Chicago, Illinois 60603 (800) 577-EURO; *World Marketing Data and Statistics.*

St. Martin's Press, Inc., 175 Fifth Avenue, New York, New York 10010 (800) 221-7945; *The Statesman's Year-Book.*

VANUATU - BUDGET

Central Intelligence Agency, Washington, D.C. 20505 (703) 482-1100, www.cia.gov; *The World Factbook.*

VANUATU - CALORIE SUPPLY

Food and Agricultural Organization of the United Nations (FAO) Via delle Terme di Caracalla, 00100 Rome, Italy (Telephone Number in U.S. (202) 653-2400); *The State of Food and Agriculture.*

VANUATU - CATTLE - See VANUATU - LIVESTOCK AND POULTRY

VANUATU - CLIMATE

St. Martin's Press, Inc., 175 Fifth Avenue, New York, New York 10010 (800) 221-7945; *The Statesman's Year-Book.*

VANUATU - COCOA PRODUCTION - See VANUATU - CROPS

VANUATU - COMMERCE

St. Martin's Press, Inc., 175 Fifth Avenue, New York, New York 10010 (800) 221-7945; *The Statesman's Year-Book.*

VANUATU - CONSTRUCTION INDUSTRY

Statistical Office of the United Nations, Publishing Service, New York, New York 10017 (800) 253-9646; *Statistical Yearbook.*

VANUATU - CONSUMER PRICE INDEX

Statistical Office of the United Nations, Publishing Service, New York, New York 10017 (800) 253-9646; *Statistical Yearbook.*

VANUATU - CONSUMER PRICES

Euromonitor International, Inc., 122 South Michigan Avenue, Suite 1200, Chicago, Illinois 60603 (800) 577-EURO; *World Marketing Data and Statistics.*

VANUATU - CORN PRODUCTION - See VANUATU - CROPS

VANUATU - CROPS

Europa Publications Limited, 18 Bedford Square, London, WC1B 3JN, England; *The Europa World Year Book.*

Food and Agricultural Organization of the United Nations (FAO) Via delle Terme di Caracalla, 00100 Rome, Italy (Telephone

Number in U.S. (202) 653-2400); *Production Yearbook;* and *The State of Food and Agriculture.*

St. Martin's Press, Inc., 175 Fifth Avenue, New York, New York 10010 (800) 221-7945; *The Statesman's Year-Book.*

Statistical Office of the United Nations, Publishing Service, New York, New York 10017 (800) 253-9646; *Statistical Yearbook.*

United Nations Conference on Trade and Development, Central Statistical Service, Palais des Nations, Geneva, Switzerland (Telephone in U.S. (800) 253-9646); *UNCTAD Commodity Yearbook.*

VANUATU - CUSTOMS DUTIES

St. Martin's Press, Inc., 175 Fifth Avenue, New York, New York 10010 (800) 221-7945; *The Statesman's Year-Book.*

VANUATU - DAIRY PRODUCTS

Europa Publications Limited, 18 Bedford Square, London, WC1B 3JN, England; *The Europa World Year Book.*

Food and Agricultural Organization of the United Nations (FAO) Via delle Terme di Caracalla, 00100 Rome, Italy (Telephone Number in U.S. (202) 653-2400); *The State of Food and Agriculture.*

VANUATU - DEATH RATES - See VANUATU - MORTALITY

VANUATU - DEMOGRAPHY

Euromonitor International, Inc., 122 South Michigan Avenue, Suite 1200, Chicago, Illinois 60603 (800) 577-EURO; *International Marketing Data and Statistics; World Marketing Data and Statistics;* and *The World Economic Factbook.*

Statistical Office of the United Nations, Publishing Service, New York, New York 10017 (800) 253-9646; *Asia-Pacific in Figures;* and *Human Development Report.*

VANUATU - DEVELOPMENT ASSISTANCE

Statistical Office of the United Nations, Publishing Service, New York, New York 10017 (800) 253-9646; *Statistical Yearbook.*

VANUATU - DIVORCE RATES

Statistical Office of the United Nations, Publishing Service, New York, New York 10017 (800) 253-9646; *Demographic Yearbook.*

VANUATU - ECONOMY

Central Intelligence Agency, Washington, D.C. 20505 (703) 482-1100,

www.cia.gov; *The World Factbook.*

Economist Intelligence Unit, 111 West 57th Street, New York, New York 10019 (800) 938-4685; *Vanuatu Country Report.*

Euromonitor International, Inc., 122 South Michigan Avenue, Suite 1200, Chicago, Illinois 60603 (800) 577-EURO; *The World Economic Factbook;* and *World Marketing Data and Statistics.*

Europa Publications Limited, 18 Bedford Square, London, WC1B 3JN, England; *The Europa World Year Book.*

St. Martin's Press, Inc., 175 Fifth Avenue, New York, New York 10010 (800) 221-7945; *The Statesman's Year-Book.*

Statistical Office of the United Nations, Publishing Service, New York, New York 10017 (800) 253-9646; *World Statistics Pocketbook.*

The World Bank, 1818 H Street, NW, Washington, D.C. 20433 (202) 477-1234; *The World Bank Atlas.*

VANUATU - EDUCATION

Euromonitor International, Inc., 122 South Michigan Avenue, Suite 1200, Chicago, Illinois 60603 (800) 577-EURO; *International Marketing Data and Statistics;* and *World Marketing Data and Statistics.*

Europa Publications Limited, 18 Bedford Square, London, WC1B 3JN, England; *The Europa World Year Book.*

St. Martin's Press, Inc., 175 Fifth Avenue, New York, New York 10010 (800) 221-7945; *The Statesman's Year-Book.*

Statistical Office of the United Nations, Publishing Service, New York, New York 10017 (800) 253-9646; *Asia-Pacific in Figures;* and *Human Development Report.*

United Nations Educational, Scientific and Cultural Organization (UNESCO), 7 Place de Fontenoy, F-75700 Paris, France (Telephone Number in U.S. (212) 963-5981); *Statistical Yearbook.*

The World Bank, 1818 H Street, NW, Washington, D.C. 20433 (202) 477-1234; *World Development Indicators.*

VANUATU - EGG PRODUCTION AND CONSUMPTION - See VANUATU - DAIRY PRODUCTS

VANUATU - ELECTRICITY

Central Intelligence Agency, Washington, D.C. 20505 (703) 482-1100, www.cia.gov; *The World Factbook.*

St. Martin's Press, Inc., 175 Fifth

Avenue, New York, New York 10010 (800) 221-7945; *The Statesman's Year-Book.*

Statistical Office of the United Nations, Publishing Service, New York, New York 10017 (800) 253-9646; *Human Development Report.*

VANUATU - EMPLOYMENT

Euromonitor International, Inc., 122 South Michigan Avenue, Suite 1200, Chicago, Illinois 60603 (800) 577-EURO; *International Marketing Data and Statistics.*

Statistical Office of the United Nations, Publishing Service, New York, New York 10017 (800) 253-9646; *Asia-Pacific in Figures.*

VANUATU - ENERGY

Euromonitor International, Inc., 122 South Michigan Avenue, Suite 1200, Chicago, Illinois 60603 (800) 577-EURO; *International Marketing Data and Statistics; World Marketing Data and Statistics;* and *The World Economic Factbook.*

Food and Agricultural Organization of the United Nations (FAO) Via delle Terme di Caracalla, 00100 Rome, Italy (Telephone Number in U.S. (202) 653-2400); *The State of Food and Agriculture.*

St. Martin's Press, Inc., 175 Fifth Avenue, New York, New York 10010 (800) 221-7945; *The Statesman's Year-Book.*

Statistical Office of the United Nations, Publishing Service, New York, New York 10017 (800) 253-9646; *Asia-Pacific in Figures; Human Development Report; World Statistics Pocketbook;* and *Statistical Yearbook.*

The World Bank, 1818 H Street, NW, Washington, D.C. 20433 (202) 477-1234; *The World Bank Atlas.*

VANUATU - ENVIRONMENT

Economist Intelligence Unit, 111 West 57th Street, New York, New York 10019 (800) 938-4685; *Vanuatu Country Report.*

Statistical Office of the United Nations, Publishing Service, New York, New York 10017 (800) 253-9646; *World Statistics Pocketbook.*

VANUATU - EXCHANGE RATES

Central Intelligence Agency, Washington, D.C. 20505 (703) 482-1100, www.cia.gov; *The World Factbook.*

Euromonitor International, Inc., 122 South Michigan Avenue, Suite 1200, Chicago, Illinois 60603 (800) 577-EURO; *International Marketing Data and Statistics;*

and *The World Economic Factbook.*

Europa Publications Limited, 18 Bedford Square, London, WC1B 3JN, England; *The Europa World Year Book.*

Statistical Office of the United Nations, Publishing Service, New York, New York 10017 (800) 253-9646; *World Statistics Pocketbook.*

VANUATU - EXPORTS

Central Intelligence Agency, Washington, D.C. 20505 (703) 482-1100, www.cia.gov; *The World Factbook.*

Economist Intelligence Unit, 111 West 57th Street, New York, New York 10019 (800) 938-4685; *Vanuatu Country Report.*

Euromonitor International, Inc., 122 South Michigan Avenue, Suite 1200, Chicago, Illinois 60603 (800) 577-EURO; *International Marketing Data and Statistics;* and *The World Economic Factbook.*

Europa Publications Limited, 18 Bedford Square, London, WC1B 3JN, England; *The Europa World Year Book.*

Food and Agricultural Organization of the United Nations (FAO) Via delle Terme di Caracalla, 00100 Rome, Italy (Telephone Number in U.S. (202) 653-2400); *The State of Food and Agriculture.*

International Monetary Fund, 700 Nineteenth Street, NW, Washington, D.C. 20431 (202) 623-7000; *Direction of Trade Statistics.*

St. Martin's Press, Inc., 175 Fifth Avenue, New York, New York 10010 (800) 221-7945; *The Statesman's Year-Book.*

United Nations Conference on Trade and Development (UNCTAD), New York, New York 10017 (800) 253-9646; *Handbook of International Trade and Development Statistics.*

The World Bank, 1818 H Street, NW, Washington, D.C. 20433 (202) 477-1234; *World Development Indicators.*

VANUATU - EXTERNAL INDEBTEDNESS

The World Bank, 1818 H Street, NW, Washington, D.C. 20433 (202) 477-1234; *World Development Indicators.*

VANUATU - EXTERNAL TRADE

Euromonitor International, Inc., 122 South Michigan Avenue, Suite 1200, Chicago, Illinois 60603 (800) 577-EURO; *World Marketing Data and Statistics.*

Food and Agricultural Organization of the United Nations (FAO) Via delle Terme

di Caracalla, 00100 Rome, Italy (Telephone Number in U.S. (202) 653-2400); *The State of Food and Agriculture;* and *Trade Yearbook.*

Statistical Office of the United Nations, Publishing Service, New York, New York 10017 (800) 253-9646; *Asia-Pacific in Figures;* and *Statistical Yearbook.*

VANUATU - FARM CROPS - See VANUATU - CROPS

VANUATU - FERTILITY RATES

Central Intelligence Agency, Washington, D.C. 20505 (703) 482-1100, www.cia.gov; *The World Factbook.*

Statistical Office of the United Nations, Publishing Service, New York, New York 10017 (800) 253-9646; *Human Development Report.*

The World Bank, 1818 H Street, NW, Washington, D.C. 20433 (202) 477-1234; *The World Bank Atlas;* and *World Development Indicators.*

VANUATU - FERTILIZER PRODUCTION AND CONSUMPTION

Food and Agricultural Organization of the United Nations (FAO), Via delle Terme di Caracalla, 00100 Rome, Italy (Telephone Number in U.S. (202) 653-2400); *Fertilizer Yearbook;* and *The State of Food and Agriculture.*

VANUATU - FETAL MORTALITY - See VANUATU - MORTALITY

VANUATU - FINANCE

Economist Intelligence Unit, 111 West 57th Street, New York, New York 10019 (800) 938-4685; *Vanuatu Country Report.*

Europa Publications Limited, 18 Bedford Square, London, WC1B 3JN, England; *The Europa World Year Book.*

St. Martin's Press, Inc., 175 Fifth Avenue, New York, New York 10010 (800) 221-7945; *The Statesman's Year-Book.*

VANUATU - FISHERIES

Food and Agricultural Organization of the United Nations (FAO) Via delle Terme di Caracalla, 00100 Rome, Italy (Telephone Number in U.S. (202) 653-2400); *The State of Food and Agriculture.*

St. Martin's Press, Inc., 175 Fifth Avenue, New York, New York 10010 (800) 221-7945; *The Statesman's Year-Book.*

Statistical Office of the United Nations, Publishing Service, New York, New York 10017 (800) 253-9646; *Statistical Yearbook.*

United Nations Conference on Trade and Development, Central Statistical Service, Palais des Nations, Geneva, Switzerland (Telephone in U.S. (800) 253-9646); *UNCTAD Commodity Yearbook.*

VANUATU - FOOD

Food and Agricultural Organization of the United Nations (FAO) Via delle Terme di Caracalla, 00100 Rome, Italy (Telephone Number in U.S. (202) 653-2400); *Production Yearbook;* and *The State of Food and Agriculture.*

Statistical Office of the United Nations, Publishing Service, New York, New York 10017 (800) 253-9646; *Human Development Report.*

United Nations Conference on Trade and Development, Central Statistical Service, Palais des Nations, Geneva, Switzerland (Telephone in U.S. (800) 253-9646); *UNCTAD Commodity Yearbook.*

VANUATU - FOREIGN TRADE

Economist Intelligence Unit, 111 West 57th Street, New York, New York 10019 (800) 938-4685; *Vanuatu Country Report.*

Euromonitor International, Inc., 122 South Michigan Avenue, Suite 1200, Chicago, Illinois 60603 (800) 577-EURO; *The World Economic Factbook.*

Europa Publications Limited, 18 Bedford Square, London, WC1B 3JN, England; *The Europa World Year Book.*

Food and Agricultural Organization of the United Nations (FAO) Via delle Terme di Caracalla, 00100 Rome, Italy (Telephone Number in U.S. (202) 653-2400); *The State of Food and Agriculture.*

St. Martin's Press, Inc., 175 Fifth Avenue, New York, New York 10010 (800) 221-7945; *The Statesman's Year-Book.*

Statistical Office of the United Nations, Publishing Service, New York, New York 10017 (800) 253-9646; *International Trade Statistics Yearbook;* and *Statistical Yearbook.*

United Nations Conference on Trade and Development, Central Statistical Service, Palais des Nations, Geneva, Switzerland (Telephone in U.S. (800) 253-9646); *UNCTAD Commodity Yearbook.*

The World Bank, 1818 H Street, NW, Washington, D.C. 20433 (202) 477-1234; *World Development Indicators.*

VANUATU - FORESTRY AND FOREST PRODUCTS

Food and Agricultural Organization of

the United Nations (FAO) Via delle Terme di Caracalla, 00100 Rome, Italy (Telephone Number in U.S. (202) 653-2400); *The State of Food and Agriculture;* and *Yearbook of Forest Products.*

St. Martin's Press, Inc., 175 Fifth Avenue, New York, New York 10010 (800) 221-7945; *The Statesman's Year-Book.*

Statistical Office of the United Nations, Publishing Service, New York, New York 10017 (800) 253-9646; *Statistical Yearbook.*

United Nations Conference on Trade and Development, Central Statistical Service, Palais des Nations, Geneva, Switzerland (Telephone in U.S. (800) 253-9646); *UNCTAD Commodity Yearbook.*

VANUATU - GENERAL MORTALITY - See VANUATU - MORTALITY

VANUATU - GOLD HOLDINGS

The World Bank, 1818 H Street, NW, Washington, D.C. 20433 (202) 477-1234; *World Development Indicators.*

VANUATU - GOVERNMENT

Central Intelligence Agency, Washington, D.C. 20505 (703) 482-1100, www.cia.gov; *The World Factbook.*

Europa Publications Limited, 18 Bedford Square, London, WC1B 3JN, England; *The Europa World Year Book.*

St. Martin's Press, Inc., 175 Fifth Avenue, New York, New York 10010 (800) 221-7945; *The Statesman's Year-Book.*

Statistical Office of the United Nations, Publishing Service, New York, New York 10017 (800) 253-9646; *Asia-Pacific in Figures;* and *National Accounts Statistics.*

The World Bank, 1818 H Street, NW, Washington, D.C. 20433 (202) 477-1234; *World Development Indicators.*

VANUATU - GRAIN PRODUCTION - See VANUATU - CROPS

VANUATU - GROSS DOMESTIC PRODUCT

Economist Intelligence Unit, 111 West 57th Street, New York, New York 10019 (800) 938-4685; *Vanuatu Country Report.*

Euromonitor International, Inc., 122 South Michigan Avenue, Suite 1200, Chicago, Illinois 60603 (800) 577-EURO; *International Marketing Data and Statistics;* and *The World Economic Factbook.*

Statistical Office of the United Nations, Publishing Service, New York, New York 10017 (800) 253-9646; *Human Development Report;* and *National*

Accounts Statistics.

The World Bank, 1818 H Street, NW, Washington, D.C. 20433 (202) 477-1234; *World Development Indicators.*

VANUATU - GROSS NATIONAL PRODUCT

Europa Publications Limited, 18 Bedford Square, London, WC1B 3JN, England; *The Europa World Year Book.*

St. Martin's Press, Inc., 175 Fifth Avenue, New York, New York 10010 (800) 221-7945; *The Statesman's Year-Book.*

The World Bank, 1818 H Street, NW, Washington, D.C. 20433 (202) 477-1234; *The World Bank Atlas;* and *World Development Indicators.*

VANUATU - GROUNDNUT PRODUCTION - See VANUATU - CROPS

VANUATU - HEALTH

Euromonitor International, Inc., 122 South Michigan Avenue, Suite 1200, Chicago, Illinois 60603 (800) 577-EURO; *World Marketing Data and Statistics.*

St. Martin's Press, Inc., 175 Fifth Avenue, New York, New York 10010 (800) 221-7945; *The Statesman's Year-Book.*

Statistical Office of the United Nations, Publishing Service, New York, New York 10017 (800) 253-9646; *Asia-Pacific in Figures; Human Development Report;* and *Statistical Yearbook.*

VANUATU - HIDE PRODUCTION

Food and Agricultural Organization of the United Nations (FAO), Via delle Terme di Caracalla, 00100 Rome, Italy (Telephone Number in U.S. (202) 653-2400); *Production Yearbook.*

VANUATU - HIGHWAYS

Central Intelligence Agency, Washington, D.C. 20505 (703) 482-1100, www.cia.gov; *The World Factbook.*

St. Martin's Press, Inc., 175 Fifth Avenue, New York, New York 10010 (800) 221-7945; *The Statesman's Year-Book.*

VANUATU - HORSES - See VANUATU - LIVESTOCK AND POULTRY

VANUATU - HOUSING AND HOUSING UNITS

Euromonitor International, Inc., 122 South Michigan Avenue, Suite 1200, Chicago, Illinois 60603 (800) 577-EURO; *World Marketing Data and Statistics.*

VANUATU - ILLITERATE POPULATION

Central Intelligence Agency, Washington, D.C. 20505 (703) 482-1100, www.cia.gov; *The World Factbook.*

Euromonitor International, Inc., 122 South Michigan Avenue, Suite 1200, Chicago, Illinois 60603 (800) 577-EURO; *The World Economic Factbook.*

Statistical Office of the United Nations, Publishing Service, New York, New York 10017 (800) 253-9646; *Asia-Pacific in Figures;* and *Human Development Report.*

VANUATU - IMPORTS

Central Intelligence Agency, Washington, D.C. 20505 (703) 482-1100, www.cia.gov; *The World Factbook.*

Economist Intelligence Unit, 111 West 57th Street, New York, New York 10019 (800) 938-4685; *Vanuatu Country Report.*

Euromonitor International, Inc., 122 South Michigan Avenue, Suite 1200, Chicago, Illinois 60603 (800) 577-EURO; *International Marketing Data and Statistics;* and *The World Economic Factbook.*

Europa Publications Limited, 18 Bedford Square, London, WC1B 3JN, England; *The Europa World Year Book.*

Food and Agricultural Organization of the United Nations (FAO) Via delle Terme di Caracalla, 00100 Rome, Italy (Telephone Number in U.S. (202) 653-2400); *The State of Food and Agriculture.*

International Monetary Fund, 700 Nineteenth Street, NW, Washington, D.C. 20431 (202) 623-7000; *Direction of Trade Statistics.*

St. Martin's Press, Inc., 175 Fifth Avenue, New York, New York 10010 (800) 221-7945; *The Statesman's Year-Book.*

United Nations Conference on Trade and Development (UNCTAD), New York, New York 10017 (800) 253-9646; *Handbook of International Trade and Development Statistics.*

The World Bank, 1818 H Street, NW, Washington, D.C. 20433 (202) 477-1234; *World Development Indicators.*

VANUATU - INDUSTRY

Central Intelligence Agency, Washington, D.C. 20505 (703) 482-1100, www.cia.gov; *The World Factbook.*

Economist Intelligence Unit, 111 West 57th Street, New York, New York 10019 (800) 938-4685; *Vanuatu Country Report.*

Euromonitor International, Inc., 122 South Michigan Avenue, Suite 1200,

Chicago, Illinois 60603 (800) 577-EURO; *World Marketing Data and Statistics.*

Europa Publications Limited, 18 Bedford Square, London, WC1B 3JN, England; *The Europa World Year Book.*

St. Martin's Press, Inc., 175 Fifth Avenue, New York, New York 10010 (800) 221-7945; *The Statesman's Year-Book.*

Statistical Office of the United Nations, Publishing Service, New York, New York 10017 (800) 253-9646; *Asia-Pacific in Figures.*

The World Bank, 1818 H Street, NW, Washington, D.C. 20433 (202) 477-1234; *World Development Indicators.*

VANUATU - INFANT AND MATERNAL MORTALITY - See VANUATU - MORTALITY

VANUATU - INTERNATIONAL RESERVES EXCLUDING GOLD

The World Bank, 1818 H Street, NW, Washington, D.C. 20433 (202) 477-1234; *World Development Indicators.*

VANUATU - LABOR

Central Intelligence Agency, Washington, D.C. 20505 (703) 482-1100, www.cia.gov; *The World Factbook.*

Euromonitor International, Inc., 122 South Michigan Avenue, Suite 1200, Chicago, Illinois 60603 (800) 577-EURO; *International Marketing Data and Statistics;* and *World Marketing Data and Statistics.*

Europa Publications Limited, 18 Bedford Square, London, WC1B 3JN, England; *The Europa World Year Book.*

Food and Agricultural Organization of the United Nations (FAO) Via delle Terme di Caracalla, 00100 Rome, Italy (Telephone Number in U.S. (202) 653-2400); *The State of Food and Agriculture.*

St. Martin's Press, Inc., 175 Fifth Avenue, New York, New York 10010 (800) 221-7945; *The Statesman's Year-Book.*

Statistical Office of the United Nations, Publishing Service, New York, New York 10017 (800) 253-9646; *Human Development Report.*

The World Bank, 1818 H Street, NW, Washington, D.C. 20433 (202) 477-1234; *The World Bank Atlas;* and *World Development Indicators.*

VANUATU - LAND USE

Central Intelligence Agency, Washington, D.C. 20505 (703) 482-1100, www.cia.gov; *The World Factbook.*

Euromonitor International, Inc., 122 South Michigan Avenue, Suite 1200, Chicago, Illinois 60603 (800) 577-EURO; *International Marketing Data and Statistics.*

Food and Agricultural Organization of the United Nations (FAO), Via delle Terme di Caracalla, 00100 Rome, Italy (Telephone Number in U.S. (202) 653-2400); *Production Yearbook.*

VANUATU - LIFE EXPECTANCY

Central Intelligence Agency, Washington, D.C. 20505 (703) 482-1100, www.cia.gov; *The World Factbook.*

Euromonitor International, Inc., 122 South Michigan Avenue, Suite 1200, Chicago, Illinois 60603 (800) 577-EURO; *The World Economic Factbook.*

Statistical Office of the United Nations, Publishing Service, New York, New York 10017 (800) 253-9646; *Asia-Pacific in Figures; Human Development Report;* and *World Statistics Pocketbook.*

The World Bank, 1818 H Street, NW, Washington, D.C. 20433 (202) 477-1234; *The World Bank Atlas.*

VANUATU - LITERACY RATE

Euromonitor International, Inc., 122 South Michigan Avenue, Suite 1200, Chicago, Illinois 60603 (800) 577-EURO; *World Marketing Data and Statistics.*

VANUATU - LIVESTOCK AND POULTRY

Europa Publications Limited, 18 Bedford Square, London, WC1B 3JN, England; *The Europa World Year Book.*

Food and Agricultural Organization of the United Nations (FAO), Via delle Terme di Caracalla, 00100 Rome, Italy (Telephone Number in U.S. (202) 653-2400); *Production Yearbook;* and *The State of Food and Agriculture.*

St. Martin's Press, Inc., 175 Fifth Avenue, New York, New York 10010 (800) 221-7945; *The Statesman's Year-Book.*

Statistical Office of the United Nations, Publishing Service, New York, New York 10017 (800) 253-9646; *Statistical Yearbook.*

United Nations Conference on Trade and Development, Central Statistical Service, Palais des Nations, Geneva, Switzerland (Telephone in U.S. (800) 253-9646); *UNCTAD Commodity Yearbook.*

VANUATU - MAIL - NUMBER OF ITEMS SENT OR RECEIVED

Statistical Office of the United Nations, Publishing Service, New York, New York

10017 (800) 253-9646; *Statistical Yearbook.*

VANUATU - MANGANESE PRODUCTION AND CONSUMPTION - See VANUATU - MINING AND MINERAL PRODUCTS

VANUATU - MANUFACTURING

The World Bank, 1818 H Street, NW, Washington, D.C. 20433 (202) 477-1234; *World Development Indicators.*

VANUATU - MARRIAGE RATES

Statistical Office of the United Nations, Publishing Service, New York, New York 10017 (800) 253-9646; *Demographic Yearbook.*

VANUATU - MEAT PRODUCTION - See VANUATU - LIVESTOCK AND POULTRY

VANUATU - MERCHANT SHIPPING

St. Martin's Press, Inc., 175 Fifth Avenue, New York, New York 10010 (800) 221-7945; *The Statesman's Year-Book.*

Statistical Office of the United Nations, Publishing Service, New York, New York 10017 (800) 253-9646; *Statistical Yearbook.*

U.S. Department of Transportation, Maritime Administration, 400 Seventh Street, SW, Washington, D.C. 20590 (202) 366-5807, www.marad.dot.gov; *A Statistical Analysis of the World's Merchant Fleets.*

VANUATU - MILITARY

Central Intelligence Agency, Washington, D.C. 20505 (703) 482-1100, www.cia.gov; *The World Factbook.*

Euromonitor International, Inc., 122 South Michigan Avenue, Suite 1200, Chicago, Illinois 60603 (800) 577-EURO; *World Marketing Data and Statistics.*

St. Martin's Press, Inc., 175 Fifth Avenue, New York, New York 10010 (800) 221-7945; *The Statesman's Year-Book.*

Statistical Office of the United Nations, Publishing Service, New York, New York 10017 (800) 253-9646; *Human Development Report.*

VANUATU - MINING AND MINERAL PRODUCTS

Europa Publications Limited, 18 Bedford Square, London, WC1B 3JN, England; *The Europa World Year Book.*

Statistical Office of the United Nations, Publishing Service, New York, New York 10017 (800) 253-9646; *Statistical Yearbook.*

United Nations Conference on Trade

and Development, Central Statistical Service, Palais des Nations, Geneva, Switzerland (Telephone in U.S. (800) 253-9646); *UNCTAD Commodity Yearbook.*

VANUATU - MONEY SUPPLY

Economist Intelligence Unit, 111 West 57th Street, New York, New York 10019 (800) 938-4685; *Vanuatu Country Report.*

The World Bank, 1818 H Street, NW, Washington, D.C. 20433 (202) 477-1234; *World Development Indicators.*

VANUATU - MORTALITY

Central Intelligence Agency, Washington, D.C. 20505 (703) 482-1100, www.cia.gov; *The World Factbook.*

Euromonitor International, Inc., 122 South Michigan Avenue, Suite 1200, Chicago, Illinois 60603 (800) 577-EURO; *International Marketing Data and Statistics;* and *The World Economic Factbook.*

Europa Publications Limited, 18 Bedford Square, London, WC1B 3JN, England; *The Europa World Year Book.*

Statistical Office of the United Nations, Publishing Service, New York, New York 10017 (800) 253-9646; *Asia-Pacific in Figures; Demographic Yearbook; Human Development Report; Statistical Yearbook;* and *World Statistics Pocketbook.*

The World Bank, 1818 H Street, NW, Washington, D.C. 20433 (202) 477-1234; *The World Bank Atlas;* and *World Development Indicators.*

VANUATU - MOTION PICTURES

Statistical Office of the United Nations, Publishing Service, New York, New York 10017 (800) 253-9646; *Statistical Yearbook.*

VANUATU - MOTOR VEHICLES IN USE

Statistical Office of the United Nations, Publishing Service, New York, New York 10017 (800) 253-9646; *Statistical Yearbook.*

VANUATU - NATALITY - See VANUATU - BIRTH RATE

VANUATU - NATIONAL ACCOUNTS

Europa Publications Limited, 18 Bedford Square, London, WC1B 3JN, England; *The Europa World Year Book.*

Statistical Office of the United Nations, Publishing Service, New York, New York 10017 (800) 253-9646; *Asia-Pacific in Figures.*

VANUATU - NATIONAL INCOME

Statistical Office of the United Nations, Publishing Service, New York, New York 10017 (800) 253-9646; *National Accounts Statistics.*

VANUATU - NEWSPAPER PRODUCTION - See VANUATU - FORESTRY AND FOREST PRODUCTS

VANUATU - PESTICIDE USE

Food and Agricultural Organization of the United Nations (FAO) Via delle Terme di Caracalla, 00100 Rome, Italy (Telephone Number in U.S. (202) 653-2400); *The State of Food and Agriculture.*

VANUATU - PETROLEUM INDUSTRY

Food and Agricultural Organization of the United Nations (FAO) Via delle Terme di Caracalla, 00100 Rome, Italy (Telephone Number in U.S. (202) 653-2400); *The State of Food and Agriculture.*

United Nations Conference on Trade and Development, Central Statistical Service, Palais des Nations, Geneva, Switzerland (Telephone in U.S. (800) 253-9646); *UNCTAD Commodity Yearbook.*

VANUATU - PIGS - See VANUATU - LIVESTOCK AND POULTRY

VANUATU - POPULATION

Central Intelligence Agency, Washington, D.C. 20505 (703) 482-1100, www.cia.gov; *The World Factbook.*

Economist Intelligence Unit, 111 West 57th Street, New York, New York 10019 (800) 938-4685; *Vanuatu Country Report.*

Euromonitor International, Inc., 122 South Michigan Avenue, Suite 1200, Chicago, Illinois 60603 (800) 577-EURO; *International Marketing Data and Statistics;* and *The World Economic Factbook.*

Europa Publications Limited, 18 Bedford Square, London, WC1B 3JN, England; *The Europa World Year Book.*

Food and Agricultural Organization of the United Nations (FAO), Via delle Terme di Caracalla, 00100 Rome, Italy (Telephone Number in U.S. (202) 653-2400); *Production Yearbook.*

St. Martin's Press, Inc., 175 Fifth Avenue, New York, New York 10010 (800) 221-7945; *The Statesman's Year-Book.*

Statistical Office of the United Nations, Publishing Service, New York, New York 10017 (800) 253-9646; *Asia-Pacific in Figures; Demographic Yearbook; Human Development Report; Statistical Yearbook;* and *World Statistics Pocketbook.*

United Nations Educational, Scientific and Cultural Organization (UNESCO), 7 Place de Fontenoy, F-75700 Paris, France (Telephone Number in U.S. (212) 963-5981); *Statistical Yearbook.*

The World Bank, 1818 H Street, NW, Washington, D.C. 20433 (202) 477-1234; *The World Bank Atlas.*

VANUATU - POST OFFICES

St. Martin's Press, Inc., 175 Fifth Avenue, New York, New York 10010 (800) 221-7945; *The Statesman's Year-Book.*

VANUATU - PRICES

Food and Agricultural Organization of the United Nations (FAO), Via delle Terme di Caracalla, 00100 Rome, Italy (Telephone Number in U.S. (202) 653-2400); *Production Yearbook;* and *The State of Food and Agriculture.*

VANUATU - RADIO RECEIVERS

St. Martin's Press, Inc., 175 Fifth Avenue, New York, New York 10010 (800) 221-7945; *The Statesman's Year-Book.*

VANUATU - RELIGION

Central Intelligence Agency, Washington, D.C. 20505 (703) 482-1100, www.cia.gov; *The World Factbook.*

St. Martin's Press, Inc., 175 Fifth Avenue, New York, New York 10010 (800) 221-7945; *The Statesman's Year-Book.*

VANUATU - RETAIL PRICE INDEX

Europa Publications Limited, 18 Bedford Square, London, WC1B 3JN, England; *The Europa World Year Book.*

VANUATU - RETAIL TRADE

Euromonitor International, Inc., 122 South Michigan Avenue, Suite 1200, Chicago, Illinois 60603 (800) 577-EURO; *World Marketing Data and Statistics.*

VANUATU - ROOT AND TUBER PRODUCTION - See VANUATU - CROPS

VANUATU - ROUNDWOOD PRODUCTION - See VANUATU - FORESTRY AND FOREST PRODUCTS

VANUATU - SAWNWOOD PRODUCTION - See VANUATU - FORESTRY AND FOREST PRODUCTS

VANUATU - SCIENCE AND TECHNOLOGY - EXPENDITURE FOR RESEARCH - See VANUATU - SCIENTISTS, TECHNICIANS AND ENGINEERS

VANUATU - SCIENTISTS, TECHNICIANS

AND ENGINEERS

Statistical Office of the United Nations, Publishing Service, New York, New York 10017 (800) 253-9646; *Statistical Yearbook.*

VANUATU - SOCIAL DATA

Statistical Office of the United Nations, Publishing Service, New York, New York 10017 (800) 253-9646; *World Statistics Pocketbook.*

VANUATU - SOCIAL SECURITY

Statistical Office of the United Nations, Publishing Service, New York, New York 10017 (800) 253-9646; *National Accounts Statistics.*

VANUATU - STOCKS - COMMODITY - MARKET PRICE - INDEX

Food and Agricultural Organization of the United Nations (FAO) Via delle Terme di Caracalla, 00100 Rome, Italy (Telephone Number in U.S. (202) 653-2400); *The State of Food and Agriculture.*

VANUATU - TAXATION

Europa Publications Limited, 18 Bedford Square, London, WC1B 3JN, England; *The Europa World Year Book.*

The World Bank, 1818 H Street, NW, Washington, D.C. 20433 (202) 477-1234; *World Development Indicators.*

VANUATU - TELEPHONES IN USE

American Telephone and Telegraph Company, 26 Parsippany Road, Whippany, New Jersey 07981 (800) 222-0300; *The World's Telephones.*

Central Intelligence Agency, Washington, D.C. 20505 (703) 482-1100, www.cia.gov; *The World Factbook.*

St. Martin's Press, Inc., 175 Fifth Avenue, New York, New York 10010 (800) 221-7945; *The Statesman's Year-Book.*

Statistical Office of the United Nations, Publishing Service, New York, New York 10017 (800) 253-9646; *World Statistics Pocketbook.*

VANUATU - TEXTILE INDUSTRY

United Nations Conference on Trade and Development, Central Statistical Service, Palais des Nations, Geneva, Switzerland (Telephone in U.S. (800) 253-9646); *UNCTAD Commodity Yearbook.*

VANUATU - TOURISM

Euromonitor International, Inc., 122 South Michigan Avenue, Suite 1200,

Chicago, Illinois 60603 (800) 577-EURO; *The World Economic Factbook;* and *World Marketing Data and Statistics.*

St. Martin's Press, Inc., 175 Fifth Avenue, New York, New York 10010 (800) 221-7945; *The Statesman's Year-Book.*

Statistical Office of the United Nations, Publishing Service, New York, New York 10017 (800) 253-9646; *Statistical Yearbook.*

World Tourism Organization, Calle Capitan Haya 42, E-28020 Madrid, Spain; *Yearbook of Tourism Statistics.*

VANUATU - TRACTORS IN USE

Statistical Office of the United Nations, Publishing Service, New York, New York 10017 (800) 253-9646; *Statistical Yearbook.*

VANUATU - TRADE - See VANUATU - FOREIGN TRADE

VANUATU - TRANSPORTATION AND COMMUNICATIONS

Central Intelligence Agency, Washington, D.C. 20505 (703) 482-1100, www.cia.gov; *The World Factbook.*

Euromonitor International, Inc., 122 South Michigan Avenue, Suite 1200, Chicago, Illinois 60603 (800) 577-EURO; *International Marketing Data and Statistics;* and *World Marketing Data and Statistics.*

St. Martin's Press, Inc., 175 Fifth Avenue, New York, New York 10010 (800) 221-7945; *The Statesman's Year-Book.*

Statistical Office of the United Nations, Publishing Service, New York, New York 10017 (800) 253-9646; *Human Development Report.*

VANUATU - UNEMPLOYMENT RATE

Central Intelligence Agency, Washington, D.C. 20505 (703) 482-1100, www.cia.gov; *The World Factbook.*

VANUATU - VITAL STATISTICS

Statistical Office of the United Nations, Publishing Service, New York, New York 10017 (800) 253-9646; *Statistical Yearbook.*

VCRS

Electronic Industries Association, 2500 Wilson Boulevard, Arlington, Virginia 22201 (703) 907-7500; *Electronic Market Data Book.*

Television Bureau of Advertising, Inc., 3 East 54th Street, New York, New York 10022 (212) 486-1111; *Trends in Television.*

VEAL - See also BEEF and MEAT AND MEAT

PRODUCTS

VEAL

U.S. Department of Agriculture, Economic Research Service, 1800 M Street, NW, Washington, D.C. 20036 (202) 694-5050, www.ers.usda.gov; *Food Consumption, Prices and Expenditures;* and *Agricultural Outlook.*

VEGETABLE OILS - See OILS

VEGETABLES - See also Individual Commodities

VEGETABLES - ACREAGE

U.S. Department of Agriculture, National Agricultural Statistics Service, Fourteenth Street and Independence Avenue, SW, Washington, D.C. 20250 (800) 727-9540, www.usda.gov/nass; *Agricultural Statistics;* and *Vegetables.*

VEGETABLES - CONSUMER EXPENDITURES

U.S. Department of Labor, Bureau of Labor Statistics, 2 Massachusetts Avenue, NE, Washington, D.C. 20212 (202) 691-5200, www.stats.bls.gov; *Consumer Expenditures in 1997,* and unpublished data.

VEGETABLES - CONSUMPTION

U.S. Department of Agriculture, Economic Research Service, 1800 M Street, NW, Washington, D.C. 20036 (202) 694-5050, www.ers.usda.gov; *Agricultural Outlook; Food, Consumption, Prices and Expenditures; Vegetables and Specialties Situations and Outlook Yearbook;* and unpublished data.

VEGETABLES - FARM MARKETINGS - SALES

U.S. Department of Agriculture, Economic Research Service, 1800 M Street, NW, Washington, D.C. 20036 (202) 694-5050, www.ers.usda.gov; *Farm Business Economic Report.*

VEGETABLES - FOREIGN TRADE

U.S. Department of Agriculture, Economic Research Service, 1800 M Street, NW, Washington, D.C. 20036 (202) 694-5050, www.ers.usda.gov; *Food Consumption, Prices, and Expenditures; Foreign Agricultural Trade of the United States; Agricultural Statistics; Vegetables and Specialties Situation and Outlook Yearbook;* and *U.S. Agricultural Trade Update.*

U.S. Department of Commerce, Bureau of the Census, Washington, D.C. 20233 (301) 457-4100, www.census.gov; *U.S. Merchandise Trade.*

VEGETABLES - GARDENS

The National Gardening Association, 180 Flynn Avenue, Burlington, Vermont 05401 (802) 863-1308; *National Gardening Survey.*

VEGETABLES - PRICES

U.S. Department of Agriculture, National Agricultural Statistics Service, Fourteenth Street and Independence Avenue, SW, Washington, D.C. 20250 (800) 727-9540, www.usda.gov/nass; *Agricultural Prices: Annual Summary.*

U.S. Department of Labor, Bureau of Labor Statistics, Two Massachusetts Avenue, NE, Washington, D.C. 20212 (202) 691-5200, www.stats.bls.gov; *Monthly Labor Review; CPI Detailed Report;* and *Producer Price Indexes.*

VEGETABLES - PRODUCTION

U.S. Department of Agriculture, Economic Research Service, 1800 M Street, NW, Washington, D.C. 20036 (202) 694-5050, www.ers.usda.gov; *Agricultural Outlook;* and *Vegetables and Specialties Situation and Outlook Yearbook.*

U.S. Department of Agriculture, National Agricultural Statistics Service, Fourteenth Street and Independence Avenue, SW, Washington, D.C. 20250 (800) 727-9540, www.usda.gov/nass; *Vegetables;* and *Agricultural Statistics.*

VEHICLES - See MOTOR VEHICLES, TRACTORS, etc.

VENEREAL DISEASES - See also AIDS

U.S. Department of Health and Human Services, Center for Disease Control, 1600 Clifton Road, NE, Atlanta, Georgia 30333 (800) 311-3435, www.cdc.gov; *Summary of Notifiable Diseases, United States, Morbidity and Mortality Weekly Report.*

Venezuela - National Statistical Office

Oficina Central de Estadistica e Informatica, Presidencia de la Republica, Aptdo. de Correos 400 Carmelitas, Caracas 1050, Venezuela.

Venezuela - Primary Statistics Source

Oficina Central de Estadistica Informatica, Presidencia de la Republica, Aptdo. de Correos 400 Carmelitas, Caracas 1050, Venezuela; *Anuario estadistico* (Statistical Yearbook).

VENEZUELA - AGRICULTURE

The Economist Intelligence Unit, 111 West 57th Street, New York, New York 10019 (800) 938-4685; *Venezuela Country Report;* and *The New Latin America Market Atlas.*

Euromonitor International, Inc., 122 South Michigan Avenue, Suite 1200, Chicago, Illinois 60603 (800) 577-EURO; *International Marketing Data and Statistics;* and *World Marketing Data and Statistics.*

Europa Publications Limited, 18 Bedford Square, London, WC1B 3JN, England; *The Europa World Year Book.*

Food and Agricultural Organization of the United Nations (FAO) Via delle Terme di Caracalla, 00100 Rome, Italy (Telephone Number in U.S. (202) 653-2400); *Production Yearbook; The State of Food and Agriculture;* and *Trade Yearbook.*

Inter-American Development Bank, 1300 New York Avenue, NW, Washington, D.C. 20577 (202) 623-1753; *Economic and Social Progress in Latin America.*

M.E. Sharpe, 80 Business Park Drive, Armonk, New York 10504 (800) 541-6563; *The Illustrated Book of World Rankings.*

St. Martin's Press, Inc., 175 Fifth Avenue, New York, New York 10010 (800) 221-7945; *The Statesman's Year-Book.*

Statistical Office of the United Nations, Publishing Service, New York, New York 10017 (800) 253-9646; *Statistical Yearbook;* and *Statistical Yearbook for Latin America and the Caribbean.*

U.C.L.A. Latin American Center Publications, University of California, Los Angeles, California 90024 (310) 825-6634; *Statistical Abstract of Latin America.*

United Nations Conference on Trade and Development, Central Statistical Service, Palais des Nations, Geneva, Switzerland (Telephone in U.S. (800) 253-9646); *UNCTAD Commodity Yearbook.*

The World Bank, 1818 H Street, NW, Washington, D.C. 20433 (202) 477-1234; *World Development Indicators.*

VENEZUELA - AIRLINE SERVICE

The Economist Intelligence Unit, 111 West 57th Street, New York, New York 10019 (800) 938-4685; *The New Latin America Market Atlas.*

Europa Publications Limited, 18 Bedford Square, London, WC1B 3JN, England; *The Europa World Year Book.*

International Civil Aviation

Organization, 999 University Street, Montreal, Quebec, Canada H3C 5H7 (514) 954-8219; *Civil Aviation Statistics of the World.*

M.E. Sharpe, 80 Business Park Drive, Armonk, New York 10504 (800) 541-6563; *The Illustrated Book of World Rankings.*

St. Martin's Press, Inc., 175 Fifth Avenue, New York, New York 10010 (800) 221-7945; *The Statesman's Year-Book.*

Statistical Office of the United Nations, Publishing Service, New York, New York 10017 (800) 253-9646; *Statistical Yearbook.*

VENEZUELA - AIRPORTS

Central Intelligence Agency, Washington, D.C. 20505 (703) 482-1100, www.cia.gov; *The World Factbook.*

VENEZUELA - ALUMINUM PRODUCTION AND CONSUMPTION - See VENEZUELA - MINING AND MINERAL PRODUCTS

VENEZUELA - ANIMAL HEALTH

Food and Agricultural Organization of the United Nations (FAO), Via delle Terme di Caracalla, 00100 Rome, Italy (Telephone Number in U.S. (202) 653-2400); *Animal Health Yearbook.*

VENEZUELA - AREA AND DENSITY OF POPULATION

Central Intelligence Agency, Washington, D.C. 20505 (703) 482-1100, www.cia.gov; *The World Factbook.*

Euromonitor International, Inc., 122 South Michigan Avenue, Suite 1200, Chicago, Illinois 60603 (800) 577-EURO; *International Marketing Data and Statistics;* and *The World Economic Factbook.*

Europa Publications Limited, 18 Bedford Square, London, WC1B 3JN, England; *The Europa World Year Book.*

Food and Agricultural Organization of the United Nations (FAO) Via delle Terme di Caracalla, 00100 Rome, Italy (Telephone Number in U.S. (202) 653-2400); *The State of Food and Agriculture.*

Inter-American Development Bank, 1300 New York Avenue, NW, Washington, D.C. 20577 (202) 623-1753; *Economic and Social Progress in Latin America.*

M.E. Sharpe, 80 Business Park Drive, Armonk, New York 10504 (800) 541-6563; *The Illustrated Book of World Rankings.*

St. Martin's Press, Inc., 175 Fifth Avenue, New York, New York 10010 (800) 221-7945; *The Statesman's Year-Book.*

Statistical Office of the United Nations, Publishing Service, New York, New York 10017 (800) 253-9646; *Statistical Yearbook.*

United Nations Educational, Scientific and Cultural Organization (UNESCO), 7 Place de Fontenoy, F-75700 Paris, France (Telephone Number in U.S. (212) 963-5981); *Statistical Yearbook.*

The World Bank, 1818 H Street, NW, Washington, D.C. 20433 (202) 477-1234; *World Development Report.*

VENEZUELA - ARMS EXPORTS AND IMPORTS - See VENEZUELA - MILITARY

VENEZUELA - BALANCE OF PAYMENTS

The Economist Intelligence Unit, 111 West 57th Street, New York, New York 10019 (800) 938-4685; *The New Latin America Market Atlas;* and *The World Market Atlas.*

Europa Publications Limited, 18 Bedford Square, London, WC1B 3JN, England; *The Europa World Year Book.*

Inter-American Development Bank, 1300 New York Avenue, NW, Washington, D.C. 20577 (202) 623-1753; *Economic and Social Progress in Latin America.*

International Monetary Fund, 700 Nineteenth Street, NW, Washington, D.C. 20431 (202) 623-7000; *Balance of Payments Yearbook.*

Organization of American States (OAS), General Secretariat, Washington, D.C. 20006 (202) 458-3533; *Statistical Bulletin of the OAS.*

Statistical Office of the United Nations, Publishing Service, New York, New York 10017 (800) 253-9646; *Economic Survey of Latin America and the Caribbean;* and *Statistical Yearbook for Latin America and the Caribbean.*

U.C.L.A. Latin American Center Publications, University of California, Los Angeles, California 90024 (310) 825-6634; *Statistical Abstract of Latin America.*

United Nations Conference on Trade and Development (UNCTAD), New York, New York 10017 (800) 253-9646; *Handbook of International Trade and Development Statistics.*

The World Bank, 1818 H Street, NW, Washington, D.C. 20433 (202) 477-1234; *World Development Report;* and *World Development Indicators.*

VENEZUELA - BANANA PRODUCTION - See VENEZUELA - CROPS

VENEZUELA - BANKING

Euromonitor International, Inc., 122 South Michigan Avenue, Suite 1200, Chicago, Illinois 60603 (800) 577-EURO; *World Marketing Data and Statistics.*

Europa Publications Limited, 18 Bedford Square, London, WC1B 3JN, England; *The Europa World Year Book.*

Inter-American Development Bank, 1300 New York Avenue, NW, Washington, D.C. 20577 (202) 623-1753; *Economic and Social Progress in Latin America.*

International Monetary Fund, 700 Nineteenth Street, NW, Washington, D.C. 20431 (202) 623-7000; *Government Finance Statistics Yearbook;* and *International Financial Statistics.*

M.E. Sharpe, 80 Business Park Drive, Armonk, New York 10504 (800) 541-6563; *The Illustrated Book of World Rankings.*

St. Martin's Press, Inc., 175 Fifth Avenue, New York, New York 10010 (800) 221-7945; *The Statesman's Year-Book.*

Statistical Office of the United Nations, Publishing Service, New York, New York 10017 (800) 253-9646; *Statistical Yearbook;* and *Statistical Yearbook for Latin America and the Caribbean.*

VENEZUELA - BARLEY PRODUCTION - See VENEZUELA - CROPS

VENEZUELA - BEER PRODUCTION - See VENEZUELA - BEVERAGES

VENEZUELA - BEVERAGES

M.E. Sharpe, 80 Business Park Drive, Armonk, New York 10504 (800) 541-6563; *The Illustrated Book of World Rankings.*

Statistical Office of the United Nations, Publishing Service, New York, New York 10017 (800) 253-9646; *Statistical Yearbook.*

VENEZUELA - BIRTH RATES

Central Intelligence Agency, Washington, D.C. 20505 (703) 482-1100, www.cia.gov; *The World Factbook.*

Euromonitor International, Inc., 122 South Michigan Avenue, Suite 1200, Chicago, Illinois 60603 (800) 577-EURO; *International Marketing Data and Statistics;* and *The World Economic Factbook.*

Europa Publications Limited, 18 Bedford Square, London, WC1B 3JN, England; *The Europa World Year Book.*

M.E. Sharpe, 80 Business Park Drive, Armonk, New York 10504 (800) 541-6563; *The Illustrated Book of World Rankings.*

Statistical Office of the United Nations, Publishing Service, New York, New York 10017 (800) 253-9646; *Demographic Yearbook; Statistical Yearbook;* and *Statistical Yearbook for Latin America and the Caribbean.*

The World Bank, 1818 H Street, NW, Washington, D.C. 20433 (202) 477-1234; *World Development Indicators.*

World Health Organization, Office of Publications, 20 Avenue Appia, CH-1211 Geneva 27, Switzerland (Telephone Number in U.S. (518) 436-9686); *World Health Statistics Annual.*

VENEZUELA - BONDS

Inter-American Development Bank, 1300 New York Avenue, NW, Washington, D.C. 20577 (202) 623-1753; *Economic and Social Progress in Latin America.*

International Monetary Fund, 700 Nineteenth Street, NW, Washington, D.C. 20431 (202) 623-7000; *Government Finance Statistics Yearbook.*

VENEZUELA - BOOK PRODUCTION

Europa Publications Limited, 18 Bedford Square, London, WC1B 3JN, England; *The Europa World Year Book.*

VENEZUELA - BROADCASTING

Billboard Limited, P.O. Box 9027, 1006 AA Amsterdam, The Netherlands (Telephone Number in U.S. (212) 764-7300); *World Radio TV Handbook.*

Central Intelligence Agency, Washington, D.C. 20505 (703) 482-1100, www.cia.gov; *The World Factbook.*

Euromonitor International, Inc., 122 South Michigan Avenue, Suite 1200, Chicago, Illinois 60603 (800) 577-EURO; *World Marketing Data and Statistics.*

M.E. Sharpe, 80 Business Park Drive, Armonk, New York 10504 (800) 541-6563; *The Illustrated Book of World Rankings.*

St. Martin's Press, Inc., 175 Fifth Avenue, New York, New York 10010 (800) 221-7945; *The Statesman's Year-Book.*

VENEZUELA - BUDGET

Central Intelligence Agency, Washington, D.C. 20505 (703) 482-1100, www.cia.gov; *The World Factbook.*

VENEZUELA - BUSINESS

Inter-American Development Bank, 1300 New York Avenue, NW, Washington, D.C. 20577 (202) 623-1753; *Economic and Social Progress in Latin America.*

VENEZUELA - BUSINESS AND PROFESSIONAL LICENSES

International Monetary Fund, 700 Nineteenth Street, NW, Washington, D.C. 20431 (202) 623-7000; *Government Finance Statistics Yearbook.*

VENEZUELA - BUTTER PRODUCTION - See VENEZUELA - DAIRY PRODUCTS

VENEZUELA - CALORIE SUPPLY

Food and Agricultural Organization of the United Nations (FAO) Via delle Terme di Caracalla, 00100 Rome, Italy (Telephone Number in U.S. (202) 653-2400); *The State of Food and Agriculture.*

Statistical Office of the United Nations, Publishing Service, New York, New York 10017 (800) 253-9646; *Statistical Yearbook for Latin America and the Caribbean.*

VENEZUELA - CAPITAL INVESTMENT

Inter-American Development Bank, 1300 New York Avenue, NW, Washington, D.C. 20577 (202) 623-1753; *Economic and Social Progress in Latin America.*

VENEZUELA - CAPITAL REVENUE

Inter-American Development Bank, 1300 New York Avenue, NW, Washington, D.C. 20577 (202) 623-1753; *Economic and Social Progress in Latin America.*

International Monetary Fund, 700 Nineteenth Street, NW, Washington, D.C. 20431 (202) 623-7000; *Government Finance Statistics Yearbook.*

VENEZUELA - CATTLE - See VENEZUELA - LIVESTOCK AND POULTRY

VENEZUELA - CAUSTIC SODA PRODUCTION - See VENEZUELA - BEVERAGES

VENEZUELA - CEMENT PRODUCTION - See VENEZUELA - MINING AND MINERAL PRODUCTS

VENEZUELA - CHEESE PRODUCTION AND CONSUMPTION - See VENEZUELA -DAIRY PRODUCTS

VENEZUELA - CHEMICAL (ORGANIC) PRODUCTION - See VENEZUELA - MINING AND MINERAL PRODUCTS

VENEZUELA - CHICKENS - See VENEZUELA - LIVESTOCK AND POULTRY

VENEZUELA - CIGAR PRODUCTION

Statistical Office of the United Nations, Publishing Service, New York, New York 10017 (800) 253-9646; *Statistical Yearbook.*

VENEZUELA - CIGARETTE PRODUCTION

M.E. Sharpe, 80 Business Park Drive, Armonk, New York 10504 (800) 541-6563; *The Illustrated Book of World Rankings.*

Statistical Office of the United Nations, Publishing Service, New York, New York 10017 (800) 253-9646; *Statistical Yearbook.*

U.C.L.A. Latin American Center Publications, University of California, Los Angeles, California 90024 (310) 825-6634; *Statistical Abstract of Latin America.*

VENEZUELA - CLIMATE

M.E. Sharpe, 80 Business Park Drive, Armonk, New York 10504 (800) 541-6563; *The Illustrated Book of World Rankings.*

St. Martin's Press, Inc., 175 Fifth Avenue, New York, New York 10010 (800) 221-7945; *The Statesman's Year-Book.*

VENEZUELA - COAL PRODUCTION - See VENEZUELA - MINING AND MINERAL PRODUCTS

VENEZUELA - COCOA (BEANS) PRODUCTION - See VENEZUELA - CROPS

VENEZUELA - COFFEE - See VENEZUELA - CROPS

VENEZUELA - COMMERCE

St. Martin's Press, Inc., 175 Fifth Avenue, New York, New York 10010 (800) 221-7945; *The Statesman's Year-Book.*

VENEZUELA - COMMUNICATIONS - See VENEZUELA - TRANSPORTATION AND COMMUNICATIONS

VENEZUELA - CONSTRUCTION INDUSTRY

The Economist Intelligence Unit, 111 West 57th Street, New York, New York 10019 (800) 938-4685; *The New Latin America Market Atlas.*

Inter-American Development Bank, 1300 New York Avenue, NW, Washington, D.C. 20577 (202) 623-1753; *Economic and Social Progress in Latin America.*

M.E. Sharpe, 80 Business Park Drive, Armonk, New York 10504 (800) 541-6563; *The Illustrated Book of World Rankings.*

U.C.L.A. Latin American Center Publications, University of California, Los Angeles, California 90024 (310) 825-6634; *Statistical Abstract of Latin America.*

Statistical Office of the United Nations, Publishing Service, New York, New York 10017 (800) 253-9646; *Statistical Yearbook.*

VENEZUELA - CONSUMER PRICE INDEX

Europa Publications Limited, 18 Bedford Square, London, WC1B 3JN, England; *The Europa World Year Book.*

Statistical Office of the United Nations, Publishing Service, New York, New York 10017 (800) 253-9646; *Statistical Yearbook.*

VENEZUELA - CONSUMER PRICES

The Economist Intelligence Unit, 111 West 57th Street, New York, New York 10019 (800) 938-4685; *The New Latin America Market Atlas.*

Euromonitor International, Inc., 122 South Michigan Avenue, Suite 1200, Chicago, Illinois 60603 (800) 577-EURO; *World Marketing Data and Statistics.*

International Labour Office, I.L.O. Publications, 1828 L Street, NW, Suite 801, Washington, D.C. 20036 (301) 638-3152; *Yearbook of Labour Statistics.*

International Monetary Fund, 700 Nineteenth Street, NW, Washington, D.C. 20431 (202) 623-7000; *International Financial Statistics.*

Organization of American States (OAS), General Secretariat, Washington, D.C. 20006 (202) 458-3533; *Statistical Bulletin of the OAS.*

U.C.L.A. Latin American Center Publications, University of California, Los Angeles, California 90024 (310) 825-6634; *Statistical Abstract of Latin America.*

VENEZUELA - CONSUMPTION

The Economist Intelligence Unit, 111 West 57th Street, New York, New York 10019 (800) 938-4685; *The New Latin America Market Atlas.*

Inter-American Development Bank, 1300 New York Avenue, NW, Washington, D.C. 20577 (202) 623-1753; *Economic and Social Progress in Latin America.*

Statistical Office of the United Nations, Publishing Service, New York, New York 10017 (800) 253-9646; *Statistical Yearbook for Latin America and the Caribbean.*

The World Bank, 1818 H Street, NW, Washington, D.C. 20433 (202) 477-1234; *World Development Report.*

VENEZUELA - COOPERATIVES

U.C.L.A. Latin American Center Publications, University of California, Los Angeles, California 90024 (310) 825-6634; *Statistical Abstract of Latin America.*

VENEZUELA - COPPER PRODUCTION AND CONSUMPTION - See VENEZUELA - MINING AND MINERAL PRODUCTS

VENEZUELA - CORN PRODUCTION - See VENEZUELA - CROPS

VENEZUELA - CORPORATE INCOME TAXES - See VENEZUELA - TAXATION

VENEZUELA - CORPORATE TAXES - See VENEZUELA - TAXATION

VENEZUELA - COTTON - See VENEZUELA - CROPS

VENEZUELA - CRIME

International Criminal Police Organization (INTERPOL), 50 quai Achille Lignon, F-69006 Lyon, France; *International Crime Statistics.*

Yale University Press, Yale Station, New Haven, Connecticut 06520 (800) 987-7323; *Violence and Crime in Cross-National Perspective.*

VENEZUELA - CROPS

Commodity Research Bureau, Inc., 30 South Wacker Drive, Chicago, Illinois 60606 (312) 454-1801; *Commodity Year Book.*

The Economist Intelligence Unit, 111 West 57th Street, New York, New York 10019 (800) 938-4685; *The New Latin America Market Atlas.*

Europa Publications Limited, 18 Bedford Square, London, WC1B 3JN, England; *The Europa World Year Book.*

Food and Agricultural Organization of the United Nations (FAO) Via delle Terme di Caracalla, 00100 Rome, Italy (Telephone Number in U.S. (202) 653-2400); *Production Yearbook;* and *The State of Food and Agriculture.*

Inter-American Development Bank, 1300 New York Avenue, NW, Washington, D.C. 20577 (202) 623-1753; *Economic and Social Progress in Latin America.*

M.E. Sharpe, 80 Business Park Drive, Armonk, New York 10504 (800) 541-6563; *The Illustrated Book of World Rankings.*

St. Martin's Press, Inc., 175 Fifth Avenue, New York, New York 10010 (800) 221-7945; *The Statesman's Year-Book.*

Statistical Office of the United Nations, Publishing Service, New York, New York 10017 (800) 253-9646; *Statistical Yearbook.*

U.C.L.A. Latin American Center Publications, University of California, Los Angeles, California 90024 (310) 825-6634; *Statistical Abstract of Latin America.*

United Nations Conference on Trade and Development, Central Statistical Service, Palais des Nations, Geneva,

Switzerland (Telephone in U.S. (800) 253-9646); *UNCTAD Commodity Yearbook*.

VENEZUELA - CUSTOMS DUTIES

Inter-American Development Bank, 1300 New York Avenue, NW, Washington, D.C. 20577 (202) 623-1753; *Economic and Social Progress in Latin America*.

International Monetary Fund, 700 Nineteenth Street, NW, Washington, D.C. 20431 (202) 623-7000; *Government Finance Statistics Yearbook*.

St. Martin's Press, Inc., 175 Fifth Avenue, New York, New York 10010 (800) 221-7945; *The Statesman's Year-Book*.

VENEZUELA - DAIRY PRODUCTS

Europa Publications Limited, 18 Bedford Square, London, WC1B 3JN, England; *The Europa World Year Book*.

Food and Agricultural Organization of the United Nations (FAO) Via delle Terme di Caracalla, 00100 Rome, Italy (Telephone Number in U.S. (202) 653-2400); *Production Yearbook;* and *The State of Food and Agriculture*.

M.E. Sharpe, 80 Business Park Drive, Armonk, New York 10504 (800) 541-6563; *The Illustrated Book of World Rankings*.

St. Martin's Press, Inc., 175 Fifth Avenue, New York, New York 10010 (800) 221-7945; *The Statesman's Year-Book*.

Statistical Office of the United Nations, Publishing Service, New York, New York 10017 (800) 253-9646; *Statistical Yearbook*.

U.C.L.A. Latin American Center Publications, University of California, Los Angeles, California 90024 (310) 825-6634; *Statistical Abstract of Latin America*.

VENEZUELA - DEATH RATES - See VENEZUELA - MORTALITY

VENEZUELA - DEBT

The Economist Intelligence Unit, 111 West 57th Street, New York, New York 10019 (800) 938-4685; *The New Latin America Market Atlas*.

VENEZUELA - DEFENSE - See VENEZUELA - MILITARY

VENEZUELA - DEMOGRAPHY

The Economist Intelligence Unit, 111 West 57th Street, New York, New York 10019 (800) 938-4685; *The World Market Atlas*.

Euromonitor International, Inc., 122 South Michigan Avenue, Suite 1200,

Chicago, Illinois 60603 (800) 577-EURO; *International Marketing Data and Statistics; World Marketing Data and Statistics;* and *The World Economic Factbook*.

M.E. Sharpe, 80 Business Park Drive, Armonk, New York 10504 (800) 541-6563; *The Illustrated Book of World Rankings*.

Statistical Office of the United Nations, Publishing Service, New York, New York 10017 (800) 253-9646; *Human Development Report*.

VENEZUELA - DEVELOPMENT ASSISTANCE

Inter-American Development Bank, 1300 New York Avenue, NW, Washington, D.C. 20577 (202) 623-1753; *Economic and Social Progress in Latin America*.

Statistical Office of the United Nations, Publishing Service, New York, New York 10017 (800) 253-9646; *Statistical Yearbook*.

VENEZUELA - DIAMOND PRODUCTION - See VENEZUELA - MINING AND MINERAL PRODUCTS

VENEZUELA - DISCOUNT RATES - See VENEZUELA - BANKING

VENEZUELA - DISEASES - See VENEZUELA - HEALTH

VENEZUELA - DIVORCE RATES

M.E. Sharpe, 80 Business Park Drive, Armonk, New York 10504 (800) 541-6563; *The Illustrated Book of World Rankings*.

Statistical Office of the United Nations, Publishing Service, New York, New York 10017 (800) 253-9646; *Demographic Yearbook;* and *Statistical Yearbook*.

VENEZUELA - ECONOMY

Central Intelligence Agency, Washington, D.C. 20505 (703) 482-1100, www.cia.gov; *The World Factbook*.

Economist Intelligence Unit, 111 West 57th Street, New York, New York 10019 (800) 938-4685; *Venezuela Country Report*.

Euromonitor International, Inc., 122 South Michigan Avenue, Suite 1200, Chicago, Illinois 60603 (800) 577-EURO; *International Marketing Data and Statistics; World Marketing Data and Statistics;* and *The World Economic Factbook*.

Europa Publications Limited, 18 Bedford Square, London, WC1B 3JN, England; *The Europa World Year Book*.

Inter-American Development Bank, 1300 New York Avenue, NW, Washington, D.C. 20577 (202) 623-1753; *Economic and Social Progress in Latin America*.

M.E. Sharpe, 80 Business Park Drive, Armonk, New York 10504 (800) 541-6563; *The Illustrated Book of World Rankings*.

Organization of American States (OAS), General Secretariat, Washington, D.C. 20006 (202) 458-3533; *Statistical Bulletin of the OAS*.

St. Martin's Press, Inc., 175 Fifth Avenue, New York, New York 10010 (800) 221-7945; *The Statesman's Year-Book*.

Statistical Office of the United Nations, Publishing Service, New York, New York 10017 (800) 253-9646; *Economic Survey of Latin America and the Caribbean;* and *World Statistics Pocketbook*.

U.C.L.A. Latin American Center Publications, University of California, Los Angeles, California 90024 (310) 825-6634; *Statistical Abstract of Latin America*.

The World Bank, 1818 H Street, NW, Washington, D.C. 20433 (202) 477-1234; *The World Bank Atlas;* and *World Development Report*.

VENEZUELA - EDUCATION

The Economist Intelligence Unit, 111 West 57th Street, New York, New York 10019 (800) 938-4685; *The New Latin America Market Atlas;* and *The World Market Atlas*.

Euromonitor International, Inc., 122 South Michigan Avenue, Suite 1200, Chicago, Illinois 60603 (800) 577-EURO; *International Marketing Data and Statistics;* and *World Marketing Data and Statistics*.

Europa Publications Limited, 18 Bedford Square, London, WC1B 3JN, England; *The Europa World Year Book*.

International Monetary Fund, 700 Nineteenth Street, NW, Washington, D.C. 20431 (202) 623-7000; *Government Finance Statistics Yearbook*.

M.E. Sharpe, 80 Business Park Drive, Armonk, New York 10504 (800) 541-6563; *The Illustrated Book of World Rankings*.

St. Martin's Press, Inc., 175 Fifth Avenue, New York, New York 10010 (800) 221-7945; *The Statesman's Year-Book*.

Statistical Office of the United Nations, Publishing Service, New York, New York 10017 (800) 253-9646; *Human Development Report;* and *Statistical Yearbook for Latin America and the Caribbean*.

U.C.L.A. Latin American Center Publications, University of California, Los Angeles, California 90024 (310) 825-6634; *Statistical Abstract of Latin America*.

United Nations Educational, Scientific and Cultural Organization (UNESCO), 7 Place de Fontenoy, F-75700 Paris, France (Telephone Number in U.S. (212) 963-5981); *Statistical Yearbook.*

The World Bank, 1818 H Street, NW, Washington, D.C. 20433 (202) 477-1234; *World Development Report;* and *World Development Indicators.*

VENEZUELA - EGG PRODUCTION AND CONSUMPTION - See VENEZUELA - DAIRY PRODUCTS

VENEZUELA - ELECTRICITY

Central Intelligence Agency, Washington, D.C. 20505 (703) 482-1100, www.cia.gov; *The World Factbook.*

The Economist Intelligence Unit, 111 West 57th Street, New York, New York 10019 (800) 938-4685; *The New Latin America Market Atlas.*

Inter-American Development Bank, 1300 New York Avenue, NW, Washington, D.C. 20577 (202) 623-1753; *Economic and Social Progress in Latin America.*

M.E. Sharpe, 80 Business Park Drive, Armonk, New York 10504 (800) 541-6563; *The Illustrated Book of World Rankings.*

Penn Well Publishing Company, 1421 South Sheridan Road, P.O. Box 1260, Tulsa, Oklahoma 74101 (800) 752-9764; *International Energy Statistics Sourcebook.*

St. Martin's Press, Inc., 175 Fifth Avenue, New York, New York 10010 (800) 221-7945; *The Statesman's Year-Book.*

Statistical Office of the United Nations, Publishing Service, New York, New York 10017 (800) 253-9646; *Electric Power in Asia and the Pacific; Human Development Report;* and *Statistical Yearbook.*

VENEZUELA - EMPLOYMENT

Euromonitor International, Inc., 122 South Michigan Avenue, Suite 1200, Chicago, Illinois 60603 (800) 577-EURO; *International Marketing Data and Statistics.*

International Labour Office, I.L.O. Publications, 1828 L Street, NW, Suite 801, Washington, D.C. 20036 (301) 638-3152; *Yearbook of Labour Statistics.*

M.E. Sharpe, 80 Business Park Drive, Armonk, New York 10504 (800) 541-6563; *The Illustrated Book of World Rankings.*

Statistical Office of the United Nations, Publishing Service, New York, New York 10017 (800) 253-9646; *Statistical Yearbook;* and *Statistical Yearbook for Latin America and the Caribbean.*

U.C.L.A. Latin American Center Publications, University of California, Los Angeles, California 90024 (310) 825-6634; *Statistical Abstract of Latin America.*

VENEZUELA - ENERGY

The Economist Intelligence Unit, 111 West 57th Street, New York, New York 10019 (800) 938-4685; *The New Latin America Market Atlas.*

Euromonitor International, Inc., 122 South Michigan Avenue, Suite 1200, Chicago, Illinois 60603 (800) 577-EURO; *International Marketing Data and Statistics; World Marketing Data and Statistics;* and *The World Economic Factbook.*

Food and Agricultural Organization of the United Nations (FAO) Via delle Terme di Caracalla, 00100 Rome, Italy (Telephone Number in U.S. (202) 653-2400); *The State of Food and Agriculture.*

M.E. Sharpe, 80 Business Park Drive, Armonk, New York 10504 (800) 541-6563; *The Illustrated Book of World Rankings.*

Penn Well Publishing Company, 1421 South Sheridan Road, P.O. Box 1260, Tulsa, Oklahoma 74101 (800) 752-9764; *International Energy Statistics Sourcebook.*

St. Martin's Press, Inc., 175 Fifth Avenue, New York, New York 10010 (800) 221-7945; *The Statesman's Year-Book.*

Statistical Office of the United Nations, Publishing Service, New York, New York 10017 (800) 253-9646; *Energy Statistics Yearbook; Human Development Report; Statistical Yearbook; World Statistics Pocketbook;* and *Statistical Yearbook for Latin America and the Caribbean.*

U.C.L.A. Latin American Center Publications, University of California, Los Angeles, California 90024 (310) 825-6634; *Statistical Abstract of Latin America.*

The World Bank, 1818 H Street, NW, Washington, D.C. 20433 (202) 477-1234; *The World Bank Atlas;* and *World Development Report.*

VENEZUELA - ENVIRONMENT

Economist Intelligence Unit, 111 West 57th Street, New York, New York 10019 (800) 938-4685; *Venezuela Country Report.*

Statistical Office of the United Nations, Publishing Service, New York, New York 10017 (800) 253-9646; *World Statistics Pocketbook.*

VENEZUELA - EXCHANGE RATES

Central Intelligence Agency, Washington, D.C. 20505 (703) 482-1100,

www.cia.gov; *The World Factbook.*

Euromonitor International, Inc., 122 South Michigan Avenue, Suite 1200, Chicago, Illinois 60603 (800) 577-EURO; *International Marketing Data and Statistics;* and *The World Economic Factbook.*

Europa Publications Limited, 18 Bedford Square, London, WC1B 3JN, England; *The Europa World Year Book.*

Inter-American Development Bank, 1300 New York Avenue, NW, Washington, D.C. 20577 (202) 623-1753; *Economic and Social Progress in Latin America.*

International Civil Aviation Organization, 999 University Street, Montreal, Quebec, Canada H3C 5H7 (514) 954-8219; *Civil Aviation Statistics of the World.*

International Monetary Fund, 700 Nineteenth Street, NW, Washington, D.C. 20431 (202) 623-7000; *International Financial Statistics.*

Organization of American States (OAS), General Secretariat, Washington, D.C. 20006 (202) 458-3533; *Statistical Bulletin of the OAS.*

Organization of Petroleum Exporting Countries, Obere Donaustrasse 93, 1020 Vienna 2, Austria; *OPEC Annual Statistical Bulletin.*

Statistical Office of the United Nations, Publishing Service, New York, New York 10017 (800) 253-9646; *Statistical Yearbook;* and *World Statistics Pocketbook.*

U.C.L.A. Latin American Center Publications, University of California, Los Angeles, California 90024 (310) 825-6634; *Statistical Abstract of Latin America.*

VENEZUELA - EXCISE TAXES - See VENEZUELA - TAXATION

VENEZUELA - EXPORTS

Central Intelligence Agency, Washington, D.C. 20505 (703) 482-1100, www.cia.gov; *The World Factbook.*

The Economist Intelligence Unit, 111 West 57th Street, New York, New York 10019 (800) 938-4685; *The New Latin America Market Atlas; Venezuela Country Report;* and *The World Market Atlas.*

Euromonitor International, Inc., 122 South Michigan Avenue, Suite 1200, Chicago, Illinois 60603 (800) 577-EURO; *International Marketing Data and Statistics;* and *The World Economic Factbook.*

Europa Publications Limited, 18 Bedford Square, London, WC1B 3JN,

England; *The Europa World Year Book.*

Food and Agricultural Organization of the United Nations (FAO) Via delle Terme di Caracalla, 00100 Rome, Italy (Telephone Number in U.S. (202) 653-2400); *The State of Food and Agriculture.*

Inter-American Development Bank, 1300 New York Avenue, NW, Washington, D.C. 20577 (202) 623-1753; *Economic and Social Progress in Latin America.*

International Monetary Fund, 700 Nineteenth Street, NW, Washington, D.C. 20431 (202) 623-7000; *Direction of Trade Statistics;* and *International Financial Statistics.*

Organization of American States (OAS), General Secretariat, Washington, D.C. 20006 (202) 458-3533; *Statistical Bulletin of the OAS.*

Organization of Petroleum Exporting Countries, Obere Donaustrasse 93, 1020 Vienna 2, Austria; *OPEC Annual Statistical Bulletin.*

St. Martin's Press, Inc., 175 Fifth Avenue, New York, New York 10010 (800) 221-7945; *The Statesman's Year-Book.*

Statistical Office of the United Nations, Publishing Service, New York, New York 10017 (800) 253-9646; *Statistical Yearbook for Latin America and the Caribbean.*

United Nations Conference on Trade and Development (UNCTAD), New York, New York 10017 (800) 253-9646; *Handbook of International Trade and Development Statistics.*

The World Bank, 1818 H Street, NW, Washington, D.C. 20433 (202) 477-1234; *World Development Report;* and *World Development Indicators.*

VENEZUELA - EXTERNAL FINANCING

Inter-American Development Bank, 1300 New York Avenue, NW, Washington, D.C. 20577 (202) 623-1753; *Economic and Social Progress in Latin America.*

Statistical Office of the United Nations, Publishing Service, New York, New York 10017 (800) 253-9646; *Statistical Yearbook for Latin America and the Caribbean.*

VENEZUELA - EXTERNAL INDEBTEDNESS

Inter-American Development Bank, 1300 New York Avenue, NW, Washington, D.C. 20577 (202) 623-1753; *Economic and Social Progress in Latin America.*

Statistical Office of the United Nations, Publishing Service, New York, New York

10017 (800) 253-9646; *Statistical Yearbook for Latin America and the Caribbean.*

The World Bank, 1818 H Street, NW, Washington, D.C. 20433 (202) 477-1234; *World Development Report;* and *World Development Indicators.*

VENEZUELA - EXTERNAL TRADE

Euromonitor International, Inc., 122 South Michigan Avenue, Suite 1200, Chicago, Illinois 60603 (800) 577-EURO; *World Marketing Data and Statistics.*

Food and Agricultural Organization of the United Nations (FAO) Via delle Terme di Caracalla, 00100 Rome, Italy (Telephone Number in U.S. (202) 653-2400); *The State of Food and Agriculture.*

Inter-American Development Bank, 1300 New York Avenue, NW, Washington, D.C. 20577 (202) 623-1753; *Economic and Social Progress in Latin America.*

Statistical Office of the United Nations, Publishing Service, New York, New York 10017 (800) 253-9646; *Statistical Yearbook;* and *Statistical Yearbook for Latin America and the Caribbean.*

VENEZUELA - FABRIC PRODUCTION - See VENEZUELA - TEXTILE INDUSTRY

VENEZUELA - FAMILY PLANNING

U.C.L.A. Latin American Center Publications, University of California, Los Angeles, California 90024 (310) 825-6634; *Statistical Abstract of Latin America.*

VENEZUELA - FARM CROPS - See VENEZUELA - CROPS

VENEZUELA - FEMALE WORKING POPULATION - See VENEZUELA - EMPLOYMENT

VENEZUELA - FERTILITY RATES

Central Intelligence Agency, Washington, D.C. 20505 (703) 482-1100, www.cia.gov; *The World Factbook.*

M.E. Sharpe, 80 Business Park Drive, Armonk, New York 10504 (800) 541-6563; *The Illustrated Book of World Rankings.*

Statistical Office of the United Nations, Publishing Service, New York, New York 10017 (800) 253-9646; *Human Development Report.*

The World Bank, 1818 H Street, NW, Washington, D.C. 20433 (202) 477-1234; *The World Bank Atlas; World Development Report;* and *World Development Indicators.*

VENEZUELA - FERTILIZER PRODUCTION AND CONSUMPTION

The Economist Intelligence Unit, 111 West 57th Street, New York, New York 10019 (800) 938-4685; *The New Latin America Market Atlas.*

Food and Agricultural Organization of the United Nations (FAO), Via delle Terme di Caracalla, 00100 Rome, Italy (Telephone Number in U.S. (202) 653-2400); *Fertilizer Yearbook;* and *The State of Food and Agriculture.*

Statistical Office of the United Nations, Publishing Service, New York, New York 10017 (800) 253-9646; *Statistical Yearbook.*

VENEZUELA - FETAL MORTALITY - See VENEZUELA - MORTALITY

VENEZUELA - FIBRE PRODUCTION - See VENEZUELA - TEXTILE INDUSTRY

VENEZUELA - FILAMENT PRODUCTION - See VENEZUELA - TEXTILE INDUSTRY

VENEZUELA - FILM - See VENEZUELA - MOTION PICTURES

VENEZUELA - FINANCE

Economist Intelligence Unit, 111 West 57th Street, New York, New York 10019 (800) 938-4685; *Venezuela Country Report.*

Europa Publications Limited, 18 Bedford Square, London, WC1B 3JN, England; *The Europa World Year Book.*

Inter-American Development Bank, 1300 New York Avenue, NW, Washington, D.C. 20577 (202) 623-1753; *Economic and Social Progress in Latin America.*

International Monetary Fund, 700 Nineteenth Street, NW, Washington, D.C. 20431 (202) 623-7000; *Government Finance Statistics Yearbook;* and *International Financial Statistics.*

M.E. Sharpe, 80 Business Park Drive, Armonk, New York 10504 (800) 541-6563; *The Illustrated Book of World Rankings.*

Organization of American States (OAS), General Secretariat, Washington, D.C. 20006 (202) 458-3533; *Statistical Bulletin of the OAS.*

St. Martin's Press, Inc., 175 Fifth Avenue, New York, New York 10010 (800) 221-7945; *The Statesman's Year-Book.*

U.C.L.A. Latin American Center Publications, University of California, Los Angeles, California 90024 (310) 825-6634; *Statistical Abstract of Latin America.*

VENEZUELA - FISHERIES

Europa Publications Limited, 18 Bedford Square, London, WC1B 3JN,

England; *The Europa World Year Book.*

Food and Agricultural Organization of the United Nations (FAO) Via delle Terme di Caracalla, 00100 Rome, Italy (Telephone Number in U.S. (202) 653-2400); *The State of Food and Agriculture;* and *Yearbook of Fishery Statistics.*

Inter-American Development Bank, 1300 New York Avenue, NW, Washington, D.C. 20577 (202) 623-1753; *Economic and Social Progress in Latin America.*

M.E. Sharpe, 80 Business Park Drive, Armonk, New York 10504 (800) 541-6563; *The Illustrated Book of World Rankings.*

St. Martin's Press, Inc., 175 Fifth Avenue, New York, New York 10010 (800) 221-7945; *The Statesman's Year-Book.*

Statistical Office of the United Nations, Publishing Service, New York, New York 10017 (800) 253-9646; *Statistical Yearbook.*

U.C.L.A. Latin American Center Publications, University of California, Los Angeles, California 90024 (310) 825-6634; *Statistical Abstract of Latin America.*

United Nations Conference on Trade and Development, Central Statistical Service, Palais des Nations, Geneva, Switzerland (Telephone in U.S. (800) 253-9646); *UNCTAD Commodity Yearbook.*

VENEZUELA - FLOUR PRODUCTION

Statistical Office of the United Nations, Publishing Service, New York, New York 10017 (800) 253-9646; *Statistical Yearbook.*

VENEZUELA - FOOD

Euromonitor International, Inc., 122 South Michigan Avenue, Suite 1200, Chicago, Illinois 60603 (800) 577-EURO; *Retail Trade International.*

Food and Agricultural Organization of the United Nations (FAO) Via delle Terme di Caracalla, 00100 Rome, Italy (Telephone Number in U.S. (202) 653-2400); *The State of Food and Agriculture.*

Statistical Office of the United Nations, Publishing Service, New York, New York 10017 (800) 253-9646; *Human Development Report.*

VENEZUELA - FOREIGN AID

Inter-American Development Bank, 1300 New York Avenue, NW, Washington, D.C. 20577 (202) 623-1753; *Economic and Social Progress in Latin America.*

VENEZUELA - FOREIGN DEBT

The Economist Intelligence Unit, 111

West 57th Street, New York, New York 10019 (800) 938-4685; *The New Latin America Market Atlas.*

Inter-American Development Bank, 1300 New York Avenue, NW, Washington, D.C. 20577 (202) 623-1753; *Economic and Social Progress in Latin America.*

International Monetary Fund, 700 Nineteenth Street, NW, Washington, D.C. 20431 (202) 623-7000; *Government Finance Statistics Yearbook.*

St. Martin's Press, Inc., 175 Fifth Avenue, New York, New York 10010 (800) 221-7945; *The Statesman's Year-Book.*

VENEZUELA - FOREIGN INDEBTEDNESS

Inter-American Development Bank, 1300 New York Avenue, NW, Washington, D.C. 20577 (202) 623-1753; *Economic and Social Progress in Latin America.*

Statistical Office of the United Nations, Publishing Service, New York, New York 10017 (800) 253-9646; *Economic Survey of Latin America and the Caribbean.*

VENEZUELA - FOREIGN INVESTMENT

The Economist Intelligence Unit, 111 West 57th Street, New York, New York 10019 (800) 938-4685; *The New Latin America Market Atlas.*

VENEZUELA - FOREIGN TRADE

The Economist Intelligence Unit, 111 West 57th Street, New York, New York 10019 (800) 938-4685; *The New Latin America Market Atlas;* and *Venezuela Country Report.*

Euromonitor International, Inc., 122 South Michigan Avenue, Suite 1200, Chicago, Illinois 60603 (800) 577-EURO; *International Marketing Data and Statistics;* and *The World Economic Factbook.*

Europa Publications Limited, 18 Bedford Square, London, WC1B 3JN, England; *The Europa World Year Book.*

Food and Agricultural Organization of the United Nations (FAO) Via delle Terme di Caracalla, 00100 Rome, Italy (Telephone Number in U.S. (202) 653-2400); *The State of Food and Agriculture.*

Inter-American Development Bank, 1300 New York Avenue, NW, Washington, D.C. 20577 (202) 623-1753; *Economic and Social Progress in Latin America.*

M.E. Sharpe, 80 Business Park Drive, Armonk, New York 10504 (800) 541-6563; *The Illustrated Book of World Rankings.*

St. Martin's Press, Inc., 175 Fifth

Avenue, New York, New York 10010 (800) 221-7945; *The Statesman's Year-Book.*

Statistical Office of the United Nations, Publishing Service, New York, New York 10017 (800) 253-9646; *Economic Survey of Latin America and the Caribbean; International Trade Statistics Yearbook;* and *Statistical Yearbook.*

U.C.L.A. Latin American Center Publications, University of California, Los Angeles, California 90024 (310) 825-6634; *Statistical Abstract of Latin America.*

United Nations Conference on Trade and Development, Central Statistical Service, Palais des Nations, Geneva, Switzerland (Telephone in U.S. (800) 253-9646); *UNCTAD Commodity Yearbook.*

The World Bank, 1818 H Street, NW, Washington, D.C. 20433 (202) 477-1234; *World Development Report;* and *World Development Indicators.*

VENEZUELA - FORESTRY AND FOREST PRODUCTS

American Forest and Paper Association, 1111 Nineteenth Street, NW, Washington, D.C. 20036 (202) 463-2700; *Wood Pulp and Fiber Statistics.*

Europa Publications Limited, 18 Bedford Square, London, WC1B 3JN, England; *The Europa World Year Book.*

Food and Agricultural Organization of the United Nations (FAO) Via delle Terme di Caracalla, 00100 Rome, Italy (Telephone Number in U.S. (202) 653-2400); *The State of Food and Agriculture;* and *Yearbook of Forest Products.*

Inter-American Development Bank, 1300 New York Avenue, NW, Washington, D.C. 20577 (202) 623-1753; *Economic and Social Progress in Latin America.*

M.E. Sharpe, 80 Business Park Drive, Armonk, New York 10504 (800) 541-6563; *The Illustrated Book of World Rankings.*

St. Martin's Press, Inc., 175 Fifth Avenue, New York, New York 10010 (800) 221-7945; *The Statesman's Year-Book.*

Statistical Office of the United Nations, Publishing Service, New York, New York 10017 (800) 253-9646; *Statistical Yearbook.*

U.C.L.A. Latin American Center Publications, University of California, Los Angeles, California 90024 (310) 825-6634; *Statistical Abstract of Latin America.*

United Nations Conference on Trade and Development, Central Statistical Service, Palais des Nations, Geneva, Switzerland (Telephone in U.S. (800) 253-

9646); *UNCTAD Commodity Yearbook*.

United Nations Educational, Scientific and Cultural Organization (UNESCO), 7 Place de Fontenoy, F-75700 Paris, France (Telephone Number in U.S. (212) 963-5981); *Statistical Yearbook*.

The World Bank, 1818 H Street, NW, Washington, D.C. 20433 (202) 477-1234; *World Development Report*.

VENEZUELA - GARLIC PRODUCTION - See VENEZUELA - CROPS

VENEZUELA - GAS AND GAS LIQUIDS PRODUCTION - See VENEZUELA - MINING AND MINERAL PRODUCTS

VENEZUELA - GENERAL INDUSTRIAL STATISTICS - See VENEZUELA - INDUSTRY

VENEZUELA - GENERAL MORTALITY - See VENEZUELA - MORTALITY

VENEZUELA - GEOGRAPHIC DATA

M.E. Sharpe, 80 Business Park Drive, Armonk, New York 10504 (800) 541-6563; *The Illustrated Book of World Rankings*.

U.C.L.A. Latin American Center Publications, University of California, Los Angeles, California 90024 (310) 825-6634; *Statistical Abstract of Latin America*.

VENEZUELA - GOATS - See VENEZUELA - LIVESTOCK AND POULTRY

VENEZUELA - GOLD HOLDINGS

International Monetary Fund, 700 Nineteenth Street, NW, Washington, D.C. 20431 (202) 623-7000; *International Financial Statistics*.

Statistical Office of the United Nations, Publishing Service, New York, New York 10017 (800) 253-9646; *Statistical Yearbook*.

The World Bank, 1818 H Street, NW, Washington, D.C. 20433 (202) 477-1234; *World Development Indicators*.

VENEZUELA - GOLD PRODUCTION AND CONSUMPTION - See VENEZUELA - MINING AND MINERAL PRODUCTS

VENEZUELA - GOLD RESERVES

The Economist Intelligence Unit, 111 West 57th Street, New York, New York 10019 (800) 938-4685; *The New Latin America Market Atlas*.

VENEZUELA - GOVERNMENT

Central Intelligence Agency, Washington, D.C. 20505 (703) 482-1100, www.cia.gov; *The World Factbook*.

Europa Publications Limited, 18 Bedford Square, London, WC1B 3JN, England; *The Europa World Year Book*.

Inter-American Development Bank, 1300 New York Avenue, NW, Washington, D.C. 20577 (202) 623-1753; *Economic and Social Progress in Latin America*.

International Monetary Fund, 700 Nineteenth Street, NW, Washington, D.C. 20431 (202) 623-7000; *Government Finance Statistics Yearbook;* and *International Financial Statistics*.

St. Martin's Press, Inc., 175 Fifth Avenue, New York, New York 10010 (800) 221-7945; *The Statesman's Year-Book*.

Statistical Office of the United Nations, Publishing Service, New York, New York 10017 (800) 253-9646; *National Accounts Statistics*.

The World Bank, 1818 H Street, NW, Washington, D.C. 20433 (202) 477-1234; *World Development Report;* and *World Development Indicators*.

VENEZUELA - GRAIN PRODUCTION - See VENEZUELA - CROPS

VENEZUELA - GRANTS

International Monetary Fund, 700 Nineteenth Street, NW, Washington, D.C. 20431 (202) 623-7000; *Government Finance Statistics Yearbook*.

VENEZUELA - GREEN PEPPER AND CHILIE PRODUCTION - See VENEZUELA - CROPS

VENEZUELA - GROSS DOMESTIC PRODUCT

The Economist Intelligence Unit, 111 West 57th Street, New York, New York 10019 (800) 938-4685; *The New Latin America Market Atlas; Venezuela Country Report;* and *The World Market Atlas*.

Euromonitor International, Inc., 122 South Michigan Avenue, Suite 1200, Chicago, Illinois 60603 (800) 577-EURO; *International Marketing Data and Statistics;* and *The World Economic Factbook*.

Europa Publications Limited, 18 Bedford Square, London, WC1B 3JN, England; *The Europa World Year Book*.

Inter-American Development Bank, 1300 New York Avenue, NW, Washington, D.C. 20577 (202) 623-1753; *Economic and Social Progress in Latin America*.

M.E. Sharpe, 80 Business Park Drive, Armonk, New York 10504 (800) 541-6563; *The Illustrated Book of World Rankings*.

Organization of American States (OAS),

General Secretariat, Washington, D.C. 20006 (202) 458-3533; *Statistical Bulletin of the OAS*.

Statistical Office of the United Nations, Publishing Service, New York, New York 10017 (800) 253-9646; *Human Development Report; National Accounts Statistics; Statistical Yearbook;* and *Statistical Yearbook for Latin America and the Caribbean*.

U.C.L.A. Latin American Center Publications, University of California, Los Angeles, California 90024 (310) 825-6634; *Statistical Abstract of Latin America*.

The World Bank, 1818 H Street, NW, Washington, D.C. 20433 (202) 477-1234; *World Development Report;* and *World Development Indicators*.

VENEZUELA - GROSS NATIONAL PRODUCT

Euromonitor International, Inc., 122 South Michigan Avenue, Suite 1200, Chicago, Illinois 60603 (800) 577-EURO; *International Marketing Data and Statistics*.

Inter-American Development Bank, 1300 New York Avenue, NW, Washington, D.C. 20577 (202) 623-1753; *Economic and Social Progress in Latin America*.

Organization of Petroleum Exporting Countries, Obere Donaustrasse 93, 1020 Vienna 2, Austria; *OPEC Annual Statistical Bulletin*.

St. Martin's Press, Inc., 175 Fifth Avenue, New York, New York 10010 (800) 221-7945; *The Statesman's Year-Book*.

U.S. Arms Control and Disarmament Agency, 320 Twenty-first Street, NW, Washington, D.C. 20451 (202) 647-8677; *World Military Expenditures and Arms Transfers*.

The World Bank, 1818 H Street, NW, Washington, D.C. 20433 (202) 477-1234; *The World Bank Atlas; World Development Report;* and *World Development Indicators*.

VENEZUELA - GROUNDNUT PRODUCTION - See VENEZUELA - CROPS

VENEZUELA - HEALTH

The Economist Intelligence Unit, 111 West 57th Street, New York, New York 10019 (800) 938-4685; *The New Latin America Market Atlas*.

Euromonitor International, Inc., 122 South Michigan Avenue, Suite 1200, Chicago, Illinois 60603 (800) 577-EURO; *World Marketing Data and Statistics*.

M.E. Sharpe, 80 Business Park Drive, Armonk, New York 10504 (800) 541-6563;

The Illustrated Book of World Rankings.

St. Martin's Press, Inc., 175 Fifth Avenue, New York, New York 10010 (800) 221-7945; *The Statesman's Year-Book.*

Statistical Office of the United Nations, Publishing Service, New York, New York 10017 (800) 253-9646; *Human Development Report; Statistical Yearbook; and Statistical Yearbook for Latin America and the Caribbean.*

U.C.L.A. Latin American Center Publications, University of California, Los Angeles, California 90024 (310) 825-6634; *Statistical Abstract of Latin America.*

United Nations Children's Fund (UNICEF), 3 United Nations Plaza, New York, New York 10017 (800) 253-9646; *State of the World's Children.*

The World Bank, 1818 H Street, NW, Washington, D.C. 20433 (202) 477-1234; *World Development Report.*

World Health Organization, Office of Publications, 20 Avenue Appia, CH-1211 Geneva 27, Switzerland (Telephone Number in U.S. (518) 436-9686); *World Health Statistics Annual.*

VENEZUELA - HEALTH EXPENDITURES

International Monetary Fund, 700 Nineteenth Street, NW, Washington, D.C. 20431 (202) 623-7000; *Government Finance Statistics Yearbook.*

VENEZUELA - HIDE PRODUCTION

Food and Agricultural Organization of the United Nations (FAO), Via delle Terme di Caracalla, 00100 Rome, Italy (Telephone Number in U.S. (202) 653-2400); *Production Yearbook.*

VENEZUELA - HIGHWAYS

Central Intelligence Agency, Washington, D.C. 20505 (703) 482-1100, www.cia.gov; *The World Factbook.*

The Economist Intelligence Unit, 111 West 57th Street, New York, New York 10019 (800) 938-4685; *The New Latin America Market Atlas.*

St. Martin's Press, Inc., 175 Fifth Avenue, New York, New York 10010 (800) 221-7945; *The Statesman's Year-Book.*

VENEZUELA - HORSES - See VENEZUELA - LIVESTOCK AND POULTRY

VENEZUELA - HOURS OF WORK - See VENEZUELA - EMPLOYMENT

VENEZUELA - HOUSING AND HOUSING UNITS

Euromonitor International, Inc., 122 South Michigan Avenue, Suite 1200, Chicago, Illinois 60603 (800) 577-EURO; *World Marketing Data and Statistics.*

M.E. Sharpe, 80 Business Park Drive, Armonk, New York 10504 (800) 541-6563; *The Illustrated Book of World Rankings.*

Statistical Office of the United Nations, Publishing Service, New York, New York 10017 (800) 253-9646; *Statistical Yearbook for Latin America and the Caribbean.*

U.C.L.A. Latin American Center Publications, University of California, Los Angeles, California 90024 (310) 825-6634; *Statistical Abstract of Latin America.*

VENEZUELA - HOUSING EXPENDITURES

International Monetary Fund, 700 Nineteenth Street, NW, Washington, D.C. 20431 (202) 623-7000; *Government Finance Statistics Yearbook.*

VENEZUELA - HYDROCHLORIC ACID PRODUCTION

Statistical Office of the United Nations, Publishing Service, New York, New York 10017 (800) 253-9646; *Statistical Yearbook.*

VENEZUELA - ILLITERATE POPULATION

Central Intelligence Agency, Washington, D.C. 20505 (703) 482-1100, www.cia.gov; *The World Factbook.*

The Economist Intelligence Unit, 111 West 57th Street, New York, New York 10019 (800) 938-4685; *The New Latin America Market Atlas;* and *The World Market Atlas.*

Euromonitor International, Inc., 122 South Michigan Avenue, Suite 1200, Chicago, Illinois 60603 (800) 577-EURO; *The World Economic Factbook.*

Statistical Office of the United Nations, Publishing Service, New York, New York 10017 (800) 253-9646; *Human Development Report;* and *Statistical Yearbook for Latin America and the Caribbean.*

United Nations Educational, Scientific and Cultural Organization (UNESCO), 7 Place de Fontenoy, F-75700 Paris, France (Telephone Number in U.S. (212) 963-5981); *Statistical Yearbook.*

VENEZUELA - IMMIGRATION

U.C.L.A. Latin American Center Publications, University of California, Los Angeles, California 90024 (310) 825-6634; *Statistical Abstract of Latin America.*

VENEZUELA - IMPORTS

Central Intelligence Agency, Washington, D.C. 20505 (703) 482-1100, www.cia.gov; *The World Factbook.*

The Economist Intelligence Unit, 111 West 57th Street, New York, New York 10019 (800) 938-4685; *The New Latin America Market Atlas; Venezuela Country Report;* and *The World Market Atlas.*

Euromonitor International, Inc., 122 South Michigan Avenue, Suite 1200, Chicago, Illinois 60603 (800) 577-EURO; *International Marketing Data and Statistics;* and *The World Economic Factbook.*

Europa Publications Limited, 18 Bedford Square, London, WC1B 3JN, England; *The Europa World Year Book.*

Food and Agricultural Organization of the United Nations (FAO) Via delle Terme di Caracalla, 00100 Rome, Italy (Telephone Number in U.S. (202) 653-2400); *The State of Food and Agriculture.*

Inter-American Development Bank, 1300 New York Avenue, NW, Washington, D.C. 20577 (202) 623-1753; *Economic and Social Progress in Latin America.*

International Monetary Fund, 700 Nineteenth Street, NW, Washington, D.C. 20431 (202) 623-7000; *Direction of Trade Statistics; Government Finance Statistics Yearbook;* and *International Financial Statistics.*

Organization of American States (OAS), General Secretariat, Washington, D.C. 20006 (202) 458-3533; *Statistical Bulletin of the OAS.*

St. Martin's Press, Inc., 175 Fifth Avenue, New York, New York 10010 (800) 221-7945; *The Statesman's Year-Book.*

Statistical Office of the United Nations, Publishing Service, New York, New York 10017 (800) 253-9646; *Statistical Yearbook for Latin America and the Caribbean.*

United Nations Conference on Trade and Development (UNCTAD), New York, New York 10017 (800) 253-9646; *Handbook of International Trade and Development Statistics.*

The World Bank, 1818 H Street, NW, Washington, D.C. 20433 (202) 477-1234; *World Development Report;* and *World Development Indicators.*

VENEZUELA - INCOME DISTRIBUTION

Statistical Office of the United Nations, Publishing Service, New York, New York 10017 (800) 253-9646; *Statistical Yearbook for Latin America and the Caribbean.*

U.C.L.A. Latin American Center

Publications, University of California, Los Angeles, California 90024 (310) 825-6634; *Statistical Abstract of Latin America.*

VENEZUELA - INCOME TAXES - See VENEZUELA - TAXATION

VENEZUELA - INDUSTRIAL METALS PRODUCTION - See VENEZUELA - MINING AND MINERAL PRODUCTS

VENEZUELA - INDUSTRY

Central Intelligence Agency, Washington, D.C. 20505 (703) 482-1100, www.cia.gov; *The World Factbook.*

Economist Intelligence Unit, 111 West 57th Street, New York, New York 10019 (800) 938-4685; *Venezuela Country Report.*

Euromonitor International, Inc., 122 South Michigan Avenue, Suite 1200, Chicago, Illinois 60603 (800) 577-EURO; *The World Economic Factbook;* and *World Marketing Data and Statistics.*

Europa Publications Limited, 18 Bedford Square, London, WC1B 3JN, England; *The Europa World Year Book.*

International Labour Office, I.L.O. Publications, 1828 L Street, NW, Suite 801, Washington, D.C. 20036 (301) 638-3152; *Yearbook of Labour Statistics.*

M.E. Sharpe, 80 Business Park Drive, Armonk, New York 10504 (800) 541-6563; *The Illustrated Book of World Rankings.*

St. Martin's Press, Inc., 175 Fifth Avenue, New York, New York 10010 (800) 221-7945; *The Statesman's Year-Book.*

Statistical Office of the United Nations, Publishing Service, New York, New York 10017 (800) 253-9646; *Economic Survey of Latin America and the Caribbean; Industrial Commodity Statistics Yearbook;* and *Statistical Yearbook.*

U.C.L.A. Latin American Center Publications, University of California, Los Angeles, California 90024 (310) 825-6634; *Statistical Abstract of Latin America.*

The World Bank, 1818 H Street, NW, Washington, D.C. 20433 (202) 477-1234; *World Development Indicators.*

World Intellectual Property Organization, 34 Chemin des Colombettes, CH-1211 Geneva 20. Switzerland; *Industrial Property Statistics.*

VENEZUELA - INFANT AND MATERNAL MORTALITY - See VENEZUELA - MORTALITY

VENEZUELA - INFLATIONARY FACTORS

Statistical Office of the United Nations, Publishing Service, New York, New York 10017 (800) 253-9646; *Economic Survey of Latin America and the Caribbean.*

VENEZUELA - INTEREST RATES

Inter-American Development Bank, 1300 New York Avenue, NW, Washington, D.C. 20577 (202) 623-1753; *Economic and Social Progress in Latin America.*

Organization of American States (OAS), General Secretariat, Washington, D.C. 20006 (202) 458-3533; *Statistical Bulletin of the OAS.*

VENEZUELA - INTERNATIONAL FINANCE

Inter-American Development Bank, 1300 New York Avenue, NW, Washington, D.C. 20577 (202) 623-1753; *Economic and Social Progress in Latin America.*

U.C.L.A. Latin American Center Publications, University of California, Los Angeles, California 90024 (310) 825-6634; *Statistical Abstract of Latin America.*

VENEZUELA - INTERNATIONAL LIQUIDITY

Inter-American Development Bank, 1300 New York Avenue, NW, Washington, D.C. 20577 (202) 623-1753; *Economic and Social Progress in Latin America.*

International Monetary Fund, 700 Nineteenth Street, NW, Washington, D.C. 20431 (202) 623-7000; *International Financial Statistics.*

VENEZUELA - INTERNATIONAL RESERVES

Inter-American Development Bank, 1300 New York Avenue, NW, Washington, D.C. 20577 (202) 623-1753; *Economic and Social Progress in Latin America.*

Organization of American States (OAS), General Secretariat, Washington, D.C. 20006 (202) 458-3533; *Statistical Bulletin of the OAS.*

VENEZUELA - INTERNATIONAL RESERVES EXCLUDING GOLD

Statistical Office of the United Nations, Publishing Service, New York, New York 10017 (800) 253-9646; *Statistical Yearbook.*

The World Bank, 1818 H Street, NW, Washington, D.C. 20433 (202) 477-1234; *World Development Indicators.*

VENEZUELA - INTERNATIONAL STATISTICS

Inter-American Development Bank, 1300 New York Avenue, NW, Washington, D.C. 20577 (202) 623-1753; *Economic and Social Progress in Latin America.*

U.C.L.A. Latin American Center Publications, University of California, Los Angeles, California 90024 (310) 825-6634; *Statistical Abstract of Latin America.*

VENEZUELA - INVESTMENT

Inter-American Development Bank, 1300 New York Avenue, NW, Washington, D.C. 20577 (202) 623-1753; *Economic and Social Progress in Latin America.*

Statistical Office of the United Nations, Publishing Service, New York, New York 10017 (800) 253-9646; *Statistical Yearbook for Latin America and the Caribbean.*

VENEZUELA - IRON ORE EXPORTS - See VENEZUELA - MINING AND MINERAL PRODUCTS

VENEZUELA - IRON ORE PRODUCTION AND CONSUMPTION - See VENEZUELA - MINING AND MINERAL PRODUCTS

VENEZUELA - IRRIGATION

Euromonitor International, Inc., 122 South Michigan Avenue, Suite 1200, Chicago, Illinois 60603 (800) 577-EURO; *International Marketing Data and Statistics.*

Inter-American Development Bank, 1300 New York Avenue, NW, Washington, D.C. 20577 (202) 623-1753; *Economic and Social Progress in Latin America.*

VENEZUELA - LABOR

Central Intelligence Agency, Washington, D.C. 20505 (703) 482-1100, www.cia.gov; *The World Factbook.*

The Economist Intelligence Unit, 111 West 57th Street, New York, New York 10019 (800) 938-4685; *The New Latin America Market Atlas.*

Euromonitor International, Inc., 122 South Michigan Avenue, Suite 1200, Chicago, Illinois 60603 (800) 577-EURO; *International Marketing Data and Statistics;* and *World Marketing Data and Statistics.*

Europa Publications Limited, 18 Bedford Square, London, WC1B 3JN, England; *The Europa World Year Book.*

Food and Agricultural Organization of the United Nations (FAO) Via delle Terme di Caracalla, 00100 Rome, Italy (Telephone Number in U.S. (202) 653-2400); *The State of Food and Agriculture.*

International Labour Office, I.L.O. Publications, 1828 L Street, NW, Suite 801, Washington, D.C. 20036 (301) 638-3152; *Yearbook of Labour Statistics.*

M.E. Sharpe, 80 Business Park Drive, Armonk, New York 10504 (800) 541-6563;

The Illustrated Book of World Rankings.

St. Martin's Press, Inc., 175 Fifth Avenue, New York, New York 10010 (800) 221-7945; *The Statesman's Year-Book.*

Statistical Office of the United Nations, Publishing Service, New York, New York 10017 (800) 253-9646; *Human Development Report.*

The World Bank, 1818 H Street, NW, Washington, D.C. 20433 (202) 477-1234; *The World Bank Atlas; World Development Report;* and *World Development Indicators.*

VENEZUELA - LAND AREA

The Economist Intelligence Unit, 111 West 57th Street, New York, New York 10019 (800) 938-4685; *The New Latin America Market Atlas.*

VENEZUELA - LAND USE

Central Intelligence Agency, Washington, D.C. 20505 (703) 482-1100, www.cia.gov; *The World Factbook.*

Euromonitor International, Inc., 122 South Michigan Avenue, Suite 1200, Chicago, Illinois 60603 (800) 577-EURO; *International Marketing Data and Statistics.*

Inter-American Development Bank, 1300 New York Avenue, NW, Washington, D.C. 20577 (202) 623-1753; *Economic and Social Progress in Latin America.*

The World Bank, 1818 H Street, NW, Washington, D.C. 20433 (202) 477-1234; *World Development Report.*

VENEZUELA - LIBRARIES

M.E. Sharpe, 80 Business Park Drive, Armonk, New York 10504 (800) 541-6563; *The Illustrated Book of World Rankings.*

United Nations Educational, Scientific and Cultural Organization (UNESCO), 7 Place de Fontenoy, F-75700 Paris, France (Telephone Number in U.S. (212) 963-5981); *Statistical Yearbook.*

VENEZUELA - LIFE EXPECTANCY RATE

Central Intelligence Agency, Washington, D.C. 20505 (703) 482-1100, www.cia.gov; *The World Factbook.*

The Economist Intelligence Unit, 111 West 57th Street, New York, New York 10019 (800) 938-4685; *The New Latin America Market Atlas.*

Euromonitor International, Inc., 122 South Michigan Avenue, Suite 1200, Chicago, Illinois 60603 (800) 577-EURO; *The World Economic Factbook.*

Statistical Office of the United Nations, Publishing Service, New York, New York 10017 (800) 253-9646; *Human Development Report; World Statistics Pocketbook;* and *Statistical Yearbook for Latin America and the Caribbean.*

The World Bank, 1818 H Street, NW, Washington, D.C. 20433 (202) 477-1234; *The World Bank Atlas;* and *World Development Report.*

VENEZUELA - LIGNITE PRODUCTION - See VENEZUELA - MINING AND MINERAL PRODUCTS

VENEZUELA - LITERACY RATE

Euromonitor International, Inc., 122 South Michigan Avenue, Suite 1200, Chicago, Illinois 60603 (800) 577-EURO; *World Marketing Data and Statistics.*

VENEZUELA - LIVESTOCK AND POULTRY

Euromonitor International, Inc., 122 South Michigan Avenue, Suite 1200, Chicago, Illinois 60603 (800) 577-EURO; *International Marketing Data and Statistics.*

Europa Publications Limited, 18 Bedford Square, London, WC1B 3JN, England; *The Europa World Year Book.*

Food and Agricultural Organization of the United Nations (FAO) Via delle Terme di Caracalla, 00100 Rome, Italy (Telephone Number in U.S. (202) 653-2400); *Production Yearbook;* and *The State of Food and Agriculture.*

M.E. Sharpe, 80 Business Park Drive, Armonk, New York 10504 (800) 541-6563; *The Illustrated Book of World Rankings.*

St. Martin's Press, Inc., 175 Fifth Avenue, New York, New York 10010 (800) 221-7945; *The Statesman's Year-Book.*

Statistical Office of the United Nations, Publishing Service, New York, New York 10017 (800) 253-9646; *Statistical Yearbook.*

United Nations Conference on Trade and Development, Central Statistical Service, Palais des Nations, Geneva, Switzerland (Telephone in U.S. (800) 253-9646); *UNCTAD Commodity Yearbook.*

VENEZUELA - LIVING LEVELS - See VENEZUELA - LIFE EXPECTANCY

VENEZUELA - MAIL - NUMBER OF ITEMS SENT AND RECEIVED

Statistical Office of the United Nations, Publishing Service, New York, New York 10017 (800) 253-9646; *Statistical Yearbook.*

VENEZUELA - MAIN ECONOMIC INDICATORS - See VENEZUELA -

ECONOMY

VENEZUELA - MANUFACTURING

The Economist Intelligence Unit, 111 West 57th Street, New York, New York 10019 (800) 938-4685; *The New Latin America Market Atlas.*

Inter-American Development Bank, 1300 New York Avenue, NW, Washington, D.C. 20577 (202) 623-1753; *Economic and Social Progress in Latin America.*

M.E. Sharpe, 80 Business Park Drive, Armonk, New York 10504 (800) 541-6563; *The Illustrated Book of World Rankings.*

Organization of American States (OAS), General Secretariat, Washington, D.C. 20006 (202) 458-3533; *Statistical Bulletin of the OAS.*

Statistical Office of the United Nations, Publishing Service, New York, New York 10017 (800) 253-9646; *Statistical Yearbook;* and *Statistical Yearbook for Latin America and the Caribbean.*

The World Bank, 1818 H Street, NW, Washington, D.C. 20433 (202) 477-1234; *World Development Indicators.*

VENEZUELA - MARRIAGE RATES

Europa Publications Limited, 18 Bedford Square, London, WC1B 3JN, England; *The Europa World Year Book.*

M.E. Sharpe, 80 Business Park Drive, Armonk, New York 10504 (800) 541-6563; *The Illustrated Book of World Rankings.*

Statistical Office of the United Nations, Publishing Service, New York, New York 10017 (800) 253-9646; *Demographic Yearbook;* and *Statistical Yearbook.*

VENEZUELA - MEAT PRODUCTION - See VENEZUELA - LIVESTOCK AND POULTRY

VENEZUELA - MEDICAL PERSONNEL

U.C.L.A. Latin American Center Publications, University of California, Los Angeles, California 90024 (310) 825-6634; *Statistical Abstract of Latin America.*

VENEZUELA - MERCHANT SHIPPING

Europa Publications Limited, 18 Bedford Square, London, WC1B 3JN, England; *The Europa World Year Book.*

Lloyd's Register of Shipping, 17 Battery Place, New York, New York 10004 (212) 425-8050; *Register of Ships.*

Organization of Petroleum Exporting Countries, Obere Donaustrasse 93, 1020 Vienna 2, Austria; *OPEC Annual Statistical*

Bulletin.

St. Martin's Press, Inc., 175 Fifth Avenue, New York, New York 10010 (800) 221-7945; *The Statesman's Year-Book.*

Statistical Office of the United Nations, Publishing Service, New York, New York 10017 (800) 253-9646; *Statistical Yearbook.*

U.S. Department of Transportation, Maritime Administration, 400 Seventh Street, SW, Washington, D.C. 20590 (202) 366-5807, www.marad.dot.gov; *A Statistical Analysis of the World's Merchant Fleets.*

VENEZUELA - MILITARY

Central Intelligence Agency, Washington, D.C. 20505 (703) 482-1100, www.cia.gov; *The World Factbook.*

The Economist Intelligence Unit, 111 West 57th Street, New York, New York 10019 (800) 938-4685; *The New Latin America Market Atlas.*

Euromonitor International, Inc., 122 South Michigan Avenue, Suite 1200, Chicago, Illinois 60603 (800) 577-EURO; *World Marketing Data and Statistics.*

The International Institute for Strategic Studies, 23 Tavistock Street, London WC2E 7NQ, England; *The Military Balance.*

International Monetary Fund, 700 Nineteenth Street, NW, Washington, D.C. 20431 (202) 623-7000; *Government Finance Statistics Yearbook.*

St. Martin's Press, Inc., 175 Fifth Avenue, New York, New York 10010 (800) 221-7945; *The Statesman's Year-Book.*

Statistical Office of the United Nations, Publishing Service, New York, New York 10017 (800) 253-9646; *Human Development Report.*

U.C.L.A. Latin American Center Publications, University of California, Los Angeles, California 90024 (310) 825-6634; *Statistical Abstract of Latin America.*

U.S. Arms Control and Disarmament Agency, 320 Twenty-first Street, NW, Washington, D.C. 20451 (202) 647-8677; *World Military Expenditures and Arms Transfers.*

VENEZUELA - MILK PRODUCTION - See VENEZUELA - DAIRY PRODUCTS

VENEZUELA - MINING AND MINERAL PRODUCTS

Commodity Research Bureau, Inc., 30 South Wacker Drive, Chicago, Illinois 60606 (312) 454-1801; *Commodity Year Book.*

The Economist Intelligence Unit, 111 West 57th Street, New York, New York 10019 (800) 938-4685; *The New Latin America Market Atlas.*

Europa Publications Limited, 18 Bedford Square, London, WC1B 3JN, England; *The Europa World Year Book.*

Inter-American Development Bank, 1300 New York Avenue, NW, Washington, D.C. 20577 (202) 623-1753; *Economic and Social Progress in Latin America.*

International Monetary Fund, 700 Nineteenth Street, NW, Washington, D.C. 20431 (202) 623-7000; *International Financial Statistics.*

M.E. Sharpe, 80 Business Park Drive, Armonk, New York 10504 (800) 541-6563; *The Illustrated Book of World Rankings.*

Organization of American States (OAS), General Secretariat, Washington, D.C. 20006 (202) 458-3533; *Statistical Bulletin of the OAS.*

Organization of Petroleum Exporting Countries, Obere Donaustrasse 93, 1020 Vienna 2, Austria; *OPEC Annual Statistical Bulletin.*

Penn Well Publishing Company, 1421 South Sheridan Road, P.O. Box 1260, Tulsa, Oklahoma 74101 (800) 752-9764; *International Energy Statistics Sourcebook.*

St. Martin's Press, Inc., 175 Fifth Avenue, New York, New York 10010 (800) 221-7945; *The Statesman's Year-Book.*

Statistical Office of the United Nations, Publishing Service, New York, New York 10017 (800) 253-9646; *Statistical Yearbook;* and *Statistical Yearbook for Latin America and the Caribbean.*

U.C.L.A. Latin American Center Publications, University of California, Los Angeles, California 90024 (310) 825-6634; *Statistical Abstract of Latin America.*

United Nations Conference on Trade and Development, Central Statistical Service, Palais des Nations, Geneva, Switzerland (Telephone in U.S. (800) 253-9646); *UNCTAD Commodity Yearbook.*

VENEZUELA - MONEY EXCHANGE RATES - See VENEZUELA - EXCHANGE RATES

VENEZUELA - MONEY RATES - MARKET

Inter-American Development Bank, 1300 New York Avenue, NW, Washington, D.C. 20577 (202) 623-1753; *Economic and Social Progress in Latin America.*

VENEZUELA - MONEY RESERVES

Euromonitor International, Inc., 122 South Michigan Avenue, Suite 1200, Chicago, Illinois 60603 (800) 577-EURO; *International Marketing Data and Statistics.*

Inter-American Development Bank, 1300 New York Avenue, NW, Washington, D.C. 20577 (202) 623-1753; *Economic and Social Progress in Latin America.*

VENEZUELA - MONEY SUPPLY

Economist Intelligence Unit, 111 West 57th Street, New York, New York 10019 (800) 938-4685; *Venezuela Country Report.*

Euromonitor International, Inc., 122 South Michigan Avenue, Suite 1200, Chicago, Illinois 60603 (800) 577-EURO; *International Marketing Data and Statistics.*

Europa Publications Limited, 18 Bedford Square, London, WC1B 3JN, England; *The Europa World Year Book.*

Inter-American Development Bank, 1300 New York Avenue, NW, Washington, D.C. 20577 (202) 623-1753; *Economic and Social Progress in Latin America.*

Statistical Office of the United Nations, Publishing Service, New York, New York 10017 (800) 253-9646; *Statistical Yearbook.*

U.C.L.A. Latin American Center Publications, University of California, Los Angeles, California 90024 (310) 825-6634; *Statistical Abstract of Latin America.*

The World Bank, 1818 H Street, NW, Washington, D.C. 20433 (202) 477-1234; *World Development Indicators.*

VENEZUELA - MORTALITY

Central Intelligence Agency, Washington, D.C. 20505 (703) 482-1100, www.cia.gov; *The World Factbook.*

The Economist Intelligence Unit, 111 West 57th Street, New York, New York 10019 (800) 938-4685; *The New Latin America Market Atlas.*

Euromonitor International, Inc., 122 South Michigan Avenue, Suite 1200, Chicago, Illinois 60603 (800) 577-EURO; *International Marketing Data and Statistics;* and *The World Economic Factbook.*

Europa Publications Limited, 18 Bedford Square, London, WC1B 3JN, England; *The Europa World Year Book.*

Statistical Office of the United Nations, Publishing Service, New York, New York 10017 (800) 253-9646; *Demographic Yearbook; Human Development Report; Statistical Yearbook; World Statistics Pocketbook;* and *Statistical Yearbook for*

Latin America and the Caribbean.

United Nations Children's Fund (UNICEF), 3 United Nations Plaza, New York, New York 10017 (800) 253-9646; *State of the World's Children.*

The World Bank, 1818 H Street, NW, Washington, D.C. 20433 (202) 477-1234; *The World Bank Atlas; World Development Report;* and *World Development Indicators.*

World Health Organization, Office of Publications, 20 Avenue Appia, CH-1211 Geneva 27, Switzerland (Telephone Number in U.S. (518) 436-9686); *World Health Statistics Annual.*

VENEZUELA - MOTION PICTURES

Statistical Office of the United Nations, Publishing Service, New York, New York 10017 (800) 253-9646; *Statistical Yearbook.*

United Nations Educational, Scientific and Cultural Organization (UNESCO), 7 Place de Fontenoy, F-75700 Paris, France (Telephone Number in U.S. (212) 963-5981); *Statistical Yearbook.*

VENEZUELA - MOTOR VEHICLE TAXES - See VENEZUELA - TAXATION

VENEZUELA - MOTOR VEHICLES IN USE

The Economist Intelligence Unit, 111 West 57th Street, New York, New York 10019 (800) 938-4685; *The New Latin America Market Atlas.*

Europa Publications Limited, 18 Bedford Square, London, WC1B 3JN, England; *The Europa World Year Book.*

Statistical Office of the United Nations, Publishing Service, New York, New York 10017 (800) 253-9646; *Statistical Yearbook.*

VENEZUELA - MOTOR VEHICLES PRODUCTION AND ASSEMBLY

Statistical Office of the United Nations, Publishing Service, New York, New York 10017 (800) 253-9646; *Statistical Yearbook.*

VENEZUELA - MULES - See VENEZUELA - LIVESTOCK AND POULTRY

VENEZUELA - MUSEUMS

M.E. Sharpe, 80 Business Park Drive, Armonk, New York 10504 (800) 541-6563; *The Illustrated Book of World Rankings.*

United Nations Educational, Scientific and Cultural Organization (UNESCO), 7 Place de Fontenoy, F-75700 Paris, France (Telephone Number in U.S. (212) 963-5981); *Statistical Yearbook.*

VENEZUELA - NATALITY - See

VENEZUELA - BIRTH RATE

VENEZUELA - NATIONAL ACCOUNTS

Europa Publications Limited, 18 Bedford Square, London, WC1B 3JN, England; *The Europa World Year Book.*

Inter-American Development Bank, 1300 New York Avenue, NW, Washington, D.C. 20577 (202) 623-1753; *Economic and Social Progress in Latin America.*

Organization of American States (OAS), General Secretariat, Washington, D.C. 20006 (202) 458-3533; *Statistical Bulletin of the OAS.*

Statistical Office of the United Nations, Publishing Service, New York, New York 10017 (800) 253-9646; *National Accounts Statistics;* and *Statistical Yearbook.*

U.C.L.A. Latin American Center Publications, University of California, Los Angeles, California 90024 (310) 825-6634; *Statistical Abstract of Latin America.*

VENEZUELA - NATIONAL INCOME

Inter-American Development Bank, 1300 New York Avenue, NW, Washington, D.C. 20577 (202) 623-1753; *Economic and Social Progress in Latin America.*

M.E. Sharpe, 80 Business Park Drive, Armonk, New York 10504 (800) 541-6563; *The Illustrated Book of World Rankings.*

Statistical Office of the United Nations, Publishing Service, New York, New York 10017 (800) 253-9646; *National Accounts Statistics; Statistical Yearbook;* and *Statistical Yearbook for Latin America and the Caribbean.*

VENEZUELA - NATIONAL PRODUCT

M.E. Sharpe, 80 Business Park Drive, Armonk, New York 10504 (800) 541-6563; *The Illustrated Book of World Rankings.*

Statistical Office of the United Nations, Publishing Service, New York, New York 10017 (800) 253-9646; *Statistical Yearbook.*

VENEZUELA - NATURAL GAS PRODUCTION - See VENEZUELA - MINING AND MINERAL PRODUCTS

VENEZUELA - NEWSPAPER PRODUCTION - See VENEZUELA - FORESTRY AND FOREST PRODUCTS

VENEZUELA - NEWSPRINT - See VENEZUELA - FORESTRY AND FOREST PRODUCTS

VENEZUELA - NITRIC ACID PRODUCTION - See VENEZUELA - MINING AND MINERAL PRODUCTS

VENEZUELA - NUTRITION

Statistical Office of the United Nations, Publishing Service, New York, New York 10017 (800) 253-9646; *Statistical Yearbook for Latin America and the Caribbean.*

VENEZUELA - OCCUPATIONS - See VENEZUELA - LABOR

VENEZUELA - ORANGES PRODUCTION - See VENEZUELA - CROPS

VENEZUELA - PAPER - See VENEZUELA - FORESTRY AND FOREST PRODUCTS

VENEZUELA - PATENTS, TRADEMARKS AND SERVICE MARKS

Statistical Office of the United Nations, Publishing Service, New York, New York 10017 (800) 253-9646; *Statistical Yearbook.*

World Intellectual Property Organization, 34 Chemin des Colombettes, CH-1211 Geneva 20. Switzerland; *Industrial Property Statistics.*

VENEZUELA - PEANUT PRODUCTION - See VENEZUELA - CROPS

VENEZUELA - PERIODICALS

United Nations Educational, Scientific and Cultural Organization (UNESCO), 7 Place de Fontenoy, F-75700 Paris, France (Telephone Number in U.S. (212) 963-5981); *Statistical Yearbook.*

VENEZUELA - PESTICIDE USE

Food and Agricultural Organization of the United Nations (FAO) Via delle Terme di Caracalla, 00100 Rome, Italy (Telephone Number in U.S. (202) 653-2400); *The State of Food and Agriculture.*

VENEZUELA - PETROLEUM INDUSTRY

Commodity Research Bureau, Inc., 30 South Wacker Drive, Suite 1810, Chicago, Illinois 60606 (312) 454-1801; *Commodity Year Book.*

The Economist Intelligence Unit, 111 West 57th Street, New York, New York 10019 (800) 938-4685; *The New Latin America Market Atlas.*

Food and Agricultural Organization of the United Nations (FAO) Via delle Terme di Caracalla, 00100 Rome, Italy (Telephone Number in U.S. (202) 653-2400); *The State of Food and Agriculture.*

Inter-American Development Bank, 1300 New York Avenue, NW, Washington, D.C. 20577 (202) 623-1753; *Economic and Social Progress in Latin America.*

M.E. Sharpe, 80 Business Park Drive,

Armonk, New York 10504 (800) 541-6563; *The Illustrated Book of World Rankings.*

Organization of American States (OAS), General Secretariat, Washington, D.C. 20006 (202) 458-3533; *Statistical Bulletin of the OAS.*

Organization of Petroleum Exporting Countries, Obere Donaustrasse 93, 1020 Vienna 2, Austria; *OPEC Annual Statistical Bulletin.*

Penn Well Publishing Company, 1421 South Sheridan Road, P.O. Box 1260, Tulsa, Oklahoma 74101 (800) 752-9764; *International Energy Statistics Sourcebook.*

St. Martin's Press, Inc., 175 Fifth Avenue, New York, New York 10010 (800) 221-7945; *The Statesman's Year-Book.*

Statistical Office of the United Nations, Publishing Service, New York, New York 10017 (800) 253-9646; *Statistical Yearbook.*

United Nations Conference on Trade and Development, Central Statistical Service, Palais des Nations, Geneva, Switzerland (Telephone in U.S. (800) 253-9646); *UNCTAD Commodity Yearbook.*

VENEZUELA - PHOSPHATE ROCK PRODUCTION - See VENEZUELA - MINING AND MINERAL PRODUCTS

VENEZUELA - PIG-IRON AND FERRO-ALLOY PRODUCTION - See VENEZUELA - MINING AND MINERAL PRODUCTS

VENEZUELA - PIGS - See VENEZUELA - LIVESTOCK AND POULTRY

VENEZUELA - PIPELINES FOR OIL AND PETROLEUM PRODUCTS

Organization of Petroleum Exporting Countries, Obere Donaustrasse 93, 1020 Vienna 2, Austria; *OPEC Annual Statistical Bulletin.*

VENEZUELA - PLASTIC AND RESIN PRODUCTION

Statistical Office of the United Nations, Publishing Service, New York, New York 10017 (800) 253-9646; *Statistical Yearbook.*

VENEZUELA - POLITICAL DATA

U.C.L.A. Latin American Center Publications, University of California, Los Angeles, California 90024 (310) 825-6634; *Statistical Abstract of Latin America.*

VENEZUELA - POPULATION

Central Intelligence Agency, Washington, D.C. 20505 (703) 482-1100, www.cia.gov; *The World Factbook.*

The Economist Intelligence Unit, 111 West 57th Street, New York, New York 10019 (800) 938-4685; *The New Latin America Market Atlas; Venezuela Country Report;* and *The World Market Atlas.*

Euromonitor International, Inc., 122 South Michigan Avenue, Suite 1200, Chicago, Illinois 60603 (800) 577-EURO; *International Marketing Data and Statistics;* and *The World Economic Factbook.*

Europa Publications Limited, 18 Bedford Square, London, WC1B 3JN, England; *The Europa World Year Book.*

Inter-American Development Bank, 1300 New York Avenue, NW, Washington, D.C. 20577 (202) 623-1753; *Economic and Social Progress in Latin America.*

International Labour Office, I.L.O. Publications, 1828 L Street, NW, Suite 801, Washington, D.C. 20036 (301) 638-3152; *Yearbook of Labour Statistics.*

M.E. Sharpe, 80 Business Park Drive, Armonk, New York 10504 (800) 541-6563; *The Illustrated Book of World Rankings.*

Organization of American States (OAS), General Secretariat, Washington, D.C. 20006 (202) 458-3533; *Statistical Bulletin of the OAS.*

St. Martin's Press, Inc., 175 Fifth Avenue, New York, New York 10010 (800) 221-7945; *The Statesman's Year-Book.*

Statistical Office of the United Nations, Publishing Service, New York, New York 10017 (800) 253-9646; *Demographic Yearbook; Human Development Report; Statistical Yearbook; World Statistics Pocketbook;* and *Statistical Yearbook for Latin America and the Caribbean.*

U.C.L.A. Latin American Center Publications, University of California, Los Angeles, California 90024 (310) 825-6634; *Statistical Abstract of Latin America.*

United Nations Educational, Scientific and Cultural Organization (UNESCO), 7 Place de Fontenoy, F-75700 Paris, France (Telephone Number in U.S. (212) 963-5981); *Statistical Yearbook.*

U.S. Arms Control and Disarmament Agency, 320 Twenty-first Street, NW, Washington, D.C. 20451 (202) 647-8677; *World Military Expenditures and Arms Transfers.*

The World Bank, 1818 H Street, NW, Washington, D.C. 20433 (202) 477-1234; *The World Bank Atlas;* and *World Development Report.*

World Health Organization, Office of Publications, 20 Avenue Appia, CH-1211

Geneva 27, Switzerland (Telephone Number in U.S. (518) 436-9686); *World Health Statistics Annual.*

VENEZUELA - POST OFFICES

M.E. Sharpe, 80 Business Park Drive, Armonk, New York 10504 (800) 541-6563; *The Illustrated Book of World Rankings.*

VENEZUELA - POTATO PRODUCTION - See VENEZUELA - CROPS

VENEZUELA - POWER PRODUCTION INDUSTRY

Statistical Office of the United Nations, Publishing Service, New York, New York 10017 (800) 253-9646; *Electric Power in Asia and the Pacific.*

VENEZUELA - PRICES

Food and Agricultural Organization of the United Nations (FAO) Via delle Terme di Caracalla, 00100 Rome, Italy (Telephone Number in U.S. (202) 653-2400); *The State of Food and Agriculture.*

International Labour Office, I.L.O. Publications, 1828 L Street, NW, Suite 801, Washington, D.C. 20036 (301) 638-3152; *Yearbook of Labour Statistics.*

International Monetary Fund, 700 Nineteenth Street, NW, Washington, D.C. 20431 (202) 623-7000; *International Financial Statistics.*

M.E. Sharpe, 80 Business Park Drive, Armonk, New York 10504 (800) 541-6563; *The Illustrated Book of World Rankings.*

Statistical Office of the United Nations, Publishing Service, New York, New York 10017 (800) 253-9646; *Economic Survey of Latin America and the Caribbean;* and *Statistical Yearbook for Latin America and the Caribbean.*

VENEZUELA - PRINTING AND WRITING PAPER - See VENEZUELA - FORESTRY AND FOREST PRODUCTS

VENEZUELA - PRODUCTION

M.E. Sharpe, 80 Business Park Drive, Armonk, New York 10504 (800) 541-6563; *The Illustrated Book of World Rankings.*

VENEZUELA - PRODUCTIVITY

Euromonitor International, Inc., 122 South Michigan Avenue, Suite 1200, Chicago, Illinois 60603 (800) 577-EURO; *International Marketing Data and Statistics.*

VENEZUELA - PROPERTY TAXES - See VENEZUELA - TAXATION

VENEZUELA - PUBLIC CONSUMPTION

FUND

Inter-American Development Bank, 1300 New York Avenue, NW, Washington, D.C. 20577 (202) 623-1753; *Economic and Social Progress in Latin America.*

VENEZUELA - PUBLIC EXPENDITURE

Inter-American Development Bank, 1300 New York Avenue, NW, Washington, D.C. 20577 (202) 623-1753; *Economic and Social Progress in Latin America.*

Organization of American States (OAS), General Secretariat, Washington, D.C. 20006 (202) 458-3533; *Statistical Bulletin of the OAS.*

Statistical Office of the United Nations, Publishing Service, New York, New York 10017 (800) 253-9646; *Statistical Yearbook for Latin America and the Caribbean.*

VENEZUELA - PUBLIC FINANCES - See VENEZUELA - FINANCE

VENEZUELA - PUBLIC REVENUES

Inter-American Development Bank, 1300 New York Avenue, NW, Washington, D.C. 20577 (202) 623-1753; *Economic and Social Progress in Latin America.*

Organization of American States (OAS), General Secretariat, Washington, D.C. 20006 (202) 458-3533; *Statistical Bulletin of the OAS.*

VENEZUELA - RADIO BROADCASTING - See VENEZUELA - BROADCASTING

VENEZUELA - RADIO RECEIVER PRODUCTION

Statistical Office of the United Nations, Publishing Service, New York, New York 10017 (800) 253-9646; *Statistical Yearbook.*

VENEZUELA - RADIO RECEIVERS

St. Martin's Press, Inc., 175 Fifth Avenue, New York, New York 10010 (800) 221-7945; *The Statesman's Year-Book.*

VENEZUELA - RAILWAYS

The Economist Intelligence Unit, 111 West 57th Street, New York, New York 10019 (800) 938-4685; *The New Latin America Market Atlas.*

Europa Publications Limited, 18 Bedford Square, London, WC1B 3JN, England; *The Europa World Year Book.*

Jane's Information Group, Sentinel House, 163 Brighton Road, Coulsdon, Surrey CR5 2NH, England (Telephone Number in U.S. (703) 683-3700); *Jane's World Railways.*

St. Martin's Press, Inc., 175 Fifth Avenue, New York, New York 10010 (800) 221-7945; *The Statesman's Year-Book.*

Statistical Office of the United Nations, Publishing Service, New York, New York 10017 (800) 253-9646; *Statistical Yearbook.*

VENEZUELA - RANCHING

U.C.L.A. Latin American Center Publications, University of California, Los Angeles, California 90024 (310) 825-6634; *Statistical Abstract of Latin America.*

VENEZUELA - RELIGION

Central Intelligence Agency, Washington, D.C. 20505 (703) 482-1100, www.cia.gov; *The World Factbook.*

M.E. Sharpe, 80 Business Park Drive, Armonk, New York 10504 (800) 541-6563; *The Illustrated Book of World Rankings.*

St. Martin's Press, Inc., 175 Fifth Avenue, New York, New York 10010 (800) 221-7945; *The Statesman's Year-Book.*

U.C.L.A. Latin American Center Publications, University of California, Los Angeles, California 90024 (310) 825-6634; *Statistical Abstract of Latin America.*

VENEZUELA - RENT PRICES

International Labour Office, I.L.O. Publications, 1828 L Street, NW, Suite 801, Washington, D.C. 20036 (301) 638-3152; *Yearbook of Labour Statistics.*

VENEZUELA - RESERVES EXCLUDING GOLD

The Economist Intelligence Unit, 111 West 57th Street, New York, New York 10019 (800) 938-4685; *The New Latin America Market Atlas.*

VENEZUELA - RETAIL TRADE

Euromonitor International, Inc., 122 South Michigan Avenue, Suite 1200, Chicago, Illinois 60603 (800) 577-EURO; *World Marketing Data and Statistics*; and *Retail Trade International.*

Inter-American Development Bank, 1300 New York Avenue, NW, Washington, D.C. 20577 (202) 623-1753; *Economic and Social Progress in Latin America.*

VENEZUELA - RICE PRODUCTION - See VENEZUELA - CROPS

VENEZUELA - ROOT AND TUBER PRODUCTION - See VENEZUELA - CROPS

VENEZUELA - ROUNDWOOD PRODUCTION - See VENEZUELA - FORESTRY AND FOREST PRODUCTS

VENEZUELA - RUBBER PRODUCTION AND CONSUMPTION

M.E. Sharpe, 80 Business Park Drive, Armonk, New York 10504 (800) 541-6563; *The Illustrated Book of World Rankings.*

VENEZUELA - SALT PRODUCTION - See VENEZUELA - MINING AND MINERAL PRODUCTS

VENEZUELA - SAWNWOOD PRODUCTION - See VENEZUELA - FORESTRY AND FOREST PRODUCTS

VENEZUELA - SCIENTISTS, TECHNICIANS AND ENGINEERS

Statistical Office of the United Nations, Publishing Service, New York, New York 10017 (800) 253-9646; *Statistical Yearbook.*

U.C.L.A. Latin American Center Publications, University of California, Los Angeles, California 90024 (310) 825-6634; *Statistical Abstract of Latin America.*

United Nations Educational, Scientific and Cultural Organization (UNESCO), 7 Place de Fontenoy, F-75700 Paris, France (Telephone Number in U.S. (212) 963-5981); *Statistical Yearbook.*

VENEZUELA - SENIOR CITIZENS

M.E. Sharpe, 80 Business Park Drive, Armonk, New York 10504 (800) 541-6563; *The Illustrated Book of World Rankings.*

VENEZUELA - SESAME SEED PRODUCTION - See VENEZUELA - CROPS

VENEZUELA - SHEEP - See VENEZUELA - LIVESTOCK AND POULTRY

VENEZUELA - SILVER PRODUCTION AND CONSUMPTION - See VENEZUELA - MINING AND MINERAL PRODUCTS

VENEZUELA - SISAL PRODUCTION - See VENEZUELA - CROPS

VENEZUELA - SOCIAL DATA

M.E. Sharpe, 80 Business Park Drive, Armonk, New York 10504 (800) 541-6563; *The Illustrated Book of World Rankings.*

Statistical Office of the United Nations, Publishing Service, New York, New York 10017 (800) 253-9646; *World Statistics Pocketbook.*

U.C.L.A. Latin American Center Publications, University of California, Los Angeles, California 90024 (310) 825-6634; *Statistical Abstract of Latin America.*

VENEZUELA - SOCIAL SECURITY

Inter-American Development Bank,

1300 New York Avenue, NW, Washington, D.C. 20577 (202) 623-1753; *Economic and Social Progress in Latin America.*

International Monetary Fund, 700 Nineteenth Street, NW, Washington, D.C. 20431 (202) 623-7000; *Government Finance Statistics Yearbook.*

Statistical Office of the United Nations, Publishing Service, New York, New York 10017 (800) 253-9646; *National Accounts Statistics.*

VENEZUELA - SOCIOECONOMIC DATA

Inter-American Development Bank, 1300 New York Avenue, NW, Washington, D.C. 20577 (202) 623-1753; *Economic and Social Progress in Latin America.*

U.C.L.A. Latin American Center Publications, University of California, Los Angeles, California 90024 (310) 825-6634; *Statistical Abstract of Latin America.*

VENEZUELA - SOYBEAN PRODUCTION - See VENEZUELA - CROPS

VENEZUELA - STAMP TAXES AND DUTIES - See VENEZUELA - TAXATION

VENEZUELA - STATE BUDGET REVENUE AND EXPENDITURES

Euromonitor International, Inc., 122 South Michigan Avenue, Suite 1200, Chicago, Illinois 60603 (800) 577-EURO; *International Marketing Data and Statistics.*

Inter-American Development Bank, 1300 New York Avenue, NW, Washington, D.C. 20577 (202) 623-1753; *Economic and Social Progress in Latin America.*

VENEZUELA - STEEL - See VENEZUELA - MINING AND MINERAL PRODUCTS

VENEZUELA - STOCKS - COMMODITY - MARKET PRICE - INDEX

Food and Agricultural Organization of the United Nations (FAO) Via delle Terme di Caracalla, 00100 Rome, Italy (Telephone Number in U.S. (202) 653-2400); *The State of Food and Agriculture.*

VENEZUELA - SUGAR PRODUCTION AND CONSUMPTION - See VENEZUELA -CROPS

VENEZUELA - SULPHURIC ACID PRODUCTION - See VENEZUELA - MINING AND MINERAL PRODUCTS

VENEZUELA - TAXATION

Europa Publications Limited, 18 Bedford Square, London, WC1B 3JN, England; *The Europa World Year Book.*

Inter-American Development Bank,

1300 New York Avenue, NW, Washington, D.C. 20577 (202) 623-1753; *Economic and Social Progress in Latin America.*

International Monetary Fund, 700 Nineteenth Street, NW, Washington, D.C. 20431 (202) 623-7000; *Government Finance Statistics Yearbook.*

Statistical Office of the United Nations, Publishing Service, New York, New York 10017 (800) 253-9646; *Statistical Yearbook for Latin America and the Caribbean.*

The World Bank, 1818 H Street, NW, Washington, D.C. 20433 (202) 477-1234; *World Development Indicators.*

VENEZUELA - TELEPHONES IN USE

American Telephone and Telegraph Company, 26 Parsippany Road, Whippany, New Jersey 07981 (800) 222-0300; *The World's Telephones.*

Central Intelligence Agency, Washington, D.C. 20505 (703) 482-1100, www.cia.gov; *The World Factbook.*

The Economist Intelligence Unit, 111 West 57th Street, New York, New York 10019 (800) 938-4685; *The New Latin America Market Atlas.*

Europa Publications Limited, 18 Bedford Square, London, WC1B 3JN, England; *The Europa World Year Book.*

St. Martin's Press, Inc., 175 Fifth Avenue, New York, New York 10010 (800) 221-7945; *The Statesman's Year-Book.*

Statistical Office of the United Nations, Publishing Service, New York, New York 10017 (800) 253-9646; *Statistical Yearbook;* and *World Statistics Pocketbook.*

VENEZUELA - TELEVISION BROADCASTING - See VENEZUELA - BROADCASTING

VENEZUELA - TELEVISION RECEIVER PRODUCTION

Statistical Office of the United Nations, Publishing Service, New York, New York 10017 (800) 253-9646; *Statistical Yearbook.*

VENEZUELA - TEXTILE INDUSTRY

American Forest and Paper Association, 1111 Nineteenth Street, NW, Washington, D.C. 20036 (202) 463-2700; *Wood Pulp and Fiber Statistics.*

Euromonitor International, Inc., 122 South Michigan Avenue, Suite 1200, Chicago, Illinois 60603 (800) 577-EURO; *Retail Trade International.*

M.E. Sharpe, 80 Business Park Drive,

Armonk, New York 10504 (800) 541-6563; *The Illustrated Book of World Rankings.*

Statistical Office of the United Nations, Publishing Service, New York, New York 10017 (800) 253-9646; *Statistical Yearbook.*

United Nations Conference on Trade and Development, Central Statistical Service, Palais des Nations, Geneva, Switzerland (Telephone in U.S. (800) 253-9646); *UNCTAD Commodity Yearbook.*

VENEZUELA - THEATRE

United Nations Educational, Scientific and Cultural Organization (UNESCO), 7 Place de Fontenoy, F-75700 Paris, France (Telephone Number in U.S. (212) 963-5981); *Statistical Yearbook.*

VENEZUELA - TIN - INDUSTRIAL PRODUCTION - See VENEZUELA -MINING AND MINERAL PRODUCTS

VENEZUELA - TIRE (MOTOR VEHICLE) PRODUCTION

Statistical Office of the United Nations, Publishing Service, New York, New York 10017 (800) 253-9646; *Statistical Yearbook.*

VENEZUELA - TOBACCO PRODUCTION

M.E. Sharpe, 80 Business Park Drive, Armonk, New York 10504 (800) 541-6563; *The Illustrated Book of World Rankings.*

Statistical Office of the United Nations, Publishing Service, New York, New York 10017 (800) 253-9646; *Statistical Yearbook.*

U.C.L.A. Latin American Center Publications, University of California, Los Angeles, California 90024 (310) 825-6634; *Statistical Abstract of Latin America.*

VENEZUELA - TOURISM

The Economist Intelligence Unit, 111 West 57th Street, New York, New York 10019 (800) 938-4685; *The New Latin America Market Atlas.*

Euromonitor International, Inc., 122 South Michigan Avenue, Suite 1200, Chicago, Illinois 60603 (800) 577-EURO; *The World Economic Factbook;* and *World Marketing Data and Statistics.*

Europa Publications Limited, 18 Bedford Square, London, WC1B 3JN, England; *The Europa World Year Book.*

M.E. Sharpe, 80 Business Park Drive, Armonk, New York 10504 (800) 541-6563; *The Illustrated Book of World Rankings.*

St. Martin's Press, Inc., 175 Fifth Avenue, New York, New York 10010 (800) 221-7945; *The Statesman's Year-Book.*

Statistical Office of the United Nations, Publishing Service, New York, New York 10017 (800) 253-9646; *Statistical Yearbook; and Statistical Yearbook for Latin America and the Caribbean.*

U.C.L.A. Latin American Center Publications, University of California, Los Angeles, California 90024 (310) 825-6634; *Statistical Abstract of Latin America.*

World Tourism Organization, Calle Capitan Haya 42, E-28020 Madrid, Spain; *Yearbook of Tourism Statistics.*

VENEZUELA - TRACTORS IN USE

The Economist Intelligence Unit, 111 West 57th Street, New York, New York 10019 (800) 938-4685; *The New Latin America Market Atlas.*

Statistical Office of the United Nations, Publishing Service, New York, New York 10017 (800) 253-9646; *Statistical Yearbook.*

VENEZUELA - TRADE - See
VENEZUELA - FOREIGN TRADE

VENEZUELA - TRADEMARKS AND SERVICE MARKS - See VENEZUELA - PATENTS, TRADEMARKS AND SERVICE MARKS

VENEZUELA - TRANSPORTATION AND COMMUNICATIONS

Central Intelligence Agency, Washington, D.C. 20505 (703) 482-1100, www.cia.gov; *The World Factbook.*

The Economist Intelligence Unit, 111 West 57th Street, New York, New York 10019 (800) 938-4685; *The New Latin America Market Atlas.*

Euromonitor International, Inc., 122 South Michigan Avenue, Suite 1200, Chicago, Illinois 60603 (800) 577-EURO; *International Marketing Data and Statistics; and World Marketing Data and Statistics.*

Europa Publications Limited, 18 Bedford Square, London, WC1B 3JN, England; *The Europa World Year Book.*

Inter-American Development Bank, 1300 New York Avenue, NW, Washington, D.C. 20577 (202) 623-1753; *Economic and Social Progress in Latin America.*

M.E. Sharpe, 80 Business Park Drive, Armonk, New York 10504 (800) 541-6563; *The Illustrated Book of World Rankings.*

St. Martin's Press, Inc., 175 Fifth Avenue, New York, New York 10010 (800) 221-7945; *The Statesman's Year-Book.*

Statistical Office of the United Nations, Publishing Service, New York, New York 10017 (800) 253-9646; *Human*

Development Report; and *Statistical Yearbook for Latin America and the Caribbean.*

U.C.L.A. Latin American Center Publications, University of California, Los Angeles, California 90024 (310) 825-6634; *Statistical Abstract of Latin America.*

VENEZUELA - UNEMPLOYMENT

Central Intelligence Agency, Washington, D.C. 20505 (703) 482-1100, www.cia.gov; *The World Factbook.*

The Economist Intelligence Unit, 111 West 57th Street, New York, New York 10019 (800) 938-4685; *The New Latin America Market Atlas.*

Euromonitor International, Inc., 122 South Michigan Avenue, Suite 1200, Chicago, Illinois 60603 (800) 577-EURO; *International Marketing Data and Statistics.*

International Labour Office, I.L.O. Publications, 1828 L Street, NW, Suite 801, Washington, D.C. 20036 (301) 638-3152; *Yearbook of Labour Statistics.*

St. Martin's Press, Inc., 175 Fifth Avenue, New York, New York 10010 (800) 221-7945; *The Statesman's Year-Book.*

Statistical Office of the United Nations, Publishing Service, New York, New York 10017 (800) 253-9646; *Statistical Yearbook.*

U.C.L.A. Latin American Center Publications, University of California, Los Angeles, California 90024 (310) 825-6634; *Statistical Abstract of Latin America.*

VENEZUELA - UTILITIES

Statistical Office of the United Nations, Publishing Service, New York, New York 10017 (800) 253-9646; *Electric Power in Asia and the Pacific.*

U.C.L.A. Latin American Center Publications, University of California, Los Angeles, California 90024 (310) 825-6634; *Statistical Abstract of Latin America.*

VENEZUELA - VITAL STATISTICS

Euromonitor International, Inc., 122 South Michigan Avenue, Suite 1200, Chicago, Illinois 60603 (800) 577-EURO; *International Marketing Data and Statistics.*

Statistical Office of the United Nations, Publishing Service, New York, New York 10017 (800) 253-9646; *Statistical Yearbook.*

VENEZUELA - WAGES

International Labour Office, I.L.O. Publications, 1828 L Street, NW, Suite 801, Washington, D.C. 20036 (301) 638-

3152; *Yearbook of Labour Statistics.*

Statistical Office of the United Nations, Publishing Service, New York, New York 10017 (800) 253-9646; *Statistical Yearbook.*

U.C.L.A. Latin American Center Publications, University of California, Los Angeles, California 90024 (310) 825-6634; *Statistical Abstract of Latin America.*

VENEZUELA - WATERMELON PRODUCTION - See VENEZUELA - CROPS

VENEZUELA - WEATHER

M.E. Sharpe, 80 Business Park Drive, Armonk, New York 10504 (800) 541-6563; *The Illustrated Book of World Rankings.*

VENEZUELA - WELFARE

Inter-American Development Bank, 1300 New York Avenue, NW, Washington, D.C. 20577 (202) 623-1753; *Economic and Social Progress in Latin America.*

International Monetary Fund, 700 Nineteenth Street, NW, Washington, D.C. 20431 (202) 623-7000; *Government Finance Statistics Yearbook.*

VENEZUELA - WHEAT PRODUCTION AND PRICES - See VENEZUELA - CROPS

VENEZUELA - WHOLESALE PRICES

Inter-American Development Bank, 1300 New York Avenue, NW, Washington, D.C. 20577 (202) 623-1753; *Economic and Social Progress in Latin America.*

Organization of American States (OAS), General Secretariat, Washington, D.C. 20006 (202) 458-3533; *Statistical Bulletin of the OAS.*

Statistical Office of the United Nations, Publishing Service, New York, New York 10017 (800) 253-9646; *Statistical Yearbook.*

VENEZUELA - WHOLESALE TRADE

Inter-American Development Bank, 1300 New York Avenue, NW, Washington, D.C. 20577 (202) 623-1753; *Economic and Social Progress in Latin America.*

VENEZUELA - WINE PRODUCTION - See VENEZUELA - BEVERAGES

VENEZUELA - WOOD AND WOOD PULP - See VENEZUELA - FORESTRY AND FOREST PRODUCTS

VENEZUELA - WOOL PRODUCTION - See VENEZUELA - TEXTILE INDUSTRY

VENEZUELA - YARN PRODUCTION - See VENEZUELA - TEXTILE INDUSTRY

VENEZUELA - ZOOS AND BOTANICAL GARDENS

United Nations Educational, Scientific and Cultural Organization (UNESCO), 7 Place de Fontenoy, F-75700 Paris, France (Telephone Number in U.S. (212) 963-5981); *Statistical Yearbook.*

VENTURE CAPITAL

Venture Economics Investor Services, 41 Pittsburgh Street, Boston, Massachusetts 02210 (617) 856-2504; *Venture Capital Journal.*

VERMICULITE

U.S. Department of the Interior, Geological Survey, Office of Minerals Information, 12201 Sunrise Valley Drive, Reston, Virginia 22092 (703) 648-4000, www.minerals.usgs.gov; *Annual Reports;* and *Mineral Commodities Summaries.*

VERMONT - See also STATE DATA (FOR INDIVIDUAL STATES)

Vermont - Primary Statistics Source

Labor Market Information, Department of Employment and Training, Post Office Box 488, Montpelier, Vermont 05602 (802) 828-4202; *Demographic and Economic Profiles.*

Vermont - State Data Centers

Center for Rural Studies, University of Vermont, 207 Morrill Hall, Burlington, Vermont 05405, Ms. Sharon Whitaker (802) 656-3021.

VESSELS - See SHIPS

VETERAN - PATRIOTIC ASSOCIATIONS

The Gale Group, 27500 Drake Road, Farmington Hills, Michigan 48331-3535 (800) 877-4253; compiled from *Encyclopedia of Associations.*

VETERANS - EXPENDITURES

U.S. Department of Health and Human Services, Health Care Financing Administration, 200 Independence Avenue, SW, Washington, D.C. 20201 (202) 690-6145, www.hcfa.gov; *Health Care Financing Review.*

U.S. Department of Veterans Affairs, 810 Vermont Avenue, NW, Washington, D.C. 20420 (202) 273-5400, www.va.gov; *Annual Report of the Secretary of Veterans Affairs; Trend Data;* and unpublished data.

VETERANS - EXPENDITURES - HOSPITAL - MEDICAL CARE

U.S. Department of Health and Human Services, Health Care Financing Administration, 200 Independence Avenue, SW, Washington, D.C. 20201 (202) 690-6145, www.hcfa.gov; *Health Care Financing Review.*

VETERANS - NUMBER

U.S. Department of Veterans Affairs, 810 Vermont Avenue, NW, Washington, D.C. 20420 (202) 273-5400, www.va.gov; *Veteran Population;* and *Annual Report of the Secretary of Veterans Affairs.*

VETERANS - PENSIONS AND OTHER BENEFITS - DISABILITY - SERVICE - CONNECTED COMPENSATION

U.S. Department of Veterans Affairs, 810 Vermont Avenue, NW, Washington, D.C. 20420 (202) 273-5400, www.va.gov; *Annual Report of the Secretary of Veterans Affairs;* and unpublished data.

VETERANS - PENSIONS AND OTHER BENEFITS - DISBURSEMENTS

Executive Office of the President, Office of Management and Budget, Executive Office Building, Washington, D.C. 20503 (202) 395-3080, www.whitehouse.gov/omb; *Historical Tables.*

Social Security Administration, 6400 Security Boulevard, Baltimore, Maryland 21235 (800) 772-1213, www.ssa.gov; *Social Security Bulletin;* and unpublished data.

U.S. Department of Commerce, Bureau of Economic Analysis, Fourteenth Street between Constitution Avenue and E Street, NW, Washington, D.C. 20230 (202) 606-9900, www.bea.doc.gov; *Survey of Current Business.*

U.S. Department of Veterans Affairs, 810 Vermont Avenue, NW, Washington, D.C. 20420 (202) 273-5400, www.va.gov; *Annual Report of the Secretary of Veterans Affairs;* and unpublished data.

VETERANS - PENSIONS AND OTHER BENEFITS - EDUCATION AND TRAINING

U.S. Department of Veterans Affairs, 810 Vermont Avenue, NW, Washington, D.C. 20420 (202) 273-5400, www.va.gov; *Annual Report of the Secretary of Veterans Affairs;* and unpublished data.

VETERANS - PENSIONS AND OTHER BENEFITS - FEDERAL AID TO STATE AND LOCAL GOVERNMENTS

Executive Office of the President, Office of Management and Budget, Executive Office Building, Washington, D.C. 20503

(202) 395-3080, www.whitehouse.gov/omb; *Historical Tables, Budget of the United States Government.*

VETERANS - PENSIONS AND OTHER BENEFITS - HEALTH EXPENDITURES

U.S. Department of Health and Human Services, Health Care Financing Administration, 200 Independence Avenue, SW, Washington, D.C. 20201 (202) 690-6145, www.hcfa.gov; *Health Care Financing Review.*

VETERANS - PENSIONS AND OTHER BENEFITS - HOSPITAL OR DOMICILIARY CARE

U.S. Department of Veterans Affairs, 810 Vermont Avenue, NW, Washington, D.C. 20420 (202) 273-5400, www.va.gov; *Annual Report of the Secretary of Veterans Affairs; Directory of VA Facilities;* and unpublished data.

VETERANS - PENSIONS AND OTHER BENEFITS - LIFE INSURANCE - FUNDS

Executive Office of the President, Office of Management and Budget, Executive Office Building, Washington, D.C. 20503 (202) 395-3080, www.whitehouse.gov/omb; *Analytical Perspectives.*

VETERANS - PENSIONS AND OTHER BENEFITS - LOANS GUARANTEED AND INSURED

U.S. Department of Veterans Affairs, 810 Vermont Avenue, NW, Washington, D.C. 20420 (202) 273-5400, www.va.gov; *Annual Report of the Secretary of Veterans Affairs;* and unpublished data.

VETERANS - PENSIONS AND OTHER BENEFITS - VETERANS OR DEPENDENTS RECEIVING

U.S. Department of Commerce, Bureau of the Census, Washington, D.C. 20233 (301) 457-4100, www.census.gov; Internet site:http://ferret.bls.census.gov/macro/031998/faminc/09000.htm.

U.S. Department of Veterans Affairs, 810 Vermont Avenue, NW, Washington, D.C. 20420 (202) 273-5400, www.va.gov; *Annual Report of the Secretary of Veterans Affairs;* and unpublished data.

VETERANS AFFAIRS - DEPARTMENT OF - BUDGET OUTLAYS

Executive Office of the President, Office of Management and Budget, Executive Office Building, Washington, D.C. 20503 (202) 395-3080, www.whitehouse.gov/omb; *Historical Tables.*

VETERANS AFFAIRS - DEPARTMENT OF - HOME LOANS

Board of Governors of the Federal Reserve System, Twentieth Street and Constitution Avenue, NW, Washington, D.C. 20551 (202) 452-3000, www.bog.frb.fed.us; *Federal Reserve Bulletin.*

Mortgage Bankers Association of America, 1125 Fifteenth Street, NW, Washington, D.C. 20005 (202) 861-6500; *National Delinquency Survey.*

U.S. Department of Veterans Affairs, 810 Vermont Avenue, NW, Washington, D.C. 20420 (202) 273-5400, www.va.gov; *Annual Report of the Secretary of Veterans Affairs.*

VETERANS AFFAIRS - DEPARTMENT OF - LAND AND BUILDINGS

General Services Administration, General Services Building, Eighteenth and F Streets, NW, Washington, D.C. 20405 (202) 708-5082, www.gsa.gov; *Inventory Report on Real Property Owned by the United States Throughout the World.*

VETERANS AFFAIRS - DEPARTMENT OF - MEDICAL CENTERS

U.S. Department of Veterans Affairs, 810 Vermont Avenue, NW, Washington, D.C. 20420 (202) 273-5400, www.va.gov; *Annual Report of the Secretary of Veterans Affairs; Directory of VA Facilities;* and unpublished data.

VETOED BILLS, CONGRESSIONAL

U. S. Congress, The Capitol, Washington, D.C. 20515 (202) 224-3121; *Calendars of the United States House of Representatives and History of Legislation.*

VIDEO GAMES

Toy Manufacturers of America, Inc., 1115 Broadway, Suite 400, New York, New York 10010; *Toy Industry Fact Book.*

Veronis Suhler and Associates, 350 Park Avenue, New York, New York 10022 (212) 935-4990; *Communications Industry Report.*

VIDEOCASSETTE RECORDERS - HOUSEHOLDS WITH

Euromonitor International, Inc., 122 South Michigan Avenue, Suite 1200, Chicago, Illinois 60603 (800) 577-EURO; *European Marketing Data and Statistics.*

Television Bureau of Advertising, Inc., 3 East 54th Street, New York, New York 10022 (212) 486-1111; *Trends in Television.*

VIOLENT CRIME - See CRIME

Vietnam (Socialist Republic Of) - National Statistical Office

General Statistical Office, 2 Hoang Van Thu Street, Hanoi, Socialist Republic of Vietnam.

Vietnam (Socialist Republic Of) - Primary Statistics Source

General Statistical Office, 2 Hoang Van Thu Street, Hanoi, Socialist Republic of Vietnam; *Nien-Giam Thong-Ke* (Statistical Yearbook).

VIETNAM (SOCIALIST REPUBLIC OF) - AGRICULTURE

Economist Intelligence Unit, 111 West 57th Street, New York, New York 10019 (800) 938-4685; *Vietnam Country Report.*

Euromonitor International, Inc., 122 South Michigan Avenue, Suite 1200, Chicago, Illinois 60603 (800) 577-EURO; *International Marketing Data and Statistics;* and *World Marketing Data and Statistics.*

Europa Publications Limited, 18 Bedford Square, London, WC1B 3JN, England; *The Europa World Year Book.*

Food and Agricultural Organization of the United Nations (FAO) Via delle Terme di Caracalla, 00100 Rome, Italy (Telephone Number in U.S. (202) 653-2400); *The State of Food and Agriculture;* and *Trade Yearbook.*

M.E. Sharpe, 80 Business Park Drive, Armonk, New York 10504 (800) 541-6563; *The Illustrated Book of World Rankings.*

St. Martin's Press, Inc., 175 Fifth Avenue, New York, New York 10010 (800) 221-7945; *The Statesman's Year-Book.*

Statistical Office of the United Nations, Publishing Service, New York, New York 10017 (800) 253-9646; *Asia-Pacific in Figures; Statistical Yearbook;* and *Statistical Yearbook for Asia and the Pacific.*

United Nations Conference on Trade and Development, Central Statistical Service, Palais des Nations, Geneva, Switzerland (Telephone in U.S. (800) 253-9646); *UNCTAD Commodity Yearbook.*

VIETNAM (SOCIALIST REPUBLIC OF) - AIRLINE SERVICE

The Economist Intelligence Unit (Asia) Limited, 10th Floor, Luk Kwok Centre, 72 Gloucester Road, Wanchai, Hong Kong (Phone Number in U.S. (800) 938-4685); *Asian Market Atlas.*

Europa Publications Limited, 18 Bedford Square, London, WC1B 3JN, England; *The Europa World Year Book.*

M.E. Sharpe, 80 Business Park Drive, Armonk, New York 10504 (800) 541-6563; *The Illustrated Book of World Rankings.*

St. Martin's Press, Inc., 175 Fifth Avenue, New York, New York 10010 (800) 221-7945; *The Statesman's Year-Book.*

VIETNAM (SOCIALIST REPUBLIC OF) - AIRPORTS

Central Intelligence Agency, Washington, D.C. 20505 (703) 482-1100, www.cia.gov; *The World Factbook.*

VIETNAM (SOCIALIST REPUBLIC OF) - ALUMINUM PRODUCTION AND CONSUMPTION - See VIETNAM (SOCIALIST REPUBLIC OF) - MINING AND MINERAL PRODUCTS

VIETNAM (SOCIALIST REPUBLIC OF) - ANIMAL HEALTH

Food and Agricultural Organization of the United Nations (FAO), Via delle Terme di Caracalla, 00100 Rome, Italy (Telephone Number in U.S. (202) 653-2400); *Animal Health Yearbook.*

VIETNAM (SOCIALIST REPUBLIC OF) - AREA AND DENSITY OF POPULATION

Central Intelligence Agency, Washington, D.C. 20505 (703) 482-1100, www.cia.gov; *The World Factbook.*

Euromonitor International, Inc., 122 South Michigan Avenue, Suite 1200, Chicago, Illinois 60603 (800) 577-EURO; *International Marketing Data and Statistics;* and *The World Economic Factbook.*

Europa Publications Limited, 18 Bedford Square, London, WC1B 3JN, England; *The Europa World Year Book.*

Food and Agricultural Organization of the United Nations (FAO) Via delle Terme di Caracalla, 00100 Rome, Italy (Telephone Number in U.S. (202) 653-2400); *The State of Food and Agriculture.*

M.E. Sharpe, 80 Business Park Drive, Armonk, New York 10504 (800) 541-6563; *The Illustrated Book of World Rankings.*

St. Martin's Press, Inc., 175 Fifth Avenue, New York, New York 10010 (800) 221-7945; *The Statesman's Year-Book.*

Statistical Office of the United Nations, Publishing Service, New York, New York 10017 (800) 253-9646; *Statistical Yearbook.*

United Nations Educational, Scientific and Cultural Organization (UNESCO), 7

Vietnam (Socialist Republic

Place de Fontenoy, F-75700 Paris, France (Telephone Number in U.S. (212) 963-5981); *Statistical Yearbook*.

The World Bank, 1818 H Street, NW, Washington, D.C. 20433 (202) 477-1234; *World Development Report*.

VIETNAM (SOCIALIST REPUBLIC OF) - ARMS EXPORTS AND IMPORTS - See VIETNAM (SOCIALIST REPUBLIC OF) - MILITARY

VIETNAM (SOCIALIST REPUBLIC OF) - BALANCE OF PAYMENTS

The Economist Intelligence Unit, 111 West 57th Street, New York, New York 10019 (800) 938-4685; *The World Market Atlas*.

International Monetary Fund, 700 Nineteenth Street, NW, Washington, D.C. 20431 (202) 623-7000; *Balance of Payments Yearbook*.

The World Bank, 1818 H Street, NW, Washington, D.C. 20433 (202) 477-1234; *World Development Report*.

VIETNAM (SOCIALIST REPUBLIC OF) - BANKING

Euromonitor International, Inc., 122 South Michigan Avenue, Suite 1200, Chicago, Illinois 60603 (800) 577-EURO; *World Marketing Data and Statistics*.

M.E. Sharpe, 80 Business Park Drive, Armonk, New York 10504 (800) 541-6563; *The Illustrated Book of World Rankings*.

St. Martin's Press, Inc., 175 Fifth Avenue, New York, New York 10010 (800) 221-7945; *The Statesman's Year-Book*.

VIETNAM (SOCIALIST REPUBLIC OF) - BARLEY PRODUCTION - See VIETNAM (SOCIALIST REPUBLIC OF) - CROPS

VIETNAM (SOCIALIST REPUBLIC OF) - BEER PRODUCTION - See VIETNAM (SOCIALIST REPUBLIC OF) - BEVERAGES

VIETNAM (SOCIALIST REPUBLIC OF) - BEVERAGES

M.E. Sharpe, 80 Business Park Drive, Armonk, New York 10504 (800) 541-6563; *The Illustrated Book of World Rankings*.

Statistical Office of the United Nations, Publishing Service, New York, New York 10017 (800) 253-9646; *Statistical Yearbook*.

VIETNAM (SOCIALIST REPUBLIC OF) - BIRTH RATES

Central Intelligence Agency, Washington, D.C. 20505 (703) 482-1100, www.cia.gov; *The World Factbook*.

The Economist Intelligence Unit (Asia) Limited, 10th Floor, Luk Kwok Centre, 72 Gloucester Road, Wanchai, Hong Kong (Phone Number in U.S. (800) 938-4685); *Asian Market Atlas*.

Euromonitor International, Inc., 122 South Michigan Avenue, Suite 1200, Chicago, Illinois 60603 (800) 577-EURO; *International Marketing Data and Statistics*; and *The World Economic Factbook*.

Europa Publications Limited, 18 Bedford Square, London, WC1B 3JN, England; *The Europa World Year Book*.

M.E. Sharpe, 80 Business Park Drive, Armonk, New York 10504 (800) 541-6563; *The Illustrated Book of World Rankings*.

Statistical Office of the United Nations, Publishing Service, New York, New York 10017 (800) 253-9646; *Asia-Pacific in Figures; Demographic Yearbook;* and *Statistical Yearbook*.

VIETNAM (SOCIALIST REPUBLIC OF) - BOOK PRODUCTION

St. Martin's Press, Inc., 175 Fifth Avenue, New York, New York 10010 (800) 221-7945; *The Statesman's Year-Book*.

United Nations Educational, Scientific and Cultural Organization (UNESCO), 7 Place de Fontenoy, F-75700 Paris, France (Telephone Number in U.S. (212) 963-5981); *Statistical Yearbook*.

VIETNAM (SOCIALIST REPUBLIC OF) - BROADCASTING

Billboard Limited, P.O. Box 9027, 1006 AA Amsterdam, The Netherlands (Telephone Number in U.S. (212) 764-7300); *World Radio TV Handbook*.

Central Intelligence Agency, Washington, D.C. 20505 (703) 482-1100, www.cia.gov; *The World Factbook*.

The Economist Intelligence Unit (Asia) Limited, 10th Floor, Luk Kwok Centre, 72 Gloucester Road, Wanchai, Hong Kong (Phone Number in U.S. (800) 938-4685); *Asian Market Atlas*.

Euromonitor International, Inc., 122 South Michigan Avenue, Suite 1200, Chicago, Illinois 60603 (800) 577-EURO; *World Marketing Data and Statistics*.

M.E. Sharpe, 80 Business Park Drive, Armonk, New York 10504 (800) 541-6563; *The Illustrated Book of World Rankings*.

St. Martin's Press, Inc., 175 Fifth Avenue, New York, New York 10010 (800) 221-7945; *The Statesman's Year-Book*.

VIETNAM (SOCIALIST REPUBLIC OF) -

BUDGET

Central Intelligence Agency, Washington, D.C. 20505 (703) 482-1100, www.cia.gov; *The World Factbook*.

VIETNAM (SOCIALIST REPUBLIC OF) - CABBAGE PRODUCTION - See VIETNAM (SOCIALIST REPUBLIC OF) - CROPS

VIETNAM (SOCIALIST REPUBLIC OF) - CALORIE SUPPLY

Food and Agricultural Organization of the United Nations (FAO) Via delle Terme di Caracalla, 00100 Rome, Italy (Telephone Number in U.S. (202) 653-2400); *The State of Food and Agriculture*.

VIETNAM (SOCIALIST REPUBLIC OF) - CASTOR BEAN PRODUCTION - See VIETNAM (SOCIALIST REPUBLIC OF) - CROPS

VIETNAM (SOCIALIST REPUBLIC OF) - CATTLE - See VIETNAM - LIVESTOCK AND POULTRY

VIETNAM (SOCIALIST REPUBLIC OF) - CAULIFLOWER PRODUCTION - See VIETNAM (SOCIALIST REPUBLIC OF) - CROPS

VIETNAM (SOCIALIST REPUBLIC OF) - CAUSTIC SODA PRODUCTION - See VIETNAM (SOCIALIST REPUBLIC OF) - BEVERAGES

VIETNAM (SOCIALIST REPUBLIC OF) - CEMENT PRODUCTION - See VIETNAM (SOCIALIST REPUBLIC OF) - MINING AND MINERAL PRODUCTS

VIETNAM (SOCIALIST REPUBLIC OF) - CHEMICAL (ORGANIC) PRODUCTION - See VIETNAM (SOCIALIST REPUBLIC OF) - MINING AND MINERAL PRODUCTS

VIETNAM (SOCIALIST REPUBLIC OF) - CHICKENS - See VIETNAM (SOCIALIST REPUBLIC OF) - LIVESTOCK AND POULTRY

VIETNAM (SOCIALIST REPUBLIC OF) - CIGAR AND CIGARETTE PRODUCTION - See VIETNAM (SOCIALIST REPUBLIC OF) - TOBACCO PRODUCTION

VIETNAM (SOCIALIST REPUBLIC OF) - CLIMATE

M.E. Sharpe, 80 Business Park Drive, Armonk, New York 10504 (800) 541-6563; *The Illustrated Book of World Rankings*.

St. Martin's Press, Inc., 175 Fifth Avenue, New York, New York 10010 (800) 221-7945; *The Statesman's Year-Book*.

VIETNAM (SOCIALIST REPUBLIC OF) - COAL PRODUCTION - See VIETNAM

(SOCIALIST REPUBLIC OF) - MINING AND MINERAL PRODUCTS

VIETNAM (SOCIALIST REPUBLIC OF) - COFFEE PRODUCTION AND CONSUMPTION - See VIETNAM (SOCIALIST REPUBLIC OF) - CROPS

VIETNAM (SOCIALIST REPUBLIC OF) - COMMERCE

St. Martin's Press, Inc., 175 Fifth Avenue, New York, New York 10010 (800) 221-7945; *The Statesman's Year-Book.*

VIETNAM (SOCIALIST REPUBLIC OF) - COMMUNICATIONS - See VIETNAM (SOCIALIST REPUBLIC OF) - TRANSPORTATION AND COMMUNICATIONS

VIETNAM (SOCIALIST REPUBLIC OF) - CONSTRUCTION INDUSTRY

M.E. Sharpe, 80 Business Park Drive, Armonk, New York 10504 (800) 541-6563; *The Illustrated Book of World Rankings.*

VIETNAM (SOCIALIST REPUBLIC OF) - CONSUMER PRICE INDEX

Statistical Office of the United Nations, Publishing Service, New York, New York 10017 (800) 253-9646; *Statistical Yearbook.*

VIETNAM (SOCIALIST REPUBLIC OF) - CONSUMER PRICES

Euromonitor International, Inc., 122 South Michigan Avenue, Suite 1200, Chicago, Illinois 60603 (800) 577-EURO; *World Marketing Data and Statistics.*

VIETNAM (SOCIALIST REPUBLIC OF) - CONSUMPTION

International Rubber Study Group, York House, Eighth Floor, Empire Way, Wembley, London HA9 0PA, England; *Rubber Statistical Bulletin.*

The World Bank, 1818 H Street, NW, Washington, D.C. 20433 (202) 477-1234; *World Development Report.*

VIETNAM (SOCIALIST REPUBLIC OF) - COPPER PRODUCTION AND CONSUMPTION - See VIETNAM (SOCIALIST REPUBLIC OF) - MINING AND MINERAL PRODUCTS

VIETNAM (SOCIALIST REPUBLIC OF) - CORN PRODUCTION - See VIETNAM (SOCIALIST REPUBLIC OF) - CROPS

VIETNAM (SOCIALIST REPUBLIC OF) - CORPORATE TAXES - See VIETNAM (SOCIALIST REPUBLIC OF) - TAXATION

VIETNAM (SOCIALIST REPUBLIC OF) - COTTON - See VIETNAM (SOCIALIST

REPUBLIC OF) - CROPS

VIETNAM (SOCIALIST REPUBLIC OF) - CROPS

Commodity Research Bureau, Inc., 30 South Wacker Drive, Suite 1810, Chicago, Illinois 60606 (312) 454-1801; *Commodity Year Book.*

Europa Publications Limited, 18 Bedford Square, London, WC1B 3JN, England; *The Europa World Year Book.*

Food and Agricultural Organization of the United Nations (FAO) Via delle Terme di Caracalla, 00100 Rome, Italy (Telephone Number in U.S. (202) 653-2400); *Production Yearbook;* and *The State of Food and Agriculture.*

M.E. Sharpe, 80 Business Park Drive, Armonk, New York 10504 (800) 541-6563; *The Illustrated Book of World Rankings.*

St. Martin's Press, Inc., 175 Fifth Avenue, New York, New York 10010 (800) 221-7945; *The Statesman's Year-Book.*

Statistical Office of the United Nations, Publishing Service, New York, New York 10017 (800) 253-9646; *Statistical Yearbook.*

United Nations Conference on Trade and Development, Central Statistical Service, Palais des Nations, Geneva, Switzerland (Telephone in U.S. (800) 253-9646); *UNCTAD Commodity Yearbook.*

VIETNAM (SOCIALIST REPUBLIC OF) - CUSTOMS DUTIES

St. Martin's Press, Inc., 175 Fifth Avenue, New York, New York 10010 (800) 221-7945; *The Statesman's Year-Book.*

VIETNAM (SOCIALIST REPUBLIC OF) - DAIRY PRODUCTS

Europa Publications Limited, 18 Bedford Square, London, WC1B 3JN, England; *The Europa World Year Book.*

Food and Agricultural Organization of the United Nations (FAO), Via delle Terme di Caracalla, 00100 Rome, Italy (Telephone Number in U.S. (202) 653-2400); *Production Yearbook;* and *The State of Food and Agriculture.*

M.E. Sharpe, 80 Business Park Drive, Armonk, New York 10504 (800) 541-6563; *The Illustrated Book of World Rankings.*

St. Martin's Press, Inc., 175 Fifth Avenue, New York, New York 10010 (800) 221-7945; *The Statesman's Year-Book.*

Statistical Office of the United Nations, Publishing Service, New York, New York 10017 (800) 253-9646; *Statistical Yearbook.*

VIETNAM (SOCIALIST REPUBLIC OF) - DEATH RATES - See VIETNAM (SOCIALIST REPUBLIC OF) - MORTALITY

VIETNAM (SOCIALIST REPUBLIC OF) - DEFENSE EXPENDITURES - See VIETNAM (SOCIALIST REPUBLIC OF) - MILITARY

VIETNAM (SOCIALIST REPUBLIC OF) - DEMOGRAPHY

The Economist Intelligence Unit, 111 West 57th Street, New York, New York 10019 (800) 938-4685; *The World Market Atlas.*

The Economist Intelligence Unit (Asia) Limited, 10th Floor, Luk Kwok Centre, 72 Gloucester Road, Wanchai, Hong Kong (Phone Number in U.S. (800) 938-4685); *Asian Market Atlas.*

Euromonitor International, Inc., 122 South Michigan Avenue, Suite 1200, Chicago, Illinois 60603 (800) 577-EURO; *International Marketing Data and Statistics;* World *Marketing Data and Statistics;* and *The World Economic Factbook.*

M.E. Sharpe, 80 Business Park Drive, Armonk, New York 10504 (800) 541-6563; *The Illustrated Book of World Rankings.*

Statistical Office of the United Nations, Publishing Service, New York, New York 10017 (800) 253-9646; *Asia-Pacific in Figures;* and *Human Development Report.*

VIETNAM (SOCIALIST REPUBLIC OF) - DIAMOND PRODUCTION - See VIETNAM (SOCIALIST REPUBLIC OF) - MINING AND MINERAL PRODUCTS

VIETNAM (SOCIALIST REPUBLIC OF) - DISEASES - See VIETNAM (SOCIALIST REPUBLIC OF) - HEALTH

VIETNAM (SOCIALIST REPUBLIC OF) - DIVORCE RATES

M.E. Sharpe, 80 Business Park Drive, Armonk, New York 10504 (800) 541-6563; *The Illustrated Book of World Rankings.*

Statistical Office of the United Nations, Publishing Service, New York, New York 10017 (800) 253-9646; *Demographic Yearbook.*

VIETNAM (SOCIALIST REPUBLIC OF) - DUCKS - See VIETNAM (SOCIALIST REPUBLIC OF) - LIVESTOCK AND POULTRY

VIETNAM (SOCIALIST REPUBLIC OF) - ECONOMY

Central Intelligence Agency, Washington, D.C. 20505 (703) 482-1100, www.cia.gov; *The World Factbook.*

Economist Intelligence Unit, 111 West 57th Street, New York, New York 10019 (800) 938-4685; *Vietnam Country Report*.

Euromonitor International, Inc., 122 South Michigan Avenue, Suite 1200, Chicago, Illinois 60603 (800) 577-EURO; *International Marketing Data and Statistics; World Marketing Data and Statistics;* and *The World Economic Factbook*.

Europa Publications Limited, 18 Bedford Square, London, WC1B 3JN, England; *The Europa World Year Book*.

M.E. Sharpe, 80 Business Park Drive, Armonk, New York 10504 (800) 541-6563; *The Illustrated Book of World Rankings*.

St. Martin's Press, Inc., 175 Fifth Avenue, New York, New York 10010 (800) 221-7945; *The Statesman's Year-Book*.

Statistical Office of the United Nations, Publishing Service, New York, New York 10017 (800) 253-9646; *World Statistics Pocketbook*.

The World Bank, 1818 H Street, NW, Washington, D.C. 20433 (202) 477-1234; *The World Bank Atlas;* and *World Development Report*.

VIETNAM (SOCIALIST REPUBLIC OF) - EDUCATION

The Economist Intelligence Unit, 111 West 57th Street, New York, New York 10019 (800) 938-4685; *The World Market Atlas*.

The Economist Intelligence Unit (Asia) Limited, 10th Floor, Luk Kwok Centre, 72 Gloucester Road, Wanchai, Hong Kong (Phone Number in U.S. (800) 938-4685); *Asian Market Atlas*.

Euromonitor International, Inc., 122 South Michigan Avenue, Suite 1200, Chicago, Illinois 60603 (800) 577-EURO; *International Marketing Data and Statistics* and *World Marketing Data and Statistics*.

M.E. Sharpe, 80 Business Park Drive, Armonk, New York 10504 (800) 541-6563; *The Illustrated Book of World Rankings*.

St. Martin's Press, Inc., 175 Fifth Avenue, New York, New York 10010 (800) 221-7945; *The Statesman's Year-Book*.

Statistical Office of the United Nations, Publishing Service, New York, New York 10017 (800) 253-9646; *Asia-Pacific in Figures;* and *Human Development Report*.

The World Bank, 1818 H Street, NW, Washington, D.C. 20433 (202) 477-1234; *World Development Report*.

VIETNAM (SOCIALIST REPUBLIC

OF) - EGG PRODUCTION AND CONSUMPTION - See VIETNAM (SOCIALIST REPUBLIC OF) - DAIRY PRODUCTS

VIETNAM (SOCIALIST REPUBLIC OF) - ELECTRICITY

Central Intelligence Agency, Washington, D.C. 20505 (703) 482-1100, www.cia.gov; *The World Factbook*.

M.E. Sharpe, 80 Business Park Drive, Armonk, New York 10504 (800) 541-6563; *The Illustrated Book of World Rankings*.

Penn Well Publishing Company, 1421 South Sheridan Road, P.O. Box 1260, Tulsa, Oklahoma 74101 (800) 752-9764; *International Energy Statistics Sourcebook*.

St. Martin's Press, Inc., 175 Fifth Avenue, New York, New York 10010 (800) 221-7945; *The Statesman's Year-Book*.

Statistical Office of the United Nations, Publishing Service, New York, New York 10017 (800) 253-9646; *Electric Power in Asia and the Pacific; Human Development Report;* and *Statistical Yearbook*.

VIETNAM (SOCIALIST REPUBLIC OF) - EMPLOYMENT

Euromonitor International, Inc., 122 South Michigan Avenue, Suite 1200, Chicago, Illinois 60603 (800) 577-EURO; *International Marketing Data and Statistics*.

M.E. Sharpe, 80 Business Park Drive, Armonk, New York 10504 (800) 541-6563; *The Illustrated Book of World Rankings*.

Statistical Office of the United Nations, Publishing Service, New York, New York 10017 (800) 253-9646; *Asia-Pacific in Figures*.

VIETNAM (SOCIALIST REPUBLIC OF) - ENERGY

Euromonitor International, Inc., 122 South Michigan Avenue, Suite 1200, Chicago, Illinois 60603 (800) 577-EURO; *International Marketing Data and Statistics; World Marketing Data and Statistics;* and *The World Economic Factbook*.

Food and Agricultural Organization of the United Nations (FAO) Via delle Terme di Caracalla, 00100 Rome, Italy (Telephone Number in U.S. (202) 653-2400); *The State of Food and Agriculture*.

M.E. Sharpe, 80 Business Park Drive, Armonk, New York 10504 (800) 541-6563; *The Illustrated Book of World Rankings*.

Penn Well Publishing Company, 1421 South Sheridan Road, P.O. Box 1260, Tulsa, Oklahoma 74101 (800) 752-9764; *International Energy Statistics Sourcebook*.

St. Martin's Press, Inc., 175 Fifth Avenue, New York, New York 10010 (800) 221-7945; *The Statesman's Year-Book*.

Statistical Office of the United Nations, Publishing Service, New York, New York 10017 (800) 253-9646; *Asia-Pacific in Figures; Human Development Report; Statistical Yearbook; World Statistics Pocketbook;* and *Statistical Yearbook for Asia and the Pacific*.

The World Bank, 1818 H Street, NW, Washington, D.C. 20433 (202) 477-1234; *The World Bank Atlas;* and *World Development Report*.

VIETNAM (SOCIALIST REPUBLIC OF) - ENVIRONMENT

Economist Intelligence Unit, 111 West 57th Street, New York, New York 10019 (800) 938-4685; *Vietnam Country Report*.

Statistical Office of the United Nations, Publishing Service, New York, New York 10017 (800) 253-9646; *World Statistics Pocketbook*.

VIETNAM (SOCIALIST REPUBLIC OF) - EXCHANGE RATES

Central Intelligence Agency, Washington, D.C. 20505 (703) 482-1100, www.cia.gov; *The World Factbook*.

The Economist Intelligence Unit (Asia) Limited, 10th Floor, Luk Kwok Centre, 72 Gloucester Road, Wanchai, Hong Kong (Phone Number in U.S. (800) 938-4685); *Asian Market Atlas*.

Euromonitor International, Inc., 122 South Michigan Avenue, Suite 1200, Chicago, Illinois 60603 (800) 577-EURO; *International Marketing Data and Statistics;* and *The World Economic Factbook*.

Europa Publications Limited, 18 Bedford Square, London, WC1B 3JN, England; *The Europa World Year Book*.

Statistical Office of the United Nations, Publishing Service, New York, New York 10017 (800) 253-9646; *World Statistics Pocketbook*.

VIETNAM (SOCIALIST REPUBLIC OF) - EXPORTS

Central Intelligence Agency, Washington, D.C. 20505 (703) 482-1100, www.cia.gov; *The World Factbook*.

The Economist Intelligence Unit, 111 West 57th Street, New York, New York 10019 (800) 938-4685; *Vietnam Country Report;* and *The World Market Atlas*.

The Economist Intelligence Unit (Asia) Limited, 10th Floor, Luk Kwok Centre, 72

Gloucester Road, Wanchai, Hong Kong (Phone Number in U.S. (800) 938-4685); *Asian Market Atlas.*

Euromonitor International, Inc., 122 South Michigan Avenue, Suite 1200, Chicago, Illinois 60603 (800) 577-EURO; *International Marketing Data and Statistics;* and *The World Economic Factbook.*

Europa Publications Limited, 18 Bedford Square, London, WC1B 3JN, England; *The Europa World Year Book.*

Food and Agricultural Organization of the United Nations (FAO) Via delle Terme di Caracalla, 00100 Rome, Italy (Telephone Number in U.S. (202) 653-2400); *The State of Food and Agriculture.*

International Monetary Fund, 700 Nineteenth Street, NW, Washington, D.C. 20431 (202) 623-7000; *Direction of Trade Statistics.*

International Rubber Study Group, York House, Eighth Floor, Empire Way, Wembley, London HA9 0PA, England; *Rubber Statistical Bulletin.*

St. Martin's Press, Inc., 175 Fifth Avenue, New York, New York 10010 (800) 221-7945; *The Statesman's Year-Book.*

The World Bank, 1818 H Street, NW, Washington, D.C. 20433 (202) 477-1234; *World Development Report.*

VIETNAM (SOCIALIST REPUBLIC OF) - EXTERNAL INDEBTEDNESS

The World Bank, 1818 H Street, NW, Washington, D.C. 20433 (202) 477-1234; *World Development Report.*

VIETNAM (SOCIALIST REPUBLIC OF) - EXTERNAL TRADE

Euromonitor International, Inc., 122 South Michigan Avenue, Suite 1200, Chicago, Illinois 60603 (800) 577-EURO; *World Marketing Data and Statistics.*

Food and Agricultural Organization of the United Nations (FAO) Via delle Terme di Caracalla, 00100 Rome, Italy (Telephone Number in U.S. (202) 653-2400); *The State of Food and Agriculture.*

Statistical Office of the United Nations, Publishing Service, New York, New York 10017 (800) 253-9646; *Asia-Pacific in Figures;* and *Statistical Yearbook for Asia and the Pacific.*

VIETNAM (SOCIALIST REPUBLIC OF) - FABRIC PRODUCTION - See VIETNAM (SOCIALIST REPUBLIC OF) - TEXTILE INDUSTRY

VIETNAM (SOCIALIST REPUBLIC OF) -

FARM CROPS - See VIETNAM (SOCIALIST REPUBLIC OF) - CROPS

VIETNAM (SOCIALIST REPUBLIC OF) - FEMALE WORKING POPULATION - See VIETNAM (SOCIALIST REPUBLIC OF) - EMPLOYMENT

VIETNAM (SOCIALIST REPUBLIC OF) - FERTILITY RATES

Central Intelligence Agency, Washington, D.C. 20505 (703) 482-1100, www.cia.gov; *The World Factbook.*

The Economist Intelligence Unit (Asia) Limited, 10th Floor, Luk Kwok Centre, 72 Gloucester Road, Wanchai, Hong Kong (Phone Number in U.S. (800) 938-4685); *Asian Market Atlas.*

M.E. Sharpe, 80 Business Park Drive, Armonk, New York 10504 (800) 541-6563; *The Illustrated Book of World Rankings.*

Statistical Office of the United Nations, Publishing Service, New York, New York 10017 (800) 253-9646; *Human Development Report.*

The World Bank, 1818 H Street, NW, Washington, D.C. 20433 (202) 477-1234; *The World Bank Atlas;* and *World Development Report.*

VIETNAM (SOCIALIST REPUBLIC OF) - FERTILIZER PRODUCTION AND CONSUMPTION

Food and Agricultural Organization of the United Nations (FAO), Via delle Terme di Caracalla, 00100 Rome, Italy (Telephone Number in U.S. (202) 653-2400); *Fertilizer Yearbook;* and *The State of Food and Agriculture.*

Statistical Office of the United Nations, Publishing Service, New York, New York 10017 (800) 253-9646; *Statistical Yearbook.*

VIETNAM (SOCIALIST REPUBLIC OF) - FETAL MORTALITY - See VIETNAM (SOCIALIST REPUBLIC OF) - MORTALITY

VIETNAM (SOCIALIST REPUBLIC OF) - FILM - See VIETNAM (SOCIALIST REPUBLIC OF) - MOTION PICTURES

VIETNAM (SOCIALIST REPUBLIC OF) - FINANCE

Economist Intelligence Unit, 111 West 57th Street, New York, New York 10019 (800) 938-4685; *Vietnam Country Report.*

Europa Publications Limited, 18 Bedford Square, London, WC1B 3JN, England; *The Europa World Year Book.*

M.E. Sharpe, 80 Business Park Drive, Armonk, New York 10504 (800) 541-6563;

The Illustrated Book of World Rankings.

St. Martin's Press, Inc., 175 Fifth Avenue, New York, New York 10010 (800) 221-7945; *The Statesman's Year-Book.*

Statistical Office of the United Nations, Publishing Service, New York, New York 10017 (800) 253-9646; *Statistical Yearbook for Asia and the Pacific.*

VIETNAM (SOCIALIST REPUBLIC OF) - FISHERIES

Europa Publications Limited, 18 Bedford Square, London, WC1B 3JN, England; *The Europa World Year Book.*

Food and Agricultural Organization of the United Nations (FAO) Via delle Terme di Caracalla, 00100 Rome, Italy (Telephone Number in U.S. (202) 653-2400); *The State of Food and Agriculture;* and *Yearbook of Fishery Statistics.*

M.E. Sharpe, 80 Business Park Drive, Armonk, New York 10504 (800) 541-6563; *The Illustrated Book of World Rankings.*

St. Martin's Press, Inc., 175 Fifth Avenue, New York, New York 10010 (800) 221-7945; *The Statesman's Year-Book.*

Statistical Office of the United Nations, Publishing Service, New York, New York 10017 (800) 253-9646; *Statistical Yearbook.*

United Nations Conference on Trade and Development, Central Statistical Service, Palais des Nations, Geneva, Switzerland (Telephone in U.S. (800) 253-9646); *UNCTAD Commodity Yearbook.*

VIETNAM (SOCIALIST REPUBLIC OF) - FOOD

Food and Agricultural Organization of the United Nations (FAO) Via delle Terme di Caracalla, 00100 Rome, Italy (Telephone Number in U.S. (202) 653-2400); *The State of Food and Agriculture.*

Statistical Office of the United Nations, Publishing Service, New York, New York 10017 (800) 253-9646; *Human Development Report;* and *Statistical Yearbook for Asia and the Pacific.*

United Nations Conference on Trade and Development, Central Statistical Service, Palais des Nations, Geneva, Switzerland (Telephone in U.S. (800) 253-9646); *UNCTAD Commodity Yearbook.*

VIETNAM (SOCIALIST REPUBLIC OF) - FOREIGN DEBT

St. Martin's Press, Inc., 175 Fifth Avenue, New York, New York 10010 (800) 221-7945; *The Statesman's Year-Book.*

VIETNAM (SOCIALIST REPUBLIC OF) - FOREIGN TRADE

Economist Intelligence Unit, 111 West 57th Street, New York, New York 10019 (800) 938-4685; *Vietnam Country Report.*

The Economist Intelligence Unit (Asia) Limited, 10th Floor, Luk Kwok Centre, 72 Gloucester Road, Wanchai, Hong Kong (Phone Number in U.S. (800) 938-4685); *Asian Market Atlas.*

Euromonitor International, Inc., 122 South Michigan Avenue, Suite 1200, Chicago, Illinois 60603 (800) 577-EURO; *International Marketing Data and Statistics;* and *The World Economic Factbook.*

Europa Publications Limited, 18 Bedford Square, London, WC1B 3JN, England; *The Europa World Year Book.*

Food and Agricultural Organization of the United Nations (FAO) Via delle Terme di Caracalla, 00100 Rome, Italy (Telephone Number in U.S. (202) 653-2400); *The State of Food and Agriculture.*

M.E. Sharpe, 80 Business Park Drive, Armonk, New York 10504 (800) 541-6563; *The Illustrated Book of World Rankings.*

St. Martin's Press, Inc., 175 Fifth Avenue, New York, New York 10010 (800) 221-7945; *The Statesman's Year-Book.*

Statistical Office of the United Nations, Publishing Service, New York, New York 10017 (800) 253-9646; *Statistical Yearbook.*

United Nations Conference on Trade and Development, Central Statistical Service, Palais des Nations, Geneva, Switzerland (Telephone in U.S. (800) 253-9646); *UNCTAD Commodity Yearbook.*

The World Bank, 1818 H Street, NW, Washington, D.C. 20433 (202) 477-1234; *World Development Report.*

VIETNAM (SOCIALIST REPUBLIC OF) - FORESTRY AND FOREST PRODUCTS

The Economist Intelligence Unit (Asia) Limited, 10th Floor, Luk Kwok Centre, 72 Gloucester Road, Wanchai, Hong Kong (Phone Number in U.S. (800) 938-4685); *Asian Market Atlas.*

Europa Publications Limited, 18 Bedford Square, London, WC1B 3JN, England; *The Europa World Year Book.*

Food and Agricultural Organization of the United Nations (FAO) Via delle Terme di Caracalla, 00100 Rome, Italy (Telephone Number in U.S. (202) 653-2400); *The State of Food and Agriculture;* and *Yearbook of Forest Products.*

M.E. Sharpe, 80 Business Park Drive, Armonk, New York 10504 (800) 541-6563; *The Illustrated Book of World Rankings.*

St. Martin's Press, Inc., 175 Fifth Avenue, New York, New York 10010 (800) 221-7945; *The Statesman's Year-Book.*

Statistical Office of the United Nations, Publishing Service, New York, New York 10017 (800) 253-9646; *Statistical Yearbook.*

United Nations Conference on Trade and Development, Central Statistical Service, Palais des Nations, Geneva, Switzerland (Telephone in U.S. (800) 253-9646); *UNCTAD Commodity Yearbook.*

United Nations Educational, Scientific and Cultural Organization (UNESCO), 7 Place de Fontenoy, F-75700 Paris, France (Telephone Number in U.S. (212) 963-5981); *Statistical Yearbook.*

The World Bank, 1818 H Street, NW, Washington, D.C. 20433 (202) 477-1234; *World Development Report.*

VIETNAM (SOCIALIST REPUBLIC OF) - GAS PRODUCTION - See VIETNAM (SOCIALIST REPUBLIC OF) - MINING AND MINERAL PRODUCTS

VIETNAM (SOCIALIST REPUBLIC OF) - GENERAL MORTALITY - See VIETNAM (SOCIALIST REPUBLIC OF) - MORTALITY

VIETNAM (SOCIALIST REPUBLIC OF) - GEOGRAPHIC DATA

M.E. Sharpe, 80 Business Park Drive, Armonk, New York 10504 (800) 541-6563; *The Illustrated Book of World Rankings.*

VIETNAM (SOCIALIST REPUBLIC OF) - GOATS - See VIETNAM (SOCIALIST REPUBLIC OF) - LIVESTOCK AND POULTRY

VIETNAM (SOCIALIST REPUBLIC OF) - GOLD PRODUCTION - See VIETNAM (SOCIALIST REPUBLIC OF) - MINING AND MINERAL PRODUCTS

VIETNAM (SOCIALIST REPUBLIC OF) - GOVERNMENT

Central Intelligence Agency, Washington, D.C. 20505 (703) 482-1100, www.cia.gov; *The World Factbook.*

Europa Publications Limited, 18 Bedford Square, London, WC1B 3JN, England; *The Europa World Year Book.*

St. Martin's Press, Inc., 175 Fifth Avenue, New York, New York 10010 (800) 221-7945; *The Statesman's Year-Book.*

Statistical Office of the United Nations, Publishing Service, New York, New York

10017 (800) 253-9646; *Asia-Pacific in Figures;* and *National Accounts Statistics.*

The World Bank, 1818 H Street, NW, Washington, D.C. 20433 (202) 477-1234; *World Development Report.*

VIETNAM (SOCIALIST REPUBLIC OF) - GRAIN PRODUCTION - See VIETNAM (SOCIALIST REPUBLIC OF) - CROPS

VIETNAM (SOCIALIST REPUBLIC OF) - GROSS DOMESTIC PRODUCT

The Economist Intelligence Unit, 111 West 57th Street, New York, New York 10019 (800) 938-4685; *Vietnam Country Report;* and *The World Market Atlas.*

The Economist Intelligence Unit (Asia) Limited, 10th Floor, Luk Kwok Centre, 72 Gloucester Road, Wanchai, Hong Kong (Phone Number in U.S. (800) 938-4685); *Asian Market Atlas.*

Euromonitor International, Inc., 122 South Michigan Avenue, Suite 1200, Chicago, Illinois 60603 (800) 577-EURO; *International Marketing Data and Statistics;* and *The World Economic Factbook.*

Europa Publications Limited, 18 Bedford Square, London, WC1B 3JN, England; *The Europa World Year Book.*

M.E. Sharpe, 80 Business Park Drive, Armonk, New York 10504 (800) 541-6563; *The Illustrated Book of World Rankings.*

Statistical Office of the United Nations, Publishing Service, New York, New York 10017 (800) 253-9646; *Human Development Report; National Accounts Statistics;* and *Statistical Yearbook.*

The World Bank, 1818 H Street, NW, Washington, D.C. 20433 (202) 477-1234; *World Development Report.*

VIETNAM (SOCIALIST REPUBLIC OF) - GROSS NATIONAL PRODUCT

Euromonitor International, Inc., 122 South Michigan Avenue, Suite 1200, Chicago, Illinois 60603 (800) 577-EURO; *International Marketing Data and Statistics.*

St. Martin's Press, Inc., 175 Fifth Avenue, New York, New York 10010 (800) 221-7945; *The Statesman's Year-Book.*

U.S. Arms Control and Disarmament Agency, 320 Twenty-first Street, NW, Washington, D.C. 20451 (202) 647-8677; *World Military Expenditures and Arms Transfers.*

The World Bank, 1818 H Street, NW, Washington, D.C. 20433 (202) 477-1234; *The World Bank Atlas;* and *World*

Development Report.

VIETNAM (SOCIALIST REPUBLIC OF) -
GROUNDNUTS PRODUCTION - See
VIETNAM (SOCIALIST REPUBLIC OF) -
CROPS

VIETNAM (SOCIALIST REPUBLIC OF) -
HEALTH

The Economist Intelligence Unit (Asia)
Limited, 10th Floor, Luk Kwok Centre, 72
Gloucester Road, Wanchai, Hong Kong
(Phone Number in U.S. (800) 938-4685);
Asian Market Atlas.

Euromonitor International, Inc., 122
South Michigan Avenue, Suite 1200,
Chicago, Illinois 60603 (800) 577-EURO;
World Marketing Data and Statistics.

M.E. Sharpe, 80 Business Park Drive,
Armonk, New York 10504 (800) 541-6563;
The Illustrated Book of World Rankings.

St. Martin's Press, Inc., 175 Fifth
Avenue, New York, New York 10010 (800)
221-7945; *The Statesman's Year-Book.*

Statistical Office of the United Nations,
Publishing Service, New York, New York
10017 (800) 253-9646; *Asia-Pacific in
Figures; Human Development Report;* and
Statistical Yearbook.

United Nations Children's Fund
(UNICEF), 3 United Nations Plaza, New
York, New York 10017 (800) 253-9646; *State
of the World's Children.*

The World Bank, 1818 H Street, NW,
Washington, D.C. 20433 (202) 477-1234;
World Development Report.

World Health Organization, Office of
Publications, 20 Avenue Appia, CH-1211
Geneva 27, Switzerland (Telephone
Number in U.S. (518) 436-9686); *World
Health Statistics Annual.*

VIETNAM (SOCIALIST REPUBLIC OF) -
HEALTH AND MEDICAL SERVICES

Statistical Office of the United Nations,
Publishing Service, New York, New York
10017 (800) 253-9646; *Statistical Yearbook.*

VIETNAM (SOCIALIST REPUBLIC OF) -
HIDE PRODUCTION

Food and Agricultural Organization of
the United Nations (FAO), Via delle Terme
di Caracalla, 00100 Rome, Italy (Telephone
Number in U.S. (202) 653-2400);
Production Yearbook.

VIETNAM (SOCIALIST REPUBLIC OF) -
HIGHWAYS

Central Intelligence Agency,

Washington, D.C. 20505 (703) 482-1100,
www.cia.gov; *The World Factbook.*

The Economist Intelligence Unit (Asia)
Limited, 10th Floor, Luk Kwok Centre, 72
Gloucester Road, Wanchai, Hong Kong
(Phone Number in U.S. (800) 938-4685);
Asian Market Atlas.

St. Martin's Press, Inc., 175 Fifth
Avenue, New York, New York 10010 (800)
221-7945; *The Statesman's Year-Book.*

VIETNAM (SOCIALIST REPUBLIC OF) -
HORSES - See VIETNAM (SOCIALIST
REPUBLIC OF) - LIVESTOCK AND
POULTRY

VIETNAM (SOCIALIST REPUBLIC OF) -
HOURS OF WORK - See VIETNAM
(SOCIALIST REPUBLIC OF) -
EMPLOYMENT

VIETNAM (SOCIALIST REPUBLIC OF) -
HOUSING AND HOUSING UNITS

Euromonitor International, Inc., 122
South Michigan Avenue, Suite 1200,
Chicago, Illinois 60603 (800) 577-EURO;
World Marketing Data and Statistics.

VIETNAM (SOCIALIST REPUBLIC OF) -
HOUSING CONSTRUCTION

M.E. Sharpe, 80 Business Park Drive,
Armonk, New York 10504 (800) 541-6563;
The Illustrated Book of World Rankings.

VIETNAM (SOCIALIST REPUBLIC OF) -
HYDROCHLORIC ACID PRODUCTION

Statistical Office of the United Nations,
Publishing Service, New York, New York
10017 (800) 253-9646; *Statistical Yearbook.*

VIETNAM (SOCIALIST REPUBLIC OF) -
ILLITERATE POPULATION

Central Intelligence Agency,
Washington, D.C. 20505 (703) 482-1100,
www.cia.gov; *The World Factbook.*

The Economist Intelligence Unit, 111
West 57th Street, New York, New York
10019 (800) 938-4685; *The World Market
Atlas.*

Euromonitor International, Inc., 122
South Michigan Avenue, Suite 1200,
Chicago, Illinois 60603 (800) 577-EURO;
The World Economic Factbook.

St. Martin's Press, Inc., 175 Fifth
Avenue, New York, New York 10010 (800)
221-7945; *The Statesman's Year-Book.*

Statistical Office of the United Nations,
Publishing Service, New York, New York
10017 (800) 253-9646; *Asia-Pacific in
Figures;* and *Human Development Report.*

VIETNAM (SOCIALIST REPUBLIC OF) -
IMPORTS

Central Intelligence Agency,
Washington, D.C. 20505 (703) 482-1100,
www.cia.gov; *The World Factbook.*

The Economist Intelligence Unit, 111
West 57th Street, New York, New York
10019 (800) 938-4685; *Vietnam Country
Report;* and *The World Market Atlas.*

The Economist Intelligence Unit (Asia)
Limited, 10th Floor, Luk Kwok Centre, 72
Gloucester Road, Wanchai, Hong Kong
(Phone Number in U.S. (800) 938-4685);
Asian Market Atlas.

Euromonitor International, Inc., 122
South Michigan Avenue, Suite 1200,
Chicago, Illinois 60603 (800) 577-EURO;
International Marketing Data and Statistics;
and *The World Economic Factbook.*

Europa Publications Limited, 18
Bedford Square, London, WC1B 3JN,
England; *The Europa World Year Book.*

Food and Agricultural Organization of
the United Nations (FAO) Via delle Terme
di Caracalla, 00100 Rome, Italy (Telephone
Number in U.S. (202) 653-2400); *The State
of Food and Agriculture.*

International Monetary Fund, 700
Nineteenth Street, NW, Washington, D.C.
20431 (202) 623-7000; *Direction of Trade
Statistics.*

International Rubber Study Group, York
House, Eighth Floor, Empire Way,
Wembley, London HA9 0PA, England;
Rubber Statistical Bulletin.

St. Martin's Press, Inc., 175 Fifth
Avenue, New York, New York 10010 (800)
221-7945; *The Statesman's Year-Book.*

The World Bank, 1818 H Street, NW,
Washington, D.C. 20433 (202) 477-1234;
World Development Report.

VIETNAM (SOCIALIST REPUBLIC OF) -
INDUSTRY

Central Intelligence Agency,
Washington, D.C. 20505 (703) 482-1100,
www.cia.gov; *The World Factbook.*

Economist Intelligence Unit, 111 West
57th Street, New York, New York 10019
(800) 938-4685; *Vietnam Country Report.*

Euromonitor International, Inc., 122
South Michigan Avenue, Suite 1200,
Chicago, Illinois 60603 (800) 577-EURO;
*International Marketing Data and Statistics;
World Marketing Data and Statistics;* and
The World Economic Factbook.

Europa Publications Limited, 18

Bedford Square, London, WC1B 3JN, England; *The Europa World Year Book.*

M.E. Sharpe, 80 Business Park Drive, Armonk, New York 10504 (800) 541-6563; *The Illustrated Book of World Rankings.*

St. Martin's Press, Inc., 175 Fifth Avenue, New York, New York 10010 (800) 221-7945; *The Statesman's Year-Book.*

Statistical Office of the United Nations, Publishing Service, New York, New York 10017 (800) 253-9646; *Asia-Pacific in Figures; Statistical Yearbook;* and *Statistical Yearbook for Asia and the Pacific.*

World Intellectual Property Organization, 34 Chemin des Colombettes, CH-1211 Geneva 20. Switzerland; *Industrial Property Statistics.*

VIETNAM (SOCIALIST REPUBLIC OF) - INFANT AND MATERNAL MORTALITY - See VIETNAM (SOCIALIST REPUBLIC OF) - MORTALITY

VIETNAM (SOCIALIST REPUBLIC OF) - INTERNAL TRADE

Statistical Office of the United Nations, Publishing Service, New York, New York 10017 (800) 253-9646; *Statistical Yearbook for Asia and the Pacific.*

VIETNAM (SOCIALIST REPUBLIC OF) - IRON ORE PRODUCTION AND CONSUMPTION - See VIETNAM (SOCIALIST REPUBLIC OF) - MINING AND MINERAL PRODUCTS

VIETNAM (SOCIALIST REPUBLIC OF) - IRRIGATION

Euromonitor International, Inc., 122 South Michigan Avenue, Suite 1200, Chicago, Illinois 60603 (800) 577-EURO; *International Marketing Data and Statistics.*

VIETNAM (SOCIALIST REPUBLIC OF) - JUTE PRODUCTION - See VIETNAM (SOCIALIST REPUBLIC OF) - CROPS

VIETNAM (SOCIALIST REPUBLIC OF) - LABOR

Central Intelligence Agency, Washington, D.C. 20505 (703) 482-1100, www.cia.gov; *The World Factbook.*

The Economist Intelligence Unit (Asia) Limited, 10th Floor, Luk Kwok Centre, 72 Gloucester Road, Wanchai, Hong Kong (Phone Number in U.S. (800) 938-4685); *Asian Market Atlas.*

Euromonitor International, Inc., 122 South Michigan Avenue, Suite 1200, Chicago, Illinois 60603 (800) 577-EURO; *International Marketing Data and Statistics;* and *World Marketing Data and Statistics.*

Food and Agricultural Organization of the United Nations (FAO) Via delle Terme di Caracalla, 00100 Rome, Italy (Telephone Number in U.S. (202) 653-2400); *The State of Food and Agriculture.*

M.E. Sharpe, 80 Business Park Drive, Armonk, New York 10504 (800) 541-6563; *The Illustrated Book of World Rankings.*

St. Martin's Press, Inc., 175 Fifth Avenue, New York, New York 10010 (800) 221-7945; *The Statesman's Year-Book.*

Statistical Office of the United Nations, Publishing Service, New York, New York 10017 (800) 253-9646; *Human Development Report.*

The World Bank, 1818 H Street, NW, Washington, D.C. 20433 (202) 477-1234; *The World Bank Atlas;* and *World Development Report.*

VIETNAM (SOCIALIST REPUBLIC OF) - LAND USE

Central Intelligence Agency, Washington, D.C. 20505 (703) 482-1100, www.cia.gov; *The World Factbook.*

Euromonitor International, Inc., 122 South Michigan Avenue, Suite 1200, Chicago, Illinois 60603 (800) 577-EURO; *International Marketing Data and Statistics.*

The World Bank, 1818 H Street, NW, Washington, D.C. 20433 (202) 477-1234; *World Development Report.*

VIETNAM (SOCIALIST REPUBLIC OF) - LIBRARIES

M.E. Sharpe, 80 Business Park Drive, Armonk, New York 10504 (800) 541-6563; *The Illustrated Book of World Rankings.*

United Nations Educational, Scientific and Cultural Organization (UNESCO), 7 Place de Fontenoy, F-75700 Paris, France (Telephone Number in U.S. (212) 963-5981); *Statistical Yearbook.*

VIETNAM (SOCIALIST REPUBLIC OF) - LIFE EXPECTANCY

Central Intelligence Agency, Washington, D.C. 20505 (703) 482-1100, www.cia.gov; *The World Factbook.*

The Economist Intelligence Unit (Asia) Limited, 10th Floor, Luk Kwok Centre, 72 Gloucester Road, Wanchai, Hong Kong (Phone Number in U.S. (800) 938-4685); *Asian Market Atlas.*

Euromonitor International, Inc., 122 South Michigan Avenue, Suite 1200, Chicago, Illinois 60603 (800) 577-EURO; *The World Economic Factbook.*

St. Martin's Press, Inc., 175 Fifth Avenue, New York, New York 10010 (800) 221-7945; *The Statesman's Year-Book.*

Statistical Office of the United Nations, Publishing Service, New York, New York 10017 (800) 253-9646; *Asia-Pacific in Figures; World Statistics Pocketbook;* and *Human Development Report.*

The World Bank, 1818 H Street, NW, Washington, D.C. 20433 (202) 477-1234; *The World Bank Atlas;* and *World Development Report.*

VIETNAM (SOCIALIST REPUBLIC OF) - LITERACY RATE

Euromonitor International, Inc., 122 South Michigan Avenue, Suite 1200, Chicago, Illinois 60603 (800) 577-EURO; *World Marketing Data and Statistics.*

VIETNAM (SOCIALIST REPUBLIC OF) - LIVESTOCK AND POULTRY

Euromonitor International, Inc., 122 South Michigan Avenue, Suite 1200, Chicago, Illinois 60603 (800) 577-EURO; *International Marketing Data and Statistics.*

Europa Publications Limited, 18 Bedford Square, London, WC1B 3JN, England; *The Europa World Year Book.*

Food and Agricultural Organization of the United Nations (FAO) Via delle Terme di Caracalla, 00100 Rome, Italy (Telephone Number in U.S. (202) 653-2400); *Production Yearbook;* and *The State of Food and Agriculture.*

M.E. Sharpe, 80 Business Park Drive, Armonk, New York 10504 (800) 541-6563; *The Illustrated Book of World Rankings.*

St. Martin's Press, Inc., 175 Fifth Avenue, New York, New York 10010 (800) 221-7945; *The Statesman's Year-Book.*

Statistical Office of the United Nations, Publishing Service, New York, New York 10017; *Statistical Yearbook.*

United Nations Conference on Trade and Development, Central Statistical Service, Palais des Nations, Geneva, Switzerland (Telephone in U.S. (800) 253-9646); *UNCTAD Commodity Yearbook.*

VIETNAM (SOCIALIST REPUBLIC OF) - LIVING LEVELS - See VIETNAM (SOCIALIST REPUBLIC OF) - LIFE EXPECTANCY

VIETNAM (SOCIALIST REPUBLIC OF) - MAIL - NUMBER OF PIECES SENT OR RECEIVED

Statistical Office of the United Nations, Publishing Service, New York, New York 10017 (800) 253-9646; *Statistical Yearbook.*

VIETNAM (SOCIALIST REPUBLIC OF) - MANPOWER

Statistical Office of the United Nations, Publishing Service, New York, New York 10017 (800) 253-9646; *Statistical Yearbook.*

VIETNAM (SOCIALIST REPUBLIC OF) - MANUFACTURING

M.E. Sharpe, 80 Business Park Drive, Armonk, New York 10504 (800) 541-6563; *The Illustrated Book of World Rankings.*

Statistical Office of the United Nations, Publishing Service, New York, New York 10017 (800) 253-9646; *Statistical Yearbook.*

VIETNAM (SOCIALIST REPUBLIC OF) - MARRIAGE RATES

M.E. Sharpe, 80 Business Park Drive, Armonk, New York 10504 (800) 541-6563; *The Illustrated Book of World Rankings.*

Statistical Office of the United Nations, Publishing Service, New York, New York 10017 (800) 253-9646; *Demographic Yearbook.*

VIETNAM (SOCIALIST REPUBLIC OF) - MEAT PRODUCTION - See VIETNAM (SOCIALIST REPUBLIC OF) - LIVESTOCK AND POULTRY

VIETNAM (SOCIALIST REPUBLIC OF) - MERCHANT SHIPPING

Europa Publications Limited, 18 Bedford Square, London, WC1B 3JN, England; *The Europa World Year Book.*

St. Martin's Press, Inc., 175 Fifth Avenue, New York, New York 10010 (800) 221-7945; *The Statesman's Year-Book.*

Statistical Office of the United Nations, Publishing Service, New York, New York 10017 (800) 253-9646; *Statistical Yearbook.*

U.S. Department of Transportation, Maritime Administration, 400 Seventh Street, SW, Washington, D.C. 20590 (202) 366-5807, www.marad.dot.gov; *A Statistical Analysis of the World's Merchant Fleets.*

VIETNAM (SOCIALIST REPUBLIC OF) - MILITARY

Central Intelligence Agency, Washington, D.C. 20505 (703) 482-1100, www.cia.gov; *The World Factbook.*

The Economist Intelligence Unit (Asia) Limited, 10th Floor, Luk Kwok Centre, 72 Gloucester Road, Wanchai, Hong Kong (Phone Number in U.S. (800) 938-4685); *Asian Market Atlas.*

Euromonitor International, Inc., 122

South Michigan Avenue, Suite 1200, Chicago, Illinois 60603 (800) 577-EURO; *World Marketing Data and Statistics.*

The International Institute for Strategic Studies, 23 Tavistock Street, London WC2E 7NQ, England; *The Military Balance.*

St. Martin's Press, Inc., 175 Fifth Avenue, New York, New York 10010 (800) 221-7945; *The Statesman's Year-Book.*

Statistical Office of the United Nations, Publishing Service, New York, New York 10017 (800) 253-9646; *Human Development Report.*

U.S. Arms Control and Disarmament Agency, 320 Twenty-first Street, NW, Washington, D.C. 20451 (202) 647-8677; *World Military Expenditures and Arms Transfers.*

VIETNAM (SOCIALIST REPUBLIC OF) - MILK PRODUCTION - See VIETNAM (SOCIALIST REPUBLIC OF) - DAIRY PRODUCTS

VIETNAM (SOCIALIST REPUBLIC OF) - MINING AND MINERAL PRODUCTS

Europa Publications Limited, 18 Bedford Square, London, WC1B 3JN, England; *The Europa World Year Book.*

M.E. Sharpe, 80 Business Park Drive, Armonk, New York 10504 (800) 541-6563; *The Illustrated Book of World Rankings.*

Penn Well Publishing Company, 1421 South Sheridan Road, P.O. Box 1260, Tulsa, Oklahoma 74101 (800) 752-9764; *International Energy Statistics Sourcebook.*

St. Martin's Press, Inc., 175 Fifth Avenue, New York, New York 10010 (800) 221-7945; *The Statesman's Year-Book.*

Statistical Office of the United Nations, Publishing Service, New York, New York 10017 (800) 253-9646; *Statistical Yearbook.*

United Nations Conference on Trade and Development, Central Statistical Service, Palais des Nations, Geneva, Switzerland (Telephone in U.S. (800) 253-9646); *UNCTAD Commodity Yearbook.*

VIETNAM (SOCIALIST REPUBLIC OF) - MONEY EXCHANGE RATES - See VIETNAM (SOCIALIST REPUBLIC OF) - EXCHANGE RATES

VIETNAM (SOCIALIST REPUBLIC OF) - MONEY RESERVES

Euromonitor International, Inc., 122 South Michigan Avenue, Suite 1200, Chicago, Illinois 60603 (800) 577-EURO; *International Marketing Data and Statistics.*

VIETNAM (SOCIALIST REPUBLIC OF) - MONEY SUPPLY

Economist Intelligence Unit, 111 West 57th Street, New York, New York 10019 (800) 938-4685; *Vietnam Country Report.*

Euromonitor International, Inc., 122 South Michigan Avenue, Suite 1200, Chicago, Illinois 60603 (800) 577-EURO; *International Marketing Data and Statistics.*

VIETNAM (SOCIALIST REPUBLIC OF) - MORTALITY

Central Intelligence Agency, Washington, D.C. 20505 (703) 482-1100, www.cia.gov; *The World Factbook.*

The Economist Intelligence Unit (Asia) Limited, 10th Floor, Luk Kwok Centre, 72 Gloucester Road, Wanchai, Hong Kong (Phone Number in U.S. (800) 938-4685); *Asian Market Atlas.*

Euromonitor International, Inc., 122 South Michigan Avenue, Suite 1200, Chicago, Illinois 60603 (800) 577-EURO; *International Marketing Data and Statistics;* and *The World Economic Factbook.*

Europa Publications Limited, 18 Bedford Square, London, WC1B 3JN, England; *The Europa World Year Book.*

Statistical Office of the United Nations, Publishing Service, New York, New York 10017 (800) 253-9646; *Asia-Pacific in Figures; Demographic Yearbook; Human Development Report; World Statistics Pocketbook;* and *Statistical Yearbook.*

United Nations Children's Fund (UNICEF), 3 United Nations Plaza, New York, New York 10017 (800) 253-9646; *State of the World's Children.*

The World Bank, 1818 H Street, NW, Washington, D.C. 20433 (202) 477-1234; *The World Bank Atlas;* and *World Development Report.*

World Health Organization, Office of Publications, 20 Avenue Appia, CH-1211 Geneva 27, Switzerland (Telephone Number in U.S. (518) 436-9686); *World Health Statistics Annual.*

VIETNAM (SOCIALIST REPUBLIC OF) - MOTION PICTURES

St. Martin's Press, Inc., 175 Fifth Avenue, New York, New York 10010 (800) 221-7945; *The Statesman's Year-Book.*

United Nations Educational, Scientific and Cultural Organization (UNESCO), 7 Place de Fontenoy, F-75700 Paris, France (Telephone Number in U.S. (212) 963-5981); *Statistical Yearbook.*

VIETNAM (SOCIALIST REPUBLIC OF) - MOTOR VEHICLES IN USE

Statistical Office of the United Nations, Publishing Service, New York, New York 10017 (800) 253-9646; *Statistical Yearbook*.

VIETNAM (SOCIALIST REPUBLIC OF) - MUSEUMS

M.E. Sharpe, 80 Business Park Drive, Armonk, New York 10504 (800) 541-6563; *The Illustrated Book of World Rankings*.

United Nations Educational, Scientific and Cultural Organization (UNESCO), 7 Place de Fontenoy, F-75700 Paris, France (Telephone Number in U.S. (212) 963-5981); *Statistical Yearbook*.

VIETNAM (SOCIALIST REPUBLIC OF) - NATALITY - See VIETNAM (SOCIALIST REPUBLIC OF) - BIRTH RATE

VIETNAM (SOCIALIST REPUBLIC OF) - NATIONAL ACCOUNTS

Europa Publications Limited, 18 Bedford Square, London, WC1B 3JN, England; *The Europa World Year Book*.

Statistical Office of the United Nations, Publishing Service, New York, New York 10017 (800) 253-9646; *Asia-Pacific in Figures; National Accounts Statistics; Statistical Yearbook;* and *Statistical Yearbook for Asia and the Pacific*.

VIETNAM (SOCIALIST REPUBLIC OF) - NATIONAL INCOME

M.E. Sharpe, 80 Business Park Drive, Armonk, New York 10504 (800) 541-6563; *The Illustrated Book of World Rankings*.

Statistical Office of the United Nations, Publishing Service, New York, New York 10017 (800) 253-9646; *National Accounts Statistics;* and *Statistical Yearbook*.

VIETNAM (SOCIALIST REPUBLIC OF) - NATIONAL PRODUCT

M.E. Sharpe, 80 Business Park Drive, Armonk, New York 10504 (800) 541-6563; *The Illustrated Book of World Rankings*.

Statistical Office of the United Nations, Publishing Service, New York, New York 10017 (800) 253-9646; *Statistical Yearbook*.

VIETNAM (SOCIALIST REPUBLIC OF) - NATURAL GAS PRODUCTION - See VIETNAM (SOCIALIST REPUBLIC OF) - MINING AND MINERAL PRODUCTS

VIETNAM (SOCIALIST REPUBLIC OF) - NEWSPAPER PRODUCTION AND CONSUMPTION - See VIETNAM (SOCIALIST REPUBLIC OF) - FORESTRY AND FOREST PRODUCTS

VIETNAM (SOCIALIST REPUBLIC OF) - NEWSPRINT PRODUCTION AND CONSUMPTION - See VIETNAM (SOCIALIST REPUBLIC OF) - FORESTRY AND FOREST PRODUCTS

VIETNAM (SOCIALIST REPUBLIC OF) - OCCUPATIONS - See VIETNAM (SOCIALIST REPUBLIC OF) - LABOR

VIETNAM (SOCIALIST REPUBLIC OF) - PATENTS, TRADEMARKS AND SERVICE MARKS

World Intellectual Property Organization, 34 Chemin des Colombettes, CH-1211 Geneva 20. Switzerland; *Industrial Property Statistics*.

VIETNAM (SOCIALIST REPUBLIC OF) - PEANUT PRODUCTION - See VIETNAM (SOCIALIST REPUBLIC OF) - CROPS

VIETNAM (SOCIALIST REPUBLIC OF) - PERIODICALS

United Nations Educational, Scientific and Cultural Organization (UNESCO), 7 Place de Fontenoy, F-75700 Paris, France (Telephone Number in U.S. (212) 963-5981); *Statistical Yearbook*.

VIETNAM (SOCIALIST REPUBLIC OF) - PESTICIDE USE

Food and Agricultural Organization of the United Nations (FAO) Via delle Terme di Caracalla, 00100 Rome, Italy (Telephone Number in U.S. (202) 653-2400); *The State of Food and Agriculture*.

VIETNAM (SOCIALIST REPUBLIC OF) - PETROLEUM INDUSTRY

Food and Agricultural Organization of the United Nations (FAO) Via delle Terme di Caracalla, 00100 Rome, Italy (Telephone Number in U.S. (202) 653-2400); *The State of Food and Agriculture*.

M.E. Sharpe, 80 Business Park Drive, Armonk, New York 10504 (800) 541-6563; *The Illustrated Book of World Rankings*.

Penn Well Publishing Company, 1421 South Sheridan Road, P.O. Box 1260, Tulsa, Oklahoma 74101 (800) 752-9764; *International Energy Statistics Sourcebook*.

United Nations Conference on Trade and Development, Central Statistical Service, Palais des Nations, Geneva, Switzerland (Telephone in U.S. (800) 253-9646); *UNCTAD Commodity Yearbook*.

VIETNAM (SOCIALIST REPUBLIC OF) - PHOSPHATE ROCK PRODUCTION - See VIETNAM (SOCIALIST REPUBLIC OF) - MINING AND MINERAL PRODUCTS

VIETNAM (SOCIALIST REPUBLIC OF) -

PIGS - See VIETNAM (SOCIALIST REPUBLIC OF) - LIVESTOCK AND POULTRY

VIETNAM (SOCIALIST REPUBLIC OF) - POPULATION

Central Intelligence Agency, Washington, D.C. 20505 (703) 482-1100, www.cia.gov; *The World Factbook*.

The Economist Intelligence Unit, 111 West 57th Street, New York, New York 10019 (800) 938-4685; *Vietnam Country Report;* and *The World Market Atlas*.

The Economist Intelligence Unit (Asia) Limited, 10th Floor, Luk Kwok Centre, 72 Gloucester Road, Wanchai, Hong Kong (Phone Number in U.S. (800) 938-4685); *Asian Market Atlas*.

Euromonitor International, Inc., 122 South Michigan Avenue, Suite 1200, Chicago, Illinois 60603 (800) 577-EURO; *International Marketing Data and Statistics*.

Europa Publications Limited, 18 Bedford Square, London, WC1B 3JN, England; *The Europa World Year Book*.

M.E. Sharpe, 80 Business Park Drive, Armonk, New York 10504 (800) 541-6563; *The Illustrated Book of World Rankings*.

St. Martin's Press, Inc., 175 Fifth Avenue, New York, New York 10010 (800) 221-7945; *The Statesman's Year-Book*.

Statistical Office of the United Nations, Publishing Service, New York, New York 10017 (800) 253-9646; *Asia-Pacific in Figures; Demographic Yearbook; Human Development Report; Statistical Yearbook; World Statistics Pocketbook;* and *Statistical Yearbook for Asia and the Pacific*.

United Nations Educational, Scientific and Cultural Organization (UNESCO), 7 Place de Fontenoy, F-75700 Paris, France (Telephone Number in U.S. (212) 963-5981); *Statistical Yearbook*.

U.S. Arms Control and Disarmament Agency, 320 Twenty-first Street, NW, Washington, D.C. 20451 (202) 647-8677; *World Military Expenditures and Arms Transfers*.

The World Bank, 1818 H Street, NW, Washington, D.C. 20433 (202) 477-1234; *The World Bank Atlas;* and *World Development Report*.

World Health Organization, Office of Publications, 20 Avenue Appia, CH-1211 Geneva 27, Switzerland (Telephone Number in U.S. (518) 436-9686); *World Health Statistics Annual*.

VIETNAM (SOCIALIST REPUBLIC OF) - POST OFFICES

M.E. Sharpe, 80 Business Park Drive, Armonk, New York 10504 (800) 541-6563; *The Illustrated Book of World Rankings.*

VIETNAM (SOCIALIST REPUBLIC OF) - POTATO PRODUCTION - See VIETNAM (SOCIALIST REPUBLIC OF) - CROPS

VIETNAM (SOCIALIST REPUBLIC OF) - PRICES

Food and Agricultural Organization of the United Nations (FAO) Via delle Terme di Caracalla, 00100 Rome, Italy (Telephone Number in U.S. (202) 653-2400); *The State of Food and Agriculture.*

International Rubber Study Group, York House, Eighth Floor, Empire Way, Wembley, London HA9 0PA, England; *Rubber Statistical Bulletin.*

M.E. Sharpe, 80 Business Park Drive, Armonk, New York 10504 (800) 541-6563; *The Illustrated Book of World Rankings.*

VIETNAM (SOCIALIST REPUBLIC OF) - PRODUCTION

International Rubber Study Group, York House, Eighth Floor, Empire Way, Wembley, London HA9 0PA, England; *Rubber Statistical Bulletin.*

M.E. Sharpe, 80 Business Park Drive, Armonk, New York 10504 (800) 541-6563; *The Illustrated Book of World Rankings.*

VIETNAM (SOCIALIST REPUBLIC OF) - PRODUCTIVITY

Euromonitor International, Inc., 122 South Michigan Avenue, Suite 1200, Chicago, Illinois 60603 (800) 577-EURO; *International Marketing Data and Statistics.*

VIETNAM (SOCIALIST REPUBLIC OF) - PUBLIC FINANCE - See VIETNAM (SOCIALIST REPUBLIC OF) - FINANCE

VIETNAM (SOCIALIST REPUBLIC OF) - RADIO

The Economist Intelligence Unit (Asia) Limited, 10th Floor, Luk Kwok Centre, 72 Gloucester Road, Wanchai, Hong Kong (Phone Number in U.S. (800) 938-4685); *Asian Market Atlas.*

VIETNAM (SOCIALIST REPUBLIC OF) - RADIO BROADCASTING - See VIETNAM (SOCIALIST REPUBLIC OF) - BROADCASTING

VIETNAM (SOCIALIST REPUBLIC OF) - RADIO RECEIVER PRODUCTION

Statistical Office of the United Nations, Publishing Service, New York, New York 10017 (800) 253-9646; *Statistical Yearbook.*

VIETNAM (SOCIALIST REPUBLIC OF) - RADIO RECEIVERS

St. Martin's Press, Inc., 175 Fifth Avenue, New York, New York 10010 (800) 221-7945; *The Statesman's Year-Book.*

VIETNAM (SOCIALIST REPUBLIC OF) - RAILWAYS

Europa Publications Limited, 18 Bedford Square, London, WC1B 3JN, England; *The Europa World Year Book.*

Jane's Information Group, Sentinel House, 163 Brighton Road, Coulsdon, Surrey CR5 2NH, England (Telephone Number in U.S. (703) 683-3700); *Jane's World Railways.*

St. Martin's Press, Inc., 175 Fifth Avenue, New York, New York 10010 (800) 221-7945; *The Statesman's Year-Book.*

Statistical Office of the United Nations, Publishing Service, New York, New York 10017 (800) 253-9646; *Statistical Yearbook.*

VIETNAM (SOCIALIST REPUBLIC OF) - RELIGION

Central Intelligence Agency, Washington, D.C. 20505 (703) 482-1100, www.cia.gov; *The World Factbook.*

M.E. Sharpe, 80 Business Park Drive, Armonk, New York 10504 (800) 541-6563; *The Illustrated Book of World Rankings.*

St. Martin's Press, Inc., 175 Fifth Avenue, New York, New York 10010 (800) 221-7945; *The Statesman's Year-Book.*

VIETNAM (SOCIALIST REPUBLIC OF) - RETAIL TRADE

Euromonitor International, Inc., 122 South Michigan Avenue, Suite 1200, Chicago, Illinois 60603 (800) 577-EURO; *World Marketing Data and Statistics.*

VIETNAM (SOCIALIST REPUBLIC OF) - RICE PRODUCTION - See VIETNAM (SOCIALIST REPUBLIC OF) - CROPS

VIETNAM (SOCIALIST REPUBLIC OF) - ROOT AND TUBER PRODUCTION - See VIETNAM (SOCIALIST REPUBLIC OF) - CROPS

VIETNAM (SOCIALIST REPUBLIC OF) - ROUNDWOOD PRODUCTION - See VIETNAM (SOCIALIST REPUBLIC OF) - FORESTRY AND FOREST PRODUCTS

VIETNAM (SOCIALIST REPUBLIC OF) - RUBBER PRODUCTION AND CONSUMPTION

Commodity Research Bureau, Inc., 30 South Wacker Drive, Suite 1810, Chicago,

Illinois 60606 (312) 454-1801; *Commodity Year Book.*

International Rubber Study Group, York House, Eighth Floor, Empire Way, Wembley, London HA9 0PA, England; *Rubber Statistical Bulletin.*

M.E. Sharpe, 80 Business Park Drive, Armonk, New York 10504 (800) 541-6563; *The Illustrated Book of World Rankings.*

Statistical Office of the United Nations, Publishing Service, New York, New York 10017 (800) 253-9646; *Statistical Yearbook.*

VIETNAM (SOCIALIST REPUBLIC OF) - SALT PRODUCTION - See VIETNAM (SOCIALIST REPUBLIC OF) - MINING AND MINERAL PRODUCTS

VIETNAM (SOCIALIST REPUBLIC OF) - SAWNWOOD PRODUCTION - See VIETNAM (SOCIALIST REPUBLIC OF) - FORESTRY AND FOREST PRODUCTS

VIETNAM (SOCIALIST REPUBLIC OF) - SCIENTISTS, TECHNICIANS AND ENGINEERS

United Nations Educational, Scientific and Cultural Organization (UNESCO), 7 Place de Fontenoy, F-75700 Paris, France (Telephone Number in U.S. (212) 963-5981); *Statistical Yearbook.*

VIETNAM (SOCIALIST REPUBLIC OF) - SENIOR CITIZENS

M.E. Sharpe, 80 Business Park Drive, Armonk, New York 10504 (800) 541-6563; *The Illustrated Book of World Rankings.*

VIETNAM (SOCIALIST REPUBLIC OF) - SESAME SEED PRODUCTION - See VIETNAM (SOCIALIST REPUBLIC OF) - CROPS

VIETNAM (SOCIALIST REPUBLIC OF) - SHEEP - See VIETNAM (SOCIALIST REPUBLIC OF) - LIVESTOCK AND POULTRY

VIETNAM (SOCIALIST REPUBLIC OF) - SILVER PRODUCTION AND CONSUMPTION - See VIETNAM (SOCIALIST REPUBLIC OF) - MINING AND MINERAL PRODUCTS

VIETNAM (SOCIALIST REPUBLIC OF) - SOCIAL DATA

M.E. Sharpe, 80 Business Park Drive, Armonk, New York 10504 (800) 541-6563; *The Illustrated Book of World Rankings.*

Statistical Office of the United Nations, Publishing Service, New York, New York 10017 (800) 253-9646; *World Statistics Pocketbook.*

VIETNAM (SOCIALIST REPUBLIC OF) - SOCIAL SECURITY

Statistical Office of the United Nations, Publishing Service, New York, New York 10017 (800) 253-9646; *National Accounts Statistics*.

VIETNAM (SOCIALIST REPUBLIC OF) - SOYBEAN PRODUCTION - See VIETNAM (SOCIALIST REPUBLIC OF) - CROPS

VIETNAM (SOCIALIST REPUBLIC OF) - STATE BUDGET REVENUE AND EXPENDITURES

Euromonitor International, Inc., 122 South Michigan Avenue, Suite 1200, Chicago, Illinois 60603 (800) 577-EURO; *International Marketing Data and Statistics*.

VIETNAM (SOCIALIST REPUBLIC OF) - STEEL - See VIETNAM (SOCIALIST REPUBLIC OF) - MINING AND MINERAL PRODUCTS

VIETNAM (SOCIALIST REPUBLIC OF) - STOCKS - COMMODITY - MARKET PRICE - INDEX

Food and Agricultural Organization of the United Nations (FAO) Via delle Terme di Caracalla, 00100 Rome, Italy (Telephone Number in U.S. (202) 653-2400); *The State of Food and Agriculture*.

VIETNAM (SOCIALIST REPUBLIC OF) - SUGAR PRODUCTION AND CONSUMPTION - See VIETNAM (SOCIALIST REPUBLIC OF) - CROPS

VIETNAM (SOCIALIST REPUBLIC OF) - TEA PRODUCTION - See VIETNAM (SOCIALIST REPUBLIC OF) - CROPS

VIETNAM (SOCIALIST REPUBLIC OF) - TELEGRAPH SERVICE

Statistical Office of the United Nations, Publishing Service, New York, New York 10017 (800) 253-9646; *Statistical Yearbook*.

VIETNAM (SOCIALIST REPUBLIC OF) - TELEPHONES IN USE

American Telephone and Telegraph Company, 26 Parsippany Road, Whippany, New Jersey 07981 (800) 222-0300; *The World's Telephones*.

Central Intelligence Agency, Washington, D.C. 20505 (703) 482-1100, www.cia.gov; *The World Factbook*.

The Economist Intelligence Unit (Asia) Limited, 10th Floor, Luk Kwok Centre, 72 Gloucester Road, Wanchai, Hong Kong (Phone Number in U.S. (800) 938-4685); *Asian Market Atlas*.

St. Martin's Press, Inc., 175 Fifth Avenue, New York, New York 10010 (800) 221-7945; *The Statesman's Year-Book*.

Statistical Office of the United Nations, Publishing Service, New York, New York 10017 (800) 253-9646; *World Statistics Pocketbook*.

VIETNAM (SOCIALIST REPUBLIC OF) - TELEVISION BROADCASTING - See VIETNAM (SOCIALIST REPUBLIC OF) - BROADCASTING

VIETNAM (SOCIALIST REPUBLIC OF) - TEXTILE INDUSTRY

St. Martin's Press, Inc., 175 Fifth Avenue, New York, New York 10010 (800) 221-7945; *The Statesman's Year-Book*.

Statistical Office of the United Nations, Publishing Service, New York, New York 10017 (800) 253-9646; *Statistical Yearbook*.

United Nations Conference on Trade and Development, Central Statistical Service, Palais des Nations, Geneva, Switzerland (Telephone in U.S. (800) 253-9646); *UNCTAD Commodity Yearbook*.

VIETNAM (SOCIALIST REPUBLIC OF) - THEATRE

United Nations Educational, Scientific and Cultural Organization (UNESCO), 7 Place de Fontenoy, F-75700 Paris, France (Telephone Number in U.S. (212) 963-5981); *Statistical Yearbook*.

VIETNAM (SOCIALIST REPUBLIC OF) - TIMBER - RESOURCE FORESTS - See VIETNAM (SOCIALIST REPUBLIC OF) - FORESTRY AND FOREST PRODUCTS

VIETNAM (SOCIALIST REPUBLIC OF) - TIRE (MOTOR VEHICLE) PRODUCTION

International Rubber Study Group, York House, Eighth Floor, Empire Way, Wembley, London HA9 0PA, England; *Rubber Statistical Bulletin*.

VIETNAM (SOCIALIST REPUBLIC OF) - TOBACCO PRODUCTION

M.E. Sharpe, 80 Business Park Drive, Armonk, New York 10504 (800) 541-6563; *The Illustrated Book of World Rankings*.

Statistical Office of the United Nations, Publishing Service, New York, New York 10017 (800) 253-9646; *Statistical Yearbook*.

VIETNAM (SOCIALIST REPUBLIC OF) - TOURISM

Euromonitor International, Inc., 122 South Michigan Avenue, Suite 1200, Chicago, Illinois 60603 (800) 577-EURO; *The World Economic Factbook;* and *World Marketing Data and Statistics*.

M.E. Sharpe, 80 Business Park Drive, Armonk, New York 10504 (800) 541-6563; *The Illustrated Book of World Rankings*.

St. Martin's Press, Inc., 175 Fifth Avenue, New York, New York 10010 (800) 221-7945; *The Statesman's Year-Book*.

VIETNAM (SOCIALIST REPUBLIC OF) - TRACTORS IN USE

Statistical Office of the United Nations, Publishing Service, New York, New York 10017 (800) 253-9646; *Statistical Yearbook*.

VIETNAM (SOCIALIST REPUBLIC OF) - TRADE - See VIETNAM (SOCIALIST REPUBLIC OF) - FOREIGN TRADE

VIETNAM (SOCIALIST REPUBLIC OF) - TRADEMARKS AND SERVICE MARKS - See VIETNAM (SOCIALIST REPUBLIC OF) - PATENTS, TRADEMARKS AND SERVICE MARKS

VIETNAM (SOCIALIST REPUBLIC OF) - TRANSPORTATION AND COMMUNICATIONS

Central Intelligence Agency, Washington, D.C. 20505 (703) 482-1100, www.cia.gov; *The World Factbook*.

The Economist Intelligence Unit (Asia) Limited, 10th Floor, Luk Kwok Centre, 72 Gloucester Road, Wanchai, Hong Kong (Phone Number in U.S. (800) 938-4685); *Asian Market Atlas*.

Euromonitor International, Inc., 122 South Michigan Avenue, Suite 1200, Chicago, Illinois 60603 (800) 577-EURO; *International Marketing Data and Statistics;* and *World Marketing Data and Statistics*.

Europa Publications Limited, 18 Bedford Square, London, WC1B 3JN, England; *The Europa World Year Book*.

M.E. Sharpe, 80 Business Park Drive, Armonk, New York 10504 (800) 541-6563; *The Illustrated Book of World Rankings*.

St. Martin's Press, Inc., 175 Fifth Avenue, New York, New York 10010 (800) 221-7945; *The Statesman's Year-Book*.

Statistical Office of the United Nations, Publishing Service, New York, New York 10017 (800) 253-9646; *Human Development Report;* and *Statistical Yearbook for Asia and the Pacific*.

VIETNAM (SOCIALIST REPUBLIC OF) - UNEMPLOYMENT

Central Intelligence Agency, Washington, D.C. 20505 (703) 482-1100, www.cia.gov; *The World Factbook*.

Euromonitor International, Inc., 122

South Michigan Avenue, Suite 1200, Chicago, Illinois 60603 (800) 577-EURO; *International Marketing Data and Statistics.*

St. Martin's Press, Inc., 175 Fifth Avenue, New York, New York 10010 (800) 221-7945; *The Statesman's Year-Book.*

VIETNAM (SOCIALIST REPUBLIC OF) - UTILITIES

Statistical Office of the United Nations, Publishing Service, New York, New York 10017 (800) 253-9646; *Electric Power in Asia and the Pacific.*

VIETNAM (SOCIALIST REPUBLIC OF) - VITAL STATISTICS

Euromonitor International, Inc., 122 South Michigan Avenue, Suite 1200, Chicago, Illinois 60603 (800) 577-EURO; *International Marketing Data and Statistics.*

World Health Organization, Office of Publications, 20 Avenue Appia, CH-1211 Geneva 27, Switzerland (Telephone Number in U.S. (518) 436-9686); *World Health Statistics Annual.*

VIETNAM (SOCIALIST REPUBLIC OF) - WAGES

Statistical Office of the United Nations, Publishing Service, New York, New York 10017 (800) 253-9646; *Statistical Yearbook for Asia and the Pacific.*

VIETNAM (SOCIALIST REPUBLIC OF) - WATERMELON PRODUCTION - See VIETNAM (SOCIALIST REPUBLIC OF) - CROPS

VIETNAM (SOCIALIST REPUBLIC OF) - WEATHER

M.E. Sharpe, 80 Business Park Drive, Armonk, New York 10504 (800) 541-6563; *The Illustrated Book of World Rankings.*

VIETNAM (SOCIALIST REPUBLIC OF) - WHEAT PRODUCTION AND PRICES - See VIETNAM (SOCIALIST REPUBLIC OF) - CROPS

VIETNAM (SOCIALIST REPUBLIC OF) - WINE PRODUCTION - See VIETNAM (SOCIALIST REPUBLIC OF) - BEVERAGES

VIETNAM (SOCIALIST REPUBLIC OF) - WOOL PRODUCTION - See VIETNAM (SOCIALIST REPUBLIC OF) - TEXTILE INDUSTRY

VIETNAM (SOCIALIST REPUBLIC OF) - YARN PRODUCTION - See VIETNAM (SOCIALIST REPUBLIC OF) - TEXTILE INDUSTRY

VIETNAMESE POPULATION

U.S. Department of Commerce, Bureau of the Census, Washington, D.C. 20233 (301) 457-4100, www.census.gov; *Census of Population, General Population Characteristics, U.S.*

Virgin Islands - Data Centers

University of the Virgin Islands, Eastern Caribbean Center, No. 2, John Brewer's Bay, Charlotte Amalie, Saint Thomas, Virgin Islands 00802, Dr. Frank Mills (340) 693-1027.

Virgin Islands Department of Economic Development, Post Office Box 6400, Charlotte Amalie, Saint Thomas, Virgin Islands 00801, Mr. Dan Inveen (809) 774-8784.

VIRGIN ISLANDS - AGRICULTURE

Europa Publications Limited, 18 Bedford Square, London, WC1B 3JN, England; *The Europa World Year Book.*

Food and Agricultural Organization of the United Nations (FAO) Via delle Terme di Caracalla, 00100 Rome, Italy (Telephone Number in U.S. (202) 653-2400); *Production Yearbook;* and *The State of Food and Agriculture.*

St. Martin's Press, Inc., 175 Fifth Avenue, New York, New York 10010 (800) 221-7945; *The Statesman's Year-Book.*

VIRGIN ISLANDS - AIRLINE SERVICE

Europa Publications Limited, 18 Bedford Square, London, WC1B 3JN, England; *The Europa World Year Book.*

St. Martin's Press, Inc., 175 Fifth Avenue, New York, New York 10010 (800) 221-7945; *The Statesman's Year-Book.*

VIRGIN ISLANDS - AIRPORTS

Central Intelligence Agency, Washington, D.C. 20505 (703) 482-1100, www.cia.gov; *The World Factbook.*

VIRGIN ISLANDS - AREA AND DENSITY OF POPULATION

Central Intelligence Agency, Washington, D.C. 20505 (703) 482-1100, www.cia.gov; *The World Factbook.*

Europa Publications Limited, 18 Bedford Square, London, WC1B 3JN, England; *The Europa World Year Book.*

Food and Agricultural Organization of the United Nations (FAO) Via delle Terme di Caracalla, 00100 Rome, Italy (Telephone Number in U.S. (202) 653-2400); *The State of Food and Agriculture.*

St. Martin's Press, Inc., 175 Fifth Avenue, New York, New York 10010 (800) 221-7945; *The Statesman's Year-Book.*

VIRGIN ISLANDS - BANKING

St. Martin's Press, Inc., 175 Fifth Avenue, New York, New York 10010 (800) 221-7945; *The Statesman's Year-Book.*

VIRGIN ISLANDS - BIRTH RATES

Central Intelligence Agency, Washington, D.C. 20505 (703) 482-1100, www.cia.gov; *The World Factbook.*

Europa Publications Limited, 18 Bedford Square, London, WC1B 3JN, England; *The Europa World Year Book.*

VIRGIN ISLANDS - BROADCASTING

Billboard Limited, P.O. Box 9027, 1006 AA Amsterdam, The Netherlands (Telephone Number in U.S. (212) 764-7300); *World Radio TV Handbook.*

Central Intelligence Agency, Washington, D.C. 20505 (703) 482-1100, www.cia.gov; *The World Factbook.*

St. Martin's Press, Inc., 175 Fifth Avenue, New York, New York 10010 (800) 221-7945; *The Statesman's Year-Book.*

United Nations Educational, Scientific and Cultural Organization (UNESCO), 7 Place de Fontenoy, F-75700 Paris, France (Telephone Number in U.S. (212) 963-5981); *Statistical Yearbook.*

VIRGIN ISLANDS - BUDGET

Central Intelligence Agency, Washington, D.C. 20505 (703) 482-1100, www.cia.gov; *The World Factbook.*

VIRGIN ISLANDS - CALORIE SUPPLY

Food and Agricultural Organization of the United Nations (FAO) Via delle Terme di Caracalla, 00100 Rome, Italy (Telephone Number in U.S. (202) 653-2400); *The State of Food and Agriculture.*

VIRGIN ISLANDS - CHEMICAL (ORGANIC) PRODUCTION - See VIRGIN ISLANDS - MINING AND MINERAL PRODUCTS

VIRGIN ISLANDS - CLIMATE

St. Martin's Press, Inc., 175 Fifth Avenue, New York, New York 10010 (800) 221-7945; *The Statesman's Year-Book.*

VIRGIN ISLANDS - COAL PRODUCTION - See VIRGIN ISLANDS - MINING AND MINERAL PRODUCTS

VIRGIN ISLANDS - COMMERCE

St. Martin's Press, Inc., 175 Fifth Avenue, New York, New York 10010 (800) 221-7945; *The Statesman's Year-Book*.

VIRGIN ISLANDS - CONSTRUCTION INDUSTRY

St. Martin's Press, Inc., 175 Fifth Avenue, New York, New York 10010 (800) 221-7945; *The Statesman's Year-Book*.

VIRGIN ISLANDS - CORN PRODUCTION - See VIRGIN ISLANDS - CROPS

VIRGIN ISLANDS - CORPORATE TAXES - See VIRGIN ISLANDS - TAXATION

VIRGIN ISLANDS - CROPS

Food and Agricultural Organization of the United Nations (FAO) Via delle Terme di Caracalla, 00100 Rome, Italy (Telephone Number in U.S. (202) 653-2400); *The State of Food and Agriculture*.

St. Martin's Press, Inc., 175 Fifth Avenue, New York, New York 10010 (800) 221-7945; *The Statesman's Year-Book*.

VIRGIN ISLANDS - CUSTOMS DUTIES

St. Martin's Press, Inc., 175 Fifth Avenue, New York, New York 10010 (800) 221-7945; *The Statesman's Year-Book*.

VIRGIN ISLANDS - DAIRY PRODUCTS

Food and Agricultural Organization of the United Nations (FAO) Via delle Terme di Caracalla, 00100 Rome, Italy (Telephone Number in U.S. (202) 653-2400); *The State of Food and Agriculture*.

St. Martin's Press, Inc., 175 Fifth Avenue, New York, New York 10010 (800) 221-7945; *The Statesman's Year-Book*.

VIRGIN ISLANDS - ECONOMY

Central Intelligence Agency, Washington, D.C. 20505 (703) 482-1100, www.cia.gov; *The World Factbook*.

Europa Publications Limited, 18 Bedford Square, London, WC1B 3JN, England; *The Europa World Year Book*.

St. Martin's Press, Inc., 175 Fifth Avenue, New York, New York 10010 (800) 221-7945; *The Statesman's Year-Book*.

Statistical Office of the United Nations, Publishing Service, New York, New York 10017 (800) 253-9646; *World Statistics Pocketbook*.

The World Bank, 1818 H Street, NW, Washington, D.C. 20433 (202) 477-1234; *The World Bank Atlas*.

VIRGIN ISLANDS - EDUCATION

Europa Publications Limited, 18 Bedford Square, London, WC1B 3JN, England; *The Europa World Year Book*.

St. Martin's Press, Inc., 175 Fifth Avenue, New York, New York 10010 (800) 221-7945; *The Statesman's Year-Book*.

United Nations Educational, Scientific and Cultural Organization (UNESCO), 7 Place de Fontenoy, F-75700 Paris, France (Telephone Number in U.S. (212) 963-5981); *Statistical Yearbook*.

VIRGIN ISLANDS - EGG PRODUCTION AND CONSUMPTION - See VIRGIN ISLANDS - DAIRY PRODUCTS

VIRGIN ISLANDS - ELECTRICITY

Central Intelligence Agency, Washington, D.C. 20505 (703) 482-1100, www.cia.gov; *The World Factbook*.

St. Martin's Press, Inc., 175 Fifth Avenue, New York, New York 10010 (800) 221-7945; *The Statesman's Year-Book*.

Statistical Office of the United Nations, Publishing Service, New York, New York 10017 (800) 253-9646; *Statistical Yearbook*.

VIRGIN ISLANDS - ENERGY

Food and Agricultural Organization of the United Nations (FAO) Via delle Terme di Caracalla, 00100 Rome, Italy (Telephone Number in U.S. (202) 653-2400); *The State of Food and Agriculture*.

St. Martin's Press, Inc., 175 Fifth Avenue, New York, New York 10010 (800) 221-7945; *The Statesman's Year-Book*.

Statistical Office of the United Nations, Publishing Service, New York, New York 10017 (800) 253-9646; *Energy Statistics Yearbook; World Statistics Pocketbook;* and *Statistical Yearbook*.

The World Bank, 1818 H Street, NW, Washington, D.C. 20433 (202) 477-1234; *The World Bank Atlas*.

VIRGIN ISLANDS - ENVIRONMENT

Statistical Office of the United Nations, Publishing Service, New York, New York 10017 (800) 253-9646; *World Statistics Pocketbook*.

VIRGIN ISLANDS - EXCHANGE RATES

Central Intelligence Agency, Washington, D.C. 20505 (703) 482-1100, www.cia.gov; *The World Factbook*.

Europa Publications Limited, 18 Bedford Square, London, WC1B 3JN, England; *The Europa World Year Book*.

Statistical Office of the United Nations, Publishing Service, New York, New York 10017 (800) 253-9646; *World Statistics Pocketbook*.

VIRGIN ISLANDS - EXPORTS

Central Intelligence Agency, Washington, D.C. 20505 (703) 482-1100, www.cia.gov; *The World Factbook*.

Europa Publications Limited, 18 Bedford Square, London, WC1B 3JN, England; *The Europa World Year Book*.

Food and Agricultural Organization of the United Nations (FAO) Via delle Terme di Caracalla, 00100 Rome, Italy (Telephone Number in U.S. (202) 653-2400); *The State of Food and Agriculture*.

St. Martin's Press, Inc., 175 Fifth Avenue, New York, New York 10010 (800) 221-7945; *The Statesman's Year-Book*.

VIRGIN ISLANDS - EXTERNAL TRADE

Food and Agricultural Organization of the United Nations (FAO) Via delle Terme di Caracalla, 00100 Rome, Italy (Telephone Number in U.S. (202) 653-2400); *The State of Food and Agriculture*.

VIRGIN ISLANDS - FARM CROPS - See VIRGIN ISLANDS - CROPS

VIRGIN ISLANDS - FERTILITY RATES

Central Intelligence Agency, Washington, D.C. 20505 (703) 482-1100, www.cia.gov; *The World Factbook*.

The World Bank, 1818 H Street, NW, Washington, D.C. 20433 (202) 477-1234; *The World Bank Atlas*.

VIRGIN ISLANDS - FERTILIZER PRODUCTION AND CONSUMPTION

Food and Agricultural Organization of the United Nations (FAO) Via delle Terme di Caracalla, 00100 Rome, Italy (Telephone Number in U.S. (202) 653-2400); *The State of Food and Agriculture*.

VIRGIN ISLANDS - FINANCE

Europa Publications Limited, 18 Bedford Square, London, WC1B 3JN, England; *The Europa World Year Book*.

St. Martin's Press, Inc., 175 Fifth Avenue, New York, New York 10010 (800) 221-7945; *The Statesman's Year-Book*.

VIRGIN ISLANDS - FISHERIES

Europa Publications Limited, 18 Bedford Square, London, WC1B 3JN, England; *The Europa World Year Book*.

Food and Agricultural Organization of the United Nations (FAO) Via delle Terme di Caracalla, 00100 Rome, Italy (Telephone Number in U.S. (202) 653-2400); *The State of Food and Agriculture.*

St. Martin's Press, Inc., 175 Fifth Avenue, New York, New York 10010 (800) 221-7945; *The Statesman's Year-Book.*

VIRGIN ISLANDS - FOOD

Food and Agricultural Organization of the United Nations (FAO) Via delle Terme di Caracalla, 00100 Rome, Italy (Telephone Number in U.S. (202) 653-2400); *The State of Food and Agriculture.*

VIRGIN ISLANDS - FOREIGN TRADE

Food and Agricultural Organization of the United Nations (FAO) Via delle Terme di Caracalla, 00100 Rome, Italy (Telephone Number in U.S. (202) 653-2400); *The State of Food and Agriculture.*

St. Martin's Press, Inc., 175 Fifth Avenue, New York, New York 10010 (800) 221-7945; *The Statesman's Year-Book.*

VIRGIN ISLANDS - FORESTRY AND FOREST PRODUCTS

Food and Agricultural Organization of the United Nations (FAO) Via delle Terme di Caracalla, 00100 Rome, Italy (Telephone Number in U.S. (202) 653-2400); *The State of Food and Agriculture.*

Statistical Office of the United Nations, Publishing Service, New York, New York 10017 (800) 253-9646; *Statistical Yearbook.*

United Nations Educational, Scientific and Cultural Organization (UNESCO), 7 Place de Fontenoy, F-75700 Paris, France (Telephone Number in U.S. (212) 963-5981); *Statistical Yearbook.*

VIRGIN ISLANDS - GOVERNMENT

Central Intelligence Agency, Washington, D.C. 20505 (703) 482-1100, www.cia.gov; *The World Factbook.*

Europa Publications Limited, 18 Bedford Square, London, WC1B 3JN, England; *The Europa World Year Book.*

St. Martin's Press, Inc., 175 Fifth Avenue, New York, New York 10010 (800) 221-7945; *The Statesman's Year-Book.*

VIRGIN ISLANDS - GRAIN PRODUCTION - See VIRGIN ISLANDS - CROPS

VIRGIN ISLANDS - GROSS NATIONAL PRODUCT

The World Bank, 1818 H Street, NW, Washington, D.C. 20433 (202) 477-1234;

The World Bank Atlas.

VIRGIN ISLANDS - HEALTH

Statistical Office of the United Nations, Publishing Service, New York, New York 10017 (800) 253-9646; *Statistical Yearbook.*

VIRGIN ISLANDS - HIDE PRODUCTION

Food and Agricultural Organization of the United Nations (FAO), Via delle Terme di Caracalla, 00100 Rome, Italy (Telephone Number in U.S. (202) 653-2400); *Production Yearbook.*

VIRGIN ISLANDS - HIGHWAYS

Central Intelligence Agency, Washington, D.C. 20505 (703) 482-1100, www.cia.gov; *The World Factbook.*

St. Martin's Press, Inc., 175 Fifth Avenue, New York, New York 10010 (800) 221-7945; *The Statesman's Year-Book.*

VIRGIN ISLANDS - ILLITERATE POPULATION

Central Intelligence Agency, Washington, D.C. 20505 (703) 482-1100, www.cia.gov; *The World Factbook.*

VIRGIN ISLANDS - IMPORTS

Central Intelligence Agency, Washington, D.C. 20505 (703) 482-1100, www.cia.gov; *The World Factbook.*

Europa Publications Limited, 18 Bedford Square, London, WC1B 3JN, England; *The Europa World Year Book.*

Food and Agricultural Organization of the United Nations (FAO) Via delle Terme di Caracalla, 00100 Rome, Italy (Telephone Number in U.S. (202) 653-2400); *The State of Food and Agriculture.*

St. Martin's Press, Inc., 175 Fifth Avenue, New York, New York 10010 (800) 221-7945; *The Statesman's Year-Book.*

VIRGIN ISLANDS - INDUSTRY

Central Intelligence Agency, Washington, D.C. 20505 (703) 482-1100, www.cia.gov; *The World Factbook.*

Europa Publications Limited, 18 Bedford Square, London, WC1B 3JN, England; *The Europa World Year Book.*

St. Martin's Press, Inc., 175 Fifth Avenue, New York, New York 10010 (800) 221-7945; *The Statesman's Year-Book.*

VIRGIN ISLANDS - LABOR

Central Intelligence Agency, Washington, D.C. 20505 (703) 482-1100,

www.cia.gov; *The World Factbook.*

Europa Publications Limited, 18 Bedford Square, London, WC1B 3JN, England; *The Europa World Year Book.*

Food and Agricultural Organization of the United Nations (FAO) Via delle Terme di Caracalla, 00100 Rome, Italy (Telephone Number in U.S. (202) 653-2400); *The State of Food and Agriculture.*

St. Martin's Press, Inc., 175 Fifth Avenue, New York, New York 10010 (800) 221-7945; *The Statesman's Year-Book.*

The World Bank, 1818 H Street, NW, Washington, D.C. 20433 (202) 477-1234; *The World Bank Atlas.*

VIRGIN ISLANDS - LAND USE

Central Intelligence Agency, Washington, D.C. 20505 (703) 482-1100, www.cia.gov; *The World Factbook.*

VIRGIN ISLANDS - LIBRARIES

United Nations Educational, Scientific and Cultural Organization (UNESCO), 7 Place de Fontenoy, F-75700 Paris, France (Telephone Number in U.S. (212) 963-5981); *Statistical Yearbook.*

VIRGIN ISLANDS - LIFE EXPECTANCY

Central Intelligence Agency, Washington, D.C. 20505 (703) 482-1100, www.cia.gov; *The World Factbook.*

Statistical Office of the United Nations, Publishing Service, New York, New York 10017 (800) 253-9646; *World Statistics Pocketbook.*

The World Bank, 1818 H Street, NW, Washington, D.C. 20433 (202) 477-1234; *The World Bank Atlas.*

VIRGIN ISLANDS - LIVESTOCK AND POULTRY

Europa Publications Limited, 18 Bedford Square, London, WC1B 3JN, England; *The Europa World Year Book.*

Food and Agricultural Organization of the United Nations (FAO), Via delle Terme di Caracalla, 00100 Rome, Italy (Telephone Number in U.S. (202) 653-2400); *Production Yearbook;* and *The State of Food and Agriculture.*

St. Martin's Press, Inc., 175 Fifth Avenue, New York, New York 10010 (800) 221-7945; *The Statesman's Year-Book.*

VIRGIN ISLANDS - MEAT PRODUCTION - See VIRGIN ISLANDS - LIVESTOCK AND POULTRY

VIRGIN ISLANDS - MERCHANT SHIPPING

St. Martin's Press, Inc., 175 Fifth Avenue, New York, New York 10010 (800) 221-7945; *The Statesman's Year-Book.*

VIRGIN ISLANDS - MILITARY

Central Intelligence Agency, Washington, D.C. 20505 (703) 482-1100, www.cia.gov; *The World Factbook.*

VIRGIN ISLANDS - MONUMENTS AND HISTORICAL SITES

United Nations Educational, Scientific and Cultural Organization (UNESCO), 7 Place de Fontenoy, F-75700 Paris, France (Telephone Number in U.S. (212) 963-5981); *Statistical Yearbook.*

VIRGIN ISLANDS - MORTALITY

Central Intelligence Agency, Washington, D.C. 20505 (703) 482-1100, www.cia.gov; *The World Factbook.*

Europa Publications Limited, 18 Bedford Square, London, WC1B 3JN, England; *The Europa World Year Book.*

Statistical Office of the United Nations, Publishing Service, New York, New York 10017 (800) 253-9646; *World Statistics Pocketbook.*

The World Bank, 1818 H Street, NW, Washington, D.C. 20433 (202) 477-1234; *The World Bank Atlas.*

VIRGIN ISLANDS - MOTOR VEHICLES IN USE

Europa Publications Limited, 18 Bedford Square, London, WC1B 3JN, England; *The Europa World Year Book.*

VIRGIN ISLANDS - MUSEUMS

United Nations Educational, Scientific and Cultural Organization (UNESCO), 7 Place de Fontenoy, F-75700 Paris, France (Telephone Number in U.S. (212) 963-5981); *Statistical Yearbook.*

VIRGIN ISLANDS - NEWSPAPER PRODUCTION - See VIRGIN ISLANDS - FORESTRY AND FOREST PRODUCTS

VIRGIN ISLANDS - OCCUPATIONS - See VIRGIN ISLANDS - LABOR

VIRGIN ISLANDS - PESTICIDE USE

Food and Agricultural Organization of the United Nations (FAO) Via delle Terme di Caracalla, 00100 Rome, Italy (Telephone Number in U.S. (202) 653-2400); *The State of Food and Agriculture.*

VIRGIN ISLANDS - PETROLEUM INDUSTRY

Food and Agricultural Organization of the United Nations (FAO) Via delle Terme di Caracalla, 00100 Rome, Italy (Telephone Number in U.S. (202) 653-2400); *The State of Food and Agriculture.*

VIRGIN ISLANDS - POPULATION

Central Intelligence Agency, Washington, D.C. 20505 (703) 482-1100, www.cia.gov; *The World Factbook.*

Europa Publications Limited, 18 Bedford Square, London, WC1B 3JN, England; *The Europa World Year Book.*

St. Martin's Press, Inc., 175 Fifth Avenue, New York, New York 10010 (800) 221-7945; *The Statesman's Year-Book.*

Statistical Office of the United Nations, Publishing Service, New York, New York 10017 (800) 253-9646; *World Statistics Pocketbook.*

The World Bank, 1818 H Street, NW, Washington, D.C. 20433 (202) 477-1234; *The World Bank Atlas.*

VIRGIN ISLANDS - PRICES

Food and Agricultural Organization of the United Nations (FAO) Via delle Terme di Caracalla, 00100 Rome, Italy (Telephone Number in U.S. (202) 653-2400); *The State of Food and Agriculture.*

VIRGIN ISLANDS - RADIO BROADCASTING - See VIRGIN ISLANDS - BROADCASTING

VIRGIN ISLANDS - RADIO RECEIVERS

St. Martin's Press, Inc., 175 Fifth Avenue, New York, New York 10010 (800) 221-7945; *The Statesman's Year-Book.*

VIRGIN ISLANDS - RELIGION

Central Intelligence Agency, Washington, D.C. 20505 (703) 482-1100, www.cia.gov; *The World Factbook.*

St. Martin's Press, Inc., 175 Fifth Avenue, New York, New York 10010 (800) 221-7945; *The Statesman's Year-Book.*

VIRGIN ISLANDS - SOCIAL DATA

Statistical Office of the United Nations, Publishing Service, New York, New York 10017 (800) 253-9646; *World Statistics Pocketbook.*

VIRGIN ISLANDS - STOCKS - COMMODITY - MARKET PRICE - INDEX

Food and Agricultural Organization of the United Nations (FAO) Via delle Terme di Caracalla, 00100 Rome, Italy (Telephone Number in U.S. (202) 653-2400); *The State*

of Food and Agriculture.

VIRGIN ISLANDS - TAXATION

St. Martin's Press, Inc., 175 Fifth Avenue, New York, New York 10010 (800) 221-7945; *The Statesman's Year-Book.*

VIRGIN ISLANDS - TELEPHONES IN USE

American Telephone and Telegraph Company, 26 Parsippany Road, Whippany, New Jersey 07981 (800) 222-0300; *The World's Telephones.*

Central Intelligence Agency, Washington, D.C. 20505 (703) 482-1100, www.cia.gov; *The World Factbook.*

Statistical Office of the United Nations, Publishing Service, New York, New York 10017 (800) 253-9646; *World Statistics Pocketbook.*

VIRGIN ISLANDS - TELEVISION BROADCASTING - See VIRGIN ISLANDS - BROADCASTING

VIRGIN ISLANDS - TOURISM

St. Martin's Press, Inc., 175 Fifth Avenue, New York, New York 10010 (800) 221-7945; *The Statesman's Year-Book.*

World Tourism Organization, Calle Capitan Haya 42, E-28020 Madrid, Spain; *Yearbook of Tourism Statistics.*

VIRGIN ISLANDS - TRADE - See VIRGIN ISLANDS - FOREIGN TRADE

VIRGIN ISLANDS - TRANSPORTATION AND COMMUNICATIONS

Central Intelligence Agency, Washington, D.C. 20505 (703) 482-1100, www.cia.gov; *The World Factbook.*

Europa Publications Limited, 18 Bedford Square, London, WC1B 3JN, England; *The Europa World Year Book.*

St. Martin's Press, Inc., 175 Fifth Avenue, New York, New York 10010 (800) 221-7945; *The Statesman's Year-Book.*

VIRGIN ISLANDS - UNEMPLOYMENT RATE

Central Intelligence Agency, Washington, D.C. 20505 (703) 482-1100, www.cia.gov; *The World Factbook.*

VIRGIN ISLANDS - WELFARE

St. Martin's Press, Inc., 175 Fifth Avenue, New York, New York 10010 (800) 221-7945; *The Statesman's Year-Book.*

VIRGIN ISLANDS - ZOOS AND BOTANICAL GARDENS

United Nations Educational, Scientific and Cultural Organization (UNESCO), 7 Place de Fontenoy, F-75700 Paris, France (Telephone Number in U.S. (212) 963-5981); *Statistical Yearbook.*

VIRGINIA - See also STATE DATA (FOR INDIVIDUAL STATES)

Virginia - Primary Statistics Source

University of Virginia, Center for Public Service, 918 Emmet Street, Suite 300, 2015 Ivy Road, Charlottesville, Virginia 22903 (804) 982-5585; *Virginia Statistical Abstract.*

Virginia - State Data Centers

Virginia Employment Commission, 703 East Main Street, Richmond, Virginia 23219, Mr. Don Lillywhite (804) 786-8026.

Center for Public Service, University of Virginia, 918 Emmet Street, North, Suite 300, Charlottesville, Virginia 22903-4823, Dr. Michael Spar (804) 982-5585.

The Library of Virginia, Documents Section, 800 E. Broad Street, Richmond, Virginia 23219-3491, Mary Clark (804) 787-2175.

VISION DEVICES

U.S. Department of Health and Human Services, National Center for Health Statistics, 3700 East-West Highway, Hyattsville, Maryland 20782 (301) 436-8500, www.cdc.gov/nchs; *Advance Data, No. 292.*

VISUAL ARTS

National Endowment for the Arts, 1100 Pennsylvania Avenue, NW, Washington, D.C. 20506 (202) 682-5400, www.arts.gov; *Survey of Public Participation in the Arts.*

VISUAL IMPAIRMENT

U.S. Department of Commerce, Bureau of the Census, Washington, D.C. 20233 (301) 457-4100, www.census.gov; Internet site: http://www.census.gov/hhes/www/disable/dissipp.html.

U.S. Department of Health and Human Services, National Center for Health Statistics, 3700 East-West Highway, Hyattsville, Maryland 20782 (301) 436-8500, www.cdc.gov/nchs; *Vital and Health Statistics; Advance Data, No. 289;* and unpublished data.

VITAL STATISTICS - See also BIRTHS and DEATHS

VITAL STATISTICS - FERTILITY AND FERTILITY RATE

U.S. Department of Health and Human Services, National Center for Health Statistics, 3700 East-West Highway, Hyattsville, Maryland 20782 (301) 436-8500, www.cdc.gov/nchs; *Vital Statistics of the United States;* and unpublished data.

VITAL STATISTICS - FOREIGN COUNTRIES

U.S. Department of Commerce, Bureau of the Census, Washington, D.C. 20233 (301) 457-4100, www.census.gov; International Data Base; and Internet site: http://www.census.gov/ipc/www/idbnew.html.

U.S. Department of Health and Human Services, National Center for Health Statistics, 3700 East-West Highway, Hyattsville, Maryland 20782 (301) 436-8500, www.cdc.gov/nchs; *Advance Data No. 303.*

World Health Organization, 20 Avenue Appia Avenue Appia, Office of Publications, CH-1211 Geneva, 27, Switzerland (Telephone Number in U.S. (518) 436-9686); *World Health Statistics Annual.*

VITAL STATISTICS - LIFE EXPECTANCY

U.S. Department of Commerce, Bureau of the Census, Washington, D.C. 20233 (301) 457-4100, www.census.gov; International Data Base; and Internet site: http://www.census.gov/ipc/www/idbnew.html.

U.S. Department of Health and Human Services, National Center for Health Statistics, 3700 East-West Highway, Hyattsville, Maryland 20782 (301) 436-8500, www.cdc.gov/nchs; *Vital Statistics of the United States; National Vital Statistics Report;* and unpublished data.

VITAL STATISTICS - MARRIAGE AND DIVORCE

U.S. Department of Health and Human Services, National Center for Health Statistics, 3700 East-West Highway, Hyattsville, Maryland 20782 (301) 436-8500, www.cdc.gov/nchs; *Vital Statistics of the United States; National Vital Statistics Report;* and unpublished data.

VITAL STATISTICS - OUTLYING AREAS

U.S. Department of Health and Human Services, National Center for Health Statistics, 3700 East-West Highway, Hyattsville, Maryland 20782 (301) 436-8500, www.cdc.gov/nchs; *Vital Statistics of the United States.*

VITAL STATISTICS - PROJECTIONS

U.S. Department of Commerce, Bureau

of the Census, Washington, D.C. 20233 (301) 457-4100, www.census.gov; *Current Population Reports;* and unpublished data.

VITAL STATISTICS - RATES - SUMMARY

U.S. Department of Health and Human Services, National Center for Health Statistics, 3700 East-West Highway, Hyattsville, Maryland 20782 (301) 436-8500, www.cdc.gov/nchs; *Vital Statistics of the United States; National Vital Statistics Report;* and unpublished data.

VITAL STATISTICS - WORLD

U.S. Department of Commerce, Bureau of the Census, Washington, D.C. 20233 (301) 457-4100, www.census.gov; International Data Base; and Internet site: http://www.census.gov/ipc/www/idbnew.html.

VITAMINS

U.S. Department of Agriculture, Center for Nutrition Policy and Promotion, 1120 20th Street, NW, North Lobby, Suite 200, Washington, D.C. 20036 (202) 418-2312, www.usda.gov/cnpp; data published by Economic Research Service in *Food Consumption, Prices, and Expenditures.*

VOCATIONAL EDUCATION

Executive Office of the President, Office of Management and Budget, Executive Office Building, Washington, D.C. 20503 (202) 395-3080, www.whitehouse.gov/omb; *Historical Tables.*

U.S. Department of Veterans Affairs, 810 Vermont Avenue, NW, Washington, D.C. 20420 (202) 273-5400, www.va.gov; *Annual Report of the Secretary of Veterans Affairs;* and unpublished data.

VOCATIONAL REHABILITATION

U.S. Department of Education, 400 Maryland Avenue, SW, Washington, D.C. 20202 (877) 424-1616, www.ed.gov; *State Vocational Rehabilitation Agency Program Data in Fiscal Years;* and *Caseload Statistics of State Vocational Rehabilitation Agencies in Fiscal Years.*

Social Security Administration, 6400 Security Boulevard, Baltimore, Maryland 21235 (800) 772-1213, www.ssa.gov; *Social Security Bulletin;* and unpublished data.

VOCATIONAL REHABILITATION - MEDICAL PAYMENTS

U.S. Department of Health and Human Services, Health Care Financing Administration, 200 Independence Avenue, SW, Washington, D.C. 20201 (202) 690-6145, www.hcfa.gov; *Health Care Financing Review.*

VOLLEYBALL

National Collegiate Athletic Association, 700 West Washington Street, Indianapolis, Indiana 46206 (317) 917-6222; *1997-98 Participation Study*.

National Federation of State High School Associations, Post Office Box 690, Indianapolis, Indiana 46206 (317) 972-6900; *The 1998-99 High School Athletics Participation Survey*.

National Sporting Goods Association, 1601 Feehanville Drive, Suite 300, Mount Prospect, Illinois 60056 (847) 296-6742; *Sports Participation in 1998*.

VOLUNTEER WORKERS

Independent Sector, 1200 18th Street, NW, Suite 200, Washington, D.C. 20036 (202) 467-6161; *Giving and Volunteering in the United States*.

VOTER REGISTRATION

Federal Election Commission, 999 E Street, NW, Washington, D.C. 20463 (800) 424-9530, www.fec.gov; *Executive Summary - Report to the Congress, June 1997*.

U.S. Department of Commerce, Bureau of the Census, Washington, D.C. 20233 (301) 457-4100, www.census.gov; *Current Population Reports;* and unpublished data.

VOTER TURNOUT

Congressional Quarterly, Inc., 1414 Twenty-second Street, NW, Washington, D.C. 20037 (202) 887-8500; *Congressional Quarterly Weekly Report*.

Federal Election Commission, 999 E Street, NW, Washington, D.C. 20463 (800) 424-9530, www.fec.gov; *Executive Summary - Report to the Congress, June 1997*.

U.S. Department of Commerce, Bureau of the Census, Washington, D.C. 20233 (301) 457-4100, www.census.gov; *Current Population Reports;* and unpublished data.

VOTES - CONGRESSIONAL

Congressional Quarterly, Inc., 1414 Twenty-second Street, NW, Washington, D.C. 20037 (202) 887-8500; *Congressional Quarterly Weekly Report;* and *America Votes*.

U.S. Department of Commerce, Bureau of the Census, Washington, D.C. 20233 (301) 457-4100, www.census.gov; *Current Population Reports*.

VOTES - GUBERNATORIAL

Congressional Quarterly, Inc., 1414 Twenty-second Street, NW, Washington, D.C. 20037 (202) 887-8500; *America Votes;* and unpublished data.

VOTES - PRESIDENTIAL

Center for Political Studies, University of Michigan, Post Office Box 1248, Ann Arbor, Michigan 48106 (313) 764-8363; unpublished data.

Congressional Quarterly, Inc., 1414 Twenty-second Street, NW, Washington, D.C. 20037 (202) 887-8500; *America Votes*.

U.S. Department of Commerce, Bureau of the Census, Washington, D.C. 20233 (301) 457-4100, www.census.gov; *Current Population Reports*.

VOTING AGE POPULATION

U.S. Department of Commerce, Bureau of the Census, Washington, D.C. 20233 (301) 457-4100, www.census.gov; *Current Population Reports;* and unpublished data.

W

WAGE EARNERS - See LABOR FORCE, EMPLOYMENT AND EARNINGS and Individual Industries

WAGES AND WAGE RATES - See EARNINGS

WAKE ISLAND - AGRICULTURE

Food and Agricultural Organization of the United Nations (FAO) Via delle Terme di Caracalla, 00100 Rome, Italy (Telephone Number in U.S. (202) 653-2400); *The State of Food and Agriculture.*

United Nations Conference on Trade and Development, Central Statistical Service, Palais des Nations, Geneva, Switzerland (Telephone in U.S. (800) 253-9646); *UNCTAD Commodity Yearbook.*

WAKE ISLAND - AIRPORTS

Central Intelligence Agency, Washington, D.C. 20505 (703) 482-1100, www.cia.gov; *The World Factbook.*

WAKE ISLAND - AREA AND DENSITY OF POPULATION

Central Intelligence Agency, Washington, D.C. 20505 (703) 482-1100, www.cia.gov; *The World Factbook.*

Food and Agricultural Organization of the United Nations (FAO) Via delle Terme di Caracalla, 00100 Rome, Italy (Telephone Number in U.S. (202) 653-2400); *The State of Food and Agriculture.*

St. Martin's Press, Inc., 175 Fifth Avenue, New York, New York 10010 (800) 221-7945; *The Statesman's Year-Book.*

Statistical Office of the United Nations, Publishing Service, New York, New York 10017 (800) 253-9646; *Statistical Yearbook.*

WAKE ISLAND - BIRTH RATES

Central Intelligence Agency, Washington, D.C. 20505 (703) 482-1100, www.cia.gov; *The World Factbook.*

Statistical Office of the United Nations, Publishing Service, New York, New York 10017 (800) 253-9646; *Demographic Yearbook.*

WAKE ISLAND - BROADCASTING

Billboard Limited, P.O. Box 9027, 1006 AA Amsterdam, The Netherlands (Telephone Number in U.S. (212) 764-7300); *World Radio TV Handbook.*

Central Intelligence Agency, Washington, D.C. 20505 (703) 482-1100, www.cia.gov; *The World Factbook.*

WAKE ISLAND - BUDGET

Central Intelligence Agency, Washington, D.C. 20505 (703) 482-1100, www.cia.gov; *The World Factbook.*

WAKE ISLAND - CALORIE SUPPLY

Food and Agricultural Organization of the United Nations (FAO) Via delle Terme di Caracalla, 00100 Rome, Italy (Telephone Number in U.S. (202) 653-2400); *The State of Food and Agriculture.*

WAKE ISLAND - CHEMICAL (ORGANIC) PRODUCTION - See WAKE ISLAND - MINING AND MINERAL PRODUCTS

WAKE ISLAND - COAL PRODUCTION - See WAKE ISLAND - MINING AND MINERAL PRODUCTS

WAKE ISLAND - CORN PRODUCTION - See WAKE ISLAND - CROPS

WAKE ISLAND - CORPORATE TAXES - See WAKE ISLAND - TAXATION

WAKE ISLAND - CROPS

Food and Agricultural Organization of the United Nations (FAO) Via delle Terme di Caracalla, 00100 Rome, Italy (Telephone Number in U.S. (202) 653-2400); *The State of Food and Agriculture.*

United Nations Conference on Trade and Development, Central Statistical Service, Palais des Nations, Geneva, Switzerland (Telephone in U.S. (800) 253-9646); *UNCTAD Commodity Yearbook.*

WAKE ISLAND - DAIRY PRODUCTS

Food and Agricultural Organization of the United Nations (FAO) Via delle Terme di Caracalla, 00100 Rome, Italy (Telephone Number in U.S. (202) 653-2400); *The State of Food and Agriculture.*

WAKE ISLAND - DEATH RATES - See WAKE ISLAND - MORTALITY

WAKE ISLAND - DIVORCE RATES

Statistical Office of the United Nations, Publishing Service, New York, New York 10017 (800) 253-9646; *Demographic Yearbook.*

WAKE ISLAND - ECONOMY

Central Intelligence Agency, Washington, D.C. 20505 (703) 482-1100, www.cia.gov; *The World Factbook.*

WAKE ISLAND - EGG PRODUCTION AND CONSUMPTION - See WAKE ISLAND - DAIRY PRODUCTS

WAKE ISLAND - ELECTRICITY

Central Intelligence Agency, Washington, D.C. 20505 (703) 482-1100, www.cia.gov; *The World Factbook.*

WAKE ISLAND - ENERGY

Food and Agricultural Organization of the United Nations (FAO) Via delle Terme di Caracalla, 00100 Rome, Italy (Telephone Number in U.S. (202) 653-2400); *The State of Food and Agriculture.*

Statistical Office of the United Nations, Publishing Service, New York, New York 10017 (800) 253-9646; *Statistical Yearbook.*

WAKE ISLAND - EXCHANGE RATES

Central Intelligence Agency, Washington, D.C. 20505 (703) 482-1100, www.cia.gov; *The World Factbook.*

WAKE ISLAND - EXPORTS

Central Intelligence Agency, Washington, D.C. 20505 (703) 482-1100, www.cia.gov; *The World Factbook.*

Food and Agricultural Organization of the United Nations (FAO) Via delle Terme di Caracalla, 00100 Rome, Italy (Telephone Number in U.S. (202) 653-2400); *The State of Food and Agriculture.*

WAKE ISLAND - EXTERNAL TRADE

Food and Agricultural Organization of the United Nations (FAO) Via delle Terme di Caracalla, 00100 Rome, Italy (Telephone Number in U.S. (202) 653-2400); *The State of Food and Agriculture.*

WAKE ISLAND - FARM CROPS - See WAKE ISLAND - CROPS

WAKE ISLAND - FERTILITY RATES

Central Intelligence Agency, Washington, D.C. 20505 (703) 482-1100, www.cia.gov; *The World Factbook.*

WAKE ISLAND - FERTILIZER

Food and Agricultural Organization of the United Nations (FAO) Via delle Terme di Caracalla, 00100 Rome, Italy (Telephone Number in U.S. (202) 653-2400); *The State of Food and Agriculture.*

WAKE ISLAND - FETAL MORTALITY - See WAKE ISLAND - MORTALITY

WAKE ISLAND - FISHERIES

United Nations Conference on Trade and Development, Central Statistical Service, Palais des Nations, Geneva, Switzerland (Telephone in U.S. (800) 253-9646); *UNCTAD Commodity Yearbook.*

WAKE ISLAND - FOOD

United Nations Conference on Trade and Development, Central Statistical Service, Palais des Nations, Geneva, Switzerland (Telephone in U.S. (800) 253-9646); *UNCTAD Commodity Yearbook.*

WAKE ISLAND - FOREIGN TRADE

Food and Agricultural Organization of the United Nations (FAO) Via delle Terme di Caracalla, 00100 Rome, Italy (Telephone Number in U.S. (202) 653-2400); *The State of Food and Agriculture.*

United Nations Conference on Trade and Development, Central Statistical Service, Palais des Nations, Geneva, Switzerland (Telephone in U.S. (800) 253-9646); *UNCTAD Commodity Yearbook.*

WAKE ISLAND - FORESTRY AND FOREST PRODUCTS

United Nations Conference on Trade and Development, Central Statistical Service, Palais des Nations, Geneva, Switzerland (Telephone in U.S. (800) 253-9646); *UNCTAD Commodity Yearbook.*

WAKE ISLAND - GENERAL MORTALITY - See WAKE ISLAND - MORTALITY

WAKE ISLAND - GOVERNMENT

Central Intelligence Agency, Washington, D.C. 20505 (703) 482-1100, www.cia.gov; *The World Factbook.*

WAKE ISLAND - GRAIN PRODUCTION - See WAKE ISLAND - CROPS

WAKE ISLAND - HIGHWAYS

Central Intelligence Agency, Washington, D.C. 20505 (703) 482-1100, www.cia.gov; *The World Factbook.*

WAKE ISLAND - ILLITERATE POPULATION

Central Intelligence Agency, Washington, D.C. 20505 (703) 482-1100, www.cia.gov; *The World Factbook.*

WAKE ISLAND - IMPORTS

Central Intelligence Agency, Washington, D.C. 20505 (703) 482-1100, www.cia.gov; *The World Factbook.*

Food and Agricultural Organization of the United Nations (FAO) Via delle Terme di Caracalla, 00100 Rome, Italy (Telephone Number in U.S. (202) 653-2400); *The State of Food and Agriculture.*

WAKE ISLAND - INDUSTRY

Central Intelligence Agency, Washington, D.C. 20505 (703) 482-1100, www.cia.gov; *The World Factbook.*

WAKE ISLAND - INFANT AND MATERNAL MORTALITY - See WAKE ISLAND - MORTALITY

WAKE ISLAND - LABOR

Central Intelligence Agency, Washington, D.C. 20505 (703) 482-1100, www.cia.gov; *The World Factbook.*

Food and Agricultural Organization of the United Nations (FAO) Via delle Terme di Caracalla, 00100 Rome, Italy (Telephone

Number in U.S. (202) 653-2400); *The State of Food and Agriculture.*

WAKE ISLAND - LAND USE

Central Intelligence Agency, Washington, D.C. 20505 (703) 482-1100, www.cia.gov; *The World Factbook.*

WAKE ISLAND - LIFE EXPECTANCY

Central Intelligence Agency, Washington, D.C. 20505 (703) 482-1100, www.cia.gov; *The World Factbook.*

WAKE ISLAND - LIVESTOCK AND POULTRY

Food and Agricultural Organization of the United Nations (FAO) Via delle Terme di Caracalla, 00100 Rome, Italy (Telephone Number in U.S. (202) 653-2400); *The State of Food and Agriculture.*

United Nations Conference on Trade and Development, Central Statistical Service, Palais des Nations, Geneva, Switzerland (Telephone in U.S. (800) 253-9646); *UNCTAD Commodity Yearbook.*

WAKE ISLAND - MARRIAGE RATES

Statistical Office of the United Nations, Publishing Service, New York, New York 10017 (800) 253-9646; *Demographic Yearbook.*

WAKE ISLAND - MEAT PRODUCTION - See WAKE ISLAND - LIVESTOCK AND POULTRY

WAKE ISLAND - MILITARY

Central Intelligence Agency, Washington, D.C. 20505 (703) 482-1100, www.cia.gov; *The World Factbook.*

WAKE ISLAND - MINING

United Nations Conference on Trade and Development, Central Statistical Service, Palais des Nations, Geneva, Switzerland (Telephone in U.S. (800) 253-9646); *UNCTAD Commodity Yearbook.*

WAKE ISLAND - MORTALITY

Central Intelligence Agency, Washington, D.C. 20505 (703) 482-1100, www.cia.gov; *The World Factbook.*

Statistical Office of the United Nations, Publishing Service, New York, New York 10017 (800) 253-9646; *Demographic Yearbook.*

World Health Organization, Office of Publications, 20 Avenue Appia, CH-1211 Geneva 27, Switzerland (Telephone Number in U.S. (518) 436-9686); *World Health Statistics Annual.*

WAKE ISLAND - NATALITY - See WAKE ISLAND - BIRTH RATE

WAKE ISLAND - NEWSPAPER PRODUCTION - See WAKE ISLAND - FORESTRY AND FOREST PRODUCTS

WAKE ISLAND - OCCUPATIONS - See WAKE ISLAND - LABOR

WAKE ISLAND - PESTICIDE USE

Food and Agricultural Organization of the United Nations (FAO) Via delle Terme di Caracalla, 00100 Rome, Italy (Telephone Number in U.S. (202) 653-2400); *The State of Food and Agriculture.*

WAKE ISLAND - PETROLEUM INDUSTRY

Food and Agricultural Organization of the United Nations (FAO) Via delle Terme di Caracalla, 00100 Rome, Italy (Telephone Number in U.S. (202) 653-2400); *The State of Food and Agriculture.*

United Nations Conference on Trade and Development, Central Statistical Service, Palais des Nations, Geneva, Switzerland (Telephone in U.S. (800) 253-9646); *UNCTAD Commodity Yearbook.*

WAKE ISLAND - POPULATION

Central Intelligence Agency, Washington, D.C. 20505 (703) 482-1100, www.cia.gov; *The World Factbook.*

St. Martin's Press, Inc., 175 Fifth Avenue, New York, New York 10010 (800) 221-7945; *The Statesman's Year-Book.*

Statistical Office of the United Nations, Publishing Service, New York, New York 10017 (800) 253-9646; *Demographic Yearbook;* and *Statistical Yearbook.*

World Health Organization, Office of Publications, 20 Avenue Appia, CH-1211 Geneva 27, Switzerland (Telephone Number in U.S. (518) 436-9686); *World Health Statistics Annual.*

WAKE ISLAND - PRICES

Food and Agricultural Organization of the United Nations (FAO) Via delle Terme di Caracalla, 00100 Rome, Italy (Telephone Number in U.S. (202) 653-2400); *The State of Food and Agriculture.*

WAKE ISLAND - RELIGION

Central Intelligence Agency, Washington, D.C. 20505 (703) 482-1100, www.cia.gov; *The World Factbook.*

WAKE ISLAND - STOCKS - COMMODITY - MARKET PRICE - INDEX

Food and Agricultural Organization of the United Nations (FAO) Via delle Terme di Caracalla, 00100 Rome, Italy (Telephone Number in U.S. (202) 653-2400); *The State of Food and Agriculture.*

WAKE ISLAND - TELEPHONES IN USE

American Telephone and Telegraph Company, 26 Parsippany Road, Whippany, New Jersey 07981 (800) 222-0300; *The World's Telephones.*

Central Intelligence Agency, Washington, D.C. 20505 (703) 482-1100, www.cia.gov; *The World Factbook.*

WAKE ISLAND - TEXTILE INDUSTRY

United Nations Conference on Trade and Development, Central Statistical Service, Palais des Nations, Geneva, Switzerland (Telephone in U.S. (800) 253-9646); *UNCTAD Commodity Yearbook.*

WAKE ISLAND - TRADE - See WAKE ISLAND - FOREIGN TRADE

WAKE ISLAND - TRANSPORTATION AND COMMUNICATIONS

Central Intelligence Agency, Washington, D.C. 20505 (703) 482-1100, www.cia.gov; *The World Factbook.*

WAKE ISLAND - UNEMPLOYMENT RATE

Central Intelligence Agency, Washington, D.C. 20505 (703) 482-1100, www.cia.gov; *The World Factbook.*

WALLIS AND FUTUNA ISLANDS - AGRICULTURE

Europa Publications Limited, 18 Bedford Square, London, WC1B 3JN, England; *The Europa World Year Book.*

Food and Agricultural Organization of the United Nations (FAO) Via delle Terme di Caracalla, 00100 Rome, Italy (Telephone Number in U.S. (202) 653-2400); *The State of Food and Agriculture.*

St. Martin's Press, Inc., 175 Fifth Avenue, New York, New York 10010 (800) 221-7945; *The Statesman's Year-Book.*

United Nations Conference on Trade and Development, Central Statistical Service, Palais des Nations, Geneva, Switzerland (Telephone in U.S. (800) 253-9646); *UNCTAD Commodity Yearbook.*

WALLIS AND FUTUNA ISLANDS - AIRLINE SERVICE

Europa Publications Limited, 18 Bedford Square, London, WC1B 3JN, England; *The Europa World Year Book.*

St. Martin's Press, Inc., 175 Fifth Avenue, New York, New York 10010 (800) 221-7945; *The Statesman's Year-Book.*

WALLIS AND FUTUNA ISLANDS - AIRPORTS

Central Intelligence Agency, Washington, D.C. 20505 (703) 482-1100, www.cia.gov; *The World Factbook.*

WALLIS AND FUTUNA ISLANDS - AREA AND DENSITY OF POPULATION

Central Intelligence Agency, Washington, D.C. 20505 (703) 482-1100, www.cia.gov; *The World Factbook.*

Europa Publications Limited, 18 Bedford Square, London, WC1B 3JN, England; *The Europa World Year Book.*

Food and Agricultural Organization of the United Nations (FAO) Via delle Terme di Caracalla, 00100 Rome, Italy (Telephone Number in U.S. (202) 653-2400); *The State of Food and Agriculture.*

St. Martin's Press, Inc., 175 Fifth Avenue, New York, New York 10010 (800) 221-7945; *The Statesman's Year-Book.*

Statistical Office of the United Nations, Publishing Service, New York, New York 10017 (800) 253-9646; *Statistical Yearbook.*

WALLIS AND FUTUNA ISLANDS - BANKING

St. Martin's Press, Inc., 175 Fifth Avenue, New York, New York 10010 (800) 221-7945; *The Statesman's Year-Book.*

WALLIS AND FUTUNA ISLANDS - BIRTH RATES

Central Intelligence Agency, Washington, D.C. 20505 (703) 482-1100, www.cia.gov; *The World Factbook.*

Statistical Office of the United Nations, Publishing Service, New York, New York 10017 (800) 253-9646; *Demographic Yearbook;* and *Statistical Yearbook.*

WALLIS AND FUTUNA ISLANDS - BROADCASTING

Billboard Limited, P.O. Box 9027, 1006 AA Amsterdam, The Netherlands (Telephone Number in U.S. (212) 764-7300); *World Radio TV Handbook.*

Central Intelligence Agency, Washington, D.C. 20505 (703) 482-1100, www.cia.gov; *The World Factbook.*

St. Martin's Press, Inc., 175 Fifth Avenue, New York, New York 10010 (800) 221-7945; *The Statesman's Year-Book.*

WALLIS AND FUTUNA ISLANDS - BUDGET

Central Intelligence Agency, Washington, D.C. 20505 (703) 482-1100, www.cia.gov; *The World Factbook.*

WALLIS AND FUTUNA ISLANDS - CALORIE SUPPLY

Food and Agricultural Organization of the United Nations (FAO) Via delle Terme di Caracalla, 00100 Rome, Italy (Telephone Number in U.S. (202) 653-2400); *The State of Food and Agriculture.*

WALLIS AND FUTUNA ISLANDS - CHEMICAL (ORGANIC) PRODUCTION - See WALLIS AND FUTUNA ISLANDS - MINING AND MINERAL PRODUCTS

WALLIS AND FUTUNA ISLANDS - COMMERCE

St. Martin's Press, Inc., 175 Fifth Avenue, New York, New York 10010 (800) 221-7945; *The Statesman's Year-Book.*

WALLIS AND FUTUNA ISLANDS - CORN PRODUCTION - See WALLIS AND FUTUNA ISLANDS - CROPS

WALLIS AND FUTUNA ISLANDS - CORPORATE TAXES - See WALLIS AND FUTUNA ISLANDS - TAXATION

WALLIS AND FUTUNA ISLANDS - CROPS

Europa Publications Limited, 18 Bedford Square, London, WC1B 3JN, England; *The Europa World Year Book.*

Food and Agricultural Organization of the United Nations (FAO) Via delle Terme di Caracalla, 00100 Rome, Italy (Telephone Number in U.S. (202) 653-2400); *The State of Food and Agriculture.*

St. Martin's Press, Inc., 175 Fifth Avenue, New York, New York 10010 (800) 221-7945; *The Statesman's Year-Book.*

United Nations Conference on Trade and Development, Central Statistical Service, Palais des Nations, Geneva, Switzerland (Telephone in U.S. (800) 253-9646); *UNCTAD Commodity Yearbook.*

WALLIS AND FUTUNA ISLANDS - DAIRY PRODUCTS

Food and Agricultural Organization of the United Nations (FAO) Via delle Terme di Caracalla, 00100 Rome, Italy (Telephone Number in U.S. (202) 653-2400); *The State of Food and Agriculture.*

St. Martin's Press, Inc., 175 Fifth Avenue, New York, New York 10010 (800) 221-7945; *The Statesman's Year-Book.*

WALLIS AND FUTUNA ISLANDS - DEATH RATES - See WALLIS AND FUTUNA ISLANDS - MORTALITY

WALLIS AND FUTUNA ISLANDS - DEVELOPMENT ASSISTANCE

Statistical Office of the United Nations, Publishing Service, New York, New York 10017 (800) 253-9646; *Statistical Yearbook.*

WALLIS AND FUTUNA ISLANDS - DIVORCE RATES

Statistical Office of the United Nations, Publishing Service, New York, New York 10017 (800) 253-9646; *Demographic Yearbook.*

WALLIS AND FUTUNA ISLANDS - ECONOMY

Central Intelligence Agency, Washington, D.C. 20505 (703) 482-1100, www.cia.gov; *The World Factbook.*

St. Martin's Press, Inc., 175 Fifth Avenue, New York, New York 10010 (800) 221-7945; *The Statesman's Year-Book.*

WALLIS AND FUTUNA ISLANDS - EDUCATION

Europa Publications Limited, 18 Bedford Square, London, WC1B 3JN, England; *The Europa World Year Book.*

St. Martin's Press, Inc., 175 Fifth Avenue, New York, New York 10010 (800) 221-7945; *The Statesman's Year-Book.*

WALLIS AND FUTUNA ISLANDS - EGG PRODUCTION AND CONSUMPTION - See WALLIS AND FUTUNA ISLANDS - DAIRY PRODUCTS

WALLIS AND FUTUNA ISLANDS - ELECTRICITY

Central Intelligence Agency, Washington, D.C. 20505 (703) 482-1100, www.cia.gov; *The World Factbook.*

St. Martin's Press, Inc., 175 Fifth Avenue, New York, New York 10010 (800) 221-7945; *The Statesman's Year-Book.*

WALLIS AND FUTUNA ISLANDS - ENERGY

Food and Agricultural Organization of the United Nations (FAO) Via delle Terme di Caracalla, 00100 Rome, Italy (Telephone Number in U.S. (202) 653-2400); *The State of Food and Agriculture.*

St. Martin's Press, Inc., 175 Fifth Avenue, New York, New York 10010 (800) 221-7945; *The Statesman's Year-Book.*

WALLIS AND FUTUNA ISLANDS - EXCHANGE RATES

Central Intelligence Agency, Washington, D.C. 20505 (703) 482-1100, www.cia.gov; *The World Factbook.*

Europa Publications Limited, 18 Bedford Square, London, WC1B 3JN, England; *The Europa World Year Book.*

WALLIS AND FUTUNA ISLANDS - EXPORTS

Central Intelligence Agency, Washington, D.C. 20505 (703) 482-1100, www.cia.gov; *The World Factbook.*

Europa Publications Limited, 18 Bedford Square, London, WC1B 3JN, England; *The Europa World Year Book.*

Food and Agricultural Organization of the United Nations (FAO) Via delle Terme di Caracalla, 00100 Rome, Italy (Telephone Number in U.S. (202) 653-2400); *The State of Food and Agriculture.*

WALLIS AND FUTUNA ISLANDS - EXTERNAL TRADE

Food and Agricultural Organization of the United Nations (FAO) Via delle Terme di Caracalla, 00100 Rome, Italy (Telephone Number in U.S. (202) 653-2400); *The State of Food and Agriculture.*

WALLIS AND FUTUNA ISLANDS - FARM CROPS - See WALLIS AND FUTUNA ISLANDS - CROPS

WALLIS AND FUTUNA ISLANDS - FERTILITY RATES

Central Intelligence Agency, Washington, D.C. 20505 (703) 482-1100, www.cia.gov; *The World Factbook.*

WALLIS AND FUTUNA ISLANDS - FERTILIZER

Food and Agricultural Organization of the United Nations (FAO) Via delle Terme di Caracalla, 00100 Rome, Italy (Telephone Number in U.S. (202) 653-2400); *The State of Food and Agriculture.*

WALLIS AND FUTUNA ISLANDS - FETAL MORTALITY - See WALLIS AND FUTUNA ISLANDS - MORTALITY

WALLIS AND FUTUNA ISLANDS - FINANCE

Europa Publications Limited, 18 Bedford Square, London, WC1B 3JN, England; *The Europa World Year Book.*

WALLIS AND FUTUNA ISLANDS - FISHERIES

Europa Publications Limited, 18 Bedford Square, London, WC1B 3JN, England; *The Europa World Year Book*.

Food and Agricultural Organization of the United Nations (FAO) Via delle Terme di Caracalla, 00100 Rome, Italy (Telephone Number in U.S. (202) 653-2400); *The State of Food and Agriculture*.

United Nations Conference on Trade and Development, Central Statistical Service, Palais des Nations, Geneva, Switzerland (Telephone in U.S. (800) 253-9646); *UNCTAD Commodity Yearbook*.

WALLIS AND FUTUNA ISLANDS - FOOD

Food and Agricultural Organization of the United Nations (FAO) Via delle Terme di Caracalla, 00100 Rome, Italy (Telephone Number in U.S. (202) 653-2400); *The State of Food and Agriculture*.

United Nations Conference on Trade and Development, Central Statistical Service, Palais des Nations, Geneva, Switzerland (Telephone in U.S. (800) 253-9646); *UNCTAD Commodity Yearbook*.

WALLIS AND FUTUNA ISLANDS - FOREIGN TRADE

Food and Agricultural Organization of the United Nations (FAO) Via delle Terme di Caracalla, 00100 Rome, Italy (Telephone Number in U.S. (202) 653-2400); *The State of Food and Agriculture*.

United Nations Conference on Trade and Development, Central Statistical Service, Palais des Nations, Geneva, Switzerland (Telephone in U.S. (800) 253-9646); *UNCTAD Commodity Yearbook*.

WALLIS AND FUTUNA ISLANDS - FORESTRY AND FOREST PRODUCTS

Food and Agricultural Organization of the United Nations (FAO) Via delle Terme di Caracalla, 00100 Rome, Italy (Telephone Number in U.S. (202) 653-2400); *The State of Food and Agriculture*.

United Nations Conference on Trade and Development, Central Statistical Service, Palais des Nations, Geneva, Switzerland (Telephone in U.S. (800) 253-9646); *UNCTAD Commodity Yearbook*.

WALLIS AND FUTUNA ISLANDS - GENERAL MORTALITY - See WALLIS AND FUTUNA ISLANDS - MORTALITY

WALLIS AND FUTUNA ISLANDS - GOVERNMENT

Central Intelligence Agency, Washington, D.C. 20505 (703) 482-1100, www.cia.gov; *The World Factbook*.

St. Martin's Press, Inc., 175 Fifth Avenue, New York, New York 10010 (800) 221-7945; *The Statesman's Year-Book*.

WALLIS AND FUTUNA ISLANDS - GRAIN PRODUCTION - See WALLIS AND FUTUNA ISLANDS - CROPS

WALLIS AND FUTUNA ISLANDS - HEALTH

St. Martin's Press, Inc., 175 Fifth Avenue, New York, New York 10010 (800) 221-7945; *The Statesman's Year-Book*.

Statistical Office of the United Nations, Publishing Service, New York, New York 10017 (800) 253-9646; *Statistical Yearbook*.

WALLIS AND FUTUNA ISLANDS - HIGHWAYS

Central Intelligence Agency, Washington, D.C. 20505 (703) 482-1100, www.cia.gov; *The World Factbook*.

St. Martin's Press, Inc., 175 Fifth Avenue, New York, New York 10010 (800) 221-7945; *The Statesman's Year-Book*.

WALLIS AND FUTUNA ISLANDS - ILLITERATE POPULATION

Central Intelligence Agency, Washington, D.C. 20505 (703) 482-1100, www.cia.gov; *The World Factbook*.

WALLIS AND FUTUNA ISLANDS - IMPORTS

Central Intelligence Agency, Washington, D.C. 20505 (703) 482-1100, www.cia.gov; *The World Factbook*.

Europa Publications Limited, 18 Bedford Square, London, WC1B 3JN, England; *The Europa World Year Book*.

Organisation for Economic Co-operation and Development (OECD), 2 rue Andre-Pascal, 75 Paris 16, France (Telephone Number in U.S. (202) 785-6323); *Textile Industry in OECD Countries*.

St. Martin's Press, Inc., 175 Fifth Avenue, New York, New York 10010 (800) 221-7945; *The Statesman's Year-Book*.

WALLIS AND FUTUNA ISLANDS - INDUSTRY

Central Intelligence Agency, Washington, D.C. 20505 (703) 482-1100, www.cia.gov; *The World Factbook*.

St. Martin's Press, Inc., 175 Fifth Avenue, New York, New York 10010 (800) 221-7945; *The Statesman's Year-Book*.

WALLIS AND FUTUNA ISLANDS - INFANT AND MATERNAL MORTALITY - See WALLIS AND FUTUNA ISLANDS - MORTALITY

WALLIS AND FUTUNA ISLANDS - LABOR

Central Intelligence Agency, Washington, D.C. 20505 (703) 482-1100, www.cia.gov; *The World Factbook*.

Food and Agricultural Organization of the United Nations (FAO) Via delle Terme di Caracalla, 00100 Rome, Italy (Telephone Number in U.S. (202) 653-2400); *The State of Food and Agriculture*.

WALLIS AND FUTUNA ISLANDS - LAND USE

Central Intelligence Agency, Washington, D.C. 20505 (703) 482-1100, www.cia.gov; *The World Factbook*.

WALLIS AND FUTUNA ISLANDS - LIFE EXPECTANCY

Central Intelligence Agency, Washington, D.C. 20505 (703) 482-1100, www.cia.gov; *The World Factbook*.

WALLIS AND FUTUNA ISLANDS - LIVESTOCK AND POULTRY

Europa Publications Limited, 18 Bedford Square, London, WC1B 3JN, England; *The Europa World Year Book*.

Food and Agricultural Organization of the United Nations (FAO) Via delle Terme di Caracalla, 00100 Rome, Italy (Telephone Number in U.S. (202) 653-2400); *The State of Food and Agriculture*.

St. Martin's Press, Inc., 175 Fifth Avenue, New York, New York 10010 (800) 221-7945; *The Statesman's Year-Book*.

United Nations Conference on Trade and Development, Central Statistical Service, Palais des Nations, Geneva, Switzerland (Telephone in U.S. (800) 253-9646); *UNCTAD Commodity Yearbook*.

WALLIS AND FUTUNA ISLANDS - MAIL - NUMBER OF ITEMS SENT OR RECEIVED

Statistical Office of the United Nations, Publishing Service, New York, New York 10017 (800) 253-9646; *Statistical Yearbook*.

WALLIS AND FUTUNA ISLANDS - MARRIAGE RATES

Statistical Office of the United Nations, Publishing Service, New York, New York 10017 (800) 253-9646; *Demographic Yearbook;* and *Statistical Yearbook*.

WALLIS AND FUTUNA ISLANDS - MEAT PRODUCTION - See WALLIS AND FUTUNA ISLANDS - LIVESTOCK AND POULTRY

WALLIS AND FUTUNA ISLANDS - MERCHANT SHIPPING

St. Martin's Press, Inc., 175 Fifth Avenue, New York, New York 10010 (800) 221-7945; *The Statesman's Year-Book.*

WALLIS AND FUTUNA ISLANDS - MILITARY

Central Intelligence Agency, Washington, D.C. 20505 (703) 482-1100, www.cia.gov; *The World Factbook.*

WALLIS AND FUTUNA ISLANDS - MINING AND MILITARY PRODUCTS

United Nations Conference on Trade and Development, Central Statistical Service, Palais des Nations, Geneva, Switzerland (Telephone in U.S. (800) 253-9646); *UNCTAD Commodity Yearbook.*

WALLIS AND FUTUNA ISLANDS - MORTALITY

Central Intelligence Agency, Washington, D.C. 20505 (703) 482-1100, www.cia.gov; *The World Factbook.*

Statistical Office of the United Nations, Publishing Service, New York, New York 10017 (800) 253-9646; *Demographic Yearbook;* and *Statistical Yearbook.*

WALLIS AND FUTUNA ISLANDS - NATALITY - See WALLIS AND FUTUNA ISLANDS - BIRTH RATE

WALLIS AND FUTUNA ISLANDS - NEWSPAPER PRODUCTION - See WALLIS AND FUTUNA ISLANDS - FORESTRY AND FOREST PRODUCTS

WALLIS AND FUTUNA ISLANDS - OCCUPATIONS - See WALLIS AND FUTUNA ISLANDS - LABOR

WALLIS AND FUTUNA ISLANDS - PESTICIDE USE

Food and Agricultural Organization of the United Nations (FAO) Via delle Terme di Caracalla, 00100 Rome, Italy (Telephone Number in U.S. (202) 653-2400); *The State of Food and Agriculture.*

WALLIS AND FUTUNA ISLANDS - PETROLEUM INDUSTRY

Food and Agricultural Organization of the United Nations (FAO) Via delle Terme di Caracalla, 00100 Rome, Italy (Telephone Number in U.S. (202) 653-2400); *The State of Food and Agriculture.*

United Nations Conference on Trade and Development, Central Statistical Service, Palais des Nations, Geneva, Switzerland (Telephone in U.S. (800) 253-9646); *UNCTAD Commodity Yearbook.*

WALLIS AND FUTUNA ISLANDS - POPULATION

Central Intelligence Agency, Washington, D.C. 20505 (703) 482-1100, www.cia.gov; *The World Factbook.*

Europa Publications Limited, 18 Bedford Square, London, WC1B 3JN, England; *The Europa World Year Book.*

St. Martin's Press, Inc., 175 Fifth Avenue, New York, New York 10010 (800) 221-7945; *The Statesman's Year-Book.*

Statistical Office of the United Nations, Publishing Service, New York, New York 10017 (800) 253-9646; *Demographic Yearbook;* and *Statistical Yearbook.*

World Health Organization, Office of Publications, 20 Avenue Appia, CH-1211 Geneva 27, Switzerland (Telephone Number in U.S. (518) 436-9686); *World Health Statistics Annual.*

WALLIS AND FUTUNA ISLANDS - POST OFFICES

St. Martin's Press, Inc., 175 Fifth Avenue, New York, New York 10010 (800) 221-7945; *The Statesman's Year-Book.*

WALLIS AND FUTUNA ISLANDS - PRICES

Food and Agricultural Organization of the United Nations (FAO) Via delle Terme di Caracalla, 00100 Rome, Italy (Telephone Number in U.S. (202) 653-2400); *The State of Food and Agriculture.*

WALLIS AND FUTUNA ISLANDS - RADIO RECEIVERS

St. Martin's Press, Inc., 175 Fifth Avenue, New York, New York 10010 (800) 221-7945; *The Statesman's Year-Book.*

WALLIS AND FUTUNA ISLANDS - RELIGION

Central Intelligence Agency, Washington, D.C. 20505 (703) 482-1100, www.cia.gov; *The World Factbook.*

St. Martin's Press, Inc., 175 Fifth Avenue, New York, New York 10010 (800) 221-7945; *The Statesman's Year-Book.*

WALLIS AND FUTUNA ISLANDS - STOCKS - COMMODITY - MARKET PRICE - INDEX

Food and Agricultural Organization of the United Nations (FAO) Via delle Terme di Caracalla, 00100 Rome, Italy (Telephone Number in U.S. (202) 653-2400); *The State of Food and Agriculture.*

WALLIS AND FUTUNA ISLANDS - TELEPHONES IN USE

American Telephone and Telegraph Company, 26 Parsippany Road, Whippany, New Jersey 07981 (800) 222-0300; *The World's Telephones.*

Central Intelligence Agency, Washington, D.C. 20505 (703) 482-1100, www.cia.gov; *The World Factbook.*

St. Martin's Press, Inc., 175 Fifth Avenue, New York, New York 10010 (800) 221-7945; *The Statesman's Year-Book.*

WALLIS AND FUTUNA ISLANDS - TEXTILE INDUSTRY

United Nations Conference on Trade and Development, Central Statistical Service, Palais des Nations, Geneva, Switzerland (Telephone in U.S. (800) 253-9646); *UNCTAD Commodity Yearbook.*

WALLIS AND FUTUNA ISLANDS - TOURISM

Europa Publications Limited, 18 Bedford Square, London, WC1B 3JN, England; *The Europa World Year Book.*

WALLIS AND FUTUNA ISLANDS - TRADE - See WALLIS AND FUTUNA ISLANDS

WALLIS AND FUTUNA ISLANDS - TRANSPORTATION AND COMMUNICATIONS

Central Intelligence Agency, Washington, D.C. 20505 (703) 482-1100, www.cia.gov; *The World Factbook.*

St. Martin's Press, Inc., 175 Fifth Avenue, New York, New York 10010 (800) 221-7945; *The Statesman's Year-Book.*

WALLIS AND FUTUNA ISLANDS - UNEMPLOYMENT RATE

Central Intelligence Agency, Washington, D.C. 20505 (703) 482-1100, www.cia.gov; *The World Factbook.*

WALLIS AND FUTUNA ISLANDS - VITAL STATISTICS

Statistical Office of the United Nations, Publishing Service, New York, New York 10017 (800) 253-9646; *Statistical Yearbook.*

World Health Organization, Office of Publications, 20 Avenue Appia, CH-1211 Geneva 27, Switzerland (Telephone Number in U.S. (518) 436-9686); *World Health Statistics Annual.*

WALNUTS

U.S. Department of Agriculture, National Agricultural Statistics Service, Fourteenth Street and Independence Avenue, SW, Washington, D.C. 20250 (800) 727-9540, www.usda.gov/nass; *Noncitrus*

Fruits and Nuts.

WAREHOUSES - See also TRUCKING

U.S. Department of Commerce, Bureau of the Census, Washington, D.C. 20233 (301) 457-4100, www.census.gov; *Current Business Reports, Motor Freight Transportation and Warehousing Survey.*

WAREHOUSES - ENERGY CHARACTERISTICS

U.S. Department of Energy, Energy Information Administration, 1000 Independence Avenue, SW, Washington, D.C. 20585 (202) 586-8800, www.eia.doe.gov; *Commercial Buildings Energy Consumption and Expenditures.*

WAREHOUSES - FLOOR SPACE

U.S. Department of Energy, Energy Information Administration, 1000 Independence Avenue, SW, Washington, D.C. 20585 (202) 586-8800, www.eia.doe.gov; *Commercial Buildings Energy Consumption Survey;* and Internet site: http://www.eia.doe.gov/emeu/cbecs/contents.html.

WAREHOUSES - INVENTORY

U.S. Department of Energy, Energy Information Administration, 1000 Independence Avenue, SW, Washington, D.C. 20585 (202) 586-8800, www.eia.doe.gov; *Commercial Buildings Energy Consumption Survey;*and Internet site: http://www.eia.doe.gov/emeu/cbecs/contents.html.

WARS - UNITED STATES TROOPS AND CASUALTIES

U.S. Department of Defense, Office of the Secretary, The Pentagon, Washington, D.C. 20301 (703) 545-6700; unpublished data.

WASHING MACHINES - HOMES WITH

Euromonitor International, Inc., 122 South Michigan Avenue, Suite 1200, Chicago, Illinois 60603 (800) 577-EURO; *European Marketing Data and Statistics.*

U.S. Department of Energy, Energy Information Administration, 1000 Independence Avenue, SW, Washington, D.C. 20585 (202) 586-8800, www.eia.doe.gov; Internet site: http://eia.doe.gov/emeu/consumption.

WASHINGTON - See also STATE DATA (FOR INDIVIDUAL STATES)

Washington - Primary Statistics Sources

Washington State Office of Financial Management, Forecasting Division, P. O. Box 43113, Olympia, Washington 98504 (360) 902-0599; *Washington State Data Book;* and *Population Trends for Washington State.*

Washington - State Data Centers

Forecasting Division Office of Financial Management, 450 Insurance Building, Box 43113, Olympia, Washington 98504-3113, Yi Zhao (360) 902-0599 .

CSSCR, University of Washington, 145 Savery Hall, DK 45, Seattle, Washington 98195, Mr. Fred Nick (206) 543-8110.

Department of Employment Security, LMEA, Post Office Box 46000, Olympia, Washington 98504-6000, Mr. Tom Norris (360) 438-3163.

Department of Sociology, Central Washington University, Applied Social Data Center, Ellensburg, Washington 98926-7545, Dr. David E. Kaufman (509) 963-1305.

Department of Sociology, Demographic Research Laboratory, Western Washington University, Bellingham, Washington 98225, Lucky Tedrow, Director (360) 650-3176.

Puget Sound Council of Governments, 1011 Western Avenue, Suite 500, South, Seattle, Washington 98104, Mr. Bob Sicko (206) 464-5325.

Social Research Center, Department of Rural Sociology, Washington State University, Pullman, Washington 99164-4006, Dr. Annabel Kirschner Cook (509) 335-4519.

WASTEPAPER

U.S. Department of Labor, Bureau of Labor Statistics, Two Massachusetts Avenue, NE, Washington, D.C. 20212 (202) 691-5200, www.stats.bls.gov; *Producer Price Indexes.*

WASTEWATER TREATMENT

Environmental Protection Agency, 1200 Pennsylvania Avenue, NW, Washington, D.C. 20460 (888) 372-8255, www.epa.gov; *Clean Water Needs Survey Report to Congress.*

WATCHES - See CLOCKS AND WATCHES, ETC.

WATER - See also WATER TRANSPORTATION SERVICES and WASTEWATER TREATMENT

WATER - AREA - UNITED STATES

U.S. Department of Commerce, Bureau of the Census, Washington, D.C. 20233 (301) 457-4100, www.census.gov; *Census of Population and Housing; Areas of the United States; Area Measurement Reports;* and unpublished data from the TIGER/GICS computer file.

WATER - POLLUTION - OIL SPILLS

Tanker Advisory Center, Incorporated, 10 East End Avenue, New York, New York 10028 (212) 628-7686; *Worldwide Tanker Casualty Returns.*

WATER - POLLUTION - RIVERS AND STREAMS

U.S. Department of the Interior, Geological Survey, National Center, 12201 Sunrise Valley Drive, Reston, Virginia 22092 (703) 648-4000, www.usgs.gov; *Water-Data Report;* and unpublished data.

U.S. Department of Transportation, United States Coast Guard, 2100 Second Street, SW, Washington, D.C. 20593 (202) 267-2229; Internet site: http://www.uscg.mil/hq/g-m/nmc/response/stats/summary.htm.

WATER - POWER

U.S. Department of Energy, Energy Information Administration, 1000 Independence Avenue, SW, Washington, D.C. 20585 (202) 586-8800, www.eia.doe.gov; *Electric Power Annual; Annual Energy Review;* and unpublished data.

U.S. Department of Energy, Federal Energy Regulatory Commission, Washington, D.C. 20585 (202) 208-0055, www.ferc.fed.us; *Hydroelectric Power Resources of the United States, Developed and Undeveloped;* and unpublished data.

U.S. Department of the Interior, Geological Survey, National Center, 12201 Sunrise Valley Drive, Reston, Virginia 22092 (703) 648-4000, www.usgs.gov; *Estimated Use of Water in the United States.*

WATER - PUBLIC SUPPLY

U.S. Department of Commerce, Bureau of the Census, Washington, D.C. 20233 (301) 457-4100, www.census.gov; *Current Housing Reports;* and *American Housing Survey.*

U.S. Department of the Interior, Geological Survey, National Center, 12201 Sunrise Valley Drive, Reston, Virginia 22092 (703) 648-4000, www.usgs.gov; *Estimated Use of Water in the United States.*

WATER - TOXIC RELEASES

Environmental Protection Agency, 1200

Pennsylvania Avenue, NW, Washington, D.C. 20460 (888) 372-8255, www.epa.gov; *Toxics Release Inventory.*

U.S. Department of the Interior, Geological Survey, National Center, 12201 Sunrise Valley Drive, Reston, Virginia 22092 (703) 648-4000, www.usgs.gov; *Estimated Use of Water in the U.S.*

WATER - WASTEWATER TREATMENT

Environmental Protection Agency, 1200 Pennsylvania Avenue, NW, Washington, D.C. 20460 (888) 372-8255, www.epa.gov; *Clean Water Needs Survey Report to Congress.*

WATER TRANSPORTATION SERVICES - EARNINGS

U.S. Department of Commerce, Bureau of the Census, Washington, D.C. 20233 (301) 457-4100, www.census.gov; *1997 Economic Census, Core Business Statistics Series, Advance Report; Census of Transportation, Communications, and Utilities;* and *County Business Patterns.*

U.S. Department of Labor, Bureau of Labor Statistics, Two Massachusetts Avenue, NE, Washington, D.C. 20212 (202) 691-5200, www.stats.bls.gov; *Employment and Earnings;* Bulletins 2445 and 2481; and Internet site: http://stats.bls.gov/ceshome.htm.

WATER TRANSPORTATION SERVICES - EMPLOYEES

U.S. Department of Commerce, Bureau of the Census, Washington, D.C. 20233 (301) 457-4100, www.census.gov; *1997 Economic Census, Core Business Statistics Series, Advance Report; Census of Transportation, Communications, and Utilities;* and *County Business Patterns.*

U.S. Department of Labor, Bureau of Labor Statistics, Two Massachusetts Avenue, NE, Washington, D.C. 20212 (202) 691-5200, www.stats.bls.gov; *Employment and Earnings;* Bulletins 2445 and 2481; and Internet site: http://stats.bls.gov/ceshome.htm.

WATER TRANSPORTATION SERVICES - FOREIGN TRADE

U.S. Department of Army, Corps of Engineers, The Pentagon, Washington, D.C. 20310 (202) 545-6700; *Waterborne Commerce of the United States.*

WATER TRANSPORTATION SERVICES - FREIGHT

Eno Transportation Foundation, One Farragut Square, South, Suite 500, Washington, D.C. 20006 (202) 879-4700; *Transportation in America.*

U.S. Department of Army, Corps of Engineers, The Pentagon, Washington, D.C. 20310 (202) 545-6700; *Waterborne Commerce of the United States.*

WATER TRANSPORTATION SERVICES - OCCUPATIONAL SAFETY

U.S. Department of Labor, Bureau of Labor Statistics, Two Massachusetts Avenue, NE, Washington, D.C. 20212 (202) 691-5200, www.stats.bls.gov; *Occupational Injuries and Illnesses in the United States by Industry.*

U.S. Department of Transportation, Bureau of Transportation Statistics, 400 Seventh Street, SW, Washington, D.C. 20590 (800) 853-1351, www.bts.gov; *National Transportation Statistics.*

WATER TRANSPORTATION SERVICES - OUTLAYS

Executive Office of the President, Office of Management and Budget, Executive Office Building, Washington, D.C. 20503 (202) 395-3080, www.whitehouse.gov/omb; *Historical Tables.*

U.S. Department of Army, Corps of Engineers, The Pentagon, Washington, D.C. 20310 (202) 761-0660; *Report of Civil Works Expenditures by State and Fiscal Year.*

WATERMELONS

U.S. Department of Agriculture, National Agricultural Statistics Service, 14th Street and Independence Avenue, SW, Washington, D.C. 20250 (800) 727-9540, www.usda.gov/nass; *Vegetables,* and *Agricultural Statistics.*

WATERPOLO

National Collegiate Athletic Association, 700 West Washington Street, Indianapolis, Indiana 46206 (317) 917-6222; *1997-98 Participation Study.*

WATERSKIING

National Sporting Goods Association, 1601 Feehanville Drive, Suite 300, Mount Prospect, Illinois 60056 (847) 296-6742; *Sports Participation in 1998: Series I and Series II.*

WEALTH - BUSINESS

U.S. Department of Commerce, Bureau of Economic Analysis, Fourteenth Street between Constitution Avenue and E Street, NW, Washington, D.C. 20230 (202) 606-9900, www.bea.doc.gov; *Survey of Current Business.*

WEALTH - FAMILIES

Board of Governors of the Federal Reserve System, 20th Street and Constitution Avenue, NW, Washington, D.C. 20551 (202) 452-3000, www.bog.frb.fed.us; *Federal Reserve Bulletin;* and unpublished data.

WEALTH - GOVERNMENT

U.S. Department of Commerce, Bureau of Economic Analysis, Fourteenth Street between Constitution Avenue and E Street, NW, Washington, D.C. 20230 (202) 606-9900, www.bea.doc.gov; *Survey of Current Business.*

WEALTH - HOUSEHOLDS

U.S. Department of Commerce, Bureau of Economic Analysis, Fourteenth Street between Constitution Avenue and E Street, NW, Washington, D.C. 20230 (202) 606-9900, www.bea.doc.gov; *Survey of Current Business.*

WEATHER

U.S. Department of Commerce, National Oceanic and Atmospheric Administration, National Climatic Data Center, 151 Patton Avenue, Asheville, North Carolina 28801 (828) 271-4800, www.ncdc.noaa.gov; *Billion Dollar U.S. Weather Disaster, 1980-1999; Comparative Climatic Data; Climatogrpahy of the U.S. No.81;* and Internet site: http://www.ncdc.noaa.gov/ol/reports/billionz.html.

WEATHER - CONDITIONS AT SELECTED STATIONS

U.S. Department of Commerce, National Oceanic and Atmospheric Administration, National Climatic Data Center, 151 Patton Avenue, Asheville, North Carolina 28801 (828) 271-4800, www.ncdc.noaa.gov; *Climatography of the United States; Billion Dollar U.S. Weather Disaster;* and *Comparative Climatic Data.*

WEATHER - FOREIGN COUNTRIES

U.S. Department of Commerce, National Oceanic and Atmospheric Administration, National Climatic Data Center, 151 Patton Avenue, Asheville, North Carolina 28801 (828) 271-4800, www.ncdc.noaa.gov; *Climates of the World.*

WEIGHTS - AVERAGE

U.S. Department of Health and Human Services, National Center for Health Statistics, 3700 East-West Highway, Hyattsville, Maryland 20782 (301) 436-8500, www.cdc.gov/nchs; unpublished data.

WELFARE SERVICES - See SOCIAL WELFARE; PUBLIC AID ASSISTANCE; and

Individual Programs

WEST VIRGINIA - See also STATE DATA (FOR INDIVIDUAL STATES)

West Virginia - Primary Statistics Sources

West Virginia Research League, Incorporated, 405 Capitol Street, Suite 414, Charleston, West Virginia 25301 (304) 346-9451; *The Statistical Handbook;* and *Economic Indicators.*

West Virginia University, College of Business and Economics, Bureau of Business and Economic Research, Post Office Box 6025, Morgantown, West Virginia 26506 (304) 293-7835; *West Virginia Statistical Abstract; County Data Profiles; Census Data Profiles;* and *West Virginia Economic Outlook.*

West Virginia - State Data Centers

West Virginia Development Office, Research and Strategic Planning Division, Capitol Complex, Building 6, room 620, Charleston, West Virginia 25305-0311, Delphine Coffey (304) 558-4010.

Bureau of Business and Economic Research, West Virginia University, Post Office Box 6025, Morgantown, West Virginia 25305, Dr. Tom Witt, Director, and Brian Lego (304) 293-7836.

Office of Health Services Research, West Virginia University Health Science Center, Medical Center Drive, Post Office Box 9145, Morgantown, West Virginia 26506-9145, Mr. Alex Lubman (304) 293-1086.

Reference Library, West Virginia State Library Committee, Science and Cultural Center, Capitol Complex, Charleston, West Virginia 25305, Robin Chesney (304) 558-2045.

WESTERN SAHARA - AGRICULTURE

Food and Agricultural Organization of the United Nations (FAO) Via delle Terme di Caracalla, 00100 Rome, Italy (Telephone Number in U.S. (202) 653-2400); *The State of Food and Agriculture.*

Statistical Office of the United Nations, Publishing Service, New York, New York 10017 (800) 253-9646; *Statistical Yearbook.*

WESTERN SAHARA - AIRPORTS

Central Intelligence Agency, Washington, D.C. 20505 (703) 482-1100, www.cia.gov; *The World Factbook.*

WESTERN SAHARA - AREA AND DENSITY OF POPULATION

Central Intelligence Agency, Washington, D.C. 20505 (703) 482-1100, www.cia.gov; *The World Factbook.*

Food and Agricultural Organization of the United Nations (FAO) Via delle Terme di Caracalla, 00100 Rome, Italy (Telephone Number in U.S. (202) 653-2400); *The State of Food and Agriculture.*

Statistical Office of the United Nations, Publishing Service, New York, New York 10017 (800) 253-9646; *Statistical Yearbook.*

WESTERN SAHARA - BARLEY PRODUCTION - See WESTERN SAHARA - CROPS

WESTERN SAHARA - BIRTH RATES

Central Intelligence Agency, Washington, D.C. 20505 (703) 482-1100, www.cia.gov; *The World Factbook.*

Statistical Office of the United Nations, Publishing Service, New York, New York 10017 (800) 253-9646; *Demographic Yearbook;* and *Statistical Yearbook.*

WESTERN SAHARA - BROADCASTING

Central Intelligence Agency, Washington, D.C. 20505 (703) 482-1100, www.cia.gov; *The World Factbook.*

WESTERN SAHARA - BUDGET

Central Intelligence Agency, Washington, D.C. 20505 (703) 482-1100, www.cia.gov; *The World Factbook.*

WESTERN SAHARA - CALORIE SUPPLY

Food and Agricultural Organization of the United Nations (FAO) Via delle Terme di Caracalla, 00100 Rome, Italy (Telephone Number in U.S. (202) 653-2400); *The State of Food and Agriculture.*

WESTERN SAHARA - CHEMICAL (ORGANIC) PRODUCTION - See WESTERN SAHARA - MINING AND MINERAL PRODUCTS

WESTERN SAHARA - COAL PRODUCTION - See WESTERN SAHARA - MINING AND MINERAL PRODUCTS

WESTERN SAHARA - CORN PRODUCTION - See WESTERN SAHARA -CROPS

WESTERN SAHARA - CORPORATE TAXES - See WESTERN SAHARA - TAXATION

WESTERN SAHARA - CROPS

Food and Agricultural Organization of the United Nations (FAO) Via delle Terme

di Caracalla, 00100 Rome, Italy (Telephone Number in U.S. (202) 653-2400); *The State of Food and Agriculture.*

Statistical Office of the United Nations, Publishing Service, New York, New York 10017 (800) 253-9646; *Statistical Yearbook.*

WESTERN SAHARA - DAIRY PRODUCTS

Food and Agricultural Organization of the United Nations (FAO) Via delle Terme di Caracalla, 00100 Rome, Italy (Telephone Number in U.S. (202) 653-2400); *The State of Food and Agriculture.*

WESTERN SAHARA - DEATH RATES - See WESTERN SAHARA - MORTALITY

WESTERN SAHARA - DIVORCE RATES

Statistical Office of the United Nations, Publishing Service, New York, New York 10017 (800) 253-9646; *Demographic Yearbook,* and *Statistical Yearbook.*

WESTERN SAHARA - ECONOMY

Central Intelligence Agency, Washington, D.C. 20505 (703) 482-1100, www.cia.gov; *The World Factbook.*

Statistical Office of the United Nations, Publishing Service, New York, New York 10017 (800) 253-9646; *World Statistics Pocketbook.*

The World Bank, 1818 H Street, NW, Washington, D.C. 20433 (800) 645-7247; *The World Bank Atlas.*

WESTERN SAHARA - EGG PRODUCTION AND CONSUMPTION - See WESTERN SAHARA - DAIRY PRODUCTS

WESTERN SAHARA - ELECTRICITY

Central Intelligence Agency, Washington, D.C. 20505 (703) 482-1100, www.cia.gov; *The World Factbook.*

Statistical Office of the United Nations, Publishing Service, New York, New York 10017 (800) 253-9646; *Statistical Yearbook.*

WESTERN SAHARA - ENERGY

Food and Agricultural Organization of the United Nations (FAO) Via delle Terme di Caracalla, 00100 Rome, Italy (Telephone Number in U.S. (202) 653-2400); *The State of Food and Agriculture.*

Statistical Office of the United Nations, Publishing Service, New York, New York 10017 (800) 253-9646; *Statistical Yearbook;* and *World Statistics Pocketbook.*

The World Bank, 1818 H Street, NW, Washington, D.C. 20433 (202) 477-1234;

The World Bank Atlas.

WESTERN SAHARA - ENVIRONMENT

Statistical Office of the United Nations, Publishing Service, New York, New York 10017 (800) 253-9646; *World Statistics Pocketbook.*

WESTERN SAHARA - EXCHANGE RATES

Central Intelligence Agency, Washington, D.C. 20505 (703) 482-1100, www.cia.gov; *The World Factbook.*

Statistical Office of the United Nations, Publishing Service, New York, New York 10017 (800) 253-9646; *World Statistics Pocketbook.*

WESTERN SAHARA - EXPORTS

Central Intelligence Agency, Washington, D.C. 20505 (703) 482-1100, www.cia.gov; *The World Factbook.*

Food and Agricultural Organization of the United Nations (FAO) Via delle Terme di Caracalla, 00100 Rome, Italy (Telephone Number in U.S. (202) 653-2400); *The State of Food and Agriculture.*

WESTERN SAHARA - EXTERNAL TRADE

Food and Agricultural Organization of the United Nations (FAO) Via delle Terme di Caracalla, 00100 Rome, Italy (Telephone Number in U.S. (202) 653-2400); *The State of Food and Agriculture.*

WESTERN SAHARA - FARM CROPS - See WESTERN SAHARA - CROPS

WESTERN SAHARA - FERTILITY RATES

Central Intelligence Agency, Washington, D.C. 20505 (703) 482-1100, www.cia.gov; *The World Factbook.*

The World Bank, 1818 H Street, NW, Washington, D.C. 20433 (202) 477-1234; *The World Bank Atlas.*

WESTERN SAHARA - FERTILIZER

Food and Agricultural Organization of the United Nations (FAO) Via delle Terme di Caracalla, 00100 Rome, Italy (Telephone Number in U.S. (202) 653-2400); *The State of Food and Agriculture.*

WESTERN SAHARA - FETAL MORTALITY - See WESTERN SAHARA - MORTALITY

WESTERN SAHARA - FISHERIES

Food and Agricultural Organization of the United Nations (FAO) Via delle Terme di Caracalla, 00100 Rome, Italy (Telephone Number in U.S. (202) 653-2400); *The State*

of Food and Agriculture.

Statistical Office of the United Nations, Publishing Service, New York, New York 10017 (800) 253-9646; *Statistical Yearbook.*

WESTERN SAHARA - FOOD

Food and Agricultural Organization of the United Nations (FAO) Via delle Terme di Caracalla, 00100 Rome, Italy (Telephone Number in U.S. (202) 653-2400); *The State of Food and Agriculture.*

WESTERN SAHARA - FOREIGN TRADE

Food and Agricultural Organization of the United Nations (FAO) Via delle Terme di Caracalla, 00100 Rome, Italy (Telephone Number in U.S. (202) 653-2400); *The State of Food and Agriculture.*

WESTERN SAHARA - FORESTRY AND FOREST PRODUCTS

Food and Agricultural Organization of the United Nations (FAO) Via delle Terme di Caracalla, 00100 Rome, Italy (Telephone Number in U.S. (202) 653-2400); *The State of Food and Agriculture.*

WESTERN SAHARA - GENERAL MORTALITY - See WESTERN SAHARA - MORTALITY

WESTERN SAHARA - GOVERNMENT

Central Intelligence Agency, Washington, D.C. 20505 (703) 482-1100, www.cia.gov; *The World Factbook.*

WESTERN SAHARA - GRAIN PRODUCTION - See WESTERN SAHARA - CROPS

WESTERN SAHARA - HEALTH

Statistical Office of the United Nations, Publishing Service, New York, New York 10017 (800) 253-9646; *Statistical Yearbook.*

WESTERN SAHARA - ILLITERATE POPULATION

Central Intelligence Agency, Washington, D.C. 20505 (703) 482-1100, www.cia.gov; *The World Factbook.*

WESTERN SAHARA - IMPORTS

Central Intelligence Agency, Washington, D.C. 20505 (703) 482-1100, www.cia.gov; *The World Factbook.*

Food and Agricultural Organization of the United Nations (FAO) Via delle Terme di Caracalla, 00100 Rome, Italy (Telephone Number in U.S. (202) 653-2400); *The State of Food and Agriculture.*

WESTERN SAHARA - INDUSTRY

Central Intelligence Agency, Washington, D.C. 20505 (703) 482-1100, www.cia.gov; *The World Factbook.*

WESTERN SAHARA - INFANT AND MATERNAL MORTALITY - See WESTERN SAHARA - MORTALITY

WESTERN SAHARA - LABOR

Central Intelligence Agency, Washington, D.C. 20505 (703) 482-1100, www.cia.gov; *The World Factbook.*

Food and Agricultural Organization of the United Nations (FAO) Via delle Terme di Caracalla, 00100 Rome, Italy (Telephone Number in U.S. (202) 653-2400); *The State of Food and Agriculture.*

WESTERN SAHARA - LAND USE

Central Intelligence Agency, Washington, D.C. 20505 (703) 482-1100, www.cia.gov; *The World Factbook.*

WESTERN SAHARA - LIFE EXPECTANCY

Central Intelligence Agency, Washington, D.C. 20505 (703) 482-1100, www.cia.gov; *The World Factbook.*

Statistical Office of the United Nations, Publishing Service, New York, New York 10017 (800) 253-9646; *World Statistics Pocketbook.*

WESTERN SAHARA - LIVESTOCK AND POULTRY

Food and Agricultural Organization of the United Nations (FAO) Via delle Terme di Caracalla, 00100 Rome, Italy (Telephone Number in U.S. (202) 653-2400); *The State of Food and Agriculture.*

Statistical Office of the United Nations, Publishing Service, New York, New York 10017 (800) 253-9646; *Statistical Yearbook.*

WESTERN SAHARA - MARRIAGE RATES

Statistical Office of the United Nations, Publishing Service, New York, New York 10017 (800) 253-9646; *Demographic Yearbook;* and *Statistical Yearbook.*

WESTERN SAHARA - MEAT PRODUCTION - See WESTERN SAHARA - LIVESTOCK AND POULTRY

WESTERN SAHARA - MERCHANT SHIPPING

Statistical Office of the United Nations, Publishing Service, New York, New York 10017 (800) 253-9646; *Statistical Yearbook.*

WESTERN SAHARA - MILITARY

Central Intelligence Agency, Washington, D.C. 20505 (703) 482-1100,

www.cia.gov; *The World Factbook.*

WESTERN SAHARA - MINING AND MINERAL PRODUCTS

Statistical Office of the United Nations, Publishing Service, New York, New York 10017 (800) 253-9646; *Statistical Yearbook.*

WESTERN SAHARA - MORTALITY

Central Intelligence Agency, Washington, D.C. 20505 (703) 482-1100, www.cia.gov; *The World Factbook.*

Statistical Office of the United Nations, Publishing Service, New York, New York 10017 (800) 253-9646; *Demographic Yearbook; Statistical Yearbook;* and *World Statistics Pocketbook.*

WESTERN SAHARA - MOTION PICTURES

Statistical Office of the United Nations, Publishing Service, New York, New York 10017 (800) 253-9646; *Statistical Yearbook.*

WESTERN SAHARA - MOTOR VEHICLES IN USE

Statistical Office of the United Nations, Publishing Service, New York, New York 10017 (800) 253-9646; *Statistical Yearbook.*

WESTERN SAHARA - NATALITY - See WESTERN SAHARA - BIRTH RATE

WESTERN SAHARA - NEWSPAPER PRODUCTION - See WESTERN SAHARA - FORESTRY AND FOREST PRODUCTS

WESTERN SAHARA - OCCUPATIONS - See WESTERN SAHARA - LABOR

WESTERN SAHARA - PESTICIDE USE

Food and Agricultural Organization of the United Nations (FAO) Via delle Terme di Caracalla, 00100 Rome, Italy (Telephone Number in U.S. (202) 653-2400); *The State of Food and Agriculture.*

WESTERN SAHARA - PETROLEUM INDUSTRY

Food and Agricultural Organization of the United Nations (FAO) Via delle Terme di Caracalla, 00100 Rome, Italy (Telephone Number in U.S. (202) 653-2400); *The State of Food and Agriculture.*

WESTERN SAHARA - PHOSPHATE ROCK PRODUCTION - See WESTERN SAHARA - MINING AND MINERAL PRODUCTS

WESTERN SAHARA - POPULATION

Central Intelligence Agency, Washington, D.C. 20505 (703) 482-1100, www.cia.gov; *The World Factbook.*

Statistical Office of the United Nations, Publishing Service, New York, New York 10017 (800) 253-9646; *Demographic Yearbook; Statistical Yearbook;* and *World Statistics Pocketbook.*

World Health Organization, Office of Publications, 20 Avenue Appia, CH-1211 Geneva 27, Switzerland (Telephone Number in U.S. (518) 436-9686); *World Health Statistics Annual.*

WESTERN SAHARA - PRICES

Food and Agricultural Organization of the United Nations (FAO) Via delle Terme di Caracalla, 00100 Rome, Italy (Telephone Number in U.S. (202) 653-2400); *The State of Food and Agriculture.*

WESTERN SAHARA - RELIGION

Central Intelligence Agency, Washington, D.C. 20505 (703) 482-1100, www.cia.gov; *The World Factbook.*

WESTERN SAHARA - SHEEP - See WESTERN SAHARA - LIVESTOCK AND POULTRY

WESTERN SAHARA - SOCIAL DATA

Statistical Office of the United Nations, Publishing Service, New York, New York 10017 (800) 253-9646; *World Statistics Pocketbook.*

WESTERN SAHARA - STOCKS - COMMODITY - MARKET PRICE - INDEX

Food and Agricultural Organization of the United Nations (FAO) Via delle Terme di Caracalla, 00100 Rome, Italy (Telephone Number in U.S. (202) 653-2400); *The State of Food and Agriculture.*

WESTERN SAHARA - TELEPHONES IN USE

Central Intelligence Agency, Washington, D.C. 20505 (703) 482-1100, www.cia.gov; *The World Factbook.*

Statistical Office of the United Nations, Publishing Service, New York, New York 10017 (800) 253-9646; *World Statistics Pocketbook.*

WESTERN SAHARA - TRACTORS IN USE

Statistical Office of the United Nations, Publishing Service, New York, New York 10017 (800) 253-9646; *Statistical Yearbook.*

WESTERN SAHARA - TRADE - See WESTERN SAHARA - FOREIGN TRADE

WESTERN SAHARA - TRANSPORTATION AND COMMUNICATIONS

Central Intelligence Agency, Washington, D.C. 20505 (703) 482-1100,

www.cia.gov; *The World Factbook.*

WESTERN SAHARA - UNEMPLOYMENT RATE

Central Intelligence Agency, Washington, D.C. 20505 (703) 482-1100, www.cia.gov; *The World Factbook.*

WESTERN SAHARA - VITAL STATISTICS

Statistical Office of the United Nations, Publishing Service, New York, New York 10017 (800) 253-9646; *Statistical Yearbook.*

World Health Organization, Office of Publications, 20 Avenue Appia, CH-1211 Geneva 27, Switzerland (Telephone Number in U.S. (518) 436-9686); *World Health Statistics Annual.*

Western Samoa - National Statistical Offices

Government Statistician, Department of Statistics, Post Office Box 1151, Apia, Western Samoa; for national statistics.

Prime Minister's Department, Post Office Box 193, Apia, Western Samoa; for foreign trade statistics.

Western Samoa - Primary Statistics Sources

Department of Statistics, Apia, Western Samoa; *Annual Statistical Abstract;* and *Statistical Bulletin.*

WESTERN SAMOA - AGRICULTURE

Asian Development Bank, P.O. Box 789, 1099 Manila, Philippines; *Key Indicators of Developing Asian and Pacific Countries.*

Economist Intelligence Unit, 111 West 57th Street, New York, New York 10019 (800) 938-4685; *Samoa Country Report.*

Euromonitor International, Inc., 122 South Michigan Avenue, Suite 1200, Chicago, Illinois 60603 (800) 577-EURO; *World Marketing Data and Statistics.*

Europa Publications Limited, 18 Bedford Square, London, WC1B 3JN, England; *The Europa World Year Book.*

St. Martin's Press, Inc., 175 Fifth Avenue, New York, New York 10010 (800) 221-7945; *The Statesman's Year-Book.*

Statistical Office of the United Nations, Publishing Service, New York, New York 10017 (800) 253-9646; *Asia-Pacific in Figures.*

The World Bank, 1818 H Street, NW, Washington, D.C. 20433 (202) 477-1234;

World Development Indicators.

WESTERN SAMOA - AIRLINE SERVICE

St. Martin's Press, Inc., 175 Fifth Avenue, New York, New York 10010 (800) 221-7945; *The Statesman's Year-Book.*

WESTERN SAMOA - AIRPORTS

Central Intelligence Agency, Washington, D.C. 20505 (703) 482-1100, www.cia.gov; *The World Factbook.*

WESTERN SAMOA - AREA AND DENSITY OF POPULATION

Central Intelligence Agency, Washington, D.C. 20505 (703) 482-1100, www.cia.gov; *The World Factbook.*

Euromonitor International, Inc., 122 South Michigan Avenue, Suite 1200, Chicago, Illinois 60603 (800) 577-EURO; *The World Economic Factbook.*

Europa Publications Limited, 18 Bedford Square, London, WC1B 3JN, England; *The Europa World Year Book.*

St. Martin's Press, Inc., 175 Fifth Avenue, New York, New York 10010 (800) 221-7945; *The Statesman's Year-Book.*

United Nations Educational, Scientific and Cultural Organization (UNESCO), 7 Place de Fontenoy, F-75700 Paris, France (Telephone Number in U.S. (212) 963-5981); *Statistical Yearbook.*

WESTERN SAMOA - BALANCE OF PAYMENTS

Europa Publications Limited, 18 Bedford Square, London, WC1B 3JN, England; *The Europa World Year Book.*

International Monetary Fund, 700 Nineteenth Street, NW, Washington, D.C. 20431 (202) 623-7000; *Balance of Payments Yearbook.*

United Nations Conference on Trade and Development (UNCTAD), New York, New York 10017 (800) 253-9646; *Handbook of International Trade and Development Statistics.*

The World Bank, 1818 H Street, NW, Washington, D.C. 20433 (202) 477-1234; *World Development Indicators.*

WESTERN SAMOA - BANKING

Asian Development Bank, P.O. Box 789, 1099 Manila, Philippines; *Key Indicators of Developing Asian and Pacific Countries.*

Euromonitor International, Inc., 122 South Michigan Avenue, Suite 1200, Chicago, Illinois 60603 (800) 577-EURO;

World Marketing Data and Statistics.

Europa Publications Limited, 18 Bedford Square, London, WC1B 3JN, England; *The Europa World Year Book.*

St. Martin's Press, Inc., 175 Fifth Avenue, New York, New York 10010 (800) 221-7945; *The Statesman's Year-Book.*

WESTERN SAMOA - BIRTH RATES

Central Intelligence Agency, Washington, D.C. 20505 (703) 482-1100, www.cia.gov; *The World Factbook.*

Euromonitor International, Inc., 122 South Michigan Avenue, Suite 1200, Chicago, Illinois 60603 (800) 577-EURO; *International Marketing Data and Statistics;* and *The World Economic Factbook.*

Europa Publications Limited, 18 Bedford Square, London, WC1B 3JN, England; *The Europa World Year Book.*

Statistical Office of the United Nations, Publishing Service, New York, New York 10017 (800) 253-9646; *Asia-Pacific in Figures.*

The World Bank, 1818 H Street, NW, Washington, D.C. 20433 (202) 477-1234; *World Development Indicators.*

WESTERN SAMOA - BONDS

Asian Development Bank, P.O. Box 789, 1099 Manila, Philippines; *Key Indicators of Developing Asian and Pacific Countries.*

WESTERN SAMOA - BROADCASTING

Billboard Limited, P.O. Box 9027, 1006 AA Amsterdam, The Netherlands (Telephone Number in U.S. (212) 764-7300); *World Radio TV Handbook.*

Central Intelligence Agency, Washington, D.C. 20505 (703) 482-1100, www.cia.gov; *The World Factbook.*

Euromonitor International, Inc., 122 South Michigan Avenue, Suite 1200, Chicago, Illinois 60603 (800) 577-EURO; *World Marketing Data and Statistics.*

St. Martin's Press, Inc., 175 Fifth Avenue, New York, New York 10010 (800) 221-7945; *The Statesman's Year-Book.*

WESTERN SAMOA - BUDGET

Central Intelligence Agency, Washington, D.C. 20505 (703) 482-1100, www.cia.gov; *The World Factbook.*

WESTERN SAMOA - CACAO EXPORTS - See WESTERN SAMOA - CROPS

WESTERN SAMOA - CALORIE SUPPLY

Asian Development Bank, P.O. Box 789, 1099 Manila, Philippines; *Key Indicators of Developing Asian and Pacific Countries.*

WESTERN SAMOA - CAPITAL INVESTMENT

Asian Development Bank, P.O. Box 789, 1099 Manila, Philippines; *Key Indicators of Developing Asian and Pacific Countries.*

WESTERN SAMOA - CAPITAL REVENUE

Asian Development Bank, P.O. Box 789, 1099 Manila, Philippines; *Key Indicators of Developing Asian and Pacific Countries.*

WESTERN SAMOA - CLIMATE

St. Martin's Press, Inc., 175 Fifth Avenue, New York, New York 10010 (800) 221-7945; *The Statesman's Year-Book.*

WESTERN SAMOA - CLOTHING EXPORTS AND IMPORTS - See WESTERN SAMOA - TEXTILE INDUSTRY

WESTERN SAMOA - COMMERCE

St. Martin's Press, Inc., 175 Fifth Avenue, New York, New York 10010 (800) 221-7945; *The Statesman's Year-Book.*

WESTERN SAMOA - CONSUMER PRICE INDEX

Asian Development Bank, P.O. Box 789, 1099 Manila, Philippines; *Key Indicators of Developing Asian and Pacific Countries.*

Europa Publications Limited, 18 Bedford Square, London, WC1B 3JN, England; *The Europa World Year Book.*

WESTERN SAMOA - CONSUMER PRICES

Euromonitor International, Inc., 122 South Michigan Avenue, Suite 1200, Chicago, Illinois 60603 (800) 577-EURO; *World Marketing Data and Statistics.*

International Monetary Fund, 700 Nineteenth Street, NW, Washington, D.C. 20431 (202) 623-7000; *International Financial Statistics.*

WESTERN SAMOA - CONSUMPTION

South Pacific Commission, Post Box D5, Noumea Cedex, New Caledonia; *Statistical Bulletin of the South Pacific: Retail Price Indexes.*

WESTERN SAMOA - COPRA EXPORTS

International Monetary Fund, 700 Nineteenth Street, NW, Washington, D.C. 20431 (202) 623-7000; *International Financial Statistics.*

WESTERN SAMOA - CORN
PRODUCTION - See WESTERN SAMOA -
CROPS

WESTERN SAMOA - CROPS

Asian Development Bank, P.O. Box 789,
1099 Manila, Philippines; *Key Indicators of
Developing Asian and Pacific Countries.*

Europa Publications Limited, 18
Bedford Square, London, WC1B 3JN,
England; *The Europa World Year Book.*

International Monetary Fund, 700
Nineteenth Street, NW, Washington, D.C.
20431 (202) 623-7000; *International
Financial Statistics.*

St. Martin's Press, Inc., 175 Fifth
Avenue, New York, New York 10010 (800)
221-7945; *The Statesman's Year-Book.*

WESTERN SAMOA - DAIRY PRODUCTS

St. Martin's Press, Inc., 175 Fifth
Avenue, New York, New York 10010 (800)
221-7945; *The Statesman's Year-Book.*

WESTERN SAMOA - DEMOGRAPHY

Euromonitor International, Inc., 122
South Michigan Avenue, Suite 1200,
Chicago, Illinois 60603 (800) 577-EURO;
*International Marketing Data and Statistics;
World Marketing Data and Statistics;* and
The World Economic Factbook.

Statistical Office of the United Nations,
Publishing Service, New York, New York
10017 (800) 253-9646; *Asia-Pacific in
Figures;* and *Human Development Report.*

WESTERN SAMOA - DEVELOPMENT
ASSISTANCE

Asian Development Bank, P.O. Box 789,
1099 Manila, Philippines; *Key Indicators of
Developing Asian and Pacific Countries.*

WESTERN SAMOA - ECONOMY

Asian Development Bank, P.O. Box 789,
1099 Manila, Philippines; *Key Indicators of
Developing Asian and Pacific Countries.*

Central Intelligence Agency,
Washington, D.C. 20505 (703) 482-1100,
www.cia.gov; *The World Factbook.*

Economist Intelligence Unit, 111 West
57th Street, New York, New York 10019
(800) 938-4685; *Samoa Country Report.*

Euromonitor International, Inc., 122
South Michigan Avenue, Suite 1200,
Chicago, Illinois 60603 (800) 577-EURO;
The World Economic Factbook; and *World
Marketing Data and Statistics.*

Europa Publications Limited, 18

Bedford Square, London, WC1B 3JN,
England; *The Europa World Year Book.*

St. Martin's Press, Inc., 175 Fifth
Avenue, New York, New York 10010 (800)
221-7945; *The Statesman's Year-Book.*

WESTERN SAMOA - EDUCATION

Euromonitor International, Inc., 122
South Michigan Avenue, Suite 1200,
Chicago, Illinois 60603 (800) 577-EURO;
International Marketing Data and Statistics;
and *World Marketing Data and Statistics.*

Europa Publications Limited, 18
Bedford Square, London, WC1B 3JN,
England; *The Europa World Year Book.*

St. Martin's Press, Inc., 175 Fifth
Avenue, New York, New York 10010 (800)
221-7945; *The Statesman's Year-Book.*

Statistical Office of the United Nations,
Publishing Service, New York, New York
10017 (800) 253-9646; *Human
Development Report.*

The World Bank, 1818 H Street, NW,
Washington, D.C. 20433 (202) 477-1234;
World Development Indicators.

WESTERN SAMOA - ELECTRICITY

Asian Development Bank, P.O. Box 789,
1099 Manila, Philippines; *Key Indicators of
Developing Asian and Pacific Countries.*

Central Intelligence Agency,
Washington, D.C. 20505 (703) 482-1100,
www.cia.gov; *The World Factbook.*

St. Martin's Press, Inc., 175 Fifth
Avenue, New York, New York 10010 (800)
221-7945; *The Statesman's Year-Book.*

Statistical Office of the United Nations,
Publishing Service, New York, New York
10017 (800) 253-9646; *Human
Development Report.*

WESTERN SAMOA - EMPLOYMENT

Euromonitor International, Inc., 122
South Michigan Avenue, Suite 1200,
Chicago, Illinois 60603 (800) 577-EURO;
International Marketing Data and Statistics.

Statistical Office of the United Nations,
Publishing Service, New York, New York
10017 (800) 253-9646; *Asia-Pacific in
Figures.*

WESTERN SAMOA - ENERGY

Euromonitor International, Inc., 122
South Michigan Avenue, Suite 1200,
Chicago, Illinois 60603 (800) 577-EURO;
*International Marketing Data and Statistics;
World Marketing Data and Statistics;* and

The World Economic Factbook.

St. Martin's Press, Inc., 175 Fifth
Avenue, New York, New York 10010 (800)
221-7945; *The Statesman's Year-Book.*

Statistical Office of the United Nations,
Publishing Service, New York, New York
10017 (800) 253-9646; *Asia-Pacific in
Figures;* and *Human Development Report.*

WESTERN SAMOA - ENVIRONMENT

Economist Intelligence Unit, 111 West
57th Street, New York, New York 10019
(800) 938-4685; *Samoa Country Report.*

WESTERN SAMOA - EXCHANGE RATES

Asian Development Bank, P.O. Box 789,
1099 Manila, Philippines; *Key Indicators of
Developing Asian and Pacific Countries.*

Central Intelligence Agency,
Washington, D.C. 20505 (703) 482-1100,
www.cia.gov; *The World Factbook.*

Euromonitor International, Inc., 122
South Michigan Avenue, Suite 1200,
Chicago, Illinois 60603 (800) 577-EURO;
International Marketing Data and Statistics;
and *The World Economic Factbook*

Europa Publications Limited, 18
Bedford Square, London, WC1B 3JN,
England; *The Europa World Year Book.*

International Monetary Fund, 700
Nineteenth Street, NW, Washington, D.C.
20431 (202) 623-7000; *International
Financial Statistics.*

WESTERN SAMOA - EXPORTS

Asian Development Bank, P.O. Box 789,
1099 Manila, Philippines; *Key Indicators of
Developing Asian and Pacific Countries.*

Central Intelligence Agency,
Washington, D.C. 20505 (703) 482-1100,
www.cia.gov; *The World Factbook.*

Economist Intelligence Unit, 111 West
57th Street, New York, New York 10019
(800) 938-4685; *Samoa Country Report.*

Euromonitor International, Inc., 122
South Michigan Avenue, Suite 1200,
Chicago, Illinois 60603 (800) 577-EURO;
International Marketing Data and Statistics;
and *The World Economic Factbook.*

Europa Publications Limited, 18
Bedford Square, London, WC1B 3JN,
England; *The Europa World Year Book.*

International Monetary Fund, 700
Nineteenth Street, NW, Washington, D.C.
20431 (202) 623-7000; *International
Financial Statistics.*

South Pacific Commission, Post Box D5, Noumea Cedex, New Caledonia; *Statistical Bulletin of the South Pacific: Overseas Trade.*

St. Martin's Press, Inc., 175 Fifth Avenue, New York, New York 10010 (800) 221-7945; *The Statesman's Year-Book.*

United Nations Conference on Trade and Development (UNCTAD), New York, New York 10017 (800) 253-9646; *Handbook of International Trade and Development Statistics.*

The World Bank, 1818 H Street, NW, Washington, D.C. 20433 (202) 477-1234; *World Development Indicators.*

WESTERN SAMOA - EXTERNAL FINANCING

Asian Development Bank, P.O. Box 789, 1099 Manila, Philippines; *Key Indicators of Developing Asian and Pacific Countries.*

WESTERN SAMOA - EXTERNAL INDEBTEDNESS

Asian Development Bank, P.O. Box 789, 1099 Manila, Philippines; *Key Indicators of Developing Asian and Pacific Countries.*

The World Bank, 1818 H Street, NW, Washington, D.C. 20433 (202) 477-1234; *World Development Indicators.*

WESTERN SAMOA - EXTERNAL TRADE

Asian Development Bank, P.O. Box 789, 1099 Manila, Philippines; *Key Indicators of Developing Asian and Pacific Countries.*

Euromonitor International, Inc., 122 South Michigan Avenue, Suite 1200, Chicago, Illinois 60603 (800) 577-EURO; *World Marketing Data and Statistics.*

Statistical Office of the United Nations, Publishing Service, New York, New York 10017 (800) 253-9646; *Asia-Pacific in Figures.*

WESTERN SAMOA - FERTILITY RATES

Central Intelligence Agency, Washington, D.C. 20505 (703) 482-1100, www.cia.gov; *The World Factbook.*

Statistical Office of the United Nations, Publishing Service, New York, New York 10017 (800) 253-9646; *Human Development Report.*

The World Bank, 1818 H Street, NW, Washington, D.C. 20433 (202) 477-1234; *World Development Indicators.*

WESTERN SAMOA - FINANCE

Asian Development Bank, P.O. Box 789, 1099 Manila, Philippines; *Key Indicators of*

Developing Asian and Pacific Countries.

Economist Intelligence Unit, 111 West 57th Street, New York, New York 10019 (800) 938-4685; *Samoa Country Report.*

Europa Publications Limited, 18 Bedford Square, London, WC1B 3JN, England; *The Europa World Year Book.*

International Monetary Fund, 700 Nineteenth Street, NW, Washington, D.C. 20431 (202) 623-7000; *International Financial Statistics.*

St. Martin's Press, Inc., 175 Fifth Avenue, New York, New York 10010 (800) 221-7945; *The Statesman's Year-Book.*

WESTERN SAMOA - FISHERIES

Europa Publications Limited, 18 Bedford Square, London, WC1B 3JN, England; *The Europa World Year Book.*

St. Martin's Press, Inc., 175 Fifth Avenue, New York, New York 10010 (800) 221-7945; *The Statesman's Year-Book.*

WESTERN SAMOA - FOOD

South Pacific Commission, Post Box D5, Noumea Cedex, New Caledonia; *Statistical Bulletin of the South Pacific: Retail Price Indexes.*

Statistical Office of the United Nations, Publishing Service, New York, New York 10017 (800) 253-9646; *Human Development Report.*

WESTERN SAMOA - FOREIGN TRADE

Asian Development Bank, P.O. Box 789, 1099 Manila, Philippines; *Key Indicators of Developing Asian and Pacific Countries.*

Economist Intelligence Unit, 111 West 57th Street, New York, New York 10019 (800) 938-4685; *Samoa Country Report.*

Euromonitor International, Inc., 122 South Michigan Avenue, Suite 1200, Chicago, Illinois 60603 (800) 577-EURO; *The World Economic Factbook.*

Europa Publications Limited, 18 Bedford Square, London, WC1B 3JN, England; *The Europa World Year Book.*

South Pacific Commission, Post Box D5, Noumea Cedex, New Caledonia; *Statistical Bulletin of the South Pacific: Overseas Trade.*

St. Martin's Press, Inc., 175 Fifth Avenue, New York, New York 10010 (800) 221-7945; *The Statesman's Year-Book.*

The World Bank, 1818 H Street, NW, Washington, D.C. 20433 (202) 477-1234;

World Development Indicators.

WESTERN SAMOA - FORESTRY AND FOREST PRODUCTS

Europa Publications Limited, 18 Bedford Square, London, WC1B 3JN, England; *The Europa World Year Book.*

St. Martin's Press, Inc., 175 Fifth Avenue, New York, New York 10010 (800) 221-7945; *The Statesman's Year-Book.*

WESTERN SAMOA - GOLD HOLDINGS

The World Bank, 1818 H Street, NW, Washington, D.C. 20433 (202) 477-1234; *World Development Indicators.*

WESTERN SAMOA - GOVERNMENT

Asian Development Bank, P.O. Box 789, 1099 Manila, Philippines; *Key Indicators of Developing Asian and Pacific Countries.*

Central Intelligence Agency, Washington, D.C. 20505 (703) 482-1100, www.cia.gov; *The World Factbook.*

Europa Publications Limited, 18 Bedford Square, London, WC1B 3JN, England; *The Europa World Year Book.*

St. Martin's Press, Inc., 175 Fifth Avenue, New York, New York 10010 (800) 221-7945; *The Statesman's Year-Book.*

Statistical Office of the United Nations, Publishing Service, New York, New York 10017 (800) 253-9646; *Asia-Pacific in Figures.*

The World Bank, 1818 H Street, NW, Washington, D.C. 20433 (202) 477-1234; *World Development Indicators.*

WESTERN SAMOA - GROSS DOMESTIC PRODUCT

Asian Development Bank, P.O. Box 789, 1099 Manila, Philippines; *Key Indicators of Developing Asian and Pacific Countries.*

Economist Intelligence Unit, 111 West 57th Street, New York, New York 10019 (800) 938-4685; *Samoa Country Report.*

Euromonitor International, Inc., 122 South Michigan Avenue, Suite 1200, Chicago, Illinois 60603 (800) 577-EURO; *International Marketing Data and Statistics;* and *The World Economic Factbook.*

Statistical Office of the United Nations, Publishing Service, New York, New York 10017 (800) 253-9646; *Human Development Report.*

The World Bank, 1818 H Street, NW,

Washington, D.C. 20433 (202) 477-1234; *World Development Indicators.*

WESTERN SAMOA - GROSS NATIONAL PRODUCT

Asian Development Bank, P.O. Box 789, 1099 Manila, Philippines; *Key Indicators of Developing Asian and Pacific Countries.*

St. Martin's Press, Inc., 175 Fifth Avenue, New York, New York 10010 (800) 221-7945; *The Statesman's Year-Book.*

The World Bank, 1818 H Street, NW, Washington, D.C. 20433 (202) 477-1234; *World Development Report;* and *World Development Indicators.*

WESTERN SAMOA - HEALTH

Euromonitor International, Inc., 122 South Michigan Avenue, Suite 1200, Chicago, Illinois 60603 (800) 577-EURO; *World Marketing Data and Statistics.*

South Pacific Commission, Post Box D5, Noumea Cedex, New Caledonia; *Statistical Bulletin of the South Pacific: Retail Price Indexes.*

St. Martin's Press, Inc., 175 Fifth Avenue, New York, New York 10010 (800) 221-7945; *The Statesman's Year-Book.*

Statistical Office of the United Nations, Publishing Service, New York, New York 10017 (800) 253-9646; *Asia-Pacific in Figures;* and *Human Development Report.*

WESTERN SAMOA - HIGHWAYS

Central Intelligence Agency, Washington, D.C. 20505 (703) 482-1100, www.cia.gov; *The World Factbook.*

St. Martin's Press, Inc., 175 Fifth Avenue, New York, New York 10010 (800) 221-7945; *The Statesman's Year-Book.*

WESTERN SAMOA - HOUSING AND HOUSING UNITS

Euromonitor International, Inc., 122 South Michigan Avenue, Suite 1200, Chicago, Illinois 60603 (800) 577-EURO; *World Marketing Data and Statistics.*

South Pacific Commission, Post Box D5, Noumea Cedex, New Caledonia; *Statistical Bulletin of the South Pacific: Retail Price Indexes.*

WESTERN SAMOA - HOUSING EXPENDITURES

South Pacific Commission, Post Box D5, Noumea Cedex, New Caledonia; *Statistical Bulletin of the South Pacific: Retail Price Indexes.*

WESTERN SAMOA - ILLITERATE POPULATION

Central Intelligence Agency, Washington, D.C. 20505 (703) 482-1100, www.cia.gov; *The World Factbook.*

Euromonitor International, Inc., 122 South Michigan Avenue, Suite 1200, Chicago, Illinois 60603 (800) 577-EURO; *The World Economic Factbook.*

Statistical Office of the United Nations, Publishing Service, New York, New York 10017 (800) 253-9646; *Asia-Pacific in Figures;* and *Human Development Report.*

WESTERN SAMOA - IMPORTS

Asian Development Bank, P.O. Box 789, 1099 Manila, Philippines; *Key Indicators of Developing Asian and Pacific Countries.*

Central Intelligence Agency, Washington, D.C. 20505 (703) 482-1100, www.cia.gov; *The World Factbook.*

Economist Intelligence Unit, 111 West 57th Street, New York, New York 10019 (800) 938-4685; *Samoa Country Report.*

Euromonitor International, Inc., 122 South Michigan Avenue, Suite 1200, Chicago, Illinois 60603 (800) 577-EURO; *International Marketing Data and Statistics;* and *The World Economic Factbook.*

Europa Publications Limited, 18 Bedford Square, London, WC1B 3JN, England; *The Europa World Year Book.*

International Monetary Fund, 700 Nineteenth Street, NW, Washington, D.C. 20431 (202) 623-7000; *International Financial Statistics.*

South Pacific Commission, Post Box D5, Noumea Cedex, New Caledonia; *Statistical Bulletin of the South Pacific: Overseas Trade.*

St. Martin's Press, Inc., 175 Fifth Avenue, New York, New York 10010 (800) 221-7945; *The Statesman's Year-Book.*

United Nations Conference on Trade and Development (UNCTAD), New York, New York 10017 (800) 253-9646; *Handbook of International Trade and Development Statistics.*

The World Bank, 1818 H Street, NW, Washington, D.C. 20433 (202) 477-1234; *World Development Indicators.*

WESTERN SAMOA - INDUSTRY

Central Intelligence Agency, Washington, D.C. 20505 (703) 482-1100, www.cia.gov; *The World Factbook.*

Economist Intelligence Unit, 111 West 57th Street, New York, New York 10019 (800) 938-4685; *Samoa Country Report.*

Euromonitor International, Inc., 122 South Michigan Avenue, Suite 1200, Chicago, Illinois 60603 (800) 577-EURO; *World Marketing Data and Statistics.*

St. Martin's Press, Inc., 175 Fifth Avenue, New York, New York 10010 (800) 221-7945; *The Statesman's Year-Book.*

Statistical Office of the United Nations, Publishing Service, New York, New York 10017 (800) 253-9646; *Asia-Pacific in Figures.*

The World Bank, 1818 H Street, NW, Washington, D.C. 20433 (202) 477-1234; *World Development Indicators.*

World Intellectual Property Organization, 34 Chemin des Colombettes, CH-1211 Geneva 20. Switzerland; *Industrial Property Statistics.*

WESTERN SAMOA - INFANT AND MATERNAL MORTALITY - See WESTERN SAMOA - MORTALITY

WESTERN SAMOA - INTERNATIONAL LIQUIDITY

International Monetary Fund, 700 Nineteenth Street, NW, Washington, D.C. 20431 (202) 623-7000; *International Financial Statistics.*

WESTERN SAMOA - INTERNATIONAL RESERVES EXCLUDING GOLD

Asian Development Bank, P.O. Box 789, 1099 Manila, Philippines; *Key Indicators of Developing Asian and Pacific Countries.*

The World Bank, 1818 H Street, NW, Washington, D.C. 20433 (202) 477-1234; *World Development Indicators.*

WESTERN SAMOA - INTERNATIONAL STATISTICS

Asian Development Bank, P.O. Box 789, 1099 Manila, Philippines; *Key Indicators of Developing Asian and Pacific Countries.*

WESTERN SAMOA - LABOR

Central Intelligence Agency, Washington, D.C. 20505 (703) 482-1100, www.cia.gov; *The World Factbook.*

Euromonitor International, Inc., 122 South Michigan Avenue, Suite 1200, Chicago, Illinois 60603 (800) 577-EURO; *International Marketing Data and Statistics;* and *World Marketing Data and Statistics.*

Europa Publications Limited, 18

Bedford Square, London, WC1B 3JN, England; *The Europa World Year Book*.

St. Martin's Press, Inc., 175 Fifth Avenue, New York, New York 10010 (800) 221-7945; *The Statesman's Year-Book*.

Statistical Office of the United Nations, Publishing Service, New York, New York 10017 (800) 253-9646; *Human Development Report*.

The World Bank, 1818 H Street, NW, Washington, D.C. 20433 (202) 477-1234; *The World Bank Atlas;* and *World Development Indicators*.

WESTERN SAMOA - LAND USE

Central Intelligence Agency, Washington, D.C. 20505 (703) 482-1100, www.cia.gov; *The World Factbook*.

Euromonitor International, Inc., 122 South Michigan Avenue, Suite 1200, Chicago, Illinois 60603 (800) 577-EURO; *International Marketing Data and Statistics*.

WESTERN SAMOA - LIFE EXPECTANCY

Central Intelligence Agency, Washington, D.C. 20505 (703) 482-1100, www.cia.gov; *The World Factbook*.

Euromonitor International, Inc., 122 South Michigan Avenue, Suite 1200, Chicago, Illinois 60603 (800) 577-EURO; *The World Economic Factbook*.

St. Martin's Press, Inc., 175 Fifth Avenue, New York, New York 10010 (800) 221-7945; *The Statesman's Year-Book*.

Statistical Office of the United Nations, Publishing Service, New York, New York 10017 (800) 253-9646; *Asia-Pacific in Figures;* and *Human Development Report*.

The World Bank, 1818 H Street, NW, Washington, D.C. 20433 (202) 477-1234; *The World Bank Atlas*.

WESTERN SAMOA - LITERACY RATE

Euromonitor International, Inc., 122 South Michigan Avenue, Suite 1200, Chicago, Illinois 60603 (800) 577-EURO; *World Marketing Data and Statistics*.

WESTERN SAMOA - LIVESTOCK AND POULTRY

Europa Publications Limited, 18 Bedford Square, London, WC1B 3JN, England; *The Europa World Year Book*.

St. Martin's Press, Inc., 175 Fifth Avenue, New York, New York 10010 (800) 221-7945; *The Statesman's Year-Book*.

WESTERN SAMOA - MANUFACTURING

Asian Development Bank, P.O. Box 789, 1099 Manila, Philippines; *Key Indicators of Developing Asian and Pacific Countries*.

The World Bank, 1818 H Street, NW, Washington, D.C. 20433 (202) 477-1234; *World Development Indicators*.

WESTERN SAMOA - MERCHANT SHIPPING

Europa Publications Limited, 18 Bedford Square, London, WC1B 3JN, England; *The Europa World Year Book*.

St. Martin's Press, Inc., 175 Fifth Avenue, New York, New York 10010 (800) 221-7945; *The Statesman's Year-Book*.

WESTERN SAMOA - MILITARY

Central Intelligence Agency, Washington, D.C. 20505 (703) 482-1100, www.cia.gov; *The World Factbook*.

Euromonitor International, Inc., 122 South Michigan Avenue, Suite 1200, Chicago, Illinois 60603 (800) 577-EURO; *World Marketing Data and Statistics*.

Statistical Office of the United Nations, Publishing Service, New York, New York 10017 (800) 253-9646; *Human Development Report*.

WESTERN SAMOA - MINING AND MINERAL PRODUCTS

Europa Publications Limited, 18 Bedford Square, London, WC1B 3JN, England; *The Europa World Year Book*.

WESTERN SAMOA - MONEY SUPPLY

Asian Development Bank, P.O. Box 789, 1099 Manila, Philippines; *Key Indicators of Developing Asian and Pacific Countries*.

Economist Intelligence Unit, 111 West 57th Street, New York, New York 10019 (800) 938-4685; *Samoa Country Report*.

Europa Publications Limited, 18 Bedford Square, London, WC1B 3JN, England; *The Europa World Year Book*.

The World Bank, 1818 H Street, NW, Washington, D.C. 20433 (202) 477-1234; *World Development Indicators*.

WESTERN SAMOA - MORTALITY

Central Intelligence Agency, Washington, D.C. 20505 (703) 482-1100, www.cia.gov; *The World Factbook*.

Euromonitor International, Inc., 122 South Michigan Avenue, Suite 1200, Chicago, Illinois 60603 (800) 577-EURO; *International Marketing Data and Statistics;*

and *The World Economic Factbook*.

Europa Publications Limited, 18 Bedford Square, London, WC1B 3JN, England; *The Europa World Year Book*.

Statistical Office of the United Nations, Publishing Service, New York, New York 10017 (800) 253-9646; *Asia-Pacific in Figures; Demographic Yearbook; Human Development Report;* and *Statistical Yearbook*.

The World Bank, 1818 H Street, NW, Washington, D.C. 20433 (202) 477-1234; *The World Bank Atlas;* and *World Development Indicators*.

WESTERN SAMOA - MOTION PICTURES

St. Martin's Press, Inc., 175 Fifth Avenue, New York, New York 10010 (800) 221-7945; *The Statesman's Year-Book*.

WESTERN SAMOA - MORTALITY

Europa Publications Limited, 18 Bedford Square, London, WC1B 3JN, England; *The Europa World Year Book*.

WESTERN SAMOA - MOTOR VEHICLES IN USE

Europa Publications Limited, 18 Bedford Square, London, WC1B 3JN, England; *The Europa World Year Book*.

WESTERN SAMOA - NATIONAL ACCOUNTS

Statistical Office of the United Nations, Publishing Service, New York, New York 10017 (800) 253-9646; *Asia-Pacific in Figures*.

WESTERN SAMOA - PATENTS, TRADEMARKS AND SERVICE MARKS

World Intellectual Property Organization, 34 Chemin des Colombettes, CH-1211 Geneva 20. Switzerland; *Industrial Property Statistics*.

WESTERN SAMOA - PETROLEUM INDUSTRY

Asian Development Bank, P.O. Box 789, 1099 Manila, Philippines; *Key Indicators of Developing Asian and Pacific Countries*.

WESTERN SAMOA - POPULATION

Asian Development Bank, P.O. Box 789, 1099 Manila, Philippines; *Key Indicators of Developing Asian and Pacific Countries*.

Central Intelligence Agency, Washington, D.C. 20505 (703) 482-1100, www.cia.gov; *The World Factbook*.

Economist Intelligence Unit, 111 West 57th Street, New York, New York 10019

(800) 938-4685; *Samoa Country Report.*

Euromonitor International, Inc., 122 South Michigan Avenue, Suite 1200, Chicago, Illinois 60603 (800) 577-EURO; *International Marketing Data and Statistics; and The World Economic Factbook.*

Europa Publications Limited, 18 Bedford Square, London, WC1B 3JN, England; *The Europa World Year Book.*

St. Martin's Press, Inc., 175 Fifth Avenue, New York, New York 10010 (800) 221-7945; *The Statesman's Year-Book.*

Statistical Office of the United Nations, Publishing Service, New York, New York 10017 (800) 253-9646; *Human Development Report;* and *National Accounts Statistics.*

United Nations Educational, Scientific and Cultural Organization (UNESCO), 7 Place de Fontenoy, F-75700 Paris, France (Telephone Number in U.S. (212) 963-5981); *Statistical Yearbook.*

The World Bank, 1818 H Street, NW, Washington, D.C. 20433 (202) 477-1234; *The World Bank Atlas.*

WESTERN SAMOA - PRICES

Asian Development Bank, P.O. Box 789, 1099 Manila, Philippines; *Key Indicators of Developing Asian and Pacific Countries.*

International Monetary Fund, 700 Nineteenth Street, NW, Washington, D.C. 20431 (202) 623-7000; *International Financial Statistics.*

South Pacific Commission, Post Box D5, Noumea Cedex, New Caledonia; *Statistical Bulletin of the South Pacific: Overseas Trade;* and *Statistical Bulletin of the South Pacific: Retail Price Indexes.*

WESTERN SAMOA - RADIO RECEIVERS

St. Martin's Press, Inc., 175 Fifth Avenue, New York, New York 10010 (800) 221-7945; *The Statesman's Year-Book.*

WESTERN SAMOA - RELIGION

Central Intelligence Agency, Washington, D.C. 20505 (703) 482-1100, www.cia.gov; *The World Factbook.*

WESTERN SAMOA - RETAIL TRADE

Euromonitor International, Inc., 122 South Michigan Avenue, Suite 1200, Chicago, Illinois 60603 (800) 577-EURO; *World Marketing Data and Statistics.*

WESTERN SAMOA - RICE PRODUCTION - See WESTERN SAMOA - CROPS

WESTERN SAMOA - SOCIAL DATA

Asian Development Bank, P.O. Box 789, 1099 Manila, Philippines; *Key Indicators of Developing Asian and Pacific Countries.*

WESTERN SAMOA - TAXATION

The World Bank, 1818 H Street, NW, Washington, D.C. 20433 (202) 477-1234; *World Development Indicators.*

WESTERN SAMOA - TELEPHONES IN USE

American Telephone and Telegraph Company, 26 Parsippany Road, Whippany, New Jersey 07981 (800) 222-0300; *The World's Telephones.*

Central Intelligence Agency, Washington, D.C. 20505 (703) 482-1100, www.cia.gov; *The World Factbook.*

Europa Publications Limited, 18 Bedford Square, London, WC1B 3JN, England; *The Europa World Year Book.*

St. Martin's Press, Inc., 175 Fifth Avenue, New York, New York 10010 (800) 221-7945; *The Statesman's Year-Book.*

WESTERN SAMOA - TEXTILE INDUSTRY

South Pacific Commission, Post Box D5, Noumea Cedex, New Caledonia; *Statistical Bulletin of the South Pacific: Retail Price Indexes.*

WESTERN SAMOA - TOBACCO PRODUCTION

South Pacific Commission, Post Box D5, Noumea Cedex, New Caledonia; *Statistical Bulletin of the South Pacific: Retail Price Indexes.*

WESTERN SAMOA - TOURISM

Euromonitor International, Inc., 122 South Michigan Avenue, Suite 1200, Chicago, Illinois 60603 (800) 577-EURO; *The World Economic Factbook;* and *World Marketing Data and Statistics.*

Europa Publications Limited, 18 Bedford Square, London, WC1B 3JN, England; *The Europa World Year Book.*

St. Martin's Press, Inc., 175 Fifth Avenue, New York, New York 10010 (800) 221-7945; *The Statesman's Year-Book.*

WESTERN SAMOA - TRADE - See WESTERN SAMOA - FOREIGN TRADE

WESTERN SAMOA - TRADEMARKS AND SERVICE MARKS - See WESTERN SAMOA - PATENTS, TRADEMARKS AND SERVICE MARKS

WESTERN SAMOA - TRANSPORTATION

AND COMMUNICATIONS

Central Intelligence Agency, Washington, D.C. 20505 (703) 482-1100, www.cia.gov; *The World Factbook.*

Euromonitor International, Inc., 122 South Michigan Avenue, Suite 1200, Chicago, Illinois 60603 (800) 577-EURO; *International Marketing Data and Statistics;* and *World Marketing Data and Statistics.*

Europa Publications Limited, 18 Bedford Square, London, WC1B 3JN, England; *The Europa World Year Book.*

South Pacific Commission, Post Box D5, Noumea Cedex, New Caledonia; *Statistical Bulletin of the South Pacific: Retail Price Indexes.*

St. Martin's Press, Inc., 175 Fifth Avenue, New York, New York 10010 (800) 221-7945; *The Statesman's Year-Book.*

Statistical Office of the United Nations, Publishing Service, New York, New York 10017 (800) 253-9646; *Human Development Report.*

WESTERN SAMOA - UNEMPLOYMENT RATE

Central Intelligence Agency, Washington, D.C. 20505 (703) 482-1100, www.cia.gov; *The World Factbook.*

WESTERN SAMOA - WHOLESALE PRICES

Asian Development Bank, P.O. Box 789, 1099 Manila, Philippines; *Key Indicators of Developing Asian and Pacific Countries.*

WHEAT - ACREAGE

U.S. Department of Agriculture, National Agricultural Statistics Service, Fourteenth Street and Independence Avenue, SW, Washington, D.C. 20250 (800) 727-9540, www.usda.gov/nass; *Agricultural Statistics; Crop Production; Crop Values; Field Crops;* and *Agricultural Outlook.*

WHEAT - FARM MARKETINGS - SALES

U.S. Department of Agriculture, Economic Research Service, 1800 M Street, NW, Washington, D.C. 20036 (202) 694-5050, www.ers.usda.gov; *Farm Business Economic Report.*

WHEAT - FARM PRICES

U.S. Department of Agriculture, National Agricultural Statistics Service, Fourteenth Street and Independence Avenue, SW, Washington, D.C. 20250 (800) 727-9540, www.usda.gov/nass; *Agricultural Statistics; Crop Production; Crop Values; Field Crops;* and *Agricultural Outlook.*

WHEAT - FOREIGN TRADE

U.S. Department of Agriculture, Economic Research Service, 1800 M Street, NW, Washington, D.C. 20036 (202) 694-5050, www.ers.usda.gov; *Food Consumption, Prices and Expenditures; Wheat Situation; U.S. Agricultural Trade Update; Foreign Agricultural Trade of the United States; Agricultural Statistics;* and unpublished data.

U.S. Department of Agriculture, Foreign Agricultural Service, Fourteenth Street and Constitution Avenue, SW, Washington, D.C. 20250 (202) 720-7115, www.fas.usda.gov; *Foreign Agricultural Commodity Circular Series.*

U.S. Department of Commerce, Bureau of the Census, Washington, D.C. 20233 (301) 457-4100, www.census.gov; *U.S. International Trade in Goods and Services.*

WHEAT - PRODUCTION

U.S. Department of Agriculture, Economic Research Service, 1800 M Street, NW, Washington, D.C. 20036 (202) 694-5050, www.ers.usda.gov; *Agricultural Statistics.*

U.S. Department of Agriculture, Foreign Agricultural Service, Fourteenth Street and Constitution Avenue, SW, Washington, D.C. 20250 (202) 720-7115, www.fas.usda.gov; *Foreign Agricultural Commodity Circular Series.*

U.S. Department of Agriculture, National Agricultural Statistics Service, Fourteenth Street and Independence Avenue, SW, Washington, D.C. 20250 (800) 727-9540; *Crop Production; Crop Values;* and *Agricultural Statistics.*

WHEAT - PRODUCTION - WORLD PRODUCTION

U.S. Department of Agriculture, Economic Research Service, 1800 M Street, NW, Washington, D.C. 20036 (202) 694-5050, www.ers.usda.gov; *Agricultural Outlook.*

WHEAT - SUPPLY AND DISAPPEARANCE

U.S. Department of Agriculture, Economic Research Service, 1800 M Street, NW, Washington, D.C. 20036 (202) 694-5050, www.ers.usda.gov; *Wheat Situation; Agricultural Supply and Demand Estimates; Agricultural Outlook;* and *Agricultural Statistics.*

WHEAT FLOUR

Statistical Office of the United Nations, Publishing Service, New York, New York 10017 (800) 253-9646; *Monthly Bulletin of Statistics.*

U.S. Department of Agriculture, Economic Research Service, 1800 M Street, NW, Washington, D.C. 20036 (202) 694-5050, www.ers.usda.gov; *Food Consumption, Prices, and Expenditures;* and *Agricultural Outlook.*

WHEELCHAIR USAGE

U.S. Department of Health and Human Services, National Center for Health Statistics, 3700 East-West Highway, Hyattsville, Maryland 20782 (301) 436-8500, www.cdc.gov/nchs; *Advance Data, Nos. 289 and 292.*

WHISKEY - See also ALCOHOLIC BEVERAGES

WHISKEY

U.S. Department of Agriculture, Economic Research Service, 1800 M Street, NW, Washington, D.C. 20036 (202) 694-5050, www.ers.usda.gov; *Food Consumption, Prices, and Expenditures;* and *Agricultural Outlook.*

U.S. Department of the Treasury, Bureau of Alcohol, Tobacco, and Firearms, 650 Massachusetts Avenue, NW, Washington, D.C. 20226 (202) 927-8500, www.atf.treas.gov; *Alcohol and Tobacco Summary Statistics;* and *Monthly Statistical Release, Distilled Spirits.*

WHITE-COLLAR WORKERS - EMPLOYMENT COST INDEX

U.S. Department of Labor, Bureau of Labor Statistics, Two Massachusetts Avenue, NE, Washington, D.C. 20212 (202) 691-5200, www.stats.bls.gov; *News; Employment Cost Index;* and Internet site: http://stats.bls.gov/ ecthome.htm.

WHITE-COLLAR WORKERS - STATE AND LOCAL GOVERNMENT WORKERS

U.S. Department of Labor, Bureau of Labor Statistics, Two Massachusetts Avenue, NE, Washington, D.C. 20212 (202) 691-5200, www.stats.bls.gov; *News, Employer costs for Employee Compensation.*

WHITING - QUANTITY AND VALUE OF CATCH

U.S. Department of Commerce, National Oceanic and Atmospheric Administration, National Marine Fisheries Service, 1335 East-West Highway, Silver Spring, Maryland 20910 (301) 427-2239, www.nmfs.noaa.gov; *Fisheries of the United States.*

WHOLESALE TRADE - CAPITAL EXPENDITURES

U.S. Department of Commerce, Bureau

of Economic Analysis, Fourteenth Street between Constitution Avenue and E Street, NW, Washington, D.C. 20230 (202) 606-9900, www.bea.doc.gov; *National Income and Product Accounts, Vol. 1;* and *Survey of Current Business.*

WHOLESALE TRADE - COMPANIES EXPORTING

U.S. Department of Commerce, Bureau of the Census, Washington, D.C. 20233 (301) 457-4100, www.census.gov; *A Profile of U.S. Exporting Companies.*

WHOLESALE TRADE - EARNINGS

U.S. Department of Commerce, Bureau of Economic Analysis, Fourteenth Street between Constitution Avenue and E Street, NW, Washington, D.C. 20230 (202) 606-9900, www.bea.doc.gov; *The National Income and Product Accounts of the United States;* and *Survey of Current Business.*

U.S. Department of Commerce, Bureau of the Census, Washington, D.C. 20233 (301) 457-4100, www.census.gov; *1997 Economic Census: Advance Summary Statistics for the U.S.; 1997 Economic Census, EC97X-CS1;Census of Wholesale Trade; County Business Patterns;* and *Economic Census of Outlying Areas.*

U.S. Department of Labor, Bureau of Labor Statistics, Two Massachusetts Avenue, NE, Washington, D.C. 20212 (202) 691-5200, www.stats.bls.gov; *Employment and Earnings;* and Internet site: http://stats.bls.gov/ ceshome.htm.

WHOLESALE TRADE - EMPLOYEES

U.S. Department of Commerce, Bureau of Economic Analysis, Fourteenth Street between Constitution Avenue and E Street, NW, Washington, D.C. 20230 (202) 606-9900, www.bea.doc.gov; *The National Income and Product Accounts of the United States;* and *Survey of Current Business.*

U.S. Department of Commerce, Bureau of the Census, Washington, D.C. 20233 (301) 457-4100, www.census.gov; *County Business Patterns; 1997 Economic Census: Advance Summary Statistics for the U.S. 1997 NAICS Basis;* and *Economic Census of Outlying Areas.*

U.S. Department of Labor, Bureau of Labor Statistics, Two Massachusetts Avenue, NE, Washington, D.C. 20212 (202) 691-5200, www.stats.bls.gov; *News, USDL 98-93; Employment and Earnings; Monthly Labor Review;* Bulletins 2445 and 2481; unpublished data; and Internet site: http://www.stats.bls. gov/ceshome.htm.

WHOLESALE TRADE - ESTABLISHMENTS

U.S. Department of Commerce, Bureau

of the Census, Washington, D.C. 20233 (301) 457-4100, www.census.gov; *1997 Economic Census: Advance Summary Statistics for the U.S. 1997 NAICS Basis; 1997 Economic Census, EC 97X-CS1; Economic Census of Outlying Areas;* and *County Business Patterns.*

WHOLESALE TRADE - FAILURES

The Dun and Bradstreet Corporation, One Diamond Hill Road, Murray Hill, New Jersey 07974 (908) 5000; *Business Failure Record.*

WHOLESALE TRADE - FOREIGN INVESTMENTS IN THE UNITED STATES

U.S. Department of Commerce, Bureau of Economic Analysis, Fourteenth Street between Constitution Avenue and E Street, NW, Washington, D.C. 20230 (202) 606-9900, www.bea.doc.gov; *Survey of Current Business;* and *Foreign Direct Investment in the U.S., Operations of Affiliates of Foreign Countries.*

WHOLESALE TRADE - GROSS DOMESTIC PRODUCT

U.S. Department of Commerce, Bureau of Economic Analysis, Fourteenth Street between Constitution Avenue and E Street, NW, Washington, D.C. 20230 (202) 606-9900, www.bea.doc.gov; *Survey of Current Business.*

WHOLESALE TRADE - HEALTH INSURANCE COVERAGE - EMPLOYEES

U.S. Department of Health and Human Services, National Center for Health Statistics, 3700 East-West Highway, Hyattsville, Maryland 20782 (301) 436-8500, www.cdc.gov/nchs; *Employer-Sponsored Health Insurance, State and National Estimates, 1997.*

WHOLESALE TRADE - INVENTORIES

U.S. Department of Commerce, Bureau of the Census, Washington, D.C. 20233 (301) 457-4100, www.census.gov; *Current Business Reports, Annual Benchmark Report for Wholesale Trade;* and unpublished data.

WHOLESALE TRADE - MERGERS AND ACQUISITIONS

Thomson Financial Securities Data, Two Gateway Center, Newark, New Jersey 07006 (973) 622-3100; *Merger and Corporate Transactions Database.*

WHOLESALE TRADE - MULTINATIONAL COMPANIES

U.S. Department of Commerce, Bureau of Economic Analysis, Fourteenth Street between Constitution Avenue and E Street,

NW, Washington, D.C. 20230 (202) 606-9900, www.bea.doc.gov; *Survey of Current Business.*

WHOLESALE TRADE - OCCUPATIONAL SAFETY

U.S. Department of Labor, Bureau of Labor Statistics, Two Massachusetts Avenue, NE, Washington, D.C. 20212 (202) 691-5200, www.stats.bls.gov; *Occupational Injuries and Illnesses in the United States by Industry.*

WHOLESALE TRADE - PROFITS

U.S. Department of the Treasury, Internal Revenue Service, 1111 Constitution Avenue, NW, Washington, D.C. 20224 (202) 874-0410, www.irs.ustreas.gov; *Statistics of Income,* various publications.

WHOLESALE TRADE - RECEIPTS

U.S. Department of Commerce, Bureau of the Census, Washington, D.C. 20233 (301) 457-4100, www.census.gov; *1997 Economic Census: Advance Summary Statistics for the U.S. 1997 NAICS Basis*

U.S. Department of the Treasury, Internal Revenue Service, 1111 Constitution Avenue, NW, Washington, D.C. 20224 (202) 874-0410, www.irs.ustreas.gov; *Statistics of Income,* various publications.

WHOLESALE TRADE - SALES

U.S. Department of Commerce, Bureau of the Census, Washington, D.C. 20233 (301) 457-4100, www.census.gov; *1997 Economic Census: Advance Summary Statistics for the U.S. 1997 NAICS Basis; 1997 Economic Census, EC97X-CS1; Census of Wholesale Trade; Current Business Reports, Annual Benchmark Report for Wholesale Trade; Economic Census of Outlying Areas;* and unpublished data.

WHOOPING COUGH

U.S. Department of Health and Human Services, Centers for Disease Control and Prevention, 1600 Clifton Road, NE, Atlanta, Georgia 30333 (800) 331-3435, www.cdc.gov; *Summary of Notifiable Diseases, United States, Morbidity and Mortality Weekly Report.*

WILDLIFE - ENDANGERED SPECIES

U.S. Department of the Interior, Fish and Wildlife Service, C Street between Eighteenth and Nineteenth Streets, NW, Washington, D.C. 20240 (202) 208-5634, www.fws.gov; *Endangered Species Technical Bulletin.*

WILDLIFE - RELATED RECREATION ACTIVITIES

U.S. Department of the Interior, Fish and Wildlife Service, C Street between Eighteenth and Nineteenth Streets, NW, Washington, D.C. 20240 (202) 208-5634, www.fws.gov; *1996 National Survey of Fishing, Hunting, and Wildlife Associated Recreation.*

WIND - ENERGY SOURCE

U.S. Department of Energy, Energy Information Administration, 1000 Independence Avenue, SW, Washington, D.C. 20585 (202) 586-8800, www.eia.doe.gov; *Annual Energy Review.*

WIND - SELECTED CITIES

U.S. Department of Commerce, National Oceanic and Atmospheric Administration, National Climatic Data Center, 151 Patton Avenue, Asheville, North Carolina 28801 (828) 271-4800, www.ncdc.noaa.gov; *Comparative Climatic Data.*

WINDSURFING

National Sporting Goods Association, 1601 Feehanville Drive, Suite 300, Mount Prospect, Illinois 60056 (847) 296-6742; *Sports Participation in 1998: Series I and II.*

WINDWARD ISLANDS - AGRICULTURE

Economist Intelligence Unit, 111 West 57th Street, New York, New York 10019 (800) 938-4685; *Windward and Leeward Islands Country Report.*

WINDWARD ISLANDS - AREA AND DENSITY OF POPULATION

St. Martin's Press, Inc., 175 Fifth Avenue, New York, New York 10010 (800) 221-7945; *The Statesman's Year-Book.*

Statistical Office of the United Nations, Publishing Service, New York, New York 10017 (800) 253-9646; *Statistical Yearbook.*

WINDWARD ISLANDS - ECONOMY

Economist Intelligence Unit, 111 West 57th Street, New York, New York 10019 (800) 938-4685; *Windward and Leeward Islands Country Report.*

WINDWARD ISLANDS - ENVIRONMENT

Economist Intelligence Unit, 111 West 57th Street, New York, New York 10019 (800) 938-4685; *Windward and Leeward Islands Country Report.*

WINDWARD ISLANDS - EXPORTS

Economist Intelligence Unit, 111 West 57th Street, New York, New York 10019 (800) 938-4685; *Windward and Leeward Islands Country Report.*

WINDWARD ISLANDS - FINANCE

Economist Intelligence Unit, 111 West 57th Street, New York, New York 10019 (800) 938-4685; *Windward and Leeward Islands Country Report.*

WINDWARD ISLANDS - FOREIGN TRADE

Economist Intelligence Unit, 111 West 57th Street, New York, New York 10019 (800) 938-4685; *Windward and Leeward Islands Country Report.*

WINDWARD ISLANDS - GROSS DOMESTIC PRODUCT

Economist Intelligence Unit, 111 West 57th Street, New York, New York 10019 (800) 938-4685; *Windward and Leeward Islands Country Report.*

WINDWARD ISLANDS - IMPORTS

Economist Intelligence Unit, 111 West 57th Street, New York, New York 10019 (800) 938-4685; *Windward and Leeward Islands Country Report.*

WINDWARD ISLANDS - INDUSTRY

Economist Intelligence Unit, 111 West 57th Street, New York, New York 10019 (800) 938-4685; *Windward and Leeward Islands Country Report.*

WINDWARD ISLANDS - MONEY SUPPLY

Economist Intelligence Unit, 111 West 57th Street, New York, New York 10019 (800) 938-4685; *Windward and Leeward Islands Country Report.*

WINDWARD ISLANDS - POPULATION

Economist Intelligence Unit, 111 West 57th Street, New York, New York 10019 (800) 938-4685; *Windward and Leeward Islands Country Report.*

St. Martin's Press, Inc., 175 Fifth Avenue, New York, New York 10010 (800) 221-7945; *The Statesman's Year-Book.*

Statistical Office of the United Nations, Publishing Service, New York, New York 10017 (800) 253-9646; *Statistical Yearbook.*

WINES - See also ALCOHOLIC BEVERAGES

WINES

Statistical Office of the United Nations, Publishing Service, New York, New York 10017 (800) 253-9646; *Statistical Yearbook;* and *Monthly Bulletin of Statistics.*

U.S. Department of Agriculture, Economic Research Service, 1800 M Street, NW, Washington, D.C. 20036 (202) 694-5050, www.ers.usda.gov; *Agricultural Outlook; U.S. Agricultural Trade Update; Food Consumption, Prices, and Expenditures; Foreign Agricultural Trade of the United States;* and unpublished data.

WIRE TAPS

Administrative Office of the United States Courts, Thurgood Marshall Federal Judiciary Building, 1 Columbus Circle, NE, Washington, D.C. 20544 (202) 502-1455, www.uscourts.gov; *Report on Applications for Orders Authorizing or Approving the Interception of Wire or Oral or Electronic Communications.*

WISCONSIN - See also STATE DATA (FOR INDIVIDUAL STATES)

Wisconsin - Primary Statistics Sources

Wisconsin Legislative Reference Bureau, Post Office Box 2037, Madison, Wisconsin 53701-2037 (608) 266-7098; *Wisconsin Blue Book.*

Wisconsin - State Data Centers

Demographic Services Center, Department of Administration, 101 East Wilson Street, Sixth Floor, Post Office Box 7868, Madison, Wisconsin 53707-7868, Mr. Robert Naylor (608) 266-1927.

Applied Population Laboratory, Department of Rural Sociology, University of Wisconsin, 1450 Linden Drive, Room 316, Madison, Wisconsin 53706, Mr. Dan Veroff (608) 265-9545.

WOMEN - ABORTIONS

Alan Guttmacher Institute, 120 Wall Street Avenue, New York, New York 10005 (212) 248-1111; *Abortion Factbook: Readings, Trends, and State and Local Data; Abortion Services in the U.S.; Family Perspectives;* and unpublished data.

U.S. Department of Health and Human Services, National Center for Health Statistics, 3700 East-West Highway, Hyattsville, Maryland 20782 (301) 436-8500; *National Vital Statistics Report.*

WOMEN - ADULT EDUCATION

U.S. Department of Education, 400 Maryland Avenue, SW, Washington, D.C. 20202 (877) 424-1616, www.ed.gov; *National Household Education Survey.*

WOMEN - ADULT EDUCATION

U.S. Department of Education, National Center for Education Statistics, 555 New Jersey Avenue, NW, Washington, D.C. 20208-5574 (202) 219-1828, http://nces.ed.gov; *National Household Education Survey.*

WOMEN - AGE

U.S. Department of Commerce, Bureau of the Census, Washington, D.C. 20233 (301) 457-4100, www.census.gov; unpublished data.

WOMEN - AIDS

U.S. Department of Health and Human Services, Centers for Disease Control and Prevention, 1600 Clifton Road, NE, Atlanta, Georgia 30333 (800) 331-3435, www.cdc.gov; *HIV/AIDS Surveillance Report.*

WOMEN - BIRTHS AND BIRTH RATES

U.S. Department of Commerce, Bureau of the Census, Washington, D.C. 20233 (301) 457-4100, www.census.gov; *Current Population Reports,* and Internet site: http://www.census.gov/ipc/www/idbnew.html.

U.S. Department of Health and Human Services, National Center for Health Statistics, 3700 East-West Highway, Hyattsville, Maryland 20782 (301) 436-8500; *Vital Statistics of the United States; National Vital Statistics Report;* and unpublished data.

WOMEN - BIRTHS AND BIRTH RATES - BIRTHS TO SINGLE WOMEN

U.S. Department of Commerce, Bureau of the Census, Washington, D.C. 20233 (301) 457-4100, www.census.gov; *Current Population Reports.*

WOMEN - BIRTHS AND BIRTH RATES - CESAREAN SECTION DELIVERIES

U.S. Department of Health and Human Services, National Center for Health Statistics, 3700 East-West Highway, Hyattsville, Maryland 20782 (301) 436-8500; *Vital and Health Statistics;* and unpublished data.

WOMEN - BIRTHS AND BIRTH RATES - CHARACTERISTICS - SELECTED

U.S. Department of Commerce, Bureau of the Census, Washington, D.C. 20233 (301) 457-4100, www.census.gov; *Current Population Reports.*

U.S. Department of Health and Human Services, National Center for Health Statistics, 3700 East-West Highway, Hyattsville, Maryland 20782 (301) 436-8500; *Vital Statistics of the United States; National Vital Statistics Report;* and unpublished data.

WOMEN - BIRTHS AND BIRTH RATES - FIRST BIRTHS

U.S. Department of Commerce, Bureau of the Census, Washington, D.C. 20233 (301) 457-4100, www.census.gov; *Current Population Reports.*

WOMEN - BUSINESS OWNERS

U.S. Department of Commerce, Bureau of the Census, Washington, D.C. 20233 (301) 457-4100, www.census.gov; *Survey of Minority-Owned Businesses.*

WOMEN - CANCER

U.S. Department of Health and Human Services, National Institutes of Health, National Cancer Institute, 9000 Rockville Pike, Bethesda, Maryland 20892 (301) 496-5737; *Cancer Statistics Review.*

WOMEN - CHILD DAY CARE

U.S. Department of Education, National Center for Education Statistics, 555 New Jersey Avenue, NW, Washington, D.C. 20208-5574 (202) 219-1828, http://nces.ed.gov; *Statistics in Brief.*

WOMEN - CHILD SUPPORT

U.S. Department of Commerce, Bureau of the Census, Washington, D.C. 20233 (301) 457-4100, www.census.gov; *Current Population Reports.*

WOMEN - CHRONIC CONDITIONS

U.S. Department of Health and Human Services, National Center for Health Statistics, 3700 East-West Highway, Hyattsville, Maryland 20782 (301) 436-8500; *Vital and Health Statistics;* and unpublished data.

WOMEN - CIGARETTE SMOKING

U.S. Department of Health and Human Services, National Center for Health Statistics, 3700 East-West Highway, Hyattsville, Maryland 20782 (301) 436-8500; *Health, United States;* and *National Vital Statistics Report.*

WOMEN - COMPUTER USE

U.S. Department of Education, National Center for Education Statistics, 555 New Jersey Avenue, NW, Washington, D.C. 20208-5574 (202) 219-1828, http://nces.ed.gov; *Digest of Education Statistics.*

WOMEN - CONTRACEPTIVE USE

U.S. Department of Health and Human Services, National Center for Health Statistics, 3700 East-West Highway, Hyattsville, Maryland 20782 (301) 436-8500; *Advance Data from Vital and Health Statistics.*

WOMEN - CRIMINAL VICTIMIZATION

U.S. Department of Justice, Bureau of Justice Statistics, 810 Seventh Street, NW, 2nd Floor, Washington, D.C. 20531 (800) 732-3277, www.ojp.usdoj.gov/bjs; *Criminal Victimization;* and *Indicators of School Crime and Safety, 1998.*

WOMEN - DEATHS AND DEATH RATES

U.S. Department of Health and Human Services, National Center for Health Statistics, 3700 East-West Highway, Hyattsville, Maryland 20782 (301) 436-8500; *National Vital Statistics Report; Vital Statistics of the United States;* and unpublished data.

WOMEN - DELIVERY PROCEDURES - BIRTHS

U.S. Department of Health and Human Services, National Center for Health Statistics, 3700 East-West Highway, Hyattsville, Maryland 20782 (301) 436-8500; *Vital and Health Statistics;* and unpublished data.

WOMEN - DISABILITY DAYS

U.S. Department of Health and Human Services, Public Health Service, 200 Independence Avenue, SW, Washington, D.C. 20201 (202) 619-1296; *Vital and Health Statistics;* and unpublished data.

WOMEN - EDUCATION - AMERICAN COLLEGE TESTING PROGRAM

American College Testing Program, Box 168, Iowa City, Iowa 52243 (319) 337-1000; *High School Profile Report.*

WOMEN - EDUCATION - ATTAINMENT

U.S. Department of Commerce, Bureau of the Census, Washington, D.C. 20233 (301) 457-4100, www.census.gov; *Current Population Reports; Census of Population;* and unpublished data.

U.S. Department of Education, National Center for Education Statistics, 555 New Jersey Avenue, NW, Washington, D.C. 20208-5574 (202) 219-1828, http://nces.ed.gov; *Digest of Education Statistics.*

U.S. Department of Labor, Bureau of Labor Statistics, Two Massachusetts Avenue, NE, Washington, D.C. 20212 (202) 691-5200, www.stats.bls.gov; *News, USDL 99-175;* Bulletin 2307; and unpublished data.

WOMEN - EDUCATION - ATTAINMENT - LABOR FORCE STATUS

U.S. Department of Labor, Bureau of Labor Statistics, Two Massachusetts Avenue, NE, Washington, D.C. 20212 (202) 691-5200, www.stats.bls.gov; *News;* Bulletin 2307; and unpublished data.

WOMEN - EDUCATION - COLLEGE ENROLLMENT

National Science Foundation, 4201 Wilson Boulevard, Arlington, Virginia 22230 (703) 306-1234, www.nsf.gov; *Survey of Graduate Science Engineering Students and Post-doctorates.*

U.S. Department of Commerce, Bureau of the Census, Washington, D.C. 20233 (301) 457-4100, www.census.gov; *Current Population Reports;* and unpublished data.

U.S. Department of Education, National Center for Education Statistics, 555 New Jersey Avenue, NW, Washington, D.C. 20208-5574 (202) 219-1828, http://nces.ed.gov; *Digest of Education Statistics; Projections of Education Statistics;* and unpublished data.

WOMEN - EDUCATION - COLLEGE ENROLLMENT - BY AGE

U.S. Department of Education, National Center for Education Statistics, 555 New Jersey Avenue, NW, Washington, D.C. 20208-5574 (202) 219-1828, http://nces.ed.gov; *Projections of Education Statistics;* and *Digest of Education Statistics..*

WOMEN - EDUCATION - COLLEGE ENROLLMENT - BY STATE

U.S. Department of Education, National Center for Education Statistics, 555 New Jersey Avenue, NW, Washington, D.C. 20208-5574 (202) 219-1828, http://nces.ed.gov; *Digest of Education Statistics.*

WOMEN - EDUCATION - DEGREES CONFERRED

National Science Foundation, 4201 Wilson Boulevard, Arlington, Virginia 22230 (703) 306-1234, www.nsf.gov; *Survey of Earned Doctorates, Selected Data on Science and Engineering Doctorate Awards.*

U.S. Department of Commerce, Bureau of the Census, Washington, D.C. 20233 (301) 457-4100, www.census.gov; unpublished data.

U.S. Department of Education, National Center for Education Statistics, 555 New Jersey Avenue, NW, Washington, D.C. 20208-5574 (202) 219-1828, http://nces.ed.gov; *Digest of Education Statistics;* and unpublished data.

WOMEN - EDUCATION - ENROLLMENT BY

LEVEL

U.S. Department of Commerce, Bureau of the Census, Washington, D.C. 20233 (301) 457-4100, www.census.gov; *Current Population Reports;* and unpublished data.

WOMEN - EDUCATION - HIGH SCHOOL DROPOUTS

U.S. Department of Commerce, Bureau of the Census, Washington, D.C. 20233 (301) 457-4100, www.census.gov; *Current Population Reports.*

WOMEN - EDUCATION - SAT TESTS

College Entrance Examination Board, 45 Columbus Avenue, New York, New York 10017 (212) 713-8000; *National College - Bound Seniors.*

WOMEN - ELECTIONS - VOTER REGISTRATION AND TURNOUT

U.S. Department of Commerce, Bureau of the Census, Washington, D.C. 20233 (301) 457-4100, www.census.gov; *Current Population Reports;* and unpublished data.

WOMEN - FERTILITY - FERTILITY RATE

U.S. Department of Commerce, Bureau of the Census, Washington, D.C. 20233 (301) 457-4100, www.census.gov; *Current Population Reports.*

U.S. Department of Health and Human Services, National Center for Health Statistics, 3700 East-West Highway, Hyattsville, Maryland 20782 (301) 436-8500; *Vital Statistics of the United States;* and unpublished data.

WOMEN - GYNECOLOGICAL SERVICES

U.S. Department of Health and Human Services, National Center for Health Statistics, 3700 East-West Highway, Hyattsville, Maryland 20782 (301) 436-8500; *Fertility, Family Planning, and Women's Health: New Data From the 1995 National Survey of Family Growth, Vital and Health Statistics;* and unpublished data.

WOMEN - HEALTH INSURANCE COVERAGE

U.S. Department of Commerce, Bureau of the Census, Washington, D.C. 20233 (301) 457-4100, www.census.gov; *Health Insurance Coverage;* and unpublished data.

WOMEN - HEIGHT DISTRIBUTION

U.S. Department of Health and Human Services, National Center for Health Statistics, 3700 East-West Highway, Hyattsville, Maryland 20782 (301) 436-8500; unpublished data.

WOMEN - HISPANIC ORIGIN POPULATION

U.S. Department of Commerce, Bureau of the Census, Washington, D.C. 20233 (301) 457-4100, www.census.gov; *Current Population Reports.*

WOMEN - HOME HEALTH AND HOSPICE CARE

U.S. Department of Health and Human Services, National Center for Health Statistics, 3700 East-West Highway, Hyattsville, Maryland 20782 (301) 436-8500; *Advance Data, No. 297.*

WOMEN - HOMICIDES

U.S. Department of Health and Human Services, National Center for Health Statistics, 3700 East-West Highway, Hyattsville, Maryland 20782 (301) 436-8500; *Vital Statistics of the United States;* and *Advance Data from Vital and Health Statistics, No. 231.*

WOMEN - HOSPITAL USE

U.S. Department of Health and Human Services, National Center for Health Statistics, 3700 East-West Highway, Hyattsville, Maryland 20782 (301) 436-8500; *Vital and Health Statistics; Advance Data, No. 304;* and unpublished data.

WOMEN - HOUSEHOLDERS

U.S. Department of Commerce, Bureau of the Census, Washington, D.C. 20233 (301) 457-4100, www.census.gov; *Current Population Reports.*

WOMEN - ILLNESS/INJURY

U.S. Department of Health and Human Services, National Center for Health Statistics, 3700 East-West Highway, Hyattsville, Maryland 20782 (301) 436-8500; *Vital and Health Statistics;* and unpublished data.

WOMEN - INCOME

U.S. Department of Commerce, Bureau of the Census, Washington, D.C. 20233 (301) 457-4100, www.census.gov; *Current Population Reports.*

WOMEN - INTERNET ACCESS

Mediamark Research, Inc., 708 Third Avenue, New York, New York 10017 (212) 599-0444; *Multimedia Audiences.*

WOMEN - LABOR FORCE AND EMPLOYMENT - AGE

U.S. Department of Labor, Bureau of Labor Statistics, Two Massachusetts Avenue, NE, Washington, D.C. 20212 (202) 691-5200, www.stats.bls.gov; *Employment*

and Earnings; Monthly Labor Review; Bulletin 2307; and unpublished data.

WOMEN - LABOR FORCE AND EMPLOYMENT - EARNINGS

U.S. Department of Commerce, Bureau of the Census, Washington, D.C. 20233 (301) 457-4100, www.census.gov; *Current Population Reports.*

U.S. Department of Labor, Bureau of Labor Statistics, Two Massachusetts Avenue, NE, Washington, D.C. 20212 (202) 691-5200, www.stats.bls.gov; *Employment and Earnings;* Bulletin 2307; and unpublished data.

WOMEN - LABOR FORCE AND EMPLOYMENT - EDUCATIONAL ATTAINMENT

U.S. Department of Labor, Bureau of Labor Statistics, Two Massachusetts Avenue, NE, Washington, D.C. 20212 (202) 691-5200, www.stats.bls.gov; unpublished data.

WOMEN - LABOR FORCE AND EMPLOYMENT - EMPLOYED

U.S. Department of Labor, Bureau of Labor Statistics, Two Massachusetts Avenue, NE, Washington, D.C. 20212 (202) 691-5200, www.stats.bls.gov; *Employment and Unemployment; News, USDL 99-75, USDL 98-93;* Bulletin 2307; and unpublished data.

WOMEN - LABOR FORCE AND EMPLOYMENT - INDUSTRY

U.S. Department of Labor, Bureau of Labor Statistics, Two Massachusetts Avenue, NE, Washington, D.C. 20212 (202) 691-5200, www.stats.bls.gov; *Employment and Earnings;* and unpublished data.

WOMEN - LABOR FORCE AND EMPLOYMENT - MARITAL STATUS

U.S. Department of Labor, Bureau of Labor Statistics, Two Massachusetts Avenue, NE, Washington, D.C. 20212 (202) 691-5200, www.stats.bls.gov; Bulletins 2217, 2340, 2307; and unpublished data.

WOMEN - LABOR FORCE AND EMPLOYMENT - OCCUPATION

U.S. Department of Commerce, Bureau of the Census, Washington, D.C. 20233 (301) 457-4100, www.census.gov; *Current Population Reports.*

U.S. Department of Labor, Bureau of Labor Statistics, Two Massachusetts Avenue, NE, Washington, D.C. 20212 (202) 691-5200, www.stats.bls.gov; Bulletin 2307; *Employment and Earnings;* and unpublished data.

WOMEN - LABOR FORCE AND EMPLOYMENT - PARTICIPATION RATES

U.S. Department of Labor, Bureau of Labor Statistics, Two Massachusetts Avenue, NE, Washington, D.C. 20212 (202) 691-5200, www.stats.bls.gov; *Employment and Earnings; Monthly Labor Review;* Bulletins 2340, 2307, 2217; and unpublished data.

WOMEN - LABOR FORCE AND EMPLOYMENT - PROJECTIONS

U.S. Department of Labor, Bureau of Labor Statistics, Two Massachusetts Avenue, NE, Washington, D.C. 20212 (202) 691-5200, www.stats.bls.gov; *Employment and Earnings; Monthly Labor Review;* Bulletin 2307; and unpublished data.

WOMEN - LABOR FORCE AND EMPLOYMENT - SCHOOL ENROLLMENT

U.S. Department of Labor, Bureau of Labor Statistics, Two Massachusetts Avenue, NE, Washington, D.C. 20212 (202) 691-5200, www.stats.bls.gov; *Bulletin 2307; News, USDL 99-75;* and unpublished data.

WOMEN - LABOR FORCE AND EMPLOYMENT - SELF-EMPLOYED

U.S. Department of Labor, Bureau of Labor Statistics, Two Massachusetts Avenue, NE, Washington, D.C. 20212 (202) 691-5200, www.stats.bls.gov; *Employment and Earnings;* Bulletin 2307; *News, USDL 98-93;* and unpublished data.

WOMEN - LABOR FORCE AND EMPLOYMENT - UNEMPLOYED

U.S. Department of Labor, Bureau of Labor Statistics, Two Massachusetts Avenue, NE, Washington, D.C. 20212 (202) 691-5200, www.stats.bls.gov; *Employment and Earnings; News, USDL 99-75;* and unpublished data.

WOMEN - LABOR FORCE AND EMPLOYMENT - UNION MEMBERSHIP

U.S. Department of Labor, Bureau of Labor Statistics, Two Massachusetts Avenue, NE, Washington, D.C. 20212 (202) 691-5200, www.stats.bls.gov; *Employment and Earnings.*

WOMEN - LABOR FORCE AND EMPLOYMENT - WORKPLACE VIOLENCE

U.S. Department of Justice, Bureau of Justice Statistics, 810 Seventh Street, NW, 2nd Floor, Washington, D.C. 20531 (800) 732-3277, www.ojp.usdoj.gov/bjs; *Workplace Violence.*

WOMEN - LIFE EXPECTANCY

U.S. Department of Health and Human Services, National Center for Health Statistics, 3700 East-West Highway, Hyattsville, Maryland 20782 (301) 436-8500; *National Vital Statistics; Vital Statistics of the United States;* and unpublished data.

WOMEN - MAMMOGRAPHY

U.S. Department of Health and Human Services, National Center for Health Statistics, 3700 East-West Highway, Hyattsville, Maryland 20782 (301) 436-8500; *Health, United States.*

WOMEN - MARITAL STATUS

U.S. Department of Commerce, Bureau of the Census, Washington, D.C. 20233 (301) 457-4100, www.census.gov; *Current Population Reports;* and unpublished data.

WOMEN - MARRIAGE AND DIVORCE

U.S. Department of Health and Human Services, National Center for Health Statistics, 3700 East West Highway, Hyattsville, Maryland 20782 (301) 436-8500; *Vital Statistics of the United States; National Vital Statistics Report; Advanced data from Vital and Health Statistics, No. 194;* and unpublished data.

WOMEN - NURSING HOME RESIDENTS

U.S. Department of Health and Human Services, National Center for Health Statistics, 3700 East West Highway, Hyattsville, Maryland 20782 (301) 436-8500; *Advance Data, No. 298.*

WOMEN - OVERWEIGHT

U.S. Department of Health and Human Services, National Center for Health Statistics, 3700 East West Highway, Hyattsville, Maryland 20782 (301) 436-8500; *Health, United States;* and unpublished data.

WOMEN - PENSION PLAN COVERAGE

U.S. Department of Commerce, Bureau of the Census, Washington, D.C. 20233 (301) 457-4100, www.census.gov; unpublished data.

WOMEN - PERSONS LIVING ALONE

U.S. Department of Commerce, Bureau of the Census, Washington, D.C. 20233 (301) 457-4100, www.census.gov; *Current Population Reports;* and unpublished data.

WOMEN - PHYSICAL ACTIVITY

U.S. Department of Health and Human Services, National Center for Chronic Disease Prevention and Health Promotion, Centers for Disease Control and Prevention, 1600 Clifton Road, NE, Atlanta, Georgia 30333 (404) 639-3311, www.cdc.gov/nccdphp; unpublished data.

WOMEN - PHYSICIANS

American Medical Association, 515 North State Street, Chicago, Illinois 60610 (312) 464-5000; *Physician Characteristics and Distribution in the United States.*

WOMEN - PHYSICIANS - VISITS TO

U.S. Department of Health and Human Services, National Center for Health Statistics, 3700 East-West Highway, Hyattsville, Maryland 20782 (301) 436-8500; *Vital and Health Statistics;* and unpublished data.

WOMEN - POPULATION

U.S. Department of Commerce, Bureau of the Census, Washington, D.C. 20233 (301) 457-4100, www.census.gov; *Census of Population;* and *Current Population Reports.*

WOMEN - PREGNANCIES

U.S. Department of Health and Human Services, National Center for Health Statistics, 3700 East-West Highway, Hyattsville, Maryland 20782 (301) 436-8500; *National Vital Statistics Report.*

WOMEN - PUBLIC OFFICIALS

Congressional Quarterly, Inc., 1414 Twenty-second Street, NW, Washington, D.C. 20037 (202) 887-8500; *Vital Statistics on Congress.*

U.S. Department of Commerce, Bureau of the Census, Washington, D.C. 20233 (301) 457-4100, www.census.gov; *Census of Governments, Popularly Elected Officials.*

WOMEN - RAPE

U.S. Department of Justice, Federal Bureau of Investigation, 935 Pennsylvania Avenue, NW, Washington, D.C. 20535 (202) 324-3691, www.fbi.gov; *Population-at-Risk Rates and Selected Crime Indicators;* and *Crime in the United States.*

WOMEN - RECREATIONAL ACTIVITIES

National Sporting Goods Association, 1601 Feehanville Drive, Suite 300, Mount Prospect, Illinois 60056 (847) 296-6742; *Sports Participation in 1998;* and *The Sporting Goods Market in 1999.*

WOMEN - SOCIAL SECURITY BENEFICIARIES AND PAYMENTS

Social Security Administration, 6400 Security Boulevard, Baltimore, Maryland 21235 (800) 772-1213; *Annual Statistical Supplement to the Social Security Bulletin;* and unpublished data.

WOMEN - SPORTS PARTICIPATION IN SCHOOL

National Collegiate Athletic Association, 700 West Washington Street, Indianapolis, Indiana 46206 (317) 917-6222; *1997-98 Participation Study.*

National Federation of State High School Associations, Post Office Box 690, Indianapolis, Indiana 46206 (317) 972-6900; *The 1998-99 High School Athletics Participation Survey.*

U.S. Department of Health and Human Services, Centers for Disease Control and Prevention, 1600 Clifton Road, NE, Atlanta, Georgia 30333 (800) 331-3435, www.cdc.gov; *Youth Risk Behavior Surveillance in the United States;* and *Morbidity and Mortality Weekly Report.*

WOMEN - SUBSTANCE ABUSE CLIENTS

U.S. Department of Health and Human Services, Substance Abuse and Mental Health Services Administration, 5600 Fishers Lane, Rockville, Maryland 20857 (301) 443-4797; *Uniform Facility Data Set: Annual Surveys.*

WOMEN - SURGICAL PROCEDURES

U.S. Department of Health and Human Services, National Center for Health Statistics, 3700 East-West Highway, Hyattsville, Maryland 20782 (301) 436-8500; *Vital and Health Statistics; Advance Data, No. 296;* and unpublished data.

WOMEN - TEACHERS

U.S. Department of Education, National Center for Education Statistics,555 New Jersey Avenue, NW, Washington, D.C. 20208-5574 (202) 219-1828, http://nces.ed.gov; *Digest of Education Statistics*; and unpublished data.

U.S. Department of Labor, Bureau of Labor Statistics, Two Massachusetts Avenue, NE, Washington, D.C. 20212 (202) 691-5200, www.stats.bls.gov; *Employment and Earnings*; and unpublished data.

WOMEN - UNEMPLOYMENT

U.S. Department of Labor, Bureau of Labor Statistics, Two Massachusetts Avenue, NE, Washington, D.C. 20212 (202) 691-5200, www.stats.bls.gov; *Employment and Earnings; News, USDL 99-75;* Bulletin 2307; and unpublished data.

WOMEN - UNEMPLOYMENT - AGE

U.S. Department of Labor, Bureau of Labor Statistics, Two Massachusetts Avenue, NE, Washington, D.C. 20212 (202) 691-5200, www.stats.bls.gov; *Employment and Earnings;* and unpublished data.

WOMEN - UNEMPLOYMENT - REASON

U.S. Department of Labor, Bureau of Labor Statistics, Two Massachusetts Avenue, NE, Washington, D.C. 20212 (202) 691-5200, www.stats.bls.gov; *Employment and Earnings;* Bulletin 2307; and unpublished data..

WOMEN - UNION MEMBERSHIP

U.S. Department of Labor, Bureau of Labor Statistics, Two Massachusetts Avenue, NE, Washington, D.C. 20212 (202) 691-5200, www.stats.bls.gov; *Employment and Earnings.*

WOMEN - VOTER REGISTRATION AND TURNOUT

U.S. Department of Commerce, Bureau of the Census, Washington, D.C. 20233 (301) 457-4100, www.census.gov; *Current Population Reports.*

WOMEN - WEIGHT DISTRIBUTION

U.S. Department of Health and Human Services, National Center for Health Statistics, 3700 East-West Highway, Hyattsville, Maryland 20782 (301) 436-8500; unpublished data.

WOOD AND WOOD PRODUCTS - See LUMBER AND WOOD PRODUCTS

WOODPULP - See also PAPER AND PAPER PRODUCTS

WOODPULP - CONSUMPTION/OUTPUT

Statistical Office of the United Nations, Publishing Service, New York, New York 10017 (800) 253-9646; *Monthly Bulletin of Statistics.*

WOODPULP - FOREIGN TRADE

U.S. Department of Agriculture, Forest Service, Post Office Box 96090, Washington, D.C. 20090 (202) 205-8333, www.fs.fed.us; *Timber Demand and Technology Assessment*; and *Agricultural Statistics.*

WOODPULP - PRODUCER PRICE INDEXES

U.S. Department of Labor, Bureau of Labor Statistics, Two Massachusetts Avenue, NE, Washington, D.C. 20212 (202) 691-5200, www.stats.bls.gov; *Producer Price Indexes.*

WOODPULP - PRODUCTION

Statistical Office of the United Nations, Publishing Service, New York, New York 10017 (800) 253-9646; *Monthly Bulletin of Statistics.*

WORK STOPPAGES

U.S. Department of Labor, Bureau of Labor Statistics, Two Massachusetts Avenue, NE, Washington, D.C. 20212 (202) 691-5200, www.stats.bls.gov; *Compensation and Working Conditions.*

WORKERS - See EMPLOYMENT AND LABOR FORCE

WORKERS' COMPENSATION PROGRAM

Social Security Administration, 6400 Security Boulevard, Baltimore, Maryland 21235 (800) 772-1213; *Annual Statistical Supplement to the Social Security Bulletin; Social Security Bulletin;* and unpublished data.

U.S. Department of Health and Human Services, Health Care Financing Administration, 200 Independence Avenue, SW, Washington, D.C. 20201 (202) 245-6113; *Health Care Financing Review.*

WORKPLACE VIOLENCE

U.S. Department of Justice, Bureau of Justice Statistics, 810 Seventh Street, NW, 2nd Floor, Washington, D.C. 20531 (800) 732-3277, www.ojp.usdoj.gov/bjs; *Workplace Violence.*

WORKSTATIONS - See COMPUTERS

WORLD SUMMARY STATISTICS - ARMED FORCES PERSONNEL

U.S. Arms Control and Disarmament Agency, 320 Twenty-first Street, NW, Washington, D.C. 20451 (202) 647-2034; *World Military Expenditures and Arms Transfers.*

WORLD SUMMARY STATISTICS - COMPARATIVE DATA (AREA, POPULATION, ETC.)

Statistical Office of the United Nations, Publishing Service, New York, New York 10017 (800) 253-9646; *Statistical Yearbook;* and *Demographic Yearbook.*

United Nations Educational, Scientific and Cultural Organization (UNESCO), 7 Place de Fontenoy, F-75700 Paris, France (Telephone Number in U.S. (212) 963-5981); *Statistical Yearbook.*

U.S. Department of Commerce, Bureau of the Census, Washington, D.C. 20233 (301) 457-4100, www.census.gov; unpublished data from the International Data Base.

WORLD SUMMARY STATISTICS - ENERGY

Statistical Office of the United Nations, New York, New York 10017 (800) 253-9646; *Energy Statistics Yearbook.*

U.S. Department of Energy, Energy

Information Administration, 1000 Independence Avenue, SW, Washington, D.C. 20585 (202) 586-8800, www.eia.doe.gov; *International Energy Annual.*

WORLD SUMMARY STATISTICS - EXPORTS OF MANUFACTURES - UNITED STATES COMPARISON

U.S. Department of Commerce, International Trade Administration, Fourteenth Street between Constitution Avenue and E Street, NW, Washington, D.C. 20230 (202) 482-2185, www.ita.doc.gov; based on *United Nations Commodity Trade Statistics; Statistical Yearbook of the Republic of China*; and unpublished data.

WORLD SUMMARY STATISTICS - FARM COMMODITIES

U.S. Department of Agriculture, Economic Research Service,1800 M Street, NW, Washington, D.C. 20036 (202) 694-5050, www.ers.usda.gov; *Agricultural Outlook.*

U.S. Department of Agriculture, Foreign Agricultural Service, Fourteenth Street and Independence Avenue, SW, Washington, D.C. 20250 (202) 720-7115, www.fas.usda.gov; *Foreign Agricultural Commodity Circular Series.*

WORLD SUMMARY STATISTICS - MERCHANT VESSELS

Lloyd's Register of Shipping, 71 Fenchurch Street, London EC3, England; *World Fleet Statistics.*

U.S. Department of Transportation, Maritime Administration, 400 Seventh Street, SW, Washington, D.C. 20590 (202) 366-5807, www.marad.dot.gov; *Merchant Fleets of the World;* and unpublished data.

WORLD SUMMARY STATISTICS - MILITARY EXPENDITURES

U.S. Arms Control and Disarmament Agency, 320 Twenty-first Street, NW, Washington, D.C. 20451 (202) 647-8677; *World Military Expenditures and Arms Transfers.*

WORLD SUMMARY STATISTICS - MINERAL PRODUCTION

U.S. Department of Energy, Energy Information Administration, 1000 Independence Avenue, SW, Washington, D.C. 20585 (202) 586-8800, www.eia.doe.gov; *Coal Industry; Quarterly Coal Report; Annual Energy Review; Monthly Energy Review; International Energy Annual; Natural Gas Annual;* and unpublished data.

WORLD SUMMARY STATISTICS - POPULATION

Statistical Office of the United Nations, Publishing Service, New York, New York 10017 (800) 253-9646; *Monthly Bulletin of Statistics.*

U.S. Department of Commerce, Bureau of the Census, Washington, D.C. 20233 (301) 457-4100, www.census.gov; Internet site: http://www.census.gov/ipc/www/worldpop.html.

WORLD SUMMARY STATISTICS - RELIGION

Encyclopedia Britannica, Incorporated, 310 South Michigan Avenue, Chicago, Illinois 60604 (312) 347-7000; *Britannica Book of the Year.*

WRESTLING

National Collegiate Athletic Association, 700 West Washington Street, Indianapolis, Indiana 46206 (317) 917-6222; *1997-98 Participation Study.*

National Federation of High School Associations, Post Office Box 20626, Kansas City, Missouri 64195-0626 (816) 464-5400; *The 1997 High School Athletics Participation Survey.*

WYOMING - See also STATE DATA (FOR INDIVIDUAL STATES)

Wyoming - Primary Statistics Sources

Department of Administration and Information, Division of Economic Analysis, 327 East Emerson Building, Cheyenne, Wyoming 82002 (307) 777-7504; *The Equality State Almanac.*

Wyoming - State Data Centers

Survey Research Center, University of Wyoming, Post Office Box 3925, Laramie, Wyoming 82071, Mr. G. Fred Doll, (307) 766-2025.

Y

Yemen - National Statistical Office

Central Statistics Organization, Ministry of Planning and Development, Sana'a, Yemen.

Yemen - Primary Statistics Source

Central Statistics Organization, Ministry of Planning and Development, Sana'a, Yemen; *Statistical Yearbook.*

YEMEN - AGRICULTURE

Economic Commission for Western Asia, Post Office Box 27, Baghdad, Iraq; *Statistical Abstract of Western Asia.*

Economist Intelligence Unit, 111 West 57th Street, New York, New York 10019 (800) 938-4685; *Yemen Country Report.*

Euromonitor International, Inc., 122 South Michigan Avenue, Suite 1200, Chicago, Illinois 60603 (800) 577-EURO; *International Marketing Data and Statistics;* and *World Marketing Data and Statistics.*

Europa Publications Limited, 18 Bedford Square, London, WC1B 3JN, England; *The Europa World Year Book.*

Food and Agricultural Organization of the United Nations (FAO) Via delle Terme di Caracalla, 00100 Rome, Italy (Telephone Number in U.S. (202) 653-2400); *Production Yearbook; The State of Food and Agriculture;* and *Trade Yearbook.*

M.E. Sharpe, 80 Business Park Drive, Armonk, New York 10504 (800) 541-6563; *The Illustrated Book of World Rankings.*

St. Martin's Press, Inc., 175 Fifth Avenue, New York, New York 10010 (800) 221-7945; *The Statesman's Year-Book.*

Statistical Office of the United Nations, Publishing Service, New York, New York

10017 (800) 253-9646; *Statistical Yearbook.*

United Nations Conference on Trade and Development, Central Statistical Service, Palais des Nations, Geneva, Switzerland (Telephone in U.S. (800) 253-9646); *UNCTAD Commodity Yearbook.*

The World Bank, 1818 H Street, NW, Washington, D.C. 20433 (202) 477-1234; *World Development Indicators.*

YEMEN - AIRLINE SERVICE

Economic Commission for Western Asia, Post Office Box 27, Baghdad, Iraq; *Statistical Abstract of Western Asia.*

International Civil Aviation Organization, 999 University Street, Montreal, Quebec, Canada H3C 5H7 (514) 954-8219; *Civil Aviation Statistics of the World.*

M.E. Sharpe, 80 Business Park Drive, Armonk, New York 10504 (800) 541-6563; *The Illustrated Book of World Rankings.*

St. Martin's Press, Inc., 175 Fifth Avenue, New York, New York 10010 (800) 221-7945; *The Statesman's Year-Book.*

YEMEN - AIRPORTS

Central Intelligence Agency, Washington, D.C. 20505 (703) (482-1100, www.cia.gov; *The World Factbook.*

YEMEN - ALUMINUM PRODUCTION AND CONSUMPTION - See YEMEN - MINING AND MINERAL PRODUCTS

YEMEN - ANIMAL HEALTH

Food and Agricultural Organization of the United Nations (FAO), Via delle Terme di Caracalla, 00100 Rome, Italy (Telephone Number in U.S. (202) 653-2400); *Animal Health Yearbook.*

YEMEN - AREA AND DENSITY OF POPULATION

Central Intelligence Agency, Washington, D.C. 20505 (703) (482-1100, www.cia.gov; *The World Factbook.*

Economic Commission for Western Asia, Post Office Box 27, Baghdad, Iraq; *Statistical Abstract of Western Asia.*

Euromonitor International, Inc., 122 South Michigan Avenue, Suite 1200, Chicago, Illinois 60603 (800) 577-EURO; *International Marketing Data and Statistics;* and *The World Economic Factbook.*

Europa Publications Limited, 18 Bedford Square, London, WC1B 3JN, England; *The Europa World Year Book.*

Food and Agricultural Organization of the United Nations (FAO) Via delle Terme di Caracalla, 00100 Rome, Italy (Telephone Number in U.S. (202) 653-2400); *The State of Food and Agriculture.*

M.E. Sharpe, 80 Business Park Drive, Armonk, New York 10504 (800) 541-6563; *The Illustrated Book of World Rankings.*

St. Martin's Press, Inc., 175 Fifth Avenue, New York, New York 10010 (800) 221-7945; *The Statesman's Year-Book.*

Statistical Office of the United Nations, Publishing Service, New York, New York 10017 (800) 253-9646; *Statistical Yearbook.*

United Nations Educational, Scientific and Cultural Organization (UNESCO), 7 Place de Fontenoy, F-75700 Paris, France (Telephone Number in U.S. (212) 963-5981); *Statistical Yearbook.*

The World Bank, 1818 H Street, NW, Washington, D.C. 20433 (202) 477-1234; *World Development Report.*

YEMEN - ARMS EXPORTS AND IMPORTS - See YEMEN - MILITARY

YEMEN - BALANCE OF PAYMENTS

Economic Commission for Western Asia, Post Office Box 27, Baghdad, Iraq;

Statistical Abstract of Western Asia.

The Economist Intelligence Unit, 111 West 57th Street, New York, New York 10019 (800) 938-4685; *The World Market Atlas.*

International Monetary Fund, 700 Nineteenth Street, NW, Washington, D.C. 20431 (202) 623-7000; *Balance of Payments Yearbook.*

United Nations Conference on Trade and Development (UNCTAD), New York, New York 10017 (800) 253-9646; *Handbook of International Trade and Development Statistics.*

The World Bank, 1818 H Street, NW, Washington, D.C. 20433 (202) 477-1234; *World Development Report;* and *World Development Indicators.*

YEMEN - BALANCE OF TRADE

Economic Commission for Western Asia, Post Office Box 27, Baghdad, Iraq; *Statistical Abstract of Western Asia.*

YEMEN - BANKING

Economic Commission for Western Asia, Post Office Box 27, Baghdad, Iraq; *Statistical Abstract of Western Asia.*

Euromonitor International, Inc., 122 South Michigan Avenue, Suite 1200, Chicago, Illinois 60603 (800) 577-EURO; *World Marketing Data and Statistics.*

International Monetary Fund, 700 Nineteenth Street, NW, Washington, D.C. 20431 (202) 623-7000; *International Financial Statistics.*

M.E. Sharpe, 80 Business Park Drive, Armonk, New York 10504 (800) 541-6563; *The Illustrated Book of World Rankings.*

YEMEN - BARLEY PRODUCTION - See YEMEN - CROPS

YEMEN - BEER PRODUCTION - See YEMEN - BEVERAGES

YEMEN - BEVERAGES

M.E. Sharpe, 80 Business Park Drive, Armonk, New York 10504 (800) 541-6563; *The Illustrated Book of World Rankings.*

YEMEN - BIRTH RATES

Central Intelligence Agency, Washington, D.C. 20505 (703) (482-1100, www.cia.gov; *The World Factbook.*

Euromonitor International, Inc., 122 South Michigan Avenue, Suite 1200, Chicago, Illinois 60603 (800) 577-EURO; *International Marketing Data and Statistics;*

and *The World Economic Factbook.*

M.E. Sharpe, 80 Business Park Drive, Armonk, New York 10504 (800) 541-6563; *The Illustrated Book of World Rankings.*

Statistical Office of the United Nations, Publishing Service, New York, New York 10017 (800) 253-9646; *Demographic Yearbook;* and *Statistical Yearbook.*

The World Bank, 1818 H Street, NW, Washington, D.C. 20433 (202) 477-1234; *World Development Indicators.*

YEMEN - BROADCASTING

Billboard Limited, P.O. Box 9027, 1006 AA Amsterdam, The Netherlands (Telephone Number in U.S. (212) 764-7300); *World Radio TV Handbook.*

Central Intelligence Agency, Washington, D.C. 20505 (703) (482-1100, www.cia.gov; *The World Factbook.*

Euromonitor International, Inc., 122 South Michigan Avenue, Suite 1200, Chicago, Illinois 60603 (800) 577-EURO; *World Marketing Data and Statistics.*

M.E. Sharpe, 80 Business Park Drive, Armonk, New York 10504 (800) 541-6563; *The Illustrated Book of World Rankings.*

St. Martin's Press, Inc., 175 Fifth Avenue, New York, New York 10010 (800) 221-7945; *The Statesman's Year-Book.*

YEMEN - BUDGET

Central Intelligence Agency, Washington, D.C. 20505 (703) (482-1100, www.cia.gov; *The World Factbook.*

YEMEN - BUTTER PRODUCTION - See YEMEN - DAIRY PRODUCTS

YEMEN - CALORIE SUPPLY

Food and Agricultural Organization of the United Nations (FAO) Via delle Terme di Caracalla, 00100 Rome, Italy (Telephone Number in U.S. (202) 653-2400); *The State of Food and Agriculture.*

YEMEN - CATTLE - See YEMEN - LIVESTOCK AND POULTRY

YEMEN - CEMENT PRODUCTION - See YEMEN - MINING AND MINERAL PRODUCTS

YEMEN - CHEESE PRODUCTION AND CONSUMPTION - See YEMEN -DAIRY PRODUCTS

YEMEN - CHEMICAL (ORGANIC) PRODUCTION - See YEMEN - MINING AND MINERAL PRODUCTS

YEMEN - CHICKENS - See YEMEN - LIVESTOCK AND POULTRY

YEMEN - CIGARETTE PRODUCTION - See YEMEN - TOBACCO PRODUCTION

YEMEN - CLIMATE

M.E. Sharpe, 80 Business Park Drive, Armonk, New York 10504 (800) 541-6563; *The Illustrated Book of World Rankings.*

St. Martin's Press, Inc., 175 Fifth Avenue, New York, New York 10010 (800) 221-7945; *The Statesman's Year-Book.*

YEMEN - COAL PRODUCTION - See YEMEN - MINING AND MINERAL PRODUCTS

YEMEN - COFFEE - See YEMEN - CROPS

YEMEN - COMMERCE

St. Martin's Press, Inc., 175 Fifth Avenue, New York, New York 10010 (800) 221-7945; *The Statesman's Year-Book.*

YEMEN - COMMUNICATIONS - See YEMEN - TRANSPORTATION AND COMMUNICATIONS

YEMEN - CONSTRUCTION INDUSTRY

M.E. Sharpe, 80 Business Park Drive, Armonk, New York 10504 (800) 541-6563; *The Illustrated Book of World Rankings.*

YEMEN - CONSUMER PRICE INDEX

Statistical Office of the United Nations, Publishing Service, New York, New York 10017 (800) 253-9646; *Statistical Yearbook.*

YEMEN - CONSUMER PRICES

Euromonitor International, Inc., 122 South Michigan Avenue, Suite 1200, Chicago, Illinois 60603 (800) 577-EURO; *World Marketing Data and Statistics.*

International Labour Office, I.L.O. Publications, 1828 L Street, NW, Suite 801, Washington, D.C. 20036 (301) 638-3152; *Yearbook of Labour Statistics.*

International Monetary Fund, 700 Nineteenth Street, NW, Washington, D.C. 20431 (202) 623-7000; *International Financial Statistics.*

YEMEN - CONSUMPTION

The World Bank, 1818 H Street, NW, Washington, D.C. 20433 (202) 477-1234; *World Development Report.*

YEMEN - COPPER PRODUCTION AND CONSUMPTION - See YEMEN - MINING AND MINERAL PRODUCTS

YEMEN - CORN PRODUCTION - See
YEMEN - CROPS

YEMEN - CORPORATE TAXES - See
YEMEN - TAXATION

YEMEN - COTTON PRODUCTION - See
YEMEN - CROPS

YEMEN - CROPS

Europa Publications Limited, 18
Bedford Square, London, WC1B 3JN,
England; *The Europa World Year Book.*

Food and Agricultural Organization of
the United Nations (FAO) Via delle Terme
di Caracalla, 00100 Rome, Italy (Telephone
Number in U.S. (202) 653-2400); *The State
of Food and Agriculture.*

M.E. Sharpe, 80 Business Park Drive,
Armonk, New York 10504 (800) 541-6563;
The Illustrated Book of World Rankings.

St. Martin's Press, Inc., 175 Fifth
Avenue, New York, New York 10010 (800)
221-7945; *The Statesman's Year-Book.*

Statistical Office of the United Nations,
Publishing Service, New York, New York
10017 (800) 253-9646; *Statistical Yearbook.*

United Nations Conference on Trade
and Development, Central Statistical
Service, Palais des Nations, Geneva,
Switzerland (Telephone in U.S. (800) 253-
9646); *UNCTAD Commodity Yearbook.*

YEMEN - CUSTOMS DUTIES

St. Martin's Press, Inc., 175 Fifth
Avenue, New York, New York 10010 (800)
221-7945; *The Statesman's Year-Book.*

YEMEN - DAIRY PRODUCTS

Economic Commission for Western
Asia, Post Office Box 27, Baghdad, Iraq;
Statistical Abstract of Western Asia.

Europa Publications Limited, 18
Bedford Square, London, WC1B 3JN,
England; *The Europa World Year Book.*

Food and Agricultural Organization of
the United Nations (FAO) Via delle Terme
di Caracalla, 00100 Rome, Italy (Telephone
Number in U.S. (202) 653-2400); *The State
of Food and Agriculture.*

M.E. Sharpe, 80 Business Park Drive,
Armonk, New York 10504 (800) 541-6563;
The Illustrated Book of World Rankings.

St. Martin's Press, Inc., 175 Fifth
Avenue, New York, New York 10010 (800)
221-7945; *The Statesman's Year-Book.*

Statistical Office of the United Nations,
Publishing Service, New York, New York

10017 (800) 253-9646; *Statistical Yearbook.*

YEMEN - DEATH RATES - See YEMEN -
MORTALITY

YEMEN - DEFENSE EXPENDITURES - See
YEMEN - MILITARY

YEMEN - DEMOGRAPHY

The Economist Intelligence Unit, 111
West 57th Street, New York, New York
10019 (800) 938-4685; *The World Market
Atlas.*

Euromonitor International, Inc., 122
South Michigan Avenue, Suite 1200,
Chicago, Illinois 60603 (800) 577-EURO;
*International Marketing Data and Statistics;
World Marketing Data and Statistics;* and
The World Economic Factbook.

M.E. Sharpe, 80 Business Park Drive,
Armonk, New York 10504 (800) 541-6563;
The Illustrated Book of World Rankings.

Statistical Office of the United Nations,
Publishing Service, New York, New York
10017 (800) 253-9646; *Human
Development Report.*

YEMEN - DEVELOPMENT ASSISTANCE

Statistical Office of the United Nations,
Publishing Service, New York, New York
10017 (800) 253-9646; *Statistical Yearbook.*

YEMEN - DIAMOND PRODUCTION - See
YEMEN - MINING AND MINERAL
PRODUCTS

YEMEN - DISEASES - See YEMEN - HEALTH

YEMEN - DIVORCE RATES

M.E. Sharpe, 80 Business Park Drive,
Armonk, New York 10504 (800) 541-6563;
The Illustrated Book of World Rankings.

Statistical Office of the United Nations,
Publishing Service, New York, New York
10017 (800) 253-9646; *Demographic
Yearbook.*

YEMEN - ECONOMY

Central Intelligence Agency,
Washington, D.C. 20505 (703) (482-1100,
www.cia.gov; *The World Factbook.*

Economist Intelligence Unit, 111 West
57th Street, New York, New York 10019
(800) 938-4685; *Yemen Country Report.*

Euromonitor International, Inc., 122
South Michigan Avenue, Suite 1200,
Chicago, Illinois 60603 (800) 577-EURO;
*International Marketing Data and Statistics;
World Marketing Data and Statistics;* and
The World Economic Factbook.

Europa Publications Limited, 18
Bedford Square, London, WC1B 3JN,
England; *The Europa World Year Book.*

M.E. Sharpe, 80 Business Park Drive,
Armonk, New York 10504 (800) 541-6563;
The Illustrated Book of World Rankings.

St. Martin's Press, Inc., 175 Fifth
Avenue, New York, New York 10010 (800)
221-7945; *The Statesman's Year-Book.*

Statistical Office of the United Nations,
Publishing Service, New York, New York
10017 (800) 253-9646; *World Statistics
Pocketbook.*

The World Bank, 1818 H Street, NW,
Washington, D.C. 20433 (202) 477-1234;
The World Bank Atlas; and *World
Development Report.*

YEMEN - EDUCATION

Economic Commission for Western
Asia, Post Office Box 27, Baghdad, Iraq;
Statistical Abstract of Western Asia.

The Economist Intelligence Unit, 111
West 57th Street, New York, New York
10019 (800) 938-4685; *The World Market
Atlas.*

Euromonitor International, Inc., 122
South Michigan Avenue, Suite 1200,
Chicago, Illinois 60603 (800) 577-EURO;
International Marketing Data and Statistics;
and *World Marketing Data and Statistics.*

M.E. Sharpe, 80 Business Park Drive,
Armonk, New York 10504 (800) 541-6563;
The Illustrated Book of World Rankings.

St. Martin's Press, Inc., 175 Fifth
Avenue, New York, New York 10010 (800)
221-7945; *The Statesman's Year-Book.*

Statistical Office of the United Nations,
Publishing Service, New York, New York
10017 (800) 253-9646; *Human
Development Report.*

United Nations Educational, Scientific
and Cultural Organization (UNESCO), 7
Place de Fontenoy, F-75700 Paris, France
(Telephone Number in U.S. (212) 963-
5981); *Statistical Yearbook.*

The World Bank, 1818 H Street, NW,
Washington, D.C. 20433 (202) 477-1234;
World Development Report; and *World
Development Indicators.*

YEMEN - EGG PRODUCTION AND
CONSUMPTION - See YEMEN - DAIRY
PRODUCTS

YEMEN - ELECTRICITY

Central Intelligence Agency,
Washington, D.C. 20505 (703) (482-1100,

www.cia.gov; *The World Factbook.*

M.E. Sharpe, 80 Business Park Drive, Armonk, New York 10504 (800) 541-6563; *The Illustrated Book of World Rankings.*

Penn Well Publishing Company, 1421 South Sheridan Road, P.O. Box 1260, Tulsa, Oklahoma 74101 (800) 752-9764; *International Energy Statistics Sourcebook.*

St. Martin's Press, Inc., 175 Fifth Avenue, New York, New York 10010 (800) 221-7945; *The Statesman's Year-Book.*

Statistical Office of the United Nations, Publishing Service, New York, New York 10017 (800) 253-9646; *Human Development Report;* and *Statistical Yearbook.*

YEMEN - EMPLOYMENT

Economic Commission for Western Asia, Post Office Box 27, Baghdad, Iraq; *Statistical Abstract of Western Asia.*

Euromonitor International, Inc., 122 South Michigan Avenue, Suite 1200, Chicago, Illinois 60603 (800) 577-EURO; *International Marketing Data and Statistics.*

International Labour Office, I.L.O. Publications, 1828 L Street, NW, Suite 801, Washington, D.C. 20036 (301) 638-3152; *Yearbook of Labour Statistics.*

M.E. Sharpe, 80 Business Park Drive, Armonk, New York 10504 (800) 541-6563; *The Illustrated Book of World Rankings.*

Statistical Office of the United Nations, Publishing Service, New York, New York 10017 (800) 253-9646; *Bulletin of Industrial Statistics for the Arab Countries;* and *Statistical Yearbook.*

YEMEN - ENERGY

Economic Commission for Western Asia, Post Office Box 27, Baghdad, Iraq; *Statistical Abstract of Western Asia.*

Euromonitor International, Inc., 122 South Michigan Avenue, Suite 1200, Chicago, Illinois 60603 (800) 577-EURO; *International Marketing Data and Statistics; World Marketing Data and Statistics;* and *The World Economic Factbook.*

Food and Agricultural Organization of the United Nations (FAO) Via delle Terme di Caracalla, 00100 Rome, Italy (Telephone Number in U.S. (202) 653-2400); *The State of Food and Agriculture.*

M.E. Sharpe, 80 Business Park Drive, Armonk, New York 10504 (800) 541-6563; *The Illustrated Book of World Rankings.*

Penn Well Publishing Company, 1421

South Sheridan Road, P.O. Box 1260, Tulsa, Oklahoma 74101 (800) 752-9764; *International Energy Statistics Sourcebook.*

St. Martin's Press, Inc., 175 Fifth Avenue, New York, New York 10010 (800) 221-7945; *The Statesman's Year-Book.*

Statistical Office of the United Nations, Publishing Service, New York, New York 10017 (800) 253-9646; *Energy Statistics Yearbook; Human Development Report; Statistical Yearbook;* and *World Statistics Pocketbook.*

The World Bank, 1818 H Street, NW, Washington, D.C. 20433 (202) 477-1234; *The World Bank Atlas;* and *World Development Report.*

YEMEN - ENVIRONMENT

Economist Intelligence Unit, 111 West 57th Street, New York, New York 10019 (800) 938-4685; *Yemen Country Report.*

Statistical Office of the United Nations, Publishing Service, New York, New York 10017 (800) 253-9646; *World Statistics Pocketbook.*

YEMEN - EXCHANGE RATES

Central Intelligence Agency, Washington, D.C. 20505 (703) (482-1100, www.cia.gov; *The World Factbook.*

Euromonitor International, Inc., 122 South Michigan Avenue, Suite 1200, Chicago, Illinois 60603 (800) 577-EURO; *International Marketing Data and Statistics;* and *The World Economic Factbook.*

Europa Publications Limited, 18 Bedford Square, London, WC1B 3JN, England; *The Europa World Year Book.*

International Civil Aviation Organization, 999 University Street, Montreal, Quebec, Canada H3C 5H7 (514) 954-8219; *Civil Aviation Statistics of the World.*

International Monetary Fund, 700 Nineteenth Street, NW, Washington, D.C. 20431 (202) 623-7000; *International Financial Statistics.*

Statistical Office of the United Nations, Publishing Service, New York, New York 10017 (800) 253-9646; *Bulletin of Industrial Statistics for the Arab Countries; Statistical Yearbook;* and *World Statistics Pocketbook.*

YEMEN - EXPORTS

Central Intelligence Agency, Washington, D.C. 20505 (703) (482-1100, www.cia.gov; *The World Factbook.*

Economic Commission for Western

Asia, Post Office Box 27, Baghdad, Iraq; *Statistical Abstract of Western Asia.*

The Economist Intelligence Unit, 111 West 57th Street, New York, New York 10019 (800) 938-4685; *Yemen Country Report;* and *The World Market Atlas.*

Euromonitor International, Inc., 122 South Michigan Avenue, Suite 1200, Chicago, Illinois 60603 (800) 577-EURO; *International Marketing Data and Statistics;* and *The World Economic Factbook.*

Food and Agricultural Organization of the United Nations (FAO) Via delle Terme di Caracalla, 00100 Rome, Italy (Telephone Number in U.S. (202) 653-2400); *The State of Food and Agriculture.*

International Monetary Fund, 700 Nineteenth Street, NW, Washington, D.C. 20431 (202) 623-7000; *Direction of Trade Statistics.*

St. Martin's Press, Inc., 175 Fifth Avenue, New York, New York 10010 (800) 221-7945; *The Statesman's Year-Book.*

Statistical Office of the United Nations, Publishing Service, New York, New York 10017 (800) 253-9646; *Bulletin of Industrial Statistics for the Arab Countries.*

United Nations Conference on Trade and Development (UNCTAD), New York, New York 10017 (800) 253-9646; *Handbook of International Trade and Development Statistics.*

The World Bank, 1818 H Street, NW, Washington, D.C. 20433 (202) 477-1234; *World Development Report;* and *World Development Indicators.*

YEMEN - EXPORTS BY COMMODITIES

Economic Commission for Western Asia, Post Office Box 27, Baghdad, Iraq; *Statistical Abstract of Western Asia.*

YEMEN - EXTERNAL INDEBTEDNESS

The World Bank, 1818 H Street, NW, Washington, D.C. 20433 (202) 477-1234; *World Development Report;* and *World Development Indicators.*

YEMEN - EXTERNAL TRADE

Euromonitor International, Inc., 122 South Michigan Avenue, Suite 1200, Chicago, Illinois 60603 (800) 577-EURO; *World Marketing Data and Statistics.*

Food and Agricultural Organization of the United Nations (FAO) Via delle Terme di Caracalla, 00100 Rome, Italy (Telephone Number in U.S. (202) 653-2400); *The State of Food and Agriculture.*

Statistical Office of the United Nations, Publishing Service, New York, New York 10017 (800) 253-9646; *Statistical Yearbook.*

YEMEN - FARM CROPS - See YEMEN - CROPS

YEMEN - FERTILITY RATES

Central Intelligence Agency, Washington, D.C. 20505 (703) (482-1100, www.cia.gov; *The World Factbook.*

M.E. Sharpe, 80 Business Park Drive, Armonk, New York 10504 (800) 541-6563; *The Illustrated Book of World Rankings.*

Statistical Office of the United Nations, Publishing Service, New York, New York 10017 (800) 253-9646; *Human Development Report.*

The World Bank, 1818 H Street, NW, Washington, D.C. 20433 (202) 477-1234; *The World Bank Atlas; World Development Report;* and *World Development Indicators.*

YEMEN - FERTILIZER

Food and Agricultural Organization of the United Nations (FAO), Via delle Terme di Caracalla, 00100 Rome, Italy (Telephone Number in U.S. (202) 653-2400); *Fertilizer Yearbook;* and *The State of Food and Agriculture.*

Statistical Office of the United Nations, Publishing Service, New York, New York 10017 (800) 253-9646; *Statistical Yearbook.*

YEMEN - FETAL MORTALITY - See YEMEN - MORTALITY

YEMEN - FINANCE

Economic Commission for Western Asia, Post Office Box 27, Baghdad, Iraq; *Statistical Abstract of Western Asia.*

Economist Intelligence Unit, 111 West 57th Street, New York, New York 10019 (800) 938-4685; *Yemen Country Report.*

Europa Publications Limited, 18 Bedford Square, London, WC1B 3JN, England; *The Europa World Year Book.*

International Monetary Fund, 700 Nineteenth Street, NW, Washington, D.C. 20431 (202) 623-7000; *International Financial Statistics.*

M.E. Sharpe, 80 Business Park Drive, Armonk, New York 10504 (800) 541-6563; *The Illustrated Book of World Rankings.*

St. Martin's Press, Inc., 175 Fifth Avenue, New York, New York 10010 (800) 221-7945; *The Statesman's Year-Book.*

YEMEN - FISHERIES

Economic Commission for Western Asia, Post Office Box 27, Baghdad, Iraq; *Statistical Abstract of Western Asia.*

Europa Publications Limited, 18 Bedford Square, London, WC1B 3JN, England; *The Europa World Year Book.*

Food and Agricultural Organization of the United Nations (FAO) Via delle Terme di Caracalla, 00100 Rome, Italy (Telephone Number in U.S. (202) 653-2400); *The State of Food and Agriculture;* and *Yearbook of Fishery Statistics.*

M.E. Sharpe, 80 Business Park Drive, Armonk, New York 10504 (800) 541-6563; *The Illustrated Book of World Rankings.*

St. Martin's Press, Inc., 175 Fifth Avenue, New York, New York 10010 (800) 221-7945; *The Statesman's Year-Book.*

Statistical Office of the United Nations, Publishing Service, New York, New York 10017 (800) 253-9646; *Statistical Yearbook.*

United Nations Conference on Trade and Development, Central Statistical Service, Palais des Nations, Geneva, Switzerland (Telephone in U.S. (800) 253-9646); *UNCTAD Commodity Yearbook.*

YEMEN - FOOD

Food and Agricultural Organization of the United Nations (FAO) Via delle Terme di Caracalla, 00100 Rome, Italy (Telephone Number in U.S. (202) 653-2400); *The State of Food and Agriculture.*

Statistical Office of the United Nations, Publishing Service, New York, New York 10017 (800) 253-9646; *Human Development Report.*

United Nations Conference on Trade and Development, Central Statistical Service, Palais des Nations, Geneva, Switzerland (Telephone in U.S. (800) 253-9646); *UNCTAD Commodity Yearbook.*

YEMEN - FOREIGN DEBT

St. Martin's Press, Inc., 175 Fifth Avenue, New York, New York 10010 (800) 221-7945; *The Statesman's Year-Book.*

YEMEN - FOREIGN TRADE

Economic Commission for Western Asia, Post Office Box 27, Baghdad, Iraq; *Statistical Abstract of Western Asia.*

Economist Intelligence Unit, 111 West 57th Street, New York, New York 10019 (800) 938-4685; *Yemen Country Report.*

Euromonitor International, Inc., 122 South Michigan Avenue, Suite 1200, Chicago, Illinois 60603 (800) 577-EURO;

International Marketing Data and Statistics; and *The World Economic Factbook.*

Europa Publications Limited, 18 Bedford Square, London, WC1B 3JN, England; *The Europa World Year Book.*

Food and Agricultural Organization of the United Nations (FAO) Via delle Terme di Caracalla, 00100 Rome, Italy (Telephone Number in U.S. (202) 653-2400); *The State of Food and Agriculture.*

International Monetary Fund, 700 Nineteenth Street, NW, Washington, D.C. 20431 (202) 623-7000; *International Financial Statistics.*

M.E. Sharpe, 80 Business Park Drive, Armonk, New York 10504 (800) 541-6563; *The Illustrated Book of World Rankings.*

St. Martin's Press, Inc., 175 Fifth Avenue, New York, New York 10010 (800) 221-7945; *The Statesman's Year-Book.*

Statistical Office of the United Nations, Publishing Service, New York, New York 10017 (800) 253-9646; *Bulletin of Industrial Statistics for the Arab Countries; International Trade Statistics Yearbook;* and *Statistical Yearbook.*

United Nations Conference on Trade and Development, Central Statistical Service, Palais des Nations, Geneva, Switzerland (Telephone in U.S. (800) 253-9646); *UNCTAD Commodity Yearbook.*

The World Bank, 1818 H Street, NW, Washington, D.C. 20433 (202) 477-1234; *World Development Report;* and *World Development Indicators.*

YEMEN - FORESTRY AND FOREST PRODUCTS

Food and Agricultural Organization of the United Nations (FAO) Via delle Terme di Caracalla, 00100 Rome, Italy (Telephone Number in U.S. (202) 653-2400); *The State of Food and Agriculture;* and *Yearbook of Forest Products.*

M.E. Sharpe, 80 Business Park Drive, Armonk, New York 10504 (800) 541-6563; *The Illustrated Book of World Rankings.*

Statistical Office of the United Nations, Publishing Service, New York, New York 10017 (800) 253-9646; *Statistical Yearbook.*

United Nations Conference on Trade and Development, Central Statistical Service, Palais des Nations, Geneva, Switzerland (Telephone in U.S. (800) 253-9646); *UNCTAD Commodity Yearbook.*

United Nations Educational, Scientific and Cultural Organization (UNESCO), 7 Place de Fontenoy, F-75700 Paris, France

(Telephone Number in U.S. (212) 963-5981); *Statistical Yearbook.*

The World Bank, 1818 H Street, NW, Washington, D.C. 20433 (202) 477-1234; *World Development Report.*

YEMEN - GAS PRODUCTION - See YEMEN - MINING AND MINERAL PRODUCTS

YEMEN - GENERAL INDUSTRIAL STATISTICS - See YEMEN - INDUSTRY

YEMEN - GENERAL MORTALITY - See YEMEN - MORTALITY

YEMEN - GEOGRAPHIC DATA

M.E. Sharpe, 80 Business Park Drive, Armonk, New York 10504 (800) 541-6563; *The Illustrated Book of World Rankings.*

YEMEN - GOATS - See YEMEN - LIVESTOCK AND POULTRY

YEMEN - GOLD HOLDINGS

International Monetary Fund, 700 Nineteenth Street, NW, Washington, D.C. 20431 (202) 623-7000; *International Financial Statistics.*

Statistical Office of the United Nations, Publishing Service, New York, New York 10017 (800) 253-9646; *Statistical Yearbook.*

The World Bank, 1818 H Street, NW, Washington, D.C. 20433 (202) 477-1234; *World Development Indicators.*

YEMEN - GOLD PRODUCTION AND CONSUMPTION - See YEMEN - MINING AND MINERAL PRODUCTS

YEMEN - GOVERNMENT

Central Intelligence Agency, Washington, D.C. 20505 (703) (482-1100, www.cia.gov; *The World Factbook.*

Economic Commission for Western Asia, Post Office Box 27, Baghdad, Iraq; *Statistical Abstract of Western Asia.*

Europa Publications Limited, 18 Bedford Square, London, WC1B 3JN, England; *The Europa World Year Book.*

International Monetary Fund, 700 Nineteenth Street, NW, Washington, D.C. 20431 (202) 623-7000; *International Financial Statistics.*

St. Martin's Press, Inc., 175 Fifth Avenue, New York, New York 10010 (800) 221-7945; *The Statesman's Year-Book.*

Statistical Office of the United Nations, Publishing Service, New York, New York 10017 (800) 253-9646; *National Accounts Statistics.*

The World Bank, 1818 H Street, NW, Washington, D.C. 20433 (202) 477-1234; *World Development Report;* and *World Development Indicators.*

YEMEN - GRAIN PRODUCTION - See YEMEN - CROPS

YEMEN - GROSS DOMESTIC PRODUCT

Economic Commission for Western Asia, Post Office Box 27, Baghdad, Iraq; *Statistical Abstract of Western Asia.*

The Economist Intelligence Unit, 111 West 57th Street, New York, New York 10019 (800) 938-4685; *Yemen Country Report;* and *The World Market Atlas.*

Euromonitor International, Inc., 122 South Michigan Avenue, Suite 1200, Chicago, Illinois 60603 (800) 577-EURO; *International Marketing Data and Statistics;* and *The World Economic Factbook.*

Europa Publications Limited, 18 Bedford Square, London, WC1B 3JN, England; *The Europa World Year Book.*

M.E. Sharpe, 80 Business Park Drive, Armonk, New York 10504 (800) 541-6563; *The Illustrated Book of World Rankings.*

Statistical Office of the United Nations, Publishing Service, New York, New York 10017 (800) 253-9646; *Bulletin of Industrial Statistics for the Arab Countries; Human Development Report; National Accounts Statistics;* and *Statistical Yearbook.*

U.S. Arms Control and Disarmament Agency, 320 Twenty-first Street, NW, Washington, D.C. 20451 (202) 647-8677; *World Military Expenditures and Arms Transfers.*

The World Bank, 1818 H Street, NW, Washington, D.C. 20433 (202) 477-1234; *World Development Report;* and *World Development Indicators.*

YEMEN - GROSS NATIONAL PRODUCT

Euromonitor International, Inc., 122 South Michigan Avenue, Suite 1200, Chicago, Illinois 60603 (800) 577-EURO; *International Marketing Data and Statistics.*

Europa Publications Limited, 18 Bedford Square, London, WC1B 3JN, England; *The Europa World Year Book.*

St. Martin's Press, Inc., 175 Fifth Avenue, New York, New York 10010 (800) 221-7945; *The Statesman's Year-Book.*

The World Bank, 1818 H Street, NW, Washington, D.C. 20433 (202) 477-1234; *The World Bank Atlas; World Development Report;* and *World Development Indicators.*

YEMEN - HEALTH

Economic Commission for Western Asia, Post Office Box 27, Baghdad, Iraq; *Statistical Abstract of Western Asia.*

Euromonitor International, Inc., 122 South Michigan Avenue, Suite 1200, Chicago, Illinois 60603 (800) 577-EURO; *World Marketing Data and Statistics.*

M.E. Sharpe, 80 Business Park Drive, Armonk, New York 10504 (800) 541-6563; *The Illustrated Book of World Rankings.*

St. Martin's Press, Inc., 175 Fifth Avenue, New York, New York 10010 (800) 221-7945; *The Statesman's Year-Book.*

Statistical Office of the United Nations, Publishing Service, New York, New York 10017 (800) 253-9646; *Human Development Report;* and *Statistical Yearbook.*

United Nations Children's Fund (UNICEF), 3 United Nations Plaza, New York, New York 10017 (800) 253-9646; *State of the World's Children.*

The World Bank, 1818 H Street, NW, Washington, D.C. 20433 (202) 477-1234; *World Development Report.*

World Health Organization, Office of Publications, Avenue Appia, CH-1211 Geneva, 27, Switzerland (Telephone Number in U.S. (518) 436-9686); *World Health Statistics: Vital Statistics and Causes of Death.*

YEMEN - HIGHWAYS

Central Intelligence Agency, Washington, D.C. 20505 (703) (482-1100, www.cia.gov; *The World Factbook.*

Economic Commission for Western Asia, Post Office Box 27, Baghdad, Iraq; *Statistical Abstract of Western Asia.*

International Road Federation, 2600 Virginia Avenue, NW, Washington, D.C. 20037 (202) 338-4641; *World Road Statistics.*

St. Martin's Press, Inc., 175 Fifth Avenue, New York, New York 10010 (800) 221-7945; *The Statesman's Year-Book.*

YEMEN - HORSES - See YEMEN - LIVESTOCK AND POULTRY

YEMEN - HOURS OF WORK - See YEMEN - EMPLOYMENT

YEMEN - HOUSING AND HOUSING UNITS

Euromonitor International, Inc., 122 South Michigan Avenue, Suite 1200, Chicago, Illinois 60603 (800) 577-EURO;

World Marketing Data and Statistics.

M.E. Sharpe, 80 Business Park Drive, Armonk, New York 10504 (800) 541-6563; *The Illustrated Book of World Rankings.*

YEMEN - ILLITERATE POPULATION

Central Intelligence Agency, Washington, D.C. 20505 (703) (482-1100, www.cia.gov; *The World Factbook.*

The Economist Intelligence Unit, 111 West 57th Street, New York, New York 10019 (800) 938-4685; *The World Market Atlas.*

Euromonitor International, Inc., 122 South Michigan Avenue, Suite 1200, Chicago, Illinois 60603 (800) 577-EURO; *The World Economic Factbook.*

Statistical Office of the United Nations, Publishing Service, New York, New York 10017 (800) 253-9646; *Human Development Report.*

United Nations Educational, Scientific and Cultural Organization (UNESCO), 7 Place de Fontenoy, F-75700 Paris, France (Telephone Number in U.S. (212) 963-5981); *Statistical Yearbook.*

YEMEN - IMPORTS

Central Intelligence Agency, Washington, D.C. 20505 (703) (482-1100, www.cia.gov; *The World Factbook.*

Economic Commission for Western Asia, Post Office Box 27, Baghdad, Iraq; *Statistical Abstract of Western Asia.*

The Economist Intelligence Unit, 111 West 57th Street, New York, New York 10019 (800) 938-4685; *Yemen Country Report;* and *The World Market Atlas.*

Euromonitor International, Inc., 122 South Michigan Avenue, Suite 1200, Chicago, Illinois 60603 (800) 577-EURO; *International Marketing Data and Statistics;* and *The World Economic Factbook.*

Food and Agricultural Organization of the United Nations (FAO) Via delle Terme di Caracalla, 00100 Rome, Italy (Telephone Number in U.S. (202) 653-2400); *The State of Food and Agriculture.*

International Monetary Fund, 700 Nineteenth Street, NW, Washington, D.C. 20431 (202) 623-7000; *Direction of Trade Statistics.*

St. Martin's Press, Inc., 175 Fifth Avenue, New York, New York 10010 (800) 221-7945; *The Statesman's Year-Book.*

Statistical Office of the United Nations, Publishing Service, New York, New York

10017 (800) 253-9646; *Bulletin of Industrial Statistics for the Arab Countries.*

United Nations Conference on Trade and Development (UNCTAD), New York, New York 10017 (800) 253-9646; *Handbook of International Trade and Development Statistics.*

The World Bank, 1818 H Street, NW, Washington, D.C. 20433 (202) 477-1234; *World Development Report;* and *World Development Indicators.*

YEMEN - INDUSTRY

Central Intelligence Agency, Washington, D.C. 20505 (703) (482-1100, www.cia.gov; *The World Factbook.*

Economist Intelligence Unit, 111 West 57th Street, New York, New York 10019 (800) 938-4685; *Yemen Country Report.*

Euromonitor International, Inc., 122 South Michigan Avenue, Suite 1200, Chicago, Illinois 60603 (800) 577-EURO; *International Marketing Data and Statistics; World Marketing Data and Statistics;* and *The World Economic Factbook.*

International Labour Office, I.L.O. Publications, 1828 L Street, NW, Suite 801, Washington, D.C. 20036 (301) 638-3152; *Yearbook of Labour Statistics.*

M.E. Sharpe, 80 Business Park Drive, Armonk, New York 10504 (800) 541-6563; *The Illustrated Book of World Rankings.*

St. Martin's Press, Inc., 175 Fifth Avenue, New York, New York 10010 (800) 221-7945; *The Statesman's Year-Book.*

Statistical Office of the United Nations, Publishing Service, New York, New York 10017 (800) 253-9646; *Bulletin of Industrial Statistics for the Arab Countries;* and *Industrial Commodity Statistics Yearbook.*

The World Bank, 1818 H Street, NW, Washington, D.C. 20433 (202) 477-1234; *World Development Indicators.*

YEMEN - INFANT AND MATERNAL MORTALITY - See YEMEN - MORTALITY

YEMEN - INTERNATIONAL LIQUIDITY

International Monetary Fund, 700 Nineteenth Street, NW, Washington, D.C. 20431 (202) 623-7000; *International Financial Statistics.*

YEMEN - INTERNATIONAL RESERVES EXCLUDING GOLD

Statistical Office of the United Nations, Publishing Service, New York, New York 10017 (800) 253-9646; *Statistical Yearbook.*

The World Bank, 1818 H Street, NW, Washington, D.C. 20433 (202) 477-1234; *World Development Indicators.*

YEMEN - IRON ORE PRODUCTION AND CONSUMPTION - See YEMEN - MINING AND MINERAL PRODUCTS

YEMEN - IRRIGATION

Euromonitor International, Inc., 122 South Michigan Avenue, Suite 1200, Chicago, Illinois 60603 (800) 577-EURO; *International Marketing Data and Statistics.*

YEMEN - LABOR

Central Intelligence Agency, Washington, D.C. 20505 (703) (482-1100, www.cia.gov; *The World Factbook.*

Economic Commission for Western Asia, Post Office Box 27, Baghdad, Iraq; *Statistical Abstract of Western Asia.*

Euromonitor International, Inc., 122 South Michigan Avenue, Suite 1200, Chicago, Illinois 60603 (800) 577-EURO; *International Marketing Data and Statistics;* and *World Marketing Data and Statistics.*

Food and Agricultural Organization of the United Nations (FAO) Via delle Terme di Caracalla, 00100 Rome, Italy (Telephone Number in U.S. (202) 653-2400); *The State of Food and Agriculture.*

International Labour Office, I.L.O. Publications, 1828 L Street, NW, Suite 801, Washington, D.C. 20036 (301) 638-3152; *Yearbook of Labour Statistics.*

M.E. Sharpe, 80 Business Park Drive, Armonk, New York 10504 (800) 541-6563; *The Illustrated Book of World Rankings.*

St. Martin's Press, Inc., 175 Fifth Avenue, New York, New York 10010 (800) 221-7945; *The Statesman's Year-Book.*

Statistical Office of the United Nations, Publishing Service, New York, New York 10017 (800) 253-9646; *Human Development Report.*

The World Bank, 1818 H Street, NW, Washington, D.C. 20433 (202) 477-1234; *The World Bank Atlas; World Development Report;* and *World Development Indicators.*

YEMEN - LAND USE

Central Intelligence Agency, Washington, D.C. 20505 (703) (482-1100, www.cia.gov; *The World Factbook.*

Economic Commission for Western Asia, Post Office Box 27, Baghdad, Iraq; *Statistical Abstract of Western Asia.*

Euromonitor International, Inc., 122

South Michigan Avenue, Suite 1200, Chicago, Illinois 60603 (800) 577-EURO; *International Marketing Data and Statistics.*

The World Bank, 1818 H Street, NW, Washington, D.C. 20433 (202) 477-1234; *World Development Report.*

YEMEN - LIBRARIES

M.E. Sharpe, 80 Business Park Drive, Armonk, New York 10504 (800) 541-6563; *The Illustrated Book of World Rankings.*

United Nations Education, Scientific and Cultural Organization (UNESCO), 7 Place de Fontenoy, F-75700 Paris, France (Telephone Number in U.S. (212) 963-5981), *Statistical Yearbook.*

YEMEN - LIFE EXPECTANCY

Central Intelligence Agency, Washington, D.C. 20505 (703) (482-1100, www.cia.gov; *The World Factbook.*

Euromonitor International, Inc., 122 South Michigan Avenue, Suite 1200, Chicago, Illinois 60603 (800) 577-EURO; *The World Economic Factbook.*

Statistical Office of the United Nations, Publishing Service, New York, New York 10017 (800) 253-9646; *Human Development Report;* and *World Statistics Pocketbook.*

The World Bank, 1818 H Street, NW, Washington, D.C. 20433 (202) 477-1234; *The World Bank Atlas;* and *World Development Report.*

YEMEN - LITERACY RATE

Euromonitor International, Inc., 122 South Michigan Avenue, Suite 1200, Chicago, Illinois 60603 (800) 577-EURO; *World Marketing Data and Statistics.*

YEMEN - LIVESTOCK AND POULTRY

Economic Commission for Western Asia, Post Office Box 27, Baghdad, Iraq; *Statistical Abstract of Western Asia.*

Euromonitor International, Inc., 122 South Michigan Avenue, Suite 1200, Chicago, Illinois 60603 (800) 577-EURO; *International Marketing Data and Statistics.*

Europa Publications Limited, 18 Bedford Square, London, WC1B 3JN, England; *The Europa World Year Book.*

Food and Agricultural Organization of the United Nations (FAO) Via delle Terme di Caracalla, 00100 Rome, Italy (Telephone Number in U.S. (202) 653-2400); *The State of Food and Agriculture.*

M.E. Sharpe, 80 Business Park Drive,

Armonk, New York 10504 (800) 541-6563; *The Illustrated Book of World Rankings.*

St. Martin's Press, Inc., 175 Fifth Avenue, New York, New York 10010 (800) 221-7945; *The Statesman's Year-Book.*

Statistical Office of the United Nations, Publishing Service, New York, New York 10017 (800) 253-9646; *Statistical Yearbook.*

United Nations Conference on Trade and Development, Central Statistical Service, Palais des Nations, Geneva, Switzerland (Telephone in U.S. (800) 253-9646); *UNCTAD Commodity Yearbook.*

YEMEN - LIVING LEVELS - See YEMEN - LIFE EXPECTANCY

YEMEN - MAIL - NUMBER OF ITEMS SENT AND RECEIVED

Statistical Office of the United Nations, Publishing Service, New York, New York 10017 (800) 253-9646; *Statistical Yearbook.*

YEMEN - MANUFACTURING

M.E. Sharpe, 80 Business Park Drive, Armonk, New York 10504 (800) 541-6563; *The Illustrated Book of World Rankings.*

Statistical Office of the United Nations, Publishing Service, New York, New York 10017 (800) 253-9646; *Bulletin of Industrial Statistics for the Arab Countries;* and *Statistical Yearbook.*

The World Bank, 1818 H Street, NW, Washington, D.C. 20433 (202) 477-1234; *World Development Indicators.*

YEMEN - MARRIAGE RATES

M.E. Sharpe, 80 Business Park Drive, Armonk, New York 10504 (800) 541-6563; *The Illustrated Book of World Rankings.*

Statistical Office of the United Nations, Publishing Service, New York, New York 10017 (800) 253-9646; *Demographic Yearbook.*

YEMEN - MEAT PRODUCTION - See YEMEN - LIVESTOCK AND POULTRY

YEMEN - MERCHANT SHIPPING

Economic Commission for Western Asia, Post Office Box 27, Baghdad, Iraq; *Statistical Abstract of Western Asia.*

Europa Publications Limited, 18 Bedford Square, London, WC1B 3JN, England; *The Europa World Year Book.*

Lloyd's Register of Shipping, 17 Battery Place, New York, New York 10004 (212) 425-8050; *Register of Ships.*

St. Martin's Press, Inc., 175 Fifth Avenue, New York, New York 10010 (800) 221-7945; *The Statesman's Year-Book.*

Statistical Office of the United Nations, Publishing Service, New York, New York 10017 (800) 253-9646; *Statistical Yearbook.*

U.S. Department of Transportation, Maritime Administration, 400 Seventh Street, SW, Washington, D.C. 20590 (202) 366-5807, www.marad.dot.gov; *A Statistical Analysis of the World's Merchant Fleets.*

YEMEN - MILITARY

Central Intelligence Agency, Washington, D.C. 20505 (703) (482-1100, www.cia.gov; *The World Factbook.*

Euromonitor International, Inc., 122 South Michigan Avenue, Suite 1200, Chicago, Illinois 60603 (800) 577-EURO; *World Marketing Data and Statistics.*

The International Institute for Strategic Studies, 23 Tavistock Street, London WC2E 7NQ, England 44 171 3797676; *The Military Balance.*

St. Martin's Press, Inc., 175 Fifth Avenue, New York, New York 10010 (800) 221-7945; *The Statesman's Year-Book.*

Statistical Office of the United Nations, Publishing Service, New York, New York 10017 (800) 253-9646; *Human Development Report.*

U.S. Arms Control and Disarmament Agency, 320 Twenty-first Street, NW, Washington, D.C. 20451 (202) 647-8677; *World Military Expenditures and Arms Transfers.*

YEMEN - MILK PRODUCTION - See YEMEN - DAIRY PRODUCTS

YEMEN - MINING AND MINERAL PRODUCTS

Economic Commission for Western Asia, Post Office Box 27, Baghdad, Iraq; *Statistical Abstract of Western Asia.*

M.E. Sharpe, 80 Business Park Drive, Armonk, New York 10504 (800) 541-6563; *The Illustrated Book of World Rankings.*

Penn Well Publishing Company, 1421 South Sheridan Road, P.O. Box 1260, Tulsa, Oklahoma 74101 (800) 752-9764; *International Energy Statistics Sourcebook.*

St. Martin's Press, Inc., 175 Fifth Avenue, New York, New York 10010 (800) 221-7945; *The Statesman's Year-Book.*

Statistical Office of the United Nations, Publishing Service, New York, New York

10017 (800) 253-9646; *Bulletin of Industrial Statistics for the Arab Countries.*

United Nations Conference on Trade and Development, Central Statistical Service, Palais des Nations, Geneva, Switzerland (Telephone in U.S. (800) 253-9646); *UNCTAD Commodity Yearbook.*

YEMEN - MONEY EXCHANGE RATE - See YEMEN - EXCHANGE RATE

YEMEN - MONEY RESERVES

Euromonitor International, Inc., 122 South Michigan Avenue, Suite 1200, Chicago, Illinois 60603 (800) 577-EURO; *International Marketing Data and Statistics.*

YEMEN - MONEY SUPPLY

Economic Commission for Western Asia, Post Office Box 27, Baghdad, Iraq; *Statistical Abstract of Western Asia.*

Economist Intelligence Unit, 111 West 57th Street, New York, New York 10019 (800) 938-4685; *Yemen Country Report.*

Euromonitor International, Inc., 122 South Michigan Avenue, Suite 1200, Chicago, Illinois 60603 (800) 577-EURO; *International Marketing Data and Statistics.*

International Monetary Fund, 700 Nineteenth Street, NW, Washington, D.C. 20431 (202) 623-7000; *International Financial Statistics.*

Statistical Office of the United Nations, Publishing Service, New York, New York 10017 (800) 253-9646; *Statistical Yearbook.*

The World Bank, 1818 H Street, NW, Washington, D.C. 20433 (202) 477-1234; *World Development Indicators.*

YEMEN - MORTALITY

Central Intelligence Agency, Washington, D.C. 20505 (703) (482-1100), www.cia.gov; *The World Factbook.*

Euromonitor International, Inc., 122 South Michigan Avenue, Suite 1200, Chicago, Illinois 60603 (800) 577-EURO; *International Marketing Data and Statistics;* and *The World Economic Factbook.*

Statistical Office of the United Nations, Publishing Service, New York, New York 10017 (800) 253-9646; *Demographic Yearbook; Human Development Report; Statistical Yearbook;* and *World Statistics Pocketbook.*

United Nations Children's Fund (UNICEF), 3 United Nations Plaza, New York, New York 10017 (800) 253-9646; *State of the World's Children.*

The World Bank, 1818 H Street, NW, Washington, D.C. 20433 (202) 477-1234; *The World Bank Atlas;* and *World Development Report.*

World Health Organization, Office of Publications, Avenue Appia, CH-1211 Geneva, 27, Switzerland (Telephone Number in U.S. (518) 436-9686); *World Health Statistics: Infectious Diseases - Cases.*

YEMEN - MOTOR VEHICLE TAXES - See YEMEN - TAXATION

YEMEN - MOTOR VEHICLES

Economic Commission for Western Asia, Post Office Box 27, Baghdad, Iraq; *Statistical Abstract of Western Asia.*

YEMEN - MOTOR VEHICLES IN USE

Europa Publications Limited, 18 Bedford Square, London, WC1B 3JN, England; *The Europa World Year Book.*

International Road Federation, 2600 Virginia Avenue, NW, Washington, D.C. 20037 (202) 338-4641; *World Road Statistics.*

Statistical Office of the United Nations, Publishing Service, New York, New York 10017 (800) 253-9646; *Statistical Yearbook.*

YEMEN - MUSEUMS

M.E. Sharpe, 80 Business Park Drive, Armonk, New York 10504 (800) 541-6563; *The Illustrated Book of World Rankings.*

YEMEN - NATALITY - See YEMEN - BIRTH RATE

YEMEN - NATIONAL ACCOUNTS

Economic Commission for Western Asia, Post Office Box 27, Baghdad, Iraq; *Statistical Abstract of Western Asia.*

Europa Publications Limited, 18 Bedford Square, London, WC1B 3JN, England; *The Europa World Year Book.*

International Monetary Fund, 700 Nineteenth Street, NW, Washington, D.C. 20431 (202) 623-7000; *International Financial Statistics.*

Statistical Office of the United Nations, Publishing Service, New York, New York 10017 (800) 253-9646; *National Accounts Statistics;* and *Statistical Yearbook.*

YEMEN - NATIONAL INCOME

M.E. Sharpe, 80 Business Park Drive, Armonk, New York 10504 (800) 541-6563; *The Illustrated Book of World Rankings.*

Statistical Office of the United Nations, Publishing Service, New York, New York 10017 (800) 253-9646; *National Accounts Statistics;* and *Statistical Yearbook.*

YEMEN - NATIONAL PRODUCT

M.E. Sharpe, 80 Business Park Drive, Armonk, New York 10504 (800) 541-6563; *The Illustrated Book of World Rankings.*

Statistical Office of the United Nations, Publishing Service, New York, New York 10017 (800) 253-9646; *Statistical Yearbook.*

YEMEN - NATURAL GAS PRODUCTION - See YEMEN - MINING AND MINERAL PRODUCTS

YEMEN - NEWSPAPER PRODUCTION - See YEMEN - FORESTRY AND FOREST PRODUCTS

YEMEN - NEWSPRINT PRODUCTION AND CONSUMPTION - See YEMEN - FORESTRY AND FOREST PRODUCTS

YEMEN - OCCUPATIONS - See YEMEN - LABOR

YEMEN - PAPER - See YEMEN - FORESTRY AND FOREST PRODUCTS

YEMEN - PATENTS, TRADEMARKS AND SERVICE MARKS

Statistical Office of the United Nations, Publishing Service, New York, New York 10017 (800) 253-9646; *Statistical Yearbook.*

YEMEN - PEANUT PRODUCTION - See YEMEN - CROPS

YEMEN - PESTICIDE USE

Food and Agricultural Organization of the United Nations (FAO) Via delle Terme di Caracalla, 00100 Rome, Italy (Telephone Number in U.S. (202) 653-2400); *The State of Food and Agriculture.*

YEMEN - PETROLEUM INDUSTRY

Food and Agricultural Organization of the United Nations (FAO) Via delle Terme di Caracalla, 00100 Rome, Italy (Telephone Number in U.S. (202) 653-2400); *The State of Food and Agriculture.*

M.E. Sharpe, 80 Business Park Drive, Armonk, New York 10504 (800) 541-6563; *The Illustrated Book of World Rankings.*

Penn Well Publishing Company, 1421 South Sheridan Road, P.O. Box 1260, Tulsa, Oklahoma 74101 (800) 752-9764; *International Energy Statistics Sourcebook.*

St. Martin's Press, Inc., 175 Fifth Avenue, New York, New York 10010 (800) 221-7945; *The Statesman's Year-Book.*

Statistical Office of the United Nations, Publishing Service, New York, New York 10017 (800) 253-9646; *Statistical Yearbook*.

United Nations Conference on Trade and Development, Central Statistical Service, Palais des Nations, Geneva, Switzerland (Telephone in U.S. (800) 253-9646); *UNCTAD Commodity Yearbook*.

YEMEN - PIGS - See YEMEN - LIVESTOCK AND POULTRY

YEMEN - POPULATION

Central Intelligence Agency, Washington, D.C. 20505 (703) (482-1100, www.cia.gov; *The World Factbook*.

Economic Commission for Western Asia, Post Office Box 27, Baghdad, Iraq; *Statistical Abstract of Western Asia*.

The Economist Intelligence Unit, 111 West 57th Street, New York, New York 10019 (800) 938-4685; *Yemen Country Report;* and *The World Market Atlas*.

Euromonitor International, Inc., 122 South Michigan Avenue, Suite 1200, Chicago, Illinois 60603 (800) 577-EURO; *International Marketing Data and Statistics;* and *The World Economic Factbook*.

Europa Publications Limited, 18 Bedford Square, London, WC1B 3JN, England; *The Europa World Year Book*.

International Labour Office, I.L.O. Publications, 1828 L Street, NW, Suite 801, Washington, D.C. 20036 (301) 638-3152; *Yearbook of Labour Statistics*.

M.E. Sharpe, 80 Business Park Drive, Armonk, New York 10504 (800) 541-6563; *The Illustrated Book of World Rankings*.

St. Martin's Press, Inc., 175 Fifth Avenue, New York, New York 10010 (800) 221-7945; *The Statesman's Year-Book*.

Statistical Office of the United Nations, Publishing Service, New York, New York 10017 (800) 253-9646; *Demographic Yearbook; Human Development Report; Statistical Yearbook;* and *World Statistics Pocketbook*.

United Nations Educational, Scientific and Cultural Organization (UNESCO), 7 Place de Fontenoy, F-75700 Paris, France (Telephone Number in U.S. (212) 963-5981); *Statistical Yearbook*.

U.S. Arms Control and Disarmament Agency, 320 Twenty-first Street, NW, Washington, D.C. 20451 (202) 647-8677; *World Military Expenditures and Arms Transfers*.

The World Bank, 1818 H Street, NW,

Washington, D.C. 20433 (202) 477-1234; *The World Bank Atlas;* and *World Development Report*.

World Health Organization, Office of Publications, Avenue Appia, CH-1211 Geneva, 27, Switzerland (Telephone Number in U.S. (518) 436-9686); *World Health Statistics: Vital Statistics and Causes of Death*.

YEMEN - POST OFFICES

M.E. Sharpe, 80 Business Park Drive, Armonk, New York 10504 (800) 541-6563; *The Illustrated Book of World Rankings*.

YEMEN - POTATO PRODUCTION - See YEMEN - CROPS

YEMEN - PRICES

Economic Commission for Western Asia, Post Office Box 27, Baghdad, Iraq; *Statistical Abstract of Western Asia*.

Food and Agricultural Organization of the United Nations (FAO) Via delle Terme di Caracalla, 00100 Rome, Italy (Telephone Number in U.S. (202) 653-2400); *The State of Food and Agriculture*.

International Labour Office, I.L.O. Publications, 1828 L Street, NW, Suite 801, Washington, D.C. 20036 (301) 638-3152; *Yearbook of Labour Statistics*.

International Monetary Fund, 700 Nineteenth Street, NW, Washington, D.C. 20431 (202) 623-7000; *International Financial Statistics*.

M.E. Sharpe, 80 Business Park Drive, Armonk, New York 10504 (800) 541-6563; *The Illustrated Book of World Rankings*.

YEMEN - PRINTING AND WRITING PAPER - See YEMEN - FORESTRY AND FOREST PRODUCTS

YEMEN - PRODUCTION

M.E. Sharpe, 80 Business Park Drive, Armonk, New York 10504 (800) 541-6563; *The Illustrated Book of World Rankings*.

YEMEN - PRODUCTIVITY

Euromonitor International, Inc., 122 South Michigan Avenue, Suite 1200, Chicago, Illinois 60603 (800) 577-EURO; *International Marketing Data and Statistics*.

YEMEN - PUBLIC FINANCE - See YEMEN - FINANCE

YEMEN - RADIO BROADCASTING - See YEMEN - BROADCASTING

YEMEN - RADIO RECEIVERS

St. Martin's Press, Inc., 175 Fifth Avenue, New York, New York 10010 (800) 221-7945; *The Statesman's Year-Book*.

YEMEN - RELIGION

Central Intelligence Agency, Washington, D.C. 20505 (703) (482-1100, www.cia.gov; *The World Factbook*.

M.E. Sharpe, 80 Business Park Drive, Armonk, New York 10504 (800) 541-6563; *The Illustrated Book of World Rankings*.

St. Martin's Press, Inc., 175 Fifth Avenue, New York, New York 10010 (800) 221-7945; *The Statesman's Year-Book*.

YEMEN - RENT PRICES

International Labour Office, I.L.O. Publications, 1828 L Street, NW, Suite 801, Washington, D.C. 20036 (301) 638-3152; *Yearbook of Labour Statistics*.

YEMEN - RETAIL TRADE

Euromonitor International, Inc., 122 South Michigan Avenue, Suite 1200, Chicago, Illinois 60603 (800) 577-EURO; *World Marketing Data and Statistics*.

YEMEN - RICE PRODUCTION - See YEMEN - CROPS

YEMEN - ROUNDWOOD PRODUCTION - See YEMEN - FORESTRY AND FOREST PRODUCTS

YEMEN - RUBBER PRODUCTION

M.E. Sharpe, 80 Business Park Drive, Armonk, New York 10504 (800) 541-6563; *The Illustrated Book of World Rankings*.

YEMEN - SALT PRODUCTION - See YEMEN - MINING AND MINERAL PRODUCTS

YEMEN - SAWNWOOD PRODUCTION - See YEMEN - FORESTRY AND FOREST PRODUCTS

YEMEN - SCIENCE AND TECHNOLOGY - EXPENDITURE FOR RESEARCH - See YEMEN - SCIENTISTS, TECHNICIANS AND ENGINEERS

YEMEN - SCIENTISTS, TECHNICIANS AND ENGINEERS

Statistical Office of the United Nations, Publishing Service, New York, New York 10017 (800) 253-9646; *Statistical Yearbook*.

YEMEN - SENIOR CITIZENS

M.E. Sharpe, 80 Business Park Drive, Armonk, New York 10504 (800) 541-6563; *The Illustrated Book of World Rankings*.

YEMEN - SHEEP - See YEMEN - LIVESTOCK

AND POULTRY

YEMEN - SILVER PRODUCTION AND CONSUMPTION - See YEMEN - MINING AND MINERAL PRODUCTS

YEMEN - SOCIAL DATA

M.E. Sharpe, 80 Business Park Drive, Armonk, New York 10504 (800) 541-6563; *The Illustrated Book of World Rankings.*

Statistical Office of the United Nations, Publishing Service, New York, New York 10017 (800) 253-9646; *World Statistics Pocketbook.*

YEMEN - SOCIAL SECURITY

Statistical Office of the United Nations, Publishing Service, New York, New York 10017 (800) 253-9646; *National Accounts Statistics.*

YEMEN - STATE BUDGET REVENUE AND EXPENDITURES

Euromonitor International, Inc., 122 South Michigan Avenue, Suite 1200, Chicago, Illinois 60603 (800) 577-EURO; *International Marketing Data and Statistics.*

YEMEN - STEEL PRODUCTION - See YEMEN - MINING AND MINERAL PRODUCTS

YEMEN - STOCKS - COMMODITY - MARKET PRICE - INDEX

Food and Agricultural Organization of the United Nations (FAO) Via delle Terme di Caracalla, 00100 Rome, Italy (Telephone Number in U.S. (202) 653-2400); *The State of Food and Agriculture.*

YEMEN - SUGAR PRODUCTION AND CONSUMPTION - See YEMEN - CROPS

YEMEN - TAXATION

Europa Publications Limited, 18 Bedford Square, London, WC1B 3JN, England; *The Europa World Year Book.*

International Road Federation, 2600 Virginia Avenue, NW, Washington, D.C. 20037 (202) 338-4641; *World Road Statistics.*

The World Bank, 1818 H Street, NW, Washington, D.C. 20433 (202) 477-1234; *World Development Indicators.*

YEMEN - TELEPHONES IN USE

American Telephone and Telegraph Company, 26 Parsippany Road, Whippany, New Jersey 07981 (800) 222-0300; *The World's Telephones.*

Central Intelligence Agency,

Washington, D.C. 20505 (703) (482-1100, www.cia.gov; *The World Factbook.*

St. Martin's Press, Inc., 175 Fifth Avenue, New York, New York 10010 (800) 221-7945; *The Statesman's Year-Book.*

Statistical Office of the United Nations, Publishing Service, New York, New York 10017 (800) 253-9646; *Statistical Yearbook;* and *World Statistics Pocketbook.*

YEMEN - TELEVISION

M.E. Sharpe, 80 Business Park Drive, Armonk, New York 10504 (800) 541-6563; *The Illustrated Book of World Rankings.*

YEMEN - TEXTILE INDUSTRY

M.E. Sharpe, 80 Business Park Drive, Armonk, New York 10504 (800) 541-6563; *The Illustrated Book of World Rankings.*

St. Martin's Press, Inc., 175 Fifth Avenue, New York, New York 10010 (800) 221-7945; *The Statesman's Year-Book.*

Statistical Office of the United Nations, Publishing Service, New York, New York 10017 (800) 253-9646; *Statistical Yearbook.*

United Nations Conference on Trade and Development, Central Statistical Service, Palais des Nations, Geneva, Switzerland (Telephone in U.S. (800) 253-9646); *UNCTAD Commodity Yearbook.*

YEMEN - TOBACCO PRODUCTION

M.E. Sharpe, 80 Business Park Drive, Armonk, New York 10504 (800) 541-6563; *The Illustrated Book of World Rankings.*

Statistical Office of the United Nations, Publishing Service, New York, New York 10017 (800) 253-9646; *Statistical Yearbook.*

YEMEN - TOURISM

Economic Commission for Western Asia, Post Office Box 27, Baghdad, Iraq; *Statistical Abstract of Western Asia.*

Euromonitor International, Inc., 122 South Michigan Avenue, Suite 1200, Chicago, Illinois 60603 (800) 577-EURO; *The World Economic Factbook;* and *World Marketing Data and Statistics.*

M.E. Sharpe, 80 Business Park Drive, Armonk, New York 10504 (800) 541-6563; *The Illustrated Book of World Rankings.*

Statistical Office of the United Nations, Publishing Service, New York, New York 10017 (800) 253-9646; *Statistical Yearbook.*

World Tourism Organization, Calle Capitan Haya 42, E-28020 Madrid, Spain; *Yearbook of Tourism Statistics.*

YEMEN - TRACTORS IN USE

Statistical Office of the United Nations, Publishing Service, New York, New York 10017 (800) 253-9646; *Statistical Yearbook.*

YEMEN - TRADE - See YEMEN - FOREIGN TRADE

YEMEN - TRADEMARKS AND SERVICE MARKS - See YEMEN - PATENTS, TRADEMARKS AND SERVICE MARKS

YEMEN - TRANSPORTATION AND COMMUNICATIONS

Central Intelligence Agency, Washington, D.C. 20505 (703) (482-1100, www.cia.gov; *The World Factbook.*

Economic Commission for Western Asia, Post Office Box 27, Baghdad, Iraq; *Statistical Abstract of Western Asia.*

Euromonitor International, Inc., 122 South Michigan Avenue, Suite 1200, Chicago, Illinois 60603 (800) 577-EURO; *International Marketing Data and Statistics.*

Europa Publications Limited, 18 Bedford Square, London, WC1B 3JN, England; *The Europa World Year Book.*

M.E. Sharpe, 80 Business Park Drive, Armonk, New York 10504 (800) 541-6563; *The Illustrated Book of World Rankings.*

St. Martin's Press, Inc., 175 Fifth Avenue, New York, New York 10010 (800) 221-7945; *The Statesman's Year-Book.*

Statistical Office of the United Nations, Publishing Service, New York, New York 10017 (800) 253-9646; *Human Development Report.*

YEMEN - UNEMPLOYMENT

Central Intelligence Agency, Washington, D.C. 20505 (703) (482-1100, www.cia.gov; *The World Factbook.*

Euromonitor International, Inc., 122 South Michigan Avenue, Suite 1200, Chicago, Illinois 60603 (800) 577-EURO; *International Marketing Data and Statistics.*

International Labour Office, I.L.O. Publications, 1828 L Street, NW, Suite 801, Washington, D.C. 20036 (301) 638-3152; *Yearbook of Labour Statistics.*

YEMEN - VITAL STATISTICS

Euromonitor International, Inc., 122 South Michigan Avenue, Suite 1200, Chicago, Illinois 60603 (800) 577-EURO; *International Marketing Data and Statistics.*

World Health Organization, Office of

Publications, Avenue Appia, CH-1211 Geneva, 27, Switzerland (Telephone Number in U.S. (518) 436-9686); *World Health Statistics: Vital Statistics and Causes of Death.*

YEMEN - WAGES

International Labour Office, I.L.O. Publications, 1828 L Street, NW, Suite 801, Washington, D.C. 20036 (301) 638-3152; *Yearbook of Labour Statistics.*

YEMEN - WEATHER - See YEMEN - CLIMATE

YEMEN - WHEAT PRODUCTION AND PRICES - See YEMEN - CROPS

YEMEN - WHOLESALE PRICES

International Monetary Fund, 700 Nineteenth Street, NW, Washington, D.C. 20431 (202) 623-7000; *International Financial Statistics.*

YEMEN - WINE PRODUCTION - See YEMEN - BEVERAGES

YEMEN - WOOL PRODUCTION - See YEMEN - TEXTILE INDUSTRY

YEMEN - YARN PRODUCTION - See YEMEN - TEXTILE INDUSTRY

YOGURT CONSUMPTION AND PRODUCTION

U.S. Department of Agriculture, Economic Research Service, 1800 M Street, NW, Washington, D.C. 20036 (202) 694-5050, www.ers.usda.gov; *Food Consumption, Prices, and Expenditures; Dairy Products;* and *Agricultural Outlook.*

U.S. Department of Agriculture, National Agricultural Statistics Service, Fourteenth Street and Independence Avenue, SW, Washington, D.C. 20250 (800) 727-9540, www.usda.usda.gov/nass; *Dairy Products; and Milk, Production, Disposition and Income.*

YOUTH EMPLOYMENT PROGRAMS

The Congress of the U.S., Congressional Research Service, 101 Independence Avenue, SE, Washington, D.C. 20540 (202) 707-5700; *Cash and Non-Cash Benefits for Persons with Limited Income: Eligibility Rules, Recipient and Expenditure Data.*

Yugoslavia - National Statistical Office

Savezni Zavod za Statistiku, Kneza Milosa, 20, Post Office Box 203, 11000 Belgrade, Yugoslavia.

Yugoslavia - Primary Statistics Sources

Savezni Zavod za Statistiku, Kneza Milosa, 20, 11000 Belgrade, Yugoslavia; *Statisticki Godisnjak Jugoslavije* (Statistical Yearbook of Yugoslavia); *Statisticki Bilten* (Statistical Bulletins); and *Statistical Pocketbook of Yugoslavia.*

YUGOSLAVIA - ABORTIONS

Statistical Office of the United Nations, Publishing Service, New York, New York 10017 (800) 253-9646; *Trends in Europe and North America: The Statistical Yearbook of the Economic Commission for Europe.*

YUGOSLAVIA - AGRICULTURE

Economist Intelligence Unit, 111 West 57th Street, New York, New York 10019 (800) 938-4685; *Yugoslavia Country Report.*

Euromonitor International, Inc., 122 South Michigan Avenue, Suite 1200, Chicago, Illinois 60603 (800) 577-EURO; *World Marketing Data and Statistics.*

Europa Publications Limited, 18 Bedford Square, London, WC1B 3JN, England; *The Europa World Year Book.*

Federal Statistical Office, Gustav-Stresemann - Ring 11, D-6200, Wiesbaden, Germany; *Jugoslawien.*

Food and Agricultural Organization of the United Nations (FAO) Via delle Terme di Caracalla, 00100 Rome, Italy (Telephone Number in U.S. (202) 653-2400); *The State of Food and Agriculture.*

M.E. Sharpe, 80 Business Park Drive, Armonk, New York 10504 (800) 541-6563; *The Illustrated Book of World Rankings.*

St. Martin's Press, Inc., 175 Fifth Avenue, New York, New York 10010 (800) 221-7945; *The Statesman's Year-Book.*

Statistical Office of the United Nations, Publishing Service, New York, New York 10017 (800) 253-9646; *Statistical Yearbook.*

United Nations Conference on Trade and Development, Central Statistical Service, Palais des Nations, Geneva, Switzerland (Telephone in U.S. (800) 253-9646); *UNCTAD Commodity Yearbook.*

The World Bank, 1818 H Street, NW, Washington, D.C. 20433 (202) 477-1234; *World Development Indicators.*

YUGOSLAVIA - AIRLINE SERVICE

Europa Publications Limited, 18 Bedford Square, London, WC1B 3JN, England; *The Europa World Year Book.*

International Civil Aviation Organization, 999 University Street, Montreal, Quebec, Canada H3C 5H7 (514) 954-8219; *Civil Aviation Statistics of the World.*

M.E. Sharpe, 80 Business Park Drive, Armonk, New York 10504 (800) 541-6563; *The Illustrated Book of World Rankings.*

St. Martin's Press, Inc., 175 Fifth Avenue, New York, New York 10010 (800) 221-7945; *The Statesman's Year-Book.*

Statistical Office of the United Nations, Publishing Service, New York, New York 10017 (800) 253-9646; *Statistical Yearbook.*

YUGOSLAVIA - ALUMINUM PRODUCTION AND CONSUMPTION - See YUGOSLAVIA - MINING AND MINERAL PRODUCTS

YUGOSLAVIA - ANTIMONY AND ANTIMONY ORE PRODUCTION AND CONSUMPTION - See YUGOSLAVIA - MINING AND MINERAL PRODUCTS

YUGOSLAVIA - APPLE PRODUCTION - See YUGOSLAVIA - CROPS

YUGOSLAVIA - AREA AND DENSITY OF POPULATION

Euromonitor International, Inc., 122 South Michigan Avenue, Suite 1200, Chicago, Illinois 60603 (800) 577-EURO; *The World Economic Factbook.*

Europa Publications Limited, 18 Bedford Square, London, WC1B 3JN, England; *The Europa World Year Book.*

Federal Statistical Office, Gustav-Stresemann - Ring 11, D-6200, Wiesbaden, Germany; *Jugoslawien.*

Food and Agricultural Organization of the United Nations (FAO) Via delle Terme di Caracalla, 00100 Rome, Italy (Telephone Number in U.S. (202) 653-2400); *The State of Food and Agriculture.*

M.E. Sharpe, 80 Business Park Drive, Armonk, New York 10504 (800) 541-6563; *The Illustrated Book of World Rankings.*

St. Martin's Press, Inc., 175 Fifth Avenue, New York, New York 10010 (800) 221-7945; *The Statesman's Year-Book.*

Statistical Office of the United Nations, Publishing Service, New York, New York 10017 (800) 253-9646; *Statistical Yearbook;* and *Trends in Europe and North America: The Statistical Yearbook of the Economic Commission for Europe.*

United Nations Educational, Scientific and Cultural Organization (UNESCO), 7 Place de Fontenoy, F-75700 Paris, France (Telephone Number in U.S. (212) 963-

5981); *Statistical Yearbook.*

YUGOSLAVIA - ARMS EXPORTS AND IMPORTS - See YUGOSLAVIA - MILITARY

YUGOSLAVIA - BALANCE OF PAYMENTS

The Economist Intelligence Unit, 111 West 57th Street, New York, New York 10019 (800) 938-4685; *The World Market Atlas.*

Europa Publications Limited, 18 Bedford Square, London, WC1B 3JN, England; *The Europa World Year Book.*

Federal Statistical Office, Gustav-Stresemann - Ring 11, D-6200, Wiesbaden, Germany; *Jugoslawien.*

International Monetary Fund, 700 Nineteenth Street, NW, Washington, D.C. 20431 (202) 623-7000; *Balance of Payments Yearbook.*

United Nations Conference on Trade and Development (UNCTAD), New York, New York 10017 (800) 253-9646; *Handbook of International Trade and Development Statistics.*

The World Bank, 1818 H Street, NW, Washington, D.C. 20433 (202) 477-1234; *World Development Indicators.*

YUGOSLAVIA - BANKING

Euromonitor International, Inc., 122 South Michigan Avenue, Suite 1200, Chicago, Illinois 60603 (800) 577-EURO; *World Marketing Data and Statistics.*

Europa Publications Limited, 18 Bedford Square, London, WC1B 3JN, England; *The Europa World Year Book.*

International Monetary Fund, 700 Nineteenth Street, NW, Washington, D.C. 20431 (202) 623-7000; *International Financial Statistics.*

M.E. Sharpe, 80 Business Park Drive, Armonk, New York 10504 (800) 541-6563; *The Illustrated Book of World Rankings.*

St. Martin's Press, Inc., 175 Fifth Avenue, New York, New York 10010 (800) 221-7945; *The Statesman's Year-Book.*

YUGOSLAVIA - BARLEY PRODUCTION - See YUGOSLAVIA - CROPS

YUGOSLAVIA - BAUXITE PRODUCTION AND CONSUMPTION - See YUGOSLAVIA - MINING AND MINERAL PRODUCTS

YUGOSLAVIA - BEER PRODUCTION - See YUGOSLAVIA - BEVERAGES

YUGOSLAVIA - BEVERAGES

M.E. Sharpe, 80 Business Park Drive, Armonk, New York 10504 (800) 541-6563; *The Illustrated Book of World Rankings.*

Statistical Office of the United Nations, Publishing Service, New York, New York 10017 (800) 253-9646; *Statistical Yearbook.*

YUGOSLAVIA - BIRTH RATES

Euromonitor International, Inc., 122 South Michigan Avenue, Suite 1200, Chicago, Illinois 60603 (800) 577-EURO; *The World Economic Factbook.*

Europa Publications Limited, 18 Bedford Square, London, WC1B 3JN, England; *The Europa World Year Book.*

M.E. Sharpe, 80 Business Park Drive, Armonk, New York 10504 (800) 541-6563; *The Illustrated Book of World Rankings.*

St. Martin's Press, Inc., 175 Fifth Avenue, New York, New York 10010 (800) 221-7945; *The Statesman's Year-Book.*

Statistical Office of the United Nations, Publishing Service, New York, New York 10017 (800) 253-9646; *Demographic Yearbook;* and *Statistical Yearbook.*

The World Bank, 1818 H Street, NW, Washington, D.C. 20433 (202) 477-1234; *World Development Indicators.*

YUGOSLAVIA - BONDS

International Monetary Fund, 700 Nineteenth Street, NW, Washington, D.C. 20431 (202) 623-7000; *Government Finance Statistics Yearbook.*

YUGOSLAVIA - BOOK PRODUCTION

Euromonitor International, Inc., 122 South Michigan Avenue, Suite 1200, Chicago, Illinois 60603 (800) 577-EURO; *European Marketing Data and Statistics.*

Europa Publications Limited, 18 Bedford Square, London, WC1B 3JN, England; *The Europa World Year Book.*

St. Martin's Press, Inc., 175 Fifth Avenue, New York, New York 10010 (800) 221-7945; *The Statesman's Year-Book.*

Statistical Office of the United Nations, Publishing Service, New York, New York 10017 (800) 253-9646; *Trends in Europe and North America: The Statistical Yearbook of the Economic Commission for Europe.*

United Nations Educational, Scientific and Cultural Organization (UNESCO), 7 Place de Fontenoy, F-75700 Paris, France (Telephone Number in U.S. (212) 963-5981); *Statistical Yearbook.*

YUGOSLAVIA - BROADCASTING

Billboard Limited, P.O. Box 9027, 1006 AA Amsterdam, The Netherlands (Telephone Number in U.S. (212) 764-7300); *World Radio TV Handbook.*

Euromonitor International, Inc., 122 South Michigan Avenue, Suite 1200, Chicago, Illinois 60603 (800) 577-EURO; *World Marketing Data and Statistics.*

M.E. Sharpe, 80 Business Park Drive, Armonk, New York 10504 (800) 541-6563; *The Illustrated Book of World Rankings.*

St. Martin's Press, Inc., 175 Fifth Avenue, New York, New York 10010 (800) 221-7945; *The Statesman's Year-Book.*

Statistical Office of the United Nations, Publishing Service, New York, New York 10017 (800) 253-9646; *Trends in Europe and North America: The Statistical Yearbook of the Economic Commission for Europe.*

United Nations Educational, Scientific and Cultural Organization (UNESCO), 7 Place de Fontenoy, F-75700 Paris, France (Telephone Number in U.S. (212) 963-5981); *Statistical Yearbook.*

YUGOSLAVIA - BUTTER - See YUGOSLAVIA - DAIRY PRODUCTS

YUGOSLAVIA - CADMIUM PRODUCTION AND CONSUMPTION - See YUGOSLAVIA - MINING AND MINERAL PRODUCTS

YUGOSLAVIA - CALORIE SUPPLY

Food and Agricultural Organization of the United Nations (FAO) Via delle Terme di Caracalla, 00100 Rome, Italy (Telephone Number in U.S. (202) 653-2400); *The State of Food and Agriculture.*

YUGOSLAVIA - CATTLE - See YUGOSLAVIA - LIVESTOCK AND POULTRY

YUGOSLAVIA - CAUSTIC SODA PRODUCTION - See YUGOSLAVIA - BEVERAGES

YUGOSLAVIA - CEMENT PRODUCTION - See YUGOSLAVIA - MINING AND MINERAL PRODUCTS

YUGOSLAVIA - CEREAL PRODUCTION - See YUGOSLAVIA - CROPS

YUGOSLAVIA - CHEESE - See YUGOSLAVIA - DAIRY PRODUCTS

YUGOSLAVIA - CHEMICAL (ORGANIC) PRODUCTION - See YUGOSLAVIA - MINING AND MINERAL PRODUCTS

YUGOSLAVIA - CHROMIUM ORE PRODUCTION AND CONSUMPTION - See YUGOSLAVIA - MINING AND MINERAL PRODUCTS

YUGOSLAVIA - CIGAR PRODUCTION - See YUGOSLAVIA - TOBACCO PRODUCTION

YUGOSLAVIA - CIGARETTE PRODUCTION - See YUGOSLAVIA - TOBACCO PRODUCTION

YUGOSLAVIA - CLIMATE

M.E. Sharpe, 80 Business Park Drive, Armonk, New York 10504 (800) 541-6563; *The Illustrated Book of World Rankings.*

St. Martin's Press, Inc., 175 Fifth Avenue, New York, New York 10010 (800) 221-7945; *The Statesman's Year-Book.*

YUGOSLAVIA - COAL PRODUCTION - See YUGOSLAVIA - MINING AND MINERAL PRODUCTS

YUGOSLAVIA - COFFEE PRODUCTION AND CONSUMPTION - See YUGOSLAVIA - CROPS

YUGOSLAVIA - COKE OVEN COKE PRODUCTION AND CONSUMPTION - See YUGOSLAVIA - MINING AND MINERAL PRODUCTS

YUGOSLAVIA - COMMERCE

St. Martin's Press, Inc., 175 Fifth Avenue, New York, New York 10010 (800) 221-7945; *The Statesman's Year-Book.*

YUGOSLAVIA - CONSTRUCTION INDUSTRY

M.E. Sharpe, 80 Business Park Drive, Armonk, New York 10504 (800) 541-6563; *The Illustrated Book of World Rankings.*

Organisation for Economic Co-operation and Development (OECD), 2 rue Andre-Pascal, 75 Paris 16, France (Telephone Number in U.S. (202) 785-6323); *Main Economic Indicators - Historical Statistics.*

St. Martin's Press, Inc., 175 Fifth Avenue, New York, New York 10010 (800) 221-7945; *The Statesman's Year-Book.*

Statistical Office of the United Nations, Publishing Service, New York, New York 10017 (800) 253-9646; *Statistical Yearbook.*

YUGOSLAVIA - CONSUMER PRICE INDEX

Statistical Office of the United Nations, Publishing Service, New York, New York 10017 (800) 253-9646; *Statistical Yearbook;* and *Trends in Europe and North America: The Statistical Yearbook of the Economic Commission for Europe.*

YUGOSLAVIA - CONSUMER PRICES

Euromonitor International, Inc., 122 South Michigan Avenue, Suite 1200, Chicago, Illinois 60603 (800) 577-EURO; *European Marketing Data and Statistics;* and *World Marketing Data and Statistics.*

International Labour Office, I.L.O. Publications, 1828 L Street, NW, Suite 801, Washington, D.C. 20036 (301) 638-3152; *Yearbook of Labour Statistics.*

International Monetary Fund, 700 Nineteenth Street, NW, Washington, D.C. 20431 (202) 623-7000; *International Financial Statistics.*

YUGOSLAVIA - CONSUMPTION

International Lead and Zinc Study Group, Metro House, 58 St. James's Street, London SW1A 1LD England; *Lead and Zinc Statistics.*

YUGOSLAVIA - COPPER AND COPPER ORE PRODUCTION AND CONSUMPTION - See YUGOSLAVIA - MINING AND MINERAL PRODUCTS

YUGOSLAVIA - CORN PRODUCTION - See YUGOSLAVIA - CROPS

YUGOSLAVIA - CORPORATE TAXES - See YUGOSLAVIA - TAXATION

YUGOSLAVIA - COTTON - See YUGOSLAVIA - CROPS

YUGOSLAVIA - CRIME

Statistical Office of the United Nations, Publishing Service, New York, New York 10017 (800) 253-9646; *Trends in Europe and North America: The Statistical Yearbook of the Economic Commission for Europe.*

Yale University Press, Yale Station, New Haven, Connecticut 06520 (800) 987-7323; *Violence and Crime in Cross-National Perspective.*

YUGOSLAVIA - CROPS

Commodity Research Bureau, 30 South Wacker Drive, Chicago, Illinois 60606 (312) 454-1801; *Commodity Year Book.*

Euromonitor International, Inc., 122 South Michigan Avenue, Suite 1200, Chicago, Illinois 60603 (800) 577-EURO; *European Marketing Data and Statistics.*

Europa Publications Limited, 18 Bedford Square, London, WC1B 3JN, England; *The Europa World Year Book.*

Food and Agricultural Organization of the United Nations (FAO) Via delle Terme di Caracalla, 00100 Rome, Italy (Telephone Number in U.S. (202) 653-2400); *The State of Food and Agriculture.*

M.E. Sharpe, 80 Business Park Drive, Armonk, New York 10504 (800) 541-6563; *The Illustrated Book of World Rankings.*

St. Martin's Press, Inc., 175 Fifth Avenue, New York, New York 10010 (800) 221-7945; *The Statesman's Year-Book.*

Statistical Office of the United Nations, Publishing Service, New York, New York 10017 (800) 253-9646; *Statistical Yearbook.*

United Nations Conference on Trade and Development, Central Statistical Service, Palais des Nations, Geneva, Switzerland (Telephone in U.S. (800) 253-9646); *UNCTAD Commodity Yearbook.*

YUGOSLAVIA - CUSTOMS DUTIES

International Monetary Fund, 700 Nineteenth Street, NW, Washington, D.C. 20431 (202) 623-7000; *Government Finance Statistics Yearbook.*

St. Martin's Press, Inc., 175 Fifth Avenue, New York, New York 10010 (800) 221-7945; *The Statesman's Year-Book.*

YUGOSLAVIA - DAIRY PRODUCTS

Europa Publications Limited, 18 Bedford Square, London, WC1B 3JN, England; *The Europa World Year Book.*

Food and Agricultural Organization of the United Nations (FAO) Via delle Terme di Caracalla, 00100 Rome, Italy (Telephone Number in U.S. (202) 653-2400); *The State of Food and Agriculture.*

M.E. Sharpe, 80 Business Park Drive, Armonk, New York 10504 (800) 541-6563; *The Illustrated Book of World Rankings.*

Organisation for Economic Co-operation and Development (OECD), 2 rue Andre-Pascal, 75 Paris 16, France (Telephone Number in U.S. (202) 785-6323); *Milk, Milk Products, and Egg Balances in OECD Member Countries.*

St. Martin's Press, Inc., 175 Fifth Avenue, New York, New York 10010 (800) 221-7945; *The Statesman's Year-Book.*

Statistical Office of the United Nations, Publishing Service, New York, New York 10017 (800) 253-9646; *Statistical Yearbook.*

YUGOSLAVIA - DEATH RATE - See YUGOSLAVIA - MORTALITY

YUGOSLAVIA - DEFENSE EXPENDITURES - See YUGOSLAVIA - MILITARY

YUGOSLAVIA - DEMOGRAPHY

The Economist Intelligence Unit, 111 West 57th Street, New York, New York 10019 (800) 938-4685; *The World Market Atlas.*

Euromonitor International, Inc., 122

South Michigan Avenue, Suite 1200, Chicago, Illinois 60603 (800) 577-EURO; *The World Economic Factbook;* and *World Marketing Data and Statistics.*

Federal Statistical Office, Gustav-Stresemann - Ring 11, D-6200, Wiesbaden, Germany; *Jugoslawien.*

M.E. Sharpe, 80 Business Park Drive, Armonk, New York 10504 (800) 541-6563; *The Illustrated Book of World Rankings.*

YUGOSLAVIA - DIAMOND PRODUCTION - See YUGOSLAVIA - MINING AND MINERAL PRODUCTS

YUGOSLAVIA - DIVORCE RATES

M.E. Sharpe, 80 Business Park Drive, Armonk, New York 10504 (800) 541-6563; *The Illustrated Book of World Rankings.*

Statistical Office of the United Nations, Publishing Service, New York, New York 10017 (800) 253-9646; *Demographic Yearbook; Statistical Yearbook;* and *Trends in Europe and North America: The Statistical Yearbook of the Economic Commission for Europe.*

YUGOSLAVIA - ECONOMY

Economist Intelligence Unit, 111 West 57th Street, New York, New York 10019 (800) 938-4685; *Yugoslavia Country Report.*

Euromonitor International, Inc., 122 South Michigan Avenue, Suite 1200, Chicago, Illinois 60603 (800) 577-EURO; *European Marketing Data and Statistics; World Marketing Data and Statistics;* and *The World Economic Factbook.*

Europa Publications Limited, 18 Bedford Square, London, WC1B 3JN, England; *The Europa World Year Book.*

Federal Statistical Office, Gustav-Stresemann - Ring 11, D-6200, Wiesbaden, Germany; *Jugoslawien.*

M.E. Sharpe, 80 Business Park Drive, Armonk, New York 10504 (800) 541-6563; *The Illustrated Book of World Rankings.*

Organisation for Economic Co-operation and Development (OECD), 2 rue Andre-Pascal, 75 Paris 16, France (Telephone Number in U.S. (202) 785-6323); *Main Economic Indicators.*

St. Martin's Press, Inc., 175 Fifth Avenue, New York, New York 10010 (800) 221-7945; *The Statesman's Year-Book.*

Statistical Office of the United Nations, Publishing Service, New York, New York 10017 (800) 253-9646; *World Statistics Pocketbook.*

The World Bank, 1818 H Street, NW, Washington, D.C. 20433 (202) 477-1234; *The World Bank Atlas.*

YUGOSLAVIA - EDUCATION

The Economist Intelligence Unit, 111 West 57th Street, New York, New York 10019 (800) 938-4685; *The World Market Atlas.*

Euromonitor International, Inc., 122 South Michigan Avenue, Suite 1200, Chicago, Illinois 60603 (800) 577-EURO; *European Marketing Data and Statistics;* and *World Marketing Data and Statistics.*

Europa Publications Limited, 18 Bedford Square, London, WC1B 3JN, England; *The Europa World Year Book.*

Federal Statistical Office, Gustav-Stresemann - Ring 11, D-6200, Wiesbaden, Germany; *Jugoslawien.*

International Monetary Fund, 700 Nineteenth Street, NW, Washington, D.C. 20431 (202) 623-7000; *Government Finance Statistics Yearbook.*

M.E. Sharpe, 80 Business Park Drive, Armonk, New York 10504 (800) 541-6563; *The Illustrated Book of World Rankings.*

St. Martin's Press, Inc., 175 Fifth Avenue, New York, New York 10010 (800) 221-7945; *The Statesman's Year-Book.*

Statistical Office of the United Nations, Publishing Service, New York, New York 10017 (800) 253-9646; *Trends in Europe and North America: The Statistical Yearbook of the Economic Commission for Europe.*

United Nations Educational, Scientific and Cultural Organization (UNESCO), 7 Place de Fontenoy, F-75700 Paris, France (Telephone Number in U.S. (212) 963-5981); *Statistical Yearbook.*

The World Bank, 1818 H Street, NW, Washington, D.C. 20433 (202) 477-1234; *World Development Indicators.*

YUGOSLAVIA - EGG PRODUCTION AND CONSUMPTION - See YUGOSLAVIA - DAIRY PRODUCTS

YUGOSLAVIA - ELECTRICITY

M.E. Sharpe, 80 Business Park Drive, Armonk, New York 10504 (800) 541-6563; *The Illustrated Book of World Rankings.*

Penn Well Publishing Company, 1421 South Sheridan Road, P.O. Box 1260, Tulsa, Oklahoma 74101 (800) 752-9764; *International Energy Statistics Sourcebook.*

St. Martin's Press, Inc., 175 Fifth Avenue, New York, New York 10010 (800)

221-7945; *The Statesman's Year-Book.*

Statistical Office of the United Nations, Publishing Service, New York, New York 10017 (800) 253-9646; *Statistical Yearbook;* and *Trends in Europe and North America: The Statistical Yearbook of the Economic Commission for Europe.*

YUGOSLAVIA - EMPLOYMENT

Euromonitor International, Inc., 122 South Michigan Avenue, Suite 1200, Chicago, Illinois 60603 (800) 577-EURO; *European Marketing Data and Statistics.*

Federal Statistical Office, Gustav-Stresemann - Ring 11, D-6200, Wiesbaden, Germany; *Jugoslawien.*

International Labour Office, I.L.O. Publications, 1828 L Street, NW, Suite 801, Washington, D.C. 20036 (301) 638-3152; *Yearbook of Labour Statistics.*

M.E. Sharpe, 80 Business Park Drive, Armonk, New York 10504 (800) 541-6563; *The Illustrated Book of World Rankings.*

Statistical Office of the United Nations, Publishing Service, New York, New York 10017 (800) 253-9646; *Statistical Yearbook;* and *Trends in Europe and North America: The Statistical Yearbook of the Economic Commission for Europe.*

YUGOSLAVIA - ENERGY

Euromonitor International, Inc., 122 South Michigan Avenue, Suite 1200, Chicago, Illinois 60603 (800) 577-EURO; *European Marketing Data and Statistics; World Marketing Data and Statistics;* and *The World Economic Factbook.*

Food and Agricultural Organization of the United Nations (FAO) Via delle Terme di Caracalla, 00100 Rome, Italy (Telephone Number in U.S. (202) 653-2400); *The State of Food and Agriculture.*

M.E. Sharpe, 80 Business Park Drive, Armonk, New York 10504 (800) 541-6563; *The Illustrated Book of World Rankings.*

Penn Well Publishing Company, 1421 South Sheridan Road, P.O. Box 1260, Tulsa, Oklahoma 74101 (800) 752-9764; *International Energy Statistics Sourcebook.*

St. Martin's Press, Inc., 175 Fifth Avenue, New York, New York 10010 (800) 221-7945; *The Statesman's Year-Book.*

Statistical Office of the United Nations, Publishing Service, New York, New York 10017 (800) 253-9646; *Energy Statistics Yearbook; Statistical Yearbook; Trends in Europe and North America: The Statistical Yearbook of the Economic Commission for Europe;* and *World Statistics Pocketbook.*

The World Bank, 1818 H Street, NW, Washington, D.C. 20433 (202) 477-1234; *The World Bank Atlas.*

YUGOSLAVIA - ENERGY EMPLOYMENT - MALE AND FEMALE - See YUGOSLAVIA - EMPLOYMENT

YUGOSLAVIA - ENVIRONMENT

Economist Intelligence Unit, 111 West 57th Street, New York, New York 10019 (800) 938-4685; *Yugoslavia Country Report.*

Statistical Office of the United Nations, Publishing Service, New York, New York 10017 (800) 253-9646; *Trends in Europe and North America: The Statistical Yearbook of the Economic Commission for Europe;* and *World Statistics Pocketbook.*

YUGOSLAVIA - EXCHANGE RATES

Euromonitor International, Inc., 122 South Michigan Avenue, Suite 1200, Chicago, Illinois 60603 (800) 577-EURO; *The World Economic Factbook.*

Europa Publications Limited, 18 Bedford Square, London, WC1B 3JN, England; *The Europa World Year Book.*

International Civil Aviation Organization, 999 University Street, Montreal, Quebec, Canada H3C 5H7 (514) 954-8219; *Civil Aviation Statistics of the World.*

International Monetary Fund, 700 Nineteenth Street, NW, Washington, D.C. 20431 (202) 623-7000; *International Financial Statistics.*

Statistical Office of the United Nations, Publishing Service, New York, New York 10017 (800) 253-9646; *Statistical Yearbook; Trends in Europe and North America: The Statistical Yearbook of the Economic Commission for Europe;* and *World Statistics Pocketbook.*

YUGOSLAVIA - EXPORTS

The Economist Intelligence Unit, 111 West 57th Street, New York, New York 10019 (800) 938-4685; *Yugoslavia Country Report;* and *The World Market Atlas.*

Euromonitor International, Inc., 122 South Michigan Avenue, Suite 1200, Chicago, Illinois 60603 (800) 577-EURO; *The World Economic Factbook.*

Europa Publications Limited, 18 Bedford Square, London, WC1B 3JN, England; *The Europa World Year Book.*

Food and Agricultural Organization of the United Nations (FAO) Via delle Terme di Caracalla, 00100 Rome, Italy (Telephone Number in U.S. (202) 653-2400); *The State*

of Food and Agriculture.

International Lead and Zinc Study Group, Metro House, 58 St. James's Street, London SW1A 1LD England; *Lead and Zinc Statistics.*

International Monetary Fund, 700 Nineteenth Street, NW, Washington, D.C. 20431 (202) 623-7000; *Direction of Trade Statistics;* and *International Financial Statistics.*

Organisation for Economic Co-operation and Development (OECD), 2 rue Andre-Pascal, 75 Paris 16, France (Telephone Number in U.S. (202) 785-6323); *Milk, Milk Products, and Egg Balances in OECD Member Countries;* and *Review of Fisheries in OECD Member Countries.*

St. Martin's Press, Inc., 175 Fifth Avenue, New York, New York 10010 (800) 221-7945; *The Statesman's Year-Book.*

Statistical Office of the United Nations, Publishing Service, New York, New York 10017 (800) 253-9646; *Trends in Europe and North America: The Statistical Yearbook of the Economic Commission for Europe.*

United Nations Conference on Trade and Development (UNCTAD), New York, New York 10017 (800) 253-9646; *Handbook of International Trade and Development Statistics.*

The World Bank, 1818 H Street, NW, Washington, D.C. 20433 (202) 477-1234; *World Development Indicators.*

YUGOSLAVIA - EXTERNAL INDEBTEDNESS

The World Bank, 1818 H Street, NW, Washington, D.C. 20433 (202) 477-1234; *World Development Indicators.*

YUGOSLAVIA - EXTERNAL TRADE

Euromonitor International, Inc., 122 South Michigan Avenue, Suite 1200, Chicago, Illinois 60603 (800) 577-EURO; *World Marketing Data and Statistics.*

Food and Agricultural Organization of the United Nations (FAO) Via delle Terme di Caracalla, 00100 Rome, Italy (Telephone Number in U.S. (202) 653-2400); *The State of Food and Agriculture.*

Statistical Office of the United Nations, Publishing Service, New York, New York 10017 (800) 253-9646; *Statistical Yearbook.*

YUGOSLAVIA - FABRIC PRODUCTION - See YUGOSLAVIA - TEXTILE INDUSTRY

YUGOSLAVIA - FARM CROPS - See YUGOSLAVIA - CROPS

YUGOSLAVIA - FERTILITY RATES

M.E. Sharpe, 80 Business Park Drive, Armonk, New York 10504 (800) 541-6563; *The Illustrated Book of World Rankings.*

Statistical Office of the United Nations, Publishing Service, New York, New York 10017 (800) 253-9646; *Trends in Europe and North America: The Statistical Yearbook of the Economic Commission for Europe.*

The World Bank, 1818 H Street, NW, Washington, D.C. 20433 (202) 477-1234; *The World Bank Atlas;* and *World Development Indicators.*

YUGOSLAVIA - FERTILIZER

Food and Agricultural Organization of the United Nations (FAO) Via delle Terme di Caracalla, 00100 Rome, Italy (Telephone Number in U.S. (202) 653-2400); *The State of Food and Agriculture.*

Statistical Office of the United Nations, Publishing Service, New York, New York 10017 (800) 253-9646; *Statistical Yearbook.*

YUGOSLAVIA - FETAL MORTALITY - See YUGOSLAVIA - MORTALITY

YUGOSLAVIA - FIBRE PRODUCTION - See YUGOSLAVIA - TEXTILE INDUSTRY

YUGOSLAVIA - FILAMENT PRODUCTION - See YUGOSLAVIA - TEXTILE INDUSTRY

YUGOSLAVIA - FILM - See YUGOSLAVIA - MOTION PICTURES

YUGOSLAVIA - FINANCE

Economist Intelligence Unit, 111 West 57th Street, New York, New York 10019 (800) 938-4685; *Yugoslavia Country Report.*

Europa Publications Limited, 18 Bedford Square, London, WC1B 3JN, England; *The Europa World Year Book.*

Federal Statistical Office, Gustav-Stresemann - Ring 11, D-6200, Wiesbaden, Germany; *Jugoslawien.*

International Monetary Fund, 700 Nineteenth Street, NW, Washington, D.C. 20431 (202) 623-7000; *International Financial Statistics.*

M.E. Sharpe, 80 Business Park Drive, Armonk, New York 10504 (800) 541-6563; *The Illustrated Book of World Rankings.*

St. Martin's Press, Inc., 175 Fifth Avenue, New York, New York 10010 (800) 221-7945; *The Statesman's Year-Book.*

YUGOSLAVIA - FISHERIES

Euromonitor International, Inc., 122 South Michigan Avenue, Suite 1200, Chicago, Illinois 60603 (800) 577-EURO; *European Marketing Data and Statistics.*

Europa Publications Limited, 18 Bedford Square, London, WC1B 3JN, England; *The Europa World Year Book.*

Federal Statistical Office, Gustav-Stresemann - Ring 11, D-6200, Wiesbaden, Germany; *Jugoslawien.*

Food and Agricultural Organization of the United Nations (FAO) Via delle Terme di Caracalla, 00100 Rome, Italy (Telephone Number in U.S. (202) 653-2400); *The State of Food and Agriculture.*

M.E. Sharpe, 80 Business Park Drive, Armonk, New York 10504 (800) 541-6563; *The Illustrated Book of World Rankings.*

Organisation for Economic Co-operation and Development (OECD), 2 rue Andre-Pascal, 75 Paris 16, France (Telephone Number in U.S. (202) 785-6323); *Review of Fisheries in OECD Member Countries.*

St. Martin's Press, Inc., 175 Fifth Avenue, New York, New York 10010 (800) 221-7945; *The Statesman's Year-Book.*

Statistical Office of the United Nations, Publishing Service, New York, New York 10017 (800) 253-9646; *Statistical Yearbook.*

United Nations Conference on Trade and Development, Central Statistical Service, Palais des Nations, Geneva, Switzerland (Telephone in U.S. (800) 253-9646); *UNCTAD Commodity Yearbook.*

YUGOSLAVIA - FLOUR PRODUCTION

Commodity Research Bureau, 30 South Wacker Drive, Chicago, Illinois 60606 (312) 454-1801; *Commodity Year Book.*

Statistical Office of the United Nations, Publishing Service, New York, New York 10017 (800) 253-9646; *Statistical Yearbook.*

YUGOSLAVIA - FOOD

Food and Agricultural Organization of the United Nations (FAO) Via delle Terme di Caracalla, 00100 Rome, Italy (Telephone Number in U.S. (202) 653-2400); *The State of Food and Agriculture.*

Organisation for Economic Co-operation and Development (OECD), 2 rue Andre-Pascal, 75 Paris 16, France (Telephone Number in U.S. (202) 785-6323); *Food Consumption Statistics.*

United Nations Conference on Trade and Development, Central Statistical Service, Palais des Nations, Geneva,

Switzerland (Telephone in U.S. (800) 253-9646); *UNCTAD Commodity Yearbook.*

YUGOSLAVIA - FOREIGN TRADE

Economist Intelligence Unit, 111 West 57th Street, New York, New York 10019 (800) 938-4685; *Yugoslavia Country Report.*

Euromonitor International, Inc., 122 South Michigan Avenue, Suite 1200, Chicago, Illinois 60603 (800) 577-EURO; *European Marketing Data and Statistics; and The World Economic Factbook.*

Europa Publications Limited, 18 Bedford Square, London, WC1B 3JN, England; *The Europa World Year Book.*

Federal Statistical Office, Gustav-Stresemann - Ring 11, D-6200, Wiesbaden, Germany; *Jugoslawien.*

Food and Agricultural Organization of the United Nations (FAO) Via delle Terme di Caracalla, 00100 Rome, Italy (Telephone Number in U.S. (202) 653-2400); *The State of Food and Agriculture.*

International Monetary Fund, 700 Nineteenth Street, NW, Washington, D.C. 20431 (202) 623-7000; *International Financial Statistics.*

M.E. Sharpe, 80 Business Park Drive, Armonk, New York 10504 (800) 541-6563; *The Illustrated Book of World Rankings.*

Organisation for Economic Co-operation and Development (OECD), 2 rue Andre-Pascal, 75 Paris 16, France (Telephone Number in U.S. (202) 785-6323); *Main Economic Indicators - Historical Statistics.*

St. Martin's Press, Inc., 175 Fifth Avenue, New York, New York 10010 (800) 221-7945; *The Statesman's Year-Book.*

Statistical Office of the United Nations, Publishing Service, New York, New York 10017 (800) 253-9646; *International Trade Statistics Yearbook; and Statistical Yearbook.*

United Nations Conference on Trade and Development, Central Statistical Service, Palais des Nations, Geneva, Switzerland (Telephone in U.S. (800) 253-9646); *UNCTAD Commodity Yearbook.*

The World Bank, 1818 H Street, NW, Washington, D.C. 20433 (202) 477-1234; *World Development Indicators.*

World Bureau of Metal Statistics, 27-A High Street, Ware Hert SG12 9BA, England; *World Metal Statistics.*

YUGOSLAVIA - FORESTRY AND FOREST PRODUCTS

American Forest and Paper Association, 1111 Nineteenth Street, NW, Washington, D.C. 20036 (202) 463-2700; *Wood Pulp and Fiber Statistics.*

Euromonitor International, Inc., 122 South Michigan Avenue, Suite 1200, Chicago, Illinois 60603 (800) 577-EURO; *European Marketing Data and Statistics.*

Europa Publications Limited, 18 Bedford Square, London, WC1B 3JN, England; *The Europa World Year Book.*

Federal Statistical Office, Gustav-Stresemann - Ring 11, D-6200, Wiesbaden, Germany; *Jugoslawien.*

Food and Agricultural Organization of the United Nations (FAO) Via delle Terme di Caracalla, 00100 Rome, Italy (Telephone Number in U.S. (202) 653-2400); *The State of Food and Agriculture; and Yearbook of Forest Products.*

M.E. Sharpe, 80 Business Park Drive, Armonk, New York 10504 (800) 541-6563; *The Illustrated Book of World Rankings.*

St. Martin's Press, Inc., 175 Fifth Avenue, New York, New York 10010 (800) 221-7945; *The Statesman's Year-Book.*

Statistical Office of the United Nations, Publishing Service, New York, New York 10017 (800) 253-9646; *Statistical Yearbook; and Trends in Europe and North America: The Statistical Yearbook of the Economic Commission for Europe.*

United Nations Conference on Trade and Development, Central Statistical Service, Palais des Nations, Geneva, Switzerland (Telephone in U.S. (800) 253-9646); *UNCTAD Commodity Yearbook.*

United Nations Educational, Scientific and Cultural Organization (UNESCO), 7 Place de Fontenoy, F-75700 Paris, France (Telephone Number in U.S. (212) 963-5981); *Statistical Yearbook.*

YUGOSLAVIA - GAS AND GAS LIQUIDS PRODUCTION - See YUGOSLAVIA - MINING AND MINERAL PRODUCTS

YUGOSLAVIA - GENERAL INDUSTRIAL STATISTICS - See YUGOSLAVIA - INDUSTRY

YUGOSLAVIA - GENERAL MORTALITY - See YUGOSLAVIA - MORTALITY

YUGOSLAVIA - GEOGRAPHIC DATA

M.E. Sharpe, 80 Business Park Drive, Armonk, New York 10504 (800) 541-6563; *The Illustrated Book of World Rankings.*

YUGOSLAVIA - GOLD HOLDINGS

International Monetary Fund, 700

Nineteenth Street, NW, Washington, D.C. 20431 (202) 623-7000; *International Financial Statistics.*

Statistical Office of the United Nations, Publishing Service, New York, New York 10017 (800) 253-9646; *Statistical Yearbook.*

The World Bank, 1818 H Street, NW, Washington, D.C. 20433 (202) 477-1234; *World Development Indicators.*

YUGOSLAVIA - GOLD PRODUCTION AND CONSUMPTION - See YUGOSLAVIA - MINING AND MINERAL PRODUCTS

YUGOSLAVIA - GOVERNMENT

Europa Publications Limited, 18 Bedford Square, London, WC1B 3JN, England; *The Europa World Year Book.*

International Monetary Fund, 700 Nineteenth Street, NW, Washington, D.C. 20431 (202) 623-7000; *Government Finance Statistics Yearbook;* and *International Financial Statistics.*

St. Martin's Press, Inc., 175 Fifth Avenue, New York, New York 10010 (800) 221-7945; *The Statesman's Year-Book.*

Statistical Office of the United Nations, Publishing Service, New York, New York 10017 (800) 253-9646; *National Accounts Statistics;* and *Statistical Yearbook.*

The World Bank, 1818 H Street, NW, Washington, D.C. 20433 (202) 477-1234; *World Development Indicators.*

YUGOSLAVIA - GRAIN PRODUCTION - See YUGOSLAVIA - CROPS

YUGOSLAVIA - GRANTS

International Monetary Fund, 700 Nineteenth Street, NW, Washington, D.C. 20431 (202) 623-7000; *Government Finance Statistics Yearbook.*

YUGOSLAVIA - GROSS DOMESTIC PRODUCT

The Economist Intelligence Unit, 111 West 57th Street, New York, New York 10019 (800) 938-4685; *Yugoslavia Country Report;* and *The World Market Atlas.*

Euromonitor International, Inc., 122 South Michigan Avenue, Suite 1200, Chicago, Illinois 60603 (800) 577-EURO; *The World Economic Factbook.*

M.E. Sharpe, 80 Business Park Drive, Armonk, New York 10504 (800) 541-6563; *The Illustrated Book of World Rankings.*

Statistical Office of the United Nations, Publishing Service, New York, New York 10017 (800) 253-9646; *National Accounts*

Statistics; *Statistical Yearbook;* and *Trends in Europe and North America: The Statistical Yearbook of the Economic Commission for Europe.*

The World Bank, 1818 H Street, NW, Washington, D.C. 20433 (202) 477-1234; *World Development Indicators.*

YUGOSLAVIA - GROSS NATIONAL PRODUCT

U.S. Arms Control and Disarmament Agency, 320 Twenty-first Street, NW, Washington, D.C. 20451 (202) 647-8677; *World Military Expenditures and Arms Transfers.*

The World Bank, 1818 H Street, NW, Washington, D.C. 20433 (202) 477-1234; *The World Bank Atlas;* and *World Development Indicators.*

YUGOSLAVIA - HEALTH

Euromonitor International, Inc., 122 South Michigan Avenue, Suite 1200, Chicago, Illinois 60603 (800) 577-EURO; *World Marketing Data and Statistics.*

Federal Statistical Office, Gustav-Stresemann - Ring 11, D-6200, Wiesbaden, Germany; *Jugoslawien.*

M.E. Sharpe, 80 Business Park Drive, Armonk, New York 10504 (800) 541-6563; *The Illustrated Book of World Rankings.*

St. Martin's Press, Inc., 175 Fifth Avenue, New York, New York 10010 (800) 221-7945; *The Statesman's Year-Book.*

Statistical Office of the United Nations, Publishing Service, New York, New York 10017 (800) 253-9646; *Statistical Yearbook;* and *Trends in Europe and North America: The Statistical Yearbook of the Economic Commission for Europe.*

United Nations Children's Fund (UNICEF), 3 United Nations Plaza, New York, New York 10017 (800) 253-9646; *State of the World's Children.*

YUGOSLAVIA - HEALTH EXPENDITURES

International Monetary Fund, 700 Nineteenth Street, NW, Washington, D.C. 20431 (202) 623-7000; *Government Finance Statistics Yearbook.*

YUGOSLAVIA - HIGHWAYS

International Road Federation, 2600 Virginia Avenue, NW, Washington, D.C. 20037 (202) 338-4641; *World Road Statistics.*

St. Martin's Press, Inc., 175 Fifth Avenue, New York, New York 10010 (800) 221-7945; *The Statesman's Year-Book.*

Statistical Office of the United Nations, Publishing Service, New York, New York 10017 (800) 253-9646; *Annual Bulletin of Transport Statistics for Europe;* and *Trends in Europe and North America: The Statistical Yearbook of the Economic Commission for Europe.*

YUGOSLAVIA - HORSES - See YUGOSLAVIA - LIVESTOCK AND POULTRY

YUGOSLAVIA - HOURS OF WORK - See YUGOSLAVIA - EMPLOYMENT

YUGOSLAVIA - HOUSING AND HOUSING UNITS

Euromonitor International, Inc., 122 South Michigan Avenue, Suite 1200, Chicago, Illinois 60603 (800) 577-EURO; *World Marketing Data and Statistics.*

M.E. Sharpe, 80 Business Park Drive, Armonk, New York 10504 (800) 541-6563; *The Illustrated Book of World Rankings.*

Statistical Office of the United Nations, Publishing Service, New York, New York 10017 (800) 253-9646; *Trends in Europe and North America: The Statistical Yearbook of the Economic Commission for Europe.*

YUGOSLAVIA - HOUSING EXPENDITURES

International Monetary Fund, 700 Nineteenth Street, NW, Washington, D.C. 20431 (202) 623-7000; *Government Finance Statistics Yearbook.*

YUGOSLAVIA - HYDROCHLORIC ACID PRODUCTION

Statistical Office of the United Nations, Publishing Service, New York, New York 10017 (800) 253-9646; *Statistical Yearbook.*

YUGOSLAVIA - ILLITERATE POPULATION

The Economist Intelligence Unit, 111 West 57th Street, New York, New York 10019 (800) 938-4685; *The World Market Atlas.*

Euromonitor International, Inc., 122 South Michigan Avenue, Suite 1200, Chicago, Illinois 60603 (800) 577-EURO; *The World Economic Factbook.*

United Nations Educational, Scientific and Cultural Organization (UNESCO), 7 Place de Fontenoy, F-75700 Paris, France (Telephone Number in U.S. (212) 963-5981); *Statistical Yearbook.*

YUGOSLAVIA - IMPORTS

The Economist Intelligence Unit, 111 West 57th Street, New York, New York 10019 (800) 938-4685; *Yugoslavia Country*

Report; and *The World Market Atlas.*

Euromonitor International, Inc., 122 South Michigan Avenue, Suite 1200, Chicago, Illinois 60603 (800) 577-EURO; *The World Economic Factbook.*

Europa Publications Limited, 18 Bedford Square, London, WC1B 3JN, England; *The Europa World Year Book.*

Food and Agricultural Organization of the United Nations (FAO) Via delle Terme di Caracalla, 00100 Rome, Italy (Telephone Number in U.S. (202) 653-2400); *The State of Food and Agriculture.*

International Lead and Zinc Study Group, Metro House, 58 St. James's Street, London SW1A 1LD England; *Lead and Zinc Statistics.*

International Monetary Fund, 700 Nineteenth Street, NW, Washington, D.C. 20431 (202) 623-7000; *Direction of Trade Statistics; Government Finance Statistics Yearbook;* and *International Financial Statistics.*

Organisation for Economic Co-operation and Development (OECD), 2 rue Andre-Pascal, 75 Paris 16, France (Telephone Number in U.S. (202) 785-6323); *Milk, Milk Products, and Egg Balances in OECD Member Countries;* and *Review of Fisheries in OECD Member Countries.*

St. Martin's Press, Inc., 175 Fifth Avenue, New York, New York 10010 (800) 221-7945; *The Statesman's Year-Book.*

Statistical Office of the United Nations, Publishing Service, New York, New York 10017 (800) 253-9646; *Trends in Europe and North America: The Statistical Yearbook of the Economic Commission for Europe.*

United Nations Conference on Trade and Development (UNCTAD), New York, New York 10017 (800) 253-9646; *Handbook of International Trade and Development Statistics.*

The World Bank, 1818 H Street, NW, Washington, D.C. 20433 (202) 477-1234; *World Development Indicators.*

YUGOSLAVIA - INCOME TAXES - See YUGOSLAVIA - TAXATION

YUGOSLAVIA - INDUSTRY

Economist Intelligence Unit, 111 West 57th Street, New York, New York 10019 (800) 938-4685; *Yugoslavia Country Report.*

Euromonitor International, Inc., 122 South Michigan Avenue, Suite 1200, Chicago, Illinois 60603 (800) 577-EURO; *The World Economic Factbook;* and *World*

Marketing Data and Statistics.

Europa Publications Limited, 18 Bedford Square, London, WC1B 3JN, England; *The Europa World Year Book.*

Federal Statistical Office, Gustav-Stresemann - Ring 11, D-6200, Wiesbaden, Germany; *Jugoslawien.*

International Labour Office, I.L.O. Publications, 1828 L Street, NW, Suite 801, Washington, D.C. 20036 (301) 638-3152; *Yearbook of Labour Statistics.*

M.E. Sharpe, 80 Business Park Drive, Armonk, New York 10504 (800) 541-6563; *The Illustrated Book of World Rankings.*

Organisation for Economic Co-operation and Development (OECD), 2 rue Andre-Pascal, 75 Paris 16, France (Telephone Number in U.S. (202) 785-6323); *Main Economic Indicators - Historical Statistics.*

St. Martin's Press, Inc., 175 Fifth Avenue, New York, New York 10010 (800) 221-7945; *The Statesman's Year-Book.*

Statistical Office of the United Nations, Publishing Service, New York, New York 10017 (800) 253-9646; *Statistical Yearbook; Industrial Commodity Statistics Yearbook;* and *Trends in Europe and North America: The Statistical Yearbook of the Economic Commission for Europe.*

The World Bank, 1818 H Street, NW, Washington, D.C. 20433 (202) 477-1234; *World Development Indicators.*

World Intellectual Property Organization, 34 Chemin des Colombettes, CH-1211 Geneva 20. Switzerland; *Industrial Property Statistics.*

YUGOSLAVIA - INFANT AND MATERNAL MORTALITY - See YUGOSLAVIA - MORTALITY

YUGOSLAVIA - INTERNAL TRADE

Statistical Office of the United Nations, Publishing Service, New York, New York 10017 (800) 253-9646; *Statistical Yearbook.*

YUGOSLAVIA - INTERNATIONAL LIQUIDITY

International Monetary Fund, 700 Nineteenth Street, NW, Washington, D.C. 20431 (202) 623-7000; *International Financial Statistics.*

YUGOSLAVIA - INTERNATIONAL RESERVES EXCLUDING GOLD

Statistical Office of the United Nations, Publishing Service, New York, New York 10017 (800) 253-9646; *Statistical Yearbook.*

The World Bank, 1818 H Street, NW, Washington, D.C. 20433 (202) 477-1234; *World Development Indicators.*

YUGOSLAVIA - IRON ORE PRODUCTION AND CONSUMPTION - See YUGOSLAVIA - MINING AND MINERAL PRODUCTS

YUGOSLAVIA - LABOR

Euromonitor International, Inc., 122 South Michigan Avenue, Suite 1200, Chicago, Illinois 60603 (800) 577-EURO; *World Marketing Data and Statistics.*

Europa Publications Limited, 18 Bedford Square, London, WC1B 3JN, England; *The Europa World Year Book.*

Food and Agricultural Organization of the United Nations (FAO) Via delle Terme di Caracalla, 00100 Rome, Italy (Telephone Number in U.S. (202) 653-2400); *The State of Food and Agriculture.*

International Labour Office, I.L.O. Publications, 1828 L Street, NW, Suite 801, Washington, D.C. 20036 (301) 638-3152; *Yearbook of Labour Statistics.*

M.E. Sharpe, 80 Business Park Drive, Armonk, New York 10504 (800) 541-6563; *The Illustrated Book of World Rankings.*

Organisation for Economic Co-operation and Development (OECD), 2 rue Andre-Pascal, 75 Paris 16, France (Telephone Number in U.S. (202) 785-6323); *Main Economic Indicators - Historical Statistics.*

St. Martin's Press, Inc., 175 Fifth Avenue, New York, New York 10010 (800) 221-7945; *The Statesman's Year-Book.*

The World Bank, 1818 H Street, NW, Washington, D.C. 20433 (202) 477-1234; *The World Bank Atlas;* and *World Development Indicators.*

YUGOSLAVIA - LAND USE

Euromonitor International, Inc., 122 South Michigan Avenue, Suite 1200, Chicago, Illinois 60603 (800) 577-EURO; *European Marketing Data and Statistics.*

YUGOSLAVIA - LEAD AND LEAD ORE PRODUCTION AND CONSUMPTION - See YUGOSLAVIA - MINING AND MINERAL PRODUCTS

YUGOSLAVIA - LIBRARIES

Euromonitor International, Inc., 122 South Michigan Avenue, Suite 1200, Chicago, Illinois 60603 (800) 577-EURO; *European Marketing Data and Statistics.*

M.E. Sharpe, 80 Business Park Drive, Armonk, New York 10504 (800) 541-6563;

The Illustrated Book of World Rankings.

Statistical Office of the United Nations, Publishing Service, New York, New York 10017 (800) 253-9646; *Trends in Europe and North America: The Statistical Yearbook of the Economic Commission for Europe.*

United Nations Educational, Scientific and Cultural Organization (UNESCO), 7 Place de Fontenoy, F-75700 Paris, France (Telephone Number in U.S. (212) 963-5981); *Statistical Yearbook.*

YUGOSLAVIA - LIFE EXPECTANCY

Euromonitor International, Inc., 122 South Michigan Avenue, Suite 1200, Chicago, Illinois 60603 (800) 577-EURO; *The World Economic Factbook.*

St. Martin's Press, Inc., 175 Fifth Avenue, New York, New York 10010 (800) 221-7945; *The Statesman's Year-Book.*

Statistical Office of the United Nations, Publishing Service, New York, New York 10017 (800) 253-9646; *Trends in Europe and North America: The Statistical Yearbook of the Economic Commission for Europe; and World Statistics Pocketbook.*

The World Bank, 1818 H Street, NW, Washington, D.C. 20433 (202) 477-1234; *The World Bank Atlas.*

YUGOSLAVIA - LIGNITE PRODUCTION - See YUGOSLAVIA - MINING AND MINERAL PRODUCTS

YUGOSLAVIA - LITERACY RATE

Euromonitor International, Inc., 122 South Michigan Avenue, Suite 1200, Chicago, Illinois 60603 (800) 577-EURO; *World Marketing Data and Statistics.*

YUGOSLAVIA - LIVESTOCK AND POULTRY

Euromonitor International, Inc., 122 South Michigan Avenue, Suite 1200, Chicago, Illinois 60603 (800) 577-EURO; *European Marketing Data and Statistics.*

Europa Publications Limited, 18 Bedford Square, London, WC1B 3JN, England; *The Europa World Year Book.*

Food and Agricultural Organization of the United Nations (FAO) Via delle Terme di Caracalla, 00100 Rome, Italy (Telephone Number in U.S. (202) 653-2400); *The State of Food and Agriculture.*

M.E. Sharpe, 80 Business Park Drive, Armonk, New York 10504 (800) 541-6563; *The Illustrated Book of World Rankings.*

St. Martin's Press, Inc., 175 Fifth Avenue, New York, New York 10010 (800) 221-7945; *The Statesman's Year-Book.*

Statistical Office of the United Nations, Publishing Service, New York, New York 10017 (800) 253-9646; *Statistical Yearbook.*

United Nations Conference on Trade and Development, Central Statistical Service, Palais des Nations, Geneva, Switzerland (Telephone in U.S. (800) 253-9646); *UNCTAD Commodity Yearbook.*

YUGOSLAVIA - MAIL - NUMBER OF ITEMS SENT AND RECEIVED

Statistical Office of the United Nations, Publishing Service, New York, New York 10017 (800) 253-9646; *Statistical Yearbook.*

YUGOSLAVIA - MANGANESE PRODUCTION AND CONSUMPTION - See YUGOSLAVIA - MINING AND MINERAL PRODUCTS

YUGOSLAVIA - MANUFACTURING

American Automobile Manufacturers Association, 1401 H Street, NW, Suite 900, Washington, D.C. 20005 (202) 326-5500; *World Motor Vehicle Data.*

M.E. Sharpe, 80 Business Park Drive, Armonk, New York 10504 (800) 541-6563; *The Illustrated Book of World Rankings.*

Statistical Office of the United Nations, Publishing Service, New York, New York 10017 (800) 253-9646; *Statistical Yearbook.*

The World Bank, 1818 H Street, NW, Washington, D.C. 20433 (202) 477-1234; *World Development Indicators.*

YUGOSLAVIA - MARRIAGE RATES

Europa Publications Limited, 18 Bedford Square, London, WC1B 3JN, England; *The Europa World Year Book.*

M.E. Sharpe, 80 Business Park Drive, Armonk, New York 10504 (800) 541-6563; *The Illustrated Book of World Rankings.*

Statistical Office of the United Nations, Publishing Service, New York, New York 10017 (800) 253-9646; *Demographic Yearbook; Statistical Yearbook; and Trends in Europe and North America: The Statistical Yearbook of the Economic Commission for Europe.*

YUGOSLAVIA - MEAT PRODUCTION - See YUGOSLAVIA - LIVESTOCK AND POULTRY

YUGOSLAVIA - MERCHANT SHIPPING

Europa Publications Limited, 18 Bedford Square, London, WC1B 3JN, England; *The Europa World Year Book.*

Lloyd's Register of Shipping, 17 Battery Place, New York, New York 10004 (212) 425-8050; *Register of Ships.*

St. Martin's Press, Inc., 175 Fifth Avenue, New York, New York 10010 (800) 221-7945; *The Statesman's Year-Book.*

Statistical Office of the United Nations, Publishing Service, New York, New York 10017 (800) 253-9646; *Annual Bulletin of Transport Statistics for Europe; and Statistical Yearbook.*

U.S. Department of Transportation, Maritime Administration, 400 Seventh Street, SW, Washington, D.C. 20590 (202) 366-5807, www.marad.dot.gov; *A Statistical Analysis of the World's Merchant Fleets.*

YUGOSLAVIA - MERCURY PRODUCTION AND CONSUMPTION - See YUGOSLAVIA - MINING AND MINERAL PRODUCTS

YUGOSLAVIA - MILITARY

The Economist Intelligence Unit, 111 West 57th Street, New York, New York 10019 (800) 938-4685; *The World Market Atlas.*

Euromonitor International, Inc., 122 South Michigan Avenue, Suite 1200, Chicago, Illinois 60603 (800) 577-EURO; *World Marketing Data and Statistics.*

International Monetary Fund, 700 Nineteenth Street, NW, Washington, D.C. 20431 (202) 623-7000; *Government Finance Statistics Yearbook.*

St. Martin's Press, Inc., 175 Fifth Avenue, New York, New York 10010 (800) 221-7945; *The Statesman's Year-Book.*

U.S. Arms Control and Disarmament Agency, 320 Twenty-first Street, NW, Washington, D.C. 20451 (202) 647-8677; *World Military Expenditures and Arms Transfers.*

YUGOSLAVIA - MILK PRODUCTION - See YUGOSLAVIA - DAIRY PRODUCTS

YUGOSLAVIA - MINING AND MINERAL PRODUCTS

Commodity Research Bureau, 30 South Wacker Drive, Chicago, Illinois 60606 (312) 454-1801; *Commodity Year Book.*

Europa Publications Limited, 18 Bedford Square, London, WC1B 3JN, England; *The Europa World Year Book.*

International Lead and Zinc Study Group, Metro House, 58 St. James's Street, London SW1A 1LD England; *Lead and Zinc Statistics.*

M.E. Sharpe, 80 Business Park Drive, Armonk, New York 10504 (800) 541-6563; *The Illustrated Book of World Rankings.*

Penn Well Publishing Company, 1421 South Sheridan Road, P.O. Box 1260, Tulsa, Oklahoma 74101 (800) 752-9764; *International Energy Statistics Sourcebook.*

St. Martin's Press, Inc., 175 Fifth Avenue, New York, New York 10010 (800) 221-7945; *The Statesman's Year-Book.*

Statistical Office of the United Nations, Publishing Service, New York, New York 10017 (800) 253-9646; *Statistical Yearbook.*

United Nations Conference on Trade and Development, Central Statistical Service, Palais des Nations, Geneva, Switzerland (Telephone in U.S. (800) 253-9646); *UNCTAD Commodity Yearbook.*

World Bureau of Metal Statistics, 27-A High Street, Ware Hert SG12 9BA, England; *World Metal Statistics.*

YUGOSLAVIA - MOLYBDENUM AND MOLYBDENUM ORE PRODUCTION AND CONSUMPTION - See YUGOSLAVIA - MINING AND MINERAL PRODUCTS

YUGOSLAVIA - MONEY EXCHANGE RATE - See YUGOSLAVIA - EXCHANGE RATE

YUGOSLAVIA - MONEY SUPPLY

Economist Intelligence Unit, 111 West 57th Street, New York, New York 10019 (800) 938-4685; *Yugoslavia Country Report.*

Europa Publications Limited, 18 Bedford Square, London, WC1B 3JN, England; *The Europa World Year Book.*

Federal Statistical Office, Gustav-Stresemann - Ring 11, D-6200, Wiesbaden, Germany; *Jugoslawien.*

International Monetary Fund, 700 Nineteenth Street, NW, Washington, D.C. 20431 (202) 623-7000; *International Financial Statistics.*

Statistical Office of the United Nations, Publishing Service, New York, New York 10017 (800) 253-9646; *Statistical Yearbook.*

The World Bank, 1818 H Street, NW, Washington, D.C. 20433 (202) 477-1234; *World Development Indicators.*

YUGOSLAVIA - MORTALITY

Euromonitor International, Inc., 122 South Michigan Avenue, Suite 1200, Chicago, Illinois 60603 (800) 577-EURO; *The World Economic Factbook.*

Europa Publications Limited, 18 Bedford Square, London, WC1B 3JN, England; *The Europa World Year Book.*

St. Martin's Press, Inc., 175 Fifth Avenue, New York, New York 10010 (800)

221-7945; *The Statesman's Year-Book.*

Statistical Office of the United Nations, Publishing Service, New York, New York 10017 (800) 253-9646; *Demographic Yearbook; Statistical Yearbook; Trends in Europe and North America: The Statistical Yearbook of the Economic Commission for Europe;* and *World Statistics Pocketbook.*

United Nations Children's Fund (UNICEF), 3 United Nations Plaza, New York, New York 10017 (800) 253-9646; *State of the World's Children.*

The World Bank, 1818 H Street, NW, Washington, D.C. 20433 (202) 477-1234; *The World Bank Atlas;* and *World Development Indicators.*

YUGOSLAVIA - MOTION PICTURES

St. Martin's Press, Inc., 175 Fifth Avenue, New York, New York 10010 (800) 221-7945; *The Statesman's Year-Book.*

United Nations Educational, Scientific and Cultural Organization (UNESCO), 7 Place de Fontenoy, F-75700 Paris, France (Telephone Number in U.S. (212) 963-5981); *Statistical Yearbook.*

YUGOSLAVIA - MOTOR VEHICLE PRODUCTION

American Automobile Manufacturers Association, 1401 H Street, NW, Suite 900, Washington, D.C. 20005 (202) 326-5500; *World Motor Vehicle Data.*

Statistical Office of the United Nations, Publishing Service, New York, New York 10017 (800) 253-9646; *Statistical Yearbook.*

YUGOSLAVIA - MOTOR VEHICLES IN USE

American Automobile Manufacturers Association, 1401 H Street, NW, Suite 900, Washington, D.C. 20005 (202) 326-5500; *World Motor Vehicle Data.*

Europa Publications Limited, 18 Bedford Square, London, WC1B 3JN, England; *The Europa World Year Book.*

International Road Federation, 2600 Virginia Avenue, NW, Washington, D.C. 20037 (202) 338-4641; *World Road Statistics.*

Statistical Office of the United Nations, Publishing Service, New York, New York 10017 (800) 253-9646; *Statistical Yearbook.*

YUGOSLAVIA - MULES - See YUGOSLAVIA - LIVESTOCK AND POULTRY

YUGOSLAVIA - MUSEUMS

Euromonitor International, Inc., 122 South Michigan Avenue, Suite 1200,

Chicago, Illinois 60603 (800) 577-EURO; *European Marketing Data and Statistics.*

M.E. Sharpe, 80 Business Park Drive, Armonk, New York 10504 (800) 541-6563; *The Illustrated Book of World Rankings.*

United Nations Educational, Scientific and Cultural Organization (UNESCO), 7 Place de Fontenoy, F-75700 Paris, France (Telephone Number in U.S. (212) 963-5981); *Statistical Yearbook.*

YUGOSLAVIA - NATALITY - See YUGOSLAVIA - BIRTH RATE

YUGOSLAVIA - NATIONAL ACCOUNTS

Europa Publications Limited, 18 Bedford Square, London, WC1B 3JN, England; *The Europa World Year Book.*

Federal Statistical Office, Gustav-Stresemann - Ring 11, D-6200, Wiesbaden, Germany; *Jugoslawien.*

International Monetary Fund, 700 Nineteenth Street, NW, Washington, D.C. 20431 (202) 623-7000; *International Financial Statistics.*

Statistical Office of the United Nations, Publishing Service, New York, New York 10017 (800) 253-9646; *National Accounts Statistics;* and *Statistical Yearbook.*

YUGOSLAVIA - NATIONAL INCOME

M.E. Sharpe, 80 Business Park Drive, Armonk, New York 10504 (800) 541-6563; *The Illustrated Book of World Rankings.*

Statistical Office of the United Nations, Publishing Service, New York, New York 10017 (800) 253-9646; *National Accounts Statistics;* and *Statistical Yearbook.*

YUGOSLAVIA - NATIONAL PRODUCT

M.E. Sharpe, 80 Business Park Drive, Armonk, New York 10504 (800) 541-6563; *The Illustrated Book of World Rankings.*

Statistical Office of the United Nations, Publishing Service, New York, New York 10017 (800) 253-9646; *Statistical Yearbook.*

YUGOSLAVIA - NATURAL GAS PRODUCTION - See YUGOSLAVIA - MINING AND MINERAL PRODUCTS

YUGOSLAVIA - NET MATERIAL PRODUCT

Statistical Office of the United Nations, Publishing Service, New York, New York 10017 (800) 253-9646; *Statistical Yearbook.*

YUGOSLAVIA - NEWSPAPER PRODUCTION - See YUGOSLAVIA - FORESTRY AND FOREST PRODUCTS

YUGOSLAVIA - NEWSPRINT PRODUCTION AND CONSUMPTION - See YUGOSLAVIA - FORESTRY AND FOREST PRODUCTS

YUGOSLAVIA - NICKEL AND NICKEL ORE PRODUCTION AND CONSUMPTION - See YUGOSLAVIA - MINING AND MINERAL PRODUCTS

YUGOSLAVIA - NITRIC ACID PRODUCTION - See YUGOSLAVIA - MINING AND MINERAL PRODUCTS

YUGOSLAVIA - OCCUPATIONS - See YUGOSLAVIA - LABOR

YUGOSLAVIA - ONION PRODUCTION - See YUGOSLAVIA - CROPS

YUGOSLAVIA - PAPER PRODUCTION - See YUGOSLAVIA - FORESTRY AND FOREST PRODUCTS

YUGOSLAVIA - PATENTS, TRADEMARKS AND SERVICE MARKS

Statistical Office of the United Nations, Publishing Service, New York, New York 10017 (800) 253-9646; *Statistical Yearbook.*

World Intellectual Property Organization, 34 Chemin des Colombettes, CH-1211 Geneva 20. Switzerland; *Industrial Property Statistics.*

YUGOSLAVIA - PEANUT PRODUCTION - See YUGOSLAVIA - CROPS

YUGOSLAVIA - PERIODICALS

United Nations Educational, Scientific and Cultural Organization (UNESCO), 7 Place de Fontenoy, F-75700 Paris, France (Telephone Number in U.S. (212) 963-5981); *Statistical Yearbook.*

YUGOSLAVIA - PESTICIDE USE

Food and Agricultural Organization of the United Nations (FAO) Via delle Terme di Caracalla, 00100 Rome, Italy (Telephone Number in U.S. (202) 653-2400); *The State of Food and Agriculture.*

YUGOSLAVIA - PETROLEUM INDUSTRY

Euromonitor International, Inc., 122 South Michigan Avenue, Suite 1200, Chicago, Illinois 60603 (800) 577-EURO; *European Marketing Data and Statistics.*

Food and Agricultural Organization of the United Nations (FAO) Via delle Terme di Caracalla, 00100 Rome, Italy (Telephone Number in U.S. (202) 653-2400); *The State of Food and Agriculture.*

M.E. Sharpe, 80 Business Park Drive, Armonk, New York 10504 (800) 541-6563; *The Illustrated Book of World Rankings.*

Penn Well Publishing Company, 1421 South Sheridan Road, P.O. Box 1260, Tulsa, Oklahoma 74101 (800) 752-9764; *International Energy Statistics Sourcebook.*

St. Martin's Press, Inc., 175 Fifth Avenue, New York, New York 10010 (800) 221-7945; *The Statesman's Year-Book.*

Statistical Office of the United Nations, Publishing Service, New York, New York 10017 (800) 253-9646; *Statistical Yearbook;* and *Trends in Europe and North America: The Statistical Yearbook of the Economic Commission for Europe.*

United Nations Conference on Trade and Development, Central Statistical Service, Palais des Nations, Geneva, Switzerland (Telephone in U.S. (800) 253-9646); *UNCTAD Commodity Yearbook.*

YUGOSLAVIA - PIG-IRON AND FERRO-ALLOYS - See YUGOSLAVIA - MINING AND MINERAL PRODUCTS

YUGOSLAVIA - PIGS - See YUGOSLAVIA - LIVESTOCK AND POULTRY

YUGOSLAVIA - PLASTIC AND RESIN PRODUCTION

Statistical Office of the United Nations, Publishing Service, New York, New York 10017 (800) 253-9646; *Statistical Yearbook.*

YUGOSLAVIA - PLATINUM PRODUCTION - See YUGOSLAVIA - MINING AND MINERAL PRODUCTS

YUGOSLAVIA - POPULATION

The Economist Intelligence Unit, 111 West 57th Street, New York, New York 10019 (800) 938-4685; *Yugoslavia Country Report;* and *The World Market Atlas.*

Euromonitor International, Inc., 122 South Michigan Avenue, Suite 1200, Chicago, Illinois 60603 (800) 577-EURO; *European Marketing Data and Statistics;* and *The World Economic Factbook.*

Europa Publications Limited, 18 Bedford Square, London, WC1B 3JN, England; *The Europa World Year Book.*

Federal Statistical Office, Gustav-Stresemann - Ring 11, D-6200, Wiesbaden, Germany; *Jugoslawien.*

International Labour Office, I.L.O. Publications, 1828 L Street, NW, Suite 801, Washington, D.C. 20036 (301) 638-3152; *Yearbook of Labour Statistics.*

M.E. Sharpe, 80 Business Park Drive, Armonk, New York 10504 (800) 541-6563; *The Illustrated Book of World Rankings.*

St. Martin's Press, Inc., 175 Fifth

Avenue, New York, New York 10010 (800) 221-7945; *The Statesman's Year-Book.*

Statistical Office of the United Nations, Publishing Service, New York, New York 10017 (800) 253-9646; *Demographic Yearbook; Statistical Yearbook; Trends in Europe and North America: The Statistical Yearbook of the Economic Commission for Europe;* and *World Statistics Pocketbook.*

United Nations Educational, Scientific and Cultural Organization (UNESCO), 7 Place de Fontenoy, F-75700 Paris, France (Telephone Number in U.S. (212) 963-5981); *Statistical Yearbook.*

U.S. Arms Control and Disarmament Agency, 320 Twenty-first Street, NW, Washington, D.C. 20451 (202) 647-8677; *World Military Expenditures and Arms Transfers.*

The World Bank, 1818 H Street, NW, Washington, D.C. 20433 (202) 477-1234; *The World Bank Atlas.*

World Health Organization, Office of Publications, Avenue Appia, CH-1211 Geneva, 27, Switzerland (Telephone Number in U.S. (518) 436-9686); *World Health Statistics: Vital Statistics and Causes of Death.*

YUGOSLAVIA - POST OFFICES

M.E. Sharpe, 80 Business Park Drive, Armonk, New York 10504 (800) 541-6563; *The Illustrated Book of World Rankings.*

St. Martin's Press, Inc., 175 Fifth Avenue, New York, New York 10010 (800) 221-7945; *The Statesman's Year-Book.*

Statistical Office of the United Nations, Publishing Service, New York, New York 10017 (800) 253-9646; *Trends in Europe and North America: The Statistical Yearbook of the Economic Commission for Europe.*

YUGOSLAVIA - POTATO PRODUCTION - See YUGOSLAVIA - CROPS

YUGOSLAVIA - POWER PRODUCTION INDUSTRY

Statistical Office of the United Nations, Publishing Service, New York, New York 10017 (800) 253-9646; *Statistical Yearbook.*

YUGOSLAVIA - PRICES

Federal Statistical Office, Gustav-Stresemann - Ring 11, D-6200, Wiesbaden, Germany; *Jugoslawien.*

Food and Agricultural Organization of the United Nations (FAO) Via delle Terme di Caracalla, 00100 Rome, Italy (Telephone Number in U.S. (202) 653-2400); *The State of Food and Agriculture.*

International Lead and Zinc Study Group, Metro House, 58 St. James's Street, London SW1A 1LD England; *Lead and Zinc Statistics.*

International Monetary Fund, 700 Nineteenth Street, NW, Washington, D.C. 20431 (202) 623-7000; *International Financial Statistics.*

M.E. Sharpe, 80 Business Park Drive, Armonk, New York 10504 (800) 541-6563; *The Illustrated Book of World Rankings.*

Organisation for Economic Co-operation and Development (OECD), 2 rue Andre-Pascal, 75 Paris 16, France (Telephone Number in U.S. (202) 785-6323); *Main Economic Indicators - Historical Statistics.*

World Bureau of Metal Statistics, 27-A High Street, Ware Hert SG12 9BA, England; *World Metal Statistics.*

YUGOSLAVIA - PRODUCTION

American Automobile Manufacturers Association, 1401 H Street, NW, Suite 900, Washington, D.C. 20005 (202) 326-5500; *World Motor Vehicle Data.*

International Lead and Zinc Study Group, Metro House, 58 St. James's Street, London SW1A 1LD England; *Lead and Zinc Statistics.*

M.E. Sharpe, 80 Business Park Drive, Armonk, New York 10504 (800) 541-6563; *The Illustrated Book of World Rankings.*

Organisation for Economic Co-operation and Development (OECD), 2 rue Andre-Pascal, 75 Paris 16, France (Telephone Number in U.S. (202) 785-6323); *Milk, Milk Products, and Egg Balances in OECD Member Countries.*

YUGOSLAVIA - PROPERTY TAXES - See YUGOSLAVIA - TAXATION

YUGOSLAVIA - PUBLIC FINANCE - See YUGOSLAVIA - FINANCE

YUGOSLAVIA - RADIO BROADCASTING - See YUGOSLAVIA - BROADCASTING

YUGOSLAVIA - RADIO RECEIVER PRODUCTION

Statistical Office of the United Nations, Publishing Service, New York, New York 10017 (800) 253-9646; *Statistical Yearbook.*

YUGOSLAVIA - RADIO RECEIVERS

St. Martin's Press, Inc., 175 Fifth Avenue, New York, New York 10010 (800) 221-7945; *The Statesman's Year-Book.*

YUGOSLAVIA - RAILWAYS

Euromonitor International, Inc., 122 South Michigan Avenue, Suite 1200, Chicago, Illinois 60603 (800) 577-EURO; *European Marketing Data and Statistics.*

Europa Publications Limited, 18 Bedford Square, London, WC1B 3JN, England; *The Europa World Year Book.*

Jane's Information Group, Sentinel House, 163 Brighton Road, Coulsdon, Surrey CR5 2NH, England (Telephone Number in U.S. (703) 683-3700); *Jane's World Railways.*

St. Martin's Press, Inc., 175 Fifth Avenue, New York, New York 10010 (800) 221-7945; *The Statesman's Year-Book.*

Statistical Office of the United Nations, Publishing Service, New York, New York 10017 (800) 253-9646; *Annual Bulletin of Transport Statistics for Europe; Statistical Yearbook;* and *Trends in Europe and North America: The Statistical Yearbook of the Economic Commission for Europe.*

YUGOSLAVIA - RELIGION

M.E. Sharpe, 80 Business Park Drive, Armonk, New York 10504 (800) 541-6563; *The Illustrated Book of World Rankings.*

YUGOSLAVIA - RETAIL TRADE

Euromonitor International, Inc., 122 South Michigan Avenue, Suite 1200, Chicago, Illinois 60603 (800) 577-EURO; *World Marketing Data and Statistics.*

Statistical Office of the United Nations, Publishing Service, New York, New York 10017 (800) 253-9646; *Statistical Yearbook.*

YUGOSLAVIA - RICE PRODUCTION - See YUGOSLAVIA - CROPS

YUGOSLAVIA - ROUNDWOOD PRODUCTION - See YUGOSLAVIA - FORESTRY AND FOREST PRODUCTS

YUGOSLAVIA - RUBBER PRODUCTION AND CONSUMPTION

M.E. Sharpe, 80 Business Park Drive, Armonk, New York 10504 (800) 541-6563; *The Illustrated Book of World Rankings.*

Statistical Office of the United Nations, Publishing Service, New York, New York 10017 (800) 253-9646; *Statistical Yearbook.*

YUGOSLAVIA - SALT PRODUCTION - See YUGOSLAVIA - MINING AND MINERAL PRODUCTS

YUGOSLAVIA - SAWNWOOD PRODUCTION - See YUGOSLAVIA - FORESTRY AND FOREST PRODUCTS

YUGOSLAVIA - SCIENCE AND

TECHNOLOGY - EXPENDITURE FOR RESEARCH - See YUGOSLAVIA - SCIENTISTS, TECHNICIANS AND ENGINEERS

YUGOSLAVIA - SCIENTISTS, TECHNICIANS AND ENGINEERS

Statistical Office of the United Nations, Publishing Service, New York, New York 10017 (800) 253-9646; *Statistical Yearbook.*

United Nations Educational, Scientific and Cultural Organization (UNESCO), 7 Place de Fontenoy, F-75700 Paris, France (Telephone Number in U.S. (212) 963-5981); *Statistical Yearbook.*

YUGOSLAVIA - SENIOR CITIZENS

M.E. Sharpe, 80 Business Park Drive, Armonk, New York 10504 (800) 541-6563; *The Illustrated Book of World Rankings.*

YUGOSLAVIA - SHEEP - See YUGOSLAVIA - LIVESTOCK AND POULTRY

YUGOSLAVIA - SILVER PRODUCTION AND CONSUMPTION - See YUGOSLAVIA - MINING AND MINERAL PRODUCTS

YUGOSLAVIA - SOCIAL DATA

M.E. Sharpe, 80 Business Park Drive, Armonk, New York 10504 (800) 541-6563; *The Illustrated Book of World Rankings.*

Statistical Office of the United Nations, Publishing Service, New York, New York 10017 (800) 253-9646; *World Statistics Pocketbook.*

YUGOSLAVIA - SOCIAL SECURITY

International Monetary Fund, 700 Nineteenth Street, NW, Washington, D.C. 20431 (202) 623-7000; *Government Finance Statistics Yearbook.*

St. Martin's Press, Inc., 175 Fifth Avenue, New York, New York 10010 (800) 221-7945; *The Statesman's Year-Book.*

Statistical Office of the United Nations, Publishing Service, New York, New York 10017 (800) 253-9646; *National Accounts Statistics.*

YUGOSLAVIA - SOYBEAN PRODUCTION - See YUGOSLAVIA - CROPS

YUGOSLAVIA - STEEL - See YUGOSLAVIA - MINING AND MINERAL PRODUCTS

YUGOSLAVIA - STOCKS - COMMODITY - MARKET PRICE - INDEX

Economic Commission for Western Asia, Post Office Box 27, Baghdad, Iraq; *Statistical Abstract of Western Asia.*

Food and Agricultural Organization of the United Nations (FAO) Via delle Terme di Caracalla, 00100 Rome, Italy (Telephone Number in U.S. (202) 653-2400); *The State of Food and Agriculture.*

World Bureau of Metal Statistics, 27-A High Street, Ware Hert SG12 9BA, England; *World Metal Statistics.*

YUGOSLAVIA - SUGAR PRODUCTION AND CONSUMPTION - See YUGOSLAVIA - CROPS

YUGOSLAVIA - SULPHURIC ACID PRODUCTION - See YUGOSLAVIA - MINING AND MINERAL PRODUCTS

YUGOSLAVIA - TAXATION

International Monetary Fund, 700 Nineteenth Street, NW, Washington, D.C. 20431 (202) 623-7000; *Government Finance Statistics Yearbook.*

International Road Federation, 2600 Virginia Avenue, NW, Washington, D.C. 20037 (202) 338-4641; *World Road Statistics.*

The World Bank, 1818 H Street, NW, Washington, D.C. 20433 (202) 477-1234; *World Development Indicators.*

YUGOSLAVIA - TELEGRAPH SERVICE

Statistical Office of the United Nations, Publishing Service, New York, New York 10017 (800) 253-9646; *Statistical Yearbook.*

YUGOSLAVIA - TELEPHONES IN USE

American Telephone and Telegraph Company, 26 Parsippany Road, Whippany, New Jersey 07981 (800) 222-0300; *The World's Telephones.*

Europa Publications Limited, 18 Bedford Square, London, WC1B 3JN, England; *The Europa World Year Book.*

St. Martin's Press, Inc., 175 Fifth Avenue, New York, New York 10010 (800) 221-7945; *The Statesman's Year-Book.*

Statistical Office of the United Nations, Publishing Service, New York, New York 10017 (800) 253-9646; *Statistical Yearbook; Trends in Europe and North America: The Statistical Yearbook of the Economic Commission for Europe;* and *World Statistics Pocketbook.*

YUGOSLAVIA - TELEVISION BROADCASTING - See YUGOSLAVIA - BROADCASTING

YUGOSLAVIA - TELEVISION RECEIVER PRODUCTION

Statistical Office of the United Nations,

Publishing Service, New York, New York 10017 (800) 253-9646; *Statistical Yearbook.*

YUGOSLAVIA - TEXTILE INDUSTRY

American Forest and Paper Association, 1111 Nineteenth Street, NW, Washington, D.C. 20036 (202) 463-2700; *Wood Pulp and Fiber Statistics.*

M.E. Sharpe, 80 Business Park Drive, Armonk, New York 10504 (800) 541-6563; *The Illustrated Book of World Rankings.*

St. Martin's Press, Inc., 175 Fifth Avenue, New York, New York 10010 (800) 221-7945; *The Statesman's Year-Book.*

Statistical Office of the United Nations, Publishing Service, New York, New York 10017 (800) 253-9646; *Statistical Yearbook.*

United Nations Conference on Trade and Development, Central Statistical Service, Palais des Nations, Geneva, Switzerland (Telephone in U.S. (800) 253-9646); *UNCTAD Commodity Yearbook.*

YUGOSLAVIA - THEATRE

United Nations Educational, Scientific and Cultural Organization (UNESCO), 7 Place de Fontenoy, F-75700 Paris, France (Telephone Number in U.S. (212) 963-5981); *Statistical Yearbook.*

YUGOSLAVIA - TIN - See YUGOSLAVIA - MINING AND MINERAL PRODUCTS

YUGOSLAVIA - TIRE (MOTOR VEHICLE) PRODUCTION

Statistical Office of the United Nations, Publishing Service, New York, New York 10017 (800) 253-9646; *Statistical Yearbook.*

YUGOSLAVIA - TOBACCO PRODUCTION

Euromonitor International, Inc., 122 South Michigan Avenue, Suite 1200, Chicago, Illinois 60603 (800) 577-EURO; *European Marketing Data and Statistics.*

M.E. Sharpe, 80 Business Park Drive, Armonk, New York 10504 (800) 541-6563; *The Illustrated Book of World Rankings.*

Statistical Office of the United Nations, Publishing Service, New York, New York 10017 (800) 253-9646; *Statistical Yearbook.*

YUGOSLAVIA - TOURISM

Euromonitor International, Inc., 122 South Michigan Avenue, Suite 1200, Chicago, Illinois 60603 (800) 577-EURO; *European Marketing Data and Statistics; World Marketing Data and Statistics;* and *The World Economic Factbook.*

Europa Publications Limited, 18

Bedford Square, London, WC1B 3JN, England; *The Europa World Year Book.*

Federal Statistical Office, Gustav-Stresemann - Ring 11, D-6200, Wiesbaden, Germany; *Jugoslawien.*

M.E. Sharpe, 80 Business Park Drive, Armonk, New York 10504 (800) 541-6563; *The Illustrated Book of World Rankings.*

St. Martin's Press, Inc., 175 Fifth Avenue, New York, New York 10010 (800) 221-7945; *The Statesman's Year-Book.*

Statistical Office of the United Nations, Publishing Service, New York, New York 10017 (800) 253-9646; *Statistical Yearbook;* and *Trends in Europe and North America: The Statistical Yearbook of the Economic Commission for Europe.*

World Tourism Organization, Calle Capitan Haya 42, E-28020 Madrid, Spain; *Yearbook of Tourism Statistics.*

YUGOSLAVIA - TRACTORS IN USE

Statistical Office of the United Nations, Publishing Service, New York, New York 10017 (800) 253-9646; *Statistical Yearbook.*

YUGOSLAVIA - TRADE - See YUGOSLAVIA - FOREIGN TRADE

YUGOSLAVIA - TRADEMARKS AND SERVICE MARKS - See YUGOSLAVIA - PATENTS, TRADEMARKS AND SERVICE MARKS

YUGOSLAVIA - TRANSPORTATION AND COMMUNICATIONS

Euromonitor International, Inc., 122 South Michigan Avenue, Suite 1200, Chicago, Illinois 60603 (800) 577-EURO; *World Marketing Data and Statistics.*

Europa Publications Limited, 18 Bedford Square, London, WC1B 3JN, England; *The Europa World Year Book.*

M.E. Sharpe, 80 Business Park Drive, Armonk, New York 10504 (800) 541-6563; *The Illustrated Book of World Rankings.*

St. Martin's Press, Inc., 175 Fifth Avenue, New York, New York 10010 (800) 221-7945; *The Statesman's Year-Book.*

Statistical Office of the United Nations, Publishing Service, New York, New York 10017 (800) 253-9646; *Annual Bulletin of Transport Statistics for Europe;* and *Trends in Europe and North America: The Statistical Yearbook of the Economic Commission for Europe.*

YUGOSLAVIA - UNEMPLOYMENT

Euromonitor International, Inc., 122 South Michigan Avenue, Suite 1200, Chicago, Illinois 60603 (800) 577-EURO; *European Marketing Data and Statistics.*

International Labour Office, I.L.O. Publications, 1828 L Street, NW, Suite 801, Washington, D.C. 20036 (301) 638-3152; *Yearbook of Labour Statistics.*

St. Martin's Press, Inc., 175 Fifth Avenue, New York, New York 10010 (800) 221-7945; *The Statesman's Year-Book.*

Statistical Office of the United Nations, Publishing Service, New York, New York 10017 (800) 253-9646; *Statistical Yearbook; and Trends in Europe and North America: The Statistical Yearbook of the Economic Commission for Europe.*

YUGOSLAVIA - URANIUM PRODUCTION AND CONSUMPTION - See YUGOSLAVIA - MINING AND MINERAL PRODUCTS

YUGOSLAVIA - VITAL STATISTICS

St. Martin's Press, Inc., 175 Fifth Avenue, New York, New York 10010 (800) 221-7945; *The Statesman's Year-Book.*

Statistical Office of the United Nations, Publishing Service, New York, New York 10017 (800) 253-9646; *Statistical Yearbook.*

World Health Organization, Office of Publications, Avenue Appia, CH-1211 Geneva, 27, Switzerland (Telephone Number in U.S. (518) 436-9686); *World Health Statistics: Vital Statistics and Causes of Death.*

YUGOSLAVIA - WAGES

Euromonitor International, Inc., 122 South Michigan Avenue, Suite 1200, Chicago, Illinois 60603 (800) 577-EURO; *European Marketing Data and Statistics.*

International Labour Office, I.L.O. Publications, 1828 L Street, NW, Suite 801, Washington, D.C. 20036 (301) 638-3152; *Yearbook of Labour Statistics.*

Organisation for Economic Co-operation and Development (OECD), 2 rue Andre-Pascal, 75 Paris 16, France (Telephone Number in U.S. (202) 785-6323); *Main Economic Indicators - Historical Statistics.*

Statistical Office of the United Nations, Publishing Service, New York, New York 10017 (800) 253-9646; *Statistical Yearbook.*

YUGOSLAVIA - WATERWAYS IN USE

Statistical Office of the United Nations, Publishing Service, New York, New York 10017 (800) 253-9646; *Annual Bulletin of Transport Statistics for Europe.*

YUGOSLAVIA - WEATHER - See YUGOSLAVIA - CLIMATE

YUGOSLAVIA - WELFARE

International Monetary Fund, 700 Nineteenth Street, NW, Washington, D.C. 20431 (202) 623-7000; *Government Finance Statistics Yearbook.*

YUGOSLAVIA - WHEAT PRODUCTION AND PRICES - See YUGOSLAVIA - CROPS

YUGOSLAVIA - WHOLESALE PRICES

Statistical Office of the United Nations, Publishing Service, New York, New York 10017 (800) 253-9646; *Statistical Yearbook.*

YUGOSLAVIA - WHOLESALE TRADE

Statistical Office of the United Nations, Publishing Service, New York, New York 10017 (800) 253-9646; *Statistical Yearbook.*

YUGOSLAVIA - WINE PRODUCTION - See YUGOSLAVIA - BEVERAGES

YUGOSLAVIA - WOOD AND WOOD PULP - See YUGOSLAVIA - FORESTRY AND FOREST PRODUCTS

YUGOSLAVIA - WOOL PRODUCTION AND CONSUMPTION - See YUGOSLAVIA - TEXTILE INDUSTRY

YUGOSLAVIA - YARN PRODUCTION - See YUGOSLAVIA - TEXTILE INDUSTRY

YUGOSLAVIA - ZINC AND ZINC ORE PRODUCTION AND CONSUMPTION - See YUGOSLAVIA - MINING AND MINERAL PRODUCTS

YUGOSLAVIA - ZOOS AND BOTANICAL GARDENS

United Nations Educational, Scientific and Cultural Organization (UNESCO), 7 Place de Fontenoy, F-75700 Paris, France (Telephone Number in U.S. (212) 963-5981); *Statistical Yearbook.*

Z

ZAIRE - See CONGO (DEMOCRATIC REPUBLIC OF)

Zambia - National Statistical Office

Central Statistical Office, Ministry of Finance, Post Office Box 31908, Lusaka, Zambia.

Zambia - Primary Statistics Sources

Central Statistical Office, Post Office Box 31908, Lusaka, Zambia; *Statistical Yearbook; Monthly Digest of Statistics;* and *Zambia in Figures.*

ZAMBIA - AGRICULTURE

Economist Intelligence Unit, 111 West 57th Street, New York, New York 10019 (800) 938-4685; *Zambia Country Report.*

Euromonitor International, Inc., 122 South Michigan Avenue, Suite 1200, Chicago, Illinois 60603 (800) 577-EURO; *International Marketing Data and Statistics;* and *World Marketing Data and Statistics.*

Europa Publications Limited, 18 Bedford Square, London, WC1B 3JN, England; *The Europa World Year Book.*

Federal Statistical Office, Gustav-Stresemann - Ring 11, D-6200, Wiesbaden, Germany; *Sambia.*

Food and Agricultural Organization of the United Nations (FAO), Via delle Terme di Caracalla, 00100 Rome, Italy (Telephone Number in U.S. (202) 653-2400); *Production Yearbook; The State of Food and Agriculture;* and *Trade Yearbook.*

M.E. Sharpe, 80 Business Park Drive, Armonk, New York 10504 (800) 541-6563; *The Illustrated Book of World Rankings.*

St. Martin's Press, Inc., 175 Fifth Avenue, New York, New York 10010 (800) 221-

7945; *The Statesman's Year-Book.*

Statistical Office of the United Nations, Publishing Service, New York, New York 10017 (800) 253-9646; *Statistical Yearbook;* and *Survey of Economic and Social Conditions in Africa.*

United Nations Conference on Trade and Development, Central Statistical Service, Palais des Nations, Geneva, Switzerland (Telephone in U.S. (800) 253-9646); *UNCTAD Commodity Yearbook.*

United Nations Economic Commission for Africa, Africa Hall, P.O. Box 3001, Addis Ababa, Ethiopia (Telephone Number in U.S. (800) 253-9646); *African Statistical Yearbook.*

The World Bank, 1818 H Street, NW, Washington, D.C. 20433 (800) 645-7247; *World Development Indicators.*

ZAMBIA - AIRLINE SERVICE

Europa Publications Limited, 18 Bedford Square, London, WC1B 3JN, England; *The Europa World Year Book.*

International Civil Aviation Organization, 999 University Street, Montreal, Quebec, Canada H3C 5H7 (514) 954-8219; *Civil Aviation Statistics of the World.*

M.E. Sharpe, 80 Business Park Drive, Armonk, New York 10504 (800) 541-6563; *The Illustrated Book of World Rankings.*

St. Martin's Press, Inc., 175 Fifth Avenue, New York, New York 10010 (800) 221-7945; *The Statesman's Year-Book.*

Statistical Office of the United Nations, Publishing Service, New York, New York 10017 (800) 253-9646; *Statistical Yearbook.*

United Nations Economic Commission for Africa, Africa Hall, P.O. Box 3001, Addis Ababa, Ethiopia (Telephone Number in U.S. (800) 253-9646); *African Statistical Yearbook.*

ZAMBIA - AIRPORTS

Central Intelligence Agency, Washington, D.C. 20505 (703) 481-1100, www.cia.gov; *The World Factbook.*

ZAMBIA - ALUMINUM PRODUCTION AND CONSUMPTION - See ZAMBIA - MINING AND MINERAL PRODUCTS

ZAMBIA - ANIMAL HEALTH

Food and Agricultural Organization of the United Nations (FAO), Via delle Terme di Caracalla, 00100 Rome, Italy (Telephone Number in U.S. (202) 653-2400); *Animal Health Yearbook.*

ZAMBIA - ANTIMONY AND ANTIMONY ORE PRODUCTION AND CONSUMPTION - See ZAMBIA - MINING AND MINERAL PRODUCTS

ZAMBIA - AREA AND DENSITY OF POPULATION

African Development Bank, 01 BP 1387, Abidjan 01, Cote D'Ivoire; *Selected Statistics on Regional Member Countries.*

Central Intelligence Agency, Washington, D.C. 20505 (703) 481-1100, www.cia.gov; *The World Factbook.*

Euromonitor International, Inc., 122 South Michigan Avenue, Suite 1200, Chicago, Illinois 60603 (800) 577-EURO; *International Marketing Data and Statistics;* and *The World Economic Factbook.*

Europa Publications Limited, 18 Bedford Square, London, WC1B 3JN, England; *The Europa World Year Book.*

Federal Statistical Office, Gustav-Stresemann - Ring 11, D-6200, Wiesbaden, Germany; *Sambia.*

Food and Agricultural Organization of the United Nations (FAO) Via delle Terme di Caracalla, 00100 Rome, Italy (Telephone Number in U.S. (202) 653-2400); *The State of Food and Agriculture.*

M.E. Sharpe, 80 Business Park Drive, Armonk, New York 10504 (800) 541-6563; *The Illustrated Book of World Rankings.*

St. Martin's Press, Inc., 175 Fifth Avenue, New York, New York 10010 (800) 221-7945; *The Statesman's Year-Book.*

Statistical Office of the United Nations, Publishing Service, New York, New York 10017 (800) 253-9646; *Statistical Yearbook;* and *Survey of Economic and Social Conditions in Africa.*

United Nations Educational, Scientific and Cultural Organization (UNESCO), 7 Place de Fontenoy, F-75700 Paris, France (Telephone Number in U.S. (212) 963-5981); *Statistical Yearbook.*

The World Bank, 1818 H Street, NW, Washington, D.C. 20433 (202) 477-1234; *World Development Report.*

ZAMBIA - ARMS EXPORTS AND EXPORTS - See ZAMBIA - MILITARY

ZAMBIA - BALANCE OF PAYMENTS

African Development Bank, 01 BP 1387, Abidjan 01, Cote D'Ivoire; *Selected Statistics on Regional Member Countries.*

The Economist Intelligence Unit, 111 West 57th Street, New York, New York 10019 (800) 938-4685; *The World Market Atlas.*

Europa Publications Limited, 18 Bedford Square, London, WC1B 3JN, England; *The Europa World Year Book.*

Federal Statistical Office, Gustav-Stresemann - Ring 11, D-6200, Wiesbaden, Germany; *Sambia.*

International Monetary Fund, 700 Nineteenth Street, NW, Washington, D.C. 20431 (202) 623-7000; *Balance of Payments Yearbook.*

United Nations Conference on Trade and Development (UNCTAD), New York, New York 10017 (800) 253-9646; *Handbook of International Trade and Development Statistics.*

United Nations Economic Commission for Africa, Africa Hall, P.O. Box 3001, Addis Ababa, Ethiopia (Telephone Number in U.S. (800) 253-9646); *African Statistical Yearbook.*

The World Bank, 1818 H Street, NW, Washington, D.C. 20433 (202) 477-1234; *World Development Report;* and *World Development Indicators.*

ZAMBIA - BANKING

Euromonitor International, Inc., 122

South Michigan Avenue, Suite 1200, Chicago, Illinois 60603 (800) 577-EURO; *World Marketing Data and Statistics.*

Europa Publications Limited, 18 Bedford Square, London, WC1B 3JN, England; *The Europa World Year Book.*

International Monetary Fund, 700 Nineteenth Street, NW, Washington, D.C. 20431 (202) 623-7000; *Government Finance Statistics Yearbook;* and *International Financial Statistics.*

M.E. Sharpe, 80 Business Park Drive, Armonk, New York 10504 (800) 541-6563; *The Illustrated Book of World Rankings.*

St. Martin's Press, Inc., 175 Fifth Avenue, New York, New York 10010 (800) 221-7945; *The Statesman's Year-Book.*

United Nations Economic Commission for Africa, Africa Hall, P.O. Box 3001, Addis Ababa, Ethiopia (Telephone Number in U.S. (800) 253-9646); *African Statistical Yearbook.*

ZAMBIA - BARLEY PRODUCTION - See ZAMBIA - CROPS

ZAMBIA - BAUXITE PRODUCTION AND CONSUMPTION - See ZAMBIA - MINING AND MINERAL PRODUCTS

ZAMBIA - BEER PRODUCTION - See ZAMBIA - BEVERAGES

ZAMBIA - BEVERAGES

M.E. Sharpe, 80 Business Park Drive, Armonk, New York 10504 (800) 541-6563; *The Illustrated Book of World Rankings.*

Statistical Office of the United Nations, Publishing Service, New York, New York 10017 (800) 253-9646; *Statistical Yearbook.*

ZAMBIA - BIRTH RATE

Central Intelligence Agency, Washington, D.C. 20505 (703) 481-1100, www.cia.gov; *The World Factbook.*

Euromonitor International, Inc., 122 South Michigan Avenue, Suite 1200, Chicago, Illinois 60603 (800) 577-EURO; *International Marketing Data and Statistics;* and *The World Economic Factbook.*

Europa Publications Limited, 18 Bedford Square, London, WC1B 3JN, England; *The Europa World Year Book.*

M.E. Sharpe, 80 Business Park Drive, Armonk, New York 10504 (800) 541-6563; *The Illustrated Book of World Rankings.*

Statistical Office of the United Nations, Publishing Service, New York, New York 10017 (800) 253-9646; *Demographic*

Yearbook; Statistical Yearbook; and *Survey of Economic and Social Conditions in Africa.*

The World Bank, 1818 H Street, NW, Washington, D.C. 20433 (202) 477-1234; *World Development Indicators.*

ZAMBIA - BONDS

International Monetary Fund, 700 Nineteenth Street, NW, Washington, D.C. 20431 (202) 623-7000; *Government Finance Statistics Yearbook.*

ZAMBIA - BOOK PRODUCTION

United Nations Educational, Scientific and Cultural Organization (UNESCO), 7 Place de Fontenoy, F-75700 Paris, France (Telephone Number in U.S. (212) 963-5981); *Statistical Yearbook.*

ZAMBIA - BROADCASTING

Billboard Limited, P.O. Box 9027, 1006 AA Amsterdam, The Netherlands (Telephone Number in U.S. (212) 764-7300); *World Radio TV Handbook.*

Central Intelligence Agency, Washington, D.C. 20505 (703) 481-1100, www.cia.gov; *The World Factbook.*

Euromonitor International, Inc., 122 South Michigan Avenue, Suite 1200, Chicago, Illinois 60603 (800) 577-EURO; *World Marketing Data and Statistics.*

M.E. Sharpe, 80 Business Park Drive, Armonk, New York 10504 (800) 541-6563; *The Illustrated Book of World Rankings.*

St. Martin's Press, Inc., 175 Fifth Avenue, New York, New York 10010 (800) 221-7945; *The Statesman's Year-Book.*

United Nations Educational, Scientific and Cultural Organization (UNESCO), 7 Place de Fontenoy, F-75700 Paris, France (Telephone Number in U.S. (212) 963-5981); *Statistical Yearbook.*

ZAMBIA - BUDGET

Central Intelligence Agency, Washington, D.C. 20505 (703) 481-1100, www.cia.gov; *The World Factbook.*

ZAMBIA - BUSINESS AND PROFESSIONAL LICENSES

International Monetary Fund, 700 Nineteenth Street, NW, Washington, D.C. 20431 (202) 623-7000; *Government Finance Statistics Yearbook.*

ZAMBIA - CADMIUM PRODUCTION AND CONSUMPTION - See ZAMBIA - MINING AND MINERAL PRODUCTS

ZAMBIA - CALORIE SUPPLY

African Development Bank, 01 BP 1387, Abidjan 01, Cote D'Ivoire; *Selected Statistics on Regional Member Countries.*

Food and Agricultural Organization of the United Nations (FAO) Via delle Terme di Caracalla, 00100 Rome, Italy (Telephone Number in U.S. (202) 653-2400); *The State of Food and Agriculture.*

ZAMBIA - CAPITAL REVENUE

International Monetary Fund, 700 Nineteenth Street, NW, Washington, D.C. 20431 (202) 623-7000; *Government Finance Statistics Yearbook.*

ZAMBIA - CATTLE - See ZAMBIA - LIVESTOCK AND POULTRY

ZAMBIA - CEMENT PRODUCTION - See ZAMBIA - MINING AND MINERAL PRODUCTS

ZAMBIA - CHEMICAL (ORGANIC) PRODUCTION - See ZAMBIA - MINING AND MINERAL PRODUCTS

ZAMBIA - CHICKENS - See ZAMBIA - LIVESTOCK AND POULTRY

ZAMBIA - CIGARETTE PRODUCTION - See ZAMBIA - TOBACCO PRODUCTION

ZAMBIA - CLIMATE

M.E. Sharpe, 80 Business Park Drive, Armonk, New York 10504 (800) 541-6563; *The Illustrated Book of World Rankings.*

St. Martin's Press, Inc., 175 Fifth Avenue, New York, New York 10010 (800) 221-7945; *The Statesman's Year-Book.*

ZAMBIA - COAL PRODUCTION AND CONSUMPTION - See ZAMBIA MINING AND MINERAL PRODUCTS

ZAMBIA - COBALT PRODUCTION AND CONSUMPTION - See ZAMBIA - MINING AND MINERAL PRODUCTS

ZAMBIA - COFFEE PRODUCTION AND CONSUMPTION - See ZAIRE -CROPS

ZAMBIA - COKE OVEN COKE PRODUCTION AND CONSUMPTION - See ZAMBIA - MINING AND MINERAL PRODUCTS

ZAMBIA - COMMERCE

St. Martin's Press, Inc., 175 Fifth Avenue, New York, New York 10010 (800) 221-7945; *The Statesman's Year-Book.*

ZAMBIA - COMMUNICATIONS - See ZAMBIA - TRANSPORTATION AND COMMUNICATION

ZAMBIA - CONSTRUCTION INDUSTRY

M.E. Sharpe, 80 Business Park Drive, Armonk, New York 10504 (800) 541-6563; *The Illustrated Book of World Rankings.*

Statistical Office of the United Nations, Publishing Service, New York, New York 10017 (800) 253-9646; *Statistical Yearbook.*

United Nations Economic Commission for Africa, Africa Hall, P.O. Box 3001, Addis Ababa, Ethiopia (Telephone Number in U.S. (800) 253-9646); *African Statistical Yearbook.*

ZAMBIA - CONSUMER PRICE INDEX

African Development Bank, 01 BP 1387, Abidjan 01, Cote D'Ivoire; *Selected Statistics on Regional Member Countries.*

Europa Publications Limited, 18 Bedford Square, London, WC1B 3JN, England; *The Europa World Year Book.*

Statistical Office of the United Nations, Publishing Service, New York, New York 10017 (800) 253-9646; *Statistical Yearbook;* and *Survey of Economic and Social Conditions in Africa.*

United Nations Economic Commission for Africa, Africa Hall, P.O. Box 3001, Addis Ababa, Ethiopia (Telephone Number in U.S. (800) 253-9646); *African Statistical Yearbook.*

ZAMBIA - CONSUMER PRICES

Euromonitor International, Inc., 122 South Michigan Avenue, Suite 1200, Chicago, Illinois 60603 (800) 577-EURO; *World Marketing Data and Statistics.*

International Labour Office, I.L.O. Publications, 1828 L Street, NW, Suite 801, Washington, D.C. 20036 (301) 638-3152; *Yearbook of Labour Statistics.*

International Monetary Fund, 700 Nineteenth Street, NW, Washington, D.C. 20431 (202) 623-7000; *International Financial Statistics.*

ZAMBIA - CONSUMPTION

African Development Bank, 01 BP 1387, Abidjan 01, Cote D'Ivoire; *Selected Statistics on Regional Member Countries.*

International Lead and Zinc Study Group, Metro House, 58 St. James's Street, London SW1A 1LD England; *Lead and Zinc Statistics.*

Statistical Office of the United Nations, Publishing Service, New York, New York 10017 (800) 253-9646; *Survey of Economic and Social Conditions in Africa.*

The World Bank, 1818 H Street, NW, Washington, D.C. 20433 (202) 477-1234; *World Development Report.*

ZAMBIA - COPPER AND COPPER ORE PRODUCTION AND CONSUMPTION - See ZAMBIA - MINING AND MINERAL PRODUCTS

ZAMBIA - CORN PRODUCTION - See ZAMBIA - CROPS

ZAMBIA - CORPORATE TAXES - See ZAMBIA - TAXATION

ZAMBIA - COTTON PRODUCTION - See ZAIRE - CROPS

ZAMBIA - CRIME

International Criminal Police Organization (INTERPOL), 50 quai Achille Lignon, F-69006 Lyon, France; *International Crime Statistics.*

Yale University Press, Yale Station, New Haven, Connecticut 06520 (203) 432-0940; *Violence and Crime in Cross-National Perspective.*

ZAMBIA - CROPS

Europa Publications Limited, 18 Bedford Square, London, WC1B 3JN, England; *The Europa World Year Book.*

Food and Agricultural Organization of the United Nations (FAO) Via delle Terme di Caracalla, 00100 Rome, Italy (Telephone Number in U.S. (202) 653-2400); *The State of Food and Agriculture.*

M.E. Sharpe, 80 Business Park Drive, Armonk, New York 10504 (800) 541-6563; *The Illustrated Book of World Rankings.*

St. Martin's Press, Inc., 175 Fifth Avenue, New York, New York 10010 (800) 221-7945; *The Statesman's Year-Book.*

Statistical Office of the United Nations, Publishing Service, New York, New York 10017 (800) 253-9646; *Statistical Yearbook.*

United Nations Conference on Trade and Development, Central Statistical Service, Palais des Nations, Geneva, Switzerland (Telephone in U.S. (800) 253-9646); *UNCTAD Commodity Yearbook.*

United Nations Economic Commission for Africa, Africa Hall, P.O. Box 3001, Addis Ababa, Ethiopia (Telephone Number in U.S. (800) 253-9646); *African Statistical Yearbook.*

ZAMBIA - CUSTOMS DUTIES

International Monetary Fund, 700 Nineteenth Street, NW, Washington, D.C. 20431 (202) 623-7000; *Government*

Finance Statistics Yearbook.

St. Martin's Press, Inc., 175 Fifth Avenue, New York, New York 10010 (800) 221-7945; *The Statesman's Year-Book.*

ZAMBIA - DAIRY PRODUCTS

Europa Publications Limited, 18 Bedford Square, London, WC1B 3JN, England; *The Europa World Year Book.*

Food and Agricultural Organization of the United Nations (FAO) Via delle Terme di Caracalla, 00100 Rome, Italy (Telephone Number in U.S. (202) 653-2400); *The State of Food and Agriculture.*

M.E. Sharpe, 80 Business Park Drive, Armonk, New York 10504 (800) 541-6563; *The Illustrated Book of World Rankings.*

St. Martin's Press, Inc., 175 Fifth Avenue, New York, New York 10010 (800) 221-7945; *The Statesman's Year-Book.*

Statistical Office of the United Nations, Publishing Service, New York, New York 10017 (800) 253-9646; *Statistical Yearbook.*

ZAMBIA - DEATH RATE - See ZAMBIA - MORTALITY

ZAMBIA - DEFENSE EXPENDITURES - See ZAMBIA - MILITARY

ZAMBIA - DEMOGRAPHY

The Economist Intelligence Unit, 111 West 57th Street, New York, New York 10019 (800) 938-4685; *The World Market Atlas.*

Euromonitor International, Inc., 122 South Michigan Avenue, Suite 1200, Chicago, Illinois 60603 (800) 577-EURO; *International Marketing Data and Statistics; World Marketing Data and Statistics;* and *The World Economic Factbook.*

Federal Statistical Office, Gustav-Stresemann - Ring 11, D-6200, Wiesbaden, Germany; *Sambia.*

M.E. Sharpe, 80 Business Park Drive, Armonk, New York 10504 (800) 541-6563; *The Illustrated Book of World Rankings.*

Statistical Office of the United Nations, Publishing Service, New York, New York 10017 (800) 253-9646; *Human Development Report;* and *Survey of Economic and Social Conditions in Africa.*

ZAMBIA - DEVELOPMENT ASSISTANCE

Statistical Office of the United Nations, Publishing Service, New York, New York 10017 (800) 253-9646; *Statistical Yearbook.*

ZAMBIA - DIAMOND PRODUCTION - See

ZAMBIA - MINING AND MINERAL PRODUCTS

ZAMBIA - DISEASES - See ZAMBIA - HEALTH

ZAMBIA - DIVORCE RATES

M.E. Sharpe, 80 Business Park Drive, Armonk, New York 10504 (800) 541-6563; *The Illustrated Book of World Rankings.*

Statistical Office of the United Nations, Publishing Service, New York, New York 10017 (800) 253-9646; *Demographic Yearbook.*

ZAMBIA - ECONOMY

African Development Bank, 01 BP 1387, Abidjan 01, Cote D'Ivoire; *Selected Statistics on Regional Member Countries.*

Central Intelligence Agency, Washington, D.C. 20505 (703) 481-1100, www.cia.gov; *The World Factbook.*

Economist Intelligence Unit, 111 West 57th Street, New York, New York 10019 (800) 938-4685; *Zambia Country Report.*

Euromonitor International, Inc., 122 South Michigan Avenue, Suite 1200, Chicago, Illinois 60603 (800) 577-EURO; *International Marketing Data and Statistics; World Marketing Data and Statistics;* and *The World Economic Factbook.*

Europa Publications Limited, 18 Bedford Square, London, WC1B 3JN, England; *The Europa World Year Book.*

Federal Statistical Office, Gustav-Stresemann - Ring 11, D-6200, Wiesbaden, Germany; *Sambia.*

M.E. Sharpe, 80 Business Park Drive, Armonk, New York 10504 (800) 541-6563; *The Illustrated Book of World Rankings.*

St. Martin's Press, Inc., 175 Fifth Avenue, New York, New York 10010 (800) 221-7945; *The Statesman's Year-Book.*

Statistical Office of the United Nations, Publishing Service, New York, New York 10017 (800) 253-9646; *Foreign Trade Statistics for Africa;* and *World Statistics Pocketbook.*

The World Bank, 1818 H Street, NW, Washington, D.C. 20433 (202) 477-1234; *The World Bank Atlas;* and *World Development Report.*

ZAMBIA - EDUCATION

African Development Bank, 01 BP 1387, Abidjan 01, Cote D'Ivoire; *Selected Statistics on Regional Member Countries.*

Euromonitor International, Inc., 122 South Michigan Avenue, Suite 1200, Chicago, Illinois 60603 (800) 577-EURO; *International Marketing Data and Statistics;* and *World Marketing Data and Statistics.*

Europa Publications Limited, 18 Bedford Square, London, WC1B 3JN, England; *The Europa World Year Book.*

Federal Statistical Office, Gustav-Stresemann - Ring 11, D-6200, Wiesbaden, Germany; *Sambia.*

International Monetary Fund, 700 Nineteenth Street, NW, Washington, D.C. 20431 (202) 623-7000; *Government Finance Statistics Yearbook.*

M.E. Sharpe, 80 Business Park Drive, Armonk, New York 10504 (800) 541-6563; *The Illustrated Book of World Rankings.*

St. Martin's Press, Inc., 175 Fifth Avenue, New York, New York 10010 (800) 221-7945; *The Statesman's Year-Book.*

Statistical Office of the United Nations, Publishing Service, New York, New York 10017 (800) 253-9646; *Human Development Report;* and *Survey of Economic and Social Conditions in Africa.*

United Nations Economic Commission for Africa, Africa Hall, P.O. Box 3001, Addis Ababa, Ethiopia (Telephone Number in U.S. (800) 253-9646); *African Statistical Yearbook.*

United Nations Educational, Scientific and Cultural Organization (UNESCO), 7 Place de Fontenoy, F-75700 Paris, France (Telephone Number in U.S. (212) 963-5981); *Statistical Yearbook.*

The World Bank, 1818 H Street, NW, Washington, D.C. 20433 (202) 477-1234; *World Development Report;* and *World Development Indicators.*

ZAMBIA - EGG PRODUCTION AND CONSUMPTION - See ZAMBIA - DAIRY PRODUCTS

ZAMBIA - ELECTRICITY

Central Intelligence Agency, Washington, D.C. 20505 (703) 481-1100, www.cia.gov; *The World Factbook.*

M.E. Sharpe, 80 Business Park Drive, Armonk, New York 10504 (800) 541-6563; *The Illustrated Book of World Rankings.*

St. Martin's Press, Inc., 175 Fifth Avenue, New York, New York 10010 (800) 221-7945; *The Statesman's Year-Book.*

Statistical Office of the United Nations, Publishing Service, New York, New York 10017 (800) 253-9646; *Human*

Development Report; Statistical Yearbook; and *Survey of Economic and Social Conditions in Africa.*

United Nations Economic Commission for Africa, Africa Hall, P.O. Box 3001, Addis Ababa, Ethiopia (Telephone Number in U.S. (800) 253-9646); *African Statistical Yearbook.*

ZAMBIA - EMPLOYMENT

Euromonitor International, Inc., 122 South Michigan Avenue, Suite 1200, Chicago, Illinois 60603 (800) 577-EURO; *International Marketing Data and Statistics.*

Federal Statistical Office, Gustav-Stresemann - Ring 11, D-6200, Wiesbaden, Germany; *Sambia.*

International Labour Office, I.L.O. Publications, 1828 L Street, NW, Suite 801, Washington, D.C. 20036 (301) 638-3152; *Yearbook of Labour Statistics.*

M.E. Sharpe, 80 Business Park Drive, Armonk, New York 10504 (800) 541-6563; *The Illustrated Book of World Rankings.*

Statistical Office of the United Nations, Publishing Service, New York, New York 10017 (800) 253-9646; *Statistical Yearbook;* and *Survey of Economic and Social Conditions in Africa.*

United Nations Economic Commission for Africa, Africa Hall, P.O. Box 3001, Addis Ababa, Ethiopia (Telephone Number in U.S. (800) 253-9646); *African Statistical Yearbook.*

ZAMBIA - ENERGY

Euromonitor International, Inc., 122 South Michigan Avenue, Suite 1200, Chicago, Illinois 60603 (800) 577-EURO; *International Marketing Data and Statistics; World Marketing Data and Statistics;* and *The World Economic Factbook.*

Food and Agricultural Organization of the United Nations (FAO) Via delle Terme di Caracalla, 00100 Rome, Italy (Telephone Number in U.S. (202) 653-2400); *The State of Food and Agriculture.*

M.E. Sharpe, 80 Business Park Drive, Armonk, New York 10504 (800) 541-6563; *The Illustrated Book of World Rankings.*

St. Martin's Press, Inc., 175 Fifth Avenue, New York, New York 10010 (800) 221-7945; *The Statesman's Year-Book.*

Statistical Office of the United Nations, Publishing Service, New York, New York 10017 (800) 253-9646; *Energy Statistics Yearbook; Human Development Report; World Statistics Pocketbook;* and *Statistical Yearbook.*

United Nations Economic Commission for Africa, Africa Hall, P.O. Box 3001, Addis Ababa, Ethiopia (Telephone Number in U.S. (800) 253-9646); *African Statistical Yearbook.*

The World Bank, 1818 H Street, NW, Washington, D.C. 20433 (202) 477-1234; *The World Bank Atlas;* and *World Development Report.*

ZAMBIA - ENVIRONMENT

Economist Intelligence Unit, 111 West 57th Street, New York, New York 10019 (800) 938-4685; *Zambia Country Report.*

Statistical Office of the United Nations, Publishing Service, New York, New York 10017 (800) 253-9646; *World Statistics Pocketbook.*

ZAMBIA - EXCHANGE RATES

African Development Bank, 01 BP 1387, Abidjan 01, Cote D'Ivoire; *Selected Statistics on Regional Member Countries.*

Central Intelligence Agency, Washington, D.C. 20505 (703) 481-1100, www.cia.gov; *The World Factbook.*

Euromonitor International, Inc., 122 South Michigan Avenue, Suite 1200, Chicago, Illinois 60603 (800) 577-EURO; *International Marketing Data and Statistics;* and *The World Economic Factbook.*

Europa Publications Limited, 18 Bedford Square, London, WC1B 3JN, England; *The Europa World Year Book.*

International Civil Aviation Organization, 999 University Street, Montreal, Quebec, Canada H3C 5H7 (514) 954-8219; *Civil Aviation Statistics of the World.*

International Monetary Fund, 700 Nineteenth Street, NW, Washington, D.C. 20431 (202) 623-7000; *International Financial Statistics.*

Statistical Office of the United Nations, Publishing Service, New York, New York 10017 (800) 253-9646; *Foreign Trade Statistics for Africa; Statistical Yearbook;* and *World Statistics Pocketbook.*

ZAMBIA - EXCISE TAXES - See ZAMBIA - TAXATION

ZAMBIA - EXPORTS

African Development Bank, 01 BP 1387, Abidjan 01, Cote D'Ivoire; *Selected Statistics on Regional Member Countries.*

Central Intelligence Agency, Washington, D.C. 20505 (703) 481-1100, www.cia.gov; *The World Factbook.*

The Economist Intelligence Unit, 111 West 57th Street, New York, New York 10019 (800) 938-4685; *The World Market Atlas;* and *Zambia Country Report.*

Euromonitor International, Inc., 122 South Michigan Avenue, Suite 1200, Chicago, Illinois 60603 (800) 577-EURO; *International Marketing Data and Statistics;* and *The World Economic Factbook.*

Europa Publications Limited, 18 Bedford Square, London, WC1B 3JN, England; *The Europa World Year Book.*

Food and Agricultural Organization of the United Nations (FAO) Via delle Terme di Caracalla, 00100 Rome, Italy (Telephone Number in U.S. (202) 653-2400); *The State of Food and Agriculture.*

International Lead and Zinc Study Group, Metro House, 58 St. James's Street, London SW1A 1LD England; *Lead and Zinc Statistics.*

International Monetary Fund, 700 Nineteenth Street, NW, Washington, D.C. 20431 (202) 623-7000; *Direction of Trade Statistics;* and *International Financial Statistics.*

St. Martin's Press, Inc., 175 Fifth Avenue, New York, New York 10010 (800) 221-7945; *The Statesman's Year-Book.*

Statistical Office of the United Nations, Publishing Service, New York, New York 10017 (800) 253-9646; *Foreign Trade Statistics for Africa;* and *Survey of Economic and Social Conditions in Africa.*

United Nations Conference on Trade and Development (UNCTAD), New York, New York 10017 (800) 253-9646; *Handbook of International Trade and Development Statistics.*

United Nations Economic Commission for Africa, Africa Hall, P.O. Box 3001, Addis Ababa, Ethiopia (Telephone Number in U.S. (800) 253-9646); *African Statistical Yearbook.*

The World Bank, 1818 H Street, NW, Washington, D.C. 20433 (202) 477-1234; *World Development Report;* and *World Development Indicators.*

ZAMBIA - EXTERNAL INDEBTEDNESS

African Development Bank, 01 BP 1387, Abidjan 01, Cote D'Ivoire; *Selected Statistics on Regional Member Countries.*

Statistical Office of the United Nations, Publishing Service, New York, New York 10017 (800) 253-9646; *Survey of Economic and Social Conditions in Africa.*

The World Bank, 1818 H Street, NW,

Washington, D.C. 20433 (202) 477-1234; *World Development Report;* and *World Development Indicators.*

ZAMBIA - EXTERNAL TRADE

African Development Bank, 01 BP 1387, Abidjan 01, Cote D'Ivoire; *Selected Statistics on Regional Member Countries.*

Euromonitor International, Inc., 122 South Michigan Avenue, Suite 1200, Chicago, Illinois 60603 (800) 577-EURO; *World Marketing Data and Statistics.*

Food and Agricultural Organization of the United Nations (FAO) Via delle Terme di Caracalla, 00100 Rome, Italy (Telephone Number in U.S. (202) 653-2400); *The State of Food and Agriculture.*

Statistical Office of the United Nations, Publishing Service, New York, New York 10017 (800) 253-9646; *Statistical Yearbook.*

ZAMBIA - FARM CROPS - See ZAMBIA - CROPS

ZAMBIA - FEMALE WORKING POPULATION - See ZAMBIA - EMPLOYMENT

ZAMBIA - FERTILITY RATES

Central Intelligence Agency, Washington, D.C. 20505 (703) 481-1100, www.cia.gov; *The World Factbook.*

M.E. Sharpe, 80 Business Park Drive, Armonk, New York 10504 (800) 541-6563; *The Illustrated Book of World Rankings.*

Statistical Office of the United Nations, Publishing Service, New York, New York 10017 (800) 253-9646; *Human Development Report;* and *Survey of Economic and Social Conditions in Africa.*

The World Bank, 1818 H Street, NW, Washington, D.C. 20433 (202) 477-1234; *The World Bank Atlas; World Development Report;* and *World Development Indicators.*

ZAMBIA - FERTILIZER

Food and Agricultural Organization of the United Nations (FAO), Via delle Terme di Caracalla, 00100 Rome, Italy (Telephone Number in U.S. (202) 653-2400); *Annual Fertilizer Review;* and *The State of Food and Agriculture.*

Statistical Office of the United Nations, Publishing Service, New York, New York 10017 (800) 253-9646; *Statistical Yearbook.*

ZAMBIA - FETAL MORTALITY - See ZAMBIA - MORTALITY

ZAMBIA - FINANCE

African Development Bank, 01 BP 1387, Abidjan 01, Cote D'Ivoire; *Selected Statistics on Regional Member Countries.*

Economist Intelligence Unit, 111 West 57th Street, New York, New York 10019 (800) 938-4685; *Zambia Country Report.*

Europa Publications Limited, 18 Bedford Square, London, WC1B 3JN, England; *The Europa World Year Book.*

Federal Statistical Office, Gustav-Stresemann - Ring 11, D-6200, Wiesbaden, Germany; *Sambia.*

International Monetary Fund, 700 Nineteenth Street, NW, Washington, D.C. 20431 (202) 623-7000; *Government Finance Statistics Yearbook;* and *International Financial Statistics.*

M.E. Sharpe, 80 Business Park Drive, Armonk, New York 10504 (800) 541-6563; *The Illustrated Book of World Rankings.*

St. Martin's Press, Inc., 175 Fifth Avenue, New York, New York 10010 (800) 221-7945; *The Statesman's Year-Book.*

United Nations Economic Commission for Africa, Africa Hall, P.O. Box 3001, Addis Ababa, Ethiopia (Telephone Number in U.S. (800) 253-9646); *African Statistical Yearbook.*

ZAMBIA - FISHERIES

Europa Publications Limited, 18 Bedford Square, London, WC1B 3JN, England; *The Europa World Year Book.*

Federal Statistical Office, Gustav-Stresemann - Ring 11, D-6200, Wiesbaden, Germany; *Sambia.*

Food and Agricultural Organization of the United Nations (FAO) Via delle Terme di Caracalla, 00100 Rome, Italy (Telephone Number in U.S. (202) 653-2400); *The State of Food and Agriculture;* and *Yearbook of Fishery Statistics.*

M.E. Sharpe, 80 Business Park Drive, Armonk, New York 10504 (800) 541-6563; *The Illustrated Book of World Rankings.*

St. Martin's Press, Inc., 175 Fifth Avenue, New York, New York 10010 (800) 221-7945; *The Statesman's Year-Book.*

Statistical Office of the United Nations, Publishing Service, New York, New York 10017 (800) 253-9646; *Statistical Yearbook;* and *Survey of Economic and Social Conditions in Africa.*

United Nations Conference on Trade and Development, Central Statistical Service, Palais des Nations, Geneva, Switzerland (Telephone in U.S. (800) 253-

9646); *UNCTAD Commodity Yearbook.*

United Nations Economic Commission for Africa, Africa Hall, P.O. Box 3001, Addis Ababa, Ethiopia (Telephone Number in U.S. (800) 253-9646); *African Statistical Yearbook.*

ZAMBIA - FLOUR PRODUCTION

Statistical Office of the United Nations, Publishing Service, New York, New York 10017 (800) 253-9646; *Statistical Yearbook.*

ZAMBIA - FOOD

African Development Bank, 01 BP 1387, Abidjan 01, Cote D'Ivoire; *Selected Statistics on Regional Member Countries.*

Food and Agricultural Organization of the United Nations (FAO) Via delle Terme di Caracalla, 00100 Rome, Italy (Telephone Number in U.S. (202) 653-2400); *The State of Food and Agriculture.*

Statistical Office of the United Nations, Publishing Service, New York, New York 10017 (800) 253-9646; *Human Development Report.*

United Nations Conference on Trade and Development, Central Statistical Service, Palais des Nations, Geneva, Switzerland (Telephone in U.S. (800) 253-9646); *UNCTAD Commodity Yearbook.*

ZAMBIA - FOREIGN DEBT

International Monetary Fund, 700 Nineteenth Street, NW, Washington, D.C. 20431 (202) 623-7000; *Government Finance Statistics Yearbook.*

St. Martin's Press, Inc., 175 Fifth Avenue, New York, New York 10010 (800) 221-7945; *The Statesman's Year-Book.*

ZAMBIA - FOREIGN TRADE

Economist Intelligence Unit, 111 West 57th Street, New York, New York 10019 (800) 938-4685; *Zambia Country Report.*

Euromonitor International, Inc., 122 South Michigan Avenue, Suite 1200, Chicago, Illinois 60603 (800) 577-EURO; *International Marketing Data and Statistics,;* and *The World Economic Factbook.*

Europa Publications Limited, 18 Bedford Square, London, WC1B 3JN, England; *The Europa World Year Book.*

Federal Statistical Office, Gustav-Stresemann - Ring 11, D-6200, Wiesbaden, Germany; *Sambia.*

Food and Agricultural Organization of the United Nations (FAO) Via delle Terme

di Caracalla, 00100 Rome, Italy (Telephone Number in U.S. (202) 653-2400); *The State of Food and Agriculture.*

International Monetary Fund, 700 Nineteenth Street, NW, Washington, D.C. 20431 (202) 623-7000; *International Financial Statistics.*

M.E. Sharpe, 80 Business Park Drive, Armonk, New York 10504 (800) 541-6563; *The Illustrated Book of World Rankings.*

St. Martin's Press, Inc., 175 Fifth Avenue, New York, New York 10010 (800) 221-7945; *The Statesman's Year-Book.*

Statistical Office of the United Nations, Publishing Service, New York, New York 10017 (800) 253-9646; *Foreign Trade Statistics for Africa; International Trade Statistics Yearbook;* and *Statistical Yearbook.*

United Nations Conference on Trade and Development, Central Statistical Service, Palais des Nations, Geneva, Switzerland (Telephone in U.S. (800) 253-9646); *UNCTAD Commodity Yearbook.*

United Nations Economic Commission for Africa, Africa Hall, P.O. Box 3001, Addis Ababa, Ethiopia (Telephone Number in U.S. (800) 253-9646); *African Statistical Yearbook.*

The World Bank, 1818 H Street, NW, Washington, D.C. 20433 (202) 477-1234; *World Development Report;* and *World Development Indicators.*

World Bureau of Metal Statistics, 27-A High Street, Ware Hert SG12 9BA, England; *World Metal Statistics.*

ZAMBIA - FORESTRY AND FOREST PRODUCTS

Europa Publications Limited, 18 Bedford Square, London, WC1B 3JN, England; *The Europa World Year Book.*

Federal Statistical Office, Gustav-Stresemann - Ring 11, D-6200, Wiesbaden, Germany; *Sambia.*

Food and Agricultural Organization of the United Nations (FAO) Via delle Terme di Caracalla, 00100 Rome, Italy (Telephone Number in U.S. (202) 653-2400); *The State of Food and Agriculture;* and *Yearbook of Forest Products.*

M.E. Sharpe, 80 Business Park Drive, Armonk, New York 10504 (800) 541-6563; *The Illustrated Book of World Rankings.*

St. Martin's Press, Inc., 175 Fifth Avenue, New York, New York 10010 (800) 221-7945; *The Statesman's Year-Book.*

Statistical Office of the United Nations, Publishing Service, New York, New York 10017 (800) 253-9646; *Statistical Yearbook.*

United Nations Conference on Trade and Development, Central Statistical Service, Palais des Nations, Geneva, Switzerland (Telephone in U.S. (800) 253-9646); *UNCTAD Commodity Yearbook.*

United Nations Economic Commission for Africa, Africa Hall, P.O. Box 3001, Addis Ababa, Ethiopia (Telephone Number in U.S. (800) 253-9646); *African Statistical Yearbook.*

United Nations Educational, Scientific and Cultural Organization (UNESCO), 7 Place de Fontenoy, F-75700 Paris, France (Telephone Number in U.S. (212) 963-5981); *Statistical Yearbook.*

The World Bank, 1818 H Street, NW, Washington, D.C. 20433 (202) 477-1234; *World Development Report.*

ZAMBIA - GAS PRODUCTION - See ZAMBIA - MINING AND MINERAL PRODUCTS

ZAMBIA - GENERAL INDUSTRIAL STATISTICS - See ZAMBIA - INDUSTRY

ZAMBIA - GENERAL MORTALITY - See ZAMBIA - MORTALITY

ZAMBIA - GEOGRAPHIC DATA

M.E. Sharpe, 80 Business Park Drive, Armonk, New York 10504 (800) 541-6563; *The Illustrated Book of World Rankings.*

ZAMBIA - GOATS - See ZAMBIA - LIVESTOCK AND POULTRY

ZAMBIA - GOLD HOLDINGS

International Monetary Fund, 700 Nineteenth Street, NW, Washington, D.C. 20431 (202) 623-7000; *International Financial Statistics.*

Statistical Office of the United Nations, Publishing Service, New York, New York 10017 (800) 253-9646; *Statistical Yearbook.*

The World Bank, 1818 H Street, NW, Washington, D.C. 20433 (202) 477-1234; *World Development Indicators.*

ZAMBIA - GOLD PRODUCTION AND CONSUMPTION - See ZAMBIA MINING AND MINERAL PRODUCTS

ZAMBIA - GOVERNMENT

Central Intelligence Agency, Washington, D.C. 20505 (703) 481-1100, www.cia.gov; *The World Factbook.*

Europa Publications Limited, 18 Bedford Square, London, WC1B 3JN, England; *The Europa World Year Book.*

International Monetary Fund, 700 Nineteenth Street, NW, Washington, D.C. 20431 (202) 623-7000; *Government Finance Statistics Yearbook;* and *International Financial Statistics.*

St. Martin's Press, Inc., 175 Fifth Avenue, New York, New York 10010 (800) 221-7945; *The Statesman's Year-Book.*

Statistical Office of the United Nations, Publishing Service, New York, New York 10017 (800) 253-9646; *National Accounts Statistics;* and *Statistical Yearbook.*

The World Bank, 1818 H Street, NW, Washington, D.C. 20433 (202) 477-1234; *World Development Report;* and *World Development Indicators.*

ZAMBIA - GRAIN PRODUCTION - See ZAMBIA - CROPS

ZAMBIA - GRANTS

International Monetary Fund, 700 Nineteenth Street, NW, Washington, D.C. 20431 (202) 623-7000; *Government Finance Statistics Yearbook.*

ZAMBIA - GROSS DOMESTIC PRODUCT

African Development Bank, 01 BP 1387, Abidjan 01, Cote D'Ivoire; *Selected Statistics on Regional Member Countries.*

The Economist Intelligence Unit, 111 West 57th Street, New York, New York 10019 (800) 938-4685; *The World Market Atlas;* and *Zambia Country Report.*

Euromonitor International, Inc., 122 South Michigan Avenue, Suite 1200, Chicago, Illinois 60603 (800) 577-EURO; *International Marketing Data and Statistics;* and *The World Economic Factbook.*

Europa Publications Limited, 18 Bedford Square, London, WC1B 3JN, England; *The Europa World Year Book.*

M.E. Sharpe, 80 Business Park Drive, Armonk, New York 10504 (800) 541-6563; *The Illustrated Book of World Rankings.*

St. Martin's Press, Inc., 175 Fifth Avenue, New York, New York 10010 (800) 221-7945; *The Statesman's Year-Book.*

Statistical Office of the United Nations, Publishing Service, New York, New York 10017 (800) 253-9646; *Human Development Report; National Accounts Statistics; Statistical Yearbook;* and *Survey of Economic and Social Conditions in Africa.*

United Nations Economic Commission for Africa, Africa Hall, P.O. Box 3001, Addis Ababa, Ethiopia (Telephone Number in U.S. (800) 253-9646); *African Statistical Yearbook.*

The World Bank, 1818 H Street, NW, Washington, D.C. 20433 (202) 477-1234; *World Development Report;* and *World Development Indicators.*

ZAMBIA - GROSS NATIONAL PRODUCT

Euromonitor International, Inc., 122 South Michigan Avenue, Suite 1200, Chicago, Illinois 60603 (800) 577-EURO; *International Marketing Data and Statistics.*

U.S. Arms Control and Disarmament Agency, 320 Twenty-first Street, NW, Washington, D.C. 20451 (202) 647-8677; *World Military Expenditures and Arms Transfers.*

The World Bank, 1818 H Street, NW, Washington, D.C. 20433 (202) 477-1234; *The World Bank Atlas; World Development Report;* and *World Development Indicators.*

ZAMBIA - GROUNDNUTS PRODUCTION - See ZAMBIA - CROPS

ZAMBIA - HEALTH

African Development Bank, 01 BP 1387, Abidjan 01, Cote D'Ivoire; *Selected Statistics on Regional Member Countries.*

Euromonitor International, Inc., 122 South Michigan Avenue, Suite 1200, Chicago, Illinois 60603 (800) 577-EURO; *World Marketing Data and Statistics.*

Federal Statistical Office, Gustav-Stresemann - Ring 11, D-6200, Wiesbaden, Germany; *Sambia.*

M.E. Sharpe, 80 Business Park Drive, Armonk, New York 10504 (800) 541-6563; *The Illustrated Book of World Rankings.*

St. Martin's Press, Inc., 175 Fifth Avenue, New York, New York 10010 (800) 221-7945; *The Statesman's Year-Book.*

Statistical Office of the United Nations, Publishing Service, New York, New York 10017 (800) 253-9646; *Human Development Report;* and *Statistical Yearbook.*

United Nations Children's Fund (UNICEF), 3 United Nations Plaza, New York, New York 10017 (800) 253-9646; *State of the World's Children.*

United Nations Economic Commission for Africa, Africa Hall, P.O. Box 3001, Addis Ababa, Ethiopia (Telephone Number in U.S. (800) 253-9646); *African Statistical Yearbook.*

The World Bank, 1818 H Street, NW, Washington, D.C. 20433 (202) 477-1234; *World Development Report.*

World Health Organization, Office of Publications, Avenue Appia, CH-1211 Geneva 27, Switzerland (Telephone Number in U.S. (518) 436-9686); *World Health Statistics Annual.*

ZAMBIA - HEALTH EXPENDITURES

International Monetary Fund, 700 Nineteenth Street, NW, Washington, D.C. 20431 (202) 623-7000; *Government Finance Statistics Yearbook.*

ZAMBIA - HIGHWAYS

Central Intelligence Agency, Washington, D.C. 20505 (703) 481-1100, www.cia.gov; *The World Factbook.*

International Road Federation, 2600 Virginia Avenue, NW, Washington, D.C. 20037 (202) 338-4641; *World Road Statistics.*

St. Martin's Press, Inc., 175 Fifth Avenue, New York, New York 10010 (800) 221-7945; *The Statesman's Year-Book.*

Statistical Office of the United Nations, Publishing Service, New York, New York 10017 (800) 253-9646; *Survey of Economic and Social Conditions in Africa.*

United Nations Economic Commission for Africa, Africa Hall, P.O. Box 3001, Addis Ababa, Ethiopia (Telephone Number in U.S. (800) 253-9646); *African Statistical Yearbook.*

ZAMBIA - HORSES - See ZAMBIA - LIVESTOCK AND POULTRY

ZAMBIA - HOURS OF WORK - See ZAMBIA - EMPLOYMENT

ZAMBIA - HOUSING AND HOUSING UNITS

Euromonitor International, Inc., 122 South Michigan Avenue, Suite 1200, Chicago, Illinois 60603 (800) 577-EURO; *World Marketing Data and Statistics.*

M.E. Sharpe, 80 Business Park Drive, Armonk, New York 10504 (800) 541-6563; *The Illustrated Book of World Rankings.*

ZAMBIA - HOUSING EXPENDITURES

International Monetary Fund, 700 Nineteenth Street, NW, Washington, D.C. 20431 (202) 623-7000; *Government Finance Statistics Yearbook.*

ZAMBIA - ILLITERATE POPULATION

Central Intelligence Agency, Washington, D.C. 20505 (703) 481-1100,

www.cia.gov; *The World Factbook.*

The Economist Intelligence Unit, 111 West 57th Street, New York, New York 10019 (800) 938-4685; *The World Market Atlas.*

Euromonitor International, Inc., 122 South Michigan Avenue, Suite 1200, Chicago, Illinois 60603 (800) 577-EURO; *The World Economic Factbook.*

Statistical Office of the United Nations, Publishing Service, New York, New York 10017 (800) 253-9646; *Human Development Report.*

United Nations Educational, Scientific and Cultural Organization (UNESCO), 7 Place de Fontenoy, F-75700 Paris, France (Telephone Number in U.S. (212) 963-5981); *Statistical Yearbook.*

ZAMBIA - IMPORTS

African Development Bank, 01 BP 1387, Abidjan 01, Cote D'Ivoire; *Selected Statistics on Regional Member Countries.*

Central Intelligence Agency, Washington, D.C. 20505 (703) 481-1100, www.cia.gov; *The World Factbook.*

The Economist Intelligence Unit, 111 West 57th Street, New York, New York 10019 (800) 938-4685; *The World Market Atlas;* and *Zambia Country Report.*

Euromonitor International, Inc., 122 South Michigan Avenue, Suite 1200, Chicago, Illinois 60603 (800) 577-EURO; *International Marketing Data and Statistics;* and *The World Economic Factbook.*

Europa Publications Limited, 18 Bedford Square, London, WC1B 3JN, England; *The Europa World Year Book.*

Food and Agricultural Organization of the United Nations (FAO) Via delle Terme di Caracalla, 00100 Rome, Italy (Telephone Number in U.S. (202) 653-2400); *The State of Food and Agriculture.*

International Lead and Zinc Study Group, Metro House, 58 St. James's Street, London SW1A 1LD England; *Lead and Zinc Statistics.*

International Monetary Fund, 700 Nineteenth Street, NW, Washington, D.C. 20431 (202) 623-7000; *Direction of Trade Statistics; Government Finance Statistics Yearbook;* and *International Financial Statistics.*

St. Martin's Press, Inc., 175 Fifth Avenue, New York, New York 10010 (800) 221-7945; *The Statesman's Year-Book.*

Statistical Office of the United Nations,

Publishing Service, New York, New York 10017 (800) 253-9646; *Foreign Trade Statistics for Africa;* and *Survey of Economic and Social Conditions in Africa.*

United Nations Conference on Trade and Development (UNCTAD), New York, New York 10017 (800) 253-9646; *Handbook of International Trade and Development Statistics.*

United Nations Economic Commission for Africa, Africa Hall, P.O. Box 3001, Addis Ababa, Ethiopia (Telephone Number in U.S. (800) 253-9646); *African Statistical Yearbook.*

The World Bank, 1818 H Street, NW, Washington, D.C. 20433 (202) 477-1234; *World Development Report;* and *World Development Indicators.*

ZAMBIA - INCOME TAXES - See ZAMBIA - TAXATION

ZAMBIA - INDUSTRIAL METALS PRODUCTION See ZAMBIA - MINING AND MINERAL PRODUCTS

ZAMBIA - INDUSTRY

Central Intelligence Agency, Washington, D.C. 20505 (703) 481-1100, www.cia.gov; *The World Factbook.*

Economist Intelligence Unit, 111 West 57th Street, New York, New York 10019 (800) 938-4685; *Zambia Country Report.*

Euromonitor International, Inc., 122 South Michigan Avenue, Suite 1200, Chicago, Illinois 60603 (800) 577-EURO; *International Marketing Data and Statistics; World Marketing Data and Statistics;* and *The World Economic Factbook.*

Europa Publications Limited, 18 Bedford Square, London, WC1B 3JN, England; *The Europa World Year Book.*

Federal Statistical Office, Gustav-Stresemann - Ring 11, D-6200, Wiesbaden, Germany; *Sambia.*

International Labour Office, I.L.O. Publications, 1828 L Street, NW, Suite 801, Washington, D.C. 20036 (301) 638-3152; *Yearbook of Labour Statistics.*

M.E. Sharpe, 80 Business Park Drive, Armonk, New York 10504 (800) 541-6563; *The Illustrated Book of World Rankings.*

St. Martin's Press, Inc., 175 Fifth Avenue, New York, New York 10010 (800) 221-7945; *The Statesman's Year-Book.*

Statistical Office of the United Nations, Publishing Service, New York, New York 10017 (800) 253-9646; *Industrial Commodity Statistics Yearbook; Statistical*

Yearbook; and *Survey of Economic and Social Conditions in Africa.*

United Nations Economic Commission for Africa, Africa Hall, P.O. Box 3001, Addis Ababa, Ethiopia (Telephone Number in U.S. (800) 253-9646); *African Statistical Yearbook.*

The World Bank, 1818 H Street, NW, Washington, D.C. 20433 (202) 477-1234; *World Development Indicators.*

World Intellectual Property Organization, 34 Chemin des Colombettes, CH-1211 Geneva 20. Switzerland; *Industrial Property Statistics.*

ZAMBIA - INFANT AND MATERNAL MORTALITY - See ZAMBIA - MORTALITY

ZAMBIA - INTERNATIONAL LIQUIDITY

International Monetary Fund, 700 Nineteenth Street, NW, Washington, D.C. 20431 (202) 623-7000; *International Financial Statistics.*

ZAMBIA - INTERNATIONAL RESERVES EXCLUDING GOLD

African Development Bank, 01 BP 1387, Abidjan 01, Cote D'Ivoire; *Selected Statistics on Regional Member Countries.*

Statistical Office of the United Nations, Publishing Service, New York, New York 10017 (800) 253-9646; *Statistical Yearbook.*

The World Bank, 1818 H Street, NW, Washington, D.C. 20433 (202) 477-1234; *World Development Indicators.*

ZAMBIA - IRON ORE PRODUCTION AND CONSUMPTION - See ZAMBIA - MINING AND MINERAL PRODUCTS

ZAMBIA - IRRIGATION

Euromonitor International, Inc., 122 South Michigan Avenue, Suite 1200, Chicago, Illinois 60603 (800) 577-EURO; *International Marketing Data and Statistics.*

ZAMBIA - LABOR

African Development Bank, 01 BP 1387, Abidjan 01, Cote D'Ivoire; *Selected Statistics on Regional Member Countries.*

Central Intelligence Agency, Washington, D.C. 20505 (703) 481-1100, www.cia.gov; *The World Factbook.*

Euromonitor International, Inc., 122 South Michigan Avenue, Suite 1200, Chicago, Illinois 60603 (800) 577-EURO; *International Marketing Data and Statistics;* and *World Marketing Data and Statistics.*

Europa Publications Limited, 18

Bedford Square, London, WC1B 3JN, England; *The Europa World Year Book.*

Food and Agricultural Organization of the United Nations (FAO) Via delle Terme di Caracalla, 00100 Rome, Italy (Telephone Number in U.S. (202) 653-2400); *The State of Food and Agriculture.*

International Labour Office, I.L.O. Publications, 1828 L Street, NW, Suite 801, Washington, D.C. 20036 (301) 638-3152; *Yearbook of Labour Statistics.*

M.E. Sharpe, 80 Business Park Drive, Armonk, New York 10504 (800) 541-6563; *The Illustrated Book of World Rankings.*

St. Martin's Press, Inc., 175 Fifth Avenue, New York, New York 10010 (800) 221-7945; *The Statesman's Year-Book.*

Statistical Office of the United Nations, Publishing Service, New York, New York 10017 (800) 253-9646; *Human Development Report.*

The World Bank, 1818 H Street, NW, Washington, D.C. 20433 (202) 477-1234; *The World Bank Atlas; World Development Report;* and *World Development Indicators.*

ZAMBIA - LAND USE

Central Intelligence Agency, Washington, D.C. 20505 (703) 481-1100, www.cia.gov; *The World Factbook.*

Euromonitor International, Inc., 122 South Michigan Avenue, Suite 1200, Chicago, Illinois 60603 (800) 577-EURO; *International Marketing Data and Statistics.*

The World Bank, 1818 H Street, NW, Washington, D.C. 20433 (202) 477-1234; *World Development Report.*

ZAMBIA - LEAD AND LEAD ORE PRODUCTION AND CONSUMPTION - See ZAMBIA - MINING AND MINERAL PRODUCTS

ZAMBIA - LIBRARIES

M.E. Sharpe, 80 Business Park Drive, Armonk, New York 10504 (800) 541-6563; *The Illustrated Book of World Rankings.*

United Nations Educational, Scientific and Cultural Organization (UNESCO), 7 Place de Fontenoy, F-75700 Paris, France (Telephone Number in U.S. (212) 963-5981); *Statistical Yearbook.*

ZAMBIA - LIFE EXPECTANCY

African Development Bank, 01 BP 1387, Abidjan 01, Cote D'Ivoire; *Selected Statistics on Regional Member Countries.*

Central Intelligence Agency,

Washington, D.C. 20505 (703) 481-1100, www.cia.gov; *The World Factbook*.

Euromonitor International, Inc., 122 South Michigan Avenue, Suite 1200, Chicago, Illinois 60603 (800) 577-EURO; *The World Economic Factbook*.

Statistical Office of the United Nations, Publishing Service, New York, New York 10017 (800) 253-9646; *Human Development Report*.

The World Bank, 1818 H Street, NW, Washington, D.C. 20433 (202) 477-1234; *The World Bank Atlas;* and *World Development Report*.

ZAMBIA - LITERACY RATE

Euromonitor International, Inc., 122 South Michigan Avenue, Suite 1200, Chicago, Illinois 60603 (800) 577-EURO; *World Marketing Data and Statistics*.

Statistical Office of the United Nations, Publishing Service, New York, New York 10017 (800) 253-9646; *Survey of Economic and Social Conditions in Africa*.

ZAMBIA - LIVESTOCK AND POULTRY

Euromonitor International, Inc., 122 South Michigan Avenue, Suite 1200, Chicago, Illinois 60603 (800) 577-EURO; *International Marketing Data and Statistics*.

Europa Publications Limited, 18 Bedford Square, London, WC1B 3JN, England; *The Europa World Year Book*.

Food and Agricultural Organization of the United Nations (FAO) Via delle Terme di Caracalla, 00100 Rome, Italy (Telephone Number in U.S. (202) 653-2400); *The State of Food and Agriculture*.

M.E. Sharpe, 80 Business Park Drive, Armonk, New York 10504 (800) 541-6563; *The Illustrated Book of World Rankings*.

St. Martin's Press, Inc., 175 Fifth Avenue, New York, New York 10010 (800) 221-7945; *The Statesman's Year-Book*.

Statistical Office of the United Nations, Publishing Service, New York, New York 10017 (800) 253-9646; *Statistical Yearbook,;* and *Survey of Economic and Social Conditions in Africa*.

United Nations Conference on Trade and Development, Central Statistical Service, Palais des Nations, Geneva, Switzerland (Telephone in U.S. (800) 253-9646); *UNCTAD Commodity Yearbook*.

United Nations Economic Commission for Africa, Africa Hall, P.O. Box 3001, Addis Ababa, Ethiopia (Telephone Number in U.S. (800) 253-9646); *African Statistical*

Yearbook.

ZAMBIA - LIVING LEVELS - See
ZAMBIA - LIFE EXPECTANCY

ZAMBIA - MAGNESIUM PRODUCTION AND CONSUMPTION - See ZAMBIA - MINING AND MINERAL PRODUCTS

ZAMBIA - MAIL - NUMBER OF PIECES SENT OR RECEIVED

Statistical Office of the United Nations, Publishing Service, New York, New York 10017 (800) 253-9646; *Statistical Yearbook*.

ZAMBIA - MANGANESE AND MANGANESE ORE PRODUCTION AND CONSUMPTION - See ZAMBIA - MINING AND MINERAL PRODUCTS

ZAMBIA - MANUFACTURING

M.E. Sharpe, 80 Business Park Drive, Armonk, New York 10504 (800) 541-6563; *The Illustrated Book of World Rankings*.

Statistical Office of the United Nations, Publishing Service, New York, New York 10017 (800) 253-9646; *Survey of Economic and Social Conditions in Africa*.

United Nations Economic Commission for Africa, Africa Hall, P.O. Box 3001, Addis Ababa, Ethiopia (Telephone Number in U.S. (800) 253-9646); *African Statistical Yearbook*.

The World Bank, 1818 H Street, NW, Washington, D.C. 20433 (202) 477-1234; *World Development Indicators*.

ZAMBIA - MARRIAGE RATES

M.E. Sharpe, 80 Business Park Drive, Armonk, New York 10504 (800) 541-6563; *The Illustrated Book of World Rankings*.

Statistical Office of the United Nations, Publishing Service, New York, New York 10017 (800) 253-9646; *Demographic Yearbook*.

ZAMBIA - MEAT PRODUCTION - See
ZAMBIA - LIVESTOCK AND POULTRY

ZAMBIA - MERCHANT SHIPPING

United Nations Economic Commission for Africa, Africa Hall, P.O. Box 3001, Addis Ababa, Ethiopia (Telephone Number in U.S. (800) 253-9646); *African Statistical Yearbook*.

U.S. Department of Transportation, Maritime Administration, 400 Seventh Street, SW, Washington, D.C. 20590 (202) 366-5807; *A Statistical Analysis of the World's Merchant Fleets*.

ZAMBIA - MILITARY

Central Intelligence Agency, Washington, D.C. 20505 (703) 481-1100, www.cia.gov; *The World Factbook*.

Euromonitor International, Inc., 122 South Michigan Avenue, Suite 1200, Chicago, Illinois 60603 (800) 577-EURO; *World Marketing Data and Statistics*.

The International Institute for Strategic Studies, 23 Tavistock Street, London WC2E 7NQ, England; *The Military Balance*.

International Monetary Fund, 700 Nineteenth Street, NW, Washington, D.C. 20431 (202) 623-7000; *Government Finance Statistics Yearbook*.

St. Martin's Press, Inc., 175 Fifth Avenue, New York, New York 10010 (800) 221-7945; *The Statesman's Year-Book*.

Statistical Office of the United Nations, Publishing Service, New York, New York 10017 (800) 253-9646; *Human Development Report*.

U.S. Arms Control and Disarmament Agency, 320 Twenty-first Street, NW, Washington, D.C. 20451 (202) 647-8677; *World Military Expenditures and Arms Transfers*.

ZAMBIA - MILK PRODUCTION - See
ZAMBIA - DAIRY PRODUCTS

ZAMBIA - MINING AND MINERAL PRODUCTS

Commodity Research Bureau, Inc., 30 South Wacker Drive, Suite 1810, Chicago, Illinois 60606 (800) 621-5271); *Commodity Year Book*.

Europa Publications Limited, 18 Bedford Square, London, WC1B 3JN, England; *The Europa World Year Book*.

International Lead and Zinc Study Group, Metro House, 58 St. James's Street, London SW1A 1LD England; *Lead and Zinc Statistics*.

International Monetary Fund, 700 Nineteenth Street, NW, Washington, D.C. 20431 (202) 623-7000; *International Financial Statistics*.

M.E. Sharpe, 80 Business Park Drive, Armonk, New York 10504 (800) 541-6563; *The Illustrated Book of World Rankings*.

St. Martin's Press, Inc., 175 Fifth Avenue, New York, New York 10010 (800) 221-7945; *The Statesman's Year-Book*.

Statistical Office of the United Nations, Publishing Service, New York, New York 10017 (800) 253-9646; *Statistical Yearbook*.

United Nations Conference on Trade

and Development, Central Statistical Service, Palais des Nations, Geneva, Switzerland (Telephone in U.S. (800) 253-9646); *UNCTAD Commodity Yearbook.*

United Nations Economic Commission for Africa, Africa Hall, P.O. Box 3001, Addis Ababa, Ethiopia (Telephone Number in U.S. (800) 253-9646); *African Statistical Yearbook.*

World Bureau of Metal Statistics, 27-A High Street, Ware Hert SG12 9BA, England; *World Metal Statistics.*

ZAMBIA - MOLYBDENUM AND MOLYBDENUM ORE PRODUCTION AND CONSUMPTION See ZAMBIA - MINING AND MINERAL PRODUCTS

ZAMBIA - MONEY EXCHANGE RATE - See ZAMBIA - EXCHANGE RATE

ZAMBIA - MONEY RESERVES

Euromonitor International, Inc., 122 South Michigan Avenue, Suite 1200, Chicago, Illinois 60603 (800) 577-EURO; *International Marketing Data and Statistics.*

ZAMBIA - MONEY SUPPLY

African Development Bank, 01 BP 1387, Abidjan 01, Cote D'Ivoire; *Selected Statistics on Regional Member Countries.*

Economist Intelligence Unit, 111 West 57th Street, New York, New York 10019 (800) 938-4685; *Zambia Country Report.*

Euromonitor International, Inc., 122 South Michigan Avenue, Suite 1200, Chicago, Illinois 60603 (800) 577-EURO; *International Marketing Data and Statistics.*

Europa Publications Limited, 18 Bedford Square, London, WC1B 3JN, England; *The Europa World Year Book.*

Federal Statistical Office, Gustav-Stresemann - Ring 11, D-6200, Wiesbaden, Germany; *Sambia.*

International Monetary Fund, 700 Nineteenth Street, NW, Washington, D.C. 20431 (202) 623-7000; *International Financial Statistics.*

Statistical Office of the United Nations, Publishing Service, New York, New York 10017 (800) 253-9646; *Statistical Yearbook.*

The World Bank, 1818 H Street, NW, Washington, D.C. 20433 (202) 477-1234; *World Development Indicators.*

ZAMBIA - MONUMENTS AND HISTORICAL SITES

United Nations Educational, Scientific and Cultural Organization (UNESCO), 7

Place de Fontenoy, F-75700 Paris, France (Telephone Number in U.S. (212) 963-5981); *Statistical Yearbook.*

ZAMBIA - MORTALITY

Central Intelligence Agency, Washington, D.C. 20505 (703) 481-1100, www.cia.gov; *The World Factbook.*

Euromonitor International, Inc., 122 South Michigan Avenue, Suite 1200, Chicago, Illinois 60603 (800) 577-EURO; *International Marketing Data and Statistics;* and *The World Economic Factbook.*

Europa Publications Limited, 18 Bedford Square, London, WC1B 3JN, England; *The Europa World Year Book.*

Statistical Office of the United Nations, Publishing Service, New York, New York 10017 (800) 253-9646; *Demographic Yearbook; Human Development Report; Statistical Yearbook; Survey of Economic and Social Conditions in Africa;* and *World Statistics Pocketbook.*

United Nations Children's Fund (UNICEF), 3 United Nations Plaza, New York, New York 10017 (800) 253-9646; *State of the World's Children.*

The World Bank, 1818 H Street, NW, Washington, D.C. 20433 (202) 477-1234; *The World Bank Atlas; World Development Report;* and *World Development Indicators.*

World Health Organization, Office of Publications, Avenue Appia, CH-1211 Geneva 27, Switzerland (Telephone Number in U.S. (518) 436-9686); *World Health Statistics Annual.*

ZAMBIA - MOTOR VEHICLE PRODUCTION

Statistical Office of the United Nations, Publishing Service, New York, New York 10017 (800) 253-9646; *Statistical Yearbook.*

ZAMBIA - MOTOR VEHICLE TAXES - See ZAMBIA - TAXATION

ZAMBIA - MOTOR VEHICLES IN USE

Europa Publications Limited, 18 Bedford Square, London, WC1B 3JN, England; *The Europa World Year Book.*

International Road Federation, 2600 Virginia Avenue, NW, Washington, D.C. 20037 (202) 338-4641; *World Road Statistics.*

Statistical Office of the United Nations, Publishing Service, New York, New York 10017 (800) 253-9646; *Statistical Yearbook;* and *Survey of Economic and Social Conditions in Africa.*

ZAMBIA - MUSEUMS

M.E. Sharpe, 80 Business Park Drive, Armonk, New York 10504 (800) 541-6563; *The Illustrated Book of World Rankings.*

United Nations Educational, Scientific and Cultural Organization (UNESCO), 7 Place de Fontenoy, F-75700 Paris, France (Telephone Number in U.S. (212) 963-5981); *Statistical Yearbook.*

ZAMBIA - NATALITY - See ZAMBIA - BIRTH RATE

ZAMBIA - NATIONAL ACCOUNTS

African Development Bank, 01 BP 1387, Abidjan 01, Cote D'Ivoire; *Selected Statistics on Regional Member Countries.*

Europa Publications Limited, 18 Bedford Square, London, WC1B 3JN, England; *The Europa World Year Book.*

Federal Statistical Office, Gustav-Stresemann - Ring 11, D-6200, Wiesbaden, Germany; *Sambia.*

International Monetary Fund, 700 Nineteenth Street, NW, Washington, D.C. 20431 (202) 623-7000; *International Financial Statistics.*

Statistical Office of the United Nations, Publishing Service, New York, New York 10017 (800) 253-9646; *National Accounts Statistics;* and *Statistical Yearbook.*

United Nations Economic Commission for Africa, Africa Hall, P.O. Box 3001, Addis Ababa, Ethiopia (Telephone Number in U.S. (800) 253-9646); *African Statistical Yearbook.*

ZAMBIA - NATIONAL INCOME

M.E. Sharpe, 80 Business Park Drive, Armonk, New York 10504 (800) 541-6563; *The Illustrated Book of World Rankings.*

Statistical Office of the United Nations, Publishing Service, New York, New York 10017 (800) 253-9646; *National Accounts Statistics;* and *Statistical Yearbook.*

ZAMBIA - NATIONAL PRODUCT

M.E. Sharpe, 80 Business Park Drive, Armonk, New York 10504 (800) 541-6563; *The Illustrated Book of World Rankings.*

Statistical Office of the United Nations, Publishing Service, New York, New York 10017 (800) 253-9646; *Statistical Yearbook.*

ZAMBIA - NATURAL GAS PRODUCTION - See ZAMBIA - MINING AND MINERAL PRODUCTS

ZAMBIA - NEWSPAPER PRODUCTION - See ZAMBIA - FORESTRY AND FOREST PRODUCTS

ZAMBIA - NEWSPRINT - See ZAMBIA - FORESTRY AND FOREST PRODUCTS

ZAMBIA - NICKEL AND NICKEL ORE PRODUCTION AND CONSUMPTION - See ZAMBIA - MINING AND MINERAL PRODUCTS

ZAMBIA - OCCUPATIONS - See ZAMBIA - LABOR

ZAMBIA - PAPER - See ZAMBIA - FORESTRY AND FOREST PRODUCTS

ZAMBIA - PATENTS, TRADEMARKS AND SERVICE MARKS

Statistical Office of the United Nations, Publishing Service, New York, New York 10017 (800) 253-9646; *Statistical Yearbook.*

World Intellectual Property Organization, 34 Chemin des Colombettes, CH-1211 Geneva 20. Switzerland; *Industrial Property Statistics.*

ZAMBIA - PEANUT PRODUCTION - See ZAMBIA - CROPS

ZAMBIA - PERIODICALS

United Nations Educational, Scientific and Cultural Organization (UNESCO), 7 Place de Fontenoy, F-75700 Paris, France (Telephone Number in U.S. (212) 963-5981); *Statistical Yearbook.*

ZAMBIA - PESTICIDE USE

Food and Agricultural Organization of the United Nations (FAO) Via delle Terme di Caracalla, 00100 Rome, Italy (Telephone Number in U.S. (202) 653-2400); *The State of Food and Agriculture.*

ZAMBIA - PETROLEUM INDUSTRY

Food and Agricultural Organization of the United Nations (FAO) Via delle Terme di Caracalla, 00100 Rome, Italy (Telephone Number in U.S. (202) 653-2400); *The State of Food and Agriculture.*

M.E. Sharpe, 80 Business Park Drive, Armonk, New York 10504 (800) 541-6563; *The Illustrated Book of World Rankings.*

Statistical Office of the United Nations, Publishing Service, New York, New York 10017 (800) 253-9646; *Statistical Yearbook.*

United Nations Conference on Trade and Development, Central Statistical Service, Palais des Nations, Geneva, Switzerland (Telephone in U.S. (800) 253-9646); *UNCTAD Commodity Yearbook.*

ZAMBIA - PIGS - See ZAMBIA - LIVESTOCK AND POULTRY

ZAMBIA - POPULATION

African Development Bank, 01 BP 1387, Abidjan 01, Cote D'Ivoire; *Selected Statistics on Regional Member Countries.*

Central Intelligence Agency, Washington, D.C. 20505 (703) 481-1100, www.cia.gov; *The World Factbook.*

The Economist Intelligence Unit, 111 West 57th Street, New York, New York 10019 (800) 938-4685; *The World Market Atlas;* and *Zambia Country Report.*

Euromonitor International, Inc., 122 South Michigan Avenue, Suite 1200, Chicago, Illinois 60603 (800) 577-EURO; *International Marketing Data and Statistics;* and *The World Economic Factbook.*

Europa Publications Limited, 18 Bedford Square, London, WC1B 3JN, England; *The Europa World Year Book.*

Federal Statistical Office, Gustav-Stresemann - Ring 11, D-6200, Wiesbaden, Germany; *Sambia.*

International Labour Office, I.L.O. Publications, 1828 L Street, NW, Suite 801, Washington, D.C. 20036 (301) 638-3152; *Yearbook of Labour Statistics.*

M.E. Sharpe, 80 Business Park Drive, Armonk, New York 10504 (800) 541-6563; *The Illustrated Book of World Rankings.*

St. Martin's Press, Inc., 175 Fifth Avenue, New York, New York 10010 (800) 221-7945; *The Statesman's Year-Book.*

Statistical Office of the United Nations, Publishing Service, New York, New York 10017 (800) 253-9646; *Demographic Yearbook; Human Development Report; Statistical Yearbook; Survey of Economic and Social Conditions in Africa;* and *World Statistics Pocketbook.*

United Nations Educational, Scientific and Cultural Organization (UNESCO), 7 Place de Fontenoy, F-75700 Paris, France (Telephone Number in U.S. (212) 963-5981); *Statistical Yearbook.*

U.S. Arms Control and Disarmament Agency, 320 Twenty-first Street, NW, Washington, D.C. 20451 (202) 647-8677; *World Military Expenditures and Arms Transfers.*

The World Bank, 1818 H Street, NW, Washington, D.C. 20433 (202) 477-1234; *The World Bank Atlas;* and *World Development Report.*

World Health Organization, Office of

Publications, Avenue Appia, CH-1211 Geneva 27, Switzerland (Telephone Number in U.S. (518) 436-9686); *World Health Statistics Annual.*

ZAMBIA - POST OFFICES

M.E. Sharpe, 80 Business Park Drive, Armonk, New York 10504 (800) 541-6563; *The Illustrated Book of World Rankings.*

ZAMBIA - POTATO PRODUCTION - See ZAMBIA - CROPS

ZAMBIA - POWER PRODUCTION INDUSTRY

Statistical Office of the United Nations, Publishing Service, New York, New York 10017 (800) 253-9646; *Statistical Yearbook.*

ZAMBIA - PRICES

Federal Statistical Office, Gustav-Stresemann - Ring 11, D-6200, Wiesbaden, Germany; *Sambia.*

Food and Agricultural Organization of the United Nations (FAO) Via delle Terme di Caracalla, 00100 Rome, Italy (Telephone Number in U.S. (202) 653-2400); *The State of Food and Agriculture.*

International Labour Office, I.L.O. Publications, 1828 L Street, NW, Suite 801, Washington, D.C. 20036 (301) 638-3152; *Yearbook of Labour Statistics.*

International Lead and Zinc Study Group, Metro House, 58 St. James's Street, London SW1A 1LD England; *Lead and Zinc Statistics.*

International Monetary Fund, 700 Nineteenth Street, NW, Washington, D.C. 20431 (202) 623-7000; *International Financial Statistics.*

M.E. Sharpe, 80 Business Park Drive, Armonk, New York 10504 (800) 541-6563; *The Illustrated Book of World Rankings.*

United Nations Economic Commission for Africa, Africa Hall, P.O. Box 3001, Addis Ababa, Ethiopia (Telephone Number in U.S. (800) 253-9646; *African Statistical Yearbook.*

World Bureau of Metal Statistics, 27-A High Street, Ware Hert SG12 9BA, England; *World Metal Statistics.*

ZAMBIA - PRINTING AND WRITING PAPER - See ZAMBIA - FORESTRY AND FOREST PRODUCTS

ZAMBIA - PRODUCTION

International Lead and Zinc Study Group, Metro House, 58 St. James's Street, London SW1A 1LD England; *Lead and Zinc*

Statistics.

M.E. Sharpe, 80 Business Park Drive, Armonk, New York 10504 (800) 541-6563; *The Illustrated Book of World Rankings.*

ZAMBIA - PRODUCTIVITY

Euromonitor International, Inc., 122 South Michigan Avenue, Suite 1200, Chicago, Illinois 60603 (800) 577-EURO; *International Marketing Data and Statistics.*

ZAMBIA - PROPERTY TAXES - See ZAMBIA - TAXATION

ZAMBIA - PUBLIC FINANCE - See ZAMBIA - FINANCE

ZAMBIA - RADIO BROADCASTING - See ZAMBIA - BROADCASTING

ZAMBIA - RADIO RECEIVER PRODUCTION

Statistical Office of the United Nations, Publishing Service, New York, New York 10017 (800) 253-9646; *Statistical Yearbook.*

ZAMBIA - RADIO RECEIVERS

St. Martin's Press, Inc., 175 Fifth Avenue, New York, New York 10010 (800) 221-7945; *The Statesman's Year-Book.*

ZAMBIA - RAILWAYS

St. Martin's Press, Inc., 175 Fifth Avenue, New York, New York 10010 (800) 221-7945; *The Statesman's Year-Book.*

Statistical Office of the United Nations, Publishing Service, New York, New York 10017 (800) 253-9646; *Survey of Economic and Social Conditions in Africa.*

United Nations Economic Commission for Africa, Africa Hall, P.O. Box 3001, Addis Ababa, Ethiopia (Telephone Number in U.S. (800) 253-9646); *African Statistical Yearbook.*

ZAMBIA - RELIGION

Central Intelligence Agency, Washington, D.C. 20505 (703) 481-1100, www.cia.gov; *The World Factbook.*

M.E. Sharpe, 80 Business Park Drive, Armonk, New York 10504 (800) 541-6563; *The Illustrated Book of World Rankings.*

St. Martin's Press, Inc., 175 Fifth Avenue, New York, New York 10010 (800) 221-7945; *The Statesman's Year-Book.*

ZAMBIA - RENT PRICES

International Labour Office, I.L.O. Publications, 1828 L Street, NW, Suite 801, Washington, D.C. 20036 (301)

638-3152; *Yearbook of Labour Statistics.*

ZAMBIA - RETAIL TRADE

Euromonitor International, Inc., 122 South Michigan Avenue, Suite 1200, Chicago, Illinois 60603 (800) 577-EURO; *World Marketing Data and Statistics.*

Statistical Office of the United Nations, Publishing Service, New York, New York 10017 (800) 253-9646; *Statistical Yearbook.*

ZAMBIA - RICE PRODUCTION - See ZAMBIA - CROPS

ZAMBIA - ROUNDWOOD PRODUCTION - See ZAMBIA - FORESTRY AND FOREST PRODUCTS

ZAMBIA - RUBBER PRODUCTION AND CONSUMPTION

M.E. Sharpe, 80 Business Park Drive, Armonk, New York 10504 (800) 541-6563; *The Illustrated Book of World Rankings.*

ZAMBIA - SAWNWOOD PRODUCTION - See ZAMBIA - FORESTRY AND FOREST PRODUCTS

ZAMBIA - SCIENCE AND TECHNOLOGY - EXPENDITURE FOR RESEARCH - See ZAMBIA - SCIENTISTS, TECHNICIANS AND ENGINEERS

ZAMBIA - SCIENTISTS, TECHNICIANS AND ENGINEERS

Statistical Office of the United Nations, Publishing Service, New York, New York 10017 (800) 253-9646; *Statistical Yearbook.*

United Nations Educational, Scientific and Cultural Organization (UNESCO), 7 Place de Fontenoy, F-75700 Paris, France (Telephone Number in U.S. (212) 963-5981); *Statistical Yearbook.*

ZAMBIA - SENIOR CITIZENS

M.E. Sharpe, 80 Business Park Drive, Armonk, New York 10504 (800) 541-6563; *The Illustrated Book of World Rankings.*

ZAMBIA - SHEEP - See ZAMBIA - LIVESTOCK AND POULTRY

ZAMBIA - SILVER PRODUCTION AND CONSUMPTION - See ZAMBIA MINING AND MINERAL PRODUCTS

ZAMBIA - SOCIAL DATA

African Development Bank, 01 BP 1387, Abidjan 01, Cote D'Ivoire; *Selected Statistics on Regional Member Countries.*

M.E. Sharpe, 80 Business Park Drive, Armonk, New York 10504 (800) 541-6563; *The Illustrated Book of World Rankings.*

Statistical Office of the United Nations, Publishing Service, New York, New York 10017 (800) 253-9646; *World Statistics Pocketbook.*

ZAMBIA - SOCIAL SECURITY

International Monetary Fund, 700 Nineteenth Street, NW, Washington, D.C. 20431 (202) 623-7000; *Government Finance Statistics Yearbook.*

Statistical Office of the United Nations, Publishing Service, New York, New York 10017 (800) 253-9646; *National Accounts Statistics.*

ZAMBIA - SOYBEAN PRODUCTION - See ZAMBIA - CROPS

ZAMBIA - STAMP TAXES AND DUTIES - See ZAMBIA - TAXATION

ZAMBIA - STATE BUDGET REVENUE AND EXPENDITURES

Euromonitor International, Inc., 122 South Michigan Avenue, Suite 1200, Chicago, Illinois 60603 (800) 577-EURO; *International Marketing Data and Statistics.*

ZAMBIA - STEEL - See ZAMBIA - MINING AND MINERAL PRODUCTS

ZAMBIA - STOCKS - COMMODITY - MARKET PRICE - INDEX

Food and Agricultural Organization of the United Nations (FAO) Via delle Terme di Caracalla, 00100 Rome, Italy (Telephone Number in U.S. (202) 653-2400); *The State of Food and Agriculture.*

International Lead and Zinc Study Group, Metro House, 58 St. James's Street, London SW1A 1LD England; *Lead and Zinc Statistics.*

World Bureau of Metal Statistics, 27-A High Street, Ware Hert SG12 9BA, England; *World Metal Statistics.*

ZAMBIA - SUGAR PRODUCTION AND CONSUMPTION - See ZAMBIA - CROPS

ZAMBIA - SULPHURIC ACID PRODUCTION - See ZAMBIA - MINING AND MINERAL PRODUCTS

ZAMBIA - TAXATION

Europa Publications Limited, 18 Bedford Square, London, WC1B 3JN, England; *The Europa World Year Book.*

International Monetary Fund, 700 Nineteenth Street, NW, Washington, D.C. 20431 (202) 623-7000; *Government Finance Statistics Yearbook.*

International Road Federation, 2600

Virginia Avenue, NW, Washington, D.C. 20037 (202) 338-4641; *World Road Statistics.*

St. Martin's Press, Inc., 175 Fifth Avenue, New York, New York 10010 (800) 221-7945; *The Statesman's Year-Book.*

The World Bank, 1818 H Street, NW, Washington, D.C. 20433 (202) 477-1234; *World Development Indicators.*

ZAMBIA - TELEGRAPH SERVICE

Statistical Office of the United Nations, Publishing Service, New York, New York 10017 (800) 253-9646; *Statistical Yearbook.*

ZAMBIA - TELEPHONES IN USE

American Telephone and Telegraph Communications, Customer Information Center, Post Office Box 19901, Indianapolis, Indiana 46219; *The World's Telephones.*

Central Intelligence Agency, Washington, D.C. 20505 (703) 481-1100, www.cia.gov; *The World Factbook.*

Europa Publications Limited, 18 Bedford Square, London, WC1B 3JN, England; *The Europa World Year Book.*

St. Martin's Press, Inc., 175 Fifth Avenue, New York, New York 10010 (800) 221-7945; *The Statesman's Year-Book.*

Statistical Office of the United Nations, Publishing Service, New York, New York 10017 (800) 253-9646; *Statistical Yearbook; and World Statistics Pocketbook.*

ZAMBIA - TELEVISION BROADCASTING - See ZAMBIA - BROADCASTING

ZAMBIA - TEXTILE INDUSTRY

M.E. Sharpe, 80 Business Park Drive, Armonk, New York 10504 (800) 541-6563; *The Illustrated Book of World Rankings.*

United Nations Conference on Trade and Development, Central Statistical Service, Palais des Nations, Geneva, Switzerland (Telephone in U.S. (800) 253-9646); *UNCTAD Commodity Yearbook.*

ZAMBIA - TIN - See ZAMBIA - MINING AND MINERAL PRODUCTS

ZAMBIA - TOBACCO PRODUCTION

M.E. Sharpe, 80 Business Park Drive, Armonk, New York 10504 (800) 541-6563; *The Illustrated Book of World Rankings.*

Statistical Office of the United Nations, Publishing Service, New York, New York 10017 (800) 253-9646; *Statistical Yearbook.*

ZAMBIA - TOURISM

Euromonitor International, Inc., 122 South Michigan Avenue, Suite 1200, Chicago, Illinois 60603 (800) 577-EURO; *The World Economic Factbook;* and *World Marketing Data and Statistics.*

Europa Publications Limited, 18 Bedford Square, London, WC1B 3JN, England; *The Europa World Year Book.*

Federal Statistical Office, Gustav-Stresemann - Ring 11, D-6200, Wiesbaden, Germany; *Sambia.*

M.E. Sharpe, 80 Business Park Drive, Armonk, New York 10504 (800) 541-6563; *The Illustrated Book of World Rankings.*

St. Martin's Press, Inc., 175 Fifth Avenue, New York, New York 10010 (800) 221-7945; *The Statesman's Year-Book.*

Statistical Office of the United Nations, Publishing Service, New York, New York 10017 (800) 253-9646; *Statistical Yearbook.*

United Nations Economic Commission for Africa, Africa Hall, P.O. Box 3001, Addis Ababa, Ethiopia (Telephone Number in U.S. (800) 253-9646); *African Statistical Yearbook.*

World Tourism Organization, Calle Capitan Haya 42, E-28020 Madrid, Spain; *Yearbook of Tourism Statistics.*

ZAMBIA - TRACTORS IN USE

Statistical Office of the United Nations, Publishing Service, New York, New York 10017 (800) 253-9646; *Statistical Yearbook.*

ZAMBIA - TRADE - See ZAMBIA - FOREIGN TRADE

ZAMBIA - TRADEMARKS AND SERVICE MARKS - See ZAMBIA - PATENTS, TRADEMARKS AND SERVICE MARKS

ZAMBIA - TRANSPORTATION AND COMMUNICATIONS

Central Intelligence Agency, Washington, D.C. 20505 (703) 481-1100, www.cia.gov; *The World Factbook.*

Euromonitor International, Inc., 122 South Michigan Avenue, Suite 1200, Chicago, Illinois 60603 (800) 577-EURO; *International Marketing Data and Statistics;* and *World Marketing Data and Statistics.*

Europa Publications Limited, 18 Bedford Square, London, WC1B 3JN, England; *The Europa World Year Book.*

Federal Statistical Office, Gustav-Stresemann - Ring 11, D-6200, Wiesbaden, Germany; *Sambia.*

M.E. Sharpe, 80 Business Park Drive, Armonk, New York 10504 (800) 541-6563; *The Illustrated Book of World Rankings.*

St. Martin's Press, Inc., 175 Fifth Avenue, New York, New York 10010 (800) 221-7945; *The Statesman's Year-Book.*

Statistical Office of the United Nations, Publishing Service, New York, New York 10017 (800) 253-9646; *Human Development Report.*

United Nations Economic Commission for Africa, Africa Hall, P.O. Box 3001, Addis Ababa, Ethiopia (Telephone Number in U.S. (800) 253-9646); *African Statistical Yearbook.*

ZAMBIA - UNEMPLOYMENT

Central Intelligence Agency, Washington, D.C. 20505 (703) 481-1100, www.cia.gov; *The World Factbook.*

Euromonitor International, Inc., 122 South Michigan Avenue, Suite 1200, Chicago, Illinois 60603 (800) 577-EURO; *International Marketing Data and Statistics.*

International Labour Office, I.L.O. Publications, 1828 L Street, NW, Suite 801, Washington, D.C. 20036 (301) 638-3152; *Yearbook of Labour Statistics.*

Statistical Office of the United Nations, Publishing Service, New York, New York 10017 (800) 253-9646; *Statistical Yearbook.*

ZAMBIA - VITAL STATISTICS

Euromonitor International, Inc., 122 South Michigan Avenue, Suite 1200, Chicago, Illinois 60603 (800) 577-EURO; *International Marketing Data and Statistics.*

Statistical Office of the United Nations, Publishing Service, New York, New York 10017 (800) 253-9646; *Statistical Yearbook.*

World Health Organization, Office of Publications, Avenue Appia, CH-1211 Geneva 27, Switzerland (Telephone Number in U.S. (518) 436-9686); *World Health Statistics Annual.*

ZAMBIA - WAGES

Federal Statistical Office, Gustav-Stresemann - Ring 11, D-6200, Wiesbaden, Germany; *Sambia.*

International Labour Office, I.L.O. Publications, 1828 L Street, NW, Suite 801, Washington, D.C. 20036 (301) 638-3152; *Yearbook of Labour Statistics.*

Statistical Office of the United Nations, Publishing Service, New York, New York 10017 (800) 253-9646; *Statistical Yearbook.*

ZAMBIA - WEATHER - See ZAMBIA - CLIMATE

ZAMBIA - WELFARE

International Monetary Fund, 700 Nineteenth Street, NW, Washington, D.C. 20431 (202) 623-7000; *Government Finance Statistics Yearbook.*

ZAMBIA - WHEAT PRODUCTION AND PRICES - See ZAMBIA - CROPS

ZAMBIA - WHOLESALE PRICES

International Monetary Fund, 700 Nineteenth Street, NW, Washington, D.C. 20431 (202) 623-7000; *International Financial Statistics.*

Statistical Office of the United Nations, Publishing Service, New York, New York 10017 (800) 253-9646; *Statistical Yearbook.*

ZAMBIA - WHOLESALE TRADE

Statistical Office of the United Nations, Publishing Service, New York, New York 10017 (800) 253-9646; *Statistical Yearbook.*

ZAMBIA - WINE PRODUCTION - See ZAMBIA - BEVERAGES

ZAMBIA - WOOL PRODUCTION - See ZAMBIA - TEXTILE INDUSTRY

ZAMBIA - ZINC AND ZINC ORE PRODUCTION AND CONSUMPTION -See ZAMBIA - MINING AND MINERAL PRODUCTS

ZAMBIA - ZOOS AND BOTANICAL GARDENS

United Nations Educational, Scientific and Cultural Organization (UNESCO), 7 Place de Fontenoy, F-75700 Paris, France (Telephone Number in U.S. (212) 963-5981); *Statistical Yearbook.*

Zimbabwe - National Statistical Office

Central Statistical Office, Kaguvi Building, 4th Street/Central Avenue, P.O. Box 8063, Causeway, Harare, Zimbabwe.

Zimbabwe - Primary Statistics Sources

Central Statistical Office, Post Office Box 8063, Causeway, Harare, Zimbabwe; *Statistical Yearbook of Zimbabwe; Annual Economic Review of Zimbabwe;* and *Monthly Digest of Statistics.*

ZIMBABWE - AGRICULTURE

Economist Intelligence Unit, 111 West 57th Street, New York, New York 10019 (800) 938-4685; *Zimbabwe Country Report.*

Euromonitor International, Inc., 122 South Michigan Avenue, Suite 1200, Chicago, Illinois 60603 (800) 577-EURO; *World Marketing Data and Statistics.*

Europa Publications Limited, 18 Bedford Square, London, WC1B 3JN, England; *The Europa World Year Book.*

Federal Statistical Office, Gustav-Stresemann - Ring 11, D-6200, Wiesbaden, Germany; *Simbabwe.*

Food and Agricultural Organization of the United Nations (FAO) Via delle Terme di Caracalla, 00100 Rome, Italy (Telephone Number in U.S. (202) 653-2400); *Production Yearbook,;* and *The State of Food and Agriculture.*

M.E. Sharpe, 80 Business Park Drive, Armonk, New York 10504 (800) 541-6563; *The Illustrated Book of World Rankings.*

St. Martin's Press, Inc., 175 Fifth Avenue, New York, New York 10010 (800) 221-7945; *The Statesman's Year-Book.*

Statistical Office of the United Nations, Publishing Service, New York, New York 10017 (800) 253-9646; *Statistical Yearbook; Survey of Economic and Social Conditions in Africa;* and *Trade Yearbook.*

United Nations Conference on Trade and Development, Central Statistical Service, Palais des Nations, Geneva, Switzerland (Telephone in U.S. (800) 253-9646); *UNCTAD Commodity Yearbook.*

United Nations Economic Commission for Africa, Africa Hall, P.O. Box 3001, Addis Ababa, Ethiopia (Telephone Number in U.S. (800) 253-9646); *African Statistical Yearbook.*

The World Bank, 1818 H Street, NW, Washington, D.C. 20433 (202) 477-1234; *World Development Indicators.*

ZIMBABWE - AIRLINE SERVICE

Europa Publications Limited, 18 Bedford Square, London, WC1B 3JN, England; *The Europa World Year Book.*

International Civil Aviation Organization, 999 University Street, Montreal, Quebec, Canada H3C 5H7 (514) 954-8219; *Civil Aviation Statistics of the World.*

M.E. Sharpe, 80 Business Park Drive, Armonk, New York 10504 (800) 541-6563; *The Illustrated Book of World Rankings.*

St. Martin's Press, Inc., 175 Fifth Avenue, New York, New York 10010 (800) 221-7945; *The Statesman's Year-Book.*

United Nations Economic Commission for Africa, Africa Hall, P.O. Box 3001, Addis Ababa, Ethiopia (Telephone Number in U.S. (800) 253-9646); *African Statistical Yearbook.*

ZIMBABWE - AIRPORTS

Central Intelligence Agency, Washington, D.C. 20505 (703) 481-1100, www.cia.gov; *The World Factbook.*

ZIMBABWE - ALUMINUM PRODUCTION AND CONSUMPTION - See ZIMBABWE - MINING AND MINERAL PRODUCTS

ZIMBABWE - ANIMAL HEALTH

Food and Agricultural Organization of the United Nations (FAO), Via delle Terme di Caracalla, 00100 Rome, Italy (Telephone Number in U.S. (202) 653-2400); *Animal Health Yearbook.*

ZIMBABWE - ANTIMONY AND ANTIMONY ORE PRODUCTION AND CONSUMPTION - See ZIMBABWE - MINING AND MINERAL PRODUCTS

ZIMBABWE - AREA AND DENSITY OF POPULATION

African Development Bank, 01 BP 1387, Abidjan 01, Cote D'Ivoire; *Selected Statistics on Regional Member Countries.*

Central Intelligence Agency, Washington, D.C. 20505 (703) 481-1100, www.cia.gov; *The World Factbook.*

Euromonitor International, Inc., 122 South Michigan Avenue, Suite 1200, Chicago, Illinois 60603 (800) 577-EURO; *The World Economic Factbook.*

Europa Publications Limited, 18 Bedford Square, London, WC1B 3JN, England; *The Europa World Year Book.*

Federal Statistical Office, Gustav-Stresemann - Ring 11, D-6200, Wiesbaden, Germany; *Simbabwe.*

Food and Agricultural Organization of the United Nations (FAO) Via delle Terme di Caracalla, 00100 Rome, Italy (Telephone Number in U.S. (202) 653-2400); *The State of Food and Agriculture.*

M.E. Sharpe, 80 Business Park Drive, Armonk, New York 10504 (800) 541-6563; *The Illustrated Book of World Rankings.*

St. Martin's Press, Inc., 175 Fifth Avenue, New York, New York 10010 (800) 221-7945; *The Statesman's Year-Book.*

Statistical Office of the United Nations, Publishing Service, New York, New York 10017 (800) 253-9646; *Statistical Yearbook;* and *Survey of Economic and Social Conditions in Africa.*

United Nations Educational, Scientific and Cultural Organization (UNESCO), 7 Place de Fontenoy, F-75700 Paris, France (Telephone Number in U.S. (212) 963-5981); *Statistical Yearbook.*

The World Bank, 1818 H Street, NW, Washington, D.C. 20433 (202) 477-1234; *World Development Report.*

ZIMBABWE - ARMS EXPORTS AND IMPORTS - See ZIMBABWE - MILITARY

ZIMBABWE - ARSENIC PRODUCTION AND CONSUMPTION - See ZIMBABWE - MINING AND MINERAL PRODUCTS

ZIMBABWE - BALANCE OF PAYMENTS

African Development Bank, 01 BP 1387, Abidjan 01, Cote D'Ivoire; *Selected Statistics on Regional Member Countries.*

The Economist Intelligence Unit, 111 West 57th Street, New York, New York 10019 (800) 938-4685; *The World Market Atlas.*

Europa Publications Limited, 18 Bedford Square, London, WC1B 3JN, England; *The Europa World Year Book.*

Federal Statistical Office, Gustav-Stresemann - Ring 11, D-6200, Wiesbaden, Germany; *Simbabwe.*

International Monetary Fund, 700 Nineteenth Street, NW, Washington, D.C. 20431 (202) 623-7000; *Balance of Payments Yearbook.*

United Nations Conference on Trade and Development (UNCTAD), New York, New York 10017 (800) 253-9646; *Handbook of International Trade and Development Statistics.*

United Nations Economic Commission for Africa, Africa Hall, P.O. Box 3001, Addis Ababa, Ethiopia (Telephone Number in U.S. (800) 253-9646); *African Statistical Yearbook.*

The World Bank, 1818 H Street, NW, Washington, D.C. 20433 (202) 477-1234; *World Development Report;* and *World Development Indicators.*

ZIMBABWE - BANKING

Euromonitor International, Inc., 122 South Michigan Avenue, Suite 1200, Chicago, Illinois 60603 (800) 577-EURO; *World Marketing Data and Statistics.*

Europa Publications Limited, 18 Bedford Square, London, WC1B 3JN, England; *The Europa World Year Book.*

M.E. Sharpe, 80 Business Park Drive, Armonk, New York 10504 (800) 541-6563; *The Illustrated Book of World Rankings.*

St. Martin's Press, Inc., 175 Fifth Avenue, New York, New York 10010 (800) 221-7945; *The Statesman's Year-Book.*

United Nations Economic Commission for Africa, Africa Hall, P.O. Box 3001, Addis Ababa, Ethiopia (Telephone Number in U.S. (800) 253-9646); *African Statistical Yearbook.*

ZIMBABWE - BARLEY PRODUCTION - See ZIMBABWE - CROPS

ZIMBABWE - BAUXITE PRODUCTION AND CONSUMPTION - See ZIMBABWE - MINING AND MINERAL PRODUCTS

ZIMBABWE - BEER PRODUCTION - See ZIMBABWE - BEVERAGES

ZIMBABWE - BEVERAGES

M.E. Sharpe, 80 Business Park Drive, Armonk, New York 10504 (800) 541-6563; *The Illustrated Book of World Rankings.*

Statistical Office of the United Nations, Publishing Service, New York, New York 10017 (800) 253-9646; *Statistical Yearbook.*

ZIMBABWE - BIRTH RATES

Central Intelligence Agency, Washington, D.C. 20505 (703) 481-1100, www.cia.gov; *The World Factbook.*

Euromonitor International, Inc., 122 South Michigan Avenue, Suite 1200, Chicago, Illinois 60603 (800) 577-EURO; *International Marketing Data and Statistics;* and *The World Economic Factbook.*

Europa Publications Limited, 18 Bedford Square, London, WC1B 3JN, England; *The Europa World Year Book.*

M.E. Sharpe, 80 Business Park Drive, Armonk, New York 10504 (800) 541-6563; *The Illustrated Book of World Rankings.*

St. Martin's Press, Inc., 175 Fifth Avenue, New York, New York 10010 (800) 221-7945; *The Statesman's Year-Book.*

Statistical Office of the United Nations, Publishing Service, New York, New York 10017 (800) 253-9646; *Demographic Yearbook; Statistical Yearbook;* and *Survey of Economic and Social Conditions in Africa.*

The World Bank, 1818 H Street, NW, Washington, D.C. 20433 (202) 477-1234;

World Development Indicators.

ZIMBABWE - BOOK PRODUCTION

Europa Publications Limited, 18 Bedford Square, London, WC1B 3JN, England; *The Europa World Year Book.*

ZIMBABWE - BROADCASTING

Billboard Limited, P.O. Box 9027, 1006 AA Amsterdam, The Netherlands (Telephone Number in U.S. (212) 764-7300); *World Radio TV Handbook.*

Central Intelligence Agency, Washington, D.C. 20505 (703) 481-1100, www.cia.gov; *The World Factbook.*

Euromonitor International, Inc., 122 South Michigan Avenue, Suite 1200, Chicago, Illinois 60603 (800) 577-EURO; *World Marketing Data and Statistics.*

M.E. Sharpe, 80 Business Park Drive, Armonk, New York 10504 (800) 541-6563; *The Illustrated Book of World Rankings.*

St. Martin's Press, Inc., 175 Fifth Avenue, New York, New York 10010 (800) 221-7945; *The Statesman's Year-Book.*

ZIMBABWE - BUDGET

Central Intelligence Agency, Washington, D.C. 20505 (703) 481-1100, www.cia.gov; *The World Factbook.*

ZIMBABWE - BUTTER PRODUCTION - See ZIMBABWE - DAIRY PRODUCTS

ZIMBABWE - CALORIE SUPPLY

African Development Bank, 01 BP 1387, Abidjan 01, Cote D'Ivoire; *Selected Statistics on Regional Member Countries.*

Food and Agricultural Organization of the United Nations (FAO) Via delle Terme di Caracalla, 00100 Rome, Italy (Telephone Number in U.S. (202) 653-2400); *The State of Food and Agriculture.*

ZIMBABWE - CATTLE - See ZIMBABWE - LIVESTOCK AND POULTRY

ZIMBABWE - CEMENT PRODUCTION - See ZIMBABWE - MINING AND MINERAL PRODUCTS

ZIMBABWE - CHEESE PRODUCTION AND CONSUMPTION - See ZIMBABWE - DAIRY PRODUCTS

ZIMBABWE - CHEMICAL (ORGANIC) PRODUCTION - See ZIMBABWE - MINING AND MINERAL PRODUCTS

ZIMBABWE - CHICKENS - See ZIMBABWE - LIVESTOCK AND POULTRY

ZIMBABWE - CHROMITE PRODUCTION AND CONSUMPTION - See ZIMBABWE - MINING AND MINERAL PRODUCTS

ZIMBABWE - CHROMIUM ORE PRODUCTION AND CONSUMPTION - See ZIMBABWE - MINING AND MINERAL PRODUCTS

ZIMBABWE - CIGARETTE PRODUCTION - See ZIMBABWE - TOBACCO PRODUCTION

ZIMBABWE - CLIMATE

M.E. Sharpe, 80 Business Park Drive, Armonk, New York 10504 (800) 541-6563; *The Illustrated Book of World Rankings.*

St. Martin's Press, Inc., 175 Fifth Avenue, New York, New York 10010 (800) 221-7945; *The Statesman's Year-Book.*

ZIMBABWE - COAL PRODUCTION - See ZIMBABWE - MINING AND MINERAL PRODUCTS

ZIMBABWE - COFFEE PRODUCTION AND CONSUMPTION - See ZIMBABWE - CROPS

ZIMBABWE - COKE PRODUCTION AND CONSUMPTION - See ZIMBABWE - MINING AND MINERAL PRODUCTS

ZIMBABWE - COMMERCE

St. Martin's Press, Inc., 175 Fifth Avenue, New York, New York 10010 (800) 221-7945; *The Statesman's Year-Book.*

ZIMBABWE - COMMUNICATIONS - See ZIMBABWE - TRANSPORTATION AND COMMUNICATIONS

ZIMBABWE - CONSTRUCTION INDUSTRY

M.E. Sharpe, 80 Business Park Drive, Armonk, New York 10504 (800) 541-6563; *The Illustrated Book of World Rankings.*

Statistical Office of the United Nations, Publishing Service, New York, New York 10017 (800) 253-9646; *Statistical Yearbook.*

United Nations Economic Commission for Africa, Africa Hall, P.O. Box 3001, Addis Ababa, Ethiopia (Telephone Number in U.S. (800) 253-9646); *African Statistical Yearbook.*

ZIMBABWE - CONSUMER PRICE INDEX

African Development Bank, 01 BP 1387, Abidjan 01, Cote D'Ivoire; *Selected Statistics on Regional Member Countries.*

Europa Publications Limited, 18 Bedford Square, London, WC1B 3JN, England; *The Europa World Year Book.*

Statistical Office of the United Nations, Publishing Service, New York, New York

10017 (800) 253-9646; *Statistical Yearbook;* and *Survey of Economic and Social Conditions in Africa.*

United Nations Economic Commission for Africa, Africa Hall, P.O. Box 3001, Addis Ababa, Ethiopia (Telephone Number in U.S. (800) 253-9646); *African Statistical Yearbook.*

ZIMBABWE - CONSUMER PRICES

Euromonitor International, Inc., 122 South Michigan Avenue, Suite 1200, Chicago, Illinois 60603 (800) 577-EURO; *World Marketing Data and Statistics.*

International Labour Office, I.L.O. Publications, 1828 L Street, NW, Suite 801, Washington, D.C. 20036 (301) 638-3152; *Yearbook of Labour Statistics.*

ZIMBABWE - CONSUMPTION

African Development Bank, 01 BP 1387, Abidjan 01, Cote D'Ivoire; *Selected Statistics on Regional Member Countries.*

Statistical Office of the United Nations, Publishing Service, New York, New York 10017 (800) 253-9646; *Survey of Economic and Social Conditions in Africa.*

The World Bank, 1818 H Street, NW, Washington, D.C. 20433 (202) 477-1234; *World Development Report.*

ZIMBABWE - COPPER AND COPPER ORE PRODUCTION AND CONSUMPTION - See ZIMBABWE - MINING AND MINERAL PRODUCTS

ZIMBABWE - CORN PRODUCTION - See ZIMBABWE - CROPS

ZIMBABWE - CORPORATE TAXES - See ZIMBABWE - TAXATION

ZIMBABWE - COTTON - See ZIMBABWE - CROPS

ZIMBABWE - CRIME

Yale University Press, Yale Station, New Haven, Connecticut 06520 (203) 432-0940; *Violence and Crime in Cross-National Perspective.*

ZIMBABWE - CROPS

Commodity Research Bureau, Inc., 30 South Wacker Drive, Suite 1810, Chicago, Illinois 60606 (800) 621-5271); *Commodity Year Book.*

Europa Publications Limited, 18 Bedford Square, London, WC1B 3JN, England; *The Europa World Year Book.*

Food and Agricultural Organization of the United Nations (FAO) Via delle Terme

di Caracalla, 00100 Rome, Italy (Telephone Number in U.S. (202) 653-2400); *The State of Food and Agriculture.*

M.E. Sharpe, 80 Business Park Drive, Armonk, New York 10504 (800) 541-6563; *The Illustrated Book of World Rankings.*

St. Martin's Press, Inc., 175 Fifth Avenue, New York, New York 10010 (800) 221-7945; *The Statesman's Year-Book.*

Statistical Office of the United Nations, Publishing Service, New York, New York 10017 (800) 253-9646; *Statistical Yearbook.*

United Nations Conference on Trade and Development, Central Statistical Service, Palais des Nations, Geneva, Switzerland (Telephone in U.S. (800) 253-9646); *UNCTAD Commodity Yearbook.*

United Nations Economic Commission for Africa, Africa Hall, P.O. Box 3001, Addis Ababa, Ethiopia (Telephone Number in U.S. (800) 253-9646); *African Statistical Yearbook.*

ZIMBABWE - CUSTOMS DUTIES

St. Martin's Press, Inc., 175 Fifth Avenue, New York, New York 10010 (800) 221-7945; *The Statesman's Year-Book.*

ZIMBABWE - DAIRY PRODUCTS

Europa Publications Limited, 18 Bedford Square, London, WC1B 3JN, England; *The Europa World Year Book.*

Food and Agricultural Organization of the United Nations (FAO) Via delle Terme di Caracalla, 00100 Rome, Italy (Telephone Number in U.S. (202) 653-2400); *The State of Food and Agriculture.*

M.E. Sharpe, 80 Business Park Drive, Armonk, New York 10504 (800) 541-6563; *The Illustrated Book of World Rankings.*

St. Martin's Press, Inc., 175 Fifth Avenue, New York, New York 10010 (800) 221-7945; *The Statesman's Year-Book.*

Statistical Office of the United Nations, Publishing Service, New York, New York 10017 (800) 253-9646; *Statistical Yearbook.*

ZIMBABWE - DEATH RATES - See ZIMBABWE - MORTALITY

ZIMBABWE - DEFENSE EXPENDITURES - See ZIMBABWE - MILITARY

ZIMBABWE - DEMOGRAPHY

The Economist Intelligence Unit, 111 West 57th Street, New York, New York 10019 (800) 938-4685; *The World Market Atlas.*

Euromonitor International, Inc., 122 South Michigan Avenue, Suite 1200, Chicago, Illinois 60603 (800) 577-EURO; *International Marketing Data and Statistics; World Marketing Data and Statistics;* and *The World Economic Factbook.*

Federal Statistical Office, Gustav-Stresemann - Ring 11, D-6200, Wiesbaden, Germany; *Simbabwe.*

M.E. Sharpe, 80 Business Park Drive, Armonk, New York 10504 (800) 541-6563; *The Illustrated Book of World Rankings.*

Statistical Office of the United Nations, Publishing Service, New York, New York 10017 (800) 253-9646; *Human Development Report;* and *Survey of Economic and Social Conditions in Africa.*

ZIMBABWE - DEVELOPMENT ASSISTANCE

Statistical Office of the United Nations, Publishing Service, New York, New York 10017 (800) 253-9646; *Statistical Yearbook.*

ZIMBABWE - DIAMOND PRODUCTION - See ZIMBABWE - MINING AND MINERAL PRODUCTS

ZIMBABWE - DIVORCE RATES

M.E. Sharpe, 80 Business Park Drive, Armonk, New York 10504 (800) 541-6563; *The Illustrated Book of World Rankings.*

Statistical Office of the United Nations, Publishing Service, New York, New York 10017 (800) 253-9646; *Demographic Yearbook.*

ZIMBABWE - ECONOMY

African Development Bank, 01 BP 1387, Abidjan 01, Cote D'Ivoire; *Selected Statistics on Regional Member Countries.*

Central Intelligence Agency, Washington, D.C. 20505 (703) 481-1100, www.cia.gov; *The World Factbook.*

Economist Intelligence Unit, 111 West 57th Street, New York, New York 10019 (800) 938-4685; *Zimbabwe Country Report.*

Euromonitor International, Inc., 122 South Michigan Avenue, Suite 1200, Chicago, Illinois 60603 (800) 577-EURO; *The World Economic Factbook;* and *World Marketing Data and Statistics.*

Europa Publications Limited, 18 Bedford Square, London, WC1B 3JN, England; *The Europa World Year Book.*

Federal Statistical Office, Gustav-Stresemann - Ring 11, D-6200, Wiesbaden, Germany; *Simbabwe.*

M.E. Sharpe, 80 Business Park Drive, Armonk, New York 10504 (800) 541-6563; *The Illustrated Book of World Rankings.*

St. Martin's Press, Inc., 175 Fifth Avenue, New York, New York 10010 (800) 221-7945; *The Statesman's Year-Book.*

Statistical Office of the United Nations, Publishing Service, New York, New York 10017 (800) 253-9646; *World Statistics Pocketbook.*

The World Bank, 1818 H Street, NW, Washington, D.C. 20433 (202) 477-1234; *The World Bank Atlas;* and *World Development Report.*

ZIMBABWE - EDUCATION

Euromonitor International, Inc., 122 South Michigan Avenue, Suite 1200, Chicago, Illinois 60603 (800) 577-EURO; *International Marketing Data and Statistics;* and *World Marketing Data and Statistics.*

Europa Publications Limited, 18 Bedford Square, London, WC1B 3JN, England; *The Europa World Year Book.*

Federal Statistical Office, Gustav-Stresemann - Ring 11, D-6200, Wiesbaden, Germany; *Simbabwe.*

M.E. Sharpe, 80 Business Park Drive, Armonk, New York 10504 (800) 541-6563; *The Illustrated Book of World Rankings.*

St. Martin's Press, Inc., 175 Fifth Avenue, New York, New York 10010 (800) 221-7945; *The Statesman's Year-Book.*

Statistical Office of the United Nations, Publishing Service, New York, New York 10017 (800) 253-9646; *Human Development Report;* and *Survey of Economic and Social Conditions in Africa.*

United Nations Economic Commission for Africa, Africa Hall, P.O. Box 3001, Addis Ababa, Ethiopia (Telephone Number in U.S. (800) 253-9646); *African Statistical Yearbook.*

United Nations Educational, Scientific and Cultural Organization (UNESCO), 7 Place de Fontenoy, F-75700 Paris, France (Telephone Number in U.S. (212) 963-5981); *Statistical Yearbook.*

The World Bank, 1818 H Street, NW, Washington, D.C. 20433 (202) 477-1234; *World Development Report;* and *World Development Indicators.*

ZIMBABWE - EGG PRODUCTION AND CONSUMPTION - See ZIMBABWE - DAIRY PRODUCTS

ZIMBABWE - ELECTRICITY

African Development Bank, 01 BP 1387, Abidjan 01, Cote D'Ivoire; *Selected Statistics on Regional Member Countries.*

Central Intelligence Agency, Washington, D.C. 20505 (703) 481-1100, www.cia.gov; *The World Factbook.*

Commodity Research Bureau, Inc., 30 South Wacker Drive, Suite 1810, Chicago, Illinois 60606 (800) 621-5271); *Commodity Year Book.*

M.E. Sharpe, 80 Business Park Drive, Armonk, New York 10504 (800) 541-6563; *The Illustrated Book of World Rankings.*

St. Martin's Press, Inc., 175 Fifth Avenue, New York, New York 10010 (800) 221-7945; *The Statesman's Year-Book.*

Statistical Office of the United Nations, Publishing Service, New York, New York 10017 (800) 253-9646; *Human Development Report.*

United Nations Economic Commission for Africa, Africa Hall, P.O. Box 3001, Addis Ababa, Ethiopia (Telephone Number in U.S. (800) 253-9646); *African Statistical Yearbook.*

ZIMBABWE - EMPLOYMENT

Euromonitor International, Inc., 122 South Michigan Avenue, Suite 1200, Chicago, Illinois 60603 (800) 577-EURO; *International Marketing Data and Statistics.*

Federal Statistical Office, Gustav-Stresemann - Ring 11, D-6200, Wiesbaden, Germany; *Simbabwe.*

International Labour Office, I.L.O. Publications, 1828 L Street, NW, Suite 801, Washington, D.C. 20036 (301) 638-3152; *Yearbook of Labour Statistics.*

M.E. Sharpe, 80 Business Park Drive, Armonk, New York 10504 (800) 541-6563; *The Illustrated Book of World Rankings.*

Statistical Office of the United Nations, Publishing Service, New York, New York 10017 (800) 253-9646; *Statistical Yearbook;* and *Survey of Economic and Social Conditions in Africa.*

United Nations Economic Commission for Africa, Africa Hall, P.O. Box 3001, Addis Ababa, Ethiopia (Telephone Number in U.S. (800) 253-9646); *African Statistical Yearbook.*

ZIMBABWE - ENERGY

Euromonitor International, Inc., 122 South Michigan Avenue, Suite 1200, Chicago, Illinois 60603 (800) 577-EURO; *International Marketing Data and Statistics; World Marketing Data and Statistics;* and

The World Economic Factbook.

Food and Agricultural Organization of the United Nations (FAO) Via delle Terme di Caracalla, 00100 Rome, Italy (Telephone Number in U.S. (202) 653-2400); *The State of Food and Agriculture.*

M.E. Sharpe, 80 Business Park Drive, Armonk, New York 10504 (800) 541-6563; *The Illustrated Book of World Rankings.*

St. Martin's Press, Inc., 175 Fifth Avenue, New York, New York 10010 (800) 221-7945; *The Statesman's Year-Book.*

Statistical Office of the United Nations, Publishing Service, New York, New York 10017 (800) 253-9646; *Energy Statistics Yearbook; Human Development Report; Statistical Yearbook;* and *World Statistics Pocketbook.*

United Nations Economic Commission for Africa, Africa Hall, P.O. Box 3001, Addis Ababa, Ethiopia (Telephone Number in U.S. (800) 253-9646); *African Statistical Yearbook.*

The World Bank, 1818 H Street, NW, Washington, D.C. 20433 (202) 477-1234; *The World Bank Atlas;* and *World Development Report.*

ZIMBABWE - ENVIRONMENT

Economist Intelligence Unit, 111 West 57th Street, New York, New York 10019 (800) 938-4685; *Zimbabwe Country Report.*

Statistical Office of the United Nations, Publishing Service, New York, New York 10017 (800) 253-9646; *World Statistics Pocketbook.*

ZIMBABWE - EXCHANGE RATES

African Development Bank, 01 BP 1387, Abidjan 01, Cote D'Ivoire; *Selected Statistics on Regional Member Countries.*

Central Intelligence Agency, Washington, D.C. 20505 (703) 481-1100, www.cia.gov; *The World Factbook.*

Euromonitor International, Inc., 122 South Michigan Avenue, Suite 1200, Chicago, Illinois 60603 (800) 577-EURO; *International Marketing Data and Statistics;* and *The World Economic Factbook.*

Europa Publications Limited, 18 Bedford Square, London, WC1B 3JN, England; *The Europa World Year Book.*

International Civil Aviation Organization, 999 University Street, Montreal, Quebec, Canada H3C 5H7 (514) 954-8219; *Civil Aviation Statistics of the World.*

Statistical Office of the United Nations, Publishing Service, New York, New York 10017 (800) 253-9646; *World Statistics Pocketbook.*

ZIMBABWE - EXPORTS

African Development Bank, 01 BP 1387, Abidjan 01, Cote D'Ivoire; *Selected Statistics on Regional Member Countries.*

Central Intelligence Agency, Washington, D.C. 20505 (703) 481-1100, www.cia.gov; *The World Factbook.*

The Economist Intelligence Unit, 111 West 57th Street, New York, New York 10019 (800) 938-4685; *The World Market Atlas;* and *Zimbabwe Country Report.*

Euromonitor International, Inc., 122 South Michigan Avenue, Suite 1200, Chicago, Illinois 60603 (800) 577-EURO; *International Marketing Data and Statistics;* and *The World Economic Factbook.*

Europa Publications Limited, 18 Bedford Square, London, WC1B 3JN, England; *The Europa World Year Book.*

Food and Agricultural Organization of the United Nations (FAO) Via delle Terme di Caracalla, 00100 Rome, Italy (Telephone Number in U.S. (202) 653-2400); *The State of Food and Agriculture.*

St. Martin's Press, Inc., 175 Fifth Avenue, New York, New York 10010 (800) 221-7945; *The Statesman's Year-Book.*

Statistical Office of the United Nations, Publishing Service, New York, New York 10017 (800) 253-9646; *Survey of Economic and Social Conditions in Africa.*

United Nations Conference on Trade and Development (UNCTAD), New York, New York 10017 (800) 253-9646; *Handbook of International Trade and Development Statistics.*

United Nations Economic Commission for Africa, Africa Hall, P.O. Box 3001, Addis Ababa, Ethiopia (Telephone Number in U.S. (800) 253-9646); *African Statistical Yearbook.*

The World Bank, 1818 H Street, NW, Washington, D.C. 20433 (202) 477-1234; *World Development Report;* and *World Development Indicators.*

ZIMBABWE - EXTERNAL INDEBTEDNESS

African Development Bank, 01 BP 1387, Abidjan 01, Cote D'Ivoire; *Selected Statistics on Regional Member Countries.*

Statistical Office of the United Nations, Publishing Service, New York, New York 10017 (800) 253-9646; *Survey of Economic and Social Conditions in Africa.*

The World Bank, 1818 H Street, NW, Washington, D.C. 20433 (202) 477-1234; *World Development Report;* and *World Development Indicators.*

ZIMBABWE - EXTERNAL TRADE

African Development Bank, 01 BP 1387, Abidjan 01, Cote D'Ivoire; *Selected Statistics on Regional Member Countries.*

Euromonitor International, Inc., 122 South Michigan Avenue, Suite 1200, Chicago, Illinois 60603 (800) 577-EURO; *World Marketing Data and Statistics.*

Food and Agricultural Organization of the United Nations (FAO) Via delle Terme di Caracalla, 00100 Rome, Italy (Telephone Number in U.S. (202) 653-2400); *The State of Food and Agriculture.*

ZIMBABWE - FARM CROPS - See ZIMBABWE - CROPS

ZIMBABWE - FERTILITY RATES

Central Intelligence Agency, Washington, D.C. 20505 (703) 481-1100, www.cia.gov; *The World Factbook.*

M.E. Sharpe, 80 Business Park Drive, Armonk, New York 10504 (800) 541-6563; *The Illustrated Book of World Rankings.*

Statistical Office of the United Nations, Publishing Service, New York, New York 10017 (800) 253-9646; *Human Development Report;* and *Survey of Economic and Social Conditions in Africa.*

The World Bank, 1818 H Street, NW, Washington, D.C. 20433 (202) 477-1234; *The World Bank Atlas; World Development Report;* and *World Development Indicators.*

ZIMBABWE - FERTILIZER

Food and Agricultural Organization of the United Nations (FAO), Via delle Terme di Caracalla, 00100 Rome, Italy (Telephone Number in U.S. (202) 653-2400); *Annual Fertilizer Review;* and *The State of Food and Agriculture.*

Statistical Office of the United Nations, Publishing Service, New York, New York 10017 (800) 253-9646; *Statistical Yearbook.*

ZIMBABWE - FETAL MORTALITY - See ZIMBABWE - MORTALITY

ZIMBABWE - FINANCE

African Development Bank, 01 BP 1387, Abidjan 01, Cote D'Ivoire; *Selected Statistics on Regional Member Countries.*

Economist Intelligence Unit, 111 West

57th Street, New York, New York 10019 (800) 938-4685; *Zimbabwe Country Report.*

Europa Publications Limited, 18 Bedford Square, London, WC1B 3JN, England; *The Europa World Year Book.*

Federal Statistical Office, Gustav-Stresemann - Ring 11, D-6200, Wiesbaden, Germany; *Simbabwe.*

M.E. Sharpe, 80 Business Park Drive, Armonk, New York 10504 (800) 541-6563; *The Illustrated Book of World Rankings.*

St. Martin's Press, Inc., 175 Fifth Avenue, New York, New York 10010 (800) 221-7945; *The Statesman's Year-Book.*

United Nations Economic Commission for Africa, Africa Hall, P.O. Box 3001, Addis Ababa, Ethiopia (Telephone Number in U.S. (800) 253-9646); *African Statistical Yearbook.*

ZIMBABWE - FISHERIES

Europa Publications Limited, 18 Bedford Square, London, WC1B 3JN, England; *The Europa World Year Book.*

Federal Statistical Office, Gustav-Stresemann - Ring 11, D-6200, Wiesbaden, Germany; *Simbabwe.*

Food and Agricultural Organization of the United Nations (FAO) Via delle Terme di Caracalla, 00100 Rome, Italy (Telephone Number in U.S. (202) 653-2400); *The State of Food and Agriculture;* and *Yearbook of Fishery Statistics.*

M.E. Sharpe, 80 Business Park Drive, Armonk, New York 10504 (800) 541-6563; *The Illustrated Book of World Rankings.*

St. Martin's Press, Inc., 175 Fifth Avenue, New York, New York 10010 (800) 221-7945; *The Statesman's Year-Book.*

Statistical Office of the United Nations, Publishing Service, New York, New York 10017 (800) 253-9646; *Statistical Yearbook;* and *Survey of Economic and Social Conditions in Africa.*

United Nations Conference on Trade and Development, Central Statistical Service, Palais des Nations, Geneva, Switzerland (Telephone in U.S. (800) 253-9646); *UNCTAD Commodity Yearbook.*

United Nations Economic Commission for Africa, Africa Hall, P.O. Box 3001, Addis Ababa, Ethiopia (Telephone Number in U.S. (800) 253-9646); *African Statistical Yearbook.*

ZIMBABWE - FOOD

African Development Bank, 01 BP 1387,

Abidjan 01, Cote D'Ivoire; *Selected Statistics on Regional Member Countries.*

Food and Agricultural Organization of the United Nations (FAO) Via delle Terme di Caracalla, 00100 Rome, Italy (Telephone Number in U.S. (202) 653-2400); *The State of Food and Agriculture.*

Statistical Office of the United Nations, Publishing Service, New York, New York 10017 (800) 253-9646; *Human Development Report.*

United Nations Conference on Trade and Development, Central Statistical Service, Palais des Nations, Geneva, Switzerland (Telephone in U.S. (800) 253-9646); *UNCTAD Commodity Yearbook.*

ZIMBABWE - FOREIGN DEBT

St. Martin's Press, Inc., 175 Fifth Avenue, New York, New York 10010 (800) 221-7945; *The Statesman's Year-Book.*

ZIMBABWE - FOREIGN TRADE

Economist Intelligence Unit, 111 West 57th Street, New York, New York 10019 (800) 938-4685; *Zimbabwe Country Report.*

Euromonitor International, Inc., 122 South Michigan Avenue, Suite 1200, Chicago, Illinois 60603 (800) 577-EURO; *The World Economic Factbook.*

Europa Publications Limited, 18 Bedford Square, London, WC1B 3JN, England; *The Europa World Year Book.*

Federal Statistical Office, Gustav-Stresemann - Ring 11, D-6200, Wiesbaden, Germany; *Simbabwe.*

Food and Agricultural Organization of the United Nations (FAO) Via delle Terme di Caracalla, 00100 Rome, Italy (Telephone Number in U.S. (202) 653-2400); *The State of Food and Agriculture.*

M.E. Sharpe, 80 Business Park Drive, Armonk, New York 10504 (800) 541-6563; *The Illustrated Book of World Rankings.*

St. Martin's Press, Inc., 175 Fifth Avenue, New York, New York 10010 (800) 221-7945; *The Statesman's Year-Book.*

Statistical Office of the United Nations, Publishing Service, New York, New York 10017 (800) 253-9646; *International Trade Statistics Yearbook;* and *Statistical Yearbook.*

United Nations Conference on Trade and Development, Central Statistical Service, Palais des Nations, Geneva, Switzerland (Telephone in U.S. (800) 253-9646); *UNCTAD Commodity Yearbook.*

United Nations Economic Commission for Africa, Africa Hall, P.O. Box 3001, Addis Ababa, Ethiopia (Telephone Number in U.S. (800) 253-9646); *African Statistical Yearbook.*

The World Bank, 1818 H Street, NW, Washington, D.C. 20433 (202) 477-1234; *World Development Report;* and *World Development Indicators.*

ZIMBABWE - FORESTRY AND FOREST PRODUCTS

Europa Publications Limited, 18 Bedford Square, London, WC1B 3JN, England; *The Europa World Year Book.*

Federal Statistical Office, Gustav-Stresemann - Ring 11, D-6200, Wiesbaden, Germany; *Simbabwe.*

Food and Agricultural Organization of the United Nations (FAO) Via delle Terme di Caracalla, 00100 Rome, Italy (Telephone Number in U.S. (202) 653-2400); *The State of Food and Agriculture;* and *Yearbook of Forest Products.*

M.E. Sharpe, 80 Business Park Drive, Armonk, New York 10504 (800) 541-6563; *The Illustrated Book of World Rankings.*

United Nations Conference on Trade and Development, Central Statistical Service, Palais des Nations, Geneva, Switzerland (Telephone in U.S. (800) 253-9646); *UNCTAD Commodity Yearbook.*

United Nations Economic Commission for Africa, Africa Hall, P.O. Box 3001, Addis Ababa, Ethiopia (Telephone Number in U.S. (800) 253-9646); *African Statistical Yearbook.*

United Nations Educational, Scientific and Cultural Organization (UNESCO), 7 Place de Fontenoy, F-75700 Paris, France (Telephone Number in U.S. (212) 963-5981); *Statistical Yearbook.*

The World Bank, 1818 H Street, NW, Washington, D.C. 20433 (202) 477-1234; *World Development Report.*

ZIMBABWE - GAS PRODUCTION - See ZIMBABWE - MINING AND MINERAL PRODUCTS

ZIMBABWE - GENERAL MORTALITY - See ZIMBABWE - MORTALITY

ZIMBABWE - GEOGRAPHIC DATA

M.E. Sharpe, 80 Business Park Drive, Armonk, New York 10504 (800) 541-6563; *The Illustrated Book of World Rankings.*

ZIMBABWE - GOATS - See ZIMBABWE - LIVESTOCK AND POULTRY

ZIMBABWE - GOLD HOLDINGS

The World Bank, 1818 H Street, NW, Washington, D.C. 20433 (202) 477-1234; *World Development Indicators.*

ZIMBABWE - GOLD PRODUCTION AND CONSUMPTION - See ZIMBABWE - MINING AND MINERAL PRODUCTS

ZIMBABWE - GOVERNMENT

Central Intelligence Agency, Washington, D.C. 20505 (703) 481-1100, www.cia.gov; *The World Factbook.*

Europa Publications Limited, 18 Bedford Square, London, WC1B 3JN, England; *The Europa World Year Book.*

St. Martin's Press, Inc., 175 Fifth Avenue, New York, New York 10010 (800) 221-7945; *The Statesman's Year-Book.*

Statistical Office of the United Nations, Publishing Service, New York, New York 10017 (800) 253-9646; *National Accounts Statistics;* and *Survey of Economic and Social Conditions in Africa.*

The World Bank, 1818 H Street, NW, Washington, D.C. 20433 (202) 477-1234; *World Development Report;* and *World Development Indicators.*

ZIMBABWE - GRAIN PRODUCTION - See ZIMBABWE - CROPS

ZIMBABWE - GROSS DOMESTIC PRODUCT

African Development Bank, 01 BP 1387, Abidjan 01, Cote D'Ivoire; *Selected Statistics on Regional Member Countries.*

The Economist Intelligence Unit, 111 West 57th Street, New York, New York 10019 (800) 938-4685; *The World Market Atlas;* and *Zimbabwe Country Report.*

Euromonitor International, Inc., 122 South Michigan Avenue, Suite 1200, Chicago, Illinois 60603 (800) 577-EURO; *International Marketing Data and Statistics;* and *The World Economic Factbook.*

Europa Publications Limited, 18 Bedford Square, London, WC1B 3JN, England; *The Europa World Year Book.*

M.E. Sharpe, 80 Business Park Drive, Armonk, New York 10504 (800) 541-6563; *The Illustrated Book of World Rankings.*

Statistical Office of the United Nations, Publishing Service, New York, New York 10017 (800) 253-9646; *Human Development Report; National Accounts Statistics; Statistical Yearbook;* and *Survey of Economic and Social Conditions in Africa.*

United Nations Economic Commission for Africa, Africa Hall, P.O. Box 3001, Addis Ababa, Ethiopia (Telephone Number in U.S. (800) 253-9646); *African Statistical Yearbook.*

The World Bank, 1818 H Street, NW, Washington, D.C. 20433 (202) 477-1234; *World Development Report;* and *World Development Indicators.*

ZIMBABWE - GROSS NATIONAL PRODUCT

Europa Publications Limited, 18 Bedford Square, London, WC1B 3JN, England; *The Europa World Year Book.*

St. Martin's Press, Inc., 175 Fifth Avenue, New York, New York 10010 (800) 221-7945; *The Statesman's Year-Book.*

U.S. Arms Control and Disarmament Agency, 320 Twenty-first Street, NW, Washington, D.C. 20451 (202) 647-8677; *World Military Expenditures and Arms Transfers.*

The World Bank, 1818 H Street, NW, Washington, D.C. 20433 (202) 477-1234; *The World Bank Atlas; World Development Report;* and *World Development Indicators.*

ZIMBABWE - GROUNDNUT PRODUCTION - See ZIMBABWE - CROPS

ZIMBABWE - HEALTH

African Development Bank, 01 BP 1387, Abidjan 01, Cote D'Ivoire; *Selected Statistics on Regional Member Countries.*

Euromonitor International, Inc., 122 South Michigan Avenue, Suite 1200, Chicago, Illinois 60603 (800) 577-EURO; *World Marketing Data and Statistics.*

Federal Statistical Office, Gustav-Stresemann - Ring 11, D-6200, Wiesbaden, Germany; *Simbabwe.*

M.E. Sharpe, 80 Business Park Drive, Armonk, New York 10504 (800) 541-6563; *The Illustrated Book of World Rankings.*

St. Martin's Press, Inc., 175 Fifth Avenue, New York, New York 10010 (800) 221-7945; *The Statesman's Year-Book.*

Statistical Office of the United Nations, Publishing Service, New York, New York 10017 (800) 253-9646; *Human Development Report;* and *Statistical Yearbook.*

United Nations Children's Fund (UNICEF), 3 United Nations Plaza, New York, New York 10017 (800) 253-9646; *State of the World's Children.*

United Nations Economic Commission for Africa, Africa Hall, P.O. Box 3001, Addis Ababa, Ethiopia (Telephone Number in U.S. (800) 253-9646); *African Statistical Yearbook.*

The World Bank, 1818 H Street, NW, Washington, D.C. 20433 (202) 477-1234; *World Development Report.*

ZIMBABWE - HIGHWAYS

Central Intelligence Agency, Washington, D.C. 20505 (703) 481-1100, www.cia.gov; *The World Factbook.*

International Road Federation, 2600 Virginia Avenue, NW, Washington, D.C. 20037 (202) 338-4641; *World Road Statistics.*

St. Martin's Press, Inc., 175 Fifth Avenue, New York, New York 10010 (800) 221-7945; *The Statesman's Year-Book.*

Statistical Office of the United Nations, Publishing Service, New York, New York 10017 (800) 253-9646; *Survey of Economic and Social Conditions in Africa.*

United Nations Economic Commission for Africa, Africa Hall, P.O. Box 3001, Addis Ababa, Ethiopia (Telephone Number in U.S. (800) 253-9646); *African Statistical Yearbook.*

ZIMBABWE - HORSES - See ZIMBABWE - LIVESTOCK AND POULTRY

ZIMBABWE - HOURS OF WORK - See ZIMBABWE - EMPLOYMENT

ZIMBABWE - HOUSING AND HOUSING UNITS

Euromonitor International, Inc., 122 South Michigan Avenue, Suite 1200, Chicago, Illinois 60603 (800) 577-EURO; *World Marketing Data and Statistics.*

M.E. Sharpe, 80 Business Park Drive, Armonk, New York 10504 (800) 541-6563; *The Illustrated Book of World Rankings.*

ZIMBABWE - ILLITERATE POPULATION

Central Intelligence Agency, Washington, D.C. 20505 (703) 481-1100, www.cia.gov; *The World Factbook.*

The Economist Intelligence Unit, 111 West 57th Street, New York, New York 10019 (800) 938-4685; *The World Market Atlas.*

Euromonitor International, Inc., 122 South Michigan Avenue, Suite 1200, Chicago, Illinois 60603 (800) 577-EURO; *The World Economic Factbook.*

St. Martin's Press, Inc., 175 Fifth Avenue, New York, New York 10010 (800) 221-7945; *The Statesman's Year-Book.*

Statistical Office of the United Nations, Publishing Service, New York, New York 10017 (800) 253-9646; *Human Development Report.*

ZIMBABWE - IMPORTS

African Development Bank, 01 BP 1387, Abidjan 01, Cote D'Ivoire; *Selected Statistics on Regional Member Countries.*

Central Intelligence Agency, Washington, D.C. 20505 (703) 481-1100, www.cia.gov; *The World Factbook.*

The Economist Intelligence Unit, 111 West 57th Street, New York, New York 10019 (800) 938-4685; *The World Market Atlas;* and *Zimbabwe Country Report.*

Euromonitor International, Inc., 122 South Michigan Avenue, Suite 1200, Chicago, Illinois 60603 (800) 577-EURO; *International Marketing Data and Statistics;* and *The World Economic Factbook.*

Europa Publications Limited, 18 Bedford Square, London, WC1B 3JN, England; *The Europa World Year Book.*

Food and Agricultural Organization of the United Nations (FAO) Via delle Terme di Caracalla, 00100 Rome, Italy (Telephone Number in U.S. (202) 653-2400); *The State of Food and Agriculture.*

St. Martin's Press, Inc., 175 Fifth Avenue, New York, New York 10010 (800) 221-7945; *The Statesman's Year-Book.*

Statistical Office of the United Nations, Publishing Service, New York, New York 10017 (800) 253-9646; *Survey of Economic and Social Conditions in Africa.*

United Nations Conference on Trade and Development (UNCTAD), New York, New York 10017 (800) 253-9646; *Handbook of International Trade and Development Statistics.*

United Nations Economic Commission for Africa, Africa Hall, P.O. Box 3001, Addis Ababa, Ethiopia (Telephone Number in U.S. (800) 253-9646); *African Statistical Yearbook.*

The World Bank, 1818 H Street, NW, Washington, D.C. 20433 (202) 477-1234; *World Development Report;* and *World Development Indicators.*

ZIMBABWE - INDUSTRIAL METALS PRODUCTION - See ZIMBABWE MINING AND MINERAL PRODUCTS

ZIMBABWE - INDUSTRY

Central Intelligence Agency, Washington, D.C. 20505 (703) 481-1100, www.cia.gov; *The World Factbook.*

Economist Intelligence Unit, 111 West 57th Street, New York, New York 10019 (800) 938-4685; *Zimbabwe Country Report.*

Euromonitor International, Inc., 122 South Michigan Avenue, Suite 1200, Chicago, Illinois 60603 (800) 577-EURO; *The World Economic Factbook;* and *World Marketing Data and Statistics.*

Europa Publications Limited, 18 Bedford Square, London, WC1B 3JN, England; *The Europa World Year Book.*

Federal Statistical Office, Gustav-Stresemann - Ring 11, D-6200, Wiesbaden, Germany; *Simbabwe.*

M.E. Sharpe, 80 Business Park Drive, Armonk, New York 10504 (800) 541-6563; *The Illustrated Book of World Rankings.*

St. Martin's Press, Inc., 175 Fifth Avenue, New York, New York 10010 (800) 221-7945; *The Statesman's Year-Book.*

Statistical Office of the United Nations, Publishing Service, New York, New York 10017 (800) 253-9646; *Survey of Economic and Social Conditions in Africa.*

United Nations Economic Commission for Africa, Africa Hall, P.O. Box 3001, Addis Ababa, Ethiopia (Telephone Number in U.S. (800) 253-9646); *African Statistical Yearbook.*

The World Bank, 1818 H Street, NW, Washington, D.C. 20433 (202) 477-1234; *World Development Indicators.*

World Intellectual Property Organization, 34 Chemin des Colombettes, CH-1211 Geneva 20. Switzerland; *Industrial Property Statistics.*

ZIMBABWE - INFANT AND MATERNAL MORTALITY - See ZIMBABWE - MORTALITY

ZIMBABWE - INTERNATIONAL RESERVES EXCLUDING GOLD

African Development Bank, 01 BP 1387, Abidjan 01, Cote D'Ivoire; *Selected Statistics on Regional Member Countries.*

The World Bank, 1818 H Street, NW, Washington, D.C. 20433 (202) 477-1234; *World Development Indicators.*

ZIMBABWE - IRON ORE PRODUCTION AND CONSUMPTION - See ZIMBABWE - MINING AND MINERAL PRODUCTS

ZIMBABWE - LABOR

African Development Bank, 01 BP 1387, Abidjan 01, Cote D'Ivoire; *Selected Statistics on Regional Member Countries.*

Central Intelligence Agency, Washington, D.C. 20505 (703) 481-1100, www.cia.gov; *The World Factbook.*

Euromonitor International, Inc., 122 South Michigan Avenue, Suite 1200, Chicago, Illinois 60603 (800) 577-EURO; *International Marketing Data and Statistics;* and *World Marketing Data and Statistics.*

Europa Publications Limited, 18 Bedford Square, London, WC1B 3JN, England; *The Europa World Year Book.*

Food and Agricultural Organization of the United Nations (FAO) Via delle Terme di Caracalla, 00100 Rome, Italy (Telephone Number in U.S. (202) 653-2400); *The State of Food and Agriculture.*

M.E. Sharpe, 80 Business Park Drive, Armonk, New York 10504 (800) 541-6563; *The Illustrated Book of World Rankings.*

St. Martin's Press, Inc., 175 Fifth Avenue, New York, New York 10010 (800) 221-7945; *The Statesman's Year-Book.*

Statistical Office of the United Nations, Publishing Service, New York, New York 10017 (800) 253-9646; *Human Development Report.*

The World Bank, 1818 H Street, NW, Washington, D.C. 20433 (202) 477-1234; *The World Bank Atlas; World Development Report;* and *World Development Indicators.*

ZIMBABWE - LAND USE

Central Intelligence Agency, Washington, D.C. 20505 (703) 481-1100, www.cia.gov; *The World Factbook.*

Euromonitor International, Inc., 122 South Michigan Avenue, Suite 1200, Chicago, Illinois 60603 (800) 577-EURO; *International Marketing Data and Statistics.*

The World Bank, 1818 H Street, NW, Washington, D.C. 20433 (202) 477-1234; *World Development Report.*

ZIMBABWE - LIBRARIES

M.E. Sharpe, 80 Business Park Drive, Armonk, New York 10504 (800) 541-6563; *The Illustrated Book of World Rankings.*

United Nations Educational, Scientific and Cultural Organization (UNESCO), 7 Place de Fontenoy, F-75700 Paris, France (Telephone Number in U.S. (212) 963-5981); *Statistical Yearbook.*

ZIMBABWE - LIFE EXPECTANCY

African Development Bank, 01 BP 1387, Abidjan 01, Cote D'Ivoire; *Selected Statistics on Regional Member Countries.*

Central Intelligence Agency, Washington, D.C. 20505 (703) 481-1100, www.cia.gov; *The World Factbook.*

Euromonitor International, Inc., 122 South Michigan Avenue, Suite 1200, Chicago, Illinois 60603 (800) 577-EURO; *The World Economic Factbook.*

St. Martin's Press, Inc., 175 Fifth Avenue, New York, New York 10010 (800) 221-7945; *The Statesman's Year-Book.*

Statistical Office of the United Nations, Publishing Service, New York, New York 10017 (800) 253-9646; *Human Development Report;* and *World Statistics Pocketbook.*

The World Bank, 1818 H Street, NW, Washington, D.C. 20433 (202) 477-1234; *The World Bank Atlas;* and *World Development Report.*

ZIMBABWE - LITERACY RATE

Euromonitor International, Inc., 122 South Michigan Avenue, Suite 1200, Chicago, Illinois 60603 (800) 577-EURO; *World Marketing Data and Statistics.*

Statistical Office of the United Nations, Publishing Service, New York, New York 10017 (800) 253-9646; *Survey of Economic and Social Conditions in Africa.*

ZIMBABWE - LIVESTOCK AND POULTRY

Europa Publications Limited, 18 Bedford Square, London, WC1B 3JN, England; *The Europa World Year Book.*

Food and Agricultural Organization of the United Nations (FAO) Via delle Terme di Caracalla, 00100 Rome, Italy (Telephone Number in U.S. (202) 653-2400); *The State of Food and Agriculture.*

M.E. Sharpe, 80 Business Park Drive, Armonk, New York 10504 (800) 541-6563; *The Illustrated Book of World Rankings.*

St. Martin's Press, Inc., 175 Fifth Avenue, New York, New York 10010 (800) 221-7945; *The Statesman's Year-Book.*

Statistical Office of the United Nations, Publishing Service, New York, New York 10017 (800) 253-9646; *Statistical Yearbook;* and *Survey of Economic and Social Conditions in Africa.*

United Nations Conference on Trade and Development, Central Statistical Service, Palais des Nations, Geneva, Switzerland (Telephone in U.S. (800) 253-9646); *UNCTAD Commodity Yearbook.*

United Nations Economic Commission for Africa, Africa Hall, P.O. Box 3001, Addis Ababa, Ethiopia (Telephone Number in

U.S. (800) 253-9646); *African Statistical Yearbook.*

ZIMBABWE - LIVING LEVELS - See ZIMBABWE - LIFE EXPECTANCY

ZIMBABWE - MAIL - NUMBER OF PIECES SENT OR RECEIVED

Statistical Office of the United Nations, Publishing Service, New York, New York 10017 (800) 253-9646; *Statistical Yearbook.*

ZIMBABWE - MANGANESE ORE PRODUCTION AND CONSUMPTION See ZIMBABWE - MINING AND MINERAL PRODUCTS

ZIMBABWE - MANUFACTURING

M.E. Sharpe, 80 Business Park Drive, Armonk, New York 10504 (800) 541-6563; *The Illustrated Book of World Rankings.*

Statistical Office of the United Nations, Publishing Service, New York, New York 10017 (800) 253-9646; *Survey of Economic and Social Conditions in Africa.*

United Nations Economic Commission for Africa, Africa Hall, P.O. Box 3001, Addis Ababa, Ethiopia (Telephone Number in U.S. (800) 253-9646); *African Statistical Yearbook.*

The World Bank, 1818 H Street, NW, Washington, D.C. 20433 (202) 477-1234; *World Development Indicators.*

ZIMBABWE - MARRIAGE RATES

M.E. Sharpe, 80 Business Park Drive, Armonk, New York 10504 (800) 541-6563; *The Illustrated Book of World Rankings.*

Statistical Office of the United Nations, Publishing Service, New York, New York 10017 (800) 253-9646; *Demographic Yearbook.*

ZIMBABWE - MEAT PRODUCTION - See ZIMBABWE - LIVESTOCK AND POULTRY

ZIMBABWE - MERCHANT SHIPPING

St. Martin's Press, Inc., 175 Fifth Avenue, New York, New York 10010 (800) 221-7945; *The Statesman's Year-Book.*

ZIMBABWE - MILITARY

Central Intelligence Agency, Washington, D.C. 20505 (703) 481-1100, www.cia.gov; *The World Factbook.*

Euromonitor International, Inc., 122 South Michigan Avenue, Suite 1200, Chicago, Illinois 60603 (800) 577-EURO; *World Marketing Data and Statistics.*

The International Institute for Strategic

Studies, 23 Tavistock Street, London WC2E 7NQ, England; *The Military Balance.*

St. Martin's Press, Inc., 175 Fifth Avenue, New York, New York 10010 (800) 221-7945; *The Statesman's Year-Book.*

Statistical Office of the United Nations, Publishing Service, New York, New York 10017 (800) 253-9646; *Human Development Report.*

United Nations Economic Commission for Africa, Africa Hall, P.O. Box 3001, Addis Ababa, Ethiopia (Telephone Number in U.S. (800) 253-9646); *African Statistical Yearbook.*

U.S. Arms Control and Disarmament Agency, 320 Twenty-first Street, NW, Washington, D.C. 20451 (202) 647-8677; *World Military Expenditures and Arms Transfers.*

ZIMBABWE - MILK PRODUCTION - See ZIMBABWE - DAIRY PRODUCTS

ZIMBABWE - MINING AND MINERAL PRODUCTS

Commodity Research Bureau, Inc., 30 South Wacker Drive, Suite 1810, Chicago, Illinois 60606 (800) 621-5271); *Commodity Year Book.*

Europa Publications Limited, 18 Bedford Square, London, WC1B 3JN, England; *The Europa World Year Book.*

M.E. Sharpe, 80 Business Park Drive, Armonk, New York 10504 (800) 541-6563; *The Illustrated Book of World Rankings.*

St. Martin's Press, Inc., 175 Fifth Avenue, New York, New York 10010 (800) 221-7945; *The Statesman's Year-Book.*

Statistical Office of the United Nations, Publishing Service, New York, New York 10017 (800) 253-9646; *Statistical Yearbook.*

United Nations Conference on Trade and Development, Central Statistical Service, Palais des Nations, Geneva, Switzerland (Telephone in U.S. (800) 253-9646); *UNCTAD Commodity Yearbook.*

United Nations Economic Commission for Africa, Africa Hall, P.O. Box 3001, Addis Ababa, Ethiopia (Telephone Number in U.S. (800) 253-9646); *African Statistical Yearbook.*

ZIMBABWE - MONEY SUPPLY

African Development Bank, 01 BP 1387, Abidjan 01, Cote D'Ivoire; *Selected Statistics on Regional Member Countries.*

Economist Intelligence Unit, 111 West 57th Street, New York, New York 10019

(800) 938-4685; *Zimbabwe Country Report.*

Europa Publications Limited, 18 Bedford Square, London, WC1B 3JN, England; *The Europa World Year Book.*

Federal Statistical Office, Gustav-Stresemann - Ring 11, D-6200, Wiesbaden, Germany; *Simbabwe.*

The World Bank, 1818 H Street, NW, Washington, D.C. 20433 (202) 477-1234; *World Development Indicators.*

ZIMBABWE - MORTALITY

Central Intelligence Agency, Washington, D.C. 20505 (703) 481-1100, www.cia.gov; *The World Factbook.*

Euromonitor International, Inc., 122 South Michigan Avenue, Suite 1200, Chicago, Illinois 60603 (800) 577-EURO; *International Marketing Data and Statistics;* and *The World Economic Factbook.*

Europa Publications Limited, 18 Bedford Square, London, WC1B 3JN, England; *The Europa World Year Book.*

St. Martin's Press, Inc., 175 Fifth Avenue, New York, New York 10010 (800) 221-7945; *The Statesman's Year-Book.*

Statistical Office of the United Nations, Publishing Service, New York, New York 10017 (800) 253-9646; *Demographic Yearbook; Human Development Report; Statistical Yearbook; Survey of Economic and Social Conditions in Africa;* and *World Statistics Pocketbook.*

United Nations Children's Fund (UNICEF), 3 United Nations Plaza, New York, New York 10017 (800) 253-9646; *State of the World's Children.*

The World Bank, 1818 H Street, NW, Washington, D.C. 20433 (202) 477-1234; *The World Bank Atlas; World Development Report;* and *World Development Indicators.*

ZIMBABWE - MOTOR VEHICLE TAXES - See ZIMBABWE - TAXATION

ZIMBABWE - MOTOR VEHICLES IN USE

Europa Publications Limited, 18 Bedford Square, London, WC1B 3JN, England; *The Europa World Year Book.*

International Road Federation, 2600 Virginia Avenue, NW, Washington, D.C. 20037 (202) 338-4641; *World Road Statistics.*

Statistical Office of the United Nations, Publishing Service, New York, New York 10017 (800) 253-9646; *Statistical Yearbook;* and *Survey of Economic and Social*

Conditions in Africa.

ZIMBABWE - MULES - See ZIMBABWE - LIVESTOCK AND POULTRY

ZIMBABWE - MUSEUMS

M.E. Sharpe, 80 Business Park Drive, Armonk, New York 10504 (800) 541-6563; *The Illustrated Book of World Rankings.*

ZIMBABWE - NATALITY - See ZIMBABWE - BIRTH RATE

ZIMBABWE - NATIONAL ACCOUNTS

African Development Bank, 01 BP 1387, Abidjan 01, Cote D'Ivoire; *Selected Statistics on Regional Member Countries.*

Europa Publications Limited, 18 Bedford Square, London, WC1B 3JN, England; *The Europa World Year Book.*

Federal Statistical Office, Gustav-Stresemann - Ring 11, D-6200, Wiesbaden, Germany; *Simbabwe.*

Statistical Office of the United Nations, Publishing Service, New York, New York 10017 (800) 253-9646; *Statistical Yearbook.*

United Nations Economic Commission for Africa, Africa Hall, P.O. Box 3001, Addis Ababa, Ethiopia (Telephone Number in U.S. (800) 253-9646); *African Statistical Yearbook.*

ZIMBABWE - NATIONAL INCOME

M.E. Sharpe, 80 Business Park Drive, Armonk, New York 10504 (800) 541-6563; *The Illustrated Book of World Rankings.*

Statistical Office of the United Nations, Publishing Service, New York, New York 10017 (800) 253-9646; *National Accounts Statistics;* and *Statistical Yearbook.*

ZIMBABWE - NATIONAL PRODUCT

M.E. Sharpe, 80 Business Park Drive, Armonk, New York 10504 (800) 541-6563; *The Illustrated Book of World Rankings.*

Statistical Office of the United Nations, Publishing Service, New York, New York 10017 (800) 253-9646; *Statistical Yearbook.*

ZIMBABWE - NATURAL GAS PRODUCTION - See ZIMBABWE - MINING AND MINERAL PRODUCTS

ZIMBABWE - NEWSPAPER PRODUCTION - See ZIMBABWE - FORESTRY AND FOREST PRODUCTS

ZIMBABWE - NEWSPRINT - See ZIMBABWE - FORESTRY AND FOREST PRODUCTS

ZIMBABWE - NICKEL AND NICKEL ORE PRODUCTION AND CONSUMPTION - See ZIMBABWE - MINING AND MINERAL PRODUCTS

ZIMBABWE - OCCUPATIONS - See ZIMBABWE - LABOR

ZIMBABWE - PAPER - See ZIMBABWE - FORESTRY AND FOREST PRODUCTS

ZIMBABWE - PATENTS, TRADEMARKS AND SERVICE MARKS

World Intellectual Property Organization, 34 Chemin des Colombettes, CH-1211 Geneva 20. Switzerland; *Industrial Property Statistics.*

ZIMBABWE - PEANUT PRODUCTION - See ZIMBABWE - CROPS

ZIMBABWE - PESTICIDE USE

Food and Agricultural Organization of the United Nations (FAO) Via delle Terme di Caracalla, 00100 Rome, Italy (Telephone Number in U.S. (202) 653-2400); *The State of Food and Agriculture.*

ZIMBABWE - PETROLEUM INDUSTRY

Food and Agricultural Organization of the United Nations (FAO) Via delle Terme di Caracalla, 00100 Rome, Italy (Telephone Number in U.S. (202) 653-2400); *The State of Food and Agriculture.*

M.E. Sharpe, 80 Business Park Drive, Armonk, New York 10504 (800) 541-6563; *The Illustrated Book of World Rankings.*

Statistical Office of the United Nations, Publishing Service, New York, New York 10017 (800) 253-9646; *Statistical Yearbook.*

United Nations Conference on Trade and Development, Central Statistical Service, Palais des Nations, Geneva, Switzerland (Telephone in U.S. (800) 253-9646); *UNCTAD Commodity Yearbook.*

ZIMBABWE - PHOSPHATE ROCK PRODUCTION - See ZIMBABWE MINING AND MINERAL PRODUCTS

ZIMBABWE - PIG-IRON AND FERRO-ALLOY PRODUCTION - See ZIMBABWE - MINING AND MINERAL PRODUCTS

ZIMBABWE - PIGS - See ZIMBABWE - LIVESTOCK AND POULTRY

ZIMBABWE - POPULATION

African Development Bank, 01 BP 1387, Abidjan 01, Cote D'Ivoire; *Selected Statistics on Regional Member Countries.*

Central Intelligence Agency, Washington, D.C. 20505 (703) 481-1100,

www.cia.gov; *The World Factbook.*

The Economist Intelligence Unit, 111 West 57th Street, New York, New York 10019 (800) 938-4685; *The World Market Atlas;* and *Zimbabwe Country Report.*

Euromonitor International, Inc., 122 South Michigan Avenue, Suite 1200, Chicago, Illinois 60603 (800) 577-EURO; *International Marketing Data and Statistics;* and *The World Economic Factbook.*

Europa Publications Limited, 18 Bedford Square, London, WC1B 3JN, England; *The Europa World Year Book.*

Federal Statistical Office, Gustav-Stresemann - Ring 11, D-6200, Wiesbaden, Germany; *Simbabwe.*

M.E. Sharpe, 80 Business Park Drive, Armonk, New York 10504 (800) 541-6563; *The Illustrated Book of World Rankings.*

St. Martin's Press, Inc., 175 Fifth Avenue, New York, New York 10010 (800) 221-7945; *The Statesman's Year-Book.*

Statistical Office of the United Nations, Publishing Service, New York, New York 10017 (800) 253-9646; *Demographic Yearbook; Human Development Report; Statistical Yearbook; Survey of Economic and Social Conditions in Africa;* and *World Statistics Pocketbook.*

United Nations Educational, Scientific and Cultural Organization (UNESCO), 7 Place de Fontenoy, F-75700 Paris, France (Telephone Number in U.S. (212) 963-5981); *Statistical Yearbook.*

U.S. Arms Control and Disarmament Agency, 320 Twenty-first Street, NW, Washington, D.C. 20451 (202) 647-8677; *World Military Expenditures and Arms Transfers.*

The World Bank, 1818 H Street, NW, Washington, D.C. 20433 (202) 477-1234; *The World Bank Atlas;* and *World Development Report.*

World Health Organization, Office of Publications, Avenue Appia, CH-1211 Geneva 27, Switzerland (Telephone Number in U.S. (518) 436-9686); *World Health Statistics Annual.*

ZIMBABWE - POST OFFICES

M.E. Sharpe, 80 Business Park Drive, Armonk, New York 10504 (800) 541-6563; *The Illustrated Book of World Rankings.*

St. Martin's Press, Inc., 175 Fifth Avenue, New York, New York 10010 (800) 221-7945; *The Statesman's Year-Book.*

ZIMBABWE - POTATO PRODUCTION - See

ZIMBABWE - CROPS

ZIMBABWE - POWER PRODUCTION INDUSTRY

Statistical Office of the United Nations, Publishing Service, New York, New York 10017 (800) 253-9646; *Statistical Yearbook.*

ZIMBABWE - PRICES

Federal Statistical Office, Gustav-Stresemann - Ring 11, D-6200, Wiesbaden, Germany; *Simbabwe.*

Food and Agricultural Organization of the United Nations (FAO) Via delle Terme di Caracalla, 00100 Rome, Italy (Telephone Number in U.S. (202) 653-2400); *The State of Food and Agriculture.*

International Labour Office, I.L.O. Publications, 1828 L Street, NW, Suite 801, Washington, D.C. 20036 (301) 638-3152; *Yearbook of Labour Statistics.*

M.E. Sharpe, 80 Business Park Drive, Armonk, New York 10504 (800) 541-6563; *The Illustrated Book of World Rankings.*

United Nations Economic Commission for Africa, Africa Hall, P.O. Box 3001, Addis Ababa, Ethiopia (Telephone Number in U.S. (800) 253-9646); *African Statistical Yearbook.*

ZIMBABWE - PRINTING AND WRITING PAPER - See ZIMBABWE - FORESTRY AND FOREST PRODUCTS

ZIMBABWE - PRODUCTION

M.E. Sharpe, 80 Business Park Drive, Armonk, New York 10504 (800) 541-6563; *The Illustrated Book of World Rankings.*

ZIMBABWE - PUBLIC FINANCE - See ZIMBABWE - FINANCE

ZIMBABWE - RADIO BROADCASTING - See ZIMBABWE - BROADCASTING

ZIMBABWE - RADIO RECEIVERS

St. Martin's Press, Inc., 175 Fifth Avenue, New York, New York 10010 (800) 221-7945; *The Statesman's Year-Book.*

ZIMBABWE - RAILWAYS

Europa Publications Limited, 18 Bedford Square, London, WC1B 3JN, England; *The Europa World Year Book.*

St. Martin's Press, Inc., 175 Fifth Avenue, New York, New York 10010 (800) 221-7945; *The Statesman's Year-Book.*

Statistical Office of the United Nations, Publishing Service, New York, New York 10017 (800) 253-9646; *Statistical Yearbook;*

and *Survey of Economic and Social Conditions in Africa.*

ZIMBABWE - RELIGION

Central Intelligence Agency, Washington, D.C. 20505 (703) 481-1100, www.cia.gov; *The World Factbook.*

M.E. Sharpe, 80 Business Park Drive, Armonk, New York 10504 (800) 541-6563; *The Illustrated Book of World Rankings.*

St. Martin's Press, Inc., 175 Fifth Avenue, New York, New York 10010 (800) 221-7945; *The Statesman's Year-Book.*

United Nations Economic Commission for Africa, Africa Hall, P.O. Box 3001, Addis Ababa, Ethiopia (Telephone Number in U.S. (800) 253-9646); *African Statistical Yearbook.*

ZIMBABWE - RENT PRICES

International Labour Office, I.L.O. Publications, 1828 L Street, NW, Suite 801, Washington, D.C. 20036 (301) 638-3152; *Yearbook of Labour Statistics.*

ZIMBABWE - RETAIL TRADE

Euromonitor International, Inc., 122 South Michigan Avenue, Suite 1200, Chicago, Illinois 60603 (800) 577-EURO; *World Marketing Data and Statistics.*

ZIMBABWE - RICE PRODUCTION - See ZIMBABWE - CROPS

ZIMBABWE - ROUNDWOOD PRODUCTION - See ZIMBABWE - FORESTRY AND FOREST PRODUCTS

ZIMBABWE - RUBBER PRODUCTION AND CONSUMPTION

M.E. Sharpe, 80 Business Park Drive, Armonk, New York 10504 (800) 541-6563; *The Illustrated Book of World Rankings.*

ZIMBABWE - SAWNWOOD PRODUCTION - See ZIMBABWE - FORESTRY AND FOREST PRODUCTS

ZIMBABWE - SENIOR CITIZENS

M.E. Sharpe, 80 Business Park Drive, Armonk, New York 10504 (800) 541-6563; *The Illustrated Book of World Rankings.*

ZIMBABWE - SHEEP - See ZIMBABWE - LIVESTOCK AND POULTRY

ZIMBABWE - SILVER PRODUCTION AND CONSUMPTION - See ZIMBABWE - MINING AND MINERAL PRODUCTS

ZIMBABWE - SOCIAL DATA

African Development Bank, 01 BP 1387,

Abidjan 01, Cote D'Ivoire; *Selected Statistics on Regional Member Countries.*

M.E. Sharpe, 80 Business Park Drive, Armonk, New York 10504 (800) 541-6563; *The Illustrated Book of World Rankings.*

ZIMBABWE - SOCIAL SECURITY

St. Martin's Press, Inc., 175 Fifth Avenue, New York, New York 10010 (800) 221-7945; *The Statesman's Year-Book.*

Statistical Office of the United Nations, Publishing Service, New York, New York 10017 (800) 253-9646; *National Accounts Statistics.*

ZIMBABWE - STEEL - See ZIMBABWE - MINING AND MINERAL PRODUCTS

ZIMBABWE - STOCKS - COMMODITY - MARKET PRICE - INDEX

Food and Agricultural Organization of the United Nations (FAO) Via delle Terme di Caracalla, 00100 Rome, Italy (Telephone Number in U.S. (202) 653-2400); *The State of Food and Agriculture.*

ZIMBABWE - SUGAR PRODUCTION AND CONSUMPTION - See ZIMBABWE - CROPS

ZIMBABWE - TAXATION

Europa Publications Limited, 18 Bedford Square, London, WC1B 3JN, England; *The Europa World Year Book.*

International Road Federation, 2600 Virginia Avenue, NW, Washington, D.C. 20037 (202) 338-4641; *World Road Statistics.*

The World Bank, 1818 H Street, NW, Washington, D.C. 20433 (202) 477-1234; *World Development Indicators.*

ZIMBABWE - TELEPHONES IN USE

American Telephone and Telegraph Communications, Customer Information Center, Post Office Box 19901, Indianapolis, Indiana 46219; *The World's Telephones.*

Central Intelligence Agency, Washington, D.C. 20505 (703) 481-1100, www.cia.gov; *The World Factbook.*

Europa Publications Limited, 18 Bedford Square, London, WC1B 3JN, England; *The Europa World Year Book.*

St. Martin's Press, Inc., 175 Fifth Avenue, New York, New York 10010 (800) 221-7945; *The Statesman's Year-Book.*

Statistical Office of the United Nations, Publishing Service, New York, New York 10017 (800) 253-9646; *Statistical Yearbook;* and *World Statistics Pocketbook.*

ZIMBABWE - TELEVISION BROADCASTING - See ZIMBABWE - BROADCASTING

ZIMBABWE - TEXTILE INDUSTRY

M.E. Sharpe, 80 Business Park Drive, Armonk, New York 10504 (800) 541-6563; *The Illustrated Book of World Rankings.*

St. Martin's Press, Inc., 175 Fifth Avenue, New York, New York 10010 (800) 221-7945; *The Statesman's Year-Book.*

United Nations Conference on Trade and Development, Central Statistical Service, Palais des Nations, Geneva, Switzerland (Telephone in U.S. (800) 253-9646); *UNCTAD Commodity Yearbook.*

ZIMBABWE - TIN - See ZIMBABWE - MINING AND MINERAL PRODUCTS

ZIMBABWE - TOBACCO PRODUCTION

M.E. Sharpe, 80 Business Park Drive, Armonk, New York 10504 (800) 541-6563; *The Illustrated Book of World Rankings.*

Statistical Office of the United Nations, Publishing Service, New York, New York 10017 (800) 253-9646; *Statistical Yearbook.*

ZIMBABWE - TOURISM

Euromonitor International, Inc., 122 South Michigan Avenue, Suite 1200, Chicago, Illinois 60603 (800) 577-EURO; *The World Economic Factbook;* and *World Marketing Data and Statistics.*

Europa Publications Limited, 18 Bedford Square, London, WC1B 3JN, England; *The Europa World Year Book.*

Federal Statistical Office, Gustav-Stresemann - Ring 11, D-6200, Wiesbaden, Germany; *Simbabwe.*

M.E. Sharpe, 80 Business Park Drive, Armonk, New York 10504 (800) 541-6563; *The Illustrated Book of World Rankings.*

St. Martin's Press, Inc., 175 Fifth Avenue, New York, New York 10010 (800) 221-7945; *The Statesman's Year-Book.*

United Nations Economic Commission for Africa, Africa Hall, P.O. Box 3001, Addis Ababa, Ethiopia (Telephone Number in U.S. (800) 253-9646); *African Statistical Yearbook.*

World Tourism Organization, Calle Capitan Haya 42, E-28020 Madrid, Spain; *Yearbook of Tourism Statistics.*

ZIMBABWE - TRACTORS IN USE

Statistical Office of the United Nations, Publishing Service, New York, New York

10017 (800) 253-9646; *Statistical Yearbook.*

ZIMBABWE - TRADE - See ZIMBABWE - FOREIGN TRADE

ZIMBABWE - TRADEMARKS AND SERVICE MARKS - See ZIMBABWE - PATENTS, TRADEMARKS AND SERVICE MARKS

ZIMBABWE - TRANSPORTATION AND COMMUNICATIONS

Central Intelligence Agency, Washington, D.C. 20505 (703) 481-1100, www.cia.gov; *The World Factbook.*

Euromonitor International, Inc., 122 South Michigan Avenue, Suite 1200, Chicago, Illinois 60603 (800) 577-EURO; *International Marketing Data and Statistics;* and *World Marketing Data and Statistics.*

Europa Publications Limited, 18 Bedford Square, London, WC1B 3JN, England; *The Europa World Year Book.*

Federal Statistical Office, Gustav-Stresemann - Ring 11, D-6200, Wiesbaden, Germany; *Simbabwe.*

M.E. Sharpe, 80 Business Park Drive, Armonk, New York 10504 (800) 541-6563; *The Illustrated Book of World Rankings.*

St. Martin's Press, Inc., 175 Fifth Avenue, New York, New York 10010 (800) 221-7945; *The Statesman's Year-Book.*

Statistical Office of the United Nations, Publishing Service, New York, New York 10017 (800) 253-9646; *Human Development Report.*

United Nations Economic Commission for Africa, Africa Hall, P.O. Box 3001, Addis Ababa, Ethiopia (Telephone Number in U.S. (800) 253-9646); *African Statistical Yearbook.*

ZIMBABWE - TUNGSTEN PRODUCTION AND CONSUMPTION - See ZIMBABWE - MINING AND MINERAL PRODUCTS

ZIMBABWE - UNEMPLOYMENT RATE

Central Intelligence Agency, Washington, D.C. 20505 (703) 481-1100, www.cia.gov; *The World Factbook.*

ZIMBABWE - VITAL STATISTICS

St. Martin's Press, Inc., 175 Fifth Avenue, New York, New York 10010 (800) 221-7945; *The Statesman's Year-Book.*

Statistical Office of the United Nations, Publishing Service, New York, New York 10017 (800) 253-9646; *Statistical Yearbook.*

World Health Organization, Office of Publications, Avenue Appia, CH-1211

Geneva 27, Switzerland (Telephone Number in U.S. (518) 436-9686); *World Health Statistics Annual.*

ZIMBABWE - WAGES

Federal Statistical Office, Gustav-Stresemann - Ring 11, D-6200, Wiesbaden, Germany; *Simbabwe.*

ZIMBABWE - WEATHER - See ZIMBABWE - CLIMATE

ZIMBABWE - WELFARE

St. Martin's Press, Inc., 175 Fifth Avenue, New York, New York 10010 (800) 221-7945; *The Statesman's Year-Book.*

ZIMBABWE - WHEAT PRODUCTION AND PRICES - See ZIMBABWE -CROPS

ZIMBABWE - WHOLESALE PRICES

Statistical Office of the United Nations, Publishing Service, New York, New York 10017 (800) 253-9646; *Statistical Yearbook.*

ZIMBABWE - WINE PRODUCTION - See ZIMBABWE - BEVERAGES

ZIMBABWE - WOOL PRODUCTION - See ZIMBABWE - TEXTILE INDUSTRY

ZIMBABWE - WOOD PULP PRODUCTION - See ZIMBABWE - FORESTRY AND FOREST PRODUCTS

ZINC - FOREIGN TRADE

U.S. Department of Commerce, Bureau of the Census, Washington, D.C. 20233 (301) 457-4608; *International Trade in Goods and Services.*

U.S. Department of the Interior, Geological Survey, Office of Minerals Information, 12201 Sunrise Valley Drive, Reston, Virginia 22092 (703) 648-7718; *Mineral Commodity Summaries.*

ZINC - MINING INDUSTRY

U.S. Department of Commerce, Bureau of the Census, Washington, D.C. 20233 (301) 457-4608; *Census of Mineral Industries.*

ZINC - PRICES

U.S. Department of the Interior, Geological Survey, Office of Minerals Information, 12201 Sunrise Valley Drive, Reston, Virginia 22092 (703) 648-7718;

Mineral Commodity Summaries; and *Annual Report.*

ZINC - PRODUCTION - WORLD

U.S. Department of the Interior, Geological Survey, Office of Minerals Information, 12201 Sunrise Valley Drive, Reston, Virginia 22092 (703) 648-7718; *Mineral Commodity Summaries;* and *Annual Reports.*

ZINC - STRATEGIC AND CRITICAL MATERIALS

U.S. Department of Defense, Defense Logistics Agency, Cameron Station, Alexandria, Virginia 22304-6100 (703) 274-6000; *Statistical Supplement, Stockpile Report to the Congress.*

Appendix A

Source Publications

This appendix provides an overview of the printed sources of information used to compile this edition of *Statistics Sources*. It consists of a complete bibliography of all the publications cited under the specific subject headings throughout both volumes. Entries in this listing are arranged alphabetically by publication title, and include the names and addresses of the issuing or publishing bodies.

ACP: Basic Statistics.
European Community Information Service, 2100 M Street, NW, Washington, D.C. 20037 (202) 862-9500

ADFL Bulletin.
Association of Departments of Foreign Languages, 10 Astor Place, New York, New York 10003 (212) 614-6319

Abortion Factbook.
Alan Guttmacher Institute, 120 Wall Street, New York, New York 10005 (212) 248-1111

Abortion Services in the United States.
Alan Guttmacher Institute, 120 Wall Street, New York, New York 10005 (212) 248-1111

Abstract of Statistics.
Central Statistics Office, Ministry of Finance, Saint George's, Grenada

Abstract of Statistics.
Department of Economic Development, Statistics Unit, Post Office Box 42, Niue Island, Niue

Abstract of Statistics.
National Statistics Office, Central Government Offices, Post Office Wards Strip, Waigani, Papua, New Guinea

Abstract of Statistics.
Statistics Office, Cathedral Square, Gibraltar

Accident Bulletin.
U.S. Department of Transportation, Federal Railroad Administration, 1120 Vermont Avenue, NW, Washington, D.C. 20590 (202) 493-6000

Accident Facts.
National Safety Council, 1121 Spring Lake Drive, Itasca, Illinois 60143-3201 (630) 285-1121

Adoption Factbook.
National Council for Adoption, 1930 17th Street, NW, Washington, D.C. 20009-6207 (202) 328-8072

Adult Education Profile.
U.S. Department of Education, National Center for Education Statistics, 555 New Jersey Avenue, NW, Washington,.D.C. 20208 (202) 219-1828

Advance Data from Vital and Health Statistics.
U.S. Department of Health and Human Services, National Center for Health Statistics, 3700 East-West Highway, Hyattsville, Maryland 20782 (301) 436-8500

Advertising Age.
Crain Communications, Inc., 740 North Rush Street, Chicago, Illinois 60611 (312) 649-5200

Aeronautics and Space Report of the President.
National Aeronautics and Space Administration, 300 E Street, SW, Washington, D.C. 20546 (202) 358-1000

Affirmative Employment Statistics.
Office of Personnel Management, 1900 E Street, NW, Washington, D.C. 20415 (202) 606-1800

Afghan Agriculture In Figures.
Central Statistics Office, Kabul, Afghanistan

Afghanistan.
Federal Statistical Office, Gustav-Stresemann-Ring 11, D-6200 Wiesbaden, Germany

Afghanistan Country Report.
Economist Intelligence Unit, 111 West 57th Street, New York, New York 10019 (800) 938-4685

Africa South of the Sahara.
Europa Publications, London, England (Available from Gale Group (800) 877-GALE)

African Development Indicators.
World Bank Publications, 1818 H Street, NW, Washington, D.C. 20043 (202) 477-1234

African Statistical Yearbook.
United Nations Economic Commission for Africa, Africa Hall, P.O Box 3001, Addis Ababa, Ethiopia (Telephone Number in U.S. (800) 253-

9646)

Agenda estadistica.
Instituto National de Estadistica, Georafia e Informatica, CP 03910, Mexico

Aging and the Family.
United Nations, Department for Economic and Social Information and Policy Analysis, New York, New York.

Agricultural Banker.
American Bankers Association, 1120 Connecticut Avenue, NW, Washington, D.C. 20036 (202) 663-5000

Agricultural Outlook.
U.S. Department of Agriculture, Economic Research Service, 1800 M Street, NW, Washington, D.C. 20036 (202) 694-5050

Agricultural Outlook.
U.S. Department of Agriculture, Office of Aquaculture, 901 D Street, SW, Washington, D.C. 20024 (202) 401-4929

Agricultural Prices: Annual Summary.
U.S. Department of Agriculture, National Agricultural Statistics Service, Fourteenth Street and Independence Avenue, SW, Washington, D.C. 20250 (800) 727-9540

Agricultural Resources and Environmental Indicators.
U.S. Department of Agriculture, Economic Research Service, 1800 M Street, NW, Washington, D.C. 20036 (202) 694-4040

Agricultural Resources: Cropland, Water, and Conservation, Situation and Outlook Report.
U.S. Department of Agriculture, Economic Research Service, 1800 M Street, NW, Washington, D.C. 20036 (202) 694-4040

Agricultural Review for Europe.
United Nations, New York, New York (Available from UNIPUB (800) 274-4888

Agricultural Statistics.
U.S. Department of Agriculture, National Agricultural Statistics Service, Fourteenth Street and Independence Avenue, SW, Washington, D.C. 20250 (800) 727-9540

Agricultural Supply and Demand Estimates.
U.S. Department of Agriculture, Economic Research Service, 1800 M Street, NW, Washington, D.C. 20036 (202) 694-4040

The Agricultural Work Force.
U.S. Department of Agriculture, Economic Research Service, 1800 M Street, NW, Washington, D.C. 20036 (202) 694-4040

Agriculture: Statistical Yearbook.
European Community Information Service, 2100 M Street, NW, Washington, D.C. 20037 (202) 862-9500

Air Carrier Financial Statistics.
U.S. Department of Transportation, Federal Aviation Administration, 800 Independence Avenue, SW, Washington, D.C. 20591 (202) 367-3484

Air Carrier Traffic Statistics.
U.S. Department of Transportation, Federal Aviation Administration, 800 Independence Avenue, SW, Washington, D.C. 20591 (202) 367-3484

Air Quality Update.
Environmental Protection Agency, 1200 Pennsylvania Avenue, NW, Washington, D.C. 20460 (888) 372-8255

Air Transport.
Air Transport Association of America, 1301 Pennsylvania Avenue, NW, Suite 1100, Washington, D.C. 20004-7017 (202) 626-4000

Air Transport Facts and Figures.
Air Transport Association of America, 1301 Pennsylvania Avenue, NW, Suite 1100, Washington, D.C. 20004 (202) 626-4000

Air Travel Consumer Report.
U.S. Department of Transportation, Office of Consumer Affairs, 400 Seventh Street, SW, Washington, D.C. 20590 (202) 366-4000

Airport Activity Statistics.
U.S. Department of Transportation, Federal Aviation Administration, 800 Independence Avenue, SW, Washington, D.C. 20591 (202) 367-3484

The Alaska Economy Performance Report.
Department of Commerce and Economic Analysis, Post Office Box 110804, Juneau, Alaska 99811 (907) 465-2017

Albania Country Report.
Economist Intelligence Unit, 111 West 57th Street, New York, New York 10019 (800) 938-4685

Albanien.
Federal Statistical Office, Gustav-Stresemann-Ring 11, D-6200 Wiesbaden, Germany

Alcohol and Tobacco Tax Collections.
U.S. Department of the Treasury, Bureau of Alcohol, Tobacco and Firearms, 650 Massachusetts Avenue, NW, Washington, D.C. 20226 (202) 927-8500

Algeria Country Report.
Economist Intelligence Unit, 111 West 57th Street, New York, New York 10019 (800) 938-4685

Algerian.
Federal Statistical Office, Gustav-Stresemann-Ring 11, D-6200 Wiesbaden, Germany

Allman Manadsstatistik.
Statiska Centralbyran, Karlavagen 100, S-115 81, Stockholm, Sweden

Almanac of the 50 States: Basic Data Profiles With Comparative Tables.
Information Publications, Palo Alto, California (415) 965-4449

America Votes.
Congressional Quarterly, Inc., 1414 22nd Street, NW, Washington, D.C. 20037 (202) 887-8500

American Banker.
American Banker, One State Street Plaza, New York, New York 10004 (800) 367-3989

American Banker Ranking the Banks.
American Banker, One State Street Plaza, New York, New York 10004 (800) 367-3989

American Cost of Living Survey: A Compilation of Price Data for Nearly 600 Goods and Services in 443 U.S. Cities from More Than 70 Sources.
Gale Group, 27500 Drake Road, Farmington Hills, Michigan 48331 (800) 877-4253

American Freshman: National Norms.
Higher Education Research Institute, University of California, Los Angeles, Graduate School of Education, Los Angeles, California 90024 (213) 825-1925

American Housing Survey.
U.S. Department of Commerce, Bureau of the Census, Washington, D.C. 20233 (301) 457-4100

American Jewish Yearbook.
American Jewish Committee, c/o Institute of Human Relations, 165 East 56th Street, New York, New York 10022 (212) 751-4000

American League Red Book.
The American League of Professional Baseball Clubs, 245 Park Avenue, New York, New York 10167 (212) 931-7600

American Library Directory.
R.R. Bowker Company, 121 Chanlon Road, New Providence, New Jersey 07974 (908) 464-6800

The American Marketplace: Demographics and Spending Patterns.
New Strategist, Ithaca, New York (607) 273-0913

American Samoa Statistical Digest.
Economic Development and Planning Office, Pago, American Samoa

American Statistics Index: A Comprehensive Guide and Index to the Statistical Publications of the United States Government.
Congressional Information Service, Bethesda, Maryland (800) 638-8380

The American Tally: Statistics and Ranking for 3,165 U.S. Cities and Towns: Covering All U.S. Cities and Towns With Populations Over 10,000.
Toucan Valley Publications, Milpitas, California (415) 956-9492

American Women: Who They Are and How They Live.
New Strategist, Ithaca, New York (607) 273-0913

America's Top Rated Cities.
Grey House

An Analysis of the Timber Situation in the United States.
U.S. Department of Agriculture, Forest Service, Post Office Box 96090, Washington, D.C. 20090 (202) 720-3760

Analysis of Class I Railroads.
Association of American Railroads, 50 F Street, NW, Washington, D.C. 20001 (202) 639-2100

Analytical Perspectives.
Executive Office of the President, Office of Management and Budget, Executive Office Building, Washington, D.C. 20503 (202) 395-3080

Angola.
Federal Statistical Office, Gustav-Stresemann-Ring 11, D-6200 Wiesbaden, Germany

Angola Country Report.
Economist Intelligence Unit, 111 West 57th Street, New York, New York 10019 (800) 938-4685

Animal Health Yearbook.
Food and Agricultural Organization of the United Nations (FAO), Via delle Terme di Caracalla, 00100 Rome, Italy (Telephone Number in the U.S. (202) 653-2400)

Annuaire Statistique.
Department de la Statistique, BP 1156, Bujumbura, Burundi

Annuaire Statistique.
Direction de la Statistique, BP 240, Nouakchott, Mauritania

Annuaire Statistique.
Direction de la Statistique et de la Comptabilite Economique, BP 2031, Brazzaville, Congo

Annuaire Statistique.
Direction de la Statistique Generale et des Etudes Economiques, BP 732, Bangui, Central African Republic

Annuaire statistique.
Direction de la Statistique, Niamey, Niger

Annuaire Statistique.
Direction Generale de la Statistique, BP 179, Libreville, Gabon

Annuaire Statistique.
Institut National de la Statistique et de l'Analyse Economique, BP 323, Cotonou, Benin

Annuaire Statistique.
Service National de la Statistique, Ministere du Plan et de la Cooperation, Post Office Box 46, Vientiane, Laos

Annuaire Statistique de Belgique.
Institut National de Statistique, National Institute of Statistics, rue de Louvain 44, 1000 Brussels, Belgium

Annuaire Statistique du Burkina Faso.
Ministere du Plan et de la Cooperation, BP 374, Ougadougou, 01, Burkina Faso

Annuaire Statistique de Djibouti.
Djibouti: Direction Nationale de la Statistique, BP 1846, Djibouti

Annuaire Statistique de Poche.
Institut National de Statistique, National Institute of Statistics, rue de Louvain 44, 1000 Brussels, Belgium

Annuaire Statistique de l'Algerie.
Sous - Direction des Statistiques, Direction des Statistiques et de la Comptabilite Nationale, BP 478, Alger, Algeria

Annuaire Statistique de la France.
Institut National de la Statistique et des Etudes Economiques (INSEE), 12 rue Boulitte, 75675 Paris Cedex 14, France

Annuaire statistique de la Guadeloupe.
Institut National de la Statistique et des Etudes Economiques, Tour Gamma A, 195 rue de Bercy, 75582, Paris Cedex 12, France

Annuaire Statistique de la Guyane.
INSEE, Observatoire Economique de Paris, Tour Gamma A, 195 rue de Bercy, 75582, Paris Cedex 12, France

Annuaire Statistique de la Martinique.
Institut National de la Statistique et des Etudes Economiques, BP 863, 97175 Pointe-a-Pitre, France

Annuaire Statistique de la Nouvelle Caledonie et Dependances.
Direction Territoriale de la Statistique et des Etudes Economiques, BP 323, Noumea, New Caledonia

Annuaire Statistique de la Suisse.
Bureau Federal de Statistique, Hallwylstrasse 15 3003 Berne, Switzerland

Annuaire Statistique de la Tunisie.
Institut National de la Statistique, 27 rue du Liban, 1002 Tunis-Belvedere, Tunis, Tunisia

Annuaire Statistique du Luxembourg.
STATEC, 19-21 Boulevard Royal, BP 304, L-2013, Luxembourg

Annuaire statistique du Mali.
Direction Nationale de la Statistique, BP12, Bamako, Mali

Annuaire statistique du Maroc.
Division de la Statistique, BP 178, Rabat, Morocco

Annuaire Statistique du Tchad.
Direction de la Statistique, BP 453, N'djamena, Chad

Annuaire statistique du Togo.
Direction de la Statistique (Department of Statistics), BP 118, Lome, Togo

Annuaire Statistique du Zaire.
Institut National de la Statistique, BP 20, Kinshasa, Gombe, Zaire

Annual Abstract of Statistics.
Central Office of Statistics, Auberge D'Italie, Valletta, Malta

Annual Abstract of Statistics.
Central Statistical Office, London, England.

Annual Abstract of Statistics.
Central Statistical Organisation, Ministry of Planning, Post Office Box 8001, Baghdad, Iraq

Annual Abstract of Statistics.
Federal Office of Statistics, 36-38 Broad Street, PMB 12528, Lagos, Nigeria

Annual Abstract of Statistics.
HM Stationery Office, Post Office Box 276, London SW8 5DT, England

Annual Abstract of Statistics.
Ministry of Finance, Central Statistical Office, Belmopan, Belize

Annual Abstract of Statistics.
Statistics Office, Post Office Box G6, Honiara, Solomon Islands

Annual Bulletin of General Energy Statistics for Europe.
Economic Commission for Europe, Geneva, Switzerland (Available from UNIPUB (800) 274-4888)

Annual Bulletin of Housing and Building Statistics for Europe and North America.
United Nations Publications, New York, New York 10017 (800) 253-9646

Annual Bulletin of Steel Statistics for Europe, America and Asia.
Statistical Office of the United Nations, Publishing Service, New York, New York 10017 (800) 253-9646

Annual Bulletin of Transport Statistics for Europe, and North America.
Statistical Office of the United Nations, Publishing Service, New York, New York 10017 (800) 253-9646

Annual Cancer Statistics Review.
U.S. Department of Health and Human Services, National Institutes of Health, National Cancer Institute, 9000 Rockville Pike, Bethesda, Maryland 20892 (301) 496-5737

Annual Digest of Statistics.
Central Statistical Office, Government Printer, Port Louis, Mauritius

Annual Economic Review.
Economic Research Center, Department of Commerce, Agana, Guam 96910

Annual Economic Review of Zimbabwe.
Central Statistical Office, Post Office Box 8063, Causeway, Harare, Zimbabwe

Annual Energy Review.
U.S. Department of Energy, Energy Information Administration, 1000 Independence Avenue, SW, Washington, D.C. 20585 (202) 586-8800

Annual Housing Survey.
U.S. Department of Commerce, Bureau of the Census, Washington, D.C. 20233 (301) 457-4100

Annual Information Exchange.
National Association of State Park Directors, 126 Mill Branch Road, Tallahassee, Florida 32312 (904) 893-4959

Annual Prospects for World Coal Trade.
U.S. Department of Energy, Energy Information Administration, 1000 Independence Avenue, SW, Washington, D.C. 20585 (202) 586-8800

Annual Report.
American Bus Association, 1100 New York Avenue, NW, Suite 1050, Washington, D.C. 20005-3934 (202) 842-1645

Annual Report.
Boy Scouts of America, 1325 West Walnut Hill Lane, Post Office Box 152079, Irving, Texas 75015 (972) 580-2000

Annual Report.
Federal Deposit Insurance Corporation, 550 Seventeenth Street, NW, Washington, D.C. 20429 (202) 393-8400

Annual Report.
Girl Scouts of the United States of America, 420 Fifth Avenue, New York, New York 10018-2702 (212) 852-8000

Annual Report.
Commodity Futures Trading Commission, 1155 21st Street, NW, Washington, D.C. 20581 (202) 418-5000

Annual Report.
Federal Communications Commission, 445 Twelfth Street SW, Washington, D.C. 20554 (888) 225-5322

Annual Report.
U.S. Library of Congress, 101 Independence Avenue, SE, Washington, D.C. 20540 (202) 707-5000

Annual Report.
National Endowment for the Arts, 1100 Pennsylvania Avenue, NW, Washington, D.C. 20506 (202) 682-5400

Annual Report.
National Endowment for the Humanities, 1100 Pennsylvania Avenue, NW, Washington, D.C. 20506 (202) 606-8400

Annual Report.
Securities and Exchange Commission, 450 Fifth Street, NW, Washington, D.C. 20549 (202) 942-4040

Annual Report of Board of Trustees, OASI, DI, HI, and SMI Trust Funds.
Social Security Administration, 6400 Security Boulevard, Baltimore, Maryland 21235 (800) 772-1213

Annual Report of the Commissioner and Chief Counsel of the Internal Revenue Service.
U.S. Department of the Treasury, Internal Revenue Service, 1111 Constitution Avenue, NW, Washington, D.C. 20224 (202) 874-0410

Annual Report of the Director.
Administrative Office of the United States Courts, Thurgood Marshall Federal Judiciary Building, One Columbus Circle, NE, Washington, D.C. 20544 (202) 502-1455

Annual Report of the National Credit Union Administration.
National Credit Union Administration, 1775 Duke Street, Alexandria,

Virginia 22314-3428 (703) 518-6300

Annual Report of the Postmaster General.
U.S. Postal Service, 475 L'Enfant Plaza West, SW, Washington, D.C. 20260-0010 (202) 268-2000

Annual Report of the Regional Airline Association.
Regional Airline Association, 2025 M Street, NW, Suite 800, Washington, D.C. 20036 (202) 367-1170

Annual Report of the Revenue Commissioners.
Government Publications Sales Office, GPO Arcade, Dublin 1, Ireland

Annual Report of the Secretary of Transportation.
U.S. Department of Transportation, United States Coast Guard, 2100 Second Street, SW, Washington, D.C. 20593 (202) 267-2229

Annual Report of the Secretary of Veterans Affairs.
U.S. Department of Veterans Affairs, 810 Vermont Avenue, NW, Washington, D.C. 20420 (202) 273-5400

Annual Report of the Territory of Norfolk Island.
Australian Government Publishing Service, Post Office Box 84, Canberra ACT 26010, Australia

Annual Report on Dental Education.
American Dental Association, 211 East Chicago Avenue, Chicago, Illinois 60611 (312) 440-2500

Annual Report on the Economic Status of the Profession.
Maryse Eymonerie Associates, Post Office Box 7893, Hilton Head, South Carolina 29938

Annual Report on the Territory of Christmas Island.
Sales and Distribution, Australian Government Publishing Service, Post Office Box 84, Canberra ACT 2601, Australia

Annual Report on the Territory of Cocos (Keeling) Islands.
Sales and Distribution, Australian Government Publishing Service, Post Office Box 84, Canberra ACT 2600, Australia

Annual Report to Congress.
U.S. Department of Education, Office of Special Education Programs, 400 Maryland Avenue, SW, Washington, D.C. 20202 (800) 872-5327.

Annual Report to Congress.
U.S. Department of Health and Human Services, Office of Child Support Enforcement, 370 L'Enfant Promenade, SW, Washington, D.C. 20447 (202) 401-9373

Annual Report to Congress on Civil Aviation Security.
U.S. Department of Transportation, Federal Aviation Administration, 800 Independence Avenue, SW, Washington, D.C. 20591 (202) 367-3484

Annual Report to the United Nations on the Administration of the Trust Territory of the Pacific Islands.
Superintendent of Documents, U.S. Government Printing Office, Washington, D.C. 20402 (202) 783-3238

Annual Reports.
U.S. Department of the Interior, Geological Survey, Office of Minerals Information, 12201 Sunrise Valley Drive, Reston, Virginia 22092 (703) 648-4000

Annual Reports of the World's Central Banks.
Chadwyck-Healey Inc., Alexandria, Virginia (800) 752-0515

Annual Retail Trade Report.
U.S. Department of Commerce, Bureau of the Census, Washington, D.C. 20233 (301) 457-4100

Annual Review of the Chief, National Guard Bureau.
U.S. National Guard Bureau, The Pentagon, Washington, D.C. 20301 (202) 433-5100

Annual Statistical Abstract.
Central Statistical Office, Ministry of Planning, Post Office Box 904, Abu Dhabi, United Arab Emirates

Annual Statistical Abstract.
Central Statistical Office, Post Office Box 26188, Safat, Kuwait

Annual Statistical Abstract.
Central Statistical Organization, Post Office Box 7283, Doha, Qatar

Annual Statistical Abstract.
Department of Statistics, Apia, Western Samoa

Annual Statistical Abstract.
Statistical Bureau, Avenue of the Republic, Post Office Box 542, Georgetown, Guyana

Annual Statistical Abstract State of Qatar.
Presidency of the Council of Ministers, Central Statistical Organisation, Doha, Qatar

Annual Statistical Bulletin.
Central Statistical Office, Post Office Box 456, Mbabane, Swaziland

Annual Statistical Bulletin.
Organization of the Petroleum Exporting Countries (OPEC), Vienna, Austria

Annual Statistical Digest.
Board of Governors of the Federal Reserve System, Twentieth Street and Constitution Avenue, NW, Washington, D.C. 20551 (202) 452-3000

Annual Statistical Digest.
Central Statistical Office, Post Office Box 98, Port of Spain, Trinidad

Annual Statistical Digest.
Central Statistics Office, Ministry of Finance, Tower Hill, Freetown, Sierra Leone

Annual Statistical Digest.
Development, Planning and Statistics Division, Premier's Office, Post Office Building, Castries, Saint Lucia

Annual Statistical Report.
American Iron and Steel Institute, 1101 17th Street, NW, Washington, D.C. 20036 (202) 452-7100

Annual Statistical Report.
U.S. Department of Justice, Drug Enforcement Administration, 600-700 Army Navy Drive, Arlington, Virginia 22202 (202) 307-1000

Annual Statistical Supplement to the Social Security Bulletin.
Social Security Administration, 6400 Security Boulevard, Baltimore, Maryland 21235 (800) 772-1213

Annual Summary of Merchant Ships Completed in the World.
Lloyd's Register of Shipping, 17 Battery Place, New York, New York 10004 (212) 425-8050

Annual Survey of Communication Services
U.S. Department of Commerce, Bureau of the Census, Washington, D.C. 20233 (301) 457-4100

Annual Survey of Corporate Contributions.
The Conference Board, 845 Third Avenue, New York, New York 10022 (212) 759-0900

Annual Survey of Hospitals.
American Hospital Association, One North Franklin, Suite 27, Chicago, Illinois 60606 (800) 242-2626

Annual Survey of Manufactures.
U.S. Department of Commerce, Bureau of the Census, Washington, D.C. 20233 (301) 457-4100

Anuario Estadistico de los Estados Unidos Mexicanos
Instituto National de Estadistica, Geografia e Informatica, CP 03910, Mexico

Annuario Statistico Italiano.
Instituto Centrale di Statistica, Via Cesare Balbo 16, 00184 Rome, Italy

Antigua: Report for the Year.
HMSO, Post Office Box 569, London SE1 9NH, England

Anuario de la Bolsa.
Colegio de Agentes de Cambio y Bolsa de Madrid, Plaza de la Lealtad, 1, Madrid-14, Spain

Anuario estatistico.
Direccao Geral de Estatistica, Bissau, Guinea Bissau

Anuario estatistico.
Direccao Nacional de Estatistica, CP 493, Maputo, Mozambique

Anuario estadistico.
Direccion de Estadisticas y Censos, Avenida Centenario 6Y8 Calles, Camayaguela DC, Honduras

Anuario estadistico.
Direccion General de Estadistica y Censos, Instituto Nacional de Estadistica y Censos, Hipolita Yrigoyen 250, Buenos Aires

Anuario Estadistico.
Direccion General de Estadistica y Censos Villa Femina, Calle Arce No 953, San Salvador, El Salvador

Anuario Estadistico.
Direccion General de Estadisticas, Cuareim, 2052, Montevideo, Uruguay

Anuario estadistico.
Instituto Nacional de Estadistica, Guatemala City, Guatemala

Anuario estadistico.
Oficina Central de Estadistica e Informatica, Presidencia de la Republica, Aptdo. de Correos 400 Carmelitas, Caracas 1050, Venezuela

Anuario estatistico.
Instituto Nacional de Estatistica (National Statistical Institute), Avenida Antonio Jose de Almeida, Lisbon, Portugal

Anuario estatistico.
Reparticao Provincial dos Servicos de Estatistica, Macau, Macau

Anuario estatistico - Annuaire statistique.
Direccao dos Servicos de Estatistica (Department of Statistical Services), Caixa Postal 1215, Luanda, Angola

Anuario estastistico.
Puerto Rico Planning Board, North Building, Box 41119, San Juan, Puerto Rico 00940

Anuario estatistico de Brasil.
Fundacao Instituto Brasileiro de Geografia e Estatistica, Avenida Franklin Roosevelt 166 20021, Rio de Janeiro, Brazil

Anuario estatistico de Cuba.

Comite Estatal de Estadisticas, Calle 46, No. 307, Gaveta Postal 6016, Miramar, Havana, Cuba

Anuario estadistico de Chile.
Instituto Nacional de Estadisticas, Casilla 7597, Correo 3, Santiago, Chile

Anuario estadistico de Espana.
Instituto Nacional de Estadistica (National Institute of Statistics), Paseo de la Castellana 183, Madrid, Spain

Anuario Estadistico de Nicaragua.
Instituto Nacional de Estadistica y Censos, Apartado 4031, Managua, Nicaragua

Annuario estadistico del Paraguay
Direccion General de Estadistica y Censos, Miguel Torres 5313, C Correos: 1118, Asuncion, Paraguay

Anuario estadistico del Peru.
Direccion General de Estadistica y Censos, Instituto Nacional de Estadistica, Avenida 28 de Julio 1056, Lima 1, Peru

Anuario general de estadistica.
DANE, Via Eldorado, Bogota, Colombia

Anuario Statistico.
Servicio Statale di Statistica, Via G Carducci 145, Repubblica di San Marino

Anuarul Statistica Al Romaniei.
Comisia Nationala Pentru Statistica, Bucharest, Romania

Aquatorialguinea.
Federal Statistical Office, Gustav-Stresemann-Ring 11, D-6200 Wiesbaden, Germany

Area Handbook for North Korea.
Superintendent of Documents, U.S. Government Printing Office, Washington, D.C. 20402 (202) 783-3238

Area Measurement Reports.
U.S. Department of Commerce, Bureau of the Census, Washington, D.C. 20233 (301) 457-4100

Areas of Acquisitions to the Territory of the United States.
U.S. Department of the Interior, 1849 C Street, NW, Washington, D.C. 20240 (202) 208-3171

Areas of the United States.
U.S. Department of Commerce, Bureau of the Census, Washington, D.C. 20233 (301) 457-4100

Argentina.
Federal Statistical Office, Gustav-Stresemann-Ring 11, D-6200 Wiesbaden, Germany

Argentina Country Report.
Economist Intelligence Unit, 111 West 57th Street, New York, New York 10019 (800) 938-4685

Argus F.C. & S. Chart.
The National Underwriter Company, 505 Gest Street, Cincinnati, Ohio 45203 (513) 721-2140

Arizona Economic Indicators.
University of Arizona, Division of Economic and Business Research, College of Business and Public Administration, Tucson, Arizona 85721 (602) 621-2155

Arizona Statistical Abstract: A 1990 Data Handbook.

University of Arizona, Division of Economic and Business Research, College of Business and Public Administration, Tucson, Arizona 85721 (602) 621-2155

Arkansas State and County Economic Data.
University of Arkansas, Little Rock, Regional Economic Analysis, Library 512, Little Rock, Arkansas 72204 (501) 659-8530

Arkansas Statistical Abstract.
University of Arkansas at Little Rock, State Data Center, Library 508, Little Rock, Arkansas 72204 (501) 659-8530

Armenia Country Report.
Economist Intelligence Unit, 111 West 57th Street, New York, New York 10019 (800) 938-4685

Arts Funding Revisited: An Update on Foundation Trends in the 1990's.
The Foundation Center, 79 Fifth Avenue, New York, New York 10003 (212) 620-4230

Aruba Country Report.
Economist Intelligence Unit, 111 West 57th Street, New York, New York 10019 (800) 938-4685

Asia-Pacific in Figures.
Statistical Office of the United Nations, Publishing Service, New York, New York 10017 (800) 253-9646

Asian Market Atlas.
The Economist Intelligence Unit (Asia) Limited, 10th Floor Luk Kwok Centre, 72 Gloucester Road, Wanchai, Hong Kong (Phone Number in the U.S. (800) 938-4685)

Atlas/Data Abstract for the United States and Selected Areas.
U.S. Department of Defense, Office of the Secretary, The Pentagon, Washington, D.C. 20301 (703) 545-6700

Atlas of the 1990 Census.
Macmillan Publishing Company, New York, New York (800) 858-7674

Athiopien.
Federal Statistical Office, Gustav-Stresemann-Ring 11, D-6200 Wiesbaden, Germany

Australia Country Report.
Economist Intelligence Unit, 111 West 57th Street, New York, New York 10019 (800) 938-4685

Australien.
Federal Statistical Office, Gustav-Stresemann-Ring 11, D-6200 Wiesbaden, Germany

Average Annual Pay by State and Industry.
U.S. Department of Labor, Bureau of Labor Statistics, Two Massachusetts Avenue, NE, Washington, D.C. 20212 (202) 691-5200

Average Annual Pay Levels in Metropolitan Areas.
U.S. Department of Labor, Bureau of Labor Statistics, Two Massachusetts Avenue, NE, Washington, D.C. 20212 (202) 691-5200

Aylik Istatistik Bulteni.
Devlet Istatistik Enstitusu, Necatibey Caddesi, 114 Ankara, Turkey

Azerbaijan Country Report.
Economist Intelligence Unit, 111 West 57th Street, New York, New York 10019 (800) 938-4685

BLS Data Diskettes.
U.S. Department of Labor, Bureau of Labor Statistics, Two Massachusetts Avenue, NE, Washington, D.C. 20212 (202) 691-5200

BLS Data Files on Tape.
U.S. Department of Labor, Bureau of Labor Statistics, Two Massachusetts Avenue, NE, Washington, D.C. 20212 (202) 691-5200

BLS News Releases On Line.
U.S. Department of Labor, Bureau of Labor Statistics, Two Massachusetts Avenue, NE, Washington, D.C. 20212 (202) 691-5200

BLS Reports on Employer Child-Care Practices.
U.S. Department of Labor, Bureau of Labor Statistics, Two Massachusetts Avenue, NE, Washington, D.C. 20212 (202) 691-5200

Bahamas.
Federal Statistical Office, Gustav-Stresemann-Ring 11, D-6200 Wiesbaden, Germany

Bahamas Country Report.
Economist Intelligence Unit, 111 West 57th Street, New York, New York 10019 (800) 938-4685

Bahrain.
Federal Statistical Office, Gustav-Stresemann-Ring 11, D-6200 Wiesbaden, Germany

Bahrain Country Report.
Economist Intelligence Unit, 111 West 57th Street, New York, New York 10019 (800) 938-4685

Balance of Payments Statistics Yearbook.
International Monetary Fund, 700 Nineteenth Street, NW, Washington, D.C. 20431 (202) 623-7000

Balance Sheet of the Farming Sector.
U.S. Department of Agriculture, Economic Research Service, 1800 M Street, NW, Washington, D.C. 20036 (202) 694-4040

Balance Sheets for United States Economy.
Board of Governors of the Federal Reserve System, Twentieth Street and Constitution Avenue, NW, Washington, D.C. 20551 (202) 452-3000

Balances of Payments of OECD Countries: 1963-1982.
Organisation for Economic Co-operation and Development (OECD), 2 rue Andre-Pascal, 75 Paris 16, France (Telephone Number in U.S. (202) 785-6323)

Bangladesch.
Federal Statistical Office, Gustav-Stresemann-Ring 11, D-6200 Wiesbaden, Germany

Bangladesh Country Report.
Economist Intelligence Unit, 111 West 57th Street, New York, New York 10019 (800) 938-4685

Bank Network News.
Faulkner and Gray, 300 South Wacker Drive, 18th Floor, Chicago, Illinois 60606 (312) 913-1334

Barbados.
Federal Statistical Office, Gustav-Stresemann-Ring 11, D-6200 Wiesbaden, Germany

Barbados Country Report.
Economist Intelligence Unit, 111 West 57th Street, New York, New York 10019 (800) 938-4685

Barbados economic report.
Barbados Statistical Service, Third Floor, National Insurance Building, Fairchild Street, Bridgetown, Barbados

Basic Statistics of the European Community.
European Community Information Service, 2100 M Street, NW,

Washington, D.C. 20037 (202) 862-9500

Belarus Country Report.
Economist Intelligence Unit, 111 West 57th Street, New York, New York 10019 (800) 938-4685

Belgien.
Federal Statistical Office, Gustav-Stresemann-Ring 11, D-6200 Wiesbaden, Germany

Belgium Country Report.
Economist Intelligence Unit, 111 West 57th Street, New York, New York 10019 (800) 938-4685

Belize.
Federal Statistical Office, Gustav-Stresemann-Ring 11, D-6200 Wiesbaden, Germany

Belize Country Report.
Economist Intelligence Unit, 111 West 57th Street, New York, New York 10019 (800) 938-4685

Benchmark Ohio.
The Ohio State University, School of Public Policy and Management, 1775 College Road, Columbus, Ohio 43210-1399 (614) 292-8696

Benin.
Federal Statistical Office, Gustav-Stresemann-Ring 11, D-6200 Wiesbaden, Germany

Benin Country Report.
Economist Intelligence Unit, 111 West 57th Street, New York, New York 10019 (800) 938-4685

Bermuda Country Report.
Economist Intelligence Unit, 111 West 57th Street, New York, New York 10019 (800) 938-4685

Bermuda Digest of Statistics.
Statistical Department, Post Office Box 177, Hamilton, Bermuda

Bevolkerung und Erwerbstatigkeit, Reihe 1.1: Stand und Entwicklung der Bevolkerung.
Statistiches Bundesamt (Allgemeiner Auskunftsdienst), Gustav-Stresemann-Ring 11, Postfach 5528, 6200 Wiesbaden 1, Germany

Bhutan Country Report.
Economist Intelligence Unit, 111 West 57th Street, New York, New York 10019 (800) 938-4685

Bibliography of American Demographic History: The Literature From 1984 to 1994.
Greenwood Press, Westport, Connecticut (203) 226-3571

Bibliography of Selected Statistical Sources of the American Nations. A Guide to the Principal Statistical Materials of the 22 American Nations Including Data Analyses, Methodology and Laws and Organization of Statistical Agencies.
Inter-American Statistical Institute, Pan American Union, Washington, D.C. (Reprinted by Blaine Ethridge Books, Detroit, Michigan)

Bibliography of Statistical Literature.
Oliver and Boyd, Edinburgh and London, England

Bibliography on Income and Wealth.
International Association for Research in Income and Wealth, New York, New York

Biennial Report of Employment by Geographic Area.
Office of Personnel Management, 1900 E Street, NW, Washington, D.C.

20415 (202) 606-1800

Bilan statistique annuel de la Guadeloupe.
INSEE, Tour Gamma A, 195 rue de Bercy, 75582 Paris Codex 12, France

Bilan Statistique de L'annee.
Institut Territorial de la Statistique, BP 395, Papeete-Tahiti, French Polynesia

Billion Dollar U.S. Weather Disaster.
U.S. Department of Commerce, National Oceanic and Atmospheric Administration, National Climatic Data Center, 151 Patton Avenue, Asheville, North Carolina 28801 (828) 271-4800

Biuletyn statystyczny
Glowny Urzad Statystyczny (Central Statistical Office), Al Niepodleglosci 208, 00-925 Warsaw, Poland

Black Americans: A Statistical Sourcebook.
Information Publications, Palo Alto, California (415) 965-4449

Black Elected Officials: A National Roster.
Joint Center for Political and Economic Studies, 1090 Vermont Avenue, NW, Suite 1100, Washington, D.C. 20005 (202) 789-3500

Black Lung Benefits Act, Annual Report.
U.S. Department of Labor, Employment Standards Administration, 200 Constitution Avenue, NW, Washington, D.C. 20210 (202) 219-6050

Boletim mensal
Direccao dos Servicos de Estatistica (Department of Statistical Services), Caixa Postal 1215, Luanda, Angola

Boletim mensal de estatistica.
Reparticao Provincial dos Servicos de Estatistica, Macau, Macau

Boletim Mensal de estatistics.
Direccao Nacional de Estatistica, CP 493, Maputo, Mozambique

Boletim trimestral de estatistica.
Direccao Geral de Estatistica, Bissau, Guinea Bissau

Boletin Anual de estatistica.
Servico Nacional de Estatistica, CP 116, Praia, Cape Verde

Boletin anuario.
Banco Central del Ecuador, Casilla 339, Quito, Ecuador

Boletin de Estadistica.
Instituto Nacional de Estadistica y Censos, Apartado 4031, Managua, Nicaragua

Boletin Economico.
Banco de Espana, Alcala, 50, Madrid-14, Spain

Boletin estadistica.
Direccion General de Estadistica, Malabo, Equatorial Guinea

Boletin estadistico.
Direccion General de Estadistica y Censos, Villa Femina, Calle Arce No. 953, San Salvador, El Salvador

Boletin estadistico.
Instituto Nacional de Estadistica, Casilla No. 6129, La Paz, Bolivia

Boletin estadistico.
Instituto Nacional de Estadistica, Guatemala City, Guatemala

Boletin estadistico del Paraguay.
Direccion General de Estadistica y Censos, Humaita 473, Asuncion, Paraguay

Boletin estadistico trimestral.
Direccion General de Estadistica y Censos, Instituto Nacional de Estadistica y Censos, Hipolita Yrigoyen 250, Buenos Aires

Boletin mensual de estadistica.
DANE, Via Eldorado, Bogota, Columbia

Boletin mensal de estatistica.
Instituto Nacional de Estatistica (National Statistical Institute), Avenida Antonio Jose de Almeida, Lisbon, Portugal

Boletin Mensual de Estadistics.
Instituto Nacional de Estadistica, Paseo de la Castellana 183, Madrid, Spain

Bolivia.
Federal Statistical Office, Gustav-Stresemann-Ring 11, D-6200 Wiesbaden, Germany

Bolivia Country Report.
Economist Intelligence Unit, 111 West 57th Street, New York, New York 10019 (800) 938-4685

Bolivia en cifras.
Instituto Nacional de Estadistica, Casilla 6129, La Paz, Bolivia

Bolletino Mensile di Statistica.
Instituto Centrale di Statistica, Via Cesare Balbo 16, 00184 Rome, Italy

Bollettino di statistica.
Servicio Statale di Statistica, Via G Carducci 145, Repubblica di San Marino

Book Industry Trends.
Book Industry Study Group, 160 Fifth Avenue, New York, New York 10010 (212) 929-1393

Book of States.
Council of State Governments, Post Office Box 11910, Lexington, Kentucky 40578 (859) 244-8000

Bosnia and Herzegovina Country Report.
Economist Intelligence Unit, 111 West 57th Street, New York, New York 10019 (800) 938-4685

Botsuana.
Federal Statistical Office, Gustav-Stresemann-Ring 11, D-6200 Wiesbaden, Germany

Botswana Country Report.
Economist Intelligence Unit, 111 West 57th Street, New York, New York 10019 (800) 938-4685

Botswana in Figures.
Central Statistics Office, Government Printer, Post Office Box 87, Gaberone, Botswana

The Bowker Annual: Library and Book Trade Almanac.
R.R. Bowker Company, 121 Chanlon Road, New Providence, New Jersey 07974 (908) 464-6800

Brasilien.
Federal Statistical Office, Gustav-Stresemann-Ring 11, D-6200 Wiesbaden, Germany

Brazil Country Report.
Economist Intelligence Unit, 111 West 57th Street, New York, New York 10019 (800) 938-4685

Britannica Book of the Year.
Encyclopedia Britannica, Inc., 310 South Michigan Avenue, Chicago,

Illinois 60604 (312) 347-7000

Britannica World Data.
Encyclopedia Britannica, Inc., 310 South Michigan Avenue, Chicago, Illinois 60604 (312) 347-7000

British Virgin Islands Country Report.
Economist Intelligence Unit, 111 West 57th Street, New York, New York 10019 (800) 938-4685

Brunei.
Federal Statistical Office, Gustav-Stresemann-Ring 11, D-6200 Wiesbaden, Germany

Brunei Country Report.
Economist Intelligence Unit, 111 West 57th Street, New York, New York 10019 (800) 938-4685

Brunei Statistical Yearbook.
Economic Planning Unit, Bandar Seri Begawan, Brunei

Budget of the United States Government.
Executive Office of the President, Office of Management and Budget, Executive Office Building, Washington, D.C. 20503 (202) 395-3080

Budget Summary.
National Aeronautics and Space Administration, 300 E Street, SW, Washington, D.C. 20546 (202) 358-1000

Buku Tahunan Perangkaan.
Department of Statistics, Jalan Cenderasari, Kuala Lumpur, Malaysia

Bulgarien.
Federal Statistical Office, Gustav-Stresemann-Ring 11, D-6200 Wiesbaden, Germany

Bulgaria Country Report.
Economist Intelligence Unit, 111 West 57th Street, New York, New York 10019 (800) 938-4685

Bulletin 2192.
U.S. Department of Labor, Bureau of Labor Statistics, Two Massachusetts Avenue, NE, Washington, D.C. 20212 (202) 691-5200

Bulletin 2217.
U.S. Department of Labor, Bureau of Labor Statistics, Two Massachusetts Avenue, NE, Washington, D.C. 20212 (202) 691-5200

Bulletin 2307.
U.S. Department of Labor, Bureau of Labor Statistics, Two Massachusetts Avenue, NE, Washington, D.C. 20212 (202) 691-5200

Bulletin 2340.
U.S. Department of Labor, Bureau of Labor Statistics, Two Massachusetts Avenue, NE, Washington, D.C. 20212 (202) 691-5200

Bulletin 2370.
U.S. Department of Labor, Bureau of Labor Statistics, Two Massachusetts Avenue, NE, Washington, D.C. 20212 (202) 691-5200

Bulletin 2429.
U.S. Department of Labor, Bureau of Labor Statistics, Two Massachusetts Avenue, NE, Washington, D.C. 20212 (202) 691-5200

Bulletin 2440.
U.S. Department of Labor, Bureau of Labor Statistics, Two Massachusetts Avenue, NE, Washington, D.C. 20212 (202) 691-5200

Bulletin de statistique.
Direction de la Statistique, Niamey, Niger

Bulletin de statistique.
Direction de la Statistique, BP 453, N'Djamena, Chad

Bulletin de Statistique.
Direction Generale de la Statistique, BP 46, Kigali, Rwanda

Bulletin de Statistique.
Institut National de la Statistique et de l'Analyse Economique, BP 323, Cotonou, Benin.

Bulletin de Statistique.
Institut National de Statistique, National Institute of Statistics, rue de Louvain 44, 1000 Brussels, Belgium

Bulletin de Statistiques.
Service National de la Statistique, Ministere du Plan et de la Cooperation, BP No 46, Vientiane, Laos

Bulletin d'informations statistiques.
Direction de la Statistique Generale et des Etudes Economiques, BP 732, Bangui, Central African Republic

Bulletin du STATEC.
STATEC, 19-21 Boulevard Royal, BP 304, L-2013, Luxembourg

Bulletin Mensuel.
Banque Nationale Suisse, Borsenstrasse 15 8022 Zurich, Switzerland

Bulletin mensuel de statistique.
Direction de la Statistique (Department of Statistics), BP 118, Lome, Togo

Bulletin mensuel de statistique.
Direction de la Statistique, BP 222, Abidjan, Cote D'Ivoire

Bulletin mensuel de statistique.
Direction de la Statistique et de la Comptabilite Nationale, BP 660, Yaounde, Cameroon

Bulletin Mensuel de Statistique.
Direction Generale de la Statistique, BP 179, Libreville, Gabon

Bulletin Mensuel de Statistique.
Direction Nationale de la statistique, BP 12, Bamako, Mali

Bulletin mensuel de statistique.
Division de la Statistique, BP 178, Rabat, Morocco

Bulletin mensuel de statistique.
Institut National de la Statistique et de la Recherche Economique, BP 38, Antananarivo, Madagascar

Bulletin Mensuel de Statistique.
Institut National de la Statistique et des Etudes Economiques, 18 boulevard Pinard, 75675 Paris Cedex 14, France

Bulletin mensuel de statistique.
Institut National de la Statistique, 27 rue du Liban, 1002 Tunis-Belvedere, Tunis, Tunisia

Bulletin mensuel des statistique.
Direction de la Statistique et de la Comptabilite Economique, BP 2031, Brazzaville, Congo

Bulletin Mensuel Statistique.
Direction de la Statistique, BP 240, Nouakchott, Mauritania

Bulletin Mensuel Statistique.
Institut National de la Statistique et des Recherches Economique, Phnom-Penh, Cambodia

Bulletin of Industrial Statistics for the Arab Countries.
Statistical Office of the United Nations, Publishing Service, New York, New York 10017 (800) 253-9646

Bulletin of International Statistical Institute.
International Statistical Institute, Voorburg, The Netherlands.

Bulletin of Statistics.
Central Statistical Services, Pretoria 0002, South Africa

Bulletin Special de Statistique.
Service de la Statistique Generale, BP 221, Conakry, Guinea

Bulletin Statistique.
Department de la Statistique, BP 1156, Bujumbura, Burundi

Bulletin Statistique.
Institut National de la Statistique et des Etudes Economiques, BP 863, 97175 Pointe-a-Pitre, France

Bulletin Statistique de la Guadeloupe.
INSEE, Tour Gamma A, 195 rue de Bercy, 75582 Paris Cedex 12, France

Bulletin statistique et economique mensuel.
Direction de la Provision et de la Statistique, BP 116, Dakar, Senegal

Bulletin Statistique Mensuel.
Direction Centrale de la Statistique, Ministere du Plan, Bir Hassan, Beirut, Lebanon

Bulletin Trimestriel de Statistique.
Direction de la Statistique Generale et des Etudes Economiques, BP 732, Bangui, Central African Republic

Bulletin Trimestriel de Statistique.
Djibouti: Direction Nationale de la Statistique, BP 1846, Djibouti

Bulletin trimestriel de Statistique.
Institut Haitien de Statistique, Cite de l'Exposition, Boulevard Harry Truman, Port-au-Prince, Haiti

Burkina Faso.
Federal Statistical Office, Gustav-Stresemann-Ring 11, D-6200 Wiesbaden, Germany

Burkina Faso Country Report.
Economist Intelligence Unit, 111 West 57th Street, New York, New York 10019 (800) 938-4685

Burma.
Federal Statistical Office, Gustav-Stresemann-Ring 11, D-6200 Wiesbaden, Germany

Burundi.
Federal Statistical Office, Gustav-Stresemann-Ring 11, D-6200 Wiesbaden, Germany

Burundi Country Report.
Economist Intelligence Unit, 111 West 57th Street, New York, New York 10019 (800) 938-4685

Bus Facts.
American Bus Association, 1100 New York Avenue, NW, Suite 1050, Washington, D.C. 20005-3034 (202) 842-1645

Business America.
U.S. Department of Commerce, International Trade Administration, Fourteenth Street between Constitution Avenue and E Street, NW, Washington, D.C. 20230 (202) 482-2185

Business Cycle Indicators.
U.S. Department of Commerce, Bureau of Economic Analysis, Fourteenth Street between Constitution Avenue and E Street, NW, Washington, D.C. 20230 (202) 606-9900

Business Failure Record.
Dun and Bradstreet Corporation, One Diamond Hill Road, Murray Hill, New Jersey 07974 (908) 665-5000

Business Information Desk Reference: Where to Find Answers to Business Questions.
MacMillan Publishing Company, New York, New York (800) 858-7674

Business Information: How to Find It, How to Use It.
Oryx Press, Westport, Connecticut (800) 279-6799

Business Starts Record.
Dun and Bradstreet Corporation, One Diamond Hill Road, Murray Hill, New Jersey 07974 (908) 665-5000

Business Statistics.
U.S. Department of Commerce, Bureau of Economic Analysis, Fourteenth Street between Constitution Avenue and E Street, NW, Washington, D.C. 20230 (202) 606-9900

Business Statistics of the United States.
Bernan Press, Lanham, Maryland (800) 865-3457

Buyers of New Cars.
Newsweek, Inc., 251 West 57th Street, New York, New York 10019 (212) 445-4000

COMECOM Data.
Greenwood Publishing Group, Westport, Connecticut (800) 225-5800

CPI Detailed Report.
U.S. Department of Labor, Bureau of Labor Statistics, Two Massachusetts Avenue, NE, Washington, D.C. 20212 (202) 691-5200

CRB Commodity Index Report.
Commodity Research Bureau, 30 South Wacker Drive, Chicago, Illinois 60606 (312) 454-1801

The Cable TV Financial Databook.
Paul Kagan Associates, Inc., 126 Clock Tower Place, Carmel, California 93923 (408) 624-1536

Calendars of the United States House of Representatives and History of Legislation.
U.S. Congress, Senate Library, The Capitol, Washington, D.C. 20510 (202) 224-3121

California Almanac.
Pacific Data Resources, Post Office Box 1911, Santa Barbara, California 93116-9954 (800) 422-2546

California Statistical Abstract.
Department of Finance, 915 L Street, 8th Floor, Sacramento, California 95814 (916) 322-2263

Cambodia Country Report.
Economist Intelligence Unit, 111 West 57th Street, New York, New York 10019 (800) 938-4685

Cameroon Country Report.
Economist Intelligence Unit, 111 West 57th Street, New York, New York 10019 (800) 938-4685

Canada Country Report.
Economist Intelligence Unit, 111 West 57th Street, New York, New York 10019 (800) 938-4685

The Canada Yearbook.
Publications Distribution, Statistics Canada, Ottawa, Ontario K1A 0T6, Canada (613) 951-8116

The Canadian Almanac and Directory.
Micromedia, Toronto, Canada (416) 362-5211

Canadian Markets, 1990.
Financial Post Information Service.

Canadian Statistical Review.
Publications Distribution, Statistics Canada, Ottawa, Ontario K1A 0T6, Canada (613) 951-8116

Cancer Statistics Review.
U.S. Department of Health and Human Services, National Cancer Institute, 9000 Rockville Pike, Bethesda, Maryland 20892 (301) 496-5737

Cape Verde Country Report.
Economist Intelligence Unit, 111 West 57th Street, New York, New York 10019 (800) 938-4685

Capital Punishment.
U.S. Department of Justice, Bureau of Justice Statistics, 810 Seventh Street, NW, Washington, D.C. 20531 (800) 732-3277

Caseload Statistics of State Vocational Rehabilitation Agencies in Fiscal Years.
U.S. Department of Education, Rehabilitation Services Administration, 400 Maryland Avenue, SW, Washington, D.C. 20202 (800) 872-5327.

Cash and Non-Cash Benefits for Persons with Limited Income: Eligibility Rules, Recipient and Expenditure Data.
The Congress of the U.S., Congressional Research Service, 10 First Street, SE, Washington, D.C. 20540 (202) 707-5700

Casualty Return.
Lloyd's Register of Shipping, 17 Battery Place, New York, New York 10004 (212) 425-8050

Catalog of Electronic Data Products from National Center for Health Statistics.
U.S. Department of Health and Human Services, National Center for Health Statistics, 3700 East-West Highway, Hyattsville, Maryland 20782 (301) 436-8500

Catalog of United States Census Publications, 1790-1945.
Greenwood Publishing Group, Westport, Connecticut (800) 225-5800

Catalogue of Statistical Materials of Developing Countries.
Institute of Developing Economics, Tokyo, Japan

Cattle, Final Estimates
U.S. Department of Agriculture, National Agricultural Statistics Service 14th Street and Independence Avenue, SW, Washington, D.C. 20250 (800) 727-9540

Cayman Islands Country Report.
Economist Intelligence Unit, 111 West 57th Street, New York, New York 10019 (800) 938-4685

Census and You.
U.S. Department of Commerce, Bureau of the Census, Washington, D.C. (301) 457-4100

Census Catalog and Guide.
U.S. Department of Commerce, Bureau of the Census, Washington, D.C. (301) 457-4100

Census CD.
GeoLytics, Inc., East Brunswick, New Jersey (732) 651-2000

Census Daily List.
U.S. Department of Commerce, Bureau of the Census, Washington, D.C. (301) 457-4100

Census of Agriculture.
U.S. Department of Commerce, Bureau of the Census, Washington, D.C. 20233 (301) 457-4100

Census of Construction Industries.
U.S. Department of Commerce, Bureau of the Census, Washington, D.C. 20233 (301) 457-4100

Census of Governments.
U.S. Department of Commerce, Bureau of the Census, Washington, D.C. 20233 (301) 457-4100

Census of Housing.
U.S. Department of Commerce, Bureau of the Census, Washington, D.C. 20233 (301) 457-4100

Census of Local Jails.
U.S. Department of Justice,, Bureau of Justice Statistics, 810 Seventh Street, NW, Washington, D.C. 20531 (800) 732-3277

Census of Manufactures.
U.S. Department of Commerce, Bureau of the Census, Washington, D.C. 20233 (301) 457-4100

Census of Mineral Industries.
U.S. Department of the Interior, Geological Survey, Office of Minerals Information, 12201 Sunrise Valley Drive, Reston, Virginia 22092 (703) 648-4000

Census of Population.
U.S. Department of Commerce, Bureau of the Census, Washington, D.C. 20233 (301) 457-4100

Census of Population and Housing.
U.S. Department of Commerce, Bureau of the Census, Washington, D.C. 20233 (301) 457-4100

Census of Population of Ireland.
Central Statistics Office, Ardee Road, Dublin 6, Ireland

Census of Public and Private Juvenile Detention, Correctional, and Shelter Facilities.
U.S. Department of Justice, Bureau of Justice Statistics, 810 Seventh Street, NW, Washington, D.C. 20531 (800) 732-3277

Census of Retail Trade.
U.S. Department of Commerce, Bureau of the Census, Washington, D.C. 20233 (301) 457-4100

Census of Service Industries.
U.S. Department of Commerce, Bureau of the Census, Washington, D.C. 20233 (301) 457-4100

Census of Transportation.
U.S. Department of Commerce, Bureau of the Census, Washington, D.C. 20233 (301) 457-4100

Census of Wholesale Trade.
U.S. Department of Commerce, Bureau of the Census, Washington, D.C. 20233 (301) 457-4100

Census Plus.
Slater Hall Information Products, Washington, D.C. (202) 682-1350 (On CD-ROM)

Censuses of Outlying Areas, Construction, Puerto Rico.
U.S. Department of Commerce, Bureau of the Census, Washington, D.C. 20233 (301) 457-4100

Censuses of Outlying Areas, Manufactures, Puerto Rico.
U.S. Department of Commerce, Bureau of the Census, Washington, D.C. 20233 (301) 457-4100

Center for Electronic Records' Title List: A Partial and Preliminary List of the Datasets in the Custody of the National Archives.
National Archives and Records Administration, 8601 Adelphi Road, College Park, Maryland 20740 (301) 713-6800

Central African Republic Country Report.
Economist Intelligence Unit, 111 West 57th Street, New York, New York 10019 (800) 938-4685

Central and South Eastern Europe.
Europa Publications (Available from The Gale Group (800) 877-GALE)

Chad Country Report.
Economist Intelligence Unit, 111 West 57th Street, New York, New York 10019 (800) 938-4685

Characteristics of Doctoral Scientists and Engineers in the United States.
National Science Foundation, 4201 Wilson Boulevard, Arlington, Virginia 22230 (703) 306-1234

Characteristics of New Housing.
U.S. Department of Commerce, Bureau of the Census, Washington, D.C. 20233 (301) 457-4100

Characteristics of the Population.
U.S. Department of Commerce, Bureau of the Census, Washington, D.C. 20233 (301) 457-4100

Characterization of Municipal Solid Waste in the United States.
Franklin Associates Limited, 4121 West 83rd Street, Suite 108, Prairie Village, Kansas 66208 (913) 649-2225

The Charitable Behavior of Americans.
Independent Sector, 1200 18th Street, NW, Suite 200, Washington, D.C. 20036 (202) 467-6161

Charts, Graphs and Stats Index 1992-1995: An Index to the Most Current Statistics Behind Today's Most Important Stories.
Highsmith Press, Fort Atkinson, Wisconsin (920) 563-9571

Chickens and Eggs.
U.S. Department of Agriculture, National Agricultural Statistics Service, Fourteenth and Independence Avenue, SW, Washington, D.C. 20250 (800) 727-9540

Child Maltreatment.
U.S. Department of Health and Human Services, National Center on Child Abuse and Neglect, 370 L'Enfant Promenade, SW, Washington, D.C. 20447 (202) 205-8586

Children in America: A Statistical Handbook.
Oryx Press, Westport, Connecticut (800) 279-ORYX

Children in Custody: Census of Public and Private Juvenile Custody Facilities.
U.S. Department of Justice, Office of Juvenile Justice and Delinquency Prevention, 633 Indiana Avenue, NW, Washington, D.C. 20531 (800) 638-8736

Chile Country Report.
Economist Intelligence Unit, 111 West 57th Street, New York, New York 10019 (800) 938-4685

China Country Report.
Economist Intelligence Unit, 111 West 57th Street, New York, New York 10019 (800) 938-4685

China Market Atlas.
The Economist Intelligence Unit (Asia) Ltd., 10th Floor, Luk Kwok Centre, 72 Gloucester Road, Wanchai, Hong Kong (Phone Number in U.S. (800) 938-4685)

China (Taiwan).
Federal Statistical Office, Gustav-Stresemann-Ring 11, D-6200 Wiesbaden, Germany

China Urban Statistics 1988.
Greenwood Publishing Group, Westport, Connecticut (800) 225-5800

China's Provincial Statistics, 1949-1989.
Westview Press, Boulder, Colorado (303) 444-3541

Churches and Church Membership in the United States.
Glenmary Research Center, 1312 Fifth Avenue, North, Nashville, Tennessee 37208 (615) 256-1905

The CIS Market Atlas.
Business International Moscow, 23 Profsoyuznaya Ulitsa, 117859, Moscow (Telephone Number in U.S. (800) 938-4685)

CIS Statistical Periodicals.
Congressional Information Service, Bethesda, Maryland (800) 638-8380

Citrus Fruits.
U.S. Department of Agriculture, National Agricultural Statistics Service, Fourteenth Street and Independence Avenue, SW, Washington, D.C. 20250 (800) 727-9540

City Data: A Catalog of Data Sources for Small Cities.
RAND, Santa Monica, California (310) 393-0411

City Employment.
U.S. Department of Commerce, Bureau of the Census, Washington, D.C. 20233 (301) 457-4100

City Government Finances.
U.S. Department of Commerce, Bureau of the Census, Washington, D.C. 20233 (301) 457-4100

Civil Aviation Statistics of the World.
International Civil Aviation Organization, 999 University Street, Montreal, Quebec H3C 5H7, Canada (514) 954-8219

The Civil Service Work Force.
National Aeronautics and Space Administration, 300 E Street, SW, Washington, DC 20546 (202) 358-1000

Climatography of the United States.
U.S. Department of Commerce, National Oceanic and Atmospheric Administration, National Climatic Data Center, 151 Patton Avenue, Asheville, North Carolina 28801 (828) 271-4800

Coal Information.
Organisation for Economic Co-operation and Development (OECD), 2 rue Andre-Pascal, 75 Paris 16, France (Telephone Number in U.S. (202) 785-6323)

Coal Production.
U.S. Department of Energy, Energy Information Administration, 1000 Independence Avenue, SW, Washington, D.C. 20585 (202) 586-8800

The Coastline of the United States.
U.S. Department of Commerce, National Oceanic and Atmospheric

Administration, National Climatic Data Center, 151 Patton Avenue, Asheville, North Carolina 28801 (828) 271-4800

Coke Plant Report.
U.S. Department of Energy, Energy Information Administration, 1000 Independence Avenue, SW Washington, D.C. 20585 (202) 586-8800

Colombia Country Report.
Economist Intelligence Unit, 111 West 57th Street, New York, New York 10019 (800) 938-4685

Colombia estadistica.
DANE, Via Eldorado, Bogota, Colombia

Combined Annual and Revised Monthly Retail Trade.
U.S. Department of Commerce, Bureau of Census, Suitland, Maryland 20233 (301) 763-2804

Commercial Atlas and Marketing Guide.
Rand McNally, Skokie, Illinois (800) 333-0136

Commercial Buildings Energy Consumption.
U.S. Department of Energy, Energy Information Administration, 1000 Independence Avenue, SW, Washington, D.C. 20585 (202) 586-8800

Commissioner of Patents and Trademarks Annual Report.
U.S. Department of Commerce, Patent and Trademark Office, 2121 Crystal Drive, Arlington, Virginia 22202 (703) 305-8341

Commodity Balance Statistics Database.
United Nations Industrial Development Organization (UNIDO), Vienna, Austria

Commodity Prices.
The Gale Group, 27500 Drake Road, Farmington Hills, Michigan 48331 (800) 877-4253

Commodity Trade and Price Trends.
The World Bank, 1818 H Street, NW, Washington, D.C. 20043 (202) 477-1234

Commodity Trade Statistics.
United Nations, Department for Economic and Social Information and Policy Analysis, New York, New York (800) 253-9646

Commodity Yearbook.
Commodity Research Bureau, 30 South Wacker Drive, Chicago, Illinois 60606 (312) 454-1801

Commonwealth of the Bahamas Statistical Abstract.
Department of Statistics, Cabinet Office, Post Office Box N3904, Nassau, Bahamas

Communications Industry Report.
Veronis, Suhler and Associates, 350 Park Avenue, New York, New York 10022 (212) 935-4990

Comoros Country Report.
Economist Intelligence Unit, 111 West 57th Street, New York, New York 10019 (800) 938-4685

Comparative Climatic Data.
U.S. Department of Commerce, National Oceanic and Atmospheric Administration, National Climatic Data Center, 151 Patton Avenue, Asheville, North Carolina 28801 (828) 271-4800

Comparative Labor Force Statistics for Ten Countries.
U.S. Department of Labor, Bureau of Labor Statistics, Two Massachusetts Avenue, NE, Washington, D.C. 20212 (202) 691-5200

Comparative Oil Company Statements.

Carl H. Pforzheimer and Company, 650 Madison Avenue, New York, New York 10022 (212) 223-6500

Comparative Statistics of Industrial and Office Real Estate Markets.
Society of Industrial and Office Realtors, 700 Eleventh Street, NW, Suite 510, Washington, D.C. 20001 (202) 383-1150

Comparative World Data: A Statistical Handbook for Social Science.
Johns Hopkins University Press, Baltimore, Maryland (800) 537-5487

Compare Minnesota: An Economic and Statistical Factbook.
Department of Trade and Economic Development, Policy Analysis Office, 500 Metro Square, Saint Paul, Minnesota 55101 (612) 296-8283

Compendio estadistico.
Direccion General de Estadistica y Censos, Instituto Nacional de Estadistica, Avenida 28 de Julio 1056, Lima 1, Peru

Compendio estadistico.
Instituto Nacional de Estadisticas, Casilla 7597, Correo 3, Santiago, Chile

Compendio Statistico Italiano.
Instituto Centrale di Statistica, Via Cesare Balbo 16, 00184 Rome, Italy

Compendium of Human Settlement Statistics.
Statistical Office of the United Nations, Publishing Service, New York, New York 10017 (800) 253-9646

Compendium of Public Employment.
U.S. Department of Commerce, Bureau of the Census, Washington, D.C. 20233 (301) 457-4100

Compendium of Social Statistics and Indicators.
Statistical Office of the United Nations, Publishing Service, New York, New York 10017 (800) 253-9646

Compensation and Working Conditions.
U.S. Department of Labor, Bureau of Labor Statistics, Two Massachusetts Avenue, NE, Washington, D.C. 20212 (202) 691-5200

Compensation Report.
Office of Personnel Management, 1900 E Street, NW, Washington, D.C. 20415 (202) 606-1800

Concise Statistical Yearbook.
Distribution Service: National Statistical Service of Greece, 14-16 Lycourgou Street, Athens 112, Greece

Concise Statistical Yearbook of Poland.
Glowny Urzad Statystyczny (Central Statistical Office), Al Niepodleglosci 208, 00-925 Warsaw, Poland

Congo Country Report.
Economist Intelligence Unit, 111 West 57th Street, New York, New York 10019 (800) 938-4685

Congo (Democratic Republic of) Country Report.
Economist Intelligence Unit, 111 West 57th Street, New York, New York 10019 (800) 938-4685

Congressional Directory.
U.S. Congress, Joint Committee on Printing, North Capitol and H Streets, NW, Washington, D.C. 20401 (202) 512-0000

Congressional District Atlas, 103rd Congress of the U.S.
U.S. Department of Commerce, Bureau of the Census, Washington, D.C. 20233 (301) 457-4100

Congressional Districts of the 103rd Congress.
U.S. Department of Commerce, Bureau of the Census, Washington,

D.C. 20233 (301) 457-4100

Congressional Quarterly Weekly Report.
Congressional Quarterly, Inc., 1414 22nd Street, NW, Washington, D.C. 20037 (202) 887-8500

Congressional Record.
U.S. Congress, The Capitol, Washington, D.C. 20510 (202) 224-3121

Conjoncture Economique.
Institut National de la Statistique, BP 20, Kinshasa, Gombe, Zaire

Connecticut Market Data.
Connecticut Department of Economic Development, 865 Brock Street, Rocky Hill, Connecticut 06067-3405

Consolidated Data Base.
Dataquest, Inc., 251 River Oak Parkway, San Jose, California 95134 (408) 468-8000

Construction Reports.
U.S. Department of Commerce, Bureau of the Census, Washington, D.C. 20233 (301) 457-4100

Construction Review.
U.S. Department of Commerce, International Trade Administration, Fourteenth Street between Constitution Avenue and E Street, NW, Washington, D.C. 20230 (202) 482-2185

Consumer Asia.
Euromonitor International, 60-61 Britton Street, London EC1M 5NA, England (Number in the U.S. (800) 577-EURO)

Consumer China.
Euromonitor International, 60-61 Britton Street, London EC1M 5NA, England (Number in the U.S. (800) 577-EURO)

Consumer Credit Delinquency Bulletin.
American Bankers Association, 1120 Connecticut Avenue, NW, Washington, D.C. 20036 (202) 663-5000

Consumer Eastern Europe.
Euromonitor International, 60-61 Britton Street, London EC1M 5NA, England (Number in the U.S. (800) 577-EURO)

Consumer Europe.
Euromonitor International, 60-61 Britton Street, London EC1M 5NA, England (Number in the U.S. (800) 577-EURO)

Consumer Expenditure Survey.
U.S. Department of Labor, Bureau of Labor Statistics, Two Massachusetts Avenue, NE, Washington, D.C. 20212 (202) 691-5200

Consumer Expenditures in 1998.
U.S. Department of Labor, Bureau of Labor Statistics, Two Massachusetts Avenue, NE, Washington, D.C. 20212 (202) 691-5200

Consumer International.
Euromonitor International, 60-61 Britton Street, London EC1M 5NA, England (Number in the U.S. (800) 577-EURO)

Consumer Japan.
Euromonitor International, 60-61 Britton Street, London EC1M 5NA, England (Number in the U.S. (800) 577-EURO)

Consumer Latin America.
Euromonitor International, 60-61 Britton Street, London EC1M 5NA, England (Number in the U.S. (800) 577-EURO)

Consumer Market Guide.
The Conference Board, 845 Third Avenue, New York, New York 10022

(212) 759-0900

Consumer Photographic Survey.
Photo Marketing Association, International, 3000 Picture Place, Jackson, Michigan 49201 (517) 788-8100

Consumer Price Index.
Central Statistics Office, St. Stephen's Green House, Earlsfort Terrace, Dublin 2, Ireland

Consumer Price Index Detailed Report.
U.S. Department of Labor, Bureau of Labor Statistics, Two Massachusetts Avenue, NE, Washington, D.C. 20212 (202) 691-5200

Consumer Research Study on Book Purchasing.
Book Industry Study Group, 160 Fifth Avenue, New York, New York 10010 (212) 929-1393

Consumer South America.
Euromonitor International, 60-61 Britton Street, London EC1M 5NA, England (Number in the U.S. (800) 577-EURO)

Consumer Southern Europe.
Euromonitor International, 60-61 Britton Street, London EC1M 5NA, England (Number in the U.S. (800) 577-EURO)

Consumer USA.
Euromonitor International, 60-61 Britton Street, London EC1M 5NA, England (Number in U.S. (800) 577-EURO)

Controlling the Risks of Government-Sponsored Enterprises.
U.S. Congress, Congressional Budget Office, Second and D Streets, SW, Washington, D.C. 20515 (202) 226-2621

Correctional Populations in the United States.
U.S. Department of Justice, Bureau of Justice Statistics, 810 Seventh Street, NW, Washington, D.C. 20531 (800) 732-3277

Costa Rica.
Federal Statistical Office, Gustav-Stresemann-Ring 11, D-6200 Wiesbaden, Germany

Costa Rica Country Report.
Economist Intelligence Unit, 111 West 57th Street, New York, New York 10019 (800) 938-4685

Cote d'Ivoire.
Federal Statistical Office, Gustav-Stresemann-Ring 11, D-6200 Wiesbaden, Germany

Cote d'Ivoire Country Report.
Economist Intelligence Unit, 111 West 57th Street, New York, New York 10019 (800) 938-4685

Cotton and Wool Outlook and Situation.
U.S. Department of Agriculture, Economic Research Service, 1800 M Street, NW, Washington, D.C. 20036 (202) 694-4040

Countries of the World and Their Leaders Yearbook.
The Gale Group, 27500 Drake Road, Farmington Hills, Michigan 48331 (800) 877-4253

Country Profiles.
Economist Intelligence Unit, New York, New York (800) 938-4685

Country Reports.
Economist Intelligence Unit, New York, New York (800) 938-4685

Country Tables - Basic Data on the Agriculture Sector.
United Nations Food and Agriculture Organization, Rome, Italy (Available from UNIPUB (800) 274-4888)

County and City Data Book.
U.S. Department of Commerce, Bureau of the Census, Washington, D.C. 20233 (301) 457-4100

County and City Extra.
Bernan Press, Lanham, Maryland (800) 274-4447.

County Business Patterns.
U.S. Department of Commerce, Bureau of the Census, Washington, D.C. 20233 (301) 457-4100

County and City Extra.
Bernan Press, Lanham, Maryland (800) 865-3457

County Government Finances.
U.S. Department of Commerce, Bureau of the Census, Washington, D.C. 20233 (301) 457-4100

County Profiles.
University of New Mexico, Bureau of Business and Economic Research, Albuquerque, New Mexico 87131 (505) 277-2216

County Profiles of Idaho.
Department of Commerce, 700 West State Street, Boise, Idaho 83720 (208) 334-2470

CPI Detailed Report.
U.S. Department of Labor, Bureau of Labor Statistics, Two Massachusetts Avenue, NE, Washington, D.C. 20212 (202) 691-5200

Crime and the Elderly.
U.S. Department of Justice, Bureau of Justice Statistics, 810 Seventh Street, NW, Washington, D.C. 20531 (800) 732-3277

Crime and the Nation's Households.
U.S. Department of Justice, Bureau of Justice Statistics, 810 Seventh Street, NW, Washington, D.C. 20531 (800) 732-3277

Crime in the United States.
U.S. Department of Justice, Federal Bureau of Investigation, 935 Pennsylvania Avenue, NW, Washington, D.C. 20535 (202) 324-3691

Criminal Victimization in the United States.
U.S. Department of Justice, Bureau of Justice Statistics, 810 Seventh Street, NW, Washington, D.C. 20531 (800) 732-3277

Croatia Country Report.
Economist Intelligence Unit, 111 West 57th Street, New York, New York 10019 (800) 938-4685

Crop Production.
U.S. Department of Agriculture, National Agricultural Statistics Service, Fourteenth Street and Independence Avenue, SW, Washington, D.C. 20250 (800) 727-9540

Crop Production: Quarterly Statistics.
European Community Information Service, 2100 M Street, NW, Washington, D.C. 20037 (202) 862-9500

Crop Values.
U.S. Department of Agriculture, National Agricultural Statistics Service, Fourteenth Street and Independence Avenue, SW, Washington, D.C. 20250 (800) 727-9540

Cuba Country Report.
Economist Intelligence Unit, 111 West 57th Street, New York, New York 10019 (800) 938-4685

Current Business Reports, Annual Benchmark Report for Wholesale Trade.
U.S. Department of Commerce, Bureau of the Census, Washington,

D.C. 20233 (301) 457-4100

Current Business Reports, Motor Freight Transportation and Warehousing Survey.
U.S. Department of Commerce, Bureau of the Census, Washington, D.C. 20233 (301) 457-4100

Current Construction Reports.
U.S. Department of Commerce, Bureau of the Census, Washington, D.C. 20233 (301) 457-4100

Current Estimates and Trends in New Hampshire's Housing Supply.
Office of State Planning, 2 ½ Beacon Street, Concord, New Hampshire 03301 (603) 271-2155

Current Housing Reports.
U.S. Department of Commerce, Bureau of the Census, Washington, D.C. 20233 (301) 457-4100

Current Industrial Reports.
U.S. Department of Commerce, Bureau of the Census, Washington, D.C. 20233 (301) 457-4100

Current Industrial Reports, Aerospace Industry (Orders, Sales, and Backlog).
U.S. Department of Commerce, Bureau of the Census, Washington, D.C. 20233 (301) 457-4100

Current Industrial Reports Manufactures' Shipments, Inventories, and Orders.
U.S. Department of Commerce, Bureau of the Census, Washington, D.C. 20233 (301) 457-4100

Current National Statistical Compendiums.
Congressional Information Service, Bethesda, Maryland (800) 638-8380

Current Population Reports.
U.S. Department of Commerce, Bureau of the Census, Washington, D.C. 20233 (301) 457-4100

Current Wage Developments.
U.S. Department of Labor, Bureau of Labor Statistics, Two Massachusetts Avenue, NE, Washington, D.C. 20212 (202) 691-5200

Cyprus Country Report.
Economist Intelligence Unit, 111 West 57th Street, New York, New York 10019 (800) 938-4685

Czech Republic Country Report.
Economist Intelligence Unit, 111 West 57th Street, New York, New York 10019 (800) 938-4685

Daily Digest.
U.S. Congress, The Capitol, Washington, D.C. 20510 (202) 224-3121

Dairy Products.
U.S. Department of Agriculture, National Agricultural Statistics Service, Fourteenth Street and Independence Avenue, SW, Washington, D.C. 20250 (800) 727-9540

Danemark.
Federal Statistical Office, Gustav-Stresemann-Ring 11, D-6200 Wiesbaden, Germany

Data Base Directory.
Knowledge Industry Publications, White Plains, New York (914) 328-9157

Data Book, Operating Banks and Branches.
Federal Deposit Insurance Corporation, 550 Seventeenth Street, NW,

Washington, D.C. 20429 (202) 393-8400

Data Developments.
U.S. Department of Commerce, Bureau of the Census, Washington, D.C. 20233 (301) 457-4100

Data Sources for Business and Market Analysis.
Scarecrow Press, Lanham, Maryland (800) 462-6420

Data: Where It Is and How To Get It.
Coleman/Morse Associates Ltd., Arnold, Maryland

Datapedia of the United States, 1790-2000, America Year by Year.
Bernan Press, Lanham, Maryland (800) 274-4447

Datos Y Cifras de Costa Rica.
Centra para la Promocion de las Exportaciones y las Inversiones, Apartado 10216, San Jose, Costa Rica

Delaware Data Book.
Delaware Development Office, 99 Kings Highway, P.O. Box 1401, Dover, Delaware 19903 (302) 739-4271

Delaware Economic Report.
University of Delaware, Bureau of Economic Research, College of Business and Economics, Newark, Delaware 19716-2730 (302) 831-8401

Demographic and Economic Profiles.
Labor Market Information, Department of Employment and Training, Montpelier, Vermont 05602 (802) 828-4202

Demographic Information Service.
The Conference Board, 845 Third Avenue, New York, New York 10022 (212) 759-0900

Demographic Statistics.
European Community Information Service, 2100 M Street, NW, Washington, D.C. 20037 (202) 862-9500

Demographic Yearbook.
St. Edmundsbury Press, Bury St. Edmunds, Suffolk, England

Demographic Yearbook.
Statistical Office of the United Nations, Publishing Service, New York, New York 10017 (800) 253-9646

Denmark Country Report.
Economist Intelligence Unit, 111 West 57th Street, New York, New York 10019 (800) 938-4685

Detailed Ancestry Groups for States.
U.S. Department of Commerce, Bureau of the Census, Washington, D.C. 20233 (301) 457-4100

Deutsche Demokratische Republik.
Federal Statistical Office, Gustav-Stresemann-Ring 11, D-6200 Wiesbaden, Germany

The Dictionary of Statistics.
The Gale Group, 27500 Drake Road, Farmington Hills, Michigan 48331 (800) 877-4253

Dictionary of U.S. Government Statistical Terms.
Information Publications, Palo Alto, California (415) 965-4449

Digest of Education Statistics.
U.S. Department of Education, National Center for Education Statistics, 555 New Jersey Avenue, NW, Washington, D.C. 20208 (202) 219-1828

Digest of Statistics.

Federal Office of Statistics, 36-38 Broad Street, PMB 12528, Lagos, Nigeria

Digest of Statistics.
Statistical Office, Ministry of Finance, Kingstown, Saint Vincent

Direction of Trade Statistics.
International Monetary Fund, 700 Nineteenth Street, NW, Washington, D.C. 20431 (202) 623-7000

Directory of Business and Financial Information Services, Special Libraries Association, Washington, D.C. (202) 234-4700

Directory of Governors of the American States, Commonwealths and Territories.
National Governors' Association, Hall of the States, 444 North Capitol Street, NW, Washington, D.C. 20001 (202) 624-5300

Directory of United Nations Databases and Information Services.
Statistical Office of the United Nations, Publishing Service, New York, New York 10017 (800) 253-9646

Directory of U.S. Government Data Files for Mainframes and Microcomputers.
National Technical Information Service, 5285 Port Royal Road, Springfield, Virginia 22161 (800) 553-6847

Directory of Veterans Administration Facilities.
U.S. Department of Veterans Affairs, 810 Vermont Avenue, NW, Washington, D.C. 20420 (202) 273-5400

Disability Statistics Compendium.
Statistical Office of the United Nations, Publishing Service, New York, New York 10017 (800) 253-9646

Djibouti Country Report.
Economist Intelligence Unit, 111 West 57th Street, New York, New York 10019 (800) 938-4685

Dodge Construction Potentials.
F.W. Dodge Division, McGraw-Hill Information Systems Company, 148 Princeton-Hightstown Road, Hightstown, New Jersey 08520-1450 (800) 393-6343

Domestic Offices, Commercial Bank Assets and Liabilities, Consolidated Report of Condition.
Board of Governors of the Federal Reserve System, Twentieth and Constitution Avenue, NW, Washington, D.C. 20551 (202) 452-3000

Domestic Uranium Mining and Milling Industry.
U.S. Department of Energy, Energy Information Administration, 1000 Independence Avenue, SW, Washington, D.C. 20585 (202) 586-8800

Dominican Republic Country Report.
Economist Intelligence Unit, 111 West 57th Street, New York, New York 10019 (800) 938-4685

Dominikanische Republik.
Federal Statistical Office, Gustav-Stresemann-Ring 11, D-6200 Wiesbaden, Germany

The Dow Jones Averages 1885-1990.
McGraw Hill, Inc., 1221 Avenue of the Americas, New York, New York 10020 (800) 722-4726

Drivers Licenses.
U.S. Department of Transportation, Federal Highway Administration, 400 Seventh Street, SW, Washington, D.C. 20590 (202) 366-0660

Drug Use Forecasting.
U.S. Department of Justice, National Institute of Justice, 633 Indiana

Avenue, NW, Washington, D.C. 20531 (202) 307-0781

Drunk Driving, Special Report.
U.S. Department of Justice, Bureau of Justice Statistics, 810 Seventh Street, NW, Washington, D.C. 20531 (800) 732-3277

Dschibuti.
Federal Statistical Office, Gustav-Stresemann-Ring 11, D-6200 Wiesbaden, Germany

EBRI Databook on Employee Benefits.
Employee Benefit Research Institute, 2121 K Street, NW, Suite 600, Washington, D.C. 20037 (202) 659-0670

Earnings in Agriculture.
European Community Information Service, 2100 M Street, NW, Washington, D.C. 20037 (202) 862-9500

The East Europe and Soviet Data Handbook: Political, Social and Developmental Indicators, 1945-1975.
Columbia University Press, 562 West 113th Street, York, New York 10014 (212) 854-1754

Eastern Europe and the Commonwealth of Independent States.
Europa Publications, London, England (Available from The Gale Group, (800) 877-GALE)

Eastern Europe, Russia and Central Asia.
Europa Publications, London, England (Available from The Gale Group, (800) 877-GALE)

Economic Abstract of Alabama.
University of Alabama, Center for Business and Economic Research, P.O. Box 870221, Tuscaloosa, Alabama 35487 (205) 348-6191

Economic Accounts for Agriculture.
Organisation for Economic Co-operation and Development (OECD), 2 rue Andre-Pascal, 75 Paris 16, France (Telephone Number in U.S. (202) 785-6323)

Economic and Social Progress in Latin America: Natural Resources.
Inter-American Development Bank, 1300 New York Avenue, NW, Washington, D.C. 20577 (202) 623-1000

Economic Census of Outlying Areas.
U.S. Department of Commerce, Bureau of the Census, Washington, D.C. 20233 (301) 457-4100

Economic Censuses of Outlying Areas, Puerto Rico.
U.S. Department of Commerce, Bureau of the Census, Washington, D.C. 20233 (301) 457-4100

Economic Data Papers - Nepal.
Economic Planning Section, Program Office, US AID, Kathmandu, Nepal

Economic Growth of OECD Countries.
U.S. Department of State, Bureau of Intelligence and Research, 2201 C Street, NW, Washington, D.C. 20520 (202) 647-1080

Economic Indicators.
Executive Office of the President, Council of Economic Advisers, Old Executive Office Building, Washington, D.C. 20500 (202) 395-5084

Economic Indicators.
West Virginia, Research League, Inc., 405 Capitol Street, Suite 414, Charleston, West Virginia 25301 (304) 346-9451

Economic Indicators Handbook.
The Gale Group, 27500 Drake Road, Farmington Hills, Michigan 48331 (800) 877-4253

Economic Indicators of the Farm Sector.
U.S. Department of Agriculture, Economic Research Service, 1800 M Street, NW, Washington, D.C. 20036 (202) 694-4040

Economic Indicators of the Farm Sector: National Financial Summary.
U.S. Department of Agriculture, Economic Research Service, 1800 M Street, NW, Washington, D.C. 20036 (202) 694-4040

Economic Indicators of the Farm Sector: Production and Efficiency Statistics.
U.S. Department of Agriculture, Economic Research Service, 1800 M Street, NW, Washington, D.C. 20036 (202) 694-4040

Economic Indicators of the Farm Sector: State Financial Summary.
U.S. Department of Agriculture, Economic Research Service, 1800 M Street, NW, Washington, D.C. 20036 (202) 694-4040

Economic Outlook.
International Monetary Fund, 700 Nineteenth Street, NW, Washington, D.C. 20431 (202) 623-7000

Economic Outlook.
Organisation for Economic Co-operation and Development (OECD), 2 rue Andre-Pascal, 75 Paris 16, France (Telephone Number in U.S. (202) 785-6323)

Economic Research Service-Finders Advisory System.
U.S. Department of Agriculture, Economic Research Service, 1800 M Street, NW, Washington, D.C. 20036 (202) 694-4040

Economic Report to the Governor.
Puerto Rico Planning Board, Area of Economic and Social Planning, Bureau of Economic Analysis and Bureau of Statistics, Santurce, Puerto Rico 00940 (809) 722-2070

Economic Report of the President.
Executive Office of the President, Council of Economic Advisers, Old Executive Office Building, Washington, D.C. 20500 (202) 395-5084

Economic Report to the Governor: State of Minnesota.
Department of Trade and Economic Development, Policy Analysis Office, 500 Metro Square Building, Saint Paul, Minnesota 55101 (612) 296-8283

Economic Survey.
Central Bureau of Statistics, Post Office Box 1098, Accra, Ghana

Economic Survey of Europe.
United Nations, New York, New York (Available from UNIPUB (800) 274-4888)

Economic Survey of Latin America and the Caribbean.
Statistical Office of the United Nations, Publishing Service, New York, New York 10017 (800) 253-9646

Economic Survey of Liberia.
Ministry of Planning and Economic Affairs, Post Office Box 9016, Monrovia, Liberia

Economics Sourcebook of Government Statistics.
The Free Press, New York, New York (800) 223-2336

Ecuador.
Federal Statistical Office, Gustav-Stresemann-Ring 11, D-6200 Wiesbaden, Germany

Ecuador Country Report.
Economist Intelligence Unit, 111 West 57th Street, New York, New York 10019 (800) 938-4685

Editor and Publisher International Year Book.

Editor and Publisher Company, 11 West 19th Street, New York, New York 10011 (212) 675-4380

Editor and Publisher Market Guide.
Editor and Publisher Company, 11 West 19th Street, New York, New York 10011 (212) 675-4380

Education at a Glance.
Organisation for Economic Co-operation and Development (OECD), 2 rue Andre-Pascal, 75 Paris 16, France (Telephone Number in U.S. (202) 785-6323)

Education in OECD Countries.
Organisation for Economic Co-operation and Development (OECD), 2 rue Andre-Pascal, 75 Paris 16, France (Telephone Number in U.S. (202) 785-6323)

Education Statistics of the United States.
Bernan Press, Lanham, Maryland (800) 865-3457

Education Statistics on Disk.
U.S. Department of Education, National Center for Education Statistics, 555 New Jersey Avenue, NW, Washington, D.C. 20208 (202) 219-1828

Educational Statistics of the Republic of China.
Ministry of Education, 5, Chungshan South Road, Taipei, Republic of China

Egypt Country Report.
Economist Intelligence Unit, 111 West 57th Street, New York, New York 10019 (800) 938-4685

EIA Publications Directory.
U.S. Department of Energy, Energy Information Administration, 1000 Independence Avenue, SW, Washington, D.C. 20585 (202) 586-8800

El Salvador.
Federal Statistical Office, Gustav-Stresemann-Ring 11, D-6200 Wiesbaden, Germany

El Salvador Country Report.
Economist Intelligence Unit, 111 West 57th Street, New York, New York 10019 (800) 938-4685

Electric Power Annual.
U.S. Department of Energy, Energy Information Administration, 1000 Independence Avenue, SW, Washington, D.C. 20585 (202) 586-8800

Electric Power in Asia and the Pacific.
Statistical Office of the United Nations, Publishing Service, New York, New York 10017 (800) 253-9646

Electric Power Monthly.
U.S. Department of Energy,, Energy Information Administration, 1000 Independence Avenue, SW, Washington, D.C. 20585 (202) 586-8800

Electronic Market Data Book.
Electronic Industries Alliance, 2500 Wilson Boulevard, Arlington, Virginia 22201 (703) 907-7500

Electronic News Service.
U.S. Department of Labor, Bureau of Labor Statistics, Two Massachusetts Avenue, NE, Washington, D.C. 20212 (202) 691-5200

Elementary-Secondary Staff Information.
Equal Employment Opportunity Commission, 1801 L Street, NW, Washington, D.C. 20507 (800) USA-EEOC

Elevations and Distances in the United States.
U.S. Department of the Interior, Geological Survey, National Center, 12201 Sunrise Valley Drive, Reston, Virginia 22092 (703) 648-4000

Emerging Stock Markets Factbook.
International Finance Corporation, 2121 Pennsylvania Avenue, NW, Washington, D.C. 20433 (202) 477-1234

Emerging Trends.
Princeton Religion Research Center, 47 Hulfish Street, Princeton, New Jersey 08542 (609) 921-8112

Emissions of Greenhouse Gases in the U.S.
U.S. Department of Energy, Energy Information Administration, 1000 Independence Avenue, SW, Washington, D.C. 20585 (202) 586-8800

Employee Benefits in Medium and Large Private Establishments.
U.S. Department of Labor, Bureau of Labor Statistics, Two Massachusetts Avenue, NE, Washington, D.C. 20212 (202) 691-5200

Employee Benefits in Small Private Establishments.
U.S. Department of Labor, Bureau of Labor Statistics, Two Massachusetts Avenue, NE, Washington, D.C. 20212 (202) 691-5200

Employee Benefits in State and Local Governments.
U.S. Department of Labor, Bureau of Labor Statistics, Two Massachusetts Avenue, NE, Washington, D.C. 20212 (202) 691-5200

Employee Retirement Systems of State and Local Governments.
U.S. Department of Commerce, Bureau of the Census, Washington, D.C. 20233 (301) 457-4100

Employer Costs for Employee Compensation.
U.S. Department of Labor, Bureau of Labor Statistics, Two Massachusetts Avenue, NE, Washington, D.C. 20212 (202) 691-5200

Employment and Earnings.
U.S. Department of Labor, Bureau of Labor Statistics, Two Massachusetts Avenue, NE, Washington, D.C. 20212 (202) 691-5200

Employment and Unemployment.
European Community Information Service, 2100 M Street, NW, Washington, D.C. 20037 (202) 862-9500

Employment and Wages, Annual Averages.
U.S. Department of Labor, Bureau of Labor Statistics, Two Massachusetts Avenue, NE, Washington, D.C. 20212 (202) 691-5200

Employment Cost Index.
U.S. Department of Labor, Bureau of Labor Statistics, Two Massachusetts Avenue, NE, Washington, D.C. 20212 (202) 691-5200

Employment, Hours and Earnings, United States, 1990-1995.
U.S. Department of Labor, Bureau of Labor Statistics, Two Massachusetts Avenue, NE, Washington, D.C. 20212 (202) 691-5200

Employment Report of United States Flag Merchant Fleet Oceangoing Vessels 1000 Gross Tons and Over.
U.S. Department of Transportation, Maritime Administration, 400 Seventh Street, SW, Washington, D.C. 20590 (202) 366-5807

Encyclopedia of Associations.
The Gale Group, 27500 Drake Road, Farmington Hills, Michigan 48331 (800) 877-4253

Encyclopedia of Business Information Sources.
The Gale Group, 27500 Drake Road, Farmington Hills, Michigan 48331 (800) 877-4253

Encyclopedia of Statistical Sciences.
John Wiley & Sons, New York, New York (800) 225-5945

Endangered Species Technical Bulletin.
U.S. Department of the Interior, Fish and Wildlife Service, C Street between Eighteenth and Nineteenth Streets, NW, Washington, D.C.

20240 (202) 208-5634

Energy Data Reports.
U.S. Department of Energy, Energy Information Administration, 1000 Independence Avenue, SW, Washington, D.C. 20585 (202) 586-8800

Energy: Monthly Statistics.
European Community Information Service, 2100 M Street, NW, Washington, D.C. 20037 (202) 862-9500

Energy Statistical Yearbook.
European Community Information Service, Washington, D.C. (Available from UNIPUB (800) 274-4888)

Energy Statistics of OECD Countries.
Organisation for Economic Co-operation and Development (OECD), 2 rue Andre-Pascal, 75 Paris 16, France (Telephone Number in U.S. (202) 785-6323)

Energy Statistics Yearbook.
European Community Information Service, 2100 M Street, NW, Washington, D.C. 20037 (202) 862-9500

Energy Statistics Yearbook.
Statistical Office of the United Nations, Publishing Service, New York, New York 10017 (800) 253-9646

Environmental Business Journal.
Environmental Business International, 4452 Park Boulevard, Suite 306, San Diego, California 92116 (619) 295-7685

The Environmental Data Book: A Guide to Statistics on the Environment and Development.
International Bank for Reconstruction and Development/World Bank, 1818 H Street, NW Washington, D.C. 20043 (202) 476-1234

Environmental Data Compendium.
Organisation for Economic Co-operation and Development, (OECD), 2 rue Andre-Pascal, 75 Paris 16, France (Telephone Number in U.S. (202) 785-6323)

EPUB.
U.S. Department of Energy, Energy Information Administration, 1000 Independence Avenue, SW, Washington, D.C. 20585 (202) 586-8800

Equatorial Guinea Country Report.
Economist Intelligence Unit, 111 West 57th Street, New York, New York 10019 (800) 938-4685

Equality State Almanac.
Department of Administration and Fiscal Control, Division of Research and Statistics, 327 East Emerson Building, Cheyenne, Wyoming 82002 (307) 777-7504

Eritrea Country Report.
Economist Intelligence Unit, 111 West 57th Street, New York, New York 10019 (800) 938-4685

ERS/NASS Bulletin Board.
U.S. Department of Agriculture, National Agricultural Statistics Service, Fourteenth Street and Independence Avenue, SW, Washington, D.C. 20250 (800) 727-9540. Accessed by modem on (202) 720-2707

Estimated Use of Water in the United States in 1985.
U.S. Department of the Interior, Geological Survey, National Center, 12201 Sunrise Valley Drive, Reston, Virginia 22092 (703) 648-4000

Estimates of School Statistics.
National Education Association, 1201 Sixteenth Street, NW, Washington, D.C. 20036 (202) 833-4000

Estonia Country Report.
Economist Intelligence Unit, 111 West 57th Street, New York, New York 10019 (800) 938-4685

Ethiopia Country Report.
Economist Intelligence Unit, 111 West 57th Street, New York, New York 10019 (800) 938-4685

Ethiopia Statistical Abstract.
Provisional Military Government of Ethiopia, Central Statistical Office, Post Office Box 1143, Addis Ababa, Ethiopia

Etudes Statistiques.
Institut National de Statistique, rue de Louvain 44, 1000 Brussels, Belgium

The Europa World Year Book.
Europa Publications Limited, 18 Bedford Square, London, England WC1B 3JN (Available from The Gale Group (800) 877-4253)

European Advertising, Marketing, and Media Data Statistics.
Euromonitor International, 60-61 Britton Street, London EC1M 5NA, England (Number in the U.S. (800) 577-EURO)

European Directory of Non-Official Statistical Sources, 1993.
Euromonitor International, 60-61 Britton Street, London EC1M 5NA, England (Number in the U.S. (800) 577-EURO)

European Historical Statistics.
European Community Information Service, 2100 M Street, NW, Washington, D.C. 20037 (202) 862-9500

European Marketing Data and Statistics.
Euromonitor International, 60-61 Britton Street, London EC1M 5NA, England (Number in the U.S. (800) 577-EURO)

Eurostatistics: Data for Short-Term Economic Analysis.
European Community Information Service, 2100 M Street, NW, Washington, D.C. 20037 (202) 862-9500

Existing Home Sales.
National Association of Realtors, 430 North Michigan Avenue, Chicago, Illinois 60611-4087 (800) 874-6500

Exports from Manufacturing Establishments.
U.S. Department of Commerce, Bureau of the Census, Washington, D.C. 20233 (301) 457-4100

Exports of Merchandise from Afghanistan.
Central Statistics Office, Kabul, Afghanistan

Exposicao: Informacao Estatistica.
Direccao de Economia e Estatistica, Sao Tome, Sao Tome e Principe

External Trade: Monthly Statistics.
European Community Information Service, 2100 M Street, NW, Washington, D.C. 20037 (202) 862-9500

External Trade: Statistical Yearbook.
European Community Information Service, 2100 M Street, NW, Washington, D.C. 20037 (202) 862-9500

FAA Statistical Handbook of Aviation.
U.S. Department of Transportation, Federal Aviation Administration, 800 Independence Avenue, SW, Washington, D.C. 20591 (202) 367-3484

FAO Production Yearbook.
Food and Agricultural Organization of the United Nations (FAO), Via delle Terme di Caracalla, 00100 Rome, Italy (Telephone Number in the U.S. (202) 653-2400)

FAO Quarterly Bulletin of Statistics.
Food and Agricultural Organization of the United Nations (FAO), Via delle Terme di Caracalla, 00100 Rome, Italy (Telephone Number in the U.S. (202) 653-2400)

FAO Trade Yearbook.
Food and Agricultural Organization of the United Nations (FAO), Via delle Terme di Caracalla, 00100 Rome, Italy (Telephone Number in the U.S. (202) 653-2400)

FAO Yearbook of Forest Products.
Food and Agricultural Organization of the United Nations (FAO), Via delle Terme di Caracalla, 00100, Rome, Italy (Telephone Number in the U.S. (202) 653-2400)

FEC Index of Independent Expenditures.
Federal Election Commission, 999 E Street, NW, Washington, D.C. 20463 (800) 424-9530

FEC Reports on Financial Activity, Final Report, Party and Non-Party Political Committees.
Federal Election Commission, 999 E Street, NW, Washington, D.C. 20463 (800) 424-9530

FEC Reports on Financial Activity, Final Report, Presidential Pre-Nomination Campaigns.
Federal Election Commission, 999 E Street, NW, Washington, D.C. 20463 (800) 424-9530

FEC Reports on Financial Activity, Final Report, U.S. Senate and House Campaigns.
Federal Election Commission, 999 E Street, NW, Washington, D.C. 20463   (800) 424-9530

Faafinta Istaatistikada bisha.
Statistical Department, State Planning Commission, Post Office Box 1742, Mogadishu, Somalia

Fact Book.
National Association of Securities Dealers, 1735 K Street, NW, Washington, D.C. 20006 (202) 728-8000

Fact Book.
New York Stock Exchange, 11 Wall Street, New York, New York 10005 (212) 656-3000

Factbook and Membership Directory.
Mortgage Insurance Companies of America, 727 15th Street, NW, Washington, D.C. 20005 (202) 393-5566

Fact Book of U.S. Agriculture.
U.S. Department of Agriculture, Washington, D.C. (800) 999-6779

Factfinder for the Nation.
U.S. Department of Commerce, Bureau of the Census, Washington, D.C. 20233 (301) 457-4100

Facts and Figures on Government Finance.
Citizens For A Sound Economy, 1250 H Street, NW, Suite 700, Washington, D.C. 20005 (202) 783-3870

Failed Bank Cost Analysis Report.
Federal Deposit Insurance Corporation, 550 Seventeenth Street, NW, Washington, D.C. 20429 (202) 393-8400

Falkland Islands and dependencies: report for the year.
H.M. Stationery Office, Post Office Box 569, London SE1 9NH, England

Falling Through the Net: Defining the Digital Divide.
U.S. Department of Commerce, National Telecommunications and

Information Administration, 1401 Constitution Avenue, NW, Washington, D.C. 20230 (202) 482-7002

Family Business Review.
Family Business Review, Boston, Massachusetts (617) 789-4200

Family Planning Perspectives.
Alan Guttmacher Institute, 120 Wall Street, New York, New York 10005 (212) 248-1111

Far East and Australia.
Europa Publications, London, England (Available from The Gale Group (800) 877-4253)

Farm Labor.
U.S. Department of Agriculture, National Agricultural Statistics Service, Fourteenth Street and Independence Avenue, SW, Washington, D.C. 20250 (800) 727-9540

Farm Management Survey.
An Foras Taluntais (The Agricultural Institute), Economics and Rural Welfare Research Centre, 19 Sandymount Avenue, Dublin 4, Ireland

Farm Numbers and Land in Farms.
U.S. Department of Agriculture, Economic Research Service, 1800 M Street, NW, Washington, D.C. 20036 (202) 694-4040

Fatal Accident Reporting System.
U.S. Department of Transportation, National Highway Traffic Safety Administration, 400 Seventh Street, SW, Washington, D.C. 20590 (202) 366-8892

Fatal and Injury Accident Rates on Public Roads in the United States.
U.S. Department of Transportation, Federal Highway Administration, 400 Seventh Street, SW, Washington, D.C. 20590 (202) 366-0660

Fats and Oils Situation.
U.S. Department of Agriculture, National Agricultural Statistics Service, Fourteenth Street and Independence Avenue, SW, Washington, D.C. 20250 (202) 720-2707

The FDIC Quarterly Banking Profile.
Federal Deposit Insurance Corporation, 550 Seventeenth Street, NW, Washington, D.C. 20429 (202) 393-8400

Federal Aid in Fish and Wildlife Restoration.
U.S. Department of the Interior, Fish and Wildlife Service, C Street between Eighteenth and Nineteenth Streets, NW, Washington, D.C. 20240 (202) 208-5634

Federal Civilian Workforce Statistics, Employment and Trends.
Office of Personnel Management, 1900 E Street, NW, Washington, D.C. 20415 (202) 606-1800

Federal Criminal Case Processing.
U.S. Department of Justice, Bureau of Justice Statistics, 810 Seventh Street, NW, Washington, D.C. 20531 (800) 732-3277

The Federal Database Finder: A Directory of Free and Fee-Based Data Bases and Files Available from the Federal Government.
Information USA Inc., Kensington, Maryland (800) 955-POWER

Federal Expenditures by State for Fiscal Year.
U.S. Department of Commerce, Bureau of the Census, Washington, D.C. 20233 (301) 457-4100

Federal Offshore Statistics.
U.S. Department of the Interior, Minerals Management Service, 1849 C Street, NW, Washington, D.C. 20240 (202) 208-3985

Federal Prosecutions of Corrupt Public Officials.
U.S. Department of Justice, 950 Pennsylvania Avenue, NW,

Washington, D.C. 20530 (202) 514-2000

Federal R & D Funding by Budget Function.
National Science Foundation, 4201 Wilson Boulevard, Arlington, Virginia 22230 (703) 306-1234

Federal Reserve Bulletin.
Board of Governors of the Federal Reserve System, Twentieth Street and Constitution Avenue, NW, Washington, D.C. 20551 (202) 452-3000

Federal Statistical Source: Where to Find Agency Experts and Personnel.
Oryx Press, Phoenix (800) 279-ORYX

Federal Support to Universities, Colleges, and Nonprofit Institutions.
National Science Foundation, 4201 Wilson Boulevard, Arlington, Virginia 22230 (703) 306-1234

Feed Situation.
U.S. Department of Agriculture, Economic Research Service, 1800 M Street, NW, Washington, D.C. 20036 (202) 694-4040

Fertilizer Yearbook.
Food and Agricultural Organization of the United Nations (FAO), Via delle Terme di Caracalla, 00100, Rome, Italy (Telephone Number in the U.S. (202) 653-2400)

Field Crops.
U.S. Department of Agriculture, National Agricultural Statistics Service, Fourteenth Street and Independence Avenue, SW, Washington, D.C. 20250 (800) 727-9540

Fiji Country Report.
Economist Intelligence Unit, 111 West 57th Street, New York, New York 10019 (800) 938-4685

Fiji Facts and Figures.
Bureau of Statistics, Government Building, P.O. Box 2221, Suva, Fiji Islands

Finances of Employee-Retirement Systems of State and Local Governments.
U.S. Department of Commerce, Bureau of the Census, Washington, D.C. 20233 (301) 457-4100

Finances of Public School Systems.
U.S. Department of Commerce, Bureau of the Census, Washington, D.C. 20233 (301) 457-4100

Financial Characteristics of U.S. Farms
U.S. Department of Agriculture, Economic Research Service, 1800 M Street, NW, Washington, D.C. 20036 (202) 694-4040

Financial Market Trends.
National Technical Information Service, 5285 Port Royal Road, Springfield, Virginia 22161 (800) 553-6847

Financial Statistics Monthly Taiwan District, The Republic of China.
Economic Research Department, The Central Bank of China, 2, Roosevelt Road, Section 1, Taipei 10757, Republic of China

Financial Statistics of Institutions of Higher Education.
U.S. Department of Education, National Center for Education Statistics, 555 New Jersey Avenue, NW, Washington,.D.C. 20208 (202) 219-1828

Financial Statistics of Selected Investor-Owned Electric Utilities.
U.S. Department of Energy, Energy Information Administration, 1000 Independence Avenue, SW, Washington, D.C. 20585 (202) 586-8800

Financing and Delivering Health Care, A Comparative Analysis of OECD Countries.
Organisation for Economic Co-operation and Development, (OECD),

2 rue Andre-Pascal, 75 Paris 16, France (Telephone Number in U.S. (202) 785-6323)

Finding Statistics Online.
Manning Publications, Greenwich, Connecticut (203) 629-2028

Finland Country Report.
Economist Intelligence Unit, 111 West 57th Street, New York, New York 10019 (800) 938-4685

Finnland.
Federal Statistical Office, Gustav-Stresemann-Ring 11, D-6200 Wiesbaden, Germany

Fire Journal.
National Fire Protection Association, One Batterymarch Park, Post Office Box 9101, Quincy, Massachusetts 02269-9101 (617) 770-3000

Fiscal Survey of the States.
National Governors' Association, Hall of the States, 444 North Capitol Street, NW, Washington, D.C. 20001 (202) 624-5300

Fisheries of the United States.
U.S. Department of Commerce, National Oceanic and Atmospheric Administration, National Marine Fisheries Service, 1315 East-West Highway, Silver Spring, Maryland 20910 (301) 713-2239

Fisheries: Yearly Statistics.
European Community Information Service, 2100 M Street, NW, Washington, D.C. 20037 (202) 862-9500

Fishery Commodities and Trade.
Food and Agricultural Organization of the United Nations (FAO), Via delle Terme di Caracalla, 00100, Rome, Italy (Telephone Number in the U.S. (202) 653-2400)

Fishery Statistics of the United States.
U.S. Department of Commerce, National Oceanic and Atmospheric Administration, National Marine Fisheries Service, 1315 East-West Highway, Silver Spring, Maryland 20910 (301) 713-2239

Fixed Reproducible Tangible Wealth in the United States.
U.S. Department of Commerce, Bureau of Economic Analysis, Fourteenth Street between Constitution Avenue and E Street, NW, Washington, D.C. 20230 (202) 606-9900

Floraculture and Environmental Horticulture Products: A Production and Marketing Statistical Review.
U.S. Department of Agriculture, Economic Research Service, 1800 M Street, NW, Washington, D.C. 20036 (202) 694-4040

Florida County Perspectives.
National Data Consultants, Post Office Box 6381, Athens, Georgia 30604 (404) 548-8460

Florida Statistical Abstract.
Bureau of Economic and Business Research, University of Florida, Gainesville, Florida 32611 (904) 392-0171

Flow of Funds Accounts.
Board of Governors of the Federal Reserve System, Twentieth Street and Constitution Avenue, NW, Washington, D.C. 20551 (202) 452-3000

Food Consumption Prices and Expenditures.
U.S. Department of Agriculture, Economic Research Service, 1800 M Street, NW, Washington, D.C. 20036 (202) 694-4040

Food Consumption Statistics.
Organisation for Economic Co-operation and Development (OECD), 2 rue Andre-Pascal, 75 Paris 16, France (Telephone Number in U.S. (202) 785-6323)

Food Cost Review.
U.S. Department of Agriculture, Economic Research Service, 1800 M Street, NW, Washington, D.C. 20036 (202) 694-4040

Foodservice Industry in Review.
National Restaurant Association, 1200 Seventeenth Street, NW, Washington, D.C. 20036 (202) 331-5900

Food Marketing Review.
U.S. Department of Agriculture, Economic Research Service, 1800 M Street, NW, Washington, D.C. 20036 (202) 694-4040

Foodservice Numbers: A Statistical Digest for the Food Service Industry.
National Restaurant Association, 1200 17th Street, NW, Washington, D.C. 20036 (202) 331-5900

The Footwear, Raw Hides and Skins, and Leather Industry in OECD Countries.
Organisation for Economic Co-operation and Development (OECD), 2 rue Andre-Pascal, 75 Paris 16, France (Telephone Number in U.S. (202) 785-6323)

Forbes Annual Report on American Industry.
Forbes, Inc., 60 Fifth Avenue, New York, New York 10011 (212) 691-6130

Forecast of Housing Activity.
National Association of Home Builders of the U.S., 1201 15th Street, NW, Washington, D.C. 20005 (202) 822-0200

Foreign Agricultural Commodity Circular Series.
U.S. Department of Agriculture, Foreign Agricultural Service, Fourteenth Street and Independence Avenue, SW, Washington, D.C. 20250 (202) 720-7115

Foreign Agricultural Trade of the United States.
U.S. Department of Agriculture, Economic Research Service, 1800 M Street, NW, Washington, D.C. 20036 (202) 694-4040

Foreign Commerce and Navigation of the United States.
U.S. Department of Commerce, Bureau of the Census, Washington, D.C. 20233 (301) 457-4100

Foreign Direct Investment in the United States.
U.S. Department of Commerce, Bureau of Economic Analysis, Fourteenth Street between Constitution Avenue and E Street, NW, Washington, D.C. 20230 (202) 606-9900

Foreign Military Construction Sales.
U.S. Department of Defense, Defense Security Assistance Agency, The Pentagon, Washington, D.C. 20301-2800 (703) 604-6604

Foreign Military Sales.
U.S. Department of Defense, Defense Security Assistance Agency, The Pentagon, Washington, D.C. 20301-2800 (703) 604-6513

Foreign Ownership of U.S. Agricultural Land Through December 31.
U.S. Department of Agriculture, Economic Research Service, 1800 M Street, NW, Washington, D.C. 20036 (202) 694-4040

Foreign Trade By Commodities.
Organisation for Economic Co-operation and Development (OECD), 2 rue Andre-Pascal, 75 Paris 16, France (Telephone Number in U.S. (202) 785-6323)

Foreign Trade Import and Export CD-ROM disc.
U.S. Department of Commerce, Bureau of the Census, Washington, D.C. 20233 (301) 457-4100

Foreign Trade of the United States.
Bernan Press, Lanham, Maryland (800) 865-3457

Foreign Trade Statistics for Africa.
Organisation for Economic Co-operation and Development (OECD), 2 rue Andre-Pascal, 75 Paris 16, France (Telephone Number in U.S. (202) 785-6323)

Foreign Trade Statistics for Africa.
Statistical Office of the United Nations, Publishing Service, New York, New York 10017 (800) 253-9646

Foreign Trade Statistics of Asia and the Pacific.
Statistical Office of the United Nations, Publishing Service, New York, New York 10017 (800) 253-9646

Forest Resources of the United States.
U.S. Department of Agriculture, Forest Service, Post Office Box 96090, Washington, D.C. 20090 (202) 720-3760

The Fortune Directories.
Time Warner, Time & Life Building, Rockefeller Center, New York, New York 10020 (212) 522-1212

Foundation Grants Index.
The Foundation Center, 79 Fifth Avenue, New York, New York 10003 (212) 620-4230

France Country Report.
Economist Intelligence Unit, 111 West 57th Street, New York, New York 10019 (800) 938-4685

Franchising in the Economy.
International Franchise Association, 1350 New York Avenue, Suite 900, Washington, D.C. 20005 (202) 628-8000

Frankreich.
Federal Statistical Office, Gustav-Stresemann-Ring 11, D-6200 Wiesbaden, Germany

Freight Commodity Statistics.
Association of American Railroads, 50 F Street, NW, Washington, D.C. 20001 (202) 639-2100

From Belief to Commitment: The Activities and Finances of Religious Congregations in the United States.
Independent Sector, 1200 18th Street, NW, Suite 200, Washington, D.C. 20036 (202) 467-6161

Gabon Country Report.
Economist Intelligence Unit, 111 West 57th Street, New York, New York 10019 (800) 938-4685

Gabun.
Federal Statistical Office, Gustav-Stresemann-Ring 11, D-6200 Wiesbaden, Germany

Gale Book of Averages.
The Gale Group, 27500 Drake Road, Farmington Hills, Michigan 48331 (800) 877-4253

Gale City and Metro Rankings Reporter.
The Gale Group, 27500 Drake Road, Farmington Hills, Michigan 48331 (800) 877-4253

Gale Country and World Rankings Reporter.
The Gale Group, 27500 Drake Road, Farmington Hills, Michigan 48331 (800) 877-4253

Gale Directory of Databases.
The Gale Group, 27500 Drake Road, Farmington Hills, Michigan 48331 (800) 877-4253

Gale Directory of Publications and Broadcast Media.
The Gale Group, 27500 Drake Road, Farmington Hills, Michigan 48331 (800) 877-4253

Gale State Rankings Reporter.
The Gale Group, 27500 Drake Road, Farmington Hills, Michigan 48331 (800) 877-4253

The Gallup Report.
Gallup Organization, Inc., 47 Hulfish Street, Princeton, New Jersey 08542 (609) 924-9600

Gambia.
Federal Statistical Office, Gustav-Stresemann-Ring 11, D-6200 Wiesbaden, Germany

Gambia Country Report.
Economist Intelligence Unit, 111 West 57th Street, New York, New York 10019 (800) 938-4685

The Gambia Trade Directory.
Banjul: Ministry of Finance and Trade, The Quadrangle, Banjul, Gambia

Ganley's Catholic Schools in America.
National Catholic Educational Association, 1077 30th Street, NW, Washington, D.C. 20007 (202) 337-6232

Gas Facts.
American Gas Association, 400 North Capitol Street, NW, Washington, D.C. 20001 (202) 824-7000

GEO-DATA: The World Geographical Encyclopedia.
The Gale Group, 27500 Drake Road, Farmington Hills, Michigan 48331 (800) 877-4253

Georgia Country Report.
Economist Intelligence Unit, 111 West 57th Street, New York, New York 10019 (800) 938-4685

The Georgia County Guide.
University of Georgia, College of Agriculture, Cooperative Extension Service, Athens, Georgia 30602 (404) 542-8938

Georgia Descriptions in Data.
Office of Planning and Budget, 254 Washington Street, SW, Atlanta, Georgia 30334 (404) 656-0911

Georgia Statistical Abstract.
Selig Center for Economic Growth, Terry College of Business, University of Georgia, Athens, Georgia 30602 (404) 542-4085

Geographic Profile of Employment and Unemployment.
U.S. Department of Labor, Bureau of Labor Statistics, Two Massachusetts Avenue, NE, Washington, D.C. 20212 (202) 691-5200

Geographical Distribution of Financial Flows to Developing Countries.
Organisation for Economic Co-operation and Development (OECD), 2 rue Andre-Pascal, 75 Paris 16, France (Telephone Number in U.S. (202) 785-6323)

Germany Country Report.
Economist Intelligence Unit, 111 West 57th Street, New York, New York 10019 (800) 938-4685

Ghana.
Federal Statistical Office, Gustav-Stresemann-Ring 11, D-6200 Wiesbaden, Germany

Ghana Country Report.
Economist Intelligence Unit, 111 West 57th Street, New York, New York

10019 (800) 938-4685

Gilbert and Ellice Islands Colony and the Central and Southern Line Islands: Report...
HM Stationery Office, Post Office Box 569, London SE1 9NH, England

Giving and Volunteering in the United States.
Independent Sector, 1200 18th Street, NW, Suite 200, Washington, D.C. 20036 (202) 467-6161

Giving U.S.A.
American Association of Fundraising Counsel, 10293 North Meridian Street, Suite 175, Indianapolis, Indiana 46290 (800) 462-2372

Global Data Locator.
Bernan Press, Lanham, Maryland (800) 274-4447

Global Development Finance.
The World Bank, 1818 H Street, NW, Washington, D.C. 20043 (202) 477-1234

The Global Economy: An Information Sourcebook.
Oryx Press, Westport, Connecticut (800) 279-ORYX

Government Finance Statistics Yearbook.
International Monetary Fund, 700 Nineteenth Street, NW, Washington, D.C. 20431 (202) 623-7000

Government Finances.
U.S. Department of Commerce, Bureau of the Census, Washington, D.C. 20233 (301) 457-4100

Government Financing of Research and Development.
European Community Information Service, 2100 M Street, NW, Washington, D.C. 20037 (202) 862-9500

Government Information on the Internet.
Bernan Press, Lanham, Maryland (800) 274-4447

Government Units.
U.S. Department of Commerce, Bureau of the Census, Washington, D.C. 20233 (301) 457-4100

Governmental Organization.
U.S. Department of Commerce, Bureau of the Census, Washington, D.C. 20233 (301) 457-4100

Greece Country Report.
Economist Intelligence Unit, 111 West 57th Street, New York, New York 10019 (800) 938-4685

Greenland.
Federal Statistical Office, Gustav-Stresemann-Ring 11, D-6200 Wiesbaden, Germany

Grenada.
Federal Statistical Office, Gustav-Stresemann-Ring 11, D-6200 Wiesbaden, Germany

Griechenland.
Federal Statistical Office, Gustav-Stresemann-Ring 11, D-6200 Wiesbaden, Germany

Guam: Annual Report to the Secretary of the Interior.
Superintendent of Documents, U.S. Government Printing Office, Washington, D.C. 20402 (202) 783-3238

The Guarantor.
Chicago Title Insurance Company, 171 North Clark Street, Chicago, Illinois 60601 (312) 630-2000

Guatemala.
Federal Statistical Office, Gustav-Stresemann-Ring 11, D-6200 Wiesbaden, Germany

Guatemala Country Report.
Economist Intelligence Unit, 111 West 57th Street, New York, New York 10019 (800) 938-4685

Guide to Economic Indicators.
M. E. Sharpe, Armonk, New York (800) 541-6563

Guide to Foreign Trade Statistics.
U.S. Department of Commerce, Bureau of the Census, Washington, D.C. 20233 (301) 457-4100

Guide to Government Statistics.
Documents Index, Manassas, Virginia (800) 899-4988

Guide to Military Installations in the U.S.
Army Times Publishing Company, 6883 Commercial Drive, Springfield, Virginia 22159 (703) 750-9000

Guide to Official Publications of Foreign Countries.
Congressional Information Service, Bethesda, Maryland (800) 638-8380

Guide to Official Statistics.
Central Statistical Office, London, England

Guide to Petroleum Statistical Information.
American Petroleum Institute, 1220 L Street, NW, Washington, D.C. 20005 (202) 682-8000

A Guide to Selected National Environmental Statistics in the U.S. Government.
Environmental Protection Agency, 1200 Pennsylvania Avenue, NW, Washington, D.C. 20460 (888) 372-8255

Guide to Service Industry Statistics and Related Data.
U.S. Department of Commerce, Bureau of the Census, Washington, D.C. 20233 (301) 457-4100

Guide to Statistical Materials Published by Governments and Associations in the United States.
Chadwyck-Healey, Alexandria, Virginia (800) 752-0515

Guide to U.S. Foundations.
The Foundation Center, 79 Fifth Avenue, New York, New York 10003 (212) 620-4230

Guide to U.S. Government Statistics.
Documents Index, Manassas, Virginia (800) 899-4988

Guinea.
Federal Statistical Office, Gustav-Stresemann-Ring 11, D-6200 Wiesbaden, Germany

Guinea Country Report.
Economist Intelligence Unit, 111 West 57th Street, New York, New York 10019 (800) 938-4685

Guinea Bissau.
Federal Statistical Office, Gustav-Stresemann-Ring 11, D-6200 Wiesbaden, Germany

Guinea Bissau Country Report.
Economist Intelligence Unit, 111 West 57th Street, New York, New York 10019 (800) 938-4685

Guns and Crime.
U.S. Department of Justice, Bureau of Justice Statistics, 810 Seventh Street, NW, Washington, D.C. 20531 (800) 732-3277

Guyana.
Federal Statistical Office, Gustav-Stresemann-Ring 11, D-6200 Wiesbaden, Germany

Guyana Country Report.
Economist Intelligence Unit, 111 West 57th Street, New York, New York 10019 (800) 938-4685

HUD Statistical Yearbook.
U.S. Department of Housing and Urban Development, 451 Seventh Street, SW, Washington, D.C. 20410 (800) 998-9999

Hagtioindi.
Statistical Bureau of Iceland, Hagstofa Islands, Hverfisgata 8-10, Reykjavik, 26699

Haiti.
Federal Statistical Office, Gustav-Stresemann-Ring 11, D-6200 Wiesbaden, Germany

Haiti Country Report.
Economist Intelligence Unit, 111 West 57th Street, New York, New York 10019 (800) 938-4685

Handbook of Economic Statistics.
Central Intelligence Agency, Washington, D.C. 20505 (703) 482-1100

Handbook of Economic Statistics.
National Technical Information Service, 5285 Port Royal Road, Springfield, Virginia 22161 (800) 553-6847

Handbook of Financial Market Indexes, Averages, and Indicators.
McGraw Hill, 1221 Avenue of the Americas, New York, New York 10020 (800) 722-4726

Handbook of Industrial Statistics.
United Nations Industrial Development Organization (UNIDO), Vienna, Austria (Available from Edward Elgar Publishing Company (800) 535-9544)

Handbook of International Economic Statistics.
Central Intelligence Agency, Washington, D.C. 20505 (703) 482-1100

Handbook of International Trade and Development Statistics.
United Nations Conference on Trade and Development (UNCTAD), New York, New York (800) 253-9646

Handbook of Labor Statistics.
U.S. Department of Labor, Bureau of Labor Statistics, Two Massachusetts Avenue, NE, Washington, D.C. 20212 (202) 691-5200

Handbook of North American Industry.
Bernan Press, Lanham, Maryland (800) 865-3457

Handbook of United States Economic and Financial Indicators.
Greenwood Publishing Group, Westport, Connecticut (800) 225-5800

Handel, Gastgewerbe, Reiseverkehr, Reihe 7.3: Urlaubs - und Erholungsreisen 1976/77.
Statistisches Bundesamt (Allgemeiner Auskunftsdienst), Gustav-Streseman-Ring 11, Postfach 5528, 6200 Wiesbaden 1, Germany

Hatchery Production - Annual.
U.S. Department of Agriculture, National Agricultural Statistics Service, Fourteenth Street and Independence Avenue, SW, Washington, D.C. 20250 (800) 727-9540

Health and Healthcare in the United States: County and Metro Area Data.
Bernan Press, Lanham, Maryland (800) 865-3457

Health Care Financing Review.
U.S. Department of Health and Human Services, Health Care Financing Administration, 200 Independence Avenue, SW, Washington, D.C. 20201 (202) 690-6145

Health Insurance Coverage.
U.S. Department of Commerce, Bureau of the Census, Washington, D.C. 20233 (301) 457-4100

Health OECD: Facts and Trends.
Organization for Economic Cooperation and Development, Publication and Information Center, 2001 L Street, NW, Washington, D.C. 20036-4095 (202) 785-6323

Health Promotion and Disease Prevention, United States.
U.S. Department of Health and Human Services, National Center for Health Statistics, 3700 East West Highway, Hyattsville, Maryland 20782 (301) 436-8500

Health Statistics: An Annotated Bibliographic Guide to Information Resources.
Scarecrow Press, Lanham, Maryland (800) 462-6420

Health, United States
U.S. Department of Health and Human Services, National Center for Health Statistics, 3700 East-West Highway, Hyattsville, Maryland 20782 (301) 436-8500

High School Profile Report.
ACT (American College Testing), 2201 North Dodge Street, Box 168, Iowa City, Iowa 52243 (319) 337-1000

Higher Education Price Indexes.
Research Associates of Washington, 1200 North Nash Street, #225, Arlington, Virginia 22209 (703) 243-3399

Highlights of United States Export and Import Trade.
U.S. Department of Commerce, Bureau of the Census, Washington, D.C. 20233 (301) 457-4100

Highway Statistics.
U.S. Department of Transportation, Federal Highway Administration, 400 Seventh Street, SW, Washington, D.C. 20590 (202) 366-0660

Hispanic Databook of U.S. Cities and Counties.
Toucan Valley Publications, Milpitas, California (415) 956-9492

Historical Corrections Statistics in the United States, 1850-1984.
Westat, Rockville, Maryland (Available from the National Criminal Justice Reference Service, 1600 Research Boulevard, Rockville, Maryland 20850 (800) 732-3277)

Historical Statistics of the States of the United States: Two Centuries of the Census, 1790-1990.
Greenwood Publishing Group, Westport, Connecticut (800) 225-5800

Historical Statistics on Governmental Finances and Employment.
U.S. Department of Commerce, Bureau of the Census, Washington, D.C. 20233 (301) 457-4100

Historical Tables, Budget of The United States Government.
Executive Office of the President, Office of Management and Budget, Executive Office Building, Washington, D.C. 20503 (202) 395-3080

Historically Planned Economies: A Guide to the Data.
World Bank Publications, 1818 H Street, NW, Washington, D.C. 20043 (202) 477-1234

HIV/AIDS Surveillance Report.
U.S. Department of Health and Human Services, Centers for Disease Control, 2600 Clifton Road, NE, Atlanta, Georgia 20333 (800) 331-3435

Hogs and Pigs, Final Estimates.
U.S. Department of Agriculture, National Agricultural Statistics Service, 14th Street and Independence Avenue, SW, Washington, D.C. 20250 (800) 727-9540

Home Sales Yearbook.
National Association of Realtors, 430 North Michigan Avenue, Chicago, Illinois 60611-4087 (800) 874-6500

Homelessness in America: A Statistical Handbook and Resource Guide.
Oryx Press, Westport, Connecticut (800) 279-ORYX (in conjunction with National Coalition for the Homeless)

Honduras.
Federal Statistical Office, Gustav-Stresemann-Ring 11, D-6200 Wiesbaden, Germany

Honduras Country Report.
Economist Intelligence Unit, 111 West 57th Street, New York, New York 10019 (800) 938-4685

Hong Kong.
Federal Statistical Office, Gustav-Stresemann-Ring 11, D-6200 Wiesbaden, Germany

Hong Kong Annual Digest of Statistics.
Census and Statistics Department, 317 des Voeux Road Central, Hong Kong, Hong Kong

Hong Kong Country Report.
Economist Intelligence Unit, 111 West 57th Street, New York, New York 10019 (800) 938-4685

Hong Kong Market Atlas.
The Economist Intelligence Unit (Asia), 10th Floor, Luk Kwok Centre, 72 Gloucester Road, Wanchai, Hong Kong (Telephone Number in U.S. (800) 938-4685)

Hong Kong Monthly Digest of Statistics.
Census and Statistics Department, 317 des Voeux Road Central, Hong Kong, Hong Kong

Hospital Statistics.
American Hospital Association, One North Franklin, Suite 27, Chicago, Illinois 60606 (800) 242-2626

Hospital Yearbook.
Statistical Office of the United Nations, Publishing Service, New York, New York 10017 (800) 253-9646

Household Energy Consumption and Expenditures.
U.S. Department of Energy, Energy Information Administration, 1000 Independence Avenue, SW, Washington, D.C. 20585 (202) 586-8800

Household Vehicles Energy Consumption.
U.S. Department of Energy, Energy Information Administration, 1000 Independence Avenue, SW, Washington, D.C. 20585 (202) 586-8800

Households Touched by Crime.
U.S. Department of Justice, Bureau of Justice Statistics, 810 Seventh Street, NW, Washington, D.C. 20531 (800) 732-3277

Housing Characteristics.
U.S. Department of Energy, Energy Information Administration, 1000 Independence Avenue, SW, Washington, D.C. 20585 (202) 586-8800

Housing Statistics of the U.S.
Bernan Press, Lanham, Maryland (800) 274-4447

Human Development Report.
Statistical Office of the United Nations, Publishing Service, New York,

New York 10017 (800) 253-9646

Hungary Country Report.
Economist Intelligence Unit, 111 West 57th Street, New York, New York 10019 (800) 938-4685

Hungary Statistical Yearbook.
Hungarian Statistical Office, 1033 Budapest, III, Kaszasdulo U.2.

Hydroelectric Power Resources of the United States, Developed and Undeveloped.
U.S. Department of Energy, Federal Energy Regulatory Commission, 1000 Independence Avenue, SW, Washington, D.C. 20585 (202) 208-0055

IEA Computers in Education Study.
University of Minnesota, Department of Sociology, Minneapolis, Minnesota 55455 (612) 625-5000

IRM Directory of Statistics of International Investment and Production.
Macmillan Publishers, Ltd., London, England (Telephone Number in the U.S. (800) 428-5331)

Iceland Country Report.
Economist Intelligence Unit, 111 West 57th Street, New York, New York 10019 (800) 938-4685

Idaho Community Profiles.
Department of Commerce, 700 West State Street, Boise, Idaho 83720 (208) 334-2470

Idaho Facts.
Department of Commerce, 700 West State Street, Boise, Idaho 83720 (208) 334-2470

Idaho Facts Data Book.
Department of Commerce, 700 West State Street, Boise, Idaho 83720 (208) 334-2470

Illinois State and Regional Economic Data Book.
Department of Commerce and Community Affairs, State Government of Illinois, 620 Adams Street, Springfield, Illinois 62701 (217) 782-1438

Illinois Statistical Abstract.
University of Illinois, Bureau of Economic and Business Research, 428 Commerce West, 1206 South 6th Street, Champaign, Illinois 61820 (217) 333-2330

The Illustrated Book of World Rankings.
M.E. Sharpe, 800 Business Park Drive, Armonk, New York 10504 (800) 541-6563

Income and Product.
Puerto Rico Planning Board, San Juan, Puerto Rico

Index - National Park System and Related Areas.
U.S. Department of the Interior, National Park Service, C Street between Eighteenth and Nineteenth Streets, NW, Washington, D.C. 20240 (202) 208-6843

Index to Health Information.
Congressional Information Service, Bethesda, Maryland (800) 638-8380

Index to International Statistics.
Congressional Information Service, Bethesda, Maryland (800) 638-8380

India Country Report.
Economist Intelligence Unit, 111 West 57th Street, New York, New York 10019 (800) 938-4685

Indiana Factbook.

Indiana University, Indiana Business Research Center, School of Business, Bloomington, Indiana 46202-5151 (317) 274-2204

Indicators of Industrial Activity.
Organisation for Economic Co-operation and Development (OECD), 2 rue Andre-Pascal, 75 Paris 16, France (Telephone Number in U.S. (202) 785-6323)

Indicators of Market Size for 117 Countries.
Economist Intelligence Unit, New York, New York (800) 938-4685

Indices - A Statistical Index to DC Services.
Office of Policy and Program Evaluation, Executive Office of the Mayor, One Judiciary Square, Suite 1000, 441 Fourth Street, Washington, D.C. 20001 (202) 727-4016

Indien.
Federal Statistical Office, Gustav-Stresemann-Ring 11, D-6200 Wiesbaden, Germany

Indikator ekonomi.
Biro Pusat Statistik, Jalan Dr. Sutomo 8, Jakarta, Indonesia

Indonesia Country Report.
Economist Intelligence Unit, 111 West 57th Street, New York, New York 10019 (800) 938-4685

Indonesian.
Federal Statistical Office, Gustav-Stresemann-Ring 11, D-6200 Wiesbaden, Germany

Industrial Commodity Statistics Yearbook.
Statistical Office of the United Nations, Publishing Service, New York, New York 10017 (800) 253-9646

Industrial Marketing Data and Statistics.
Euromonitor International, 60-61 Britton Street, London EC1M 5NA, England (Number in the U.S. (800) 577-EURO)

Industrial Outlook.
U.S. Department of Commerce, International Trade Administration, Fourteenth Street between Constitution Avenue and E Street, NW, Washington, D.C. 20230 (202) 482-2185

Industrial Production and Capacity Utilization.
Board of Governors of the Federal Reserve System, Twentieth Street and Constitution Avenue, NW, Washington, D.C. 20551 (202) 452-3000

Industrial Production: Quarterly Statistics.
European Community Information Service, 2100 M Street, NW, Washington, D.C. 20037 (202) 862-9500

Industrial Property Statistics.
World Intellectual Property Organization, 34 Chemin des Colombettes, CH-1211 Geneva 20, Switzerland

Industrial Statistics Yearbook.
United Nations, New York, New York (Available from UNIPUB (800) 274-4888

Industrial Structure Statistics.
Organisation for Economic Co-operation and Development (OECD), 2 rue Andre-Pascal, 75 Paris 16, France (Telephone Number in U.S. (202) 785-6323)

Inflation Measures for Schools and Colleges.
Research Associates of Washington, 1200 North Nash Street, #225, Arlington, Virginia 22209 (703) 243-3399

Information Industry Directory.

The Gale Group, 27500 Drake Road, Farmington Hills, Michigan 48331 (800) 877-4253

Information Please Almanac.
Houghton Mifflin, Boston, Massachusetts (800) 352-5455

Informe estadistico.
Direccion General de Estadistica y Censos, Instituto Nacional de Estadistica, Avenida 28 de Julio 1056, Lima 1, Peru

Inside the Recording Industry: A Statistical Overview.
Recording Industry Association of America, 1330 Connecticut Avenue, NW, Suite 300, Washington, D.C. 20036 (202) 775-0101

Instat: International Statistics Sources: Subject Guide to Sources of International Comparative Statistics
Routledge, 24 West 35th Street, New York, New York 10001 (212) 216-7843

Insurance Facts.
Insurance Information Institute, 110 William Street, New York, New York 10038 (212) 669-9200

Intergovernmental AIDS Reports.
AIDS Policy Center, Intergovernmental Health Policy Project, George Washington University, 444 North Capital Street, Suite 515, Washington, D.C. 20001 (202) 624-8698

International Business Information, How to Find It, How to Use It.
Oryx Press, Westport, Connecticut (800) 279-ORYX

International Comparisons of Manufacturing Productivity and Labor Cost Trends.
U.S. Department of Labor, Bureau of Labor Statistics, Two Massachusetts Avenue, NE, Washington, D.C. 20212 (202) 691-5200

International Crime Statistics.
International Criminal Police Organization (INTERPOL), 50 quai Achille Lignon, F-69006 Lyon, France

International Direct Investment Statistics Yearbook.
Organisation for Economic Co-operation and Development (OECD), 2 rue Andre-Pascal, 75 Paris 16, France (Telephone Number in U.S. (202) 785-6323)

International Directory of Non-Official Statistical Sources.
Euromonitor International, 60-61 Britton Street, London EC1M 5NA, England (Number in the U.S. (800) 577-EURO)

International Economic Indicators.
Center for International Business Cycle Research, Columbia University, Graduate School of Business, 808 Uris Hall, New York, New York 10027 (212) 280-2916

International Economic Indicators.
Foundation for International Business and Economic Research, 60 East 42nd Street, New York, New York 10165 (212) 983-2222

International Economic Indicators.
U.S. Department of Commerce, International Trade Administration, Fourteenth Street between Constitution Avenue and E Street, NW, Washington, D.C. 20230 (202) 482-2185

International Encyclopedia of Statistics.
Macmillan Publishing Company, New York, New York (800) 858-7674

International Energy Annual.
U.S. Department of Energy, Energy Information Administration, 1000 Independence Avenue, SW, Washington, D.C. 20585 (202) 586-8800

International Energy Review.
U.S. Department of Energy, Energy Information Administration, 1000 Independence Avenue, SW, Washington, D.C. 20585 (202) 586-8800

International Energy Statistics Sourcebook.
Penn Well Publishing Company, 1421 South Sheridan Road, Tulsa, Oklahoma 74101 (800) 752-9764

International Financial Statistics.
International Monetary Fund, 700 Nineteenth Street, NW, Washington, D.C. 20431 (202) 623-7000

International Historical Statistics, Africa and Asia.
International Labour Office, I.L.O. Publications, CH-1211, Geneva 22, Switzerland

International Historical Statistics Europe 1750-1988.
Stockton Press, New York, New York (800) 221-2123

International Historical Statistics The Americas and Australasia.
Euromonitor International, 60-61 Britton Street, London EC1M 5NA, England (Number in the U.S. (800) 577-EURO)

International Marketing Data and Statistics.
Euromonitor International, 60-61 Britton Street, London EC1M 5NA, England (Number in the U.S. (800) 577-EURO)

International Petroleum Annual.
U.S. Department of Energy, Energy Information Administration, 1000 Independence Avenue, SW, Washington, D.C. 20585 (202) 586-8800

International Science and Technology Data Update.
National Science Foundation, 4201 Wilson Boulevard, Arlington, Virginia 22230 (703) 306-1234

International Sea-Borne Trade Statistics Yearbook.
Statistical Office of the United Nations, Publishing Service, New York, New York 10017 (800) 253-9646

International Trade Statistics Yearbook.
International Monetary Fund, Nineteenth and H Streets, NW, Washington, D.C. 20431 (202) 623-7000

International Trade Statistics Yearbook.
Statistical Office of the United Nations, Publishing Service, New York, New York 10017 (800) 253-9646

Internet Access in Public Schools and Classrooms.
U.S. Department of Education, National Center for Education Statistics, 555 New Jersey Avenue, NW, Washington, D.C. 20208 (202) 219-1828

Internet Blue Pages: The Guide to Federal Government Web Sites.
Cyberage Books, Information Today, 143 Old Marlton Pike, Medford, New Jersey 08055 (609) 654-6266

The Interstudy Edge.
Interstudy, 5715 Christmas Lake, Excelsior, Minnesota 55331 (612) 474-1176

Inventory Report on Real Property Owned by the United States Throughout the World.
General Services Administration, General Services Building, Eighteenth and F Streets, NW, Washington, D.C. 20405 (202) 708-5082

Investment Statistics Locator.
Oryx Press, Westport, Connecticut (800) 279-ORYX

Iran.
Federal Statistical Office, Gustav-Stresemann-Ring 11, D-6200 Wiesbaden, Germany

Iran Country Report.
Economist Intelligence Unit, 111 West 57th Street, New York, New York 10019 (800) 938-4685

Irak.
Federal Statistical Office, Gustav-Stresemann-Ring 11, D-6200 Wiesbaden, Germany

Iraq Country Report.
Economist Intelligence Unit, 111 West 57th Street, New York, New York 10019 (800) 938-4685

Ireland Country Report.
Economist Intelligence Unit, 111 West 57th Street, New York, New York 10019 (800) 938-4685

Irish Statistical Bulletin.
Central Statistics Office, Earlsfort Terrace, Dublin 2, Ireland

The Iron and Steel Industry.
Organisation for Economic Co-operation and Development (OECD), 2 rue Andre-Pascal, 75 Paris 16, France (Telephone Number in U.S. (202) 785-6323)

Iron and Steel Statistical Yearbook.
European Community Information Service, 2100 M Street, NW, Washington, D.C. 20037 (202) 862-9500

IRS Data Book.
U.S. Department of the Treasury, Internal Revenue Service, 1111 Constitution Avenue, NW, Washington, D.C. 20224 (202) 874-0410

The Irwin Business and Investment Almanac.
Richard D. Irwin, Inc., 1333 Burr Ridge Parkway, Burr Ridge, Illinois 60521 (630) 789-4000

Israel.
Federal Statistical Office, Gustav-Stresemann-Ring 11, D-6200 Wiesbaden, Germany

Israel Country Report.
Economist Intelligence Unit, 111 West 57th Street, New York, New York 10019 (800) 938-4685

Italien.
Federal Statistical Office, Gustav-Stresemann-Ring 11, D-6200 Wiesbaden, Germany

Italy Country Report.
Economist Intelligence Unit, 111 West 57th Street, New York, New York 10019 (800) 938-4685

Jaacijfers voor Suriname.
General Bureau of Statistics, Post Office Box 244, Paramaribo, Suriname

Jail Inmates.
U.S. Department of Justice, Bureau of Justice Statistics, 810 Seventh Street, NW, Washington, D.C. 20531 (800) 732-3277

Jamaica Country Report.
Economist Intelligence Unit, 111 West 57th Street, New York, New York 10019 (800) 938-4685

Jamaika.
Federal Statistical Office, Gustav-Stresemann-Ring 11, D-6200 Wiesbaden, Germany

Jane's World Railways.
Jane's Information Group, Sentinel House, 163 Brighton Road,

Coulsdon, Surrey CR5 2NH, England

Japan.
Federal Statistical Office, Gustav-Stresemann-Ring 11, D-6200 Wiesbaden, Germany

Japan Country Report.
Economist Intelligence Unit, 111 West 57th Street, New York, New York 10019 (800) 938-4685

Japan Statistical Yearbook.
Management and Coordination Agency, Statistics Bureau, Tokyo, Japan

Joint Association Survey on Drilling Costs.
American Petroleum Institute, 1220 L Street, NW, Washington, D.C. 20005 (202) 682-8000

Jordan Country Report.
Economist Intelligence Unit, 111 West 57th Street, New York, New York 10019 (800) 938-4685

Jordanien.
Federal Statistical Office, Gustav-Stresemann-Ring 11, D-6200 Wiesbaden, Germany

Journal of Commerce.
U.S. Department of Commerce, Bureau of the Census, Washington, D.C. 20233 (301) 457-4100

Journal of Philippine Statistics.
Publications Division, Bureau of the Census and Statistics, Post Office Box 779, Manila, Philippines

Jugoslawien.
Federal Statistical Office, Gustav-Stresemann-Ring 11, D-6200 Wiesbaden, Germany

Justice Expenditure and Employment in the U.S.
U.S. Department of Justice, Bureau of Justice Statistics, 810 Seventh Street, NW, Washington, D.C. 20531 (800) 732-3277

Juvenile Court Statistics.
National Center for Juvenile Justice, 701 Forbes Avenue, Pittsburgh, Pennsylvania 15219 (412) 227-6950

Kamerun.
Federal Statistical Office, Gustav-Stresemann-Ring 11, D-6200 Wiesbaden, Germany

Kanada.
Federal Statistical Office, Gustav-Stresemann-Ring 11, D-6200 Wiesbaden, Germany

Kansas Statistical Abstract.
University of Kansas, Institute for Public Policy and Business Research, 607 Blake Hall, Lawrence, Kansas 66045-2960 (913) 864-3701

Kap Verde.
Federal Statistical Office, Gustav-Stresemann-Ring 11, D-6200 Wiesbaden, Germany

Katar.
Federal Statistical Office, Gustav-Stresemann-Ring 11, D-6200 Wiesbaden, Germany

Kazakhstan Country Report.
Economist Intelligence Unit, 111 West 57th Street, New York, New York 10019 (800) 938-4685

Kenia.
Federal Statistical Office, Gustav-Stresemann-Ring 11, D-6200 Wiesbaden, Germany

Kentucky Economic Statistics.
Department of Existing Business and Industry Capital Plaza Office Tower, Frankfort, Kentucky 40601

Kenya Country Report.
Economist Intelligence Unit, 111 West 57th Street, New York, New York 10019 (800) 938-4685

Kenya Statistical Digest.
Central Bureau of Statistics, Ministry of Economic Planning and Development, Post Office Box 30266, Nairobi, Kenya

Key Indicators of Developing Asian and Pacific Countries.
Asian Development Bank, Post Office Box 789, 1099 Manila, Philippines

Kiribati.
Federal Statistical Office, Gustav-Stresemann-Ring 11, D-6200 Wiesbaden, Germany

Kolumbien.
Federal Statistical Office, Gustav-Stresemann-Ring 11, D-6200 Wiesbaden, Germany

Kongo.
Federal Statistical Office, Gustav-Stresemann-Ring 11, D-6200 Wiesbaden, Germany

Koobaha Staatistikada.
Central Statistical Department, Post Office Box 1742, Mogadishu, Somalia

Korea Country Report.
Economist Intelligence Unit, 111 West 57th Street, New York, New York 10019 (800) 938-4685

Korea (Democratic Volksrepublic).
Federal Statistical Office, Gustav-Stresemann-Ring 11, D-6200 Wiesbaden, Germany

Korea (Republik).
Federal Statistical Office, Gustav-Stresemann-Ring 11, D-6200 Wiesbaden, Germany

Korea Statistical Yearbook.
National Statistical Office, Seoul, Korea

Kuba.
Federal Statistical Office, Gustav-Stresemann-Ring 11, D-6200 Wiesbaden, Germany

Kuwait.
Federal Statistical Office, Gustav-Stresemann-Ring 11, D-6200 Wiesbaden, Germany

Kuwait Country Report.
Economist Intelligence Unit, 111 West 57th Street, New York, New York 10019 (800) 938-4685

Kyrgyz Republic Country Report.
Economist Intelligence Unit, 111 West 57th Street, New York, New York 10019 (800) 938-4685

La Vie Economique: Rapports Economiques et de Statistique Sociale.
Office Federale de la Statistique, Hallwylstrasse 15, CH-3005 Berne, Switzerland

Labor Force Sample Survey.
European Community Information Service, 2100 M Street, NW, Washington, D.C. 20037 (202) 862-9500

Labour Force Statistics.
Organisation for Economic Co-operation and Development (OECD), 2 rue Andre-Pascal, 75 Paris 16, France (Telephone Number in U.S. (202) 785-6323)

Labour Force Survey.
Central Statistics Office, Ardee Road, Dublin 6, Ireland

Labour Statistics.
Organisation for Economic Co-operation and Development (OECD), 2 rue Andre-Pascal, 75 Paris 16, France (Telephone Number in U.S. (202) 785-6323)

LaFleur's Lottery World.
TLF Publications, Inc. (LaFleur's), Boyds, Maryland 20841 (301) 540-0123

Land Areas of the National Forest System.
U.S. Department of Agriculture, Forest Service, Post Office Box 96090, Washington, D.C. 20090 (202) 205-8333

Landshagir.
Statistical Bureau of Iceland, Skuggasund 3, 15-150, Reykjavik

Laos.
Federal Statistical Office, Gustav-Stresemann-Ring 11, D-6200 Wiesbaden, Germany

Laos Country Report.
Economist Intelligence Unit, 111 West 57th Street, New York, New York 10019 (800) 938-4685

Largest Rivers in the United States.
U.S. Department of the Interior, Geological Survey, National Center, 12201 Sunrise Valley Drive, Reston, Virginia 22092 (703) 648-4000

Latvia Country Report.
Economist Intelligence Unit, 111 West 57th Street, New York, New York 10019 (800) 938-4685

Latvijas Statistikas Gadagramata.
Latvijas Republikas Valsts Statistikas Komiteja, Riga Latvia

Law Enforcement Officers Killed and Assaulted.
U.S. Department of Justice, Federal Bureau of Investigation, 935 Pennsylvania Avenue, NW, Washington, D.C. 20535 (202) 324-3691

Lawyer Statistical Report: The U.S. Legal Profession in the 1990's.
American Bar Foundation, 750 North Lake Shore Drive, Chicago, Illinois 60611 (312) 988-6500

Layers and Egg Production - Annual.
U.S. Department of Agriculture, National Agricultural Statistics Service, Fourteenth Street and Independence Avenue, SW, Washington, D.C. 20250 (800) 727-9540

Lead and Zinc Statistics.
International Lead and Zinc Study Group, Metro House, 58 St. James's Street, London SW1A 1LD England

Learning Mathematics and Learning Science.
U.S. Department of Education, National Center of Education Statistics, 1990 K Street, NW, Washington,.D.C. 20006 (202) 502-7300.

Lebanon Country Report.
Economist Intelligence Unit, 111 West 57th Street, New York, New York

10019 (800) 938-4685

Le Cameroon en Chiffres.
Direction de la Statistique et de la Comptabilite Nationale, BP 660, Yaounde, Cameroon

L'Economie de la Tunisie en Chiffres.
Institut National de la Statistique, 27 rue du Liban, 1002 Tunis-Belvedere, Tunis, Tunisia

Les Banques Suisses.
Banque Nationale Suisse, Borsenstrasse 15 8022 Zurich, Switzerland

Lesotho.
Federal Statistical Office, Gustav-Stresemann-Ring 11, D-6200 Wiesbaden, Germany

Lesotho Country Report.
Economist Intelligence Unit, 111 West 57th Street, New York, New York 10019 (800) 938-4685

Lesotho Statistical Yearbook.
Bureau of Statistics, Post Office Box 455, Maseru 100, Lesotho

Libanon.
Federal Statistical Office, Gustav-Stresemann-Ring 11, D-6200 Wiesbaden, Germany

Liberia.
Federal Statistical Office, Gustav-Stresemann-Ring 11, D-6200 Wiesbaden, Germany

Liberia Country Report.
Economist Intelligence Unit, 111 West 57th Street, New York, New York 10019 (800) 938-4685

Library Journal.
R.R. Bowker Company, 121 Chanlon Road, New Providence, New Jersey 07974 (908) 464-6800

Libya Country Report.
Economist Intelligence Unit, 111 West 57th Street, New York, New York 10019 (800) 938-4685

Libyen.
Federal Statistical Office, Gustav-Stresemann-Ring 11, D-6200 Wiesbaden, Germany

Liechtenstein.
Federal Statistical Office, Gustav-Stresemann-Ring 11, D-6200 Wiesbaden, Germany

Life Insurance Fact Book.
American Council of Life Insurance, 1001 Pennsylvania Avenue, NW, Washington, D.C. 20004-2599 (202) 624-2000

Lithuania Country Report.
Economist Intelligence Unit, 111 West 57th Street, New York, New York 10019 (800) 938-4685

Lithuania's Statistics Yearbook.
Lithuanian Department of Statistics, Vilnius, Lithuania

Lives Saved by Child Restraints.
U.S. Department of Transportation, National Highway Traffic Safety Administration, 400 Seventh Street, SW, Washington, D.C. 20590 (202) 366-8892

Livestock and Meat Statistics.
U.S. Department of Agriculture, National Agricultural Statistics Service,

Fourteenth Street and Independence Avenue, SW, Washington, D.C. 20250 (800) 727-9540

Local Area Personal Income.
U.S. Department of Commerce, Bureau of Economic Analysis, Fourteenth Street between Constitution Avenue and E Street, NW, Washington, D.C. 20230 (202) 606-9900

Luxembourg.
Federal Statistical Office, Gustav-Stresemann-Ring 11, D-6200 Wiesbaden, Germany

Luxembourg Country Report.
Economist Intelligence Unit, 111 West 57th Street, New York, New York 10019 (800) 938-4685

Macau.
Federal Statistical Office, Gustav-Stresemann-Ring 11, D-6200 Wiesbaden, Germany

Macau Country Report.
Economist Intelligence Unit, 111 West 57th Street, New York, New York 10019 (800) 938-4685

Macedonia Country Report.
Economist Intelligence Unit, 111 West 57th Street, New York, New York 10019 (800) 938-4685

Madagascar Country Report.
Economist Intelligence Unit, 111 West 57th Street, New York, New York 10019 (800) 938-4685

Madagaskar.
Federal Statistical Office, Gustav-Stresemann-Ring 11, D-6200 Wiesbaden, Germany

Main Economic Indicators.
Organisation for Economic Co-operation and Development (OECD), 2 rue Andre-Pascal, 75 Paris 16, France (Telephone Number in U.S. (202) 785-6323)

Maine: A Statistical Summary.
Maine Department of Economic and Community Development, State House Station 59, Augusta, Maine 04333 (207) 289-2656

Major Programs of the Bureau of Labor Statistics.
U.S. Department of Labor, Bureau of Labor Statistics, Two Massachusetts Avenue, NE, Washington, D.C. 20212 (202) 691-5200

Major U.S. Statistical Series: Definitions, Publications, Limitations.
ALA Books, Chicago, Illinois (800) 545-2433

Malawi.
Federal Statistical Office, Gustav-Stresemann-Ring 11, D-6200 Wiesbaden, Germany

Malawi Country Report.
Economist Intelligence Unit, 111 West 57th Street, New York, New York 10019 (800) 938-4685

Malawi Statistical Yearbook.
National Statistical Office, Post Office Box 333, Zomba, Malawi

Malaysia.
Federal Statistical Office, Gustav-Stresemann-Ring 11, D-6200 Wiesbaden, Germany

Malediven.
Federal Statistical Office, Gustav-Stresemann-Ring 11, D-6200 Wiesbaden, Germany

Mali.
Federal Statistical Office, Gustav-Stresemann-Ring 11, D-6200 Wiesbaden, Germany

Mali Country Report.
Economist Intelligence Unit, 111 West 57th Street, New York, New York 10019 (800) 938-4685

Malta.
Federal Statistical Office, Gustav-Stresemann-Ring 11, D-6200 Wiesbaden, Germany

Malta Country Report.
Economist Intelligence Unit, 111 West 57th Street, New York, New York 10019 (800) 938-4685

Maly rocznik statystyczny.
Glowny Urzad Statystyczny (Central Statistical Office), Al Niepodleglosci 208, 00-925 Warsaw, Poland

Manufacturing and Trade Inventories and Sales.
U.S. Department of Commerce, Bureau of the Census, Washington, D.C. 20233 (301) 457-4100

Manufacturing Climate Study.
Grant/Thorton, One Prudential Plaza, Chicago, Illinois 60601 (773) 381-0790

Manufacturing Energy Consumption.
U.S. Department of Energy, Energy Information Administration, 1000 Independence Avenue, SW, Washington, D.C. 20585 (202) 586-8800

Manufacturing Profiles.
U.S. Department of Commerce, Bureau of the Census, Washington, D.C. 20233 (301) 457-4100

Maritime Transport.
European Community Information Service, 2100 M Street, NW, Washington, D.C. 20037 (202) 862-9500

Maritime Transport.
Lloyd's Register of Shipping, 17 Battery Place, New York, New York 10004 (212) 425-8050

Maritime Transport.
Organisation for Economic Co-operation and Development (OECD), 2 rue Andre-Pascal, 75 Paris 16, France (Telephone Number in U.S. (202) 785-6323)

Market Data Book.
Oncor International, 1747 Pennsylvania Avenue, NW, Suite 350, Washington, D.C. 20006 (800) 231-7224

Market Share Reports.
U.S. Department of Commerce, International Trade Administration, Fourteenth Street between Constitution Avenue and E Street, NW, Washington, D.C. 20230 (202) 482-2185

A Marketer's Guide to Discretionary Income.
U.S. Department of Commerce, Bureau of the Census, Washington, D.C. 20233 (301) 457-4100

Marketing Know-How: Your Guide to the Best Marketing Tools and Sources.
American Demographics Press, Ithaca, New York (607) 273-6343

Marketplace Update.
Access Research, Inc., 8 Griffen Road North, Windsor, Connecticut 06095 (860) 688-8821

Marokko.
Federal Statistical Office, Gustav-Stresemann-Ring 11, D-6200 Wiesbaden, Germany

Maryland Statistical Abstract.
Department of Economic and Employment Development, 217 East Redwood Street, Baltimore, Maryland 21202 Inquiries: (410) 333-6953; copies: (410) 333-6955

A Matter of Fact.
Pierian Press, Ann Arbor, Michigan (800) 678-2435

Mauretanien.
Federal Statistical Office, Gustav-Stresemann-Ring 11, D-6200 Wiesbaden, Germany

Mauritania Country Report.
Economist Intelligence Unit, 111 West 57th Street, New York, New York 10019 (800) 938-4685

Mauritius.
Federal Statistical Office, Gustav-Stresemann-Ring 11, D-6200 Wiesbaden, Germany

Mauritius Country Report.
Economist Intelligence Unit, 111 West 57th Street, New York, New York 10019 (800) 938-4685

Measuring Health Care, Expenditures, Costs, and Performance.
Organisation for Economic Cooperation and Development, (OECD), 2 rue Andre-Pascal, 75 Paris 16, France (Telephone Number in U.S. (202) 785-6323)

Meat Animals - Production, Disposition and Income.
U.S. Department of Agriculture, National Agricultural Statistics Service, Fourteenth Street and Independence Avenue, SW, Washington, D.C. 20250 (800) 727-9540

Meat Balances in OECD Member Countries.
Organisation for Economic Co-operation and Development (OECD), 2 rue Andre-Pascal, 75 Paris 16, France (Telephone Number in U.S. (202) 785-6323)

The Medicare and Medicaid Data Book.
U.S. Department of Health and Human Services, Health Care Financing Administration, 200 Independence Avenue, SW, Washington, D.C. 20201 (202) 690-6145

Medicare Program Statistics.
U.S. Department of Health and Human Services, Health Care Financing Administration, 200 Independence Avenue, SW, Washington, D.C. 20201 (202) 690-6145

Merchant Fleets of the World.
U.S. Department of Transportation, Maritime Administration, 400 Seventh Street, SW, Washington, D.C. 20590 (202) 366-5807

Merger and Corporate Transactions Database.
Thomson Financial Securities Data, 2 Gateway Center, Newark, New Jersey 07006 (973) 622-3100

Metals Week.
McGraw-Hill, Inc., 1221 Avenue of the Americas, New York, New York 10020 (800) 722-4726

Mexico Country Report.
Economist Intelligence Unit, 111 West 57th Street, New York, New York 10019 (800) 938-4685

Mexiko.

Federal Statistical Office, Gustav-Stresemann-Ring 11, D-6200 Wiesbaden, Germany

Michigan Statistical Abstract.
School of Business Administration, Bureau of Business Research, Wayne State University, Detroit, Michigan 48202

Microcomputers in Schools.
Market Data Retrieval, One Forest Parkway, Shelton, Connecticut 06484 (203) 926-4800

Middle East and North Africa.
Europa Publications, London, England (Available from The Gale Group, 27500 Drake Road, Farmington Hills, Michigan 48331 (800) 877-4253)

Military Assistance Facts.
U.S. Department of Defense, Defense Security Assistance Agency, The Pentagon, Washington, D.C. 20301-2800 (703) 604-6604

The Military Balance.
The International Institute for Strategic Studies, 23 Tavistock Street, London WC2E 7NQ, England

The Military Budget and National Economic Priorities.
U.S. Congress, Joint Economic Committee, U.S. Capitol Building, Washington, D.C. 20515

Milk Cows and Production, Final Estimates.
U.S. Department of Agriculture, National Agricultural Statistics Service, 14th Street and Independence Avenue, SW, Washington, D.C. 20250 (800) 727-9540

Milk, Milk Products and Egg Balances in OECD Member Countries.
Organisation for Economic Co-operation and Development (OECD), 2 rue Andre-Pascal, 75 Paris 16, France (Telephone Number in U.S. (202) 785-6323)

Milk Production, Disposition and Income.
U.S. Department of Agriculture, National Agricultural Statistics Service, Fourteenth Street and Independence Avenue, SW, Washington, D.C. 20250 (800) 727-9540

Mineral Commodity Summaries.
U.S. Department of the Interior, Geological Survey, Office of Minerals Information, 12201 Sunrise Valley Drive, Reston, VA 20292 (703) 648-4000

Mineral Facts and Problems.
U.S. Department of the Interior, Geological Survey, Office of Minerals Information, 12201 Sunrise Valley Drive, Reston, VA 22092 (703) 648-4000

Minerals Yearbook.
U.S. Department of the Interior, Geological Survey, Office of Minerals Information, 12201 Sunrise Valley Drive, Reston, VA 22092 (703) 648-4000

Minimum Wage and Maximum Hours Standards Under the Fair Labor Standards Act.
U.S. Department of Labor, Employment Standards Administration, 200 Constitution Avenue, NW, Washington, D.C. 20210 (202) 219-6050

Minnesota Population and Household Estimates.
Office of State Demographer, State Planning Agency, 300 Centennial Building, Saint Paul, Minnesota 55155 (612) 296-2557

Minority Owned Businesses.
U.S. Department of Commerce, Bureau of the Census, Washington, D.C. 20233 (301) 457-4100

Mississippi Statistical Abstract.
Mississippi State University, College of Business and Industry, Division of Research, Mississippi State, Mississippi 39762 (601) 325-3817

Moldova Country Report.
Economist Intelligence Unit, 111 West 57th Street, New York, New York 10019 (800) 938-4685

Money and Finance.
European Community Information Service, 2100 M Street, NW, Washington, D.C. 20037 (202) 862-9500

Money Stock, Liquid Assets, and Debt Measures.
Board of Governors of the Federal Reserve System, Twentieth Street and Constitution Avenue, NW, Washington, D.C. 20551 (202) 452-3000

Mongolei.
Federal Statistical Office, Gustav-Stresemann-Ring 11, D-6200 Wiesbaden, Germany

Mongolia Country Report.
Economist Intelligence Unit, 111 West 57th Street, New York, New York 10019 (800) 938-4685

Montana County Profiles.
Montana Department of Commerce, Census and Economic Information Center, Capitol Station, Helena, Montana 59620 (406) 444-2896

Monthly Abstract of Statistics.
Government Bookshop, Mulgrave Street, Wellington, New Zealand

Monthly Bulletin of Statistics.
Central Bureau of Statistics, Hakirya, Romema, Jerusalem, Israel

Monthly Bulletin of Statistics.
National Statistical Office, Post Office Box 333, Zomba, Malawi

Monthly Bulletin of Statistics.
Statistical Office of the United Nations, Publishing Service, New York, New York 10017 (800) 253-9646

Monthly Commodity Price Bulletin.
United Nations, Geneva, Switzerland (800) 253-9646

Monthly Digest of Statistics.
Barbados Statistical Service, Third Floor, National Insurance Building, Fairchild Street, Bridgetown, Barbados

Monthly Digest of Statistics.
Central Statistical Office, Post Office Box 8063, Causeway, Harare, Zimbabwe

Monthly Digest of Statistics.
Central Statistical Office, Post Office Box 31908, Lusaka, Zambia

Monthly Digest of Statistics.
Central Statistical Office, Post Office Box 26188, Safat, Kuwait

Monthly Digest of Statistics.
Department of Statistics, 8 Shenton Way 10-01, Treasury Building, Singapore, 0106

Monthly Digest of Statistics.
HM Stationery Office, Post Office Box 276, London SW8 5DT, England

Monthly Energy Review.
U.S. Department of Energy, Energy Information Administration, 1000 Independence Avenue, SW, Washington, D.C. 20585 (202) 586-8800

Monthly Failure Report.
Dun and Bradstreet Corporation, One Diamond Hill Road, Murray Hill, New Jersey 07974 (908) 665-5000

Monthly Industrial Survey.
Confederation of Irish Industry, Confederation House, Kildare Street, Dublin 2, Ireland

Monthly Labor Review.
U.S. Department of Labor, Bureau of Labor Statistics, Two Massachusetts Avenue, NE, Washington, D.C. 20212 (202) 691-5200

Monthly Product Announcement.
U.S. Department of Commerce, Bureau of the Census, Washington, D.C. 20233 (301) 457-4100

Monthly Retail Trade Report.
U.S. Department of Commerce, Bureau of the Census, Washington, D.C. 20233 (301) 457-4100

Monthly Statistical Bulletin.
National Statistical Service of Greece, 14-1G Lycourgou Street, Athens 112, Greece

Monthly Statistical Bulletin of Bangladesh.
Bureau of Statistics, Bangladesh Secretariat School Building, Dacca, Bangladesh

Monthly Statistics of Foreign Trade.
Organisation for Economic Co-operation and Development, (OECD), 2 rue Andre-Pascal, 75 Paris 16, France (Telephone Number in U.S. (202) 785-6323)

Monthly Statistics of Japan.
Management and Coordination Agency, Statistics Bureau, Tokyo, Japan

Monthly Statistics of Korea.
National Statistical Office, Seoul, Korea

Monthly Statistics of the Republic of China.
Directorate - General of Budget, Accounting and Statistics, Executive Yuan, Republic of China

Monthly Summary of Statistics.
Australian Bureau of Statistics, Post Office Box 10, Belconnen, Canberra ACT 2616, Australia

Morbidity and Mortality Weekly Report.
U.S. Department of Health and Human Services, Centers for Disease Control, 1600 Clifton Road, NE, Atlanta, Georgia 30333 (800) 331-3435

Morocco Country Report.
Economist Intelligence Unit, 111 West 57th Street, New York, New York 10019 (800) 938-4685

Motor Vehicles Defect Recall Campaigns.
U.S. Department of Transportation, National Highway Traffic Safety Administration, 400 Seventh Street, SW, Washington, D.C. 20590 (202) 366-8892

Mosambik.
Federal Statistical Office, Gustav-Stresemann-Ring 11, D-6200 Wiesbaden, Germany

Mozambique Country Report.
Economist Intelligence Unit, 111 West 57th Street, New York, New York 10019 (800) 938-4685

MSA Profile Metropolitan Area Forecasts to 2020.

Woods and Poole Economics, Inc., Washington, D.C. (800) 786-1915

Multimedia Audiences.
Mediamark Research Inc., 708 Third Avenue, New York, New York 10017 (212) 599-0444

Municipal New Issues Database.
Thomson Financial Securities Data, 2 Gateway Center, Newark, New Jersey 07006 (973) 622-3100

Mutual Fund Fact Book.
Investment Company Institute, 1401 H Street, NW, Suite 600, Washington, D.C. 20005 (202) 326-5800

Myanmar Country Report.
Economist Intelligence Unit, 111 West 57th Street, New York, New York 10019 (800) 938-4685

NADA Data.
National Automobile Dealers Association, 8400 Westpark Drive, McLean, Virginia 22102 (703) 821-7000

NASA News.
National Aeronautics and Space Administration, 300 E Street, SW, Washington, D.C. 20546 (202) 358-1000

NASBO State Expenditure Report.
National Association of State Budget Officers,, Hall of the States, 444 North Capitol Street, NW, Suite 642, Washington, D.C. 20001 (202) 624-5382

NFPA Reports on U.S. Fire Loss.
National Fire Protection Association, One Batterymarch Park, Post Office Box 9101, Quincy, Massachusetts 02269-9101 (617) 770-3000

NLN Data Book.
National League for Nursing, 61 Broadway, 33rd Floor, New York, New York 10006 (212) 363-5555

Namibia.
Federal Statistical Office, Gustav-Stresemann-Ring 11, D-6200 Wiesbaden, Germany

Namibia Country Report.
Economist Intelligence Unit, 111 West 57th Street, New York, New York 10019 (800) 938-4685

Narodnoe Khoziaistvo Rossiiskoi Federatsii: Statisticheskii Ezhegodnik.
Gosudarstvennyi komitet Rossiiskoi Federatsii po Statistike, Moscow, Russia

Narodnoye Khozyaystvo SSR: Statisticheskiy Yezhegodnik.
Central Statistical Board of the Council of Ministers of the Soviet Union, Moscow, Russia

National Accounts.
Organisation for Economic Co-operation and Development (OECD), 2 rue Andre-Pascal, 75 Paris 16, France (Telephone Number in U.S. (202) 785-6323)

National Accounts of OECD Countries.
Organisation for Economic Co-operation and Development, (OECD), 2 rue Andre-Pascal, 75 Paris 16, France (Telephone Number in U.S. (202) 785-6323)

National Accounts Statistics.
Statistical Office of the United Nations, Publishing Service, New York, New York 10017 (800) 253-9646

National Air Pollutant Emission Trends.

Environmental Protection Agency, 1200 Pennsylvania Avenue, NW, Washington, D.C. 20460 (888) 372-8255

National Air Quality and Emissions Trends Report.
Environmental Protection Agency, 1200 Pennsylvania Avenue, NW, Washington, D.C. 20460 (888) 372-8255

National Ambient Air Quality and Emissions Trends Report.
Environmental Protection Agency, 1200 Pennsylvania Avenue, NW, Washington, D.C. 20460 (888) 372-8255

National Analysis of Official Child Neglect and Abuse Reporting.
American Humane Association, Animal Protection Division, 63 Inverness Drive, East, Englewood, Colorado 80112 (303) 792-9900

National Archive of Criminal Justice Data.
Sponsored by the Bureau of Justice Statistics, U.S. Department of Justice, and operated by the Inter-University Consortium for Political and Social Research, Washington, D.C. (800) 999-0960

National Child Abuse and Neglect Data System, Working Paper 2, Summary Data Component.
U.S. Department of Health and Human Services, National Center on Child Abuse and Neglect, 370 L'Enfant Promenade, SW, Washington, D.C. 20447 (202) 205-8586

National College - Bound Senior.
College Entrance Examination Board, 45 Columbus Avenue, New York, New York 10017 (212) 713-8000

National Credit Union Administration Year-End Statistics.
National Credit Union Administration, 1775 Duke Street, Alexandria, Virginia 22314-3428 (703) 518-6300

The National Data Book of Foundations.
The Foundation Center, 79 Fifth Avenue, New York, New York 10003 (212) 620-4230

National Delinquency Survey.
Mortgage Bankers Association of America, 1125 15th Street, NW, Washington, D.C. 20005 (202) 861-6500

National Development Plan.
Statistics Office, Ministry of Finance, Post Office Box 67, Bariki, Tarawa, Kiribati

National Economy of the MPR for 60 Years.
Central Statistical Office, Ulan Bator, Mongolia

National Economy of the Republic of Belarus.
State Committee of the Republic of Belarus on Statistics and Analysis, Minsk, Belarus

National Food Review.
U.S. Department of Agriculture, Economic Research Service, 1800 M Street, NW, Washington, D.C. 20036 (202) 694-4040

National Gardening Survey.
National Gardening Association, 1100 Dorset Street, South, Burlington, Vermont 05403 (802) 863-5215

National Health Interview Survey.
U.S. Department of Health and Human Services, National Center for Health Statistics, 3700 East-West Highway, Hyattsville, Maryland 20782 (301) 436-8500

National Household Education Survey.
U.S. Department of Education, 400 Maryland Avenue, SW, Washington, D.C. 20202 (877) 424-1616

National Household Survey on Drug Abuse.
U.S. Department of Health and Human Services, Substance Abuse and Mental Health Services Administration, 5600 Fishers Lane, Rockville, Maryland 20857 (800) 729-6686

The National Income and Product Accounts of the United States.
U.S. Department of Commerce, Bureau of Economic Analysis, Fourteenth Street between Constitution Avenue and E Street, NW, Washington, D.C. 20230 (202) 606-9900

National League Green Book.
National League of Professional Baseball Clubs, 245 Park Avenue, 28th Floor, New York, New York 10167 (212) 931-7700

National Park Statistical Abstract.
U.S. Department of the Interior, National Park Service, C Street between Eighteenth and Nineteenth Streets, NW, Washington D.C. 20240 (202) 208-6843

The National Parks: Index.
U.S. Department of the Interior, National Park Service, C Street between Eighteenth and Nineteenth Streets, NW, Washington, D.C. 20240 (202) 208-6843

National Patterns of Science and Technology Resources.
National Science Foundation, 4201 Wilson Boulevard, Arlington, Virginia 22230 (703) 306-1234

National Payroll Hours.
U.S. Postal Service, 475 L'Enfant Plaza West, SW, Washington, D.C. 20260-0010 (202) 268-2000

National Restaurant Association Foodservice Industry Forecast.
National Restaurant Association, 1200 Seventeenth Street, NW, Washington, D.C. 20036 (202) 331-5900

National Roster of Hispanic Elected Officials.
National Association of Latino Elected and Appointed Officials, 311 Massachusetts Avenue, NE, Washington, D.C. 20002 (202) 546-2536

National Study on Child Neglect and Abuse Reporting.
American Humane Association, Animal Protection Division, 63 Inverness Drive, East, Englewood, Colorado 80112 (303) 792-9900

National Survey of Hunting, Fishing, and Wildlife - Associated Recreation.
U.S. Department of the Interior, Fish and Wildlife Service, C Street between Eighteenth and Nineteenth Streets, NW, Washington, D.C. 20240 (202) 208-5634

National Survey of Salaries and Wages in Public Schools.
Educational Research Service, 2000 Clarendon Boulevard, Arlington, Virginia 22201 (703) 243-2100

National Trade Data Bank: The Export Connection on CD-ROM.
U.S. Department of Commerce, International Trade Administration, Fourteenth Street between Constitution Avenue and E Street, NW, Washington, D.C. 20230 (202) 482-2185

National Transportation Statistics.
U.S. Department of Transportation, Bureau of Transportation Statistics, 400 Seventh Street, SW, Washington, D.C. 20590 (800) 853-1351

National Vital Statistics Report.
U.S. Department of Health and Human Services, National Center for Health Statistics, 3700 East-West Highway, Hyattsville, Maryland 20782 (301) 436-8500

Nations Within a Nation.
Greenwood Publishing Group, Westport, Connecticut (800) 225-5800

Natural Gas Annual.
U.S. Department of Energy, Energy Information Administration, 1000 Independence Avenue, SW, Washington, D.C. 20585 (202) 586-8800

Natural Gas Monthly.
U.S. Department of Energy, Energy Information Administration, 1000 Independence Avenue, SW, Washington, D.C. 20585 (202) 586-8800

Nauru.
Federal Statistical Office, Gustav-Stresemann-Ring 11, D-6200 Wiesbaden, Germany

NCJRS Electronic Bulletin Board.
U.S. Department of Justice, National Criminal Justice Reference Service, 1600 Research Boulevard, Rockville, Maryland 20850 (800) 732-3277 (Access by modem on (301) 738-8895)

Nebraska Statistical Handbook.
Department of Economic Development, Division of Research, Box 94666, Lincoln, Nebraska 68509 (402) 471-3779

Nepal.
Federal Statistical Office, Gustav-Stresemann-Ring 11, D-6200 Wiesbaden, Germany

Nepal Country Report.
Economist Intelligence Unit, 111 West 57th Street, New York, New York 10019 (800) 938-4685

Netherlands Country Report.
Economist Intelligence Unit, 111 West 57th Street, New York, New York 10019 (800) 938-4685

Netherlands Antilles Country Report.
Economist Intelligence Unit, 111 West 57th Street, New York, New York 10019 (800) 938-4685

Nevada Statistical Abstract.
Department of Administration, Planning Division, Capitol Complex, Carson City, Nevada 89710 (702) 687-4065

New Book of American Rankings, The.
Facts on File, 460 Park Avenue, South, New York, New York (212) 967-8800

New Business Incorporations.
Dun and Bradstreet Corporation, One Diamond Hill Road, Murray Hill, New Jersey 07974 (908) 665-5000

New Caledonia Country Report.
Economist Intelligence Unit, 111 West 57th Street, New York, New York 10019 (800) 938-4685

New Hebrides Anglo-French Condominium: Report for the Year.
HM Stationery Office, Post Office Box 569, London SE1, England

New Jersey Source Book.
New Jersey State Data Center, New Jersey Department of Labor, CN 388, Trenton, New Jersey 08625-0388 (609) 984-2593

New Jersey Statistical Factbook.
New Jersey State Data Center, New Jersey Department of Labor, CN 388, Trenton, New Jersey 08625-0388 (609) 984-2593

The New Latin American Market Atlas.
The Economist Intelligence Unit, 111 West 57th Street, New York, New York 10019 (800) 938-4685

New Mexico Statistical Abstract.
University of New Mexico, Bureau of Business and Economic

Research, Albuquerque, New Mexico 87131 (505) 277-2216

New Motorcycle Registrations by States.
R.L. Polk and Company, 26955 Norwestern Highway, Southfield, Michigan 48034 (248) 728-7000

New One-Family Houses Sold and For Sale.
U.S. Department of Commerce, Bureau of the Census, Washington, D.C. 20233 (301) 457-4100

New Ship Construction.
U.S. Department of Transportation, Maritime Administration, 400 Seventh Street, SW, Washington, D.C. 20590 (202) 366-5807

New York State Statistical Yearbook.
Nelson Rockefeller Institute of Government, 411 State Street, Albany, New York 12203 (518) 472-1300

New Zealand Country Report.
Economist Intelligence Unit, 111 West 57th Street, New York, New York 10019 (800) 938-4685

New Zealand Official Yearbook.
Government Bookshop, Mulgrave Street, Wellington, New Zealand

New Zealand Pocket Digest of Statistics.
Government Bookshop, Mulgrave Street, Wellington, New Zealand

News.
U.S. Department of Labor, Bureau of Labor Statistics, Two Massachusetts Avenue, NE, Washington, D.C. 20212 (202) 691-5200

Nicaragua.
Federal Statistical Office, Gustav-Stresemann-Ring 11, D-6200 Wiesbaden, Germany

Nicaragua Country Report.
Economist Intelligence Unit, 111 West 57th Street, New York, New York 10019 (800) 938-4685

Niederlands.
Federal Statistical Office, Gustav-Stresemann-Ring 11, D-6200 Wiesbaden, Germany

Nien-Giam Thong-Ke.
General Statistical Office, 2 Hoang Van Thu Street, Hanoi, Socialist Republic of Vietnam

Niger.
Federal Statistical Office, Gustav-Stresemann-Ring 11, D-6200 Wiesbaden, Germany

Niger Country Report.
Economist Intelligence Unit, 111 West 57th Street, New York, New York 10019 (800) 938-4685

Nigeria.
Federal Statistical Office, Gustav-Stresemann-Ring 11, D-6200 Wiesbaden, Germany

Nigeria Country Report.
Economist Intelligence Unit, 111 West 57th Street, New York, New York 10019 (800) 938-4685

The Non-Ferrous Metals Industry.
Organisation for Economic Co-operation and Development (OECD), 2 rue Andre-Pascal, 75 Paris 16, France (Telephone Number in U.S. (202) 785-6323)

Non-Voter Study.

Committee for the Study of the American Electorate, 421 New Jersey Avenue, SE, Washington, D.C. 20003 (202) 546-3221

Noncitrus Fruit and Nuts.
U.S. Department of Agriculture, National Agricultural Statistics Service, Fourteenth Street and Independence Avenue, SW, Washington, D.C. 20250 (800) 727-9540

Nonresidential Buildings Energy Consumption Survey: Characteristics of Commercial Buildings.
U.S. Department of Energy, Energy Information Administration, 1000 Independence Avenue, SW, Washington, D.C. 20585 (202) 586-8800

Nonresidential Buildings Energy Consumption Survey: Commercial Buildings, Consumption and Expenditures.
U.S. Department of Energy, Energy Information Administration, 1000 Independence Avenue, SW, Washington, D.C. 20585 (202) 586-8800

Norway Country Report.
Economist Intelligence Unit, 111 West 57th Street, New York, New York 10019 (800) 938-4685

Norwegen.
Federal Statistical Office, Gustav-Stresemann-Ring 11, D-6200 Wiesbaden, Germany

Note Annuelle de Statistique.
Direction de la Satistique et de la Comptabilite Nationale, BP 660, Yaounde, Cameroon

Nucleonics Week.
McGraw-Hill, Inc., 1221 Avenue of the Americas, New York, New York 10020 (800) 722-4726

Numeric Databases.
Ablex Publishing Corporation, Norwood, New Jersey (201) 767-8450

OECD Economic Outlook.
Organisation for Economic Co-operation and Development (OECD), 2 rue Andre-Pascal, 75 Paris 16, France (Telephone Number in U.S. (202) 785-6323)

OECD Economic Surveys.
Organisation for Economic Co-operation and Development (OECD), 2 rue Andre-Pascal, 75 Paris 16, France (Telephone Number in U.S. (202) 785-6323)

OECD Economic Surveys: Australia.
Organisation for Economic Co-operation and Development (OECD), 2 rue Andre-Pascal, 75 Paris 16, France (Telephone Number in U.S. (202) 785-6323)

OECD Economic Surveys: Austria.
Organisation for Economic Co-operation and Development (OECD), 2 rue Andre-Pascal, 75 Paris 16, France (Telephone Number in U.S. (202) 785-6323)

OECD Economic Surveys: Belgium-Luxembourg.
Organisation for Economic Co-operation and Development (OECD), 2 rue Andre-Pascal, 75 Paris 16, France (Telephone Number in U.S. (202) 785-6323)

OECD Economic Surveys: Canada.
Organisation for Economic Co-operation and Development (OECD), 2 rue Andre-Pascal, 75 Paris 16, France (Telephone Number in U.S. (202) 785-6323)

OECD Economic Surveys: Denmark.
Organisation for Economic Co-operation and Development (OECD), 2 rue Andre-Pascal, 75 Paris 16, France (Telephone Number in U.S. (202)

785-6323)

OECD Economic Surveys: Finland.
Organisation for Economic Co-operation and Development (OECD), 2 rue Andre-Pascal, 75 Paris 16, France (Telephone Number in U.S. (202) 785-6323)

OECD Economic Surveys: France.
Organisation for Economic Co-operation and Development (OECD), 2 rue Andre-Pascal, 75 Paris 16, France (Telephone Number in U.S. (202) 785-6323)

OECD Economic Surveys: Germany.
Organisation for Economic Co-operation and Development (OECD), 2 rue Andre-Pascal, 75 Paris 16, France (Telephone Number in U.S. (202) 785-6323)

OECD Economic Surveys: Greece.
Organisation for Economic Co-operation and Development (OECD), 2 rue Andre-Pascal, 75 Paris 16, France (Telephone Number in U.S. (202) 785-6323)

OECD Economic Surveys: Iceland.
Organisation for Economic Co-operation and Development (OECD), 2 rue Andre-Pascal, 75 Paris 16, France (Telephone Number in U.S. (202) 785-6323)

OECD Economic Surveys: Ireland.
Organisation for Economic Co-operation and Development (OECD), 2 rue Andre-Pascal, 75 Paris 16, France (Telephone Number in U.S. (202) 785-6323)

OECD Economic Surveys: Italy.
Organisation for Economic Co-operation and Development (OECD), 2 rue Andre-Pascal, 75 Paris 16, France (Telephone Number in U.S. (202) 785-6323)

OECD Economic Surveys: Japan.
Organisation for Economic Co-operation and Development (OECD), 2 rue Andre-Pascal, 75 Paris 16, France (Telephone Number in U.S. (202) 785-6323)

OECD Economic Surveys: Netherlands.
Organisation for Economic Co-operation and Development (OECD), 2 rue Andre-Pascal, 75 Paris 16, France (Telephone Number in U.S. (202) 785-6323)

OECD Economic Surveys: New Zealand.
Organisation for Economic Co-operation and Development (OECD), 2 rue Andre-Pascal, 75 Paris 16, France (Telephone Number in U.S. (202) 785-6323)

OECD Economic Surveys: Norway.
Organisation for Economic Co-operation and Development (OECD), 2 rue Andre-Pascal, 75 Paris 16, France (Telephone Number in U.S. (202) 785-6323)

OECD Economic Surveys: Portugal.
Organisation for Economic Co-operation and Development (OECD), 2 rue Andre-Pascal, 75 Paris 16, France (Telephone Number in U.S. (202) 785-6323)

OECD Economic Surveys: Spain.
Organisation for Economic Co-operation and Development (OECD), 2 rue Andre-Pascal, 75 Paris 16, France (Telephone Number in U.S. (202) 785-6323)

OECD Economic Surveys: Sweden.
Organisation for Economic Co-operation and Development (OECD), 2 rue Andre-Pascal, 75 Paris 16, France (Telephone Number in U.S.

(202) 785-6323)

OECD Economic Surveys: Switzerland.
Organisation for Economic Co-operation and Development (OECD), 2 rue Andre-Pascal, 75 Paris 16, France (Telephone Number in U.S. (202) 785-6323)

OECD Economic Surveys: Turkey.
Organisation for Economic Co-operation and Development (OECD), 2 rue Andre-Pascal, 75 Paris 16, France (Telephone Number in U.S. (202) 785-6323)

OECD Economic Surveys: United Kingdom.
Organisation for Economic Co-operation and Development (OECD), 2 rue Andre-Pascal, 75 Paris 16, France (Telephone Number in U.S. (202) 785-6323)

OECD Employment Outlook.
Organisation for Economic Co-operation and Development (OECD), 2 rue Andre-Pascal, 75 Paris 16, France (Telephone Number in U.S. (202) 785-6323)

OECD Environmental Data.
Organisation for Economic Co-operation and Development (OECD), 2 rue Andre-Pascal, 75 Paris 16, France (Telephone Number in U.S. (202) 785-6323)

OECD Financial Statistics.
Organisation for Economic Co-operation and Development (OECD), 2 rue Andre-Pascal, 75 Paris 16, France (Telephone Number in U.S. (202) 785-6323)

OECD Health Systems: Facts and Trends.
Organisation for Economic Co-operation and Development (OECD), 2 rue Andre-Pascal, 75 Paris 16, France (Telephone Number in U.S. (202) 785-6323)

OECD Import-Export Mocrotables.
Organisation for Economic Co-operation and Development (OECD), 2 rue Andre-Pascal, 75 Paris 16, France (Telephone Number in U.S. (202) 785-6323)

OECD Industrial Structure Statistics.
Organisation for Economic Co-Operation and Development (OECD), 2 rue Andre-Pascal, 75 Paris 16, France (Telephone Number in U.S. (202) 785-6323)

OECD Main Science and Technology Indicators.
Organisation for Economic Co-operation and Development (OECD), 2 rue Andre-Pascal, 75 Paris 16, France (Telephone Number in U.S. (202) 785-6323)

OERI Electronic Bulletin Board.
U.S. Department of Education, Office of Educational Research and Improvement, 400 Maryland Avenue, SW, Washington, D.C. 20202 (877) 424-1616

OPEC Annual Statistical Bulletin.
Organization of Petroleum Exporting Countries, Obere Donaustrasse 93, 1020 Vienna 2, Austria

Occupational Injuries and Illnesses in the U.S. by Industry.
U.S. Department of Labor, Bureau of Labor Statistics, Two Massachusetts Avenue, NE, Washington, D.C. 20212 (202) 691-5200

Occupations of Federal White-Collar and Blue- Collar Workers.
Office of Personnel Management, 1900 E Street, NW, Washington, D.C. 20415 (202) 606-1800

Office Market Data Book.

ONCOR International, 1747 Pennsylvania Avenue, NW, Suite 350, Washington, D.C. 20006 (800) 231-7224

Official Guard and Reserve Manpower Strengths and Statistics.
U.S. Department of Defense, Office of the Secretary, The Pentagon, Washington, D.C. 20301 (703) 545-6700

The Official Guide to American Incomes.
New Strategist, Ithaca, New York (607) 273-0913

The Official Guide to Racial and Ethnic Diversity.
New Strategist, Ithaca, New York (607) 273-0913

Official Professional Rodeo Media Guide.
Professional Rodeo Cowboys Association, 101 Prorodeo Drive, Colorado Springs, Colorado 80910 (719) 593-8840

Oil and Gas Information.
Organisation for Economic Co-operation and Development (OECD), 2 rue Andre-Pascal, 75 Paris 16, France (Telephone Number in U.S. (202) 785-6323)

Oil and Gas Journal.
Penn Well Publishing Company, 1421 South Sheridan Road, Tulsa, Oklahoma 74101 (800) 752-9764

Oil Statistics.
Organisation for Economic Co-operation and Development (OECD), 2 rue Andre-Pascal, 75 Paris 16, France (Telephone Number in U.S. (202) 785-6323)

Okonomisk utsyn.
Statistisk Sentralbyra (Central Bureau of Statistics), Skippergate 15, P.B. 8131, DEP N-0033, Oslo 1, Norway

Oman.
Federal Statistical Office, Gustav-Stresemann-Ring 11, D-6200 Wiesbaden, Germany

Oman Country Report.
Economist Intelligence Unit, 111 West 57th Street, New York, New York 10019 (800) 938-4685

Open Doors.
Institute of International Education, 809 United Nations Plaza, New York, New York 10017 (212) 984-5400

Opera America Profile.
Opera America, 1156 Fifteenth Street, NW, Suite 810, Washington, D.C. 20005 (202) 293-4466

Oregon Blue Book.
Oregon Secretary of State, State Capitol Building, Salem, Oregon 97310

Osterreich.
Federal Statistical Office, Gustav-Stresemann-Ring 11, D-6200 Wiesbaden, Germany

PTV Programming Survey.
Corporation for Public Broadcasting, 901 E Street, NW, Washington, D.C. 20004-2006 (202) 879-9600

The Pacific Basin: An Economic Handbook.
Euromonitor International, 60-61 Britton Street, London EC1M 5NA, England (Number in the U.S. (800) 577-EURO)

Pacific Islands Country Report.
Economist Intelligence Unit, 111 West 57th Street, New York, New York 10019 (800) 938-4685

Pakistan.
Federal Statistical Office, Gustav-Stresemann-Ring 11, D-6200 Wiesbaden, Germany

Pakistan Country Report.
Economist Intelligence Unit, 111 West 57th Street, New York, New York 10019 (800) 938-4685

Palau Country Report.
Economist Intelligence Unit, 111 West 57th Street, New York, New York 10019 (800) 938-4685

Palestinian Statistical Abstract.
Palestine Liberation Organization, Economic Department, Central Bureau of Statistics, Damascus, Syria

Panama.
Federal Statistical Office, Gustav-Stresemann-Ring 11, D-6200 Wiesbaden, Germany

Panama Country Report.
Economist Intelligence Unit, 111 West 57th Street, New York, New York 10019 (800) 938-4685

Panama en Cifras.
Direccion de Estadistica y Censo, Apartado 5213, Panama 5 RP, Panama

Papua-Neuguinea.
Federal Statistical Office, Gustav-Stresemann-Ring 11, D-6200 Wiesbaden, Germany

Papua New Guinea Country Report.
Economist Intelligence Unit, 111 West 57th Street, New York, New York 10019 (800) 938-4685

Paraguay.
Federal Statistical Office, Gustav-Stresemann-Ring 11, D-6200 Wiesbaden, Germany

Paraguay Country Report.
Economist Intelligence Unit, 111 West 57th Street, New York, New York 10019 (800) 938-4685

Patenting Trends in the United States, State Country Report.
U.S. Department of Commerce, Patent and Trademark Office, 2121 Crystal Drive, Arlington, Virginia 22202 (703) 305-8341

Pay Structure of the Federal Civil Service.
Office of Personnel Management, 1900 E Street, NW, Washington, D.C. 20415 (202) 606-1800

Payload Flight Assignments NASA Mixed Fleets.
National Aeronautics and Space Administration, 300 E Street, SW, Washington, D.C. 20546 (202) 358-1000

Pennsylvania Statistical Abstract.
Pennsylvania State Data Center, Pennsylvania State University of Harrisburg, 777 West Harrisburg Pike, Middleton, Pennsylvania 15057

Performance Profiles of Major Energy Producers.
U.S. Department of Energy, Energy Information Administration, 1000 Independence Avenue, SW Washington, D.C. 20585 (202) 586-8800

Peru.
Federal Statistical Office, Gustav-Stresemann-Ring 11, D-6200 Wiesbaden, Germany

Peru Country Report.
Economist Intelligence Unit, 111 West 57th Street, New York, New York

10019 (800) 938-4685

Petroleum Marketing Monthly.
U.S. Department of Energy, Energy Information Administration, 1000 Independence Avenue, SW, Washington, D.C. 20585 (202) 586-8800

Petroleum Statement Annual.
U.S. Department of Energy, Energy Information Administration, 1000 Independence Avenue, SW Washington, D.C. 20585 (202) 586-8800

Petroleum Supply Annual.
U.S. Department of Energy, Energy Information Administration, 1000 Independence Avenue, SW, Washington, D.C. 20585 (202) 586-8800

Petroleum Supply Monthly.
U.S. Department of Energy, Energy Information Administration, 100 Independence Avenue, SW, Washington, D.C. 20585 (202) 586-8800

Philippine.
Federal Statistical Office, Gustav-Stresemann-Ring 11, D-6200 Wiesbaden, Germany

Philippine Statistical Yearbook.
Publications Division, Bureau of the Census and Statistics, Post Office Box 779, Manila, Philippines

Philippines Country Report.
Economist Intelligence Unit, 111 West 57th Street, New York, New York 10019 (800) 938-4685

Physician Characteristics and Distribution in the United States.
American Medical Association, 515 North State Street, Chicago, Illinois 60610 (312) 464-5000

Places, Towns, and Townships.
Bernan Press, Lanham, Maryland (800) 865-3457

Plant and Equipment Expenditures and Plans.
U.S. Department of Commerce, Bureau of the Census, Washington, D.C. 20233 (301) 457-4100

Pocket Statistics.
National Aeronautics and Space Administration, 300 E Street, SW, Washington, D.C. 20546 (202) 358-1000

Pocket Year Book Australia.
Australian Bureau of Statistics, Post Office Box 10, Belconnen, Canberra ACT 2616, Australia

Poland Country Report.
Economist Intelligence Unit, 111 West 57th Street, New York, New York 10019 (800) 938-4685

Polen.
Federal Statistical Office, Gustav-Stresemann-Ring 11, D-6200 Wiesbaden, Germany

Population Abstract of the United States.
Documents Index, Manassas, Virginia (800) 899-4988

Population and Vital Statistics Report.
Statistical Office of the United Nations, Publishing Service, New York, New York 10017 (800) 253-9646

Population-at-Risk Rates and Selected Crime Indicators.
U.S. Department of Justice, U.S. Federal Bureau of Investigation, Federal Bureau of Investigation, 935 Pennsylvania Avenue, NW, Washington, D.C. 20535 (202) 324-3691

Population Estimates for New Hampshire Cities and Towns, New

Hampshire Population Projections for Cities and Towns.
Office of State Planning, 2 1/2 Beacon Street, Concord, New Hampshire 03301 (603) 271-2155

Population Index.
Office of Population Research, Princeton University and the Population Association of America, Princeton, New Jersey (609) 258-4873

Population Information in Twentieth Century Census Volumes: 1950-1980.
Oryx Press, Westport, Connecticut (800) 279-ORYX

Population of the United States.
Macmillan Publishing Company, New York, New York (800) 858-7674

Population Trends for Washington State.
Washington State Office of Financial Management, Forecasting Division, Post Office Box 43113, Olympia, Washington 98504-3113 (360) 902-0599

Portugal.
Federal Statistical Office, Gustav-Stresemann-Ring 11, D-6200 Wiesbaden, Germany

Portugal Country Report.
Economist Intelligence Unit, 111 West 57th Street, New York, New York 10019 (800) 938-4685

Poultry - Production and Value.
U.S. Department of Agriculture, National Agricultural Statistics Service, Fourteenth Street and Independence Avenue, SW, Washington, D.C. 20250 (800) 727-9540

Power Production, Fuel Consumption, and Installed Capacity Data.
U.S. Department of Energy, Energy Information Administration, 1000 Independence Avenue, SW, Washington, D.C. 20585 (202) 586-8800

Presidential Primaries and Caucuses.
Congressional Quarterly, Inc., 1414 22nd Street, NW, Washington, D.C. 20037 (202) 887-8500

Price Trends for Federal-Aid Highway Construction.
U.S. Department of Transportation, Federal Highway Administration, 400 Seventh Street, SW, Washington, D.C. 20590 (202) 366-0660

Prime Contract Awards.
U.S. Department of Defense, Office of the Secretary, The Pentagon, Washington, D.C. 20301 (703) 545-6700

Prisoners in 1992.
U.S. Department of Justice, Bureau of Justice Statistics, 810 Seventh Street, NW, Washington, D.C. 20531 (800) 732-3277

Prisoners in State and Federal Institution on December 31.
U.S. Department of Justice, Bureau of Justice Statistics, 810 Seventh Street, NW, Washington, D.C. 20531 (800) 732-3277

Private Pension Plan Bulletin.
U.S. Department of Labor, Pension and Welfare Benefits Administration, 200 Constitution Avenue, NW, Washington, D.C. 20210 (202) 219-8921

Probation and Parole.
U.S. Department of Justice, Bureau of Justice Statistics, 810 Seventh Street, NW, Washington, D.C. 20531 (800) 732-3277

Producer Price Indexes.
U.S. Department of Labor, Bureau of Labor Statistics, Two Massachusetts Avenue, NE, Washington, D.C. 20212 (202) 691-5200

Product Alert Weekly.
Marketing Intelligence Service Limited, 6473 D Route 64, Naples, New York 14512 (716) 374-6326

Products and Services.
Department of Development, Office of Statistical Research, Post Office Box 1001, Columbus, Ohio 43226-0101 (614) 466-2115

Production Yearbook.
Food and Agricultural Organization of the United Nations (FAO), Via delle Terme di Caracalla, 00100 Rome, Italy (Telephone Number in the U.S. (202) 653-2400)

Productivity Measures for Selected Industries and Government Services.
U.S. Department of Labor, Bureau of Labor Statistics, Two Massachusetts Avenue, NE, Washington, D.C. 20212 (202) 691-5200

Profile of Rural Idaho.
Department of Commerce, 700 West State Street, Boise, Idaho 83720 (208) 334-2470

Profile of State and Local Law Enforcement Agencies.
U.S. Department of Justice, Bureau of Justice Statistics, 810 Seventh Street, NW, Washington, D.C. 20531 (800) 732-3277

Projected Total Population and Age Distribution for 2000 and 2005: Massachusetts Cities and Towns.
Massachusetts Institute for Social and Economic Research, 128 Thompson Hall, University of Massachusetts at Amherst, Amherst Massachusetts 01003 (413) 545-3460

Projections of Education Statistics.
U.S. Department of Education, National Center for Education Statistics, 555 New Jersey Avenue, NW, Washington,.D.C. 20208 (202) 219-1828

Public Broadcasting Income, Fiscal Year.
Corporation for Public Broadcasting, 901 E Street, NW, Washington, D.C. 20004-2006 (202) 879-9600

Public Education Finances.
U.S. Department of Commerce, Bureau of the Census, Washington, D.C. 20233 (301) 457-4100

Public Employment.
U.S. Department of Commerce, Bureau of the Census, Washington, D.C. 20233 (301) 457-4100

Public Land Statistics.
U.S. Department of the Interior, Bureau of Land Management, C Street between Eighteenth and Nineteenth Streets, NW, Washington, D.C. 20240 (202) 452-5125

Publishers Weekly.
R. R. Bowker Company, 121 Chanlon Road, New Providence, New Jersey 07974 (908) 464-6800

Puerto Rico Country Report.
Economist Intelligence Unit, 111 West 57th Street, New York, New York 10019 (800) 938-4685

The Pulp and Paper Industry.
Organisation for Economic Co-operation and Development (OECD), 2 rue Andre-Pascal, 75 Paris 16 France (Telephone Number in U.S. (202) 785-6323)

Qatar Country Report.
Economist Intelligence Unit, 111 West 57th Street, New York, New York 10019 (800) 938-4685

Quarterly Abstract of Statistics.

Statistical Institute of Jamaica, Nine Swallowfield Road, Kingston 5, Jamaica

Quarterly Abstract of Statistics.
Statistics Office, Post Office Box 125, Takamoa, Raratonga, Cook Islands

Quarterly Bulletin of Statistics.
Census and Statistical Department, Secretariat of Planning, 40 Sharia Damascus, Tripoli, Libya

Quarterly Bulletin of Statistics.
Central Statistical Organization, Six-Story Building, Strand Road, Rangoon, Myanmar

Quarterly Bulletin of Statistics.
National Statistical Office, Bangkok, Thailand

Quarterly Coal Report.
U.S. Department of Energy, Energy Information Administration, 1000 Independence Avenue, SW. Washington, D.C. 20585 (202) 586-8800

Quarterly Digest of Statistics.
Central Bureau of Statistics, Post Office Box 1098, Accra, Ghana

Quarterly Digest of Statistics.
Central Office of Statistics, Auberge D'Italie, Valletta, Malta

Quarterly Digest of Statistics.
Central Statistical Office, Post Office Box 456, Mbabane, Swaziland

Quarterly Digest of Statistics.
Statistics Office, Post Office G6, Honiara, Solomon Islands

Quarterly Economic and Statistical Bulletin.
Statistics Division, Ministry of Planning, Government Printer, Post Office Box 33, Entebbe, Uganda

Quarterly Financial Report for Manufacturing, Mining and Trade Corporations.
U.S. Department of Commerce, Bureau of the Census, Washington, D.C. 20233 (301) 457-4100

Quarterly Oil Statistics and Energy Balances.
Organisation for Economic Co-operation and Development (OECD), 2 rue Andre-Pascal, 75 Paris 16, France (Telephone Number in U.S. (202) 785-6323)

Quarterly Public Assistance Statistics.
U.S. Department of Health and Human Services, Administration for Children and Families, 370 L'Enfant Promenade, SW, Washington, D.C. 20447 (202) 401-9200

Quarterly Statistical Bulletin.
Bureau of Statistics, Government Publications Agency, Post Office Box 1801, Dar es Salaam, Tanzania

Quarterly Statistical Bulletin.
Bureau of Statistics, Post Office Box MS 455, Maseru, Lesotho

Quarterly Statistical Bulletin of Liberia.
Ministry of Planning and Economic Affairs, Post Office Box 9016, Monrovia, Liberia

Quarterly Statistical Digest.
Statistical Bureau, Post Office Box 542, Avenue of the Republic, Georgetown, Guyana

Quarterly Statistical Digest.
Statistics and Research Department, Nicosia, Cyprus

Quarterly Statistical Summary.
Department of Statistics, Cabinet Office, Post Office Box N3904, Nassau, Bahamas

Quarterly Survey of Capital Appropriations.
The Conference Board, 845 Third Avenue, New York, New York 10022 (212) 759-0900

Quarterly Survey of Capital Investment and Supply Conditions in Manufacturing.
The Conference Board, 845 Third Avenue, New York, New York 10022 (212) 759-0900

Quarterly Thrift Financial Aggregates.
U.S. Department of the Treasury, Office of Thrift Supervision, 1700 G Street, NW, Washington, D.C. 20552 (202) 906-6000

RMA Monthly Tire Report.
The Rubber Manufacturers Association, 1400 K Street, NW, Washington, D.C. 20005 (202) 682-4800

RV's. . . A Year End Report.
Recreation Vehicle Industry Association, Post Office Box 2999, 1896 Preston White Drive, Reston, Virginia 22090 (703) 620-6003

Radio Facts.
Radio Advertising Bureau, 261 Madison Avenue, 23rd Floor, York, New York 10016 (212) 681-7200

Railroad Facts, Statistics of Railroads of Class I.
Association of American Railroads, 50 F Street, NW, Washington, D.C. 20001 (202) 639-2100

Rankings of the States.
National Education Association, 1201 Sixteenth Street, NW, Washington, D.C. 20036 (202) 833-4000

Real Estate Outlook: Market Trends and Insights.
National Association of Realtors, 430 North Michigan Avenue, Chicago, Illinois 60611-4087 (800) 874-6500

Reducing the Health Consequences of Smoking.
U.S. Department of Health and Human Services, Centers for Disease Control, Office of Smoking and Health, 1600 Clifton Road, NE, Atlanta, Georgia 30333 (800) 331-3435

Regions: Statistical Yearbook.
European Community Information Service, 2100 M Street, NW, Washington, D.C. 20037 (202) 862-9500

Register of Ships.
Lloyd's Register of Shipping, 17 Battery Place, New York, New York 10004 (212) 425-8050

Religion in America.
Gallup Organization, Inc., 47 Hulfish Street, Princeton, New Jersey 08542 (609) 924-9600

Report of Civil Works Expenditures by State and Fiscal Year.
U.S. Department of the Army, Corps of Engineers, The Pentagon, Washington, D.C. 20310 (703) 695-2442

Report of the AFL-CIO Executive Council.
American Federation of Labor And Congress of Industrial Organizations, 815 16th Street, NW, Washington, D.C. 20006 (202) 637-5000

Report of the Hospital Nursing Personnel Survey.
American Hospital Association, One North Franklin, Suite 27, Chicago, Illinois 60606 (800) 242-2626

Report on Applications for Orders Authorizing or Approving the Interception of Wire, Oral or Electronic Communications.
Administrative Office of the United States Courts, Thurgood Marshall Federal Judiciary Building, 1 Columbus Circle, NE, Washington, D.C. 20544 (202) 502-1455

Report to Congress on the Activities and Operations of the Public Integrity Section.
U.S. Department of Justice, 950 Pennsylvania Avenue, NW, Washington, D.C. 20530 (202) 514-2000

The Republic of China Monthly of Financial Statistics.
Department of Statistics, Ministry of Finance, 2, Aikuo West Road, Taipei, Republic of China

Republic of Kenya Statistical Abstract.
Central Bureau of Statistics, Ministry of Economic Planning and Development, Post Office Box 30266, Nairobi, Kenya

Republica Dominicana en Cifras (The Dominican Republic in Figures).
Oficina Nacional de Estadistica y Censos, Avenida Mexico, Santo Domingo, Dominican Republic

Research and Development In Industry.
National Science Foundation, 4201 Wilson Boulevard, Arlington, Virginia 22230 (703) 306-1234

Resena estadistica de la Republica de Guinea Ecuatorial.
Direccion General de Estadistica, Malabo, Equatorial Guinea

Residential Energy Consumption Survey.
U.S. Department of Energy, Energy Information Administration, 1000 Independence Avenue, SW, Washington, D.C. 20585 (202) 586-8800

Resumen estadistico.
Instituto Nacional de Estadistica, Casilla 6129, La Paz, Bolivia

Retail Trade International.
Euromonitor International, Inc., 122 South Michigan Avenue, Suite 1200, Chicago, Illinois 60603 (800) 577-EURO

Revenue Statistics of OECD Member Countries.
Organisation for Economic Co-operation and Development (OECD), 2 rue Andre-Pascal, 75 Paris 16, France (Telephone Number in U.S. (202) 785-6323)

Review of Fisheries in OECD Member Countries.
Organisation for Economic Co-operation and Development (OECD), 2 rue Andre-Pascal, 75 Paris 16, France (Telephone Number in U.S. (202) 785-6323)

Revista de Estadistica.
Direccion General de Estadistica, Balderas 71, Mexico 1, DF, Mexico

Rhode Island Basic Economic Statistics.
Department of Economic Development, 7 Jackson Walkway, Providence, Rhode Island 02903 (401) 277-2601

Roadway Congestion in Major Urban Areas.
Texas Transportation Institute, Texas A&M University, Riverside Campus, Building 7751, Safety Division, College Station, Texas 77843 (409) 845-8408

Rocznik statystyczny.
Glowny Urzad Statystyczny, Al Niepodleglosci 208, 00-925 Warsaw, Poland

Romania Country Report.
Economist Intelligence Unit, 111 West 57th Street, New York, New York

10019 (800) 938-4685

Ruanda.
Federal Statistical Office, Gustav-Stresemann-Ring 11, D-6200 Wiesbaden, Germany

Rubber Statistical Bulletin.
International Rubber Study Group, York House, 8th Floor, Empire Way, Wembley, London HA9 0PA, England

Rumanien.
Federal Statistical Office, Gustav-Stresemann-Ring 11, D-6200 Wiesbaden, Germany

Russia and Eurasia Facts and Figures Annual.
Academic International Press, Box 1111, Gulf Breeze, Florida 32562

Russia Country Report.
Economist Intelligence Unit, 111 West 57th Street, New York, New York 10019 (800) 938-4685

Russische Federation.
Federal Statistical Office, Gustav-Stresemann-Ring 11, D-6200 Wiesbaden, Germany

Rwanda Country Report.
Economist Intelligence Unit, 111 West 57th Street, New York, New York 10019 (800) 938-4685

SPA Software Sales Report.
Software Publishers Association, 1730 M Street, NW, Washington, D.C. 20036 (202) 452-1600

STATBASE Locator on Disk: UNSTAT's Guide to International Computerized Statistical Databases: World Statistics in Brief-Special Issue.
Statistical Office of the United Nations, Publishing Service, New York, New York 10017 (800) 253-9646

Saint Kitts and Nevis.
Federal Statistical Office, Gustav-Stresemann-Ring 11, D-6200 Wiesbaden, Germany

Saint Kitts-Nevis-Anguilla: Report.
HM Stationery Office, Post Office Box 569, London SE1 9NH, England

Saint Lucia.
Federal Statistical Office, Gustav-Stresemann-Ring 11, D-6200 Wiesbaden, Germany

Saint Vincent und die Grenadinen.
Federal Statistical Office, Gustav-Stresemann-Ring 11, D-6200 Wiesbaden, Germany

Sambia.
Federal Statistical Office, Gustav-Stresemann-Ring 11, D-6200 Wiesbaden, Germany

Samoa.
Federal Statistical Office, Gustav-Stresemann-Ring 11, D-6200 Wiesbaden, Germany

Samoa Country Report.
Economist Intelligence Unit, 111 West 57th Street, New York, New York 10019 (800) 938-4685

Sao Tome and Principe Country Report.
Economist Intelligence Unit, 111 West 57th Street, New York, New York 10019 (800) 938-4685

Saudi Arabia Country Report.
Economist Intelligence Unit, 111 West 57th Street, New York, New York 10019 (800) 938-4685

Saudi Arabien.
Federal Statistical Office, Gustav-Stresemann-Ring 11, D-6200 Wiesbaden, Germany

Savings and Home Financing Source Book.
U.S. Department of the Treasury, Office of Thrift Supervision, 1700 G Street, NW, Washington, D.C. 20552 (202) 906-6000

School Price Index.
Research Associates of Washington, 1200 North Nash Street, #225, Arlington, Virginia (703) 243-3399

Schweden.
Federal Statistical Office, Gustav-Stresemann-Ring 11, D-6200 Wiesbaden, Germany

Schweiz.
Federal Statistical Office, Gustav-Stresemann-Ring 11, D-6200 Wiesbaden, Germany

Science and Engineering Indicators.
National Science Foundation, 4201 Wilson Boulevard, Arlington, Virginia 22230 (703) 306-1234

Sea and Inland Fisheries Report.
Department of Fisheries and Forestry, Government Publication Sales Office, GPO Arcade, Dublin 1, Ireland

Secondary Information Service Statistics.
National Federation of Abstracting and Indexing Services (NFAIS), Philadelphia, Pennsylvania (215) 893-1561

Securities Industry Association Fact Book.
Securities Industry Association, 120 Broadway, New York, New York 10271 (212) 608-1500

Selected Highway Statistics and Charts.
U.S. Department of Transportation, National Highway Traffic Safety Administration, 400 Seventh Street, SW, Washington, D.C. 20590 (202) 366-8892

Selected Manpower Statistics.
U.S. Department of Defense, Office of the Secretary, The Pentagon, Washington, D.C. 20301 (703) 545-6700

Selected Social and Economic Characteristics.
University of South Dakota, State Data Center, Vermillion, South Dakota 57069 (605) 677-5287

Selected Statistics on Regional Member Countries.
African Development Bank, 01 BP 13 87, Abidjan 01, Cote d'Ivoire

Senegal.
Federal Statistical Office, Gustav-Stresemann-Ring 11, D-6200 Wiesbaden, Germany

Senegal Country Report.
Economist Intelligence Unit, 111 West 57th Street, New York, New York 10019 (800) 938-4685

Serie estadistica.
Instituto Nacional de Estadistica, 10 de Agosto 229, Quito, Ecuador

Service Annual Survey.
U.S. Department of Commerce, Bureau of the Census, Washington, D.C. 20233 (301) 457-4100

Seychellen.
Federal Statistical Office, Gustav-Stresemann-Ring 11, D-6200 Wiesbaden, Germany

Seychelles Country Report.
Economist Intelligence Unit, 111 West 57th Street, New York, New York 10019 (800) 938-4685

Shopping Centers Today.
International Council of Shopping Centers, 1221 Avenue of the Americas, New York, New York 10020 (646) 728-3800

Sierra Leone.
Federal Statistical Office, Gustav-Stresemann-Ring 11, D-6200 Wiesbaden, Germany

Sierra Leone Country Report.
Economist Intelligence Unit, 111 West 57th Street, New York, New York 10019 (800) 938-4685

Simbabwe.
Federal Statistical Office, Gustav-Stresemann-Ring 11, D-6200 Wiesbaden, Germany

Singapore Country Report.
Economist Intelligence Unit, 111 West 57th Street, New York, New York 10019 (800) 938-4685

Singapur.
Federal Statistical Office, Gustav-Stresemann-Ring 11, D-6200 Wiesbaden, Germany

Sintesi Statistica Socio-economica.
Servicio Statale di Statistica, Via G Carducci 145, Repubblica di San Marino

Sintesis estadistica.
Instituto Nacional de Estadisticas, Casilla 7597, Correo 3, Santiago, Chile

Situation economique du Senegal.
Direction de la Prevision et de la Statistique, BP 116, Dakar, Senegal

Situation economique, financiere et Sociale de la Republique Gabonaise.
Direction Generale de la Statistique, BP 179, Libreville, Gabon

Slovakia Country Report.
Economist Intelligence Unit, 111 West 57th Street, New York, New York 10019 (800) 938-4685

Slovenia Country Report.
Economist Intelligence Unit, 111 West 57th Street, New York, New York 10019 (800) 938-4685

Social Security Bulletin.
Social Security Administration, 6400 Security Boulevard, Baltimore, Maryland 21235 (800) 772-1213

Social Security Programs Throughout the World.
Social Security Administration, 6400 Security Boulevard, Baltimore, Maryland 21235 (800) 772-1213

Social Statistics in Use.
Russell Sage Foundation, New York, New York (212) 750-6000

Socioeconomic Characteristics of Medical Practice.
American Medical Association, 515 North State Street, Chicago, Illinois 60610 (312) 464-5000

Socio-Economic Indicators by Census Tract.
Office of Planning, Data, Management Division, Presidential Building, 415 12th Street, NW, Washington, D.C. 20004 (202) 727-6533

Socio-Economic Indicators of Change by Census Tract.
Office of Planning, Data, Management Division, Presidential Building, 415 12th Street, NW, Washington, D.C. 20004 (202) 727-6533

Socioeconomic Statistics.
Puerto Rico Planning Board, San Juan, Puerto Rico

Solar Collector Manufacturing Activity.
U.S. Department of Energy, Energy Information Administration, 1000 Independence Avenue, SW, Washington, D.C. 20585 (202) 586-8800

Solomon Islands Country Report.
Economist Intelligence Unit, 111 West 57th Street, New York, New York 10019 (800) 938-4685

Somalia.
Federal Statistical Office, Gustav-Stresemann-Ring 11, D-6200 Wiesbaden, Germany

Somalia Country Report.
Economist Intelligence Unit, 111 West 57th Street, New York, New York 10019 (800) 938-4685

Sourcebook of Criminal Justice Statistics.
U.S. Department of Justice, National Criminal Justice Reference Service, 1600 Research Boulevard, Rockville, Maryland 20850 (800) 732-3277

Source Book of Health Insurance Data.
Health Insurance Association of America, 555 13th Street, NW, Suite 600 East, Washington, D.C. 20004 (202) 824-1600

Sourcebook of ZIP Code Demographics.
CACI, Arlington, Virginia (Available from The Gale Group, 27500 Drake Road, Farmington Hills, Michigan 48331 (800) 877-4253)

Sources of European Economic and Business Information.
Gower Publishing Company, Farnborough, England (Telephone Number in the U.S. (802) 276-3162)

Sources of Unofficial UK Statistics.
Gower Publishing Company, Farnborough, England (Telephone Number in the U.S. (802) 276-3162)

South Africa Country Report.
Economist Intelligence Unit, 111 West 57th Street, New York, New York 10019 (800) 938-4685

South Africa: Official Yearbook of the Republic of South Africa.
Department of Foreign Affairs and Information, PBX 152, Pretoria 0001, South Africa

South African Statistics.
Central Statistical Services, Pretoria, 0002 South Africa

South America, Central America, and the Caribbean.
Europa Publications, London, England (Available from The Gale Group, 27500 Drake Road, Farmington Hills, Michigan 48331 (800) 877-4253)

South Carolina Statistical Abstract.
Division of Research and Statistical Services, Budget and Control Board, R.C. Dennis Building, Room 425, Columbia, South Carolina 29201 (803) 734-3781

South Dakota Community Abstracts.

University of South Dakota, State Data Center, Vermillion, South Dakota 57069 (605) 677-5287

Soviet Statistics Since 1950.
Saint Martin's Press, New York, New York (800) 817-2525

Space Activities of the United States, CIS and Other Launching Countries/Organization.
The Congress of the United States, Congressional Research Service, 10 First Street, SE, Washington, D.C. 20540 (202) 707-5700

Space Shuttle Flights.
National Aeronautics and Space Administration, 300 E Street, SW, Washington, D.C. 20546 (202) 358-1000

Spain.
Federal Statistical Office, Gustav-Stresemann-Ring 11, D-6200 Wiesbaden, Germany

Spain Country Report.
Economist Intelligence Unit, 111 West 57th Street, New York, New York 10019 (800) 938-4685

Special Issues Index.
Greenwood Publishing Group, Westport, Connecticut (800) 225-5800

The Sporting Goods Market in 1999.
National Sporting Goods Association, 1601 Feehanville Drive, Suite 300, Mount Prospect, Illinois 60056 (847) 296-6742

Sports Participation in 1998.
National Sporting Goods Association, 1601 Feehanville Drive, Suite 300, Mount Prospect, Illinois 60056 (847) 296-6742

Sri Lanka Country Report.
Economist Intelligence Unit, 111 West 57th Street, New York, New York 10019 (800) 938-4685

Sri Lanka Yearbook.
Department of Census and Statistics, No. 6, Albert Crescent, Colombo 7, Sri Lanka

Standard and Poor's Corporation, Trade and Securities: Statistics.
Standard and Poor's Corporation, New York, New York (212) 208-8000

Standard and Poor's Outlook.
Standard and Poor's Corporation, 25 Broadway, New York, New York 10004 (212) 208-8000

Stat Fact.
Newsbank, New Canaan, Connecticut (800) 762-8182

State Aid to Local Government.
National Association of State Budget Officers, Hall of the States, 444 North Capitol Street, NW, Suite 642, Washington, D.C. 20001 (202) 624-5382

State and Local Government Information Report.
Equal Employment Opportunity Commission, 1801 L Street, NW, Washington, D.C. 20507 (800) USA-EEOC

State and Local Statistics Sources.
The Gale Group, 27500 Drake Road, Farmington Hills, Michigan 48331 (800) 877-4253

State and Metropolitan Area Data Book (A Statistical Abstract Supplement).
U.S. Department of Commerce, Bureau of the Census, Washington, D.C. 20233 (301) 457-4100

State Approved Schools of Nursing, RN.
National League for Nursing, 61 Broadway, 33rd Floor, New York, New York 10006 (212) 363-5555

The State Economic, Demographic and Fiscal Handbook.
American Association of Retired Persons, Public Policy Institute, Washington, D.C. (202) 434-2277

State Elective Officials and the Legislatures.
Council of State Governments, P.O. Box 11910, Lexington, Kentucky 40578 (859) 244-8000

State Energy Data Report.
U.S. Department of Energy, Energy Information Administration, 1000 Independence Avenue, SW, Washington, D.C. 20585 (202) 586-8800

State Energy Price and Expenditure Report.
U.S. Department of Energy, Energy Information Administration, 1000 Independence Avenue, SW, Washington, D.C. 20585 (202) 586-8800

State Government Finances.
U.S. Department of Commerce, Bureau of the Census, Washington, D.C. 20233 (301) 457-4100

State Government Tax Collections.
U.S. Department of Commerce, Bureau of the Census, Washington, D.C. 20233 (301) 457-4100

State Legislatures.
National Conference of State Legislatures, 1560 Broadway, Suite 700, Denver, Colorado 80202 (303) 830-2200

The State of Charter Schools.
U.S. Department of Education, Office of Education Research and Improvement, 400 Maryland Avenue, SW, Washington, D.C. 20202 (877) 424-1616

The State of Food and Agriculture.
Food and Agricultural Organization of the United Nations (FAO), Via Delle Terme di Caracalla, 00100 Rome, Italy (Telephone Number in the U.S. (202) 653-2400)

The State of Hawaii Data Book: A Statistical Abstract.
Hawaii State Department of Business and Economic Development and Tourism, P.O. Box 2359, Honolulu, Hawaii 96804 (808) 586-2481

The State of Small Business: A Report of the President.
Small Business Administration, 409 Third Street, SW, Washington, D.C. 20416 (800) UASK-SBA

State of the Cellular Industry.
Cellular Telecommunications Industry Association, 1250 Connecticut Avenue, NW, Suite 800, Washington, D.C. 20036 (202) 785-0081

The State of the Environment 1985.
Organisation for Economic Co-operation and Development (OECD), 2 rue Andre-Pascal, 75 Paris 16, France (Telephone Number in U.S. (202) 785-6323)

State of the World's Children.
United Nations Children's Fund (UNICEF), 3 United Nations Plaza, New York, New York, 10017 (800) 253-9646

State Profile.
Woods and Poole Economics, Inc., Washington, D.C. (800) 786-1915

State Profiles: Financing Public Higher Education.
Research Associates of Washington, 1200 North Nash Street, #225, Arlington, Virginia (703) 243-3399

State Profiles: The Population and Economy of Each U.S. State.
Bernan Press, Lanham, Maryland (800) 865-3457

State Projections to 2000.
U.S. Department of Education, National Center for Education Statistics, 555 New Jersey Avenue, NW, Washington,.D.C. 20208 (202) 219-1828

State Vocational Rehabilitation Agency Program Data in Fiscal Years.
U.S. Department of Education, Rehabilitation Services Administration, 400 Maryland Avenue, SW, Washington, D.C. 20202 (800) 872-5327.

The Statesman's Yearbook.
Macmillan, London (Available from HPS (888) 330-8477

Statistical Abstract.
Bureau of Statistics, Government Publications Agency, Post Office Box 1801, Dar es Salaam, Tanzania

Statistical Abstract.
Central Bureau of Statistics, Abel-Malek Bin Marwan Street, Malki Quarter, Damascus, Syrian Arab Republic

Statistical Abstract.
Central Bureau of Statistics, Ministry of Economic Planning and Development, Post Office Box 30266, Nairobi, Kenya

Statistical Abstract.
Central Statistical Office, Post Office Box 206, Victoria, Mahe, Seychelles

Statistical Abstract.
Central Statistics Organization, Post Office Box 5835, Manama, Bahrain

Statistical Abstract.
Consultancy Services Division, Nepal Industrial Development Corporation, Kathmandu, Nepal

Statistical Abstract.
HM Stationary Office, Post Office Box 569, London SE1 9NH, England

Statistical Abstract.
Statistical Institute of Jamaica, Nine Swallowfield Road, Kingston 5, Jamaica

Statistical Abstract.
Statistics Department, Post Office Box 149, Nuku'alofa, Tonga

Statistical Abstract.
Statistics and Research Department, Nicosia, Cyprus

Statistical Abstract for Missouri.
Business and Public Administration Research Center, University of Missouri, Columbia, Missouri 65211 (314) 882-4805

Statistical Abstract for the Democratic Republic of the Sudan.
Department of Statistics, Post Office Box 700, Khartoum, Sudan

Statistical Abstract: India.
Central Statistical Organization, New Delhi, India

Statistical Abstract of Colorado.
University of Colorado, Business Research Division, Campus Box 420, Boulder, Colorado 80309 (303) 492-8227

Statistical Abstract of Ethiopia.
Central Statistical Office, Post Office Box 1143, Addis Ababa, Ethiopia
Statistical Abstract of Ireland.
Central Statistics Office, Earlsfort Terrace, Dublin 2, Ireland

Statistical Abstract of Israel.

Central Bureau of Statistics, Hakirya, Romema, Jerusalem, Israel

Statistical Abstract of Latin America.
U.C.L.A. Latin American Center Publications, University of California, Los Angeles, California 90024 (310) 825-6634

Statistical Abstract of Libya.
Census and Statistical Department, Secretariat of Planning, 40 Sharia Damascus, Tripoli, Libya

Statistical Abstract of Louisiana.
Division of Business and Economic Research, University of New Orleans, New Orleans, Louisiana 70148 (504) 286-6248

Statistical Abstract of North Carolina Counties.
Office of State Planning, Office of the Governor, 116 West Jones Street, Raleigh, North Carolina 27603-8005 (919) 733-4131

The Statistical Abstract of North Dakota.
University of North Dakota, Bureau of Business and Economic Research, Grand Forks, North Dakota 58202 (701) 777-2637

Statistical Abstract of Oklahoma.
Center for Economic and Management Research, University of Oklahoma, 307 West Brooks Street, Room 4, Norman, Oklahoma 73109 (405) 325-2931

Statistical Abstract of the Arab Republic of Egypt.
Central Agency for Public Mobilization and Statistics, Post Office Box 2086, Cairo, Egypt

Statistical Abstract of the British Virgin Islands.
Statistical Division, Planning Unit, Chief Minister's Office, Tortola, British Virgin Islands

Statistical Abstract of the Democratic Socialist Republic of Sri Lanka.
Department of Census and Statistics, No. 6, Albert Crescent, Colombo 7

Statistical Abstract of the Government of the Cayman Islands.
Department of Finance and Development, Administration Building, Georgetown, Grand Cayman, Cayman Islands

Statistical Abstract of the United States.
U.S. Department of Commerce, Bureau of the Census, Washington, D.C. 20233 (301) 457-4100

Statistical Abstract of Utah.
Bureau of Economic and Business Research, 401 Kendall D. Garff Building, University of Utah, Salt Lake City, Utah 84112 (801) 581-6333

Statistical Abstract of Western Asia.
Economic Commission for Western Asia, Post Office Box 27, Baghdad, Iraq

Statistical Abstract of the World.
The Gale Group, 27500 Drake Road, Farmington Hills, Michigan 48331 (800) 877-4253

Statistical Brief.
U.S. Department of Commerce, Bureau of the Census, Washington, D.C. 20233 (301) 457-4100

Statistical Bulletin.
Central Statistics Office, Ministry of Finance, Tower Hill, Freetown, Sierra Leone

Statistical Bulletin.
Central Statistics Office Government Printer, P.O. Box 87, Gaberone, Botswana

The Statistical Bulletin.
The Conference Board, 845 Third Avenue, New York, New York 10022 (212) 759-0900

Statistical Bulletin.
Department of Statistics, Apia, Western Samoa

Statistical Bulletin.
HM Stationary Office, Post Office Box 569, London SE1 9NH, England

Statistical Bulletin.
Manager of Publications, Government of Pakistan, Block Number 44, Shahrah-e-iraq, Karachi, Pakistan

Statistical Bulletin of the OAS.
Organization of American States (OAS), General Secretariat, 17th Street and Constitution Avenue, NW, Washington, D.C. 20006 (202) 458-3000

Statistical Bulletin of the South Pacific: Overseas Trade.
South Pacific Commission, Post Box D5, Noumea Cedex, New Caledonia

Statistical Bulletin of the South Pacific: Retail Price Indexes.
South Pacific Commission, Post Box D5, Noumea Cedex, New Caledonia

Statistical Data on Korea.
Korean Overseas Information Service, Ministry of Culture and Information, Seoul 110, Republic of Korea

Statistical Digest.
Statistical Division, 22 Bath Road, Roseau, Dominica

Statistical Digest.
Statistics Office, Post Office Box 292, Plymouth, Montserrat

Statistical Digest.
National Statistics Office, Central Government Offices, P.O. Wards Strip, Waigani, Papua New Guinea

Statistical Forecasts of the United States.
The Gale Group, 27500 Drake Road, Farmington Hills, Michigan 48331 (800) 877-4253

Statistical Handbook.
West Virginia Research League, Inc., 405 Capitol Street, Suite 414, Charleston, West Virginia 25301 (304) 346-9451

Statistical Handbook of Working America.
The Gale Group, 27500 Drake Road, Farmington Hills, Michigan 48331 (800) 877-4253

Statistical Handbook on Aging Americans.
Oryx Press, Westport, Connecticut (800) 279-ORYX

Statistical Handbook on the American Family.
Oryx Press, Westport, Connecticut (800) 279-ORYX

Statistical Handbook on Consumption and Wealth in the United States.
Oryx Press, Westport, Connecticut (800) 279-ORYX

Statistical Handbook on Poverty in the Developing World.
Oryx Press, Westport, Connecticut (800) 279-ORYX

Statistical Handbook on Racial Groups in the United States.
Oryx Press, Westport, Connecticut (800) 279-ORYX

Statistical Handbook on Technology.
Oryx Press, Westport, Connecticut (800) 279-ORYX

Statistical Handbook on U.S. Hispanics.
Oryx Press, Westport, Connecticut (800) 279-ORYX

Statistical Handbook on Violence in America.
Oryx Press, Westport, Connecticut (800) 279-ORYX

Statistical Handbook on Women in America.
Oryx Press, Westport, Connecticut (800) 279-ORYX

Statistical Handbook: States of the Former USSR.
The World Bank, 1818 H Street, NW, Washington, D.C. 20043 (202) 477-1234

Statistical Indicators for Asia and the Pacific.
Statistical Office of the United Nations, Publishing Service, New York, New York 10017 (800) 253-9646

Statistical Indicators of Short-Term Changes in ECE Countries.
Statistical Office of the United Nations, Publishing Service, New York, New York 10017 (800) 253-9646

Statistical Indicators on Social Life.
Management and Coordination Agency, Statistics Bureau, Tokyo, Japan

Statistical Pocketbook.
Netherlands Central Bureau of Statistics, 428 Prinses Beatrixlaan, 2270 AZ Voorburg, The Hague, Netherlands

Statistical Pocketbook.
Central Bureau voor de Statistiek, Kloosterweg 1, Postbus 4481, 6401 C2 Heerlen, Netherlands

Statistical Pocketbook.
Central Statistical Office, International Division, 2P, Volov Street, Sofia, Bulgaria

Statistical Pocketbook.
Central Statistical Organization, Ministry of Planning, Post Office Box 8001, Baghdad, Iraq

Statistical Pocketbook.
Central Statistical Organization, Six-Storey Building, Strand Road, Rangoon, Myanmar

Statistical Pocketbook of Hungary.
Kozponti Statisztikai Hivatal, Keleti Karoly Utca 5-7, 1024 Budapest 11, Hungary

Statistical Pocketbook of India.
Central Statistical Organization, New Delhi, India

Statistical Pocketbook of Pakistan.
Manager of Publications, Government of Pakistan, Block Number 44, Shahrah-e-iraq, Karachi, Pakistan

Statistical Pocketbook of the Democratic Socialist Republic of Sri Lanka.
Department of Census and Statistics, No. 6, Albert Crescent, Colombo 7, Sri Lanka

Statistical Pocketbook of the Philippines.
Publications Division, Bureau of the Census and Statistics, Post Office Box 779, Manila, Philippines

Statistical Pocketbook of Yugoslavia.
Savezni Zavod Za Statistiku, Kneza Milosa 20, 11000 Belgrade, Yugoslavia

Statistical Profile of Iowa.
Iowa Department of Economic Development Research Bureau, 200

East Grand Avenue, Des Moines, Iowa 50309

Statistical Record of Asian Americans.
The Gale Group, 27500 Drake Road, Farmington Hills, Michigan 48331
(800) 877-4253

Statistical Record of Black America.
The Gale Group, 27500 Drake Road, Farmington Hills, Michigan 48331
(800) 877-4253

Statistical Record of Children.
The Gale Group, 27500 Drake Road, Farmington Hills, Michigan 48331
(800) 877-4253

Statistical Record of Health and Medicine.
The Gale Group, 27500 Drake Road, Farmington Hills, Michigan 48331
(800) 877-4253

Statistical Record of Hispanic Americans.
The Gale Group, 27500 Drake Road, Farmington Hills, Michigan 48331
(800) 877-4253

Statistical Record of Native North Americans.
The Gale Group, 27500 Drake Road, Farmington Hills, Michigan 48331
(800) 877-4253

Statistical Record of Older Americans.
The Gale Group, 27500 Drake Road, Farmington Hills, Michigan 48331
(800) 877-4253

Statistical Record of Religion in America.
The Gale Group, 27500 Drake Road, Farmington Hills, Michigan 48331
(800) 877-4253

Statistical Record of the Environment.
The Gale Group, 27500 Drake Road, Farmington Hills, Michigan 48331
(800) 877-4253

Statistical Record of Women Worldwide.
The Gale Group, 27500 Drake Road, Farmington Hills, Michigan 48331
(800) 877-4253

Statistical Reference Index.
Congressional Information Service, Bethesda, Maryland (800) 638-8380

Statistical Reflection of the Islamic Republic of Iran.
Iranian Statistical Centre, D. Fatemi Avenue, Tehran, Iran

Statistical Report.
U.S. Department of Justice, Bureau of Prisons, 320 First Street, NW, Washington, D.C. 20534 (202) 307-3198

Statistical Review of Government in Utah.
Utah Foundation, 10 West 100 South 323, Salt Lake City, Utah 84101 (801) 364-1837

Statistical Source Directory for New Jersey State Government.
New Jersey State Data Center, New Jersey Department of Labor, CN 388, Trenton, New Jersey 08625-0388 (609) 984-2593

Statistical Supplement, Stockpile Report to the Congress.
U.S. Department of Defense, Defense Logistics Agency, 8725 John Kingman Road, Fort Belvoir, Virginia 22060 (703) 767-6666

Statistical Tables.
Lloyd's Register of Shipping, 17 Battery Place, New York, New York 10004 (212) 425-8050

Statistical Yearbook.

Central Department of Statistics, Ministry of Finance and National Economy, Riyadh, Saudi Arabia

Statistical Yearbook.
Central Statistical Organization, Post Office Box 1272, Steamer Point, Aden, Yemen

Statistical Yearbook.
Central Statistical Organization, Six-Storey Building, Strand Road, Rangoon, Myanmar

Statistical Yearbook.
Central Statistical Office, Post Office Box 31908, Lusaka, Zambia

Statistical Yearbook.
Central Statistics Organization, Ministry of Planning and Development, Sana'a, Yemen

Statistical Yearbook.
Department of Statistics, Post Office Box 2015, Amman, Jordan

Statistical Yearbook.
Department of Statistics, Post Office Box 700, Khartoum, Sudan

Statistical Yearbook.
Direccao dos Servicos de Estatistica, CP 1215, Luanda, Angola

Statistical Yearbook.
Directorate General of The National Statistics, Post Office Box 881, Muscat, Oman

Statistical Yearbook.
Food and Agricultural Organization of the United Nations (FAO), Via delle Terme di Caracalla, 00100 Rome, Italy (Telephone Number in the U.S. (202) 653-2400)

Statistical Yearbook.
Inter-American Development Bank, 1300 New York Avenue, NW, Washington, D.C. 20577 (202) 623-1000

Statistical Yearbook.
International Monetary Fund, 700 Nineteenth Street, NW, Washington, D.C. 20431 (202) 623-7000

Statistical Yearbook.
Iranian Statistical Centre, Dr. Fatemi Avenue, Tehran, Iran

Statistical Yearbook.
Korean Overseas Information Service, Ministry of Culture and Information, Seoul 110, Republic of Korea

Statistical Yearbook.
Lloyd's Register of Shipping, 17 Battery Place, New York, New York 10004 (212) 425-8050

Statistical Yearbook.
Organisation for Economic Co-operation and Development (OECD), 2 rue Andre-Pascal, 75 Paris 16, France (Telephone Number in U.S. (202) 785-6323)

Statistical Yearbook.
Organization of American States (OAS), General Secretariat, 17th Street and Constitution Avenue, NW, Washington, D.C. 20006 (202) 458-3000

Statistical Yearbook.
Statistical Division, Ministry of Finance, Redcliffe Street, St. John's, Antigua

Statistical Yearbook.
Statistical Office of the United Nations, Publishing Service, New York,

New York 10017 (800) 253-9646

Statistical Yearbook.
Statistiches Bundesamt (Allgemeiner Auskunftsdienst), Gustav-Stresemann-Ring 11, Postfach 5528, 6200 Wiesbaden 1, Germany

Statistical Yearbook.
Statistics Office, Post Office Box G6, Honiara, Solomon Islands

Statistical Yearbook.
U.S. Department of Justice, Immigration and Naturalization Service, 425 I Street, NW, Washington, D.C. 20536 (202) 305-1613

Statistical Yearbook.
United Nations Educational, Scientific and Cultural Organization (UNESCO), 7 Place de Fontenoy, F-75700 Paris, France (Telephone Number in U.S. (212) 963-5981)

Statistical Yearbook: Arab Republic of Egypt.
Central Agency for Public Mobilization and Statistics, Post Office Box 2086, Cairo, Egypt

Statistical Yearbook for Asia and the Pacific.
Statistical Office of the United Nations, Publishing Service, New York, New York 10017 (800) 253-9646

Statistical Yearbook for Latin America and the Caribbean.
Statistical Office of the United Nations, Publishing Service, New York, New York 10017 (800) 253-9646

Statistical Yearbook of Albania.
Drejtoria e Statistikes, Tirane, Albania

Statistical Yearbook of Algeria.
Direction des Stahstiques et de la Comptabilite Nationale, BP 478, Alber, Algeria

Statistical Yearbook of Bangladesh.
Bureau of Statistics, Bangladesh Secretariat, School Building, No. 12, Dacca, Bangladesh

Statistical Yearbook of Bhutan.
Central Statistical Office, Planning Commission, Thimphu, Bhutan

Statistical Yearbook of Bulgaria.
Central Statistical Office, International Division, 2 P Volov Street, Sofia, Bulgaria

Statistical Yearbook of Greece.
National Statistical Service of Greece, 14-16 Lycourgou Street, Athens 112, Greece

Statistical Yearbook of Jamaica.
Statistical Institute of Jamaica, Nine Swallowfield Road, Kingston 5, Jamaica

Statistical Yearbook of Maldives.
Ministry of Planning and Development, Maldives

Statistical Yearbook of Municipal Finances.
Bond Market Association, 40 Broad Street, 12th Floor, New York, New York 10004-2373 (212) 809-7000

Statistical Year Book of Nepal.
Central Bureau of Statistics, National Planning Commission Secretariat, Ramshah Path, Thapathali, Katmandu, Nepal

Statistical Yearbook of the Electric Utility Industry.
Edison Electric Institute, 701 Pennsylvania Avenue, NW, Washington,

D.C. 20004-2696 (202) 508-5000

Statistical Yearbook of the Netherlands.
Netherlands Central Bureau of Statistics, 428 Prinses, Beatrixlaan, 2270 AZ Voorburg, The Hague, Netherlands

Statistical Yearbook of Thailand.
National Statistical Office, Bangkok, Thailand

Statistical Yearbook of Zimbabwe.
Central Statistical Office, Post Office Box 8063, Causeway, Harare, Zimbabwe

Statistiches Jahrbuch der Schweiz: Annuaire statistique de la Suisse.
Office Federale de la Statistique, Hallwylstrasse 15, CH-3005 Berne, Switzerland

Statistiches Jahrbuch fur die Republik Osterreich
Osterreichisches Statistiches Zentralamt, Hintere Zollamtsstrasse 2B, A1033 Vienna, Austria

Statisticka rocenka Ceske A Slovenske Federativni Republiky.
Federalni Statisticky Urad (Federal Statistical Office), Sokolovska 142, Praha 8-Karlin, Czechoslovakia

Statisticke prehledy.
Federalni Statisticky Urad (Federal Statistical Office), Sokolovska 142, Praha 8-Karlin, Czechoslovakia

Statisticki Bilten.
Savezni Zavod Za Statistiku, Kneza Milosa 20, 11000 Belgrade, Yugoslavia

Statisticki Godisnjak Jugoslavije.
Savezni Zavod Za Statistiku, Kneza Milosa, 20, 11000 Belgrade, Yugoslavia

Statistics and Indicators on Women in Africa.
Statistical Office of the United Nations, Publishing Service, New York, New York 10017 (800) 253-9646

Statistics at a Glance: Bhutan.
Central Statistical Office, Planning Commission, Post Office Box 338, Thimphu, Bhutan

Statistics Canada Catalogue.
Statistics Canada, Ottawa, Ontario, K1A 0T6 Canada (613) 951-8116

Statistics Canada Index.
Micromedia Limited, Toronto, Canada (416) 362-5211

Statistics Europe: Sources for Economic, Social and Market Research.
CBD Research Ltd., Beckenham, Kent, England (Available from The Gale Group, 27500 Drake Road, Farmington Hills, Michigan 48331 (800) 877-4253)

Statistics for the 21st Century.
Dun & Bradstreet Corporation, One Diamond Hill Road, Murray Hill, New Jersey 07974 (908) 665-5000

Statistics of Communication Common Carriers.
Federal Communications Commission, 445 Twelfth Street SW, Washington, D.C. 20554 (888) 225-5322

Statistics of Foreign Trade.
Organisation for Economic Co-operation and Development (OECD), 2 rue Andre-Pascal, 75 Paris 16, France (Telephone Number in U.S. (202) 785-6323)

Statistics of Income.

U.S. Department of the Treasury, Internal Revenue Service, 1111 Constitution Avenue, NW, Washington, D.C. 20224 (202) 874-0410

Statistics of Income Bulletin.
U.S. Department of the Treasury, Internal Revenue Service, 1111 Constitution Avenue, NW, Washington, D.C. 20224 (202) 874-0410

Statistics of Income, Corporation Income Tax Returns.
U.S. Department of the Treasury, Internal Revenue Service, 1111 Constitution Avenue, NW, Washington, D.C. 20224 (202) 874-0410

Statistics of Income, Individual Income Tax Returns.
U.S. Department of the Treasury, Internal Revenue Service, 1111 Constitution Avenue, NW, Washington, D.C. 20224 (202) 874-0410

Statistics of Income, Partnership Returns.
U.S. Department of the Treasury, Internal Revenue Service, 1111 Constitution Avenue, NW, Washington, D.C. 20224 (202) 874-0410

Statistics of Interstate Natural Gas Pipeline Companies.
U.S. Department of Energy, Energy Information Administration, 1000 Independence Avenue, SW, Washington, D.C. 20585 (202) 586-8800

Statistics of Paper, Paperboard and Woodpulp.
American Forest and Paper Association, 1111 Nineteenth Street, NW, Washington, D.C. 20036 (202) 463-2700

Statistics of the Communications Industry in the U.S.
Federal Communications Commission, 445 Twelfth Street SW, Washington, D.C. 20554 (888) 225-5322

Statistics of the Local Exchange Carriers.
United States Telephone Association, 1401 H Street, NW, Suite 600, Washington, D.C. 20005 (202) 326-7300

Statistics of the Presidential and Congressional Election.
U.S. Congress, Clerk of the House, The Capitol, Washington, D.C. 20515 (202) 224-3121

Statistics of the Telephone Industry.
United States Telephone Association, 1401 H Street, NW, Suite 600, Washington, D.C. 20005 (202) 326-7300

Statistics Office, Ministry of Finance, Tortola, British Virgin Islands.
HM Stationery Office, Post Office Box 569, London, England SE1 9NH

Statistics on Alcohol, Drug and Tobacco Use.
The Gale Group, 27500 Drake Road, Farmington Hills, Michigan 48331 (800) 877-4253

Statistics on Banking.
Federal Deposit Insurance Corporation, 550 Seventeenth Street, NW, Washington, D.C. 20429 (202) 393-8400

Statistik Indonesia.
Biro Pusat Statistik, Jalan Dr. Sutomo 8, Jakarta, Indonesia

Statistiques annuelles.
Services des Statistiques et des Etudes Economiques, 4 rue des Iris, Monte Carlo, Monaco

Statistiques: revue de l'Office National des Statistiques.
Office National de la Statistiques, 8/10 Rue des Moussebiline, B.P. 55 Alger, Algeria

Statistisch jaarboek: Nederlandse Antillen.
Central Bureau of Statistics, Willemstad, Curacao, Netherlands Antilles

Statistiches Jahrbuch.
Amt fur Volkswirtschaft des furstichen Regierung, FL-9490 Vaduz,

Liechtenstein

Statistisches, Jahrbuch der Deutschen Demokratischen Republik.
Staatsverlag der DDR, Otto-Grotewohl-Strasse 17, 108 Berlin, Germany

Statistisches Jahrbuch fur die Bundes Republik Deutschland.
Statistisches Bundesamt Federal Statistical Office, Gustav-Stresemann-Ring 11, Postfach 5528, 6200 Wiesbaden, Germany

Statistisches Taschebuch.
Statistisches Bundesamt Federal Statistical Office, Gustav-Stresemann-Ring 11, Postfach 5528, 6200 Wiesbaden, Germany

Statistisches Taschenbuch der Deutschen Demokratischen Republik.
Staatsverlag der DDR, Otto-Grotewohl-Strasse 17, 108 Berlin, Germany

Statistisk Arbog.
Danmarks Statistik, Sejrogade 11, Postboks 2250, 2100 Kobenhavn 0, Denmark

Statistisk arbok.
Statistisk Sentralbyra (Central Bureau of Statistics), Skippergate 15, P.B. 8131, DEP –0033, Oslo 1, Norway

Statistisk Arbor.
Danmarks Statistik, Sejrogade 11, Kobenhavn, Denmark

Statistisk Arsbuk for Sverige.
Statistiska Centralbyran, Karlavagen 100, S-115 81, Stokholm, Sweden

Statistisk manedshefte.
Statistisk-Sentralbyra (Central Bureau of Statistics), Skippergate 15, P.B. 8131, DEP-0033, Oslo 1, Norway

Statistisk Manedsoversigt.
Danmarks Statistik, Sejrogadell, Postboks 2250, 2100 Kobenhavn 0, Denmark

Statistiske Efterretninger.
Danmarks Statistik, Sejrogadell, Postboks 2250, 2100 Kobenhavn 0, Denmark

Statisztikai evkonyv.
Kozponti Statisztikai Hivatal, Keleti Karoly Utca 5-7, 1024 Budapest 11, Hungary

Statisztikai havi kozlemenyek.
Kozponti Statisztikai Hivatal, Keleti Karoly Utca 5-7, 1024 Budapest 11, Hungary

Statmaster.
Oryx Press, Westport, Connecticut (800) 279-ORYX
Steel Statistical Yearbook.
International Iron and Steel Institute, 120, rue Colonel Bourg, B-1140 Brussels, Belgium

Storm Data.
U.S. Department of Commerce, National Oceanic and Atmospheric Administration, National Climatic Data Center, 151 Patton Avenue, Asheville, North Carolina 28801 (828) 271-4800

Student Financing of Graduate and Professional Education.
U.S. Department of Education, National Center for Education Statistics, 555 New Jersey Avenue, NW, Washington, .D.C. 20208 (202) 219-1828

Sudan.
Federal Statistical Office, Gustav-Stresemann-Ring 11, D-6200 Wiesbaden, Germany

Sudan Country Report.

Economist Intelligence Unit, 111 West 57th Street, New York, New York 10019 (800) 938-4685

Summary of Notifiable Diseases, United States, Morbidity and Mortality Weekly Report.
U.S. Department of Health and Human Services, Centers for Disease Control, 1600 Clifton Road, NE, Atlanta, Georgia 30333 (800) 331-3435

Summary of Statistics.
National Statistics Office, Central Government Offices, Post Office Wards Strip, Waigana, Papua New Guinea

Suomen tilastollin Vuosikirja.
Statistics Finland, Box 504, Annankatu, 44, SF-00100 Helsinki, Finland

Supplementary Materials: National Priorities List, Proposed Rule.
Environmental Protection Agency, 1200 Pennsylvania Avenue, NW, Washington, D.C. 20460 (888) 372-8255

Supplementary Report, Metropolitan Statistical Areas.
U.S. Department of Commerce, Bureau of the Census, Washington, D.C. 20233 (301) 457-4100

Suriname.
Federal Statistical Office, Gustav-Stresemann-Ring 11, D-6200 Wiesbaden, Germany

Suriname Country Report.
Economist Intelligence Unit, 111 West 57th Street, New York, New York 10019 (800) 938-4685

The Survey of Buying Power Data Service.
Market Statistics, 355 Park Avenue, New York, New York 10010 (212) 592-6250

Survey of Current Business.
U. S. Department of Commerce, Bureau of Economic Analysis, Fourteenth Street between Constitution Avenue and E Street, NW, Washington, D.C. 20230 (202) 606-9900

Survey of Earned Doctorates, Selected Data on Science and Engineering Doctorate Awards.
National Science Foundation, 4201 Wilson Boulevard, Arlington, Virginia 22230 (703) 306-1234

Survey of Economic and Social Conditions in Africa.
Statistical Office of the United Nations, Publishing Service, New York, New York 10017 (800) 253-9646

Survey of Employer Anti-drug Programs.
U.S. Department of Labor, Bureau of Labor Statistics, Two Massachusetts Avenue, NE, Washington, D.C. 20212 (202) 691-5200

Survey of Federal Support to Universities, Colleges, and Selected Nonprofit Institutions.
National Science Foundation, 4201 Wilson Boulevard, Arlington, Virginia 22230 (703) 306-1234

Survey of Graduate Science and Engineering Students and Postdoctorates.
National Science Foundation, 4201 Wilson Boulevard, Arlington, Virginia 22230 (703) 306-1234

Survey of Hospital Semi-Private Room Charges.
Health Insurance Association of America, 555 13th Street, NW, Suite 600 East, Washington, D.C. 20004 (202) 824-1600

Survey of Minority-Owned Business Enterprises.
U.S. Department of Commerce, Bureau of the Census, Washington, D.C. 20233 (301) 457-4100

Survey of Progress.
Central Statistics Office, Block No. 4, Microrayon, Kabul, Afghanistan

Survey of Scientific and Engineering Expenditures at Universities and Colleges.
National Science Foundation, 4201 Wilson Boulevard, Arlington, Virginia 22230 (703) 306-1234

Survey of State Prison Inmates.
U.S. Department of Justice, Bureau of Justice Statistics, 810 Seventh Street, NW, Washington, D.C. 20531 (800) 732-3277

Survey of Women-Owned Businesses.
U.S. Department of Commerce, Bureau of the Census, Washington, D.C. 20233 (301) 457-4100

Swasiland.
Federal Statistical Office, Gustav-Stresemann-Ring 11, D-6200 Wiesbaden, Germany

Swaziland Country Report.
Economist Intelligence Unit, 111 West 57th Street, New York, New York 10019 (800) 938-4685

Sweden Country Report.
Economist Intelligence Unit, 111 West 57th Street, New York, New York 10019 (800) 938-4685

Syria Country Report.
Economist Intelligence Unit, 111 West 57th Street, New York, New York 10019 (800) 938-4685

Syrien.
Federal Statistical Office, Gustav-Stresemann-Ring 11, D-6200 Wiesbaden, Germany

Tableau Economique de La Reunion.
Institut National de la Statistique et des Etudes Economiques, 4 rue de l'Ecole, Sainte, Clothilde, Reunion 97490

Taiwan Agricultural Yearbook.
Department of Agriculture and Forestry, Taiwan Provincial Government, Chung-hsing Village, Nantou, Nantou Hsien, Taiwan, Republic of China

Taiwan Country Report.
Economist Intelligence Unit, 111 West 57th Street, New York, New York 10019 (800) 938-4685

Taiwan Statistical Data Book.
Council for Economic Planning and Development, 9th Floor, 87 Nanking East Road, Section 2, Taipei, Republic of China

Tajikistan Country Report.
Economist Intelligence Unit, 111 West 57th Street, New York, New York 10019 (800) 938-4685

Tansania.
Federal Statistical Office, Gustav-Stresemann-Ring 11, D-6200 Wiesbaden, Germany

Tanzania Country Report.
Economist Intelligence Unit, 111 West 57th Street, New York, New York 10019 (800) 938-4685

Tax Rates and Tax Burdens in the District of Columbia: A Nationwide Comparison.
Government of the District of Columbia, Department of Finance and Revenue, 441 Fourth Street, NW, Washington, D.C. 20001 (202) 727-6103

Tchad.
Federal Statistical Office, Gustav-Stresemann-Ring 11, D-6200 Wiesbaden, Germany

Teacher Use of Computers and the Internet in Schools.
U.S. Department of Education, National Center for Education Statistics, 555 New Jersey Avenue, Washington, D.C. 20208 (202) 219-1828

Technology Assessment and Forecast Database.
U.S. Department of Commerce, Patent and Trademark Office, 2121 Crystal Drive, Arlington, Virginia 22202 (703) 305-8341

Telecommunication Statistics.
International Telecommunication Union, Place des Nations, CH-1211 Geneva 20, Switzerland

Telephone Subscribership in the U.S.
Federal Communications Commission, 445 Twelfth Street SW, Washington, D.C. 20554 (888) 225-5322

Television and Cable Factbook.
Warren Communication News, Inc., 2115 Ward Court, NW, Washington, D.C. 20037 (202) 872-9200

Tennessee Statistical Abstract.
Center for Business and Economic Research, University of Tennessee, Knoxville, Tennessee 37996-4170 (615) 974-5441

Texas Almanac.
Dallas Morning News, Communications Center, Post Office Box 655237, Dallas, Texas 75265 (214) 977-8261

Texas Fact Book.
Bureau of Business Research, University of Texas, College of Business Administration, Post Office Box 7459, Austin, Texas 78713 (512) 471-1616

The Textile Industry: An Information Sourcebook.
Oryx Press, Westport, Connecticut (800) 279-ORYX

Textile Industry in OECD Countries.
Organisation for Economic Co-operation and Development (OECD), 2 rue Andre-Pascal, 75 Paris 16, France (Telephone Number in U.S. (202) 785-6323)

Thailand.
Federal Statistical Office, Gustav-Stresemann-Ring 11, D-6200 Wiesbaden, Germany
Thailand Country Report.
Economist Intelligence Unit, 111 West 57th Street, New York, New York 10019 (800) 938-4685

Thailand Statistical Yearbook.
National Statistical Office, Bangkok, Thailand
Tilastokeskus.
Statistics Finland, Box 504, Annankatu, 44, SF-00100 Helsinki, Finland

Timber Demand and Technology Assessment.
U.S. Department of Agriculture, Forest Service, Post Office Box 96090, Washington, D.C. 20090 (202) 205-8333

Titanium Ingot, Mill Products, and Castings.
U.S. Department of Commerce, Bureau of the Census, Washington, D.C. 20233 (301) 457-4100

Tobacco Situation.
U.S. Department of Agriculture, Economic Research Service, 1800 M Street, NW, Washington, D.C. 20036 (202) 694-4040

Togo.

Federal Statistical Office, Gustav-Stresemann-Ring 11, D-6200 Wiesbaden, Germany

Togo Country Report.
Economist Intelligence Unit, 111 West 57th Street, New York, New York 10019 (800) 938-4685

Tonga Country Report.
Economist Intelligence Unit, 111 West 57th Street, New York, New York 10019 (800) 938-4685

Top-line Reports.
Mediamark Research, Inc., 708 Third Avenue, New York, New York 10017 (212) 599-0444

Tourism: Annual Statistics.
European Community Information Service, Washington, D.C. (Available from UNIPUB (800) 274-4888)

Tourism and the Travel Industry: An Information Sourcebook.
Oryx Press, Westport, Connecticut (800) 279-ORYX

Tourism Policy and International Tourism in OECD Member Countries.
Organisation for Economic Co-operation and Development (OECD), 2 rue Andre-Pascal, 75 Paris 16, France (Telephone Number in U.S. (202) 785-6323)

Tourism Statistics: Annual Report.
Civil Aviation and Tourism Authority, Afghan Tourist Organization, Kabul, Afghanistan

Toxics Release Inventory Public Data Release.
Environmental Protection Agency, 1200 Pennsylvania Avenue, NW, Washington, D.C. 20460 (888) 372-8255

Trade by Commodities.
Organisation for Economic Co-operation and Development (OECD), 2 rue Andre-Pascal, 75 Paris 16, France (Telephone Number in U.S. (202) 785-6323)

Trade Production.
Food and Agricultural Organization of the United Nations (FAO), Via delle Terme di Caracalla, 00100, Rome, Italy (Telephone Number in the U.S. (202) 653-2400)

Trade Statistics of Ireland.
Central Statistics Office, St. Stephen's Green House, Earlsfort Terrace, Dublin 2, Ireland

Trade Yearbook.
Food and Agricultural Organization of the United Nations (FAO), Via delle Terme di Caracalla, 00100, Rome, Italy (Telephone Number in the U.S. (202) 653-2400)

Traffic Safety Facts.
U.S. Department of Transportation, National Highway Traffic Safety Administration, 400 Seventh Street, SW, Washington, D.C. 20590 (202) 366-8892

Trinidad Country Report.
Economist Intelligence Unit, 111 West 57th Street, New York, New York 10019 (800) 938-4685

Transit Fact Book.
American Public Transportation Association, 1201 New York Avenue, NW, Suite 400, Washington, D.C. 20005 (202) 898-4000

Transport Annual Statistics.
European Community Information Service, 2100 M Street, NW, Washington, D.C. 20037 (202) 862-9500

Transportation in America.
Eno Transportation Foundation, One Farragut Square, South, Suite 500, Washington, D.C. 20006 (202) 879-4700

Transportation Safety Information Report.
U.S. Department of Transportation, Transportation Systems Center, Kendall Square, Cambridge, Massachusetts 02142 (617) 494-2224

Travel and Tourism Data: A Comprehensive Research Handbook on World Travel.
Oryx Press, Westport, Connecticut (800) 279-ORYX

Treasury Bulletin.
U.S. Department of the Treasury, Fifteenth Street and Pennsylvania Avenue, NW, Washington, D.C. 20220 (202) 622-2000

Trend Data.
U.S. Department of Veterans Affairs, 810 Vermont Avenue, NW, Washington, D.C. 20420 (202) 273-5400

The Trend of Employment and Unemployment.
Central Statistics Offices, Ardee Road, Dublin 6, Ireland

Trends in Europe and North America: The Statistical Yearbook of the Economic Commission for Europe.
Statistical Office of the United Nations, Publishing Service, New York, New York 10017 (800) 253-9646

Trends in Family Income.
U.S. Congress, Congressional Budget Office, Second and D Streets, SW, Washington, D.C. 20515 (202) 226-2600

Trends in Telephone Service.
U.S. Federal Communications Commission, 445 12th Street, SW, Washington, D.C. 20554 (888) 225-5322

Trends in Television.
Television Bureau of Advertising, Inc., 3 East 54th Street, New York, New York 10022 (212) 486-1111

Trinidad and Tobago.
Federal Statistical Office, Gustav-Stresemann-Ring 11, D-6200 Wiesbaden, Germany

Tschechoslowakei.
Federal Statistical Office, Gustav-Stresemann-Ring 11, D-6200 Wiesbaden, Germany

Tunesien.
Federal Statistical Office, Gustav-Stresemann-Ring 11, D-6200 Wiesbaden, Germany

Turkei.
Federal Statistical Office, Gustav-Stresemann-Ring 11, D-6200 Wiesbaden, Germany

Turkey Country Report.
Economist Intelligence Unit, 111 West 57th Street, New York, New York 10019 (800) 938-4685

Turkeys.
U.S. Department of Agriculture, National Agricultural Statistics Service, Fourteenth Street and Independence Avenue, SW, Washington, D.C. 20250 (800) 727-9540

Turkiye Istatistik Cep Yilligi.
Devlet Istatistik Enstitusu, Necatibey Caddesi, 114 Ankara, Turkey

Turkiye Istatistik Yilligi.
Devlet Istatistik Enstitusu, Necatibey Caddesi, 114 Ankara, Turkey

Turkmenistan Country Report.
Economist Intelligence Unit, 111 West 57th Street, New York, New York 10019 (800) 938-4685

Turks and Caicos Islands Country Report.
Economist Intelligence Unit, 111 West 57th Street, New York, New York 10019 (800) 938-4685

Tuvalu.
Federal Statistical Office, Gustav-Stresemann-Ring 11, D-6200 Wiesbaden, Germany

Typical Electric Bills.
U.S. Department of Energy, Energy Information Administration, 1000 Independence Avenue, SW, Washington, D.C. 20585 (202) 586-8800

2002: Country by Country.
Economist Intelligence Unit, 111 West 57th Street, New York, New York (800) 938-4685

UNCTAD Commodity Yearbook.
United Nations Conference on Trade and Development (UNCTAD), Central Statistical Service, Palais des Nations, Geneva, Switzerland (Telephone in U.S. (800) 253-9646)

UNCTAD Statistical Pocket Book.
United Nations Conference on Trade and Development (UNCTAD), New York, New York (800) 253-9646

UNESCO Statistical Yearbook.
United Nations Educational, Scientific and Cultural Organization (UNESCO), 7 Place de Fontenoy, Paris, France (Available from UNIPUB (800) 274-4888)

USDA.
U.S. Department of Agriculture, Forest Service, Post Office Box 96090, Washington, D.C. 20090 (202) 205-8333

Uganda.
Federal Statistical Office, Gustav-Stresemann-Ring 11, D-6200 Wiesbaden, Germany

Uganda Country Report.
Economist Intelligence Unit, 111 West 57th Street, New York, New York 10019 (800) 938-4685

Ukraine.
Federal Statistical Office, Gustav-Stresemann-Ring 11, D-6200 Wiesbaden, Germany

Ukraine Country Report.
Economist Intelligence Unit, 111 West 57th Street, New York, New York 10019 (800) 938-4685

Uniform Crime Reports for the United States.
U.S. Department of Justice, Federal Bureau of Investigation, 935 Pennsylvania Avenue, NW, Washington, D.C. 20535 (202) 324-3691

Undergraduate Financing of Postsecondary Education.
U.S. Department of Education, 400 Maryland Avenue, SW, Washington, D.C. 20202 (877) 424-1616

Undergraduate General Education and Humanities Requirements.
U.S. Department of Education, 400 Maryland Avenue, SW, Washington, D.C. 20202 (877) 424-1616

Understanding the Census: A Guide for Marketers, Planners, Grant-Writers and Other Data Users.
Oryx Press, Westport, Connecticut (800) 279-ORYX

Unemployment Insurance, Financial Data.
U.S. Department of Labor, Employment and Training Administration, 200 Constitution Avenue, NW, Washington, D.C. 20210 (202) 219-6871

Unemployment Insurance Financial Handbook.
U.S. Department of Labor, Employment and Training Administration, 200 Constitution Avenue, NW, Washington, D.C. 20210 (202) 219-6871

Ungarn.
Federal Statistical Office, Gustav-Stresemann-Ring 11, D-6200 Wiesbaden, Germany

Union List of African Censuses, Development Plans and Statistical Abstracts.
K. G. Saur, New Jersey (908) 665-3576

United Arab Emirates Country Report.
Economist Intelligence Unit, 111 West 57th Street, New York, New York 10019 (800) 938-4685

United Kingdom Country Report.
Economist Intelligence Unit, 111 West 57th Street, New York, New York 10019 (800) 938-4685

United Kingdom Statistical Sources.
The Library Association, London, England

United Nations Statistical Yearbook.
Statistical Office of the United Nations, Publishing Service, New York, New York 10017 (800) 253-9646

United Nations Women's Indicators and Statistics Database on CD-ROM (WISTAT): Version 3.
Statistical Office of the United Nations, Publishing Service, New York, New York 10017 (800) 253-9646

United States Census of Agriculture.
U.S. Department of Commerce, Bureau of the Census, Washington, D.C. 20233 (301) 457-4100

United States Census of Construction Industries.
U.S. Department of Commerce, Bureau of the Census, Washington, D.C. 20233 (301) 457-4100

United States Census of Governments.
U.S. Department of Commerce, Bureau of the Census, Washington, D.C. 20233 (301) 457-4100

United States Census of Housing.
U.S. Department of Commerce, Bureau of the Census, Washington, D.C. 20233 (301) 457-4100

United States Census of Manufactures.
U.S. Department of Commerce, Bureau of the Census, Washington, D.C. 20233 (301) 457-4100

United States Census of Mineral Industries.
U.S. Department of Commerce, Bureau of the Census, Washington, D.C. 20233 (301) 457-4100

United States Census of Outlying Areas.
U.S. Department of Commerce, Bureau of the Census, Washington, D.C. 20233 (301) 457-4100

United States Census of Outlying Areas, Manufactures, Puerto Rico.
U.S. Department of Commerce, Bureau of the Census, Washington, D.C. 20233 (301) 457-4100

United States Census of Outlying Areas, Selected Services Industries, Puerto Rico.

U.S. Department of Commerce, Bureau of the Census, Washington, D.C. 20233 (301) 457-4100

United States Census of Population.
U.S. Department of Commerce, Bureau of the Census, Washington, D.C. 20233 (301) 457-4100

United States Census of Population, Persons of Spanish Origin.
U.S. Department of Commerce, Bureau of the Census, Washington, D.C. 20233 (301) 457-4100

United States Census of Retail Trade.
U.S. Department of Commerce, Bureau of the Census, Washington, D.C. 20233 (301) 457-4100

United States Census of Selected Service Industries.
U.S. Department of Commerce, Bureau of the Census, Washington, D.C. 20233 (301) 457-4100

United States Census of Service Industries, Geographic Area Series.
U.S. Department of Commerce, Bureau of the Census, Washington, D.C. 20233 (301) 457-4100

United States Census of Transportation.
U.S. Department of Commerce, Bureau of the Census, Washington, D.C. 20233 (301) 457-4100

United States Census of Wholesale Trade.
U.S. Department of Commerce, Bureau of the Census, Washington, D.C. 20233 (301) 457-4100

United States Crude Oil, Natural Gas and Natural Gas Liquids Reserves.
U.S. Department of Energy, Energy Information Administration, 1000 Independence Avenue, SW, Washington, D.C. 20585 (202) 586-8800

United States Domestic Postage Rates: Recent History.
U.S. Postal Service, 475 l'Enfant Plaza West, SW, Washington, D.C. 20260-0100 (202) 268-2000

United States Economic Census of Outlying Areas.
U.S. Department of Commerce, Bureau of the Census, Washington, D.C. 20233 (301) 457-4100

United States Immunization Survey.
U.S. Department of Health and Human Services, Centers for Disease Control, 1600 Clifton Road, NE, Atlanta, Georgia 30333 (800) 331-3435

United States Imports for Consumption and General Imports, TSUSA Commodity and Country.
U.S. Department of Commerce, Bureau of the Census, Washington, D.C. 20233 (301) 457-4100

United States Industrial Outlook.
U.S. Department of Commerce, International Trade Administration, Fourteenth Street between Constitution Avenue and E Street, NW, Washington, D.C. 20230 (202) 482-2185

United States International Travel Statistics.
U.S. Department of Transportation, Transportation Systems Center, Kendall Square, Cambridge, Massachusetts 02142 (617) 494-2224

United States Life Tables and Actuarial Tables.
U.S. Department of Health and Human Services, National Center for Health Statistics, 3700 East-West Highway, Hyattsville, Maryland 20782 (301) 436-8500

United States Merchandise Trade: Exports, General Imports, and Imports for Consumption.
U.S. Department of Commerce, Bureau of the Census, Washington,

D.C. 20233 (301) 457-4100

United States Merchandise Trade: Selected Highlights.
U.S. Department of Commerce, Bureau of the Census, Washington, D.C. 20233 (301) 457-4100

United States Merchant Marine Data Sheet.
U.S. Department of Transportation, Maritime Administration, 400 Seventh Street, SW, Washington, D.C. 20590 (202) 366-5807

United States Overseas Loans and Grants and Assistance from International Organizations.
U.S. Agency for International Development 1300 Pennsylvania Avenue, NW, Washington, D.C. 20523-0001 (202) 712-0000

United States Pet Ownership and Demographics Sourcebook.
American Veterinary Medical Association, 1931 North Meacham Road, Suite 100, Schaumburg, Illinois 60173 (847) 925-8070

United States Scientists and Engineers.
National Science Foundation, 4201 Wilson Boulevard, Arlington, Virginia 22230 (703) 306-1234

United States/Soviet Military Balance, Statistical Trends.
The Congress of the U.S., Congressional Research Service, 10 First Street, SE, Washington, D.C. 20540 (202) 707-5700

United States Trade with Puerto Rico and United States Possessions.
U.S. Department of Commerce, Bureau of the Census, Washington, D.C. 20233 (301) 457-4100

United States Waterborne Exports and General Imports.
U.S. Department of the Army, The Pentagon, Washington, D.C. 20310 (703) 695-2442

Uranium Industry Annual.
U.S. Department of Energy, Energy Information Administration, 1000 Independence Avenue, SW, Washington, D.C. 20585 (202) 586-8800

Uruguay.
Federal Statistical Office, Gustav-Stresemann-Ring 11, D-6200 Wiesbaden, Germany

Uruguay Country Report.
Economist Intelligence Unit, 111 West 57th Street, New York, New York 10019 (800) 938-4685

USA/USSR: Facts and Figures.
U.S. Bureau of the Census and Information - Publication Center, State Committee on Statistics of the U.S.S.R., Washington, D.C. (301) 763-2804

U.S. Direct Investment Abroad.
U.S. Department of Commerce, Bureau of Economic Analysis, 14th Street between Constitution Avenue and E Street, NW, Washington, D.C. 20230 (202) 606-9900

U.S. Global Trade Outlook, 1995-2000.
U.S. Department of Commerce, International Trade Administration, Fourteenth Street between Constitution Avenue and E Street, NW, Washington, D.C. 20230 (202) 482-2185

U.S. Government on the Web: Getting the Information You Need.
Libraries Unlimited, Post Office Box 6633, Englewood, Colorado 80155 (800) 237-6124

U.S. Industrial Outlook.
U.S. Department of Commerce, International Trade Administration, Fourteenth Street between Constitution Avenue and E Street, NW, Washington, D.C. 20230 (202) 482-2185

U.S. Merchandise Trade: Selected Highlights.
U.S. Department of Commerce, Bureau of the Census, Washington, D.C. 20233 (301) 457-4100

USA Counties on CD-ROM.
U.S. Department of Commerce, Bureau of the Census, Washington, D.C. 20233 (301) 457-4100

User's Guide to BEA Information.
U.S. Department of Commerce, Bureau of Economic Analysis, Fourteenth Street between Constitution Avenue and E Street, NW, Washington, D.C. 20230 (202) 606-9900

Using Government Information Sources: Print and Electronic.
Oryx Press, Westport, Connecticut (800) 279-ORYX

Uzbekistan Country Report.
Economist Intelligence Unit, 111 West 57th Street, New York, New York 10019 (800) 938-4685

Vanuatu Country Report.
Economist Intelligence Unit, 111 West 57th Street, New York, New York 10019 (800) 938-4685

Vegetables.
U.S. Department of Agriculture, National Agricultural Statistics Service, Fourteenth Street and Independence Avenue, SW, Washington, D.C. 20250 (800) 727-9540

Venezuela.
Federal Statistical Office, Gustav-Stresemann-Ring 11, D-6200 Wiesbaden, Germany

Venezuela Country Report.
Economist Intelligence Unit, 111 West 57th Street, New York, New York 10019 (800) 938-4685

Venture Capital Journal.
Venture Economics Investor Services, 41 Pittsburgh Street, Boston, Massachusetts 02210 (617) 856-2504

Vereinigte Arabische Emirate.
Federal Statistical Office, Gustav-Stresemann-Ring 11, D-6200 Wiesbaden, Germany

Vessel Entrances and Clearances.
U.S. Department of Commerce, Bureau of the Census, Washington, D.C. 20233 (301) 457-4100

Veteran Population.
U.S. Department of Veterans Affairs, 810 Vermont Avenue, NW, Washington, D.C. 20420 (202) 273-5400

Vietnam.
Federal Statistical Office, Gustav-Stresemann-Ring 11, D-6200 Wiesbaden, Germany

Vietnam Country Report.
Economist Intelligence Unit, 111 West 57th Street, New York, New York 10019 (800) 938-4685

Violence and Crime in Cross-National Perspective.
Yale University Press, Yale Station, New Haven, Connecticut 06520 (800) 987-7323

Virginia Statistical Abstract
University of Virginia, Center for Public Service, Dynamics Building, Fourth Floor, 2015 Ivy Road, Charlottesville, Virginia 22903 (804) 924-3921

Vital Health Statistics.
U.S. Department of Health and Human Services, National Center for Health Statistics, 3700 East-West Highway, Hyattsville, Maryland 20782 (301) 436-8500

Vital Statistics in Corrections.
American Correctional Association, Lanham, Maryland (800) 222-5646

Vital Statistics of the United States.
U.S. Department of Health and Human Services, National Center for Health Statistics, 3700 East-West Highway, Hyattsville, Maryland 20782 (301) 436-8500

Vital Statistics on Congress.
Congressional Quarterly, Inc., 1414 22nd Street, NW, Washington, D.C. 20037 (202) 887-8500

Voluntary Support of Education.
Council for Aid to Education, 342 Madison Avenue, Suite 1532, New York, New York 10073 (212) 661-5800

Washington State Data Book.
Washington State Office of Financial Management, Forecasting Division, Post Office Box 43113, Olympia, Washington 98504 (360) 902-0599

Water-Data Report.
U.S. Department of Interior, Geological Survey, National Center, 12201 Sunrise Valley Drive, Reston, Virginia 22092 (703) 648-4000

Waterborne Commerce of the United States.
U.S. Department of the Army, Corps of Engineers, The Pentagon, Washington, D.C. 20310 (703) 695-2442

Weekly Railroad Traffic.
Association of American Railroads, 50 F Street, NW, Washington,, D.C. 20001 (202) 639-2100

West Virginia Economic Outlook.
West Virginia University, College of Business and Economics, Post Office Box 6025, Morgantown, West Virginia 26506 (304) 293-7835

West Virginia Statistical Abstract.
West Virginia University, College of Business and Economics, Bureau of Business and Economic Research, Post Office Box 6025, Morgantown, West Virginia 26506 (304) 293-7835

Western Europe.
Europa Publications, London, England (Available from The Gale Group, 27500 Drake Road, Farmington Hills, Michigan 48331 (800) 877-4253)

Western European Censuses, 1960, An English Language Guide.
University of California, Institute of International Studies, Berkeley, California (Reprinted by Greenwood Press, Westport, Connecticut (800) 225-5800)

Wheat Situation.
U.S. Department of Agriculture, National Agricultural Statistics Service, Fourteenth Street and Independence Avenue, SW, Washington, D.C. 20250 (800) 727-9540

Whitaker's Almanac.
J. Whitaker and Sons, London, England (Distributed in the U.S. by The Gale Group, 27500 Drake Road, Farmington Hills, Michigan 48331 (800) 877-4253)

Who Knows What: A Guide to Experts.
Washington Researchers, Washington, D.C. (202) 333-3499

Windward and Leeward Islands Country Report.
Economist Intelligence Unit, 111 West 57th Street, New York, New York 10019 (800) 938-4685

Wirtschaft und Statistik.
Statistiches Bundesamt Federal Statistical Office, Gustav-Stresemann-Ring 11, 6200 Wiesbaden, Postfach 5528, Germany

Wisconsin Blue Book.
Wisconsin Legislative Reference Bureau, P.O. Box 2037, Madison, Wisconsin 53701-2037 (608) 266-0341

Women and Minorities in Science and Engineering.
National Science Foundation, 4201 Wilson Boulevard, Arlington, Virginia 22230 (703) 306-1234

Wood Pulp and Fiber Statistics.
American Forest and Paper Association, 1111 19th Street, NW, Washington, D.C. 20036 (202) 463-2700

World Agriculture Supply and Demand Estimates.
U.S. Department of Agriculture, Economic Research Service, 1800 M Street, NW, Washington, D.C. 20036 (202) 694-4040

World Agriculture - Trends and Indicators.
U.S. Department of Agriculture, Foreign Agricultural Service, Fourteenth Street and Independence Avenue, SW, Washington, D.C. 20250 (202) 720-7115

World Almanac and Book of Facts.
Funk & Wagnalls, Mahwah, New Jersey (201) 529-6900

World Bank Atlas.
The World Bank, 1818 H Street, NW, Washington, D.C. 20043 (202) 477-1234

World Development Indicators.
The World Bank, 1818 H Street, NW, Washington, D.C. 20043 (202) 477-1234

World Development Report.
Oxford University Press, New York, New York (published for the International Bank for Reconstruction and Development and The World Bank) (800) 645-7247

World Economic Data.
ABC-CLIO, Santa Barbara, California (800) 422-2546

The World Economic Factbook.
Euromonitor International, 60-61 Britton Street, London EC1M 5NA, England (Number in the U.S. (800) 577-EURO)

World Economic Survey.
United Nations, New York, New York (Available from UNIPUB (800) 274-4888)

The World Factbook.
Central Intelligence Agency, Washington, D.C. 20505 (703) 482-1100

World Handbook of Political and Social Indicators.
Yale University Press, Yale Station, New Haven, Connecticut 06520 (800) 987-7323

World Health Statistics Annual.
World Health Organization, 20 Avenue Appia, Office of Publications, CH-1211 Geneva 27, Switzerland (Telephone Number in U.S. (518) 436-9686)

World Index of Economic Forecasts: Including Industrial Tendency Surveys and Development Plans.

Gower Publishing Company, Farnborough, England (Telephone Number in the U.S. (802) 276-3162)

World Livestock Situation.
U.S. Department of Agriculture, Foreign Agricultural Service, Fourteenth Street and Independence Avenue, SW, Washington, D.C. 20250 (202) 720-7115

World Lottery Almanac.
TLF Publications, Inc. (LaFleur's), Boyds, Maryland 20841 (301) 540-0123

World Marketing Data and Statistics.
Euromonitor International, Inc., 122 South Michigan Avenue, Suite 1200, Chicago, Illinois 60603 (80) 577-EURO

World Metal Statistics.
World Bureau of Metal Statistics, 27-A High Street, Ware Herts, SG12 9BA, England

World Military Expenditures and Arms Transfers.
U.S. Arms Control and Disarmament Agency, 320 Twenty-first Street, NW, Washington, D.C. 20451 (202) 647-8677

World of Information Asia and Pacific Review.
Walden Publishing Ltd., Two Market Street, Saffron Walden Essex, CB10 1HZ, England

World Population Profile.
U.S. Department of Commerce, Bureau of the Census, Washington, D.C. 20233 (301) 457-4100

World Poultry Situation.
U.S. Department of Agriculture, Foreign Agricultural Service, Fourteenth Street and Independence Avenue, SW, Washington, D.C. 20250 (202) 720-7115

World Radio TV Handbook.
Billboard Limited, Post Office Box 9027, 1006 AA Amsterdam, The Netherlands (Telephone Number in U.S. (212) 764-7300)

World Road Statistics.
International Road Federation, 2600 Virginia Avenue, NW, Washington, D.C. 20037 (202) 338-4641

World Statistics in Brief: United Nations Statistical Pocketbook.
Statistical Office of the United Nations, Publishing Service, New York, New York 10017 (800) 253-9646

World Statistics Pocketbook.
Statistical Office of the United Nations, Publishing Service, New York, New York 10017 (800) 253-9646

World Telecommunication Indicators.
International Telecommunication Union, Palais des Nations, CH-1211, Geneva 20, Switzerland

World's Top Tourism Earners.
World Tourism Organization, Madrid, Spain

Worldwide Tanker Casualty Returns.
Tanker Advisory Center, 10 East End Avenue, New York, New York 10028 (212) 628-7686

The World's Jet and Turboprop Airliner Fleet.
AVMARK, 1500 Wilson Boulevard, Suite 515, Arlington, Virginia 22209 (703) 528-5610

The World's Telephones.
American Telephone and Telegraph Company, 26 Parsippany Road, Whippany, New Jersey 07981 (800) 222-0300

The World's Women, 1995: Trends and Statistics.
Statistical Office of the United Nations, Publishing Service, New York, New York 10017 (800) 253-9646

Year Book Australia.
Australian Bureau of Statistics, Post Office Box 10, Belconnen, Canberra ACT 2616, Australia

Yearbook of American and Canadian Churches.
National Council of the Churches of Christ in the United States of America, 475 Riverside Drive, New York, New York 10115 (212) 870-2227

Yearbook of Fishery Statistics.
Food and Agricultural Organization of the United Nations (FAO), Via delle Terme di Caracalla, 00100 Rome, Italy (Telephone Number in the U.S. (202) 653-2400)

Yearbook of Forest Products.
Food and Agricultural Organization of the United Nations (FAO), Via delle Terme di Caracalla, 00100, Rome, Italy (Telephone Number in the U.S. (202) 653-2400)

Yearbook of Forest Statistics.
Food and Agricultural Organization of the United Nations (FAO), Via delle Terme di Caracalla, 00100, Rome, Italy (Telephone Number in the U.S. (202) 653-2400)

Yearbook of International Statistics.
Statistical Office of the United Nations, Publishing Service, New York, New York 10017 (800) 253-9646

Yearbook of International Trade Statistics.
Statistical Office of the United Nations, Publishing Service, New York, New York 10017 (800) 253-9646

Yearbook of Labour Statistics.
International Labour Office, I.L.O. Publications, CH-1211, Geneva 22, Switzerland (Telephone Number in U.S. (518) 436-9686)

Yearbook of Statistics Singapore.
Department of Statistics, 8 Shenton Way 10-01, Treasury Building, Singapore, 0106

Yearbook of Tourism Statistics.
World Tourism Organization, Calle Capitan Haya 42, E-28020 Madrid, Spain

Year-end Review and Forecast.
Aerospace Industries Association of America, 1250 I Street, NW, Washington, D.C. 20005 (202) 371-8400

Yemen Country Report.
Economist Intelligence Unit, 111 West 57th Street, New York, New York 10019 (800) 938-4685

Yugoslavia Country Report.
Economist Intelligence Unit, 111 West 57th Street, New York, New York 10019 (800) 938-4685

Zambia Country Report.
Economist Intelligence Unit, 111 West 57th Street, New York, New York 10019 (800) 938-4685

Zambia in Figures.
Central Statistical Office, Post Office Box 31908, Lusaka, Zambia

Zentral afrikanische Republik.
Federal Statistical Office, Gustav-Stresemann-Ring 11, D-6200 Wiesbaden, Germany

Zimbabwe Country Report.
Economist Intelligence Unit, 111 West 57th Street, New York, New York 10019 (800) 938-4685

Appendix B

Sources of Nonpublished Statistical Data

This appendix provides an overview of the agencies, institutions, and other organizational sources of nonpublished statistical information used to compile this edition of *Statistics Sources*. It consists of a complete listing of all such organizations cited under the specific subject headings throughout both volumes. Entries are arranged alphabetically by organization name, and include addresses.

Administrative Office of the United States Courts, Thurgood Marshall Federal Judiciary Building, One Columbus Circle, NE, Washington, D.C. 20544 (202) 502-1455.

Air Transport Association of America, 1301 Pennsylvania Avenue, NW, Washington, D.C. 20004-7017 (202) 626-4000.

Alabama Department of Economic and Community Affairs, Office of State Planning, Post Office Box 5690, 3465 Norman Bridge Road, Montgomery, Alabama 36103-5690 (205) 242-5493.

Alabama Public Library Service, 6030 Monticello Drive, Montgomery, Alabama 36130 (205) 277-7330.

Alaska State Data Center, Research and Analysis, Department of Labor, Post Office Box 25504, Juneau, Alaska 99802-5504 (907) 465-6026.

Algemeen Bureau Voor de Statistiek, Post Office Box 244, Paramaribo, Suriname.

Amateur Softball Association of America, 2801 NE 50th Street, Oklahoma City, Oklahoma 73111-7203 (405) 424-5266.

American Association of Colleges of Osteopathic Medicine, 5550 Friendship Boulevard, Suite 310, Chevy Chase, Maryland 20815 (301) 968-4100.

American Association of Tissue Banks, 1350 Beverly Road, Suite 220-A, McLean, Virginia 22101 (703) 827-9582.

American Banker, One State Street Plaza, New York, New York 10004 (800) 367-3989.

American Bowling Congress, 5301 South 76th Street, Greendale, Wisconsin 53129 (414) 421-9000.

American Council of Life Insurance, 1001 Pennsylvania Avenue, NW, Washington, D.C. 20004-2599 (202) 624-2000.

American Enterprise Institute for Public Policy Research, 1150 Seventeenth Street, NW, Washington, D.C. 20036 (202) 862-5800.

American Forest and Paper Association, 1111 Nineteenth Street, NW, Washington, D.C. 20036 (202) 463-2700.

American Hospital Association, One North Franklin, Suite 27, Chicago, Illinois 60606 (800) 242-2626.

American Humane Association, Animal Protection Division, 63 Inverness Drive, East, Englewood, Colorado 80112 (303) 792-9900.

American Osteopathic Association, 142 East Ontario Street, Chicago, Illinois 60611 (800) 621-1773.

American Symphony Orchestra League, 33 West 60th Street, New York, New York 10023 (212) 262-5161.

American Telephone and Telegraph Company, 26 Parsippany Road, Whippany, New Jersey 07981 (800) 222-0300.

Amt fur Volkswirtschaft des furstlichen Regierung, FL-9490 Vaduz, Liechtenstein.

Applied Population Laboratory, Department of Rural Sociology, University of Wisconsin, 1450 Linden Drive, Room 316, Madison, Wisconsin 53706 (608) 265-3044.

Applied Social Data Center, Department of Sociology, Central Washington University, Ellensburg, Washington 98926 (509) 963-1305.

The Arbitron Company, 142 West 57th Street, New York, New York 10019 (212) 887-1300.

Arizona Department of Security, First Floor, Southeast Wing, 1789 West Jefferson Street, Phoenix, Arizona 85007 (602) 542-5984.

Arkansas State Library, 1 Capitol Mall, Little Rock, Arkansas 72201 (501) 682-2864.

Association of Bay Area Governments, Metro Center, Eighth and Oak Streets, Post Office Box 2050, Oakland, California 94604-2050 (510) 464-7937.

Association of Monterey Bay Area Governments, 445 Reservation Road, Suite G, Post Office Box 838, Marina, California 93933 (408) 883-3750.

Association of Racing Commissioners International, Two Paragon Centre, 2343 Alexandria Drive, Suite 200, Lexington, Kentucky 40504 (606) 224-7070.

Australian Bureau of Statistics, Post Office Box 10, Belconnen, Canberra ACT 2616, Australia.

Banco Central de Ecuador, Division de Investigacciones Economicas, Avenue 10 de Agosto Y Briceno, Quito, Ecuador.

Bangladesh Bureau of Statistics, Room No. 12, School Building, Bangladesh Secretariat, Dhaka 2, Bangladesh.

Bank of Thailand, Bangkhunprom, Bangkok 10200, Thailand.

Barbados Statistical Service, Third Floor, National Insurance Building, Fairchild Street, Bridgetown, Barbados.

Battery Council International, 401 North Michigan Avenue, Chicago, Illinois 60611 (312) 644-6610.

Biblioteca Carnegie, Avenue Ponce De Leon-Parada 1, San Juan, Puerto Rico 00901 (809) 724-1046.

Biro Pusat Statistik, Jalan Dr. Sutomo 9, Jakarta, Indonesia.

Board of Governors of the Federal Reserve System, Twentieth Street and Constitution Avenue, NW, Washington, D.C. 20551 (202) 452-3000.

Bond Market Association, 40 Broad Street, 12th Floor, New York, New York 10004-2373 (212) 809-7000

Bureau de la Statistique de Quebec, Centre d'information et de Documentation, 117 St. Andre, ler etage, Quebec, PQG1K 3Y3, Canada (418) 691-2401 and (800) 463-4090.

Bureau of Business and Economic Research, University of Montana, Missoula, Montana 59812 (406) 243-5113.

Bureau of Business and Economic Research, University of New Mexico, 1920 Lomas, NE, Albuquerque, New Mexico 87131 (505) 277-6626.

Bureau of Economic Analysis, Florida Department of Commerce, 107 West Gaines Street, 315 Collins Building, Tallahassee, Florida 32399-2000 (904) 487-2971.

Bureau of Governmental Research and Service, University of Oregon, Hendricks Hall, Room 331, 1408 University Street, Post Office Box 3177, Eugene, Oregon 97403 (503) 346-5235.

Bureau of Statistics, Alberta Treasury, Sixth Floor, Park Plaza, 10611 98 Avenue, Edmonton, Alberta T5K 2R7, Canada (403) 427-3058.

Bureau of Statistics, Census Administrator and Principal Statistician, Vanuatu Government, Private Mail Bag 19, Port Vila, Vanuatu.

Bureau of Statistics, Department of Finance, Post Office Box 1320, Yellowknife, Northwest Territories X1A 2L9, Canada (403) 873-7147.

Bureau of Statistics, Economic Planning Board, 90 Gyoungwoon-dong, Jongro-Ku, Seoul, Korea.

Bureau of Statistics, Government Buildings, Post Office Box 2221, Suva, Fiji.

Bureau of Statistics, Ministry of Planning and Economic Affairs, Post Office Box 9016, Monrovia, Liberia.

Bureau of Statistics, Post Office Box 796, Dar es Salaam, United Republic of Tanzania.

Bureau of Statistics, Post Office Box 455, Maseru 100, Lesotho.

Business Committee for the Arts, 1775 Broadway, Suite 510, New York, New York 10019 (212) 664-0600.

Business Research Bureau, School of Business, Patterson Hall, University of South Dakota, 414 East Clark, Vermillion, South Dakota 57069 (605) 677-5287.

Business Research Division, Graduate School of Business Administration, University of Colorado-Boulder, Boulder, Colorado 80309 (303) 492-8227.

Business Statistics Office, Government Buildings, Cardiff Road, Newport, Gwent NP9 1XC, United Kingdom.

Campbell County Library, 2101 Four J Road, Gillette, Wyoming 82716 (307) 682-3223.

Canadian Pulp and Paper Association, 1155 Metcalfe Street, 19th Floor, Montreal, Quebec H3B 4T6, Canada (514) 866-6621.

Cape Cod Community Library, Library/Learning Resource Center, Route 132, West Barnstable, Massachusetts 02668 (508) 362-8638.

Capitol Region Council of Governments, 221 Main Street, Hartford, Connecticut 06106 (203) 522-2217.

CENCI Uruguay, Misiones 1361, ESC 14, Casilla de Correo 1510, Montevideo, Uruguay.

Census and Data Users Services, Department 4690, Research Services Building, Suite A, Illinois State University, Normal, Illinois 61790-4950 (309) 438-5946.

Census and Economic Information Center, Montana Department of Commerce, 1424 Ninth Avenue, Capitol Station, Helena, Montana 59620-0501 (406) 444-2896.

Census and Statistics Department, Wanchai Tower I, 12 Harbor Road, Wanchai, Hong Kong.

Census Data Center, Department of Education, Grimes State Office Building, Des Moines, Iowa 50319 (515) 281-4730.

Census Services, Iowa State University, 320 East Hall, Ames, Iowa 50011 (515) 294-8337.

Center for Applied Urban Research, The University of Nebraska-Omaha, Peter Kiewit Conference Center, 1313 Farnam-on-the-Mall, Omaha, Nebraska 68182 (402) 595-2311.

Center for Business and Economic Research, College of Business Administration, University of Tennessee, Room 100, Glocker Hall, Knoxville, Tennessee 37996-4170 (615) 974-5441.

Center for Business and Economic Research, Northeast Louisiana University, Monroe, Louisiana 71209 (318) 342-1215.

Center for Business and Economic Research, University of Alabama, Box 870221, Tuscaloosa, Alabama 35487-0221 (205) 348-6191.

Center for Business Research, College of Business Administration, Arizona State University, Tempe, Arizona 85287 (602) 965-3961.

Center for Business Research and Services, Campus Box 8450, Idaho State University, Pocatello, Idaho 83209 (208) 236-3409.

Center for Computer and Information Services, Rutgers University, CCIS-

Hill Center, Busch Campus, Post Office Box 879, Piscataway, New Jersey 08854 (732) 932-9384.

Center for Economic Development and Business Research, Box 48, Wichita State University, Wichita, Kansas 67208 (316) 689-3225.

The Center for Economic Research, West Virginia University, 323 Business and Economic Building, Morgantown, West Virginia 26506-6025 (304) 293-7832.

Center for Geographic Information, Office of State Planning, Post Office Box 27687, Raleigh, North Carolina 27611 (919) 733-2090.

Center for Governmental Studies, Northern Illinois University, Social Science Research Building, DeKalb, Illinois 60115 (815) 753-0922.

Center for Health Policy and Statistics, South Dakota Department of Health, Foss Building 523 East Capitol, Pierre, South Dakota 57501 (605) 773-3693.

Center for Life Course and Population Studies, Department of Sociology, Room 126, Stubbs Hall, Louisiana State University, Baton Rouge, Louisiana 70803-5411 (504) 388-5359.

Center for Political Studies, University of Michigan, Post Office Box 1248, Ann Arbor, Michigan 48106 (313) 764-8363.

Center for Population Research and Census, Portland State University, Post Office Box 751, Portland, Oregon 97207-0751 (503) 725-5159.

Center for Population Studies, University of Mississippi, Bondurant Building, Room 3W, University, Mississippi 38677 (601) 232-7288.

Center for Public Affairs Research, Nebraska State Data Center, Room 203-Annex 26, University of Nebraska at Omaha, Omaha, Nebraska 68182 (402) 595-2311.

Center for Public Service, University of Virginia, 918 Emmet Street, North, Suite 300, Charlottesville, Virginia 22903-1795 (804) 982-5585.

Center for Rural Studies, University of Vermont, 207 Morrill Hall, Burlington, Vermont 05405-0106 (802) 656-3201.

Center for Social and Behavioral Research, University of Northern Iowa, Cedar Falls, Iowa 50614 (319) 273-2105.

Center for Social Organization of Schools, The Johns Hopkins University, 3505 North Charles Street, Baltimore, Maryland 21218 (410) 338-7570.

Center for the American Woman and Politics, The Eagleton Institute of Politics, Rutgers University, New Brunswick, New Jersey 08901 (908) 828-2210.

Center for the Study of Population, Institute for Social Research, 654 Bellemy Building, Florida State University, Tallahassee, Florida 32306-4063 (904) 644-1762.

Center for Urban and Economic Research, College of Business and Public Administration, University of Louisville, Louisville, Kentucky 40292 (502) 588-7990.

Central Agency for Public Mobilisation and Statistics, Salah Salem Street, Nasr City, Cairo, Egypt.

Central Bureau of Statistics, Abdel-Malek Bin Marwan Street, Malki Quarter, Damascus, Syrian Arab Republic.

Central Bureau of Statistics, Willemstad, Curacao, Netherlands Antilles.

Central Bureau of Statistics, Post Office Box 13015, Jerusalem 91130, Israel.

Central Bureau of Statistics, National Planning Commission Secretariat, Ramshah Path, Thapathali, Kathmandu, Nepal.

Central Bureau of Statistics, Post Office Box 1098, Accra, Ghana.

Central Bureau of Statistics, Post Office Box 3, Jakarta 10002, Indonesia.

Central Bureau of Statistics, Pyongyang, Democratic People's Republic of Korea.

Centraal Bureau Voor de Statistiek, Windstraat 21, Oranjestad, Aruba.

The Central Data Processing Division, Department of Administration Services, 301 Centennial Mall South, Lower Level, Post Office Box 95045, Lincoln, Nebraska 68509-5045 (402) 471-4862.

Central Department of Statistics, Ministry of Finance and National Economy, Post Office Box 3735, Riyadh, Saudi Arabia.

Central Intelligence Agency, Washington, D.C. 20505 (703) 482-1100.

Central Office of Statistics, Auberge D'Italie, Valletta, Malta.

Central Planning Division, Ministry of Finance and Planning, Kingstown, Saint Vincent and the Grenadines.

Central Planning Organization, Statistics Organization, Ministry of Planning and Development, Sana'a, Yemen.

Central Statistical Office, Post Office Box 456, Mbabane, Swaziland.

Central Statistical Office, 23 Park Street, Post Office Box 98, Port of Spain, Trinidad.

Central Statistical Office, Great George Street, London SW1P 3AQ United Kingdom.

Central Statistical Office, International Division, 2P, Volov Street, Sofia, Bulgaria.

Central Statistical Office, Ministry of Development and Planning, Tripoli, Libya.

Central Statistical Office, Ministry of Economic Planning and Development, Royal Road, Port Louis, Mauritius.

Central Statistical Office, Ministry of Finance, Post Office Box 31908, Lusaka, Zambia.

Central Statistical Office, The Ministry of Planning, Post Office Box 26188, Safat, Kuwait.

Central Statistical Office, National Planning Commission, 6th Floor, Government Offices, Private Bag 13356, Windhoek, Namibia.

Central Statistical Office, Planning Commission, Post Office Box Number 338, Thimphu, Bhutan.

Central Statistical Office, Post Office Box 1143, Addis Ababa, Ethiopia.
Central Statistical Office, Post Office Box 8063, Causeway, Harare, Zimbabwe.

Central Statistical Office, Ulan Bator, Mongolian People's Republic.

Central Statistical Office of Finland, Box 504, Annankatu 44 SF-00100 Helsinki, Finland.

Central Statistical Organisation, Ministry of Planning, Post Office Box 8001, Baghdad, Iraq.

Central Statistical Organisation, Post Office Box 7283, Doha, Qatar.

Central Statistical Organisation, Sardar Patel Bhavan, Parliament Street, New Delhi, India.

Central Statistical Organization, Ministry of Planning and Finance, Six-Storeyed Building, Strand Road, Yangoon, Myanmar.

Central Statistical Services, Private Bag X44, Pretoria 0001, South Africa.

Central Statistics Department, Old Treasury Building, 32 Buckle Street, Banjul, Gambia.

Central Statistics Office, Ardee Road, Dublin 6, Ireland.

Central Statistics Office, Block No. 4, Mikrorayon, Kabul, Afghanistan.
Central Statistics Office, Ministry of Development and Economic Planning, Tower Hill, Freetown, Sierra Leone.

Central Statistics Office, Private Bag 0024, Gaborone, Botswana.

Central Statistics Office, Saint Stephen's Green House, Earlsfort Terrace, Dublin 2, Ireland.

Central Statistics Organisation, Post Office Box 5835, Bahrain.

Central Statistics Organisation, Post Office Box 1272, Steamer Point, Aden, Yemen.

Centre for Industrial Statistics Information and Research, Industrial Economics and Planning Division, Ministry of Industry, Rama 6 Road, Bangkok 10400, Thailand.

Centre National de la Statistique et des Etudes Economiques, BP 2031, Brazzaville, People's Republic of Congo.

Centro Nacional de informatica de Andorra, Avda Meritxell 86B, Andorra La Vella, Andorra.

Chicago Area Geographic Information Study, Department of Geography, M/C 092, 1007 West Harrison Street, Room 2102, University of Illinois at Chicago, Chicago, Illinois 60607 (312) 996-5274.

Chief Government Statistician, Department of Statistics, Ministry of Planning and Economic Development, Post Office Box 13, Entebbe, Uganda.

The Chief Secretary, Chief Secretary's Office, Grand Turk, Turks and Caicos Islands.

Chief Statistician, Economic Planning Unit, Jalan Elizabeth, Kedua, Bandar Seri Begawan, Brunei.

Chief Statistician, Post Office Box 206, Victoria, Mahe, Seychelles.

CIT - Information Services, Princeton University, 87 Prospect Avenue, Princeton, New Jersey 08544 (609) 258-6052.

Cleveland State University, Northern Ohio Data and Information Service, 1737 Euclid Avenue, Cleveland, Ohio 44115 (216) 687-2209.

College of Business Administration, Northern Arizona University, Box 15066, Flagstaff, Arizona 86011 (602) 523-7313.

College of Urban Affairs and Public Policy, University of Delaware, Graham Hall, Room 286, Academy Street, Newark, Delaware 19716 (302) 451-8406.

Colorado Division of Local Government, Department of Local Affairs, 1313 Sherman Street, Room 521, Denver, Colorado 80203 (303) 866-2156.

Comite Estatal de Estadisticas, Almendares No. 156, Civdad de la Habana, Cuba.

Community Development Division, Governor's Office of Community and Industrial Development, Capitol Complex, Building 6, Room 553, Charleston, West Virginia 25305 (304) 348-4010.

Competitive Media Reporting, 11 West 42nd Street, New York, New York 10036 (212) 789-1400.

Computer Science Center, University of Maryland, College Park, Maryland 20742 (301) 405-3037.

Connecticut Department of Economic Development, 865 Brook Street, Building #1, Rocky Hill, Connecticut 06067-3405 (203) 258-4219.

Connecticut Office of Policy and Management, Policy Development and Planning Division, 80 Washington Street, Hartford, Connecticut 06106 (203) 566-8285.

Cornell University, CISER Data Archive, 201 Caldwell Hall, Ithaca, New York 14853 (607) 255-4801.

Corporation for Public Broadcasting, 901 E Street, NW, Washington, D.C. 20004-2006 (202) 879-9600.

Danmarks Statistik, Post Boks 2550 Sejrogade 11, 2100 Copenhagen 0, Denmark.

Data Services, University of Georgia Libraries, Sixth Floor, Athens, Georgia 30602 (404) 542-0727.

Data Services Division, Mayor's Office of Planning, Room 570, Presidential Building, 415 Twelfth Street, NW, Washington, D.C. 20004 (202) 727-6533.

Dataquest Inc., 251 River Oak Parkway, San Jose, California 95134 (408) 468-8000.

Delaware Development Office, 99 Kings Highway, Post Office Box 1401, Dover, Delaware 19903 (302) 739-4271.

Demographic Services Center, Department of Administration, 101 East Wilson, Sixth Floor, Post Office Box 7868, Madison, Wisconsin 53707-7868 (608) 266-1927.

Department of Administration, Office of Municipal Affairs, One Capitol Hill, Providence, Rhode Island 02908-5873 (401) 277-6493.

Department of Administration and Fiscal Control, Research and Statistics Division, Emerson Building, Cheyenne, Wyoming 82002-0060 (307) 777-7504.

Department of Agricultural Economics, North Dakota State University, Morrill Hall, Room 224, Post Office Box 5636, Fargo, North Dakota 58105 (701) 237-8621.

Department of Commerce, 590 South Marine Drive, Suite 601, 6th Floor GITC Building, Tamuning, Guam 96911 (671) 646-5841.

Department of Commerce and Labor, Saipan, M.P. 96950, Commonwealth of the Northern Mariana Islands.

Department of Commercial Intelligence and Statistics, One Council House Street, Calcutta, India.

Department of Community and Economic Development, 324 South State Street, Suite 500, Salt Lake City, Utah 84111 (801) 538-8897.

Department of Community and Regional Affairs, Division of Municipal and Regional Assistance, Post Office Box BH, Juneau, Alaska 99811 (907) 465-4750.

Department of Economics, New Mexico State University, Box 30001, Las Cruces, New Mexico 88003 (505) 646-2112.

Department of Education, Division of Libraries and Museums, Alaska State Library, Pouch G, Juneau, Alaska 99811 (907) 465-2927.

Department of Employment Security, 140 East 300 South, Post Office Box 11249, Salt Lake City, Utah 84147 (801) 536-7813.

Department of Employment Security, Post Office Box 9046, Olympia, Washington 98504 (206) 438-4804.

Department of Finance and Development, Administration Building, George Town, Grand Cayman, Cayman Islands.

Department of Geography, University of North Dakota, Grand Forks, North Dakota 58202 (701) 777-4246.

Department of Island Development and Industry, Government Offices, Yaren District, Republic of Nauru, Central Pacific.

Department of Rural Sociology, Texas A & M University System, Special Services Building, College Station, Texas 77843-2125 (409) 845-5115 or 5332.

Department of Sociology, Demographic Research Laboratory, Western Washington University, Bellingham, Washington 98225 (206) 676-3176.

Department of Statistics, Post Office Box 2015, Amman, Jordan.

Department of Statistics, Post Office Box 1151, Apia, Samoa.

Department of Statistics, Ministry of Trade and Industry, 8 Shenton Way, 10-01, Treasury Building, Singapore, 0106.

Department of Statistics, Post Office Box 2922, Wellington, New Zealand.

Department of Statistics, Bangunan Perseketuan, Jalan Mat Salleh, Post Office Box 500, Kota Kinabalu, Sabah.

Department of Statistics, 5th Floor Bangunan Tun Datuk Patinggi Tuanku Haji Bujang, Jalan Simpang Tiga, Kuching, Sarawak.

Department of Statistics, Jalan Cenderasari 50514, Kuala Lumpur, Malaysia.

Department of Statistics, Ministry of Finance and Economic Planning, Post Office Box 700, Khartoum, Sudan.

Departmento Administrativo Nacional de Estadistica, Avenida Eldorado, Bogota DE, Colombia.

Departmento de Estudios Economicos del Banco Central del Paraguay, Pablo Vl y San Rafael, Barrio Santo Domingo, Asuncion, Paraguay.

Departamento de Relaciones Internacionales, Comite Estatal de Estadisticas, Paseo y 5a, Vedado, Ciudad de La Habana, Cuba.

Devlet Istatistik Enstitusu, Necatibey Caddesi, 114 Ankara, Turkey.

Direccao - Geral de Estatistica, C.P. 116, Praia, Cape Verde.

Direccao de Estatistica, CP 256, Sao Tome, Sao Tome e Principe.

Direccao de Services de Estatistica e Census, Post Office Box 3022, Macau.

Direccion de Estadistica y Censo, Apartado 5213, Panama 5, Panama.

Direccion General de Estadistica, Centro Nacional de Informacion, Edificio America, 8 Calle 9-55, Zona 1, Guatemala City, Guatemala.

Direccion General de Estadistica y Censos, Avenida Centenario GY8 Calles, Comayaguela DC, Honduras, Honduras.

Direccion General de Estadistica y Censos, Cuareim 2052, Montevideo, Uruguay.

Direccion General de Estadistica y Censos, Miquel Torres 5313, C Correos: 1118, Asuncion, Paraguay.

Direccion General de Estadistica y Censos la Calle P Y 45 Ave Norte, San Salvador, El Salvador.

Direccion General de Estadistics y Censos, Apartado 10216, San Jose, Costa Rica.

Directeur General de la Statistique et des Etudes Economiques, BP 2119, Libreville, Gabon.

Directia Centrala de Statistica, Str. Stavropoleos No. 6, Bucharest, Romania.

Direction Central de la Statistique, Bir Hassan, Beirut, Lebanon.

Direction de la Statistique, Ministere de l'Economie et des Finances, BP 116, Dakar, Senegal.

Direction de la Statistique, BP 118, Lome, Togo.

Direction de la Statistique, BP 453, N'Djamena, Chad.

Direction de la Statistique, BP 178, Rabat, Morocco.

Direction de la Statistique, Commissariat d'Etat du Development Economique et du Plan, Bissau, Guinea Bissau.

Direction de la Statistique, BP V55, Abidjan, Cote d'Ivoire.

Direction de la Statistique et de la Comptabilite Nationale, Ministere de Plan et de l'Amenagement du Territoire, Yaounde, Cameroon.

Direction de la Statistique, et de la Demographie, BP 240, Nouakchott, Mauritania.

Direction de la Statistique Generale et des Etudes Economiques, BP 732, Bangui, Central African Republic.

Direction de la Statistiques, Ministere du Plan BP 467, Niamey, Niger.

Direction Generale de la Banque des Donnees d L'Etat, BP 485, Antananarivo, Madagascar.

Direction Generale de la Statistique, Ministere du Plan, BP 46, Kigali, Rwanda.

Direction Generale de la Statistique, Ministere du Plan et Cooperation Internationale, Conakry, Guinea.

Direction Nationale de la Statistique, BP 67, Djibouti.

Direction Nationale des Statistiques de Commerce Exterieur, Centre de Renseignements Statistiques, 192 Rue St. Honore, 75056 Paris RP, France.

Direction Nationale de L'Informatique, Ministere du Plan, B.P. 12, Bamako, Mali.

Direction Territoriale de la Statistique et des Etudes Economiques, BP 823, Noumea, New Caledonia.

The Director, Department of Census and Statistics, 6 Albert Crescent, Colombo 7, Sri Lanka.

Director of Central Statistics Department, Ministry of Planning, Post Office Box 904, Abu Dhabi, United Arab Emirates.

Director of Statistics, Abu Dhabi Emirate, Department of Planning, Post Office Box 12, Abu Dhabi, United Arab Emirates.

Director of Statistics, Bahamas Government, Department of Statistics, Post Office Box N3904, Nassau, Bahamas.

Directorate General of National Statistics, Development Council, Post Office Box 881, Muscat, Oman.

Directorate of Economics and Statistics, Ministry of Agriculture, Krishi Bhavan, Dr. Rajendra Prasad Road, New Delhi, India.

Directorate of Statistics, Ministry of Planning, Phnom Penh, Cambodia.

Distilled Spirits Council of the United States, 1250 I Street NW, Suite 900, Washington, D.C. 20005 (202) 628-3544.

Division de la Statistique du Commerce, Direction Generale des Douanes, Monbijoustrasse 40, CH-3011 Berne, Switzerland.

Division of Business and Economic Research, University of New Orleans, Lake Front, New Orleans, Louisiana 70148 (504) 286-6980.

Division of Business Research, Louisiana Tech University, Post Office Box 10318, Ruston, Louisiana 71272 (318) 257-3701.

Division of Demographic and Statistical Services, Georgia Office of Planning and Budget, 254 Washington Street, SW, Room 640, Atlanta, Georgia 30334 (404) 656-0911.

Division of Economic Analysis and Research, Maine Department of Labor, 20 Union Street, Augusta, Maine 04330 (207) 289-2271.

Division of Economic and Business Research, College of Business and Public Administration, University of Arizona, Tucson, Arizona 85721 (602) 621-2155.

Division of Equalization and Assessment, 16 Sheridan Avenue, Albany, New York 12210 (518) 474-6742.

Division of Labor Market and Demographic Research, New Jersey Department of Labor, CN 388-John Fitch Plaza, Trenton, New Jersey 08625-0388 (609) 984-2593.

Division of Local Government, Colorado Department of Local Affairs, 1313 Sherman Street, Room 521, Denver, Colorado 80203 (303) 866-2156.

Division of Planning and Financial Analysis, Illinois Bureau of the Budget, William Stratton Building, Room 605, Springfield, Illinois 62706 (217) 782-1381.

Division of Policy and Research, Department of Economic Development, 1 Commerce Plaza, Room 905, 99 Washington Avenue, Albany, New York 12245 (518) 474-1141.

Division of Research and Information Systems, Department of Economic and Community Development, 1200 Walter Sillas Building, Post Office Box 849, Jackson, Mississippi 39205 (601) 359-2674.

Division of Research and Statistical Services, South Carolina Budget and Control Board, Rembert C. Dennis Building, Room 425, Columbia, South Carolina 29201 (803) 734-3780.

Division of State Library, 109 East Jones Street, Raleigh, North Carolina 27611 (919) 733-3683.

Division of the Budget, Room 152-E, State Capitol Building, Topeka, Kansas 66612 (913) 296-0025.

Documents Department, The Libraries, Colorado State University, Fort Collins, Colorado 80523 (303) 491-1880.

Documents Department, South Dakota State Library, Department of Education and Cultural Affairs, 800 Governors Drive, Pierre, South Dakota 57501-2294 (605) 773-3131.

Documents Librarian, Georgia State University, University Plaza, Atlanta, Georgia 30303 (404) 651-2185.

Documents Librarian, State Data Center Program, Albany State College, 504 College Drive, Albany, Georgia 31705 (912) 430-4799.

Documents Librarian, State Data Center Program, Georgia Southern College, Statesboro, Georgia 30460 (912) 681-5117.

Documents Section, Washington State Library AJ-11, Olympia, Washington 98504 (206) 753-4027.

Dow Jones and Company, Inc., 200 Liberty Street, New York, New York 10006 (212) 597-5600.

Drejtoria e Statisikes, Tirana, Albania.

Economic Development Department, 1100 St. Francis Drive, Santa Fe, New Mexico 87503 (505) 827-0182.

Economic Development Planning Office, Pago Pago, American Samoa 96799.

Economic Planning and Statistics Office, Cathedral Square, Gibraltar.

Economics, Statistics and Fiscal Analysis Division, Department of Provincial Treasury, Post Office Box 2000, Charlottetown, Prince Edward Island C1A 7N8, Canada (902) 368-4030.

Employee Benefit Research Institute, 2121 K Street, NW, Suite 600, Washington, D.C. 20037 (202) 659-0670.

Employment Security Division, Connecticut Department of Labor, 200 Folly Brook Boulevard, Wethersfield, Connecticut 06109 (203) 566-2120.

Environmental Protection Agency, 1200 Pennsylvania Avenue, NW,, Washington, D.C. 20460 (888) 372-8255.

Executive Council Office, Bureau of Statistics, Post Office Box 2703, Whitehorse, Yukon Territory Y1A 2C6, Canada (403) 667-5640.

Executive Office of the President, Office of Management and Budget, Executive Office Building, Washington, D.C. 20503 (202) 395-3080.

Eye Bank Association of America, 1015 18th Street, NW, Suite 1010, Washington, D.C. 20036-5504 (202) 775-4999.

Federal Bureau of Statistics, Ministry of Finance and Economic Affairs, 5-SLIC Building, Blue Area, F-6/4, Islamabad, Pakistan.

Federal Communications Commission, 445 Twelfth Street, NW, Washington, D.C. 20554 (888) 225-5322.

Federal Deposit Insurance Corporation, 550 Seventeenth Street, NW, Washington, D.C. 20429 (202) 393-8400.

Federal Documents Librarian, Nebraska Library Commission, The Atrium, 1200 North Street, Suite 120, Nebraska 68508-2006 (402) 471-2045.

Federal Documents Section, Department of Library, Archives, and Public Records, 1700 West Washington, 2nd Floor, Phoenix, Arizona 85007 (602) 542-4121.

Federal Election Commission, 999 E Street, NW, Washington, D.C. 20463 (800) 424-9530.

Federal Office of Statistics, 36-38 Broad Street, PM Bag 12528, Lagos, Nigeria.

Federalni Statisticky Urad, Sokolovska 142, 186 13 Prague 8, Czechoslovakia.

Florida State Data Center, Executive Office of the Governor, REA/OPB, The Capitol, Room 1604, Tallahassee, Florida 32399-0001 (904) 487-2814.

Food and Agricultural Organization of the United Nations (FAO), Via delle Terme di Caracalla, 00100, Rome Italy (Telephone Number in U.S. (202) 653-2400).

Foreign Relations Department, States Statistical Committee, Ulitsa Kirova 39, Moscow 103450, Russia.

Fundacao Instituto Brasileiro de Geografia e Estatistica, Av Franklin Roosevelt, 166/10 andar, 20 021 Rio de Janeiro RJ, Brazil.

Future Computing/Datapro, Inc., 600 Delran Parkway, Delran, New Jersey 08075 (859) 764-0100.

Gallup Organization, Inc., 47 Hulfish Street, Princeton, New Jersey 08542 (609) 924-9600.

Gartner Group, Inc., 56 Top Gallant Road, Stamford, Connecticut 06902 (203) 964-0096.

Geographic Resources Center, University of Missouri-Columbia, 17 Stewart Hall, Columbia, Missouri 65211 (314) 882-1404.

Georgia Department of Community Affairs, Office of Coordinated Planning, 100 Peachtree Street, N.E. #1200, Atlanta, Georgia 30303 (404) 656-5526.

Government Documents, Connecticut State Library, 231 Capitol Avenue, Hartford, Connecticut 06106 (203) 566-4971.

Government of Niue, Post Office Box 67, Alofi, Niue, South Pacific.

Government Statistician, Department of Statistics, Post Office Box 1151, Apia, Western Samoa.

Governor's Office of Community and Industrial Development, Community Development Division, Capitol Complex, Building 6, Room 553, Charleston, West Virginia 25305 (304) 348-4010.

Governor's Office of Federal-State Programs, Department of Community Development, 301 West Pearl Street, Jackson, Mississippi 39203-3096 (601) 949-2219.

Gtowny Urzad Statystyczny (Central Statistical Office), Al Niepodegosci 208, 00-925 Warsaw, Poland.

Guam Department of Commerce, 590 South Marine Drive, Suite 601, Sixth Floor, GITC Building, Tamuning, Guam 96911 (671) 646-5841.

Guttmacher Institute, Alan, 120 Wall Street Avenue, New York, New York 10005 (212) 248-1111.

Haute Commissariat du Plan et Cooperation, Presidence de la Republique, Bangui, Central African Republic.

Hawaii State Data Center, Department of Business & Economic Development and Tourism, 220 South King Street, Suite 400, Honolulu, Hawaii 96813 (808) 586-2493.

Idaho Department of Commerce, 700 West State Street, Boise, Idaho 83720 (208) 334-2470.

The Idaho State Library, 325 West State Street, Boise, Idaho 83702 (208) 334-2150.

Illinois Bureau of the Budget, William Stratton Building, Room 605, Springfield, Illinois 62706 (217) 782-1381.

Indiana Business Research Center, Indiana University, Tenth and Fee Lane, Bloomington, Indiana 47405 (812) 855-5507.

Indiana Business Research Center, 801 West Michigan, B.S. 4015, Indianapolis, Indiana 46202-5151 (317) 274-2205.

Indiana State Data Center, Indiana State Library, 140 North Senate Avenue, Indianapolis, Indiana 46204 (317) 232-3733.

Information and Communication Services Division, State Department of Budget and Finance, Kalanimoku Building, 1151 Punchbowl Street, Honolulu, Hawaii 96813 (808) 568-1940.

Information Officer, Broadway House, Saint Helena.

Inspectorate General of Customs, Ministry of Finance, 85 Hsim-Hseng South Road, Section 1, Taipei, Republic of China.

Institut Haitien de Statistique et d'Informatique, Cite de l'Exposition, Boulevard Harry Truman, Port-au-Prince, Haiti.

Institut National de la Statistique, BP 20, Kinshasa, Zaire.

Institut National de la Statistique et de l'Analyse Economique, Ministere du Plan, de la Statistique, BP 323, Cotonou, Benin.

Institut National de la Statistique et des Etudes Economiques, 18 Boulevard Adolphe Pinard, 75675 Paris Cedex 14, France.

Institut National de Statistique, 27 rue du Liban, 1002 Tunis-Belvedere, Tunis, Tunisia.

Institut National de Statistique, rue de Louvain 44, 1000 Brussels, Belgium.

Institut Territorial de la Statistique, BP 395, Papeete, Tahiti, French Polynesia.

Institute for Public Policy and Business Research, 607 Blake Hall, The University of Kansas, Lawrence, Kansas 66045-2960 (913) 864-3123.

Institute for Research in Social Science, University of North Carolina, Manning Hall CB 3355, Chapel Hill, North Carolina 27599-3355 (919) 962-0512.

Institute for Social and Economic Research, University of Alaska, 3211 Providence Drive, Anchorage, Alaska 99508 (907) 786-7710.

Institute of State and Regional Affairs, Pennsylvania State Data Center, Pennsylvania State University at Harrisburg, Middletown, Pennsylvania 17057-4898 (717) 948-6336.

Institutional Research, Room 319, Business Building, Boise State University, Boise, Idaho 83725 (208) 385-1613.

Instituto Nacional de Estadistica, Casilla 6129, Plaza Mario Guzman Aspiazu No. 1, La Paz, Bolivia.

Instituto Nacional de Estadistica, 10 Avenue de Agosto 229, Quito, Ecuador.

Instituto Nacional de Estadistica, Avenida 28 de Julio 1056, Lima 1, Peru.

Instituto Nacional de Estatistica, Avenida Antonio Jose de Almeida, 1078 Lisbon 1, Portugal.

Instituto Nacional de Estadistica, Ministerio de Economia y Hacienda, Paseo de la Castellana 183, Madrid 28046, Spain.

Instituto Nacional de Estadistica y Censos, Hipolito Yrigoyen 250, Piso 12, Of 1210, 1310 Buenos Aires, Argentina.

Instituto Nacional de Estatisticas, Caixa Postal 1215, Luanda, Angola.
Instituto Nacional de Estadisticas, Casilla 498-3, Santiago, Chile.

Instituto Nacional de Estadisticas y Censos, Apartado 4031, Managua, Nicaragua.

Instituto Nacional de Estadistica, Geografia e Informatica, Patriotismo No. 711, PH, CP 03910 Mexico.

Instituto Nazionale di Statistica, Via Cesare Balbo 16, 00100 Rome, Italy.

Interagency Resource and Information Center, Department of Education, 501 Capitol Square Building, St. Paul, Minnesota 55101 (612) 296-6684.

International Monetary Fund, 700 Nineteenth Street, NW, Washington, D.C. 20431 (202) 623-7000.

International Snowmobile Industry Association, 3975 University Drive, Suite 310, Fairfax, Virginia 22030 (703) 273-9606.

Iowa Social Science Institute, University of Iowa, 345 Shaeffer Hall, Iowa City, Iowa 52242 (319) 335-2371.

Iranian Statistical Centre, Dr Fatemi Avenue, Tehran, Iran.

Kenya Customs and Excise Department, Ministry of Finance, Ministry of Finance, Post Office Box 40160, Nairobi, Kenya.

Kozponti Statisztikai Hivatal (Central Statistical Office), Post Office Box 51, Keleti Karoly Utca 5-7, 1024 Budapest 11, Hungary.

Labor Market Information Center, South Dakota Department of Labor, 420 South Roosevelt, Box 4730, Aberdeen, South Dakota 57402-4730 (605) 622-2314.

Land Resources Information Service, Division of Land Resources, Post Office Box 27687, Raleigh, North Carolina 27611 (919) 733-2090.

The Library of Michigan, Government Documents Service, Post Office Box 30007, 717 West Allegan Street, Lansing, Michigan 48909 (517) 373-0640.

Louisiana State Office of Planning and Budget, Division of Administration, Post Office Box 94095, Baton Rouge, Louisiana 70804 (504) 342-7410.

L'Union Economique Belgo-Luxembourgeoise, Institut National de Statistique, rue de Louvain 44, 1000 Brussels, Belgium.

Magazine Publishers of America, 919 Third Avenue, New York, New York 10022 (212) 872-3700.

Main Library, University of Georgia, Athens, Georgia 30602 (404) 542-0664.

Maine State Library, State House Station 64, Augusta, Maine 04333 (207) 289-5600.

Major League Baseball Players Association, 12 East 49th Street, 24th Floor, New York, New York 10017 (212) 826-0808.

Manitoba Bureau of Statistics, #333, 260 St. Mary Avenue, Winnipeg, Manitoba R3C 0M6, Canada (204) 945-2985.

Market Data Retrieval, One Forest Parkway, Shelton, Connecticut 06484 (203) 926-4800.

Maryland Department of State Planning, 301 West Preston Street, Baltimore, Maryland 21201 (410) 225-4450.

Massachusetts Institute for Social and Economic Research, 128 Thompson Hall, University of Massachusetts, Amherst, Massachusetts 01003 (413) 545-3460.

Massachusetts Institute for Social and Economic Research, Box 219, Saltonstall State Office Building, Room 1103, 100 Cambridge Street, Boston, Massachusetts 02133 (617) 727-4537.

Mediamark Research, Inc., 708 Third Avenue, New York, New York 10017 (212) 599-0444.

Metals Week, McGraw-Hill Publications Company, Inc., 1221 Avenue of the Americas, New York, New York 10020 (212) 512-2000.

Metropolitan Council Research, 230 East Fifth Street, St. Paul, Minnesota 55101 (612) 291-8140.

Metropolitan Life Insurance Company, One Madison Avenue, New York, New York 10010 (212) 889-8804.

Metropolitan Washington Council of Governments, 777 North Capitol Street, Suite 300, Washington, D.C. 20002-4201 (202) 962-3200.

Michigan Information Center, Department of Management and Budget, Office of Revenue and Tax Analysis, Post Office Box 30026, Lansing, Michigan 48909 (517) 373-7910.

MIMIC/Center for Urban Studies, Wayne State University, Faculty/Administration Building, 656 West Kirby, Detroit, Michigan 48202 (313) 577-8359.

Ministere de la Planification et du Developpement Populaire, Institut National de la Statistique et de la Demographie, BP 7050 Ouagadougou, Burkina Faso.

Ministere du Plan et de la Statistique, Bureau du Premier Ministre, Conakry, Guinea.

Ministerio de Economia y Hacienda, Direccion General de Aduanas, Seccion de Estadistica, San Francisco de Sales 6, Madrid 3, Spain.

Ministerio de Planificacion y DeSarrollo Economico, Direccion General de Estadistica, Malabo, Equatorial Guinea.

Ministry of Economic Affairs, Department of Statistics, 15 Foochow Street, Taipei, Taiwan.

Ministry of Economic Planning and Development, Post Office Box 30266, Nairobi, Kenya.

Ministry of Economy, Planning and Finance, Post Office Box 46, Vientiane, Laos.

Ministry of Finance and Corporate Relations, Central Statistics Branch, 553 Superior Street, First Floor, Victoria, British Columbia V8V 1X4, Canada (604) 387-1502.

Ministry of Foreign Affairs, 8 Lenin Street Minsk, Belarus.

Ministry of Planning and Environment, Male 20-05, Republic of Maldives.

Ministry of Planning and National Development, Post Office Box 30266,

Nairobi, Kenya.

Missouri Small Business Development Centers, 300 University Place, Columbia, Missouri 65211 (314) 882-0344.

Missouri State Library, 600 West Main Street, Post Office Box 387, Jefferson City, Missouri 65102 (314) 751-1823.

Montana State Library, 1515 East Sixth Avenue, Capitol Station, Helena, Montana 59620 (406) 444-3004.

Motion Picture Association of America, 15503 Venture Blvd, Encino, California 91436 (818) 995-6600.

Motorcycle Industry Council, 2 Jenner Street, Suite 150, Irvine, California 92718 (949) 727-4211.

National Archives and Records Administration, 8601 Adelphi Road, College Park, Maryland 20740 (301) 713-6800.

National Assembly of State Arts Agencies, 1029 Vermont Avenue, NW, 2nd Fl., Washington, D.C. 20005 (202) 347-6352.

National Association of Home Builders of the U.S., 1201 Fifteenth Street, NW, Washington, D.C. 20005 (202) 822-0200.

National Association of Latino Elected and Appointed Officials, NALEO Education Fund, 311 Massachusetts Avenue, NE, Washington, D.C. 20002 (202) 546-2536.

National Association of Securities Dealers, 1735 K Street, NW, Washington, D.C. 20006 (202) 728-8000.

National Basketball Association, 645 Fifth Avenue, Tenth Floor, New York, New York 10022 (212) 826-7000.

National Center for Children in Poverty, Columbia University, 154 Haven Avenue, Manhattan, New York 10032 (212) 304-7100.

National Center for Employee Ownership, 1736 Franklin Street, 8th Fl., Oakland, California 94612 (510) 208-1300.

National Center for Juvenile Justice, 710 Fifth Avenue, Pittsburgh, Pennsylvania 15219 (412) 227-6950.

National Collegiate Athletic Association, 700 West Washington Street, Indianapolis, Indiana 46206 (317) 917-6222.

National Council for Adoption, 1930 Seventeenth Street, NW, Washington, D.C. 20009-6207 (202) 328-8072.

National Credit Union Administration, 1775 Duke Street, Alexandria, Virginia 22314-3428 (703) 518-6300.

National Directorate of Statistics, Ministerio do Plano, Av Ahmed Sekou Toure 21, CP 493, Maputo, Mozambique.

National Education Association, 1201 Sixteenth Street, NW, Washington, D.C. 20036 (202) 833-4000.

National Football League, 2021 L Street, NW, 6th Floor, Washington, D.C. 20036 (202) 463-2200.

National Football League Players Association, 2021 L Street, NW, Washington, D.C. 20036 (202) 463-2200.

National Gardening Association, 1100 Dorset Street, South, Burlington, Vermont 05403 (802) 863-5215.

National Golf Foundation, 1150 South U.S. Highway One, Jupiter, Florida 33477 (407) 744-6006.

National Hockey League, 1251 Avenue of the Americas, New York, New York 10020 (212) 730-1413.

National Hockey League Players Association, 777 Bay Street, Suite 2400, Toronto, Ontario, Canada M5G 2C8 (416) 408-4040.

National Marine Manufactures Association, 1819 L Street, NW, Suite 700, Washington, D.C. 20036 (202) 861-1180.

National Republican Congressional Committee, 320 First Street, SE, Washington, D.C. 20003 (202) 479-7000.

National Safety Council, 1121 Spring Lake Drive, Itasca, Illinois 60143-3201 (630) 285-1121.

National Science Foundation, 4201 Wilson Boulevard, Arlington, Virginia 22230 (703) 306-1234.

National Statistical Coordination Board, Marvin Plaza Building, 2153 Pasong Tamo Street, Makati, Metro Manila, Republic of the Philippines.

National Statistical Office, Larn Luang Road, Bangkok 10100, Thailand.

National Statistical Office, 90 Kyongun-dong, Chong-gu, Seoul, Korea.

National Statistical Office, Post Office Box 333, Zomba, Malawi.

National Statistical Service of Greece, 14-16 Lykourgou Street, 10166 Athens, Greece.

National Statistics Office, Central Government Offices, Post Office Wards Strip, Waigani, Papua New Guinea.

Natural Resources and Economics, Department of Agriculture, Colorado State University, Fort Collins, Colorado 80523 (303) 491-5706.

Natural Resources Commission, 301 Centennial Mall South, Post Office Box 94876, Lincoln, Nebraska 68509-4876 (402) 471-2081.

Nebraska Department of Labor, 550 South Sixteenth Street, Post Office Box 94600, Lincoln, Nebraska 68509-4600 (402) 471-2518.

Nelson A. Rockefeller, Institute of Government, 411 State Street, Albany, New York 12203 (518) 443-5258.

Netherlands Central Bureau of Statistics, 428 Prinses Beatrixlaan, 2270 AZ Voorburg, The Hague, Netherlands.

Nevada State Library, Capitol Complex, 100 Stewart Street, Carson City, Nevada 89710 (702) 687-8327.

New Brunswick Statistics Agency, Post Office Box 6000, Fredericton, New Brunswick E3B 5H1, Canada (506) 453-2381.

New Hampshire State Library, 20 Park Street, Concord, New Hampshire 03301-6303 (603) 271-2060.

New Jersey Department of Labor, Division of Labor Market and Demographic Research, CN 388-John Fitch Plaza, Trenton, New Jersey 08625-0388 (609) 984-2593.

New Jersey State Library, 185 West State Street, CN 520, Trenton, New Jersey 08625-0520 (609) 292-6259.

New Mexico State Library, 325 Don Gaspar Avenue, Post Office Box 1629, Santa Fe, New Mexico 87503 (505) 827-3824.

New York State Department of Economic Development, Division of Policy and Research, One Commerce Plaza, Room 905, 99 Washington Avenue, Albany, New York 12245 (518) 474-6005.

New York State Library, Cultural Education Center, Empire State Plaza, Albany, New York 12230 (518) 474-3940.

Newfoundland Statistics Agency, Executive Council, 10th Floor, Confederation Building, Post Office Box 8700, St. John's, Newfoundland A1B 4J6, Canada (709) 729-2913.

North Carolina Office of State Planning, 116 West Jones Street, Raleigh, North Carolina 27603-8005 (919) 733-3683.

North Dakota State Library, Liberty Memorial Building, Capitol Grounds, Bismarck, North Dakota 58505 (701) 224-2490.

Northeastern Illinois Planning Commission, Research Services, 400 West Madison Street, Chicago, Illinois 60606-2642 (312) 454-0400.

Office des Changes, Division des Etudes et de la Balance des Paiements, Place Moulay Hassan, BP 71, Rabat, Morocco.

Office Federale de la Statistique, Hallwylstrasse 15, CH-3003 Berne, Switzerland.

Office National des Statistiques, 8/10 Rues des Moussebiline, B.P. 55 Alger, Algeria.

Office of Administration, 124 Capitol Building, Post Office Box 809, Jefferson City, Missouri 65102 (314) 751-2345.

Office of Administration Services, South Dakota Department of Health, 445 East Capitol Avenue, Pierre, South Dakota 57501-3185 (605) 773-3693.

Office of Biometrics, University of New Hampshire Pettee Hall, Durham, New Hampshire 03824 (603) 862-3930.

Office of Computing, University of Missouri-St. Louis, 8001 Natural Bridge Road, Room 451 CCB, St. Louis, Missouri 63121 (314) 553-6014.

Office of Financial Management, Forecasting Division, 450 Insurance Building, Box 43113, Olympia, Washington 98504 (206) 586-2504.

Office of Health Services Research, Department of Community Medicine, Health Science Center, West Virginia University, Morgantown, West Virginia 26506 (304) 293-1086.

Office of Health Statistics, Rhode Island Department of Health, 3 Capitol Hill, Providence, Rhode Island 02908 (401) 277-2550.

Office of Intergovernmental Assistance, State Capitol, Fourteenth Floor, Bismarck, North Dakota 58505 (701) 224-2094.

Office of Management and Budget, Division of Policy, Pouch AD, Juneau, Alaska 99811 (907) 465-3640.

Office of Personnel Management, 1900 E Street, NW, Washington, D.C. 20415 (202) 606-1800.

Office of Planning and Budget, Division of Administration, Post Office Box 94095, 1051 North Third Street, Baton Rouge, Louisiana 70804 (504) 342-7410.

Office of Planning and Budget, State Capitol, Room 116, Salt Lake City, Utah 84114 (801) 538-1550.

Office of Planning and Statistics, Majuro, Republic of the Marshall Islands 96960.

Office of Planning and Statistics, Post Office Box 100, Koror, Republic of Palau, Western Caroline Islands 96940.

Office of Planning and Statistics, Post Office Box PS4, National

Government Federated States of Micronesia, Palikir, Pohnpei FAM 96941.

Office of Policy and Management, State of Kentucky, Capitol Annex, Frankfort, Kentucky 40601 (502) 564-7300.

Office of Policy Research and Coordination, Pavilion Office Building, 109 State Street, Montpelier, Vermont 05609 (802) 828-3326.

Office of Population Censuses and Surveys, Head Office, St. Catherines House, 10 Kingsway, London WC2B 6JP, United Kingdom.

Office of Social and Economic Data Analysis, University of Missouri-Columbia, 224 Lewis Hall, Columbia, Missouri 65211 (314) 882-7396.

Office of State Planning, 2 1/2 Beacon Street, Concord, New Hampshire 03301 (603) 271-2155.

Oficina Central de Estadistica e Informatica, Presidencia de la Republica, Aptdo. de Correos 400 Carmelitas, Caracas 1050, Venezuela.

Oficina Nacional de Estadistica Apartado de Correos No. 1342, Santo Domingo D.N., Dominican Republic.

Ohio Data Users Center, Ohio Department of Development, Post Office Box 1001, Columbus, Ohio 43266-0101 (614) 466-2115.

Ohio State University Library/Census Data Center, 126 Main Library, 1858 Neil Avenue Mall, Columbus, Ohio 43210 (614) 292-6175.

Oklahoma Department of Libraries, 200 N.E. Eighteenth Street, Oklahoma City, Oklahoma 73105 (405) 521-2502.

Oklahoma State Data Center, Oklahoma Department of Commerce, 6601 Broadway Extension, Post Office Box 26980, Oklahoma City, Oklahoma 73126-0980 (405) 841-5184.

Oregon Housing Agency, 1600 State Street, Suite 100, Salem, Oregon 97310-0161 (503) 378-4730.

Oregon State Library, State Library Building, Salem, Oregon 97310 (503) 378-4277.

Organisation for Economic Co-operation and Development, (OECD), 2 rue Andre-Pascal, 75 Paris 16, France (Telephone Number in U.S. (202) 785-6323).

Osterreichisches Statistisches Zentralamt, Hintere Zollamtsstrasse 2b, A 1033 Vienna, Austria.

Penn State at Harrisburg Acquisitions, Heindel Library, Middletown, Pennsylvania 17057 (717) 948-6074.

Pennsylvania State Data Center, Institute of State and Regional Affairs, Pennsylvania State University at Harrisburg, Middletown, Pennsylvania 17057 (717) 948-6336.

Pennsylvania State Library, Forum Building, Harrisburg, Pennsylvania 17105 (717) 787-2327.

Planning and Statistics Division, Ministry of Finance, Post Office Box 33, Viaku, Tuvalu.

Planning Unit, Ministry of Finance, Belmopan, Belize.

Policy Development and Planning Division, Connecticut Office of Policy and Management, 80 Washington Street, Hartford, Connecticut 06106-4459 (203) 566-8285.

Policy Research Office, Post Office Box 94601, State Capitol, Room 1319, Lincoln, Nebraska 68509-4601 (402) 471-2414.

Population and Resources Laboratory, Department of Sociology, Kansas State University, Manhattan, Kansas 66506 (913) 532-5984.

Population Division of the United Nations, New York, New York 10017 (800) 253-9646.

Population Research Laboratory, Utah State University, UMC 07, Logan, Utah 84322 (801) 750-1231.

Price Gilbert Memorial Library, Georgia Institute of Technology, Atlanta, Georgia 30332 (404) 894-4519.

Prime Minister's Department, Post Office Box 193, Apia, Western Samoa.

Publishers Information Bureau, 919 Third Avenue, New York, New York 10022 (212) 872-3700.

Puerto Rico Department of Labor and Human Resources, Bureau of Labor Statistics, San Juan, Puerto Rico.

Puerto Rico Planning Board, Minillas Government Center, North Building, Avenida De Diego, Post Office Box 41119, San Juan, Puerto, Rico 00940-9985 (809) 728-4430.

Puget Sound Council of Governments, 216 First Avenue South, Seattle, Washington 98104 (206) 464-5355.

Recinto Universitario De Mayaguez, Edificio Anexo Pineiro, Carretera Num 2, Mayaguez, Puerto Rico 00708 (809) 834-4040.

Reference Department, Louisiana State Library, Post Office Box 131, Baton Rouge, Louisiana 70821 (504) 342-4920.

Reference Library, West Virginia State Library Commission, Science and Cultural Center, Capitol Complex, Charleston, West Virginia 25305 (304) 348-2045.

Regional Research and Development Service, Southern Illinois University at Edwardsville, Box 1456, Edwardsville, Illinois 62026-1456 (618) 692-2278.

Research and Analysis Bureau, Employment Policy Division, Montana Department of Labor and Industry, Post Office Box 1728, Helena, Montana 59624 (406) 444-2430.

Research and Analysis Section, Arkansas Employment Security Division, Post Office Box 2981, Little Rock, Arkansas 72203 (501) 682-3159.

Research and Planning Division, Minister's Secretariat, Ministry of Finance, 1-1 Kasumigaseki 3-chome, Chiyoda-ku, Tokyo 100, Japan.

Research Division, Indiana Department of Commerce, 1 North Capitol, Suite 700, Indianapolis, Indiana 46204 (317) 232-8959.

Research Library, Department of Library, Archives and Public Records, 1700 West Washington, Second Floor, Phoenix, Arizona 85007 (602) 542-3701.

Research Section, Iowa Department of Economic Development, 200 East Grand Avenue, Des Moines, Iowa 50309 (515) 281-3005.

Rhode Island Department of Economic Development, 7 Jackson Walkway, Providence, Rhode Island 02903 (401) 277-2601.

Rhode Island Department of Education, 22 Hayes Street, Providence, Rhode Island 02908 (401) 277-3126.

Rhode Island Department of State Library Services, 300 Richmond Street, Providence Rhode Island 02903 (401) 277-2726.

Robert W. Woodruff Library for Advanced Studies, Emory University, Atlanta, Georgia 30322 (404) 727-6880.

Rockefeller, Nelson A., Institute of Government, 411 State Street, Albany, New York 12203 (518) 472-1300.

Roper Center, Institute for Social Injury, University of Connecticut, U-164, Storrs, Connecticut 06269-1164 (203) 486-4440.

Rutgers University - The State University, Kilmer Campus, Lucy Stone Hall, B Wing, New Brunswick, New Jersey 08903 (908) 932-3822.

Sacramento Area COG, 106 K Street, Suite 300, Sacramento, California 95816 (916) 457-2264.

San Diego Association of Governments, First Federal Plaza, 401 B Street, Suite 800, San Diego, California 92101 (619) 236-5300.

Saskatchewan Bureau of Statistics, Fifth Floor, 2350 Albert Street, Regina, Saskatchewan S4P 4A6, Canada (306) 787-6327.

Savezni Zavod za Statistiku, Kneza Milosa, 20, Post Office Box 203, 11000 Belgrade, Yugoslavia.

The Secretariat, Stanley, Falkland Islands.

Securities and Exchange Commission, 450 Fifth Street, NW, Washington, D.C. 20549 (202) 942-4040.

Service Central de la Statistique et des Etudes Economiques, 19-21 Boulevard Royal, BP 304, L2013, Luxembourg.

Service National Des Etudes et Statistiques, Ministere du Plan, BP 1156, Bujumbura, Burundi.

Services des Statistiques, et des Etudes Economiques, 4 rue des Iris, Monte Carlo, Monaco.

Shipbuilders Council of America, 1600 Wilson Boulevard, Suite 100, Arlington, Virginia 22209 (703) 351-6734.

Slovensky Statisticky Urad Mileticova 3, 800 00 Bratislava, Czechoslovakia.

Small Business Administration, 409 Third Street, SW, Washington, D.C. 20416 (800) UASK-SBA.

Small Business Development Center, 217 East Redwood Street, Ninth Floor, Baltimore, Maryland 21202 (410) 333-6995.

Social Research Center, Department of Rural Sociology, Washington State University, Pullman, Washington 99164-4006 (509) 335-4519.

Social Science Data Center, Brown University, Post Office Box 1916, Providence, Rhode Island 02912 (401) 863-2550.

Social Security Administration, 6400 Security Boulevard, Baltimore, Maryland 21235 (800) 772-1213.

South Carolina State Library, Post Office Box 11469, Columbia, South Carolina 29211 (803) 734-8666.

South Dakota State University, Rural Sociology Department, Scobey Hall 226, Box 504, Brookings, South Dakota 57007 (605) 688-4132.

Southern California Association of Governments, 818 West Seventh Street, Twelfth Floor, Los Angeles, California 90017 (213) 236-1800.

Specialty Vehicle Institute of America, Two Jenner Street, Suite 150, Irvine, California 92718 (714) 727-3727.

Staatliche Zentralverwaltung fur Statistik (State Central Administration for Statistics), 1026 Berlin, Hans-Beimler-Strasse 70/72, Germany.

State Census Data Center, Department of Finance, 915 L Street, Sacramento, California 95814 (916) 322-4651.

State Committee of Azerbaijan on Statistics, 10 Chapaena Street, Baku 370008, Azerbaijan.

State Committee of Republic of Kirgizstan on Statistics, 374 Frunze Street, Bishkek 720884, Kirgizstan.

State Committee of Republic of Tajikstan on Statistics, 127 Ayini Street, Dushanbe - 29, 734029, Tajikistan.

State Committee of Republic of Turkmenistan on Statistics, 72 Makhtumkuli Avenue, Ashkhabad 744000, Turkmenistan.

State Data Center, Texas Department of Commerce, 9th and Congress Streets, Post Office Box 12728, Capitol Station, Austin, Texas 78711 (512) 320-9667.

State Data Center, University of Arkansas-Little Rock, 2801 South University, Little Rock, Arkansas 72204 (501) 569-8530.

State Data Center, Texas Department of Commerce, Ninth and Congress Streets, Post Office Box 12728, Capitol Station, Austin, Texas 78711 (512) 320-9683.

State Data Center, University of Arkansas-Little Rock, 2801 South University, Little Rock, Arkansas 72204 (501) 569-8530.

State Data Center Program, Mercer University Law Library, Mercer University, Macon, Georgia 31207 (912) 752-2668.

State Data Center Program, University of California-Berkeley, 2538 Channing Way, Berkeley, California 94720 (510) 642-6571.

State Demographer's Office, Minnesota Planning, 300 Centennial Office Building, 658 Cedar Street, St. Paul, Minnesota 55155 (612) 296-2557.

State Library, State Capitol Building, Room 343-N, Topeka, Kansas 66612 (913) 296-3296.

State Library Division, Department for Libraries and Archives, 300 Coffeetree Road, Post Office Box 537, Frankfort, Kentucky 40601 (502) 875-7000.

State Library, North Carolina Department of Cultural Resources State Library, 109 East Jones Street, Raleigh, North Carolina 27611 (919) 733-3270.

State Library of Florida, R.A. Gray Building, Tallahassee, Florida 32399-0250 (904) 487-2651.

State Library of Iowa, East Twelfth and Grand, Des Moines, Iowa 50319 (515) 281-4350.

State Library of Ohio, 65 South Front Street, Columbus, Ohio 43215 (614) 644-7051.

State Library Resource Center, Pratt Library, 400 Cathedral Street, Baltimore, Maryland 21201 (410) 396-1789.

State Service Center for Geographic Information Systems, Department of Energy Building, 625 Marion Street, NE, Salem, Oregon 97310 (503) 378-4036.

State Statistical Bureau, 38 Yuetan Nanjie, Sanlihe, Beijing, People's Republic of China.

Statistical Bureau, Ministry of Economic Planning and Finance, Post Office Box 542, Georgetown, Guyana.

Statistical Bureau of Iceland, Skuggasund 3, 15-150, 101 Reykjavik, Iceland.

Statistical Department, Ministry of Trade, Industry, and Tourism, Post Office Building, Castries, Saint Lucia.

Statistical Department, State Planning Commission, Post Office Box 1742, Mogadishu, Somalia.

Statistical Department, The Treasury, The Valley, Anguilla.

Statistical Division, Ministry of Finance, Post Office Box 67, Bariki, Tarawa, Gilbert Islands.

Statistical Division, Ministry of Finance, Upper Redcliffe Street, Saint John's, Antigua.

Statistical Institute of Jamaica, Nine Swallowfield Road, Kingston 5, Jamaica.

Statistical Office, Ministry of Finance, 22 Bath Road, Roseau, Dominica.

Statistical Office, Church Street, Basseterre, Saint Kitts.

Statistical Office, Ministry of Finance and National Economy, Post Office Box 3735, Riyadh, Saudi Arabia.

Statistical Office of the United Nations, Publishing Service, New York, New York 10017 (800) 253-9646.

Statistical Office, Post Office Box 125, Avarua, Raratonga, Cook Islands.
Statistical Service, Post Office Box 1098, Accra, Ghana.

Statistical Services Branch, Department of Economic Development, Post Office Box 519, Halifax, Nova Scotia B3J 2R7, Canada (902) 424-5691.

Statistician's Office, Church Street, Hamilton 5, Bermuda.

Statistics and Research Department, Ministry of Finance, 13 Lord Byron Avenue, Nicosia, Cyprus.

Statistics Bureau, Management and Coordination Agency, 19-1 Waka-Matsucho, Shinjuku, Tokyo 162, Japan.

Statistics Canada, Ottawa, Ontario K1A 0T6, Canada (613) 951-8116.
Statistics Department, Ministry of Finance, Post Office Box 149, Nuku'alofa, Tonga.

Statistics Department, Ministry of Finance, Saint George's, Grenada.
Statistics Division, Planning Unit, Ministry of Finance, Church Street, Post Office Box 186, Basseterre, Saint Kitts and Nevis.

Statistics Group, Sectoral and Community Economic Policy Branch, Ministry of Treasury and Economics, Frost Building, North Third Floor, Toronto, Ontario M7A 1Y9, Canada (416) 325-1544.

Statistics Office, Chief Statistician, Government Headquarters, Plymouth, Montserrat.

Statistics Office, Ministry of Finance and Economic Planning, Post Office Box 67, Bariki, Tarawa, Kiribati.

Statistics Office, NPSO, Vila, Vanuatu.

Statistics Office, Ministry of Finance and Economic Planning, Post Office Box G6, Honiara, Solomon Islands.

Statistics Office, Post Office Box 125, Rarotonga, Cook Islands.

Statistiska Central Byran, Karlavagen 5 - 115 81 Stockholm, Sweden.

Statistisches Bundesamt, 1 Gustav-Stresemann-Ring 11, Postfach 5528, 6200 Wiesbaden, Germany.

Statistisk Sentralbyra, Skippergate 15, Postboks 8131, DEP N - 0033, Oslo, Norway.

Supreme Court of the United States, Office of the Clerk, United States Supreme Court Building, One First Street, NE, Washington, D.C. 20543 (202) 479-3000.

Survey Research Center, University of Wyoming, Post Office Box 3925, Laramie, Wyoming 82071 (307) 766-2931.

Survey Research Center, Wilson Hall, Room 1-108, Montana State University, Bozeman, Montana 59717 (406) 994-4481.

T C Basbakanlik Devlet Istatistik Enstitusu, Necatibey Caddesi 114, Ankara, Turkey.

Techniques and Statistics Division, Customs Department, Sunthornkosa Road, Klong Toey, Bangkok 10110, Thailand.

Television Bureau of Advertising, Inc.,3 East 54th Street, 10th Floor, New York, New York 10022 (212) 486-1111.

Tennessee State Planning Office, John Sevier State Office Building, 500 Charlotte Avenue, Suite 307, Nashville, Tennessee 37243-0001 (615) 741-1676.

Texas Natural Resources Information System (TNRIS), Post Office Box 13231, Austin, Texas 78711 (512) 463-8399.

Texas State Library and Archive Commission, Post Office Box 12927, Capitol Station, Austin, Texas 78711 (512) 463-5455.

Theatre Communications Group, 355 Lexington Avenue, New York, New York 10017 (212) 697-5230.

Tilastokeskus, Annankatu 44, 00100 Helsinki 10, Finland.

Tong Cuc Thong Ke Vietnam, 6B Hoang Dieu, Hanoi, Socialist Republic of Vietnam.

Ufficio Statale di Statistica, Via Antonio Onofri 87, Repubblica de San Marino.

United Nations, Department for International Economic and Social Affairs, New York, New York 10017.

U.S. Congress, Clerk of the House, The Capitol, Washington, D.C. 20515 (202) 224-3121.

U.S. Congress, Congressional Budget Office, Second and D Streets, SW, Washington, D.C. 20515 (202) 226-2600.

U.S. Congress, Joint Committee on Printing, North Capitol and H Streets, NW, Washington, D.C. 20401 (202) 512-0000.

U.S. Department of Agriculture, Economic Research Service, 1800 M Street, NW, Washington, D.C. 20036 (202) 694-5050.

U.S. Department of Agriculture, Food and Nutrition Service, 3101 Park Center Drive, Alexandria, Virginia 22302 (703) 305-2286.

U.S. Department of Agriculture, Forest Service, Post Office Box 96090, Washington, D.C. 20090 (202) 205-8333.

U.S. Department of Agriculture, National Agricultural Statistics Service, Fourteenth Street and Independence Avenue, SW, Washington, D.C. 20250 (800) 727-9540.

U.S. Department of Commerce, Bureau of Economic Analysis, Fourteenth Street between Constitution Avenue and E Street, NW, Washington, D.C. 20230 (202) 606-9900.

U.S. Department of Commerce, Bureau of the Census, Washington, D.C. 20233 (301) 457-4100.

U.S. Department of Commerce, International Trade Administration, Fourteenth Street between Constitution Avenue and E Street, NW, Washington, D.C. 20230 (202) 482-2185.

U.S. Department of Defense, Defense Security Cooperation Agency, The Pentagon, Washington, D.C. 20301 (703) 604-6604.

U.S. Department of Defense, Office of the Comptroller, The Pentagon, Washington, D.C. 20301 (703) 545-6700.

U.S. Department of Defense Office of the Secretary, The Pentagon, Washington, D.C. 20301 (703) 545-6700.

U.S. Department of Education, 400 Maryland Avenue, SW, Washington, D.C. 20202 (877) 424-1616.

U.S. Department of Education, National Center for Education Statistics, 555 New Jersey Avenue, NW, Washington, D.C. 20208 (202) 219-1828.

U.S. Department of Education, Office of Postsecondary Education, 1990 K Street, NW, Washington, D.C. 20006 (800) 872-5327.

U.S. Department of Education, Office of Special Education Programs, 600 Independence Avenue, SW, Washington, D.C. 20202 (800) 872-5327.

U.S. Department of Energy, Energy Information Administration, 1000 Independence Avenue, SW, Washington, D.C. 20585 (202) 586-8800.

U.S. Department of Energy, Federal Energy Regulatory Commission, 1000 Independence Avenue, SW, Washington, D.C. 20585 (202) 208-0055.

U.S. Department of Health and Human Services, Centers for Disease Control, 1600 Clifton Road, NE, Atlanta, Georgia 30333 (800) 311-3435.

U.S. Department of Health and Human Services, Health Care Financing Administration, 200 Independence Avenue, SW, Washington, D.C. 20201 (202) 690-6145.

U.S. Department of Health and Human Services, Health Resources and Services Administration, 5600 Fishers Lane, Rockville, Maryland 20857 (301) 443-3376.

U.S. Department of Health and Human Services, National Center for Health Statistics, 3700 East-West Highway, Hyattsville, Maryland 20782 (301) 436-8500.

U.S. Department of Health and Human Services, National Institute of Mental Health, 5600 Fishers Lane, Rockville, Maryland 20857 (301) 443-3877.

U.S. Department of Health and Human Services, Public Health Service, 200 Independence Avenue, SW, Washington, D.C. 20201 (202) 690-7694.

U.S. Department of Health and Human Services, Substance Abuse and Mental Health Administration, 5600 Fisher's Lane, Rockville, Maryland 20857 (800) 729-6686.

U.S. Department of Housing and Urban Development, 451 Seventh Street, SW, Washington, D.C. 20410 (800) 998-9999.

U.S. Department of Justice, Bureau of Justice Statistics, 810 Seventh Street, NW, Washington, D.C. 20531 (800) 732-3277.

U.S. Department of Justice, Federal Bureau of Investigation, 935 Pennsylvania Avenue, NW, Washington, D.C. 20535 (202) 324-3691.

U.S. Department of Justice, Immigration and Naturalization Service, 425 I Street, NW, Washington, D.C. 20536 (202) 305-1613.

U.S. Department of Justice, Office of Juvenile Justice and Delinquency Prevention, 633 Indiana Avenue, NW, Washington, D.C. 20531 (800) 638-8736.

U.S. Department of Labor, Bureau of Labor Statistics, Two Massachusetts Avenue, NE, Washington, D.C. 20212 (202) 691-5200.

U.S. Department of Labor, Employment and Training Administration, 200 Constitution Avenue, NW, Washington, D.C. 20210 (202) 219-6871.

U.S. Department of Labor, Employment Standards Administration, 200 Constitution Avenue, NW, Washington, D.C. 20210 (202) 219-6050.

U.S. Department of Labor, Mine Safety and Health Administration, 4015 Wilson Boulevard, Arlington, Virginia 22203 (703) 235-1452.

U.S. Department of State, 2201 C Street, NW, Washington, D.C. 20520 (202) 647-4000.

U.S. Department of State, Bureau of Intelligence and Research, 2201 C Street, NW, Washington, D.C. 20520 (202) 647-1080.

U.S. Department of the Army, The Pentagon, Washington, D.C. 20310 (703) 695-2442.

U.S. Department of the Interior, Bureau of Indian Affairs, C Street between Eighteenth and Nineteenth Streets, NW, Washington, D.C. 20240 (202) 208-3710.

U.S. Department of the Interior, Geological Survey, National Center, 12201 Sunrise Valley Drive, Reston, Virginia 22092 (703) 648-4000.

U.S. Department of the Interior, National Park Service, C Street between Eighteenth and Nineteenth Streets, NW, Washington, D.C. 20240 (202) 208-6843.

U.S. Department of the Treasury, Fifteenth Street and Pennsylvania Avenue, NW, Washington, D.C. 20220 (202) 622-2000.

U.S. Department of the Treasury, Internal Revenue Service, 1111 Constitution Avenue, NW, Washington, D.C. 20224 (202) 874-0410.

U.S. Department of Transportation, Federal Aviation Administration, 800 Independence Avenue, SW, Washington, D.C. 20591 (202) 367-3484.

U.S. Department of Transportation, Federal Highway Administration, 400 Seventh Street, SW, Washington, D.C. 20590 (202) 366-0660.

U.S. Department of Transportation, Maritime Administration, 400 Seventh Street, SW, Washington, D.C. 20590 (202) 366-5807.

U.S. Department of Transportation, National Highway Traffic Safety Administration, 400 Seventh Street, SW, Washington, D.C. 20590 (202) 366-8892.

U.S. Department of Transportation, U.S. Coast Guard, 2100 Second Street, SW, Washington, D.C. 20593 (202) 267-2229.

U.S. Department of Veterans Affairs, 810 Vermont Avenue, NW, Washington, D.C. 20420 (202) 273-5400.

U.S. Postal Service, 475 L'Enfant Plaza West, SW, Washington, D.C. 20260-0010 (202) 268-2000.

U.S. Tennis Association, Post Office Box 5046, White Plaines New York 10602 (914) 696-7000.

United Way of Rhode Island, 229 Waterman Street, Providence, Rhode Island 02908 (401) 521-9000.

University of Cincinnati, Southwest Ohio Regional Data Center, Institute for Policy Research, Mail Loc 132, Cincinnati, Ohio 45221 (513) 556-5082.

University of Massachusetts, Documents Library, 100 Morrissey Boulevard, Boston, Massachusetts 02125 (617) 287-5935.

University of Utah, Bureau of Economic and Business Research, 401 KDGB Building, Salt Lake City, Utah 84112 (801) 581-3353.

University of The Virgin Islands, Eastern Caribbean Center, Charlotte Amalie, Saint Thomas, Virgin Islands 00802 (809) 776-9200.

University of Washington, 145 Savery Hall, DK45, Seattle, Washington 98195 (206) 543-8110.

Urban Information Center, University of Missouri-St. Louis, 8001 Natural Bridge Road, St. Louis, Missouri 63121 (314) 553-6014.

Urban Studies Center, College of Urban and Public Affairs, University of Louisville, Louisville, Kentucky 40292 (502) 588-7990.

Vermont Department of Libraries, 109 State Street, Montpelier, Vermont 05609 (802) 828-3261.

Vermont Travel Department, 134 State Street, Montpelier, Vermont 05602 (802) 828-3217.

Virgin Islands Department of Economic Development, Post Office Box 6400, Charlotte Amalie, St. Thomas, Virgin Islands 00801 (809) 774-8784.

Virginia Employment Commission, 703 East Main Street, Richmond, Virginia 23219 (804) 786-8308.

Virginia State Library, Documents Section, Eleventh Street at Capitol Square, Richmond, Virginia 23219-3491 (804) 786-2303.

Waring, John A., 4830 Ponderosa Drive, Annandale,, Virginia 22203 (703) 425-0762.

Woodruff, Robert W., Library for Advanced Studies, Emory University, Atlanta, Georgia 30322 (404) 727-6880.

World Health Organization, 20 Avenue Appia, Office of Publications, CH-1211 Geneva 27, Switzerland (Telephone Number in U.S. (518) 436-9686).